YEARBOOK OF THE UNITED NATIONS 2005

Volume 59

Yearbook of the United Nations, 2005

Volume 59   Sales No. E.07.I.1

Prepared by the Yearbook Unit of the Academic Initiative Section of the Department of Public Information, United Nations, New York. Although the *Yearbook* is based on official sources, it is not an official record.

Chief Editor: Peter Jackson

Senior Editors: Federigo Magherini, Jullyette Ukabiala

Editors/Writers: Judith Gehler, Melissa Gorelick, Lawri Moore, John R. Sebesta, Namrita Talwar

Contributing Editors: Kathryn Gordon, Juanita B. Phelan

Contributing Writers: Luisa Balacco, Jacqueline Bouscher, Shirley Brownell, Maria Carlino, Frank Carrére-Bencimon, Mathieu Faupin, Jessamy Garver-Affeldt, Ryan Daniel Kolb, Kimberly Willis

Copy Editors: Donna Culpepper, Charlotte Maitre

Senior Typesetter: Sunita Chabra

Researcher/Copy Coordinator: Rodney Pascual

Administrative Assistant: Carmelita Aquilizan

Editorial Assistants: Beata Gloza, Nicole Rodriguez

Indexer: David Golante

Jacket Design: Graphic Design Unit

YEARBOOK
OF THE
UNITED
NATIONS
2005

Volume 59

Department of Public Information
United Nations, New York

COPYRIGHT © 2008 UNITED NATIONS

Yearbook of the United Nations, 2005
Vol. 59
ISBN: 978-92-1-100967-5
ISSN: 0082-8521

UNITED NATIONS PUBLICATIONS
SALES NO. E.07.I.1

Printed in Canada

A s we mark the 60th year of the publication of *The Yearbook of the United Nations*, I am delighted to contribute my first foreword to this indispensable and authoritative reference work on the Organization. This milestone edition documents the results of the 2005 World Summit, an unprecedented gathering of more than 150 Heads of State and Government who collectively took bold decisions in the areas of security, human rights, United Nations reform and the Millennium Development Goals.

The 2005 World Summit pledged to "enhance the relevance, effectiveness, efficiency, accountability and credibility of the United Nations system." It set the stage for major advances, including the creation of the Peacebuilding Commission and the Human Rights Council, the adoption of a global counter-terrorism strategy, and the establishment of a Central Emergency Response Fund to expedite humanitarian relief. The vision forged in 2005 continues to animate our work as we move, in the phrase of this *Yearbook's* theme, "towards development, security and human rights for all".

Ban Ki-moon

Secretary-General of the United Nations
New York, December 2007

Contents

Part One: *Political and security questions*

Part Two: *Human Rights*

Part Three: *Economic and social questions*

Part Four: *Legal questions*

Part Five: *Institutional, administrative and budgetary questions*

Part Six: *Intergovernmental organizations related to the United Nations*

Appendices

Indexes

About the 2005 edition of the *Yearbook*

This volume of the *YEARBOOK OF THE UNITED NATIONS* continues the tradition of providing the most comprehensive coverage of the activities of the United Nations. It is an indispensable reference tool for the research community, diplomats, government officials and the general public seeking readily available information on the UN system and its related organizations.

Efforts by the Department of Public Information to achieve a more timely publication have resulted in having to rely on provisional documentation and other materials to prepare the relevant articles. Largely, Economic and Social Council resolutions and some other texts in the present volume are provisional.

Structure and scope of articles

The *Yearbook* is subject-oriented and divided into six parts covering political and security questions; human rights issues; economic and social questions; legal questions; institutional, administrative and budgetary questions; and intergovernmental organizations related to the United Nations. Chapters and topical headings present summaries of pertinent UN activities, including those of intergovernmental and expert bodies, major reports, Secretariat activities and, in selected cases, the views of States in written communications.

Activities of United Nations bodies. All resolutions, decisions and other major activities of the principal organs and, on a selective basis, those of subsidiary bodies are either reproduced or summarized in the appropriate chapter. The texts of all resolutions and decisions of substantive nature adopted in 2005 by the General Assembly, the Security Council and the Economic and Social Council are reproduced or summarized under the relevant topic. These texts are preceded by procedural details giving date of adoption, meeting number and vote totals (in favour–against–abstaining) if any; and an indication of their approval by a sessional or subsidiary body prior to final adoption. The texts are followed by details of any recorded or roll-call vote on the resolution/decision as a whole.

Major reports. Most reports of the Secretary-General, in 2005, along with selected reports from other UN sources, such as seminars and working groups, are summarized briefly.

Secretariat activities. The operational activities of the United Nations for development and humanitarian assistance are described under the relevant topics. For major activities financed outside the UN regular budget, selected information is given on contributions and expenditures.

Views of States. Written communications sent to the United Nations by Member States and circulated as documents of the principal organs have been summarized in selected cases, under the relevant topics. Substantive actions by the Security Council have been analysed and brief reviews of the Council's deliberations given, particularly in cases where an issue was taken up but no resolution was adopted.

Related organizations. The *Yearbook* also briefly describes the 2005 activities of the specialized agencies and other related organizations of the UN system.

Multilateral treaties. Information on signatories and parties to multilateral treaties and conventions is taken from *Multilateral Treaties Deposited with the Secretary-General: Status as at 31 December 2005* (ST/LEG/ SER.E/24 (vols. I & II)), Sales No. E.06.V.2.

Terminology

Formal titles of bodies, organizational units, conventions, declarations and officials are given in full on first mention in an article or sequence of articles. They are also used in resolution/decision texts, and in the SUBJECT INDEX under the key word of the title. Short titles may be used in subsequent references.

How to find information in the *Yearbook*

The user may locate information on the United Nations activities contained in this volume by the use of the Table of Contents, the Subject Index, the Index of Resolutions and Decisions and the Index of Security Council presidential statements. The volume also has five appendices: Appendix I comprises a roster of Member States; Appendix II reproduces the Charter of the United Nations, including the Statute of the International Court of Justice; Appendix III gives the structure of the principal organs of the United Nations; Appendix IV provides the agenda for each session of the principal organs in 2005; and Appendix V gives the addresses of the United Nations information centres and services worldwide.

For more information on the United Nations and its activities, visit our Internet site at:

www.un.org

ABBREVIATIONS COMMONLY USED IN THE *YEARBOOK*

ACABQ	Advisory Committee on Administrative and Budgetary Questions
AU	African Union
CEB	United Nations System Chief Executives Board for Coordination
CIS	Commonwealth of Independent States
CPC	Committee for Programme and Coordination
DPKO	Department of Peacekeeping Operations
DPRK	Democratic People's Republic of Korea
DRC	Democratic Republic of the Congo
ECA	Economic Commission for Africa
ECE	Economic Commission for Europe
ECLAC	Economic Commission for Latin America and the Caribbean
ECOWAS	Economic Community of West African States
ESCAP	Economic and Social Commission for Asia and the Pacific
ESCWA	Economic and Social Commission for Western Asia
EU	European Union
FAO	Food and Agriculture Organization of the United Nations
FYROM	The former Yugoslav Republic of Macedonia
GDP	gross domestic product
GNP	gross national product
HIV/AIDS	human immunodeficiency virus/acquired immunodeficiency syndrome
IAEA	International Atomic Energy Agency
ICAO	International Civil Aviation Organization
ICC	International Criminal Court
ICJ	International Court of Justice
ICRC	International Committee of the Red Cross
ICT	information and communication technology
ICTR	International Criminal Tribunal for Rwanda
ICTY	International Tribunal for the Former Yugoslavia
IDA	International Development Association
IFAD	International Fund for Agricultural Development
IFC	International Finance Corporation
ILO	International Labour Organization
IMF	International Monetary Fund
IMO	International Maritime Organization
ITU	International Telecommunication Union
JIU	Joint Inspection Unit
LDC	least developed country
MDGs	Millennium Development Goals
MINURSO	United Nations Mission for the Referendum in Western Sahara
MINUSTAH	United Nations Stabilization Force in Haiti
MONUC	United Nations Organization Mission in the Democratic Republic of the Congo
MRU	Mano River Union
MYFF	multi-year Funding Framework
NATO	North Atlantic Treaty Organization
NGO	non-governmental organization
NSGT	Non-Self-Governing Territory
OAS	Organization of American States
OCHA	Office for the Coordination of Humanitarian Affairs
ODA	official development assistance
OECD	Organisation for Economic Co-operation and Development
OHCHR	Office of the United Nations High Commissioner for Human Rights
OIOS	Office of Internal Oversight Services
ONUB	United Nations Operation in Burundi
OSCE	Organization for Security and Cooperation in Europe
PA	Palestinian Authority
PRSPs	poverty-reduction strategy papers
UNAIDS	Joint United Nations Programme on HIV/AIDS
UNAMA	United Nations Assistance Mission in Afghanistan
UNAMI	United Nations Assistance Mission for Iraq
UNAMSIL	United Nations Mission in Sierra Leone
UNCTAD	United Nations Conference on Trade and Development
UNDOF	United Nations Disengagement Observer Force (Golan Heights)
UNDP	United Nations Development Programme
UNEP	United Nations Environment Programme
UNESCO	United Nations Educational, Scientific and Cultural Organization
UNFICYP	United Nations Peacekeeping Force in Cyprus
UNFPA	United Nations Population Fund
UN-Habitat	United Nations Human Settlements Programme
UNHCR	Office of the United Nations High Commissioner for Refugees
UNIC	United Nations Information Centre
UNICEF	United Nations Children's Fund
UNIDO	United Nations Industrial Development Organization
UNIFIL	United Nations Interim Force in Lebanon
UNMEE	United Nations Mission in Ethiopia and Eritrea
UNMIK	United Nations Interim Administration Mission in Kosovo
UNMIL	United Nations Mission in Liberia
UNMOGIP	United Nations Military Observer Group in India and Pakistan
UNMOVIC	United Nations Monitoring, Verification and Inspection Commission
UNOCI	United Nations Operation in Côte d'Ivoire
UNODC	United Nations Office on Drugs and Crime
UNOMIG	United Nations Observer Mission in Georgia
UNOPS	United Nations Office for Project Services
UNRWA	United Nations Relief and Works Agency for Palestine Refugees in the Near East
UNTSO	United Nations Truce Supervision Organization
WFP	World Food Programme
WHO	World Health Organization
WIPO	World Intellectual Property Organization
WMDs	weapons of mass destruction
WMO	World Meteorological Organization
WTO	World Trade Organization
YUN	*Yearbook of the United Nations*

EXPLANATORY NOTE ON DOCUMENTS

References in square brackets in each chapter of Parts One to Five of this volume give the symbols of the main documents issued in 2005 on the topic. The following is a guide to the principal document symbols:

A/- refers to documents of the General Assembly, numbered in separate series by session. Thus, A/60/- refers to documents issued for consideration at the sixtieth session, beginning with A/60/1. Documents of special and emergency special sessions are identified as A/S- and A/ES-, followed by the session number.

A/C.- refers to documents of the Assembly's Main Committees, e.g. A/C.1/- is a document of the First Committee, A/C.6/-, a document of the Sixth Committee. A/BUR/- refers to documents of the General Committee. A/AC.- documents are those of the Assembly's ad hoc bodies and A/CN.-, of its commissions; e.g. A/AC.105/- identifies documents of the Assembly's Committee on the Peaceful Uses of Outer Space, A/CN.4/-, of its International Law Commission. Assembly resolutions and decisions since the thirty-first (1976) session have been identified by two arabic numerals; the first indicates the session of adoption; the second, the sequential number in the series. Resolutions are numbered consecutively from 1 at each session. Decisions since the fifty-seventh session are numbered consecutively, from 401 for those concerned with elections and appointments, and from 501 for all other decisions. Decisions of special and emergency special sessions are numbered consecutively, from 11 for those concerned with elections and appointments, and from 21 for all other decisions.

E/- refers to documents of the Economic and Social Council, numbered in separate series by year. Thus, E/2005/- refers to documents issued for consideration by the Council at its 2005 sessions, beginning with E/2005/1. E/AC.-, E/C.- and E/CN.-, followed by identifying numbers, refer to documents of the Council's subsidiary ad hoc bodies, committees and commissions. For example, E/CN.5/- refers to documents of the Council's Commission for Social Development, E/C.2/-, to documents of its Committee on Non-Governmental Organizations. E/ICEF/- documents are those of the United Nations Children's Fund (UNICEF). Symbols for the Council's resolutions and decisions, since 1978, consist of two arabic numerals: the first indicates the year of adoption and the second, the sequential number in the series. There are two series: one for resolutions, beginning with 1 (resolution 2005/1); and one for decisions, beginning with 201 (decision 2005/201).

S/- refers to documents of the Security Council. Its resolutions are identified by consecutive numbers followed by the year of adoption in parentheses, beginning with resolution 1(1946).

ST/-, followed by symbols representing the issuing department or office, refers to documents of the United Nations Secretariat.

Documents of certain bodies bear special symbols, including the following:

CD/-	Conference on Disarmament
CERD/-	Committee on the Elimination of Racial Discrimination
DC/-	Disarmament Commission
DP/-	United Nations Development Programme
HS/-	Commission on Human Settlements
ITC/-	International Trade Centre
TD/-	United Nations Conference on Trade and Development
UNEP/-	United Nations Environment Programme

Many documents of the regional commissions bear special symbols, which are sometimes preceded by the following:

E/ECA/-	Economic Commission for Africa
E/ECE/-	Economic Commission for Europe
E/ECLAC/-	Economic Commission for Latin America and the Caribbean
E/ESCAP/-	Economic and Social Commission for Asia and the Pacific
E/ESCWA/-	Economic and Social Commission for Western Asia

"L" in a symbol refers to documents of limited distribution, such as draft resolutions; "CONF." to documents of a conference; "INF." to those of general information. Summary records are designated by "SR.", verbatim records by "PV.", each followed by the meeting number.

United Nations sales publications each carry a sales number with the following components separated by periods: a capital letter indicating the language(s) of the publication; two arabic numerals indicating the year; a Roman numeral indicating the subject category; a capital letter indicating a subdivision of the category, if any; and an arabic numeral indicating the number of the publication within the category. Examples: E.05.II.A.2; E/F/R.05.II.E.7; E.05.X.1.

Documents cited in the text in square brackets may be obtained through the UN Official Document System by logging on to: http://documents.un.org.

Report of the Secretary-General

Report of the Secretary-General on the work of the Organization

*Following is the Secretary-General's report on the work of the Organization [A/60/1], dated 25 August 2005, submitted to the sixtieth session of the General Assembly. The Assembly took note of it on 29 September (**decision 60/504**).*

Introduction

1. Every year, this comprehensive report on the work of the Organization provides me with an opportunity to review the progress of the United Nations in meeting the Charter objectives of maintaining international peace and security; developing friendly relations among nations; achieving international cooperation in solving economic, social, cultural or humanitarian problems; and encouraging respect for human rights and fundamental freedoms for all. Success in fulfilling the purposes of the United Nations requires the full commitment and support of its Member States, civil society and the private sector, as well as the peoples of the world.

2. This past year has witnessed both progress and setbacks not just for the United Nations, but also for the world. There have been positive developments in the area of peace and security, such as the end of the North-South conflict in the Sudan, democratic elections in Afghanistan and Iraq, improvements in relations between India and Pakistan. Such developments strengthen our determination to continue our efforts in other conflict situations.

3. Vicious terrorist attacks in Egypt, Iraq, the United Kingdom of Great Britain and Northern Ireland and elsewhere have dramatized the magnitude of the threat of terrorism. No cause or belief can possibly justify the use of terror and indiscriminate violence against civilians. Terrorism is not the product of any particular religion or ideology, nor is it directed only at certain countries or people. It is a menace affecting all of us, and the international community must continue to work together to confront and defeat it.

4. Together with the Organization's efforts to maintain peace and security, promoting sustainable development remains at the centre of our actions. Our generation is the first to have the knowledge and resources to eradicate extreme poverty, so there is no longer any excuse for leaving over a billion of our fellow human beings in that state. Meeting the goals of the Millennium Declaration, agreed upon by all Member States as a blueprint for building a better world in the twenty-first century, is at the core of our global mission. In this context, I am particularly encouraged by the recent commitments on official development assistance and debt cancellation by the European Union and the Group of Eight. All States, both developed and developing, must do their part to intensify the fight against poverty and disease. We need a major global effort to meet the Millennium Development Goals by 2015 and to ensure that the benefits of globalization are more equally shared among the world's peoples.

5. An unprecedented Indian Ocean tsunami in December 2004 spread death and destruction over 14 countries on two continents. The disaster confirmed a disturbing trend during the past decade: the number of people killed by natural disasters has increased by almost 50 per cent. The outpouring of support from Governments, civil society, the private sector and individuals and the quick mobilization of resources set a new standard for humanitarian response. I hope that the global outpouring of solidarity and generosity will become a model for the response to other ongoing or future humanitarian crises.

6. Human rights abuses sadly persist in many parts of the world. Clearly, enormous efforts are still needed to make human rights a reality for all. The tragedy in Darfur and the appalling suffering of the civilian population represents one of the most flagrant violations of human rights. United Nations system agencies have made valiant efforts to provide humanitarian assistance to the population. The United Nations is supporting the efforts of the African Union, whose troops are helping to protect the population from further atrocities. I am pleased that the Security Council has now agreed to ask the International

Criminal Court to play an essential role in holding to account those accused of war crimes. The crisis in Darfur is not simply an African problem. It concerns the entire international community.

7. During the past year, United Nations reform has been high on my agenda. The concrete reform measures that have been put in place since I became Secretary-General in 1997 have already made the United Nations a more effective and efficient organization. The system shows greater coherence, and its disparate elements now work better together. However, there is much that remains to be done to adapt the Organization's structures and institutional culture to new expectations and new challenges.

8. Last March I put before the Member States a set of proposals in my report entitled "In larger freedom", a phrase which comes from the Preamble to the Charter of the United Nations. I put forward bold yet achievable interlinked proposals on development, security and human rights, as well as a series of institutional reforms covering the intergovernmental organs, Secretariat management and coordination of the wider United Nations system. I hope that at the High-level Plenary Meeting of the General Assembly, to be held in New York in September, leaders from all Member States of the United Nations will take concrete decisions to improve the prosperity, security and dignity of peoples everywhere and to strengthen the Organization itself as an instrument for achieving these noble objectives.

9. I submit this ninth annual report of mine in accordance with the Charter and in the hope that, through our collective efforts, the dream of a more secure, prosperous and just world embodied in the Charter will become a reality for all.

Chapter I

Achieving peace and security

10. The United Nations worked tirelessly around the globe throughout the year to prevent and resolve conflicts and to consolidate peace. From Afghanistan to Burundi, from Iraq to the Sudan, from Haiti to the Middle East, the tools employed were as diverse as the circumstances. My envoys used their good offices in seeking peace agreements or in trying to prevent disputes from violently escalating. Peacekeepers deployed to conflict zones in record numbers and in complex multidimensional operations—working not only to provide security, but also to disarm, demobilize and reintegrate former fighters; to permit the safe and sustainable return of refugees and internally displaced persons; and to help war-torn countries, write constitutions, hold elections and strengthen human rights and the rule of law. United Nations agencies, funds and programmes tailored their assistance to the special needs of post-conflict societies.

Conflict prevention and peacemaking

11. Nowhere were the stakes higher and the challenges to global peace and security greater than in **Iraq**. The international community has a shared and vital responsibility to achieve a successful transition that will lead to national reconciliation and a better life for all Iraqis. For both Iraq and the world at large, success is the only option.

12. The United Nations has been doing everything it can to help. Under the leadership of my Special Representative for Iraq and the United Nations Assistance Mission for Iraq, the United Nations has worked on many different fronts: to promote an inclusive, participatory and transparent political transition process; to provide reconstruction, development and humanitarian assistance; and to promote the protection of human rights, national reconciliation and judicial and legal reform. Although insecurity remains a constraint, I have consistently sought ways to work within the prevailing circumstances in order to carry out United Nations activities.

13. Our contributions to the political transition are numerous and ongoing. In August 2004 the United Nations helped to convene a national conference at which an Interim National Council was selected. The United Nations also played a leading role in assisting the Independent Electoral Commission of Iraq in its successful management of the historic elections in January 2005. Following the convening of the Transitional National Assembly in March and the formation of the Transitional Government in April, Iraq's political transition has entered a decisive phase. The United Nations is helping the Iraqis draft a permanent constitution and to prepare for a constitutional referendum and elections for a permanent Government in accordance with the timetable endorsed by the Security Council in its resolution 1546(2004).

14. At the international conference on Iraq, held in Brussels in June 2005, representatives from more than 80 countries and organizations emphasized the leading role of the United Nations in supporting the political process. They also welcomed the decision of the Transitional Government to establish an Iraqi-led donor coordination mechanism with the support of the United Nations. I hope the conference will help build momentum for greater international burden-sharing for Iraq's political and economic reconstruction.

15. Violence dropped sharply in the **Israeli-Palestinian conflict**, as actions by leaders on both sides generated new hopes for peace. The summit meeting held at Sharm el-Sheikh, Egypt, on 8 February 2005 produced a series of commitments—including a halt to violence and military activities—aimed at rebuilding trust and breaking the cycle of bloodshed. Although formal negotiations were not resumed, the two parties agreed to hold direct discussions to coordinate the Israeli withdrawal from the Gaza Strip and parts of the northern West Bank, scheduled to take place in August.

16. I welcomed the new momentum with cautious optimism, aware there would likely be setbacks and delays. During a visit to Israel and the occupied Palestinian territory in March 2005, I urged the two sides to seek further progress through direct dialogue and negotiations. In May, I appointed a new Special Coordinator for the Middle East Peace Process and Personal Representative to the Palestinian Authority and the Palestine Liberation Organization. The United Nations has also remained engaged through its participation in the Quartet for Middle East peace, which has met five times in the period since September 2004, and in April 2005 I appointed a Special Envoy for Gaza Disengagement. Despite the improved climate for peace, I continued to express grave concern about the Israeli barrier and its humanitarian impact. In response to a request from the General Assembly, I proposed a framework for a registry of damage caused by the barrier.

17. **Lebanon** became a focus of international attention following the adoption of Security Council resolution 1559(2004) in September and the shocking bomb attack that killed former Prime Minister Rafik Hariri and 20 others in Beirut in February 2005. I designated a Special Envoy for the implementation of Security Council resolution 1559(2004), which called, among other things, for the withdrawal of foreign forces from the country and the disbanding and disarmament of militias. A team of military experts I dispatched to Lebanon at the end of April concluded to the best of its ability that Syrian military assets, except in one disputed border area, had been withdrawn fully from Lebanon. I sent the team back in June to clarify allegations that Syrian intelligence operatives continued to operate in the country.

18. The assassination of Mr. Hariri, occurring only months before planned parliamentary elections, raised fears that Lebanon would return to its violent past. In condemning the attack, the Security Council requested that I report to it urgently on its causes, circumstances and conse-quences. Within days I dispatched a mission of inquiry, which concluded that an international commission should independently investigate the crime. The Council agreed, calling for such a commission to be created to assist the Lebanese authorities in investigating the bombing. By June, the United Nations International Independent Investigation Commission was fully operational. I also responded positively to a request of the Lebanese Government for electoral assistance by deploying a mission to help authorities prepare for the parliamentary elections and to coordinate the work of international electoral observers. The holding of these elections on time and in a credible manner has been a key element in a transition in which the Lebanese people have been expressing their determination to shape their own future, strengthen political institutions and restore their full sovereignty.

19. Turning to Africa, there was a major breakthrough in the **Sudan** with the signing on 9 January of the Comprehensive Peace Agreement between the Government and the Sudan People's Liberation Movement (SPLM). The accord ended two decades of North-South fighting that had killed and uprooted millions of people. During the negotiations, my Special Adviser provided support to the parties and to the mediation by the Intergovernmental Authority on Development (IGAD). The agreement permitted the United Nations Mission in the Sudan to be established, replacing the United Nations Advance Mission in the Sudan, which had been created in June 2004 to prepare for the anticipated peace-keeping operation as well as to provide further support to the parties in the final months leading up to the signing of the Peace Agreement. While attending the historic swearing-in of the new Government of National Unity on 9 July in Khartoum, I was encouraged that the two former adversaries, President Omer Hassan A. Al-Bashir and First Vice-President John Garang, pledged to seek wider political participation in the interim Government as well as to pursue peace and reconciliation in the regions of the Sudan that remained wracked by instability and conflict. The tragic and untimely death of First Vice-President Garang just three weeks later on 30 July was a terrible loss for the Sudan. However, since that date, I have been greatly reassured by the speed with which SPLM named Dr. Garang's successor, Commander Salva Kiir, as the head of the Movement and his subsequent inauguration as the First Vice-President of the Sudan. Crucially, both parties have quickly and authoritatively reaffirmed their commitment to the implementation of the Comprehensive Peace Agreement.

20. Peace between North and South did not, however, resolve the dire situation in the western **Darfur** region of the Sudan where, amid continuing human rights abuses and ceasefire violations, the United Nations provided massive humanitarian assistance to a brutalized population. The United Nations also actively supported and encouraged the African Union in its efforts to mediate a peace agreement for Darfur through the Abuja process and in its deployment of troops and police to monitor the ceasefire and improve security on the ground. The African Union mission has performed admirably under extraordinarily difficult circumstances and with limited means. As a result, the terrible violence that has afflicted the region has largely stopped in areas where the mission operates. However, while I found reasons to be encouraged during my visit to the region in May, the situation in Darfur remains intolerable. The parties to the conflict must comply with their commitments, guarantee the safety of civilians and make every effort to conclude a full-fledged peace agreement by the end of 2005. Only then can real security begin to take hold and the people of Darfur begin to rebuild their lives. The signing in Abuja on 5 July of the Declaration of Principles for the Resolution of the Sudanese Conflict in Darfur was an important step in the right direction, as the Declaration gives shape to future negotiations on issues such as unity, religion, power-sharing, wealth-sharing, security arrangements and the key question of land use and ownership.

21. The Security Council took an important stand against impunity in Darfur when it decided in March 2005 to refer charges of war crimes charges to the International Criminal Court. The Court should benefit from the ground already laid by the International Commission of Inquiry that I established. In addition, the United Nations High Commissioner for Human Rights and my Special Adviser on the Prevention of Genocide visited Darfur at my request and offered recommendations to the Security Council on protecting civilians and preventing massive violations of human rights and international humanitarian law.

22. Hopes were rekindled for peace in **Somalia** after the Somali National Reconciliation Conference concluded successfully in October 2004 with the formation of a Transitional Federal Government based in Nairobi. The United Nations supported the IGAD-led negotiating process and was asked to play a leading role in coordinating international support for implementing the terms of the transitional federal charter that came out of the Conference. While this has been the most inclusive peace effort to date, insecurity and ongoing disputes have prevented the Transitional Federal Government from relocating to Somalia. Seeing a need for higher profile United Nations leadership, I appointed a Special Representative, who will head an expanded United Nations Political Office for Somalia.

23. Efforts to end the violence in northern **Uganda** edged forward in December 2004 with the first face-to-face meeting between the Government of Uganda and the "Lord's Resistance Army". Those efforts, facilitated by a national mediator and supported by the United Nations and others in the international community, continued in 2005 with a view to finding a peaceful resolution to the 19-year-old conflict.

24. Political transitions were marred by violence in some African countries, prompting good offices efforts by the United Nations and others to prevent disputes from escalating into armed conflicts. The United Nations supported regional initiatives by the Economic Community of West African States (ECOWAS) and the African Union to ensure respect for constitutionality during the transitional process in Togo upon the sudden death of President Gnassingbé Eyadema. The United Nations peacebuilding offices in **Guinea-Bissau** and the **Central African Republic** were active in promoting peaceful transitions in those countries. I dispatched a Special Envoy to Guinea-Bissau to help ensure that presidential elections were conducted peacefully and transparently in June.

25. I continued to work closely with the Heads of State of **Cameroon** and **Nigeria** in peacefully settling their territorial dispute. In a three-way meeting in May, both Presidents renewed to me their commitment to moving the process forward in accordance with the ruling of the International Court of Justice. The United Nations also continued to help **Equatorial Guinea** and **Gabon** mediate a settlement of their dispute over the island of Mbanie.

26. As called for in the July 2004 report of the Security Council mission to **West Africa**, my Special Representative for West Africa continued to hold regular meetings of the heads of the United Nations presences in the region. He pursued preventive diplomacy missions to help defuse tension in several countries, while also engaging ECOWAS, Governments, civil society organizations and donors in developing an integrated regional conflict-prevention strategy.

27. Civilians bore the brunt of continued fighting in **Colombia** With some 2 million internally displaced persons, the situation has not improved. Violence increased in the first half of 2005, particularly attacks against indigenous communities. Regrettably, peacemaking efforts

did not lead to a resumption of negotiations. While allowing the mandate of my Special Adviser to expire in April, given the unfavourable climate for peace talks, I made it clear that United Nations good offices remained available to Colombia.

28. The United Nations Verification Mission in **Guatemala** closed at the end of 2004, successfully completing 10 years of dedicated support to the Guatemalan peace process As a follow-on mechanism to strengthen human rights and the rule of law, the Office of the United Nations High Commissioner for Human Rights agreed with the Government to establish an office in Guatemala. On the other hand, the Constitutional Court rejected a 2004 agreement between the Government and the United Nations to create a special investigative commission on illegal groups and clandestine security organizations.

29. Following the outcome of the April referendums in **Cyprus**, my good offices were dormant, and I encouraged all parties to engage in a period of reflection. In late May and early June 2005, the Under-Secretary-General for Political Affairs visited Cyprus, Greece and Turkey to ascertain the views of all parties in order to assist me in determining the priority, resources and intensity with which to pursue my good offices in the future.

30. I continue to be encouraged by the steady and meaningful progress achieved by **India** and **Pakistan** in their bilateral dialogue. The launch, in April 2005, of the landmark bus service across the line of control was a powerful gesture of peace. Leaders of the two countries assured me of their commitment to working to resolve all outstanding issues, including that of Jammu and Kashmir.

31. In **Nepal**, the United Nations system is making efforts to strengthen its presence and ability to respond to the deteriorating situation caused by the ongoing conflict and political crisis. I hope that the establishment of a monitoring presence of the Office of the High Commissioner for Human Rights will lead to improvements in human rights, which in turn could enhance the prospects for peace talks. In my contacts with King Gyanendra, I continue to urge a prompt return to constitutional rule and to reiterate the readiness of the United Nations to help to peacefully resolve the conflict. As part of such efforts, my Special Adviser visited Nepal from 10 to 15 July and met with King Gyanendra, senior Government officials, leaders of political parties and a cross-section of representatives of Nepalese society.

32. Insecurity grew in **Central Asia**, where there was political upheaval in Kyrgyzstan in

March and an outbreak of violence in Uzbekistan in May. I informed the members of the Security Council of my intention to establish in Turkmenistan the United Nations Regional Centre for Preventative Diplomacy for Central Asia as a response to the growing instability and as a tool for strengthening cooperation on issues ranging from the fight against drug trafficking and terrorism to strengthening democratic institutions and respect for human rights. In Tajikistan, with assistance from the United Nations Tajikistan Office of Peacebuilding (UNTOP), the Government took further steps to consolidate the peace.

33. During a visit to **Sri Lanka** in January 2005, I encouraged a collective commitment to recovering from the Indian Ocean tsunami tragedy and to reinvigorating the peace process. The United Nations continued to support efforts backed by the Government of Norway to revive peace negotiations and stands ready to assist the process in any way necessary.

34. The United Nations Observer Mission in **Bougainville** concluded its mandate successfully in June 2005 following peaceful, transparent elections and the inauguration of the first autonomous Bougainville Government. With these achievements, Bougainville has reached a major milestone in its peace process.

35. My good offices efforts in **Myanmar** continued, albeit with little progress. My Special Envoy has not been able to visit the country since March 2004. I met Senior General Than Shwe, Chairman of the State Peace and Development Council, during the Asia-Africa Summit in Jakarta in April and emphasized that the transition process must include all parties.

36. In **Indonesia**, I am hopeful that peace talks between the Government and the Free Aceh Movement, facilitated by the Chairman of the Board of the Crisis Management Initiative and former President of Finland, will succeed. Regarding the serious human rights violations committed in 1999 in **Timor-Leste**, I established an Independent Commission of Experts in February to review the prosecution of those crimes. The Commission submitted its report to me at the end of May and I transmitted it to the Security Council. I still firmly believe that the perpetrators must be brought to justice.

37. I remain concerned about the situation on the **Korean peninsula**. I am pleased, however, that after a long period of intensive diplomatic efforts to revitalize the Beijing process, the Governments concerned demonstrated flexibility and goodwill and agreed to resume the six-party talks. I will continue doing my best to mobilize international support for this multilateral approach towards a nuclear-free peninsula. I will

also look for practical ways in which the Organization can strengthen its humanitarian and development work in the Democratic People's Republic of Korea.

38. Meanwhile, in seven countries of Africa, Latin America and Asia—**Ecuador, Ghana, Guyana, Kenya, Namibia, Yemen** and **Zimbabwe**— a joint programme of the Department of Political Affairs and the United Nations Development Programme (undp) was actively helping Governments, political parties and members of civil society to acquire the skills they need to resolve disputes peacefully before they lead to violence. Separately, my Special Adviser on the Prevention of Genocide worked to develop a system for early warning of situations potentially involving massive violations of human rights and international humanitarian law.

39. As requested by the Security Council in 2004, I intend, by October, to present an action plan for the implementation throughout the United Nations system of resolution 1325 (2000), by which the Council called upon the Organization and its Member States to involve women more systematically and at the highest levels in the pursuit of international peace and security.

Peacekeeping and peacebuilding

40. The past year has brought tremendous challenges for United Nations peacekeeping, whose scale of operations has reached a historic high. Even as major commitments in Sierra Leone and Timor-Leste were reduced, the Security Council established a new 10,000-person-strong peacekeeping operation in the Sudan. Approximately 80,000 military, civilian police and civilian personnel served in 16 peacekeeping operations and in the special political missions in Afghanistan and Timor-Leste.

41. I was deeply disturbed by the reports during the year of sexual exploitation and abuse committed by United Nations peacekeepers in several missions, including in the Democratic Republic of the Congo. I have enacted a policy of zero tolerance towards such offences, which applies to all personnel engaged in United Nations operations. I strongly encourage Member States to support the enforcement of this policy with respect to their national contingents.

42. The challenges facing the new operation in the **Sudan** are enormous, given the complexity of the situation, the potential for interference from "spoilers" outside the peace process, the sheer size of Africa's largest country, the absence of infrastructure in many areas and the prevalence of landmines. Creating conditions for the safe and sustainable return of more than 500,000 refugees and some 4 million internally displaced

persons will be one of the keys to consolidating peace. Despite these challenges, I was encouraged during my visit to the region in May by the commitment of the parties to the Comprehensive Peace Agreement. Implementation will not come without a price. Governments must deliver on the generous pledges of support they made to the Sudan at the April 2005 donor conference in Oslo.

43. In **Côte d'Ivoire**, many of the provisions of the Linas-Marcoussis Agreement signed by the Ivorian parties in January 2003 have yet to be implemented. The November 2004 military operation by the National Armed Forces of Côte d'Ivoire against Forces nouvelles positions in the north of the country and the ensuing violence in Abidjan and elsewhere dealt a severe blow to the peace process. The United Nations is working in close cooperation with the African Union and ECOWAS in support of the peace process. The United Nations Operation in Côte d'Ivoire is playing an important role in enhancing security. The mission is also monitoring the use of the media to incite hate and violence as well as the arms embargo imposed by the Security Council in November 2004. The mediation efforts of the President of South Africa, initiated on behalf of the African Union after the November 2004 crisis, resulted in an agreement signed in Pretoria on 6 April, which calls upon the United Nations to play a major role in the disarmament, demobilization and reintegration of combatants, the preparation of presidential elections, scheduled for October, and the restoration of security in the north. However, implementation of the Pretoria Agreement has proceeded only slowly. In July I appointed a High Representative for the Elections in Côte d'Ivoire, who will certify all stages of the electoral process and verify that the elections are free, fair and transparent.

44. In **Liberia**, steady progress has been made with the support of the United Nations Mission in Liberia (UNMIL) and the United Nations country team in disarming, demobilizing, rehabilitating and reintegrating ex-combatants and in starting the large-scale return of refugees and internally displaced persons. Preparations for the 11 October elections remained on course, and the restructuring of the Liberian police service also advanced. The National Transitional Government of Liberia made slow progress in restoring administration throughout the country. It will need continued assistance so that it can deliver basic services and extend its authority nationwide while addressing concerns about the lack of transparency in the collection and use of public revenues.

45. While undergoing further personnel reductions, the United Nations Mission in **Sierra Leone** continued to make progress in accomplishing the benchmarks established for it by the Security Council, which include strengthening the capacity of the armed forces and police to maintain security and stability; consolidating State authority throughout the country; and helping UNMIL to fully deploy in neighbouring Liberia. After assessing the situation, I recommended that the presence of the United Nations Mission in Sierra Leone (UNAMSIL) be extended for a final period of six months, until the end of 2005. A strong and integrated presence of the United Nations system will be needed after the departure of UNAMSIL in order to help Sierra Leone consolidate peace. In collaboration with the Government of Sierra Leone, the Office of the Special Adviser on Africa convened a conference on disarmament, demobilization, reintegration and stability in Freetown from 21 to 23 June. The conference focused on examining the extent to which current disarmament, demobilization and reintegration programmes genuinely contribute to stability and identifying the necessary preconditions for the success of such programmes.

46. I regret that no progress was made in overcoming the deadlock in **Western Sahara**. The Security Council twice extended the mandate of the United Nations Mission for the Referendum in Western Sahara (MINURSO), which currently runs to October 2005. I continue to stand ready to help the parties move towards a political solution that would permit the people of Western Sahara to exercise their right to self-determination. Meanwhile, MINURSO continued to support confidence-building measures led by the United Nations High Commissioner for Refugees, including the exchange of family visits between Western Sahara and the Tindouf area refugee camps in Algeria.

47. The **Burundi** peace process advanced considerably, following the deployment of the United Nations Operation in Burundi (UNOB) in June 2004. After twice being postponed, the referendum on a post-transitional constitution was held successfully on 28 February 2005, with support from UNOB. Communal elections were successfully concluded in June, despite some violence at polling stations in two western provinces. The three-year transitional period was extended to 26 August 2005. By mid-year more than 10,000 former combatants had participated in the disarmament, demobilization and reintegration programme. Laws establishing a new integrated army and police force were promulgated, and the cantonment process was completed in May. The armed parties and movements that signed the Arusha Peace and Reconciliation Agreement registered as political parties. Improved security eased the return and reintegration of refugees and internally displaced persons.

48. Stalemate persisted in the peace process between **Eritrea** and **Ethiopia**, although relative calm prevailed in the temporary security zone and its adjacent areas. The United Nations Mission in Ethiopia and Eritrea continued to monitor the zone, chairing the Military Coordination Commission and coordinating humanitarian, human rights and demining activities, including the clearance of roads. It is imperative that the parties begin a peaceful dialogue to address outstanding issues while proceeding to demarcate the border without further delay.

49. In the **Democratic Republic of the Congo**, despite some progress by the Transitional Government in extending its authority, power-sharing was complicated by the fragile relations among its members. Some progress was made in preparing for elections, although necessary legislation had not been adopted. The United Nations Organization Mission in the Democratic Republic of the Congo (MONUC) worked to ensure that the country's constitutional framework and its electoral laws were consistent with internationally accepted principles. The Mission also helped to strengthen the operational capacity of the Congolese National Police. On 13 May 2005 the National Assembly approved a draft constitution, to be put to a referendum later in the year. The transitional period was extended by six months, through December. Voter registration commenced on 20 June in Kinshasa.

50. United Nations peacekeepers were able to take a more robust approach towards protecting civilians after the Security Council, in October 2004, authorized the deployment of 5,900 additional troops and civilian police to reinforce the Mission's military and security capacity. Combined military and political pressure resulted in the disarmament of 14,000 militiamen in the Ituri district. Regrettably, 11 peacekeepers were killed in the line of duty.

51. The March 2005 announcement by the Forces démocratique de libération du Rwanda (FDLR) of its intention to renounce violence and to enter the process of disarmament, demobilization and reintegration was an important development. Despite MONUC preparations for repatriating the remaining FDLR combatants, there had been no tangible progress since the announcement. Meanwhile, the United Nations High Commissioner for Refugees continued to help repatriate Rwandan refugees from the rainforest of the eastern part of the Democratic Republic of the Congo.

52. In **Afghanistan**, progress continued in implementing the Bonn Agreement's benchmarks, with the support of the United Nations Assistance Mission in Afghanistan. President Hamid Karzai and a new cabinet took office in December 2004, following presidential elections held without major security incidents. The benchmarks will be completed later in the year, following parliamentary and provincial elections scheduled for September 2005. Nevertheless, Afghan institutions of security and justice and the provision of basic services are still extremely weak and dependent on the international community. Opium production has increased. Accordingly, I am giving thought to a possible post-Bonn agenda, to be worked out in close consultation with the Afghan authorities and their international partners.

53. The United Nations Interim Force in **Lebanon** continued to monitor the Blue Line between Israel and Lebanon. The past year has seen a limited number of armed exchanges between Hizbollah and the Israel Defense Forces, the worst of which resulted in the death of an Israeli soldier and a United Nations military observer. Israel frequently violated Lebanese airspace and, in a new development, Hizbollah drones twice penetrated Israeli airspace. My representatives in the region and I have continued to urge the parties to respect the Blue Line and to abide fully by their obligations. We have also continued to emphasize the pressing need for the Lebanese Government to exert control over the use of force throughout its entire territory and to prevent attacks from Lebanon across the Blue Line.

54. In **Timor-Leste**, the United Nations continued to provide capacity-building assistance in public administration, law enforcement, democratic governance and human rights, while the role of United Nations agencies increased in those areas. The United Nations Office in Timor-Leste was established by the Security Council with a one-year mandate to 20 May 2006, succeeding the United Nations Mission of Support in East Timor. The operation was further reduced and its tasks revised to enable a smooth transition, by the end of the mandate, from a special political mission to a framework for sustainable development assistance.

55. The United Nations Observer Mission in **Georgia** continued to monitor the ceasefire between the Georgian and Abkhaz sides and to promote a comprehensive political settlement of the conflict. After elections produced a new leadership in Sukhumi, both sides met again under United Nations auspices in April 2005 and agreed to resume dialogue on issues related to security, the return of displaced persons and economic cooperation.

56. The United Nations Interim Administration Mission in **Kosovo** transferred additional powers to the provisional institutions of self-government. The new Kosovo Government and the provisional institutions showed a greater commitment to implementing the Standards for Kosovo, which are central to the policy of the international community in Kosovo and which aim to lay foundations for a sustainable multi-ethnic, democratic society in which all can live in dignity and without fear. On 3 June I appointed a Special Envoy to carry out a comprehensive review of Kosovo, as indicated in my recent report on the United Nations Interim Administration Mission in Kosovo, endorsed by the Security Council on 27 May. The comprehensive review is being carried out in accordance with resolution 1244 (1999) and the relevant presidential statements of the Security Council. It consists of consultations with the parties and the international community and is broad in scope in order to assess the current situation and the conditions for the possible next steps in the process.

57. The United Nations Stabilization Mission in **Haiti** (MINUSTAH) continued to carry out its mandate to help ensure a secure and stable environment within which the constitutional and political processes can go forward. Despite ongoing criminality, overall security conditions improved gradually following successful operations by MINUSTAH troops and police, jointly with the Haitian National Police. Preparations are under way to help organize presidential, legislative and local elections in the third quarter of 2005. The lack of a legal framework impeded the disarmament, demobilization and reintegration of former combatants. Moreover, the Transitional Government maintained its ambiguous position vis-à-vis the former military. The human rights situation remained of utmost concern.

58. The Security Council endorsed my recommendations for an amended concept of operations and force level of the United Nations Peacekeeping Force in **Cyprus**, including the downsizing of the military personnel and an increase in its police component. The mission was extended with the new concept of operations and force strength until 15 December 2005.

Cooperation with regional organizations

59. Regional organizations have become essential partners of the United Nations in promoting international peace and security. The sixth high-level meeting between the United Nations and regional organizations, held in New York on

25 and 26 July 2005, provided an important opportunity to strengthen those bonds.

60. Cooperation was particularly strong in Africa, where in many cases the United Nations assumed a supporting role in peacemaking and preventive action led by the African Union and African subregional organizations, such as ECOWAS and IGAD. In Darfur and elsewhere, we have seen how peacekeeping by regional organizations is making a growing and valuable contribution. The United Nations and the African Union are working together closely through the deployment of a United Nations assistance cell in Addis Ababa, through close cooperation between the Special Representatives of the two organizations in Khartoum and ever more closely on the ground in Darfur. Staff exchange programmes were conducted with the African Union and ECOWAS, and discussions are under way for similar arrangements with the Economic Community of Central African States. The increased regional role in peacekeeping also implies new requirements for coordination, cooperation and assistance from external partners, as discussed in my report of November 2004 on enhancement of African peacekeeping capacity. It is important that such capacity be developed in a way that complements the unique and indispensable resource of United Nations peacekeeping.

61. In November 2004 I attended the first Summit of Heads of State and Government of the International Conference on the Great Lakes Region, held in Dar es Salaam under the auspices of the United Nations and the African Union. The Summit adopted a declaration of principles that addressed the interlinked issues of peace, security, development, governance and humanitarian affairs.

62. Cooperation with the European Union deepened over the past year, as demonstrated by my presence in December 2004 at the European Council in Brussels and the meetings held by the Deputy Secretary-General in Strasbourg and Brussels in February 2005 with officials from the European Parliament, the European Commission and the Council of the European Union. Working-level dialogue also continued, permitting the sharing of political assessments and fostering greater coordination on the ground.

63. Cooperation in economic and social fields has intensified as well. Under a framework agreement reached in May 2004 between the European Commission and 10 United Nations entities, strategic partnership agreements have thus far been signed with the International Labour Organization (ILO), the World Health Organization (WHO), UNDP, the Food and Agriculture Organization of the United Nations (FAO) and the Office of the United Nations High Commissioner for Refugees (UNHCR).

64. The United Nations and the European Union continued their collaboration in peace operations on the ground, including in particular in the Democratic Republic of the Congo and in Kosovo. This was supplemented by ongoing dialogue on policy issues, including meetings of the United Nations-European Union steering committee in November 2004 and June 2005 and United Nations participation in a European Union peacekeeping "exercise study" in April 2005.

65. Contacts on peace and security in southeastern Asia increased between the United Nations and the Association of Southeast Asian Nations. The United Nations and the Commonwealth of Independent States (CIS) sought to strengthen cooperation in the area of conflict prevention. A memorandum of understanding was signed to that effect between the UNTOP and the CIS Executive Secretariat.

Terrorism

66. Terrorism is a threat to all that the United Nations stands for: respect for human rights, the rule of law, the protection of civilians, tolerance among peoples and nations and the peaceful resolution of conflict. The United Nations must speak loudly and clearly in denouncing terrorism and be an effective international forum for combating it.

67. In an address to the International Summit on Democracy, Terrorism and Security, held in Madrid in March 2005, I set out a five-part strategy to combat terrorism. I stressed that terrorism was neither an acceptable nor an effective way to advance any cause and urged Member States to conclude a comprehensive convention against terrorism. I also emphasized that the fight against terrorism must not infringe on human rights and fundamental freedoms.

68. Since 2001 I have sought to prioritize the Organization's activities in combating terrorism and to provide strategic guidance in order to ensure that the United Nations system functions more coherently and effectively in the struggle against terrorism. As I indicated in my remarks in Madrid, departments and agencies across the United Nations can and must contribute to implementing a comprehensive strategy against terrorism. I have recently established an implementation task force, under my office, to coordinate this work.

69. Cooperation is particularly important among the United Nations bodies most directly engaged in the fight against terrorism—including Security Council subsidiary organs and their

expert panels, the Counter-Terrorism Committee Executive Directorate and the Terrorism Prevention Branch of the United Nations Office on Drugs and Crime. In the same vein, and given the increasing links between terrorism and drug trafficking, I continue to urge Member States to sign and ratify the 13 existing anti-terrorism conventions—including the International Convention for the Suppression of Acts of Nuclear Terrorism adopted by the General Assembly in April 2005—and to work closely to implement them.

Electoral assistance

70. The past year witnessed several landmark elections in countries going through complex transitions to peace—elections in which the United Nations played a key role, both by giving technical assistance and by facilitating negotiations leading to the establishment of electoral institutions and laws. Credible elections have become an essential element in peacemaking, peacebuilding and the prevention of conflict.

71. Eighteen months of intense preparations culminated successfully in the Afghan presidential elections of October 2004. Despite threats and intimidation from extremist groups targeting the electoral process, voter turnout was high even in the most vulnerable conflict areas. Women participated heavily, determined to take part in the political life of their country, and were assisted by an extensive voter registration exercise and targeted education campaigns. Building on that success, the United Nations will be assisting with the coming parliamentary and provincial elections, which had to be postponed until September 2005 owing to technical and financial difficulties.

72. United Nations electoral experts also provided crucial support to the historic election in Iraq on 30 January 2005 for its Transitional National Assembly. The high voter turnout defied expectations, given the levels of violence and intimidation from insurgents attempting to disrupt the process.

73. Electoral support was important to the mandates of peacekeeping operations and the political agreements in numerous countries, including Burundi, Côte d'Ivoire, the Democratic Republic of the Congo, Haiti and Liberia. Assistance was provided to establish and develop national electoral institutions; to institute proper electoral legislation and an effective system for complaints and appeals; to promote civil and voter registration; and to carry out civic education and media campaigns.

74. Of course, an election by itself cannot resolve deep-seated problems, particularly in a society traumatized by conflict. A United Nations University study shows that ill-timed or poorly designed elections in volatile situations can actually fuel chaos and reverse progress towards democracy. Exacerbating existing tensions, they can result in support for extremists or encourage patterns of voting that reflect wartime allegiances.

Disarmament

75. New challenges and threats heightened international concern about weapons of mass destruction. Among them were cases of non-compliance with nuclear non-proliferation commitments, evidence of the existence of a clandestine nuclear network, ambivalent commitment to disarmament and the threat of weapons of mass destruction falling into the hands of terrorists. Multilateral instruments to prevent proliferation and to promote disarmament must be revitalized if they are to continue to contribute to international peace and security.

76. In May the 2005 Review Conference of the Parties to the Treaty on the Non-Proliferation of Nuclear Weapons failed to reach agreement on any substantive issues. The opportunity was missed to address the most pressing problems of not only the nuclear non-proliferation regime, but also of international security more broadly. I urge Member States to act with greater determination on this important issue and to give it further consideration in the coming months.

77. The Conference on Disarmament remains deadlocked. It will fail to regain its importance as the multilateral negotiating body on disarmament treaties unless Member States proceed to substantive negotiations on items relevant to the current international security environment.

78. States continued their discussions to promote better implementation of the Biological Weapons Convention. While steady progress has been achieved in the destruction of declared chemical arsenals, a great deal more remains to be done. The Comprehensive Nuclear-Test-Ban Treaty requires further efforts to realize its entry into force. There has been progress in the substantive examination of the 118 national reports submitted so far under Security Council resolution 1540(2004) on the non-proliferation of weapons of mass destruction. Significant progress has been made towards establishing a nuclear-weapon-free zone in Central Asia.

79. Estimated global military expenditures exceeded $1 trillion in 2004 and were projected to keep rising. While participation has improved in the United Nations Register of Conventional Arms and the Standardized Instrument for Reporting Military Expenditures, greater progress

with a view to universal participation is needed, particularly on military expenditures.

80. I am encouraged by the recent agreement reached on the text of a politically binding international instrument to enable States to identify and trace in a timely and reliable manner illicit small arms and light weapons, to be presented to the General Assembly for adoption at its sixtieth session. Its acceptance is another positive step forward in the realization of the political commitments made in the United Nations Programme of Action to Prevent, Combat and Eradicate the Illicit Trade in Small Arms and Light Weapons in All Its Aspects. I urge Member States to take all action necessary to ensure the early and effective implementation of the instrument. Its adoption also augurs well for maintaining the momentum of active dialogue among Member States on tackling the issue of illicit brokering in small arms and light weapons.

81. The Nairobi Summit on a Mine-Free World, held in November and December 2004, provided the first opportunity for a review by the parties of the 1997 Convention on the Prohibition of the Use, Stockpiling, Production and Transfer of Anti-Personnel Mines and on Their Destruction. The resulting Nairobi Action Plan for 2005-2009 set as its top priority meeting the deadlines for clearing mined areas.

Sanctions

82. During the past year, the Security Council created two new sanctions committees: on Côte d'Ivoire, pursuant to resolution 1572 (2004), and on the Sudan, pursuant to resolution 1591(2005). The measures imposed by the two resolutions were designed to provide incentives for peace, in that arms embargos were immediately applied for the entire territory of Côte d'Ivoire and the Darfur region of the Sudan, whereas sanctions targeted at individuals and related entities (in the form of a travel ban and assets freeze) were not to enter into force until 30 days after the adoption of the respective resolutions. This gap of one month provided an incentive to the parties to re-engage quickly in the peace process in order to avoid the application of further sanctions measures. Although the Côte d'Ivoire and Sudan committees have not yet designated any individuals or entities, the possibility serves as a continued incentive.

83. Targeted sanctions lists have been drawn up by and continue to play an important role in the work of the Al-Qaida and Taliban sanctions Committee, the Liberia sanctions Committee and the Security Council Committee established pursuant to resolution 1518 (2003), which is concerned with individuals and entities associated

with the former Government of Iraq. By the end of 2004, the preparation of new or revised guidelines was under way in the Al-Qaida and Taliban, Liberia and Côte d'Ivoire sanctions committees. The adoption of revised guidelines would assist the committees concerned in managing targeted sanctions lists in a uniform and transparent way.

84. In a related development, the Security Council, in its resolution 1566(2004), decided to establish a working group to examine practical measures to be imposed upon individuals, groups or entities involved in or associated with terrorist activities, other than those designated by the Al-Qaida and Taliban sanctions Committee. The resolution also raised the possibility of establishing an international fund to compensate victims of terrorist acts and their families.

85. The Security Council continued to receive detailed information regarding its sanctions regimes from expert groups tasked with monitoring States' compliance and investigating alleged sanctions violations. These included the Panel of Experts on Somalia, the Analytical Support and Sanctions Monitoring Team on Al-Qaida and the Taliban, the Panel of Experts on Liberia, the Group of Experts on the Democratic Republic of the Congo, the Group of Experts on Côte d'Ivoire, and the Panel of Experts concerning the Sudan. More attention should be paid to implementing the valuable recommendations of these expert groups.

Chapter II

Cooperating for development

Achieving the Millennium Development Goals

86. The framework for the development activities of the United Nations provided by the Millennium Declaration and the eight Millennium Development Goals was given added focus and impetus by the issuance of the report of the United Nations Millennium Project, *Investing in Development: A Practical Plan to Achieve the Millennium Development Goals*, as well as my report for the High-level Plenary Meeting, "In larger freedom: towards development, security and human rights for all" (A/59/2005 and Add.1-3). The Millennium Project report offered a comprehensive analysis and a set of proposals on how to achieve the Millennium Development Goals at the country, regional and global levels. I welcomed the proposals and presented Member States with a set of priorities to move the development agenda forward.

87. During the past months, the member agencies of the United Nations Development

Group (UNDG) continued to implement its four-pillar strategy to support the achievement of the Millennium Development Goals. The four pillars are: *(a)* integrating the Goals into all aspects of the United Nations system's work at the country level; *(b)* assisting developing countries in preparing Millennium Development Goal progress reports; *(c)* working with the Millennium Project and the Millennium Campaign to build global support for the Goals; and *(d)* supporting advocacy and awareness-raising efforts based on national strategies and national needs.

88. The Millennium Campaign has been mobilizing and reinforcing political support for the Millennium Declaration by working with parliamentary networks, local authorities, the media, faith-based organizations, youth organizations, the business sector, non-governmental organizations (NGOs) and other entities. In 2004 the Campaign and its partners in civil society helped to secure a major breakthrough with the launch of the Global Call to Action against Poverty, the largest campaign coalition against poverty assembled in recent years. While the Campaign was one among several partners who made this achievement possible, its advocacy and facilitating role did make a significant contribution to the coalition-building process.

89. To track global, regional and national progress, a wide-ranging system of monitoring and reporting has also been put in place. Monitoring progress towards the Millennium Development Goals at the global level has involved the collaboration of international agencies and regional commissions and close consultation with national experts and statisticians. The Inter-Agency and Expert Group on Millennium Development Goal Indicators coordinates the efforts of United Nations entities and national statistical services, as well as regional and international statistical bodies from outside the United Nations system. It coordinates the compilation and analysis of the indicators, reviewing methodologies and supporting countries in the collection, analysis and reporting of data for Millennium Development Goal indicators. The results of this work have been reflected in the statistics and analysis prepared as a basis for my annual reports to the General Assembly on the implementation of the Millennium Declaration and in the Millennium Development Goal indicators country series, an annually revised database comprising the most up-to-date series provided by the designated lead agency for the indicator in question. On 9 June I launched *The Millennium Development Goals Report 2005*, containing the most comprehensive and up-to-date statistics on targets and indicators associated with the Millennium Development

Goals compiled through a collaborative effort by 25 United Nations agencies and global organizations.

90. The availability of high-quality statistical data and the capacity of Governments, donors and international organizations to systematically measure, monitor and report reliable indicators lies at the heart of development policy and the achievement of the Millennium Development Goals. An important contribution to building national statistical capacity is the Organization's work in providing technical assistance to national statistical offices and training of national statisticians in the production and use of indicators. DevInfo, a software tool developed by the United Nations system for the collection and analysis of both standard and specific user-defined indicators, is finding wider application. Governments, United Nations country teams, academic institutions and others increasingly make use of it to provide standardized and comparable reporting on the Millennium Development Goals. Regional commissions have also been providing support to national capacity-building in monitoring and reporting on the Goals through workshops and tools such as an Arabic version of the UNDG handbook "Indicators for Monitoring the Millennium Development Goals". To build national capacity to monitor the Goals and to improve the use of evidence-based methodologies for the management of development policy, UNDP developed a project on building capacity and statistical literacy for Millennium Development Goal monitoring at the country level, which is moving steadily into its implementation phase.

91. UNDP is the lead agency for monitoring at the country level. It has been assisting Governments and country teams in the preparation and dissemination of their reports. As at March 2005, 93 countries and territories had produced 104 such reports, ranging from middle-income countries to some of the lowest-income least developed countries. Eight countries have produced their second reports (Albania, Armenia, Bolivia, Cambodia, Egypt, Lithuania, Mauritius and Senegal) and two other countries, Cameroon and Viet Nam, have released their third annual reports. Three regional Millennium Development Goal reports were published in 2004 in cooperation with other United Nations entities, complementing national reports with data and analysis on the status and trends in the Arab States, Central Europe and the Caribbean region, bringing the total number of regional reports prepared to date to six.

92. A major contribution of the United Nations development system to achievement of the Millennium Development Goals has been the

growing number of ongoing and new inter-agency initiatives. In response to the challenge of fighting hunger and achieving food security, United Nations food and agricultural agencies have strengthened their collaboration. Jointly, the agencies are pursuing a twin-track approach that seeks to provide direct assistance to the hungry to meet their immediate food and nutrition needs while simultaneously addressing longer-term agricultural and rural development issues by providing support for sustainable growth, including improved infrastructure, sound natural resource management and increased access to land, water, credit and social services.

93. The majority, or three quarters of the world's poor women, men and children, live and work in rural areas. In order to achieve the Millennium Development Goals, it is essential that poverty reduction interventions focus on the rural poor and that significant investments be made in rural and agricultural development. Some parts of the United Nations system are pursuing this goal by strengthening the capacity of the rural poor and their organizations, improving equitable access to productive natural resources and technology and increasing access to financial services and markets. Other parts are investing the vast majority of their resources in countries reported by the United Nations to be struggling the most to achieve the Millennium Development Goals and countries where a lack of data suggests major capacity problems.

94. The capacity to innovate can be developed to contribute to the poverty reduction and sustainability targets of the Millennium Development Goals. The United Nations University Institute for New Technologies in Maastricht, the Netherlands, examines how this can be done by looking at successful examples, such as flower production in Colombia and Kenya, shrimp production in Bangladesh and horticulture in Ghana, activities which, starting from a base of almost zero 20 years ago, are now among the top export earners for their countries.

95. There is certainly a need to address urban poverty by promoting the role of cities as engines of economic growth and social development. Several United Nations system organizations are working together to help eradicate poverty in urban areas, to promote sustainable urbanization and to enhance industrial development.

96. There is a need to make further efforts to ensure progress in the realization of the education-related Millennium Development Goals, namely universal primary education and the elimination of gender disparity in primary and secondary education. Various United Nations system organizations have teamed up in joint activities to help achieve those goals. A number of initiatives have been set in motion to generate sustained global commitment and support for country-level efforts in implementing Education for All, coordinated by the United Nations Educational, Scientific and Cultural Organization (UNESCO). Those initiatives include the Education for All Global Monitoring Report, which has become a standard reference document for all partners in the field of education; the Collective Consultation of NGOs on Education for All; national and regional Education for All Forums; and the annual meetings of the High-level Group on Education for All and the Working Group on Education for All. Other initiatives include the Education for All Fast-Track Initiative, which is improving efficiency in the allocation of resources to primary education service delivery, system expansion, system financing and spending for primary education; supporting the Initiative through school feeding; using the Millennium Development Goal indicators relating to education to ensure that all children have access to primary schooling in refugee camps; and a new series of reports of the United Nations Children's Fund (UNICEF) entitled "Progress for children", which are report cards on children's issues related to the Millennium Development Goals.

97. Over the years, organizations of the system have scored major successes in immunizing children and reducing child mortality. In 2004 an inter-agency working group on integrated management of childhood illness was established. The Child Survival Partnership is another multi-agency initiative aimed at providing a forum for coordinated action to address the major conditions that affect children's health. The Partnership enables Governments and other stakeholders to agree on consistent approaches and stimulates concerted efforts to implement them.

98. Organizations of the system have also long recognized that the eradication of extreme poverty and hunger cannot succeed if questions of population and reproductive health are not addressed effectively. Making sexual and reproductive health services accessible to all is essential for meeting goals related to child and maternal mortality, HIV/AIDS and gender equality and to ensuring the right of all women, men and children to the highest attainable standards of health.

99. Greater attention to the Millennium Development Goals is required in countries emerging from conflict. Within the context of the joint United Nations-World Bank needs assessments and recovery planning, the Goals provide important targets and indicators for planning the transition out of conflict. For example, relevant Mil-

lennium Development Goal targets and indicators are being used for the delivery of humanitarian relief to refugees and other displaced persons. In post-conflict countries, shorter-term humanitarian relief must help form the basis for longer-term development efforts to achieve the Goals.

The United Nations development agenda

100. While the Millennium Development Goals provide a compelling platform from which to mobilize the international community, they must be pursued as part of a larger development agenda that also encompasses the needs of the middle-income developing countries, questions of growing inequality and the wider dimensions of human development. Social integration and issues that require long-term approaches must be addressed equally, such as the differential impact of globalization and increasing the participation of developing countries in global economic governance.

101. The aforementioned issues and the basic objective of integrating economic, social and environmental goals were addressed in depth by the United Nations conferences and summits. Their outcomes reflect a broad-based consensus that various parts of the United Nations system should pursue the full scope of the United Nations development agenda, including the Millennium Development Goals. Progress towards the goals thus set is reviewed in detail each year by the functional commissions of the Economic and Social Council, while the Council itself takes a cross-cutting, integrated view.

102. At its forty-third session, held in New York from 9 to 18 February 2005, the Commission for Social Development reviewed progress in implementing the commitments of the World Summit for Social Development over the past 10 years, including global performance in promoting full and productive employment. Various United Nations system entities are working on such projects as making employment part of United Nations country programming processes in developing countries, fighting rural unemployment and helping with the development of skills. The Youth Employment Network, which I launched in 2001 in partnership with the heads of the World Bank and ILO, has been promoting the preparation of national action plans for youth employment in an increasing number of countries.

103. Promoting social integration was one of the core issues addressed by the World Summit for Social Development in 1995. The Copenhagen Declaration, a key outcome of the Summit, contains a specific commitment to advance social integration by fostering societies that are stable, safe, just and tolerant and that respect diversity. The Millennium Declaration also subsumes social integration in its synthesis of peace, security, development and human rights. While some progress has been made in such areas as accession to legal instruments dealing with economic, social and cultural rights and the elimination of discrimination, the concept of social integration has yet to be fully incorporated into the general development discourse. The challenge is to ensure that the concept of social integration is at the centre of all policies and to find practical ways and means of achieving a "society for all".

104. The Commission for Social Development emphasized the need for more integrated efforts to achieve the Millennium Development Goals and implement the broader Copenhagen commitments. There remains a shortage of comprehensive and systematic national plans to address the special concerns of youth and vulnerable groups, including indigenous peoples, the elderly, those living with disabilities and internally displaced persons. There is thus a need to ensure that policy interventions to achieve the Millennium Development Goals of halving poverty and hunger should take into account the needs and concerns of those vulnerable groups. The Department of Economic and Social Affairs supports activities to enhance social integration, overcome exclusion and increase the participation of social groups in national development and decision-making. To help implement the Madrid Plan of Action on Ageing, the main outcome of the Second World Assembly on Ageing (8-12 April 2002), the Department assisted Governments in ensuring that the older poor were explicitly integrated into development processes, including Millennium Development Goal programmes.

105. UNDG adopted, in October 2004, a Guidance Note on Durable Solutions for Displaced Persons. This marked the first time that a common policy was adopted among United Nations development actors on the importance of attaining durable solutions for displaced persons and on how to incorporate them into joint planning and implementation strategies. The Guidance Note has been included in the existing UNDG guidelines on common country assessment and in the United Nations Development Assistance Framework.

106. At its forty-ninth session, held in New York from 28 February to 11 March 2005, the Commission on the Status of Women reviewed progress towards implementation of the 1995 Beijing Declaration and Platform for Action and the outcomes of the twenty-third special session

of the General Assembly, held in 2000. Ten years after the Beijing conference, there remain many areas in which progress is lacking. For example, high rates of violence against women afflict all parts of the world, including zones of armed conflict. There is an increasing incidence of HIV/AIDS among women, gender inequality in employment, a lack of sexual and reproductive health rights and a lack of equal access under the law to land and property, among other things. The Commission's final declaration emphasized that the full and effective implementation of the Beijing Declaration and Platform for Action was essential to achieving the internationally agreed development goals, including those contained in the Millennium Declaration.

107. In order to achieve all six Education for All goals by 2015, the issues of access to and quality of education are inseparable and must be addressed concurrently and improved through both national and international initiatives. The High-level Group on Education for All, meeting in Brasilia in November 2004, focused on quality education. The United Nations Decade of Education for Sustainable Development(2005-2014), in follow-up to the World Summit on Sustainable Development, contributes to improving the quality and relevance of education.

108. Progress towards achieving the goals set in 2002 in Johannesburg, South Africa, at the World Summit on Sustainable Development continues to be made through the efforts of the United Nations system and the implementation of the various multilateral environmental agreements. The thirteenth session of the Commission on Sustainable Development, held in New York from 11 to 22 April 2005, was attended by over 75 Government ministers with such diverse portfolios as finance, development, planning, trade, housing, water, health and the environment. It focused on the multidisciplinary issues of water and sanitation and human settlements. Over 150 organizations of other major groups of stakeholders also took part in the session. Agreement was reached on a set of practical policy options intended to boost global efforts to implement the Johannesburg commitments to provide clean water, basic sanitation and decent housing.

109. The goal pledged in the Millennium Declaration of ensuring the entry into force of the Kyoto Protocol of the United Nations Framework Convention on Climate Change was finally realized in February 2005 following its ratification by the Russian Federation, thus ensuring the continuity of mitigation efforts into the next decade. The tenth session of the Conference of the Parties to the Convention, held in Buenos Aires from 6 to 17 December 2004, marking 10 years of action under the Convention, adopted a package of measures aimed at helping countries to prepare for climate change. The Stockholm Convention on Persistent Organic Pollutants held its first Conference of the Parties in Punta del Este, Uruguay, from 2 to 6 May 2005, marking the start of an ambitious international effort to rid the world of polychlorinated biphenyls, dioxins and furans, as well as nine highly dangerous pesticides, including DDT.

110. At its twenty-third session, held in Nairobi from 21 to 25 February 2005, the Governing Council of the United Nations Environment Programme (UNEP) and Global Ministerial Environment Forum gave new impetus to the implementation of the environmental agenda across a wide range. Governments also formally adopted the Bali Strategic Plan for Technology Support and Capacity-Building, which will help focus the work of UNEP, including support for developing countries, thus serving its overall objective of combating poverty by promoting the concept of "environment for development".

111. Implementing the Monterrey Consensus, the main outcome of the 2002 International Conference on Financing for Development, remains critical for furthering the global development agenda, including the Millennium Development Goals. The Monterrey Consensus recognized that economically effective and socially sensitive macroeconomic policies were needed to achieve the outcomes of United Nations conferences.

112. In April 2005 the Economic and Social Council hosted its annual special high-level meeting with the Bretton Woods institutions, the World Trade Organization (WTO) and the United Nations Conference on Trade and Development (UNCTAD). The overall theme of the meeting was "coherence, coordination and cooperation in the context of the implementation of the Monterrey Consensus: achieving the internationally agreed development goals, including those contained in the Millennium Declaration". In my view, this annual meeting is a unique platform for promoting coherence within the system on economic and financial issues in support of the United Nations development agenda, including the Millennium Development Goals. The High-level Dialogue on Financing for Development, held in New York on 27 and 28 June 2005, further contributed to identifying the tasks ahead in the overall implementation of the Monterrey Consensus, which are of particular importance in the run-up to the High-level Plenary Meeting in September.

113. The Monterrey Consensus recognized trade as a powerful driver of economic growth and poverty reduction. Various organizations of the United Nations system have been collaborat-

ing to build trade-related capacity, particularly in the least developed countries, so as to better integrate those countries into the global economy and enable them to reap greater benefits from globalization. A notable example of this collaboration is the Integrated Framework for Trade-Related Technical Assistance, combining the efforts of the International Monetary Fund (IMF), the International Trade Centre UNCTAD/WTO (ITC), UNCTAD, UNDP, the World Bank and WTO, in partnership with bilateral donors and recipient countries. The Integrated Framework supports national development plans with diagnostic studies to identify and respond to trade development needs. Experience shows that reforming formal trade policies is not enough to stimulate growth. There is a need to address a range of obstacles, including weak institutions, deficient infrastructure and trade barriers in key markets.

114. The Monterrey Consensus viewed microcredit as an innovative source of development finance. The International Year of Microcredit, 2005, which was launched by the General Assembly in November 2004, has brought together various United Nations agencies, civil society organizations and the private sector to promote microfinance and microcredit as a key instrument for reducing poverty and achieving the Millennium Development Goals.

115. An important cross-cutting dimension of the United Nations development agenda is the promotion of good governance at the global and national levels. The strong focus of UNDP on democratic governance responds to a growing demand for support from many developing countries in realization of the importance of effective, accountable and inclusive institutions and processes for achieving the Millennium Development Goals and the other internationally agreed development goals.

116. At its fourth session, held in New York from 4 to 8 April 2005, the United Nations Committee of Experts on Public Administration stressed ensuring integrity, transparency and accountability in pro-poor policies. National poverty reduction strategies offer space for an accountable and participatory process that is aligned with the United Nations development goals, including those contained in the Millennium Declaration, namely, a stable macroeconomic environment, a robust role for the private sector in line with developmental objectives and dialogue with civil society to mainstream the concerns of the poor into public policy.

117. Both the Johannesburg Declaration on Sustainable Development and the Monterrey Consensus explicitly recognized that corruption was one of the serious threats to sustainable development and called for anti-corruption measures to be put in place at all levels as a priority. The first global and legally binding convention against corruption, adopted by the General Assembly in October 2003, has been signed so far by 118 countries and ratified by 15. It will enter into force upon the deposit of the thirtieth instrument of ratification. The ratification of the Convention and its entry into force will enable States parties to employ the instrument and, consequently, to prevent, detect and combat corruption more effectively, at both the national and international levels.

118. The United Nations Office on Drugs and Crime launched a global programme against corruption in February 1999 as a vehicle to provide technical assistance to Member States. The purpose of the programme is to strengthen legal and institutional frameworks and develop policy guidance, as well as to enhance cooperation across agencies active in anti-corruption policy, advocacy and enforcement. To date, the programme is managing some 15 technical assistance projects supporting Member States in preventing and controlling corruption. The projects focus mainly on strengthening judicial integrity and criminal justice, a unique strategic niche, particularly in post-conflict States, where actions to return the rule of law have a potentially high impact and an overall stabilizing effect. The Office has also helped Member States to implement international standards to combat money-laundering and terrorist financing through direct technical assistance.

119. The cultivation of illicit drug crops remains a serious impediment to the sustainable development of some countries. Joint action between the United Nations and host Governments is undertaken to carry out annual crop surveys in the countries concerned. Those surveys provide illicit drug production trend analyses to the international community. They also make available reliable information upon which development strategies can be based in order to offer alternative sustainable livelihoods to farmers dependent on such illicit cultivation.

The special needs of Africa

120. The United Nations system continues to provide support for Africa's development. The independent panel of eminent persons that I established last year to recommend ways to mobilize international support for the New Partnership for Africa's Development (NEPAD) submitted its first report in April 2005.

121. In an effort to promote private sector involvement in the implementation of NEPAD and

to mobilize private sector resources, the Office of the Special Adviser on Africa organized two meetings, a panel discussion on promoting the domestic private sector in October 2004 and, jointly with the NEPAD secretariat, an expert group meeting on the contribution of the private sector to the implementation of the New Partnership, in March 2005. Studies presented at the latter meeting detailed the nature and scope of private sector involvement, including taking equity, forming public-private partnerships and fostering other types of joint ventures.

122. The technical staff of the Economic Commission for Africa and UNDP actively participated in the support missions of the NEPAD African Peer Review Mechanism to a number of countries, such as Ghana (May 2004), Rwanda (June 2004), Mauritius (June 2004), Kenya (July 2004) and Uganda (February 2005). Subsequent missions are planned for Mali, Mozambique and South Africa. As part of its institutional support, UNDP has been actively involved in the planning and has provided direct technical and administrative support to the African peer review panel and secretariat. It is supporting all the country preparations of member States, including institutional support to the African peer review focal points and, the setting up of national structures to oversee the process (such as national African Peer Review Mechanism commissions), as well as the organization of sensitization workshops.

123. The Department of Economic and Social Affairs has provided a wide range of technical and advisory services in support of the NEPAD governance agenda, including support to the design of the NEPAD governance and capacity-building programmes on public administration, on leadership for public sector performance and on managing conflict; strategies for mainstreaming professionalism and ethics in the African public service; strengthening Africa's parliaments; and the Africa Governance Inventory web portal, developed by the Department, which is the main organizer for the Pan-African Conference of Ministers of Public Service, a biennial meeting held in conjunction with the NEPAD secretariat.

124. The Office of the United Nations High Commissioner for Refugees convenes the United Nations sub-cluster on humanitarian response and post-conflict recovery, which advances the promotion and implementation of integrated programmes in post-conflict countries to contribute to reconstruction and sustain peace and stability. UNHCR is currently analysing 14 transitional situations in Africa in order to identify critical gaps and determine how to improve the effectiveness of its efforts. The analysis will inform future programme initiatives and contribute to the work of NEPAD, and United Nations entities.

125. The United Nations Development Fund for Women provided support for the first regional women's meeting, held in Kigali in October 2004, in preparation for the International Conference on the Great Lakes Region, convened in Dar es Salaam in November 2004. The meeting addressed the specific needs of women in matters pertaining to peace and security, democracy and governance, economic and regional integration and humanitarian and social affairs. The meeting resulted in the Kigali Declaration, which was later incorporated into the Dar es Salaam outcome document adopted by the heads of State and Government at the International Conference.

126. The Department of Economic and Social Affairs provided advisory services and sponsored technical cooperation programmes to support African Governments in meeting their obligations under international agreements and treaties, including the Beijing Platform for Action and the Convention on the Elimination of All Forms of Discrimination against Women. Those efforts were aimed in particular at enhancing national capacity to implement the Convention and at building the capacity of judges to apply international human rights law at the domestic level. The Department also worked with national machineries for the advancement of women to support countries emerging from conflict to meet their obligations under the Convention.

127. The World Food Programme (WFP) and NEPAD jointly carried out a study on national food reserve systems in Africa and how they could be improved to better contribute to improving food security and coping capacities for dealing with food crises. The United Nations Industrial Development Organization (UNIDO) provided support in the articulation of the African Productive Capacity Initiative, which was adopted by the African Union summit, in July 2004, as the policy framework for Africa's industrial development. UNESCO has developed the Literacy Initiative for Empowerment, which will be implemented in countries with an illiteracy rate of over 50 per cent or 10 million illiterates. UNEP, in partnership with the NEPAD secretariat and the African Ministerial Conference on the Environment, is assisting African countries to prepare the five subregional environmental action plans of NEPAD. The United Nations Human Settlements Programme (UN-Habitat) formulated the NEPAD cities programme as a means of achieving "quick wins". To further strengthen

the programme, the African Ministerial Conference on Housing and Urban Development, held in Durban, South Africa, from 31 January to 4 February 2005, agreed on an enhanced framework of implementation for overcoming the challenges of shelter and urbanization.

128. A cluster of United Nations agencies and entities is also supporting NEPAD in the areas of agriculture, trade and market access through knowledge management, advocacy and capacity-building. A continuing major challenge for United Nations organizations in Africa is achieving greater effectiveness, avoiding duplication and overlap, cutting costs and, more generally, improving policy and operational coherence and strengthening the regional coordination mechanism in support of the implementation of the priorities of NEPAD.

The needs of least developed countries, landlocked developing countries and small island developing States

129. The international community continues to focus on the development needs and challenges faced by the most vulnerable countries. While the overall indicators for the least developed countries, landlocked developing countries and small island developing States show improvement in many respects, progress has been uneven. At the present pace of development, many of those countries will not be able to reach the Millennium Development Goals. The Office of the High Representative for the Least Developed Countries, Landlocked Developing Countries and Small Island Developing States continued to assist me in mobilizing the efforts of all parts of the United Nations system in ensuring coordinated follow-up of the outcomes of the conferences and summits related to those groups of countries.

130. The emergence of a domestic entrepreneurial class, the strengthening of production and commercial exchange capacity and the provision of lasting debt relief are essential to allow trade to play its due role in alleviating poverty in the least developed countries. UNCTAD has contributed to this task in a variety of ways. Following the publication of its *Least Developed Countries Report 2004* on the linkages between trade and poverty alleviation, UNCTAD has continued to analyse what the international community has done for the least developed countries in the areas of trade policy, development finance and technical cooperation. UNCTAD has also been providing extensive training to and building the capacity of the least developed countries in trade negotiations and commercial diplomacy, including on issues related to accession to WTO. Jointly,

UNCTAD, UNDP, IMF, the World Bank, WTO and ITC have assisted a number of least developed countries in their efforts to mainstream trade in national development strategies, using their Integrated Framework for Trade-related Technical Assistance.

131. FAO, in providing field programme assistance to the least developed countries, met a wide range of needs, from emergency assistance and agricultural rehabilitation to policy assistance and programme support for food security, sustainable agricultural growth and rural development. UNIDO activities for the least developed countries concentrated on building productive capacity to enable those countries to integrate into the global economy. The African Productive Capacity Initiative, for example, was approved by the African Heads of State as a NEPAD component for sustainable industrial development.

132. The United Nations Capital Development Fund continued to strengthen and refine its programmes to provide greater support to the needs of least developed countries in meeting the Millennium Development Goals through its local development and microfinance programmes. In microfinance alone, the Fund approved a new $42 million seven-year initiative to tackle constraints and harness opportunities to invigorate economies and deepen the financial sectors in 20 African least developed countries. The World Intellectual Property Organization assisted least developed countries in technological capacity-building and in the areas of legislative advice, collective management of copyright and related rights and small- and medium-sized enterprise. The Least Developed Countries Fund of the Global Environment Facility provides funds for the enhancement of those countries' adaptive capacity and the implementation of their national adaptation plans of action and grants for their environmental projects.

133. At the regional level, the Economic and Social Commission for Asia and the Pacific has continued to support the most vulnerable countries through a variety of activities, such as the regional poverty alleviation programme, its project of strengthening national capabilities in poverty alleviation and conflict negotiation skills, an advocacy project on multisectoral responses to fight HIV/AIDS in Asia, capacity-building for effective participation in the multilateral trading system and external debt management.

134. With their small populations, often long maritime and air transportation routes, and mono-crop cultures, small island developing States are particularly vulnerable to the impact of both economic trends in the rest of the world and natural phenomena. The December 2004 tsu-

nami, which affected many categories of countries, served to highlight the special vulnerability of the small island developing States, which suffered enormous human and material loss. The disaster showed the importance of heeding the warning signs, coming together in advance of the calamity and sustaining a collective effort to end human misery and lay solid foundations for peace and development. I have therefore called for a global warning system, covering not only tsunamis but also other natural disasters, such as storm surges and cyclones.

135. In the aftermath of the tsunami, the United Nations and its various agencies, funds and programmes mobilized rapidly to mount a coordinated response, providing immediate humanitarian relief—food aid; water purification, emergency health and sanitation kits; temporary shelters; and supplies for emergency obstetrical care, safe blood transfusions and vaccinations—and coordinating efforts for long-term rehabilitation and reconstruction of the affected areas.

136. Coming on the heels of the tragedy, the International Meeting to Review the Implementation of the Programme of Action for the Small Island Developing States in January 2005, hosted by the Government of Mauritius with the support of the Office of the High Representative for the Least Developed Countries, Landlocked Developing Countries and Small Island Developing States, the Department of Economic and Social Affairs, UNCTAD, the regional economic commissions and UNDP, provided a timely venue for the international community to come together in renewed support of those countries. The meeting received considerable international attention and saw active participation from civil society, the private sector and other stakeholders. The social, economic and environmental vulnerabilities of the small island developing States were re-emphasized, and donor support was sought to further implement the agreed international programme for small island developing States. The Mauritius Declaration and Strategy provide a clear navigational chart for international and national efforts for the development of small island States. United Nations organizations and the small island developing States are now embarking on developing their road maps for the implementation of the Strategy.

137. The High-level Meeting on the Role of International, Regional and Subregional Organizations for the Implementation of the Almaty Programme of Action for Landlocked Developing Countries, convened by the Office of the High Representative for the Least Developed Countries, Landlocked Developing Countries and Small Island Developing States in Almaty, Kazakhstan, in March 2005, adopted a joint communiqué in which international and regional partners identified further measures to assist landlocked developing countries through coordinated strategies.

138. Landlocked developing countries incur significant additional transport costs for their exports and imports arising from inefficient transportation arrangements linked directly to their geographically disadvantaged status. During the past year, agencies of the United Nations system strengthened their partnership to implement the Almaty Programme of Action: Addressing the Needs of Landlocked Developing Countries within a New Global Framework for Transit Transport Cooperation for Landlocked and Transit Developing Countries. UNCTAD research shows that the international transport costs for imports of landlocked African countries account for an average of 20.7 per cent of the value of the imports, as compared with the world average of 5.1 per cent and the average of African countries of 12.7 per cent. In 2004, several landlocked developing countries, with advisory support from regional commissions and other United Nations entities, implemented measures to increase the efficiency of transit transport operations.

Combating HIV/AIDS

139. HIV/AIDS is both an emergency and a long-term development issue. The epidemic risks undoing past and present efforts to achieve the internationally agreed development goals, including the Millennium Development Goals, and as such it must be made a firm priority for action.

140. The Commission on Population and Development, at its thirty-eighth session, held in New York in April 2005, focused in particular on HIV/AIDS and its connection with poverty. It emphasized the need to strengthen policy and programme linkages and coordination between HIV/AIDS and sexual and reproductive health, incorporating them in national development plans, including poverty reduction strategies, as a necessary step for addressing the HIV/AIDS epidemic. The report on the impact of AIDS submitted to the Commission revealed that since the first AIDS case was diagnosed in 1981, more than 20 million people had died from the disease. As at the end of 2004, approximately 39.4 million people were living with HIV. The AIDS epidemic takes a heavy toll on women and adolescent girls, who account for some 57 per cent of all people living with HIV in sub-Saharan Africa and about 50 per cent on average worldwide. The AIDS epidemic is spreading as a result of underlying causes, including the disempowerment of women and stigma and discrimination against

people living with HIV. In addition, the vast majority of people in need of treatment lack access to affordable antiretroviral drugs.

141. The United Nations continues to develop joint and comprehensive approaches to HIV/AIDS, including in the areas of prevention, treatment, care, the fight against discrimination and the mitigation of impact. Significant progress has been made in expanding treatment through the WHO-led "3 by 5 Initiative" to provide 3 million people living with HIV/AIDS in developing and middle-income countries with life-prolonging antiretroviral treatment by the end of 2005. The number of people receiving such treatment has more than doubled, from 400,000 in December 2003 to approximately 1 million in June 2005. Concurrently, the Joint United Nations Programme on HIV/AIDS (UNAIDS) is working to ensure that prevention remains a priority through a broad initiative and a complementary UNESCO-led Global Initiative on Education and HIV/AIDS to scale up education-sector responses to the epidemic. New policies on prevention were endorsed at the seventeenth meeting of the UNAIDS Programme Coordinating Board (27-29 June), with a view to bridging the current HIV prevention gap, particularly among women and young people.

142. The United Nations is working in close partnership with the Global Fund to Fight AIDS, Tuberculosis and Malaria to strengthen capacity at the country level. As a token of this partnership, I have agreed to chair the replenishment meeting of the Global Fund, to be held on 5 and 6 September in London, which is aimed at increasing the predictability of the Fund's resource-mobilization efforts.

143. Joint efforts to address the multifaceted challenges posed by HIV/AIDS cover a wide array of activities, ranging from awareness-raising and advocacy to resource mobilization, capacity-building and health service delivery. FAO, UNICEF and WFP supported the improvement of food and nutrition security, as well as care for orphans and other children living with HIV/AIDS in Southern Africa. Through the Southern Africa Capacity Initiative, UNDP worked with United Nations agencies, including the United Nations Volunteers Programme and WHO, to counter the devastating loss of capacity due to HIV/AIDS across Governments, civil society and the private sector. ILO promoted and facilitated the management and mitigation of HIV/AIDS in the workplace with its national tripartite constituents, namely Governments, employers and workers' organizations.

144. In 2004 UNHCR became the tenth co-sponsoring organization of UNAIDS and adopted, in March 2005, a three-year strategic plan to combat HIV/AIDS among returnees, refugees and other displaced persons.

145. On 2 June the General Assembly, at its high-level meeting on HIV/AIDS, reviewed progress on the Declaration of Commitment adopted at its special session held in June 2001. On 18 July the Security Council, at its meeting on HIV/AIDS, focused on the strong collaboration between UNAIDS and the Department of Peacekeeping Operations in making sure that HIV prevention efforts are part of all United Nations peacekeeping operations.

146. As at 2005, the World AIDS Campaign, led since 1997 by UNAIDS, has become a global civil society movement aimed at promoting the Declaration of Commitment on HIV/AIDS. The Campaign will now be led by a civil society global steering group, with UNAIDS as a non-voting member. I welcome this milestone in the involvement of civil society in the global governance of development issues.

147. One remaining challenge is a simplified approach to accessing the United Nations system's support and assistance mechanisms. In December 2004, UNDG and the UNAIDS secretariat provided further guidance for" United Nations implementation support plans to country responses on HIV/AIDS". In March 2005 leaders from donor and developing country Governments, civil society, United Nations agencies and other multilateral and international institutions agreed to form a global task team to develop a set of recommendations on improving the institutional architecture of the response to HIV/AIDS to reduce the burden placed on countries. The team's recommendations were approved by the UNAIDS Programme Coordinating Board in June 2005.

148. During the past year, my Special Envoys for HIV/AIDS continued to assist me in four regions of the world—Africa, Asia, the Caribbean and Eastern Europe—in promoting key issues and to advocate for an expanded response to HIV/AIDS in their regions.

Chapter III

Meeting humanitarian commitments

149. Large-scale human suffering continues as a result of a number of ongoing crises and humanitarian emergencies around the world, such as those in Colombia and the Democratic Republic of the Congo. At the same time, in Nepal and the Darfur region of the Sudan, an increasing number of people are affected by conflict and insecurity. Several devastating natural disasters

have also occurred in the past year, including hurricanes in the Caribbean, locusts in the Sahel and the tsunami in the Indian Ocean.

150. The outpouring of international support for relief and recovery operations in countries affected by the tsunami has been both generous and unprecedented in its scale. Sadly, many other crises continue to suffer from neglect. By December 2004, a year after the devastating earthquake in Bam, Islamic Republic of Iran, only 11 per cent of pledged funds had been disbursed. In Côte d'Ivoire, the Democratic Republic of the Congo and Somalia, funding continues to be well below what is required, even after considerable effort by United Nations agencies and their partners to better assess needs and prioritize activities. Once again, I call upon the donor community to ensure that funding is provided more consistently across humanitarian emergencies and that it better address the needs of all sectors, including in the area of protection.

Protecting and assisting refugees and displaced populations

151. The consolidation of peace in a number of conflicts during 2004 encouraged the return of refugees and displaced people to their homes. More than 1.5 million refugees were aided in their voluntary repatriation last year, 35 per cent more than in 2003. UNHCR estimates that in 2004 the global number of refugees dropped to 9.2 million, its lowest level since 1980. That number does not, however, include an estimated 4.2 million Palestine refugees, who continued to receive assistance and services from the United Nations Relief and Works Agency for Palestine Refugees in the Near East (UNRWA), among them an estimated 1.6 million living in the occupied Palestinian territory. In spite of the decrease in the number of refugees, the total population of concern to UNHCR increased from 17 million people at the end of 2003 to 19.2 million by the end of 2004. The latter figure includes 4.8 million internally displaced persons, a fraction of the worldwide total. Globally an estimated 25 million people have been displaced internally because of conflict or human rights violations.

152. The largest number of returns last year occurred in Afghanistan with more than 940,000 refugees alone returning home. Economic improvements and successful elections reinforced interventions to ensure the reintegration of more than 4.1 million refugees and internally displaced people who had returned home since the end of 2001. Mine-action programmes continue to facilitate return and the delivery of assistance by opening vital routes into communities at risk. Using a community-based approach to ensure

local support, UNICEF has been addressing the particular needs of returning child soldiers. More than 4,000 underage soldiers have been demobilized and reintegrated into their communities through programmes combining informal education, skills training and psycho-social support. Despite progress, however, an estimated 160,000 people remain displaced in Afghanistan owing to insecurity or drought in their place of origin. An estimated 1 million Afghans remain in the Islamic Republic of Iran, while another 960,600 are living in camps in Pakistan. According to a February 2005 Government census, an additional 1.9 million Afghans are living in urban areas in Pakistan, some of whom may be refugees.

153. Returns also continued in Africa. Under the UNHCR organized return programme, nearly 90,000 Angolans returned home in 2004—an increase over the corresponding figure for 2003 (43,000)—bringing the total to more than 338,000 since the conflict ended there in the first quarter of 2002. In Burundi, some 90,000 refugees returned home in 2004 as part of UNHCR assisted repatriation programmes, bringing the total number of assisted returns to 226,000 since the start of the programmes in April 2002. In Liberia, a total of 269,000 refugees and internally displaced people had returned home since October 2004. In Sierra Leone, the repatriation of refugees has come to an end. Some 270,000 refugees have returned home since the conflict ended, an estimated 179,000 of whom were assisted by UNHCR.

154. In eastern Africa, the conclusion of a peace agreement between the Government of the Sudan and the Sudan People's Liberation Movement has opened the door to significant levels of return. By mid-March 2005 an estimated 600,000 Sudanese had returned home, including 200,000 people who had repatriated spontaneously from neighbouring countries and 400,000 who had returned from other areas of the Sudan. Mine education and clearance in the Nuba region facilitated the resettlement of returnees there. As many as 550,000 refugees are expected to return in the coming months from neighbouring countries where they are being registered by UNHCR for organized repatriation. To continue providing effective protection and assistance, UNHCR has expanded its presence in southern Sudan.

155. The optimism generated by the resolution of the conflict in southern Sudan has been dampened, however, by continuing violence in Darfur, where more than 1.6 million people have fled their homes since the beginning of armed conflict. UNHCR continues to provide for more

than 200,000 Sudanese refugees residing in 12 camps in Chad. Through a UNICEF-led campaign, 81,000 refugees and local children have been vaccinated against measles.

156. The conflict in Colombia continues to generate new displacement, with more than 138,000 Colombians having fled their homes last year in search of safety elsewhere in the country. With a negotiated settlement to the conflict still elusive, prospects for durable solutions are not likely in 2005 for an estimated 2 million internally displaced persons and more than 40,000 Colombian refugees. On a more positive note, 20 Latin American Governments commemorated the twentieth anniversary of the Cartagena Declaration in November 2004 and recommitted themselves to upholding the comprehensive refugee protection standards contained therein.

157. In order to strengthen the response to internal displacement, the Inter-Agency Standing Committee issued, in September 2004, a policy package on implementing the collaborative response to situations of internal displacement. The package provides guidance to humanitarian and resident coordinators and United Nations country teams and sets out a road map for implementing the collaborative response. The Office for the Coordination of Humanitarian Affairs, through its inter-agency Internal Displacement Division, also continued its efforts to support the effective implementation of a collaborative response.

158. Ensuring effective security for refugees and internally displaced persons continues to be a pressing and vital need, as demonstrated by the massacre of 156 Congolese refugees at the Gatumba camp in Burundi in August 2004, and the continuing use of sexual violence as a tool of war in places like Darfur and the eastern part of the Democratic Republic of the Congo. The "Convention Plus" initiative, launched in 2003 by UNHCR to complement the 1951 Convention relating to the Status of Refugees, led to the development in 2004 of tools to enhance State responsibility and international burden-sharing for refugee protection. Such tools, like the Multilateral Framework of Understandings on Resettlement, for example, provide a means of making international cooperation on refugee-related challenges more robust and effective.

159. To counter gender-based violence, the Inter-Agency Standing Committee adopted, in January 2005, a statement of commitment on action to prevent gender-based violence, ensure appropriate care for survivors and work towards holding perpetrators accountable. UNHCR is increasing the number of women in leadership positions within camp committees to improve prevention of gender-based violence. It is also working to increase the participation of women in assessments of its programmes to enhance its gender-focused protection measures. To better assist survivors of gender-based violence, UNHCR and the United Nations Population Fund (UNFPA) have started a pilot programme in the United Republic of Tanzania for the provision of post- exposure prophylaxis. UNFPA has also developed a training programme on the clinical management of rape survivors.

160. The incidence of sexual and gender-based violence has been appallingly high in the Democratic Republic of the Congo. For the prevention of such incidents and the treatment of the victims, the Government of Belgium and the United Nations system have launched the first-ever comprehensive programme focusing on health, judicial reform, psycho-social assistance and livelihood support. The four-year project will benefit 25,000 women, young people and children in three provinces and will include the participation of key Congolese ministries, the Congolese military and police and local NGOs with expertise in addressing sexual violence. UNICEF has also expanded its interventions for preventing and responding to sexual violence, providing assistance to more than 15,000 children and women survivors in the most-affected eastern area of the country. Those activities, however, are focused primarily on response. More needs to be done in terms of prevention, targeting impunity and reinforcing accountability.

Humanitarian assistance

161. The past three years have been turbulent ones for the humanitarian community, as conflicts in Afghanistan, Iraq and Darfur and the disaster in the Indian Ocean have tested its ability to guarantee a response that is effective and appropriate. The expectation that large crises will continue to demand greater capacity, quality and accountability in humanitarian response requires that the United Nations examine and strengthen the systems, tools and competencies it has in place. To that end, the Office for the Coordination of Humanitarian Affairs has commissioned a review of the international humanitarian response system.

162. In Africa, the conflict in Darfur, Sudan, has led to the internal displacement of more than 1.6 million persons. Another 200,000 people have been driven across the border to Chad. United Nations system agencies at present provide nearly 28,000 tons of food per month to nearly 2 million people. They have also supported interventions that provide 850,000 internally displaced people with access to safe drinking water and assisted in a major Government

immunization campaign in Darfur in which more than 2 million children were vaccinated against measles. An early warning and response network has been established throughout Darfur to warn against a possible outbreak of disease, and support is provided for the early resumption of farming activities, as well as community-based animal health initiatives, land tenure policy reform and natural resources management. A mine information office has been established in Darfur to help humanitarian agencies conduct operations safely.

163. In Uganda, 2.1 million displaced people living in settlements were dependent on WFP food assistance as at June 2005. UNICEF has supported the construction of 27 temporary schools in camps for the internally displaced, trained 800 displaced teachers in psycho-social counselling and established 18 early childhood development centres. UNICEF is also providing emergency shelter, household items and access to clean water and sanitation facilities for nearly 12,000 "night commuters", children who move each evening from vulnerable rural areas into more secure towns to avoid abduction by the Lord's Resistance Army.

164. The largest outbreak of Marburg haemorrhagic fever in history struck the northern Angolan province of Uige in March. WHO and other partners quickly moved to support the Angolan Ministry of Health in its efforts to contain the dangerous virus. In Liberia, UNICEF has been instrumental in the disarmament, demobilization and reintegration process for children associated with fighting forces. Thus far, more than 11,780 children have benefited from demobilization programmes. The UNICEF back-to-school campaign has enabled more than 600,000 students to return to school, bringing a sense of stability and hope to many urban and rural communities across the country. In the Democratic Republic of the Congo, the ongoing FAO relief programmes support the food security and livelihoods of nearly 500,000 conflict-affected farming households. To open up markets for rural inhabitants, FAO is also rehabilitating hundreds of kilometres of small roads, while WFP provides food rations to the project workforce.

165. In the Middle East, United Nations system agencies are working with the Iraqi Ministry of Health to revitalize health systems in the country by repairing, restocking and restarting essential facilities. Iraqi health professionals are being trained, policies and regulations for water quality are being established and water-testing systems are being updated. Furthermore, $60 million worth of projects covering irrigation, veterinary services, livestock production and cottage industries are being implemented.

166. In the same region, the United Nations Relief and Works Agency for Palestine Refugees in the Near East (UNRWA) is continuing its regular programme of assistance for the 4.2 million Palestine refugees registered in Jordan, Lebanon, the Syrian Arab Republic and the West Bank and Gaza Strip. The Agency enrols some 500,000 students in 652 schools, operates 125 health clinics, supports 250,000 poor refugees, works with 102 community-based centres and operates an extensive microcredit programme. UNRWA also continues to provide emergency support to Palestinians in the occupied Palestinian territory, where poverty rates are as high as 70 per cent. In 2004, for instance, UNRWA provided food aid to more than 1.1 million Palestinians in the occupied Palestinian territory. The Agency also constructed some 300 new shelters in southern Gaza, where Israeli forces had demolished over 730 shelters. UN-Habitat has also started a special human settlements programme for the Palestinian people. Despite such efforts, developments such as the extension of the Israeli barrier in the West Bank have exacerbated the deteriorating socio-economic conditions of the Palestinian population.

167. In those emergencies and some 27 others, the Office for the Coordination of Humanitarian Affairs is providing support to United Nations country teams through the resident and humanitarian coordinators. In 2004 the Office facilitated the preparation and launch, in November, of consolidated humanitarian appeals for 18 crises. Through those appeals the United Nations and its partners requested $4.4 billion to cover the immediate relief and recovery needs of some 35 million people. Six months after the appeals were launched, however, only 38 per cent of requirements had been met. If the generous support to the appeal for the tsunami-affected areas is excluded, only 24 per cent of requirements had been met for the rest of the appeals. Of the 14 appeals for Africa, 8 had received less than 20 per cent as at May 2005.

168. The way humanitarian crises are funded affects the ability of the United Nations to respond promptly, effectively and in a principled manner. As events during the reporting period have made clear, there are many situations in which crises develop or escalate quickly, where the rapid deployment of staff in critical sectors is required or where the needs in underreported emergencies or sectors may go unnoticed but still require substantial support. Timely, adequate and predictable funding improves the ability of the United Nations to further develop and main-

tain response capacity commensurate to the needs on the ground.

169.   Early recovery is one sector that is frequently underfunded, especially when it comes to support for building the capacity of national institutions. A sustainable transition from conflict to peace, however, depends on the prompt re-establishment of national capacities that have been eroded by conflict. Several activities of UNDP focus on this area. For example, in Guinea-Bissau, UNDP helped the Government to establish an economic emergency management fund to help with the temporary payment of civil servants' salaries, which in turn enabled the Government to stabilize priority areas of public administration and resume its delivery of social services.

Natural disaster management

170.   The incidence and severity of disasters associated with natural hazards continues to increase. According to the Centre for Research on the Epidemiology of Disasters, more than 246,000 people were killed between April 2004 and April 2005 as a result of natural disasters. Another 157 million were injured, displaced or otherwise adversely affected. An estimated $100 billion worth of property damage also occurred, which in many countries eroded hard-won development gains. Ongoing climate change, environmental degradation, unplanned urbanization and mitigation systems that do not adequately address those factors are the likely cause of the increase in both the incidence and the severity of disasters.

171.   Of the disasters that have occurred in the past year, the 26 December 2004 earthquake and tsunami in the Indian Ocean was by far the largest. In the immediate aftermath of the tsunami, the Office for the Coordination of Humanitarian Affairs facilitated the preparation and launch of an inter-agency "flash" appeal covering the urgent needs of some 5 million people for six months. Of the $1 billion requested, nearly 90 per cent had been pledged by May 2005. As a result of the swift and generous support provided by Governments and private citizens around the world, the immediate humanitarian situation in the affected areas was quickly stabilized. No major outbreaks of communicable disease occurred, and affected communities received the necessary food and other support. Extensive damage to local infrastructure caused delays in the most immediate response. A massive logistics operation was soon established, however, with military assets from over 17 countries, which enabled local authorities and humanitarian organizations to assist stricken communities. The effort was one of the most complex in the history of

WFP, which spearheaded the coordination of logistics on behalf of the United Nations system through the Joint Logistics Centre. Within days, helicopters were continuously ferrying food down Sumatra's hard-hit western coast. By 7 January, WFP was feeding 750,000 people in Sri Lanka, and by 3 May it had reached almost 1.9 million people across the region and had dispatched 90,000 tons of food. UNHCR provided tents, plastic sheeting, blankets, kitchen sets and other household goods to more than 100,000 people in Sumatra and 160,000 people in Sri Lanka.

172.   In response to the tsunami, WHO coordinated a large, multi-agency assessment of health needs along the west coast of Aceh. Early warning systems were promptly established in affected areas and the Global Outbreak Alert and Response Network was triggered. Clinics, hospitals and laboratories reported weekly communicable disease figures and daily alerts. UNICEF distributed emergency health supplies for 800,000 people and by mid-May was providing 850,000 people with safe drinking water. UNICEF and its partners have also constructed and rehabilitated sanitation facilities for 550,000 people. Approximately 400,000 children were immunized against measles and provided with vitamin A supplements. UNICEF and its partners also facilitated the registration, tracing and reunification of separated and unaccompanied children. Thanks to the vigilance of the international community and affected Governments, children have been protected against exploitation and trafficking.

173.   Operations are now moving from relief to recovery efforts. With initial inputs from UNHCR in some countries and support from UN-Habitat, shelter reconstruction programmes have begun. FAO is helping affected countries to coordinate and plan the rehabilitation of their agriculture, fisheries and forestry sectors, with an emphasis on rebuilding sustainable livelihood opportunities to enhance food security and incomes. To facilitate the transition to recovery, I have appointed a Special Envoy for Tsunami Recovery, who is working to sustain global attention to and cooperation in long-term recovery and reconstruction.

174.   In Africa, despite considerable warnings nine months prior, a massive desert locust upsurge infested 10 West and North African countries in the summer of 2004, threatening millions of hectares of crops. FAO and the Governments of the affected countries mounted a major control operation, treating more than 12 million hectares of infested land to protect crops.

175.   A number of hurricanes hit the Caribbean between August and October 2004, causing

substantial damage. Hurricane Ivan, the most powerful to hit the region in 10 years, caused damage to 90 per cent of the homes in Grenada, leaving some 60,000 people homeless. Hurricane Jeanne hit Haiti, killing an estimated 1,500 people. Another 300,000 were injured or suffered property damage. FAO is helping to restore agricultural and fisheries production throughout the region with diverse interventions, including the repair of fishing boats, the distribution of tools, seeds and fertilizers and the rehabilitation of irrigation infrastructure. UNDP is also supporting recovery efforts in five Caribbean countries. A principal aim of this support is to ensure that recovery and reconstruction efforts avoid risks that may have contributed to the disaster in the first place, such as building in high-risk areas using inappropriate construction techniques.

176. Reducing risk by strengthening disaster management must be a principal aim of the international community. To that end, the United Nations and the Government of Japan organized the World Conference on Disaster Reduction in Kobe in January 2005. The Conference resulted in the Hyogo Framework for Action 2005-2015: Building the Resilience of Nations and Communities to Disasters. Translating the framework into results will be a significant challenge for the United Nations system, as well as Governments, regional entities and NGOs. The Framework calls for targeted increases in official development assistance and national budgets towards reducing underlying risk factors. The secretariat of the International Strategy for Disaster Reduction is coordinating strategic guidelines to support national and regional efforts through the Inter-Agency Task Force on Disaster Reduction.

177. The Office for the Coordination of Humanitarian Affairs is continuing its efforts to improve disaster management by broadening participation in the disaster assessment and coordination teams. Increasingly, such teams include emergency managers from disaster-prone countries. This allows the United Nations to build local response capacity and deal with more disasters more quickly. For example, during the Caribbean storms in 2004, the United Nations deployed four such teams simultaneously to the Dominican Republic, Grenada, Haiti, Jamaica and the Cayman Islands consisting of a total of 24 members from 12 countries and organizations working in three languages. A few months later, during the Indian Ocean tsunami, five disaster assessment and coordination teams were deployed to Indonesia, Maldives, Somalia, Sri Lanka and Thailand, consisting of a total of 44 members from 16 countries and four international organizations. Disaster management and

risk-reduction efforts have also been strengthened by the launch, in December 2004, of the Humanitarian Early Warning Service website (www.hewsweb.org). Developed by WFP on behalf of the Inter-Agency Standing Committee, the website provides easy public access to early warning analysis and forecasts on a variety of natural hazards.

178. Recent events have demonstrated that natural disasters also create protection needs for affected populations, but this remains a largely neglected area. For example, in the immediate aftermath of the tsunami there were concerns over trafficking of orphaned children. The International Federation of Red Cross and Red Crescent Societies is seeking to codify the laws relating to natural disasters in the international disaster response law project. For the time being, however, the protection framework for the victims of natural disasters is less well developed than the protection afforded to civilians affected by armed conflict.

Protection of civilians in armed conflict

179. Over the past few years there has been increasing international recognition that, in many humanitarian crises, material assistance used to safeguard lives and livelihoods is only one element of the support that affected populations require. A number of crises—some regional in nature, as in West Africa, others country-specific, as in Darfur—have been characterized as crises of protection. In response, the United Nations system, Member States and civil society have increasingly become aware that the existing international framework needs to be enhanced to better address the complex emergencies we are facing today. To that end, the General Assembly, the Economic and Social Council and the Security Council have passed a series of resolutions urging Member States and other parties to conflicts to fully respect their international commitments under international humanitarian, refugee and human rights law.

180. More and more, the challenge is to translate the overall legal and policy framework into practice in the field. I am pleased to report that significant progress has been made in this regard during the reporting period. The Security Council, for example, has increasingly incorporated concerns for protection issues in the mandates of peacekeeping missions. More importantly, such missions are now better staffed and structured to address protection needs. The Office for the Coordination of Humanitarian Affairs has worked with a number of countries currently or formerly affected by armed conflict to find common approaches to creating more secure environments

for civilians. In Uganda, for example, the Government, humanitarian organizations, affected parties, the military and civil society all agreed to a common approach and joint or complementary actions that each would undertake to improve the protection of civilians. This achievement led to specific and positive changes on the ground in northern Uganda, including increased access for humanitarian staff. A similar dialogue has been started in the northern Caucasus to address post-conflict protection challenges.

181. Recent developments have also underscored the importance of engaging with regional and other intergovernmental organizations on protection issues. In Darfur, for example, women collecting firewood outside villages were becoming increasingly vulnerable to rape and sexual abuse as the conflict worsened. The African Union, which has been engaged with the Office for the Coordination of Humanitarian Affairs on protection issues, placed its monitors and troops along routes taken by women, thus contributing to a decrease in the number of rapes and other attacks.

182. Supporting national Governments in their efforts to strengthen domestic judicial structures and undertake security sector reform is central to anchoring protection gains made during the crisis and ensuring their sustainability. As part of its emergency response programme for Darfur, UNDP has partnered with local and international non-governmental organizations to train more than 1,400 stakeholders in the region, including members of the judiciary, Sudanese NGOs, and security personnel. The training includes an introduction to international standards on human rights and criminal law, humanitarian law, gender justice, child protection and codes of conduct.

Chapter IV

The international legal order and human rights

Human rights developments

183. In follow-up to my report of September 2002 entitled "Strengthening of the United Nations: an agenda for further change" (A/57/387 and Corr.1) and the resulting action 2 initiative, the Office of the United Nations High Commissioner for Human Rights (OHCHR) placed greater emphasis on strengthening national systems of human rights protection. This led to greater engagement at the country level and in particular through cooperation with and capacity-building for United Nations country teams. Technical cooperation and advisory services continued in all parts of the world, with a focus in particular on the development of national human rights action plans, human rights education and strengthening the capacity of national human rights institutions.

184. At its 2005 session, the Commission on Human Rights agreed to permit accredited national human rights institutions to speak within their mandates and to address the Commission under all items of its agenda. This is a significant development, which enhances the status and effectiveness of national institutions within the international human rights system.

185. In an effort to address human rights violations and promote better protection, OHCHR continued to undertake monitoring and fact-finding missions. An agreement between the High Commissioner for Human Rights and the Government of Nepal, signed on 10 April 2005, established an OHCHR office in Nepal with a broad mandate to protect and promote human rights, including by conducting monitoring activities throughout the country. The High Commissioner will submit periodic analytical reports on the human rights situation in the country to the Commission on Human Rights, the General Assembly and me.

186. In the Sudan, as part of the United Nations emergency 90-day plan of action, OHCHR deployed human rights observers to Darfur in mid-August 2004. The Security Council, in its resolution 1564(2004), authorized the establishment of the International Commission of Inquiry for Darfur, which was substantively and administratively supported by OHCHR. The Commission submitted a report on its findings to me on 25 January 2005.

187. OHCHR supported the Commission of Inquiry in Côte d'Ivoire, established under the Linas-Marcoussis Agreement at the request of the Government of Côte d'Ivoire and the Security Council in its presidential statement of 25 May 2004 (S/PRST/2004/17). The Commission submitted its report in December 2004. In October, the Truth and Reconciliation Commission of Sierra Leone, whose operations were fully supported by OHCHR, submitted its report to the President of Sierra Leone. OHCHR activities in support of the implementation of the recommendations of the Commission are continuing.

188. The special procedures mechanisms of the Commission on Human Rights continued to make valuable contributions to the protection of human rights, including some 100 reports addressing a variety of human rights issues submitted to the Commission, over 1,000 confidential communications addressed to the Governments of some 140 countries for urgent

action, and 40 country visits by mandate holders in the framework of their fact-finding activities.

189. The Commission on Human Rights at its sixty-first session established new special procedures on the use of mercenaries, minority issues, human rights and international solidarity, human rights and transnational corporations, protection of human rights and fundamental freedoms while countering terrorism and the situation of human rights in the Sudan. The Commission also adopted, after 15 years of elaboration, the basic principles and guidelines on the right to a remedy and reparation for victims of gross violations of international human rights law and serious violations of international humanitarian law. The Independent Expert of the Commission on Human Rights on Impunity also updated the Set of Principles for the protection and promotion of human rights through action to combat impunity.

190. The work of the expert bodies established under the human rights treaties continues to be of critical importance. From August 2004 to July 2005, the Human Rights Committee, the Committee on Economic, Social and Cultural Rights, the Committee on the Elimination of Racial Discrimination, the Committee on the Rights of the Child, the Committee on the Elimination of Discrimination against Women and the Committee against Torture considered the reports of 94 States parties. The treaty bodies continue to harmonize their working methods and to consider means to assist States parties to fulfil their substantive commitments and meet their reporting obligations. Over the past year, treaty bodies have also adopted well over 100 decisions and views on individual cases.

191. While the sixty-first session of the Commission on Human Rights attracted more than 3,000 participants, including a record 88 senior Government officials addressing the high-level segment, the politicization of the Commission's debates and the lack of consideration of certain situations involving grave human rights violations remains a deep concern. Reflecting the high level of interest on the issue of reform, the Commission held an informal meeting on the human rights sections of my report entitled "In larger freedom". Member States across regional groups as well as non-governmental organizations expressed a wide spectrum of views on my proposals, in particular the establishment of a new Human Rights Council.

192. OHCHR provided a plan of action on 20 May 2005 following the issuance of my above-mentioned report, which lays out a strategic plan to strengthen and focus the work of the Office. With the emphasis placed on implementation,

OHCHR is further equipping itself for a programme of effective dialogue and engagement with countries, which will be supported by, inter alia, strengthened geographic and thematic expertise, greater deployments at the regional and subregional levels and more in-country offices. Protecting human rights and empowering people will be the main objectives of OHCHR as it takes the lead in moving the human rights agenda from rhetoric to reality.

International Criminal Court

193. By its resolution 58/318, the General Assembly approved the Relationship Agreement between the United Nations and the International Criminal Court, which had been approved by the Assembly of States Parties to the Rome Statute of the International Criminal Court on 7 September 2004. The Relationship Agreement, which entered into force on 4 October 2004, sets out the legal framework for cooperation between the United Nations and the Court to facilitate the effective discharge of their respective responsibilities.

194. Under the Relationship Agreement, the United Nations undertakes to cooperate with the Court with due regard to its responsibilities and competence under the Charter and subject to its rules. At the request of the Court or the Prosecutor, the United Nations may provide information and documents that are relevant to the work of the Court. In addition, the United Nations may agree to provide the Court with other forms of cooperation and assistance. The Relationship Agreement also anticipates the conclusion of supplementary arrangements to implement its terms. On the basis of such arrangements, the United Nations has already rendered assistance to the Office of the Prosecutor on a number of occasions.

195. Through its approval of the Relationship Agreement, the General Assembly further decided that the International Criminal Court may attend and participate in the work of the General Assembly in the capacity of observer. All expenses that may accrue to the United Nations as a result of the implementation of the Relationship Agreement shall be paid in full to the Organization.

196. By its resolution 1593(2005) the Security Council, acting under Chapter VII of the Charter, decided "to refer the situation in Darfur since 1 July 2002 to the Prosecutor of the International Criminal Court". Pursuant to that decision, I provided several documents to the Prosecutor, including a sealed envelope containing a list of suspects, which I had received

from the Chairman of the International Commission of Inquiry for Darfur (see para. 186).

International criminal tribunals

International Tribunal for the Former Yugoslavia

197. During the reporting period, the Tribunal continued to implement measures to ensure the fulfilment of its mandate by 2010. The Tribunal began the process of transferring cases back to the States of the former Yugoslavia. Currently, 10 requests involving 18 accused are pending. The establishment of the War Crimes Chamber of the Court of Bosnia and Herzegovina in 2005 provided further capacity to try war crimes in the region. In addition, investigation files were transferred to the Prosecutor of Bosnia and Herzegovina. In the light of the referral of cases to local courts, rule 11 bis of the Rules of Procedure and Evidence was amended. Amendments were also made to rules 98 bis and 124.

198. As at 23 June 2005, six trials involving a total of nine accused were ongoing before the Tribunal's trial chambers. At that time, 30 other cases involving 51 accused were in the pretrial phase. In the trial chambers a total of three judgements were delivered. In the Appeals Chamber four judgements were delivered. As at 23 June 2005, 58 persons were being detained at the Tribunal's detention facility, and 21 persons were on provisional release. The Tribunal transferred three convicted persons to Denmark, Spain and the United Kingdom to serve their sentences. The Tribunal attained a record of 23 indictees taken into its custody during the period from October 2004 to April 2005. As a result, the number of accused who remain at large has been reduced to 10. Nevertheless, among them there are still high-profile officials such as Radovan Karadziæ and Ratko Mladiæ, at large for nearly 10 years. In this respect the cooperation of the international community, especially of the States of the former Yugoslavia, remains essential in bringing the accused to justice. Nevertheless, the Tribunal continues to move towards fulfilling its mandate to ensure that all 163 indictees are brought to justice.

International Criminal Tribunal for Rwanda

199. The trial chambers' activities are now at an all-time high, with an unprecedented number of trials in progress. Thanks to the full use of the nine ad litem judges working with the nine permanent judges, as well as a fourth courtroom funded by the Governments of Norway and the United Kingdom, the output has continued to increase. Judgements concerning 25 accused have been delivered, and 25 others are on trial. In two of those trials, which involve 10 accused, the defence is presenting its evidence. In another trial, concerning four accused, the prosecution has called all witnesses. Sixteen detainees are awaiting trial. Their cases will start as soon as trial chamber capacity allows. The Appeals Chamber delivered three judgements during the reporting period involving four accused, as well as numerous interlocutory decisions.

200. The Office of the Prosecutor concluded its investigations with respect to those suspected of committing genocide. The last indictments are expected to be submitted for confirmation by the Chambers by the middle of 2005. The process of referring cases to national jurisdictions has commenced, with the Prosecutor in February 2005 handing over to the Government of Rwanda 15 dossiers on persons who had been under investigation. Greater effort is being devoted to the tracking and apprehension of fugitives. The Tracking Unit of the Office of the Prosecutor was reorganized and strengthened and its mode of operation revised. There is an active programme to enhance State cooperation through contacts by the prosecutor with authorities in various countries.

201. The Registry continues its steadfast support for the judicial process by servicing the other organs of the Tribunal and the defence. It also gathers support from States and/or international institutions for the smooth conduct of the proceedings. Agreements are concluded with States and institutions to fund activities not covered by the regular budget, to ensure the movement of witnesses and their safety and to find places where convicted persons will serve their sentences.

Special Court for Sierra Leone

202. As the Special Court for Sierra Leone approaches its fourth year of operation, all nine accused persons who are in custody in Freetown are currently on trial. On 17 January 2005 three judges were appointed to the second trial chamber and the trial in the case of the Armed Forces Revolutionary Council started on 7 March. Meanwhile, the first trial chamber continues to alternate the trials regarding the Civil Defence Forces and the Revolutionary United Front, which began on 3 June and 5 July 2004 respectively. Two other cases are still pending before the Special Court. The whereabouts of Johnny Paul Koroma, Chairman of the Armed Forces Revolutionary Council, remain unknown. Charles Taylor resigned as President of Liberia on 11 August 2003 and since that date has been in Nigeria.

203. In October 2004 the Special Court adopted its completion strategy, which the President presented to the Security Council on 24 May 2005. The Registrar signed agreements on the enforcement of sentences with two countries, and negotiations are ongoing with a number of others. During the post-completion phase, the Court will continue certain "residual activities" after it no longer exists in its current form and with its current capacity.

204. To date, the Special Court has received approximately $54.9 million in voluntary contributions from 33 States against a four-year budget of $104 million. In order to supplement insufficient voluntary contributions, I sought a subvention of up to $40 million for the biennium 2004-2005. The General Assembly, in its resolution 59/276, authorized me to enter into commitments not exceeding $20 million to supplement the financial resources of the Special Court for the period from 1 January to 30 June 2005. In my report of 18 April 2005 (A/59/ 534/Add.4), I proposed an additional subvention of up to $13 million to finance the first six months of the fourth year of operations of the Court, until December 2005, and stated my intention to propose an additional subvention of up to $7 million for the Court in 2006. The General Assembly, on 22 June 2005, adopted resolution 59/294, in which it approved commitment authority for up to $13 million for the period from 1 July 2005 to 31 December 2005.

Enhancing the rule of law

205. On 6 October 2004, the Security Council held an open meeting to discuss my report on the rule of law and transitional justice in conflict and post-conflict societies (S/2004/ 616). The Council stressed the importance and urgency of restoring justice and the rule of law in post-conflict societies, not only to help them come to terms with past abuses, but also to promote national reconciliation and prevent a return to conflict. The Council underlined the importance of tailoring solutions to local circumstances and, more importantly, of involving local actors. It accordingly emphasized the need to give consideration to the full range of transitional justice mechanisms, not just courts. Finally, in terms of concrete action, the Council urged the Secretariat to make proposals for implementing the various practical recommendations set out in my report.

206. Over the past year I have continued work to put in place the arrangements necessary for the entry into force of the Agreement between the United Nations and the Royal Government of Cambodia concerning the Prosecution under Cambodian Law of Crimes Committed During the Period of Democratic Kampuchea. In December 2004 I sent a third planning mission to Phnom Penh to complete work on identifying the probable requirements of the Extraordinary Chambers.

207. On 28 March I convened a pledging conference with a view to seeking the $43 million needed to fund the United Nations commitment under the Agreement and received sufficient contributions and pledges to meet the Organization's obligations. On 28 April I consequently notified the Government of Cambodia that the legal requirements on the part of the United Nations for the entry into force of the Agreement had been complied with, and the Agreement accordingly entered into force the following day.

208. Upon the request of the Government of Burundi that the Security Council establish an international judicial commission of inquiry as provided for in the Arusha Peace and Reconciliation Agreement for Burundi, I dispatched an assessment mission to consider the advisability and feasibility of establishing such an international commission for the purpose of clarifying the truth and bringing to justice those responsible for the crime of genocide, crimes against humanity and war crimes committed in Burundi since its independence. The assessment mission recommended the establishment of a twin mechanism: a non-judicial accountability mechanism in the form of a truth commission and a judicial accountability mechanism in the form of a special chamber within the court system of Burundi.

209. Regarding the Sudan, pursuant to Security Council resolution 1564(2004), I established an international commission of inquiry in order to investigate reports of violations of international humanitarian law in Darfur by all parties, to determine also whether or not acts of genocide had occurred and to identify the perpetrators of such violations with a view to ensuring that those responsible were held accountable. In its report (S/2005/60), the Commission found that the crimes committed in Darfur did not amount to genocide and characterized them as crimes against humanity. It further recommended that the Security Council refer the situation in Darfur to the International Criminal Court.

210. With respect to Timor-Leste, on 11 January 2005 I established an independent Commission of Experts to review the prosecution of serious human rights violations committed in Timor-Leste in 1999 and to assess the progress made by the Indonesian Ad Hoc Human Rights Court in Jakarta and by the Serious Crimes Unit and the Special Panels for Serious Crimes in Dili.

The Commission, which was supported by OHCHR, submitted its report on 26 May 2005.

211. Consistent with the goal of advancing the international rule of law and to encourage wider participation in the multilateral treaty framework, in 2000 I initiated an annual treaty event. In March I invited Governments to participate in this year's treaty event, entitled "Focus 2005: responding to global challenges", to be held during the high-level plenary meeting of the sixtieth session of the General Assembly. During the reporting period, three new multilateral treaties were added to the 506 active treaties already deposited with me. In addition, 11 treaties relating to the environment, health, telecommunications and transport entered into force.

212. A meeting of experts organized by the United Nations University in cooperation with the Office of Legal Affairs concluded that the pressure of contemporary problems could sometimes hide the reality of progress made in international criminal justice. Fifteen years ago, no leader would have had cause to fear international criminal prosecution. Today no leader can be confident of impunity. This is an astonishing amount of progress in a remarkably short period of time in human history.

Legal affairs

213. During its fifty-ninth session, the General Assembly adopted by consensus the United Nations Convention on Jurisdictional Immunities of States and Their Property (resolution 59/38) and the International Convention for the Suppression of Acts of Nuclear Terrorism (resolution 59/290). The adoption of the latter represents a significant step forward in the strengthening of the international legal framework against terrorism. In addition, On 8 March, the General Assembly approved the United Nations Declaration on Human Cloning (resolution 59/280), thus concluding its discussion of a highly complex item that had been on its agenda since 2001.

214. With respect to the law of the sea, the Open-ended Informal Consultative Process on Oceans and the Law of the Sea at its sixth meeting discussed fisheries and their contribution to sustainable development. At its initial meeting, in January 2005, the United Nations Ocean and Coastal Areas network, the general mechanism for inter-agency cooperation in ocean affairs, established four task forces dealing with, among other things, the tsunami disaster and marine biodiversity beyond national jurisdiction. An important initiative was the establishment of a new capacity-building team that developed a training manual on article 76 of the United Nations Convention on the Law of the Sea and on how to make submissions to the Commission on the Limits of the Continental Shelf.

215. During the past year, the Office of Legal Affairs has continued to provide legal advice and assistance in relation to a broad and diverse range of the Organization's activities. With respect to the United Nations presence in Iraq, the Office advised me on issues arising from the bombing of the United Nations headquarters in Baghdad on 19 August 2003; the winding down of the oil-for-food programme, including questions related to the Independent Inquiry Committee; and the activities of the United Nations Assistance Mission for Iraq. In relation to the Organization's peace-keeping operations more generally, the Office continued to provide advice and assistance with respect to the interpretation and implementation of mandates, the preparation of rules of engagement and the negotiation and implementation of status-of-forces agreements.

216. The International Trade Law Division assisted in the adoption of a legislative guide on insolvency law designed to help countries establish fair and transparent systems to address commercial failure. With respect to matters internal to the Organization, the Office facilitated a comprehensive review of United Nations general conditions of contract; assisted in the development of general principles for accepting pro bono goods and services; prepared guidelines on the use of information and communication technology resources and data; revised the financial regulations of certain United Nations funds; and represented the Secretary-General before the United Nations Administrative Tribunal.

Chapter V

Management

Administration and management

217. The Organization maintained a strong emphasis on improving client orientation in the delivery of services and implemented measures to produce better results in all areas, with a renewed focus on accountability through both performance measurement and strengthened reporting. In an effort to enhance accountability by reporting more effectively on the implementation of recommendations made by the oversight bodies and by providing analyses of the decisions made by the United Nations Administrative Tribunal, the relevant functions of the Department of Management were rationalized and consolidated.

218. The Organization's sponsorship of the Global Compact Leaders Summit in June 2004

highlighted the paradox that the Secretariat itself could do more to ensure that its own administrative practices were fully aligned with Global Compact principles. Accordingly, the Department of Management convened a working group that took action to implement changes in vendor relations and facilities management and to research practical measures for pension investments and human resources policies that would reconcile fiduciary responsibility, our own regulations and the Global Compact principles.

219. The Organization built new capacities and pursued concrete measures to ensure the security and safety of United Nations staff and property. Most significantly in institutional terms, an internal review process and extensive discussions with Member States resulted in the unification of United Nations security functions within a new Department of Safety and Security. A staff security plan was completed and put in place at the Headquarters complex, tamper-proof holographic building passes were introduced, a crisis management plan was put in place at all duty stations and anti-blast film was installed on all windows in the Secretariat building and all the annex buildings in New York.

220. Several security rehearsals, including a complete evacuation, were used to test the updated and revalidated crisis management operational plan for the Headquarters complex. The current year will bring the United Nations complex into full compliance with the minimum operating security standards. Security involves more than tangible, preventive measures, and in that spirit the Organization funded and implemented training for 40 designated senior officers responsible for security at their duty stations and their security management teams. In addition, the counselling services carried out stress management training missions in 34 countries and provided individual stress counselling to 3,500 staff members and dependants.

Common support services

221. The Organization continued to pursue opportunities to cut costs through volume discounts and to create service efficiencies through process redesign. The newly initiated Inter-Agency Travel Network promotes a global airline agreement signed with a major international carrier; as a result, for the first time, smaller offices can obtain discounts. By introducing e-commerce philatelic products and other innovations, the United Nations Postal Administration has become profitable for the first time since 1994; further revenue increases are projected as the Administration's new market profile is further enhanced.

Information and communication technology strategy

222. In the ongoing effort to upgrade the wide-area network infrastructure, the network equipment in the Secretariat building has been brought up to the new standard and the design for upgrading the electrical facilities in the annex buildings was completed. By the first quarter of 2005, both Headquarters and offices away from New York were prepared to do business using this highly cost-effective method, which brings offices around the globe into closer collaboration. Once these enhancements have been completed, the Organization may begin to consolidate administrative functions, which are currently decentralized and replicated throughout all offices away from Headquarters. With the constitution of the Project Review Committee for information and communication technology initiatives, all offices comply with a process that requires preparation of a business case to justify investments and ensure consistency with technical standards. Our information technologists re-engineered and implemented a new Secretariat-wide Intranet to increase staff productivity and efficiency by enabling organizational units to share information without having specialized technical knowledge.

Human resources management

223. Further embedding and broadening of the principles of human resources management reform in the Secretariat continued to be the main focus. Greater attention has been given to making progress on geographical and gender balance, harmonizing conditions of service of staff assigned to the field, streamlining administrative procedures and increasing the efficiency of existing human resources-related information technology systems such as the electronic performance appraisal system and the Galaxy electronic staffing system. Improved inter-agency cooperation on HIV/AIDS issues has resulted in the design and implementation of "HIV/AIDS in the workplace" orientation sessions for staff from the Secretariat, as well as United Nations funds, programmes and specialized agencies. A new programme for senior women leaders and new organizational development tools that model effective managers and departments were introduced.

224. Preparation for mobility, including a comprehensive communication campaign Secretariat-wide, a voluntary managed reassignment exercise, attention to work-life issues and development of career support programmes, has been a major priority. Monitoring of human resources has been strengthened, as evidenced by the establishment of human resources action plans for 26 departments and offices. On-site monitoring of

delegated authority for human resources management has been done in six departments and offices, two tribunals and three peacekeeping missions.

Capital master plan

225. While significant technical work has gone forward on design, construction planning, and space programming in support of the urgent and inevitable refurbishment of the Headquarters complex, many of the assumptions that underlie the capital master plan project and its costing, approved by the General Assembly in 2003, have been called into question by political and financial dynamics. Refurbishment of the core complex can proceed only upon the acquisition of transitional accommodations—so-called "swing space"—for staff and operations, including Secretariat functions and conference space, but the site originally proposed appears to be unavailable. A number of alternative options are being explored. In the meantime, the General Assembly is to take a decision on the host country's loan offer of $1.2 billion, combined with my request for authorization to conclude an agreement that would afford the United Nations full discretion in borrowing and drawing down funds.

Financial management

226. The United Nations budget process is on its way to assuming a more logical structure, with significant benefits for strategic planning. The new biennial budget for 2006-2007 is clearly linked to the new two-year programme plan. The planning and budgetary processes were aligned and simplified through the use of the same results-based-budgeting logical framework for both the budget and the biennial programme plan. For programme managers, the budget website continued to play a key role in ensuring the availability of key planning and budgetary data.

227. Regarding peacekeeping budgets, those for the financial period 2004/05 featured more measurable indicators of achievement and outputs and improved linkages between the results-based budgeting frameworks and resource requirements. For the first time, the budgets of peacekeeping operations have indicated how many personnel (military, police and civilian staff, comprising on average 69 per cent of total resources), are attributable to individual components. Variances in human resources have been justified by reference to specific elements in the results-based-budgeting frameworks. Furthermore, for the support component of peacekeeping budgets, measurable outputs have been identified for each of the main operational cost categories (e.g., facilities, ground transportation, air transportation, information technology and communications).

228. In another area with implications for field operations, the first phase of a comprehensive cash-management project has been implemented, namely, the automation of the disbursement functions. Electronic systems have been upgraded and integrated for use for the Headquarters overseas bank accounts utilizing the SWIFT (Society for Worldwide Interbank Financial Telecommunication) network. In addition, the Treasury has implemented a set of measures to assist peacekeeping missions in reducing local bank charges, finding alternative means of transporting money into and within mission areas by United Nations personnel and reducing cash-in-transit insurance premiums.

229. Within the Secretariat, with respect to services provided to staff members, the accounting and payroll services have focused on client orientation. Improved techniques for the review and consolidation of data were developed, which helped in the preparation of the final consolidated financial statements, and new tax reimbursement and quarterly tax advance systems were put in place.

Financial situation

230. The financial situation of the United Nations remains very fragile. Despite lower arrears in contributions to the regular budget and the international tribunals in 2004, a substantial amount of assessed contributions, a legal obligation of Member States, remained unpaid. As a result, our reserves were regularly depleted and the Organization was obliged to delay reimbursements to Member States that had contributed troops and equipment to peacekeeping operations. In addition, the Organization was obliged periodically to resort to cross-borrowing from the accounts of closed peacekeeping operations for the regular budget, the tribunals and some ongoing peacekeeping operations. This is not only an inherently undesirable practice, but the pool of funds available in those accounts is limited and shrinking as the surpluses are returned to Member States. The solution to the continuing financial problems of the Organization is for Member States to fully meet their financial obligations to the United Nations in a timely manner.

Security for United Nations staff

231. United Nations staff members continue to face serious and often escalating threats in carrying out their duties in the field. In Afghanistan, for example, they have been the targets of abduction, assassination or improvised explosive

devices. A protracted hostage situation involving United Nations staff in Afghanistan was successfully resolved during the months of October and November 2004. Also in November, the degraded security situation in Côte d'Ivoire necessitated the relocation of dependants and the evacuation of non-essential United Nations staff. In February 2005, nine United Nations peacekeepers were brutally murdered in Bunia, Democratic Republic of the Congo. Over the past year, humanitarian assistance workers have operated in a high-risk environment in responding to the crisis in Darfur, Sudan. Detentions, hostage-taking, murder and looting of relief supplies have increasingly characterized the security conditions there.

232. Against this background, my longstanding efforts to reinforce the Organization's security structure were realized through the establishment of the Department of Safety and Security, responsible for the safety and security of more than 100,000 United Nations staff members and an estimated 300,000 dependants serving at more than 150 duty stations worldwide. My report to the General Assembly at its fifty-ninth session on a strengthened and unified security management system for the United Nations was supported by Assembly resolution 59/276, which established the Department of Safety and Security effective 1 January 2005. The new Department, headed by an Under-Secretary-General, amalgamates the former Office of the United Nations Security Coordinator, the Security and Safety Service and the security component of the Department of Peacekeeping Operations.

233. The Department of Safety and Security is responsible for providing leadership, operational support and oversight of the security management system to facilitate the safest and most efficient conduct of the programmes and activities of the United Nations system. Under the leadership of the new Under-Secretary-General, who assumed his post in February 2005, every effort is being made to have the major elements of the Department in place and running by the sixtieth session of the General Assembly. The overarching goal is to ensure that the Department has the operational ability to make it possible to carry out the United Nations mandate in the most demanding locations on the globe.

234. In its resolution 59/276, the General Assembly specified measures to strengthen the security and safety of the United Nations system, including field-security arrangements at all duty stations worldwide, and to unify the separate security structures into the Department of Safety and Security. The ongoing structural changes include the establishment of distinct capacities for policy, planning and coordination; compliance, evaluation and monitoring; and training and standardization, as well as strengthening of the Critical Incident Stress Management Unit. The administrative capacity of the Department will be strengthened through the creation of an Executive Office. A Division of Headquarters Security and Safety Services has been set up to provide policy and operational guidance to major duty stations and regional commissions and to coordinate personal protection functions. A Division of Regional Operations with an enhanced threat and risk-assessment capacity and a round-the-clock communications centre will strengthen the ability of the United Nations to ensure its own security.

Accountability and oversight

235. As a result of its five-year review of the mandate of the Office of Internal Oversight Services, the General Assembly, in its resolution 59/272, adopted new measures aimed at strengthening the Office's independence and reporting mechanism. This, together with my announcement to establish a Management Oversight Committee and other initiatives to strengthen integrity, accountability and oversight, provides a solid foundation for an improved internal governance framework for the Organization. In addition, the Office of Internal Oversight Services assisted in the drafting of the Organization's first whistle-blowing protection policy, which, among other things, promulgates the establishment of an Ethics Office to receive reports of reprisals or threats against complainants and witnesses who cooperate in an investigation.

Monitoring, evaluation and consultation

236. The Office of Internal Oversight Services continued its activities to strengthen monitoring and evaluation in the context of results-based management, including the provision of training and an evaluation manual, which is available on its website. The Office established a Secretariat-wide Working Group on Monitoring and Evaluation, which submitted proposals to the Deputy-Secretary-General on the strengthening and monitoring of programme performance and evaluation, which were also included in the report of the Office to the General Assembly (A/60/73), drafted in collaboration with the Joint Inspection Unit.

237. In its evaluation of UN-Habitat (E/AC.51/2005/3), the Office recommended narrowing the focus of the programme and im-

proving the management of some of its activities. The Office also conducted evaluations of the United Nations Voluntary Fund for Victims of Torture (E/CN.4/2005/55) and a pilot thematic evaluation, which focused on Headquarters-field linkages for poverty eradication (E/AC.51/2005/2). The Office continued to provide change-management consulting services, including to the Department for General Assembly and Conference Management aimed at enhancing the effectiveness of the document slotting system. Because of limited resources, the Office was unable to make certain necessary enhancements to the Integrated Monitoring and Documentation Information System and to provide training to staff at offices away from Headquarters.

Internal audit

238. The Office conducted approximately 160 audits and issued seven reports to the General Assembly dealing with a wide range of issues, including peacekeeping operations; safety and security; the appeals process of the administrative justice system; the procurement of air services for peacekeeping missions; the capital master plan; information technology; the activities of the Office of the United Nations High Commissioner for Refugees; the United Nations libraries; and the mission subsistence allowance.

239. Following the bombing of United Nations offices in Baghdad, the Office conducted a comprehensive global audit of security management at Headquarters and at 20 field missions (A/59/702). The Peacekeeping Service undertook a number of audits, including of procurement, vacancy rates and the state of discipline at various missions. A management review of the appeals process at Headquarters, Geneva, Vienna and Nairobi (A/59/408) determined that the timeliness of appeals could be improved by streamlining the process at most duty stations. Audits of the UNHCR emergency operations in Burundi, Chad and the Sudan identified a need to improve procurement and general management. Limited resources prevented the Office from undertaking horizontal performance audits, such as an audit of the activities of the United Nations system on HIV/AIDS and the advancement of women.

Investigations

240. The Office received a total of 560 matters and issued 91 investigative reports, including 20 on sexual exploitation and abuse at the United Nations Organization Mission in the Democratic Republic of the Congo. The General Assembly affirmed the need for a comprehensive strategy to eliminate future sexual exploitation and abuse

in United Nations peacekeeping operations. Following its review of the report of the Office on strengthening the investigative functions in the United Nations (A/58/708), the General Assembly assigned specific responsibility for the investigation of serious misconduct, including sexual exploitation and abuse, to the Office, and requested that I establish an administrative mechanism for the mandatory reporting by programme managers of allegations of misconduct to the Office (resolution 59/287). As indicated previously, I have already enacted a policy of zero tolerance towards such offences.

241. The resources of the Office were stretched to the limit to handle the MONUC sexual exploitation cases, to provide liaison services for the Independent Inquiry Committee, headed by Paul Volcker, and to deal with the backlog of cases in peacekeeping operations.

Strengthening the Organization

242. As I reported last year, most of the reform elements contained in my "agenda for further change" of 2002 have now been implemented. We have seen some very clear benefits: a thoroughly revised programme budget for 2004-2005, a shorter, more efficient cycle of planning and budgeting for the biennium 2006-2007, a reduction in the quantity of reports and meetings and greater integration of human rights elements in the work of United Nations country teams. Nevertheless, progress in a number of other areas has been slow. That is one of the reasons I have launched a two-track package of Secretariat reform in 2005. I am pursuing one track vigorously under my own authority, and the other is to be taken up in the context of the wider proposals contained in my reform report, "In larger freedom", to be taken up at the High-level Plenary Meeting in September. I hope that together they demonstrate my commitment to continuous improvement and to strengthening the Organization to meet the needs of the twenty-first century.

243. The current phase of reform comes at a particularly crucial time for the United Nations. The Secretariat has faced an unprecedented series of organizational challenges that have exposed flaws in the way it does business. I am moving ahead with a package of small yet important measures for immediate implementation. I anticipate that most of them will have been fully implemented by September. While preparation for many of the steps predates problems revealed over the past year, the initiatives also explicitly seek to address both the serious concerns expressed by United Nations staff in the integrity perception survey and the recommendations of

the Independent Inquiry Committee investigating the oil-for-food programme. Broadly, these fit into the following four categories:

- Improving the performance of senior management
- Enhancing oversight and accountability
- Ensuring ethical conduct
- Increasing transparency

244. The Senior Management Group, an internal information-sharing and coordination tool that I instituted upon taking office, has proven too large for effective and timely decision-making. As a result, two smaller senior committees—one for policy issues and the other for management and reform matters—have been created. I have also introduced a much more transparent system for the selection of new United Nations senior leaders—with an open selection process based on predetermined criteria. I am also introducing a much more structured system of induction to ensure that senior officials are properly briefed on the broader system of United Nations rules, regulations, codes of conduct and managerial systems.

245. The need for better tools to ensure accountability has also been identified. I have created a small Management Performance Board that will systematically assess the performance of individual senior managers and advise me on suggested corrective action where necessary. A new Oversight Committee is also being established to ensure that appropriate management action is taken to implement the recommendations of the various oversight bodies.

246. Concerns about fairness and integrity were raised by staff in the 2004 integrity survey. We are moving ahead with a series of measures to strengthen ethical conduct. First, I am introducing a robust new policy for the protection of whistle-blowers so that staff can feel sufficiently protected to come forward with concerns about conduct without reprisal. Second, the Organization is moving swiftly to take appropriate disciplinary action against all proven cases of sexual misconduct. At the same time, measures to improve training, to impose a unified standard of conduct, to establish credible complaint mechanisms and to review welfare and recreational needs for personnel in the field are well under way. Third, a more expansive requirement for financial disclosure by senior officials and better dissemination of code of conduct requirements are being introduced.

247. In terms of increasing transparency, the Organization is developing a clear and consistent policy for sharing different categories of United Nations information, which will increase the transparency of our work while ensuring confidentiality where needed. Work is also under way to validate our procurement system to ensure that it meets the highest global standards and to develop policy guidance on the provision of pro bono goods and services.

248. At the same time, I hope that the outcome of the High-level Plenary Meeting in September will allow for a more fundamental strengthening of the Secretariat. I proposed three key reforms in my report of March 2005 (A/59/2005), which, if approved, will go a long way to enhance the efficiency and effectiveness of the Organization. First, I have proposed that all mandates older than five years be reviewed by Member States and considered for deletion. Second, and inextricably linked to the mandate review, I have proposed a one-time buy-out for United Nations personnel whose skills and profile no longer match the new needs of the Secretariat. Third, I have asked the General Assembly to approve a thorough review of all the budgetary and human resources rules that govern the Secretariat. I believe these reforms are long overdue and, if done properly, could have a major impact on modernizing the Organization and making it more responsive.

Chapter VI

Partnerships

Communications

249. The past year has certainly challenged United Nations communicators and, although it has not been a particularly good year for public perceptions of the United Nations in some Member States, I believe that our communication processes have demonstrated a new fluidity and our communicators have shown considerable skill in rising to meet those challenges.

250. In my previous annual report, I spoke of 2003 as a year of consolidation for the Department of Public Information. The Department's reorientation and the other changes I had instituted in its structure have certainly been tested in the forge of public opinion. Its capacity to mobilize resources quickly and efficiently to address priority issues was much needed and is now well established. Throughout the past year, the Department of Public Information has provided advice, support and information on numerous urgent projects to ensure that the public hears of our efforts to address managerial problems at Headquarters and in the field.

251. In the face of a number of crises and bitter and often unjust criticism, the Department

strengthened its media monitoring and reinforced its media response capacity. Several public information initiatives were launched to counter misinformation in the media, and a crisis communications team was mobilized, which included senior staff from my Office, the Spokesman's Office and the Department. This team now sets daily priorities that guide not only the Organization's response to media concerns, but also its promotion of important international issues.

252. Guided by this strategy, senior spokes persons are aided in their efforts to make the views of the United Nations known through television and radio appearances and the publication of opinion pieces, interviews and letters in high-impact print media. Information is now provided rapidly to our civil society partners when they express interest in engaging the public on priority issues. In addition, the network of United Nations information centres is employed to ensure that our message is heard all around the world, through interviews and the placement of articles in local media in the regions they serve.

253. I have become increasingly convinced that the Organization must do more to ensure that its staff are informed of our efforts to promote issues and address our critics, and the Department of Public Information has played an important role in improving our internal communications using a new Intranet website entitled "Hot Issues, Cold Facts" and developing and distributing briefing material on major issues to staff in the field and at Headquarters.

254. Throughout the year, the Department of Public Information undertook a series of outreach initiatives that bolstered United Nations efforts to promote tolerance and understanding, most notably through three major seminars addressing specific manifestations of intolerance. The first of them, the "Unlearning Intolerance" seminar on anti-Semitism, held in June 2004, raised the profile of an important problem that the Department addressed again early in 2005, when it hosted a major exhibition from Israel's Yad Vashem (the Holocaust Martyrs' and Heroes' Remembrance Authority) concurrently with the special session of the General Assembly commemorating the liberation of the death camps. The second seminar focused on Islamophobia and drew an equally inspiring cast of experts from across the religious and political spectrum.

255. The Department has also made it a priority to ensure that civil society is informed of the ongoing process of revitalization and reform of the United Nations and, where possible, is engaged in that process. Information about the various proposals in the reports that I have commissioned or encouraged, including the report of the High-level Panel on Threats, Challenges and Change and the report of the Millennium Project, *Investing in Development*, were vigorously promoted. Since the launch of my own report, "In larger freedom", in March 2005, the focus has shifted to providing information on its recommendations to civil society actors to allow them to be effectively engaged in the review process.

256. As I have stated elsewhere, I believe that the Millennium Development Goals are the framework around which United Nations development activities must be aligned. In addition to providing information about significant relevant events, like the Global Compact Leaders Summit and the Mauritius meeting on the sustainable development of small island developing States, the Department worked with the Millennium Campaign Office to launch a new campaign to generate support for the Millennium Development Goals, featuring a specially designed logo and the catch phrase "keep the promise".

257. The Millennium Development Goals and the role of civil society in achieving them were the primary topics of discussion when 2,000 representatives of non-governmental organizations from around the world attended the fifty-seventh annual Department of Public Information/NGO Conference in September 2004. An even larger turnout is expected for the 2005 conference, which will focus on ways to revitalize the architecture of the international system at whose centre the United Nations stands.

258. Conscious of the need to ensure public support at a time when the United Nations faces an unprecedented surge in demand for peacekeeping operations, the Department of Public Information worked with the Department of Peacekeeping Operations on strategies to inform Member States, decision makers and the public about our operations. Communications experts from Headquarters were sent to peacekeeping missions to review their information programmes, assess their resource requirements and determine what support from Headquarters would best help them to play an effective role in implementing their mission's mandate. Information campaigns aimed at informing United Nations staff, troop contributors and peacekeepers of the seriousness of my determination to prevent unacceptable behaviour by peacekeeping personnel were also instituted, and information on standards of conduct has been produced and distributed to all missions.

259. Following a successful pilot training project in 2004 for peacekeeping information staff, a second training course was held in May 2005. The objective of such exercises is to strengthen United Nations capacity to conduct

effective information campaigns at the start of new peacekeeping missions. I intend to continue this training to ensure that the United Nations has a solid cadre of versatile and well-trained public information staff available when required.

260. I continue to examine the network of United Nations information centres with a view to improving their capacity to function effectively. Several significant obstacles have emerged that make it clear that it will not be possible to create regional hubs in other regions comparable to the model for Western Europe. As a consequence, I have recalibrated the proposals I made in 2004 and set out a new modus operandi that aims to rationalize the network of centres based on strategic communications imperatives (see my report to the Committee on Information, A/AC.198/2005/3). I await the advice of the General Assembly on this new approach.

261. The interests of Africa remained at the forefront of the Department of Public Information's priorities, with its revamped publication *Africa Renewal* now reaching more than a million people (in English or French) and two new radio programmes specifically about Africa added to the Department's regular roster.

262. New media and civil society partnerships play a key role in the Department's efforts to increase the reach of its information products. Under the terms of an arrangement negotiated during the past year, the International Association of University Presidents will now distribute United Nations radio programmes to 100 of its 700 affiliates worldwide by the end of 2005.

263. New partnerships have also been established with radio, television and cable networks and media production companies around the world. One such partnership has resulted in the daily transmission by satellite of a video package of United Nations news footage to more than 500 broadcasters worldwide. Much of the footage from the field distributed under this arrangement is at present produced by UNICEF and other agencies, but as the Department's technical capacities expand I expect that video reports from peacekeeping missions will supplement this material. At the same time, a new digital storage system that is now in operation should make it possible to make high-resolution professional-quality photographs available via the United Nations website.

264. Continuing its efforts to draw attention to vital stories that fall off the media's radar screen, the Department issued its second annual list of 10 stories the world should hear more about. The list included tales of troubling humanitarian emergencies and fragile post-conflict situations, as well as encouraging stories about human rights, health and development. The level of press attention the project has attracted, as well as positive feedback from Member States and others, demonstrates that the top-10 stories project has become a valuable tool for drawing the attention of the media and the world at large to urgent matters of international concern.

265. The United Nations website continues to grow, with about 1 million pages of information, in all six official languages, viewed by users around the globe every day: a 50 per cent increase over 2002 figures. A significant step towards multilingualism on the website has been achieved through the introduction of public access to the Official Document System (ODS) through the Web. Anyone with Internet access can now access official documents in all six official languages electronically.

266. The Internet is now an increasingly important source for news, and the Department continues to strengthen its main online news portal, the UN News Centre, which covers breaking stories on United Nations activities and offers easy access to a wide range of related sources. The News Centre is one of the most heavily visited areas of the United Nations website and is frequently cited as a resource by major media outlets. The list of subscribers to the associated e-mail news service continues to grow steadily, as does the number of news media sites that have established direct links to the UN News Centre.

267. Webcasting of United Nations events is now an integral part of the daily work of the United Nations. In addition to daily webcasts of General Assembly and Security Council meetings and my spokesman's press briefings, the Department of Public Information now webcasts events in connection with conferences held away from Headquarters. In addition to providing millions with immediate virtual access to the deliberative and legislative bodies of the United Nations, the webcasts are now archived on the Web, and more than 10,000 video clips are currently accessed from those archives every day.

268. The involvement of the United Nations in *The Interpreter* culminated in the premiere of the feature film in April 2005. Based on the large number of interview requests and the media response in general, the desired outcome—an increased awareness of the United Nations among a broad audience—was certainly attained.

269. Outreach to educational institutions continued throughout the past year, with new partnerships with universities and other schools having been established. One result of those outreach efforts was that the number of visitors taking the Headquarters guided tour has returned

to pre-11 September 2001 levels, reaching 360,000 in 2004. The largest increase was in the number of students touring the complex. They now make up 42 per cent of the total number of visitors. To highlight the Organization's sixtieth anniversary, the Department of Public Information has launched new promotional campaigns encouraging schools to take the tours and engage with the Organization in other creative ways.

270. The special United Nations website for students, the Cyberschoolbus, was selected as one of the 101 best sites for teachers. It now hosts the most comprehensive website on the Millennium Development Goals developed explicitly for a younger audience. It also launched a new feature, GA Newsflash, providing information about the work of the fifty-ninth session of the General Assembly to a younger audience. The documentaries and web material of the award-winning UN Works programme are also being distributed to schools and educators.

271. An internal reform of the Dag Hammarskjöld Library, currently under way, will foster a culture of knowledge management throughout the Organization, enhance effectiveness and align the Library's activities, services and outputs more closely with the goals and objectives of the Organization.

United Nations Fund for International Partnerships

272. The successful partnership between the United Nations Fund for International Partnerships (UNFIP) and the United Nations Foundation (UNF) entered its eighth year in March 2005. From the inception of the partnership in 1998 to the end of 2004, a total of $637 million has been allocated to fund 324 projects with activities in 122 countries and involving 37 United Nations organizations. The cumulative amount of co-financing from other funding partners, such as multilateral and bilateral donors, has been $237 million, or more than one third of the total. Projects have covered the following programme areas: children's health; population and women; biodiversity; renewable energy and climate change; and peace, security and human rights.

273. The UNF-UNFIP partnership has continued to focus on grant-making and on telling the story of programmes and projects and the work of the United Nations in general. UNF has continued to provide an important platform for advocacy on behalf of the Organization, including strengthening United States-United Nations relations. The Foundation's contributions are available for use in ways that the Organization's core funds are not—opening up possibilities for inno-

vation and creativity. In response to UNF matching and challenge grants, new partners have come forward to collaborate and existing partners have increased their engagement in United Nations causes such as emergency humanitarian assistance and HIV/AIDS prevention.

274. Building on a series of innovative initiatives, UNF, the Coalition for Environmentally Responsible Economies and UNFIP hosted the Second Institutional Investor Summit on Climate Risk in May 2005. The Summit brought together international pension fund managers, Government officials, business executives and treasurers—collectively responsible for managing well over $5 trillion in assets—with nongovernmental organizations and senior United Nations officials to explore the connection between climate risk and fiduciary responsibility. It concluded with a call for action to manage climate risk and capture opportunities.

275. The growing interest from the private sector and foundations in the work of the United Nations has led to a substantial increase in enquiries about partnerships with entities of the United Nations system: UNFIP receives an average of five substantive enquiries per week from companies, foundations, individual philanthropists, academic institutions and civil society. The UNFIP office now functions as a one-stop service for opportunities to form partnerships to achieve the Millennium Development Goals. It has helped to create innovative alliances with a number of institutions, foundations and corporations, including Domini, Vodafone and the United States Chamber of Commerce. UNFIP facilitated a partnership between the producers of the film *Hotel Rwanda*, UNF and UNDP and established the International Fund for Rwanda, channelling profits from the film and entertainment industry to assist in the country's recovery and reconciliation.

276. In December 2004 UNFIP hosted an event for members of the European Foundation Centre to encourage closer collaboration between European foundations and the United Nations. UNFIP also launched the Power Users of Information and Communication Technology initiative in collaboration with the Education Development Centre to harness the power of technically talented youth worldwide. In response to the Indian Ocean tsunami, UNF provided $5 million of its core funds and, with UNFIP support, was able to leverage an additional $35 million from a range of partners, including the American Red Cross.

277. The International Year of Sport and Physical Education(2005) has provided a useful opportunity for UNFIP to promote field-level

projects using sport as a tool for development, as it continues to provide support to my Special Adviser on Sport for Development and Peace.

Project services

278. The year 2004 was one of further transition and recovery for the United Nations Office for Project Services (UNOPS). A realignment of the Office's structure to bring services closer to clients proceeded and a comprehensive programme to improve financial conditions and the internal control framework and to streamline business processes and technologies to meet changing client and market needs cost-effectively and efficiently was initiated. UNOPS experienced growing demand for its services, particularly for project management services supporting large-scale, complex programme activities in post-conflict and transitional situations. The increased diversification of its client base is of note, and the UNDP/UNFPA Executive Board approved resolutions extending UNOPS service outreach to regional and subregional development banks as well as host Governments in the provision of services to infrastructure and public works programmes.

279. In terms of 2004 performance, UNOPS acquired $739 million in new business, representing the highest level of business acquisition since 1998. Total project delivery for 2004 amounted to $495.22 million, with revenue totalling $45.27 million and expenditures $57.08 million. In addition to ongoing administrative costs, expenditures cover non-recurring investments for the roll-out of a new enterprise resource programme, Atlas, jointly implemented by UNDP/ UNFPA and UNOPS, and expenses associated with change initiatives, to recast UNOPS as a financially viable client-centred organization.

Civil society and business partnerships

280. Since the inception of the United Nations 60 years ago, civil society has always been a key partner of the Organization, whether at the country level delivering humanitarian assistance or at the global level participating in intergovernmental debates. The presence and participation of civil society has clearly enhanced the legitimacy, accountability and transparency of the United Nations.

281. The exponential growth in both numbers and influence over the past two decades or so prompted me to establish the Panel of Eminent Persons on United Nations-Civil Society Relations to assess and draw lessons from United Nations interaction with civil society and recom-

mend ways to improve it. The Panel submitted its report in June 2004 (A/58/817 and Corr.1).

282. I issued a report (A/59/354) in September 2004 in response to the report of the Panel. I commended the report of the Panel to the attention of the General Assembly and made specific recommendations on how it could be implemented. Follow-up actions have already been initiated in a number of areas. The General Assembly decided to hold informal interactive hearings on 23 and 24 June 2005 with representatives of NGOs, civil society organizations and the private sector. I hope this will become an annual meeting held just before the opening of each General Assembly session. The United Nations Development Group is increasing its efforts to strengthen the capacity of the United Nations resident coordinator system to engage with civil society and other relevant local actors at the country level. To that end, UNDG has constituted a working group on civil society to develop terms of reference for the civil society focal point in the resident coordinator system and define a set of programme activities at the country level that will be funded by a trust fund to be established. I am currently looking into ways of putting the Non-Governmental Liaison Service on a stronger institutional and financial footing, but it will take some time to arrive at an acceptable solution. Finally, access to official documents by civil society has become much easier since ODS was made available to the public, on 31 December 2004.

283. On the other hand, I have decided not to pursue the proposed Partnership Office. While we had obtained the concurrence of the Advisory Committee on Administrative and Budgetary Questions for the establishment of a post for the head of the office at the Assistant Secretary-General level, it has not been possible to raise sufficient voluntary funds from donors to ensure its long-term viability. Moreover, some of the expected constituents of the proposed office were not very supportive.

284. So far, the General Assembly has not adopted a resolution in response to the two reports on civil society. Thus, I reiterated in my report to the high-level plenary meeting of the General Assembly to be held in September 2005 (A/59/2005) that the Assembly should engage much more actively with civil society. I sincerely hope that the Member States will act on these recommendations.

285. During the past year the Global Compact has continued its impressive growth while at the same time taking strategic steps to improve quality management. The Global Compact today includes more than 2,000 companies from over 80 countries. At the Global Compact Leaders Sum-

mit that I convened in June 2004, the largest gathering of business and civil society representatives ever held at the United Nations, participants from all sectors agreed that the initiative had reached a stage requiring an intensified focus on quality assurance, brand management and governance at both the global and local levels.

286. To that end the Global Compact Office fully implemented during the past year its policy on communication on progress whereby corporate participants are required to submit annually a prominent communication outlining their implementation of the 10 principles or risk being identified as inactive on the Global Compact website. The overall objective is to increase the transparency and public accountability of the initiative. The Global Compact Office communicated directly with all participating chief executive officers concerning this requirement, while also engaging the many country networks to mobilize local participants in that regard. To assist in the effort, the Global Compact Office, in collaboration with key partners, published the Practical Guide to Communication on Progress. As the 30 June 2005 deadline for submissions approached, more than 80 per cent of the largest corporations engaged in the Global Compact had submitted their communications—many of exemplary quality. However, at the same time, the majority of participants—most of them in the developing world—had not yet submitted their communications. An overriding challenge moving forward, therefore, will be to encourage more companies to develop this important communication, understanding hurdles that include language issues as well as fundamental differences in business culture and attitudes with respect to implementation versus communication. Indeed, it is clear that many Global Compact participants have impressive track records in terms of turning the 10 principles into practice, but are unclear why the Global Compact is now placing such importance on communicating those activities. Thus, we must better explain the rationale, as well as provide those companies with a simple model to follow as they get started.

287. The past year also witnessed important developments with respect to Global Compact country networks, now numbering more than 40. A key meeting of country networks was co-convened by the Government of the United Kingdom in December 2004 at which some networks agreed to form formal governance structures while others opted for looser structures. The networks agreed to work with participants in relation to encouraging the development of communications on progress, as well as becoming more ro-

bust and dynamic with respect to brand management, the recruitment of new participants and initiating more programmes and activities to broaden implementation. One challenge moving forward will indeed be to encourage "sleepy" networks either to become more active or simply fade way. During the year there were impressive examples of country network activity. For example, the Global Compact Egypt network held a series of seminars on implementation, while the Global Compact Society India helped convene a two-day Global Compact Regional Conclave in South Asia in Jamshedpur, which drew more than 200 participants and focused on the issue of business and poverty.

288. With respect to improving brand management, the Global Compact Office also published a new and more comprehensive policy on the use of the Global Compact logo, introducing a second, modified logo for use by participants and other supporters.

289. During the year, the Global Compact Office—at my request—entered the next phase of its governance review, which included the development and circulation to participants of discussion papers relating to overall governance as well as more refined integrity measures. The process was completed in August 2005. While the governance of the Global Compact will continue to be directed from the Global Compact Office, the initiative's participants will take over greater ownership through the many country networks that have been established. At the country level, participants will focus on broader and deeper implementation of the principles and utilize quality-assurance mechanisms to ensure that commitments are translated into concrete action.

290. The Global Compact Office also played a major role in the development of Business Contributions to United Nations Emergency Relief: An Orientation Guide, which it launched with the Office for the Coordination of Humanitarian Affairs at a landmark conference on 25 April, attended by former United States President Bill Clinton. The Guide has been designed to assist businesses in identifying effective ways to support United Nations emergency relief efforts. As the response to the tsunami relief effort demonstrated, we can do a better job at the United Nations in helping to channel the enormous generosity of the private sector amid global crises.

291. In terms of specific issue areas, the Global Compact Office on 28 April launched two related publications—*Enabling Economies of Peace: Public Policy for Conflict-Sensitive Business*, published by the Global Compact, and *Conflict-Sensitive Business Practice: Guidance for Extractive*

Industries, published by the NGO International Alert. I welcome these contributions, as one urges Governments to strengthen efforts to assist businesses in promoting peace, while the other encourages high-impact industries to more aggressively develop conflict-sensitive business practices.

292. Also during the year, the Global Compact stepped up its efforts with respect to engaging the financial markets. Under the umbrella of the Who Cares Wins initiative, launched in June 2004 at the Leaders Summit, a group of mainstream investment companies met in working groups during the year and will publish in 2005 a report and tool that will assist financial analysts in the integration of environmental and social factors to help make markets more inclusive and sustainable. At the same time, the Global Compact and UNEP launched the Principles for Responsible Investment initiative, which is currently mobilizing the chief executive officers of the world's largest pension funds to advance responsible investment globally. In both cases, the challenge will be the adoption of such approaches and guidelines by a critical mass of financial sector actors.

293. The past year also saw the launch of *Compact Quarterly*, an electronic newsletter containing articles and updates on the Global Compact and its issue areas. During its short life, the newsletter has already enjoyed a readership of more than 3,000 participants, policymakers and thought leaders from around the world.

294. Finally, the Global Compact Office secured the support of the Government of China to convene the Global Compact China Summit on 30 November and 1 December 2005. This promises to be a historic event, bringing Chinese business and Government heads together with the leaders of foreign companies and other organizations to advance responsible corporate citizenship in China and beyond.

295. The past year also saw concrete follow-up to the report of the Commission on the Private Sector and Development entitled "Unleashing Entrepreneurship: Making Business Work for the Poor", presented in March 2004 under the auspices of UNDP. The report was officially launched in more than 30 countries, engaging Heads of State, key policymakers, local Governments and private sector players, both foreign and domestic. The launches were complemented by a series of workshops and new project developments, concrete initiatives embodying the recommendations of the report. The year also saw expansion of the Growing Sustainable Business initiative, a key programme that takes the findings of the Commission's report and pushes the envelope of innovative strategies at the nexus of markets and development. Inspired by the Global Compact's 2002 policy dialogue on business and sustainable development, this initiative facilitates business-led enterprise solutions to poverty reduction. It has amassed a portfolio of over 15 leading global businesses and has further pushed its expansion in Africa, Asia and Latin America. Cited by the recent World Economic Forum, NEPAD and Commission for Africa reports as a ground-breaking contribution to the business and development landscape, I look to its continued growth in inspiring innovative business approaches to advance the Millennium Development Goals.

Conclusion

296. The activities described in the present report cover a broad range of issues of direct relevance to the world's peoples, from peace and security to development, human rights and the rule of law. In all these areas, the United Nations is responding imaginatively to the ever-changing needs of the international community. The Organization is a symbol and an instrument of our shared commitment to working together in pursuit of common objectives. Despite its imperfections, the United Nations embodies humanity's hope for a peaceful and equitable world order.

297. In this sixtieth anniversary year of the United Nations, it is important to recognize the many achievements of the Organization since its founding in San Francisco in 1945. But it must also be a time of reflection on how we can better fulfil our duties and responsibilities. Change is nothing new for the Organization, and change has never been more important. At the High-level Plenary Meeting in September, leaders of Member States will have the opportunity to take bold decisions to make our world fairer and freer, more prosperous and more secure, and to strengthen the United Nations. I am confident they will rise to the occasion for our own sake and for the sake of future generations.

2005 UNITED NATIONS WORLD SUMMIT

United Nations Headquarters, New York

60TH ANNIVERSARY OF THE UNITED NATIONS

United Nations

60

A Time for Renewal

"Today, as we celebrate sixty years of our United Nation
we must recognize that the world today is very differen
from that of our founders. The United Nations must
reflect this new age, and respond to its challenges.

Kofi Annan

The 2005 World Summit of the United Nations General Assembly

Gathering of world leaders. From 14 to 16 September, world leaders gathered at United Nations Headquarters in New York for a World Summit (a High-level Plenary Meeting of the United Nations General Assembly) to commemorate the sixtieth anniversary of the founding of the Organization and to chart its future course in a changed world. Convened at the commencement of its sixtieth (2005) session, in response to General Assembly resolution 58/291 [YUN 2004, p. 1363], the World Summit was organized around six plenary meetings and four interactive roundtable sessions. During those three days, world leaders from over 170 countries reviewed the status of implementation of the Millennium Declaration, adopted at the 2000 Millennium Summit [YUN 2000, p. 49], as well as the integrated follow-up to other major United Nations conferences and summits in the economic, social and related fields.

The World Summit was preceded by the resumed fifty-ninth session of the Assembly (15 April), which considered the preparations for the event; a High-level Dialogue on Financing for Development (New York, 27-28 June) (see p. 1065); informal interactive hearings with representatives of civil society and private sector organizations (New York, 23-24 June) (see p. 75); and the Second World Conference of Speakers of Parliament (New York, 7-9 September) (see p. 76).

To assist the World Summit's preparations and negotiations, the Secretary-General submitted to the General Assembly a March report entitled "In larger freedom: towards development, security and human rights for all" [A/59/2005 & Corr. 1] (see p. 67). Three addenda to the report contained explanatory notes on his proposals for the creation of a Peacebuilding Commission [A/59/2005/Add.2], a Human Rights Council [A/59/2005/Add.1], and a letter to the Assembly President containing the Plan of Action for the Human Rights Council submitted by the United Nations High Commissioner for Human Rights [A/59/2005/Add.3]. He also transmitted, by a March note [A/59/727], the overview of the UN Millennium Project's final report, entitled "Investing in Development: A Practical Plan to Achieve the Millennium Development Goals" (see p. 70), prepared by 265 of the world's leading development experts, headed by the Secretary-General's Special Adviser on the Millennium Development Goals (MDGs), Professor Jeffrey D. Sachs (United States).

The World Summit was opened on 14 September by Göran Persson, Prime Minister of Sweden and Co-Chairperson of the Summit, who told the gathering: "five years ago, at the outset of the new millennium, we met here to address key challenges for the future of mankind. Our response included a set of ambitious, yet realistic goals for development. It is time to take stock and evaluate. What have we achieved? Where have we failed?" Good progress in several areas, he added, indicated that eliminating global poverty was not a forlorn hope. It could be done. The challenge was to make development work everywhere. "Let us take advantage of this great opportunity, and our presence here, to live up to our commitments in the Millennium Declaration and the Development Goals. Let each and every one of us do whatever we can to contribute to the great enterprise of building a better United Nations for the benefit of all mankind," he urged.

The President of Gabon, El Hadj Omar Bongo Ondimba, who also Co-Chaired the Summit, said "today, we must acknowledge that we are far from our goal" and drew attention to persisting problems regarding peace and collective security, owing to increasing acts of violence throughout the world, including in the Middle East, Africa and Asia. "Disease and poverty continued to weigh heavily on millions of people in developing countries", he observed, noting that, "clearly, the declaration to be adopted at the end of this summit must not be just another statement. I hope that a new impetus will be born and a new commitment imbued with pragmatism to respond tangibly to the challenges that face us . . . It is therefore our duty to act together to give future generations a better world."

United States President George W. Bush, in his address as the host country President, said "the advance of freedom and security is the calling of our time. It is the mission of the United Nations . . . to spread the hope of liberty, to fight poverty and disease and to help secure human rights and human dignity for all the world's people. To help make those promises real, the United Nations must be strong and efficient, free from corruption and accountable to the people it serves. The

United Nations must stand for integrity—and live by the high standards it sets for others. Meaningful institutional reform must include measures to improve internal oversight, identify cost savings and ensure that precious resources are used for their intended purpose."

The Secretary-General, in his address to the Summit, said that, in marking its sixtieth anniversary, the Organization remained fully engaged in conflict resolution, peacekeeping, humanitarian assistance, defence of human rights and development around the world. However, there were still deep divisions among Member States and the underperformance of their collective institutions were preventing them from coming together to meet the threats they faced and to seize the opportunities before them. The reports of the High-level Panel on Threats, Challenges and Change [YUN 2004, p. 54] and on the UN Millennium Project [A/59/727] had set the agenda for reform, along with a balanced set of proposals he had put forward for decisions at the World Summit (see p. 69), which were ambitious, but necessary and achievable.

The draft Summit outcome document, which had been negotiated, while being a far-reaching package of changes, had not achieved the sweeping and fundamental reform that was required, due to sharp differences of opinion, some of which were substantive and legitimate. The package, however, was a good start and the Organization should turn to the next stages in the reform process. First, it should implement what had been agreed, including getting the Peacebuilding Commission and the Human Rights Council up and running, concluding a comprehensive convention on terrorism and ensuring that the Democracy Fund (see p. 655) was working effectively. Second, the Organization should continue to work with determination on the tough issues on which progress was urgent. A healthy, effective United Nations was vital in the service of all the world's peoples. That was why the reform process mattered and had to continue. He urged world leaders to keep working on the reform agenda, to have the patience to persevere and the vision to forge a real consensus.

On 16 September, after three days of statements, debate and exchange of views in round-table sessions (see p. 71), consultations and negotiations, the General Assembly (see below) adopted the draft outcome document of its 2005 High-level Plenary Meeting (World Summit), **resolution 60/1**, contained in the annex to its **resolution 59/314** of 13 September, which was adopted during its resumed fifty-ninth session. In resolution 60/1, world leaders reaffirmed their faith in the United Nations and their com-

mitment to the purposes and principles of the Charter of the United Nations and outlined a set of principles and a vision for providing multilateral solutions to problems in the areas of development, peace and collective security, human rights and the rule of law and strengthening of the United Nations. The Secretary-General had also submitted to the Summit on 14 September [A/60/355] a statement of the programme budget implications of draft Summit outcome document, in the amount of $80 million, for consideration in the context of the review of the programme budgets for the biennia 2004-2005 and 2006-2007.

Before the adoption of resolution 60/1, the Venezuelan representative, in an explanation of position, said that the outcome document was conceived in darkness and brought forth from the shadows to be approved, in violation of the basic democratic process. The analysis and preparation of the document were restricted to a small group of 32 persons, and subsequently to a smaller group of 15, and thereafter, to an even smaller group. That, he purported, represented an increasing and dangerous curtailment of the exercise of democracy in the Assembly.

2005 World Summit Outcome

A five-part 2005 World Summit Outcome, set out in **resolution 60/1** [draft: A/60/L.1], was adopted by the General Assembly on 16 September [meeting 8] without vote [agenda items 48 and 121].

The General Assembly,
Adopts the following 2005 World Summit Outcome:

I. Values and principles
1. We, Heads of State and Government, have gathered at United Nations Headquarters in New York from 14 to 16 September 2005.
2. We reaffirm our faith in the United Nations and our commitment to the purposes and principles of the Charter of the United Nations and international law, which are indispensable foundations of a more peaceful, prosperous and just world, and reiterate our determination to foster strict respect for them.
3. We reaffirm the United Nations Millennium Declaration, which we adopted at the dawn of the twenty-first century. We recognize the valuable role of the major United Nations conferences and summits in the economic, social and related fields, including the Millennium Summit, in mobilizing the international community at the local, national, regional and global levels and in guiding the work of the United Nations.
4. We reaffirm that our common fundamental values, including freedom, equality, solidarity, tolerance, respect for all human rights, respect for nature and shared responsibility, are essential to international relations.
5. We are determined to establish a just and lasting peace all over the world in accordance with the pur-

poses and principles of the Charter. We rededicate ourselves to support all efforts to uphold the sovereign equality of all States, respect their territorial integrity and political independence, to refrain in our international relations from the threat or use of force in any manner inconsistent with the purposes and principles of the United Nations, to uphold resolution of disputes by peaceful means and in conformity with the principles of justice and international law, the right to self-determination of peoples which remain under colonial domination and foreign occupation, non-interference in the internal affairs of States, respect for human rights and fundamental freedoms, respect for the equal rights of all without distinction as to race, sex, language or religion, international cooperation in solving international problems of an economic, social, cultural or humanitarian character and the fulfilment in good faith of the obligations assumed in accordance with the Charter.

6. We reaffirm the vital importance of an effective multilateral system, in accordance with international law, in order to better address the multifaceted and interconnected challenges and threats confronting our world and to achieve progress in the areas of peace and security, development and human rights, underlining the central role of the United Nations, and commit ourselves to promoting and strengthening the effectiveness of the Organization through the implementation of its decisions and resolutions.

7. We believe that today, more than ever before, we live in a global and interdependent world. No State can stand wholly alone. We acknowledge that collective security depends on effective cooperation, in accordance with international law, against transnational threats.

8. We recognize that current developments and circumstances require that we urgently build consensus on major threats and challenges. We commit ourselves to translating that consensus into concrete action, including addressing the root causes of those threats and challenges with resolve and determination.

9. We acknowledge that peace and security, development and human rights are the pillars of the United Nations system and the foundations for collective security and well-being. We recognize that development, peace and security and human rights are interlinked and mutually reinforcing.

10. We reaffirm that development is a central goal in itself and that sustainable development in its economic, social and environmental aspects constitutes a key element of the overarching framework of United Nations activities.

11. We acknowledge that good governance and the rule of law at the national and international levels are essential for sustained economic growth, sustainable development and the eradication of poverty and hunger.

12. We reaffirm that gender equality and the promotion and protection of the full enjoyment of all human rights and fundamental freedoms for all are essential to advance development and peace and security. We are committed to creating a world fit for future generations, which takes into account the best interests of the child.

13. We reaffirm the universality, indivisibility, interdependence and interrelatedness of all human rights.

14. Acknowledging the diversity of the world, we recognize that all cultures and civilizations contribute to the enrichment of humankind. We acknowledge the importance of respect and understanding for religious and cultural diversity throughout the world. In order to promote international peace and security, we commit ourselves to advancing human welfare, freedom and progress everywhere, as well as to encouraging tolerance, respect, dialogue and cooperation among different cultures, civilizations and peoples.

15. We pledge to enhance the relevance, effectiveness, efficiency, accountability and credibility of the United Nations system. This is our shared responsibility and interest.

16. We therefore resolve to create a more peaceful, prosperous and democratic world and to undertake concrete measures to continue finding ways to implement the outcome of the Millennium Summit and the other major United Nations conferences and summits so as to provide multilateral solutions to problems in the four following areas:

- Development
- Peace and collective security
- Human rights and the rule of law
- Strengthening of the United Nations

II. Development

17. We strongly reiterate our determination to ensure the timely and full realization of the development goals and objectives agreed at the major United Nations conferences and summits, including those agreed at the Millennium Summit that are described as the Millennium Development Goals, which have helped to galvanize efforts towards poverty eradication.

18. We emphasize the vital role played by the major United Nations conferences and summits in the economic, social and related fields in shaping a broad development vision and in identifying commonly agreed objectives, which have contributed to improving human life in different parts of the world.

19. We reaffirm our commitment to eradicate poverty and promote sustained economic growth, sustainable development and global prosperity for all. We are encouraged by reductions in poverty in some countries in the recent past and are determined to reinforce and extend this trend to benefit people worldwide. We remain concerned, however, about the slow and uneven progress towards poverty eradication and the realization of other development goals in some regions. We commit ourselves to promoting the development of the productive sectors in developing countries to enable them to participate more effectively in and benefit from the process of globalization. We underline the need for urgent action on all sides, including more ambitious national development strategies and efforts backed by increased international support.

Global partnership for development

20. We reaffirm our commitment to the global partnership for development set out in the Millennium Declaration, the Monterrey Consensus and the Johannesburg Plan of Implementation.

21. We further reaffirm our commitment to sound policies, good governance at all levels and the rule of

law, and to mobilize domestic resources, attract international flows, promote international trade as an engine for development and increase international financial and technical cooperation for development, sustainable debt financing and external debt relief and to enhance the coherence and consistency of the international monetary, financial and trading systems.

22. We reaffirm that each country must take primary responsibility for its own development and that the role of national policies and development strategies cannot be overemphasized in the achievement of sustainable development. We also recognize that national efforts should be complemented by supportive global programmes, measures and policies aimed at expanding the development opportunities of developing countries, while taking into account national conditions and ensuring respect for national ownership, strategies and sovereignty. To this end, we resolve:

(a) To adopt, by 2006, and implement comprehensive national development strategies to achieve the internationally agreed development goals and objectives, including the Millennium Development Goals;

(b) To manage public finances effectively to achieve and maintain macroeconomic stability and long-term growth and to make effective and transparent use of public funds and ensure that development assistance is used to build national capacities;

(c) To support efforts by developing countries to adopt and implement national development policies and strategies through increased development assistance, the promotion of international trade as an engine for development, the transfer of technology on mutually agreed terms, increased investment flows and wider and deeper debt relief, and to support developing countries by providing a substantial increase in aid of sufficient quality and arriving in a timely manner to assist them in achieving the internationally agreed development goals, including the Millennium Development Goals;

(d) That the increasing interdependence of national economies in a globalizing world and the emergence of rule-based regimes for international economic relations have meant that the space for national economic policy, that is, the scope for domestic policies, especially in the areas of trade, investment and industrial development, is now often framed by international disciplines, commitments and global market considerations. It is for each Government to evaluate the trade-off between the benefits of accepting international rules and commitments and the constraints posed by the loss of policy space. It is particularly important for developing countries, bearing in mind development goals and objectives, that all countries take into account the need for appropriate balance between national policy space and international disciplines and commitments;

(e) To enhance the contribution of non-governmental organizations, civil society, the private sector and other stakeholders in national development efforts, as well as in the promotion of the global partnership for development;

(f) To ensure that the United Nations funds and programmes and the specialized agencies support the efforts of developing countries through the common country assessment and United Nations Development Assistance Framework process, enhancing their support for capacity-building;

(g) To protect our natural resource base in support of development.

Financing for development

23. We reaffirm the Monterrey Consensus and recognize that mobilizing financial resources for development and the effective use of those resources in developing countries and countries with economies in transition are central to a global partnership for development in support of the achievement of the internationally agreed development goals, including the Millennium Development Goals. In this regard:

(a) We are encouraged by recent commitments to substantial increases in official development assistance and the Organization for Economic Cooperation and Development estimate that official development assistance to all developing countries will now increase by around 50 billion United States dollars a year by 2010, while recognizing that a substantial increase in such assistance is required to achieve the internationally agreed goals, including the Millennium Development Goals, within their respective time frames;

(b) We welcome the increased resources that will become available as a result of the establishment of timetables by many developed countries to achieve the target of 0.7 per cent of gross national product for official development assistance by 2015 and to reach at least 0.5 per cent of gross national product for official development assistance by 2010 as well as, pursuant to the Brussels Programme of Action for the Least Developed Countries for the Decade 2001-2010, 0.15 per cent to 0.20 per cent for the least developed countries no later than 2010, and urge those developed countries that have not yet done so to make concrete efforts in this regard in accordance with their commitments;

(c) We further welcome recent efforts and initiatives to enhance the quality of aid and to increase its impact, including the Paris Declaration on Aid Effectiveness, and resolve to take concrete, effective and timely action in implementing all agreed commitments on aid effectiveness, with clear monitoring and deadlines, including through further aligning assistance with countries' strategies, building institutional capacities, reducing transaction costs and eliminating bureaucratic procedures, making progress on untying aid, enhancing the absorptive capacity and financial management of recipient countries and strengthening the focus on development results;

(d) We recognize the value of developing innovative sources of financing, provided those sources do not unduly burden developing countries. In that regard, we take note with interest of the international efforts, contributions and discussions, such as the Action against Hunger and Poverty, aimed at identifying innovative and additional sources of financing for development on a public, private, domestic or external basis to increase and supplement traditional sources of financing. Some countries will implement the International Finance Facility. Some countries have launched the International Finance Facility for immunization. Some countries will implement in the near future, utilizing their national authorities, a contribution on airline tickets to enable the financing of development projects, in particular in the health sector, directly or through financing of the International Finance Facility. Other countries are considering whether and to what extent they will participate in these initiatives;

(e) We acknowledge the vital role the private sector can play in generating new investments, employment and financing for development;

(f) We resolve to address the development needs of low-income developing countries by working in competent multilateral and international forums, to help them meet, inter alia, their financial, technical and technological requirements;

(g) We resolve to continue to support the development efforts of middle-income developing countries by working, in competent multilateral and international forums and also through bilateral arrangements, on measures to help them meet, inter alia, their financial, technical and technological requirements;

(h) We resolve to operationalize the World Solidarity Fund established by the General Assembly and invite those countries in a position to do so to make voluntary contributions to the Fund;

(i) We recognize the need for access to financial services, in particular for the poor, including through microfinance and microcredit.

Domestic resource mobilization

24. In our common pursuit of growth, poverty eradication and sustainable development, a critical challenge is to ensure the necessary internal conditions for mobilizing domestic savings, both public and private, sustaining adequate levels of productive investment, increasing human capacity, reducing capital flight, curbing the illicit transfer of funds and enhancing international cooperation for creating an enabling domestic environment. We undertake to support the efforts of developing countries to create a domestic enabling environment for mobilizing domestic resources. To this end, we therefore resolve:

(a) To pursue good governance and sound macroeconomic policies at all levels and support developing countries in their efforts to put in place the policies and investments to drive sustained economic growth, promote small and medium-sized enterprises, promote employment generation and stimulate the private sector;

(b) To reaffirm that good governance is essential for sustainable development; that sound economic policies, solid democratic institutions responsive to the needs of the people and improved infrastructure are the basis for sustained economic growth, poverty eradication and employment creation; and that freedom, peace and security, domestic stability, respect for human rights, including the right to development, the rule of law, gender equality and market-oriented policies and an overall commitment to just and democratic societies are also essential and mutually reinforcing;

(c) To make the fight against corruption a priority at all levels and we welcome all actions taken in this regard at the national and international levels, including the adoption of policies that emphasize accountability, transparent public sector management and corporate responsibility and accountability, including efforts to return assets transferred through corruption, consistent with the United Nations Convention against Corruption. We urge all States that have not done so to

consider signing, ratifying and implementing the Convention;

(d) To channel private capabilities and resources into stimulating the private sector in developing countries through actions in the public, public/private and private spheres to create an enabling environment for partnership and innovation that contributes to accelerated economic development and hunger and poverty eradication;

(e) To support efforts to reduce capital flight and measures to curb the illicit transfer of funds.

Investment

25. We resolve to encourage greater direct investment, including foreign investment, in developing countries and countries with economies in transition to support their development activities and to enhance the benefits they can derive from such investments. In this regard:

(a) We continue to support efforts by developing countries and countries with economies in transition to create a domestic environment conducive to attracting investments through, inter alia, achieving a transparent, stable and predictable investment climate with proper contract enforcement and respect for property rights and the rule of law and pursuing appropriate policy and regulatory frameworks that encourage business formation;

(b) We will put into place policies to ensure adequate investment in a sustainable manner in health, clean water and sanitation, housing and education and in the provision of public goods and social safety nets to protect vulnerable and disadvantaged sectors of society;

(c) We invite national Governments seeking to develop infrastructure projects and generate foreign direct investment to pursue strategies with the involvement of both the public and private sectors and, where appropriate, international donors;

(d) We call upon international financial and banking institutions to consider enhancing the transparency of risk rating mechanisms. Sovereign risk assessments, made by the private sector should maximize the use of strict, objective and transparent parameters, which can be facilitated by high-quality data and analysis;

(e) We underscore the need to sustain sufficient and stable private financial flows to developing countries and countries with economies in transition. It is important to promote measures in source and destination countries to improve transparency and the information about financial flows to developing countries, particularly countries in Africa, the least developed countries, small island developing States and landlocked developing countries. Measures that mitigate the impact of excessive volatility of short-term capital flows are important and must be considered.

Debt

26. We emphasize the high importance of a timely, effective, comprehensive and durable solution to the debt problems of developing countries, since debt financing and relief can be an important source of capital for development. To this end:

(a) We welcome the recent proposals of the Group of Eight to cancel 100 per cent of the outstanding debt of eligible heavily indebted poor countries owed to the

International Monetary Fund, the International Development Association and African Development Fund and to provide additional resources to ensure that the financing capacity of the international financial institutions is not reduced;

(b) We emphasize that debt sustainability is essential for underpinning growth and underline the importance of debt sustainability to the efforts to achieve national development goals, including the Millennium Development Goals, recognizing the key role that debt relief can play in liberating resources that can be directed towards activities consistent with poverty eradication, sustained economic growth and sustainable development;

(c) We further stress the need to consider additional measures and initiatives aimed at ensuring long-term debt sustainability through increased grant-based financing, cancellation of 100 per cent of the official multilateral and bilateral debt of heavily indebted poor countries and, where appropriate, and on a case-by-case basis, to consider significant debt relief or restructuring for low- and middle-income developing countries with an unsustainable debt burden that are not part of the Heavily Indebted Poor Countries Initiative, as well as the exploration of mechanisms to comprehensively address the debt problems of those countries. Such mechanisms may include debt for sustainable development swaps or multicreditor debt swap arrangements, as appropriate. These initiatives could include further efforts by the International Monetary Fund and the World Bank to develop the debt sustainability framework for low-income countries. This should be achieved in a fashion that does not detract from official development assistance resources, while maintaining the financial integrity of the multilateral financial institutions.

Trade

27. A universal, rule-based, open, non-discriminatory and equitable multilateral trading system, as well as meaningful trade liberalization, can substantially stimulate development worldwide, benefiting countries at all stages of development. In that regard, we reaffirm our commitment to trade liberalization and to ensure that trade plays its full part in promoting economic growth, employment and development for all.

28. We are committed to efforts designed to ensure that developing countries, especially the least-developed countries, participate fully in the world trading system in order to meet their economic development needs, and reaffirm our commitment to enhanced and predictable market access for the exports of developing countries.

29. We will work towards the objective, in accordance with the Brussels Programme of Action, of duty-free and quota-free market access for all least developed countries' products to the markets of developed countries, as well as to the markets of developing countries in a position to do so, and support their efforts to overcome their supply-side constraints.

30. We are committed to supporting and promoting increased aid to build productive and trade capacities of developing countries and to taking further steps in that regard, while welcoming the substantial support already provided.

31. We will work to accelerate and facilitate the accession of developing countries and countries with economies in transition to the World Trade Organization consistent with its criteria, recognizing the importance of universal integration in the rules-based global trading system.

32. We will work expeditiously towards implementing the development dimensions of the Doha work programme.

Commodities

33. We emphasize the need to address the impact of weak and volatile commodity prices and support the efforts of commodity-dependent countries to restructure, diversify and strengthen the competitiveness of their commodity sectors.

Quick-impact initiatives

34. Given the need to accelerate progress immediately in countries where current trends make the achievement of the internationally agreed development goals unlikely, we resolve to urgently identify and implement country-led initiatives with adequate international support, consistent with long-term national development strategies, that promise immediate and durable improvements in the lives of people and renewed hope for the achievement of the development goals. In this regard, we will take such actions as the distribution of malaria bed nets, including free distribution, where appropriate, and effective anti-malarial treatments, the expansion of local school meal programmes, using home-grown foods where possible, and the elimination of user fees for primary education and, where appropriate, health-care services.

Systemic issues and global economic decision-making

35. We reaffirm the commitment to broaden and strengthen the participation of developing countries and countries with economies in transition in international economic decision-making and norm-setting, and to that end stress the importance of continuing efforts to reform the international financial architecture, noting that enhancing the voice and participation of developing countries and countries with economies in transition in the Bretton Woods institutions remains a continuous concern.

36. We reaffirm our commitment to governance, equity and transparency in the financial, monetary and trading systems. We are also committed to open, equitable, rule-based, predictable and non-discriminatory multilateral trading and financial systems.

37. We also underscore our commitment to sound domestic financial sectors, which make a vital contribution to national development efforts, as an important component of an international financial architecture that is supportive of development.

38. We further reaffirm the need for the United Nations to play a fundamental role in the promotion of international cooperation for development and the coherence, coordination and implementation of development goals and actions agreed upon by the international community, and we resolve to strengthen coordination within the United Nations system in close cooperation with all other multilateral financial, trade and development institutions in order to support

sustained economic growth, poverty eradication and sustainable development.

39. Good governance at the international level is fundamental for achieving sustainable development. In order to ensure a dynamic and enabling international economic environment, it is important to promote global economic governance through addressing the international finance, trade, technology and investment patterns that have an impact on the development prospects of developing countries. To this effect, the international community should take all necessary and appropriate measures, including ensuring support for structural and macroeconomic reform, a comprehensive solution to the external debt problem and increasing the market access of developing countries.

South-South cooperation

40. We recognize the achievements and great potential of South-South cooperation and encourage the promotion of such cooperation, which complements North-South cooperation as an effective contribution to development and as a means to share best practices and provide enhanced technical cooperation. In this context, we note the recent decision of the leaders of the South, adopted at the Second South Summit and contained in the Doha Declaration and the Doha Plan of Action, to intensify their efforts at South-South cooperation, including through the establishment of the New Asian-African Strategic Partnership and other regional cooperation mechanisms, and encourage the international community, including the international financial institutions, to support the efforts of developing countries, inter alia, through triangular cooperation. We also take note with appreciation of the launching of the third round of negotiations on the Global System of Trade Preferences among Developing Countries as an important instrument to stimulate South-South cooperation.

41. We welcome the work of the United Nations High-Level Committee on South-South Cooperation and invite countries to consider supporting the Special Unit for South-South Cooperation within the United Nations Development Programme in order to respond effectively to the development needs of developing countries.

42. We recognize the considerable contribution of arrangements such as the Organization of Petroleum Exporting Countries Fund initiated by a group of developing countries, as well as the potential contribution of the South Fund for Development and Humanitarian Assistance, to development activities in developing countries.

Education

43. We emphasize the critical role of both formal and informal education in the achievement of poverty eradication and other development goals as envisaged in the Millennium Declaration, in particular basic education and training for eradicating illiteracy, and strive for expanded secondary and higher education as well as vocational education and technical training, especially for girls and women, the creation of human resources and infrastructure capabilities and the empowerment of those living in poverty. In this context, we reaffirm the Dakar Framework for Action adopted at the World Education Forum in 2000 and recognize the importance of the United Nations Educational, Scientific and Cultural Organization strategy for the eradication of poverty, especially extreme poverty, in supporting the Education for All programmes as a tool to achieve the millennium development goal of universal primary education by 2015.

44. We reaffirm our commitment to support developing country efforts to ensure that all children have access to and complete free and compulsory primary education of good quality, to eliminate gender inequality and imbalance and to renew efforts to improve girls' education. We also commit ourselves to continuing to support the efforts of developing countries in the implementation of the Education for All initiative, including with enhanced resources of all types through the Education for All fast-track initiative in support of country-led national education plans.

45. We commit ourselves to promoting education for peace and human development.

Rural and agricultural development

46. We reaffirm that food security and rural and agricultural development must be adequately and urgently addressed in the context of national development and response strategies and, in this context, will enhance the contributions of indigenous and local communities, as appropriate. We are convinced that the eradication of poverty, hunger and malnutrition, particularly as they affect children, is crucial for the achievement of the Millennium Development Goals. Rural and agricultural development should be an integral part of national and international development policies. We deem it necessary to increase productive investment in rural and agricultural development to achieve food security. We commit ourselves to increasing support for agricultural development and trade capacity-building in the agricultural sector in developing countries. Support for commodity development projects, especially market-based projects, and for their preparation under the Second Account of the Common Fund for Commodities should be encouraged.

Employment

47. We strongly support fair globalization and resolve to make the goals of full and productive employment and decent work for all, including for women and young people, a central objective of our relevant national and international policies as well as our national development strategies, including poverty reduction strategies, as part of our efforts to achieve the Millennium Development Goals. These measures should also encompass the elimination of the worst forms of child labour, as defined in International Labour Organization Convention No. 182, and forced labour. We also resolve to ensure full respect for the fundamental principles and rights at work.

Sustainable development: managing and protecting our common environment

48. We reaffirm our commitment to achieve the goal of sustainable development, including through the implementation of Agenda 21 and the Johannesburg Plan of Implementation. To this end, we commit ourselves to undertaking concrete actions and measures at all levels and to enhancing international cooperation, taking into account the Rio principles. These efforts will also promote the integration of the

three components of sustainable development—economic development, social development and environmental protection—as interdependent and mutually reinforcing pillars. Poverty eradication, changing unsustainable patterns of production and consumption and protecting and managing the natural resource base of economic and social development are overarching objectives of and essential requirements for sustainable development.

49. We will promote sustainable consumption and production patterns, with the developed countries taking the lead and all countries benefiting from the process, as called for in the Johannesburg Plan of Implementation. In that context, we support developing countries in their efforts to promote a recycling economy.

50. We face serious and multiple challenges in tackling climate change, promoting clean energy, meeting energy needs and achieving sustainable development, and we will act with resolve and urgency in this regard.

51. We recognize that climate change is a serious and long-term challenge that has the potential to affect every part of the globe. We emphasize the need to meet all the commitments and obligations we have undertaken in the United Nations Framework Convention on Climate Change and other relevant international agreements, including, for many of us, the Kyoto Protocol. The Convention is the appropriate framework for addressing future action on climate change at the global level.

52. We reaffirm our commitment to the ultimate objective of the Convention: to stabilize greenhouse gas concentrations in the atmosphere at a level that prevents dangerous anthropogenic interference with the climate system.

53. We acknowledge that the global nature of climate change calls for the widest possible cooperation and participation in an effective and appropriate international response, in accordance with the principles of the Convention. We are committed to moving forward the global discussion on long-term cooperative action to address climate change, in accordance with these principles. We stress the importance of the eleventh session of the Conference of the Parties to the Convention, to be held in Montreal in November 2005.

54. We acknowledge various partnerships that are under way to advance action on clean energy and climate change, including bilateral, regional and multilateral initiatives.

55. We are committed to taking further action through practical international cooperation, inter alia:

(*a*) To promote innovation, clean energy and energy efficiency and conservation; improve policy, regulatory and financing frameworks; and accelerate the deployment of cleaner technologies;

(*b*) To enhance private investment, transfer of technologies and capacity-building to developing countries, as called for in the Johannesburg Plan of Implementation, taking into account their own energy needs and priorities;

(*c*) To assist developing countries to improve their resilience and integrate adaptation goals into their sustainable development strategies, given that adaptation to the effects of climate change due to both natural and human factors is a high priority for all nations, particu-

larly those most vulnerable, namely, those referred to in article 4.8 of the Convention;

(*d*) To continue to assist developing countries, in particular small island developing States, least developed countries and African countries, including those that are particularly vulnerable to climate change, in addressing their adaptation needs relating to the adverse effects of climate change.

56. In pursuance of our commitment to achieve sustainable development, we further resolve:

(*a*) To promote the United Nations Decade of Education for Sustainable Development and the International Decade for Action, "Water for Life";

(*b*) To support and strengthen the implementation of the United Nations Convention to Combat Desertification in Those Countries Experiencing Serious Drought and/or Desertification, Particularly in Africa, to address causes of desertification and land degradation, as well as poverty resulting from land degradation, through, inter alia, the mobilization of adequate and predictable financial resources, the transfer of technology and capacity-building at all levels;

(*c*) That the States parties to the Convention on Biological Diversity and the Cartagena Protocol on Biosafety should support the implementation of the Convention and the Protocol, as well as other biodiversity-related agreements and the Johannesburg commitment for a significant reduction in the rate of loss of biodiversity by 2010. The States parties will continue to negotiate within the framework of the Convention on Biological Diversity, bearing in mind the Bonn Guidelines, an international regime to promote and safeguard the fair and equitable sharing of benefits arising out of the utilization of genetic resources. All States will fulfil commitments and significantly reduce the rate of loss of biodiversity by 2010 and continue ongoing efforts towards elaborating and negotiating an international regime on access to genetic resources and benefit-sharing;

(*d*) To recognize that the sustainable development of indigenous peoples and their communities is crucial in our fight against hunger and poverty;

(*e*) To reaffirm our commitment, subject to national legislation, to respect, preserve and maintain the knowledge, innovations and practices of indigenous and local communities embodying traditional lifestyles relevant to the conservation and sustainable use of biological diversity, promote their wider application with the approval and involvement of the holders of such knowledge, innovations and practices and encourage the equitable sharing of the benefits arising from their utilization;

(*f*) To work expeditiously towards the establishment of a worldwide early warning system for all natural hazards with regional nodes, building on existing national and regional capacity such as the newly established Indian Ocean Tsunami Warning and Mitigation System;

(*g*) To fully implement the Hyogo Declaration and the Hyogo Framework for Action 2005-2015 adopted at the World Conference on Disaster Reduction, in particular those commitments related to assistance for developing countries that are prone to natural disasters and disaster-stricken States in the transition phase towards sustainable physical, social and economic recovery, for risk-reduction activities in post-disaster recovery and for rehabilitation processes;

(*h*) To assist developing countries' efforts to prepare integrated water resources management and water efficiency plans as part of their national development strategies and to provide access to safe drinking water and basic sanitation in accordance with the Millennium Declaration and the Johannesburg Plan of Implementation, including halving by 2015 the proportion of people who are unable to reach or afford safe drinking water and who do not have access to basic sanitation;

(*i*) To accelerate the development and dissemination of affordable and cleaner energy efficiency and energy conservation technologies, as well as the transfer of such technologies, in particular to developing countries, on favourable terms, including on concessional and preferential terms, as mutually agreed, bearing in mind that access to energy facilitates the eradication of poverty;

(*j*) To strengthen the conservation, sustainable management and development of all types of forests for the benefit of current and future generations, including through enhanced international cooperation, so that trees and forests may contribute fully to the achievement of the internationally agreed development goals, including those contained in the Millennium Declaration, taking full account of the linkages between the forest sector and other sectors. We look forward to the discussions at the sixth session of the United Nations Forum on Forests;

(*k*) To promote the sound management of chemicals and hazardous wastes throughout their life cycle, in accordance with Agenda 21 and the Johannesburg Plan of Implementation, aiming to achieve that by 2020 chemicals are used and produced in ways that lead to the minimization of significant adverse effects on human health and the environment using transparent and science-based risk assessment and risk management procedures, by adopting and implementing a voluntary strategic approach to international management of chemicals, and to support developing countries in strengthening their capacity for the sound management of chemicals and hazardous wastes by providing technical and financial assistance, as appropriate;

(*l*) To improve cooperation and coordination at all levels in order to address issues related to oceans and seas in an integrated manner and promote integrated management and sustainable development of the oceans and seas;

(*m*) To achieve significant improvement in the lives of at least 100 million slum-dwellers by 2020, recognizing the urgent need for the provision of increased resources for affordable housing and housing-related infrastructure, prioritizing slum prevention and slum upgrading, and to encourage support for the United Nations Habitat and Human Settlements Foundation and its Slum Upgrading Facility;

(*n*) To acknowledge the invaluable role of the Global Environment Facility in facilitating cooperation with developing countries; we look forward to a successful replenishment this year along with the successful conclusion of all outstanding commitments from the third replenishment;

(*o*) To note that cessation of the transport of radioactive materials through the regions of small island developing States is an ultimate desired goal of small island developing States and some other countries and recognize the right of freedom of navigation in accordance with international law. States should maintain dialogue and consultation, in particular under the aegis of the International Atomic Energy Agency and the International Maritime Organization, with the aim of improved mutual understanding, confidence-building and enhanced communication in relation to the safe maritime transport of radioactive materials. States involved in the transport of such materials are urged to continue to engage in dialogue with small island developing States and other States to address their concerns. These concerns include the further development and strengthening, within the appropriate forums, of international regulatory regimes to enhance safety, disclosure, liability, security and compensation in relation to such transport.

HIV/AIDS, malaria, tuberculosis and other health issues

57. We recognize that HIV/AIDS, malaria, tuberculosis and other infectious diseases pose severe risks for the entire world and serious challenges to the achievement of development goals. We acknowledge the substantial efforts and financial contributions made by the international community, while recognizing that these diseases and other emerging health challenges require a sustained international response. To this end, we commit ourselves to:

(*a*) Increasing investment, building on existing mechanisms and through partnership, to improve health systems in developing countries and those with economies in transition with the aim of providing sufficient health workers, infrastructure, management systems and supplies to achieve the health-related Millennium Development Goals by 2015;

(*b*) Implementing measures to increase the capacity of adults and adolescents to protect themselves from the risk of HIV infection;

(*c*) Fully implementing all commitments established by the Declaration of Commitment on HIV/AIDS through stronger leadership, the scaling up of a comprehensive response to achieve broad multisectoral coverage for prevention, care, treatment and support, the mobilization of additional resources from national, bilateral, multilateral and private sources and the substantial funding of the Global Fund to Fight AIDS, Tuberculosis and Malaria as well as of the HIV/AIDS component of the work programmes of the United Nations system agencies and programmes engaged in the fight against HIV/AIDS;

(*d*) Developing and implementing a package for HIV prevention, treatment and care with the aim of coming as close as possible to the goal of universal access to treatment by 2010 for all those who need it, including through increased resources, and working towards the elimination of stigma and discrimination, enhanced access to affordable medicines and the reduction of vulnerability of persons affected by HIV/AIDS and other health issues, in particular orphaned and vulnerable children and older persons;

(*e*) Ensuring the full implementation of our obligations under the International Health Regulations adopted by the fifty-eighth World Health Assembly in May 2005, including the need to support the Global Outbreak Alert and Response Network of the World Health Organization;

(f) Working actively to implement the "Three Ones" principles in all countries, including by ensuring that multiple institutions and international partners all work under one agreed HIV/AIDS framework that provides the basis for coordinating the work of all partners, with one national AIDS coordinating authority having a broad-based multisectoral mandate, and under one agreed country-level monitoring and evaluation system. We welcome and support the important recommendations of the Global Task Team on Improving AIDS Coordination among Multilateral Institutions and International Donors;

(g) Achieving universal access to reproductive health by 2015, as set out at the International Conference on Population and Development, integrating this goal in strategies to attain the internationally agreed development goals, including those contained in the Millennium Declaration, aimed at reducing maternal mortality, improving maternal health, reducing child mortality, promoting gender equality, combating HIV/AIDS and eradicating poverty;

(h) Promoting long-term funding, including public-private partnerships where appropriate, for academic and industrial research as well as for the development of new vaccines and microbicides, diagnostic kits, drugs and treatments to address major pandemics, tropical diseases and other diseases, such as avian flu and severe acute respiratory syndrome, and taking forward work on market incentives, where appropriate through such mechanisms as advance purchase commitments;

(i) Stressing the need to urgently address malaria and tuberculosis, in particular in the most affected countries, and welcoming the scaling up, in this regard, of bilateral and multilateral initiatives.

Gender equality and empowerment of women

58. We remain convinced that progress for women is progress for all. We reaffirm that the full and effective implementation of the goals and objectives of the Beijing Declaration and Platform for Action and the outcome of the twenty-third special session of the General Assembly is an essential contribution to achieving the internationally agreed development goals, including those contained in the Millennium Declaration, and we resolve to promote gender equality and eliminate pervasive gender discrimination by:

(a) Eliminating gender inequalities in primary and secondary education by the earliest possible date and at all educational levels by 2015;

(b) Guaranteeing the free and equal right of women to own and inherit property and ensuring secure tenure of property and housing by women;

(c) Ensuring equal access to reproductive health;

(d) Promoting women's equal access to labour markets, sustainable employment and adequate labour protection;

(e) Ensuring equal access of women to productive assets and resources, including land, credit and technology;

(f) Eliminating all forms of discrimination and violence against women and the girl child, including by ending impunity and by ensuring the protection of civilians, in particular women and the girl child, during and after armed conflicts in accordance with the obligations of States under international humanitarian law and international human rights law;

(g) Promoting increased representation of women in Government decision-making bodies, including through ensuring their equal opportunity to participate fully in the political process.

59. We recognize the importance of gender mainstreaming as a tool for achieving gender equality. To that end, we undertake to actively promote the mainstreaming of a gender perspective in the design, implementation, monitoring and evaluation of policies and programmes in all political, economic and social spheres, and further undertake to strengthen the capabilities of the United Nations system in the area of gender.

Science and technology for development

60. We recognize that science and technology, including information and communication technology, are vital for the achievement of the development goals and that international support can help developing countries to benefit from technological advancements and enhance their productive capacity. We therefore commit ourselves to:

(a) Strengthening and enhancing existing mechanisms and supporting initiatives for research and development, including through voluntary partnerships between the public and private sectors, to address the special needs of developing countries in the areas of health, agriculture, conservation, sustainable use of natural resources and environmental management, energy, forestry and the impact of climate change;

(b) Promoting and facilitating, as appropriate, access to and the development, transfer and diffusion of technologies, including environmentally sound technologies and corresponding know-how, to developing countries;

(c) Assisting developing countries in their efforts to promote and develop national strategies for human resources and science and technology, which are primary drivers of national capacity-building for development;

(d) Promoting and supporting greater efforts to develop renewable sources of energy, such as solar, wind and geothermal;

(e) Implementing policies at the national and international levels to attract both public and private investment, domestic and foreign, that enhances knowledge, transfers technology on mutually agreed terms and raises productivity;

(f) Supporting the efforts of developing countries, individually and collectively, to harness new agricultural technologies in order to increase agricultural productivity through environmentally sustainable means;

(g) Building a people-centred and inclusive information society so as to enhance digital opportunities for all people in order to help bridge the digital divide, putting the potential of information and communication technologies at the service of development and addressing new challenges of the information society by implementing the outcomes of the Geneva phase of the World Summit on the Information Society and ensuring the success of the second phase of the Summit, to be held in Tunis in November 2005; in this regard, we welcome the establishment of the Digital Solidarity Fund and encourage voluntary contributions to its financing.

Migration and development

61. We acknowledge the important nexus between international migration and development and the need to deal with the challenges and opportunities that migration presents to countries of origin, destination and transit. We recognize that international migration brings benefits as well as challenges to the global community. We look forward to the high-level dialogue of the General Assembly on international migration and development to be held in 2006, which will offer an opportunity to discuss the multidimensional aspects of international migration and development in order to identify appropriate ways and means to maximize their development benefits and minimize their negative impacts.

62. We reaffirm our resolve to take measures to ensure respect for and protection of the human rights of migrants, migrant workers and members of their families.

63. We reaffirm the need to adopt policies and undertake measures to reduce the cost of transferring migrant remittances to developing countries and welcome efforts by Governments and stakeholders in this regard.

Countries with special needs

64. We reaffirm our commitment to address the special needs of the least developed countries and urge all countries and all relevant organizations of the United Nations system, including the Bretton Woods institutions, to make concerted efforts and adopt speedy measures for meeting in a timely manner the goals and targets of the Brussels Programme of Action for the Least Developed Countries for the Decade 2001-2010.

65. We recognize the special needs of and challenges faced by landlocked developing countries and therefore reaffirm our commitment to urgently address those needs and challenges through the full, timely and effective implementation of the Almaty Programme of Action: Addressing the Special Needs of Landlocked Developing Countries within a New Global Framework for Transit Transport Cooperation for Landlocked and Transit Developing Countries and the São Paulo Consensus adopted at the eleventh session of the United Nations Conference on Trade and Development. We encourage the work undertaken by United Nations regional commissions and organizations towards establishing a time-cost methodology for indicators to measure the progress in implementation of the Almaty Programme of Action. We also recognize the special difficulties and concerns of landlocked developing countries in their efforts to integrate their economies into the multilateral trading system. In this regard, priority should be given to the full and timely implementation of the Almaty Declaration and the Almaty Programme of Action.

66. We recognize the special needs and vulnerabilities of small island developing States and reaffirm our commitment to take urgent and concrete action to address those needs and vulnerabilities through the full and effective implementation of the Mauritius Strategy adopted by the International Meeting to Review the Implementation of the Programme of Action for the Sustainable Development of Small Island Developing States, the Barbados Programme of Action and the outcome of the twenty-second special session of the General Assembly. We further undertake to promote greater international cooperation and partnership for the implementation of the Mauritius Strategy through, inter alia, the mobilization of domestic and international resources, the promotion of international trade as an engine for development and increased international financial and technical cooperation.

67. We emphasize the need for continued, coordinated and effective international support for achieving the development goals in countries emerging from conflict and in those recovering from natural disasters.

Meeting the special needs of Africa

68. We welcome the substantial progress made by the African countries in fulfilling their commitments and emphasize the need to carry forward the implementation of the New Partnership for Africa's Development to promote sustainable growth and development and deepen democracy, human rights, good governance and sound economic management and gender equality and encourage African countries, with the participation of civil society and the private sector, to continue their efforts in this regard by developing and strengthening institutions for governance and the development of the region, and also welcome the recent decisions taken by Africa's partners, including the Group of Eight and the European Union, in support of Africa's development efforts, including commitments that will lead to an increase in official development assistance to Africa of 25 billion dollars per year by 2010. We reaffirm our commitment to address the special needs of Africa, which is the only continent not on track to meet any of the goals of the Millennium Declaration by 2015, to enable it to enter the mainstream of the world economy, and resolve:

(*a*) To strengthen cooperation with the New Partnership for Africa's Development by providing coherent support for the programmes drawn up by African leaders within that framework, including by mobilizing internal and external financial resources and facilitating approval of such programmes by the multilateral financial institutions;

(*b*) To support the African commitment to ensure that by 2015 all children have access to complete, free and compulsory primary education of good quality, as well as to basic health care;

(*c*) To support the building of an international infrastructure consortium involving the African Union, the World Bank and the African Development Bank, with the New Partnership for Africa's Development as the main framework, to facilitate public and private infrastructure investment in Africa;

(*d*) To promote a comprehensive and durable solution to the external debt problems of African countries, including through the cancellation of 100 per cent of multilateral debt consistent with the recent Group of Eight proposal for the heavily indebted poor countries, and, on a case-by-case basis, where appropriate, significant debt relief, including, inter alia, cancellation or restructuring for heavily indebted African countries not part of the Heavily Indebted Poor Countries Initiative that have unsustainable debt burdens;

(*e*) To make efforts to fully integrate African countries in the international trading system, including through targeted trade capacity-building programmes;

(*f*) To support the efforts of commodity-dependent African countries to restructure, diversify and strengthen the competitiveness of their commodity sectors and decide to work towards market-based arrangements with the participation of the private sector for commodity price-risk management;

(*g*) To supplement the efforts of African countries, individually and collectively, to increase agricultural productivity, in a sustainable way, as set out in the Comprehensive Africa Agriculture Development Programme of the New Partnership for Africa's Development as part of an African "Green Revolution";

(*h*) To encourage and support the initiatives of the African Union and subregional organizations to prevent, mediate and resolve conflicts with the assistance of the United Nations, and in this regard welcomes the proposals from the Group of Eight countries to provide support for African peacekeeping;

(*i*) To provide, with the aim of an AIDS-, malaria- and tuberculosis-free generation in Africa, assistance for prevention and care and to come as close as possible to achieving the goal of universal access by 2010 to HIV/AIDS treatment in African countries, to encourage pharmaceutical companies to make drugs, including antiretroviral drugs, affordable and accessible in Africa and to ensure increased bilateral and multilateral assistance, where possible on a grant basis, to combat malaria, tuberculosis and other infectious diseases in Africa through the strengthening of health systems.

III. Peace and collective security

69. We recognize that we are facing a whole range of threats that require our urgent, collective and more determined response.

70. We also recognize that, in accordance with the Charter, addressing such threats requires cooperation among all the principal organs of the United Nations within their respective mandates.

71. We acknowledge that we are living in an interdependent and global world and that many of today's threats recognize no national boundaries, are interlinked and must be tackled at the global, regional and national levels in accordance with the Charter and international law.

72. We therefore reaffirm our commitment to work towards a security consensus based on the recognition that many threats are interlinked, that development, peace, security and human rights are mutually reinforcing, that no State can best protect itself by acting entirely alone and that all States need an effective and efficient collective security system pursuant to the purposes and principles of the Charter.

Pacific settlement of disputes

73. We emphasize the obligation of States to settle their disputes by peaceful means in accordance with Chapter VI of the Charter, including, when appropriate, by the use of the International Court of Justice. All States should act in accordance with the Declaration on Principles of International Law concerning Friendly Relations and Cooperation among States in accordance with the Charter of the United Nations.

74. We stress the importance of prevention of armed conflict in accordance with the purposes and principles of the Charter and solemnly renew our commitment to promote a culture of prevention of armed conflict as a means of effectively addressing the interconnected security and development challenges faced by peoples throughout the world, as well as to strengthen the capacity of the United Nations for the prevention of armed conflict.

75. We further stress the importance of a coherent and integrated approach to the prevention of armed conflicts and the settlement of disputes and the need for the Security Council, the General Assembly, the Economic and Social Council and the Secretary-General to coordinate their activities within their respective Charter mandates.

76. Recognizing the important role of the good offices of the Secretary-General, including in the mediation of disputes, we support the Secretary-General's efforts to strengthen his capacity in this area.

Use of force under the Charter of the United Nations

77. We reiterate the obligation of all Member States to refrain in their international relations from the threat or use of force in any manner inconsistent with the Charter. We reaffirm that the purposes and principles guiding the United Nations are, inter alia, to maintain international peace and security, to develop friendly relations among nations based on respect for the principles of equal rights and self-determination of peoples and to take other appropriate measures to strengthen universal peace, and to that end we are determined to take effective collective measures for the prevention and removal of threats to the peace and for the suppression of acts of aggression or other breaches of the peace, and to bring about by peaceful means, in conformity with the principles of justice and international law, the adjustment or settlement of international disputes or situations that might lead to a breach of the peace.

78. We reiterate the importance of promoting and strengthening the multilateral process and of addressing international challenges and problems by strictly abiding by the Charter and the principles of international law, and further stress our commitment to multilateralism.

79. We reaffirm that the relevant provisions of the Charter are sufficient to address the full range of threats to international peace and security. We further reaffirm the authority of the Security Council to mandate coercive action to maintain and restore international peace and security. We stress the importance of acting in accordance with the purposes and principles of the Charter.

80. We also reaffirm that the Security Council has primary responsibility in the maintenance of international peace and security. We also note the role of the General Assembly relating to the maintenance of international peace and security in accordance with the relevant provisions of the Charter.

Terrorism

81. We strongly condemn terrorism in all its forms and manifestations, committed by whomever, wherever and for whatever purposes, as it constitutes one of the most serious threats to international peace and security.

82. We welcome the Secretary-General's identification of elements of a counter-terrorism strategy. These elements should be developed by the General Assem-

bly without delay with a view to adopting and implementing a strategy to promote comprehensive, coordinated and consistent responses, at the national, regional and international levels, to counter terrorism, which also takes into account the conditions conducive to the spread of terrorism. In this context, we commend the various initiatives to promote dialogue, tolerance and understanding among civilizations.

83. We stress the need to make every effort to reach an agreement on and conclude a comprehensive convention on international terrorism during the sixtieth session of the General Assembly.

84. We acknowledge that the question of convening a high-level conference under the auspices of the United Nations to formulate an international response to terrorism in all its forms and manifestations could be considered.

85. We recognize that international cooperation to fight terrorism must be conducted in conformity with international law, including the Charter and relevant international conventions and protocols. States must ensure that any measures taken to combat terrorism comply with their obligations under international law, in particular human rights law, refugee law and international humanitarian law.

86. We reiterate our call upon States to refrain from organizing, financing, encouraging, providing training for or otherwise supporting terrorist activities and to take appropriate measures to ensure that their territories are not used for such activities.

87. We acknowledge the important role played by the United Nations in combating terrorism and also stress the vital contribution of regional and bilateral cooperation, particularly at the practical level of law enforcement cooperation and technical exchange.

88. We urge the international community, including the United Nations, to assist States in building national and regional capacity to combat terrorism. We invite the Secretary-General to submit proposals to the General Assembly and the Security Council, within their respective mandates, to strengthen the capacity of the United Nations system to assist States in combating terrorism and to enhance the coordination of United Nations activities in this regard.

89. We stress the importance of assisting victims of terrorism and of providing them and their families with support to cope with their loss and their grief.

90. We encourage the Security Council to consider ways to strengthen its monitoring and enforcement role in counter-terrorism, including by consolidating State reporting requirements, taking into account and respecting the different mandates of its counter-terrorism subsidiary bodies. We are committed to cooperating fully with the three competent subsidiary bodies in the fulfilment of their tasks, recognizing that many States continue to require assistance in implementing relevant Security Council resolutions.

91. We support efforts for the early entry into force of the International Convention for the Suppression of Acts of Nuclear Terrorism and strongly encourage States to consider becoming parties to it expeditiously and acceding without delay to the twelve other international conventions and protocols against terrorism and implementing them.

Peacekeeping

92. Recognizing that United Nations peacekeeping plays a vital role in helping parties to conflict end hostilities and commending the contribution of United Nations peacekeepers in that regard, noting improvements made in recent years in United Nations peacekeeping, including the deployment of integrated missions in complex situations, and stressing the need to mount operations with adequate capacity to counter hostilities and fulfil effectively their mandates, we urge further development of proposals for enhanced rapidly deployable capacities to reinforce peacekeeping operations in crises. We endorse the creation of an initial operating capability for a standing police capacity to provide coherent, effective and responsive start-up capability for the policing component of the United Nations peacekeeping missions and to assist existing missions through the provision of advice and expertise.

93. Recognizing the important contribution to peace and security by regional organizations as provided for under Chapter VIII of the Charter and the importance of forging predictable partnerships and arrangements between the United Nations and regional organizations, and noting in particular, given the special needs of Africa, the importance of a strong African Union:

(a) We support the efforts of the European Union and other regional entities to develop capacities such as for rapid deployment, standby and bridging arrangements;

(b) We support the development and implementation of a ten-year plan for capacity-building with the African Union.

94. We support implementation of the 2001 Programme of Action to Prevent, Combat and Eradicate the Illicit Trade in Small Arms and Light Weapons in All Its Aspects.

95. We urge States parties to the Anti-Personnel Mine Ban Convention and Amended Protocol II to the Convention on Certain Conventional Weapons to fully implement their respective obligations. We call upon States in a position to do so to provide greater technical assistance to mine-affected States.

96. We underscore the importance of the recommendations of the Adviser to the Secretary-General on Sexual Exploitation and Abuse by United Nations Peacekeeping Personnel, and urge that those measures adopted in the relevant General Assembly resolutions based upon the recommendations be fully implemented without delay.

Peacebuilding

97. Emphasizing the need for a coordinated, coherent and integrated approach to post-conflict peacebuilding and reconciliation with a view to achieving sustainable peace, recognizing the need for a dedicated institutional mechanism to address the special needs of countries emerging from conflict towards recovery, reintegration and reconstruction and to assist them in laying the foundation for sustainable development, and recognizing the vital role of the United Nations in that regard, we decide to establish a Peacebuilding Commission as an intergovernmental advisory body.

98. The main purpose of the Peacebuilding Commission is to bring together all relevant actors to marshal resources and to advise on and propose integrated strategies for post-conflict peacebuilding and recovery. The Commission should focus attention on the reconstruction and institution-building efforts necessary for recovery from conflict and support the development of integrated strategies in order to lay the foundation for sustainable development. In addition, it should provide recommendations and information to improve the coordination of all relevant actors within and outside the United Nations, develop best practices, help to ensure predictable financing for early recovery activities and extend the period of attention by the international community to post-conflict recovery. The Commission should act in all matters on the basis of consensus of its members.

99. The Peacebuilding Commission should make the outcome of its discussions and recommendations publicly available as United Nations documents to all relevant bodies and actors, including the international financial institutions. The Peacebuilding Commission should submit an annual report to the General Assembly.

100. The Peacebuilding Commission should meet in various configurations. Country-specific meetings of the Commission, upon invitation of the Organizational Committee referred to in paragraph 101 below, should include as members, in addition to members of the Organizational Committee, representatives from:

(a) The country under consideration;

(b) Countries in the region engaged in the post-conflict process and other countries that are involved in relief efforts and/or political dialogue, as well as relevant regional and subregional organizations;

(c) The major financial, troop and civilian police contributors involved in the recovery effort;

(d) The senior United Nations representative in the field and other relevant United Nations representatives;

(e) Such regional and international financial institutions as may be relevant.

101. The Peacebuilding Commission should have a standing Organizational Committee, responsible for developing its procedures and organizational matters, comprising:

(a) Members of the Security Council, including permanent members;

(b) Members of the Economic and Social Council, elected from regional groups, giving due consideration to those countries that have experienced post-conflict recovery;

(c) Top providers of assessed contributions to the United Nations budgets and voluntary contributions to the United Nations funds, programmes and agencies, including the standing Peacebuilding Fund, that are not among those selected in (a) or (b) above;

(d) Top providers of military personnel and civilian police to United Nations missions that are not among those selected in (a), (b) or (c) above.

102. Representatives from the World Bank, the International Monetary Fund and other institutional donors should be invited to participate in all meetings of the Peacebuilding Commission in a manner suitable to their governing arrangements, in addition to a representative of the Secretary-General.

103. We request the Secretary-General to establish a multi-year standing Peacebuilding Fund for post-conflict peacebuilding, funded by voluntary contributions and taking due account of existing instruments. The objectives of the Peacebuilding Fund will include ensuring the immediate release of resources needed to launch peacebuilding activities and the availability of appropriate financing for recovery.

104. We also request the Secretary-General to establish, within the Secretariat and from within existing resources, a small peacebuilding support office staffed by qualified experts to assist and support the Peacebuilding Commission. The office should draw on the best expertise available.

105. The Peacebuilding Commission should begin its work no later than 31 December 2005.

Sanctions

106. We underscore that sanctions remain an important tool under the Charter in our efforts to maintain international peace and security without recourse to the use of force, and resolve to ensure that sanctions are carefully targeted in support of clear objectives, to comply with sanctions established by the Security Council and to ensure that sanctions are implemented in ways that balance effectiveness to achieve the desired results against the possible adverse consequences, including socio-economic and humanitarian consequences, for populations and third States.

107. Sanctions should be implemented and monitored effectively with clear benchmarks and should be periodically reviewed, as appropriate, and remain for as limited a period as necessary to achieve their objectives and should be terminated once the objectives have been achieved.

108. We call upon the Security Council, with the support of the Secretary-General, to improve its monitoring of the implementation and effects of sanctions, to ensure that sanctions are implemented in an accountable manner, to review regularly the results of such monitoring and to develop a mechanism to address special economic problems arising from the application of sanctions in accordance with the Charter.

109. We also call upon the Security Council, with the support of the Secretary-General, to ensure that fair and clear procedures exist for placing individuals and entities on sanctions lists and for removing them, as well as for granting humanitarian exemptions.

110. We support efforts through the United Nations to strengthen State capacity to implement sanctions provisions.

Transnational crime

111. We express our grave concern at the negative effects on development, peace and security and human rights posed by transnational crime, including the smuggling of and trafficking in human beings, the world narcotic drug problem and the illicit trade in small arms and light weapons, and at the increasing vulnerability of States to such crime. We reaffirm the need to work collectively to combat transnational crime.

112. We recognize that trafficking in persons continues to pose a serious challenge to humanity and requires a concerted international response. To that end, we urge all States to devise, enforce and strengthen effective measures to combat and eliminate all forms of

trafficking in persons to counter the demand for trafficked victims and to protect the victims.

113. We urge all States that have not yet done so to consider becoming parties to the relevant international conventions on organized crime and corruption and, following their entry into force, to implement them effectively, including by incorporating the provisions of those conventions into national legislation and by strengthening criminal justice systems.

114. We reaffirm our unwavering determination and commitment to overcome the world narcotic drug problem through international cooperation and national strategies to eliminate both the illicit supply of and demand for illicit drugs.

115. We resolve to strengthen the capacity of the United Nations Office on Drugs and Crime, within its existing mandates, to provide assistance to Member States in those tasks upon request.

Women in the prevention and resolution of conflicts

116. We stress the important role of women in the prevention and resolution of conflicts and in peacebuilding. We reaffirm our commitment to the full and effective implementation of Security Council resolution 1325(2000) of 31 October 2000 on women and peace and security. We also underline the importance of integrating a gender perspective and of women having the opportunity for equal participation and full involvement in all efforts to maintain and promote peace and security, as well as the need to increase their role in decision-making at all levels. We strongly condemn all violations of the human rights of women and girls in situations of armed conflict and the use of sexual exploitation, violence and abuse, and we commit ourselves to elaborating and implementing strategies to report on, prevent and punish gender-based violence.

Protecting children in situations of armed conflict

117. We reaffirm our commitment to promote and protect the rights and welfare of children in armed conflicts. We welcome the significant advances and innovations that have been achieved over the past several years. We welcome in particular the adoption of Security Council resolution 1612(2005) of 26 July 2005. We call upon States to consider ratifying the Convention on the Rights of the Child and the Optional Protocol to the Convention on the Rights of the Child on the involvement of children in armed conflict. We also call upon States to take effective measures, as appropriate, to prevent the recruitment and use of children in armed conflict, contrary to international law, by armed forces and groups, and to prohibit and criminalize such practices.

118. We therefore call upon all States concerned to take concrete measures to ensure accountability and compliance by those responsible for grave abuses against children. We also reaffirm our commitment to ensure that children in armed conflicts receive timely and effective humanitarian assistance, including education, for their rehabilitation and reintegration into society.

IV. Human rights and the rule of law

119. We recommit ourselves to actively protecting and promoting all human rights, the rule of law and democracy and recognize that they are interlinked and mutually reinforcing and that they belong to the universal and indivisible core values and principles of the United Nations, and call upon all parts of the United Nations to promote human rights and fundamental freedoms in accordance with their mandates.

120. We reaffirm the solemn commitment of our States to fulfil their obligations to promote universal respect for and the observance and protection of all human rights and fundamental freedoms for all in accordance with the Charter, the Universal Declaration of Human Rights and other instruments relating to human rights and international law. The universal nature of these rights and freedoms is beyond question.

Human rights

121. We reaffirm that all human rights are universal, indivisible, interrelated, interdependent and mutually reinforcing and that all human rights must be treated in a fair and equal manner, on the same footing and with the same emphasis. While the significance of national and regional particularities and various historical, cultural and religious backgrounds must be borne in mind, all States, regardless of their political, economic and cultural systems, have the duty to promote and protect all human rights and fundamental freedoms.

122. We emphasize the responsibilities of all States, in conformity with the Charter, to respect human rights and fundamental freedoms for all, without distinction of any kind as to race, colour, sex, language or religion, political or other opinion, national or social origin, property, birth or other status.

123. We resolve further to strengthen the United Nations human rights machinery with the aim of ensuring effective enjoyment by all of all human rights and civil, political, economic, social and cultural rights, including the right to development.

124. We resolve to strengthen the Office of the United Nations High Commissioner for Human Rights, taking note of the High Commissioner's plan of action, to enable it to effectively carry out its mandate to respond to the broad range of human rights challenges facing the international community, particularly in the areas of technical assistance and capacity-building, through the doubling of its regular budget resources over the next five years with a view to progressively setting a balance between regular budget and voluntary contributions to its resources, keeping in mind other priority programmes for developing countries and the recruitment of highly competent staff on a broad geographical basis and with gender balance, under the regular budget, and we support its closer cooperation with all relevant United Nations bodies, including the General Assembly, the Economic and Social Council and the Security Council.

125. We resolve to improve the effectiveness of the human rights treaty bodies, including through more timely reporting, improved and streamlined reporting procedures and technical assistance to States to enhance their reporting capacities and further enhance the implementation of their recommendations.

126. We resolve to integrate the promotion and protection of human rights into national policies and to support the further mainstreaming of human rights throughout the United Nations system, as well as closer cooperation between the Office of the United Nations High Commissioner for Human Rights and all relevant United Nations bodies.

127. We reaffirm our commitment to continue making progress in the advancement of the human rights of the world's indigenous peoples at the local, national, regional and international levels, including through consultation and collaboration with them, and to present for adoption a final draft United Nations declaration on the rights of indigenous peoples as soon as possible.

128. We recognize the need to pay special attention to the human rights of women and children and undertake to advance them in every possible way, including by bringing gender and child-protection perspectives into the human rights agenda.

129. We recognize the need for persons with disabilities to be guaranteed full enjoyment of their rights without discrimination. We also affirm the need to finalize a comprehensive draft convention on the rights of persons with disabilities.

130. We note that the promotion and protection of the rights of persons belonging to national or ethnic, religious and linguistic minorities contribute to political and social stability and peace and enrich the cultural diversity and heritage of society.

131. We support the promotion of human rights education and learning at all levels, including through the implementation of the World Programme for Human Rights Education, as appropriate, and encourage all States to develop initiatives in this regard.

Internally displaced persons

132. We recognize the Guiding Principles on Internal Displacement as an important international framework for the protection of internally displaced persons and resolve to take effective measures to increase the protection of internally displaced persons.

Refugee protection and assistance

133. We commit ourselves to safeguarding the principle of refugee protection and to upholding our responsibility in resolving the plight of refugees, including through the support of efforts aimed at addressing the causes of refugee movement, bringing about the safe and sustainable return of those populations, finding durable solutions for refugees in protracted situations and preventing refugee movement from becoming a source of tension among States. We reaffirm the principle of solidarity and burden-sharing and resolve to support nations in assisting refugee populations and their host communities.

Rule of law

134. Recognizing the need for universal adherence to and implementation of the rule of law at both the national and international levels, we:

(*a*) Reaffirm our commitment to the purposes and principles of the Charter and international law and to an international order based on the rule of law and international law, which is essential for peaceful coexistence and cooperation among States;

(*b*) Support the annual treaty event;

(*c*) Encourage States that have not yet done so to consider becoming parties to all treaties that relate to the protection of civilians;

(*d*) Call upon States to continue their efforts to eradicate policies and practices that discriminate against women and to adopt laws and promote practices that protect the rights of women and promote gender equality;

(*e*) Support the idea of establishing a rule of law assistance unit within the Secretariat, in accordance with existing relevant procedures, subject to a report by the Secretary-General to the General Assembly, so as to strengthen United Nations activities to promote the rule of law, including through technical assistance and capacity-building;

(*f*) Recognize the important role of the International Court of Justice, the principal judicial organ of the United Nations, in adjudicating disputes among States and the value of its work, call upon States that have not yet done so to consider accepting the jurisdiction of the Court in accordance with its Statute and consider means of strengthening the Court's work, including by supporting the Secretary-General's Trust Fund to Assist States in the Settlement of Disputes through the International Court of Justice on a voluntary basis.

Democracy

135. We reaffirm that democracy is a universal value based on the freely expressed will of people to determine their own political, economic, social and cultural systems and their full participation in all aspects of their lives. We also reaffirm that while democracies share common features, there is no single model of democracy, that it does not belong to any country or region, and reaffirm the necessity of due respect for sovereignty and the right of self-determination. We stress that democracy, development and respect for all human rights and fundamental freedoms are interdependent and mutually reinforcing.

136. We renew our commitment to support democracy by strengthening countries' capacity to implement the principles and practices of democracy and resolve to strengthen the capacity of the United Nations to assist Member States upon their request. We welcome the establishment of a Democracy Fund at the United Nations. We note that the advisory board to be established should reflect diverse geographical representation. We invite the Secretary-General to help to ensure that practical arrangements for the Democracy Fund take proper account of existing United Nations activity in this field.

137. We invite interested Member States to give serious consideration to contributing to the Fund.

Responsibility to protect populations from genocide, war crimes, ethnic cleansing and crimes against humanity

138. Each individual State has the responsibility to protect its populations from genocide, war crimes, ethnic cleansing and crimes against humanity. This responsibility entails the prevention of such crimes, including their incitement, through appropriate and necessary means. We accept that responsibility and will act in accordance with it. The international community should, as appropriate, encourage and help States to exercise this responsibility and support the United Nations in establishing an early warning capability.

139. The international community, through the United Nations, also has the responsibility to use appropriate diplomatic, humanitarian and other peaceful means, in accordance with Chapters VI and VIII of the Charter, to help to protect populations from genocide, war crimes, ethnic cleansing and crimes against

humanity. In this context, we are prepared to take collective action, in a timely and decisive manner, through the Security Council, in accordance with the Charter, including Chapter VII, on a case-by-case basis and in cooperation with relevant regional organizations as appropriate, should peaceful means be inadequate and national authorities are manifestly failing to protect their populations from genocide, war crimes, ethnic cleansing and crimes against humanity. We stress the need for the General Assembly to continue consideration of the responsibility to protect populations from genocide, war crimes, ethnic cleansing and crimes against humanity and its implications, bearing in mind the principles of the Charter and international law. We also intend to commit ourselves, as necessary and appropriate, to helping States build capacity to protect their populations from genocide, war crimes, ethnic cleansing and crimes against humanity and to assisting those which are under stress before crises and conflicts break out.

140. We fully support the mission of the Special Adviser of the Secretary-General on the Prevention of Genocide.

Children's rights

141. We express dismay at the increasing number of children involved in and affected by armed conflict, as well as all other forms of violence, including domestic violence, sexual abuse and exploitation and trafficking. We support cooperation policies aimed at strengthening national capacities to improve the situation of those children and to assist in their rehabilitation and reintegration into society.

142. We commit ourselves to respecting and ensuring the rights of each child without discrimination of any kind, irrespective of the race, colour, sex, language, religion, political or other opinion, national, ethnic or social origin, property, disability, birth or other status of the child or his or her parent(s) or legal guardian(s). We call upon States to consider as a priority becoming a party to the Convention on the Rights of the Child.

Human security

143. We stress the right of people to live in freedom and dignity, free from poverty and despair. We recognize that all individuals, in particular vulnerable people, are entitled to freedom from fear and freedom from want, with an equal opportunity to enjoy all their rights and fully develop their human potential. To this end, we commit ourselves to discussing and defining the notion of human security in the General Assembly.

Culture of peace and initiatives on dialogue among cultures, civilizations and religions

144. We reaffirm the Declaration and Programme of Action on a Culture of Peace as well as the Global Agenda for Dialogue among Civilizations and its Programme of Action adopted by the General Assembly and the value of different initiatives on dialogue among cultures and civilizations, including the dialogue on interfaith cooperation. We commit ourselves to taking action to promote a culture of peace and dialogue at the local, national, regional and international levels and request the Secretary-General to explore enhancing implementation mechanisms and to follow up on those initiatives. In this regard, we also welcome the Alliance of Civilizations initiative announced by the Secretary-General on 14 July 2005.

145. We underline that sports can foster peace and development and can contribute to an atmosphere of tolerance and understanding, and we encourage discussions in the General Assembly for proposals leading to a plan of action on sport and development.

V. Strengthening the United Nations

146. We reaffirm our commitment to strengthen the United Nations with a view to enhancing its authority and efficiency, as well as its capacity to address effectively, and in accordance with the purposes and principles of the Charter, the full range of challenges of our time. We are determined to reinvigorate the intergovernmental organs of the United Nations and to adapt them to the needs of the twenty-first century.

147. We stress that, in order to efficiently perform their respective mandates as provided under the Charter, United Nations bodies should develop good cooperation and coordination in the common endeavour of building a more effective United Nations.

148. We emphasize the need to provide the United Nations with adequate and timely resources with a view to enabling it to carry out its mandates. A reformed United Nations must be responsive to the entire membership, faithful to its founding principles and adapted to carrying out its mandate.

General Assembly

149. We reaffirm the central position of the General Assembly as the chief deliberative, policymaking and representative organ of the United Nations, as well as the role of the Assembly in the process of standard-setting and the codification of international law.

150. We welcome the measures adopted by the General Assembly with a view to strengthening its role and authority and the role and leadership of the President of the Assembly and, to that end, we call for their full and speedy implementation.

151. We call for strengthening the relationship between the General Assembly and the other principal organs to ensure better coordination on topical issues that require coordinated action by the United Nations, in accordance with their respective mandates.

Security Council

152. We reaffirm that Member States have conferred on the Security Council primary responsibility for the maintenance of international peace and security, acting on their behalf, as provided for by the Charter.

153. We support early reform of the Security Council—an essential element of our overall effort to reform the United Nations—in order to make it more broadly representative, efficient and transparent and thus to further enhance its effectiveness and the legitimacy and implementation of its decisions. We commit ourselves to continuing our efforts to achieve a decision to this end and request the General Assembly to review progress on the reform set out above by the end of 2005.

154. We recommend that the Security Council continue to adapt its working methods so as to increase the involvement of States not members of the Council in its work, as appropriate, enhance its accountability to the membership and increase the transparency of its work.

Economic and Social Council

155. We reaffirm the role that the Charter and the General Assembly have vested in the Economic and Social Council and recognize the need for a more effective Economic and Social Council as a principal body for coordination, policy review, policy dialogue and recommendations on issues of economic and social development, as well as for implementation of the international development goals agreed at the major United Nations conferences and summits, including the Millennium Development Goals. To achieve these objectives, the Council should:

(a) Promote global dialogue and partnership on global policies and trends in the economic, social, environmental and humanitarian fields. For this purpose, the Council should serve as a quality platform for high-level engagement among Member States and with the international financial institutions, the private sector and civil society on emerging global trends, policies and action and develop its ability to respond better and more rapidly to developments in the international economic, environmental and social fields;

(b) Hold a biennial high-level Development Cooperation Forum to review trends in international development cooperation, including strategies, policies and financing, promote greater coherence among the development activities of different development partners and strengthen the links between the normative and operational work of the United Nations;

(c) Ensure follow-up of the outcomes of the major United Nations conferences and summits, including the internationally agreed development goals, and hold annual ministerial-level substantive reviews to assess progress, drawing on its functional and regional commissions and other international institutions, in accordance with their respective mandates;

(d) Support and complement international efforts aimed at addressing humanitarian emergencies, including natural disasters, in order to promote an improved, coordinated response from the United Nations;

(e) Play a major role in the overall coordination of funds, programmes and agencies, ensuring coherence among them and avoiding duplication of mandates and activities.

156. We stress that in order to fully perform the above functions, the organization of work, the agenda and the current methods of work of the Economic and Social Council should be adapted.

Human Rights Council

157. Pursuant to our commitment to further strengthen the United Nations human rights machinery, we resolve to create a Human Rights Council.

158. The Council will be responsible for promoting universal respect for the protection of all human rights and fundamental freedoms for all, without distinction of any kind and in a fair and equal manner.

159. The Council should address situations of violations of human rights, including gross and systematic violations, and make recommendations thereon. It should also promote effective coordination and the mainstreaming of human rights within the United Nations system.

160. We request the President of the General Assembly to conduct open, transparent and inclusive negotiations, to be completed as soon as possible during the sixtieth session, with the aim of establishing the mandate, modalities, functions, size, composition, membership, working methods and procedures of the Council.

Secretariat and management reform

161. We recognize that in order to effectively comply with the principles and objectives of the Charter, we need an efficient, effective and accountable Secretariat. Its staff shall act in accordance with Article 100 of the Charter, in a culture of organizational accountability, transparency and integrity. Consequently we:

(a) Recognize the ongoing reform measures carried out by the Secretary-General to strengthen accountability and oversight, improve management performance and transparency and reinforce ethical conduct, and invite him to report to the General Assembly on the progress made in their implementation;

(b) Emphasize the importance of establishing effective and efficient mechanisms for responsibility and accountability of the Secretariat;

(c) Urge the Secretary-General to ensure that the highest standards of efficiency, competence, and integrity shall be the paramount consideration in the employment of the staff, with due regard to the principle of equitable geographical distribution, in accordance with Article 101 of the Charter;

(d) Welcome the Secretary-General's efforts to ensure ethical conduct, more extensive financial disclosure for United Nations officials and enhanced protection for those who reveal wrongdoing within the Organization. We urge the Secretary-General to scrupulously apply the existing standards of conduct and develop a system-wide code of ethics for all United Nations personnel. In this regard, we request the Secretary-General to submit details on an ethics office with independent status, which he intends to create, to the General Assembly at its sixtieth session;

(e) Pledge to provide the United Nations with adequate resources, on a timely basis, to enable the Organization to implement its mandates and achieve its objectives, having regard to the priorities agreed by the General Assembly and the need to respect budget discipline. We stress that all Member States should meet their obligations with regard to the expenses of the Organization;

(f) Strongly urge the Secretary-General to make the best and most efficient use of resources in accordance with clear rules and procedures agreed by the General Assembly, in the interest of all Member States, by adopting the best management practices, including effective use of information and communication technologies, with a view to increasing efficiency and enhancing organizational capacity, concentrating on those tasks that reflect the agreed priorities of the Organization.

162. We reaffirm the role of the Secretary-General as the chief administrative officer of the Organization, in accordance with Article 97 of the Charter. We request the Secretary-General to make proposals to the General Assembly for its consideration on the conditions and measures necessary for him to carry out his managerial responsibilities effectively.

163. We commend the Secretary-General's previous and ongoing efforts to enhance the effective management of the United Nations and his commitment to update the Organization. Bearing in mind our responsibility as Member States, we emphasize the need to decide on additional reforms in order to make more efficient use of the financial and human resources available to the Organization and thus better comply with its principles, objectives and mandates. We call on the Secretary-General to submit proposals for implementing management reforms to the General Assembly for consideration and decision in the first quarter of 2006, which will include the following elements:

(a) We will ensure that the United Nations budgetary, financial and human resource policies, regulations and rules respond to the current needs of the Organization and enable the efficient and effective conduct of its work, and request the Secretary-General to provide an assessment and recommendations to the General Assembly for decision during the first quarter of 2006. The assessment and recommendations of the Secretary-General should take account of the measures already under way for the reform of human resources management and the budget process;

(b) We resolve to strengthen and update the programme of work of the United Nations so that it responds to the contemporary requirements of Member States. To this end, the General Assembly and other relevant organs will review all mandates older than five years originating from resolutions of the General Assembly and other organs, which would be complementary to the existing periodic reviews of activities. The General Assembly and the other organs should complete and take the necessary decisions arising from this review during 2006. We request the Secretary-General to facilitate this review with analysis and recommendations, including on the opportunities for programmatic shifts that could be considered for early General Assembly consideration;

(c) A detailed proposal on the framework for a one-time staff buyout to improve personnel structure and quality, including an indication of costs involved and mechanisms to ensure that it achieves its intended purpose.

164. We recognize the urgent need to substantially improve the United Nations oversight and management processes. We emphasize the importance of ensuring the operational independence of the Office of Internal Oversight Services. Therefore:

(a) The expertise, capacity and resources of the Office of Internal Oversight Services in respect of audit and investigations will be significantly strengthened as a matter of urgency;

(b) We request the Secretary-General to submit an independent external evaluation of the auditing and oversight system of the United Nations, including the specialized agencies, including the roles and responsibilities of management, with due regard to the nature of the auditing and oversight bodies in question. This evaluation will take place within the context of the comprehensive review of the governance arrangements. We ask the General Assembly to adopt measures during its sixtieth session at the earliest possible stage, based on the consideration of recommendations of the evaluation and those made by the Secretary-General;

(c) We recognize that additional measures are needed to enhance the independence of the oversight structures. We therefore request the Secretary-General to submit detailed proposals to the General Assembly at its sixtieth session for its early consideration on the creation of an independent oversight advisory committee, including its mandate, composition, selection process and qualification of experts;

(d) We authorize the Office of Internal Oversight Services to examine the feasibility of expanding its services to provide internal oversight to United Nations agencies that request such services in such a way as to ensure that the provision of internal oversight services to the Secretariat will not be compromised.

165. We insist on the highest standards of behaviour from all United Nations personnel and support the considerable efforts under way with respect to the implementation of the Secretary-General's policy of zero tolerance regarding sexual exploitation and abuse by United Nations personnel, both at Headquarters and in the field. We encourage the Secretary-General to submit proposals to the General Assembly leading to a comprehensive approach to victims' assistance by 31 December 2005.

166. We encourage the Secretary-General and all decision-making bodies to take further steps in mainstreaming a gender perspective in the policies and decisions of the Organization.

167. We strongly condemn all attacks against the safety and security of personnel engaged in United Nations activities. We call upon States to consider becoming parties to the Convention on the Safety of United Nations and Associated Personnel and stress the need to conclude negotiations on a protocol expanding the scope of legal protection during the sixtieth session of the General Assembly.

System-wide coherence

168. We recognize that the United Nations brings together a unique wealth of expertise and resources on global issues. We commend the extensive experience and expertise of the various development-related organizations, agencies, funds and programmes of the United Nations system in their diverse and complementary fields of activity and their important contributions to the achievement of the Millennium Development Goals and the other development objectives established by various United Nations conferences.

169. We support stronger system-wide coherence by implementing the following measures:

Policy

- Strengthening linkages between the normative work of the United Nations system and its operational activities

- Coordinating our representation on the governing boards of the various development and humanitarian agencies so as to ensure that they pursue a coherent policy in assigning mandates and allocating resources throughout the system

- Ensuring that the main horizontal policy themes, such as sustainable development, human rights and gender, are taken into account in decision-making throughout the United Nations

Operational activities

- Implementing current reforms aimed at a more effective, efficient, coherent, coordinated and better-performing United Nations country presence with a strengthened role for the senior resident official, whether special representative, resident coordinator or humanitarian coordinator, including appropriate authority, resources and accountability, and a common management, programming and monitoring framework
- Inviting the Secretary-General to launch work to further strengthen the management and coordination of United Nations operational activities so that they can make an even more effective contribution to the achievement of the internationally agreed development goals, including the Millennium Development Goals, including proposals for consideration by Member States for more tightly managed entities in the fields of development, humanitarian assistance and the environment

Humanitarian assistance

- Upholding and respecting the humanitarian principles of humanity, neutrality, impartiality and independence and ensuring that humanitarian actors have safe and unhindered access to populations in need in conformity with the relevant provisions of international law and national laws
- Supporting the efforts of countries, in particular developing countries, to strengthen their capacities at all levels in order to prepare for and respond rapidly to natural disasters and mitigate their impact
- Strengthening the effectiveness of the United Nations humanitarian response, inter alia, by improving the timeliness and predictability of humanitarian funding, in part by improving the Central Emergency Revolving Fund
- Further developing and improving, as required, mechanisms for the use of emergency standby capacities, under the auspices of the United Nations, for a timely response to humanitarian emergencies

Environmental activities

- Recognizing the need for more efficient environmental activities in the United Nations system, with enhanced coordination, improved policy advice and guidance, strengthened scientific knowledge, assessment and cooperation, better treaty compliance, while respecting the legal autonomy of the treaties, and better integration of environmental activities in the broader sustainable development framework at the operational level, including through capacity-building, we agree to explore the possibility of a more coherent institutional framework to address this need, including a more integrated structure, building on existing institutions and internationally agreed instruments, as well as the treaty bodies and the specialized agencies

Regional organizations

170. We support a stronger relationship between the United Nations and regional and subregional organizations, pursuant to Chapter VIII of the Charter, and therefore resolve:

(*a*) To expand consultation and cooperation between the United Nations and regional and subregional organizations through formalized agreements between the respective secretariats and, as appropriate, involvement of regional organizations in the work of the Security Council;

(*b*) To ensure that regional organizations that have a capacity for the prevention of armed conflict or peacekeeping consider the option of placing such capacity in the framework of the United Nations Standby Arrangements System;

(*c*) To strengthen cooperation in the economic, social and cultural fields.

Cooperation between the United Nations and parliaments

171. We call for strengthened cooperation between the United Nations and national and regional parliaments, in particular through the Inter-Parliamentary Union, with a view to furthering all aspects of the Millennium Declaration in all fields of the work of the United Nations and ensuring the effective implementation of United Nations reform.

Participation of local authorities, the private sector and civil society, including non-governmental organizations

172. We welcome the positive contributions of the private sector and civil society, including non-governmental organizations, in the promotion and implementation of development and human rights programmes and stress the importance of their continued engagement with Governments, the United Nations and other international organizations in these key areas.

173. We welcome the dialogue between those organizations and Member States, as reflected in the first informal interactive hearings of the General Assembly with representatives of non-governmental organizations, civil society and the private sector.

174. We underline the important role of local authorities in contributing to the achievement of the internationally agreed development goals, including the Millennium Development Goals.

175. We encourage responsible business practices, such as those promoted by the Global Compact.

Charter of the United Nations

176. Considering that the Trusteeship Council no longer meets and has no remaining functions, we should delete Chapter XIII of the Charter and references to the Council in Chapter XII.

177. Taking into account General Assembly resolution 50/52 of 11 December 1995 and recalling the related discussions conducted in the General Assembly, bearing in mind the profound cause for the founding of the United Nations and looking to our common future, we resolve to delete references to "enemy States" in Articles 53, 77 and 107 of the Charter.

178. We request the Security Council to consider the composition, mandate and working methods of the Military Staff Committee.

Speaking after the adoption of resolution 60/1, the United States representative said that his country had joined the consensus on the outcome document and was pleased that Member States had agreed to denounce terrorism in all its forms, advance the cause of development, reform the management of the United Nations, establish a Peacebuilding Commission and create a Human Rights Council. However, the United States understood that reference to the International Conference on Population and Development [YUN 1994, p. 955], the Beijing Declaration and Platform for Action [YUN 1995, p. 1170] and the use of the phrase "reproductive health" in the outcome document did not constitute support, endorsement or promotion of abortion.

The Prime Minister of Sweden and Co-Chairperson of the Summit stated that, during the debate, leaders reaffirmed their strong commitment to international cooperation as a tool for meeting global challenges. The World Summit Outcome document took decisive steps to strengthen the United Nations and the collective security system and reaffirmed the commitment to achieving the MDGs by 2015. He said that the momentum created had to be maintained for the months and years ahead, and urged all political leaders to remain committed in order to ensure that the decisions taken would be turned into reality.

Special meeting on Financing for Development

On 14 September [meeting 3], the General Assembly, in accordance with resolution 59/291 (see p. 72), held a separate meeting on Financing for Development, as part of its High-level Plenary Meeting (World Summit). The meeting had before it the Assembly President's summary of the deliberations of the second High-level Dialogue on Financing for Development (New York, 27-28 June) [A/60/219] (see p. 1064), which reviewed the implementation of the Monterrey Consensus adopted at the 2002 International Conference on Financing for Development [YUN 2002, p. 953], and discussed ways to advance efforts in that regard.

President Bongo Ondimba, Co-Chairperson of the World Summit, in his opening remarks to the meeting, said that, although the Monterrey Consensus provided a framework for mobilizing financial resources for development, resources allocated for that purpose were still far from the minimum necessary and seriously jeopardized implementation of the commitments made in 2002 [ibid.]. He welcomed the decision of the Group of Eight (G-8) most industrialized countries to cancel the debt of 18 developing countries, the steps taken by the European Union (EU) to increase official development assistance (ODA) and the decision of Heads of State and Govern-

ment in June in Doha, Qatar, to create a development fund. He said that all other initiatives aimed at providing more equitable trade measures within the context of the World Trade Organization (WTO) Doha round of multilateral trade negotiations (see p. 1041), including those aimed at finding new resources of financing for development, should be encouraged.

Prime Minister Göran of Sweden, Co-Chairperson of the Summit, observed at the meeting that poverty was one of the major threats facing humanity and he expected the Summit to reaffirm the recognition that poverty was a common challenge and required action by all parties. He noted that while progress had been made over the past five years in halving poverty, it was unevenly distributed between and within countries. Africa remained a region of great concern, but other areas in the world lagged behind also. He said the progress in countries that were performing well benefited only a few, and that a good average did not necessarily translate into prosperity for the poorest. He called on world leaders to renew their pledges and intensify efforts to honour their commitments.

Addressing the meeting, the Secretary-General said that the past quarter century had seen a dramatic reduction in extreme poverty, yet international solidarity had fallen well short of need. The challenge was to transform the breakthroughs of the past few years into a Monterrey-based MDG performance pact. At the national level, States needed to practise good governance, mobilize domestic resources and devise strategies to meet the MDGs and other important development objectives. The international community should support those steps through wide-ranging global reforms, more and better aid, trade policies that gave a fair chance to developing countries, and the opening up of institutions to allow the developing world a greater voice. The General Assembly and the Economic and Social Council should play a stronger role in monitoring performance, offering advice and issuing warnings.

The meeting also heard statements from several Heads of State and Government, as well as the President of the World Bank and the Managing Director of the International Monetary Fund.

"In larger freedom: towards development, security and human rights for all"

In his March report [A/59/2005] to the General Assembly entitled "In larger freedom: towards development, security and human rights for all", the Secretary-General, as requested by Assembly resolution 55/2 [YUN 2000, p. 49], gave a broad review of the implementation of the Millennium Declaration that was adopted at the United Nations Millennium Summit [ibid.] and proposed an agenda to be taken up at the 2005 World Summit. The Secretary-General said that a point-by-point report on the implementation of the Millennium Declaration would miss the larger point that new circumstances demanded that consensus be revitalized on key challenges and priorities, and that such consensus be converted into collective action. He said much had happened since the adoption of the Millennium Declaration to compel such an approach.

The report did not include all areas in which progress was important or desirable but only those items in which action was both vital and achievable in the months ahead. The name of the report stressed the enduring relevance of the UN Charter and emphasized that its purposes had to be advanced in the lives of individual men and women, encapsulating the idea that development, security and human rights went hand in hand. Unless all those causes were advanced, none would succeed. The report discussed the historic opportunity presented in 2005 for taking ambitious and urgent action to advance global change and to reform the Organization under the headings: freedom from want; freedom from fear; freedom to live in dignity; and proposals for strengthening the United Nations.

In the annex to the report, entitled "For decision by Heads of State and Government", the Secretary-General set out his reform proposals under the various headings.

Under **"Freedom from want"**, in order to reduce poverty and promote global prosperity for all, he urged Heads of State and Government to: reaffirm, and commit themselves to implementing the development consensus agreed in 2002 at the International Conference on Financing for Development [YUN 2002, p. 953], and at the World Summit on Sustainable Development [ibid., p. 821]. Within the context of the MDGs, he recommended that: developing countries recommit themselves to taking primary responsibility for their own development by strengthening governance, combating corruption and putting in place policies and investments to drive private sector-led growth and maximize domestic resources to fund national development strategies; developed countries should support those efforts through increased development assistance, a more development-oriented trading system and wider and deeper debt relief, recognizing the special needs of Africa; developing countries affected by extreme poverty should, by 2006, adopt and begin to implement a comprehensive national strategy

to meet the 2015 MDGs targets; developed countries that had not already done so, should establish timetables to achieve the 0.7 per cent target of gross national income (GNI) for ODA by 2015; they should also redefine debt sustainability as the level of debt that allowed a country to achieve both the MDGs and reach 2015 without an increase in its debt ratios, which meant exclusive grant-based finance and 100 per cent debt cancellation for most heavily indebted poor countries (HIPC), and significantly more debt reduction to many heavily indebted non-HIPC and middle-income countries. The Secretary-General also proposed that leaders complete the WTO Doha round of multilateral trade negotiations no later than 2006, with full commitment to realizing its development focus; launch, in 2005, an International Financial Facility to support an immediate front-loading of ODA, consider other innovative sources of finance for development to supplement the Facility in the longer term; and launch a series of "quick win" initiatives to realize major immediate progress towards the MDGs. The international community should urgently provide the resources for an expanded and comprehensive response to HIV and AIDS and full funding for the Global Fund to fight AIDS, tuberculosis and malaria. World leaders should reaffirm gender equality; recognize the need for significantly increased international support for scientific research and development to address the special needs of the poor in the areas of health, agriculture, natural resource and environmental management, energy and climate; resolve to develop a more inclusive international framework for climate change beyond 2012; establish a worldwide early warning system for all natural hazards; and decide that, starting in 2005, developing countries that put forward sound, transparent and accountable national strategies and required increased development assistance should receive a sufficient increase in aid to enable them to achieve the MDGs.

Under **"Freedom from fear"**, the Secretary-General urged Heads of State and Government to commit themselves to agreeing on and implementing comprehensive strategies for confronting the range of threats to international peace and security, including those relating to weapons of mass destruction, terrorism, State collapse, civil conflict, deadly infectious diseases, extreme poverty and the destruction of the environment. In that context, he further urged Heads to pledge full compliance with the Treaty on the Non-Proliferation of Nuclear Weapons (NPT) (see p. 597), the Convention on the Prohibition of the Development, Production and Stockpiling of Bacteriological (Biological) and Toxin Weapons and on Their Destruction (Biological Weapons Convention) (see p. 615) and the Convention on the Prohibition of the Development, Production, Stockpiling and Use of Chemical Weapons and on Their Destruction (Convention on Chemical Weapons) (see p. 616), in order to further strengthen the multilateral framework for non-proliferation and disarmament. Heads should also reaffirm their commitment to a moratorium on nuclear test explosions and to the entry into force of the Comprehensive Nuclear-Test-Ban Treaty (CTBT) (see p. 593). He further urged leaders to: develop legally binding international instruments to regulate the marking, tracing and illicit brokering of small arms and light weapons, and to ensure the effective monitoring and enforcement of UN arms embargoes; affirm that no cause or grievance justified the targeting and deliberate killing of civilians and non-combatants, and declare that any action that was intended to cause death or serious bodily harm to civilians or non-combatants constituted an act of terrorism; resolve to implement the comprehensive UN counter-terrorism strategy (see p. 101), that he had presented, which would deny terrorists access to funds and materials, deter States from sponsoring terrorism, develop State capacity to defeat terrorism while defending human rights; and resolve to accede to all international conventions against terrorism, conclude a convention on nuclear terrorism as a matter of urgency, as well as a comprehensive convention on terrorism before the end of the Assembly's sixtieth (2005) session.

Member States should: accede to all relevant international conventions on organized crime and corruption, and implement them effectively; request the Security Council to set out the principles for the use of force and affirm its intention to be guided by them when authorizing or mandating such use; establish a Peacebuilding Commission and a voluntary standing fund for peacebuilding; create strategic reserves for UN peacekeeping; support efforts by the European Union (EU) and the African Union (AU) and others to establish standby capacities as part of an interlocking system of peacekeeping capacities; establish a UN civilian police standby capacity; and ensure that Council sanctions were effectively enforced.

Under **"Freedom to live in dignity"**, the Secretary-General exhorted Heads of State and Government to reaffirm their commitment to human dignity by strengthening the rule of law, ensuring respect for human rights and fundamental freedoms and promoting democracy. In this respect, they should embrace the "responsibility to protect" as a basis for collective action

against genocide, ethnic cleansing and crimes against humanity, and agree to act on that responsibility. He also urged them to support the 2005 Treaty-signing Event (see p. 75), which focused on 31 multilateral treaties, and encouraged Governments that had not done so to ratify and implement all treaties relating to the protection of civilians. Leaders should also support democracy in their own countries, regions and the world, and resolve to strengthen UN capacity to assist emerging democracies, and to that end, welcome the creation of a Democracy Fund to provide funding and technical assistance to countries seeking to establish or strengthen their democracy. They should recognize the important role of the International Court of Justice in adjudicating disputes among countries and consider how to strengthen the Court's work.

Under **"the imperative for collective action: strengthening the United Nations"**, in order to make the United Nations a more efficient instrument for forging a united response to shared threats and needs, the Secretary-General urged Heads of State and Government to reform, restructure and revitalize its major organs and institutions. The General Assembly should adopt, at its sixtieth session, a comprehensive package of reforms that included rationalizing its work and speeding up its deliberative process, streamlining its agenda, committee structure and procedures for plenary debates and for requesting reports, and strengthening the role and authority of its President; it should focus on addressing the major substantive issues of the day on its agenda; and establish mechanisms for engaging fully and systematically with civil society.

The Security Council should be made more representative of the international community and current geopolitical realities by expanding its membership. It should consider the two options—models A and B—proposed in the current report, as well as any other viable proposals and decisions taken on the issue before the World Summit.

The Economic and Social Council should be mandated to: hold annual ministerial-level assessments of progress towards agreed development goals, particularly the MDGs; serve as a high-level development cooperation forum; convene timely meetings to assess threats to development such as famines, epidemics and major natural disasters, and to promote coordinated responses to them; and regularize its work in post-conflict management by working with the proposed Peacebuilding Commission.

The Secretary-General also recommended that the Commission on Human Rights should be replaced with a smaller standing Human Rights

Council, as a principal organ of the United Nations or subsidiary body of the General Assembly, and that the Secretariat be reformed by endorsing his request that the Assembly review the continued relevance of all mandates older than five years to see if the activities concerned were still needed or whether resources assigned to them could be reallocated in response to new and emerging challenges.

Heads should give the Secretary-General the authority and resources to pursue a one-time staff buyout so as to refresh and realign the staff to meet current needs and undertake a comprehensive review of the budget and human resources rules. They should endorse the Secretary-General's package of management reforms and commission a comprehensive review of the Office of Internal Oversight Services. They should further ensure stronger system-wide coherence by coordinating their representatives on the governing boards of the various development and humanitarian agencies; commit themselves to protecting humanitarian space and ensuring that humanitarian actors had safe and unimpeded access to vulnerable populations; accelerate humanitarian response by developing new funding arrangements; and support the Secretary- General's effort to strengthen the inter-agency and country-level responses to the needs of internally displaced persons.

Heads of State and Government should: recognize the need for a more integrated structure for environmental standard-setting, scientific discussion and monitoring, and treaty compliance that assigned environmental activities at the operational level to the development agencies to ensure an integrated approach to sustainable development; support a stronger relationship between the United Nations and regional organizations, including by developing and implementing a 10-year plan for capacity-building with the AU, and by ensuring that regional organizations with conflict prevention or peacekeeping capacity considered placing such capacities in the framework of the United Nations Standby Arrangements System; eliminate references to "enemy States" from the Charter; and delete Article 47 on the Military Staff Committee and the references to it, as well as Chapter XIII on the Trusteeship Council.

A practical plan to achieve the MDGs

In March [A/59/727], the Secretary-General transmitted to the General Assembly a report on "Investing in Development: A Practical Plan to Achieve the Millennium Development Goals", an overview of the final report of the UN Millennium Project, an independent advisory body he had appointed in 2002, headed by his Special Adviser on the Millennium Development Goals, Professor Jeffrey Sachs, and supported by the United Nations Development Programme (UNDP). The report was prepared jointly by 10 task forces established under the Project, made up of 265 development practitioners and experts from academia, Governments, UN agencies, international and financial institutions, non-governmental organizations (NGOs), donor agencies and the private sector. The report described why the MDGs were important and the varied progress made in achieving them, and offered a diagnosis of why progress had been mixed across regions and Goals. It made recommendations for implementation at the country level, focusing on the processes, investments, policies and scale-up strategies required to achieve the MDGs and estimated the costs and benefits of achieving them.

According to the report, the world had made significant progress in achieving many of the Goals, but there were huge disparities across and within countries. Sub-Saharan Africa was the epicentre of crisis and faced continuing food insecurity, a rise in extreme poverty, high child and maternal mortality, large numbers of people living in slums and widespread shortfall in most of the MDGs. While Asia recorded the fastest progress, hundreds of millions of people remained in extreme poverty and even some of the fastest-growing countries in that region failed to achieve non-income Goals. Other regions had mixed records, notably Latin America, the transition economies, the Middle East and North Africa, often with slow or no progress on some Goals and persistent inequalities undermining progress in others. Overall, the proportion of undernourished people remained high in many parts of the world; progress was made in primary education in most regions, but sub-Saharan Africa and South Asia remained significantly off track; gender equality remained unfulfilled and the education parity target for 2005 would be missed in many countries; child mortality rates had generally declined with progress slowed in many regions and even reversed in others; maternal mortality remained unacceptably high in every region, reflecting low public attention to women's needs; HIV/AIDS, which currently affected 40 million people, continued to pose a serious threat along with malaria; the population with access to improved drinking-water supply increased substantially in most regions; the world was not on track to meet the sanitation Goal; about 900 million people were living in slum-like conditions, characterized by insecure tenure, inadequate housing and lack of access to water or sanitation; and, all regions experienced environmental degradation.

The report identified four overarching reasons why the Goals were not being achieved: poor governance, corruption, poor economic policy choices and the denial of human rights. It recommended that developing country Governments adopt, by 2006, bold MDG-based poverty reduction strategies in order to meet the 2015 deadline. Those strategies should anchor the scaling-up of public investments, capacity-building, domestic resource mobilization and official development assistance (ODA) and provide a framework for strengthening governance, promoting human rights, engaging civil society and promoting the private sector. Those strategies should also be developed and implemented in transparent and inclusive processes. International donors should identify at least a dozen MDG "fast-track" countries for a rapid scaling-up of ODA in 2005, and developed and developing countries should jointly launch, in the same year, a group of "Quick Win" actions to save and improve millions of lives and to promote economic growth. Developing country governments should align national strategies with such regional initiatives as the New Partnership for Africa's Development (see p. 1003) and the Caribbean Community and Common Market, and regional groups should receive increased direct donor support for regional projects. High-income countries should increase ODA from 0.25 per cent of their GNP to around 0.44 per cent in 2006 and 0.54 per cent in 2015. They should also open their markets to developing country exports in accordance with the World Trade Organization (WHO) Doha Round of multilateral trade negotiations and help least developed countries raise export competitiveness through investments in critical trade-related infrastructure, including electricity, roads and ports. The Doha Development Agenda should be fulfilled and the Doha Round completed by 2006. The Secretary-General and the United Nations Development Group should strengthen the coordination of UN agencies, funds and programmes to support the MDGs at Headquarters and at the country level.

Round-table sessions

More open and in-depth discussions of the Summit's agenda took place in four interactive round-table sessions, each chaired by a Head of State or Government. Each regional group (Africa, Asia, Eastern Europe, Latin America and the Caribbean, Western Europe and other States) was represented in the round tables, in accordance with General Assembly resolution 59/291 (see p. 72). During the Summit's concluding plenary, the Chairpersons of the four round table sessions made oral presentations on the deliberations of their respective groups.

Round Table 1. The Chairman of Round Table I, John Howard, Prime Minister of Australia, in his statement read by that country's Deputy Permanent Representative to the United Nations, said that the broad sentiment shared in the Round Table was a sense of optimism for the future of the United Nations, despite some ambivalent comments on the draft outcome document. Participants felt that the document excluded many things which should have been at its heart and had not gone far enough in other matters. The major disappointment related to the neglect of the issues of disarmament and the risk of nuclear proliferation. On the positive side, strong support was expressed for the Peacebuilding Commission, the revamping of the UN human rights machinery and the recognition of the mutual interdependence of the developed and developing worlds. There was also a strong emphasis on poverty eradication and meeting the commitments for the realization of the MDGs.

Round Table 2. The Chairman of Round Table 2, Aleksander Kwasniewski, President of Poland, in his summary said that world leaders emphasized the importance of multilateralism in responding to the challenges and threats of the increasingly interdependent and globalized age of the twenty-first century. There was a call to make the World Summit one of: solidarity, especially with Africa; broad partnership for development; progress on human rights and the new Human Rights Council; and courage to accelerate reform of the United Nations. Participants strongly supported the idea of enhancing efforts to promote development, including making the MDGs an operational reality, and for strengthening human rights and democracy, including the consolidation of the Democracy Fund and the Human Rights Council.

Round Table 3. The Chairman of Round Table 3, Winston B. Spenser, Prime Minister of Antigua and Barbuda, reported that participants focused on development, stressing the importance of the MDGs and their use by national institutions to assess and guide public policies in the economic and social fields, and the need to strengthen global partnership to implement them. Speakers also underlined the need for a coherent policy on trade and aid. The unique challenges of landlocked countries and small island developing nations were addressed, as well as the potential of information and communication technologies (ICT) in helping to achieve the MDGs and the importance of improving developing countries' access to ICT. Of concern were the lack of progress in addressing the debt problem of middle-income countries and the issue of conditionality attached to debt cancellation and its impact on the quality of aid. The importance of making international trade a real engine for development was emphasized, for which the early completion of the Doha round of multilateral trade negotiations was considered essential. Also highlighted were the link between humanitarian assistance and development and the need for greater international cooperation to establish the context for evolving durable solutions and addressing the root causes of crises, abuse and instability.

Round Table 4. The Chairman of Round Table 4, Olusegun Obasanjo, President of Nigeria, said that the draft outcome document clearly emphasized the vital role that the United Nations had to play in the twenty-first century. He pointed out that many gaps and omissions remained, including the failure to agree on the reform of the Security Council and on measures to further non-proliferation and disarmament. There was disappointment that the high expectations on a broad range of issues, including the concept of impunity and the role of the International Criminal Court, were not met. Participants reiterated their condemnation of terrorism as one of the greatest threats to international peace and security and emphasized the importance of redoubling efforts towards a global convention against terrorism. The need to assist developing countries that lacked the capacity to combat terrorism was also discussed and specific reference made to assistance in the area of safe transportation by sea and air. He also said that development had to remain at the centre of trade negotiations, and globalization made more inclusive and equitable. The specific needs of developing countries should be taken into consideration and favourable access to markets granted to small countries and special efforts made to help them, especially those in Africa, to build an environment for attracting foreign investment. Concern was expressed regarding the capacity of low- and middle-income countries to reach the MDGs. In that regard, it was suggested that those countries' access to international monetary and financial institutions should be facilitated and other systemic imbalances fixed to ensure equitable development. A broad consensus had also emerged with regard to the need to strengthen and reform the United Nations so that it could effectively play its role in addressing the multidimensional challenges of the twenty-first century.

Closing session. During the closing session on 16 September, the World Summit also heard statements by the Co-Chairpersons, and by representatives of the League of Arab States, the Euro-pean Commission, the Organization of the Islamic Conference, the World Conference of Speakers of Parliaments of the Inter-Parliamentary Union, the Shanghai Cooperation Organization, the International Union for the Conservation of Nature and Natural Resources, the Council of Europe, the Commonwealth Secretariat, the Asian Development Bank, the African Development Bank, the International Confederation of Free Trade Unions, the Flora Tristan Centre for Peruvian Women, a national women's organization, and BHI Holdings Limited, a private business enterprise concerned with development ventures.

World Summit preparatory meetings

The General Assembly, at its resumed fifty-ninth (2005) session on 13 April, considered and took decisions on the preparations for and organization of the High-level Plenary Meeting of the General Assembly (see resolution below) and at its September session adopted the draft outcome document for submission to the World Summit.

On 15 April [meeting 92], the Assembly adopted **resolution 59/291** [draft: A/59/L.60] without vote [agenda items 45 and 55].

Preparation for and organization of the High-level Plenary Meeting of the General Assembly

The General Assembly,

Recalling its resolution 58/291 of 6 May 2004 in which it, inter alia, decided to convene in New York in 2005, at the commencement of the sixtieth session of the General Assembly, a high-level plenary meeting of the Assembly with the participation of Heads of State and Government, on dates to be decided by the Assembly at its fifty-ninth session,

Recalling also its resolution 59/145 of 17 December 2004, in which it welcomed the report of the Secretary-General entitled "Modalities, format and organization of the high-level plenary meeting of the sixtieth session of the General Assembly" requested in its resolution 58/291, and following informal consultations convened by the President of the General Assembly and being convinced that the High-level Plenary Meeting would constitute a significant event,

1. *Expresses satisfaction* with the open, inclusive and transparent manner in which the President of the General Assembly is conducting the preparatory process for the High-level Plenary Meeting, which should lead to the adoption of a balanced document;

2. *Welcomes* the submission by the Secretary-General on 21 March 2005 of the comprehensive report entitled "In larger freedom: towards development, security and human rights for all";

3. *Invites,* owing to the importance of the High-level Plenary Meeting, the Head of State of the country of the President of the General Assembly at its fifty-ninth session and the Head of State or Government of the country of the President of the General Assembly at its sixtieth session to jointly preside over the High-level Plenary Meeting;

4. *Decides* that the Holy See, in its capacity as observer State, and Palestine, in its capacity as observer, shall participate in the High-level Plenary Meeting;

5. *Decides also* that the plenary meetings shall be organized in accordance with the modalities set forth in annex I to the present resolution and that the list of speakers for the plenary meetings shall be established in accordance with the procedure set forth in that annex;

6. *Decides further* that the round-table sessions shall be organized in accordance with the modalities set forth in annex II to the present resolution;

7. *Decides* that the separate meeting on Financing for Development to be held within the framework of the High-level Plenary Meeting shall be held on 14 September 2005, immediately following the adjournment of the opening plenary meeting;

8. *Decides also* that the President of the General Assembly shall preside over the informal interactive hearings to be held on 23 and 24 June 2005 with representatives of non-governmental organizations, civil society organizations and the private sector, and that the hearings shall be organized in accordance with the modalities set forth in annex III to the present resolution, and requests the President of the Assembly to prepare a summary of the hearings to be issued as an Assembly document prior to the High-level Plenary Meeting in September 2005;

9. *Requests* the Secretary-General to establish a trust fund to enhance the participation in the hearings of representatives of non-governmental organizations and civil society organizations from developing countries, and calls upon Member States and others to support the trust fund generously and speedily;

10. *Encourages* Member States to attend the hearings at the ambassadorial level to facilitate interaction between the Member States and the representatives of non-governmental organizations, civil society organizations and the private sector;

11. *Requests* the President of the General Assembly to continue to hold open, inclusive and transparent consultations with all Member States with a view to reaching the broadest possible agreement on all major issues relating to the High-level Plenary Meeting, taking into account the views expressed by Member States.

Annex I

Organization of the plenary meetings and establishment of the list of speakers for the High-level Plenary Meeting of the General Assembly

1. The High-level Plenary Meeting will consist of a total of six meetings, on the basis of two meetings a day, as follows:

Wednesday, 14 September 2005, from 9 a.m. to 10 a.m. and from 3 p.m. to 7 p.m.;
Thursday, 15 September 2005, from 9 a.m. to 1 p.m. and from 3 p.m. to 7 p.m.;
Friday, 16 September 2005, from 9 a.m. to 1 p.m. and from 3 p.m. to 7 p.m.

2. The podium in the General Assembly Hall will have three seats to accommodate the two Co-Chairpersons and the Secretary-General. In the absence of the Head of State of the country of the President of the General Assembly at its fifty-ninth session or the Head of State or Government of the country of the President of the General Assembly at its sixtieth session, the President of the Assembly at its fifty-ninth session or the President of the Assembly at its sixtieth session will sit instead.

3. At the opening plenary meeting, on Wednesday morning, 14 September 2005, the speakers will be the two Co-Chairpersons, the Secretary-General and the head of the delegation of the host country of the Organization.

4. The separate meeting on Financing for Development will be held from 10 a.m. to 1 p.m. immediately following the adjournment of the opening plenary meeting. Statements will be made by the head of the delegation of the host country of the International Conference on Financing for Development, major institutional stakeholders, individual delegations, in particular delegations that are proposing key initiatives in the Financing for Development process, one representative from civil society and one representative from the private sector, in consultation with the President of the General Assembly.

5. The list of speakers for the High-level Plenary Meeting will therefore be established on the basis of five meetings. The afternoon meeting on Wednesday, 14 September 2005, the morning and afternoon meetings on Thursday, 15 September 2005, and the morning meeting on Friday, 16 September 2005, will each have 40 speaking slots. The Friday afternoon meeting will have 32 speaking slots since the last hour will be devoted to the closing of the High-level Plenary Meeting.

6. The list of speakers for the High-level Plenary Meeting will be established initially as follows:

(a) The representative of the Secretary-General will draw one name from a first box containing the names of all Member States that will be represented by Heads of State, Heads of Government, vice-presidents, crown princes/princesses, and of the Holy See, in its capacity as observer State, and Palestine, in its capacity as observer, should they be represented by their highest-ranking officials. This procedure will be repeated until all names have been drawn from the box, thus establishing the order in which participants will be invited to choose their meetings and select their speaking slots. The representative of the Secretary-General will then draw from a second box the names of those not contained in the first box in accordance with the same procedure;

(b) Five boxes will be prepared, each one representing a meeting and each one containing numbers corresponding to speaking slots at that meeting;

(c) Once the name of a Member State, the Holy See, in its capacity as observer State, or Palestine, in its capacity as observer, has been drawn by the representative of the Secretary-General, that Member State, the Holy See, in its capacity as observer State, or Palestine, in its capacity as observer, will be invited first to choose a meeting and then to draw from the appropriate box the number indicating the speaking slot in the meeting.

7. The initial list of speakers for the High-level Plenary Meeting as outlined in paragraph 6 above will be established at a meeting to be scheduled as soon as possible in the month of May 2005.

8. Subsequently, when each category of speakers is organized following the order resulting from the selection process outlined in paragraph 6 above, the list of speakers for each meeting will be rearranged in accordance with the established practice of the General Assembly:

(*a*) Heads of State will thus be accorded first priority, followed by Heads of Government; vice-presidents, crown princes/princesses; the highest-ranking official of the Holy See, in its capacity as observer State, and of Palestine, in its capacity as observer; ministers; and permanent representatives;

(*b*) In the event that the level at which a statement is to be made is subsequently changed, the speaker will be moved to the next available speaking slot in the appropriate category at the same meeting;

(*c*) Participants may arrange to exchange their speaking slots in accordance with the established practice of the General Assembly;

(*d*) Speakers who are not present when their speaking turn comes will be automatically moved to the next available speaking slot within their category.

9. In order to accommodate all speakers at the High-level Plenary Meeting, statements will be limited to five minutes, on the understanding that this will not preclude the distribution of more extensive texts.

10. Without prejudice to other organizations which have observer status in the General Assembly, a representative of each of the following may also be included in the list of speakers for the plenary meetings of the High-level Plenary Meeting:

League of Arab States

African Union

European Community

Organization of the Islamic Conference

World Conference of Speakers of Parliament of the Inter-Parliamentary Union.

11. Representatives of non-governmental organizations in consultative status with the Economic and Social Council, civil society organizations and the private sector, one from each grouping, selected during the informal interactive hearings of June 2005, may also be included in the list of speakers for the plenary meetings of the High-level Plenary Meeting in consultation with the President of the General Assembly, time permitting.

12. Other than for Member States, the list of speakers for the plenary meetings of the High-level Plenary Meeting will be closed on Monday, 1 August 2005.

13. The arrangements set out above shall in no way create a precedent.

Annex II

Organization of the interactive round-table sessions for the High-level Plenary Meeting of the General Assembly

1. The High-level Plenary Meeting will hold four interactive round-table sessions, as follows:

Wednesday, 14 September 2005, from 3 p.m. to 6 p.m.;

Thursday, 15 September 2005, from 10 a.m. to 1 p.m. and from 3 p.m. to 6 p.m.;

Friday, 16 September 2005, from 10 a.m. to 1 p.m.

2. The four round-table sessions will have at least 40 seats each and will be chaired by a Head of State or Government.

3. The chairpersons of the four round-table sessions will be from the African States, the Asian States, the Eastern European States and the Latin American and Caribbean States. Those four chairpersons will be selected by their respective regional groups in consultation with the President of the General Assembly.

4. Following the selection of the chairpersons of the round-table sessions, each regional group will determine which of its members will participate in each round-table session, ensuring that equitable geographical distribution will be maintained, allowing for some flexibility. The chairpersons of the regional groups will communicate to the President of the General Assembly the list of countries from their respective regions that will participate in each round-table session. Member States are encouraged to be represented at the round tables at the level of Head of State or Government.

5. All four round-table sessions will cover the entire agenda of the High-level Plenary Meeting.

6. Each Head of State or Head of Government or head of delegation attending the round-table sessions may be accompanied by two advisers.

7. The composition of the four round-table sessions will be subject to the principle of equitable geographical distribution. Thus, for each regional group, the distribution of its members for participation in each round-table session will be as follows:

(*a*) African States: fifteen Member States;

(*b*) Asian States: fifteen Member States;

(*c*) Eastern European States: seven Member States;

(*d*) Latin American and Caribbean States: ten Member States;

(*e*) Western European and other States: nine Member States.

8. A Member State that is not a member of any of the regional groups may participate in a round-table session to be determined in consultation with the President of the General Assembly. The Holy See, in its capacity as observer State, and Palestine, in its capacity as observer, as well as the organizations listed in paragraph 10 of annex I to the present resolution, may also participate in different round-table sessions to be determined also in consultation with the President of the Assembly.

9. Heads of entities of the United Nations system may also participate in the round-table sessions, in consultation with the President of the General Assembly.

10. The list of participants in each round-table session will be made available in due course.

11. The round-table sessions will be closed to the media and the general public. Accredited delegates and observers will be able to follow the proceedings of the round-table sessions via a closed-circuit television in the overflow room.

12. Summaries of the deliberations of the four round-table sessions will be presented orally by the chairpersons of the round-table sessions during the concluding plenary meeting of the High-level Plenary Meeting.

Annex III

Organization of the informal interactive hearings

1. The President of the General Assembly will preside over the informal interactive hearings to be held on 23 and 24 June 2005. The hearings shall consist of a

brief opening plenary meeting followed by four sequential sessions of the hearings on the basis of two sessions a day, from 10 a.m. to 1 p.m., and from 3 p.m. to 6 p.m. Each session will consist of presentations by invited participants from non-governmental organizations in consultative status with the Economic and Social Council, civil society organizations and the private sector and an exchange of views with Member States.

2. The hearings will be attended by representatives of non-governmental organizations in consultative status with the Economic and Social Council, civil society organizations, the private sector, Member States and observers.

3. The President of the General Assembly will determine the list of invited participants and the exact format and organization of the hearings, in consultation with Member States and representatives of non-governmental organizations in consultative status with the Economic and Social Council, civil society organizations and the private sector.

4. The themes for the hearings will be based on the comprehensive report of the Secretary-General of 21 March 2005 and the clusters defined therein.

5. The President of the General Assembly will consult with representatives of non-governmental organizations in consultative status with the Economic and Social Council, civil society organizations and the private sector, and with Member States, as appropriate, on the list of representatives of non-governmental organizations, civil society organizations and the private sector that may participate in the plenary meetings of the High-level Plenary Meeting of September 2005.

On 13 September [meeting 118], the Assembly adopted **resolution 59/314** [draft: A/59/L.70] without vote [agenda items 45 and 55], which contained the draft outcome document of the September 2005 High-level Plenary Meeting of the Assembly.

Other World Summit events

Treaty-signing ceremony

During the World Summit (14-16 September), the General Assembly held a Treaty-signing Event—"Focus 2005: Responding to Global Challenges"—during which 99 countries and the European Community signed, ratified or acceded to a number of UN treaties. Fifty-two countries participated at the level of Head of State or Government and over 40 at the level of Minister of Foreign Affairs. A total of 265 treaty actions were undertaken during the event. The treaties that attracted the most attention were: the International Convention for the Suppression of Acts of Nuclear Terrorism (see p. 1410), which was opened for signature during the event (82 signatures); the United Nations Convention against Corruption, adopted by General Assembly resolution 58/4 [YUN 2003, p. 1127] (seven signatures, two ratifications and one accession), and which entered into force on 14 December; the Optional Protocol to the Convention against Torture and Other Cruel, Inhuman or Degrading Treatment or Punishment, adopted by Assembly resolution 57/199 [YUN 2002, p. 631] (nine signatures and two ratifications); the World Health Organization Framework Convention on Tobacco Control [YUN 2003, p. 1251] (five ratifications and two accessions); and the United Nations Convention on Jurisdictional Immunities of States and Their Property, adopted by Assembly resolution 59/38 [YUN 2004, p. 1304] (nine signatures). One State, Liberia, undertook a record 83 treaty actions on 16 September.

Related World Summit gatherings

The occasion of the World Summit also provided an opportunity for several other bodies to gather, in order for their views and proposals to be taken into account by the Heads of State and Government, during their deliberations and finalization of the Summit's outcome document. Those gatherings included the informal interactive session of the General Assembly with representatives of non-governmental organizations (NGOs), civil society organizations and the private sector [A/60/331]; the second High-level Dialogue on Financing for Development (New York, 27-28 June) (see p. 1065); the second World Conference of Speakers of Parliament [A/60/398]; and other related regional meetings.

Informal interactive hearings

For the first time in its history, the General Assembly held informal interactive hearings with representatives of NGOs, civil society organizations and the private sector (New York, 23-24 June) [A/60/331], in accordance with Assembly resolutions 59/291 and 59/293 (see pp. 72 & 1064). The hearings were organized by the Assembly President, Jean Ping (Gabon), as an input to the preparatory process of the High-level Plenary Meeting of the General Assembly (World Summit).

The hearings, based on the Secretary-General's report "In larger freedom: towards development, security and human rights for all" (see p. 67), were conducted in five interactive sessions, on the themes: "Freedom from want: the MDGs one to seven; Freedom from want: MDG eight and issues regarding financing for development; Freedom from fear; Freedom to live in dignity; and Strengthening the United Nations".

A summary of the hearings [A/60/331], transmitted to the Assembly by its President, outlined the main messages emerging from the sessions. There was a shared feeling that development, peace and security and human rights were interconnected and that the World Summit presented a unique opportunity to make headway in bringing about a more prosperous, fair and safe world. The hearings emphasized: a human rights-based approach to development, peace and security and the need to elevate human rights within the United Nations; that gender equality, empowering women and protecting their human rights were prerequisites for achieving the MDGs; and that the draft outcome document of the World Summit gave more attention to the rights, needs and contributions of such groups as indigenous peoples, those facing racial discrimination and disabilities, children, youth and older people.

Concerning MDG eight (trade and financing for development), the hearings expressed the need to challenge the trade liberalization agenda of the Doha multilateral trade negotiations (see p. 1041) and to prioritize development concerns. There was a call for keeping the commitment to devote 0.7 per cent of GNP to ODA, innovative sources of financing and ensuring immediate and wide-ranging debt relief and cancellation. It was felt that the outcome document should give greater attention to the need to enhance democracy and accountability in international decision-making. The need to move towards a culture of conflict prevention was recognized and it was felt that the outcome document should give serious attention to disarmament and a new legal instrument to control arms trade.

Member States were urged to recognize the responsibilities that accompanied sovereignty, including a commitment to prevent genocide and massive human rights violations. Civil society participation in the United Nations needed to be strengthened, and there was widespread agreement on the need for a strengthened United Nations and support for the proposed Peacebuilding Commission and Human Rights Council. Key issues raised on Secretariat reform included the need for increased resources and the preservation of the Secretariat's independence and integrity.

IPU World Conference of Speakers of Parliaments

The second World Conference of Speakers of Parliament of the Inter-Parliamentary Union (IPU) was held at United Nations Headquarters from 7 to 9 September. The Final Declaration of the Conference "Bridging the democracy gap in international relations: a stronger role for parliaments", was transmitted to the General Assembly on 16 September [A/60/398] by the IPU President. The Declaration stated that the Conference was convened to take stock of action effected by parliaments since their first meeting in 2000 [YUN 2000, p. 67], and to examine how to support

better international cooperation and the United Nations, in order to help bridge the democracy gap in international relations. It also stated that the United Nations had to remain the cornerstone of global cooperation and urged all parliaments to debate the reform proposals contained in the Secretary-General's report "In larger freedom: towards development, security and human rights for all" (see p. 67) and engage with their respective Governments to create the momentum for action.

The Conference welcomed the UN decision to grant observer status to IPU [YUN 2002, p. 1445] and noted that the time had come for a strategic partnership between the two institutions. It would also welcome more substantive cooperation with the United Nations and called on the world body to resort more frequently to the political and technical expertise which IPU and its Member Parliaments could provide, particularly in postconflict institution-building. It also welcomed the debate on how best to establish more meaningful and structured interaction between the United Nations and national parliaments. The Conference encouraged IPU to ensure that national parliaments were better informed about UN activities, to develop further parliamentary hearings and specialized meetings at the United Nations, and to cooperate more closely with regional parliamentary assemblies and organizations, with a view to enhancing coherence and efficiency in global and interregional parliamentary cooperation. Participants pledged to increase the capacity of their parliaments to bring their influence to bear on the work of the United Nations, enhance its transparency and accountability and to provide an impetus to the reforms under way. They encouraged every parliament to organize, around the same time each year, an "International Day of Parliaments" and to hold a parliamentary debate on one of the recommendations included in the Final Declaration of the Conference.

The IPU Secretary-General, Anders Johnsson, in reporting to the World Summit on the outcome of the Conference, said that the Declaration had taken up the subject of UN reform, as the Speakers of Parliamentarians wanted to see the reform proposals debated, and acted on immediately by their Governments. They wanted comprehensive reform that would recognize the intrinsic link between democracy, security development and human rights, and a stronger United Nations. They called on States to demonstrate leadership and political will to provide the Organization with more efficient mechanisms, appropriate human and financial resources and real management reform.

Regional contributions to the World Summit

Communications. On 5 August [A/59/900], Lebanon, on behalf of the Arab Group at the United Nations, transmitted to General Assembly President resolution No. 314 and a Declaration on the pursuit of the implementation of the Millennium Development Goals, issued by a Joint Ministerial Conference of Arab Ministers of Social Affairs and Planning on the Millennium Development Goals (Cairo, Egypt, 30 June).

On 22 August [A/60/313], Indonesia transmitted to the General Assembly President the Jakarta Declaration on the Millennium Development Goals in Asia and the Pacific: the Way Forward 2015, adopted at a Ministerial Regional Meeting (Jakarta, Indonesia, 3-5 August).

On 9 September [A/60/368], Guatemala transmitted to the Secretary-General its second progress report on the MDGs, for submission to the High-level Plenary of the Assembly's sixtieth session.

Implementation of the World Summit Outcome

Report of Secretary-General. The Secretary-General, in an October report [A/60/430] on the implementation of those decisions contained in the World Summit Outcome requiring specific action by him, noted that the Outcome document provided comprehensive policy guidance for the ongoing work of the Secretariat and UN agencies, funds and programmes, all of which would be reviewing their programmes accordingly. He informed Member States of the programmatic and management-related workplan and overall framework he established for implementing the Summit Outcome, and the basic processes and time lines expected in each area of activity. The implementation of mandated actions would be under his direct leadership, with a number of individual programmatic elements falling to the lead UN department or entity, which would work with relevant parts of the UN system to prepare further proposals and implementation plans for the General Assembly's consideration.

The implementation activity fell into four broad clusters: work related to institutional innovations, including support to the intergovernmental process discussing the Peacebuilding Commission and Human Rights Council, and finalizing details and/or beginning the implementation of such new entities as the Peacebuilding Support Office and Peacebuilding Fund, as well as the analysis and recommendations requested in support of the review of programmatic and institutional mandates older than five years; the

overhaul of oversight and audit arrangements, including the creation of an ethics office and strengthened financial disclosure regulations and the development of new oversight arrangements, including a new oversight committee reporting to the Assembly; the review of existing financial and human resources regulations, rules and policies and the development of the proposed staff buy-out programme; and the review of system-wide coherence, including ensuring greater policy and operational coordination across specialized agencies, funds and programmes, and the development of proposals for more tightly managed entities in the fields of development, humanitarian assistance and the environment. The financial implications of the Summit's decisions were calculated, and submitted to the Assembly in November (see p. 1476). Budgetary implications for the proposed Peacebuilding Commission and the Human Rights Council were submitted separately.

The report also described the actions taken under specific subject areas to implement the Summit Outcome decisions. Those actions addressed economic and social development (see also CEB consideration below), peaceful settlement of disputes, particularly regarding the preparation of proposals to further support national efforts and capacity to prevent conflict and enhancement of the capacity of the Department of Political Affairs for mediation and other activities in support of the Secretary-General's good offices function and the work of his special envoys. The Secretary-General stated that he had formed a Counter-Terrorism Implementation Task Force and would submit proposals in 2006 to further strengthen the UN system capacity to assist States in combating terrorism and to enhance coordination in that regard. In the area of peacekeeping, the Department of Peacekeeping Operations presented a proposal for a strategic reserves concept and would continue to engage with Member States on that and other options for enhanced rapidly deployable capacities to reinforce peacekeeping operations in crisis. The Secretariat was proceeding with the design and terms of reference of the Peacebuilding Fund, which was expected to be established by the end of November, and work had commenced to prepare the Peacebuilding Support Office. Considering the Summit's decision that the Security Council improve the monitoring of the implementation and effects of sanctions, the Office of Legal Affairs was tasked with developing proposals and guidelines for the Council's consideration, and with respect to the need to strengthen the UN Office on Drugs and Crime to carry out its mandate, financial implications would be submitted in November. The Office of the United Nations High Commissioner for Human Rights was working with the Department for General Assembly and Conference Management to ensure that support arrangements were in place for the Human Rights Council as soon as the Assembly took a decision on that matter. The Secretary-General also highlighted efforts to strengthen the rule of law in UN activities and to develop a system-wide code of ethics for all UN staff. With regard to Secretariat reform, he had initiated the review of all mandates older than five years to assist the Assembly to update and focus the work of the Organization, based on which a strategic framework for 2008-2009 would be proposed subsequent to the Assembly's approval of the review. Work was also under way to strengthen the capacity of the Office of Internal Oversight Services, and proposals would be submitted to the Assembly, based on the recommendations of the CEB High-level Committee on Management, for an independent external evaluation of the auditing, oversight, roles and responsibilities of the management of the United Nations and the specialized agencies. The Secretariat was also preparing proposals for the creation of an independent oversight advisory committee to enhance the independence of UN oversight structures. The Secretary-General said he intended to review and discuss options for strengthening management and coordination of UN operational activities, and the Office for the Coordination of Humanitarian Affairs was developing proposals to improve the timeliness and predictability of humanitarian funding.

The Secretary-General concluded that work was under way to implement many of the Summit's decisions along with a number of steps he had already taken in that regard. However, progress in some key areas would depend on decisions that had to be taken by Member States and he underscored the urgent need for them to complete discussions on those issues.

The Secretary-General issued separate reports on the establishment of the ethics office, comprehensive review of governance arrangements, including an independent external evaluation of the auditing and oversight system and the independent audit advisory committee [A/60/568 & Corr. 1, 2] (see p. 1496).

CEB consideration. The Chief Executives Board for Coordination (CEB), at its second regular session (New York, 28 October) [CEB/2005/2], discussed the implications of, and follow-up to, the outcome of the 2005 World Summit. It had before it a background note entitled "United Nations system follow-up to the 2005 World Summit", which analysed the Outcome under the

headings: development; peace and collective security, human rights and the rule of law and humanitarian assistance; and management reform. The Secretary-General drew the Board's attention to the four broad clusters of his workplan for the remainder of 2005 and the first quarter of 2006 and beyond (see above). He said the fourth cluster—system-wide coherence— was of particular importance to CEB, as its implementation posed a range of coherence issues that needed to be addressed collectively. He said work could not be rushed nor held to the deadline of the first quarter of 2006 or earlier, as the other clusters. The process needed to be inclusive with ample opportunity for discussion and input. He undertook to consult with Member States on how the World Summit Outcome follow-up in that area might be organized, following consultations with CEB. The Chairman of the High-level Committee on Programmes (HLCP), reporting on the Committee's tenth session (Frascati, Italy, 6-8 October) [CEB/2005/7], said that on the overall issue of system-wide coherence, HLPC emphasized that issues of development, peace and security and human rights had to be tackled in an integrated manner and that the main horizontal themes of sustainable development, human rights and gender had to be mainstreamed in the policies of all organizations. HLCP member organizations suggested that the Outcome document be placed before their governing bodies as a basis for more coherent and coordinated follow-up by Member States and the UN system. The Committee raised the possibility of developing a road map with appropriate indicators and milestones for the system's follow-up to the Outcome.

The Executive Heads welcomed the Outcome as an expression of the importance of multilateral cooperation and the crucial role of the UN system. CEB would pursue all matters in which system-wide coordination and coherence were involved, including developing proposals for strengthened management and coordination of operational activities, particularly in relation to the World Summit's call for more tightly managed entities in the fields of development, humanitarian assistance and the environment; fully utilizing HLPC, in collaboration with UNDG, for advancing policy and operational coherence at Headquarters and in the field; drawing on the CEB report prepared in the lead-up to the Summit, entitled "One United Nations—Catalyst for Progress and Change", in elaborating a system-wide approach to ensuring coherent and coordinated follow-up of the Outcome; encouraging UN system organizations to bring the Outcome to the attention of their governing bodies; providing support for the strengthened role of the

Economic and Social Council, particularly in relation to the holding of annual ministerial-level substantive reviews to assess progress in reaching the internationally agreed development goals and the convening of a biennial high-level development cooperation forum.

Assembly and Security Council actions. In December, the General Assembly (**resolution 60/180**) and the Security Council (**resolutions 1645(2005)** and **1646(2005)**) (see p. 94) took action to establish the Peacebuilding Commission.

Other implementation matters. In a 10 June letter [A/59/842], China welcomed the report of the High-Level Panel on Threats, Challenges and Change [YUN 2004, p. 54], the UN Millennium Project Report (see p. 70) and the comprehensive report of the Secretary-General (see p. 67). It maintained, among other things, that UN reforms should observe the principles of multilateralism, sovereign equality, non-interference in internal affairs and peaceful resolution of conflicts; reforms should be all-dimensional and multisectoral; and they should accommodate the propositions and concerns of all UN members, especially those from developing countries.

In a 16 September statement, issued by the Office of the Spokesman [SG/SM/10100], the Secretary-General welcomed the initiative of the Prime Minister of Sweden to create a "Leaders' Network in support of UN reform". The Secretary-General encouraged other countries to support the initiative and expressed hope that the Network could help translate the commitments made at the World Summit into effective action.

On 26 September [A/60/394], Iran transmitted to the Secretary-General the Tehran communiqué, adopted at the International Conference on United Nations Reform (Tehran, Iran, 17-18 July).

On 27 September [A/60/412], Mexico, on behalf of the Group of Friends for the Reform of the United Nations (Algeria, Australia, Canada, Chile, Colombia, Germany, Japan, Kenya, Mexico, New Zealand, the Netherlands, Pakistan, Singapore, Spain, Sweden), said, in a letter to the Secretary-General, that the crucial phase of the implementation of the outcome document of the 2005 World Summit was about to begin. If the Organization failed to turn its words into actions, multilateralism would not be able to produce the solutions that societies demanded all over the world. It urged the Secretary-General to continue working to implement the commitments and agreements reached during the High-level Plenary Meeting and assured him that the Group of Friends would continue to take the necessary actions to attain the goal of bringing about a comprehensive and sound United Nations.

Other matters

Request for legal opinion

On 7 October [A/60/438], Venezuela, in a letter to the General Assembly President, reiterated its objections to the process leading to the Assembly's adoption of draft resolutions A/59/L.70 and A/60/L.1 relating to the World Summit Outcome. It requested that the matter be referred to the UN Office of Legal Affairs to determine whether the procedure followed in the negotiation and adoption of the final outcome document of the World Summit complied with the United Nations Charter and the Assembly's rules of procedure.

In a 1 November reply [A/60/535], the Assembly President told Venezuela that he had been informed by the Office of Legal Affairs that, as a matter of policy and practice, it provided legal advice only at the request of a UN organ and not from individual Member States. Moreover, it was incumbent on the Office of the President and Member States to implement the document, which was adopted without vote by more than 150 Heads of State and Government.

PART ONE

Political and security questions

Chapter I

International peace and security

In 2005, the United Nations celebrated its sixtieth anniversary in an international environment, which continued to face interconnected threats to peace and security stemming from war and conflict, civil violence, international organized crime, terrorism and arms proliferation, including weapons of mass destruction, persistent poverty, deadly infectious diseases and environmental degradation. In September, at the 2005 World Summit, a High-level Plenary Meeting of the General Assembly to mark that milestone, world leaders articulated the need for a new security consensus that would address those threats preventively, including a new global strategy for preventing catastrophic terrorism from ever becoming a reality. They also approved the Secretary-General's proposal for the creation of an intergovernmental Peacebuilding Commission and a Peacebuilding Support Office to strengthen the management of UN peace operations worldwide, which he had articulated in his report to the Summit, entitled "In larger freedom: towards development, security and human rights for all".

The Security Council, which also met in September at the level of Heads of State and Government to discuss threats to international peace and security, adopted additional measures for Member States to reinforce ongoing efforts to prevent terrorism. To help countries break the cycle of relapsing into conflict, the Council adopted a declaration on strengthening its effectiveness in conflict prevention, particularly in Africa. The Council also addressed the role that civil society could play and stressed the need for a broad strategy of conflict prevention that addressed the root causes of armed conflict and political and social crises comprehensively. Conscious of the invaluable contribution of regional organizations to UN peace efforts, the Council held a High-level meeting with regional organizations in October and expressed its determination to further develop cooperation between the United Nations and those organizations in the maintenance of peace and security.

Throughout the year, the United Nations worked tirelessly to prevent and resolve conflicts and to consolidate peace. Those efforts resulted in the successful transition from peacekeeping to peacebuilding in Sierra Leone and Timor Leste,

support for the organization of elections in Burundi, the Democratic Republic of the Congo (DRC), Haiti and Liberia, and facilitated complex political transition processes in those countries, and in Afghanistan.

The year 2005 was particularly devastating with regard to international terrorism, having witnessed an increase in tragic terrorist attacks worldwide, including in Egypt, India, Indonesia, Iraq, Lebanon and London. In a series of statements, the Council condemned those acts and called for the prosecution of the perpetrators. The General Assembly, in the outcome document of its 2005 World Summit, welcomed the identification by the Secretary-General of elements for a counter-terrorism strategy, and in April, adopted the International Convention for the Suppression of Acts of Nuclear Terrorism.

During the year, the United Nations continued to strengthen its peacekeeping capacity worldwide. In June, the Assembly considered and took action on a number of cross-cutting issues related to the administrative and budgetary aspects of UN peacekeeping operations, including a request to the Office of Internal Oversight Services to review the practices and management structure of the Department of Peacekeeping Operations. The Council and the Assembly also confronted the issue of sexual abuse and exploitation by peacekeepers, with the Assembly endorsing the recommendations contained in the report of the Secretary-General's Adviser on Sexual Exploitation and Abuse by United Nations Peacekeeping Personnel, entitled "A comprehensive strategy to eliminate future sexual exploitation and abuse in United Nations peacekeeping operations".

The Organization maintained 12 political and peacebuilding missions and 18 peacekeeping operations. At the end of 2005, some 85,000 military and civilian personnel were serving under UN command, compared to 64,701 the previous year.

The financial position of UN peacekeeping operations continued to improve during the year, as expenditures increased to $4,074.3 million, compared to $2,933.8 million in 2004, a 39 per cent increase, mostly attributable to expanded operations in the DRC and the full-year impact of four other missions. Unpaid assessed contributions amounted to $1.7 billion, compared to $1.5 billion the previous year.

Promotion of international peace and security

A new concept of collective security

In his 21 March report entitled "In larger freedom: towards development, security and human rights for all" [A/59/2005 & Add.1], submitted to the 2005 World Summit (see p. 48), the Secretary-General endorsed the broad vision of the role of the United Nations in providing collective security and the case for a more comprehensive concept of such collective action, as articulated in the 2004 report of the High-level Panel on Threats, Challenges and Change [YUN 2004, p. 54]. He said that threats to peace and security in the twenty-first century included not just international war and conflict, but civil violence, organized crime, terrorism, weapons of mass destruction, poverty, deadly infectious disease and environmental degradation. In a globalized world, the threats were interconnected, and as such, a new security consensus had to be found to address them all preventively, acting at a sufficiently early stage with the full range of available instruments. An essential part of the new consensus had to be agreement on when and how much force could be used to defend international peace and security, particularly the right to use it preemptively against imminent threats, and preventively against latent or non-imminent threats. He recommended that the Security Council adopt a resolution setting out the principles for using force and expressing its intention to be guided by them when deciding to authorize or mandate such use. The Secretary-General said that the time had come to transform the United Nations into the effective instrument for preventing conflict that it was meant to be, by acting on several key policy and institutional priorities. In that context, a new global strategy was needed to avert catastrophic terrorism. The multilateral frameworks for handling threats from nuclear, biological and chemical weapons should be revitalized to ensure continued progress on disarmament and to address the growing risk of a cascade of proliferation, especially in the nuclear field, and efforts should be continued to reduce the prevalence and risk of war. The Secretary-General appealed to Member States to do more to ensure that the United Nations had effective capacities for peacekeeping, commensurate with the de-

mands placed upon it. Noting that the time was ripe for an interlocking system of peacekeeping capacities to enable the Organization to work with relevant regional organizations, he proposed the creation of an intergovernmental Peacebuilding Commission and Peacebuilding Support Office (see p. 93).

The World Summit, in its outcome document (**resolution 60/1** of 16 September) (see p. 48), decided to establish the Peacebuilding Commission and endorsed the creation of an initial operating capability for a standing police capacity for the policing component of UN peacekeeping operations.

Maintenance of international peace and security

On 12 July [meeting 5225], the Security Council held a debate on the role of the Council in humanitarian crises: challenges, lessons learned, and the way ahead. Greece, in an explanatory non-paper of 6 July [S/2005/434], said that the debate was to focus on recent Council efforts to break the cycle of conflict affecting societies and to prevent them from relapsing into such crises. Attention was to be placed particularly on the three key pillars of post-conflict security: the promotion of the rule of law; security sector reform; and the disarmament, demobilization and reintegration of ex-combatants.

In opening the debate, the Council President noted that the early prevention of humanitarian crises had become a political and moral imperative for the Council, and that the United Nations should strengthen its capacity to move from reaction to prevention of crises before they reached critical mass. While the responsibility for the protection of civilian populations rested primarily with States concerned, in cases of extreme violations and atrocities, the international community had an obligation to the victims of such violence. The United Nations, particularly the Council, had to take effective action to alleviate the suffering of civilians and to avert the occurrence of humanitarian disasters.

The Secretary-General, in his statement to the Council, observed that Member States needed to take early action in a crisis situation to prevent human suffering and said it was important to prevent future conflicts by addressing their root causes. He also addressed the problems of providing security and justice in post-conflict situations, based on the rule of law, which he said could not be imposed from outside. Local actors had to understand that only confidence in the rule of law would ensure lasting security, by enabling different factions or communities to rely on the forces of the State, rather than on factional militias for protection. The role of the international community was to galvanize and provide technical assistance to that process, while making sure all national actors were included in it. Different parts of the UN system, including international financial institutions, needed to cooperate closely with each other, bilateral donors and troop contributors. Ensuring such coordination was one of the roles he hoped to see fulfilled by the new Peacebuilding Commission.

In his address, the Under-Secretary-General for Peacekeeping Operations, Jean-Marie Guéhenno, while also reflecting on post-conflict situations, stressed that, if peace were to be lasting, the short-, medium- and long-term security and justice needs of both the State and its population had to be addressed equally. UN efforts in the security and justice sectors tended to be driven by peace agreements, which addressed those issues in the context of ending a conflict. While being an important element, it did not lay a strong basis for the consolidation of State and human security in the post-conflict setting. Insufficient attention was given to a comprehensive national security review process that identified threats to State and human security and the development of a security architecture that was responsive to those threats. As a result, both the international community and host countries were ill-prepared to tackle critical challenges, such as corruption, cross-border narcotics and arms, and human trafficking. Peace agreement-driven approaches had, in some instances, even led the international community to support the reform of State institutions that had lost their legitimacy in the eyes of the population. It was, therefore, not surprising that those same countries had a high propensity for relapsing into conflict.

Furthermore, international efforts related to the security and justice sectors were often disjointed, leading to uneven or duplicative assistance, and within the United Nations, there was no single system-wide approach to those issues. International approaches in support of security sector reform in post-conflict countries mostly applied foreign models and standards that were often politically unpalatable, unsuitable or unrealistic in the light of the realities of the situation.

To address those challenges, the international community should reconsider whether it was always realistic to seek to rebuild, reform or restructure a country's defence, police, courts and penal system while simultaneously seeking to re-establish security, keep the political process on track, facilitate the return of displaced populations, conduct elections and restore basic services.

In some cases, it might be appropriate to start early on complex tasks, such as rebuilding courts and training police, while in others, the sequence of activities might need to be re-examined to enable the peacekeeping operation to focus on stabilization while a proper assessment of threats and needs was conducted and appropriate international, regional and local partners were identified to rebuild the security infrastructure and institutions. Those questions needed to be thought through carefully to ensure that efforts and resources were spent on viable processes and institutions that could be sustained beyond the brief lifespan of a peacekeeping operation.

For the UN system, another key to better delivery was to continue to strive to carry out its mandates in as integrated a manner as possible, including with development partners at the initial stages of planning for peacekeeping operations, to ensure that joint efforts were guided by a coherent, long-term strategy, and allowed for smooth handovers to national and development partners once the peacekeeping mandate was over. At the same time, there should be greater integration of capacities within the UN system, with assignment of clear responsibility for specific activities; the development of repositories of best practices, including diverse models of reforming the security sector; and effective coordination of United Nations, bilateral and other efforts.

There should also be a differentiation between areas where the UN system had, or should further develop, its capacity to carry out operational tasks and deliver programmes, and other areas where it could most usefully engage knowledgeably with host countries and bilateral and multilateral partners that had the requisite experience or capacity. As such, the UN's role should be to advocate for assistance and to ensure that what was promised and delivered responded to the actual needs of the host country. One key area that deserved examination was defence reform, where the United Nations currently had limited capacity.

SECURITY COUNCIL ACTION

On 12 July [meeting 5225], following consultations among Security Council members, the President made statement **S/PRST/2005/30** on behalf of the Council:

> The Security Council reaffirms the purposes and principles enshrined in the Charter of the United Nations and bears in mind its primary responsibility under the Charter for the maintenance of international peace and security.
>
> The Council remains deeply concerned by the devastating humanitarian, political and economic consequences of armed conflicts and stresses the overriding political and moral imperatives to prevent the outbreak and escalation of armed conflicts

and humanitarian crises, and the benefits therein for peace and development and friendly relations among all States.

The Council acknowledges the importance of helping to prevent future conflicts through addressing their root causes in a legitimate and fair manner.

The Council reiterates the importance it attaches to the promotion and urgent restoration of justice and the rule of law in post-conflict societies and in promoting national reconciliation, democratic development, and human rights. The Council recognizes that ending impunity is important in peace agreements and can contribute to efforts to come to terms with past abuses and to achieve national reconciliation to prevent future conflict. The Council recalls that it has repeatedly emphasized the responsibility of States to end impunity and bring to justice those responsible for genocide, war crimes, crimes against humanity and serious violations of international humanitarian law.

The Council further recognizes the increasing importance of civilian aspects of conflict management in addressing complex crisis situations and in preventing the recurrence of conflict and acknowledges the importance of civilian-military cooperation in crisis management. When approving a United Nations operation, the Council should take into account the essential role of military and civilian police in assisting the stabilization of crisis situations and the maintenance of security. At the same time, the Council acknowledges that the special representative of the Secretary-General, assisted by civilian advisers, could play a key coordination role in the provision of humanitarian assistance, the re-establishment of public order, the functioning of public institutions, as well as rehabilitation, reconstruction and peacebuilding, which lead to long-term sustainable development.

The Council stresses the need to ensure adequate and timely financing for peacebuilding priorities at all stages of the peace process and stresses the need for sustained financial investment in peacebuilding over the medium to longer-term period of recovery. It recognizes the importance of rapid initiation of peacebuilding activities to meet immediate needs and encourages the building of capabilities that can be incorporated rapidly.

The Council takes note with interest of the important proposal by the Secretary-General to establish a peacebuilding commission and shares the objective of improving United Nations capacity to coordinate with donors and troop contributors and to perform peacebuilding activities, in particular from the start of peacekeeping operations through stabilization, reconstruction and development. The Council recognizes the important role that this body could play to bridge the gap between maintenance of international peace and security and the work of humanitarian and economic development assistance.

The Council acknowledges that in post-conflict societies, successful peacebuilding rests on the premise that protection of civilians, the promotion of the rule of law and transitional justice, disarmament, demobilization, repatriation, reintegration and rehabilitation of former combatants, security sector and democratic, economic and social reform

are integrated elements and that national ownership plays an important role which should be supported by the international community, including the regional organizations.

The Council emphasizes that security sector reform is an essential element of any stabilization process in post-conflict environments, underlines the fact that it is inextricably linked with promotion of the rule of law, transitional justice, disarmament, demobilization and reintegration and the protection of civilians, among others, and acknowledges the need for more adequate preparation, including mobilization of necessary planning resources, and more coherent approaches by the United Nations and the international community in addressing these issues.

The Council acknowledges the need to give adequate attention to security sector reform in the future, drawing on best practices that have been developed in this area. The Council also stresses the need seriously to consider the promotion of the rule of law and transitional justice, the disarmament, demobilization and reintegration process and security sector reform, their interlinkage and the availability of adequate resources, when approving the necessary mandates for United Nations operations.

Conflict prevention

Prevention of armed conflict

On 14 September [meeting 5261], the Security Council met at the level of Heads of State and Government to discuss threats to international peace and security, particularly international terrorism and the prevention of armed conflict, especially in Africa.

The Council unanimously adopted **resolution 1625(2005)**. The draft [S/2005/578] was prepared in consultations among Council members.

The Security Council,

Decides to adopt the attached declaration on strengthening the effectiveness of the role of the Security Council in conflict prevention, particularly in Africa.

Annex

The Security Council,

Meeting on 14 September 2005 at the level of Heads of State and Government to discuss how to strengthen the effectiveness of the role of the Security Council in the prevention of armed conflict, particularly in Africa,

Reaffirming its commitment to the purposes and principles of the Charter of the United Nations,

Bearing in mind its primary responsibility for the maintenance of international peace and security,

Deeply concerned by the high human cost and material losses caused by armed conflicts and recognizing that peace, security and development are mutually reinforcing, including in the prevention of armed conflict,

Reaffirming the importance of adhering to the principles of refraining, in international relations, from the threat or the use of force in any manner inconsistent with the purposes of the United Nations, and of peaceful settlement of international disputes,

Reaffirming also the need to adopt a broad strategy of conflict prevention which addresses the root causes of armed conflict and political and social crises in a comprehensive manner, including by promoting sustainable development, poverty eradication, national reconciliation, good governance, democracy, gender equality, the rule of law and respect for and protection of human rights,

Recognizing the need to strengthen the important role of the United Nations in the prevention of violent conflicts, and to develop effective partnerships between the Council and regional organizations, in particular the African Union and its subregional organizations, in order to enable early responses to disputes and emerging crises,

Recalling the Constitutive Act of the African Union, the Protocol relating to the establishment of the Peace and Security Council of the African Union, and the African Union Non-Aggression and Common Defence Pact adopted in Abuja on 31 January 2005, as well as the African Union position on unconstitutional changes of governments, as stated in the 1999 Algiers Decision and the 2000 Lomé Declaration,

Recognizing the important supporting roles played by civil society, men and women, in conflict prevention, and the need to take into account all possible contributions from civil society,

1. *Expresses its determination* to enhance the effectiveness of the United Nations in preventing armed conflicts and to monitor closely situations of potential armed conflict;

2. *Affirms its determination* to strengthen United Nations conflict prevention capacities by:

(a) Assessing regularly the developments in regions at risk of armed conflict and encouraging the Secretary-General to provide information to the Security Council on such developments pursuant to Article 99 of the Charter of the United Nations;

(b) Promoting the follow-up of preventive diplomacy initiatives of the Secretary-General;

(c) Supporting regional mediation initiatives in close consultation with regional and subregional organizations concerned;

(d) Supporting regional and subregional capacities for early warning to help them in working out appropriate mechanisms to enable prompt action in reaction to early warning indicators;

(e) Requesting as necessary and appropriate information and assistance from the Economic and Social Council in accordance with Article 65 of the Charter;

(f) Taking measures to contribute to combating the illicit trade in arms in all its aspects and the use of mercenaries;

(g) Helping to enhance durable institutions conducive to peace, stability and sustainable development;

(h) Supporting efforts of African States to build independent and reliable national judicial institutions;

3. *Requests* the Secretary-General:

(a) To provide to the Security Council regular reports and analysis of developments in regions of potential armed conflicts, particularly in Africa, and, as appropriate, a presentation of ongoing preventive diplomacy initiatives;

(b) To assist countries at risk of armed conflict in performing strategic conflict risk assessments, in implementing the measures agreed to by the concerned countries, in enhancing national dispute management capacities, and in addressing the root causes of armed conflict;

(c) To promote coordination with regional conflict management machinery in Africa which would provide the Council with additional reliable and timely information to facilitate rapid decision-making;

4. *Stresses* the importance of establishing effective comprehensive strategies of conflict prevention, focused on averting negative developments in the security, economic, social and humanitarian sectors and in the field of governance and human rights in countries which are facing crises, with special attention to:

(a) Developing quick-win activities to prevent conflicts arising from competition for economic resources and to monitoring tension arising from economic and social issues;

(b) Encouraging United Nations regional offices to facilitate the implementation of strategies aimed at curbing illicit cross-border activities;

(c) Strengthening the capacities of civil society groups, including women's groups, working to promote a culture of peace, and to mobilize donors to support these efforts;

(d) Developing policy measures to foster good governance and the protection of human rights in order to strengthen weakened or collapsed governance mechanisms and to end the culture of impunity;

(e) Promoting the fairness and transparency of electoral processes;

5. *Stresses also* the critical importance of a regional approach to conflict prevention, particularly to programmes of disarmament, demobilization and reintegration, as well as the effective and sustainable reintegration of ex-combatants;

6. *Reaffirms its determination* to take action against illegal exploitation of and trafficking in natural resources and high-value commodities in areas where it contributes to the outbreak, escalation or continuation of armed conflict;

7. *Calls for* the strengthening of cooperation and communication between the United Nations and regional or subregional organizations or arrangements, in accordance with Chapter VIII of the Charter, particularly with respect to mediation initiatives;

8. *Encourages* all African States to adhere to the African Union Non-Aggression and Common Defence Pact adopted in Abuja on 31 January 2005, and to sign, where appropriate, subregional pacts on peace, security, democracy, good governance and development, and calls upon the United Nations system and the international community to support the implementation of the pacts;

9. *Encourages* African countries to continue to work closely with the United Nations Secretariat and United Nations regional offices in the implementation of measures aimed at securing peace, security, stability, democracy and sustainable development consistent with the objectives of the New Partnership for Africa's Development;

10. *Urges* the international community, including the United Nations system and International Financial

Institutions to support African countries in their efforts to achieve the above objectives, and in this respect welcomes the decisions taken at the summit of the Group of Eight, held in Gleneagles, United Kingdom of Great Britain and Northern Ireland, from 6 to 8 July 2005, for combating poverty in Africa;

11. *Urges* all African States and the international community to cooperate fully in developing the capacities of African regional and subregional organizations to deploy both civilian and military assets quickly when needed, including the development of the African Union's African Standby Force, welcomes bilateral and multilateral programmes developed to this end, and expresses its support for the proposal of the Secretary-General to establish a ten-year capacity-building programme for the African Union;

12. *Decides* to remain seized of the matter.

By **decision 59/568** of 12 September, the General Assembly deferred consideration of the item "Prevention of armed conflict", and included it in the agenda of its sixtieth (2005) session.

Role of civil society in conflict prevention and pacific settlement of disputes

The Security Council, on 20 September [meeting 5264], discussed the role of civil society in conflict prevention and the pacific settlement of disputes. In accordance with rule 39 of the Council's provisional rules of procedure, the Executive Director of the European Centre for Conflict Prevention, Chair of the Columbia University Seminar on Conflict Resolution and faculty coordinator of the Columbia University Conflict Resolution Network, and the Executive Director of the African Centre for the Constructive Resolution of Disputes were invited to attend the meeting.

The Philippines, in a 7 September letter to the Secretary-General [S/2005/594], said that non-governmental organizations (NGOs), civil society, local authorities and the private sector could contribute to the promotion and implementation of development, security and human rights programmes, and it was important that they be engaged with Governments, the United Nations and other international organizations in those key areas. Coordination with civil society organizations in the peaceful settlement of disputes was beneficial and necessary, given their strength as neutral actors whose knowledge, abilities, experience, links with key constituencies, influence and resources contributed greatly to creating confidence among parties concerned.

Specific civil society sectors that could be tapped to assist parties in the search for peaceful solution to disputes, tensions and frictions included the academe, NGOs dedicated to conflict prevention, and the religious sector. The Council therefore needed to address: ways to harness the actual and potential contributions of non-governmental and civil society organizations in developing a strategy for comprehensive conflict prevention and the pacific settlement of disputes in line with Chapter VI of the UN Charter; how it could collaborate with those organizations in overall conflict prevention strategies and in the various stages of dispute settlement; how it could mobilize them to play a more active role in pursuit of "other peaceful means" to settle disputes, such as informal dialogues and contacts between and among parties to disputes; and, in addition to existing mechanisms as the Arria formula (Security Council informal consultative arrangement), what cooperative framework could be fostered in order for the Council and those organizations to have a smooth working relationship to safeguard international peace and security.

The Secretary-General, in his statement to the Council, delivered on his behalf by Assistant Secretary-General, Tuliameni Kalomoh, of the Department of Political Affairs, said that civil society's role in conflict prevention needed to be fully recognized, and both the United Nations and regional organizations had to do more to tap into the comparative advantages of that role. Local ownership and participation were essential for the success of peace processes, and civil society was often far out in front in identifying new threats and concerns. That was certainly one of its most important roles. Civil society organizations were also indispensable in "track-two" and "people-to-people" diplomacy, which was often integral to successful official diplomacy and post-conflict political and reconciliation processes. At times, they could reach parties on the ground that Governments or the United Nations could not and they could also complement the work of the United Nations by: offering valuable analyses originating in the field, forging partnerships to implement UN decisions, increasing the sustainability of UN operations and creating networks to advocate for peacebuilding. For those reasons, civil society organizations would have an important role to play in the deliberations of the Peacebuilding Commission.

SECURITY COUNCIL ACTION

On 20 September [meeting 5264], following consultations among Security Council members, the President made statement **S/PRST/2005/42** on behalf of the Council:

Recognizing the complex nature of threats to international peace and security, the Security Council underlined the need for a broad strategy for conflict prevention and pacific settlement of disputes in line with Chapter VI of the Charter of the United Nations.

The Council stressed that the essential responsibility for conflict prevention rests with national governments, and that the United Nations and the international community can play an important role in support of national efforts for conflict prevention and can assist in building national capacity in this field, and recognized the important supporting role of civil society.

The Council reaffirmed the need for this strategy to be based on engagement with governments, regional and subregional organizations as well as civil society organizations, as appropriate, reflecting the widest possible range of opinions.

The Council underlined the potential contributions of a vibrant and diverse civil society in conflict prevention, as well as in the peaceful settlement of disputes. It noted that a well-functioning civil society has the advantage of specialized knowledge, capabilities, experience, links with key constituencies, influence and resources, which can assist parties in conflict to achieve a peaceful solution to disputes.

The Council noted that a vigorous and inclusive civil society could provide community leadership, help shape public opinion, and facilitate as well as contribute to reconciliation between conflicting communities. The Council also underscored the role that these actors could play in providing a bridge to dialogue and other confidence- building measures between parties in conflict.

The Council underscored and will strengthen its relationship with civil society, including as appropriate, through, inter alia, the use of "Arria-formula" meetings and meetings with local civil society organizations during Council missions.

The Council agreed to keep this item under review.

Conflict diamonds

Kimberley Process. At its 2005 regular session, the Plenary Meeting of the Kimberley Process (Moscow, Russian Federation, 15-17 November) reviewed the implementation of the Kimberley Process Certification Scheme (KPCS), established in 2003 [YUN 2003, p. 55] to stop the use of conflict diamonds in fuelling armed conflict, protect the legitimate diamond industry and ensure implementation of resolutions on trade in conflict diamonds.

The Plenary was informed that, in 2005, Indonesia was included in the list of Kimberley Process participants and Lebanon rejoined KPCS. It noted with concern evidence of ongoing illicit production of diamonds in the Northern rebel-controlled regions of Côte d'Ivoire and adopted a resolution outlining measures to prevent the introduction of conflict diamonds from that country into the legitimate trade. It also agreed to conduct a detailed assessment, with the United Nations and other participants, to identify where diamonds from Côte d'Ivoire were entering into the trade.

The Plenary noted the progress made in implementing the KPCS peer review process. At the time of the meeting, 19 Participants had received review visits and six more were expected to receive such visits by the end of the year. Having received the report of the Working Group on Statistics on aspects of national methodologies that constrained statistical reporting, the Plenary decided that Participants should use Kimberley Process Certificate-based data when submitting trade data, thereby improving the comparability of statistics provided by them. The Working Group was to study the issue of public release of statistical information and report in 2006.

The Plenary adopted a declaration setting out recommendations for effective internal controls over alluvial diamond mining, in order to improve the traceability of alluvial production and to further the effective implementation of KPCS. It agreed to renew the mandate of the ad hoc subgroup on alluvial production, which was to report at intervals on the progress achieved towards implementing those recommendations. The Plenary also adopted terms of reference for the review of KPCS to be carried out by the ad hoc Working Group on the Review of KPCS, and mandated it to report in 2006.

Botswana and the European Community were elected Chair and Vice-Chair, respectively, of the Kimberley Process for 2006.

The report of the Plenary meeting was transmitted to the General Assembly President, in December [A/60/589 & Corr.1], by the Russian Federation, in its capacity as Chair of the Kimberley Process, in accordance with General Assembly resolution 59/144 [YUN 2004, p. 995].

GENERAL ASSEMBLY ACTION

On 20 December [meeting 67], the General Assembly adopted **resolution 60/182** [draft: A/60/L.42 & Add.1] without vote [agenda item 11].

The role of diamonds in fuelling conflict: breaking the link between the illicit transaction of rough diamonds and armed conflict as a contribution to prevention and settlement of conflicts

The General Assembly,

Recognizing that the trade in conflict diamonds is a matter of serious international concern, which can be directly linked to the fuelling of armed conflict, the activities of rebel movements aimed at undermining or overthrowing legitimate Governments and the illicit traffic in and proliferation of armaments, especially small arms and light weapons,

Recognizing also the devastating impact of conflicts fuelled by the trade in conflict diamonds on the peace, safety and security of people in affected countries, and the systematic and gross human rights violations that have been perpetrated in such conflicts,

Noting the negative impact of such conflicts on regional stability and the obligations placed upon States by the Charter of the United Nations regarding the maintenance of international peace and security,

Recognizing, therefore, that continued action to curb the trade in conflict diamonds is imperative,

Recognizing also the positive benefits of the legitimate diamond trade to producing countries, and underlining the need for continued international action to prevent the problem of conflict diamonds from negatively affecting the trade in legitimate diamonds, which makes a critical contribution to the economies of many of the producing, exporting and importing States, especially developing States,

Noting that the vast majority of rough diamonds produced in the world are from legitimate sources,

Recalling the Charter and all the relevant resolutions of the Security Council related to conflict diamonds, and determined to contribute to and support the implementation of the measures provided for in those resolutions,

Recalling also Security Council resolution 1459(2003) of 28 January 2003, in which the Council strongly supported the Kimberley Process Certification Scheme as a valuable contribution against trafficking in conflict diamonds,

Welcoming the important contribution of the Kimberley Process, which was initiated by African diamond-producing countries,

Believing that the implementation of the Kimberley Process Certification Scheme should substantially reduce the opportunity for conflict diamonds to play a role in fuelling armed conflict and should help to protect legitimate trade and ensure the effective implementation of the relevant resolutions on trade in conflict diamonds,

Recalling its resolutions 55/56 of 1 December 2000, 56/263 of 13 March 2002, 57/302 of 15 April 2003, 58/290 of 14 April 2004 and 59/144 of 15 December 2004, in which it called for the development and implementation of proposals for a simple, effective and pragmatic international certification scheme for rough diamonds,

Welcoming, in this regard, the implementation of the Kimberley Process Certification Scheme in such a way that it does not impede the legitimate trade in diamonds or impose an undue burden on Governments or industry, particularly smaller producers, and does not hinder the development of the diamond industry,

Welcoming also the decision of countries and one regional economic integration organization to address the problem of conflict diamonds by participating in the Kimberley Process and to implement the Kimberley Process Certification Scheme,

Welcoming further the important contribution made by the diamond industry, in particular the World Diamond Council, as well as civil society, to assist international efforts to stop the trade in conflict diamonds,

Welcoming the voluntary self-regulation initiatives for the diamond industry announced by the World Diamond Council, and recognizing that a system of such voluntary self-regulation will contribute, as described in the Interlaken Declaration of 5 November 2002 on the Kimberley Process Certification Scheme for Rough Diamonds, to ensuring the effectiveness of national systems of internal control for rough diamonds,

Noting with appreciation that the Kimberley Process has pursued its deliberations on an inclusive basis, involving concerned stakeholders, including producing, exporting and importing States, the diamond industry and civil society,

Recognizing that State sovereignty should be fully respected and that the principles of equality, mutual benefits and consensus should be adhered to,

Recognizing also that the Kimberley Process Certification Scheme, which came into effect on 1 January 2003, will be credible only if all participants have established internal systems of control designed to eliminate the presence of conflict diamonds in the chain of producing, exporting and importing rough diamonds within their own territories, while taking into account that differences in production methods and trading practices, as well as differences in institutional controls thereof, may require different approaches to meet minimum standards,

1. *Reaffirms its strong and continuing support* for the Kimberley Process Certification Scheme;

2. *Recognizes* that the Kimberley Process Certification Scheme can help to ensure the effective implementation of relevant resolutions of the Security Council containing sanctions on the trade in conflict diamonds, and calls for the full implementation of existing Council measures targeting the illicit trade in rough diamonds that play a role in fuelling conflict;

3. *Also recognizes* the important contributions that the international efforts to address the problem of conflict diamonds, including the Kimberley Process Certification Scheme, have made to the settlement of conflicts in Angola, the Democratic Republic of the Congo, Liberia and Sierra Leone, and the ongoing value of the Certification Scheme as a mechanism for the prevention of future conflicts;

4. *Stresses* that the widest possible participation in the Kimberley Process Certification Scheme is essential and should be encouraged, and urges all Member States to participate actively in the Certification Scheme by complying with its undertakings;

5. *Takes note with appreciation* of the report of the Chair of the Kimberley Process submitted pursuant to resolution 59/144, and congratulates the Governments, regional economic integration organization representatives, the organized diamond industry and civil society participating in the Kimberley Process for contributing to the development and implementation of the Kimberley Process Certification Scheme;

6. *Notes* the decision of the General Council of the World Trade Organization of 15 May 2003 granting a waiver with respect to the measures taken to implement the Kimberley Process Certification Scheme, effective from 1 January 2003 to 31 December 2006;

7. *Welcomes* the adoption by the plenary meeting of the Kimberley Process, held in Moscow from 15 to 17 November 2005, of a resolution on the subject of illicit diamond production in Côte d'Ivoire that outlines a series of measures to prevent the introduction of conflict diamonds from Côte d'Ivoire into legitimate trade, including a detailed assessment of the volume of rough diamonds produced in and exported from Côte d'Ivoire, to be carried out in cooperation with the United Nations, and encourages cooperation between the Kimberley Process and the United Nations, particularly the United Nations Operation in Côte d'Ivoire;

8. *Also welcomes* the adoption by the plenary meeting of the Kimberley Process of a declaration on improving internal controls over alluvial diamond production, which sets out recommendations for effective internal controls over alluvial diamond mining and encourages potential donors to provide capacity-building assistance to further the effective implementation of the Kimberley Process Certification Scheme;

9. *Notes with appreciation* the contribution of the Kimberley Process and of its Chair to the work of the Security Council Committee established pursuant to resolution 1521(2003) concerning Liberia, including the submission of a report on the results of the Kimberley Process expert mission to Liberia;

10. *Welcomes* the agreement reached at the plenary meeting of the Kimberley Process on terms of reference for the three-year review of the Kimberley Process Certification Scheme;

11. *Also welcomes* the important progress made in the implementation of the peer review mechanism in the Kimberley Process Certification Scheme, and encourages all remaining participants to receive voluntary review visits;

12. *Further welcomes* the progress made towards the collection and submission of statistical reports on the production and trade in rough diamonds, and encourages all the Kimberley Process participants to enhance the quality of data, with a view to ensuring effective implementation of the Kimberley Process Certification Scheme;

13. *Acknowledges with great appreciation* the important contribution that the Russian Federation, as Chair of the Kimberley Process in 2005, has made to the efforts to curb the trade in conflict diamonds, and welcomes the succession of Botswana as Chair and the European Community as Vice-Chair of the Process for 2006;

14. *Requests* the Chair of the Kimberley Process to submit a report on the implementation of the Process to the General Assembly at its sixty-first session;

15. *Decides* to include in the provisional agenda of its sixty-first session the item entitled "the role of diamonds in fuelling conflict".

Implementation of 1970 Declaration

The General Assembly, by **decision 60/520** of 8 December, included in the provisional agenda of its sixty-second (2007) session the item entitled "Review of the implementation of the Declaration on the Strengthening of International Security" [YUN 1970, p. 105].

Peacemaking and peacebuilding

Post-conflict peacebuilding

On 26 May [meeting 5187], the Security Council discussed the issue of post-conflict peacebuilding. It had before it a 16 May [S/2005/316] discussion paper submitted by Denmark, which urged the Council to discuss the current policy, institutional and financial challenges in post-conflict peacebuilding, with a view to strengthening coherence and consistency of Council action, while keeping in mind that it was only one of several players in the field.

Denmark, in opening the debate, noted that, although the United Nations had made progress in strengthening its coherence in post-conflict situations, significant challenges remained in the policy, institutional and financial fields. Regarding policy, the Organization needed to ensure local ownership of the process of devising and implementing post-conflict peacebuilding strategies, so as to make them sustainable, with participatory dialogues between the United Nations and local stakeholders, to highlight the fact that the country in question and its people carried the main responsibility for their future. As the regional perspective was often underestimated in addressing a particular conflict, comprehensive strategies were needed that addressed the specifics of the conflict and its regional dimensions, as well as cross-cutting issues such as small arms; demobilization, disarmament and the reintegration (DDR) of former combatants; the protection of women and children; and the repatriation of refugees and internally displaced persons.

In West Africa, where soldiers of fortune, mercenaries and sanctions-busters were taking their deadly business from one theatre of conflict to the next, the United Nations should focus more on tackling cross-border issues by, among other ways, aiming for a comprehensive subregional DDR strategy.

Regional organizations in different parts of the world, especially the European Union (EU) and the African Union (AU), were taking on greater responsibilities in peacebuilding, and it was important to involve and support them in taking a leadership role.

Most post-conflict situations had a "rule-of-law vacuum" and the United Nations had to be able to more effectively help fill that vacuum, by helping to build national judicial institutions, strengthening governance and ensuring transitional justice for crimes committed during conflicts. Denmark said that it would welcome thoughts on creating a focal point for the rule of law.

At the institutional level, it stressed that all relevant actors should be involved to ensure systematic contributions from UN development and humanitarian agencies in the integrated mission planning process for post-conflict situations. Accordingly, a system of recording and disseminating best practices should be devised.

Overall, the United Nations needed to develop peacebuilding strategies that aimed for local ownership and regional engagement, which were coordinated between all actors in the field and at Headquarters, made efficient use of the available resources within and outside the United Nations and ensured sufficient financial means and long-term donor commitment.

The Deputy Secretary-General, in his statement, said that strategies for ending war should also tackle the question of relapse, ensure that peace agreements were implemented in a sustainable manner and that critical stabilization activities, such as the reintegration and rehabilitation of demobilized combatants, were adequately financed and carefully implemented. The United Nations should help societies and markets recover their vitality and strengthen the capacity of State and social institutions to provide security and justice based on the rule of law.

To improve the peacebuilding success rate, four things were vital. building on existing national institutions and capacities, both of the State and of civil society; ensuring that the UN system, especially its operations on the ground, and its principal organs, functioned in a coherent fashion; involving international financial institutions, bilateral donors and regional actors in UN peacebuilding efforts; and providing more resources for both immediate needs and medium-term recovery.

Recalling that the Secretary-General had proposed the establishment of a Peacebuilding Commission and a Peacebuilding Support Office (see p. 93) to help meet those needs, the Deputy Secretary-General emphasized that the Commission would bring together international financial institutions, bilateral donors and regional actors, and harmonize peacebuilding activity across the multilateral system.

SECURITY COUNCIL ACTION

On 26 May [meeting 5113], following consultations among Security Council members, the President made statement **S/PRST/2005/20** on behalf of the Council:

The Security Council reaffirms its commitment to the purposes and principles enshrined in the Charter of the United Nations and recalls its primary responsibility for the maintenance of international peace and security. The Council considers post-conflict peacebuilding closely linked to its primary responsibilities.

The Council recognizes that intra-State conflicts and States emerging from conflict are among the most complex challenges facing the international community and that responding to these challenges in most instances requires a coherent and integrated mix of peacebuilding and peacekeeping activities, including political, military, civilian, humanitarian and development activities.

The Council acknowledges that serious attention to the longer-term process of peacebuilding in all its multiple dimensions is critically important and that adequate support for peacebuilding activities can help to prevent countries from relapsing into conflict.

The Council underlines the fact that priorities in the post-conflict environment should include, where appropriate: protection of civilians; disarmament, demobilization, repatriation, reintegration and rehabilitation of former combatants; security sector and economic and social reform; the end of impunity; establishment and re-establishment of the institutions of Government, the rule of law and transitional justice, respect for human rights; and economic revitalization.

The Council recognizes the key role played by the United Nations, including the United Nations funds, programmes and specialized agencies, in peacebuilding alongside the international financial institutions, in particular the World Bank, bilateral donors and troop contributors. It also acknowledges the role the private sector can play in countries emerging from conflict. The Council underlines the fact that a successful outcome of post-conflict peacebuilding activities depends on the sustained commitment of all relevant actors to the process, through the involvement of these actors and the coordination of their activities in all phases from planning through implementation. In this regard, the Council also stresses the importance of pursuing coherent policies and resource allocation between these United Nations entities taking into account their respective mandates. The Council recalls the report of the Panel on United Nations Peace Operations and the recommendations therein, and welcomes the progress made since the publication of the report, not least as regards planning of peacekeeping operations.

The Council underlines the fact that for countries emerging from conflict, significant international assistance for economic and social rehabilitation and reconstruction is indispensable. In this regard, the Council acknowledges the role the Economic and Social Council plays, including in sustainable development, and reiterates its willingness to improve cooperation with United Nations bodies and organs directly concerned with peacebuilding.

The Council underlines the importance of national ownership of the transition process from the end of a conflict to the attainment of lasting peace and sustainable development and the need for the international community to support nationally owned peacebuilding priorities. The Council recognizes the positive role played by local stakeholders and encourages dialogue between the United Nations and relevant national actors. The Council encourages capacity-building in order to respond to the country-specific circumstances of each conflict situation. One goal of this capacity-building—and of peacebuilding generally—should be to promote the establishment of self-supporting national authorities and thus the evolution of international assistance from peace support to longer-term development.

The Council recognizes the crucial role of regional and subregional organizations in post-conflict peacebuilding and their involvement at the earliest possible stage. The Council realizes that a clear regional perspective is necessary as most conflicts have interlocking political, security, humanitarian and economic dynamics across borders. The Council underscores in this respect the need for enhanced cooperation and, where appropriate, coordination between United Nations and regional and subregional organizations in peacebuilding, based on a more integrated approach and with the aim of maximizing use of available resources and capabilities.

The Council stresses the importance of a comprehensive international and regional approach to disarmament, demobilization and reintegration of former combatants that is not limited to the political and security aspects, but also addresses its social and economic aspects, including special needs of child soldiers and women.

The Council stresses the special needs of Africa in post-conflict situations and encourages the international community to pay particular attention to those needs. It welcomes the ever-closer partnership between the African Union, the African subregional organizations and the United Nations in the area of peacemaking and peacekeeping and stresses the importance of extending this partnership to peacebuilding efforts.

The Council underscores the importance of cooperation between United Nations peacekeeping operations and the United Nations funds, programmes and specialized agencies. The Council stresses the importance of ensuring that planning and implementation of United Nations humanitarian, peacekeeping, political and developmental activities at country level are well coordinated system-wide, including through the development of shared strategic objectives. The Council stresses that the United Nations should function as one integrated entity at country level under effective overall leadership in post-conflict peacebuilding.

The Council stresses the need to ensure adequate and timely financing for peacebuilding priorities at all stages of the peace process and stresses the need for sustained financial investment in peacebuilding over the medium to longer-term period of recovery. It recognizes the importance of rapid initiation of peacebuilding activities to meet immediate needs and encourages the building of capabilities that can be incorporated rapidly.

The Council welcomes the submission of the report of the Secretary-General of 21 March 2005 entitled "In larger freedom: towards development, security and human rights for all" and of the report by the High-level Panel on Threats, Challenges and Change entitled "A more secure world: our shared responsibility". The Council acknowledges institutional gaps, identified in the reports, in the United Nations institutional machinery with respect to effectively, coherently and comprehensively helping countries with the transition from conflict to lasting peace and sustainable development.

The Council takes note with interest of the important proposal by the Secretary-General to establish a peacebuilding commission and shares the objective of improving United Nations capacity to coordinate with donors and troop contributors and to perform peacebuilding activities, in particular from the start

of peacekeeping operations through stabilization, reconstruction and development. The Council recognizes the important role that this body could play to bridge the gap between maintenance of international peace and security and the work of humanitarian and economic development assistance.

Establishment of Peacebuilding Commission

In May [A/59/2005/Add.2], the Secretary-General set out the modalities for the establishment of the Peacebuilding Commission, which he had proposed in the main part of his report entitled "In larger freedom: towards development, security and human rights for all" (see p. 67). He stated that the proposed Commission would provide a central node for helping to create and promote comprehensive peacebuilding strategies. It should also encourage coherent decision-making on peacebuilding by Member States and the UN Secretariat, agencies and programmes, and provide a forum in which UN system representatives, major bilateral donors, troop contributors, relevant actors and organizations, international financial institutions and the national or transitional authorities of the country concerned could share information about post-conflict recovery.

The Commission should provide information to the Security Council and focus attention on development and institution-building efforts necessary for recovery; help ensure predictable financing for early recovery activities, partly by providing an overview of assessed, voluntary and standing funding mechanisms; periodically review progress towards medium-term recovery goals; ensure sustained financing of recovery and development activities and extend the period of political attention to post-conflict recovery; strengthen UN preventive efforts by providing better tools for helping States and societies reduce the risk of conflict; develop best practice on cross-cutting peacebuilding issues; and improve the coordination of UN funds, programmes and agencies.

To support the Commission's work, a Peacebuilding Support Office would be established to prepare the substantive inputs for Commission meetings; provide high-quality inputs to the planning process for peacebuilding operations, working with lead departments, UN field presences and others; and conduct best practices analysis and develop policy guidance. A Standing Fund for Peacebuilding would also be established, possibly on a voluntary, replenishable basis, to provide critical targeted support to nascent authorities and to early peacebuilding activities. In terms of the institutional structure, the Commission would advise the Security Council and the Economic and Social Council. Its core membership should comprise Security Council and Economic and Social Council members, major donors and leading troop contributors. In country specific operations, the Commission should involve the national or transitional authorities, relevant regional actors and organizations, troop contributors and the major donors to the specific country.

In terms of modalities, the Commission should be advisory in nature, meet on a quarterly basis, with country-specific meetings held at regular intervals, and should be flexible in allowing participation by national actors and field- and capital-based representatives.

The General Assembly, in **resolution 60/1** of 16 September (see p. 48), agreed to establish the Peacebuilding Commission.

SECURITY COUNCIL ACTION

On 20 December [meeting 5335], the Security Council, acting concurrently with the General Assembly in **resolution 60/180** (see below for text of resolution), unanimously adopted **resolution 1645(2005)**. The draft [S/2005/803] was prepared in consultations among Council members.

On the same date, the Council unanimously adopted **resolution 1646(2005)**. The draft [S/2005/806] was prepared in consultations among Council members.

The Security Council,

Recalling its resolution 1645(2005) of 20 December 2005,

1. *Decides,* pursuant to paragraph 4 (*a*) of resolution 1645(2005), that the permanent members listed in article 23, paragraph 1, of the Charter of the United Nations shall be members of the Organizational Committee of the Peacebuilding Commission and that, in addition, the Security Council shall select annually two of its elected members to participate in the Organizational Committee;

2. *Decides also* that the annual report referred to in paragraph 15 of resolution 1645(2005) shall also be submitted to the Council for an annual debate.

GENERAL ASSEMBLY ACTION

On 20 December [meeting 66], the General Assembly, acting concurrently with the Security Council in **resolution 1645(2005)**, adopted **resolution 60/180** [draft: A/60/L.40] without vote [agenda items 46 and 120].

The Peacebuilding Commission

The General Assembly,

Guided by the purposes and principles enshrined in the Charter of the United Nations,

Reaffirming the 2005 World Summit Outcome,

Recalling, in particular, paragraphs 97 to 105 of the World Summit Outcome,

Recognizing that development, peace and security and human rights are interlinked and mutually reinforcing,

Emphasizing the need for a coordinated, coherent and integrated approach to post-conflict peacebuilding and reconciliation with a view to achieving sustainable peace,

Recognizing the need for a dedicated institutional mechanism to address the special needs of countries emerging from conflict towards recovery, reintegration and reconstruction and to assist them in laying the foundation for sustainable development,

Recognizing also the vital role of the United Nations in preventing conflicts, assisting parties to conflicts to end hostilities and emerge towards recovery, reconstruction and development and in mobilizing sustained international attention and assistance,

Reaffirming the respective responsibilities and functions of the organs of the United Nations as defined in the Charter and the need to enhance coordination among them,

Affirming the primary responsibility of national and transitional Governments and authorities of countries emerging from conflict or at risk of relapsing into conflict, where they are established, in identifying their priorities and strategies for post-conflict peacebuilding, with a view to ensuring national ownership,

Emphasizing, in that regard, the importance of supporting national efforts to establish, redevelop or reform institutions for the effective administration of countries emerging from conflict, including capacity-building efforts,

Recognizing the important role of regional and subregional organizations in carrying out post-conflict peacebuilding activities in their regions, and stressing the need for sustained international support for their efforts and capacity-building to that end,

Recognizing also that countries that have experienced recent post-conflict recovery would make valuable contributions to the work of the Peacebuilding Commission,

Recognizing further the role of Member States supporting the peacekeeping and peacebuilding efforts of the United Nations through financial, troop and civilian police contributions,

Recognizing the important contribution of civil society and non-governmental organizations, including women organizations, to peacebuilding efforts,

Reaffirming the important role of women in the prevention and resolution of conflicts and in peacebuilding, and stressing the importance of their equal participation and full involvement in all efforts for the maintenance and promotion of peace and security and the need to increase their role in decision-making with regard to conflict prevention and resolution and peacebuilding,

1. *Decides,* acting concurrently with the Security Council, in accordance with Articles 7, 22 and 29 of the Charter of the United Nations, with a view to operationalizing the decision by the 2005 World Summit, to establish the Peacebuilding Commission as an intergovernmental advisory body;

2. *Also decides* that the following shall be the main purposes of the Commission:

(*a*) To bring together all relevant actors to marshal resources and to advise on and propose integrated strategies for post-conflict peacebuilding and recovery;

(b) To focus attention on the reconstruction and institution-building efforts necessary for recovery from conflict and to support the development of integrated strategies in order to lay the foundation for sustainable development;

(c) To provide recommendations and information to improve the coordination of all relevant actors within and outside the United Nations, to develop best practices, to help to ensure predictable financing for early recovery activities and to extend the period of attention given by the international community to post-conflict recovery;

3. *Further decides* that the Commission shall meet in various configurations;

4. *Decides* that the Commission shall have a standing Organizational Committee, responsible for developing its own rules of procedure and working methods, comprising:

(a) Seven members of the Security Council, including permanent members, selected according to rules and procedures decided by the Council;

(b) Seven members of the Economic and Social Council, elected from regional groups according to rules and procedures decided by the Council, giving due consideration to those countries that have experienced post-conflict recovery;

(c) Five top providers of assessed contributions to United Nations budgets and of voluntary contributions to United Nations funds, programmes and agencies, including a standing peacebuilding fund, that are not among those selected in *(a)* or *(b)* above, selected by and from among the ten top providers, giving due consideration to the size of their contributions, according to a list provided by the Secretary-General, based on the average annual contributions in the previous three calendar years for which statistical data are available;

(d) Five top providers of military personnel and civilian police to United Nations missions that are not among those selected in *(a)*, *(b)* or *(c)* above, selected by and from among the ten top providers, giving due consideration to the size of their contributions, according to a list provided by the Secretary-General, based on the average monthly contributions in the previous three calendar years for which statistical data are available;

(e) Giving due consideration to representation from all regional groups in the overall composition of the Committee and to representation from countries that have experienced post-conflict recovery, seven additional members shall be elected according to rules and procedures decided by the General Assembly;

5. *Emphasizes* that a Member State can only be selected from one category set out in paragraph 4 above at any one time;

6. *Decides* that members of the Organizational Committee shall serve for renewable terms of two years, as applicable;

7. *Also decides* that country-specific meetings of the Commission, upon invitation of the Organizational Committee referred to in paragraph 4 above, shall include as members, in addition to members of the Committee, representatives from:

(a) The country under consideration;

(b) Countries in the region engaged in the post-conflict process and other countries that are involved in relief efforts and/or political dialogue, as well as relevant regional and subregional organizations;

(c) The major financial, troop and civilian police contributors involved in the recovery effort;

(d) The senior United Nations representative in the field and other relevant United Nations representatives;

(e) Such regional and international financial institutions as may be relevant;

8. *Further decides* that a representative of the Secretary-General shall be invited to participate in all meetings of the Commission;

9. *Decides* that representatives from the World Bank, the International Monetary Fund and other institutional donors shall be invited to participate in all meetings of the Commission in a manner suitable to their governing arrangements;

10. *Emphasizes* that the Commission shall work in cooperation with national or transitional authorities, where possible, in the country under consideration with a view to ensuring national ownership of the peacebuilding process;

11. *Also emphasizes* that the Commission shall, where appropriate, work in close consultation with regional and subregional organizations to ensure their involvement in the peacebuilding process in accordance with Chapter VIII of the Charter;

12. *Decides* that the Organizational Committee shall, giving due consideration to maintaining a balance in addressing situations in countries in different regions in accordance with the main purposes of the Commission as stipulated above, establish the agenda of the Commission based on the following:

(a) Requests for advice from the Security Council;

(b) Requests for advice from the Economic and Social Council or the General Assembly with the consent of a concerned Member State in exceptional circumstances on the verge of lapsing or relapsing into conflict and with which the Security Council is not seized in accordance with Article 12 of the Charter;

(c) Requests for advice from Member States in exceptional circumstances on the verge of lapsing or relapsing into conflict and which are not on the agenda of the Security Council;

(d) Requests for advice from the Secretary-General;

13. *Also decides* that the Commission shall make the outcome of its discussions and recommendations publicly available as United Nations documents to all relevant bodies and actors, including the international financial institutions;

14. *Invites* all relevant United Nations bodies and other bodies and actors, including the international financial institutions, to take action on the advice of the Commission, as appropriate and in accordance with their respective mandates;

15. *Decides* that the Commission shall submit an annual report to the General Assembly and that the Assembly shall hold an annual debate to review the report;

16. *Underlines* that in post-conflict situations on the agenda of the Security Council with which it is actively seized, in particular when there is a United Nations–mandated peacekeeping mission on the ground or under way and given the primary responsibility of the

Council for the maintenance of international peace and security in accordance with the Charter, the main purpose of the Commission will be to provide advice to the Council at its request;

17. *Also underlines* that the advice of the Commission to provide sustained attention as countries move from transitional recovery towards development will be of particular relevance to the Economic and Social Council, bearing in mind its role as a principal body for coordination, policy review, policy dialogue and recommendations on issues of economic and social development;

18. *Decides* that the Commission shall act in all matters on the basis of consensus of its members;

19. *Notes* the importance of participation of regional and local actors, and stresses the importance of adopting flexible working methods, including use of videoconferencing, meetings outside of New York and other modalities, in order to provide for the active participation of those most relevant to the deliberations of the Commission;

20. *Calls upon* the Commission to integrate a gender perspective into all of its work;

21. *Encourages* the Commission to consult with civil society, non-governmental organizations, including women organizations, and the private sector engaged in peacebuilding activities, as appropriate;

22. *Recommends* that the Commission terminate its consideration of a country-specific situation when foundations for sustainable peace and development are established or upon the request of national authorities of the country under consideration;

23. *Reaffirms its request* to the Secretary-General to establish, within the Secretariat, from within existing resources, a small peacebuilding support office staffed by qualified experts to assist and support the Commission, and recognizes in that regard that such support could include gathering and analysing information relating to the availability of financial resources, relevant United Nations in-country planning activities, progress towards meeting short and medium-term recovery goals and best practices with respect to cross-cutting peacebuilding issues;

24. *Also reaffirms its request* to the Secretary-General to establish a multi-year standing peacebuilding fund for post-conflict peacebuilding, funded by voluntary contributions and taking due account of existing instruments, with the objective of ensuring the immediate release of resources needed to launch peacebuilding activities and the availability of appropriate financing for recovery;

25. *Requests* the Secretary-General to report to the General Assembly on the arrangements for establishing the peacebuilding fund during its sixtieth session;

26. *Calls upon* relevant bodies and Member States referred to in paragraph 4 above to communicate the names of members of the Organizational Committee to the Secretary-General to enable him to convene the first constituting meeting of the Committee as soon as possible following the adoption of the present resolution;

27. *Decides* that the arrangements set out above will be reviewed five years after the adoption of the present resolution to ensure that they are appropriate to fulfil the agreed functions of the Commission and that such a review and any changes as a result thereof

will be decided following the same procedure as set out in paragraph 1 above;

28. *Also decides* to include in the provisional agenda of its sixty-first session an item titled "Report of the Peacebuilding Commission".

Cooperation with regional organizations

High-level meeting between the UN and regional organizations. The sixth high-level meeting between the United Nations and regional organizations (New York, 25-26 July) was held under the theme "United Nations–regional organizations: partnership for a more secure world". Twenty regional organizations participated in the meeting, which discussed the findings of the High-level Panel on Threats, Challenges and Change [YUN 2004, p. 54] and the Secretary-General's report entitled "In larger freedom: towards development, security and human rights for all" (see p. 67). As Chairman of the meeting, the Secretary-General transmitted the meeting's conclusions in identical letters to the Presidents of the General Assembly and the Security Council on 29 August [A/60/341-S/2005/567]. The participants condemned the spate of terrorist bombings of recent months (see p. 103), and held the view that human and State security depended on combating terrorism while respecting civil liberties and addressing the root causes of conflict and terrorism. Structural prevention needed to be complemented by effective operational prevention, based on effective regional-global cooperation in conflict prevention and resolution, peacekeeping and peacebuilding. To that end, the systemic weaknesses of the global system, such as absolute poverty, natural resource depletion and environmental degradation, health pandemics and the social ills of crime and corruption, needed to be seriously addressed as issues of international peace and security.

Participants expressed satisfaction at the work done since the fifth high-level meeting [YUN 2003, p. 58] to strengthen the UN–regional organizations partnership, and endorsed the proposals of the six working groups that had been established on peacekeeping, civilian protection, respect for human rights in counter-terrorism, dialogue among civilizations, disarmament and the implications of United Nations reform for the partnership. They supported the further development of organizational capacities in conflict prevention and resolution, peacekeeping and peacebuilding, particularly the proposed 10-year capacity-building plan for the African Union (AU), approved by the Assembly in resolution 60/1 (see p. 48). Future meetings would accord special attention to African needs.

In the light of the trauma experienced by the peoples of so many regions in the wake of the Indian Ocean tsunami and other national disasters, participants agreed to include disaster relief and related risk-reduction on their agenda for future cooperation. They recognized that a more structured relationship between the United Nations and regional and other intergovernmental organizations was needed, and endorsed the Secretary-General's intention to conclude agreements with individual organizations. They agreed to convene annually to monitor developments in international security and promote UN goals; ensure that their high-level meetings coincided with the Security Council's meetings with regional organizations; establish a standing committee to, among other things, ensure implementation of their decisions; identify one high-level official in each organization to liaise with the United Nations and with one another; recognize that interested regional and subregional organizations should pursue joint activities under the umbrella of high-level meetings under Chapter VIII of the Charter, while other intergovernmental organizations should partner with the United Nations under the other Charter provisions; and strengthen the secretariat of the high-level meetings to assist the new standing committee and the working groups. Participants supported the establishment of the Human Rights Council and the Peacebuilding Commission by the General Assembly in resolution 60/1 (see p. 48), and adopted a statement on a partnership among civilizations, which was appended to its report.

Security Council public meeting. On 17 October [meeting 5282], the Security Council met with representatives of the AU, the Association of Southeast Asian Nations, the Commonwealth of Independent States, the Council of Europe, the League of Arab States, the North Atlantic Treaty Organization, the Organization of American States and the Organization for Security and Cooperation in Europe to consider cooperation between the United Nations and regional organizations in maintaining international peace and security.

In a discussion paper forwarded to the Secretary-General on 10 October [S/2005/638], Romania stated that the relationship between the United Nations and regional organizations was pursued on an ad hoc basis, despite its widely acknowledged importance and day-to-day impact on Council activities. Given the significant participation of those organizations in maintaining peace and security all over the world, the time was right for the relationship to become more focused and organized. Romania proposed that the

meeting take measures to deepen and better structure the Council's relationship with regional organizations; follow up in the Council's areas of responsibility on the understandings reached at the World Summit in that regard; and draw attention to the opinions of regional organizations on the subject, with a view to enhancing their contributions to maintaining international peace and security.

On 17 October [meeting 5282], the Security Council unanimously adopted **resolution 1631(2005)**. The draft [S/2005/649] was prepared in consultations among Council members.

The Security Council,

Recalling Chapter VIII of the Charter of the United Nations,

Reaffirming its previous relevant resolutions and the statement by its President,

Welcoming the adoption of the 2005 World Summit Outcome,

Recalling its invitation of 28 January 1993 to regional organizations to improve coordination with the United Nations, the Declaration on the Enhancement of Cooperation between the United Nations and Regional Arrangements or Agencies in the Maintenance of International Peace and Security adopted by the General Assembly on 9 December 1994, the meeting of the Security Council on the theme "The Security Council and regional organizations: facing the new challenges to international peace and security", held on 11 April 2003 under the presidency of Mexico, and its debate on the theme "Cooperation between the United Nations and regional organizations in stabilization processes", held on 20 July 2004 under the presidency of Romania,

Welcoming the Conclusions of the Chairman of the sixth high-level meeting between the United Nations and regional and other intergovernmental organizations, held in New York on 25 and 26 July 2005,

Reiterating its primary responsibility for the maintenance of international peace and security,

Emphasizing that the growing contribution made by regional organizations in cooperation with the United Nations can usefully complement the work of the Organization in maintaining international peace and security, and stressing in this regard that such contribution must be made in accordance with Chapter VIII of the Charter,

Recognizing the necessity to support capacity-building and cooperation at the regional and subregional levels in maintaining international peace and security, and noting in particular the importance of strengthening the capacity of African regional and subregional organizations,

Acknowledging the resolve of Heads of State and Government of the 2005 World Summit to expand, as appropriate, the involvement of regional organizations in the work of the Security Council, and to ensure that regional organizations that have a capacity for the prevention of armed conflict or peacekeeping consider the option of placing such capacity in the framework of the United Nations Standby Arrangements System,

Welcoming the decision in the 2005 World Summit Outcome to establish a Peacebuilding Commission, and looking forward to it as an important opportunity for cooperation and close contact with regional and subregional organizations in post-conflict peace-building and recovery,

1. *Expresses its determination* to take appropriate steps for the further development of cooperation be-tween the United Nations and regional and sub-regional organizations in maintaining international peace and security, consistent with Chapter VIII of the Charter of the United Nations, and invites regional and subregional organizations that have a capacity for conflict prevention or peacekeeping to place such ca-pacities in the framework of the United Nations Standby Arrangements System;

2. *Urges* all States and relevant international organ-izations to contribute to strengthening the capacity of regional and subregional organizations, in particular of African regional and subregional organizations, in conflict prevention and crisis management, and in post-conflict stabilization, including through the pro-vision of human, technical and financial assistance, and welcomes in this regard the establishment by the European Union of the African Peace Facility;

3. *Stresses* the importance for the United Nations of developing the ability of regional and subregional or-ganizations to deploy peacekeeping forces rapidly in support of United Nations peacekeeping operations or other operations mandated by the Security Council, and welcomes relevant initiatives taken in this regard;

4. *Stresses also* the potential role of regional and subregional organizations in addressing the illicit trade in small arms and light weapons and the need to take into account in the mandates of peacekeeping op-erations, where appropriate, the regional instruments enabling States to identify and trace illegal small arms and light weapons;

5. *Reiterates* the need to encourage regional co-operation, including through the involvement of re-gional and subregional organizations in the peaceful settlement of disputes, and to include, where appro-priate, specific provisions with this aim in future man-dates of peacekeeping and peacebuilding operations authorized by the Council;

6. *Welcomes* the efforts undertaken by its subsidiary bodies with responsibilities in counter-terrorism to foster cooperation with regional and subregional or-ganizations, notes with appreciation the efforts made by an increasing number of regional and subregional organizations in the fight against terrorism, and urges all relevant regional and subregional organizations to enhance the effectiveness of their counter-terrorism efforts within their respective mandates, including with a view to develop their capacity to help Member States in their efforts to tackle the threats to interna-tional peace and security posed by acts of terrorism;

7. *Expresses its intention* to hold regular meetings, as appropriate, with heads of regional and subregional organizations in order to strengthen the interaction and cooperation with these organizations in maintain-ing international peace and security, ensuring, if possi-ble, that such meetings coincide with the annual high-level meetings held by the United Nations with

regional and other intergovernmental organizations for better efficiency of participation and substantive complementarity of agendas;

8. *Recommends* better communication between the United Nations and regional and subregional organi-zations through, notably, liaison officers and the hold-ing of consultations at all appropriate levels;

9. *Reiterates* the obligation for regional organiza-tions, under article 54 of the Charter, to keep the Council fully informed of their activities for the main-tenance of international peace and security;

10. *Invites* the Secretary-General to submit a report to the Council on the opportunities and challenges fac-ing the cooperation between the United Nations and regional and subregional organizations in maintaining international peace and security, and encourages the Secretary-General to explore with regional organi-zations the possibility of agreements establishing a framework for regional organizations' cooperation with and contributions to United Nations-led peace-keeping operations, taking into due consideration the cooperation guidelines already identified between the United Nations and certain regional organizations;

11. *Requests* the Secretary-General, where appropri-ate, to include in his regular reporting to the Council on peacekeeping and peacebuilding operations under its mandate, assessments of progress on the coopera-tion between the United Nations and regional and sub-regional organizations;

12. *Decides* to remain seized of the matter.

Reports of Secretary-General. The Secretary-General, in his report on the work of the Organi-zation [A/60/1], described UN cooperation activi-ties with regional organizations in the areas of peace and security and development. In his re-port entitled "In larger freedom: towards devel-opment, security and human rights for all" [A/59/2005], submitted to the 2005 World Summit, he said that the United Nations and regional organi-zations should play complementary roles in fac-ing the challenges of international peace and security. In that context, donor countries should pay particular attention to the need for a 10-year plan for capacity-building with the AU.

To improve coordination between the United Nations and regional organizations, he intended to introduce memoranda of understanding with individual organizations, governing the sharing of information, expertise and resources, and would invite regional organizations to participate in UN system meetings, when issues of interest to them were being discussed. The Secretary-General also proposed that the rules of UN peacekeeping budgets be amended to give the Organization the option, in exceptional circum-stances, to use assessed contributions to finance Council-authorized regional operations or the participation of regional organizations in multi-pillar peace operations under the overall um-brella of the United Nations.

Political and peacebuilding missions in 2005

During 2005, 12 UN political and peace-building missions were in operation: six in Africa, five in Asia and the Pacific and one in the Middle East. With regard to the missions in Africa, the mandates of the United Nations Peacebuilding Office in the Central African Republic and the United Nations Peacebuilding Support Office in Guinea-Bissau were extended until 31 December 2006. The mandate of the United Nations Advance Mission in the Sudan was extended until 24 March 2005. On the same day, the Security Council established the United Nations Mission in the Sudan for an initial period of six months and asked the Secretary-General to transfer all functions performed by the United Nations advance mission to the new mission. The activities of the United Nations Political Office for Somalia were extended for the 2006-2007 biennium, and on 31 August, the Security Council requested the Secretary-General to establish the United Nations Integrated Office in Sierra Leone (UNIOSIL) for a period of 12 months, beginning 1 January 2006. In other Council action, the mandate of the United Nations Office for West Africa was extended for three years from 1 January 2005 to 31 December 2007.

In Asia and the Pacific, the Council established the United Nations Office in Timor-Leste (UNOTIL), which would operate for one year, until 20 May 2006. The Council extended the mandates of the United Nations Tajikistan Office of Peacebuilding until 1 June 2006, the United Nations Assistance Mission in Afghanistan was extended until 24 March 2006, and the United Nations Assistance Mission for Iraq until 11 August 2006. In the Democratic People's Republic of Korea, the United Nations Command continued to implement the maintenance of the 1953 Armistice Agreement [YUN 1953, p. 136].

(For the financing of UN political and peacebuilding missions, see PART FIVE, Chapter II.)

Roster of 2005 political and peacebuilding offices

The figures for mission strength listed for the following missions and offices are as at 1 December 2005.

UNPOS

United Nations Political Office for Somalia
Established: 15 April 1995.
Mandate: To monitor the situation in Somalia and keep the Security Council informed, particularly about developments affecting the humani-tarian and security situation, repatriation of refugees and impacts on neighbouring countries.
Head of Office: François Lonseny Fall (Guinea).
Strength: 5 international civilian staff, 3 local civilian staff.

Great Lakes region

Office of the Special Representative of the Secretary-General for the Great Lakes Region
Established: 19 December 1997.
Mandate: To monitor developments in the region and their implications for peace and security and to contribute to regional efforts in the prevention or peaceful settlement of conflicts.
Special Representative of the Secretary-General: Ibrahima Fall (Senegal).
Strength: 8 international civilian staff, 8 local civilian staff.

UNOGBIS

United Nations Peacebuilding Support Office in Guinea-Bissau
Established: 3 March 1999.
Mandate: To assist in the transition from conflict management to post-conflict peacebuilding and reconstruction; to promote national reconciliation and assist in the holding of elections and security and justice sectors reform. That mandate was revised in 2005 to help the country consolidate democratic gains.
Head of Office: João Bernardo Honwana (Mozambique).
Strength: 11 international civilian staff, 2 military advisers, 1 civilian police adviser, 13 local civilian staff.

UNSCO

Office of the United Nations Special Coordinator for the Middle East
Established: 1 October 1999.
Mandate: To act as the focal point for the United Nations contribution to the implementation of the peace agreements and to enhance UN assistance.
Special Coordinator of the Middle East Peace Process and Personal Representative of the Secretary-General and Special Representative: Alvaro de Soto (Peru).
Strength: 27 international civilian staff, 23 local civilian staff.

BONUCA

United Nations Peace-building Office in the Central African Republic
Established: 15 February 2000.

Mandate: To support efforts to consolidate peace and promote national reconstruction and economic recovery.

Head of Office: General Lamine Cissé (Senegal).

Strength: 25 international civilian staff, 5 military advisers, 6 civilian police, 44 local civilian staff, 2 UN volunteers.

UNTOP

United Nations Tajikistan Office of Peacebuilding

Established: 1 June 2000.

Mandate: To provide a political framework and leadership for post-conflict peacebuilding.

Representative of the Secretary-General: Vladimir Sotirov (Bulgaria).

Strength: 10 international civilian staff, 18 local civilian staff, 1 civilian police adviser.

UNOWA

Office of the Special Representative of the Secretary-General for West Africa

Established: March 2002.

Mandate: To ensure the strengthening of harmonization and coordination of UN system activities in an integrated regional perspective and development of a partnership with the Economic Community of West African States, other sub-regional organizations and international and national actors, including civil society.

Special Representative: Ahmedou Ould-Abdallah (Mauritania).

Strength: 7 international civilian staff, 7 local civilian staff.

UNAMA

United Nations Assistance Mission in Afghanistan

Established: 28 March 2002.

Mandate: To fulfil the tasks and responsibilities entrusted to the United Nations in the Bonn Agreement; promote national reconciliation and rapprochement; mange all UN humanitarian relief, recovery and reconstruction activities; and assist in the promotion of the political process.

Special Representative of the Secretary-General: Jean Arnault (France).

Strength: 185 international civilian staff, 751 local civilian staff, 11 military observers; 7 civilian police, 42 UN volunteers.

UNAMI

United Nations Assistance Mission for Iraq

Established: 14 August 2003.

Mandate: To support the Secretary-General in the fulfilment of his mandate under Security Council resolution 1483(2003).

Special Representative of the Secretary-General: Ashraf Jehangir Qazi (Pakistan).

Strength: 222 international civilian staff, 365 local civilian staff, 5 military advisers (including staff in Jordan and Kuwait).

UNOMB

United Nations Observer Mission in Bougainville (Papua New Guinea)

Established: 1 January 2004.

Ended: 30 June 2005.

Mandate: To assist in the promotion of the political process under the Lincoln Agreement.

Head of Office: Tor Stenbock (Norway).

Strength: 2 international civilian staff.

UNAMIS

United Nations Advance Mission in Sudan

Established: 11 June 2004.

Ended: 24 March 2005.

Mandate: To prepare for the international monitoring foreseen in the 2003 Naivasha Agreement on Security Arrangements, to facilitate contacts with the parties concerned and to prepare for the introduction of a peace support operation following the signing of a comprehensive peace agreement.

Special Representative of the Secretary-General: Johannes Pronk (Netherlands).

UNOTIL

United Nations Office in Timor Leste

Established: 28 April 2005.

Mandate: To support the development of critical State institutions, support the further development of the police and provide training in the observance of democratic governance and human rights.

Special Representative of the Secretary-General: Sukehiro Hasegawa (Japan).

Strength: 158 international civilian staff, 281 local civilian staff, 15 military advisers, 57 civilian police, 36 UN volunteers (Staff in Jordan and Kuwait were included).

Threats to international peace and security

International terrorism

Report of Secretary-General to the World Summit. The Secretary-General, in his report to the 2005 World Summit [A/59/2005] (see p. 67) entitled "In larger freedom: towards development, security and human rights for all", said that terrorism was a threat to all that the United Nations stood for, including respect for human rights and the rule of law, the protection of civilians, tolerance among peoples and nations, and the peaceful resolution of conflict. Transnational networks of terrorist groups had global reach and made common cause to pose a universal threat, desired to acquire nuclear, biological and chemical weapons and to inflict mass casualties. The strategy against the problem had to be comprehensive and based on five pillars: dissuading people from resorting to terrorism or supporting it; denying terrorists access to funds and materials; deterring States from sponsoring terrorism; developing State capacity to defeat terrorism; and defending human rights. He urged Member States and civil society organizations everywhere to join in that strategy. He said that the moral authority of the United Nations and its strength in condemning terrorism had been hampered by the inability of Member States to agree on a comprehensive convention that included a definition of terrorism. The Secretary-General fully endorsed the call of the High-level Panel on Threats, Challenges and Change [YUN 2004, p. 54] for such a definition, which would make it clear that, in addition to actions already proscribed by existing conventions, any action constituted terrorism that was intended to cause death or serious bodily harm to civilians or non-combatants with the purpose of intimidating a population or compelling a Government or an international organization to do or abstain from doing something. He believed that the proposal had a clear moral force and strongly urged world leaders to unite behind it and to conclude a comprehensive convention on terrorism before the end of the General Assembly's sixtieth (2005) session. The Secretary-General also urged Member States to complete, without delay, an international convention for the suppression of acts of nuclear terrorism (see p. 1410), and to appoint a special rapporteur to report to the Commission on Human Rights on the compatibility of counter-terrorism measures with international human rights laws.

The General Assembly, in resolution 60/1 (see p. 48), which contained the World Summit Outcome, welcomed the Secretary-General's identification of elements of a counter-terrorism strategy, which the Assembly should develop, adopt and implement.

Summit meeting of the Security Council

By a 2 September note [S/2005/562], the Security Council President issued a statement on the Council's behalf, informing the media that Council members had agreed to take advantage of the presence of Heads of State and Government in New York to hold a meeting on 14 September, to consider the subject of international peace and security.

On 14 September [meeting 5261], the Council held a summit-level meeting at the level of Heads of State or Government to discuss threats to international peace and security. It adopted two resolutions, the first of which was on the prevention of terrorism (1624(2005)) (see below) and the other on enhanced steps to prevent armed conflict, particularly in Africa (1625(2005)) (see p. 155).

Speaking after the vote, the Secretary-General, elaborating on the elements of his proposed counter-terrorism strategy, said that the international community should complete a comprehensive convention that outlawed terrorism in all its forms. He also hoped that States would accede without delay to the International Convention for the Suppression of Acts of Nuclear Terrorism adopted by the Assembly (see p. 1410). In terms of developing State capacity to prevent terrorism, including the promotion of good governance and the rule of law, he welcomed the establishment of the Democracy Fund (see p. 655). The Secretary-General urged that the victims of terrorism should not be forgotten, noting that the Security Council had agreed to explore the possibility of an international fund to compensate victims and their families, which should be financed in part with assets seized from terrorist organizations.

President Vladimir Putin of the Russian Federation said that the common task was to create a truly solid front in the fight against terrorism, and any attempt to condone it or to use terrorists for different political purposes should be condemned unanimously. Those who advocated terrorism and propagated the ideologies of racism and ethnic or religious intolerance should be fought, not only using the power of the State but also engaging civil society, the mass media, humanitarian cooperation and interreligious dialogue. He said that the issues of fighting terrorism and its roots needed further cooperation and should be permanent items on the agenda of the United Nations, including the Security Council and other UN bodies.

United States President, George Bush, said that Council members had a solemn obligation to stop terrorism in its early stages, to defend their citizens against terrorism, to attack terrorist networks and deprive them of a safe haven, and to promote an ideology of freedom and tolerance that would refute the dark vision of the terrorist. They should do all they could to disrupt each stage of planning and support for terrorist acts, be consistent with past Council resolutions to freeze terrorist assets, deny them freedom of movement and prevent them from acquiring weapons, including weapons of mass destruction. The United States would continue to work with and through the Council to help all nations meet those commitments.

China's President, Hu Jinato, said that China supported an important role for the Security Council in responding to terrorism and other non-traditional threats to security. However, the international community should act in strict accordance with the purposes and principles of the Charter and work closely in a more effective fight against terrorism in all its forms and manifestations. It was also essential to promote dialogue among civilizations and to earnestly address problems of poverty, ignorance and social justice in order to eliminate the breeding ground for terrorism.

United Kingdom Prime Minister, Anthony Blair, told the Council that the terrorism, which had disfigured countries in every continent, at every stage of development, with every conceivable mix of races and religions, was a movement. It had an ideology and a strategy, which was not just to kill, but to cause chaos and instability and to divide and confuse nations. It would not be defeated until the international community's determination was as complete as theirs, its defence of freedom as absolute as their fanaticism, and its passion for the democratic way as great as their passion for tyranny. It was a doctrine of fanaticism, and the international community should unite to uproot it by cooperating on security, taking action against those who incited, preached or taught extremism and eliminating ambivalence by fighting not just the methods of terrorism but also the motivation, reasoning and excuses for terror.

SECURITY COUNCIL ACTION

On 14 September [meeting 5261], the Security Council unanimously adopted **resolution 1624 (2005)**. The draft [S/2005/577] was prepared in prior consultations among Council members.

The Security Council,

Reaffirming its resolutions 1267(1999) of 15 October 1999, 1373(2001) of 28 September 2001, 1535(2004) of 26 March 2004, 1540(2004) of 28 April 2004, 1566 (2004) of 8 October 2004 and 1617(2005) of 29 July 2005, the declaration annexed to its resolution 1456 (2003) of 20 January 2003, as well as its other resolutions concerning threats to international peace and security caused by acts of terrorism,

Reaffirming also the imperative to combat terrorism in all its forms and manifestations by all means, in accordance with the Charter of the United Nations, and also stressing that States must ensure that any measures taken to combat terrorism comply with all their obligations under international law, and should adopt such measures in accordance with international law, in particular international human rights law, refugee law and humanitarian law,

Condemning in the strongest terms all acts of terrorism irrespective of their motivation, whenever and by whomsoever committed, as one of the most serious threats to peace and security, and reaffirming the primary responsibility of the Security Council for the maintenance of international peace and security under the Charter,

Condemning in the strongest terms also the incitement of terrorist acts, and repudiating attempts at the justification or glorification (*apologie*) of terrorist acts that may incite further terrorist acts,

Deeply concerned that the incitement of terrorist acts motivated by extremism and intolerance poses a serious and growing danger to the enjoyment of human rights, threatens the social and economic development of all States, undermines global stability and prosperity, and must be addressed urgently and proactively by the United Nations and all States, and emphasizing the need to take all necessary and appropriate measures in accordance with international law at the national and international levels to protect the right to life,

Recalling the right to freedom of expression reflected in article 19 of the Universal Declaration of Human Rights adopted by the General Assembly on 10 December 1948 ("the Universal Declaration"), and recalling also the right to freedom of expression set out in article 19 of the International Covenant on Civil and Political Rights adopted by the Assembly on 16 December 1966 and that any restrictions thereon shall only be such as are provided by law and are necessary on the grounds set out in article 19, paragraph 3, of the Covenant,

Recalling also the right to seek and enjoy asylum reflected in article 14 of the Universal Declaration and the non-refoulement obligation of States under the Convention relating to the Status of Refugees adopted on 28 July 1951, together with its Protocol adopted on 31 January 1967 ("the Refugees Convention and its Protocol"), and also recalling that the protections afforded by the Refugees Convention and its Protocol shall not extend to any person with respect to whom there are serious reasons for considering that he has been guilty of acts contrary to the purposes and principles of the United Nations,

Reaffirming that acts, methods and practices of terrorism are contrary to the purposes and principles of the United Nations and that knowingly financing, planning and inciting terrorist acts are also contrary to the purposes and principles of the United Nations,

Deeply concerned by the increasing number of victims, especially among civilians of diverse nationalities and beliefs, of terrorism motivated by intolerance or extremism in various regions of the world, reaffirming its profound solidarity with the victims of terrorism and their families, and stressing the importance of assisting victims of terrorism and providing them and their families with support to cope with their loss and grief,

Recognizing the essential role of the United Nations in the global effort to combat terrorism, and welcoming the identification by the Secretary-General of elements of a counter-terrorism strategy to be considered and developed by the General Assembly without delay with a view to adopting and implementing a strategy to promote comprehensive, coordinated and consistent responses at the national, regional and international levels to counter terrorism,

Stressing its call upon all States to become party, as a matter of urgency, to the international counter-terrorism conventions and protocols whether or not they are party to regional conventions on the matter, and to give priority consideration to signing the International Convention for the Suppression of Nuclear Terrorism adopted by the General Assembly on 13 April 2005,

Re-emphasizing that continuing international efforts to enhance dialogue and broaden understanding among civilizations, in an effort to prevent the indiscriminate targeting of different religions and cultures, and addressing unresolved regional conflicts and the full range of global issues, including development issues, will contribute to strengthening the international fight against terrorism,

Stressing the importance of the role of the media, civil and religious society, the business community and educational institutions in those efforts to enhance dialogue and broaden understanding, and in promoting tolerance and coexistence and fostering an environment which is not conducive to incitement of terrorism,

Recognizing the importance, in an increasingly globalized world, of States acting cooperatively to prevent terrorists from exploiting sophisticated technology, communications and resources to incite support for criminal acts,

Recalling that all States must cooperate fully in the fight against terrorism, in accordance with their obligations under international law, in order to find, deny safe haven to and bring to justice, on the basis of the principle of extradite or prosecute, any person who supports, facilitates, participates or attempts to participate in the financing, planning, preparation or commission of terrorist acts or provides safe havens,

1. *Calls upon* all States to adopt such measures as may be necessary and appropriate and in accordance with their obligations under international law:

(a) To prohibit by law incitement to commit a terrorist act or acts;

(b) To prevent such conduct;

(c) To deny safe haven to any persons with respect to whom there is credible and relevant information giving serious reasons for considering that they have been guilty of such conduct;

2. *Also calls upon* all States to cooperate, inter alia, to strengthen the security of their international borders, including by combating fraudulent travel documents and, to the extent attainable, by enhancing terrorist screening and passenger security procedures with a view to preventing those guilty of the conduct in paragraph 1 (a) above from entering their territory;

3. *Further calls upon* all States to continue international efforts to enhance dialogue and broaden understanding among civilizations, in an effort to prevent the indiscriminate targeting of different religions and cultures, and to take all measures as may be necessary and appropriate and in accordance with their obligations under international law to counter incitement of terrorist acts motivated by extremism and intolerance

and to prevent the subversion of educational, cultural and religious institutions by terrorists and their supporters;

4. *Stresses* that States must ensure that any measures taken to implement paragraphs 1, 2 and 3 of the present resolution comply with all of their obligations under international law, in particular international human rights law, refugee law and humanitarian law;

5. *Calls upon* all States to report to the Security Council Committee established pursuant to resolution 1373(2001) concerning counter-terrorism (the Counter-Terrorism Committee), as part of their ongoing dialogue, on the steps that they have taken to implement the present resolution;

6. *Directs* the Counter-Terrorism Committee:

(a) To include in its dialogue with Member States their efforts to implement the present resolution;

(b) To work with Member States to help to build capacity, including by spreading best legal practice and promoting exchange of information in this regard;

(c) To report back to the Council in twelve months on the implementation of the present resolution;

7. *Decides* to remain actively seized of the matter.

2005 terrorist attacks

In 2005, there was an unprecedented rise in the number of terrorist attacks worldwide. The Security Council met on 10 occasions to condemn such acts and to express sympathy and condolences to the victims and affected Governments and its determination to combat terrorism in all its forms.

London

On 7 July, a series of bombs exploded in London's public transport system during the morning rush hour, killing 52 persons, including the four perpetrators, and wounding 700. The incident was the deadliest single act of terrorism since the 1988 bombing of Pan Am flight 103 over Lockerbie, Scotland. The four terrorists, Mohammed Sidique Khan, Shehzad Tanweer, Germaine Lindsay and Hasib Hussain, belonged to an Al-Qaida affiliated organization named the Secret Organization of Al-Qaida in Europe, which later claimed responsibility for the attacks.

The Secretary-General deplored the atrocious bombings as an attack on humanity itself and urged that such violence should not be allowed to derail efforts to combat poverty and address the aspirations of billions of people worldwide.

SECURITY COUNCIL ACTION

On 7 July [meeting 5223], the Security Council unanimously adopted **resolution 1611(2005)**. The draft [S/2005/437] was prepared in consultation among Council members.

The Security Council,

Reaffirming the purposes and principles of the Charter of the United Nations and its relevant resolutions, in particular resolutions 1373(2001) of 28 September 2001 and 1566(2004) of 8 October 2004,

Reaffirming also the need to combat by all means, in accordance with the Charter, threats to international peace and security caused by terrorist acts,

1. *Condemns without reservation* the terrorist attacks in London on 7 July 2005, and regards any act of terrorism as a threat to peace and security;

2. *Expresses its deepest sympathy and condolences* to the victims of these terrorist attacks and their families, and to the people and Government of the United Kingdom of Great Britain and Northern Ireland;

3. *Urges* all States, in accordance with their obligations under resolution 1373(2001), to cooperate actively in efforts to find and bring to justice the perpetrators, organizers and sponsors of these barbaric acts;

4. *Expresses its utmost determination* to combat terrorism, in accordance with its responsibilities under the Charter of the United Nations.

Communication. On 8 July [S/2005/450], Saudi Arabia transmitted to the Council President a statement on the bombings in London, issued by the Grand Mufti of the Kingdom of Saudi Arabia and Chairman of the Committee of Senior Ulema and of the Department of Scientific Research and Ifta', declaring that the incidents of individual and collective killing, explosions, destruction of property and the terrorizing of peace-loving people were forbidden by Islam and that any attribution of those acts to Islam was unjust. Islam forbade the unjust killing of human beings and Islamic scholars had repeatedly expressed their censure of such abominable acts and had stated time and again that those acts had nothing to do with Islam.

Iraq

On 7 July [S/2005/438], Egypt informed the Security Council that its recently appointed Ambassador to Iraq, Ihab El Sherif, was killed that day, four days after being kidnapped in Baghdad by a group of terrorists. Egypt said that while it continued to support the people of Iraq at its critical political juncture, it was regrettable that there still existed some groups that disrespected the sacredness of human life. It called on the Council to condemn the surge of violence against foreign diplomats in Iraq, in particular the killing of Ambassador El Sherif.

SECURITY COUNCIL ACTION

On 8 July [meeting 5224], following consultations among Security Council members, the President made statement **S/PRST/2005/29** on behalf of the Council:

The Security Council condemns in the strongest possible terms the assassination of the recently appointed Head of the Egyptian Mission to Iraq, Ambassador Ihab El Sherif, on 7 July 2005 and expresses its condolences to the family of the victim and to the Government and people of Egypt.

The Council also condemns all terrorist attacks in Iraq, including the attempted assassinations of diplomats from Bahrain and Pakistan and attacks against other civilian personnel.

The Council emphasizes that there can be no justification for such terrorist acts and underlines the need to bring to justice the perpetrators.

The Council reaffirms its unwavering support for the Iraqi people in their political transition, as outlined in its resolution 1546(2004). The Council also reaffirms the independence, sovereignty, unity and territorial integrity of Iraq and calls upon the international community to stand by the Iraqi people in their pursuit of peace, stability and democracy.

The Council welcomes Egypt's continued commitment in this regard, as stated in the letter dated 7 July 2005 from the Permanent Representative of Egypt to the United Nations addressed to the President of the Council, and recognizes the important role of Egypt and other neighbouring countries in supporting the political process, helping to control transit across Iraq's borders, and extending other support to the Iraqi people.

On 27 July [meeting 5240], following consultations among Council members, the President made statement **S/PRST/2005/37** on behalf of the Council:

The Security Council condemns in the strongest possible terms the assassination, today, 27 July 2005, of the two Algerian diplomats accredited to the Algerian Embassy to Iraq, Mr. Ali Belaroussi and Mr. Azzedine Belkadi, and expresses its condolences to the families of the victims and to the Government and people of Algeria.

The Council emphasizes that there can be no justification for such terrorist acts and underlines the need to bring to justice the perpetrators.

The Council reaffirms its unwavering support for the Iraqi people in their political transition, as outlined in resolution 1546(2004). The Council also reaffirms the independence, sovereignty, unity and territorial integrity of Iraq and calls upon the international community to stand by the Iraqi people in their pursuit of peace, stability and democracy.

On 4 August [meeting 5246], the Security Council unanimously adopted **resolution 1618(2005)**. The draft [S/2005/494] was submitted by Romania, the United Kingdom and the United States.

The Security Council,

Reaffirming all its previous relevant resolutions on Iraq, in particular resolution 1546(2004) of 8 June 2004,

Reaffirming its unwavering support for the Iraqi people in their political transition, as outlined in resolution 1546(2004), further reaffirming Iraq's independence, sovereignty, unity and territorial integrity, and calling upon the international community to stand by the Iraqi people in their pursuit of peace, stability and democracy,

Reaffirming the purposes and principles of the Charter of the United Nations and its relevant resolutions, in particular resolutions 1373(2001) of 28 September 2001, 1566(2004) of 8 October 2004, and 1267(1999) of 15 October 1999 and subsequent resolutions,

Reaffirming also the need to combat by all means, in accordance with the Charter, threats to international peace and security caused by terrorist acts,

Commending the courage of the Iraqi people who are working bravely in support of the political and economic transition currently taking place in spite of the grave threat of terrorism,

Welcoming the active steps undertaken by the Government of Iraq towards achieving national dialogue and unity, and encouraging the continuation of those efforts,

1. *Condemns without reservation and in the strongest terms* the terrorist attacks that have taken place in Iraq, and regards any act of terrorism as a threat to peace and security;

2. *Takes note in particular* of the shameless and horrific attacks in recent weeks which have resulted in over one hundred deaths, including thirty-two children, employees of the Independent Electoral Commission of Iraq, and a member and an expert adviser of the Commission charged with drafting a permanent constitution for a new, democratic Iraq, Mr. Mijbil Sheikh Issa and Mr. Dhamin Hussein Ubaidi;

3. *Notes with great concern* that attacks on foreign diplomats in Iraq have increased in number and have resulted in the murder or kidnapping of such diplomats;

4. *Expresses its deepest sympathy and condolences* to the victims of these terrorist attacks and their families, and to the people and Government of Iraq;

5. *Affirms* that acts of terrorism must not be allowed to disrupt Iraq's political and economic transition currently taking place, including the constitutional drafting process and its referendum, as outlined in resolution 1546(2004);

6. *Reaffirms* the obligations of Member States under resolutions 1373(2001), 1267(1999), 1333(2000) of 19 December 2000, 1390(2002) of 16 January 2002, 1455 (2003) of 17 January 2003, 1526(2004) of 30 January 2004 and 1617(2005) of 29 July 2005 and other relevant international obligations with respect, inter alia, to terrorist activities in and from Iraq or against its citizens, and, specifically, strongly urges Member States to prevent the transit of terrorists to and from Iraq, arms for terrorists, and financing that would support terrorists, and re-emphasizes the importance of strengthening the cooperation of the countries in the region, particularly neighbours of Iraq, in this regard;

7. *Urges* all States, in accordance with their obligations under resolution 1373(2001), to cooperate actively in efforts to find and bring to justice the perpetrators, organizers and sponsors of these barbaric acts;

8. *Expresses its utmost determination* to combat terrorism, in accordance with its responsibilities under the Charter of the United Nations;

9. *Calls upon* the international community to support fully the Government of Iraq in exercising its responsibilities to provide protection to the diplomatic community, United Nations staff and other foreign civilian personnel working in Iraq;

10. *Decides* to remain seized of the matter.

Egypt

On 23 July, a series of bomb attacks targeted the Egyptian resort city of Sharm El-Sheikh on the southern tip of the Sinai Peninsula. Some 88 people were killed and over 150 wounded. Among them were nationals from the Czech Republic, France, Germany, Israel, Kuwait, the Netherlands, Qatar, the Russian Federation, Spain, the United Kingdom and the United States. It was the deadliest terrorist attack in that country's history.

SECURITY COUNCIL ACTION

On 27 July [meeting 5239], following consultations among Security Council members, the President made statement **S/PRST/2005/36** on behalf of the Council:

> The Security Council unequivocally condemns the terrorist attacks that took place in Sharm El-Sheikh, Egypt, on 23 July 2005, and expresses its deepest sympathy and condolences to the victims of these attacks and their families, and to the people and Government of Egypt as well as to all other countries whose citizens have been killed or injured in these attacks.
>
> The Council underlines the need to bring the perpetrators, organizers, financers and sponsors of this horrendous act to justice and urges all States, in accordance with their obligations under international law and resolution 1373(2001), to cooperate actively with the Egyptian authorities in this regard.
>
> The Council reaffirms that terrorism in all its forms and manifestations constitutes one of the most serious threats to international peace and security and that any acts of terrorism are criminal and unjustifiable, regardless of their motivation, whenever and by whomsoever committed.
>
> The Council further reaffirms the need to combat by all means, in accordance with the Charter of the United Nations, threats to international peace and security caused by terrorist acts.
>
> The Council reiterates its determination to combat all forms of terrorism, in accordance with its responsibilities under the Charter.

Indonesia

On 1 October, a series of explosions occurred at Jimbaran and Kuta in Bali, Indonesia, killing 23 people, including the three bombers, and wounding some 129 persons.

On 4 October [meeting 5274], following consultations among Security Council members, the President made statement **S/PRST/2005/45** on behalf of the Council:

> The Security Council condemns in the strongest terms the terrorist bombings that took place on 1 Oc-

tober 2005 in Bali, Indonesia, which has again fallen victim to a heinous act of terrorism.

The Council expresses its deepest sympathy and condolences to the victims of these attacks and their families, and to the people and the Government of Indonesia.

The Council underlines the need to bring the perpetrators, organizers, financers and sponsors of these intolerable acts to justice, and urges all States, in accordance with their obligations under international law and resolution 1373(2001), to cooperate with and provide support and assistance, as appropriate, to the Government of Indonesia in this regard.

The Council reaffirms that terrorism in all its forms and manifestations constitutes one of the most serious threats to international peace and security, and that any acts of terrorism are criminal and unjustifiable, regardless of their motivation, wherever, whenever and by whomsoever committed.

The Council further reaffirms the need to combat by all means, in accordance with the Charter of the United Nations, threats to international peace and security caused by terrorist acts.

The Council reiterates its determination to combat all forms of terrorism, in accordance with its responsibilities under the Charter.

India

On 29 October, three explosions at the Sarojini Nagar marketplace, the Paharganj marketplace and on a bus in the Govindpuri area in Delhi, India, killed 61 people and injured some 92 others. Responsibility for the attack, which took place just before the important festival of Diwali, was claimed by a Pakistan-based organization called the Islamic Inquilab Mahaz.

SECURITY COUNCIL ACTION

On 31 October [meeting 5298], following consultations among Security Council members, the President made statement **S/PRST/2005/53** on behalf of the Council:

The Security Council strongly condemns the series of bomb attacks that occurred in New Delhi on 29 October 2005, causing numerous deaths and injuries, and expresses its deepest condolences to the victims of these heinous acts of terrorism and their families, and to the people and the Government of India.

The Council stresses the importance of bringing the perpetrators, organizers, financers and sponsors of these reprehensible acts of violence to justice, and urges all States, in accordance with their obligations under international law and resolutions 1373(2001) and 1624(2005), to cooperate actively with the Indian authorities in this regard.

The Council reaffirms that terrorism in all its forms and manifestations constitutes one of the most serious threats to international peace and security, and that any acts of terrorism are criminal and unjustifiable, regardless of their motivation, wherever, whenever and by whomsoever committed.

The Council further reaffirms the need to combat by all means, in accordance with the Charter of the United Nations, threats to international peace and security caused by terrorist acts.

The Council reiterates its determination to combat all forms of terrorism, in accordance with its responsibilities under the Charter.

Jordan

On 9 November, Al-Qaida in Iraq claimed responsibility for coordinated bomb attacks at the Grand Hyatt Hotel, the Radisson SAS Hotel and the Days Inn in Amman, Jordan, which killed a total of 60 persons and the three suicide bombers, and injured 115 others.

SECURITY COUNCIL ACTION

On 10 November [meeting 5303], following consultations among Security Council members, the President made statement **S/PRST/2005/55** on behalf of the Council:

The Security Council condemns in the strongest terms the terrorist bombings that took place in Amman on 9 November 2005.

The Council expresses its deepest sympathy and condolences to the victims of these attacks and their families, and to the people and the Government of Jordan.

The Council underlines the need to bring the perpetrators, organizers, financers and sponsors of these intolerable acts to justice, and urges all States, in accordance with their obligations under international law and resolutions 1373(2001) and 1624 (2005), to cooperate with and provide support and assistance, as appropriate, to the Government of Jordan in this regard.

The Council reaffirms that terrorism in all its forms and manifestations constitutes one of the most serious threats to international peace and security, and that any acts of terrorism are criminal and unjustifiable, regardless of their motivation, wherever, whenever and by whomsoever committed.

The Council further reaffirms the need to combat by all means, in accordance with the Charter of the United Nations, threats to international peace and security caused by terrorist acts. The Council reminds States that they must ensure that any measures taken to combat terrorism comply with all their obligations under international law, in particular international human rights, refugee and humanitarian law.

The Council reiterates its determination to combat all forms of terrorism, in accordance with its responsibilities under the Charter.

Lebanon

On 15 February [meeting 5122], the Security Council, in statement **S/PRST/2005/4** (see p. 551), condemned the 14 February terrorist bombing in Beirut, Lebanon, which killed the former Lebanese Prime Minister, Rafiq Hariri and others, and inflicted serious injury on dozens of people, including former Minister Basil Fleihan.

On 7 June [meeting 5197], the Council, in statement **S/PRST/2005/22** (see p. 560), condemned the 2 June terrorist bombing in Beirut that killed Lebanese journalist, Samir Qassir, and welcomed the determination of the Government to bring the perpetrators to justice.

On 12 December [meeting 5320], the Council, in statement **S/PRST/2005/61** (see p. 560), condemned the terrorist bombing on that same day in the suburbs of Beirut, which killed Lebanese member of Parliament and journalist, Gebrane Tueni.

Measures to eliminate international terrorism

During 2005, the United Nations pursued actions on several fronts to combat and eliminate terrorism. The Security Council, by **resolution 1617(2005)** of 29 July (see p. 410), adopted measures to tighten the sanctions imposed against Al-Qaida, the Taliban and their associates.

The General Assembly, in **resolution 59/290** of 13 April, adopted the International Convention for the Suppression of Acts of Nuclear Terrorism (see p. 1411); and in **resolution 60/43** of 8 December (see p. 1417), it called on all States to prevent and suppress terrorist acts and asked the Terrorism Prevention Branch of the United Nations Office on Drugs and Crime to continue to enhance the capabilities of the United Nations in the prevention of terrorism. In **resolution 60/78** (see p. 602) of the same date, the Assembly requested the Secretary-General to report on measures already taken by international organizations on issues regarding the linkage between the fight against terrorism and the proliferation of weapons of mass destruction, and to seek the views of Member States on additional measures for tackling that threat.

Communications. On 10 March [A/59/754-S/2005/197], Croatia transmitted to the Secretary-General the Zagreb Declaration on International Cooperation on Counter-Terrorism, Corruption and the Fight against Transnational Organized Crime, adopted at an expert workshop on the subject (Zagreb, Croatia, 7-9 March).

On 11 April [A/59/775-S/2005/238], Spain transmitted to the Secretary-General the Madrid Agenda adopted at the International Summit on Democracy, Terrorism and Security (Madrid, Spain, 8-11 March), organized by the Madrid Club (a body of former presidents and prime ministers of democratic countries dedicated to the promotion of democracy). The Agenda contained a number of recommendations for combating international terrorism.

The Permanent Observer of the League of Arab States to the United Nations transmitted to the Security Council President on 10 May [S/2005/309] the "Recommendations of the Arab Regional Seminar on Combating Terrorism" (Cairo, Egypt, 16-17 February).

On 18 May [A/59/811], Mauritius transmitted to the Secretary-General the Port Louis Declaration, adopted by the Regional Ministerial Conference of French-speaking Countries of Africa for the promotion of the ratification and implementation of the UN conventions on combating terrorism, corruption and transnational organized crime and of the universal counter-terrorism instruments (Port Louis, Mauritius, 25-27 October 2004).

Cuba, on 24 May [A/59/812-S/2005/341], transmitted to the Secretary-General a document containing "Summary of main points concerning the presence of terrorist Luis Posada Carriles in the United States".

On 25 July [A/59/882-S/2005/488], Cape Verde transmitted to the Secretary-General the action plan adopted by a regional expert workshop on the ratification and implementation of the universal instruments against terrorism, transnational organized crime and corruption, as well as the drafting of reports to the United Nations Counter-Terrorism Committee (Praia, Cape Verde, 8-10 December 2004).

On 12 August [A/59/895-S/2005/527], Egypt transmitted to the Secretary-General the recommendations adopted by a national workshop on the legal instruments to fight terrorism (Cairo, Egypt, 21-22 December 2004). On 1 September [A/60/329], Egypt also transmitted to the Secretary-General a letter by its Minister for Foreign Affairs, proposing the convening of a special session of the General Assembly to examine and adopt an action plan for cooperation against terrorism.

Counter-Terrorism Committee

In 2005, the Chairman of the Counter-Terrorism Committee (CTC), established by Security Council resolution 1373(2001) [YUN 2001, p. 61], submitted CTC's work programmes for the 90-day periods from 1 January to 31 March [S/2005/22], 1 April to 30 June [S/2005/266], 1 July to 30 September [S/2005/421] and 1 Ocotber to 31 December [S/2005/663]. The Council considered those work programmes at meetings held on 18 January, 25 April, 20 July and 26 October.

Security Council consideration (January). The CTC Chairman, reporting on 18 January [meeting 5113] to the Security Council on the Committee's work, said that the Committee had received 551 reports from Member States and other entities by 31 December 2004. He reported two problems that required attention: the shortage of experts to review reports submitted by Member States and the increasing number of those failing to submit their reports on time. He emphasized that the Committee, operating through the CTC Executive Directorate (CTED), was prepared to provide Member States with the necessary assistance and guidelines on issues relating to the implementation of resolution 1373(2002) and had begun to review the problem in a broader context. CTC continued to develop new approaches to providing technical assistance and was undertaking analytical work to assess the assistance needs of Member States. It would also continue to update the Directory of Counter-Terrorism Information and Sources of Assistance and the Assistance Matrix. CTC would also continue to encourage Member States to accede to the 12 relevant international conventions and protocols relating to terrorism [YUN 2001, p. 69] and regularly monitor progress in that area.

During that period, the Committee completed preparations for its initial visit to several Member States in implementation of resolutions 1535 (2004) [YUN 2004, p. 79] on the revitalization of the Committee and 1566(2004) [ibid., p. 74], emphasizing the urgent need to strengthen international cooperation in combating terrorism. The visits were to help develop a more direct dialogue with national Governments, to enhance monitoring of the implementation of resolution 1373(2001) and to ensure a more accurate assessment of the capacities of States and their technical assistance needs.

CTC prepared for its fourth special meeting with international, regional and subregional organizations, and commended the proposal of the Commonwealth of Independent States (CIS) to organize that meeting in Almaty, Kazakhstan, from 26 to 28 January. It maintained cooperation between CTC experts and those of the Monitoring Group on sanctions against Al-Qaida and the Taliban, and would seek to establish contacts with the newly appointed experts under resolution 1540(2004) [YUN 2004, p. 544].

SECURITY COUNCIL ACTION

On 18 January [meeting 5113], following consultations among Security Council members, the President made statement **S/PRST/2005/3** on behalf of the Council:

The Security Council welcomes the briefing by the Chairman of the Security Council Committee established pursuant to resolution 1373(2001) concerning counter-terrorism (the Counter-Terrorism Committee) on the work of the Committee.

The Council reaffirms that terrorism in all its forms and manifestations constitutes one of the most serious threats to peace and security and that any acts of terrorism are criminal and unjustifiable, regardless of their motivation, whenever and by whomsoever committed.

The Council recalls the statement by its President of 19 October 2004, which indicated the intention of the Council to review the structure and activities of the Counter-Terrorism Committee, resolution 1535 (2004) on the revitalization of the Committee and resolution 1566(2004) emphasizing the urgent need to strengthen international cooperation in combating terrorism.

The Council invites the Counter-Terrorism Committee to pursue its agenda as set out in the work programme for the Committee for the fourteenth 90-day period. It invites the Committee, in particular, to ensure that Counter-Terrorism Committee Executive Directorate becomes fully operational in the shortest possible time, and to take additional measures to enhance cooperation with the Security Council Committee established pursuant to resolution 1267(1999) concerning Al-Qaida and the Taliban and associated individuals and entities and the Security Council Committee established pursuant to resolution 1540(2004) and to initiate contacts with the Security Council Working Group established pursuant to resolution 1566(2004).

The Council notes the importance of continuing the efforts of the Counter-Terrorism Committee in the following key areas: to enhance the capabilities of Member States to combat terrorism, to identify and address the problems faced by States in implementing resolution 1373(2001), to facilitate the provision of technical assistance and cooperation adjusted to the recipient countries' needs, to encourage the largest possible number of States to become parties to the international conventions and protocols related to counter-terrorism, and to strengthen its dialogue and cooperation with international, regional and subregional organizations acting in the areas outlined in resolution 1373(2001).

The Council welcomes the intention of the Counter-Terrorism Committee to hold its fourth special meeting with international, regional and subregional organizations from 26 to 28 January 2005 in Almaty, Kazakhstan.

The Council invites the Counter-Terrorism Committee to accelerate the preparation of assessments of Member States' assistance needs so that these can be shared with the relevant States and, in due course, with interested donor States and organizations. The Council invites the Committee to conduct the first of its visits to Member States in March 2005 in order to enhance the monitoring by the Committee of the implementation of resolution 1373(2001) and to facilitate the provision of technical and other assistance for such implementation.

The Council notes that, as of 16 December 2004, 75 States had not submitted their respective reports to the Counter-Terrorism Committee on time as set out in resolution 1373(2001). It calls upon them urgently to do so, in order to maintain the universality of response which the threat of terrorism and the implementation of resolution 1373(2001) require.

The Council invites the Counter-Terrorism Committee to continue reporting on its activities at regular intervals.

Communication. On 3 February [S/2005/87], CTC Chairman transmitted to the Council President summaries provided by international, regional and subregional organizations and bodies and UN specialized agencies, funds and programmes that participated in the CTC/CIS fourth special meeting (26-28 January) regarding their activities and experiences in counter-terrorism and developments in their work in that regard since 2003.

Security Council consideration (April). The CTC Chairman, reporting to the Council on 25 April, together with the Chairmen of the Security Council Committee established pursuant to resolution 1267(1999) concerning Al-Qaida and the Taliban and associated individuals and entities, and the Security Council Committee established pursuant to resolution 1540 (2004), on the work of CTC, said that 75 States were late in submitting their reports, due to the lack of available technical capacity and "reporting fatigue". CTC's visit to Member States were initiated by a visit to Morocco (14-18 March), with similar visits to Albania, Kenya and Thailand planned. The Committee encouraged respective Member States to welcome those visits. With regard to technical needs assessments, a methodology on their preparation and review was developed and agreed upon. So far, 51 assessments were prepared and 11 endorsed by CTC and forwarded for review by Member States.

For technical reasons, CTED had not yet become fully operational and that seriously limited CTC's ability to sustain dialogue with Member States. CTC, as requested by the Council in resolution 1566(2004), was developing a set of best practices to assist States in implementing the provisions of resolution 1373(2001) relating to the financing of terrorism. It had also taken steps towards its own revitalization, in accordance with resolution 1535(2004). As set out in the work programme for April to June, it would continue efforts to complete the revitalization process, particularly in terms of developing a fully functional CTED.

SECURITY COUNCIL ACTION

On 25 April [meeting 5168], following consultations among Security Council members, the Council President made **statement S/PRST/ 2005/16** on behalf of the Council:

The Security Council welcomes the briefings by the Chairmen of the Security Council Committee established pursuant to resolution 1267(1999) concerning Al-Qaida and the Taliban and associated individuals and entities, the Security Council Committee established pursuant to resolution 1373(2001) on counter-terrorism and the Security Council Committee established pursuant to resolution 1540 (2004), on the work of the three Committees.

The Council reaffirms that terrorism in all its forms and manifestations constitutes one of the most serious threats to peace and security and that any acts of terrorism are criminal and unjustifiable, regardless of their motivations, whenever and by whomsoever committed.

The Council also reaffirms that proliferation of nuclear, chemical and biological weapons, as well as their means of delivery, constitutes a threat to international peace and security as stressed in resolution 1540(2004). The Council recalls its grave concern about the risk posed by non-State actors that attempt to develop, acquire, manufacture, possess, transport, transfer or use nuclear, chemical and biological weapons and their means of delivery.

The Council welcomes the adoption by the General Assembly on 13 April 2005 of the International Convention for the Suppression of Acts of Nuclear Terrorism by consensus.

The Council stresses the different mandates of the three Committees. The Council reaffirms its call for enhanced cooperation among the Committees, as well as their respective groups of experts, in monitoring implementation by States of provisions of the Council resolutions relevant to the three Committees, and invites the Committees, including their respective groups of experts, to strengthen further their cooperation through enhanced information sharing, coordinated visits to countries and other issues of relevance to the three Committees. The Council also invites the three Committees to continue cooperation with the working group established pursuant to resolution 1566(2004).

The Council recalls the obligation of Member States to report to the three Committees in a timely manner on steps they have taken or intend to take to implement resolutions 1267(1999), 1373(2001), and 1540(2004) and related resolutions, and encourages the three Committees to consider, if appropriate, how to deal with late submission of reports to these Committees in a coordinated manner.

The Council reaffirms that the responsibility for implementing its resolutions relevant to the mandates of the three Committees, including preparation of reports to the respective Committees, rests with the States. The Council encourages international, regional and subregional organizations to enhance their efforts to further the implementation by their members of these resolutions, and further encourages such organizations, as well as States, where appropriate, to provide technical assistance to enhance the capacity of States to implement these resolutions.

The Council welcomes the important contribution made by relevant international, regional and subregional organizations in the fight against terrorism and to ensure that non-State actors do not develop, acquire, manufacture, possess, transport, transfer or use nuclear, chemical and biological weapons and their means of delivery. The Council encourages the three Committees to further strengthen their cooperation with such organizations.

The Council further welcomes the important contribution made to the work of the Committee established pursuant to resolution 1267(1999) by the Analytical Support and Sanctions Monitoring Team established pursuant to Council resolution 1526 (2004) in application of its mandate annexed to that resolution; to the work of the Committee established pursuant to resolution 1540(2004) by its experts; and, to the work of the Counter-Terrorism Committee established pursuant to resolution 1373(2001) by the Counter-Terrorism Committee Executive Directorate established by resolution 1535(2004), and notes with satisfaction the completion by the Counter-Terrorism Committee Executive Directorate of its first field mission to a Member State as contemplated by resolution 1535(2004).

The Council invites the Counter-Terrorism Committee to pursue its agenda as set out in the work programme for its fifteenth 90-day period. The Council encourages all parts of the United Nations to do their utmost to ensure that the Counter-Terrorism Committee Executive Directorate becomes fully operational in the shortest possible time.

The Council also invites the Committee established pursuant to resolution 1540(2004) to pursue its undertakings as provided for in the first trimestrial programme of work approved by the Committee on 22 April 2005. The Council welcomes the submission by 113 Member States so far of reports on steps they have taken or intend to take to implement resolution 1540(2004), and calls upon States that have not yet submitted a report to do so as soon as possible. The Council welcomes the recruitment of experts of the Committee, and notes that they have begun to support the Committee in the consideration of the first reports submitted by Member States pursuant to resolution 1540(2004).

The Council invites the three Committees to continue reporting on their activities at regular intervals and, where appropriate, in a coordinated manner.

Report of CTC Chairman (July). Reporting to the Security Council on 20 July [meeting 5229], the CTC Chairman stated that CTED had visited Kenya in May and Albania and Thailand in June and obtained a thorough understanding of the situation in those countries and a better insight into the difficulties facing States seeking to ensure full implementation of resolution 1373 (2001). To guarantee follow-up to those visits, CTC was committed to ensuring that the technical needs identified during the visits were met.

Noting that, as at July, 67 States were behind in their reporting to CTC, the Chairman said CTC would continue discussions with the other two sanctions committees on how best to address reporting issues in a coordinated manner. CTC decided to further identify assistance needs in the process of evaluating States' reports. It would continue discussions on meeting requests made,

including by further developing cooperation with potential donors. Regarding the need to provide clarity and transparency on what it took to implement resolution 1373(2001), CTC discussed the usefulness of developing best practices to guide States. In that regard, it welcomed work already done by international, regional and subregional organizations.

SECURITY COUNCIL ACTION

On 20 July [meeting 5229], following consultations among Security Council members, the Council President made statement **S/PRST/2005/34** on behalf of the Council:

The Security Council reaffirms that terrorism in all its forms and manifestations constitutes one of the most serious threats to peace and security and that any acts of terrorism are criminal and unjustifiable regardless of their motivations, whenever and by whomsoever committed. The Council reiterates its condemnation of the Al-Qaida network and other terrorist groups for ongoing and multiple criminal terrorist acts, aimed at causing death and destruction of property, and undermining stability. The Council also reaffirms that proliferation of nuclear, chemical and biological weapons, as well as their means of delivery, constitutes a threat to international peace and security, and recalls its grave concern about the risk posed by non-State actors that attempt to develop, acquire, manufacture, possess, transport, transfer or use nuclear, chemical and biological weapons and their means of delivery.

The Council reiterates its call upon all Member States to become parties to all 12 international conventions against terrorism, and in this context draws attention to the treaty event being held in New York in September, and encourages Member States to take that opportunity also to sign the International Convention for the Suppression of Acts of Nuclear Terrorism. The Council calls upon Member States to cooperate on an expedited basis to resolve all outstanding issues, with a view to adopting the draft comprehensive convention on international terrorism.

The Council urges all States to cooperate to bring to justice, in accordance with the principle of extradite or prosecute, the perpetrators, organizers and sponsors of acts of terrorism. Recent events, as condemned by the Council in its resolution 1611(2005) and the statement by its President of 8 July 2005, stress the urgency and necessity of redoubling efforts to combat terrorism.

The Council welcomes the briefings by the Chairmen of the Security Council Committee established pursuant to resolution 1267(1999) concerning Al-Qaida and the Taliban and associated individuals and entities, the Security Council Committee established pursuant to resolution 1373(2001) on counter-terrorism and the Security Council Committee established pursuant to resolution 1540(2004), on the work of the three Committees. The Council reaffirms the importance and the urgency it attaches to the implementation of the provisions of the resolutions relevant to the three Committees, as well as to the fulfilment of the mandates of the three Committees. The Council therefore strongly encourages Member States as well as the respective Committees to redouble their efforts to seek ways to further strengthen the implementation of resolutions 1267 (1999), 1373(2001) and 1540(2004), in accordance with the provisions of these and other relevant resolutions.

The Council reaffirms its call for enhanced cooperation among the three Committees, as well as their respective group of experts, in monitoring implementation by States of the provisions of the relevant Council resolutions, with due respect for their different mandates, including through enhanced information sharing, coordinated response to late submission of reports by States to the three Committees, and other issues of relevance to the three Committees. The Council also invites the three Committees to continue cooperation with the working group established pursuant to resolution 1566(2004).

The Council urges Member States to redouble their efforts to implement the provisions of the resolutions relevant to the work of the three Committees. While reaffirming that the responsibility for implementing the provisions of these resolutions rests with the States, the Council encourages States to seek the necessary assistance to ensure that the necessary capacity to implement the resolutions is available.

The Council reiterates that relevant international, regional and subregional organizations can play a crucial role in supporting the goals of these resolutions, raising awareness of their importance, and helping their members implement them. The Council encourages such organizations, as or when proposed by the relevant Committee, where appropriate, to provide the necessary technical assistance. Moreover, the Council encourages its Counter-Terrorism Committee, its Al-Qaida/Taliban Sanctions Committee, and, when appropriate its Committee established pursuant to resolution 1540 (2004), as well as relevant organizations, to enhance cooperation with a view to identifying, promoting, and developing, as appropriate, best practices to provide clarity and guidance to States on the implementation of the provisions of the relevant resolutions.

The Council encourages Member States in a position to do so to make technical assistance available on a priority basis.

The Council invites the three Committees to continue reporting on their activities at regular intervals and, where appropriate, in a coordinated manner.

Report of CTC Chairman (October). The CTC Chairman, at the Council's 26 October meeting [meeting 5293], reported that CTED was fully staffed and urged States to take advantage of the resources available and request the assistance needed to further their counter-terrorism efforts. Over the past three months, the Committee's priorities were: engaging with regional organizations that had developed a counter-terrorism agenda; clearing the backlog of reports from States; continuing to examine ways to better facilitate technical assistance; continuation of

visits to States; enhancing dialogue and cooperation with international, regional and subregional organizations, through their involvement in the CTC visits to States and by engaging them to help strengthen the Committee's capacity to promote the implementation of resolution 1373(2001) among other things; taking steps to ensure follow-up to Security Council resolution 1624 (2005) (see p. 102) on incitement of terrorism adopted at the Council's summit meeting in September; and engaging in policy discussions aimed at giving CTED the guidance foreseen in the revitalization documents.

Specifically, CTC and its CTED were ready to guide and assist international and regional organizations, and would make greater efforts to reach out to them. CTC encouraged those organizations to consider ways to enhance their bilateral cooperation in order to assist each other in developing their counter-terrorism agenda. It would also consider how to follow up on the latest special meeting (see p. 108) with international, regional and subregional groups and on how to approach future meetings in order to ensure their usefulness to everyone concerned.

Regarding the elimination of the backlog of reports from States on their implementation of resolution 1373(2001), the Committee examined ways of updating the reporting regime, including ensuring that all aspects of resolution 1373(2001) were included in future dialogues with States. It would also discuss with other related Council committees ways to jointly address the claim of reporting fatigue in the light of the World Summit's call for the Council to consider streamlining its reporting procedure (see p. 48).

In terms of assistance needs, the Committee assessed requirements and obtained agreement to share its findings with potential donors for 25 States. It also started sharing the needs assessments with the Counter-Terrorism Action Group. CTC intended to strengthen its dialogue with States to determine what each one needed in order to reach agreement on such needs and to stress the importance of achieving them. In that process, CTC would also enhance its cooperation with relevant international organizations and examine how its dialogue with potential donors could become more result-oriented.

The Committee would continue its discussions on ways to provide transparent guidance on the implementation of resolution 1373(2001) through the development of best practices and on how a human rights perspective might be incorporated into the Committee's policy and substantive work, while respecting the various aspects of its Council mandate. In that regard, the Committee intended to take steps to prepare for the

Council's comprehensive review of CTED, in line with resolution 1535(2004).

Comprehensive review of CTC Executive Directorate

On 15 December [S/2005/800], the CTC Chairman submitted the Committee's report for consideration by the Security Council, as part of its comprehensive review of the Counter-Terrorism Committee Executive Directorate (CTED). The review, requested by the Council in resolution 1535(2004) [YUN 2004, p. 79], by which CTED was created, assessed the Directorate's assistance to CTC, particularly in attaining the goals of the revitalization process set out in the CTC Chairman's 2004 report to the Council [ibid.]. It also reviewed the extent to which both the mandate and functioning of CTED would enable it best to fulfil that role in the future.

CTC stated that, as CTED only became fully staffed in September, it had not had the full benefit of CTED's expertise, thus making the results of the review not as comprehensive as intended. During that time, however, it had provided CTC with valuable support. CTC recommended that the Council clarify CTED's reporting lines, within the framework of Council resolution 1535(2004) and indicate its readiness to work with the Secretary-General on the matter. CTC agreed to develop policy guidance in all key areas of CTED's mandate, to update that guidance as necessary and to review it annually. CTC agreed on the need for CTED to develop and carry out implementation plans for each area of policy guidance, with clear objectives and targets, within an appropriate time line. Progress towards the objectives of the policy guidance would form part of CTC's quarterly reports to the Council on the implementation of resolution 1373(2001).

CTED, whose guiding principles were cooperation, transparency, even-handedness and consistency of approach, would have as its future focus high-priority areas such as: providing in-depth analysis of the implementation of resolution 1373(2001); enhancing dialogue with States, through a more tailored approach to their individual circumstances, including through letters, direct dialogue and more flexibility regarding visits; reviewing and proposing ways to update the reporting regime and taking into account the 2005 World Summit Outcome recommendation, contained in General Assembly resolution 60/1 (see p. 48), on consolidating reporting requirements in cooperation with other Security Council counter-terrorism-related subsidiary bodies; close cooperation with other relevant Council subsidiary bodies, particularly the Security Council Committees established pursuant to resolutions 1267(1999) and 1540(2004), including on information-sharing, visits and technical assistance; continuing effective capacity-building work, through strengthening the facilitation of technical assistance, with a view to creating measurable results to enable more States to receive the assistance needed to further their implementation of resolution 1373(2001); improving the assistance provided to Member States through publishing and developing best practices in all areas of resolution 1373 (2001); and reviewing and proposing how to further develop cooperation with international, regional and subregional organizations to enhance the synergy between their work and that of the Committee in furthering the implementation of resolution 1373(2001).

The Committee reaffirmed its responsibility to include the implementation of Council resolution 1624(2005) in its dialogue with Member States and resolve to help build capacity in that regard, including through spreading best legal practices and promoting the exchange of information. It recommended that the Security Council request that another comprehensive review of CTED be prepared by CTC by 31 December 2006.

SECURITY COUNCIL ACTION

On 21 December [meeting 5338], following consultations among Security Council members, the President made statement **S/PRST/2005/64** on behalf of the Council:

The Security Council reaffirms that terrorism in all its forms and manifestations constitutes one of the most serious threats to international peace and security, and that any acts of terrorism are criminal and unjustifiable, regardless of their motivation, wherever, whenever and by whomsoever committed.

The Council recalls its resolution 1535(2004), by which it decided to establish the Counter-Terrorism Committee Executive Directorate (hereinafter "CTED") as a special political mission under the policy guidance of the Security Council Committee established pursuant to resolution 1373(2001) concerning counter-terrorism (the Counter-Terrorism Committee) to enhance the ability of the Committee to monitor implementation of resolution 1373(2001) and effectively continue the capacity-building work in which it was engaged. At the same time, the Council decided to carry out a comprehensive review of CTED by 31 December 2005.

During today's consultations, the Council undertook this review and came to the following conclusions:

The Council endorsed the report prepared by the Counter-Terrorism Committee and forwarded to the Council, and agreed with the conclusions contained therein.

The Council noted that CTED had only been fully staffed since 6 September 2005 and welcomed the start that CTED had made on its objectives as set out in the revitalization process. It welcomed the fact that the Counter-Terrorism Committee, in consultation with the Secretary-General, had decided to declare CTED operational on 15 December 2005.

The Council recalled that the mandate of CTED flows from that of the Counter-Terrorism Committee and reaffirmed that the Committee has the sole responsibility for providing policy guidance to CTED. It also welcomed the fact that such guidance would be accompanied by implementation plans to enhance the ability of the Committee to effectively implement its mandate.

The Council agreed with the Secretary-General and with the Counter-Terrorism Committee that there was a need to clarify CTED's reporting lines, within the framework of resolution 1535(2004), and welcomed the Secretary-General's initiative in this regard. The Council expressed its readiness to work with him on this matter.

The Council welcomed the integration into the work of the Counter-Terrorism Committee of the issue of implementation by Member States of resolution 1624(2005).

The Council decided to carry out another comprehensive review of CTED by 31 December 2006, prepared by the Counter-Terrorism Committee.

Reports of States. Between January and December, the CTC Chairman transmitted to the Council President reports submitted by Member States on action they had taken or planned to implement resolution 1373(2001) and letters from the Committee requesting follow-up information: [S/2005/33-34, S/2005/61-63, S/2005/70-71, S/2005/90-95 & Add.1, S/2005/107-123, S/2005/161-166, S/2005/191-194, S/2005/213, S/2005/224-225, S/2005/231, S/2005/239, S/2005/255-260, S/2005/264-265 & Add.1, S/2005/276-277, S/2005/286-296, S/2005/347, S/2005/366-367, S/2005/370, S/2005/425, S/2005/441-443, S/2005/445, S/2005/455-456, S/2005/461, S/2005/466, S/2005/479, S/2005/481-484, S/2005/501-502 & Add.1, S/2005/516-519, S/2005/524, S/2005/551, S/2005/573, S/2005/583, S/2005/595, S/2005/671, S/2005/705, S/2005/822 & Corr.1-823, S/2005/846].

Action by Commission
on Crime Prevention and Criminal Justice

The Commission on Crime Prevention and Criminal Justice, at its fourteenth session (23-27 May) [E/2005/30], recommended to the Economic and Social Council for approval a draft resolution entitled "Strengthening international cooperation and technical assistance in promoting the implementation of the universal conventions and protocols related to terrorism within the framework of the activities of the United Nations Office on Drugs and Crime". That resolution was approved by the Council as **resolution 2005/19** (see p. 1232).

IAEA action

The General Conference of the International Atomic Energy Agency (IAEA), at its forty-ninth session (Vienna, Austria, 26-30 September) (see p. 1563), adopted resolution GC(49)/RES/10 on measures to protect against nuclear terrorism, in which it called for an early entry into force of the International Convention for the Suppression of Acts of Nuclear Terrorism, adopted by the General Assembly in resolution 59/290 of 13 April (see p. 1411). It also called on the Director-General to continue to implement Agency activities relevant to nuclear and radiological security and protection against nuclear and radiological terrorism.

Peacekeeping operations

In 2005, the General Assembly and the Security Council continued to oversee the management and operation of UN peacekeeping missions. The Council addressed key issues aimed at strengthening and streamlining the overall conduct of those operations, reviewed the mandates of several ongoing operations and created new ones to deal with new security concerns. The Assembly took action on a number of financial and administrative matters. In December, acting in concurrence with the Council, the Assembly established the Peacebuilding Commission and the Peacebuilding Support Office.

The Department of Peacekeeping Operations (DPKO) continued to implement the recommendations of the Special Committee on Peacekeeping Operations, whose mandate was to review the whole question of peacekeeping operations in all their aspects, as well as those of the Assembly.

General aspects of UN peacekeeping

Military information
management in peacekeeping operations

In November [A/60/596], the Secretary-General transmitted the report of the Office of Internal Oversight Services (OIOS) on the review of the effectiveness of military information management in UN peacekeeping operations. OIOS assessed the effectiveness of information management by the military component of peacekeeping operations in terms of reducing operational and security risks and enhancing mission performance. It also and examined DPKO's information management capability and effectiveness in mission planning and performance. The report addressed, in particular, the role of information management in contemporary peacekeeping, its organization, inter-mission information flow and management, backstopping support for information management, promotion of organizational learning and best practice, and the use of information technology.

OIOS found that the requirement for information management existed in all peacekeeping missions, but the size and composition of the management entity varied depending on the mandate, size of force and structure of the mission. Observing that information flow in peacekeeping appeared to be an excessively complex and tangled network, OIOS stated that mission-wide collaboration was essential for information management. It noted DPKO's efforts to simplify the flow of information in peacekeeping by establishing integrated central information collation and processing centres at the mission level by conceptualizing a Joint Mission Analysis Cell (JMAC) as a multidisciplinary entity analysing information from all sources and providing strategic information and assessments to senior mission management. A JMAC type organization had already been established in seven missions and DPKO had established a working group to develop a policy for the concept and structure of JMACs.

Regarding capacity for effective information management, OIOS found that in most peacekeeping operations staff functions at force headquarters did not have any specific order of battle, knowledge, experience or adequate skills for using the products of overt information management for tactical and strategic purposes. In the opinion of OIOS, the reluctance of the United Nations to acknowledge intelligence operations as an operational and strategic resource had limited staff functions to their most basic and generic tasks, preventing key mission staff from employing intelligence as a vital component and virtual substitute for the use of force, manpower and time.

OIOS therefore recommended that DPKO establish an integrated information management system, such as a JMAC, in all multidimensional peacekeeping operations and develop strategic guidance, relevant policies and guidelines for JMACs, with system-wide uniform application. The function and role of a JMAC should be distinct from that of the military information cell/force G2 branch (military information cell) as a mission-level asset for strategic information support. DPKO should review the field policy and guide peacekeeping operations to develop a specific order of battle and standard operating procedures. It should also develop clear guidelines

for the recruitment and selection of civilian and military staff to JMAC and the force G2 branch and a standardized training module for in-mission training; provide clear guidance to missions on the interface between JMAC and the public information officer in the framework of mission information management; and develop guidelines for integrating the functions of the military public information officer and the public information officer.

DPKO should further provide field missions with the requisite human, technical and financial resources to bolster, through publications and radio broadcasts, the mission's public information outreach and generate goodwill; institutionalize mechanisms for troop-contributing countries to communicate vital information inputs that could impact operational decisions; issue directives and guidelines for establishing and operating joint mission information management committees in regions where there was a UN regional office for information-sharing between field missions; and develop an institutional capacity for backstopping field missions by strengthening the monitoring and assessment capacity in the Situation Centre or the Current Military Operations Service. It should also develop mission-tailored packages containing templates, draft standard operating procedures, standard database formats and sample documents on information management; a compendium of best practices and lessons learned in information management; and a policy for providing technological support for information collection and for enhancing mission capacity for information analysis and synthesis. DPKO should provide a capability to perform and produce geographical and terrain analysis and to manage digital/analog geographic data, and review policies on communications monitoring and electronic countermeasures to enhance security and improve mission preparedness to deal with unexpected situations.

Military involvement in civil assistance in peacekeeping operations

In December [A/60/588], the Secretary-General transmitted the OIOS report on the review of military involvement in civil assistance in peacekeeping operations. The report focused on support provided to humanitarian activities by the military components of peacekeeping operations at the request of humanitarian organizations and agencies, and community support projects (CSPs) conducted. It addressed the coordination of such assistance with overall mission objectives and the enhancement of its effectiveness and efficiency.

OIOS found that, in addition to providing security, civil assistance had become a common activity of the military component in all missions, which led to the broadening of contemporary peacekeeping mandates in the context of multi-dimentional peace operations. While support for humanitarian activities was provided on request, CSPs were generally initiated and carried out by the military component itself. However, without a coherent and comprehensive approach to planning and strategy, coordination, guidance and support, continued improvisation would hamper the capacity of military components to support humanitarian activities and local communities. The current weaknesses in guidance to contingents on CSPs in missions, combined with disappointing feedback from humanitarian organizations and agencies regarding the efforts of military components to support local communities needed to be addressed in order to maximize the benefits of cooperation and synergy in the field. OIOS was confident that the results of discussions on integrated missions and civil-military coordination in missions, especially between DPKO and the Office for the Coordination of Humanitarian Affairs (OCHA), would be translated into clear instructions for military components in the near future. The next challenge was to build on the experience gained by military components supporting humanitarian activities and to pursue changes that addressed military involvement in civil assistance throughout the stages of a peacebuilding operation beyond the humanitarian emergency phase. Such efforts would equally require a comprehensive approach that took into account implications for planning, strategy, coordination, guidance and support.

OIOS recommended that DPKO ensure that, in mission planning, opportunities for military support to humanitarian organizations and agencies were identified and considered, in consultation with relevant partners; that mission-level planning documents included a strategy for CSPs that took into account the needs of the population on the ground and overall mission objectives; provide missions with guidance for coordinating CSPs and quick-impact projects; and review with OCHA the terms of reference and structural location of civilian officers responsible for civil-military coordination in missions to enhance their effectiveness and avoid duplication.

It also recommended that peacekeeping operations should inform humanitarian organizations and agencies in the mission area to submit their requests for military support to a specific point of contact, which would prioritize such requests from a humanitarian perspective and forward them to the military component for action,

and that such points should be established for different levels of command or different areas within the mission. DPKO should also promulgate its revised policy on civil-military coordination and ensure that it was fully reflected in all other relevant guidance material and served as the basis for the preparation of a generic standard operating procedure.

DPKO should complement the terms of reference for quick-impact projects with additional instructions on the preparation of mission-specific strategies and on their management, implementation and evaluation; advise missions, in consultation with OCHA, about their point of contact for advice on military involvement in civil assistance; and ensure that an adequate number of qualified personnel and a sufficient amount of support equipment were provided to missions for an effective civil-military coordination function at force, sector headquarters and contingent levels; update the generic training module on civil-military coordination contained in the standard generic training module level 1 to include more detail on the role of the military component in implementing CSPs and quick-impact projects, and the standard training module level 3 to include a separate module on civil-military coordination.

DPKO said that it agreed with and supported each recommendation and was already taking steps to implement some of them, which could form a support basis for some of its policy initiatives.

Operational capacity of UN military observers

In its report on the review of the operational capacity of UN Military Observers (UNMOs), transmitted to the General Assembly by the Secretary-General in April [A/59/764], OIOS noted that UNMOs played a crucial role in peacekeeping operations, which had evolved from monitoring compliance with ceasefire agreements to more complex tasks, including governance, humanitarian and human rights issues. However, the complexity of the environment and those new tasks did not appear to result in a commensurate revision of UNMOs role and operational modalities. OIOS reviewed the operational capacity of UNMOs, with a view to enhancing their effectiveness and efficiency in the context of multi-dimensional peacekeeping, focusing on command and control, selection and training, deployment, rotation and repatriation, use of advanced technology and administrative and logistics support. It also examined UNMO's role in missions vis-à-vis the armed contingents and how that effected their security and safety, and their cooperation and coordination with other mission components.

In terms of command and control, OIOS noted that, among the 13 missions with UNMOs, four different organizational structures were used: in the first structure, the Chief Military Observer (CMO) exercised full operational authority over the UNMOs; in the second, there was a separate chain of command for UNMOs who reported directly to the head of mission; the third followed the principle of "unity of command" with all military units under the operational authority of the Force Commander; and the fourth reflected a greater integration in UNMOs into the command and control chain of the contingent force. Among the difficulties reported were the lack of an effective flow of information in some missions, and the physical separation of the UNMOs chain of command from that of armed contingents resulting in structural restrictions for coordination at the lower tactical levels. OIOS believed that, to ensure effective integration, there should be a common communications plan and standard operating and reporting procedures, with priority given to a single and unified chain of command.

In the area of selection and training, the most pressing challenges were the different levels of military skills, training and experience of team members, language proficiency, driving, radio communications and map-reading skills.

Regarding safety and security, UNMOs were normally unarmed in forward locations, making them vulnerable to attack, hostage-taking and harassment. Their most common concerns were the availability of safe, reliable and efficient communications and their deployment to remote locations in small numbers, where they had to make independent arrangements for accommodation within local communities, which posed a major security risk.

OIOS also found that disruptions in cooperation and coordination between military units in general, and UNMOs and armed contingents in particular, often resulted from the lack of common understanding of their respective roles in the mission.

To improve the overall operational effectiveness of UNMOs in peacekeeping operations, OIOS recommended that DPKO develop a more generic and streamlined command and control structure for its peacekeeping missions with UNMOs and armed contingents that allowed effective integration of UNMOs at the Force Headquarters level through a single unified chain of command, while maintaining operational independence at sector and lower levels. It should also develop: a mechanism that ensured that UNMOs attended a recognized military observers' course at a na-

tional peacekeeping training centre prior to deployment; a system that helped identify troop-contributing countries that provided UNMOs who consistently performed poorly and recommended steps that improved standards and ensured compliance, and encouraged greater participation of female UNMOs in peacekeeping missions. DPKO should explore the use of a standby roster for improving its initial deployment of UNMOs, develop a system for staggering their arrival, rotation and repatriation, streamline the induction and checkout procedures, and develop a comprehensive security plan for UNMOs to help ensure that they operated within range of the VHF/HF communications systems of the armed contingents and were provided with armed escorts. Armed contingents should maintain a quick reaction team, with stand-by ground-to-air communications in each sector for response to emergency extraction/evacuation situations. Mission directives should emphasize that the responsibility for the security of UNMOs rested with the armed contingents, and UNMOs should be provided with a distinct identity to distinguish them from armed contingents in order to emphasize their unarmed status.

Mission plans should include an effective information reporting structure and a comprehensive communications plan to facilitate effective integration of UNMOs with other mission components. Proficient translators/interpreters should be made available to UNMO teams as required and each mission should have an exit strategy for UNMOs that built on established benchmarks and links with the post-peacekeeping phase. DPKO should also establish a focal point in the Military Adviser's office for UNMO policy issues.

HIV/AIDS and international peacekeeping operations

On 18 July [meeting 5228], the Security Council considered the question of HIV/AIDS in international peacekeeping operations. The Under-Secretary-General for Peacekeeping Operations, Jean-Marie Guéhenno, in briefing the Council on the subject, said that, since the adoption of resolution 1308(2000) [YUN 2000, p. 82] on the impact of AIDS on peace and security, a comprehensive strategy had been developed to reduce the risk of peacekeepers contracting or transmitting the virus while on mission. The key elements of that strategy were: the creation of specific mission capacity to address AIDS; ensuring the availability of condoms and observing universal medical precautions; developing voluntary counselling and testing capacities in missions; establishing monitoring and evaluation mechanisms; and setting up projects for outreach to local communities and mainstreaming the issue of AIDS into mission mandates. In terms of progress achieved in those areas, there were currently 10 AIDS advisers, compared to just four in 2000 deployed at major peacekeeping operations, supported by United Nations Volunteers and host country professionals, and focal points in the smaller missions. Since awareness-training was central to the strategy, DPKO was working closely with troop-contributing countries and the Joint United Nations Programme on HIV/AIDS (UNAIDS) to establish at least a basic level of AIDS awareness among all those working in peacekeeping operations and AIDS awareness-training was routinely included in all "train the trainer" courses, in military observer programmes and in other sessions organized and sponsored by DPKO to enhance national peacekeeping capabilities. AIDS awareness-training was also central to pre-deployment training for mission-specific personnel and formed part of induction training for all civilian personnel. The AIDS training module was revised to ensure that the issues of gender, codes of conduct and sexual abuse were fully reflected.

As the strategy also aimed at reinforcing support for AIDS prevention and mobilizing all DPKO personnel to deal with it, AIDS was high on the agenda of the conference of all force commanders and would continue to be part of the senior leadership training for those serving in peacekeeping operations. Training modules were tailored for specific occupational groups, such as public information officers and stress counsellors serving in the most difficult missions.

To assess the effectiveness of the training programmes, DPKO piloted an HIV/AIDS knowledge, attitude and practice survey in Liberia (May/June), in collaboration with the United States Centers for Disease Control and Prevention and UNAIDS, involving over 660 uniformed peacekeepers. The preliminary findings showed that awareness was generally high, with over 87 per cent of those in a mission for at least one month having received AIDS-awareness training since their arrival. However, only a small number had received training from within their battalions or detachments, and less than 2 per cent had been briefed on AIDS by their commanding officers while in the mission area.

To create greater capacity among peacekeepers, AIDS advisers conducted peer education programmes, drawing on UNAIDS peer education kit and awareness cards. UNAIDS and DPKO were also examining ways to create a network to maintain the capacity of peer educators when they returned home. The survey showed that of the peacekeepers surveyed, over 92 per cent were

tested for HIV as part of their preparation for deployment. DPKO's efforts focused not only on how to reduce the risk of HIV transmission, but also on how to capitalize on the positive potential of peacekeepers as agents of change.

Despite the lessons learned over the past five years, answers were still required to ascertain whether enough was done, whether the basic strategy was the right one and what additional investments were needed to sustain and strengthen those efforts.

The UNAIDS Executive Director, Peter Piot, reporting to the Council on the implementation of resolution 1308(2000), said that, in response to resolution 1308(2000), an Office on AIDS, Security and Humanitarian Response was established in the UNAIDS secretariat, with support from Denmark. Some one million AIDS-awareness cards were distributed in 13 languages through peacekeepers and national security forces, and a peer education kit, available in 11 languages, had become an integral part of the military training curricula in several troop-contributing countries. With the increasing focus on regional troop and mission management for peacekeeping, UNAIDS was engaged with key regional bodies and was supporting the African Union (AU) with its AIDS programmes for AU peacekeeping forces. UNAIDS was also working with the North Atlantic Treaty Organization and the Caribbean Community secretariat in developing comprehensive AIDS programmes for uniformed services.

UNAIDS was assisting 53 Member States with comprehensive programmes to address AIDS among uniformed services, and had signed formal partnership agreements with 15 ministries of defence, covering about 1.3 million active uniformed personnel. For the future, two great tasks related to AIDS and security had to be faced: expanding the knowledge of the broader impact of AIDS on human security and national stability in the most-affected countries and those in conflict and post-conflict situations; and dealing with classic security matters. The unstated goal underpinning resolution 1308(2000) that all peacekeepers and uniformed personnel be given the knowledge and means to protect themselves and others from HIV had not yet been achieved. The Executive Director expressed the hope that the Council would make that an explicit and time-bound goal and ensure that peacekeeping missions were given the means to meet their responsibilities with respect to HIV, and that they were held accountable for their performance in responding to AIDS.

SECURITY COUNCIL ACTION

On 18 July [meeting 5228], following consultations among Security Council members, the President made statement **S/PRST/2005/33** on behalf of the Council:

The Security Council reaffirms its commitment to the full implementation of resolution 1308(2000). The Council also recalls the Declaration of Commitment on HIV/AIDS adopted at the twenty-sixth special session of the General Assembly on 27 June 2001.

The Council welcomes the collaboration between the Department of Peacekeeping Operations of the Secretariat and the Joint United Nations Programme on HIV/AIDS and its co-sponsors to address HIV/AIDS awareness among peacekeeping personnel, both uniformed and civilian. The Council commends the Joint Programme for developing, in cooperation with interested States, national programmes to address HIV/AIDS among their uniformed personnel. The Council recognizes the significant number of direct and indirect beneficiaries of the programmes worldwide.

The Council recognizes that men and women in the uniformed services are vital elements in the fight against HIV/AIDS. The Council welcomes the efforts by Member States, including through existing national programmes, the Department of Peacekeeping Operations, the Joint Programme and other stakeholders, to counter the spread of the disease. The Council encourages Member States, in the preparation of their personnel for participation in peacekeeping operations, to employ best practices in HIV/AIDS education, prevention, awareness, countering stigma and discrimination, voluntary confidential counselling and testing, and care and treatment.

The Council also recognizes that United Nations peacekeeping personnel can be important contributors to the response to HIV/AIDS, particularly for vulnerable communities in post-conflict environments. The Council welcomes the action taken by the Secretary-General and the United Nations peacekeeping missions to integrate HIV/AIDS awareness in their mandated activities and outreach projects for vulnerable communities and urges them to pay particular attention to the gender dimensions of HIV/AIDS. In this context, the Council encourages further cooperation between the Department of Peacekeeping Operations and the Joint Programme and its co-sponsors, non-governmental organizations and civil society, bilateral and multilateral donors and national Governments.

The Council further recognizes that significant progress has been made in implementation of resolution 1308(2000) but that many challenges remain. The Council expresses its readiness to further promote and support the implementation of this resolution. In order to maintain and consolidate momentum, the Council welcomes regular briefings, as needed, by the Department of Peacekeeping Operations and the Joint Programme on the progress made, as a measure to strengthen commitment and accountability at the highest levels and ensure sustained monitoring and evaluation of the impact of programmes. The Council reaffirms its intention to

contribute, within its competence, to the attainment of the relevant objectives in the Declaration adopted at the twenty-sixth special session of the General Assembly in carrying out the Council's work, in particular in its follow-up to resolution 1308(2000).

Sexual exploitation and abuse in UN peacekeeping operations

OIOS report. On 5 January [A/59/661], the Secretary-General transmitted to the General Assembly the report of the Office of Internal Oversight Services (OIOS) on the investigation into numerous allegations of sexual exploitation and abuse of Congolese women and girls by UN peacekeepers serving with the United Nations Organization Mission in the Democratic Republic of the Congo (MONUC) (see p. 165). OIOS found that many of the 72 allegations originally reported could not be substantiated or even fully investigated because of their non-specific nature. It, however, compiled 20 case reports, 19 of which involved peacekeepers from three contingents. Six cases were fully substantiated, in two others, the identification of the perpetrator was not fully corroborated, and in the 11 remaining cases, the victims and witnesses were unable to clearly identify the perpetrators. OIOS therefore made a number of recommendations for corrective actions.

Special Committee consideration (January/ February). The Special Committee on Peacekeeping Operations (New York, 31 January–25 February) [A/59/19/Rev.1], expressed outrage at the large number of alleged sexual misconduct by military and civilian personnel at MONUC. The Special Committee felt that the issue needed to be viewed within a broader and systemic context and, in that respect, recommended a comprehensive and balanced approach to the problem. It emphasized the need for reinforced efforts and measures by the United Nations and Member States to ensure that military, civilian police and civilian personnel in UN peacekeeping missions were fully aware of their duties and obligations.

The Special Committee supported the Secretary-General's efforts to address the problem, and the need to strengthen the implementation of UN zero tolerance policy and standards of conduct, in order to provide clear and effective guidelines for all Member States contributing military, civilian police and personnel. The Special Committee requested the Secretary-General to submit a comprehensive report with recommendations on the issue by April, following which it would reconvene to review the report and submit its findings for consideration by the

Fifth (Administrative and Budgetary) Committee and the General Assembly.

The Assembly, in resolution 59/281 (see p. 129), endorsed the Special Committee's recommendations.

Report of Adviser to Secretary-General. On 24 March [A/59/710], the Secretary-General, in response to the Special Committee's request, submitted the report of his Adviser on Sexual Exploitation and Abuse by United Nations Peacekeeping Personnel, His Royal Highness Prince Zeid Ra'ad Zeid Al-Hussein (Jordan), entitled "A comprehensive strategy to eliminate future sexual exploitation and abuse in United Nations peacekeeping operations". The report discussed the problem under four main themes: the rules on standards of conduct; the investigative process; organizational, managerial and command responsibility; and individual disciplinary, financial and criminal accountability. It stated that in 2003, DPKO had investigated allegations of sexual exploitation and abuse implicating five staff and 19 military personnel. The Secretariat was aware that the data gathered on those cases might not reflect the true extent of those incidents; the complaint procedures and victim support mechanisms were not adequate; and a system for systematically reporting misconduct was required. Following improvements in the Organization's complaint mechanism, the number of allegations received against peacekeeping personnel increased significantly. In 2004, DPKO received 105 allegations, 16 of which were against civilians, 9 against civilian police and 80 against military personnel. Forty-five per cent of those allegations related to sex with persons under 18 years of age, 31 per cent with adult prostitutes, while rape and sexual assault comprised 13 and 5 per cent, respectively. The remaining 6 per cent was related to other forms of sexual abuse and exploitation, as defined in the Secretary-General's bulletin on the subject [YUN 2004, p. 107].

The report noted that efforts to address the problem were ad hoc and inadequate, and a radical change was needed in the way it was addressed in peacekeeping contexts. During the Adviser's visit to the Democratic Republic of the Congo (DRC), women's organizations drew attention to several external factors they believed contributed to the problem, including the erosion of the social fabric by the ongoing conflict, the lack of income-generation possibilities, the high incidence of sexual violence against women and children during the conflict, discrimination, exploitative behaviour against them, and the lack of a well-functioning legal and judicial system, thereby encouraging impunity. On the other hand, MONUC personnel seemed to share a perception that little was being done to deal effectively with the problem, and that whistle-blowers would not be protected. There was little awareness of UN standards of conduct, inadequate recreational facilities and protracted periods of separation from families and communities.

Regarding the Organization's rules, the report concluded that the difficulty of dealing with sexual exploitation and abuse was compounded by the many categories of personnel in a mission, each governed by different rules. However, although the responsibility for the conduct and discipline of troops rested with troop-contributing countries, the Assembly should apply the rules set out in the Secretary-General's bulletin on special measures for protection from sexual exploitation and abuse to all categories of UN peacekeeping personnel. Those standards, as well as those set out in the publications entitled "Ten Rules: Code of Personal Conduct for Blue Helmets" and "We Are United Nations Peacekeepers", should be included in each memorandum of understanding signed with each troop-contributing country, whose obligation should be to ensure that those rules were binding on their national contingents. The rules should also be readily available to all members of a peacekeeping mission, including in card form and in the languages of the various contingents.

Concerning investigations into alleged sexual exploitation and abuse conducted by the Organization, the report recommended that a permanent professional mechanism be established to investigate complex cases of serious misconduct in that regard. An expert in military law should participate in any investigation to ensure that evidence was gathered in accordance with national law. Troop-contributing countries should share information obtained through its contingent's investigations and hold on-site courts martial to facilitate access to witnesses and evidence in the peacekeeping area. Those countries whose legislation did not so permit should consider reforming their legislation.

In relation to organizational, managerial and command accountability, a series of measures were recommended, including extensive training, an effective programme of outreach to the local community, a data collection system to track the investigation and resolution of allegations and the establishment of full-time positions at Headquarters and in the field to coordinate action by missions on those issues. Mission-specific measures were also recommended to deal with the problem and to help make life at the missions less difficult. In addition, the United Nations should offer basic assistance to alleged victims.

There should be strict disciplinary accountability for peacekeeping personnel who violated the Organization's rules relating to sexual exploitation and abuse, and in that context, the Assembly should define acts of sexual exploitation and abuse as serious misconduct in the Staff Regulations and request the Secretary-General to introduce expedited procedures to deal with such cases. Troop-contributing countries should also endeavour to bring implicated members of their contingent to justice.

UN peacekeeping personnel should be held financially accountable for harm caused to victims as a result of their acts of sexual exploitation and abuse. In particular, the Assembly should authorize DNA and other tests to establish paternity and obligate peacekeeping personnel to provide financial support to so-called peacekeeper babies. The model memorandum of understanding should require troop-contributing countries to ensure that their contingents respected local law and to exercise criminal jurisdiction over their troops. The Secretary-General should appoint a group of experts to advise on the feasiblility of drafting an international instrument or the use of other means to ensure that UN personnel were subject to criminal prosecution for defined crimes of sexual exploitation and abuse.

Special Committee consideration (April). The Special Committee on Peacekeeping Operations, at its resumed session (New York, 4-8 April) [A/59/19/Rev.1], having considered the report of the Secretary-General's Special Adviser (see above), recognized the shared responsibility of the Secretariat and Member States in preventing sexual exploitation and abuse by all categories of personnel in UN peacekeeping missions and in enforcing UN standards of conduct. The Special Committee was committed to implementing fundamental, systematic changes as a matter of urgency and adopted a number of recommendations, which were without prejudice to the right of troop-contributing countries to exercise exclusive jurisdiction over their own contingents.

The Special Committee welcomed the standards set out in the Secretary-General's bulletin on special measures for protection from sexual exploitation and abuse and recommended that the Assembly endorse them for all categories of UN peacekeeping personnel. The Secretary-General should issue the standards in a manner convenient to troop-contributing countries, in the languages of contingent members and in UN official languages. DPKO should provide training on the requisite standards of conduct, particularly on the detailed prohibitions in the Secretary-General's bulletin.

The Special Committee urged the full integration of the Office of the Special Adviser on Gender Issues and Advancement of Women in efforts to encourage the reporting of abuse and to promote an environment that discouraged such acts. It highlighted the need for welfare and recreational services to be made available to all categories of personnel in peacekeeping missions. In that regard, the Secretary-General should carry out a comprehensive review, including a cost-benefit analysis, of welfare and recreational needs. That should also include: a review of the rules on rest and recreation and the classification of duty stations as family or non-family for UN civilian staff; the need for welfare officers and stress counsellors; the development of minimum standards of welfare and recreational facilities for all categories of personnel; and the effectiveness of the system of welfare payments. Related proposals should be made to the Assembly's sixtieth (2005) session.

The Secretary-General should establish a data collection and management system at Headquarters and in the field to track allegations of sexual exploitation and abuse and responses of missions to those allegations, which should ensure that prior offenders were not rehired, and track nonspecific allegations since they might indicate a problem requiring managerial response.

The Special Committee recommended: the strengthening of DPKO's capacity to address all cases of misconduct, including sexual exploitation and abuse, provide prompt advice to missions, ensure the coherent application of UN procedures, and provide guidance and advice for all categories of civilian and uniformed personnel; measures to protect persons disclosing sexual exploitation and abuse from intimidation; and the establishment of a professional and independent investigative capacity to investigate alleged sexual exploitation and abuse and other allegations of misconduct of a similar grave nature. DPKO, in cooperation with the Department of Public Information, should establish an effective outreach programme to explain the Organization's policy relating to sexual exploitation and abuse, and effective mechanisms to allow individuals to make related complaints in a confidential setting. DPKO should also provide feedback to alleged victims on the outcome of their complaints and of the mission's investigation, giving due regard to the privacy laws of Member States.

The Secretary-General should provide the Special Committee, at its 2006 session, with a comprehensive strategy for assisting victims of sexual exploitation and abuse, including financial compensation. In the meantime, missions should provide emergency assistance to victims within mission budgets. Staff Regulations and contracts with United Nations Volunteers, consultants and individual contractors should be amended to specifically provide that acts of sexual exploitation and abuse constituted serious misconduct.

The Special Committee, noting that the report of the Secretary-General's Adviser included recommendations on the content of the model memorandum of understanding between the United Nations and troop-contributing countries, said it was informed that the model, which was last reported to the Assembly in 1997 [YUN 1997, p. 55], had not been adopted as a basis for negotiation with individual troop-contributing countries. The Committee therefore recommended that the Secretary-General prepare a revised draft model memorandum of understanding, and submit it to the Special Committee for consideration in 2006.

The Secretary-General should appoint a group of legal experts to prepare and submit to the Assembly at its sixtieth (2005) session, a comprehensive report providing advice on: the best way to ensure that the original intent of the Charter would be achieved, namely that UN staff and experts on missions would not be effectively exempted from the consequences of criminal acts committed at their duty station, nor unjustly penalized, in accordance with due process; whether, and if so, how, the standards in the Secretary-General's bulletin could bind contingent members in the period prior to the conclusion of a memorandum of understanding or other agreement or action by a troop-contributing country that incorporated those standards under its national law; and to study and propose ways of standardizing the norms of conduct applicable to all categories of peacekeeping personnel, paying particular attention to the issue of sexual exploitation and abuse. He should also provide a progress report on the implementation of the recommendations as part of his annual report to the Special Committee at its next regular (2006) session.

Security Council consideration. On 31 May [meeting 5191], the Security Council considered the reports of the Special Committee and the Secretary-General's Adviser on the subject. In his briefing to the Council, the Secretary-General's Adviser said that it was well known that, in the early 1960s, the United Nations Operation in the Congo had faced difficulties relating to discipline of some of its personnel, and since 1989, similar reports had surfaced in practically every subsequent mission. Over the past 60 years, Member States had refrained from opening that subject to public discourse because of pride and a deep sense of embarrassment, which only produced outright denials. Not only were abuses by peacekeepers repugnant, they struck at the credibility of the operation in question and the Organization as a whole. In order to overcome those difficulties, Member States had to resolve to recognize the truth openly, however painful that might be. While highlighting actions being taken to implement the recommendations of the Special Committee, the Secretary-General's Adviser indicated that it would be prudent to expect that further allegations could emerge in the future due to the Secretariat's strengthening of the system for lodging complaints. DPKO and OIOS would continue to coordinate on developing a standing procedure for launching investigations, and the relationship between OIOS and troop-contributing countries on investigations would need further refinement. The Adviser expressed hope that in 2006, the Special Committee would take up those recommendations and ideas in his report that were not addressed at its resumed session. He intended to propose again the holding of in-mission courts martial for the worst offences.

The Under-Secretary-General for Peacekeeping Operations, Jean-Marie Guéhenno, told the Council that combating sexual exploitation and abuse was one of DPKO's highest priorities and it had made significant progress in investigating related allegations and putting in place wide-ranging measures to prevent the problem. Over the past year, field missions had instituted numerous measures to prevent misconduct and enforce UN standards of conduct, such as providing training on aspects of those standards relating to sexual exploitation and abuse at missions in Côte d'Ivoire, Liberia and Sierra Leone and there were plans to make such training mandatory for all peacekeeping personnel arriving at missions. In 2004, DPKO issued a policy on human trafficking that was accompanied by a resource manual on the issue and included a training module and practical guidance for peacekeeping operations. In early 2005, awareness-raising posters on sexual exploitation and abuse and brochures on human trafficking were distributed to all missions.

Citing the Secretary-General's 9 February letter to the Council [S/2005/79], Mr. Guéhenno noted that MONUC had put in place mission-specific measures to minimize misconduct and was strengthening managerial accountability by requiring regional heads of office to prepare workplans for preventing sexual exploitation and abuse. At Headquarters, DPKO had established a task force to develop guidance and tools for peacekeeping operations to address sexual exploitation and abuse effectively, and was co-chairing, with the United Nations Office for the Coordination of Humanitarian Affairs, an inter-agency task force aimed at developing an organizational culture throughout the UN system that prevented such acts. It was also developing common policies and guidance on victim assistance. The Department was cooperating closely with OIOS to develop suggestions for discussion with troop-contributing countries on how to facilitate their participation in OIOS investigations involving military peacekeeping personnel.

In 2005, DPKO reported 340 new allegations of which 217 were against uniformed personnel (involving 193 military and 24 civilian police officers), while about 123 were against civilian staff. Eighty allegations involved UN staff and 42 were related to other UN civilian personnel, which included individual contractors, consultants, Junior Professional Officers and UN Volunteers. With regard to cases involving DPKO and other civilian personnel, as at December, four allegations were deemed as requiring no further action and 68 were investigated, 33 of which were sent to Headquarters for disciplinary action, 1 was pending investigation, 14 were substantiated and four were unsubstantiated. Sixteen cases involving civilian personnel were sent to Boards of Inquiry for investigation. As of September 2005, cases of sexual exploitation and abuse from DPKO's field missions were referred to OIOS.

SECURITY COUNCIL ACTION

On 31 May [meeting 5191], following consultations among Security Council members, the President made statement **S/PRST/2005/21** on behalf of the Council:

> The Security Council recognizes the vital role that United Nations peacekeeping operations have played for decades in bringing peace and stability to countries emerging from war. The Council further recognizes that, with few exceptions, the women and men who serve in United Nations peacekeeping operations do so with the utmost professionalism, dedication and, in some cases, make the ultimate sacrifice.
>
> The Council is deeply concerned about the allegations of sexual misconduct by United Nations peacekeeping personnel. The distinguished and honourable record of accomplishment in United Nations peacekeeping is being tarnished by the acts of a few individuals.
>
> The Council condemns, in the strongest terms, all acts of sexual abuse and exploitation committed by United Nations peacekeeping personnel. The Council reiterates that sexual exploitation and abuse are unacceptable and have a detrimental effect on the fulfilment of mission mandates.
>
> The Council, while confirming that the conduct and discipline of troops is primarily the responsibil-

ity of troop-contributing countries, recognizes the shared responsibility of the Secretary-General and all Member States to take every measure within their purview to prevent sexual exploitation and abuse by all categories of personnel in United Nations peacekeeping missions and to enforce United Nations standards of conduct in this regard. The Council reiterates the importance of ensuring that sexual exploitation and abuse are properly investigated and appropriately punished.

> The Council underlines the fact that the provision of an environment in which sexual exploitation and abuse are not tolerated is primarily the responsibility of managers and commanders.
>
> The Council welcomes the comprehensive report on sexual exploitation and abuse by United Nations peacekeeping personnel, prepared by the Adviser to the Secretary-General on this issue, Prince Zeid Ra'ad Zeid Al-Hussein, Permanent Representative of the Hashemite Kingdom of Jordan to the United Nations. The Council also welcomes the report of the Special Committee on Peacekeeping Operations and its Working Group on its resumed session.
>
> The Council urges the Secretary-General and troop-contributing countries to ensure that the recommendations of the Special Committee, which fall within their respective responsibilities, are implemented without delay.
>
> The Council will consider including relevant provisions for prevention, monitoring, investigation and reporting of misconduct cases in its resolutions establishing new mandates or renewing existing mandates. In this regard, the Council calls upon the Secretary-General to include, in his regular reporting on peacekeeping missions, a summary of the preventive measures taken to implement a zero-tolerance policy and of the outcome of actions taken against personnel found culpable of sexual exploitation and abuse.

GENERAL ASSEMBLY ACTION

On 22 June [meeting 104], the General Assembly, on the recommendation of the Fourth (Special Political and Decolonization) Committee [A/59/472/Add.2], adopted **resolution 59/300** without vote [agenda item 77].

Comprehensive review of a strategy to eliminate future sexual exploitation and abuse in United Nations peacekeeping operations

The General Assembly,

Recalling its resolution 2006(XIX) of 18 February 1965 and all other relevant resolutions,

Recalling in particular its resolution 58/315 of 1 July 2004,

Recalling its resolution 59/281 of 29 March 2005, in which it endorsed the recommendation in paragraph 56 of the report of the Special Committee on Peacekeeping Operations that the Secretary-General make available to the United Nations membership, no later than the first week of April 2005, a comprehensive report on the issue of sexual exploitation and abuse by military, civilian police and civilian personnel in United Nations peacekeeping operations,

Noting that the Secretary-General, on 24 March 2005, transmitted to the President of the General Assembly a report of his Adviser concerning sexual exploitation and abuse by United Nations peacekeeping personnel,

Affirming the need for the Organization to adopt without delay a comprehensive strategy to eliminate future sexual exploitation and abuse in United Nations peacekeeping operations as recommended by the Special Committee and the Adviser to the Secretary-General,

Convinced of the need for the United Nations to take strong and effective steps in this regard,

1. *Welcomes* the report of the Adviser to the Secretary-General;

2. *Endorses* the proposals, recommendations and conclusions of the Special Committee on Peacekeeping Operations, contained in chapter II of the report on its 2005 resumed session;

3. *Urges* Member States, the Secretariat and the relevant organs of the United Nations to take all necessary steps to implement the proposals, recommendations and conclusions of the Special Committee, and supports the request of the Special Committee to the Secretary-General that he provide a progress report on the implementation of the recommendations of the Special Committee at its next regular session;

4. *Requests* the Special Committee to include this issue in its report to the General Assembly at its sixtieth session.

On the same date, the Assembly took further action on the question of sexual exploitation and abuse in section XIV of **resolution 59/296** on the administrative and budgetary aspects of UN peacekeeping operations: cross-cutting issues (see p. 133).

Strengthening operational capacity

The Secretary-General, in his report on the implementation of the recommendations of the Special Committee on Peacekeeping Operations [A/59/608 & Corr.1], outlined proposals for filling the gaps in UN peacekeeping capabilities. He proposed a strategic reserve for UN peacekeeping, comprising a number of task forces of some 1,250 troops each. Each task force would be held within the national command of a troop contributor and would be a combined-arms force, with enabling units capable of sustained operations. The task forces would be drawn from a geographical range of troop-contributing countries, each of which would secure prior political and legislative agreement to deploy, obviating the time-consuming process of securing agreement immediately prior to deployment. The task forces would be configured in a structure of "graduated readiness", and once deployed, would come under the command of the Force Commander. The strategic reserve would be deployed for a specific duration and task, and would return to the troop-contributing country upon the completion of that task. It would focus mainly on stabilization, but could provide an interim capability pending deployment of other forces.

The Secretary-General also proposed a standing civilian police capacity for two to three years and comprising up to 100 police officers, to be deployed in teams of 10 to 20 in mission areas to support early planning and needs assessments, the building up of mission headquarters, the setting up of a well functioning civilian police component to develop sustainable local police structures and periodic evaluations related to mandate implementation.

The Special Committee, at its 2005 substantive session [A/59/19/Rev.1], while noting the unprecedented increase in peacekeeping operations, recognized that the current level of resources limited the scope and number of missions that DPKO could effectively undertake and manage. It recommended that DPKO evaluate how and to what extent the complexity of peacekeeping mandates affected the operational efficiency of peacekeeping missions, with a view to reporting its findings to the Special Committee in 2006. The Special Committee noted with concern the Secretary-General's assessment that UN peacekeeping continued to face significant gaps, particularly in regard to enabling and niche capabilities and strategic lift operations.

While recognizing that the UN's ability to rapidly deploy and support forces continued to improve, the Special Committee noted that initiatives to strengthen regional arrangements would provide readily available and deployable forces to reduce deployment time lines. It believed that a definitive review of the effectiveness of the UN standby arrangement system was necessary, and while supporting the call for rapid deployment, urged the Secretariat to optimize all aspects of pre-mandate operational preparedness and deployment. It called for a more efficient management of the financial and logistical aspects of peacekeeping operations at Headquarters and in the field, in order to make deployment both rapid and effective. To overcome the contingent-owned equipment and sustainability shortfall faced by some troop-contributing countries, the Special Committee recommended that DPKO continue to facilitate various enabling arrangements, including through other Member States and bilateral arrangements.

The Special Committee welcomed initiatives to improve the operational effectiveness of UN peacekeeping operations, including the creation of tactical and force-level reserves in mission areas, and took note of the Secretary-General's strategic reserve initiative to provide existing peacekeeping missions with a robust and capable reserve, to be called upon if required (see above). Furthermore, questions such as the composition of task forces, the decision-making processes for deployment, command and control arrangements, complementarity with other crisis response initiatives, sustainability and financial implications, among others, had to be answered before the Special Committee could reach firm conclusions on related proposals. The Special Committee recommended that DPKO work closely with Member States to answer those questions.

Civilian rapid deployment roster

In a March report [A/59/763], submitted in response to General Assembly resolution 58/298 [YUN 2004, p. 96], the Secretary-General described the status of the pilot civilian rapid deployment roster, established in 2003 [YUN 2003, p. 99] as a mechanism whereby UN staff members were selected and included in a roster for deployment at short notice for a limited time to perform critical functions at start-up, surge or liquidation phases of peacekeeping operations. The report also analysed the achievements and shortcomings of the mechanism and made recommendations to improve its utility.

As at July 2004, 57 staff members on the roster had been deployed to six missions. The operation of the mechanism was evaluated internally by the Personnel Management and Support Service and further reviewed by the Peacekeeping Best Practices Unit, during which various aspects were examined, including communications, process and commitment, the composition of the roster, applications, the selection and clearance process, deployment, medical clearance, length of deployment, the training programme and management and resources.

The reviews revealed, among other findings, that the actual purpose and implementation of the roster, its administration, funding and the permissible length of deployment, remained unclear. Some releasing missions were reluctant to release selected staff, while some receiving missions questioned the qualifications of the staff member selected. Critical posts were left vacant or without a sufficient number of candidates, and wide differences were observed between the qualifications of applicants included on the roster and the technical skills required.

Addressing the way forward, the Secretary-General observed that the value of a civilian rapid deployment roster mechanism was clearly demonstrated, despite the constraints identified. The roster would be extended to fully encompass the needs of missions during the start-up, surge and liquidation phases, and the team structure replaced by a single integrated roster, with a revised list of critical functions for which a specific number of staff would be selected. The new roster would comprise approximately 365 civilian staff members.

Comprehensive revised procedures would be communicated to all field missions and DPKO would explain the mechanism and its implementation modalities, clarifying that the roster facility was not a transfer or promotion mechanism, nor a substitute for the regular recruitment process. To ensure a larger pool of candidates, particularly for senior positions and functions, the application process would be extended to other Secretariat offices and possibly to UN Volunteers. The Secretary-General recommended that the civilian rapid deployment facility be closely linked to other DPKO rapid deployment initiatives.

Other major changes would be introduced in the revised selection and clearance process, which would enable DPKO or the missions to nominate staff members for inclusion on the roster. Individual staff members could also continue to voluntarily request inclusion in the roster. Staff would remain on the roster for one year, and the maximum deployment period would be extended to 120 days. With the concurrence of both the receiving and releasing missions, roster staff might apply for a position in the receiving mission but would have to return to their parent mission for a minimum period of three months. An evaluation mechanism would be built into the new procedures.

A rapid deployment roster management capacity would be established within the Personnel Management and Support Service to coordinate the selection and clearance process, monitor the roster, identify gaps and issue application request announcements to ensure that the roster remained populated and updated, and meet with staff and supervisors to promote and discuss the programme. Focal points would also be appointed in each technical entity in the Secretariat to provide technical advice and help to locate candidates. The roster would be renewed annually.

The Secretary-General concluded that the roster was one way of meeting DPKO's urgent operational requirements. The Department would report on efforts to build such a cadre in its comprehensive report on the conditions of field service.

In April [A/59/736], ACABQ considered the Secretary-General's report on the status of the civilian rapid deployment roster. Taking note of the selection criteria for the mechanism, the findings of an internal evaluation and review of its operation and the Secretary-General's recommendations for improving its utility, ACABQ encouraged the maximum use of existing personnel management and database systems, including the Galaxy recruitment system, in managing the roster, particularly in terms of improving its efficiency and reducing management costs. It requested the Secretariat to increase cooperation with UN agencies, funds and programmes in establishing the humanitarian, development and disarmament, demobilization and reintegration components of the roster to ensure that the requirements of integrated missions were fully met.

Strategies for complex peacekeeping operations

The Special Committee on Peacekeeping Operations, at its 2005 substantive session (31 January–25 February) [A/59/19/Rev.1], recognized the need for DPKO to plan peacekeeping missions so as to facilitate an effective approach to peacebuilding and long-term prevention of the recurrence of armed conflict. It encouraged the Secretariat to develop coherent strategies and early integrated mission planning based on lessons learned in the areas of disarmament, demobilization and reintegration, strengthening of the rule of law, security sector reform, quick-impact projects and mine action, with a view to restoring immediate security and stability in post-conflict societies.

Underlining the need for clear and well-defined mandates and exit strategies for complex peacekeeping operations, the Special Committee called for the inclusion of peacebuilding elements in complex mandates to generate enabling conditions to prevent the recurrence of armed conflict. In that regard, it looked forward to the detailed review of UN system capacity to be included in the Secretary-General's report to the General Assembly's resumed fifty-ninth (2005) session on the implementation of resolution 57/337 [YUN 2003, p. 50].

The Special Committee welcomed DPKO's intention to develop guidance and training for civil/military cooperation in peacebuilding activities and called on the Secretary-General to report on best practices for the peacekeeping, humanitarian/development interface for Member States' consideration.

The Special Committee stressed the need for effective planning for the transition from peacekeeping to peacebuilding and to long-term development and to strengthen the financing of post-conflict assistance. It also encouraged cooperation with the business community, including the provision of employment opportunities to demobilized fighters as a contribution to reconstruction and post-conflict resolution.

The Special Committee called for long-term donor commitment to support disarmament, demobilization and reintegration programmes, and requested the Secretary-General to identify the additional resources needed to support donor capacity in that regard. It welcomed progress by DPKO and other UN agencies in developing UN integrated standards on disarmament, demobilization and reintegration as well as on a comprehensive weapons management strategy, encouraged them to complete those processes. The Special Committee also took note of the Stockholm Initiative on Disarmament, Demobilization and Reintegration launched in 2004 by 23 countries and 14 organizations, including UN agencies, to review current practice in that area and to strengthen intervention that supported peace processes. The initiative was examined and further defined during subsequent meetings. A final conference (Stockholm, Sweden, 17-18 November) discussed the Initiative's aims, outline and recommendations.

Recognizing the importance of quick-impact projects in addressing local needs, building and sustaining confidence and supporting peacekeeping operations, the Special Committee recommended that the selection procedure for those projects be addressed at the field level, that resources for them directly support the mission's mandate, and that they either respond to needs not covered by existing development and humanitarian assistance efforts, or serve as a catalyst to broaden those efforts.

Noting that a UN peacekeeping mission might be mandated to assist in building or reforming rule of law capacities, it encouraged the Secretariat to work towards the strategic and operational planning of peacekeeping operations to fulfil such mandates. It also encouraged DPKO to give special attention to the protection, welfare and rights of children in armed conflict.

The Special Committee looked forward to the Secretary-General's comprehensive strategy and action plan for mainstreaming gender perspectives into all peacekeeping activities and to reviewing that strategy in 2006, and DPKO's status reports on those initiatives. It commended the introduction of mandatory pre-deployment gender training for military, civilian and civilian police personnel and the issuance of guidance on human trafficking. It also encouraged Member States and the Secretariat to increase the participation of women in all aspects and levels of peacekeeping operations and stressed the need for ongoing reporting by the Secretary-General on the implementation of gender mainstreaming in the field and at Headquarters.

The Special Committee also recommended that, within the integrated mission planning process, DPKO should provide the concept of operations and the operational plan for the information of potential troop-contributing countries and regional organizations as early as possible in the mission planning process in order to facilitate national planning prior to submitting recommendations to the Security Council.

Safety and security

Security Council action. On 2 March, the Security Council, in statement **S/PRST/2005/ 10** (see p. 167), condemned a 25 February attack against a patrol of the United Nations Mission in the Democratic Republic of the Congo (MONUC), which resulted in the death of nine Bangladeshi peacekeepers.

Special Committee consideration. The Special Committee on Peacekeeping Operations, at its 2005 substantive session [A/59/19/Rev.1], expressed concern about the precarious security environment in many field missions and called on the Secretariat to give priority to enhancing the safety and security of United Nations and associated personnel in the field. It condemned the killing of military and civilian police officers in several missions and recognized that those attacks and other acts of violence constituted a major challenge to UN field operations. The Department of Safety and Security and DPKO needed to coordinate activities in order to provide integrated, unified security assessments and operational advice and support to crisis management to peacekeeping missions. The Secretariat should improve its capacity for the collection, analysis and dissemination of information and provide a concept definition or policy paper on joint mission analysis cells, setting out, among other things, the details of their structure, functions and role, with the aim of providing information on the various components in the context of both new and existing peacekeeping operations.

The Special Committee was concerned about the safety and security of military observers and other unarmed UN personnel deployed in UN peacekeeping operations and asked the Secretariat to provide greater clarity on measures taken to enhance their security. It stressed the need for correct risk assessments prior to the deployment of military observers and other unarmed UN personnel in difficult areas and called upon the Secretariat to ensure that they were provided with adequate security.

Welcoming improved information flow to troop-contributing countries, the Committee encouraged the Secretariat to maintain that flow. It agreed that, as the United Nations enhanced its capacity to gather field information and assess risks, all forms of technical monitoring and surveillance means, particularly aerial monitoring, should be explored to ensure the safety of peacekeepers, especially in volatile and dangerous conditions and in situations too dangerous for visual ground monitoring. The Secretary-General should provide in his next report to the Committee a comprehensive assessment in that regard, based on lessons learned.

The Special Committee stressed the need for DPKO to incorporate in measures to deal with aerial accidents the lessons learned from past incidents and to maintain the highest possible standards of air safety, especially when subcontracting air transport.

OIOS report. During the year, OIOS conducted a global audit of field security management at 15 field missions managed by DPKO and five political and peacebuilding missions administered by the Department of Political Affairs. As stated in the OIOS report [A/59/702], the audit, which assessed the effectiveness of field security management, aimed to help enhance the security of UN personnel in the field during a period of heightened risk. The audit found that basic security arrangements were being improved in the majority of missions and that good practices prevailed in some duty stations. The Office of the United Nations Security Coordinator (UNSECOORD) and DPKO had cooperated in strengthening security management. However, improvements were needed both at Headquarters and in field security structures, as well as in security plans and policies and their implementation, deployment and personnel administration, budgeting and resourcing, coordination with host Governments and external military forces and among UN agencies, and physical security. Other major findings included the need to clarify the roles and responsibilities of various security governing bodies, and that country-wide security organization in various countries needed to be re-examined, and reporting lines of security officers clearly defined. In some duty stations, no official memorandum of understanding or protocol (status of forces/mission agreement) on security issues was signed with the host Government and/or the external military forces, and the attendance by agencies at country-wide security management team meetings was poor. In other duty stations, the security plan was either incomplete or out of date and, in many cases, not tested or rehearsed. The security warden system was deficient, internal communications between staff and the mission security section was poor and there was inadequate awareness of the importance of security arrangements among UN personnel while the minimum operating security standards recommended by UNSECOORD had not yet been established by DPKO as a policy requirement.

Some missions had insufficient resources to ensure compliance with security requirements, as there was no separate budget line for security costs in mission budgets. The vacancy rate for security posts was high in many missions, and security training was often inadequate. In some missions, security arrangements for officials designated as "at risk" were inadequate, close protection was not always provided to high-ranking officials and perimeter security and access control procedures for visitors needed to be improved.

OIOS recommended that the Secretary-General issue a single policy document/manual incorporating all security-related directives and procedures, clearly identifying the roles and responsibilities of those expected to carry out security functions in the field and with additional clarification of those functions provided to missions when necessary. UNSECOORD and DPKO should direct all designated officials and heads of mission to improve security training for all UN staff at duty stations and to increase their awareness of the security arrangements; ensure that the composition and performance of the security management teams at the countrywide and mission levels met relevant UN policy requirements; improve the security warden system in duty stations and ensure that missions maintained updated staff lists, including dependants and contact information for each person. They should also ensure that mission and countrywide security plans were complete, updated and tested and that missions adhered to guidelines and requirements for providing close protection to senior officials.

DPKO should ensure that proper reporting lines and accountability mechanisms for security matters in field missions were established and review the practices for recruiting chief security officers; require peacekeeping missions to use UNSECOORD minimum operating security standards when implementing security management programmes; and request the Controller to establish separate budget lines in peacekeeping missions' budgets for the security function to facilitate the planning and monitoring of security-related expenditures. It should also address the understaffing of security posts and take immediate remedial action; streamline the procedure for acquiring essential security and safety equip-

ment; ensure that the strategic deployment stocks at the UN Logistics Base at Brindisi, Italy, had essential security equipment available for rapid deployment to new missions; that designated officials took action to improve coordination at the countrywide and mission levels and strengthen communication and cooperation with the respective host Governments and external military forces; and clarify the authority and mechanisms regarding the declaration and revision of security phases.

DPKO and the Department of Safety and Security agreed with the majority of the recommendations, some of which they had already taken action to implement.

By **decision 60/551** of 23 December, the General Assembly deferred until its resumed sixtieth session consideration of the OIOS report on the global audit of field security management.

Cooperation with regional organizations

The Special Committee on Peacekeeping Operations [A/59/19/Rev.1], recognizing that regional arrangements had unique and complementary capacities to offer within the context of cooperation with UN peacekeeping operations, urged the United Nations to strengthen its operational linkages and partnerships with those organizations. It called on DPKO to continue to explore the concept of trilateral arrangements among the United Nations, regional arrangements and donor countries, with a view to enhancing regional peacekeeping capacity. The Special Committee welcomed the continued efforts of the European Union to cooperate with the United Nations in crisis management situations and to develop crisis management capabilities.

Women and peacekeeping

On 27 October [meeting 5294], the Security Council discussed the question of women and peace and security. It had before it a concept paper [S/2005/664] on the subject submitted by Romania and the Secretary-General's report [S/2005/636] on the preparation of a system-wide action plan for implementing resolution 1325 (2000) on women, peace and security [YUN 2000, p. 1113].

The Under-Secretary-General for Peacekeeping Operations, reporting on progress made and the remaining challenges in implementing resolution 1325(2000), said that DPKO had integrated a gender perspective in the disarmament, demobilization and reintegration process in Liberia, resulting in the demobilization of over 21,000 women, many of whom provided important information on hidden arms caches. In

Burundi, 231 of the 485 disarmed female ex-combatants were recruited into the newly restructured police force as part of their reintegration. Gender advisers trained police personnel of restructured police forces to ensure that victims of rape and other forms of gender-based violence had access to confidential and gender-sensitive case reporting. The first specialist police unit to deal with gender-based violent crimes in peacekeeping missions was established in Timor-Leste, and similar units in other missions. Considerable work had also been done to promote women's participation in transitional government institutions.

Gender units were also supporting capacity development of national counterparts in the governmental and non-governmental sectors in all mission areas. In Afghanistan, that included capacity development of women's affairs departments in 29 provinces across the country. In Côte d'Ivoire, the gender unit was supporting the mobilization of women's groups representing political parties, trade unions and non-governmental organizations (NGOs) to create a common platform to promote women's participation in decision-making. Gender units also supported the integration of gender perspectives into the judicial and legal sectors.

However, there were some setbacks such as the revelation of sexual exploitation by peacekeepers of women and girls (see p. 118), which highlighted the importance incorporating a gender perspective into DPKO's work. A significant proportion of peacekeeping personnel still did not have a conceptual understanding of gender mainstreaming, which partly explained why many gender mainstreaming strategies had not been institutionalized and the limited progress made in increasing the number of female personnel in peacekeeping, particularly in uniformed functions and in senior leadership positions. The perspectives of women were still not adequately harnessed to inform planning and operational activities.

The Under-Secretary-General stated that, in recognition of those shortcomings, he had issued a policy statement on gender mainstreaming in peacekeeping that provided an operational framework at the field and Headquarters levels for implementing resolution 1325(2000). As part of that policy, DPKO was finalizing a comprehensive action plan for implementing that resolution, built on the system-wide action plan outlined in the Secretary-General's report before the Council.

In renewing DPKO's commitment to the implementation of resolution 1325(2000), the Department intended to focus on ensuring that respon-

sibility for implementing the resolution was not limited to gender advisers or female staff alone; all men and women, particularly at senior levels at Headquarters and in the field, were responsible for implementing the resolution; all DPKO policies and guidance incorporated the relevant provisions of the resolution; gender mainstreaming was emphasized within all reporting and accountability mechanisms; marked progress was made towards increasing the number of women in peacekeeping; and partnership frameworks that guided collaboration with UN agencies and Member States in the implementation of the resolution were reviewed and refined. Strategic objectives and actions of individual DPKO offices would be consolidated into one Department-wide plan.

To further the implementation of resolution 1325(2000), the Under-Secretary-General suggested that Council members engage with the issue of women and peace and security on an ongoing basis and that its visits to peacekeeping missions provide for meaningful discussions with women leaders and representatives of women's organizations. The Council should also consider designing an action plan to guide its role in monitoring the implementation of resolution 1325(2000).

The Council President, in statement **S/PRST/2005/52** of 27 October (see p. 1255), welcomed the UN System-wide Action Plan for the implementation of resolution 1325(2000) and reaffirmed the Council's commitment to integrate gender perspectives into the terms of reference of Council visits and missions and to include gender specialists in its teams.

Comprehensive review of peacekeeping

Special Committee on Peacekeeping Operations

As requested by the General Assembly in resolution 58/315 [YUN 2004, p. 90], the Special Committee on Peacekeeping Operations and its Working Group continued their comprehensive review of the whole question of peacekeeping operations in all their aspects [A/59/19/Rev.1]. In response to the Committee's request, the Secretary-General submitted a report on the implementation of the Committee's 2004 [A/59/608 & Corr.1] and 2005 [A/60/640 & Add.1] recommendations.

The Special Committee held two sessions in 2005, its substantive session (New York, 31 January–25 February) and a resumed session (New York, 4-8 April). During the general debate of its resumed substantive session, the Special Committee considered uniform standards, training, the participation of women in peacekeeping missions, planning, organizational, management and command responsibility, welfare and recreation, data management, capacity to address misconduct, investigations, public information and communications, victim assistance, individual disciplinary, financial and criminal accountability, memorandum of understanding and the group of legal experts (for details, see respective sections).

It also considered the report [A/59/710] on a comprehensive strategy to eliminate future sexual exploitation and abuse in UN peacekeeping operations (see p. 118).

GENERAL ASSEMBLY ACTION

On 29 March [meeting 84], the General Assembly, on the recommendation of the Fourth Committee [A/59/472/Add.1], adopted **resolution 59/281** without vote [agenda item 77].

Comprehensive review of the whole question of peacekeeping operations in all their aspects

The General Assembly,

Recalling its resolution 2006(XIX) of 18 February 1965 and all other relevant resolutions,

Recalling in particular its resolution 58/315 of 1 July 2004,

Affirming that the efforts of the United Nations in the peaceful settlement of disputes, including through its peacekeeping operations, are indispensable,

Convinced of the need for the United Nations to continue to improve its capabilities in the field of peacekeeping and to enhance the effective and efficient deployment of its peacekeeping operations,

Considering the contribution that all States Members of the United Nations make to peacekeeping,

Noting the widespread interest in contributing to the work of the Special Committee on Peacekeeping Operations expressed by Member States, in particular troop-contributing countries,

Bearing in mind the continuous necessity of preserving the efficiency and strengthening the effectiveness of the work of the Special Committee,

1. *Welcomes* the report of the Special Committee on Peacekeeping Operations;

2. *Endorses* the proposals, recommendations and conclusions of the Special Committee, contained in paragraphs 22 to 154 of its report;

3. *Urges* Member States, the Secretariat and relevant organs of the United Nations to take all necessary steps to implement the proposals, recommendations and conclusions of the Special Committee;

4. *Reiterates* that those Member States that become personnel contributors to the United Nations peacekeeping operations in years to come or participate in the future in the Special Committee for three consecutive years as observers shall, upon request in writing to the Chairman of the Special Committee, become members at the following session of the Special Committee;

5. *Decides* that the Special Committee, in accordance with its mandate, shall continue its efforts for a comprehensive review of the whole question of peacekeeping operations in all their aspects and shall review the implementation of its previous proposals and consider any new proposals so as to enhance the capacity of the United Nations to fulfil its responsibilities in this field;

6. *Requests* the Special Committee to submit a report on its work to the General Assembly at its sixtieth session;

7. *Decides* to include in the provisional agenda of its sixtieth session the item entitled "Comprehensive review of the whole question of peacekeeping operations in all their aspects".

By **decision 60/523** of 8 December, the Assembly took note of the report of the Fourth Committee [A/60/478] on its consideration of the agenda item "Comprehensive review of the whole question of peacekeeping operations in all their aspects".

Operations in 2005

As at 1 January 2005, there were 16 peacekeeping missions in operation—7 in Africa, 1 in the Americas, 2 in Asia, 3 in Europe and the Mediterranean and 3 in the Middle East. During the year, two missions were closed (in Sierra Leone and Timor-Leste), and one new mission launched (in the Sudan), bringing the total number of missions in operation at year's end to 15.

Africa

In Africa, the mandate of the United Nations Mission in Sierra Leone (UNAMSIL) was extended for a final period of six months until 31 December. The Security Council also extended the mandates of the United Nations Organization Mission in the Democratic Republic of the Congo (MONUC) until 30 September 2006; the United Nations Mission for the Referendum in Western Sahara (MINURSO) until 30 April 2006; the United Nations Mission in Ethiopia and Eritrea (UNMEE) until 15 March 2006; the United Nations Operations in Côte d'Ivoire (UNOCI) until 24 January 2006; the United Nations Operation in Burundi (ONUB) until 1 July 2006; and the United Nations Mission in Liberia (UNMIL) to 31 March 2006. On 24 March, the Council established the United Nations Mission in Sudan (UNMIS) to support the implementation of the Comprehensive Peace Agreement signed between the Government and the Sudan People's Liberation Movement/Army on 9 January (see p. 301), with an authorized strength of 10,000 military personnel and 715 civilian police. In September, the Council extended the mission's mandate until 24 March 2006.

Americas

In the Americas, the Security Council extended the mandate of the United Nations Stabilization Mission in Haiti (MINUSTAH) until 15 February 2006.

Asia

In Asia, the United Nations Military Observer Group in India and Pakistan (UNMOGIP), established in 1949, continued to monitor the ceasefire in Jammu and Kashmir, while the Council's mandate for the United Nations Mission of Support in East Timor (UNMISET) ended on 20 May.

In related action, the Council extended, in September, the authorization of the International Security Assistance Force in Afghanistan for a further period of twelve months beyond October 2005 (**resolution 1623(2005)** (see p. 409).

Europe and the Mediterranean

In Europe and the Mediterranean, the Security Council extended the mandates of the United Nations Observer Mission in Georgia (UNOMIG) until 31 January 2006 and of the United Nations Peacekeeping Force in Cyprus (UNFICYP) until 15 June 2006. The United Nations Interim Administration Mission in Kosovo (UNMIK), Serbia and Montenegro, remained in place. The Council also authorized Member States, acting through or in cooperation with the European Union, to establish for a further period of 12 months a multinational stabilization force (EUFOR) in Bosnia and Herzegovina, as a legal successor to the stabilization force (SFOR), within the context of international efforts to implement the Peace Agreement in the country.

Middle East

Three long-standing operations continued in the Middle East: the United Nations Truce Supervision Organization (UNTSO), which continued to observe the truce in Palestine; the United Nations Interim Force in Lebanon (UNIFIL), whose mandate was extended until 31 January 2006; and the United Nations Disengagement Observer Force (UNDOF), whose mandate was renewed until 30 June 2006.

Roster of 2005 operations

UNTSO

United Nations Truce Supervision Organization
Established: June 1948.

Mandate: To assist in supervising the observance of the truce in Palestine.
Strength as at December 2005: 150 military observers.

UNMOGIP

United Nations Military Observer Group in India and Pakistan
Established: January 1949.
Mandate: To supervise the ceasefire between India and Pakistan in Jammu and Kashmir.
Strength as at December 2005: 42 military observers.

UNFICYP

United Nations Peacekeeping Force in Cyprus
Established: March 1964.
Mandate: To prevent the recurrence of fighting between the two Cypriot communities.
Strength as at December 2005: 840 troops, 69 civilian police.

UNDOF

United Nations Disengagement Observer Force
Established: June 1974.
Mandate: To supervise the ceasefire between Israel and the Syrian Arab Republic and the disengagement of Israeli and Syrian forces in the Golan Heights.
Strength as at December 2005: 1,047 troops.

UNIFIL

United Nations Interim Force in Lebanon
Established: March 1978.
Mandate: To restore peace and security and assist the Lebanese Government in ensuring the return of its effective authority in the area.
Strength as at December 2005: 1,989 troops.

MINURSO

United Nations Mission for the Referendum in Western Sahara
Established: April 1991.
Mandate: To monitor and verify the implementation of a settlement plan for Western Sahara and assist in the holding of a referendum in the Territory.
Strength as at December 2005: 31 troops, 195 military observers; 6 civilian police.

UNOMIG

United Nations Observer Mission in Georgia
Established: August 1993.
Mandate: To verify compliance with a ceasefire agreement between the parties to the conflict in

Georgia and investigate ceasefire violations; expanded in 1994 to include monitoring the implementation of an agreement on a ceasefire and separation of forces and observing the operation of a multinational peacekeeping force.

Strength as at December 2005: 122 military observers, 12 civilian police.

UNMIK

United Nations Interim Administration Mission in Kosovo

Established: June 1999.

Mandate: To promote, among other things, the establishment of substantial autonomy and self-government in Kosovo, perform basic civilian administrative functions, organize and oversee the development of provisional institutions, facilitate a political process to determine Kosovo's future status, support reconstruction of key infrastructure, maintain civil law and order, protect human rights and assure the return of refugees and displaced persons.

Strength as at December 2005: 2,146 civilian police, 37 military observers.

UNAMSIL

United Nations Mission in Sierra Leone

Established: October 1999.

Ended: 31 December 2005.

Mandate: To cooperate with the Government of Sierra Leone and other parties in the implementation of the Peace Agreement signed in Lomé, Togo, on 7 July 1999, including, among other things, to assist in the implementation of the disarmament, demobilization and reintegration plan, monitor adherence to the ceasefire agreement of 18 May 1999 and facilitate the delivery of humanitarian assistance.

MONUC

United Nations Organization Mission in the Democratic Republic of the Congo

Established: November 1999.

Mandate: To establish contacts with the signatories to the Ceasefire Agreement, provide technical assistance in the implementation of the Agreement, provide information on security conditions, plan for the observation of the ceasefire, facilitate the delivery of humanitarian assistance and assist in the protection of human rights.

Strength as at December 2005: 15,046 troops, 707 military observers, 1,038 civilian police.

UNMEE

United Nations Mission in Ethiopia and Eritrea

Established: July 2000.

Mandate: To establish and put into operation the mechanism for verifying the cessation of hostilities and to assist the Military Coordination Commission in tasks related to demining and in administrative support to its field offices.

Strength as at December 2005: 3,130 troops, 202 military observers.

UNMISET

United Nations Mission of Support in East Timor

Established: 17 May 2002.

Ended: 20 May 2005.

Mandate: To provide assistance to the core administrative structures and interim law enforcement and public security of East Timor (renamed Timor-Leste), including assisting in the development of the East Timor Police Service and contribute to the maintenance of East Timor's external and internal security.

UNMIL

United Nations Mission in Liberia

Established: 19 September 2003.

Mandate: To support the implementation of the ceasefire agreement and the peace process; protect UN staff, facilities and civilians; support humanitarian and human rights activities; and assist in national security reform, including national police training and formation of a new restructured military.

Strength as at December 2005: 14,824 troops, 197 military observers, 1,091 civilian police.

UNOCI

United Nations Operation in Côte d'Ivoire

Established: April 2004.

Mandate: To monitor the implementation of the 3 May 2003 comprehensive ceasefire agreement and the movement of armed groups; assist in disarmament, demobilization, reintegration, repatriation and resettlement; protect UN personnel, institutions and civilians; support humanitarian assistance; support implementation of the peace process; assist in the promotion of human rights, public information, and law and order.

Strength as at December 2005: 6,698 troops, 195 military observers, 696 civilian police.

MINUSTAH

United Nations Stabilization Mission in Haiti

Established: 1 June 2004.

Mandate: To ensure a secure and stable environment in support of the Transitional Government; to support the constitutional and political process, to support the Transitional Government in bringing about national dialogue, conducting free and fair elections, and extending State authority throughout the country; promote and protect human rights and coordinate with the Transitional Government in the provision of humanitarian assistance.

Strength as at December 2005: 7,286 troops, 1,748 civilian police.

ONUB

United Nations Operation in Burundi
Established: 1 June 2004.

Mandate: To monitor the implementation of ceasefire agreements; promote the re-establishment of confidence between Burundian forces; assist in disarmament and demobilization; monitor the quartering of the Armed Forces of Burundi and their heavy weapons; create security conditions for the provision of humanitarian assistance and the voluntary return of refugees; assist in the electoral process; protect civilians under threat and UN personnel and facilities.

Strength as at December 2005: 5,170 troops, 187 military observers, 82 civilian police.

UNMIS

United Nations Mission in the Sudan
Established: 24 March 2005.

Mandate: To support the implementation of the Comprehensive Peace Agreement signed between the Government of the Sudan and the Sudan People's Liberation Movement/Army on 9 January 2005; facilitate and coordinate the voluntary return of refugees and internally displaced persons, and humanitarian assistance; assist with humanitarian demining; and protect and promote human rights.

Strength as at December 2005: 4,009 troops, 467 military observers, 289 civilian police.

Financial and administrative aspects of peacekeeping operations

Financing

Expenditures for UN peacekeeping operations for the period 1 July 2004 to 30 June 2005 totalled $4,074.3 million, compared to $2,933.8 million for the previous 12-month period. The 39 per cent increase in expenditure was attributable to the expanded operations of MONUC, the full-year impact of four peacekeeping missions (UNMIL, UNOCI, MINUSTAH, ONUB), established in 2004, and the recent addition of UNMIS, partly offset by the lower expenditure levels in UNAMSIL and UNMISET.

In terms of the overall financial situation during the year, assessments, unpaid assessments and expenditures of active missions all increased on account of the increased activity, with a corresponding decrease in liquidity. Outstanding unpaid assessments for active peacekeeping missions rose by $147.5 million or 15 per cent. Unpaid assessments for closed missions did not change significantly. As at 30 June 2005, total unpaid assessments amounted to $1.7 billion, compared to $1.5 billion in the previous financial period.

Available cash for active missions totalled $1,245 million, while liabilities reached $1,704 million. For closed missions, available cash totalled $310.7 million, while liabilities were $322.1 million. Closed missions with cash surplus continued to be the only available source of lending to active peacekeeping missions. New loans totalling $244 million were made during the reporting period, bringing total loans outstanding as at 30 June 2005 to $41.6 million.

Notes of Secretary-General. In March [A/C.5/59/18], the Secretary-General, in accordance with General Assembly resolution 49/233 A [YUN 1994, p. 1338], submitted to the Assembly's Fifth (Administrative and Budgetary) Committee updated information on the approved budgetary levels for the period from 1 July 2004 to 30 June 2005 for all current peacekeeping operations, including requirements for the United Nations Logistics Base (UNLB), and the support account for peacekeeping operations, amounting to $3,878,821,200. That figure took into account the 2004 Assembly decisions in respect of UNMISET, MINUSTAH, ONUB, UNAMSIL and UNOCI.

In April [A/C.5/59/29], the Secretary-General submitted proposed budgetary requirements for all peacekeeping operations (except MONUC and UNMIS), UNLB and the support account for peacekeeping operations for the period from 1 July 2005 to 30 June 2006, amounting to $3,555,741,900. In June [A/C.5/59/33], that information was updated to include the commitment authorities for MONUC for the period 1 July to 31 October 2005 in the amount of $3,021,273,700.

In June [A/C.5/59/34], the Secretary-General, taking into account further financing actions by the Assembly, provided a breakdown of resources approved for all 15 peacekeeping operations, the support account for peacekeeping operations and UNLB in the amount of $3,521,456,500.

The Secretary-General also submitted a May note [A/C.5/59/31], which provided the working definitions used by DPKO in the preparation of mission budgets that included a disarmament, demobilization and reintegration component. The definitions, which addressed each element of that component, were being discussed by the United Nations interagency working group on disarmament, demobilization and reintegration, with a view to standardizing them across the UN system. While the Secretariat might continue to include operational costs related to disarmament and demobilization, including reinsertion, in the budgets of relevant peacekeeping missions, financial support for reintegration would continue to be resourced through voluntary contributions and managed by the appropriate agencies, funds and programmes.

The Advisory Committee on Administrative and Budgetary Questions (ACABQ), in its overview of the report of the Board of Auditors on the administrative and budgetary aspects of the financing of UN peacekeeping operations [A/59/736], welcomed the continued progress in the presentation of peacekeeping budgets using results-based budgeting techniques, but noted that some areas required further improvements. There was a need to formulate sufficiently representative and comprehensive indicators of achievement to better indicate progress in attaining expected accomplishments of logistical, administrative and security support. ACABQ made a number of other recommendations for improving the results-based budgeting presentation.

The Committee was concerned about the unevenness in the quality of presentation in the budget documentation submitted to it and held the view that the ultimate responsibility for maintaining standards with regard to presentation and related issues rested with Headquarters. It was also concerned about the tendency on the part of the Administration to use peacekeeping budgets to introduce initiatives with policy implications, rather than first seeking the necessary policy guidance from the Assembly.

ACABQ also considered a number of reports by the Secretary-General and OIOS on various cross-cutting issues relating to the administrative and budgetary aspects of the financing of UN peacekeeping operations. Those reports and ACABQ comments thereon were discussed under subsequent subheadings of this chapter.

By **decision 59/562** of 22 June, the Assembly, having considered the Secretary-General's May statement [A/C.5/59/32] on the programme budget implications of draft resolution [A/C.5/59/L.53] entitled "Administrative and budgetary aspects of the financing of the United Nations peacekeeping operations: cross-cutting issues", noted that an additional appropriation of $466,600 would be required for the support account for peacekeeping operations for the period from 1 July 2005 to 30 June 2006, should it adopt that draft resolution.

On 22 June [meeting 104], the General Assembly, on the recommendation of the Fifth Committee [A/59/532/Add.1], adopted **resolution 59/296** without vote [agenda item 123].

Administrative and budgetary aspects of the financing of the United Nations peacekeeping operations: cross-cutting issues

The General Assembly,

Recalling its resolutions 49/233 A of 23 December 1994, 49/233 B of 31 March 1995, 51/218 E of 17 June 1997 and 57/290 B of 18 June 2003,

Having considered the general report of the Advisory Committee on Administrative and Budgetary Questions on the report of the Board of Auditors concerning the administrative and budgetary aspects of the financing of the United Nations peacekeeping operations,

I

1. *Appreciates* the efforts of all peacekeeping personnel in dealing with the current unprecedented surge in peacekeeping operations;

2. *Endorses* the conclusions and recommendations contained in the general report of the Advisory Committee on Administrative and Budgetary Questions, subject to the provisions of the present resolution;

3. *Requests* the Secretary-General to submit an annual overview report on the financing of peacekeeping missions, reporting, inter alia, on trends in the size, composition and funding of the peacekeeping missions, relevant developments in peacekeeping operations, efforts to improve the management and functioning of peacekeeping operations and the management priorities for the coming year as well as actions taken to implement the provisions of the present resolution;

4. *Also requests* the Secretary-General to provide relevant information in the individual budget submissions of peacekeeping operations for the financial period 2006/07 on the efficiencies resulting from the implementation of the applicable provisions of the present resolution;

II

Results-based budgeting

1. *Reaffirms* its resolution 55/231 of 23 December 2000;

2. *Recognizes* the continued progress in the presentation of the peacekeeping budgets using results-based budgeting techniques;

3. *Decides* that the progressive implementation of results-based budgeting shall be in full compliance with its resolution 55/231;

4. *Recalls* that in paragraph 9 of its resolution 55/231, the General Assembly requested the Secretary-General to ensure that, in presenting the programme budget, expected accomplishments and, where possible, indicators of achievement are included to measure achievements in the implementation of the programmes of the Organization and not those of individual Member States;

5. *Notes* that some indicators of achievement reflected in the budgets and budget performance reports appear to measure the performance of Member

States, and requests the Secretary-General to ensure that the purpose of the indicators of achievement is not to assess the performance of Member States but, where possible, to reflect the contributions by peacekeeping missions to the expected accomplishments and objectives in keeping with their respective mandates;

6. *Requests* the Secretary-General to submit his future budget proposals in full compliance with its resolution 55/231;

7. *Encourages* the Secretary-General to continue to refine the existing results-based budgeting framework and to provide clearer financial information on all components of the missions;

8. *Requests* the Secretary-General to integrate operational, logistical and financial aspects fully in the planning phase of peacekeeping operations by linking results-based budgeting to the mandate implementation plans of peacekeeping operations;

III

Budget presentation

1. *Reiterates* paragraph 5 of its resolution 57/290 B;

2. *Notes with concern* the unevenness in the quality of presentation in the documentation submitted, and reiterates its request to the Secretary-General to provide in the budget documents the necessary information available that fully justifies his resource requirements;

3. *Reaffirms* rule 153 of the rules of procedure of the General Assembly, and requests the Secretary-General, in the context of the overview report, to provide detailed information on major policy changes having an impact on resource levels, human resources management policies or operational requirements that require the approval of the Assembly;

4. *Welcomes* the use, in the proposed budgets for 2005/06, of a new methodology for budgeting international staff costs;

5. *Requests* the Secretary-General to ensure that the Department of Peacekeeping Operations of the Secretariat and all missions make every effort to introduce strict budgetary discipline and enforce adequate controls over budget implementation;

6. *Also requests* the Secretary-General to entrust the Office of Internal Oversight Services of the Secretariat with conducting a business process review of the preparation of peacekeeping budget proposals, including the respective roles of staff in missions and at Headquarters and to submit its findings, including recommendations to streamline the process, to the General Assembly in the context of the report requested in section IV of the present resolution;

7. *Decides* that, in view of the critical importance of budgets for the effective functioning of missions, the submission of budget proposals from missions to Headquarters should constitute part of the leadership and accountability functions of the Head of Mission/Special Representative;

8. *Reaffirms* the necessity to provide peacekeeping operations with adequate financial resources, especially in their start-up and expanded phases, to enable the timely, full and effective implementation of their mandates in accordance with the relevant resolutions of the Security Council;

9. *Affirms* that budget submissions should, to the extent possible, reflect management improvements and efficiency gains to be achieved and articulate future strategies in this regard;

10. *Requests* the Secretary-General to undertake the review of the functions of the posts as an ongoing exercise and to determine the level of posts according to changing operational requirements as well as the actual responsibilities and functions performed, with a view to ensuring the most cost-effective use of resources;

IV

Review of the management structure of all peacekeeping operations

Recalling its decision 59/507 of 29 October 2004,

Having considered the note by the Secretary-General on the review of the management structure of all peacekeeping operations,

1. *Recalls* its previous request for several complex peacekeeping operations to review their structures, bearing in mind the complexities, mandates and specificities of each, and notes that some operations have undertaken the revision, and requests the Secretary-General to ensure that the remaining complex operations conduct the requested review and streamline their structures and to report thereon in the context of the relevant budget submissions;

2. *Requests* the Secretary-General to monitor the evolution of structures in individual peacekeeping operations to avoid the duplication of functions and an excessive proportion of higher-grade posts, bearing in mind the mandates, complexities and specificities of each mission;

3. *Recalls*, in this context, its resolution 59/272 of 23 December 2004;

4. *Requests* the Secretary-General, as a matter of priority, to entrust the Office of Internal Oversight Services with a comprehensive management audit to review the practices of the Department of Peacekeeping Operations and to identify risks and exposures to duplication, fraud and abuse of authority in the following operational areas: finance, including budget preparation; procurement; human resources, including recruitment and training; and information technology, and to report thereon to the General Assembly at its sixtieth session;

5. *Also requests* the Secretary-General to entrust the Office of Internal Oversight Services, in the light of the increasing demands with which the Department of Peacekeeping Operations is faced and the burden this is putting on its functioning, with carrying out a review of the management structures of the Department, while taking into account the Security Council mandates and existing recommendations formulated on previous occasions by the Office of Internal Oversight Services and the Board of Auditors and paying specific attention to the interaction, coordination and cooperation of the Department with other Secretariat departments and offices, including but not limited to the Department of Political Affairs, the Department of Public Information, the Office of Programme Planning, Budget and Accounts and the Department of Management, as well as the relevant funds and programmes, and to report thereon to the General Assembly at its sixty-first session;

6. *Urges* the Secretary-General to review, streamline and simplify procedures, on a continuing basis, as

well as to recommend changes to regulations and rules, as appropriate, in order to support more effective and efficient administrative processes, with a view to achieving economies in requirements for human and other resources;

7. *Notes* the observation of the Advisory Committee on Administrative and Budgetary Questions regarding the need for the full and timely implementation of recommendations of all oversight bodies, and urges the Secretary-General to expedite the establishment of the high-level follow-up mechanism and to report thereon to the General Assembly at its sixtieth session;

8. *Stresses* the need to improve the cooperation and coordination between the peacekeeping missions and Headquarters with regard to lessons learned and areas of common interest that could be used by all missions;

9. *Requests* the Secretary-General to ensure that all relevant financial regulations and rules, staff regulations and rules and administrative issuances are fully complied with by all missions and that appropriate disciplinary actions are taken in all cases of non-compliance;

10. *Also requests* the Secretary-General to finalize the process for the establishment of guidelines for the enforcement of basic standards of conduct and behaviour for all United Nations system personnel;

11. *Encourages* the Secretary-General to take additional measures to ensure the safety and security of all personnel under the auspices of the United Nations participating in peacekeeping missions, bearing in mind paragraphs 5 and 6 of Security Council resolution 1502(2003) of 26 August 2003;

12. *Requests* the Secretary-General to review the level and functions of the protocol officers, bearing in mind the relevant observations of the Advisory Committee, and to report thereon in the context of the relevant budget submissions;

V

Shared funding of posts of Deputy Special Representatives of the Secretary-General

1. *Takes note* of paragraph 62 of the report of the Advisory Committee on Administrative and Budgetary Questions, and in this regard decides that the position of the Deputy Special Representative of the Secretary-General, who heads the humanitarian pillar and serves as Resident Coordinator, will be funded through a cost-sharing arrangement with the United Nations Development Programme;

2. *Requests* the Secretary-General to report, in the context of the overview report, on the outcome of the exchange of letters, specifying agreed generic job profiles, organizational structure and cost-sharing arrangements with the United Nations Development Programme;

3. *Also requests* the Secretary-General to report the necessary reimbursement for the transition period, reflecting the effective start date of the cost-sharing arrangements, in the context of the budget performance reports;

VI

Disarmament, demobilization (including reinsertion) and reintegration

1. *Takes note* of the note by the Secretary-General;

2. *Notes* that reinsertion activities are part of the disarmament and demobilization process, as outlined in the note by the Secretary-General;

3. *Emphasizes* that disarmament, demobilization and reintegration programmes are a critical part of peace processes and integrated peacekeeping operations, as mandated by the Security Council, and supports strengthening the coordination of those programmes in an integrated approach;

4. *Stresses* the importance of a clear description of respective roles of peacekeeping missions and all other relevant actors;

5. *Also stresses* the need for strengthened cooperation and coordination between the various actors within and outside the United Nations system to ensure effective use of resources and coherence on the ground in implementing disarmament, demobilization and reintegration programmes;

6. *Requests* the Secretary-General, when submitting future budget proposals containing mandated resource requirements for disarmament, demobilization and reinsertion, to provide clear information on these components and associated post and non-post costs;

7. *Notes* that the components used by the Secretary-General for budgeting for disarmament, demobilization and reinsertion activities are set out in the note by the Secretary-General, recognizing ongoing discussions on these concepts;

8. *Notes also* the intention of the Secretary-General to submit integrated disarmament, demobilization and reintegration standards to the General Assembly at its sixtieth session;

VII

Quick-impact projects

Requests the Secretary-General to streamline the process of implementation of quick-impact projects and to ensure that they are fully implemented within the planned time frames;

VIII

Training, recruitment and staff in the field

Recalling its resolutions 56/293 of 27 June 2002 and 57/318 of 18 June 2003,

Having considered the report of the Secretary-General on the training policy and evaluation system of the Department of Peacekeeping Operations, and the relevant paragraphs of the report of the Advisory Committee on Administrative and Budgetary Questions,

Having also considered the reports of the Secretary-General on the criteria used for recruitment to support account posts, on greater use of national staff in field missions, on measures to expedite recruitment for field missions, taking into account the delegation of recruitment authority to field missions, including the use of fair and transparent recruitment procedures and monitoring mechanisms, on measures that would better streamline the policy guidelines related to the temporary duty assignment of staff in peacekeeping missions, on the status of the civilian rapid deployment roster, on the staffing of field missions, including the use of 300- and 100-series appointments and the relevant section of the report of the Advisory Committee,

Having further considered the notes by the Secretary-General transmitting the reports of the Office of In-

ternal Oversight Services on the audit of the policies
and procedures for recruiting Department of Peacekeeping Operations staff and on the follow-up audit of
the policies and procedures of the Department of
Peacekeeping Operations for recruiting international
civilian staff for field missions,

1. *Emphasizes* the importance of finalizing the comprehensive training strategy, and decides to restrict
training away from mission headquarters of civilian
staff to training specific to the implementation of the
mandate of the mission, the effective functioning of
the mission, the function of a post or, where it is cost-
effective, until the finalization of the strategy;

2. *Requests* the Secretary-General to report on the
finalization and implementation of the comprehensive
training strategy along with the framework of the evaluation of training to the General Assembly at its sixtieth session in the context of his overview report;

3. *Also requests* the Secretary-General to ensure that
the comprehensive training strategy includes the training needs of national staff for the purpose of capacity-
building in the mission area;

4. *Further requests* the Secretary-General to ensure
that staff in all United Nations peacekeeping operations have access to relevant training opportunities;

5. *Requests* the Secretary-General to make greater
use of national staff;

6. *Recalls* section X, paragraph 7, of its resolution
59/266 of 23 December 2004, decides to establish an
overall target of no more than 5 per cent of authorized
General Service/Field Service posts across missions,
with the exception of those missions in a start-up
phase, and other exceptional circumstances, to be
filled by staff on assignment from Headquarters, and
requests the Secretary-General to report on the progress towards reaching this target;

7. *Affirms* that locally recruited mission staff may
be recruited as international staff only through the
normal recruitment process in which they compete for
international posts in another mission along with
other external candidates;

8. *Requests* the Secretary-General to ensure that the
highest standards of efficiency, competence and integrity serve as the paramount consideration in the employment of staff, with due regard for the principle of
equitable geographical distribution, in accordance
with Article 101, paragraph 3, of the Charter of the
United Nations;

9. *Reiterates its request* to the Secretary-General to
make every effort to fill vacant posts in peacekeeping
operations expeditiously;

10. *Decides* that generic vacancy announcements
posted in Galaxy shall be accompanied by information
on the location of current specific vacancies and that
this would apply to all international vacancies in peacekeeping missions;

11. *Notes with concern* the observations of the
Advisory Committee on Administrative and Budgetary
Questions, in paragraphs 55 and 56 of its report, regarding the practice of hiring individual contractors
or individuals on procurement contracts to perform
functions of a continuing nature, and requests the
Secretary-General to revert to the General Assembly
for its consideration of the creation of a post if the
function is ongoing and is so warranted;

12. *Takes note* of the report of the Secretary-General
on criteria used for recruitment to support account
posts, and requests the Secretary-General to update
the information and to submit a report thereon to the
General Assembly at its sixty-first session for its consideration in the context of human resources management;

13. *Recalls* section X of its resolution 59/266;

14. *Regrets* that the report of the Secretary-General
on the staffing of field missions, including the use of
300- and 100-series appointments, did not fully provide the information requested in section X, paragraphs 2 and 3, of resolution 59/266, and in this context reiterates its request to the Secretary-General in
section X, paragraph 3, of its resolution 59/266;

15. *Decides* to continue to suspend the application
of the four-year maximum limit for appointments of
limited duration under the 300 series of the Staff
Rules in peacekeeping operations until 30 June 2006;

16. *Authorizes* the Secretary-General, bearing in
mind paragraph 15 above, to reappoint under the 100
series of the Staff Rules those mission staff whose service under 300-series contracts has reached the four-
year limit by 30 June 2006, provided that their functions have been reviewed and found necessary and
their performance has been confirmed as fully satisfactory, and requests the Secretary-General to report
thereon to the General Assembly at the second part of
its resumed sixtieth session;

17. *Notes* the fact that 278 of 346 eligible staff were
judged to have performed "fully satisfactorily", and requests the Secretary-General to apply rigorously the
criteria set out in its resolution 59/266;

18. *Requests* the Secretary-General to continue the
practice of using 300-series contracts as the primary instrument for the appointment of new mission staff;

IX

Conditions of service

1. *Recalls* section X, paragraphs 5 and 6, of its resolution 59/266, in which the General Assembly requested the International Civil Service Commission
and the Secretary-General to review conditions of service in the field and to report to the Assembly at its
sixty-first session;

2. *Decides* to limit conversion of General Service
posts to the Field Service category pending receipt of
that review;

3. *Also decides* that the review of the field service is
the appropriate mechanism for possible recognition of
hardship, if warranted;

X

Mission subsistence allowance

Recalling its resolution 58/258 of 23 December
2003,

Having considered the report of the Office of Internal
Oversight Services on the audit of mission subsistence
allowance policies and procedures and the note by the
Secretary-General transmitting his comments thereon,

1. *Requests* the Secretary-General to ensure that the
Office of Internal Oversight Services continues to audit the mission subsistence allowance rates to ensure
their reasonableness in comparison with the actual
subsistence costs in the various mission areas and with

the daily subsistence allowance set by the International Civil Service Commission in the same areas;

2. *Decides* to revert to the question of mission subsistence allowance rates and the recommendations of the Office of Internal Oversight Services in the context of the review of conditions of service in the field, requested by the General Assembly in section X, paragraphs 5 and 6, of its resolution 59/266;

3. *Also decides* that specific guidelines and criteria for the setting of miscellaneous or incidental costs as a component of the mission subsistence allowance should be developed, taking into account that mission subsistence allowance rates should not, as a general principle, exceed those of the daily subsistence allowance in the same locality;

XI

Participation of United Nations Volunteers

Recalling its resolution 54/245 A of 23 December 1999,

Having considered the report of the Secretary-General on the participation of United Nations Volunteers in peacekeeping operations, the report of the Joint Inspection Unit on the evaluation of the United Nations Volunteers Programme and the note by the Secretary-General transmitting his comments thereon, and the related reports of the Advisory Committee on Administrative and Budgetary Questions,

1. *Takes note* of the report of the Secretary-General on the participation of United Nations Volunteers in peacekeeping operations, the report of the Joint Inspection Unit on the evaluation of the United Nations Volunteers Programme and the note by the Secretary-General transmitting his comments thereon, and endorses the observations and recommendations of the Advisory Committee on Administrative and Budgetary Questions, as contained in paragraphs 70 to 72 of its report;

2. *Acknowledges* the valuable contribution of United Nations Volunteers in the United Nations system;

3. *Recognizes* that Volunteers should not be used as a substitute for staff to be recruited against authorized posts for the implementation of mandated programmes and activities and should not be sought for financial reasons;

4. *Takes note* of paragraph 25 of the report of the Secretary-General and the intention of the Department of Peacekeeping Operations to continue its efforts to exploit the potential for increased use of United Nations Volunteers in peacekeeping operations in those functions or skills which are not normally available in the Secretariat or which are limited;

5. *Requests* the Secretary-General to continue to ensure that Volunteers are subject to the same obligations and responsibilities, including standards of conduct, that the United Nations staff are subject to;

6. *Also requests* the Secretary-General to take into account greater use of national staff in peacekeeping operations, when feasible;

XII

Military component

1. *Requests* the Secretary-General to make every effort to reimburse Member States that have provided troops and equipment to United Nations peacekeeping operations in a timely manner;

2. *Also requests* the Secretary-General to ensure that the deployment of troops and contingent-owned equipment is well coordinated so that troops are not deployed without their equipment;

XIII

Regional investigators

Having considered the note by the Secretary-General transmitting the report of the Office of Internal Oversight Services on the first year of experience of regional investigators in two hubs, Vienna and Nairobi,

Takes note of the findings and recommendations contained in the report of the Office of Internal Oversight Services on the first year of experience of regional investigators in two hubs, Vienna and Nairobi, and emphasizes in particular the utilization of resident investigators to do investigations in the large peacekeeping missions and regional investigators to do investigations in the other missions and to provide support for complex cases in the large missions;

XIV

Sexual exploitation and abuse

Recalling its resolution 59/300 of 22 June 2005,

Reaffirming its resolutions 48/218 B of 29 July 1994, 54/244 of 23 December 1999, 59/272 of 23 December 2004 and 59/287 of 13 April 2005,

Having considered the report of the Secretary-General on special measures for protection from sexual exploitation and sexual abuse and the report on the investigation by the Office of Internal Oversight Services into allegations of sexual exploitation and abuse in the United Nations Organization Mission in the Democratic Republic of the Congo,

1. *Takes note* of the report of the Secretary-General on special measures for protection from sexual exploitation and sexual abuse and the report on the investigation by the Office of Internal Oversight Services into allegations of sexual exploitation and abuse in the United Nations Organization Mission in the Democratic Republic of the Congo;

2. *Emphasizes* the need for the development of a comprehensive, well-defined and coherent policy, taking into account also the relevant provisions of resolution 59/300, addressing, inter alia, the various managerial aspects of preventing and addressing allegations of sexual exploitation and abuse in all United Nations activities;

3. *Affirms* that the implementation of a zero-tolerance policy and procedures towards acts of sexual exploitation and abuse should be clearly defined as a core management function, in particular also addressing clear lines of responsibility and accountability relating to the non-implementation and non-enforcement of codes of conduct, policies and preventive measures, and should ensure that adequate mechanisms are in place in this regard;

4. *Requests* the Secretary-General to submit to the General Assembly at its sixtieth session a comprehensive report based on a thorough analysis of the aspects referred to in paragraphs 2 and 3 of the present section, as well as addressing the following:

(a) Systematic consideration of the full continuum of personnel conduct issues, including policy development, training, community relations, compliance supervision, accountability, discipline and investigation;

(b) Clear demonstration that existing expertise and resources in the Organization, both at Headquarters and in the field, including on child protection, gender, public information and other components within their specific roles and mandates, as well as human resources management and training, are fully utilized, and that relevant resource requests avoid duplication of resources and functions and enhance coordination among relevant departments and offices, while ensuring the effective implementation of the mandates of the missions;

(c) Clear reporting lines and proposals for the placement of the proposed capacity dealing with personnel conduct issues, bearing in mind that the Special Representative of the Secretary-General is ultimately accountable;

(d) Full justification of resource requirements, both at Headquarters and in the field, taking into account the specificities of each mission and based on empirical data on the actual number of allegations and cases of sexual exploitation and abuse;

XV

Global audit of field security management

Having considered the report of the Office of Internal Oversight Services on the global audit of field security management,

Decides to defer until its sixtieth session consideration of the report of the Office of Internal Oversight Services in the context of its consideration of a strengthened and unified security management system for the United Nations;

XVI

Procurement

Recalling its resolutions 57/290 B of 18 June 2003, 58/297 of 18 June 2004 and section A of its resolution 59/288 of 13 April 2005,

Having considered the reports of the Secretary-General on procurement and contract management for peacekeeping operations and the related report of the Advisory Committee on Administrative and Budgetary Questions,

Having also considered the reports of the Secretary-General on the analysis of establishing a global procurement hub for all peacekeeping missions at Brindisi, Italy, and on the implementation of the strategic deployment stocks, including the functioning of the existing mechanisms and the award of contracts for procurement, and the related reports of the Advisory Committee on Administrative and Budgetary Questions,

Having further considered the note by the Secretary-General transmitting the report of the Office of Internal Oversight Services on the procurement of goods and services through letters of assist,

1. *Requests* the Secretary-General, in order to improve the transparency and efficiency of procurement in peacekeeping operations, to ensure implementation of and compliance with the mechanisms aimed at facilitating the compilation by all missions of an assessment of progress and final performance of vendors and its immediate transmission to the United Nations Procurement Service at Headquarters;

2. *Notes* progress towards the harmonization of Headquarters and mission procurement databases, and in this regard welcomes the continued efforts towards improved transparency and accountability of a comprehensive procurement system, including the availability of peacekeeping procurement data for Member States, as currently displayed on the United Nations Procurement Service web site;

3. *Requests* the Secretary-General to continue to improve reporting procurement data to Member States and to consider procurement system processes utilized in the government and private sectors;

4. *Notes* the efforts made by the Secretary-General to increase procurement opportunities for developing countries and countries with economies in transition, and requests the Secretary-General:

(a) To continue to simplify the vendor registration process, taking into account access to the Internet;

(b) To take further steps to sensitize the business community to procurement opportunities within the United Nations system, including:

(i) The holding of additional business seminars;

(ii) Inviting the Inter-Agency Procurement Working Group to hold more meetings in developing countries;

(iii) Including the issue of diversity of sources of procurement as an agenda item at the annual meetings of the Inter-Agency Procurement Working Group;

5. *Requests* the Secretary-General to ensure that all peacekeeping missions operate with reference to their procurement plans in order to realize the benefits offered by proper procurement planning;

6. *Encourages* the Secretary-General to continue to monitor and address causes of excessive procurement lead times at peacekeeping missions;

7. *Also encourages* the Secretary-General to continue to ensure that all peacekeeping missions formally identify the training needs of all procurement officers and communicate these needs to Headquarters in order to ensure that training follows proper planning and evaluation of its effectiveness;

XVII

Asset management

1. *Reiterates* that the Department of Peacekeeping Operations should ensure that all missions implement an assets replacement programme in a cost-effective manner and in strict compliance with the guidelines on the life expectancy of assets;

2. *Requests* the Secretary-General to ensure that the heads of the peacekeeping operations take effective measures to ensure inventory control, replenishment of stocks and reasonable write-off procedures for the disposal of assets no longer required or useful;

3. *Also requests* the Secretary-General to ensure that formal written agreements are in place, which include elements such as financial reimbursement and liability, with other United Nations bodies before loaning out to them resources belonging to a peacekeeping operation;

4. *Commends* the ongoing efforts to increase cooperation between missions, particularly those in the same region, and stresses that any agreement on the loan or sharing of mission assets should be clearly understood and documented by the missions involved, bearing in mind that individual operations should remain responsible for preparing and overseeing their

own budgets as well as for controlling their own assets and logistical operations;

XVIII

Information technology

Having considered the reports of the Secretary-General on the functional requirements of field missions for communication and information technology and on the information and communications technology strategy: arrangements for the Galaxy system and the relevant section of the report of the Advisory Committee on Administrative and Budgetary Questions,

1. *Requests* the Secretary-General to take fully into account the return on investment for information and communication technology and to report on its impact on the resource requirements for the support account for peacekeeping operations;

2. *Also requests* the Secretary-General to ensure the full implementation of the information and communications technology strategy adopted by the General Assembly in order to avoid unnecessary redundancies;

3. *Further requests* the Secretary-General to implement the Galileo system in all peacekeeping operations in order to unify peacekeeping operations inventory;

XIX

Air operations

Recalling section B of its resolution 59/288,

1. *Requests* the Secretary-General to take all necessary actions to ensure that staff members involved in air operations are adequately trained, as specified in the Air Operations Manual;

2. *Also requests* the Secretary-General to continue to conduct aviation quality inspections and aviation assessments at missions to confirm that established standards are being fully complied with;

3. *Further requests* the Secretary-General to improve the formulation of resource requirements for air operations in budget submissions to make them more reflective of actual operations, bearing in mind the overbudgeting of air transportation requirements in some peacekeeping operations;

4. *Requests* the Secretary-General to undertake an analysis of the impact of the new costing structure relating to air operations, bearing in mind the relevant observations and recommendations of the Advisory Committee on Administrative and Budgetary Questions and the Board of Auditors, and to report thereon in the context of his next overview report;

XX

Ground transportation

1. *Requests* the Secretary-General to provide the General Assembly with a cost-benefit analysis on the issue of the transfer of vehicles with high mileage to the United Nations Logistics Base at Brindisi, Italy, to other missions and to upcoming missions, taking into account the cost of freight, and to report thereon to the Assembly at its sixtieth session;

2. *Also requests* the Secretary-General, in the context of his overview report, to provide detailed information on the implementation of the vehicle policy, as requested in paragraph 86 of the report of the Advisory Committee on Administrative and Budgetary Questions;

3. *Further requests* the Secretary-General to develop a standard policy with regard to the purchase and assignment of standard civilian and specially equipped armoured vehicles, as well as representational vehicles;

XXI

Ratios of vehicles and information technology equipment to staff

1. *Notes with concern* the lack of information on the implementation of ratios of vehicles to staff and discrepancies in the implementation of standard ratios;

2. *Requests* the Secretary-General to ensure that peacekeeping operations adhere to the standard ratios, bearing in mind the mandate, complexities and size of individual peacekeeping operations;

3. *Also requests* the Secretary-General to ensure that in all missions the actual ratio of heavy/medium vehicles is no greater than the established standard ratio of 1:1 and to justify any departure from this standard ratio;

4. *Further requests* the Secretary-General to review the policies on standard ratios of vehicles to staff and to provide the General Assembly, in the context of the overview report, with information on the outcome of the review and efforts to ensure that individual peacekeeping operations adhere to the standard ratios, while bearing in mind the mandate, complexity and size of individual operations;

5. *Requests* the Secretary-General to apply greater economies in the provision of 4x4 vehicles for civilian staff in missions, in particular but not limited to senior staff at the D-1 level and above, bearing in mind that the existing ratio for 4x4 vehicles must not be exceeded, and to report on the implementation thereof to the General Assembly at its sixtieth session in the context of the overview report;

6. *Encourages* the Secretary-General progressively to reduce the allocation of one printer per work station and to implement, with immediate effect, where it is cost-effective and feasible, the ratio of printers to desktop computers of 1:4 for all work stations in peacekeeping missions, at Headquarters and in the field;

7. *Decides* to defer consideration of new provisions for desktop computers, printers and laptops at Headquarters and in the field with the exception of new missions and those missions undergoing expansion according to Security Council mandates as well as for replacement purposes in strict compliance with the General Assembly resolution, pending the report of the Office of Internal Oversight Services on the comprehensive management audit to review the practices of the Department of Peacekeeping Operations, mentioned in section IV, paragraph 4, of the present resolution;

XXII

Rations contracts

1. *Requests* the Secretary-General to undertake a cost-benefit analysis of the delivery of food rations by air assets, without prejudice to the delivery of food to the troops, and to implement the most viable and cost-effective option in each peacekeeping operation;

2. *Also requests* the Secretary-General to ensure that all missions monitor and evaluate the quality management systems of rations contractors to ensure that food

quality and hygienic conditions are in accordance with established standards;

3. *Further requests* the Secretary-General to undertake a cost-benefit analysis of the use of an independent inspection mechanism to verify the fulfilment by contractors and vendors of all contract specifications regarding quality, hygiene and delivery plans.

Peacekeeping support account

In February [A/59/714 & Add.1], the Secretary-General submitted the financial performance report on the budget of the support account for peacekeeping operations for the period from 1 July 2003 to 30 June 2004. Expenditure for the period totalled $111,201,000 against approved resources of $112,075,800, resulting in an unencumbered balance of $874,800, attributable mainly to underexpenditure in respect of consultants, official travel, facilities and infrastructure and other supplies, services and equipment. The Secretary-General recommended that the unencumbered balance and other income and adjustments of $1,873,000 be applied to the 2005/2006 budget. In March [A/59/730], he submitted the budget for the support account for the period from 1 July 2005 to 30 June 2006 in the amount of $150,743,200, which provided for 761 continuing posts, 100 new posts and 10 existing Resident Auditor posts transferred from mission budgets.

In April [A/59/784], ACABQ, noting that peacekeeping missions had evolved into complex, multidimensional operations, with considerable authority delegated by Headquarters to the field, was of the opinion that such development should have an impact on the level of backstopping required. The level of the support account should not increase indefinitely, nor be used to establish posts that were not approved under the regular budget, or to propose the establishment of posts that should properly be done under the regular budget. It recommended that the Secretary-General analyse the evolution of the support account, starting with the original concept of overload, and describe changing needs to justify departures from that concept. ACABQ reiterated that reports on the support account should justify the totality of resources requested and not just additional requests for posts and non-post requirements. As to the backstopping of special political missions, it was important to revisit the issue of coordination and cooperation between DPKO and the Department of Political Affairs to ensure complementarity, avoid potential duplication and overlap and to consider the possible redistribution of resources to bring them in line with changes in activities and priorities.

ACABQ also recommended approval of 69 posts out of the 110 proposed, and reductions

amounting to $7,052,300 gross ($6,760,800 net) in the proposed budget for the support account for the period from 1 July 2005 to 30 June 2006, and that the unencumbered balance of $874,800 for the period 1 July 2003 to 30 June 2004 and other income of $1,873,000 related to the period ended 30 June 2004 be applied to the resources required for the new budget period.

GENERAL ASSEMBLY ACTION

On 22 June [meeting 104], the General Assembly, on the recommendation of the Fifth Committee [A/59/532/Add.1], adopted **resolution 59/301** without vote [agenda item 123].

Support account for peacekeeping operations

The General Assembly,

Recalling its resolutions 45/258 of 3 May 1991, 47/218 A of 23 December 1992, 48/226 A of 23 December 1993, 56/241 of 24 December 2001, 56/293 of 27 June 2002, 57/318 of 18 June 2003, 58/298 of 18 June 2004 and 59/287 of 13 April 2005, its decisions 48/489 of 8 July 1994, 49/469 of 23 December 1994 and 50/473 of 23 December 1995 and other relevant resolutions of the General Assembly,

Having considered the reports of the Secretary-General on the financing of the support account for peacekeeping operations and the related reports of the Advisory Committee on Administrative and Budgetary Questions,

Recognizing the importance of the United Nations being able to respond and deploy rapidly to a peacekeeping operation upon adoption of a relevant resolution of the Security Council, within thirty days for traditional peacekeeping operations and ninety days for complex peacekeeping operations,

Recognizing also the need for adequate support during all phases of peacekeeping operations, including the liquidation and termination phases,

Mindful that the level of the support account should broadly correspond to the mandate, number, size and complexity of peacekeeping missions,

1. *Takes note* of the reports of the Secretary-General on the financing of the support account for peacekeeping operations;

2. *Reaffirms* the need for effective and efficient administration and financial management of peacekeeping operations, and urges the Secretary-General to continue to identify measures to increase the productivity and efficiency of the support account;

3. *Also reaffirms* the need for adequate funding for the backstopping of peacekeeping operations, as well as the need for full justification for that funding in support account budget submissions;

4. *Requests* the Secretary-General to ensure the full implementation of the relevant provisions of General Assembly resolution 59/296 of 22 June 2005;

5. *Endorses* the conclusions and recommendations contained in the relevant report of the Advisory Committee on Administrative and Budgetary Questions, subject to the provisions of the present resolution;

6. *Requests* the Secretary-General to rejustify the need for the P-5 post in the Executive Office of the Secretary-General at the sixtieth session;

7. *Decides* to maintain, for the period from 1 July 2005 to 30 June 2006, the funding mechanism for the support account used in the current period, from 1 July 2004 to 30 June 2005, as approved in paragraph 3 of its resolution 50/221 B of 7 June 1996;

8. *Reaffirms* the need for the Secretary-General to ensure that delegation of authority to the Department of Peacekeeping Operations of the Secretariat and field missions is in strict compliance with relevant resolutions and decisions and the relevant rules and procedures of the General Assembly on this matter;

9. *Decides* to provide general temporary assistance to implement and monitor the environmental protection programmes in the field, and requests the Secretary-General to rejustify this position by providing additional information on the necessity of the backstopping capacity at Headquarters and on the ongoing cooperative arrangements with the United Nations Environment Programme in the area of environmental protection;

10. *Approves* the establishment of the post of Police Generation Officer (P-4) in the Civilian Police Division;

11. *Decides* to provide general temporary assistance for the P-3 post for the secretariat of the Fifth Committee;

12. *Requests* the Secretary-General to entrust the Office of Internal Oversight Services to conduct an audit of standard costs applied to headquarters overheads such as furniture and rental of premises, providing comparative costs on current market prices for these items, and to submit its findings to the General Assembly at the second part of its resumed sixtieth session;

13. *Decides* that all future requests for additional headquarters capacity linked to new or expanded peacekeeping or peace support missions must be accompanied by an analysis of spare capacity created by any downsizing or liquidation of other missions;

14. *Also decides* that following the end of mandate of missions, mission-specific posts in the Office of Operations of the Department of Peacekeeping Operations should be disestablished or redeployed and reflected accordingly in the next support account proposal;

15. *Further decides* not to provide funds in the amount of 350,000 United States dollars for the independent review of the Department of Peacekeeping Operations, as requested in paragraph 63 of the report of the Secretary-General;

16. *Decides* not to provide funds for Enterprise Content Management and Customer Relationship Management pilot projects, with the exception of the resources of 149,000 dollars sought for the Archives and Records Management Section in paragraph 366 of the report of the Secretary-General;

17. *Notes* that as a result of the expanded range of activities in the Situation Centre, there is a need for a broader and balanced range of skills and qualifications, including but not limited to knowledge of operational military and civilian police issues, among the Situation Centre officers, and in this regard requests the Secretary-General to ensure that the 11 Operations Officer (P-3) posts are available for incumbency to all qualified candidates, including officers seconded from Member States, keeping in mind the importance of representation of major troop-contributing countries;

18. *Decides* to approve the post of Chief of the Unit (P-5) to strengthen the Criminal Law and Judicial Advisory Unit;

Financial performance report for the period from 1 July 2003 to 30 June 2004

19. *Takes note* of the report of the Secretary-General on the financial performance of the support account for peacekeeping operations for the period from 1 July 2003 to 30 June 2004;

Budget estimates for the period from 1 July 2005 to 30 June 2006

20. *Approves* the support account requirements in the amount of 146,935,200 dollars for the period from 1 July 2005 to 30 June 2006, including 761 continuing and 70 new temporary posts and their related post and non-post requirements;

Financing of the budget estimates

21. *Decides* that the requirements for the support account for peacekeeping operations for the period from 1 July 2005 to 30 June 2006 shall be financed as follows:

(a) The unencumbered balance of 874,800 dollars for the period from 1 July 2003 to 30 June 2004 and other income of 1,873,000 dollars related to the period ended 30 June 2004, to be applied to the resources required for the period from 1 July 2005 to 30 June 2006;

(b) The amount of 13,790,000 dollars in excess of the authorized level of the Peacekeeping Reserve Fund in respect of the period ended 30 June 2004 to be applied to the resources required for the period from 1 July 2005 to 30 June 2006;

(c) The balance of 130,397,400 dollars to be prorated among the budgets of the active peacekeeping operations for the period from 1 July 2005 to 30 June 2006;

(d) The net estimated staff assessment income of 18,431,600 dollars, comprising the amount of 18,444,600 dollars for the period from 1 July 2005 to 30 June 2006, 26,400 dollars and 400,300 dollars for the requirements presented in the statements by the Secretary-General and the decrease of 439,700 dollars in respect of the financial period ended 30 June 2004, to be set off against the balance referred to in subparagraph *(c)* above, to be prorated among the budgets of the individual active peacekeeping operations.

Peacekeeping Reserve Fund

In April, the General Assembly considered the Secretary-General's 2004 [YUN 2004, p. 97] and 2005 [A/59/787] reports on the level of the Peacekeeping Reserve Fund, established in 1992 [YUN 1992, p. 1022] to ensure the rapid deployment of peacekeeping operations. From a level of $163.79 million, comprising a reserve of $150 million and an accumulated surplus of $13.79 million as at 30 June 2004, the balance of the Fund had increased, as at 31 March 2005, to $165.02 million, prior to the recording of investment income for the first quarter of the year. The Secretary-General recommended that the excess of $13.79 million over the authorized Fund level of $150 million be applied to the 2005/2006 budget of the support account for peacekeeping operations.

ACABQ, in an April report [A/59/791], said that the recommendation to use the excess in that fashion should be considered on a case-by-case basis and that it would be more prudent to determine whether or not to utilize any excess over the authorized Fund level with reference to actual cash on hand rather than a Fund balance that included credits from long-outstanding loans. It therefore recommended that, instead of using the excess balance as proposed by the Secretary-General, it should be maintained in the Fund.

GENERAL ASSEMBLY ACTION

On 22 June [meeting 104], the General Assembly, on the recommendation of the Fifth Committee [A/59/532/Add.1], adopted **resolution 59/297** without vote [agenda item 123].

Peacekeeping Reserve Fund

The General Assembly,

Having considered the reports of the Secretary-General on the Peacekeeping Reserve Fund and the related reports of the Advisory Committee on Administrative and Budgetary Questions,

Recalling its resolution 47/217 of 23 December 1992 on the establishment of the Peacekeeping Reserve Fund and its resolutions 49/233 A of 23 December 1994 and 51/218 E of 17 June 1997,

Reaffirming the general principles underlying the financing of United Nations peacekeeping operations, as stated in General Assembly resolutions 1874(S-IV) of 27 June 1963, 3101(XXVIII) of 11 December 1973 and 55/235 of 23 December 2000,

1. *Takes note* of the status of contributions to the Peacekeeping Reserve Fund as at 31 December 2004;

2. *Also takes note* of the reports of the Advisory Committee on Administrative and Budgetary Questions;

3. *Decides* that the excess balance of 13,790,000 United States dollars in respect of the financial period ended 30 June 2004 shall be applied to meet the financing of the support account for peacekeeping operations for the period from 1 July 2005 to 30 June 2006.

Funds from closed missions

In March [A/59/752], the Secretary-General, in response to the General Assembly's request in resolution 57/323 [YUN 2003, p. 85], that he postpone the return of 50 per cent of the net cash available for credit to Member States as a result of the closure of a number of peacekeeping missions, reported that the amount available for that purpose as at 30 June 2004 was $92,898,000. He recommended that, since the available cash in the Peacekeeping Reserve Fund ($134.1 million), as at 28 February 2005, was not sufficient to meet all foreseeable cash requirements, particularly the

start-up of UNMIS and the expansion of MONUC and pending the payment of assessed contributions, the balance of $92,898,000 from closed missions should be retained. He indicated that he would report to the Assembly on the matter at its sixtieth (2005) session.

ACABQ recommended acceptance of the Secretary-General's proposals [A/59/790].

By **decision 59/563** of 22 June, the Assembly took note of the Secretary-General's report on the updated financial position of closed peacekeeping missions and the related ACABQ report and decided to consider the updated financial position of those missions as at 30 June 2005 during the main part of its sixtieth session.

The Assembly also decided that the updated information on the financial position of the United Nations Angola Verification Mission (UNAVEM) and the United Nations Observer Mission in Angola (MONUA) should be included in the report it would consider at its sixtieth (2005) session on the updated financial position of closed peacekeeping missions, under the item entitled "Administrative and budgetary aspects of the financing of the United Nations peacekeeping operations" (**decision 59/564**).

In October [A/60/437], the Secretary-General, updating the information on the financial position of closed missions, including UNAVEM and MONUA, stated that, as at 30 June, the net cash available for credit to Member States amounted to $126,304,000. Owing to the high level of outstanding assessments in the special accounts of some ongoing peacekeeping missions, there was a continuing need to borrow from closed missions. Moreover, the Assembly had only provided commitment authority for the period 1 July to 31 October for MONUC and UNMIS. The full budgets for those missions were still to be reviewed by the Assembly. The Secretary-General recommended that the Assembly approve the retention of the available cash balance of $126,304,000 for the 13 closed peacekeeping missions, in the light of the Organization's experience in respect of cash requirements during 2004/2005.

ACABQ, in November [A/60/551], stated that the postponement of the return of "available cash" to Member States was a policy decision to be determined by the Assembly. It drew attention to the fact that cash from closed missions appeared to be the only source for temporary cross-borrowing and was a source of funding for new or expanded missions, in addition to the Peacekeeping Reserve Fund. The Assembly might wish to take the Committee's observations into account in reaching its decision.

By **decision 60/551** of 23 December, the Assembly deferred until its resumed sixtieth (2006) session the Secretary-General's October report on the subject and the related ACABQ report.

Consolidation of peacekeeping accounts

In April [A/59/795], the Secretary-General expressed regret that, owing to the unprecedented surge in peacekeeping operations, the Secretariat had not been able to prepare the comprehensive report on the feasibility of consolidating the accounts of the various peacekeeping operations, as requested by the General Assembly in resolution 57/319 [YUN 2003, p. 90]. Further analysis was required to consider the efficiency aspects of streamlining the processes for the financing of peacekeeping operations while permitting more consistent and timely reimbursement to troop-contributing Governments. The Secretary-General intended to submit the report to the Assembly's sixtieth (2005) session.

Accounts and auditing

At its resumed fifty-ninth (2005) session, the General Assembly considered the financial report and audited financial statements for UN peacekeeping operations for 1 July 2003 to 30 June 2004 [A/59/5 (vol. II)/Corr.1], the Secretary-General's report on the implementation of the recommendations of the Board of Auditors [A/59/704] and the related ACABQ report [A/59/736].

GENERAL ASSEMBLY ACTION

On 22 June [meeting 104], the General Assembly, on the recommendation of the Fifth Committee [A/59/588/Add.1], adopted **resolution 59/264 B** without vote [agenda item 106].

Financial reports and audited financial statements, and reports of the Board of Auditors

B

The General Assembly,

Having considered the financial report and audited financial statements for the twelve-month period from 1 July 2003 to 30 June 2004 and the report of the Board of Auditors on United Nations peacekeeping operations, the related section of the report of the Advisory Committee on Administrative and Budgetary Questions and the report of the Secretary-General on the implementation of the recommendations of the Board of Auditors concerning United Nations peacekeeping operations in respect of that period,

1. *Accepts* the audited financial statements on the United Nations peacekeeping operations for the period from 1 July 2003 to 30 June 2004;

2. *Takes note* of the observations and endorses the recommendations contained in the report of the Board of Auditors;

3. *Also takes note* of the observations and endorses the recommendations contained in the report of the Advisory Committee on Administrative and Budgetary

Questions related to the report of the Board of Auditors, subject to the provisions of the present resolution;

4. *Commends* the Board of Auditors for the quality of its report and the streamlined format thereof;

5. *Takes note* of the report of the Secretary-General on the implementation of the recommendations of the Board of Auditors concerning United Nations peacekeeping operations in respect of the financial period ended 30 June 2004;

6. *Requests* the Secretary-General to indicate an expected time frame for the implementation of the recommendations of the Board of Auditors as well as the priorities for their implementation, including the office holders to be held accountable;

7. *Also requests* the Secretary-General to report to the General Assembly at its sixtieth session on measures undertaken to implement paragraph 6 above;

8. *Further requests* the Secretary-General to ensure the full implementation of the recommendations of the Board of Auditors, including those relating to the issue of the management of rations in peacekeeping operations as a whole and the management of air operations, and the related recommendations of the Advisory Committee in a prompt and timely manner;

9. *Requests* the Secretary-General, in implementing the recommendations referred to in paragraph 81 of the report of the Board of Auditors, to take into account that this relates solely to the recommendations of the Panel on United Nations Peace Operations as adopted by the General Assembly which have not been fully implemented to date.

On the same day, the Assembly also considered and took action on the Secretary-General's report [YUN 2004, p. 98] on the first year of experience of regional investigators in two hubs, Vienna and Nairobi, in section XIII of **resolution 59/296** (see p. 133).

Reimbursement issues

Equipment

The General Assembly, at its resumed fifty-ninth (2005) session, considered the Secretary-General's report on reformed procedures for determining reimbursement to Member States for contingent-owned equipment [YUN 2004, p. 98] and the findings and recommendations of the 2004 Working Group on Contingent-Owned Equipment [ibid.]. ACABQ, in its February 2005 report on the subject [A/59/708], recommended approval of the checklist attached to the Secretary-General's report defining the criteria for reimbursement of commercial pattern support vehicles as military pattern vehicles, and his proposed reimbursement rates for the new items of major equipment. The Contingent-Owned Equipment Manual should be amended to reflect that and the undated Manual distributed as an official UN document. As suggested by the Secretary-General, ACABQ also recommended approval of the Secretariat's proposal that the next Working Group on Contingent-Owned Equipment be held in 2008, instead of 2007, to review the contingent-owned equipment system, in accordance with the formats established by the Phase V Working Group, and establish a methodology for conducting rate reimbursement reviews.

ACABQ further recommended that the next Working Group review and make recommendations on the costing and medical staffing level of the modular medical concept; and that the Assembly approve the updated format for major medical equipment, as proposed by the Secretary-General for collecting national cost data on medical equipment for review by the next Working Group. It also recommended that consideration be given to having a diverse group of qualified, experienced and impartial individuals make proposals on the factors and elements on which the reimbursement of troop costs could be based.

GENERAL ASSEMBLY ACTION

On 22 June [meeting 104], the General Assembly, on the recommendation of the Fifth Committee [A/59/532/Add.1], adopted **resolution 59/298** without vote [agenda item 123].

Reformed procedures for determining reimbursement to Member States for contingent-owned equipment

The General Assembly,

Recalling its resolution 55/274 of 14 June 2001,

Having considered the report of the Secretary-General on the reformed procedures for determining reimbursement to Member States for contingent-owned equipment, the letter dated 12 March 2004 from the Chairman of the 2004 Working Group on Contingent-Owned Equipment to the Chairman of the Fifth Committee and the related reports of the Advisory Committee on Administrative and Budgetary Questions,

1. *Takes note* of the report of the Secretary-General on the reformed procedures for determining reimbursement to Member States for contingent-owned equipment, the letter dated 12 March 2004 from the Chairman of the 2004 Working Group on Contingent-Owned Equipment to the Chairman of the Fifth Committee and the related reports of the Advisory Committee on Administrative and Budgetary Questions;

2. *Endorses* the conclusions and recommendations contained in the reports of the Advisory Committee on Administrative and Budgetary Questions, subject to the provisions of the present resolution;

3. *Regrets* that the 2004 Working Group on Contingent-Owned Equipment was unable to reach consensus on, inter alia, a review of the rates of reimbursement for contingent-owned equipment and self-sustainment;

4. *Decides* to approve the proposal of the Secretary-General that the next Working Group on Contingent-Owned Equipment, which will meet in 2008, carry out a comprehensive review of the contingent-owned equipment system, as per the formats established by the Phase V Working Group, for a period of not less than fourteen working days;

5. *Urges* the Secretary-General to explore the possibility of holding the Working Group meeting earlier than 2008, if feasible;

6. *Decides* that the next Working Group on Contingent-Owned Equipment will consider, without prejudice to the comprehensive review of the contingent-owned equipment system, in recommending any revision of rates of reimbursement for contingent-owned equipment and self-sustainment, the fact that there was no revision of such rates for the period 2004 to 2008 owing to the lack of consensus on an increase in the rates and on the methodology of the 2004 Working Group;

7. *Notes that,* in addition to maintaining all existing components of the current methodology, the Secretary-General had proposed the inclusion of peacekeeping-related training costs and post-deployment medical costs in the troop reimbursement methodology;

8. *Regrets* that the 2004 Working Group on Contingent-Owned Equipment was unable to reach consensus on the components for inclusion in the troop-cost reimbursement methodology;

9. *Notes* that the report of the Secretary-General on the rates of reimbursement to the Governments of troop-contributing countries did not address all elements of the request made in paragraph 8 of General Assembly resolution 55/274;

10. *Reiterates* its request contained in paragraph 8 of its resolution 55/274, and requests the Secretary-General to submit to the General Assembly at its sixtieth session a comprehensive report thereon, addressing all elements;

11. *Notes* that the Secretary-General, in preparing the comprehensive report, may utilize, as appropriate, external expertise;

12. *Decides* to review the daily allowance for troops at its resumed sixtieth session, based on information to be provided in the context of the comprehensive report referred to in paragraph 10 above;

13. *Also decides* to set up a channel of communication between the Secretariat and the Member States on the contingent-owned equipment system, strictly for the exchange of information and for seeking clarification and not for reaching decisions that are within the mandate of the Working Group on Contingent-Owned Equipment and relevant intergovernmental bodies.

Management of peacekeeping assets

UN Logistics Base

The General Assembly, at its resumed fifty-ninth (2005) session, considered the financial performance report of the United Nations Logistics Base (UNLB) at Brindisi, Italy, for the period from 1 July 2003 to 30 June 2004 [A/59/681]. Expenditure for the period totalled $22,059,100 gross ($20,682.000 net) against total appropriations of $22,208,100 gross ($20,949,600 net), resulting in an unencumbered balance of $149,000.

The Assembly was asked to decide on the treatment of that balance and other income adjustments amounting to $2,292,000.

The Assembly also had before it the proposed budget for the period from 1 July 2005 to 30 June 2006 [A/59/691], in the amount of $37,691,900, an increase of $9,269,900 in total resources over the previous twelve-month period. Overall, the proposed budget reflected increases of 21.4 per cent in operational costs, 52.9 per cent in personnel costs and 50.8 per cent in staff assessment, and provided for the deployment of 42 international and 167 national staff. It also provided for the completion of phase 1 of the three-phase refurbishment plan, including completion of the hardstanding and associated infrastructure at San Vito to replace the San Pancrazio facilities.

ACABQ, in April [A/59/736/Add.2], recommended that the unencumbered balance and other income/adjustments for the period ended 30 July 2004 be credited to Member States in a manner to be determined by the Assembly, and that the estimated budget requirement be reduced from $37,691,900 to $31,513,100.

In June [A/C.5/59/33], the Secretary-General submitted to the Fifth Committee a note on the amounts to be appropriated in respect of each peacekeeping mission, including the prorated share of UNLB for the period from 1 July 2005 to 30 June 2006.

GENERAL ASSEMBLY ACTION

On 22 June [meeting 104], the General Assembly, on the recommendation of the Fifth Committee [A/59/532/Add.1], adopted **resolution 59/299** without vote [agenda item 123].

Financing of the United Nations Logistics Base at Brindisi, Italy

The General Assembly,

Recalling section XIV of its resolution 49/233 A of 23 December 1994,

Recalling also its decision 50/500 of 17 September 1996 on the financing of the United Nations Logistics Base at Brindisi, Italy, and its subsequent resolutions and decisions thereon, the latest of which was resolution 58/297 of 18 June 2004,

Recalling further its resolution 56/292 of 27 June 2002 concerning the establishment of the strategic deployment stocks and its subsequent resolutions 57/315 of 18 June 2003 and 58/297 of 18 June 2004 on the status of the implementation of the strategic deployment stocks,

Having considered the reports of the Secretary-General on the financing of the United Nations Logistics Base and on the implementation of the strategic deployment stocks, including the functioning of the existing mechanisms and the award of contracts for procurement, and the related reports of the Advisory Committee on Administrative and Budgetary Questions,

Reiterating the importance of establishing an accurate inventory of assets,

1. *Notes with appreciation* the facilities provided by the Government of Italy to the United Nations Logistics Base at Brindisi;

2. *Endorses* the conclusions and recommendations contained in the report of the Advisory Committee on Administrative and Budgetary Questions, and requests the Secretary-General to ensure their full implementation;

3. *Notes* the proposal of the Secretary-General to expand the Logistics Base, and requests the Secretary-General to include in the budget submission for 2006/07 detailed information on the financial and legal implications, as well as on the expected benefits that may arise from the expansion;

4. *Encourages* the Secretary-General to ensure the active participation of the Department of Peacekeeping Operations of the Secretariat in the negotiations between the World Food Programme and the Government of Italy concerning the release of the San Vito Base;

5. *Requests* the Secretary-General to ensure the full implementation of the relevant provisions of General Assembly resolution 59/296 of 22 June 2005;

6. *Also requests* the Secretary-General to undertake a further analysis of how the Logistics Base could best be utilized to provide efficient and economical communications and information technology services, as well as other services, for United Nations peacekeeping and Headquarters clients;

7. *Reiterates* the need to implement, as a matter of priority, an effective inventory management standard, especially in respect of peacekeeping operations involving high inventory value;

Strategic deployment stocks

8. *Takes note* of the report of the Secretary-General on the implementation of the strategic deployment stocks, including the functioning of the existing mechanisms and the award of contracts for procurement;

9. *Also takes note* of the deficiencies in the contingent-owned equipment of rehatted troops, and requests the Secretary-General to review options for the effective rehatting of contingents and provide recommendations in this regard;

10. *Approves* the use of savings derived from the liquidation of prior-period obligations and the unspent balance of the strategic deployment stocks to cover losses in currency exchange and the replenishment of the stocks;

11. *Also approves* the inclusion of strategic deployment stocks replenishment within the commitment authority described in section IV, paragraph 1, of General Assembly resolution 49/233 A;

12. *Requests* the Secretary-General to ensure the implementation of the existing policies and procedures relating to stock control and inventory and replenishment, regarding strategic deployment;

Financial performance report for the period from 1 July 2003 to 30 June 2004

13. *Takes note* of the report of the Secretary-General on the financial performance of the United Nations Logistics Base for the period from 1 July 2003 to 30 June 2004;

**Budget estimates for the period from
1 July 2005 to 30 June 2006**

14. *Approves* the cost estimates for the United Nations Logistics Base amounting to 31,513,100 United States dollars for the period from 1 July 2005 to 30 June 2006;

Financing of the budget estimates

15. *Decides* that the requirements for the United Nations Logistics Base for the period from 1 July 2005 to 30 June 2006 shall be financed as follows:

(*a*) The unencumbered balance and other income in the total amount of 2,441,000 dollars in respect of the financial period ended 30 June 2004 to be applied against the resources required for the period from 1 July 2005 to 30 June 2006;

(*b*) The balance of 29,072,100 dollars to be prorated among the budgets of the active peacekeeping operations for the period from 1 July 2005 to 30 June 2006;

(*c*) The net estimated staff assessment income of 2,351,700 dollars, comprising the amount of 2,233,100 dollars for the period from 1 July 2005 to 30 June 2006 and the increase of 118,600 dollars in respect of the financial period ended 30 June 2004, to be set off against the balance referred to in subparagraph (*b*) above, to be prorated among the budgets of the individual active peacekeeping operations;

16. *Also decides* to consider at its sixtieth session the question of the financing of the United Nations Logistics Base at Brindisi, Italy.

Strategic deployment stocks

In response to resolution 58/297 [YUN 2004, p. 99], the Secretary-General submitted a February report [A/59/701] on the implementation of the strategic deployment stocks (SDS), including the functioning of the existing mechanism and the award of contracts for procurement. He indicated that the two-year project for establishing SDS had been effectively completed. Its management at the Secretariat and at UNLB was fully functional, the procurement of equipment and materials completed and stocks utilized to support multiple mission start-ups and expansions. Since the establishment of SDS in July 2002 [YUN 2002, p. 63], $132 million worth of equipment had been issued to various operations.

Total expenditure on the project between 2002 and 2004 amounted to $141,536 million. Total unliquidated obligations, as at 30 June 2004, amounted to $20,845,243, 70 per cent of which were disbursed during 1 July 2004 and 31 January 2005, with the remaining $6.3 million to be disbursed by 30 June 2005. Outstanding contributions from Member States to SDS as at 31 December 2004 amounted to $13.6 million, 99 per cent of which was related to the special assessed contribution of one Member State. Savings as a result of the liquidation of prior obligations stood at $397,322, which could be used, together with the unspent balance of $9,033, to cover currency exchange losses and replenishment of stocks.

The total value of procurement in support of SDS amounted to $140,639,492. Contracts valued at $12 million were awarded to companies from developing countries and countries with economies in transition, and contracts for 1.9 million awarded to companies in Africa.

The Secretary-General asked the Assembly to note the completion of the strategic deployment programme, approve the use of savings and the unspent balance to cover losses on currency exchange and the replenishment of stocks, and the inclusion of SDS replenishment within the $50 million commitment authority. He also asked that the Assembly authorize him, on an exceptional basis, and with ACABQ's concurrence, to enter into commitments over and above the $50 million for the replenishment of SDS in respect of the start-up phase of a new peacekeeping mission, to be financed from the Peacekeeping Reserve Fund.

ACABQ, in its April report [A/59/736/Add.2], recommended approval of the Secretary-General's recommendations.

The General Assembly took action on the recommendations in **resolution 59/299** of 22 June (see p. 145).

Ground and air transportation

ACABQ, in its April report [A/59/736], considered the variety of armoured personnel carriers used in missions, and efforts made to obtain them by negotiating contingent-owned equipment with troop- and police-contributing countries. A limited number of armoured personnel carriers reported as part of inventory were provided by troop-contributing countries, ownership of which was later transferred to the United Nations under the old methodology for reimbursement of contingent-owned equipment. ACABQ also noted the persistent use of outdated vehicles, which were expensive to maintain, and recommended that the cost-effectiveness of utilizing such vehicles be reviewed as a matter of priority.

ACABQ, having been informed that the use of representational vehicles was mission-specific, noted that in some missions two or more vehicles, including specially equipped armoured vehicles, were assigned to the Secretary-General's Special Representative and that other vehicles of both types were distributed among the civilian staff without a standard policy regarding their entitlement to or need for such vehicles. The Committee had also addressed that issue in its reports on the relevant peacekeeping operations. In view of the high cost involved, it was of the view that DPKO should develop a policy with regard to the purchase and assignment of both standard civilian and specially equipped armoured vehicles, as well as representational vehicles. Representational and specially equipped vehicles, it stressed, should not be utilized as status symbols, but should be assigned on the basis of demonstrated need and in accordance with an established policy.

Regarding air transportation in peacekeeping missions, ACABQ analysed the costing structure relating to air operations contracts and efforts by DPKO to move away from the commercial industry approach of block-hours costing to one based on actual flight hours utilized. Noting that contracts were still being issued or renewed on the basis of block-hours costing if the terms were favourable to the Organization, the Committee urged a prudent approach that took into account the cooperation of vendors who had agreed to work with the Organization on the basis of the new costing structure. It requested DPKO to analyse the impact of the new pricing structure in order to assess its cost-effectiveness and to report thereon at the next opportunity.

The General Assembly, by **resolution 59/288 B** of 13 April (see p. 1471), took action on the 2004 OIOS report [YUN 2004, p. 101] on the audit of safeguarding air safety standards while procuring air services for United Nations peacekeeping missions.

Procurement

The General Assembly, at its resumed fifty-ninth (2005) session, considered the OIOS report [YUN 2003, p. 95] on the procurement of goods and service through letters of assist and the Secretary-General's 2004 [YUN 2004, p. 101] and February 2005 [A/59/688] reports on procurement and contract management for peacekeeping operations. The February report examined developments relating to ethics guidance, assistance to newly established peacekeeping missions, procurement training, vendor management and other measures to improve procurement and contract management for peacekeeping operations.

The Secretariat had developed ethical guidelines for staff involved in the procurement process to assist those serving in peacekeeping missions to determine how to conduct themselves in dealing with suppliers and other entities. The Procurement Service also drafted, in consultation with the Office of Human Resources Management and the Office of Legal Affairs (OLA), a Declaration of Ethical Responsibilities, which addressed the issue of confidentiality and conflict of interest, and should be signed by all staff engaged in procurement activities. The Procurement Service was also promulgating a UN vendor code of conduct, addressing the issue of corporate social responsibility, environmental and sustainable procurement and corruption, which would be communicated to all suppliers interested in doing business with the UN system. OLA was also coordinating an inter-agency working group to promulgate a revised United Nations General Conditions of Contract.

In addition, although the Procurement Service had released senior staff members to assist a number of peacekeeping missions, the retention of high-quality procurement staff for sustained periods in those missions remained an issue. The Secretariat was helping to develop a UN system-wide procurement training and certification programme to ensure consistency in knowledge and facilitate staff mobility between Headquarters and missions and within the UN system as a whole.

To streamline the approval process for field requirements, the Procurement Service was developing with DPKO and the Headquarters Committee on Contracts a standard personal delegation of authority document to be used across field missions and offices away from Headquarters. The revised delegation of authority, the level of which was raised to $1 million, would be issued by the first quarter of 2005 for the procurement of "core requirements", essential goods and services, which, by their nature or owing to market conditions, lent themselves to local procurement.

The Procurement Service was working to reduce the lead times for the provision of goods and services to peacekeeping missions, and with OLA, to develop model lease and contract templates to facilitate the work of procurement officials at those missions. In addition to vendor performance reporting, which the Procurement Service required from peacekeeping missions for the purposes of vendor management and contract renewals, the Service was working with UN system organizations to enhance the functioning of the United Nations Global Marketplace through information-sharing among all participating organizations. The Global Marketplace, in use at the Secretariat since February 2004, would be introduced in peacekeeping missions in 2005. The observance of reporting requirements relating to vendor performance remained an issue in peacekeeping missions, but the Secretariat had instituted measures to improve compliance and all missions were required to complete quarterly evaluations on vendor performance levels for headquarters contracts. A comprehensive review of vendor management conducted in 2004 made recommendations for simplifying, streamlining and harmonizing the vendor registration process, and the Procurement Service was developing, with other UN system organizations, the business process and implementing those recommendations. The new arrangements, which were to commence by 1 May, would significantly improve the efficiency and effectiveness of vendor management through standardized registration, reduce administrative duplication and institute dependable and professional evaluations of vendors' capabilities.

In March [A/59/722], ACABQ urged the Secretary-General to finalize, promulgate and implement expeditiously the guidelines on ethical principles and the declaration of independence and to report the results to the Assembly at its resumed fifty-ninth (2005) session. It also recommended expeditious finalization and promulgation of the code of conduct for suppliers and the revised General Conditions, and that the Secretary-General report to the Assembly during the main part of its sixtieth (2005) session. ACABQ underlined the importance of revisiting procurement plans on a quarterly basis to ensure that they were updated in accordance with mission operational requirements, and the need to enforce the use of procurement plans and tools to facilitate effective and efficient procurement management. While welcoming the developments in respect of procurement lead times and model leases and contract templates, ACABQ recommended that, instead of across-the-board averages, benchmarks for lead times be established by clusters of commodities or services to provide realistic data and to better illustrate achievements in that regard. It encouraged DPKO and the Department of Management to review and streamline the vendor performance, monitoring and reporting process, and asked that information on the delegation of authority be provided to the Assembly at its resumed fifty-ninth (2005) session.

Global procurement hub

As requested by ACABQ [YUN 2004, p. 101] and endorsed by the General Assembly in resolution 58/297 [ibid., p. 99], the Secretary-General submitted a February report [A/59/703] on the merit of establishing a global procurement hub for all peacekeeping missions at UNLB in Brindisi, Italy. The comprehensive review, conducted with the assistance of an external international consulting firm, assessed the implications of relocating the procurement and logistics function to UNLB, taking into consideration the current volatile operational environment and the evolving role of UNLB in support of field missions, particularly in the context of strategic deployment stock operations. It specifically examined the extent to which changes would translate into improved service

and support for peacekeeping missions, the reallocation of responsibilities and transfer of skills, the interdependence between Headquarters-based procurement and logistics functions and those currently carried out at UNLB.

The review found that the relocation of functions would imply a division of the procurement function, and duplicate functions both at Headquarters and UNLB, reconfigure the procurement management structure and relocate or duplicate other related support functions, such as those of the Headquarters Committee on Contracts, the Office of Legal Affairs and accounts payable. Certain management and oversight functions, such as those provided by OIOS, might also need to be duplicated at Headquarters and UNLB. The relocation of the procurement function would also negatively affect communication with some outside interlocutors and the commercial section of Member States' consulates.

A survey of UNLB revealed that its existing infrastructure was inadequate to accommodate the functions and staff associated with the proposed procurement and logistics hub. The financial benefits of the relocation of the logistics and procurement functions from New York to UNLB would be limited, with modest savings in operating costs of less than five per cent and a return-on-investment period of nine years. Relocation would require significant reorganization at Headquarters and UNLB, and the terms of the memorandum of understanding with the host Government and the various domestic priorities of the region placed limitations on UNLB.

The Secretary-General concluded that a relocation of procurement and operational logistics functions to UNLB would have a negative impact on operational effectiveness and the financial case for such a move was weak. He was concerned that removal of critical logistics functions from the highly integrated structures in the Secretariat would negatively impact the Organization's overall capacity to rapidly and effectively deploy new missions and to provide effective logistical support to the 32 ongoing peacekeeping and peacebuilding operations.

ACABQ, in its April report on the administrative and budgetary aspects of UN peacekeeping operations [A/59/736], stated that notwithstanding the disadvantages described by the Secretary-General of relocating staff and related resources to UNLB, it was convinced that there was a greater potential to maximize the benefits from the considerable investment in information and communication technology (ICT) at UNLB and elsewhere. Further analysis should be made of how UNLB could best be utilized to provide efficient and economical ICT and other services for UN peacekeeping and Headquarters clients, and the cost-effectiveness of reducing reliance on commercial providers in favour of increasing UNLB's role.

Restructuring issues

Responding to General Assembly decision 59/507 [YUN 2004, p. 94], requesting a report on the review of the management structure of all peace-keeping operations, the Secretary-General, in an April note [A/59/794], expressed regret that the Secretariat was unable to provide the report requested. The Secretariat was in the process of reconciling the staffing tables of all peace-keeping missions and consolidating data on staffing and organizational structures that were critical elements in the analysis required to produce the report. Once the data collection was completed, the comprehensive review and analysis would be undertaken and the report submitted to the Assembly at the second part of its resumed sixtieth (2006) session.

ACABQ, in April [A/59/736], said that, while it understood the pressure of work under which the Secretariat found itself, such a review had little value if undertaken after the budgets and management structures had been approved and put in place. It recommended that the Secretariat proceed with the review, which should be completed in time for the next round of peacekeeping budgets preparation.

The Assembly, in section IV of **resolution 59/296** (see p. 133), requested the Secretary-General, as a matter of priority, to entrust to OIOS the conduct of a comprehensive management audit of DPKO practices and to review its management structure.

Personnel matters

During the year, the General Assembly considered a number of reports relating to personnel matters, including the Secretary-General's report on the DPKO training policy and evaluation system [A/58/753], the criteria used for the recruitment of support account posts [YUN 2004, p. 103], greater use of national staff in the field, taking into account the delegation of recruitment authority to field missions, including the fair and transparent recruitment procedures and monitoring mechanisms [A/58/764], measures that would better streamline the policy guidelines relating to the temporary duty assignment of staff in peacekeeping missions [YUN 2003, p. 99], the status of civilian rapid deployment roster, the staffing of field missions, including the use of 300- and 100-series appointments, and relevant sections of ACABQ report (see below). It also considered OIOS reports on the audit of the policies and

procedures for recruiting DPKO staff [YUN 2004, p. 103] and on the follow-up audit of DPKO policies and procedures for recruiting international civilian staff for field missions [ibid., p. 104].

The Assembly also considered the Secretary-General's report on special measures for protection from sexual exploitation and sexual abuse [A/59/782] (see p. 1526) and the OIOS report into allegations of sexual exploitation and abuse in MONUC [A/59/661] (see p. 118).

In considering those reports, ACABQ [A/59/736] recognized that the United Nations was developing a framework and methodology for evaluating training, the final model of which would be specifically suited to the organizational qualities and particular skill requirements of the United Nations and its peacekeeping activities and connected to existing staff evaluation. ACABQ considered it essential to have in place a mechanism to evaluate the effectiveness of training and to track competency gaps. It pointed out that training national staff of a particular mission for service in another was a new policy that should be thoroughly assessed and considered by the Assembly before being applied, since such staff would be serving as international staff and might be performing functions that could be carried out by national staff in that mission area. A better approach might be to reform the Field Service category of staff to meet the demands faced by peacekeeping operations.

Noting the Secretary-General's intention to review arrangements for regularizing the budgetary and technical support of the Galaxy e-staffing system and for transferring responsibility from DPKO to the Department of Management, ACABQ recommended that the lessons learned and experiences acquired during the development, implementation and roll-out phases of Galaxy by information technology specialists and users and applicants be fully documented and analysed. The experiences of other large organizations with similar systems should also be reviewed and consideration given to sharing the applications developed or acquired. The results should be reflected in the Secretary-General's report to the Assembly's sixtieth (2005) session, which should also evaluate the impact of the proposed changes on the UN's ICT strategy on interactions and interfaces with other systems, users and applicants. Special attention should be paid to the modalities of the transition and planning for a seamless change without disruption of services, and to a clear definition of the phases during which there would be an overlap of responsibilities between DPKO and the Department of Management. In addition, an analysis of the human resources requirements in terms of both UN staff and consultants and other financial implications should be provided.

Concerning recruitment for field missions, ACABQ welcomed the Secretariat's intention to develop flexible and creative staffing strategies to expand the use of National Professional Officers in those missions, and encouraged it to review the current criteria and made proposals for consideration by the International Civil Service Commission.

On the question of sexual exploitation and abuse, ACABQ called for a comprehensive approach [A/C.4/59/L.21] to the problem for all UN activities, both at Headquarters and in the field, and for an analysis of the related resource requirements to implement a consistent policy in that area. It would await the results of that analysis and revert to the matter during consideration of the proposed programme budget and other relevant matters.

ACABQ was informed that arrangements with the United Nations Development Programme (UNDP) for the shared funding of the position of the Deputy Special Representative of the Secretary-General who led the humanitarian pillar and also served as Resident Coordinator had not yet been put into effect. Also, no formal agreement existed between DPKO and UNDP for the cost-sharing of Deputy Special Representative posts in peacekeeping missions, which were determined on a case-by-case basis. ACABQ saw no reason why the arrangements discussed with UNDP would not be applied to all missions concerned, irrespective of the level that was eventually determined for the posts. It expected that an undertaking that UNDP would fund the posts up to the Director (D-2) level would be confirmed and put into practice, and requested to be informed accordingly before the 2006/2007 budgets were submitted.

Staffing of field missions

As requested by the General Assembly in resolution 59/266 [YUN 2004, p. 1418], the Secretary-General reported in April [A/59/762] on the staffing of field missions, including the use of 300 and 100 series appointments. As a follow-up to his 2004 report on the subject [YUN 2004, p. 105], the April report provided information on mission staff reappointed from 300 to 100 series contracts after reaching the four-year limit of their 300 series contracts and made proposals for the further use of those appointment instruments in field missions.

The report observed that, as at 30 June 2005, 346 international staff had reached, or exceeded four years of service under the 300 series appointment of limited duration, and were consid-

ered for reappointment under the 100 series contract, in accordance with the criteria set out in section X of resolution 59/266, that their functions be reviewed and found necessary and that their performance be confirmed as fully satisfactory. As a result of that review, 287 staff met the criteria set out in resolution 59/266, 48 did not, due either to anticipated downsizing or mission closure and remained under the 300 series contract, 4 reached the mandatory age of separation, 5 had not met the necessary performance criteria and 2 were still pending consideration.

DPKO proposed that the 100 series appointment be used for the employment of staff performing functions that were not, by their nature, temporary or limited in duration, and for which the Department had a continuing need for one year or longer, and the 300 series appointment for functions of a temporary nature, with a limited duration of under one year, such as electoral assistance, border monitoring and short-term projects. The use of the 100 series appointment for functions of a continuing nature would also help to harmonize the conditions of service between different groups of staff in field missions, including Secretariat field staff and their counterparts from UN agencies, funds and programmes. The Secretary-General sought the Assembly's agreement to that request and, pending consideration of the proposal, approval to continue reappointing serving staff under 100 series contracts on a case-by-case basis after they had reached the maximum period of service permitted under a 300 series appointment, provided there was a continuing need for their services and they had a fully satisfactory performance record.

ACABQ [A/59/736] was of the opinion that the conditions of service for all staff in field missions should be harmonized and looked forward to receiving the Secretary-General's comprehensive report on the subject before considering the next round of peacekeeping financing proposals. In the meantime, it recommended that the Secretary-General be authorized to make 100 series appointments as he had requested, trusting that the criteria would be rigorous and consistently applied. However, no action should be taken on the general issue of appointing staff under the 100 series, pending consideration of the Secretary-General's comprehensive report.

Mission subsistence allowance

Pursuant to General Assembly resolution 58/258 [YUN 2003, p. 97], the Secretary-General submitted, in February [A/59/698], the OIOS report on the audit of mission subsistence allowance (MSA) rates, the daily allowance paid to

United Nations international civilian staff, military observers and civilian police in special peacekeeping missions to cover subsistence costs. OIOS reviewed those rates in several of the largest peacekeeping missions and followed up on recommendations contained in the Secretary-General's 2001 report on the subject [YUN 2001, p. 104]. OIOS noted, among other things, that its views and those of the Office of Human Resources Management (OHRM) and DPKO differed markedly concerning the most appropriate relationship between MSA and daily subsistence allowance (DSA) rates. OIOS maintained that MSA rates should always be lower than DSA rates, while OHRM argued that the conditions of life in many duty stations were sufficiently arduous to warrant higher MSA rates.

During extended discussions with OIOS, OHRM expressed strong resistance to lowering MSA rates automatically when DSA rates dropped. Consequently, there was no point in OIOS making recommendations that would continue to be resisted strongly by departments. It noted that the comprehensive review requested by the Special Committee on Peacekeeping Operations in 2002 [YUN 2002, p. 85] of the allowance structure, which was to take into account the adverse conditions of life and work affecting personnel in UN peacekeeping operations and related request that a fair service package be developed, had not been undertaken. To resolve its differences of opinion with OHRM and DPKO regarding MSA, OIOS recommended that the comprehensive review be undertaken in a spirit of openness and transparency, and that the review consider establishing a two-component MSA structure, with one component for subsistence (food, accommodation and incidentals) and the other to compensate for particular living conditions in duty stations. OHRM and DPKO had accepted that recommendation.

OIOS also recommended that OHRM undertake a monthly comparative analysis of MSA and DSA rates, and that the difference should trigger the adjustment of MSA rates in the mission concerned. OHRM should also apply a consistent policy in promulgating revised MSA rates, by making them effective from the first day of the month following the issuance of its final MSA report.

The Secretary-General, in his comments on the OIOS report [A/59/698/Add.1], agreed with most of the recommendations. However, regarding the recommendation calling for a monthly analysis of the two rates, with consequential adjustment of MSA rates, he noted that the two rates served different purposes. While DSA was designed to cover expenditures incurred during short-term official travel under normal circumstances, MSA was defined as the total UN contribution towards living expenses incurred in connection with a special mission assignment. He did not feel that there was justification for using an across-the-board formula to determine MSA by reference to DSA. The Secretary-General noted, however, that for monitoring purposes only, OHRM was undertaking monthly comparisons of both rates in localities where there were special peacekeeping missions.

UN Volunteers

The General Assembly, at its resumed fifty-ninth (2005) session, considered the Secretary-General's report on the participation of UN Volunteers in peacekeeping operations [YUN 2001, p. 814] and the related ACABQ report [ibid., p. 94], as well as the report of the Joint Inspection Unit (JIU) on the evaluation of the Programme [YUN 2003, p. 1388] and the Secretary-General's comments thereon [A/59/68/Add.1].

ACABQ, in its April report [A/59/736], while noting the successful cooperation between UN Volunteers and DPKO, observed that the functions and responsibilities of volunteers were not always clearly defined. It recommended that the Programme and DPKO define clear parameters of employment for volunteers working with the Department and that the Assembly request the Programme to intensify its follow-up with the Office of Legal Affairs to ensure that the privileges and immunities of volunteers were clearly defined. It agreed with JIU that UNDP should introduce a regular cycle for the Programme to ensure objective risk control and management oversight.

Chapter II

Africa

In 2005, Africa showed measured progress towards resolving the many ongoing conflict situations that had beset the continent over the past decade, although there were grim reminders of the need for firmer international action to help resolve fully those conflicts and bring peace and prosperity to the populations concerned. The year witnessed the successful transition from peacekeeping to peacebuilding in several countries in Central Africa and the Great Lakes region, thereby facilitating the complex transition processes in those countries. The United Nations, in partnership with the African Union (AU) and other regional organizations and international actors, supported elections in Burundi in June and July. That paved the way for the election of Pierre Nkurunziza as President by the Joint Parliamentary Congress, whose inauguration marked the formal conclusion of the transitional process to a democratically elected Government. Similarly, in the Central African Republic, the election of General François Bozizé in June as President marked that country's return to constitutional order. Meanwhile, in the Democratic Republic of the Congo, preparations were under way for national elections scheduled to be held in 2006. In preparation for that event, the country successfully held a referendum on a new Constitution in December. However, key challenges remained, including the daunting task of consolidating peace by bringing the rebel groups into the peace process, concluding the disarmament, demobilization and reintegration programmes for ex-combatants, promoting national reconciliation and creating conditions for economic and social rehabilitation and development.

In West Africa, several countries were on the path towards economic and democratic reforms as the intensity of conflicts lessened. Elections were successfully held in Liberia, which were won by Ellen Johnson-Sirleaf, thereby becoming the President-elect. Her inauguration in early 2006 would also mark a return to constitutional government in Liberia. Progress was also made in restoring State authority and addressing concerns about corruption in the National Transitional Government. In that regard, a governance and economic management assistance programme was developed to help the country regain control of its vital natural resources. The apprehension of former Liberian leader Charles Taylor for prosecution by the Special Court for Sierra Leone was deemed a priority by the Security Council. In Sierra Leone, the United Nations continued to help in laying the foundation for the country to achieve lasting stability, democracy and prosperity. Sierra Leone made further progress in meeting the benchmarks set by the Council to allow the United Nations Mission in Sierra Leone to continue to implement its plan for withdrawing its forces deployed there. At the request of the President of Sierra Leone, and given the continuing instability in the Mano River Basin subregion, the Council established the United Nations Office in Sierra Leone to assist the Government in consolidating peace, building national conflict prevention capacity and preparing for elections in 2007. The Government was able to take control of its diamond-mining sector, repatriate some 272,000 refugees and establish a national human rights commission. Cameroon and Nigeria continued to cooperate in resolving their border issues. Both countries, despite some delays, took action to begin, with international assistance, the planned withdrawal and transfer of authority in the Bakassi Peninsula and to begin the demarcation of the land boundary. However, those developments were overshadowed by the continuing conflict in Côte d'Ivoire, where the parties failed to live up to their commitments. Key benchmarks in the implementation of the 2003 Linas-Marcoussis Agreement were not met, such as the target date for the completion of demobilization and the constitutional deadline for holding presidential elections in October. In those circumstances, the AU and the Economic Community of West African States extended President Gbagbo's term for one year, appointed a Prime Minister and established bodies to oversee the peace process. In Guinea-Bissau, controversies over the eligibility of the two presidential candidates and the election results later in the year created a highly polarized atmosphere in the country. The Secretary-General revised the mandate of the United Nations Office in Guinea-Bissau to facilitate its new role in the transition process. The United Nations also supported the Government of Togo in addressing the political crisis arising from the sudden death of President

Gnassingbé Eyadema, in preserving the stability of the country and ensuring a peaceful transition of power consistent with the Constitution and rule of law. Political upheavals and incidents of violence occurred following the elections, amidst allegations of human rights violations. Based on the report of a fact-finding mission dispatched to Togo by the United Nations High Commissioner for Human Rights to investigate those allegations, the Government indicated its willingness to take action to prevent further violence and address the problems leading to such misconduct.

The ongoing conflicts in the Horn of Africa continued to take centre stage, as the United Nations and the international community spared no effort in trying to resolve them. In the Sudan, the 21-year civil war between the north and south of the country ended in January with the signing by the parties of the Comprehensive Peace Agreement, setting out new arrangements for power- and wealth-sharing. The Government of National Unity was established in September and the government of southern Sudan in December. In March, the Security Council set up the United Nations Mission in Sudan to oversee the implementation of the Comprehensive Peace Agreement. Hopes that the new political arrangement would lead to a solution to the crisis in the Darfur region in western Sudan were not realized, as the conflict there continued unabated. The Council tightened its sanctions in the face of the continued refusal of the Government to accept a UN peacekeeping force to assist the AU Force deployed there. The Council sent an assessment mission to Darfur to examine the human rights situation and, based on its recommendations, decided to refer the cases of violation of international human rights and humanitarian law to the International Criminal Court. In Somalia, the fledgling Transitional Federal Government based in Nairobi, Kenya, relocated to Somalia, but was not operational for most of the year due to a dispute over the site of the relocation and the composition of the interim peace support mission sponsored by the Intergovernmental Authority on Development. The border dispute between Eritrea and Ethiopia remained unsettled. The Eritrea-Ethiopia Boundary Commission failed to advance its demarcation activities, stalled since 2003 by Ethiopia's rejection of significant parts of the Commission's 2002 final and binding delimitation decision and Eritrea's insistence on its implementation. Eritrea, contrary to the Council's demand, increased its restrictions on the United Nations Mission in Ethiopia and Eritrea, including the request for certain nationalities to leave the country. The Council agreed to

relocate its staff to Ethiopia until it reviewed future plans for the Mission.

The question of the future of the Western Sahara remained unresolved. In an effort to break the deadlock, the Secretary-General appointed a new Personal Envoy to explore with the parties and neighbours how best to achieve a mutually acceptable solution. Morocco continued to refuse to accept a referendum that would include the option of independence, while the Frente Popular para la Liberación de Saguía El-Hamra y de Río de Oro continued to insist that the only way forward was to implement the 2003 peace plan proposed by the Special Envoy or the 1991 settlement plan proposed by the Secretary-General.

Promotion of peace in Africa

In 2005, the United Nations continued ongoing efforts to identify and tackle the root causes of conflict in Africa and to consider ways to promote sustainable peace and development on the continent. In March, the Security Council discussed the African dimension of its work and explored how to improve its effectiveness in addressing related issues. Several Council members highlighted the root causes of conflicts on the continent and the need to combine peace and security efforts with long-term development strategies and to strengthen cooperation with regional and subregional organizations, particularly the African Union (AU), in conflict prevention and management on the continent. In September, the Council adopted a declaration on strengthening the effectiveness of its role in conflict prevention, particularly in Africa. The Secretary-General reported on the implementation of his 1998 recommendations for tackling the root causes of conflict and the promotion of durable peace in Africa, highlighting progress made and remaining challenges. The Office of the Special Adviser on Africa (OSAA), headed by Ibrahim Gambari (Nigeria), continued to serve as the focal point for monitoring the implementation of those recommendations and for enhancing international efforts to promote peace on the continent. In December, the Secretary-General extended the appointment of his Geneva-based Special Adviser on Africa, Mohamed Sahnoun (Algeria), until 31 December 2006.

Working Group. On 5 January [S/2005/4], the Security Council President said that following consultations among Council members, it was agreed that Mr. Joël W. Adechi (Benin) would serve as Chairman of the Ad Hoc Working Group on Conflict Prevention and Resolution in Africa until the end of 2005. However, on 26 June, Mr. Adechi relinquished the office and Mr. Jean-Francis R. Zinsou (Benin) took over as Acting Chairman until 19 October. By a 20 October note [S/2005/660], the Council President announced that Council members had agreed that Mr. Simon Bodéhoussè Idohou (Benin) would serve as Chairman of the Group until the end of 2005. On 21 December [S/2005/814], the President said that Council members had agreed that the Group would continue its work until 31 December 2006.

The Working Group, established in 2002 [YUN 2002, p. 93] to monitor the implementation of Council recommendations relating to its role in conflict prevention and resolution in Africa, reported in December [S/2005/833] on its 2005 activities. It monitored and contributed to the Council's work on improving ways to better address crises in Africa by promoting a common understanding of related issues. In particular, it forged a larger consensus on the need to develop a culture of proactive prevention of conflict. It accorded particular attention to the importance of peacebuilding in Africa, within the context of discussions on the establishment of a Peacebuilding Commission that might help improve cooperation between the Security Council and the Economic and Social Council in addressing relevant matters.

During the year, the Working Group held two major events: a policy forum (New York, 13 June) on the role of the Security Council in enhancing UN capacity for conflict prevention, which underlined the need to shift from a culture of reaction to crises to that of prevention, both in pre- and post-conflict situations; and a seminar (New York, 15 December) on cooperation between the United Nations and African regional organizations in the field of peace and security [S/2005/828], which outlined concrete steps to support the African Peace and Security Architecture of the African Union and to integrate it fully into the system of collective peace and security established by the UN Charter.

Security Council consideration. The Security Council, on 30 March [meeting 5156], discussed the African dimension of its work on how to improve its effectiveness in addressing African issues and its current agenda and methods of work. To facilitate the deliberations, the Council President prepared a background document [S/2005/188] outlining the objectives and scope of the discussion. Several Council members, pointing to the many conflict situations in Africa and the associated threats to international peace and security, noted that the continent was the main host of UN peacekeeping operations and the focus of much

of the Council's monthly deliberations. Noting that the Council could do more to help address conflicts and related problems in Africa, delegates stressed, among other things, the need to strengthen cooperation with African regional and subregional organizations, particularly the African Union (AU), in preventing and managing conflicts on the continent and the importance of combining peace and security efforts with long-term development strategies. References were made to the importance of institutional dialogue among the principal bodies of the United Nations, particularly the Security Council and the Economic and Social Council, and to the greater involvement of international financial institutions, programmes and agencies. Delegations also referred to the Secretary-General's recommendations contained in his report entitled "In larger freedom" (see p. 67), especially regarding the establishment of a peacebuilding commission.

The Council President, speaking in his capacity as the representative of Brazil, noted that the Council had held up to 25 meetings in 24 days on Africa during the month of March, which indicated that the Council had not been effective enough in early crisis identification and conflict avoidance. The Council, therefore, needed to evolve from the logic of conflict resolution to that of prevention, and a new dimension—sustainability—needed to be added to its approach to work. He emphasized that the Council was responsible for peace and security that could be sustained over time and not for a year or two or the short period when a peacekeeping operation was deployed. Council efforts to provide security and ensure that fragile peace processes flourished demanded military action and parallel concrete measures to lead people out of the vicious circle of hopelessness and provide for sustainable peace. The Council's decision-making process would be substantially improved by making use of first-hand information regarding conflicts in Africa, as was provided recently when the Council was briefed by the representative of AU Mediators on the crisis in Côte d'Ivoire. Further improvement could be ensured through more Council missions to countries in conflict, which often provided a unique opportunity for members to engage in the realities of the conflicts with which the Council was seized. Dialogue with international and local non-governmental organizations (NGOs) or civil society representatives should also be initiated. The Council President stressed the need for closer cooperation between peacekeeping and political missions deployed on the continent, increased international support in terms of the requisite resources for facilitating peace processes in Africa and combating impunity by bringing perpetrators of wrongdoing to justice in local courts and international criminal tribunals.

On 30 June [meeting 5220], the Council deliberated on Africa's food crisis as a threat to peace and security. Addressing the Council, the Executive Director of the World Food Programme (WFP) said the greatest humanitarian crisis currently facing the world was not in Darfur (Sudan) or Afghanistan or the Democratic People's Republic of Korea. It was the gradual disintegration of the social structures in southern Africa, and hunger was at its core. The lethal mix of AIDS, recurring drought and failing governance and capacity was eroding social and political stability. The AIDS pandemic, in particular, which claimed one million lives in the region in 2004 and which had reduced life expectancy there by 20 years, was directly undermining the capacity of communities to produce enough food for themselves. It was currently estimated that some 8.3 million people would need food aid in southern Africa, largely owing to the lack of adequate rainfall between January and March, and for the continent as a whole, one out of every three Africans had been malnourished in the past 10 years. The Executive Director defined hunger as a symptom of failed harvest and of the failure to cope with natural disaster and overcome social inequities, ethnic strife and racial hatred. He noted that the relationship between hunger and conflict was similar to that between hunger and poverty, as hunger was both a cause and effect of poverty and political conflict. In that regard, competition for limited food resources could ignite violence and instability, as illustrated in a number of conflict situations in Africa, notably in the Sudan (Darfur), Mauritania and Senegal. He described adequate food aid as a critical component for facilitating peace processes in many African countries emerging from conflict, particularly with regard to disarmament, demobilization and reintegration efforts. It was also a tool to support education, help rebuild communities and afford people the means to safeguard their own welfare. The Executive Director described the extent of WFP's food aid delivery programme in Africa and addressed related concerns and questions raised by Council members. On the question of what was required to cover the total needs of Africa, the Executive Director estimated that an annual sum of $5 billion would be required to look after some 115 million people on the continent who needed help, comprising 93 million children and their mothers. To achieve that, there was a need for a global movement which would adopt the position that it was no longer acceptable for children to go hungry.

In a 19 December briefing to the Council [meeting 5332], the Chairman of the Ad Hoc Working Group on Conflict Prevention and Resolution in Africa said that the Group's activities in 2005 emphasized ways and means of meeting the challenge of preventing threats to the collective security of the international community and of addressing the related question of conflict prevention and resolution, within the contexts of ongoing UN reform efforts and of implementing the Millennium Development Goals. As several African countries continued to suffer from conflict situations and the continent faced complex difficulties that could cause those emerging from conflict to relapse into violence, the Group felt that it should take an active part in the debate on how to reform the UN and enhance its effectiveness in the area of conflict prevention and resolution in Africa. In doing so, it had contributed to forging a consensus on important issues of relevance to its work and had drawn up a programme of work identifying some general or specific issues raised in the Council in order to highlight the need to develop a comprehensive strategy for conflict prevention and to harmonize the approach to African questions by the United Nations, particularly the Security Council.

SECURITY COUNCIL ACTION

On 14 September [meeting 5261], the Security Council unanimously adopted **resolution 1625 (2005)**. The draft [S/2005/578] was prepared in consultations among Council members.

The Security Council,

Decides to adopt the attached declaration on strengthening the effectiveness of the role of the Security Council in conflict prevention, particularly in Africa.

Annex

The Security Council,

Meeting on 14 September 2005 at the level of Heads of State and Government to discuss how to strengthen the effectiveness of the role of the Security Council in the prevention of armed conflict, particularly in Africa,

Reaffirming its commitment to the purposes and principles of the Charter of the United Nations,

Bearing in mind its primary responsibility for the maintenance of international peace and security,

Deeply concerned by the high human cost and material losses caused by armed conflicts, and recognizing that peace, security and development are mutually reinforcing, including in the prevention of armed conflict,

Reaffirming the importance of adhering to the principles of refraining, in international relations, from the threat or the use of force in any manner inconsistent with the purposes of the United Nations, and of peaceful settlement of international disputes,

Reaffirming also the need to adopt a broad strategy of conflict prevention which addresses the root causes of armed conflict and political and social crises in a comprehensive manner, including by promoting sustainable development, poverty eradication, national reconciliation, good governance, democracy, gender equality, the rule of law and respect for and protection of human rights,

Recognizing the need to strengthen the important role of the United Nations in the prevention of violent conflicts, and to develop effective partnerships between the Council and regional organizations, in particular the African Union and its subregional organizations, in order to enable early responses to disputes and emerging crises,

Recalling the Constitutive Act of the African Union, the Protocol relating to the Establishment of the Peace and Security Council of the African Union, and the African Union Non-Aggression and Common Defence Pact adopted in Abuja on 31 January 2005, as well as the African Union position on unconstitutional changes of government, as stated in the 1999 Algiers Decision and the 2000 Lomé Declaration,

Recognizing the important supporting roles played by civil society, men and women, in conflict prevention, and the need to take into account all possible contributions from civil society,

1. *Expresses its determination* to enhance the effectiveness of the United Nations in preventing armed conflicts and to monitor closely situations of potential armed conflict;

2. *Affirms its determination* to strengthen United Nations conflict prevention capacities by:

(*a*) Assessing regularly the developments in regions at risk of armed conflict and encouraging the Secretary-General to provide information to the Security Council on such developments pursuant to Article 99 of the Charter of the United Nations;

(*b*) Promoting the follow-up of preventive diplomacy initiatives of the Secretary-General;

(*c*) Supporting regional mediation initiatives in close consultation with regional and subregional organizations concerned;

(*d*) Supporting regional and subregional capacities for early warning to help them in working out appropriate mechanisms to enable prompt action in reaction to early warning indicators;

(*e*) Requesting, as necessary and appropriate, information and assistance from the Economic and Social Council in accordance with Article 65 of the Charter;

(*f*) Taking measures to contribute to combating the illicit trade in arms in all its aspects and the use of mercenaries;

(*g*) Helping to enhance durable institutions conducive to peace, stability and sustainable development;

(*h*) Supporting efforts of African States to build independent and reliable national judicial institutions;

3. *Requests* the Secretary-General:

(*a*) To provide to the Security Council regular reports and analysis of developments in regions of potential armed conflict, particularly in Africa, and, as appropriate, a presentation of ongoing preventive diplomacy initiatives;

(*b*) To assist countries at risk of armed conflict in performing strategic conflict risk assessments, in implementing the measures agreed to by the concerned countries, in enhancing national dispute management capacities, and in addressing the root causes of armed conflict;

(*c*) To promote coordination with regional conflict management machinery in Africa which would provide the Council with additional reliable and timely information to facilitate rapid decision-making;

4. *Stresses* the importance of establishing effective comprehensive strategies of conflict prevention, focused on averting negative developments in the security, economic, social and humanitarian sectors and in the field of governance and human rights in countries which are facing crises, with special attention to:

(*a*) Developing quick-win activities to prevent conflicts arising from competition for economic resources, and to monitoring tension arising from economic and social issues;

(*b*) Encouraging United Nations regional offices to facilitate the implementation of strategies aimed at curbing illicit cross-border activities;

(*c*) Strengthening the capacities of civil society groups, including women's groups, working to promote a culture of peace, and to mobilize donors to support these efforts;

(*d*) Developing policy measures to foster good governance and the protection of human rights in order to strengthen weakened or collapsed governance mechanisms and to end the culture of impunity;

(*e*) Promoting the fairness and transparency of electoral processes;

5. *Stresses also* the critical importance of a regional approach to conflict prevention, particularly to programmes of disarmament, demobilization and reintegration, as well as the effective and sustainable reintegration of ex-combatants;

6. *Reaffirms its determination* to take action against illegal exploitation of and trafficking in natural resources and high-value commodities in areas where it contributes to the outbreak, escalation or continuation of armed conflict;

7. *Calls for* the strengthening of cooperation and communication between the United Nations and regional or subregional organizations or arrangements, in accordance with Chapter VIII of the Charter, particularly with respect to mediation initiatives;

8. *Encourages* all African States to adhere to the African Union Non-Aggression and Common Defence Pact adopted in Abuja on 31 January 2005, and to sign, where appropriate, subregional pacts on peace, security, democracy, good governance and development, and calls upon the United Nations system and the international community to support the implementation of the pacts;

9. *Encourages* African countries to continue to work closely with the United Nations Secretariat and United Nations regional offices in the implementation of measures aimed at securing peace, security, stability, democracy and sustainable development consistent with the objectives of the New Partnership for Africa's Development;

10. *Urges* the international community, including the United Nations system and international financial institutions, to support African countries in their efforts to achieve the above objectives, and in this respect welcomes the decisions taken by the summit of the Group of Eight, held in Gleneagles, United King-

dom of Great Britain and Northern Ireland, from 6 to 8 July 2005, for combating poverty in Africa;

11. *Urges* all African States and the international community to cooperate fully in developing the capacities of African regional and subregional organizations to deploy both civilian and military assets quickly when needed, including the development of the African Union's African Standby Force, welcomes bilateral and multilateral programmes developed to this end, and expresses its support for the proposal of the Secretary-General to establish a ten-year capacity-building programme for the African Union;

12. *Decides* to remain seized of the matter.

Office of the Special Adviser on Africa

In 2005, the New York-based Office of the Special Adviser on Africa (OSAA), established by the terms of General Assembly resolutions 57/7 [YUN 2002, p. 910] and 57/300 [YUN 2002, p. 1353], continued efforts to support the Organization's deliberations on Africa, to enhance international efforts to promote peace and development on the continent through analytical and advocacy-oriented activities and to assist the Secretary-General in related matters. In particular, OSAA continued to serve as the focal point for monitoring the implementation of the recommendations contained in the Secretary-General's 1998 report [YUN 1998, p. 66] on the causes of conflict and the promotion of durable peace and sustainable development in Africa. In that regard, it played a lead role in preparing the Secretary-General's 2005 progress report on the implementation of the recommendations in his 1998 report (see below), which highlighted the need for special attention to post-conflict reconstruction and peacebuilding and for increased conflict prevention and resolution efforts. Analytical work undertaken by OSAA within the year on related topics focused on "human security in Africa"—the concept of protecting and empowering people at the individual and community levels—as an essential condition to national and international security; "peace consolidation in Africa: challenges and opportunities", which reflected on post-conflict civilian and military efforts by external and internal actors to prevent the recurrence of conflict and establish the conditions for durable peace and sustainable development; and "conflict in Africa and the role of disarmament, demobilization and reintegration in post-conflict reconstruction", which recognized the significance of disarmament and demobilization programmes for the re-establishment of peace, security and stability in post-conflict situations.

OSAA organized an international conference, in cooperation with Sierra Leone (Freetown, 21-23 June), on disarmament, demobilization and reintegration and stability in Africa to share experiences and ideas on improving the design and implementation of those programmes to better sustain peace on the continent, and took initiatives to promote and facilitate UN system support for Africa's economic recovery within the framework of the New Partnership for Africa's Development (NEPAD) (see p. 1003).

In December, the General Assembly, in **resolution 60/223** (see p. 158), stressed the importance of enabling the Office of the Special Adviser on Africa to better fulfil its role as the focal point within the Secretariat for monitoring the implementation of the recommendations contained in the Secretary-General's report on the causes of conflict and promotion of durable peace and sustainable development in Africa.

Implementation of Secretary-General's 1998 recommendations on promotion of peace

Report of Secretary-General. In response to General Assembly resolution 59/255 [YUN 2004, p. 112], the Secretary-General submitted on 1 August a report [A/60/182] on the implementation of the recommendations contained in his 1998 report on the causes of conflict and promotion of durable peace and sustainable development in Africa [YUN 1998, p. 66]. Updating developments since his follow-up report on the subject [YUN 2004, p. 111], the report reviewed recent action taken in implementing those recommendations, particularly regarding progress made in peace-making and peacekeeping. It also highlighted remaining challenges and constraints and proposed measures to better consolidate peace on the continent.

The report noted that many recent trends in Africa had been positive, especially the fact that the number of major conflicts on the continent had further dropped from six in 2004 to three in 2005, a tremendous improvement from 1998 when the number stood at 14. Furthermore, most African countries enjoyed relatively stable political conditions and the majority had democratically elected Governments. Other encouraging developments included the establishment of the AU African Peer Review Mechanism, created to support national efforts to enhance political, economic and corporate governance, and the continent's improved growth rates, although not sufficient to ensure the achievement of the Millennium Development Goal of halving extreme poverty by 2015. The report described initiatives taken and the progress achieved towards enhancing the environment for peace through peace-making and conflict prevention; peacekeeping by the United Nations and regional organizations, as well as UN support to the latter; and a variety of post-conflict peacebuilding and reconstruction activities, including the promotion of human security and human rights in Africa and support in reestablishing governmental structures and the rule of law. Other activities concerned the promotion of a culture of peace, controlling the illicit traffic in small arms and light weapons, disarmament, demobilization and reintegration and stability, addressing economic and social challenges, and mobilizing resources for the reintegration of refugees and internally displaced persons. Notable progress was also made in terms of enhancing the role of women in conflict prevention and resolution and peacebuilding, as well as in financial and technical assistance to address the underlying causes of conflict and to support sustainable development.

Despite those advances, the conditions required for sustained peace and development had yet to be consolidated throughout the continent. Civil strife in the Democratic Republic of the Congo and in the Darfur region of the Sudan had resulted in great and horrific loss of life, brutality and human dislocation, and the international community's response to those crises had been slow and inadequate. The Secretary-General's High-level Panel on Threats, Challenges and Change [YUN 2004, p. 54] had identified economic and social threats, including poverty, infectious diseases and environmental degradation, and internal conflicts, including civil war, genocide and other large-scale atrocities, as the most harmful threats to durable peace and sustainable development in Africa. As such, continuing efforts and support by the international community, including UN organizations, were necessary to reduce poverty and disease, raise governmental capacity to provide services and security, and sustain peace and development on a longterm basis. It was important for the world community to increase financial, human and technical resources to advance regional, subregional and national security development efforts in Africa, ensuring that an adequate allocation was dedicated to the capacity-building of regional organizations. The AU should establish, as a matter of priority, a continental early warning system to be complemented with enhanced collaboration with the United Nations. To help strengthen the AU's capacity to take the lead in peacekeeping efforts in Africa, the necessary financial support from the international community was vital. More technical and institutional support to African organizations was needed in order to develop common standards and operating procedures for all peacekeeping operations. In that regard, careful consideration should be given to the establishment of a revolving fund to enable African States to obtain strategic sea and airlift capabilities. The

report also highlighted the need for close coordination of all peacekeeping and peace support activities on the continent, with the active involvement of the United Nations.

GENERAL ASSEMBLY ACTION

On 23 December [meeting 69], the General Assembly adopted **resolution 60/223** [draft: A/60/L.45 & Add.1] without vote [agenda item 66 *(b)*].

Implementation of the recommendations contained in the report of the Secretary-General on the causes of conflict and the promotion of durable peace and sustainable development in Africa

The General Assembly,

Recalling the report of the Open-ended Ad Hoc Working Group on the Causes of Conflict and the Promotion of Durable Peace and Sustainable Development in Africa, and its resolutions 53/92 of 7 December 1998, 54/234 of 22 December 1999, 55/217 of 21 December 2000, 56/37 of 4 December 2001, 57/296 of 20 December 2002, 57/337 of 3 July 2003, 58/235 of 23 December 2003 and 59/255 of 23 December 2004, as well as resolution 59/213 of 20 December 2004 on cooperation between the United Nations and the African Union,

Recalling also, in this context, Security Council resolutions 1325(2000) of 31 October 2000 on women and peace and security, 1366(2001) of 30 August 2001 on the role of the Council in the prevention of armed conflicts, and 1625(2005) of 14 September 2005 on strengthening the effectiveness of the Council's role in conflict prevention, especially in Africa,

Recalling further the creation by the Economic and Social Council, by its resolution 2002/1 of 15 July 2002, of ad hoc advisory groups on African countries emerging from conflict,

Having considered the progress report of the Secretary-General on the implementation of the recommendations contained in his report on the causes of conflict and the promotion of durable peace and sustainable development in Africa,

Recalling the 2005 World Summit Outcome, through which world leaders reaffirmed their commitment to addressing the special needs of Africa,

Recognizing that development, peace and security and human rights are interlinked and mutually reinforcing,

Noting that conflict prevention and the consolidation of peace would benefit from the coordinated, sustained and integrated efforts of the United Nations system and Member States, and regional and subregional organizations, as well as international and regional financial institutions,

Reaffirming that the implementation of the recommendations contained in the report of the Secretary-General on the causes of conflict and the promotion of durable peace and sustainable development in Africa must remain a priority in the agenda of the United Nations system and for Member States,

Stressing that the responsibility for peace and security in Africa, including the capacity to address the root causes of conflict and to resolve conflicts in a peaceful manner, lies primarily with African countries, while recognizing the need for support from the international community,

Underlining the need to address the negative implications of the illegal exploitation of natural resources in all its aspects on peace, security and development in Africa, noting, in this context, the relevant recommendations contained in the progress report of the Secretary-General,

Underscoring the need to further strengthen political will so as to ensure the financial and technical support required for the effective implementation of the recommendations included in the reports of the Secretary-General,

Reaffirming the need to strengthen the synergies between Africa's economic and social development programmes and its peace and security agenda,

1. *Takes note with appreciation* of the progress report of the Secretary-General on the implementation of the recommendations contained in his report on the causes of conflict and the promotion of durable peace and sustainable development in Africa, including recent efforts in peacemaking and peacekeeping operations and the need for special attention to post-conflict reconstruction and peacebuilding;

2. *Welcomes* the continuing progress in the reduction of major conflicts on the continent and the sustained efforts in recent times by the African Union, as well as by African regional and subregional organizations, to mediate and resolve conflicts, and notes that despite the positive trends and advances in Africa, the conditions required for sustained peace and development have yet to be consolidated throughout the continent;

3. *Notes with concern* the continuation on the continent, of many situations characterized by various forms of civil strife, including those caused by ethnic, religious and economic factors, and the role of illegal exploitation of natural resources in fuelling conflicts in Africa;

4. *Supports* Africa's goal of achieving a conflict-free Africa by 2010;

5. *Welcomes* the commitments in the areas of peace and stability made by the Group of Eight countries in the context of the Gleneagles communique adopted at their annual summit, held at Gleneagles, United Kingdom of Great Britain and Northern Ireland, from 6 to 8 July 2005, and looks forward to the early implementation of these commitments;

6. *Also welcomes* the determination of the African Union to strengthen its peacekeeping capacity and to take the lead in peacekeeping in the continent, in accordance with Chapter VIII of the Charter of the United Nations and in close coordination with the United Nations, through the Peace and Security Council, as well as ongoing efforts to develop a continental early warning system, enhanced mediation capacity, including through the establishment of the Panel of the Wise, and an African standby force;

7. *Urges* African countries, the United Nations system and the international community to increase, coordinate and sustain their efforts aimed at addressing the full range of causes of conflict in Africa by strengthening conflict prevention and resolution and post-conflict peacebuilding measures and activities, including the strengthening of African peacekeeping capacity;

8. *Urges* the United Nations and other relevant partners to support the establishment of the African Union continental early warning system as a matter of priority;

9. *Urges* the United Nations and invites other development partners to increase their support for the African Union in order to enhance its capacity and effectiveness in the planning, deployment and management of peacekeeping operations and the provision of advanced training to African peacekeepers, recognizes the important role of the good offices of the Secretary-General in Africa, and encourages the Secretary-General to use mediation as often as possible to help to solve conflicts peacefully, taking due consideration of the work performed by the African Union and other subregional organizations in that regard;

10. *Welcomes* the use of the African Peace Facility of the European Union, and initiatives by members of the Group of Eight to build African peacekeeping capacity, such as the Global Peace Operations Initiative of the United States of America and the Reinforcement of African Peacekeeping Capacities programme of France, as well as efforts by other international partners to support the implementation of peace initiatives undertaken by the African Union and African subregional organizations;

11. *Also welcomes* the decision taken in the 2005 World Summit Outcome to establish a Peacebuilding Commission as an intergovernmental advisory body to address the special needs of countries emerging from conflict towards recovery, reintegration and reconstruction and to assist them in laying the foundation for sustainable development, and notes that the Commission should begin its work no later than 31 December 2005;

12. *Invites* the Commission of the African Union, the secretariat of the New Partnership for Africa's Development and the United Nations Secretariat to coordinate their actions with a view to implementing an African-led agenda, deriving from the strategic policy framework for post-conflict reconstruction being developed by the African Union to tackle post-conflict peacebuilding and reconstruction, addressing the linkages among security, development and humanitarian dimensions of peace in Africa;

13. *Calls upon* the United Nations system and invites Member States to assist African countries emerging from conflict in their efforts to restore security, provide for the safe return of internally displaced persons and refugees, promote and monitor human rights and increase income-generating activities, especially for youth and demobilized ex-combatants;

14. *Stresses* the critical importance of a regional approach to conflict prevention, particularly regarding cross-border issues such as disarmament, demobilization and reintegration programmes, prevention of illegal exploitation and trafficking of natural resources and high-value commodities, and emphasizes the potential role of the African Union and subregional organizations in addressing the issue of the illicit trade in small arms and light weapons in all its aspects;

15. *Notes with concern* the tragic plight of children in conflict situations in Africa, particularly the growing phenomenon of child soldiers, and reiterates the need for post-conflict counselling, rehabilitation and education;

16. *Also notes with concern* that violence against women continues and often increases, even as armed conflicts draw to an end, and urges further progress in the implementation of policies and guidelines relating to protection of and assistance for women in conflict and post-conflict situations;

17. *Calls for* the enhancement of the role of women in conflict prevention, conflict resolution, and post-conflict peacebuilding and for expanding gender mainstreaming in the work of United Nations organizations involved in peacemaking, peacekeeping and post-conflict reconstruction;

18. *Decides* to continue to monitor the implementation of the recommendations contained in the report of the Secretary-General on the causes of conflict and the promotion of durable peace and sustainable development in Africa;

19 *Stresses* the importance of enabling the Office of the Special Adviser on Africa to better fulfil its role as the focal point within the Secretariat for monitoring the implementation of the recommendations contained in the report of the Secretary-General referred to in paragraph 18 above;

20. *Requests* the Secretary-General to submit to the General Assembly at its sixty-first session a progress report on the implementation of the present resolution.

African peacekeeping capacity

The Special Committee on Peacekeeping Operations, at its 2005 substantive session (New York, 31 January–25 February) [A/59/19/Rev.1], continued discussions on the enhancement of African peacekeeping capabilities. Welcoming AU efforts to strengthen its crisis management and progress towards the development of an African standby force, the Special Committee called upon the international community to support those efforts. It advocated, in particular, that the United Nations and key strategic partners should increase support for AU efforts to undertake and manage peacekeeping operations in Africa, and supported the development of a joint action plan to address the systemic constraints identified by African States, including in the areas of common doctrine and training standards, logistical support, funding and institutional capacity. For the effectiveness of such joint action, the Special Committee stressed the importance of enhanced coordination between the United Nations, the AU and subregional organizations and non-African partners, including the European Union (EU) and Group of Eight (G-8) major industrialized countries. It welcomed the Secretary-General's recommendations for enhancing African peacekeeping capacity, such programmes as staff exchanges and the secondment of UN peacekeeping personnel to help the AU and subregional organizations build a cadre of qualified civilian and military training staff, and for the possibility of UN logistical support to AU peacekeeping missions until the Union developed fully its own capacity. The Special Committee recognized that the United Nations could make available to the AU a small core planning and advisory capacity to facilitate the initial planning and start-up processes of an AU-led peacekeeping mission. Such core capacity could consist of representatives from the Department of Peacekeeping Operations and its field missions, and could be temporarily attached to the AU headquarters.

On 14 September, the Security Council, in **resolution 1625(2005)** (see p. 155), urged African States and the international community to fully cooperate in developing the capacities of African regional and subregional organizations to deploy both civilian and military assets quickly when needed, including the development of the AU African Standby Force, and welcomed bilateral and multilateral programmes developed towards that end.

Central Africa and Great Lakes region

The United Nations and the wider international community continued in 2005 to assist the States of Central Africa and the Great Lakes region to resolve chronic conflicts and achieve political stability. The United Nations kept in place its peacekeeping missions in the Democratic Republic of the Congo (DRC), Burundi and the Central African Republic in support of the ongoing electoral and peace processes in those countries. As it had done in the previous five years, the Security Council dispatched a mission to assess the overall situation in the region and make recommendations. The United Nations Standing Advisory Committee on Security Questions in Central Africa held its yearly meetings also to assess the geopolitical and security situation in the region. More importantly, the 11 core States of the 2004 International Conference on Peace, Security, Democracy and Development in the Great Lakes Region, in collaboration with AU, made preparations for a second summit Conference in 2006, intended to adopt a regional security, stability and development pact.

Burundi, which had been moving its transitional process progressively forward, approved its Constitution by referendum in February, and, for the first time since gaining independence in 1962, successfully held national elections in June and July. In August, a Joint Parliamentary Congress elected Pierre Nkurunziza as President, whose inauguration in the same month marked the formal conclusion of the transitional process to a democratically elected Government. Similarly, the Central African Republic, in an electoral process deemed free, reliable, fair and transparent by national and international observers, voted for and confirmed General François Bozizé as President and Head of State in June, marking the country's return to constitutional order since the coup d'état in 2003. The national electoral process was completed in September, when elections at the *colline* level were held.

In the DRC, where preparations for national elections were under way, organizational problems resulted in delays, necessitating the Government of National Unity and Transition to extend the transition period, as allowed under the terms of the 2002 Global and All-Inclusive Agreement on the Transition in the Democratic Republic of the Congo; the revised electoral timetable called for elections by 30 June 2006. In December, the DRC successfully held a referendum on the new Constitution. Meanwhile, the Council increased the strength of the United Nations Organization Mission in the Democratic Republic of the Congo to provide logistics and security during the electoral period. To bolster the efforts of the DRC and the Mission to exert military pressure on the armed groups and movements operating in the eastern part of the country to give up their arms and disband, and to stem the flow of illegal arms into the area, the Council, in April, expanded the scope of its 2003 arms embargo imposed on those groups and movements and, in August, renewed the embargo until 31 July 2006. At the request of the Council, the Secretary-General re-established the Group of Experts monitoring the arms embargo twice, the second time, until 31 January 2006.

Among the key challenges confronting the newly elected Government of Burundi in its efforts to consolidate peace was to bring the rebel group, Parti pour la libération du peuple hutu-Forces nationales de libération, referred to as FNL (Rwasa), or Palipehutu-FNL, into the peace process. In the DRC, the Forces démocratiques de libération du Rwanda, an anti-Rwanda armed group operating in the eastern part of the country, issued a statement in March by which the group, in addition to condemning the 1994 Rwanda genocide, undertook to renounce the use of force and cease all offensive operations against Rwanda—a statement which the Council regarded as a significant opportunity to move towards the return of peace in the DRC, national reconciliation in Rwanda, and full normalization of relations between the two countries. Another armed group called the ex-FAR/Interahamwe

(elements of the former Rwandan regime, including former soldiers of the Forces Armées Rwandaises), also operating in the eastern DRC, made known its intention to disarm unconditionally and return to Rwanda. Those statements remained to be put into action.

The United Nations Peace-building Support Office in the Central African Republic (BONUCA) continued to support the Republic's efforts to return to stability and achieve reconciliation and reconstruction, following the 2003 coup d'état. With the agreement of the Security Council, the Secretary-General extended the mandate of BONUCA for an additional year, until 31 December 2006, to help the country build on the success of its recent elections.

In December, the General Assembly requested the Secretary-General to establish an outreach programme entitled "The Rwanda Genocide and the United Nations", as well as measures to mobilize civil society for Rwanda genocide victim remembrance and education.

International Conference on Great Lakes Region

Preparations for second summit

On 15 November [S/2005/793], the Secretary-General noted that, since the first summit of the International Conference on Peace, Security, Democracy and Development in the Great Lakes Region [YUN 2004, p. 116], the 11 core countries of the Conference (Angola, Burundi, Central African Republic, Congo, Democratic Republic of the Congo (DRC), Kenya, Rwanda, Sudan, the United Republic of Tanzania, Uganda, Zambia) had worked to translate the Declaration adopted by the Conference [ibid.] into common programmes of action and protocols under the four Conference themes of peace and security, governance and democracy, economic development and regional integration, and social and humanitarian issues. A number of those were selected as priorities, which, together with the Declaration, were to form a stability and development pact for the Great Lakes region to be proposed for consideration by the upcoming second summit of the Conference. The extent of implementation of the proposed pact as a regional peacebuilding initiative, when adopted, would be the real measure of the success of the Conference.

The Regional Inter-Ministerial Committee, set up by the Conference [ibid.] to prepare draft protocols and programmes of action, met twice during the year. At its first meeting (Kigali, Rwanda, 15-18 February), the Committee approved its structure and functioning, as well as that of the Regional Preparatory Committee; the terms of reference of the draft protocols; programmes of action and projects; and the plan of activities for the summit. At its second meeting (Lusaka, Zambia, 22-23 July), it reviewed and prioritized the draft programmes of action and projects and discussed follow-up to the second summit.

The Regional Preparatory Committee met twice (Kigali, 14-16 February; Lusaka, 18-21 July) to prepare for the Inter-Ministerial Committee meetings. Thereafter, it held an extraordinary meeting (Luanda, Angola, 26-30 September) to review the draft documents for submission to a third and final Inter-Ministerial Committee meeting, rescheduled for 2006, following postponement of the second summit until after 30 June 2006, when the political transition in the DRC was expected to conclude.

Special Representative for Great Lakes Region

On 15 November [S/2005/793], the Secretary-General notified the Security Council that the mandate of his Special Representative for the Great Lakes Region, Ibrahima Fall, would expire on 31 December. In view of the Special Representative's involvement with the first (2004) summit of the International Conference on the Great Lakes Region [YUN 2004, p. 116] and the ongoing preparations for the second (2006) summit, the Secretary-General affirmed his intention to extend the mandate until 31 December 2006.

On 15 December [S/2005/794], the Council requested further clarification of the intended extension of the mandate, detailing the expected activities of the Special Representative and his office to support the Conference process, based on the assessment of his role and performance over the previous eight years. By a further exchange of letters between the Secretary-General and the Council on 23 [S/2005/849] and 30 December [S/2005/850], the Special Representative's mandate was extended until 31 March 2006, although the information requested was not available by the end of 2005.

Security Council mission to Central Africa

On 27 October [S/2005/682], the Security Council informed the Secretary-General that it was sending a mission to Central Africa from 4 to 10 November, headed by Jean-Marc de La Sablière (France). The mission would visit Burundi, the DRC, Rwanda, Uganda and the United Republic of Tanzania. Under its general terms of reference, the mission would underscore the importance of the resources committed by the United Nations to peacekeeping in the DRC and Burundi and the need for an unequivocal commitment on the part of national and regional actors; stress the importance of achieving sustainable peace, security and stability for all countries in the region; and encourage the peaceful resolution of differences through dialogue and the establishment of confidence-building measures and mechanisms. The mission would welcome investigative and preventive action by the United Nations Organization Mission in the Democratic Republic of the Congo (MONUC) and the United Nations Operation in Burundi (UNOB) in cases of alleged sexual exploitation and abuse by UN personnel, and would reaffirm the need for troop-contributing States to take the necessary disciplinary and judicial measures, and to attend fully to the victims. It would examine also the question of the use of children in armed conflict. Specific terms of reference were also outlined for each of the countries to be visited.

Mission report. On 14 November [S/2005/716], the mission reported on its visit, the sixth in as many years. In the DRC, the mission observed the progress made in the peace and transition process. President Joseph Kabila and the four Vice-Presidents stressed that their relationship had improved since the Government of National Unity and Transition was installed. The mission insisted on strict adherence to the electoral timeline for the political transition, which should culminate in the holding of free elections by 30 June 2006, and stressed the need to create socio-economic and political conditions to ensure stability in the post-transitional period. It insisted that progress in security sector reform was critical to the immediate and long-term stability of the DRC, particularly with regard to the acceleration of operations to disarm and repatriate foreign armed groups on its territory, and the resumption of the demobilization, training and integration of former combatants into a restructured DRC army.

In Burundi, the mission noted the challenges facing the new Government in the post-transitional period in its efforts to consolidate peace under its key priorities of reconstruction, development, good governance, human rights and the return of refugees from neighbouring countries. Regarding Burundi's suggestion that the UN peacekeeping component could be gradually reduced because security had returned to a major part of the country, the mission cautioned against an untimely disengagement of peacekeepers, as that had led, in similar situations, to a weakening of the overall security and political situation. In that regard, the mission expressed concern over the increase in insecurity and attacks on civilians, reportedly by the rebel Forces nationales de libération (Palipehutu-FNL), which repeated Government efforts had failed to bring into the peace process. Despite the difficulties it faced in reconciling its commitment to downsize public administration with the constitutional requirement to include Burundi's 36 political parties, the Government promised to make every effort to ensure their representation in the administration.

In meetings with President Yoweri Kaguta Museveni of Uganda and President Paul Kagame of Rwanda, the mission reiterated the Council's concern regarding the continued presence of foreign armed groups in eastern DRC, and underlined the importance of supporting and reinforcing the integration of the Forces armées de la République démocratique du Congo (FARDC) to enable it to tackle those armed groups robustly, with MONUC support. The Presidents agreed that, while successful elections in the DRC would contribute to the stability of the country and of the region as a whole, the issue of the presence of Ugandan and Rwandan armed groups in the eastern DRC, had to be resolved as they posed a threat not only to the DRC but also to Uganda and Rwanda. President Museveni reiterated the call made by the Tripartite Plus Joint Commission that the Forces démocratiques pour la libération du Rwanda (FDLR) be forcibly disarmed; President Kagame insisted that MONUC conduct operations against FDLR in the provinces of North Kivu and South Kivu as robustly as against Congolese militias in the district of Ituri.

The mission highlighted its concerns over the humanitarian situation in northern Uganda, the recent attacks on humanitarian workers and the security challenges faced by aid agencies. It encouraged Uganda to expedite the arrest of five leaders of the defeated Lord's Resistance Army (LRA), for whom the International Criminal Court had issued arrest warrants, while finding a peaceful solution for other LRA elements, some of whom remained active and contributed to insecurity in northern Uganda. The mission urged Uganda to extend amnesty to rank-and-file LRA combatants and to help them reintegrate into their communities. It emphasized that the use of force in the territory of a foreign State without the latter's consent would be a violation of the UN Charter.

The mission expressed concern over reports of continuing violations of the arms embargo imposed by Security Council resolution 1493(2003) [YUN 2003, p. 130] and urged Uganda and Rwanda to improve their cooperation with the Group of Experts established under resolution 1533(2004) [YUN 2004, p. 137] to monitor arms flows into the region. It also urged them to reinforce measures to prevent and deny the entry of arms into the east-

ern part of the DRC through their respective territories. Rwanda confirmed that it had established an inter-ministerial committee to monitor implementation of the embargo and to strengthen cooperation with the Group of Experts. The mission encouraged the Group to continue its investigations and called upon all States concerned to cooperate fully with it.

The United Republic of Tanzania shared the mission's concerns regarding the security situation in Burundi, including the risks that could arise from an untimely withdrawal of ONUB. In that regard, President Benjamin Mkapa and his Foreign Minister called for additional support for the integration of Burundi's army. The President reiterated Tanzania's commitment to cooperate with the Office of the United Nations High Commissioner for Refugees (UNHCR) in support of the voluntary return of Burundian and Congolese refugees in the United Republic of Tanzania to their respective countries.

The mission made a series of recommendations for consideration by the Council that were specific to each of the countries visited and for regional cooperation.

Uganda, on 7 December [S/2005/770], conveyed its observations on a number of the mission's recommendations as they related to Uganda, as well as a detailed account of the exchange of views between the head of the mission and Uganda's President and of their joint press conference.

Security Council consideration. The Council, on 15 November [meeting 5305], heard a briefing by the head of the mission, who said that the mission found in the DRC commendable progress in the preparations for the referendum on the constitution and for the legislative and presidential elections, for which 20 million voters had been registered. Several problems remained, however. First, the election preparations had been delayed, making the electoral timetable tight. The mission emphasized the imperative of opening the elections to everyone, adhering to the election date of 30 June 2006, and promulgating the electoral law the day after the adoption of the constitution on 18 December 2005. Second, despite progress in the demobilization of ex-combatants and restructuring of the army and police, the armed forces integration programme was interrupted after the first phase, and only six of the nine brigades planned had been integrated. The DRC was asked to redouble its efforts in starting the second integration phase and to ensure that the newly integrated brigades received the necessary equipment and were paid regularly and adequately. Third, the mission reiterated that the priority of re-establishing State authority had to be carried out with respect for the rule of law. Additional problems concerned the armed groups in the eastern part of the DRC, regarding which the mission stressed the need for every country concerned to respect the sovereignty of their neighbours, ensure that those groups received no cross-border support, respect the arms embargo, and no longer tolerate the illegal exploitation of natural resources that financed arms trafficking.

In Burundi, where a post-transition Government was already in place, the issue of disengaging the military component of ONUB was raised. The United Nations and Burundi might wish to consider a plan for a phased disengagement and transition from peacekeeping to peacebuilding. The mission felt it advisable for Burundi to establish a dialogue with the international community, the best channel for which would be the proposed Peacebuilding Commission (see p. 93). As to Palipehutu-FNL, the remaining active rebel group in the country, the Government remained open to resuming negotiations to bring the group into the peace process. The briefing recalled the previously expressed readiness of the Council (in its resolution 1577 (2004) [YUN 2004, p. 155]) to consider appropriate measures against individuals who threatened Burundi's peace and national reconciliation process, an option that the mission reminded Burundi was still available.

The head of the mission introduced the mission's report (see above) for consideration by the Council on 6 December [meeting 5315], which took note of the report and endorsed its recommendations on 21 December [meeting 5340] in resolution 1649(2005) (see p. 187).

Standing Advisory Committee on Security Questions

The United Nations Standing Advisory Committee on Security Questions in Central Africa held its twenty-second and twenty-third ministerial meetings in Brazzaville, Congo, on 14-18 March [A/59/769-S/2005/212] and on 29 August-2 September [A/60/393-S/2005/616], with all Committee members (Angola, Burundi, Cameroon, Central African Republic, Chad, Congo, DRC, Equatorial Guinea, Gabon, Rwanda, Sao Tome and Principe) participating. At both meetings, the Committee reviewed the geopolitical and security situation in Burundi, the Central African Republic, the DRC and Chad, as well as the situation between the DRC and Rwanda. The Committee noted considerable improvement in the security situation in Central Africa as a whole and in the countries reviewed in particular. Having led to free and democratic elections, the peace processes under way in most of those countries remained fragile, however, and the countries concerned and others of the subregion, together with the international community, needed to redouble their efforts to consolidate peace. In that regard, the Committee appealed to the subregion to become more closely involved in the settlement of conflicts and to support the ongoing peace processes.

The Committee condemned all forms of violence committed against women and children in conflict or in post-conflict situations, and recommended strengthening the mechanisms to punish those responsible. It exchanged experiences in the implementation of disarmament, demobilization and reintegration programmes for ex-combatants, and urgently appealed for funds to enable timely implementation. It adopted two declarations: one on mercenary activity in Central Africa that had become a serious obstacle to subregional peace, stability and development; and the other on the role of the Economic Community of Central African States in the implementation of the 2004 Declaration on Peace, Security, Democracy and Development in the Great Lakes Region [YUN 2004, p. 116]. The Committee reviewed Central Africa's contribution to the second biennial meeting of States to consider the implementation of the Programme of Action adopted by the 2001 UN Conference on small arms [YUN 2001, p. 499] and noted the activities of the Subregional Centre for Human Rights and Democracy in Central Africa.

The Committee, concerned at the continued tensions and incidents along the DRC-Rwanda border, particularly the presence of Rwandan armed groups in the eastern regions of the DRC, urged the AU Peace and Security Council to implement its 10 January decision to provide a military force to assist the DRC in disarming the anti-Rwandan rebel group ex-FAR/Interahamwe and other hostile forces operating in the DRC. It welcomed the bilateral and tripartite measures agreed upon at the high-level tripartite meeting among Cameroon, the Central African Republic and Chad (Yaoundé, Cameroon, 25-26 August) on the long-term prevention and/or containment of insecurity along their common borders caused by roadblocks set up by armed gangs and others.

The Secretary-General, in response to General Assembly resolution 59/96 [YUN 2004, p. 571], submitted a July report [A/60/166] on the Committee's activities regarding regional confidence-building measures taken at its twenty-second ministerial meeting, updating an earlier report [A/59/182] on the Committee's twentieth [YUN 2003, p. 111] and twenty-first [YUN 2004, p. 118] meetings.

Democratic Republic of the Congo

In 2005, the peace process in the DRC continued to move forward in the context of the 2002 Global and All-Inclusive Agreement on the Transition in the Democratic Republic of the Congo [YUN 2002, p. 125]. The Agreement provided for a two-year transitional period, which started from the formation of a transitional Government, inaugurated on 30 June 2003 as the Government of National Unity and Transition (Transitional Government) [YUN 2003, p. 129], and ended on 30 June 2005. Owing to problems related to the organization of the elections, the National Assembly and Senate jointly decided on 17 June to extend the transitional period for six months, as from 1 July. The period would be renewable once and would expire on the inauguration of the President following national elections, which were to be completed in 2006. The transition and election preparations were supported by the International Committee in Support of the Transition, comprising the five permanent Security Council members, plus Belgium and Canada; four African countries (Angola, Gabon, South Africa and Zambia); the EU and the AU; and MONUC (see below).

As of 17 December, over 25 million citizens of an estimated electorate of 22 to 28 million had registered to vote. On 18 and 19 December, a referendum on the DRC Constitution was held successfully.

By resolution 1596(2005), the Council expanded the scope of the arms embargo it had imposed by resolution 1493(2003) [YUN 2003, p. 130] on armed groups operating in the DRC. By resolution 1616(2005), it renewed the provisions of the embargo until 31 July 2006 and requested the Secretary-General to re-establish the Group of Experts monitoring the flows of arms in the region for a period expiring on 31 January 2006.

MONUC

The United Nations Organization Mission in the Democratic Republic of the Congo (MONUC), established by Security Council resolution 1279 (1999) [YUN 1999, p. 92], was headed by William Lacy Swing (United States), Special Representative of the Secretary-General for the Democratic Republic of the Congo. MONUC continued in 2005 to discharge its mandate, as enhanced by Council resolution 1565(2004) [YUN 2004, p. 129], to provide operational and security support to guarantee the advancement of the transitional processes in the DRC towards elections and the establishment of a democratically elected Government. Its mandate was extended by the Council twice during the year, the first time until 1 October 2005 and the second until 30 September 2006. MONUC was headquartered in the DRC capital, Kinshasa.

Following its consideration of the Secretary-General's special report on the election process, the Council, by resolution 1621(2005) (see p. 181), increased the strength of MONUC by 841 personnel (five formed police units of 125 officers each plus 216 additional police) and authorized MONUC, in close coordination with UNDP, to provide additional support to the Independent Electoral Commission (IEC) for the transport of electoral materials within the DRC. By resolution 1635(2005) (see p. 186), the Council further increased MONUC's military strength by 300 to provide additional security within its area of operations during the electoral period. By its resolution 60/121, the General Assembly authorized the full deployment to MONUC of 507 additional personnel in support of the DRC elections.

Appointment. By an exchange of letters between the Secretary-General and the Security Council on 4 [S/2005/151] and 9 March [S/2005/152], Lieutenant General Babacar Gaye (Senegal) was appointed Force Commander of MONUC, replacing Major General Somaila Isliya (Nigeria), who completed his assignment on 28 February.

Sexual exploitation and abuse

In a 9 February letter to the Security Council [S/2005/79], the Secretary-General discussed the UN response to allegations of sexual exploitation and misconduct by MONUC civilian and military personnel. He reiterated that the United Nations could not tolerate even one instance of a UN peacekeeper victimizing the most vulnerable. Such behaviour did great harm to the distinguished tradition of UN peacekeepers, to troop-contributing Member States and to the reputation and honour of fellow peacekeepers. Most importantly, it violated the fundamental "duty of care" that peacekeepers owed to the very people they were sent to protect and serve. On the basis of the report of Prince Zeid Ra'ad Zeid Al-Hussein (Jordan), the Secretary-General's Adviser on Sexual Exploitation and Abuse by United Nations Peacekeeping Personnel, the United Nations was developing ways for troop-contributing countries to assist in eliminating sexual exploitation and abuse.

In January, the Office of Internal Oversight Services (OIOS) released the report on its investigation into alleged sexual misconduct by peacekeepers serving in Bunia (see p. 118). It identified 72 allegations, of which 20 warranted follow-up action; of those 20, seven individual cases (all military personnel) were fully substantiated. As most of those individuals had been rotated out of the Mission or repatriated, their cases were forwarded to the relevant Member States for action, with a request for information on follow-up measures taken. Additional investigations, carried out by MONUC into allegations against six other military personnel were completed; of those, four were repatriated, one was exonerated and one rotated home before the investigation was concluded. A joint team from the UN Office of Human Resources Management and DPKO investigated another five individuals, all civilians: one was in custody and awaiting trial in his home country, one was reassigned, one was cleared, one was disciplined and one was still under investigation. Also in January, DPKO sent a multidisciplinary team, headed by its Assistant Secretary-General to MONUC, to conduct further investigations and assist MONUC in developing an effective and sustainable response to the issue. The team completed nine investigations, was still investigating 10 others and had closed several files. MONUC had taken a number of measures to eliminate sexual exploitation and abuse: it had adopted a strict non-fraternization policy, imposed a curfew for military contingents, conducted comprehensive training and awareness-raising for all Mission personnel, and put forward proposals for improving contingent welfare facilities.

The Secretary-General appealed to the Council to assist in strengthening MONUC's capacity to conduct self-monitoring and enforcement programmes.

In his March report on MONUC (see p. 172), the Secretary-General said that the Headquarters-based task force on sexual exploitation and abuse had clarified existing policies and provided new guidelines to MONUC and other peacekeeping operations. The multidisciplinary team deployed to MONUC (see above) was increased in February by five highly skilled investigators and would be further strengthened to meet medium-term investigation requirements. The team was working closely with civilian and military colleagues in MONUC to consolidate the investigation process, decrease duplication, provide specialized techniques specific to the prevention of sexual exploitation and abuse, and improve the review process on which disciplinary recommendations were based. It established a sexual exploitation and abuse focal point network with all UN agencies, funds and programmes in the DRC. The MONUC code of conduct was revised to define and clarify behaviour constituting sexual exploitation and abuse.

By its resolution 1592(2005) (see p. 174), the Council urged troop-contributing countries to carefully review the report of the Secretary-

General's Special Adviser entitled "A comprehensive strategy to eliminate future sexual exploitation and abuse in UN peacekeeping operations" (see p. 119), and to take appropriate action to prevent sexual exploitation and abuse by their personnel in the Mission, including pre-deployment awareness-training, and to take disciplinary and other action to ensure full accountability in cases of such misconduct.

In his August report (see p. 179), the Secretary-General stated that the MONUC Office for Addressing Sexual Exploitation and Abuse was established on 1 March. Its activities included investigating allegations of sexual misconduct involving MONUC personnel; developing and implementing policies that emphasized prevention of sexual exploitation and abuse and assistance to victims of such misconduct; training MONUC personnel in that regard; and raising awareness of the issue among the Congolese public. By the end of June, some 400 persons of all categories of MONUC personnel had attended MONUC-conducted training on the prevention of sexual exploitation and abuse.

In his September report (see p. 182), the Secretary-General said that the inter-agency focal point network on sexual exploitation and abuse, chaired by MONUC, was developing common standards and procedures for: the code of conduct; training materials and strategies; the referral of complaints; community outreach; the implementing partners of UN agencies and MONUC, in compliance with the Secretary-General's bulletin [ST/SGB/2003/13] on special measures for protection from sexual exploitation and abuse; and the transmission of complaints received by one agency about incidents involving staff of another agency. MONUC established a Sexual Violence Working Group, which was developing training and advocacy packages for the Congolese military, police and judiciary, and reviewing existing relevant legislation. MONUC also established a database to facilitate the provision of assistance to individual victims.

In his December report (see p. 189), the Secretary-General stated that, in accordance with General Assembly resolution 59/287 (see p. 1474), the MONUC Office for Addressing Sexual Exploitation and Abuse formally handed over all pending cases and new allegations to OIOS on 4 October. From 25 December 2004 to mid-October 2005, 111 investigations into allegations of sexual exploitation and abuse, involving 167 MONUC personnel, were completed; allegations were substantiated against 78 (over 46 per cent of the alleged perpetrators), representing 0.4 per cent of all MONUC personnel in all levels and categories. On 8 November, the MONUC Conduct and Discipline Team was established to ensure the prevention of all types of personnel misconduct, with emphasis on sexual exploitation and abuse, and compliance with and enforcement of UN standards of conduct among all categories of Mission personnel. By 16 November, the Team had held 60 briefings for over 1,500 MONUC personnel.

Attack on peacekeepers

The Secretary-General, in describing the security situation in the district of Ituri, north east of the DRC, as contained in his March report on MONUC, stated that, on 22 February, the Union des patriotes congolais (UPC) attacked MONUC peacekeepers in Nizi, wounding two Pakistani soldiers. On 25 February, nine Bangladeshi peacekeepers protecting a camp of internally displaced persons were killed near the town of Kafé, 80 kilometres north of Bunia, on Lake Albert. The attack might have been in response to the increasing pressure by MONUC on militia groups over the previous weeks, notably the 24 February arrest of numerous militia members of the Front des nationalistes et intégrationistes (FNI) in their Datule stronghold. It might also have been designed to discourage the International Committee in Support of the Transition (CIAT) [YUN 2004, p. 119], which was in Bunia as part of efforts to ensure the extension of State administration to the area.

In response, MONUC and CIAT asked the Transitional Government to arrest the FNI leaders, in particular its President, Floribert Njabu, its former military leader, Goda Sukpa, and its current military commander, Etienne Lona; the head of the UPC/L faction, Thomas Lubanga, and its military commander, Bosco Ntaganda; and the head of the Front de résistance patriotique de l'Ituri (FRPI), Germain Katanga. Etienne Lona, who surrendered to MONUC, was arrested by the Government in Bunia on 1 March. MONUC also asked that the Transitional Government send clear orders to the armed groups in Ituri that they had to join the disarmament process immediately.

Also on 1 March, MONUC successfully mounted a large-scale cordon-and-search operation with attack-helicopter support to dismantle an FNI headquarters in Loga (north-east of Bunia), in Ituri. In the exchange of fire, between 50 and 60 FNI militia were killed and two Pakistani MONUC soldiers were injured.

SECURITY COUNCIL ACTION (March)

On 2 March [meeting 5133], following consultations among Security Council members, the President made statement **S/PRST/2005/10** on behalf of the Council:

The Security Council condemns with the utmost firmness the attack against a patrol of the United Nations Mission in the Democratic Republic of the Congo by the Front des Nationalistes et Intégrationnistes in Ituri, which occurred on 25 February 2005 near the town of Kafé, resulting in the murder of nine Bangladeshi peacekeepers. It offers its condolences to the victims' families and to the authorities of Bangladesh. It commends the dedication of the Mission's personnel, who operate in particularly hazardous conditions. It welcomes the action of the Mission against the militia groups responsible for these killings and the Mission's continued robust action in pursuit of its mandate.

The Council considers this aggression, by its intentional and well-planned nature, to be an unacceptable outrage. It calls upon the Government of National Unity and Transition immediately to take all necessary measures to bring to justice the perpetrators, sponsors and authors of this attack, and welcomes the first arrests undertaken by the Government. It endorses in this regard the serious concern expressed in Kinshasa on 28 February 2005 by the International Committee for Support to the Transition over the illegal and criminal activities of militia in Ituri and their military and political leaders, in particular Floribert Ndjabu, Goda Sukpa, Etienne Lona, Thomas Lubanga, Bosco Tanganda and Germain Katanga. It expresses its concern that the integration of Ituri militia officers into the Congolese armed forces has failed to lead to the disarmament of their troops which should proceed without delay.

The Council calls upon the Government of National Unity and Transition to strengthen its support for the implementation of the disarmament and community reintegration programme for Ituri militiamen. It considers those who try to impede this programme as a threat to the political process in the Democratic Republic of the Congo. It also calls upon the Government of National Unity and Transition urgently to deploy additional integrated troops and police units to Ituri, and invites donors to provide support for this vital undertaking.

The Council reminds all States in the region of their responsibility to ensure compliance for the arms embargo imposed by resolution 1493(2003) and is considering additional measures it might take to reinforce implementation and monitoring of the embargo. It further urges those States to ensure that their territories cannot be used by any Congolese armed group, notably the Ituri militia, whose activities perpetuate a climate of insecurity that affects the whole region.

The Council reaffirms its full support for the Mission, and urges it to continue to fulfil its mandate with determination. It notes the importance for the Mission to continue to strengthen its action in Ituri and in North and South Kivu.

Responding to the foregoing presidential statement, the DRC informed the Security Council on 21 March [S/2005/190] that, on that date, Thomas Lubanga was detained and immediately transferred to Makala prison; Floribert Ndjabu,

Goda Sukpa and Germain Katanga were already under arrest; and Etienne Lona had reportedly surrendered to MONUC. Bosco Ntaganda remained at large and continued to cause trouble in an area in Ituri not under the control of the Congolese authorities. The DRC requested all possible assistance from the Council and MONUC for his capture.

Financing

In April, during its resumed fifty-ninth session, the General Assembly considered the Secretary-General's revised budget for MONUC for the period 1 July 2004 to 30 June 2005 [A/59/707], amounting to $962,012,400 against the initial appropriation of $709,123,200, together with the related report of the Advisory Committee on Administrative and Budgetary Questions (ACABQ) [A/59/735].

GENERAL ASSEMBLY ACTION (April, June, December)

On 13 April [meeting 91], the General Assembly, on the recommendation of the Fifth (Administrative and Budgetary) Committee [A/59/771], adopted **resolution 59/285 A** without vote [agenda item 127].

Financing of the United Nations Organization Mission in the Democratic Republic of the Congo

A

The General Assembly,

Having considered the report of the Secretary-General on the financing of the United Nations Organization Mission in the Democratic Republic of the Congo and the related report of the Advisory Committee on Administrative and Budgetary Questions,

Recalling Security Council resolutions 1258(1999) of 6 August 1999 and 1279(1999) of 30 November 1999 regarding, respectively, the deployment to the Congo region of military liaison personnel and the establishment of the United Nations Organization Mission in the Democratic Republic of the Congo, and the subsequent resolutions by which the Council extended the mandate of the Mission, the latest of which was resolution 1565(2004) of 1 October 2004, by which the Council authorized an increase in the Mission's strength by 5,900 personnel, including up to 341 civilian police,

Recalling also its resolution 54/260 A of 7 April 2000 on the financing of the Mission and its subsequent resolutions thereon, the latest of which was resolution 58/259 B of 18 June 2004,

Reaffirming the general principles underlying the financing of United Nations peacekeeping operations, as stated in General Assembly resolutions 1874(S-IV) of 27 June 1963, 3101(XXVIII) of 11 December 1973 and 55/235 of 23 December 2000,

Noting with appreciation that voluntary contributions have been made to the Mission,

Mindful of the fact that it is essential to provide the Mission with the financial resources necessary to enable it to fulfil its responsibilities under the relevant resolutions of the Security Council,

1. *Takes note* of the status of contributions to the United Nations Organization Mission in the Democratic Republic of the Congo as at 15 March 2005, including the contributions outstanding in the amount of 309.4 million United States dollars, representing some 13 per cent of the total assessed contributions, notes with concern that only forty-five Member States have paid their assessed contributions in full, and urges all other Member States, in particular those in arrears, to ensure payment of their outstanding assessed contributions;

2. *Expresses its appreciation* to those Member States which have paid their assessed contributions in full, and urges all other Member States to make every possible effort to ensure payment of their assessed contributions to the Mission in full;

3. *Expresses concern* at the financial situation with regard to peacekeeping activities, in particular as regards the reimbursement of troop contributors, which bear additional burdens owing to overdue payments by Member States of their assessments;

4. *Also expresses concern* at the delay experienced by the Secretary-General in deploying and providing adequate resources to some recent peacekeeping missions, in particular those in Africa;

5. *Emphasizes* that all future and existing peacekeeping missions shall be given equal and non-discriminatory treatment in respect of financial and administrative arrangements;

6. *Also emphasizes* that all peacekeeping missions shall be provided with adequate resources for the effective and efficient discharge of their respective mandates;

7. *Reiterates its request* to the Secretary-General to make the fullest possible use of facilities and equipment at the United Nations Logistics Base at Brindisi, Italy, in order to minimize the costs of procurement for the Mission;

8. *Endorses* the conclusions and recommendations contained in the report of the Advisory Committee on Administrative and Budgetary Questions and requests the Secretary-General to ensure their full implementation;

9. *Requests* the Secretary-General to include in the proposed budget for the Mission for the period from 1 July 2005 to 30 June 2006 the resources necessary to ensure the integration of gender perspectives into the entire electoral process;

10. *Also requests* the Secretary-General to take all action necessary to ensure that the Mission is administered with a maximum of efficiency and economy, particularly with regard to air transport;

11. *Further requests* the Secretary-General, in order to reduce the cost of employing General Service staff, to continue efforts to recruit local staff for the Mission against General Service posts, commensurate with the requirements of the Mission;

**Revised budget estimates
for the period from 1 July 2004 to 30 June 2005**

12. *Decides* to appropriate to the Special Account for the United Nations Organization Mission in the Democratic Republic of the Congo the additional amount of 245,642,900 dollars for the maintenance of the Mission for the period from 1 October 2004 to 30 June 2005, inclusive of the amount of 49,950,000 dollars previously authorized by the Advisory Committee on Administra-

tive and Budgetary Questions under the terms of section IV of General Assembly resolution 49/233 A of 23 December 1994, taking into account the total amount of 746,072,500 dollars already appropriated and apportioned for the period from 1 July 2004 to 30 June 2005 under the provisions of its resolution 58/259 B;

Financing of the appropriation

13. *Decides also* to apportion among Member States the additional amount of 163,761,932 dollars for the period from 1 October 2004 to 31 March 2005, in accordance with the levels set out by the General Assembly in its resolution 55/235, as adjusted by the Assembly in its resolution 55/236 of 23 December 2000 and updated in its resolution 58/256 of 23 December 2003, and taking into account the scale of assessments for 2004 and 2005, as set out in its resolution 58/1 B of 23 December 2003;

14. *Decides further* to apportion among Member States the additional amount of 81,880,968 dollars at a monthly rate of 27,293,656 dollars for the period from 1 April to 30 June 2005, in accordance with the scheme set out in paragraph 13 above and taking into account the scale of assessments for 2005, as set out in General Assembly resolution 58/1 B, subject to the decision of the Security Council to extend the mandate of the Mission;

15. *Emphasizes* that no peacekeeping mission shall be financed by borrowing funds from other active peacekeeping missions;

16. *Encourages* the Secretary-General to continue to take additional measures to ensure the safety and security of all personnel under the auspices of the United Nations participating in the Mission;

17. *Invites* voluntary contributions to the Mission in cash and in the form of services and supplies acceptable to the Secretary-General, to be administered, as appropriate, in accordance with the procedure and practices established by the General Assembly;

18. *Decides* to keep under review during its fifty-ninth session the item entitled "Financing of the United Nations Organization Mission in the Democratic Republic of the Congo".

In June, the Assembly considered a further report of the Secretary-General [A/59/779] requesting commitment authority with assessment in the amount of $383,187,800 to cover MONUC operational and human resource requirements from 1 July to 31 October 2005, pending submission to the Assembly's sixtieth session of a full budget for MONUC for the period 1 July 2005 to 30 June 2006. ACABQ recommended approval of the request [A/59/736/ Add.16].

On 22 June [meeting 104], the Assembly, on the recommendation of the Fifth Committee [A/59/771/Add.1], adopted **resolution 59/285 B** without vote [agenda item 127].

Financing of the United Nations Organization Mission in the Democratic Republic of the Congo

B

The General Assembly,

Having considered the report of the Secretary-General on the financing of the United Nations Or-

ganization Mission in the Democratic Republic of the Congo and the related reports of the Advisory Committee on Administrative and Budgetary Questions,

Recalling Security Council resolutions 1258(1999) of 6 August 1999 and 1279(1999) of 30 November 1999 regarding, respectively, the deployment to the Congo region of military liaison personnel and the establishment of the United Nations Organization Mission in the Democratic Republic of the Congo, and the subsequent resolutions by which the Council extended the mandate of the Mission, the latest of which was resolution 1592(2005) of 30 March 2005,

Recalling also its resolution 54/260 A of 7 April 2000 on the financing of the Mission, and its subsequent resolutions thereon, the latest of which was resolution 59/285 A of 13 April 2005,

Reaffirming the general principles underlying the financing of United Nations peacekeeping operations, as stated in General Assembly resolutions 1874(S-IV) of 27 June 1963, 3101(XXVIII) of 11 December 1973 and 55/235 of 23 December 2000,

Noting with appreciation that voluntary contributions have been made to the Mission,

Mindful of the fact that it is essential to provide the Mission with the necessary financial resources to enable it to fulfil its responsibilities under the relevant resolutions of the Security Council,

1. *Requests* the Secretary-General to entrust the Head of Mission with the task of formulating future budget proposals in full accordance with the provisions of General Assembly resolution 59/296 of 22 June 2005, as well as other relevant resolutions;

2. *Takes note* of the status of contributions to the United Nations Organization Mission in the Democratic Republic of the Congo as at 15 April 2005, including the contributions outstanding in the amount of 52.7 million United States dollars, representing some 2 per cent of the total assessed contributions, notes with concern that only fifty-two Member States have paid their assessed contributions in full, and urges all other Member States, in particular those in arrears, to ensure payment of their outstanding assessed contributions;

3. *Expresses its appreciation* to those Member States which have paid their assessed contributions in full, and urges all other Member States to make every possible effort to ensure payment of their assessed contributions to the Mission in full;

4. *Expresses concern* at the financial situation with regard to peacekeeping activities, in particular as regards the reimbursements to troop contributors that bear additional burdens owing to overdue payments by Member States of their assessments;

5. *Also expresses concern* at the delay experienced by the Secretary-General in deploying and providing adequate resources to some recent peacekeeping missions, in particular those in Africa;

6. *Emphasizes* that all future and existing peacekeeping missions shall be given equal and non-discriminatory treatment in respect of financial and administrative arrangements;

7. *Also emphasizes* that all peacekeeping missions shall be provided with adequate resources for the effective and efficient discharge of their respective mandates;

8. *Reiterates its request* to the Secretary-General to make the fullest possible use of facilities and equipment at the United Nations Logistics Base at Brindisi, Italy, in order to minimize the costs of procurement for the Mission;

9. *Endorses* the conclusions and recommendations contained in the report of the Advisory Committee on Administrative and Budgetary Questions, and requests the Secretary-General to ensure their full implementation;

10. *Requests* the Secretary-General to ensure the full implementation of the relevant provisions of its resolution 59/296;

11. *Emphasizes* that the Special Representative of the Secretary-General should be responsible for the implementation of the policies of the Organization regarding personnel conduct, and requests the Secretary-General to ensure that the Special Representative remains fully engaged in all such matters;

12. *Requests* the Secretary-General to take all necessary action to ensure that the Mission is administered with a maximum of efficiency and economy;

13. *Also requests* the Secretary-General, in order to reduce the cost of employing General Service staff, to continue efforts to recruit local staff for the Mission against General Service posts, commensurate with the requirements of the Mission;

Budget estimates
for the period from 1 July to 31 October 2005

14. *Authorizes* the Secretary-General to enter into commitments in an amount not exceeding 383,187,800 dollars for the maintenance of the Mission for the period from 1 July to 31 October 2005;

Financing of the commitment authority

15. *Decides* to apportion among Member States the amount of 265,322,580 dollars for the period from 1 July to 1 October 2005, in accordance with the levels updated in General Assembly resolution 58/256 of 23 December 2003, and taking into account the scale of assessments for 2005, as set out in its resolution 58/1 B of 23 December 2003;

16. *Decides also* that, in accordance with the provisions of its resolution 973(X) of 15 December 1955, there shall be set off against the apportionment among Member States, as provided for in paragraph 15 above, their respective share in the Tax Equalization Fund of 4,235,325 dollars, representing the estimated staff assessment income approved for the Mission for the period from 1 July to 1 October 2005;

17. *Decides further* to apportion among Member States the amount of 84,677,420 dollars for the period from 2 to 31 October 2005, in accordance with the scheme set out in paragraph 15 above, subject to a decision of the Security Council to extend the mandate of the Mission;

18. *Decides* that, in accordance with the provisions of its resolution 973(X), there shall be set off against the apportionment among Member States, as provided for in paragraph 17 above, their respective share in the Tax Equalization Fund of 1,351,700 dollars, representing the estimated staff assessment income approved for the Mission for the period from 2 to 31 October 2005;

Estimates for the support account for peacekeeping operations and the United Nations Logistics Base for the period from 1 July 2005 to 30 June 2006

19. *Decides also* to appropriate to the Special Account for the United Nations Organization Mission in the Democratic Republic of the Congo the amount of 20,220,700 dollars for the period from 1 July 2005 to 30 June 2006, comprising 16,534,400 dollars for the support account for peacekeeping operations and 3,686,300 dollars for the United Nations Logistics Base;

Financing of the appropriation

20. *Decides further* to apportion among Member States the amount of 20,220,700 dollars, in accordance with the levels updated in General Assembly resolution 58/256, and taking into account the scale of assessments for 2005 and 2006, as set out in its resolution 58/1 B;

21. *Decides* that, in accordance with the provisions of its resolution 973(X), there shall be set off against the apportionment among Member States, as provided for in paragraph 20 above, their respective share in the Tax Equalization Fund of 2,635,300 dollars, comprising the prorated share of 2,337,100 dollars of the estimated staff assessment income approved for the support account and the prorated share of 298,200 dollars of the estimated staff assessment income approved for the United Nations Logistics Base;

22. *Emphasizes* that no peacekeeping mission shall be financed by borrowing funds from other active peacekeeping missions;

23. *Encourages* the Secretary-General to continue to take additional measures to ensure the safety and security of all personnel under the auspices of the United Nations participating in the Mission, bearing in mind paragraphs 5 and 6 of Security Council resolution 1502(2003) of 26 August 2003;

24. *Invites* voluntary contributions to the Mission in cash and in the form of services and supplies acceptable to the Secretary-General, to be administered, as appropriate, in accordance with the procedure and practices established by the General Assembly;

25. *Decides* to include in the provisional agenda of its sixtieth session the item entitled "Financing of the United Nations Organization Mission in the Democratic Republic of the Congo".

In December, at its sixtieth session, the Assembly considered the Secretary-General's financial performance report on the MONUC budget for the period 1 July 2003 to 30 June 2004 [A/59/657], showing total expenditures of $636,485,400, against an appropriation of $641,038,300; his proposed MONUC budget for 1 July 2005 to 30 June 2006 [A/60/389], amounting to $1,147,530,000, which incorporated the $383,187,800 authorized by Assembly resolution 59/285 B above; and the related report of ACABQ [A/60/536].

On 8 December [meeting 62], the Assembly, on the recommendation of the Fifth Committee [A/60/574], adopted **resolution 60/121 A** without vote [agenda item 140].

Financing of the United Nations Organization Mission in the Democratic Republic of the Congo

The General Assembly,

Having considered the reports of the Secretary-General on the financing of the United Nations Organization Mission in the Democratic Republic of the Congo and the related report of the Advisory Committee on Administrative and Budgetary Questions,

Recalling Security Council resolutions 1258(1999) of 6 August 1999 and 1279(1999) of 30 November 1999 regarding, respectively, the deployment to the Congo region of military liaison personnel and the establishment of the United Nations Organization Mission in the Democratic Republic of the Congo, and the subsequent resolutions by which the Council extended the mandate of the Mission, the latest of which was resolution 1635(2005) of 28 October 2005,

Recalling also its resolution 54/260 A of 7 April 2000 on the financing of the Mission, and its subsequent resolutions thereon, the latest of which was resolution 59/285 B of 22 June 2005,

Reaffirming the general principles underlying the financing of United Nations peacekeeping operations, as stated in General Assembly resolutions 1874(S-IV) of 27 June 1963, 3101(XXVIII) of 11 December 1973 and 55/235 of 23 December 2000,

Noting with appreciation that voluntary contributions have been made to the Mission,

Mindful of the fact that it is essential to provide the Mission with the necessary financial resources to enable it to fulfil its responsibilities under the relevant resolutions of the Security Council,

1. *Requests* the Secretary-General to entrust the Head of Mission with the task of formulating future budget proposals in full accordance with the provisions of General Assembly resolution 59/296 of 22 June 2005, as well as other relevant resolutions;

2. *Takes note* of the status of contributions to the United Nations Organization Mission in the Democratic Republic of the Congo as at 31 October 2005, including the contributions outstanding in the amount of 220.9 million United States dollars, representing some 7.8 per cent of the total assessed contributions, notes with concern that only forty Member States have paid their assessed contributions in full, and urges all other Member States, in particular those in arrears, to ensure payment of their outstanding assessed contributions;

3. *Expresses its appreciation* to those Member States which have paid their assessed contributions in full, and urges all other Member States to make every possible effort to ensure payment of their assessed contributions to the Mission in full;

4. *Expresses concern* at the financial situation with regard to peacekeeping activities, in particular as regards the reimbursements to troop contributors that bear additional burdens owing to overdue payments by Member States of their assessments;

5. *Also expresses concern* at the delay experienced by the Secretary-General in deploying and providing adequate resources to some recent peacekeeping missions, in particular those in Africa;

6. *Emphasizes* that all future and existing peacekeeping missions shall be given equal and non-discriminatory treatment in respect of financial and administrative arrangements;

7. *Also emphasizes* that all peacekeeping missions shall be provided with adequate resources for the effective and efficient discharge of their respective mandates;

8. *Expresses deep concern* at the very high rate of attrition and related difficulties in recruitment, and requests the Secretary-General to intensify his ongoing efforts to rectify this situation, including through innovative approaches, and to ensure the expeditious filling of all vacant posts;

9. *Reiterates its request* to the Secretary-General to make the fullest possible use of facilities and equipment at the United Nations Logistics Base at Brindisi, Italy, in order to minimize the costs of procurement for the Mission;

10. *Welcomes* the establishment and development of the logistics base at Entebbe, Uganda, as a regional hub for common use by missions in the region to enhance the efficiency and responsiveness of logistical support operations, and requests the Secretary-General to report to the General Assembly in the context of his overview report, to be submitted during the second part of its resumed sixty-first session, on economies and efficiencies realized through its utilization and on the increased effectiveness of regional support for peacekeeping operations;

11. *Also welcomes* the measures put in place in the Mission for the prevention and identification of and responses to instances of misconduct by its personnel, and encourages the Secretary-General to intensify his efforts to ensure compliance by all personnel with the zero-tolerance policy and procedures in accordance with the relevant resolutions of the General Assembly;

12. *Emphasizes* that the Special Representative of the Secretary-General should be responsible for the implementation of the policies of the Organization regarding personnel conduct, and requests the Secretary-General to ensure that the Special Representative remains fully engaged in all such matters;

13. *Endorses* the conclusions and recommendations contained in the report of the Advisory Committee on Administrative and Budgetary Questions, subject to the provisions of the present resolution, and requests the Secretary-General to ensure their full implementation;

14. *Recalls its previous requests* for a review of the structure of the Mission, and, noting with concern that the review has not been completed, requests the Secretary-General to ensure that the review is finalized as a matter of urgency and that its conclusions and recommendations are reflected in the budget submission for the Mission for 2006/07;

15. *Reaffirms* the critical role of the Mission, including in public information, in the preparation and conduct of the referendum and elections, and requests the Secretary-General, when preparing the budget proposals for 2006/07, to also take into account all previous relevant resolutions of the General Assembly and to ensure that resource requirements reflect any revisions in the mandate of the Mission that may arise due to developments in the post-election period, including all those personnel, support and operational components that are directly related to election activities;

16. *Stresses* the imperative nature of the successful conduct of electoral operations, and authorizes the full deployment of 507 additional personnel in support of

the elections while making best use of existing staffing resources, bearing in mind the need to ensure that the deployment schedule responds to developments on the ground;

17. *Authorizes* the Secretary-General to utilize until 30 June 2006 general temporary assistance for the functions provided by the 395 individual contractors, and requests the Secretary-General to fully justify any proposed conversion of these 395 individual contractors in the context of the results of the comprehensive review to be included in the proposed budget for 2006/07;

18. *Requests* the Secretary-General to ensure the full implementation of the relevant provisions of its resolution 59/296;

19. *Also requests* the Secretary-General to take all necessary action to ensure that the Mission is administered with a maximum of efficiency and economy;

20. *Further requests* the Secretary-General to ensure that the Mission effectively utilizes the available rail and inland waterway transport modes where they are more reliable and cost-effective than air transportation and safe to use;

21. *Requests* the Secretary-General, in order to reduce the cost of employing General Service staff, to continue efforts to recruit local staff for the Mission against General Service posts, commensurate with the requirements of the Mission;

**Financial performance report
for the period from 1 July 2003 to 30 June 2004**

22. *Takes note* of the report of the Secretary-General on the financial performance of the Mission for the period from 1 July 2003 to 30 June 2004;

**Budget estimates
for the period from 1 July 2005 to 30 June 2006**

23. *Decides* to appropriate to the Special Account for the United Nations Organization Mission in the Democratic Republic of the Congo the amount of 1,133,672,200 dollars for the maintenance of the Mission for the period from 1 July 2005 to 30 June 2006, inclusive of the amount of 383,187,800 dollars previously authorized by the General Assembly under the terms of its resolution 59/285 B for the period from 1 July to 31 October 2005, and in addition to the amount of 20,220,700 dollars already appropriated under the terms of the same resolution for the support account for peacekeeping operations and the United Nations Logistics Base for the period from 1 July 2005 to 30 June 2006;

Financing of the appropriation

24. *Decides also,* taking into account the amount of 350 million dollars already apportioned under the terms of its resolution 59/285 B for the maintenance of the Mission for the period from 1 July to 31 October 2005, to apportion among Member States the additional amount of 783,672,200 dollars for the maintenance of the Mission for the period from 1 November 2005 to 30 June 2006, in accordance with the levels updated in General Assembly resolution 58/256 of 23 December 2003, and taking into account the scale of assessments for 2005 and 2006, as set out in its resolution 58/1 B of 23 December 2003;

25. *Decides further* that, in accordance with the provisions of its resolution 973(X) of 15 December 1955,

there shall be set off against the apportionment among Member States, as provided for in paragraph 24 above, their respective share in the Tax Equalization Fund of the amount of 15,664,375 dollars, representing the estimated additional staff assessment income approved for the Mission for the period from 1 November 2005 to 30 June 2006;

26. *Decides* that, for Member States that have fulfilled their financial obligations to the Mission, there shall be set off against their apportionment, as provided for in paragraph 24 above, their respective share of the unencumbered balance and other income in the amount of 32,836,900 dollars in respect of the financial period ended 30 June 2004, in accordance with the levels updated in its resolution 58/256, and taking into account the scale of assessments for 2004, as set out in its resolution 58/1 B;

27. *Decides also* that, for Member States that have not fulfilled their financial obligations to the Mission, there shall be set off against their outstanding obligations their respective share of the unencumbered balance and other income in the amount of 32,836,900 dollars in respect of the financial period ended 30 June 2004, in accordance with the scheme set out in paragraph 26 above;

28. *Decides further* that the increase of 466,700 dollars in the estimated staff assessment income in respect of the financial period ended 30 June 2004 shall be added to the credits from the amount of 32,836,900 dollars referred to in paragraphs 26 and 27 above;

29. *Emphasizes* that no peacekeeping mission shall be financed by borrowing funds from other active peacekeeping missions;

30. *Encourages* the Secretary-General to continue to take additional measures to ensure the safety and security of all personnel under the auspices of the United Nations participating in the Mission, bearing in mind paragraphs 5 and 6 of Security Council resolution 1502(2003) of 26 August 2003;

31. *Invites* voluntary contributions to the Mission in cash and in the form of services and supplies acceptable to the Secretary-General, to be administered, as appropriate, in accordance with the procedure and practices established by the General Assembly;

32. *Decides* to keep under review during its sixtieth session the item entitled "Financing of the United Nations Organization Mission in the Democratic Republic of the Congo".

Political developments and MONUC activities

Report of Secretary-General (March). In response to Security Council resolution 1565(2004) [YUN 2004, p. 129], the Secretary-General issued his seventeenth (March) report on MONUC [S/2005/167], covering major developments in the Mission area and progress in the implementation of the MONUC mandate since December 2004 [ibid., p. 134]. He reported some progress in the implementation of the transitional agenda, but no significant improvement in the difficult relationship between the components of the Transitional Government. Implementation of some major aspects of the transition, including security-sector reform and the legislative agenda, had experienced considerable delays. By 3 January, Parliament had adopted laws on the armed forces, nationality and voter registration. However, legislation on the constitutional referendum and amnesty, the status of the political opposition, the financing of political parties, the draft constitution and the electoral law remained outstanding. A preliminary draft of the constitution was discussed in the Senate, including such issues as the balance of power between the President and the Prime Minister, and between the central Government and provincial governments.

On 7 January, the IEC President indicated to the press that, in his view, it would not be feasible to hold elections in June and that a date later in the year should be considered. The statement fuelled popular suspicion that the Transitional Government wanted to postpone the elections. That led to demonstrations on 9 and 10 January in Kinshasa, Goma and Mbuji-Mayi, which resulted in nine civilian deaths

Progress was made by the DRC-Rwanda Joint Verification Mechanism in addressing cross-border issues, and by the DRC-Rwanda-Uganda Tripartite Joint Commission in de-escalating regional tensions—both established in 2004 [YUN 2004, p. 134]. Joint verification teams were established in Goma and Bukavu by the DRC and Rwanda and facilitated by MONUC and the AU. The Goma team investigated 18 allegations, two of which were confirmed, including the presence of FDLR in Lusamambo and an internally displaced persons camp at Ngungu in the Kalehe territory near the Rwandan border. The team confirmed that a Rwandan soldier was being detained by FARDC elements in Kashebere, whose return was demanded by Rwanda. MONUC encouraged the parties to address those issues jointly. The Bukavu team became operational on 8 February; it carried out two verification missions, to Kalonge and Mule in the DRC, to investigate allegations of FDLR activities in the area, but which it could not corroborate.

The Tripartite Joint Commission met in Washington, D.C., on 2 February, with ministerial-level officials of the DRC, Rwanda and Uganda in attendance; the United Nations was also represented. The meeting discussed the use of pre-existing mechanisms to settle disputes and agreed to set up subcommissions on security and defence issues and on diplomatic affairs. At a further meeting (Kampala, Uganda, 23 February), the Commission agreed to establish a joint intelligence fusion, operations and analysis cell, through which they would share information on security issues and take appropriate action.

Regarding the security situation in Ituri, military operations by various armed groups had increased, particularly in the Tchomia and Kasenyi areas. MONUC adopted a four-pronged, proactive strategy that included pressing the Transitional Government to take decisive measures against any military group that opposed disarmament and the extension of State authority; strengthening coordination of the disarmament and community reintegration process, so as to conclude the process by 31 March; increasing political and financial support for the District Commissioner's office; and supporting legitimate authorities in re-establishing control over customs revenue. The Transitional Government had yet to put in place a transparent revenue collection system to end the fighting over the control of parallel tax and custom structures.

In early January, isolated attacks between UPC/L and FNI in the area of Djugu evolved into a wider confrontation between the two groups in the Tchomia and Kasenyi regions. In late January, Lendu fighters and FNI militia attacked Hema villages in the Tche area of Djugu; in response, MONUC launched several operations to enhance security there. On 24 February, MONUC launched a cordon-and-search operation at Ariwara, disarming 116 soldiers of the Forces armées du peuple congolais (FAPC) and collecting 118 weapons and ammunition. It also arrested 30 FNI militia and confiscated weapons in the village of Datule.

The security situation in North and South Kivu remained tense. In response to Rwanda's threats in December 2004 [YUN 2004, p. 135] to enter the DRC to disarm FDLR forcibly, the DRC sent additional FARDC troops to the area, resulting in increased inter-FARDC clashes. Reports were received of collaboration between FDLR and the Mayi-Mayi and between FDLR and FARDC elements. In North Kivu, the cease-fire between opposing FARDC units around Kanyabayonga held, but tensions remained high. In mid-January, MONUC withdrew on schedule from the 10-kilometre security zone it had established in December 2004 on the Kirumba-Mighobwe axis and reinforced its positions between Mighobwe and Kanyabayonga and in Butembo. In the Rutshuru territory, nine soldiers and one civilian were killed in FDLR raids between mid-January and early February.

As to the national disarmament, demobilization and reintegration programme, the Supreme Defence Council, on 25 January, revised its estimate of the number of FARDC combatants from 300,000 to 250,000. Subsequently, the Structure militaire d'intégration issued a revised plan for the emergency disarmament or mixing and retraining of troops, under which 10 disarmament centres would be opened before the end of March and MONUC would register arms handed in during the disarmament process, destroy unserviceable weapons and turn over the serviceable ones to the integrated army. Disarmament centres had so far been opened at Mushaki, Nyaleke (North Kivu), Kamina (Katanga) and Kitona (Bas-Congo). An estimated 11,500 troops had arrived at the centres and had handed in their weapons.

In accordance with resolution 1565(2004) [YUN 2004, p. 129], three joint commissions, on essential legislation, security-sector reform and elections, were established. The Joint Commission on Essential Legislation met twice, beginning on 24 January, with a focus on supporting the transitional institutions to adopt, as a priority, a draft post-transitional Constitution and the electoral law. The Joint Commission on Security Sector Reform held its first meeting on 26 January.

IEC, with the support of the EU, MONUC and other international donors, prepared a budget of some $285 million for the electoral process, which was endorsed by the World Bank Consultative Group in December 2004. The funds would be managed through a UNDP trust fund. The Secretary-General requested DPKO and the Electoral Assistance Division to field a mission to the DRC to work jointly with MONUC in finalizing a comprehensive operational election plan.

The number of foreign combatants and their dependants repatriated to Uganda, Rwanda and Burundi totalled 11,410. Progress in repatriation remained slow due to the continued resistance by the hard-line leadership of the armed groups and the persistent military tension and instability in the Kivus. The presence and activities on Congolese territory of ex-FAR/Interahamwe remained a destabilizing factor in the relations between the DRC and Rwanda. In that regard, MONUC, in consultation with Congolese authorities, key Member States and Rwanda, was implementing a strategy of political and military pressure in conjunction with a reliance on justice. In February, Transitional Government officials met with the FDLR leadership to persuade them to renounce publicly the use of force against Rwanda, condemn the 1994 genocide in that country [YUN 1994, p. 282] and agree to disarm voluntarily and be repatriated. With its deployment of two brigades to the Kivus, MONUC would step up military pressure by conducting operations to disrupt and weaken FDLR formations, thereby to limit their area of operations. It was also assisting FARDC in developing a concept of operations for the forcible disarmament of FDLR, including logistic support.

Regarding the human rights situation in the DRC, a special MONUC team continued to monitor gross violations of human rights in North Kivu. Investigations determined that ex-Armée nationale congolaise (ex-ANC) elements of FARDC were responsible for the arbitrary killings of at least 30 unarmed civilians at Buramba and of dozens more in the Masisi territory, following the group's occupation of Nyabiondo in December 2004. The North Kivu Governor, who initiated commissions of inquiry into the violations, denied that FARDC (ex-ANC) troops were responsible. MONUC investigated attacks on villages in Rutshuru, near the Ugandan border, where sexual violence was widely reported. In Ituri, arbitrary killings, sexual violence and abductions by militia groups continued on a daily basis.

The Secretary-General said he was deeply disturbed by the general deterioration of security and unabated abuse of human rights in Ituri. He called on the Transitional Government to make visible progress towards the holding of elections, most importantly through the adoption of the draft constitution and electoral law and the commencement of voter registration. He also called on the Congolese leaders to ensure that the Constitution and the electoral law provided for an inclusive political process, with a clear balance of power between the executive and legislative branches of Government, as well as for an independent judiciary, a representative legislature and clear lines of accountability. He called on the international community to step up its efforts and financial and logistic support with regard to security sector reform, and to provide logistics and training support for FARDC units. He stressed that the establishment of an integrated and professional army and police force was key to the MONUC exit strategy, and urged the international community to organize itself around a lead country to support those efforts. The Secretary-General recommended that the Council extend MONUC's mandate for a period of one year, until 31 March 2006.

SECURITY COUNCIL ACTION

On 30 March [meeting 5155], the Security Council unanimously adopted **resolution 1592(2005)**. The draft [S/2005/207] was prepared in consultations among Council members.

The Security Council,

Recalling its previous resolutions and the statements by its President concerning the Democratic Republic of the Congo, in particular resolution 1565(2004) of 1 October 2004, and the statement of 2 March 2005,

Reaffirming its commitment to respect the sovereignty, territorial integrity and political independence of the Democratic Republic of the Congo as well as of all

States in the region, and its support for the process of the Global and All-Inclusive Agreement on the Transition in the Democratic Republic of the Congo, signed in Pretoria on 17 December 2002, and calling upon all the Congolese parties to honour their commitments in this regard, in particular so that free, fair and peaceful elections can take place,

Reiterating its serious concern regarding the continuation of hostilities by armed groups and militias in the eastern part of the Democratic Republic of the Congo, particularly in the provinces of North and South Kivu and in the Ituri district, and by the grave violations of human rights and of international humanitarian law that accompany them, calling upon the Government of National Unity and Transition to bring the perpetrators to justice without delay, and recognizing that the continuing presence of ex-Forces armées rwandaises and Interahamwe elements remains a threat for the local civilian population and an impediment to good-neighbourly relations between the Democratic Republic of the Congo and Rwanda,

Welcoming, in this regard, the African Union's support for efforts to further peace in the eastern part of the Democratic Republic of the Congo, and calling upon the African Union to work closely with the United Nations Organization Mission in the Democratic Republic of the Congo in defining its role in the region,

Recalling its condemnation of the attack by one of these militias against members of the Mission on 25 February 2005, and welcoming the first steps taken to date to bring them to justice, in particular the arrests of militia leaders suspected of bearing responsibility for human rights abuses,

Reiterating its call upon the Congolese parties, when selecting individuals for key posts in the Government of National Unity and Transition, including the armed forces and national police, to take into account the record and commitment of those individuals with regard to respect for international humanitarian law and human rights,

Recalling that all the parties bear responsibility for ensuring security with respect to civilian populations, in particular women, children and other vulnerable persons, and expressing concern at the continuing levels of sexual violence,

Reaffirming its full support for the Mission and for its personnel, who operate in particularly hazardous conditions, and welcoming the robust action it is undertaking in pursuit of its mandate,

Bearing in mind the third special report of the Secretary-General of 16 August 2004 on the Mission and its recommendations, and aware of the importance of keeping under review the situation in the Katanga and KasaV provinces,

Recalling the link between the illicit exploitation and trade of natural resources in certain regions and the fuelling of armed conflicts, condemning categorically the illegal exploitation of natural resources and other sources of wealth of the Democratic Republic of the Congo, and urging all States, especially those in the region including the Democratic Republic of the Congo itself, to take appropriate steps in order to end these illegal activities,

Taking note of the seventeenth report of the Secretary-General of 15 March 2005 on the Mission,

and looking forward to the special report on the electoral process announced by the Secretary-General in paragraph 34 of his seventeenth report,

Noting that the situation in the Democratic Republic of the Congo continues to constitute a threat to international peace and security in the region,

Acting under Chapter VII of the Charter of the United Nations,

1. *Decides* to extend the mandate of the United Nations Organization Mission in the Democratic Republic of the Congo, as contained in resolution 1565(2004), until 1 October 2005, with the intention to renew it for further periods;

2. *Reaffirms its demand* that all parties cooperate fully with the operations of the Mission and that they ensure the safety of, as well as unhindered and immediate access for, United Nations and associated personnel in carrying out their mandate, throughout the territory of the Democratic Republic of the Congo, and in particular that all parties provide full access to Mission military observers, including to all ports, airports, airfields, military bases and border crossings, and requests the Secretary-General to report without delay any failure to comply with these demands;

3. *Urges* the Government of National Unity and Transition to do its utmost to ensure the security of civilians, including humanitarian personnel, by effectively extending State authority throughout the territory of the Democratic Republic of the Congo, and in particular in North and South Kivu and in Ituri;

4. *Calls upon* the Government of National Unity and Transition to carry out the reform of the security sector, through the expeditious integration of the armed forces and of the national police of the Democratic Republic of the Congo and in particular by ensuring adequate payment and logistical support for their personnel, and stresses the need in this regard to implement without delay the national disarmament, demobilization and reintegration programme for Congolese combatants;

5. *Also calls upon* the Government of National Unity and Transition to develop with the Mission a joint concept of operations for the disarmament of foreign combatants by the armed forces of the Democratic Republic of the Congo, with the assistance of the Mission, within its mandate and capabilities;

6. *Calls upon* the donor community, as a matter of urgency, to continue to engage firmly in the provision of assistance needed for the integration, training and equipping of the armed forces and of the national police of the Democratic Republic of the Congo, and urges the Government of National Unity and Transition to promote all possible means to facilitate and to expedite cooperation to this end;

7. *Emphasizing* that the Mission is authorized to use all necessary means, within its capabilities and in the areas where its armed units are deployed, to deter any attempt at the use of force to threaten the political process, and to ensure the protection of civilians under imminent threat of physical violence, from any armed group, foreign or Congolese, in particular the ex-Forces armées rwandaises and Interahamwe, encourages the Mission in this regard to continue to make full use of its mandate under resolution 1565(2004) in the eastern part of the Democratic Republic of the Congo, and stresses that, in accordance with its mandate, the

Mission may use cordon and search tactics to prevent attacks on civilians and to disrupt the military capability of illegal armed groups that continue to use violence in those areas;

8. *Calls upon* all the parties to the transition in the Democratic Republic of the Congo to make concrete progress towards the holding of elections, as provided for by the Global and All-Inclusive Agreement on the Transition in the Democratic Republic of the Congo, in particular in furthering the early adoption of the constitution and of the electoral law, as well as the registration of voters;

9. *Demands* that the Governments of Uganda, Rwanda, as well as the Democratic Republic of the Congo put a stop to the use of their respective territories in support of violations of the arms embargo imposed by resolution 1493(2003) of 28 July 2003 or of activities of armed groups operating in the region;

10. *Urges* all States neighbouring the Democratic Republic of the Congo to impede any kind of support to the illegal exploitation of Congolese natural resources, particularly by preventing the flow of such resources through their respective territories;

11. *Reaffirms its concern* regarding acts of sexual exploitation and abuse committed by United Nations personnel against the local population, and requests the Secretary-General to ensure compliance with the zero tolerance policy he has defined and with the measures put in place to prevent and investigate all forms of misconduct, discipline those found responsible and provide support to the victims, and to pursue active training and awareness-raising of all Mission personnel, and further requests the Secretary-General to keep the Council regularly informed of the measures implemented and their effectiveness;

12. *Urges* troop-contributing countries carefully to review the letter dated 24 March 2005 from the Secretary-General to the President of the Security Council and to take appropriate action to prevent sexual exploitation and abuse by their personnel in the Mission, including the conduct of predeployment awareness-training, and to take disciplinary action and other action to ensure full accountability in cases of such misconduct involving their personnel;

13. *Decides* to remain actively seized of the matter.

Declarations of intent to disarm

Rwanda, by a 1 April communiqué [S/2005/223], informed the Security Council that it had received information that the ex-FAR/Interahamwe forces (also known as FDLR/FOCA) operating in the eastern DRC had decided to disarm unconditionally and to return to Rwanda. Rwanda urged the DRC and the international community to act with dispatch to ensure the expeditious disarmament and return of those forces. It remained ready to receive all former combatants returning to Rwanda and to assist in their reintegration. Rwanda welcomed the commitment of the Sant' Egidio community in its role as mediator to join the international community in working for a speedy disarmament and demobilization of those groups. It expressed grave concern that the United

Nations, the EU and some countries planned to hold discussions with ex-FAR/Interahamwe, and that the political leadership of groups responsible for the 1994 genocide was based in Belgium with an official address.

A 24 June assessment of the Security Council's work under the Presidency of China [S/2005/415] included information that the Council was briefed on 7 April by the Assistant Secretary-General for Peacekeeping Operations on the 31 March FDLR statement issued in Rome, in which FDLR condemned the 1994 genocide in Rwanda [YUN 1994, p. 282] and committed itself to renounce the use of force and cease all offensive operations against Rwanda.

The thirty-third meeting of the AU Peace and Security Council (Addis Ababa, Ethiopia, 24 June) [S/2005/429] reiterated the AU's determination to contribute to the effective disarmament and neutralization of ex-FAR/Interahamwe and other armed groups in the eastern DRC and encouraged the DRC, the other countries of the region and the international community to do their utmost to persuade FDLR to honour unconditionally and without delay its commitments made in Rome on 31 March.

SECURITY COUNCIL ACTION

On 12 April [meeting 5162], following consultations among Security Council members, the President made statement **S/PRST/2005/15** on behalf of the Council:

The Security Council welcomes the statement issued by the Forces démocratiques de libération du Rwanda in Rome, on 31 March 2005, in which they condemn the 1994 genocide and commit themselves to renounce the use of force and cease all offensive operations against Rwanda. It considers this encouraging statement as a significant opportunity to move towards the return of peace in the Democratic Republic of the Congo, national reconciliation in Rwanda, and full normalization of relations between the two countries. It commends the role of independent mediator played by the Sant'Egidio community.

The Council calls upon the Forces démocratiques de libération du Rwanda to turn their positive words into action and to demonstrate their commitment to peace by immediately handing all their arms to the United Nations Organization Mission in the Democratic Republic of the Congo and by taking part in the programme put in place for their earliest voluntary and peaceful return to Rwanda or resettlement, as well as by assisting the International Criminal Tribunal for Rwanda in Arusha to fulfil its mandate, particularly with regard to the arrest and transfer to its custody of indictees who remain at large.

The Council encourages all other armed groups in the Democratic Republic of the Congo that have not yet done so to renounce likewise the use of force and to take part without delay in the programmes of disarmament, demobilization and reintegration.

The Council urges the Governments of the Democratic Republic of the Congo and Rwanda to work together, in close cooperation with the Mission, to make use of the chance given to them to contribute to peace and stability in the whole Great Lakes region of Africa.

The Council welcomes the commitment of the Government of Rwanda to receive former combatants, and urges the Government of Rwanda to guarantee the return and reintegration of members of the Forces démocratiques de libération du Rwanda and their dependents to be repatriated, in accordance with applicable standards of international law and with respect for the rights and freedoms of the human being.

The Council recalls the need for an effective programme of reintegration to be quickly implemented with the support, as appropriate, of the international community.

Press statement. According to a 26 April press statement by the Security Council President [SC/8369], the Council was briefed by the Under-Secretary-General for Peacekeeping Operations that political developments in the DRC were at a point when the transition process was entering a key phase. The possibility that the Council might send a number of its ambassadors on a mission to the DRC capital, Kinshasa, was discussed, a decision which would be taken at an appropriate stage. The Council encouraged the Congolese parties to carry through their political process in full respect of the principles set out in the 2002 Global and All-Inclusive Agreement [YUN 2002, p. 125]. The Council remained committed to supporting the process, including through its strong support for the action by the Special Representative and CIAT in Kinshasa.

Election preparations

In a May special report [S/2005/320], the Secretary-General provided an overview of progress towards the holding of elections in the DRC, including the legislative and operational framework, the political situation and the security environment. Based on the findings of an April UN mission to the DRC to assess electoral preparations, the report also presented MONUC's plans for assisting the Congolese people to achieve a viable and open electoral process.

The Secretary-General said that, while considerable difficulties had been encountered during the previous two years, the Transitional Government had made significant strides in implementing the objectives of 2002 Global and All-Inclusive Agreement, and the Congolese people were increasingly focused on the forthcoming national elections, the first in the DRC since 1965. The elections faced a number of challenges: the logistical task of reaching all eligible voters in a country the size of Europe with virtually no roads; a population without identity cards and no census since 1984; political tensions and insecurity from armed groups; and pressure from the public's high expectations for change. The electoral process would also be affected by a number of key transitional issues on which progress was significantly delayed, in particular the integration and reform of the army and police, the legislative agenda, the extension of State administration, and the financial management of the country. The Secretary-General said it was essential that the elections be sufficiently credible in the eyes of the Congolese electorate and that the political parties encourage broad acceptance of the process and its results. At a March seminar for political parties, IEC presented a draft code of conduct for the electoral process, which was adopted by general consensus by all parties present and was being finalized for their signature. The Secretary-General said Congolese leaders should be urged to pledge publicly, on behalf of their respective political parties and followers, to accept the results of the elections and condemn any use of violence, intimidation or corruption during the electoral process; the international community should ensure that those commitments were respected.

To address reports of growing and widespread misuse of State resources, and to help strengthen public confidence in the transition process, some Member States had suggested the establishment of a joint mechanism of Congolese officials and international donors to support the transparent management of State resources. Strongly supporting the idea, the Secretary-General said the mechanism could take the form a "Group of Friends on Good Governance" and include the World Bank Group, the International Monetary Fund (IMF) and UNDP; he asked his Special Representative to explore the concept with his Congolese interlocutors and donors.

The Secretary-General observed that, despite the security, operational and political challenges, elections could be held in the DRC within a reasonable period of time, given sufficient focus and support by the Transitional Government and assistance from international partners. It was primarily the responsibility of the Transitional Government to create the conditions necessary for stability in the post-transition period and for the success of the electoral process. The Secretary-General strongly urged the transitional leaders to enter into the commitments recommended, including the signing of a code of conduct and the establishment of a "Group of Friends on Good Governance". He remained deeply concerned over the state of security sector reform, stating that the Transitional Government should not allow armed elements of former factions to be politically manipulated during the electoral period. It had to ensure transparent payment of salaries and financial support to a viable "brassage" process, as well as support to the new integrated brigades. The Secretary-General urged donors to transform their commitments to the electoral budget into actual disbursements to avoid bottlenecks in the electoral operations.

In the context of MONUC's role in disarming more than 12,000 combatants in Ituri and in increasing security in North Kivu and South Kivu, the Secretary-General recommended that the Council consider: increasing MONUC's military strength by some 2,590 all ranks to a total of 19,290—the additional military personnel to be deployed temporarily during and in the immediate period following the elections; strengthening the civilian police component by an additional 261 civilian police and five formed police units to undertake training and institution-building activities; and mandating MONUC to provide logistical support, as requested by IEC, for the transport of electoral material from Kinshasa to the 145 territories (into which the districts were subdivided) and 21 cities in the DRC.

In a July addendum to his report [S/2005/320/Add.1], the Secretary-General informed the Council that the financial implications arising from the recommended support by MONUC for the elections were projected at some $188.8 million for the 12-month period.

Extension of transition period. On 17 June [S/2005/408], the DRC National Assembly and Senate, in a joint decision, extended the transition period in the DRC for six months as from 1 July, in accordance with the Transitional Constitution. The period would be renewable once and would expire on the inauguration of the DRC President after the elections. Annexed to the decision was a tentative schedule of elections drawn up by IEC.

SECURITY COUNCIL ACTION (June)

On 29 June [meeting 5218], following consultations among Security Council members, the President made statement **S/PRST/2005/27** on behalf of the Council:

> The Security Council takes note of the joint decision reached by the two Houses of Parliament of the Democratic Republic of the Congo on 17 June 2005 to extend for a period of six months, renewable once, the transitional period that was to expire on 30 June 2005, in accordance with the provisions of the Global and All-Inclusive Agreement on the Transition in the Democratic Republic of the Congo, signed in Pretoria on 17 December 2002, and with article 196 of the transitional Constitution.

> The Council calls upon all Congolese parties to respect this decision, which aims to allow the elections provided for by the Agreement to take place in satisfactory logistic and security conditions. It encourages the Congolese people to mobilize for and conduct the electoral process in a peaceful manner, and urges, in particular, candidates and political parties to refrain from any action that might disrupt the process. It takes note, in this regard, of the recommendation contained in the special report of the Secretary-General of 26 May 2005 on elections in the Democratic Republic of the Congo that all political parties should sign and commit themselves to respect the agreed code of conduct for the electoral process. The Council urges all parties and transitional institutions to make every effort to respect scrupulously the timetable for polls developed by the Independent Electoral Commission, and in particular to begin preparations for the referendum on the draft Constitution as soon as possible.

> The Council welcomes the progress made so far in the preparation of the elections, in particular the adoption and promulgation of the referendum law, and the start of voter registration in Kinshasa, which marks an historic and important step in the electoral process in the Democratic Republic of the Congo. The Council calls upon the transitional authorities to accelerate those reforms remaining to be carried out, in particular drafting of the electoral law and integration of the security forces.

> The Council underlines the importance of elections as the foundation for the longer term restoration of peace and stability, national reconciliation, and establishment of the rule of law in the Democratic Republic of the Congo. It calls upon the Congolese authorities to exercise efficient, transparent and comprehensive control over State finances, ensuring that there is no impunity for those responsible for acts of embezzlement or corruption. In this regard, the Council encourages the Congolese authorities to continue consultations with their international partners, in full respect for the sovereignty of the Democratic Republic of the Congo, and to put in place credible arrangements to strengthen support for good governance and transparent economic management.

Massacres

As described in a later communication from the Secretary-General to the Security Council [S/2006/28], a group of armed Rwandan elements attacked the village of Kabingu in Ntulu-Mamba in South Kivu on 9 July. A MONUC multidisciplinary team that investigated the attack, from 12 to 20 July, confirmed that over 50 civilians were killed, more than 40 of whom, mostly women and children, were either burned alive in their huts or killed by machete blows while trying to escape; 15 others were injured, 6 of whom later died of their injuries; 11 women were raped. Widespread looting was also reported. Eyewitnesses indicated that the perpetrators were a group of about 30 well-armed Rwandans from an area near Kahuzi-Biega National Park, approximately 20 kilometres north-west of Bukavu—the same group whom local sources claimed was responsible for the 23 May massacre of at least 14 civilians in Nindja in Kabare territory. Witnesses suggested that the attack on Kabingu might have been a reprisal for the population's collaboration with FARDC and MONUC.

On 12 July [S/2005/451], the DRC condemned the attack on the village of Ntulu-mamba and those attacks carried out by FDLR, ex-FAR/Interahamwe, Rasta and other armed gangs, as well as attacks on the villages of Nyamirima, Nyakakoma and Ishasha, 150 kilometres north of Goma in North Kivu, which it said resulted in more than 30 deaths, over 50 wounded and 39 huts burned down. The DRC recalled that, despite FDLR's commitment of 31 March (see p. 176) to abandon its military activities and return to Rwanda, it had not yet done so. The DRC had always held that whatever potential threat the armed gangs posed to their countries of origin, they were a permanent danger and cause of insecurity to the Congolese populations. With UN support, the DRC was determined to intensify its operations to secure the regions affected by the attacks and forcibly disarm the gangs. It expected the firm support of the international community in that regard.

SECURITY COUNCIL ACTION (July)

On 13 July [meeting 5226], following consultations among Security Council members, the President made statement **S/PRST/2005/31** on behalf of the Council:

> The Security Council condemns with the utmost firmness the massacre of some 50 people, most of them women and children, which occurred on 9 July 2005 in Ntulu-Mamba, in the Democratic Republic of the Congo.
>
> The Council requests the Special Representative of the Secretary-General for the Democratic Republic of the Congo to establish the facts and report to the Council as quickly as possible.
>
> The Council calls upon the Congolese authorities to prosecute and bring to justice expeditiously the perpetrators and those responsible for these crimes, and requests the United Nations Organization Mission in the Democratic Republic of the Congo to provide all necessary support. The Council encourages the Congolese authorities to continue their efforts to ensure the protection of civilians and respect for human rights within their territory.
>
> The Council stresses the need to bring to an end, particularly in the Kivus and Ituri, attacks by armed groups on local populations, which not only cause further suffering to civilians but also threaten the stability of the entire region, as well as the holding of elections in the Democratic Republic of the Congo. The Council demands that the Force démocratique de libération du Rwanda abide by the commitment made in Rome, on 31 March 2005, renounce the use of force and settle without delay the issue of the return to Rwanda of their combatants.
>
> The Council reaffirms its full support for the Mission. It welcomes the robust actions the Mission is undertaking in pursuit of its mandate, and the assistance it provides to the armed forces of the Democratic Republic of the Congo in reinforcing the safety of the population.

The extended transition period

Report of Secretary-General (August). In his eighteenth (August) report on MONUC [S/2005/506] the Secretary-General reported that, at the end of June, when the transition period was originally to end, and into the first weeks of its six-month extended period, the Transitional Government maintained public order amid calls for violent disturbances and heightened tension due to the debate over the future of the transition process. That debate had divided the Congolese people into two major camps: those participating in the transitional institutions, who favoured an extension of the transition; and those largely not represented in the transitional institutions, who accused the Transitional Government of failing to organize the elections on time, opposed an automatic extension of the transition and called for public demonstrations to stop the transitional process. While the large-scale actions called for by the Union pour la démocratie et le progrès social (UDPS), the lead party of the groups opposing the automatic extension, did not materialize, clashes between demonstrators and security forces between 29 June and 1 July resulted in a number of deaths in Kinshasa, Tshikapa and Mbuji-Mayi. Nonetheless, by 30 June, almost 250,000 voters had received their electoral cards in Kinshasa, a tangible proof that the transition was making progress and that the electoral process was under way.

On 13 May, the National Assembly adopted the draft constitution, which was to be submitted to a referendum on 27 November (see p. 189); on 23 June, the President promulgated the referendum law. A preliminary draft of the electoral law prepared by IEC and the Ministry of the Interior was under review by national and international experts. On 18 June, 186 of the 221 registered political parties signed the code of conduct prepared by IEC, outlining the principles for conducting the electoral process in a transparent, equitable, credible and non-violent manner; UDPS and the Parti du peuple pour la reconstruction et la démocratie (PPRD) had yet to sign the code. For security reasons, voter registration was being implemented throughout the country in five stages, beginning with Kinshasa (20 June) and in Province Orientale and Bas-Congo (25 July); Katanga,

Kasai Oriental and Kasai Occidental; Maniema, North and South Kivu; and ending with Bandundu and Equateur by 30 September. By 26 July, more than 2.7 million voters had registered.

The shortfall in available funds to finance the upcoming elections was of serious concern. Of the estimated total budget of $422 million, only $272.8 million had been pledged, and additional requirements of $103 million were still pending a decision of the Security Council. If the funds were not approved, the electoral timetable could experience considerable delays. In addition, the Transitional Government estimated that some $48 million would be needed for electoral security, and a further $14.25 million for a communications system.

IEC launched a civic education campaign on 18 June, and disseminated most of the major legal texts relating to the elections, in the four national languages (Swahili, Lingala, Tshiluba and Kikongo). MONUC, in partnership with the UNDP and Appui au processus électoral au Congo, produced four videos on the electoral process in those languages.

Some progress was made towards de-escalating regional tensions as a result of the meeting of the Foreign Ministers of the DRC, Rwanda and Uganda (Lubumbashi, DRC, 21 April) under their 2004 tripartite agreement on regional security [YUN 2004, p. 134]. The parties reaffirmed their commitment to ending the presence and activities of foreign armed groups in the eastern DRC; agreed to support FARDC efforts to disarm, demobilize and repatriate FDLR combatants to Rwanda, with MONUC support, and to establish a "fusion cell" for the exchange and analysis of information on border security.

The security situation in Ituri remained volatile, despite robust measures taken by FARDC, with MONUC support, to disarm combatants. Moreover, the Transitional Government had yet to extend its authority throughout the district. On 24 May, a joint FARDC-MONUC operation forcefully expelled the Lubanga wing of UPC/L from its stronghold in Katoto. Under the disarmament and community reintegration programme, which ended on 25 June, 15,607 combatants of various militia groups, including 4,395 children (840 of whom were girls) were disarmed, and some 6,200 weapons collected. The sustainability of the programmes for the reintegration of ex-combatants into civilian life and of ex-militiamen into FARDC was a major challenge. Two thirds of ex-combatants were unemployed, and, without prospects for long-term socio-economic opportunities, were likely to be tempted to take up arms again. The implementation of reinsertion projects, costing some $3 mil-

lion, was progressing slowly. As a result of the disarmament exercise, FAPC and the Kisembo wing of UPC ceased to exist. Reports indicated, however, that other groups, including UPC/L and FNI, were consolidating their remaining forces under a new alliance called the Mouvement révolutionnaire congolais (MRC). In that connection, the Secretary-General strongly urged neighbouring States to ensure that remaining militia groups were not allowed to use their territories as rear bases, safe havens or supply routes for illegal arms trafficking. MONUC urged the Transitional Government to issue international arrest warrants for militia leaders who might have taken refuge in a neighboring country.

The MONUC brigade in North Kivu carried out operations in close coordination with FARDC against armed elements in the province to facilitate free and safe access for civilians, and joint MONUC-FARDC operations were conducted in FDLR-held territory to limit FDLR's freedom of movement. In Katanga and the Kasais, the threat to the electoral process posed by political tensions and uncontrolled armed groups remained of serious concern.

In early May, the FDLR President, Ignace Murwanashyaka, travelled to Kinshasa and to North and South Kivu, apparently to sensitize the estimated 40,000 FDLR combatants and dependants believed to be operating in those provinces and prepare them to implement the FDLR 31 March declaration. He left the country in mid-May without, however, issuing orders for them to enter the disarmament, demobilization, repatriation and rehabilitation programme, for which MONUC had prepared six temporary assembly areas. There followed a slight increase in voluntary programme participation, but no large-scale repatriation. Between January 2003 and 27 June 2005, a total of 11,729 foreign combatants and their dependants were registered as having returned to their countries.

The Secretary-General noted that, despite tensions at the end of the first transition period on 30 June, that date passed without major disruptions to the peace process. He urged the Security Council to approve the requests and recommendations detailed in his special report on elections (see p. 177) in order to allow strict adherence to the electoral timetable.

The Secretary-General called on the Congolese authorities to show leadership and political commitment to make certain that the reform and restructuring of the security services, particularly the armed forces and national police, were effectively addressed, and asked donors to continue to coordinate their support in that regard.

The Secretary-General, concerned about the continuing volatility in Ituri and its repercussions for the security of the Great Lakes region, asked the Transitional Government and its partners to prepare urgently a comprehensive plan for integrating Ituri into the nation and end the illegal exploitation of resources in the DRC. He urged national and international action to prevent violations of the arms embargo imposed by Council resolution 1493(2003) [YUN 2003, p. 130] and as extended in scope by resolution 1596(2005) (see p. 192). He also urged the Transitional Government and its international partners to follow up urgently his recommendation to set up an arrangement between donors, international financial institutions and the Transitional Government to promote good governance, and accountable and transparent economic management. The Secretary-General appealed to Member States to maintain pressure on all relevant parties to ensure that the disarmament and repatriation of FDLR combatants proceeded without further delay.

Security Council briefing. In his briefing to the Security Council on 11 August on progress in the election preparations, the Assistant Secretary-General for Peacekeeping Operations stressed the need to strengthen MONUC with a view to mandating it to provide logistical support for the election process, as requested in the Secretary-General's special report on the elections.

Communications. The Secretary-General, on 22 August [S/2005/543], drew to the Council's attention that the DRC effectively had entered the electoral phase of its transitional process following the launch of voter registration in the capital, Kinshasa. The registration, which closed on 31 July with over 2.9 million registered, marked the first stage of the nationwide registration programme to be extended to all provinces. The Secretary-General understood that the Council had reached agreement in principle to approve his recommendation to furnish MONUC with the resources required to allow it to provide logistical support to the Congolese electoral process. To ensure the successful completion of ongoing registration activities in time for the 27 November constitutional referendum, the Secretary-General said he intended to begin immediately to provide such support, pending the Council's consideration and approval of his recommendations.

The Council took note of that intention on 26 August [S/2005/544].

SECURITY COUNCIL ACTION (September)

On 6 September [meeting 5255], the Security Council unanimously adopted **resolution 1621**

(2005). The draft [S/2005/555] was prepared in consultations among Council members.

The Security Council,

Recalling its previous resolutions and the statements by its President concerning the Democratic Republic of the Congo, in particular resolutions 1565(2004) of 1 October 2004 and 1592(2005) of 30 March 2005 and the statement of 29 June 2005,

Reaffirming its commitment to respect for the sovereignty, territorial integrity and political independence of the Democratic Republic of the Congo as well as of all States in the region, and its support for the process of the Global and All-Inclusive Agreement on the Transition in the Democratic Republic of the Congo, signed at Pretoria on 17 December 2002,

Underlining the importance of elections as the foundation for the longer-term restoration of peace and stability, national reconciliation and establishment of the rule of law in the Democratic Republic of the Congo,

Calling upon the transitional institutions and all Congolese parties to ensure that free, fair and peaceful elections take place and that the timetable for polls developed by the Independent Electoral Commission is scrupulously respected,

Paying tribute to the donor community for the assistance they provide to the electoral process in the Democratic Republic of the Congo, and encouraging them to maintain it,

Welcoming the interest and commitment shown by the Congolese authorities to promote good governance and transparent economic management, and encouraging them to continue their efforts in this regard,

Reiterating its serious concern regarding the continuation of hostilities by armed groups and militias in the eastern part of the Democratic Republic of the Congo, at the violations of human rights and of international humanitarian law that accompany them, and at the threat they pose to the holding of elections in the Democratic Republic of the Congo,

Taking note of the special report of the Secretary-General of 26 May 2005 on elections in the Democratic Republic of the Congo and of the recommendations contained therein,

Noting that the situation in the Democratic Republic of the Congo continues to constitute a threat to international peace and security in the region,

Acting under Chapter VII of the Charter of the United Nations,

1. *Approves* the recommendations and the concept of operations described in paragraphs 50 to 57 of the special report of the Secretary-General, and authorizes an increase in the strength of the United Nations Organization Mission in the Democratic Republic of the Congo of 841 personnel, including up to five formed police units of 125 officers each and the additional police personnel;

2. *Underlines* the temporary character of the deployments referred to in paragraph 1 above, and requests the Secretary-General to take the necessary steps with a view to downsizing or repatriating these additional personnel from 1 July 2006 at the latest, and to report to the Security Council before 1 June 2006 on the assessment mentioned in paragraph 47 of his special report;

3. *Approves* the recommendation made by the Secretary-General in paragraphs 58 and 59 of his special report, and authorizes the Mission, in accordance with that recommendation and with its mandate as defined in paragraphs 5(*f*) and 7(*c*) of resolution 1565 (2004), and acting in close coordination with the United Nations Development Programme, to provide additional support to the Independent Electoral Commission for the transport of electoral materials;

4. *Encourages* the Mission, within its capacity and in accordance with its mandate, to provide advice and assistance as well as the necessary support to the setting up by the Transitional Government, international financial institutions and donors of an arrangement to strengthen support for good governance and transparent economic management;

5. *Decides* to remain actively seized of the matter.

Statements and communication. Speaking before the General Assembly on 21 September [meeting 18], Uganda said no attention was being given to creating institutions and infrastructure to sustain the DRC, and the integration of armed factions into a single national armed force was halfhearted. Advocating the concept of provisional immunity, Uganda advised that all factions should first be integrated and those guilty of offences punished later. What was being witnessed was a rush to elections and political agendas in the DRC without due regard to the institutions and infrastructure necessary for the long-term sustainability of peace. The 1999 Lusaka Ceasefire Agreement [YUN 1999, p. 87], which provided a strong mechanism to enable the region and the DRC to play complementary roles in the peace process, had been abandoned; and, for over five years, MONUC had made no significant effort to ensure demobilization and disarmament of the negative forces recognized by that accord, thus leaving in place the seeds of future conflict.

The DRC, responding on 23 September [meeting 23], said Uganda's comments were disrespectful and unacceptable. It referred to what it called Uganda's irredentist designs on the DRC, aimed at "making a grab" for the country's eastern province. It said Uganda's objective was to gain control of the significant reserves of raw materials and strategic minerals in Congolese territory. The DRC believed that, to persuade Uganda to embark sincerely on the road to peace, the international community had to impose a comprehensive embargo on the sale of arms and suspend bilateral and multilateral assistance to that country.

In the exercise of its right of reply, Uganda, in a 29 September statement to the Assembly [A/60/400], said it was out of concern and in the spirit of friendship that it proffered its advice on how the international community could move the peace process forward in the DRC, especially in the country's eastern part. Similar advice was offered by Uganda's President to the Secretary-General during the high-level plenary meeting of the Assembly on 13 September and in a 22 August letter to the Security Council President; namely, that efforts be made to integrate militia leaders into the Government of National Unity; that provisional immunity be extended to the various rebel groups to ensure immediate peace; and that once peace and security were established, justice could be pursued. Uganda drew the Assembly's attention to an incident on 13 June, when some Congolese militia leaders entered Uganda. In the absence of a regional process under which they could be handed over to the DRC, all Uganda could do in fulfilment of its international obligation was to declare them personae non gratae. On a bilateral level, Uganda and the DRC were working closely to address outstanding problems. An intelligence-sharing mechanism existed between the two countries and a regional intelligence fusion cell was about to be launched with United States assistance.

Further political developments

Report of Secretary-General (September). The Secretary-General, in his nineteenth (September) report on MONUC [S/2005/603], stated that significant progress was made in voter registration for the elections, along with some progress in the integration of military units in the DRC armed forces and training of the national police. Cooperation among the parties represented in the Transitional Government increased, resulting in enhanced policy coordination. Overall relations between the DRC and neighbouring States had also improved. Only limited progress had been made by donors in providing the resources pledged in support of security for the electoral process to the UNDP-managed basket fund: out of $48.4 million pledged, only $7.6 million had been received by 6 September. Meanwhile, the Transitional Government had disbursed $1.6 million of the $4 million it had pledged.

UDPS, claiming it had not been properly registered as a political party by the Ministry of Interior, called for a boycott of the electoral process and continued to foment tensions in Katanga and the Kasais, where its supporters protested voter registration activities; efforts to persuade UDPS leaders to join the process were unsuccessful. As at 17 September, more than 11 million voters had registered, including 2.9 million in Kinshasa, out of an estimated electorate of 20 to 25 million. Although nationwide registration was to end on 25 September, registration timelines were extended in several areas, as in Katanga and the Kasais, due to logistical difficulties and the slow rate of registration. Despite massive international community support for the electoral process, only $165 million out of the $274 million pledged for the electoral budget had been received from donors as of 6 September.

On 10 August, DRC Vice-President Azarias Ruberwa met with Uganda's President Museveni in Kampala on the issue of the armed groups operating in the DRC. On 23 August, Uganda declared the six MRC leaders personae non gratae and expelled them from Uganda (see p. 184). However, the potential of MRC to undermine progress in stabilizing Ituri remained, given the Transitional Government's incapacity to bring armed group leaders to justice and prevent their movement into and from Uganda.

The DRC, Rwanda and Uganda held a meeting (Kigali, 24-25 August) within the framework of the Tripartite Joint Commission, with Burundi, the AU Commission, the EU Presidency and MONUC attending as observers. Expressing serious concern at the failure of FDLR to disarm and repatriate in accordance with its 31 March declaration (see p. 176), the meeting agreed that the Transitional Government should maintain contact with FDLR to ensure implementation of its declaration and that failure to do so by 30 September would have serious consequences, including the imposition of sanctions. The meeting also agreed to step up pressure to disarm militias operating in the eastern DRC and to negotiate bilateral extradition treaties concerning the remnant militia leaders. At a ministerial level meeting of the Tripartite Joint Commission (New York, 16 September), Burundi became a full participant; thus the Commission was renamed the Tripartite Plus Joint Commission; a summary of the decisions taken at the meeting was attached to Security Council presidential statement S/PRST/2005/46 (see p. 185).

In Ituri, militia remnants continued to commit human rights violations against the local population in areas where MONUC or FARDC was not present. Regular joint FARDC-MONUC operations resulted in the apprehension of some militia elements, seizure of illegal arms and ammunition, and limiting the militias' operational area. Despite the disarmament of 15,600 ex-combatants in Ituri, the National Commission for Demobilization and Reinsertion continued to face difficulties in discharging its responsibilities, in particular the payment of demobilization allowances to ex-combatants.

While the situation in North and South Kivu remained tense, voter registration started in the two provinces on 21 August and generally proceeded smoothly. On 26 August, tensions escalated near Rutshuru in North Kivu following repeated clashes between Mayi-Mayi elements and ex-Rassemblement congolais pour la démocratie-Goma (RCD-G) elements who had yet to participate in the disarmament process. On 25 August, a statement attributed to General Laurent Nkunda, one of the main perpetrators of the May 2004 Bukavu crisis [YUN 2004, p. 124], was published in Goma, in which he threatened to bring down the Transitional Government. The Council of Ministers responded with a special decree on 2 September, by which it stripped the General of his rank, removed him from the army and decided to prosecute him. Joint or parallel MONUC and FARDC operations resulted in an improved security situation in South Kivu. MONUC investigated a number of attacks by armed groups on villages in South Kivu. In North Kivu, MONUC teams continued to monitor the volatile security situation in the Rutshuru and Masisi territories. Frequent clashes between FARDC troops and armed groups operating in the area resulted in numerous civilian casualties. MONUC investigated several cases of killing, rape and abduction of civilians in Katanga.

Law and order problems continued to contribute to the fragility of the security situation in some areas of Katanga where the Transitional Government had not established effective security mechanisms for the protection of civilians. Despite calls by UDPS for a boycott of voter registration, the process continued in Katanga in a generally peaceful fashion. In northern and central Katanga, most Mayi-Mayi commanders refused to join the disarmament process; lawlessness continued to prevail in 10 out of Katanga's 21 territories. On 10 and 11 August, FARDC exchanged fire with a Mayi-Mayi group near the Lunga gold mine, about 200 kilometres from Kalemie, and took control of the area. The Secretary-General again recommended that the Council consider authorizing the deployment to MONUC of an additional brigade of 2,580 personnel.

A special humanitarian action plan for the DRC was being developed, with a preliminary budget of $800 million. The plan's major objectives were to save lives, reduce vulnerability and facilitate the transition, with reintegration as a cross-cutting issue.

The Secretary-General urged donors to accelerate the disbursement of their pledges for financing. However, the Transitional Government needed to work closely with its international partners to ensure the sound, transparent and accountable management of public finances and address corruption effectively. He called on the Congolese authorities to allocate adequate financial resources for strengthening the justice sector in the 2006 State budget and appealed to donors to increase their support in that area. He urged donors to support the development of the 2006 humanitarian action plan (see above) and to provide additional resources in response to the 2005 Consolidated Appeal for the DRC (see p. 996). He also called for increased support by international partners for the security sector reform, including for the main requirements of the FARDC brigades.

The Secretary-General recommended that MONUC's mandate be extended for one year, until 1 October 2006, which would include the period up to the elections and the immediate post-transitional period following the installation of the new Government.

Uganda, in its observations on the Secretary-General's foregoing report on MONUC, forwarded to the Council on 4 October [S/2005/633], fully endorsed the Secretary-General's request for 2,580 additional personnel for MONUC and his call on the international community to increase its assistance to the DRC in all areas, especially security reform.

SECURITY COUNCIL ACTION (September)

On 30 September [meeting 5272], the Security Council unanimously adopted **resolution 1628 (2005)**. The draft [S/2005/614] was prepared in consultations among Council members.

The Security Council,

Recalling its resolutions on the Democratic Republic of the Congo, in particular resolutions 1565(2004) of 1 October 2004, 1592(2005) of 30 March 2005, 1596 (2005) of 18 April 2005 and 1621(2005) of 6 September 2005,

Reaffirming its commitment to respect for the sovereignty, territorial integrity and political independence of the Democratic Republic of the Congo, and its readiness to support the peace and national reconciliation process in that country, in particular through the United Nations Organization Mission in the Democratic Republic of the Congo,

Noting that the situation in the Democratic Republic of the Congo continues to constitute a threat to international peace and security in the region,

1. *Decides* to extend the mandate of the United Nations Organization Mission in the Democratic Republic of the Congo, as contained in resolutions 1565(2004), 1592(2005), 1596(2005) and 1621(2005), adopted under Chapter VII of the Charter of the United Nations, until 31 October 2005;

2. *Decides also* to remain seized of the matter.

Communications. The DRC, in a 3 October letter to the Security Council [S/2005/620], protested the Ugandan President's statement that the Ugandan army would cross the border into the DRC if in two months' time the DRC Government and MONUC failed to disarm the Ugandan rebels of LRA, who had come from the Sudan and in-

stalled themselves in the Garamba National Park, in the eastern DRC. The DRC called the statement an affront to the international community and a violation of the Charter. The DRC reiterated that it harboured no hidden agenda against any of its neighbours, and had given the LRA rebels an ultimatum to leave the country immediately. The DRC reminded the Council of its various resolutions and presidential statements expressing concern over the proven support of Uganda for the militia in the DRC, particularly in Ituri.

The DRC was firmly committed to the peace process; faced with the new Ugandan threat, however, it would have no choice but to act within the framework of international legality and of Article 51 of the Charter on the inherent right of individual or collective self-defence in the event of an armed attack. The DRC asked the Council to impose appropriate sanctions on Uganda, including an embargo on arms sales to that country, and to demand that it refrain from any action likely to disrupt the DRC peace process.

Uganda, on 7 October [S/2005/645], strongly protested and called false the DRC allegations. It pointed out that the main threat to international peace and security was posed by negative forces, mainly LRA, stationed in the DRC and using it as a base from which to attack Uganda and terrorize its citizens. Uganda had an obligation to defend itself if attacked, in accordance with Article 51 of the Charter. Uganda asserted, however, that there was no attack planned on the DRC and none was envisaged. The DRC had an international obligation to make sure its territory was not used as a base from which anti-Uganda elements could attack Uganda.

Uganda stressed that its businessmen did not trade in arms; it did not support any Congolese militia. Its sole interest and unequivocal demand was that the LRA terrorists be promptly disarmed, arrested and brought to justice. It was encouraged that the DRC had taken steps to act against them and was confident that the DRC would continue to do so. Uganda added that at no time had it attempted to enter the DRC in order to attack the LRA terrorists.

Uganda requested the Council to ensure that the DRC and MONUC were given the necessary assistance to disarm and demobilize the negative forces.

SECURITY COUNCIL ACTION (October)

On 4 October [meeting 5275], following consultations among Security Council members, the President made statement **S/PRST/2005/46** on behalf of the Council:

The Security Council takes note of the report of the Secretary-General of 26 September 2005 on the

United Nations Organization Mission in the Democratic Republic of the Congo. It expresses its concern over the presence of foreign armed groups which continue to pose a serious threat to stability in the eastern part of the country.

The Council deplores in this regard the failure of the Forces démocratiques de libération du Rwanda to proceed with the disarmament and repatriation of their combatants, and exhorts them to do so without further delay and in accordance with the declaration that they signed at Rome on 31 March 2005.

The Council recognizes the attached decision, taken on 16 September 2005 by the Democratic Republic of the Congo, Uganda, Rwanda and Burundi, acting within the framework of the Tripartite Plus Joint Commission, to set the deadline of 30 September 2005 for the Forces démocratiques de libération du Rwanda to disarm or otherwise to face measures intended to compel them to do so. The Forces démocratiques de libération du Rwanda can no longer remain as an armed group in the Democratic Republic of the Congo.

The Council demands that the Forces démocratiques de libération du Rwanda seize this opportunity to proceed voluntarily with their disarmament and return to Rwanda without any delay or preconditions.

The Council commends the political and military pressure placed on the Forces démocratiques de libération du Rwanda by the Government of the Democratic Republic of the Congo and the United Nations Organization Mission in the Democratic Republic of the Congo.

The Council welcomes the steps taken by the Government of Rwanda, with the support of the international community, to peacefully repatriate members of the Forces démocratiques de libération du Rwanda returning to Rwanda, in accordance with the applicable norms of international law and with respect for the rights and freedoms of the human person. The Council encourages the Government of Rwanda to continue to give the widest publicity to its commitments.

The Council demands the full cooperation of the Forces démocratiques de libération du Rwanda with the International Criminal Tribunal for Rwanda, particularly with regard to the arrest and transfer of indictees who remain at large.

Moreover, the Council notes with concern the incursion of members of the Lord's Resistance Army into the Democratic Republic of the Congo and welcomes the intention of the Congolese armed forces to disarm this group in cooperation with the Mission and in accordance with the mandate of the Mission as set out in resolution 1565(2004).

Further, the Council calls upon all armed groups in the Great Lakes region of Africa to act without delay to lay down their arms and join the processes of political transition under way in the region.

The Council calls upon the States of the region to deepen their cooperation with a view to putting an end to the activities of illegal armed groups. It recalls its adherence to respect for the sovereignty of all States and underlines that any recourse to the threat or use of force against the territorial integrity of a State is contrary to the purposes and principles set out in the Charter of the United Nations.

Attachment

Tripartite Plus Joint Commission Ministerial
Waldorf Astoria Hotel
New York
16 September 2005

Summary of decisions

Members of the Tripartite Commission commended Burundi's successful political transition, officially welcomed Burundi as a full participant and adopted the new name Tripartite Plus Joint Commission.

The Tripartite Plus members

— Reiterated their commitment to prevent negative elements from using their respective territories to destabilize neighbouring countries;

— Agreed to continue military and political pressure on the Forces démocratiques de libération du Rwanda (FDLR) to ensure that it fulfils its commitment to disarm and repatriate;

— Agreed to continue military and diplomatic pressure on all other militias to ensure their disarmament and repatriation or reintegration;

— Agreed to retain 30 September 2005, as the deadline for voluntary disarmament and repatriation or reintegration and that failure to do so would trigger imposition of sanctions;

— Agreed that the Tripartite Joint Commission has contributed to the reduction of tension in the Great Lakes region and that additional confidence-building measures are necessary to bring stability to the area, including:

  • Authorization by the Democratic Republic of the Congo of a Ugandan office in Beni to encourage, in conjunction with the United Nations Organization Mission in the Democratic Republic of the Congo (MONUC) and the Democratic Republic of the Congo, the disarmament and repatriation or reintegration of the Allied Democratic Forces (ADF), the National Army for the Liberation of Uganda (NALU) and the People's Redemption Army (PRA);

  • Consideration of how to extradite Mutebusi, Nkunda and other leaders of armed groups;

  • Articulation of the mechanisms the United States of America and the European Union should employ against all militias operating in eastern Democratic Republic of the Congo by Tripartite members;

— Agreed to have the European Union, in conjunction with the Government of Rwanda, draft an information package for distribution to FDLR that outlines measures to encourage their disarmament and repatriation or reintegration;

— Welcomed the African Union's announcement of plans for an October reconnaissance mission that will lead to recommendations on how to proceed with the establishment of an African Union force in eastern Democratic Republic of the Congo;

— Welcomed the continued effort of the international community to augment and build the capacity of the Armed Forces of the Democratic

Republic of the Congo (FARDC) in order to bring stability to eastern Democratic Republic of the Congo;
— Agreed that MONUC's response in eastern Democratic Republic of the Congo had improved, but that additional capacity was necessary to enforce its mandate;
— Agreed that the facilitator will draft a timeline of actions by the Tripartite members and Contact Group through 31 December 2005 that are aimed at ensuring stability in the Great Lakes region, to include:
  • Develop sanctions that will be imposed on militias after 30 September 2005 should voluntary disarmament not occur.
  • Install Tripartite Fusion Cell in Kisangani and Tripartite Plus member capitals.
  • Develop and distribute an incentive package to encourage FDLR and other militias to return to their country of origin.
  • Undertake an African Union reconnaissance mission in the Democratic Republic of the Congo.

Communication. Following a meeting of the Tripartite Plus Joint Commission (Kampala, 20-21 October), the Ministers of the partner States of the Commission (Burundi, the DRC, Rwanda and Uganda), in a 21 October letter to the Security Council [S/2005/667], proposed that the draft resolution before the Council on the renewal of MONUC's mandate (see below) be strengthened to include the identification by name of all armed groups currently operating in the eastern DRC; the disarmament of all armed groups and militias in that area, using all means necessary; and a redoubling of the donor community's efforts to support the integration, training and equipping of the DRC armed forces and national police. Attached to the letter was a text of an amendment to the draft resolution incorporating those points.

In resolution 1649(2005) (see p. 187), the Council took note of the letter and requested the Secretary-General to submit his observations and, if deemed necessary, his recommendations.

SECURITY COUNCIL ACTION (October and December)

On 28 October [meeting 5296], the Security Council unanimously adopted **resolution 1635 (2005)**. The draft, [S/2005/665] was prepared in consultations among Council members.

The Security Council,

Recalling its resolutions and the statements by its President on the Democratic Republic of the Congo, in particular resolutions 1565(2004) of 1 October 2004, 1592(2005) of 30 March 2005, 1596(2005) of 18 April 2005, 1621(2005) of 6 September 2005 and 1628(2005) of 30 September 2005, and the statement of 4 October 2005,

Reaffirming its commitment to respect for the sovereignty, territorial integrity and political independence of the Democratic Republic of the Congo as well as of

all States in the region, and its support for the process of the Global and All-Inclusive Agreement on the Transition in the Democratic Republic of the Congo, signed at Pretoria on 17 December 2002,

Underlining the importance of elections as the foundation for the longer-term restoration of peace and stability, national reconciliation and establishment of the rule of law in the Democratic Republic of the Congo,

Paying tribute to the donor community for the assistance they provide to the Democratic Republic of the Congo, and in particular to the electoral process, and encouraging them to maintain it,

Welcoming the interest and commitment shown by the Congolese authorities to promote good governance and transparent economic management, and urging all the components of the Government of National Unity and Transition to strengthen their efforts in continuing to build consensus in this regard,

Reiterating its serious concern regarding the continuation of hostilities by militias and foreign armed groups in the eastern part of the Democratic Republic of the Congo, and at the threat they pose to the holding of elections in the Democratic Republic of the Congo,

Deploring the violations of human rights and international humanitarian law carried out by these militias and groups, and stressing the urgent need for those responsible for these crimes to be brought to justice,

Recognizing the link between the illegal exploitation of natural resources, the illicit trade in such resources and the proliferation of and trafficking in arms as one of the factors fuelling and exacerbating conflicts in the Great Lakes region of Africa, and in particular in the Democratic Republic of the Congo,

Taking note of the nineteenth report of the Secretary-General on the United Nations Organization Mission in the Democratic Republic of the Congo, of 26 September 2005, and of the recommendations contained therein,

Noting that the situation in the Democratic Republic of the Congo continues to constitute a threat to international peace and security in the region,

Acting under Chapter VII of the Charter of the United Nations,

1. *Decides* to extend the mandate of the United Nations Organization Mission in the Democratic Republic of the Congo until 30 September 2006;

2. *Having taken note* of the recommendations described in paragraphs 27 to 29 of the report of the Secretary-General, authorizes an increase of 300 personnel in the military strength of the Mission to allow for the deployment of an infantry battalion in Katanga, with enabling assets, including its own air mobility and appropriate medical support, to provide additional security within its area of operations during the electoral period;

3. *Underlines* the temporary character of the increase referred to in paragraph 2 above, and requests the Secretary-General to take the necessary steps with a view to downsizing or repatriating this additional strength from 1 July 2006 at the latest, and to report to the Security Council before 1 June 2006 on the assessment to be made for that purpose;

4. *Calls upon* the transitional institutions and all Congolese parties to ensure that free, fair and peaceful elections take place and that the timetable for polls de-

veloped by the Independent Electoral Commission is scrupulously respected, and underlines in this regard the fact that it is the responsibility of the Congolese authorities to adopt the necessary legislation without further delay;

5. *Calls upon* the Government of National Unity and Transition to carry out reform of the security sector, through the expeditious integration of the Armed Forces and of the National Police of the Democratic Republic of the Congo and in particular by ensuring adequate payment and logistical support for their personnel;

6. *Calls upon* the donor community, as a matter of urgency, to continue to engage firmly in the provision of assistance needed for the integration, training and equipping of the Armed Forces and of the National Police of the Democratic Republic of the Congo, and urges the Government of National Unity and Transition to promote all possible means to facilitate and expedite cooperation to this end;

7. *Requests* the Mission, within its capacity and mandate, and in consultation with international financial institutions and donors, to continue to provide advice and assistance, as well as the necessary support, to the effective follow-up to the meeting held on 21 September 2005 between the Espace présidentiel and the International Committee in Support of the Transition, to strengthen support for good governance and transparent economic management;

8. *Welcomes* the action taken by the Mission in investigating and dealing with instances of sexual exploitation and abuse and its efforts to put in place preventive measures, requests the Secretary-General to continue to take the necessary measures to achieve actual compliance in the Mission with the United Nations zero-tolerance policy on sexual exploitation and abuse and to keep the Council informed, and urges troop-contributing countries to take appropriate preventive action, including predeployment awareness training, and other action to ensure full accountability in cases of such conduct involving their personnel;

9. *Decides* to remain actively seized of the matter.

On 21 December [meeting 5340], the Council, having considered the report of the Security Council mission to Central Africa in November (see p. 162) and the 21 October letter of the Tripartite Plus Joint Commission (see p. 186), unanimously adopted **resolution 1649(2005)**. The draft [S/2005/810] was prepared in consultations among Council members.

The Security Council,

Recalling its resolutions and the statements by its President concerning the Democratic Republic of the Congo, in particular resolutions 1533(2004) of 12 March 2004, 1565(2004) of 1 October 2004, 1592(2005) of 30 March 2005, 1596(2005) of 18 April 2005, 1616(2005) of 29 July 2005, 1621(2005) of 6 September 2005 and 1628(2005) of 30 September 2005, and the statements of 2 March and 4 October 2005,

Reaffirming its commitment to respect for the sovereignty, territorial integrity and political independence of the Democratic Republic of the Congo as well as all States in the region, and its support for the process of

the Global and All-Inclusive Agreement on the Transition in the Democratic Republic of the Congo, signed at Pretoria on 17 December 2002, and underlining the importance of elections as the foundation for the longer-term restoration of peace and stability, national reconciliation and establishment of the rule of law in the Democratic Republic of the Congo,

Reiterating its serious concern regarding the continuation of hostilities by militias and foreign armed groups in the eastern part of the Democratic Republic of the Congo, and at the threat they pose to civilians and to the holding of elections in the Democratic Republic of the Congo and to stability in the region,

Deploring the violations of human rights and international humanitarian law committed by these groups and militias, and stressing the urgent need for those responsible for these crimes to be brought to justice,

Welcoming the robust action taken by the United Nations Organization Mission in the Democratic Republic of the Congo against these groups and militias, and commending the dedication of the personnel of the Mission, who are operating in particularly hazardous conditions,

Calling upon all armed groups in the Great Lakes region of Africa, such as the Forces démocratiques de libération du Rwanda, the Parti pour la libération du peuple hutu-Forces nationales de libération and the Lord's Resistance Army, to act without delay to lay down their arms, enter demobilization programmes and support efforts to consolidate peace that are under way in the region,

Having noted the decision, taken on 16 September 2005 by the Democratic Republic of the Congo, Uganda, Rwanda and Burundi, acting within the framework of the Tripartite Plus Joint Commission, to retain the deadline of 30 September 2005 for the voluntary disarmament of the Forces démocratiques de libération du Rwanda, on the understanding that sanctions would be imposed should they fail to respect this deadline,

Taking note of the letter dated 21 October 2005 from the ministers representing Burundi, the Democratic Republic of the Congo, Rwanda and Uganda on the Tripartite Plus Joint Commission addressed to the President of the Security Council,

Calling upon the States of the region to deepen their cooperation with a view to putting an end to the activities of illegal armed groups, and underlining the fact that any recourse to the threat or use of force against the territorial integrity of a State is contrary to the Charter of the United Nations,

Urging, in this regard, participants in the International Conference on Peace, Security, Democracy and Development in the Great Lakes Region of Africa to convene the second summit as soon as possible,

Aware that the link between the illegal exploitation of natural resources, the illicit trade in those resources and the proliferation of and trafficking in arms is one of the factors fuelling and exacerbating conflicts in the Great Lakes region of Africa, in particular in the Democratic Republic of the Congo,

Paying tribute to the donor community for the assistance it is providing to the Democratic Republic of the Congo, and encouraging it to maintain that assistance,

Taking note of the report of the Security Council mission which visited the region of Central Africa from 4

to 11 November 2005, and endorsing its recommendations,

Noting that the situation in the Democratic Republic of the Congo continues to pose a threat to international peace and security in the region,

Acting under Chapter VII of the Charter,

1. *Deplores* the fact that foreign armed groups present in the eastern part of the Democratic Republic of the Congo have not yet laid down their arms, and demands that all such groups engage voluntarily and without any delay or preconditions in their disarmament and in their repatriation and resettlement;

2. *Decides* that, for a period expiring on 31 July 2006, the provisions of paragraphs 13 to 16 of resolution 1596(2005) shall extend to the following individuals, as designated by the Security Council Committee established pursuant to resolution 1533(2004) ("the Committee"):

(a) Political and military leaders of foreign armed groups operating in the Democratic Republic of the Congo who impede the disarmament and the voluntary repatriation or resettlement of combatants belonging to those groups;

(b) Political and military leaders of Congolese militias receiving support from outside the Democratic Republic of the Congo, and in particular those operating in Ituri, who impede the participation of their combatants in disarmament, demobilization and reintegration processes;

3. *Decides also* that the measures imposed under paragraph 2 above as well as those under paragraph 13 of resolution 1596(2005) shall not apply where the Committee authorizes in advance, and on a case-by-case basis, the transit of individuals returning to the territory of the State of their nationality, or participating in efforts to bring to justice perpetrators of grave violations of human rights or international humanitarian law;

4. *Decides further* that the tasks of the Committee set out in paragraph 18 of resolution 1596(2005) shall extend to the provisions set out in paragraph 2 above;

5. *Requests* the Secretary-General and the Group of Experts established pursuant to resolution 1533 (2004), within its capabilities and without prejudice to the execution of the other tasks in its mandate, to assist the Committee in the designation of the leaders referred to in paragraph 2 above;

6. *Decides* that the provisions of paragraphs 2 to 5 above shall enter into force on 15 January 2006, unless the Secretary-General informs the Council that the process of disarmament of those foreign armed groups and Congolese militias operating in the Democratic Republic of the Congo is being completed;

7. *Decides also* that, no later than 31 July 2006, it shall review the measures set forth in paragraph 2 above, in the light of progress accomplished in the peace and transition process in the Democratic Republic of the Congo, in particular with regard to the disarmament of foreign armed groups;

8. *Urges* the Government of National Unity and Transition to do its utmost to ensure the security of civilians, including humanitarian personnel, by effectively extending State authority throughout the territory of the Democratic Republic of the Congo, and in particular in the provinces of North Kivu and South Kivu and in the Ituri district;

9. *Recalls* that, by its resolution 1565(2004), the Council has mandated the United Nations Organization Mission in the Democratic Republic of the Congo to support operations led by the Armed Forces of the Democratic Republic of the Congo to disarm foreign combatants, and to facilitate the voluntary repatriation of disarmed foreign combatants and their dependants;

10. *Requests*, in this regard, the Secretary-General, in close coordination with all relevant stakeholders and in particular the Government of National Unity and Transition, to submit to the Council for its consideration, by 15 March 2006, a comprehensive and integrated strategy for the disarmament, repatriation and resettlement of foreign combatants, incorporating military, political, economic and justice-related aspects, including the contribution of the Mission within its current mandate, in accordance with the applicable norms of international law and with respect for the rights and freedoms of the human person;

11. *Emphasizes* that, as per resolution 1565(2004), the Mission is authorized to use all necessary means, within its capabilities and in the areas where its armed units are deployed, to deter any foreign or Congolese armed group from attempting to use force to threaten the political process, and to ensure the protection of civilians under imminent threat of physical violence;

12. *Urges* the Government of National Unity and Transition to carry out reform of the security sector, through the expeditious integration of the Armed Forces and of the National Police of the Democratic Republic of the Congo, and in particular by ensuring adequate and timely payment and logistical support for their personnel, with a view to allowing them, inter alia, to expedite the disarmament of armed groups operating on Congolese territory, taking note, as appropriate, of the recommendations of the European Union Mission of Assistance for Security Sector Reform mentioned in the report of the Security Council mission to Central Africa;

13. *Reiterates its call upon* the donor community, as a matter of urgency, to continue to engage firmly in the provision of assistance needed for the integration, training and equipping of the Armed Forces and of the National Police of the Democratic Republic of the Congo, and urges the Government of National Unity and Transition to promote all possible means to facilitate and expedite cooperation to this end;

14. *Requests* the Secretary-General to submit his observations and, if he deems it necessary, recommendations concerning the letter dated 21 October 2005 from the ministers representing Burundi, the Democratic Republic of the Congo, Rwanda and Uganda on the Tripartite Plus Joint Commission addressed to the President of the Security Council;

15. *Demands* that the Governments of Uganda, Rwanda, the Democratic Republic of the Congo and Burundi take measures to prevent the use of their respective territories in support of violations of the arms embargo imposed by resolutions 1493(2003) of 28 July 2003 and 1596(2005), and renewed by resolution 1616 (2005), or in support of activities of armed groups present in the region;

16. *Demands also* that all States neighbouring the Democratic Republic of the Congo, as well as the Government of National Unity and Transition, impede any kind of support to the illegal exploitation of Con-

golese natural resources, in particular by preventing the flow of such resources through their respective territories;

17. *Requests* States concerned and in particular those in the region to take additional measures with regard to the political and military leaders of the foreign armed groups present in their respective territories, including, where necessary, by taking action to bring them to justice or by taking appropriate measures of international cooperation and judicial assistance;

18 *Reiterates its call upon* the Congolese authorities to bring to justice without delay perpetrators of grave violations of human rights and international humanitarian law, and reiterates that the mandate of the United Nations Organization Mission in the Democratic Republic of the Congo, as set out in resolution 1565(2004), includes cooperation with efforts to bring such perpetrators to justice;

19. *Demands* that all parties cooperate fully with the International Criminal Tribunal for Rwanda, particularly with regard to the arrest and transfer of indictees who remain at large;

20. *Decides* to remain actively seized of the matter.

Constitutional referendum

The referendum on the draft constitution, originally scheduled for 27 November, but postponed owing to the need to extend the period of voter registration, particularly in the provinces of Bandundu and Equateur, was successfully held on 18 and 19 December with minimal security incidents country-wide. Turnout was moderate and somewhat low in the opposition strongholds of the Kasais and in parts of Kinshasa, but appreciably higher in the eastern provinces. The referendum was preceded by a formal information campaign, from 2 to 16 December, as required by the referendum law. Several months prior to that, IEC, MONUC, most political parties and several NGOs carried out civic education programmes. Civic and voter education activities were generally believed to have been insufficient, however, and would need to be stepped up in the lead-up to the elections.

SECURITY COUNCIL ACTION

On 21 December [meeting 5340], following consultations among Security Council members, the President made statement **S/PRST/2005/66** on behalf of the Council:

The Security Council commends the people of the Democratic Republic of the Congo for the successful holding of the referendum on the draft Constitution. The large number of voters demonstrated a genuine aspiration to peace and national reconciliation.

The Council pays tribute to the work of the Independent Electoral Commission, which was able, with unprecedented and outstanding logistical support from the United Nations Organization Mission in the Democratic Republic of the Congo and with the assistance of the international community, to take up this challenge.

The Council recalls its support for the holding of elections in the coming months, which must take place before the end of the transitional period on 30 June 2006. It urges the Government of National Unity and Transition to live up to the expectations of the Congolese people and to do its utmost to ensure that the next polls are held in accordance with the timetable of the Independent Electoral Commission.

The EU, on 22 December [S/2005/853], issued a statement congratulating the Congolese people, IEC and MONUC on the successful holding of the referendum on the Constitution on 18 December and reiterated its strong commitment to help the Congolese people to achieve the goal of completing the transition to full democratic Government as soon as possible.

Situation at end of year

The twentieth (December) report of the Secretary-General on MONUC [S/2005/832] noted that the electoral process gained further momentum. Voter registration was completed in all provinces, with over 25 million citizens, of an estimated electorate of 22 to 28 million having been registered by 17 December. On 7 November, President Kabila submitted to the National Assembly the draft electoral law, adopted by the Council of Ministers on 25 October. The draft provided for elections to the national and provincial assemblies to be conducted under a proportional representation system, with a closed list of candidates; to that end, 186 districts would be established, based on the existing administrative units (territories, towns and, for Kinshasa, communes). A joint commission of National Assembly and Senate members considered the draft text to help bridge differences on some of its essential provisions, including the options of using open and closed lists. It recommended an amended draft providing for a combination of three electoral systems, depending on the number of seats in each constituency. On 29 November, the National Assembly adopted the law granting amnesty for all political offences, including attempts on the life of a Head of State, as envisaged in the 2002 Global and All-Inclusive Agreement [YUN 2002, p. 125].

The security situation in Ituri, although significantly improved, remained fragile. An FARDC integrated brigade, with MONUC support, was deployed to the gold-mining areas of Kilo and Mongwalu in mid-October. By early November, close to 1,000 MRC militia had surrendered, of whom 300 were transported to Kisangani to be disarmed and demobilized. As a result of a joint

FADRC-MONUC operation launched in mid-November in Irumu territory, south of Bunia, some 200 MRC elements fled towards North Kivu, where they surrendered to FARDC and were disarmed. Another 100 militia fled to Uganda and handed over their weapons to the Ugandan Peoples' Defence Forces (UPDF); their repatriation was being organized by Uganda and the DRC. Security in the border areas deteriorated, particularly in the Aru and Faradje territories, reportedly infiltrated by LRA and Sudanese criminal elements and UPDF troops from the Sudan and Uganda. The situation improved following a joint FADRC-MONUC operation around Aba, on the border with the Sudan, and a mid-November meeting there between FARDC and the Sudanese People's Liberation Movement/Army (SPLM/A).

The Transitional Government intensified military pressure on foreign armed groups and Mayi-Mayi elements in the Kivus who persisted in their refusal to enter the disarmament process. Military operations in the Kivus focused on, among other things, addressing concentrations of militia, especially FDLR and the Allied Democratic Forces/National Army for the Liberation of Uganda, ensuring flexible logistic MONUC support to enable rapid FARDC deployment, conducting joint FARDC-MONUC operations and supporting the operations of the integrated FARDC brigades. In late September, FARDC captured Bwahungu and Tubimbi, in Walungu territory in South Kivu, occupied for almost two months by FDLR and allied ex-Mayi-Mayi elements. In reprisal, FDLR/Rastas on 9 October attacked civilians in and around Buba in Walungu, causing 25 deaths. On 25 October, FARDC, with MONUC support, launched operations against renegade Mayi-Mayi in Virunga National Park, disarming 359 of them, destroying five camps and confiscating 167 weapons, as well as capturing 14 FDLR elements. While the operations improved security in several areas, they also caused the displacement of some 5,000 civilians from their homes in Bulundule, Bulindi and the adjoining villages to Kanyabayonga.

The security situation in northern and central Katanga continued to suffer from the activities of uncontrolled armed groups and FARDC elements. Mayi-Mayi militia reportedly killed a Catholic priest, looted villages and perpetrated human rights abuses in Moba, Manono and Kabala, causing the displacement of some 2,000 persons. An additional source of insecurity in the area were FARDC elements, particularly in connection with illegal tax collection and disputes with the provincial authorities. In the Nyunzu-Kabalo-Kongolo area, ex-Mayi-Mayi groups were reported to have expanded their territorial control, including over the Lunga gold mines. Outside the main cities, illegal roadblocks were set up, and gross human rights violations by Mayi-Mayi, FARDC, the national police, and intelligence and security services continued unabated.

The Transitional Government, with MONUC support, intensified its operations forcibly to disarm and repatriate Rwandan and Ugandan armed groups in the DRC. Several operations were carried out in the North and South Kivus, and about 60 Rwandan combatants and their dependants agreed to enter the demobilization process. As to the three-phase disarmament of former FARDC factional forces, only the first phase was completed with the integration of six brigades. The second phase, which was to have begun in September, was delayed by the slow pace in moving troops to the disarmament centres and by a shortfall of about 30,000 troops entering the process. Despite efforts to address the backlog, the national disarmament, demobilization and reintegration of ex-combatants into society remained slow.

The Secretary-General congratulated the people of the DRC on their successful constitutional referendum, the first important step to the elections. He urged all Congolese and international stakeholders to continue working together towards meeting the outstanding objectives of the transitional agenda. He also urged the Parliament to accelerate its review and approval of the electoral law, and the Transitional Government to promulgate an electoral timetable and step up the related civic education. He called on the Government to work with its partners to implement their proposals to address issues related to security sector reform, and with the international community to increase the capacity of the judicial system nationwide and to ensure humane conditions of detention. He strongly urged donors to consider his request for the minimum resources necessary for FARDC to conduct military operations with MONUC to disarm the foreign armed groups in the DRC. He also pointed to the strengthening of the Government's sovereignty, including its ability to manage the country's natural resources and provide basic services to the population, as requiring serious attention.

Arms embargo

In February [S/2005/81], the Security Council Committee established pursuant to resolution 1533(2004) [YUN 2004, p. 137] (Security Council Committee on the DRC) to review and monitor the arms embargo imposed by resolution 1493 (2003) [YUN 2003, p. 130] reported on its activities from 12 March to 31 December 2004, during which it held one formal and four informal meetings. The Committee received replies from 34 States and the EU to the request contained in resolution 1533(2004) that all States inform the Committee of measures they had taken to comply with the arms embargo. It also received notifications in advance from three States regarding exceptions to the embargo, on which the Committee took no action.

Report of Group of Experts (January). In accordance with Security Council resolution 1552(2004) [YUN 2004, p. 141], the Group of Experts on the Democratic Republic of the Congo, established pursuant to resolution 1533(2004), submitted its first report in January [S/2005/30]. As described by the report, the political and military realities in the eastern part of the DRC and on either side of it were such as to make the arms embargo susceptible to a variety of interpretations; hence, the need for a reappraisal of its geographical scope and targets. Many of the areas in the region suffered from the absence of State authority and thus from the extension of law and order. Moreover, the intertwining of shared interests and objectives on both sides of the DRC's eastern border rendered the arms embargo subject to abuse. The Group focused its investigations on three sectors connected to weapons supply and logistical support, namely, civil aviation, customs and immigration, and border commerce, and gave a detailed account of its findings.

Given the complexity of the political landscape in the DRC and the varying allegiances within the Transitional Government, the Group recommended that the target of the embargo, as defined in Council resolution 1493(2003), be revisited with a view to clarifying its terms and exemptions; that the état-major intégré of the armed forces of the DRC in Kinshasa, in which all parties to the 2002 Global and All-Inclusive Agreement [YUN 2002, p. 125] were represented and which, in principle, functioned as the decision-making body of the integrated army, be instituted as the sole procuring and authorizing agent on behalf of the Transitional Government and of the integrated army for military hardware and other forms of military equipment; and that the Council extend the arms embargo to the entire territory of the DRC, with the exception of the état-major and MONUC and for supplies of non-lethal material and training for humanitarian or protective use. Monitoring should extend until the end of the embargo. A Group liaison officer should be integrated into the Joint Mission Analysis Cell at MONUC headquarters for the duration of any future mandate to coordinate the activities of the Group and MONUC and the flow of information between them.

MONUC should standardize inspection and data collection procedures and establish baseline data on weapons seized or acquired. As to the monitoring of airports and air operations, MONUC should conduct regular ad hoc inspections of aircraft, including relevant documentation, at strategic airports, and share the information obtained with the DRC civil aviation authorities, the International Civil Aviation Organization (ICAO) and the Group for further action. The Ubwari Peninsula on the Congolese side of Lake Tanganyika was, in the Group's opinion, a conduit for arms smuggling and a hub for illicit military activity and should be monitored.

Modalities for integration into the DRC national army and police should include prior notification to MONUC of the internal movements of arms and related materiel for the use of the integrated units. The Council should consider resourcing a small arms component within UNOB or a UN agency, and baseline data and a weapons inventory should be established in connection with the disarmament programme in Burundi. The Group called on the commander of the DRC tenth military region to sensitize those who denied access to MONUC and the Group during an airport inspection in Bukavu, as well as all FARDC personnel under his command, to the need to abide by UN resolutions; to prevent similar instances in the future, the état-major should send clear instructions to all FARDC military regions to cooperate with MONUC in its inspections.

Given the large number of illicit aircraft operating to and from the eastern DRC, a coordinated, aggressive campaign should be launched by the Transitional Government, ICAO, MONUC and neighbouring Governments to divest the region of aircraft and air cargo companies involved in illegal aviation practices. The DRC civil aviation authorities should regularly verify the validity of aircrafts and pilots' documents to stop the use of false documents. The Group recommended that Uganda regularize the status of civilian aircraft using the military apron at Entebbe Airport and that Burundi investigate the dual use of the registration 9U-BHR by aircraft of Volga Atlantic and Aigle Aviation.

The Group's recommendations relating to border controls called for, among other measures: the imposition by the Council of a travel ban and asset freeze on high-ranking leaders of the Ituri armed groups, and the extension of State authority to customs and immigration in all of the DRC, especially in the embargoed areas; the mobilization by Uganda of sufficient manpower, including police and immigration officials, along key border crossings; and the strict regulation of

Uganda's gold export trade and Rwanda's import of mineral resources.

The Group underscored the need to rectify the ambiguous relations between the military regions in the eastern DRC. The eighth and tenth military regional command structures, although officially part of an integrated FARDC, were in conflict with one another in the field. Accordingly, the Group called for sanctions against General Obedi, commander of the eighth military region who had been reluctant to oust the dissident General Nkunda and Colonel Nakabaka, an ex-Mayi-Mayi commander found supplying arms to FNL and FDLR from FARDC stores. It also called on the état-major to send clear instructions to the commanders of the eighth and tenth military regions to thwart cohabitation between FARDC troops and FDLR units in their respective areas of responsibility and to give priority to apprehending General Nkunda and extraditing the dissident Colonel Mutebutsi and his renegade forces to the DRC to face charges.

Finally, the Group recommended that the DRC, Rwanda and Uganda adhere to their 2004 tripartite agreement on regional security [YUN 2004, p. 134]. The Tripartite Plus Joint Commission and the 2004 Joint Verification Mechanism signed by the DRC and Rwanda [ibid.] should serve as the appropriate forums for addressing allegations of foreign military interference in the internal affairs of another country. Member States should strive to identify members of the FDLR diaspora based in their respective countries and contributing to the financing of FDLR activities in order to sever such assistance.

Communications. In a 31 January letter [S/2005/73], Rwanda informed the Security Council Committee on the DRC that the Group's report had been completed without its input and that it had been deliberately denied the opportunity to share information with the Group in a meaningful manner. It claimed that the Rwanda section of the report was "riddled with inconsistencies, ambiguity and innuendo". Rwanda addressed some of the issues dealt with in the report, including civil aviation, allegations of Rwandan support for dissident forces, Rwanda's alleged "residual" presence in the DRC, and the negative forces of FDLR. It concluded that FDLR/Forces combattantes Abacunguzi presented the greatest threat to regional peace and security, and recommended that the embargo and its monitoring be extended to the entire territory of the DRC. It also recommended that the Group's report and the evidence on which it was based be subject to critical review by either the Joint Verification Mechanism or the Tripartite Plus Joint Commission.

On 23 February [S/2005/210], Uganda, while welcoming the report, found sections that were of concern to it, including the report's methodology, allegations that Uganda maintained contact with leaders of armed groups in the embargoed region, illegal flights between Uganda and the DRC, Uganda's negligible customs supervision along its border with the DRC, arms transfers from Uganda to dissident forces in the DRC, and denying the Group a visit to military facilities. Uganda further outlined measures it had taken to comply with the Group's recommendations.

SECURITY COUNCIL ACTION (April)

On 18 April [meeting 5163], the Security Council unanimously adopted **resolution 1596(2005)**. The draft [S/2005/245] was prepared in consultations among Council members.

The Security Council,

Recalling its resolutions concerning the Democratic Republic of the Congo, in particular resolutions 1493 (2003) of 28 July 2003, 1533(2004) of 12 March 2004, 1552(2004) of 27 July 2004, 1565(2004) of 1 October 2004 and 1592(2005) of 30 March 2005, and recalling also the statements by its President concerning the Democratic Republic of the Congo, in particular the statement of 7 December 2004,

Reiterating its serious concern regarding the presence of armed groups and militias in the eastern part of the Democratic Republic of the Congo, particularly in the provinces of North and South Kivu and in the Ituri district, which perpetuate a climate of insecurity in the whole region,

Welcoming the fact that some of these groups and militias have started to submit an inventory of arms and related materiel in their possession, as well as their location, with a view to their participation in the programmes of disarmament, and encouraging those who have not yet done so rapidly to do so,

Expressing its readiness to review the provisions of its resolutions 918(1994) of 17 May 1994, 997(1995) of 9 June 1995 and 1011(1995) of 16 August 1995 in a broader perspective, taking into account the implications of continued instability in the eastern part of the Democratic Republic of the Congo for peace and security in the Great Lakes region of Africa,

Condemning the continuing illicit flow of weapons within and into the Democratic Republic of the Congo, and declaring its determination to continue closely monitoring implementation of the arms embargo imposed by resolution 1493(2003),

Recalling the importance for the Government of National Unity and Transition to implement without delay the integration for which it bears responsibility of the armed forces of the Democratic Republic of the Congo by continuing to work within the framework of the Joint Commission on Security Sector Reform, and encouraging the donor community to provide coordinated financial and technical assistance for this task,

Commending the efforts made by the Secretary-General, the African Union and other actors concerned to restore peace and security in the Democratic Republic of the Congo, and welcoming in this regard the Declaration adopted in Dar es Salaam on 20 November 2004 at the conclusion of the first summit of the International Conference on Peace, Security, Democracy and Development in the Great Lakes Region,

Taking note of the reports of the Group of Experts established by paragraph 10 of resolution 1533(2004), of 15 July 2004 and 25 January 2005, transmitted by the Security Council Committee established in accordance with paragraph 8 of the same resolution (hereinafter "the Committee"), and of their recommendations,

Noting that the situation in the Democratic Republic of the Congo continues to constitute a threat to international peace and security in the region,

Acting under Chapter VII of the Charter of the United Nations,

1. *Reaffirms* the measures established by paragraph 20 of resolution 1493(2003) and extended until 31 July 2005 by resolution 1552(2004), decides that these measures shall from now on apply to any recipient in the territory of the Democratic Republic of the Congo, and reiterates that assistance includes financing and financial assistance related to military activities;

2. *Decides* that the measures above shall not apply to:

   (a) Supplies of arms and related materiel or technical training and assistance intended solely for support of or use by units of the army and police of the Democratic Republic of the Congo, provided that the said units:

   —Have completed the process of their integration; or

   —Operate under the command, respectively, of the état-major intégré of the armed forces or of the national police of the Democratic Republic of the Congo; or

   —Are in the process of their integration, in the territory of the Democratic Republic of the Congo outside the provinces of North and South Kivu and the Ituri district;

   (b) Supplies of arms and related materiel as well as technical training and assistance intended solely for support of or use by the United Nations Organization Mission in the Democratic Republic of the Congo;

   (c) Supplies of non-lethal military equipment intended solely for humanitarian or protective use, and related technical assistance and training, as notified in advance to the Committee in accordance with paragraph 8 (e) of resolution 1533(2004);

3. *Requests* the Mission, within its existing capabilities and without prejudice to the performance of its current mandate, and the Group of Experts referred to in paragraph 21 below to continue to focus their monitoring activities in North and South Kivu and in Ituri;

4. *Decides* that all future authorized shipments of arms and related materiel consistent with such exemptions noted in paragraph 2 (a) above shall only be made to receiving sites as designated by the Government of National Unity and Transition, in coordination with the Mission, and notified in advance to the Committee;

5. *Demands* that all parties other than those referred to in paragraph 2 (a) above with military capabilities in Ituri, in North Kivu or in South Kivu, help the Government of National Unity and Transition implement its commitments regarding disarmament, demobilization and reintegration of foreign and Congolese combatants, and regarding security sector reform;

6. *Decides* that, during the period of enforcement of the measures referred to in paragraph 1 above, all Governments in the region, and in particular those of the Democratic Republic of the Congo and of States bordering Ituri and the Kivus, shall take the necessary measures:

   (a) To ensure that aircraft operate in the region in accordance with the Convention on International Civil Aviation, signed in Chicago on 7 December 1944, in particular by verifying the validity of documents carried in aircraft and the licences of pilots;

   (b) To prohibit immediately in their respective territories operation of any aircraft inconsistent with the conditions in that Convention or the standards established by the International Civil Aviation Organization, in particular with respect to the use of falsified or out-of-date documents, and to notify the Committee, and to maintain such prohibition until the Committee is informed by States or by the Group of Experts that these aircraft meet the said conditions and standards set forth in chapter V of the Chicago Convention and determines that they will not be used for a purpose inconsistent with the resolutions of the Security Council;

   (c) To ensure that all civilian and military airports or airfields on their respective territories will not be used for a purpose inconsistent with the measures imposed by paragraph 1 above;

7. *Also decides* that each Government in the region, in particular those of States bordering Ituri and the Kivus, as well as that of the Democratic Republic of the Congo, shall maintain a registry for review by the Committee and the Group of Experts of all information concerning flights originating in their respective territories en route to destinations in the Democratic Republic of the Congo, as well as flights originating in the Democratic Republic of the Congo en route to destinations in their respective territories;

8. *Calls upon* the Government of National Unity and Transition to strengthen the monitoring of the activity of all airports and airfields, in particular those located in Ituri and in the Kivus, to ensure in particular that only customs airports are used for international air service, and requests the Mission, in airports and airfields where it has a permanent presence, to cooperate within its existing capability with the competent Congolese authorities, with a view to enhancing the capability of those authorities to monitor and control the use of airports;

9. *Recommends*, in this context, to States in the region, and in particular to those parties to the Declaration adopted in Dar es Salaam on 20 November 2004, to promote regional cooperation in the field of air traffic control;

10. *Decides* that, during the period of enforcement of the measures referred to in paragraph 1 above, the Government of the Democratic Republic of the Congo on the one hand, and those of States bordering Ituri and the Kivus on the other hand, shall take the necessary measures:

   (a) To strengthen, as far as each of them is concerned, customs controls on the borders between Ituri or the Kivus and the neighbouring States;

(b) To ensure that all means of transport on their respective territories will not be used in violation of the measures taken by Member States in accordance with paragraph 1 above, and to notify the Mission of such actions;
and requests the Mission and the United Nations Operation in Burundi, in accordance with their respective mandates, to provide assistance to this end, where they have a permanent presence, to the competent customs authorities of the Democratic Republic of the Congo and of Burundi;

11. *Reiterates its call upon* the international community, in particular the specialized international organizations concerned, notably the International Civil Aviation Organization and the World Customs Organization, to provide financial and technical assistance to the Government of National Unity and Transition, with a view to helping it exercise effective control over its borders and its airspace, and invites in this regard the International Monetary Fund and the World Bank to provide assistance with a view to evaluating and improving the performance and enhancing the capacity of the Customs of the Democratic Republic of the Congo;

12. *Urges* all States to conduct inquiries into the activities of their nationals who operate or are associated with the operation of aircraft or other means of transport such as those referred to in paragraphs 6 and 10 above used for the transfer of arms or related materiel in violation of the measures imposed by paragraph 1 above, and if necessary to institute the appropriate legal proceedings against them;

13. *Decides* that, during the period of enforcement of the measures referred to in paragraph 1 above, all States shall take the necessary measures to prevent the entry into or transit through their territories of all persons designated by the Committee as acting in violation of the measures taken by Member States in accordance with paragraph 1 above, provided that nothing in this paragraph shall oblige a State to refuse entry into its territory to its own nationals;

14. *Decides also* that the measures imposed by the previous paragraph shall not apply where the Committee determines in advance and on a case-by-case basis that such travel is justified on the grounds of humanitarian need, including religious obligation, or where the Committee concludes that an exemption would further the objectives of the Council's resolutions, that is peace and national reconciliation in the Democratic Republic of the Congo and stability in the region;

15. *Decides further* that all States shall, during the period of enforcement of the measures referred to in paragraph 1 above, immediately freeze the funds, other financial assets and economic resources which are on their territories from the date of adoption of the present resolution, which are owned or controlled, directly or indirectly, by persons designated by the Committee pursuant to paragraph 13 above, or that are held by entities owned or controlled, directly or indirectly, by any persons acting on their behalf or at their direction, as designated by the Committee, and decides further that all States shall ensure that no funds, financial assets or economic resources are made available by their nationals or by any persons within their territories, to or for the benefit of such persons or entities;

16. *Decides* that the provisions of the previous paragraph do not apply to funds, other financial assets and economic resources that:

(a) Have been determined by relevant States to be necessary for basic expenses, including payment for foodstuffs, rent or mortgage, medicines and medical treatment, taxes, insurance premiums, and public utility charges, or for payment of reasonable professional fees and reimbursement of incurred expenses associated with the provision of legal services, or fees or service charges, in accordance with national laws, for routine holding or maintenance of frozen funds, other financial assets and economic resources, after notification by the relevant States to the Committee of the intention to authorize, where appropriate, access to such funds, other financial assets and economic resources and in the absence of a negative decision by the Committee within four working days of such notification;

(b) Have been determined by relevant States to be necessary for extraordinary expenses, provided that such determination has been notified by the relevant States to the Committee and has been approved by the Committee; or

(c) Have been determined by relevant States to be the subject of a judicial, administrative or arbitration lien or judgement, in which case the funds, other financial assets and economic resources may be used to satisfy that lien or judgement provided that the lien or judgement was entered prior to the date of the present resolution, is not for the benefit of a person or entity designated by the Committee pursuant to paragraph 15 above, and has been notified by the relevant States to the Committee;

17. *Decides also* that, no later than 31 July 2005, it shall review the measures set forth in paragraphs 1, 6, 10, 13 and 15 above, in the light of progress made in the peace and transition process in the Democratic Republic of the Congo, in particular with regard to the integration of the armed forces and of the national police;

18. *Decides further* that the Committee shall undertake, in addition to the tasks listed in paragraph 8 of resolution 1533(2004), the following tasks:

(a) To designate persons and entities with respect to the measures set forth in paragraphs 6, 10, 13 and 15 above, including aircraft and airlines, and regularly to update its list;

(b) To seek from all States concerned, and particularly those in the region, information regarding the actions taken by them to enforce the measures imposed by paragraphs 1, 6, 10, 13 and 15 above, and any further information it may consider useful, including by providing all States with an opportunity to send representatives to meet the Committee to discuss in more detail any relevant issues;

(c) To call upon all States concerned, and particularly those in the region, to provide the Committee with information regarding the actions taken by them to investigate and prosecute, as appropriate, individuals designated by the Committee, pursuant to subparagraph (a) above;

(d) To consider and decide on requests for the exemptions set out in paragraphs 14 and 16 above;

(e) To promulgate guidelines as may be necessary to facilitate the implementation of paragraphs 6, 10, 13 and 15 above;

19. *Demands* that all parties and all States cooperate fully with the work of the Group of Experts referred to in paragraph 21 below and of the Mission, and that they ensure:

(a) The safety of their members;

(b) Unhindered and immediate access for the members of the Group of Experts, in particular by supplying them with any information on possible violations of the measures taken by Member States in accordance with paragraphs 1, 6, 10, 13 and 15 above, and by facilitating access of the Group of Experts to persons, documents and sites it deems relevant to the execution of its mandate;

20. *Requests* all States concerned, in particular those in the region, to report to the Committee, within forty-five days from the date of adoption of the present resolution, on the actions they have taken to implement the measures imposed by paragraphs 6, 10, 13 and 15 above, and authorizes the Committee thereafter to request from all Member States any information it may consider necessary to fulfil its mandate;

21. *Requests* the Secretary-General, in consultation with the Committee, to re-establish, within thirty days from the date of adoption of the present resolution and for a period expiring on 31 July 2005, the Group of Experts referred to in paragraph 10 of resolution 1533(2004) with the addition of a fifth expert for financial issues, and requests further that the Secretary-General provide the Group of Experts with the necessary resources to fulfil its mandate;

22. *Requests* the Group of Experts to report to the Council in writing before 1 July 2005, through the Committee, inter alia on the implementation of the measures set forth in paragraphs 1, 6, 10, 13 and 15 above;

23. *Decides* to remain seized of the matter.

Press statement and communication. According to a 26 April press statement [SC/8368], the Security Council Committee on the DRC had been apprised of allegations pertaining to the work of the Group of Experts. It noted with concern that the allegations appeared to have been circulated in breach of contractual undertakings on confidentiality and in complete disregard for the security and safety of those involved with the work of the Group, undermining its future investigations. The Committee thoroughly examined the allegations calling into question the Group's investigative methodology and some of its findings and carefully considered the Group's explanations, with which it was fully satisfied. The Committee reaffirmed its full support for the work of the Group and encouraged it to continue to observe the highest procedural and evidentiary standards in conducting its work.

Rwanda, on 21 July [S/2005/263], reiterated its concerns, (see p. 192) regarding the Rwanda section of the Group's January report (see p. 191). It said those concerns had been corroborated by the UN independent consultant who reviewed the Group's work and concluded that, with respect to Rwanda, the experts had failed to conduct a thorough investigation. In many cases, they did not meet their own evidentiary standards, misrepresented facts and situations, and omitted significant information in reporting specific incidents to support their predetermined conclusions. The Group's poor working methods and lack of integrity and transparency suggested that its appointing authority and the Security Council should ensure that the Group's mandate was fulfilled in a strictly professional and non-prejudiced manner. Rwanda reiterated its request of 15 April to the Secretary-General that the Group's reports be subjected to an independent and transparent review.

Re-establishment of Group. The Secretary-General, on 17 May [S/2005/322], informed the Security Council that, in accordance with paragraph 21 of resolution 1596(2005) above, he had re-established the Group of Experts for a period expiring on 31 July 2005, and appointed five experts, among them a finance expert, to constitute the Group.

Report of Group of Experts (July). The second report of the Group of Experts, submitted in July [S/2005/436], noted that the short mandate period of the Group compelled it to focus on a limited number of issues relating to the implementation of the arms embargo. The Group reported that it was unable to collect irrefutable evidence of new violations of the embargo, but was investigating a suspected shipment of dual-use material crossing the border between Zambia and the DRC. It continued to receive reports of weapons flows and illegal armed group activities in the DRC and neighbouring States, but was unable to investigate the specific methods used to acquire, transport, and transfer those arms and to finance those activities, or the procurement of associated military material. The extent to which armed groups received logistical support and arms shipments across the border between Ituri and Uganda required further investigation, as did the way arms embargo violators continued to profit from the insufficient control of the DRC airspace and landing sites in Ituri. The Transitional Government, with MONUC support, was reasserting its authority over the border, in particular in Ituri district, as evidenced by the stationing of 27 border control officials at critical border crossings with Uganda. In its inspection of the Ituri crossings at Aru and Ariwara, however, the Group found that the Government's authority was weak and undermined by the overwhelming presence of illicit commercial networks with ties to dissident Ituri armed factions. The weak border controls allowed for lucrative alliances between leaders of armed groups and unscrupulous businessmen, and for the diversion of wealth to fund arms-related activities and destabilization efforts in the eastern DRC. The Group received satisfactory assistance from the concerned Governments in its investigation of civil aviation operations, but concluded that DRC supervision of those operations was of an unacceptably low standard.

The Group's interaction with the DRC, Uganda and Rwanda took place in a climate of cooperation and trust. However, owing to the time constraints of the Group's limited mandate, the DRC Transitional Government could not satisfy fully the Group's requests for information. The same was true of the meetings with Uganda. The meetings with Rwanda were likewise conducted in a constructive and open spirit but, except in the area of civil aviation, little of the other information requested by the Group was provided. The Group continued to examine the financial means sustaining embargoed parties, including revenue generated from the trade of precious metals; in so doing, it reviewed statistics from all three Governments on the production, import and export of precious metals and found significant inconsistencies.

The Group observed that inter-State cooperation in the Great Lakes region was one of the most powerful tools for countering violations of the arms embargo, which demanded a flexible and permanent mechanism for unambiguous information-sharing and cooperative action between States at the tactical and political levels.

The Group recommended maintaining the sanctions regime well into the post-electoral period; allocating sufficient means to MONUC for deployment on the borders and in DRC airports to support national customs structures and for monitoring its airspace and airport activities. It called for the development, under the Government's direction, of enhanced traceability systems for all important natural resources of the DRC, with the participation of Rwanda and Uganda, the World Bank and IMF, regional participants such as the Multi-country Demobilization and Reintegration Programme and the International Conference in the Great Lakes Region, along with relevant industry participants and other interested partners; and for regular reporting by the DRC to the Security Council Committee on the DRC on developments and implementation of those systems. The Group further recommended that the DRC request ICAO for technical expertise to improve national aviation security standards, and that the World Bank, ICAO and other multilateral organizations assist the Transitional Government in developing the capacity of the national civil aviation authority.

SECURITY COUNCIL ACTION

On 29 July [meeting 5243], the Security Council unanimously adopted **resolution 1616(2005)**. The draft [S/2005/493] was prepared in consultations among Council members.

The Security Council,

Recalling its previous resolutions and the statements by its President concerning the Democratic Republic of the Congo, in particular resolutions 1493(2003) of 28 July 2003, 1533(2004) of 12 March 2004, 1552(2004) of 27 July 2004, 1565(2004) of 1 October 2004, 1592 (2005) of 30 March 2005 and 1596(2005) of 18 April 2005,

Reiterating its serious concern regarding the presence of armed groups and militias in the eastern part of the Democratic Republic of the Congo, particularly in the provinces of North Kivu and South Kivu and in the Ituri district, which perpetuate a climate of insecurity in the whole region,

Condemning the continuing illicit flow of weapons within and into the Democratic Republic of the Congo, and declaring its determination to closely monitor compliance with the arms embargo imposed by resolution 1493(2003) and expanded by resolution 1596(2005), and to enforce the measures provided for in paragraphs 13 and 15 of resolution 1596(2005) against persons and entities acting in violation of the embargo,

Recognizing the linkage between the illegal exploitation of natural resources, illicit trade in such resources and the proliferation and trafficking of arms as one of the factors fuelling and exacerbating conflicts in the Great Lakes region of Africa,

Taking note of the report of the Group of Experts referred to in paragraph 10 of resolution 1533(2004) and paragraph 21 of resolution 1596(2005) (hereinafter "the Group of Experts"), of 5 July 2005, transmitted by the Security Council Committee established in accordance with paragraph 8 of resolution 1533 (2004) (hereinafter "the Committee"),

Noting that the situation in the Democratic Republic of the Congo continues to constitute a threat to international peace and security in the region,

Acting under Chapter VII of the Charter of the United Nations,

1. *Reaffirms* the demands of paragraphs 15, 18 and 19 of resolution 1493(2003) and of paragraphs 5 and 19 of resolution 1596(2005);

2. *Decides*, in the light of the failure by the parties to comply with the demands of the Council, to renew until 31 July 2006 the provisions of paragraphs 20 to 22 of resolution 1493(2003), as amended and expanded by paragraph 1 of resolution 1596(2005), and reaffirms paragraphs 2, 6, 10 and 13 to 16 of resolution 1596 (2005);

3. *Expresses its intention* to modify or to remove those provisions if it determines that the demands noted above have been satisfied;

4. *Requests* the Secretary-General, in consultation with the Committee, to re-establish the Group of Experts within thirty days from the date of adoption of the present resolution and for a period expiring on 31 January 2006, drawing, as appropriate, on the expertise of the members of the Group of Experts established pursuant to resolution 1596(2005);

5. *Requests* the Group of Experts to continue fulfilling its mandate as defined in resolutions 1533(2004) and 1596(2005), to update the Committee on its work by 10 November 2005, and to report to the Council in writing before 10 January 2006, through the Committee, inter alia on the implementation of the measures imposed by paragraph 20 of resolution 1493(2003) and expanded by resolution 1596(2005), with recommendations in this regard, in particular concerning the lists provided for by paragraph 10(*g*) of resolution 1533(2004), and including information on the sources of financing, such as from natural resources, which are funding the illicit trade in arms;

6. *Decides* to remain actively seized of the matter.

Re-establishment of Group. The Secretary-General, on 2 September [S/2005/566], informed the Security Council that, in accordance with paragraph 4 of the foregoing resolution, he re-established the Group of Experts until 31 January 2006, and appointed five experts to constitute the Group.

Communications. Following adoption of Security Council resolution 1596(2005) (see p. 192), a number of States informed the Security Council Committee on the DRC of measures they had taken to comply with the requirements contained in the resolution: Brazil [S/AC.43/2005/15], Burundi [S/AC.43/2005/13], Canada [S/AC.43/2005/2], DRC [S/AC.43/2005/14], Japan [S/AC.43/2005/16], Lithuania [S/AC.43/2005/10], Norway [S/AC.43/2005/4], Portugal [S/AC.43/2005/11], Russian Federation [S/AC.43/2005/9], Rwanda [S/AC.43/2005/1], Sri Lanka [S/AC.43/2005/8], Switzerland [S/AC.43/2005/3], South Africa [S/AC.43/2005/5], Uganda [S/AC.43/2005/6 & Add.1], United Kingdom [S/AC.43/2005/7], United Republic of Tanzania [S/AC.43/2005/12].

Brazil, in a later addendum [S/AC.43/2005/15/Add.1], informed the Committee of the measures it had taken to comply with the provisions of resolution 1616(2005) (see above).

Burundi

Several positive developments took place in Burundi in 2005, culminating in the successful conclusion of the transition period and the peaceful transfer of authority to representative and democratically elected government and institutions. With the assistance of the United Nations Operation in Burundi (ONUB), the referendum on the post-transition Constitution was conducted successfully on 28 February. On 3 June, for the first time since Burundi's independence in 1962, elections were held for communal councillors. Elections for the National Assembly were held on 4 July, and indirect Senate elections on 29 July. On 19 August, Pierre Nkurunziza, leader of the largest former political armed group called Conseil national pour la défense de la démocratie-Forces pour la défense de la démocratie, was elected President by a Joint Parliamentary Congress. His inauguration on 26 August marked the formal conclusion of the transitional process.

In March, an assessment mission dispatched by the Secretary-General in 2004 to consider the possible establishment of an international judicial commission of inquiry, as provided for in the 2000 Arusha Agreement on Peace and Reconciliation, recommended the establishment of two accountability mechanisms, negotiations for which were under way: a non-judicial one in the form of a national truth commission and a judicial one in the form of a special chamber within the Burundi court system.

On 15 May, Domitien Ndayizeye, President of the Transitional Government of Burundi, and Agathon Rwasa, leader of a faction of the Parti pour la libération du peuple hutu-Forces nationales de libération (FNL (Rwasa), also known as Palipehutu-FNL), signed a declaration to cease hostilities immediately, establish technical teams to decide on the mechanisms for a permanent ceasefire and promptly begin negotiations. Negotiations had not taken place by year's end and FNL remained outside the peace process.

The Implementation Monitoring Committee, established under the terms of the Arusha Agreement to monitor, supervise and coordinate the implementation of the Agreement, had played a critical role since September 2000 in Burundi's peace process and was dissolved with the installation of the new Government of Burundi. On the basis of a proposal by the Secretary-General, ONUB in October launched the Burundi Partners' Forum, an international mechanism to support the new Government in its efforts to consolidate peace and promote recovery and development in the country.

Burundi believed that the significant improvement in the overall situation in the country no longer warranted the continuation of a peacekeeping presence; hence, at its request, ONUB began to draw down 40 per cent of its military force in December. Consultations were held between ONUB and the Burundian authorities to determine modalities for the withdrawal.

ONUB

The United Nations Operation in Burundi, established in 2004 by Security Council resolution 1545(2004) [YUN 2004, p. 145], was extended until 1 July 2006 by resolution 1650(2005) (see p. 214). Among the many tasks specified by its mandate, ONUB was to ensure respect of the ceasefire agreements; promote the re-establishment of confidence between the Burundian forces; carry out the disarmament and demobilization portions of the national programme of disarmament, demobilization and reintegration of combatants; monitor the quartering of the Armed Forces of Burundi (FAB) and their heavy weapons, and the illegal flow of arms and movements of combatants across Burundi's borders; contribute to the successful completion of the electoral process, and to the creation of security conditions for the provision of humanitarian assistance; facilitate the voluntary return of refugees and internally displaced persons; protect civilians under imminent threat of violence; and to ensure the protection of UN personnel, facilities and equipment, as well as the security and freedom of movement of ONUB personnel.

Headquartered in the Burundi capital of Bujumbura, ONUB was headed by the Special Representative of the Secretary-General for Burundi, Carolyn McAskie (Canada). Its military observers were deployed to 27 team sites across the country; its infantry battalions were deployed to the following areas of operation: Cibitoké, Gitega, Bubanza, Bujumbura and Makamba. It maintained five regional offices, in Bujumbura Rurale, Gitega, Makamba, Muyinga and Ngozi. The electoral, human rights, civilian police, civil affairs and public information personnel in each office operated under the leadership of a Regional Coordinator.

The Status of Forces Agreement for ONUB, requested in resolution 1545(2004), was signed by the United Nations and the Transitional Government in Bujumbura on 17 June.

The mandate of ONUB was extended thrice during the year, the third time until 1 July 2006.

Sexual exploitation and abuse. The Special Representative moved proactively to enforce the Secretary-General's zero-tolerance policy with regard to undesirable behaviour, abuse and sexual exploitation by UN personnel in Burundi. The code of conduct officer of ONUB, accompanied by the Special Representative and the Force Commander, gave briefings for all contingent commanders and senior officers. The few complaints of misconduct by UN personnel were promptly addressed and were under investigation. In June, the Deputy Secretary-General visited Burundi to deliver a special message on the code of conduct and sexual exploitation and abuse. She also acknowledged the efforts and commitment of ONUB to upholding the highest possible standards of conduct.

Financing

In June, during its resumed fifty-ninth session, the General Assembly considered the Secretary-General's report on the ONUB budget for 1 July 2005 to 30 June 2006 totalling $296,654,700 and expenditure report for the period 21 April to 30 June 2004 indicating expenditures of $40,246,100 against an appropriation of $49,709,300 [A/59/748]. It also considered ACABQ's related report [A/59/736/Add.12], containing its recommendations and observations.

GENERAL ASSEMBLY ACTION

On 22 June [meeting 104], the General Assembly, on the recommendation of the Fifth Committee [A/59/528/Add.1], adopted **resolution 59/15 B** without vote [agenda item 153].

Financing of the United Nations Operation in Burundi

B

The General Assembly,

Having considered the report of the Secretary-General on the financing of the United Nations Operation in Burundi and the related reports of the Advisory Committee on Administrative and Budgetary Questions,

Recalling Security Council resolution 1545(2004) of 21 May 2004, by which the Council authorized, for an initial period of six months as from 1 June 2004, with the intention to renew it for further periods, the deployment of a peacekeeping operation called the United Nations Operation in Burundi, and the subsequent resolution 1577(2004) of 1 December 2004, by which the Council extended the mandate of the Operation until 1 June 2005,

Recalling also its resolution 58/312 of 18 June 2004 on the financing of the Operation and its subsequent resolution 59/15 A of 29 October 2004,

Reaffirming the general principles underlying the financing of United Nations peacekeeping operations, as stated in General Assembly resolutions 1874(S-IV) of 27 June 1963, 3101(XXVIII) of 11 December 1973 and 55/235 of 23 December 2000,

Mindful of the fact that it is essential to provide the Operation with the necessary financial resources to enable it to fulfil its responsibilities under the relevant resolutions of the Security Council,

1. *Requests* the Secretary-General to entrust the Head of Mission with the tasks of formulating future budget proposals in full accordance with the provisions of General Assembly resolution 59/296 of 22 June 2005, as well as other relevant resolutions;

2. *Takes note* of the status of contributions to the United Nations Operation in Burundi as at 15 April 2005, including the contributions outstanding in the amount of 88.7 million United States dollars, representing some 25 per cent of the total assessed contributions, notes with concern that only forty-three Member States have paid their assessed contributions in full, and urges all other Member States, in particular those in arrears, to ensure payment of their outstanding assessed contributions;

3. *Expresses its appreciation* to those Member States which have paid their assessed contributions in full, and urges all other Member States to make every possi-

ble effort to ensure payment of their assessed contributions to the Operation in full;

4. *Expresses concern* at the financial situation with regard to peacekeeping activities, in particular as regards the reimbursements to troop contributors that bear additional burdens owing to overdue payments by Member States of their assessments;

5. *Also expresses concern* at the delay experienced by the Secretary-General in deploying and providing adequate resources to some recent peacekeeping missions, in particular those in Africa;

6. *Emphasizes* that all future and existing peacekeeping missions shall be given equal and non-discriminatory treatment in respect of financial and administrative arrangements;

7. *Also emphasizes* that all peacekeeping missions shall be provided with adequate resources for the effective and efficient discharge of their respective mandates;

8. *Reiterates its request* to the Secretary-General to make the fullest possible use of facilities and equipment at the United Nations Logistics Base at Brindisi, Italy, in order to minimize the costs of procurement for the Operation;

9. *Endorses* the conclusions and recommendations contained in the report of the Advisory Committee on Administrative and Budgetary Questions, and requests the Secretary-General to ensure their full implementation;

10. *Requests* the Secretary-General to ensure the full implementation of the relevant provisions of its resolution 59/296;

11. *Notes with concern* that the Status of Forces Agreement remains unsigned, and requests that this be finalized as a matter of urgency;

12. *Requests* the Secretary-General to take all necessary action to ensure that the Operation is administered with a maximum of efficiency and economy;

13. *Also requests* the Secretary-General, in order to reduce the cost of employing General Service staff, to continue efforts to recruit local staff for the Operation against General Service posts, commensurate with the requirements of the Operation;

Expenditure report
for the period from 21 April to 30 June 2004

14. *Takes note* of the expenditure report for the Operation for the period from 21 April to 30 June 2004;

15. *Decides* to appropriate to the Special Account for the United Nations Operation in Burundi the amount of 49,709,300 dollars previously authorized and apportioned for the establishment of the Operation for the period from 21 April to 30 June 2004 under the terms of its resolution 58/312;

Budget estimates
for the period from 1 July 2005 to 30 June 2006

16. *Decides also* to appropriate to the Special Account for the United Nations Operation in Burundi the amount of 307,693,100 dollars for the period from 1 July 2005 to 30 June 2006, inclusive of 292,272,400 dollars for the maintenance of the Operation, 12,609,400 dollars for the support account for peacekeeping operations and 2,811,300 dollars for the United Nations Logistics Base;

Financing of the appropriation

17. *Decides further* to apportion among Member States the amount of 307,693,100 dollars at a monthly rate of 25,641,091 dollars, in accordance with the levels updated in General Assembly resolution 58/256 of 23 December 2003 and taking into account the scale of assessments for 2005 and 2006, as set out in its resolution 58/1 B of 23 December 2003, subject to a decision of the Security Council to extend the mandate of the Operation;

18. *Decides* that, in accordance with the provisions of its resolution 973(X) of 15 December 1955, there shall be set off against the apportionment among Member States, as provided for in paragraph 17 above, their respective share in the Tax Equalization Fund of 10,306,800 dollars, comprising the estimated staff assessment income of 8,297,100 dollars approved for the Operation for the period from 1 July 2005 to 30 June 2006, the prorated share of 1,782,300 dollars of the estimated staff assessment income approved for the support account and the prorated share of 227,400 dollars of the estimated staff assessment income approved for the United Nations Logistics Base;

19. *Decides also* that, for Member States that have fulfilled their financial obligations to the Operation, there shall be set off against their apportionment, as provided for in paragraph 17 above, their respective share of the unencumbered balance and interest income in the amount of 9,470,200 dollars in respect of the financial period ended 30 June 2004, in accordance with the levels updated in its resolution 58/256, and taking into account the scale of assessments for 2004, as set out in its resolution 58/1 B;

20. *Decides further* that, for Member States that have not fulfilled their financial obligations to the Operation, there shall be set off against their outstanding obligations their respective share of the unencumbered balance and interest income in the amount of 9,470,200 dollars in respect of the financial period ended 30 June 2004, in accordance with the scheme set out in paragraph 19 above;

21. *Decides* that the decrease of 33,900 dollars in the estimated staff assessment income in respect of the financial period ended 30 June 2004 shall be set off against the credits from the amount of 9,470,200 dollars referred to in paragraphs 19 and 20 above;

22. *Emphasizes* that no peacekeeping mission shall be financed by borrowing funds from other active peacekeeping missions;

23. *Encourages* the Secretary-General to continue to take additional measures to ensure the safety and security of all personnel under the auspices of the United Nations participating in the Operation, bearing in mind paragraphs 5 and 6 of Security Council resolution 1502(2003) of 26 August 2003;

24. *Invites* voluntary contributions to the Operation in cash and in the form of services and supplies acceptable to the Secretary-General, to be administered, as appropriate, in accordance with the procedure and practices established by the General Assembly;

25. *Decides* to include in the provisional agenda of its sixtieth session the item entitled "Financing of the United Nations Operation in Burundi".

Political and military developments

Political developments and ONUB activities

Report of Secretary-General (March). In response to Security Council resolution 1577(2004) [YUN 2004, p. 154], the Secretary-General issued his March report on UNOB [S/2005/149] covering developments since November 2004 [YUN 2004, p. 153]. He said the six-month extension of the transition period, which began on 1 November 2004 [ibid.], had allowed the Burundian parties to advance the peace process despite some delays in the electoral calendar. The President had promulgated a law to establish a National Truth and Reconciliation Commission and decreed a limited right of assembly during the campaign on the constitution. The constitutional referendum would be conducted in accordance with the 1993 national election law. On 2 February 2005, the President's Office indicated that the texts of the proposed electoral code and communal law, both prerequisites for the conduct of elections, were ready for submission to the Council of Ministers, before being introduced to the National Assembly and Senate.

On 6 January, the transitional President sought and promptly received the Constitutional Court's interpretation that would allow him to submit a revision to the constitution for direct referendum or through the National Assembly and Senate. He had asked the Court to determine his authority directly to amend those articles of the constitution prohibiting transitional presidents from running in the first presidential election; requiring the National Assembly and the Senate to elect the first president of the post-transitional period; and providing for the co-option of an additional 18 to 21 Assembly members under specific circumstances. The President's party, the Front for Democracy in Burundi (FRODEBU), called for an endorsement of the constitution in the referendum but opposed any pre-referendum amendments. On 12 January, the FRODEBU parliamentary group issued a statement stressing that the proposed amendments would be inconsistent with the 2000 Arusha Agreement on Peace and Reconciliation in Burundi [YUN 2000, p. 146]. The Conseil national pour la défense de la démocratie-Forces pour la défense de la démocratie (CNDD-FDD(Nkurunziza)) issued a statement accusing President Ndayizeye of trying to delay elections, and warned that a "return to war" remained an option. By a 17 January joint communiqué, 11 political parties, including FRODEBU, condemned the President's attempts to amend the constitution. On the other hand, the Vice-President's party, the Union for National Progress, Burundi (UPRONA), sup-

ported the President, advocating strongly for an amendment. During that period, the Special Representative met with the President and other leaders on numerous occasions to discuss the proposed amendments, impressing upon them the importance of adhering to the Arusha Agreement. On 25 and 26 January, the Facilitator of the Burundi peace process (the Deputy President of South Africa) travelled to Bujumbura to convey a message from the Great Lakes region to all parties against amending the constitution before the referendum, likewise reminding them of their obligations under the Arusha Agreement. On 4 February, President Ndayizeye announced that he would no longer seek a constitutional amendment. UPRONA expressed dissatisfaction and, along with two other Tutsi-dominated parties—the Rally for Democracy and Economic and Social Development (RADDES) and the Party for National Redress (PARENA)—called for a vote against the constitution in the referendum. Despite two postponements by the Independent National Electoral Commission (CENI), the referendum on the post-transition Constitution took place on 28 February (see p. 202).

On 25 January, FNL (Rwasa) announced its willingness to restart peace talks with the Transitional Government, the first such indication since formal negotiations ended after FNL claimed responsibility for the August 2004 Gatumba massacre [YUN 2004, p. 149]. FNL's willingness to negotiate was also made known, through an intermediary, to the Special Representative. The Secretary-General affirmed UN preparedness to extend to the Great Lakes Regional Peace Initiative on Burundi and the Facilitator, the mediators of the Burundian peace process, any assistance that would help achieve a comprehensive ceasefire and sustainable peace in Burundi.

The Implementation Monitoring Committee, at its twenty-fifth session (24-25 January), welcomed the progress in the peace process, specifically the publication of voter lists, the promulgation at the end of 2004 of the laws on the new National Defence Force and national police service, and the registration early in January of the former armed political movements as political parties. It examined the new law on the National Truth and Reconciliation Commission, noting the need to avoid overlapping jurisdictions between the Commission and the proposed international judicial commission of inquiry (see p. 205). It held two special meetings in February to examine matters pertaining to the return of Burundian refugees, other vulnerable populations, land reform and political prisoners.

In keeping with the 3 January communiqué, expressing its intention to normalize relations with the DRC, Burundi's Foreign Minister visited Kinshasa (10-12 February) and concluded a bilateral agreement on the normalization of relations and security cooperation with DRC. The Secretary-General requested his Special Representative to discuss with the two Governments and MONUC an action plan to increase security along the Burundi-DRC border.

The security situation in Burundi remained generally stable, but armed clashes between the joint FAB/CNDD-FDD and FNL (Rwasa) continued in the provinces of Bujumbura Rurale, Bubanza and Cibitoké. On 23 January, the Governor of Bubanza and his bodyguard were killed when his entourage was stopped by unidentified assailants. ONUB issued a statement on 25 January deploring the murder; its subsequent investigation into the incident failed to ascertain the motive or find the perpetrators.

With regard to security sector reform, the laws promulgated by President Ndayizeye at the end of 2004 for the establishment of the new National Defence Force and national police service required considerable work to define their operational modalities and to enact the necessary legal instruments and regulations.

The Secretary-General reported some progress in the disarmament, demobilization and reintegration programme. Following the successful training and integration of 1,800 joint FAB/CNDD-FDD security units at the Tenga training centre at the end of 2004, an agreement with the Government was reached on 13 January 2005 to begin the training and integration of an additional 2,700 ex-combatants. As of 4 February, 4,441 ex-combatants, who were not to be integrated into the security forces, had been disarmed and demobilized at the Gitega, Bubanza and Muramvya demobilization centres, where they also received elementary skills training and financial assistance. By 20 February, 12,950 ex-combatants, predominantly from CNDD-FDD and ex-FAB, entered designated cantonment sites in preparation for their relocation to a demobilization centre. Given the generally poor conditions in those sites, on 22 February, the Joint Ceasefire Commission, the Executive Secretariat and ONUB met to address specific concerns pertaining to conditions at the Buramata cantonment site; in subsequent meetings, all parties agreed to begin the initial demobilization of ex-combatants from that site. The remaining ex-combatants had not yet begun their full-scale transfer from the pre-disarmament assembly area to the cantonment sites, pending the harmonization of ranks, appointment of their representatives in the Na-

tional Defence Force high command, approval of an operational plan for integration into the national security structures, and the return of FAB soldiers to barracks. ONUB, the Executive Secretariat and FAB agreed that the return of FAB soldiers to barracks would take place simultaneously with the entry of the armed political parties/movements to the cantonment sites, where their security would be monitored by ONUB military observers, in coordination with the joint security units and joint liaison teams comprising members from all parties.

The first and second phases of the demobilization of child soldiers ended by 31 December 2004, with 2,260 FAB and *gardiens de la paix* child soldiers demobilized by UNICEF and its partners through the Child Soldiers National Structure. An additional 618 children from the six armed political parties/movements were demobilized and reintegrated with their families or were in community care.

On 19 January, the Minister of Public Security signed a paper jointly elaborated by the Transitional Government and ONUB entitled "Concept for the Integration of the Burundi National Police". The paper set forth the reform and integration of the national police in two phases: the first phase was to ensure security during the elections, to be provided by the national police and defence forces; the second was to consist of various consolidation activities and long-term reform and capacity development initiatives. The paper also identified the responsibilities of the different actors involved and provided a basic framework for donors to provide assistance. On 18 February, during the first phase, ONUB began a 10-day training-of-trainers course for 70 Burundian civilian police trainers selected from officers of the Government and of the armed political parties/movements.

Besides monitoring the ceasefire agreements and the implementation of disarmament and demobilization activities, ONUB assisted with the nationwide distribution of electoral material and provided security daily to personnel of ONUB, UN agencies and programmes and NGOs, as well as to food convoys to the various assembly/cantonment sites throughout Burundi. It increased patrols close to the refugee camps in Mwaro and Muyinga and the former transit site at Ngagara (Bujumbura Mairie), where Congolese Banyamulenge refugees were located. It conducted a series of military operations aimed at deterring foreign combatants from infiltrating the border with the DRC, curtailing the flow of illegal weapons and assisting in the monitoring of the DRC arms embargo, in coordination with MONUC.

The Secretary-General observed that despite delays in the electoral calendar, there had been continued progress in the peace process, especially with regard to the extension of the transition, preparation for elections, and the demobilization, disarmament and reintegration process. He pointed out the key tasks to be completed without delay as the transitional process was entering its final and most crucial phase: the promulgation of an electoral code and communal law; the establishment of technically realistic dates in the electoral calendar; and the commencement of meaningful military and police integration. The inclusion of FNL (Rwasa) in the peace process also needed to be carefully assessed in order to achieve sustainable peace and stability throughout Burundi. The Secretary-General reiterated his call on all political and military leaders to stay the course, to respect the letter and spirit of the Arusha Agreement and to conclude the transitional process expeditiously and in good faith. He instructed the Special Representative to explore with the Burundian parties and regional and international partners ideas on how the United Nations and the international community could continue to support the consolidation of peace after elections. A decisive donor response would also be required in the post-transitional period to help stabilize the country. The extent of human rights violations in Burundi continued to be of concern; and the culture of impunity, which had contributed to the conflict, had to be addressed decisively, in order to lay the foundation of lasting peace and national reconciliation.

Constitutional referendum

The referendum on the post-transition Constitution was conducted successfully without major incident on 28 February. Of the 3.3 million registered voters, 92.4 per cent, or 2,894,372 Burundians, exercised their right to vote for the first time since 1994; and about 90.1 per cent of voters endorsed the Constitution. On 6 March, the Constitutional Court confirmed the referendum results and formally adopted the Constitution. International donors provided full funding for the referendum and ONUB provided extensive transportation assistance, including the transport by land and air of electoral materials to polling stations.

By a press statement of 1 March [SG/SM/9742], the Secretary-General congratulated the Transitional Government and the Burundian people for the successful conduct of the referendum. He called on all Burundian parties to build on that positive momentum and ensure the early conduct of the national elections that would conclude the transitional process in Burundi.

The EU, in a 4 March statement [S/2005/146], welcomed the successful holding of the referendum and the high voter turnout. It encouraged Burundi to complete as swiftly as possible the remaining stages of the electoral process and urged all political forces to take part in that process and to accept unreservedly the expression of the will of the people.

SECURITY COUNCIL ACTION (March)

On 14 March [meeting 5141], following consultations among Security Council members, the President made statement **S/PRST/2005/13** on behalf of the Council:

> The Security Council welcomes the approval by the Burundian people of the post-transitional Constitution, through the referendum of 28 February 2005, the final results of which have just been declared. The very broad participation of the citizens of Burundi, who have voted in favour of the Constitution in large numbers, is the sign of their support to the peace process. It is an important event for Burundi and for the whole region of the Great Lakes of Africa.
>
> The Council calls upon all Burundians to remain committed to the course of national reconciliation, for further steps remain to be taken. It invites, in particular, the political leadership in the country to work together towards the common goal of holding, expeditiously, local and national elections that are free and fair. It encourages the donor community to continue providing its assistance to this end.

Report of Secretary-General (May). In his fourth report on ONUB, issued on 19 May [S/2005/328], the Secretary-General noted that, in furtherance of the transitional process, the Chairman of the Regional Peace Initiative on Burundi, President Museveni of Uganda, convened a summit (Entebbe, Uganda, 22 April) attended by the Facilitator and the Presidents of Burundi, Kenya, the United Republic of Tanzania and Zambia, together with high-level representatives of Ethiopia, Rwanda and the AU, and the Special Representative of the Secretary-General. The summit endorsed a revised electoral calendar presented by CENI, and extended the transition period for the second time, until 26 August. It called for strict adherence to the new electoral timeline, which set the communal elections for 3 June; the legislative elections for 4 July; the Senate elections for 29 July; and the election by Parliament of a post-transition president for 19 August. Elections at the *colline* (village) level were to be held after the end of the transition period, on 23 September. The summit also endorsed the efforts of the Tanzanian President in his contacts with FNL (Rwasa), and mandated the Facilitator to resolve outstanding issues between President Ndayizeye and CNDD-FDD (Nkurunziza).

As national elections drew near, tensions mounted, especially between FRODEBU and CNDD-FDD (Nkurunziza), leading the latter to suspend its participation in cabinet meetings at the end of April. Tensions began when President Ndayizeye rejected the CNDD-FDD nominee for the post of Minister of the Interior (reserved for CNDD-FDD), requesting that several candidates be submitted for the post, which had fallen vacant with the death in March of the incumbent Minister. To resolve the problem, the Facilitator invited President Ndayizeye and CNDD-FDD leader Pierre Nkurunziza to a meeting (Pretoria, South Africa, 9 May), at which it was agreed that close consultations between the two leaders were necessary; in keeping with President Ndayizeye's undertaking, he appointed an alternative Interior Minister nominated by CNDD-FDD on 11 May.

The electoral code and the communal law, which were submitted to the National Assembly in early March, were promulgated on 20 April. By 8 May, 32 political parties had submitted their lists of candidates for the communal elections, with an average of 11 competing parties per commune. Submission of similar lists for the legislative elections was expected to be completed by 20 May.

The Implementation Monitoring Committee, at its twenty-sixth and twenty-seventh regular sessions, called on the Transitional Government to ensure the adoption of the necessary legal framework, including a decree on the harmonization of military ranks, in order to allow for the reintegration of former armed political parties/movements into the new national defence and police forces. The Committee, which had played a critical role in the peace process since September 2000, was expected to be dissolved at the end of the transition. Consequently, the Special Representative began consultations on the possible establishment of an international support mechanism to assist the elected Government during its first term.

Overall, the security situation in Burundi remained stable except for minor clashes with armed FNL (Rwasa) elements, and acts of banditry and looting. In Mubimbi and Kabezi, communes in Bujumbura Rurale, acts of criminality reportedly increased after CNDD-FDD combatants withdrew to cantonment sites. Security improved with the reinforcement of ONUB patrols in those areas in March and April, and its deployment of National Defence Force units at the end of April.

As to security sector reform, the last pre-disarmament assembly area closed in April, following the transfer of all combatants of the armed political parties/movements to cantonment sites. Combatants from the Gashingwa and Mabanda sites were transferred to the military regions to undergo joint training with former FAB units before their formal integration into the new National Defence Force. That process had been yet to be completed for combatants in the Kibuye cantonment sites. In addition, two brigades and one special protection unit, with a total of 6,000 personnel, were established and deployed through direct integration. On 11 May, President Ndayizeye signed a decree regulating the harmonization of military ranks, setting out the mechanism for the demobilization of officers and regulating the status of officers to be integrated into the National Defence Force and national police. The Executive Secretariat of the National Commission for Demobilization, Reinsertion and Reintegration established 10 provincial offices in support of ex-combatant reinsertion.

The Secretary-General stated that it was incumbent on the Burundian parties to demonstrate the political will necessary for the successful conclusion of the transitional process, and to ensure the strictest adherence to the new electoral calendar. He invited all Burundian leaders to reinforce the message that sectarian interests could no longer define modern Burundian society, which should build on the gains of the peace process and move towards national reconciliation, stability and development. The Secretary-General believed that the international community should play an active role in supporting the elected Government and endorsed efforts of the United Republic of Tanzania to facilitate an agreement between the Government and FNL (Rwasa). In the meantime, Burundi had to find a solution to its devastating debt burden if it was to enter the reconstruction and development phase in earnest. Ethnic and regional division, at the core of human rights abuses, needed to be resolutely addressed in the post-transition period.

In his belief that the role of ONUB in Burundi continued to be vital, especially during the electoral period, the Secretary-General recommended extending the mandate of the Operation at its current strength for an additional period of six months, until 1 December 2005.

Declaration of 15 May

Following consultations with member States of the Regional Peace Initiative, the United Nations and international partners, the United Republic of Tanzania held meetings with an FNL (Rwasa) delegation (Dar es Salaam, the United Republic of Tanzania, 4-12 April), which concluded with a statement by the delegation expressing FNL's intention to negotiate with the Transitional Government, cease hostilities, and provide a written explanation for its involvement in the 2004 Gatumba massacre [YUN 2004, p. 149]. The Deputy Chairperson of the Regional Peace Initiative (President Benjamin Mkapa of the United Republic of Tanzania) subsequently met with FNL leader Agathon Rwasa (Dar es Salaam, 25 April), who reiterated his group's commitment to begin negotiations. To that end, the United Republic of Tanzania arranged a meeting between President Ndayizeye and the FNL leader in Dar es Salaam on 15 May. At the meeting, the two parties signed a declaration [S/2005/325] by which they agreed on an immediate cessation of hostilities and to establish within a period of not more than one month technical teams to decide on the mechanisms of the permanent ceasefire; to begin negotiations as early as possible; and to negotiate without disrupting the current electoral process.

The Secretary-General later reported, however, that 15 FNL elements were killed the previous day in circumstances suggesting premeditated violence. The claim by the National Defence Force that they were killed in combat was contested by some witnesses. Those deaths and subsequent clashes with FNL undermined the parties' confidence in further negotiations. On 9 June, the United Republic of Tanzania convened talks in Dar es Salaam between the National Defence Force and FNL in the presence of regional, international and UN observers. The talks led to the issuance on 14 June of a joint communiqué committing the parties to respect the 15 May declaration and to identify core responsibilities and establish a mechanism for its implementation. Nonetheless, hostilities between the National Defence Force and FNL continued, as did FNL's forcible recruitment of combatants, including children.

SECURITY COUNCIL ACTION (23 and 31 May)

On 23 May [meeting 5184], following consultations among Security Council members, the President made statement **S/PRST/2005/19** on behalf of the Council:

The Security Council takes note with satisfaction of the declaration signed on 15 May 2005 in Dar es Salaam, United Republic of Tanzania, by the President of the Republic of Burundi, Mr. Domitien Ndayizeye, and by the leader of the rebel group Parti pour la libération du peuple hutu-Forces nationales de libération, Mr. Agathon Rwasa. The Council takes note in particular of the commitment by both parties to immediately cease hostilities, agree within a month on a permanent ceasefire, and negotiate without disturbing the electoral process.

The Council shares the understanding that this declaration is a first step that should allow the Forces nationales de libération to be rapidly integrated, in a negotiated manner, into the transitional process

currently in progress in Burundi. The Council remains convinced that the participation of the Forces nationales de libération in this process will facilitate the holding of the forthcoming elections, in accordance with the timetable confirmed at the last meeting of member States of the Regional Peace Initiative on Burundi, held in Entebbe, Uganda, on 22 April 2005.

The Council commends the mediation of President Benjamin Mkapa and of the Government of the United Republic of Tanzania and, more generally, the efforts of States of the Regional Initiative chaired by President Yoweri Museveni of the Republic of Uganda and of the Facilitation led by Deputy President Jacob Zuma of the Republic of South Africa, as well as those made by the Special Representative of the Secretary-General, to bring the peace and national reconciliation process in Burundi to a successful conclusion. The Council reiterates that putting an end to the climate of impunity in Burundi and the Great Lakes region is essential to that process.

The Council urges all Burundian parties to exert greater efforts to ensure the success of the transition, national reconciliation and the stability of the country in the longer term.

On 31 May [meeting 5193], the Security Council unanimously adopted **resolution 1602(2005)**. The draft [S/2005/345] was prepared in consultations among Council members.

The Security Council,

Recalling its relevant resolutions on Burundi, in particular resolutions 1545(2004) of 21 May 2004, 1565 (2004) of 1 October 2004, 1577(2004) of 1 December 2004 and 1596(2005) of 18 April 2005, as well as the statements by its President, in particular those of 15 August 2004 and 14 March and 23 May 2005,

Reaffirming its strong commitment to the sovereignty, independence, territorial integrity and unity of Burundi, and recalling the importance of the principles of good-neighbourliness and non-interference, and of regional cooperation,

Reaffirming its full support for the process of the Arusha Peace and Reconciliation Agreement for Burundi, signed at Arusha, United Republic of Tanzania, on 28 August 2000 (hereinafter "the Arusha Agreement"), calling upon all the Burundian parties to fully honour their commitments, and assuring them of its determination to support Burundi's efforts to bring the transition to an end successfully through the holding of free and fair elections,

Welcoming the positive achievements that have been made so far by the Burundian parties, including since the deployment of the United Nations Operation in Burundi on 1 June 2004,

Welcoming in particular the approval by the Burundian people of the post-transitional Constitution in the referendum of 28 February 2005,

Taking note with satisfaction of the declaration signed on 15 May 2005 in Dar es Salaam, United Republic of Tanzania, by the President of the Republic of Burundi, Mr. Domitien Ndayizeye, and by the leader of the rebel group Parti pour la libération du peuple hutu-Forces nationales de libération, Mr. Agathon Rwasa, and taking note in particular of the commitment by both parties to cease hostilities immediately, agree within a month on a permanent ceasefire, and negotiate without disturbing the electoral process,

Urging the international community to take advantage of these positive political developments to increase its assistance for social and economic development in Burundi,

Welcoming the imminent holding of elections as provided for in the Arusha Agreement, taking note with satisfaction of the electoral timetable confirmed at the last meeting of member States of the Regional Peace Initiative on Burundi, held in Entebbe, Uganda, on 22 April 2005, calling upon the transitional authorities strictly to adhere to this timetable for the holding of each poll, and urging all Burundian parties and candidates to ensure respect for the electoral code of conduct, refrain from any actions that may disrupt the process and accept the result of the elections,

Encouraging the Transitional Government to continue, with the cooperation of the United Nations Operation in Burundi, to enhance the participation of women in the political process,

Taking note of the progress achieved in the reform of the security sector, as well as in the disarmament and demobilization of former combatants, and stressing in this regard the need to implement without delay a national reintegration strategy in order to further consolidate peace and stability,

Paying tribute to the efforts of the member States of the Regional Peace Initiative on Burundi, especially Uganda and the United Republic of Tanzania, and the Facilitation of South Africa, to support the peace process in Burundi, and encouraging them to continue to assist the efforts of the Burundian parties,

Encouraging the international donor community to respond to requests from the Government of Burundi to strengthen its national judicial institutions and rule-of-law capacity,

Condemning all acts of violence, any threat of the use of force, as well as violations of human rights and international humanitarian law, and stressing the need for the Burundian authorities to ensure the safety of civilian populations, in particular with regard to women, children and other vulnerable persons,

Reiterating its strong condemnation of the Gatumba massacre of 13 August 2004, and its commitment that perpetrators of such crimes, as well as all persons responsible for violations of human rights and international humanitarian law, be brought to justice,

Considering that putting an end to the climate of impunity in Burundi, as well as in the Great Lakes of Africa as a whole, is essential for building lasting peace in the region,

Taking note with satisfaction of the report of the Secretary-General of 19 May 2005,

Noting that factors of instability remain in Burundi, and determining that the situation in that country continues to constitute a threat to international peace and security in the region,

Acting under Chapter VII of the Charter of the United Nations,

1. *Decides* to extend the mandate of the United Nations Operation in Burundi until 1 December 2005;

2. *Calls upon* all Burundian parties to exert greater efforts to ensure the success of the transition, national reconciliation and the stability of the country in the longer term, in particular by refraining from any actions which may affect the cohesion of the Arusha Agreement process;

3. *Looks forward* to the recommendations to be made by the Secretary-General by 15 November 2005 on the role of the United Nations in supporting Burundi, including on the possible adjustment of the mandate and force strength of the United Nations Operation in Burundi, in accordance with progress made on the ground;

4. *Also looks forward* to the submission by the Secretary-General of his detailed proposal, as described in paragraphs 53 and 54 of his report, for the establishment of an international support mechanism during the post-transitional period in Burundi;

5. *Requests* the Secretary-General to continue to keep the Security Council informed in his reports on the situation in Burundi of actions taken in the fight against impunity;

6. *Welcomes* efforts undertaken by the United Nations Operation in Burundi to implement the Secretary-General's zero-tolerance policy on sexual exploitation and abuse, and to ensure full compliance of its personnel with the United Nations code of conduct, requests the Secretary-General to continue to take all necessary action in this regard and to keep the Council informed, and urges troop-contributing countries to take appropriate preventive and disciplinary action to ensure that such acts are properly investigated and punished in cases involving their personnel;

7. *Decides* to remain actively seized of the matter.

Establishment of commission of inquiry

Report of assessment mission. In March [S/2005/158], the Secretary-General submitted the report of the assessment mission authorized by the Security Council in 2004 in response to Burundi's request [YUN 2004, p. 142], with the objective of considering the advisability and feasibility of establishing an international judicial commission of inquiry in post-conflict Burundi, as provided for in the 2000 Arusha Agreement. The mission, which visited Burundi from 16 to 24 May, was led by Tuliameni Kalomoh, Assistant Secretary-General for Political Affairs, and included representatives of the UN Department of Political Affairs (DPA), the Office of the United Nations High Commissioner for Human Rights (OHCHR), UNHCR and the Office of the United Nations Security Coordinator (UNSECOORD). It held consultations with representatives of the Government and local authorities, political parties, religious leaders and civil society. It also visited courts and met with judicial authorities and members of the legal profession.

The report discussed the nature and added value of an international judicial commission of inquiry; the possibility of limiting the temporal competence of the commission to specific events or periods; the existing National Truth and Reconciliation Commission and its relationship to the proposed international judicial commission of inquiry; the implications of "provisional immunity"and its scope and legal validity before the national and international commissions, and before Burundian national courts; and the implementation of the judicial reforms provided for in the Arusha Agreement and the capacity of the Burundian judicial system to bring to trial those responsible for the crimes of genocide, crimes against humanity and war crimes in an impartial, fair and effective manner.

The mission recommended the establishment of two accountability mechanisms: a non-judicial one in the form of a national truth commission of mixed composition, including both national and international members; and a judicial one in the form of a special chamber within Burundi's court system. It recognized that the proposed mechanisms deviated from the letter, though not the spirit, of the Arusha Agreement; however, it was convinced that the establishment of the two mechanisms in parallel, as envisioned by the Agreement, would create the almost certain risk of overlapping jurisdictions, contradictory findings, wasted resources and, more importantly, marginalize the national truth and reconciliation commission.

The mission recommended that the proposed national truth commission be composed of five commissioners (three international and two national), with the mandate to establish the historical facts and determine the causes and nature of the conflict in Burundi, classify the crimes committed since independence in 1962 to the date of the signature in 2000 of the Arusha Agreement and identify those responsible. It would be carried out by an investigative unit responsible for investigating the crimes and identifying those responsible, and a research unit responsible for establishing the causes and facts of the conflict and the nature of the crimes committed in the different cycles of violence. The composition of the units would be mixed, with a substantial international component to include investigators, forensic experts, historians, political scientists and other experts, as appropriate. The commission would establish its main office in Bujumbura and a number of regional offices throughout the country.

In deciding to recommend a special chamber within the Burundi court system, the mission opted for a judicial accountability mechanism not only located in the country but forming part of that court system (a "court within a court"), with a view to strengthening the judicial sector in material and human resources and to leaving behind a legacy of trained judges, prosecutors, defence counsels and experienced court managers. The special chamber would have the competence to prosecute those bearing the greatest responsibility for the crime of genocide, crimes against humanity and war crimes committed in Burundi. Its temporal jurisdiction would be limited to specific phases of the conflict and would include, as a minimum, the events that occurred between 1972 and 1993. The special chamber would consist of a trial panel (or panels) of three judges and an appellate panel of five. The composition of the special chamber would be mixed, with a majority of international judges, an international prosecutor and a registrar.

The truth commission and the special chamber would be established as national law entities; as such, they would not be UN bodies and would not normally be financed through assessed contributions. In Burundi's circumstances, however, the establishment of any accountability mechanism would have to rely entirely on international funding in the form of voluntary contributions, or partly through assessed contributions.

In his observations, the Secretary-General said that the establishment of the two accountability mechanisms should be placed within the context of the overall judicial reform and capacity-building in Burundi, and pursued in complementarity with other justice and rule of law initiatives. ONUB and OHCHR should engage, within their respective mandates under Council resolution 1545(2004) [YUN 2004, p. 145], in the establishment and operation of the international truth commission and in strengthening the capacity of Burundi's judicial sector. The mission's proposal was the first in a two-stage process of establishing judicial and non-judicial accountability mechanisms in Burundi. If acceptable, the Council should mandate the Secretary-General to engage in negotiations with Burundi on the proposal's practical implementation. At the second stage and in parallel with the first, a broad-based, genuine and transparent consultation process should be conducted with a range of national actors and civil society at large to ensure that the general legal framework for the establishment of the mechanisms reflected the views and wishes of the people of Burundi and that the sense of national ownership was deep and genuine.

Security Council consideration. At its meeting on 15 June [meeting 5203], the Security Council was briefed by the Assistant Secretary-General for Legal Affairs, Ralph Zacklin, on the foregoing mission report, focusing his remarks on the recommended judicial and non-judicial mechanisms and placing them in their national and international contexts. He pointed out that the establishment of an international judicial commission of inquiry, foreseen in the Arusha Agreement, had to be considered in the light of Burundi's history of ethnic conflict, the events that had occurred since the conclusion of the Agreement in 2000 and the experience gained by the United Nations in promoting justice and the rule of law over the past 12 years. It should also be examined against the background of four international commissions of inquiry dispatched to Burundi between 1993 and 1995 [YUN 1993, p. 264; YUN 1994, p. 277; YUN 1995, pp. 340 & 346], three at the request of the Council.

For all their differences, the four commissions shared similar features: their subject matter and temporal jurisdiction were limited to the 1993 coup d'état in Burundi, the assassination of its President and the ensuing massacres. As the earlier 1972 massacre of Hutus was not within their mandate, a legal determination that the crime of genocide had been committed in Burundi was made only in respect of the 1993 massacres of Tutsis. While all four commissions recommended that to eradicate impunity those responsible should be brought to account, no action had been taken on the recommendation by any UN organ.

In connection with the legal basis for the establishment of the special chamber and the applicable law governing its operation, i.e., the Burundian law, with necessary modifications, the Assistant Secretary-General pointed out that, based on existing UN practice, in order for the United Nations to cooperate in the establishment of the special chamber, its founding instrument would have to exclude the death penalty from the sentencing framework and declare any amnesty given to genocide, crimes against humanity and war crimes invalid before the chamber. He said the expeditious establishment of the truth commission for Burundi would ensure that, by the time a special chamber was established, the results of the commission's investigations could be shared with the prosecutor of the special chamber. He also stressed that whatever mode of financing was utilized for the mechanisms, it was important that the funding be viable and sustained to permit them to take root, fulfil their mandates, and create the desired legacy of truth, reconciliation and justice.

In its statement before the Council, Burundi supported the mission's recommendations as meeting the dual concerns of the political negotiators of the Arusha Agreement and the people of Burundi to establish the truth and bring the guilty to justice and punish them. As the new version of the truth commission did not sufficiently highlight the aspect of reconciliation, Burundi requested that the Council give priority to that aspect in discussions on the commission. With respect to the judicial mechanism, Burundi pointed to the need to accelerate the ongoing reform of the judicial system to enable it to discharge its new mission. The final document on the judicial mechanism should clarify the relationship between the truth commission and the special chamber, and the Council should specify the financing modalities of the two mechanisms.

SECURITY COUNCIL ACTION

On 20 June [meeting 5207], the Security Council unanimously adopted **resolution 1606(2005)**. The draft [S/2005/396] was prepared in consultations among Council members.

The Security Council,

Reaffirming its support for the process of the Arusha Peace and Reconciliation Agreement for Burundi, signed at Arusha, United Republic of Tanzania, on 28 August 2000 (hereinafter "the Arusha Agreement"),

Convinced of the need, for the consolidation of peace and reconciliation in Burundi, to establish the truth, investigate the crimes, and identify and bring to justice those bearing the greatest responsibility for crimes of genocide, crimes against humanity and war crimes committed in Burundi since independence, to deter future crimes of this nature, and to put an end to the climate of impunity, in Burundi and in the region of the Great Lakes of Africa as a whole,

Emphasizing that appropriate international assistance to Burundi is needed to help the Burundian people to end impunity, promote reconciliation and establish a society and government under the rule of law,

Having taken note of the letter dated 24 July 2002 from the then President of the Republic of Burundi, Pierre Buyoya, to the Secretary-General requesting the establishment of an international judicial commission of inquiry, as provided for in the Arusha Agreement,

Having taken note also of the report transmitted by the Secretary-General to the Security Council on 11 March 2005, following on the assessment mission he had dispatched to Burundi, from 16 to 24 May 2004, to consider the advisability and feasibility of establishing such a commission,

Having heard the opinion of the Transitional Government of Burundi, presented by its Minister of Justice, Didace Kiganahe, on 15 June 2005, on the recommendations contained in the report, which aim at the creation of a mixed truth commission and a special chamber within the court system of Burundi,

Acknowledging the crucial importance of reconciliation for peace and national unity in Burundi, and sharing the view that a future truth commission should contribute to it,

1. *Requests* the Secretary-General to initiate negotiations with the Government and consultations with all Burundian parties concerned on how to implement his recommendations, and to report to the Security Council by 30 September 2005 on details of implementation, including costs, structures and time frame;

2. *Decides* to remain seized of the matter.

The Secretary-General reported to the Security Council on 11 October [S/2005/644], as requested in resolution 1606(2005)(above), that a number of developments in Burundi had delayed the negotiations called for. Although the Transitional Government had appointed a commission in July to negotiate with the United Nations for the establishment of the truth commission and the special chamber within the court system of Burundi, negotiations could not take place owing to the activities involved in the electoral process and the subsequent inauguration of President Pierre Nkurunziza on 26 August, as well as the consequent disbandment of the commission established by the Transitional Government, with the installation of the new Government (below).

In meetings with ONUB in early September, President Nkurunziza and the new Minister of Justice expressed the Government's support in principle for the establishment of the two accountability mechanisms; the truth commission was to be established before the special chamber. They indicated their intention to nominate a committee to liaise with the United Nations on the details of the proposed legal framework for the two mechanisms, but made clear that Burundi would not be ready to engage in substantive negotiations before 30 September.

In preparation for the negotiations, consultations among Secretariat departments and offices, and between the Secretariat and relevant NGOs, were held at UN Headquarters to coordinate their respective roles in elaborating the operational modalities of the mechanisms and, their interrelationship and sequencing. In parallel, OHCHR undertook a preparatory mission to Burundi (27 September–1 October) to discuss coordination of activities between it and ONUB in relation to the establishment of a truth commission, the initiation of an information campaign, the design of a national consultative process on the two mechanisms, and the organization of a national conference on transitional justice. On the basis of the preliminary results of the consultative process, the preparatory discussions with Burundi and its readiness to start the negotiating process, a UN mission would be dispatched to Burundi to negotiate the practical implementation of the legal framework and report in due course to the Council.

Elections

On 3 June, for the first time since the country's independence in 1962, elections were held in Burundi for communal councillors. Some 80 per cent of the registered voters participated, and candidates were nominated by 35 political parties, as reported by the Secretary-General in Sep-

tember [S/2005/586]. CNDD-FDD (Nkurunziza) won 93 of the 129 communes, gaining 57.3 per cent of the national vote; FRODEBU took 23.3 per cent; UPRONA, 6.3 per cent; Leonard Nyangoma's faction of CNDD (CNDD (Nyangoma)), 4.1 per cent; MRC, 2.1 per cent; and PARENA, 1.8 per cent. In general, the electoral campaign was conducted peacefully, except in Kayanza province, where tensions between FRODEBU and CNDD-FDD supporters resulted in several acts of violence. The communal elections were held without any serious disruption in 15 of Burundi's 17 provinces, but violence in Bubanza and Bujumbura Rurale caused the early closure of 133 polling stations. With UN assistance, the elections in the affected communes were successfully concluded on 7 June.

Elections for the National Assembly were held as scheduled on 4 July, in a peaceful atmosphere, with the participation of some 77 per cent of the registered voters. CNDD-FDD (Nkurunziza) received 57.8 per cent of the national vote; FRODEBU, 21.6 per cent; UPRONA, 7.1 per cent; CNDD (Nyangoma), 4.9 per cent; and MRC, 2.1 per cent. Indirect Senate elections, in which ballots were cast by the 3,225 newly elected communal councillors, were held on 29 July. The Senate was composed of 41 members: one Hutu and one Tutsi representing each of the 17 provinces; three co-opted representatives from the Batwa community; and the four former Heads of State.

On 19 August, Pierre Nkurunziza, leader of CNDD-FDD, was elected President by a Joint Parliamentary Congress comprising members of the National Assembly and the Senate. On 26 August, the inauguration of Mr. Nkurunziza, the first democratically elected President in over a decade, marked the formal conclusion of the transitional process in Burundi. The final round of elections at the *colline* level was to be held on 23 September.

In his inaugural speech, President Nkurunziza signalled his intention to crack down on corruption, crime and lawlessness; fight the spread of HIV/AIDS; improve security; and promote economic growth. He promised free primary education for all children and urged all Burundians to help rebuild the country.

On 29 August, the National Assembly and the Senate confirmed President Nkurunziza's nominees for first Vice-President and second Vice-President. On 30 August, the President nominated ministers for the 20-member Cabinet; its composition generally complied with the Constitution and with the power-sharing arrangements in the Government agreed upon in the Arusha Agreement, which envisaged a Government consisting of 60 per cent Hutu, 40 per cent Tutsi and 30 per cent women representatives. Donors provided $22 million for the elections through the UNDP-managed trust fund.

Press statement of Secretary-General. By a press statement of 19 August [SG/SM/10053], the Secretary-General congratulated the Burundians on the election of their first post-transitional President. He wished the President-elect every success as he faced the challenging tasks ahead, including continuing the major reforms currently under way, the consolidation of peace, national reconciliation, reconstruction and development.

SECURITY COUNCIL ACTION

On 30 August [meeting 5252], following consultations among Security Council members the President made statement **S/PRST/2005/41** on behalf of the Council:

> The Security Council acknowledges the election of Mr. Pierre Nkurunziza as President of the Republic of Burundi, on 19 August 2005. This vote marks the welcome final step of the transitional process in Burundi. The conclusion of this transitional process represents an important milestone for the future of Burundi as well as the Great Lakes region as a whole.
>
> The Council pays tribute to the spirit of peace and dialogue demonstrated by the Burundian people throughout the transitional period, and commends them for their encouraging participation in the electoral process. The Council calls upon all parties to respect the will of the Burundian people, the elected Government and the commitments agreed upon during the transitional process. It encourages the new authorities to continue on the course of stability and national reconciliation and to promote social concord. It reaffirms in this regard that it is essential to put an end to the climate of impunity.
>
> The Council commends the critical contribution of the Regional Peace Initiative on Burundi, the African Union and the United Nations Operation in Burundi to the peace process. It calls upon all international partners of Burundi, including the States of the Regional Initiative and the main donors, to remain committed, and encourages them to agree with the Burundian authorities on the most appropriate framework to coordinate their support to reforms currently under way and to the consolidation of peace.

Communication. The AU Peace and Security Council, by a communiqué adopted at its thirty-seventh meeting (Addis Ababa, 8 September) [S/2005/580], welcomed the conclusion of the transitional period in Burundi, the successful conduct of the electoral process, the peaceful transfer of power to democratically elected institutions, the election of Mr. Nkurunziza as President and the establishment of new institutions based on the principles defined in the Burundian

Constitution. It encouraged the Government to work resolutely towards consolidating the progress made and concluding the peace process, urged renewed efforts towards concluding a ceasefire agreement with Palipehutu-FNL, and appealed to all of Burundi's partners to provide the requisite financial and socio-economic assistance for post-conflict reconstruction and development.

Further political developments

Report of Secretary-General (September). In his special report of 14 September [S/2005/586], the Secretary-General focused on the conclusion of the transitional process and the proposed international arrangements for providing support to the new Government.

At meetings held on 20 and 21 June and on 18 and 19 July, the Implementation Monitoring Committee reiterated its call for the Transitional Government to implement pending defence and security sector reforms, and called on the CENI to ensure the free and fair conduct of the elections, including strict adherence to the electoral calendar. On 8 and 9 August, the Committee held its final meeting in Bujumbura. It issued a statement drawing the attention of the new Government and the international community to several outstanding provisions of the Arusha Agreement and called on the Government expeditiously to complete the implementation of those relating to the repatriation of refugees and rehabilitation of civilians affected by conflict; the release of political prisoners; reconstruction and economic and social development; the reform of the defence and security sectors and of the justice system; and ending impunity.

The Transitional Government concluded the harmonization of all military and police ranks for both the demobilization of personnel and their reintegration into either the new National Defence Force or the national police. Integration of ex-combatants of armed groups into the National Defence Force was completed. In May, ONUB, in cooperation with international donors, finalized a plan for the comprehensive reform of the security sector. The plan was communicated to the Transitional Government, which welcomed the initiative, but noted that it should be further developed in coordination with the incoming Government.

By 15 August, 16,491 combatants of the former Armed Forces of Burundi and of the armed political parties/movements had entered the national demobilization process, including 2,909 children and 485 female combatants. Another 11,400 former soldiers were expected to be demobilized by December. The Ministry of Defence reaffirmed its commitment to continue demobilization until the National Defence Force was reduced to 30,000 personnel.

During the reporting period, the continuing military confrontations between the National Defence Force and FNL had severe consequences for the civilian population in Bujumbura and Bubanza provinces. FNL continued targeting civilians suspected of no longer supporting it or of supporting CNDD-FDD, some of whom were beheaded or otherwise mutilated. On 16 June, five civilians attending a religious service in Bujumbura Rurale were killed, and at least 10 others were wounded by grenades and gunfire. In Bujumbura and Bujumbura Rurale, ONUB documented an increase in summary executions of suspected FNL supporters, reportedly by National Defence Force soldiers. During the electoral period, the Defence Force carried out mass arbitrary arrests of suspected FNL supporters, and several deaths resulting from torture and ill-treatment were reported; however, most detainees were released after questioning.

A total of 116,799 Burundians continued to live in 160 displacement sites nationwide, the majority in Kayanza, Ngozi, Kirundo, Muyinga and Gitega provinces. Furthermore, 26,077 Burundian refugees returned to Burundi between January and August, most to Makamba, Muyinga and Ruyigi provinces. UNHCR facilitated 25,030 returns.

The Secretary-General observed that, despite the progress achieved in consolidating peace, significant challenges remained. He underscored some of the key areas requiring sustained and enhanced international engagement and donor support: reconstruction, development, job creation, rehabilitation of the national health and education sectors, promotion of reconciliation, putting an end to impunity, conclusion of the security sector and judicial reform programmes and ensuring sound governance. He was encouraged by President Nkurunziza's willingness to pursue negotiations with FNL and called on FNL to act without further delay and in good faith to reach a peaceful settlement with the Government.

Burundi Partners' Forum. The Secretary-General, elaborating on his proposal for an international mechanism to support the new Government, stated that such a mechanism should support the reform processes under way, including those relating to the security sector, the judiciary and land ownership. It should address civilian disarmament issues and the management of large-scale refugee returns; ensure coordination among donors for reconstruction and development funding; support national efforts to consolidate peace through reconciliation; and assure the people of Burundi of the international community's commitment to ensuring democratic, transparent and accountable governance. The forum, which would have a small secretariat, would be chaired by the Special Representative and include representatives of the Regional Peace Initiative, the international donor community, the AU and the United Nations. It would meet monthly and hold regular meetings with the Government. At a 13 September meeting of the Heads of State of Burundi and of the member States of the Regional Peace Initiative, the AU, donors and other international stakeholders, chaired jointly by the Secretary-General and the President of Uganda, agreement was reached in principle on the establishment of the proposed mechanism in the form of a partners' forum, whose mandate and composition would be further elaborated in consultation with Burundi.

SECURITY COUNCIL ACTION (September)

On 22 September [meeting 5268], following consultations among Security Council members, the President made statement **S/PRST/2005/43** on behalf of the Council:

The Security Council takes note of the special report of the Secretary-General of 14 September 2005 on the United Nations Operation in Burundi, in particular the proposal to establish a partners' forum as an international support mechanism.

The Council also takes note of the declaration adopted on 13 September 2005 in New York during the summit on Burundi, co-chaired by the Secretary-General and the President of the Republic of Uganda, in his capacity as Chairman of the Regional Peace Initiative on Burundi.

The Council welcomes the decision taken during the summit to establish a forum of Burundi's partners and encourages the Special Representative of the Secretary-General for Burundi to conclude discussions with all concerned partners in order to establish the forum as soon as possible.

The forum should work with the Government of Burundi in consolidating peace and national reconciliation in Burundi, supporting reforms being undertaken by the Government and enhancing donor coordination, and should work in close coordination with the Peacebuilding Commission once it is operational.

The Council also reiterates its call upon the donor community to pursue bilateral and multilateral efforts to support the country.

Subsequently, ONUB convened an informal meeting (Bujumbura, 18 October), at which the Burundi Partners' Forum was launched bringing together representatives of the AU, the Regional Peace Initiative, neighbouring countries, the United Nations and donors. In addition to holding regular meetings, the Forum would also hold periodic meetings with the participation of all interested international partners.

Security Council consideration. The Council heard briefings by the head of its mission to Central Africa on 15 November [meeting 5305] and on 6 December [meeting 5315]. In introducing the mission's report at the December meeting, the head of the mission remarked that the transition in Burundi had been a success and that the peace and national reconciliation process had set a stunning example for the region. The United Nations, whose support had been crucial to that success, had to withdraw and make way for others. The problem of FNL's non-participation in the peace process continued to pose a challenge; the mission hoped that, with the encouragement of Tanzania, FNL would return to the negotiating table without delay.

Situation at end of year

Report of Secretary-General (November). In response to Security Council resolution 1602 (2005) (see p. 204), the Secretary-General issued his fifth report on ONUB on 21 November [S/2005/728], updating major developments in the peace consolidation process and presenting his recommendations on the role of ONUB in supporting Burundi in its post-transition phase, including possible adjustments to the Operation's mandate and force strength.

Elections at the *colline* level were held as scheduled on 23 September in a generally peaceful atmosphere, with a moderate voter turnout. Some 44,724 independent candidates competed for 14,560 *colline* administrator posts. ONUB provided technical and logistical assistance to CENI in organizing the elections and coordinated closely with the Government on the provision of security. Those elections completed the national electoral process.

The new Cabinet, meeting for the first time on 9 September, identified the following tentative priorities for the Government: restoring peace and democracy, completing security sector reform, combating corruption, improving living conditions, addressing security issues and promoting regional cooperation. Steps were taken to curb public expenditure, and accountability measures were introduced for government officials, including declaring their financial assets.

On 29 October, the newly elected President of FRODEBU, Léonce Ngendakumana, announced that his party was considering withdrawing from the Government unless the decision-making process became more inclusive. On 4 November, the FRODEBU parliamentary group issued a statement expressing concern over the arbitrary arrests of some of its members accused of belong-

ing to FNL. In a 30 October statement, CNDD (Nyangoma) also expressed concern over continuing insecurity in the country, including incidents of arbitrary arrests, torture and human rights violations, despite the new Government's promises for a tangible improvement in the human rights situation.

On 10 September, contrary to its previous position, FNL indicated that it would negotiate with the Government but only with the involvement of the international community. On 14 September, it announced the formation of an 80-member delegation to participate in negotiations, but with the precondition that violations of the 15 May agreement on the cessation of hostilities (see p. 203) be investigated. On 8 October, elements claiming to be from FNL and headed by Jean-Bosco Sindayigaya, a former deputy to FNL leader Agathon Rwasa, proclaimed that the leadership of FNL had been suspended and that the new faction was prepared to negotiate with the Government. The situation regarding the FNL leadership remained unclear. On 6 October, the Government announced that, unless FNL agreed to enter into negotiations before 31 October, it would take measures to bring it to the negotiating table, willingly or by force. It also announced on 29 October that measures would be taken to curb FNL activities. At the request of the Regional Peace Initiative, the United Republic of Tanzania continued its efforts to facilitate talks between the Government and FNL.

Meanwhile, the Tripartite Plus Joint Commission held a meeting (New York, 16 September) at which the members agreed to continue military and diplomatic pressure on all militias operating in their territories to ensure the disarmament and repartition or reintegration of those militias, and to impose sanctions on them if they refused to disarm voluntarily before 30 September. At a further meeting (Kampala, Uganda, 21 October), the Commission agreed to take measures against the armed groups, including FNL, that were operating in the eastern DRC and neighbouring countries. The measures would include prosecution and extradition of the groups' leaders, the imposition of travel bans and financial restrictions against them, and their possible designation as terrorist groups.

While the security situation in most areas of the country remained generally stable, attacks by FNL and clashes between it and the National Defence Force increased in the western provinces. As a result, the population, particularly in Bujumbura Rurale and Bubanza provinces, continued to suffer from violence and intimidation.

Multidisciplinary assessment mission. A multidisciplinary UN assessment mission, led by DPKO and comprising representatives of DPA, the Department of Safety and Security, the Office for the Coordination of Humanitarian Affairs, UNDP, the United Nations Development Group, OHCHR, UNHCR and the World Bank, visited Burundi from 16 to 23 October. The mission met with a wide cross-section of Burundian and international stakeholders and evaluated the security situation on the ground, the overall peace consolidation and national recovery process, and the UN role in the post-transition phase.

The mission examined key security challenges that needed to be addressed urgently for the restoration of stability in Burundi: bringing FNL into the peace process; building the capacity of the security sector, namely, the National Defence Force and the national police; completing the disarmament and demobilization process and reintegrating former combatants; reintegrating refugees and internally displaced persons; and resolving regional issues. Other challenges to be addressed effectively to ensure the consolidation of durable peace included: promoting democracy and good governance and strengthening State administration; strengthening the rule of law; fostering respect for human rights; transitional justice through the establishment of a national truth commission and a special chamber within Burundi's court system (see p. 206); and developing strategies for poverty reduction and humanitarian relief, promoting economic recovery and development, resolving disputes over land and property rights, and developing action plans for clearing mines and other explosive remnants of war.

The mission found that some progress had been achieved towards reforming the security sector. Success of the reintegration process was evidenced by a National Defence Force that currently comprised some 33,000 military personnel, which would be further reduced to 25,000 by December 2007, as it was important that the force be reduced to a size that was financially sustainable. Some 20,000 officers had been integrated into the national police force, of whom 1,012 were women. As to the disarmament and demobilization programme, by 16 October, 17,459 combatants of the former Armed Forces of Burundi and members of the armed political parties/movements had been demobilized, including 3,007 children and 482 women. By 10 October the Government had disarmed and paid allowances to 2,849 members of the *gardiens de la paix* and to 1,704 *militants combattants*; nonetheless, the process had been repeatedly interrupted owing to problems concerning the accuracy of lists of the *gardiens*, and was again suspended in mid-October. Despite the establishment (by the Transitional Government in

April) of a National Commission for Civilian Disarmament to address the problem of the large number of small arms in the hands of the civilian population, little progress had been achieved. Refugee returns rose to over 18,000 in October, bringing the total number of returnees to more than 60,000. With UNHCR assistance, 281,731 Burundian refugees returned from the United Republic of Tanzania; some 426,521 more remained in the DRC, Rwanda and Tanzania. The number of internally displaced persons decreased from 145,000 in 2004 to 117,000 in 2005.

Drawdown of ONUB military component. In discussions with the assessment mission, the Government was of the view that, since security had been restored in most areas of the country, international support, including UN support, should focus on institutional capacity-building and on recovery, reconstruction and development. It therefore favoured an early withdrawal of the ONUB military component, while acknowledging the important role that it could continue to play in other critical areas. A joint Government-ONUB technical working group held extensive consultations (Bujumbura, 4-14 November) to consider the nature of ONUB support in the next phase. The Government indicated its strong preference for an early disengagement of ONUB's military and police and that its other areas of responsibility should be progressively assumed by the UN country team and other international partners during 2006. It further indicated the readiness of the National Defence Force and the national police to address security challenges, and to assume as soon as possible all security responsibilities currently undertaken by ONUB in the 14 provinces where security had generally been restored.

It was proposed that the ONUB military component could begin drawing down in December, starting with one national contingent. The phased withdrawal of two battalions, a level II hospital and an aviation unit from the provinces of Kirundo, Ngozi, Cankuzo, Ruyigi, Rutana, Makamba, Gitega, Karuzi and Muyinga could be completed from April to June 2006. During that period, troops could also be withdrawn or redeployed from Mwaro, Muramvya and Bururi. The result would be a reduction of approximately 2,000 personnel, or 40 per cent of ONUB's current authorized military strength. The number of military observers deployed throughout the country would also be reduced from the current authorized strength of 200 to 120 by the end of April 2006. The balance of the ONUB force would remain temporarily deployed in the three border provinces of Bujumbura Rurale (including Bujumbura city), Bubanza and Cibitoké, where FNL remained active and would continue to monitor and enhance security along the Burundi-DRC border, including Lake Tanganyika, in coordination with the National Defence Force and MONUC. A mechanism would be established to coordinate activities of the National Defence Force and the ONUB force related to border control and the progressive transfer of all security responsibilities from ONUB to the national army and police, including the protection of civilians in those provinces.

While it was envisaged that the withdrawal of the ONUB force could, at the request of the Government, be completed in the second half of 2006, a detailed drawdown plan for the approximately 3,000 remaining ONUB troops would be developed after a joint assessment by ONUB and the National Defence Force in January 2006.

The Government proposed that the ONUB police component be reduced from its current authorized strength of 120 to about 15 police trainers, to be based in Bujumbura, by the end of March 2006. ONUB could also play an important role in monitoring the implementation of a possible ceasefire agreement with FNL; supporting the ongoing disarmament, demobilization and reintegration, and security sector reform processes; and monitoring and promoting human rights, particularly through national capacity-building. The Government also requested ONUB support in the area of transitional justice, including for the establishment of a truth and reconciliation commission and special chamber (see p. 206). Many of those tasks were envisaged to be either completed or continued through other bilateral and multilateral assistance programmes before the end of 2006.

The Secretary-General encouraged Burundi and its international and regional partners to adopt a common approach to resolving the armed conflict with FNL and urged Burundi to continue its efforts to engage in talks with FNL, and the FNL leaders to seize the opportunity to join the peace process. He suggested that, if efforts to bring FNL to the negotiating table failed, the Security Council and the region might wish to consider the use of targeted measures against the FNL leaders who continued to obstruct a peaceful solution.

The Secretary-General encouraged Burundi to identify as a matter of urgency the priority areas in which assistance was needed to support the National Defence Force and the national police, and donors to give expeditious, positive consideration to helping meet the shortfalls, especially of equipment, logistics, housing, transport and training. The United Nations stood ready to assist the Government in establishing the truth and reconciliation commission and special cham-

ber and to help ensure that they functioned effectively. The Secretary-General urged the Government to address as a priority the increasing human rights violations in the country and ensure that perpetrators were brought to justice.

The Secretary-General did not believe that ONUB should be maintained for longer than needed. However, in view of the major outstanding challenges, combined with a general lack of resources to address them, he cautioned the Security Council against a hasty or premature international disengagement. He appealed to the regional and international stakeholders, as well as international donors, to remain committed to Burundi in the next critical phase in that country, including by increasing bilateral and multilateral assistance. Taking into consideration the proposed adjustment in the military strength of ONUB, the Secretary-General recommended that its mandate be extended for a further six-month period, until 31 May 2006.

Burundian position. On 23 November [S/2005/736], Burundi transmitted its report to the Security Council on the conclusions of the talks between its Government and ONUB, following the UN assessment mission in October on the evolution of the ONUB mandate (see p. 211). The report outlined the modalities for the gradual withdrawal of ONUB forces as described in the Secretary-General's report (see p. 211) and the agreed areas of cooperation between ONUB and Burundi, as follows: monitoring Burundi's borders with the DRC, including Lake Tanganyika; support for the completion of the disarmament, demobilization and reintegration process and security sector reform; support for the promotion of human rights; support for transitional justice in the context of the establishment of the truth and reconciliation commission and the special chamber (see p. 206); protection of ONUB personnel and equipment; demining; and support for the World Food Programme (WFP) and UNHCR humanitarian operations. The report noted that Burundi would continue to cooperate with ONUB by working with the teams that were not part of the first withdrawal in the areas and within the limits of what was agreed. In March 2006, Burundi and ONUB would assess the situation on the ground and progress made in the agreed areas of cooperation.

Security Council consideration. During the 30 November meeting [meeting 5311] of the Security Council to discuss the reports of the Secretary-General and Burundi, the Foreign Minister of Burundi stated that the country, strengthened by its achievements, was working to address the challenges of reconstruction and development. There was peace throughout most of the country, with the exception of a few pockets in Bujumbura Rurale, Cibitoké and Bubanza, where the crime rate remained high and atrocities were sometimes perpetrated by members of Palipehutu-FNL. The National Defence Force and the national police were working hard to put an end to such actions with encouraging results: in November, 707 FNL members left the movement and surrendered to Burundian authorities; many of them had rejoined their families. Burundi was emerging from a long period of economic stagnation and a sense of confidence had returned. The last few months had seen a significant increase in tax yield due to the strict collection of duties and taxes. The Foreign Minister stressed, however, the urgent need to strengthen financially multilateral agencies, including UN agencies, to enable them to shift from humanitarian to development support of post-conflict Burundi.

SECURITY COUNCIL ACTION (November)

On 30 November [meeting 5311], the Security Council unanimously adopted **resolution 1641 (2005)**. The draft [S/2005/741] was prepared in consultations among Council members.

The Security Council,

Recalling its relevant resolutions on Burundi, and in particular resolution 1545(2004) of 21 May 2004,

Reaffirming its strong commitment to the sovereignty, independence, territorial integrity and unity of Burundi, and recalling the importance of the principles of good-neighbourliness, non-interference and co-operation in the relations between States in the region,

Noting that factors of instability remain in Burundi, which continue to constitute a threat to international peace and security in the region,

Acting under Chapter VII of the Charter of the United Nations,

1. *Decides* to extend the mandate of the United Nations Operation in Burundi until 15 January 2006;

2. *Decides also* to remain actively seized of the matter.

Also on 30 November, the Council President in a press statement [SC/8567], said that the extension of the ONUB mandate to 15 January 2006 was of a technical nature to allow time for discussion on the future of the Operation. By the statement, Council members encouraged the new Burundian authorities to continue on the course of stability and national reconciliation and to promote social concord in the country. They reiterated their support for ONUB, which, together with the Burundi Partners' Forum, continued to have an important role to play in support of the Government's efforts towards the consolidation of peace. The Council would review ONUB's mandate, taking into account developments in Burundi and the region, and the numerous remaining challenges. They recognized the importance of a gradual disengagement of ONUB and encouraged the Burundian authorities and ONUB to consult closely on the matter. Council members again called on Palipehutu-FNL to join the peace process without further delay or conditions, and welcomed the willingness shown by the Government to achieve a peaceful solution.

SECURITY COUNCIL ACTION (December)

On 21 December [meeting 5341], the Security Council unanimously adopted **resolution 1650 (2005)**. The draft [S/2005/811] was prepared in consultations among Council members.

The Security Council,

Recalling its resolutions and the statements by its President on Burundi, and in particular resolution 1545(2004) of 21 May 2004,

Reaffirming its strong commitment to the sovereignty, independence, territorial integrity and unity of Burundi, and recalling the importance of the principles of good-neighbourliness, non-interference and co-operation in the relations among States in the region,

Congratulating the people of Burundi for the successful conclusion of the transitional period and the peaceful transfer of authority to representative and democratically elected government and institutions,

Expressing its gratitude to the States of the Regional Peace Initiative on Burundi, the African Union and the United Nations Operation in Burundi for their significant contribution to the success of the political transition,

Encouraging the new authorities and all Burundian political actors to continue on the course of stability and national reconciliation and to promote social concord in their country, while recognizing that numerous challenges remain to be addressed,

Stressing the need to put in place the reforms provided for in the Arusha Peace and Reconciliation Agreement for Burundi, signed on 28 August 2000,

Encouraging in particular the Burundian authorities to continue to work with the Special Representative of the Secretary-General for Burundi, including on the establishment of the mixed truth commission and the special chamber within the court system of Burundi referred to in resolution 1606(2005) of 20 June 2005,

Reiterating its support for the United Nations Operation in Burundi, which continues to have an important role to play in support of the efforts of the Government of Burundi towards the consolidation of peace,

Recognizing the important role of the Partners' Forum established during the summit on Burundi, held in New York on 13 September 2005, in the consolidation of peace and reconciliation in Burundi and in supporting reform being undertaken by the Government,

Encouraging the Government to work with its international partners, in particular with a view to mobilizing assistance for the reconstruction of the country,

Taking note of the position of the Government on the evolution of the mandate of the United Nations Operation in Burundi, as recorded in the letter dated 23 November 2005 from the Chargé d'affaires a.i. of the Permanent Mission of Burundi to the United Nations addressed to the President of the Security Council and as presented to the Council on 30 November 2005 by

Mrs. Antoinette Batumubwira, Minister for Foreign Affairs and International Cooperation of Burundi,

Taking note also of the report of the Security Council mission which visited the region of Central Africa from 4 to 11 November 2005, and endorsing the recommendations contained therein,

Expressing its serious concern at the continuation of hostilities by the Parti pour la libération du peuple hutu-Forces nationales de libération, and at the threat it poses to civilians,

Noting that, although there has been an improvement in the security situation since the completion of the transitional period, factors of instability remain in Burundi and in the Great Lakes region of Africa, which continue to constitute a threat to international peace and security in the region,

Acting under Chapter VII of the Charter of the United Nations,

1. *Takes note* of the fifth report of the Secretary-General on the United Nations Operation in Burundi, of 21 November 2005, and in particular of the recommendations contained in paragraphs 57 to 60 thereof;

2. *Decides* to extend the mandate of the United Nations Operation in Burundi until 1 July 2006;

3. *Welcomes* the readiness expressed by the Secretary-General to continue to consult closely with the Government of Burundi, with a view to determining, on the basis of the recommendations referred to in the letter dated 23 November 2005 from the Chargé d'affaires a.i. of the Permanent Mission of Burundi to the United Nations addressed to the President of the Security Council, the modalities for implementing a gradual disengagement of the United Nations peacekeeping presence and an adjustment to its mandate, taking into account all the circumstances, as well as the merits of a United Nations contribution and support to the consolidation of peace in Burundi;

4. *Looks forward* to receiving the report of the Secretary-General on the joint assessment mentioned in paragraph 60 of his fifth report on the United Nations Operation in Burundi, by 15 March 2006;

5. *Authorizes*, subject to the following conditions, the temporary redeployment of military and civilian police personnel between the United Nations Operation in Burundi and the United Nations Organization Mission in the Democratic Republic of the Congo, taking into account the need to ensure effective performance of the current mandates of those missions, and requests in this regard the Secretary-General to begin consultations with the countries contributing military and civilian police personnel to those missions:

(a) The Secretary-General shall receive the prior agreement of the countries contributing military and civilian police personnel and of the Governments concerned;

(b) He shall inform the Council in advance of his intention to proceed with such a redeployment, and in particular of its proposed scope and duration;

(c) Any such redeployment shall require a corresponding prior decision of the Council;

6. *Underlines* the fact that any personnel redeployed in accordance with paragraph 5 above shall continue to be counted against the authorized ceiling on military and civilian police personnel of the mission from which they are being transferred, and that any such transfer shall not have the effect of extending the deployment of

personnel after the expiration of the mandate of their original mission, unless the Council decides otherwise;

7. *Urges* the Government to complete the implementation of the programme of disarmament, demobilization and reintegration, including the effective reintegration of former combatants;

8. *Welcomes* the willingness shown by the Government to achieve a peaceful solution with the Parti pour la libération du peuple hutu-Forces nationales de libération, and reiterates its call upon this movement to join the peace and national reconciliation process without further delays or conditions, and its intention to consider appropriate measures that might be taken against those individuals who threaten this process;

9. *Expresses its deep concern* at the violations of human rights reported by the Secretary-General, and urges the Government and other parties concerned to take the necessary steps to prevent further violations and to ensure that those responsible for such violations are brought to justice without delay;

10. *Urges* the international partners for the development of Burundi, including the United Nations bodies concerned, to continue to provide their support for the reconstruction of the country, particularly through an active participation in the donors conference to be organized in early 2006;

11. *Decides* to remain actively seized of the matter.

Further report of Secretary-General. Reporting on developments in Burundi during November and December [S/2006/163], the Secretary-General noted that Parliament adopted nine out of 37 draft laws presented to it during its first session, which ended in December. It also approved the national budget for 2006, totalling $417 million. The budget was linked to the poverty reduction strategy and envisaged an increase in funding for health, education, public investment and wages, and a slight reduction in the allocation for the security sector.

The President announced the Government's 2006 priorities, which included economic recovery, reconstruction, reconciliation, governance, trade, education and environmental protection. He reiterated his commitment to resolving the issues of prison overcrowding and political prisoners, and to combating corruption and mismanagement. He pledged to strengthen the capacity of the security sector, reorganize judicial institutions, disarm civilians, and reintegrate returnees and former combatants. Taxes on basic food items were reduced. Membership of the Burundi Partners' Forum was expanded to include all international representatives accredited to Burundi. In addition, a National Committee for Aid Coordination was established in December.

Following the appointment of a commission to identify political prisoners, the President announced in December the conditional release of all prisoners detained for more than two years without charge and those who had served at least a quarter of their sentence, except those who had committed serious crimes. By presidential decree, provisional immunity was granted to all political prisoners identified by the commission; 1,457 detainees were subsequently released. The decision raised serious concerns among political parties and human rights organizations over the lack of transparency in the work of the commission, in particular regarding the criteria on which the releases were based. The lack of preparation of the communities to which released detainees would return also raised concerns. The Government had since launched a sensitization campaign to explain its decision on political prisoners and to promote reconciliation in their communities.

In December, ONUB destroyed unserviceable ammunition collected through the disarmament process during a public ceremony organized by the Government and ONUB. With World Bank support, 96 per cent of former combatants received reinsertion allowances for the first 18 months following their demobilization. However, the delivery of longer-term economic reintegration assistance, including micro-projects, vocational training and apprenticeships had been seriously delayed. As at December, a total of 5,295 former combatants were receiving reintegration assistance, over half of them under the national programme. Meanwhile, in November, the National Defence Force began basic training on core military duties at the company level.

With regard to the return and reintegration of refugees and displaced persons, UNHCR facilitated 5,409 and 1,250 returns in November and December, respectively, bringing the total number of refugee returns to 68,000 during 2005.

At the request of the Government, ONUB began the drawdown of 40 per cent of its military force in December. As requested by Security Council resolution 1650(2005) (see p. 214), ONUB consulted with the Burundian authorities to determine the modalities for implementing the withdrawal of ONUB, on the basis of the recommendations made by Burundi in its 23 November report (see p. 213).

(For action by the Economic and Social Council on the reports of its Ad Hoc Advisory Group on the humanitarian and economic needs of Burundi, see p. 1008.)

Rwanda

Assistance to survivors of 1994 genocide

On 23 December [meeting 69], the General Assembly adopted **resolution 60/225** [draft: A/60/L.34 & Add.1] without vote [agenda item 73 (*a*)].

Assistance to survivors of the 1994 genocide in Rwanda, particularly orphans, widows and victims of sexual violence

The General Assembly,

Guided by the Charter of the United Nations and the Universal Declaration of Human Rights,

Recalling the 2005 World Summit Outcome, particularly its recognition that all individuals, in particular vulnerable people, are entitled to freedom from fear and freedom from want, with an equal opportunity to enjoy all their rights and fully develop their human potential,

Recalling also its resolution 59/137 of 10 December 2004, in which it requested the Secretary-General to encourage relevant agencies, funds and programmes of the United Nations system to continue to work with the Government of Rwanda to develop and implement programmes aimed at supporting vulnerable groups that continue to suffer from the effects of the 1994 genocide,

Recalling further the findings and recommendations of the independent inquiry commissioned by the Secretary-General, with the approval of the Security Council, into the actions of the United Nations during the 1994 genocide in Rwanda,

Recalling the report containing the findings and recommendations of the International Panel of Eminent Personalities commissioned by the Organization of African Unity to investigate the genocide in Rwanda and the surrounding events, entitled "Rwanda: The Preventable Genocide",

Recalling also its resolution 58/234 of 23 December 2003, by which it declared 7 April 2004 the International Day of Reflection on the Genocide in Rwanda,

Recognizing the numerous difficulties faced by survivors of the 1994 genocide in Rwanda, particularly the orphans, widows and victims of sexual violence, who are poorer and more vulnerable as a result of the genocide, especially the many victims of sexual violence who have contracted HIV and have since either died or become seriously ill with AIDS,

Firmly convinced of the necessity to restore the dignity of the survivors of the 1994 genocide in Rwanda, which would help to promote reconciliation and healing in Rwanda,

Commending the tremendous efforts of the Government and people of Rwanda and civil society organizations, as well as international efforts, to provide support for restoring the dignity of the survivors, including the allocation by the Government of Rwanda of 5 per cent of its national budget every year to support genocide survivors,

1. *Requests* the Secretary-General to encourage the relevant agencies, funds and programmes of the United Nations system to implement resolution 59/137 expeditiously;

2. *Encourages* all Member States to provide assistance to genocide survivors and other vulnerable groups in Rwanda in support of the present resolution;

3. *Expresses its appreciation* for development assistance and support for the reconstruction and rehabilitation of Rwanda after the 1994 genocide, and calls upon Member States to continue to support the development of Rwanda, inter alia, through programmes under the poverty reduction strategy;

4. *Urges* Member States to develop educational programmes that will inculcate future generations with

the lessons of the genocide in Rwanda in order to help to prevent future acts of genocide;

5. *Requests* the Secretary-General to establish a programme of outreach entitled "The Rwanda Genocide and the United Nations" as well as measures to mobilize civil society for Rwanda genocide victim remembrance and education, in order to help to prevent future acts of genocide, and to report to the General Assembly on the establishment of the programme within six months from the date of the adoption of the present resolution;

6. *Also requests* the Secretary-General, in view of the critical situation of the survivors of the 1994 genocide in Rwanda, particularly orphans, widows and victims of sexual violence, to take all necessary and practicable measures for the implementation of the present resolution and to report thereon to the General Assembly at its sixty-second session;

7. *Requests* the General Committee to consider including in the provisional agenda of the General Assembly at its sixty-second session an additional item entitled "Assistance to survivors of the 1994 genocide in Rwanda, particularly orphans, widows and victims of sexual violence".

Arms embargo

On 7 February [S/2005/76], the Security Council Committee established pursuant to resolution 918(1994) [YUN 1994, p. 285] concerning the arms embargo against Rwanda issued a report covering its activities from 1 January to 31 December 2004. In the absence of a specific monitoring mechanism to ensure implementation of the arms embargo, the Committee recalled its previous observation [YUN 2004, p. 160] that it relied solely on the cooperation of States and organizations in a position to provide information on violations of the embargo. During the reporting period, no violations were brought to the Committee's attention.

Central African Republic

The United Nations Peacebuilding Office in the Central African Republic (BONUCA) had continued since 2000 to support the efforts of the Government to return the country to stability and achieve reconciliation and reconstruction, following the 2003 coup d'état. With the assistance of BONUCA and the international community, the first and second rounds of legislative and presidential elections were held successfully in March and May, and, in June, General François Bozizé, President of the Transitional Government, was confirmed President and Head of State of the Central African Republic, marking a return to constitutional order. As it assumed office, the new Government confronted several continuing major challenges, including insecurity in the north and west of the country due to the presence of armed groups, the human

rights situation, and economic fragility. A Committee of Foreign Partners, including BONUCA, was established to monitor developments in the political, security and human rights situation and in respect of democracy in the country.

In November, the Secretary-General, with the agreement of the Security Council, extended BONUCA's mandate for an additional year, until 31 December 2006, to help the country build on the success of its recent elections. At the same time, he raised the rank of the Representative of the Secretary-General in the Central African Republic to that of Special Representative.

BONUCA mandate

On 30 November [S/2005/758], the Secretary-General informed the Security Council that the Central African authorities had advised his Representative that they wanted BONUCA, established by Security Council presidential statement S/PRST/2000/5 [YUN 2000, p. 162], to continue to assist them in building lasting peace. Since prospects for lasting stability in the Central African Republic were more encouraging than ever, the Secretary-General recommended that BONUCA's mandate be extended until 31 December 2006, to enable it to help the country build on the success of its recent elections. Support from BONUCA, particularly with regard to strengthening political dialogue and promoting the rule of law, would help create a climate conducive to reconstruction and development.

The Central African authorities, together with neighbouring countries, had also requested BONUCA and the Representative to serve as facilitators in their search for a common solution to security threats caused by the upsurge of banditry and the proliferation of weapons in the sub-region. In view of those additional responsibilities and recent encouraging developments, the Secretary-General intended to raise the rank of his Representative in the Central African Republic to that of Special Representative, at the Assistant Secretary-General level.

The Council, on 2 December [S/2005/759], took note of the Secretary-General's recommendation and intention.

Political and security developments

The Security Council President, in a 6 January press statement [SC/8283], said that the Representative of the Secretary-General in the Central African Republic, General Lamine Cissé, had briefed the Council on the situation in Central Africa and on BONUCA activities. The Council reiterated its full support of the Representative's action in the country and noted the progress made by Central Africans in the transitional process towards the restoration of constitutional legality and the rule of law. The Council encouraged the country's international partners to continue to support that process, particularly by funding the forthcoming elections. It noted the difficulties arising from the recent ruling by the Transitional Constitutional Court to exclude certain candidates from the presidential elections, but were encouraged by the decision of the Head of State, General François Bozizé, to accept three of those who had been excluded. The Council invited General Bozizé and all other political actors to find promptly a consensual solution to save the electoral process and to create an environment conducive to the organization of free, transparent and democratic elections.

The Council requested the Secretary-General to inform it of any new developments in the country and to assess the situation through his Representative no later than the end of March.

Elections

The Secretary-General reported in June [S/2005/414] that the first and second rounds of presidential and legislative elections in the Central African Republic were held on 13 March and 8 May, respectively. Apart from some organizational problems and cases of attempted or actual electoral fraud, the elections took place in an atmosphere of calm. Of the 11 candidates in the first round of the presidential elections, two advanced to the second round: Head of State General Bozizé and former Prime Minister Martin Ziguélé. Of the 909 candidates, including 135 women, running in the legislative elections, 18 were elected in the first round and 325 advanced to the second. On 24 May, despite large-scale rigging alleged by the Union des forces vives de la nation, the Mixed and Independent Electoral Commission (CEMI), established in 2004 to ensure implementation of the Electoral Code [YUN 2004, p. 161], felt that the allegations did not undermine the credibility of the electoral process and announced the final results, declaring elected, along with 86 parliament members, General Bozizé as President, with 64.6 per cent of the vote, compared to 35.4 per cent for Mr. Ziguélé. On 11 June, after considering requests for annulment, the Transitional Constitutional Court confirmed the presidential election results and proceeded with the investiture of General Bozizé as President and Head of State of the Central African Republic. The election was observed by 269 national and 28 international observers working under the technical coordination of the International Organization of la Francophonie (OIF). In their joint report, the observers indicated that the reported shortcomings did not constitute irregularities and concluded that the electoral process had been free, reliable, fair and transparent.

On 3 June, the new National Assembly met to elect its officers and standing committees and to adopt its rules of procedure. The Assembly was dominated by the Convergence Kwa Na Kwa party, accounting for 77 of the 105 new seats. On 11 June, the President appointed Elie Doté (former head of the Agriculture and Development Division of the African Development Bank) to the post of Prime Minister.

Communications. The Security Council President, in a press statement of 12 April [SC/8357], said that the Council had been briefed by the Representative of the Secretary-General on the situation in the Central African Republic after the first round of presidential and legislative elections held on 13 March. He said that Council members welcomed the assistance that international partners continued to provide to the country, in particular for the electoral process. They unanimously welcomed the fact that the first round of elections was held with respect for democratic values, and noted with satisfaction that Central Africans demonstrated responsibility on that occasion.

The AU Peace and Security Council, by a communiqué adopted at its thirty-third meeting (Addis Ababa, Ethiopia, 24 June) [S/2005/429], welcomed the positive evolution of the situation in the Central African Republic, in particular the holding of legislative and presidential elections, which marked the country's return to constitutional rule. In the light of that development, the Peace and Security Council decided to lift the 2003 suspension of the Central African Republic from the activities of AU policy organs, imposed by the Central Organ of the OAU Mechanism for Conflict Prevention, Management and Resolution [YUN 2003, p. 158], following the 2003 coup d'état [ibid., p. 156].

Reports of Secretary-General

Report of Secretary-General (June). The Secretary-General, responding to presidential statement S/PRST/2001/25 [YUN 2001, p. 156], submitted a 27 June report [S/2005/414] on the situation in the Central African Republic and BONUCA activities during the first half of 2005.

Of concern was the security situation, particularly in the capital, Bangui, and in the northern areas of the country. Some areas experienced renewed attacks by armed gangs operating as roadblockers, mostly targeting livestock breeders, commercial transport operators or diamond collectors. The attacks displaced about 800 people who had left for the country's major townships and neighbouring Cameroon and Chad. The authorities were concerned that the gangs might be used to destabilize the new Government and its defence and security forces. Despite those threats, the restructuring of the armed forces continued, with France providing support for the training of three battalions. The BONUCA military team also worked with UNDP in the implementation of a project for the reintegration of former combatants, alongside the National Disarmament, Demobilization and Reintegration Commission. The Civilian Police Section of BONUCA continued to monitor the security situation in the capital and in the hinterland, and trained a total of 110 policemen and 286 gendarmes.

With the return to constitutional order and the expected resumption of cooperation between the country and its major donor partners, economic growth was expected to resume in most sectors in 2005, although overall economic activity was fragile. National public finances remained in deep crisis owing to the lack of good governance, the narrowness of the tax base and paucity of revenue. The country was increasingly dependent on budget support from its bilateral and multilateral partners, including France, China, the EU and the Central African Economic and Monetary Community (CEMAC), for its basic needs. It would not be able to meet its 2005 payment obligations without immediate additional budgetary support.

The humanitarian situation continued to deteriorate, from a situation of extreme poverty to a humanitarian emergency, especially in Ouham, Ouham-Pendé, Nana-Grébizi and Kémo prefectures, where resumption of normal activities was impeded by insecurity. In close cooperation with international NGOs and with additional funding from Norway, Sweden and the World Bank, the country team pursued activities to improve access to social services as a matter of urgency and enhance protection of the most vulnerable segments of the population. Other initiatives were launched to improve access to health services, boost school enrolment and revitalize agricultural production.

Serious human rights violations continued during the first half of 2005 in Bangui and in the hinterland, including torture and cruel, inhuman and degrading treatment, rape, kidnapping and forced disappearances for ransom, and summary executions. Harassment, threats, intimidation and cases of abuse of authority by law enforcement agencies were also noted during the electoral campaign.

The Secretary-General congratulated the international partners that provided financial and/or technical support to CEMI during the electoral process. With the emergency situation ended, the electoral process completed and new institutions in place, the Central African Republic had the tools to embark on the path to peace, reconstruction and sustainable development. The Secretary-General encouraged the new authorities to do everything possible to ensure respect for human rights. He appealed to the goodwill and generosity of the country's partners to provide considerable and immediate financial assistance to the economic reconstruction effort under way. The United Nations would provide technical assistance for the formulation of a poverty reduction strategy.

SECURITY COUNCIL ACTION

On 22 July [meeting 5232], following consultations among Security Council members, the President made statement **S/PRST/2005/35** on behalf of the Council:

> The Security Council heard a briefing by the Representative of the Secretary-General, General Lamine Cissé, on the situation in the Central African Republic and the activities of the United Nations Peacebuilding Support Office in the Central African Republic. It reiterated its full support for the action of the Representative of the Secretary-General.
>
> The Council is deeply gratified by the successful holding of the presidential and legislative elections, and welcomes the establishment of the newly elected institutions whose stability is necessary to ensure lasting peace in the Central African Republic.
>
> The Council acknowledges the efforts by the Central African defence and security forces to guarantee satisfactory security conditions during the electoral process, and commends the Multinational Force of the Central African Economic and Monetary Community, France, the European Union, China and Germany for providing decisive support to them.
>
> The Council appreciates the vital role played in the process by the Multinational Force of the Central African Economic and Monetary Community to date, and expresses its support for continuing efforts by the Force to back the consolidation of the constitutional order, which has thus been re-established, and the rebuilding of the rule of law. In this regard, it welcomes the decision of the States of the Central African Economic and Monetary Community to extend the mandate of the Force.
>
> The Council invites the Government of the Central African Republic, and all the political and social forces, to consolidate the national dialogue and to ensure national reconciliation with a view to achieving sustainable development in their country.
>
> The Council calls upon international donors and the international financial institutions to continue to assist the Central African Republic generously. It emphasizes that their support will be indispensable for the country's economic and social recovery, and encourages them to formulate, in close consultation with the United Nations system and the Govern-

ment of the Central African Republic, a concerted development strategy.

The Council requests the Secretary-General to explore, in close consultation with the authorities of the Central African Republic and the country's development partners, the possibility of setting up a follow-up committee or enlarging the Committee of Foreign Partners to Follow Up on the Electoral Process in order to support the reconstruction efforts initiated by the Central Africans. It invites the Secretary-General to report to it on his consultations, through his Representative in the Central African Republic, no later than 31 October 2005.

The Council expresses its concern at the insecurity reigning in the north and the west of the country owing to the presence of armed groups in these regions, and invites relevant States to consult with sub-regional and regional organizations and with the United Nations Peacebuilding Support Office in the Central African Republic on the action required to respond collectively to the threat posed by these armed groups to the stability of the Central African Republic and certain countries of the subregion.

The Council expresses also its deep concern at the continued deterioration of the humanitarian situation in the Central African Republic, in particular in the north of the country. It calls upon the international community to contribute generously to meet the humanitarian needs of the Central African Republic.

Report of Secretary-General (October). In response to the foregoing presidential statement, the Secretary-General, in his October report [S/2005/679], highlighted the results of his consultations with foreign partners and the Central African Republic on either setting up a follow-up committee, or enlarging the Committee of Foreign Partners to Follow Up on the Electoral Process, to support Central Africa's reconstruction efforts.

The Secretary-General said that the poverty reduction strategy paper for the country, once finalized, would become the framework for action, programming and reference for partners, under government coordination and with UN system support. The framework plan, based on the priorities determined with the Central African authorities, focused on democratic governance, resumption of post-conflict programmes, and the fight against HIV/AIDS. The plan was revised by BONUCA, UN agencies and the Government in the light of the new priorities determined by the Government, as contained in the general policy paper presented to the National Assembly by the Prime Minister on 8 August. Short-term (2005-2006) priorities included: streamlining of public finances by improving the collection of receivables; resolving the external debt-servicing problem through the early conclusion of an appropriate programme with the International Monetary Fund; introducing a transparent management

and good governance mechanism; limiting the number of civil servants and State officials to control the wage bill; improving the management and functioning of public financial administrations through foreign technical assistance; providing security throughout the national territory by strengthening the defence and security forces; and expanding private sector development by improving the existing legal, judicial and regulatory framework. Medium-term (2007-2010) priorities included rehabilitating the basic infrastructure, particularly transport, energy and water supply; modernizing the telecommunication sector and its spatial and territorial expansion; modernizing the agricultural sector; increasing the exploitation of mineral and forestry resources; and promoting a policy of national unity based on tolerance, a culture of peace, dialogue and justice. The new Government was receiving assistance from its foreign partners and the UN system for the implementation of those priority actions.

At the political level, BONUCA would mediate and strengthen the dialogue between the political actors, and support the Government's efforts in promoting national unity and reconciliation. It would continue to provide technical assistance to strengthen the capacity of the defence and security forces and support efforts to restructure the army and eradicate the problem of cross-border insecurity, in keeping with the proposals made at the high-level tripartite meeting on that issue (Yaoundé, Cameroon, 25-26 August) by Cameroon, the Central African Republic and Chad. The recommendations adopted at that meeting provided, at the bilateral and trilateral levels, for increased exchanges of security intelligence and information, aerial border surveillance, reactivation of mixed commissions, increased contacts between civilian and military border authorities, joint operations and evaluation of the security situation. At a quadripartite meeting of BONUCA, Cameroon, the Central African Republic and Chad, organized by UNHCR (Geneva, 6 October), the three countries agreed to intensify security measures along their common borders and to launch large-scale humanitarian programmes without regard for their national borders, in order to facilitate the settlement of their populations and adoption of a special integrated development plan for the region. BONUCA would facilitate cooperation among those countries in order to eliminate permanently cross-border insecurity created by armed groups and those who set up roadblocks. It would continue to monitor security along the common borders of the three countries, and also the border between the Sudan and the DRC, in order to prevent serious conflict or humanitarian crises from spilling over from one country to the other.

BONUCA would provide greater support for the Government's efforts to promote and protect human rights and assist in implementing its commitment to restore the rule of law and respect its international obligations. As to reconstruction and economic governance and recovery, the UN system would support efforts to inform and mobilize donors and friends of the Central African Republic, with a view to securing technical and financial support. In the area of finance, the country's partners would help the Government to modernize public financial administrations; improve the monitoring and control of company taxes; introduce an economic and financial good governance charter that officials would be required to sign upon assuming office; and promote greater public awareness of public property. In the social and humanitarian fields, the UN system would focus on upgrading health services, improving access to potable water, raising school attendance and promoting subsistence farming.

Following consultations and exchanges among BONUCA, the country team, the Government and development partners, a Committee of Foreign Partners was established, comprising China, France, Germany, the Russian Federation and the United States; BONUCA, CEMAC and its Multinational Force in Central Africa, the EU, OIF, and the World Bank; and the United Nations Resident and Humanitarian Coordinator. With the Secretary-General's Representative and the High Representative of France as Co-Chairmen, the Committee would monitor developments in the political, security and human rights areas and issues related to respect for democracy.

The Secretary-General observed that the Central African Republic was gradually returning to peace, economic recovery, reconstruction and sustainable development, which required, a comprehensive approach and joint action with the country's development partners. Existing cooperation frameworks, such as the United Nations Development Assistance Framework and the consolidated appeal process, should be strengthened so as to provide greater support to the country's economic recovery efforts and to prevent any deterioration in the socio-economic situation.

Report of Secretary-General (December). The Secretary-General, reporting on 29 December [S/2005/831] on the situation in the Central African Republic and on BONUCA activities in the second half of the year, said that the period was marked by the progressive establishment of republican institutions. The President's appointment on 26 August of a National Ombudsman, in accordance with constitutional provisions, was seen by the Central African people as an important step towards peacebuilding and the strengthening of national political life.

The settlement of electoral disputes by the Transitional Constitutional Court resulted in a change in representation in the National Assembly. The Assembly, at its special session (5-13 August), adopted the Prime Minister's general political programme (see p. 220); at its regular session, it approved the 2005 supplementary budget and adopted the 2006 finance act. The judicial branch was also restructured, especially at the level of the courts and tribunals. The permanent Constitutional Court was established on 8 September, replacing the Transitional Constitutional Court.

Economic activity was heavily affected in 2005 by the negative consequences of earlier politico-military crises and insufficient external assistance. The latest figures suggested a modest recovery of less than 2 per cent, as compared with a forecast of 2.6 per cent. Slight improvements were recorded in fiscal revenues as a result of a census of State officials and civil servants conducted from 25 August through 5 September, which detected close to 1,700 irregularities. Nevertheless, public finances remained in deep crisis, the main effect of which was a new accumulation of salary arrears. The State had been able to pay salaries for six months, only four of which were for 2005; those payments were enabled by the assistance of France and China. The budgetary shortfall had engendered a series of strikes that paralysed a number of public services. In the post-election phase, the anticipated external budgetary assistance was an absolute necessity if the Central African Republic was to overcome its difficulties. Thus, a cooperation agreement between the Central African authorities and the international financial institutions needed to be concluded quickly. However, external assistance alone would not revive the country's economy. The Government had to step up the pace of reform and take strict measures to control public expenditure, expand the tax base and improve transparency in the management of State finances through a more effective anti-corruption drive.

Those parts of the UN system responsible for operational development activities acted within an integrated approach combining response to humanitarian emergencies, reconstruction and development activities, and improvement of the security situation. The revised United Nations Development Assistance Framework for the period 2004-2006, which identified as strategic priorities democratic governance, reconstruction, post-conflict recovery and combating HIV/AIDS, remained the reference point for programming. During the reporting period, the UN system stepped up action to stem the deterioration in humanitarian indicators, in collaboration with international NGOs and with financial support from Ireland, Norway, Sweden, the United States and the World Bank.

The overall human rights situation had been improving, although slowly, since the country's return to constitutional legality. Nevertheless, human rights were often flagrantly violated. Prison conditions were deteriorating and did not meet the minimum standards set by the international human rights instruments ratified by the Government. Violations of press and broadcast freedom continued. The recent arrest of a parliamentarian and of the president of the High Council for Communication, and abuses by the defence forces against the civilian population were brought to the attention of the BONUCA Human Rights Section.

The security situation had been precarious since the elections, in particular in the western and north-eastern regions of the country. Armed gangs continued to interfere with agricultural and commercial activities, causing significant population displacements to neighbouring Chad and Cameroon. The crisis in Darfur, Sudan (see p. 315), and the porous borders had exacerbated the proliferation and movement of light arms and psychotropic drugs. The restructuring of the armed forces continued. The Military Section of BONUCA participated in organizing training courses for battalion command post observers and officers, auto mechanics and small-calibre weapons technicians; its Civilian Police Section continued to monitor the country's security situation and trained 158 national policemen and 98 gendarmes.

The Secretary-General commended the people of the Central African Republic for their patience and political maturity during the post-election period. He said the immensity of the task to be accomplished was beyond the capacity of the Republic alone, which was still recovering from the effects of the recent crises and social tensions; the support of the international community was therefore crucial.

West Africa

In 2005, despite the positive developments achieved in West Africa, daunting challenges remained ahead. While several States were on the path towards economic and democratic reforms and the intensity of conflicts had lessened, the subregion remained vulnerable. The reintegration of former combatants and security sector reform were among the priorities still to be addressed. In March, the Secretary-General presented a progress report on ways to combat subregional and cross-border problems in West Africa, as well as efforts by the United Nations Office for West Africa (UNOWA) and the international community to address subregional cross-border issues. A collaborative EU/Economic Community of West African States (ECOWAS/UNOWA) working group was established to develop a plan of action for their activities and a regional conflict prevention policy.

The United Nations continued efforts to move the peace process forward in Côte d'Ivoire, through the implementation of the 2003 Linas-Marcoussis Agreement [YUN 2003, p. 166] and the 2004 Accra III Agreements [YUN 2004, p. 182]. The May 2003 ceasefire monitored by the United Nations Operation in Côte d'Ivoire (UNOCI) continued to hold, with no major violations of the UN-imposed arms embargo. However, key benchmarks were not met, such as the targeted date for the completion of the demobilization of combatants and the constitutional deadline for holding presidential elections on 30 October 2005. The rebel movement Forces nouvelles retained control over the north of the country, while the south remained under Government control. Agreements were brokered in Pretoria, South Africa, on elections and disarmament issues in April and June, but in each case, the parties failed to live up to their commitments, and new disagreements emerged over the work and composition of the Independent Electoral Commission. ECOWAS and the AU extended President Gbagbo's term for a year, appointed a Prime Minister and established bodies to oversee the peace process. Optimism prevailed that Côte d'Ivoire's new road map would move the country beyond the impasse of no-war-no-peace and toward holding national elections by October 2006.

Events in Liberia were dominated by electoral activities. The United Nations Mission in Liberia (UNMIL) supported various aspects of the process, including security services. Elections were held in October, in a peaceful manner, in which Ellen Johnson-Sirleaf obtained the majority vote. While progress was made in restoring State authority, concerns about corruption in the National Transitional Government led to the establishment of an investigative committee, which concluded that there had been administrative and financial malpractices. A governance and economic management assistance programme was developed to address such issues. Violent demonstrations and protests by ex-combatants and reports of their recruitment from neighbouring countries to participate in conflicts, remained an ongoing threat to stability. The apprehension and transfer of former President Charles Taylor to Sierra Leone for prosecution by the Special Court was added to the UNMIL mandate, which was extended through 31 March 2006.

Concerted efforts were made in Sierra Leone to implement the provisions of the 2000 Agreement on the Ceasefire and Cessation of Hostilities (Abuja Agreement) and to lay the foundation for the country to achieve lasting stability, democracy and prosperity. The security situation remained stable, facilitating the implementation of the drawdown plan to reduce troops of the United Nations Mission in Sierra Leone (UNAMSIL), and of the benchmarks set by the Security Council. Due to the fragile situation in the Mano River Basin subregion and shortfalls in security sector reform, the President of Sierra Leone requested a follow-on UN presence after the withdrawal of UNAMSIL. The Security Council therefore established the United Nations Integrated Office in Sierra Leone (UNIOSIL) to assist the Government to consolidate peace, build the national capacity for conflict prevention and prepare for the 2007 elections. An international training team led by the United Kingdom would continue to provide training until 2010. Other progress included further Government control of the diamond-mining sector, the repatriation of some 272,000 Sierra Leonean refugees, the establishment of a national human rights commission and the Security Council Committee's recommendation to revisit the legal basis of the sanctions against Sierra Leone.

In Guinea-Bissau, controversies over the eligibility of two presidential candidates and the election results later in the year created a highly polarized atmosphere in the country. The United Nations Peace-building Support Office in Guinea-Bissau (UNOGBIS) and regional organizations, such as the AU and ECOWAS, provided support throughout the electoral process. In May, the Supreme Court validated the applications of both former Presidents Vieira and Yala, paving the way for the holding of the first and second round of presidential elections in June and July. However, one candidate rejected the final results, causing tensions to escalate. Although the inauguration of President-elect Vieira took place in October, by year's end, the rift had deepened further. By presidential decrees, Mr. Vieira dismissed the Government, appointed a Prime Minister and named a new Government, creating two blocs in the National Popular Assembly: one supporting the Government appointed by President Vieira and the other allied to the previous Government. To facilitate the new role of UNOGBIS in the transition process, the Secretary-General revised its mandate and recommended an extension for one year, until 31 December 2006.

Cameroon and Nigeria cooperated to resolve the border issue, with UN assistance, through the Cameroon-Nigerian Mixed Commission. Activities focused on completing and consolidating the transfers of authority, finding solutions to the outstanding maritime boundary issues and carrying out the demarcation process. In May, the Presidents of the two countries renewed their commitment to pursue the peaceful implementation of the 2002 International Court of Justice ruling [YUN 2004, p. 1265]. However, delays occurred in the planned withdrawal and transfer of authority in the Bakassi Peninsula and in the demarcation exercise.

The United Nations supported the Government of Togo in addressing the political crisis arising from the sudden death of President Gnassingbé Eyadéma, and in taking measures to preserve stability in the country and in ensuring a peaceful transfer of power consistent with the Constitution and the rule of law. Peaceful and orderly elections were conducted in April. However, the political upheaval and incidents of violence that occurred before, during and after the elections, resulted in allegations of human rights violations. The United Nations High Commissioner for Human Rights dispatched a fact-finding mission to Togo to assess the situation. The Government indicated that it would examine the Commissioner's recommendations to prevent the cycles of violence and unrest that had often marred elections in Togo, and to redress the problems leading to such misconduct.

Regional issues

The Secretary-General noted that in 2005 West Africa presented a mixed picture. Several States were on the path to economic and democratic reforms; conflicts were less intense, with fewer people killed. Nonetheless, the subregion remained acutely vulnerable. Some conflicts showed little sign of abating; small arms and light weapons continued to proliferate; human rights abuses were perpetrated with impunity; youth unemployment was soaring; corruption was pervasive; rural exodus into urban areas was fueling explosive population growth in cities, undermining prospects for per capita growth; and in many countries HIV/AIDS and other infectious diseases continued to spread.

Among the key organizations assisting in confronting the problems undermining the subregion's development and security was the 15-nation Economic Community of West African States (ECOWAS), with its growing capacity for economic integration and conflict management and prevention.

In his message [SG/SM/9862] to the ECOWAS summit early in the year (Accra, Ghana, 19 January), the Secretary-General cautioned that, despite positive developments in the subregion during the previous 12 months, daunting challenges lay ahead. He cited the adverse political and economic effects of the crisis in Côte d'Ivoire on much of West Africa; the situation in Guinea-Bissau and Liberia, which demanded sustained attention, especially with regard to security sector reform and the reintegration of former combatants into society; and lawlessness in certain border zones.

While encouraging development partners to explore ways of assisting ECOWAS to focus attention on security sector reform, the Secretary-General hoped ECOWAS would also continue the fight against corruption and impunity, consult more systematically with civil society organizations, and engage fully in discussions on the reform proposals contained in the report of the High-level Panel on Threats, Challenges and Change [YUN 2004, p. 54]. He said that ECOWAS needed to be reinforced further to give it real authority to deal with the problems facing the subregion and affirmed UN support in that effort.

UNOWA

The United Nations Office for West Africa (UNOWA), established by the Secretary-General in 2001 [YUN 2001, p. 162], was extended for three years from 1 January 2005 to 31 December 2007, on the recommendation of the Secretary-General [YUN 2004, p. 170] and with the concurrence of the Security Council [S/2004/858]. Headed by the Special Representative for West Africa, Ahmedou Ould-Abdallah (Mauritania) since 2002, UNOWA maintained its headquarters in Dakar, Senegal.

In keeping with his intention to strengthen UNOWA, the Secretary-General, on 11 January 2005 [S/2005/16], transmitted to the Council a copy of the enhanced mandate, which the Council took note of on 11 January [S/2005/17]. The functions entrusted to UNOWA under the mandate were to promote an integrated subregional approach and facilitate coordination and information exchange, with due regard to specific mandates of UN organizations, peacekeeping operations and peacebuilding support offices; liaise with and assist ECOWAS and the Mano River Union (see p. 228); perform good offices roles

and special assignments in conflict prevention and peacebuilding; report to UN Headquarters on key subregional developments; and execute additional tasks assigned by the Secretary-General and the Security Council, including support to the work of the Cameroon-Nigeria Mixed Commission (see p. 296) and follow-up of the relevant recommendations contained in the report of the 2004 Security Council mission to West Africa [YUN 2004, p. 169] and of the Council's recommendations on cross-border issues in the subregion [ibid., p. 167].

Activities

During the year, UNOWA held regular meetings with the heads of UN operations and political offices in West Africa to develop an integrated subregional approach to conflict prevention and management, and to promote peace, security and development in the subregion. It continued to monitor the crisis in Côte d'Ivoire in order to update the Council on developments, and convened regional meetings aimed at formulating basic principles and guidelines for a harmonized approach to disarmament, demobilization and reintegration in West Africa. It worked to develop a regional strategy to tackle the problem of youth unemployment and launched a study entitled "Youth Unemployment and Regional Insecurity in West Africa" on the eve of the Afrique-France Summit (Dakar, 1 December). It convened a meeting (Timbuktu, Mali, April) to devise an integrated strategy for stabilizing the Mauritania/Mali/Niger border cluster area. Joint UNOWA/ECOWAS activities included, among others, the ECOWAS workshop on lessons learned from peacekeeping operations (Accra, 10-11 February) and the development of the ECOWAS/EU/UNOWA Framework of Action for Peace and Security at the seventh EU/ECOWAS Ministerial Troika meeting (Luxembourg, 18 May).

Threats to peace and security

Report of Secretary-General (February). On 11 February [S/2005/86], the Secretary-General submitted a report on progress made towards the implementation of the Security Council's recommendations contained in presidential statement S/PRST/2004/7 [YUN 2004, p. 167] on ways to combat subregional and cross-border problems in West Africa and those made by its 2004 mission to West Africa [ibid., p. 169].

The report outlined steps taken or envisaged to develop an integrated and coordinated approach to conflict prevention. Through the collaborative efforts of UN entities, those steps included: regular liaison between the Special

Representative and other UN presences in the subregion to facilitate information exchange and analysis, devise integrated strategies to coordinate periodic meetings among the five UN peacekeeping and political missions in the subregion; and the UN Consolidated Inter-Agency Appeal for West Africa 2005 (see p. 999), which focused on alleviating the deterioration of human security, hence the ongoing close collaboration among the humanitarian, political and military actors. With UN support, the States in the Mano River basin—Guinea, Liberia and Sierra Leone—were reactivating the Mano River Union to enhance regular institutional cooperation among them and among the Union, the subregion and international partners; a reactivated Union would make possible the resumption of consultations among its members, particularly on ways to deal with mercenaries. ECOWAS and UNOWA concluded a cooperation agreement and a joint work programme on preventing unconstitutional seizure of power, and improving the capacity of ECOWAS in conflict prevention, crisis management and post-conflict prevention. ECOWAS and UNOWA would be working closely with the EU on many of those activities. A related action plan was under development. UNICEF received funding from the Humanitarian Aid Office of the European Commission for a subregional child protection project to reinforce the coordination of child protection initiatives in the subregion. UN entities had increasingly invited civil society organizations, particularly women's groups, to participate in the elaboration and implementation of action plans on cross-border issues and to undertake advocacy work, especially in remote areas. Through the efforts of a UNDP-funded civil society focal point within the ECOWAS secretariat, civil society organizations created the West Africa Civil Society Forum as an umbrella institution for regional integration, peace and security.

The report also outlined action taken to address cross-border issues in the following areas: combating the proliferation of small arms and light weapons; harmonization of disarmament, demobilization and reintegration, especially for child soldiers; finding durable solutions to the problem of refugees and displaced persons; security sector reform; and developing integrated strategies in sensitive border zones. The Programme for Coordination and Assistance for Security and Development was replaced by the ECOWAS Small Arms Control Programme to facilitate the conversion of the 1998 ECOWAS moratorium on the importation, exportation and manufacture of small arms and light weapons [YUN 1998, p. 537] into a legally binding instrument, build the capacity of national commissions and

assist them in developing national action plans. UN presences in West Africa undertook a major collaborative exercise on ways to harmonize the national programmes on disarmament, demobilization and reintegration and eliminate inconsistencies among them. Such a strategy should help reduce the cross-border movement of combatants and weapons and consolidate peace processes throughout the subregion. Workshops for UN peace missions and agencies and development partners in the subregion were held (Dakar, Senegal, May and August 2004) to identify key aspects in which cross-border collaboration and policy harmonization were deemed essential: child, foreign and female combatants; militia groups; disarmament, demobilization and reintegration in countries not at war but deeply affected by armed conflict in neighbouring countries; and the monetary component. A key objective was the repatriation of foreign child combatants to their countries of origin, a strategy which was the subject of a meeting (Dakar, June 2004) of UNICEF and child protection agencies. ECOWAS and UNHCR agreed on a series of joint activities on four main themes: addressing security issues in refugee camps; prevention-mitigation preparedness and response; reviewing ECOWAS treaties and protocols with a view to harmonizing refugee policies in West Africa; and addressing refugee, returnee and development issues. The Humanitarian Coordination Section of the United Nations Mission in Liberia (UNMIL) organized a workshop on property rights of returnees, with emphasis on protecting widows' rights to property, with the aim to minimizing property disputes that could threaten social peace and cohesion. The UN presences in West Africa, working closely with development partners, continued to support ECOWAS in its efforts to reform the security sector of its member States. Senior officers of the subregion's military and security forces, UN agencies, international development partners and West African civil society organizations held a meeting (Dakar, 22-23 November 2004) to develop a common understanding of security sector reform in the West African context and reviewed reform projects in areas of health, particularly HIV/AIDS in the armed and security forces; security forces and mismanagement in the administration of justice; and weakness in the fight against criminal activities. ECOWAS, in collaboration with the United Nations Office on Drugs and Crime, examined ways to improve its border control mechanisms by strengthening the flow of information among national law enforcement authorities, regional networking and cooperation in law enforcement issues. A joint initiative, known as "Integrated strategies for sensitive border areas in West Africa", headed by UNOWA and the Office for the Coordination of Humanitarian Affairs, and including concerned UN country teams and peace missions, ECOWAS, development partners and civil society groups in the region, was launched in October 2004 to address problems of West African border areas. Draft integrated strategies for four particular clusters were developed: Guinea/Cote d'Ivoire/Liberia/Sierra Leone; Mali/Burkina Faso/Côte d'Ivoire/Ghana; Mauritania/Mali/Niger; and Senegal/Gambia/Guinea-Bissau.

The Secretary-General noted the constructive partnership among the UN system, development partners and ECOWAS, as well as some Governments, civil society organizations and local communities in West Africa. He also noted the steps taken towards the development of truly collaborative arrangements for addressing cross-border problems. He called on ECOWAS and development partners to begin work on establishing a register of small arms. He pointed out that of special benefit to West Africa would be the recommendation of the 2004 High-level Panel on the establishment of a sizeable standing fund for peacebuilding that could be used to fund rehabilitation and reintegration programmes. The Secretary-General stressed that measures to reduce the high levels of youth unemployment were vital for rehabilitation, peacebuilding and development; that the 2005 consolidated appeals process for West Africa should underline the need to fund a regional humanitarian response strategy and development partners should fund the project proposals providing a range of cross-border support services; and that UNOWA, in consultation with its partners in West Africa, should produce, before the end of 2005, a regionally integrated programme for security sector reform with concrete projects that development partners could fund.

Security Council consideration. At its meeting on 25 February [meeting 5131], the Security Council considered the foregoing progress report of the Secretary-General, who said the report highlighted areas requiring immediate and longer-term actions; its recommendations were directed at a wide range of players, including the Council and other parts of the UN system, development partners, ECOWAS and civil society organizations, calling on all to practice prevention and to address at an early stage the root causes of conflict. He singled out ECOWAS efforts to address the complex challenges facing the subregion and drew attention to the growing cooperation among security agencies in cracking down on cross-border crime, as well as the efforts under way to protect children, to stem small-arms

flows and to involve civil society groups more regularly in peacebuilding and other initiatives.

The Special Representative of the Secretary-General and Head of UNOWA said that the Office would continue to facilitate coherent and integrated approaches to peacebuilding among UN entities in West Africa; strengthen its partnership with West African States and subregional organizations, especially with ECOWAS; carry out preventive diplomacy and early warning missions; and devise policy recommendations that provided a basis for effective crisis management. In partnership with West African Governments, civil society organizations, the private sector and other international actors, it would initiate outreach activities to address persistent and emerging challenges to peace and security.

To strengthen action within the framework of its mandate, UNOWA focused on three broad challenges: the institutional, which called for further strengthening of collaboration among the UN entities in West Africa; the methodological, which required prioritizing issues, areas and objectives; and the doctrinal, which called for concentrating on countries at war and strongly supporting those which were not at war but which remained fragile.

SECURITY COUNCIL ACTION

On 25 February [meeting 5131], following consultations among Security Council members, the President made statement **S/PRST/2005/9** on behalf of the Council:

The Security Council has carefully reviewed the progress report of the Secretary-General of 11 February 2005 on the implementation of the recommendations of the Council on cross-border and subregional problems in West Africa, and reaffirms the statement by its President of 25 March 2004.

The Council notes with appreciation the enhanced cooperation among the various United Nations political and peacekeeping missions in the subregion and looks forward to receiving the forthcoming report of the Secretary-General on inter-mission cooperation. The Council also welcomes the growing and constructive partnership between the United Nations system, the Economic Community of West African States, individual Member States, key bilateral and multilateral development partners, as well as civil society organizations, including women's organizations, aimed at addressing the many complex challenges confronting the West African subregion.

The Council reiterates its belief that action on cross-border and subregional issues should take place as part of a wider strategy of conflict prevention, crisis management and peacebuilding in the subregion. The Council thus also encourages the United Nations Office for West Africa further to promote an integrated and joint subregional approach with the Economic Community of West African States and the African Union, as well as with other key international partners and civil society organizations.

The Council welcomes the encouraging prospects for the reactivation of the Mano River Union and the resumption of dialogue among its member States, notably on ways to deal with mercenaries. It also welcomes initiatives taken by the Economic Community of West African States to establish a Small Arms Unit and to adopt a new Small Arms Control Programme and its ongoing efforts to transform the moratorium on the import, export and manufacture of small arms and light weapons, signed in Abuja on 31 October 1998, into a binding convention.

The Council welcomes the decision of the European Commission on 2 December 2004 to assist the Economic Community of West African States in implementing its plans to combat the illicit dissemination of small arms. The Council reiterates its call upon all Member States and organizations, in a position to do so, to extend further assistance to the Economic Community of West African States in this field. The Council calls upon arms producing and exporting countries and West African States to explore ways in which they can ensure the implementation of the moratorium.

The Council calls upon Member States and key international partners to explore practical ways of assisting the Economic Community of West African States in enhancing its capacities in the areas of conflict prevention, peacemaking and peacekeeping, including through the provision of technical expertise, training programmes, and logistical and financial resources. In this connection, the Council reaffirms the crucial importance of the reintegration of ex-combatants, taking into account the special needs of child soldiers and women, in order to reverse the culture of violence and create an enabling environment for national reconciliation in countries emerging from conflict, and reiterates its call to the international community to provide adequate funding to this end.

The Council underlines the fact that ongoing or emerging crises in West Africa are a threat to subregional stability, and, in this regard, notes with deep concern the emerging and ongoing tensions in some countries over the transfer of power, involving members of security and armed forces, and which may further obstruct efforts to stabilize the subregion.

The Council recalls in this regard the African Union position on unconstitutional changes of governments, as stated in the 1999 Algiers Declaration and the 2000 Lomé Declaration.

The Council welcomes the action taken by the Economic Community of West African States and the African Union to address these issues.

The Council expresses its deep concern about the involvement of individuals including those from security and armed forces in such illicit activities as smuggling of arms, drugs and natural resources, human trafficking, extortion at roadblocks and money laundering, in the context of mismanagement in the administration of justice, and weak government capacity to fight against criminal activities and impunity. The Council stresses the need to pay special attention to those critical issues that have a direct bearing on efforts to enhance peace, stability and democratic governance in West African countries.

The Council emphasizes the need to pursue security sector reforms aiming at improving civil-military relations in countries emerging from conflict situations and creating a culture of peace and stability and promoting the rule of law. In this regard, the Council requests the United Nations Office for West Africa to further explore with interested governments and organizations ways in which security sector reforms could be formulated and implemented.

In this regard, the Council welcomes the ongoing efforts of the Economic Community of West African States, in collaboration with the United Nations Office on Drugs and Crime, to improve border control mechanisms in West Africa by facilitating the flow of information among national law enforcement authorities, as well as regional networking and cooperation in law enforcement issues.

The Council reiterates the importance of curbing the growing risks of instability along some border areas. The Council, therefore, encourages the United Nations Office for West Africa to facilitate, in close cooperation with the Executive Secretariat of the Economic Community of West African States and its member States concerned, the implementation of strategies developed for sensitive border zones in the subregion, and calls upon donors to support these efforts.

The Council stresses the need to help West African States to curb illicit cross-border activities and to strengthen the capacities of the civil society groups working to promote a cross-border culture of non-violence and peace.

The Council further emphasizes the need to generate economic activities and to foster development as a means of promoting sustainable peace in the subregion. It urges international donors to assist the Economic Community of West African States to address that need.

The Council reaffirms the urgency of finding lasting solutions to the problem of youth unemployment in order to prevent the recruitment of such youth by illegal armed groups. In this connection, the Council requests the Secretary-General to include in his next progress report practical recommendations on how best to tackle the problem of youth unemployment.

The Council urges donor countries, international organizations and civil society to address the dire humanitarian situation in many parts of the subregion and to provide adequate resources within the framework of the consolidated appeals process 2005 for West Africa as part of a regional humanitarian response strategy to improve the human security of the people in dire need of protection or those whose coping capacities are close to exhaustion.

The Council expresses its intention to keep these issues under review, and requests the Secretary-General to report on them regularly through his reports on the United Nations missions in the subregion.

Mano River Union. At a special summit of the Mano River Union, comprising Guinea, Liberia and Sierra Leone (Freetown, Sierra Leone, 28 July), the Heads of State and Government of the member countries considered security issues within the Mano River basin and the revival of the Union's secretariat. They reaffirmed their commitments to support initiatives promoting confidence-building measures along border areas and strengthening security in the sub-region and to pursue a peaceful solution to the border issue along the Makona-Moa River in conformity with the 2004 memorandum or understanding signed in Conakry, Guinea [YUN 2004, p. 217], stipulating that the village of Yenga belonged to Sierra Leone and the Makona-Moa River to Guinea, as contained in the Anglo-French Treaty of 1912 and renewed by the 1974 Agreement between Sierra Leone and Guinea. They affirmed that the agreement should be concretized by the demarcation of the border areas by experts from both countries and begin in August. They appealed to the United Nations and the international community, including the EU, to provide assistance for the reactivation of the Union's secretariat.

Inter-mission cooperation in West Africa

Report of Secretary-General (March). In his March report [S/2005/135] on inter-mission cooperation among the United Nations Mission in Sierra Leone (UNAMSIL), the United Nations Mission in Liberia (UNMIL) and the United Nations Operation in Côte d'Ivoire (UNOCI), the Secretary-General noted that the presence of those three peacekeeping missions, under the aegis of UNOWA, provided an opportunity to pursue a coordinated subregional approach to addressing a number of linked key issues at the national and subregional levels.

The Secretary-General, in addition to describing ongoing inter-mission cooperation activities among UNAMSIL, UNMIL and UNOCI, presented recommendations on potential areas for future cooperation. Among them were: information sharing and joint strategy formulation to support the peace processes in Côte d'Ivoire, Liberia and Sierra Leone, together with the establishment of fully functional and inclusive joint mission analysis cells for effective information management; cross-border military operations, including "hot pursuit" operations, joint air patrolling, shared routine cross-border patrolling and periodic patrol visits at border crossing checkpoints, extended areas of border responsibility, prearranged coordinated military operations, and the possible establishment of an operational-level subregional reserve force capable of rapid deployment, with a command and control centre;

sharing of experiences in planning, harmonizing and implementing disarmament, demobilization and reintegration programmes, and working closely with Governments and partners to support the repatriation of foreign ex-combatants, including women and children formerly associated with armed forces; sharing of information on combating the proliferation of small arms and light weapons, including on types and country of origin of weapons collected, arms flows and small arms and light weapons control programmes in each mission area; and sharing of technical expertise among the missions' civilian police operations on cross-border issues (trafficking in natural resources, arms and drugs) and drawing on expertise of international or subregional police mechanisms.

Other suggested areas of cooperation were in human rights, child protection, humanitarian assistance, civil affairs, the rule of law, public information and administration and logistics.

The Secretary-General pointed out that to conduct some of the inter-mission operations identified above, the Security Council would need to adjust the mandates of the individual missions. That entailed addressing a number of political and legal considerations: the consent of Governments in which the missions were deployed; agreement of troop-contributing countries for the use of their troops and equipment in more than one mission area, with consequent adjustments to the related memorandums of understanding; and arrangements for the extension of the protection, privileges and immunities, exemptions and facilities in the mission's respective status-of-forces agreements to UN personnel and property from other missions that might be deployed in the State concerned as part of inter-mission operations. Also to be addressed were financial and staffing constraints, changes to the budgetary process and estimates, and coordination with UN Headquarters on the subregional reallocation of assets so as to keep in line with global peacekeeping priorities and requirements.

The Secretary-General observed that, while the above agenda would require persistent effort, its benefits would stretch beyond West Africa as similar principles of inter-mission cooperation could be applied wherever there were other contiguous UN presences.

Côte d'Ivoire

In 2005, the United Nations, the Economic Community of West African States (ECOWAS), the African Union (AU) and the international community continued efforts to move Côte d'Ivoire's peace process forward through the implementation of the 2003 Linas-Marcoussis Agreement [YUN 2003, p. 166] and the 2004 Accra III Agreement [YUN 2004, p. 182]. A Zone of Confidence separated troops belonging to the National Armed Forces of Côte d'Ivoire (FANCI), deployed in the Government, controlled south of the country, and those of the Forces nouvelles, deployed in the rebel-controlled north. The main responsibility for peacekeeping rested with the Licorne (French forces), whose deployment was endorsed by the Security Council in resolution 1464(2003) [ibid., p. 168]. Those efforts were supported by the United Nations Operation in Côte d'Ivoire, established by the Council in resolution 1528(2004) [YUN 2004, p. 173] to, among other things, monitor the May 2003 ceasefire and movements of armed groups, assist in the disarmament, demobilization, reintegration and repatriation and resettlement of ex-combatants and support humanitarian assistance and implementation of the peace process. The Mission was headed by the Special Representative of the Secretary-General. In June, the Council authorized an increase in UNOCI's military strength by 850 troops, bringing the Mission's military strength to just over 7,090. It also raised the number of UN police officers to 725.

During the year, the ceasefire monitored by UNOCI and the French Licorne forces continued to hold, with no major violations of the UN-imposed arms embargo. However, the target dates by which combatants were to be disarmed, demobilized and reintegrated into society were not met, nor was the 30 October deadline for the holding of presidential elections. In an effort to break the political stalemate, the Ivorian parties, at a meeting convened in April by the AU Mediator, South African President Thabo Mbeki, signed the Pretoria Agreement, which addressed a number of contentious issues on elections and disarmament. Under the accord, the two sides agreed not to veto the presidential candidates put forward by the signatories of the 2003 Linas-Marcoussis Agreement. It also allowed both former rebel and Government forces to withdraw heavy weapons from the frontline on each side of the Zone of Confidence. However, in June, the Forces nouvelles announced that it would not disarm until pro-Government militias laid down their weapons, thus delaying the peace process.

By September, it had become clear that elections could not be held by the end of October as scheduled. Combatants had not disarmed; the registration of voters had been delayed; and the country was still divided. As the deadline approached, new disagreements emerged over the work and composition of the Independent Electoral Commission. With a missed electoral dead-

line, leaders of ECOWAS and the AU agreed to extend President Laurent Gbagbo's term of office for a year. Significant powers would be entrusted to a Prime Minister who would oversee a power-sharing government and the transition to fresh elections by October 2006. ECOWAS and the AU also created two new bodies, the International Working Group and a Mediation Group, to oversee the peace process; both bodies were co-chaired by the UN Special Representative in Côte d'Ivoire. The Security Council endorsed those decisions in October.

In early December, the AU Chairperson, President Olusegun Obasanjo of Nigeria, the Chairperson of ECOWAS, President Mamadou Tandja of Niger, and the AU Mediator, President Mbeki, brokered the appointment of Charles Konan Banny, the Governor of the Central Bank for West African States, as the new Prime Minister.

In the latter months of 2005, a number of senior UN officials visited Côte d'Ivoire, including the Chairman of the UN Sanctions Committee on Côte d'Ivoire, who warned leaders that sanctions would be imposed against anyone obstructing the peace process. Despite setbacks in the Ivorian peace process in 2005, optimism remained that Côte d'Ivoire's new road map, drawn up by the International Working Group, would move the country out of the current impasse of no-war-no-peace and result in the disarmament of combatants, dismantlement of militias, restoration of State authority throughout the country, and, ultimately, to the holding of national elections by October 2006.

Political and security developments

Communications. On 10 January [S/2005/29], the AU Peace and Security Council, in a communiqué issued at its twenty-third meeting (Libreville, Gabon), endorsed the plan [YUN 2004, p. 189] submitted by the AU Mediator, South African President Thabo Mbeki, to help Côte d'Ivoire emerge from the crisis (the December 2004 road map), which called for the adoption of all the texts emanating from the Linas-Marcoussis Agreement, the implementation of the disarmament, demobilization and reintegration programme, the effective functioning of the Government of National Reconciliation, and the establishment throughout the national territory of a climate conducive to the restoration of peace and security in the country. It renewed President Mbeki's mandate and urged the Ivorian parties to cooperate with him and honour the commitments made within the framework of the December 2004 road map.

On 13 January [S/2005/28], Côte d'Ivoire transmitted to the UN Security Council President a progress report "Moving the peace process forward: an update on the implementation of the December 2004 road map", outlining action it had taken in respect of the legislative programme, the disarmament, demobilization and reinsertion programme, efforts to create a climate conducive to free political activity, the functioning of the Government of National Reconciliation and the restoration of social services and redeployment of Government administration in the whole territory.

In another letter of the same date [S/2005/27], Côte d'Ivoire informed the Council President that it did not want France to initiate the Council's resolutions and declarations concerning Côte d'Ivoire, given the bias of the French force (Operation Licorne) in destroying all of the country's military aircraft and bombarding its presidential palaces in November 2004 [YUN 2004, p. 186]. It also wanted the French forces to be integrated into UNOCI.

In separate letters of 26 January [S/2005/55, A/59/693] addressed to the Council and the General Assembly, Côte d'Ivoire expressed concern over the tone of the opposition press. The priority should be to foster a return to dialogue, allay tensions and avoid the spread of false information.

Report of Secretary-General. The Secretary-General, in his fourth progress report on UNOCI [S/2005/186], highlighted major developments in the peace process at the beginning of the year. He said that much of the focus was on the efforts of President Thabo Mbeki, who led an AU mediation initiative, in January, in close cooperation with the United Nations and ECOWAS. Several rounds of consultations took place in Côte d'Ivoire and Pretoria, South Africa, with the Ivorian parties, including President Laurent Gbagbo, Prime Minister Seydou Diarra, the Secretary-General of the Forces nouvelles, Guillaume Soro, senior Government officials and opposition party leaders, focusing on how to advance the plan of action (see above) agreed upon by the Ivorian parties during President Mbeki's visit to Côte d'Ivoire in December 2004 [YUN 2004, p. 187]. Other interrelated issues dealt with the enactment of legislative reforms envisaged in the Linas-Marcoussis Agreement and ensuring the effective functioning of the Government of National Reconciliation.

In other developments, the Government extended until 11 June the ban on street marches and demonstrations in Abidjan, instituted in December 2004 [ibid., p. 190]. The Forces nouvelles, whose ministers had not participated in the Government since the November 2004 crisis [ibid., p. 185] indicated, in discussions with the AU mediation team, UNOCI and the Licorne forces, its wish to be allowed to bring their own close protection units to Abidjan. The effective functioning of the Government was also affected by a lack of clarity regarding the delegation of powers from the President to the Prime Minister and other ministers. The absence of civil servants remained a major contributing factor to the continued deterioration in the humanitarian situation, particularly in the north. Meanwhile, UNOCI continued to support efforts for the redeployment of State administration, which needed some $506 million to facilitate the return of civil servants and other Government personnel to their respective areas of responsibility.

On 18 January, the Forces nouvelles and FANCI resumed cooperation with the National Commission for Disarmament, Demobilization and Reintegration, which reported that an estimated 10,000 militia members still remained active in Côte d'Ivoire, and their growing numbers continued to be a major cause of concern. However, the Forces nouvelles efforts to formalize the national disarmament, demobilization and reintegration plan, which included the restructuring of FANCI, were derailed when it was attacked by militias at its checkpoint at Logoualé on 28 February.

Concerning the holding of elections, Prime Minister Seydou Diarra had sought to reactivate the national identification exercise in an effort to move the election preparations forward. The Independent Electoral Commission, on 8 February, adopted its programme of work, but the G-7 group of opposition political parties rejected the legislation revising the Commission's structure and composition as not being in conformity with the Linas-Marcoussis Agreement. The law establishing the Commission was challenged in court, as a result of which its main activities had to be suspended. On 18 February, several political parties expressed their wish that the United Nations organize the Ivorian elections. The Secretary-General, while expressing concern over the protracted delays in the organization and preparation of the presidential and legislative elections, stated that the request for an enhanced UN role in the electoral process had to be agreed upon to by all Ivorian parties.

The security situation remained tense, with a marked increase in criminality, especially in Abidjan and the Zone of Confidence. In the light of the volatile security situation, the Secretary-General recommended that UNOCI's mandate be extended for a period of 12 months, until 4 April 2006.

Security Council consideration. The Security Council was briefed on 28 March [meeting 5152] on the situation in Côte d'Ivoire by the Deputy Special Representative, Alan Doss (United Kingdom), who stated that the December 2004 road map remained largely unachieved. The Government of National Reconciliation remained bereft of Forces nouvelles ministers and the military dialogue had been interrupted, delaying the disarmament, demobilization and reintegration process.

In February, the Forces nouvelles reorganized the areas under their control, creating five new territorial entities under the command of new warlords. At the same time, its Secretary-General, Guillaume Soro, announced the opening of a new police and customs academy, as well as a new bank in Bouaké, actions that, even though they did not indicate an immediate intention to secede, revealed that they saw the crisis as one of long duration. In the absence of judicial authority in the Zone of Confidence, UNOCI proposed that the national authorities take exceptional measures to fill the gap, including the nomination of temporary administrators and the reactivation of the joint brigade composed of impartial forces, national forces and Forces nouvelles to patrol and combat rising crime in the Zone. Forces nouvelles had yet to accept the proposal because of suspicion that the central power would seek to establish itself in the Zone through that mechanism. UNOCI, supported by the Licorne forces, remained vigilant in the Zone, amid rising tensions.

On behalf of the AU Mediation Mission in Côte d'Ivoire, the South African Deputy Foreign Minister, Aziz Pahad, said that, to resolve the outstanding challenges with regard to the implementation of the road map and to ensure lasting peace in Côte d'Ivoire, a meeting between President Mbeki and the country's principal political leaders was planned for 3 April in South Africa (see p. 232). The AU mediation would report to the UN Security Council about the outcome. Meanwhile, an AU mediation legal team visited Côte d'Ivoire and had extensive interactions with the parties to determine the compliance of adopted legislation with the Linas-Marcoussis Agreement. The team confirmed that significant progress had been made in that regard, although there were differences among the parties on the appropriate legislative texts, mainly related to the interpretation of the Linas-Marcoussis Agreement, rather than a reluctance to implement it. There were areas where the Agreement was not in line with international practice. The findings were largely received by the parties.

The representative of Côte d'Ivoire complained that the Secretary-General's report showed considerable sympathy for the point of view of Forces nouvelles, the former rebels and opposition parties, while that of the legitimate authorities was systematically called into question. That risked giving comfort to the former rebels in their intention to change the country's institutions by violence and encourage other rebellions in the subregion.

SECURITY COUNCIL ACTION

On 4 April [meeting 5159], the Security Council unanimously adopted **resolution 1594(2005)**. The draft [S/2005/221] was prepared in consultations among Council members.

The Security Council,

Recalling its resolutions 1528(2004) of 27 February 2004, 1572(2004) of 15 November 2004 and 1584(2005) of 1 February 2005, as well as the relevant statements by its President, in particular those of 6 November and 16 December 2004,

Reaffirming its strong commitment to the sovereignty, independence, territorial integrity and unity of Côte d'Ivoire, and recalling the importance of the principles of good-neighbourliness, non-interference and regional cooperation,

Recalling that it endorsed the agreement signed by the Ivorian political forces at Linas-Marcoussis, France, on 23 January 2003 (the Linas-Marcoussis Agreement) and approved by the Conference of Heads of State on Côte d'Ivoire, held in Paris on 25 and 26 January 2003, and the agreement signed at Accra on 30 July 2004 (the Accra III Agreement),

Welcoming the efforts of the Secretary-General, the African Union and the Economic Community of West African States towards re-establishing peace and stability in Côte d'Ivoire, and reaffirming in this regard its full support to the ongoing facilitation mission undertaken by the President of the Republic of South Africa, Mr. Thabo Mbeki, on behalf of the African Union,

Taking note of the report of the Secretary-General of 18 March 2005,

Determining that the situation in Côte d'Ivoire continues to pose a threat to international peace and security in the region,

Acting under Chapter VII of the Charter of the United Nations,

1. *Decides* that the mandate of the United Nations Operation in Côte d'Ivoire and of the French forces supporting it shall be extended for a period of one month, until 4 May 2005;

2. *Calls upon* all Ivorian parties immediately and actively to pursue a just and lasting solution to the current crisis, particularly through the African Union mediation led by President Thabo Mbeki;

3. *Decides* to remain actively seized of the matter.

Appointments. On 25 February [S/2005/133], the Secretary-General informed the Security Council of his intention to appoint Mr. Pierre Schori (Sweden) as his Special Representative and Head of UNOCI. On 2 March [S/2005/134], the Council took note of his intention.

The Pretoria Agreement

The AU mediation mission, led by South African President and Mediator, Thabo Mbeki, convened a meeting in Pretoria, South Africa from 3 to 6 April to discuss the December 2004 road map with President Laurent Gbagbo; Prime Minister Seydou Diarra; Henri Konan Bédié, President of the Democratic Party of Côte d'Ivoire; Alassane Ouattara, President of the Rally of Republicans; and Guillaume Soro, Secretary-General of the Forces nouvelles. The meeting resulted in the signing, on 6 April, of the Pretoria Agreement on the Peace Process in Côte d'Ivoire. The text of the Agreement, together with the Mediator's letter of determination on article 35 of the Constitution of Côte d'Ivoire addressed to the Ivorian leaders, were transmitted to the Security Council President by South Africa on 25 April [S/2005/270].

In the Agreement, the parties declared the immediate and final cessation of hostilities and the end of the war throughout the national territory; agreed to proceed with the disarmament and dismantling of militia throughout the country; that the Chiefs of Staff of FANCI and of the Armed Forces of the Forces nouvelles ensure the implementation of the National Disarmament, Demobilization and Reintegration Plan and make recommendations for the formation of one army; adopted a number of interim measures to guarantee the security of people and assets as soon as the cantonment of the Forces nouvelles in the North commenced; accepted the plan proposed by the AU mediation ensuring the security for the Forces nouvelles Ministers in the Government of National Reconciliation, including the return of the Forces nouvelles to the Government; reaffirmed the authority of the Prime Minister; agreed on amendments in the composition, organization and functioning of the Independent Electoral Commission; and mandated the Mediator to request UN assistance in organizing the elections. They also agreed to restore the status of the Ivorian Radio and Television (RTI) to that enjoyed prior to 24 December 2004, covering the whole country; and to finalize by 31 April, texts for the amendment of laws that were not in conformity with the Linas-Marcoussis Agreement. Agreement was also reached on the financing of political parties and national reconciliation. Concerning the eligibility of the Presidency in the upcoming elections, the Mediator undertook to make a determination on the matter (see below).

The Mediator, in his 25 April letter to the Ivorian parties with respect to the revision of article 35 of the Constitution relating to the eligibility of the Presidency, determined that, for the 2005 presidential elections, the Constitutional Council should accept the eligibility of the candidates who might be presented by the political parties that were signatories to the Linas-Marcoussis Agreement and requested President Gbagbo, under the powers granted to him by article 48 of the Constitution to give legal force to that determination.

SECURITY COUNCIL ACTION

On 4 May [meeting 5173], the Security Council unanimously adopted **resolution 1600(2005)**. The draft [S/2005/282] was prepared in consultations among Council members.

The Security Council,

Recalling its resolutions 1528(2004) of 27 February 2004, 1572(2004) of 15 November 2004, 1584(2005) of 1 February 2005 and 1594(2005) of 4 April 2005, as well as the relevant statements by its President, in particular those of 6 November and 16 December 2004,

Reaffirming its strong commitment to the sovereignty, independence, territorial integrity and unity of Côte d'Ivoire, and recalling the importance of the principles of good-neighbourliness, non-interference and regional cooperation,

Recalling that it endorsed the agreement signed by the Ivorian political forces at Linas-Marcoussis, France, on 23 January 2003 (the Linas-Marcoussis Agreement) and approved by the Conference of Heads of State on Côte d'Ivoire, held in Paris on 25 and 26 January 2003, and the agreement signed at Accra on 30 July 2004 (the Accra III Agreement),

Welcoming the efforts of the Secretary-General, the African Union and the Economic Community of West African States towards re-establishing peace and stability in Côte d'Ivoire, and reaffirming in this regard its full support to the ongoing facilitation mission undertaken by the President of the Republic of South Africa, Mr. Thabo Mbeki, on behalf of the African Union,

Determining that the situation in Côte d'Ivoire continues to pose a threat to international peace and security in the region,

Acting under Chapter VII of the Charter of the United Nations,

1. *Welcomes* the signing by the Ivorian parties at Pretoria on 6 April 2005 of the agreement on the peace process in Côte d'Ivoire (the Pretoria Agreement), under the auspices of the President of South Africa, Mr. Thabo Mbeki, commends President Mbeki for the essential role he has played, on behalf of the African Union, to restore peace and stability in Côte d'Ivoire, and reaffirms its full support for his mediation efforts;

2. *Calls* on all parties to implement fully the Pretoria Agreement and reminds them that they have decided in the Agreement to refer to the mediator, President Thabo Mbeki, any differences which may arise in the interpretation of any part of the Agreement;

3. *Welcomes* further the decision taken by President Thabo Mbeki with regard to eligibility for the Presidency of the Republic, as described in his letter dated 11 April 2005 to Mr. Laurent Gbagbo, President of the Republic of Côte d'Ivoire, and takes note with satisfaction of the announcement made by President Gbagbo on 26 April 2005 that all candidates nominated by the

political parties signatory to the Linas-Marcoussis Agreement would be eligible for the Presidency;

4. *Urges* all the Ivorian parties to take all necessary steps to ensure that the forthcoming general elections are free, fair and transparent;

5. *Decides* that the mandate of the United Nations Operation in Côte d'Ivoire and of the French forces supporting it shall be extended for a period of one month, until 4 June 2005;

6. *Decides also* to remain actively seized of the matter.

On 23 May [S/2005/340], President Mbeki, in his capacity as the Mediator for the peace process in Côte d'Ivoire, expressed the hope that the Council would agree on the appointment of a competent authority to oversee the upcoming elections and that the United Nations would assist the Ivorian people in its organization.

On 3 June [meeting 5194], the Security Council unanimously adopted **resolution 1603(2005).** The draft [S/2005/359] was prepared in consultations among Council members.

The Security Council,

Recalling its previous resolutions and the statements by its President relating to the situation in Côte d'Ivoire,

Reaffirming its strong commitment to the sovereignty, independence, territorial integrity and unity of Côte d'Ivoire, and recalling the importance of the principles of good-neighbourliness, non-interference and regional cooperation,

Recalling that it endorsed the agreement signed by the Ivorian political forces at Linas-Marcoussis, France, on 23 January 2003 (the Linas-Marcoussis Agreement) and approved by the Conference of Heads of State on Côte d'Ivoire, held in Paris on 25 and 26 January 2003, and the agreement signed at Accra on 30 July 2004 (the Accra III Agreement),

Welcoming the efforts of the Secretary-General, the African Union and the Economic Community of West African States towards re-establishing peace and stability in Côte d'Ivoire,

Welcoming in particular the mediation efforts undertaken by Mr. Thabo Mbeki, President of the Republic of South Africa, on behalf of the African Union, and reaffirming its full support for him,

Welcoming the signing by the Ivorian parties at Pretoria on 6 April 2005 of the agreement on the peace process in Côte d'Ivoire (the Pretoria Agreement), under the auspices of President Thabo Mbeki, and expressing its satisfaction with the first steps which have been undertaken by the Ivorian parties in order to implement the Agreement, in particular with the agreement on the disarmament, demobilization and reintegration process reached on 14 May 2005 and the restoration of the status of the Ivorian Radio and Television to that which it enjoyed before 24 December 2004,

Reaffirming its resolution 1325(2000) of 31 October 2000 on women and peace and security, its resolutions 1379(2001) of 20 November 2001 and 1460(2003) of 30 January 2003 on children and armed conflict, as well as its resolutions 1265(1999) of 17 September 1999 and 1296(2000) of 19 April 2000 on the protection of civilians in armed conflict,

Expressing grave concern at the allegations of misconduct of some peacekeeping troops deployed in African countries, including sexual exploitation, affirming that these troops should comply with their code of conduct, and reaffirming that there will be a zero tolerance policy of any misconduct or sexual exploitation in all peacekeeping troops,

Having taken note of the report of the Secretary-General of 18 March 2005,

Having taken note also of the letter dated 23 May 2005 from the Permanent Representative of South Africa to the United Nations addressed to the President of the Security Council,

Expressing its concern at the continued deterioration of the security and humanitarian situation, in particular in the west of the country,

Determining that the situation in Côte d'Ivoire continues to pose a threat to international peace and security in the region,

Acting under Chapter VII of the Charter of the United Nations,

1. *Endorses* the Pretoria Agreement, and demands that all the signatories to the Agreement and all the Ivorian parties concerned implement it fully and without delay;

2. *Stresses*, in this regard, that non-respect, by the signatories to the Pretoria Agreement, or by any other Ivorian party concerned, of any of the commitments made in Pretoria in the presence of the President of South Africa, Mr. Thabo Mbeki, would endanger the peace process in Côte d'Ivoire and would constitute an obstacle to the implementation of the Linas-Marcoussis Agreement and the Accra III Agreement, and therefore reaffirms its readiness to implement paragraphs 9 and 11 of its resolution 1572(2004) of 15 November 2004 if the parties fail to meet their commitments under the Linas-Marcoussis and Pretoria Agreements;

3. *Commends* President Thabo Mbeki for the essential role he has played, on behalf of the African Union, to restore peace and stability in Côte d'Ivoire, reaffirms its full support for his mediation efforts, reminds the signatories to the Pretoria Agreement that, in the event of differences in the interpretation of all or part of the Agreement, they should seek a ruling from President Mbeki, and encourages the Secretary-General, President Mbeki and the African Union to continue to collaborate closely in the implementation of the Agreement;

4. *Takes note with satisfaction* of the provisions of the Pretoria Agreement reaffirming the determination of the signatories to the Agreement regarding the need to organize presidential elections in October 2005 and legislative elections following immediately thereafter, as well as their agreement to invite the United Nations to participate in the work of the Independent Electoral Commission and the Constitutional Council and in the organization of the general elections, and of the decision by the Council of Ministers on 28 April 2005 to hold the first round of the presidential elections on 30 October 2005;

5. *Welcomes* the decision taken by President Thabo Mbeki with regard to eligibility for the Presidency of the Republic, as described in his letter dated 11 April

2005 to Mr. Laurent Gbagbo, President of the Republic of Côte d'Ivoire, and takes note with satisfaction of the announcement made by President Gbagbo on 26 April 2005 that all candidates nominated by the political parties signatory to the Linas-Marcoussis Agreement would be eligible for the presidential elections;

6. *Demands* that all the Ivorian parties take all necessary steps to ensure that the forthcoming general elections are free, fair and transparent;

7. *Requests* the Secretary-General, on the basis of the Pretoria Agreement, to designate, as an exceptional arrangement, after consultations with the African Union and President Thabo Mbeki, a High Representative for the elections in Côte d'Ivoire, autonomous from the United Nations Operation in Côte d'Ivoire, to assist in particular in the work of the Independent Electoral Commission and the Constitutional Council, without prejudice to the responsibilities of the Special Representative of the Secretary-General for Côte d'Ivoire and with the following mandate:

(a) To verify, on behalf of the international community, that all stages of the electoral process, including the establishment of a register of voters and the issuance of voters' cards, provide all the necessary guarantees for the holding of open, free, fair and transparent presidential and legislative elections within the time limits laid down in the Constitution of the Republic of Côte d'Ivoire;

(b) To provide, in close cooperation with the United Nations Operation in Côte d'Ivoire and the mediation, all necessary advice and guidance to the Constitutional Council, the Independent Electoral Commission and other relevant agencies or institutions to help them to prevent and resolve any difficulty which may jeopardize the holding of open, free, fair and transparent elections within the time limits laid down in the Constitution, with the authority to make necessary determinations in this regard;

(c) To report immediately to the Security Council through the Secretary-General, and to inform the mediator of the African Union, President Thabo Mbeki, of any difficulty which may jeopardize the holding of open, free, fair and transparent elections, and to submit to them, as appropriate, such recommendations as he may see fit to make;

(d) To keep the Council, through the Secretary-General, and President Thabo Mbeki regularly informed of all aspects of his mandate;

(e) To request and receive information and technical advice from the United Nations Operation in Côte d'Ivoire as well as from other sources;

8. *Decides* that the mandate of the High Representative as referred to in paragraph 7 above will end after the forthcoming general elections in Côte d'Ivoire;

9. *Calls upon* the donor community to provide all the necessary financial resources to the High Representative to support the full implementation of his mission;

10. *Takes note* of the agreement on the disarmament, demobilization and reintegration process and on the restructuring of the armed forces signed at Yamoussoukro on 14 May 2005 by the chiefs of staff of the National Armed Forces of Côte d'Ivoire and the armed forces of the Forces nouvelles, demands that the parties implement fully this agreement so that the disarmament, demobilization and reintegration process

can start without delay, reaffirms in this regard paragraphs 9 and 11 of its resolution 1572(2004), reaffirms also paragraph 8 of its resolution 1584(2005) of 1 February 2005 regarding the establishment of a comprehensive list of armaments in their possession, and demands the immediate disarmament and dismantling of militias throughout the national territory;

11. *Decides* that the mandate of the United Nations Operation in Côte d'Ivoire and of the French forces supporting it shall be extended until 24 June 2005, with a view to renewing it, in this specific instance, for a period of seven months;

12. *Authorizes* the Secretary-General to begin the necessary planning and preparations, including troop and police generation as well as required support and other arrangements, to facilitate a timely deployment in the event that the Council decides to increase the authorized strength of troops and police for the United Nations Operation in Côte d'Ivoire and to adjust its mandate;

13. *Underlines* the importance of mainstreaming the gender perspective in peacekeeping operations and post-conflict peacebuilding and of appropriate expertise in this regard, and encourages the United Nations Operation in Côte d'Ivoire to actively address this issue;

14. *Urges* donors and international financial institutions to provide the necessary support to the implementation of the Pretoria Agreement, in particular the disarmament, demobilization and reintegration programme and the electoral process, through the expeditious allocation of financial resources;

15. *Calls upon* all parties to cooperate fully in the deployment and operations of the United Nations Operation in Côte d'Ivoire, in particular by guaranteeing the safety, security and freedom of movement of United Nations personnel as well as associated personnel throughout the territory of Côte d'Ivoire;

16. *Welcomes* the efforts undertaken by the United Nations Operation in Côte d'Ivoire to implement the Secretary-General's zero tolerance policy on sexual exploitation and to ensure full compliance of its personnel with the United Nations code of conduct, requests the Secretary-General to continue to take all necessary action in this regard and to keep the Council informed, and urges troop-contributing countries to take appropriate preventive action, including conducting predeployment awareness training, and to take disciplinary action and other action to ensure full accountability in cases of such conduct involving their personnel;

17. *Requests* the Secretary-General to continue to keep the Council regularly informed of the developments in the situation in Côte d'Ivoire, the implementation of the mandate of the United Nations Operation in Côte d'Ivoire and of the Linas-Marcoussis and Pretoria Agreements, and to report to it in this regard every three months;

18. *Requests* France to continue to report to the Council periodically on all aspects of its mandate in Côte d'Ivoire;

19. *Invites* the African Union to keep the Council regularly informed of the implementation of the provisions of the Pretoria Agreement and to make recommendations to the Council as it deems necessary;

20. *Expresses its full support* to the Special Representative of the Secretary-General for Côte d'Ivoire;

21. *Decides* to remain actively seized of the matter.

On 19 July, the Secretary-General informed the Council of his intention to appoint Ambassador António Monteiro (Portugal) to the post of High Representative for the elections in Côte d'Ivoire, which the Council noted on 22 July [S/2005/486, S/2005/487].

Implementation of the Pretoria Agreement

Report of Secretary-General. In his fifth report on UNOCI [S/2005/398 & Add.1], issued in June, the Secretary-General stated that the momentum gained in the peace process following the signing of the Pretoria Agreement had slowed as only limited progress was made towards its implementation. As a result of the Agreement, FANCI and the Forces nouvelles, meeting in Bouaké from 14 to 16 April, issued a communiqué indicating that a seminar would be held in Yamoussoukro on the national disarmament, demobilization and reintegration programme and the restructuring of the armed forces. Following a meeting (Daoukro, 19 April) of the Quadripartite Commission (comprising FANCI, the Forces nouvelles, UNOCI and the Licorne forces), FANCI and the Forces nouvelles withdrew their heavy weapons from the boundaries of the Zone of Confidence between 21 and 24 April to agreed locations.

As follow-up to the resolution of the question of eligibility for the presidential elections, President Gbagbo consulted with national stakeholders on the issue, and on 26 April declared that all candidates nominated by the political parties would be allowed to participate in the elections. He also announced, under the same special powers granted to him by the Pretoria Agreement, that the production of voters' lists and registration cards would be the sole responsibility of the National Institute of Statistics, a decision that was strongly criticized by the opposition parties, who objected to such use of those powers as being outside those granted to him by the Agreement. On 20 May, Alassane Ouattara, President of the Rally of Republicans, and Henri Konan Bédié, President of the Democratic Party of Côte d'Ivoire, requested President Mbeki to make an additional determination on the issue.

Some progress was made in the revision of laws that were not in conformity with the Linas-Marcoussis Agreement, such as the law concerning the Independent Electoral Commission and the funding of political parties, but there were still divergent views within the Council of Ministers as to whether those laws should be amended. Prime Minister Diarra sought confirmation from President Mbeki on the need to revise other key pieces of legislation, including the nationality code and the laws on identification and land tenure.

On 14 May, the chiefs of staff of FANCI and the Forces nouvelles agreed on the timing and modalities of the national disarmament, demobilization and reintegration programme, which was to take place from 27 June to 10 August, and that a special commission should develop a plan for restructuring the armed forces by 26 September. The cost of the programme was estimated at $150 million. However, on 18 May, the Forces nouvelles indicated that they would not disarm, until a number of conditions had been met, including the disarmament and dismantling of militias and the adoption by the National Assembly of the amended law on the composition of the Independent Electoral Commission, the nationality code and the law on identification. It also insisted on adequate security guarantees during the process and that the requisite funding be secured before the start of the process. As to the disarmament and dismantling of the militias, while a symbolic handover of weapons by four of the main pro-Government militias operating in the west took place in Guiglo on 25 May, under the supervision of the chief of staff of FANCI, several of the militia members expressed a reluctance to disarm in the absence of adequate guarantees for their future. UNOCI was assisting the Prime Minister in developing a disarmament plan and was developing a training programme for the 600 Forces nouvelles members who would provide security in the north as soon as the cantonment of their forces began. On 28 April, President Gbagbo restored Ivorian Radio and Television to its original status and reinstated its board of directors.

In connection with the elections, an electoral review mission, led by the Electoral Assistance Division of the Department of Political Affairs, was deployed to Côte d'Ivoire from 20 May to 3 June to assess and review election preparations and make recommendations on further UN support. The mission found that the preparations for the elections had been subjected to delays and, unless the current slow pace of implementation was significantly increased, it would not be possible to meet the scheduled date of 30 October. Moreover, the Independent Electoral Commission did not enjoy the full support of all political actors, as the revised law on its composition had yet to be adopted. The situation was further compounded by the ambiguity surrounding the respective roles and responsibilities of the National Institute of Statistics and the Commission. As a result, preparing a budget for the electoral process was not possible and donors were reluctant to provide funds. On 18 April, in Paris, four opposition parties—the Rally of Republicans, the Democratic Party of Côte d'Ivoire, the Movement of Forces of the Future and the Union for Democracy and Peace in Côte d'Ivoire—created a common electoral platform known as the "Rally of Houphouëtistes for Democracy and Peace".

The continuing violence in the western part of Côte d'Ivoire remained a major cause for concern. Between 30 April and 2 May, 25 people were killed and 41 injured in Duékoué, Yrozon, Blody and Tao Zeo, and more than 9,000 were displaced. On 31 May, traditional hunters attacked the villages of Guetrozon and Petit Duékoué, killing some 41 people and injuring 61 others. It appeared that FANCI soldiers in Guetrozon did little to stop the initial attacks. On 1 June, UNOCI personnel helped the Ivorian Defence and Security Forces stabilize the situation. UNOCI reinforced its presence in and around Duékoué in support of those forces. To address the critical situation in the west, the Special Representative met with the Government to discuss ways to strengthen security in and around Duékoué, and on 8 June, he called on the Ivorian authorities to investigate the Duékoué attacks.

The Secretary-General observed that the maintenance of security nationwide was essential for the implementation of the Pretoria Agreement to proceed smoothly. The recent killings in the Duékoué area underscored the need to reinforce UNOCI urgently to prevent any further deterioration of the situation in the west. He therefore requested the Council to authorize the deployment of an additional 2,076 troops and three formed police units comprising 375 officers. The Secretary-General hoped that the additional troops would be redeployed throughout the country to provide support for the elections. He urged donor countries to give urgent consideration to the provision of the needed resources, in particular technical and financial assistance for the disarmament, demobilization and reintegration and electoral processes and also for the restoration of State authority. The United Nations would continue to work closely with the AU, ECOWAS and other key partners in support of the implementation of the key provisions of the Pretoria Agreement.

In a later addendum [S/2005/398/Add.1], the Secretary-General reported that the financial implications of the additional personnel for nine months would amount to $86.1 million.

SECURITY COUNCIL ACTION

On 24 June [meeting 5213], the Security Council unanimously adopted **resolution 1609(2005)**.

The draft [S/2005/405] was prepared in consultations among Council members.

The Security Council,

Recalling its previous resolutions and the statements by its President relating to the situation in Côte d'Ivoire,

Recalling also its resolution 1561(2004) of 17 September 2004 on the situation in Liberia and its resolution 1562(2004) of 17 September 2004 on the situation in Sierra Leone,

Reaffirming its strong commitment to the sovereignty, independence, territorial integrity and unity of Côte d'Ivoire, and recalling the importance of the principles of good-neighbourliness, non-interference and regional cooperation,

Recalling that it endorsed the agreement signed by the Ivorian political forces at Linas-Marcoussis, France, on 23 January 2003 (the Linas-Marcoussis Agreement) and approved by the Conference of Heads of State on Côte d'Ivoire, held in Paris on 25 and 26 January 2003, the agreement signed at Accra on 30 July 2004 (the Accra III Agreement) and the agreement signed at Pretoria on 6 April 2005 (the Pretoria Agreement),

Having taken note of the report of the Secretary-General of 17 June 2005 and of his report of 2 March 2005 on inter-mission cooperation and possible cross-border operations between the United Nations Mission in Sierra Leone, the United Nations Mission in Liberia and the United Nations Operation in Côte d'Ivoire,

Expressing its serious concern at the continued deterioration of the security and humanitarian situation, in particular after the tragic events that occurred in the west of the country,

Determining that the situation in Côte d'Ivoire continues to pose a threat to international peace and security in the region,

Acting under Chapter VII of the Charter of the United Nations,

1. *Decides* that the mandate of the United Nations Operation in Côte d'Ivoire and of the French forces supporting it shall be extended, in this specific instance, for a period of seven months, until 24 January 2006;

2. *Also decides* that the United Nations Operation in Côte d'Ivoire shall have the following mandate from the date of adoption of the present resolution:

Monitoring of the cessation of hostilities and movements of armed groups

(a) To observe and monitor the implementation of the joint declaration of the end of the war of 6 April 2005 and of the comprehensive ceasefire agreement of 3 May 2003, to prevent, within its capabilities and its areas of deployment, any hostile action, in particular within the Zone of Confidence, and to investigate violations of the ceasefire;

(b) To liaise with the National Armed Forces of Côte d'Ivoire and the military elements of the Forces nouvelles in order to promote, in coordination with the French forces, the re-establishment of trust among all the Ivorian forces involved;

(c) To assist the Government of National Reconciliation in monitoring the borders, with particular attention to the situation of Liberian refugees and to any cross-border movement of combatants;

Disarmament, demobilization, reintegration, repatriation and resettlement

(d) To assist the Government of National Reconciliation in undertaking the regrouping of all the Ivorian forces involved and to assist in ensuring the security of their disarmament, cantonment and demobilization sites;

(e) To support the Government of National Reconciliation in the implementation of the national programme for the disarmament, demobilization and reintegration of combatants, paying special attention to the specific needs of women and children;

(f) To coordinate closely with the United Nations missions in Sierra Leone and in Liberia in the implementation of a voluntary repatriation and resettlement programme for foreign ex-combatants, paying special attention to the specific needs of women and children, in support of the efforts of the Government of National Reconciliation and in cooperation with the Governments concerned, relevant international financial institutions, international development organizations and donor nations;

(g) To ensure that the programmes mentioned in subparagraphs (e) and (f) above take into account the need for a coordinated regional approach;

(h) To secure, neutralize or destroy any weapons, ammunition or any other materiel surrendered by the former combatants;

Disarmament and dismantling of militias

(i) To assist the Prime Minister of the Government of National Reconciliation in formulating and monitoring the implementation of the Joint Operation Plan for the disarmament and dismantling of militias envisaged in paragraph 4 of the Pretoria Agreement;

(j) To secure, neutralize or destroy all weapons, ammunition and other materiel surrendered by militias;

Protection of United Nations personnel, institutions and civilians

(k) To protect United Nations personnel, installations and equipment, ensure the security and freedom of movement of United Nations personnel and, without prejudice to the responsibility of the Government of National Reconciliation, to protect civilians under imminent threat of physical violence, within its capabilities and its areas of deployment;

(l) To support, in coordination with the Ivorian and South African authorities, the provision of security for members of the Government of National Reconciliation;

Monitoring of the arms embargo

(m) To monitor the implementation of the measures imposed by paragraph 7 of resolution 1572(2004) of 15 November 2004, in cooperation with the Group of Experts established pursuant to resolution 1584 (2005) of 1 February 2005 and, as appropriate, with the United Nations Mission in Liberia, the United Nations Mission in Sierra Leone and Governments concerned, including by inspecting, as they deem it necessary and without notice, the cargo of aircraft and of any transport vehicle using the ports, airports, airfields, military bases and border crossings of Côte d'Ivoire;

(n) To collect, as appropriate, arms and any related materiel brought into Côte d'Ivoire in violation of the measures imposed by paragraph 7 of resolution 1572 (2004), and to dispose of such arms and related materiel as appropriate;

Support for humanitarian assistance

(o) To facilitate the free flow of people, goods and humanitarian assistance, inter alia, by helping to establish the necessary security conditions and taking into account the special needs of vulnerable groups, especially women, children and elderly people;

Support for the redeployment of State administration

(p) To facilitate, with the assistance of the African Union, the Economic Community of West African States and other international partners, the re-establishment by the Government of National Reconciliation of the authority of the State throughout Côte d'Ivoire, which is essential for the social and economic recovery of the country;

Support for the organization of open, free, fair and transparent elections

(q) To provide all necessary technical assistance to the Government of National Reconciliation, the Independent Electoral Commission and other relevant agencies or institutions, with the support of the African Union, the Economic Community of West African States and other international partners, for the organization of open, free, fair and transparent presidential and legislative elections within the time frames envisaged in the Constitution of the Republic of Côte d'Ivoire;

(r) To provide technical information, advice and assistance, as appropriate, to the High Representative referred to in paragraph 7 of resolution 1603(2005) of 3 June 2005;

(s) To contribute, within its capabilities and its areas of deployment, to the security of the areas where voting is to take place;

Assistance in the field of human rights

(t) To contribute to the promotion and protection of human rights in Côte d'Ivoire, with special attention to violence committed against children and women, to monitor and help to investigate human rights violations with a view to ending impunity, and to keep the Security Council Committee established pursuant to resolution 1572(2004) regularly informed of developments in this regard;

Public information

(u) To promote understanding of the peace process and the role of the United Nations Operation in Côte d'Ivoire among local communities and the parties, through the mission's public information capacity, including its radio broadcasting capability;

(v) To monitor the Ivorian mass media, in particular with regard to any incidents of incitement by the media to hatred, intolerance and violence, and to keep the Security Council Committee established pursuant to resolution 1572(2004) regularly informed of the situation in this regard;

Law and order

(w) To assist the Government of National Reconciliation, in conjunction with the African Union, the Economic Community of West African States and other international organizations, in restoring a civilian policing presence throughout Côte d'Ivoire, to advise the Government of National Reconciliation on the restructuring of the internal security services, and to assist the Ivorian parties in the implementation of temporary and interim security measures in the northern part of the country, as provided for in paragraph 6 of the Pretoria Agreement;

(x) To assist the Government of National Reconciliation, in conjunction with the African Union, the Economic Community of West African States and other international organizations, in re-establishing the authority of the judiciary and the rule of law throughout Côte d'Ivoire;

3. *Authorizes*, for the period specified in paragraph 1 above, an increase in the military component of the United Nations Operation in Côte d'Ivoire of up to 850 additional personnel, as well as an increase in the civilian police component of up to a ceiling of 725 civilian police personnel, including three formed police units, and the necessary additional civilian personnel;

4. *Authorizes* the Secretary-General to take all the necessary steps in order to implement, as appropriate, relevant measures envisaged in paragraphs 19 to 23 and 76 (*b*) to (*e*) of his report of 2 March 2005 on intermission cooperation and possible cross-border operations between the United Nations Mission in Sierra Leone, the United Nations Mission in Liberia and the United Nations Operation in Côte d'Ivoire, subject to the agreement of the troop-contributing countries and, where relevant, of the Governments concerned and without prejudice to the performance of the mandates of those United Nations missions;

5. *Requests* the Secretary-General to seek the agreement of the countries contributing military and civilian police personnel to the United Nations Mission in Liberia, the United Nations Mission in Sierra Leone and the United Nations Operation in Côte d'Ivoire to redeploy such personnel as may be needed on a temporary basis to reinforce another of the above three missions, as appropriate, taking account of the need to ensure effective performance of the current mandates of those missions;

6. *Authorizes*, subject to the necessary prior steps referred to in paragraphs 4 and 5 above, including the agreement of the troop-contributing countries and, where relevant, the Governments concerned, the temporary redeployment of military and civilian police personnel among the United Nations Mission in Liberia, the United Nations Mission in Sierra Leone and the United Nations Operation in Côte d'Ivoire to deal with challenges which cannot be handled within the authorized personnel ceiling of a given mission, subject to the following conditions:

(*a*) The Secretary-General shall inform the Security Council in advance of his intention to proceed with such a redeployment, including its scope and duration, with the understanding that the implementation of the above-mentioned reinforcement will require a corresponding decision of the Council;

(*b*) Any forces redeployed shall continue to be counted against the authorized ceiling on military and civilian personnel of the mission from which they are being transferred and shall not count against the ceiling of the mission to which they are being transferred;

(*c*) Any such transfer shall not result in any increase in the total combined ceilings on military and civilian personnel deployed in the United Nations Operation in Côte d'Ivoire, the United Nations Mission in Sierra Leone and the United Nations Mission in Liberia determined by the Council in the respective mandates of the three missions;

(*d*) Any such transfer shall not have the effect of extending the deployment period of personnel deployed under the mandate of their original mission, unless the Council decides otherwise;

7. *Decides* to review the troop level of the United Nations Operation in Côte d'Ivoire by 31 December 2005, including the civilian police component, in the light of the situation in Côte d'Ivoire after the forthcoming general elections and on the basis of the tasks remaining to be carried out, with a view to further reduction as appropriate;

8. *Authorizes* the United Nations Operation in Côte d'Ivoire to use all necessary means to carry out its mandate, within its capabilities and its areas of deployment;

9. *Requests* the United Nations Operation in Côte d'Ivoire to carry out its mandate in close liaison with the United Nations missions in Sierra Leone and in Liberia, including, especially, in the prevention of movements of arms and combatants across shared borders and the implementation of disarmament and demobilization programmes;

10. *Underlines* the importance of mainstreaming the gender perspective in peacekeeping operations and post-conflict peacebuilding and of appropriate expertise in this regard, and encourages the United Nations Operation in Côte d'Ivoire to actively address this issue;

11. *Welcomes* the efforts undertaken by the United Nations Operation in Côte d'Ivoire to implement the Secretary-General's zero tolerance policy on sexual exploitation and abuse and to ensure full compliance of its personnel with the United Nations code of conduct, requests the Secretary-General to continue to take all necessary action in this regard and to keep the Council informed, and urges troop-contributing countries to take appropriate preventive action, including conducting predeployment awareness training, and to take disciplinary action and other action to ensure that such acts are properly investigated and punished in cases involving their personnel;

12. *Authorizes*, from the date of adoption of the present resolution, the French forces to use all necessary means in order to support the United Nations Operation in Côte d'Ivoire in accordance with the agreement reached between the United Nations Operation in Côte d'Ivoire and the French authorities, and in particular:

(*a*) To contribute to the general security of the area of activity of the international forces;

(*b*) To intervene at the request of the United Nations Operation in Côte d'Ivoire in support of its elements whose security may be threatened;

(*c*) In consultation with the United Nations Operation in Côte d'Ivoire, to intervene against belligerent actions, if security conditions so require, outside the areas of deployment of the United Nations Operation in Côte d'Ivoire;

(*d*) To help to protect civilians in the deployment areas of their units;

(*e*) To contribute to monitoring the arms embargo established by resolution 1572(2004), in accordance with paragraphs 2 and 3 of resolution 1584(2005);

13. *Decides* to remain actively seized of the matter.

Tripartite Monitoring Group

The Tripartite Monitoring Group, set up to review progress in the implementation of the Accra III Agreement, signed by the parties in 2004 [YUN 2004, p. 182], which provided a framework and timetable for the reactivation of the peace process, issued six reports in 2005 covering the periods from 18 December 2004 to 28 February 2005 [S/2005/82, S/2005/175], 1 March to 30 June [S/2005/395, S/2005/463], and 1 July to 31 August [S/2005/539, S/2005/611]. As of June, the Group's work was extended to reviewing implementation of the Pretoria Agreement.

Monitoring Group report (July). On 15 July [S/2005/463], the Secretary-General forwarded to the Security Council the fifteenth report of the Tripartite Monitoring Group on the implementation of the Accra III Agreement and the Pretoria Agreement. According to the report, although the Pretoria Agreement emphasized the critical importance of adopting the laws stemming from the Linas-Marcoussis Agreement, the disarmament process leading to the reunification of the country, and the creation of conditions conducive to the holding of elections in October, the outbreak of pockets of inter-communal violence and political bickering had brought the peace process to a standstill. Aside from the invocation by President Gbagbo of the exceptional powers under Article 48 of the Constitution to authorize the candidacy of Alassane Ouattara, and the signing of decrees restoring the Ivorian Radio and Television to its pre-November 2004 status, no further progress was recorded in the implementation of the legislative components of the Agreement.

Meanwhile, President Mbeki convened another meeting of the signatories to the Pretoria Agreement on 28 and 29 June in order to take stock of the progress in the implementation of the Agreement. After intensive discussions, the parties issued a "Declaration on the Implementation of the Pretoria Agreement on the peace process in Côte d'Ivoire". In the Declaration, in addition to reaffirming the importance of moving speedily towards the holding of elections in October, the parties agreed that the dismantling and disarmament of militias should be completed by 20 August, and that the Troika, comprising UNOCI, the Office of the Ivorian Prime Minister and the AU mediation, would determine any additional measures that might be required to expedite the process.

Regarding the disarmament, demobilization and reintegration of ex-combatants, the parties agreed that the chiefs of staff of FANCI and the Forces nouvelles would meet on 7 July to finalize a disarmament, demobilization and reintegration timetable. The parties also called on the National Assembly to adopt by 15 July, amendments to laws on the Independent Electoral Commission, the financing of political parties, nationality, identification, the Human Rights Commission, the print media and audio-visual communication. Failing to do so, the Mediator would be authorized to decide on "exceptional measures", which President Gbagbo would take to ensure the adoption of the amendments. The parties also agreed that the AU should impose sanctions against those who failed to implement the Pretoria Agreement and blocked the peace process. In that regard, the Mediator would recommend that the Security Council impose the targeted sanctions envisaged in resolution 1572(2004) [YUN, 2004, p. 172].

SECURITY COUNCIL ACTION

On 6 July [meeting 5221], following consultations among Security Council members, the President made statement **S/PRST/2005/28** on behalf of the Council:

> The Security Council has taken note with interest of the Declaration on the implementation of the Pretoria Agreement on the peace process in Côte d'Ivoire signed on 29 June 2005 at Pretoria under the auspices of the African Union mediator, President Thabo Mbeki.
>
> The Council welcomes the efforts undertaken by the African Union mediation so that the forthcoming elections in Côte d'Ivoire are credible and are held as planned, and reiterates its full support to the African Union mediator.
>
> The Council recalls that it has endorsed the Pretoria Agreement signed on 6 April 2005.
>
> The Council demands that all the signatories to this Agreement and all the Ivorian parties concerned implement fully and without delay all the commitments made with the African Union mediation and comply scrupulously with the timetable agreed on 29 June 2005 in Pretoria.
>
> The Council affirms that it stands ready, in close consultation with the African Union mediation, to implement individual sanctions provided for in paragraphs 9 and 11 of resolution 1572(2004) against those who do not comply with those commitments or who constitute an obstacle to their full implementation.

Further developments

Visit of High Representative to Côte d'Ivoire. The High Representative for the elections in

Côte d'Ivoire, António Monteiro, in response to Security Council resolution 1603(2005), visited Côte d'Ivoire from 8 to 18 August. In his report, transmitted by the Secretary-General on 12 September [S/2005/584], the High Representative said that, in his meetings with a wide spectrum of actors, diplomatic representatives and international organizations, two principal issues were of concern to him—the conformity of the legislative package adopted by President Gbagbo with the relevant agreements, and the urgency of appointing a reconstituted Independent Electoral Commission. During the discussions, the G-7 opposition parties conveyed their dissatisfaction with certain aspects of the legislative package but made a clear commitment to designate their representatives on the reconstituted Independent Electoral Commission. The Forces nouvelles, on 18 August, following internal consultations, indicated to the High Representative their firm commitment to nominate their representative to the Commission.

In his meeting with President Mbeki, the High Representative discussed concerns expressed by the parties that the legislative package did not fully respect the Linas-Marcoussis and Pretoria Agreements and those grey areas requiring clarification. They arrived at an agreement on those issues about which they would write President Gbagbo. On the question of funding the electoral process, the High Representative drew attention to the $31 million still needed in the electoral budget, the result of institutional uncertainty and donor reticence because of the apparent lack of a genuine political commitment to push the peace process forward. He urged the Security Council to approach major donors for the necessary funding.

The High Representative stated that he had been advised by technical experts that the feasibility of holding elections by 30 October seemed increasingly problematic and that it would be preferable to leave the debate on that question until after the establishment of the Independent Electoral Commission, by which time a decision could be taken on a new date. In the meantime, the Commission's main task would be to draft and promote acceptance by all parties of an electoral code of conduct.

Communiqué of AU Peace and Security Council. The AU Peace and Security Council, in a communiqué issued at its eighth meeting (New York, 14 September) [S/2005/598], expressed concern over the lack of political will by the Ivorian parties to fully implement the various agreements reached, especially concerning the dismantling and disarming of militias, the disarmament, demobilization and rehabilitation programme and the creation of conditions conducive to elections. It called on them to honour their obligations and expressed its readiness to continue to cooperate with the United Nations on the best ways to support and advance the peace process.

Report of Secretary-General. The Secretary-General, in his September report [S/2005/604] on UNOCI, submitted in response to resolution 1603(2005), said that, since the signing of the Declaration on the Implementation of the Pretoria Agreement, some progress was made in carrying out the legislative reforms envisaged in the Linas-Marcoussis and Pretoria Agreements. On 10 July, realizing that the National Assembly would not pass the amended laws on time, due to continued resistance from the majority party, the Ivorian Popular Front, President Mbeki formally requested President Gbagbo to use his exceptional powers under article 48 of the Ivorian Constitution to ensure the adoption of the amended laws within the time frame stipulated by the Declaration. On 15 July, in response to that request, the President signed a series of decrees promulgating revised versions of the laws on the Independent Electoral Commission, nationality, identification, the Human Rights Commission, and the print media and audio-visual communications.

The Forces nouvelles and the members of the G-7 opposition parties expressed strong reservations on several of the revised texts, claiming that they still did not conform to the spirit of the Linas-Marcoussis Agreement. In the light of those concerns, President Gbagbo, on 29 August, promulgated new versions of the law on the Electoral Commission, the nationality code and the naturalization law, bringing them into conformity with the Linas-Marcoussis Agreement. However, controversy over the political process continued. On 1 September, in response to a statement by the South African Deputy Foreign Minister, Aziz Pahad, blaming the opposition forces for blocking the peace process, the Forces nouvelles declared that they would no longer work with the AU mediation, as it was biased towards President Gbagbo, and called on the AU Chairman, Nigerian President, Olusegun Obasanjo, to determine how best to move the peace process forward. On 30 October, the Forces nouvelles Secretary-General stated that President Gbagbo would no longer be President and called on all concerned to work together to put in place a transitional government.

Meanwhile, efforts continued towards the rehabilitation of the disarmament sites. At a meeting held in Yamoussoukro (7-9 July), the chiefs of staff of FANCI and the Forces nouvelles agreed on a timetable for starting the pre-cantonment of forces on 31 July and the actual disarmament and demobilization of combatants between 26 September and 3 October. They also agreed on linking implementation of the various phases of the disarmament, demobilization and reintegration of forces to other key provisions of the Pretoria Agreement and to establish a joint committee for the restructuring of the defence and security forces. According to the Office of the Prime Minister, as at 26 August, five of the nine disarmament sites in the north and five of the six sites in the south had already been rehabilitated. Some 2,000 militia members in the west were expected to be integrated into the programme.

The security situation in Côte d'Ivoire remained unpredictable and volatile. Following the attacks, in early June, on the villages of Guetrozon and Petit Duékoué in the west of the country, UNOCI strengthened its presence in the area and conducted joint patrols with FANCI. UNOCI's efforts to maintain a secure and stable environment were severely hampered by increased obstruction of the Mission's movements and operations in various parts of the country. Tensions were exacerbated by inflammatory statements made by the former FANCI chief of staff, calling for the departure of President Gbagbo and threatening to resort to "all necessary means" if the international community failed to ensure his departure. The Special Representative protested those obstructions to President Gbagbo, who, in a nationwide address, called on all Ivorians to allow the impartial forces to move freely throughout the country.

Concerning the elections, on 25 August, the Forces nouvelles declared that the elections could not be held on 30 October since the necessary conditions, including the identification of all Ivorians, had not been met and that a political transition would be required. It reaffirmed its willingness to designate its representatives to the Independent Electoral Commission, subject to certain conditions, including participation in the Commission's local organs and the exclusion of the National Institute of Statistics from the electoral process. On 29 August, in Abidjan, the political opposition also declared that it would not be possible to hold the elections on 30 October, while stressing the need for a transitional period, during which President Gbagbo would not be in power.

Under the current circumstances, the Secretary-General agreed that the elections could not be held on 30 October as required by the Ivorian Constitution, and urged that the parties agree on a new time frame for that process. He urged all Ivorian parties to exercise the utmost restraint and to cooperate fully with all key stakeholders.

International partners were urged to remain engaged and support the peace process, humanitarian needs and long-term development.

Decision of AU Peace and Security Council (October). The AU Peace and Security Council, meeting in Addis Ababa, Ethiopia, at the level of Heads of State and Government, in a communiqué issued on 6 October [S/2005/639], endorsed the observations of the ECOWAS Extraordinary Summit (Abuja, Nigeria, 30 September) on the end of the mandate of President Laurent Gbagbo on 30 October, and the impossibility, recognized by all Ivorian parties, of organizing presidential elections on the scheduled date; and its decision that the arrangements agreed upon in the Linas-Marcoussis Agreement should continue from 31 October 2005 to 31 October 2006, during which President Gbagbo would continue as Head of State. A new Prime Minister, acceptable by all Ivorian parties, would be appointed and the Government would continue to discharge its responsibilities. The Prime Minister would not be eligible to stand for election. To assist the Government, a ministerial International Working Group (IWG) would be established to evaluate, monitor and follow up the peace process, including the road map agreed upon in Pretoria, and the parties invited to a Forum for National Dialogue in Yamoussoukro. It also decided to submit its decision to the UN Security Council and to dispatch a high-level delegation to Côte d'Ivoire, comprising the Presidents of Nigeria and South Africa to meet with President Gbagbo and other Ivorian parties.

Security Council consideration. The Security Council, meeting on 13 October [meeting 5278] to discuss the situation in Côte d'Ivoire, was briefed by Nigeria's Minister for Foreign Affairs, Oluyemi Adeniji, AU Commissioner Said Djinnit, the Secretary-General's Special Representative for Côte d'Ivoire, Pierre Schori, and the High Representative for elections in Côte d'Ivoire, António Monteiro.

As requested by the AU Peace and Security Council, Foreign Minister Oluyemi Adeniji submitted its 6 October decision (above) to the UN Security Council, drawing particular attention to the request that the Council consider a substantial increase in UNOCI strength.

The AU Commissioner, in his briefing, said that the AU Peace and Security Council, in adopting its 6 October decision, aimed to inject new impetus into the peace process. He observed that the Ivorian parties and the international community needed to take full advantage of the 12-month period decided by the Peace and Security Council to address all outstanding issues. The international community, together with the UN Security Council, needed to convey a strong signal to the parties as to their determination and cohesion. The United Nations should strengthen its role and presence, both in terms of providing UNOCI with the means to discharge its mandate effectively and reinforcing the authority of the High Representative for elections. The parties had to comply with their commitments and obligations and the international community had to exert more pressure and sanctions against the defaulting parties.

The Secretary-General's Special Representative urged the Council to endorse the 6 October AU decision to send a strong message of the unity of purpose of the international community and encourage the urgent convening of IWG to define a new timetable, with key benchmarks, for the implementation of the remaining provisions of the Pretoria Agreement. The Prime Minister and the Government should be in place as soon as possible and recommendations made on the role of the legislature after December. Presidents Obasanjo and Mbeki should be supported in their visit to Côte d'Ivoire, and the UN role should be clarified.

Reporting on the election process, the High Representative for the elections in Côte d'Ivoire said that, with the composition of the Independent Electoral Commission finalized, additional time was needed to allow for the application of all legal formalities and to resolve the issue of multiple nominations by one party. On 29 September, President Gbagbo signed a decree establishing the new Independent Electoral Commission, the first meeting of which was scheduled to be held on 19 October. The High Representative said that the Commission's most difficult tasks would be the identification question and the criteria for voter eligibility. He was exploring with political leaders the idea of voters' cards, with photograph and fingerprint. The High Representative concluded that the 12-month period proposed by the AU was largely sufficient for the preparation and holding of free and fair elections.

SECURITY COUNCIL ACTION

On 14 October [meeting 5281], following consultations among Security Council members, the President made statement **S/PRST/2005/49** on behalf of the Council:

The Security Council heard briefings by the Minister for Foreign Affairs of Nigeria, Mr. Oluyemi Adeniji, the Commissioner for Peace and Security of the African Union, Mr. Said Djinnit, the Special Representative of the Secretary-General for Côte d'Ivoire, Mr. Pierre Schori, and the High Representative for the elections in Côte d'Ivoire, Mr. António

Monteiro, during its meeting held on 13 October 2005.

The Security Council appreciates the efforts of the African Union, in particular President Thabo Mbeki of the Republic of South Africa and President Olusegun Obasanjo of the Federal Republic of Nigeria, Chairman of the African Union, the Economic Community of West African States, the leaders of the region, the Special Representative of the Secretary-General and the High Representative for the elections to promote peace and stability in Côte d'Ivoire, and reiterates its full support for those efforts.

The Security Council endorses the decision of the Peace and Security Council of the African Union on the situation in Côte d'Ivoire adopted at its 40th meeting, held at the level of Heads of State and Government in Addis Ababa on 6 October 2005, expresses its intention to take rapidly all necessary measures to support, as appropriate, its implementation, in order to organize free, fair, open, transparent and credible elections as soon as possible and no later than 31 October 2006, and looks forward to regular reports on its implementation in accordance with paragraph 10 (v), of the decision of the Peace and Security Council.

The Security Council takes note, in particular, of the request of the Peace and Security Council for an increase in the strength of the United Nations Operation in Côte d'Ivoire, without prejudice to any future decision or commitment of the Security Council in this regard. The Council expresses its intention to consider whether to provide additional resources to the United Nations Operation in Côte d'Ivoire, based on careful study of conditions in the country and evidence of meaningful progress towards implementation of the commitments made under the Linas-Marcoussis Agreement and other relevant agreements.

The Security Council reaffirms that it endorsed the Linas-Marcoussis Agreement, the Accra III Agreement and the Pretoria Agreement and demands that all the Ivorian parties signatories to those Agreements, as well as all the Ivorian parties concerned, implement fully and without delay their commitments under those Agreements, in accordance with the decision of the Peace and Security Council.

The Security Council welcomes the forthcoming visit of a high-level delegation to Côte d'Ivoire led by Presidents Obasanjo and Mbeki, expresses its full support for it and urges all the Ivorian parties to cooperate fully and in good faith with this delegation, in particular in order to ensure the rapid implementation of the decision of the Peace and Security Council and the early appointment of a Prime Minister acceptable to all parties and to guarantee, with the support of the United Nations, the organization of free, fair, open, transparent and credible elections.

The Security Council also expresses its full support for the forthcoming visit to the region of the Chairman of the Security Council Committee established pursuant to resolution 1572(2004) and underlines that the purpose of this visit is to assess the progress made by all parties towards the implementation of their commitments, bearing in mind the mandate of the Committee under paragraphs 9 and 11 of resolution 1572(2004), and to remind all Ivorian parties of their responsibilities for the full and rapid implementation of the peace process.

On 21 October [meeting 5288], the Council unanimously adopted **resolution 1633(2005)**. The draft [S/2005/661] was prepared in consultations among Council members.

The Security Council,

Recalling its previous resolutions and the statements by its President relating to the situation in Côte d'Ivoire,

Reaffirming its strong commitment to the sovereignty, independence, territorial integrity and unity of Côte d'Ivoire, and recalling the importance of the principles of good-neighbourliness, non-interference and regional cooperation,

Recalling that it endorsed the agreement signed by the Ivorian political forces at Linas-Marcoussis, France, on 23 January 2003 ("the Linas-Marcoussis Agreement") and approved by the Conference of Heads of State on Côte d'Ivoire, held in Paris on 25 and 26 January 2003, the agreement signed at Accra on 30 July 2004 ("the Accra III Agreement") and the agreement signed at Pretoria on 6 April 2005 ("the Pretoria Agreement"),

Reaffirming that the Linas-Marcoussis, Accra III and Pretoria Agreements remain the appropriate framework for the peaceful and lasting solution to the crisis in Côte d'Ivoire,

Having taken note of the decision of the Peace and Security Council of the African Union adopted at its fortieth meeting, held at the level of Heads of State and Government in Addis Ababa on 6 October 2005 ("the decision of the Peace and Security Council"),

Having taken note also of the creation of an International Working Group at the ministerial level ("the International Working Group") and of a day-to-day mediation undertaken by representatives of the International Working Group ("the Mediation Group"),

Having heard on 13 October 2005 briefings by the Minister for Foreign Affairs of Nigeria and the Commissioner for Peace and Security of the African Union on behalf of the African Union, the Special Representative of the Secretary-General for Côte d'Ivoire and the High Representative for the elections in Côte d'Ivoire,

Expressing its serious concern at the persistence of the crisis and the deterioration of the situation in Côte d'Ivoire,

Reiterating its firm condemnation of all violations of human rights in Côte d'Ivoire,

Determining that the situation in Côte d'Ivoire continues to pose a threat to international peace and security in the region,

Acting under Chapter VII of the Charter of the United Nations,

1. *Commends* the continued efforts of the African Union, in particular President Olusegun Obasanjo of the Federal Republic of Nigeria, Chairman of the African Union, and President Thabo Mbeki of the Republic of South Africa, Mediator of the African Union, the Economic Community of West African States and the leaders of the region to promote peace and stability in Côte d'Ivoire, and reiterates its full support for them;

2. *Commends also* the constant efforts of the Special Representative of the Secretary-General for Côte d'Ivoire, Mr. Pierre Schori, and of the High Representative for the elections in Côte d'Ivoire, Mr. António Monteiro, and reiterates its full support for them, including for the arbitration and certification role of the High Representative for the elections;

3. *Reaffirms its endorsement* of the observation of the Economic Community of West African States and of the Peace and Security Council of the African Union on the end of the mandate of President Laurent Gbagbo on 30 October 2005 and the impossibility of organizing presidential elections on the scheduled date, and of the decision of the Peace and Security Council, including its decision on the fact that President Gbagbo shall remain Head of State from 31 October 2005 for a period not exceeding twelve months, and demands that all the parties signatories to the Linas-Marcoussis Agreement, the Accra III Agreement and the Pretoria Agreement as well as all the Ivorian parties concerned implement it fully and without delay;

4. *Supports* the establishment of the International Working Group at the ministerial level and the Mediation Group, which should both be co-chaired by the Special Representative of the Secretary-General, urges the International Working Group to meet as soon as possible, and affirms that the secretariat of the International Working Group shall be coordinated by the United Nations, in accordance with paragraph 10 (vi) of the decision of the Peace and Security Council;

5. *Urges* the Chairman of the African Union, the Chairman of the Economic Community of West African States and the African Union Mediator to consult immediately with all the Ivorian parties in order to ensure that a new Prime Minister acceptable to all the Ivorian parties signatories to the Linas-Marcoussis Agreement is appointed by 31 October 2005, in accordance with paragraph 10 (ii) of the decision of the Peace and Security Council, and to maintain close contact with the Secretary-General throughout the process;

6. *Expresses its full support* for paragraph 10 (iii) of the decision of the Peace and Security Council, which stresses that the ministers shall be accountable to the Prime Minister, who shall have full authority over his or her Cabinet;

7. *Reiterates* the importance of having all ministers participate fully in the Government of National Reconciliation as underscored in the statement by its President of 25 May 2004, considers, therefore, that, when a minister is not participating fully in the Government, his or her portfolio should be assumed by the Prime Minister and requests the International Working Group to monitor closely the situation in this regard;

8. *Stresses* that the Prime Minister must have all the necessary powers according to the Linas-Marcoussis Agreement and all the governmental financial, material and human resources, particularly with regard to security, defence and electoral matters, to ensure the effective functioning of the Government, to guarantee security and the redeployment of the administration and public services throughout the territory of Côte d'Ivoire, to lead the programme of disarmament, de-

mobilization and reintegration and the operations of disarmament and dismantling of militias, and to ensure the fairness of the identification process and of voter registration, leading to the organization of free, open, fair and transparent elections, with the support of the United Nations;

9. *Calls upon* all Ivorian parties to ensure that the Prime Minister has all powers and resources described in paragraph 8 above and faces no hindrance or difficulty in implementing his or her tasks;

10. *Requests* the International Working Group, on the basis of paragraphs 10 (iii) and (v) of the decision of the Peace and Security Council, to verify that the Prime Minister has all the necessary powers and resources described in paragraph 8 above and immediately to report to the Security Council any hindrance or difficulty which the Prime Minister may face in implementing his or her tasks and to identify those responsible;

11. *Invites* the International Working Group, noting that the mandate of the National Assembly will end by 16 December 2005, to consult with all the Ivorian parties, in liaison, as appropriate, with the Forum for National Dialogue as referred to in paragraph 11 of the decision of the Peace and Security Council, with a view to ensuring that the Ivorian institutions function normally until the holding of the elections in Côte d'Ivoire, and to keep the Security Council and the Peace and Security Council informed in that regard;

12. *Considers*, as noted by the Peace and Security Council in paragraph 9 of its decision, that additional measures are required to expedite the implementation of some provisions of the Linas-Marcoussis, Accra III and Pretoria Agreements, in particular the disarmament, demobilization and reintegration process, the dismantling and disarmament of militias and the creation of conditions for holding free, fair, open and transparent elections, including the identification process and the registration of voters;

13. *Requests*, therefore, the International Working Group to draw up as soon as possible a road map in consultation with all Ivorian parties, with a view to holding free, fair, open and transparent elections as soon as possible and no later than 31 October 2006, concerning in particular:

(a) The appointment of a new Prime Minister as provided for in paragraph 5 above;

(b) The implementation of all outstanding issues as referred to in paragraph 12 above, recalling in this regard that the concomitant implementation of the identification process and of the cantonment of the forces, as provided for in the national programme for disarmament, demobilization, reintegration and rehabilitation signed at Yamoussoukro on 14 May 2005, would expedite the creation of conditions for holding free, fair, open and transparent elections;

14. *Demands* that the Forces nouvelles proceed without delay with the disarmament, demobilization and reintegration programme in order to facilitate the restoration of the authority of the State throughout the national territory, the reunification of the country and the organization of the elections as soon as possible;

15. *Affirms* that the identification process must also start without delay;

16. *Demands* that all Ivorian parties stop all incitement to hatred and violence in radio and television broadcasting as well as in any other media;

17. *Demands also* the immediate disarmament and dismantling of militias throughout the national territory;

18. *Recalls* paragraphs 5 and 7 of the decision of the Peace and Security Council, and demands that all Ivorian parties refrain from any use of force and violence, including against civilians and foreigners, and from all kinds of disruptive street protests;

19. *Urges* countries neighbouring Côte d'Ivoire to prevent any cross-border movement of combatants or arms into Côte d'Ivoire;

20. *Reiterates its serious concern* at all violations of human rights and international humanitarian law in Côte d'Ivoire, and urges the Ivorian authorities to investigate those violations without delay in order to put an end to impunity;

21. *Condemns* the serious attacks against the personnel of the United Nations Operation in Côte d'Ivoire and the unacceptable obstacles to the freedom of movement of the United Nations Operation in Côte d'Ivoire and French forces, demands that all Ivorian parties cooperate fully in their operations, in particular by guaranteeing the safety, security and freedom of movement of their personnel, as well as associated personnel, throughout the territory of Côte d'Ivoire, and affirms that any obstacle to their freedom of movement or to the full implementation of their mandates would not be tolerated;

22. *Takes note* of paragraph 13 of the decision of the Peace and Security Council, recalls the statement by its President of 14 October 2005 and its decisions under resolution 1609(2005) of 24 June 2005, including paragraphs 4, 5 and 6 thereof, and expresses its intention to review the troop level of the United Nations Operation in Côte d'Ivoire by the end of its mandate on 24 January 2006, in the light of the situation in Côte d'Ivoire;

23. *Recalls* paragraph 12 of the decision of the Peace and Security Council and its support for the individual measures provided for in paragraphs 9 and 11 of resolution 1572(2004) of 15 November 2004, and reaffirms its readiness to impose those measures against any person who blocks the implementation of the peace process, as defined in particular by the road map mentioned in paragraph 13 above, who is determined to be responsible for serious violations of human rights and international humanitarian law in Côte d'Ivoire, who publicly incites hatred and violence, or against any person or entity who is determined to be in violation of the arms embargo;

24. *Urges* the International Working Group, which shall receive regular reports from the Mediation Group, and the Security Council Committee established pursuant to resolution 1572(2004) to evaluate, monitor and follow up closely the progress made with regard to the issues mentioned in paragraphs 14 to 18 above;

25. *Decides* to remain actively seized of the matter.

Communications. On 3 November [S/2005/707], the Secretary-General informed the Council President that, in accordance with resolution

1603(2005) (see p. 233), his High Representative for the elections in Côte d'Ivoire had significantly contributed to the resolution of some of the key issues pertaining to the organization of the elections and had briefed the Council on 13 October (see above) on those issues. UNDP had put in place a project to receive donor contributions to support the work of the High Representative and had advanced $600,000 to the project against future contributions from donors. Those anticipated contributions had not yet materialized. The Secretary-General therefore appealed to Council members, in particular, to take the lead in fulfilling their responsibilities.

Implementation of resolution 1633(2005)

International Working Group meeting (October). The International Working Group (IWG), created by the AU Peace and Security Council on 6 October, and supported by the Security Council in resolution 1633(2005) (see p. 243), to assist the Ivorian Government in the implementation of its programme and consolidate and strengthen existing follow-up mechanisms, held its first meeting on 8 November in Abidjan. In a communiqué issued on the same date, and transmitted by the Secretary-General on 28 November [S/2005/744], the Group, comprising Ministers from Benin, Ghana, Guinea, the Niger, France, the United Kingdom, the EU and the United States, noted that resolution 1633(2005), which was binding on all Ivorians, was the primary basis of the process, as it granted the soon-to-be-appointed Prime Minister inherent powers and all the necessary resources to fully and effectively carry out his mandate. It identified and agreed on the specific duties and authority of the Prime Minister over the cabinet. Accordingly, the Group prepared a road map for the holding of elections no later than 31 October 2006. The road map, which included a timetable for action, covered issues of governance; the political process; disarmament, demobilization and reinsertion of ex-combatants; disarmament and disbanding of militias; redeployment of administration; identification and citizenship; electoral process; restoration of security; respect for human rights; sanctions and hindrance to freedom of movement; media monitoring; and humanitarian action.

SECURITY COUNCIL ACTION

On 30 November [meeting 5314], following consultations among Security Council members, the President made statement **S/PRST/2005/58** on behalf of the Council:

The Security Council affirms that the rapid appointment of a Prime Minister of Côte d'Ivoire is crucial to relaunch the peace process leading to the holding of free, fair, open and transparent elections no later than 31 October 2006, and to implement fully the road map established by the International Working Group at its first meeting, held in Abidjan on 8 November 2005.

Therefore, the Council expresses its deep concern at the persistent disagreements among Ivorian parties on the appointment of the Prime Minister and considers that the Prime Minister must be designated without any further delay. The Council stresses once again that the Prime Minister must have all the necessary powers and resources described in paragraph 8 of resolution 1633(2005).

The Council commends the initiatives undertaken by the Chairman of the African Union, the Chairman of the Economic Community of West African States and the African Union Mediator, and notes that their consultations with the parties signatories to the Linas-Marcoussis Agreement have been held, as provided for by the decision of the Peace and Security Council of the African Union of 6 October 2005 and by resolution 1633(2005). It reiterates its full support for them and urges them to expedite their efforts. The Security Council urges them to identify as soon as possible the candidate for the office of Prime Minister that they deem acceptable to all parties signatories to the Linas-Marcoussis Agreement, given the consultations they have held.

The Council expresses its full support for the International Working Group, endorses its final communiqué of 8 November 2005, welcomes its decision to hold its second meeting in Abidjan on 6 December 2005, and urges the Group to keep the Council informed of the conclusions of its work.

The Council commends also the continuing efforts of the Special Representative of the Secretary-General for Côte d'Ivoire and the High Representative for the elections in Côte d'Ivoire, and reiterates its support for them. In particular, it encourages the Ivorian parties to cooperate fully with the High Representative to resolve the current dispute concerning the Independent Electoral Commission and reaffirms that the High Representative, in accordance with paragraph 7 of resolution 1603(2005), can make all the necessary determinations in order to help the electoral process to move forward.

The Council reaffirms its readiness, in close consultation with the African Union Mediation, to impose individual measures provided for in paragraphs 9 and 11 of resolution 1572(2004) and in resolution 1633(2005).

Report of Secretary-General. The Secretary-General, updating the Security Council on developments in Côte d'Ivoire, in a later report on UNOCI [S/2006/2], said that following the adoption of resolution 1633(2005), his Special Representative met with the Ivorian parties to explain its legal and political implications. The regional leaders appointed to facilitate consultations with the parties on the issue of the appointment of a new Prime Minister, as provided under that resolution, were unable to travel to Côte d'Ivoire before 31 October. The absence of a new Prime Minister, as the mandate of President Gbagbo came to an end on 30 October, resulted in a situation of uncertainty and heightened tensions in the country. On that date, President Gbagbo, in an address to the nation, stated that he would remain in power in view of the continued occupation of part of the country by the Forces nouvelles, based on a ruling made by the Constitutional Council on 29 October. The opposition parties and the Forces nouvelles rejected that interpretation and suspended their participation in the Council of Ministers. Both the opposition and the ruling party organized rallies in Abidjan to underscore their respective positions on the expiry of the President's mandate. The Forces nouvelles also organized demonstrations in Bouaké and other areas in the north, demanding that President Gbagbo step down. To help calm the situation, the Secretary-General issued a statement on 29 October calling on the Ivorian parties to exercise restraint, and based on consultations with Presidents Mbeki and Obasanjo, explained that Prime Minister Seydou Diarra would remain in office until a new Prime Minister was appointed. He also appealed to the parties to cooperate with the international partners in implementing resolution 1633(2005).

The regional leaders subsequently held a series of consultations with the Ivorian parties on the appointment of a new Prime Minister, including a visit by President Obasanjo to Côte d'Ivoire on 4 November, during which the parties submitted a list of 16 candidates for the post, which was later reduced to a shortlist of four. Presidents Mbeki, Obasanjo and Mamadou Tandja of the Niger conducted further consultations with the parties in Abidjan on 22 November, but no agreement was reached on a candidate acceptable to all. Presidents Mbeki and Obasanjo returned to Abidjan on 4 December for the final round of consultations, at the end of which they announced the appointment of Charles Konan Banny, the Governor of the Central Bank for West African States, as the Prime Minister for the transition period. The Forces nouvelles and the ruling party, the Front Populaire Ivoirien, welcomed his appointment and shortly after, former Prime Minister Seydou Diarra and the Government of National Reconciliation tendered their resignations. Mr. Banny was sworn into office on 7 December. The formation of the new Government, which was announced on 28 December, paved the way for the implementation of the peace agreements.

International Working Group meeting (December). At its second meeting held on 6 December [S/2005/768], IWG assured Prime Minister designate Charles Konan Banny of its full support, and invited the AU Mediation Group to verify and report to it as to whether the Prime Minister held all powers and resources described in paragraph 8 of Security Council resolution 1633 (2005) and reaffirmed in its 30 November presidential statement (see p. 245). Should it become necessary during the transition period to enact legislation to ensure the expeditious implementation of the Government's programme, the Council of Ministers would adopt decisions, which the Prime Minister would present within two days to the Head of State for signature within a maximum of five days.

The Group expressed concern over the protracted delay in the working of the Independent Electoral Commission, which had yet to become operational. It gave its full support to the High Representative on the consultations he had initiated to allow the Commission to function without delay as well as, if necessary, to use arbitration powers with regard to the constitution of the bureau, in accordance with resolutions 1603(2005) and 1633(2005) and the 30 November statement of the Council President. It resolved to help overcome any hindrance relating to the application of the individual sanctions imposed by the Council. It urged the Ivorian media to abstain from any publication, radio or television broadcasting that undermined the peace and reconciliation process and encouraged the Prime Minister to take steps to improve the media environment. The Group updated the road map for holding the elections (see p. 245) with a view to organizing the elections by 31 October 2006.

SECURITY COUNCIL ACTION

On 9 December [meeting 5318], following consultations among Security Council members, the President made statement **S/PRST/2005/60** on behalf of the Council:

> The Security Council welcomes the appointment of Mr. Charles Konan Banny as Prime Minister of Côte d'Ivoire, and expresses its full support for him. It also commends the continued and decisive efforts of Presidents Olusegun Obasanjo, Thabo Mbeki and Mamadou Tandja, and reiterates its full support for them.
>
> The Council endorses the final communiqué of the International Working Group of 6 December 2005. It recalls the previous final communiqué of the International Working Group, of 8 November 2005, which states, in particular, that the fundamental basis of the peace and national reconciliation process is enshrined in resolution 1633(2005) and that the International Working Group will provide all necessary support to the new Prime Minister and the Government that he will establish. The Council also reaffirms its support for the decision of the Peace and Security Council of the African Union, which

stresses that the ministers shall be accountable to the Prime Minister, who shall have full authority over his Cabinet.

The Council recalls and reaffirms that the Prime Minister must have all the necessary powers and resources described in resolution 1633(2005), and stresses the importance of the full implementation of that resolution by the Ivorian parties under the monitoring of the International Working Group. Therefore, the Council urges the establishment without delay of the Government so that the Prime Minister can implement as soon as possible the road map defined by the International Working Group, and requests the Mediation Group and the International Working Group to monitor this matter closely.

The Council reiterates its full support for the Special Representative of the Secretary-General for Côte d'Ivoire and the High Representative for the elections in Côte d'Ivoire.

Communication. The EU, on 13 December [S/2005/829], expressed satisfaction over the nomination of Charles Konan Banny to the post of Prime Minister and considered it necessary that Mr. Banny should be able to effectively exercise the powers granted by the Council.

Later developments. In a later report [S/2006/2], the Secretary-General said that the High Representative for the elections was consulted on the outline of an electoral schedule, which would form part of the road map for the overall peace process. On 30 November, he proposed an outline to the AU Mediation Group, which envisaged that the substantive work on the preparations for the elections would commence by the end of December, by which time the reconstituted Independent Electoral Commission was to be fully operational. The development of the legal framework for the electoral operations, including the identification and registration of voters and the distribution of electoral identity cards, would also begin.

Meanwhile, the Independent Electoral Commission encountered internal problems, resulting in serious delays in the envisaged schedule. The reconstituted Commission was sworn into office on 17 October, but was not able to function as some members boycotted it, protesting the procedures under which its bureau was elected on 19 October. The Front Populaire Ivoirien, the ruling party, took the dispute to the Supreme Court, which, on 25 November, nullified the election of the Commission's bureau. The High Representative consulted with the parties and the Prime Minister on ways of resolving the dispute. He reported to IWG, which, in its communiqué of 6 December (see p. 246), expressed its full support for his initiative and affirmed that, if necessary, he should use his arbitration powers to assist in the constitution of the bureau.

At the expert meeting on disarmament, demobilization and reintegration, held on 8 November, specific recommendations were made to the Mediation Group on the need to update the disarmament, demobilization and reintegration timetable at the monthly IWG meetings; adopt measures for an immediate commencement of pre-cantonment of combatants and the disarmament and dismantling of the militias as soon as possible, as called for by Security Council resolution 1633(2005); create a task force to monitor and support the process of dismantling and disarmament of the militia groups; and create a disarmament, demobilization and reintegration team coordinated by UNOCI and comprising representatives of the AU, ECOWAS, the AU mediation, the World Bank and the Licorne forces. The team would serve as a forum for the exchange of information and would facilitate the development of a concerted and integrated approach to the disarmament, demobilization and reintegration process in Côte d'Ivoire.

The Secretary-General called upon the political parties to work with the Prime Minister and the High Representative for the elections in resolving the dispute within the Independent Electoral Commission. He fully supported the IWG view that, if need be, the High Representative should invoke his arbitration authority to decisively settle the matter.

With regard to the end of the mandate of the National Assembly on 16 December, the Mediation Group consulted with the Ivorian parties on the IWG decision concerning the procedure for dealing with emergency legislation during the transition period, following calls for the Assembly's mandate to be extended.

The Secretary-General stated that the effective implementation of the road map for the transition period required that the Ivorian parties fully comply with their obligations under the various peace agreements.

Sanctions

The Security Council Committee established pursuant to resolution 1572(2004) [YUN 2004, p. 187] concerning Côte d'Ivoire, continued to monitor implementation of the arms embargo, travel restrictions and freeze of assets on designated individuals and entities imposed by that resolution. In 2005, the Committee held 7 formal meetings and 13 informal consultations. During the reporting period the Committee received several notes verbales from Member States period from 19 January to 9 August [S/AC.45.2005/1-38] on the implementation of the sanctions.

It considered reports submitted by Member States, in accordance with their obligations under resolution 1572(2004), containing information on measures they had taken to implement the resolution [S/AC.45/2005/1-38]. In a report on its activities during 2005 [S/2006/55], the Committee Chairman informed that, on 13 June 2005, the Committee adopted guidelines for its work, including procedures for listing and delisting individuals and entities subject to the targeted sanctions. It considered several arms embargo monitoring reports and media monitoring reports prepared by UNOCI. The Committee considered the interim and final reports of the Group of Experts established by the Council under resolution 1584(2005) to assess compliance with the sanctions and on 14 December, began consideration of the Group's updated report, in accordance with resolution 1632(2005) (see p. 250). The Committee Chairman visited Côte d'Ivoire from 18 to 21 October to assess progress made by all parties towards implementation of their commitments and submitted his report to the Council (see p. 251).

SECURITY COUNCIL ACTION

On 1 February [meeting 5118], the Security Council unanimously adopted **resolution 1584(2005)**. The draft [S/2005/54] was prepared in consultations among Council members.

The Security Council,

Recalling its resolutions 1528(2004) of 27 February 2004 and 1572(2004) of 15 November 2004, as well as the relevant statements by its President, in particular those of 5 August, 6 November and 16 December 2004,

Reaffirming its strong commitment to the sovereignty, independence, territorial integrity and unity of Côte d'Ivoire, and recalling the importance of the principles of good-neighbourliness, non-interference and regional cooperation,

Recalling that it endorsed the agreement signed by the Ivorian political forces at Linas-Marcoussis, France, on 23 January 2003 (the Linas-Marcoussis Agreement) and approved by the Conference of Heads of State on Côte d'Ivoire, held in Paris on 25 and 26 January 2003, and the agreement signed at Accra on 30 July 2004 (the Accra III Agreement),

Deploring once again the repeated violations of the ceasefire agreement of 3 May 2003,

Strongly recalling the obligations of all Ivorian parties, the Government of Côte d'Ivoire as well as the Forces nouvelles, to comply fully with the ceasefire agreement of 3 May 2003, to refrain from any violence, in particular against civilians, including foreign citizens, and to cooperate fully with the activities of the United Nations Operation in Côte d'Ivoire,

Welcoming the efforts of the Secretary-General, the African Union and the Economic Community of West African States towards re-establishing peace and stability in Côte d'Ivoire, and reaffirming in this regard its full support to the ongoing facilitation mission undertaken by Mr. Thabo Mbeki, President of the Republic of South Africa, on behalf of the African Union,

Welcoming also the decision of the Peace and Security Council of the African Union on Côte d'Ivoire taken on 10 January 2005 in Libreville, and noting its communiqué issued on that occasion,

Determining that the situation in Côte d'Ivoire continues to pose a threat to international peace and security in the region,

Acting under Chapter VII of the Charter of the United Nations,

1. *Reaffirms* its decision in paragraph 7 of resolution 1572(2004) that all States, particularly those bordering Côte d'Ivoire, shall take the necessary measures to prevent the direct or indirect supply, sale or transfer to Côte d'Ivoire of arms or any related materiel as well as the provision of any assistance, advice or training related to military activities;

2. *Authorizes* the United Nations Operation in Côte d'Ivoire and the French forces supporting it, within their capacity and without prejudice to their mandate set out in resolution 1528(2004) and paragraph 3 below:

(*a*) To monitor the implementation of the measures imposed by paragraph 7 of resolution 1572(2004), in cooperation with the group of experts referred to in paragraph 7 below, and, as appropriate, with the United Nations Mission in Liberia, the United Nations Mission in Sierra Leone and Governments concerned, including by inspecting, as they deem it necessary and, as appropriate, without notice, the cargo of aircraft and of any transport vehicle using the ports, airports, airfields, military bases and border crossings of Côte d'Ivoire;

(*b*) To collect, as appropriate, arms and any related materiel brought into Côte d'Ivoire in violation of the measures imposed by paragraph 7 of resolution 1572 (2004), and to dispose of such arms and related materiel as appropriate;

3. *Requests* the French forces supporting the United Nations Operation in Côte d'Ivoire, in addition to their mandate set out in resolution 1528(2004), to provide, as appropriate, security assistance to the United Nations Operation in Côte d'Ivoire in carrying out the tasks set out in paragraph 2 above;

4. *Acknowledges* that the appropriate civilian expertise within the United Nations Operation in Côte d'Ivoire is needed to fulfil the tasks set out in paragraph 2 above, to the extent that no additional resources are required;

5. *Demands* that all Ivorian parties, including the Government of Côte d'Ivoire and the Forces nouvelles, provide unhindered access, particularly to equipment, sites and installations referred to in paragraph 2 above, to the United Nations Operation in Côte d'Ivoire and French forces supporting it to enable them to carry out the tasks set out in paragraphs 2 and 3 above;

6. *Requests* the Secretary-General and the Government of France to report immediately to the Security Council, through the Security Council Committee established pursuant to paragraph 14 of resolution 1572 (2004) (the Committee), any hindrance or difficulty in implementing the tasks described in paragraph 2 (*b*) above, so that the Council can consider all appropriate measures against any individual or group that hinders the implementation of those tasks;

7. *Requests* the Secretary-General, in consultation with the Committee, to create, as referred to in para-

graph 17 of resolution 1572(2004), within thirty days of the date of adoption of the present resolution, and for a period of six months, a group of experts consisting of no more than three members (the Group of Experts), having the necessary skills to perform the following mandate:

(a) To examine and analyse information gathered by the United Nations Operation in Côte d'Ivoire and the French forces in the context of the monitoring mandate set out in paragraph 2 above;

(b) To gather and analyse all relevant information in Côte d'Ivoire, in countries of the region and, as necessary, in other countries, in cooperation with the Governments of those countries, on flows of arms and related materiel, and provision of assistance, advice or training related to military activities, as well as networks operating in violation of the measures imposed by paragraph 7 of resolution 1572(2004);

(c) To consider and recommend, where appropriate, ways of improving the capabilities of States, in particular those in the region, to ensure the effective implementation of the measures imposed by paragraph 7 of resolution 1572(2004);

(d) To report to the Council in writing within ninety days of its establishment, through the Committee, on the implementation of the measures imposed by paragraph 7 of resolution 1572(2004), with recommendations in this regard;

(e) To keep the Committee regularly updated on its activities;

(f) To exchange with the United Nations Operation in Côte d'Ivoire and the French forces, as appropriate, information that might be of use in fulfilling its monitoring mandate set out in paragraph 2 above;

(g) To provide the Committee in its reports with a list, with supporting evidence, of those found to have violated the measures imposed by paragraph 7 of resolution 1572(2004), and those found to have supported them in such activities, for possible future measures by the Council;

(h) To cooperate with other relevant groups of experts, in particular the group of experts on Liberia established pursuant to resolutions 1521(2003) of 22 December 2003 and 1579(2004) of 21 December 2004;

8. *Calls upon* the Government of Côte d'Ivoire and the Forces nouvelles, specifically their armed forces, to cooperate with the United Nations Operation in Côte d'Ivoire in establishing, within forty-five days of the date of adoption of the present resolution, a comprehensive list of armaments in the possession of those armed forces and in possession of paramilitary troops and militias associated with them, as well as their location, in particular aircraft and their armament of any kind, missiles, explosive devices, artillery of any calibre, including anti-aircraft artillery, and armoured and non-armoured vehicles, in order to help the United Nations Operation in Côte d'Ivoire to fulfil the tasks set out in paragraph 2 above and to assist in undertaking the regrouping of all the Ivorian forces involved and in implementing the national programme for the disarmament, demobilization and reintegration of combatants in accordance with resolution 1528(2004);

9. *Requests* the Secretary-General to communicate as appropriate to the Council, through the Committee, information gathered by the United Nations Opera-

tion in Côte d'Ivoire and, when possible, reviewed by the Group of Experts, about the supply of arms and related materiel to Côte d'Ivoire;

10. *Requests* also the Government of France to communicate as appropriate to the Council, through the Committee, information gathered by the French forces and, when possible, reviewed by the Group of Experts, about the supply of arms and related materiel to Côte d'Ivoire;

11. *Urges* all States, relevant United Nations bodies and, as appropriate, other organizations and interested parties, to cooperate fully with the Committee, the Group of Experts, the United Nations Operation in Côte d'Ivoire and the French forces, in particular by supplying any information at their disposal on possible violations of the measures imposed by paragraph 7 of resolution 1572(2004);

12. *Expresses its grave concern* at the use of mercenaries by both Ivorian parties, and urges both sides immediately to desist from this practice;

13. *Recalls* its request, set out in paragraph 15 of resolution 1572(2004), to all States, in particular those in the region, to report to the Committee on steps they have taken to implement the measures imposed by paragraph 7 of resolution 1572(2004);

14. *Expresses its intention* to consider the recommendations of the Secretary-General contained in his report of 9 December 2004, and the addendum thereto;

15. *Decides* to remain actively seized of the matter.

On 29 March [S/2005/211], the Secretary-General, as requested in resolution 1584(2005) (above), informed the Council of his intention to appoint, in consultation with the Council's Committee established in accordance with resolution 1572(2004) [YUN 2004, p. 187], Gilbert Charles Barthe (Switzerland), Atabou Bodian (Senegal) and Alex Vines (United Kingdom) to the Group of Experts concerning Côte d'Ivoire. On 3 June [S/2005/368], he informed the Council of the appointment of Jean-Pierre Witty (Canada) to replace Gilbert Charles Barthe, who was unable to take up his appointment.

Report of Group of Experts (July). In accordance with resolutions 1572(2004) and 1584(2005), the Group of Experts issued a July interim report [S/2005/470] on the situation in Côte d'Ivoire. The Panel, which began its mandate on 18 April, visited France and the United Kingdom and held consultations in New York before visiting Côte d'Ivoire's neighbours (Guinea, Mali, Burkina Faso and Senegal). In May it visited Portugal and Côte d'Ivoire. In Côte d'Ivoire, the Panel liaised closely with political, police and military branches of UNOCI. It also met with the French Licorne forces. The Panel visited all the country's airports and took into account the Secretary-General report's [S/2005/135] on inter-mission cooperation.

On 18 October [meeting 5283], the Council unanimously adopted **resolution 1632(2005)**. The draft [S/2005/653] was prepared in consultations among Council members.

The Security Council,

Recalling its previous resolutions concerning the situation in Côte d'Ivoire, in particular resolutions 1572(2004) of 15 November 2004, 1584(2005) of 1 February 2005 and 1609(2005) of 24 June 2005, and the relevant statements by its President,

Welcoming the ongoing efforts of the Secretary-General, the African Union and the Economic Community of Western African States towards re-establishing peace and stability in Côte d'Ivoire,

Recalling the interim report of the Group of Experts created by the Secretary-General pursuant to paragraph 7 of resolution 1584(2005), and anticipating the receipt of its final report,

Determining that the situation in Côte d'Ivoire continues to constitute a threat to international peace and security in the region,

Acting under Chapter VII of the Charter of the United Nations,

1. *Decides* to extend the mandate of the Group of Experts until 15 December 2005, and requests the Secretary-General to take the necessary administrative measures;

2. *Requests* the Group of Experts to submit to the Security Council, through the Committee established pursuant to paragraph 14 of resolution 1572(2004), before 1 December 2005, a brief written update on the implementation of the measures imposed by paragraph 7 of resolution 1572(2004) and reaffirmed by paragraph 1 of resolution 1584(2005), with recommendations in this regard;

3. *Decides* to remain actively seized of the matter.

On 2 November [S/2005/696], the Secretary-General informed the Council of his intentions to reappoint members of the Group of Experts, in accordance with resolution 1584(2005), until 15 December.

Report of Group of Experts (November). In November [S/2005/699], the Chairman of the Security Council Committee established pursuant to resolution 1572(2004) transmitted to the Council President the final report of the Group of Experts on the situation in Côte d'Ivoire. The report examined the political context, defence expenditure and natural resources, the effectiveness of the sanctions and possible violations of the arms embargo. The Group found that, despite rumours of fresh supplies of weapons and ammunition reaching the militias, there was no evidence of recent deliveries to those groups. It noted during its visits to Côte d'Ivoire many speculative articles in the Ivorian press alleging massive violations of the embargo, most of which were inaccurate. It reported that a number of countries had suspended or blocked the export of military goods and services to Côte d'Ivoire and many were forthcoming with information that assisted the Group in its task. However, there

was widespread frustration on the part of Member States at not being able to implement fully resolution 1572(2004) because the Sanctions Committee had failed to provide them with the names of individuals or organizations for an assets freeze or travel ban. The Group noted that the Committee needed to urgently clarify that issue.

The Group noted that Côte d'Ivoire defence expenditure was high and urged the Council to call upon the Government to submit a comprehensive breakdown of those expenditures for 2005 as a matter of urgency. As for Forces nouvelles, it noted that the natural resources under its control funded its military activities, especially the proceeds from cocoa, cotton and diamonds. The Panel indicated that the fruit terminal at the port of Abidjan was a strategic location for the unloading of military goods and equipment and highlighted the need for better declaration procedures and the strengthening of UNOCI monitoring capabilities. Meanwhile, the Group noted that, even though the export of diamonds from Côte d'Ivoire was illegal, there was no credible evaluation of illicit export volumes of rough diamonds. UNOCI and the secretariat of the Kimberley Process (an international arrangement for the certification of rough diamonds) needed to investigate the production and illicit export of diamonds and make public reports of their findings. The Council should also call upon the Government to commission an audit of all cocoa agencies to be completed by May 2006.

The Group concluded that neither the Government nor the Forces nouvelles had a strategic need for, or the financial capability to procure heavy and light weapons. Their immediate needs were for transport, including helicopters. While UNOCI was vigilant concerning air assets importations, it was less focused on the increasing number of vehicles imported for military use by FANCI and the Forces nouvelles. The Group highlighted what it called a "dual-use loophole" and called for its remedy through the drafting of a tighter definition by the Council. It recommended that the Committee request Belarus, Bulgaria, Côte d'Ivoire and Togo to report on the ownership of certain aircraft at Lomé airport. The Group noted that Côte d'Ivoire had not made submissions to the United Nations Register of Conventional Arms and recommended that it submit a baseline statement of acquisitions in its possession. It welcomed the establishment by the Government of Côte d'Ivoire, in May, of the National Commission for the ECOWAS Moratorium on Small Arms and Light Weapons and hoped that it would play an active role in the negotiations to transform the moratorium into a binding regional convention.

Report of Committee Chairman. The Committee Chairman, Adamantios Th. Vassilakis, visited Côte d'Ivoire from 18 to 21 October. His report, submitted to the Council on 9 December [S/2005/790], assessed the progress made by all parties towards the implementation of their commitments. The Chairman stated that the sanctions had proved to be an effective tool and deterrent, although there was scepticism among some regarding their positive effects, in particular about their power to change the behaviour of targeted individuals. There was strong agreement that individual sanctions should be applied without further delay to force the parties to implement the agreements reached and to prevent incitement to hatred and violence, human rights violations and abuses. Although the Group of Experts on Côte d'Ivoire did not find major violations of the arms embargo, there were indications that large quantities of arms were at the disposal of the population.

The Chairman recommended that the Council and the Committee should keep the situation under close review until resolution 1633(2005) (see p. 243) was fully and unconditionally implemented and the disarmament of the Forces nouvelles, the militias and the defence groups completed. The Committee should consider taking prompt action against any individuals hindering the peace process, violating the arms embargo, inciting hatred, violence or intolerance or committing violations or abuses of human rights or humanitarian law. He suggested that the Council should consider the report of the International Commission of Inquiry for Côte d'Ivoire [YUN 2004, p. 117] and that the Sanctions Committee discuss the annexes, as suggested by the Secretary-General, with a view to putting an end to impunity.

While the request of the AU and the Mediator to withhold action that would have a negative effect on the peace process was justified, the Council should not leave unanswered any actions that might give the impression that it allowed impunity.

SECURITY COUNCIL ACTION

On 14 December [meeting 5327], the Security Council adopted unanimously **resolution 1643 (2005)**. The draft [S/2005/786] was prepared in consultations among Council members.

The Security Council,

Recalling its previous resolutions and the statements by its President relating to the situation in Côte d'Ivoire,

Reaffirming its strong commitment to the sovereignty, independence, territorial integrity and unity of Côte d'Ivoire, and recalling the importance of the principles of good-neighbourliness, non-interference and regional cooperation,

Recalling that it endorsed the agreement signed by the Ivorian political forces at Linas-Marcoussis, France, on 23 January 2003 (the Linas-Marcoussis Agreement) and approved by the Conference of Heads of State on Côte d'Ivoire, held in Paris on 25 and 26 January 2003, the agreement signed at Accra on 30 July 2004 (the Accra III Agreement) and the agreement signed at Pretoria on 6 April 2005 (the Pretoria Agreement), as well as the decision of the Peace and Security Council of the African Union on the situation in Côte d'Ivoire adopted at its fortieth meeting, held at the level of Heads of State and Government in Addis Ababa on 6 October 2005,

Commending the efforts of the Secretary-General, the African Union, in particular President Olusegun Obasanjo of the Federal Republic of Nigeria, Chairman of the African Union, and President Thabo Mbeki of the Republic of South Africa, Mediator of the African Union, President Mamadou Tandja of the Republic of the Niger, Chairman of the Economic Community of West African States, and the leaders of the region to promote peace and stability in Côte d'Ivoire, and reiterating its full support for them,

Recalling the final communiqué of the International Working Group of 8 November 2005, which states in particular that the fundamental basis of the peace and national reconciliation process is enshrined in resolution 1633(2005) of 21 October 2005, and recalling also the final communiqué of the International Working Group of 6 December 2005,

Strongly recalling the obligations of all Ivorian parties, the Government of Côte d'Ivoire as well as the Forces nouvelles, to refrain from any violence, in particular against civilians, including foreign citizens, and to cooperate fully with the activities of the United Nations Operation in Côte d'Ivoire,

Expressing its serious concern at the persistence of the crisis in Côte d'Ivoire and of obstacles to the peace and national reconciliation process from all sides,

Reiterating its firm condemnation of all violations of human rights and international humanitarian law, including the use of child soldiers, in Côte d'Ivoire,

Taking note of the final communiqué of the Kimberley Process issued following its plenary meeting held in Moscow from 15 to 17 November 2005, and of the resolution adopted by Kimberley Process participants at that meeting setting out concrete measures to prevent the introduction of diamonds from Côte d'Ivoire into the legitimate diamond trade, and recognizing the linkage between the illegal exploitation of natural resources, such as diamonds, illicit trade in such resources, and the proliferation of and trafficking in arms and the recruitment and use of mercenaries as one of the sources of fuelling and exacerbating conflicts in West Africa,

Taking note also of the report of the Group of Experts on Côte d'Ivoire submitted on 7 November 2005,

Determining that the situation in Côte d'Ivoire continues to pose a threat to international peace and security in the region,

Acting under Chapter VII of the Charter of the United Nations,

1. *Decides* to renew until 15 December 2006 the provisions of paragraphs 7 to 12 of resolution 1572(2004) of 15 November 2004;

2. *Reaffirms* paragraphs 4 and 6 of resolution 1572(2004), paragraph 5 of resolution 1584(2005) of 1 February 2005, and paragraphs 3, 9, 14, 19 and 21 of resolution 1633(2005), reaffirms also paragraph 8 of resolution 1584(2005), and, in this regard, demands that the Forces nouvelles establish without delay a comprehensive list of armaments in their possession, in accordance with their obligations;

3. *Reaffirms its readiness* to impose the individual measures provided for in paragraphs 9 and 11 of resolution 1572(2004), including against any person designated by the Security Council Committee established pursuant to paragraph 14 of resolution 1572(2004) (the Committee) who blocks the implementation of the peace process as enshrined in resolution 1633(2005) and in the final communiqué of the International Working Group, who is determined to be responsible for serious violations of human rights and international humanitarian law committed in Côte d'Ivoire since 19 September 2002, who publicly incites hatred and violence, and who is determined to be in violation of the arms embargo;

4. *Decides* that any serious obstacle to the freedom of movement of the United Nations Operation in Côte d'Ivoire and of the French forces supporting it, or any attack on or obstruction to the action of the United Nations Operation in Côte d'Ivoire, of the French forces, of the High Representative for the elections in Côte d'Ivoire or of the International Working Group constitutes a threat to the peace and national reconciliation process for the purposes of paragraphs 9 and 11 of resolution 1572(2004);

5. *Requests* the Secretary-General and the Government of France to report to the Council immediately, through the Committee, any serious obstacle to the freedom of movement of the United Nations Operation in Côte d'Ivoire and of the French forces supporting it, including the names of those responsible, and requests the High Representative and the International Working Group to report to it immediately, through the Committee, any attack or obstruction to their action;

6. *Decides* that all States shall take the necessary measures to prevent the import of all rough diamonds from Côte d'Ivoire to their territory, welcomes the measures agreed upon by participants in the Kimberley Process Certification Scheme to this effect, and calls upon the States in the region which are not participants in the Kimberley Process to intensify their efforts to join the Kimberley Process in order to increase the effectiveness of monitoring the import of diamonds from Côte d'Ivoire;

7. *Requests* all States concerned, in particular those in the region, to report to the Committee, within ninety days of the date of adoption of the present resolution, on the actions that they have taken to implement the measures imposed by paragraphs 7, 9 and 11 of resolution 1572(2004) and by paragraphs 4 and 6 above, and authorizes the Committee to request whatever further information it may consider necessary;

8. *Decides* that, at the end of the period mentioned in paragraph 1 above, the Council shall review the measures imposed by paragraphs 7, 9 and 11 of resolu-

tion 1572(2004) and by paragraphs 4 and 6 above, in the light of progress accomplished in the peace and national reconciliation process in Côte d'Ivoire, and expresses its readiness to consider the modification or termination of those measures before the aforesaid period only if the provisions of resolution 1633(2005) have been fully implemented;

9. *Requests* the Secretary-General, in consultation with the Committee, to re-establish, within thirty days of the date of adoption of the present resolution and for a period of six months, a group of experts consisting of no more than five members (the Group of Experts), with the appropriate range of expertise, in particular on arms, diamonds, finance, customs, civil aviation and any other relevant expertise, to perform the following mandate:

(a) To exchange information with the United Nations Operation in Côte d'Ivoire and the French forces in the context of their monitoring mandate set out in paragraphs 2 and 12 of resolution 1609(2005) of 24 June 2005;

(b) To gather and analyse all relevant information in Côte d'Ivoire and elsewhere, in cooperation with the Governments of those countries, on flows of arms and related materiel, on provision of assistance, advice or training related to military activities, on networks operating in violation of the measures imposed by paragraph 7 of resolution 1572(2004), and on the sources of financing, including from the exploitation of natural resources in Côte d'Ivoire, for purchases of arms and related materiel and activities;

(c) To consider and recommend, where appropriate, ways of improving the capabilities of States, in particular those in the region, to ensure the effective implementation of the measures imposed by paragraph 7 of resolution 1572(2004) and by paragraph 6 above;

(d) To seek further information regarding the action taken by States with a view to implementing effectively the measures imposed by paragraph 6 above;

(e) To report to the Council in writing within ninety days of its establishment, through the Committee, on the implementation of the measures imposed by paragraph 7 of resolution 1572(2004) and by paragraph 6 above, with recommendations in this regard;

(f) To keep the Committee regularly updated on its activities;

(g) To provide the Committee in its reports with evidence of any violations of the measures imposed by paragraph 7 of resolution 1572(2004) and by paragraph 6 above;

(h) To cooperate with other relevant groups of experts, in particular the group of experts on Liberia established pursuant to resolutions 1521(2003) of 22 December 2003 and 1579(2004) of 21 December 2004;

(i) To monitor the implementation of the individual measures set out in paragraphs 9 and 11 of resolution 1572(2004);

10. *Also requests* the Secretary-General to communicate, as appropriate, to the Council, through the Committee, information gathered by the United Nations Operation in Côte d'Ivoire and, when possible, reviewed by the Group of Experts, about the supply of arms and related materiel to Côte d'Ivoire and about the production and illicit export of diamonds;

11. *Requests* the Government of France to communicate, as appropriate, to the Council, through the Com-

mittee, information gathered by the French forces and, when possible, reviewed by the Group of Experts, about the supply of arms and related materiel to Cote d'Ivoire and about the production and illicit export of diamonds;

12. *Requests* the Kimberley Process to communicate, as appropriate, to the Council, through the Committee, information, when possible, reviewed by the Group of Experts, about the production and illicit export of diamonds;

13. *Urges* all States, relevant United Nations bodies and other organizations and interested parties, including the Kimberley Process, to cooperate fully with the Committee, the Group of Experts, the United Nations Operation in Côte d'Ivoire and the French forces, in particular by supplying any information at their disposal on possible violations of the measures imposed by paragraphs 7, 9 and 11 of resolution 1572(2004) and by paragraphs 4 and 6 above;

14. *Decides* to remain actively seized of the matter.

UNOCI financing

In March [A/59/750], the Secretary-General submitted the UNOCI budget for the period from 1 July 2005 to 30 June 2006, in the amount of $371,835,600. The report also contained an expenditure report for the period from 4 April to 30 June 2004.

ACABQ, in its April report [A/59/736/Add.15], recommended that the budget be reduced by $4,225,600 to $367,610,000.

GENERAL ASSEMBLY ACTION

On 22 June [meeting 104], the General Assembly, on the recommendation of the Fifth Committee [A/59/529/Add.1], adopted **resolution 59/16 B** without vote [agenda item 154].

Financing of the United Nations Operation in Côte d'Ivoire

B

The General Assembly,

Having considered the report of the Secretary-General on the financing of the United Nations Operation in Côte d'Ivoire and the related reports of the Advisory Committee on Administrative and Budgetary Questions,

Recalling Security Council resolution 1528(2004) of 27 February 2004, by which the Council established the United Nations Operation in Côte d'Ivoire for an initial period of twelve months as from 4 April 2004, and the subsequent resolutions by which the Council extended the mandate of the Operation, the latest of which was resolution 1600(2005) of 4 May 2005,

Recalling also its resolution 58/310 of 18 June 2004 on the financing of the Operation and its subsequent resolution 59/16 A of 29 October 2004,

Reaffirming the general principles underlying the financing of United Nations peacekeeping operations, as stated in General Assembly resolutions 1874(S-IV) of 27 June 1963, 3101(XXVIII) of 11 December 1973 and 55/235 of 23 December 2000,

Mindful of the fact that it is essential to provide the Operation with the necessary financial resources to enable it to fulfil its responsibilities under the relevant resolutions of the Security Council,

1. *Requests* the Secretary-General to entrust the Head of Mission with the task of formulating future budget proposals in full accordance with the provisions of General Assembly resolution 59/296 of 22 June 2005, as well as other relevant resolutions;

2. *Takes note* of the status of contributions to the United Nations Operation in Côte d'Ivoire as at 15 April 2005, including the contributions outstanding in the amount of 43.8 million United States dollars, representing some 11 per cent of the total assessed contributions, notes with concern that only fifty-three Member States have paid their assessed contributions in full, and urges all other Member States, in particular those in arrears, to ensure payment of their outstanding assessed contributions;

3. *Expresses its appreciation* to those Member States which have paid their assessed contributions in full, and urges all other Member States to make every possible effort to ensure payment of their assessed contributions to the Operation in full;

4. *Expresses concern* at the financial situation with regard to peacekeeping activities, in particular as regards the reimbursements to troop contributors that bear additional burdens owing to overdue payments by Member States of their assessments;

5. *Also expresses concern* at the delay experienced by the Secretary-General in deploying and providing adequate resources to some recent peacekeeping missions, in particular those in Africa;

6. *Emphasizes* that all future and existing peacekeeping missions shall be given equal and non-discriminatory treatment in respect of financial and administrative arrangements;

7. *Also emphasizes* that all peacekeeping missions shall be provided with adequate resources for the effective and efficient discharge of their respective mandates;

8. *Reiterates its request* to the Secretary-General to make the fullest possible use of facilities and equipment at the United Nations Logistics Base at Brindisi, Italy, in order to minimize the costs of procurement for the Operation;

9. *Endorses* the conclusions and recommendations contained in the report of the Advisory Committee on Administrative and Budgetary Questions, and requests the Secretary-General to ensure their full implementation;

10. *Requests* the Secretary-General to ensure the full implementation of the relevant provisions of its resolution 59/296;

11. *Also requests* the Secretary-General to take all necessary action to ensure that the Operation is administered with a maximum of efficiency and economy;

12. *Further requests* the Secretary-General, in order to reduce the cost of employing General Service staff, to continue efforts to recruit local staff for the Operation against General Service posts, commensurate with the requirements of the Operation;

Expenditure report for the period from 4 April to 30 June 2004

13. *Takes note* of the expenditure report for the Operation for the period from 4 April to 30 June 2004;

Budget estimates for the period from 1 July 2005 to 30 June 2006

14. *Decides* to appropriate to the Special Account for the United Nations Operation in Côte d'Ivoire the amount of 386,892,500 dollars for the period from 1 July 2005 to 30 June 2006, inclusive of 367,501,000 dollars for the maintenance of the Operation, 15,856,300 dollars for the support account for peacekeeping operations and 3,535,200 dollars for the United Nations Logistics Base;

Financing of the appropriation

15. *Decides also* to apportion among Member States the amount of 386,892,500 dollars at a monthly rate of 32,241,041 dollars, in accordance with the levels updated in General Assembly resolution 58/256 of 23 December 2003, and taking into account the scale of assessments for 2005 and 2006, as set out in Assembly resolution 58/1 B of 23 December 2003, subject to a decision of the Security Council to extend the mandate of the Operation;

16. *Decides further* that, in accordance with the provisions of its resolution 973(X) of 15 December 1955, there shall be set off against the apportionment among Member States, as provided for in paragraph 15 above, their respective share in the Tax Equalization Fund of 10,150,900 dollars, comprising the estimated staff assessment income of 7,623,600 dollars approved for the Operation for the period from 1 July 2005 to 30 June 2006, the prorated share of 2,241,300 dollars of the estimated staff assessment income approved for the support account and the prorated share of 286,000 dollars of the estimated staff assessment income approved for the United Nations Logistics Base;

17. *Decides* that, for Member States that have fulfilled their financial obligations to the Operation, there shall be set off against their apportionment, as provided for in paragraph 15 above, their respective share of the unencumbered balance and other income in the amount of 13,328,900 dollars in respect of the financial period ended 30 June 2004, in accordance with the levels updated in its resolution 58/256, and taking into account the scale of assessments for 2004, as set out in its resolution 58/1 B;

18. *Decides also* that, for Member States that have not fulfilled their financial obligations to the Operation, there shall be set off against their outstanding obligations their respective share of the unencumbered balance and other income in the amount of 13,328,900 dollars in respect of the financial period ended 30 June 2004, in accordance with the scheme set out in paragraph 17 above;

19. *Decides further* that the decrease of 219,600 dollars in the estimated staff assessment income in respect of the financial period ended 30 June 2004 shall be set off against the credits from the amount of 13,328,900 dollars referred to in paragraphs 17 and 18 above;

20. *Emphasizes* that no peacekeeping mission shall be financed by borrowing funds from other active peacekeeping missions;

21. *Encourages* the Secretary-General to continue to take additional measures to ensure the safety and security of all personnel under the auspices of the United Nations participating in the Operation, bearing in mind paragraphs 5 and 6 of Security Council resolution 1502(2003) of 26 August 2003;

22. *Invites* voluntary contributions to the Operation in cash and in the form of services and supplies acceptable to the Secretary-General, to be administered, as appropriate, in accordance with the procedure and practices established by the General Assembly;

23. *Decides* to include in the provisional agenda of its sixtieth session the item entitled "Financing of the United Nations Operation in Côte d'Ivoire".

On 20 September [A/60/364], the Secretary-General submitted a revised budget amounting to $423,130,600, including an increase of $55,629,600 to accommodate the increase in UNOCI strength, authorized by the Security Council in resolution 1609(2005) (see p. 236).

ACABQ, in its October report [A/60/420], recommended a reduction of $4,353,000, bringing the total budget to $418,777,000, on account of the delayed deployment schedule for additional civilian staff.

GENERAL ASSEMBLY ACTION

On 23 November [meeting 53], the General Assembly, on the recommendation of the Fifth Committee [A/60/540], adopted **resolution 60/17 A** without vote [agenda item 138].

Financing of the United Nations Operation in Côte d'Ivoire

A

The General Assembly,

Having considered the report of the Secretary-General on the financing of the United Nations Operation in Côte d'Ivoire and the related report of the Advisory Committee on Administrative and Budgetary Questions,

Recalling Security Council resolution 1528(2004) of 27 February 2004, by which the Council established the United Nations Operation in Côte d'Ivoire for an initial period of twelve months as from 4 April 2004, and the subsequent resolutions by which the Council extended the mandate of the Operation, the latest of which was resolution 1609(2005) of 24 June 2005,

Recalling also its resolution 58/310 of 18 June 2004 on the financing of the Operation and its subsequent resolutions thereon, the latest of which was resolution 59/16 B of 22 June 2005,

Reaffirming the general principles underlying the financing of United Nations peacekeeping operations, as stated in General Assembly resolutions 1874(S-IV) of 27 June 1963, 3101(XXVIII) of 11 December 1973 and 55/235 of 23 December 2000,

Mindful of the fact that it is essential to provide the Operation with the necessary financial resources to enable it to fulfil its responsibilities under the relevant resolutions of the Security Council,

1. *Requests* the Secretary-General to entrust the Head of Mission with the task of formulating future budget proposals in full accordance with the provisions of General Assembly resolution 59/296 of 22 June 2005, as well as other relevant resolutions;

2. *Takes note* of the status of contributions to the United Nations Operation in Côte d'Ivoire as at 30 September 2005, including the contributions outstanding in the amount of 153.8 million United States dollars, representing some 22 per cent of the total assessed contributions, notes with concern that only twenty-seven Member States have paid their assessed contributions in full, and urges all other Member States, in particular those in arrears, to ensure payment of their outstanding assessed contributions;

3. *Expresses its appreciation* to those Member States which have paid their assessed contributions in full, and urges all other Member States to make every possible effort to ensure payment of their assessed contributions to the Operation in full;

4. *Expresses concern* at the financial situation with regard to peacekeeping activities, in particular as regards the reimbursements to troop contributors that bear additional burdens owing to overdue payments by Member States of their assessments;

5. *Also expresses concern* at the delay experienced by the Secretary-General in deploying and providing adequate resources to some recent peacekeeping missions, in particular those in Africa;

6. *Emphasizes* that all future and existing peacekeeping missions shall be given equal and non-discriminatory treatment in respect of financial and administrative arrangements;

7. *Also emphasizes* that all peacekeeping missions shall be provided with adequate resources for the effective and efficient discharge of their respective mandates;

8. *Reiterates its request* to the Secretary-General to make the fullest possible use of facilities and equipment at the United Nations Logistics Base at Brindisi, Italy, in order to minimize the costs of procurement for the Operation;

9. *Endorses* the conclusions and recommendations contained in the report of the Advisory Committee on Administrative and Budgetary Questions, and requests the Secretary-General to ensure their full implementation;

10. *Requests* the Secretary-General to ensure the full implementation of the relevant provisions of its resolution 59/296;

11. *Also requests* the Secretary-General to take all necessary action to ensure that the Operation is administered with a maximum of efficiency and economy;

12. *Further requests* the Secretary-General, in order to reduce the cost of employing General Service staff, to continue efforts to recruit local staff for the Operation against General Service posts, commensurate with the requirements of the Operation;

Revised budget estimates
for the period from 1 July 2005 to 30 June 2006
13. *Decides* to appropriate to the Special Account for the United Nations Operation in Côte d'Ivoire the amount of 51,276,000 dollars for the maintenance of the Operation for the period from 1 July 2005 to 30 June 2006, in addition to the amount of 386,892,500 dollars already appropriated for the same period under the terms of its resolution 59/16 B;

Financing of the appropriation
14. *Also decides*, taking into account the amount of 386,892,500 dollars previously apportioned for the period from 1 July 2005 to 30 June 2006 under the terms of its resolution 59/16 B, to apportion among Member States the additional amount of 28,946,129 dollars for the period from 1 July 2005 to 24 January 2006, in accordance with the levels updated in General Assembly resolution 58/256 of 23 December 2003, and taking into account the scale of assessments for 2005 and 2006, as set out in its resolution 58/1 B of 23 December 2003;

15. *Further decides* that, in accordance with the provisions of its resolution 973(X) of 15 December 1955, there shall be added to the apportionment among Member States, as provided for in paragraph 14 above, their respective share in the Tax Equalization Fund of the amount of 4,064 dollars, representing the estimated decrease in staff assessment income approved for the Operation for the period from 1 July 2005 to 24 January 2006;

16. *Decides* to apportion among Member States the additional amount of 22,329,871 dollars at a monthly rate of 4,273,000 dollars for the period from 25 January to 30 June 2006, in accordance with the scheme set out in paragraph 14 above, and taking into account the scale of assessments for 2006 as set out in its resolution 58/1 B, subject to a decision of the Security Council to extend the mandate of the Operation;

17. *Also decides* that, in accordance with the provisions of its resolution 973(X), there shall be added to the apportionment among Member States, as provided for in paragraph 16 above, their respective share in the Tax Equalization Fund of the amount of 3,136 dollars, representing the estimated decrease in staff assessment income approved for the Operation for the period from 25 January to 30 June 2006;

18. *Emphasizes* that no peacekeeping mission shall be financed by borrowing funds from other active peacekeeping missions;

19. *Encourages* the Secretary-General to continue to take additional measures to ensure the safety and security of all personnel under the auspices of the United Nations participating in the Operation, bearing in mind paragraphs 5 and 6 of Security Council resolution 1502(2003) of 26 August 2003;

20. *Invites* voluntary contributions to the Operation in cash and in the form of services and supplies acceptable to the Secretary-General, to be administered, as appropriate, in accordance with the procedure and practices established by the General Assembly;

21. *Decides* to keep under review during its sixtieth session the item entitled "Financing of the United Nations Operation in Côte d'Ivoire".

Liberia

In 2005, Liberia marked a major milestone in its efforts towards the restoration of peace and stability, with the successful holding of both legislative and presidential elections on 11 October. The elections, which saw Ellen Johnson-Sirleaf become the President-elect, marked one of the final steps towards completing the two-year transition period stipulated in the 2004 Comprehensive Peace Agreement [YUN 2004, p. 192]. With the assistance of the United Nations Mission in

Liberia, the Economic Commission of West African States and other regional and international actors, Liberia made progress in the disarmament of combatants, the disbandment of former factions, the establishment of a stable environment throughout the country, the partial restoration of State authority in the counties, the resettlement of a significant number of refugees, the establishment of the Truth and Reconciliation Commission, the launching of security sector reform and the agreement to establish the Governance and Economic Management Assistance Programme.

However, significant problems faced the new Government to be installed in 2006. Concerns about the performance of the National Transitional Government of Liberia, particularly its lack of transparency in the collection and use of revenues, as well as corruption, had led to the establishment of an investigative committee. The committee concluded that there had been administrative and financial malpractices and recommended that remedial measures be taken. The security situation in the country remained calm, but fragile. Demonstrations and protest marches by ex-combatants demanding rehabilitation and reintegration opportunities or protesting the non-payment of salary arrears posed a threat to stability, in addition to the civil unrest which arose from alleged ritual killings. The discovery of diamonds in Sinoe County sparked a rush of over 20,000 people to the site and gave rise to violations of UN sanctions. The situation in neighbouring countries continued to be monitored, as the recruitment of Liberian ex-combatants from Côte d'Ivoire, Guinea and Sierra Leone remained a concern.

The Panel of Experts established to conduct an assessment on the implementation, impact and effectiveness of the arms, travel, timber and diamond sanctions imposed on Liberia concluded that the assets freeze had not been implemented and reports were received of violations of the travel ban, including by former President Charles Taylor. Sanctions on timber had been effective, but the Forest Review Committee had recommended the cancellation of all concessions and that the sector be reformed. The Panel identified developments that were undermining Liberia's efforts to meet the Security Council's requirements for lifting the embargo on exporting rough diamonds. The Panel also found that Government administration was weak, with archaic internal controls and little external oversight, and if the sanctions on diamonds and timber were to be lifted, it was unlikely that Government revenues would enter the budget process for the benefit of the Liberian people. The Security Council therefore renewed the arms and travel measures for a further 12 months and the diamonds and timber measures for six months.

Governments and human rights organizations continued to call on the Government of Nigeria to hand over former President Charles Taylor to the Special Court for Sierra Leone. The Council, following allegations that Taylor had been meddling in Liberian politics and had violated the conditions of his asylum in Nigeria, indicated that his return to Liberia would constitute a threat to international peace and security in the region and amended the UNMIL mandate to include the apprehension and detainment of Mr. Taylor, in the event of a return to Liberia, and his transfer to Sierra Leone for prosecution before the Special Court for Sierra Leone.

The National Transitional Government of Liberia made some human rights advances with the signing of the Truth and Reconciliation Commission Act into law in and the establishment of the Independent National Commission. UNMIL spearheaded the formulation of a five-year national human rights action plan for Liberia.

In December, the Security Council extended UNMIL's mandate until 31 March 2006 and authorized a temporary increase in the personnel ceiling to 15,250 troops.

UNMIL

The United Nations Mission in Liberia (UNMIL), established by Security Council resolution 1509(2003) [YUN 2003, p. 194], was mandated to support the implementation of the 2003 Agreement on Ceasefire and Cessation of Hostilities [ibid., p. 189] and of the peace process; protect UN staff, facilities and civilians; support humanitarian and human rights activities; and assist in national security reform, including national police training and the formation of a new, restructured military.

By resolution 1638(2005) (see p. 267), the Council decided that the mandate should include the apprehension and detention of former President Charles Taylor in the event of his return to Liberia and to transfer him to the Special Court for Sierra Leone. By resolution 1626(2005) (see p. 264), the Council extended UNMIL's mandate until 31 March 2006.

Headquartered in the Liberian capital, Monrovia, UNMIL was headed by the Special Representative of the Secretary-General for Liberia, Jacques Paul Klein (United States), from July 2003 to April 2005. He was succeeded in that capacity by Alan Doss (United Kingdom), who was appointed with effect from 15 August [S/2005/464 & S/2005/465].

Lieutenant General Joseph Olorungbon Owonibi (Nigeria), Deputy Force Commander of UNMIL since November 2003, was appointed Force Commander as of 1 January 2005 [S/2005/19 & S/2005/18]; and Lieutenant General Chikadibia Isaac Obiakor (Nigeria) was appointed Force Commander as of 1 January 2006 [S/2005/738 & S/2005/739].

Also by resolution 1626(2005), the Council supported the Secretary-General's recommendation to return to the ceiling of 15,000 UN military personnel authorized by resolution 1509(2003) [YUN 2003, p. 194] by 31 March 2006.

Financing

In June, at its resumed fifty-ninth (2005) session, the General Assembly considered the performance report on the UNMIL budget for 1 August 2003 to 30 June 2004 [A/59/624], showing expenditures amounting to $548,178,700 against a total appropriation of $564,494,300, and the proposed budget for UNMIL for 1 July 2005 to 30 June 2006 [A/59/630] of $722,633,600, together with the related ACABQ report [A/59/736/Add.11].

GENERAL ASSEMBLY ACTION

On 22 June [meeting 104], the General Assembly, on the recommendation of the Fifth Committee [A/59/836], adopted **resolution 59/305** without vote [agenda item 134].

Financing of the United Nations Mission in Liberia

The General Assembly,

Having considered the reports of the Secretary-General on the financing of the United Nations Mission in Liberia and the related reports of the Advisory Committee on Administrative and Budgetary Questions,

Recalling Security Council resolution 1497(2003) of 1 August 2003, by which the Council declared its readiness to establish a United Nations stabilization force to support the transitional government and to assist in the implementation of a comprehensive peace agreement in Liberia,

Recalling also Security Council resolution 1509(2003) of 19 September 2003, by which the Council decided to establish the United Nations Mission in Liberia for a period of twelve months, and the subsequent resolution 1561(2004) of 17 September 2004, by which the Council extended the mandate of the Mission until 19 September 2005,

Recalling further its resolution 58/261 A of 23 December 2003 on the financing of the Mission and its subsequent resolution 58/261 B of 18 June 2004,

Reaffirming the general principles underlying the financing of United Nations peacekeeping operations, as stated in General Assembly resolutions 1874(S-IV) of 27 June 1963, 3101(XXVIII) of 11 December 1973 and 55/235 of 23 December 2000,

Noting with appreciation that voluntary contributions have been made to the Mission,

Mindful of the fact that it is essential to provide the Mission with the necessary financial resources to enable it to fulfil its responsibilities under the relevant resolutions of the Security Council,

1. *Requests* the Secretary-General to entrust the Head of Mission with the task of formulating future budget proposals in full accordance with the provisions of General Assembly resolution 59/296 of 22 June 2005, as well as other relevant resolutions;

2. *Takes note* of the status of contributions to the United Nations Mission in Liberia as at 15 April 2005, including the contributions outstanding in the amount of 96 million United States dollars, representing some 7 per cent of the total assessed contributions, notes with concern that only sixty-three Member States have paid their assessed contributions in full, and urges all other Member States, in particular those in arrears, to ensure payment of their outstanding assessed contributions;

3. *Expresses its appreciation* to those Member States that have paid their assessed contributions in full, and urges all other Member States to make every possible effort to ensure payment of their assessed contributions to the Mission in full;

4. *Expresses concern* at the financial situation with regard to peacekeeping activities, in particular as regards the reimbursements to troop contributors that bear additional burdens owing to overdue payments by Member States of their assessments;

5. *Also expresses concern* at the delay experienced by the Secretary-General in deploying and providing adequate resources to some recent peacekeeping missions, in particular those in Africa;

6. *Emphasizes* that all future and existing peacekeeping missions shall be given equal and non-discriminatory treatment in respect of financial and administrative arrangements;

7. *Also emphasizes* that all peacekeeping missions shall be provided with adequate resources for the effective and efficient discharge of their respective mandates;

8. *Reiterates its request* to the Secretary-General to make the fullest possible use of facilities and equipment at the United Nations Logistics Base at Brindisi, Italy, in order to minimize the costs of procurement for the Mission;

9. *Endorses* the conclusions and recommendations contained in the report of the Advisory Committee on Administrative and Budgetary Questions, and requests the Secretary-General to ensure their full implementation;

10. *Requests* the Secretary-General to ensure the full implementation of the relevant provisions of its resolution 59/296;

11. *Also requests* the Secretary-General to entrust the Special Representative of the Secretary-General to intensify his/her coordination and collaboration efforts with the agencies, funds and programmes in Liberia and to develop a workplan containing an integrated list of priorities, and further requests the Secretary-General to report to the General Assembly on actions taken as well as progress made in the context of the Mission budget for the period from 1 July 2006 to 30 June 2007;

12. *Further requests* the Secretary-General to take all necessary action to ensure that the Mission is administered with a maximum of efficiency and economy;

13. *Requests* the Secretary-General, in order to reduce the cost of employing General Service staff, to continue efforts to recruit local staff for the Mission against General Service posts, commensurate with the requirements of the Mission;

Financial performance report for the period from 1 August 2003 to 30 June 2004

14. *Takes note* of the report of the Secretary-General on the financial performance of the Mission for the period from 1 August 2003 to 30 June 2004;

Budget estimates for the period from 1 July 2005 to 30 June 2006

15. *Decides* to appropriate to the Special Account for the United Nations Mission in Liberia the amount of 760,567,400 dollars for the period from 1 July 2005 to 30 June 2006, inclusive of 722,422,100 dollars for the maintenance of the Mission, 31,191,200 dollars for the support account for peacekeeping operations and 6,954,100 dollars for the United Nations Logistics Base;

Financing of the appropriation

16. *Decides also* to apportion among Member States the amount of 166,902,291 dollars for the period from 1 July to 19 September 2005, in accordance with the levels updated in General Assembly resolution 58/256 of 23 December 2003, and taking into account the scale of assessments for 2005 as set out in its resolution 58/1 B of 23 December 2003;

17. *Decides further* that, in accordance with the provisions of its resolution 973(X) of 15 December 1955, there shall be set off against the apportionment among Member States, as provided for in paragraph 16 above, their respective share in the Tax Equalization Fund of 3,552,213 dollars, comprising the estimated staff assessment income of 2,461,223 dollars approved for the Mission, the prorated share of 967,552 dollars of the estimated staff assessment income approved for the support account and the prorated share of 123,438 dollars of the estimated staff assessment income approved for the United Nations Logistics Base;

18. *Decides* to apportion among Member States the amount of 593,665,109 dollars for the period from 20 September 2005 to 30 June 2006 at a monthly rate of 63,380,616 dollars, in accordance with the levels updated in General Assembly resolution 58/256, and taking into account the scale of assessments for 2005 and 2006 as set out in its resolution 58/1 B, subject to a decision of the Security Council to extend the mandate of the Mission;

19. *Decides also* that, in accordance with the provisions of its resolution 973(X), there shall be set off against the apportionment among Member States, as provided for in paragraph 18 above, their respective share in the Tax Equalization Fund of 12,635,087 dollars, comprising the estimated staff assessment income of 8,754,477 dollars approved for the Mission, the prorated share of 3,441,548 dollars of the estimated staff assessment income approved for the support account and the prorated share of 439,062 dollars of the estimated staff assessment income approved for the United Nations Logistics Base;

20. *Decides further* that, for Member States that have fulfilled their financial obligations to the Mission, there shall be set off against their apportionment, as provided for in paragraph 16 above, their respective share of the unencumbered balance and other income in the total amount of 17,034,600 dollars in respect of the financial period ended 30 June 2004, in accordance with the levels updated in General Assembly resolution 58/256, and taking into account the scale of assessments for 2004 as set out in its resolution 58/1 B;

21. *Decides* that, for Member States that have not fulfilled their financial obligations to the Mission, there shall be set off against their outstanding obligations their respective share of the unencumbered balance and other income in the total amount of 17,034,600 dollars in respect of the financial period ended 30 June 2004, in accordance with the scheme set out in paragraph 20 above;

22. *Decides also* that the decrease of 2,096,900 dollars in the estimated staff assessment income in respect of the financial period ended 30 June 2004 shall be set off against the credits from the amount of 17,034,600 dollars referred to in paragraphs 20 and 21 above;

23. *Emphasizes* that no peacekeeping mission shall be financed by borrowing funds from other active peacekeeping missions;

24. *Encourages* the Secretary-General to continue to take additional measures to ensure the safety and security of all personnel under the auspices of the United Nations participating in the Mission, bearing in mind paragraphs 5 and 6 of Security Council resolution 1502(2003) of 26 August 2003;

25. *Invites* voluntary contributions to the Mission in cash and in the form of services and supplies acceptable to the Secretary-General, to be administered, as appropriate, in accordance with the procedure and practices established by the General Assembly;

26. *Decides* to include in the provisional agenda of its sixtieth session the item entitled "Financing of the United Nations Mission in Liberia".

Peacebuilding efforts

Implementation of Comprehensive Peace Agreement and UNMIL activities

Report of Secretary-General (March). The Secretary-General, on 17 March, submitted his sixth progress report on UNMIL [S/2005/177] covering developments since his December 2004 report [YUN 2004, p. 200]. He noted the various advancements made in the implementation of the 2003 Comprehensive Peace Agreement [YUN 2003, p. 192]: preparations for the October 2005 elections were under way; former armed factions either formed new political parties or associated themselves with existing ones; increased numbers of internally displaced persons and refugees were returning to their homes; the training programme for the new Liberian police service was moving forward; and the process of restoring county administration continued, albeit at a slow pace. Limited progress was made in efforts to entrench the rule of law and improve the human rights situation; however, the National Transitional Government continued to function, notwithstanding serious internal tensions.

The Implementation Monitoring Committee and the International Contact Group, the two mechanisms monitoring implementation of the 2003 Comprehensive Peace Agreement, continued to meet regularly. Subregional engagement with the peace process remained strong, notably by ECOWAS, which visited Liberia in February/March to assess progress in the peace process and election preparations.

The Government, responding to donor concerns about its performance, particularly its lack of transparency in the collection and use of revenues and resistance to reforms and audits to fight corruption, set up a Task Force on Corruption and a Cash Management Committee. The National Transitional Legislative Assembly also set up a committee in January to investigate allegations of administrative and financial impropriety involving its leadership; it presented its report in March, confirming existent administrative and financial malpractices and recommending remedial measures. A proposal to suspend the Assembly leadership for up to seven months (which went into effect on 14 March) degenerated into a fracas; UNMIL had to intervene to restore calm.

In contravention of an article of the Comprehensive Peace Agreement barring principal cabinet ministers from running for elective office in the 11 October elections, two such officials declared their intention to run for the presidency and a senatorial seat, one arguing that the article was inconsistent with another article of the Agreement that he invoked. UNMIL and the International Contact Group on Liberia found no contradiction between the two articles—a finding reaffirmed by the National Elections Commission and the ECOWAS Mediator, General Abdulsalami Abubakar.

The overall security situation remained calm but fragile. Several incidents of lawlessness and violent unrest occurred, but no major disturbances. Large student demonstrations protesting the closure of schools were staged in Monrovia in December 2004, as were protests by civil servants against the non-payment of salaries in arrears and, in January and February 2005, by ex-combatants who were growing increasingly restive while awaiting rehabilitation and reintegration opportunities. Disturbances also occurred at rubber plantations. Incidents of mob violence erupted in Maryland County in January, following allegations attributing the disappearance of certain persons to ritual killings. As a result, the Transitional Government imposed a dusk-to-

dawn curfew, and UNMIL troops and police acted quickly to restore calm.

As of 1 March, the number of formally disarmed combatants totalled 101,495, including women, boys and girls. With UNICEF assistance, 98 per cent of former child combatants were rejoined with their families. UNMIL destroyed all weapons and ammunition collected during the disarmament process. It encouraged communities to divulge information on arms caches and, with UNDP, launched a community arms collection and destruction project. Some 612 ex-combatants identified as foreign nationals during the disarmament and demobilization process were still awaiting repatriation. In addition to 50 children already repatriated to Liberia from Sierra Leone, the two countries reached an agreement for the repatriation by 31 March of 435 Liberian ex-combatants in internment camps in Sierra Leone. The most pressing challenge was to create long-term reintegration opportunities for more than 100,000 ex-combatants. Only 25,591 were participating in reintegration projects funded by the relevant UNDP-managed trust fund, the European Commission and the United States Agency for International Development; a number of projects in the pipeline would provide immediate opportunities for another 44,502, but many of them had yet to begin, owing to a lack of funding. The Secretary-General appealed to the international community for funds to reduce the $40 million shortfall.

As to the restructuring of the national police, some 1,134 trainees were enrolled in the National Police Academy training programme. As of 1 March, 200 police officers were deployed in the 12 counties with minimal or no police presence, and command structures were established with the deployment of police commanders to five regional police centres in Kakata, Tubmanburg, Gbarnga, Zwedru and Harper. For those outlying deployments to be sustainable, an estimated $871,000 was urgently required for basic equipment, renovations of police stations, including detention cells and security measures. The United States continued to take the lead in coordinating plans for the restructuring of the Liberian military, for which a preliminary budget was estimated at $87.5 to $200 million. Unfortunately, the restructuring exercise could not proceed until the existing personnel from the Armed Forces of Liberia had been decommissioned. In that regard, the Government's list of 14,084 personnel was being verified against the UNMIL database to determine their eligibility benefits for terminal. An estimated minimum of $8.5 million in donor assistance would be needed to cover the cost of their severance and pension packages.

Reform of the justice sector continued at a slow pace. Circuit courts functioned in only eight counties and only 60 per cent of the magistrate courts were operational. UNMIL conducted four training courses throughout the country for prosecutors and law enforcement officers. At the initiative of UNMIL, a case flow management committee was established to address the problem of pretrial detainees held for excessive periods. The recruitment of correctional officers, expected to take place every three months, had begun, with UNMIL providing technical advice and on-the-job training, as well as assisting in developing draft national policies on prisoner discipline and adjudication and admission procedures. About $130,000 was urgently required for the training of correctional officers and $800,000 for prison refurbishment and security upgrades.

Limited progress was made in the restoration of State authority and in the rehabilitation of government institutions. As of 18 February, the National Task Force for the Restoration of State authority completed consultations for the selection of Superintendent and Assistant Superintendent nominees in all 15 counties. The Transitional Government deployed 564 government officials across the country, including internal revenue collectors, customs officers and some 250 immigration and naturalization officers. UNMIL supported government efforts to ensure financial transparency and accountability by liaising with the General Audit Office on audits of ministries and State-owned enterprises. Concerns persisted over the Government's limited capacity to deliver basic services. A dearth of official vehicles and office accommodation, combined with other logistical constraints, undermined the ability of recently deployed county superintendents to perform their duties. Also, most regional officials had to travel to Monrovia to collect their salaries. UNMIL was working with the Central Bank of Liberia to establish rural branches and with the World Bank and the Government to find a short-term solution to the problem.

UNMIL continued to support the Government in asserting control over the country's land-based and marine natural resources. The Government lacked the capacity to police illegal fishing in its territorial waters and was powerless to prevent offshore dumping of waste by foreign vessels. UNMIL provided advice to the technical working group on fishing and undertook reconnaissance of Liberian waters to monitor illegal fishing. It also assisted government institutions in regulating issues of ownership, land tenure, management and functioning in respect of rubber and timber plantations. The Government was fo-cused on ensuring compliance by the diamond-mining sector with the Kimberley Process Certification Scheme [YUN 2000, p. 76]. A review team of international experts on the Scheme that visited the country in February was to present its recommendations to the Panel of Experts dealing with sanctions on Liberia (see p. 269). UNMIL trained guards from the Forestry Development Authority and conducted an environmental baseline survey.

In the humanitarian area, UNHCR continued to facilitate the voluntary repatriation of Liberian refugees from Ghana, Guinea, Côte d'Ivoire, Nigeria and Sierra Leone. An estimated 100,000 refugees had returned spontaneously, while 8,113 returned with UNHCR assistance. As of 1 March, 67,644 internally displaced persons returned to their respective counties and were provided with return packages. Assistance provided by other UN agencies included food aid by WFP; agricultural support to farm families from FAO; and the re-establishment of country health teams by WHO. In addition to providing basic health care for 100,000 internally displaced persons and enabling the immunization services for 2.47 million children, UNICEF trained 13,000 teachers in "emergency" education as part of its back-to-school campaign.

The Secretary-General observed that the main pillars of the transition process had been successfully erected. However, if not provided with the necessary support and advice during that critical period, Liberia faced the risk of repeating the pattern of abuse of power, institutional breakdown and violence that had plagued the country for the past 25 years. It was therefore imperative that the Government proceed without delay to institute fundamental reforms and that the international community provide the required resources to allow for the consolidation of gains made so far. The Government also needed to eliminate corrupt practices and institute transparent arrangements for the management of public funds and take disciplinary actions against Government officials resisting institutional reforms to fight corruption. It should play a more proactive role in urgently finding a solution to the problems of the inadequate payment of salaries and provision of logistics for the national police, which might perpetuate a culture of corruption in the police service. The Government, along with the international community, should give due consideration to providing the $8.5 million required to complete the programme for restructuring the Armed Forces of Liberia.

The Secretary-General underscored other concerns, including the need to convene a national consultative forum prior to the elections to discuss reforms, particularly those on land use and property rights; measures to ensure free and fair elections; the growing disaffection among former combatants, unemployed youth, students and government workers; the activities of close associates of former President Charles Taylor; and negative developments in Côte d'Ivoire and their impact on efforts to stabilize Liberia.

EU evaluations. In a 21 March statement on evaluations [S/2005/222] carried out by the European Commission in Liberia, the EU, noting that the country was at a crucial point in its transition process, called on all political forces and the Liberian transitional authorities to cooperate to ensure strict compliance with the timetable and framework for the conduct of the October elections. It expressed concern about the significant level of corruption brought to light in recent reports and evaluations that was largely going unpunished, saying such corruption damaged the country's image and ongoing democratic process, and could jeopardize the conduct and international recognition of the elections.

Report of Secretary-General (June). In his June progress report on UNMIL [S/2005/391], the Secretary-General stated that the United Nations, the European Commission, the World Bank, the International Monetary Fund, ECOWAS and the United States met (Copenhagen, Denmark, 11 May) to address the issue of improving Liberia's economic governance. It reviewed the audit reports of the Central Bank of Liberia and five State-owned enterprises, and noted that the technical and policy advice on economic governance-related issues given to the Government over the previous 18 months had not achieved the desired results due to its unwillingness to institute reforms. Concluding that financial malfeasance and a lack of transparency and accountability were undermining the implementation of the Comprehensive Peace Agreement, they decided to develop an economic governance action plan for the Government's implementation, to be submitted to the Security Council for consideration.

With the agreement of the Chairman of the Transitional Government, Charles Gyude Bryant, ECOWAS earlier had dispatched a team of investigators to look into allegations of corruption within the Government. The team encountered resistance from some Ministers and other officials, as well as from the Liberian Institute of Certified Public Accountants, which petitioned the Supreme Court for a writ of prohibition restraining public officers from cooperating with the investigation on the grounds that it was a violation of Liberia's sovereignty. The writ was refused by the Supreme Court. Tensions stemming from the 14 March suspension of four members

of the National Transitional Legislative Assembly—the Speaker, Deputy Speaker, the Chairperson of the Ways and Means Committee and Chairperson of the Rules and Orders Committee—for administrative and financial malpractice continued. A petition filed by the suspended officials for a reversal of their suspension was pending before the Supreme Court. The Assembly, which maintained that the judiciary had no jurisdiction over its internal processes, continued to function under the newly elected Acting Speaker and Deputy Speaker.

The Implementation Monitoring Committee and the International Contact Group continued to meet regularly to review progress in the peace process and to address emerging issues. The second meeting of the ECOWAS Coordination Mechanism (Abuja, Nigeria, 26 May), jointly held by the Government and the United Nations, examined progress and remaining challenges in the implementation of the Comprehensive Peace Agreement; welcomed the decision of Liberia's international partners to develop an economic governance action plan (above); emphasized that security sector reform should include the rehabilitation of the judicial, penal and immigration sectors; and called for the adoption of clear, well-defined and transparent criteria for the inclusion in or exclusion of individuals from the sanctions list on travel ban and assets freeze. The meeting also called for evidence from those alleging that the former President of Liberia was in violation of the terms of his asylum in Nigeria by actively interfering in Liberia's forthcoming presidential elections.

The security situation was marred by several incidents. Unemployed ex-combatants, susceptible to exploitation by political elements, held violent demonstrations to demand reintegration benefits and opportunities and also threatened to disrupt the elections and attack UNMIL personnel. Organized ex-combatant groups linked to influential members of the former armed factions were illegally occupying the State-owned Guthrie Rubber Plantation, located on the border of Bomi and Grand Cape Mount Counties. Other groups held protests demanding that their enrolment in schools they had formerly attended be facilitated. On 15 April, the first referral and counselling office for demobilized ex-combatants opened in Monrovia. Other threats to security were: the "coalition of unwilling political forces" composed of individuals barred by the Comprehensive Peace Agreement from running in the 11 October elections, those on the Security Council travel-ban and assets-freeze lists and those benefiting economically from Liberia's instability and lack of Government authority; and ethnic clashes. UNMIL troops continued to provide umbrella security throughout the country in order to create a stable environment for the electoral process. It took over security responsibilities at Monrovia's Freeport to enable it to meet international ship and port facility standards and enhance its security and operations.

In support of security sector reform, the programme to develop the new professional Liberian National Police made steady progress. In-kind support was provided by Belgium (weapons and ammunition), China (motorcycles and radios) and the United States (uniforms and funding for operational costs and trainee stipends). In May, UNMIL launched a training programme for senior law enforcement managers, who would serve as a core group of trainers when the new police service, to be established formally on 1 July, was to assume responsibility for running the Academy's training programme.

The programme for the recruitment and training of the new armed forces was expected to begin after the completion of the decommissioning and retirement process for the existing Armed Forces of Liberia. By an executive order signed on 15 May by the Chairman of the Transitional Government, that process would begin on 31 May; it was expected to be completed by September. The decommissioning exercise, estimated at $16.4 million, had a shortfall of some $5.4 million.

Other UNMIL activities included building the capacity of the justice sector in terms of training the various categories of judicial personnel, providing legal aid services to defendants, assisting in convening a meeting of a legislative drafting working group, and providing support to the Bureau of Corrections and Rehabilitation towards the rehabilitation of corrections infrastructure. UNMIL increased programming on human rights, transitional justice and humanitarian activities and carried out community-level live broadcasts with public participation on issues related to the peace process. It assisted in the return of Government officials to their duty stations, thereby to restore State authority, especially in the interior of the country; in providing advice to the relevant institutions and authorities on measures to ensure proper management of natural resources and monitoring sites where natural resource exploitation was taking place; spearheading the formulation of a five-year national human rights action plan; and accelerating the return of internally displaced persons and refugees to their counties of origin.

The annual review meeting on the Results-Focused Transitional Framework (Copenhagen, 9-10 May), attended by the Government and its international partners, identified priorities for 2005: addressing corruption, ensuring transparency and integrity in fiscal management and providing basic services in the interior of the country to sustain the return of internally displaced persons and refugees. The meeting recognized the need to extend the Framework into 2006 to ensure a structured transition from the Framework to a poverty reduction strategy based on the Millennium Development Goals [YUN 2000, p. 51].

The Secretary-General noted the encouraging progress achieved in Liberia in the past three months. He stressed the importance of the remaining six months of the transition period for laying the foundations for a peaceful and democratic Liberia; any efforts to disrupt the electoral process should be expeditiously addressed. He reiterated his March recommendation that the Security Council favourably consider authorizing an additional formed police unit of 120 officers, for an interim period of six months beginning in August, to assist in dealing with security emergencies during the electoral period.

Report of Secretary-General (September). In his September report on UNMIL [S/2005/560], the Secretary-General stated that the National Transitional Government took measures against a number of reported cases of Government corruption, suspending the Commissioner of the Bureau of Maritime Affairs, following allegations of fraud and dismissing Liberia's representative to the International Maritime Organization (IMO). Along with two others from the Bureau, they were alleged to have misappropriated more than $4 million and were charged with "economic sabotage and fraud of the internal revenue of Liberia". The ECOWAS team dispatched to investigate corruption within the Government (see p. 261) submitted its report to the ECOWAS Heads of State. Meanwhile, draft legislation on the establishment of a Liberian anti-corruption agency had been prepared.

The leadership crisis at the Transitional Legislative Assembly was resolved on 2 August, when the Supreme Court ruled that the 14 March suspension of four of its members violated neither the Comprehensive Peace Agreement, nor the Constitution, nor the standing rules of the Assembly, and that the Assembly had followed due process. One member, who had sought the Secretary-General's intervention to facilitate his reinstatement, or lift the Agreement's restriction barring him from running in the elections, was informed that the United Nations respected the Court's ruling and the sanctity of the legislature, and that it had no authority to modify the Agreement.

During the reporting period, diamond deposits discovered in the Sanquin District of Sinoe County resulted in an influx to the site of some 20,000 people who began illegal alluvial diamond mining. The presence of such a large group of youths, including ex-combatants, posed a threat to security. Cholera broke out in the area, claiming 29 lives. A security assessment team recommended evacuation of the area, while WHO delivered cholera treatment kits for 10,000 people. Other security concerns were the simmering ethnic tensions, property disputes and election-related violence.

The programme for the establishment of a new Liberian police service was on course to complete the basic training of 1,800 national police in time for the October elections. By 24 August, 756 police officers had completed the full basic training programme. Some 263 Special Security Service personnel and 116 Liberian Seaport Police had also graduated from the training programme. In July, 208 more police officers were deployed to various locations in the country, bringing to 918 the number of officers redeployed to police stations in the counties. The United States pledged $1.7 million to allow training at the Police Academy to continue for a further year. Funding shortfalls hampered efforts to rehabilitate police infrastructure, re-equip specialized units and decommission personnel from the Liberian National Police and the Special Security Services who were ineligible to join the new restructured services

By 24 August, 8,164 of the 9,086 irregular armed forces personnel had been demobilized. The demobilization programme, however, faced a funding shortfall of $11.5 million for the demobilization of 4,095 regular personnel of the Armed Forces of Liberia. Demobilized soldiers would be eligible to apply for the new military force during a 45-day recruitment period. The new force, originally intended to be 4,000 strong, was reduced to 2,000 for lack of funds. Also by 24 August, 37,500 demobilized ex-combatants had been placed in rehabilitation and reintegration projects and another 35,448 accommodated in projects covered by the UNDP-managed Disarmament, Demobilization, Reintegration and Rehabilitation Trust Fund. Nonetheless, 26,000 ex-combatants were still awaiting participation in the rehabilitation and reintegration programme, which was also facing a shortage of about $18.5 million. UNMIL and UNDP began registering ex-combatants illegally occupying the Guthrie Rubber Plantation (see p. 261) for reintegration opportunities. Ex-combatants numbering 5,187 who were unarmed and therefore did not enter the disarmament and demobilization

programme would be placed in community-based recovery programmes.

The judicial system reform saw significant progress with the conclusion of the nomination, vetting and appointment processes for circuit court judges, specialized court judges and magistrates. UNMIL collaborated with the Liberian National Bar Association to ensure transparency in the selection and vetting procedures. The courts in operation were handling an increased number of cases: in July alone, six criminal jury trials were concluded, which equalled the total concluded during the whole of 2004. UNMIL continued to assist the Bureau of Corrections in improving conditions at corrections institutions and deployed corrections advisers to Zwedru and Harper, where courts recently opened with no detention facilities. UNMIL quick-impact projects also financed projects for water, sanitation and physical exercise in Monrovia and Gbarnga prisons.

In the area of human rights, on 10 June, the Chairman of the Transitional Government signed into law the Truth and Reconciliation Commission Act and, on 14 July, the ECOWAS Mediator presided over the inauguration of the selection panel for the Commission. The panel would recommend 15 candidates, from among whom the Chairman would select and appoint up to nine commissioners by 10 September. They would be assisted by three international technical advisers selected by OHCHR and ECOWAS. Following a visit to Liberia (9-13 July), the United Nations High Commissioner for Human Rights, Louise Arbour, expressed the view that the weakest link in the Liberian transitional process was the justice system and recommended that the international community do more to encourage the Liberian judiciary to open up to international assistance. UNMIL hosted a workshop (21-23 July) on transitional justice for African peacekeeping missions, facilitated activities to raise human rights awareness and conducted a nationwide survey of human rights violations in the agricultural sector, with a focus on rubber plantations.

To extend and consolidate State authority in all 15 counties, the Government completed the commissioning of all 15 county superintendents in mid-July. Almost 95 per cent of civil servants had returned to their duty stations in the counties and at border posts; their salaries could be paid by offices of the Central Bank of Liberia in Kakata, Buchanan and Gbarnga, recently constructed with UNMIL assistance. To assist the Government to regain full control over the exploitation of the country's natural resources, particularly over artisanal diamond-mining activities, UNMIL continued to report to the Government the findings of its aerial and ground surveillance of areas where illegal diamond-mining was being carried out. On 28 July, the Government announced a draft action plan to meet the requirements for lifting the sanctions imposed by the Security Council on diamond mining and the export of rough diamonds from Liberia, which recommended an increased UNMIL presence in diamond-mining areas. The report of the Forest Concession Review Committee, endorsed by the European Commission, the United States and UNMIL, recommended the cancellation of all 70 forestry concession agreements for failure to meet the basic operational requirements and the debarment of 12 companies for complicity in the country's civil war. A committee would be established to monitor implementation of the reform programme. On 17 August, UNMIL assisted the Ministry of Internal Affairs to evacuate an estimated 1,000 people illegally residing, mining and hunting in Sapo National Park.

The Secretary-General commended the Liberian people for their determination to participate in the polls and the National Elections Commission for keeping the electoral process on track. He emphasized that the political parties, the candidates and their supporters needed to ensure that the electoral campaigns were conducted peaceably and freely, and that voters could participate in credible polls without any threat of violence. He called on the Government to redouble its efforts to raise the requisite funds for demobilizing security personnel and decommissioning former armed forces personnel who were ineligible to join the restructured security services. The Secretary-General appealed to donors to close the funding gap for the reintegration programme for ex-combatants. He stated that the proposed governance and economic management assistance programme would be an important tool for ensuring the Government's control over its revenues and expenditures, assisting in national recovery efforts, helping Liberia meet the requirements for the lifting of sanctions imposed by the Security Council and retaining the confidence of donors. He urged the Government to reach an early agreement on the programme for consideration by the Council. Although the transitional process prescribed by the Comprehensive Peace Agreement would conclude upon the inauguration of the newly elected Government in January 2006, the Secretary-General said that the peace process would still face many challenges.

In the light of the new phase of UNMIL operations, the Secretary-General recommended that its mandate be extended for a period of 12 months, until 19 September 2006.

The Secretary-General also proposed a temporary increase in UNMIL troop strength of some 250 troops, from 15 November 2005 to 31 March 2006, to provide security both at the Special Court for Sierra Leone after the withdrawal of UNAMSIL, and throughout Liberia in the sensitive period following the October elections and the inauguration of the newly-elected Government of Liberia, scheduled for January 2006.

SECURITY COUNCIL ACTION

On 19 September [meeting 5263], the Security Council unanimously adopted **resolution 1626 (2005)**. The draft [S/2005/591] was prepared in consultations among Council members.

The Security Council,

Recalling its previous resolutions and the statements by its President concerning the situation in Liberia and in Sierra Leone, in particular resolutions 1509(2003) of 19 September 2003, 1610(2005) of 30 June 2005 and 1620(2005) of 31 August 2005,

Welcoming the report of the Secretary-General of 1 September 2005,

Welcoming progress made in the preparations for the October 2005 presidential and legislative elections,

Welcoming the further extension of State authority, including progress in the establishment of a new Liberian police service and the appointment of new judges and magistrates,

Expressing its appreciation for the indispensable and continuing contributions to the Liberian peace process by the Economic Community of West African States and the African Union, and for financial and other assistance provided by the international community,

Welcoming the signing by the National Transitional Government of Liberia and the International Contact Group on Liberia of the Governance and Economic Management Assistance Program, which is designed to ensure prompt implementation of the Comprehensive Peace Agreement signed at Accra on 18 August 2003 and to expedite the lifting of measures imposed by resolution 1521(2003) of 22 December 2003,

Reiterating its appreciation for the essential work of the Special Court for Sierra Leone and its vital contributions to the establishment of the rule of law in Sierra Leone and the subregion, and encouraging all States to cooperate fully with the Court as it implements its completion strategy,

Noting that the United Nations Mission in Sierra Leone is scheduled to end its operations on 31 December 2005,

Recalling the briefing by the President of the Special Court for Sierra Leone to the Security Council on 24 May 2005, in which he stressed the need for a continuing international security presence to provide protection for the Court after the departure of the Mission, and welcoming the recommendations of the Secretary-General in this regard,

Determining that the situation in Liberia continues to constitute a threat to international peace and security in the region,

Acting under Chapter VII of the Charter of the United Nations,

1. *Decides* that the mandate of the United Nations Mission in Liberia shall be extended until 31 March 2006;

2. *Calls upon* all Liberian parties to demonstrate their full commitment to a democratic process of government by ensuring that the upcoming presidential and legislative elections are peaceful, transparent, free and fair;

3. *Calls upon* the international community to respond to continuing needs for resources for the rehabilitation and reintegration of ex-combatants and for security sector reform;

4. *Looks forward* to the implementation of the Governance and Economic Management Assistance Programme by the National Transitional Government of Liberia and succeeding governments of Liberia in collaboration with their international partners, and requests the Secretary-General to include information on the progress of this implementation in his regular reports on the Mission;

5. *Authorizes* the Mission, subject to the consent of the troop-contributing countries concerned and of the Government of Sierra Leone, to deploy from November 2005 up to 250 United Nations military personnel to Sierra Leone to provide security for the Special Court for Sierra Leone, as recommended in paragraphs 90 to 94 of the report of the Secretary-General of 1 September 2005;

6. *Authorizes* a temporary increase in the personnel ceiling of the Mission, to a total of 15,250 United Nations military personnel, for the period from 15 November 2005 to 31 March 2006 in order to ensure that the support provided to the Court does not reduce the capabilities of the Mission in Liberia during its political transition period;

7. *Authorizes* the Mission, subject to the consent of the troop-contributing countries concerned and of the Government of Sierra Leone, to deploy an adequate number of military personnel to Sierra Leone, if and when needed, to evacuate military personnel of the Mission deployed to Sierra Leone pursuant to paragraph 5 of the present resolution and officials of the Court in the event of a serious security crisis affecting those personnel and the Court;

8. *Requests* the United Nations Integrated Office in Sierra Leone, once established, to assist in providing logistics support for military personnel of the Mission deployed to Sierra Leone pursuant to the present resolution;

9. *Requests* the Secretary-General and the Government of Sierra Leone to conclude an agreement regarding the status of military personnel of the Mission deployed to Sierra Leone pursuant to the present resolution, taking into account General Assembly resolution 59/47 of 2 December 2004 on the scope of legal protection under the Convention on the Safety of United Nations and Associated Personnel, and decides that, pending the conclusion of such an agreement, the model status-of-forces agreement dated 9 October 1990 shall apply provisionally;

10. *Supports* the recommendation of the Secretary-General to return to the ceiling of United Nations military personnel authorized in resolution 1509(2003) by 31 March 2006;

11. *Encourages* the United Nations missions in the region, within their capabilities and areas of deployment and without prejudice to their mandates, to continue their efforts towards enhancing inter-mission cooperation, especially with regard to the prevention of cross-border movement of arms and combatants and the illicit exploitation of natural resources and in the implementation of disarmament, demobilization and reintegration programmes;

12. *Welcomes* the efforts undertaken by the Mission to implement the Secretary-General's zero-tolerance policy on sexual exploitation and abuse and to ensure full compliance of its personnel with the United Nations code of conduct, and requests the Secretary-General to take all necessary action in this regard and to keep the Security Council informed, and urges troop-contributing countries to take appropriate preventive action, including conducting predeployment awareness training, and to take disciplinary action and other action to ensure that allegations of sexual exploitation or abuse against their personnel are properly investigated and, if substantiated, punished;

13. *Requests* the Secretary-General to provide recommendations on a drawdown plan for the Mission, including specific benchmarks and a tentative schedule, in his March 2006 report;

14. *Also requests* the Secretary-General to continue to keep the Council regularly informed on the progress of the Mission in the implementation of its mandate;

15. *Decides* to remain actively seized of the matter.

Elections

Pre-election activities. The Secretary-General reported in March [S/2005/177] that with the signing into law of the Electoral Reform Bill in December 2004, the National Elections Commission developed the legal and policy framework for the elections by adopting guidelines on the registration of political parties, independent candidates, and coalitions and alliances. With UNMIL assistance, it formulated regulations on voter registration, a code of conduct for Commission staff and accreditation guidelines for national and international observers. It introduced a process whereby political parties would draft their own code of conduct. The Commission began the civic education campaign in January and, on 7 February, announced the electoral timetable: voter registration would take place from 25 April to 21 May and the voter registers would be exhibited from 27 June to 1 July; elections would be held on 11 October and the results would be announced by 26 October.

Election messages targeting various segments of the population, including women, youth and ex-combatants, were prepared and media development training provided to radio station managers and journalists. UNMIL was to deploy its electoral staff to 11 counties by mid-March and set up electoral offices in 17 major locations by 21 March. Its troops provided security for the establishment of county electoral offices and identification of voter registration locations, as well as escort for electoral officials and logistics support for the distribution of election materials throughout the country. The Secretary-General strongly recommended the deployment of a fifth formed police unit for six months beginning in August, to reinforce UNMIL capacity to maintain a secure environment during the electoral period. The UNMIL Gender Unit, in cooperation with relevant partners and stakeholders, was working to ensure fair and genuine representation of women in the electoral process.

The Secretary-General reported in June [S/2005/391] that the voter registration process, held from 25 April to 21 May, was a notable success. Some 1.3 million voter registration forms were received from the 1,511 registration centres, which were supported by 1,039 static and mobile teams deployed nationwide to conduct the registration. Returning refugees were allowed an additional two-week period to register.

The Secretary-General reported in September [S/2005/560] that 22 political parties had been registered; eight others were registered under the umbrella of two alliances and one coalition, namely, the Alliance for Peace and Democracy, the United Democratic Alliance and the Coalition for the Transformation of Liberia. Several key milestones were reached, including the issuance of the Writ of Election on 13 July, the publication of the electoral districts on 15 July, the nomination of candidates from 21 July to 6 August, and the beginning of the campaign period on 15 August. The voters' register was exhibited from 30 June to 2 July, followed by the determination of rejections and challenges and consequent adjustments to the register. As of 1 September, the number of registered voters stood at 1,353,556.

The official list of candidates was published on 15 August. The National Elections Commission approved 22 presidential candidates, 22 vice-presidential candidates, 205 candidates for the Senate and 513 to the House of Representatives. Earlier, on 25 July, the Commission approved regulations on complaints and appeals, establishing its original jurisdiction over specified electoral offences; campaign finance guidelines and forms; directives to magistrates on their legal obligations in the electoral process; polling and counting procedures and related guidelines and regulations.

UNMIL and the UN country team assisted the Commission in overcoming the significant operational challenges of holding three elections on the same day during the rainy season in conditions of poor road networks. Direct technical assistance to the Commission was provided by the European Commission and the International Foundation for Election Systems.

Elections. The voting on 11 October was orderly and peaceful with no serious security incidents reported. Voter turnout was 74.9 per cent. Nine political parties and three independent candidates won seats in the 30-seat Senate. Five of the newly elected Senators were women (16.7 per cent). Eleven political parties and seven independent candidates obtained seats in the 64-seat House of Representatives. As none of the presidential candidates received more than 50 per cent of the votes in the first-round election, the National Elections Commission scheduled a run-off election on 8 November between the two candidates with the most votes: George Weah of the Congress for Democratic Change (CDC) (28.3 per cent) and Ellen Johnson-Sirleaf of the Unity Party (19.8 per cent). Although negative campaigning contributed to a somewhat tense political atmosphere, the run-off election took place in a peaceful atmosphere. On 9 November, as the National Elections Commission released the results, Mr. Weah's party, CDC, claimed having evidence of "massive and systematic" fraud during the run-off, submitted its complaints to the Commission and filed a petition with the Supreme Court to suspend ballot counting. CDC supporters held demonstrations in Monrovia, requesting a rerun of the elections. To calm the situation, the Secretary-General telephoned the two candidates to urge their supporters to exercise patience and allow the vote counting to be completed. On 16 November, the Elections Commission began open hearings on 16 complaints alleging irregularities; UNMIL initiated a review aimed at tracking the movement of all ballot papers.

On 23 November, the final official results of the run-off, as certified by the Board of Commissioners of the National Elections Commission, were announced: Mrs. Johnson-Sirleaf obtained 59.4 per cent of the vote and Mr. Weah, 40.6 per cent out of 805,572 valid votes cast. Voter turnout was 61 per cent. In keeping with the Electoral Reform Law, the parties were allowed one week to protest the declaration of the results, and the Elections Commission one month to respond. The complainants could also appeal the ruling of the Commission with the Supreme Court.

The first round of the elections was monitored by 436 international electoral observers, and the second by 302, who characterized them as peaceful, orderly, free, fair and transparent.

The Secretary-General later reported [S/2006/159] that, on 16 December, the National Elections Commission concluded its hearings on the CDC's complaints of irregularities and ruled that, while minor technical errors might have occurred in the electoral process, there had been no intent to commit fraud. On 21 December, following appeals from several regional leaders, Mr. Weah announced that he would not challenge the Commission's ruling in the Supreme Court. That paved the way for arrangements for the installation of the President-elect, Mrs. Johnson-Sirleaf.

EU statement. The EU, in an 11 November statement [S/2005/802], called upon the candidates, their parties and supporters to continue to demonstrate the responsible attitude they had shown during the campaigning and voting, and to abide by established procedures. It also reiterated the importance for the new Government, Senate and House of Representatives to cooperate fully with the international community in ensuring that the former President of Liberia was brought before the Special Court for Sierra Leone.

UNMIL mandate to apprehend former President of Liberia

The Secretary-General noted in his September report (above) that some Governments and human rights organizations continued to call on Nigeria to hand over to the Special Court for Sierra Leone the former President of Liberia, Charles Taylor, under indictment by the Court and in asylum in Nigeria (see p. 287). The Minister of Justice of Liberia, in a 5 July statement, alleged that Mr. Taylor had been meddling in Liberian politics and thus called for a review of the agreement for his asylum, a statement from which the National Transitional Government dissociated itself. The July special summit of the Mano River Union (see p. 228) issued a communiqué indicating that a review or a referral of the matter by Nigeria to ECOWAS might be necessary. For its part, Nigeria reaffirmed its commitment to honour the asylum agreement and hand over Mr. Taylor only at the request of the incoming Government of Liberia.

SECURITY COUNCIL ACTION

On 11 November [meeting 5304], the Security Council unanimously adopted **resolution 1638 (2005)**. The draft [S/2005/710] was submitted by Denmark, the United Kingdom and the United States.

The Security Council,

Recalling its previous resolutions and the statements by its President concerning Liberia, Sierra Leone and West Africa,

Affirming its commitment to the sovereignty, political independence and territorial integrity of Liberia,

Expressing its appreciation to Nigeria and its President, Mr. Olusegun Obasanjo, for their contributions to restoring stability in Liberia and the West African subregion, and acknowledging that Nigeria acted with broad international support when it decided to provide for the temporary stay in Nigeria of former President Charles Taylor,

Stressing that former President Taylor remains under indictment by the Special Court for Sierra Leone, and determining that his return to Liberia would constitute an impediment to stability and a threat to the peace of Liberia and to international peace and security in the region,

Acting under Chapter VII of the Charter of the United Nations,

1. *Decides* that the mandate of the United Nations Mission in Liberia shall include the following additional element: to apprehend and detain former President Charles Taylor in the event of a return to Liberia and to transfer him or facilitate his transfer to Sierra Leone for prosecution before the Special Court for Sierra Leone, and to keep the Government of Liberia, the Government of Sierra Leone and the Security Council fully informed;

2. *Decides also* to remain actively seized of the matter.

Further peace process developments

Report of Secretary-General (December). The Secretary-General, in his December progress report on UNMIL [S/2005/764], describing developments related to the October presidential and legislative elections (see p. 266) and further progress made in the implementation of the 2003 Comprehensive Peace Agreement and the factors that hampered completion of a number of the priorities set out in the Agreement.

The report pointed out that, in the prevailing calm but fragile security environment, potentially serious security challenges could come from the armed forces personnel not satisfied with their demobilization and retirement benefits; restive ex-combatants awaiting reintegration opportunities; CDC supporters disgruntled over the run-off elections; members of the former Anti-Terrorist Unit wanting to participate in the demobilization programme; and security problems in western Côte d'Ivoire.

Further progress was made in the training and restructuring of the Liberian National Police. The previously announced target of 1,800 trained police was achieved by the time of the October elections. More than 300 Special Security Service personnel and 152 Liberian Seaport Police had graduated from the UN training programme. The Government approved a new structure for the Special Security Service, reducing its current strength of 1,287 to 395, including 35 civilian staff. Under the programme to restructure the Armed Forces of Liberia, led by the United States, the first phase of the demobilization of 9,400 irregular personnel recruited into the armed forces after the outbreak of the civil war in 1989 was successfully completed on 10 September. The second phase, under which 4,273 regular personnel recruited before the conflict were to be retired, began on 17 October; only 2,227 had been retired by 1 December, as funding for that phase was $3 million short. In that regard, recruitment and training for the new armed forces could not begin before completion of the second phase. Due to acute budgetary constraints, the projection of overall troop strength for the new Armed Forces of Liberia was reduced from 4,000 to 2,000—a level to be kept under review to take account, not only of resource availability, but also of long-term national requirements and potential external threats. UNMIL continued to work with the Government on the restructuring of other law enforcement agencies.

To bring the Truth and Reconciliation Commission into operation, the Government on 18 October appointed nine commissioners from a list of 150 publicly nominated candidates. In addition, OHCHR submitted the name of one of three international technical advisers to support the Commission's operations; ECOWAS would designate the other two. The independent expert on the promotion and protection of human rights in Liberia, during his second visit to the country (25 September–7 October), expressed concern about the weak state of the rule of law and welcomed the inception of the Commission. UNMIL also launched its first bimonthly public report on the human rights situation in Liberia

The Government achieved mixed progress in gaining full control over the exploitation of the country's natural resources. To fulfil the conditions for admission to the Kimberley Process Certification Scheme for the export of rough diamonds, a chief implementing officer was appointed and 120 mineral agents and inspectors were deployed throughout the country. However, in Gbarpolu and Nimba counties, where diamond deposits had been recently discovered, local officials were reportedly engaged in the illegal sale of mining permits. In the forestry sector, the Government referred fraudulently granted concessions to the Ministry of Justice for action, and lifted the ban on pit-sawing imposed in 2004 by the Forestry Development Authority to reduce the level of deforestation. The World Bank disbursed $1 million through the Global Environment Facility for a project to support the Authority's activities to protect Sapo National Park, following the evacuation of over 1,000 people illegally residing, hunting and mining there.

The Secretary-General observed that the elections constituted the penultimate step towards completing the two-year transition period stipu-lated in the Comprehensive Peace Agreement, which would end in January 2006 with the installation of the new Government, and congratulated Mrs. Johnson-Sirleaf on her victory in the presidential election. He said the achievements made during the transition period—the disarmament of combatants, the disbandment of the former armed factions, the establishment of a stable security environment throughout the country, the partial restoration of State authority in the counties, the resettlement of a substantial number of internally displaced persons and returning refugees, the establishment of the Truth and Reconciliation Commission, the launching of the security sector reform programme and the agreement to establish the Governance and Economic Management Assistance Programme—all had laid a good foundation upon which the new Government should build.

The challenges ahead were formidable for a country still in the early stages of reconstruction and rehabilitation, as major residual tasks from the transition period remained to be completed, including the reintegration of war-affected persons and ex-combatants; consolidation of State authority throughout the country; promotion of human rights; rehabilitation of the judicial system; advancement of security sector reform and implementation of the economic governance programme. Other pressing priorities not part of the transition programme that required attention were constitutional reform, economic recovery, poverty reduction and the provision of such basic services as water and electricity.

From the outset, the new Government would need to focus on economic governance issues, particularly in the management of funds and natural resources. With the mandate of the Governance Reform Commission expiring in January 2006, Liberia's international partners stood ready to discuss a successor arrangement to move the governance reform process forward. The Contracts and Monopolies Commission was to be replaced by the Public Procurement and Concessions Commission as from 1 January 2006.

The Secretary-General hoped the new Government would promptly open an effective and sustained dialogue with the people of Liberia, focusing on programmes to improve their living conditions in the shortest possible time and on policy and institutional reforms pivotal to political stability and economic progress. Under the leadership of his Special Representative, UNMIL and the UN country team were developing a peacebuilding framework to guide UN support for the new Government.

Appointment. On 28 December [SG/A/966], the Secretary-General appointed Jordan Ryan (United

States) as his Deputy Special Representative for Recovery and Good Governance for Liberia, with effect from 1 January 2006. He would also serve as the United Nations Resident Coordinator and Humanitarian Coordinator in the country.

Sanctions

The Security Council received several reports on the implementation of sanctions imposed on Liberia pursuant to Council resolutions 1521 (2003) [YUN 2003, p. 208] and 1579(2004) [YUN 2004, p. 210]. Those sanctions banned arms and related materiel, military training, the export of Liberian timber products and rough diamonds, and international travel by individuals so designated, who constituted a threat to the peace process in Liberia and the subregion. Financial sanctions had also been imposed on former President Charles Taylor and his immediate family by resolution 1532(2004) [ibid., p. 204].

Appointment of Panel. On 17 January [S/2005/35], the Secretary-General informed the Council of his appointment of five members of the Panel of Experts established pursuant to resolution 1579(2004), which was mandated to conduct an assessment mission to Liberia and neighbouring States in order to report on the implementation of resolution 1521(2003) and any violations of the sanctions imposed by that resolution and those imposed by resolution 1532(2004); progress made towards meeting the conditions for lifting the sanctions; and the humanitarian and socio-economic impact of the measures imposed by resolution 1521(2003).

An 11 February press statement [SC/8308] chronicled the fifth meeting (New York, 4 February) of the Security Council Committee established pursuant to resolution 1521(2003), at which the Panel of Experts presented their programme of work, which was scheduled to run through 21 June 2005. In Liberia, the Panel would hold meetings with individuals inside and outside the Government and visit a number of relevant sites.

Implementation of sanctions regime

Report of Expert Panel (March). The Panel of Experts established pursuant to Security Council resolutions 1521(2003) and 1579(2004) concerning Liberia transmitted a March interim report [S/2005/176] to the Council, which contained the assessment on diamonds. Having visited the country in February and worked closely with the Kimberley Process expert mission, as well as the Liberian Ministry of Lands, Mines and Energy, the Panel identified developments that were

undermining Liberia's endeavours to meet the requirements of the Security Council for lifting the embargo on exporting rough diamonds.

The training of outstation personnel for the Bureau of Mines, including regional coordinators, mining agents and mineral inspectors, continued but a lack of funding prevented them from being placed on the payroll and deployed to the field. The issuance of all diamond-mining licences and permits was suspended, effective from 14 January, which essentially outlawed all diamond-mining activity, and a moratorium placed on alluvial diamond prospecting. While the Panel commended the Ministry of Lands, Mines and Energy initiative to combat the illegal export of diamonds, the legality of the suspension under the Liberian Constitution had been questioned. Furthermore, the Ministry lacked the institutional capacity and authority to enforce the policy in remote mining areas. Slow funding had curtailed progress on a capacity-building project designed to improve implementation of the Kimberley Process Certification Scheme and on the completion of the facilities to house the assaying and computer equipment for the Scheme. Aerial surveys of established mining areas in Nimba County and the Upper Lofa River region were conducted by the Panel with UNMIL assistance. Despite the mining moratorium in force, the Panel estimated illegal domestic diamond production at $350,000 per month.

The Kimberley Process expert mission visited Liberia from 14 to 18 February and assessed steps taken by the Government to apply for participation in the Kimberley Process Certification Scheme. The expert mission found that Liberia had not met the requirements for participating in the scheme, as the country lacked functional internal controls and monitoring systems. Furthermore, the absence of UNMIL peacekeepers, State security and government administration in the diamond-producing regions in the west, was contributing to illegal mining activities in the country. The Panel of Experts shared the view of the expert mission and concluded that Liberia was not yet in a position to make a successful application for participation in the Kimberley Process.

Report of Expert Panel (June). The Panel of Experts submitted a June report [S/2005/360], pursuant to paragraph 8 (*f*) of Security Council resolution 1579(2004), which contained an assessment on all sanctions. The Panel noted that UN forces, including civilian police, had discovered a substantial number of weapons and ammunition, including a weapons cache discovered in February in Vahun, Lofa County. A local civilian source and an UNMIL security officer were of the opinion that more caches existed. Unfortunately, in some cases, all or part of the weapons caches reported to UNMIL for investigation were moved before UNMIL forces arrived, due to information leaks. Reports of the recruitment of former combatants for Côte d'Ivoire, Guinea and Sierra Leone remained a concern, which threatened stability in the subregion. The Special Court for Sierra Leone had reported its suspicions to the Panel that Charles Taylor had gone to Burkina Faso from Nigeria in violation of the travel ban and had been in permanent phone contact with his accomplices in Liberia. The Panel could not verify those reports.

The Panel recommended that UNMIL units in charge of criminal investigations be given a special mandate to undertake independent inquiries in order to recover weapons and monitor the possible recruitment of former combatants and to investigate violations of any of the sanctions, including diamonds, timber, the travel ban and seizures of assets. A witness protection programme should be established and legal protection from prosecution should be given to undercover agents and informants.

Despite repeated denials to the contrary by the Ministry of Lands, Mines and Energy, the Panel was able to confirm that a mining cooperatives support/mineral purchase agreement between Liberia and the West Africa Mining Corporation Limited (WAMCO) had been signed on 19 January. The contract was not subject to an open, competitive tender process, nor was it referred to the Monopolies and Contracts Commission. The sweeping rights awarded WAMCO under the contract for the exclusive purchase of virtually all minerals in Liberia to the west of the St. Paul River would adversely impact market competition, deny diggers a fair price for their goods, and ultimately encourage diamond smuggling to more favourable markets in neighbouring countries. The secrecy surrounding the WAMCO agreement had stalled the Government's progress in meeting the Security Council requirements for lifting the embargo on rough diamond exports. In particular, funding pledged by the United States and international donors for the implementation of internal control structures, as well as the provision of equipment and technical assistance had been put on hold. Furthermore, the mining moratorium had failed to curb illegal activity, which was steadily increasing and had risen to some $500,000 per month. The Panel had also received reports that Liberian diamonds were being trafficked through Guinea and Sierra Leone, and that Banjul and Bamako had become key trans-shipment points for uncertified diamonds.

As funding to implement mechanisms for participation in the Kimberley Process Certification Scheme would remain suspended until outstanding questions regarding the WAMCO deal had been answered, the Panel recommended that international donors interested in diamond sector reform work quickly with the Government and WAMCO to resolve the issue. It concluded that levels of illegal mining and export of Liberian diamonds would continue to grow steadily. As the Government lacked the capacity to deal with the problem and unchecked mining activity would pose an increasing threat to security and stability in the mining areas, the Panel recommended that UNMIL be given a robust mandate to assist the Government with its control of illegal mining in order to maintain security. It also advised that an external independent supervisory management structure for Liberia's mineral resources would be the best solution to problems concerning managerial professionalism and administrative transparency.

While the Panel indicated that there had been no evidence of timber exports or any detection of industrial logging, pit-sawing—the processing of logs using chainsaws—had been increasing, in spite of the ban on that activity since 15 September 2000. The Panel concluded that, while the export sanctions were effective, the domestic industry continued to operate illegally and few of the necessary reforms had been implemented. In addition to its previous recommendations, the Panel proposed that a management organization to control the forestry sector should be established.

The Panel determined that the Government's financial administration was weak, with non-existent internal control systems and ineffective external oversight. A lack of transparency and accountability in the system allowed import revenue to leak from Government coffers and the method used in siphoning off Government revenues appeared to be the same as during the regime of Charles Taylor, who continued to be provided, according to unconfirmed reports, with monetary support from those funds.

The Panel concluded that the assets freeze had been ineffective. The Government had not taken action to implement it and the time lag between the travel ban resolution and the issuance of the assets freeze list had allowed time for concerned individuals to transfer funds

Report of Secretary-General (June). Also in June [S/2005/376], pursuant to Security Council resolution 1579(2004), the Secretary-General submitted a report on progress made by Liberia in meeting the conditions of resolution 1521

(2003) relating to the arms embargo, travel ban, diamond sanctions and timber sanctions.

The Secretary-General observed that the Government continued to take steps towards meeting the conditions contained in resolution 1521 (2003). With regard to the arms embargo, the ending of the disarmament and demobilization process and the dissolution of the armed factions had signalled the completion of the implementation of the ceasefire agreement. However, a key condition for lifting the arms embargo and travel ban was full implementation of the Comprehensive Peace Agreement, including the holding of national elections (see p. 266), installation of a new Liberian Government, scheduled to take place in 2006, and the laying of foundations for sustainable development and good governance. Furthermore, delays in the restructuring of the armed forces and the provision of reintegration opportunities for former combatants remained a threat to stability and the success of the transitional process.

Despite some progress in meeting the conditions for lifting the diamond sanctions, such as the training and deployment of mineral inspectors and the construction of a centre for appraising and certifying rough diamonds, the Government lacked the capacity to ensure effective control over diamond-producing areas and Liberia's borders. As UNMIL lacked both the mandate and the troop levels to perform such a role, the Secretary-General recommended that the Security Council consider broadening the mandate and increasing UNMIL's resources to enable the Mission to assist the Government in providing security in the diamond and timber-producing areas. With respect to the timber industry, governmental reforms to ensure that revenues were used for legitimate purposes had not been implemented. The Secretary-General recommended that the Government invite an internationally recognized forestry management team to temporarily oversee operations in the forestry sector.

SECURITY COUNCIL ACTION

On 21 June [meeting 5208], the Security Council unanimously adopted **resolution 1607(2005)**. The draft [S/2005/401] was prepared in consultations among Council members.

The Security Council,

Recalling its previous resolutions and statements by its President on the situation in Liberia and West Africa,

Taking note of the reports of the Panel of Experts on Liberia of 17 March and 13 June 2005, and the report of the Secretary-General of 7 June 2005, submitted pursuant to resolution 1579(2004) of 17 June 2004,

Recognizing the linkage between the illegal exploitation of natural resources such as diamonds and timber,

the illicit trade in such resources, and the proliferation and trafficking of arms and the recruitment and use of mercenaries as one of the sources of fuelling and exacerbating conflicts in West Africa, particularly in Liberia,

Recalling that the measures imposed under resolution 1521(2003) of 22 December 2003 were designed to prevent such illegal exploitation from fuelling a resumption of the conflict in Liberia, as well as to support the implementation of the Comprehensive Peace Agreement signed at Accra on 18 August 2003 and the extension of the authority, throughout Liberia, of the National Transitional Government of Liberia,

Expressing its concern that, while the deployment of the United Nations Mission in Liberia has contributed to the improvement of security throughout Liberia, the National Transitional Government of Liberia has not yet established its authority throughout Liberia,

Emphasizing the need for the international community to help the National Transitional Government of Liberia to increase its capacity to establish its authority throughout Liberia, particularly to establish its control over the diamond-producing and timber-producing areas and Liberia's borders,

Expressing deep concern at information that former President of Liberia Charles Taylor and others still closely associated with him continue to engage in activities that undermine peace and stability in Liberia and the region,

Having reviewed the measures imposed by paragraphs 2, 4, 6 and 10 of resolution 1521(2003) and paragraph 1 of resolution 1532(2004) of 12 March 2004 and the progress made towards meeting the conditions set forth in paragraphs 5, 7 and 11 of resolution 1521 (2003),

Welcoming the assessment of the Panel of Experts that there is no evidence of illegal timber being exported from Liberia, but noting with concern that few of the reforms in the National Transitional Government of Liberia road map necessary to meet the conditions set forth in paragraph 11 of resolution 1521(2003) for lifting the measures on timber imposed by paragraph 10 of resolution 1521(2003) have been implemented,

Acknowledging the recent completion of the Forest Concession Review, and welcoming the report of the Forest Concession Review Committee,

Welcoming the progress made by the National Transitional Government of Liberia in the training of diamond mining officials, but noting with serious concern the increase in unlicensed mining and illegal exports of diamonds and the agreement to, and lack of transparency in, granting exclusive mining rights to a single company by the National Transitional Government,

Noting with concern the limited progress made by the National Transitional Government of Liberia towards establishing transparent financial management systems that will help ensure that government revenues are not used to fuel conflict or otherwise used in violation of the resolutions of the Council but are used for legitimate purposes for the benefit of the Liberian people, including development,

Taking note of the ongoing discussions regarding a Liberia Economic Governance Action Plan, designed to ensure prompt implementation of the Comprehensive Peace Agreement and to expedite the lifting of measures imposed by resolution 1521(2003), and expressing its intention to consider, as appropriate, the Action Plan,

Emphasizing that, despite completion of demobilization and disarmament, significant challenges remain in completing the reintegration and repatriation of ex-combatants and the restructuring of the security sector, as well as establishing and maintaining stability in Liberia and the subregion,

Determining that the situation in Liberia continues to constitute a threat to international peace and security in the region,

Acting under Chapter VII of the Charter of the United Nations,

1. *Decides*, on the basis of its assessments above of progress made by the National Transitional Government of Liberia towards meeting the conditions for lifting the measures imposed by resolution 1521(2003), to renew the measures on diamonds imposed by paragraph 6 of resolution 1521(2003) for a further period of six months from the date of adoption of the present resolution;

2. *Urges* the National Transitional Government of Liberia to intensify its efforts, with the support of the United Nations Mission in Liberia, to establish its authority over the diamond-producing areas and to work towards establishing an official certificate-of-origin regime for trade in rough diamonds that is transparent and internationally verifiable, with a view to joining the Kimberley Process;

3. *Reiterates* the Council's readiness to terminate all measures imposed by resolution 1521(2003) once the conditions set forth in paragraphs 5, 7 and 11 of that resolution have been met;

4. *Calls upon* the National Transitional Government of Liberia urgently to intensify its efforts to reform the Forestry Development Authority, to implement the Liberia Forest Initiative and to implement the recommendations of the Forest Concession Review Committee for reform, which will ensure transparency, accountability and sustainable forest management and contribute towards the lifting of the measures on timber set forth in paragraph 10 of resolution 1521(2003);

5. *Invites* the National Transitional Government of Liberia to consider, with the assistance of international partners and for a specific time period, the possibility of commissioning independent external advice on the management of Liberia's diamond and timber resources, in order to increase investor confidence and attract additional donor support;

6. *Notes* that the measures imposed by paragraph 1 of resolution 1532(2004) remain in force to prevent former President of Liberia Charles Taylor, his immediate family members, senior officials of the former Taylor regime, or other close allies or associates from using misappropriated funds and property to interfere in the restoration of peace and stability in Liberia and the subregion, and reconfirms its intention to review these measures at least once a year;

7. *Reiterates its intention* to consider whether and how to make available to the Government of Liberia the funds, other financial assets and economic resources frozen pursuant to paragraph 1 of resolution 1532(2004), once that Government has established

transparent accounting and auditing mechanisms to ensure the responsible use of government revenue to benefit directly the people of Liberia;

8. *Emphasizes its concern* that the National Transitional Government of Liberia has taken no action to implement its obligations under paragraph 1 of resolution 1532(2004), and calls upon the Government to take such action immediately, particularly by adopting the necessary domestic legislation, with technical support provided by Member States;

9. *Notes* that the measures on arms, travel and timber imposed by paragraphs 2, 4 and 10 respectively of resolution 1521(2003) and renewed by paragraph 1 of resolution 1579(2004) remain in force until 21 December 2005;

10. *Urges* the Mission to intensify its efforts, as mandated in resolution 1509(2003) of 19 September 2003, to assist the National Transitional Government of Liberia in re-establishing its authority throughout Liberia, including diamond-producing and timber-producing areas, and restoring proper administration of natural resources;

11. *Reiterates* the importance of the Mission to continue to provide assistance to the National Transitional Government of Liberia, the Security Council Committee established pursuant to paragraph 21 of resolution 1521(2003) (hereinafter "the Committee") and the Panel of Experts, within its capabilities and areas of deployment and without prejudice to its mandate, in the following areas:

(*a*) Monitoring the implementation of the measures in paragraphs 2, 4, 6 and 10 of resolution 1521(2003) in accordance with paragraph 23 of that resolution;

(*b*) Supporting efforts by the National Transitional Government to prevent violations of those measures, and reporting any such violations;

(*c*) Collecting, as appropriate, arms and any related materiel brought into Liberia in violation of the measures taken by States to implement paragraph 2 of resolution 1521(2003), and disposing of such arms and related materiel as appropriate;

(*d*) Assisting the National Transitional Government in monitoring the recruitment and movement of ex-combatants, and reporting any relevant information to the Panel of Experts and the Committee, in order to reduce the opportunity for ex-combatants to undermine the peace process or provoke renewed instability in Liberia and the subregion;

(*e*) Developing a strategy, in conjunction with the Economic Community of West African States and other international partners, to consolidate a national legal framework as mandated in resolution 1509(2003), including the implementation by the National Transitional Government of the measures in paragraph 1 of resolution 1532(2004);

12. *Calls upon* the United Nations Mission in Liberia, the United Nations Mission in Sierra Leone and the United Nations Mission in Côte d'Ivoire to intensify their cooperation, within their capabilities and areas of deployment and without prejudice to their mandates, to monitor arms trafficking and recruitment of mercenaries within the subregion;

13. *Reiterates its call upon* the international donor community to continue to provide assistance to the peace process, including for reintegration of ex-combatants and reconstruction, to contribute generously to consol-

idated humanitarian appeals, to disburse as soon as possible the pledges made at the International Reconstruction Conference on Liberia, held in New York on 5 and 6 February 2004, and to respond to the financial, administrative and technical needs of the National Transitional Government of Liberia, in particular to assist the Government to meet the conditions referred to in paragraph 3 above, so that the measures can be lifted as soon as possible;

14. *Decides* to re-establish the Panel of Experts appointed pursuant to resolution 1579(2004) for a further period until 21 December 2005 to undertake the following tasks:

(*a*) To conduct a follow-up assessment mission to Liberia and neighbouring States in order to investigate and compile a report on the implementation, and any violations, of the measures imposed by resolution 1521(2003), including any information relevant to the designation by the Committee of the individuals described in paragraph 4 *(a)* of resolution 1521(2003) and paragraph 1 of resolution 1532(2004), and including the various sources of financing, such as from natural resources, for the illicit trade of arms;

(*b*) To assess the impact and effectiveness of the measures imposed by paragraph 1 of resolution 1532 (2004);

(*c*) To assess the progress made towards meeting the conditions for lifting the measures imposed by resolution 1521(2003);

(*d*) To assess the humanitarian and socio-economic impact of the measures imposed by paragraphs 2, 4, 6 and 10 of resolution 1521(2003);

(*e*) To report to the Council by 7 December 2005, through the Committee, on all the issues listed in the present paragraph, and to provide informal updates to the Committee, as appropriate, before that date, especially on progress made towards meeting the conditions for lifting the measures imposed by paragraphs 6 and 10 of resolution 1521(2003);

(*f*) To cooperate with other relevant groups of experts, in particular the group of experts on Côte d'Ivoire established pursuant to resolution 1584(2005) of 1 February 2005;

15. *Requests* the Secretary-General, acting in consultation with the Committee, to appoint as soon as possible no more than five experts, with the appropriate range of expertise, in particular on arms, timber, diamonds, finance, humanitarian and socio-economic and any other relevant issues, drawing as much as possible on the expertise of the members of the Panel of Experts established pursuant to resolution 1579(2004), and further requests the Secretary-General to make the necessary financial and security arrangements to support the work of the Panel;

16. *Calls upon* all States and the National Transitional Government of Liberia to cooperate fully with the Panel of Experts;

17. *Decides* to remain seized of the matter.

The Secretary-General, on 22 July [S/2005/480], informed the Security Council of the names of the five experts he had appointed to the Panel of Experts pursuant established by resolution 1607(2005) (see above).

Report of Expert Panel (December). The Panel of Experts transmitted a report [S/2005/745] to the Security Council on 7 December, pursuant to resolution 1607(2005), containing an assessment of all sanctions, including diamonds, timber, arms and travel, as well as updates on financial matters, the assets freeze and the humanitarian and socio-economic impact of the sanctions on Liberia. On 22 June, following a directive by a 90 per cent shareholder, WAMCO officially terminated its mining contract with the Ministry of Lands, Mines and Energy. The Ministry, in collaboration with an international mineral exploration company, established laboratories for geological testing and mapping, completed the training and deployment of outstation personnel and issued invitations to international companies to bid for work necessary to achieve compliance with the Kimberley Process Certification Scheme. As a result of the WAMCO issue (see p. 270) the $1.4 million pledged for disbursement by the United States for training, acquisition of Kimberley Process certificates and database production would not be available until the new Government took office in January 2006. The Panel concluded that, as Liberia was not in a position to make a successful application to participate in the Kimberley Process, Liberian production threatened the credibility of the certification schemes in neighbouring States. Encouraging donors to disburse funding for structural reform, the Panel recommended that UNMIL mandate be extended to assist Liberia in restoring the rule of law in mining areas and that the international community provide technical and material assistance to non-diamond-producing States to enable them to participate in the Kimberley Process.

Sanctions on timber had been effective and there were no reports of major exports. However, given the perceived conspiracy between the Government and the timber industry over the past 25 years, the Forest Concession Review Committee recommended cancellation of each concession and that the sector be completely reformed.

Concerns regarding the arms embargo focused on the recruitment of ex-combatants from neighbouring States and the potential cross-border movement of recruits, in particular between Côte d'Ivoire and Liberia. The Panel continued to receive reports of organized recruitment. Although there had been no major discoveries in Liberia since the previous report of the Panel, small but regular flows of weapons and ammunition had been remitted to UNMIL outside the disarmament programme. In August, a waiver had been granted to allow the import of weapons for the training and equipping of the New Armed Forces of Liberia (NAFL). The travel ban documented a number of violations, as well as the fraudulent use of Liberian passports. The Panel recommended a review of the passport system.

One and a half years after its imposition, the assets freeze had yet to be implemented. The Panel recommended that the international community should pressure the incoming Government to implement the freeze. A midterm review of the assets of designated persons should be conducted and the necessary legal action to confiscate their assets undertaken.

On economic matters, the Panel recommended that international donors take note of the desperate state of the country's economy, and allocate resources to speed up rehabilitation of the infrastructure, as well as rehabilitation programmes. It also recommended that the newly elected Government cooperate proactively with the international community in implementing the Governance and Economic Management Programme.

The Panel indicated that the Government's financial administration continued to be weak. The Panel concluded that, should the sanctions on diamonds and timber be lifted, it was unlikely that Government revenues would enter the budget process for the benefit of the Liberian people. It recommended comprehensive audits of various executive offices; completion of the financial accounts of all major revenue-generating State-owned enterprises; and filling of positions in the Governance and Economic Management Programme on a priority basis, with time-bound objectives prescribed for each position.

SECURITY COUNCIL ACTION

On 20 December [meeting 5336], the Security Council unanimously adopted **resolution 1647 (2005)**. The draft [S/2005/792] was submitted by Denmark, France, Japan, Romania, the United Kingdom and the United States.

The Security Council,

Recalling its previous resolutions and the statements by its President on the situation in Liberia and West Africa,

Welcoming the peaceful and orderly conduct of the recent elections in Liberia, an important step in Liberia's progress towards lasting peace and stability,

Welcoming also the commitment of the President-elect of the Republic of Liberia, Mrs. Ellen Johnson-Sirleaf, to rebuilding Liberia for the benefit of all Liberians, with the support of the international community,

Stressing the continuing importance of the United Nations Mission in Liberia in improving security throughout Liberia and helping the new Government to establish its authority throughout the country, particularly in the diamond- and timber-producing areas and border areas,

Taking note of the report of the Panel of Experts on Liberia of 25 November 2005,

Having reviewed the measures imposed by paragraphs 2, 4, 6 and 10 of resolution 1521(2003) of 22 December 2003 and paragraph 1 of resolution 1532(2004) of 12 March 2004 and the progress towards meeting the conditions set out in paragraphs 5, 7 and 11 of resolution 1521(2003), and concluding that insufficient progress has been made towards that end,

Underlining its determination to support the new Government of Liberia in its efforts to meet those conditions, and encouraging donors to do likewise,

Determining that the situation in Liberia continues to constitute a threat to international peace and security in the region,

Acting under Chapter VII of the Charter of the United Nations,

1. *Decides*, on the basis of its assessment of progress made to date towards meeting the conditions for lifting the measures imposed by resolution 1521(2003):

   (a) To renew the measures on arms and travel imposed by paragraphs 2 and 4 of resolution 1521(2003) for a further period of twelve months from the date of adoption of the present resolution;

   (b) To renew the measures on diamonds and timber imposed by paragraphs 6 and 10 of resolution 1521(2003) for a further period of six months from the date of adoption of the present resolution;

   (c) To review any of the above measures at the request of the new Government of Liberia, once the Government reports to the Security Council that the conditions set out in resolution 1521(2003) for terminating the measures have been met, and provides the Council with information to justify its assessment;

2. *Reiterates* the Council's readiness to terminate these measures once the conditions set forth in paragraphs 5, 7 and 11 of resolution 1521(2003) have been met;

3. *Welcomes* the determination of the President-elect of Liberia, Mrs. Ellen Johnson-Sirleaf, to meet the conditions for terminating the measures thus renewed, and encourages the new Government of Liberia:

   (a) To reform the Forestry Development Authority, to implement the Liberia Forest Initiative and to implement the recommendations of the Forest Concession Review Committee for reform and cancellation of existing logging concessions, which will ensure transparency, accountability and sustainable forest management and contribute towards the lifting of the measures on timber in accordance with paragraphs 11 and 12 of resolution 1521(2003);

   (b) To consider, with the assistance of international partners and for a specific time period, the possibility of commissioning independent external advice on the management of Liberia's diamond resources, in order to increase revenue and investor confidence and to attract additional donor support;

4. *Encourages* the new Government of Liberia to implement the Governance and Economic Management Assistance Program, designed to ensure prompt implementation of the Comprehensive Peace Agreement signed at Accra on 18 August 2003 and expedite the lifting of the measures imposed by resolution 1521 (2003);

5. *Welcomes* the assistance provided by the United Nations Mission in Liberia to the Government of Liberia in re-establishing its authority throughout the country, and encourages the Mission to continue its joint patrols with the Forestry Development Authority;

6. *Notes* that the measures imposed by paragraph 1 of resolution 1532(2004) remain in force, and reconfirms its intention to review those measures at least once a year;

7. *Emphasizes its concern* that the National Transitional Government of Liberia took no action to implement its obligations under paragraph 1 of resolution 1532(2004), and calls upon the incoming Government to take such action immediately, particularly by adopting the necessary domestic legislation, with technical support provided by Member States;

8. *Calls upon* the international donor community to support the incoming Government of Liberia by providing generous assistance to the peace process, including for the reintegration of ex-combatants, reconstruction and humanitarian appeals, and by responding to the financial, administrative and technical needs of the Government, in particular to assist the Government to meet the conditions referred to in paragraph 2 above, so that the measures can be lifted as soon as possible;

9. *Decides* to re-establish the Panel of Experts appointed pursuant to resolution 1607(2005) of 21 June 2005 for a further period until 21 June 2006 to undertake the following tasks:

(a) To conduct a follow-up assessment mission to Liberia and neighbouring States in order to investigate and compile a report on the implementation, and any violations, of the measures imposed by resolution 1521(2003), including any information relevant to the designation by the Security Council Committee established pursuant to resolution 1521(2003) of the individuals described in paragraph 4 *(a)* of resolution 1521 (2003) and the individuals and entities described in paragraph 1 of resolution 1532(2004), and including the various sources of financing, such as from natural resources, for the illicit trade in arms;

(b) To assess the impact and effectiveness of the measures imposed by paragraph 1 of resolution 1532 (2004);

(c) To assess the progress made towards meeting the conditions for lifting the measures imposed by resolution 1521(2003);

(d) To assess the humanitarian and socio-economic impact of the measures imposed by paragraphs 2, 4, 6 and 10 of resolution 1521(2003);

(e) To report to the Council, through the Committee, by 7 June 2006 on all the issues listed in the present paragraph, and to provide informal updates to the Committee, as appropriate, before that date, especially on progress made towards meeting the conditions for lifting the measures imposed by paragraphs 6 and 10 of resolution 1521(2003);

(f) To cooperate with other relevant groups of experts, in particular the group of experts on Côte d'Ivoire established pursuant to resolution 1643(2005) of 15 December 2005, and with the Kimberley Process Certification Scheme;

10. *Requests* the Secretary-General, acting in consultation with the Committee, to appoint as soon as possible no more than five experts, with the appropriate expertise, in particular on arms, timber, diamonds, finance, and humanitarian and socio-economic issues, drawing as much as possible on the expertise of the members of the Panel of Experts established pursuant to resolution 1607(2005), and further requests the Secretary-General to make the necessary financial and security arrangements to support the work of the Panel;

11. *Calls upon* all States and the Government of Liberia to cooperate fully with the Panel of Experts;

12. *Decides* to remain seized of the matter.

Security Council Committee. The Security Council Committee established pursuant to resolution 1521(2003) concerning Liberia submitted a report [S/2006/464] on its activities for the period 1 January to 31 December 2005. During the reporting period, the Committee held two formal meetings and 12 informal consultations.

The Committee received two requests for exemptions to the arms embargo. It approved a request to allow for the equipping and training of the Liberian armed forces and police. However, the second request, which involved the import of sidearms for the Liberian police, remained in limbo as, at the end of the year, the Committee had not received a waiver request from any exporting State in that connection. It also received and approved the export of non-lethal military equipment for the drilling of boreholes to provide water to outlying villages.

The Committee considered nine requests for travel ban waivers, of which four were granted. It held quarterly reviews of the travel ban list initially issued on 16 March 2004 [YUN 2004, p. 211], retaining the names of 52 persons listed as at 31 December 2004, and adding seven more in 2005. The Committee conducted one six-month review of the assets freeze list in June, and on 30 November, it added the names of two individuals and 30 entities to the list.

Harmonization of the contents of both the travel-ban and assets-freeze lists was concluded in May, thereby presenting identical information on individuals inscribed on both lists. The Committee received two replies from States on actions taken to implement the sanctions provided for in resolution 1521(2003) and four replies from States on actions taken to trace and freeze the funds, other financial assets and economic resources described in resolution 1532(2004).

Sierra Leone

In 2005, Sierra Leone continued to maintain strict adherence to the 2000 Agreement on the Ceasefire and Cessation of Hostilities [YUN 2000, p. 210] and accelerated its efforts to meet the benchmarks laid down by the Security Council in

2004 for the completion of the country's transition phase and the corresponding drawdown of the United Nations Mission in Sierra Leone. With the gradual achievement of the benchmarks, the Mission began drawing down further in mid-September, while ensuring a seamless transition from peacekeeping to peacebuilding. By the completion of its withdrawal at the end of December, the Mission left behind a country with great potential to achieve lasting stability, democracy and prosperity. The Mission's collaborative effort with the partnerships it had forged during its six years of operation had placed Sierra Leone on a firm path to its next phase of post-conflict recovery and peacebuilding.

To assist the Government to consolidate peace, build the national capacity for conflict prevention and prepare for the 2007 elections, the Council requested the Secretary-General to establish the United Nations Integrated Office in Sierra Leone, for an initial 12-month period beginning on 1 January 2006, on the basis of his recommendation. To complete the restructuring and training of the Sierra Leone security forces, which had assumed full responsibility for the maintenance of security in the country, the United Kingdom committed the International Military Advisory and Training Team, which it led, to providing continued training to the armed forces until at least 2010.

The Special Court for Sierra Leone continued to try those bearing the greatest responsibility for serious violations of international humanitarian and Sierra Leonean laws committed in the territory of Sierra Leone since 1996. In a statement before the Council, the President of the Court emphasized the importance of the expeditious apprehension and trial of two indictees who remained at large for the credibility of the Court and for its contribution to combating the culture of impunity. He estimated that the trials would be completed by the end of 2006 and that the appeals stage would take another four to six months. With the departure of the Mission, which provided security for the Court, the Council, by resolution 1626(2005), authorized the United Nations Mission in Liberia to assume that responsibility from November, as recommended by the Secretary-General.

In the light of the favourable security environment in Sierra Leone, and no reported violations or alleged violations of the sanctions regime in the country for at least two years, its Chairman recommended that the Council revisit the legal basis of the sanctions in force in Sierra Leone.

UNAMSIL

The United Nations Mission in Sierra Leone (UNAMSIL), established by Security Council resolution 1270(1999) [YUN 1999, p. 165], continued to be headed by the Special Representative of the Secretary-General for Sierra Leone, Daudi Ngelautwa Mwakawago (United Republic of Tanzania). The Deputy Special Representative, Victor da Silva Angelo, also served as Resident Representative of UNDP and UN Resident Coordinator in Sierra Leone.

In accordance with Council resolution 1537 (2004) [YUN 2004, p. 214], which defined the configuration of the Mission's residual presence in the country for an initial six-month period to 30 June 2005, the Mission completed its transition to such presence at the end of February 2005, having reduced its troop strength from the December 2004 level of 5,000 to 3,250 troops, 141 military observers and 80 civilian police. By Council resolution 1610(2005), the mandate of the Mission was extended for a final period of six months, until 31 December 2005.

As Sierra Leone prepared to enter its next peacebuilding phase, the Mission's planned withdrawal of its 3,200-strong force, which began in mid-September, was carried out in three phases, starting with closing the UN military observers' team sites, then withdrawing the force, and finally closing UNAMSIL headquarters. Meanwhile, a media campaign designed by UNAMSIL and other stakeholders was under way to raise national and international awareness about the achievements and exit strategy of the Mission and the mandate of the incoming United Nations Integrated Office in Sierra Leone (UNIOSIL) (see p. 281). Activities outlined in the joint UNAMSIL/UN country team transition plan continued, aimed at ensuring a seamless transition from peacekeeping to peacebuilding in Sierra Leone, while facilitating the Mission's exit strategy and preparing the ground for the establishment of UNIOSIL.

The UNAMSIL withdrawal was scheduled for completion by the end of December. As of 1 December, some 1,160 troops and 69 military observers remained in Freetown; 46 military police continued to operate from team sites in Freetown, Kenema, Bo, Makeni and Lungi, which would remain operational until 31 December, when all police personnel would be repatriated. A team of 10 officers would be retained temporarily to facilitate a smooth transition to UNIOSIL. Some 87 administrative support staff would also be retained to carry out the liquidation of UNAMSIL between 1 January and 30 June 2006.

By presidential statement S/PRST/2005/63 (see p. 286), the Council commended UNAMSIL for its invaluable contribution over the past six years to Sierra Leone's recovery from conflict and its progress towards peace, democracy and prosperity, as well as the Secretary-General's Special Representatives and all who had made the Mission a success, especially those who had helped it recover from its 2000 crisis [YUN 2000, p. 194].

Financing

In June, during its resumed fifty-ninth (2005) session, the General Assembly considered the performance report on the UNAMSIL budget for 1 July 2003 to 30 June 2004 [A/59/635 & Corr.1], showing expenditures of $448,734,400 against a total appropriation of $520,053,600; the proposed budget for 1 July 2005 to 30 June 2006 [A/59/758 & Corr.1], totalling $107,159,700, together with the Secretary-General's related note on maintenance and liquidation costs [S/2005/273/Add.1]; the proposed donation of assets to the Government of Sierra Leone with an inventory value of $8,406,072 and a corresponding residual value of $3,829,178 [A/59/759]; and the related ACABQ report [A/59/736/Add.9].

ACABQ recommended approval of the proposed budget. Noting that UNAMSIL was the first mission to have established an Asset Disposal and Environmental Protection Unit, ACABQ asked the Department of Peacekeeping Operations (DPKO) to integrate the lessons learned into its best practices documentation for sharing with other missions; it also recommended acceptance of the Secretary-General's proposed donation of assets to the Government of Sierra Leone.

GENERAL ASSEMBLY ACTION

On 22 June [meeting 104], the General Assembly, on the recommendation of the Fifth Committee [A/59/527/Add.1], adopted **resolution 59/14 B** without vote [agenda item 136].

Financing of the United Nations Mission in Sierra Leone

B

The General Assembly,

Having considered the reports of the Secretary-General on the financing of the United Nations Mission in Sierra Leone and the related reports of the Advisory Committee on Administrative and Budgetary Questions,

Bearing in mind Security Council resolution 1270 (1999) of 22 October 1999, by which the Council established the United Nations Mission in Sierra Leone, and the subsequent resolutions by which the Council revised and extended the mandate of the Mission, the latest of which was resolution 1562(2004) of 17 September 2004,

Recalling its resolution 53/29 of 20 November 1998 on the financing of the United Nations Observer Mission in Sierra Leone and subsequent resolutions on the financing of the United Nations Mission in Sierra Leone, the latest of which was resolution 59/14 A of 29 October 2004,

Reaffirming the general principles underlying the financing of United Nations peacekeeping operations, as stated in General Assembly resolutions 1874(S-IV) of 27 June 1963, 3101(XXVIII) of 11 December 1973 and 55/235 of 23 December 2000,

Noting with appreciation that voluntary contributions have been made to the Mission,

Mindful of the fact that it is essential to provide the Mission with the necessary financial resources to enable it to fulfil its responsibilities under the relevant resolutions of the Security Council,

1. *Requests* the Secretary-General to entrust the Head of Mission with the task of formulating future budget proposals in full accordance with the provisions of General Assembly resolution 59/296 of 22 June 2005, as well as other relevant resolutions;

2. *Takes note* of the status of contributions to the United Nations Observer Mission in Sierra Leone and the United Nations Mission in Sierra Leone as at 15 April 2005, including the contributions outstanding in the amount of 94.5 million United States dollars, representing some 3 per cent of the total assessed contributions, notes with concern that only forty-three Member States have paid their assessed contributions in full, and urges all other Member States, in particular those in arrears, to ensure payment of their outstanding assessed contributions;

3. *Expresses its appreciation* to those Member States which have paid their assessed contributions in full, and urges all other Member States to make every possible effort to ensure payment of their assessed contributions to the Mission in full;

4. *Expresses concern* at the financial situation with regard to peacekeeping activities, in particular as regards the reimbursements to troop contributors that bear additional burdens owing to overdue payments by Member States of their assessments;

5. *Also expresses concern* at the delay experienced by the Secretary-General in deploying and providing adequate resources to some recent peacekeeping missions, in particular those in Africa;

6. *Emphasizes* that all future and existing peacekeeping missions shall be given equal and non-discriminatory treatment in respect of financial and administrative arrangements;

7. *Also emphasizes* that all peacekeeping missions shall be provided with adequate resources for the effective and efficient discharge of their respective mandates;

8. *Reiterates its request* to the Secretary-General to make the fullest possible use of facilities and equipment at the United Nations Logistics Base at Brindisi, Italy, in order to minimize the costs of procurement for the Mission;

9. *Endorses* the conclusions and recommendations contained in the report of the Advisory Committee on Administrative and Budgetary Questions, and requests the Secretary-General to ensure their full implementation;

10. *Requests* the Secretary-General to ensure the full implementation of the relevant provisions of its resolution 59/296;

11. *Also requests* the Secretary-General to take all necessary action to ensure that the Mission is administered with a maximum of efficiency and economy;

12. *Further requests* the Secretary-General, in order to reduce the cost of employing General Service staff, to continue efforts to recruit local staff for the Mission against General Service posts, commensurate with the requirements of the Mission;

Financial performance report for the period from 1 July 2003 to 30 June 2004

13. *Takes note* of the report of the Secretary-General on the financial performance of the Mission for the period from 1 July 2003 to 30 June 2004;

14. *Decides* to reduce the appropriation authorized for the Mission for the period from 1 July 2003 to 30 June 2004 under the terms of its resolution 57/291 B of 18 June 2003 from 543,489,900 dollars to 509,436,300 dollars, the amount apportioned among Member States in respect of the same period;

Budget estimates for the period from 1 July 2005 to 30 June 2006

15. *Decides also* to appropriate to the Special Account for the United Nations Mission in Sierra Leone the amount of 113,216,400 dollars, inclusive of 89,606,400 dollars for the maintenance of the Mission for the period from 1 July to 31 December 2005, 17,932,900 dollars for the liquidation of the Mission for the period from 1 January to 30 June 2006, 4,642,100 dollars for the support account for peacekeeping operations and 1,035,000 dollars for the United Nations Logistics Base;

Financing of the appropriation

16. *Decides further* to apportion among Member States the amount of 113,216,400 dollars at a monthly rate of 9,434,700 dollars, in accordance with the levels updated in General Assembly resolution 58/256 of 23 December 2003, and taking into account the scale of assessments for 2005 and 2006, as set out in its resolution 58/1 B of 23 December 2003, subject to a decision of the Security Council to extend the mandate of the Mission;

17. *Decides* that, in accordance with the provisions of its resolution 973(X) of 15 December 1955, there shall be set off against the apportionment among Member States, as provided for in paragraph 16 above, their respective share in the Tax Equalization Fund of 4,047,700 dollars, comprising the estimated staff assessment income of 3,307,800 dollars approved for the Mission for the period from 1 July 2005 to 30 June 2006, the prorated share of 656,100 dollars of the estimated staff assessment income approved for the support account and the prorated share of 83,800 dollars of the estimated staff assessment income approved for the United Nations Logistics Base;

18. *Decides also* that, for Member States that have fulfilled their financial obligations to the Mission, there shall be set off against their apportionment, as provided for in paragraph 16 above, their respective share of the unencumbered balance and other income in the amount of 54,054,600 dollars in respect of the financial period ended 30 June 2004, in accordance with the levels updated in General Assembly resolution 58/256, and taking into account the scale of assessments for 2004, as set out in its resolution 58/1 B;

19. *Decides further* that, for Member States that have not fulfilled their financial obligations to the Mission, there shall be set off against their outstanding obligations their respective share of the unencumbered balance and other income in the amount of 54,054,600 dollars in respect of the financial period ended 30 June 2004, in accordance with the scheme set out in paragraph 18 above;

20. *Decides* that the increase of 239,200 dollars in the estimated staff assessment income in respect of the financial period ended 30 June 2004 shall be added to the credits from the amount of 54,054,600 dollars referred to in paragraphs 18 and 19 above;

Donation of assets to the Government of Sierra Leone

21. *Approves* the donation of the assets of the Mission, with a total inventory value of 8,406,072 dollars and corresponding residual value of 3,829,178 dollars, to the Government of Sierra Leone;

22. *Emphasizes* that no peacekeeping mission shall be financed by borrowing funds from other active peacekeeping missions;

23. *Encourages* the Secretary-General to continue to take additional measures to ensure the safety and security of all personnel under the auspices of the United Nations participating in the Mission, bearing in mind paragraphs 5 and 6 of Security Council resolution 1502(2003) of 26 August 2003;

24. *Invites* voluntary contributions to the Mission in cash and in the form of services and supplies acceptable to the Secretary-General, to be administered, as appropriate, in accordance with the procedure and practices established by the General Assembly;

25. *Decides* to include in the provisional agenda of its sixtieth session the item entitled "Financing of the United Nations Mission in Sierra Leone".

UNAMSIL activities

Assessment mission

Report of Secretary-General (April). In his April report on UNAMSIL [S/2005/273], the Secretary-General provided an update on the implementation of the benchmarks established by Security Council resolution 1537(2004) [YUN 2004, p. 214] for the residual Mission presence in Sierra Leone, as well as his recommendations concerning the continued UN presence in the country after the Mission's withdrawal and termination, based on the findings of a UN interdepartmental assessment mission that visited Sierra Leone from 20 to 28 March. The mission evaluated progress on the security situation, strengthening the capacity of the Sierra Leone armed forces and police, consolidating State authority throughout the country, and consolidating the deployment in neighbouring Liberia of the United Nations Mission in Liberia (UNMIL).

The report indicated that, with the aid of UNAMSIL and other bilateral and multilateral partners, the Government of Sierra Leone had made considerable progress in implementing the benchmarks. The security situation in the country had been calm and stable, with no incidents requiring support from UNAMSIL since September 2004 [ibid., p. 218], when it turned over primary responsibility for security to the Government. Nevertheless, major shortfalls remained in the security sector, especially in the country-wide consolidation of State administration and the restoration of full government control over diamond-mining activities.

With the support of the International Military Advisory and Training Team, led by the United Kingdom, the Government continued to implement a contingency programme aimed at increasing the capacity of the armed forces to deal with external security threats and backstop the police in maintaining law and order. The programme included the deployment of three armed forces brigades to the provinces and border areas; the continued restructuring of the armed forces to reduce their troop strength from some 13,000 to 10,500 by 2007; the establishment of nationwide security and intelligence committees to provide a framework for cooperation in security matters; and the construction of army barracks in the provinces and border areas. However, the programme to prepare the armed forces to assume responsibility for the country's security was behind schedule as their operational effectiveness was hampered by such logistic shortfalls as the lack of communications equipment and accommodation for the soldiers. In March 2005, the Secretary-General appealed to potential donors to provide assistance in that regard.

The police force, whose strength stood at 8,200 in March, made notable improvements in maintaining internal security with the support of UNDP, the Mission's civilian police and an international training team. The completed construction of classrooms and dormitories at the Police Training School allowed for an increase in the number of recruits from 400 to 600 per trainee group. Lack of Government funding for training, however, thwarted the chances of reaching the benchmark of 9,500 trained police officers by year's end. UNAMSIL also increased the capacity of the police through in-service specialist training and the development of training manuals. Since 2003, some 729 middle-management police officers, 109 field-coaching officers and 150 training instructors had been trained. While the Office of National Security had improved its effectiveness and intelligence-gathering capacity, the effectiveness of the central security structures was restricted by limited resources.

The assessment of the security sector in the context of the fragile security situation in the wider Mano River basin, comprising Côte d'Ivoire, Guinea, Liberia and Sierra Leone, brought to the fore potential threats to Sierra Leone's security from possible tensions in Liberia in connection with its forthcoming October elections, setbacks in the Côte d'Ivoire peace process, instability in Guinea and the unresolved territorial dispute between Guinea and Sierra Leone over the border village of Yenga. President Ahmad Tejan Kabbah and senior security officials informed UNAMSIL that to withdraw on the expiration of its mandate at the end of June would be premature, as the security sector could not effectively assume primary responsibility for the security of the country until the end of 2005.

Further strides were made in the consolidation of State authority through the continuing decentralization process, which provided a framework for the devolution of power and responsibilities between the central and local governments. With the support of the World Bank, UN agencies and UNAMSIL, training and capacity-building programmes were conducted for the recently elected local councils, making them functional; their capacity to deliver services to their communities was seriously curtailed, however, by lack of qualified personnel, funding, logistics and infrastructure. The judiciary was undergoing a gradual but slow consolidation. The administration of justice at the chiefdom level was reinforced with the appointment of 200 chairpersons of customary courts nationwide. At least one magistrates' court was operational in each of the 12 administrative districts, and government officials were functioning in all of them. Of great concern were the slow pace in addressing undue delays in the trial and adjudication of cases and the lack of judicial personnel, which were exacerbated by the lack of codified opinions of the Supreme Court and statutory laws. An increased police presence in the provinces had considerably improved the maintenance of law and order.

The Government made considerable progress in controlling the diamond-mining sector by implementing measures to curb illicit mining, including implementation of the Kimberley Process Certification Scheme [YUN 2000, p. 76]. A total of 2,300 diamond-mining licences were issued in 2004, compared to 800 in 2001, and official diamond exports increased from $10 million in 2000 to $127 million in 2004. Also under implementation was the core minerals policy adopted in December 2004, aimed at creating an enabling legal, fiscal and institutional framework for the development of the country's mineral resources.

Furthermore, a national cadastral system to facilitate the settlement of disputes over mining rights, territorial boundaries and mining sites was being established.

With respect to regional events, the report noted that, at a summit of the Mano River Union (Koindu, Sierra Leone, 20 February), Guinea, Liberia and Sierra Leone pledged to promote regional peace and security and improve economic cooperation. Under a 24 March memorandum of understanding between Sierra Leone and Liberia on the mutual repatriation of ex-combatants, 387 such persons were repatriated to Liberia in April. The urgency of resolving the Sierra Leone–Guinea dispute over Yenga was repeatedly stressed to the assessment mission. Despite the 2 September 2004 statement issued by the two countries reaffirming that Yenga belonged to Sierra Leone, the withdrawal of Guinea's troops from Yenga and the demarcation of the boundary between them had yet to take place.

The report also highlighted the repatriation of some 271,991 Sierra Leonean refugees since 2001, largely with UNHCR assistance; the establishment of human rights committees in nine of the 12 administrative districts; the expected follow-up to the recommendations of the Truth and Reconciliation Commission contained in its final report to the President in October 2004 [YUN 2004, p. 217]; and an update on the trials at the Special Court for Sierra Leone (see p. 286).

The Secretary-General indicated areas requiring attention to further enhance stability in Sierra Leone: political and electoral reform; good governance; issues related to youth, women and children; justice sector reform; capacity-building of the security structure; development of a public information strategy; and sustained support for economic initiatives.

Given the risk of civil unrest from the lack of improvement in the economy and living standards of the majority of the population, national and international stakeholders emphasized the need for the continued deployment of the residual UNAMSIL presence until the end of 2005. A joint transition plan, developed by UNAMSIL and the UN country team for the continued involvement of the international community in Sierra Leone was being implemented. The Secretary-General proposed a study of the logistical, political and legal implications of the cross-border commitment of UNMIL after the withdrawal of UNAMSIL.

The Secretary-General observed that, while the country had advanced towards meeting the benchmarks for stabilization and for the withdrawal of UNAMSIL, much remained to be done to address the underlying causes of conflict in the

country so as to attain durable stability. In particular, the strengthening of the security sector required special, long-term attention. He therefore recommended that the Security Council extend the UNAMSIL mandate for a final period of six months, until the end of 2005, and that the drawdown of the Mission be completed by 31 December and its liquidation within six months thereafter.

SECURITY COUNCIL ACTION

On 30 June [meeting 5219], the Security Council unanimously adopted **resolution 1610(2005)**. The draft [S/2005/418] was prepared in consultations among Council members.

The Security Council,

Recalling its previous resolutions and the statements by its President concerning the situation in Sierra Leone,

Affirming the commitment of all States to respect the sovereignty, political independence and territorial integrity of Sierra Leone,

Emphasizing the importance of the continued support of the United Nations and the international community for the long-term security and development of Sierra Leone,

Having considered the report of the Secretary-General of 26 April 2005, and noting with approval his observations in paragraph 65 on the drawdown schedule of the United Nations Mission in Sierra Leone and in paragraphs 63 and 64 on the need for a strong United Nations system presence in Sierra Leone after the withdrawal of the Mission,

Commending the work of the Truth and Reconciliation Commission, and encouraging the Government of Sierra Leone to disseminate widely the Commission's report and the Government's response to it,

Expressing its appreciation for the essential work of the Special Court for Sierra Leone, noting its vital contribution to the establishment of the rule of law in Sierra Leone, and in this regard underlining the importance of ensuring that all those indicted by the Court appear before it, in order to strengthen the stability of Sierra Leone and the subregion and to bring an end to impunity, and encouraging all States to cooperate fully with the Court,

Determining that the situation in Sierra Leone continues to constitute a threat to international peace and security in the region,

Acting under Chapter VII of the Charter of the United Nations,

1. *Decides* that the mandate of the United Nations Mission in Sierra Leone shall be extended for a final period of six months until 31 December 2005;

2. *Requests* the Secretary-General to finalize the necessary planning for an appropriate integrated United Nations system presence in Sierra Leone, as recommended in paragraphs 63 and 64 of his report, with the capacity and expertise to coordinate the activities of the United Nations agencies, funds and programmes, to cooperate with the donor community, and to continue to support the efforts of the Govern-

ment of Sierra Leone at peace consolidation and long-term development, after the Mission has withdrawn;

3. *Encourages* the Mission and the United Nations country team in Sierra Leone to continue their close collaboration to ensure a seamless transition from peacekeeping to peacebuilding, including through the implementation of their joint transition plan;

4. *Recalls* that the Sierra Leone security forces shall effectively assume full responsibility for security in the country after the withdrawal of the Mission;

5. *Underlines* the importance of providing effective security for the Special Court for Sierra Leone after the Mission has withdrawn, and requests the Secretary-General to make recommendations thereon to the Security Council as soon as possible;

6. *Urges* the Government of Sierra Leone to continue its efforts to develop an effective, affordable and sustainable police force, armed forces, penal system and independent judiciary, and further to promote good governance and strengthen mechanisms to tackle corruption, and encourages donors and the Mission, in accordance with its mandate, to assist the Government in this regard, as well as in restoring public services throughout the country;

7. *Encourages* the United Nations missions in the region to continue their efforts towards enhancing inter-mission cooperation, especially in the prevention of movements of arms and combatants across borders and in the implementation of disarmament, demobilization and reintegration programmes;

8. *Welcomes* the efforts undertaken by the Mission to implement the Secretary-General's zero tolerance policy on sexual exploitation and abuse and to ensure full compliance of its personnel with the United Nations code of conduct, requests the Secretary-General to continue to take all necessary action in this regard and to keep the Security Council informed, and urges troop-contributing countries to take appropriate preventive action including the conduct of pre-deployment awareness training, and to take disciplinary action and other action to ensure that such acts are properly investigated and punished in cases involving their personnel;

9. *Welcomes* the Secretary-General's intention to keep the security, political, humanitarian and human rights situation in Sierra Leone under close review and to report regularly to the Council, after due consultations with troop-contributing countries and the Government of Sierra Leone;

10. *Decides* to remain actively seized of the matter.

UNIOSIL

In his April report [S/2005/273], the Secretary-General noted that, although stability had been successfully restored in Sierra Leone, serious challenges to building durable peace in the country remained. Considerable capacity-building was needed to enhance the Government's capability to discharge its functions related to political and economic governance and conflict prevention. Hence, after the termination of UNAMSIL, a strong UN presence was likely to be needed to assist in that regard. A number of options were being considered to ensure that the

UN system was able to develop and implement in a fully coordinated and integrated manner, and in close consultation with national stakeholders, a viable peace consolidation strategy for Sierra Leone.

As requested by the Security Council in resolution 1610(2005) above, the Secretary-General's recommendations for the continued UN presence in Sierra Leone were submitted in a July addendum to his report [S/2005/273/Add.2], following extensive consultations among the UN Departments of Peacekeeping Operations, Political Affairs, and Economic and Social Affairs, the Office for the Coordination of Humanitarian Affairs, UNDP, the Office of the United Nations High Commissioner for Human Rights (OHCHR), UNAMSIL, the UN country team, the Government of Sierra Leone and other national and international stakeholders.

Recommended was a modestly sized UN integrated office in Sierra Leone to be established for an initial period of 12 months, beginning on 1 January 2006. The office would further develop and consolidate the continuing initiatives of the UN country team. Its mandate would be to assist the Government, inter alia, to build the capacity of State institutions to address the root causes of the conflict and the main problems facing the country; develop a national action plan for human rights and establish a national human rights commission; enhance good governance and transparency and accountability; improve budgetary and expenditure processes; build the capacity of the National Electoral Commission (NEC) to conduct the national electoral process in 2007; strengthen the judiciary; develop political and economic empowerment initiatives for youth and initiatives for the rights and well-being of war-affected and vulnerable children and adolescents; build an independent and capable public radio capacity; liaise with the security sector and further strengthen the capacity of the police; and coordinate with the Special Court for Sierra Leone.

The office would be headed by the Executive Representative of the Secretary-General, who would also serve as the UNDP Resident Representative and the United Nations Resident and Humanitarian Coordinator, to ensure a cohesive and coordinated approach within the whole UN family in Sierra Leone. It would comprise a small office to support the Executive Representative and five sections on the key areas of its mandate: good governance and peace consolidation, human rights and rule of law, civilian police and military assistance, development, and public information. The sections would be staffed, respectively, by: eight peace and governance advisers, five international human rights officers supported by national officers and UN volunteers, 20 civilian police and 10 military liaison officers, the UN country team, the Office of the Resident and Humanitarian Coordinator and one senior coordination adviser, and three international public information officers and a number of national officers.

In reiterating that a sustained commitment of the United Nations, working in close partnership with the Government, would be required after the withdrawal of UNAMSIL, the Secretary-General hoped the Council would give serious consideration to his recommendations.

Communication. By a 21 June letter [S/2005/419], the President of Sierra Leone commended the work of UNAMSIL in bringing about peace and stability in Sierra Leone and said that, after the withdrawal of the Mission, a follow-on UN presence in the country would be indispensable, especially in the period leading up to the national elections in 2007.

SECURITY COUNCIL ACTION

On 31 August [meeting 5254], the Security Council unanimously adopted **resolution 1620(2005)**. The draft [S/2005/554] was prepared in consultations among Council members.

The Security Council,

Recalling its previous resolutions and the statements by its President concerning the situation in Sierra Leone,

Commending the valuable contribution that the United Nations Mission in Sierra Leone has made to the recovery of Sierra Leone from conflict and to the country's peace, security and development,

Having considered the report of the Secretary-General of 26 April 2005, and the addendum thereto of 28 July 2005, and welcoming his recommendation that a United Nations integrated office be established in Sierra Leone after the withdrawal of the United Nations Mission in Sierra Leone at the end of 2005, in order to continue to assist the Government of Sierra Leone to consolidate peace by enhancing political and economic governance, building the national capacity for conflict prevention, and preparing for elections in 2007,

Taking note of the letter dated 21 June 2005 from the President of the Republic of Sierra Leone to the Secretary-General, which likewise emphasizes the need for a United Nations integrated office to support the above objectives,

Emphasizing the importance of a smooth transition between the United Nations Mission in Sierra Leone and the new United Nations integrated office, and of the effective and efficient operation of the office,

Emphasizing also the importance of the continued support of the United Nations and the international community for the long-term security and development of Sierra Leone, particularly in building the capacity of the Government of Sierra Leone,

Reiterating its appreciation for the essential work of the Special Court for Sierra Leone and its vital contribution to the establishment of the rule of law in Sierra Leone and the subregion, underlining its expectation that the Court will finish its work in accordance with its completion strategy, and, in this regard, encouraging all States to cooperate fully with the Court and to provide it with the necessary financial resources,

Welcoming the publication of the report of the Sierra Leone Truth and Reconciliation Commission, and encouraging the Government of Sierra Leone to take further steps to implement its recommendations,

1. *Requests* the Secretary-General to establish the United Nations Integrated Office in Sierra Leone, as recommended in the addendum to his report, for an initial period of twelve months, beginning on 1 January 2006, with the following key tasks:

(a) To assist the Government of Sierra Leone in:

(i) Building the capacity of State institutions to address further the root causes of the conflict, provide basic services and accelerate progress towards the Millennium Development Goals through poverty reduction and sustainable economic growth, including through the creation of an enabling framework for private investment and systematic efforts to address HIV/AIDS;

(ii) Developing a national action plan for human rights and establishing the national human rights commission;

(iii) Building the capacity of the National Electoral Commission to conduct a free, fair and credible electoral process in 2007;

(iv) Enhancing good governance, transparency and accountability of public institutions, including through anti-corruption measures and improved fiscal management;

(v) Strengthening the rule of law, including by developing the independence and capacity of the justice system and the capacity of the police and corrections system;

(vi) Strengthening the Sierra Leonean security sector, in cooperation with the International Military Advisory and Training Team and other partners;

(vii) Promoting a culture of peace, dialogue and participation in critical national issues through a strategic approach to public information and communication, including by building an independent and capable public radio capacity;

(viii) Developing initiatives for the protection and well-being of youth, women and children;

(b) To liaise with the Sierra Leonean security sector and other partners, to report on the security situation and to make recommendations concerning external and internal security threats;

(c) To coordinate with United Nations missions and offices and regional organizations in West Africa in dealing with cross-border challenges such as the illicit movement of small arms, human trafficking and smuggling and illegal trade in natural resources;

(d) To coordinate with the Special Court for Sierra Leone;

2. *Emphasizes* the primary responsibility of the Government of Sierra Leone for the consolidation of peace and security in the country, and urges continued

support from international donors for the efforts of the Government in this regard;

3. *Underlines* the importance of establishing a fully integrated office with effective coordination of strategy and programmes between the United Nations agencies, funds and programmes in Sierra Leone, between the United Nations and other international donors, and between the integrated office, the Economic Community of West African States and other United Nations missions in the region;

4. *Welcomes* the recommendation made by the Secretary-General in the addendum to his report that the integrated office should be headed by an Executive Representative of the Secretary-General and his intention that he or she should also serve as the Resident Representative of the United Nations Development Programme and United Nations Resident Coordinator;

5. *Requests* the Secretary-General to continue planning for security for the Special Court for Sierra Leone on the basis outlined in paragraphs 15 to 24 of the addendum to his report, and looks forward to further details on the proposed arrangements;

6. *Also requests* the Secretary-General to keep the Security Council regularly informed of progress in establishing the integrated office, and thereafter in the implementation of the present resolution;

7. *Decides* to remain actively seized of the matter.

Appointment. By an exchange of letters between the Secretary-General and the Security Council on 7 and 12 December, respectively [S/2005/779, S/2005/780], the Deputy Special Representative for Sierra Leone, Victor da Silva Angelo (Portugal), was appointed Executive Representative for UNIOSIL. He would continue to serve as the Resident Representative of UNDP and UN Resident Coordinator in Sierra Leone.

Financing. The Secretary-General, in his December report [A/60/585] on estimates in respect of special political missions, good offices and other political activities authorized by the General Assembly and/or the Security Council, submitted proposed requirements for UNIOSIL in the amount of $23,298,600 for the period 1 January to 31 December 2006 under section 3, Political affairs of the 2006-2007 programme budget.

The Assembly, in section VI of **resolution 60/248** of 23 December (see p. 1495), approved, as recommended by ACABQ [A 60/7/Add. 24], for UNIOSIL a prorated amount out of the charge of $100 million for the 26 special political missions for the period 1 January to 30 April 2006.

Further UNAMSIL activities

Report of Secretary-General (September). In his September report on UNAMSIL [S/2005/596], the Secretary-General outlined the withdrawal plan for UNAMSIL and described the media campaign on the achievements and exit strategy of the Mission, as well as the plans for a seamless transition from peacekeeping to peacebuilding.

The Secretary-General described the security environment in Sierra Leone as generally calm and stable. The Government took further steps towards assuming full responsibility for the maintenance of security. The performance of the Office of National Security improved, particularly its coordination capacity. Progress was limited, however, in addressing the serious threats to the country's stability: corruption, ineffective governance, widespread poverty, massive youth unemployment and consequent public discontent. Although the political situation in Liberia was stabilizing as preparations for the October elections were proceeding peacefully, and as its border with Sierra Leone continued to be jointly monitored by UNMIL and UNAMSIL, the fragile security situation in the subregion remained a potential threat.

Implementation of the benchmarks progressed further, as demonstrated by the enhanced capacity of the security forces, increased public confidence in the police and the successful recruitment, training and deployment of some 3,000 police officers, bringing the police force strength to 9,000 against the benchmark of 9,500. The armed forces continued to be constrained by a lack of communications equipment and shortages of accommodation, rations, fuel, ammunition, medical supplies, water and uniforms.

Further advances were made in the consolidation of State authority. The Government continued devolving major State administrative services in education, health and agriculture to the local councils. Relations between the local councils and the chiefdom system were evolving satisfactorily. The Government and local councils, in collaboration with UNAMSIL and civic organizations, began a new mediation initiative at the provincial and district levels for dispute settlement among chiefdoms. With UNAMSIL support, the Government was proceeding with the launch in October of the diamond-mining cadastral system in the district of Kono, which would be expanded to other diamond-mining areas. Although diamond exports rose to $82 million in the first half of 2005, close monitoring of the mines and diamond extraction needed to be maintained in view of UNAMSIL surveys showing that more than 50 per cent of diamond mining remained unlicensed, and reports that illegal diamond smuggling was considerable. On electoral reform, the restructuring and capacity-building of the National Electoral Commission continued with the appointment of a chairperson in May and a commitment by the Government of $8 million for staff recruitment and to facilitate further restructuring. International partners set up a basket fund to mobilize the $18.4 million required to complete the Commission's electoral tasks for the conduct of credible elections in 2007.

The Mano River Union countries (Guinea, Liberia and Sierra Leone), at their recent summit (Freetown, 28 July), reaffirmed their commitment to pursue a peaceful solution to the Yenga border issue, and agreed that demarcation of the border between Guinea and Sierra Leone would start on 20 August. The summit devoted considerable attention to the promotion of confidence-building measures in border areas and on the strengthening of security in the subregion.

Following the July visit of the United Nations High Commissioner for Human Rights, Louise Arbour, to Sierra Leone, the Government showed renewed interest in the establishment of a national human rights commission. With the support of UNAMSIL and OHCHR, preparatory work to that end was begun by the Attorney General and the Minister of Justice. The final report of the Truth and Reconciliation Commission was published and, on 8 August, UNAMSIL began nationwide distribution and sensitization of its findings and recommendations. The Government published a white paper reflecting most of the recommendations but had yet to implement them.

The Secretary-General observed that the Government had made commendable efforts towards consolidating constitutional order and State authority throughout Sierra Leone. However, it had yet to address many of the root causes of the conflict in the country, such as poverty, youth unemployment, illiteracy and lack of basic infrastructure. He also noted the commendable progress in the diamond-mining sector, adding that the Government should be encouraged to continue to build on initiatives aimed at generating additional revenue from that vital sector. He said further efforts, including by the international community, were required to help resolve the potential source of conflict posed by the Yenga border dispute, and instructed his Special Representative to intensify mediation efforts to reach a solution before the termination of UNAMSIL.

Report of Secretary-General (December). In his final report on UNAMSIL [S/2005/777], the Secretary-General observed that the tasks before the country as it advanced into the post-conflict peacebuilding phase were challenging. Public expectation of peace dividends was high at the same time that perception of government responsiveness to the population's needs was generally low; whence the need for a strategy to communicate the Government's vision and programmes to the public and to involve the participation of civic organizations and the private sector in enhancing democratic governance. Although the political situation was calm and stable, signs of tension were surfacing as political parties began preparing for the 2007 national elections. The two main parties, the ruling Sierra Leone People's Party (SLPP) and the All People's Congress (APC) selected Vice-President Solomon Berewa and APC leader Ernest Bai Koroma, respectively, as their presidential candidates. In the process, both parties experienced intra-party divisions that resulted in splinter groups. A faction of APC challenged the party's elected leadership in the courts, while Charles Margai, a prominent SLPP member, formed his own political party, the People's Movement for Democratic Change (PMDC), having failed to be selected as the SLPP presidential nominee. UNAMSIL promoted inter-party dialogue, reconciliation and tolerance among the political parties and bi-partisan approaches to national issues in the legislature. Other political developments included the appointment of a new Chairman of the Anti-Corruption Commission, which had investigated corruption charges against six cabinet ministers; and the formalization of the Political Parties Registration Commission with the approval of its composition by Parliament on 1 December.

Short-term indicators of internal security were positive, with little probability of a return to civil conflict, and criminal activities were expected to remain at manageable levels. The increased capacity of the security sector to restore law and order was exemplified by its efficient handling of three serious security incidents without UNAMSIL assistance: the violent riots resulting from the 7 November murder in Kenema of two motorcycle transportation operators and the death on 18 November in Koidu of a third operator in a traffic accident; and the disruption on 19 November by the supporters of Charles Margai of a commemorative ceremony at a college in Bo, where Vice-President Berewa was the guest of honour. No major external threats to the country's security occurred during the reporting period. Efforts to resolve the Yenga border dispute were in progress; Guinea and Sierra Leone conducted an on-site inspection of the disputed area and held consultations at Koindu.

In anticipation of the start of UNIOSIL operations on 1 January 2006, a UN interdepartmental team led by UNDP, and in collaboration with the Government and relevant partners, developed a draft peace consolidation strategy that would provide the framework for the implementation of the UNIOSIL mandate. Building upon the work accomplished under the joint UNAMSIL/UN country team transition plan for 2005, the strategy would focus on peace consolidation, as well as on complementing the Government's poverty reduction strategy and the revised UN development assistance framework. The third review of the transition plan, conducted in October, pointed to the successful completion of the initiatives taken by the UN system towards laying the foundation for post-conflict peacebuilding in Sierra Leone.

Towards the completion of its withdrawal by the end of December, UNMIL assumed command of the military unit protecting the Special Court for Sierra Leone on 1 December; it would be relieved on 15 January 2006 by a military guard force from Mongolia. UNMIL would also earmark a rapid reaction force to be deployed from the Liberian capital of Monrovia to Freetown.

Ongoing restructuring of Sierra Leone's armed forces slowed considerably due to a shortage of resources. The army training and restructuring programme required additional resources to enable it to be completed on schedule. The Sierra Leone police were deployed throughout the country in 74 police stations and 112 police posts. Police strength reached the benchmark figure of 9,500, some 4,000 of whom had received training from UNAMSIL.

The increasing trend towards respect for human rights and fundamental freedoms continued, especially for civil and political rights. Efforts were in progress to repeal or amend the provisions of the Public Order Act to eliminate undue limits on freedom of expression. The Government authorized the Ministry of Justice to proceed with the establishment of a national human rights commission. UNAMSIL collaborated with the Ministry on the selection and appointment of commissioners, while OHCHR contracted for the advisory services of a consultant. UNAMSIL, which produced an abridged version of the Truth and Reconciliation Commission's final report, continued its dissemination and conducted workshops on its findings and recommendations. To date, the Government had not prepared an action plan for implementing the recommendations. A stakeholders conference was held (6-8 December, Freetown) to review the human rights situation in Sierra Leone, assess tasks to be undertaken in the post-UNAMSIL phase and develop a work plan for the human rights component of UNIOSIL.

The Secretary-General observed that the completion of the peacekeeping phase of UN involvement in Sierra Leone and the departure of UNAMSIL at the end of December marked a turning point for the country. During its six years of operation, UNAMSIL had forged an effective partnership with the UN country team, the countries in the subregion, the donor community, humanitarian organizations, the Government and civil society in order to steer Sierra Leone on the path to post-conflict recovery. The formidable challenges posed by the socio-economic situation notwithstanding, the prospects for Sierra Leone were promising. The Secretary-General was encouraged by recent pledges of support by donors at the Fourth Consultative Group Meeting (London, 29-30 November) held by the World Bank and by the enthusiasm of political parties in preparing for the 2007 elections.

The Secretary-General highlighted the fact that UNAMSIL had broken new ground as the first peacekeeping mission to absorb a parallel subregional peacekeeping force and to enter into a backstopping arrangement with a Member State, namely, the United Kingdom, which had simultaneously launched a security sector reform programme to complement the Mission's efforts. He also highlighted the integrated mission concept, introduced for the first time in UNAMSIL, whose Deputy Special Representative held three integrative offices (see p. 283); the innovative approach of the Security Council to the UNAMSIL exit strategy, based on a carefully calibrated drawdown of its military component in step with the fulfilment of specified benchmarks; the establishment of UNIOSIL with its integrated nature and comprehensive peacebuilding mandate; and the regional approach to peacekeeping operations through inter-mission cooperation between UNAMSIL and other UN presences in the subregion.

The Secretary-General noted that the presence of both UNAMSIL and UNMIL had enabled the countries of the Mano River basin to begin rebuilding peaceful and mutually beneficial relationships. He hoped that Sierra Leone, Côte d'Ivoire, Guinea and Liberia would construct new mechanisms for security cooperation among them and that key stabilizing factors would prevail to ensure peace and stability in the West Africa subregion.

Security Council consideration. The Security Council, at its 20 December meeting [meeting 5334] to consider the Secretary-General's foregoing report, heard a briefing by the Special Representative for Sierra Leone and Head of UNAMSIL, who commended the country's gradual rise from a decade-long conflict and remarkable turnaround towards a future of hope and promise for a better life for its population. That UNAMSIL had completed most of the tasks assigned to it was a source of pride. One of the most satisfying achievements had been the realization of the benchmark to strengthen the Sierra Leone police to its pre-war level of 9,500 personnel under the supervision of the UN police. The Special Representative drew attention not only to the dramatic increase in revenue collection, citing that by November diamond exports had already amounted to some $131 million, but also to specific aspects of control over the diamond industry that were imperative. He pointed out, however, some of the problems that could destabilize the country in the post-UNAMSIL phase: funding gaps for meeting running costs of the security sector and support services, the possible intensification of inter- and intra-party rivalry as the 2007 elections approached, the backlog in court trials, unemployment and poverty.

The Special Representative remarked that, at the request of the Peacekeeping Best Practices Section of DPKO, a public opinion survey directed by Jean Krasno of the City College of New York and Yale University revealed that a large number of Sierra Leoneans had a positive perception of the work done by UNAMSIL since its inception. He was convinced that the Mission had provided a model for future peacekeeping missions. He thanked all concerned for their collaborative effort without which UNAMSIL could have faltered or failed.

SECURITY COUNCIL ACTION

On 20 December [meeting 5334], following consultations among Security Council members, the President made statement **S/PRST/2005/63** on behalf of the Council:

The Security Council commends the United Nations Mission in Sierra Leone for its invaluable contribution over the last six years to Sierra Leone's recovery from conflict and its progress towards peace, democracy and prosperity. The Council is grateful to the Secretary-General, his Special Representatives and all the individuals from the United Nations and from troop- and police-contributing countries who have made the Mission a success, especially those who helped the Mission to recover from the crisis it faced in May 2000. The Council also deeply appreciates the cooperation extended by the Government and the people of Sierra Leone to the Mission and the members of the United Nations family operating in the country.

The Council notes with satisfaction the innovations in the Mission's methods of operation that may prove useful best practice in making other United Nations peacekeeping operations more effective and efficient, including an exit strategy based on specific benchmarks for drawdown; an integrated mission with a Deputy Special Representative managing governance, development and humanitarian elements; and substantial, regular cooperation and coordination with other United Nations peacekeeping operations and offices in the region.

At the request of the Council, the Secretary-General has established the new United Nations Integrated Office in Sierra Leone in order to provide continued support to the Government as it tackles the many challenges ahead, including good governance, sustainable economic development, job creation and delivery of public services. The Government will need the sustained help of donors and development partners, particularly in addressing difficult but essential issues such as security sector reform, fighting corruption, the reinforcement of governance mechanisms, including the judiciary, and equal rights for women and girls. The Council therefore encourages Sierra Leone's development partners to continue their support in all these areas, and notes with satisfaction the outcome of the recent meeting of the donors' Consultative Group on Sierra Leone, held in London on 29 and 30 November 2005.

With Sierra Leone now stable and at peace, the Council sees a great opportunity for the development of a mature and vibrant political culture. Achieving this will require tolerance, cooperation from all sides and a shared commitment to act responsibly and avoid inflammatory rhetoric. To that end, government and political leaders should reaffirm their commitment to the basic principles of democratic governance. This will pave the way for fair, transparent and peaceful elections in 2007.

The Council reiterates its appreciation for the work of the Special Court for Sierra Leone and its vital contribution to reconciliation and the rule of law in the country and the subregion, and encourages all States, particularly States in the subregion, to cooperate fully with the Court and to provide it with the necessary financial resources.

The Council continues to emphasize the importance of a regional approach to the countries of West Africa. The Council hopes that Sierra Leone's neighbours will intensify their cooperation, not least through the Mano River Union and the Economic Community of West African States, especially in the area of peace and security, and with the continued support of the United Nations and development partners.

Special Court for Sierra Leone

The Special Court for Sierra Leone, jointly established by the Government of Sierra Leone and the United Nations in 2002 [YUN 2002, p. 164] in accordance with Security Council resolution 1315(2000) [YUN 2000, p. 205], continued in 2005 to try those bearing the "greatest responsibility" for serious violations of international humanitarian and Sierra Leonean laws committed in the territory of Sierra Leone since 1996. The Secretary-General reported in April [S/2005/273] that former Chairman of the Armed Forces Revolutionary Council (AFRC) Johnny Paul Koroma, under a 17-count indictment, remained at large, and that efforts were continuing to apprehend former Liberian President Charles Taylor, indicted in 2003 [YUN 2003, p. 216] on 17 counts of crimes against humanity, violations of article 3 common to the Geneva Conventions and of Additional Protocol II and other serious violations of international humanitarian law and currently in asylum in Nigeria. On 24 February, the European Parliament unanimously adopted a resolution calling on the EU member States to take immediate action to bring about the appearance of Charles Taylor before the Special Court.

Security Council consideration. On 24 May [meeting 5185], the President of the Special Court for Sierra Leone, Judge Emanuel Ayoola, briefed the Security Council on the progress of the Court in relation to its revised completion strategy (see below). He said that of 13 indictments issued, two were withdrawn due to the death of the accused, leaving 11 proper indictments active. Nine of the 11 accused were in the custody of the Court in Freetown and two remained at large (see above). The Prosecutor indicated the possibility of additional indictments that could be linked to existing indictees, but their number would be limited. As to the three joint trials under way, namely, of AFRC, the Civil Defence Forces (CDF) and the Revolutionary United Front (RUF), Judge Ayoola estimated that, at the trial stage, the trials of the first two would be completed by the end of 2005 or early 2006, and the third by the end of 2006, plus an estimated additional four to six months for the appeals stage.

The Judge stressed that several factors could adversely affect the progress of the trials and thus the completion strategy, such as the number of witnesses required or the sudden illness or unavailability of key individual participants, as well as funding, security and cooperation of States (principally Nigeria and Liberia) in transferring the two accused who were at large. He said the importance of the expeditious apprehension and trial of Messrs. Koroma and Taylor could not be overemphasized for the credibility of the Court and for its contribution to combating the culture of impunity, which was essential for the consolidation of peace and development of the rule of law in Sierra Leone. On the question of funding for the Court, he was aware that the Fifth Committee was considering a commitment authority for the period 31 July–31 December 2005 but that funds beyond 2005 had not been assured.

The Council, by **resolution 1638(2005)** (see p. 267) of 11 November, authorized UNMIL to apprehend and detain Charles Taylor, should he return to Liberia, and transfer him to Sierra Leone for prosecution before the Special Court.

Completion strategy

By identical letters of 26 May to the General Assembly and the Security Council [A/59/816-S/2005/350], the Secretary-General presented the revised completion strategy prepared by the Special Court and endorsed by the Court's Management Committee on 18 May. The strategy specified that the Court's mandate would be carried out in two phases: the completion phase of the trials, during which the Court would render final judgements against all accused in custody and transfer those convicted to appropriate prisons in or outside Sierra Leone to serve their sentences, and concurrently downsize its staff and transfer and liquidate its assets; and the post-completion phase, during which the Court, through a mechanism that would need to be created, would continue certain residual activities: supervising sentence enforcement, providing witness support and protection, and conducting contempt and review proceedings and proceedings against any accused who later surrendered or was apprehended.

In addition, the completion strategy paper updated Court activities, including the swearing in of three additional judges in January; introducing initiatives to improve trial management efficiency in the form of a second Trial Chamber that began functioning in March, and the creation of a Judicial Services Co-ordinating Committee, the estimated completion dates of the trials and the status of enforcement agreements. The paper also pointed to ongoing efforts to develop a fundraising strategy for the Court's completion and post-completion phases from January 2006 onwards, the need to retain key personnel and ensure the security of the Court's premises, and the concern of the Court that supporters of the detainees posed a security threat to it so that the continued presence of international troops to protect the Court and its staff until the end of trial proceedings was critical to the completion strategy.

Security arrangements

In keeping with Security Council resolution 1610(2005) (see p. 280), the Secretary-General, on 28 July [S/2005/273/Add.2], following consultations among the Special Court, UNAMSIL and UNMIL on various options for providing reliable security for the Court after UNAMSIL's withdrawal at the end of the year, indicated that while the overall security of the Court would continue to be provided by the Sierra Leonean Government, the only feasible and cost-effective option would be to transfer that responsibility from UNAMSIL to UNMIL. Therefore, subject to the consent of troop-contributing countries, the Secretary-General recommended that a company-size military unit from UNAMSIL be retained in Freetown upon its departure to continue to protect the Court, and that UNMIL assume command, control and support of the unit. He said his recommendations were fully consistent with resolution

1609(2005) (see p. 236) authorizing, subject to certain conditions, the temporary redeployment of military and civilian police personnel among UNMIL, UNAMSIL and UNOCI to deal with challenges that could not be handled within the authorized personnel ceiling of a given mission in the region; approval of his recommendation would enhance inter-mission cooperation, as proposed in his report [S/2005/135] on such cooperation and possible cross-border operations among the three missions. The UN Secretariat, UNAMSIL and UNMIL had already consulted with potential troop-contributing countries, the Governments of Liberia and Sierra Leone, and the Special Court, and implementation proposals were being prepared.

Financing

Report of Secretary General. The Secretary-General indicated in an 18 April report [A/59/534/Add.4] that, for the period from 1 July 2004 to 30 June 2005, expenditures for the Special Court would total approximately $26.6 million. He estimated that the commitment authority of $20 million authorized by General Assembly resolution 59/276 [YUN 2004, p. 1383] to supplement the Court's financial resources for the period 1 January to 30 June 2005 would be fully utilized and that an additional subvention of $13 million would be required for the period from 1 July to 31 December 2005. Accordingly, the Secretary-General requested the Assembly to appropriate $33 million as a subvention to the Court for the period from 1 January to 31 December 2005 under special political missions of section 3, Political affairs, of the 2004-2005 programme budget. A further subvention of $7 million would be required in 2006 to allow the Court to complete the existing trials, which the Secretary-General would request under the same section in the 2006-2007 programme budget during the sixtieth (2005) session of the General Assembly.

ACABQ [A/59/569/Add.4] encouraged the Court's Management Committee to raise voluntary contributions and recommended that the Secretary-General, in concert with the Committee, intensify efforts to raise voluntary contributions to support the work of the Court.

By section II of **resolution 59/294** of 22 June (see p. 1488), the Assembly authorized an additional $13 million subvention to supplement the finance resources of the Court for the period 1 July to 31 December 2005, bringing the total subvention to $33 million for the period 1 January to 31 December 2005.

Sanctions

The Security Council Committee established pursuant to resolution 1132(1997) [YUN 1997, p. 135] concerning Sierra Leone submitted two reports in 2005: one on 25 January [S/2005/44] covering its 2004 [YUN 2004, p. 223] activities and the other on 30 December [S/2005/843] covering its 2005 activities to monitor and implement the 1998 embargo on the sale or supply of arms to Sierra Leone and the travel ban on leading members of the former military junta in Sierra Leone and of RUF, imposed by resolution 1171(1998) [YUN 1998, p. 169].

During 2005, the Committee did not meet, but its members were able to take all necessary decisions through the no-objection procedure. It noted that, as of the reporting date, the travel ban list included the names of 30 individuals designated as leading members of the former military junta, AFRC and RUF. Since the list was last revised in September 2004, no further information or recommendation had been received from Sierra Leone. In 2005, the Committee received a 2 August notification from Greece of its proposed export of a diesel electric generator to Sierra Leone by a South African power company; the Committee replied that since the equipment was not an embargoed item, it was not subject to the Committee's consideration. On 22 August [S/2005/561], the United Kingdom notified the Committee of its plan to export blank ammunition and demolition stores to the Sierra Leone armed forces. On 3 November [S/2005/724], the United Kingdom further notified the Committee of the request for a trade licence to export armoured cars from Jordan to Sierra Leone for use by the Special Court for Sierra Leone.

The Chairman of the Committee was of the view that, following the completion of the drawdown of UNAMSIL from Sierra Leone, the time would be appropriate for the Security Council to revisit the legal basis of its measures concerning Sierra Leone.

Security Council consideration. At the meeting of the Security Council on 19 December [meeting 5332], the Security Council Committee Chairman, Ronaldo Mota Sardenberg, in his briefing of the Council, summarized the history of the sanctions imposed in Sierra Leone, beginning with Council resolution 1132(1997), based on the Council's determination that the situation in the country constituted a threat to international peace and security. Taking into consideration the fact that UNAMSIL had since forged effective partnerships and placed Sierra Leone on a firm path to post-conflict recovery, and in the context of the Government's further progress towards consolidating constitutional order and assuming full responsibility for the maintenance of the country's security, Mr. Sardenberg said that the Council might soon start to review the Sierra Leone sanctions regime with a view to updating its legal basis and streamlining the measures currently in place, as well as the Committee's mandate. Consultations within the Committee and with the Government of Sierra Leone would contribute towards that end.

Guinea-Bissau

The United Nations Peace-building Support Office in Guinea-Bissau (UNOGBIS) continued in 2005 to assist Guinea-Bissau in the implementation of the provisions of the September 2003 Political Transition Charter for the restoration of constitutional order [YUN 2003, p. 227], interrupted by a military mutiny in October 2004.

For most of the first half of 2005, the political situation in the country was dominated by preparations for the presidential elections held in two rounds: the first on 19 June and the second on 24 July, culminating in the election of João Bernardo "Nino" Vieira and his investiture on 1 October as the new President of Guinea-Bissau. The event marked the completion of the electoral process that began in March 2004, ending a transitional period that had been in progress since the coup d'état of 14 September 2003.

The conduct of the elections, observed by international observers and coordinated by UNOGBIS country-wide, was peaceful and deemed free, fair and transparent. The pre-election stage, however, was marred by tensions sparked by the question as to whether one of two candidates who were former Presidents was eligible to run under the terms of the Transition Charter. Tensions mounted in the immediate post-election period as the runner-up persisted in rejecting the voting results and twice appealed to the Supreme Court of Justice for their annulment. The Court ruled to confirm the results on the first appeal; it could not rule on the second owing to "insufficient judicial elements". The investiture of the President was thus able to proceed.

Relations between the President and Prime Minister were difficult, notwithstanding their publicly stated willingness to work together. On 28 October, the President dismissed the Government, citing tensions among the organs of State sovereignty that rendered the Government dysfunctional. Shortly after, he appointed a new Prime Minister and, on 9 November, named a new Government. Those actions deepened the divisions generated during the elections, as reflected in a National Popular Assembly that became polarized into two camps: one supporting the Government appointed by the President and the other allied to the Government formed in May 2004 and dismissed by the President. The balance of power remained fluid, with neither side able to assure sustainable support in Parliament.

Throughout the electoral process, UNOGBIS used its good offices to promote dialogue among political, military and civil society actors. The Secretary-General noted that the aspects of its mandate relating to the full restoration of constitutional order, the holding of peaceful, free and fair presidential elections and the elaboration of a UN peacebuilding strategy for Guinea-Bissau had been successfully implemented. The engagement of key national stakeholders and international partners on the question of security sector reform within the broader framework of public administration reform was under way, and the basis of a national initiative to address the challenge posed by illicit small arms and light weapons had been established. In view of those developments, the Secretary-General, with the concurrence of the Security Council, adjusted the mandate of UNOGBIS and its resource base and staffing, in its new role of supporting the Government's efforts to consolidate constitutional rule, promote national reconciliation and respect for the rule of law and human rights, and of working with the other UN agencies to mobilize international financial assistance to enable the Government to meet its immediate financial needs.

UNOGBIS

The United Nations Peace-building Support Office in Guinea-Bissau (UNOGBIS), a political mission established in 1999 by decision of the Secretary-General and supported by Security Council resolution 1233(1999) [YUN 1999, p. 140], was extended until 22 December 2005. Its mandate had been revised by resolution 1580(2004) [YUN 2004, p. 229] in the face of intensified political turmoil and uncertainty in 2004. The Support Office was headed by the Representative of the Secretary-General for Guinea-Bissau, João Bernardo Honwana (Mozambique).

In line with resolution 1580(2004), the Secretary-General reported, in March [S/2005/174], that a UN multidisciplinary mission visited Guinea-Bissau from 12 to 17 February to conduct a review of UNOGBIS with a view to adjusting the Mission's capacities to meet the requirements of its mandate. Its broad objectives were to assess those aspects of the mandate that could foster political dialogue, ensure credible elections to take place in 2005, enhance respect for the rule of law and promote transitional justice, enhance the administration of justice, develop local conflict resolution mechanisms, promote security sector reform, initiate programmes to eradicate the proliferation of small arms and mobilize international support for the country.

In the light of work that remained to put the country's peacebuilding process on a steady forward-looking track, and taking account of the findings of the review mission, the Secretary-General recommended that, within the framework of its revised mandate, as outlined in Council resolution 1580(2004), UNOGBIS should focus on the promotion of political dialogue, development of stable civil-military relations, promotion of the implementation of the Programme of Action adopted by the 2001 UN Conference on small arms [YUN 2001, p. 499] as an urgent priority, advancement of a comprehensive and integrated UN peacebuilding strategy, and adjustment of the use of available UNOGBIS human and financial resources to enable it to respond more effectively to the requirements of its revised mandate. In that regard, some existing posts might need to be adjusted and new posts created.

In view of the completion of the country's transition phase that culminated in the presidential elections, the Secretary-General, in September [S/2005/575], proposed that UNOGBIS mandate be revised to include the following functions: to support efforts to consolidate constitutional rule, enhance political dialogue and promote national reconciliation and respect for the rule of law and human rights; to assist in strengthening the capacity of national institutions to maintain constitutional order; to encourage and support national efforts to reform the security sector; to encourage the Government to implement fully the Programme of Action on small arms; within the framework of a comprehensive peacebuilding strategy, to work closely with the Resident Coordinator and the UN country team to mobilize international financial assistance to enable the Government to meet its immediate financial and logistical needs; and to enhance cooperation and coordination with the AU, ECOWAS, the Community of Portuguese-speaking Countries (CPLP) and other international partners, and intermission cooperation. The emphasis of the revised mandate would be on initiatives meeting the requirements of self-sustainability and national ownership; the development of synergies and complementarities with UN agencies, particularly UNDP and the Bretton-Woods institutions (the World Bank Group and the International Monetary Fund), and with the AU, ECOWAS and CPLP; and political dialogue, governance, human rights, security sector reform and resource mobilization. The Secretary-General reiterated the resource base and personnel requirements as indicated in March (above).

On 2 December [S/2005/795], the Secretary-General advised the Council of a 21 November letter from the new President of Guinea-Bissau stating that, while UNOGBIS had achieved an important element in its mandate with the conclusion of the political transition in the country, it still had a decisive role to play in the consolidation of peace and stability and requested an extension of UNOGBIS mandate. The Secretary-General furthermore referred to his proposals (above) for the adjustment of the mandate and recommended that it be extended for one year, until 31 December 2006, which the Council noted on 15 December [S/2005/796]. The Council had issued a press statement on the previous day [SC/8581], stating that an agreement was reached for the mandate's revision and renewal as recommended.

Political and security developments and UNOGBIS activities

Report of Secretary-General (March). In his March report [S/2005/174] on developments in Guinea-Bissau and UNOGBIS activities, the Secretary-General noted that the country had improved noticeably since his December 2004 report [YUN 2004, p. 228], despite tremendous challenges. The country was peaceful, although the political situation remained complex and difficult. The Government was preparing for the holding of presidential elections by 7 May, as envisaged in the 2003 Political Transition Charter [YUN 2003, p. 227], which was one of the key benchmarks for the full restoration of constitutional normality. However, the slow pace of the preparations and the transition processes, which were interrupted by the 6 October 2004 military mutiny [YUN 2004, p. 227], and the demands by most political parties for a completely new voter register resulted in the election date being postponed. Since some 20 political parties had challenged the accuracy of the 2004 voter register and demanded a new registration exercise, the National Election Commission and political parties agreed to revise the register and to issue new voting cards. Agreement on that critical measure led to a subsequent consensus that the elections would be held in June 2005. Meanwhile, the Government obtained Parliament's approval of the 2005 State budget, re-engaged in dialogue with its development partners and continued efforts towards restoring the rule of law and improving fiscal management. Despite a continuing difficult financial situation, it managed to pay salaries up to December 2004, thereby removing the potential for social unrest.

The National Popular Assembly, at its new session (28 February–28 March), considered a proposed amnesty bill for all involved in various military interventions from 1980 to 6 October 2004 and proposed amendments to the Electoral Registration and the National Election Commission laws. During the session, on 1 March, the Representative of the Secretary-General in Guinea-Bissau briefed the Assembly on the political significance and practical implications of Security Council resolution 1580(2004), especially with regard to the need to uphold the principles of justice and to continue the fight against impunity.

As to military and security aspects, the Chief of General Staff held several sensitization meetings to promote reconciliation of the different military factions. He visited his counterparts in neighbouring Guinea and Senegal in February to discuss bilateral security issues and modalities of cooperation among their armed forces. Both countries provided non-lethal military assistance to the Guinea-Bissau armed forces. UNOGBIS continued to encourage the military leadership to initiate reform, to which the Chief of General Staff had several times reiterated his commitment. Three committees were set up to examine the Defence Act and military regulations, retirement for members of the armed forces and their physical deployment. UNOGBIS and UNDP were finalizing preparations to establish a technical team to support the Government and the armed forces to plan and implement military reform. An initial contribution for security sector reform was raised at a donor mini-conference (Lisbon, Portugal, 11 February). The Secretary-General dispatched a fact-finding and project development mission (7-11 March) to examine the challenge posed by the proliferation of small arms and light weapons in Guinea-Bissau. The mission, in collaboration with UNOGBIS, the UN country team, the Government and relevant civil society bodies, established the operational and conceptual capacity-building needs for the national implementation of the 2001 Programme of Action on small arms.

The International Organization of Migration (IOM) continued to provide administrative and financial management support to the demobilization, reinsertion and reintegration programme, which was in its last phase. Of the 7,182 beneficiaries, 2,406 had been reintegrated and 2,031 were expected to do so by June. The programme requested an extension to December 2005 to allow it to complete all its reintegration activities.

Progress towards the elimination of mine-related risks continued under the supervision of the UNDP-supported national mine-action coordination authority. By February, 2,545 anti-personnel mines, 64 anti-tank mines and 40,439 pieces of unexploded ordnance had been removed and 789,075 square metres cleared.

The economic situation improved slightly in 2004, the gross domestic product having increased to 4.3 per cent. Nonetheless, the Government remained unable to pay the backlog of civil service salary arrears from 2003, domestic debt, or salaries for January 2005. The 11 February donor mini-conference (above) was held to prepare for the Donor Round Table Conference to be held in the last quarter of 2005 and to mobilize resources to cover the gap of some $40 million in the 2005 State budget; funds were to be channelled through the UNDP-managed Emergency Economic Management Fund.

The Secretary-General observed that the country still faced tremendous challenges and was still floundering and unable to address effectively the basic needs of the populace, accomplish military reform or build a common vision among national stakeholders on how to foster peace, justice and reconciliation. The old sources of conflict persisted. The forthcoming presidential elections, scheduled for 19 June, would formally end the transition and mark the full restoration of constitutional order. If poorly prepared and managed, however, the elections could be an additional source of tension and further instability. The Secretary-General therefore urged national stakeholders to endeavour to create an environment conducive to peaceful, transparent, free and fair elections; a good beginning had been made by reaching consensus on the election date. UNOGBIS and the UN country team would continue to support the organization of the elections, concentrating on helping to lower tensions within and among political parties and promoting the adoption of a code of conduct by all parties during the electoral period. The Secretary-General said that the proposal to have Parliament grant a blanket amnesty to all involved in military actions raised concerns among large segments of the population, including civil society organizations.

The Secretary-General called on the international community to support Guinea-Bissau's efforts to complete the political transition, manage conflict, reform its institutions and relaunch the economy. He welcomed the extension of the mandate of the Ad Hoc Advisory Group on Guinea-Bissau of the Economic and Social Council and trusted that it would continue to support the country to address its pressing short- and longer-term development goals.

(For action by the Economic and Social Council on the reports of its Ad Hoc Advisory Group on Guinea-Bissau with respect to the country's humanitarian and economic needs, see p. 1009.)

On 31 March [meeting 5157], following consultations among Security Council members, the President made statement **S/PRST/2005/14** on behalf of the Council:

The Security Council recognizes some progress made in some areas in Guinea-Bissau, including the electoral process, and urges all political actors in the country to show unequivocal commitment to a peaceful electoral process, leading to peaceful, transparent, free and fair elections, by refraining from inspiring or promoting any sort of ethnic or religious hostilities, particularly with a view to obtaining political gains. In this regard, the Council strongly condemns any attempts to incite violence and to impede ongoing efforts towards peace, stability and social and economic development.

The Council expresses its growing concern at recent political developments in Guinea-Bissau, in particular the decision by the Partido da Renovaçno Social to select ex-President Koumba Yalá as its presidential candidate. Any decision, such as this, which challenges the Political Transition Charter has the potential to jeopardize the successful conclusion of the transitional process and forthcoming presidential elections.

The Council also expresses its deep concern at the fact that peace efforts have not yet generated sufficient social and economic benefits for the population that could discourage the use of force.

The Council stresses, at the same time, the urgent need for international support to the electoral process. It recalls previous appeals for increased international assistance to Guinea-Bissau, including to the forthcoming presidential elections, as part of an urgently needed peacebuilding strategy in that country.

The Council calls upon Guinea-Bissau's international development partners, including all concerned agencies of the United Nations system, to cooperate fully with the Government of Guinea-Bissau, which has been fully engaged in the implementation of the Political Transition Charter and in efforts to promote transparency and good governance. It welcomes, in this regard, the holding on 11 February 2005, in Lisbon, of the meeting of Guinea-Bissau's partners to prepare for the round-table conference and stresses the importance of strong participation in the donor round-table conference scheduled for October 2005.

The Council welcomes initial measures taken by the Chief of General Staff regarding the process of reform of the Armed Forces and the promotion of reconciliation among the military. The Council further encourages full inclusiveness and renewed commitment to reconciliation in the Armed Forces, and development of constructive civilian-military relations based on the Armed Forces as an institution subordinated to the elected civilian authorities. In accordance with its mandate in resolution 1580 (2004), it reaffirms the role of the United Nations

Peacebuilding Support Office in Guinea-Bissau in encouraging and supporting national efforts to reform the security sector.

Report of Secretary-General (June). In his June report [S/2005/380] on Guinea-Bissau and UNOGBIS, the Secretary-General noted that tensions over the election preparations (see p. 291) demonstrated the fragility of peace and stability in the country. A mid-April strike by teachers protesting the non-payment of salaries also demonstrated the continued high level of social dissatisfaction.

Reconciliation and reintegration of the different military factions continued, with the armed forces Commission on Reconciliation and Reintegration holding a series of awareness-raising meetings (28 February–6 April) to promote the idea and content of a comprehensive security sector reform package. A census taken by the military forces in May concluded that 5,100 military personnel were in active service; the Ministry of Public Administration also completed two censuses of the police, border guards and customs officials based in Bissau.

Arrangements were formalized to enable interested Member States to contribute to security sector reform through the UNDP Thematic Trust Fund for Crisis Prevention and Recovery. The fact-finding mission on illicit small arms that visited Guinea-Bissau in March (see p. 291) developed a project proposal for assistance towards the establishment of a national small arms commission to spearhead and coordinate national efforts to address the problem, and for the execution of a pilot small arms collection and destruction programme in the city of Bissau. While the level of criminality in Guinea-Bissau was relatively low, seizures of illicit weapons and cocaine suggested an increase in organized crime operators; the Police Commissioner expressed concern about the lack of resources to address the problem.

Regarding the proposed general amnesty (see p. 291), the National Popular Assembly referred the matter to the Parliamentary Commission on National Reconciliation and to the Committee for Legal and Constitutional Affairs. UNOGBIS partially funded a two-day seminar organized by civil society organizations to promote a better understanding of the legal aspects of the proposal.

The Secretary-General said he was encouraged by the renewed commitment of the national authorities to hold the elections on schedule and called on all candidates to do their utmost to ensure a peaceful election and to accept the results. He welcomed the process of reconciliation within the armed forces and the increasingly republican attitude adopted by the military, as well as the re-affirmation by the military leadership of its sub-ordination to civilian authority. He encouraged the AU, ECOWAS, CPLP and other partners of Guinea-Bissau to continue their critical role in promoting peace and stability in the country. Re-iterating that Guinea-Bissau continued to face tremendous political, social and economic chal-lenges, he noted that the UN country team and UNOGBIS had concluded the review of the UN comprehensive peacebuilding strategy for Guinea-Bissau, which combined peace, security and development agendas and defined the activi-ties to be implemented.

Presidential elections

Presidential candidates. As reported by the Secretary-General [S/2005/380], legal controver-sies surrounding the eligibility of two former Presidents, João Bernardo "Nino" Vieira and Koumba Yalá, to run for the presidency created a highly polarized atmosphere during the prepara-tions for the presidential elections scheduled for 19 June. Mr. Vieira, who returned to Guinea-Bissau on 7 April for the first time since his over-throw in a 1999 coup [YUN 1999, p. 142], was wel-comed by supporters, including a section of the governing African Party for the Independence of Guinea and Cape Verde (PAIGC). Mr. Yalá, on the other hand, nominated on 26 March by the Party of Social Renewal, filed his candidacy with the Supreme Court of Justice, in spite of a provi-sion in the Political Transition Charter banning his participation in political activities for five years.

Communications. The EU, in an 8 April state-ment [S/2005/249], expressed its growing concern at recent developments in the country, particularly Mr. Yalá's decision to run in the 19 June presiden-tial elections and his public declarations that could undermine the efforts and progress achieved thus far in Guinea-Bissau. It called on regional organi-zations, such as CPLP and ECOWAS, to remain actively engaged in support of the country's efforts to achieve political stability.

A press statement issued on 13 April on behalf of the Secretary-General [SG/SM/9818] stated his concern at the mounting political and social ten-sions as the country prepared for presidential elections. Accordingly, he directed his Represen-tative in Guinea-Bissau to facilitate dialogue among all of the country's political actors, on whom he called to refrain from any action or statement that could jeopardize the elections.

The AU Peace and Security Council, by a com-muniqué issued at its thirty-first meeting (Addis Ababa, Ethiopia, 8 June) [S/2005/381], urged all presidential candidates and their supporters to refrain from any act that might disrupt the elec-toral process and to commit themselves to accept-ing the election results; welcomed the decision of the Commission on the Situation in Guinea-Bissau to deploy an observer mission to monitor the elections; called for accelerating preparations for the Donor Round Table Conference in No-vember; and agreed in principle to the proposed establishment of an AU liaison office that would support efforts to promote stability and socio-economic development, and enhance democracy and respect for the rule of law and human rights in Guinea-Bissau.

Pre-election events. On 29 April, the Secretary-General appointed the former Pres-ident of Mozambique, Joaquim Alberto Chissano, as his Special Envoy for Guinea-Bissau to facili-tate the holding of peaceful and credible elec-tions and to help bring the ongoing transition to a successful conclusion and thus to the restoration of constitutional order. During his visit to the country (2-10 May), Mr. Chissano met with actors involved in the electoral process and secured the publicly stated commitments of the armed forces and the Ministry of Defence to respect the Con-stitution and not to interfere in the electoral pro-cess. In a ruling announced on 18 May, the Su-preme Court validated the applications of 17 of the 21 candidates, including former Presidents Vieira and Yalá. Although criticized by some, the ruling was accepted by the society at large. Ten-sions mounted again on 15 May, when Mr. Yalá announced that the Court's decision to allow him to stand had created a constitutional power vac-uum in the country; consequently, he decided to resume his presidential term and postpone the elections. The authorities reacted by reaffirming the Government's commitment to hold elections as scheduled; the Military Committee Chairman publicly pledged his allegiance to Interim Pres-ident Pereira Rosa; and, on 17 May, thousands of school children and students, led by their teach-ers, held a "march for peace". Similar marches were also held in the interior of the country. Fol-lowing the alleged 25 May attempt by Mr. Yalá to occupy a building of the presidential compound, which he denied, Government authorities and the National Election Commission issued state-ments reaffirming their commitment to hold elections as scheduled. An electoral needs assessment mission dispatched by the Secretary-General to the country (18-25 May) concluded that the necessary technical conditions were in place for the holding of the first round of elec-tions. On 28 May, the official candidates began their electoral campaign in Bissau. By the end of May, donors had committed over 2.6 million euros to fund the elections through UNDP and directly to the Government. The EU also committed up to 1.5 million euros to cover costs of its Election Observation Mission already deployed in Guinea-Bissau.

Elections. The first round of the presidential elections took place on 19 June as scheduled. It was described as peaceful by the Secretary-General, who commended the people of Guinea-Bissau for turning out in large numbers [SG/SM/9942]. The second round, held on 24 July, was also described by the Secretary-General as peaceful, free, fair and transparent. The provisional results were announced by the national election authorities on 28 July: the majority vote, 52.35 per cent, had gone to Nino Vieira, compared with 47.65 per cent for Mr. Malam Bacai Sanhá, which Mr. Sanhá and his party, PAIGC, rejected. The Secretary-General appealed for calm during the counting process prior to the announcement of the final results and stressed the need to employ legal means to address any electoral grievances [SG/SM/10018]. Tension persisted as Mr. Sanhá again rejected the final results announced on 10 August. Following mediation efforts by the AU, Mr. Sanhá filed an official appeal with the Supreme Court of Justice, indicating that he would accept the Court's ruling. The international community, particularly ECOWAS, CPLP, the AU and the United Nations, had cooperated closely and coordinated their efforts to reduce electoral tension.

Communication. Earlier, the EU, by a 1 August statement [S/2005/514], expressed pleasure that the second round of the presidential elections was considered by international observers, particularly by the European Union Election Observation Mission (EU EOM), to have been peaceful and generally well organized in a transparent and inclusive manner, in line with principles for democratic elections, and that the voters were able to exercise their franchise freely, despite a tense pre-election period. Noting the provisional results published on 28 July, the EU called on all political parties and stakeholders to ensure completion of the remaining part of the election process in line with constitutional and other legal provisions.

SECURITY COUNCIL ACTION

On 19 August [meeting 5248], following consultations among Security Council members, the President made statement **S/PRST/2005/39** on behalf of the Council:

The Security Council acknowledges with satisfaction the successful holding of the presidential elections in Guinea-Bissau and the announcement by the National Electoral Commission of the final results of the ballot. This marks an important step towards the restoration of constitutional order. The Council takes note of the appeal filed with the Supreme Court of Justice by one of the contenders and strongly encourages all parties to honour their commitments and accept the final ruling of the Court. The Council urges them to refrain from any actions that could jeopardize the efforts towards peace and stability in Guinea-Bissau.

The Council commends the people of Guinea-Bissau for their encouraging participation in the electoral process.

The Council pays tribute to Guinea-Bissau's partners and neighbours, who provided indispensable support for the holding of the elections. The Council also congratulates international observers on the essential role they played throughout the country, and welcomes their statement recognizing the presidential elections as free, fair and transparent.

The Council expresses its appreciation for the contribution made by the African Union, the Community of Portuguese-speaking Countries, the Economic Community of West African States, the European Union, the Special Envoy of the Secretary-General, the Special Envoy of the Chairperson of the African Union, the Representative of the Secretary-General in Guinea-Bissau and the United Nations Peacebuilding Support Office in Guinea-Bissau, bilateral partners and international financial institutions. The Council underlines the importance of their timely diplomatic efforts aimed at promoting national dialogue and respect for the rule of law.

Considering the challenges still facing Guinea-Bissau, the Council urges all relevant national and international parties to reaffirm their commitment to peace and democracy in Guinea-Bissau, and calls upon bilateral development partners of Guinea-Bissau, international financial institutions and United Nations agencies to increase their support for economic and social development and the consolidation of national institutions, as well as the promotion of good governance and human rights, in particular by providing emergency financial assistance and technical support, in the short run, and by participating actively in the Donor Round Table Conference to be held in November 2005.

The Council therefore welcomes the decision taken by the Economic and Social Council on 26 July 2005 to extend the mandate of the Ad Hoc Advisory Group on Guinea-Bissau, and commends the Advisory Group for its work.

The Council invites the Secretary-General to present recommendations in his next report regarding the updating of the mandate of the Support Office and its role in the consolidation of peace and stability in Guinea-Bissau in the post-transition period.

Also on 19 August, the Supreme Court of Justice confirmed the final results of the second round of the presidential elections. On the same date, the EU EOM released a statement confirming that the elections had met international principles for democratic elections and that, in accordance with the electoral law of Guinea-Bissau, all legal resources had been exhausted.

Nevertheless, on 20 August, Mr. Sanhá and Prime Minister Carlos Gomes Júnior, the PAIGC president, persisted in rejecting the Court's ruling. On 23 August, the Secretary-General took note of the Court's ruling and called on all parties to accept it [SG/SM/10055]. On 26 August, the Supreme Court rejected Mr. Sanhá's second request for annulment of the poll, declaring that due to "insufficient judicial elements" it could not rule on the request.

In New York, on 21 September, the Secretary-General met with the Prime Minister to impress upon him the need to abide by his commitment made before the General Assembly on 16 September that the President-elect would be inaugurated on 1 October 2005 [SG/SM/10117]. As confirmed to the Assembly, President-elect Vieira was sworn in on 1 October as the new President of Guinea-Bissau, marking the formal end of the transitional period, which the country had been undergoing since the coup d'état of 14 September 2003.

Post-electoral situation

Report of Secretary-General (September). In his September report [S/2005/575] on developments in Guinea-Bissau and UNOGBIS activities, the Secretary-General said that the political situation in the country remained fragile. Although the aftermath of the polling was marked by bitterness and sharp political divisions over the provisional election results, there were some positive aspects of the electoral process: the political neutrality of the armed forces, deemed crucial in guaranteeing a peaceful environment for the elections; the appeals by national civil society organizations to candidates and their supporters to practice civil tolerance; and the use by UNOGBIS of its good offices to promote dialogue among the political, military and civil society actors throughout the electoral process.

From March to August, UNOGBIS focused its activities on managing and resolving crises inherent in the political transition, and building working relationships with national stakeholders and international partners in preparation for the post-transition consolidation phase. It would also facilitate the development of self-sustainable national peacebuilding mechanisms and initiatives and resume its advocacy and good offices roles, as well as training and capacity-building activities, especially in conflict management and resolution.

A draft comprehensive peacebuilding strategy was prepared and discussed with national stakeholders, which aligned the short-term political objectives of consolidating peace and stability with the medium- to long-term objectives of promoting sustainable socio-economic development. Its objectives were: to promote self-sustaining dialogue; enhance governance, the rule of law and respect for human rights; foster harmonious relations between organs of sovereignty, assist in the creation of indigenous conflict prevention and national reconciliation mechanisms; support security sector reform and the implementation of the 2001 Programme of Action on small arms; and mobilize international support for quick-impact projects.

In his summary of developments so far, the Secretary-General noted that the aspects of the UNOGBIS mandate relating to the full restoration of constitutional order, the holding of peaceful, free and fair presidential elections and the elaboration of a UN peacebuilding strategy for Guinea-Bissau had been successfully implemented. The engagement of key national stakeholders and international partners on the question of security sector reform within the broader framework of public administration reform was under way, and the basis of a national initiative to address the challenge posed by illicit small arms and light weapons had been established and required resource mobilization.

In view of those developments, the Secretary-General proposed a revision of the UNOGBIS mandate and an increase in its resources base and personnel requirements (see p. 289).

Report of Secretary-General (December). In his December report on Guinea-Bissau and UNOGBIS [S/2005/752], the Secretary-General noted the strained political situation in the country. The persistent rejection of the election results by Mr. Sanhá and the stalling until 1 October of the inauguration of President Vieira raised internal tensions and worried the country's external partners. Because of the deep divisions over the elections, the Guinea-Bissau political class remained highly polarized, resulting in a realignment of political forces in Parliament caused by splits within the governing party. The rift in PAIGC arose over support by a faction of the party for the electoral campaign of President Vieira and deepened further when the party leadership, headed by former Prime Minister Carlos Gomes Júnior, sought to maintain sanctions applied against 14 PAIGC parliamentarians who had backed the Vieira campaign, including the PAIGC vice-president, Aristides Gomes. In an attempt to create a new majority in Parliament, the 14 suspended PAIGC parliamentarians and other parties and individuals supporting President Vieira formed the Forum for the Convergence of Development. Shortly after President Vieira took office, he and Prime Minister Carlos Gomes Júnior publicly stated their willingness to work together but their relations continued to be difficult. Thus, following intensive consultations, the President issued a decree on 28 October dismissing the Government, citing continuing tensions among the organs of State sovereignty, which hampered the smooth functioning of State institutions and weakened the Government's capacity to survive in Parliament. PAIGC denounced the decision as "arbitrary and unconstitutional". On 2 November, the President issued another decree appointing Aristides Gomes as Prime Minister, drawing further adverse reaction from the PAIGC leadership, who contested the decision in the Supreme Court of Justice, insisting that the Prime Minister should come from PAIGC as the party majority in Parliament. On 9 November, the President named a new Government, which was expected to present its programme and the 2006 budget to the regular month-long parliamentary session.

UNOGBIS continued to use its good offices, often in tandem with ECOWAS, to help calm tensions and to focus on helping to develop self-sustaining national peacebuilding mechanisms.

The Secretary-General, noting that political tensions along personality and party lines continued to cast a shadow on the prospects for stability in Guinea-Bissau, warned that the lingering political instability not only hampered further democratic progress, but could lead donors to withhold urgently needed assistance to meet the country's reconstruction and development needs. He called upon all political actors and the society at large to respect the Supreme Court's ruling, once rendered, over the constitutionality of the President's government changes.

Further developments. In a later report [S/2006/162], the Secretary-General said that the stand-off between the Government and the opposition in Parliament had hampered progress in the normalization of relations among State institutions. The bitter divisions were mirrored in a National Popular Assembly polarized into two blocs: one, a dissident PAIGC faction supporting the Government appointed by the President on 2 November; the other, allied to the previous PAIGC Government dismissed by the President on 28 October. The balance of power remained fluid, with neither side able to assure sustainable support in Parliament. UNOGBIS led joint efforts with CPLP and ECOWAS to get the two sides to negotiate their differences constructively. A process initiated to bring together senior presidential advisers, government representatives, parliamentary parties and the Permanent Commission of the National Popular Assembly resulted in the participants' commitment to constructive dialogue and reconciliation, yet the will to move to joint problem-solving was lacking.

UNOGBIS continued its support of national efforts towards security sector reform. In December, it presented to the Government the report of the United Kingdom Security Sector Development Advisory Team that visited the country in October. Based on one of the recommendations in the report, the Prime Minister issued a decree creating an inter-ministerial committee on security sector reform.

Cameroon–Nigeria

In 2005, Cameroon and Nigeria continued to cooperate peacefully to advance progress in implementing the 2002 ruling of the International Court of Justice on the land and maritime boundary between them through the Cameroon-Nigeria Mixed Commission. The Secretary-General, through his good offices and with UN Secretariat support, continued to facilitate implementation. During the year, the withdrawal and transfer of authority along the land boundary were completed, as was a field assessment pilot project to establish the modus operandi of the complex survey of the land boundary. Demarcation of the land boundary began in early November southward from Lake Chad, spanning the distance from the mouth of the river Ebeji to Lawa/Wulba [UNOWA/CNMC/2005/09].

At their fourth meeting with the Secretary-General in May, the Heads of State of the two parties renewed their commitment to pursue to completion of the outstanding aspects of the implementation, including the Bakassi peninsula and the maritime boundary into the Gulf of Guinea.

Cameroon–Nigeria Mixed Commission

The Cameroon-Nigeria Mixed Commission, the mechanism established by the Secretary-General on 15 November 2002 [YUN 2002, p. 1265] at the request of the Presidents of Nigeria and Cameroon to facilitate the peaceful implementation of the 10 October 2002 ruling of the International Court of Justice (ICJ) on the border dispute between them [ibid., p. 1265], remained under the chairmanship of the Special Representative of the Secretary-General for West Africa, Ahmedou Ould-Abdallah (Mauritania). The Commission was responsible for the demarcation of the land boundary between the two countries; the withdrawal of civil administration, military and police forces and transfer of authority in relevant areas along the boundary; the eventual demilitarization of the Bakassi peninsula; the protection of the rights of the affected populations; the development of projects to promote joint economic ventures and cross-border cooperation; and the reactivation of the five-member Lake Chad Basin Commission (Cameroon, Central African Republic, Chad, Niger and Nigeria), created in 1964 for the regulation and planning of the uses of the Lake and other natural resources of the conventional basin.

The Mixed Commission established two sub-commissions: one responsible for the demarcation of the 1,600-kilometre land boundary between the two countries, with a joint technical team to carry out field assessments of the boundary and to supervise the demarcation work to be undertaken by outside contractors; the other to assess the situation of the affected populations and to consider ways to ensure the protection of their rights. Of the Commission's three working groups, those on the withdrawal of civil administration and military and police forces and the transfer of authority in the Lake Chad area, and on withdrawals and transfers of authority in the land boundary, completed their work in December 2003 and July 2004, respectively. The third working group, on maritime boundary, remained in place. An observer team was responsible for following up on the withdrawals and transfers of authority in the Lake Chad area and the land boundary. A UN team based in Dakar, Senegal, provided technical and logistical assistance and substantive support to the Commission and its subsidiary bodies. The mandate of the United Nations Office for West Africa also called for support to the work of the Mixed Commission (see p. 224).

The activities of the Mixed Commission in 2005 focused on three core tasks: completing and consolidating the transfers of authority undertaken in 2004 through monitoring, assessment and support activities on behalf of the affected populations placed under new administration along the final land boundary; finding solutions to the outstanding maritime boundary issues; and carrying out the demarcation process to its conclusion [A/59/534/Add.1].

Activities

Progress report. On 1 August [S/2005/528], the Secretary-General informed the Security Council of the latest achievements and activities undertaken by the Mixed Commission to implement the 2002 ICJ ruling. He reported that, since his progress report of 17 March 2004 [YUN 2004, p. 230], Cameroon and Nigeria had made encouraging and significant progress with support from the United Nations.

To consolidate the withdrawal and transfer of authority in the Lake Chad area and along the land boundary, the Commission deployed a team of civilian observers from Cameroon, Nigeria and the United Nations for a 12-month period from the withdrawal date. The team reported that the situation in the two areas remained calm and the issues raised by the affected populations were being addressed by the new authorities in the transferred areas. To foster confidence among the parties, the Commission identified projects aimed at promoting cross-border cooperation and joint economic activities. It sought financing for those projects from several multilateral financial and development organizations and obtained voluntary contributions to cover costs related to the work of two military advisers and a legal expert on the maritime boundary. In-kind contributions in the form of accommodations and transportation were provided by the two countries for the Commission's meetings and field visits to the Lake Chad area, the land boundary and the Bakassi peninsula. Both countries made a number of reciprocal official visits and discussed cross-border cooperation.

The first phase of the demarcation activities was a pilot field assessment undertaken from March to May (on a 62-kilometre stretch) to verify the location of the physical boundary line as depicted on preliminary maps produced by the United Nations and to determine pillar sites. The exercise sought to establish the technical modalities of the survey of the 1,600-kilometre land boundary. The field assessment was to be followed by the emplacement of pillars, a final survey and a final mapping. A workplan on the maritime boundary agreed upon by the two parties in June 2004 included the delineation of the maritime boundary, as delimited by the 2002 ICJ decision, and the production of a map on that basis. It was expected that the delimitation process would continue in the second half of 2005.

At the Secretary-General's fourth meeting with the Presidents of Cameroon and Nigeria (Geneva, 10-11 May) to review the work of the Commission, the Presidents renewed their commitment to pursue the peaceful implementation of the ICJ ruling and move the process forward to its completion. The withdrawal and transfer of authority in the Bakassi Peninsula, which had been planned for 15 September 2004, were delayed due to technical reasons raised by one of the parties. The demarcation of the land boundary, expected to last about 96 weeks, began on 8 November 2005 by a team of experts from Cameroon, Nigeria and the United Nations.

Of an estimated budget of $12 million for the demarcation of the land boundary, the Mixed Commission raised $8.15 million in voluntary contributions. In addition to the logistical support provided by the parties, Canada, Italy,

Norway, Sweden and Uruguay also provided substantive and technical support in the form of military and legal experts. The Secretary-General underscored that the Mixed Commission was funded entirely from extrabudgetary funds from its inception to 2003. During the 2004-2005 biennium, however, some $9 million was provided from the UN regular budget. Given the Commission's remaining tasks, he intended to ask for additional funds from the regular budget for the Commission for 2006.

On 12 August [S/2005/529], the Security Council took note of the foregoing information from the Secretary-General and of his intention to continue the activities of the UN support team to the Cameroon-Nigeria Mixed Commission with funding from the UN regular budget. The Council urged the parties to the Mixed Commission to work with international donors to seek further voluntary contributions.

Earlier, on 13 July [S/2005/475], the EU expressed concern at reports of security incidents in the Bakassi peninsula. It urged Nigeria and Cameroon to work constructively to establish the facts, defuse tension and meet under the auspices of the Mixed Commission as soon as practicable.

Financing

The General Assembly, by section VII of resolution 59/276 [YUN 2004, p. 1385], approved requirements for the Cameroon-Nigeria Mixed Commission for the period 1 January to 31 December 2005 in the amount of $3,938,200. In December 2005, the Secretary-General, in his report on estimates in respect of special political missions, good offices and other political initiatives authorized by the General Assembly and/or the Security Council [A/60/585 & Corr.1], proposed resource requirements for the Commission of $7,339,000 for the period 1 January to 31 December 2006.

The Assembly, in section VI of **resolution 60/248** of 23 December (see p. 1495), acting on ACABQ's recommendation [A/607/Add.24], approved a prorated amount for the Commission out of the $100 million authorized for the 26 special political missions and decided to reconsider the issue at its resumed sixtieth (2006) session.

Togo

During 2005, the West African State of Togo underwent a political crisis that arose from the question of succession due to the death of its President on 5 February and the absence from the country of the President of the National Assembly, who, under the Constitution, would have assumed office as Acting President pending elections within 60 days. The appointment on 9 Feb-

ruary of Fauré Gnassingbé, the late President's son, as Interim President, sparked widespread demonstrations and mounting pressure from the United Nations, the EU, the AU and ECOWAS for Togo to hold presidential elections consistent with the Constitution and the rule of law. Mr. Gnassingbé stepped down on 25 February and ran in the presidential elections, held on 24 April.

Although the elections proper were orderly, serious political violence and human rights violations followed the announcement of the election results on 26 April, declaring Mr. Gnassingbé the winner. A fact-finding mission dispatched by the United Nations High Commissioner for Human Rights to assess the situation published its report in September. The Government said it would consider the recommendations within the framework of the national reconciliation process and other efforts to strengthen democracy and the rule of law, which it was determined to pursue.

Transfer of presidential power

The Secretary-General, by a press statement issued on 5 February [SG/SM/9706] on the death of President Gnassingbé Eyadéma of Togo, extended his condolences to the bereaved family, the Government and the people of Togo. Noting that the late President had played a central role in the governance of the country for almost 40 years and had contributed significantly to the peaceful settlement of disputes in Africa in general and in West Africa in particular, the Secretary-General trusted the Togolese authorities to take all necessary measures to preserve stability in the country and ensure a peaceful transfer of power. Two days later, [SG/SM/9711], he expressed concern that the transfer of power had not been done in full respect of the Constitution.

Togo explained, in a memorandum of 8 February [A/59/697], that uncertainty and insecurity gripped the country owing to the power vacuum created by the death of the President and by the absence from the country of the President of the National Assembly, Fambaré Ouattara Natchaba, who in such an event would serve as Acting President pending elections. After consultations within the military and security forces and among the leaders of the ruling party, the Rassemblement du peuple togolais (RPT), on how to preserve national stability and safeguard civil order, the Parliament met in special session and unanimously relieved the absent Assembly President of his duties. Minister Faure Gnassingbé, son of the late President and a member of the National Assembly before being appointed Minister, was proposed by the military for the presidency. To that end, he resigned his ministerial position and resumed his Assembly seat; he was then elected President of the National Assembly and, as such, temporarily assumed the duties as President of Togo. Parliament also amended the constitutional requirement under article 65 that elections be held within 60 days, a period deemed insufficient given the political climate in the country.

In his address to the nation on 9 February [A/59/700], President Fauré Gnassingbé enumerated the late President's major achievements. He stated that he had been appointed to the presidency as a matter of urgency and pledged to carry out fully the responsibilities conferred upon him by the Constitution. He then announced his decision to reduce by one quarter the sentences of those imprisoned for ordinary offences, invited Togolese nationals living abroad to return at any time, and asked the Government to carry on dialogue with the opposition in a new spirit. He said that the 22 commitments made by Togo in Brussels on 14 April 2004 would remain the country's basic guidelines (see below).

Resignation of appointed President

On 12 February [SG/SM/9716], the Secretary-General expressed concern over the deteriorating security situation in Togo and the deaths and injuries caused by violence in the capital, Lomé, where demonstrators protested the unconstitutional succession of Fauré Gnassingbé to the presidency. He called on all sides to exercise maximum restraint while the search for an early and peaceful solution to the crisis continued. On 19 February [SG/SM/9728], concerned that talks between ECOWAS and the Togolese authorities on the country's constitutional crisis had not advanced, and noting that ECOWAS had suspended Togo from that regional body, the Secretary-General reiterated his call for urgent efforts to find a peaceful solution.

By a 23 February statement [S/2005/136], the EU expressed great alarm at developments in Togo. While it welcomed the positive signals given by the announcement of presidential elections within 60 days and restoration of the freedom to demonstrate, it condemned the violation of constitutional and legal provisions in the continued maintenance of Mr. Fauré Gnassingbé as Interim President. The EU demanded an immediate return to constitutional and legal order to open the way for free and transparent presidential elections and supported the actions of the AU and ECOWAS in that regard.

The Secretary-General, on 25 February [SG/SM/9737], welcomed Mr. Gnassingbé's decision to step down as Head of State of Togo and the subsequent designation by the National Assembly of an Interim Head of State who would oversee the organization of the forthcoming elections in accordance with the Constitution. He noted that because of those positive developments, ECOWAS lifted the sanctions it had imposed on Togo.

The EU on 4 March [S/2005/147] stated its readiness to assist in facilitating free and transparent elections. It insisted that the Government honour the 22 undertakings it had made in the framework of the consultations held under article 96 of the 2000 Cotonou Declaration [YUN 2000, p. 544] on peace, security, democracy and development, particularly in the holding of a national dialogue to set up an electoral framework acceptable to all parties for the conduct of presidential and parliamentary elections.

Presidential elections

Pre-election events. On 20 April [SG/SM/9831], following fatal clashes between supporters and opponents of RPT, the Secretary-General called on political leaders to avoid any actions or statements that could incite or contribute to violence before, during or after the 24 April presidential vote. In the light of the many concerns already raised about the electoral process, he urged the authorities to ensure that citizens were able to vote freely and peacefully. He reiterated the readiness of the United Nations to work with all segments of the society to promote national reconciliation and socio-economic development following a peaceful electoral process.

On 21 April [HR/4829], two UN human rights experts expressed concern over reports of violent clashes during demonstrations by sympathizers of the various political parties that resulted in casualties and in the arrest of a number of demonstrators, of the media being prevented from covering the electoral campaigns, and of irregularities in the context of the organization of the elections.

Elections. By a press statement issued on 24 April [SG/SM/9836], the day of the presidential elections, the Secretary-General commended the peaceful and orderly manner in which the Togolese turned out in large numbers to cast their votes in the elections, as well as the sense of political and civic responsibility demonstrated by the leaders and the population. He appealed for calm while the official results were being awaited and urged parties to refer any electoral disputes to the appropriate authorities as provided for in the Electoral Code. In a statement two days later [SG/SM/9841], he expressed grave concern over reports of violence in Lomé following the voting on 24 April and the announcement of the preliminary results on 26 April. He called on political leaders and their supporters to refrain from actions inciting further violence, hatred and divisions; he also called on the security forces to exercise similar restraint. He commended efforts by regional leaders and institutions, particularly ECOWAS, to promote peace, and welcomed the AU initiative to encourage dialogue and national reconciliation.

Post-electoral period. On 28 April, UNHCR announced the deployment of an emergency team to neighbouring Benin, where more than 3,600 refugees had fled due to insecurity in Togo following the announcement of the election results, and that an additional 450 Togolese had sought refuge in Ghana.

According to a 10 June press statement [HR/4855], the United Nations High Commissioner for Human Rights established a fact-finding mission to look into allegations of human rights violations in Togo between 5 February and 5 May. The mission was to assess human rights issues arising from the conduct of the presidential elections, verify reports of alleged violations and compile information on perpetrators. The mission was to arrive in Togo on 13 June for about two weeks of field work.

The Government of Togo issued a 27 September communiqué [A/60/392] by which it took note of the publication of the final report of the fact-finding mission, indicating that before and during the presidential elections on 24 April, and despite the climate of tension and conflict, only a few acts of violence and minor incidents, such as the clashes of 15 April between coalition and RPT militants, had occurred between the death of the late President on 5 February and 24 April.

Togo drew attention to the report's conclusions regarding the post-electoral period, from 26 to 29 April, according to which militants belonging to the opposition were responsible for a number of actions which led to reactions from the security forces and RPT militants. The announcement on 26 April by the Independent National Electoral Commission of the provisional election results indicating that the RPT candidate, Faure Gnassingbé, had won, unleashed an outbreak of the most serious acts of political violence and systematic violations of human rights. Clashes again broke out from 27 to 29 April in Lomé and in the interior, resulting in many deaths and injuries. Togo disputed as unsubstantiated the statements of witnesses putting the number of deaths at between 400 and 500, adding that the report made no distinction between deaths caused by one side or the other in order to establish responsibility.

With respect to the report's recommendation enjoining the Togolese, particularly the political leadership, to heed the republican values of mutual respect and respect for public and private property, and of the urgent need to combat impunity, Togo noted that the mandate of the Special National Inquiry Commission included the assessment of the damages incurred by the State and those by all other victims, with a view to taking adequate measures. The Government was determined to pursue the institutional reforms already under way, particularly those related to justice, the restoration of public confidence in the institutions of the country and the creation of conditions favourable to an all-inclusive political dialogue.

The EU, taking note of the fact-finding mission report on 25 October [S/2005/711], reiterated its condemnation of acts of violence and called on the Togolese authorities to deal thoroughly and fairly with the issue of human rights by prosecuting those responsible for such violence so as to end any sense of impunity. It further renewed its call for genuine dialogue involving all political forces in the country.

Horn of Africa

The political landscape in the Horn of Africa, which continued to be characterized by complex interlocking conflicts and rebellions, underwent a number of changes in 2005.

In the Sudan, the largest country in the region, the 21-year civil war officially ended in January with the signing by the Government and the Sudan Peoples' Liberation Movement/Army of the Comprehensive Peace Agreement between them, setting forth a new relationship between the north and the south based on power- and wealth-sharing arrangements. Under those terms, the Government of National Unity was established in September and the Government of southern Sudan in December; the restructured political system provided for a referendum in 2011 in which the south would decide whether to secede from the rest of the country. In March, the Security Council established the United Nations Mission in the Sudan (UNMIS) to help the parties implement the Peace Agreement. In addition, UNMIS helped to support the African Union Mission in the Sudan in its efforts to monitor the ceasefire in the Darfur region and to broker a deal to end the fighting between the rebel groups there. The hope that the new political arrangements might lead to a solution to the crisis in Darfur was not realized.

In Somalia, the fledgling Transitional Federal Government, established in 2004, based first in Nairobi, Kenya, and by mid-year in Somalia, was not operational for most of the year due to an impasse between the President and the Prime Minister on the one hand, and the Speaker of Parliament and some parliamentarians and ministers on the other, regarding the relocation site of the Government and the composition of an interim peace support mission, sponsored by the Intergovernmental Authority on Development and endorsed by the AU, in response to a request by the President. The United Nations Political Office for Somalia pursued its contacts with Somali leaders and other entities concerned in order to advance the peace and reconciliation process. The Monitoring Group on Somalia, charged by the Council with investigating violations of the arms embargo imposed on the country, continued to discharge its mandate on a renewable six-month basis.

The border dispute between Eritrea and Ethiopia remained unsettled. The United Nations Mission in Ethiopia and Eritrea continued to monitor the border region designated as the Temporary Security Zone and to support the work of the five-member Eritrea-Ethiopia Boundary Commission, the neutral body mandated under the terms of the 2000 Agreement on Cessation of Hostilities and Comprehensive Peace Agreement to delimit and demarcate the colonial treaty border. The Commission attempted but failed to advance its demarcation activities, stalled since 2003, due to the continued rejection by Ethiopia of significant parts of the Commission's 2002 final and binding delimitation decision and to Eritrea's insistence on adherence to that decision. The Commission thus suspended its activities and closed its field offices. Meanwhile, each country strengthened its military posture adjacent to its side of the Zone. As demanded by the Council, Ethiopia subsequently withdrew its troops to their previous deployment levels; Eritrea maintained it had no troops to withdraw. Contrary to the Council's demand that it lift its restrictions on the freedom of movement of the Mission, Eritrea increased them and, moreover, in December, asked certain nationalities of its staff to leave the country. The Council, in consultation with the Secretary-General, agreed to relocate the Mission's civilian and military staff temporarily to Ethiopia, while it reviewed future plans for the Mission.

Sudan

In 2005, the situation in the Sudan was marked by hope and disappointment. While efforts to resolve the conflict between the north and the south were successfully concluded, ending a 21-year civil war, the security situation in the Darfur region of the western part of the country deteriorated significantly, and the political process for finding a solution to that conflict remained mired in a stalemate.

In January, the Comprehensive Peace Agreement signed by the Government and the Sudan People's Liberation Movement/Army (SPLM/A) laid the basis for a new relationship between the north and the south based on arrangements for power-sharing and wealth-sharing, the establishment of a Government of National Unity and the government of southern Sudan, as well as the adoption of a new constitution. The restructured political system, based on democracy and respect for human rights, provided for a final decision on secession to be made by the south at the end of six years. The Security Council established the United Nations Mission in the Sudan (UNMIS) to help the parties implement the Peace Agreement, with the assistance of the international community. However, the optimism generated by that historic event was overshadowed by the death of John Garang, the SPLM/A Chairman and First Vice-President in the National Unity Government in a helicopter crash. Contrary to expectations, Mr. Garang's death did not derail implementation of the Peace Agreement and his successor, Salva Kiir, promised to adhere to all the agreements reached.

The signing of the Comprehensive Peace Agreement and the establishment of the Government of National Unity raised hopes for finding a solution to the crisis in the Darfur region, where two local rebel groups, the Justice and Equality Movement (JEM) and the Sudanese Liberation Movement/Army (SLM/A), were still fighting Government forces and allied militia groups.

The African Union Mission in the Sudan (AMIS), supported by the United Nations, particularly UNMIS, the European Union (EU), the United States, the North Atlantic Treaty Organization and other donors, increased its military deployment to more than 6,300 troops. In addition to monitoring the fragile ceasefire in Darfur, the AU stepped up its mediation efforts to broker a deal to end the fighting between the rebel groups. However, despite several rounds of talks in Abuja, Nigeria, a solution remained elusive as divisions within the rebel movement widened and the parties remained uncompromising in their positions on the issues of power-sharing, wealth-sharing and security.

Comprehensive Peace Agreement

Report of Secretary-General. In his 7 January report on the Sudan [S/2005/10], the Secretary-General welcomed the initialling on 31 December 2004 [YUN 2004, p. 256] by the Government of the Sudan and the Sudan People's Liberation Movement/Army (SPLM/A) of the last two agreements of the north-south peace process: the Agreement on the Implementation Modalities of the Protocols and Agreements, and the Agreement on the Permanent Ceasefire and Security Agreements Implementation Modalities, both of which were part of the Comprehensive Peace Agreement. The Secretary-General said that he looked forward to the signing of the Comprehensive Peace Agreement and indicated that the United Nations was prepared to play a significant role in its implementation. He was nevertheless concerned that there was no agreed basis to allow the UN advance mission in the Sudan to start its pre-deployment activities in the SPLM/A controlled areas. The Secretary-General expected that the signing of the Comprehensive Peace Agreement would improve capacity to solve the problems in the Darfur region (see p. 315).

Terms of Comprehensive Peace Agreement. The Comprehensive Peace Agreement was signed on 9 January in Nairobi, Kenya, by the Government of the Sudan, represented by Vice-President Ali Osman Mohamed Taha, and SPLM/A, represented by Chairman John Garang de Mabior. It was witnessed by several African and international representatives, including the Presidents of Kenya and Uganda, the United States Secretary of State and the United Kingdom Secretary of State for International Development, the AU Chairperson and the EU representative. The Agreement, transmitted to the Council President by the Sudan on 8 February [S/2005/78], consisted of four protocols, two framework agreements and two annexes regarding implementation modalities: the Machakos Protocol, signed on 20 July 2002 [YUN 2002, p. 217]; the Protocol on Power Sharing, signed on 26 May 2004 [YUN 2004, p. 236]; the Agreement on Wealth Sharing during the Pre-Interim and Interim Period, dated 7 January 2004; Principles of Agreement for the resolution of the Abyei conflict, signed on 26 May 2004 [ibid.]; the Protocol on the Resolution of the Conflict in Southern Kordofan and Blue Nile States, signed on 26 May 2004 [ibid.]; and the Framework Agreement on Security Arrangements during the Interim Period, dated 25 September 2003 [YUN 2003, p. 257]. Annexed to the Agreement were the Permanent Ceasefire and Security Arrangements Implementation Modalities and Appendices [YUN 2004, p. 256]; and Implementation Modalities and Global Implementation Matrix and Appendices, both signed on 31 December 2004 [ibid.]. In the chapeau to the Comprehensive Peace Agreement, the parties agreed to the beginning of the Interim Period

and appealed to the regional and international communities, organizations and States that had witnessed the signing of the Agreement to provide and affirm their unwavering support for its implementation and make available resources for its programmes and activities in the transition to peace.

Security Council consideration. In briefing the Security Council on 11 January [meeting 5109], the Secretary-General's Special Representative for the Sudan, Jan Pronk, said that the signing of the Comprehensive Peace Agreement heralded the definitive end to nearly four decades of conflict, the uprooting and displacement of 4 million people and half a million refugees in neighbouring countries. However, it was not the end. Former combatants would have to be disarmed and demobilized; displaced people and refugees would need to return and participate in the economy and society, claiming a share of the resources, including land; other southern militant groups that did not participate in the peace talks would have to be incorporated into the new structures; and people's expectations concerning welfare, growth, education and other social and economic needs would have to be met.

Communication. The EU Presidency, in an 11 January statement [S/2005/37], welcomed the signing of the Agreement and reiterated its support for international efforts to consolidate it, in close cooperation with the United Nations, the AU and the Intergovernmental Authority on Development (IGAD).

Implementation of Comprehensive Peace Agreement

Report of Secretary-General (January). On 31 January, the Secretary-General, in his report on the Sudan [S/2005/57], said that harmonizing all aspects of the Comprehensive Peace Agreement would be a complex task. Some grey areas and potentially difficult issues remained, with the parties having differing interpretations of the texts that could prove controversial at a later stage. Some complicated issues had been left for the Presidency to decide and some decisions deferred to a later date. The creation of the Assessment and Evaluation Commission, the body to monitor the Agreement's implementation, as provided for in the Machakos Protocol, had been delayed until the adoption of the Interim National Constitution and the establishment of the Presidency. In addition, the government of southern Sudan faced the challenge of raising funds to pay its army and to achieve proportional downsizing. At the same time, political solutions would have to be found for other marginalized and unstable regions, such as Darfur. The integration of other armed groups in both the north and south was another challenge, to be carried out in good faith with international support. SPLM/A would have to engage with southern constituencies forming the south-south dialogue to jointly discuss the creation of southern institutions and public policies and to forge a shared vision for southern Sudan in line with the Comprehensive Peace Agreement. At the same time, the South Sudan Defence Force (a coalition of southern factions) would need assurances that the south-south dialogue would be carried out in good faith and result in a fair share of political and socio-economic power. In the north, traditional power structures would have to shift to accommodate the new alignment.

The Secretary-General welcomed the parties' engagement with a broad spectrum of the opposition to begin developing a consensus on peace implementation. He supported the convening of an all-inclusive national conference to discuss future governance in the Sudan, to be articulated in the national constitution and federal arrangements.

To assist in the implementation of the Comprehensive Peace Agreement, the Secretary-General recommended the establishment of the United Nations Advance Mission in Sudan (UNAMIS), whose main tasks would be to support implementation of the Comprehensive Peace Agreement; ensure security and freedom of movement for UN personnel and protect civilians; and provide governance assistance, as well as humanitarian and development assistance. UNAMIS mandate would be for seven years, including the pre-interim and interim periods, followed by a phase-out period. The Mission, to be headed by the Secretary-General's Special Representative, would have authority over all UN entities in the field, providing overall management and policy guidance, and coordinating all UN activities throughout the country. The Special Representative would be assisted by two deputies, one of whom would work with the Special Representative in matters relating to good offices and political support for the peace process and governance, and the other would act as the Resident Coordinator and Humanitarian Coordinator. The Force Commander would be responsible for the deployment and operation of UN military personnel. The Mission's area of operation would include six sectors (the Equatorial area, the Bahr el Ghazal area, the Upper Nile area, the Nuba Mountains area, Southern Blue Nile and the Abyei area). The mission's headquarters would be based in Khartoum, with a special office in Rumbek, the southern capital or wherever the southern government might choose to relo-

cate. The Mission would include the following political components: public information, military, civilian police, rule of law, human rights, civil affairs, and electoral assistance. The military component would have a troop strength of 10,130, comprising 750 military observers, 160 staff officers, up to 5,070 enabling units, a force protection component of 4,150 and 755 civilian police.

The Secretary-General also emphasized that substantial resources were required for relief and recovery, including the return, repatriation and resettlement of internally displaced persons and refugees, as well as for the development activities envisaged by the joint assessment mission. Member States were urged to fund fully the work plan for 2005 and to make their contributions early, so as to allow for substantial recovery programming that could quickly demonstrate to the Sudanese people the dividends of peace. He recommended that the Security Council authorize the deployment of a multinational peace support operation with the mandate as he had proposed.

Security Council consideration (4 February). During the Security Council's consideration of the Secretary-General's report [S/2005/57], on 4 February [meeting 5119], the Special Representative for the Sudan affirmed that measures were being prepared to support the parties in their implementation of the Peace Agreement through the United Nations Advance Mission in Sudan (UNAMIS), established in 2004 [YUN 2004, p. 247]. Plans for the establishment of an institutional framework for the United Nations in south Sudan were already under way and consultations and briefings were held with both the Government and SPLM on those issues. The logistical and operational plan was developed to deploy just over 10,000 troops for monitoring and verification.

The Special Representative noted that, despite the signing of the Agreement, some areas still remained to be agreed upon (see p. 302). That process would be completed by the new presidency of the Sudan, which was to be composed of President Al-Bashir and Vice-Presidents Taha and Garang. He warned that if solutions were not found to the conflicts in Darfur and elsewhere in the Sudan, any peace support operation limited to south Sudan would be affected by the consequences of such conflicts. Therefore, for peace to be sustainable, the Government and the people of the Sudan would have to choose a comprehensive approach to address all the causes of conflict in a holistic and balanced way. The peace support operation would also have to be comprehensive and balanced. Tasks and priorities would be regularly assessed in the light of changing circumstances.

The indivisibility of peace in the Sudan also had consequences for UN peace efforts. In accordance with Council resolutions 1555(2004) [ibid. p. 127] and 1564(2004) [ibid. p.245], the Secretary-General had incorporated contingency planning for Darfur into the mission.

Security Council consideration (8 February). At its February 8 meeting [meeting 5120], the Council President welcomed the sense of ownership demonstrated by the Sudanese parties in the achievement of the Comprehensive Peace Agreement, and expected them to demonstrate likewise in its implementation. The Council endorsed Norway's initiative to convene a donor's conference in Oslo for the mobilization of resources. Council members were preparing a draft resolution to address all aspects of the situation in the Sudan, in particular the establishment of a UN peace support operation. The Council supported the Secretary-General's recommendations that the proposed mission cooperate with the AU and support its efforts to resolve the ongoing conflicts in the Darfur region.

The Sudan's First Vice-President, Ali Osman Taha, informed the Council that the Comprehensive Peace Agreement had been endorsed by the legislative institutions and actual implementation had begun. In that regard, Sudan was ready to discuss with the United Nations the details of its proposed mission (see p. 303). He appealed for the lifting of economic and trade restrictions or sanctions; the writing off of the Sudan's foreign debt; and generous donations at the upcoming donors conference to get the economic development process under way. The Government was firm in its commitment to apply the basic principles endorsed in the 1998 Constitution and the Comprehensive Peace Agreement to all states of the Sudan and to undertake a final settlement on the basis of those principles.

SPLM/A Chairman Garang told the Council that SPLM's National Liberation Council, the Movement's highest legislative body, had unanimously ratified the Comprehensive Peace Agreement on 24 January and the National Assembly on 1 February. In preparation for the Agreement's implementation, SPLM/A had established several committees to work out mechanisms to transform its various organs of guerilla warfare and armed opposition into institutions of good governance. It was holding discussions with the Government of the Sudan and planned to send advance teams to Khartoum, Juba, Malaka, Wau, Kadugli, Damazien and Abyei, as specified in the Agreement, to facilitate coordination of its implementation. Both sides were also evaluating the drafts of their respective joint assessment missions for presentation at the upcoming Oslo conference, and were also working jointly on an initial draft of the interim national constitution for presentation to and adoption by their respective legislative authorities. The interim constitution would launch the Government of National Unity, the government of southern Sudan and other structures stipulated in the Comprehensive Peace Agreement. He urged the international community to help with the enormous task of the voluntary return, reintegration and rehabilitation of returning refugees and internally displaced persons. SPLM/A supported, in principle, the deployment of a UN peace support mission and requested discussions with the United Nations of the details of that mission

He said that he was encouraged to believe that the Comprehensive Peace Agreement could be successfully applied and adapted to the conflicts in Darfur and eastern Sudan so that a comprehensive peace agreement might be achieved for the whole of the country.

SECURITY COUNCIL ACTION (10-17 March)

On 10 March [meeting 5137], the Security Council unanimously adopted **resolution 1585(2005)**. The draft [S/2005/154] was prepared in consultations among Council members.

The Security Council,

Recalling its resolutions 1547(2004) of 11 June 2004, 1556(2004) of 30 July 2004 and 1574(2004) of 19 November 2004,

Reaffirming its readiness to support the peace process,

1. *Decides* to extend the mandate of the United Nations Advance Mission in the Sudan, established by its resolution 1547(2004), until 17 March 2005;

2. *Decides* to remain actively seized of the matter.

On 17 March, the Council [meeting 5143] unanimously adopted **resolution 1588(2005)**. The draft [S/2005/173] was prepared in consultations with Council members.

The Security Council,

Recalling its resolutions 1547(2004) of 11 June 2004, 1556(2004) of 30 July 2004, 1574(2004) of 19 November 2004 and resolution 1585(2005) of 10 March 2005,

Reaffirming its readiness to support the peace process,

1. *Decides* to extend the mandate of the United Nations Advance Mission in the Sudan, established by its resolution 1547(2004), until 24 March 2005;

2. *Decides* to remain actively seized of the matter.

Establishment of UNMIS

On 24 March [meeting 5151], the Security Council unanimously adopted **resolution 1590(2005)**. The draft [S/2005/198] was prepared in consultations among Council members.

The Security Council,

Recalling its resolutions 1547(2004) of 11 June 2004, 1556(2004) of 30 July 2004, 1564(2004) of 18 September 2004, 1574(2004) of 19 November 2004, 1585(2005) of 10 March 2005 and 1588(2005) of 17 March 2005, and the statements by its President concerning the Sudan,

Reaffirming its commitment to the sovereignty, unity, independence and territorial integrity of the Sudan, and recalling the importance of the principles of good-neighbourliness, non-interference and regional cooperation,

Welcoming the signing of the Comprehensive Peace Agreement between the Government of the Sudan and the Sudan People's Liberation Movement/Army in Nairobi on 9 January 2005,

Recalling the commitments made by the parties in the N'Djamena ceasefire agreement of 8 April 2004 and the Humanitarian and Security Protocols of 9 November 2004 signed in Abuja between the Government of the Sudan, the Sudan Liberation Movement/Army and the Justice and Equality Movement, and recalling the commitments made in the joint communiqué of 3 July 2004 of the Government of the Sudan and the Secretary-General,

Expressing its determination to help the people of the Sudan to promote national reconciliation, lasting peace and stability, and to build a prosperous and united Sudan in which human rights are respected and the protection of all citizens is assured,

Taking note of the statements by Mr. Ali Osman Taha, First Vice-President of the Government of the Sudan and Mr. John Garang de Mabior, Chairman of the Sudan People's Liberation Movement/Army, at the meeting of the Security Council on 8 February 2005, and their strong will and determination to find a peaceful resolution to the conflict in Darfur, as expressed at the meeting,

Recognizing that the parties to the Comprehensive Peace Agreement must build on the Agreement to bring peace and stability to the entire country, and calling upon all Sudanese parties, in particular those party to the Agreement, to take immediate steps to achieve a peaceful settlement to the conflict in Darfur and to take all necessary action to prevent further violations of human rights and international humanitarian law and to put an end to impunity, including in the Darfur region,

Expressing its utmost concern over the dire consequences of the prolonged conflict for the civilian population in the Darfur region as well as throughout the Sudan, in particular the increase in the number of refugees and internally displaced persons,

Considering that the voluntary and sustainable return of refugees and internally displaced persons will be a critical factor for the consolidation of the peace process,

Expressing its deep concern for the security of humanitarian workers and their access to populations in need, including refugees, internally displaced persons and other war-affected populations,

Condemning the continued violations of the N'Djamena ceasefire agreement and the Abuja Protocols by all sides in Darfur and the deterioration of the security situation and the negative impact this has had on humanitarian assistance efforts,

Strongly condemning all violations of human rights and international humanitarian law in the Darfur region, in particular the continuation of violence against civilians and sexual violence against women and girls since the adoption of resolution 1574(2004), urging all parties to take necessary steps to prevent further violations, and expressing its determination to ensure that those responsible for all such violations are identified and brought to justice without delay,

Recalling the demands in resolutions 1556(2004), 1564(2004) and 1574(2004) that all parties to the conflict in Darfur refrain from any violence against civilians and cooperate fully with the African Union mission in Darfur,

Commending the efforts of the African Union, in particular its Chairman, acknowledging the progress made by the African Union in the deployment of an international protection force, police and military observers, and calling upon all Member States to contribute generously and urgently to the African Union mission in Darfur,

Commending also the efforts of the Intergovernmental Authority on Development, in particular the Government of Kenya as Chair of the Subcommittee on the Sudan,

Reaffirming its resolutions 1325(2000) of 31 October 2000 on women and peace and security, 1379(2001) of 20 November 2001 and 1460(2003) of 30 January 2003 on children and armed conflict, as well as resolutions 1265(1999) of 17 September 1999 and 1296(2000) of 19 April 2000 on the protection of civilians in armed conflict and resolution 1502(2003) of 26 August 2003 on the protection of United Nations personnel, associated personnel and humanitarian personnel in conflict zones,

Welcoming the efforts by the United Nations to sensitize United Nations personnel in the prevention and control of HIV/AIDS and other communicable diseases in all its established operations,

Expressing grave concern at the allegations of sexual exploitation and misconduct by United Nations personnel in United Nations established operations, and welcoming the letter dated 9 February 2005 from the Secretary-General to the Council in this regard, affirming that there will be a zero-tolerance policy toward sexual exploitation and abuse of any kind in all United Nations peacekeeping missions,

Recognizing that international support for implementation of the Comprehensive Peace Agreement is critically important to its success, emphasizing that progress towards resolution of the conflict in Darfur would create conditions conducive for delivery of such assistance, and alarmed that the violence in Darfur nonetheless continues,

Taking note of the reports of the Secretary-General of 31 January 2005, 4 February 2005, and 4 March 2005, as well as the report of 25 January 2005 of the International Commission of Inquiry for Darfur,

Taking note also of the request of the parties to the Comprehensive Peace Agreement for the establishment of a peace support mission,

Expressing appreciation for the important contributions of the Standby High-Readiness Brigade towards the planning, preparation and initial deployment of a peacekeeping operation, as well as the preparatory work by the United Nations Advance Mission in the Sudan,

Determining that the situation in the Sudan continues to constitute a threat to international peace and security,

1. *Decides* to establish the United Nations Mission in the Sudan for an initial period of six months and further decides that the Mission will consist of up to 10,000 military personnel and an appropriate civilian component including up to 715 civilian police personnel;

2. *Requests* that the Mission closely and continuously liaise and coordinate at all levels with the African Union Mission in the Sudan with a view to expeditiously reinforcing the effort to foster peace in Darfur, especially with regard to the Abuja peace process and the African Union Mission in the Sudan;

3. *Requests* the Secretary-General, through his Special Representative for the Sudan, to coordinate all the activities of the United Nations system in the Sudan, to mobilize resources and support from the international community for both immediate assistance and the long-term economic development of the Sudan and to facilitate coordination with other international actors, in particular the African Union and the Intergovernmental Authority on Development, of activities in support of the transitional process established by the Comprehensive Peace Agreement, and to provide good offices and political support for the efforts to resolve all ongoing conflicts in the Sudan;

4. *Decides* that the mandate of the Mission shall be the following:

(a) To support implementation of the Comprehensive Peace Agreement by performing the following tasks:

(i) To monitor and verify the implementation of the N'Djamena ceasefire agreement and to investigate violations;

(ii) To liaise with bilateral donors on the formation of joint integrated units;

(iii) To observe and monitor movement of armed groups and redeployment of forces in the areas of deployment of the Mission in accordance with the ceasefire agreement;

(iv) To assist in the establishment of the disarmament, demobilization and reintegration programme as called for in the Comprehensive Peace Agreement, with particular attention to the special needs of women and child combatants, and its implementation through voluntary disarmament and weapons collection and destruction;

(v) To assist the parties to the Comprehensive Peace Agreement in promoting understanding of the peace process and the role of the Mission by means of an effective public information campaign, targeted at all sectors of society, in coordination with the African Union;

(vi) To assist the parties to the Comprehensive Peace Agreement in addressing the need for a national inclusive approach, including the role of women, towards reconciliation and peace-building;

(vii) To assist the parties to the Comprehensive Peace Agreement, in coordination with bilateral and multilateral assistance programmes, in restructuring the police service in the Sudan, consistent with democratic policing, to develop a police training and evaluation programme, and to otherwise assist in the training of civilian police;

(viii) To assist the parties to the Comprehensive Peace Agreement in promoting the rule of law, including an independent judiciary, and the protection of human rights of all people of the Sudan through a comprehensive and coordinated strategy with the aim of combating impunity and contributing to long-term peace and stability and to assist the parties to the Agreement to develop and consolidate the national legal framework;

(ix) To ensure an adequate human rights presence, capacity and expertise within the Mission to carry out human rights promotion, civilian protection and monitoring activities;

(x) To provide guidance and technical assistance to the parties to the Comprehensive Peace Agreement, in cooperation with other international actors, to support the preparations for and conduct of elections and referendums provided for by the Agreement;

(b) To facilitate and coordinate, within its capabilities and in its areas of deployment, the voluntary return of refugees and internally displaced persons, and humanitarian assistance, inter alia, by helping to establish the necessary security conditions;

(c) To assist the parties to the Comprehensive Peace Agreement, in cooperation with other international partners in the mine-action sector, by providing humanitarian demining assistance, technical advice and coordination;

(d) To contribute towards international efforts to protect and promote human rights in the Sudan, as well as to coordinate international efforts towards the protection of civilians with particular attention to vulnerable groups including internally displaced persons, returning refugees, and women and children, within the Mission's capabilities and in close cooperation with other United Nations agencies, related organizations and non-governmental organizations;

5. *Requests* the Secretary-General to report to the Council within thirty days on options for how the Mission can reinforce the effort to foster peace in Darfur through appropriate assistance to the African Union Mission in the Sudan, including logistical support and technical assistance, and to identify ways in liaison with the African Union to utilize the Mission's resources, particularly logistical and operations support elements, as well as reserve capacity towards this end;

6. *Calls upon* all parties to cooperate fully in the deployment and operations of the Mission, in particular by guaranteeing the safety, security and freedom of movement of United Nations personnel as well as associated personnel throughout the territory of the Sudan;

7. *Emphasizes* that there can be no military solution to the conflict in Darfur, and calls upon the Government of the Sudan and the rebel groups, particularly the Justice and Equality Movement and the Sudan Liberation Movement/Army to resume the Abuja talks rapidly, without preconditions, and negotiate in good faith to speedily reach agreement, and urges the par-

ties to the Comprehensive Peace Agreement to play an active and constructive role in support of the Abuja talks and take immediate steps to support a peaceful settlement to the conflict in Darfur;

8. *Calls upon* all Member States to ensure the free, unhindered and expeditious movement to the Sudan of all personnel, as well as equipment, provisions, supplies and other goods, including vehicles and spare parts, which are for the exclusive and official use of the Mission;

9. *Calls upon* all parties to ensure, in accordance with relevant provisions of international law, the full, safe and unhindered access of relief personnel to all those in need, and delivery of humanitarian assistance, in particular to internally displaced persons and refugees;

10. *Requests* that the Secretary-General transfer all functions performed by the United Nations Advance Mission in the Sudan to the Mission, together with staff and logistics of the office as appropriate, on the date when the Mission is established, and to ensure a seamless transition between the United Nations and existing monitoring missions, namely the Verification Monitoring Team, the Joint Monitoring Commission and the Civilian Protection Monitoring Team;

11. *Also requests* the Secretary-General to keep the Council regularly informed of the progress in implementing the Comprehensive Peace Agreement, respect for the ceasefire and the implementation of the mandate of the Mission, including a review of the troop level, with a view to its adjusted reduction, taking account of the progress made on the ground and the tasks remaining to be accomplished, and to report to the Council in this regard every three months;

12. *Further requests* that the Secretary-General continue to report on a monthly basis on the situation in Darfur;

13. *Urges* the joint assessment mission of the United Nations, the World Bank and the parties, in association with other bilateral and multilateral donors, to continue their efforts to prepare for the rapid delivery of an assistance package for the reconstruction and economic development of the Sudan, including official development assistance and trade access, to be implemented once implementation of the Comprehensive Peace Agreement begins, welcomes the initiative of the Government of Norway to convene an international donors conference for the reconstruction and economic development of the Sudan, and urges the international community accordingly to donate generously, including to address the needs of internally displaced persons and refugees;

14. *Requests* the Secretary-General to take the necessary measures to achieve actual compliance in the Mission with the United Nations zero-tolerance policy towards sexual exploitation and abuse, including the development of strategies and appropriate mechanisms to prevent, identify and respond to all forms of misconduct, including sexual exploitation and abuse, and the enhancement of training for personnel to prevent misconduct and ensure full compliance with the United Nations code of conduct, requests the Secretary-General to take all necessary action in accordance with the Bulletin on special measures for protection from sexual exploitation and sexual abuse and to keep the Council informed, and urges troop-contributing countries to take appropriate preventive action, including the conduct of predeployment awareness training, and to take disciplinary action and other action to ensure full accountability in cases of such conduct involving their personnel;

15. *Reaffirms* the importance of appropriate expertise on issues relating to gender in peacekeeping operations and post-conflict peacebuilding in accordance with resolution 1325(2000), recalls the need to address violence against women and girls as a tool of warfare, and encourages the Mission, as well as the Sudanese parties to actively address these issues;

16. *Acting* under Chapter VII of the Charter of the United Nations,

(a) Decides that the Mission is authorized to take the necessary action, in the areas of deployment of its forces and as it deems within its capabilities, to protect United Nations personnel, facilities, installations and equipment, ensure the security and freedom of movement of United Nations personnel, humanitarian workers, joint assessment mechanism and assessment and evaluation commission personnel, and, without prejudice to the responsibility of the Government of the Sudan, to protect civilians under imminent threat of physical violence; and

(b) Requests that the Secretary-General and the Government of the Sudan, following appropriate consultation with the Sudan People's Liberation Movement, conclude a status-of-forces agreement within thirty days of adoption of the present resolution, taking into consideration General Assembly resolution 58/82 of 9 December 2003 on the scope of legal protection under the Convention on the Safety of United Nations and Associated Personnel, and notes that pending the conclusion of such an agreement, the model status-of-forces agreement dated 9 October 1990 shall apply provisionally;

17. *Underscores* the immediate need to rapidly increase the number of human rights monitors in Darfur, and urges the Secretary-General and the United Nations High Commissioner for Human Rights to undertake to accelerate the deployment of human rights monitors to Darfur and augment their numbers and also to move forward with the formation of civilian monitoring protection teams, and expects that the Secretary-General will report on progress on the formation of these teams in his reports to the Council as outlined in paragraph 11 above;

18. *Decides* to remain seized of the matter.

Further political developments

Report of Secretary-General (June). In a 23 June report [S/2005/411], the Secretary-General, in an assessment of the overall situation in the country since the signing of the Comprehensive Peace Agreement and the commencement of the implementation process, said that, at the start of the interim period of six and a half years of shared responsibility between the Government and SPLM/A, many of the political players in the north, as well as some forces in the south of the Sudan, were still hesitant to commit themselves to an agreement to which they were not party, especially its provisions on wealth-sharing arrangements. However, on 18 June (Cairo, Egypt), after months of effort and inconclusive talks, an agreement was finalized by the National Democratic Alliance and the Government, including Mr. Garang, that would enable the Alliance to participate in its implementation. As a sign of increasing engagement, more than 100 political leaders and civil society representatives attending a South-South Dialogue Conference (Nairobi, Kenya, April), at which they signed a covenant pledging to defend the Agreement and declaring their commitment to a process of reconciliation and national healing. They also adopted a number of resolutions that addressed various steps to be taken in support of the Agreement's implementation. However, on 1 June, 15 Sudanese political parties, including the Umma National Party and the Popular National Congress, signed a political declaration pledging to work together, but not in the context of the Agreement.

The Joint National Transition Team commenced its duties related to the Agreement's implementation, playing a crucial role in preparing for the establishment of governments at the national, southern Sudan and state/regional levels. It also developed fund-raising strategies for the smooth and timely commencement of the interim period, including the finalization of the joint Government-SPLM/A position for the donors' conference held in Oslo on 11 April. In addition, SPLM/A began to establish its presence in Khartoum, as well as in southern areas under the Government's control to set up SPLM/A political structures and had started working with the National Congress and local authorities.

On 30 April, the National Constitutional Review Commission was inaugurated. Composed of representatives from the Government, SPLM/A and some northern- and southern-based political opposition parties, the Commission met in both Khartoum and Rumbek. The conclusion of its work would pave the way for the establishment of the Government of National Unity.

The Abyei area, having been accorded special administrative status under the Agreement during the interim period, and considered the bridge between the north and the south, required particular attention. The Abyei Boundaries Commission, which was constituted in Nairobi, visited the region in April and May. The Secretary-General expressed concern over the obstruction of the Commission's activities by rogue elements resulting in a number of security incidents. Moreover, numerous armed groups in southern Sudan posed a potential security threat and risked jeopardizing the Agreement's implementation. To address the problem, SPLM and the Government convened an initial meeting of the Collaborative Committee of Other Armed Groups, but no further progress was made. The Joint Media Commission, established by the parties in early March, worked to improve the population's awareness of the Agreement's provisions, address the issue of hostile propaganda and help develop a cooperative relationship between the parties in the area of information. UNMIS assisted the Commission in its work. Concerning the joint integrated units to be deployed in the ceasefire areas and in Khartoum, the Government and SPL/A identified their participants and held discussions in the Nuba Mountains on the formation of units in southern Kordofan.

Communication. On 24 June [S/2005/413], the Secretary-General drew the attention of the Security Council President to the urgent need for additional donor support for the Sudan, in the light of a shortfall of over $1 billion for all sectors and areas of the country. He said that failure to meet the humanitarian challenges facing the country could place the Comprehensive Peace Agreement in jeopardy. Five months since the signing of the Agreement and two months after the pledge of $4.5 billion in humanitarian assistance made at the Oslo Conference, a large percentage of the pledges for 2005 had yet to materialize and pledges for more immediate assistance were urgently needed.

Death of First Vice-President

Report of Secretary-General (September). In a later report [S/2005/579], the Secretary-General said that President Omar Al-Bashir, First Vice-President Garang and Vice-President Ali Osman Taha were sworn in on 9 July. The President issued a decree on the same day to establish a caretaker Government, pending the establishment of the Government of National Unity. The new Interim National Constitution was also signed by President Al-Bashir and the state of emergency was lifted in all states except Darfur, Kassala and Red Sea. However, implementation of the Agreement was put to the test with the death of First Vice-President and SPLM Chairman John Garang on 30 July. His death sparked violence in Khartoum, Juba and Malakal in southern Sudan, resulting in a significant number of deaths, arson and damage to property. SPLM moved swiftly to confirm Salva Kiir as its new Chairman who, with Sudanese President Omar al-Bashir and a number of Sudanese and other world leaders, appealed for calm and unity. By the time Mr. Garang's funeral was held on 6 August, the tense atmosphere had dissipated somewhat and the caretaker Government had established committees to investigate both the helicopter crash and the violence. Salva Kiir was sworn in as First Vice-President of the Sudan on 11 August. During the inauguration ceremony, President Al-Bashir vowed to join hands with SPLM to continue working towards "harmony and co-existence", while the new First Vice-President pledged to continue the vision of the late SPLM leader and to work for unity for all southerners over the interim period. He called for the inclusion of all Sudanese political forces within the Comprehensive Peace Agreement. On 19 August, Riek Machar was appointed Vice-President of southern Sudan in accordance with SPLM succession procedures.

SECURITY COUNCIL ACTION

On 2 August [meeting 5245], the Security Council met to consider the death, on 30 July, of First Vice-President and SPLM Chairman John Garang de Mabior in a helicopter crash near New Cush, southern Sudan. Following consultations among Council members, the President made statement **S/PRST/2005/38** on behalf of the Council:

> The Security Council expresses its profound regret over the death of the First Vice-President of the Sudan Mr. John Garang de Mabior in a helicopter crash on 30 July 2005. The Council offers its deepest sympathy and condolences to the family of Mr. Garang and to the people and Government of the Sudan.
>
> This is a time for the world community to come together to support Mr. Garang's vision of a united and peaceful Sudan. The Council commends the perseverance and commitment which the parties in the Sudan demonstrated in achieving the Comprehensive Peace Agreement and the promise of a new future. Over the last few years, Mr. Garang's courageous efforts were instrumental in ending the over 21-year civil war that cost the lives of millions of Sudanese. His leadership offered hope for democracy and peace for all people of the Sudan.
>
> The Council calls upon all Sudanese to honour his memory by restoring peace and calm throughout the Sudan. The Council trusts that, despite the sudden death of Mr. Garang, the people of the Sudan remain united and continue to work for the consolidation of peace in the country by implementing the Comprehensive Peace Agreement, for which Mr. Garang worked unstintingly.
>
> The Council stresses that the death of Mr. Garang should not deter the struggle of the Sudanese people for justice and dignity, and encourages the people of the Sudan to refrain from violence and maintain peace in the midst of mourning.
>
> The Council reiterates its determination to assist the Sudanese people in their efforts to promote national reconciliation, resolve the conflict in Darfur and restore peace and stability throughout the country, and to build a prosperous and united Sudan.
>
> The Council looks to the international community to continue its support for the people of the Sudan to implement the Comprehensive Peace Agreement, to resolve the humanitarian crisis in Darfur, and to proceed with the reconstruction and rehabilitation process.

Further implementation of Peace Agreement

The Secretary-General, in his September report [S/2005/597], said that Mr. Garang's death led to delays in the implementation of the Comprehensive Peace Agreement, including the appointment of the Council of Ministers, which was to have been completed by 9 August. There were reports of tension within the caretaker Government between the parties over portfolios and prolonged delays over the allocation of the key "sovereign" and economic ministries. At the same time, many commissions and committees anticipated in the Comprehensive Peace Agreement, in areas such as human rights and the civil service, remained to be created. However, on 30 August, President Al-Bashir established the Ceasefire Political Commission, whose functions would include supervising, monitoring and overseeing the Agreement's implementation, as well as providing a political forum for continuous dialogue between the parties and the international community. Meanwhile, the mandate and composition of the Assessment and Evaluation Commission were reviewed by the Presidency.

While the Government of National Unity remained to be finalized, the two chambers of the national legislature, the National Assembly and the Council of States, were inaugurated on 31 August. Three pieces of legislation were introduced for its review and approval: the Bank of Sudan Act, the Constitutional Court Act, and the Judicial Service Commission Act. Among other positive developments were the nomination by the Government and SPLM of officers to form the Joint Integrated Units, which would constitute the nucleus of the future Sudanese National Armed Forces and encouraging signs that political parties that were not signatories to the Agreement, including the National Democratic Alliance, were ready to participate in the Government of National Unity.

In the south, the SPLM legislative council was dissolved on 18 July and a caretaker administration established. On 27 August, the Southern Sudan Constitutional Drafting Committee was established to examine and adopt the draft of the southern Sudanese constitution based on the Comprehensive Peace Agreement and the Interim National Constitution. A south-south dialogue meeting (Nairobi, 30 June), facilitated by the Moi Africa Institute, brought together senior SPLM/A security officials and commanders of various militia groups active in southern Sudan for the first time since the 1991 SPLM/A split, but failed to resolve the fundamental differences between the Southern Sudan Defence Force and SPLM/A. However, Major General Paulino Matip, leader of the Southern Sudan Defence Force, sent encouraging signals following Mr. Kiir's accession to the SPLM/A leadership and his inauguration as First Vice-President. For his part, Mr. Kiir expressed readiness to discuss outstanding issues with the Southern Sudan Defence Force, including those yet to be resolved by the south-south dialogue.

On 14 July, the Abyei Boundaries Commission defined and demarcated the area of the nine Ngok Dinka chiefdoms transferred to Kordofan in 1905, prompting protests from some members of the Missiriya tribe. UNMIS contacted the parties in both Khartoum and Abyei to ensure that the resolution of the Abyei question was concluded on the basis of the Comprehensive Peace Agreement. The Special Representative undertook initiatives to reduce tension in the area. The Commission presented its report to the Presidency, which was being discussed.

On 4 August, President Al-Bashir issued a provisional order to promulgate a decree on the organization of humanitarian and voluntary work, which provided wide powers to the Ministry of Humanitarian Affairs and the Humanitarian Affairs Commission to oversee and control the activities of national and international non-governmental and civil society organizations.

The Secretary-General observed that much had been achieved in the implementation of the Comprehensive Peace Agreement, despite a number of complications and challenges. He deeply regretted the death of First Vice-President Garang and the ensuing loss of life during the subsequent riots. He was, however, reassured by the determination to recover from the setback and the desire to stay the course of the peace process. It was essential that Government positions be swiftly agreed upon and that the remaining commissions and other bodies anticipated in the Agreement be established as soon as possible. While noting that the ceasefire was holding, he called on the parties to submit to the Ceasefire Joint Military Committee detailed lists of the size and location of their troops, and to ensure that timely notification of troop dispositions and redeployments was submitted.

In the east, the Government and the Eastern Front had shown willingness to engage in direct talks, but it was taking a long time for those face-to-face talks to begin. In the meantime, the Front had given the United Nations access to the area to undertake a security and humanitarian assessment in Hameshkoreib and had agreed to discuss the details of that access with UNMIS. SPLM/A faced tremendous challenges in establishing the

government of southern Sudan, and while UNMIS had responded with logistical and material assistance, the Mission would find it increasingly difficult to continue doing so without compromising its other mandated tasks. The Secretary-General appealed to the international community, in the light of the scale of the immense challenge facing the government of southern Sudan, to provide adequate support so as to consolidate peace in the Sudan. He recommended that the Council renew UNMIS mandate until 24 September 2006.

SECURITY COUNCIL ACTION (September)

On 23 September [meeting 5269], the Security Council unanimously adopted **resolution 1627 (2005)**. The draft [S/2005/599] was prepared in consultations among Council members.

The Security Council,

Recalling its previous resolutions, in particular resolution 1590(2005) of 24 March 2005, and the statements by its President concerning the Sudan,

Reaffirming its commitment to the sovereignty, unity, independence and territorial integrity of the Sudan,

Reiterating its expression of sympathy and condolences on the death of First Vice-President John Garang de Mabior on 30 July 2005, and commending the Government of the Sudan and First Vice-President Salva Kiir Mayardit for continued efforts for the consolidation of peace in the Sudan,

Welcoming implementation by the Government of the Sudan and the Sudan People's Liberation Movement/Army of the Comprehensive Peace Agreement of 9 January 2005, and in particular welcoming the formation of the Government of National Unity as a significant and historic step towards lasting peace in the Sudan,

Urging the parties to meet their outstanding commitments under the Comprehensive Peace Agreement, including, as a priority, the establishment of the Assessment and Evaluation Commission,

Determining that the situation in the Sudan continues to constitute a threat to international peace and security,

Acknowledging the commitments by troop-contributing countries in support of the United Nations Mission in the Sudan, and encouraging deployment in order for the Mission to support timely implementation of the Comprehensive Peace Agreement,

1. *Decides* to extend the mandate of the United Nations Mission in the Sudan until 24 March 2006, with the intention to renew it for further periods;

2. *Requests* the Secretary-General to report to the Security Council every three months on the implementation of the mandate of the Mission, including its work to reinforce the efforts of the African Union Mission in the Sudan to foster peace in Darfur;

3. *Urges* troop-contributing countries to review carefully the letter dated 24 March 2005 from the Secretary-General to the President of the General Assembly and to take appropriate action to prevent sexual exploitation and abuse by their personnel in the United Nations Mission in the Sudan, including pre-deployment awareness training, and to take disci-

plinary action and other action to ensure full accountability in cases of such misconduct involving their personnel;

4. *Decides* to remain actively seized of the matter.

Report of Secretary-General (December). In December [S/2005/821], the Secretary-General reported that implementation of the Comprehensive Peace Agreement gained some momentum despite the delays following the death of former First Vice-President John Garang. After considerable dispute over the allocation of some ministerial portfolios, most notably that of energy and mining, the Government of National Unity was established on 20 September. Members of the National Democratic Alliance subsequently agreed to join the Government and was allocated a number of executive positions and seats in parliament, but other northern parties decided to stay in opposition, although they did state their respect for the Comprehensive Peace Agreement and desire for a more inclusive political process. Some southern parties, other than SPLM, also joined the Government of National Unity.

Meanwhile, the government of southern Sudan was established on 22 October as a caretaker government, pending the adoption of the Interim Constitution of Southern Sudan, which was subsequently signed into law on 5 December. Ten southern Sudan state governors were also appointed during this period. However, although the government of southern Sudan included a number of small southern parties, it had been criticized by some as not being fully representative of the south. Some members of the Southern Sudan Legislative Assembly alleged an ethnic imbalance in the government of southern Sudan.

A number of key commissions were established and staffed, and some of the legislation for creating the remaining commissions was adopted. The presidency issued decrees to establish the Assessment and Evaluation Commission, the National Petroleum Commission, the Fiscal and Financial Allocation and Monitoring Commission and the Technical Ad Hoc Border Committee. The Assessment and Evaluation Commission, chaired by Norway, held its first two meetings. The membership of the Ceasefire Political Commission, announced in November, comprised representatives of NCP, SPLM, IGAD, the IGAD Partners Forum and the United Nations as a full member.

At the same time, the delay in implementing the Abyei Boundary Commission's decision defining the borders of the Abyei area contributed to a tense situation in that part of the country. The situation on the ground was further complicated by a sudden upsurge of returns, and a military build-up by the Sudanese Armed Forces (SAF), the Sudan People's Liberation Army (SPLA) and the South Sudan Defence Force. Due to concern that the start of the migration season could lead to clashes between the Missiriya and Dinka tribes, UNMIS increased its presence in Abyei and completed the deployment of the UN protection force there. The Mission encouraged the authorities to establish both the Executive Council and the Joint Integrated Unit in Abyei to normalize the situation and contribute to confidence-building measures. It also convened meetings with the parties to discuss areas of mutual concern, including security and migratory routes. UN agencies also started to plan humanitarian and developmental programmes in Abyei to help promote peaceful coexistence.

In the meantime, the problem of other armed groups remained of crucial importance in southern Sudan. Negotiations continued between First Vice-President Salva Kiir and leaders of other armed groups on their participation in southern state governments, some of whom had been offered government positions. However, many others did not meet the Comprehensive Peace Agreement standard of "incorporation", leaving a considerable number of them completely outside the process, including the remaining "independents" who were a source of growing concern, as the 9 January 2006 deadline for full integration approached. Meanwhile, extortion schemes, illegal taxation, forced recruitment and violence attributed to other armed groups still continued in some areas.

The Secretary-General urged the Government of National Unity and the government of southern Sudan to tackle the insecurity in southern Sudan, while the Government there should encourage continuing reconciliation throughout the region. The withdrawal of SPLA from the Hameshkoreib region of eastern Sudan on the border with Eritrea risked creating a power vacuum. He urged the eastern leaders to facilitate a security and humanitarian assessment of the area so as to allow humanitarian access from within the Sudan. Most importantly, direct talks on the situation in the east had to begin so that a political agreement could be reached. In the light of the fluidity of the situation on the ground, the United Nations would need to maintain a multifunctional presence in eastern Sudan beyond the 9 January 2006 deadline for the redeployment of SPLA.

UNMIS activities

In accordance with resolution 1590(2005), UNMIS provided good offices and political support to assist the parties in implementing the

Comprehensive Peace Agreement and resolve all ongoing conflicts in the Sudan. It met regularly with officials of the Government of National Unity, the government of southern Sudan and opposition groups in an effort to encourage wider participation in and support for the peace process. The military elements began deployment during the first week of April and established the force headquarters in Khartoum and the Joint Military Monitoring Coordination Office responsible for supporting the Ceasefire Joint Military Committee. The Committee held 15 meetings during the year under the chairmanship of the UNMIS Force Commander. Military deployment remained behind schedule, owing largely to delays in the force-generation process. As at December, the military strength stood at 4,291 personnel, or 40 per cent of the expected total of 9,880. By September, it had established full-time military observer presence in Juba, Wau, Malakal, Kadugli, Ed Damazin, Abyei and Kassala. UNMIS had also begun to monitor the movement of armed groups and the redeployment of forces in its operational area. The first monitored redeployment took place on 3 and 4 September when 993 SPLA troops moved from Kassala to Khartoum with their weapons and equipment to make up the future Khartoum Joint Inspection Unit.

UNMIS facilitated, supported and encouraged local reconciliation initiatives in areas of conflict within the Sudan, including encouraging dialogue in relevant areas, identifying the needs of the new public administration and helping to defuse tension. UNDP was supporting state- and country-level public administration through technical assistance and in-service training. In Abyei, UNMIS hosted the first meeting in many years between Dinka Ngok and Missiriya leaders to discuss the seasonal migration of Missiriya nomads through the Dinka Ngok farming areas, and other issues that could lead to conflict between the two tribes. In southern Sudan, the Lord's Resistance Army operating out of Uganda perpetrated several vicious attacks on villages, and since the issue of indictments by the International Criminal Court of its leaders, had started targeting UN personnel and NGOs, hampering their activities. UNMIS coordinated its activities with others in the area to address the situation.

UNMIS supported the interim disarmament, demobilization and reintegration authorities for the north and the south in key assessment surveys. Disarmament of child combatants was planned to start in December. Japan and the United Kingdom had contributed $ 6.9 million and 2 million pounds, respectively, to implement the special groups' needs. However, serious challenges remained to the full implementation of the disarm-

ament, demobilization and reintegration programme and the establishment of the related national coordination councils and commissions for northern and southern Sudan.

The deployment of UN police suffered from delays due to a lack of facilities, especially in Kadugli, Abyei and Juba. As at December, 215 police from 27 countries had been deployed. The police monitored, advised and reported on the activities of the local police in southern Sudan, including criminal investigation and correctional reform.

UNMIS also liaised with the African Union Mission in the Sudan (AMIS) to reinforce AU-led efforts to foster peace in Darfur through technical and logistical assistance to AMIS.

Financing

On 1 March [S/2005/57/Add.1], the Secretary-General informed the Security Council that the financial implications of UNMIS deployment were projected at $1,009.8 million for a 12-month period.

On 29 March [A/57/756 & Corr. 1, 2], pending the submission of a full budget for UNMIS at the General Assembly's sixtieth (2005) session, the Secretary-General requested commitment authority with assessment in the amount of $595.5 million to cover the requirements of the Mission for the period from 1 July 2004 to the date of the establishment of the Mission and immediate start-up requirements to 31 October 2005.

ACABQ, in its April report [A/59/768], recommended approval of the Secretary-General's proposal.

GENERAL ASSEMBLY ACTION

On 21 April, the General Assembly, on the recommendation of the Fifth Committee [A/59/780], adopted **resolution 59/292** without vote [agenda item 151].

Financing of the United Nations Mission in the Sudan

The General Assembly,

Having considered the report of the Secretary-General on the financing of the United Nations Mission in the Sudan and the related report of the Advisory Committee on Administrative and Budgetary Questions,

Recalling Security Council resolution 1590(2005) of 24 March 2005, by which the Council established the United Nations Mission in the Sudan for an initial period of six months from 24 March 2005,

Recognizing that the costs of the Mission are expenses of the Organization to be borne by Member States in accordance with Article 17, paragraph 2, of the Charter of the United Nations,

Reaffirming the general principles underlying the financing of United Nations peacekeeping operations, as stated in its resolutions 1874(S-IV) of 27 June 1963, 3101(XXVIII) of 11 December 1973 and 55/235 of 23 December 2000,

Mindful of the fact that it is essential to provide the Mission with the necessary financial resources to enable it to fulfil its responsibilities under the relevant resolution of the Security Council,

1. *Expresses concern* about the financial situation with regard to peacekeeping activities, in particular as regards the reimbursements to troop contributors that bear additional burdens owing to overdue payments by Member States of their assessments;

2. *Also expresses concern* at the delay experienced by the Secretary-General in deploying and providing adequate resources to some recent peacekeeping missions, in particular those in Africa;

3. *Emphasizes* that all future and existing peacekeeping missions shall be given equal and non-discriminatory treatment in respect of financial and administrative arrangements;

4. *Also emphasizes* that all peacekeeping missions shall be provided with adequate resources for the effective and efficient discharge of their respective mandates;

5. *Reiterates its request* to the Secretary-General to make the fullest possible use of facilities and equipment at the United Nations Logistics Base at Brindisi, Italy, in order to minimize the costs of procurement for the Mission;

6. *Endorses* the conclusions and recommendations contained in the report of the Advisory Committee on Administrative and Budgetary Questions, and requests the Secretary-General to ensure their full implementation;

7. *Notes* that the General Assembly has never pronounced itself on the use of assessed peacekeeping contributions for the purposes stated in paragraph 15 of the report of the Advisory Committee, and decides to revert to this issue in the context of its consideration of item 123, entitled "Administrative and budgetary aspects of the financing of the United Nations peacekeeping operations", during the second part of its resumed fifty-ninth session in the light of the additional information to be provided thereon by the Secretary-General;

8. *Requests* the Secretary-General to take all action necessary to ensure that the Mission is administered with a maximum of efficiency and economy;

9. *Also requests* the Secretary-General, in order to reduce the cost of employing General Service staff, to continue efforts to recruit local staff for the Mission against General Service posts, commensurate with the requirements of the Mission;

Budget estimates for the period from 1 July 2004 to 31 October 2005

10. *Authorizes* the Secretary-General to establish a special account for the United Nations Mission in the Sudan for the purpose of accounting for the income received and expenditure incurred in respect of the Mission;

11. *Also authorizes* the Secretary-General to enter into commitments for the Mission for the period from 1 July 2004 to 31 October 2005 in a total amount not exceeding 595,498,500 United States dollars for the initial establishment of the Mission, comprising, for the period from 1 July 2004 to 30 June 2005, the amount of 279,501,300 dollars, inclusive of the amount of 99,999,400 dollars previously authorized by the Advisory Committee, and, for the period from 1 July to 31 October 2005, the amount of 315,997,200 dollars, under the terms of section IV of General Assembly resolution 49/233 A of 23 December 1994;

Financing of the commitment authority

12. *Decides* to apportion among Member States the total amount of 497,873,300 dollars for the period from 1 July 2004 to 23 September 2005, comprising the amount of 279,501,300 dollars for the period from 1 July 2004 to 30 June 2005 and the amount of 218,372,000 dollars for the period from 1 July to 23 September 2005, in accordance with the levels set out by the General Assembly in its resolution 55/235, as adjusted by the Assembly in its resolution 55/236 of 23 December 2000 and updated in its resolution 58/256 of 23 December 2003, taking into account the scale of assessments for 2004 and 2005, as set out in its resolution 58/1 B of 23 December 2003;

13. *Decides also* that, in accordance with the provisions of its resolution 973(X) of 15 December 1955, there shall be set off against the apportionment among Member States, as provided for in paragraph 12 above, their respective share in the Tax Equalization Fund of 1,635,000 dollars, representing the estimated staff assessment income approved for the Mission for the period from 1 July 2004 to 30 June 2005, and 2,042,500 dollars, representing the estimated staff assessment income approved for the Mission for the period from 1 July to 23 September 2005;

14. *Decides further* to apportion among Member States the amount of 97,625,200 dollars for the period from 24 September to 31 October 2005, at a monthly rate of 78,999,300 dollars, in accordance with the scheme set out in paragraph 12 above, taking into account the scale of assessments for 2005, as set out in its resolution 58/1 B, subject to a decision of the Security Council to extend the mandate of the Mission;

15. *Decides* that, in accordance with the provisions of its resolution 973(X), there shall be set off against the apportionment among Member States, as provided for in paragraph 14 above, their respective share in the Tax Equalization Fund of 913,100 dollars, representing the estimated staff assessment income approved for the Mission for the period from 24 September to 31 October 2005;

16. *Emphasizes* that no peacekeeping mission shall be financed by borrowing funds from other active peacekeeping missions;

17. *Encourages* the Secretary-General to continue to take additional measures to ensure the safety and security of all personnel under the auspices of the United Nations participating in the Mission;

18. *Invites* voluntary contributions to the Mission in cash and in the form of services and supplies acceptable to the Secretary-General, to be administered, as appropriate, in accordance with the procedure and practices established by the General Assembly;

19. *Decides* to include in the provisional agenda of its sixtieth session the item entitled "Financing of the United Nations Mission in the Sudan".

In August [A/60/190], the Secretary-General submitted the budget for UNMIS from 1 July 2004 to 30 June 2006, comprising $222,031,700 for the period from 1 July 2004 to 30 June 2005 and $1,017,602,600 for the period from 1 July 2005 to 30 June 2006. ACABQ's comments and recommendations thereon were contained in its October report [A/60/428].

On 8 December [meeting 62], the Assembly, on the recommendation of the Fifth Committee [A/60/562], adopted **resolution 60/122** without vote [agenda item 151].

Financing of the United Nations Mission in the Sudan

The General Assembly,

Having considered the report of the Secretary-General on the financing of the United Nations Mission in the Sudan and the related report of the Advisory Committee on Administrative and Budgetary Questions,

Recalling Security Council resolution 1590(2005) of 24 March 2005, by which the Council established the United Nations Mission in the Sudan for an initial period of six months as from 24 March 2005, and the subsequent resolution 1627(2005) of 23 September 2005 by which the Council extended the mandate of the Mission until 24 March 2006,

Recalling also its resolution 59/292 of 21 April 2005 on the financing of the Mission,

Reaffirming the general principles underlying the financing of United Nations peacekeeping operations, as stated in its resolutions 1874(S-IV) of 27 June 1963, 3101(XXVIII) of 11 December 1973 and 55/235 of 23 December 2000,

Mindful of the fact that it is essential to provide the Mission with the necessary financial resources to enable it to fulfil its responsibilities under the relevant resolutions of the Security Council,

1. *Requests* the Secretary-General to entrust the Head of Mission with the task of formulating future budget proposals in full accordance with the provisions of General Assembly resolution 59/296 of 22 June 2005, as well as other relevant resolutions;

2. *Takes note* of the status of contributions to the United Nations Mission in the Sudan as at 30 September 2005, including the contributions outstanding in the amount of 127.9 million United States dollars, representing some 26 per cent of the total assessed contributions, notes with concern that only sixty-six Member States have paid their assessed contributions in full, and urges all other Member States, in particular those in arrears, to ensure payment of their outstanding assessed contributions;

3. *Expresses its appreciation* to those Member States which have paid their assessed contributions in full, and urges all other Member States to make every possible effort to ensure payment of their assessed contributions to the Mission in full;

4. *Expresses concern* at the financial situation with regard to peacekeeping activities, in particular as regards the reimbursements to troop contributors that bear additional burdens owing to overdue payments by Member States of their assessments;

5. *Also expresses concern* at the delay experienced by the Secretary-General in deploying and providing adequate resources to some recent peacekeeping missions, in particular those in Africa;

6. *Emphasizes* that all future and existing peacekeeping missions shall be given equal and non-discriminatory treatment in respect of financial and administrative arrangements;

7. *Also emphasizes* that all peacekeeping missions shall be provided with adequate resources for the effective and efficient discharge of their respective mandates;

8. *Reiterates its request* to the Secretary-General to make the fullest possible use of facilities and equipment at the United Nations Logistics Base at Brindisi, Italy, in order to minimize the costs of procurement for the Mission;

9. *Endorses* the conclusions and recommendations contained in the report of the Advisory Committee on Administrative and Budgetary Questions subject to the provisions of the present resolution, and requests the Secretary-General to ensure their full implementation;

10. *Reaffirms* its resolution 59/296, and requests the Secretary-General to ensure the full implementation of its relevant provisions;

11. *Recognizes* that the activities on disarmament, demobilization and reintegration are in conformity with its resolution 59/296, and authorizes the Secretary-General to utilize the proposed resources for disarmament, demobilization and reintegration in conformity with the provisions of that resolution;

12. *Welcomes* the steps taken to ensure the coordination and collaboration of efforts with the agencies, funds and programmes, as spelled out in paragraph 120 of the report of the Secretary-General, and to implement a unified workplan including, inter alia, disarmament, demobilization and reintegration, and requests the Secretary-General to report to the General Assembly on further actions taken, as well as progress made and to provide a clear description of respective roles and responsibilities in future budgets submissions commencing with the 2006/07 budget;

13. *Decides* to establish the 740 security posts requested in paragraphs 38 to 65 of the report of the Secretary-General, authorizes the Secretary-General, bearing in mind paragraph 29 of the report of the Advisory Committee on Administrative and Budgetary Questions, to utilize redeployment to meet the evolving security requirements in the Mission area and requests him to report thereon in the context of the Mission budget proposals for 2006/07;

14. *Welcomes* the review undertaken by the Mission on the proposed structure of the Mission, and requests the Secretary-General, bearing in mind the relevant observations of the Advisory Committee on Administrative and Budgetary Questions, to further elaborate on management efficiencies achieved, as well as on the strengthened monitoring and accountability system in the context of a unified, area-based and decentralized organizational structure and to report thereon in future budgets submissions commencing with the 2006/07 budget;

15. *Recalls* section XVII, paragraph 4, of its resolution 59/296 and, in this context, requests the Secretary-General to pursue, through collaboration

between the United Nations peacekeeping operations in the region, opportunities for optimizing, where possible, the provision and management of support resources and service delivery, while ensuring the effective provision of such resources and service delivery for peacekeeping operations in the region, and to report thereon in the context of the respective 2006/07 budgets;

16. *Welcomes* the use of the Entebbe installation to enhance the efficiency and responsiveness of its logistical support operations for peacekeeping missions in the regions;

17. *Requests* the Secretary-General to take all necessary action to ensure that the Mission is administered with a maximum of efficiency and economy;

18. *Also requests* the Secretary-General, in order to reduce the cost of employing General Service staff, to continue efforts to recruit local staff for the Mission against General Service posts, commensurate with the requirements of the Mission;

Budget estimates for the period
from 1 July 2004 to 30 June 2005

19. *Decides* to appropriate to the Special Account for the United Nations Mission in the Sudan the amount of 222,031,700 dollars for the period from 1 July 2004 to 30 June 2005 for the establishment of the Mission;

20. *Decides also* to approve the increase in the estimated staff assessment income for the period from 1 July 2004 to 30 June 2005 from 1,635,000 dollars to 2,313,100 dollars;

Budget estimates
for the period from 1 July 2005 to 30 June 2006

21. *Decides further* to appropriate to the Special Account for the Mission the amount of 969,468,800 dollars for the maintenance of the Mission for the period from 1 July 2005 to 30 June 2006, inclusive of the amount of 315,997,200 dollars for the period from 1 July to 31 October 2005 previously authorized by the General Assembly under the terms of its resolution 59/292;

22. *Decides* to approve the increase in the estimated staff assessment income for the period from 1 July 2005 to 30 June 2006 from 2,955,600 dollars to 12,661,600 dollars;

Financing of the appropriation

23. *Decides also*, to apply the amount of 57,469,600 dollars, representing the difference between the amount of 279,501,300 dollars already apportioned by the General Assembly for the period from 1 July 2004 to 30 June 2005 under the terms of its resolution 59/292 and the amount of 222,031,700 dollars indicated in paragraph 19 above, to the resources required for the period from 1 July 2005 to 30 June 2006;

24. *Decides further*, taking into account the amount of 315,997,200 dollars already apportioned by the General Assembly for the period from 1 July to 31 October 2005 under the terms of its resolution 59/292 and the amount of 57,469,600 dollars indicated in paragraph 23 above, to apportion among Member States the additional amount of 355,679,000 dollars for the period from 1 November 2005 to 24 March 2006, in accordance with the levels updated in General Assembly resolution 58/256 of 23 December 2003, and taking into

account the scale of assessments for 2005 and 2006, as set out in its resolution 58/1 B of 23 December 2003;

25. *Decides* that, in accordance with the provisions of its resolution 973(X) of 15 December 1955, there shall be set off against the apportionment among Member States, as provided for in paragraph 24 above, their respective share in the Tax Equalization Fund of the amount of 5,792,000 dollars, representing the estimated additional staff assessment income approved for the Mission for the period from 1 November 2005 to 24 March 2006;

26. *Decides also* to apportion among Member States the additional amount of 240,323,000 dollars for the period from 25 March to 30 June 2006, in accordance with the scheme set out in paragraph 24 above, and taking into account the scale of assessments for 2006, as set out in its resolution 58/1 B, subject to a decision of the Security Council to extend the mandate of the Mission;

27. *Decides further*, that in accordance with the provisions of its resolution 973(X), there shall be set off against the apportionment among Member States, as provided for in paragraph 26 above, their respective share in the Tax Equalization Fund of the amount of 3,914,000 dollars, representing the estimated additional staff assessment income approved for the Mission for the period from 25 March to 30 June 2006;

28. *Emphasizes* that no peacekeeping mission shall be financed by borrowing funds from other active peacekeeping missions;

29. *Encourages* the Secretary-General to continue to take additional measures to ensure the safety and security of all personnel under the auspices of the United Nations participating in the Mission;

30. *Invites* voluntary contributions to the Mission in cash and in the form of services and supplies acceptable to the Secretary-General, to be administered, as appropriate, in accordance with the procedure and practices established by the General Assembly;

31. *Decides* to keep under review during its sixtieth session the item entitled "Financing of the United Nations Mission in the Sudan".

In December [A/60/626], the Secretary-General submitted the performance report for the UNMIS budget for the period from 1 July 2004 to 30 June 2005.

Situation in Darfur

Report of Secretary-General (January). In his January report [S/2005/10], submitted pursuant to Security Council resolutions 1556(2004) [YUN 2004, p. 240], 1564(2004) [ibid., p. 245] and 1574(2004) [ibid., p. 252], the Secretary-General, while hailing the conclusion of the Comprehensive Peace Agreement in the north-south peace process in the Sudan, noted the political stalemate in the situation in the Darfur region of the country. He said that the security situation was very poor, as new security problems had arisen. On 3 January, an attack by Government forces on a Sudanese Liberation Movement/Army (SLM/A) position in northern Darfur had been reported. Violence

was seeping into the camps of internally displaced persons and was directly affecting humanitarian workers. Groups were also rearming and
the conflict was spreading outside Darfur. Large
quantities of arms had been carried into Darfur
and the build-up of arms and intensification of
violence, including air attacks, suggested that the
security situation was deteriorating. The pressures on the parties to abide by their commitments were not having a perceptible effect on the
ground, which led him to conclude that the
Council should reconsider measures for achieving improved security and protection for the internally displaced persons.

Talks between the parties, within the Abuja
peace process (10-22 December, 2004) had not
yielded concrete results or a narrowing of the gap
on the issues between them, and despite statements to the contrary, they had not committed
themselves in practice to the implementation of
the N'Djamena Humanitarian Ceasefire Agreement [YUN 2004, p. 235]. A move from the current
fragile ceasefire to a resolution to the conflict in
Darfur depended on the accomplishment of six
tasks: the parties had to be persuaded, by a combination of pressure and assurances; that it was in
their interest to pursue a peace settlement; respect the ceasefire; communicate their troop locations to the AU Ceasefire Commission; and
agree on a plan of separation of forces. The parties should also minimize attacks by armed personnel on civilians by identifying practical means
to ensure that their forces' basic survival needs
were met without violating the ceasefire. The
composition and modalities of the Joint Commission provided for under the Humanitarian
Ceasefire Agreement had to be amended so as to
improve its credibility and effectiveness. There
had to be proactive follow-up on the implementation of previous commitments and obligations so
as to reduce the level of violence on the ground
and build confidence in the peace process and
the international community had to help the AU
force to accelerate the rate of its deployment. Perpetrators of violations of human rights law and
crimes under international humanitarian law
should not be allowed to go unpunished.

Regarding the political process, action in three
areas could be key to putting it on the right track:
the parties should commit themselves to proceeding with political talks without further delay; the Council should assist the parties of the
north-south dialogue to agree on a declaration of
principles that addressed the core issues of power
and wealth-sharing, as well as the integration of
the Darfur peace talks into the wider process of
peacemaking in the Sudan; and, while the current negotiation process between the Govern-

ment, SLM/A and the Justice and Equality Movement (JEM) should proceed, it would be useful to
start thinking of ways to create a broad and strong
support base for sustainable peace.

Restoring peace in Darfur would require reconciliation and restoration of the social fabric in
that region. Reconciliation would have to include
all social groups and segments, especially non-
armed groups and victims of the current violence. The only alternative to finding new measures was to find a way to deploy as many personnel on the ground as possible. The AU force had
done more than any other outside agent to improve the security situation on the ground, and
whatever actions and new initiatives were undertaken, the AU would remain, for the foreseeable
future, the best mechanism for promoting peace
in Darfur.

Security Council consideration (11 January).
On 7 January [meeting 5109], the Security Council
discussed the situation in the Sudan, especially
the signing, on 9 January, of the Comprehensive
Peace Agreement. The Special Representative of
the Secretary-General for the Sudan, Jan Pronk,
in his briefing to the Council, said that, although
the security situation in Darfur had not improved, the signature of the north-south peace
Comprehensive Peace Agreement was an opportunity to improve the capacity to solve that conflict. In that regard, he suggested that any future
talks on Darfur's political future be separated
from those on security and humanitarian access,
which should be relegated to the AU Ceasefire
Commission and the Joint Commission; the
Darfur ceasefire institutions should be empowered to enable them to authorize independent assessment of any ceasefire breaches and to make
binding recommendations requiring unconditional implementation; and, with AU assistance,
insist that both the Government and the rebel
movements exercise full restraint and avert any
attacks or retaliations; and the Government and
the rebel movements should withdraw behind
the lines prevailing before 8 December 2004 and
the AU should protect the areas concerned; the
Government should make a new start by disarming the Popular Defence Forces; the rebel movements should commit themselves to not blocking
or disrupting the seasonal movement of nomadic
tribes; and the Government should control and
restrain the militias through force or tribal reconciliation and arrest those responsible for human
rights violations.

The Special Representative suggested that it
was time to prepare a national conference, with a
view to reaching a consensus about the modalities of a peaceful future for the country, thereby
integrating the Darfur peace talks into the wider

peacemaking process. However, the Darfur talks should not wait until such a national conference was feasible.

Communication. On 27 January [S/2005/56], Australia, Canada and New Zealand informed the Security Council President that they were gravely concerned by the deteriorating situation in Darfur and for the safety of persons living there. Believing that the Council was uniquely placed to assist in protecting civilians in the Darfur region, they proposed that it establish a committee to monitor the implementation of the arms embargo called for in resolution 1556(2004) [YUN 2004, p. 240] and address, with the assistance of a panel of experts, the origins of arms flows to those actors covered therein. The committee would, among other things, determine the financiers of the armed militias in Darfur, including pro-government militias, rebel movements and other emerging movements. It could also help to ensure that existing Council resolutions were being properly implemented and identify areas where further Council attention might be necessary. The Council should design targeted measures to bring greater pressure to bear on all parties to the conflict to comply with their undertakings and with its resolutions, including individual travel bans and the freezing of assets. The Secretary-General, in his next report on Darfur, should assess further the extent to which the parties to the conflict had respected the obligations imposed on them by earlier Council resolutions.

Also, should the International Commission of Inquiry established pursuant to resolution 1564 (2004) [ibid., p. 245] determine that crimes within the jurisdiction of the International Criminal Court had been committed, the Council should refer the matter to the Court as the most appropriate body to investigate such crimes.

Report of the Secretary-General (February). In his 4 February report [S/2005/68], the Secretary-General said that the past six months had seen the Government of the Sudan progressively implement some of the elements of its obligations in the security, human rights, humanitarian and political spheres. However, that progress had been neither steady nor even, and some areas had been completely neglected. Fighting in Darfur involving Government forces, the armed movements and militias allied to the Government continued. On the eve of the December 2004 Abuja talks, the Government began a series of offensive operations termed "road clearing", particularly in southern Darfur. Those operations, which included de facto coordination with militia, involved clearing, burning of villages and looting. In January 2005, the authorities informed the United Nations and its partners that it intended to launch a similar operation in northern Darfur. Responding to UN concerns, the Government postponed or suspended the "clearing" provided the AU carried out road patrols. Operations resumed in mid-January, coinciding with militia attacks, such as those on Hamada village on 13 January and on Gereida and Shangil Tobai on 26 January.

Concerning human rights, the report of the Commission of Inquiry to Investigate Alleged Human Rights Violations Committed by Armed Groups in the Darfur States established by the Government of the Sudan in 2004 was released in January 2005 [S/2005/80]. It stated that serious violations of human rights were committed in the three Darfur States by all parties. However, genocide did not occur and the number of persons killed was exaggerated. Rape and crimes of sexual violence were not widespread or systematic and did not amount to crimes against humanity. The National Commission of Inquiry recommended that judicial investigation committees be established. The President directed that a Judicial Inquiry Committee and an Inventory of Losses and Reparations Committee be formed. The Secretary-General pointed out that the Committee's report differed substantially from the findings of the International Commission of Inquiry (see p. 323) regarding the scale and systematic nature of the crimes committed and the responsibility of the Government of the Sudan.

The Secretary-General suggested that future talks in the Abuja process de-link security and humanitarian issues from political ones, allowing the parties to focus their attention on designing the implementing institutions that would follow an agreement.

N'Djamena Joint Commission meeting (February). The seventh high-level meeting of the Joint Commission met in N'Djamena on 16 and 17 February [S/2005/140]. The meeting, attended by the Presidents of Chad, Gabon, the Democratic Republic of the Congo and the Sudan, the Chairman of the AU Commission, and ministerial representation from Egypt, the Libyan Arab Jamahiriya and Nigeria, and the Secretary-General's Special Representative, was presented with a report by the Chairman of the Ceasefire Commission detailing ceasefire violations since January. The report faulted the Government and rebels for the violations and criticized the lack of commitment to the Humanitarian Ceasefire Agreement. The Ceasefire Commission made recommendations to the Joint Commission on ways to improve the security situation in Darfur, among which were that the status of AMIS units making up the protection force be upgraded from a company to a battalion; that SLM/A and

JEM unconditionally release to the AU-Ceasefire Commission the locations of their combatants; and that the Government of the Sudan review and resubmit its plan for the disarmament of the armed militia operating in Darfur. The Joint Commission supported the sending of a survey team to Darfur to delineate the areas of control held by the various forces and called upon the AU Peace and Security Council to reinforce its Ceasefire Commission in order to find a solution to the crisis within an African framework. The joint commission also called for the rapid resumption of the next round of peace talks.

Sudan's proposals on Darfur. On 25 February [S/2005/128], Sudan transmitted to the Security Council President Al-Bashir proposals on the situation in Darfur to the February N'Djamena Summit (above). Those proposals centred on expediting the negotiation process, enhancing the security situation, strengthening the AU mission, and improving the humanitarian situation and the political dialogue. Among his main proposals, President Al-Bashir suggested that negotiations in Abuja, Nigeria, resume before the end of February, with representation from the two rebel movements. Believing that the best way to address the security situation was to identify the active armed elements in Darfur so that responsibility could be accurately determined, he called for the adoption of criterion for doing so, which he had proposed. He also informed that Government forces had suspended all attacks and had been directed to exercise utmost restraint. The Government had also withdrawn its air bombers from Darfur and demobilized 30 per cent of the Popular Defence Forces (PDF) (paramilitary forces mobilized when there was a threat to national security) and proposed demobilizing a further 20 per cent. The demobilization would come to a zero level when the rebels started implementing fully their commitments. He also proposed measures for dealing with the armed civilians among the tribes, strengthening the role of the Ceasefire Commission, and for strengthening humanitarian access.

The President believed that the Comprehensive Peace Agreement provided the basis for settling the Sudan, political and economic problems and was committed to a final settlement based on the principles set out in the Agreement.

AU mediation team. On 1 March, [S/2005/139], the Sudan informed the Council President that, as part of efforts to achieve a political solution to the Darfur conflict, an AU mediation team had concluded a three-day visit to the country, during which it held consultations with the Sudanese parties on the best way to rapidly resume the Abuja talks as called for by the AU. At the end of the consultations, the mediation team informed its interlocutors that a draft Framework Protocol on the resolution of the conflict in Darfur would be prepared in the light of the positions expressed by them. The mediation team would hold similar consultations in Nairobi, Kenya and Asmara, Eritrea, with the SLM/A and JEM leaders.

Report of Secretary-General (March). Reporting on developments in the Sudan, the Secretary-General, on 4 March [S/2005/140], said that, although there had been fewer clashes in Darfur between the Government and armed movement in February than in previous two months, the security situation remained fragile. SLM/A and Government forces clashed twice in February in northern Darfur. The AU confirmed that the Government had started removing Antonov bombers from El-Fasher and Nyala, although it kept its military helicopters in Darfur. Although the Government did not resume the "road clearing" operations, its forces remained in several areas they had occupied during those operations. At the same time, SLM/A forces maintained their presence in nearby locations. Fighting between militia or Janjaweed and rebel groups occurred in February. The Janjaweed attacked SLM/A forces on 2 and 19 February, while a Janjaweed-rebel conflict reportedly took place on 21 February.

In South Darfur, civilians were attacked in villages and on roads, particularly in the east of Nyala. Further incidents of rape and sexual violence continued to be reported throughout Darfur. Areas outside many of the displaced persons' camps remained particularly insecure. There were also reports of arrests by the police of unmarried women in the Mukjar area (West Darfur) who had become pregnant as a result of rape. There was no meaningful investigation into the reported killings of over 100 civilians and the mass rape of over 30 women and girls in the village of Hamada (South Darfur) on 13 and 14 January. Two of the committees established by the Government following the recommendations of the National Committee of Inquiry—the Judicial Inquiry Committee and the Reparations Committee—had begun visiting Darfur states. In terms of humanitarian access, relief agencies had gained access to areas previously closed due to security concerns. However, humanitarian operations continued to be impeded by the continued harassment of workers, including arrests, detention and abductions of national staff, especially in South Darfur, and attacks by armed groups on commercial trucks carrying humanitarian assistance.

The Secretary-General observed that there were no significant advances in searching for a political solution to the crisis in Darfur. The Government had not stopped militia from attacking civilians, while the rebel movements had done little to seize the political opportunities created since the signing of the Agreement. On the ground, their forces harassed the relief workers, fired on AU and WFP helicopters and refused to reveal their positions to the AU Ceasefire Commission. At the political level, the rebel movements appeared to be increasingly divided, resulting in a diminished capacity to engage in serious political negotiations.

The Secretary-General reported that he met with the Chairperson of the AU Commission, Alpha Oumar Konaré, on 28 February, and agreed that an AU-led assessment of peacekeeping requirements in Darfur would be undertaken as a matter of urgency, with the participation of the United Nations and its key partners (see p. 327). He was also sending a UN team to the region to make a full assessment of options for strengthening the peacekeeping presence in Darfur. In the meantime, the international community should not miss the opportunity to strengthen the position of the AU force in Darfur.

Security Council consideration (24 March). At the Security Council's 24 March meeting [meeting 5151] to consider the reports of the Secretary-General on Darfur, the Under-Secretary-General for Peacekeeping Operations, Jean-Marie Guéhenno, told the Council that it was clear that the current state of affairs in Darfur was unacceptable. The violence and destruction had to stop, and impunity ended. If the security did not improve quickly, the rape and killings would continue. It had to be made clear to those responsible that they would be held accountable. Humanitarian workers and the AU mission were on the front line of the international community's response to the Darfur crisis. The Council owed it to them to act with courage and determination.

Imposition of travel ban and assets freeze

On 29 March [meeting 5153], the Security Council adopted by vote (12-0-3) **resolution 1591 (2005)**. The draft [S/2005/206] was submitted by the United States.

The Security Council,

Recalling its resolutions 1547(2004) of 11 June 2004, 1556(2004) of 30 July 2004, 1564(2004) of 18 September 2004, 1574(2004) of 19 November 2004, 1585(2005) of 10 March 2005, 1588(2005) of 17 March 2005 and 1590(2005) of 24 March 2005, and statements by its President concerning the Sudan,

Reaffirming its commitment to the sovereignty, unity, independence and territorial integrity of the Sudan,

and recalling the importance of the principles of good-neighbourliness, non-interference and regional cooperation,

Recalling the commitments made by the parties in the N'Djamena ceasefire agreement of 8 April 2004 and the Humanitarian and Security Protocols of 9 November 2004 signed in Abuja between the Government of the Sudan, the Sudan Liberation Movement/Army and the Justice and Equality Movement, and recalling the commitments made in the joint communique of 3 July 2004 of the Government of the Sudan and the Secretary-General,

Welcoming the signing of the Comprehensive Peace Agreement between the Government of the Sudan and the Sudan People's Liberation Movement/Army in Nairobi on 9 January 2005,

Recognizing that the parties to the Comprehensive Peace Agreement must build on the Agreement to bring peace and stability to the entire country, and calling upon all Sudanese parties, in particular those party to the Agreement, to take immediate steps to achieve a peaceful settlement to the conflict in Darfur and to take all necessary action to prevent further violations of human rights and international humanitarian law and to put an end to impunity, including in the Darfur region,

Expressing its utmost concern over the dire consequences of the prolonged conflict for the civilian population in the Darfur region as well as throughout the Sudan, in particular the increase in the number of refugees and internally displaced persons,

Considering that the voluntary and sustainable return of refugees and internally displaced persons will be a critical factor for the consolidation of the peace process,

Expressing its deep concern for the security of humanitarian workers and their access to populations in need, including refugees, internally displaced persons and other war-affected populations,

Condemning the continued violations of the N'Djamena ceasefire agreement and the Abuja Protocols by all sides in Darfur and the deterioration of the security situation and negative impact this has had on humanitarian assistance efforts,

Strongly condemning all violations of human rights and international humanitarian law in the Darfur region, in particular the continuation of violence against civilians and sexual violence against women and girls since the adoption of resolution 1574(2004), urging all parties to take necessary steps to prevent further violations, and expressing its determination to ensure that those responsible for all such violations are identified and brought to justice without delay,

Recognizing that international support for implementation of the Comprehensive Peace Agreement is critically important to its success, emphasizing that progress towards resolution of the conflict in Darfur would create conditions conducive for delivery of such assistance, and alarmed that the violence in Darfur nonetheless continues,

Recalling the demands, in resolutions 1556(2004), 1564(2004) and 1574(2004), that all parties to the conflict in Darfur refrain from any violence against civilians and cooperate fully with the African Union mission in Darfur,

Welcoming the N'Djamena summit on Darfur held on 16 February 2005 and the continued commitment of the African Union to play a key role in facilitating a resolution to the conflict in Darfur in all respects, and the announcement by the Government of the Sudan on 16 February 2005 that it would take immediate steps, including withdrawal of its forces from Labado, Qarifa, and Marla in Darfur, and the withdrawal of its Antonov aircraft from Darfur,

Commending the efforts of the African Union, in particular its Chairman, acknowledging the progress made by the African Union in the deployment of an international protection force, police and military observers, and calling upon all Member States to contribute generously and urgently to the African Union mission in Darfur,

Reaffirming its resolutions 1325(2000) of 31 October 2000 on women and peace and security, 1379(2001) of 20 November 2001 and 1460(2003) of 30 January 2003 on children and armed conflict, as well as resolutions 1265(1999) of 17 September 1999 and 1296(2000) of 19 April 2000 on the protection of civilians in armed conflict and resolution 1502(2003) of 26 August 2003 on the protection of United Nations personnel, associated personnel and humanitarian personnel in conflict zones,

Taking note of the reports of the Secretary-General of 3 December 2004, 31 January 2005, 4 February 2005 and 4 March 2005, as well as the report of 25 January 2005 of the International Commission of Inquiry for Darfur,

Determining that the situation in the Sudan continues to constitute a threat to international peace and security,

Acting under Chapter VII of the Charter of the United Nations,

1. *Strongly deplores* the fact that the Government of the Sudan and rebel forces and all other armed groups in Darfur have failed to comply fully with their commitments and the demands of the Security Council referred to in resolutions 1556(2004), 1564(2004) and 1574(2004), condemns the continued violations of the N'Djamena ceasefire agreement and the Abuja Protocols, including air strikes by the Government of the Sudan in December 2004 and January 2005 and rebel attacks on Darfur villages in January 2005, and the failure of the Government of the Sudan to disarm Janjaweed militiamen and apprehend and bring to justice Janjaweed leaders and their associates who have committed violations of human rights and international humanitarian law and other atrocities, and demands that all parties take immediate steps to fulfil all their commitments to respect the N'Djamena ceasefire agreement and the Abuja Protocols, including notification of force positions, to facilitate humanitarian assistance, and to cooperate fully with the African Union mission;

2. *Emphasizes* that there can be no military solution to the conflict in Darfur, and calls upon the Government of the Sudan and the rebel groups, particularly the Justice and Equality Movement and the Sudan Liberation Movement/Army to resume the Abuja talks rapidly, without preconditions, and negotiate in good faith to speedily reach agreement, and urges the parties to the Comprehensive Peace Agreement to play an active and constructive role in support of the Abuja talks and take immediate steps to support a peaceful settlement to the conflict in Darfur;

3. *Decides*, in the light of the failure of all parties to the conflict in Darfur to fulfil their commitments:

(a) To establish, in accordance with rule 28 of its provisional rules of procedure, a committee of the Council consisting of all the members of the Council (hereinafter "the Committee") to undertake the following tasks:

(i) To monitor implementation of the measures referred to in subparagraphs *(d)* and *(e)* of the present paragraph and paragraphs 7 and 8 of resolution 1556(2004), and paragraph 7 below;

(ii) To designate those individuals subject to the measures imposed by subparagraphs *(d)* and *(e)* of the present paragraph and to consider requests for exemptions in accordance with subparagraphs *(f)* and *(g)* of the present paragraph;

(iii) To establish such guidelines as may be necessary to facilitate the implementation of the measures imposed by subparagraphs *(d)* and *(e)* of the present paragraph;

(iv) To report at least every ninety days to the Council on its work;

(v) To consider requests from and, as appropriate, provide prior approval to the Government of the Sudan for the movement of military equipment and supplies into the Darfur region in accordance with paragraph 7 below;

(vi) To assess reports from the panel of experts established under subparagraph *(b)* of the present paragraph, and Member States, in particular those in the region, on specific steps they are taking to implement the measures imposed by subparagraphs *(d)* and *(e)* of the present paragraph and paragraph 7 below;

(vii) To encourage a dialogue between the Committee and interested Member States, in particular those in the region, including by inviting representatives of such States to meet with the Committee to discuss implementation of the measures;

(b) To request the Secretary-General, in consultation with the Committee, to appoint for a period of six months, within thirty days of adoption of the present resolution, a panel of experts comprised of four members and based in Addis Ababa to travel regularly to El-Fasher and other locations in the Sudan, and to operate under the direction of the Committee to undertake the following tasks:

(i) To assist the Committee in monitoring implementation of the measures in subparagraphs *(d)* and *(e)* of the present paragraph, paragraphs 7 and 8 of resolution 1556(2004), and paragraph 7 below, and to make recommendations to the Committee on actions the Council may want to consider;

(ii) To provide a midterm briefing on its work to the Committee and an interim report no later than ninety days after adoption of the present resolution, and a final report no later than thirty days prior to termination of its mandate to the Council through the Committee with its findings and recommendations; and

(iii) To coordinate its activities as appropriate with ongoing operations of the African Union Mission in the Sudan;

(c) That those individuals, as designated by the Committee established by subparagraph *(a)* of the present paragraph, based on the information provided by Member States, the Secretary-General, the United Nations High Commissioner for Human Rights or the Panel of Experts established under subparagraph *(b)* of the present paragraph, and other relevant sources, who impede the peace process, constitute a threat to stability in Darfur and the region, commit violations of international humanitarian or human rights law or other atrocities, violate the measures implemented by Member States in accordance with paragraphs 7 and 8 of resolution 1556(2004) and paragraph 7 below as implemented by a State, or are responsible for offensive military overflights described in paragraph 6 below, shall be subject to the measures identified in subparagraphs *(d)* and *(e)* of the present paragraph;

(d) That all States shall take the necessary measures to prevent entry into or transit through their territories of all persons as designated by the Committee pursuant to subparagraph *(c)* of the present paragraph, provided that nothing in the present subparagraph shall obligate a State to refuse entry into its territory to its own nationals;

(e) That all States shall freeze all funds, financial assets and economic resources that are on their territories on the date of adoption of the present resolution or at any time thereafter, that are owned or controlled, directly or indirectly, by the persons designated by the Committee pursuant to subparagraph *(c)* of the present paragraph, or that are held by entities owned or controlled, directly or indirectly, by such persons or by persons acting on their behalf or at their direction, and decides also that all States shall ensure that no funds, financial assets or economic resources are made available by their nationals or by any persons within their territories to or for the benefit of such persons or entities;

(f) That the measures imposed by subparagraph *(d)* of the present paragraph shall not apply where the Committee established by subparagraph *(a)* of the present paragraph determines on a case by case basis that such travel is justified on the grounds of humanitarian need, including religious obligation, or where the Committee concludes that an exemption would otherwise further the objectives of the Council's resolutions for the creation of peace and stability in the Sudan and the region;

(g) That the measures imposed by subparagraph *(e)* of the present paragraph do not apply to funds, other financial assets and economic resources:

(i) That have been determined by relevant States to be necessary for basic expenses, including payment for foodstuffs, rent or mortgage, medicines and medical treatment, taxes, insurance premiums and public utility charges or for payment of reasonable professional fees and reimbursement of incurred expenses associated with the provision of legal services, or fees or service charges, in accordance with national laws, for routine holding or maintenance of frozen funds, other financial assets and economic resources, after notification by the relevant States to the Committee of the intention to authorize, where appropriate, access to such funds, other financial assets and economic resources and in the absence of a negative decision by the Committee within two working days of such notification;

(ii) That have been determined by relevant States to be necessary for extraordinary expenses, provided that such determination has been notified by the relevant States to the Committee and has been approved by the Committee; or

(iii) That have been determined by relevant States to be the subject of a judicial, administrative or arbitral lien or judgment, in which case the funds or other financial assets and economic resources may be used to satisfy that lien or judgment provided that the lien or judgment was entered prior to the date of the present resolution, is not for the benefit of a person or entity designated by the Committee, and has been notified by the relevant States to the Committee;

4. *Decides also* that the measures referred to in subparagraphs 3 *(d)* and *(e)* above shall enter into force thirty days from the date of adoption of the present resolution, unless the Council determines before then that the parties to the conflict in Darfur have complied with all the commitments and demands referred to in paragraph 1 above and paragraph 6 below;

5. *Expresses its readiness* to consider the modification or termination of the measures under paragraph 3 above, on the recommendation of the Committee or at the end of a period of twelve months from the date of adoption of the present resolution, or earlier if the Council determines before then that the parties to the conflict in Darfur have complied with all the commitments and demands referred to in paragraph 1 above and paragraph 6 below;

6. *Demands* that the Government of the Sudan, in accordance with its commitments under the N'Djamena ceasefire agreement and the Abuja Security Protocol, immediately cease conducting offensive military flights in and over the Darfur region, and invites the African Union Ceasefire Commission to share pertinent information as appropriate in this regard with the Secretary-General, the Committee, or the Panel of Experts established under paragraph 3 *(b)* above;

7. *Reaffirms* the measures imposed by paragraphs 7 and 8 of resolution 1556(2004) and decides that these measures shall, immediately upon adoption of the present resolution, also apply to all the parties to the N'Djamena ceasefire agreement and any other belligerents in the states of Northern Darfur, Southern Darfur and Western Darfur; decides that these measures shall not apply to the supplies and related technical training and assistance listed in paragraph 9 of resolution 1556(2004); decides also that these measures shall not apply with respect to assistance and supplies provided in support of implementation of the Comprehensive Peace Agreement; decides further that these measures shall not apply to movements of military equipment and supplies into the Darfur region that are approved in advance by the Committee established under paragraph 3 *(a)* above upon a request by the Government of the Sudan; and invites the African Union Ceasefire Commission to share pertinent information as appropriate in this regard with the

Secretary-General, the Committee or the Panel of Experts established under paragraph 3 *(b)* above;

8. *Reiterates* that, in the event the parties fail to fulfil their commitments and demands as outlined in paragraphs 1 and 6 above, and the situation in Darfur continues to deteriorate, the Council will consider further measures as provided for in Article 41 of the Charter of the United Nations;

9. *Decides* to remain seized of the matter.

RECORDED VOTE ON RESOLUTION 1591:

In favour: Argentina, Benin, Brazil, Denmark, France, Greece, Japan, Philippines, Romania, United Kingdom, United Republic of Tanzania, United States.
Against: None.
Abstaining: Algeria, China, Russian Federation.

Algeria, in its explanation of vote, said that, while it supported the approach to send a strong message to the parties to respect their commitments, it had, with other delegations, made proposals to "rebalance" the text, which were in line with the position of the African Group. It had doubts concerning the relevance and usefulness of certain of the resolution's measures. Also, the resolution did not take into consideration the early signs of a trend towards both parties respecting the ceasefire. It regretted that efforts were not made to promote a consensus.

The Russian Federation said that it was unable to support the draft resolution because it was not convinced that the potential political and diplomatic measures to defuse the conflict in Darfur had been exhausted, especially at the beginning of the deployment of a UN peacekeeping operation in the south of the Sudan. It was important to give the Government of National Unity of the Sudan time to show itself in a positive light, including with regard to Darfur.

China said that it had serious reservations about the resolution. While Council resolution 1590(2005) of 24 March (see p. 305) authorizing the deployment of a peacekeeping operation in southern Sudan would help the Sudanese people achieve peace and stability, just maintaining the pressure without regard to the complexity of the Darfur crisis could end up further complicating the situation and would not help efforts to find a political solution. China had always taken a cautious approach to sanctions and had repeatedly stressed that the Council should exercise great caution with respect to "measures" that could make negotiations more difficult and had a negative impact on the peace process.

The United Republic of Tanzania regretted that the situation in Darfur compelled the adoption of the resolution, after months of waiting for the Abuja peace process to resume. That process remained stalled and there was no significant improvement on the ground with regard to the humanitarian situation. It appealed to all parties to respond to the Council's and the international

community's concerns by making a bold and decisive move towards peace in Darfur before the measures adopted became effective. The Council should review those measures as soon as the new Government was in place.

The Sudan said that, while it did not deny that the Council should address the situation in the Sudan and the events in Darfur, its unwise resolutions might make the situation worse. The Council talked about supporting the AU, but its resolution would complicate the situation both for the AU and on the ground. The sponsors of the draft resolution refused to show flexibility to reach a consensus, justified by reference to a resolution of the United States Congress, which, according to the Sudan, did not know the history and culture of the country and went against Africa's position.

The United States said that the resolution was adopted by 12 Council members, including two African States, and that the members of the United States Congress cared deeply about Darfur and many of them had gone there and had first-hand experience working with some of the NGOs in the area. The United States hoped that the resolution would contribute to an end to the violence in Darfur and to a successful resolution of the Abuja peace process.

Note by Security Council President. On 5 May [S/2005/297], the Council President informed that, following consultations among its members on 29 April and 4 May, the Council elected Mr. Adamantios Th. Vassilakis (Greece) as the Chairman of the Security Council Committee concerning the Sudan, established pursuant to resolution 1591(2005), for a period ending 31 December 2005, and two Vice-Chairmen from Argentina and the Philippines.

On 30 June [S/2005/428], the Secretary-General informed the Council President of the appointment of the four members to serve on the Panel of Experts to be established in accordance with paragraph 3 of Council resolution 1591(2005).

SECURITY COUNCIL ACTION (December)

On 21 December [meeting 5342], the Security Council unanimously adopted **resolution 1651 (2005)**. The draft [S/2005/812] was prepared in consultations among Council members.

The Security Council,

Recalling its previous resolutions concerning the situation in the Sudan, in particular resolutions 1556 (2004) of 30 July 2004 and 1591(2005) of 29 March 2005, and the statements by its President concerning the Sudan,

Stressing its firm commitment to the cause of peace throughout the Sudan, including through the African Union-led inter-Sudanese peace talks in Abuja ("Abuja Talks"), full implementation of the Comprehensive Peace Agreement, and an end to the violence and atrocities in Darfur,

Urging all parties to the Abuja Talks to reach without further delay an agreement that will establish a basis for peace, reconciliation, stability and justice in the Sudan,

Recalling the midterm briefing of 7 October 2005 by the Panel of Experts appointed by the Secretary-General pursuant to paragraph 3 *(b)* of resolution 1591 (2005), and anticipating the receipt of its final report,

Emphasizing the need to respect the provisions of the Charter of the United Nations concerning privileges and immunities, and the Convention on the Privileges and Immunities of the United Nations, as applicable to United Nations operations and persons engaged in such operations,

Reaffirming its commitment to the sovereignty, unity, independence and territorial integrity of the Sudan, and recalling the importance of the principles of good-neighbourliness, non-interference and cooperation in the relations among States in the region,

Determining that the situation in the Sudan continues to constitute a threat to international peace and security in the region,

Acting under Chapter VII of the Charter,

1. *Decides* to extend the mandate of the Panel of Experts appointed pursuant to resolution 1591(2005) until 29 March 2006, and requests the Secretary-General to take the necessary administrative measures;

2. *Requests* the Panel of Experts to report and make recommendations to the Security Council, through the Committee established pursuant to paragraph 3 *(a)* of resolution 1591(2005), prior to the termination of its mandate, on the implementation of the measures imposed by paragraphs 7 and 8 of resolution 1556(2004) and paragraphs 3, 6 and 7 of resolution 1591(2005);

3. *Decides* to remain actively seized of the matter.

Report of International Commission of Inquiry

On 31 January [S/2005/60], the Secretary-General transmitted the report of the five-member Commission of Inquiry, established pursuant to Security Council resolution 1564(2004) [YUN 2004, p. 245], on the violations of international humanitarian law and human rights law in Darfur.

The Commission, headed by Antonio Cassese (Italy), was mandated to investigate reports of violations of international humanitarian law and human rights law in Darfur by all parties; determine whether or not acts of genocide had occurred; and name the perpetrators with a view to ensuring that they were held accountable. The Commission, which visited the Sudan from 8 to 20 November 2004 and from 9 to 16 January 2005, held extensive meetings with representatives of the Government, the Governors of the Darfur states and other senior officials in the capital and at the provincial and local levels, internally displaced persons, victims and witnesses of violations, NGOs and UN representatives.

Based on its investigations, the Commission established that the Government of the Sudan and the Janjaweed were responsible for serious violations of international human rights and humanitarian law amounting to crimes under international law. In particular, Government forces and militias conducted indiscriminate attacks, including the killing of civilians, torture, enforced disappearances, destruction of villages, rape and other forms of sexual violence, pillaging and forced displacement, throughout Darfur. Those acts were conducted on a widespread and systematic basis and might amount to crimes against humanity.

Government officials stated that any attacks carried out by their armed forces in Darfur were for counter-insurgency purposes and conducted on the basis of military imperatives. However, the findings revealed that most attacks were deliberately and indiscriminately directed against civilians. While it did not find a systematic or a widespread pattern to those violations, it found credible evidence that rebel forces, namely, SLA members and JEM, also were responsible for serious violations of international human rights and humanitarian law which might amount to war crimes.

The Commission concluded that the Government of the Sudan had not pursued a policy of genocide. The crucial element of genocidal intent appeared to be missing, at least as far as the central Government authorities were concerned. The policy of attacking, killing and forcibly displacing members of some tribes did not evince a specific intent to annihilate, in whole or in part, a group distinguished on racial, ethnic, national or religious grounds. Rather, it seemed that those who planned and organized attacks on villages pursued the intent to drive the victims from their homes, primarily for purposes of counter-insurgency warfare. That conclusion should not be taken in any way as detracting from the gravity of the crimes perpetrated in that region. Those identified as possibly responsible for those violations consisted of individual perpetrators, including Government officials, members of militia forces, members of rebel groups, and certain foreign army officers acting in their personal capacity. Some Government officials, as well as militia forces, had also been named as possibly responsible for joint criminal enterprise to commit international crimes, and others of involvement in planning and/or ordering the commission of such crimes, or in aiding and abetting them. The Commission would list the names of those persons in a sealed file to be placed in the Secretary-General's custody, with the recommendation that it be handed over to the International Criminal Court (ICC). The evidentiary material collected would be handed over to the United Nations High Commissioner for Human Rights.

The Commission recommended that the Council immediately refer the Darfur situation to ICC, as the alleged crimes documented in Darfur met the thresholds of article 13(*b*) of the Rome Statute establishing the Court [YUN 1998, p. 1209]. The Sudanese justice system was unable and unwilling to address the situation in Darfur, which had been significantly weakened during the last decade. The measures taken so far by the Government to address the crisis had been both grossly inadequate and ineffective, which contributed to the climate of almost total impunity for human rights violations in Darfur.

It also recommended the establishment of a Compensation Commission to grant reparation to the victims, whether or not the perpetrators of such crimes had been identified. It urged the Sudanese Government to undertake a number of measures, including ending impunity for war crimes and crimes against humanity committed in Darfur; strengthening the independence and impartiality of the judiciary; empowering courts to address human rights violations; granting full and unimpeded access by the International Committee of the Red Cross (ICRC) and UN human rights monitors to all those detained in relation to the situation in Darfur; ensuring the protection of all victims and witnesses; enhancing the capacity of the Sudanese judiciary through training; respecting the rights of internally displaced persons and fully implementing the Guiding Principles on Internal Displacement; fully cooperating with relevant UN and AU human rights bodies and mechanisms; and creating a truth and reconciliation commission once peace was established in Darfur.

The Commission also recommended the reestablishment by the Commission on Human Rights of the mandate of the Special Rapporteur on human rights in the Sudan, and public and periodic reports on the human rights situation in Darfur by the High Commissioner for Human Rights.

Communications. On 10 February [S/2005/77], the Sudan, in its response to the Commission's report, said that it had grave reservations as to the Commission's methodology for preparing its report and reaching conclusions, particularly the definition of the "Janjaweed" phenomenon. It was concerned with the judicial standards of evidence. In addition, despite evidence to the contrary, the Commission nonetheless held the Government responsible for attacks perpetrated by armed groups outside of its control. The Government strongly objected to the Commission's recommendations that the Darfur issue be referred

to ICC. It said it doubted the accuracy of many of the Commission's findings and that its judicial system was competent to bring the perpetrators of human rights abuse and violations to justice.

On 18 February [S/2005/100], the Sudan complained about the non-circulation of the report of its National Commission of Inquiry (see p. 317) transmitted to the Council President on 23 January for circulation to Council members.

Security Council Consideration (February). The Security Council, on 16 February [meeting 5125], considered the report of the International Commission of Inquiry (see above). The Secretary-General told the Council that the call to urgent action in Darfur did not stop at the Commission's recommendation for referring the situation there to ICC, for the attacks on villages, the killing of civilians, rape, pillaging and forced displacement continued in Darfur. The international community, led by the Council, had to find a way to halt the killing and protect the vulnerable through a full range of options, including targeted sanctions, stronger peacekeeping efforts, new measures to protect civilians and increased pressure on both sides for a lasting political solution.

The United Nations High Commissioner for Human Rights, Louise Arbour, said the Commission's recommendations provided a blueprint for action. Their implementation would not only do justice for the victims of the massive crimes committed, but might actually contribute to reducing the exposure of thousands of prospective victims. Any new initiative proposed by the Government of the Sudan to address those crimes could not be supported in the light of the Commission's conclusions, especially the extent of involvement of Government officials.

Further communication (March). On 22 March [S/2005/196], Switzerland urged Council members to refer the situation in Darfur to ICC, as recommended by the International Commission of Inquiry on Darfur.

Referral of Darfur situation to ICC

SECURITY COUNCIL ACTION

On 31 March [meeting 5158], the Security Council adopted resolution **1593(2005)** by vote (11-0-4). The draft [S/2005/218] was prepared in consultations among Council members.

The Security Council,

Taking note of the report of the International Commission of Inquiry for Darfur on violations of international humanitarian law and human rights law in Darfur,

Recalling article 16 of the Rome Statute of the International Criminal Court, under which no investigation or prosecution may be commenced or proceeded with by the International Criminal Court for a period of twelve months after a Security Council request to that effect,

Also recalling articles 75 and 79 of the Rome Statute, and encouraging States to contribute to the International Criminal Court's Trust Fund for Victims,

Taking note of the existence of agreements referred to in article 98, paragraph 2, of the Rome Statute,

Determining that the situation in the Sudan continues to constitute a threat to international peace and security,

Acting under Chapter VII of the Charter of the United Nations,

1. *Decides* to refer the situation in Darfur since 1 July 2002 to the Prosecutor of the International Criminal Court;

2. *Decides also* that the Government of the Sudan and all other parties to the conflict in Darfur shall cooperate fully with and provide any necessary assistance to the International Criminal Court and the Prosecutor pursuant to the present resolution and, while recognizing that States not party to the Rome Statute of the Court have no obligation under the Statute, urges all States and concerned regional and other international organizations to cooperate fully;

3. *Invites* the Court and the African Union to discuss practical arrangements that will facilitate the work of the Prosecutor and of the Court, including the possibility of conducting proceedings in the region, which would contribute to regional efforts in the fight against impunity;

4. *Encourages* the Court, as appropriate and in accordance with the Rome Statute, to support international cooperation with domestic efforts to promote the rule of law, protect human rights and combat impunity in Darfur;

5. *Emphasizes* the need to promote healing and reconciliation, and encourages in this respect the creation of institutions, involving all sectors of Sudanese society, such as truth and/or reconciliation commissions, in order to complement judicial processes and thereby reinforce the efforts to restore long-lasting peace, with African Union and international support as necessary;

6. *Decides* that nationals, current or former officials or personnel from a contributing State outside the Sudan which is not a party to the Rome Statute shall be subject to the exclusive jurisdiction of that contributing State for all alleged acts or omissions arising out of or related to operations in the Sudan established or authorized by the Security Council or the African Union, unless such exclusive jurisdiction has been expressly waived by that contributing State;

7. *Recognizes* that none of the expenses incurred in connection with the referral, including expenses related to investigations or prosecutions in connection with that referral, shall be borne by the United Nations and that such costs shall be borne by the parties to the Rome Statute and those States that wish to contribute voluntarily;

8. *Invites* the Prosecutor to address the Council within three months of the date of adoption of the present resolution and every six months thereafter on actions taken pursuant to the present resolution;

9. *Decides* to remain seized of the matter.

RECORDED VOTE ON RESOLUTION 1593:

In favour: Argentina, Benin, Denmark, France, Greece, Japan, Philippines, Romania, Russian Federation, United Kingdom, United Republic of Tanzania.

Against: None.

Abstaining: Algeria, Brazil, China, United States.

The United States, in an explanation of vote, said that it strongly supported the bringing to justice of those responsible for the crimes and atrocities that had occurred in Darfur and ending the climate of impunity there, but could not agree to referring the Darfur situation to ICC because of its continuing fundamental objection to the view that ICC should exercise jurisdiction over the nationals, including government officials, of States not party to the Rome Statute. It had not dropped, and indeed continued to maintain its long-standing objection and concerns regarding ICC.

Algeria said that the process of fighting impunity was a crucial element for peace and stability and should aim at restoring harmonious relations between the populations of Darfur and serve the cause of peace. Algeria believed that the AU was best placed to take charge of that delicate and sensitive undertaking of satisfying the requirements for peace without sacrificing the requirements for justice. It regretted that the Council had declined to consider Nigerian President Obasanjo's proposal for reconciling those two fundamental requirements.

China stated that it would prefer to see perpetrators of gross violations of human rights stand trial in the Sudanese judicial system, which had recently taken legal action against a number of individuals involved. China was not a party to the Rome Statute and was not in favour of referring the question of Darfur to ICC without the consent of the Sudanese Government since that would only complicate efforts to secure an early settlement of the Darfur issue and have unforeseeable consequences for the north-south peace process.

The United Kingdom welcomed the Council's decision, which it considered the most efficient and effective means available to deal with impunity and to ensure justice for the people of Darfur.

Brazil said that, while it supported referring the Darfur situation to ICC, the number of substantial issues raised would not contribute to the strengthening of ICC. Brazil had consistently rejected initiatives to extend exemptions of certain categories of individuals from ICC jurisdiction and it maintained its position to prevent efforts that might dismantle the achievements reached in international justice.

Establishment of special criminal court on Darfur

On 18 June [S/2005/403], the Sudan, in a press release of the same date, informed the Security Council President that, on 7 June, the Chief Justice had issued a decree establishing the Special Criminal Court on the Events in Darfur. The Chief Justice, with other judges and the Deputy Minister of Justice, had visited the three Darfur states the previous week to assess the performance of the judiciary and the judicial system and to address reports of attacks against persons, property and honour in those states. He had therefore decided to establish the Court to examine those reports and any report transmitted to the investigation committees, whose establishment had been recommended by Sudan's Commission of Inquiry to Investigate Alleged Human Rights Violations Committed by Armed Groups in the Darfur States (see p. 317).

The Court would be headed by an experienced Supreme Court judge and composed of judges of the Court of Appeal, including a woman judge, given the nature of some of the reports. Appeals would be heard by a special court of appeal to be set up by the Chief Justice.

Further developments in Darfur

Report of Secretary-General on Darfur (April). The Secretary-General, in an April report on Darfur [S/2005/240], said that the positive trends that were evident in February stalled, as a result of violent confrontations between the rebel movements and Government forces, who were operating jointly with armed tribal militia. Attacks and threats against humanitarian workers and supplies remained a major concern, as well as attacks on the AMIS. SLM/A and JEM fought with the Government army and Janjaweed on at least seven occasions, the most recent on 26 March, when Government troops and tribal militias attacked SLM/A positions in western Darfur. The third, and least active armed rebel group in Darfur, the National Movement for Reform and Development (NMRD), also fought Government forces in that region. The fighting resulted in an undetermined number of casualties, including civilians.

The increased intensity of the fighting in West Darfur raised concerns that the Government was still trying to control the Jebel Moon and Jebel Marra regions, despite the human cost of such a campaign into the heart of rebel territory. Reports continued to be received of Janjaweed and SLM/A attacks on civilians. At the same time, security in the camps for internally displaced persons remained unstable. Kalma camp saw continued harassment and intimidation, as well as random shootings by the police. The gravity of

sexual and gender-based violence in Darfur was highlighted in a report released on 8 May by the NGO, Médecins sans frontières, which said it had treated some 500 rape victims between October 2004 and February 2005. On 6 March, the establishment of a committee to combat sexual violence was announced by a Governor's decree. The United Nations had raised questions about the committee's mandate, but agreed to participate in its work as an observer to bring concerns to the committee's attention and advise on improving response, should the mandate be amended.

Meanwhile, the AU continued its efforts with the parties to the Darfur conflict in search of a framework for a political settlement. A draft framework agreement prepared by the mediation team was being reviewed by the parties. The Special Representative held talks with them, including the rebel movements, on assisting the AU peace process. Earlier, he had travelled to Asmara to meet with the leadership of Eritrea, SLM/A and JEM. That meeting revealed a strong consensus that the Abuja peace process remained a primary forum for negotiations and participants repeated their stated position that the judicial process called for by the International Commission of Inquiry (see p. 324) should move forward in advance or in step with the political negotiations. On 27 March, the Special Representative met with the Sudan's First Vice-President to discuss the Asmara meetings and the peace process generally. The Secretary-General discussed with the AU Commission Chairman, Alpha Oumar Konaré, steps to strengthen AMIS-UNMIS cooperation.

Report of Secretary-General (May). On 10 May [S/2005/305], the Secretary-General reported that during April, troop movements and the illegal occupation of new positions increased, as did harassment, burning of unoccupied villages, kidnapping, banditry, including carjacking, armed robbery and theft of livestock, attacks on civilians and rape by militia. Reports also suggested that the Government had tried to restrain its Popular Defence Forces militia and prevent criminal acts by issuing warnings and arresting perpetrators. Those efforts were inadequate, however, judging by the widespread reports of abuse by those groups in much of the non-rebel-held areas of Darfur.

Most of the militia activities involved small bands targeting civilians and internally displaced persons. However, on 7 April, a militia of the Missiriya tribe carried out the most serious attack since the sacking of Hamada in January. A militia under the command of Nasir Al-Tijani Adel Kaadir carried out a day-long raid of Khor

Abeche in southern Darfur in retaliation for an earlier incident in which 10 members of the Missiriya people were killed and cattle stolen by SLA elements. In a joint statement, the AU and the United Nations determined that, pursuant to resolution 1591(2005), the name of Nasir Al-Tijani Adel Kaadir and his identified collaborators would be passed on to the relevant sanctions committee. Prior to the attacks, approximately 7,000 displaced persons were registered in Khor Abeche, a town with a population of about 3,000. A joint UN/AU assessment found the village had been substantially burned and looted and practically all of the population had fled. The Wali of South Darfur established a committee to investigate the attack and announce its findings within 15 days.

SLA and JEM carried out attacks on police and militia in April and continued to take commercial, private and NGO vehicles at gunpoint to be converted into battlefield platforms, on a scale that suggested that those acts were approved by their leadership.

Enhancing the AU Mission in the Sudan

AU Mission in the Sudan. In May [S/2005/285], the Secretary-General submitted, pursuant to Security Council resolution 1590(2005), a report on UN assistance to AMIS. He said that, in response to that resolution, he met with the AU Commission Chairperson on 28 February, and they agreed to dispatch a mission to Darfur to assess the security situation and AMIS deployment, consider requirements for enhancing peace support in Darfur, and explore UNMIS options for reinforcing AMIS, in particular in the areas of logistical support and technical assistance.

The mission (10-22 March and 1-4 May), led by the AU, and including the United Nations, the EU and the United States, assessed that since AMIS had been effective in the areas where it was deployed, it needed to be strengthened. That was to take place in two phases: phase I would allow AMIS to reach its full operational capability within its authorized strength of 3,320, by May; and phase II, involving deployments from June to August, would expand AMIS personnel to 7,447, including 5,887 military personnel and 1,560 police, plus civilian staff. That phase would entail improved compliance with the N'Djamena Humanitarian Ceasefire Agreement and the Abuja humanitarian and security protocols, providing a secure environment for internally displaced persons in and around camps and those not yet displaced to permit humanitarian access.

A phase III, involving a complex, multidimensional operation of more than 12,000 military and police personnel, was also envisaged to provide a secure environment throughout Darfur to permit the return of displaced persons. A decision on that phase would be made in September.

On 28 April, the AU Peace and Security Council, in a communiqué on the enhancement of AMIS, decided to increase its strength to 6,171 military personnel, with an appropriate civilian component, including up to 1,560 civilian police. It appealed to all AU partners to continue providing support to meet the requirements for the strengthening and sustainment of AMIS. At the Secretary-General's request, his Special Adviser, Lakhdar Brahimi, in a meeting with the AU Commission Chairperson, following the AU Peace and Security Council meeting, agreed that the two organizations should discuss ways in which the United Nations could assist with military and logistics planning, in appealing for funding for AMIS expansion, and in organizing and co-hosting a pledging conference to mobilize resources for that purpose.

The Secretary-General said that, while the assistance UNMIS could provide at that stage was limited, because of its focus on implementing the Comprehensive Peace Agreement, the United Nations and UNMIS could: assist in identifying qualified police personnel in support of completing phase I; assist the AU to develop a detailed operational plan for AMIS expansion; provide technical advice in logistics, planning and management; and provide training support for AU personnel in selecting police personnel for phase II and in convening troop contributor, and pledging conferences.

The Secretary-General observed that AMIS had been a groundbreaking initiative for the AU and its supporters within the international community. The Mission had accomplished a remarkable amount in a very short time, despite significant constraints. It was critical for all concerned to do their part. The Secretary-General recommended that AU States members identify personnel to join AMIS, the AU Commission strengthen planning and management capacity in order to support an expanded mission, and partners provide the AU with the means to carry out a costly and challenging task.

SECURITY COUNCIL ACTION

On 12 May [meeting 5177], following consultations among Security Council members, the President made statement **S/PRST/2005/18** on behalf of the Council:

> The Security Council welcomes the report of the Secretary-General of 3 May 2005 on assistance by the United Nations Mission in the Sudan to the African Union Mission in the Sudan and the proposals

therein on support the United Nations could make available to the African Union Mission.

The Council applauds the vital leadership role the African Union is playing in Darfur and the work of the African Union Mission on the ground. The Council supports the findings of the joint assessment mission, led by the African Union from 10 to 22 March 2005, which included the United Nations and other partners. The Council also supports the subsequent decision taken by the Peace and Security Council of the African Union on 28 April 2005 to expand its mission in Darfur to 7,731 personnel by the end of September 2005.

The Council welcomes the ongoing deployment of the United Nations Mission in the Sudan and looks forward to close coordination and cooperation between the Mission and the African Union Mission in the Sudan. In this context, the Council recalls its request in resolution 1590(2005) for the United Nations Mission in the Sudan to closely and continuously liaise and coordinate, at all levels, with the African Union Mission in the Sudan with a view towards expeditiously reinforcing the effort to foster peace in Darfur, especially with regard to the Abuja peace process and the African Union Mission in the Sudan.

The Council welcomes the role played by the African Union's partners in support of the African Union Mission in the Sudan and underlines the active role played by the European Union and by other bilateral donors.

The Council emphasizes the importance of increased coordinated international assistance for the African Union effort in Darfur and emphasises the readiness of the United Nations to continue playing a key role. In this context, the Council welcomes the second joint assessment mission from 1 to 4 May 2005, which included representatives from the African Union, the United Nations and other partners. The Council looks forward to continuing contacts in order to facilitate provision of assistance as requested by the African Union. The Council welcomes, in this regard, the effort and intention of the Secretary-General to consult closely with the African Union on the scope and nature of possible United Nations support to the African Union Mission in the Sudan.

Developments in Darfur between May and June

Report of Secretary-General on Darfur (May). On 10 May [S/2005/305], the Secretary-General said that, while there had been comparatively few systematic attacks in April, troop movements and illegal occupation of new positions increased, as had harassment, burning of unoccupied villages, kidnapping, banditry, attacks on civilians and rape by the militia. The border area of western Darfur saw an elevated level of military activity due to the movement of armed groups across the border with Chad. The non-fatal shooting of a Chadian consul en route from the border to Geneina, on 16 April, added to the tensions.

As to the Darfur political process, the AU focused its efforts on garnering the support of the parties for its proposed draft framework protocol for the resolution of conflict in Darfur. An AU negotiating team travelled to Khartoum to discuss the draft protocol with Government officials, including the Vice-President. It also contacted representatives of the armed movements. However, because of a lack of confidence between them, the parties refrained from taking a clear position on the proposed draft framework protocol.

Meanwhile, following the adoption of Security Council resolutions 1591(2005) and 1593(2005), tension in the Darfur states and Khartoum increased, with the risks of hostile action against the UN and other elements of the international presence in Darfur. The Secretary-General urged the Government to make clear its acceptance of all recent resolutions relating to the Sudan and Darfur, and to ensure that a cooperative policy was reflected at all levels.

Report of Secretary-General (June). The Secretary-General visited Darfur in May, where he found that the security situation had improved and the overall violence against civilians had dropped in comparison to the 2004 levels. According to his June report [S/2005/378], the trend was, however, not entirely positive, as increased fighting was reported between the Government and SLM/A forces. The Government forces were on the defensive, in most cases, as rebel movements conducted small-scale attacks against Government convoys or small units of army or police personnel.

Meanwhile, the Jebel Marra area had become inaccessible to relief operations, as insecurity and the rains made the road to most localities in rebel-held areas unsafe. In northern Darfur, SLA ambushed several convoys and vehicles engaged in humanitarian work along the Kabkabiya-El-Fasher-road, while in southern Darfur, insecurity and banditry on the Ed Daein-Nyala road seriously hampered access for humanitarian relief operations.

The AU announced that the next round of the Darfur peace talks was to resume in Abuja, Nigeria, on 10 June and the appointment of Salim A. Salim as its Special Envoy for the Inter-Sudanese Peace Talks on Darfur. The Sudanese leaders had assured the Secretary-General during his visit to Darfur that the Naivasha Agreement [YUN 2004, p. 236] would serve as the model and framework for an agreement in Darfur, with arrangements for power and wealth-sharing, a land commission and a reconciliation process. He urged the Government to commence an effective programme of disarmament and demobilization of the tribal militias that continued to terrorize the civilian population of Darfur.

Joint Implementation Mechanism missions to Darfur

The Joint Implementation Mechanism, established to oversee implementation of the terms of the 3 July 2004 communiqué [YUN 2004, p. 239] signed by the United Nations and the Government of the Sudan, undertook three missions to Darfur (western Darfur (15-16 June) and northern and southern Darfur (22-23 June)) to evaluate their compliance with it. The Mechanism's report, annexed to the Secretary-General's July report on Darfur [S/2005/467], examined humanitarian issues, human rights, security and political issues.

The missions found that the overall situation in Darfur had improved considerably since the signing of the joint communiqué in 2004, with progress having been achieved in all areas. However, the remaining obstacles had to be acknowledged and addressed. Substantial gaps in the response of humanitarian assistance still persisted, despite the increase in humanitarian assistance. The number of conflict-affected people in Darfur had risen from 1,090,000 to more than 2,730,000, due in part to the return of internally displaced persons to areas closer to their homes because of localized improvements in security. Assistance also had to be widened to reach affected groups outside the camps. The easing of restrictions on humanitarian operations had resulted in a significant increase in humanitarian presence and delivery, but humanitarian workers still faced difficulties in visa processing, and reports continued to be made of harassment, arbitrary arrests and restrictions on their movement. The provision of humanitarian assistance to internally displaced person in some camps was hampered also by the resistance of local camp leaders to the head count necessary for registration.

Although the Government had taken a number of positive steps in the area of human rights, including cooperation with the international human rights officers that had been deployed, and established a National Judicial Committee to investigate human rights violations in Darfur and a Special Criminal Court for Darfur Crimes, those instruments had not yet contributed to the establishment of accountability for human rights and the ending of impunity.

While the security situation had improved, especially in the camps, it remained volatile and unpredictable. The reported presence of militias around the camps highlighted the need to improve the security environment and not just provide safe havens to which the civilian population

could be confined. With respect to disarmament, while some steps had been taken in that regard, the missions found limited indications of a systematic and sustained effort by the authorities to address the disarmament of the Janjaweed and other armed groups.

The missions concluded that, despite the progress, efforts were needed to end the harassment of aid workers in southern Darfur and ensure that the policies adopted at the national and state levels were implemented. More needed to be done to address impunity and disarmament. Both the civilian police and AMIS troops received strong support from the displaced population, as their limited deployment had helped restore confidence. While recognizing that protecting the population remained the responsibility of the local authorities, cooperation with AMIS would help improve the security situation and offer better protection for internally displaced persons.

Further political and security developments in Darfur

Reports of Secretary-General (August/October). The fifth round of the AU-led Abuja talks aimed at reaching a political agreement between the Government and the two armed movements opened on 10 June, the Secretary-General stated in his July report [S/2005/467]. On 5 July, the three parties agreed on the Declaration of Principles for the Resolution of the Sudanese Conflict in Darfur, which contained important provisions regarding the shape of future negotiations on matters such as unity, religion, power-sharing, wealth-sharing, security arrangements and land use and ownership. The Declaration of Principles was favourably received in Darfur, the Secretary-General said in his August report on Darfur [S/2005/523]. The third armed movement in Darfur, NMRD, had been quoted as agreeing to abide by the Declaration of Principles when it met the Government in El-Fasher on 19 July. Meanwhile, the Darfur Forum, a broad-based unaffiliated Sudanese civil society organization, in a meeting with the Special Representative in July, argued that the armed movements did not represent all the people of Darfur and sought participation in talks with the Government. The Declaration of Principles provided for the start of comprehensive inter-Darfur dialogue following the Abuja talks to allow the concerns, beyond those of the parties, such as the non-fighting groups and civil society, to be addressed. The Special Representative and his staff were already discussing with such parties the conditions under which such a dialogue would lead to a sustainable peace.

The AU mediator intended to contact the partners in the run-up to the next round of Abuja talks scheduled to start on 24 August to discuss the way forward. At the same time, UNMIS was exploring ways to further support the AU, substantively and technically, through the provision of experts and logistical support for participants attending the talks. Although internal divisions within SLM/A posed a challenge to the next round of talks, the signing of an agreement between SLM/A and JEM in Tripoli, Libyan Arab Jamahiriya, on 18 July, would in some measure help to unify the rebels' positions on key issues. However, renewed fighting between the Government of the Sudan and SLM/A on 23 July threatened to complicate further the next round of talks.

The Special Criminal Court for the events in Darfur began proceedings in August, with four cases before it dealing with rape, armed robbery, illegal possession of firearms and unlawful killing of persons in custody. Two of the cases involved charges brought against members of the Government armed forces and military intelligence. However, none of the cases addressed the major violations of human rights and international humanitarian law, nor the criminal responsibility of senior officials. The Secretary-General expressed concern also that the Special Court had no special procedures in place for protecting minors.

As at 1 July, the number of people needing humanitarian assistance had risen to 3.2 million. Flooding, due to heavy rains, prompted the relocation of internally displaced persons in some camps and emergency intervention to safeguard minimum sanitary conditions in all three Darfur states, and hindered road access to various parts of the region. At a time when humanitarian assistance had to rely increasingly on air operations, funding gaps risked constraining the delivery of that assistance. As to security in the camps, the registration process was violently disrupted on 8 July in seven of the eight camps around Geneina. Violent attacks took place again on 16 July during food distribution in the Mornei camp, with exchanges of fire between armed elements and Government police. On both occasions, there was strong evidence of incitement by sheikhs within the camps, whose manipulation of the ration-card system was threatened by the registration process.

Meanwhile, AMIS continued to take the lead in international efforts to address security concerns in Darfur. The Secretary-General urged major AU partners to fill the funding gap for AMIS and encouraged the AU Commission to establish clear priorities within its budget so that critical needs could be addressed.

Reports of Secretary-General (September/October). In mid-August, the Special Representative resumed his visit to Darfur to continue contacts with SLM/A leaders on the Darfur peace negotiations and to discuss with them the security problems facing humanitarian assistance convoys. During an earlier trip to Darfur, the Special Representative met SLM/A Secretary-General Minni Minawi and several field commanders to discuss some of the problems facing SLM/A. Mr. Minawi requested UN financial, logistical and technical assistance in organizing a conference of the movement's military and political leadership to clarify its structure. While the Special Representative did not rule out the possibility of such assistance, he emphasized the need for the Abuja negotiations to resume on schedule. Elements of SLM/A sympathetic to Mr. Minawi called for a delay in the Abuja talks in order to convene that conference. While that conference did not take place, it would be important for SLM/A to adopt a unified position for the negotiations, the Secretary-General noted in his September report [S/2005/592].

The sixth round of Inter-Sudanese Peace Talks on Darfur resumed in Abuja on 15 September. The talks opened with technical workshops on power-sharing, wealth-sharing and security (15-21 September) the Secretary-General reported in October [S/2005/650]. At the AU's request, the United Nations provided air transportation to the talks for some JEM and SLM/A delegates and a group of SLA commanders. Nevertheless, the talks opened with uncertainty regarding the cohesion of the SLM/A delegation and the degree to which SLM/A's Secretary-General Minawi's faction was participating.

The workshops and the talks were negatively affected by reports of a Government attack on SLM/A positions in Jebel Marra and near El-Fasher and violence in Shaeria on 19 September (see below). Nonetheless, at the urging of the AU mediator and international partners, all the parties continued to attend the workshops until their conclusion. Negotiations did not begin until the end of September. Internal division within SLM paralysed the talks for one week, during which discussions were limited to procedural matters. Neither SLM faction seemed willing to negotiate substance, despite urgent appeals by the AU mediator and representatives of the international community.

In September, the Secretary-General also reported an alarming deterioration in the security situation in all three Darfur states. The frequency and intensity of the violence committed by the Sudanese Armed Forces and the Popular Defence Forces, Government-aligned tribal militias and the armed movements, including in particular SLM/A, reached levels unseen since January. In northern Darfur, tribal militia struck villages in a number of locations, including in Shangil Tobayi area, Um Maharek and south of Tawilla town. In southern Darfur, one of the more devastating clashes occurred on 19 September when SLM/A attacked Sudanese Armed Forces positions in and around the village of Shaeria, forcing many civilians to seek shelter outside the town. The Sudanese Armed Forces suffered dozens of casualties and SLM/A made off with quantities of arms, munitions, fuel and other supplies. On 29 September, Government police and Sudanese Armed Forces units entered Tawilla town and the adjacent Dali IDP camp, firing at civilians indiscriminately and without provocation.

The security situation in western Darfur worsened dramatically as well. Banditry and hijacking along roads from Geneina reached such dire levels that all roads leading south, west and east from the town were "off-limits" for UN staff and critical movements could proceed only with authorized armed escorts. Indications showed that local authorities were increasingly unwilling or incapable of controlling the tribal militia and armed gangs operating in the area. The police were often challenged by armed gangs or militia members and did not appear to have the capacity to enforce laws.

While banditry and lawlessness were the primary cause of insecurity in western Darfur, there was also politically motivated violence, with the largest and deadliest of those incidents being the unprovoked attack by tribal militia on the Aro Sharow camp and the villages of Gosmino and Ardja in the Kulbus area of western Darfur near the border with Chad on 28 September. The latest information available indicated that 35 internally displaced persons were killed and 10 wounded in the violence, and over 4,000 forced to flee. The volatile security situation during September also took a toll on international personnel working in Darfur.

Evidence showed that Government forces triggered some of the incidents, and there were clear indications that, in many cases, the tribal militia operated with enabling support from the Government. Those attacks were confirmed by the Head of AMIS, Baba Gana Kingibe, who announced in a press conference on 1 October that the Sudanese Armed Forces had conducted "coordinated offensive operations" with tribal militia on four occasions since 18 September. That assessment was corroborated by evidence

gathered from survivors of the militia attacks on villages.

Communications. The EU Presidency, in a 23 September statement [S/2005/630], expressed concern about reports of serious clashes in Darfur, including most recently on the eastern slopes of the Jebel Marra and in Shaeria, South Darfur. It called on all belligerents to reign in their fighters and to ensure their forces respected international law, as well as the N'Djamena Ceasefire Agreement and the Abuja protocols.

The AU Peace and Security Council, in a 10 October communiqué [S/2005/643], expressed concern over the deteriorating security situation throughout Darfur since August. It condemned the killing and abduction of AMIS soldiers and the attacks by SLM/A in Turba on 23 August and on the Government's military camp in Shaeria on 19 September, and Janjaweed attacks on Tawilla town and its camps on 29 September. The Council requested the AU Commission to examine ways to strengthen the mechanisms for effective compliance by the Sudanese parties with all agreements, as well as the decisions of the Ceasefire Commission and the Joint Commission and to submit proposals on the best way forward. It supported the Chairperson's decision to send a high-level military team to Darfur to assess the situation and make recommendations on how to prevent a recurrence of such incidents. It also decided to bring the situation in Darfur to the attention of the UN Security Council.

On 20 October [S/2005/676], the AU Peace and Security Council extended AMIS mandate for three months until 20 January 2006, and appealed to AU member States and partners to provide financial and logistical support to enable it to execute its mandate.

SECURITY COUNCIL ACTION

On 13 October [meeting 5277], following consultations among Security Council members, the President made statement **S/PRST/2005/48** on behalf of the Council:

The Security Council expresses its grave concern at recent reports of an upsurge of violence in Darfur by all sides and insists that all parties strictly abide by the demands and commitments made in the N'djamena ceasefire agreement of 8 April 2004, the resolutions of the Council and the Abuja Protocols. The Council strongly condemns the attack of 8 October 2005 reportedly by the Sudan Liberation Movement/Army on personnel of the African Union Mission in the Sudan in Darfur, which killed four Nigerian peacekeepers and two civilian contractors and wounded three others near Menawasha, and the attack of 9 October 2005 reportedly by the Justice and Equality Movement in Tine in Northern Darfur, which resulted in the ambush and detention of approximately 35 Mission personnel. The Council extends its deepest condolences to the families of those killed.

The Council also condemns the attack of 25 September 2005 in Modaina, Chad, by armed groups coming from the Sudan, which killed 75 people, the majority of them civilians. The Council joins with the African Union in expressing particular outrage at the attack of 19 September 2005 by Darfur rebels against the town of Sheiara, the attack by Janjaweed militias on the camp for displaced persons at Aro Sharow on 28 September 2005, during which 29 people were killed and many more wounded, and the attack on the village of Tawilla by Sudanese government forces on 29 September 2005.

The Council expresses its deep concern at the humanitarian impact that these developments cause and at the restrictions imposed on humanitarian operations in Darfur. The Council insists that restrictions end immediately and strongly urges all parties to ensure unhindered humanitarian access in Darfur.

The Council also expresses its concern that in the report of the Secretary-General of 19 September 2005 it was stated that there had been 'no visible effort by the Government [of the Sudan] to disarm the militia or hold them to account in accordance with past agreements and Security Council resolutions [...]. The SLM/A [Sudan Liberation Movement/Army] and the Justice and Equality Movement (JEM) are also failing to abide by the commitments made under past agreements and are doing far too little to control their men under arms.' The Council recalls the obligation undertaken by the Government of the Sudan to disarm and control militias. It demands that the Sudan Liberation Movement/Army, the Justice and Equality Movement and the Government of the Sudan immediately cease violence, comply with the N'djamena ceasefire agreement, end impediments to the peace process and cooperate fully with the African Union Mission in the Sudan. The Council again emphasizes the need to bring to justice those who perpetrate violence.

The Council recalls the provisions of its resolution 1591(2005) concerning the Sudan. It urges the African Union to share the results of its investigations into recent attacks with the Council for possible referral to the Sudan sanctions committee in order to assist in the implementation of the provisions of the relevant Council resolutions.

The Council expresses its unequivocal support for the African Union Mission in the Sudan, and recalls that the Government of the Sudan and Darfur rebel movements have to take the necessary steps to facilitate the deployment and effectiveness of the Mission.

The Council remains firmly committed to the cause of peace in all of the Sudan, including through the Abuja talks and through full implementation of the Comprehensive Peace Agreement. It encourages the Government of National Unity and the Darfur rebels to engage in the search for a solution to the Darfur conflict. It urges all parties to make rapid progress at the Abuja talks to conclude a peace agreement without further delay.

Reports of Secretary-General (November/ December). In his November report [S/2005/719], the Secretary-General stated that the sixth round of the inter-Sudanese peace talks on Darfur held in Abuja ended on 20 October following weeks of difficult negotiations among the Government, SLM/A and JEM. The parties adopted a joint communiqué, in which they expressed their commitment "to make the next round", due to start on 21 November, "a decisive one". The start of the actual negotiations was delayed due to the dispute over the legitimacy of SLM/A representatives to the talks. Both SLM/A Chairman Wahid and Secretary-General Minawi had sent separate lists of delegates to the talks. A group of 10 field commanders, representing different tribal groups, and 3 representatives from Mr. Minawi's office in Asmara, arrived in Abuja on 25 September, stressing the "neutrality" of their group in the ongoing disagreement between the SLM/A Chairman and Secretary-General and promising to promote unity within the movement. Despite week-long consultations, SLM/A leadership failed to find a compromise. On 29 October, an SLM reconciliation conference was convened in northern Darfur, which was attended by Mr. Minawi but not by Mr. Wahid, who sent a delegation.

Despite the SLM split, the talks started on 3 October, first with the power-sharing commission and later on the wealth-sharing and the security commission. Although negotiations on the three main elements of the talks should have been conducted in parallel, SLM/A and JEM, which formed a united delegation throughout the talks, cited a lack of capacity within the movements to discuss some of them, in particular wealth-sharing. Nevertheless, before the adjournment of the talks, the agenda on wealth-sharing was adopted. Some progress was made on three of nine items on the power-sharing agenda: general principles on power-sharing; human rights and fundamental freedoms; and the criteria and guidelines for power-sharing. Discussions began on the fourth agenda item, the federal system and all levels of Government, although the positions of the two sides still differed considerably. In particular, there were lingering concerns that the movements might continue to withhold their recognition of either the Comprehensive Peace Agreement or the Interim National Constitution on the grounds that they were not party to their negotiation.

The ninth meeting of the Joint Commission, established by the 2004 N'Djamena Protocol, was held in the Chadian capital on 13 and 14 October, the first since February 2005. The meeting took place in parallel to the Abuja talks, and both meetings influenced each other positively. During the meeting, the Government and SLM/A were criticized for significant ceasefire violations and the militia groups for attacks on civilians. The Joint Commission noted that the Government had made no progress in disarming the Janjaweed and that the movements had failed to identify their positions and separate their forces on the ground. It urged the parties to give written indications of their respective positions to the Ceasefire Commission; reiterated its call for the immediate disarmament of the Janjaweed, and urged the Government to allow the entry into Darfur of 105 armoured personnel carriers made available by Canada to AMIS. The Government signalled its readiness to allow only 35 armoured personnel carriers into the region but indicated a willingness to consider the entry of the remaining 70. Finally, it was agreed that the Joint Commission would meet on a regular basis, possibly monthly.

The Secretary-General observed that, to ensure the success of the peace process, continued coordination among international partners was required, especially for those activities that would have to be carried out after a successful conclusion of the peace talks. They included: bridging the relief-development gap; assisting voluntary returns; ceasefire monitoring; disarmament, demobilization and reintegration; policing; and rule of law and human rights monitoring. Moreover, the Darfur-Darfur dialogue and reconciliation were core issues that should be addressed both during and after the talks if the peace settlement was to be truly inclusive. International community support for a Darfur peace agreement would also depend on several factors, including its consistency with the Comprehensive Peace Agreement and the Interim National Constitution and respect for the constitutional arrangements worked out for southern Sudan; its potential application to other conflict areas in the country, such as eastern Sudan; and the inclusion of measures to effectively enforce a permanent ceasefire in Darfur.

In his December report [S/2005/825], the Secretary-General informed that, following the adjournment of the sixth round of the inter-Sudanese peace talks on Darfur, the Minawi element of the SLM/A leadership called a conference in Haskanita, in eastern Darfur, on 29 October. Although the conference, was well attended, the SLM/A Chairman Abdul Wahid Al-Nur and the majority of his supporters refused to participate. The Haskanita conference culminated in the election of Minni Minawi as the new SLM/A Chairman, which was rejected by Abdul Wahid. Several important initiatives were undertaken to repair the SLM/A rift and help create a conducive environment for the seventh round of Abuja talks, which resumed on 29 November. The first was a meeting of senior officials from donor countries and the United Nations (London, 1 November), convened by the United Kingdom, to, among other things, discuss how to unite positions within SLM/A ahead of the talks, proposals to end the violence in Darfur, and the post-Abuja period. UNMIS also participated in a meeting (Nairobi, 8-9 November), convened by the United States, to reconcile Abdul Wahid and Minni Minawi. Although Abdul Wahid attended the meeting, Minni Minawi did not, but sent a delegation to represent him.

On 12 November, a meeting of Special Envoys convened by the Special Representative in Khartoum, attended by representatives from the AU, the EU, Canada, France, Germany, the Netherlands, Norway, the United Kingdom and the United States, discussed how to facilitate a more unified position within SLM before the talks began, and humanitarian and development issues that would have to be addressed after the conclusion of a peace agreement. An UNMIS paper presented to the Special Envoys, focused on the post-Abuja process and discussed the characteristics that would be required of any peace agreement to make it credible and sustainable. At the meeting, the importance for the international community to engage the parties on key post-conflict issues that needed to be defined in the peace agreement was also recognized, some of which could also be addressed in more detail in the Darfur-Darfur dialogue, to be held after the conclusion of a final peace agreement on Darfur. That dialogue should also include a strategy for sustainable reconciliation among all communities in Darfur.

On 19 November, following the Envoys' meeting in Khartoum, United States Assistant Secretary of State for African Affairs, Jendayi Frazer, and the Head of AMIS, Ambassador Baba Gana Kingibe, jointly facilitated a meeting between Abdul Wahid and Minni Minawi to urge them again to participate constructively and with a united purpose in the seventh round of the Abuja talks, notwithstanding the disagreements within the movement. A further initiative was led by the Government of Chad, assisted by the Libyan Arab Jamahiriya, Eritrea and the AU, in N'Djamena on 25 and 26 November. Both Abdul Wahid and Minni Minawi agreed to present a common negotiating platform, to be coordinated with JEM.

The Special Representative also held two bilateral meetings with Mr. Minawi, during which he underlined the international community's position that divisions within SLM should not detract from the overarching mission of achieving peace and reconciliation in Darfur before the end of 2005. He urged Mr. Minawi to refrain from detaining dissenting commanders, made clear that the United Nations could not take a stance in the movement's internal dispute and called on him to cooperate with Abdul Wahid to ensure that the signing of a peace agreement reached during the next round would result in the cessation of military activities by all.

The seventh round of inter-Sudanese peace talks on Darfur opened in Abuja on 29 November. All parties pledged to negotiate in good faith, with a view to reaching an agreement by the end of the year. Talks were held on power-sharing and on wealth-sharing and security arrangements. While the parties identified priority areas of concern in the power-sharing discussions, their position still remained far apart, which the AU mediation was attempting to bridge through compromise solutions.

In preparation for those talks, the AU Peace and Security Council (Addis Ababa, Ethiopia, 22 November) [S/2005/765] issued a communiqué expressing concern over developments on the ground. It demanded that the SLM/A leadership should be addressed collectively to resolve the conflict in a democratic and transparent manner. The AU Council decided, in consultation with the UN Security Council, to consider future measures, including sanctions, to be taken against any party that undermined or constituted an obstacle to the Darfur peace process. It appealed to all international partners to support the AU position on an all-inclusive peace process, and the peace talks, as well as AMIS deployment in Darfur.

Concerning the security situation, the Secretary-General said in his November report that the security situation in western Darfur remained very precarious in October. Even after promises by the state government to implement joint military and police patrols on the highways to ensure security, lawlessness and banditry reached such dangerous levels that all roads out of Geneina remained open to UN staff only with approved armed escorts. The tense situation within Geneina itself warranted a reduction of non-essential UN personnel on 12 October. The poor security situation was compounded by issues that straddled the Sudan-Chad border. Reports of defections from the Chadian army highlighted the risk of transborder tribal ties internationalizing the conflict in Darfur. Moreover, criminal cross-border activities added another dimension to the already challenging security environment.

October also marked a milestone for AMIS, as five of its members were killed on 8 October, the mission's first such deaths, during a firefight with an armed group that had earlier ambushed and killed two civilian contractors in southern Darfur. The AMIS patrol stated that the attackers appeared to be members of the SLM/A, while the movement's leadership denied any involvement. That event was followed the next day by a large-scale, though short-term, detention of AMIS personnel and advisers by a splinter faction of JEM near Tine, northern Darfur. On 27 October, an AMIS patrol was shot at near Tama, southern Darfur, by unknown gunmen. The escalation of targeted violence against AMIS underscored the serious dangers and risks facing the AU force and the need for all parties to guarantee their safety and security in Darfur.

In early November, the freedom of movement of members of the panel of experts appointed by the Security Council to monitor the implementation of Council resolution 1591(2005) was affected during the panel's latest visit to El-Fasher, where they were harassed by Government security agents. On 10 November, the State Minister admitted that the behaviour of military intelligence "had been wrong" and assured the Special Representative that the panel members had freedom of movement in the pursuit of their mandated activities.

In his December report, the Secretary-General said that the confirmed number of civilian deaths due to violence had almost doubled, due to both politically motivated attacks and criminal banditry. In particular, two political developments significantly contributed to violence and insecurity during the reporting period. First, the internal struggle within SLM/A created a leadership vacuum in certain areas of Darfur, leading to speculation that the split would spur inter-tribal clashes between the Fur and the Zaghawa, the respective tribes of the two rival SLM/A leaders, Abdul Wahid and Minni Minawi. Second, a recent influx of military deserters from Chad into western Darfur had further destabilized the complex security situation in the region. They joined Chadian armed opposition groups based in Darfur who engaged in a wide range of destructive activities, including cross-border smuggling, cattle-rustling and banditry. There were also serious inter-tribal clashes in southern Darfur between the Falata and the Massalit. Militia attacks on more than a dozen Massalit villages south-west of Gereida occurred from 6 to 17 November, resulting in an estimated 60 deaths, and the displacement of 15,000 people.

In northern Darfur, SLM/A internal difficulties translated into an increasing number of inter-tribal incidents on 11 November between the Zaghawa and Meidop tribes. On 13 November, confrontation between the two tribes resulted in the death of at least 15 people.

Western Darfur presented the most complex security environment of the three States, as splinters of various armed groups and significant numbers of infiltrators from Chad engaged in criminally and politically motivated violence. On 18 November, the Sudanese Armed Forces carried out operations in the Jebel Moon area, allegedly against Chadian deserters who had moved into the area. That incident was confirmed a week later by an UNMIS assessment team visiting the area on a fact-finding mission. Furthermore, there was no sign of Chadian deserters as alleged by the Government.

The Secretary-General noted that the situation in Darfur had not changed since 2004: the vast majority of armed militia had not been disarmed, nor any major steps taken by the Government to bring to justice or even identify any of the militia leaders or the perpetrators of attacks, contributing to a prevailing climate of impunity. He urged the Government of the Sudan once again to take decisive steps to address those issues. The current round of the Abuja talks was critical and had to be decisive, despite the serious difficulties encountered, as a result of the division within SLM. Further procrastination should not be accepted. The international community, including his Special Representative, had begun engaging the parties on key post-conflict issues that needed to be defined in a peace agreement. However, a peace agreement could result in security and protection only if it was widely accepted among the various elements in Darfur, including those not represented at the Abuja talks. Sustained dialogue among all parties and an inclusive and long-term reconciliation strategy therefore would have to follow an agreement in Abuja. All parties would have to demonstrate their political determination for genuine reconciliation. Those and other steps would have to go hand in hand with an enhanced international security presence, which should address adequately the deteriorating security situation on the ground.

The Secretary-General said that he was pleased that the AU had decided to lead a second assessment mission from 10 to 20 December (see below), including a team from the United Nations. The mission's recommendations on the way forward would help inform the AU, its partners and the Security Council as they considered the next steps to take. In the meantime, everything possible should be done to sustain and strengthen the AU Mission and to further enhance protection efforts throughout the region. He also appealed to the donor community to respond generously to the massive humanitarian needs in Darfur, which were outlined in the 2006 workplan for the Sudan, and presented on 2 December.

AU assessment team to Darfur (December)

The AU-led assessment team to Darfur arrived there on 10 December to review AMIS operations, assess the implementation of the recommendations of the March assessment mission (see p. 327) and evaluate the security situation.

In its assessment, transmitted by Nigeria to the Security Council President on 22 December [S/2005/834], the mission concluded that the AMIS presence had contributed to reducing the number of ceasefire violations and afforded some level of protection for the delivery of humanitarian assistance. Its "firewood patrols" and field sorties enabled internally displaced persons to cultivate and harvest crops in certain areas, and that, together with a sustained humanitarian effort by the international community, had considerably reduced malnutrition and mortality rates in Darfur. Several AMIS commanders had also engaged in local reconciliation efforts ("military diplomacy"), thus contributing to reducing tensions and preventing many incidents. The deployment of the civilian police component, which had started 24-hour operations in some locations, also helped to improve significantly the security in the camps for internally displaced persons and their immediate vicinity.

The team noted, however, that the prevailing security situation did not allow for the return of internally displaced persons and refugees in any significant numbers. Banditry, harassment of civilians, and tensions and skirmishes between ethnic communities were rife throughout Darfur and remained an unresolved security challenge.

The team paid tribute to the fallen AMIS soldiers in the Khor Abeche area in southern Darfur and those injured near the Chadian border. The mission noted that AMIS personnel, whose total strength, as at 13 December, stood at 6,932 (5,623 military personnel and 1,309 civilian police), were conducting their tasks with increasing effectiveness and great commitment.

The findings of the assessment mission would form the basis of the AU Commission's recommendations to the Peace and Security Council in January 2006 on how to further enhance the effectiveness of the AU forces in Darfur and to provide pointers on the way forward.

Year-end developments

In a later report [S/2006/59], the Secretary-General indicated that the seventh round of the inter-Sudanese peace talks, which started in

Abuja on 29 November, made slow progress. Work in the power-sharing commission was delayed for a week, as the parties were unable to reach a compromise on the four key issues of agenda item 4, namely: whether Darfur should become a region or remain divided into three separate states; the inclusion of a Darfurian representative in the structure of the presidency; Darfurian representation at the national capital level; and the application of the 1 January 1956 boundaries to Darfur. After extensive consultations with both sides, the power-sharing commission resumed work on 19 December in a somewhat improved atmosphere and was continuing to debate the four issues.

In the wealth-sharing commission, further progress was made. The movements called for a joint assessment mission by both sides, with international community participation, to assess the effects of the war on the ground. While it was established that this could not take place without the appropriate security conditions, the parties nevertheless agreed to call upon international partners to participate in such a mission with the least possible delay. Despite concerted efforts to move matters forward in the commission on security arrangements, the agenda for discussion was only adopted on 23 December. Little progress was made, given the failure of the parties, particularly the movements, to separate their formal negotiating position from an agreement on the substance of the agenda. There was a growing feeling that some of the protagonists were deliberately stalling in support of their belief that they could achieve a military solution.

From 19 to 21 December, the National Congress Party (NCP) components within the Darfur state governments organized an all-Darfur conference, to which the armed movements, Darfurians in the diaspora and in political movements across the Sudan were invited. However, other major political parties, including SLM, boycotted the conference, citing differences in views with NCP. Internally displaced persons in the Abo-Shouk and El-Salam camps in El-Fasher also boycotted the conference, arguing that they were not sufficiently represented. The conference adopted a wide range of recommendations in the economic, political and social areas.

Concerning the security situation, the Secretary-General reported that December witnessed a continuation of very high levels of violence and insecurity in Darfur, including banditry, a new round of militia attacks on villages and camps, intensive Government combat operations and the deliberate destruction of significant areas of farmland. In addition, the rapid deterioration of the situation along the Chad-Sudan border and concern about a possible conflict between those two neighbouring countries further exacerbated the climate of insecurity.

Both SLM/A and the Government seriously flouted the ceasefire agreements. On 3 December, armed militia attacked the SLA at Um Kunya, south of Nyala, resulting in 11 civilian deaths and up to 7,500 people displaced. On 4 December, in an apparent retaliation, SLA forces attacked the Sudanese Armed Forces garrison at Donkey Dereaisa, while Sudanese Armed Forces attacked their positions in the Masteri area, south-west of Geneina. Heavy fighting continued for three days, forcing the relocation of NGOs from the area. Government forces and rebels also fought in Masteri, Kongo Haraza and Beida, together with militia attacks in the Jebel Moon, Silea and Kulbus areas.

The level and intensity of inter-tribal and militia clashes also increased. On 19 December, hundreds of armed militia attacked the village of Abu Sorouj, in western Darfur, burning dozens of huts and looting livestock. A total of 19 villagers, including several women and children, were reported killed in the attack.

The security situation in western Darfur was again being negatively affected by the rapidly deteriorating situation along the Chad-Sudan border. On 18 December, major clashes took place between Chadian rebel groups and Chadian armed forces in the border town of Adre. Since then, there was a worrying build-up of armed forces of the two states and local militias on both sides of the border.

In the area of human rights, unidentified armed elements continued to launch attacks on camps during December, while elements associated with the Sudanese Armed Forces continued to harass and intimidate them. At Kalma camp, on 15 December, the Government lifted the commercial blockade that had been imposed on the camp for more than six months. The blockade prevented the flow of critical goods and materials into the camp and led to a dramatic increase in tensions and violence there. The lifting of the ban, combined with the more regular AMIS presence in the camp, had significantly reduced the number of security incidents reported from Kalma.

Field missions and investigations conducted by UN human rights officers in December also revealed serious abuses against civilians in the context of major attacks by the Sudanese Armed Forces and/or armed militias. Documented violations included forced displacement, arbitrary arrest, prolonged detention, torture by national security officials and the indiscriminate use of force in military operations.

Communications. The EU Presidency, in a 21 December statement [S/2005/852], welcomed the progress made in the seventh round of the Abuja talks in the wealth-sharing commission, but expressed concern at the lack of progress on power-sharing and security arrangements. The EU was deeply concerned by the continuing violations of the ceasefire agreements in Darfur and called on all sides to stop such attacks and refrain from any action that might aggravate the situation in Darfur and Chad.

On 22 December [S/2005/835], the Spokesman for the AU mediation issued a statement, in which the AU Special Envoy for Darfur and Chief Negotiator expressed outrage at the attack on Abu Sorouj in western Darfur on 19 December. The Special Envoy stressed that the perpetrators should be made to face the full force of the law and urged the Sudanese authorities and others concerned to ensure that justice was done. He also called on the Government of the Sudan and all parties to the conflict to ensure the protection of the civilian population in Darfur.

SECURITY COUNCIL ACTION

On 21 December [meeting 5342], following consultations among Security Council members, the President made statement **S/PRST/2005/67** on behalf of the Council:

> The Security Council welcomes the commencement in Abuja of the seventh round of the African Union-led inter-Sudanese peace talks on Darfur, and expresses its appreciation to the African Union, the international community and the other donors.
>
> The Council is encouraged by the active participation of representatives from all invited groups of the Sudan Liberation Movement/Army and the Justice and Equality Movement, as well as members of the Sudan People's Liberation Movement, as part of the Government of National Unity, and urges their continued cooperation with the African Union Mission in the Sudan and with the United Nations Mission in the Sudan.
>
> The Council calls upon all parties to the conflict to fulfil their commitments to conclude a just and full peace accord without further delay. The Council demands that all parties refrain from violence and put an end to atrocities on the ground, especially those committed against civilians, including women and children, humanitarian workers and international peacekeepers.
>
> The Council recalls the demands on the Government of the Sudan and the rebel forces, as well as other armed groups, to respect fully their commitments referred to in its recent resolutions. The Council demands, in particular, that the Sudan Liberation Movement/Army, the Justice and Equality Movement and the Government of the Sudan immediately cease violence, comply with the N'djamena ceasefire agreement, end impediments to the peace process and cooperate fully with the African Union

Mission in the Sudan, and that the Government of the Sudan disarm and control militias. It further demands that those responsible for violations of human rights and international humanitarian law be brought to justice without delay.

> The Council recalls its concern that the persisting violence in Darfur might further negatively affect the region, in particular the security of Chad. It firmly condemns, in this context, recent attacks perpetrated by armed elements within Chad and in particular the attack of 18 December 2005 on positions of the Chadian national army in the town of Adré, and supports efforts to reduce tensions on the border.
>
> The Council reaffirms its determination to make full use of existing measures under its relevant resolutions on the Sudan, including holding accountable those responsible for violence and violations of the arms embargo, and those who impede the peace process.
>
> The Council expresses its gratitude to the African Union and its Mission in the Sudan for the positive role that its forces have played in reducing violence and promoting the restoration of order in Darfur.
>
> The Council also appeals to donors to continue both to support the crucial work of the African Union Mission in the Sudan in stemming the violence in this suffering region and to provide critical humanitarian assistance to millions of war-afflicted civilians in Darfur and across the border in Chad.
>
> In the broader Sudan context, the Council welcomes further progress achieved in the implementation of the Comprehensive Peace Agreement, in particular the signing of the Constitution for Southern Sudan and the formation of the Government of Southern Sudan.

Eritrea-Sudan

On 27 June [S/2005/416], the Sudan accused Eritrea of acts of aggression and sabotage designed to undermine the peace agreements achieved in southern Sudan and to destabilize and threaten national security. It also accused Eritrea of organizing conferences of Sudanese opposition groups in Eritrea and offering political, training and logistic support to those organizations. It called on the Security Council to address the situation, which it warned was soon reaching that point when it would be forced to exercise its legitimate right to defend its sovereignty, territorial integrity and security.

Eritrea, in a 28 June response [S/2005/417], detailed its historic efforts to promote internal peace and stability in the Sudan, and said that the groundless accusations were either pretexts by the Government to derail the entire peace process and renege on its commitments, or a deliberate diversion to foment problems in the region.

Somalia

The Transitional Federal Government of Somalia, established at the end of 2004, following the successful conclusion of the Somali National Conference, began 2005 with the endorsement by Parliament of a Cabinet. Shortly thereafter, the Government, in addressing the two immediate priorities, namely, its relocation from Nairobi to Somalia and the establishment of an interim peace support mission pending deployment to the country of a peacekeeping mission, caused a rift within the leadership of the transitional federal institutions that resulted in a political impasse for most of the year.

On the one hand, President Abdullahi Yusuf Ahmed and Prime Minister Ali Mohammed Gedi planned to start functioning in Jawhar until it was safe to relocate to the capital, Mogadishu; on the other, the Speaker of Parliament, Sharif Hassan Sheik Adan, and some ministers insisted on immediate relocation to Mogadishu. Although no agreement was reached, relocation got under way by midyear, with each side relocating to its chosen site. Also contentious was the composition of an interim peace support mission, sponsored by the Intergovernmental Authority on Development and endorsed by the African Union, in response to a request by the President. As the impasse persisted, each side proceeded to engage in unilateral actions that the other rejected, leading to heightened tension and reported military build-up by both sides. The Security Council cautioned that a peace support mission had to be carefully planned and required the support of the Somali people; it called on all Somali leaders to exercise maximum restraint and stressed that a resort to military force was unacceptable.

Meanwhile, the United Nations Political Office for Somalia remained in contact with Somali leaders, civic organizations and the States and organizations concerned in order to advance the peace and reconciliation process. In November, the Secretary-General outlined to the Council the specifics of an expanded role for the United Nations in the country, which the Government, States in the region and the international community had requested.

The Monitoring Group on Somalia, charged by the Council with investigating violations of the arms embargo imposed on the country, reported in August a dramatic rise in violations that involved the leaders of the two opposing sides, which corresponded to their increased militarization activities in central and southern Somalia. At the request of the Council, the Secretary-General, in March and November, re-established the Group, each time for a six-month period, in order to continue its functions.

Insecurity remained prevalent in Mogadishu and in other parts of the country, as intermittent violence, factional and inter-clan conflicts and militia rivalries continued, which not only exacerbated the threat to the viability of the transitional institutions but also prevented implementation of UN programmes in the country and hampered delivery of humanitarian assistance to the Somali communities in crisis.

The self-proclaimed republic of "Somaliland" in the north-west continued to press for international recognition of its status as an independent State. "Somaliland" and the self-declared autonomous north-east region of "Puntland" were relatively stable throughout the year.

(For assistance for humanitarian relief and the economic and social rehabilitation of Somalia, see p. 996.)

United Nations Political Office for Somalia

The United Nations Political Office for Somalia (UNPOS), established in 1995 [YUN 1995, p. 400], continued to assist in advancing the cause of peace and reconciliation in Somalia. The Secretary-General, in his February report (see p. 339), stated that the Transitional Federal Government, the countries in the region and the international community had asked the United Nations to take the lead in coordinating support to the Government to implement the agreements reached by the Somali National Reconciliation Conference, which concluded in October 2004 with the election of the President [YUN 2004, p. 261], and to establish peace and stability in Somalia. The Secretary-General recalled having previously pointed to the need, at that stage of the Somali peace process, for an expanded UN political presence and proposed an incremental expansion based on discussions with the Transitional Federal Government. That called for a higher profile leadership by UNPOS and an increase in its staff in the areas of political and military liaison, information, civil police, disarmament, demobilization and reintegration, and human rights. The Security Council, in welcoming the efforts of UNPOS, concurred with the need for an expanded UN role in Somalia as proposed (see p. 341).

On 16 November [S/2005/729], the Secretary-General confirmed to the Council that the expanded role for the United Nations would include assisting in the continuous dialogue among Somali parties for reconciliation; assisting in effort to address the issue of "Somaliland"; coordinating support for the peace process with Somalia's neighbours and other international partners; and chairing the Coordination and Monitoring Committee, as well as playing a leading political role in peacebuilding activities. The main objectives of UNPOS during 2006-2007 would be to foster inclusive dialogue and reconciliation among the transitional federal institutions (TFIs); support the establishment of governance structures and institutions and develop action plans for them, in close coordination with the Transitional Federal Government; and coordinate international political and financial support to the nascent Somali institutions.

The Council took note of the information on 21 November [S/2005/730].

Appointment. By an exchange of letters between the Secretary-General and the Security Council [S/2005/280, S/2005/279], François Lonseny Fall (Guinea) was appointed Special Representative of the Secretary-General for Somalia and Head of UNPOS, to succeed Winston A. Tubman (Liberia), who had served in that capacity until March. Mr. Fall assumed his duties in Nairobi on 27 May.

Financing

The Secretary-General, in his April report [A/59/534/Add.4] on estimates in respect of the special political missions, good offices and other political initiatives authorized by the General Assembly and/or the Security Council, presented additional resource requirements for the expanded operation of UNPOS for the period 1 June to 31 December 2005, estimated at $5,017,400 net ($5,394,600 gross). Of that amount, $845,700 would be met from the unencumbered balance against existing appropriations for the period ending on 31 May 2005, thus reducing the overall additional requirements for UNPOS to $4,171,700 net ($4,548,900 gross).

On 22 April [A/59/569/Add.4], ACABQ recommended approval of the resources requested, but was aware that savings might be achieved as events dictated possible movements.

The General Assembly, in section II of **resolution 59/294** of 22 June (see p. 1488), approved the UNPOS budget for the period 1 June to 31 December 2005 in the amount set out in the Secretary-General's report.

In December [A/60/585 & Corr. 1], the Secretary-General, in his budget submission for the 26 special political missions authorized by the Assembly and or the Security Council, proposed requirements for UNPOS for 2006 in the amount of $7,129.2 million. The Assembly, in section VI of **resolution 60/248** of 23 December (see p. 1495), approved $100 million for those missions and decided to continue consideration of the Secretary-General's request at its resumed sixtieth (2006) session.

National reconciliation process and security situation

As requested by Security Council presidential statement S/PRST/2001/30 [YUN 2001, p. 210], the Secretary-General submitted quarterly reports during the year updating developments on the situation in Somalia since his October 2004 report [YUN 2004, p. 260].

Report of Secretary-General (February). In his February report [S/2005/89], the Secretary-General stated that the new Cabinet proposed by the Prime Minister, composed of 92 ministers, assistant ministers and ministers of State, was endorsed by Parliament on 13 January. The unusually large number of appointments drew criticism, which the Prime Minister defended as necessary to ensure inclusivity. At its first meeting, on 15 January, the Cabinet set up committees to handle cooperation with the international community and to work on the relocation of the Transitional Federal Government from Nairobi to Somalia. The relocation plan called for relocating to Somalia 987 people, including the Government and Parliament members, and delegates to the Somali National Reconciliation Conference; peacebuilding and reconciliation through the organization of peacebuilding conferences in 92 districts; establishment of provisional regional and district administrations pending full realization of the federal structure; encampment and retraining of 53,000 militia members; and formation of a police force of 10,000. The plan, costing some 94,375,572 euros, was expected to last over three months, from mid-February. The plan was presented on 2 February to the new Coordination and Monitoring Committee [YUN 2004, p. 262], created as a mechanism through which donor countries and regional and subregional organizations provided support to the efforts of the Transitional Federal Government. The Committee's Declaration of Principles and Structured Coordination Modalities, which served as the highest level of information-sharing and policy discussion in the partnership between the international community and the Government, was signed on 9 February by the Transitional Federal Government and the United Nations, representing the international community.

On 6 February, two delegations of 73 Parliamentarians led by the Speaker of Parliament and the Second Deputy Speaker visited Mogadishu to discuss the relocation and security issues with local leaders, clan elders and other stakeholders. The visits were supported by the United Nations Trust Fund for Peacebuilding in Somalia, the United Nations Development Programme (UNDP) and the European Commission. For their part, the President and the Prime Minister, while still residing in Nairobi, had undertaken a number of diplomatic missions to countries of the region towards the end of the previous year to discuss those issues.

On 31 January, the Intergovernmental Authority on Development (IGAD) issued a communiqué expressing the willingness of Djibouti, Ethiopia, Kenya, the Sudan and Uganda to participate in a future African Union (AU) peace support mission to Somalia. On 7 February, the AU Peace and Security Council authorized IGAD to deploy such a mission to Somalia. A large demonstration led by a number of sheikhs and militias under the Sharia courts had been mounted, on 8 January, against the deployment in Somalia of what they considered foreign troops in support of the Transitional Federal Government. Heavy weapons, including anti-aircraft guns and armoured vehicles were reportedly being purchased for use against such troops.

The intermittent fighting and violence in Somalia continued to prevent the United Nations from implementing programmes in many areas of the country. Large-scale violations of the arms embargo by extremist groups, militias and some Parliament members were reported. Of concern was the proliferation of small arms and heavy weapons, such as tanks, artillery, anti-aircraft guns, rocket launchers and heavy mortars. Because of insecurity in Mogadishu, where violent crime remained common and clan disputes occasionally occurred, the Transitional Federal Government had been obliged to consider a phased approach for its return to the capital and perhaps to start functioning in Baidoa or Jawhar. Widespread inter-clan fighting and banditry continued to have a severe impact on southern and central Somalia.

Confrontation continued between "Somaliland" (the north-western regions) and "Puntland" (north-eastern Somalia) over control of the north-western regions of Sool and Sanaag. An electoral law passed by the "Somaliland" House of Representatives and by the House of Elders on 18 January and 5 February, respectively, provided for the demarcation of district and regional boundaries; the holding of elections in all "Somaliland" regions (including Sool and Sanaag) and a population census; and the completion of voter registration and issuance of identity cards to all "Somalilanders" before elections. The law raised concern over the possibility of renewed tensions between "Somaliland" and "Puntland" during those elections, scheduled for 28 March. In "Puntland" on 8 January, General Adda Musse was elected President.

Given that stabilizing the humanitarian situation in Somalia constituted an essential component for the peace and reconciliation process, the report also described the efforts to that end, including assistance to the drought-affected regions of the north and south-central zones and along the Somali coastline that had been affected by the 2004 Indian Ocean tsunami [YUN 2004, p. 952], as well as to the estimated 400,000 Somalis displaced by drought conditions and clan conflicts. Further detailed were UNDP operational activities to promote peace and stability in the areas of governance, livelihoods, health, water and environmental protection, child protection, HIV/AIDS, internally displaced persons and refugees, and education. The Secretary-General called on the Office for the Coordination of Humanitarian Affairs and UN agencies to accelerate their efforts to reach out to non-traditional donors, and for the expansion of community-based peace and reconciliation initiatives currently being undertaken in the humanitarian context.

SECURITY COUNCIL ACTION

On 7 March [meeting 5135], following consultations among Security Council members, the President made statement **S/PRST/2005/11** on behalf of the Council:

The Security Council reaffirms all its previous decisions concerning the situation in Somalia, in particular the statement by its President of 19 November 2004.

The Council welcomes the report of the Secretary-General of 18 February 2005, and reaffirms its commitment to a comprehensive and lasting settlement of the situation in Somalia and its respect for the sovereignty, territorial integrity, political independence and unity of Somalia, consistent with the purposes and principles of the Charter of the United Nations.

The Council welcomes the progress made in the Somali National Reconciliation Process, in particular the ongoing relocation efforts of the Transitional Federal Government, expects further progress in this regard and stresses the need for the international community to provide strong political, financial and capacity-building support for these efforts.

The Council commends the efforts of the African Union and the Intergovernmental Authority on Development in support of the Transitional Federal Government. The Council reiterates its support for the efforts of the African Union in assisting the process of transition in Somalia. The Council recognizes the African Union's readiness to play an important role in a future peace support mission in Somalia. Such a mission must be carefully considered and planned and would require the support of the Somali people.

The Council urges all Somali factions and militia leaders to cease hostilities and encourages them and the Transitional Federal Government to enter into immediate negotiations for a comprehensive and verifiable ceasefire agreement leading to final disarmament, and welcomes the willingness of the United Nations to provide advice in this regard.

The Council expresses its gratitude to all those donors who have supported the peace process in Somalia and encourages donor countries and regional and subregional organizations to contribute to the reconstruction and rehabilitation of Somalia, in particular through efforts coordinated by United Nations agencies.

The Council welcomes the establishment of the Coordination and Monitoring Committee, chaired jointly by the Prime Minister of the Transitional Federal Government and the United Nations, through which donor countries and regional and subregional organizations can provide support to the efforts of the Government.

The Council stresses that improving the humanitarian situation is an essential component of support for the peace and reconciliation process. The Council strongly believes that ensuring humanitarian access to all Somalis in need and providing guarantees for the safety and security of aid workers is an immediate priority and obligation of the Transitional Federal Government.

The Council welcomes the efforts of the United Nations Political Office for Somalia and its leading role in coordinating support for the Transitional Federal Government to implement the agreements reached at the Somali National Reconciliation Conference and establish peace and stability in Somalia. The Council takes note of the need to expand the United Nations presence as proposed in the report of the Secretary-General of 18 February 2005. The Council concurs with the Secretary-General that a further enhanced role for the Organization in Somalia must be incremental and should be based on the outcome of discussions with the Government.

The Council reaffirms its full support for the peace process in Somalia and the commitment of the United Nations to assist the regional and subregional efforts in this regard.

Communications. The European Union (EU), in a 7 April statement issued by its Presidency [S/2005/248], urged all Somali parties inside and outside the TFIs to refrain immediately from further hostilities and armed confrontations, and called for an immediate dialogue among all the parties within the TFIs with a view to having the Council of Ministers and Parliament reach an agreement on a new comprehensive proposal on relocation and security.

By a joint statement of 12 May [S/2005/326], the EU and the United States stressed the urgent need for a viable agreement on relocation and security, to be endorsed by the TFIs. They welcomed the Somali efforts on relocation, including those of the Somali parties to facilitate demilitarization in Mogadishu, which should be incorporated into a national plan as soon as possible.

Report of Secretary-General (June). The Secretary-General's June report [S/2005/392] noted that the two issues of relocation and security had proved controversial within the Transitional Federal Government. Serious concern was expressed among Somalis and the international community that, almost eight months after the conclusion of the Somali National Reconciliation Conference, the transitional institutions were still in Nairobi rather than in Somalia. Controversy on the first issue caused a rift between President Yusuf and Prime Minister Gedi, on the one hand, who argued that the Government should relocate temporarily to Baidoa or Jawhar until Mogadishu was made safe; and Speaker of Parliament Sharif Hassan Sheikh Adan and those associated with him, on the other, who insisted on immediate relocation to Mogadishu. Consequently, relocation could not begin in mid-February as planned. However, Parliament members and ministers gradually began leaving Nairobi for Mogadishu beginning in late March through the middle of June. By the reporting date, over 100 parliamentarians were in Mogadishu. The President arrived in the city of Jawhar on 26 July, which he and the Prime Minister used as the de facto temporary seat of the Transitional Federal Government.

Controversy on the second issue centered on the inclusion of troops from the front line States—Djiouti, Ethiopia and Kenya—in a future AU/IGAD peace support mission requested by the President. Again, a large number of Parliament members, Cabinet ministers and other leaders who were later joined by the Speaker, while welcoming AU troops, categorically opposed the inclusion of troops from those States and insisted on the endorsement by Parliament of the mission's composition and mandate. The opposing sides held demonstrations in the capital in early March in support of their respective views. The IGAD Council of Ministers met on the issue on 17 and 18 March, following Parliament's debate on it. The Ministers reaffirmed their commitment to execute their 31 January decision to deploy an IGAD peace support mission to Somalia (see p. 340). Deployment would take place in two phases: during phase I, troops from the Sudan and Uganda would provide security and support to the Government to ensure its relocation to Somalia, while the remaining IGAD countries would provide logistics, equipment and training to the Somali army and police; during phase II, troop deployment would be undertaken by the remaining IGAD countries pending the deployment of AU troops. The Ministers welcomed the decision of the Ministers for Foreign Affairs of the League of Arab States (LAS) to participate in the mission and to assist IGAD and the AU in that regard.

An AU/IGAD fact-finding mission had visited Somalia earlier (14-26 February) to hold consultations with different segments of the population in many parts of the country, including Mogadishu. The mission elicited mixed reactions, but, on the whole, most Somalis supported the deployment of foreign troops, except troops from neighbouring States. In an emergency session of Parliament called by the President on 11 May, two motions submitted by the Prime Minister—to deploy the IGAD peace support mission, authorized on 17 February (see p. 340), and to approve the Cabinet's decision to relocate to Baidoa or Jawhar, with an office in Mogadishu, pending stabilization of the capital—were approved by votes of 145 and 141, respectively. The votes were declared null and void by the Speaker.

The AU Peace and Security Council, following its consideration of the fact-finding mission's report at its twenty-ninth meeting (Addis Ababa, Ethiopia, 12 May), issued a communiqué [S/2005/315] authorizing the deployment under phase I of the IGAD peace support mission, which was to facilitate the relocation of the Transitional Federal Government and provide protection as appropriate; to assist the Government and the Somali parties in security sector reform and disarmament, demobilization and reintegration efforts; and to facilitate humanitarian operations within its capabilities. The AU Council also requested the Security Council to authorize an exemption for the peace support mission from the arms embargo imposed on Somalia by Security Council resolution 733(1992) [YUN 1992, p. 199].

In addition to the activities of IGAD, the AU and LAS to help establish a functional Government, Sweden held consultations related to the coordination of international support to the Government relocation plan. The Director of the Africa Division of the UN Department of Political Affairs visited Nairobi in April to stress the need to resolve the current differences within the Transitional Federal Government. Citing the impossibility of ensuring security for the Government by external troops alone, he pointed to the need for a comprehensive ceasefire agreement with the possible formation of a core Somali security force that was initially to be recruited on the basis of the "4.5 formula" for clan representation and quickly trained. The TFIs could gradually move from Nairobi to Mogadishu, while the President could travel to different locations in Somalia.

UNPOS likewise encouraged dialogue between the Transitional Federal Government members in Mogadishu and those in Nairobi (see p. 344). It visited possible facilities for the relocation and identified a number of project proposals for several peacebuilding activities under the United Nations Trust Fund for Peacebuilding in Somalia.

In Mogadishu, despite the rapprochement between many of the faction leaders there, violent crime and occasional inter-clan incidents continued at such levels that the city remained at UN security phase V. In the South of the country, aid operations were seriously hampered by the proliferation of checkpoints manned by uncontrolled militia who restricted staff and supply movement. In contrast, administrations in both "Somaliland" and "Puntland" were able to control such activities, allowing delivery of aid over a wide area. In "Somaliland" in May, a visiting AU delegation was briefed by authorities there on the determination of "Somaliland" to protect its sovereignty, stressing that its recognition was within the purview of the AU. A United Kingdom official had visited Hargeysa in the previous month to discuss the forthcoming parliamentary elections. The reporting period saw no significant incidents between "Somaliland" and "Puntland" in the contested regions of Sool and Sanaa, although no progress towards a political solution had been achieved.

The Secretary-General updated information on developments in the various operational activities mentioned in his first report (see p. 339), including the training of youth groups in good governance to enhance their participation in district-based local governance processes. The United Nations had also developed policy and operational plans for countrywide disarmament, demobilization and reintegration. As to security sector reform, the United Nations was registering and surveying over 15,000 security forces and militia in "Puntland" and "Somaliland", where demobilization and reintegration of several thousand forces were under way. Pilot projects and planning would continue in central and southern Somalia pending large-scale demobilization, in partnership with the Transitional Federal Government. Under development were small-arms and light-weapons control strategies, including a legal framework for the curtailment of weapons proliferation in the country.

The Secretary-General underlined the importance of including a humanitarian and human rights component in training programmes envisaged for foreign troops and Somali security forces. He said the United Nations would continue to support disarmament, demobilization and reintegration efforts and to build on experiences of UN agencies already involved in such programmes.

SECURITY COUNCIL ACTION (July)

On 14 July [meeting 5227], following consultations among Security Council members, the President made statement **S/PRST/2005/32** on behalf of the Council:

The Security Council reaffirms all its previous decisions concerning the situation in Somalia, in particular the statements by its President of 19 November 2004 and 7 March 2005.

The Council welcomes the report of the Secretary-General of 16 June 2005, and reaffirms its commitment to a comprehensive and lasting settlement of the situation in Somalia and its respect for the sovereignty, territorial integrity, political independence and unity of Somalia, consistent with the purposes and principles of the Charter of the United Nations.

The Council is encouraged by the relocation now under way of the transitional federal institutions to Somalia, urges further progress in this regard and calls upon the Somali leaders to continue to work towards reconciliation, through inclusive dialogue and consensus-building within the framework of the transitional federal institutions, in accordance with the Transitional Federal Charter of the Somali Republic adopted in February 2004.

The Council expresses its concern at the recent disagreements and increased tensions among Somali leaders, which threaten the viability of the transitional federal institutions. The Council calls upon all leaders in Somalia to exercise maximum restraint and take immediate effective steps to reduce tension. Violence or military action by any members of the transitional federal institutions or other parties is unacceptable as the means for dealing with the current differences within the transitional federal institutions. The Council reiterates that any members of the transitional federal institutions or other parties who persist on the path of confrontation and conflict, including military action, will be held accountable.

The Council urges the transitional federal institutions to conclude without delay a national security and stabilization plan, to include a comprehensive and verifiable ceasefire agreement leading to final disarmament, and welcomes the willingness of the United Nations to provide advice in this regard.

The Council commends the commitment of the African Union and the Intergovernmental Authority on Development in support of the relocation to Somalia of the transitional federal institutions and reiterates its support for those efforts in assisting the process of transition in Somalia. The Council welcomes the readiness of the African Union and the Intergovernmental Authority on Development to reinforce their continued support for the establishment of a functioning central government of Somalia, including the possible deployment of a peace support mission to Somalia, and encourages the Peace and Security Council of the African Union to keep the Security Council informed of all developments. The Council expects the African Union and the Intergovernmental Authority on Development to work out a detailed mission plan in close coordination with, and with the broad consensus of, the transitional federal institutions and consistent with a national security and stabilization plan.

The Council takes note of the request by the Peace and Security Council to the Security Council for the authorization of an exemption from the arms embargo imposed against Somalia by resolution 733 (1992) of 23 January 1992, contained in the communiqués issued by the Peace and Security Council on 12 May and 3 July 2005. The Security Council stands ready to consider this matter in due course on the basis of information on the above-mentioned mission plan.

The Council further reminds all parties in Somalia, including all members of the transitional federal institutions, as well as all Member States, of their obligation to implement and enforce the arms embargo imposed by the Council under resolution 733(1992). Continued non-compliance with this measure undermines the efforts of those who seek to establish peace in Somalia. There can be no effective and lasting progress in Somalia as long as arms and ammunition flow unchecked across Somalia's borders. A stable and secure environment in Somalia is essential to the future success of the national reconciliation process.

The Council welcomes the continued engagement of donors in supporting the establishment of a functioning government in Somalia through the mechanism of the Coordination and Monitoring Committee and in fulfilment of the Declaration of Principles. The Council encourages donor countries and regional and subregional organizations to continue to contribute to the reconstruction and rehabilitation of Somalia, in particular through the mechanism of the Rapid Assistance Programme and efforts coordinated by the United Nations.

The Council stresses that improving the humanitarian situation is an essential component of support for the peace and reconciliation process. The Council reiterates that ensuring humanitarian access to all Somalis in need and providing guarantees for the safety and security of aid workers is an immediate priority and obligation of the transitional federal institutions. The Council further welcomes the ongoing efforts and work of the business community, humanitarian organizations, non-governmental organizations, civil society and women's groups to facilitate the demilitarization of Somalia.

The Council deplores the recent hijacking of a vessel off the coast of Somalia that had been chartered by the World Food Programme and was carrying food aid for tsunami victims, and notes the subsequent decision by the Programme to suspend all shipments of humanitarian assistance to Somalia. The Council expresses its concern at the impact of these developments, and calls for the quick and appropriate resolution of this incident. The Council condemns in the strongest terms the brutal murder of Somali peace activist Abdulkadir Yahya Ali in Mogadishu on 11 July 2005. The Council calls for the incident to be investigated immediately and for those responsible to be held fully accountable.

The Council welcomes the steps being taken to strengthen the capacity of the United Nations Political Office for Somalia and reaffirms its strong support for the leadership of the Special Representative of the Secretary-General in his efforts in fostering inclusive dialogue among the leaders of the transitional federal institutions. The Council calls upon all Somali parties and Member States to extend to him their fullest cooperation in this regard.

The Council reaffirms its full support for the peace process in Somalia and the commitment of the United Nations to assist the regional and subregional efforts in this regard.

Report of Secretary-General (October). The Secretary-General's report of 11 October [S/2005/642] indicated no progress in resolving the differences between the TFI leaders on four broad issues: the relocation of the TFIs; a national security and stabilization plan; national reconciliation; and the peace support mission envisaged by the AU and IGAD. Instead, tensions worsened between the President and the Prime Minister, who were based in Jawhar, and the Speaker of Parliament and ministers based in Mogadishu, with the opposing parties proceeding to take unilateral actions.

At a meeting of some Parliament members in Nairobi on 12 June, chaired by the First Deputy Speaker, the President announced a two-month recess of Parliament; the Speaker, who did not attend, questioned the legitimacy of the meeting and the President's declaration of such a recess. On 8 August, the Prime Minister announced the composition of committees on national security, economic affairs and social affairs, which the Minister for National Security refused to recognize as having been constituted without the consultations required by the Transitional Federal Charter. Some Parliament members who met in Mogadishu on 13 August under the Speaker's chairmanship, announced the creation of a 59-member committee to restore peace and stability in Mogadishu; they then summoned the full Parliament to a meeting on 27 August, also in Mogadishu, so as to establish parliamentary subcommittees. That meeting did not take place. On 27 August, the Prime Minister announced to reporters that the Government would soon start offering oil, gas and mineral concessions to foreign firms and called on such firms to avoid dealings with no other authority than the Transitional Federal Government.

Mediation efforts between the two parties were mounted by Yemen, the Deputy Prime Minister and the Minister of Interior, as well as by the Special Representative, jointly with Kenya's Minister for Regional Cooperation and East Africa Affairs. On the basis of Security Council presidential statement S/PRST/2005/32 (above), the Special Representative intensified his contacts with the leadership of the TFIs to foster an inclusive dialogue. On 1 August, he visited Jawhar and presented the President and the Prime Minister with a proposed road map for dialogue which would address the key issues of an agreement on the safe relocation of the TFIs, a national security and stabilization plan, modalities for the deployment of an AU/IGAD peace support mission, and national reconciliation. A sequencing chart, prepared by IGAD, the AU and the EU, was also presented. It proposed that, upon successful conclusion of the dialogue, the Council of Ministers and a full session of Parliament should be called to establish a national security commission to draw up the modalities for the deployment of a peace support mission.

On 3 August, the Special Representative visited Mogadishu and presented to the Speaker, ministers and members of Parliament a copy of the road map and sequencing chart. They expressed support for the initiative but voiced their concerns that the President and the Prime Minister might resort to an armed confrontation with them. While committing themselves to dialogue, they emphasized that the agenda, venue and composition of delegations for the talks had to be agreed to in advance. The Prime Minister announced at a press conference on 19 August that the Government was open for dialogue within the TFIs. The Speaker, for his part, gave an undertaking to the Special Representative not to use any Parliament meetings to undermine the prospects for dialogue, and, on 26 August, reiterated his willingness to enter into dialogue within the framework of the TFIs, stressing the need to respect the Transitional Federal Charter.

On 13 September, the Prime Minister informed the Transitional Federal Government of his intentions, after consultations, to begin holding meetings of the Council of Ministers in Mogadishu. The Special Representative welcomed the initiative and expressed the hope that the meetings would be preceded by consultations and followed by a full session of Parliament, in accordance with the Transitional Federal Charter. In his discussions with high-level officials in the subregion, the Special Representative impressed upon his interlocutors the need to foster dialogue with the TFIs and encouraged them to use their influence towards that end. He subsequently held talks with European Governments to impress upon them the need for the international community to speak with one voice on the issues of an inclusive dialogue and of a functional parliament as essential for the legitimacy of the Transitional Federal Government.

The Heads of Mission of the EU countries in Nairobi welcomed the Prime Minister's proposal to resolve the differences within the TFIs at three levels: the leadership (President, Prime Minister and Speaker), the Cabinet (ministers), and Parliament. They emphasized that, if a resolution through dialogue was successful, more financial assistance would be forthcoming from their countries.

The Secretary-General expressed deep concern that the political tensions between the TFI leaders had led to military preparations. On 6 July, the President announced the creation of a Somali national army, which began to be assembled soon thereafter from various regions of Somalia. When troops loyal to him arrived in Jawhar in early September, the Mogadishu-based leaders responded by deploying their troops in the direction of Jawhar. By a 7 September press release, they warned all humanitarian agencies and diplomats to suspend their presence in Jawhar and cautioned all aircraft to cease landing there. On 8 September, the United Nations relocated its international humanitarian staff to Nairobi and Wajid, a move criticized by the President. On 12 September, the offices of the United Nations Children's Fund were ordered closed by the faction leader controlling Jawhar.

Meanwhile, in "Somaliland" on 27 June, the "President" there, speaking on the occasion of the forty-fifth anniversary of independence from the United Kingdom, expressed optimism for gaining international recognition for "Somaliland". At the request of the electoral commission, he also postponed the parliamentary elections to 29 September.

Mogadishu remained insecure, in spite of unprecedented pre-disarmament efforts to encamp militiamen, canton "technicals" (armed vehicles), and dismantle checkpoints. Killings and politically-linked assassinations in the capital included the assassination of a Somali reporter working for Horn Afrik Radio (5 June) and of the long-standing peace activist, Abdul Qadir Yahya, who was also a senior member of the Center for Research and Dialogue (11 July). Lack of security in most of the country remained a significant problem also for aid agencies. The increased inflow of weapons, in continued violation of the UN arms embargo on Somalia (see p. 346), the inter- and intra-clan fighting, especially in central and southern Somalia, and fighting between rival militias all made for difficult humanitarian access to the critical communities in need of emergency assistance.

As later reported by the Secretary-General [S/2006/122], the Prime Minister led a ministerial delegation to Mogadishu on 6 November, to make good his intention of holding a meeting of the Council of Ministers in an effort to break the deadlock within the Transitional Federal Government. Soon after arriving in the north of the city, his motorcade was attacked by an explosive device; although he was unhurt, the blast killed nine people and wounded at least 10 others. Nonetheless, the Prime Minister called a Cabinet meeting on 8 November, but only those ministers already supporting him attended; those based in Mogadishu declined to attend, as the meeting was not preceded by consultations between the two sides.

Another initiative for reconciliation was undertaken in early November by the Chairman of the Juba Alliance in control of Kismayo, who proposed a two-phased approach to parliamentary dialogue: the first would involve a meeting in Kismayo of 16 parliamentarians each from Jawhar and Mogadishu to discuss technical modalities; the second would involve a full session of Parliament. Owing to lack of consensus on the question of venue, the initiative was not realized.

SECURITY COUNCIL ACTION (November)

On 9 November [meeting 5302], following consultations among Security Council members, the President made statement **S/PRST/2005/54** on behalf of the Council:

> The Security Council reaffirms all previous statements by its President and its resolutions concerning the situation in Somalia, in particular the statement by its President of 14 July 2005 and its resolution 1630(2005) of 14 October 2005.
>
> The Council welcomes the report of the Secretary-General of 11 October 2005, and reaffirms its commitment to a comprehensive and lasting settlement of the situation in Somalia and its respect for the sovereignty, territorial integrity, political independence and unity of Somalia, consistent with the purposes and principles of the Charter of the United Nations.
>
> The Council expresses its concern over recent reported military activities and hostile rhetoric, and emphasizes that any resort to military force as a means of dealing with the current differences within the transitional federal institutions is unacceptable. The Council condemns in the strongest terms the assassination attempt on 6 November 2005 against Prime Minister Ali Mohammed Gedi in Mogadishu.
>
> The Council expresses its concern and disappointment over the lack of progress in ameliorating the contention between the leaders of the transitional federal institutions, and over the non-functioning of the Transitional Federal Parliament, which has an essential role in promoting the peace process. The Council calls upon all Somali parties and the leaders of the transitional federal institutions to take concrete steps towards reaching a consensus agreement through inclusive dialogue without delay. The Council commends the Prime Minister's initiative for the early convening of a full Council of Ministers in Mogadishu, to be followed by a full session of Parliament. The Council underlines the fact that the primary responsibility for progress in restoring an effective functioning govern-

ment to Somalia lies with the leaders and members of the transitional federal institutions.

The Council underlines its strong support for the Special Representative of the Secretary-General for Somalia in his efforts at facilitating the peace process in Somalia, supporting ongoing Somali-owned internal initiatives. The Council calls upon all Member States to provide their full and active support in this regard.

The Council commends the neighbouring countries, the Intergovernmental Authority on Development, the African Union, the League of Arab States, the European Union and concerned Member States for their keen interest and persistent efforts in support of the peace process in Somalia. The Council urges them to use their influence and leverage through a common approach to ensure that the transitional federal institutions resolve their differences and build trust, through an inclusive dialogue, and to move ahead on the key issues of security and national reconciliation.

The Council affirms its continuing support to the transitional federal institutions and reiterates the need for a national security and stabilization plan to be agreed, through which any efforts to rebuild the security sector should be directed.

The Council condemns the increased inflow of weapons into Somalia and the continuous violations of the United Nations arms embargo. The Council further reminds all States of their obligations to comply fully with the measures imposed by resolution 733(1992) and urges them to take all necessary steps to hold violators accountable.

The Council expresses serious concern over the increasing incidents of piracy off the coast of Somalia. The Council condemns recent hijackings of vessels in the area, particularly of ships carrying humanitarian supplies to Somalia. The Council urges the transitional federal institutions, regional actors and relevant international organizations to work together to address this problem.

The Council expresses its growing concern over the situation of one million Somalis in a state of humanitarian emergency or suffering from severe livelihood distress and the rising civil and food insecurity in parts of southern Somalia, where malnutrition levels have increased. The Council stresses that improving humanitarian access to all Somalis in need is an essential component of durable peace and reconciliation.

The Council recognizes the role of civil society, in particular women's groups, and their contribution to progress in demobilizing militias and improving the humanitarian situation in Somalia.

The Council strongly urges the transitional federal institutions to ensure humanitarian access and provide guarantees for the safety and security of aid workers. The Council condemns in the strongest terms the killing of a United Nations national security officer in Kismayo on 3 October 2005. The Council calls for those responsible to be held accountable.

The Council reaffirms its full support for the peace process in Somalia and the commitment of the United Nations to assist in this regard.

Arms embargo

Report of Monitoring Group (March). As requested by Security Council resolution 1558 (2004) [YUN 2004, p. 264], the Monitoring Group of four experts re-established by the Secretary-General for a period of six months [ibid., p. 265], continued to investigate violations of the arms embargo covering access to Somalia by land, air and sea, to assess progress of its full implementation by States in the region, and to make recommendations.

The Group issued its report [S/2005/153] on 14 February, which the Security Council Committee established pursuant to resolution 751 (1992) concerning Somalia (Committee on sanctions against Somalia) [YUN 1992, p. 202] transmitted to the Council on 8 March. The Group reported that violations of the arms embargo continued to occur at a brisk and alarming rate. Since February 2004, it had uncovered 34 separate arms shipments in violation of the embargo, which ranged from individual weapons, such as large anti-aircraft guns, to ocean freight containers full of arms ranging from explosives and ammunition to small arms, mines and anti-tank weapons.

Information gathered by the Group indicated the existence of a sophisticated financial network operating inside and outside Somalia that might be directly involved in arms purchases. Recent arms shipments had strengthened the military capacity of well organized and funded opposition elements within Somalia, who had publicly expressed their intent to violently oppose the Government and any international supporters that might provide military support to it inside Somalia.

The report drew attention to two major arms markets that continued to help fuel and perpetuate the violent clashes and instability prevalent in the country: the Bakaaraha arms market inside Somalia, particularly in Mogadishu, and an arms market located in Yemen that the Group was convinced was the source of a continuous supply of arms for the Bakaaraha market. Those markets were also a main cause of the many arms-related problems in the front line States. The increased clandestine arms shipments to Somalia relied less on air and more on sea and road transport. The Group's findings included arms shipments offloaded from container ships at a neighbouring country's seaport and transported to Somalia by road and by dhows. Organized criminal groups involved in the clandestine movement of arms shipments from source to recipient had consistently circumvented the customs and police authorities of the various States responsible for interdicting such shipments. As a result, the continued heavy flow of arms into Somalia, mostly directed to those elements opposed to the newly established Transitional Federal Government (temporarily based in Nairobi), posed a serious threat to its peaceful establishment in Somalia.

Among the Group's recommendations were the continued monitoring of the arms embargo, especially at border crossings and along the Somali coastline, which were the linchpins of the embargo violations; updating of the draft list of violators; and establishing a more formally structured Transitional Federal Government relationship with the AU, IGAD and possibly the front-line States to facilitate information exchange and cooperation. With international and regional support, the Transitional Federal Government should be encouraged to take prompt and decisive steps to regulate or stop arms sales through the Bakaaraha market. Increased arms enforcement and interdiction by the customs, police and security organs of the regional and front-line States should be promoted. The Transitional Federal Government should work with the International Civil Aviation Organization, through the Civil Aviation Caretaker Authority for Somalia, to enable it to undertake its responsibilities for curtailing the transport of arms by air. The Committee on sanctions against Somalia, through the Monitoring Group and in collaboration with the International Maritime Organization and neighbouring States, should develop projects for the effective control of maritime activities along the Somali coastline; regional and front-line States should continue to monitor aggressively aircraft movements to and from Somalia, in coordination with the Civil Aviation Caretaker Authority; and neighbouring States should enforce the embargo by closely monitoring their common borders and regulating the flow of vehicular traffic.

The Transitional Federal Government was to be encouraged to establish its own customs border enforcement upon its relocation to Somalia, and special operations against illicit cross-border arms movement were to be conducted by regional customs authorities. The Group recommended that steps be taken to regulate the production of charcoal and establish adequate legal financial channels for the revenues derived from its export, without which large sums of money would continue to be indiscriminately used by warlords to strengthen their positions in the Somali conflict; and that financial and law enforcement authorities in countries where counterfeit Somali shillings were being printed undertake joint operations to address the practice and the smuggling of such currency into Somalia. Organizations giving donations to Somali charities and NGOs should reinforce their post-donation audit to ensure that donations were not diverted to warlords or extremist groups.

Communication. By a letter of 8 June to the Council [S/2005/390], Yemen annexed a detailed response to all the statements and references, implied or otherwise, to the country in the Group's February report above. It made clear that the reported arms market inside Yemen had ceased to exist legally as from the beginning of 2003, when it was abolished by the Government and the permits granted for its operation were cancelled. Although the reference to a neighbouring country's seaport from which arms shipments were offloaded for transport to Somalia was unclear, Yemen pointed out that it had no land borders with Somalia across which weapons might be transported to that country by land; Yemen was not among other parties having the capacity to carry out such combined sea-and-land activity.

SECURITY COUNCIL ACTION (March)

On 15 March [meeting 5142], the Security Council unanimously adopted **resolution 1587(2005)**. The draft [S/2005/160] was prepared in consultations among Council members.

The Security Council,

Reaffirming its previous resolutions and the statements by its President concerning the situation in Somalia, in particular resolution 733(1992) of 23 January 1992, which established an embargo on all deliveries of weapons and military equipment to Somalia (hereinafter referred to as "the arms embargo"), and resolutions 1519(2003) of 16 December 2003 and 1558(2004) of 17 August 2004,

Welcoming further progress in the process of national reconciliation in Somalia, and expecting further steps by the Transitional Federal Government towards establishing effective national governance in Somalia,

Reaffirming the importance of the sovereignty, territorial integrity, political independence and unity of Somalia,

Commending the efforts of the African Union and the Intergovernmental Authority on Development in support of the Transitional Federal Government, and welcoming the continued support of the African Union for reconciliation in Somalia,

Taking note of the report of the Monitoring Group of 14 February 2005, submitted pursuant to paragraph 3 *(e)* of resolution 1558(2004), and the observations and recommendations contained therein,

Condemning the continued flow of weapons and ammunition supplies to and through Somalia, in violation of the arms embargo, and expressing its determination that violators should be held accountable,

Reiterating the importance of the implementation of the arms embargo by Member States and the enhancement of the monitoring of the arms embargo in Somalia through persistent and vigilant investigation into the violations, bearing in mind that strict enforcement of the arms embargo will improve the overall security situation in Somalia,

Determining that the situation in Somalia constitutes a threat to international peace and security in the region,

Acting under Chapter VII of the Charter of the United Nations,

1. *Stresses* the obligation of all States to comply fully with the measures imposed by resolution 733(1992);

2. *Expresses its intention* to give the report of the Monitoring Group of 14 February 2005 due consideration in order to improve implementation of and compliance with the measures imposed by resolution 733(1992);

3. *Requests* the Secretary-General, in consultation with the Security Council Committee established pursuant to resolution 751(1992) concerning Somalia (hereinafter referred to as "the Committee"), to re-establish within thirty days of the date of the adoption of the present resolution, and for a period of six months, the Monitoring Group referred to in paragraph 3 of resolution 1558(2004), with the following mandate:

(*a*) To continue investigating the implementation of the arms embargo by Member States and violations, inter alia, through field-based investigations in Somalia, where possible, and, as appropriate, in other States, in particular, those in the region;

(*b*) To assess actions taken by Somali authorities, as well as Member States, in particular those in the region, to implement fully the arms embargo;

(*c*) To make specific recommendations based on detailed information in relevant areas of expertise related to violations and measures to give effect to and strengthen the implementation of the arms embargo in its various aspects;

(*d*) To continue refining and updating information on the draft list of those individuals and entities who violate the measures implemented by Member States in accordance with resolution 733(1992), inside and outside Somalia, and their active supporters, for possible future measures by the Council, and to present such information to the Committee as and when the Committee deems appropriate;

(*e*) To continue making recommendations based on its investigations, on the previous reports of the Panel of Experts appointed pursuant to resolutions 1425 (2002) of 22 July 2002 and 1474(2003) of 8 April 2003, and on the previous reports of the Monitoring Group appointed pursuant to resolutions 1519(2003) and 1558 (2004);

(*f*) To work closely with the Committee on specific recommendations for additional measures to improve overall compliance with the arms embargo;

(*g*) To assist in identifying areas where the capacities of States in the region can be strengthened to facilitate the implementation of the arms embargo;

(*h*) To provide to the Council, through the Committee, a midterm briefing within ninety days of its establishment;

(*i*) To submit to the Council through the Committee, no later than thirty days prior to the termination of its mandate, a final report covering all the tasks set out above, which the Committee will subsequently consider and convey to the Council prior to the expiration of its mandate;

4. *Also requests* the Secretary-General to make the necessary financial arrangements to support the work of the Monitoring Group;

5. *Reaffirms* paragraphs 4, 5, 7, 8 and 10 of resolution 1519(2003);

6. *Requests* the Committee, in accordance with its mandate and in consultation with the Monitoring Group and other relevant United Nations entities, to consider and recommend to the Council ways to improve implementation of and compliance with the arms embargo, including ways to develop the capacity of States in the region to implement the arms embargo, in response to continuing violations;

7. *Also requests* the Committee to consider, when appropriate, a visit to Somalia and/or the region by its Chairman and those he may designate, as approved by the Committee, to demonstrate the determination of the Council to give full effect to the arms embargo;

8. *Decides* to remain actively seized of the matter.

On 6 April [S/2005/229], the Secretary-General informed the Council that, after consultations with the Committee on sanctions against Somalia, he had re-established the Monitoring Group and appointed the four experts to constitute its membership.

Report of Monitoring Group (October). In accordance with the foregoing Security Council resolution, the Monitoring Group issued its report on 22 August [S/2005/625], which the Committee on sanctions against Somalia transmitted to the Council on 5 October. The Group reported that the previous six-month period saw a dramatic and sustained rise in the number of arms embargo violations that involved members of the Transitional Federal Government and those of the opposition in Mogadishu. The greatly increased arms flows into Somalia reflected the ongoing militarization in central and southern Somalia by the two sides (see p. 346). The opposition members who committed violations were the same individuals previously identified by the Group as warlords who did not want the establishment in Somalia of a Government that would infringe or overturn their personal political and economic vested interests. The Bakaraaha arms market in Mogadishu continued to play a major role as an intermediary for channelling arms to members of the opposition. States in the region provided direct arms support to both sides as well.

The Group identified two key generators of revenue that accrued to certain powerful local administrations to help maintain their militias and purchase arms: the fishing industry, driven principally by foreign interests with whom local administrations or faction leaders concluded licensing arrangements for the unrestrained exploitation of marine resources in Somali coastal waters; and the export from Somalia of large commercial quantities of charcoal, which represented a considerable source of revenue for factions engaged in arms embargo violations.

Therefore, to reduce the financial capacity of such local administrations to buy arms, the Group recommended that the Council consider adopting an integrated arms embargo that would reaffirm and maintain the existing arms embargo on Somalia and include an embargo on the export of Somali charcoal, a ban on foreign vessels fishing in Somali waters, and an embargo on the export of fish from those waters.

SECURITY COUNCIL ACTION (October)

On 14 October [meeting 5280], the Security Council unanimously adopted **resolution 1630(2005)**. The draft [S/2005/646] was prepared in consultations among Council members.

The Security Council,

Reaffirming its previous resolutions and the statements by its President concerning the situation in Somalia, in particular resolution 733(1992) of 23 January 1992, which established an embargo on all deliveries of weapons and military equipment to Somalia (hereinafter referred to as "the arms embargo"), and resolutions 1519(2003) of 16 December 2003, 1558(2004) of 17 August 2004 and 1587(2005) of 15 March 2005,

Reaffirming also the importance of the sovereignty, territorial integrity, political independence and unity of Somalia,

Reiterating the urgent need for all Somali leaders to take tangible steps to begin political dialogue,

Reaffirming its strong support for the leadership of the Special Representative of the Secretary-General for Somalia in his efforts at fostering inclusive dialogue, particularly through his road map for dialogue among the leaders of the transitional federal institutions,

Stressing the need for the transitional federal institutions to continue working towards establishing effective national governance in Somalia,

Commending the efforts of the African Union and the Intergovernmental Authority on Development in support of the transitional federal institutions, and welcoming the continued support of the African Union for national reconciliation in Somalia,

Taking note of the report of the Monitoring Group of 22 August 2005, submitted pursuant to paragraph 3 *(i)* of resolution 1587(2005)and the observations and recommendations contained therein,

Condemning the significant increase in the flow of weapons and ammunition supplies to and through Somalia, which constitutes a violation of the arms embargo and a serious threat to the Somali peace process,

Reiterating its insistence that all Member States, in particular those in the region, should refrain from any action in contravention of the arms embargo and should take all necessary steps to hold violators accountable,

Reiterating and underscoring the importance of enhancing the monitoring of the arms embargo in Somalia through persistent and vigilant investigation into the violations, bearing in mind that strict enforcement of the arms embargo will improve the overall security situation in Somalia,

Determining that the situation in Somalia constitutes a threat to international peace and security in the region,

Acting under Chapter VII of the Charter of the United Nations,

1. *Stresses* the obligation of all Member States to comply fully with the measures imposed by resolution 733(1992);

2. *Expresses its intention,* in the light of the report of the Monitoring Group of 22 August 2005, to consider specific actions to improve implementation of and compliance with the measures imposed by resolution 733(1992);

3. *Decides* to request the Secretary-General, in consultation with the Security Council Committee established pursuant to resolution 751(1992) (hereinafter referred to as "the Committee"), to re-establish within thirty days of the date of adoption of the present resolution, and for a period of six months, the Monitoring Group referred to in paragraph 3 of resolution 1558 (2004), with the following mandate:

(a) To continue the tasks outlined in paragraphs 3 *(a)* to *(c)* of resolution 1587(2005);

(b) To continue to investigate, in coordination with relevant international agencies, all activities, including in the financial, maritime and other sectors, which generate revenues used to commit arms embargo violations;

(c) To continue to investigate any means of transport, routes, seaports, airports and other facilities used in connection with arms embargo violations;

(d) To continue refining and updating information on the draft list of those individuals and entities who violate the measures implemented by Member States in accordance with resolution 733(1992), inside and outside Somalia, and their active supporters, for possible future measures by the Council, and to present such information to the Committee as and when the Committee deems appropriate;

(e) To continue making recommendations based on its investigations, on the previous reports of the Panel of Experts appointed pursuant to resolutions 1425 (2002) of 22 July 2002 and 1474(2003) of 8 April 2003, and on the previous reports of the Monitoring Group appointed pursuant to resolutions 1519(2003), 1558 (2004)and 1587(2005);

(f) To work closely with the Committee on specific recommendations for additional measures to improve overall compliance with the arms embargo;

(g) To assist in identifying areas where the capacities of States in the region can be strengthened to facilitate the implementation of the arms embargo;

(h) To provide to the Council, through the Committee, a midterm briefing within ninety days of its establishment;

(i) To submit, through the Committee, for consideration by the Council, a final report covering all the tasks set out above, no later than fifteen days prior to the termination of the mandate of the Monitoring Group;

4. *Requests* the Secretary-General to make the necessary financial arrangements to support the work of the Monitoring Group;

5. *Reaffirms* paragraphs 4, 5, 7, 8 and 10 of resolution 1519(2003);

6. *Requests* the Committee, in accordance with its mandate and in consultation with the Monitoring Group and other relevant United Nations entities, to consider and recommend to the Council ways to improve implementation of and compliance with the arms embargo, in response to continuing violations;

7. *Also requests* the Committee to consider, when appropriate, a visit to Somalia and/or the region by its Chairman and those he may designate, as approved by the Committee, to demonstrate the determination of the Council to give full effect to the arms embargo;

8. *Decides* to remain actively seized of the matter.

As requested, the Secretary-General advised the Council on 2 November [S/2005/695] that, after consultations with the Committee on sanctions against Somalia, he had re-established the Monitoring Group and appointed the four experts to constitute its membership.

Report of Committee on sanctions. In accordance with a 1995 Security Council note, the Chairman of the Committee on sanctions against Somalia transmitted the annual report of the Committee [S/2005/813] summarizing its activities during 2005. The Committee held nine informal and three formal meetings. At the informal meetings, it met separately with representatives of Somalia's neighbouring countries: Ethiopia, Eritrea and Kenya; discussed actions to follow up the meetings with those countries; met with the members of the Monitoring Group; discussed the AU communiqué of 12 May [S/2005/315] seeking exemption from the arms embargo for the proposed AU/IGAD peace support mission so as to allow it to bring military equipment to Somalia (see p. 341); and heard a briefing by the Chairman on his visit to Kenya, Ethiopia and Yemen (26 November–4 December), as requested by Council resolution 1630(2005). Discussions at the formal meetings concerned the findings and recommendations of the Group as contained in its two reports.

The Committee's strong support for the work of the Monitoring Group, its active dialogue with and engagement of Somalia's neighbouring States, and the Chairman's recent visit to the region were evidence of its firm commitment to further strengthen the arms embargo on Somalia. As in the past, the Committee continued to rely on the cooperation of States and organizations in a position to provide information on violations of the arms embargo.

Eritrea–Ethiopia

The United Nations, in 2005, maintained its presence in Eritrea and Ethiopia in order to assist the countries in the implementation of their 2000 Agreement on Cessation of Hostilities and Comprehensive Peace Agreement, both signed in Algiers (the Algiers Agreements), which regulated their border dispute that had led to armed conflict in 1998 and subsequent intermittent fighting. The United Nations Mission in Ethiopia and Eritrea (UNMEE), established in 2000, continued to monitor the border region designated as the Temporary Security Zone and to support the work of the five-member Eritrea-Ethiopia Boundary Commission, the neutral body mandated under the terms of the Peace Agreement to delimit and demarcate the colonial treaty border.

During the year, the Boundary Commission attempted but failed to advance its demarcation activities, stalled in 2003, following the rejection by Ethiopia of significant parts of the Commission's 2002 final and binding delimitation decision, previously accepted by both parties. Ethiopia declined to attend a meeting called by the Commission and remained firm in its insistence on preconditions for the implementation of the demarcation in the form of procedural impediments, whereas Eritrea insisted on adherence to the delimitation decision. In view of the impasse, the Commission decided in May to suspend activities and close its field offices; it expressed readiness to proceed with and complete the demarcation process whenever circumstances permitted.

Ethiopia continued to reinforce its troop build-up close to the southern boundary of the Zone, begun at the end of the previous year, while Eritrea continued to conduct military exercises north of it. UNMEE had successfully maintained the integrity of the Zone, despite restrictions imposed by both parties on its freedom of movement. However, Eritrea imposed additional operational and administrative restrictions and, in October, banned all UNMEE helicopter flights within its airspace, thus severely inhibiting UNMEE capacity to implement its monitoring mandate. The fact-finding mission dispatched by the Security Council to the region in November to assess the situation involving UNMEE resulted in Council resolution 1640(2005) demanding that the parties immediately return to the 16 December 2004 levels of deployment, that Ethiopia accept fully the Commission's delimitation decision, and that Eritrea immediately reverse all restrictions imposed on UNMEE operations. Ethiopia complied with the demand on troop redeployment; Eritrea maintained it had no troops to redeploy. The other demands of the resolution remained unfulfilled by year's end.

Eritrea, instead of reversing its restrictions, asked that UNMEE staff of certain nationalities leave the country with effect from 6 December.

On 14 December, the Council, in consultation with the Secretary-General, agreed to temporarily relocate UNMEE civilian and military staff to Ethiopia; it intended to maintain the military presence of the Mission in Eritrea during its review of future plans for the Mission, whose mandate had been extended until 15 March 2006.

UNMEE

The United Nations Mission in Ethiopia and Eritrea (UNMEE), established by Security Council resolution 1312(2000) [YUN 2000, p. 174], continued in 2005 to monitor and verify implementation of the June 2000 Agreement on Cessation of Hostilities between Ethiopia and Eritrea [ibid., p. 173]. Its core operations, as revised by resolutions 1320 (2000) [ibid., p. 176] and 1430(2002) [YUN 2002, p. 189], were devoted to observation, reporting, analysis, identification of potential flashpoints and preventive action, chairing the Military Coordination Commission and assisting the Boundary Commission (see below). The area under constant monitoring was within and around the Temporary Security Zone, a 25-kilometre-wide buffer zone separating Eritrea and Ethiopia, which for operational purposes, was divided into Sector West, Sector Centre and Sub-Sector East (formerly Sector East). UNMEE was headquartered in Addis Ababa and Asmara and maintained an office in Adigrat, Ethiopia.

In accordance with resolution 1560(2004) [YUN 2004, p. 270], which approved the two-phased adjustments to the configuration of the Mission, as proposed by the Secretary-General [ibid., p. 269], the Mission's operations were streamlined beginning in December 2004 and completed by the end of January 2005. Its force was reduced from three to two battalions, and the former Sector East was reorganized into the new Sub-Sector East under the operational command of Sector Centre.

On the recommendation of the Secretary-General, the Council extended the mandate of UNMEE twice during the year, each for a six-month period: the first time until 15 September 2005 and the second until 15 March 2006.

Appointments. The Special Representative of the Secretary-General for Eritrea and Ethiopia, Legwaila Joseph Legwaila (Botswana), who had headed UNMEE since 2000, was assisted by two Deputy Special Representatives appointed by the Secretary-General in 2005: Joël W. Adechi (Benin), on 25 May [SG/A/925-AFR/1171], who was to take up his duties in the Eritrean capital, Asmara, in early June; and Azouz Ennifar (Tunisia), on 29 July [SG/A/936-AFR/1222], who was to be based in the Ethiopian capital, Addis Ababa. The latter succeeded Cheikh-Tidiane Gaye (Senegal), who had left the Mission area earlier in the year.

Financing

At its resumed fifty-ninth session, the General Assembly considered the Secretary-General's performance report on the budget of UNMEE for 1 July 2003 to 30 June 2004 [A/59/616] showing expenditures totalling $183,600,200 out of an apportionment of $188,400,000, a variance of $4,799,800, or 2.5 per cent; the proposed UNMEE budget for 1 July 2005 to 30 June 2006 [A/59/636 & Corr.1], amounting to $176,716,200; and the related report of ACABQ [A/59/736/Add. 10].

GENERAL ASSEMBLY ACTION

On 22 June [meeting 104], the General Assembly, on the recommendation of the Fifth Committee [A/59/833], adopted **resolution 59/303** without vote [agenda item 130].

Financing of the United Nations Mission in Ethiopia and Eritrea

The General Assembly,

Having considered the reports of the Secretary-General on the financing of the United Nations Mission in Ethiopia and Eritrea and the related reports of the Advisory Committee on Administrative and Budgetary Questions,

Bearing in mind Security Council resolution 1312(2000) of 31 July 2000, by which the Council established the United Nations Mission in Ethiopia and Eritrea, and the subsequent resolutions by which the Council extended the mandate of the Mission, the latest of which was resolution 1586(2005) of 14 March 2005,

Recalling its resolution 55/237 of 23 December 2000 on the financing of the Mission and its subsequent resolutions thereon, the latest of which was resolution 58/302 of 18 June 2004,

Reaffirming the general principles underlying the financing of United Nations peacekeeping operations, as stated in General Assembly resolutions 1874(S-IV) of 27 June 1963, 3101(XXVIII) of 11 December 1973 and 55/235 of 23 December 2000,

Noting with appreciation that voluntary contributions have been made to the Mission,

Mindful of the fact that it is essential to provide the Mission with the necessary financial resources to enable it to fulfil its responsibilities under the relevant resolutions of the Security Council,

1. *Requests* the Secretary-General to entrust the Head of Mission with the task of formulating future budget proposals in full accordance with the provisions of General Assembly resolution 59/296 of 22 June 2005, as well as other relevant resolutions;

2. *Takes note* of the status of contributions to the United Nations Mission in Ethiopia and Eritrea as at 15 April 2005, including the contributions outstanding in the amount of 18.9 million United States dollars, representing some 2 per cent of the total assessed contributions, notes with concern that only thirty-one Member States have paid their assessed contributions

in full, and urges all other Member States, in particular those in arrears, to ensure payment of their outstanding assessed contributions;

3. *Expresses its appreciation* to those Member States which have paid their assessed contributions in full, and urges all other Member States to make every possible effort to ensure payment of their assessed contributions to the Mission in full;

4. *Expresses concern* at the financial situation with regard to peacekeeping activities, in particular as regards the reimbursements to troop contributors that bear additional burdens owing to overdue payments by Member States of their assessments;

5. *Also expresses concern* at the delay experienced by the Secretary-General in deploying and providing adequate resources to some recent peacekeeping missions, in particular those in Africa;

6. *Emphasizes* that all future and existing peace-keeping missions shall be given equal and non-discriminatory treatment in respect of financial and administrative arrangements;

7. *Also emphasizes* that all peacekeeping missions shall be provided with adequate resources for the effective and efficient discharge of their respective mandates;

8. *Reiterates its request* to the Secretary-General to make the fullest possible use of facilities and equipment at the United Nations Logistics Base at Brindisi, Italy, in order to minimize the costs of procurement for the Mission;

9. *Endorses* the conclusions and recommendations contained in the report of the Advisory Committee on Administrative and Budgetary Questions, and requests the Secretary-General to ensure their full implementation;

10. *Requests* the Secretary-General to ensure the full implementation of the relevant provisions of its resolution 59/296;

11. *Also requests* the Secretary-General to take all necessary action to ensure that the Mission is administered with a maximum of efficiency and economy;

12. *Further requests* the Secretary-General, in order to reduce the cost of employing General Service staff, to continue efforts to recruit local staff for the Mission against General Service posts, commensurate with the requirements of the Mission;

**Financial performance report
for the period from 1 July 2003 to 30 June 2004**

13. *Takes note* of the report of the Secretary-General on the financial performance of the Mission for the period from 1 July 2003 to 30 June 2004;

**Budget estimates for the period
from 1 July 2005 to 30 June 2006**

14. *Decides* to appropriate to the Special Account for the United Nations Mission in Ethiopia and Eritrea the amount of 185,993,300 dollars for the period from 1 July 2005 to 30 June 2006, inclusive of 176,664,400 dollars for the maintenance of the Mission, 7,628,200 dollars for the support account for peacekeeping operations and 1,700,700 dollars for the United Nations Logistics Base;

Financing of the appropriation

15. *Decides also* to apportion among Member States the amount of 38,748,604 dollars for the period from 1 July to 15 September 2005, in accordance with the

levels updated in General Assembly resolution 58/256 of 23 December 2003, and taking into account the scale of assessments for 2005, as set out in its resolution 58/1 B of 23 December 2003;

16. *Decides further* that, in accordance with the provisions of its resolution 973(X) of 15 December 1955, there shall be set off against the apportionment among Member States, as provided for in paragraph 15 above, their respective share in the Tax Equalization Fund of 1,186,104 dollars, comprising the estimated staff assessment income of 932,812 dollars approved for the Mission, the prorated share of 224,625 dollars of the estimated staff assessment income approved for the support account, and the prorated share of 28,667 dollars of the estimated staff assessment income approved for the United Nations Logistics Base;

17. *Decides* to apportion among Member States the amount of 147,244,696 dollars for the period from 16 September 2005 to 30 June 2006 at a monthly rate of 15,499,441 dollars, in accordance with the levels updated in General Assembly resolution 58/256, and taking into account the scale of assessments for 2005 and 2006, as set out in its resolution 58/1 B, subject to a decision of the Security Council to extend the mandate of the Mission;

18. *Decides also* that, in accordance with the provisions of its resolution 973(X), there shall be set off against the apportionment among Member States, as provided for in paragraph 17 above, their respective share in the Tax Equalization Fund of 4,507,196 dollars, comprising the estimated staff assessment income of 3,544,688 dollars approved for the Mission, the prorated share of 853,575 dollars of the estimated staff assessment income approved for the support account and the prorated share of 108,933 dollars of the estimated staff assessment income approved for the United Nations Logistics Base;

19. *Decides further* that for Member States that have fulfilled their financial obligations to the Mission, there shall be set off against their apportionment, as provided for in paragraph 15 above, their respective share of the unencumbered balance and other income in the total amount of 20,184,500 dollars in respect of the financial period ended 30 June 2004, in accordance with the levels updated in General Assembly resolution 58/256, and taking into account the scale of assessments for 2004, as set out in its resolution 58/1 B;

20. *Decides* that, for Member States that have not fulfilled their financial obligations to the Mission, there shall be set off against their outstanding obligations their respective share of the unencumbered balance and other income in the total amount of 20,184,500 dollars in respect of the financial period ended 30 June 2004, in accordance with the scheme set out in paragraph 19 above;

21. *Decides also* that the increase of 744,800 dollars in the estimated staff assessment income in respect of the financial period ended 30 June 2004 shall be added to the credits from the amount referred to in paragraphs 19 and 20 above;

22. *Emphasizes* that no peacekeeping operation shall be financed by borrowing funds from other active peacekeeping operations;

23. *Encourages* the Secretary-General to continue to take additional measures to ensure the safety and security of all personnel under the auspices of the United

Nations participating in peacekeeping operations, bearing in mind paragraphs 5 and 6 of Security Council resolution 1502(2003) of 26 August 2003;

24. *Invites* voluntary contributions to the Mission in cash and in the form of services and supplies acceptable to the Secretary-General, to be administered, as appropriate, in accordance with the procedure and practices established by the General Assembly;

25. *Decides* to include in the provisional agenda of its sixtieth session the item entitled "Financing of the United Nations Mission in Ethiopia and Eritrea".

The Secretary-General submitted on 22 and 28 December, respectively, the performance report on the UNMEE budget for 1 July 2004 to 30 June 2005 [A/60/615] and the UNMEE budget for 1 July 2006 to 30 June 2007 [A/60/636 & Corr.1].

Implementation of Algiers Agreements

Report of Secretary-General (March). The Secretary-General, in his March report [S/2005/142] updating developments in the peace process to which Ethiopia and Eritrea were committed under the terms of the 2000 Algiers Agreements, stated that, since his last report [YUN 2004, p. 272], Ethiopia had been steadily massing troops towards the southern boundary of the Temporary Security Zone. UNMEE confirmed the deployment of six to seven additional divisions at points ranging from 25 to 45 kilometres from that boundary, and training exercises and troop movements in Sector West. While Ethiopia described those activities as part of a reorganization of its armed forces to improve its defence capability, Eritrea regarded them as provocative. No significant movement of the Eritrean Defence Forces had been observed, however, except for some adjustments in areas near the Zone to cover the main roads linking both countries.

Concerned about a consequent rise in tensions along the parties' common border, the Secretary-General appealed to Ethiopia to redeploy its troops in order to reinstate the situation obtaining prior to 16 December 2004. With Ethiopia's troop build-up and hostile rhetoric from the two parties, the continuing threat to military stability due to the lack of progress in the Ethiopia-Eritrea peace process remained. Nonetheless, both generally cooperated with UNMEE, thus enabling it to maintain the integrity of the Zone.

The Military Coordination Commission, at its twenty-eighth meeting (Nairobi, 17 January), reviewed the functioning of the sector-level military coordination commissions and discussed the Ethiopian troop deployment and its potential impact on the peace process.

Restrictions on UNMEE's freedom of movement in areas adjacent to the Zone had been reduced to some extent by Eritrea. However, its continued closure of the Asmara-Keren-Barentu road—the best supply route for UN troops in Sector West—constituted a major impediment to UNMEE operations, although it was reopened briefly from 12 to 26 January to facilitate the rotation of the Jordanian battalion. Moreover, Eritrea's position in denying UNMEE a direct flight route between the capitals of both countries remained unchanged; UNMEE aircraft thus continued to fly via Djibouti, resulting in additional costs and work hours, and increased risk to staff safety and security. On the Ethiopian side of the Zone, restrictions were also encountered, especially in Sub-Sector East.

The UNMEE Mine Action Coordination Centre continued to provide support for the maintenance of a well-coordinated mine action response within the Zone and nearby areas, where landmines and unexploded ordnance posed a major danger and thus an obstacle to the resettlement there of the populations of both countries. During the reporting period, the Centre's field teams provided mine-risk education, assistance and advice to almost 4,000 people. Three people were reported killed and 11 injured resulting from five accidental mine/ordnance explosions, three in Sector Centre and two in Sector West.

The overall humanitarian situation in Eritrea continued to deteriorate. Successive years of drought and existing economic policies had so seriously undermined crop and livestock production that about two thirds of the population required varying levels of food assistance throughout the year. Some 19,000 internally displaced persons who had recently returned to the Zone required social services and sustainable reintegration. In Ethiopia, the 2005 joint humanitarian appeal was launched in December 2004 (see p. 1032), just as the Government embarked on its Productive Safety Nets Programme. Despite the previous year's reported bumper harvest, large areas of the country remained severely affected by drought and food insecurity.

UNMEE implemented numerous small-scale, quick-impact projects for safe water, sanitation, and health and education services, with funding through the Trust Fund to Support the Peace Process in Ethiopia and Eritrea. It regularly monitored the situation of the more than 8,000 Eritrean refugees in the Shimelba camp, near Shiraro in Ethiopia, who faced critical humanitarian needs; monitored the human rights situation within the Zone, investigating border crossings and abduction of minors; undertook preliminary needs assessments in Ethiopia for technical cooperation projects to assist in capacity-building efforts in human rights, and planned to do the same in Eritrea; and regularly conducted human rights promotional and training activities for target groups in both countries.

The Secretary-General reiterated his appeal to Ethiopia and Eritrea to refrain from any action that could jeopardize the fragile and relative stability that had so far prevailed in the Zone, as well as the importance for both countries to accept demarcation of the boundary in accordance with the Boundary Commission's instructions (see below). He suggested that the Council might find it opportune to reaffirm and demonstrate its 2002 commitment to support the peace process [YUN 2002, p. 184] by returning to visit the two countries. He again appealed to Eritrea to cooperate with his Special Envoy for Ethiopia and Eritrea, Lloyd Axworthy (Canada), to enable him to facilitate implementation of the Algiers Agreements and the 13 April 2002 delimitation decision of the Commission [ibid., p. 187].

The Secretary-General, affirming the stabilizing role of UNMEE in the Ethiopia-Eritrea conflict, recommended that its mandate be extended until 15 September 2005.

Boundary Commission (February). The sixteenth report of the Boundary Commission [S/2005/142, annex I], issued in February and covering its activities from 15 December 2004 to 28 February 2005, stated that, despite its efforts, it had not been able to secure a resumption of the demarcation process, stalled since the Commission's eleventh (2003) report [YUN 2003, p. 241].

By a 26 January letter to Ethiopia and Eritrea, the Commission, stating the imperative of being enabled to continue and complete its mission, called on both parties to assist it to that end without any preconditions, and provided a framework of specific steps that needed to be taken. The Commission subsequently invited the parties to meet with it in London on 22 February. Since the invitation was accepted only by Eritrea and not by Ethiopia, the Commission cancelled that meeting but held its own meeting on that date. The Commission outlined the principal developments that had led to the current impasse and identified the conduct that had prevented it from completing its mandate.

In summary, the Commission said it found itself confronted by the situation whereby Eritrea was insisting on adherence to the Commission's 13 April 2002 delimitation decision [YUN 2002, p. 187]. It was willing to meet with the Commission and Ethiopia to discuss the unconditional renewal of the demarcation process, but was not prepared to accept Ethiopia's 2003 proposal [YUN 2003, p. 240]—that the Security Council set up an alternative mechanism to demarcate the contested parts of the boundary (principally Badme, found

by the Commission to lie on the Eritrean side of the boundary, and parts of Sector Centre) in a just and legal manner—for the completion of demarcation in the Eastern Sector, unless there was at the same time a clear assurance from Ethiopia that the rest of the boundary would also be demarcated. Ethiopia, on the other hand, was not prepared to allow demarcation to continue in the manner laid down in the demarcation directions and in the timeline set by the Commission. While insisting on prior dialogue, Ethiopia had rejected the opportunity for such dialogue within the framework of the demarcation process provided by the Commission in its 26 January letter. That, the Commission said, was the latest in a series of obstructive actions taken since the summer of 2002 and belied the frequently professed acceptance by Ethiopia of the delimitation decision.

In view of the situation, the Commission said it was taking immediate steps to close its field offices; they could be reactivated, if Ethiopia abandoned its insistence on preconditions for the implementation of the demarcation. The Commission remained ready to proceed with and complete the demarcation process whenever circumstances permitted.

SECURITY COUNCIL ACTION (March)

On 14 March [meeting 5139], the Security Council unanimously adopted **resolution 1586(2005)**. The draft [S/2005/157] was prepared in consultations among Council members.

The Security Council,

Reaffirming all its previous resolutions and statements pertaining to the situation between Ethiopia and Eritrea, and the requirements contained therein, including in particular resolution 1560(2004) of 14 September 2004,

Stressing its unwavering commitment to the peace process, including through the role played by the United Nations Mission in Ethiopia and Eritrea, and to the full and expeditious implementation of the comprehensive Peace Agreement signed on 12 December 2000 at Algiers by the Governments of Ethiopia and Eritrea (hereinafter referred to as "the parties") and the preceding Agreement on Cessation of Hostilities signed on 18 June 2000 ("the Algiers Agreements"), and the delimitation decision of the Eritrea-Ethiopia Boundary Commission of 13 April 2002, embraced by the parties as final and binding in accordance with the Algiers Agreements,

Welcoming the Secretary-General's determination that the Mission has been able to maintain the integrity of the Temporary Security Zone,

Expressing concern regarding the recent high concentration of Ethiopian troops in the areas adjacent to the Temporary Security Zone,

Recalling that lasting peace between Ethiopia and Eritrea, as well as in the region, cannot be achieved without the full demarcation of the border between the parties,

Seriously concerned with the decision of the Boundary Commission to take immediate steps to close down its field offices, due to the lack of progress made in the demarcation of the border, as reflected in the sixteenth report on the work of the Commission, of 24 February 2005,

Expressing its concern about Ethiopia's ongoing rejection of significant parts of the decision of the Boundary Commission and its current lack of cooperation with the Commission, including the refusal to participate in the meeting of 22 February 2005,

Expressing its disappointment about the continuing refusal of Eritrea to engage with the Special Envoy of the Secretary-General for Ethiopia and Eritrea, whose good offices represent a concrete opportunity for both parties to move the peace process forward,

Recalling the recent increase in United Nations peacekeeping activities and the need to allocate peacekeeping resources in the most effective manner, and recalling in this regard the additional burden caused by the delays in the demarcation process,

Welcoming Eritrea's unconditional acceptance of the decision of the Boundary Commission,

Welcoming also Ethiopia's five-point peace proposal of 25 November 2004,

Having considered the report of the Secretary-General of 7 March 2005, and welcoming the observations made therein,

1. *Decides* to extend the present mandate of the United Nations Mission in Ethiopia and Eritrea until 15 September 2005;

2. *Calls upon* the parties to refrain from any increase of troops in the areas adjacent to the Temporary Security Zone, to give serious consideration to returning to the 16 December 2004 levels of deployment and, more generally, to refrain from any threat of use of force against each other;

3. *Also calls upon* the parties to cooperate fully and expeditiously with the Mission in the implementation of its mandate, to ensure the security of all staff of the Mission, and to remove immediately and unconditionally all restrictions on and impediments to the work and to the full and free movement of the Mission and its staff;

4. *Takes note* of positive developments in some areas of relations between the Mission and the parties, in this regard urges Eritrea to take immediate steps, in consultation with the Mission, towards implementing the direct flights between Addis Ababa and Asmara, and also calls upon Eritrea to reopen the Asmara to Barentu road;

5. *Stresses* that Ethiopia and Eritrea have the primary responsibility for the implementation of the Algiers Agreements and the decision of the Eritrea-Ethiopia Boundary Commission, and calls upon the parties to show political leadership to achieve a full normalization of their relationship, including through political dialogue for the adoption of further confidence-building measures and to consolidate progress achieved so far, by making full use of the existing framework of the Commission;

6. *Reiterates its call upon* the parties to cooperate fully and promptly with the Boundary Commission and to create the necessary conditions for demarcation to proceed expeditiously, including through the complete appointment by Ethiopia of its field liaison officers;

7. *Calls upon* Ethiopia without preconditions to start the implementation of demarcation, by taking the necessary steps to enable the Boundary Commission to demarcate the border completely and promptly;

8. *Expresses its concern* at the worsening humanitarian situation in Ethiopia and Eritrea and the implications this could have for the peace process, and calls upon Member States to continue to provide prompt and generous support for humanitarian operations in Ethiopia and Eritrea;

9. *Reiterates its full support* for the Special Envoy of the Secretary-General for Ethiopia and Eritrea, Mr. Lloyd Axworthy, in his efforts to facilitate the implementation of the Algiers Agreements, the decision of the Boundary Commission and the normalization of diplomatic relations between the two countries through his good offices, and emphasizes that this appointment does not constitute an alternative mechanism;

10. *Calls upon* Eritrea to accept the good offices of the Secretary-General and cooperate with his Special Envoy;

11. *Calls upon* the witnesses to the Algiers Agreements to play a more concerted and active role to facilitate their full implementation;

12. *Decides* to continue monitoring closely the steps taken by the parties in the implementation of their commitments under the relevant resolutions of the Security Council and under the Algiers Agreements, including through the Boundary Commission, and to review any implications for the Mission;

13. *Requests* the Secretary-General to continue to monitor the situation closely, to review the mission's mandate in the light of progress made in the peace process and changes made to the Mission;

14. *Decides* to remain actively seized of the matter.

Report of Secretary-General (June). In his 20 June report [S/2005/400], the Secretary-General noted that Ethiopia maintained its troop deployment close to the southern boundary of the Temporary Security Zone and that Eritrea remained engaged in military training exercises nearby. In a demonstration of transparency, Ethiopia gave UNMEE details of its current military positions, while Eritrea escorted the Force Commander to its operational locations in Sub-Sector East and Sector West. In addition to the usual cross-border incursions involving livestock rustling and individual strayings into the Zone, three shooting incidents occurred in Sector West, allegedly between armed Ethiopians and Eritrean militia, on 9, 11 and 26 April, which resulted in the deaths of four Ethiopians and one Eritrean militiaman. Those incidents notwithstanding, UNMEE was able to maintain the integrity of the Zone.

UNMEE ground patrols operating on the Eritrean side adjacent to the Zone continued to encounter restrictions. Its personnel had also been subjected to unwarranted arrests and detention by Eritrean authorities, who had moreover imposed restrictions on the military police contingent in Asmara, in contravention of the 1946 Convention on the Privileges and Immunities of the United Nations [YUN 1946-47, p. 100, GA res. 179 A (I), annex, 13 Feb. 1946], and of the model status-of-forces agreement in force between the United Nations and the Government of Eritrea.

The Military Coordination Commission, at its twenty-ninth and thirtieth meetings (Nairobi, 25 March and 11 May), discussed the prevailing military situation, the cross-border incidents and existing restrictions on UNMEE's freedom of movement.

The Secretary-General noted that the national and regional elections held in Ethiopia on 15 May were generally peaceful. The elections were monitored by more than 300 foreign observers and were covered by over 800 accredited national and international journalists. The delay in announcing the final vote counts resulted in some demonstrations, however, in which a number of demonstrators were shot and killed by security forces.

The period from March through May saw eight incidents of mine or unexploded ordnance within the Zone that killed one person in Sector Centre and injured eight others in Sector West, near the Ethiopian side of which four newly laid mines on certain roads were also discovered. UNMEE, together with the commercial contractors, destroyed eight mines and 704 items of unexploded ordnance, and demined 1,385,156 square metres of land and 457 kilometres of road.

The Secretary-General expressed concern over the recent shootings in the Zone, which he felt could easily escalate into situations that would compromise military stability, as well as the continuing stalemate in the peace process, which he considered unsustainable in the long term. He said that the attainment of durable peace between Ethiopia and Eritrea rested primarily with both of them, and fulfilment of that responsibility was a debt they owed to their peoples.

Boundary Commission (May). The seventeenth report of the Boundary Commission [S/2005/400, annex I], issued on 30 May and covering the period 1 March to 30 May, stated that the Commission had suspended all its activities in the area, closed its field offices and terminated its staff contracts. For the time being, its field assets were in UNMEE's custody. There had been no further demarcation activity.

Report of Secretary-General (August). In an August report [S/2005/553], the Secretary-General stated that the integrity of the Temporary Security Zone continued to be successfully maintained by UNMEE, even as Ethiopia's troops remained in

their forward positions to the south of the Zone and Eritrea's military exercises continued.

Improved cooperation by Ethiopia and Eritrea with UNMEE resulted in a decline in the restrictions imposed by both parties on the Mission's freedom of movement. The Asmara-Keren-Barentu road remained closed, however, with no indication from Eritrea as to when it would reopen. Eritrea's continuing restrictions on UNMEE police in Asmara, preventing the Italian contingent from resuming its activities there led to the contingent's withdrawal in July. Kenyan military police were to take over and deploy as early as possible. As to the long-standing request for a direct flight route between Asmara and Addis Ababa, although Ethiopia had agreed to allow UN aircraft to fly directly from Addis Ababa to Asmara, UNMEE had yet to receive a positive response from the authorities in Asmara.

At the thirty-first meeting of the Military Coordination Commission (Nairobi, 16 July), the Eritrean and Ethiopian delegates, in addition to discussing the current military situation and functioning of the sector military coordination commissions, reiterated their willingness to cooperate fully with UNMEE to resolve outstanding issues relating to the maintenance of the Zone.

From June to mid-August, three accidents from unexploded ordnance occurred in Sector West and two in Sector Centre that killed one child and injured four persons. UNMEE demining assets and commercial contractors destroyed 10 mines and 285 pieces of unexploded ordnance, besides clearing 1,079,195 square metres of land and 574 kilometres of road. UNMEE continued to work with commercial contractors to implement an integrated approach to demining operations inside the Zone focusing on minefields in the Shilalo region of Eritrea, in Sector West. UNMEE Mine Action Coordination Centre provided mine-risk education to 1,978 internally displaced persons returning to that region.

In the area of human rights, UNMEE followed up cases of cross-border abductions and missing persons from Ethiopia and Eritrea; monitored the repatriation of 298 persons to Ethiopia and 163 to Eritrea under the auspices of the International Committee of the Red Cross; visited Shimelba refugee camp in northern Ethiopia, where international aid agencies addressed the needs of 9,327 refugees for food, water, sanitation, health and education services; and continued its technical cooperation activities in Ethiopia, including training projects for law enforcement officials, civil society organizations and national human rights institutions. The Secretary-General once again invited Eritrea to assist UNMEE in extending its technical cooperation in human rights work in the country.

The Secretary-General, stating that the protracted stalemate in the Ethiopia-Eritrea peace process was inherently destabilizing, reiterated his strong appeal to the witnesses to the Algiers Agreements—Algeria, the EU, OAU (now the AU), the United Nations and the United States—especially those with influence on the parties, to play a more concerted role in assisting them to resolve the stalemate. He also called on the international community to spare no effort in bringing the parties together to engage in constructive dialogue aimed at moving the peace process forward and normalizing bilateral relations between them.

The Secretary-General recommended that UNMEE's mandate be extended for a further six months, until 15 March 2006, and that the authorized number of its military observers be increased by 10, to a total of 230, within the existing authorized strength of 3,404 military personnel. Given the progress made in integrating demining operations in the Mission area, the difficulties facing the Eritrean national demining programme and of the fact that demining support to the Eritrea-Ethiopia Boundary Commission remained on hold, the Secretary-General also recommended that UNMEE assist the parties, in continuing cooperation with other international partners in the mine action sector, by providing humanitarian demining assistance, technical advice and coordination in and around the Zone.

Boundary Commission (August). The eighteenth report of the Boundary Commission [S/2005/553/Add.1], issued on 31 August and covering the period 1 June to 31 August, advised that there had been no change in the demarcation situation since its report of 30 May (see p. 356).

SECURITY COUNCIL ACTION (September)

On 13 September [5259], the Security Council unanimously adopted **resolution 1622(2005)**. The draft [S/2005/569] was prepared in consultations among Council members.

The Security Council,

Reaffirming all its previous resolutions and the statements by its President pertaining to the situation between Ethiopia and Eritrea, and the requirements contained therein, including in particular resolution 1586 (2005) of 14 March 2005,

Stressing its unwavering commitment to the peace process, including through the role played by the United Nations Mission in Ethiopia and Eritrea, and to the full and expeditious implementation of the comprehensive Peace Agreement signed by the Governments of Ethiopia and Eritrea (hereinafter referred to as the parties) on 12 December 2000 and the preceding Agreement on Cessation of Hostilities signed on 18 June 2000 ("the Algiers Agreements"), and the delimitation decision of the Eritrea-Ethiopia Boundary Commission of 13 April 2002, embraced by the parties as final and binding in accordance with the Algiers Agreements,

Stressing that lasting peace between Ethiopia and Eritrea, as well as in the region, cannot be achieved without the full demarcation of the border between the parties,

Deeply concerned by the continuing lack of progress in the implementation of the final and binding decision of the Boundary Commission, and by Ethiopia's ongoing rejection of significant parts of the decision of the Boundary Commission,

Noting with deep concern the continuing high concentration of troops in the areas adjacent to the Temporary Security Zone,

Having considered the report of the Secretary-General, and welcoming the observations made therein,

Noting that possible options to resolve the stalemate in the peace process include, when appropriate, a visit to Ethiopia and Eritrea, as suggested by the Secretary-General in paragraph 38 of his report, as well as a meeting of the witnesses to the signing of the Algiers Agreements,

Welcoming the action taken by the Mission to address the issue of sexual exploitation and abuse, particularly the efforts towards prevention through training, and also the action taken to address HIV and AIDS,

1. *Decides* to extend the mandate of the United Nations Mission in Ethiopia and Eritrea until 15 March 2006;

2. *Approves* the reconfiguration of the military component of the Mission, including an increase in the number of military observers by 10, within the existing overall mandated strength of the Mission, and the assistance to the parties in the mine action sector, as recommended by the Secretary-General in paragraphs 11 and 42 of his report;

3. *Calls upon* both parties to refrain from any action which may lead to an escalation of the tension, and in this respect urges both parties to give serious consideration to returning to the 16 December 2004 levels of deployment and, more generally, to refrain from any threat of use of force against each other;

4. *Reaffirms* that Ethiopia and Eritrea have the primary responsibility for the implementation of the Algiers Agreements and the decision of the Eritrea-Ethiopia Boundary Commission, by making full use of the existing framework of the Boundary Commission;

5. *Calls upon* Ethiopia to accept fully the decision of the Boundary Commission and to enable, without preconditions, the Commission to demarcate the border completely and promptly;

6. *Calls upon* the parties to implement completely and without further delay the decision of the Boundary Commission and to create the necessary conditions for demarcation to proceed expeditiously;

7. *Takes note* of the continuing improvement in the climate of cooperation between the Mission and the parties, calls upon both parties to cooperate fully and expeditiously with the Mission in the implementation of its mandate, to ensure the security of all the staff of the Mission, and to remove immediately and uncondi-

tionally all restrictions on and impediments to the work and to the full and free movement of the Mission and its staff, and in this regard strongly urges Eritrea to remove the restrictions on the military police of the Mission in Asmara;

8. *Urges* Eritrea to take immediate steps, in consultation with the Mission, towards implementing direct United Nations flights between Addis Ababa and Asmara and to reopen the road from Asmara to Barentu to Mission traffic;

9. *Calls upon* both parties to achieve a full normalization of their relations, including through political dialogue between them for the adoption of further confidence-building measures and to consolidate progress achieved so far;

10. *Expresses its concern* at the ongoing food insecurity in Ethiopia and Eritrea and its potential to create greater instability, and calls upon Member States to continue to provide generous support for both humanitarian and development activities to improve food security in Ethiopia and Eritrea;

11. *Calls upon* Eritrea to lift all restrictions imposed on the operations of aid organizations, to enable them to carry out their humanitarian activities;

12. *Decides* to continue monitoring closely the steps taken by the parties in the implementation of their commitments under the relevant resolutions of the Security Council and under the Algiers Agreements, including through the Boundary Commission, and to review any implications for the Mission;

13. *Requests* the Secretary General to take the necessary measures to achieve actual compliance in the Mission with the United Nations zero-tolerance policy on sexual exploitation and abuse, including the development of strategies and appropriate mechanisms to prevent, identify and respond to all forms of misconduct, including sexual exploitation and abuse, and the enhancement of training for personnel to prevent misconduct and ensure full compliance with the United Nations code of conduct, also requests the Secretary-General to take all necessary action in accordance with the Secretary-General's bulletin on special measures for protection from sexual exploitation and sexual abuse and to keep the Council informed, and urges troop-contributing countries to take appropriate preventive action, including conducting predeployment awareness training, and to take disciplinary action and other action to ensure full accountability in cases of such conduct involving their personnel;

14. *Also requests* the Secretary-General to continue to monitor the situation closely, to review the mission's mandate in the light of progress made in the peace process and changes made to the Mission;

15. *Decides* to remain actively seized of the matter.

Restrictions on UNMEE

On 4 October [meeting 5276], following consultations among Security Council members, the President made statement **S/PRST/2005/47** on behalf of the Council:

The Security Council expresses its grave concern at the decision of the Government of Eritrea to restrict all types of United Nations Mission in Ethiopia and Eritrea helicopter flights within Eritrean air-

space or coming to Eritrea, effective from 5 October 2005, which will have serious implications for the ability of the Mission to carry out its mandate and for the safety of the staff.

Recalling all its previous resolutions and the statements by its President regarding the situation between Ethiopia and Eritrea, the Council emphasizes that the aforementioned decision of the Government of Eritrea gravely contravenes the Council's call upon the parties, in resolution 1312(2000), to provide the Mission with the access, assistance, support and protection required for the performance of its duties, as well as the Agreement on Cessation of Hostilities signed at Algiers on 18 June 2000 by the Government of the Federal Democratic Republic of Ethiopia and the Government of the State of Eritrea.

The Council further underlines the need for implementation of the decision of the Eritrea-Ethiopia Boundary Commission without further delay, which will enable the Mission to fulfil its mandate.

The Council reaffirms that both parties bear the primary responsibility for the implementation of the Algiers Agreements and the decision of the Boundary Commission.

The Council calls upon the Government of Eritrea to immediately reverse its decision and to provide the Mission with the access, assistance, support and protection required for the performance of its duties. It also calls upon both parties to cooperate fully and expeditiously with the Mission in the implementation of its mandate.

The Council also calls upon both parties to show maximum restraint and to refrain from any threat of use of force against each other.

The Council reiterates its call upon both parties to achieve a full normalization of their relations, including through political dialogue between them for the adoption of further confidence-building measures and to consolidate progress achieved so far.

Communications. The Secretary-General informed the Security Council President on 24 October [S/2005/668] that the situation with regard to UNMEE had seriously deteriorated, stating that the current state of affairs constituted a crisis requiring the international community's full attention and urgent and specific action, without which the situation could escalate and lead to another round of devastating hostilities. He said the Council had been thoroughly briefed on the latest turn of events affecting UNMEE, most recently on 19 October, both in informal consultations and at a special meeting with the troop-contributing countries.

Underlined at those briefings was Eritrea's decision to restrict all types of UNMEE helicopter flights within Eritrean airspace, thus severely inhibiting the Mission's capacity to implement its monitoring mandate, as requested by the parties in the June 2000 Agreement on Cessation of Hostilities and authorized by Council resolutions 1312(2000) and 1320(2000) [YUN 2002, pp. 173, 174, 176]. As such, the decision also seriously affected prospects for the implementation of the December 2000 comprehensive Peace Agreement between Eritrea and Ethiopia [ibid., p. 180]. In addition, the Eritrean restriction dramatically affected the security of UN peacekeepers and their operations to the extent that 18 out of 40 observation posts and deployment sites in isolated places had become unsustainable and no longer operationally viable.

At the meeting with the troop-contributing countries, India and Jordan expressed alarm at the implications of the helicopter ban and other restrictions, which their Governments regarded as unacceptable. They appealed for a strong and unequivocal message from the Council to reverse the untenable situation. At the same time, Ethiopia stated to the press that members of the Eritrean Defence Force had infiltrated the Temporary Security Zone and urged the United Nations to "take measures to restore the status quo".

The Secretary-General said that he had conveyed his serious concern about the restrictions to the President of Eritrea, who replied on 20 October that the Council and the Secretary-General had forfeited their "relevance" on matters relating to the peace process.

The Secretary-General further expressed concern over the restrictions on humanitarian operations in Eritrea, including significant delays in relief food distributions, the impoundment of UN project vehicles and lack of access to some of the UN warehouses and containers.

He called on the Council to exert its maximum influence to avert a further deterioration of the situation and to secure the lifting of the restrictions. He said it was imperative for the Council to address the underlying causes of the stalemate in the peace process, including those relating to the Ethiopian position on the delimitation decision of the Boundary Commission. He stood ready to work with the Council collectively and with key stakeholders individually to bring the crisis to an end, to conclude the peace process, and to re-establish vital humanitarian activities in Eritrea.

Eritrea, on 28 October [S/2005/688], drew attention to what it called the Council's failure to carry out its obligations to maintain regional peace and security under the Charter of the United Nations and the Algiers Agreements. Citing Ethiopia's repeated obstruction of the work of the Boundary Commission, Eritrea claimed those acts were condoned by the Council, which took no remedial action to ensure the rule of law in that regard. It referred to Ethiopia's presence in Badme and other areas north of the delimitation line as forcible occupation of sovereign Eritrean territory, and to Ethiopia's disregard of the 2002

Council instructions to dismantle its illegal settlements [YUN 2002, p. 189]. Eritrea said it had suffered immeasurably from Ethiopia's occupation of almost six years, which had held its people hostage, condemned them to live in makeshift camps under traumatic physical and psychological conditions, and hampered Eritrea's development objectives, with resultant substantial losses to its economy.

Eritrea further said that the Council's unwillingness to enforce the rule of law and to ensure respect for the sovereignty and territorial integrity of a UN Member State had compromised the Council's credibility and legal and moral authority. Eritrea had shown maximum patience and restraint throughout the Ethiopian occupation; the measures it was taking to protect its sovereignty and territorial integrity were legal acts of self-defence, recognized as such by the Charter. It could not be blamed for the grave situation currently facing the region, and attempts by the Council to blame it were legally and politically unwarranted.

Eritrea attached its letters of 2 and 15 March 2004: the first reiterated its views on the appointment of the Special Envoy for Ethiopia and Eritrea [YUN 2004, p. 266], namely, that the appointment was tantamount to establishing a "new mechanism" that would only cause unnecessary complications; the second questioned the actions of the Special Envoy.

Ethiopia, on 31 October [S/2005/690], laid out its view on what it called Eritrea's violation of the Agreement on Cessation of Hostilities between them. Ethiopia said its opinion of the 2002 delimitation decision by the Boundary Commission would never change: it was unfair, unjust and indefensible. Ethiopia recalled its repeated statement that its acceptance of the decision "in principle" did not mean a return to the drawing board, nor did it imply the introduction of a precondition; its request for dialogue on the implementation of the demarcation was consistent with international demarcation practice. The crisis between it and Eritrea did not grow out of their dispute over the boundary, and to claim that normalization and durable peace could be achieved only with the completion of the demarcation process, would be naive and dishonest; at the root of the crisis were more weighty issues that needed to be addressed. It was this conviction that prompted Ethiopia to present its comprehensive five-point peace proposal [YUN 2004, p. 271]. Despite Eritrea's latest steps to cripple UNMEE and degrade its capacity for monitoring the Zone, Ethiopia reassured the troop-contributing countries and the Council that it would continue to do whatever was humanly possible to support

UNMEE to fulfil its obligation; it would not allow itself to be provoked by Eritrea.

Fact-finding mission. On 2 November [S/2005/694], the Security Council informed the Secretary-General that it had authorized Kenzo Oshima (Japan), in his capacity as Chairman of the Council's Working Group on Peacekeeping Operations, to conduct a fact-finding mission in Ethiopia and Eritrea, from 6 to 9 November, regarding the current situation involving UNMEE.

In his report on the mission, transmitted to the Council on 16 November [S/2005/723], Mr. Oshima stated that he had exchanged views with UNMEE officials and those representing the troop contributors, as well as with the Foreign Minister of Ethiopia, in Addis Ababa, on 7 November; and with the Acting Commissioner of the Military Coordination Commission and the Director of the Office of the President of Eritrea, in Asmara, on 8 November. On his way to Asmara, he visited Sub-Sector East headquarters in Assab, Eritrea.

His discussions with Special Representative Legwaila and briefings from the Force Commander of UNMEE revealed that the situation was tense and potentially volatile, and could deteriorate further. Ethiopia had been reinforcing its military in areas adjacent to the Zone; Eritrea could be doing the same outside the Zone, which UNMEE could not verify owing to the restrictions imposed on it by Eritrea. The restrictions, especially the ban on helicopter flights, had reduced UNMEE's monitoring capabilities by 60 per cent and seriously affected medical evacuations. UNMEE was concerned that, if the two sides continued to strengthen their military postures, a possible resumption of armed conflict through miscalculation could not be excluded. Troop contributing countries were unified in their appeal for the urgent removal of the restrictions. Many believed that UNMEE's withdrawal would have devastating consequences.

The Foreign Minister of Ethiopia reiterated his country's position as set out in his 31 October letter (above). In response to a request for clarification of Ethiopia's acceptance "in principle" of the Boundary Commission's delimitation decision, the Minister stressed that Ethiopia was not asking for partial or total renegotiation of the decision, but rather for implementation of the decision in a practical rather than in a mechanical manner, pointing to locations to be reviewed where Ethiopian and Eritrean communities would be affected. As to the Council's concern over the situation in and around the Zone, he stated that Ethiopia would exercise maximum restraint: it would not be the first to fire nor would it allow itself to be provoked.

The Eritrean Director stressed that only the full and faithful implementation of the Boundary Commission's decision could resolve the impasse. He criticized the Council for failing to compel Ethiopia to accept the border ruling, as provided for in the Algiers Agreements, and to proceed with demarcation without preconditions. He rejected the idea of a special envoy, as well as the expansion of the mandate of the Special Representative of the Secretary-General to include political matters. The Director took note of the Council's concern over the situation, of Mr. Oshima's urging for the exercise of maximum restraint, and of the issue of the risks to UNMEE personnel resulting from the helicopter flight ban. The Director pointed out that Ethiopia's military build-up was provocative, and that a large number of Eritreans living near the border could be affected if armed conflict resumed because of the Council's continuing failure to address the major issue of demarcation.

Mr. Oshima observed that, to avoid a resumption of hostilities, the Council needed to: give serious attention to the question of how to help break the stalemate between the two countries; consider a new resolution strongly urging Eritrea to lift its restrictions, and another urging Ethiopia to accept and implement fully the Boundary Commission's decision; and ask the Secretary-General and the countries with influence on the two parties to launch a new series of vigorous diplomatic initiatives to break the stalemate. As the idea of a special envoy was unacceptable to one of the parties, diplomatic efforts should continue to engage both to end the crisis; a Council resolution in support of those efforts should be carefully crafted.

SECURITY COUNCIL ACTION (November)

On 23 November [meeting 5308], the Security Council unanimously adopted **resolution 1640 (2005)**. The draft [S/2005/732] was prepared in consultations among Council members.

The Security Council,

Reaffirming all its previous resolutions and the statements by its President pertaining to the situation between Eritrea and Ethiopia, and the requirements contained therein, including in particular resolution 1622(2005) of 13 September 2005 and the statement by its President of 4 October 2005,

Expressing once again its grave concern at the decision of the Government of Eritrea of 4 October 2005 to restrict all types of United Nations Mission in Ethiopia and Eritrea helicopter flights within Eritrean airspace or coming to Eritrea, effective from 5 October 2005, and the additional restrictions on the freedom of movement of the Mission imposed since then, which have serious implications for the ability of the Mission to carry out its mandate and for the safety of its staff and the forces of the troop contributors,

Alarmed by the implications and potential impact of the aforementioned decision made and restrictions imposed by the Government of Eritrea with regard to the maintenance of peace and security between Eritrea and Ethiopia, and the principles governing United Nations peacekeeping operations,

Reaffirming the integrity of the Temporary Security Zone as provided for in the Agreement on Cessation of Hostilities of 18 June 2000, and recalling the objectives behind its establishment,

Stressing that lasting peace between Eritrea and Ethiopia, as well as in the region, cannot be achieved without the full demarcation of the border between the parties,

Expressing its grave concern at the Government of Ethiopia's failure, to date, to accept without preconditions the implementation of the final and binding decision of the Eritrea-Ethiopia Boundary Commission of 13 April 2002,

Expressing its appreciation to Ambassador Kenzo Oshima for his visit to Ethiopia and Eritrea from 6 to 9 November 2005, in his capacity as Chairman of the Security Council Working Group on Peacekeeping Operations, taking note of his report, and welcoming the observations made therein,

Noting with deep concern the high concentration of troops on both sides of the Temporary Security Zone, and stressing that the continuation of the situation would constitute a threat to international peace and security,

1. *Deeply deplores* the continued imposition by Eritrea of restrictions on the freedom of movement of the United Nations Mission in Ethiopia and Eritrea, and demands that the Government of Eritrea reverse, without further delay or preconditions, its decision to ban Mission helicopter flights, as well as additional restrictions imposed on the operations of the Mission, and provide the Mission with the access, assistance, support and protection required for the performance of its duties;

2. *Calls upon* both parties to show maximum restraint and to refrain from any threat or use of force against each other, and demands that both parties return to the 16 December 2004 levels of deployment, beginning with immediate effect and completing this redeployment within thirty days, in order to prevent aggravation of the situation;

3. *Requests* the Secretary-General to monitor compliance by the parties with the demands in paragraphs 1 and 2 above and to report to the Security Council forty days after the adoption of the present resolution;

4. *Expresses its determination* to consider further appropriate measures, including under Article 41 of the Charter of the United Nations, if one or both parties fail to comply with the demands in paragraphs 1 and 2 above;

5. *Demands* that Ethiopia accept fully and without further delay the final and binding decision of the Eritrea-Ethiopia Boundary Commission and take immediately concrete steps to enable, without preconditions, the Commission to demarcate the border completely and promptly, and expresses its determination to monitor closely the actions of both parties in relation to the demarcation of the border and to keep this matter under consideration;

6. *Expresses its deep appreciation* for the contribution and dedication of the troop-contributing countries to the work of the Mission and, in the light of the risk of further deterioration of the situation, appeals to them to persevere in maintaining their presence and contribution to the activities of the Mission, despite the immense difficulties which they are facing;

7. *Calls upon* both parties to work, without preconditions, to break the current stalemate through diplomatic efforts;

8. *Decides* to remain actively seized of the matter.

Communications. Following adoption of the foregoing resolution, Eritrea issued a press release on 24 November [S/2005/737] accusing the Security Council of adopting yet another deplorable resolution on the Eritrea-Ethiopia conflict, which was lopsided in favour of Ethiopia. Eritrea recounted Ethiopia's repeated violations of the comprehensive Peace Agreement and the Council's failure in each case to exercise its responsibility and take remedial action, all of which had led to the stoppage of demarcation activities and closure of the Commission's offices. Eritrea said that, in a perverted logic, the Council would not invoke, as it should, Chapter VII in the face of Ethiopia's continued violation of the Peace Agreement and the Charter. It had chosen instead to focus on derivative and secondary clauses and arrangements to impose sanctions on Eritrea.

Ethiopia, commenting on resolution 1640 (2005), in a statement addressed to the Council on 9 December [S/2205/774], stressed that the ongoing crisis had been created by Eritrea, which should not be rewarded for escalating tensions along the border. Ethiopia had reacted with consistent moderation in the face of Eritrea's continuing bellicose actions. Unlike Eritrea, which had violated the integrity of the Temporary Security Zone, Ethiopia had no troops within the Zone, and its current troop deployment was fully consistent with its obligations under the Algiers Agreement. In the interests of peace, Ethiopia was prepared to redeploy its forces in compliance with paragraph 2 of the resolution, even if doing so could put its security at risk. Should Eritrea take advantage of that unilateral compliance and cause harm to Ethiopia's security, Ethiopia was convinced that the Council would shoulder its responsibility by taking the necessary action.

Ethiopia wrote the Secretary-General, also on 9 December, to convey the same information.

Further report of Secretary-General. The Secretary-General later reported [S/2006/1] that, on 18 November, elements of Ethiopia's armed forces took up position at Peak 885, a site inside the Temporary Security Zone in Sub-Sector East vacated by UNMEE the day before, but withdrew on 23 November following formal protests by UNMEE. They again made a brief incursion into the area of Adi Melele in Sector West on 29 November. Until the adoption of Security Council resolution 1640(2005), Ethiopia had continued reinforcing its troops and conducting military exercises near the southern boundary of the Zone. Eritrea had also engaged in considerable troop movements towards the northern boundary.

On 6 December, Eritrea wrote UNMEE requesting that its personnel of Canadian, European, Russian Federation and United States nationality leave the country within 10 days, giving no reason for the decision. In a statement issued on 7 December, the Secretary-General condemned the decision and once again appealed to Asmara to reverse all restrictions imposed on UNMEE. At his request, the Under-Secretary-General for Peacekeeping Operations, Jean-Marie Guéhenno, together with the Department of Peacekeeping Operations military adviser, visited the region (16-21 December) to meet with the parties, the diplomatic community and UNMEE personnel to discuss the current situation and how to move the peace process forward. Although Ethiopia's Prime Minister received Mr. Guéhenno, no senior Eritrean official agreed to do so, nor did Eritrea respond to his two letters urging a reconsideration of its decision to withdraw certain UNMEE staff from the country. Likewise, Eritrea did not respond to the Secretary-General's calls to rescind that decision.

On 15 and 16 December, UNMEE temporarily redeployed 77 of its civilian staff—including those specified by Eritrea and others who could no longer perform their functions effectively in Asmara owing to Eritrea's restrictions—and 61 military personnel from Eritrea to Ethiopia. The move was with the agreement of the Council, which expressed its intention to review options for UNMEE's future deployment and functions, in the context of its original purpose. (See presidential statement S/PRST/2005/62 on p. 363.)

Implementation of Security Council resolution 1640(2005). The meeting of the Military Coordination Commission (Nairobi, 25 November) discussed the demands of resolution 1640(2005) on the parties, principally the lifting of all restrictions on UNMEE, the need to show maximum restraint and a return to the pre-16 December 2004 levels of military deployment within 30 days. While the Ethiopian delegation agreed to redeploy its troops accordingly, the Eritrean delegation argued that the provision did not apply to Eritrea as it had not moved any troops forward.

Upon Ethiopia's presentation on 27 November of the plan for redeploying its forces to the levels specified, UNMEE developed a monitoring and verification plan of the troops to be pulled back, and ascertained their presence at the forward positions and scheduled pull back. UNMEE confirmed the departures and, where possible, the arrivals at the designated pre-16 December 2004 locations; thereafter, it reconfirmed that each of the vacated locations had not been reoccupied by Ethiopia. The entire exercise was conducted by UNMEE military observers in cooperation with Ethiopian authorities. On 23 December, UNMEE confirmed that Ethiopia had completed the planned withdrawal of eight of its divisions from the forward positions. On the same date, Ethiopia informed the Council that it had responded "receptively" to the resolution; it would refrain from initiating any armed hostilities and would work to resolve its differences with Eritrea peacefully, adding, however, that "the range of possibilities open to Ethiopia" would be "limited" until Eritrea demonstrated a similar resolve, including normal diplomatic dialogue.

Eritrea reversed neither its ban on UNMEE helicopter flights nor the additional restrictions, as demanded by the resolution. Instead of providing the Mission with access, support and protection required for the performance of its duties, Eritrea had put in place additional restrictions on ground patrols, especially in large areas of Sector West and Sector Centre, where they were restricted to main roads and precluded from night patrolling. Challenge inspections were blocked by Eritrean militia at a number of locations. In Eritrea's view, the demand for redeployment of troops to the 16 December 2004 levels did not apply to it. Eritrea had taken no observable steps towards such redeployment, and vacant military locations in areas adjacent to the Zone were presumed vacated by Eritrean troops for destinations undetermined by the Mission. At the same time, armed Eritrean personnel had been observed in 15 to 17 locations inside the Zone, in numbers ranging from 80 to 150 per location. Some who claimed to be militia refused to show identity cards. Eritrea insisted that it had no soldiers inside the Zone, merely some militia engaged in agricultural activities.

SECURITY COUNCIL ACTION (7 and 14 December)

On 7 December [meeting 5317], following consultations among Security Council members, the President made statement **S/PRST/2005/59** on behalf of the Council:

The Security Council condemns the decision of the Government of Eritrea to request some members of the United Nations Mission in Ethiopia and Eritrea to leave the country within 10 days, effective from 6 December 2005, which is inconsistent with the obligations of the Government of Eritrea to respect the exclusively international nature of the peacekeeping operation. In this regard, the Council unequivocally demands that Eritrea immediately reverse its decision without preconditions.

The Council recalls that, in its resolution 1640 (2005), it demanded that the Government of Eritrea reverse all restrictions imposed on the operations of the Mission.

The Council will be consulting on how to respond to this completely unacceptable action by Eritrea.

On 14 December [meeting 5326], following consultations among Council members, the President made statement **S/PRST/2005/62** on behalf of the Council:

The Security Council has agreed, in consultation with the Secretary-General, to temporarily relocate military and civilian staff of the United Nations Mission in Ethiopia and Eritrea from Eritrea to Ethiopia. The Council intends to maintain a military presence of the Mission in Eritrea during the period in which it is reviewing future plans for the Mission.

The Council has approved this decision solely in the interests of the safety and security of Mission staff. The lack of cooperation with the Mission by the Eritrean authorities has produced conditions on the ground which prevent the Mission from implementing its mandate satisfactorily.

The Council strongly condemns Eritrea's unacceptable actions and restrictions on the Mission, which have drastically reduced any meaningful operational capacity for the mission and will have, if they are sustained, implications for the future of the Mission. The Council recalls its demand, expressed in resolution 1640(2005), that Eritrea reverse such restrictions and provide the Mission with the access, assistance, support and protection required for the performance of its duties.

In this regard, the Council intends, with the Secretariat, to review promptly all options for the deployment and functions of the Mission in the context of its original purpose, its capacity to act effectively and the different military options available.

The view of the Council on the fundamental issue of implementation of the delimitation decision of the Eritrea-Ethiopia Boundary Commission remains unchanged and the Council emphasizes the urgent need for progress in implementation of the decision of the Boundary Commission.

North Africa

Western Sahara

For another year in 2005, the United Nations Mission for the Referendum in Western Sahara successfully monitored compliance by Morocco and the Frente Popular para la Liberación de Saguía El-Hamra y de Río de Oro (Frente Polisario) with the 1991 ceasefire that ended their armed hostilities over their dispute regarding

the governance of the Territory of Western Sahara, thus maintaining the conditions conducive to the achievement of an agreed political solution. All UN efforts to that end notwithstanding, a solution remained elusive.

In a bid to break the long-standing political deadlock on the question, the Secretary-General, in July, appointed a new Personal Envoy, Peter van Walsum (Netherlands), to explore with the two parties, as well as with Algeria, where thousands of Saharans had sought asylum from the conflict, and the other neighbouring countries, how best to achieve a mutually acceptable solution. During the Envoy's exploratory mission, Morocco reiterated its non-acceptance of a referendum that would include the option of independence. For Frente Polisario, the only way forward was to implement either the 2003 peace plan proposed by the previous Personal Envoy, James Baker III, or the 1991 settlement plan proposed by the Secretary-General, both approved by the Security Council and both providing for self-determination through a referendum, with independence as an option.

A significant and encouraging development during the year was the release in August of the last remaining 404 prisoners of war held by Frente Polisario, some for over 20 years. In that connection, the Council called on both parties, in cooperation with the International Committee of the Red Cross, to resolve the fate of persons unaccounted for since the beginning of the conflict.

Following a comprehensive review of the administrative and operational structure of the Mission, the military and civilian components of the Mission were reorganized in order to integrate their activities, thereby to enhance their effectiveness. The Council extended the Mission's mandate twice, the second time until 30 April 2006.

The Council and the General Assembly again called for the full cooperation of the parties and States of the region with the Secretary-General and his Personal Envoy to end the current impasse and achieve progress towards a political solution.

MINURSO

The United Nations Mission for the Referendum in Western Sahara (MINURSO), established by Security Council resolution 690(1991) [YUN 1991, p. 794], continued in 2005 to monitor compliance with the 1991 formal ceasefire between Frente Polisario and Morocco [ibid., p. 796]. Monitoring was carried out by the Mission's military observers through a combination of ground and air patrols and observation posts, and through inspections of larger-than-company-size military units of the Frente Polisario forces and the Royal

Moroccan Army (RMA). The main focus was on military activities close to the "berm" cutting across Western Sahara, extending from the north-east corner down to the south-west, near the Mauritanian border.

Military agreement No.1, signed between MINURSO and separately with the parties [YUN 1998, p. 194], remained the basic legal instrument governing the ceasefire monitoring of the five parts into which, for operational purposes, the disputed Territory of Western Sahara was divided: one five-kilometre-wide buffer strip to the east and south of the berm; two restricted areas—one, 25 kilometres wide east of the berm and the other, 30 kilometres wide west of it; and two areas with limited restrictions that encompassed the remainder of the Territory. Bilateral military agreements Nos. 2 and 3 [YUN 1999, p. 180], committing both parties to cooperate with MINURSO in the exchange of mine-related information, marking of mined areas, and clearance and destruction of mines and unexploded ordnance, remained in force.

MINURSO maintained its headquarters in Laayoune, Western Sahara; a liaison office in Tindouf, Algeria, and nine military-observer team sites located across the Territory, four on the Moroccan-controlled side and five on the Frente Polisario side.

On the recommendation of the Secretary-General, the Council extended the mandate of MINURSO twice during the year, the first time until 31 October 2005 and the second until 30 April 2006.

Appointments. By an exchange of letters between the Secretary-General and the Security Council on 4 and 8 August [S/2005/511 & S/2005/512], Francesco Bastagli (Italy) was appointed Special Representative of the Secretary-General for Western Sahara and Head of MINURSO, with effect from 1 September.

By a further exchange of letters on 6 and 9 September [S/2005/570 & S/2005/571], Brigadier General Kurt Mosgaard (Denmark) was appointed Force Commander of MINURSO, from 12 September, to succeed Major General Gyorgy Szaraz (Hungary), who completed his tour of duty on 11 August.

Restructuring. During the year, MINURSO, in cooperation with the Department of Peacekeeping Operations, developed a new concept of operations that went into effect on 1 October, which fully integrated military and civilian activities so as to enhance the Mission's operational effectiveness. The military structure was reorganized by closing two sector headquarters and redeploying their military observers to the nine team sites, thus increasing MINURSO's patrol ca-

pabilities. The military headquarters was restructured to include a joint civilian-military mission analysis centre and a joint operations centre to enhance data collection and information management. Night observation patrols and temporary observation posts were to be introduced, for which night vision equipment would be provided.

A comprehensive review of the structure of the Mission's administrative and other civilian components was also completed. Its recommendations included a reduction by 57 posts (47 international and 10 local), to be offset by an increase of 18 posts (international) and the creation of 24 United Nations Volunteer posts. The recommendations were to be phased in and completed by mid-2006.

Financing

The General Assembly, at its resumed fifty-ninth session, considered the performance report on the MINURSO budget for 1 July 2003 to 30 June 2004 [A/59/619], showing a total expenditure of $38,850,800 for the period out of an apportionment of $41,529,500, resulting in an unencumbered balance of $2,678,700; the MINURSO budget for 1 July 2005 to 30 June 2006 [A/59/629] showing estimated requirements of $46,328,400; and the related report of ACABQ [A/59/736/Add.5].

GENERAL ASSEMBLY ACTION

On 22 June [meeting 104], the General Assembly, on the recommendation of the Fifth Committee [A/59/839], adopted **resolution 59/308** without vote [agenda item 137].

Financing of the United Nations Mission for the Referendum in Western Sahara

The General Assembly,

Having considered the reports of the Secretary-General on the financing of the United Nations Mission for the Referendum in Western Sahara and the related reports of the Advisory Committee on Administrative and Budgetary Questions,

Recalling Security Council resolution 690(1991) of 29 April 1991, by which the Council established the United Nations Mission for the Referendum in Western Sahara, and the subsequent resolutions by which the Council extended the mandate of the Mission, the latest of which was resolution 1598(2005) of 28 April 2005,

Recalling also its resolution 45/266 of 17 May 1991 on the financing of the Mission and its subsequent resolutions and decisions thereon, the latest of which was resolution 58/309 of 18 June 2004,

Reaffirming the general principles underlying the financing of United Nations peacekeeping operations, as stated in General Assembly resolutions 1874(S-IV) of 27 June 1963, 3101(XXVIII) of 11 December 1973 and 55/235 of 23 December 2000,

Noting with appreciation that voluntary contributions have been made to the Mission,

Mindful of the fact that it is essential to provide the Mission with the necessary financial resources to enable it to fulfil its responsibilities under the relevant resolutions of the Security Council,

1. *Requests* the Secretary-General to entrust the Head of Mission with the task of formulating future budget proposals in full accordance with the provisions of General Assembly resolution 59/296 of 22 June 2005, as well as other relevant resolutions;

2. *Takes note* of the status of contributions to the United Nations Mission for the Referendum in Western Sahara as at 15 April 2005, including the contributions outstanding in the amount of 43.1 million United States dollars, representing some 7 per cent of the total assessed contributions, notes with concern that only sixty Member States have paid their assessed contributions in full, and urges all other Member States, in particular those in arrears, to ensure payment of their outstanding assessed contributions;

3. *Expresses its appreciation* to those Member States that have paid their assessed contributions in full, and urges all other Member States to make every possible effort to ensure payment of their assessed contributions to the Mission in full;

4. *Expresses concern* at the financial situation with regard to peacekeeping activities, in particular as regards the reimbursements to troop contributors that bear additional burdens owing to overdue payments by Member States of their assessments;

5. *Also expresses concern* at the delay experienced by the Secretary-General in deploying and providing adequate resources to some recent peacekeeping missions, in particular those in Africa;

6. *Emphasizes* that all future and existing peacekeeping missions shall be given equal and non-discriminatory treatment in respect of financial and administrative arrangements;

7. *Also emphasizes* that all peacekeeping missions shall be provided with adequate resources for the effective and efficient discharge of their respective mandates;

8. *Reiterates its request* to the Secretary-General to make the fullest possible use of facilities and equipment at the United Nations Logistics Base at Brindisi, Italy, in order to minimize the costs of procurement for the Mission;

9. *Endorses* the conclusions and recommendations contained in the report of the Advisory Committee on Administrative and Budgetary Questions, and requests the Secretary-General to ensure their full implementation;

10. *Requests* the Secretary-General to ensure the full implementation of the relevant provisions of its resolution 59/296;

11. *Decides* that the posts of Chief of Staff, Legal Officer, Information Officer, Assistant in Facilities Management Services and Information Technology Assistant, which are filled respectively at the levels of D-1, P-4, P-3, G-7 and FS-5, shall be budgeted at those levels, pending the management review;

12. *Requests* the Secretary-General to take all necessary action to ensure that the Mission is administered with a maximum of efficiency and economy;

13. *Also requests* the Secretary-General, in order to reduce the cost of employing General Service staff, to continue efforts to recruit local staff for the Mission against General Service posts, commensurate with the requirements of the Mission;

**Financial performance report
for the period from 1 July 2003 to 30 June 2004**

14. *Takes note* of the report of the Secretary-General on the financial performance of the Mission for the period from 1 July 2003 to 30 June 2004;

**Budget estimates
for the period from 1 July 2005 to 30 June 2006**

15. *Decides* to appropriate to the Special Account for the United Nations Mission for the Referendum in Western Sahara the amount of 47,948,400 dollars for the period from 1 July 2005 to 30 June 2006, inclusive of 45,540,400 dollars for the maintenance of the Mission, 1,969,000 dollars for the support account for peacekeeping operations and 439,000 dollars for the United Nations Logistics Base;

Financing of the appropriation

16. *Decides also* to apportion among Member States the amount of 15,982,800 dollars for the period from 1 July to 31 October 2005, in accordance with the levels updated in General Assembly resolution 58/256 of 23 December 2003, and taking into account the scale of assessments for 2005 as set out in its resolution 58/1 B of 23 December 2003;

17. *Decides further* that, in accordance with the provisions of its resolution 973(X) of 15 December 1955, there shall be set off against the apportionment among Member States, as provided for in paragraph 16 above, their respective share in the Tax Equalization Fund of 940,600 dollars, comprising the estimated staff assessment income of 836,000 dollars approved for the Mission, the prorated share of 92,767 dollars of the estimated staff assessment income approved for the support account and the prorated share of 11,833 dollars of the estimated staff assessment income approved for the United Nations Logistics Base;

18. *Decides* to apportion among Member States the amount of 31,965,600 dollars for the period from 1 November 2005 to 30 June 2006, at a monthly rate of 3,995,700 dollars, in accordance with the levels updated in General Assembly resolution 58/256, and taking into account the scale of assessments for 2005 and 2006 as set out in its resolution 58/1 B, subject to a decision of the Security Council to extend the mandate of the Mission;

19. *Decides also* that, in accordance with the provisions of its resolution 973(X), there shall be set off against the apportionment among Member States, as provided for in paragraph 18 above, their respective share in the Tax Equalization Fund of 1,881,200 dollars, comprising the estimated staff assessment income of 1,672,000 dollars approved for the Mission, the prorated share of 185,533 dollars of the estimated staff assessment income approved for the support account and the prorated share of 23,667 dollars of the estimated staff assessment income approved for the United Nations Logistics Base;

20. *Decides further* that, for Member States that have fulfilled their financial obligations to the Mission, there shall be set off against their apportionment, as

provided for in paragraph 16 above, their respective share of the unencumbered balance and other income in the total amount of 3,872,700 dollars in respect of the financial period ended 30 June 2004, in accordance with the levels updated in General Assembly resolution 58/256, and taking into account the scale of assessments for 2004, as set out in its resolution 58/1 B;

21. *Decides* that, for Member States that have not fulfilled their financial obligations to the Mission, there shall be set off against their outstanding obligations their respective share of the unencumbered balance and other income in the total amount of 3,872,700 dollars in respect of the financial period ended 30 June 2004, in accordance with the scheme set out in paragraph 20 above;

22. *Decides also* that the decrease of 598,200 dollars in the estimated staff assessment income in respect of the financial period ended 30 June 2004 shall be set off against the credits from the amount of 3,872,700 dollars referred to in paragraphs 20 and 21 above;

23. *Emphasizes* that no peacekeeping mission shall be financed by borrowing funds from other active peacekeeping missions;

24. *Encourages* the Secretary-General to continue to take additional measures to ensure the safety and security of all personnel under the auspices of the United Nations participating in the Mission, bearing in mind paragraphs 5 and 6 of Security Council resolution 1502(2003) of 26 August 2003;

25. *Invites* voluntary contributions to the Mission in cash and in the form of services and supplies acceptable to the Secretary-General, to be administered, as appropriate, in accordance with the procedure and practices established by the General Assembly;

26. *Decides* to include in the provisional agenda of its sixtieth session the item entitled "Financing of the United Nations Mission for the Referendum in Western Sahara".

In December [A/60/634], the Secretary-General submitted the performance report on the MINURSO budget for 1 July 2004 to 30 June 2005.

Peacemaking efforts

In response to Security Council resolution 1570(2004) [YUN 2004, p. 277], the Secretary-General submitted three interim reports during the year on the evolving situation concerning Western Sahara and the status of MINURSO as it related to the political and operational environment. The reports consistently noted that Western Sahara and Morocco remained deadlocked regarding the 2003 peace plan for self-determination for the people of Western Sahara [YUN 2003, p. 259]. They also underscored the continued support and cooperation provided by the AU to MINURSO throughout the reporting periods.

Report of Secretary-General (January). In his January report [S/2005/49], the Secretary-General stated that MINURSO continued its ground and air patrols to visit and inspect units larger than company size of RMA and Frente Polisario military forces, in accordance with military agreement No. 1 (see p. 364). Both forces continued to conduct routine maintenance and training activities. Frente Polisario remained insistent on limiting the Mission's ground and air patrolling of the Territory east of the berm, which it controlled. A smaller-than-company-size Frente Polisario unit was observed in the area known as Spanish fort within the restricted area east of the berm, as were activities to enhance RMA radar monitoring capability along the berm. Those actions were undertaken ostensibly to deter the movement of illegal migrants and smugglers. MINURSO drew the parties' attention to the prohibitions under the agreement of troop movements and tactical reinforcement of equipment within the restricted areas. The parties agreed in principle to inform MINURSO in detail of their proposed actions to address the problem of illegal migration and to cooperate with it to diminish any possible friction between them as a result of such actions.

Because of the significant increase in the smuggling of migrants through Western Sahara in the previous two years, the parties had requested the Mission to increase its patrolling of known smuggling routes. The International Organization for Migration (IOM) confirmed, on 3 November, the successful repatriation to Bangladesh and India of 23 migrants found near Mijek in 2004. Frente Polisario informed the Mission that of the 21 migrants found near Tifariti, it had released 20, who were Pakistanis, to the border with Mauritania; arrangements for the repatriation of the remaining migrant, a Bangladeshi, were under consideration.

A relief and recovery programme for Western Saharan refugees, budgeted at some $40 million for the two-year period from September 2004 to August 2006, continued to be carried out by the World Food Programme (WFP). WFP and the Office of the United Nations High Commissioner for Refugees (UNHCR) had been increasing their monitoring and logistical capacity in the Tindouf refugee camps, a programme to which the EU had contributed 5.5 million euros.

An evaluation of the pilot phase (March-August 2004) of the confidence-building programme, led by UNHCR with MINURSO support and aimed at facilitating person-to-person contacts between the refugees in the Tindouf camps and their relatives in the Territory, yielded positive results. The parties expressed support for continuing the exchange of family visits and telephone service under existing arrangements. Since its inception in March 2004, a total of 1,476 persons, 754 from the refugee camps and 722 from the Territory, had benefited from the programme.

The Secretary-General noted that the 1991 ceasefire continued to be respected by the parties and monitored by MINURSO to the extent of its ability. He remained concerned, however, that the prolonged political deadlock might lead to a deterioration of the situation in Western Sahara. In that regard, he would examine the parties' reiteration of their desire for increasing the Mission's strength and reinforcing its patrolling capacity.

Report of Secretary-General (April). According to the April report of the Secretary-General [S/2005/254], Morocco protested the occasional demonstrations in the buffer strip by Frente Polisario civilian supporters (mainly from outside the region) allegedly escorted by armed military personnel. For its part, Frente Polisario protested the alleged shooting of a civilian from across the berm and the mistreatment of clandestine migrants by Morocco. Investigation of the allegations by MINURSO were inconclusive. In March, MINURSO completed a database of the parties' compliance with the military agreements that facilitated the tracking and analysis of information obtained by military observers. In that regard, MINURSO confirmed that compliance with military agreement No. 1 had seriously deteriorated. RMA continued installing and upgrading its radar and surveillance capability in over 40 locations along the entire length of the berm, improving its defence infrastructure, including constructing a second strand of the berm, and conducting live-fire military exercises that occasionally extended to the restricted areas towards the north-east corner of the Territory. Frente Polisario continued deployment of a unit of armed personnel with anti-aircraft weapons in the Spanish fort, repeated incursions into the buffer strip by vehicles carrying armed military personnel, and restricting the Mission's freedom of movement. Both parties, instead of submitting prior notifications or requests for engaging in regulated or restricted actions, submitted their requests after the fact.

In addition to the continuing cooperation of the parties with MINURSO in marking and disposing of mines and unexploded ordnance, MINURSO was cooperating with the Geneva International Centre for Humanitarian Demining to develop an information management system for mine action and a comprehensive database to support a wider mine action campaign.

On 22 March, MINURSO transported the Bangladeshi found in the Tifariti area (above) to Mauritania, where he was transferred to IOM for repatriation; it visited an additional 46 migrants, reportedly from Bangladesh, also stranded in Tifariti since April. MINURSO's capacity to assist in the repatriation operation of illegal migrants was limited to lending logistical support on a humanitarian basis.

A joint WFP and UNHCR monitoring mission (5-12 March) to the Tindouf refugee camps was organized to look into the recurrent breakdown of food distribution mechanisms there. Together with MINURSO, the two agencies also facilitated a visit by donors (16-19 March).

In early January, following consultations with the Special Representative, UNHCR submitted a new action plan for implementing the 2005 phase of the confidence-building measures programme. UNHCR hosted a donors meeting (Geneva, 3 February), which by the reporting date had resulted in $1.8 million in contributions received and pledged. Frente Polisario and Algeria had approved the plan, while Morocco intended to consider it further.

The Secretary-General expressed concern at the scale of the violations of military agreement No. 1 and felt the need for the parties to reconfirm their commitment to the ceasefire and military agreements. He also registered his concern over the recently reported statement by the Frente Polisario leadership that a "return to arms" might be "closer than ever". In view of the gravity of some of the violations described, consideration could be given to strengthening MINURSO. He therefore recommended the extension of its mandate for a further six months, to 31 October 2005.

SECURITY COUNCIL ACTION (April)

On 28 April [meeting 5170], the Security Council unanimously adopted **resolution 1598(2005)**. The draft [S/2005/275] was prepared in consultations among Council members.

The Security Council,

Recalling all its previous resolutions on Western Sahara, including resolutions 1495(2003) of 31 July 2003, 1541(2004) of 29 April 2004 and 1570(2004) of 28 October 2004,

Reaffirming its commitment to assist the parties to achieve a just, lasting and mutually acceptable political solution which will provide for the self-determination of the people of Western Sahara in the context of arrangements consistent with the principles and purposes of the Charter of the United Nations, and noting the role and responsibilities of the parties in this respect,

Reiterating its call upon the parties and States of the region to continue to cooperate fully with the United Nations to end the current impasse and to achieve progress towards a political solution,

Urging the Frente Popular para la Liberación de Seguía El-Hamra y de Río de Oro to release without further delay all remaining prisoners of war in compliance with international humanitarian law, and calling upon Morocco and the Frente Popular para la Liberación de Seguía El-Hamra y de Río de Oro to continue to cooperate with the International Committee of the Red Cross to resolve the fate of persons who are unaccounted for since the beginning of the conflict,

Having considered the report of the Secretary-General of 19 April 2005, and taking note of his interim report of 27 January 2005,

1. *Decides* to extend the mandate of the United Nations Mission for the Referendum in Western Sahara until 31 October 2005;

2. *Affirms* the need for full respect of the military agreements reached with the Mission with regard to the ceasefire;

3. *Calls upon* Member States to consider voluntary contributions to fund confidence- building measures that allow for increased contact between separated family members, especially family unification visits;

4. *Looks forward* to receiving the results of the comprehensive review of the structure of the administrative and other civilian components of the Mission, as outlined in the report of the Secretary-General of 19 April 2005;

5. *Requests* that the Secretary-General provide a report on the situation concerning Western Sahara before the end of the mandate period;

6. *Decides* to remain seized of the matter.

Personal Envoy of Secretary-General. By an exchange of letters between the Secretary-General and the Security Council on 25 and 28 July [S/2005/497 & S/2005/498], Peter van Walsum (Netherlands) was appointed Personal Envoy of the Secretary-General for Western Sahara to help assess the situation and to explore how best to overcome the current political impasse. As a first step, the Secretary-General requested his Personal Envoy to establish contacts with the parties, neighbouring States and other stakeholders to ascertain their views on the best way forward.

As later reported by the Secretary-General [S/2006/249], the Personal Envoy, following his preliminary discussions in New York with representatives of the two parties and of Algeria and Mauritania, undertook an exploratory mission to the region from 11 to 17 October.

The Personal Envoy informed the Secretary-General that there continued to be a total lack of agreement on how to enable the people of Western Sahara to exercise their right to self-determination. Morocco had reiterated it would not accept a referendum that would include the option of independence; it strongly advocated negotiations with a view to achieving a just, lasting and mutually acceptable political solution, but made clear that negotiations would have to be about the autonomy status of Western Sahara. The position of Frente Polisario, with the general support of Algeria, was that the only way forward was to implement either the 2003 peace plan

for the self-determination of the people of Western Sahara or the 1991 settlement plan [YUN 1991, p. 793], both of which provided for self-determination through a referendum, with independence as one of the options. Any other course would not be acceptable to Frente Polisario. Mauritania reiterated its strict neutrality.

On his return from the region, the Personal Envoy held consultations with authorities in Madrid, Paris and Washington, D.C., on 18, 22 and 25 October, respectively.

Communications. Morocco, on 23 September [S/2005/602], drew attention to continued grave violations of the rights of thousands of Moroccan detainees in prison and civilians in camps in Algeria, the country of asylum. Apart from its limited presence in the refugee camps, UNHCR had been unable to conduct a census of that population because Algeria made such a census conditional upon the settlement of the Western Saharan dispute. Morocco spoke of the existence of detention centres and military barracks within the camps and of peoples held hostage there in violation of the principles governing the right of asylum. As to the photographic montages made of inmates in Laayoune prison, Morocco said they were the manipulated images of persons imprisoned for such crimes as homicide, rape or drug trafficking, and were part of a propaganda campaign against it.

Algeria, on 26 September [S/2005/605], referred to Morocco's letter as directly or tacitly implicating Algeria in some aspects of the Western Sahara conflict. It said that Morocco, caught in the act of repressing Sahrawi civilians and accused by NGOs and the international media of grave crimes and acts of torture against Sahrawi political prisoners, was reacting like any occupying or colonial power by cordoning off the Territory it had been occupying since 1975 and prohibiting by military force NGOs, the media, outside observers and parliamentarians from entering the Territory. Regarding the "thousands of Moroccan civilians still in the camps", Algeria said they included Sahrawi refugees duly identified as such by UNHCR who had had no choice but to flee from their occupied homeland and to whom Algeria had generously offered asylum.

Algeria noted that, given the very serious situation prevailing in Western Sahara, where 151 POWs were being held by Morocco, several hundred Sahrawi civilians remained missing, and 37 prisoners had been staging a hunger strike since 8 August (see below) to obtain political prisoner status, it called on the Security Council to appeal to Morocco concerning the disappeared Sahrawi civilians and the plight of the 37 political prisoners. It should not allow Morocco to stall progress indefinitely, paralyse the Organization and frustrate the hopes of the international community.

Report of Secretary-General (October). In his October report [S/2005/648], the Secretary-General stated that there had been some unrest in the Territory, where several demonstrations were organized in Laayoune and other main towns in support of the self-determination of Western Saharans and respect for their human rights. Violent confrontations between the demonstrators and the Moroccan security forces ensued, resulting in arrests and detentions. A number of detainees went on a hunger strike from early August to 29 September. Tensions ran particularly high following the death of a demonstrator from injuries inflicted by police during a 29 October protest in Laayoune. Two police officers involved in the incident were being held pending completion of a judicial inquiry by Morocco into the circumstances surrounding that death.

In response to the demonstrations, Morocco increased its security and police presence in all the main towns of the Territory and, in December, deployed army troops there for the first time since 1999. In letters of 17 November and 14 and 20 December to the UN Secretary-General, the Frente Polisario Secretary-General called on the United Nations to intervene to protect the Saharan citizens and guarantee their human rights, condemned the intervention of the Moroccan police and military in the demonstrations and warned that deployment of the troops to Western Sahara constituted a dangerous development that could lead to deadly confrontations between Moroccan and Saharan civilians.

New violations of military agreement No. 1 occurred during the reporting period. From 14 April to 14 September, MINURSO observed 13 violations by RMA and 10 by Frente Polisario. They included brief incursions into the buffer strip by armed elements from both sides, construction of new physical structures and movement of military units without prior notification or MINURSO approval. MINURSO pointed out that the civilian demonstrations by Frente Polisario supporters in the buffer strip, while not constituting a breach of the agreement, contributed to increased tensions along the berm.

In keeping with military agreements Nos. 2 and 3, the parties continued to extend a high level of cooperation to MINURSO in the marking and disposal of mines and unexploded ordnance. Between the first and third reporting periods, MINURSO had discovered and marked 407 of such items and monitored the destruction of 3,693. In addition, it monitored 54 disposal operations, all carried out by RMA.

One of the most painful chapters of the Frente Polisario–Morocco conflict was brought to a close on 18 August, when, through the mediation of the United States, Frente Polisario released the last 404 Moroccan POWs in its custody to ICRC for repatriation to Morocco. ICRC continued to pursue the question of persons who remained unaccounted for as a result of the conflict.

With regard to assistance to Western Saharan refugees, by a joint UNHCR-WFP decision communicated to Frente Polisario and to Algeria, as the country of asylum, the number of assisted beneficiaries was reduced from 158,000 to 90,000 as at 1 September, with assistance targeted to the most vulnerable of the population in the Tindouf refugee camps. That number would be used for planning purposes, pending a comprehensive registration of the refugee population. While donor support for humanitarian programmes had risen to over $5 million in 2005, additional international assistance would be required to provide supplementary food to improve the health of the refugees.

The exchange of family visits between the Territory and the Tindouf refugee camps under the confidence-building programme did not resume during the reporting period. Although Frente Polisario and Algeria had approved the action plan for the 2005 phase, Morocco had suggested some amendments that were discussed with UNHCR, after which Morocco accepted the plan; the programme was to resume in early November.

The Secretary-General expressed concern over the alleged human rights abuses in the Territory and in the Tindouf refugee camps (see p. 368). He pointed out that MINURSO had neither the mandate nor the resources to address the issue, but the High Commissioner for Human Rights intended to approach the parties and Algeria, as the country of asylum, with a view to exploring what action might be taken in that regard.

In the belief that MINURSO continued to play an important role in monitoring the ceasefire and stabilizing the situation on the ground, the Secretary-General recommended that its mandate be extended for a further period of six months, until 30 April 2006.

SECURITY COUNCIL ACTION (October)

On 28 October [meeting 5295], the Security Council unanimously adopted **resolution 1634 (2005)**. The draft [S/2005/677] was prepared in consultations among Council members.

The Security Council,
Recalling all its previous resolutions on Western Sahara, including resolutions 1495(2003) of 31 July 2003,

1541(2004) of 29 April 2004 and 1598(2005) of 28 April 2005,

Reaffirming its commitment to assist the parties to achieve a just, lasting and mutually acceptable political solution which will provide for the self-determination of the people of Western Sahara in the context of arrangements consistent with the purposes and principles of the Charter of the United Nations, and noting the role and responsibilities of the parties in this respect,

Reiterating its call upon the parties and States of the region to continue to cooperate fully with the United Nations to end the current impasse and to achieve progress towards a political solution,

Taking note of the release on 18 August 2005 of the remaining four hundred and four Moroccan prisoners of war by the Frente Popular para la Liberación de Saguía el-Hamra y de Río de Oro in compliance with international humanitarian law, and calling upon the parties to continue to cooperate with the International Committee of the Red Cross to resolve the fate of persons who are unaccounted for since the beginning of the conflict,

Welcoming the appointment of the Personal Envoy of the Secretary-General for Western Sahara Mr. Peter van Walsum, and noting that he recently completed consultations in the region,

Having considered the report of the Secretary-General of 13 October 2005,

1. *Reaffirms* the need for full respect of the military agreements reached with the United Nations Mission for the Referendum in Western Sahara with regard to the ceasefire;

2. *Calls upon* Member States to consider voluntary contributions to fund confidence-building measures that allow for increased contact between separated family members, especially family unification visits;

3. *Decides* to extend the mandate of the Mission until 30 April 2006;

4. *Requests* that the Secretary-General provide a report on the situation concerning Western Sahara before the end of the mandate period, and requests the Personal Envoy of the Secretary-General to provide a briefing, within three months of the adoption of the present resolution, on the progress of his efforts;

5. *Decides* to remain seized of the matter.

GENERAL ASSEMBLY ACTION

The General Assembly, in December, examined the Secretary-General's July report summarizing his 1 July 2004–30 June 2005 reports to the Security Council on the question of Western Sahara [A/60/116] and the relevant chapter in the report of the Special Committee on decolonization for 2005 [A/60/23] (see p. 658).

On 8 December [meeting 62], the Assembly, on the recommendation of the Fourth (Special Political and Decolonization) Committee [A/60/472], adopted **resolution 60/114** without vote.

Question of Western Sahara

The General Assembly,

Having considered in depth the question of Western Sahara,

Reaffirming the inalienable right of all peoples to self-determination and independence, in accordance with the principles set forth in the Charter of the United Nations and General Assembly resolution 1514 (XV) of 14 December 1960 containing the Declaration on the Granting of Independence to Colonial Countries and Peoples,

Recalling its resolution 59/131 of 10 December 2004,

Recalling also all resolutions of the General Assembly and the Security Council on the question of Western Sahara,

Recalling further Security Council resolutions 658 (1990) of 27 June 1990 and 690(1991) of 29 April 1991, by which the Council approved the settlement plan for Western Sahara,

Recalling Security Council resolutions 1359(2001) of 29 June 2001 and 1429(2002) of 30 July 2002, as well as 1495(2003) of 31 July 2003, in which the Council expressed its support of the peace plan for self-determination of the people of Western Sahara as an optimum political solution on the basis of agreement between the two parties, and resolutions 1541(2004) of 29 April 2004, 1570(2004) of 28 October 2004 and 1598(2005) of 28 April 2005,

Taking note of the responses of the parties and neighbouring States to the Personal Envoy of the Secretary-General concerning the peace plan contained in the report of the Secretary-General of 23 May 2003,

Reaffirming the responsibility of the United Nations towards the people of Western Sahara,

Noting with satisfaction the entry into force of the ceasefire in accordance with the proposal made by the Secretary-General, and stressing the importance it attaches to the maintenance of the ceasefire as an integral part of the settlement plan,

Underlining, in this regard, the validity of the settlement plan, while noting the fundamental differences between the parties in its implementation,

Stressing that the lack of progress in the settlement of the dispute on Western Sahara continues to cause suffering to the people of Western Sahara, remains a source of potential instability in the region and obstructs the economic development of the Maghreb region and that, in view of this, the search for a political solution is critically needed,

Welcoming the efforts of the Secretary-General and his Personal Envoy in search of a mutually acceptable political solution, which will provide for self-determination of the people of Western Sahara,

Having examined the relevant chapter of the report of the Special Committee on the Situation with regard to the Implementation of the Declaration on the Granting of Independence to Colonial Countries and Peoples,

Having also examined the report of the Secretary-General,

1. *Takes note* of the report of the Secretary-General;

2. *Underlines* Security Council resolution 1495 (2003), in which the Council expressed its support of the peace plan for self-determination of the people of Western Sahara as an optimum political solution on the basis of agreement between the two parties;

3. *Underlines also* that the parties reacted differently to this plan;

4. *Continues to support strongly* the efforts of the Secretary-General and his Personal Envoy to achieve a

mutually acceptable political solution to the dispute over Western Sahara;

5. *Commends* the Secretary-General and his Personal Envoy for their outstanding efforts and the two parties for the spirit of cooperation they have shown in the support they provide for those efforts;

6. *Calls upon* all the parties and the States of the region to cooperate fully with the Secretary-General and his Personal Envoy;

7. *Reaffirms* the responsibility of the United Nations towards the people of Western Sahara;

8. *Calls upon* the parties to cooperate with the International Committee of the Red Cross in its efforts to solve the problem of the fate of the people unaccounted for, and calls upon the parties to abide by their obligations under international humanitarian law to release without further delay all those held since the start of the conflict;

9. *Requests* the Special Committee on the Situation with regard to the Implementation of the Declaration on the Granting of Independence to Colonial Countries and Peoples to continue to consider the situation in Western Sahara and to report thereon to the General Assembly at its sixty-first session;

10. *Invites* the Secretary-General to submit to the General Assembly at its sixty-first session a report on the implementation of the present resolution.

Other issues

Zimbabwe

In May, the Government of Zimbabwe launched a clean-up operation of its cities known Operation Murambatsvina (Operation Restore Order), designed to stop all forms of alleged illegal activities in areas such as vending, illegal structures, illegal cultivation, among others, in its cities. The number of people affected by the Operation was estimated at 2.4 million, with some 700,000 having lost their homes. The campaign was condemned by several UN Member States, Zimbabwean opposition parties, church groups and NGOs.

Concerned by the adverse impact of the Operation on the lives of the urban poor, on 20 June, the Secretary-General appointed Anna Kajumulo Tibaijuka, Executive Director of the United Nations Human Settlement Programme (UN-Habitat), as his Special Envoy to lead a fact-finding mission to Zimbabwe to assess the scope and impact of Operation Murambatsvina. The Special Envoy visited Zimbabwe between 26 June and 8 July. The mission reported that the Operation was carried out in an indiscriminate and unjustified manner. The humanitarian consequences were enormous and any humanitarian response would only be meaningful if it contributed to long-term recovery and reconstruction

efforts. The mission made a number of recommendations for the Government of Zimbabwe, the United Nations and the wider international community to address the situation.

Communication (July). On 26 July [S/2005/490], Australia, Canada and New Zealand expressed concern at the growing humanitarian and human rights crisis in Zimbabwe. They said that the report of the Secretary-General's Special Envoy had documented the failure of the Government of Zimbabwe to protect its people and was responsible for the situation. The Government had to take urgent action to implement the recommendations contained in the Special Envoy's report. However, they noted that the reaction of the Government of Zimbabwe to the report gave little confidence that it would do so. Noting that the report stated that there would be far-reaching and long-term social, economic, political and institutional consequences, the three States were of the view that for too long the United Nations had been unable to take up the deteriorating situation in Zimbabwe and called on the Security Council to be seized of the situation as a matter of urgency and to engage actively with the Government of Zimbabwe to bring the situation to an end.

Security Council consideration. On 27 July [meeting 5237], at the request of the United Kingdom [S/2005485, S/2005/489], the Council met in a closed session to hear a briefing by the Secretary-General's Special Envoy. The representative of Zimbabwe was invited to participate in the meeting. At the request of the Russian Federation, the agenda was put to the vote and was adopted by a vote of nine in favour, five against and one abstention.

Communications. In a 31 October press statement [SG/SM/10195], the Secretary-General said that he remained concerned by the humanitarian crisis in Zimbabwe as the United Nations continued to receive reports that tens of thousands of people were still homeless and in need of assistance, months after the May eviction campaign. He was dismayed to learn of the Government's rejection of offers of UN assistance and its claim that there was no humanitarian crisis and that its interventions had addressed the most urgent needs. The Secretary-General noted that the Government's decision to decline assistance came despite extensive consultations on relief with the United Nations. In the light of the impending rainy season, he appealed to the Government to ensure that those who were out in the open without shelter and means of sustaining their livelihoods were provided with humanitarian assistance in collaboration with the United Nations and the humanitarian community in order to avert a further deterioration of the humanitarian situation.

The European Union (EU), in a 7 November statement of its Presidency [S/2005/712], noted the Secretary-General's statement and shared his concern over the grave humanitarian situation in Zimbabwe. It called on the Government of Zimbabwe to work with the United Nations and the international community to get aid and shelter to those in need and to implement all the recommendation contained in the report of the Secretary-General's Special Envoy (see above).

In another statement issued on 19 December [S/2005/830], the EU Presidency welcomed the visit (3-7 December) to Zimbabwe by the United Nations Under-Secretary-General for Huamnitarian Affairs, Jan Egleland, and the agreements signed by UN agencies and Zimbabwe for food assistance and HIV/AIDS programmes. It noted the exchanges between the United Nations and Zimbabwe over the need for assistance with shelter. The EU called on Zimbabwe to build on those efforts and to allow the United Nations and other international donors unrestricted access in order to provide urgently needed humanitarian assistance.

Mauritania

Mauritania, on 31 May [S/2005/362], drew the attention of the Security Council to arrests it had made of a number of Islamic extremists in the country, from whom it had elicited information that Mauritanian youths had been trained outside the country by the Algerian Salafist Group for Preaching and Combat, which had ties to an international terrorist network connected with Al-Qaida. Some of the trainees had returned to the country, while others were still in training.

Mauritania further transmitted a press release on 6 June [S/2005/374], reporting an armed attack by the Salafist Group on a national army unit in the village of Limgheiti, killing 15 soldiers and wounding 17 others; two were missing. It also reported that, of 20 Mauritanians recently trained by the Group, 10 had returned to the country, 7 of whom were arrested and 3 were at large.

By a statement issued on 4 August [SG/SM/10030], the Secretary-General condemned the coup d'état in Mauritania the previous day, ousting President Maauya Ould Sid' Ahmed Taya. The Secretary-General called for the restoration of constitutional order and underlined the need for the full respect for human rights and the rule of law.

The AU Peace and Security Council, by a communiqué issued at its thirty-seventh meeting (Addis Ababa, Ethiopia, 8 September) [S/2005/581], stated that it took note of developments since the 3 August coup and the commitments made by the new Mauritanian authorities towards the swift restoration of constitutional order through a process that should culminate in presidential and legislative elections before 3 August 2007.

Cooperation between the AU and the UN system

On 17 October 2005 [meeting 5282], during consideration by the Security Council of the question of cooperation between the United Nations and regional organizations in maintaining peace and security (see p. 96), the Secretary-General welcomed the commitment by the 2005 World Summit to support a 10-year programme aimed at strengthening the capacity of the AU (see p. 59).

The representative of the Chairperson of the African Union Commission said that cooperation between the AU and the United Nations was both political and economic and based on a number of agreements and resolutions, citing UN collaboration with the AU and subregional organizations, such as the Economic Community of West African States, in addressing conflict prevention and peacekeeping operations on the African continent, and on the ongoing crises in Côte d'Ivoire, the Sudan and Somalia. He called for increased support for the consolidation of the African Union Commission in terms of long-term consultants and training programmes, strengthening the organs of the AU and establishment of specialized committees to enable the AU to perform effectively in the area of regional stabilization. He said that regional stabilization was about, among other things, effective conflict management and resolution. Thus, in welcoming the Summit commitment to address the special needs of Africa (see p. 57), the AU representative said that the stabilization of the continent required the swift implementation of the measures proposed to that end.

Chapter III

Americas

During 2005, the United Nations continued to advance the cause of lasting peace, human rights, sustainable development and the rule of law in the Americas. With the ending of the mandate of the United Nations Verification Mission in Guatemala at the end of 2004, the Guatemalan peace process had matured into a new phase in which national actors had assumed fuller responsibility for monitoring and promoting the accords. A joint agreement in May between the Government of Guatemala and the Office of the United Nations High Commissioner for Human Rights resulted in the establishment of an office for monitoring and reporting on human rights in that country.

Despite efforts by the United Nations Stabilization Mission in Haiti (MINUSTAH) and the Haitian National Police to ensure a secure and stable environment in Haiti, the security situation remained precarious. Outbreaks of violence and illegal activities of armed groups continued to be a serious concern. The risk of retaliation against MINUSTAH and UN personnel increased, hampering the Mission's ability to carry out its mandate, including preparations for elections. The Mission's mandate was extended and its capacity expanded to address the increased political and security challenges prior to and after the elections. The Security Council sent a mission to Haiti, in conjunction with the Ad Hoc Advisory Group of the Economic and Social Council, to assess the situation and to make recommendations on how the international community could help Haiti restore good governance and economic and social stability. The Transitional Government launched the electoral process, which was to be completed in time for the installation of a new President in February 2006, but political and technical difficulties caused delays. It also launched a national dialogue and adopted a disarmament, demobilization and reintegration programme, the success of which depended on the willingness of armed groups to lay down their weapons.

In other developments in the region, the Ibero-American Secretariat was established at the Fifteenth Summit of the Heads of State and Government of the Ibero-American community of nations. Costa Rica filed an application with the International Court of Justice instituting proceedings against Nicaragua in a dispute concerning navigational and related rights on the San Juan River. The General Assembly again called on States to refrain from promulgating laws and measures, such as the ongoing embargo against Cuba by the United States. The Assembly granted observer status to the Ibero-American community of nations and the Latin American Integration Association.

Central America

The situation in Central America

Report of Secretary-General. As requested by the General Assembly in resolution 58/239 [YUN 2003, p. 276], the Secretary-General submitted an August report on the situation in Central America [A/60/218], which summarized progress achieved by countries in building democratic, equitable and peaceful societies. The report described activities by the United Nations Development Programme (UNDP) and other UN bodies to support the efforts of Central American countries in achieving sustainable development.

The Secretary-General stated that the electoral processes in some countries highlighted the need for further electoral reforms, particularly in the area of political parties and their financing mechanisms. El Salvador and Guatemala held presidential elections in which former actors in the countries' civil wars played a principal role. However, political parties in both countries were unable to garner citizen participation. The electoral campaign in El Salvador in March 2004, had pitted the ruling Alianza Republicana Nacionalista (ARENA) against the Frente Farabundo Martí para la Liberación Nacional (FMLN), with other political parties unable to pose a significant challenge. ARENA won its fourth consecutive term in office, an outcome that had significant repercussions on El Salvador's political system and deepened its polarization. In Guatemala's second democratic transfer of government since 1966, Óscar Berger was sworn in as the country's President on 15 January 2004. In the first months of the new Government, Congress approved electoral reforms called for in the 1996 Agreement on a Firm and Lasting Peace [YUN 1996, p. 168]. Electoral reforms in Honduras also progressed, with the implementation of regulations on the issuance of separate lists for presidential, congressional and mayoral elections; the participation of small political parties; alliances among parties; and the duration and financing of electoral campaigns. Voters elected Manuel Zelaya as President on 27 November 2004. In Nicaragua, the electoral system needed profound transformation to ensure impartiality and transparency for the November 2006 elections.

As violence in Central America had become widespread, with the homicide rate in some countries reaching epidemic levels, public security was a central concern. Youth gangs were a major security threat in the region, with an estimated 200 to 400 gangs in Guatemala, comprising some 150,000 to 200,000 members between 10 and 17 years old. The youth-gang phenomenon was due to widespread migration as a result of the breakdown in family structures, a young population, 74 per cent of which was under the age of 35 in 2000, the impact of poverty on adolescents' prospects, and the availability of weapons. Organized crime had also afflicted the region, with some countries becoming transit points for illegal drug-trafficking. Efforts to address the public security crisis included joint operations by the police and military in El Salvador, Guatemala and Honduras. The Secretary-General expressed concern about the potential for blurring the line between security and national defence matters and urged that the distinction between the two be upheld.

While the region had advanced in establishing peace through the eradication of violence, discrimination, impunity and inequities, UN human rights mechanisms continued to observe deficits in those areas. Women and children in Central America were often the victims of violence, and human rights defenders and journalists had become the target of threats and persecution. Many obstacles hampered efforts to bring perpetrators of human rights abuses to justice, and cases of torture, disappearances and extrajudicial executions continued to go unpunished. Inadequate Government funding of national human rights institutions had also slowed progress. The Special Rapporteur on violence against women, in visits to Guatemala and El Salvador in 2004, cited impunity as one of the most prominent concerns in both countries. As recommended by the Special Rapporteur, the Government of El Salvador increased the 2005 budgets of the Salvadoran Institute for the Development

of Women and the Office of the Human Rights Procurator.

A joint agreement in May 2005 between the Government of Guatemala and the Office of the United Nations High Commissioner for Human Rights (OHCHR) resulted in the establishment of an OHCHR office for monitoring and reporting on the national human rights situation. The office, which became operational in July, would continue the work done by the United Nations Verification Mission in Guatemala (MINUGUA) (see p. 376), advise the Government on human rights policies and assist national institutions. The new administration also made efforts to address discrimination against the indigenous population, support a reparation programme for victims of human rights violations, and publicly recognize State responsibility for past human rights violations.

Despite progress achieved in the area of judicial reform, marginalized sectors of Central America had limited access to justice, resulting in widespread impunity. Lack of independence from other State powers, deficient funding and poor coordination were issues prevalent in several judiciaries. In Guatemala, while centres for the administration of justice had been opened in isolated, indigenous areas and there were more mediation centres, poor inter-institutional coordination and unclear policies on hiring bilingual staff for Guatemala's indigenous population, half of whom did not necessarily speak Spanish, had affected their effectiveness. Although the Honduran judicial system had been modernized since the 1990s, resulting in a lessening of corruption, improved access to justice was not included in the reform. In El Salvador, an agreement between the Supreme Court of Justice and the National Council on the Judiciary to establish a judicial training programme marked a positive development towards resolving tension between the two institutions. A climate of mistrust of the justice system prevailed in Nicaragua, especially concerning the lack of political independence. A 2004 judicial career law regulating the judiciary's administrative and financial management granted the politicized Supreme Court discretionary power to name a number of judges.

In the area of governance, the Secretary-General said that corruption was endemic in Central America, although unprecedented steps had been taken to address it. Corruption scandals in Costa Rica involving three former Presidents; the alleged misuse of some $16 million by the former Guatemalan President during his tenure; and the sentencing of the former Nicaraguan President, Arnoldo Alemán, to 20 years in prison for various corruption crimes exemplified the situation. Encouraged that all countries in the region had signed the United Nations Convention against Corruption, adopted by the Assembly in resolution 58/4 [YUN 2003, p. 1127], the Secretary-General urged countries that had not yet ratified it to do so. In the light of Guatemala's failure to ratify a 2004 agreement with the United Nations to establish the Commission for the Investigation of Illegal Groups and Clandestine Security Organizations, he also urged that Government to address the issue of impunity, particularly as it related to those aspects.

In institution-building, progress was achieved in the Central American integration process both within and outside the region. The outward drive stemmed from the signing of the Central American Free Trade Agreement (CAFTA), and from the expectations of a possible agreement of association between the European Union (EU) and Central America, which could translate into a free trade agreement. At the Twenty-first Ministerial Conference on Political Dialogue and Economic Cooperation between the EU and the Central American Integration System (SICA) (Luxembourg, 26 May), ministers reaffirmed that such an agreement would give new impetus to the regional economic integration process. Efforts continued in the designing of regional strategies for integrating the region into the world economy to ensure sustainable development in all Central American countries. In that regard, the Puebla-Panama Plan [YUN 2001, p. 240] had evolved into a mechanism for facilitating, coordinating and articulating eight regional initiatives on tourism, transport, energy, telecommunications, competitiveness and integration, sustainable development, human development and disaster prevention and migration. Further progress had been achieved in regional integration with the political commitment for the creation of a customs union, and the decision by the leaders of El Salvador, Guatemala, Honduras and Nicaragua at the SICA meeting in June to introduce a regional arrest warrant, as well as a Central American passport and common visa requirements.

While Central America had not experienced a large-scale disaster since Hurricane Mitch [YUN 1998, p. 876] and the earthquakes in El Salvador in 2001 [YUN 2001, p. 858], those and past disasters had a long-term effect on development. Resources for development had been absorbed by post-disaster relief work and by investments required to rebuild stocks and infrastructure, but the reconstruction processes had not restored conditions to pre-disaster levels. Seasonal phenomena and climatic variations had also negatively affected development in Central America. The Secretary-General highlighted the need for the region to strengthen national and local capacity to respond to emergencies and to promote policies that improved risk management.

Border disputes between Central American countries continued their course in the International Court of Justice (ICJ) (see PART FOUR, Chapter I). The Belize-Guatemala territorial dispute was resolved with facilitation by the Organization of American States (OAS). In July, Belize and Guatemala adopted a new agreement on confidence-building measures and a new framework for negotiations. The Secretary-General emphasized that bringing closure to their territorial issues was a key step in creating long-term stability in the region. Concerning the Nicaraguan-Honduran disagreement, resulting from the 1999 López-Ramírez Treaty between Honduras and Colombia, an ICJ decision was expected by year's end or in 2006.

Cooperation activities carried out by UNDP and other UN organizations and programmes to achieve sustainable development in Central American countries were focused on poverty eradication, agricultural development, health and nutrition, public finance and economic growth, environment, support for consensus-building processes and the strengthening of democratic institutions.

The Secretary-General observed that the Alliance for Sustainable Development of Central America [YUN 1994, p. 389]—a regional strategy for cooperation and integration—had been falling behind as an institutional basis for programme development. He indicated that there was little interest in having a regional conceptual and strategic framework for the development of Central America and some bodies and leaders preferred to harmonize the region's institutions under the aegis of CAFTA. He said that the UN system had made significant efforts to coordinate its work in Central America within the framework of the Millennium Development Goals (MDGs), particularly in strengthening the coordination and leadership role of national Governments to ensure that foreign assistance responded to national priorities and needs. The Secretary-General emphasized the importance of international cooperation for strengthening the integration of the Central American region within the context of globalization.

On 31 October [meeting 41], in a statement to the Assembly, Nicaragua, on behalf of SICA, said that Central America was a changed region. The decades of armed violence and acute economic and social crises had been overcome and all Governments enjoyed the legitimacy acquired through free elections. Their economies were growing and their political systems had become more open and democratic. In the light of the progress achieved, there was no longer a need to introduce a draft resolution under the agenda item.

The Assembly, by **decision 60/508** of 31 October, decided that the item entitled "The situation in Central America: progress in fashioning a region of peace, freedom, democracy and development" would remain on the agenda, for consideration upon notification by a Member State, beginning with the sixty-first (2006) session.

Communications. By a 21 October letter [A/60/447], Spain transmitted to the Secretary-General the Salamanca Declaration, adopted by Heads of State and Government of the Ibero-American community of nations (Salamanca, 14-15 October), as well as communiqués on the integration process in Latin America and the Caribbean and on support for negotiations between the EU and Central America and the Andean Community.

Nicaragua, on behalf of SICA, transmitted to the Secretary-General the Declaration of León [A/60/613], adopted at the Twenty-seventh Ordinary Meeting of Heads of State and Government of SICA (León Santiago de los Caballeros, Nicaragua, 2 December), which outlined measures for further consolidating SICA and for strengthening it as a region of peace, freedom, democracy and development.

On 28 December [A/60/672], El Salvador transmitted the text of the Declaration of San Salvador, adopted by SICA on the occasion of the Fourth Central American Congress on sexually transmitted infections (STIs) and HIV/AIDS, the Fourth Central American Meeting of People Living with HIV/AIDS and the Third Latin American and Caribbean Forum on STIs and HIV/AIDS (San Salvador, 11 November).

Guatemala

In 2005, Guatemala continued to consolidate peace and build upon the foundation developed in previous years, which had resulted in successful elections in 2003 [YUN 2003, p. 282] and the handover of power in January 2004 [YUN 2004, p. 286]. The departure of the United Nations Verification Mission in Guatemala at the end of 2004 marked the beginning of a new phase in the country, with the opportunity for Guatemalans to shape their own destiny through further development of the peace process and nation-building.

MINUGUA

The United Nations Verification Mission in Guatemala (MINUGUA), established in 1994 to verify implementation of the Comprehensive Agreement on Human Rights [YUN 1994, p. 408]

and extended in 1996 to verify the Agreement on a Firm and Lasting Peace [YUN 1996, p. 168], completed its operations on 31 December 2004 [YUN 2004, p. 287].

The Secretary-General, in a March end-of-mission report [A/59/746], submitted in response to General Assembly resolution 58/238 [YUN 2003, p. 283], described its work throughout the various stages of the Guatemalan peace process. The report also highlighted the innovative transition strategy implemented during the Mission's last two years of operation to build national capacity to promote the peace accords agenda after MINUGUA's departure.

The Secretary-General said that, operating in the multi-ethnic, multicultural and multilingual environment of Guatemala—with its deeply entrenched racism and abandonment of Mayan, Xinca and Garifuna indigenous communities, which comprised at least half the population—had been one of the most difficult challenges for MINUGUA. Great cultural sensitivity on the part of MINUGUA had been required to ensure effective operations. He indicated that MINUGUA staff, representing dozens of nationalities and fields of work, had performed admirably under difficult circumstances and that international and Guatemalan staff had worked side by side in innovative ways. With the departure of MINUGUA and the end of international verification, the Guatemalan peace process had matured into a new and important phase in which national actors were assuming fuller responsibility for monitoring and promoting the goals of the peace accords. He added that current and future UN operations could benefit from lessons learned from MINUGUA, as a successful example of multidimensional peacebuilding.

Haiti

During 2005, Haiti continued to be beset by political, economic and social challenges, resulting from a combination of weak governance and poverty. In the light of the violence that had erupted in 2004 following the departure of former President Jean-Bertrand Aristide from the country, tensions remained high between his Fanmi Lavalas party and the Transitional Government. Fanmi Lavalas had denounced the pact [YUN 2004, p. 293] signed by the Interim Government, civil society organizations and political groups on measures to be undertaken during the transition period, including the holding of local and national elections, and remained outside the political process. Violence between the Haitian National Police (HNP) and former soldiers of the disbanded armed forces continued. The Security Council decided to send a mission to Haiti, in conjunction with the Ad Hoc Advisory Group of the Economic and Social Council, to assess the situation. The mandate of the United Nations Stabilization Mission in Haiti (MINUSTAH), established by Security Council resolution 1542(2004) [ibid., p. 294], was expanded to address the political and security concerns related to the preparation and holding of elections scheduled for the end of the year. In addition to providing security support, MINUSTAH also focused on training and reforming HNP, monitoring the human rights situation, providing humanitarian assistance, and coordinating with the OAS in election preparations.

Political and security situation

Security Council consideration (January). On 12 January [meeting 5110], the Security Council met to discuss the Secretary-General's November 2004 report on MINUSTAH [YUN 2004, p. 298]. The Special Representative of the Secretary-General and Head of MINUSTAH, Mr. Juan Gabriel Valdés, in his briefing before the Council, said that, although security threats and challenges remained serious, the level of violence had been reduced and MINUSTAH's ability to handle situations that risked jeopardizing security had improved substantially. Within its security concept of legitimate use of force, balanced by a focus on the most urgent problems affecting the more vulnerable people of Haiti, MINUSTAH embarked on a new phase of its mission. It took steps to stabilize the security situation, forcing groups of former soldiers who defied the authority of the State and the Mission to back down, and causing other illegally armed groups to lose ground. As a result of the success of "Operation Liberty" conducted in December 2004 [ibid., p. 300] in the Cité Soleil district of Port-au-Prince, two police stations were opened and the deployment of MINUSTAH patrols and the activities of the Haitian civil service created conditions for the initiation of a variety of quick-impact projects. The Mission was convinced that gradual progress in health, sanitation and education, as well as the prompt launching of the disarmament, demobilization and reintegration (DDR) initiative would qualitatively change the Cité Soleil area and neighbourhood and help eliminate the armed bands active there. To that end, MINUSTAH had started planning and organizing the DDR programme and welcomed the creation of a disarmament committee as announced by Prime Minister Latortue. At the same time, it was closely

following the Transitional Government's policy of making compensation and severance pay to former members of the Haitian armed forces. In addition, all the armed former soldiers who had participated in the 15 December 2004 [ibid.] attempt to illegally take possession of the abandoned private residence of former President Aristide had been disarmed and had agreed to participate in reintegration programmes.

Concerning the electoral process, the Special Representative said that the basic technical elements for proceeding with the 2005 electoral timetable were in place, including the swearing in on 6 January of the new representative of the Catholic Church, thereby reinstating full membership of the Provisional Electoral Council, the Transitional Government's decision to allocate additional funding and to establish a mechanism to disburse those funds through UNDP, and the disbursal of the financing pledges by Canada and the EU. The Provisional Electoral Council completed the preparation of the electoral law and the OAS, in cooperation with MINUSTAH, started voter registration in March. The release of some Fanmi Lavalas leaders should be viewed as a step that could positively impact national dialogue and the elimination of violence. However, the Special Representative expressed concern over the imprisonment of former Prime Minister, Yvon Neptune, for nearly a year without trial, and the fact that human rights violations and crimes were being committed with an apparent link to HNP. He reiterated the demands he had made at the Contact Group meeting in December 2004 that the Transitional Government should select a few projects for priority implementation and the international community should simplify its financing mechanisms to allow infrastructure projects to be undertaken in 2005 so as to give hope to thousands of Haitians. He welcomed the World Bank's decision to release $73 million, following the repayment of arrears by the Transitional Government, the announcement by Canada to fund the electoral process and the reiteration of the EU's funding pledge.

Haiti's Minister for Foreign Affairs, Yvon Siméon, said that the Secretary-General's recommendation that the international community should make a long-term commitment to Haiti was justified, as the DDR process was a long-term effort requiring resources in excess of the country's capacity. The security situation, particularly in the working-class neighbourhoods, had deteriorated in recent months and the combined shortage of HNP personnel and the delayed deployment of MINUSTAH troops had complicated efforts to deal with gangs and restore order in dangerous areas. However, HNP, with MINUSTAH assistance, regained control of several illegally occupied police stations and efforts to neutralize gang and criminal activity were being enhanced. The Government, in an effort to establish a stable and secure environment through the disarmament of armed groups, had given special attention to demobilized military personnel. The commission responsible for those matters had been reorganized with encouraging results. The first instalment of pension payments to members of Haiti's armed forces had been made and it was hoped that the full amount due could be provided to all former military personnel, thereby meeting one of their main demands. Efforts were also under way to address human rights issues.

On elections, Mr. Siméon said that the Government was making every effort to facilitate the work of the Provisional Electoral Council and to fulfil its commitment to restore an elected Government by 7 February 2006. Haiti needed the support of its bilateral and multilateral partners and he hoped that the international community's commitment would not be limited to the political transition.

SECURITY COUNCIL ACTION

On 12 January [meeting 5110], following consultations among Security Council members, the President made statement **S/PRST/2005/1** on behalf of the Council:

The Security Council reaffirms the comprehensive mandate of the United Nations Stabilization Mission in Haiti as set forth in resolutions 1542 (2004) and 1576(2004), and expresses its support for a United Nations presence in Haiti as long as necessary.

The Council underlines the fact that national reconciliation, security and economic development remain key to stability in Haiti, and in that regard stresses that all Member States and international organizations, especially those in the region, should support the Transitional Government of Haiti in those efforts.

The Council underlines the important role of the Mission in ensuring a secure environment and commends the recent joint operations by the Mission and the Haitian National Police, in particular against all illegal armed groups. It notes, however, that further urgent action is needed to continue to improve the security situation. The Council again calls upon all parties in Haiti to respect human rights and to renounce the use of violence to advance their goals.

The Council encourages the Transitional Government to create without delay the national commission on disarmament, demobilization and reintegration to address all armed groups, particularly former members of the military, in a comprehensive manner. It notes that any compensation should be part of a comprehensive and durable solution.

The Council renews its appeal for the prompt disbursement of the funds pledged by international financial institutions and donor countries at the International Donors Conference on Haiti, held in July 2004. It recognizes the need for the Mission, other organs of the United Nations system, international financial institutions and Member States to assist the Transitional Government in the preparation and implementation of development projects in Haiti, as well as quick-impact projects. The Council reiterates the need to assist the Transitional Government in establishing a long-term development strategy for Haiti, in accordance with the priorities set forth in the Interim Cooperation Framework.

The Council welcomes recent steps taken by the Transitional Government to release some individuals being held without formal charge or trial, and calls upon the Transitional Government to review all such cases in order to ensure full respect for due process and the rule of law. In this regard, the Council calls upon the Mission to continue its support for the provision of human rights training to Haitian judicial, police and correctional authorities to ensure adherence to international norms and standards.

The Council encourages the Transitional Government to continue to take steps towards a comprehensive and inclusive national dialogue and reconciliation process, and calls upon all political actors in Haiti to renounce violence and join this dialogue without delay. The Council fully supports the Mission's continuing facilitation of this process.

The Council calls upon the Transitional Government, with the assistance of the Mission and the Organization of American States, urgently to take the necessary measures to ensure the holding of free and fair elections in 2005 and the subsequent transfer of power to elected authorities, and welcomes the recent decisions of the Provisional Electoral Council in its preparations. It encourages all political parties that have rejected violence to participate in the electoral process.

The Council expresses its intention to organize a mission to Haiti before 1 June 2005, possibly in conjunction with a mission of the Ad Hoc Advisory Group on Haiti of the Economic and Social Council.

The Council expresses its gratitude to the countries that have contributed personnel to the Mission. It urges troop and police-contributing countries to complete the authorized strength of the Mission as soon as possible, stressing that prompt completion of this step is an essential requirement for the continuing success of the operation.

The Council expresses its full support for the Special Representative of the Secretary-General for Haiti, Mr. Juan Gabriel Valdés, and commends the work done by the Mission and all of its personnel.

Report of Secretary-General (February). In his February report on MINUSTAH [S/2005/124], the Secretary-General indicated that, although the Mission's troop level had increased significantly and its capacity to respond to threats had produced noticeable results, the security situation remained precarious. Illegal activities of armed groups continued to be a serious concern and the risk of retaliation against MINUSTAH and UN personnel had increased due to the Mission's crackdown on gang members and former soldiers. On 7 January, to thwart ongoing shooting, including attacks against the Mission's presence in Cité Soleil, MINUSTAH arrested 96 suspects and placed them in HNP custody. MINUSTAH also maintained a presence in Bel-Air, a poor district affected by gang violence. In January, it launched three clean-up operations in the area to remove accumulated waste that restricted security patrols.

The security situation was further complicated by the Transitional Government's launch, in 2004, of a $2.8 million compensation programme for demobilized former military personnel [YUN 2004, p. 301]. Despite their willingness to accept the indemnity, the former soldiers refused to disarm, demanding the creation of an interim security force. MINUSTAH advised that any further payments should be linked to disarmament and entry into the DDR process, but no official position had been taken by the Haitian authorities. However, funding pledged for DDR activities remained limited, and additional support from the Transitional Government and the international community was needed.

Due to its increased strength, the MINUSTAH civilian police component was able to focus on the training and capacity-building of HNP through a co-location programme aimed at mentoring, advising and assisting the force at all levels. On 21 January, 200 newly trained officers graduated, together with 193 former military who were to be reintegrated into HNP. Training for 370 new recruits began on 10 January, and for 96 inspectors and 25 commissioners on 14 February.

In January, the Provisional Electoral Council presented the proposed electoral calendar to the Transitional Government, which provided for local elections on 9 October, parliamentary and presidential elections on 13 November and 18 December, instalment of Parliament on 9 January 2006, and the swearing in of the new President on 7 February 2006. The presidential decree adopting the new electoral law was published by the Transitional Government on 11 February. On 10 January, a global funding agreement totalling $44.3 million was signed for conducting the elections. On 4 February, a memorandum of understanding was signed between UNDP and the United Nations Office for Project Services for the conduct of a security and logistical assessment mission, to be led by MINUSTAH. The mission, launched on 9 February, evaluated the security and logistical conditions for the elections. In his address to the nation, the interim Prime Minister, Mr. Gérard Latortue, invited all illegally armed groups to disarm and participate in the country's reconstruction process and requested the support of political parties in the transition process. He specifically invited Fanmi Lavalas in the election process.

An ad hoc group (Groupe de réflexion et de promotion du dialogue national) on national dialogue submitted a report to the Prime Minister on 31 December. Discussions among political actors and civil society continued on inclusiveness, structure and timing of the dialogue in its relation to the electoral process. MINUSTAH submitted to the interim President and Prime Minister a working paper on approaches relating to national dialogue, based on consultations by the Secretary-General's Special Representative with sectors throughout the country. On 14 February, the Transitional Government, MINUSTAH and UNDP signed an agreement to launch a $1.7 million project to support national dialogue.

The Secretary-General observed that the political transition was at a sensitive phase and preparations for the elections had to be accelerated. Encouraged by the Prime Minister's invitation to Fanmi Lavalas to participate in the electoral process and anticipating the official launch of the national dialogue, he called on all political parties and Haitian voters to join the electoral process. The Secretary-General remained concerned about the human rights situation in the country, and called on the Haitian authorities to investigate allegations of human rights abuses, including those attributed to HNP officers and to take appropriate action. He also called on the Transitional Government to establish the national commission on DDR.

Security Council mission

On 31 March [S/2005/220], the Security Council President informed the Secretary-General that the Council had decided to send a mission to Haiti from 13-16 April, in conjunction with the Economic and Social Council's Ad Hoc Advisory Group on Haiti (see p. 390). The mission, to be led by Ronaldo Mota Sardenberg (Brazil) [S/2005/235], would, among other things, assess the level of MINUSTAH coordination in each aspect of its mandate and between the capital and outlying regions of Haiti; review progress achieved and determine the needs required in the areas of security, political transition, human rights, development, institution-building and the humanitarian situation; and convey to local actors the Council's message of support for MINUSTAH and the UN presence in Haiti, the long-term commitment of the international community in Haiti, and the steps the Transitional Government and all the parties needed to take, including rejecting violence and respecting human rights, engaging fully in the electoral process, and launching an inclusive national dialogue.

Report of Security Council mission. The report of the Security Council mission to Haiti (13-16 April) was issued on 6 May [S/2005/302]. The mission, the first by the Council to Latin America, or the Caribbean, visited Port-au-Prince and the cities of Cap-Haïtien and Gonaïves. The mission met with the Transitional Government, the Provisional Electoral Council, representatives of political parties and civil society, MINUSTAH, and members of the Core Group on Haiti [YUN 2004, p. 299].

The mission found that, while the security situation had improved, it remained fragile and had to be addressed to ensure a stable political transition process and socio-economic development. Some interlocutors believed that the insecurity stemmed from violence by supporters of former President Aristide, former military personnel and armed gangs with ties to criminal activities, such as drug trafficking and illegal arms-dealing, and shifting affiliations, while others felt that it was less of a threat and had been exaggerated by the media. Despite criticisms of its operation, it was agreed that the presence of MINUSTAH military and police forces was essential to prevent the situation from deteriorating and assist in the stabilization process. However, those forces felt handicapped by the lack of reliable tactical intelligence. Joint MINUSTAH/HNP security operations had successfully undermined alliances between illegally armed groups and gangs associated with former President Aristide's supporters and the former military personnel. The security challenges to be faced included retaliation against information sources, collusion between illegal actors and some police officers, the urban environment in which illegal gangs operated and the need to enhance coordination and cooperation.

The mission ascertained that HNP could not adequately exercise public security functions over the entire country due to a lack of personnel, equipment and training, as well as a limited budget and corruption, and called for its immediate reform. Increased international assistance would be required to implement the reforms of the force, the professionalization of which was a long-term task. MINUSTAH, whose mandate was to assist in restructuring and reforming HNP, was hampered by the ambiguous attitude of the police toward serious reform, the diversion of MINUSTAH resources to more immediate security-related operational tasks, and the lack of French-speaking civilian police and specialists in MINUSTAH.

The mission found that, while challenges remained, a promising attitude towards DDR was evolving, with an increased willingness by some members of the former military to participate, although some were more interested in being reabsorbed into public sector positions than accept the benefits offered in a DDR programme. The mission was concerned that promises made by the Transitional Government of indemnity payments, pensions and State employment to members of the former military were not linked to DDR, particularly the need to disarm. Some of the promises had not been kept, which could destabilize the situation and exacerbate frustrations and alienation. The political situation presented promises and challenges. It was dominated by such concerns as the insecurity in the capital, the debate over the imprisonment of former Prime Minister Yvon Neptune and former Interior Minister Jocelerme Privert and controversial issues surrounding the media. The situation was also very complex, with some 90 registered parties and a myriad of civil society organizations, which did not appear to have clearly identifiable political platforms. The possible linkages between some political parties and illegally armed groups remained a source of concern. The mission was reminded of the considerable challenges in conducting elections, such as security, technical issues, possible discrimination against independent candidates, and the need for early adoption of legislation to provide, among other things, for public funding for political parties and the adoption of a national identity card. The mission was concerned that many logistical aspects of organizing elections, arising from the Provisional Electoral Council's lack of capacity, could complicate the timely preparation of the elections.

The mission noted reports that a culture of impunity remained pervasive, as a result of which the population continued to view the national police with fear and lack of respect, and that human rights investigations were hampered by the instability of the situation and the security concerns of victims and witnesses.

The mission, in its recommendations, said that the Haitian authorities and the international community should continue to prepare for Haiti's medium- and long-term institution-building and development, and Haitians themselves, particularly the Transitional Government, should seize the opportunity to take full ownership of their future.

It urged the Haitian authorities to prepare for elections and to ensure their smooth operation, and that sufficient funds were identified for that purpose. The elections should be open to all political parties that publicly renounced violence.

MINUSTAH should provide donors with a budget and integrated timeline for all electoral activities, while the Transitional Government should commence a broad-based civic education programme to ensure the broadest possible participation of the Haitian population. An international coordinated presence, working with the Haitian authorities, should help to ensure that the registration and voting processes conformed with democratic standards, and that arrangements were established for international electoral observation.

The mission requested the Department of Peacekeeping Operations (DPKO) to conduct a comprehensive review of the security situation and MINUSTAH resources, make recommendations on the need for additional police and military resources, and improve the rules of engagement of the civilian police to provide, among other things, for operational support to HNP, in order to increase global security and protection during the electoral period.

MINUSTAH should continue to support the Transitional Government to ensure a secure and stable environment, including improving coordination procedures with HNP. The mission stressed the need for better coordination between MINUSTAH civil police and military components, and for the MINUSTAH Joint Mission Analysis Cell to become operational as soon as possible in order to pool and better operationalize the information available to its military, police and civilian components.

The political dialogue initiated by the Transitional Government should focus on the needs of the upcoming elections, and allow for broader grass-roots participation. The mission supported a long-term dialogue aimed at developing a common vision for the country's future, involving all sectors of Haitian society.

The Haitian authorities should implement without delay the DDR programme proposed by MINUSTAH (p. 377) and clarify its intention vis-à-vis the status of former military personnel, and payments to any groups should be made only as part of a DDR programme. Concerned about the reported funding gap for DDR, the mission called upon MINUSTAH and DPKO to provide detailed information to the Council on whether further international resources were required and upon the donor community to provide the necessary resources.

The mission stressed the urgency of accelerating HNP reform so that they could establish the trust of Haitian citizens and be counted upon to provide public security in Haiti. That reform should be planned and executed by the Transitional Government with the support of MINUSTAH and bilateral partners.

The international community should provide assistance for rebuilding Haiti's institutions, many of which were barely functioning, such as the judicial and penal systems. The mission recommended that additional measures to assist the judicial system be examined with Haitian authorities, and that MINUSTAH's mandate be amended to allow international experts to participate and assist in that effort.

All actors had to abide by human rights standards, and combating impunity and promoting respect for human rights were urgently demanded by both the Haitian people and the international community. The Haitian authorities were urged to address, as a matter of priority, the most flagrant, sensitive or visible cases, including by investigating alleged human rights violations by HNP.

Stressing that there could be no genuine stability in the country without strengthening its economy, the mission renewed its appeal for the accelerated disbursement of the funds pledged by international financial institutions since the 2004 International Donors Conference on Haiti [YUN 2004, p. 301], and supported the Cayenne (French Guiana) follow-up donor conference to be held by July. The need to urgently implement highly visible quick-impact projects was emphasized, and donors were called upon to resume full cooperation with Haiti, especially in supporting such priority areas as infrastructure, energy and the environment.

To improve the Haitian population's understanding of its mandate and role, the mission recommended that MINUSTAH develop and implement a proactive communications and public relations strategy. It also reaffirmed the Council's view that a long-term UN presence in Haiti was required.

Security Council consideration (April/May). On 20 April [meeting 5164], the Security Council was provided with an oral report on the mission's activities and findings by the head of the mission, Ronaldo Mota Sardenberg. On 13 May [meeting 5178], the Council considered the mission's final report (see above). Mr. Sardenberg, in introducing the report to the Council, said that, notwithstanding the deep-seated root causes of unrest in Haiti, including poverty, the situation required a long-term approach, while at the same time dealing with a number of very serious issues in the short and medium term. The holding of elections was the most pressing and visible challenge for Haitians and the international community in the short term. Free, fair and inclusive elections had to take place in accordance with the established timetable, as they were essential for the formation of a legitimate Government. However, additional resources would be required to cover an estimated $22 million funding gap so that those elections could take place.

Haiti's representative told the Council that the Interim Government's priority remained the holding of free and democratic elections at the end of 2005, and laying the foundation for the country's socio-economic development. He drew the Council's attention to the measures the Government intended to take in that regard, including conducting operations to gain control of some armed gangs, restoring the State's authority throughout the country and regaining control of police stations. Moreover, the national dialogue had been officially initiated and an official commission created to implement DDR programmes. However, the funds required to carry out the latter exercise exceeded available government funding and pledged contributions remained limited. The Interim Government wanted to reaffirm its commitment to working for the respect of human rights and was responsive to the comments and criticisms of human rights organizations. It was working with the international community to rebuild and strengthen State institutions and intended to carry out the reforms of the judiciary and police. To accomplish those things, the ongoing assistance of the international community and MINUSTAH would remain essential. Accordingly, Haiti hoped that MINUSTAH's mandate would be renewed as recommended by the mission.

National dialogue and election preparations

Report of Secretary-General (May). The Secretary-General, in his May report on MINUSTAH activities [S/2005/313 & Add.1], stated that the two main processes of the political transition—national dialogue and elections—were launched by the Transitional Government and the Provisional Electoral Council, respectively, but internal divisions and limited capacity hampered their ability to decisively move the transition forward, putting into question the inclusiveness, transparency, credibility and legitimacy of those processes. While the Transitional Government had been in office for a year, it continued to be criticized by leading political and civil society groups. As the political discourse failed to offer a clear vision for Haiti's future beyond the elections, the political class remained polarized. Fanmi Lavalas maintained its position to remain outside the transition process, as a result of, among other reasons, the 28 February fatal shooting of a demonstrator by HNP and the continued detention of high-profile party figures, such as

Interior Minister Jocelerme Privert. That party itself was internally fractured, with hardliners calling for the return of former President Aristide; moderate elements of the party not ruling out participation; and leaders participating in open discussions with the interim Prime Minister, the Secretary-General's Special Representative and other political parties at a March seminar.

The 7 April launch of national dialogue by interim President Boniface Alexandre had sparked mixed reactions. Outlined in a presidential decree, the dialogue aimed to create an environment conducive to holding the elections; ensure the proper governance of the country after the elections; develop a clear vision for national development; and reinforce mechanisms of good governance. A 12-member preparatory commission would assist the interim President in establishing institutions to lead the dialogue. However, differences remained on what the focus of the dialogue should be and whether a longer-term dialogue should begin before the upcoming elections. Some civil society organizations and political parties were concerned by provisions in the decree, which barred any changes to the Transitional Government, the Consensus on the Political Transition Pact [YUN 2004, p. 293], the electoral calendar or the Constitution. MINUSTAH continued to meet with key political actors, including factions of Fanmi Lavalas, to ensure that the dialogue served the long-term aim of national reconciliation and the holding of credible and inclusive elections.

The electoral law, which was published on 11 February, provided for local elections to be held on 9 October and the first round of parliamentary and presidential elections on 13 November, with a second round on 18 December, if necessary. Voter registration began on 25 April, and by 9 May, 15 of the 409 planned registration offices had opened and more than 16,000 citizens had registered, out of approximately 4 million eligible voters. The deadline for completing the registration process was 9 August. MINUSTAH was concerned about the constitutionality of certain provisions of the electoral law, which it had made known to the Transitional Government, and the fact that necessary decrees, such as those on the funding of political parties and on the official status of the new national identification card, had not yet been adopted. Other concerns included security, highlighted by the attacks on 24 and 29 March on the headquarters of the Provisional Electoral Council, and the shortfall of $22 million out of a total revised electoral budget of $60.7 million. On 1 April, the Prime Minister created an Electoral Security Commission to prepare a comprehensive security plan for the elections and to supervise its execution. The Provisional Electoral Council agreed to establish a corps of 3,600 local electoral assistants, to be armed with non-lethal weapons, to provide security at registration and polling centres alongside MINUSTAH and HNP.

The security situation in Port-au-Prince remained volatile with an increased number of violent acts by various armed groups. The 19 February incident at the National Penitentiary in Port-au-Prince, where a group of unidentified armed men forced their way into the prison and enabled 493 detainees to escape, was a public security setback. Kidnappings reported in Port-au-Prince had also increased. Outside the capital the situation remained generally calm, with only a few incidents reported in Cap-Haïtien, Gonaïves, Hinche and Petit-Goâve. To ensure a stable and secure environment, MINUSTAH undertook a number of successful operations, including the recovery of police stations in Petit-Goâve and Terre-Rouge in March. However, the situation in Cité Soleil presented severe challenges. A joint HNP/MINUSTAH operation to restrict the movements of gang members and the circulation of weapons and ammunition was met with strong resistance. Three MINUSTAH soldiers were killed during the reporting period and there were other instances where MINUSTAH personnel had been targeted. The HNP Director-General said that 45 police officers had been killed in the past year. MINUSTAH monitored public demonstrations mostly organized by Fanmi Lavalas supporters.

An encouraging development in the area of DDR was the adoption by the Transitional Government of the national DDR programme, developed jointly by the Transitional Government, MINUSTAH, UNDP and other stakeholders through the Interim Cooperation Framework Sectoral Round Table on disarmament. However, the programme was not operational and its legal status was still unclear. Other positive developments were the 13 March surrender by 227 former soldiers in Cap-Haïtien of a symbolic number of weapons, and their agreement to be reintegrated into society. MINUSTAH continued its sensitization campaign with other illegal armed groups on a community-by-community basis and members of some urban gangs in Les Cayes and Port-au-Prince had expressed an interest in handing over their weapons in exchange for community development initiatives.

The report also highlighted the 15 March adoption of the HNP 2004-2008 strategic development plan by the Conseil supérieur de la police nationale; implementation by MINUSTAH of a co-location programme for training and capacity-building of the police; supervision and assistance by MINUSTAH police advisers in the training of new HNP recruits; and participation by MINUSTAH in the implementation of the joint HNP vetting programme.

The Secretary-General recommended that the Transitional Government do more to secure broad participation in the electoral process and ensure that legislation conducive to such participation was in place. It should also address the concerns raised regarding the electoral law, while the donor community should ensure that the necessary financial means were available to support the electoral process. Although there had been signs of improvement in the security situation following successful MINUSTAH/HNP operations to curb the activities of illegal armed groups, those efforts had to be maintained to eliminate potential threats to the electoral process. Urging prompt implementation of a comprehensive DDR programme by the Transitional Government, the Secretary-General expressed concern that, unless progress could be achieved in that area, the security situation would remain fragile. He appealed to the Transitional Government to investigate human rights violations allegedly committed by HNP officers, and to explore means by which the international community could assist in expediting some of the most sensitive cases. He advised that reform of the justice and penal systems be pursued in parallel to the efforts to professionalize HNP. In the area of police reform, he urged the Transitional Government to ensure that the technical advice and recommendations provided by MINUSTAH's civilian police officers were implemented by HNP officers at all levels.

Extension and expansion of MINUSTAH mandate

In view of the expectation that security challenges would increase in the months leading up to and following the elections, the Secretary-General indicated [S/2005/313] that a review by his Special Representative and MINUSTAH leadership had concluded that the Mission's structure would need to be enhanced. The proposals included: the development of standard procedures for the police and military components; enhancement of the Joint Operations Centre; development of a mission-wide Joint Mission Analysis Cell; addition of an infantry battalion of 750 troops to address gang violence in Cité Soleil; strengthening of the Mission's "surge" capacity to handle the potentially volatile security environment in the eastern part of the Central District; and creation of a new sector headquarters for the military component for the Port-au-

Prince region, which would require an additional 50 staff officers. Further proposals focused on the need to reorient MINUSTAH resources to enhance coverage of the country with formed police units; and to professionalize HNP by strengthening its involvement in the vetting programme, election-related activities and investigations of human rights abuses or other security incidents. Those activities would require an additional 275 police personnel. Total proposed MINUSTAH requirements would raise from 6,700 to 7,500 troops and from 1,622 to 1,897 police officers. MINUSTAH would also provide support to the judiciary to expedite judicial procedures for all cases of prolonged pre-trial detention, including through the establishment of ad hoc commissions to review the cases of detainees, and to help the Transitional Government overcome deficiencies in the justice and penal sectors. The Secretary-General recommended that the Security Council approve the adjustments to MINUSTAH's mandate and extended it for a further 12 months, until after the elections and the establishment of the newly elected Government.

Security Council consideration (23 May). The Security Council, in a closed meeting on 23 May [meeting 5183] with the troop-contributing countries, heard a briefing by the Special Representative of the Secretary-General and head of MINUSTAH.

SECURITY COUNCIL ACTION

On 31 May [meeting 5192], the Security Council unanimously adopted **resolution 1601(2005)**. The draft [S/2005/354] was prepared in consultations among Council members.

The Security Council,

Reaffirming resolutions 1542(2004) of 30 April 2004 and 1576(2004) of 29 November 2004, and recalling resolution 1529(2004) of 29 February 2004, relevant statements by its President, as well as the report of the Security Council on its mission to Haiti from 13 to 16 April 2005,

Determining that the situation in Haiti continues to constitute a threat to international peace and security in the region,

Acting under Chapter VII of the Charter of the United Nations, as described in paragraph 7, section I, of resolution 1542(2004),

1. *Decides* to extend the mandate of the United Nations Stabilization Mission in Haiti, as contained in resolution 1542(2004), until 24 June 2005, with the intention to renew for further periods;

2. *Welcomes* the report of the Secretary-General;

3. *Decides* to remain seized of the matter.

The Security Council met on 7 June [meeting 5196] in a private meeting with Haiti's interim Prime Minister, Gérard Latortue, who described the situation in the country and put forward

ideas on how to better address the security situation, particularly through cooperation between MINUSTAH and HNP [A/60/2].

SECURITY COUNCIL ACTION

On 22 June [meeting 5210], the Council unanimously adopted **resolution 1608(2005)**. The draft [S/2005/402] was prepared in consultations among Council members.

The Security Council,

Reaffirming resolutions 1542(2004) of 30 April 2004 and 1576(2004) of 29 November 2004, and recalling resolution 1529(2004) of 29 February 2004, relevant statements by its President, as well as the report of the Security Council on its mission to Haiti from 13 to 16 April 2005,

Reaffirming its strong commitment to the sovereignty, independence, territorial integrity and unity of Haiti,

Stressing that free and fair elections, open to all political parties that have renounced violence and with the broadest possible participation of the Haitian people, must take place in 2005 in accordance with the established timetable, and that the democratically elected authorities must take office on 7 February 2006,

Affirming its determination to ensure a secure and stable environment in which the electoral process can take place,

Condemning all violations of human rights, including lack of due process and prolonged pretrial detentions, and urging the Transitional Government of Haiti to take all necessary measures to put an end to impunity and to ensure progress in the respect for the rule of law, including by pursuing reforms in the Haitian National Police and in the justice and correctional systems,

Reaffirming the importance of appropriate expertise on issues relating to gender in peacekeeping operations and post-conflict peacebuilding in accordance with resolution 1325(2000) of 31 October 2000, recalling the need to address violence against women and children, and encouraging the United Nations Stabilization Mission in Haiti, as well as the Transitional Government, to actively address these issues,

Underlining the fact that pervasive poverty is an important root cause of unrest in Haiti, and stressing that there can be no genuine stability without strengthening its economy, including through a long-term strategy for sustainable development and the strengthening of Haitian institutions,

Welcoming the approval of a national programme on disarmament, demobilization and reintegration by the Transitional Government, the United Nations Development Programme and the Mission, and emphasizing that its implementation is imperative for broader stabilization efforts to succeed,

Recalling that security, political reconciliation and economic reconstruction efforts remain key to the stability of Haiti,

Noting that the Haitian people must take responsibility for achieving stability, social and economic development and law and order,

Determining that the situation in Haiti continues to constitute a threat to international peace and security,

Acting under Chapter VII of the Charter of the United Nations, as described in paragraph 7, section I, of resolution 1542(2004),

1. *Decides* to extend the mandate of the United Nations Stabilization Mission in Haiti, as contained in resolution 1542(2004), until 15 February 2006, with the intention to renew for further periods;

2. *Welcomes* the report of the Secretary-General of 13 May 2005 on the Mission, and supports the recommendations of the Secretary-General as outlined in paragraphs 44 to 52 thereof, as follows:

(a) A temporary increase, during the electoral period and subsequent political transition, of 750 personnel to the currently authorized military strength of the Mission in order to create a rapid reaction force in Haiti to provide increased security, in particular in and around Port-au-Prince;

(b) An increase of 50 military personnel in order to create a sector headquarters in Port-au-Prince, with the understanding that the Mission will optimize at all levels the coordination between military and police components to ensure efficient and better-integrated operations, including by posting United Nations staff civilian police officers in this headquarters;

(c) A temporary increase, during the electoral period and subsequent political transition, of 275 personnel to the current strength of the Mission's civilian police component to provide increased security;

(d) An assessment of the Haitian judiciary and correctional systems, including to explore possibilities for greater international community support, and a more active role of the Mission, to be submitted to the Security Council as soon as possible;

3. *Decides* that for a temporary period, the Mission will consist of a military component of up to 7,500 troops of all ranks and of up to 1,897 civilian police, and requests the Secretary-General to devise, in a timely manner, a progressive drawdown strategy of the Mission force levels for the post-election period, in accordance with the situation on the ground;

4. *Requests* the Secretary-General to share with the Council the overall plan for the successful holding of elections in Haiti, including voter registration, security, logistics, civic education, observation, and detailed budget information, urges Haitian authorities to increase and accelerate efforts to prepare for and ensure the smooth conduct of the elections, and calls upon international donors to provide the necessary resources to support the electoral process;

5. *Also requests* the Secretary-General to share with the Council the reform plan for the Haitian National Police, formulated by the Mission and the Haitian authorities, that includes the anticipated size, standards, implementation timetable and resources;

6. *Requests* that the Mission concentrate the use of its resources, including civilian police, towards increasing security and protection during the electoral period, including a review, as appropriate, of the rules of engagement of the individual civilian police officers;

7. *Also requests* that the Mission and the Haitian authorities take all necessary steps to achieve optimal coordination between the Mission's civilian police and the Haitian National Police;

8. *Reaffirms* the authority of the Mission to vet and certify new and existing Haitian National Police personnel for service, and urges the Transitional Government of Haiti to ensure that police personnel do not serve unless certified and to ensure that technical advice and recommendations provided by the Mission are fully implemented by Haitian authorities at all levels without delay;

9. *Calls upon* the Mission to make the Joint Mission Analysis Cell operational as soon as possible in order to pool and better use the information available to the military, police and civilian components of the Mission, and also calls for the use of the Mission's aviation assets in an efficient and effective manner in support of security operations;

10. *Urges* the Transitional Government to conduct thorough and transparent investigations into cases of human rights violations, particularly those allegedly involving Haitian National Police officers, and requests that in order to support this effort the Mission make the Joint Special Investigation Unit operational as soon as possible;

11. *Welcomes* the launching on 7 April 2005 of the "national dialogue" by the Transitional Government and stresses that such a dialogue should serve the long-term aim of national reconciliation and, in the shorter term, the holding of credible and inclusive elections, urges the Transitional Government to redouble its efforts for this essential process, and invites all Haitians to participate in this dialogue without delay;

12. *Urges* the Transitional Government and the Mission to begin immediately effective implementation of the disarmament, demobilization and reintegration programme, and calls upon all Member States to provide timely financial, human and technical resources in support of this programme;

13. *Renews its appeal* for the accelerated disbursement of the funds pledged by international financial institutions and donors at the International Donors Conference on Haiti on 19 and 20 July 2004, supports the Cayenne follow-up donor conference held in Montreal, Canada, on 16 and 17 June 2005, and calls upon all donors to continue to assist Haiti;

14. *Requests* the Mission to strengthen its capacity to implement quick-impact projects, and calls for increased coordination between the various development actors in Haiti in order to ensure greater efficiency in development efforts;

15. *Invites* the Bretton Woods institutions to consider the issue of debt sustainability and the implications of the Highly Indebted Poor Countries Initiative for Haiti;

16. *Urges* the Mission to urgently develop and implement a proactive communications and public relations strategy, in order to improve the Haitian population's understanding of the mandate of the Mission and its role in Haiti;

17. *Welcomes* efforts undertaken by the Mission to implement the Secretary-General's zero-tolerance policy on sexual exploitation and abuse and to ensure full compliance of its personnel with the United Nations code of conduct, requests the Secretary-General to continue to take all necessary action in this regard and to keep the Council informed, and urges troop-contributing countries to take appropriate preventive and disciplinary action to ensure that such acts are properly investigated and punished in cases involving their personnel;

18. *Requests* the Secretary-General to report to the Council on the effectiveness of the implementation of the mandate of the Mission at least once every three months, and requests that the Secretariat keep the Council members informed, on a regular basis, on the status of electoral preparations, including party and voter registration figures and other relevant data;

19. *Decides* to remain seized of the matter.

Further political and security developments

Report of Secretary-General (October). In an October report [S/2005/631] on MINUSTAH, the Secretary-General said that the Transitional Government and MINUSTAH continued to be confronted with serious political and security challenges. To develop a strategy to combat armed gang violence and strengthen confidence in the Transitional Government and the electoral process, Prime Minister Latortue organized closed meetings with political leaders and the private sector. Other developments included the 14 June resignation of the Minister of Justice and Public Security and the ensuing inauguration of a new cabinet on 22 June; the appointment of a new HNP Director General; and the 25 June presentation by the Council of Eminent Persons to the Transitional Government of a road map outlining priorities for the successful continuation of the transition process.

Political tensions and security concerns peaked when a well-known journalist and poet, Jacques Roche, who had been kidnapped four days earlier, was found murdered on 14 July. Father Gérard Jean-Juste, a Lavalas activist, was taken into protective custody following his appearance at Mr. Roche's funeral on 21 July and was later arrested and charged with participating in the kidnapping and murder of Mr. Roche. On 31 August, he was transferred to the National Penitentiary.

MINUSTAH organized a series of meetings of political parties to create a positive environment for the electoral process. On 17 May, the leaders of 34 political parties signed the "Port-au-Prince declaration against corruption", which called for the development of an ethical code of conduct for political parties, and on 14 June, 17 political parties, including sectors of Fanmi Lavalas, signed an electoral code of conduct barring the use of violence in the pursuit of political power. On 27 September, 12 parties signed a "pacte de stabilité et de gouvernabilité" committing them to cooperating and collaborating before and after the elections. With UNDP, MINUSTAH and the Transitional Government organized a workshop for some 60 political leaders to discuss key governance issues. The Provisional Electoral Council approved the registration of 45 political parties and 32 presidential candidates, including former

President René Préval. Considerable progress was made in voter registration, led by OAS. As at 29 September, over 2.9 million people, more than 70 per cent of the estimated 4 million eligible voters, had registered. The deadline for voter registration was extended four times, the latest until 30 September. A few setbacks had hindered progress in the election preparations. The Provisional Electoral Council announced in September a change in the dates for the legislative and presidential elections to 20 November and 3 January 2006, and local and municipal elections on 11 December 2005. The calendar had not been promulgated by the Transitional Government and its feasibility was publicly contested. Prime Minister Latortue asked the Council to review the calendar in the light of the constitutional requirement to swear in the President by 7 February 2006. As the Provisional Electoral Council continued to suffer from structural and operational shortcomings, its ability to organize and administer the elections in a timely manner remained an issue of concern. To support the process, MINUSTAH and OAS identified 10 key decisions and actions to be urgently taken by the Haitian authorities, including providing the Council with an effective executive structure and staff; confirming the electoral calendar; revising the electoral decree; and determining the location and number of polling sites. As no action had been taken by the national authorities to implement the 10 priority measures, it was anticipated that MINUSTAH might need to play a more active role in the electoral process than originally envisaged.

A marked rise in violence and criminality in Port-au-Prince, including 59 kidnappings in June and the killing of 17 people in a 1 July arson attack against the main marketplace, had generated serious public anxiety. On 6 July, in a large-scale operation in Cité Soleil aimed at apprehending a prominent gang leader, Emmanuel Wilmer, MINUSTAH encountered heavy gunfire. While it was believed that Mr. Wilmer and his associates had been killed during the operation, there was concern that, due to the densely populated urban nature of the terrain and the strength of the armed response, civilians might have been caught in the crossfire as MINUSTAH troops were withdrawing. There were unconfirmed reports from HNP and other sources that gangs were seen killing civilians following the operation. Security in other parts of the country remained fragile, but generally stable. Conditions in Bel-Air had improved significantly enough to allow the reopening of HNP community stations in the area.

MINUSTAH developed an electoral security plan, defining responsibilities and security arrangements for the election period, which included increased military and police capacities. It also continued to persuade groups of former soldiers to disarm voluntarily, with no progress being made. The National Commission on Disarmament, with MINUSTAH assistance, devised a modus operandi for negotiating eligibility criteria. In the area of the rule of law, the lack of strong and professional institutions continued to be a concern, particularly in relation to the alleged misconduct of HNP officers. Their alleged involvement in the execution of nine individuals on 20 August at a football game in the Martissant area of Port-au-Prince was under investigation by MINUSTAH. The release of Louis Jodel Chamblain, the second-in-command of a paramilitary group who had been convicted of various crimes in 1993 and 1994, had further tarnished the credibility of the justice system.

In his observations of prospects for a credible electoral process, the Secretary-General indicated that, although a significant number of voters had registered and progress had been made in dealing with urgent security threats, the gains attained were fragile and other issues needed to be addressed, such as the technical problems to the electoral process, the possibility of increased violence during the campaign period, and the persisting impunity and disregard for human rights. The Transitional Government should also address concerns regarding the electoral law and take measures to facilitate inclusive and participatory elections to avoid any perception that the judicial process was being used to adversely affect political participation. The 10 priority actions identified by MINUSTAH and OAS to overcome technical and organizational challenges needed to be taken urgently, with a focus on strengthening the Provisional Electoral Council. He emphasized that the international community should stand ready to play a greater role in organizing the electoral process to ensure its success. The Secretary-General stated that, given the possible increase in tension during the electoral process, a message of reassurance and deterrence could be conveyed if one or more Member States were ready to back up MINUSTAH through the deployment of an offshore presence.

Security Council consideration (October). On 18 October [meeting 5284], the Security Council met to discuss the question concerning Haiti and heard a briefing from interim Prime Minister Gérard Latortue. The Council had before it the Secretary-General's October report on MINUSTAH (see above).

Mr. Latortue reaffirmed the Transitional Government's commitment to ensure the transfer of power on 7 February 2006 and said that the political situation in Haiti had evolved in the right direction. He informed the Council that, although there were more than 40 political parties and 30 presidential candidates, the political parties had been working well together and had signed a governability pact to demonstrate their commitment to working with whichever party was elected and whosoever might become President. He announced the installation of a new Director General of the Provisional Electoral Council, who would oversee implementation of all the major decisions of the Council, and his intention to submit a new electoral timetable to guarantee the handover of power by 7 February 2006. Mr. Latortue also indicated that the Government had observed that some gangs were working in complicity with HNP agents and warned that, despite the apparent calm, there were still forces opposed to democracy and the transfer of power through transparent and free elections. He emphasized that the recent arrest of 15 corrupt police officers had demonstrated the HNP Director General's courage to clean house and the Government's resolve to ensure respect for human rights. He alerted the Security Council to the fact that MINUSTAH's mandate would expire on 15 February 2006, only eight days after the installation of the new Government. Haiti would therefore still require MINUSTAH's assistance for a period of time.

SECURITY COUNCIL ACTION

On 18 October [meeting 5285], following consultations among Security Council members, the President made statement **S/PRST/2005/50** on behalf of the Council:

> The Security Council expresses its full support for the work of the United Nations Stabilization Mission in Haiti and the Special Representative of the Secretary-General for Haiti, Mr. Juan Gabriel Valdés.
>
> The Council stresses the primary importance of ensuring that Haiti benefits from transparent, inclusive, free and fair elections, in accordance with international democratic standards and open to all political candidates that have renounced violence, thereby enabling legitimate leadership at the national and local levels. The Council conveys its concern regarding the risk of delays in the electoral process, and underlines international expectations that the first round of national elections should take place in 2005, and all efforts should be undertaken so that the democratically elected authorities take office on 7 February 2006 in accordance with the Haitian Constitution. The Council notes with appreciation that, so far, more than 3 million people have been registered. The Council praises the Organization of

American States and other relevant international stakeholders for their contribution to that process. The Council welcomes the representation of a broad range of Haitian political opinion in the electoral process and underlines the importance of a collaborative approach by political leaders. National reconciliation and political dialogue should continue to be promoted as a means to ensure long-term stability and good governance.

The Council notes with concern that important challenges to the preparations for the elections remain yet to be overcome. While welcoming the recent steps taken by the Transitional Government and the Provisional Electoral Council, the Security Council urges them to perform the ten urgent tasks required to ensure that elections will take place this year, which were endorsed by the Transitional Government on 17 September 2005 and reiterated by the Core Group on Haiti on 18 October 2005. The Council calls for effective and prompt decision-making in key areas by the relevant Haitian authorities, and urges the Haitian authorities to make full use of the advice and assistance of the Mission in the organization of elections. The Council calls upon them to work with the Mission to develop a phased electoral plan as a matter of priority, with a view to finalizing a feasible electoral calendar. The Council also urges the Haitian authorities to publish swiftly the final list of candidates for the elections, and to agree in consultation with the Mission upon a list of voting centres that ensures voter access and takes into account budgetary, security and logistical implications.

The Council strongly supports the Mission's endeavours to ensure a secure and stable environment in Haiti, which is crucial for the country's progress, and to enable the electoral process to take place. The Council recognizes the contribution of the Mission to the restoration and maintenance of the rule of law in the country, and underlines the need for strong and coordinated assistance to enable the reform and restructuring of Haiti's rule-of-law institutions. To this end, the Council urges the Transitional Government, working with the Mission, to put into effect the initiatives called for in resolution 1608(2005) concerning the Haitian National Police reform and restructuring plan as well as the reform of the judicial system, in order to end impunity and ensure due process. The Council welcomes the improvements in the security situation, due to the resolve of the Mission to act in support of the Transitional Government. The Council expresses concern regarding reports of involvement of some officers of the Haitian National Police in serious crimes and human rights violations and stresses the need to investigate fully any allegations of serious crimes and human rights violations. The Council welcomes the deployment of the additional military and police personnel of the Mission, in accordance with resolution 1608(2005), and expresses its gratitude to troop- and police-contributing countries.

The Council reiterates the need for the Transitional Government and the Mission to begin immediately effective implementation of a disarmament, demobilization and reintegration programme. The Council stresses the need to implement high-visibility, quick-impact projects that create jobs. The Coun-

cil also recognizes the need to maintain stability in the period immediately following the elections, including through a continued international presence, and to ensure that key Haitian institutions can function adequately, especially those institutions addressing the rule of law and development. The Council recognizes the importance of the upcoming donor conference to be held in Brussels on 20 and 21 October 2005, and calls upon donors to continue to disburse the pledged funds. The Council recognizes further that this conference constitutes an important opportunity to further elaborate on short-, medium- and long-term strategies, within a unified framework, to ensure coordination and continuity in a coherent and well prioritized response to Haitian problems. Haiti is at a critical juncture. While ultimately the responsibility for Haiti's future lies with its Government and people, the international community must continue to provide support.

Communication. On 21 October [A/60/447], Spain transmitted a communiqué adopted by the Heads of State and Government of the Ibero-American community of nations (Salamanca, Spain, 14-15 October), supporting the implementation of MINUSTAH's mandate and requesting the Ibero-American Secretary-General to carry out a mission to Haiti to assess the situation and, in conjunction with the United Nations and other international bodies, encourage the authorities to hold the elections as planned.

Further developments. In a later report [S/2006/60], the Secretary-General stated that the activities of the Haitian authorities and MINUSTAH continued to focus on ensuring the organization of credible and timely elections. However, political and technical difficulties in the decision-making process caused more delays. Disputes arose from the creation of a "commission on nationalities", which had recommended against several candidacies, including that of Dumarsais Siméus, a presidential candidate of the "Tet Ansanm" political party. On 8 December, the Supreme Court, which had previously indicated that Mr. Siméus' candidacy should be retained, refused a request by the Provisional Electoral Council to reverse its decision. The decision by the interim President, on 9 December, to order the retirement of five Supreme Court judges and nominate five others to replace them was considered a serious human rights concern. The United Nations High Commissioner for Human Rights stressed full respect for the separation of powers.

While voter registration had concluded at the end of October, all technical and logistical arrangements had not been completed. Presidential elections were being contested by 33 candidates approved by the Provisional Electoral Council, following weeks of controversy over the eligibility of presidential candidates holding dual nationality, and parliamentary seats by 1,409 candidates. Due to concerns over possible links between political parties and armed groups, technical issues that could impede voter access and transparency of the voting and tabulation processes, and questions of the independence of electoral workers, the Secretary-General stressed the importance of the presence of international observers to ensure credible elections. By early December, observers of the International Mission for Monitoring Haitian Elections had been deployed to all 10 provinces. MINUSTAH maintained contact with observers around the country through regular meetings and briefings and provided logistical and security assistance, in emergency cases.

The overall security environment remained relatively stable in most of the country and in areas of Port-au-Prince that had been problematic, such as the Bel-Air district. However, the situation deteriorated in Cité Soleil and the adjacent Route Nationale 1 during December, and gangs remained active in areas outside the capital in Artibonite and Ouanaminthe. Kidnappings increased sharply during the final months of the year, with 56 in September, 63 in October, 74 in November and 241 in December. A confrontation in October between HNP and armed gangs in Gonaives led to arson, looting and the death of two people over the course of three days. Criminal activities, such as illegal arms and drug trafficking, persisted along Haiti's porous land and sea borders. On 12 December, Haiti and the Dominican Republic reached agreement on the reactivation of the Haitian-Dominican mixed commission in an effort to better manage security at the border. MINUSTAH continued to play a pivotal role in the security and stability of the country, but it had also suffered five fatalities and injury to two military peacekeepers in a 16 December ambush in Plaisance. Although conditions for a comprehensive DDR programme remained elusive, MINUSTAH, in conjunction with the National Commission on Disarmament, established community violence reduction and development committees in some of the more volatile districts. An initial group of 14 disarmed gang members entered the Reintegration Orientation Centre on 11 November, followed by a group of 18 in December. Fifteen former military personnel formally entered the disarmament process on 20 October.

Professional, logistical and technical shortcomings of the HNP continued to inhibit its effectiveness. However, staged demonstrations against the HNP General Director and the spray-painting of MINUSTAH vehicles with slogans, fol-

lowing the 4 November arrest of two senior HNP officers for alleged obstruction of the investigation into the Martissant killings (see p. 387) in August, illustrated the potential resistance to reform measures.

MINUSTAH

In 2005, the United Nations Stabilization Mission in Haiti (MINUSTAH), established by Security Council resolution 1542(2004) [YUN 2004, p. 294], continued to focus on ensuring a secure and stable environment, supporting the political process, and protecting and promoting human rights. In June, pursuant to Security Council resolution 1608(2005), the structure of the Mission was enhanced and its mandate extended to 15 February 2006 (see p. 384).

MINUSTAH activities

During 2005, the Secretary-General reported to the Security Council on the activities of MINUSTAH and developments in Haiti for the periods 18 November 2004 to 24 February 2005 [S/2005/124], 25 February to 12 May [S/2005/313 & Add.1], and 13 May to 5 October [S/2005/631]. Activities for the remainder of the year were contained in a later report [S/2006/60]. In addition to the political and security aspects, the reports summarized MINUSTAH activities dealing with human rights; child protection; the humanitarian situation and development; gender; the prevention of HIV/AIDS; the implementation of the Interim Cooperative Framework (ICF) and quick-impact projects; coordination with international organizations, such as the Caribbean Community (CARICOM) and OAS; and Mission support.

Human rights. The human rights situation remained alarming, with reported cases of summary executions, prolonged pre-trial detentions, arbitrary arrest, disregard for due process, rape and the alleged torture of children in the detention facilities of the Judicial Police. A hunger strike, which began in February, by Yvon Neptune and Jocelerme Privert, protesting their prolonged pre-trial detentions, resulted in their hospitalization. Although it was reported in May that Mr. Neptune's health had seriously deteriorated, he and Mr. Privert remained in detention through the end of the year. The independent expert on the situation of human rights in Haiti, Louis Joinet, who visited the country in March and November, presented a report [E/CN.4/2006/115] covering those visits to the Commission on Human Rights (see p. 740).

Child protection. MINUSTAH and the United Nations Children's Fund (UNICEF) continued to draw attention to violence against children. By

May, another 50 had died from gang violence, while others had been victims of rape. The alleged killing by HNP of two minors in Cité de Dieu and a 4-year-old girl in Pétion-Ville were under investigation by MINUSTAH and UNICEF. Human rights organizations and the main hospital in Cité Soleil reported that 30 to 40 children had died due to gang violence. To address violations of children's rights, MINUSTAH signed an agreement with HNP for the provision of comprehensive child-protection training for all new police recruits. It also organized focus groups to develop ways to reintegrate juvenile members of the armed groups into their communities.

Humanitarian situation. MINUSTAH continued to respond to the humanitarian situation in Haiti. The effects of severe drought early in the year and the ensuing agricultural loss were further exacerbated by Hurricanes Dennis and Emily, which killed 32 people and damaged 15 schools, 400 houses, 3 water-supply systems and 1 bridge in the southern peninsula. Security challenges, particularly in Port-au-Prince, had also hampered the work of humanitarian organizations, requiring MINUSTAH and aid organizations to coordinate their activities.

Development. Further implementation of the ICF [YUN 2004, p. 296] and quick-impact projects progressed. As at 9 May, 57 projects were being implemented in agriculture, education, health, HIV/AIDS, water and sanitation; five of those had been implemented by MINUSTAH troops, mainly in infrastructure rehabilitation. By October, 40 of the 98 projects approved by MINUSTAH for the 2004/05 fiscal year had been implemented. At a ministerial meeting on assistance to Haiti (18 March, Cayenne, French Guiana), the donor community pledged to finance 380 ICF high-impact projects at an estimated cost of 750 million euros. At a donor conference later in the year (20-21 October, Brussels), it was decided that the time frame for ICF would be extended from September 2006 to the end of 2007.

Gender. MINUSTAH supported women's organizations and their recommendations on the draft electoral law, including one granting a two-thirds reduction of the registration fee for candidates from a political party or coalition that had at least 30 per cent female candidates. Following its activities to promote women's participation in the electoral process, MINUSTAH, as a member of the National Coordination Committee on the Prevention of Violence Against Women, intensified its work in that area. The Mission participated in the development of the UN inter-agency national plan on sexual violence against women (see p. 1250); launched a poster campaign in all MINUSTAH offices on the prohibition of sexual ex-

ploitation and abuse; and required new staff members to receive compulsory training on UN policy regarding sexual abuse and exploitation.

HIV/AIDS. The MINUSTAH HIV/AIDS Unit provided HIV/AIDS awareness training to its personnel and that of HNP. The Joint United Nations Programme on HIV/AIDS (UNAIDS) and MINUSTAH developed an HIV/AIDS peer leader training programme to engage MINUSTAH personnel in prevention, education and communication activities and to establish partnerships with HIV/AIDS response organizations. MINUSTAH continued to participate in the ICF Sectoral Round-Table on HIV/AIDS and was involved in community outreach activities related to "World AIDS Day" on 1 December, including the training of former gang members and their families on HIV/AIDS prevention, awareness training for 481 Bel-Air community members and the allocation of television spots with a message on HIV/AIDS from MINUSTAH leaders and heads of UN agencies.

Other activities. The reports also chronicled MINUSTAH activities and coordination efforts with OAS and CARICOM. OAS assisted in election preparations, particularly in voter registration. While CARICOM supported the dialogue initiatives and humanitarian relief efforts in Haiti, it had not yet recognized the Transitional Government as a legitimate representative of Haiti within the organization. The Special Representative attended a CARICOM conference (16-17 February, Paramaribo, Suriname), which discussed regional issues, including Haiti. As MINUSTAH operated from shared common offices and other temporary premises at several locations since its establishment, it experienced operational difficulties. In early 2005, a site for an integrated headquarters was selected and by 27 June had been fully established. A later report indicated that renovations of the Mission headquarters were completed and MINUSTAH had erected facilities for the expanded force elements.

Programme of support for Haiti

Ad Hoc Advisory Group. The Ad Hoc Advisory Group on Haiti, which had been mandated by resolution 2004/322 [YUN 2004, p. 939] to follow and advise on the long-term development of the country, submitted its May report [E/2005/66] to the Economic and Social Council. Acknowledging that the new Government would face immense challenges when installed in February 2006, the Group highlighted possible elements to build on, such as progress in macroeconomic stability and economic governance. The report summarized the activities of the Group, including its April visit to Haiti in conjunction with the Security Council mission (see p. 379); the status of the MDGs; an update on international support to Haiti; priority areas for action; and implications for the long-term development of Haiti. The Group also made recommendations addressed to the Council, MINUSTAH and the UN country team, the Haitian authorities and the donor community.

Communication. On 27 June [E/2005/86], Haiti transmitted to the Economic and Social Council a letter from the interim Prime Minister, Gérard Latortue, in which he supported the recommendations of the Ad Hoc Advisory Group and requested that the Group's mandate be renewed. Mr. Latortue warned the Council not to underestimate the scope of the follow-up activities in the area of DDR. He announced the establishment of a strategic "think tank" to work in collaboration with the Ad Hoc Advisory Group to prepare a programme of work and budget.

On 27 July, the Council adopted **resolution 2005/46** on the Ad Hoc Advisory Group on Haiti (see p. 1012).

Financing of missions

MINUSTAH

On 18 March [A/59/745], the Secretary-General submitted to the General Assembly the budget for MINUSTAH for the period from 1 July 2005 to 30 June 2006 and the expenditure report for the Mission for the period 1 May to 30 June 2004. The budget, which amounted to $478,055,100, provided for the deployment of 6,700 military personnel, 1,622 civilian police officers, 489 international staff, 621 national staff and 179 United Nations Volunteers (UNVs). Total expenditure for the establishment of the Mission for the period 1 May to 30 June 2004 amounted to $34,556,100 gross.

ACABQ report (April). In a 19 April report [A/59/736/Add.13], the Advisory Committee on Administrative and Budgetary Questions (ACABQ) identified reductions totalling $7,947,000. It therefore recommended that the General Assembly appropriate $470,108,100 for the period 1 July 2005 to 30 June 2006; and that the unencumbered balance of $14,703,700 for the period 1 May to 30 June 2004 be credited to Member States in a manner to be determined by the Assembly.

GENERAL ASSEMBLY ACTION

On 22 June [meeting 104], the General Assembly, on the recommendation of the Fifth (Administrative and Budgetary) Committee [A/59/530/Add.1], adopted **resolution 59/17 B** without vote [agenda item 155].

Financing of the United Nations Stabilization Mission in Haiti

B

The General Assembly,

Having considered the report of the Secretary-General on the financing of the United Nations Stabilization Mission in Haiti and the related reports of the Advisory Committee on Administrative and Budgetary Questions,

Recalling Security Council resolution 1529(2004) of 29 February 2004, by which the Council declared its readiness to establish a United Nations stabilization force to support continuation of a peaceful and constitutional political process and the maintenance of a secure and stable environment in Haiti,

Recalling also Security Council resolution 1542 (2004) of 30 April 2004, by which the Council decided to establish the United Nations Stabilization Mission in Haiti for an initial period of six months, and the subsequent resolution 1576(2004) of 29 November 2004, by which the Council extended the mandate of the Mission until 1 June 2005,

Recalling further its resolution 58/311 of 18 June 2004 on the financing of the Mission and its subsequent resolution 59/17 A of 29 October 2004,

Reaffirming the general principles underlying the financing of United Nations peacekeeping operations, as stated in General Assembly resolutions 1874 (S-IV) of 27 June 1963, 3101(XXVIII) of 11 December 1973 and 55/235 of 23 December 2000,

Mindful of the fact that it is essential to provide the Mission with the necessary financial resources to enable it to fulfil its responsibilities under the relevant resolutions of the Security Council,

1. *Requests* the Secretary-General to entrust the Head of Mission with the task of formulating future budget proposals in full accordance with the provisions of General Assembly resolution 59/296 of 22 June 2005, as well as other relevant resolutions;

2. *Takes note* of the status of contributions to the United Nations Stabilization Mission in Haiti as at 15 April 2005, including the contributions outstanding in the amount of 80.8 million United States dollars, representing some 35 per cent of the total assessed contributions, notes with concern that only forty-eight Member States have paid their assessed contributions in full, and urges all other Member States, in particular those in arrears, to ensure payment of their outstanding assessed contributions;

3. *Expresses its appreciation* to those Member States which have paid their assessed contributions in full, and urges all other Member States to make every possible effort to ensure payment of their assessed contributions to the Mission in full;

4. *Expresses concern* at the financial situation with regard to peacekeeping activities, in particular as regards the reimbursements to troop contributors that bear additional burdens owing to overdue payments by Member States of their assessments;

5. *Also expresses concern* at the delay experienced by the Secretary-General in deploying and providing adequate resources to some recent peacekeeping missions, in particular those in Africa;

6. *Emphasizes* that all future and existing peacekeeping missions shall be given equal and non-

discriminatory treatment in respect of financial and administrative arrangements;

7. *Also emphasizes* that all peacekeeping missions shall be provided with adequate resources for the effective and efficient discharge of their respective mandates;

8. *Reiterates its request* to the Secretary-General to make the fullest possible use of facilities and equipment at the United Nations Logistics Base at Brindisi, Italy, in order to minimize the costs of procurement for the Mission;

9. *Endorses* the conclusions and recommendations contained in the report of the Advisory Committee on Administrative and Budgetary Questions, and requests the Secretary-General to ensure their full implementation, subject to the provisions of the present resolution;

10. *Requests* the Secretary-General to ensure the full implementation of relevant provisions of its resolution 59/296;

11. *Notes paragraph 20 of the report of the* Advisory Committee on Administrative and Budgetary Questions;

12. *Requests* the Secretary-General to address, as a matter of urgency, structural and management problems that remain to be thoroughly resolved as previously determined by the General Assembly;

13. *Decides* that the protocol functions shall be absorbed within the existing staff strength of the Mission;

14. *Requests* the Secretary-General to utilize expertise existing within the United Nations system that could support the Mission in carrying out substantive activities mandated by the Security Council;

15. *Also requests* the Secretary-General to take all necessary action to ensure that the Mission is administered with a maximum of efficiency and economy;

16. *Further requests* the Secretary General, in order to reduce the cost of employing General Service staff, to continue efforts to recruit local staff for the Mission against General Service posts, commensurate with the requirements of the Mission;

**Expenditure report for the period
from 1 May to 30 June 2004**

17. *Takes note* of the expenditure report for the Mission for the period from 1 May to 30 June 2004;

**Budget estimates for the period
from 1 July 2005 to 30 June 2006**

18. *Decides* to appropriate to the Special Account for the United Nations Stabilization Mission in Haiti the amount of 494,887,000 dollars for the period from 1 July 2005 to 30 June 2006, inclusive of 470,073,600 dollars for the maintenance of the Mission, 20,289,800 dollars for the support account for peacekeeping operations and 4,523,600 dollars for the United Nations Logistics Base;

Financing of the appropriation

19. *Decides also* to apportion among Member States the amount of 494,887,000 dollars at a monthly rate of 41,240,583 dollars, in accordance with the levels updated in General Assembly resolution 58/256 of 23 December 2003, taking into account the scale of assessments for 2005 and 2006 as set out in its resolution 58/1 B of 23 December 2003, subject to a decision of the Security Council to extend the mandate of the Mission;

20. *Decides further* that, in accordance with the provisions of its resolution 973(X) of 15 December

1955, there shall be set off against the apportionment among Member States, as provided for in paragraph 19 above, their respective share in the Tax Equalization Fund of 13,303,300 dollars, comprising the estimated staff assessment income of 10,069,500 dollars approved for the Mission, the prorated share of 2,867,900 dollars of the estimated staff assessment income approved for the support account and the prorated share of 365,900 dollars of the estimated staff assessment income approved for the United Nations Logistics Base;

21. *Decides* that, for Member States that have fulfilled their financial obligations to the Mission, there shall be set off against their apportionment, as provided for in paragraph 19 above, their respective share of the unencumbered balance of 14,703,700 dollars in respect of the financial period ended 30 June 2004, in accordance with the levels updated in General Assembly resolution 58/256, taking into account the scale of assessments for 2004 as set out in its resolution 58/1 B;

22. *Decides also* that, for Member States that have not fulfilled their financial obligations to the Mission, there shall be set off against their outstanding obligations their respective share of the unencumbered balance of 14,703,700 dollars in respect of the financial period ended 30 June 2004, in accordance with the scheme set out in paragraph 21 above;

23. *Decides further* that the decrease of 326,300 dollars in the estimated staff assessment income in respect of the financial period ended 30 June 2004 shall be set off against the credits from the amount of 14,703,700 dollars referred to in paragraphs 21 and 22 above;

24. *Emphasizes* that no peacekeeping mission shall be financed by borrowing funds from other active peacekeeping missions;

25. *Encourages* the Secretary-General to continue to take additional measures to ensure the safety and security of all personnel under the auspices of the United Nations participating in the Mission, bearing in mind paragraphs 5 and 6 of Security Council resolution 1502(2003) of 26 August 2003;

26. *Invites* voluntary contributions to the Mission in cash and in the form of services and supplies acceptable to the Secretary-General, to be administered, as appropriate, in accordance with the procedure and practices established by the General Assembly;

27. *Decides* to include in the provisional agenda of its sixtieth session the item entitled "Financing of the United Nations Stabilization Mission in Haiti".

Report of Secretary General (August). In a 1 August report [A/60/176 & Corr.1], the Secretary-General submitted a revised budget for MINUSTAH for the period 1 July 2005 to 30 June 2006, in the amount of $518,828,500 gross, representing an increase of $48,754,900, which provided for an additional 800 military contingent personnel, 275 civilian police officers and 17 temporary international staff, 30 national staff and 18 UNVs.

ACABQ report (September). In a September report [A/60/386], ACABQ reviewed the revised budget proposals and after identifying reductions totalling $2,340,000, recommended that the Assembly appropriate an additional amount of $46,414,900 for the period 1 July 2005 to 30 June 2006.

GENERAL ASSEMBLY ACTION

On 23 November [meeting 53], the General Assembly, on the recommendation of the Fifth Committee [A/60/541], adopted **resolution 60/18** without vote [agenda item 145].

Financing of the United Nations Stabilization Mission in Haiti

The General Assembly,

Having considered the report of the Secretary-General on the financing of the United Nations Stabilization Mission in Haiti and the related report of the Advisory Committee on Administrative and Budgetary Questions,

Recalling Security Council resolution 1529(2004) of 29 February 2004, by which the Council declared its readiness to establish a United Nations stabilization force to support continuation of a peaceful and constitutional political process and the maintenance of a secure and stable environment in Haiti,

Recalling also Security Council resolution 1542 (2004) of 30 April 2004, by which the Council decided to establish the United Nations Stabilization Mission in Haiti for an initial period of six months, and the subsequent resolutions by which the Council extended the mandate of the Mission, the latest of which was resolution 1608(2005) of 22 June 2005, by which the Council extended the mandate of the Mission until 15 February 2006 and authorized an increase for a temporary period in the military and civilian police components of the Mission,

Recalling further its resolution 58/311 of 18 June 2004 on the financing of the Mission and its subsequent resolutions thereon, the latest of which was resolution 59/17 B of 22 June 2005,

Reaffirming the general principles underlying the financing of United Nations peacekeeping operations, as stated in General Assembly resolutions 1874(S-IV) of 27 June 1963, 3101(XXVIII) of 11 December 1973 and 55/235 of 23 December 2000,

Mindful of the fact that it is essential to provide the Mission with the necessary financial resources to enable it to fulfil its responsibilities under the relevant resolutions of the Security Council,

1. *Requests* the Secretary-General to entrust the Head of Mission with the task of formulating future budget proposals in full accordance with the provisions of General Assembly resolution 59/296 of 22 June 2005, as well as other relevant resolutions;

2. *Takes note* of the status of contributions to the United Nations Stabilization Mission in Haiti as at 31 August 2005, including the contributions outstanding in the amount of 190 million United States dollars, representing some 34 per cent of the total assessed contributions, notes with concern that only twenty Member States have paid their assessed contributions in full, and urges all other Member States, in particular those in arrears, to ensure payment of their outstanding assessed contributions;

3. *Expresses its appreciation* to those Member States which have paid their assessed contributions in full and urges all other Member States to make every possible effort to ensure payment of their assessed contributions to the Mission in full;

4. *Expresses concern* at the financial situation with regard to peacekeeping activities, in particular as regards the reimbursements to troop contributors that bear additional burdens owing to overdue payments by Member States of their assessments;

5. *Also expresses concern* at the delay experienced by the Secretary-General in deploying and providing adequate resources to some recent peacekeeping missions, in particular those in Africa;

6. *Emphasizes* that all future and existing peacekeeping missions shall be given equal and non-discriminatory treatment in respect of financial and administrative arrangements;

7. *Also emphasizes* that all peacekeeping missions shall be provided with adequate resources for the effective and efficient discharge of their respective mandates;

8. *Reiterates its request* to the Secretary-General to make the fullest possible use of facilities and equipment at the United Nations Logistics Base at Brindisi, Italy, in order to minimize the costs of procurement for the Mission;

9. *Endorses* the conclusions and recommendations contained in the report of the Advisory Committee on Administrative and Budgetary Questions, subject to the provisions of the present resolution, and requests the Secretary-General to ensure their full implementation;

10. *Decides* not to endorse paragraph 22 of the report of the Advisory Committee on Administrative and Budgetary Questions;

11. *Decides* to reduce the overall level of operational costs by 2,340,000 dollars, taking into account the reductions proposed in paragraphs 18 and 21 of the report of the Advisory Committee on Administrative and Budgetary Questions;

12. *Requests* the Secretary-General to ensure the full implementation of relevant provisions of its resolution 59/296;

13. *Also requests* the Secretary-General to take all necessary action to ensure that the Mission is administered with a maximum of efficiency and economy;

14. *Further requests* the Secretary-General, in order to reduce the cost of employing General Service staff, to continue efforts to recruit local staff for the Mission against General Service posts, commensurate with the requirements of the Mission;

Revised budget estimates for the period from 1 July 2005 to 30 June 2006

15. *Decides* to appropriate to the Special Account for the United Nations Stabilization Mission in Haiti the amount of 46,414,900 dollars for the maintenance of the Mission for the period from 1 July 2005 to 30 June 2006, in addition to the amount of 494,887,000 dollars already appropriated for the same period under the terms of its resolution 59/17 B;

Financing of the appropriation

16. *Also decides*, taking into account the amount of 494,887,000 dollars previously apportioned at a monthly rate of 41,240,583 dollars for the period from 1 July 2005 to 30 June 2006 under the terms of its resolution 59/17 B, to apportion among Member States the additional amount of 29,147,500 dollars for the period from 1 July 2005 to 15 February 2006, in

accordance with the levels updated in General Assembly resolution 58/256 of 23 December 2003 and taking into account the scale of assessments for 2005 and 2006, as set out in its resolution 58/1 B of 23 December 2003;

17. *Further decides* that, in accordance with the provisions of its resolution 973(X) of 15 December 1955, there shall be set off against the apportionment among Member States, as provided for in paragraph 16 above, their respective share in the Tax Equalization Fund of the additional amount of 104,100 dollars approved for the Mission for the period from 1 July 2005 to 15 February 2006;

18. *Decides* to apportion among Member States the additional amount of 17,267,400 dollars for the period from 16 February to 30 June 2006 at a monthly rate of 3,867,900 dollars, in accordance with the levels updated in General Assembly resolution 58/256 and taking into account the scale of assessments for 2006, as set out in its resolution 58/1 B, subject to a decision of the Security Council to extend the mandate of the Mission;

19. *Also decides* that, in accordance with the provisions of its resolution 973(X), there shall be set off against the apportionment among Member States, as provided for in paragraph 18 above, their respective share in the Tax Equalization Fund of the additional amount of 61,600 dollars approved for the Mission;

20. *Emphasizes* that no peacekeeping mission shall be financed by borrowing funds from other active peacekeeping missions;

21. *Encourages* the Secretary-General to continue to take additional measures to ensure the safety and security of all personnel under the auspices of the United Nations participating in the Mission, bearing in mind paragraphs 5 and 6 of Security Council resolution 1502(2003) of 26 August 2003;

22. *Invites* voluntary contributions to the Mission in cash and in the form of services and supplies acceptable to the Secretary-General, to be administered, as appropriate, in accordance with the procedure and practices established by the General Assembly;

23. *Decides* to keep under review during its sixtieth session the item entitled "Financing of the United Nations Stabilization Mission in Haiti".

Other questions

Costa Rica–Nicaragua

On 29 September [A/60/417-S/2005/632], Costa Rica transmitted to the Secretary-General a statement relating to the filing before the International Court of Justice (ICJ) by Costa Rica of a case against Nicaragua concerning navigational rights of Costa Rica on the San Juan River (see p. 1385). Costa Rica said that, despite the progress achieved as a result of the September 2002 Agreement between the two countries, its rights with respect to the San Juan River remained in dispute and that it had brought the issue before the highest international judicial body so as to resolve once and for all the only source of disagreement with Nicaragua.

Cuba–United States

On 21 October [A/60/447], Spain transmitted a communiqué protesting the implementation of the Helms-Burton Act and requesting the United States to end the economic, commercial and financial blockade against Cuba.

In a letter dated 1 November [A/60/531], Cuba transmitted the declaration by organizations that had participated in the "Third Forum of Cuban civil society against the embargo and the annexation" (Havana, 31 October), which indicated that the United States embargo against Cuba had adversely impacted the country's economy, and if not dismantled, would continue to be a fundamental obstacle to Cuba's development. The declaration also demanded that the United States Government proceed with the immediate extradition of alleged terrorist Luis Clemente Posada Carriles to Venezuela and the immediate release of five imprisoned Cuban anti-terrorist fighters.

Report of Secretary-General. On 10 August [A/60/213], in response to General Assembly resolution 59/11 [YUN 2004, p. 305], the Secretary General forwarded information received by Governments as at 15 July 2005 on the implementation of that resolution. That text had called on States to refrain from unilateral application of economic and trade measures against other States, and urged them to repeal or invalidate such measures. In addition to the replies from 84 States, the report included statements from the EU and from 10 UN bodies and 10 specialized agencies.

GENERAL ASSEMBLY ACTION

On 8 November [meeting 45], the General Assembly adopted **resolution 60/12** [draft: A/60/L.9], by recorded vote (182-4-1) [agenda item 18].

Necessity of ending the economic, commercial and financial embargo imposed by the United States of America against Cuba

The General Assembly,

Determined to encourage strict compliance with the purposes and principles enshrined in the Charter of the United Nations,

Reaffirming, among other principles, the sovereign equality of States, non-intervention and non-interference in their internal affairs and freedom of international trade and navigation, which are also enshrined in many international legal instruments,

Recalling the statements of the Heads of State or Government at the Ibero-American Summits concerning the need to eliminate the unilateral application of economic and trade measures by one State against another that affect the free flow of international trade,

Concerned at the continued promulgation and application by Member States of laws and regulations, such as that promulgated on 12 March 1996 known as the "Helms-Burton Act", the extraterritorial effects of which affect the sovereignty of other States, the legitimate interests of entities or persons under their jurisdiction and the freedom of trade and navigation,

Taking note of declarations and resolutions of different intergovernmental forums, bodies and Governments that express the rejection by the international community and public opinion of the promulgation and application of regulations of the kind referred to above,

Recalling its resolutions 47/19 of 24 November 1992, 48/16 of 3 November 1993, 49/9 of 26 October 1994, 50/10 of 2 November 1995, 51/17 of 12 November 1996, 52/10 of 5 November 1997, 53/4 of 14 November 1998, 54/21 of 9 November 1999, 55/20 of 9 November 2000, 56/9 of 27 November 2001, 57/11 of 12 November 2002, 58/7 of 4 November 2003 and 59/11 of 28 October 2004,

Concerned that, since the adoption of its resolutions 47/19, 48/16, 49/9, 50/10, 51/17, 52/10, 53/4, 54/21, 55/20, 56/9, 57/11, 58/7 and 59/11, further measures of that nature aimed at strengthening and extending the economic, commercial and financial embargo against Cuba continue to be promulgated and applied, and concerned also at the adverse effects of such measures on the Cuban people and on Cuban nationals living in other countries,

1. *Takes note* of the report of the Secretary-General on the implementation of resolution 59/11;

2. *Reiterates its call upon* all States to refrain from promulgating and applying laws and measures of the kind referred to in the preamble to the present resolution in conformity with their obligations under the Charter of the United Nations and international law, which, inter alia, reaffirm the freedom of trade and navigation;

3. *Once again urges* States that have and continue to apply such laws and measures to take the necessary steps to repeal or invalidate them as soon as possible in accordance with their legal regime;

4. *Requests* the Secretary-General, in consultation with the appropriate organs and agencies of the United Nations system, to prepare a report on the implementation of the present resolution in the light of the purposes and principles of the Charter and international law and to submit it to the General Assembly at its sixty-first session;

5. *Decides* to include in the provisional agenda of its sixty-first session the item entitled "Necessity of ending the economic, commercial and financial embargo imposed by the United States of America against Cuba".

RECORDED VOTE ON RESOLUTION 60/12:

In favour: Afghanistan, Albania, Algeria, Andorra, Angola, Antigua and Barbuda, Argentina, Armenia, Australia, Austria, Azerbaijan, Bahamas, Bahrain, Bangladesh, Barbados, Belarus, Belgium, Belize, Benin, Bhutan, Bolivia, Bosnia and Herzegovina, Botswana, Brazil, Brunei Darussalam, Bulgaria, Burkina Faso, Burundi, Cambodia, Cameroon, Canada, Cape Verde, Central African Republic, Chad, Chile, China, Colombia, Comoros, Congo, Costa Rica, Côte d'Ivoire, Croatia, Cuba, Cyprus, Czech Republic, Democratic People's Republic of Korea, Democratic Republic of the Congo, Denmark, Djibouti, Dominica, Dominican Republic, Ecuador, Egypt, Equatorial Guinea, Eritrea, Estonia, Ethiopia, Fiji, Finland, France, Gabon, Gambia, Georgia, Germany, Ghana, Greece, Grenada, Guatemala, Guinea, Guinea-Bissau, Guyana, Haiti, Honduras, Hungary, Iceland, India, Indonesia, Iran, Ireland, Italy, Jamaica, Japan, Jordan, Kazakhstan, Kenya, Kiribati, Kuwait, Kyrgyzstan, Lao People's Democratic Republic, Latvia, Lebanon, Lesotho, Liberia, Libyan Arab Jamahiriya, Liechtenstein, Lithuania, Luxembourg, Madagascar, Malawi, Malaysia, Maldives, Mali, Malta, Mauritania, Mauritius, Mexico, Monaco, Mongolia, Mozambique, Myanmar, Namibia, Nauru, Nepal, Netherlands, New Zealand, Niger, Nigeria, Norway, Oman, Pakistan, Panama, Papua New Guinea, Paraguay, Peru, Philippines, Poland, Portugal, Qatar, Republic of Korea, Republic of Moldova, Romania, Russian Federation, Rwanda, Saint Kitts and Nevis, Saint Lucia, Saint Vincent and the Grenadines, Samoa, San Marino, Sao Tome and Principe, Saudi Arabia, Senegal, Serbia and Montenegro, Seychelles, Sierra Leone, Singapore, Slovakia, Slovenia, Solomon Islands, Somalia, South Africa, Spain, Sri Lanka, Sudan, Suriname, Swaziland, Sweden, Switzerland, Syrian Arab Republic, Tajikistan, Thailand, the former Yugoslav Republic of Macedonia, Timor-Leste, Togo, Tonga, Trinidad and Tobago, Tunisia, Turkey, Turkmenistan, Tuvalu, Uganda, Ukraine, United Arab Emirates, United Kingdom, United Republic of Tanzania, Uruguay, Uzbekistan, Vanuatu, Venezuela, Viet Nam, Yemen, Zambia, Zimbabwe.

Against: Israel, Marshall Islands, Palau, United States.

Abstaining: Micronesia.

Communications. On 21 May [A/59/808-S/2005/330], Cuba transmitted the text of a 20 May address by President Fidel Castro pertaining to alleged terrorist acts that had taken place in the country. Other letters from Cuba [A/59/812-S/2005/341, A/59/907-S/2005/565, A/60/408-S/2005/626] dealt with the situation of alleged terrorist Luis Posada Carriles. Venezuela also transmitted letters on 15 June [A/59/849-S/2005/394] and 29 September [A/60/406-S/2005/624] in reference to Mr. Carriles.

Ibero-American community

On 21 October [A/60/447], Spain transmitted the Salamanca Declaration, adopted on 15 October by the Heads of State and Government of the Ibero-American community of nations at its Fifteenth Summit (Salamanca, Spain, 14-15 October), establishing the Ibero-American secretariat as a permanent organ to support the institutionalization of the Ibero-American Conference.

Observer status

On 23 November, the General Assembly granted observer status to the Ibero-American Conference (**resolution 60/28**) (see p. 1543) and to the Latin American Integration Association (**resolution 60/25**) (see p. 1542) in the work of the Assembly.

Chapter IV

Asia and the Pacific

In 2005, the United Nations continued to face great political and security challenges in Asia, especially in Afghanistan and Iraq, in its efforts to restore peace and stability, and promote economic and social development in that region.

In Afghanistan, the political transition provided for under the Bonn Agreement [YUN 2001, p. 263] was completed with the holding of parliamentary and provincial council elections on 18 September and the inauguration of the National Assembly on 19 December. In recognition of the fact that Afghanistan would require international assistance to meet security, economic and humanitarian challenges, the Afghan Government and the United Nations, following the parliamentary elections, initiated consultations with international actors to reach a consensus on the strategy to address them.

The International Security Assistance Force (ISAF), a multinational force established by Security Council resolution 1386(2001) [ibid., p. 267], continued to assist the Afghan Government in the maintenance of security in Kabul and its surrounding areas. The North Atlantic Treaty Organization (NATO) continued its role as lead command for ISAF throughout 2005. In December, NATO adopted a revised ISAF operational plan, which expanded its presence to the southern regions of Afghanistan.

In July, the Council further refined its sanctions measures against Osama bin Laden, Al-Qaida, the Taliban and their associates, and provided more clarity regarding who could be placed on the Al-Qaida and Taliban Sanctions Committee's consolidated list, which remained a critical tool for implementing all sanctions measures. The mandate of the Analytical Support and Sanctions Monitoring Committee was extended for 17 months. The Monitoring Team submitted two reports on the implementation of the sanctions measures by States.

The Economic and Social Council, in July, adopted resolution 2005/24 on support to the Government of Afghanistan in its efforts to implement the counter-narcotics implementation plan (see p. 1357). By resolution 60/179, the General Assembly, in December, called on the international community to support the Afghan Government in ensuring the effective implementation of that plan (ibid.). The Council, in July,

adopted resolution 2005/8 on the situation of women and girls in Afghanistan (see p. 1259).

Nowhere were the stakes higher and the challenges to global peace and security greater than in Iraq. The United Nations continued to promote an inclusive, participatory and transparent political transition process, despite great security constraints due to an ever increasing level of violence.

During the year, the Iraqi people exercised their right to vote on three different occasions. In January, elections for the Transitional National Assembly, 18 governorate councils and the Kurdistan National Assembly took place. Following the election, Ibrahim al-Jaafari was elected Prime Minister of the Iraqi Transitional Government. The constitutional referendum was held on 15 October, resulting in the adoption of a new constitution, and on 15 December, elections were held for a new Parliament, the Council of Representatives. Though final elections results were expected to be announced in January 2006, the transition timetable set forth in the Transitional Administrative Law and endorsed by resolution 1546(2004) was completed with the holding of those elections. However, while Iraq met all the key benchmarks of that timetable, it continued to face formidable political, security and economic challenges. The political transition was accompanied by an increasingly sophisticated and complex insurgency, underscored by high levels of ethnic and sectarian violence, intimidation and murder, including the assassination of foreign diplomats. The security environment constrained both the UN presence and its ability to operate effectively in Iraq. UN staff continued to rely to a large degree on the multinational force for security and information.

The high-level Independent Inquiry Committee of the Iraq oil-for-food programme, headed by Paul A. Volcker, reported evidence of misadministration in the programme and of corruption within the United Nations and by affiliated contractors. The Committee also found that the programme's general management was characterized by weak administrative practices and inadequate control and auditing. The Committee, however, did note that the programme succeeded in restoring minimal standards of nutrition and health in Iraq, while helping to maintain the international effort to prevent the former regime of Saddam Hussein from acquiring weapons of mass destruction. The Secretary-General took full responsibility for his personal failings, as well as the Organization's.

With the establishment of two liaison detachments in Basra and Erbil, the United Nations Assistance Mission for Iraq (UNAMI) continued to operate from three countries, with offices in Baghdad, Amman, Jordan, and Kuwait City. Given the prevailing security situation inside Iraq, UNAMI relied on the Multinational Force for logistical support and personnel security.

The United Nations Monitoring, Verification and Inspection Commission and the International Atomic Energy Agency continued to assess material that was in the public domain pertaining to Iraq's alleged weapons of mass destruction.

Despite greater cooperation from the Iraqi authorities, progress towards the resolution of the issue of the repatriation and return of all Kuwaiti and third-country nationals or their remains was slow. Kuwait continued to face no small task in locating mass graves and in recovering mortal remains.

In 2005, Timor-Leste continued to strengthen its national institutions with help from the United Nations Mission of Support in East Timor (UNMISET) and the newly established United Nations Office in Timor-Leste (UNOTIL). As State institutions and security structures were not yet strong enough to stand alone at the close of UNMISET's mandate on 20 May, UNOTIL was created as a follow-on mission, with a scaled-down structure, for a period of one year, to support and monitor progress in the development of critical state institutions and to observe democratic governance and human rights. After a law on restructuring the Government was promulgated, a new Government was selected and sworn in on 28 July. Local elections were completed in all 13 districts. UN support of the serious crimes process, tasked with investigating and prosecuting crimes against humanity committed in 1999, came to a close with the termination of UNMISET's mandate. Significant progress was made towards the demarcation of the land border between Indonesia and Timor-Leste. An agreement between Timor-Leste and Australia over the sharing of Timor Sea oil and gas resources was also close to finalization.

The Papua New Guinea province of Bougainville made significant progress towards the fulfilment of the 2001 Bougainville Peace Agreement. With the support of the United Nations Observer Mission in Bougainville (UNOMB), the weapons disposal process was completed and elections to establish the first Autonomous Bougainville Government were held. Joseph C. Kabui, former President of the Bougainville's People's Congress, was elected to the presidency. Following the elections, UNOMB's mandate, having been fully implemented, was terminated on 30 June.

Among other concerns in the region brought to the attention of the United Nations, were growing instability in Central Asia; developments in the Democratic People's Republic of Korea; the situation in Myanmar; tensions in Nepal; and the issue of the Greater Tunb, Lesser Tunb and Abu Musa islands in the Persian Gulf. The activities of the United Nations Tajikistan Office of Peacebuilding were extended for another year, until 1 June 2006, in order to continue to support Tajikistan in its post-conflict peacebuilding efforts. The General Assembly adopted a resolution welcoming Mongolia's efforts to celebrate its eight hundredth anniversary of statehood in 2006, emphasizing the concept of dialogue among civilizations.

Afghanistan

Implementation of the Bonn Agreement

In 2005, the United Nations continued to assist the Government of Afghanistan in implementing the 2001 Agreement on Provisional Arrangements in Afghanistan Pending the Reestablishment of Permanent Government Institutions (the Bonn Agreement) [YUN 2001, p. 263], with support provided by the United Nations Assistance Mission in Afghanistan (UNAMA), under the direction of the Special Representative of the Secretary-General and Head of Mission, and by the International Security Assistance Force (ISAF), led by the North Atlantic Treaty Organization (NATO). Implementation of the Bonn process was completed with the holding of parliamentary elections on 18 September.

The Secretary-General submitted two progress reports to the General Assembly and the Security Council on the implementation of the Bonn Agreement and on UNAMA activities for the period from January to August [A/59/744-S/2005/183, A/60/224-S/2005/525]. Developments for the latter part of the year were contained in a later report [A/60/712-S/2006/145]. ISAF activities were reported to the Council by the NATO Secretary-General through the UN Secretary-General [S/2005/131, S/2005/230, S/2005/431, S/2005/634]. The Council extended UNAMA's mandate until 24 March 2006 (**resolution 1589(2005)**) (see p. 400) and ISAF's authorization until 13 October 2006 (**resolution 1623(2005)**) (see p. 409).

On 21 December, the Council took note of the Secretary-General's intention to appoint Tom Koenigs (Germany) as his Special Representative for Afghanistan and Head of UNAMA to replace Jean Arnault (France) [S/2005/819, S/2005/820].

Security Council consideration (January). At the Security Council's 10 January meeting [meeting 5108] to discuss the situation in Afghanistan, the Special Representative of the Secretary-General, in his briefing on developments in Afghanistan and plans for the coming months, said that the 2004 presidential elections and the appointment of a cabinet [YUN 2004, p. 321] had given a new momentum to the Afghan Peace process. Afghans and the international community had to take full advantage of that circumstance to move the Bonn Agenda forward and fulfil as much as possible, in 2005, the broad objectives of the transition. He noted that parliamentary elections were expected to take place between 21 April and 21 May, following the establishment of the Independent Electoral Commission (see below). In order to meet the April-May target date, the Government and the electoral authorities had to decide on: the participation of refugees and nomads; the demarcation of district boundaries; the population figures for each province; the preparation of voter lists; and the revision of the electoral law. The most urgent of those decisions concerned the assignment of population settlements to districts, a task which, under the electoral law, had to be completed 120 days before election day. The Ministry of Interior indicated that good progress had been made in that regard.

With regard to the management of the electoral process, the United Nations had streamlined international support, with United Nations Development Programme (UNDP) overseeing trust fund management and donor relations, in addition to supporting electoral observation, and the United Nations Office for Project Services (UNOPS) acting as executing agency for all budget lines. It was estimated that between $120 and $130 million would be needed to cover the three elections, with an additional $30 million if it was decided to hold out-of-country elections as well.

On the issue of security, the national army and professional police would be deployed for the parliamentary elections, for which close to 400 district elections would need to be secured. The strength of the Afghan National Army (ANA) was expected to increase from 28 to 32 battalions by April and to 39 by July, and that of the Afghan National Police (ANP) from approximately 30,000 to more than 45,000 members by July. International forces would provide security and back up

national agencies. The United Nations Country Team carried out a comprehensive security assessment to ascertain the type of security challenges that the United Nations itself would be facing. It concluded that, as the security situation remained very diverse in different parts of the country, adequate measures had to be taken to provide UN agencies and electoral operations with access to risk-prone regions.

The narcotics industry and the accompanying corruption remained one of the biggest threats to the building of an effective, democratic Afghan State and to the country's long-term peace and stability. The central Government had shown a commitment to tackling the problem through the establishment of the new Ministry of Counter-Narcotics, and the launch of the national narcotics eradication programme [YUN 2004, p. 328], which was to focus on seven key provinces. To counterbalance the potentially negative impact of eradication initiatives, it was critical that alternative livelihood programmes be strengthened and made known to affected communities, and that the Government develop further its counter-narcotics public information campaign through traditional and community-based channels.

Disarmament, demobilization and reintegration had been a key consideration in deciding the date and modalities of the elections. That concern applied particularly to local elections, where a web of political interests and armed groups could significantly distort the electoral process.

Report of Secretary-General (March). In his March report on the situation in Afghanistan and its implications for international peace and security [A/59/744-S/2005/183], submitted in response to Security Council resolution 1536(2004) [YUN 2004, p. 313] and General Assembly resolutions 59/112 A [ibid., p. 323] and 59/112 B [ibid., p. 917], the Secretary-General summarized key developments in Afghanistan since his 26 November 2004 report [ibid., p. 323]. He said that, on 24 January, President Hamid Karzai established the Independent Electoral Commission, which, with international electoral experts would constitute the Joint Electoral Management Body (JEMB) to oversee the elections.

The overall security situation was relatively calm for almost four months as the severe winter season significantly impeded the operations of extremists, terrorists, factional forces and criminal elements. In areas least affected by winter conditions, particularly the south-eastern and southern regions, coalition forces, ANA and Government institutions continued to be targeted by extremists employing anti-tank mines, small unit ambushes and rocket attacks. The Afghan Government, with international community support, had to tackle the problem of illegal armed groups operating throughout the country, which included ex-combatants from decommissioned units who did not enter the disarmament, demobilization and reintegration process. Those groups perpetuated the drug industry, imposed illegal taxes on individuals in reconstruction programmes and impeded the progress of State expansion. Through a pilot project under the leadership of the National Security Council, UNAMA was working with national and international security agencies to map and categorize more than 1,000 such groups.

The training of the reformed ANA continued to make progress, but sustaining an effective police force proved challenging. Key areas yet to be effectively addressed included: in-depth reform and expansion of the structure of the police force, and post-deployment monitoring. Measures were also required to identify and exclude corrupt and anti-government elements in the force.

The Secretary-General observed that a number of post-conflict peacebuilding tasks had yet to be fulfilled, including the restoration of countrywide security, the full resettlement of refugees and internally displaced persons, the rehabilitation of key economic and social infrastructure and the establishment of functional State institutions across the country. Some of the important tasks relating to post-conflict rehabilitation had hardly started, such as the settlement of conflicting land claims, property rights, national reconciliation, and transitional justice.

Implementation of the Bonn Agreement would be complete with the holding of elections later in 2005, but in order to move forward with the next phase of the peace process, Afghans would need the sustained engagement of the international community. After more than three years of intensive engagement by the United Nations in Afghanistan, a number of lessons learned had been identified. They included multiple needs for: an extended presence of international forces to overcome a number of bottlenecks that continued to affect the pace and scope of reconstruction, such as a massive skills deficit; a comprehensive approach to the creation or recreation of key State institutions, in particular a national police force, civil service and justice system; sustainability; a stronger link between post-conflict reconstruction and economic growth; and improvements in regional cooperation.

All UN specialized agencies and programmes were expected to play a supportive role in building State capacity in education, health, agriculture, national and subnational administration, among others. While considerable efforts were being made to identify the UN's role following the parliamentary elections, the Afghan leadership, the Parliament, and other relevant parties would have to be consulted before a definitive recommendation could be submitted to the Security Council. In the meantime, the Secretary-General recommended that UNAMA's mandate be extended for 12 months, until March 2006.

Security Council consideration (March). On 22 March [meeting 5145], the Security Council discussed the situation in Afghanistan. The Special Representative of the Secretary-General for Afghanistan and Head of UNAMA, Jean Arnault, said that the Afghan electoral authorities had decided that parliamentary and provincial elections would be held on 18 September, four months later than originally anticipated. That would allow for more in-depth civic education of the public, which, in turn, would enhance participation, give more time to complete the disarmament, demobilization and reintegration process, place more and better trained army and police units at the disposal of the electoral process, and prepare for the establishment of the future National Assembly.

With regard to security, the two roadside bombs that killed six and injured 31 in Kandahar on 16 March were a reminder that, while the security situation overall had improved, complacency was not in order, particularly for the United Nations, since the two attacks were directed at its humanitarian convoys. It was hoped that a new initiative, entitled "Consolidation of Peace", aimed at allowing rank and file Taliban and other fighters from extremist organizations to disarm and resettle in their communities, could help reduce violence in 2005. The initiative provided for low- and mid-level fighters to enter a reconciliation process under the responsibility of the provincial governors and community leaders. It did not offer, however, unconditional amnesty and did not apply to the worst offenders among Taliban commanders and other senior leaders from extremist groups, whose capture and prosecution would remain a priority for international forces and domestic security agencies. For individuals whose status deserved special measures, reintegration would take place under close monitoring by security agencies.

SECURITY COUNCIL ACTION

On 24 March [meeting 5148], the Security Council unanimously adopted **resolution 1589(2005).** The draft [S/2005/195] was prepared in consultation among Council members.

The Security Council,

Recalling its previous resolutions on Afghanistan, in particular resolution 1536(2004) of 26 March 2004 extending the mandate of the United Nations Assistance Mission in Afghanistan through 26 March 2005,

Reaffirming its strong commitment to the sovereignty, independence, territorial integrity and national unity of Afghanistan,

Welcoming once again the successful holding of the presidential election on 9 October 2004,

Recognizing the urgent need to tackle the ongoing challenges in Afghanistan, including the fight against narcotics, the lack of security in certain areas, terrorist threats, comprehensive nationwide disarmament, demobilization and reintegration of the Afghan Militia Forces and disbandment of illegal armed groups, timely preparation for the parliamentary, provincial and district elections, development of Afghan government institutions, acceleration of justice sector reform, promotion and protection of human rights, and economic and social development,

Reaffirming, in this context, its continued support for the implementation of the provisions of the Bonn Agreement of 5 December 2001 and of the Berlin Declaration of 1 April 2004, including the annexes thereto, and pledging its continued support thereafter for the Government and people of Afghanistan as they rebuild their country, strengthen the foundations of a constitutional democracy and assume their rightful place in the community of nations,

Recalling and emphasizing the importance of the Declaration on Good-neighbourly Relations, signed in Kabul on 22 December 2002, and encouraging all States concerned to continue to follow up on the Kabul Declaration and the Declaration on Encouraging Closer Trade, Transit and Investment Cooperation, signed in Dubai, United Arab Emirates, on 22 September 2003,

Expressing its appreciation and strong support for the ongoing efforts of the Secretary-General and his Special Representative for Afghanistan, and stressing the central and impartial role that the United Nations continues to play in promoting peace and stability in Afghanistan,

1. *Welcomes* the report of the Secretary-General of 18 March 2005;

2. *Decides* to extend the mandate of the United Nations Assistance Mission in Afghanistan for an additional period of twelve months from the date of adoption of the present resolution;

3. *Stresses* the importance of urgently establishing a framework for the holding at the earliest possible date of free and fair elections, welcomes in this regard the announcement of the Joint Electoral Management Body that elections for the lower house of the parliament (Wolesi Jirga) and provincial councils will be held on 18 September 2005, calls upon the Mission to continue to provide necessary support in order to facilitate timely elections with the broadest possible participation, and urges the donor community to promptly make available the necessary financial support based on that framework, in close coordination with the Government of Afghanistan and the Mission, and to consider contributing to electoral observer missions;

4. *Also stresses* the importance of security for credible parliamentary, provincial and district elections,

and to this end calls upon Member States to contribute personnel, equipment and other resources to support the expansion of the International Security Assistance Force and the establishment of provincial reconstruction teams in other parts of Afghanistan, and to coordinate closely with the Mission and the Government of Afghanistan;

5. *Welcomes* the international efforts to assist in setting up the new Afghan Parliament and ensure its efficient functioning, which will be critical to the political future of Afghanistan and the steps towards a free and democratic Afghanistan;

6. *Also welcomes* the substantial progress in the disarmament, demobilization and reintegration process in accordance with the Bonn Agreement, encourages the Government of Afghanistan to continue its active efforts to accelerate the process towards its completion by June 2006, to disband the illegal armed groups and to dispose of the ammunition stockpile, and requests the international community to further extend assistance for these efforts;

7. *Further welcomes* the effort to date of the Government of Afghanistan to implement its National Drug Control Strategy, adopted in May 2003, including through the launch of the Counter-narcotics Implementation Plan, in February 2005, which reflects a new determination of the Government to tackle the cultivation, production and trafficking of drugs, urges the Government to take decisive action to stop the processing and trade of drugs and to pursue the specific measures set out in that plan in the fields of: building institutions; information campaigns; alternative livelihoods; interdiction and law enforcement; criminal justice; eradication; demand reduction and treatment of addicts; and regional cooperation, and calls upon the international community to provide every possible assistance to the Government in pursuing full implementation of all aspects of the plan;

8. *Supports* the fight against the illicit trafficking in drugs and precursors within Afghanistan and in neighbouring States and countries along trafficking routes, including increased cooperation among them to strengthen anti-narcotic controls to curb the drug flow, and welcomes in this context the signing on 1 April 2004 of the Berlin Declaration on Counter-Narcotics within the framework of the Kabul Declaration on Good-neighbourly Relations;

9. *Requests* the Mission to continue to support the ongoing effort for the establishment of a fair and transparent justice system, including the reconstruction and reform of the prison sector, in order to strengthen the rule of law throughout the country;

10. *Calls for* full respect for human rights and international humanitarian law throughout Afghanistan, and in this regard requests the Mission, with the support of the Office of the United Nations High Commissioner for Human Rights, to continue to assist in the full implementation of the human rights provisions of the new Afghan Constitution, in particular those regarding the full enjoyment by women of their human rights, commends the Afghan Independent Human Rights Commission for its courageous efforts to monitor respect for human rights in Afghanistan as well as to foster and protect these rights, welcomes in this regard the Commission's report of 29 January 2005 and the proposed national strategy for transi-

tional justice, and requests international support for that endeavour;

11. *Welcomes* the development of the Afghan National Army and Afghan National Police and the ongoing efforts to increase their capabilities as important steps towards the goal of Afghan security forces providing security and ensuring the rule of law throughout the country;

12. *Calls upon* the Government of Afghanistan, with the assistance of the international community, including the Operation Enduring Freedom Coalition and the International Security Assistance Force, in accordance with their respective designated responsibilities as they evolve, to continue to address the threat to the security and stability of Afghanistan posed by Al-Qaida operatives, the Taliban and other extremist groups, factional violence among militia forces and criminal activities, in particular violence involving the drug trade;

13. *Requests* the Secretary-General to report to the Council in a timely manner on developments in Afghanistan, and to make recommendations on the future role of the Mission, after the parliamentary elections;

14. *Decides* to remain actively seized of the matter.

Security Council consideration (June). On 24 June [meeting 5215], the Security Council discussed the situation in Afghanistan and was briefed on the latest developments by the Special Representative of the Secretary-General for Afghanistan and by the Executive Director of the United Nations Office on Drugs and Crime (UNODC). The Special Representative said that, since his March report (see p. 398) the security situation in Afghanistan had deteriorated, especially in the southern and eastern part of the country, jeopardizing rebuilding efforts and obliging UN agencies to keep a very low profile. Drugs, local rivalry, corruption and ordinary criminal acts added to the violence, but the decisive factor in the escalation of violence was the offensive by extremist groups, including the Taliban. They had more money, more effective weaponry, more powerful means of disseminating radio propaganda, and were more aggressive vis-à-vis civilians and demonstrated greater cruelty and indiscriminate violence. International response to thwart that policy of destabilization had to focus on attacking the financing of fundamentalist elements, the safe havens where they trained and the networks that supported them.

Despite the security situation, preparations for the elections were encouraging. The electoral administration had been deployed countrywide, with offices being fully operational in Kabul and in the eight regional centres, as well as in all 34 provincial capitals. An independent Electoral Complaints Commission was created to handle and adjudicate all electoral complaints and challenges. Nominations, which took place between 4 and 26 May, saw more than 6,000 candidates submitting their applications for the 249 seats in the lower house and the 420 seats in the 34 provincial councils, 12 per cent of whom were women. At the same time, a countrywide assessment carried out by UNAMA and the Afghan Independent Human Rights Commission concluded that there was a broad perception that people linked to armed groups were determined to use violence and intimidation to succeed in getting elected. Measures therefore had to be taken to neutralize them and to reassure the majority of candidates and the population at large that they could vote in September without the risk of reprisals.

Communications. On 30 June [A/59/863-S/2005/427], the Russian Federation transmitted the text of the statement by the Heads of State of Armenia, Belarus, Kazakhstan, Kyrgyzstan, the Russian Federation and Tajikistan, which was adopted by the Council on Collective Security of the Collective Security Treaty Organization, calling on interested countries and international and regional organizations to coordinate action relating to the post-conflict settlement in Afghanistan, with a central role played by the United Nations.

On 13 July [A/60/129], Kazakhstan transmitted to the Secretary-General the text of the declaration adopted by the Heads of State of the Shangai Cooperation Organization (SCO) at their summit meeting (Astana, Kazakhstan, 5 July). In the light of the completion of the active military phase of counter-terrorism operations in Afghanistan, SCO believed those of its members that had made available their ground infrastructure for the temporary accommodation of the coalition members' military contingents and had granted the use of their territories and airspace for military transit to facilitate counter-terrorism operations, should establish end dates for the temporary use of those facilities and the presence of the military contingents in the territories of SCO countries.

Report of Secretary-General (August). The Secretary-General, in his August report on Afghanistan [A/60/224-S/2005/525], said that President Karzai signed, on 27 April, a revised electoral law requiring the Central Statistics Office to release population figures province by province, which were to be used to allocate seats to the Wolesi Jirga (lower house of parliament) and the provincial councils. A voter registration drive took place between 25 June and 21 July and the official electoral campaign began on 17 August. Civic education efforts were also undertaken. However, some $31 million was still required to fill a funding gap and avoid any delay in the holding of the elections.

The Secretary-General observed that, although significant gains had been made in meeting the objectives of the political agenda, the implementation of the institutional agenda of the Bonn Agreement had been uneven across sectors. Many critical State institutions at both the national and provincial levels remained weak and susceptible to corruption. While initiatives had been taken to reform civil administration at the central level, reforms below that level had proved more difficult. In particular, insufficient resources were dedicated to developing effective public administration at the provincial and district levels, which were also plagued by a lack of capacity and corruption, and an uncertain security environment.

In discussions held in June on cooperation between Afghanistan and the international community after the September parliamentary elections, the Government and UNAMA recognized that sustained international community support was required to achieve security, full disarmament, justice and a competent civil administration in all provinces, to implement a robust development strategy and the Afghan constitution and to promote human rights. They elaborated a number of key principles, designed to enhance further cooperation between Afghanistan and the international community.

The security situation in Afghanistan continued to be of paramount concern. Since March, the level of the insurgency had risen, as had the sophistication of the weaponry. The tactics used were more brutal and effective. The southern and parts of the eastern regions of the country had borne the brunt of the upsurge in violence. In a significant departure from their previous tactics, which focused on provincial authorities, international and national forces and election workers, insurgents started targeting local communities and their leaders. The Afghan National Army and the coalition forces intensified their operations in the south and parts of the east of the country, engaging insurgents in often prolonged combat. In the north, north-east, central highlands, central and most of the western region, minor factional clashes and criminal activity continued to be reported. A public demonstration, on 11 May, in Jalalabad (Nangarhar province), turned violent, causing widespread damage, with several casualties reported. With regard to electoral security, there had been multiple attacks against local JEMB employees and other Afghan electoral workers. Various measures were put in place by international military forces and the Government to help contain any upsurge in violence and to mitigate security risks to which the electoral process might be exposed.

The Secretary-General said that following the elections, he would consult with the Afghan Government and international actors to determine the post-electoral agenda. At the conclusion of those discussions, and prior to the expiration of UNAMA's mandate in March 2006, he would make specific proposals to the Council on the future UN role in Afghanistan.

Security Council consideration (August). On 23 August [meeting 5249], the Security Council discussed the situation in Afghanistan. The Secretary-General's Special Representative for Afghanistan told the Council that bringing extremist violence and other forms of insecurity under control after the 18 September elections would remain at the top of the agenda for the Afghan Government. Post-election objectives included the strengthening of key State institutions, such as the police, justice and civilian administration; the development of a comprehensive reconstruction strategy; and the elimination of the narcotics industry. The international community appeared committed to working with Afghan authorities towards an extended compact, with benchmarks and timelines for the achievement of its objectives. In the next phase, international financial, technical and security resources would be indispensable to the Afghan State's own political will and fiscal efforts. In that respect, the Afghan Government had proposed that a high-level conference on the post-Bonn compact be held in January 2006, shortly after the anticipated inauguration of the National Assembly. The proposed conference could also lead to closer links between Afghanistan and its neighbours in all fields, including security cooperation, trade, development and counter-narcotics efforts.

SECURITY COUNCIL ACTION

On 23 August [meeting 5249], following consultations among Security Council members, the President made statement **S/PRST/2005/40** on behalf of the Council:

The Security Council welcomes the progress in the preparations for the parliamentary (Wolesi Jirga) and provincial council elections scheduled for 18 September 2005, including the compilation of the final candidate list and updating of voter registration, and encourages all Afghan participants, especially the candidates and their supporters, to work constructively to ensure that the ongoing electoral campaigns are conducted peacefully, in an environment free of intimidation, and that the elections can be held successfully. The Council calls upon the international community to extend additional financial assistance in order to fill the gap of 29.6 million United States dollars for these elections.

The Council expresses grave concern about the increased attacks by the Taliban, Al Qaida and other extremist groups in Afghanistan over the past few months. The Council condemns the attempts to disrupt the political process by terrorist acts or other forms of violence in Afghanistan. The Council, in this regard, endorses the effort of the Government of Afghanistan, with the support of the ISAF and the Operation Enduring Freedom coalition, within their respective responsibilities, to improve the safety and stability of the country.

The Council also stresses the importance of continued cooperation and increased dialogue between neighbouring States and the Government of Afghanistan to promote regional development and the long-term peace and stability of Afghanistan.

The Council notes the progress made to date, in particular in security sector reform, and in this regard welcomes the completion of the disarmament of the Afghan Military Forces. The Council expresses its strong view that the international community must maintain a high level of commitment to assist Afghanistan in addressing its remaining challenges, including the security situation, disbandment of illegal armed groups, production of and trafficking in drugs, development of Afghan government institutions, acceleration of justice sector reform, promotion and protection of human rights, and sustainable economic and social development.

The Council welcomes the desire of the international community and the Government of Afghanistan to agree to a new framework for international engagement beyond the completion of the Bonn political process. The Council expresses, in this regard, its readiness to review, based on the report of the Secretary-General to be submitted in accordance with its resolution 1589(2005), and in the light of consultations that the United Nations will have with the Government of Afghanistan and all concerned international actors, the mandate of the United Nations Assistance Mission in Afghanistan after the completion of the electoral process, in order to allow the United Nations to continue to play a vital role in the post-Bonn period. The Council is also ready to consider the renewal of the mandate of the International Security Assistance Force prior to its expiration, upon the request of the Government of Afghanistan.

Communication. By a 17 October letter to the Secretary-General [A/60/440-S/2005/658], Yemen transmitted the final communiqué of the annual coordination meeting of the Ministers for Foreign Affairs of the States members of the Organization of the Islamic Conference (OIC) (New York, 23 September). OIC member States that had pledged donations to the Afghan People Assistance Fund were called upon to expedite the remittance of their donations.

Elections

On 18 September 2005, some 6.4 million Afghans, representing a little over 50 per cent of registered voters, went to the polls to elect representatives to the Lower House of the National Assembly and the 34 provincial councils. The Secretary-General, in a later report [A/60/712-S/2006/145], said that 54 candidates were excluded from the electoral process by the Electoral Complaints Commission. The Commission also adjudicated 3,300 of the some 5,400 complaints lodged, including 575 high-priority cases, most of them alleging fraud. It imposed fines in 22 cases, banned nine officials from serving in future electoral administrations and excluded 74 ballot boxes (2.5 per cent) from the count because of clear indications of fraud. Having received notification from the Electoral Complaints Commission that no remaining complaints could materially alter the outcome of the elections, JEMB announced the final certified results on 12 November. The new Lower House reflected Afghanistan's political and ethnic diversity, including a large number of professionals, liberals, some former commanders, jihadis, a small number of reconciled Taliban, and some individuals accused of human rights abuses. Twenty-seven per cent of all seats were occupied by women, who also were elected to 121 of the 420 seats available in the provincial councils. In November, each provincial council elected from among its members two representatives to serve in the Upper House. The full complement of the National Assembly was reached on 9 December, with the certification by JEMB of the 34 members, including 17 women, nominated by President Karzai. The electoral process was concluded on 19 December with the inauguration of the National Assembly.

Despite fears that violence would disrupt the process, especially given the trend of attacks in the preceding months, which included the murder of eight candidates, security incidents did not significantly affect the polling. However, the counting and the complaints processes that followed took place in a climate of tension and distrust, due to their complexity. More significantly, the tension was fuelled by thousands of defeated candidates, many of whom were reluctant to acknowledge their electoral defeat. Significant protests and demonstrations took place in Kunduz, Kandahar, Nangarhar and Kabul, which resulted in some disruption to the counting process.

SECURITY COUNCIL ACTION (November)

On 23 November [meeting 5309], following consultations among Security Council members, the President made statement **S/PRST/2005/56** on behalf of the Council:

The Security Council congratulates the people of Afghanistan on the confirmation of the final results of the parliamentary and provincial council elections. The successful holding of these elections has demonstrated the broad commitment of Afghan voters to democracy and freedom in their country, and the Council welcomes the fact that the completion of the confirmation process has paved the way toward the timely inauguration of the new parliament and thus to the conclusion of the Bonn political process.

The Council commends all Afghans for having taken this step and calls upon them, and, in particular, the representatives-elect and other former candidates, to remain fully committed to peace, the Constitution, the rule of law and democracy in Afghanistan.

The Council, in this connection, reiterates its appreciation to all those who contributed to the electoral process, and extends special appreciation to the Joint Electoral Management Body and the United Nations Assistance Mission in Afghanistan for their dedication. The Council also reiterates its endorsement of the efforts of the Afghan security forces, with the support of the International Security Assistance Force and the Operation Enduring Freedom coalition, within their respective responsibilities, to improve the safety and stability of the country.

The Council hopes for the prompt appointment of all members of the House of Elders (Meshrano Jirga).

The Council reaffirms the importance for the international community to maintain a high level of commitment to assisting Afghanistan in addressing its remaining challenges, in particular in the fields of security, including fighting terrorist and narcotics threats, governance and development.

The Council supports the central and impartial role that the United Nations continues to play for the consolidation of peace and stability in Afghanistan and coordination of the relevant international efforts and welcomes consultations initiated by the Government of Afghanistan and the United Nations on the post-Bonn process.

Finally, the Council stresses that violence in any form intended to disrupt the democratic process in Afghanistan will not be tolerated. The Council unequivocally condemns all recent attacks in Afghanistan, including the attacks against the International Security Assistance Force, and expresses its deepest sympathies to the victims, both Afghan and international, and their families, as well as to the troop contributors of the Force.

Later developments

In a later report on the situation in Afghanistan [A/60/712-S/2006/145], the Secretary-General said that, during the last months of 2005, the operational tempo and tactical sophistication of insurgent and other anti-Government elements continued to develop. Violence and threats against local officials, religious leaders, teachers, staff and facilities of the education system intensified, in particular in the south and south-east of the country. Corruption, the menace of a criminalized economy, dominated by drug and other organized criminal networks, and the presence of illegally armed groups, undermined the authority of the legitimately elected Government. In addition, there was a marked increase in suicide bombings. Up to November, a significant proportion of security related incidents involved clashes between anti-Government elements and security forces, primarily international military forces. Since most of those incidents resulted in the defeat of anti-Government elements, attacks against foreign military forces decreased in favour of attacks against Afghan security forces and soft targets (Government and social institutions) that were difficult to detect or identify.

Communication. On 2 December [A/60/578-S/2005/754], the Russian Federation transmitted to the Secretary-General the text of the Declaration adopted by the Ministers for Foreign Affairs of the member States of the Collective Security Treaty Organization (Moscow, Russian Federation, 30 November). The members said that, in view of the serious situation caused by the sharp increase in drug trafficking worldwide, there was an urgent need to establish under UN auspices, an effective global anti-drug partnership, which should make every effort to set up security zones along the Afghan border.

GENERAL ASSEMBLY ACTION

On 30 November [meeting 58], the General Assembly adopted **resolution 60/32 A** [draft: A/60/L.27 & Add.1, as orally revised] without vote [agenda items 17 and 73 *(e)*].

The situation in Afghanistan and its implications for international peace and security

The General Assembly,

Recalling its resolution 59/112 A of 8 December 2004 and all its previous relevant resolutions,

Recalling also all relevant Security Council resolutions and statements by the President of the Council on the situation in Afghanistan, in particular the most recent resolutions 1589(2005) of 24 March 2005 and 1623(2005) of 13 September 2005, as well as the statement by the President of the Council of 23 August 2005,

Reaffirming its strong commitment to the sovereignty, independence, territorial integrity and national unity of Afghanistan, and respecting its multicultural, multiethnic and historical heritage,

Applauding the holding of parliamentary and provincial council elections on 18 September 2005, leading to the completion of the Bonn process,

Emphasizing the importance of the Government being representative of the ethnic, cultural and geographical diversity of the country,

Recalling Security Council resolution 1325(2000) of 31 October 2000 on women and peace and security, and applauding the substantive progress achieved in the empowerment of women in Afghan politics as historic milestones in the political process, which will help to consolidate durable peace and national stability in Afghanistan,

Recognizing the urgent need to tackle the remaining challenges in Afghanistan, including terrorist threats, the fight against narcotics, the lack of security in certain areas, the comprehensive nationwide disbandment of illegal armed groups and the reintegration of the Afghan Military Forces, the development of Afghan Government institutions, including at the subnational level, the strengthening of the rule of law, the acceleration of justice sector reform, the promotion of national reconciliation and an Afghan-led transitional justice process, the safe and orderly return of Afghan refugees, the promotion and protection of human rights, and economic and social development,

Reaffirming in this context its continued support for the spirit and the provisions of the Bonn Agreement of 5 December 2001, and of the Berlin Declaration, including the annexes thereto, of 1 April 2004, and pledging its continued support, after the successful completion of the political transition, to the Government and people of Afghanistan as they rebuild their country, strengthen the foundations of a constitutional democracy and resume their rightful place in the community of nations,

Expressing its appreciation and strong support for the central and impartial role that the Secretary-General and his Special Representative continue to play for the consolidation of peace and stability in Afghanistan, and welcoming consultations initiated by the Government of Afghanistan and the United Nations on the post-Bonn process,

Expressing in this context its deep concern over attacks against both Afghan and foreign nationals committed to supporting the consolidation of peace, stability and development in Afghanistan, in particular United Nations and diplomatic staff, national and international humanitarian and development personnel, the International Security Assistance Force and the Operation Enduring Freedom coalition,

Noting that, despite improvements in building the security sector, increased terrorist attacks caused by Al-Qaida operatives, the Taliban and other extremist groups, particularly in the south and in parts of the east of Afghanistan over the past months, and the lack of security caused by criminal activity and the illicit production of and trafficking in drugs, still remain a serious challenge, threatening the democratic process as well as reconstruction and economic development,

Noting also that the responsibility for providing security and law and order throughout the country resides with the Government of Afghanistan supported by the Assistance Force and the Operation Enduring Freedom coalition, recognizing the progress achieved in this respect, and stressing the importance of further extending central government authority to all parts of Afghanistan,

Commending the Afghan national army and police, the Assistance Force and the Operation Enduring Freedom coalition for their contributions in improving security conditions, including for the electoral process, in Afghanistan,

Deeply concerned about the continued cultivation, production of and trafficking in narcotic drugs in Afghanistan, which is undermining stability and security as well as the political and economic reconstruction of Afghanistan and which has dangerous repercussions in the region and far beyond, and commending in that context the reaffirmed commitment of the Government of Afghanistan to rid the country of this pernicious production and trade, including by decisive law enforcement measures and by combating corruption, which have led to a decrease in opium cultivation in 2005,

Recognizing that the social and economic development of Afghanistan, specifically the development of alternative gainful and sustainable livelihoods in the formal productive sector, is an important element of the successful implementation of the comprehensive Afghan national drug control strategy and depends to a large extent on enhanced international cooperation with the Government of Afghanistan,

1. *Welcomes* the report of the Secretary-General and the recommendations contained therein;

2. *Congratulates* the people of Afghanistan on the parliamentary and provincial council elections on 18 September 2005, which have demonstrated the broad commitment of Afghan voters towards a democratic future for their country;

3. *Expresses its appreciation* for the support of the United Nations Assistance Mission in Afghanistan and of the international community, including from countries neighbouring Afghanistan, which facilitated the holding of parliamentary and provincial council elections through providing security assistance, funds, election personnel and observers;

4. *Recognizes* the upcoming completion of the political transition according to the Bonn process, with the establishment of the National Assembly of Afghanistan, as well as the challenges lying ahead, and calls upon the international community to continue to provide sustained support;

5. *Endorses* the key principles for cooperation between the Government of Afghanistan and the international community during the post-Bonn process as set out in the report of the Secretary-General, including the leadership role of Afghanistan in the reconstruction process, the just allocation of domestic and international reconstruction resources across the country, regional cooperation, lasting capacity- and institution-building, combating corruption and the promotion of transparency and accountability, public information and participation, and the continued central role of the United Nations in the post-Bonn process, which should also include fields in which the United Nations offers the best expertise available;

6. *Welcomes* the readiness of the Government of Afghanistan to prepare an interim national development strategy, which is to be considered at a conference in London planned for January 2006, where a new engagement between the international community and the Government of Afghanistan is also due to be concluded, and urges the international community actively to support this process by, where possible, aligning their support behind this strategy;

7. *Stresses* the importance of the provision of sufficient security in the post-Bonn process, and to that end calls upon Member States to continue contributing personnel, equipment and other resources to the International Security Assistance Force and to further develop the provincial reconstruction teams in close coordination with the Government of Afghanistan and the Assistance Mission;

8. *Welcomes* the progress made since the commencement of the disarmament, demobilization and reintegration process in October 2003, in particular the completion of the disarmament and demobilization of the Afghan Military Forces, and stresses the need to reintegrate former combatants for the success of the programme;

9. *Stresses* the importance of advancing the disbandment of illegal armed groups throughout the country, while ensuring further coordination and coherence with other relevant efforts regarding security sector reform and community development;

10. *Welcomes* the development of the new professional Afghan national army and Afghan national police and the progress made in the creation of a fair and effective justice system as important steps towards the goal of strengthening the Government of Afghanistan, providing security, ensuring the rule of law and eliminating corruption throughout the country, and urges the international community to continue to support the efforts of the Government of Afghanistan in these areas in a coordinated manner;

11. *Calls upon* the Government of Afghanistan, with the assistance of the international community, including through the Operation Enduring Freedom coalition and the Assistance Force, in accordance with their respective designated responsibilities, to continue to address the threat to the security and stability of Afghanistan posed by Al-Qaida operatives, the Taliban and other terrorist or extremist groups as well as by criminal violence, in particular violence involving the drug trade;

12. *Calls for* full respect for human rights and international humanitarian law throughout Afghanistan and, with the assistance of the Afghan Independent Human Rights Commission and of the Assistance Mission, full implementation of the human rights provisions of the new Afghan Constitution, including those regarding the full enjoyment by women of their human rights, and commends the commitment of the Government of Afghanistan in this respect;

13. *Welcomes* the efforts to date of the Afghan authorities to carry out their comprehensive counternarcotics implementation plan presented on 16 February 2005, and urges the Government of Afghanistan to take decisive action, in particular to stop the processing of and trade in drugs, by pursuing the concrete steps set out in the work plan of the Government of Afghanistan, presented at the International Conference on Afghanistan, held in Berlin on 31 March and 1 April 2004;

14. *Calls upon* the international community to assist the Government of Afghanistan in carrying out its comprehensive counter-narcotics implementation plan, aimed at eliminating illicit poppy cultivation, including through support for increased law enforcement, interdiction, demand reduction, eradication of illicit crops, crop substitution and other alternative livelihood and development programmes, increasing public awareness and building the capacity of drug control institutions, and encourages the channelling of increased counter-narcotics funding through the Government of Afghanistan counter-narcotics trust fund;

15. *Supports* the fight against the illicit trafficking in drugs and precursors within Afghanistan and in neighbouring States and countries along trafficking routes, including increased cooperation among them to strengthen anti-narcotic controls to curb the drug flow, and welcomes, in this context, the signing on 1 April 2004 of the Berlin Declaration on Counter-Narcotics within the framework of the Kabul Declaration on Good-neighbourly Relations of 22 December 2002;

16. *Commends* the continuing efforts of the signatories of the Kabul Declaration on Good-neighbourly Relations to implement their commitments under the Declaration, including, within that framework, those under the Declaration on Encouraging Closer Trade, Transit and Investment Cooperation of 22 September 2003, and calls upon all other States to respect and support the implementation of those provisions and to promote regional stability;

17. *Appreciates* the efforts of the members of the Tripartite Commission, namely, Afghanistan, Pakistan and the United States of America, to continue to address cross-border activities in accordance with its mandate;

18. *Calls for* the provision of continued international assistance to the vast number of Afghan refugees and internally displaced persons to facilitate their safe and orderly return and sustainable reintegration into society so as to contribute to the stability of the entire country;

19. *Requests* the Secretary-General to report to the General Assembly every six months during its sixtieth session on developments in Afghanistan, including on parliamentary and provincial elections and on consultations on the post-Bonn process as well as on the progress made in the implementation of the present resolution;

20. *Decides* to include in the provisional agenda of its sixty-first session an item entitled the situation in Afghanistan.

On the same date, the Assembly adopted **resolution 60/32 B** on emergency international assistance for peace, normalcy and reconstruction of war-stricken Afghanistan (see p. 1000).

Sectoral issues

Judicial system and the rule of law

The United Nations continued to support the reform agenda drawn up by the Judicial Reform Commission, established under the Bonn Agreement. In the light of the lack of clarity in the Commission's mandate and capacity to lead the reform, the Government was gradually shifting responsibility for reform from the Commission to the Supreme Court, the Attorney-General's office and the Ministry of Justice. Those bodies coordinated their efforts through the Consultative Group for Justice, which had become an active player in shaping the reform strategy. The Group, with UNDP and UNAMA support, was developing a comprehensive needs assessment to serve as a basis for future justice sector reform efforts. The strategy would have to address critical issues, including finding an appropriate balance between capacity development and institutional reform. With UNDP support, the Ministry of Justice and the Attorney-General made significant progress in the implementation of the Government's public administrative reform programme. In June, the Law on the Organization and Jurisdiction of the Courts came into force and the Juvenile Justice Code and the Law on Prisons and Detention Centres were adopted. A number of justice sector facilities were rehabilitated and work was under way on new court houses in Herat and in other regions. The Ministry of Justice and the Attorney-General's office, assisted by UNDP, completed the first phase of the Government's priority reform and restructuring process and had commenced the second phase, which required merit-based recruitment of all Ministry of Justice staff under a revised structure. In June, the Judicial Education and Training Committee was established, which was to develop a more coordinated approach to the planning, implementation and evaluation of programmes for judges. In October, the Government endorsed a strategic framework for justice sector reform, entitled "Justice for All", developed by the Consultative Group on Justice. The framework was divided into five areas: law reform, institution-building, access to justice programmes, traditional justice and coordination.

Security sector reform

The reform of the security sector was in its fourth and final phase, making the sector more representative of the demographic realities of the country. Some 965 junior officers within the Ministry of Defence were to be appointed in an attempt to redress previous imbalances in the composition of the Ministry. Training of the reformed Afghan Army continued, with the United States, assisted by France, acting as lead nation. The training schedule was accelerated, allowing five battalions to be trained simultaneously. Plans to train six battalions at a time, to be implemented in March, would enable the Army to reach its target of 70,000 troops by December 2006.

In June, Germany and United States—lead coalition forces—proposed a major new police reform and mentoring programme to the Government and the international community. In December, as part of the restructuring of police leadership, and following an extensive selection process, 31 generals were identified and had taken up senior police positions in the Ministry of Interior.

Disarmament, demobilization and reintegration

On 7 July, Afghanistan's New Beginnings Programme for disarmament, demobilization and reintegration ended, with more than 63,380 (all ranks) Afghan Military Forces troops disarmed. Of those, more than 59,290 were demobilized and over 57,590 had chosen to enter the reintegration process. The Programme enabled the Government to remove all Afghan Military Forces personnel from the Ministry of Defence payroll, resulting in an estimated saving to the national budget of a recurrent cost of over $120 million and effectively dissolving the Afghan Military Forces. The Programme was currently focused on ensuring the sustainable reintegration of ex-combatants into their communities and the legal economy, which included a project to monitor and evaluate the progress made by those who had completed the reintegration programme.

A crucial outcome of the disarmament, demobilization and reintegration process was the safe removal and cantonment of over 10,880 heavy weapons. Cities such as Jalalabad, Kandahar, Gardiz, Mazar-e-Sharif and Bamian were largely free of operational heavy weapons. Progress in disarmament, demobilization and reintegration helped to improve the political environment for the organization of elections, and together with the creation of the Afghan National Army, furthered the goal of ensuring that military assets and weaponry belonged to the State of Afghanistan alone. Progress was made in the design of the successor project to disarmament, demobilization and reintegration, which would concentrate on enhancing security, governance, access to justice and community-based economic and social benefits.

Counter-narcotics activities

The illicit narcotics industry continued to pose a threat to peace and stability in Afghanistan, which remained the largest supplier of opium worldwide. Government-led eradication and interdiction efforts had yielded modest results in some areas; however, that had been offset by higher crop yields. In January, the Executive Director of UNODC encouraged the Government and major partners to make development assistance available to farmers to offset their income losses and to make joint efforts to provide mutual legal assistance and create conditions for the extradition of major traffickers. On 16 February, the Government of Afghanistan and the United Kingdom, the lead nation on counter-narcotics, launched the 2005 counter-narcotics implementation plan in Kabul. With 60 per cent of Afghanistan's opium being produced in the provinces of Badakhshan, Helmand and Nangarhar, the new plan initially concentrated Afghan and international efforts on eradication and the creation of alternative livelihoods in those provinces, as well as in Kandahar.

Following the large-scale Government-led anti-cultivation campaign, land under poppy cultivation was estimated to have dropped by 21 per cent. Nevertheless, the average yield of the poppy crop increased to an estimated 39 kilograms per hectare in 2005, compared with 32 kilograms per hectare in 2004. Eradication efforts by provincial governors in 2005 did not achieve the expected success; only some 4,000 hectares (or 4 per cent of the total poppy fields under cultivation) were eradicated. In December, a UNODC survey indicated that some 920,000 Afghans (3.8 per cent of the population) were drug users. In recognition of the urgent need to stem the cycle of insecurity promoted by the narcotics industry, the Government adopted a new Counter-Narcotics Law on 17 December, containing criminal and procedural provisions, including investigation, prosecution and trial, and established the jurisdiction of the Central Narcotics Tribunal.

Recovery, rehabilitation and reconstruction

The economic and developmental challenges facing Afghanistan remained daunting. Although the International Monetary Fund reported that the Afghan economy grew at a rate of 7.5 per cent in 2004-2005, the Government estimated that a growth rate of 9 per cent was required to achieve recovery. In January, the UN country team started developing the United Nations Development Assistance Framework for Afghanistan, which identified those development activities that UN agencies would undertake for the 2006-2008 period. The country's first national human development report entitled "Security with a Human Face" was launched on 21 February. As the country devised its long-term development strategy, the report recommended addressing links between poverty reduction, democracy and conflict prevention to lay the foundation for sustained economic growth and stability. In September, the Government endorsed a report on the MDGs, which provided the framework for the Interim Afghanistan National Development Strategy. In December, the country programme action plans of UNDP, UNICEF and the United Nations Population Fund, as well as the World Food Programme relief and recovery operation, were agreed upon with the Minister for Foreign Affairs.

Social aspects

The human rights situation in Afghanistan remained challenging, owing to the security situation and weaknesses in governance. Impunity of factional commanders and former warlords undermined any improvements. The significant upsurge in violence in some parts of the country limited access to those areas by both international humanitarian actors and Government representatives, denying the population entitlements, services and protection. Complaints of serious human rights violations committed by representatives of national security institutions, including arbitrary arrest, illegal detention and torture were numerous. In January, the United Nations High Commissioner visited Afghanistan and, in February, the Secretary-General's Independent Expert on the situation of human rights in Afghanistan also visited the country (see p. 733). In the months prior to the parliamentary elections, just as was the case in 2004 for the presidential elections, a joint political rights verification exercise was carried out by the Afghanistan Independent Human Rights Commission and UNAMA to bring human rights concerns to the attention of the Government, the public and the international community.

A welcome development was the issuance of an order by the Ministry of Interior on 30 November, outlining expectations regarding police adherence to international human rights standards and the terms of reference for new human rights offices to be established within provincial Afghan National Police headquarters. On 12 December, the Government adopted the National Action Plan on Peace, Reconciliation and Justice, which was based on recommendations made by the Afghanistan Independent Human Rights Commission. Following the adoption of the plan, which set out a three-year comprehensive strategy on transitional justice, a three-day conference on truth-seeking and reconciliation was hosted by the Office of the United Nations High Commissioner for Human Rights (OHCHR), with support from UNAMA and the Afghanistan Independent Human Rights Commission. The conference was attended by representatives of local government and civil society. Participants said the highest priority should be given to: ending impunity, prosecuting and removing human rights abusers from public service and other positions of authority.

UNAMA

The United Nations Assistance Mission in Afghanistan was established by Security Council resolution 1401(2002) [YUN 2002, p. 264] to promote, among other things, national reconciliation and the responsibilities entrusted to the United Nations under the Bonn Agreement. It comprised the Office of the Special Representative, which included four special advisers in the fields of human rights, demobilization, gender and the rule of law, as well as three sub-components: two substantive pillars, one political (Pillar I) and one relief, recovery and reconstruction (Pillar II), and an administrative component. UNAMA was headquartered in Kabul, with regional offices in Bamiyan, Gardez, Herat, Jalalabad, Kandahar, Kunduz and Mazar-e-Sharif and three sub-offices in Faizabad, Maimana and Panjao. UNAMA was headed by the Special Representative of the Secretary-General. In December, the Secretary-General appointed Tom Koenings (Germany) as Special Representative and Head of UNAMA to replace Jean Arnault (France). By **resolution 1589(2005)** (see p. 399), the Security Council extended UNAMA's mandate until 24 March 2006.

International Security Assistance Force

During the year, the Secretary-General submitted to the Security Council, in accordance with Council resolution 1386(2001) [YUN 2001, p. 267] and 1510(2003) [YUN 2003, p. 310], reports on the activities of ISAF in February [S/2005/131], April [S/2005/230], July [S/2005/431] and October [S/2005/634]. Activities from October to the end of the year were covered in a later report [S/2006/318].

ISAF continued to implement the activities mandated by Council resolution 1386(2001) to assist the Afghan Government in the maintenance of security in Kabul and its surrounding areas and, by resolution 1510(2003), to provide support for and to strengthen the ability of the Government to ensure a more secure environment throughout the country. It executed its security tasks in association with the Afghan National Army and the Kabul police.

As at 30 August, the Force, operating under NATO leadership, comprised 11,551 personnel from 26 NATO nations, plus 309 from 11 non-NATO nations.

The overall security situation in Kabul and its environs remained relatively calm but unstable, with continual warnings of attacks against ISAF, coalition forces and the Afghan Government. The northern area of ISAF operations experienced a steady rise in criminal activity and factional fighting. The western area, where opposing militant forces were less active, remained relatively free of terrorism and crime. The security situation outside ISAF area of operations, mainly in the southern and eastern regions of the country, remained tense due to the activity of those forces.

ISAF increased its military presence in the country in preparation for and in support of the 18 September elections in order to verify procedures and enhance security. ISAF also carried out a strategic assessment of air operations to identify airfields, air capabilities and infrastructure for ISAF to continue its mission in the medium to long term. However, NATO intended to hand over the entire responsibility for Kabul International Airport to the Afghan authorities in the longer term. To that end, a clearing house mechanism was set up to coordinate efforts for the rehabilitation of Afghan airspace management.

ISAF civil-military cooperation shifted its focus from quick-reaction projects and short-term assessment to a more long-term vision aimed at meeting Afghan needs and harmonizing the activities of the international community. Improving civil administration remained the first priority. ISAF helped identify actual needs, promoted the use of respective functional specialists, and acted as a mediator for training and funding issues. Progress was also being made in the reform of the justice sector, including training, facility-building and restoration, as well as the reform of the Ministry of Justice, the Supreme Court and the Office of the General Prosecutor.

Among other things, ISAF established links with counter-narcotics forces and agencies. The Afghan Government counter-narcotics implementation plan (see p. 1357) was coordinated with ISAF, coalition forces and embassy counter-narcotics specialists. The plan adopted an eight-pillar approach, focusing on building institutions, information campaigns, alternative livelihoods, law enforcement, criminal justice, eradication, demand reduction, treatment of addicts and regional cooperation.

Afghanistan, in a 1 September [S/2005/574] letter to the Secretary-General, said that it looked forward to ISAF's future expansion to the south and east of the country and hoped that the Security Council would continue to reflect in its resolutions the importance of fulfilling ISAF's mandate.

The Secretary-General, in a later report on the situation in Afghanistan [A/60/712], reported that, on 8 December, the NATO Foreign Ministers adopted a revised ISAF operational plan which provided for ISAF's expansion to the southern regions of Afghanistan.

Extension of ISAF mandate

On 13 September [meeting 5260], the Security Council unanimously adopted **resolution 1623 (2005)**. The draft [S/2005/576] was prepared in consultations among Council members.

The Security Council,

Reaffirming its previous resolutions on Afghanistan, in particular resolutions 1386(2001) of 20 December 2001, 1413(2002) of 23 May 2002, 1444(2002) of 27 November 2002, 1510(2003) of 13 October 2003 and 1563 (2004) of 17 September 2004,

Reaffirming its strong commitment to the sovereignty, independence, territorial integrity and national unity of Afghanistan,

Reaffirming its resolutions 1368(2001) of 12 September 2001 and 1373(2001) of 28 September 2001, and reiterating its support for international efforts to root out terrorism in accordance with the Charter of the United Nations,

Recognizing that the responsibility for providing security and law and order throughout the country resides with the Afghans themselves, and welcoming the cooperation of the Government of Afghanistan with the International Security Assistance Force,

Recalling the importance of the Bonn Agreement of 5 December 2001 and the Berlin Declaration of 1 April 2004, in particular annex 1 to the Bonn Agreement, which, inter alia, provides for the progressive expansion of the Force to other urban centres and other areas beyond Kabul,

Stressing the importance of extending central government authority to all parts of Afghanistan, of respect for democratic values, of full completion of the disarmament, demobilization and reintegration process, of the disbandment of illegal armed groups, of justice sector reform, of security sector reform, including reconstitution of the Afghan National Army and Police, and of combating narcotics trade and production, and recognizing certain progress that has been made in these and other areas with the help of the international community,

Recognizing the challenges facing Afghanistan with regard to the security situation in parts of the country,

Welcoming, in this context, the commitment by lead nations of the North Atlantic Treaty Organization to establish further Provincial Reconstruction Teams,

Further welcoming the role played by the Force and the Operation Enduring Freedom coalition in assisting in securing the conduct of national elections,

Expressing its appreciation to Italy for taking over the lead from Turkey in commanding the Force, and to those nations who contributed to Eurocorps, and recognizing with gratitude the contributions of many nations to the Force,

Taking note of the letter dated 1 September 2005 from Mr. Abdullah Abdullah, Minister for Foreign Affairs of Afghanistan, to the Secretary-General,

Determining that the situation in Afghanistan still constitutes a threat to international peace and security,

Determined to ensure the full implementation of the mandate of the Force, in consultation with the Government of Afghanistan,

Acting, for these reasons, under Chapter VII of the Charter,

1. *Decides* to extend the authorization of the International Security Assistance Force, as defined in resolutions 1386(2001) and 1510(2003), for a period of twelve months beyond 13 October 2005;

2. *Authorizes* the Member States participating in the Force to take all necessary measures to fulfil its mandate;

3. *Recognizes* the need to strengthen the Force, and in this regard calls upon Member States to contribute personnel, equipment and other resources to the Force, and to make contributions to the trust fund established pursuant to resolution 1386(2001);

4. *Calls upon* the Force to continue to work in close consultation with the Government of Afghanistan and the Special Representative of the Secretary-General for Afghanistan as well as with the Operation Enduring Freedom coalition in the implementation of the mandate of the Force;

5. *Requests* the leadership of the Force to provide quarterly reports on the implementation of the mandate of the Force to the Security Council through the Secretary-General;

6. *Decides* to remain actively seized of the matter.

Sanctions

In 2005, the Security Council adopted new measures against Osama bin Laden, Al-Qaida, the Taliban, their associates and associated entities. By resolution 1617(2005) (see below), the Council further refined the financial measures, travel ban and arms embargo imposed on those persons identified in the consolidated list created pursuant to resolution 1267(1999) [YUN 1999, p. 265].

Pursuant to that resolution, the Secretary-General, on 2 September [S/2005/563], informed the Council President that he had appointed eight experts to the Analytical Support and Sanctions Monitoring Team, established in accordance with resolution 1526(2004) [YUN 2004, p. 332].

SECURITY COUNCIL ACTION (July)

On 29 July [meeting 5244], the Security Council unanimously adopted **resolution 1617(2005)**. The draft [S/2005/495] was submitted by Algeria, Argentina, Denmark, France, Greece, Japan, Romania, the Russian Federation, the United Republic of Tanzania, the United Kingdom and the United States.

The Security Council,

Recalling its resolutions 1267(1999) of 15 October 1999, 1333(2000) of 19 December 2000, 1363(2001) of 30 July 2001, 1373(2001) of 28 September 2001, 1390 (2002) of 16 January 2002, 1452(2002) of 20 December 2002, 1455(2003) of 17 January 2003, 1526(2004) of 30 January 2004 and 1566(2004) of 8 October 2004, and the relevant statements by its President,

Reaffirming that terrorism in all its forms and manifestations constitutes one of the most serious threats to peace and security and that any acts of terrorism are criminal and unjustifiable regardless of their motivations, whenever and by whomsoever committed, and reiterating its unequivocal condemnation of Al-Qaida, Osama bin Laden, the Taliban—and associated individuals, groups, undertakings and entities—for ongoing and multiple criminal terrorist acts aimed at causing the death of innocent civilians and other victims, destruction of property and greatly undermining stability,

Expressing its concern over the use of various media, including the Internet, by Al-Qaida, Osama bin Laden and the Taliban, and their associates, including for terrorist propaganda and inciting terrorist violence, and urging the Security Council Working Group established pursuant to resolution 1566(2004) to consider these issues,

Reaffirming the need to combat by all means, in accordance with the Charter of the United Nations and international law, threats to international peace and security caused by terrorist acts, stressing in this regard the important role the United Nations plays in leading and coordinating this effort,

Emphasizing the obligation placed upon all Member States to implement, in full, resolution 1373(2001), including with regard to the Taliban or Al-Qaida, and any individuals, groups, undertakings or entities associated with Al-Qaida, Osama bin Laden or the Taliban who have participated in financing, planning, facilitating, recruiting for, preparing, perpetrating, or otherwise supporting terrorist activities or acts, as well as to facilitate the implementation of counter-terrorism obligations in accordance with relevant Security Council resolutions,

Stressing the importance of clarifying which individuals, groups, undertakings and entities are subject to listing in the light of information regarding the changing nature of, and threat from, Al-Qaida, particularly as reported by the Analytical Support and Sanctions Monitoring Team of the Security Council Committee established pursuant to resolution 1267(1999) (the "Monitoring Team"),

Underscoring the importance of Member State designations pursuant to relevant resolutions and robust implementation of existing measures as a significant preventive measure in combating terrorist activity,

Noting that, in giving effect to the measures outlined in paragraph 4 *(b)* of resolution 1267(1999), paragraph 8 *(c)* of resolution 1333(2000) and paragraphs 1 and 2 of resolution 1390(2002), full account is to be taken of the provisions of paragraphs 1 and 2 of resolution 1452(2002),

Welcoming the efforts of the International Civil Aviation Organization to prevent travel documents from being made available to terrorists and their associates,

Encouraging Member States to work within the framework of Interpol, in particular through the use of the Interpol database of stolen and lost travel documents, to reinforce the implementation of the measures against Al-Qaida, Osama bin Laden and the Taliban, and their associates,

Expressing its concern over the possible use by Al-Qaida, Osama bin Laden or the Taliban, and their associates, of man-portable air defence systems, commercially available explosives and chemical, biological, radiation or nuclear weapons and material, and encouraging Member States to consider possible action to reduce these threats,

Urging all States, international bodies and regional organizations to allocate sufficient resources, including through international partnership, to meet the ongoing and direct threat posed by Al-Qaida, Osama bin Laden and the Taliban, and individuals, groups, undertakings and entities associated with them,

Stressing the importance of meeting the ongoing threat that Al-Qaida, Osama bin Laden and the Taliban, and individuals, groups, undertakings and entities associated with them represent to international peace and security,

Acting under Chapter VII of the Charter,

1. *Decides* that all States shall take the measures as previously imposed by paragraph 4 *(b)* of resolution 1267(1999), paragraph 8 *(c)* of resolution 1333(2000) and paragraphs 1 and 2 of resolution 1390(2002) with respect to Al-Qaida, Osama bin Laden and the Taliban and other individuals, groups, undertakings and entities associated with them, as referred to in the list created pursuant to resolutions 1267(1999) and 1333 (2000) ("the Consolidated List"):

(a) Freeze without delay the funds and other financial assets or economic resources of those individuals, groups, undertakings and entities, including funds derived from property owned or controlled, directly or indirectly, by them or by persons acting on their behalf or at their direction, and ensure that neither these nor any other funds, financial assets or economic resources are made available, directly or indirectly, for the benefit of such persons, by their nationals or by any persons within their territory;

(b) Prevent the entry into or the transit through their territories of those individuals, provided that nothing in the present paragraph shall oblige any State to deny entry into or require the departure from its territories of its own nationals and that the present paragraph shall not apply where entry or transit is necessary for the fulfilment of a judicial process or the Security Council Committee established pursuant to resolution 1267(1999) ("the Committee") determines on a case-by-case basis only that entry or transit is justified;

(c) Prevent the direct or indirect supply, sale or transfer, to those individuals, groups, undertakings and entities from their territories or by their nationals outside their territories, or using their flag vessels or aircraft, of arms and related materiel of all types, including weapons and ammunition, military vehicles and equipment, paramilitary equipment and spare parts for the aforementioned, and technical advice, assistance, or training related to military activities;

2. *Also decides* that acts or activities indicating that an individual, group, undertaking or entity is "associated with" Al-Qaida, Osama bin Laden or the Taliban include:

(a) Participating in the financing, planning, facilitating, preparing or perpetrating of acts or activities by, in conjunction with, under the name of, on behalf of, or in support of;

(b) Supplying, selling or transferring arms and related materiel to;

(c) Recruiting for; or

(d) Otherwise supporting acts or activities of;

Al-Qaida, Osama bin Laden or the Taliban, or any cell, affiliate, splinter group or derivative thereof;

3. *Further decides* that any undertaking or entity owned or controlled, directly or indirectly, by, or otherwise supporting, such an individual, group, undertaking or entity associated with Al-Qaida, Osama bin Laden or the Taliban shall be eligible for designation;

4. *Decides* that, when proposing names for the Consolidated List, States shall act in accordance with paragraph 17 of resolution 1526(2004) and henceforth also shall provide to the Committee a statement of case describing the basis of the proposal, and further encour-

ages States to identify any undertakings and entities owned or controlled, directly or indirectly, by the proposed subject;

5. *Requests* relevant States to inform, to the extent possible, and in writing where possible, individuals and entities included in the Consolidated List of the measures imposed on them, the guidelines of the Committee, and, in particular, the listing and delisting procedures and the provisions of resolution 1452(2002);

6. *Decides* that the statement of case submitted by the designating State referred to in paragraph 4 above may be used by the Committee in responding to queries from Member States whose nationals, residents or entities have been included on the Consolidated List, decides also that the Committee may decide on a case-by-case basis to release the information to other parties, with the prior consent of the designating State, for example, for operational reasons or to aid the implementation of the measures, and decides further that States may continue to provide additional information which shall be kept on a confidential basis within the Committee unless the submitting State agrees to the dissemination of such information;

7. *Strongly urges* all Member States to implement the comprehensive, international standards embodied in the Forty Recommendations and the nine Special Recommendations on Terrorist Financing of the Financial Action Task Force on Money Laundering;

8. *Requests* the Secretary-General to take the necessary steps to increase cooperation between the United Nations and Interpol in order to provide the Committee with better tools to fulfil its mandate more effectively and to give Member States better tools to implement the measures referred to in paragraph 1 above;

9. *Urges* all Member States, in their implementation of the measures called for in paragraph 1 above, to ensure that stolen and lost passports and other travel documents are invalidated as soon as possible and to share information on those documents with other Member States through the Interpol database;

10. *Calls upon* all Member States to use the checklist contained in annex II to the present resolution to report to the Committee by 1 March 2006 on specific actions that they have taken to implement the measures outlined in paragraph 1 above with regard to individuals and entities henceforth added to the Consolidated List, and thereafter at intervals to be determined by the Committee;

11. *Directs* the Committee to encourage the submission of names and additional identifying information from Member States for inclusion on the Consolidated List;

12. *Calls upon* the Committee, working in cooperation with the Security Council Committee established pursuant to resolution 1373(2001) ("the Counter-Terrorism Committee") to inform the Council of specific additional steps that States could take to implement the measures outlined in paragraph 1 above;

13. *Reiterates* the need for ongoing close cooperation and exchange of information between the Committee, the Counter-Terrorism Committee and the Security Council Committee established pursuant to resolution 1540(2004), as well as their respective groups of experts, including enhanced information-sharing, coordinated visits to countries, technical assistance and other issues of relevance to all three committees;

14. *Also reiterates* the importance of having the Committee follow up via oral and/or written communications with Member States regarding effective implementation of the sanctions measures and provide Member States with an opportunity, at the request of the Committee, to send representatives to meet with the Committee for more in-depth discussion of relevant issues;

15. *Requests* the Committee to consider, where and when appropriate, visits to selected countries by the Chairman and/or Committee members to enhance the full and effective implementation of the measures referred to in paragraph 1 above, with a view to encouraging States to comply fully with the present resolution and resolutions 1267(1999), 1333(2000), 1390 (2002), 1455(2003) and 1526(2004);

16. *Also requests* the Committee to report orally, through its Chairman, at least every one hundred and twenty days to the Council on the overall work of the Committee and the Monitoring Team, and, as appropriate, in conjunction with the reports by the Chairmen of the Counter-Terrorism Committee and the Committee established pursuant to resolution 1540 (2004), including briefings for all interested Member States;

17. *Reminds* the Committee of its responsibilities as outlined in paragraph 14 of resolution 1455(2003) and paragraph 13 of resolution 1526(2004), and calls upon the Committee to provide the Council, no later than 31 July 2006, with an update of the written assessment referred to in paragraph 13 of resolution 1526(2004) of actions taken by Member States to implement the measures described in paragraph 1 above;

18. *Requests* that the Committee continue its work on its guidelines, including on listing and de-listing procedures, and implementation of resolution 1452 (2002), and requests the Chairman, in his periodic reports to the Council pursuant to paragraph 16 above, to provide progress reports on the work of the Committee on these issues;

19. *Decides*, in order to assist the Committee in the fulfilment of its mandate, to extend the mandate of the New York-based Monitoring Team for a period of seventeen months, under the direction of the Committee, with the responsibilities outlined in annex I to the present resolution;

20. *Requests* the Secretary-General, upon adoption of the present resolution and acting in close consultation with the Committee, to appoint, consistent with United Nations rules and procedures, no more than eight members, including a coordinator, to the Monitoring Team, taking into account the areas of expertise referred to in paragraph 7 of resolution 1526(2004);

21. *Decides* to review the measures described in paragraph 1 above with a view to their possible further strengthening in seventeen months, or sooner if necessary;

22. *Also decides* to remain actively seized of the matter.

Annex I to resolution 1617(2005)

In accordance with paragraph 19 of this resolution, the Monitoring Team shall operate under the direction of the Security Council Committee established pursuant to resolution 1267(1999) and shall have the following responsibilities:

(a) To collate, assess, monitor and report on and make recommendations regarding implementation of the measures, to pursue case studies, as appropriate; and to explore in depth any other relevant issues as directed by the Committee;

(b) To submit a comprehensive programme of work to the Committee for its approval and review, as necessary, in which the Monitoring Team should detail the activities envisaged in order to fulfil its responsibilities, including proposed travel, based on close coordination with the Counter-Terrorism Committee Executive Directorate to avoid duplication and reinforce synergies;

(c) To submit, in writing, three comprehensive, independent reports to the Committee, the first by 31 January 2006, the second by 31 July 2006, and the third by 10 December 2006, on implementation by States of the measures referred to in paragraph 1 of this resolution, including specific recommendations for improved implementation of the measures and possible new measures, as well as reporting on listing, de-listing, and exemptions pursuant to resolution 1452(2002);

(d) To analyse reports submitted pursuant to paragraph 6 of resolution 1455(2003), the checklists submitted pursuant to paragraph 10 of this resolution, and other information submitted by Member States to the Committee as instructed by the Committee;

(e) To work closely and share information with the Counter-Terrorism Committee Executive Directorate and the group of experts of the Security Council Committee established pursuant to resolution 1540(2004) to identify areas of convergence and to help to facilitate concrete coordination among the three Committees;

(f) To develop a plan to assist the Committee with addressing non-compliance with the measures referred to in paragraph 1 of this resolution;

(g) To present to the Committee recommendations, which could be used by Member States to assist them with the implementation of the measures referred to in paragraph 1 of this resolution and in preparing proposed additions to the Consolidated List;

(h) To consult with Member States in advance of travel to selected Member States, based on its programme of work as approved by the Committee;

(i) To encourage Member States to submit names and additional identifying information for inclusion on the Consolidated List, as instructed by the Committee;

(j) To study and report to the Committee on the changing nature of the threat of Al-Qaida and the Taliban and the best measures to confront it;

(k) To consult with Member States, including regular dialogue with representatives in New York and in capitals, taking into account comments from Member States, especially regarding any issues that might be contained in the reports of the Monitoring Team referred to in paragraph *(c)* of this annex;

(l) To report to the Committee, on a regular basis or when the Committee so requests, through oral and/or written briefings on the work of the Monitoring Team, including its visits to Member States and its activities;

(m) To assist the Committee in preparing oral and written assessments to the Council, in particular the analytical summaries referred to in paragraphs 17 and 18 of this resolution;

(n) Any other responsibility identified by the Committee.

Annex II to resolution 1617(2005)

1267 Committee Checklist

Please provide to the United Nations 1267 (Al-Qaida/Taliban Sanctions) Committee by XXX date information on the following individuals, groups, undertakings, and entities added in the last six months to the Committee's Consolidated List of those subject to the sanctions described in Security Council resolution 1267(1999) and successor resolutions.

This information is provided by the Government of _____ on XXX date.

(See checklist on p. 414)

Sanctions Committee activities

The Al-Qaida and Taliban Sanctions Committee, established pursuant to resolution 1267(1999) [YUN 1999, p. 265], submitted a report [S/2006/22] covering its activities from 1 January to 31 December 2005. During that period, the Committee held seven formal meetings and 36 informal consultations at the expert level.

The Security Council, in resolution 1617(2005) (see above), provided more clarity regarding the mandatory sanctions measures and their implementation. The resolution provided an explanation of the term "associated with", in reference to association with Al-Qaida, Osama bin Laden and the Taliban, thus clarifying who could be subject to placement on the Committee's Consolidated List. Annex II of the resolution contained a checklist for monitoring sanctions implementation by States. The Council also extended the mandate of the Analytical Support and Sanctions Monitoring Team for a period of 17 months, to be discharged under the direction of the Sanctions Committee.

The Committee considered the recommendations contained in the Monitoring Team's second and third reports (see below). Some of the recommendations contained in the third report were referred to the Counter-Terrorism Committee (CTC) for further action and some to the Committee established pursuant to resolution 1540(2004) [YUN 2004, p. 544] for information. The Committee also identified a number of recommendations, such as listing and de-listing issues, that would require its further consideration. For the first time, the Committee decided to issue, as a letter from the Chairman (see below), its comments and observations on the recommendations contained in the third report, that should be brought to the attention of all States.

	YES	NO

1. Mr. Doe (Number _____ on Consolidated List)
    A. Name added to visa lookout list?
    B. Any visas denied?
    C. Financial institutions notified?
    D. Any assets frozen?
    E. Arms embargo ban implemented?
    F. Any attempts to purchase arms?
    Additional information, if available:

	YES	NO

2. The Doe Corp. (Number _____ on Consolidated List)
    A. Financial institutions notified?
    B. Any assets frozen?
    C. Arms embargo ban implemented?
    D. Any attempts to purchase arms?
    Additional information, if available:

To comply with its obligation to submit a written analytical assessment of Member State implementation of relevant sanctions measures pursuant to paragraph 13 of resolution 1526(2004) [ibid., p. 332], the Committee requested the Monitoring Team to assist it by providing a preliminary analysis, which it received on 11 July. Based on the information provided in the analysis, the Committee submitted its assessment (see below) with the expectation that it would serve as feedback for Member States that had submitted their implementation reports and as a source inspiration for the 46 non-reporting States.

The Committee continued to consider notifications and requests submitted by Member States pursuant to resolution 1452(2002) [YUN 2002, p. 280], seeking exceptions to the sanctions measures. It also updated its Consolidated List of individuals and entities belonging to or associated with Al-Qaida and the Taliban on the basis of relevant information provided by Member States. The Committee increased cooperation with the International Criminal Police Organization (Interpol). The UN Secretariat and Interpol also elaborated a supplementary agreement to implement the cooperation agreement between the two organizations.

Monitoring Team

The Analytical Support and Sanctions Monitoring Team (the Monitoring Team), established by Security Council resolution 1526(2004) [YUN 2004, p. 332], had the mandate of collating, assessing, monitoring, reporting on and making recommendations regarding the implementation of measures imposed in that resolution.

Report of Monitoring Team (February). Pursuant to Council resolution 1526(2004), the Sanctions Committee Chairman, on 14 February [S/2005/83], transmitted to the Council President the second report of the Monitoring Team. The report noted that there had been no let-up in the determination of Al-Qaida, the Taliban and their associates to continue their campaign of terror, with further escalation in terms of the brutality of attacks. Although the Team's focus was to examine the implementation of existing sanctions, it noted that, by themselves, they could only hope to limit Al-Qaida activity, not end it.

The Team, drawing on its assessment of Member States' reports and other evidence, suggested a list of specific criteria, among other factors, for measuring compliance and implementation at the national level, and proposed various strategies to enhance implementation, including that the Council ask States to complete a compliance checklist after each additional listing. The assets freeze was perhaps the most implemented of the sanctions on a global scale, and constituted the most effective mechanism for preventing large-scale terrorist operations. Member States had generally reformed their official banking systems to prevent listed parties from receiving or transferring money, but there were many unofficial ways to circumvent those restrictions. Cash couriers, alternative remittance systems and charities could all be exploited to finance terrorism, and the challenge for the international community was finding a proper balance between restricting the flow of money to terrorists and allowing legitimate transactions to continue freely.

In terms of the arms embargo, the Team believed the world community had, in some senses, been the victim of its own success. Although embargoes might have impeded terrorists from obtaining military-style weapons and arms, they had not stopped their attacks. The Team considered three areas for action: man-portable anti-aircraft missile systems, commercially available materials that could be turned into explosives and weapons of mass destruction.

Implementation of the travel ban could be viewed as a success to the extent that no Member State had reported any violation. However, it was unlikely that no listed individual crossed a national border in the three years since it was enacted. The Team suggested that the travel ban be refined and clarified to deal with overt attempts by those listed to travel, and proposed new initiatives to prevent covert travel. The Team discussed those topics with Interpol, among others, and proposed a joint partnership between the United Nations and Interpol on matters of common concern, including stolen, lost and fraudulent travel documents, international arrest warrants and additional information on listed persons that Interpol might possess.

Annexed to the report were several annexes containing additional case studies, summaries of sanctions-related litigation and other supplementary information.

Report of Monitoring Team (September). Pursuant to Security Council resolution 1526 (2004), the Sanctions Committee Chairman, on 2 September [S/2005/572], transmitted to the Council President the third report of the Monitoring Team. The Team found that Al-Qaida continued to evolve and adapt to the pressures and opportunities of the world around it, and the threat of a significant attack remained real in all areas. At the same time, there had been a revival of the threat from the Taliban. The international consensus against Al-Qaida and the Taliban remained firm, helped by a common understanding of the high level of the threat and of the international consequences of a successful major attack. States increasingly saw the advantage of making the sanctions regime as effective as possible, and more of them wished to participate in shaping its development. While the Consolidated List, the assets freeze, the arms embargo and the travel ban continued to provide the basis for an effective regime, there was scope to further improve implementation of those measures and to make them more powerful. More States had proposed names for the Consolidated List, or improvements to existing entries, and reported activity with regard to implementation. Although there had been further reports of assets freezing,

the combination of sanctions had still not achieved its full potential and the Monitoring Team made further recommendations for improvement. The report also addressed two issues of concern to many States: the need for greater fairness in the application of the sanctions and the lack of sufficient identifiers on the Consolidated List. Concerning the assets freeze, apart from the lack of identifiers, it suffered from the ability of terrorists and their supporters to use alternative and often illegal means to raise and transfer money. The Team made specific proposals to deal with the abuse by listed persons and other terrorists of, for example, charities and other non-profit organizations and alternative remittance systems.

As terrorist tactics had evolved, the Team believed the arms embargo should change accordingly, taking into account, among other tactics, how their fundamental objective to influence public opinion through the media affected their choice of weapons. It suggested that the scope of the embargo and its links to other international non-proliferation agreements could provide fruitful areas for future work by the Council and the Committee. Concerning the implementation of the travel ban and similar national prohibitions, the Team supported initiatives to increase the use of biometrics in travel documents and to enhance regional and international cooperation in matters relating to security and the travel of listed persons and other terrorists.

Sanctions Committee observations (December). On 1 December [S/2005/760], the Sanctions Committee's Chairman transmitted to the Council President the Committee's comments and observations on the recommendations contained in the Monitoring Team's third report (see above). The Committee found that many of the recommendations should be brought to the attention of Member States, as they could significantly improve their implementation of the sanctions measures. However, while acknowledging the value of the Team's recommendations, the Committee arrived at its own conclusions, not necessarily shared by the Team.

The Committee supported the Team's recommendation to render the List in both English transliteration and in the language of the original documents, which would lead to greater accuracy and clarity and thus better implementation of sanctions. The Committee had already requested the Team to work with relevant States in ensuring an accurate rendition of the names in their original language and hoped to update the List with that information before the end of December.

The Committee also agreed to replace the current numbering system, which changed each time an individual or entity was added, with a permanent reference number, in order to ease communication between Member States and the Committee.

In its efforts to improve implementation of the sanctions regime, the Committee supported the recommendation that Member States be reminded of the meaning of a UN listing. A criminal conviction or indictment was not a prerequisite for inclusion on the List, and States needed not wait until national administrative, civil, or criminal proceedings could be brought or concluded against an individual or entity before proposing names for the List. Delays in implementing sanctions only allowed Al-Qaida or Taliban supporters an opportunity to circumvent sanctions.

As recommended by the Team, the Committee encouraged States that had not done so to enact legislation, or other measures, to allow for the freezing of assets of parties on the List, without the need for criminal offences or criminal standards of evidence to be demonstrated. While some Member States drew attention to the need to present sufficient evidence to judicial authorities as a condition for the freezing of assets, the Committee noted that such a procedure was not in conformity with Member States' obligations under Chapter VII of the UN Charter and urged States to ensure that assets were frozen as soon as the Committee added the name of an individual or an entity to its List.

The Committee noted the broad nature of the Team's recommendations regarding the implementation of the assets freeze, which would be useful not only in the implementation of sanctions against Al-Qaida and the Taliban, but also in general counter-terrorism efforts. It would therefore forward the recommendations to the Security Council's CTC (see p. 107).

The Committee supported the recommendation that States should improve or adopt measures to deal with the evasion of the travel ban through the issuance of new passports. Such measures could include a requirement that individuals applying for a new passport provide details of any previous identities and travel documents under those names, and mandatory monitoring (with possible referral to law enforcement) of cases of repeat passport requests by individuals.

Assessment of sanctions implementation

In response to Security Council resolution 1526(2004) [YUN 2004, p. 332], the Sanctions Committee Chairman, on 1 December [S/2005/761], transmitted to the Council President an analytical assessment of Member States' implementation of the measures referred to in paragraph 1 of that resolution, with a view to recommending further measures for the Council's consideration. An analysis provided by the Monitoring Team to the Committee on 11 July, based on all reports submitted by Member States in accordance with Council resolution 1455(2003) [YUN 2003, p. 311], reports from the Monitoring Team's and the Chairman's visits to selected States, contacts with Member States, CTC and its Executive Directorate and other sources, was annexed to the Committee's assessment.

The Monitoring Team's analysis noted that all States had a counter-terrorism policy and the great majority showed awareness of Al-Qaida and the Taliban, though many might not have had the Consolidated List as their primary focus. Those States did not necessarily separate action taken against persons on the List from that taken against all those generally regarded as terrorists. States were not likely to voluntarily report that their implementation of the sanctions regime was less than complete, and while the Team could not say that any State had demonstrated a clear lack of political will, the depth of commitment might, in some cases, need further examination, since an apparent lack of capacity might conceal a lack of will.

The Monitoring Team's contacts with Member States suggested that commitment to the sanctions would be enhanced by greater relevance and accuracy in the List and a sense that the sanctions regime was dynamic in tracking the changing nature of the Al-Qaida/Taliban threat. On behalf of the Committee, the Team had written to 85 States with a connection to names on the List to encourage updates. Thirty-seven had replied, 23 of which had supplied additional information. The Committee accepted 146 amendments concerning 63 names, and was considering many others. It was also considering how best to ensure that listed individuals and entities did not have time to move their assets before banks received notification of their listing. Controls beyond the banking sector were more difficult to implement and enforce and listed terrorists were still managing to raise and receive funds from sympathizers outside their immediate circle.

The travel ban would be helped by greater accuracy and relevance of the List, and closer cooperation with Interpol, but considerable international effort would be needed to solve the problem of false and stolen documents. The proper circulation of the List to vulnerable border crossings would need sustained analysis and assistance before solutions were found. Likewise the arms embargo would be more effective as analysis of the ways listed terrorists managed to acquire the means to launch attacks filtered through to help fine-tune international efforts to stem the flow.

In its assessment, the Committee observed that Member States still needed to further improve their implementation of sanctions. It continued to place emphasis on the submission of reports from Member States, especially since there were 47 non-reporting States.

Iraq

Situation in Iraq

In 2005, the United Nations, through the Secretary-General's Special Representative for Iraq and the United Nations Assistance Mission for Iraq (UNAMI), continued to assist Iraq in its transition to democratic governance and reconstruction and reconciliation, despite the ever growing escalation of violence.

Communication (January). By a 19 January letter to the Secretary-General [A/59/679-S/2005/41], Turkey said that Iraq was at a crucial turning point in its political transition with the first free Iraqi elections in many decades to be held on 30 January. The UN Mission had been doing exemplary work and the Organization's seal on the elections would make its results more legitimate for the Iraqis and the international community. However, security, especially in central Iraq, remained elusive. One large segment of Iraqi society was either unwilling or felt unable to take part in the elections, despite Turkey's efforts to persuade that group to make a strong electoral showing. The international community's objective had been, and remained, to transfer sovereign authority to a transition government conferred by popular mandate. As the drafting of the new Iraqi constitution would get under way in the next phase, the participation of all Iraqis in that undertaking would become all the more important.

Meeting of countries neighbouring Iraq. The Ministers for Foreign Affairs of the countries neighbouring Iraq, at their seventh meeting (Amman, Jordan, 5-6 January), attended by Bahrain, Jordan, Saudi Arabia, Iraq, Turkey, the Syrian Arab Republic and Iran, agreed on the importance of the elections for Iraq's political transition, including the drafting of a constitution, the subsequent referendum and the election of a constitutional Government. In the concluding communiqué, participants confirmed their readiness to cooperate with the Interim Government of Iraq, to broaden political participation in the spirit of national dialogue and consensus-

building and to promote Iraq's transition to a united, democratic and pluralistic State, with a federal structure, if so decided by the Iraqi people.

The follow-up meeting to the 2004 International Ministerial Meeting of the Countries Neighbouring Iraq [YUN 2004, p. 358] was held in Cairo, Egypt, on 11 January. The meeting was attended by Iraq, Jordan, Kuwait, Saudi Arabia, the Syrian Arab Republic and Turkey, as well as by Canada, China, France, Germany, Italy, Japan, the Netherlands, the Russian Federation, the United States and the United Kingdom. The United Nations, the League of Arab States (LAS) and the EU also attended the meeting. In addition to reaffirming the call on all Iraqis to participate in the elections, several delegates emphasized the need for the political process to create conditions conducive to greater stability and reconstruction efforts.

January elections

On 30 January, more than 8.5 million Iraqis, out of a voter population of over 14 million, exercised their democratic right to vote, despite concerns about the security environment, attempts at disruption and ongoing violence and concerns about the credibility of the elections, the Secretary-General stated in his March report on Iraq [S/2005/141 & Corr.1]. He affirmed that the conduct of the elections for the Transitional National Assembly, 18 Governorate Councils and the Kurdistan National Assembly met recognized international standards and the number of serious irregularities and complaints conveyed to the Independent Electoral Commission was relatively small, all of which were being investigated and addressed by the Commission. The Commission was supported in its work by an electoral assistance team led by the United Nations. It accredited more than 2,000 Iraqi, international and Arabic media personnel throughout the country, 33,141 national observers, 622 international observers and 61,725 agents of political parties and entities to observe the electoral process. The United Nations actively encouraged the development of election observer groups and established a project for that purpose.

The uncertain political environment and security conditions necessitated a range of contingencies and special measures. The Commission worked extensively with national and international security forces to provide a viable security framework for the elections. The security plan put in place, including the closure of borders and a ban on vehicle movements, created a security environment that permitted electoral staff to carry out their work. Of the planned

5,243 polling centres, 5,199 were able to open and operate on polling day.

From 111 competing political entities and co-alitions, 275 representatives were elected to the Transitional National Assembly from a total of 7,785 candidates. Over 31 per cent of seats were awarded to female candidates, surpassing the goal established in the Transitional Administrative Law.

Security Council consideration (February). On 16 February [meeting 5123], the Security Council was briefed by the Under-Secretary-General for Political Affairs, Kieran Prendergast. The Secretary-General attended the meeting.

The Under-Secretary-General said that the simultaneous holding of three elections on 30 January was a momentous event for Iraq and the international community and marked a significant development in Iraq's transition to democratic government. The electoral system—proportional representation with a single national constituency—was chosen in order to facilitate a wide range of representation, though turnout was low in areas with a high percentage of Sunni Arabs.

The Under-Secretary-General said that the key to forging a national discussion and understanding was the drafting of the new constitution. Iraq's most immediate challenges were forming a transitional Government that was broadly representative of Iraqi society and finding ways to bring together all Iraqi constituencies in a national effort to define the future of their country. Prominent political leaders in Iraq had signalled their sensitivity to the fact that certain constituencies, particularly among Arab Sunnis and other Arab nationalists, were likely to find themselves underrepresented in the Transitional National Assembly due to the low turnout in some regions. Those leaders had indicated their determination to assuage any fears of political alienation, including by raising the possibility of inviting representatives of groups that did not, or could not, take part in the elections to participate both in the transitional Government and in the constitution-drafting process. Conversely, some political elements that had urged a boycott or postponement of elections appeared to be insisting that their views be included in any future dialogue and that they participate fully in the drafting of a permanent constitution.

The new transitional institutions of Iraq would need the active support and engagement of the international community. The United Nations was ready to offer technical assistance and public information support, as well as political facilitation. The Secretary-General, for his part, would continue to foster greater regional and international convergence in support of Iraq's political transition.

SECURITY COUNCIL ACTION (February)

On 16 February [meeting 5124], following consultations among Security Council members, the President made statement **S/PRST/2005/5** on behalf of the Council:

The Security Council congratulates the people of Iraq on the successful elections of 30 January 2005. These elections represent a historic moment for Iraq and a positive step in its political transition. In turning out to the polls, Iraqis demonstrated their respect for the rule of law and non-violence. They voted for democracy and full ownership of their affairs. The Council commends the Iraqi people for having taken this step to exercise their right to freely determine their own political future and encourages them to continue to do so in moving ahead with their political transition.

The Council congratulates the newly-elected coalitions and individuals in these elections.

The elections took place under difficult conditions, and the Council salutes the bravery of the Iraqi people who demonstrated their commitment to democracy, defying the terrorists. The Council commends the tens of thousands of Iraqis who ran as candidates, administered the elections, staffed the polls, observed the elections and provided security. The Council gives special recognition to the Independent Electoral Commission of Iraq for its fortitude and organizational skill in administering the elections.

The Council commends the Secretary-General and the United Nations for successfully assisting election preparations, including advice and support extended to the Iraqis by the Special Representative of the Secretary-General for Iraq Ashraf Jehangir Qazi, the United Nations Assistance Mission for Iraq, particularly the lead electoral adviser Carlos Valenzuela, the United Nations Electoral Assistance Division and its Director Carina Perelli. The Council also appreciates the assistance given by other international actors, including European Union electoral experts.

The Council also notes the commendable role played by the Iraqi security forces and the Multinational Force-Iraq in providing security for the elections.

These elections are an important step for Iraq's political transition, as outlined in Council resolution 1546(2004). The Council looks forward to the seating of the Transitional National Assembly and the formation of a new Transitional Government of Iraq in the near future. A Constitution of Iraq, to be drafted under the authority of the Transitional National Assembly, is expected to be put to a referendum by October 2005 and followed by general elections by December 2005 under the new Constitution. The Council affirms its continuing support for the Iraqi people in their political transition and reaffirms the independence, sovereignty, unity and territorial integrity of Iraq.

Underlining the importance of the maximum possible participation of all components of Iraqi society in the political process, the Council stresses the need for sustained political efforts aimed at making the next steps of the transition, in particular the coming constitutional process, as inclusive, participatory and transparent as possible. The Council welcomes the statements recently made by Iraqi leaders in this regard, and strongly encourages the Transitional Government of Iraq and the Transitional National Assembly to reach out broadly to all segments of Iraqi society, with a view to promoting genuine political dialogue and national reconciliation and to ensuring that all Iraqis are duly represented and have a voice in the political process and the drafting of the Iraqi Constitution.

The Council reaffirms the leading role of the Special Representative of the Secretary-General for Iraq and the United Nations Assistance Mission for Iraq set out in resolution 1546(2004) in support of Iraq's own efforts and as requested by the Government of Iraq, to promote national dialogue and consensus-building on the drafting of a national constitution. In this regard, the Council urges the United Nations to prepare itself rapidly and encourages the members of the international community to provide advisers and technical support to the United Nations to help it to fulfil this role.

The Council condemns, in the strongest possible terms, acts of terrorism in Iraq, which should not be allowed to disrupt Iraq's political and economic transition. The Council calls upon those who use violence in an attempt to subvert the political process to lay down their arms and participate in the political process. It encourages the Iraqi authorities to engage with all those who renounce violence and to create a political atmosphere conducive to national reconciliation and political competition through peaceful means.

The Council stresses the continued importance of Iraq's neighbouring countries and regional organizations in supporting the political process, cooperating with the Iraqi authorities to control transit across Iraq's borders and extending other support for the people of Iraq in their efforts to achieve security and prosperity.

Consistent with resolution 1546(2004), the Council reaffirms its support for a federal, democratic, pluralist and unified Iraq, in which there is full respect for human rights. It welcomes the support of the international community to Iraq and underlines the importance of enhanced and expeditious assistance from all States and relevant international organizations in support of Iraq's further implementation of the political transition process and efforts to achieve national reconciliation, economic reconstruction and stability, in accordance with resolution 1546(2004).

Communications (March-June). On 13 March [A/59/761-S/2005/215], the Ministerial Council of the Gulf Cooperation Council (GCC), at its ninety-fourth session (Riyadh, Saudi Arabia, 13 March), welcomed the success of the Iraqi electoral process and underlined the importance of involving the entire political spectrum in shaping Iraq's future.

On 23 March [S/2005/274], the Council of LAS, at its seventeenth session (Algiers, Algeria, 22-23 March), adopted a resolution affirming the necessity of participation by all segments of the Iraqi people in the political process, in particular the drafting of a permanent Constitution based on national consensus, the holding of a referendum thereon and participation in the legislative elections scheduled for December. LAS also decided to provide training for Iraqis, including for the police and armed forces, in order to enable the Iraqi Government to terminate the foreign military presence.

On 30 April [S/2005/298], the Ministers for Foreign Affairs of the countries neighbouring Iraq, in a joint statement issued at their eighth official meeting (Istanbul, Turkey, 29-30 April), welcomed the holding of the 30 January Iraqi general elections, the subsequent appointment of Prime Minister al-Jaafari and the formation and endorsement of the Transitional National Government. They added that the United Nations should play a pivotal role in the new transitional phase, which would include the holding of the constitutional referendum and parliamentary elections and that UNAMI should serve as the focal point in receiving and processing political and donor assistance to the transition process.

On 5 April [A/59/824-S/2005/363], the Joint Council and Ministerial Meeting between GCC States and the EU, at their fifteenth session (Manama, Bahrain, 5 April), issued a joint communiqué reaffirming their willingness to work with the new Transitional National Assembly and stressing the importance of the continuing implementation of Council resolution 1546(2004) and, in particular, the drafting of a permanent constitution, leading to a constitutionally elected government by 31 December.

On 11 June [A/59/845-S/2005/386], the GCC Ministerial Council, at the ninety-fifth session (Riyadh, 11 June), reviewed the deterioration of the security and humanitarian situation and the increasing cycle of violence in Iraq. It condemned all terrorist acts that targeted Iraqi civilians and military, humanitarian and religious institutions, in addition to the abduction and torture of innocent persons. It also condemned the deliberate mass killing of Iraqis and prisoners of war, including Kuwaiti nationals and nationals of other States, perpetrated by the former Iraqi regime.

UN Assistance Mission for Iraq

The United Nations Assistance Mission for Iraq (UNAMI), established by Security Council resolution 1500(2003) [YUN 2003, p. 346], continued to support the Secretary-General in the fulfilment of his mandate under resolution 1483 (2003) [ibid., p. 338]. UNAMI's mission was expanded by Council resolution 1546(2004) [YUN 2004, p. 348] to include assisting in the convening of a national conference to select a Consultative Council, advising on the holding of elections, promoting national dialogue and consensus-building on the drafting of a new constitution, advising on the development of effective civil and social services and contributing to the coordination and delivery of reconstruction, development and humanitarian assistance. The Special Representative of the Secretary-General and his substantive, security and administrative support staff were based in Baghdad, while the majority of humanitarian project planning and management activities were conducted from Amman, Jordan. The primary logistics support base was in Kuwait, while two small liaison detachments were deployed in Erbil and Basra.

On 6 May, the Secretary-General appointed Michael von der Schulenburg as Deputy Special Representative for Political Affairs in Iraq to further strengthen UNAMI's political presence in Baghdad.

During the year, the Secretary-General submitted four reports on UNAMI's activities [S/2005/141, S/2005/373, S/2005/585, S/2005/766].

Report of Secretary-General (March). In response to resolution 1546(2004), the Secretary-General submitted a March report [S/2005/141 & Corr.1] on UNAMI's activities in Iraq since his December 2004 report [YUN 2004, p. 358]. The Secretary-General stated that, since the elections, a number of Iraqi political leaders from successful electoral lists had signalled their willingness to invite prominent representative leaders from Arab Sunni communities to participate in the Transitional Government and in the constitution-making process, so as to ensure balanced representation in both. Similarly, several Arab Sunni and Arab nationalist political entities that did not participate in the elections, or had urged a boycott or postponement, had declared that their points of view had to be included in the next steps of the transition and that they had the right to participate fully in the drafting of a permanent constitution. Efforts were under way to prepare for the convening of the Transitional National Assembly.

Progress in the political process remained heavily influenced by the security situation. The large number of casualties among Iraqi police, security forces and civilians, as well as inadequate judicial protection, were serious impediments to law enforcement. Daily attacks against Iraqis and foreigners resumed immediately after the elections, including a terrorist attack in Hillah on 28 February, during which over 120 persons were killed and 140 injured. Curfews, restrictions on movement and other measures were imposed and eased at regular intervals in most parts of the country. At the end of February, the multinational force (MNF) and Iraqi security forces mounted a counter-insurgency campaign in Anbar province, including Ramadi. The Special Representative conveyed to the Interim Government and MNF concern over the potential political and humanitarian consequences of an escalation of the situation.

UN personnel in Iraq continued to be constrained by security conditions, necessitating extremely well-protected living and working facilities within heavily guarded areas. Movement outside the Baghdad international zone, or similarly well-protected compounds in other parts of the country, continued to be extremely hazardous and therefore dependent on MNF's protection. Under those conditions, any expansion of the UN presence in Iraq would be limited by the number of persons who could be accommodated in the Baghdad international zone, and those who could be protected by the small security liaison detachments deployed to MNF cantonments at Basra and Erbil, which were dispatched there in February to facilitate periodic visits, prepare UN facilities and assess the security conditions required for any expansion of its presence in Iraq.

The trust fund for Iraq, established by the Secretary-General in 2004 [YUN 2004, p. 357], had received contributions totalling $8.3 million as at 1 March 2005, from 11 Member States. A mechanism for the disbursement of funds to Member States providing troops to the distinct entity was being finalized. The United States informed the United Nations that the first troop contingent contributed to the distinct entity by Georgia, would be deployed to Baghdad in March 2005.

The Secretary-General observed that the 30 January elections marked the completion of an important first step in Iraq's political transition to the restoration of full sovereignty and the return of peace and stability. Priority attention had to be given to addressing the basic needs of all Iraqis. Security, job creation, infrastructural improvements, institutional capacity-building and effective delivery of basic services were essential for making the political and security context more conducive to a successful transition process. To meet those challenges, the new transitional institutions of Iraq would need continued and active support from the international community. The United Nations would do everything possible to implement its mandate under Security Council resolution 1546(2004), as circumstances permitted. The next step in Iraq's transition was the constitution-making process. Full Iraqi ownership of that process would be particularly important. The Secretary-General's Special Representative was consulting with a wide range of Iraqi representatives to promote dialogue and consensus-building in support of the political transition, including the constitution-making process. The United Nations could provide technical assistance, public information support and coordination of international assistance. UNAMI's work in the reconstruction, development and humanitarian areas was driven by Iraqi demands and priorities; 23 UN agencies, programmes and funds were working from both inside and outside the country to ensure a coordinated and efficient effort in providing reconstruction and humanitarian assistance to Iraq.

Security Council consideration (11 April). On 11 April [meeting 5161], the Council was briefed by the Secretary-General's Special Representative for Iraq, Ashraf Jehangir Qazi, and by the United States representative on behalf of MNF.

Mr. Qazi said that the Transitional National Assembly, which convened for the first time on 16 March, had elected a new president and two vice-presidents. Although there had been a reduction in the number of violent incidents since the elections, the tactics and lethality of the insurgency continued to evolve and were cause for concern. The faster Iraqi security forces could be trained, the sooner they would be able to take charge of the country's security. The international community could provide critical support to Iraq's transition by stepping up reconstruction and developmental assistance through the International Reconstruction Fund Facility, and UNAMI was prepared to play an enhanced coordinating role between donors and the Iraqi authorities. Iraqi interlocutors wanted the United Nations to assume greater responsibilities and greater visibility in Iraq. Liaison offices had been opened in Erbil and Basra for the deployment of an initial number of humanitarian and development staff. The United Nations would assess the scope for increased humanitarian and development initiatives. The arrival of newly contributed guard units assigned to provide UN security in Baghdad and Basra would, it was hoped, encourage other countries to support the expansion of UN activities in Iraq.

The United States said that Iraq remained a very difficult security environment. Terrorists and insurgents were determined to thwart the country's progress towards peace and democracy. They continued a campaign of attacks and intimidation against Iraqi leaders and citizens, security forces and private citizens, as well as against aid workers and MNF. Iraqis continued to volunteer in large numbers to serve their country in the Iraqi security forces, over 150,000 of whom had been equipped and trained. Interior Ministry troops numbered some 85,000, including regular police, members of special police commandos, public order and mechanized battalions, border guard units and dignitary-protection elements. Defence Ministry forces numbered 65,000 and included troops from the regular Iraqi army, air force, navy and special operations. Though progress had been made in building up the Iraqi security forces, more time and continued support from MNF were needed before they could reach full operational capacity. What had changed since the December 2004 report [YUN 2004, p. 357] was the increasing use of Iraqi security forces, supported by MNF as required. Military forces and civil affairs personnel, in coordination with the Iraqi Government, international donors and international and national non-governmental organizations (NGOs), also worked to provide civil, humanitarian and reconstruction assistance throughout Iraq. MNF also disbursed funds to build and improve infrastructure, provide for the welfare of the citizens and support education. The United States said that the elections of 30 January were an essential step in the Iraqi people's path towards stability and self-governance. Transparency and broad-based participation in the drafting of Iraq's new constitution would be critical to developing a stable and thriving democracy. Noting that security for UNAMI was a necessary condition for the United Nations to fulfil its mandate in Iraq, the United States acknowledged those countries that had pledged more than $15 million towards funding for the distinct entity under MNF's unified command that provided security for the United Nations in Baghdad. The United States encouraged countries to provide additional assistance to the entity through the provision of funds or troops to meet the security needs of expanded UN activities. It welcomed the deployment of UN liaison teams to Basra and Erbil and wished to see the United Nations expand the implementation of its responsibilities for economic and humanitarian reconstruction assistance in Iraq.

The representative of Iraq said that the country had just marked the two-year anniversary of the fall of the previous regime. The journey had not been easy, nor would it have been possible without outside help. However, Iraq needed to be relieved from the shackles and burdens of the previous regime. It was time for the Council to dismantle the relevant legal, bureaucratic and other relevant structures that it had imposed on Iraq before 2003.

Report of Secretary-General (June). The Secretary-General, in his June report [S/2005/373] on Iraq said that, after delays in reaching an agreement, the Transitional National Assembly was formally inaugurated on 16 March, but it was not until 6 April that the Assembly elected Hajim Al-Hasani as its President and Hussain Sharistani and Aref Taifour as Vice-Presidents. The Assembly's 275 members comprised the United Iraqi Alliance (140 seats), the Kurdistan Alliance List (75 seats), the Iraqi List (40 seats), the Iraqis (five seats), Turkman Iraqi Front (three seats), National Independent Cadres and Elites (three seats), National Union (two seats), Islamic Group of Kurdistan/Iraq (two seats), Islamic Action Organization in Iraq (two seats), National Democratic Alliance (one seat), Al Rafideen National List (one seat), Liberation and Reconciliation Gathering (one seat).

To ensure adequate and legitimate representation of Arab Sunnis in the Transitional Government, many of whom did not participate in the January elections, and were therefore underrepresented in the Assembly, the two main political groupings in the Assembly, the Kurdistan Alliance and the United Iraqi Alliance, negotiated, resulting in a memorandum of understanding that laid the basis for the formation of the new government. On 28 April, the Transitional National Assembly endorsed the Transitional Government, comprised of 32 ministerial and 4 deputy ministerial posts, under the premiership of Ibrahim al-Jaafari. The Presidency Council was made up of Jalal Talabani, who was sworn in as President of Iraq on 7 April, and Ghazi al-Yawar and Adel Abdul Medhi as Vice-Presidents.

On 10 May, the Transitional National Assembly established the Constitution Drafting Committee to draft a permanent constitution by 15 August, which would then be presented to the Iraqi people for approval in a general referendum to be held no later than 15 October. The Drafting Committee established a subcommittee to identify mechanisms for making the constitution-making process more inclusive and two more Committees on Federalism and human rights.

At the international level, the United States and the EU, at the request of the Transitional Government, offered to co-host an international conference on Iraq in Brussels, Belgium, in June (see p. 423). The conference would be an opportunity for the newly formed Iraqi Government to present its priorities and strategic directions related to the political process, including the constitution-making process, the upcoming electoral events, reconstruction and development issues and security and public order issues.

The new phase of Iraq's political transition took place in a security environment that had yet to show signs of improvement. Since the inauguration of the Transitional Government, attacks against both Iraqi civilians and public officials had increased significantly. Bombings, strikes against Iraqi and MNF installations and convoys, attacks on aircraft, hostage-takings and targeted assassinations against Iraqi civilians, including public figures, many with increasing sophistication, continued to be centred on Baghdad, Mosul, Ramadi and Tikrit. Iraqi police recruitment centres were particular targets, and indiscriminate attacks against civilians continued to cause growing numbers of casualties, with the apparent intent of demonstrating the weakness and inability of the new Government to control the security situation and of exacerbating sectarian tensions. Ground movement between the Baghdad international zone and airport had occasionally been interrupted. A major attack against local security forces in Erbil and incidents in other parts of Iraq demonstrated a sustained ability of hostile elements to select and coordinate attack targets throughout the country. The significant rise in insurgent attacks in April and May had taken a particularly heavy toll on civilians, but accurate reporting of incidents was problematic and figures concerning the number of casualties remained uncertain. MNF and Iraqi security forces stepped up their anti-insurgent campaigns in and around Baghdad, as well as in western Iraq. There were reports of high casualty rates and alleged violations of civil liberties and human rights by all sides. In response to the security situation, the Transitional Government, on 13 May, extended the Order for Safeguarding National Security to all parts of Iraq, except the three northern governorates, for another 30 days.

To strengthen security arrangements for UN staff in Iraq, a third UN personal security detail was to be deployed in mid-June.

On 30 May, Iraq requested the United Nations and the international donor community, to provide technical assistance in helping to promote national dialogue between the Constitutional Drafting Committee and the Iraqi people, and build consensus nationwide for the draft constitution. UNAMI organized its assistance programme in the areas of facilitation and good offices for promoting inclusiveness and consensus-building; institutional support; knowledge sharing; public outreach; and coordination of international assistance. It also led a joint comprehensive review of the UN-Iraqi assistance strategic framework on 24 March, which outlined the main priority areas for future reconstruction and rehabilitation in Iraq. The United Nations also played an increasingly important role in donor coordination.

The Secretary-General observed that the United Nations had been able, under challenging circumstances, to help Iraq meet each benchmark of its political transition process. The Transitional National Assembly had requested that the Organization provide technical assistance for the Constitutional process. UNAMI had developed a comprehensive support programme and was engaged with the members of the Constitution Drafting Committee and other relevant actors to help make that process a success. However, the volatile security situation remained a formidable challenge to the transition process. The Secretary-General expressed concern about the potential for escalation of inter- and intra-communal tensions into ethnic or sectarian strife and the regional ramifications thereof.

Security Council consideration (June). On 16 June [meeting 5204], the Council was briefed on the situation in Iraq by the Assistant Secretary-General for Political Affairs, Danilo Türk.

Mr. Türk said that the security environment remained extremely challenging, particularly the ever-increasing level of sectarian violence. Security initiatives, in order to work, needed to form part of a broader credible political process that could address the underlying political problems. Two years after the demise of the former regime, it was imperative for the new Government, with the support of the international community, to deliver basic services effectively and to do more to promote the rule of law and respect for human rights.

International Conference on Iraq

On 22 June, the EU and the United States jointly hosted the Iraq International Conference in Brussels. More than 80 countries and organizations, including the United Nations, attended the Conference. The preparatory process was led by a steering group composed of the EU, the United States, Iraq, Egypt, Japan, the Russian Federation and the United Nations. A preparatory meeting took place in Cairo, Egypt on 2 June. The International Conference focused on building a renewed international partnership with Iraq based on a comprehensive approach that involved supporting Iraq's political transition process, encouraging its economic recovery and reconstruction, and helping to establish the rule of law and public order in the country. The Transitional Government of Iraq set out its vision and strategy in those areas, stressing priority activities. Participants resolved to support the Tran-

sitional Government in accordance with resolution 1546(2004). The Secretary-General, who attended the conference, expressed the hope that the new partnership forged at the meeting would mean wider and deeper consensus in the Security Council in support of resolution 1546(2004).

Assassination of diplomats and escalation of violence

On 7 July [S/2005/438], Egypt informed the Council President that the Head of the Egyptian Mission to Iraq, Ambassador Ihab El Sherif, had been abducted and killed in Baghdad by a group of terrorists. Egypt also reaffirmed its commitment to the Iraqi people.

On 8 July [S/2005/449], Saudi Arabia said that the killing of Ambassador El Sherif was wrongly and falsely couched under the guise of religion.

The Security Council, in statement **S/PRST/2005/29** of 8 July (see p. 1155), condemned the assassination of Ambassador El Sherif, as well as terrorist attacks in Iraq, including the attempted assassinations of diplomats from Bahrain and Pakistan.

In related action, the Council, in statement **S/PRST/2005/37** of 27 July (see p. 1100), condemned the assassination of two Algerian diplomats.

Concerned with the escalation of violence, the Council, in **resolution 1618(2005)** of 4 August (see p. 104), took note of the attacks that had taken place in July, which resulted in over 100 deaths, including 32 children. It expressed concern regarding the increasing attacks on foreign diplomats, including murder or kidnapping.

Communication. On 25 July, Foreign Ministers of the Organization of the Islamic Conference (OIC) (Sana'a, Yemen, 28-30 June) [A/59/884-S/2005/522], adopted a resolution on Iraq, in which they stressed, among other things, the necessity for Iraq's neighbours to take effective measures to control their borders, in order to prevent the movement of terrorists from and into Iraq. They also decided to cancel all of the country's arrears to OIC up to the 2004-2005 financial year.

Extension of UNAMI's mandate

On 3 August [S/2005/509], the Secretary-General informed the Security Council President that, despite severe operational and security constraints, UNAMI had grown in size and expanded its activities in Baghdad since it resumed operations in Iraq in August 2004. It had 260 UNAMI civilian and military personnel based in Iraq and those numbers were expected to rise further in 2005, with the operational use of new facilities in

Erbil and Basra, and increased reconstruction, development and humanitarian activities in those areas. UNAMI's electoral and constitutional support would continue beyond the scheduled completion of the timetable outlined in resolution 1546(2004), if so requested by the Iraqi Government. Similarly, UNAMI was ready to continue to assist in reconstruction, development and humanitarian assistance as long as the Iraqi Government deemed it necessary. Adequate support and resources would be required for UNAMI to continue to implement its mandated tasks. In that regard, the Secretary-General welcomed the spirit of international cooperation, evidenced at the Brussels Conference on Iraq on 22 June (see above), and hoped it would translate into increased support for UN efforts inside Iraq. He recommended that UNAMI's mandate be extended for a further period of 12 months.

SECURITY COUNCIL ACTION

On 11 August [meeting 5247], the Security Council unanimously adopted **resolution 1619(2005)**. The draft [S/2005/515] was prepared in consultations among Council members.

The Security Council,

Recalling all its previous relevant resolutions on Iraq, in particular resolutions 1500(2003) of 14 August 2003, 1546(2004) of 8 June 2004 and 1557(2004) of 12 August 2004,

Reaffirming the independence, sovereignty, unity and territorial integrity of Iraq,

Recalling that the United Nations Assistance Mission for Iraq was established on 14 August 2003 and extended on 12 August 2004, and reaffirming that the United Nations should play a leading role in assisting the efforts of the Iraqi people and Government in developing institutions for representative government, and in promoting national dialogue and unity,

Stressing that this Iraqi national dialogue, which the Mission should assist, is crucial for the political stability and unity of Iraq,

Taking note of the letter dated 3 August 2005 from the Secretary-General addressed to the President of the Security Council,

1. *Decides* to extend the mandate of the United Nations Assistance Mission for Iraq for another period of twelve months from the date of the present resolution;

2. *Expresses its intention* to review the mandate of the Mission in twelve months or sooner, if requested by the Government of Iraq;

3. *Decides* to remain seized of the matter.

Further political and security developments

Report of Secretary-General (September). The Secretary-General, in his 7 September [S/2005/585] report on UNAMI's operations and on the progress made towards the political transition in Iraq, said that Iraq's evolving transition was dominated by the writing of a permanent constitution, preparations for the referendum on the constitution and elections for a permanent government. The delays in convening the Transitional National Assembly and forming the Transitional Government reduced the time available for completing the draft constitution by the 15 August deadline. Additional time was therefore required to make the Constitution Drafting Committee more inclusive of the aspirations of all Iraqi political constituencies. Some 15 Sunnis and 10 advisers were brought into the process and the Committee held its first meeting on 5 July.

The security situation in Iraq affected the constitution-making process. Among other incidents, representatives of the Sunni Conference were repeatedly threatened because of their participation in the constitutional proceedings and a Sunni Arab representative to the Committee was assassinated on 19 July. On 1 August, the Constitution Drafting Committee decided not to request an extension and to aim at completing the draft by the 15 August deadline. President Jalal Talabani convened a leadership conference on 7 August that brought Iraq's political leaders together to forge a political compact on outstanding issues. The Transitional National Assembly voted twice to extend the deadline. On 28 August, the text of the draft constitution was resubmitted to the Assembly, but agreement on several issues remained elusive and negotiations between the parties continued.

In other developments, on 12 June, the inaugural session of the Kurdistan National Assembly elected Massoud Barzani to a four-year term as President of the Kurdistan Regional Government. At the request of the Iraqi Electoral Commission, the UN Electoral Division deployed a needs assessment mission to Iraq from 5 to 26 June to review electoral planning issues. As a result of the mission's recommendations and a meeting held in Jordan (28-30 June), a "critical path" document outlining tasks, deadlines and resources for UN assistance to the Electoral Commission was drawn up. The Transitional National Assembly and the Independent Electoral Commission began preparations for the constitutional referendum on 15 October. On 25 July, the Assembly adopted the referendum law, which was signed by the President. On 8 August, the Assembly requested UN assistance in drafting a new electoral law. At the request of the Transitional Government, the United Nations initiated steps towards a national census.

At the fourth meeting of regional donors to the International Reconstruction Fund Facility for Iraq (18-19 July, Dead Sea, Jordan), Iraq presented its 2005-2007 development strategy. In the area of human rights, on 8 August, the Transitional Government reinstated capital punishment, which had been abolished by a decree of the Coalition Provisional Authority, and authorized the execution on 17 August of three men convicted of kidnapping, killing and rape.

The Secretary-General observed that the constitutional process had engaged the Iraqi people in an unprecedented debate on key challenges facing their country, which generated significant political momentum despite the difficult circumstances in which the process had taken place. However, continuing acts of terrorism, violent crimes, including kidnappings and torture, and the adverse actions of security forces and paramilitary groups, represented a disconcerting source of human rights violations in the country. Deficiencies in the administration of the justice system posed a major challenge and the lack of basic services and economic prospects furthered the perception among many Iraqis that the political process had yet to fully deliver on its promise of a better life. Developing the capacity of the Iraqi security forces to assume full responsibility for their country's security remained a crucial task and the full reintegration of local militias and paramilitary forces into the new Iraqi security apparatus had to be part of that effort. National reconciliation would remain the major challenge for the Iraqi people. It was incumbent upon the Iraqi political parties and groups to develop mutually beneficial approaches to resolving differences and responding to the demands of all constituencies. While pursuing their respective policy interests, communities had to build bridges of hope and trust between one another with a view to strengthening their sense of nationhood and preserving the unity, territorial integrity, sovereignty and political independence of Iraq. Otherwise, rising sectarian tensions and violence held the potential for escalation into serious civil strife.

Security Council consideration (September). On 21 September [meeting 5266], the Council was briefed by the Special Representative of the Secretary-General for Iraq and by the United States representative on behalf of MNF.

The Special Representative said that the text by the Transitional National Assembly of a draft constitution was not designated until 28 August, which continued to be discussed and changed. Changes to the text were finally read out to the National Assembly on 18 September. Major points of contention were the issue of federalism, modalities for the formation of regions in addition to the existing Kurdistan region, the identity of the State, the role of Islam as a source of law, and the distribution of powers with respect to natural resources, including oil and water. Several important constitutional arrangements were deferred to the next elected national assembly for legislative action. A copy of the constitutional text to be put to the Iraqi people on 15 October was formally communicated to the Special Representative, with a request that UNAMI facilitate its publication and distribution. Preparations were also being made for general elections. The Special Representative said that, while the referendum and the elections were necessary instruments in Iraq's transition to democracy, they were only staging posts along an evolving transition. Irrespective of their outcome, a number of overarching challenges remained, including promoting national reconciliation; respecting Iraqi ownership of the political process and strengthening the security of the State; developing good governance practices and institutional capacity-building; and encouraging international and regional engagement and consensus in support of Iraq's transition.

The United States said that the number of terror incidents had been relatively steady in the post-election period, with attacks concentrated in four of Iraq's 18 provinces. The frequency of attacks on Iraq's infrastructure, such as electricity generation and oil facilities, decreased since the election, but they continued to have an adverse impact on the availability of electricity and on oil revenues. The capacity of Iraqi Security Forces was increasing, reducing the influence and effectiveness of insurgents, and strengthening Iraqi rule-of-law capabilities. As at 19 September, there were 193,000 trained and equipped Iraqi security forces, including 104,000 police, highway patrol and other forces under the Ministry of the Interior, and 89,000 in the army, air force and navy. Those forces, in partnership with MNF, increasingly conducted the full spectrum of counter-insurgency operations to isolate and neutralize former regime extremists and foreign terrorists. To stem the flow of foreign fighters, priority had been placed on securing the Iraqi-Syrian border. MNF and the Iraqi Government were developing a conditions-based security plan to define the environment necessary for further and greater transfers of responsibility from MNF to the Iraqi security forces.

On the same day, in a closed meeting [meeting 5267], the Security Council had a constructive exchange of views with the Minister for Foreign Affairs of Iraq, Hoshyar Zebari.

Referendum on the constitution. The Secretary-General, in his December report on Iraq [S/2005/66], stated that further amendments to the Iraqi constitution were put before the Assembly on 12 October. Those related to the federal and united character of Iraq, the use of Iraq's two official languages in federal and official institutions in the Kurdistan region, Iraqi citizenship, the administration of "national treasures", the question of de-Baathification, and the institution of a constitutional review process, which provided for a comprehensive review of the new constitution following the convening of the new parliament and the Council of Representatives, after the 15 December elections. On 13 October, which was declared National Constitution Day, the amended draft constitution was endorsed by the Transitional Government. The referendum, which was successfully organized by the Independent Electoral Commission, with the assistance of the United Nations and the International Electoral Assistance Team, was held on 15 October.

According to the final certified results released by the Electoral Commission, there was a 64.6 per cent voter turnout, with 79 per cent voting in favour and 21 per cent against. Two governorates (Al Anbar and Salahaddin) voted by more than two thirds to reject the draft constitution. Based on those results, the Board of Commissioners therefore decided that the draft constitution was adopted.

Overall, referendum day saw a high level of voter turnout throughout the country and among all the main political constituencies, despite the difficult security situation. That result marked a change from the elections held in January (see p. 417), where the turnout was significantly low in some areas and among some groups, particularly Arab Sunnis.

Report of Secretary-General (December). In response to resolution 1546(2004), the Secretary-General submitted a December report [S/2005/766] on UNAMI's operations and on developments in the political transition process since his September report (see p. 424). The Secretary-General visited Iraq on 12 November, where he met with political and community leaders. He reiterated the UN's commitment to supporting Iraq's political and economic reconstruction, as well as the need for national dialogue and reconciliation. He also emphasized the need for Iraqis to ensure free and credible elections on 15 December, and that a credible political process ultimately offered the best prospects for improving the security situation. An improvement in the basic living conditions of the Iraqi people and in the human rights situation also remained critical in that regard. The trip also allowed the Secretary-General to meet with UN staff in Baghdad and to better measure the challenges the mission faced on a day-to-day basis, particularly in terms of security, accommodation and movement. He also honoured the memory of the 22 colleagues killed

in the attack against the UN headquarters in Baghdad on 19 August 2003 [YUN 2003, p. 346].

A preparatory meeting for the Conference on Iraqi National Accord was held at LAS headquarters in Cairo, Egypt from 19 to 21 November 2005. The meeting was attended by a wide spectrum of Iraqi political and community leaders, government representatives from the region, as well as from regional, international and other organizations. The meeting agreed to convene the Conference on Iraqi National Accord in early 2006 in Baghdad, and requested the cooperation of the United Nations in that regard. The preparatory meeting was a significant event in that, for the first time, a broad range of representatives of Iraq's different communities came together to discuss national reconciliation and the future of their country.

The political transition and attempts to maintain security by the Iraqi Security Forces and MNF were accompanied by an increasingly sophisticated and complex insurgency, underscored by high levels of violence, intimidation and murder. Public instability and insecurity were compounded by an increase in sectarian strife. While the number of attacks during the latter half of the reporting period was lower than average, the lethal character of those attacks had increased, with large numbers of casualties.

The Secretary-General observed that, with the adoption of a new constitution, Iraq was moving towards the scheduled completion of its political transition process outlined in resolution 1546 (2004). The fact that the political process remained on target against an ambitious timetable was a considerable achievement in itself, given the difficult conditions under which it had taken place. Despite meeting those benchmarks, however, Iraq remained beset with formidable security, political and economic challenges. Inside Iraq, promoting an inclusive, participatory and transparent political process that responded to the aspirations of all of Iraq's communities continued to offer the best prospect for improving the overall security situation.

Communications. The ninety-sixth regular session of the GCC Ministerial Council (Jeddah, Saudi Arabia, 6-7 September) [A/60/388-S/2005/612], in a press statement, noted the further deterioration of the security and humanitarian situation in Iraq, and condemned all terrorist acts that targeted civilians and the kidnapping of innocent persons.

The final communiqué of the annual coordination meeting of OIC Ministers for Foreign Affairs (New York, 23 September) [A/60/440-S/2005/658 & Corr.2] condemned all calls based on sectarianism which caused discord among Iraqi people, in particular calls by terrorist groups for Iraqis to fight against each other.

By a 2 December letter to the Secretary-General [A/60/577-S/2005/753], Turkey said that the willingness of the United Nations to work in partnership with the Iraqi Government to assist the Iraqi people in whatever way possible remained a key element for the success of the political transition process.

The Third Extraordinary Session of the Islamic Summit Conference (Makkah Al-Mukkarramah, Saudi Arabia, 7-8 December) [A/60/633-S/2005/826], in the final communiqué, expressed the hope that the legislative elections, scheduled for 15 December (see below), would lead to a constitutional Iraqi Government so as to safeguard the country's unity and territorial integrity and ensure peace, security and stability.

Security Council consideration (December). On 14 December [meeting 5325], the Security Council was briefed on the situation in Iraq by the Under-Secretary-General for Political Affairs and by the United States representative.

The Under-Secretary-General said that the 15 December general election was about to bring to a conclusion the political process outlined in resolution 1546(2004), even though much remained to be done about the security situation. Irrespective of the outcome of the election, the need for national dialogue and reconciliation was of the utmost importance. Moreover, after three years of dramatic change and decades of deprivation, Iraqis were still looking to their leaders for tangible improvements to better their lives and further stabilize their country. It was therefore in the interest of the region and the international community to continue to provide long-term support to Iraq. While in resolution 1637(2005) (see p. 429) the Council reaffirmed the leading role of the United Nations in assisting Iraq with further political and economic development, it had to be recognized that the UN's capacity in Iraq depended on the commitment and support of States Members. In that regard, an agreement was signed on 8 December between the United Nations and the United States for the provision of security for UNAMI, formalizing the security arrangements that were already in place for the United Nations in Iraq.

The United States representative said that, as had happened in the run-up to the October referendum, insurgent attacks increased leading up to the 15 December election. Although about 80 per cent of all attacks were directed against MNF, about 80 per cent of all casualties were Iraqis. While attacks on Iraq's infrastructure accounted for a small portion of total attacks, they continued to have a significant impact on the Iraqi Govern-

ment's oil revenue and provoked public dissatisfaction with essential services. MNF's operations disrupted key insurgent cells, limited their movement and facilitated progress in reconstruction and democracy-building. Despite persistent security challenges, significant progress was made in wresting territory from enemy control due to MNF and Iraqi-led operations. MNF continued to work with the Iraqi Government to train and equip the Iraqi security forces. The goal was to complete total force generation by August 2007. Despite repeated attacks against volunteers, recruiting from the Shia and Kurdish communities, as well as from Sunni areas, continued to outpace demand. Iraqi units were increasingly able to take the lead in combat operations against the insurgency and were responsible for security in Najaf, Karbala and much of Baghdad province. More than 102,000 Iraqi soldiers, sailors and airmen had been trained and equipped, in addition to 75,000 police and highway patrol officers. However, Iraqi forces were not yet ready to conduct independent operations without MNF's assistance. MNF and its Iraqi partners faced multiple challenges in the security sphere, including countering the intimidation and brutality of enemies; building representative Iraqi security forces and institutions whose first loyalties were to the Iraqi Government; neutralizing the actions of such countries as Syria and Iran, which provided support to terrorists in Iraq; understanding the composition of and relationships between terrorists and other enemy networks; addressing the militias and armed groups that were outside the formal security sector and central Government command; ensuring that the security ministries had the capacity to sustain Iraq's new army and police forces; and integrating political, economic and security tools, and synchronizing them with Iraqi Government efforts to foster good and transparent governance, the rule of law, respect for human rights and the well-being of all Iraqi citizens.

Parliamentary elections

The December election for a new Parliament, the Council of Representatives, marked the beginning of the last phase of the political transition processes set out in the Transitional Administrative Law [YUN 2004, p. 346]. The election, held on 15 December, was the third major national electoral event in Iraq in 2005. A total of 307 political entities and 19 coalitions encompassing more than 7,500 candidates representing almost all Iraqi communities and political affiliations entered the contest for the 275 seats in the Council of Representatives. Despite security concerns, voter turnout was high throughout the country, with a participation rate of over 75 per cent, a significant increase from the voter turnout in the January election, which was approximately 58 per cent. In addition, compared to January, Sunni Arab voters participated in significantly greater numbers.

On 19 and 20 December, the Independent Electoral Commission announced partial election results. In response, 43 parties—mainly belonging to the Iraqi National Front, the Iraqi Accord Front and the National Dialogue Front—formed a group to protest against intimidation, ballot stuffing, over-registration, improper apportionment of seats to governorates and other election-related practices, and to lodge complaints against the Electoral Commission. Amid growing protests over the announced partial results, including calls by political parties for an external investigation, the Electoral Commission welcomed the decision of the International Mission for Iraq Elections, an international non-governmental body composed mainly of independent electoral management bodies, to deploy a monitoring team on 1 January 2006 as part of its observation mandate. Final elections results were expected to be announced in January 2006.

Communication. The final communiqué and the Abu Dhabi Declaration adopted by the GCC Supreme Council at its twenty-sixth session (Abu Dhabi, United Arab Emirates, 18-19 December) [A/60/80-S/2006/108] welcomed the 15 December Iraqi parliamentary elections and urged the Iraqi people to continue their dialogue with a view to achieving national reconciliation.

Multinational force

On 24 May [S/2005/337], Iraq noting that, in accordance with Security Council resolution 1546(2004), the mandate of the multinational force (MNF) was due for review, formally requested the Council to allow for the continuation of that mandate until the completion of the political process, or until Iraq could provide for its own security needs.

Security Council consideration (May). On 31 May [meeting 5189], the Council was briefed by the United States representative on MNF's efforts and progress in Iraq.

The United States representative said that MNF's mandate authorized the multinational force to take all necessary measures for maintaining security and stability in Iraq, including preventing and deterring terrorism, so as to allow the Iraqi people to implement freely and without intimidation the timetable and programme for the political process and to benefit from reconstruction and rehabilitation activities. MNF, with its 28 member countries and 160,000 personnel,

also provided assistance in building the capacity of the Iraqi security forces and institutions through recruiting, training, equipping, mentoring and monitoring, and provided security for the United Nations. MNF's key goals were to develop increasingly capable Iraqi security forces and to transfer more and more security responsibilities to them. MNF was committed to staying the course in Iraq and to coordinating with the Iraqi Government more effective tactics to defeat the insurgents and prevent their attacks.

MNF was making progress in its goal of helping Iraqi security forces move towards self-reliance. Some 165,000 Iraqi soldiers and police officers had been trained and equipped and the Iraqi army had over 90 battalion-level units conducting operations. Some of those forces carried on independent security operations, and others operated alongside or with MNF support. Iraqi police and military forces were shouldering the burden in 12 of Iraq's 18 provinces. MNF would continue to focus on partnering, mentoring, teaching and capacity-building. Joint headquarters were established at the national and provincial levels to coordinate MNF, Iraqi Ministry of Defence and Iraqi Ministry of Interior operations.

MNF, in coordination with the Iraqi Government and security forces, international donors, and national and international NGOs, continued to support reconstruction and assistance activities, including building schools and hospitals, improving the infrastructure of roads, water and sanitation, and removing landmines and unexploded ordnance. MNF also recognized the difficult security challenges that Iraq posed to the United Nations, and welcomed UNAMI's willingness and UN Secretariat staff to work closely with MNF to ensure that UN personnel faced minimum risk and delivered maximum support to Iraq. MNF units from Georgia and Romania, with United States and United Kingdom support, protected UN facilities and staff in Baghdad and Basra. In addition, the Czech Republic, Denmark, Finland, Germany, Japan, Luxembourg, the Netherlands, Portugal, Slovenia and Sweden made financial contributions for UNAMI protection.

A specific timeline for the withdrawal of MNF could not be set, but the force would not remain in Iraq any longer than necessary, nor would it leave until the Iraqis could meet the serious security challenges they faced. Any decision regarding force size would be driven by events on the ground.

On the same day [meeting 5190], the Council had a constructive discussion with the Minister for Foreign Affairs of Iraq.

MNF mandate extension

On 31 October [S/2005/687], Iraq noted that, with the holding on 15 October of the referendum to approve a new Constitution for Iraq (see p. 425), the country had taken an important step in building a strong democratic future and was approaching the completion of its political transformation. However, there still remained an extensive agenda for reconstruction and political development, the realization of which would require security and stability. Iraq was confronted by forces of terrorism that incorporated foreign elements and carried out horrific attacks in an attempt to thwart political and economic development in Iraq. The Iraqi security forces needed more time to fill out their ranks, fully equip themselves and complete their training, with a view to assuming responsibility for all security matters. Until such time as the Iraqi security forces could assume full responsibility for the country's security, continued international support would be needed, including the participation of MNF. Iraq therefore requested the Council to extend for a period of 12 months, starting 31 December 2005, MNF's mandate, as provided for in Council resolution 1546(2004), with the provision that the Council would review that mandate upon being so requested by the Iraqi Government or at the end of eight months from the date of the resolution. It would also declare, in the extension, that it would terminate the mandate earlier if requested by the Iraqi Government. Iraq also believed that the provisions of resolution 1546(2004) relating to the deposit of proceeds into the Development Fund for Iraq and the role of the International Advisory and Monitoring Board (IAMB) (see p. 431) would help to ensure that Iraq's natural resources were used for the benefit of the Iraqi people. Iraq requested the Council to extend the validity of those terms for an additional 12 months, subject to review.

On the same date [S/2005/691], the United States said that, consistent with Iraq's request, MNF was prepared to continue to undertake a broad range of tasks to contribute to the maintenance of security and stability and to ensure force protection.

SECURITY COUNCIL ACTION

On 8 November [meeting 5300], the Security Council unanimously adopted **resolution 1637 (2005)**. The draft [S/2005/704] was submitted by Denmark, Japan, Romania, the United Kingdom and the United States.

The Security Council,

Welcoming the beginning of a new phase in Iraq's transition, and looking forward to the completion of the political transition process as well as to the day that Iraqi forces assume full responsibility for the maintenance of security and stability in their country, thus allowing the completion of the multinational force mandate,

Recalling all of its previous relevant resolutions on Iraq,

Reaffirming the independence, sovereignty, unity and territorial integrity of Iraq,

Reaffirming also the right of the Iraqi people freely to determine their own political future and control their own natural resources,

Welcoming the commitment of the Transitional Government of Iraq to work towards a federal, democratic, pluralistic and unified Iraq in which there is full respect for political and human rights,

Calling upon the international community, particularly countries in the region and Iraq's neighbours, to support the Iraqi people in their pursuit of peace, stability, security, democracy and prosperity, and noting the contribution that the successful implementation of the present resolution will bring to regional stability,

Welcoming the assumption of full governmental authority by the Interim Government of Iraq on 28 June 2004, the direct democratic election of the Transitional National Assembly on 30 January 2005, the drafting of a new constitution for Iraq and the recent approval of the draft constitution by the people of Iraq on 15 October 2005,

Noting that the Government of Iraq established as a result of the election scheduled to take place by 15 December 2005 will play a critical role in continuing to promote national dialogue and reconciliation and in shaping the democratic future of Iraq, and reaffirming the willingness of the international community to work closely with the Government of Iraq with respect to efforts to assist the Iraqi people,

Calling upon those who use violence in an attempt to subvert the political process to lay down their arms and participate in the political process, including in the election scheduled for 15 December 2005, and encouraging the Government of Iraq to engage with all those who renounce violence and to promote a political atmosphere conducive to national reconciliation and political competition through peaceful democratic means,

Reaffirming that acts of terrorism must not be allowed to disrupt Iraq's political and economic transition, and further reaffirming the obligations of Member States under resolution 1618(2005) of 4 August 2005 and other relevant resolutions and international obligations with respect, inter alia, to terrorist activities in and from Iraq or against its citizens,

Recognizing the request, conveyed in the letter dated 27 October 2005 from the Prime Minister of Iraq to the President of the Security Council, which is annexed to the present resolution, to retain the presence of the multinational force in Iraq, and further recognizing the importance of the consent of the sovereign Government of Iraq for the presence of the multinational force and of close coordination between the multinational force and that Government,

Welcoming the willingness of the multinational force to continue efforts to contribute to the maintenance of security and stability in Iraq, including participating in the provision of humanitarian and reconstruction assistance, as described in the letter dated 29 October

2005 from the Secretary of State of the United States of America to the President of the Security Council, which is annexed to the present resolution,

Recognizing the tasks and arrangements set out in the letters annexed to resolution 1546(2004) of 8 June 2004 and the cooperative implementation by the Government of Iraq and the multinational force of those arrangements,

Affirming the importance that all forces promoting the maintenance of security and stability in Iraq act in accordance with international law, including obligations under international humanitarian law, and cooperate with relevant international organizations, and welcoming their commitments in this regard,

Recalling the establishment of the United Nations Assistance Mission for Iraq on 14 August 2003, underlining the particular importance of the Mission's assistance for the upcoming election by 15 December 2005 of a Government pursuant to a newly adopted Constitution, and affirming that the United Nations should continue to play a leading role in assisting the Iraqi people and Government with further political and economic development, including advising and supporting the Government of Iraq, as well as the Independent Electoral Commission of Iraq, contributing to the coordination and delivery of reconstruction, development and humanitarian assistance, and promoting the protection of human rights, national reconciliation, as well as judicial and legal reform in order to strengthen the rule of law in Iraq,

Recognizing that international support for security and stability is essential to the well-being of the people of Iraq as well as the ability of all concerned, including the United Nations, to carry out their work on behalf of the people of Iraq, and expressing its appreciation for contributions by Member States in this regard under resolutions 1483(2003) of 22 May 2003, 1511 (2003) of 16 October 2003 and 1546(2004),

Recognizing also that the Government of Iraq will continue to have the primary role in coordinating international assistance to Iraq, and reaffirming the importance of international assistance and development of the Iraqi economy and the importance of coordinated donor assistance,

Recognizing further the significant role of the Development Fund for Iraq and the International Advisory and Monitoring Board in helping the Government of Iraq to ensure that Iraq's resources are being used transparently and equitably for the benefit of the people of Iraq,

Determining that the situation in Iraq continues to constitute a threat to international peace and security,

Acting under Chapter VII of the Charter of the United Nations,

1. *Notes* that the presence of the multinational force in Iraq is at the request of the Government of Iraq and, having regard to the letters annexed to the present resolution, reaffirms the authorization for the multinational force as set forth in resolution 1546(2004), and decides to extend the mandate of the multinational force as set forth in that resolution until 31 December 2006;

2. *Decides* that the mandate of the multinational force shall be reviewed at the request of the Government of Iraq or no later than 15 June 2006, and de-

clares that it will terminate this mandate earlier if requested by the Government of Iraq;

3. *Decides also* to extend until 31 December 2006 the arrangements established in paragraph 20 of resolution 1483(2003) for the deposit into the Development Fund for Iraq of proceeds from export sales of petroleum, petroleum products and natural gas and the arrangements referred to in paragraph 12 of resolution 1483(20003) and paragraph 24 of resolution 1546 (2004) for the monitoring of the Development Fund for Iraq by the International Advisory and Monitoring Board;

4. *Decides further* that the provisions in paragraph 3 above for the deposit of proceeds into the Development Fund for Iraq and for the role of the International Advisory and Monitoring Board shall be reviewed at the request of the Government of Iraq or no later than 15 June 2006;

5. *Requests* that the Secretary-General continue to report to the Security Council on the operations in Iraq of the United Nations Assistance Mission for Iraq on a quarterly basis;

6. *Requests* that the United States of America, on behalf of the multinational force, continue to report to the Council on the efforts and progress of the force on a quarterly basis;

7. *Decides* to remain actively seized of the matter.

Annex I

Letter dated 27 October 2005 from Mr. Ibrahim Aleshaiker al Jaafari, Prime Minister of Iraq, to the President of the Security Council

On 15 October 2005 Iraq voted in a general referendum held at the national level for the purpose of approving a new Constitution for Iraq. The country thus took another important step towards building a strong democratic future and establishing a Government elected in accordance with a permanent Constitution. At the same time, Iraq is approaching the completion of its political transformation through the process of electing its future legislative authority and forming a new Government, which is to take place in December 2005. There still remains an extensive agenda for reconstruction and political development, the realization of which will require security and stability.

We are proceeding towards political stability and economic prosperity and taking fundamental steps towards restoring security and stability. Yet Iraq is still confronted by forces of terrorism that incorporate foreign elements which carry out horrific attacks and terrorist acts in an attempt to thwart political and economic development in Iraq. The Iraqi security forces, which are growing in size, capacity and experience day by day, need more time to fill out their ranks, fully equip themselves and complete their training with a view to assuming responsibility for all security matters and providing adequate security for the Iraqi people. Until such time as the Iraqi security forces assume full responsibility for Iraq's security, we need the continued support of the international community, including the participation of the Multinational Force, in order to establish lasting peace and security in Iraq. We understand that the Multinational Force is willing to continue its efforts. We therefore request the Security Council to extend, for a period of 12 months starting 31 December 2005, the mandate of the Multinational Force, as provided in Council resolution 1546(2004), including the tasks and arrangements specified in the letters annexed thereto, with the proviso that the Council shall review that mandate upon being so requested by the Government of Iraq or at the end of a period of eight months from the date of the resolution and declare, in the extension, that it will terminate the mandate before the expiry of that period should the Government of Iraq so request.

The Government of Iraq believes that the provisions of resolution 1546(2004) relating to the deposit of proceeds into the Development Fund for Iraq and the role of the International Advisory and Monitoring Board will help to ensure that Iraq's natural resources are used for the benefit of the Iraqi people. We understand that the funds deposited in the Development Fund for Iraq belong to Iraq and will continue to enjoy the immunities and privileges of the Fund, given the importance of those terms for the Iraqi people during this critical period. We request the Security Council to extend the validity of those terms for an additional 12 months and to review them upon being so requested by the Government of Iraq or at the end of a period of eight months from the date of the resolution.

The Iraqi people are determined to establish for themselves a stable, peaceful democracy, which will provide the basis for the establishment of a vibrant economy. This vision of Iraq's future can become a reality with the help of the international community.

It is my understanding that the sponsors intend to have the present letter annexed to the resolution on Iraq currently being drafted. In the meantime, I should be grateful if you would have copies of this letter circulated to the members of the Security Council as soon as possible.

Annex II

Letter dated 29 October 2005 from Ms. Condoleezza Rice, Secretary of State of the United States of America, to the President of the Security Council

Having reviewed the request of the Government of Iraq to extend the mandate of the Multinational Force (MNF) in Iraq and following consultations with the Government of Iraq, I am writing to confirm, consistent with this request, that the MNF under unified command stands ready to continue to fulfil its mandate as set out in Security Council resolution 1546 (2004).

Since the end of the occupation on 28 June 2004, the Government of Iraq and the MNF have developed an effective and cooperative security partnership to address the evolving nature of Iraq's security environment, including the continuing need to prevent and deter acts of terrorism. This partnership plays a critical role in the daily efforts to improve security throughout Iraq. In the context of this partnership, the MNF is prepared to continue to undertake a broad range of tasks to contribute to the maintenance of security and stability and to ensure force protection, acting under the authorities set forth in resolution 1546(2004), including the tasks and arrangements set out in the letters annexed thereto, and in close cooperation with the Government of Iraq. The forces that make up the MNF will remain committed to acting consistently with their obligations under international law, including the law of armed conflict.

Substantial progress has already been made in helping to build and train the Iraqi Security Forces (ISF), allowing them to take on increasing security responsibilities. The Government of Iraq and the MNF are developing a security plan to set forth the conditions necessary for transfer of security responsibility from the MNF to the ISF. Conditions permitting, we look forward to notable progress in the next year. Together, we will build towards the day when the Iraqi forces assume full responsibility for the maintenance of security and stability in Iraq.

The co-sponsors intend to annex the present letter to the resolution on Iraq under consideration. In the meantime, I request that you provide copies of the present letter to members of the Council as quickly as possible.

International Advisory and Monitoring Board

The International Advisory and Monitoring Board for Iraq (IAMB), established by Security Council resolution 1483(2003) [YUN 2003, p. 338] to ensure that the Development Fund for Iraq was used in a transparent manner for the purpose set out in paragraph 14 of that resolution and that the Iraqi export sales of petroleum products and natural gas were consistent with international market best practices, continued to oversee the auditing of the Fund.

IAMB report (January). In a 7 January letter [S/2005/12] submitted by the Secretary-General to the Council President, the Secretary-General's representative on IAMB reported on an external audit report on the Fund's operations and Iraq's oil export sales, covering the period from its inception up to the transition of authority by the Coalition Provisional Authority (CPA) to the Interim Government of Iraq on 28 June 2004 [YUN 2004, p. 346]. The audit firm concluded that all known oil proceeds, reported frozen assets and transfers from the oil-for-food programme had been properly and transparently accounted for in the Fund. However, on the basis of a review of the audit reports, IAMB believed that controls were insufficient to provide reasonable assurance for the completeness of export sales of petroleum and petroleum products and whether all Fund disbursements were made for the purposes intended. The priority findings of the audit report included: weaknesses in controls over oil extraction, including the absence of metering, resulting in the audit firm qualifying its audit opinions of the Fund's statements of cash receipts and payments; control weaknesses in the administration of resources handled by CPA, including inadequate record-keeping and accounting systems, and the uneven application of agreed-upon contracting procedures; and inadequate controls identified at Iraqi spending ministries, including the absence of reconciliation procedures, insufficient payroll records, deviation from tendering procedures and inadequate contract monitoring by CPA relating to payments on behalf of the Iraqi ministries. The audit reports were submitted to the Iraqi Council of Ministers and CPA for attention and follow-up. As a matter of priority, the financial reporting and control systems needed to be improved in key Iraqi disbursing ministries, including the State Oil Marketing Organization and the regional Governments, and controls strengthened over oil extraction.

The Board received six audit reports prepared by the United States Defense Contract Audit Agency on sole-sourced contracts which it had previously sought. IAMB agreed to the terms of reference for a special audit of those contracts by an independent auditor.

Communication. On 26 May [S/2005/344], Iraq requested the Council to approve the continuation of the Development Fund for Iraq and IAMB, as those mechanisms had demonstrated that Iraq's oil resources were being used transparently for the benefit of the Iraqi people and reassured donors and creditors that Iraq was managing its resources and its debts in a responsible manner. Moreover, IAMB had helped identify areas where stewardship of the Fund could be improved.

IAMB report (June). In a 13 June letter [S/2005/384] submitted by the Secretary-General to the Council President, the Secretary-General's representative on IAMB reported on the Board's activities since January. IAMB received, on 21 May, the reports by an independent auditor covering the audit of Iraq's oil export sales and the Fund's operations for the period from 29 June to 31 December 2004. The audit reports pointed out some weaknesses, including incomplete fund accounting records; untimely recording, reporting, reconciliation and follow-up of spending by Iraqi ministries; incomplete records maintained by United States agencies, including disbursements that were not recorded in the Iraqi budget; lack of documented justification for limited competition for contracts at the Iraqi ministries; unreconciled quantities of oil and oil products exported, indicating a lack of control and possible misappropriation of oil revenues, and significant difficulties in ensuring completeness and accuracy of Iraqi budgets and controls over expenditures; and the non-deposit of proceeds of export sales of petroleum products into the appropriate accounts in contravention of Council resolution 1483(2003) [YUN 2003, p. 338]. IAMB drew to the attention of the Iraqi Government the weaknesses identified in the audit reports and invited it to act on the audit recommendations to strengthen the Fund's financial controls and administration. IAMB also met with Iraqi officials to address

issues and concerns raised in the two previous audits covering the period from May 2003 to June 2004. On 15 April 2005, the United States informed IAMB that an independent auditor had been selected to carry out a special audit of sole-sourced contracts.

Security Council Committee established pursuant to resolution 1518(2003)

On 23 December [S/2005/827], the Chairman of the Security Council Committee established pursuant to resolution 1518(2003) [YUN 2003, p. 362] submitted to the Council President the Committee's annual report for 2005. The Committee was established to continue to identify, in accordance with paragraphs 19 and 23 of resolution 1483 (2003) [ibid., p. 338], individuals and entities associated with the former Iraqi regime whose funds, other financial assets and economic resources should be frozen and transferred to the Development Fund for Iraq. During the reporting period, the Committee held four informal meetings and reviewed, among other things, its draft guidelines for the de-listing of individuals and entities from its assets-freeze and transfer list.

UN Monitoring, Verification and Inspection Commission and IAEA activities

UNMOVIC

On 19 May [S/2005/333] and 23 August [S/2005/540], the Secretary-General proposed to the Security Council the appointments of Stephen G. Rademaker (United States) to the UNMOVIC College of Commissioners, replacing Susan F. Burk (United States); and Lu Yongshou (China), replacing Chen Weixiong (China). The Council agreed to the Secretary-General's proposals [S/2005/334, S/2005/541].

Reports of UNMOVIC (February, May). As called for in resolution 1284(1999) [YUN 1999, p. 230], UNMOVIC submitted to the Council, through the Secretary-General, four quarterly reports on its activities. Throughout the year, the Executive Chairman continued to provide monthly briefings to the Council President and kept the Secretary-General informed about the Commission's activities.

The February report [S/2005/129] stated that, during the period from 1 December 2004 to 28 February 2005, UNMOVIC imagery analysts continued the ongoing review of the status of sites subject to inspection and monitoring in Iraq. Of the 411 sites inspected, Commission experts examined post-war high-resolution imagery of 353. Of that number, approximately 70 showed varying degrees of bomb damage, and about 90 contained dual-use equipment and materials that had been stripped and/or razed. Commission experts also noted that repairs and new construction had commenced at 10 sites.

An UNMOVIC working group of technical experts was convened to prepare an initial study on monitoring procedures of small quantities of weapons of mass destruction (WMD) and to review the history of incidents involving small quantities of biological and chemical agents. The study would serve as the basis for a more in-depth assessment of the matter within UNMOVIC. The group considered the types and range of small quantities of agents; the capabilities needed for the acquisition of such quantities, including the quantity of precursors and capacity of equipment; and the possible points for acquiring, producing and transporting small quantities of agents for WMD, or associated primary precursors. It was noted that, although the ongoing monitoring and verification regime for Iraq included the monitoring of small-scale production activities in the biological and chemical disciplines and that relevant materials were subject to notification, it was possible that small quantities of such materials could be acquired through clandestine procurement networks. Accordingly, the group felt that some changes in emphasis and reporting thresholds in the current monitoring and verification regime might be needed, including more activity-based monitoring of sites and less reliance on specific quantities as triggers. UNMOVIC also continued to enhance its information technology system for inspectors and analysts. It noted the continuing uncertainty over the possible existence in Iraq of biological seed stocks (reference strains of micro-organisms provided by culture collections, as well as to master and working seed stocks) that could be used in the future for the production of biological weapon agents. The College of Commissioners discussed, among other things, confirmation of disarmament, monitoring and the possible need for end-use verification of imports of dual-use items into Iraq for a defined period, and recognized that those issues, including its mandate, were ultimately matters for the Council to decide.

In the May report [S/2005/351] covering the period from 1 March to 31 May, UNMOVIC said that Iran had notified the Commission that no dual-use equipment and materials subject to monitoring, which were known to have been present at Iraqi sites, had been found on Iranian soil. UNMOVIC imagery analysts continued to review the status of sites subject to inspection and monitoring in Iraq. The analysis revealed that dual-use items had been removed totally from 52 sites and partially from 44 others which had suffered

less damage. Additionally, at 13 sites, some items that were stored in the open had been removed. No conclusion could be drawn concerning the presence or absence of equipment or materials inside undamaged buildings, nor the destination of all items removed. The report examined some of the most significant dual-use equipment removed from the 109 sites under review with respect to categories, numbers and utilities.

A series of addenda to the October 2004 United States–led Iraq Survey Group report [YUN 2004, p. 362] were released in April 2005. The Group had found that reports of WMD in Iraq were usually scams or resulted from the misidentification of materials or activities. In a very limited number of cases they related to findings of old chemical munitions produced before 1990. Overall, the addenda did not change the previous assessment and comments made by UNMOVIC with regard to the October 2004 comprehensive report, although some information presented differed in detail from that in the Commission's possession. However, it appeared that most of the information came from interviews with individuals and was based mainly on their recollections. On the issue of the status of dual-use items and former weapons sites subject to monitoring, the limited assessments of the Iraq Survey Group corroborated information already obtained by the Commission through satellite imagery assessment.

In 2005, the results of an independent review of the biological provisions and associated annex of the monitoring and verification plan, carried out by a panel of external non-governmental technical experts, were submitted. The panel, first convened by UNMOVIC in November 2004 [YUN 2004, p. 362], suggested that Iraq could be assisted in the drafting and implementation of national legislation and compliance with international obligations, as well as in the establishment of a good records and documentation system which would help the monitoring and verification process. The panel also identified criteria to be the triggers for declarations under the monitoring plan, which pertained to containment, activities, international transfer, equipment and agents. UNMOVIC compiled its first draft of the compendium of Iraq's proscribed weapons and programmes in March. The draft provided a detailed technical description of Iraq's proscribed weapons and programmes with an emphasis on lessons that could be drawn from both the nature of the programmes and the experience gained in the process of their verification by UN inspectors. Examples of such lessons on specific issues were outlined in an appendix to the report.

In the August report [S/2005/545] covering the period from 1 June to 31 August, UNMOVIC said that, in June, the Commission convened a panel of external technical experts to conduct a technical review of the missile provisions and the associated list of dual-use items, equipment and technology. The panel made recommendations regarding the missile provisions, in the light of the UN monitoring and verification experience, the changed situation in Iraq and technical advances in unmanned delivery systems that could be associated with the delivery of weapons of mass destruction. An overview of the biological weapons programme of Iraq was annexed to the report.

The November report [S/2005/742] covering the period from 1 September to 30 November noted that UNMOVIC's imagery analysts had been assessing activities at sites by analysing images of specific locations over successive time frames. Imagery from September showed that agricultural activity had started inside the perimeter of the former Muthanna State Establishment, once Iraq's prime chemical weapons production site, where the majority of chemical weapons destruction also took place. UNMOVIC continued to follow up on dual-use technology developments and to assess the implications for its mandate and the application of new technologies in detection, monitoring and verification. An overview of Iraq's procurement for its WMD programmes was annexed to the report.

Escrow account

On 20 June [S/2005/406], the Secretary-General proposed to the Security Council that an amount of $200,000,000 be transferred from UNMOVIC's escrow account established under Council resolution 1284(1999) [YUN 1999, p. 230] and related resolutions to the Development Fund for Iraq, and $20,256,697 credited against assessments issued in respect of the obligations of the Iraqi Government for UN regular budget, peacekeeping and international Tribunal activities. On 24 June [S/2005/407], the Council approved the Secretary-General's proposal.

On 2 November [S/2005/702], the Secretary-General proposed that $2,182,168 plus 226,493 euros be transferred from the UNMOVIC escrow account to settle Iraq's outstanding arrears with IAEA. On 9 November [S/2005/703], the Council approved the Secretary-General's proposal.

IAEA

IAEA reports (April and October). In accordance with Security Council resolution 1051(1996) [YUN 1996, p. 218], IAEA submitted to the Council,

through the Secretary-General, two consolidated six-monthly reports, on 13 April [S/2005/243] and 14 October [S/2005/652], on the Agency's verification activities in Iraq.

In April, IAEA said that, since 17 March 2003, it had not been in a position to implement its mandate in Iraq under Council resolution 687(1991) [YUN 1991, p. 172] and related resolutions. Given the adoption of Council resolution 1546(2004) [YUN 2004, p. 348], IAEA's mandate pursuant to those resolutions remained valid until the Council decided otherwise. IAEA stood ready to resume verification activities in Iraq and maintained a core team with the necessary competence required for the fulfilment of that mandate. During the period under review, IAEA continued to consolidate, restructure and further analyse the information collected by it since 1991, so as to identify lessons learned and secure data in paper and electronic archives for improved future access and maintenance of knowledge, while at the same time developing strategies for future verification activities in Iraq, should the Council direct the Agency to do so. The information obtained was derived principally from open sources and commercial satellite imagery of locations of interest to IAEA for potential future verification in Iraq. The imagery showed that there had been extensive removal of equipment and that one site, which contained buried contaminated rubble, had been extensively excavated.

In October, IAEA reported that, pursuant to the Safeguards Agreement between Iraq and IAEA in connection with the 1968 Treaty on the Non-Proliferation of Nuclear Weapons [YUN 1968, p. 17], it carried out on 17 and 18 September its annual physical inventory verification of the nuclear material in Iraq located at the store facility near the Tuwaitha complex south of Baghdad. IAEA inspectors were able to verify all nuclear material subject to safeguards. The Iraq Nuclear Verification Office had focused on the further development of an archive system for the storage and retrieval of electronic and hard-copy information collected and generated by IAEA in the course of its Council-mandated activities in Iraq. Satellite imagery of the most significant sites continued to be collected and assessed.

Iraq-Kuwait

Oil-for-food programme: high-level Independent Inquiry Committee

The oil-for-food programme, established by Security Council resolution 986(1995) [YUN 1995,

p. 475] authorizing the sale of Iraqi petroleum and petroleum products as a temporary measure to finance humanitarian assistance, thereby alleviating the adverse consequences of the sanctions regime imposed by the Council, was phased out on 21 November 2003 [YUN 2003, p. 362]. In March 2004 [YUN 2004, p. 364], the Secretary-General informed the Council of his intention to establish an independent, high-level inquiry concerning matters arising from public news reports and commentaries that had called into question the administration and management of the programme, including allegations of fraud and corruption. The independent inquiry, according to its terms of reference, was to determine whether UN procedures for the processing and approving of contracts under the programme, the monitoring of the sale and delivery of petroleum and related products and the purchase of and delivery of humanitarian goods had been violated; and whether any UN official, personnel, agent or contractor had engaged in any illicit or corrupt activities in the carrying out of their respective roles in relation to the programme. In April 2004 [ibid., p. 364], the high-level Independent Inquiry Committee (IIC), headed by Paul A. Volcker, was formed. (For further information, see Part V, Chapter I.)

On 7 September, IIC submitted its final report, "The Management of the United Nations Oil-for-Food Programme", to the Council (see p. 1475).

Security Council consideration (September). On 7 September [meeting 5256], the Council was briefed by IIC Chairman, Paul Volcker on the broad conclusions and recommendations of the Committee's report. The Secretary-General attended the meeting.

Mr. Volcker said that IIC found evidence of mismanagement in the oil-for-food programme and of corruption within the United Nations and by contractors. The responsibility for the failures had to be broadly shared, starting with Member States and the Council itself. In the first place, the programme left too much initiative with Iraq. That basic difficulty was compounded by a failure to clearly define the complex administrative responsibilities shared between the Security Council Committee established by resolution 661 (1990) [YUN 1990, p. 192] (Committee on Sanctions) and the UN Secretariat, and by continuing political differences. The result was that no one seemed clearly in command and delays in and evasion of decision-making were chronic. The administrative structure and practices of the Secretariat and some agencies were not up to the challenge presented by the programme. Those weaknesses were aggravated by unethical and corrupt behaviour at key points at the higher lev-

els of the Office of the Iraq Programme and in the purchasing department. There was a pervasive absence of effective auditing and administrative controls, as well as weak planning, inadequate funding and too few professional staff. The absence of truly independent status for the auditing and control functions was a critical deficiency. Close cooperation among various UN organs apparently went against the grain for agencies with their own funding, management and oversight. On the positive side, an expert study commissioned by the Committee confirmed that the programme had averted malnutrition and a further collapse of medical services in Iraq. That was no small achievement, especially when combined with the support that the programme had provided for maintaining the basic sanctions against Iraq and its inability to obtain WMDs.

IIC conclusions and recommendations called for a stronger operational capacity and authority and a new chief operating officer with a clear mandate and authority for administration; strong and independent auditing control and investigatory functions; and a strong independent oversight board.

Mr. Volcker said that IIC's conclusions could not be dismissed as simply reporting aberrations in one programme or something that could be smoothed over with patchwork changes. The problems were symptomatic of deep-seated systemic issues. Those issues arose in an Organization designed 60 years ago for a simpler time, without large and complex operational challenges alongside its political and diplomatic responsibilities. The Organization's credibility and confidence were challenged by the travails of the oil-for-food programme and, to some degree, the Organization had been weakened. Reform was therefore urgent and the Council and the General Assembly should set benchmarks for progress.

The Secretary-General said that the report was critical of him personally, which he accepted. The Committee had previously concluded that he did not influence, or attempt to influence, the procurement process. However, he did accept, with regret, the conclusion that he was not diligent or effective enough in pursuing an investigation after the fact, when he learned that the company that employed his son had won the humanitarian inspection contract. The evidence of actual corruption among a small number of UN staff was also disappointing. On the positive side, the Committee noted that the programme did succeed in restoring and maintaining minimal standards of nutrition and health in Iraq, while helping to maintain the international effort to prevent Saddam Hussein from acquiring WMDs.

Secondly, it observed that the wholesale corruption within the programme took place among private companies manipulated by Saddam Hussein's Government. More important, however, were the Committee's findings about the general management of the programme, which was characterized by weak administrative practices and inadequate control and auditing, which reflected on the system of decision-making, accountability and management throughout the Organization. Here too, the Secretary-General took responsibility for the failings revealed, both in the implementation of the programme and, more generally, in the functioning of the Secretariat.

The Secretary-General said that the report also found that many of those problems were rooted in an unclear demarcation of roles and responsibilities among the Council, its Committee on Sanctions and the Secretariat, and in particular, in the Council's decision to retain substantial elements of operational control within the Committee on Sanctions, composed of national diplomats working under highly politicized instructions from their home Governments, yet willing to take decisions only when there was unanimous consent among all of its 15 members.

The Inquiry's findings underscored the importance of management reforms, many of which were already being considered in the General Assembly as part of a broader agenda of political and institutional change. The Secretary-General had already embarked on new reforms in areas where he had discretion to improve the performance of senior management, strengthen oversight and accountability, increase transparency and ensure the highest standards of ethics, notably by creating a new ethics office. In addition, it was vital to review the rules governing the Organization's budgetary and human resources, to build a stronger and better-resourced oversight structure and ensure that it was fully independent both from the Secretariat and from political interference by Member States. The Secretary-General should be allowed to carry out his functions effectively, taking decisions on the deployment of staff and resources without having to wait for prior approval from the Assembly, the Council or their various committees. As stated in the report, one of the fundamental problems with the oil-for-food programme was that neither the Council nor the Secretariat's leadership was clearly in command, and that turned out to be a recipe for the dilution of Secretariat authority and the evasion of personal responsibility at all levels. The Secretary-General stated that Member States, the Secretariat, agencies, funds and programmes could not be proud

of what IIC had found. Reform was imperative if the United Nations was to regain and retain the measure of respect among the international community that its work required.

Communication of Secretary-General. On 20 December [S/2005/847], the Secretary-General informed the Council President that the United Nations had received requests from the IIC Chairman and the Government of Iraq to maintain the Committee's operation until the end of March 2006. Given Iraq's support for that proposal and in view of the volume of inquiries to the Committee for the cooperation by Member States seeking to follow up on the findings of its final report, the Secretary-General decided to accede to the IIC Chairman's request. The basis for the extension and other details on the follow-up functions of IIC and related matters were annexed to the Secretary-General's letter. The Committee, once it had completed its investigation, would not retain any investigative capacity or authority.

On 30 December [S/2005/848], the Council took note of the Secretary-General's information and decision, in particular that the extension would be exclusively to assist national bodies investigating the cases resulting from the Committee's work, manage access to the Committee archives and ensure its preservation and disposition.

United Nations Iraq Account: letters of credit

The Secretary-General, in response to Security Council resolution 1483(2003) [YUN 2003, p. 338] terminating all activities under the oil-for-food programme on 21 November 2003, had informed the Council [ibid., p. 366] that the United Nations would retain beyond the termination date, and until they were executed or expired, responsibility for the administration and execution of letters of credit issued under the programme by the bank for the United Nations Iraq Account (UNIA) for the purchase of humanitarian supplies for the south/centre of Iraq.

In an 8 August letter to the Council President [S/2005/535], the Secretary-General addressed the issue of the management of those letters of credit so that the termination of the oil-for-food programme could be continued in an orderly manner. As at 31 July, 549 letters of credit were reported by the bank as being "open", due to difficulties in processing the authentication documents required for payment to the vendor, resulting in funds being retained in UNIA for the expired letters of credit. To overcome those difficulties and since most of the letters had already expired, the Secretary-General submitted proposals for reinstating or extending the letters of credit, including those that had expired by 31

December 2004, those expiring in 2005, and those due to expire in 2006 and 2007. He also made proposals for resolving a number of related issues.

On 19 August [S/2005/536], the Council welcomed the Secretary-General's proposal and requested him to report orally to the Council on the implementation of those arrangements by mid-October.

On 17 October [S/2005/656], the Secretary-General said that consultations on the termination of the ongoing operations of the oil-for-food programme were conducted by the UN Controller with the relevant Iraqi authorities on 3 October. Of the 549 letters of credit reported as open as at 8 August, 44 had been paid, 17 reinstated for the purpose of making payments and two cancelled. However, the rate of processing of the authentication documents for the arrival of goods in Iraq had not improved. The Secretary-General outlined his course of action for dealing with the remaining letters of credit.

On 11 November [S/2005/713], the Council President said that the Secretary-General's letter concerning the termination of operations relating to the letters of credit raised against UNIA had been brought to the attention of the Council during private consultations held on 19 October with the Controller. The Council welcomed the 3 October meeting between the UN and the relevant Iraqi authorities and took note of the new arrangements proposed by the Secretary-General. It requested him to inform the Council on the implementation of those arrangements by mid-December.

In a 19 December update [S/2005/807], the Secretary-General informed the Council that some progress had been made on the amendments to the letters of credit by the relevant Iraqi authorities. Since his letter of 17 October, Iraq had provided the United Nations with 127 formal requests for amendments and reinstatements of letters of credit. However, little progress had been made with regard to the processing of authentication documents. Bearing in mind the timetable envisaged in the previous letters, the Secretary-General provided an update on the implementation of the new arrangements concerning the termination of operations relating to the letters of credit raised against UNIA.

POWs, Kuwaiti property and missing persons

On 18 April [S/2005/251], the Council President stated that, following consultations held on 11 April, the Council had agreed that issues relating to the return of all Kuwaiti property, the repatriation or return of all Kuwaiti and third-country nationals or their remains, and the United Nations Compensation Commission would be considered under the agenda item entitled "The situation between Iraq and Kuwait". Other issues that did not fall under that category would be considered under the agenda item entitled "The situation concerning Iraq".

Reports of Secretary-General (April/June). In response to Security Council resolution 1284 (1999) [YUN 1999, p. 230], the Secretary-General submitted reports in April [S/2005/233 & Corr.1], June [S/2005/377], August [S/2005/513], and December [S/2005/769] on Iraq's compliance with its obligations regarding the repatriation or return of all Kuwaiti and third-country nationals or their remains, and on the return of all Kuwaiti property, including archives, seized by Iraq during its occupation of Kuwait, which began in August 1990 [YUN 1990, p. 189]. The High-level Coordinator for compliance by Iraq with its obligations regarding the return of Kuwaiti nationals and property, Yuli M. Vorontsov (Russian Federation), briefed the Council throughout the year.

In April, the Secretary-General observed that the search for Kuwaiti POWs and third-country nationals had not progressed substantially since the submission of his December 2004 report [YUN 2004, p. 365]. However, the identification of remains had continued. He supported the determination of the Kuwaiti Government to pursue the issue of Kuwaiti POWs and third-country nationals until all files were closed. The new Iraqi authorities had taken a constructive stance in meeting Iraq's international obligations in accordance with resolution 1284(1999).

In June, the Secretary-General said that the Kuwaiti national archives had still not been found. He welcomed the agreement of the Iraqi Government to send a joint Kuwaiti-Iraqi mission of experts to Tunisia to deal with the issue of spare parts belonging to Kuwait Airways Corporation (KAC) found on board two Iraqi aircrafts stationed in Tunisia.

In his August report, the Secretary-General said that different sources continued to provide information about the location of grave sites possibly containing the remains of Kuwaiti and third-country nationals. Kuwaiti assessment teams visited Iraq between March and May. Iraqi representatives took part in the joint assessment and investigative efforts.

In December, the Secretary-General said that improvement in Iraq's cooperation could speed up the search for the remains of Kuwaiti and third-country missing persons. However, given the security situation in Iraq and the technical difficulties in the identification process, progress in resolving the issue had been slow. The Secretary-General supported Kuwait's call for expertise from specialized laboratories worldwide to resolve the problems of identification. He also reported that the mission of experts, led by the High-level Coordinator to Tunisia (12-16 September), ascertained that the aircraft spare parts and engine found in Tunisia belonged to Kuwait, which was further evidence of the illegal removal of items from Kuwait by the previous Iraqi regime.

UN Iraq-Kuwait Observation Mission

The United Nations Iraq-Kuwait Observation Mission (UNIKOM) discharged its functions until 6 October 2003, in accordance with its terms of reference, as expanded by resolution 806(1993) [YUN 1993, p. 406].

The Secretary-General submitted to the General Assembly a report on UNIKOM financing [A/59/614], providing details on the final disposition of its assets, the inventory value of which amounted to $23,916,522, as at 3 July 2003. In April 2005 [A/59/736 & Add.14], ACABQ considered the Secretary-General's report on UNIKOM's financing.

On 22 June, the Assembly took note of the Secretary-General's report (**decision 59/565**).

UN Compensation Commission and Fund

The United Nations Compensation Commission (UNCC), established in 1991 [YUN 1991, p. 195] for the resolution and payment of claims against Iraq for losses and damage resulting from its 1990 invasion and occupation of Kuwait [YUN 1990, p. 189], continued in 2005 to expedite the prompt settlement of claims through the United Nations Compensation Fund, which was established at the same time as the Commission.

Governing Council. The Commission's Governing Council held four sessions in Geneva during the year—the fifty-fifth (8-10 March) [S/2005/169], the fifty-sixth (28-30 June) [S/2005/507], the fifty-seventh (27-29 September) [S/2005/686] and the fifty-eighth (6-8 December) [S/2005/815]—at which it considered the reports and recommendations of the Panels of Commissioners appointed to review specific instalments of various categories of claims. The Governing Council also acted on the Executive Secretary's report submitted at each session, which, in addition to providing a summary of the previous period's activities, covered the processing, withdrawal and payment of claims.

Other matters considered by the Council included the processing and payment of claims, ensuring payments were made into the Compensation Fund, the distribution of payments and the return of undistributed funds. It also decided that it would not give any further consideration to claims preparation costs.

Oversight activities

On 29 December [S/2005/840], the Secretary-General transmitted to the Security Council the report of the Board of Auditors, updated as at 31 July 2005, on the implementation of its 2004 recommendations [YUN 2004, p. 367] relating to the Compensation Commission for the 2002-2003 biennium. The Board found that eight of its 20 recommendations had been implemented by June 2005, though the Board had yet to validate the implementation of two of them; nine remained under implementation and the Board had yet to validate the degree of implementation for three of them; and three had not been implemented.

Timor-Leste

In 2005, the Security Council established the United Nations Office in Timor-Leste (UNOTIL) by resolution 1599(2005) (see p. 440) as a follow-on mission to the United Nations Mission of Support in East Timor (UNMISET), which came to an end on 20 May. UNOTIL was charged with supporting and monitoring progress in the development of critical state institutions, the police and the Border Patrol Unit and observance of democratic governance and human rights.

Commission of Experts. Pursuant to Council resolution 1573(2004) [YUN 2004, p. 376] reaffirming the need to fight against impunity in Timor-Leste, the Secretary-General on 11 January [S/2005/96] informed the Council of the establishment of an independent Commission of Experts to review the prosecution of serious crimes against humanity committed in East Timor in 1999. The Commission, consisting of three experts, would assess the progress made by the Indonesian judicial process involving the ad hoc Human Rights Tribunal in the Indonesian Capital, Jakarta, and the serious crimes process, involving the Serious Crimes Unit and the Special Panels for Serious Crimes in Timor-Leste's capital, Dili, and identify obstacles and difficulties encountered. It would evaluate the extent to which justice and accountability for the crimes committed in East Timor had been achieved and recommend further measures so that perpetrators could be held accountable and reconciliation promoted.

On 26 January [S/2005/97], the Council President informed the Secretary-General that the Council had noted his decision to establish a Commission of Experts. On 17 February [S/2005/104], the Secretary-General informed the Council of the appointment of Prafullachandra Bhagwati (India), Yozo Yokota (Japan) and Shaista Shameem (Fiji) to the Commission of Experts.

UN Mission of Support in East Timor

Prior to its closure on 20 May, UNMISET, which was established under Security Council resolution 1410(2002) [YUN 2002, p. 321], continued to carry out its mandate in Timor-Leste by providing assistance to the administrative, law enforcement and public security structures critical to the viability and political stability of Timor-Leste, in addition to contributing to the maintenance of its external and internal security.

Report of Secretary-General (February). In response to Security Council resolution 1573 (2004) [YUN 2004, p. 376], the Secretary-General submitted a February report [S/2005/99] covering UNMISET activities since his November 2004 report [YUN 2004, p. 374]. During that period, the overall situation in Timor-Leste remained calm and stable despite the reported incursion of an armed ex-militia group in January and clashes between the military and police.

While the National Parliament continued to strengthen the country's legal framework through the adoption of key legislation, no progress was made in the selection of the Provedor for Human Rights and Justice. The delay was a cause for concern, especially in the light of an increase in reported cases of abuse of police power, especially in dealing with political opposition. Despite efforts to improve the relationship between the Timorese armed forces and the national police, problems continued to arise, and members of the two groups had clashed in past months. Sightings of alleged ex-militia groups, especially in border areas, had also been reported. On 20 January, the Prime Minister, Mari Alkatiri, publicly stated that it should not be assumed that the ex-militia infiltrators were acting at the behest of the Indonesian army. Nevertheless, the Tactical Coordination Line remained porous and disputes between opposing villages, illegal trading, smuggling, illegal border crossings and minor criminal activities continued to occur.

Relations between Timor-Leste and Indonesia continued to improve, with frequent high-level meetings being held during the reporting period. During his visit to Jakarta from 27 to 29 January, Timor-Leste President, Xanana Gusmão, discussed with Indonesian President, Susilo Bambang Yudhoyono, the formation of the Truth and Friendship Commission, decided on in 2004 [YUN 2004, p. 377] to deal with human rights abuses perpetrated in 1999, as well as other bilateral issues. The Commission's terms of reference were reviewed at a meeting (7-9 February) between the Timor-Leste Minister for Foreign Affairs, José Ramos-Horta, and his Indonesian counterpart, Hassan Wirajuda.

As regards security, work on the defence plan known as "Defence 2020" was ongoing, and further progress was expected at the end of workshops to be held in May. The military liaison group continued to foster close collaboration between the Timorese and Indonesian border security agencies by holding weekly meetings at which the two countries discussed and resolved border issues and disputes. Nevertheless, working relations between the respective border security agencies remained at the developmental stage, reinforcing the continued need for military liaison officers. Additional training by the military liaison group, in cooperation with UNMISET civilian police advisers, would be needed to bring the Timorese border security agencies up to the required level of self-sufficiency. Military liaison officers would also be required to facilitate communication between the two parties, especially since a formal agreement on the demarcation of the border had not been reached. The military liaison arrangement between the Indonesian army and UNMISET was due to expire on 20 May. However, a successor arrangement between Indonesia and Timor-Leste, under which the Tactical Coordination Line would remain in place but the Border Patrol Unit would replace UNMISET's military component, had yet to be endorsed by either side. The Secretary-General urged them to expeditiously resolve, by 20 May, a final agreement on the demarcation of the land border or a border management agreement similar to the military liaison arrangement. Timor-Leste therefore requested that a 41-person military liaison component continue to be deployed beyond 20 May. As advised by UNMISET, the Secretary-General recommended retaining 35 military liaison officers to continue facilitating contacts between the Timorese and Indonesian border security agencies, providing additional training to the Timorese border security agencies and monitoring security-related developments along the border. In addition, the continued deployment of a small international security force, of some 144 troops, including logistic support and air mobility, would be required to protect the military liaison officers and other UN personnel. As the Timorese Police Reserve Unit had become operational, the 125-person International Response Unit would be removed, resulting in a significant reduction of the military component.

The eight transition working groups constituted by the Special Representative in August 2004 [YUN 2004, p. 375] to identify assistance requirements and assess progress made in institutional capacity-building completed their work. While their findings and conclusions did not represent a consensus of all participants, they reflected an objective assessment of the key concerns remaining in the areas covered by the UNMISET mandate, namely the development of a professional police service, the deficiencies of the Timorese security sector and the overall capacity development of State and Government institutions, including the development of a functioning justice sector. Also addressed were the continuing requirements for enhancing transparency and accountability, the future of the serious crimes process and the need to support marginalized groups.

The Secretary-General observed that tangible progress had been made in establishing sustainable State institutions and in promoting democracy, transparency, accountability and respect for human rights during the UNMISET consolidation phase, which started in May 2004 [YUN 2004, p. 368]. Nevertheless, significant challenges remained and the provision of international assistance beyond the expiration of UNMISET's current mandate on 20 May would be crucial for the long-term security, stability and sustainable development of the country. The Secretary-General, noting Timor-Leste's request (see below) for the continuation of UNMISET's mandate, recommended maintaining a UN mission with a scaled-down structure for 12 months, until 20 May 2006.

Communication (February). On 20 January [S/2005/103], Timor-Leste's Prime Minister requested that UNMISET's mandate be extended for another year, with some 41 military liaison officers, 58 civilian trainers and 62 police trainers in order to support the further development of Timorese capacity. He also hoped for a coordinated structure for the provision of that assistance which would be a single focal point of contact and include human rights and other advisers. He requested that the Secretary-General recommend those measures to the Security Council.

Security Council consideration (February). On 28 February [meeting 5132], the Security Council considered the Secretary General's February report (see above). In his briefing to the Council,

the Secretary-General's Special Representative to Timor-Leste, Mr. Hasegawa, said that, although progress had been registered in the area of institution-building, as some State institutions, for instance banking institutions, were less dependent on international experts, it had become clear that several ministries and institutions continued to require international advisers, particularly for justice, legal and security matters, as well as in the finance and monetary sector, where highly specialized expertise was required. The Prime Minister had therefore requested the retention of 58 "most critical" posts, and while UNMISET recognized the need for many of those posts, it suggested that 45 posts might be sufficient. The United Nations Development Programme (UNDP) and the World Bank were making arrangements to fund some posts, but there had been no other firm commitments. Without some form of continued international assistance, it was almost certain that several State institutions would not be able to discharge their sovereign functions adequately after May.

Legal advisers had pointed out the urgent need to lay out basic legal frameworks for several ministries. Similarly, the Timorese authorities sought guidance on how to combat emerging corruption.

While a provisional line comprising more than 95 per cent of the borderline had been agreed upon at the technical level, Timor-Leste and Indonesia were unable to resolve the remaining issues and to establish a transportation corridor linking the enclave of Oecussi located inside West Timor with the rest of Timor-Leste.

In the area of law enforcement, UN police continued to play an advisory role, focusing on the improvement of policing capability, professional development and the institutional strengthening of the Timor-Leste national police. The professional skills development plan was concluding its second phase of training national police officers in all 13 districts, and UN police advisers and bilateral partners were working closely on a "training the trainers" course and a course for station commanders. Despite significant progress made in training officers of the Timor-Leste national police on human rights issues, the excessive use of force and professional misconduct by the national police remained major challenges. UN police technical advisers were advising and training national police officers to deal with a large backlog of professional ethics cases at the national police headquarters.

SECURITY COUNCIL ACTION

On 28 April [meeting 5171], the Security Council unanimously adopted **resolution 1599(2005)**.

The draft [S/2005/267] was prepared in consultations among council members.

The Security Council,

Reaffirming its previous resolutions on the situation in Timor-Leste, in particular resolutions 1543(2004) of 14 May 2004 and 1573(2004) of 16 November 2004,

Having considered the report of the Secretary-General of 18 February 2005,

Commending the people and the Government of Timor-Leste for the peace and stability they have achieved in the country, as well as for their continuing efforts towards consolidating democracy and strengthening State institutions,

Commending the United Nations Mission of Support in East Timor, under the leadership of the Special Representative of the Secretary-General, and welcoming the continuing progress made towards the completion of key tasks inscribed in its mandate, particularly during its consolidation phase, in accordance with resolutions 1543(2004) and 1573(2004),

Paying tribute to Timor-Leste's bilateral and multilateral partners for their invaluable assistance, particularly with regard to institutional capacity-building and social and economic development,

Expressing its appreciation to those Member States which have provided support to the Mission,

Having considered the letter dated 20 January 2005 from the Prime Minister of Timor-Leste to the Secretary-General,

Noting the Secretary-General's analysis of the need for a United Nations presence to remain in Timor-Leste after 20 May 2005, although at a reduced level,

Noting also that the emerging institutions in Timor-Leste are still in the process of consolidation and that further assistance is required to ensure sustained development and strengthening of key sectors, mainly rule of law, including justice, human rights, and support for the Timor-Leste police, and other public administration,

Acknowledging the excellent communication and goodwill that have characterized relations between Timor-Leste and Indonesia, including the decision to establish a Truth and Friendship Commission, and their land border agreement signed in Dili on 8 April 2005, which covers approximately 96 per cent of the land border, and encouraging continued efforts by both Governments towards resolving this and all pending bilateral issues,

Acknowledging also the decision of the Secretary-General outlined in his letter dated 11 January 2005 to the Security Council to send a Commission of Experts to Timor-Leste and Indonesia to review the serious crimes accountability processes and recommend further measures as appropriate,

Remaining fully committed to the promotion of long-lasting stability in Timor-Leste,

1. *Decides* to establish a one-year follow-on special political mission in Timor-Leste, the United Nations Office in Timor-Leste, which will remain in Timor-Leste until 20 May 2006;

2. *Decides also* that the Office will have the following mandate:

(*a*) To support the development of critical State institutions through provision of up to forty-five civilian advisers;

(*b*) To support further development of the police through provision of up to forty police advisers, and support for development of the Border Patrol Unit through provision of up to thirty-five additional advisers, fifteen of whom may be military advisers;

(*c*) To provide training in observance of democratic governance and human rights through provision of up to ten human rights officers; and

(*d*) To monitor and review progress in (*a*) to (*c*) above;

3. *Requests* that, when implementing its mandate, the Office emphasize proper transfer of skills and knowledge in order to build the capacity of the public institutions of Timor-Leste to deliver their services in accordance with international principles of the rule of law, justice, human rights, democratic governance, transparency, accountability and professionalism;

4. *Also requests* that the Office be led by a Special Representative of the Secretary-General, who will direct the operations of the mission and coordinate all United Nations activities in Timor-Leste through his office, with due attention to safety of personnel, and facilitated by appropriate levels of logistics support, including transportation assets, such as air transport when necessary;

5. *Further requests* that the Secretary-General deploy some of the advisers, authorized in paragraph 2 (*b*) above, to assist the National Police of Timor-Leste in developing procedures for and in training the Border Patrol Unit and to assist the Government of Timor-Leste in coordinating contacts with the Indonesian military, with the objective of transferring skills to the Border Patrol Unit to assume full responsibility for such coordination as soon as possible;

6. *Underlines* the fact that United Nations assistance to Timor-Leste should be coordinated with the efforts of bilateral and multilateral donors, regional mechanisms, non-governmental organizations, private sector organizations and other actors from within the international community, and encourages the Special Representative of the Secretary-General to establish and chair a consultative group, made up of these stakeholders in Timor-Leste, that will meet regularly for that purpose;

7. *Urges* the donor community, as well as the United Nations agencies and multilateral financial institutions, to continue providing resources and assistance for the implementation of projects towards sustainable and long-term development in Timor-Leste, and urges the donor community to actively participate in the donors conference scheduled to be held in April 2005;

8. *Encourages,* in particular, the Government of Timor-Leste, the Office, the United Nations Secretariat, United Nations development and humanitarian agencies, and multilateral financial institutions to start immediately planning for a smooth and rapid transition in Timor-Leste from a special political mission to a sustainable development assistance framework;

9. *Reaffirms* the need for credible accountability for the serious human rights violations committed in East Timor in 1999, and in this regard underlines the need for the Secretariat, in agreement with the authorities of Timor-Leste, to preserve a complete copy of all the records compiled by the Serious Crimes Unit, calls upon all parties to cooperate fully with the work of the Secretary-General's Commission of Experts, and looks

forward to the Commission's upcoming report exploring possible ways to address this issue, including ways of assisting the Truth and Friendship Commission which Indonesia and Timor-Leste have agreed to establish;

10. *Requests* the Secretary-General to keep the Council closely and regularly informed of developments on the ground and of the implementation of the mandate of the Office, and the planning for a transition to a sustainable development assistance framework, and to submit a report within four months of the date of adoption of the present resolution and every four months thereafter, with recommendations for any modifications such progress might allow to size, composition, mandate and duration of the presence of the Office;

11. *Decides* to remain actively seized of the matter.

Report of Secretary-General (May). The Secretary-General, in his May end of mandate report [S/2005/310] reviewing the activities of UNMISET since February, said that occasional problems continued to arise between the Timorese armed forces and the national police, including an altercation near a nightclub in Dili which remained under investigation. The problem posed by the proliferation of weapons in Timor-Leste was highlighted by an assault upon the manager of the Australia–New Zealand Bank and his wife outside their residence in Dili. Violence perpetrated by martial arts groups also increased during the reporting period, as did illegal cross-border activities.

Local elections were successfully held in the eastern districts of Baucau, Lautem and Manatuto in two phases, on 17 and 23 March, respectively. The technical and logistical difficulties encountered in the first phase of the elections, including errors in the voter roll, invalid voter registration cards and inadequate transportation to the polling stations, were mostly overcome in the second phase. While the ruling Fretilin party dominated the elections in the Baucau district, independent and opposition candidates won a significant number of seats in the other two districts.

Relations between Timor-Leste and Indonesia were further reinforced by the visit of the President of Indonesia, Susilo Bambang Yudhoyono, to Timor-Leste on 8 and 9 April. In an address to the Timorese Parliament, President Yudhoyono stressed Indonesia's commitment to resolve the outstanding issues between the two countries, including the status of East Timorese refugees residing in western Timor, security in border areas, and the common land and maritime boundaries. Indonesia intended to establish a land connection route between Oecussi and mainland Timor-Leste, continue the scholarship programme for Timorese students studying in Indonesia, and provide training for 100 Timorese police officers in Indonesia. In a symbolic gesture of reconciliation, President Yudhoyono ended his visit by laying a wreath at the Santa Cruz cemetery. During that visit, the Foreign Ministers of Timor-Leste and Indonesia signed the Provisional Agreement on the Borderline, as finalized by the Technical Subcommittee on Border Demarcation and Regulation at its meeting in Bogor, Indonesia, on 28 and 29 March. The Agreement, which came into effect on 8 May, established a provisional borderline covering approximately 96 per cent of the entire land border. The Technical Subcommittee was due to meet again shortly thereafter to discuss the surveys to be carried out on the remaining 4 per cent of the border, most of which was located along the Oecussi enclave border, as well as additional ground surveys to further refine the agreed provisional line.

On 29 March, the National Parliament endorsed Sebastiao Dias Ximenes as the first Provedor (Ombudsman) for Human Rights and Justice of Timor-Leste, paving the way for that office to begin its work. Advances in strengthening the Timorese legal system included the promulgation on 17 February of the law on the Superior Council for Defence and Security.

In accordance with Security Council resolution 1543(2004) [YUN 2004, p. 372], UN support for the serious crimes process was to cease on 20 May. The Secretary-General received, on 29 April, a letter from the Commission of Experts requesting that the liquidation of the Serious Crimes Unit be suspended and that measures be considered to safeguard the institutional knowledge of the serious crimes process until the findings of the Commission had been submitted to and considered by the Security Council. In response to that request, 10 staff of the Serious Crimes Unit, including an international judge, a prosecutor, a legal officer and administrative assistants, were to be retained during the UNMISET liquidation phase. During the reporting period, the Special Panels for serious crimes completed eight trials involving 11 defendants, leaving no pending trials. The Special Panels had tried a total of 87 defendants, 84 of whom were convicted of crimes against humanity and other charges, while three were acquitted of all charges. The Court of Appeal heard six serious crimes cases, while six others were still pending.

With a view to increasing the accountability and professionalism of the police, professional ethics offices were opened in the districts to assist in the investigation of complaints of misconduct. During the reporting period, such complaints, including violations of human rights, decreased; 43 cases of misconduct were reported from February to April 2005, compared to 78 cases from November 2004 to January 2005.

The relationship between the Indonesian Armed Forces and the Border Patrol Unit continued to develop with assistance from the Military Liaison Group. On 21 April, however, the Border Patrol Unit exchanged gunfire with Indonesian military personnel, who were reportedly pursuing a group of smugglers at the Tactical Coordination Line. UNMISET facilitated several meetings between the two groups in order to exchange information and assisted both sides in conducting an impartial investigation. However, the Indonesian Armed Forces cancelled a third meeting, indicating that it would not participate in further talks with the Unit until the Timorese police were prepared to share the results of their investigation.

The Secretary-General welcomed the adoption of Security Council resolution 1599(2005) (see p. 440), in which the Council reaffirmed its continuing commitment to Timor-Leste through the establishment of a one-year follow-on mission in the country, the United Nations Office in Timor-Leste (UNOTIL). Noting that the Council did not authorize the deployment of the 144-strong backup security force, as he had recommended (see p. 439), the Secretary-General warned that the withdrawal of the last uniformed UN troops from Timor-Leste could have a negative impact on the overall security situation in the country, as it would eliminate a significant deterrent to criminal activities, especially in border areas. The withdrawal of the military engineering unit, which ensured the maintenance of the land route between Dili and the border, was also a matter for concern. It was expected that, without such intervention, the route would become impassable, especially during the rainy season. He indicated that further international assistance would be essential, beyond the support provided through UNOTIL, including assistance with security needs. Additionally, the advisory support available through UNOTIL to strengthen administrative and police structures would need to be supplemented with bilateral and multilateral assistance to ensure sustainable progress.

Security Council consideration (May). On 16 May [meeting 5180], the Security Council considered the Secretary-General's end of mandate report on UNMISET (see above). The Assistant Secretary-General for Peacekeeping Operations, Hédi Annabi, summarized developments pertaining to the political and security situation and briefed the Council on his visit to Timor-Leste between 26 April and 2 May. He commended the Timorese and UNMISET on the progress they had

achieved towards building a stable and democratic State, but recognized the need for additional support from the international community in order to consolidate those gains.

Report of Commission of Experts

On 24 June [S/2005/458], the Secretary-General transmitted to the Security Council President the report of the Commission of Experts reviewing the prosecution of human rights violations committed during the events of 1999 [YUN 1999, p. 707], as well as a summary of that report. The report contained a comprehensive analysis of the judicial processes in question, as well as a wide range of recommendations.

The Commission conducted a fact-finding mission to Timor-Leste from 5 to 10 April to meet with the President and national and local government authorities, the judiciary and UNMISET staff, victims' groups and NGOs. At the invitation of Indonesia, it visited Jakarta from 18 to 20 May.

The Commission found that the serious crimes process in Timor-Leste had ensured a notable degree of accountability for those responsible for the crimes committed in 1999. Investigations and prosecutions had generally met international standards. The process had also significantly contributed to strengthening respect for the rule of law and encouraging community participation in the process of reconciliation and justice. The existence of an effective and credible judicial process, such as the Special Panels, had also discouraged retributive and vengeful attacks. However, there was frustration about the inability of the judicial process to bring to justice those outside the country's jurisdiction, particularly high-level indictees. The Commission concluded that the serious crimes process had not yet achieved full accountability of those who bore the greatest responsibility for serious violations of human rights in 1999, due to several factors, including lack of sufficient resources. The lack of access to evidence and suspects in Indonesia also impeded progress, and there was no extradition agreement between Indonesia and Timor-Leste or any form of effective mutual legal assistance framework to enable the arrest and transfer of indictees. The judicial process before the Ad Hoc Human Rights Court for Timor-Leste was not effective in delivering justice, and many aspects of the ad hoc judicial process revealed scant respect for, or conformity to, relevant international standards.

The Commission recommended that the Council retain the Serious Crimes Unit, the Special Panels and the Defence Lawyers Unit until the Secretary-General and the Council could examine the Commission's recommendations, or alternatively, set up mechanisms for completing the investigation and prosecution of serious human rights violations. It made a number of recommendations relevant to Timor-Leste and Indonesia. If those recommendations were not initiated by the respective Governments, the Council should, under Chapter VII of the UN Charter, create an ad hoc international criminal tribunal for Timor-Leste, to be located in a third State, or use the International Criminal Court. Member States also had the obligation under their respective national laws, to pursue investigation and prosecution of those persons responsible for serious violations of human rights in East Timor in 1999.

On 14 July [S/2005/459], the Secretary-General transmitted to the Council President two 22 June letters from the President and Prime Minister of Timor-Leste containing their comments regarding the final report of the Commission of Experts. Although appreciative of the Secretary-General's efforts in appointing the Commission of Experts, Timor-Leste was disappointed that the Commission had failed to provide legally sound and feasible recommendations for the advancement of the investigations of serious crimes and for the enhancement of the proposed Commission for Truth and Friendship. More importantly, the Commission of Experts failed to consider ways in which its analysis might assist both Governments in enhancing their agreed commitments and in elaborating a mechanism to advance the objectives of the Commission for Truth and Friendship.

On 28 September [S/2005/613], the Council President informed the Secretary-General that his 24 June letter (see above), transmitting the summary and full report of the Commission of Experts, had been brought to the Council's attention. Before further consideration of the report, the Council requested that the Secretary-General, in close consultation with his Special Representative, submit a report on justice and reconciliation for Timor-Leste, containing a practically feasible approach, taking into account both the report of the Commission of Experts and the views expressed by Indonesia and Timor-Leste.

United Nations Office in Timor-Leste

By resolution 1599(2005) of 28 April (see p. 440), the Security Council established a one-year follow-on mission to UNMISET, known as the United Nations Office in Timor-Leste (UNOTIL). The mission, to be headed by the Secretary-General's Special Representative, would comprise 40 police trainers to support further development of the police, 20 additional police advisers and 15

military advisers to support the development of the Border Patrol Unit, 45 civilian advisers to help develop critical State institutions, 10 human rights officers to provide training in the observance of democratic governance and human rights and a small office to support the Special Representative and coordinate the work of the mission with UN system partners.

On 27 May [S/2005/356], the Secretary-General informed the Council President of his intention to appoint Sukehiro Hasegawa (Japan) as his Special Representative for Timor-Leste and Head of UNOTIL, with effect from 21 May. On 1 June [S/2005/357], the Council took note of the Secretary-General's intention.

Report of Secretary-General (August). In August, the Secretary-General submitted a report [S/2005/533] covering developments on the ground since his May report (see p. 442) and describing UNOTIL activities since its inception.

During the reporting period, in order to curb the violent activities of martial arts groups, a series of initiatives was undertaken, with the support of President Gusmão, which culminated in the signing of a joint declaration by 14 groups on 30 June. The signatories to the declaration committed themselves to preventing, reducing and eradicating acts of violence between martial arts groups. On 22 July, six members of a political opposition group were detained in Lautem district following violent clashes with the local community. The following week, the Timorese naional police conducted coordinated search operations of that group's premises across the eastern part of the country, reportedly seizing items, including military uniforms, machetes, knives, flags, a firearm and ammunition. Subsequently, the coordinator of the group complained to the Provedor for Human Rights and Justice.

Local elections were held in two phases in the districts of Cova Lima, Ermera and Viqueque, on 12 and 18 May, and in those of Ainaro, Aileu and Manufahi, on 27 June and 2 July. While the ruling party won a relative majority, opposition and independent candidates also fared well. Despite some technical difficulties, primarily involving voter verification, improvements were noted in voter education and in cooperation between the secretariat for the Technical Administration of Elections, the local authorities and the police.

Relations between Timor-Leste and Indonesia continued to improve. Following meetings in June and July, agreement was reached, among other things, on the completion of negotiations on the unresolved segments of the common land boundary by the end of the year; the establishment of a new border management mechanism between Timor-Leste and Indonesia's border security agencies; the opening of a bus line from the Oecussi enclave to mainland Timor-Leste; and the issuance of border passes to border area residents. The 10 members of the bilateral Commission for Truth and Friendship were officially announced on 1 August. The Commission met for the first time in Denpasar, Bali (4-5 August), to discuss matters related to its internal structures, working procedures and its programme of work. On 11 August, the Presidents of the two countries signed a memorandum of understanding on the establishment of the Commission.

Further advances were made towards strengthening the Timorese institutional and legal framework. Two important organs provided for in the Constitution, namely the Superior Council for Defence and Security and the Council of State, were inaugurated on 12 and 17 May, respectively. The Provedor for Human Rights and Justice and his two Deputies were also sworn in by the National Parliament, which approved the statute of the Office of the Public Prosecutor on 25 July. On 29 July, it authorized the adoption of the penal code and of the penal and civil procedure codes by government decree. On 28 June, a decree law on restructuring the Government was promulgated, raising the total number of ministries from 10 to 15 and establishing, among other things, five new Secretary of State posts for the coordination of regional development and investment programmes. On 27 July, Prime Minister Mari Alkatiri officially announced the composition of the new Government, comprising 41 members, seven of whom were women and two with strong ties to the opposition. The new Government was sworn in by President Gusmão on 28 July.

Despite significant progress towards the development of a viable justice sector, Timor-Leste continued to rely on international advisers to perform line functions at both the Court of Appeal and the district courts to help reduce the backlog of cases. UNOTIL advisers trained 15 judges, 15 prosecutors and 10 public defenders, most of whom would assume their duties in the national courts by May 2006, with a probable need for continued on-the-job mentoring.

With continued support from UNOTIL's military training advisers, the Border Patrol Unit began direct dialogue with its Indonesian counterpart. UNOTIL's military training advisers would continue to support both parties in finalizing the border management agreement and establishing a mechanism to facilitate the resolution of border incidents. A joint concept of operations was developed to ensure close cooperation between the police and the military training advisers tasked

with further developing the Border Patrol Unit. Joint operations and reporting mechanisms had been established at UNOTIL headquarters, where police and military training advisers planned and coordinated their border activities while maintaining regular contact with the Timorese national police headquarters.

UNOTIL placed special emphasis on the coordination of donor assistance and encouraged the implementation of measures for the sustainable long-term development in Timor-Leste. Towards that end, the Special Representative established a consultative group to coordinate the assistance of stakeholders.

Security Council consideration (August). On 29 August [meeting 5251], the Security Council considered the Secretary-General's August report (see above) and was briefed on the situation in Timor-Leste by his Special Representative, who reported that, as local elections were coming to a close, public attention was focused on the presidential and national parliamentary elections to be held in 18 months. President Gusmão and Prime Minister Alkatiri requested UN assistance in the drafting of electoral laws to establish a legal framework for the nationwide elections. In addition, Timorese authorities requested external assistance to set up database-management systems and administrative support.

New opportunities and challenges had emerged in the economic sphere, with revenues from Timor Sea oil and gas resources starting to flow, which compensated for declining budgetary support from development partners. The National Parliament unanimously passed, on 13 July, the Petroleum Fund Act and the law on petroleum taxation, and on 23 August, the law on petroleum activities.

Regarding the serious crimes process, the first pre-trial hearing of former militia members indicted in Timor Leste took place on 4 August and the Dili district court scheduled trial for 3 September. UNOTIL produced a copy of the records compiled by the Serious Crimes Unit with the support of experts from the UN Department of Management, and was discussing with the Timorese Government the draft agreement on the preservation of serious crimes records. Although the Serious Crimes Unit had made an important contribution to achieving justice, it was able to investigate fewer than half of the estimated 1,450 murders committed in 1999.

While Timorese counterparts had increased their ownership of the functional responsibilities carried out by their offices, the effectiveness of UNOTIL's civilian advisers in transferring skills and knowledge continued to be hindered by the lack of national capacity in such technical and specialized sectors as justice and finance, as well as by the difficulty faced by State institutions in establishing and implementing a viable career development system. To meet those challenges, UNOTIL developed a new strategy, in close cooperation with stakeholders, for strengthening the capacity of key sovereign State institutions responsible for public administration, law and order, justice, human rights and democratic governance.

Further developments. In a later report [S/2006/24], the Secretary-General covered developments in Timor-Leste through the end of the year.

He reported that the fifth round of local elections was held in the districts of Dili and Liquica, on 20 and 30 September, marking the final round of village and sub-village elections in all 13 districts. Overall, the elections were conducted in a peaceful and orderly manner and the average voter turnout reached over 80 per cent, with several political parties fielding candidates. The ruling party won a large majority. Re-elections were held on 21 December for 18 village council positions in 10 districts, following an order from the Court of Appeals, citing technical irregularities during the earlier elections. Preparations for parliamentary and presidential elections in 2007 were already under way, with nine parties registered under the 2004 Law on Political Parties. In response to the request by the Timorese Government for assistance with the 2007 elections, an electoral assistance needs assessment mission was sent to Timor-Leste in November. Based on the mission's recommendations, UNOTIL provided advisory assistance for the preparation of the elections. The mission also recommended that prior to the drafting of electoral laws, discussions should take place within Timor-Leste regarding fundamental issues, such as the role and functions of an independent electoral supervisory body, terms of office for the President and members of Parliament and the timing of the elections. It was also strongly recommended that international assistance be provided, including support to voter registration, electoral administration and provision of resources.

Further progress was achieved in delineating the land border between Timor-Leste and Indonesia. On 30 August, Timor-Leste and Indonesia commenced demarcation of the 96 per cent of the land border agreed to in the Provisional Agreement on the Borderline signed by the foreign ministers in Dili in April (see p. 442). In December, significant progress was made in negotiations between the two sides on the remaining 4 per cent of the border. A number of cross-border incidents occurred in September and October, including the burning of farmland and stone-throwing incidents, mainly as a result of local disputes between villagers living on either side of the border. In response, UNOTIL facilitated exchanges between the Indonesian army and the Timorese police, in which the two sides agreed on joint measures to prevent the recurrence of further incidents. Although the situation had stabilized and a number of community-level meetings aimed at promoting cross-border cultural and economic exchanges had taken place, concerted efforts were nevertheless needed by both sides to inform the population in the border districts about the agreed boundary.

The bilateral Commission for Truth and Friendship, which commenced work in August, focused primarily on the analysis of documents provided by the Ad Hoc Human Rights Tribunal in Jakarta. The Commission requested the Timor-Leste Government to review the records compiled by the former United Nations Serious Crimes Unit in Dili. On 31 October, after close to five years of operation, the Commission for Reception, Truth and Reconciliation transmitted to President Gusmão its final report on human rights abuses in the country between 1974 and 1999, which he submitted to the National Parliament on 28 November, and to Prime Minister Mari Alkatiri on 30 November.

In the area of police development, UNOTIL was planning to complete all training programmes for Timorese national police by 20 May 2006. During the reporting period, the Rapid Intervention Unit completed comprehensive training programmes, and had shown remarkable improvements, especially with regard to professionalism, discipline and observance of human rights. The Immigration Unit also made considerable progress towards self-sufficiency. In addition, three new specialized units, namely the Counter-Terrorism Unit, the Explosive Ordnance Disposal Unit and the Public Information Office, were established. UNOTIL provided basic training in counter-terrorism and explosive ordnance to those units, to be followed by advanced training in the coming months. UNOTIL police advisers and Timorese police leaders were jointly preparing a long-term plan for the Timorese police, known as "Plan 2020", which would provide the Timorese police leadership with an opportunity to think strategically and to plan and organize their future activities. The police advisers also worked in close cooperation with Timorese police leaders in the formulation of operational and training manuals for various units.

Financing of UN operations

During 2005, the General Assembly considered the financing of three UN missions in Timor-Leste—UNMISET, UNOTIL and the United Nations Mission in East Timor (UNAMET). UNMISET was established by Council resolution 1410(2002) [YUN 2002, p. 321] to provide assistance to the administrative, law enforcement and public security structures critical to the viability and political stability of Timor-Leste, in addition to contributing to the maintenance of its external and internal security. UNOTIL was established by Council resolution 1599(2005) as a follow-on mission to UNMISET, charged with supporting and monitoring progress in the development of critical state institutions, the police and BPU and observance of democratic governance and human rights. UNAMET was established by Council resolution 1246(1999) [YUN 1999, p. 283] to conduct the 1999 popular consultations on East Timor's autonomy [ibid., p. 288]; its mandate ended on 30 November 1999, in accordance with resolution 1262 (1999) [ibid., p. 287].

UNMISET and UNOTIL

On 22 June [meeting 104], the General Assembly, considered the UNMISET performance report for the period from 1 July 2003 to 30 June 2004 [A/59/655], UNMISET's budget for the period from 1 July 2005 to 30 June 2006 [A/59/637] and the related ACABQ report [A/59/736/Add.17]. The Assembly, on the recommendation of the Fifth Committee [A/59/531/Add. 1], adopted **resolution 59/13 B** without vote [agenda item 129].

Financing of the United Nations Mission of Support in East Timor

B

The General Assembly,

Having considered the reports of the Secretary-General on the financing of the United Nations Mission of Support in East Timor and the related reports of the Advisory Committee on Administrative and Budgetary Questions,

Recalling Security Council resolution 1272(1999) of 25 October 1999 regarding the establishment of the United Nations Transitional Administration in East Timor and the subsequent resolutions by which the Council extended the mandate of the Transitional Administration, the last of which was resolution 1392 (2002) of 31 January 2002, by which the mandate was extended until 20 May 2002,

Recalling also Security Council resolution 1410(2002) of 17 May 2002, by which the Council established the United Nations Mission of Support in East Timor as of 20 May 2002 for an initial period of twelve months, and the subsequent resolutions by which the Council extended the mandate of the Mission, the last of which was resolution 1573(2004) of 16 November 2004, by which the Council extended the mandate of the Mission for a final period of six months until 20 May 2005,

Recalling further its resolution 54/246 A of 23 December 1999 on the financing of the United Nations Transitional Administration in East Timor and its subsequent resolutions on the financing of the United Nations Mission of Support in East Timor, the latest of which was resolution 59/13 A of 29 October 2004,

Reaffirming the general principles underlying the financing of United Nations peacekeeping operations, as stated in General Assembly resolutions 1874(S-IV) of 27 June 1963, 3101(XXVIII) of 11 December 1973 and 55/235 of 23 December 2000,

Noting with appreciation that voluntary contributions have been made to the Mission and to the Trust Fund for the United Nations Transitional Administration in East Timor,

Mindful of the fact that it is essential to provide the Mission with the necessary financial resources to enable it to complete its administrative liquidation,

1. *Takes note* of the status of contributions to the United Nations Transitional Administration in East Timor and the United Nations Mission of Support in East Timor as at 15 April 2005, including the contributions outstanding in the amount of 66.4 million United States dollars, representing some 4 per cent of the total assessed contributions, notes with concern that only fifty-one Member States have paid their assessed contributions in full, and urges all other Member States, in particular those in arrears, to ensure payment of their outstanding assessed contributions;

2. *Expresses its appreciation* to those Member States that have paid their assessed contributions in full, and urges all other Member States to make every possible effort to ensure payment of their assessed contributions to the Transitional Administration and the Mission in full;

3. *Expresses concern* at the financial situation with regard to peacekeeping activities, in particular as regards the reimbursements to troop contributors that bear additional burdens owing to overdue payments by Member States of their assessments;

4. *Also expresses concern* at the delay experienced by the Secretary-General in deploying and providing adequate resources to some recent peacekeeping missions, in particular those in Africa;

5. *Emphasizes* that all future and existing peacekeeping missions shall be given equal and non-discriminatory treatment in respect of financial and administrative arrangements;

6. *Also emphasizes* that all peacekeeping missions shall be provided with adequate resources for the effective and efficient discharge of their respective mandates;

7. *Endorses* the conclusions and recommendations contained in the report of the Advisory Committee on Administrative and Budgetary Questions;

Financial performance report for the period from 1 July 2003 to 30 June 2004

8. *Takes note* of the report of the Secretary-General on the financial performance of the Mission for the period from 1 July 2003 to 30 June 2004;

Budget estimates for the period from 1 July 2005 to 30 June 2006

9. *Decides* to appropriate to the Special Account for the United Nations Mission of Support in East Timor the amount of 1,757,800 dollars, inclusive of 1,662,200 dollars for the administrative liquidation of the Mis-

sion for the period from 1 July to 31 October 2005 and 78,200 dollars for the support account for peacekeeping operations and 17,400 dollars for the United Nations Logistics Base for the period from 1 July 2005 to 30 June 2006;

Financing of the appropriation

10. *Decides also* to apportion among Member States the amount of 1,662,200 dollars for the Mission for the period from 1 July to 31 October 2005, in accordance with the levels updated in General Assembly resolution 58/256 of 23 December 2003, and taking into account the scale of assessments for 2005, as set out in its resolution 58/1 B of 23 December 2003;

11. *Decides further* that, in accordance with the provisions of its resolution 973(X) of 15 December 1955, there shall be set off against the apportionment among Member States, as provided for in paragraph 10 above, their respective share in the Tax Equalization Fund of 119,400 dollars, representing the estimated staff assessment income approved for the Mission for the period from 1 July to 31 October 2005;

12. *Decides* to apportion among Member States the amount of 78,200 dollars for the support account and the amount of 17,400 dollars for the United Nations Logistics Base for the period from 1 July 2005 to 30 June 2006, in accordance with the levels updated in General Assembly resolution 58/256, and taking into account the scale of assessments for 2005 and 2006, as set out in its resolution 58/1 B;

13. *Decides also* that, in accordance with the provisions of its resolution 973(X), there shall be set off against the apportionment among Member States, as provided for in paragraph 12 above, their respective share in the Tax Equalization Fund of 12,400 dollars for the period from 1 July 2005 to 30 June 2006, comprising the prorated share of 11,000 dollars of the estimated staff assessment income approved for the support account and the prorated share of 1,400 dollars of the estimated staff assessment income approved for the United Nations Logistics Base;

14. *Decides further* that for Member States that have fulfilled their financial obligations to the Mission, there shall be set off against their apportionment, as provided for in paragraph 10 above, their respective share of the unencumbered balance and other income in the amount of 18,065,900 dollars in respect of the financial period ended 30 June 2004, in accordance with the levels updated in its resolution 58/256, and taking into account the scale of assessments for 2004, as set out in its resolution 58/1 B;

15. *Decides* that for Member States that have not fulfilled their financial obligations to the Mission, there shall be set off against their outstanding obligations their respective share of the unencumbered balance and other income in the amount of 18,065,900 dollars in respect of the financial period ended 30 June 2004, in accordance with the scheme set out in paragraph 14 above;

16. *Decides also* that the increase of 392,100 dollars in the estimated staff assessment income in respect of the financial period ended 30 June 2004 shall be added to the credits from the amount of 18,065,900 dollars referred to in paragraphs 14 and 15 above;

17. *Emphasizes* that no peacekeeping mission shall be financed by borrowing funds from other active peacekeeping missions;

18. *Encourages* the Secretary-General to continue to take additional measures to ensure the safety and security of all personnel under the auspices of the United Nations participating in the Mission, bearing in mind paragraphs 5 and 6 of Security Council resolution 1502(2003) of 26 August 2003;

19. *Invites* voluntary contributions to the Mission in cash and in the form of services and supplies acceptable to the Secretary-General, to be administered, as appropriate, in accordance with the procedure and practices established by the General Assembly;

20. *Decides* to include in the provisional agenda of its sixtieth session the item entitled "Financing of the United Nations Mission of Support in East Timor".

In October [A/60/425], the Secretary-General submitted to the Assembly a report on estimates in respect of special political missions, good offices and other political initiatives authorized by the General Assembly and/or the Security Council. The Secretary-General proposed resource requirements for UNOTIL for the period from 21 May to 31 December 2005, estimated at $22,027,700 ($23,890,200 gross). Requirements for the period beyond December 2005 would be presented in a consolidated report containing the budget proposals for all special political missions at the first part of the sixtieth session of the General Assembly. The ongoing operation of UNOTIL was being funded partly through the utilization of savings realized under the United Nations Advance Mission in the Sudan (UNAMIS) and partly through the use of commitments granted by ACABQ under the terms of General Assembly resolution 58/273 [YUN 2003, p. 1422]. The total requirements being sought amounted to $15,726,000 net ($17,588,500 gross).

In November [A/60/7/Add.10], ACABQ recommended that UNOTIL's estimated budget requirement for the period from 21 May to 31 December be reduced from $22,027,700 to $21,939,900.

On 23 December [meeting 69], the General Assembly, on the recommendation of the Fifth Committee [A/60/593], adopted **resolution 60/244** without vote [agenda item 123].

Estimates in respect of special political missions, good offices and other political initiatives authorized by the General Assembly and/or the Security Council: United Nations Office in Timor-Leste

The General Assembly,

Having considered the report of the Secretary-General on estimates in respect of special political missions, good offices and other political initiatives authorized by the General Assembly and/or the Security Council and the related report of the Advisory Committee on Administrative and Budgetary Questions,

1. *Takes note* of the report of the Secretary-General and the related report of the Advisory Committee on Administrative and Budgetary Questions;

2. *Endorses* the conclusions and recommendations of the Advisory Committee contained in its report, subject to the provisions of the present resolution;

3. *Decides* to approve the position of Chief of Staff at the D-1 level;

4. *Requests* the Secretary-General to ensure appropriate coordination of gender mainstreaming activities;

5. *Also requests* the Secretary-General to make every effort to achieve savings in operational costs, taking into account the recommendations of the Advisory Committee;

6. *Approves* the budget for the United Nations Office in Timor-Leste in the amount of 23,782,100 United States dollars gross (21,939,900 dollars net) for the period from 21 May to 31 December 2005;

7. *Notes* that requirements for the United Nations Office in Timor-Leste, after taking into account the utilization of savings of 6,301,700 dollars under the United Nations Advance Mission in the Sudan, amount to 17,480,400 dollars gross (15,638,200 dollars net);

8. *Decides* to appropriate, under the procedure provided for in paragraph 11 of annex I to General Assembly resolution 41/213 of 19 December 1986, an amount of 15,638,200 dollars under section 3, Political affairs, of the programme budget for the biennium 2004-2005, for the United Nations Office in Timor-Leste;

9. *Also decides* to appropriate an amount of 1,842,200 dollars under section 34, Staff assessment, of the programme budget for the biennium 2004-2005, to be offset by a corresponding amount under income section 1, Income from staff assessment.

UNAMET

On 12 September, the General Assembly deferred consideration of the item on the financing of UNAMET and included it in the draft agenda of its sixtieth (2005) session (**decision 59/570**).

Other matters

Cambodia

In 2005, the Secretary-General continued to put in place the arrangements for the entry into force of the Agreement between the United Nations and the Royal Government of Cambodia concerning the Prosecution under Cambodian Law of Crimes Committed During the Period of Democratic Kampuchea. The Agreement, approved by the General Assembly in resolution 57/228 B [YUN 2003, p. 385], regulated cooperation between the United Nations and the Royal Gov-

ernment of Cambodia in bringing to trial senior leaders of Democratic Kampuchea and those who were most responsible for the crimes committed during the period from 17 April 1975 to 6 January 1979. The Agreement provided, among other things, the legal basis and the principles and modalities for such cooperation. On 28 March, the Secretary-General convened a pledging conference in New York with a view to seeking the $43 million needed to fund the UN's commitment under the Agreement and received sufficient contributions and pledges to meet the Organization's obligations. On 28 April, the Government of Cambodia was notified that the legal requirements on the part of the United Nations for the entry into force of the Agreement had been complied with, and the Agreement accordingly entered into force the following day. On 14 October, the Secretary-General appointed Michelle Lee as international Deputy Director of the Office of Administration

In a November report [A/60/565], the Secretary-General reviewed progress towards the establishment of Extraordinary Chambers for the Prosecution under Cambodian Law of Crimes Committed during the period of Democratic Kampuchea. The Assembly was requested to take note of the report and decide that the international judges, the international co-prosecutor and the international co-investigating judge be deemed to be UN officials for the purpose of their terms and conditions of service.

India-Pakistan

During the year, steady and meaningful progress was achieved by India and Pakistan in their bilateral dialogue, agreed to in 2004 [YUN 2004, p. 382]. The April 2005 launch of a bus service across the line of control between the two countries was an important gesture of peace, and the leaders of both countries assured the Secretary-General of their commitment to work towards resolving all outstanding issues, including that of Jammu and Kashmir.

The United Nations Military Observer Group in India and Pakistan (UNMOGIP) continued in 2005 to monitor the situation in Jammu and Kashmir. On 2 December [S/2005/772], the Secretary-General informed the Security Council President of his intention to appoint Major General Dragutin Repinc (Croatia) as Chief Military Observer of UNMOGIP, replacing Major General Guido Dante Palmieri (Italy), who relinquished his post on 13 September. The Council took note of the Secretary-General's intention on 8 December [S/2005/773].

Korea

The Secretary-General, in his report on the work of the Organization [A/60/1], said that, while concerns remained about the situation on the Korean peninsula, some progress was noted in 2005, as intensive diplomatic efforts to revitalize the Beijing process had resulted in the resumption of the six-party talks (China, the Democratic People's Republic of Korea (DPRK), Japan, the Republic of Korea, the Russian Federation and the United States), aimed at achieving a nuclear-weapon free peninsula and a comprehensive settlement on related issues. The Secretary-General said that he would continue to mobilize international support for that multilateral approach towards a nuclear-weapon free peninsula, as well as look for practical ways in which the United Nations could strengthen its humanitarian and development work in the DPRK.

On 13 July [S/2005/474], the EU welcomed the announcement that the six-party talks were to be resumed. It urged the DPRK to dismantle its nuclear programmes and offered support in achieving that goal.

In separate letters of 23 September [CD/1759, CD/1760], the DPRK and the Republic of Korea transmitted to the Secretary-General of the Conference on Disarmament the joint statement adopted by the six parties (see above), in which they unanimously reaffirmed their goal of the verifiable denuclearization of the Korean peninsula in a peaceful manner.

The DPRK, in a 28 October letter [A/C.1/60/5], objected to urgings by the United States and the United Kingdom that it abandon its nuclear programme first, rather than as part of a process of simultaneous actions undertaken by itself, the United States and the Republic of Korea, as was agreed upon by the six parties. On 9 November, the fifth round of those talks commenced (Beijing, 9-11 November).

In other matters, by a 7 March letter [A/59/732-S/2005/150] to the Secretary-General, the DPRK registered its objection to Japan's attempt to occupy a permanent seat on the Security Council.

Kyrgyzstan

The Secretary-General, in his report on the work of the Organization [A/60/1], said that political upheaval in Kyrgyzstan reflected the growing instability in Central Asia. Responding to that instability, he had established in Turkmenistan the United Nations Regional Centre for Preventive Diplomacy for Central Asia as a tool for strengthening cooperation on issues ranging from the fight against drug trafficking and terrorism to strengthening democratic institutions and respect for human rights.

On 4 April [S/2005/247], the EU said that, in collaboration with the Organization for Security and Cooperation in Europe (OSCE), it was closely following developments in Kyrgyzstan, and had taken note of the resignation of Kyrgyz Prime Minister Tanayev and his government. It appealed to the newly appointed leaders to restore public order as soon as possible, start a dialogue with all political forces involved and implement a policy of national reconciliation. The new Kyrgyz leaders were also called upon to respect democratic values and human rights, and take all necessary measures to guarantee security and stability in the country. The EU was willing to cooperate with the new leaders in that context, and would support OSCE efforts to achieve that goal. The decision of the Kyrgyz Parliament to organize presidential elections within three months and parliamentary elections within six months was noted by the EU.

Mongolia

GENERAL ASSEMBLY ACTION

On 14 November [meeting 52], the General Assembly adopted **resolution 60/16** [draft: A/60/L.17 & Add.1] without vote [agenda item 42].

Eight hundred years of Mongolian statehood

The General Assembly,

Recalling its resolution 56/6 of 9 November 2001 on the Global Agenda for Dialogue among Civilizations,

Reaffirming that civilizational achievements constitute the collective heritage of mankind, providing a source of inspiration and progress for humanity at large,

Emphasizing the need to achieve an objective understanding of all civilizations and enhance constructive interaction and cooperative engagement among civilizations,

Recognizing the richness of nomadic civilization and its important contribution to promoting dialogue and interaction among all forms of civilization,

Recognizing also that nomadic civilization influenced, inter alia, societies across Asia and Europe and, in turn, absorbed influences from both East and West in a true interchange of human values,

Recognizing further the important role played by a strong and persistent nomadic culture in the development of extensive trade networks and the creation of large administrative, cultural, religious and commercial centres,

Mindful of the ever-increasing significance and relevance of a culture of living in harmony with nature, which is inherent in nomadic civilization, in today's world,

1. *Welcomes* the efforts of Member States, including Mongolia, to preserve and develop nomadic culture and traditions in modern societies;

2. *Also welcomes* the efforts undertaken by the Government of Mongolia to celebrate the eight hundredth anniversary of Mongolian statehood in 2006;

3. *Invites* Member States, the United Nations, its specialized agencies and other organizations of the United Nations system, as well as relevant intergovernmental and non-governmental organizations, regional organizations and foundations, and academia, to take part actively in the events to be organized by Mongolia in celebration of this anniversary.

Speaking before the vote, the representative of Mongolia said that his nation's traditions, values and culture, as well as its mentality and self-identity, stemmed from its nomadic roots. The eight hundredth anniversary of statehood provided Mongolia with an opportunity to look back at the legacies of its forefathers and to closely study nomadic civilization. The draft resolution sought to reinforce the concept of dialogue among civilizations, bringing the role and contribution of nomadic civilization into the global agenda. It also reaffirmed the importance of preserving and developing the centuries-old traditions and culture of nomadic peoples in modern societies. In addition, it sought to encourage renewed interest in studying various aspects of nomadic civilization on the part of relevant international organizations, civil society and academia, thus contributing to mutual understanding among civilizations and cultures.

Myanmar

In 2005, the Secretary-General continued to provide his good offices in the pursuit of national reconciliation and democratization in Myanmar, but encountered difficulties as the ousting of then Prime Minister General Khin Nyunt in 2004 had significantly reduced political contact between the Myanmar authorities and the United Nations. The UN Special Envoy and the Special Rapporteur for the Commission on Human Rights had still not been allowed into the country. According to the Special Rapporteur, over 1,100 political prisoners reportedly remained in Myanmar, and the release of 249 of them on 6 July had been tempered by the continuation of the arrests, detention and harsh sentences meted out to civilians and democracy advocates for peaceful political activities. The practice of administrative detention continued, and National League for Democracy (NLD) General-Secretary, Daw Aung San Suu Kyi, remained under house arrest. While Myanmar had embarked upon the process laid out in the Government's 2003 seven-point road map towards democratization, it had not done so in a genuinely all-inclusive manner. In a meeting with the Chairman of the State

Peace and Development Council, Senior General Than Shwe, held during the Asia-Africa Summit (Jakarta, 22-23 April), the Secretary-General emphasized that the transition process had to include all parties.

In his 10 October report on the situation of human rights in Myanmar [A/60/422] (see p. 892), the Secretary-General maintained that the seven-point road map towards democracy and the National Convention had the potential to generate positive change. However, the Convention was not adhering to the recommendations made by successive General Assembly resolutions. The Convention, responsible for elaborating the basic principles for the drafting of a firm and stable constitution, was reconvened from 17 February to 31 March, but without the involvement of a number of political parties, including NLD. The exclusion of important and representative political actors from the process, the restrictions placed on their involvement, the lack of tolerance towards critical voices and the intimidation and detention of pro-democracy activists rendered any notion of a democratic process devoid of meaning. The Secretary-General called upon the Myanmar authorities to resume dialogue with the representatives of all ethnic nationality groups and political leaders and to allow his Special Envoy to recommence visits to Myanmar.

On 24 October [A/C.3/60/2], Myanmar called into question various assertions made in the Secretary-General's 10 October report (see above). The report was said to contain important factual errors and overreached the parameters mandated by Assembly resolution 59/263 [YUN 2004, p. 812].

The Secretary-General, responding on 7 November [A/60/422/Add.1], stated that information in his report came from the public domain, or was provided to him by his Special Envoy, who could not verify the accuracy of the information, as he had been denied access to Myanmar since March 2004. The Secretary-General reiterated his commitment to providing his good offices aimed at facilitating national reconciliation and democratization in Myanmar.

On 2 November [A/C.3/60/6], Myanmar transmitted to the Secretary-General a memorandum on the situation of human rights in the country, which addressed, among other things, recent political developments.

On 28 January, the Executive Board of the United Nations Development Programme/United Nations Population Fund took note of the report of the assessment mission to Myanmar [DP/2005/6] and the report submitted by the independent assessment mission to the country [E/2005/35 (dec. 2005/3)].

Nepal

In Nepal, the UN system strengthened its presence and capacity to respond to the deteriorating situation caused by the ongoing conflict and political crisis. The Secretary-General continued to urge a prompt return to constitutional rule, and reiterated the UN's readiness to help peacefully resolve the conflict. As part of those efforts, the Special Adviser of the Secretary-General, Lakdhar Brahimi, visited Nepal from 10 to 15 July and met with King Gyanendra, senior Government officials, leaders of political parties and a cross-section of Nepalese society.

On 28 February [S/2005/137], the EU, recalling the 2 February statement of its Presidency, expressing deep concern about the dissolution of the multiparty Government in Nepal and the assumption by the King of executive powers, stated that the action taken by the King was a serious setback to the prospects for a negotiated and democratic solution to the conflict in Nepal. It urged the King to take early measures to restore democratic freedoms and civil liberties and to lift the emergency powers he had introduced following the takeover of power on 1 February. In particular, the EU called for the restoration of representative democracy; the fast release of all political and other prisoners detained under emergency ordinances; unrestricted access without the need for prior notice to all detainees by the National Human Rights Commission and its representatives; political parties and civil society organizations to be granted the freedom to organize and operate; the lifting of reporting restrictions on the media; assurances of continued independence for the Commission for the Investigation of Abuse of Authority; and the restoration of the right to assembly and other fundamental rights. The EU was also mindful of the impact the new political situation might have on security conditions in the country and on donors' ability to provide development assistance to Nepal.

On 8 September [S/2005/629], the EU welcomed the statement by the Communist Party of Nepal (Maoist) (CPN(M)) of a unilateral ceasefire. It urged the CPN(M) to cease using violence for political ends and called upon all political forces to work towards a democratically based peace process leading to a durable negotiated solution, involving a national consensus and the reintegration of the CPN(M) into a multiparty democracy.

In a 28 October statement [S/2005/751], the EU condemned the seizure, carried out at gunpoint by the security forces, of radio equipment from the Kantipur FM station in Kathmandu. Amendments contained in the new media ordinance also caused concern, as they infringed upon the right to freedom of expression. The EU called upon the Government of Nepal to uphold the fundamental rights guaranteed by the Constitution of the Kingdom of Nepal and to allow the Nepalese people their right to freedom of expression.

On 5 December [S/2005/804], the EU recognized the efforts of the political parties in Nepal in securing an agreement with the Maoists which could form the basis for a peace process in the country. It continued to support the transition of the Maoists into mainstream politics, but urged them to renounce violence, including by putting their weapons verifiably beyond use. As a first step, the EU called on the Maoists to extend their current ceasefire and to work to create the right conditions for peace talks to resume. It also urged the King and the Government to begin serious engagement on a negotiated settlement to the conflict. In a further statement dated 5 December [S/2005/805], the EU condemned the 27 November seizure, carried out at gunpoint by the security forces, of radio equipment from the Sagamartha FM station in Kathmandu. It once again called upon the Government of Nepal to uphold the fundamental rights of the people of Nepal, including the right to freedom of expression.

Papua New Guinea

In 2005, Bougainville (Papua New Guinea) made substantial progress towards peace and stability through the successful completion of elections and the establishment of the first Autonomous Bougainville Government. Up to its closure on 30 June, the United Nations Observer Mission in Bougainville (UNOMB) continued to assist in the implementation of the 2001 Bougainville Peace Agreement, concluded between the Papua New Guinea Government and the Bougainville parties. The Agreement, which established the framework for a peace process, including a permanent ceasefire, as provided for in the 1998 Lincoln Agreement [YUN 1998, p. 319] and its annex, the Arawa Agreement [ibid.], covered issues of autonomy, the holding of a referendum and agreements on weapons disposal.

Report of Secretary-General (March). On 28 March, in response to a December 2004 Security Council request [YUN 2004, p. 386], the Secretary-General submitted a report [S/2005/204] reviewing the progress achieved by the parties to the 2001 Bougainville Peace Agreement in the preparations for elections, reconciliation with the leaders of the "no-go zone", maintenance of law and order, weapons disposal, and post-conflict peacebuilding. The report also elaborated on UNOMB's closure plan.

The Bougainville Provincial Administration, with the support of the National Election Commission, had made plans for the upcoming elections which would bring about the establishment of the first Autonomous Bougainville Government. The Administration finalized a report on the boundaries of provincial constituencies, and was updating and consolidating the common roll of the province, including the "no-go zone" (mountainous region controlled by rebel leader Francis Ona and his Me'ekamui Defence Force (MDF)). The Transitional Consultative Committee, composed of members of the Bougainville Interim Provincial Government and the Bougainville People's Congress, decided that polling in the elections for the presidency and the Bougainville legislature would be held from 20 May to 2 June. The legislature, to be known as the House of Representatives, would consist of 33 members representing their respective constituencies, along with one woman and one former combatant to be elected for each of Bougainville's three regions (North, Central and South). The President would be elected directly on a Bougainville-wide ballot, while the Speaker would be elected from candidates outside the House by its members.

With the facilitation of UNOMB, community leaders and volunteers from among the former combatants were carrying out an election public-awareness campaign with rank-and-file MDF members in the "no-go zone". As a result of that campaign, a significant number of MDF members had expressed support for and willingness to take part in the elections. Both the national Government and the Bougainville leaders expressed their desire to have international observers present during the elections in order to enhance the confidence of the Bougainville people regarding the peace process and their ability to vote freely.

On 8 March, UNOMB facilitated a meeting that brought together, for the first time, several Bougainville political leaders, former military leaders and combatants of the Bougainville Revolutionary Army and the Bougainville Resistance Force to discuss the peace process with 100 key MDF players. The meeting decided that similar exchanges should be held in the near future to sort out differences and to work together for the future of Bougainville. The MDF representatives also pledged not to interrupt the electoral process. At the second meeting (Arawa, 17 March), the participants discussed the upcoming elections, the lifting of the last roadblock at Morgan Junction and reconciliation between Francis Ona, the leader in the "no-go zone", and Joseph Kabui, President of the Bougainville People's Congress. Mr. Kabui had expressed his readiness

to meet Mr. Ona to initiate the reconciliation process, and sources close to Mr. Ona had informed UNOMB that he was ready to reciprocate. That would signify a breakthrough in relations between their factions, and would bode well for a potential opening of the "no-go zone" and the provision of government services to the population living there. UNOMB would continue to provide logistical and other support to the parties in the matter.

Regarding security, the general situation on the ground was steadily improving. UNOMB had destroyed most of the 2,014 weapons originally placed in containers in accordance with the weapons disposal plan, and was working through community leaders to persuade former combatants to destroy the remaining weapons, which were kept in secure storage. The deployment of Bougainville regular police had produced good results, and the people of Bougainville repeatedly commented on security improvements and increased freedom of movement as tangible outcomes of the successful implementation of the Peace Agreement. In the province, over 116 Bougainville Police were on active duty, and 50 more would be graduating from the Police Academy in Bomana, Port Moresby, by the end of the month. They would be deployed before the beginning of the election. Additionally, 383 community police officers were functioning in their respective villages in most areas of the island.

The National Court resumed hearings in Buka for the first time in four years to try a backlog of cases. Although some progress had been achieved, the establishment of correctional institutions was lagging behind, thereby impinging on human rights issues. To remedy the situation, the Provincial Administration was working in close cooperation with the representatives of the Law and Justice Programme, funded by regional donors, to expedite the construction and renovation of the required institutions.

Because of the enormous rehabilitation and recovery challenges the Autonomous Bougainville Government would face upon its establishment, capacity-building needed to be one of its priorities, requiring the continued assistance of UN agencies and programmes and donors. UNDP would implement its Bougainville Planning and Community Support Programme project and the United Nations Children's Fund planned expanding its volunteer teacher training programme. Donor assistance would be channelled through the Governance and Implementation Fund. The agreed steps and priorities of that implementation were provided for in the Joint Working Plan of the Papua New Guinea Government and the Bougainville Administration.

UNDP and major donors were encouraging the Bougainville Administration to take the lead in coordinating the distribution of international assistance in accordance with the priorities specified in the Joint Working Plan.

Given the progress achieved by the parties in weapons disposal and in the preparations for elections, and barring any unforeseen complications, UNOMB would complete its mandate and formally close its activities on 30 June, at which point it was expected that an Autonomous Bougainville Government would already have been set up. In the interim, the Mission would continue to monitor the situation to verify the handing over of weapons and that the level of security was conducive to the holding of elections. Upon the closure of UNOMB, UN developmental and humanitarian agencies and the donor community would take the lead in helping the Autonomous Bougainville Government to implement its rehabilitation and capacity-building programmes.

Elections

The United Nations had been requested by the national Government of Papua New Guinea, in concurrence with the Bougainville leaders, to coordinate the work of the international electoral observers invited by the Papua New Guinea Government. The resultant UN election coordination unit gave extensive briefings to the observers prior to their deployment in Bougainville and, in close cooperation with UNOMB, facilitated their movement by helicopter to 29 of the 33 constituencies throughout the three regions of Bougainville. The United Nations also supported the airlift of polling boxes, electoral officers and observers. International observers from Australia, Fiji, Japan, New Zealand, Samoa, Trinidad and Tobago and Vanuatu, as well as representatives of the Commonwealth and Pacific Islands Forum secretariats, concluded that the elections had been conducted in accordance with the electoral laws and in a calm and peaceful environment.

As declared by the international observers, the outcome of the elections accurately reflected the will of the people of Bougainville. Of the 112,000 voters enlisted on the common roll, 69,343 cast their ballots, constituting 62 per cent of the whole electorate. The presidential campaign was won by Joseph C. Kabui, former President of the Bougainville People's Congress, receiving close to 15,000 more votes than the runner-up, former Governor John Momis. Two key government positions—a senior minister and the Deputy Speaker—were held by women, and a number of former combatants were elected as constituency members. The new Government was inaugurated on 15 June.

SECURITY COUNCIL ACTION

On 15 June [meeting 5201], following consultations among Security Council members, the President made statement **S/PRST/2005/23** on behalf of the Council:

The Security Council welcomes the first general elections for the president and members of the House of Representatives of the Autonomous Region of Bougainville held from 20 May through 9 June 2005, and considers that they were competently and transparently conducted, as noted by the international observer team. The Council congratulates the Autonomous Bougainville Government and the people of Bougainville on this achievement, and takes note that these elections, which reflect the expressed will of the people of Bougainville, mark a significant and historical landmark in the Bougainville peace process and make it possible to enter into a new stage for further implementation of the Bougainville Peace Agreement.

The Council further welcomes the inauguration of the Autonomous Bougainville Government in its full capacity, and affirms its continuing support for the people of Bougainville.

The Council urges those who did not participate in the electoral process to respect the outcome of the elections and support without delay the Autonomous Bougainville Government in its peacebuilding efforts.

The Council pays tribute to the efforts of the Government of Papua New Guinea and the Bougainville leaders for fully implementing the Bougainville Peace Agreement. The Council commends the support by the international community, in particular the significant contributions made by the countries in the region, partners in the donor community, as well as the United Nations. The Council also expresses its appreciation for the commendable role played by the Commonwealth and the Pacific Islands Forum in dispatching electoral observers for the smooth conduct of the elections.

The Council notes with satisfaction that the performance of the United Nations Observer Mission in Bougainville, as well as that of its preceding United Nations Political Office in Bougainville, demonstrated that a small United Nations special political mission with a clearly defined mandate can make a critical contribution to a regional conflict resolution effort in an efficient and effective manner.

The Council encourages the ongoing support and commitment by the international community to the efforts made by the Government of Papua New Guinea and the people of Bougainville in pursuit of their economic and social development as well as sustainable peace in the region.

Security Council consideration (July). On 6 July [meeting 5222], the Security Council was briefed by the Assistant Secretary-General for Political Affairs, Danilo Türk, on the main developments that had taken place in Bougainville since 7 April. Mr. Türk noted that UNOMB's mandate had been fully implemented. On 19 May, UNOMB informed the parties to the Bougainville Peace Agreement that the weapons disposal plan incorporated into the Agreement had been implemented. Of a total of 2,016 weapons kept in containers, 1,896 were destroyed. UNOMB collected and destroyed an additional 155 weapons, bringing the total to 2,051 weapons. It therefore determined that the parties had substantially complied with the implementation of the plan, paving the way for the holding of elections (see p. 454). The parties agreed that it would be up to the Autonomous Bougainville Government to address the issue of the remaining weapons that had not been placed in containers, or that had been stolen out of them during the implementation of phases II and III of the plan.

On 14 June, the parties to the Peace Agreement convened the final meeting of the Peace Process Consultative Committee. Having resolved that the objectives of the Committee under the Lincoln and Bougainville Peace Agreements had been achieved, the parties agreed to dissolve it. Relations between the national and Bougainville Governments would be managed through the permanent Joint Supervisory Body, which would supervise and check on the implementation of the autonomy arrangements. That and other mechanisms were in place to resolve any disputes that might emerge between the parties. The national and autonomous Governments intended to work together to address the challenges facing them through consultation and cooperation at the appropriate levels.

Following the completion of the weapons disposal plan and the implementation of the autonomous arrangements, there remained the third main pillar of the Peace Agreement—the holding of a referendum on Bougainville's political status 10 to 15 years in the future, which would include the choice of independence for Bougainville. Responsibility for the conduct of the referendum would be shared between the Bougainville and national Governments. In accordance with the Agreement and the Papua New Guinea Constitution, the final decision on the referendum would be left to the Papua New Guinea Parliament and to subsequent consultations with the Autonomous Bougainville Government.

In his inauguration speech, President Kabui indicated that his Government would start negotiations with the national Government and the Bougainville Copper Limited mining company on the transfer of the company's assets and prospecting authority to the Autonomous Bougainville Government. Given the sensitivity of the involvement of Bougainville Copper Limited

in Bougainville, the Government might in the future hold wide consultations with the people on the potential resumption of exploration and mining operations.

The success of the elections and the unity of the newly formed Government provided a strong base from which to redesign the laws of the administration and region, improve service delivery and allow for economic development. The Bougainville administration was putting together a coherent development plan for the whole region, but continued support from the United Nations and other international actors would also be crucial in meeting the expectations of the people of Bougainville. UNDP was taking the lead in helping the administration to develop a donor coordination system, and other UN agencies were engaged in a range of activities.

The Papua New Guinea representative noted the challenges that still remained, namely the development of an economy capable of sustaining autonomy, provision of opportunities for individuals and communities to help themselves, promotion of good governance, and encouragement of ongoing reconciliation and mutual respect in the community. While there were still concerns about the continued existence of weapons in Bougainville, and the presence of Francis Ona and his supporters in the "no-go zone", it was recognized that peacebuilding had to be viewed as an ongoing process.

Tajikistan

In 2005, with the assistance of the United Nations Tajikistan Office of Peacebuilding (UNTOP), the Government of Tajikistan took further steps to consolidate the peace. In view of the important role being played by UNTOP and Tajikistan's continuing need for support in its post-conflict peacebuilding efforts, the Secretary-General announced, on 10 May [S/2005/323], his intention to continue the UNTOP activities for a further year, until 1 June 2006. On 18 May [S/2005/324] the Security Council took note of his intention.

UNTOP, established in 2000 [YUN 2000, p. 315] following the withdrawal of the United Nations Mission of Observers in Tajikistan (UNMOT), continued in 2005 to facilitate national dialogue and reconciliation, assist in strengthening democratic institutions and conflict prevention mechanisms, promote the rule of law and build human rights capacity. At the recommendation of a UN Electoral Needs Assessment Mission, UNTOP developed and supervised the implementation of a technical assistance project for the parliamentary elections of February 2005, training more than 13,000 poll workers and 300 district election commissioners across all districts of the country, as well as 250 local media representatives. In other training activities, Tajik instructors were trained in conflict prevention and resolution mechanisms. To assist in the reform and transition of national law enforcement agencies to peacetime policing, UNTOP trained staff of the Ministry of the Interior in human rights standards, forensic techniques and modern practices in law enforcement.

Tibet

On 6 July [S/2005/462], the EU welcomed the fourth round of talks between the envoys of the Dalai Lama and members of the Chinese Government (Berne, Switzerland, 30 June–1 July). The EU strongly supported the continuation of dialogue and hoped to see serious negotiations leading to a peaceful, sustainable and mutually agreeable solution for Tibet.

United Arab Emirates-Iran

Greater Tunb, Lesser Tunb and Abu Musa

In a series of communications between 7 March and 20 September [S/2005/144, S/2005/274, S/2005/597], the League of Arab States (LAS) informed the Security Council President of the adoption of two decisions and one resolution denouncing the Iranian occupation of Greater Tunb, Lesser Tunb and Abu Musa, and affirming the full sovereignty of the United Arab Emirates over the three islands. LAS also called upon the Secretary-General and Council President to maintain the issue among the matters of which the Security Council was seized until Iran ended its occupation of the islands.

In a series of letters transmitted between 16 March and 30 December [S/2005/189, S/2005/232, S/2005/300, S/2005/301, S/2005/468, S/2005/697, S/2005/851], Iran stated that the three islands were integral and eternal parts of the Iranian territory and rejected any claims to the contrary. It continued to emphasize the importance of negotiations between itself and the United Arab Emirates to improve bilateral relations and remove any misunderstanding between the two countries.

In other communications issued between March and September [A/59/761-S/2005/215, A/59/845-S/2005/386, A/60/388-S/2005/612], Bahrain transmitted to the Secretary-General statements made by the Ministerial Council of the Gulf Cooperation Council throughout the year, reiterating its support of the sovereignty of the United Arab Emirates over the three islands.

The United Arab Emirates, in a 3 May letter to the Secretary-General [S/2005/283], requested that the Security Council retain on its agenda for 2005 the item entitled "Letter dated 3 December 1971 from the Permanent Representatives of Algeria, Iraq, the Libyan Arab Jamahiriya and the People's Democratic Republic of Yemen to the United Nations addressed to the President of the Security Council (S/10409)", concerning Iran's occupation of Greater Tunb, Lesser Tunb, and Abu Musa, until a settlement of the dispute was achieved by direct peaceful means and negotiation or through recourse to the International Court of Justice.

Uzbekistan

On 25 May [A/59/817], Uzbekistan informed the Secretary-General of events that took place in the Andijan region on 12 and 13 May, in which 30 armed criminals attacked the patrol and sentry service and a military unit. Preliminary reports indicated that the attack was carried out by members of the Islamic group Akromiya, which was directly linked to the religious extremist organization, Hizb ut-Tahrir, whose activities were prohibited in many countries. Early investigation showed a possible link between the fighters and extremist organizations active in certain countries of the region, as well as terrorist groups that were hiding in Afghanistan.

Uzbekistan called upon UN Member States and Governing bodies to be restrained and responsible in evaluating the events in Andijan, and to wait for the results of the official investigation. On 23 May, the Uzbek Parliament set up an independent parliamentary commission to conduct a comprehensive investigation of the circumstances connected with the events in Andijan and an in-depth analysis, determination of the reasons and conditions which led to the tragic events, conduct a comprehensive analysis and legal assessment of the actions by the Government of Uzbekistan and the security structures and inform the Parliament and the public about the course of the investigation.

On 7 November [A/C.3/60/8], Uzbekistan informed the Secretary-General of measures being taken to liberalize the court-judicial system.

On 8 November [S/2005/750], the EU expressed alarm at reports of the detention and harassment of journalists and others, including human rights defenders, who had questioned the Uzbek authorities' version of events in Andijan, and called on the Uzbek Government to discontinue such practices. On 18 November [S/2005/749], the EU expressed concern about the trial of 15 individuals in relation to the 12 and 13 May events in

Andijan. The EU said that it had serious doubts about the credibility of the case presented by the prosecution, and believed that the defence procedures were inadequate to ensure a fair trial. The EU continued to place primary importance on a credible and transparent independent international inquiry into the events of 12 and 13 May, and welcomed an opportunity to discuss its concerns with the Uzbek Government.

In a 9 December response [A/60/587-S/2005/778], Uzbekistan called the EU's comments unfair and biased. The Supreme Court of Uzbekistan stated that the judicial proceedings relating to the 15 individuals accused of committing terrorist acts in Andijan in May were conducted in accordance with Uzbek legislation, which itself complied with the standards and requirements of international law. Also on 14 December [A/60/590-S/2005/787], Uzbekistan stated that the EU 8 November statement bore no relation to the facts.

Regional meetings

On 11 March [A/59/741-S/2005/172], Kazakhstan transmitted to the Secretary-General a joint communiqué of the meeting of the Council of Ministers for Foreign Affairs of the States members of the Shanghai Cooperation Organization (SCO) (Astana, Kazakhstan, 25 February). At the meeting, representatives from China, Kazakhstan, the Kyrgyz Republic, the Russian Federation, Tajikistan and Uzbekistan discussed the broadening of cooperation and international questions of mutual concern.

On 13 July [A/60/129], Kazakhstan submitted to the Secretary-General a declaration by SCO Heads of State (Astana, Kazakhstan, 5 June), noting that the organization was expanding multilateral cooperation among its member States and was actively cooperating with other international organizations and countries.

Following the Ministerial Regional Meeting on the Millennium Development Goals (MDGs) in Asia and the Pacific (Jakarta, Indonesia, 3-5 August), Indonesia transmitted to the Secretary-General and the General Assembly President the text of the Jakarta Declaration on MDGs in Asia and the Pacific: the Way Forward 2015 [A/60/313], in which countries in the region strengthened their commitment and reaffirmed their solidarity to achieving the MDGs by 2015.

Chapter V

Europe and the Mediterranean

In 2005, the restoration of peace and stability in the post-conflict countries of Europe and the Mediterranean gained momentum as the advances made in re-establishing their institutions and social and economic infrastructure were further consolidated. However, many political issues and situations remained unresolved.

Bosnia and Herzegovina, with the assistance of the international community, led by the European Union (EU), continued to reform its institutions, allowing it to meet the requirements of the EU Stabilization and Association Process and the North Atlantic Treaty Organization Partnership for Peace Programme, and thus move closer to full integration into Europe.

In Kosovo (Serbia and Montenegro), the United Nations continued to assist in building a modern, multi-ethnic society through the United Nations Interim Administration Mission in Kosovo (UNMIK). Significant progress was made by the Provisional Institutions of Self-Government in implementing the standards established in 2002 that Kosovo had to attain, despite some delays and setbacks. That allowed UNMIK to further transfer authority to those institutions, including police and justice responsibilities to the new ministries of interior and justice. In May, the Secretary-General appointed a Special Envoy to assess whether the conditions were right to begin the political process for determining Kosovo's future status. Based on that review and the Secretary-General's recommendation, the Security Council decided, on 24 October, to launch that process. Advances were also made in normalizing relations between the authorities in Pristina (Kosovo's capital) and Belgrade (Serbia and Montenegro).

Renewed efforts were made to end the stalemate in the Georgian/Abkhaz peace process. Senior officials of the Group of Friends of the Secretary-General (France, Germany, Russian Federation, United Kingdom, United States) tried to get the two parties to restart dialogue on the basis of the 2001 Basic Principles for the Distribution of Competences between Tbilisi (Georgian Government) and Sukhumi (the Abkhaz leadership). That initiative was boosted when the discussions on security matters led to the signing of a protocol and adoption of measures to strengthen the 1994 Agreement on a Ceasefire and Separation of Forces (Moscow Agreement). However, the complex political situations between the two sides prevailed, as evidenced by Georgia's call for the withdrawal of the security forces of the Commonwealth of Independent States and for a UN-led international force.

No progress was made towards a settlement of the conflict between Armenia and Azerbaijan over the Nagorny Karabakh region in Azerbaijan.

In the Mediterranean, the situation in Cyprus remained unresolved, following the failed 2004 peace efforts. The Secretary-General, having assessed the situation, determined that progress had been negligible between the Greek Cypriots and the Turkish Cypriots, and concluded that further clarifications were needed before negotiations could be resumed. He also reviewed the mandate and concept of operations of the United Nations Force in Cyprus.

The former Yugoslavia

UN operations

In 2005, the United Nations maintained one peacekeeping mission in the territories of the former Yugoslavia. Through the United Nations Interim Administration Mission in Kosovo, it continued efforts to restore peace and stability to the Serbia and Montenegro province of Kosovo. Peace activities in Bosnia and Herzegovina were conducted by the European Union, through the European Union Police Mission and the European Union Force.

**Financial status and liquidation
of closed peacekeeping operations**

UNMIBH

In March [A/59/751], the Secretary-General submitted the final performance report on the budget of the United Nations Mission in Bosnia and Herzegovina (UNMIBH), which ended on 31 December 2002, in which he recommended that the General Assembly retain the cash balance of $7,182,000 available in the UNMIBH special account as at 30 June 2004.

The Advisory Committee on Administrative and Budgetary Questions (ACABQ), in its 18 April report [A/59/736/Add.8], recommended approval of the Secretary-General's recommendations.

GENERAL ASSEMBLY ACTION

On 22 June [meeting 104], the General Assembly, on the recommendation of the Fifth (Administrative and Budgetary) Committee [A/59/832], adopted **resolution 59/302** without vote [agenda item 125].

Financing of the United Nations Mission in Bosnia and Herzegovina

The General Assembly,

Having considered the report of the Secretary-General on the financing of the United Nations Mission in Bosnia and Herzegovina and the related report of the Advisory Committee on Administrative and Budgetary Questions,

1. *Takes note* of the proposal of the Secretary-General contained in paragraph 13 of his report and his intention to report to the General Assembly at its sixtieth session on the matter;

2. *Also takes note* of the status of outstanding contributions to the United Nations Mission in Bosnia and Herzegovina as at 15 April 2005 in the amount of 27.9 million United States dollars, representing some 3 per cent of the total assessed contributions, notes with concern that only one hundred and fifteen Member States have paid their assessed contributions in full, and urges all other Member States, in particular those in arrears, to ensure payment of their outstanding assessed contributions;

3. *Expresses its appreciation* to those Member States that have paid their assessed contributions in full, and urges all other Member States to make every possible effort to ensure payment of their assessed contributions to the Mission in full;

4. *Endorses* the conclusions and recommendation contained in the report of the Advisory Committee on Administrative and Budgetary Questions;

5. *Decides* to postpone the return of the net cash balance of 7,182,000 dollars available as at 30 June 2004 in the Special Account for the United Nations Mission in Bosnia and Herzegovina;

6. *Also decides* that updated information on the financial position of the Mission shall be included in the report to be considered by the General Assembly at its sixtieth session on the updated position of closed peacekeeping missions under the agenda item entitled "Administrative and budgetary aspects of the financing of the United Nations peacekeeping operations";

7. *Further decides* that the item entitled "Financing of the United Nations Mission in Bosnia and Herzegovina" shall be deleted from its agenda.

Bosnia and Herzegovina

In 2005, efforts to assist the two entities comprising the Republic of Bosnia and Herzegovina—the Federation of Bosnia and Herzegovina (where mainly Bosnian Muslims (Bosniacs) and Bosnian Croats resided) and Republika Srpska (where mostly Bosnian Serbs resided)—in implementing the 1995 General Framework Agreement for Peace in Bosnia and Herzegovina and the annexes thereto (the Peace Agreement) [YUN 1995, p. 544] were conducted by the European Union (EU). Those efforts were accomplished through the activities of the Office of the High Representative for the Implementation of the Peace Agreement on Bosnia and Herzegovina, responsible for the Agreement's civilian aspects [YUN 1996, p. 293], and the European Union Police Mission in Bosnia and Herzegovina (EUPM). The EU Force (EUFOR) mission executed the responsibilities for the Agreement's military aspects, which were transferred to it by the North Atlantic Treaty Organization (NATO) in December 2004 [YUN 2004, p. 401]. The Peace Implementation Council (PIC) and its Steering Board continued to oversee and facilitate the Agreement's implementation.

The High Representative reported on the progress made in the implementation process and related political developments in the country during the year in the context of his mission implementation plan, which set out a number of core tasks to be accomplished [YUN 2003, p. 401]. Bosnia and Herzegovina undertook a number of reforms, particularly in areas of the rule of law, refugee return, police restructuring, defence reform and economic development, in accordance with European standards, and also continued to work towards full integration into Europe through the EU Stabilization and Association process and NATO's Partnership for Peace requirements. Having made sufficient progress in completing legislative and other requirements of the European Commission feasibility study [ibid., p. 402], the European Council launched formal talks on a stabilization and association agreement on 25 November.

Implementation of Peace Agreement

Civilian aspects

The civilian aspects of the 1995 Peace Agreement entailed a wide range of activities, including humanitarian aid, infrastructure rehabilitation, establishment of political and constitutional institutions, promoting respect for human rights and the holding of free and fair elections. The High Representative for the Implementation of the Peace Agreement, who chaired the PIC Steering Board and other key implementation bodies, was the final authority with regard to implementing the civilian aspects of the Peace Agreement [YUN 1995, p. 547]. The reports on EUPM activities were submitted by the EU Secretary-General and High Representative for the Common Foreign and Security Policy, Javier Solana, to the Security Council President through the UN Secretary-General.

Office of the High Representative

Reports of High Representative. The High Representative, Lord Paddy Ashdown (United Kingdom), reported to the Security Council through the Secretary-General on the peace implementation process for the periods 1 January to 30 June 2005 [S/2005/706] and 1 July 2005 to 31 January 2006 [S/2006/75], describing progress in the implementation of the Peace Agreement's civilian aspects. (For details on specific topics in the report see below)

The Council, on 23 March, considered the High Representative's report covering the latter half of 2004 [YUN 2004, p. 392] and, on 15 November, his report covering the first half of 2005.

On 29 December [S/2006/40], Lord Ashdown informed the Council, through the Secretary-General, that the PIC Steering Board had chosen Dr. Christian Schwarz-Schilling (Germany) to succeed him as the High Representative for Bosnia and Herzegovina, effective 31 January 2006.

Mission implementation plan

The High Representative, in his briefing to the Security Council on 23 March [meeting 5147], during consideration of his report covering the latter half of 2004 [YUN 2004, p. 392], stated that Republika Srpska had, for the first time in 10 years, transferred five of the major war crimes indictees to the International Tribunal for the Former Yugoslavia (ICTY) (see p. 1387), including General Vinko Pandurevic, the third most senior indictee. However, that did not constitute the full cooperation required by ICTY and the international community. The process would not end until Radovan Karadzic, Ratko Mladic and all the other main indictees were in custody.

In terms of the country's future within the EU and NATO, cooperation with ICTY was non-negotiable. The country's application to join NATO's Partnership for Peace Programme was due to be reconsidered again in April and the EU had made it clear that it hoped to decide on Bosnia and Herzegovina's readiness to begin negotiations on a stabilization and association process in May.

The European Union Enlargement Commissioner, Olli Rehn, indicated to Bosnia and Herzegovina that, in addition to cooperation with ICTY, the other cardinal issue on which progress

was expected was police restructuring. In January, the Police Restructuring Commission presented its recommendations, which included the establishment of a single State-level police structure, based on operational efficiency, rather than on political control.

Progress in other areas of reform included the opening in March of the new War Crimes Chamber and maximum security prison facilities, the full operationalization of the Taxation Authority in January, and the assumption of defence reform by NATO, with the aim of creating a single State-wide Ministry of Defence. However, the financial sustainability of Bosnia and Herzegovina's government structures was cause for concern, in the face of massive and unsustainable deficits, signalling the need for functional reform to increase governance efficiency.

In his November report [S/2005/706], the High Representative stated that, since the introduction of the first mission implementation plan in 2003 [YUN 2003, p. 401], two core tasks had been completed (ensuring that extreme nationalists, war criminals and their organized criminal networks could not reverse peace implementation; and promoting the sustainable return of refugees and displaced persons), leaving four ongoing (entrenching the rule of law; reforming the economy; institution-building; and defence reform).

To accelerate further progress in the mission implementation plan, the Office of the High Representative instituted a new system whereby a detailed action plan was commissioned for each outstanding item, outlining a critical path to the item's completion, and identification of those responsible for taking action.

In a later report [S/2006/75], the High Representative stated that the action planning process helped to clear the accumulated backlog in the mission implementation plan. Of the outstanding rule of law items, all but one were tied to the police restructuring process, which would likely stretch into early 2008, while those related to economic reform and institution-building included a broad range of reform priorities.

Civil affairs

The High Representative, in his reports covering 1 January to 30 June [S/2005/706] and from 1 July to 31 December [S/2006/75], stated that Bosnia and Herzegovina was the only country in the region without a contractual relationship with the EU. The EU Special Representative had explained to the country's authorities and population the tough conditions they had to meet, including improved cooperation with ICTY, respect for the Constitutional Charter, police restructuring and public broadcast reform, in order to move ahead on the EU stabilization and association agreement. They also had to put in place laws ensuring the legal and technical framework of the Indirect Taxation Authority, if the value added tax were to be introduced on time in January 2006.

In other areas, the Defence Reform Commission reached final agreement on the abolition of the entity armies and defence ministries and the model for an integrated and democratically controlled army at the State level, enabling Bosnia and Herzegovina to participate in NATO's Partnership for Peace Programme and its full membership in that organization.

Under the reforms adopted by the entity parliaments, entities would cede their remaining defence responsibilities to the State on 1 January 2006. The phased implementation of the reforms was expected to take two years to complete, and a team of experts, assisted by NATO, would coordinate the transition.

Meanwhile, the political situation remained volatile. In response to measures taken by the High Representative, the United States and EUFOR, following NATO's refusal in December 2004 to admit Bosnia and Herzegovina to the Partnership for Peace Programme, the Republika Srpska government and two of the four Serb members of the Council of Ministers resigned in protest. By mid-February, a new government was formed in Banja Luka, with all State-level ministers agreeing to remain in their positions. In April, there was further instability following the indictments of a number of political figures, particularly Dragan Cavic, the Croat member of the State Presidency, and Branko Dokic, the State Transport Minister. On the insistence of the High Representative, Dokic resigned his post but Cavic was removed from office. The Parliamentary Assembly elected the Croat National Union candidate, Ivo Miro Jovic, to replace Cavic, who was subsequently elected president of the main Croat nationalist party.

The political climate was also affected by the long-running failure of the Council of Ministers to agree on the appointment of the head of the State Investigation and Protection Agency. The decision by the High Representative to appoint the best-qualified candidate, a Serb applicant, rather than the Croat, backed by most of the Ministers, led to further resignations.

By the end of the year, the Bosnia and Herzegovina governments had agreed on and enacted reforms in a number of fields, including the rule of law, human rights, taxation, competition, transport, narcotics control, the information society and the media. The major achievement regarding the rule of law was the agreement on police restructuring, which provided for the legislative and budgetary competences for all police matters to be vested at the State level; no political interference with operational policing; and for the determination of functional local police areas using technical policing criteria in areas where operational command was exercised at the local level. The Directorate for Police Restructuring Implementation was established on 8 December and its steering and executive boards were appointed on 29 December.

Cooperation between the Bosnia and Herzegovina authorities and ICTY was enhanced. Of the 18 fugitives wanted by ICTY at the beginning of 2005, only four remained at large, including the two most wanted indictees, Radovan Karadic and Ratko Mladic.

Progress continued towards the unification of Mostar city's administration. Formerly ethnically divided institutions were unified, civil service appointments made in line with the new civil service law, a unified city budget passed and efforts made to recover uncollected revenues inherited from former city municipalities. The long-stalled plan to move several Federation government ministries from Sarajevo to Mostar also gained momentum. The Mostar Implementation Unit completed its mandate and handed over responsibility for supporting and monitoring the finalization of outstanding unification tasks to the Office of the High Representative.

The Brcko District of Bosnia and Herzegovina celebrated its fifth anniversary in March, with its first popularly elected assembly and government in place. Only a few items stemming from the 1999 Final Arbitral Award of the Brcko Arbitral Tribunal [YUN 1999, p. 324] remained to be completed, the most important of which was the elimination of the residual legal traces of the former Inter-Entity Boundary Line in the District, which signalled that the laws and regulations inherited from the two entities and the three former municipalities had been harmonized. Efforts continued to put relations between the State and the Brcko District on a firm footing. In November, an agreement was signed between Bosnia and Herzegovina's Council of Ministers and the Brcko government to open a Brcko District office within the Council of Ministers, ensuring that the District had appropriate representation at the State level.

Judicial reform

The Office of the High Representative continued to assist in strengthening the capacity of the Bosnia and Herzegovina Court. It oversaw the transfer of almost all the legal staff from its Rule of Law Department to the Court. The High Representative indicated that, since Bosnia and Herzegovina currently had laws and legal institutions necessary to inculcate and maintain the rule of law, his Office's Rule of Law Department, as well as its Anti-Crime and Corruption Unit closed at the end of 2005. The latter transferred its files to the requisite local authorities.

Emphasis was also placed on strengthening the capacity of local prosecutors at the district and cantonal levels. The Office completed a survey of criminal and civil asset forfeiture laws to support the Ministry of Justice in dealing with the proceeds of crime.

Economic reforms

The High Representative reported that the Bosnia and Herzegovina authorities took significant steps towards increasing intergovernmental coordination on fiscal matters. On 11 February, they launched the Working Group on Fiscal Sustainability to advise on and make policy recommendations for achieving significant savings at all levels of government. Also, on 14 May, the State and entities established the Bosnia and Herzegovina Fiscal Council, one of whose main tasks was to ensure that the country's consolidated budget included funding for its security institutions and its EU aspirations. In June, the Parliamentary Assembly passed the law on railways. Entity legislation enabling the registration of businesses was also passed.

The overall macroeconomic situation remained positive, with growth in gross domestic product reaching 5.7 per cent, which was among the highest in the region. Industrial production rebounded, but agricultural reform lagged as the country still lacked a coherent agricultural policy. In that regard, the Office of the High Representative recommended that a working group responsible for implementing related EU recommendations be established.

Despite some individual successes during the first half of the year, the overall privatization effort remained lackluster, compounded by fractured administrative responsibility for privatization, especially in the Federation.

Public administration reform

All the outstanding European Commission-funded "functional reviews" of the public sector in Bosnia and Herzegovina were completed and their results publicized. The National Public Administration Reform Coordinator was charged with overseeing the follow-up. Public administration reform was also incorporated in the Bosnia and Herzegovina European Partnership programme. A number of amendments to the Civil Service Law aimed at enhancing staff qual-

ity and speeding up the recruitment process, prepared by the Office of the High Representative, in cooperation with the Bosnia and Herzegovina Civil Service Agency, were adopted in June. The Agency, which was working at full capacity since January 2005, reviewed 1,214 civil service posts in 77 Federation bodies.

Media development

On 1 February, the Council of Ministers adopted the draft public broadcasting system law, creating a common system made up of three multi-ethnic services, broadcasting in all three official languages (Bosnian, Croatian, Serbian). The Bosnia and Herzegovina House of Representatives passed the Law on Public Broadcasting Service on 18 May and the State parliament endorsed it on 21 December. To bring their own legislation in line with State law, the Federation and the Republika Srpska governments adopted draft legislation in mid-December, which was forwarded to their respective parliaments for adoption.

On 5 October, the Bosnia and Herzegovina Parliamentary Assembly passed the state framework legislation—the Law on the Radio and Television System of Bosnia and Herzegovina.

Relations with other countries

While relations between Bosnia and Herzegovina and its neighbours remained cordial overall, some key peace implementation issues remained unresolved. The country's borders with both Croatia and Serbia and Montenegro were still undefined by treaty, and access to Croatia's Adriatic port of Ploce remained unsettled. The High Representative asked the PIC Steering Board for permission to remove those issues from the mission implementation plan and that they be dealt with bilaterally with the countries concerned. However, many Bosnia and Herzegovina citizens were also citizens of Croatia or Serbia and Montenegro and the constitutional provisions of those countries on the extradition of their citizens meant that the regional battle against organized crime and the pursuit of war criminals not indicted by ICTY were both impeded.

The issue of the final status of the Kosovo province of Serbia and Montenegro (see p. 467) had already had some effect in the country. In June, Serbia and Montenegro's Foreign Minister stated that independence for Kosovo would inevitably raise questions about the status of Republika Srpska within Bosnia and Herzegovina. That issue and the future of the State union of Serbia and Montenegro would likely dominate regional politics.

Security Council consideration (November).

The Security Council, on 15 November [meeting 5306], considered recent developments in Bosnia and Herzegovina's path to European Union integration. The High Representative, Lord Ashdown, said that the major obstacles to Bosnia and Herzegovina's Euro-Atlantic integration had been overcome. On 8 November, EU foreign ministers welcomed the European Commission's recommendation to commence drawing up a negotiating mandate for the country's Stabilization and Association Agreement, negotiations for which were expected to be approved on 21 November in Brussels, precisely 10 years after the signing of the Peace Agreement.

The EU, backed by the international community, especially the United States, made it clear that the remaining conditions for Bosnia and Herzegovina to begin stabilization talks were non-negotiable. While the aspiration of EU membership had been a powerful draw, it had taken consistent international pressure over the past 10 years to bring the country closer to the EU and NATO. This was clearly evident in cooperation with ICTY. However, while the transfer of 12 indictees in 2005 to ICTY was a huge step forward, another anniversary of the massacre at Srebrenica [YUN 1995, p. 529] had passed without the transfer of Radovan Karadzic and Ratko Mladic. The opening of the Stabilization and Association Agreement negotiations demonstrated that the reform process was moving from the peace implementation phase to that of achieving European standards.

European Union missions in Bosnia and Herzegovina

EUPM

Report of EU Secretary-General. As invited by the Security Council in presidential statement S/PRST/2002/33 [YUN 2002, p. 363], EU Secretary-General and High Representative for the Common Foreign and Security Policy reported, through the UN Secretary-General, on the activities of the EU Police Mission (EUPM) covering the period 1 January to 31 December [S/2006/125].

The report stated that in 2005, considerable progress was made in setting up the State Investigation and Protection Agency. EUPM monitored and advised on the selection and recruitment process and assisted the Agency in developing its human resources strategy. The structure of the State Border Service (SBS) was brought in line with the other State-level agencies, with clearer procedures and powers given to police officers on the border. EUPM also helped SBS in manage-

ment training and worked to solve the issue of the failure by the Council of Ministers to appoint a Director of the Service, as that affected implementation of EUPM projects. Following the intervention of the High Representative, Vinko Dumancic was appointed Director. In September, the European Commission and Bosnia and Herzegovina signed a memorandum of understanding on the funding of the new SBS headquarters near Sarajevo airport.

The Police Restructuring Commission presented its report to the High Representative/EU Special Representative in January, with recommendations on the establishment of a single police structure. In October, the Republika Srpska National Assembly adopted the Agreement on Police Restructuring, thus removing one of the last obstacles for Bosnia and Herzegovina to start negotiations with the EU on the Stabilization and Association Agreement. EUPM and the Office of the High Representative/EU Special Representative also developed a framework for the establishment of the Directorate for Implementation of Police Restructuring.

In July, the Ministry of Security presented to the Council of Ministers a strategic agreement with Europol (European Police Office) to facilitate cooperation between EU members and Bosnia and Herzegovina in preventing and combating international crime. EUPM supported efforts to make the nationwide intelligence system more effective, by ensuring that it operated across all entities and police agencies in Bosnia and Herzegovina.

To help achieve financial viability and sustainability of the local police, EUPM also made progress in developing local capacity regarding salary scales, budget planning for organizational units, revising maintenance costs of premises, rationalization of the use of police equipment, control over inventories and payrolls, and general budget implementation and management.

As at 31 December, the Mission numbered 801 personnel, of whom 410 were seconded police officers, 61 international civilians and 330 national staff. The European Council agreed on 24 November to continue EUPM for another two years from 1 January 2006 to 31 December 2007, with a refocus on the coordination of policing efforts under the European security and defence policy in the fight against organized crime, in addition to helping establish in Bosnia and Herzegovina a sustainable, professional and multi-ethnic police service. All 25 EU member States, together with nine non-EU contributing States, participated in the Mission in 2005. Brigadier General Vincenzo Coppola (Italy) was appointed Head of Mission/Police Commissioner from January 2006 to succeed Commissioner Kevin Carty (Ireland), whose tour of duty ended on 31 December 2005.

Police certification

The European Commission for Democracy through Law (the "Venice Commission"), in a 25 October opinion on a possible solution to the issue of decertification of police officers in Bosnia and Herzegovina, concluded that the International Police Task Force (IPTF) responsible for the police certification process instituted in 2001 [YUN 2001, p. 332], while implementing the vetting procedure of local police officers, failed to provide the relevant police officers with a public, adversarial, impartial and independent examination of their rights. The review mechanism also appeared to be abortive for the most part. The Venice Commission, therefore, recommended that the United Nations review the decisions that denied certification, and those that had been challenged before domestic authorities after the end of 2002, when IPTF's mission ended.

EUFOR

The EU Force (EUFOR) mission in Bosnia and Herzegovina executed the military aspects of the Peace Agreement as specified in annexes 1-A and 2, which were transferred to it by NATO in December 2004 [YUN 2004, p. 401]. Its activities were recorded in four reports covering the periods 2 December 2004 to 28 February 2005 [S/2005/226], 1 March to 31 May [S/2005/440], 1 June to 15 September [S/2005/698], and 16 September to 30 November [S/2006/12], submitted by the EU Secretary-General and High Representative for the Common Foreign and Security Policy of the European Union, in accordance with resolution 1575(2004) [YUN 2004, p. 401].

As at 30 November, EUFOR's strength stood at 6,200 troops from 22 EU member States and 11 third countries, deployed in three multinational task forces throughout the country.

EUFOR continued to conduct multiple operations, including patrolling in sensitive and remote areas, local liaison and observation team activities, collection of illegal weapons and promoting cooperation with the local authorities to ensure compliance with the Peace Agreement. Routine liaison activities were conducted to assist and support capacity-building in the local police and other agencies. The EUFOR Integrated Police Unit assisted the State Border Service in preventing illegal activities along the borders and the unauthorized entry of people and goods into the country. EUFOR also carried out large-scale operations to assist Bosnia and Herzegovina authorities in cracking down on organized crime networks, including the smuggling of heroin, and human trafficking. Throughout the year, it conducted, in conjunction with appropriate authorities, operations to collect voluntarily surrendered illegal arms and ammunition under amnesty conditions, and when necessary, in more invasive operations. It also helped to maintain a safe and secure environment, especially during the observance of the tenth anniversary of the Srebrenica massacre, developed cooperation with local authorities and conducted well-coordinated operations on the ground.

SECURITY COUNCIL ACTION

On 21 November [meeting 5307], the Security Council unanimously adopted **resolution 1639 (2005)**. The draft [S/2005/727] was prepared in consultations among Council members.

The Security Council,

Recalling all its previous relevant resolutions concerning the conflicts in the former Yugoslavia and the relevant statements by its President, including resolutions 1031(1995) of 15 December 1995, 1088(1996) of 12 December 1996, 1423(2002) of 12 July 2002, 1491(2003) of 11 July 2003, 1551(2004) of 9 July 2004 and 1575(2004) of 22 November 2004,

Reaffirming its commitment to the political settlement of the conflicts in the former Yugoslavia, preserving the sovereignty and territorial integrity of all States there within their internationally recognized borders,

Emphasizing its full support for the continued role in Bosnia and Herzegovina of the High Representative for the Implementation of the Peace Agreement on Bosnia and Herzegovina,

Underlining its commitment to support the implementation of the General Framework Agreement for Peace in Bosnia and Herzegovina and the annexes thereto (collectively the "Peace Agreement"), as well as the relevant decisions of the Peace Implementation Council,

Recalling all the agreements concerning the status of forces referred to in appendix B to annex 1-A of the Peace Agreement, and reminding the parties of their obligation to continue to comply therewith,

Recalling also the provisions of its resolution 1551 (2004) concerning the provisional application of the status-of-forces agreements contained in appendix B to annex 1-A of the Peace Agreement,

Emphasizing its appreciation to the High Representative, the Commander and personnel of the multinational stabilization force (the European Union Force), the Senior Military Representative and personnel of the North Atlantic Treaty Organization Headquarters Sarajevo, the Organization for Security and Cooperation in Europe, the European Union and the personnel of other international organizations and agencies in Bosnia and Herzegovina for their contributions to the implementation of the Peace Agreement,

Emphasizing that a comprehensive and coordinated return of refugees and displaced persons throughout the region continues to be crucial to lasting peace,

Recalling the declarations of the ministerial meetings of the Peace Implementation Council,

Recognizing that full implementation of the Peace Agreement is not yet complete, while paying tribute to the achievements of the authorities at State and entity level in Bosnia and Herzegovina and of the international community in the ten years since the signing of the Peace Agreement,

Emphasizing the importance of Bosnia and Herzegovina's progress towards Euro-Atlantic integration on the basis of the Peace Agreement, while recognizing the importance of Bosnia and Herzegovina's transition to a functional, reform-oriented, modern and democratic European country,

Taking note of the reports of the High Representative, including his latest report of 2 November 2005,

Determined to promote the peaceful resolution of the conflicts in accordance with the purposes and principles of the Charter of the United Nations,

Recalling the relevant principles contained in the Convention on the Safety of United Nations and Associated Personnel of 9 December 1994 and the statement by its President of 9 February 2000,

Welcoming and encouraging efforts by the United Nations to sensitize peacekeeping personnel in the prevention and control of HIV/AIDS and other communicable diseases in all its peacekeeping operations,

Taking note of the conclusions of the Ministers for Foreign Affairs of the European Union at their meeting held in Luxembourg on 13 June 2005 which refer to the requirement for the European Union Force to remain in Bosnia and Herzegovina beyond 2005, and confirm the intention of the European Union to take the steps necessary to that end,

Recalling the letters between the European Union and the North Atlantic Treaty Organization sent to the Security Council on 19 November 2004, on how those organizations will cooperate together in Bosnia and Herzegovina in which both organizations recognize that the European Union Force will have the main peace stabilization role under the military aspects of the Peace Agreement,

Recalling also the confirmation by the Presidency of Bosnia and Herzegovina, on behalf of Bosnia and Herzegovina, including its constituent entities, of the arrangements for the European Union Force and the North Atlantic Treaty Organization Headquarters presence,

Welcoming the increased engagement of the European Union in Bosnia and Herzegovina and the continued engagement of the North Atlantic Treaty Organization,

Further welcoming tangible signs of Bosnia and Herzegovina's progress towards the European Union, and, in particular, the decision by the European Union to open negotiations with Bosnia and Herzegovina on a Stabilization and Association Agreement, and calling upon the authorities in Bosnia and Herzegovina to implement in full their undertakings, including on police reform, as part of that process,

Determining that the situation in the region continues to constitute a threat to international peace and security,

Acting under Chapter VII of the Charter,

1. *Reaffirms once again its support* for the General Framework Agreement for Peace in Bosnia and Herzegovina and the annexes thereto (collectively the "Peace Agreement"), as well as for the Dayton Agreement on Implementing the Federation of Bosnia and Herzegovina of 10 November 1995, and calls upon the parties to comply strictly with their obligations under those Agreements;

2. *Reiterates* that the primary responsibility for the further successful implementation of the Peace Agreement lies with the authorities in Bosnia and Herzegovina themselves and that the continued willingness of the international community and major donors to assume the political, military and economic burden of implementation and reconstruction efforts will be determined by the compliance and active participation by all the authorities in Bosnia and Herzegovina in implementing the Peace Agreement and rebuilding a civil society, in particular in full cooperation with the International Tribunal for the Prosecution of Persons Responsible for Serious Violations of International Humanitarian Law Committed in the Territory of the Former Yugoslavia since 1991, in strengthening joint institutions, which foster the building of a fully functioning self-sustaining State able to integrate itself into the European structures, and in facilitating returns of refugees and displaced persons;

3. *Reminds* the parties once again that, in accordance with the Peace Agreement, they have committed themselves to cooperate fully with all entities involved in the implementation of this peace settlement, as described in the Peace Agreement, or which are otherwise authorized by the Security Council, including the International Tribunal for the Former Yugoslavia, as it carries out its responsibilities for dispensing justice impartially, and underlines the fact that full cooperation by States and entities with the Tribunal includes, inter alia, the surrender for trial or apprehension of all persons indicted by the Tribunal and the provision of information to assist in Tribunal investigations;

4. *Emphasizes its full support* for the continued role of the High Representative for the Implementation of the Peace Agreement on Bosnia and Herzegovina in monitoring the implementation of the Peace Agreement and giving guidance to and coordinating the activities of the civilian organizations and agencies involved in assisting the parties to implement the Peace Agreement, and reaffirms that, under annex 10 of the Peace Agreement, the High Representative is the final authority in theatre regarding the interpretation of civilian implementation of the Peace Agreement and that, in case of dispute, he may give his interpretation and make recommendations, and make binding decisions as he judges necessary on issues as elaborated by the Peace Implementation Council in Bonn, Germany, on 9 and 10 December 1997;

5. *Expresses its support* for the declarations of the ministerial meetings of the Peace Implementation Council;

6. *Reaffirms* its intention to keep implementation of the Peace Agreement and the situation in Bosnia and Herzegovina under close review, taking into account the reports submitted pursuant to paragraphs 18 and 21 below, and any recommendations that those reports might include, and its readiness to consider the imposition of measures if any party fails significantly to meet its obligations under the Peace Agreement;

7. *Recalls* the support of the authorities of Bosnia and Herzegovina for the European Union Force and the continued North Atlantic Treaty Organization

presence and their confirmation that both are the legal successors to the Stabilization Force for the fulfilment of their missions for the purposes of the Peace Agreement, its annexes and appendices and relevant Security Council resolutions and can take such actions as are required, including the use of force, to ensure compliance with annexes 1-A and 2 of the Peace Agreement and relevant Council resolutions;

8. *Pays tribute* to those Member States which participated in the multinational stabilization force (the European Union Force) and in the continued North Atlantic Treaty Organization presence, established in accordance with its resolution 1575(2004), and welcomes their willingness to assist the Parties to the Peace Agreement by continuing to deploy a multinational stabilization force (the European Union Force) and by maintaining a continued North Atlantic Treaty Organization presence;

9. *Welcomes* the intention of the European Union to maintain European Union military operation to Bosnia and Herzegovina from November 2005;

10. *Authorizes* the Member States acting through or in cooperation with the European Union to establish for a further period of twelve months, starting from the date of adoption of the present resolution, a multinational stabilization force (the European Union Force) as a legal successor to the Stabilization Force under unified command and control, which will fulfil its missions in relation to the implementation of annexes 1-A and 2 of the Peace Agreement in cooperation with the North Atlantic Treaty Organization Headquarters presence in accordance with the arrangements agreed between the North Atlantic Treaty Organization and the European Union as communicated to the Security Council in their letters of 19 November 2004, which recognize that the European Union Force will have the main peace stabilization role under the military aspects of the Peace Agreement;

11. *Welcomes* the decision of the North Atlantic Treaty Organization to continue to maintain a presence in Bosnia and Herzegovina in the form of a North Atlantic Treaty Organization Headquarters in order to continue to assist in implementing the Peace Agreement in conjunction with the European Union Force, and authorizes the Member States acting through or in cooperation with the North Atlantic Treaty Organization to continue to maintain a North Atlantic Treaty Organization Headquarters as a legal successor to the Stabilization Force under unified command and control, which will fulfil its missions in relation to the implementation of annexes 1-A and 2 of the Peace Agreement in cooperation with the European Union Force in accordance with the arrangements agreed between the North Atlantic Treaty Organization and the European Union as communicated to the Security Council in their letters of 19 November 2004, which recognize that the European Union Force will have the main peace stabilization role under the military aspects of the Peace Agreement;

12. *Reaffirms* that the Peace Agreement and the provisions of its previous relevant resolutions shall apply to and in respect of both the European Union Force and the North Atlantic Treaty Organization presence as they have applied to and in respect of the Stabilization Force and that, therefore, references in the Peace Agreement, in particular in annex 1-A and the appendices thereto, and in relevant resolutions to the Implementation Force and/or the Stabilization Force, the North Atlantic Treaty Organization and the North Atlantic Council shall be read as applying, as appropriate, to the North Atlantic Treaty Organization presence, the European Union Force, the European Union and the Political and Security Committee and Council of the European Union, respectively;

13. *Expresses its intention* to consider the terms of further authorization as necessary in the light of developments in the implementation of the Peace Agreement and the situation in Bosnia and Herzegovina;

14. *Authorizes* the Member States acting under paragraphs 10 and 11 above to take all necessary measures to effect the implementation of and to ensure compliance with annexes 1-A and 2 of the Peace Agreement, stresses that the parties shall continue to be held equally responsible for compliance with those annexes and shall be equally subject to such enforcement action by the European Union Force and the North Atlantic Treaty Organization presence as may be necessary to ensure implementation of those annexes and the protection of the European Union Force and the North Atlantic Treaty Organization presence;

15. *Authorizes* Member States to take all necessary measures, at the request of either the European Union Force or the North Atlantic Treaty Organization Headquarters, in defence of the European Union Force or the North Atlantic Treaty Organization presence, respectively, and to assist both organizations in carrying out their missions, and recognizes the right of both the European Union Force and the North Atlantic Treaty Organization presence to take all necessary measures to defend themselves from attack or threat of attack;

16. *Authorizes* the Member States acting under paragraphs 10 and 11 above, in accordance with annex 1-A of the Peace Agreement, to take all necessary measures to ensure compliance with the rules and procedures governing command and control of airspace over Bosnia and Herzegovina with respect to all civilian and military air traffic;

17. *Demands* that the parties respect the security and freedom of movement of the European Union Force, the North Atlantic Treaty Organization presence, and other international personnel;

18. *Requests* the Member States acting through or in cooperation with the European Union and the Member States acting through or in cooperation with the North Atlantic Treaty Organization to report to the Security Council on the activity of the European Union Force and the North Atlantic Treaty Organization Headquarters presence, respectively, through the appropriate channels and at least at three-monthly intervals;

19. *Invites* all States, in particular those in the region, to continue to provide appropriate support and facilities, including transit facilities, for the Member States acting under paragraphs 10 and 11 above;

20. *Reiterates its appreciation* for the deployment by the European Union of its Police Mission to Bosnia and Herzegovina since 1 January 2003;

21. *Requests* the Secretary-General to continue to submit to the Security Council reports from the High Representative, in accordance with annex 10 of the Peace Agreement and the conclusions of the Peace Implementation Conference held in London on 4 and 5

December 1996, and later Peace Implementation Conferences, on the implementation of the Peace Agreement and in particular on compliance by the parties with their commitments under that Agreement;

22. *Decides* to remain seized of the matter.

Serbia and Montenegro

In 2005, the United Nations continued to assist the authorities and people of the Kosovo province of Serbia and Montenegro in building a multiethnic society. The United Nations Interim Administration Mission in Kosovo (UNMIK) led efforts, along with the Kosovo authorities, in strengthening the Provisional Institutions of Self-Government, mainly the Kosovo Assembly and the Kosovo Government, and in transferring authority to those institutions, in accordance with the 2001 Constitutional Framework for Provisional Self-Government [YUN 2001, p. 352]. It also monitored progress towards the fulfilment of the eight standards set out in the 2003 "standards for Kosovo" document [YUN 2003, p. 420], under which Kosovo was expected to develop stable democratic institutions under UNMIK administration before any decision could be made on its future status. The standards also included promoting human rights, establishing the rule of law, protecting minority rights, dialogue with Belgrade and the Kosovo Protection Corps (KPC).

For most of 2005, progress in strengthening Kosovo's fledgling institutions was inconsistent. Significant steps were taken to improve the security situation; however, implementation in the areas of the rule of law, protection of minority rights and return of internally displaced persons was slow. In March, the International Criminal Tribunal for the Former Yugoslavia (ICTY) issued an indictment for the Prime Minister of Kosovo, Ramush Haradinaj, who resigned his post and voluntarily agreed to go to the Hague. He was succeeded by Bajram Kosumi.

Meanwhile, in September, UNMIK started working on six priority areas: continued implementation of the standards, a comprehensive reform of local government, improving security, building local capacity, maintaining a safe and secure environment and restructuring of the mission. It initiated informal, technical-level talks with the European Union (EU) and the Organization for Security and Cooperation in Europe (OSCE) on contingency planning for their possible involvement in Kosovo following the determination of the province's future status. By the end of 2005, the Mission commenced the transfer of

some of its police and justice responsibilities to the new ministries of interior and justice.

Situation in Kosovo

The United Nations continued to work towards the full implementation of Security Council resolution 1244(1999) [YUN 1999, p. 353], which set out the modalities for a political solution to the crisis in the Serbia and Montenegro province of Kosovo, and of resolutions 1160(1998) [YUN 1998, p. 369], 1199(1998) [ibid., p. 377], 1203(1998) [ibid., p. 382] and 1239 (1999) [YUN 1999, p. 349]. The civilian aspects of resolution 1244(1999) were being implemented by UNMIK and the military aspects by the international security presence (KFOR), led by NATO.

Report of Secretary-General (February). The Secretary-General, in his February report on UNMIK activities [S/2005/88], said that there had been encouraging and tangible progress in the commitment of the Provisional Institutions of Self-Government to the implementation of the "standards-before-status" policy. However, none of the eight standards had been completely fulfilled. The continued unwillingness of the Kosovo Serbs to engage in dialogue and support the implementation of the standards hampered the ability to move forward, although the participation of their leader in the decentralization working group on 24 January was encouraging. Meanwhile, the transition from the October 2004 elections [YUN 2004, p. 416] to the installation of the new coalition Government, headed by the Prime Minister of Kosovo, Ramush Haradinaj, showed growing political maturity. Agreement was reached on the distribution of chairmanships of the 10 new Assembly committees and the major opposition parties had committed themselves to playing an important role. Kosovo's President, Ibrahim Rugova, confirmed his respect for the Constitutional Framework by resigning as president of his party, the Democratic League of Kosovo (LDK.).

The security situation remained stable, with no serious inter-ethnic crime, especially against Kosovo Serbs, since June 2004. Although the security of minorities had improved since the violence of March 2004 [YUN 2004, p. 405], freedom of movement remained precarious and Kosovo Serbs, in particular, continued to consider themselves at risk. Their fears were fed by isolated incidents that were not always condemned or addressed by the local political leadership. The Government did not take sufficient action to punish ethnically targeted crimes, or put in place a system to monitor and censure violations of the language laws, or promote a culture of human rights and tolerance. The Provisional Institutions had yet to demonstrate their willingness to assume responsibility for the security of Kosovo Serbs and other communities. The reconstruction programme had not been completed, and many of the newly constructed houses remained unoccupied. Some municipalities delayed the drafting of return strategies, the appointment of return officers and other support measures, and none of them had finalized a development plan.

At the same time, most authorities in Belgrade were not supportive of Kosovo Serb participation in the Provisional Institutions, or in processes to address their special needs. The working group on direct dialogue between Pristina and Belgrade had not met since March 2004, mainly because of obstacles raised by Belgrade.

Some progress was achieved regarding the economy. The Government, with UNMIK, finalized the draft 2005 budget within tight macroeconomic constraints and established an independent tax and customs review board, a credit information centre and an insurance communication platform. The privatization process also continued. Given the increased capability of the Provisional Institutions in the economic area, the Special Representative announced further transfers of economic Competences.

The Secretary-General observed that, while noteworthy steps were taken in some areas, overall progress on the implementation of the standards remained uneven. Further sustained effort was required in areas of importance to minority communities, notwithstanding the lack of engagement by Kosovo Serbs in the Provisional Institutions. The Secretary-General called upon all parties to immediately follow through on their commitment to recommence participation in the direct dialogue working group on missing persons.

Security Council consideration (February). The Special Representative, in his briefing to the Security Council on 24 February [meeting 5130], reported that, while the security situation continued to improve, it remained fragile. He therefore welcomed NATO's decision to maintain KFOR's operational capabilities during the year. The new Government was proceeding with the devolution of authority to the local level, and agreed on five pilot municipalities, two of which were of particular interest to Kosovo Serbs. The next step would be to define the exact nature of additional municipal competences. At the central level, the transfer of competences from UNMIK to the Provisional Institutions accelerated. Three new ministries were established (Communities and Returns, Local Government Administration, Energy and Mining) and were becoming opera-

tional. To ensure that transferred competences could be exercised effectively, UNMIK encouraged donors to coordinate and better target their efforts to help build capacity across all areas. Economic stagnation remained a serious concern, with widespread unemployment and the absence of a social safety net. After 12 months of boycott by Belgrade, direct dialogue between Pristina and Belgrade was about to resume. The working group on missing persons was scheduled to meet on 10 March. It was hoped that recent positive signals from Belgrade would result in an intensification of direct dialogue.

The Special Representative informed that, following his next technical assessment of the implementation of standards, a comprehensive review of those standards was planned for mid-2005 (see below). Should that review conclude that sufficient progress had been made, the international community should be prepared to embark on the process leading to status talks. There was broad agreement on a clear way forward and a clear timetable that could lead to negotiations on final status in the second half of 2005.

Communications. The EU Presidency, in a 10 March statement [S/2005/200], noted the indictment by ICTY (see p. 1388) of Kosovo's Prime Minister, Ramush Haradinaj, and welcomed his decision to resign his post and go voluntarily to The Hague. It called on Kosovo's political forces to form as quickly as possible a new government determined to continue implementation of the standards set by the United Nations. In a further statement of 16 March [S/2005/201], the EU welcomed the increasing number of voluntary surrenders and transfer of indictees from Serbia and Montenegro, including Kosovo, and from Bosnia and Herzegovina to ICTY, a trend that should lead to all indictees being brought before the Tribunal. It repeated that the Governments of the region bore the key responsibility in that process and their cooperation with ICTY was essential for further progress towards closer EU relations.

Serbia and Montenegro, on 18 May [S/2005/329], drew attention to the fact that, on 26 April, without consultation, UNMIK and Germany, despite the bilateral Readmission Agreement between Germany and Serbia and Montenegro, which provided that the displaced non-Albanian population would not be forcibly repatriated to Kosovo and Metohija before security and safety standards were met, signed a bilateral agreement stipulating conditions for the deportation of Askalias, Egyptians and Roma from Germany to Kosovo and Metohija. Serbia and Montenegro, while welcoming all opportunities for the return of displaced persons, was concerned over attempts to force displaced non-Albanians, mostly

Roma, to return to Kosovo and Metohija without their consent. Serbia and Montenegro urged UNMIK to begin carrying out its international obligations and thus enable all citizens of Kosovo and Metohija to enjoy international legal protection.

Report of Secretary-General (May). The Secretary-General, in his May report [S/2005/335], said that the smooth transition to a new Government led by Prime Minister Bajram Kosumi, following Mr. Haradinaj's resignation, was accompanied by a renewed commitment to carry out the standards implementation programme of the previous Government. The reconfigured coalition of LDK and the Alliance for the Future of Kosovo (AAK) also emphasized and focused on those standards relating to sustainable multi-ethnicity. However, tensions between the governing and opposition parties intensified, as the latter sharpened their criticism of the Kosovo Assembly, alleging repeated violations of Assembly rules to stifle open debate, and walking out of Assembly proceedings on a number of occasions. The Special Representative urged them to work towards Kosovo-wide consensus on issues vital to the territory's future. Kosovo Serb participation in the political process remained low, with the only top central-level government position held by a Kosovo Serb being that of Minister of Returns and Communities. However, minority employment was rising in central Provisional Institutions amidst expanded recruitment activity.

Significant progress was made on the issue of cultural heritage, with the signing by representatives of the Serbian Orthodox Church and the Provisional Institutions of a new memorandum of understanding on the reconstruction of Serbian Orthodox religious sites damaged during the March 2004 riots [YUN 2004, p. 405]. Efforts by the international community in the area of restoration and reconstruction of cultural heritage in Kosovo, including through a donor conference (Paris, France, 13 May), were advanced. Local government reform was further delayed, as the major opposition parties continued to oppose the government-approved work programme for that purpose. Improvements in freedom of movement and a diminishing reliance of Kosovo minorities on escorts when travelling across majority areas were encouraging. KFOR continued to dismantle units providing static protection of designated sites.

The Secretary-General welcomed the offer by Serbian President, Boris Tadic, to meet with Kosovo's President Ibrahim Rugova, and the expressed intention of their respective Prime Ministers to also meet. He was encouraged by the resumption of direct dialogue on practical matters between Pristina and Belgrade. He believed that a comprehensive review of the situation in Kosovo should be initiated and, in that regard, he intended to appoint a Special Envoy to conduct that review.

Security Council consideration. In his briefing to the Council on 27 May [meeting 5188], the Special Representative reported that, in order to manage tension between political parties, and in view of the critical period ahead for Kosovo and the significant political issues to be discussed, party leaders had agreed to his proposal to come together in a forum to enhance constructive dialogue and ensure the maximum possible consensus on critical issues. While regretting that, after 15 months, there was no clear signal from Belgrade to the Kosovo Serbs to participate in the Provisional Institutions, he believed that progress in Kosovo would continue even without meaningful participation by the Kosovo Serbs, but progress in establishing a fully multi-ethnic Kosovo and integrating all communities would be limited.

Comprehensive review of policies and practices

Following the announcement in his May report on UNMIK (see above) to appoint a Special Envoy to initiate a comprehensive review of the situation in Kosovo, in keeping with Security Council resolution 1244(1999) [YUN 1999, p. 353] and relevant presidential statements, the Secretary-General informed the Council President on 27 May [S/2005/364] of the appointment of Ambassador Kai Eide (Norway) to undertake that assessment. The review would assess the current situation and conditions for the next steps in the political process, looking at actual political realities and the formal preconditions for launching the future status process. The Council noted the Secretary-General's intention on 2 June [S/2005/365].

In his report [S/2005/635], transmitted to the Council by the Secretary-General in October, Ambassador Eide said that, following a period of political stagnation and frustration, Kosovo had entered a new dynamic phase of development. Standards implementation, although uneven, had made progress in developing new institutional frameworks. The institutional vacuum that existed after the end of the conflict in 1999 [YUN 1999, p. 342] was replaced by a comprehensive set of institutions. Much progress was also made in the development of a sustainable legal framework. Meanwhile, Kosovo Serbs remained outside the central political institutions, maintaining parallel structures for health and educational services out of fear that they would become a decoration to any central-level political institution. The

Kosovo Albanians had done little to dispel that fear.

The current economic situation remained bleak. Unemployment was high and poverty widespread, compounded by the lack of public income and an antiquated energy sector. The privatization process, while it could have a positive impact on Kosovo's economy—as many of the socially owned enterprises had been idle—could lead to discrimination in employment along ethnic lines.

The rule of law was hampered by a lack of ability and readiness to enforce legislation at all levels. Although the Kosovo Police Service (KPS) was gradually taking on new and more demanding tasks, crimes of a more serious nature or with ethnic dimensions remained difficult for it to address. The Kosovo justice system was the weakest of the institutions, with an increasing backlog of thousands of civil cases. While organized crime and corruption were the biggest threats to the stability and sustainability of institutions, the Government had not taken the administrative and legislative action to fight them. The Special Envoy noted that, given the weakness of the police and judiciary, further transfer of competences in those areas should be considered with great caution, and the continued presence of international police with executive powers in sensitive areas was still needed. The current reduction in the number of international judges and prosecutors was premature and should be urgently reconsidered.

The overall security situation was stable, yet fragile. Low-level inter-ethnic violence and incidents were frequently unreported. The situation with regard to founding a multi-ethnic society was grim. Property rights were neither respected nor ensured, and a great number of agricultural and commercial properties remained illegally occupied, representing an obstacle to the return process and sustainable livelihoods. Meanwhile, the overall return process had virtually come to a halt, as the general atmosphere in many areas was not conducive to return. The process was further hampered by the fact that assistance was only provided to those returning to their home of origin. The continued existence of displaced persons camps inside Kosovo remained a sore point for the governing structures and for the international community, especially the plight of Roma camps in Plementina and Zitkovac.

The Special Envoy concluded that the time had come to commence the process of addressing Kosovo's future status, as postponing it was unlikely to lead to further tangible results in standards implementation. There was a shared expectation in Kosovo and Belgrade that the future status process would commence soon. However, all sides needed clarity with regard to Kosovo's future status: the Kosovo Albanians needed greater clarity on the framework of Kosovo's political and economic development, while the Kosovo Serbs needed clarity to make informed decisions about their future lives. For Belgrade, determining Kosovo's future status would remove an important source of internal political instability and facilitate the realization of Serbia's European perspective. The process needed to take place while the international community was still present in sufficient strength in Kosovo and could work to bring minority communities into the process. In that regard, Kosovo Serbs would have to be party to the process and mechanisms found to include the smaller communities, as well as neighbouring States, to ensure regional stability. The demarcation of the border with The former Yugoslav Republic of Macedonia would be of particular significance and should be resolved before the process ended.

Kosovo's future status process had to move forward with caution, with all parties brought together and kept together throughout the process, and with a clear and common agenda. The end result should be stable and sustainable, with no artificial deadlines. Direct talks between Belgrade and Pristina on decentralization and cultural and religious matters would be essential elements of any future status process and would serve as a confidence-building measure.

The international community, in particular the EU, would have to play a prominent role in Kosovo, along with the continued presence of NATO and the involvement of the Organization for Security and Cooperation in Europe (OSCE). With the United Nations eventually stepping down from its current role, a High Representative or a similar arrangement would have to be considered, firmly anchored in the EU. A road map for integration into international structures would provide Kosovo with real prospects for the future, while Belgrade would need incentives for integration into Euro-Atlantic cooperation frameworks.

The Secretary-General, in his letter transmitting the Special Envoy's report, said that he accepted its conclusion and intended to appoint a Special Envoy to lead the future status process.

Security Council consideration. The Council met on 24 October [meeting 5289] to consider the report on the comprehensive review. In introducing the results of his work, the Special Envoy said that he supported the commencement of the status process because it was important to keep the political process from stagnating. Furthermore, all would benefit from clarity on the status issue and the commencement of the process would give enhanced leverage to the further implementation of standards.

The Special Representative and Head of UNMIK, in his briefing to the Council, said that the start of the status process would be a galvanizing moment in Kosovo. The resolution of Kosovo's status could have only a positive effect on the wider region in terms of political stability and economic growth. In any case, continuing the status quo was not a viable option. However, there was much work to be done outside the status talks as they proceeded.

With that in mind, UNMIK had identified six priority areas for its work in the coming months: continuing with the implementation of standards, especially in the key areas of movement, returns and the economy; supporting the Provisional Institutions in pursuing comprehensive local government reform; pursuing a comprehensive security agenda, including the transfer of competences from UNMIK to the new Provisional Ministries of Public Order and Justice by the end of 2005; strengthening capacity-building to ensure that, regardless of the outcome of status talks, Kosovo's institutions would be fully capable of taking on their future responsibilities; continuing UNMIK's restructuring, with a view to having an optimal set-up throughout the status process, while cooperating with international partners to develop a phased and well-managed transition to eventual future arrangements; and ensuring the maintenance of a safe and secure environment for everyone in Kosovo.

Serbia and Montenegro's Prime Minister, Vojislav Kostunica, emphasized to the Council his country's preparedness to assume its share of responsibility in resolving the issue of Kosovo and Metohija. It was committed to a compromise solution and was willing to ensure substantial autonomy for the province as part of the State of Serbia and Montenegro. The future status process would have the best likelihood of success if it took the form of direct talks between the two sides, mediated by the Special Envoy.

SECURITY COUNCIL ACTION (October)

On 24 October [meeting 5290], following consultations among Security Council members, the President made statement **S/PRST/2005/51** on behalf of the Council:

> The Security Council welcomes the report of the Secretary-General's standards review envoy, Mr. Kai Eide, on the comprehensive review of the implementation of standards, as well as of the overall situation in and relating to Kosovo, Serbia and Montenegro, forwarded by the Secretary-General on 7 October

2005. The Council pays tribute to Mr. Eide's work in compiling his important report.

The Council recalls the report of the Secretary-General of 23 May 2005 in which he initiated the comprehensive review conducted by Mr. Eide. In the light of the findings in Mr Eide's report, the Council stresses that further, more sustained progress is required, and that the implementation of standards in Kosovo must continue with undiminished energy and a stronger sense of commitment, as underlined by the Secretary-General in his letter. It urges Kosovo's leaders to increase their efforts to ensure the implementation of standards at all levels, allowing tangible results to be delivered to all Kosovo's citizens. Particular and time-conscious attention should be given to protecting minorities, developing further the process of decentralization, creating the necessary conditions to allow sustainable returns, preservation of cultural and religious heritage in Kosovo, and promoting reconciliation. The Council also urges the authorities in Belgrade to do their utmost to facilitate this process, and to engage constructively. The Council reaffirms its full support for the Special Representative of the Secretary-General for Kosovo, Mr. Soren Jessen-Petersen, and the United Nations Interim Administration in Kosovo in their continuing work to support the implementation of standards, which must continue during the future status process and will be an important factor in determining the degree of progress.

The Council agrees with Mr. Eide's overall assessment that, notwithstanding the challenges still facing Kosovo and the wider region, the time has come to move to the next phase of the political process. The Council therefore supports the intention of the Secretary-General to start a political process to determine the future status of Kosovo, as foreseen in Council resolution 1244(1999). The Council reaffirms the framework of the resolution, and welcomes the Secretary-General's readiness to appoint a special envoy to lead the future status process. It looks forward to an early appointment. The Council offers its full support to this political process, which would determine the future status of Kosovo, and further reaffirms its commitment to the objective of a multi-ethnic and democratic Kosovo, which must reinforce regional stability.

The Council welcomes the intention of the Contact Group (France, Germany, Italy, the Russian Federation, the United Kingdom of Great Britain and Northern Ireland and the United States of America) to remain closely engaged in the political process that will be led by the United Nations, and to support the Secretary-General's future status envoy. The Council calls upon interested regional and international organizations to cooperate closely in the process to determine the future status of Kosovo. The Council also supports the meaningful involvement and cooperation of countries in the region.

The Council requests that the Secretary-General provide regular updates on progress in determining the future status of Kosovo, as defined by Council resolution 1244(1999), and will remain actively seized of the matter.

Future status process

Appointment of Special Envoy. On 31 October [S/2005/708], the Secretary-General informed the Security Council of his intention to appoint Mr. Martti Ahtisaari (Finland) as his Special Envoy to lead the future status process for Kosovo, and Mr. Albert Rohan (Austria) as his deputy, which the Council welcomed on 10 November [S/2005/709].

Guiding principles. By the same letter of 10 November [S/2005/709], the Council also transmitted the guiding principles for the future status process for Kosovo, agreed to by the Contact Group (France, Germany, Italy, Russian Federation, United Kingdom, United States). The Contact Group called on the parties to engage in good faith, refrain from unilateral steps and reject any form of violence. They should establish unified negotiating teams and agree on common positions. The process should provide for the effective participation of the Kosovo Serbs and other Kosovo citizens and communities. The implementation of the standards should continue during the status process and would be a factor in determining progress. The final decision on the status of Kosovo should be endorsed by the Security Council.

The status process should be based on the following principles: the settlement of the Kosovo issue should be fully compatible with international standards of human rights, democracy and international law and contribute to regional security; conform to democratic values and European standards and contribute to realizing Kosovo's European perspective, in particular, its progress in the stabilization and association process, as well as the integration of the entire region into Euro-Atlantic institutions; ensure sustainable multi-ethnicity in Kosovo, including constitutional guarantees and mechanisms to ensure the implementation of human rights for all citizens; ensure the participation of all communities in government, at both the central and local levels; and include safeguards for the protection of cultural and religious heritage, including provisions specifying the status of Serbian Orthodox Church institutions and sites and other patrimony in Kosovo.

The settlement of Kosovo's status should also strengthen regional security and stability, with no changes in its current territory, meaning no partition and no union with any country or part of any country. It should ensure Kosovo's security and that it did not pose a military or security threat to its neighbours; promote mechanisms to strengthen Kosovo's ability to enforce the rule of law, fight organized crime and terrorism and safeguard the multi-ethnic character of the police and the judiciary; ensure sustainable economic

and political development, and maintain an international civilian and military presence to supervise compliance with the provisions of the status settlement; ensure security and protection of minorities; and monitor and support the authorities in the continued implementation of standards.

Future status preparations. The Secretary-General, in his report on UNMIK [S/2006/45] describing developments in the latter part of the year, said that his Special Envoy for the future status process, Mr. Ahtisaari, held initial consultations in the region, including in Kosovo, from 21 to 27 November. Since then, the Kosovo Albanian leaders had made significant progress in preparing for the status process. In September, President Rugova established a negotiating team, which met on 6 October, and a political group to prepare specific position papers. In the meantime, Kosovo Albanian political and institutional leaders had welcomed the Contact Group's guiding principles (see above).

At a plenary meeting on 17 November, the Kosovo Assembly unanimously adopted a resolution reconfirming the political will of the people of Kosovo for an independent and sovereign state of Kosovo, and provided a mandate for Kosovo's delegation to the future status process. A similar resolution was adopted by Serbia and Montenegro's Parliament on 21 November. On 22 November, the Kosovo negotiating team met with the Special Envoy and submitted a document outlining its platform for status negotiations, including its commitment to equal rights for majority and minority communities, based on the rule of law. On 9 December, the negotiating team established a Consultative Committee for Minorities to advise on minority issues. The negotiating team and its political group were making progress in preparing Pristina for the status process, although detailed proposals on specific issues had yet to be agreed.

Other developments

Reporting on other developments during the latter part of the year [S/2006/45], the Secretary-General said that the comprehensive review of the situation in Kosovo (see p. 469) had encouraged the Provisional Institutions to make progress on both the implementation of standards and on a number of important processes, including dialogue between the communities and local government reform. However, the participation of Kosovo Serb leaders in the political process had declined. As the main Kosovo Serb party (the Serbian List for Kosovo and Metohija (SLKM)) remained outside the Provisional Institutions, the Serbian National Council of North Kosovo engaged more actively with UNMIK to fill the gap left by SLKM as the international community's main local interlocutor. The mid-September appointment of a new head of the Serbian Coordination Centre in Belgrade, Sanda Raskovic-Ivic, was seen as an expression of Serbia's intention to take a more assertive role in political decisions related to Kosovo and in promoting their implementation through the Centre's coordinators on the ground.

Meanwhile, the security situation remained generally stable, despite the continuation of violent attacks, the most significant of which were the shooting of a KPS senior officer on 28 September, the murder of a Kosovo Serb student on 30 November and a 3 December rocket-propelled grenade attack on a bus with 11 passengers en route to Belgrade, but which failed to explode. There were also reports of illegal checkpoints being set up in remote locations.

Progress in local government reform remained uneven. In August, the Special Representative established the territorial delineation of five pilot municipal units, two in Kosovo Albanian, two in Kosovo Serb and one in Kosovo Turkish-majority areas. With UNMIK support, the units in the Kosovo Albanian and Kosovo Turkish-majority areas were successfully launched. Although the Assemblies of those three units lacked adequate premises, they met regularly. However, the establishment of the Kosovo Serb units was held up by the refusal of the Provisional Institutions to map out those units that would be dominated by a Kosovo Serb majority, and by Kosovo Serb insistence that two of the units be overwhelmingly Kosovo Serb before they would consider participation.

Dialogue between Belgrade and Pristina showed some progress at the political level, but stagnated at the technical level. In addition to the Ministerial-level meeting in Vienna on decentralization, the respective Ministers of Culture met in Belgrade on 23 September and in Bulgaria on 8 and 9 December. At the technical level, the four direct dialogue working groups for technical co-operation continued to meet on the issues of energy, missing persons, returns, and transport and communications, however, progress was limited since September, and, with the initiation of the future status process, the parties were increasingly reluctant to engage constructively in direct dialogue.

Work on repairing and protecting Serbian Orthodox cultural and religious heritage proceeded well. Reconstruction work on Serbian Orthodox churches began on 10 October and the first phase of the consolidation and protection of 30 cultural heritage sites was completed by the end of the year. The United Nations Educational, Scientific and Cultural Organization held the first session (Paris, France, 9 December) of the Experts Committee on the Rehabilitation and Safeguarding of the Cultural Heritage in Kosovo, which decided to implement 14 projects at a cost of over $3 million.

UNMIK transferred more competences to the Provisional Institutions, particularly those relating to the rule of law and security. Five out of Kosovo's six regions currently had KPS commanders and all 33 police stations had undergone the transition to KPS operational command. In addition, several prisons and detention centres had local commanders. The promulgation in December of an UNMIK regulation establishing new Ministries of Justice and Internal Affairs marked a key step forward. Another regulation was signed on the KPS framework and guiding principles, which provided for the legal and ethical basis for a transitioned service and guarantees for minorities and paved the way for the creation of new public safety institutions, such as the Police Inspectorate and the Kosovo Academy for Public Service Education and Development.

Future international involvement in Kosovo

Consequent upon the recognition in the Contact Group's guiding principles for the Kosovo future status process that an international civilian and military presence would be required in Kosovo, the Special Representative initiated consultations in October, with a view to preparing a technical assessment of the needs of such an involvement, without prejudice to the actual outcome of the process. The assessment, conducted by UNMIK, in collaboration with OSCE and NATO, as well as with UN funds and agencies and bilateral donors, focused on four main areas: the rule of law; good governance; democratization, human rights and minority issues; and economic and fiscal issues.

Progress on standards implementation

The Secretary-General transmitted to the Security Council the technical assessments of progress in implementing the eight standards for Kosovo (functioning democratic institutions, rule of law, freedom of movement, returns and integration, economy, property rights, dialogue with Belgrade and the Kosovo Protection Corps), which it had to meet to comply with Council resolution 1244(1999) [YUN 1999, p. 353], the Constitutional Framework for Provisional Self-Government [YUN 2001, p. 352], the original standards/benchmarks statement endorsed by the Council in presidential statement S/PRST/

2002/11 [YUN 2002, p. 369] and the 2004 Kosovo Standards Implementation Plan [YUN 2004, p. 408]. Those assessments, prepared by the Special Representative, were annexed to the Secretary-General's reports on UNMIK covering the periods November 2004 to January 2005 [S/2005/88], February to April [S/2005/335], and May to December [S/2006/45].

Functioning of democratic institutions. Kosovo's political institutions demonstrated deepening maturity by electing a new Government quickly after the resignation of the former Prime Minister, Mr. Haradinaj (see p. 468). Minority community members participating in the Government increased to four (Kosovo Serb and Bosniac Ministers, Kosovo Egyptian and Turk Deputy Ministers). Three further positions (Minister, Deputy Minister and Assembly Presidency) reserved for Kosovo Serbs awaited nominations by their political parties. The Assembly adopted improved rules of procedure and continued to rely on UNMIK support to amend legislation to ensure technical adequacy and compliance with the constitutional framework and international human rights instruments. Ten laws adopted by the Assembly were being reviewed by UNMIK for conformity with international standards, five of which needed revision to comply with the constitutional framework. The Law on Freedom of Association of Non-Governmental Organizations was adopted by the Assembly and was awaiting promulgation. The Government approved a progressive law on the use of languages and established a language compliance monitoring mechanism, which was functioning effectively for the central government and 12 municipalities. The Independent Media Commission law was promulgated and appointments to the Commission's Council were progressing. The Assembly passed, at first reading, the law on the public broadcaster, which was reviewed by relevant Assembly committees. All the main daily and weekly newspapers endorsed the press code and a Press Council was established to monitor its implementation. The Government also adopted a strategic plan for minority media, as well as codes of conduct for elected officials and civil servants, comprehensive government rules of procedure and terms of reference for the new Ministries. Municipal minority employment increased as 15 of 27 municipalities met or exceeded their targets. The Government initiated a special recruitment campaign that reserved and advertised 103 central institution positions for minorities.

Rule of law. Local crime prevention councils were operating in every municipality, and crime clearance rates remained broadly comparable for majority and minority victims. Central and municipal political leaders' condemnation of serious crimes and encouragement to cooperate fully with the police increased markedly. KPS continued to assume greater responsibilities. Seven police stations (total of 27 out of 32) and the first regional command centre (Gnjilane) made the transition to KPS command.

As at December, 426 people were charged for offences relating to the violence in March 2004, 209 of which had been convicted, 12 acquitted, 95 cases dropped and 110 pending. The action plan to combat trafficking in persons was approved and work started on its implementation, including the opening of a toll-free telephone line for victims and a victims' resource centre.

Freedom of movement. Freedom of movement improved in every municipality, except northern Mitrovica. Of the 583 minority community members surveyed, 83 per cent said that they had travelled outside their area of residence to other parts of Kosovo. Their perception of their freedom of movement had also improved. Regular military escorts ceased and KFOR's fixed guarding positions were reduced from 50 before March 2004 to 14. As of July, the Austerlitz Bridge joining northern and southern Mitrovica was opened to traffic 24 hours a day. Five inter-urban bus lines subsidized by the Kosovo consolidated budget were opened, connecting minority communities in Prishtine/Pristina, Mitrovica/Prizren and Gjilan/Gnjilane regions.

Returns and reintegration. The Government and most municipalities significantly increased official support for returns, and undertook a wide-ranging outreach programme to strengthen and support freedom of movement, returns and dialogue and tolerance building. The Prime Minister, Ministers and many municipal leaders actively engaged with internally displaced persons. On 25 February, the Prime Minister and 23 Kosovo Albanian majority municipalities adopted a joint declaration urging the displaced to return and the majority population to accept and implement its responsibilities towards minority communities. It also called for the protection of property rights and the release of illegally occupied property. The Government allocated 10.5 million euros for returns from the 2005 consolidated budget and an additional 2.2 million euros for the reconstruction of houses damaged or destroyed in March 2004. UNHCR documented 1,925 voluntary returns between 1 January to 30 November 2005, one third of which were Kosovo Serbs. Return projects were ongoing in 18 municipalities, 25 had endorsed municipal returns strategies and 28 had functioning municipal returns officers. The Ministry of Labour and Social Welfare assumed humanitarian responsibility for all eligible internally displaced persons. The strategic framework on communities and returns was launched in July and a protocol on returns was agreed to at the technical level between Pristina and Belgrade in September.

On 25 January [S/2005/47], Serbia and Montenegro brought to the Security Council's attention the difficult situation prevailing in Kosovo and Metohija, resulting from harsh winter conditions that had deprived several Serbian villages of power supply. Serbia and Montenegro said that depriving the remaining Serb population of power at the height of winter further discouraged returns and brought additional pressure on them to leave Kosovo and Metohija.

Economy. Five pieces of basic economic legislation were promulgated. Eight laws and regulations were in place, and nine were in the legislative process. A regulatory framework for mines and minerals was established and a Regulation establishing an Independent Commission for Mines and Minerals was adopted, opening the way for investment. Twenty-four per cent of the budget was allocated to public investment, a three per cent increase since 2004. The Government instructed spending agencies to comply with the International Monetary Fund (IMF) recommendations, particularly in reducing recurrent expenditure, and promulgated a system for monitoring spending agencies' expenditures, imposing fiscal discipline and ensuring efficient allocation of expenditures. Budget management was also strengthened, unauthorized budget transfers identified and reversed, and attempted transfers corrected by the Ministry of Finance and Economy. Chairmanship of the Economic Fiscal Council was transferred to the Prime Minister. A letter of intent was signed with IMF on Kosovo's medium-term economic and fiscal policy framework, committing the Government to stricter public expenditure controls and limits on the budget deficit, public sector employment and benefits and growth in government spending. A new excise code, a law to support small and medium-sized enterprises and a revised procedure for appointments to the Kosovo Pension Savings Trust were promulgated.

Property rights. The promulgation of a Regulation on the allocation of socially owned immovable property managed by municipalities laid the foundation for more effective efforts to regularize informal settlements and provide social housing. Political leadership against illegal occupation and use of property was more marked. A working group was created to develop a public information campaign on the issue and the Government developed plans for a new data collec-

tion system for property rights by tracking court-adjudicated illegal occupation/repossession claims and related actions. Although there was no evidence of ethnic bias in either property-related court decisions or their execution, efforts were needed to make the related legislation more coherent, consistent and compliant with international human rights and European standards. All administrative instructions to implement the law on spacial planning and the situational analysis of informal settlements and the draft guidelines for spacial planning to protect and begin to regularize informal settlements were completed also. Ninety-four per cent of the residential property caseload of the Housing and Property Directorate had been adjudicated, and was expected to be completed by the end of the year. A joint Provisional Institutions-Housing and Property Directorate forum was established to improve coordination of and increase in public support for implementation of the Directorate's decisions. The backlog of property-related cases in the courts rose to 8,486. UNMIK and the Government agreed on a mechanism to resolve outstanding conflict-related property claims.

Cultural heritage. An action plan for cooperation with the Council of Europe on cultural heritage was drafted, including joint elaboration of a heritage policy (2006-2010) on the preservation of cultural heritage and capacity-building for cultural institutions. A public awareness campaign on the importance of the cultural heritage sites of all Kosovo communities was started. Fieldwork on the inventory of cultural heritage sites was completed, but work on the official inventory stalled. A total of 4.2 million euros was again allocated from the consolidated budget for initial reconstruction of Serbian Orthodox sites damaged in March 2004. A Reconstruction Implementation Commission was established to lead reconstruction of those sites; 30 priority sites had been agreed upon.

Dialogue with Belgrade. Direct dialogue with Belgrade resumed during the year. The working group on missing persons met in Belgrade in March, June, October and December. The working group on energy met in May and November and the working group on returns held an ad hoc meeting in September. Progress was made in establishing a working group on the environment.

Kosovo Protection Corps. The Kosovo Protection Corps (KPC) continued to comply with the rule of law, act in accordance with its mandate as a civilian emergency organization and make significant additional standards efforts. A vigorous minority recruitment and retention campaign continued. A total of 161 minorities actively participated, including 31 Ashkali, 18 Bosniacs,

8 Egyptians, 9 Croats, 14 Muslims, 2 Roma, 48 Serbs, 30 Turks and a Goran.

By the end of the year, KPC teams had cleared over 1.7 million square metres of land of unexploded ordnance. The Civil Protection Brigade was inaugurated and its members received specialized training in the handling of hazardous materials, crisis management and firefighting.

UN Interim
Administration Mission in Kosovo

The United Nations Interim Administration Mission in Kosovo (UNMIK), established in 1999 [YUN 1999, p. 357] to facilitate a political process to determine Kosovo's political future, comprised five components referred to as pillars: interim administration (led by the United Nations); institution-building (led by OSCE); economic reconstruction (led by the EU); humanitarian affairs (led by UNHCR); and police and justice (led by the United Nations). UNMIK was headed by the Special Representative of the Secretary-General, Soren Jessen-Petersen.

The Secretary-General reported to the Security Council on the activities of UNMIK and developments in Kosovo for the periods 1 November 2004 to 31 January 2005 [S/2005/88] and 1 February to 30 April 2005 [S/2005/335] (see above). Activities for the remainder of the year were covered in a later report [S/2006/45].

Financing

On 13 April [meeting 91], the General Assembly, having considered the Secretary-General's request for an additional appropriation of $33,744,100 for the maintenance of UNMIK for the period 1 July 2004 to 30 June 2005 [A/59/692] and the comments and recommendation of ACABQ thereon [A/59/728], adopted, on the recommendation of the Fifth Committee [A/59/772], **resolution 59/286 A** without vote [agenda item 133].

Financing of the United Nations Interim Administration Mission in Kosovo

A

The General Assembly,

Having considered the note by the Secretary-General on the financing arrangements for the United Nations Interim Administration Mission in Kosovo for the period from 1 July 2004 to 30 June 2005 and the related report of the Advisory Committee on Administrative and Budgetary Questions,

Recalling Security Council resolution 1244(1999) of 10 June 1999 regarding the establishment of the United Nations Interim Administration Mission in Kosovo,

Recalling also its resolution 53/241 of 28 July 1999 on the financing of the Mission and its subsequent resolutions thereon, the latest of which is resolution 58/305 of 18 June 2004,

Acknowledging the complexity of the Mission,

Reaffirming the general principles underlying the financing of United Nations peacekeeping operations, as stated in General Assembly resolutions 1874(S-IV) of 27 June 1963, 3101(XXVIII) of 11 December 1973 and 55/235 of 23 December 2000,

Mindful of the fact that it is essential to provide the Mission with the necessary financial resources to enable it to fulfil its responsibilities under the relevant resolution of the Security Council,

1. *Takes note* of the status of contributions to the United Nations Interim Administration Mission in Kosovo as at 28 February 2005, including the contributions outstanding in the amount of 132.4 million United States dollars, representing some 7 per cent of the total assessed contributions, notes with concern that only sixty-eight Member States have paid their assessed contributions in full, and urges all other Member States, in particular those in arrears, to ensure payment of their outstanding assessed contributions;

2. *Expresses its appreciation* to those Member States which have paid their assessed contributions in full, and urges all other Member States to make every possible effort to ensure payment of their assessed contributions to the Mission in full;

3. *Expresses concern* at the financial situation with regard to peacekeeping activities, in particular as regards the reimbursements to troop contributors that bear additional burdens owing to overdue payments by Member States of their assessments;

4. *Also expresses concern* at the delay experienced by the Secretary-General in deploying and providing adequate resources to some recent peacekeeping missions, in particular those in Africa;

5. *Emphasizes* that all future and existing peacekeeping missions shall be given equal and non-discriminatory treatment in respect of financial and administrative arrangements;

6. *Also emphasizes* that all peacekeeping missions shall be provided with adequate resources for the effective and efficient discharge of their respective mandates;

7. *Reiterates its request* to the Secretary-General to make the fullest possible use of facilities and equipment at the United Nations Logistics Base at Brindisi, Italy, in order to minimize the costs of procurement for the Mission;

8. *Endorses* the conclusions and recommendations contained in the report of the Advisory Committee on Administrative and Budgetary Questions, and requests the Secretary-General to ensure their full implementation;

9. *Requests* the Secretary-General to take all necessary action to ensure that the Mission is administered with a maximum of efficiency and economy;

10. *Also requests* the Secretary-General, in order to reduce the cost of employing General Service staff, to continue efforts to recruit local staff for the Mission against General Service posts, commensurate with the requirements of the Mission;

Revised budget estimates for the period from 1 July 2004 to 30 June 2005

11. *Decides* to appropriate to the Special Account for the United Nations Interim Administration Mission in Kosovo the additional amount of 30 million

dollars for the maintenance of the Mission for the period from 1 July 2004 to 30 June 2005, taking into account the total amount of 278,413,700 dollars already appropriated for the Mission for the same period under the provisions of General Assembly resolution 58/305;

Financing of the appropriation

12. *Decides also* to apportion among Member States the amount of 30 million dollars, taking into account the amount of 278,413,700 dollars already apportioned by the General Assembly in its resolution 58/305 for the period from 1 July 2004 to 30 June 2005, in accordance with the levels set out by the Assembly in its resolution 55/235, as adjusted in its resolution 55/236 of 23 December 2000 and updated in its resolution 58/256 of 23 December 2003, the scale of assessments for 2004 and 2005, as set out in its resolution 58/1 B of 23 December 2003, to be applied against a portion thereof, that is, 15 million dollars, which is the amount pertaining to the period ended 31 December 2004, and to be applied also against the balance, that is, 15 million dollars for the period from 1 January to 30 June 2005;

13. *Decides further* that, in accordance with the provisions of its resolution 973(X) of 15 December 1955, there shall be set off against the apportionment among Member States, as provided for in paragraph 12 above, their respective share in the Tax Equalization Fund of the additional amount of 3,850,800 dollars, approved for the Mission for the period from 1 July 2004 to 30 June 2005;

14. *Emphasizes* that no peacekeeping mission shall be financed by borrowing funds from other active peacekeeping missions;

15. *Encourages* the Secretary-General to continue to take additional measures to ensure the safety and security of all personnel under the auspices of the United Nations participating in the Mission;

16. *Invites* voluntary contributions to the Mission in cash and in the form of services and supplies acceptable to the Secretary-General, to be administered, as appropriate, in accordance with the procedure and practices established by the General Assembly;

17. *Decides* to keep under review during its fifty-ninth session the item entitled "Financing of the United Nations Interim Administration Mission in Kosovo".

On 22 June [meeting 104], the Assembly, having considered UNMIK's financial performance report for the period from 1 July 2003 to 30 June 2004 [A/59/736], the proposed budget for the period from 1 July 2005 to 30 June 2006 [YUN 2004, p. 418] and ACABQ's comments and recommendations thereon [A/59/736/Add.1], adopted, on the recommendation of the Fifth Committee [A/59/772/Add.1], **resolution 59/286 B** without vote [agenda item 133].

B

The General Assembly,

Having considered the reports of the Secretary-General on the financing of the United Nations Interim Administration Mission in Kosovo and the related reports of the Advisory Committee on Administrative and Budgetary Questions,

Recalling Security Council resolution 1244(1999) of 10 June 1999 regarding the establishment of the United Nations Interim Administration Mission in Kosovo,

Recalling also its resolution 53/241 of 28 July 1999 on the financing of the Mission and its subsequent resolutions thereon, the latest of which was resolution 59/286 A of 13 April 2005,

Acknowledging the complexity of the Mission,

Reaffirming the general principles underlying the financing of United Nations peacekeeping operations, as stated in General Assembly resolutions 1874(S-IV) of 27 June 1963, 3101(XXVIII) of 11 December 1973 and 55/235 of 23 December 2000,

Mindful of the fact that it is essential to provide the Mission with the necessary financial resources to enable it to fulfil its responsibilities under the relevant resolution of the Security Council,

1. *Requests* the Secretary-General to entrust the Head of Mission with the task of formulating future budget proposals in full accordance with the provisions of General Assembly resolution 59/296 of 22 June 2005, as well as other relevant resolutions;

2. *Takes note* of the status of contributions to the United Nations Interim Administration Mission in Kosovo as at 15 April 2005, including the contributions outstanding in the amount of 82.7 million United States dollars, representing some 4 per cent of the total assessed contributions, notes with concern that only seventy-four Member States have paid their assessed contributions in full, and urges all other Member States, in particular those in arrears, to ensure payment of their outstanding assessed contributions;

3. *Expresses its appreciation* to those Member States which have paid their assessed contributions in full, and urges all other Member States to make every possible effort to ensure payment of their assessed contributions to the Mission in full;

4. *Expresses concern* at the financial situation with regard to peacekeeping activities, in particular as regards the reimbursements to troop contributors that bear additional burdens owing to overdue payments by Member States of their assessments;

5. *Also expresses concern* at the delay experienced by the Secretary-General in deploying and providing adequate resources to some recent peacekeeping missions, in particular those in Africa;

6. *Emphasizes* that all future and existing peacekeeping missions shall be given equal and non-discriminatory treatment in respect of financial and administrative arrangements;

7. *Also emphasizes* that all peacekeeping missions shall be provided with adequate resources for the effective and efficient discharge of their respective mandates;

8. *Reiterates its request* to the Secretary-General to make the fullest possible use of facilities and equipment at the United Nations Logistics Base at Brindisi, Italy, in order to minimize the costs of procurement for the Mission;

9. *Endorses* the conclusions and recommendations contained in the report of the Advisory Committee on Administrative and Budgetary Questions, and requests

the Secretary-General to ensure their full implementation;

10. *Requests* the Secretary-General to ensure the full implementation of the relevant provisions of its resolution 59/296;

11. *Notes,* as pointed out by the Advisory Committee on Administrative and Budgetary Questions in paragraphs 20 and 21 of its report, that the functions of a large number of posts have been performed by staff at grades lower than the budgeted levels, and requests the Secretary-General to take appropriate action;

12. *Requests* the Secretary-General to take all necessary action to ensure that the Mission is administered with a maximum of efficiency and economy;

13. *Also requests* the Secretary-General, in order to reduce the cost of employing General Service staff, to continue efforts to recruit local staff for the Mission against General Service posts, commensurate with the requirements of the Mission;

**Financial performance report for
the period from 1 July 2003 to 30 June 2004**

14. *Takes note* of the report of the Secretary-General on the financial performance of the Mission for the period from 1 July 2003 to 30 June 2004;

**Budget estimates for the
period from 1 July 2005 to 30 June 2006**

15. *Decides* to appropriate to the Special Account for the United Nations Interim Administration Mission in Kosovo the amount of 252,551,800 dollars for the period from 1 July 2005 to 30 June 2006, inclusive of 239,889,800 dollars for the maintenance of the Mission, 10,353,700 dollars for the support account for peacekeeping operations and 2,308,300 dollars for the United Nations Logistics Base;

Financing of the appropriation

16. *Decides also* to apportion among Member States the amount of 252,551,800 dollars, at a monthly rate of 21,045,983 dollars in accordance with the levels updated in General Assembly resolution 58/256 of 23 December 2003, and taking into account the scale of assessments for 2005 and 2006, as set out in its resolution 58/1 B of 23 December 2003;

17. *Decides further* that, in accordance with the provisions of its resolution 973(X) of 15 December 1955, there shall be set off against the apportionment among Member States, as provided for in paragraph 16 above, their respective share in the Tax Equalization Fund of the amount of 21,704,300 dollars, comprising the estimated staff assessment income of 20,054,100 dollars approved for the Mission, the prorated share of 1,463,500 dollars of the estimated staff assessment income approved for the support account and the prorated share of 186,700 dollars of the estimated staff assessment income approved for the United Nations Logistics Base;

18. *Decides* that, for Member States that have fulfilled their financial obligations to the Mission, there shall be set off against their apportionment, as provided for in paragraph 16 above, their respective share of the unencumbered balance and other income in the amount of 4,470,000 dollars in respect of the financial period ended 30 June 2004, in accordance with the levels updated in General Assembly resolution 58/256, and taking into account the scale of assessments for 2004, as set out in its resolution 58/1 B;

19. *Decides also* that, for Member States that have not fulfilled their financial obligations to the Mission, there shall be set off against their outstanding obligations their respective share of the unencumbered balance and other income in the amount of 4,470,000 dollars in respect of the financial period ended 30 June 2004, in accordance with the scheme set out in paragraph 18 above;

20. *Decides further* that the increase of 3,763,200 dollars in the estimated staff assessment income in respect of the financial period ended 30 June 2004 shall be added to the credits from the amount of 4,470,000 dollars referred to in paragraphs 18 and 19 above;

21. *Emphasizes* that no peacekeeping mission shall be financed by borrowing funds from other active peacekeeping missions;

22. *Encourages* the Secretary-General to continue to take additional measures to ensure the safety and security of all personnel under the auspices of the United Nations participating in the Mission, bearing in mind paragraphs 5 and 6 of Security Council resolution 1502(2003) of 26 August 2003;

23. *Invites* voluntary contributions to the Mission in cash and in the form of services and supplies acceptable to the Secretary-General, to be administered, as appropriate, in accordance with the procedure and practices established by the General Assembly;

24. *Decides* to include in the provisional agenda of its sixtieth session the item entitled "Financing of the United Nations Interim Administration Mission in Kosovo".

In December, the Secretary-General submitted the performance report for UNMIK for the period from 1 July to 30 June 2005 [A/60/637 & Corr.1].

International security presence

The Secretary-General transmitted to the Security Council, in accordance with resolution 1244(1999) [YUN 1999, p. 353], reports on the activities of the international security presence in Kosovo (KFOR), also known as Operation Joint Guard, covering the periods 1 January to 31 January [S/2005/352], 1 February to 31 May [S/2005/241, S/2005/308, S/2005/348, S/2005/420], 1 August to 31 August [S/2005/689] and 1 November to 31 December [S/2006/167]. As at 31 December, the force, which operated under NATO leadership, comprised 17,751 troops, including 2,768 from non-NATO countries.

KFOR continued operations to prevent ethnic violence and protect patrimonial sites and remained vigilant to deter possible threats directed against international organizations and military bases. The force continued to improve its crowd and riot control capabilities so as to be better prepared to counter any resurgence of violence.

Georgia

In 2005, renewed efforts were made to end the stalemate in the Georgian/Abkhaz peace process and to restart dialogue on the basis of the 2001 paper known as Basic Principles for the Distribution of Competences between Tbilisi (Georgia's Government) and Sukhumi (the Abkhaz leadership) [YUN 2001, p. 386], which was intended to serve as a framework for substantive negotiations over the status of Abkhazia as a sovereign entity within the State of Georgia.

In April, for the first time since July 2003, high-level representatives of the Group of Friends of the Secretary-General (Russia, Germany, France, United Kingdom, United States) met in Geneva, with the participation of the parties. Although those discussions revealed the differing priorities of the Georgian and Abkhaz delegations, they did lead to further cooperation in practical issues. Discussions on security matters were held and a protocol signed, including measures to strengthen implementation of the 1994 Moscow Agreement on a Ceasefire and Separation of Forces. Draft documents on the non-resumption of hostilities and the safe and dignified return of refugees were finalized for discussion, and meetings of the so-called Sochi working groups on the Sochi-Tbilisi railway and on the return of displaced persons and refugees resumed. In October, the latter working group endorsed in principle documents prepared by the Office of the United Nations High Commissioner for Refugees on the verification and registration of displaced persons and refugees.

However, those positive developments took place against the backdrop of an increasingly difficult and complex situation on the ground, including a call by the Georgian side for the withdrawal of the security forces of the Commonwealth of Independent States and for a UN-led international force.

UN Observer Mission in Georgia

The United Nations Observer Mission in Georgia (UNOMIG), established by Security Council resolution 858(1993) [YUN 1993, p. 509], continued to monitor compliance with the 1994 Agreement on a Ceasefire and Separation of Forces (Moscow Agreement) [YUN 1994, p. 583] and to fulfil other tasks as mandated by Council resolution 937(1994) [ibid., p. 584]. At the request of the parties [ibid., p. 583], the Mission operated in close collaboration with the collective peacekeeping force of the Commonwealth of Independent

States (CIS) located in the zone of conflict since 1994. The Council extended the Mission's mandate twice during the year, the first time until 31 July 2005, and the second, until 31 January 2006.

UNOMIG's main headquarters was located in Sukhumi (Abkhazia, Georgia), with some administrative headquarters in Pitsunda, a liaison office in the Georgian capital of Tbilisi and team bases and a sector headquarters in each of the Gali and Zugdidi sectors. A team base in the Kodori Valley was manned by observers operating from Sukhumi. As at 31 December 2005, UNOMIG's strength stood at 122 military observers and 12 civilian police officers.

Heidi Tagliavini (Switzerland) continued as the Secretary-General's Special Representative for Georgia and Head of UNOMIG. She was assisted by Major General Hussein Ghobashi (Egypt), UNOMIG's Chief Military Observer, who was succeeded on 13 August by Major General Niaz Muhammad Khan Khattak (Pakistan).

Political aspects of the conflict

Report of Secretary-General (January). The Secretary-General, in his January report [S/2005/32] on the situation in Abkhazia, Georgia, and UNOMIG's operations there, noted that recent efforts to advance dialogue for resolving the conflict had encountered serious challenges. UNOMIG's main efforts were focused on finding ways to re-establish dialogue and avoid further regression. The December 2004 high-level meeting of the Group of Friends [YUN 2004, p. 429] had provided an opportunity to reflect on how best to address those challenges in pursuit of a lasting and comprehensive solution.

The Secretary-General hoped that the political situation would stabilize and that dialogue in the priority areas of economic cooperation, the return of refugees and internally displaced persons and political and security matters would resume, accompanied by relevant confidence-building measures. As UNOMIG's presence was critical to maintaining stability in the conflict zone and advancing the peace process, the Secretary-General recommended that its mandate be extended until 31 July 2005.

Communication. In a 26 January letter to the Security Council President [S/2005/45], Georgia reiterated its readiness to resume negotiations with the Abkhaz side, but regretted the lack of a similar willingness on their part. Georgia said that the longer the conflict remained unresolved, the more difficult it would be to find a compromise. It therefore invited the Council to increase its involvement in the conflict-resolution process, including through a field visit to Georgia to learn first-hand of the reality on the ground and to get the process out of the current stalemate.

SECURITY COUNCIL ACTION

On 28 January [meeting 5116], the Security Council unanimously adopted **resolution 1582(2005)**. The draft [S/2005/48] was prepared in consultations among Council members.

The Security Council,

Recalling all its relevant resolutions, in particular resolution 1554(2004) of 29 July 2004,

Welcoming the report of the Secretary-General of 17 January 2005,

Recalling the conclusions of the summits of the Organization for Security and Cooperation in Europe held in Lisbon in December 1996 and in Istanbul on 18 and 19 November 1999, regarding the situation in Abkhazia, Georgia,

Recalling also the relevant principles contained in the Convention on the Safety of United Nations and Associated Personnel adopted on 9 December 1994,

Deploring the fact that the perpetrators of the shooting down of a helicopter of the United Nations Observer Mission in Georgia on 8 October 2001, which resulted in the death of nine people on board, have still not been identified,

Stressing that the continued lack of progress on key issues of a comprehensive settlement of the conflict in Abkhazia, Georgia, is unacceptable,

Welcoming, however, the positive momentum given to the United Nations-led peace process by regular high-level meetings of the Group of Friends of the Secretary-General in Geneva and the Georgian-Russian summit meetings,

Welcoming also the important contributions made by the Mission and the collective peacekeeping force of the Commonwealth of Independent States in stabilizing the situation in the zone of conflict, and stressing its attachment to the close cooperation existing between them in the performance of their respective mandates,

1. *Reaffirms* the commitment of all Member States to the sovereignty, independence and territorial integrity of Georgia within its internationally recognized borders, and the necessity to define the status of Abkhazia within the State of Georgia in strict accordance with these principles;

2. *Commends and strongly supports* the sustained efforts of the Secretary-General and his Special Representative, with the assistance of the Russian Federation in its capacity as facilitator as well as of the Group of Friends of the Secretary-General and of the Organization for Security and Cooperation in Europe, to promote the stabilization of the situation and the achievement of a comprehensive political settlement, which must include a settlement of the political status of Abkhazia within the State of Georgia;

3. *Reiterates its strong support* for the document entitled "Basic Principles for the Distribution of Competences between Tbilisi and Sukhumi" and for its letter of transmittal, finalized by, and with the full support of, all members of the Group of Friends;

4. *Deeply regrets* the continued refusal of the Abkhaz side to agree to a discussion on the substance of that document, again strongly urges the Abkhaz side to receive the document and its letter of transmittal, urges both parties thereafter to give them full and open consideration and to engage in constructive negotiations on their substance, and urges those having influence with the parties to promote this outcome;

5. *Regrets* the lack of progress on the initiation of political status negotiations, and recalls, once again, that the purpose of those documents is to facilitate meaningful negotiations between the parties, under the leadership of the United Nations, on the status of Abkhazia within the State of Georgia, and is not an attempt to impose or dictate any specific solution to the parties;

6. *Notes* its position on Abkhaz elections as expressed in its resolution 1255(1999) of 30 July 1999;

7. *Calls upon* both sides to participate in constructive negotiations towards a political settlement of the conflict and to spare no efforts to overcome their ongoing mutual mistrust, and underlines the fact that the process of negotiation leading to a lasting political settlement acceptable to both sides will require concessions from both sides;

8. *Welcomes* the commitment by the Georgian side to a peaceful resolution of the conflict, and calls upon both parties further to publicly dissociate themselves from all militant rhetoric and demonstrations of support for military options;

9. *Reminds* all concerned to refrain from any action that might impede the peace process;

10. *Welcomes* the convening of regular meetings of senior representatives of the Group of Friends and the United Nations in Geneva, and encourages both sides to participate actively in the next meeting;

11. *Urges* the parties to participate in a more active, regular and structured manner in the task forces established in the first Geneva meeting (to address issues in the priority areas of economic cooperation, the return of internally displaced persons and refugees, and political and security matters) and complemented by the working groups established in Sochi, Russian Federation, in March 2003, and reiterates that results-oriented activities in these three priority areas remain key to building common ground between the Georgian and Abkhaz sides and ultimately for concluding meaningful negotiations on a comprehensive political settlement based on the document entitled "Basic Principles for the Distribution of Competences between Tbilisi and Sukhumi" and its letter of transmittal;

12. *Encourages* the sides, in that respect, to continue their discussion on security guarantees with the participation of the Group of Friends;

13. *Calls again upon* the parties to take concrete steps to revitalize the peace process in all its major aspects, including their work in the Coordinating Council and its relevant mechanisms, to build on the results of the third meeting on confidence-building measures between the Georgian and Abkhaz sides, held in Yalta, Ukraine, on 15 and 16 March 2001, and to implement the proposals agreed on that occasion in a purposeful and cooperative manner, with a view to holding a fourth meeting on confidence-building measures, and welcomes the intention expressed by Germany to host such a meeting pending progress in the conflict resolution process;

14. *Notes* that contacts at the level of civil society can reinforce mutual confidence, and calls upon both sides to facilitate such contacts;

15. *Stresses* the urgent need for progress on the question of the refugees and internally displaced persons, calls upon both sides to display a genuine commitment to make returns the focus of special attention and to undertake this task in close coordination with the United Nations Observer Mission in Georgia and in consultation with the Office of the High Commissioner for Refugees, and the Group of Friends;

16. *Calls for* the rapid finalization and signature of the letter of intent on returns proposed by the Special Representative of the Secretary-General, and welcomes the meetings, with the participation of the Special Representative and the Office of the High Commissioner of the Sochi working group on refugees and internally displaced persons;

17. *Reaffirms* the unacceptability of the demographic changes resulting from the conflict, reaffirms also the inalienable right of all refugees and internally displaced persons affected by the conflict to return to their homes in secure and dignified conditions, in accordance with international law and as set out in the Quadripartite Agreement on the Voluntary Return of Refugees and Displaced Persons of 4 April 1994 and the Yalta Declaration;

18. *Recalls* that the Abkhaz side bears a particular responsibility to protect the returnees and to facilitate the return of the remaining displaced population;

19. *Welcomes* the continuing activities of the United Nations Development Programme in the Gali, Ochamchira and Tkvarcheli districts and the opening of offices by the United Nations Development Programme in Sukhumi and Gali;

20. *Urges* the parties, once again, to implement the recommendations of the joint assessment mission of November 2000 to the Gali sector, regrets that there has been no progress to that effect despite the positive consideration by the parties given to those recommendations in the first Geneva meeting, and calls again upon the Abkhaz side to agree to the opening as soon as possible of the Gali branch of the human rights office in Sukhumi and to provide security conditions for its unhindered functioning;

21. *Reiterates its concern* that despite the start of the deployment of a civilian police component as part of the Mission, as endorsed in resolution 1494(2003) of 30 July 2003, and agreed upon by the parties, the deployment of the remaining officers in the Gali sector is still outstanding, and calls upon the Abkhaz side to allow for a swift deployment of the police component in that region;

22. *Calls in particular upon* the Abkhaz side to improve law enforcement involving the local population and to address the lack of instruction in their mother tongue for the ethnic Georgian population;

23. *Welcomes* the measures taken by the Georgian side to put an end to the activities of illegal armed groups, and encourages the maintenance of these efforts;

24. *Condemns* any violations of the provisions of the Agreement on a Ceasefire and Separation of Forces signed in Moscow on 14 May 1994;

25. *Welcomes* the continuing relative calm in the Kodori Valley, and condemns the killings and abductions of civilians in the Gali district;

26. *Urges* the parties to abide by the provisions of the protocols on security issues in the Gali district signed on 8 October 2003 and 19 January 2004, to continue their regular meetings and to cooperate more closely with each other to improve security in the Gali sector, and takes note of the resumption of Abkhaz participation in the quadripartite meetings and the Joint Investigation Group;

27. *Reiterates its call upon* the Georgian side to provide comprehensive security guarantees to allow for independent and regular monitoring of the situation in the upper Kodori Valley by joint patrols of the Mission and the collective peacekeeping force of the Commonwealth of Independent States;

28. *Underlines* the fact that it is the primary responsibility of both sides to provide appropriate security and to ensure the freedom of movement of the Mission, the collective peacekeeping force and other international personnel;

29. *Strongly condemns*, in that respect, the repeated abductions of personnel of those missions in the past, deeply deplores the fact that none of the perpetrators have ever been identified or brought to justice, reiterates that it is the responsibility of the parties to end this impunity, and calls upon them to take action;

30. *Calls upon* the parties, once again, to take all necessary steps, to identify those responsible for the shooting down of a Mission helicopter on 8 October 2001, to bring them to justice, and to inform the Special Representative of the steps taken in particular in the criminal investigation;

31. *Decides* to extend the mandate of the Mission for a new period terminating on 31 July 2005, subject to a review, as appropriate, of its mandate by the Council in the event of changes in the mandate of the collective peacekeeping force;

32. *Requests* the Secretary-General to continue to keep the Council regularly informed and to report three months from the date of the adoption of the present resolution on the situation in Abkhazia, Georgia;

33. *Decides* to remain actively seized of the matter.

Meeting of Group of Friends (April). For the first time since July 2003, high-level representatives of the Group of Friends of the Secretary-General (Russian Federation, Germany, France, United Kingdom, United States) met (Geneva, 7-8 April) with the participation of the parties. Separate consultations were held with each side to discuss their respective concerns and possible areas for follow-up discussions. The meetings revealed the differing priorities of the Georgian and Abkhaz delegations. The Georgian representatives underscored their willingness to discuss economic issues with the Abkhaz side, but emphasized the right of refugees and internally displaced persons to return and, in that context, the need for measures to address human rights and security in the Gali district. The Abkhaz side undertook to pursue the opening of a UNOMIG human rights branch office and Georgian-language instruction in the Gali district, but highlighted their security concerns and urged Tbilisi to avoid militant rhetoric. They also urged the lifting of restrictions imposed by CIS in 1996 [YUN 1996, p. 359] and encouraged joint economic projects, such as the reopening of the Sochi-Tbilisi railway, to boost confidence among all parties.

Both sides responded positively to proposals by the Office of the United Nations High Commissioner for Refugees (UNHCR) for building trust and confidence at the grass-roots level, verifying the number and needs of the displaced population, developing mechanisms for monitoring and protection, addressing basic social and economic needs and creating conditions conducive to future returns.

The Group of Friends also discussed Germany's offer to host a conference on economic confidence-building and cooperation.

Report of Secretary-General (April). In a 25 April report [S/2005/269] on the situation in Abkhaz, Georgia, the Secretary-General stated that his Special Representative continued active dialogue with the two sides, supported by the Group of Friends. In Sukhumi, the new leadership, following the inauguration of Sergey Bagapsh as de facto President on 12 February, paved the way for renewed discussions, while in Tbilisi, the appointment by Georgian President Mikhail Saakashvili of a new Special Representative for a Georgian-Abkhaz settlement underlined the Government's continued desire for renewed engagement in the peace process. However, that optimism was clouded by naval incidents near Sukhumi on 16 March, and Abkhaz officials accusing the Georgian side of complicating the negotiation process. Following the high-level meeting of the Group of Friends in April (see above), the Special Representative led a joint visit (9-13 April) of senior Georgian and Abkhaz representatives to Italy to study the successful experience in institution-building and economic transformation in the autonomous region of Trentino–South Tyrol.

The Secretary-General said that he was encouraged by signals from the two sides, for while basic differences in their underlying positions remained, the renewed spirit of cooperation and dialogue was welcome and should be encouraged. To maintain momentum, he encouraged them to resume discussions in the relevant task forces and working groups. He welcomed their positive reaction to the UNHCR proposals (see above), which should pave the way for the verification exercise.

Security Council consideration. On 4 May, during consideration of the Secretary-General's report in closed session [meeting 5174], the Security Council heard briefings by the Under-Secretary-General for Peacekeeping Operations and the Special Envoy of the President of Georgia, Irakli Alasania. The Council President, in an assessment of the Council's work during May [S/2005/500], said that the Council took stock of the recent positive developments in the peace process after the high-level meeting of the Group of Friends in Geneva.

Report of Secretary-General (July). Reporting in July on the situation in Abkhazia, Georgia [S/2005/453], the Secretary-General said that, on 10 May, United States President George Bush, during his visit to Tbilisi, emphasized the need for the peaceful settlement of conflicts and urged the Georgian leadership to work with the Abkhaz and South Ossetian leaderships towards that end. He pledged his country's support for and cooperation with the United Nations in resolving the Georgian-Abkhaz conflict. On 30 May, the Foreign Ministers of Georgia and the Russian Federation, in a joint declaration on the modalities of functioning and withdrawal of Russian bases from Georgia, affirmed their cooperation in the achievement of a peaceful settlement of the conflicts in Georgia.

On 12 May, the Special Representative brought together the Georgian and Abkhaz representatives at the operational level at UNOMIG's Gali headquarters to discuss security issues. The discussions concluded with the signing of a protocol, which included measures to strengthen the implementation of the Moscow Agreement. The parties undertook to submit information on the strength of their armed personnel in the conflict zone, samples of their identification documents and proposals for establishing additional hotlines between law enforcement agencies across the ceasefire line. They also agreed to maintain a minimum distance between the positions of law enforcement agencies and the ceasefire line, establish groups on each side to monitor the situation in the security zone, share information on criminal activities, resume patrolling in the Kodori Valley, improve the human rights situation and ensure support for the safety of international staff in the region. They agreed to meet on 20 and 21 July to discuss security guarantees, in line with the commitments made at the April meeting of the Group of Friends (see p. 481).

The Russian Federation convened (15-16 June) the so-called Sochi working groups on the rehabilitation of the Sochi-Tbilisi railway and on the return of refugees and internally displaced persons. The Special Representative, the Commander of the CIS peacekeeping force and the head of UNHCR's Tbilisi office participated. Concerning the return of refugees and internally displaced persons, the parties expressed support for the documents prepared by UNHCR, including a draft questionnaire and plan for the verification and registration of returnees to the Gali district and its paper on strategic directions for confidence-building activities in the context of returns. Regarding railway rehabilitation, they agreed that an expert group would discuss the security and practical aspects of conducting a technical survey of the Psou-Inguri section of the railway. At the 2 July meeting of the group, the parties agreed to establish joint mobile groups, which would include representatives from both sides and the Russian Federation, and to finalize all related practical matters to begin the survey in mid-July.

The Secretary-General, welcoming the incremental progress made, expressed hope that each side would muster the political will for a more meaningful and pragmatic re-engagement and pledged UN assistance in that regard. He urged the Georgian side to be forthcoming in meeting Abkhaz security concerns and the Abkhaz side to effectively address practical and security concerns of the local population and returnees. The Secretary-General therefore recommended that UNOMIG's mandate be extended until 31 January 2006.

SECURITY COUNCIL ACTION

On 27 July [meeting 5238], the Security Council met in closed session to consider the Secretary-General's report on the situation in Georgia [S/2005/453]. It heard a briefing from the Secretary-General's Special Representative, Ms. Heidi Tagliavini and a statement by the Special Envoy of the President of Georgia, Mr. Irakli Alasania.

On 29 July [meeting 5242], the Council unanimously adopted **resolution 1615(2005)**. The draft [S/2005/492] was prepared by France, Germany, Romania, the Russian Federation, the United Kingdom and the United States.

The Security Council,

Recalling all its relevant resolutions, in particular resolution 1582(2005) of 28 January 2005,

Welcoming the report of the Secretary-General of 13 July 2005,

Recalling the conclusions of the summits of the Organization for Security and Cooperation in Europe held in Lisbon in December 1996 and in Istanbul on 18 and 19 November 1999 regarding the situation in Abkhazia, Georgia,

Recalling also the relevant principles contained in the Convention on the Safety of United Nations and Associated Personnel of 9 December 1994,

Deploring the fact that the perpetrators of the shooting down of a helicopter of the United Nations Observer Mission in Georgia on 8 October 2001, which resulted in the death of nine people on board, have still not been identified,

Stressing that the continued lack of progress on key issues of a comprehensive settlement of the conflict in Abkhazia, Georgia, is unacceptable,

Welcoming, however, the positive momentum given to the United Nations-led peace process by regular high-level meetings of the Group of Friends of the Secretary-General in Geneva and the Georgian-Russian summit meetings,

Welcoming also the important contributions made by the Mission and the collective peacekeeping forces of the Commonwealth of Independent States in stabilizing the situation in the zone of conflict, and stressing its attachment to the close cooperation existing between them in the performance of their respective mandates,

1. *Reaffirms* the commitment of all Member States to the sovereignty, independence and territorial integrity of Georgia within its internationally recognized borders, and the necessity to define the status of Abkhazia within the State of Georgia in strict accordance with these principles;

2. *Commends and strongly supports* the sustained efforts of the Secretary-General and his Special Representative, with the assistance of the Russian Federation in its capacity as facilitator as well as of the Group of Friends of the Secretary-General and of the Organization for Security and Cooperation in Europe, to promote the stabilization of the situation and the achievement of a comprehensive political settlement, which must include a settlement of the political status of Abkhazia within the State of Georgia;

3. *Reiterates its strong support* for the document entitled "Basic Principles for the Distribution of Competences between Tbilisi and Sukhumi" and for its letter of transmittal, finalized by, and with the full support of, all members of the Group of Friends;

4. *Deeply regrets* the continued refusal of the Abkhaz side to agree to a discussion on the substance of that document, again strongly urges the Abkhaz side to receive the document and its letter of transmittal, urges both parties thereafter to give them full and open consideration and to engage in constructive negotiations on their substance, and urges those having influence with the parties to promote this outcome;

5. *Regrets* the lack of progress on the initiation of political status negotiations, and recalls, once again, that the purpose of those documents is to facilitate meaningful negotiations between the parties, under the leadership of the United Nations, on the status of Abkhazia within the State of Georgia, and is not an attempt to impose or dictate any specific solution to the parties;

6. *Calls upon* both sides to participate in constructive negotiations towards a political settlement of the conflict and to spare no efforts to overcome their ongoing mutual mistrust, and underlines the fact that the process of negotiation leading to a lasting political settlement acceptable to both sides will require concessions from both sides;

7. *Welcomes* the commitment by the Georgian side to a peaceful resolution of the conflict, and calls upon

both parties further to publicly dissociate themselves from all militant rhetoric and demonstrations of support for military options;

8. *Reminds* all concerned to refrain from any action that might impede the peace process;

9. *Welcomes* the convening of regular meetings of senior representatives of the Group of Friends and the United Nations in Geneva as well as the participation of both sides in the last meeting, held on 7 and 8 April 2005, and the commitments expressed by the parties during this meeting, and strongly urges both sides to continue to participate constructively in future meetings;

10. *Urges* the parties to participate in a more active, regular and structured manner in the task forces established in the first Geneva meeting (to address issues in the priority areas of economic cooperation, the return of internally displaced persons and refugees, and political and security matters) and complemented by the working groups established in Sochi, Russian Federation, in March 2003, and reiterates that results-oriented activities in these three priority areas remain key to building common ground between the Georgian and Abkhaz sides and ultimately for concluding meaningful negotiations on a comprehensive political settlement based on the document entitled "Basic Principles for the Distribution of Competences between Tbilisi and Sukhumi" and its letter of transmittal;

11. *Regrets* the cancellation of the meeting on security guarantees planned for July 2005, and expects that such a meeting with the full participation of both sides will be held as soon as possible;

12. *Welcomes* the signing on 12 May 2005 of a Protocol with measures to strengthen the implementation of the Agreement on Ceasefire and Separation of Forces signed in Moscow on 14 May 1994;

13. *Calls again upon* the parties to take concrete steps to revitalize the peace process in all its major aspects, including their work in the Coordinating Council and its relevant mechanisms, to build on the results of the third meeting on confidence-building measures between the Georgian and Abkhaz sides, held in Yalta, Ukraine, on 15 and 16 March 2001, and to implement the proposals agreed on that occasion in a purposeful and cooperative manner, with a view to holding a fourth meeting on confidence-building measures, and welcomes the intention expressed by Germany to host such a meeting pending progress in the conflict resolution process;

14. *Welcomes* the positive developments towards the reopening of the railways between Sochi and Tbilisi and towards the return of refugees and internally displaced persons;

15. *Notes* that contacts at the level of civil society can reinforce mutual confidence, and calls upon both sides to facilitate such contacts;

16. *Stresses* the urgent need for progress on the question of the refugees and internally displaced persons, calls on both sides to display a genuine commitment to make returns the focus of special attention and to undertake this task in close coordination with the United Nations Observer Mission in Georgia and in consultation with the Office of the United Nations High Commissioner for Refugees and the Group of Friends;

17. *Calls for* the rapid finalization and signature of the letter of intent on returns proposed by the Special Representative of the Secretary-General, and welcomes the meetings with the participation of the Special Representative and the Office of the High Commissioner of the Sochi working group on refugees and internally displaced persons;

18. *Reaffirms* the unacceptability of the demographic changes resulting from the conflict, reaffirms also the inalienable rights of all refugees and internally displaced persons affected by the conflict, and stresses that they have the right to return to their homes in secure and dignified conditions, in accordance with international law and as set out in the Quadripartite Agreement of 4 April 1994 and the Yalta Declaration;

19. *Recalls* that the Abkhaz side bears a particular responsibility to protect the returnees and to facilitate the return of the remaining displaced population;

20. *Welcomes* the continuing activities of the United Nations Development Programme in the Gali, Ochamchira and Tkvarcheli districts and the opening of offices by the United Nations Development Programme in Sukhumi and Gali;

21. *Urges* the parties once again to implement the recommendations of the joint assessment mission of November 2000 to the Gali sector, regrets that there has been no progress to that effect despite the positive consideration by the parties given to those recommendations in the first Geneva meeting, and calls again upon the Abkhaz side to agree to the opening as soon as possible of the Gali branch of the human rights office in Sukhumi and to provide security conditions for its unhindered functioning;

22. *Reiterates its concern* that despite the start of the deployment of a civilian police component as part of the Mission, as endorsed in resolution 1494(2003) of 30 July 2003 and agreed upon by the parties, the deployment of the remaining officers in the Gali sector is still outstanding, and calls upon the Abkhaz side to allow for a swift deployment of the police component in that region;

23. *Calls in particular upon* the Abkhaz side to improve law enforcement protection of the local population and to address the lack of instruction in their mother tongue for the ethnic Georgian population;

24. *Welcomes* the measures taken by the Georgian side to put an end to the activities of illegal armed groups, and encourages the maintenance of these efforts;

25. *Condemns* any violations of the provisions of the Agreement on a Ceasefire and Separation of Forces signed in Moscow on 14 May 1994;

26. *Welcomes* the continuing relative calm in the Kodori Valley, and condemns the continuing criminal activities, including killings and abductions of civilians, in the Gali and Zugdidi districts;

27. *Urges* the parties to abide by the provisions of the protocols on security issues in the Gali district signed on 8 October 2003 and 19 January 2004, to continue their regular meetings and to cooperate more closely with each other to improve security in the Gali sector, and takes note of the resumption of Abkhaz participation in the quadripartite meetings and the Joint Investigation Group;

28. *Reiterates its call upon* the Georgian side to provide comprehensive security guarantees to allow for independent and regular monitoring of the situation in the upper Kodori Valley by joint patrols of the Mission and the peacekeeping force of the Commonwealth of Independent States;

29. *Underlines* the fact that it is the primary responsibility of both sides to provide appropriate security and to ensure the freedom of movement of the Mission, the collective peacekeeping force and other international personnel, and calls upon both sides to fulfil their obligations in this regard;

30. *Strongly condemns*, in that respect, the repeated abductions of personnel of those missions in the past, deeply deplores the fact that none of the perpetrators have ever been identified or brought to justice, reiterates that it is the responsibility of the parties to end this impunity, and calls upon them to take action;

31. *Calls upon* the parties, once again, to take all necessary steps to identify those responsible for the shooting down of a Mission helicopter on 8 October 2001, to bring them to justice, and to inform the Special Representative of the steps taken in particular in the criminal investigation;

32. *Welcomes* the efforts being undertaken by the Mission to implement the zero-tolerance policy of the Secretary-General on sexual exploitation and abuse and to ensure full compliance of its personnel with the United Nations code of conduct, requests the Secretary-General to continue to take all necessary action in this regard and to keep the Security Council informed, and urges troop-contributing countries to take appropriate preventive action, including the conduct of predeployment awareness training, and to take disciplinary action and other action to ensure full accountability in cases of such conduct involving their personnel;

33. *Decides* to extend the mandate of the Mission for a new period terminating on 31 January 2006, subject to a review, as appropriate, of its mandate by the Council in the event of changes in the mandate of the collective peacekeeping force;

34. *Requests* the Secretary-General to continue to keep the Council regularly informed and to report three months from the date of the adoption of the present resolution on the situation in Abkhazia, Georgia;

35. *Decides* to remain actively seized of the matter.

Communication. In identical letters of 23 September [A/60/379-S/2005/606], Georgia brought to the attention of the Secretary-General and the Council President the celebration by the Tskhinvali separatist authorities, on 20 September, of the "independence" of the self-proclaimed republic of South Ossetia. It said that the presence of representatives of the separatist regimes of Abkhazia, Transniestria and Nagorno Karabakh (Azerbaijan), as well as of the State Duma of the Russian Federation was a flagrant violation of universally recognized norms and principles.

Report of Secretary-General (October). In his October report [S/2005/657] on the situation in Abkhazia, Georgia, the Secretary-General stated that his Special Representative, in her continuing dialogue with the two sides of the Georgian/Abkhaz conflict and with the Group of Friends, focused on the issue of security guarantees. A planned meeting of 22 July with the two sides was postponed after Abkhazia protested the detention of a cargo vessel en route to Sukhumi by the Georgian Navy on 3 July, for violating Georgian maritime space. The ship was released by the Georgian authorities on 31 July and transported with UNOMIG's assistance to Sukhumi, following the Special Representative's intervention. At the meeting, which was subsequently held on 4 August with the participation of the Group of Friends and OSCE, the two sides agreed on the need to reconfirm their commitment to the non-resumption of hostilities and for the safe and dignified return of internally displaced persons and refugees to the Gali district, in the light of the change of their respective leadership. They also discussed a draft joint document on the non-resumption of hostilities, and confirmed their readiness to accept the UNHCR proposals (see p. 482) on the return and registration of refugees to the Gali district. Maritime security issues were also addressed and the two sides agreed to continue discussions on the subject and to submit their views and proposals to UNOMIG before the next meeting which was to be held in October. On 10 August, the Tbilisi-based Ambassadors of the Group of Friends visited Sukhumi to discuss the results of the meeting on security guarantees and to encourage the Abkhaz leadership to engage meaningfully in the priority areas of the peace process.

The so-called Sochi working group on the rehabilitation of the Sochi-Tbilisi railway held follow-up meetings in Tbilisi and Sukhumi on 11 and 19 July, respectively, to discuss further the modalities of a technical survey, which began on 10 August by Russian and Abkhaz specialists. As a result of problems relating to their immigration status, Georgian experts were only able to join them in October. At the October meeting (6-7 October) of the working group on the return of internally displaced persons and refugees, the parties endorsed, in principle, the UNHCR approach to the return of refugees and internally displaced persons and planned activities for the next two years, and discussed modalities for the registration of returnees to Gali and the issue of the language of instruction in schools there.

In other developments, Georgia protested the large-scale Abkhaz military exercises held from 15 to 19 August, while the Abkhaz side continued to question Tbilisi's intentions to seek closer relations with the Russian Federation. On 11 October, the Georgian Parliament adopted a resolution on the possible withdrawal of peacekeeping forces from the Georgian-South Ossetian and Georgian-Abkhaz conflict zones in 2006. During the reporting period, UNOMIG reported three violations of the 1994 Moscow Agreement on the Abkhaz side of the ceasefire line. Two cases related to restrictions placed on the movement of UNOMIG patrols by Abkhaz soldiers on 16 July and 2 August and the third to the presence of 6 Abkhaz tanks and several artillery pieces in the restricted weapons zone during a military exercise.

Communications. On 27 October [S/2005/678], Georgia noted the positive developments in the conflict-resolution process, as outlined in the Secretary-General's report (see above), but stressed that those developments were marred by the largest Abkhaz post-war military exercise held in the zone of responsibility of the Russian peacekeeping force. It also drew attention to the unresolved issues of the establishment of a UNOMIG human rights sub-office in Gali, the full deployment of its civilian police and the banning of instruction in the Georgian language in Gali schools.

Georgia also stated that the role of the Russian-led peacekeeping operation had been exhausted and called for a full-scale international UN-led peacekeeping operation. It also drew attention to the Georgian-South Ossetian peace plan announced by the Georgian Prime Minister on 26 October [A/60/547].

In identical letters of 9 November [A/60/552, S/2005/718] addressed to the Secretary-General and the Council President, Georgia transmitted an 11 October resolution adopted by its Parliament, which gave a negative assessment of the operations of the peacekeeping forces in Abkhazia and South Ossetia and seriously questioned its mandate, and instructed the Government to intensify negotiations with the Russian Federation, international organizations and interested countries on the fulfilment of obligations undertaken by those forces in Abkhazia and to report by 1 July 2006. If the assessment proved negative, it would demand a cessation of the operation and the withdrawal of Russian peacekeeping forces. The Government was also to submit a peace plan for Abkhazia by 1 May 2006.

Further report of Secretary-General. In a report covering developments on the situation in Abkhazia, Georgia, during late 2005 [S/2006/19], the Secretary-General stated that his Special Representative's contacts with the Group of Friends, the Russian Federation and the two sides were centred on the draft documents on the non-resumption of hostilities and the safe and dignified return of internally displaced persons. She

convened meetings (6-7 December) in Sukhumi between the Georgian State Minister for Conflict Resolution and Abkhazia's de facto Foreign Minister, during which an understanding was reached on those documents, with both sides undertaking to secure their approval and signature. Georgian President Saakashvili reiterated his readiness to discuss without preconditions economic, humanitarian, confidence-building and security issues and to possibly sign the joint documents. The de facto Abkhaz President did not exclude the likelihood of such a meeting after a document on the non-resumption of hostilities had been initialled by the sides.

At its first meeting (Sukhumi, Georgia, 6 December), the Steering Committee for the rehabilitation programme in the conflict zone launched the first phase of the programme at an estimated cost of 4 million euros, thereby opening a new chapter in the economic dimension of the peace process. The two-year joint programme, financed by the European Commission and implemented by UNOMIG and the United Nations Development Programme (UNDP), aimed at improving the living conditions of the local population most affected by the conflict through the restoration of basic services, building confidence and enhancing security and stability in the area.

The Special Representative also facilitated a visit to Georgia from 21 to 24 December (see p. 870) by the Secretary-General's Representative on the human rights of internally displaced persons, who discussed with the Georgian and the de facto Abkhaz authorities ways to enhance the human rights of displaced persons in the zone of conflict.

On 19 November, the Secretary-General met with the Georgian President in Tbilisi and reiterated the UN's commitment to work closely with both sides and with the Group of Friends in search of a peaceful settlement to the conflict.

Those developments took place against the backdrop of an increasingly difficult and complex situation on the ground. The Georgian side called upon the international community to condemn human rights violations committed by the de facto Abkhaz authority and the lack of action by the CIS peacekeeping forces. Meanwhile, the promulgation of a new de facto law on Abkhaz citizenship raised concerns of the local Georgian population that those wishing to remain in Abkhazia would be forced to renounce their Georgian citizenship. The conscription of ethnic Georgians into the Abkhaz military created further tensions between both sides. Georgia protested those actions as attempts to establish a fait accompli prior to a comprehensive settlement of the conflict. The Abkhaz side responded that the escalated tension resulted from the activities of Georgian partisan groups, cross-ceasefire criminal elements and incorrect media reports. They also raised concerns over Georgia's increased military expenditure and the modernization of its armed forces, including the establishment of a military base in Senaki near the Zugdidi restricted weapons zone. The Special Representative discussed with both sides the new de facto Abkhaz law on citizenship and Georgian parliamentary action (see above) on the withdrawal of the CIS peacekeeping force from the conflict zone.

Situation on the ground

Kodori Valley

In early 2005, UNOMIG patrols in the Kodori Valley—the upper part of which was controlled by Georgia and the lower part by the de facto Abkhaz authorities—which were suspended because of inadequate security from both sides, resumed. UNOMIG conducted joint patrols with the CIS peacekeeping force in the lower part of the valley to assess the damage to the main road due to flooding and to monitor the situation on the ground. In December, UNOMIG engineers, with the CIS force, jointly repaired the road.

During the year, UNOMIG also continued to review the feasibility of resuming regular patrols in the upper valley and continued negotiations with the Georgian side to secure adequate security in that regard.

The Mission's patrolling capacity was greatly improved by the donation of two vehicles by the Swiss Government.

Gali and Zugdidi sectors

The overall military situation in the Gali sector was generally calm, but there was an increase in criminal activities throughout 2005. The de facto Abkhaz State Security Service increased its presence in the security zone by establishing three additional temporary posts that were later removed. In May and June, several incidents between the local population and Abkhaz armed personnel, including the forced removal of between 25 and 30 young men from the village of Okumi by Abkhaz military recruitment authorities, significantly increased tension in the area.

On 18 June, two UNOMIG patrol teams were robbed by armed gunmen, forcing UNOMIG to increase its security level in the lower Gali sector. In late 2005, violent attacks increased significantly, including the targeting of a de facto Abkhaz taxation representative and a de facto head of administration on 27 November and 18 Decem-

ber, respectively, the detonation of remotely controlled explosives, and the killing of the de facto Abkhaz chief of security of the Inguri hydro power station on 11 December. Criminal incidents, including smuggling, increased during the year. On 30 January, Georgian police were ambushed during an anti-smuggling operation and on 4 June Georgian police exchanged fire with a group of smugglers from the Abkhaz-controlled side of the ceasefire line.

A Georgian Interior Ministry special-purpose unit deployed near the ceasefire line detained four CIS peacekeeping soldiers on 21 March, who, according to Georgian officers, lacked clearly marked CIS insignia. They were released the same day after their identity was confirmed. The following day, the CIS peacekeeping force temporarily surrounded the headquarters of the Georgian unit and opposed their deployment in close proximity to the ceasefire line. UNOMIG officials mediated a meeting between the Georgian State Minister for Conflict Resolution and the Commander of the CIS peacekeeping force, which agreed that a joint fact-finding group would examine the situation. Subsequent discussions by the Joint Fact-Finding Group resulted in the Georgian unit being moved 150 metres away from the ceasefire line. Relations between the CIS peacekeeping force and the Georgian side were strained further by political tensions, resulting in several demonstrations against the force at its headquarters and at the main Inguri River bridge.

Humanitarian situation and human rights

United Nations agencies, international and non-governmental organizations (NGOs) continued to assist vulnerable groups affected by the conflict in Abkhazia, Georgia, by providing food, medical aid and infrastructure assistance, building capacities of local organizations, developing peace education, empowering women and creating economic opportunities. On 30 September, the Special Representative, the Head of the European Commission delegation to Georgia and Armenia and the UNDP Resident Representative in Georgia signed a memorandum of understanding on the funding and implementation of a programme for the Gali, Tkvarcheli, Ochamchira and Zugdidi districts, the first phase of which would focus on rehabilitation projects in the health and infrastructure sectors. UNDP, with funds provided by the European Commission and Norway, facilitated income generation through agriculture and the rehabilitation of drinking water and irrigation systems. UNHCR, in partnership with other organizations, launched confidence-building measures containing both protection and assistance activities, while the United Nations Children's Fund continued to provide rehabilitated schools with student and teacher supplies, as well as vaccines, immunization equipment and essential drugs, maternity, surgical and emergency health equipment to Abkhaz hospitals. The United Nations Development Fund for Women assisted in raising awareness about gender-based violence and reproductive health and promoted support for women's legal rights. The World Food Programme promoted community-based food-for-work activities, focusing on the rehabilitation of basic agricultural infrastructure and the upgrading of livelihoods of poor households through improved land use and assets.

UNOMIG continued to implement the programme for the protection and promotion of human rights in Abkhazia, Georgia. The human rights office in Sukhumi collected information from victims, witnesses and other reliable sources and followed up on cases related to due process, citizenship, arbitrary detention, treatment of detainees, impunity, involuntary disappearances, arbitrary evictions and property rights violations. The office continued to conduct regular visits to detention facilities, provide legal advisory services to the local population and monitor court trials. The de facto Abkhaz authorities still had not agreed to allow the Mission to open a human rights sub-office in the Gali district.

UNOMIG facilitated the first visit (19 and 20 February) to Sukhumi by the Special Rapporteur of the Commission on Human Rights on torture and other cruel, inhuman or degrading treatment or punishment (see p. 813). The office followed up with local residents and Abkhaz authorities on several alleged cases of involuntary disappearance, religious intolerance and ill-treatment in detention. Cases of denied access to detainees and the reluctance of the de facto authorities to cooperate with the office were registered. Together with local NGOs, the office commenced implementation of an Abkhazia-wide human rights programme, funded by Switzerland. In the Sukhumi militia training centre, UNOMIG staff and police advisers conducted a seven-week training course in human rights and law enforcement.

Financing

The General Assembly considered the UNOMIG financial performance report for the period from 1 July 2003 to 30 June 2004 [A/59/622], the Mission's budget for the period from 1 July 2005 to 30 June 2006 [A/59/634], and ACABQ's related comments and recommendations thereon [A/59/736/Add.17].

On 22 June [meeting 104], the Assembly, on the recommendation of the Fifth Committee [A/59/834], adopted **resolution 59/304** without vote [agenda item 131].

Financing of the United Nations Observer Mission in Georgia

The General Assembly,

Having considered the reports of the Secretary-General on the financing of the United Nations Observer Mission in Georgia and the related reports of the Advisory Committee on Administrative and Budgetary Questions,

Recalling Security Council resolution 854(1993) of 6 August 1993, by which the Council approved the deployment of an advance team of up to ten United Nations military observers for a period of three months and the incorporation of the advance team into a United Nations observer mission if such a mission was formally established by the Council,

Recalling also Security Council resolution 858(1993) of 24 August 1993, by which the Council established the United Nations Observer Mission in Georgia, and the subsequent resolutions by which the Council extended the mandate of the Observer Mission, the latest of which was resolution 1582(2005) of 28 January 2005,

Recalling further its decision 48/475 A of 23 December 1993 on the financing of the Observer Mission and its subsequent resolutions and decisions thereon, the latest of which was resolution 58/303 of 18 June 2004,

Reaffirming the general principles underlying the financing of United Nations peacekeeping operations, as stated in General Assembly resolutions 1874(S-IV) of 27 June 1963, 3101(XXVIII) of 11 December 1973 and 55/235 of 23 December 2000,

Mindful of the fact that it is essential to provide the Observer Mission with the necessary financial resources to enable it to fulfil its responsibilities under the relevant resolutions of the Security Council,

1. *Requests* the Secretary-General to entrust the Head of Mission with the task of formulating future budget proposals in full accordance with the provisions of General Assembly resolution 59/296 of 22 June 2005, as well as other relevant resolutions;

2. *Takes note* of the status of contributions to the United Nations Observer Mission in Georgia as at 15 April 2005, including the contributions outstanding in the amount of 11 million United States dollars, representing some 4 per cent of the total assessed contributions, notes with concern that only thirty-four Member States have paid their assessed contributions in full, and urges all other Member States, in particular those in arrears, to ensure payment of their outstanding assessed contributions;

3. *Expresses its appreciation* to those Member States which have paid their assessed contributions in full, and urges all other Member States to make every possible effort to ensure payment of their assessed contributions to the Observer Mission in full;

4. *Expresses concern* at the delay experienced by the Secretary-General in deploying and providing adequate resources to some recent peacekeeping missions, in particular those in Africa;

5. *Emphasizes* that all future and existing peacekeeping missions shall be given equal and non-

discriminatory treatment in respect of financial and administrative arrangements;

6. *Also emphasizes* that all peacekeeping missions shall be provided with adequate resources for the effective and efficient discharge of their respective mandates;

7. *Reiterates its request* to the Secretary-General to make the fullest possible use of facilities and equipment at the United Nations Logistics Base at Brindisi, Italy, in order to minimize the costs of procurement for the Observer Mission;

8. *Endorses* the conclusions and recommendations contained in the report of the Advisory Committee on Administrative and Budgetary Questions, and requests the Secretary-General to ensure their full implementation;

9. *Requests* the Secretary-General to ensure the full implementation of the relevant provisions of its resolution 59/296;

10. *Also requests* the Secretary-General to take all action necessary to ensure that the Observer Mission is administered with a maximum of efficiency and economy;

11. *Further requests* the Secretary-General, in order to reduce the cost of employing General Service staff, to continue efforts to recruit local staff for the Observer Mission against General Service posts, commensurate with the requirements of the Mission;

Financial performance report for the period from 1 July 2003 to 30 June 2004

12. *Takes note* of the report of the Secretary-General on the financial performance of the Observer Mission for the period from 1 July 2003 to 30 June 2004;

Budget estimates for the period from 1 July 2005 to 30 June 2006

13. *Decides* to appropriate to the Special Account for the United Nations Observer Mission in Georgia the amount of 36,380,000 dollars for the period from 1 July 2005 to 30 June 2006, inclusive of 34,562,100 dollars for the maintenance of the Observer Mission, 1,486,500 dollars for the support account for peacekeeping operations and 331,400 dollars for the United Nations Logistics Base;

Financing of the appropriation

14. *Decides also* to apportion among Member States the amount of 3,031,667 dollars for the period from 1 to 31 July 2005, in accordance with the levels updated in General Assembly resolution 58/256 of 23 December 2003, and taking into account the scale of assessments for 2005, as set out in its resolution 58/1 B of 23 December 2003;

15. *Decides further* that, in accordance with the provisions of its resolution 973(X) of 15 December 1955, there shall be set off against the apportionment among Member States, as provided for in paragraph 14 above, their respective share in the Tax Equalization Fund of 207,575 dollars, comprising the estimated staff assessment income of 187,833 dollars approved for the Observer Mission, the prorated share of 17,508 dollars of the estimated staff assessment income approved for the support account and the prorated share of 2,234 dollars of the estimated staff assessment income approved for the United Nations Logistics Base;

16. *Decides* to apportion among Member States the amount of 33,348,333 dollars for the period from 1 August 2005 to 30 June 2006 at a monthly rate of 3,031,666 dollars, in accordance with the levels updated in General Assembly resolution 58/256, and taking into account the scale of assessments for 2005 and 2006, as set out in its resolution 58/1 B, subject to a decision of the Security Council to extend the mandate of the Observer Mission;

17. *Decides also* that, in accordance with the provisions of its resolution 973(X), there shall be set off against the apportionment among Member States, as provided for in paragraph 16 above, their respective share in the Tax Equalization Fund of 2,283,325 dollars, comprising the estimated staff assessment income of 2,066,167 dollars approved for the Observer Mission, the prorated share of 192,592 dollars of the estimated staff assessment income approved for the support account and the prorated share of 24,566 dollars of the estimated staff assessment income approved for the United Nations Logistics Base;

18. *Decides further* that, for Member States that have fulfilled their financial obligations to the Observer Mission, there shall be set off against their apportionment, as provided for in paragraphs 14 and 16 above, their respective share of the unencumbered balance and other income in the amount of 1,104,100 dollars in respect of the financial period ended 30 June 2004, in accordance with the levels updated in General Assembly resolution 58/256, and taking into account the scale of assessments for 2004, as set out in its resolution 58/1 B;

19. *Decides* that, for Member States that have not fulfilled their financial obligations to the Observer Mission, there shall be set off against their outstanding obligations their respective share of the unencumbered balance and other income in the total amount of 1,104,100 dollars in respect of the financial period ended 30 June 2004, in accordance with the scheme set out in paragraph 18 above;

20. *Decides also* that the increase of 179,600 dollars in the estimated staff assessment income in respect of the financial period ended 30 June 2004 shall be added to the credits from the amount of 1,104,100 dollars referred to in paragraphs 18 and 19 above;

21. *Emphasizes* that no peacekeeping mission shall be financed by borrowing funds from other active peacekeeping missions;

22. *Encourages* the Secretary-General to continue to take additional measures to ensure the safety and security of all personnel under the auspices of the United Nations participating in the Observer Mission, bearing in mind paragraphs 5 and 6 of Security Council resolution 1502(2003) of 26 August 2003;

23. *Invites* voluntary contributions to the Observer Mission in cash and in the form of services and supplies acceptable to the Secretary-General, to be administered, as appropriate, in accordance with the procedure and practices established by the General Assembly;

24. *Decides* to include in the provisional agenda of its sixtieth session the item entitled "Financing of the United Nations Observer Mission in Georgia".

Armenia and Azerbaijan

In 2005, the Organization for Security and Co-operation in Europe (OSCE) Minsk Group (France, Russian Federation, United States) continued to mediate the dispute between Armenia and Azerbaijan, which had erupted in armed conflict in 1992 [YUN 1992, p. 388], after four years of sporadic fighting in the Nagorny Karabakh region of Azerbaijan. There was no change in the position of either country with regard to the conflict during the year. Both sides continued to address communications to the Secretary-General, clarifying their positions regarding the conflict or lodging complaints against the actions of the other. Nagorny Karabakh's communications were transmitted by Armenia.

The General Assembly, by **decision 59/571** of 12 September, decided to defer consideration of the item entitled "The situation in the occupied territories of Azerbaijan" and to include it in the agenda of its sixtieth (2005) session.

Communications. On 2 February [A/59/689-S/2005/64], Azerbaijan transmitted to the Secretary-General two resolutions adopted on 25 January by the Parliamentary Assembly of the Council of Europe regretting that, after more than a decade, the Nagorny Karabakh conflict remained unresolved and calling on the OSCE Minsk Group Co-Chairs to take immediate steps to negotiate a political settlement and on the parties to submit to each other, through the Minsk Group, constructive proposals for the peaceful settlement of the conflict. Should negotiations fail, Armenia and Azerbaijan should consider submitting them to the International Court of Justice, in accordance with Article 36, paragraph 1 of the Court's statute. The two countries should also foster political reconciliation by increasing inter-parliamentary cooperation and the Secretary-General of the Council should draw up an action plan for specific support to the two countries targeted at mutual reconciliation processes.

On 24 February [A/59/713-S/2005/125], Azerbaijan transmitted to the Secretary-General an appeal of refugees from Khodjaly to the United Nations, the Council of Europe and OSCE, to bring the truth of the genocide of February 1992 [YUN 1992, p. 388] to the attention of the world community and to call for a legal-political assessment of that crime. In its letter of transmittal, Azerbaijan regretted that, on the occasion of the thirteenth anniversary of that incident, the international community's response remained inadequate, a fact, it said, was noted by Congressman Dan Burton on 17 February in the United States House of Representatives. In a fur-

ther letter of 28 February [A/59/720-S/2005/132 & Corr.1], Azerbaijan transmitted to the Secretary-General video films witnessing the Government-supported transfer of Armenians from Yerevan to the occupied Lachin region of Azerbaijan and satellite images of the occupied territories of Azerbaijan. Hard copies of the images were also attached to the letter.

For its part, Armenia, on 7 March [A/59/729-S/2005/145] said that Azerbaijan's actions had threatened the peace process and the relative stability established. Armenia had demonstrated its willingness and readiness to cooperate and to work towards finding a lasting solution to the Nagorny Karabakh conflict, which was possible only through a reduction in tension and discontinuation of hate propaganda. On 8 March [A/59/743-S/2005/184], Armenia refuted Azerbaijan's version of the 1992 incident contained in its February 24 letter (see above), reaffirming that its armed forces had no involvement in the 1992 incident and citing Azerbaijani accounts annexed to the letter to support its contention that the incident was part of Azerbaijan's internal power struggle. On 15 March [A/59/740-S/2005/171], Armenia forwarded to the Secretary-General an 8 March press statement issued by the Ministry of Defence of Nagorny Karabakh, informing of an attempt by an Azerbaijani intelligence-diversionary group to penetrate the rear of the army of Nagorny Karabakh in the north-east section of the contact line near Seysulan, in the Martakert region of Nagorny Karabakh. The statement appealed to Azerbaijan to strictly follow the ceasefire regime and not to threaten peace and security in the region.

Report of OSCE fact-finding mission. The Co-Chairs of OSCE Minsk Group went on a fact-finding mission (31 January–5 February) to the occupied territories of Azerbaijan surrounding Nagorny Karabakh. The mission, first proposed by Azerbaijan in a 1994 draft resolution in the General Assembly, was agreed to by the parties following a series of discussions organized by the Minsk Group Co-Chairs between the Foreign Ministers of Azerbaijan and Armenia. The Mission found evidence of the presence of settlers in the territories examined, but did not determine that such settlements resulted from a deliberate policy by Armenia. While there was evidence of varying degrees of support by the Nagorny Karabakh authorities to settlers in some regions, the Co-Chairs did not assess the extent to which there was coordination between the Government of Armenia and the Nagorny Karabakh authorities, who stated that they did indeed encourage settlements in Lachin (or Berdzor in Armenian maps), located in the narrow strip of territory between Nagorny Karabakh and Armenia. The Co-

Chairs noted that Lachin had been treated as a separate case in previous negotiations.

The Co-Chairs concluded that there was little disagreement between the two sides on the number of settlers and the nature of the settlements, but they did disagree on the question of government sponsorship and the place of origin of the settlers. The areas in question had undergone complete destruction and any settlement allowing the return of internally displaced persons and refugees would require substantial international assistance for reconstruction of shelter and infrastructure. Although most settlers expressed the desire to return to the areas from which they had fled, it was clear that the longer they remained in the occupied territories, the deeper their roots and attachment became. Prolonged continuation of the situation could lead to a fait accompli that could seriously complicate the peace process.

The Co-Chairs recommended that further settlement of the occupied territories be discouraged and urged the parties, as part of negotiations towards a political settlement, to address the problem of settlers and to avoid changes in the region's demographic structure. Relevant international agencies should re-evaluate the needs and funding assessments in the region for resettlement purposes. The Co-Chairs urged the parties to allow direct contact between interested communities as a way of ensuring the preservation of the cultural heritage and sacred sites of the affected regions, to develop practical confidence-building measures between the parties and the communities and to work with their public to prepare the groundwork for a peaceful settlement.

The report of the Co-chairs of the Minsk Group Fact-Finding Mission, together with the letter of transmittal to the OSCE Permanent Council, was transmitted to the Secretary-General by Armenia [A/59/742-S/2005/182] and Azerbaijan [A/59/747-S/2005/187] on 16 and 18 March, respectively.

EU statement. On 4 April [S/2005/246], Luxembourg forwarded to the Secretary-General a 30 March statement issued by the EU Presidency welcoming Azerbaijan's decree of 20 March pardoning 115 prisoners, 53 of whom were designated "political prisoners" by Council of Europe experts. It also expressed concern about the remaining political prisoners and called for their immediate release.

Cyprus

In 2005, the Cyprus problem remained unresolved, following the disappointing result in 2004

of the Secretary-General's mission of good offices, and little prospect of negotiations restarting in the near future. The Secretary-General continued to closely monitor the situation and dispatched a high-level UN official in May and June to Cyprus to assess whether the climate was conducive to a renewal of his mission of good offices. After consultations with both parties and with Greece and Turkey, the Secretary-General determined that progress was negligible at best and the conditions surrounding a resumption of negotiations needed to be further clarified. Despite the call by the parties for the resumption of those negotiations, the Secretary-General considered doing so inopportune. Meanwhile, the military situation on the island remained stable with only a few minor disturbances and small, unsuccessful attempts by each side to alter the status quo. The United Nations Peacekeeping Force in Cyprus (UNFICYP) implemented a new concept of operations in February, which included a reduction of the Mission's military component and the introduction of a more mobile framework. The Secretary-General recommended that the Security Council extend UNFICYP's mandate, as revised, until June 2006.

Incidents and position statements

Communications. Throughout 2005, the Secretary-General received letters from the Government of Cyprus and from the Turkish Cypriot authorities containing charges and counter-charges, protests and accusations, and explanations of positions regarding the question of Cyprus. Letters from the "Turkish Republic of Northern Cyprus" were transmitted by Turkey.

In communications dated between 7 January and 16 November, Cyprus reported violations of its national airspace and unauthorized intrusion into Nicosia's flight information region by Turkish military jets and civilian aircraft, while those from the "Turkish Republic of Northern Cyprus" claimed the existence of two independent States on the island of Cyprus and that the flights mentioned took place within the sovereign airspace of the "Turkish Republic of Northern Cyprus" [A/59/696-S/2005/75, A/59/755-S/2005/205, A/59/804-S/2005/319, A/59/815-S/2005/349, A/59/892-S/2005/510, A/59/903-S/2005/547, A/60/381-S/2005/607, A/60/411-S/2005/618, A/60/434-S/2005/654, A/60/445-S/2005/670, A/60/554-S/200/714, A/60/564-S/2005/733].

In other communications, the "Turkish Republic of Northern Cyprus" authorities objected strongly to the mistreatment of Turkish Cypriots visiting the southern portion of the island, which they claimed was the result of a rising trend of racism, chauvinism and ultra-nationalism among the Greek Cypriots. They also objected to the decision by the Greek Cypriot Government to declare 2005 "The Year for Remembrance and Honouring of EOKA Liberation Struggle", a right-wing nationalist group that supported the complete annexation of the island to Greece [A/59/760-S/2005/214, A/60/442-S/2005/666, A/60/557-S/2005/721].

Cyprus brought to the attention of the Secretary-General on 8 April a decision by the European Court of Human Rights concerning property rights in Cyprus, which rejected Turkey's objections on jurisdiction of a Greek Cypriot's property claim in the northern area of the island and considered that the remedies established to compensate losses in the "Turkish Republic of Northern Cyprus" could not be regarded as "effective" or "adequate" means for redressing the applicant's complaints [A/59/777-S/2005/234]. The "Turkish Republic of Northern Cyprus", in a 31 May response [A/59/821-S/2005/358], noted that the Court's decision was preliminary, based on admissibility, and recounted that the "Comprehensive Settlement of the Cyprus Problem" [YUN 2004, p. 438] provided for the establishment of a property board, and recognized that the situation was too complicated to be settled by individual application to the Court. It emphasized that the property issue in Cyprus needed a political solution.

In a 14 June letter [A/59/846-S/2005/387], Cyprus alerted the Secretary-General to the Turkish military actions to reinforce its presence in the northern part of the island, which were refuted, on 28 June [A/59/866-S/2005/439], by the "Turkish Republic of Northern Cyprus". Other letters related to claims by Cyprus of the destruction of cultural heritage [A/60/404-S/2005/622], disturbing statements reportedly made by the Commander of land forces of the Turkish army during his January visit to the occupied areas of Cyprus [A/59/699-S/2005/85], Cyprus's response to Turkish Cypriot claims of racism, chauvinism and ultra-nationalism (see above) [A/60/558-S/2005/722], violations of the military status quo by the Turkish occupation forces [A/60/446-S/2005/675], and statements reportedly made by the de facto Turkish Cypriot leader concerning the latest efforts to resolve the Cyprus problem [A/59/899-S/2005/537].

Letters from the "Turkish Republic of Northern Cyprus" refuted distortions and misinformation regarding the intentions of the de facto Turkish Cypriot leadership [A/60/375-S/2005/601], and contained accusations relating to the Greek Cypriot policy of the continuation of the usurped "Republic of Cyprus" and its goal of extending its authority to northern Cyprus [A/59/906-S/2005/538].

Good offices mission

In 2005, the overall situation in Cyprus remained stable. Official contacts between the Greek Cypriot and the Turkish Cypriot sides, which had ceased since the April 2004 referenda [YUN 2004, p. 440] on the "Comprehensive Settlement of the Cyprus Problem" [ibid., p. 438], had not resumed and there was little sign of an improvement in relations. Differences on core issues of the Cyprus problem were evident during the regular monthly meetings of the political leaders of the two sides, and separate meetings with leaders of political parties of both sides produced no tangible results beyond general declarations of support for a just settlement. However, on 9 May, the Secretary-General held informal consultations with the President of Cyprus, Tassos Papadopoulos, and Turkey's Prime Minister, Recep Tayyip Erdogan. Subsequently, the Under-Secretary-General for Political Affairs, held preliminary discussions in New York (16-20 May) with a Greek Cypriot delegation to explore the possibility of resuming negotiations. At the Secretary-General's request, the Under-Secretary-General also held consultations in Cyprus, Greece and Turkey between 30 May and 7 June to seek their respective views on the UN's role in the current circumstances.

Security Council consideration. In his briefing to the Security Council on 22 June [meeting 5211] on the results of those discussions, the Under-Secretary-General reported that Mr. Papadopoulos, while expressing his eagerness for negotiations to resume under the auspices of the Secretary-General, cautioned that they should be carefully prepared but not open-ended, with no deadlines and no arbitration of important issues by the United Nations or any other third party, and that only a settlement agreed by the parties should be submitted to referendum. He believed that future negotiations would be successful only if the Turkish Cypriot side and Turkey were prepared to meet outstanding Greek Cypriot concerns during those negotiations, which included areas of governance, security, citizenship, residency, property, territory, economic and financial issues, transition periods and guarantees of implementation. The Under-Secretary-General indicated to him that, while the United Nations understood those concerns, their breadth and depth might be daunting for the other side, and advised that he produce a list of focused, finite, manageable and prioritized proposals, which he declined to do.

The Turkish Cypriot leader, Mehmet Ali Talat, also wanted negotiations under the auspices of the Secretary-General to resume as soon as possible, based on the Comprehensive Settlement, but with clear time limits for negotiations, since he was concerned that talks might drag on indefinitely. His concerns related to territory, property, resettlement of Turkish Cypriots, financing and guarantees against usurpation of the settlement arrangement by either side. He expressed his disappointment at the failure of the Council and the international community to react to the Secretary-General's May 2004 good offices report [ibid., p. 440] describing the negotiating process and assessing its outcome, and the lack of action to help ease the unjustifiable isolation and punishment of the Turkish Cypriots. Mr. Talat regarded the Greek Cypriot concerns as unacceptable and outside the parameters of the Comprehensive Settlement.

The Under-Secretary-General, in his conclusions, noted the acceptance by the parties that negotiations should resume on the basis of the Comprehensive Settlement, the wide gap between their stated positions, and the low level of confidence between them. He suggested that a prioritized and exhaustive list of concrete proposals for further negotiations would be an important advance in the process. However, while the persistence of the status quo on the island was unacceptable, launching an intensive new process prematurely would be inadvisable. The Secretary-General, therefore, intended to reflect on the future of his mission of good offices, taking into account the Council's reaction and developments on the ground, particularly the evolving positions of the respective parties.

Statement by President of Cyprus. On 18 September [meeting 11], the Cyprus President, in his address during the General Assembly's general debate, said that the Comprehensive Settlement was rejected because it did not provide for and could not bring about the reunification of the country, its society and institutions. However, since the 2004 referenda, the priority had been on revisiting the content, product and shortcomings of the last negotiating process and on dispelling certain misconceptions. He declared that, contrary to general opinion, the Secretary-General's mandate for the good offices mission had not ended but had entered a new phase. It was an ongoing and sustained process, through which a negotiated settlement could be brokered without arbitration and deadlines. Cyprus remained committed to holding those negotiations under UN auspices and to creating conditions for making them fruitful. In that context, Cyprus had been implementing substantial practical measures to build confidence and promote the economic development of the Turkish Cypriots, with the hope of making progress on other aspects of the Cyprus problem, especially the fate of missing persons and the welfare of those in the enclaves. The Cyprus problem was at a critical juncture. Revival of the talks required thorough preparation and an honest assessment that the prospect of success was at least credible.

Communication. In a 4 October letter transmitted to the Secretary-General by Turkey [A/60/414-S/2005/628], the "Turkish Republic of Northern Cyprus" refuted the statements made by President Papadopoulus to the Assembly on 18 September. It suggested that the Cypriot President, in asserting that the Comprehensive Settlement was divisive and could not bring about reunification, was implying that the United Nations had somehow finalized a plan that was outside the parameters of the Council's resolution and did not envisage the reunification of the island. Furthermore, the demand for a new UN process, free of arbitration and deadlines, was a recipe for another 40 years of inconclusive negotiations. Lingering Greek Cypriot concerns about security and implementation of the Comprehensive Settlement needed to be articulated with clarity and finality. The Turkish Cypriot people had demonstrated their will and resolution for the reunification of the island in line with international treaties on Cyprus and UN parameters, but they were equally resolute in rejecting a minority status in the island in a Greek-run "Republic of Cyprus".

Report of Secretary-General (November). In his November report on UNFICYP [S/2005/743 & Corr.1], the Secretary-General informed the Council that, in meetings with the Greek Cypriot (16 September) and the Turkish Cypriot (31 October) leaders, supported by Greece and Turkey, both sides had requested him to resume his mission of good offices and to consider holding a new round of negotiations. The Turkish Cypriot leader, Mr. Talat, also raised the issue of ending the isolation of the Turkish Cypriots. However, the Secretary-General advised that the time was not right to resume his mission of good offices, or to appoint a full-time person dedicated to the Cyprus problem, since the conditions surrounding such a resumption required further clarification, but he would continue to dispatch, on an ad hoc basis, senior Secretariat officials to visit Cyprus, Greece and Turkey to assess the situation on the ground.

UNFICYP

In 2005, the United Nations Peacekeeping Force in Cyprus (UNFICYP), established in 1964 [YUN 1964, p. 165], continued to monitor the ceasefire lines between the Turkish and Turkish Cypriot forces on the northern side and the Cypriot

National Guard on the southern side of the island; maintain the military status quo and prevent a recurrence of fighting; and undertake humanitarian and economic activities. In the absence of a formal ceasefire agreement, UNFICYP's task was to judge whether changes in military positions constituted violations of the military status quo, as recorded by the Force in 1974. UNFICYP, under the overall authority of the Secretary-General's Special Representative and Chief of Mission, Zbigniew Wlosowicz (Poland), continued to keep the area between the ceasefire lines, known as the buffer zone, under constant surveillance through a system of observation posts and air, vehicle and foot patrols.

The Secretary-General informed the Security Council on 12 September [S/2005/589] of his intention to appoint Michael Moller (Denmark) to replace Mr. Wlosowicz, whose assignment ended on 30 November, which the Council noted on 15 September [S/2005/590].

As at 31 December, UNFICYP, under the command of Major General Herbert Joaquin Figoli Almandos (Uruguay), comprised 840 troops and 69 civilian police.

Activities

Report of Secretary-General (May). In his May report [S/2005/353] covering UNFICYP activities from 25 September 2004 to 20 May 2005, the Secretary-General indicated that the military security situation in Cyprus remained stable and the overall number of incidents along the ceasefire lines decreased. Since November 2004, over 250,000 square metres of Greek Cypriot National Guard minefields in the buffer zone were cleared and 400 anti-personnel and some 900 anti-tank mines removed. On 19 May, the Turkish Cypriot side lifted restrictions imposed since July 2000 on UNFICYP's movement in the north, thereby enabling the Force to effectively restore operations in and around the buffer zone.

On 7 February, the Force commenced the new concept of operations (concentration with mobility) announced in 2004 [YUN 2004, p. 445], reducing its operational sites from 12 to 4 camps, its permanent observation posts from 17 to 2, and its patrol bases from 21 to 9. Patrols were increased in frequency (from 50 to 200 per day) and extended in duration to prevent operational gaps resulting from the closure of static observation posts. A joint UNFICYP/Headquarters review team visited the island (6-11 May) to assess UNFICYP's restructuring and the implementation of the new concept of operations. The review team found that the changes had allowed UNFICYP to maintain the same level of mandate implementation, while the introduction of a military observer and liaison group had increased the emphasis on liaison, observation and mediation rather than on the interposition of forces. The civilian police and civil affairs tasks continued to increase in number and complexity, as had requests from both sides for assistance. Regarding the possibility of further reductions in force strength, the review team concluded that more time and experience was needed to assess the full impact of the new concept before taking decisions in that regard. The Secretary-General, while agreeing with the team's observation, noted that delays in the recruitment and deployment of staff had not allowed the new concept to reach its full potential.

UNFICYP's support of projects in the buffer zone continued, especially in the areas of infrastructure, farming and ecology. It also continued its humanitarian assistance and provided facilities for 57 bicommunal events, bringing together some 2,500 Greek Cypriots and Turkish Cypriots. While the movement of people across the buffer zone was steady, trade was limited by technical and political hurdles. In February, the European Council raised the ceiling on the value of personal goods to 135 euros and expanded the list of personal items and agricultural goods that could be taken across the line. The Turkish Cypriot side took reciprocal action with regard to personal goods.

The European Commission's recommendation of a 259 million euro aid package for the north of the island was yet to be acted upon, for while the Greek Cypriot side supported it, the Turkish Cypriot side agreed to accept it only together with the Commission's recommendation on direct trade between the north of the island and the EU.

Cyprus' EU membership had raised other concerns. In the area of property, it had opened new fronts of litigation and acrimony, with hundreds of Greek Cypriots' claims against Turkey for loss of property rights pending before the European Court of Human Rights. In addition, Greek Cypriots had approached courts in the south for EU arrest warrants against foreigners buying or selling Greek Cypriot property in the north. The prospect of an increase of people-to-people litigation in property cases posed a serious threat to the reconciliation process.

The Secretary-General recommended that the Council extend UNFICYP's mandate until 15 December 2005.

SECURITY COUNCIL ACTION

On 15 June [meeting 5202], the Security Council unanimously adopted **resolution 1604(2005)**.

The draft [S/2005/382] was submitted by the United Kingdom.

The Security Council,

Welcoming the report of the Secretary-General of 27 May 2005 on the United Nations operation in Cyprus,

Reiterating its call to the parties to assess and address the humanitarian issue of missing persons with due urgency and seriousness, and welcoming in this regard the resumption of the activities of the Committee on Missing Persons since August 2004,

Welcoming the Secretary-General's review of the United Nations Peacekeeping Force in Cyprus, pursuant to resolution 1568(2004) of 22 October 2004,

Noting that the Government of Cyprus has agreed that in view of the prevailing conditions on the island it is necessary to keep the Force beyond 15 June 2005,

Taking note of the assessment of the Secretary-General that the security situation on the island continues to be stable and that the situation along the Green Line remains calm, and, nonetheless, that there were problems in a few sensitive areas, and welcoming in this context the further decrease in the overall number of incidents involving the two sides,

Welcoming the Secretary-General's intention to keep the operations of the Force under close review, continuing to take into account developments on the ground and the views of the parties, and to revert to the Council with recommendations for further adjustments as appropriate to the mandate, force levels and concept of operation of the Force once he judges that sufficient time has passed since the implementation of its new concept of operations to make this assessment,

Taking note with satisfaction of the lifting of restrictions of movement of the Force by the Turkish Cypriot side and the Turkish forces, and taking note in this connection that the Force enjoys good cooperation from both sides,

Welcoming the fact that over seven million crossings by Greek Cypriots to the north and Turkish Cypriots to the south have taken place, and encouraging the opening of additional crossing points,

Expressing concern at the increase in crime across the ceasefire line and urging both sides to increase cooperation in order to address this issue,

Welcoming all efforts to promote bicommunal contacts and events, including on the part of the United Nations, and urging the two sides to promote further bicommunal contacts and to remove any obstacles to such contacts,

Echoing the Secretary-General's gratitude to the Government of Cyprus and the Government of Greece for their voluntary contributions to the funding of the Force, and his request for further voluntary contributions from other countries and organizations,

Welcoming and encouraging efforts by the United Nations to sensitize peacekeeping personnel in the prevention and control of HIV/AIDS and other communicable diseases in all its peacekeeping operations,

1. *Reaffirms* all its relevant resolutions on Cyprus, in particular resolution 1251(1999) of 29 June 1999 and subsequent resolutions;

2. *Decides* to extend the mandate of the United Nations Peacekeeping Force in Cyprus for a further period ending 15 December 2005;

3. *Calls upon* the Turkish Cypriot side and Turkish forces to restore in Strovilia the military status quo which existed there prior to 30 June 2000;

4. *Requests* the Secretary-General to submit a report by 1 December 2005 on the implementation of the present resolution;

5. *Welcomes* the efforts being undertaken by the Force to implement the Secretary-General's zero-tolerance policy on sexual exploitation and abuse and to ensure full compliance of its personnel with the United Nations code of conduct, requests the Secretary-General to continue to take all necessary action in this regard and to keep the Security Council informed, and urges troop-contributing countries to take appropriate preventive action, including the conduct of predeployment awareness training, and to take disciplinary action and other action to ensure full accountability in cases of such conduct involving their personnel;

6. *Decides* to remain seized of the matter.

Communication. On 16 August [A/59/897-S/2005/531], the "Turkish Republic of Northern Cyprus", responding to the Secretary-General's report (see p. 494) and the Council's resolution, provided information on what it considered a number of inaccuracies and misrepresentations contained in the report.

Earlier, on 31 May [A/59/820-S/2005/355], the "Turkish Republic of Northern Cyprus" had called for the lifting of all restrictions on the territory and made known its proposals, on 30 May, for reaching a just, durable and comprehensive solution to the Cyprus problem. They included the free movement of people, goods and services to and from the Turkish Cypriot side and between the north and the south; the lifting of all restrictions applied to seaports and airports, including direct flights; the elimination of restrictions regarding third-country nationals; special arrangements for the direct inclusion of the north as an economic entity in the EU's customs union and for the enjoyment of its full benefits by all Turkish Cypriots; and the removal of obstacles that prevented the Turkish Cypriot side from participating in international sports, cultural and other activities.

Cyprus, in a 29 June response [A/59/857-S/2005/422], said that those proposals contravened international law and Council resolutions by attempting to upgrade the status of the illegal entity established by the use of forces in the northern part of Cyprus and elaborate policies for which Turkey had been repeatedly condemned. Over the past two years, the Government of Cyprus had been providing Turkish Cypriots with a generous package of measures, including social benefits, free medical care and employment opportunities. It had also advocated that the 259 million euros earmarked for 2004-2006 by the

European Commission for the Turkish Cypriots, in the event of a Cyprus settlement, be made available to them immediately, and that the number of crossing points for persons and goods at the dividing line be increased.

Report of Secretary-General (November). In a 29 November report on UNFICYP [S/2005/743 & Corr.1], the Secretary-General stated that, although the number of incidents continued to decrease since the implementation of the new concept of operations, a few of them raised significant concerns, especially an incursion by Turkish Forces into the buffer zone in the Louroujina Pocket, the placement of buoys by Turkish Forces close to the western maritime security line, the entry into the buffer zone and the removal of a Turkish flag from a Turkish Cypriot observation post by a Greek Cypriot civilian, and shots fired at UNFICYP personnel by a Greek Cypriot hunter. For the first time since 2001, military exercises were held in November by both the Cypriot National Guard and the Turkish Forces/Turkish Cypriot security forces.

The clearing of mines continued. On 5 August, UNFICYP secured an agreement to begin clearing Turkish minefields in Nicosia and the surrounding areas within the buffer zone. Since May, some 78,132 square metres were cleared and more than 470 anti-personnel and approximately 430 anti-tank mines destroyed.

UNFICYP continued to promote confidence-building activities between the two sides and worked to open more border crossing points in order to promote bilateral trade. In August, it facilitated the temporary opening of the Astromeritis/Bostanci crossing point until the completion of the EU-funded road construction project within the buffer zone. During the reporting period, UNFICYP police and military components conducted 62 humanitarian convoys, money runs and humanitarian visits. In September, UNFICYP assisted with the delivery of textbooks for Greek Cypriot primary and secondary schools in the north and facilitated the appointment of seven teachers at the secondary level.

UNFICYP civilian police increased contacts with both sides as a result of increased staffing and monitored and followed up on approximately 100 cases of Greek Cypriots and Turkish Cypriots involved in criminal court proceedings on both sides of the buffer zone.

The Committee on Missing Persons in Cyprus held 20 meetings throughout the year in Cyprus. On 30 June, it reached agreement in principle on a common programme of exhumations and identification scheduled to begin in 2006. Further agreements were reached in September and No-

vember on the establishment of an anthropological laboratory in the buffer zone, where collected remains from both sides could be stored. The project, which would be staffed by the Inforce Foundation Centre for Forensic Science, Technology and Law based in the United Kingdom and financed by voluntary contributions, was expected to last for three to four years.

The Secretary-General, in his conclusions, said that the early completion of the work of the Committee on Missing Persons in Cyprus and a solution to that problem would greatly contribute to reconciliation. He therefore urged all concerned to redouble their efforts and put aside political considerations in order to close that painful humanitarian chapter and end the suffering of the relatives of missing persons. He recommended that UNFICYP's mandate be extended until 15 June 2006.

SECURITY COUNCIL ACTION

On 14 December [meeting 5324], the Security Council unanimously adopted **resolution 1642 (2005)**. The draft [S/2005/784] was submitted by the United Kingdom.

The Security Council,

Welcoming the report of the Secretary-General of 29 November 2005 on the United Nations operation in Cyprus,

Reiterating its call to the parties to assess and address the humanitarian issue of missing persons with due urgency and seriousness, and welcoming in this regard the resumption of the activities of the Committee on Missing Persons in Cyprus since August 2004, as well as the intention of the Secretary-General to appoint a third member as of January 2006 and to reinforce his office,

Noting that the Government of Cyprus has agreed that, in view of the prevailing conditions on the island, it is necessary to keep the United Nations Peacekeeping Force in Cyprus beyond 15 December 2005,

Taking note of the assessment of the Secretary-General that the security situation on the island continues to be stable and that the situation along the Green Line remains calm, welcoming in this context the further decrease in the overall number of incidents involving the two sides, while noting nonetheless that there were incidents of significant concern,

Urging both sides to avoid any action which could lead to an increase in tension, and taking note with concern, in this context, of the conduct, for the first time since 2001, of the "Nikiforos" military exercise, and, afterwards, the "Toros" military exercise,

Regretting that progress towards a political solution has been negligible at best, and urging both sides to work towards the resumption of negotiations for a comprehensive settlement,

Welcoming the continuous engagement of the Secretary-General in the search for a comprehensive settlement of the Cyprus problem,

Welcoming also all demining activity in the buffer zone, including the agreement to begin the clearing of

Turkish Forces minefields in Nicosia and surrounding areas within the buffer zone,

Expressing its concern that, since the release of the report of the Secretary-General, differences have arisen over construction activity related to the proposed additional crossing point at Ledra Street, and urging both sides to cooperate with the Force to resolve this issue,

Welcoming the intention of the Secretary-General to keep the operations of the Force under close review while continuing to take into account developments on the ground and the views of the parties, and to revert to the Security Council with recommendations, as appropriate, for further adjustments of the mandate, force levels and concept of operation of the Force as soon as warranted,

Welcoming also the fact that over nine million crossings by Greek Cypriots to the north and Turkish Cypriots to the south have taken place, and encouraging the opening of additional crossing points,

Welcoming further all efforts to promote bicommunal contacts and events, including, inter alia, on the part of the United Nations, and urging the two sides to promote further bicommunal contacts and to remove any obstacles to such contacts,

Echoing the Secretary-General's gratitude to the Government of Cyprus and the Government of Greece for their voluntary contributions to the funding of the Force, and his request for further voluntary contributions from other countries and organizations,

Welcoming and encouraging efforts by the United Nations to sensitize peacekeeping personnel in the prevention and control of HIV/AIDS and other communicable diseases in all its peacekeeping operations,

1. *Reaffirms* all its relevant resolutions on Cyprus, in particular resolution 1251(1999) of 29 June 1999 and subsequent resolutions;

2. *Expresses its full support* for the United Nations Peacekeeping Force in Cyprus, and decides to extend its mandate for a further period ending 15 June 2006;

3. *Calls upon* the Turkish Cypriot side and Turkish forces to restore in Strovilia the military status quo which existed there prior to 30 June 2000;

4. *Requests* the Secretary-General to submit a report on the implementation of the present resolution by 1 June 2006;

5. *Welcomes* the efforts being undertaken by the Force to implement the Secretary-General's zero-tolerance policy on sexual exploitation and abuse and to ensure full compliance of its personnel with the United Nations code of conduct, requests the Secretary-General to continue to take all necessary action in this regard and to keep the Security Council informed, and urges troop-contributing countries to take appropriate preventive action, including conducting predeployment awareness training, and to take disciplinary action and other action to ensure full accountability in cases of such conduct involving their personnel;

6. *Decides* to remain seized of the matter.

Financing

On 13 April [meeting 91], the General Assembly, having considered the Secretary-General's report on UNFICYP's financial performance for the period from 1 July 2004 to 30 June 2005

[A/59/718], and ACABQ's related comments and recommendations [A/59/734], adopted, on the recommendation of the Fifth Committee [A/59/770 & Add.1], **resolution 59/284 A** without vote [agenda item 126].

Financing of the United Nations Peacekeeping Force in Cyprus

A

The General Assembly,

Having considered the note by the Secretary-General on the financing arrangements for the United Nations Peacekeeping Force in Cyprus and the related report of the Advisory Committee on Administrative and Budgetary Questions,

Recalling Security Council resolution 186(1964) of 4 March 1964, regarding the establishment of the Force, and the subsequent resolutions by which the Council extended the mandate of the Force, the latest of which is resolution 1568(2004) of 22 October 2004,

Recalling also its resolution 47/236 of 14 September 1993 on the financing of the Force for the period beginning 16 June 1993 and its subsequent resolutions and decisions thereon, the latest of which is resolution 58/301 of 18 June 2004,

Reaffirming the general principles underlying the financing of United Nations peacekeeping operations as stated in General Assembly resolutions 1874(S-IV) of 27 June 1963, 3101(XXVIII) of 11 December 1973 and 55/235 of 23 December 2000,

Noting with appreciation that voluntary contributions have been made to the Force by certain Governments,

Noting that voluntary contributions were insufficient to cover all the costs of the Force, including those incurred by troop-contributing Governments prior to 16 June 1993, and regretting the absence of an adequate response to appeals for voluntary contributions, including that contained in the letter dated 17 May 1994 from the Secretary-General to all Member States,

Mindful of the fact that it is essential to provide the Force with the necessary financial resources to enable it to fulfil its responsibilities under the relevant resolutions of the Security Council,

1. *Takes note* of the note by the Secretary-General on the financing arrangements for the United Nations Peacekeeping Force in Cyprus and the related report of the Advisory Committee on Administrative and Budgetary Questions;

2. *Also takes note* of the status of contributions to the Force as at 28 February 2005, including the contributions outstanding in the amount of 24.1 million United States dollars, representing some 10 per cent of the total assessed contributions, notes with concern that only forty-one Member States have paid their assessed contributions in full, and urges all other Member States, in particular those in arrears, to ensure payment of their outstanding assessed contributions;

3. *Expresses its appreciation* to those Member States which have paid their assessed contributions in full, and urges all other Member States to make every possible effort to ensure payment of their assessed contributions to the Force in full;

4. *Expresses concern* at the financial situation with regard to peacekeeping activities, in particular as regards the reimbursements to troop contributors that

bear additional burdens owing to overdue payments by Member States of their assessments;

5. *Also expresses concern* at the delay experienced by the Secretary-General in deploying and providing adequate resources to some recent peacekeeping missions, in particular those in Africa;

6. *Emphasizes* that all future and existing peacekeeping missions shall be given equal and non-discriminatory treatment in respect of financial and administrative arrangements;

7. *Also emphasizes* that all peacekeeping missions shall be provided with adequate resources for the effective and efficient discharge of their respective mandates;

8. *Reiterates its request* to the Secretary-General to make the fullest possible use of facilities and equipment at the United Nations Logistics Base at Brindisi, Italy, in order to minimize the costs of procurement for the Force;

9. *Endorses* the observations and recommendations of the Advisory Committee on Administrative and Budgetary Questions, and requests the Secretary-General to ensure their full implementation;

10. *Requests* the Secretary-General to expedite negotiations with the host Government on issues surrounding the relocation of military contingent personnel as well as other personnel of the Force, in accordance with the provisions of the March 1964 Agreement between the United Nations and the Government of Cyprus;

11. *Also requests* the Secretary-General to take all necessary action to ensure that the Force is administered with a maximum of efficiency and economy;

12. *Further requests* the Secretary-General, in order to reduce the cost of employing General Service staff, to continue efforts to recruit local staff for the Force against General Service posts, commensurate with the requirements of the Force;

13. *Decides* to continue to maintain as separate the account established for the Force for the period prior to 16 June 1993, invites Member States to make voluntary contributions to that account, and requests the Secretary-General to continue his efforts in appealing for voluntary contributions to the account;

14. *Emphasizes* that no peacekeeping mission shall be financed by borrowing funds from other active peacekeeping missions;

15. *Encourages* the Secretary-General to continue to take additional measures to ensure the safety and security of all personnel under the auspices of the United Nations participating in the Force;

16. *Invites* voluntary contributions to the Force in cash and in the form of services and supplies acceptable to the Secretary-General, to be administered, as appropriate, in accordance with the procedure and practices established by the General Assembly;

17. *Decides* to keep under review during its fifty-ninth session the item entitled "Financing of the United Nations Peacekeeping Force in Cyprus".

On 22 June [meeting 104], the Assembly, having considered the performance report on UNFICYP's budget for the period from 1 July 2003 to 30 June 2004 [A/59/620], its budget for the period from 1 July 2005 to 30 June 2006 [A/59/656 & Add.1] and

the ACABQ report thereon [A/59/736/ Add.6], adopted, on the recommendation of the Fifth Committee [A/59/770/Add.1], **resolution 59/284 B**, without vote [agenda item 126].

B

The General Assembly,

Having considered the reports of the Secretary-General on the financing of the United Nations Peacekeeping Force in Cyprus and the related reports of the Advisory Committee on Administrative and Budgetary Questions,

Recalling Security Council resolution 186(1964) of 4 March 1964 regarding the establishment of the Force and the subsequent resolutions by which the Council extended the mandate of the Force, the latest of which was resolution 1568(2004) of 22 October 2004,

Recalling also its resolution 47/236 of 14 September 1993 on the financing of the Force for the period beginning 16 June 1993 and its subsequent resolutions and decisions thereon, the latest of which were resolutions 58/301 of 18 June 2004 and 59/284 A of 13 April 2005,

Reaffirming the general principles underlying the financing of United Nations peacekeeping operations as stated in General Assembly resolutions 1874(S-IV) of 27 June 1963, 3101(XXVIII) of 11 December 1973 and 55/235 of 23 December 2000,

Noting with appreciation that voluntary contributions have been made to the Force by certain Governments,

Noting that voluntary contributions were insufficient to cover all the costs of the Force, including those incurred by troop-contributing Governments prior to 16 June 1993, and regretting the absence of an adequate response to appeals for voluntary contributions, including that contained in the letter dated 17 May 1994 from the Secretary-General to all Member States,

Mindful of the fact that it is essential to provide the Force with the necessary financial resources to enable it to fulfil its responsibilities under the relevant resolutions of the Security Council,

1. *Requests* the Secretary-General to entrust the Head of Mission with the task of formulating future budget proposals, in full accordance with the provisions of General Assembly resolution 59/296 of 22 June 2005, as well as other relevant resolutions;

2. *Takes note* of the status of contributions to the United Nations Peacekeeping Force in Cyprus as at 15 April 2005, including the contributions outstanding in the amount of 14.1 million United States dollars, representing some 6 per cent of the total assessed contributions, notes with concern that only fifty-five Member States have paid their assessed contributions in full, and urges all other Member States, in particular those in arrears, to ensure payment of their outstanding assessed contributions;

3. *Expresses its appreciation* to those Member States that have paid their assessed contributions in full, and urges all other Member States to make every possible effort to ensure payment of their assessed contributions to the Force in full;

4. *Expresses concern* at the financial situation with regard to peacekeeping activities, in particular as regards the reimbursements to troop contributors that bear additional burdens owing to overdue payments by Member States of their assessments;

5. *Also expresses concern* at the delay experienced by the Secretary-General in deploying and providing adequate resources to some recent peacekeeping missions, in particular those in Africa;

6. *Emphasizes* that all future and existing peacekeeping missions shall be given equal and non-discriminatory treatment in respect of financial and administrative arrangements;

7. *Also emphasizes* that all peacekeeping missions shall be provided with adequate resources for the effective and efficient discharge of their respective mandates;

8. *Reiterates its request* to the Secretary-General to make the fullest possible use of facilities and equipment at the United Nations Logistics Base at Brindisi, Italy, in order to minimize the costs of procurement for the Force;

9. *Endorses* the observations and recommendations contained in the report of the Advisory Committee on Administrative and Budgetary Questions, and requests the Secretary-General to ensure their full implementation;

10. *Requests* the Secretary-General to ensure full implementation of the relevant provisions of its resolution 59/296;

11. *Also requests* the Secretary-General to take all necessary action to ensure that the Force is administered with a maximum of efficiency and economy;

12. *Further requests* the Secretary-General, in order to reduce the cost of employing General Service staff, to continue efforts to recruit local staff for the Force against General Service posts, commensurate with the requirements of the Force;

Financial performance report for the period from 1 July 2003 to 30 June 2004

13. *Takes note* of the report of the Secretary-General on the financial performance of the Force for the period from 1 July 2003 to 30 June 2004;

14. *Decides* to appropriate to the Special Account for the United Nations Peacekeeping Force in Cyprus the amount of 1,665,400 dollars for the maintenance of the Force for the period from 1 July 2003 to 30 June 2004, in addition to the amount of 45,772,600 dollars already appropriated for the Force for the same period under the terms of its resolution 57/332 of 18 June 2003;

Financing of the additional appropriation for the period from 1 July 2003 to 30 June 2004

15. *Notes with appreciation* that a one-third share of the net additional appropriation, equivalent to 500,800 dollars, will be funded through voluntary contributions from the Government of Cyprus;

16. *Decides*, taking into account the amount of 24,705,100 dollars already apportioned under the terms of its resolution 57/332, to apportion among Member States the additional amount of 1,164,600 dollars for the maintenance of the Force for the period from 1 July 2003 to 30 June 2004, in accordance with the levels updated in General Assembly resolution 58/256 of 23 December 2003, and taking into account the scale of assessments for 2004, as set out in its resolution 58/1 B of 23 December 2003;

17. *Decides also* that, in accordance with the provisions of its resolution 973(X) of 15 December 1955, there shall be set off against the apportionment among Member States, as provided for in paragraph 16 above,

their respective share in the Tax Equalization Fund of the amount of 163,000 dollars, representing the additional staff assessment income for the Force for the period from 1 July 2003 to 30 June 2004;

18. *Decides further* that, for Member States that have fulfilled their financial obligations to the Force, there shall be set off against their apportionment, as provided for in paragraph 16 above, their respective share of other income in the amount of 701,231 dollars in respect of the financial period ended 30 June 2004, in accordance with the scheme set out in paragraph 16 above;

19. *Decides* that, for Member States that have not fulfilled their financial obligations to the Force, there shall be set off against their outstanding obligations their respective share of other income in the amount of 701,231 dollars in respect of the financial period ended 30 June 2004, in accordance with the scheme set out in paragraph 16 above;

20. *Decides also*, taking into account its voluntary contribution for the financial period ended 30 June 2004, that one third of other income in the amount of 451,300 dollars in respect of the financial period ended 30 June 2004 shall be returned to the Government of Cyprus;

21. *Decides further*, taking into account its voluntary contribution for the financial period ended 30 June 2004, that the prorated share of other income in the amount of 201,369 dollars in respect of the financial period ended 30 June 2004 shall be returned to the Government of Greece;

Budget estimates for the period from 1 July 2005 to 30 June 2006

22. *Decides* to appropriate to the Special Account for the United Nations Peacekeeping Force in Cyprus the amount of 46,512,600 dollars for the period from 1 July 2005 to 30 June 2006, inclusive of 44,184,300 dollars for the maintenance of the Force, 1,903,800 dollars for the support account for peacekeeping operations and 424,500 dollars for the United Nations Logistics Base;

Financing of the appropriation for the period from 1 July 2005 to 30 June 2006

23. *Notes with appreciation* that a one-third share of the net appropriation, equivalent to 14,699,000 dollars, will be funded through voluntary contributions from the Government of Cyprus and the amount of 6.5 million dollars from the Government of Greece;

24. *Decides* to apportion among Member States the amount of 25,313,600 dollars at a monthly rate of 2,109,466 dollars, in accordance with the levels updated in General Assembly resolution 58/256, and taking into account the scale of assessments for 2005 and 2006, as set out in its resolution 58/1 B, subject to a decision of the Security Council to extend the mandate of the Force;

25. *Decides also* that, in accordance with the provisions of its resolution 973(X), there shall be set off against the apportionment among Member States, as provided for in paragraph 24 above, their respective share in the Tax Equalization Fund of 2,415,600 dollars, comprising the estimated staff assessment income of 2,112,100 dollars approved for the Force, the prorated share of 269,100 dollars of the estimated staff assessment income approved for the support account

and the prorated share of 34,400 dollars of the estimated staff assessment income approved for the United Nations Logistics Base;

26. *Decides further* to continue to maintain as separate the account established for the Force for the period prior to 16 June 1993, invites Member States to make voluntary contributions to that account and requests the Secretary-General to continue his efforts in appealing for voluntary contributions to the account;

27. *Emphasizes* that no peacekeeping mission shall be financed by borrowing funds from other active peacekeeping missions;

28. *Encourages* the Secretary-General to continue to take additional measures to ensure the safety and security of all personnel under the auspices of the United Nations participating in the Force, bearing in mind paragraphs 5 and 6 of Security Council resolution 1502(2003) of 26 August 2003;

29. *Invites* voluntary contributions to the Force in cash and in the form of services and supplies acceptable to the Secretary-General, to be administered, as appropriate, in accordance with the procedure and practices established by the General Assembly;

30. *Decides* to include in the provisional agenda of its sixtieth session the item entitled "Financing of the United Nations Peacekeeping Force in Cyprus".

In December, the Secretary-General further submitted the performance report on UNFICYP's budget for the period form 1 July 2004 to 30 June 2005 [A/60/584] and the budget for the period from 1 July 2006 to 30 June 2007 [A/60/592].

Other issues

Strengthening of security and cooperation in the Mediterranean

In response to General Assembly resolution 59/108 [YUN 2004, p. 448], the Secretary-General submitted a July report [A/60/118] containing replies received from Albania, Burkina Faso and Turkey to his 25 February note verbale requesting the views of States and intergovernmental organizations on ways to strengthen cooperation in the Mediterranean region.

GENERAL ASSEMBLY ACTION

On 8 December [meeting 62], the General Assembly, on the recommendation of the First (Disarmament and International Security) Committee [A/60/468], adopted **resolution 60/94** without vote [agenda item 102].

Strengthening of security and cooperation in the Mediterranean region

The General Assembly,

Recalling its previous resolutions on the subject, including resolution 59/108 of 3 December 2004,

Reaffirming the primary role of the Mediterranean countries in strengthening and promoting peace, security and cooperation in the Mediterranean region,

Bearing in mind all the previous declarations and commitments, as well as all the initiatives taken by the riparian countries at the recent summits, ministerial meetings and various forums concerning the question of the Mediterranean region,

Recognizing the indivisible character of security in the Mediterranean and that the enhancement of cooperation among Mediterranean countries with a view to promoting the economic and social development of all peoples of the region will contribute significantly to stability, peace and security in the region,

Recognizing also the efforts made so far and the determination of the Mediterranean countries to intensify the process of dialogue and consultations with a view to resolving the problems existing in the Mediterranean region and to eliminating the causes of tension and the consequent threat to peace and security, and their growing awareness of the need for further joint efforts to strengthen economic, social, cultural and environmental cooperation in the region,

Recognizing further that prospects for closer Euro-Mediterranean cooperation in all spheres can be enhanced by positive developments worldwide, in particular in Europe, in the Maghreb and in the Middle East,

Reaffirming the responsibility of all States to contribute to the stability and prosperity of the Mediterranean region and their commitment to respecting the purposes and principles of the Charter of the United Nations as well as the provisions of the Declaration on Principles of International Law concerning Friendly Relations and Cooperation among States in accordance with the Charter of the United Nations,

Noting the peace negotiations in the Middle East, which should be of a comprehensive nature and represent an appropriate framework for the peaceful settlement of contentious issues in the region,

Expressing its concern at the persistent tension and continuing military activities in parts of the Mediterranean that hinder efforts to strengthen security and cooperation in the region,

Taking note of the report of the Secretary-General,

1. *Reaffirms* that security in the Mediterranean is closely linked to European security as well as to international peace and security;

2. *Expresses its satisfaction* at the continuing efforts by Mediterranean countries to contribute actively to the elimination of all causes of tension in the region and to the promotion of just and lasting solutions to the persistent problems of the region through peaceful means, thus ensuring the withdrawal of foreign forces of occupation and respecting the sovereignty, independence and territorial integrity of all countries of the Mediterranean and the right of peoples to self-determination, and therefore calls for full adherence to the principles of non-interference, non-intervention, non-use of force or threat of use of force and the inadmissibility of the acquisition of territory by force, in accordance with the Charter and the relevant resolutions of the United Nations;

3. *Commends* the Mediterranean countries for their efforts in meeting common challenges through coordinated overall responses, based on a spirit of multilateral partnership, towards the general objective of turn-

ing the Mediterranean basin into an area of dialogue, exchanges and cooperation, guaranteeing peace, stability and prosperity, encourages them to strengthen such efforts through, inter alia, a lasting multilateral and action-oriented cooperative dialogue among States of the region, and recognizes the role of the United Nations in promoting regional and international peace and security;

4. *Recognizes* that the elimination of the economic and social disparities in levels of development and other obstacles as well as respect and greater understanding among cultures in the Mediterranean area will contribute to enhancing peace, security and cooperation among Mediterranean countries through the existing forums;

5. *Calls upon* all States of the Mediterranean region that have not yet done so to adhere to all the multilaterally negotiated legal instruments related to the field of disarmament and non-proliferation, thus creating the necessary conditions for strengthening peace and cooperation in the region;

6. *Encourages* all States of the region to favour the necessary conditions for strengthening the confidence-building measures among them by promoting genuine openness and transparency on all military matters, by participating, inter alia, in the United Nations system for the standardized reporting of military expenditures and by providing accurate data and information to the United Nations Register of Conventional Arms;

7. *Encourages* the Mediterranean countries to strengthen further their cooperation in combating terrorism in all its forms and manifestations, taking into account the relevant resolutions of the United Nations, and in combating international crime and illicit arms transfers and illicit drug production, consumption and trafficking, which pose a serious threat to peace, security and stability in the region and therefore to the improvement of the current political, economic and social situation and which jeopardize friendly relations among States, hinder the development of international cooperation and result in the destruction of human rights, fundamental freedoms and the democratic basis of pluralistic society;

8. *Requests* the Secretary-General to submit a report on means to strengthen security and cooperation in the Mediterranean region;

9. *Decides* to include in the provisional agenda of its sixty-first session the item entitled "Strengthening of security and cooperation in the Mediterranean region".

Cooperation with the Organization for Security and Cooperation in Europe

On 2 September [A/59/908], Slovenia, on behalf of the member States of the Organization for Security and Cooperation in Europe (OSCE), requested that consideration of the sub-item "Cooperation between the United Nations and the Organization for Security and Cooperation in Europe" be deferred to the General Assembly's sixtieth (2005) session and be included in the agenda of that session, as no agreement had been reached on the text of a draft resolution on the subject. The request was made on the understanding that, without setting a precedent, the sub-item would again be considered under the item entitled "Cooperation between the United Nations and regional and other organizations", which was to be included in the agenda of the sixty-first (2006) session and be considered biennially, pursuant to Assembly resolution 55/285 [YUN 2001, p. 1287].

By **decision 59/567** of 12 September, the Assembly agreed to that request.

Chapter VI

Middle East

The conflict in the Middle East abated somewhat during the first months of 2005, as actions by Israeli and Palestinians leaders generated new hopes for peace. The summit meeting held at Sharm el-Sheikh, Egypt, on 8 February, produced a series of commitments, including a halt to violence and military activities, aimed at rebuilding trust and breaking the cycle of bloodshed. Although formal negotiations were not resumed, the two parties agreed to coordinate the Israeli withdrawal from the Gaza Strip and parts of the northern West Bank. Israel's disengagement from those areas, which took place between 15 August and 12 September, marked a watershed in that it constituted the first removal of Israeli settlements in the Occupied Palestinian Territory. However, the disengagement failed to revive the peace process due to a resurgence of violence during the last months of 2005. A November Agreement on Movement and Access between Israel and the Palestinian Authority (PA), which called, among other things, for the continuous operation of the border crossings between Gaza and Israel, was not fully implemented by the end of the year. Israel's ongoing construction of the separation wall in the occupied territories and restrictions on movement in the form of checkpoints, curfews and the permit system greatly contributed to the continuing humanitarian and socio-economic crisis in the Palestinian areas.

The Palestinian presidential election, the first to be held since 1996, took place, on 9 January, in the West Bank and Gaza Strip. Voters elected the Chairman of the Palestine Liberation Organization (PLO), Mahmoud Abbas, as the new President of the PA to replace Yasser Arafat, who died on 11 November 2004. Four rounds of municipal elections were also held throughout the year. President Abbas repeatedly called for an end to violence and promoted Palestinian reforms, especially in the security sector. He faced major fiscal and budgetary problems, which threatened to paralyze the PA's administration. In addition, a number of unintegrated Palestinian militia groups, clans and individual force commanders continued to wield undue influence. The political wing of the Islamic organization, Hamas, took part in the municipal elections, though it boycotted the presidential one. Legislative elections were scheduled to take place in January 2006.

In Israel, Prime Minister Ariel Sharon carried out the disengagement plan, originally announced in February 2004, despite strong domestic opposition. The international community commended the Israeli Government for the smooth and professional execution of the disengagement operation. Throughout 2005, Israel expressed concern over the inability by the PA to control Palestinian terrorist organizations and dismantle their infrastructure.

The Quartet, a coordinating mechanism for international peace efforts, comprising the Russian Federation, the United States, the European Union and the United Nations, continued to promote the road map initiative as the best solution to the conflict. The road map, which was endorsed by the Security Council in 2003, aimed to achieve progress through parallel and reciprocal steps by Israel and the PA in the political, security, economic, humanitarian and institution-building areas, under an international monitoring system. In April, the Quartet principals named James D. Wolfensohn as their Special Envoy for Gaza Disengagement, whose mandate focused on the non-security aspects of the Israeli withdrawal, including trade, and the revival of the Palestinian economy.

In March, the United Kingdom hosted a meeting on supporting the PA, which was attended by representatives of the Quartet, including the Secretary-General. The participants agreed to support the Palestinian leadership in its efforts to strengthen the PA's institutions.

During a visit to Israel and the Occupied Palestinian Territory in March, the Secretary-General urged the two sides to seek further progress through direct dialogue and negotiations. In May, he appointed Alvaro de Soto as the United Nations Special Coordinator for the Middle East Peace Process and his Personal Representative to the Palestine Liberation Organization and the PA.

In February, a bomb attack killed former Lebanese Prime Minister Rafik Hariri and 20 others in Beirut. The Secretary-General designated a Special Envoy for the implementation of Security Council resolution 1559(2004), which called, among other measures, for the withdrawal of foreign forces from the country and the disbanding and disarmament of militias. In addition, the Secretary-General dispatched a team of military experts to Lebanon at the end of April to verify whether Syrian military assets, except in one disputed border area, had been withdrawn fully from Lebanon. He sent the team back in June to clarify allegations that Syrian intelligence operatives continued to operate in the country. The assassination of Mr. Hariri, occurring only months before planned parliamentary elections, raised fears that Lebanon would return to its violent past. In condemning the attack, the Security Council requested that the Secretary-General report on the causes, circumstances and consequences of the attack. A UN mission of inquiry, which was dispatched by the Secretary-General, concluded that an international commission should independently investigate the crime. The Council established the United Nations International Independent Investigation Commission (UNIIIC). In resolution 1636(2005), it took note, with concern, of the Commission's conclusion that there was converging evidence pointing to the involvement of both Lebanese and Syrian officials in Mr. Hariri's assassination, and insisted that Syria should not interfere in Lebanese domestic affairs.

The mandates of the United Nations Interim Force in Lebanon and of the United Nations Disengagement Observer Force in the Golan Heights were extended twice during the year, and the United Nations Truce Supervision Organization continued to assist both peacekeeping operations in their tasks.

The United Nations Relief and Works Agency for Palestine Refugees in the Near East continued to provide education and health and social services to over four million Palestinian refugees living both in and outside camps in the West Bank and the Gaza Strip, as well as in Jordan.

During the year, the Special Committee to Investigate Israeli Practices Affecting the Human Rights of the Palestinian People and Other Arabs of the Occupied Territories reported to the Assembly on the situation in the West Bank, including East Jerusalem, the Gaza Strip and the Golan Heights. The Committee on the Exercise of the Inalienable Rights of the Palestinian People continued to mobilize international support for the Palestinians.

Peace process

Overall situation

The Secretary-General, in a November report on the peaceful settlement of the question of Palestine [A/60/539-S/2005/701] (see also p. 535), said that, despite setbacks, 2005 witnessed the successful completion of the Israeli disengagement from the Gaza Strip and parts of the northern West Bank, first announced by prime Minister Ariel Sharon in February 2004 [YUN 2004, p. 455]. On 12 September, Israel withdrew the last of its military personnel and installations from the Gaza Strip, and by 20 September from four settlements in the northern West Bank, thereby putting an end to its permanent presence in the area. As Israel's first withdrawal from the Occupied Palestinian Territory since the occupation began in 1967, it was a landmark in Israeli-Palestinian relations, setting an important precedent for the eventual realization of the two-State solution.

In the aftermath of the Israeli withdrawal, the Quartet's Special Envoy for Gaza Disengagement, James D. Wolfensohn, who had helped to enhance crucial channels of coordination between the parties during the disengagement process, continued to follow up on a six-point agenda: border crossings and trade corridors; movement between the West Bank and Gaza; movement within the West Bank; the Gaza airport and seaport; the houses in the Israeli settlements; and their agricultural assets. Many of those issues remained unresolved. Mr. Wolfensohn identified three key areas for the Palestinian Authority (PA) to address: the PA's fiscal crisis and development of a fiscal stabilization plan to be included in the 2006 budget; the creation of a general development plan related to a fiscally sound financial plan for 2006-2008; and the design of quick-impact economic programmes for short-term employment generation. Those issues were important elements of the foundations for economic recovery, good governance and eventual statehood.

The Palestinian presidential election, held in January, was complicated by the continuing Israeli occupation and restrictions on freedom of movement imposed in the Occupied Palestinian Territory. However, voter turnout was high. Mahmoud Abbas, who won with 62.5 per cent of the votes, was elected President. Elections for the Palestinian Legislative Council were scheduled to be held in January 2006. The PA leadership sought to encourage groups engaged in terrorism to abandon that course and engage in the democratic process.

At the Sharm el-Sheikh summit in February 2005, convened by Egypt and with the participation of Jordan, the parties pledged to end all violence. Israel agreed to release a number of Palestinian prisoners and transfer control of five West Bank cities to the PA. However, while Israel released a number of prisoners, it transferred control of only two of the five cities agreed upon and resumed its policy of extrajudicial killings. Nevertheless, the Israeli Defence Force (IDF) exercised restraint in its military activities in the period prior to disengagement, despite incidents of Palestinian violence and halted its policy of demolishing Palestinian houses.

The Palestinian security services remained divided, weak, overstaffed, badly motivated and under-armed. A number of unintegrated forces, Palestinian clans and individual force commanders continued to wield undue influence. They were also hampered by corruption, institutional hierarchies, cults of personality and lack of cohesive training. The security services were consolidated into three main branches—the national forces, the intelligence forces and the police—under the supervision of the Ministry of Interior. New heads of those services were appointed and the security retirement law implemented. President Abbas stressed his commitment to work towards the PA's monopoly on the use of force.

Israel, for its part, did not make progress in implementing its core commitments under the June 2003 road map [YUN 2003, p. 461]. Settlement expansion and lack of action on removing illegal settlement outposts erected since 2001 undermined trust in Israel's intentions. In early 2005, Israel announced plans to construct 3,500 new housing units in Ma'ale Adumim and two other settlement blocs in the West Bank.

On 6 May [S/2005/306], the Secretary-General informed the Security Council President of his intention to appoint Alvaro de Soto (Peru) as the United Nations Special Coordinator for the Middle East Peace Process and as his Personal Representative to the Palestinian Liberation Organization (PLO) and the PA. He succeeded Terje Roed-Larsen (Norway), who served in that position from 1 October 1999 to 31 December 2004. Mr. de Soto would coordinate all UN activities on the ground related to the Middle East peace process; ensure that the Organization's contribution was fully integrated and coordinated; represent the Secretary-General in all meetings and structures involving the parties and the international community and provide political guidance to the UN family. On 10 May [S/2005/307], the Council took note of the Secretary-General's intention.

Occupied Palestinian Territory

Presidential elections and related developments

Security Council consideration (January). The Security Council met on 13 January [meeting 5111] to discuss the situation in the Middle East, including the Palestinian question.

The Under-Secretary-General for Political Affairs, Kieran Prendergast, said that a real opportunity existed to start implementing the road map and moving toward a settlement of the conflict. The election of a new PA President, Mahmoud Abbas, on 9 January, in a politically competitive, yet peaceful atmosphere, marked the successful completion by the Palestinians of another critical step in the democratic transition in the Occupied Palestinian Territory. Israel played a commendable part in facilitating the elections. Its forces generally allowed free movement and reduced their own activity inside the Palestinian areas on election day.

The United Nations continued to support the Palestinian Central Elections Commission and provided technical assistance for the preparation and conduct of the elections. The United Nations Liaison Support Unit facilitated contacts with Palestinian and Israeli authorities and assisted the international observers. UN technical support to the Palestinians would continue for the elections to the Palestinian Legislative Council. A new Israeli coalition Government was also in place to tackle the implementation of Prime Minister Ariel Sharon's 2004 withdrawal plan [YUN 2004, p. 455]. The new Cabinet was expected to decide in late January on the evacuation of settlements in the Gaza Strip and parts of the northern West Bank. Prime Minister Sharon's plan should be implemented as part of the road map [YUN 2003, p. 464] and in coordination with the new Israeli Government and the new Palestinian leadership.

In the period prior to the 9 January elections, Palestinian militants fired some 210 Qassam rockets and mortar shells against Israeli settlements in Gaza and civilian targets inside Israel. The marked increase in attacks came despite public calls by PLO Chairman Abbas to end rocket attacks against Israeli targets. During the same period, Israeli forces conducted 40 military incursions and bulldozing operations, causing death and injury to Palestinian civilians, as well as militants. On 4 January [A/ES-10/293-S/2005/2], eight Palestinian civilians were killed, including at least five children from the same family, when an Israeli tank shell hit an agricultural area in Beit Lahia.

As requested by the General Assembly in resolution ES-10/15 [YUN 2004, p. 465], the Secretary-General, on 11 January, sent a letter to the Assembly President setting out a framework for the establishment of a register of damage in connection with the barrier. It would consist of an independent board, legal and technical experts and a small secretariat—a registry. The board would have overall responsibility for the register and would establish rules and regulations governing the registry's work. The registry would focus on the technical task of gathering claims of damage relating to the construction of the barrier.

The construction of the barrier and restrictions on movement in the form of checkpoints, curfews and the permit system were the chief reasons for the continuing socio-economic crisis in the Palestinian areas. Lifting those restrictions on freedom of movement was indispensable to economic recovery. The PA's stability—and with it, prospects for real and tangible reform and political progress—was crucially dependent on a sound fiscal base. Despite its strong 2004 revenue performance, the PA remained under pressure, owing to lower than expected disbursement of external budget support and a growing wage bill. December 2004 salaries could be paid only as a result of a $20 million contribution from the United States and the release of arrears of tax remittances by Israel.

Both parties had important steps to take. Israeli settlement activity—including the natural growth of settlements—had not been frozen, as Israel was obliged to do under the road map. In 2004, the number of people living in the West Bank and Gaza strip settlements rose by 6 per cent. On the Palestinian side, there was the need to establish credible and reformed institutions and to put an end to the violence and terror. It was crucial that Palestinian reform efforts be supported, especially in the areas of security and governance, and that the PA was financially secure and able to meet the humanitarian needs of the population. In that context, the United Nations welcomed the initiative of United Kingdom Prime Minister, Tony Blair, to convene an international meeting (see p. 507) to discuss important issues on the agenda of the new Palestinian leadership. Coordination between the parties and active support from the international community were needed to achieve a successful disengagement plan that would lead to further steps in the implementation of the road map and the resumption of full peace negotiations.

SECURITY COUNCIL ACTION (January)

On 13 January [meeting 5111], following consultations among Security Council members, the President made statement **S/PRST/2005/2** on behalf of the Council:

> The Security Council welcomes the Palestinian presidential election held on 9 January 2005. It commends the credible and fair character of the vote and congratulates the Palestinian people who demonstrated their commitment to democracy by participating in the election under challenging conditions. The Council pays tribute to the Central Elections

Commission which played a key role in ensuring the successful conclusion of the election, and expresses its appreciation for the contribution of international observers and for the support of the United Nations.

> The Council congratulates the newly elected President of the Palestinian Authority on his election.

> The Council looks forward to the convening of the Palestinian legislative elections in the near future, and affirms its continuing support for the Palestinian people in their democratic process.

> The Council supports the Palestinian Authority and its efforts to pursue the process of strengthening institutions.

> The Council underlines the importance of enhanced and expeditious international assistance to the Palestinian people and the Palestinian Authority.

> The Council stresses the need for the full implementation of the Quartet Road map, as endorsed by the Council in its resolution 1515(2003), for the creation of an independent, viable, democratic and sovereign State of Palestine living side by side with Israel in peace and security.

> The Council calls upon Israelis and Palestinians to relaunch a genuine political process and advance towards a just and lasting peace in the region.

Communications (18-26 January). The Permanent Observer of Palestine, in an 18 January letter to the Secretary-General and the Council President [A/ES-10/295-S/2005/38], said that the situation in the Occupied Palestinian Territory continued to be marred by instability, escalating tensions and violence. Israeli forces continued to raid and launch military attacks against civilian areas. The situation in the Gaza Strip, in particular, continued to be critical. On 15 and 16 January, four Palestinians were killed and two others wounded by Israeli forces in Gaza. IDF had also closed all border crossings into and out of Gaza. On 26 January [A/ES-10/296-S/2005/46], the Permanent Observer said that IDF, on that day, killed four Palestinian civilians. In addition, Israel had resumed construction of a section of the separation wall by the settlement of Ariel, located 12 miles into the West Bank, despite the 2004 advisory opinion by the International Court of Justice (ICJ) on its illegality [YUN 2004, p. 465]. Israel also continued to confiscate Palestinian land in Jerusalem and to enact unlawful measures in its drive to entrench its annexation of the city.

For its part, Israel said that between 9 and 18 January [A/59/678-S/2005/40], Palestinian gunmen killed eight Israelis and wounded some 15 others. The worst attack occurred on 13 January in northern Gaza, when six Israeli civilians were killed and five wounded. Israel said that there was little evidence that the new Palestinian leadership was serious about confronting Palestinian terrorism. The window of opportunity for progress in the peace process would close if the Palestinian leaders continued to fail to abide by their road map's obligations.

Sharm el-Sheikh meeting

A summit meeting between President Abbas and Prime Minister Sharon took place in Sharm el-Sheikh, Egypt, on 8 February, hosted by Egyptian President Hosni Mubarak, in the presence of Jordan's King Abdullah II. At the meeting, President Abbas and Prime Minister Sharon reaffirmed their commitment to the road map and agreed that "all Palestinians [would] stop all acts of violence against Israelis everywhere" and that "Israel [would] cease all its military activity against all Palestinians everywhere".

SECURITY COUNCIL ACTION (February)

On 16 February [meeting 5126], following consultations among Security Council members, the President made statement **S/PRST/2005/6** on behalf of the Council:

> The Security Council welcomes the summit held in Sharm El-Sheikh, Egypt, on 8 February 2005, and the resumption of direct talks between the Prime Minister of Israel, Mr. Ariel Sharon, and the President of the Palestinian Authority, Mr. Mahmoud Abbas. The Council expresses its appreciation to Mr. Hosni Mubarak, President of the Arab Republic of Egypt, for the invitation to both parties to the summit, and to King Abdullah II bin Al Hussein of Jordan for his participation.
>
> The Council underlines the understandings reached by the Government of Israel and the Palestinian Authority, in particular that all Palestinians will stop all acts of violence against all Israelis everywhere and that Israel will cease all its military activities against all Palestinians everywhere. The Council calls for the full respect by the parties of their commitments in this regard.
>
> The Council recognizes these understandings, along with other recent positive developments, as primary steps towards restoring confidence between the two parties and as a significant opportunity to enhance a new spirit of cooperation and to promote an atmosphere conducive to the establishment of peace and coexistence in the region.
>
> The Council commends the role being played by Egypt and Jordan in facilitating a successful resumption of dialogue between the Government of Israel and the Palestinian Authority within the framework of the road map.
>
> The Council welcomes the initiative of the Government of the United Kingdom of Great Britain and Northern Ireland in convening an international meeting in London on 1 March 2005 to support Palestinian efforts to prepare the ground for a viable Palestinian State. The Council also welcomes the upcoming meeting of the Quartet at the ministerial level which will convene in the margins of the London meeting.
>
> The Council looks forward to further engagement by the Quartet with the two parties to ensure continued progress in the peace process and the full implementation of the road map and relevant Council resolutions, including resolutions 242(1967), 338(1973), 1397(2002) and 1515(2003), towards the creation of an independent, viable, democratic and sovereign State of Palestine living side by side with Israel in peace and security.
>
> The Council looks forward to the establishment of a just, lasting and comprehensive peace in the Middle East.

Post-electoral period.

Communication (22 February). In identical letters to the Secretary-General and the Security Council President [A/ES-10/297-S/2005/101], the Permanent Observer of Palestine said that, on 20 February, the Israeli Government approved the final route of the separation wall. If completed, the new route of the wall would result in the de facto annexation of at least seven per cent of the total area of the West Bank, not including the area of East Jerusalem. The wall was severing and isolating cities, towns and villages in the West bank, imprisoning thousands of civilians in walled enclaves and causing the complete encirclement of East Jerusalem, isolating it from the rest of the West Bank.

Security Council consideration (February). The Security Council, on 22 February [meeting 5128], discussed the situation in the Middle East, including the Palestinian question.

The Under-Secretary-General for Political Affairs, Mr. Prendergast, said that the latest developments had rekindled hopes for progress towards peace between Israel and the Palestinians. Israel announced that it would release 900 prisoners and withdraw from five West Bank cities and the surrounding areas. On 21 February, 500 Palestinian prisoners were released. Israel also halted punitive house demolitions, reopened three crossing points into Gaza and issued more work permits. Most significantly, Prime Minister Sharon reiterated his readiness to coordinate with the Palestinians the disengagement plan from the Gaza Strip and parts of the northern West Bank. The first meetings to that effect had taken place between Israel's Vice Premier, Shimon Peres, and senior Palestinian officials to begin coordinating the civilian and economic aspects of Israel's withdrawal. On 20 February, the Israeli Cabinet approved in principle the evacuation of settlements under the disengagement plan. The Knesset (Parliament) also demonstrated support for the Prime Minister by passing, on 16 February, the Compensation and Evacuation Law, which represented an essential step in carrying out the withdrawal plan.

On the Palestinian side, the PA deployed 1,000 security officers along the Gaza Strip's northern border with Israel, and hundreds more in the central and southern districts of Gaza. Fulfilling an important obligation under the road map, President Abbas restructured the security services into three main branches (see p. 504), all of which would report to the PA Minister of the Interior.

During the period under review, 54 Palestinians and 8 Israelis were killed, and 150 Palestinians and 46 Israelis injured. On 13 January, Hamas, the Popular Resistance Committees and the Al-Aqsa Martyrs Brigade attacked the Karni crossing between Israel and the Gaza Strip, killing six Israeli civilians (see above). In response, Israel announced that it would temporarily cut all ties with the PA, and renewed military incursions into Palestinian areas, which had been suspended since the Palestinian presidential elections.

On 20 February, the Israeli Cabinet approved the revised route of Israel's barrier in the West Bank, which, although it had been moved closer to the Green Line, still incorporated a large amount of Palestinian land. To the south of Jerusalem, the new route placed the Gush Etzion settlement block on the Israeli side of the barrier and surrounded four Palestinian villages, plus a sizeable amount of Palestinian agricultural land. Barrier construction restarted in the Salfit area of the northern West Bank around the settlement of Ariel, raising concerns that large amounts of Palestinian territory might end up being incorporated on the Israeli side. Barrier activity also intensified in the Jerusalem area, where a large number of confiscation orders were served to landowners.

The Under-Secretary-General stated that the United Nations recognized Israel's right and duty to protect its people against terrorist attacks, but urged it to address its legitimate security needs in ways that did not increase suffering among Palestinians, prejudge final status issues or threaten longer-term prospects for peace by making the creation of a viable and contiguous Palestinian state more difficult.

London meetings

On 1 March, the United Kingdom hosted the 2005 London Meeting on Supporting the PA, which was attended by representatives of the Quartet, including the Secretary-General. PA President Abbas presented his plans for building the institutions needed to underpin a future viable Palestinian State. The central aim of the Meeting was to help the Palestinian leadership strengthen PA institutions. The Quartet, the World Bank, the International Monetary Fund, the Arab League and 20 national delegations

agreed to, among other things, support the PA's plans on governance, security and economic development; address the PA's short-term economic priorities and hold an international donors' meeting to address the long-term challenges; galvanise international private sector involvement; and streamline the international structures for supporting Palestinian reform and economic development. The international community also agreed to support Palestinian efforts to prepare for Israeli withdrawal from Gaza and parts of the West Bank.

Quartet meeting (1 March). Following the London Meeting on Supporting the PA (see above), representatives of the Quartet met in London. They condemned the terrorist attack that occurred in Tel Aviv on 25 February (see above). The Quartet welcomed President Abbas' condemnation of that attack and his pledge to act against those responsible, and stressed the need for further action by the PA to prevent acts of terrorism. The Quartet recognized the importance of the Sharm el-Sheikh summit of 8 February (see p. 506) at which both parties called for a halt to violence and military activities. It commended the Israeli cabinet's decision to withdraw from Gaza and parts of the West Bank and reiterated that withdrawal from those areas should be full and complete and undertaken in a manner consistent with the road map. The Quartet reiterated its view that no party should undertake unilateral actions that could prejudge the resolution of final status issues. It welcomed the London Meeting and urged the international community to review and energize donor coordination structures, with a view to increasing their effectiveness.

SECURITY COUNCIL ACTION (9 March)

On 9 March [meeting 5136], following consultations among Security Council members, the President made statement **S/PRST/2005/12** on behalf of the Council:

> The Security Council welcomes the conclusions of the London Meeting on Supporting the Palestinian Authority, held on 1 March 2005. The Council supports the objectives of the London Meeting to help the Palestinian leadership to strengthen the institutions needed for a viable and independent Palestinian State.
>
> The Council hopes that the London Meeting will be part of the longer-term process of international support to the Palestinian people and the Palestinian Authority and a contribution to helping both sides to implement the road map endorsed by the Council in its resolution 1515(2003) and agreed to by the parties as the path towards a lasting comprehensive negotiated settlement to the Middle East conflict, based on Council resolutions 242(1967), 338 (1973) and 1397(2002).

The Council stresses the crucial importance of security, good governance and development of the Palestinian economy. In this context, the Council welcomes President Abbas's comprehensive plan presented at the London Meeting for strengthening the institutions of the Palestinian Authority in these three areas.

The Council stresses the key role of the international community in assisting the Palestinian Authority in taking forward this plan. The Council welcomes the international community's commitments to respond to the plans of the Palestinian Authority by providing financial and political support. The Council recognizes the important role of the Quartet in international efforts aimed at providing assistance to the Palestinian Authority in the fields of security, economic development and governance.

The Council supports the proposals for follow-up to the London Meeting and looks forward to their early implementation.

The Council supports the Joint Statement of the Quartet issued following the meeting of the Quartet held in the margins of the London Meeting, and looks forward to the Quartet's active engagement over the forthcoming period, while recognizing also the important role of other interested parties.

The Council reiterates its call for full respect by the Government of Israel and the Palestinian Authority of understandings reached at the Sharm El-Sheikh summit on 8 February 2005, in particular that all Palestinians will stop all acts of violence against all Israelis everywhere and that Israel will cease all its military activities against all Palestinians everywhere.

The Council reiterates its call upon both Israel and the Palestinian Authority to ensure continued progress in the peace process towards full implementation of the road map in direct contact with the Quartet. It stresses the need for concerted and sustained action by the Palestinian Authority to fulfil its security-related commitments and welcomes in this context President Abbas' commitment to exert every effort towards that end. The Council stresses also the need for Israel to implement its road map commitments.

The Council reiterates its demand for immediate cessation of all acts of violence, including all acts of terror, provocation, incitement and destruction.

The Council reiterates its commitment to the vision of two States, Israel and Palestine, living side by side in peace and security.

Further political and security developments

Communication (23 March). On 23 March [A/ES-10/298-S/2005/202], the Permanent Observer of Palestine said that on 21 March, the Israeli Government confirmed its approval of plans to build 3,500 more housing units in the Ma'ale Adumim settlement, the largest Israeli settlement in the Occupied Palestinian Territory.

Security Council consideration (March). The Security Council, on 24 March [meeting 5149], met to discuss the situation in the Middle East, including the Palestinian question.

The Under-Secretary-General for Political Affairs reported that the Secretary-General visited Israel and the Occupied Palestinian Territory from 13 to 16 March, at the invitation of the Israeli Government, to attend the inauguration of the new Holocaust History Museum at Yad Vashem. The Secretary-General used the occasion to hold meetings with Israeli and Palestinian leaders, including Prime Minister Sharon and President Abbas. During those discussions, Israeli leaders emphasized that their overriding concern was for the PA to move from words to action and to take steps to bring to justice those who organized and perpetrated terrorist acts, noting that the dismantlement of terrorist organizations and infrastructure was a Palestinian obligation under the road map.

PA leaders expressed frustration over Israel's refusal to ease closures significantly or to release large numbers of prisoners, particularly those with significant influence among Palestinians, and over the delays in the full implementation of 8 February Sharm el-Sheikh commitments. Without such confidence-building steps, they would be unable to consolidate popular support for the peace process. Palestinian interlocutors were also concerned by what they described as continuing unilateral acts by Israel. The respective presentations by the parties impressed on the Secretary-General the immediate and urgent need to rebuild trust and restore confidence. He urged the parties to engage in direct dialogue and negotiations. The Secretary-General also said that the United Nations remained committed to supporting the PA in the areas of security reform and elections.

The Israeli disengagement plan was discussed extensively. The Secretary-General was left with a strong impression of Prime Minister Sharon's determination to proceed with the plan, even in the face of serious domestic opposition. The Secretary-General emphasized the importance of all aspects of the withdrawal being fully coordinated and that the withdrawal was an important step in a broader process and should be consistent with the road map and its goals. Prime Minister Sharon cautioned that the timely implementation of the withdrawal initiative could be jeopardized if the Knesset failed to approve the budget·before the end of March, which would cause the Government to fall and new elections to be held automatically.

After his visit to Israel, the Secretary-General travelled to Algiers to attend the Arab Summit (see below). He welcomed the decision taken by Arab leaders to relaunch the Arab peace initiative, as approved at the 2002 Beirut Summit [YUN

2002, p. 419], as Arab involvement in the peace process was essential.

The Under-Secretary-General said that the United Nations continued to be concerned over Israel's failure to dismantle settlement outposts and freeze their expansion. The Israeli Government's report on outposts by former Chief State Prosecutor Talia Sasson found that various ministries, as well as IDF and the World Zionist Organization, had supported construction of unauthorized outposts. The Cabinet approved the report on 13 March, including the core recommendation that the Government should take responsibility for what was happening in the outposts in the territories. However, there were unofficial reports of a Government decision to approve the building of at least 3,500 new settlement housing units in 2005, linking the major Israeli settlement of Ma'ale Adumim to Jerusalem. A halt to such actions was needed to preserve hope of a viable future for the Palestinian people.

During the reporting period, implementation of the commitments made at the 8 February Sharm el-Sheikh summit continued, but not as quickly as expected. It was only on 16 March that outstanding issues related to the handover of Jericho—the first of five West Bank cities and their environs to be transferred to Palestinian control—were fully resolved. Tulkarem was handed over on 21 March after similar delays. Negotiations on the transfer of Bethlehem, Qalqiliya and Ramallah were under way, but difficulties remained. The transfer of three other major urban centres in the West Bank—Nablus, Jenin and Hebron—would be discussed by the parties at a later date. Meanwhile, the joint Israeli-Palestinian ministerial committee on Palestinian prisoners did not reach agreement on the release of an additional 400 Palestinian prisoners. Only 16 out of 60 Palestinian deportees were allowed to return to Bethlehem so far.

Communications. On 20 April [A/ES-10/301-S/2005/262], the Chairman of the Committee on the Exercise of the Inalienable Rights of the Palestinian People (Committee on Palestinian Rights) expressed deep concern at Israel's settlement activities in the Occupied Palestinian Territory. He said that, on 18 April, the Israel Lands Authority announced that tenders had been issued for the construction of 50 homes in the settlement of "Elkana" in the West Bank. In March, the Israeli Government had made public its intention to construct some 3,500 homes in the area between East Jerusalem and the Ma'ale Adumim settlement, effectively cutting off East Jerusalem from the rest of the West Bank. In mid-April, construction activity in Ma'ale Adumim continued, despite international criticism. Israel's pol-

icy precluded the possibility of establishing a viable and contiguous Palestinian State, prejudged the outcome of final status negotiations and undermined international efforts at achieving a comprehensive, just and lasting peace in the Middle East.

On 18 April [S/2005/274], the Permanent Observer of the League of Arab States (LAS) transmitted to the Council President the texts of the resolutions and the Algiers Declaration adopted by the LAS Council at its seventeenth session (Algiers, Algeria, 22-23 March), which the Secretary-General attended. The LAS Council reaffirmed that the 2002 Arab peace initiative was fundamental to a peaceful, just, comprehensive and lasting settlement in the region. The Council rejected all efforts to pre-empt the outcome of final status negotiations, and stressed that the Israeli withdrawal from the Gaza Strip and parts of the West Bank had to take place in the framework of the road map. The Council, among other things, invited all Arab States to support the PA's budget.

Security Council consideration (April). At the Security Council's 21 April meeting [meeting 5166] to discuss the situation in the Middle East, including the Palestinian question, the Under-Secretary-General for Political Affairs said that, on 14 April, the Quartet principals named James D. Wolfensohn (United States) as their Special Envoy to coordinate the international community's efforts in support of Israel's disengagement initiative. His task was to promote coordination and cooperation between Israel and the PA. (For further information on the Special Envoy, see p. 513.)

Meanwhile, Prime Minister Sharon had overcome the remaining official challenges to his withdrawal initiative. On 28 March, the Knesset rejected draft legislation to introduce a national referendum on disengagement and the next day passed the 2005 State budget, thereby averting the need for new elections. Israeli preparations for evacuating and relocating Israeli settlers went ahead, notwithstanding continued opposition from a militant minority.

On the Palestinian side, both President Abbas and Prime Minister Ahmed Qurei announced that the PA was prepared to coordinate the withdrawal with Israel, despite the PA's political concerns regarding the plan. President Abbas established a ministerial committee for coordination, headed by the Prime Minister, with ministers assigned to sectoral subcommittees tasked with preparing for the pullout and developing longer-term strategies for the post disengagement period. PA Prime Minister Qurei and Israeli Defence Minister Mofaz and Minister Dahlam met on 21 April to discuss the economic and military aspects of the disengagament.

Despite the doubts and the difficult challenges ahead, the hope and optimism of the past months remained. That was confirmed by the continued overall decline in casualties, violence and military operations. However, there was an apparent failure to break the tendency towards retributive violence, so that even one incident carried with it the risk of escalation. Israel justified its military incursions, arrest campaigns, curfews and movement restrictions as necessary to confront and preempt security threats. Israel charged that the PA was not taking serious action against violence and militants. Palestinian leaders, for their part, claimed that they were taking action but acknowledged the slow and difficult nature of the process. They believed that Israeli military operations were counterproductive, in that they made it more difficult for the PA to disarm or arrest militants and threatened the viability of the ceasefire. At the same time, Al-Aqsa militants had become the main disrupters of law and order, threatening PA officials and ordinary citizens alike. In response, President Abbas declared a state of alert and reshuffled the security forces in the West Bank. He subsequently announced his intention to disarm those Fatah militants who were on Israel's wanted list and to integrate them into the PA's security agencies. In addition, President Abbas issued a presidential decree enforcing the security forces pension bill, which would lead to the retirement of some 2,000 security staff.

The Under-Secretary-General observed that, although those actions and announcements were positive, they were not enough. Security reform and a visible and sustained effort to stop all violent activity were basic requirements of the road map. As such, they could not be a matter for compromise and the will to act had to come from the PA. However, there was also much that Israel could do to support, rather than hinder, President Abbas' ability to take difficult steps. The joint Israeli-Palestinian committees dealing with fugitives, prisoners and the transfer of major urban centres in the West Bank did not meet in the past month. Security control was not transferred in any of the Palestinian cities during that period; nor were any prisoners released. The United Nations also noted with great concern that Prime Minister Sharon had publicly reiterated his commitment to implementing a plan aimed at connecting Jerusalem with Ma'ale Adumim, the largest West Bank settlement and the announcement (see p. 509) that bids were being invited for the construction of 50 housing units in the West Bank settlement of Elkan. In that connection, United States President George Bush, after a meeting with Prime Minister Sharon, said that Israel should not undertake any activity that contravened road map obligations or prejudiced final status negotiations, and that Israel should meet its road map obligations regarding settlements in the West Bank and remove unauthorized outposts. The Under-Secretary-General said that President Bush's statement represented the position of all four members of the Quartet.

Quartet meeting (9 May). Representatives of the Quartet—the UN Secretary-General, the Russian Foreign Minister, the United States Secretary of State and the High Representative for European Common Foreign Policy and Security Policy—met in Moscow, the Russian Federation, on 9 May to review developments in the Middle East. The Quartet, in a statement issued at the end of its meeting [A/59/803-S/2005/314], urged Israel and the PA to renew efforts to fulfil the commitments they had agreed to at the Sharm el-Sheikh summit in order to maintain momentum. It reiterated its commitment to the two-state solution and to Israeli withdrawal as a way to re-energize the road map. The Quartet affirmed that a new Palestinian state had to be truly viable, with contiguity in the West Bank, that a state of scattered territories would not work and that no party should take unilateral actions that could prejudge final status issues. The Quartet also affirmed that the two-state vision and the road map were the best means of achieving a negotiated settlement leading to permanent peace and an end to the occupation.

The Quartet expressed its full support for James Wolfensohn, its Special Envoy for Gaza Disengagement, whose task was to focus on the non-security aspects of withdrawal, particularly disposition of assets; passages, access and trade; and revival of the Palestinian economy during and after the Israeli withdrawal. In that regard, both Israel and the Palestinians would have to cooperate closely to identify and implement actions and policies that would ensure a smooth and successful implementation of the Israeli initiative. The Palestinian side would have to demonstrate a strong commitment to security reform and performance, and to building transparent, accountable government institutions and an investor-friendly climate, with a view to restoring growth. The Israeli side would need to relieve the economic hardships faced by the Palestinian people, facilitate rehabilitation and reconstruction by easing the system of restrictions on the movement of Palestinian people and goods, and take further steps to respect the dignity of the Palestinian people and improve their quality of life, while not endangering Israeli security.

The Quartet recognized that economic development and progress on security went hand in hand, as security reforms and the re-establishment of the rule of law were necessary to creating an enabling environment for economic growth and political progress. The Quartet also recognized the need for continued efforts by the international community to assist the PA in accomplishing those tasks, including rebuilding the capabilities of the Palestinian security services. It expressed its full support for General William Ward, United States Security Coordinator, who was assisting the Palestinians in reforming and reconstructing their security forces and coordinating international assistance in that regard. The Quartet welcomed the steps taken by President Abbas to reform the Palestinian security services and stressed the need for continued implementation of those reforms in order to reinstate permanently law and order in Gaza and the West Bank.

Communication (17 May). On 17 May [A/ES-10/302-S/2005/321], the Permanent Observer of Palestine said that the Israeli Government had announced its intention to continue with its plans to extend the wall around the Ma'ale Adumim settlement and to begin construction of another section connecting the "Gush Etzion" settlement to Jerusalem from the South.

Security Council consideration (May). The Security Council, on 18 May [meeting 5181], heard a briefing by the Under-Secretary-General for Political Affairs. He said that, on 9 May, Prime Minister Sharon announced a three-week delay of the Gaza disengagement because of a traditional Jewish period of mourning. The practical preparations for the withdrawal, however, were progressing, as were the Israeli Government's efforts to find acceptable solutions for the relocation of settlers. Direct talks were renewed on 21 April between Israel and the PA on the disengagement plan.

The level of violence between Palestinians and Israelis remained far below that which prevailed before the Sharm el-Sheikh summit. However, there were reports of a slow but steady increase in violent incidents, including attacks by Palestinian militants against Israelis, clashes between Israeli security forces and Palestinian protestors and Israeli arrest operations against wanted militants.

As to the implementation of the Sharm el-Sheikh commitments, the Under-Secretary-General worried that further delays in handing over the remaining three Palestinian cities and in releasing prisoners threatened to undermine President Abbas. It would be difficult for the PA to undertake sustained and sustainable action on

security unless it was aided and supported in its efforts to rein in the militants. A significant step forward in that regard was Israel's reported approval of the deployment of hundreds of armed Palestinian police in all West Bank cities in order to strengthen the PA ahead of the transfer of further areas to Palestinian security control.

On 5 May, Palestinians held a second round of local elections in 84 municipalities in Gaza and the West Bank. Hamas won a substantial share of the vote and of the municipal councils, which was an indication of the support the militants enjoyed among the Palestinian population, partly as a result of their engagement in social welfare activities. At the same time, it also reflected popular frustration with the PA. As part of preparations for the 17 July legislative elections, the Palestinian Legislative Council approved a revised electoral law, which envisioned a mix of constituency-based and national representation.

The United Nations remained concerned about the continued construction of Israel's barrier in the West Bank. On Monday, 16 May, the Israeli High Court of Justice rescinded the temporary injunctions it had previously imposed on the construction of the barrier around the West Bank settlement of Ariel.

Communications (19 May–7 June). The fifteenth session of the Ministerial Meeting between the Gulf Cooperation Council States (GCC) and the EU (Manama, Bahrain, 5 April) [A/59/805-S/2005/327] welcomed, in a 19 May joint communiqué, the prospect of Israel's withdrawal from Gaza and from certain parts of the northern West Bank as an initial stage in the process towards achieving a lasting peace in the Middle East. They also welcomed the steps taken by the PA to address the security issue and called on it to continue in that regard. Both sides called on the Israeli Government to take further action to alleviate the suffering of the Palestinians by lifting prohibitions on movement, and reversing its settlement policy and the construction of the so-called security fence in the Palestinian territory, including in and around East Jerusalem.

On 6 June [A/ES-10/303-S/2005/372], in identical letters addressed to the Secretary-General and the Council President, the Permanent Observer of Palestine said that 5 June 2005 marked 38 years since the onset of Israel's occupation of Palestinian territory, including East Jerusalem. Israel continued to undertake unilateral and concrete measures that were altering the situation on the ground and would negatively influence the outcome of any final settlement between the two sides.

The ninety-fifth regular session of the Ministerial Council of GCC (Riyadh, Saudi Arabia, 11

June) [A/59/845-S/2005/386] noted that a just and comprehensive peace in the Middle East would not be achieved unless the principle of land for peace was applied and a lasting independent Palestinian State established with Jerusalem as its capital, existing alongside the State of Israel in peace and security, in addition to Israel's withdrawal from the occupied Syrian Golan to the line of 4 June 1967.

Security Council consideration (June). The Under-Secretary-General for Political Affairs, in his 17 June [meeting 5206] briefing to the Security Council, said that Israeli and Palestinian authorities were slowly, and not without difficulty, coordinating the implementation of Israel's withdrawal from Gaza and parts of the northern West Bank. Confidence-building measures were also being discussed. A variety of bilateral meetings were also held to discuss questions such as the assets of settlements and their eventual fate. Israelis and Palestinians agreed to continue their coordination on security matters at the ministerial, planning and operational levels. According to the United States Security Coordinator, an improved atmosphere and increased willingness to engage in coordination characterized the latest cooperative efforts between the parties. On the Palestinian side, an integrated team comprising top-level personnel from the three security services was set up, and planning was proceeding based on a timeline provided by the Israeli side. Some progress was also made on the implementation of the February Sharm el-Sheikh understandings. On 29 May, the Israeli cabinet approved the release of an additional 400 Palestinian prisoners, 398 of whom were released on 2 June.

In Israel, opponents to the disengagement were still vocal and resorted to protests, demonstrations and, in some cases, acts of sabotage and civil disobedience. The Government nevertheless pressed ahead with its plans to relocate the evacuated settlers and remained committed to the full and timely withdrawal. The PA also faced a number of serious internal challenges, partly as a result of its efforts to institute comprehensive security reform. On 2 June, Palestinian military intelligence forces went on a rampage in the Gaza Strip.

Against the backdrop of increased internal challenges and disorder, violence between Palestinians and Israelis continued to pose a serious threat to the safety and security of both peoples. Of particular concern, was the escalation in rocket and mortar attacks by Palestinian militants against Israeli targets. During the reporting period, IDF resumed the practice of targeting from the air Palestinian militants engaged in suspicious activity. Despite the serious nature of those various incidents, there was evidence of a serious effort on the Palestinian side to maintain the calm and, on the Israeli side, of determination not to overreact to isolated incidents. The Under-Secretary-General expressed concern, however, over statements by some Palestinian factions that they no longer felt bound by their earlier pledge to maintain a ceasefire. He also repeated his concern that Israel was not living up to its road map obligations. In particular, Israel's construction of the barrier encroached upon Palestinian land and threatened to prejudge eventual bilateral negotiations between the parties.

Quartet meeting (23 June). Representatives of the Quartet, meeting in London on 23 June, reaffirmed their support for the Israeli withdrawal from Gaza and parts of the northern West Bank and an orderly Palestinian takeover in those areas. Noting that less than two months remained until the announced start of the disengagement, the Quartet called on Israelis and Palestinians to work together towards that end. It reiterated its full support for the Quartet's Special Envoy for Gaza Disengagement in his efforts to assist with the non-security aspects of disengagement and revival of the Palestinian economy: strengthening the overall capacity of the PA; facilitating legal and judicial reform; completing the reform of the financial system to establish a sound, transparent regulatory regime; and implementing anti-corruption efforts, a comprehensive budget strategy and wage and pension reform. Private sector job creation and a vibrant civil society sector were also critical. The Quartet urged Israel to take immediate steps, without endangering its security, to relieve the economic hardships faced by the Palestinian people and to facilitate rehabilitation and reconstruction by easing the flow of goods and people in and out of Gaza and the West Bank and between them.

The Quartet noted that peace and security were essential for political and economic revival and stressed that the Palestinians had to confront violence and terror in order for political and economic life to flourish. It urged both parties to avoid and prevent any escalation in violence so that the Israeli withdrawal could proceed peacefully. The Quartet condemned the upsurge in violence in Gaza, including the firing of mortars and Qassam rockets into Israeli towns and homes. In that regard, the Quartet welcomed the PA's full cooperation with General William Ward, the United States Security Coordinator, in assisting them to reform and restructure their security forces. Rapid reform of the security services and restructuring of the rule of law were essential for improving security for Palestinians and Israelis alike. The Quartet also expressed its concern over settlement activity.

Quartet Special Envoy. On 28 June [S/2005/432], the Secretary-General requested the Security Council President to confirm support for the establishment of an office in Jerusalem for the Quartet's Special Envoy for Gaza Disengagement, Mr. Wolfensohn. He would also provide logistical, technical and financial assistance to support the office. The Envoy's mandate began on 1 June and was due to end on 31 December 2005. On 5 July [S/2005/433], the Council confirmed support for the arrangements proposed by the Secretary-General.

On 13 December [S/2005/797], the Secretary-General informed the Council President that the Quartet had decided to extend Mr. Wolfensohn's mandate for a further three months until 31 March 2006. The Quartet's Special Envoy would continue to work on issues related to disengagement and to coordinate the international community's efforts to ensure recovery of the economy in Gaza, in preparation for a Consultative Group meeting of donors scheduled for 21 March 2006. On 16 December [S/2005/798], the Council welcomed the proposed arrangements set out in the Secretary-General's letter.

Security situation

In communications dated between 28 February and 18 August [A/ES-10/293-S/2005/2, A/59/717-S/2005/130, A/ES-10/298-S/2005/202, A/ES-10/299-S/2005/237, A/59/829-S/2005/375, A/59/854-S/2005/410, A/59/870-S/2005/452, A/59/873-S/2005/457, A/ES-10/305-S/2005/530, A/59/905-S/2005/552], both Israel and Palestine brought to the attention of the Secretary-General and the Security Council President information on attacks committed by either side.

Israel said that on 25 February a Palestinian suicide bomber blew himself up in Tel Aviv, killing five civilians and wounding 50 others. The terrorist organization Islamic Jihad announced responsibility for the attack from its headquarters in Damascus, Syria. Despite the toll in Israeli lives claimed by the attack, Israel continued to exercise restraint and hoped that the new Palestinian leadership would meet its obligations and adopt a zero tolerance policy for terrorism. On 19 May, Palestinian terrorists fired over 40 mortar shells at Israeli communities in the Gaza Strip. The PA was notified of those attacks, but did not successfully prevent further attacks, or arrest the terrorists involved. On 7 June, Hamas terrorists fired a volley of rockets at the Israeli town of Sderot, wounding three civilians. Several other attacks occured on the same day, including the shelling of the Israeli community of Ganei

Tal by the Islamic Jihad terrorist organization, in which three workers were killed and six others wounded. On 20 June, IDF thwarted a planned Palestinian suicide bombing. That incident occured on the same day that two Israelis were killed and three wounded in other Palestinian terrorist attacks. In the Gaza Strip, the average number of terrorist attacks per week had risen to between 50 and 80, as opposed to an average of 10 to 15 in early February. On 12 July, another Palestinian suicide bomber killed four Israeli civilians and wounded 90 others at a shopping mall in the Israeli town of Netanya. On 14 July, terrorists affiliated with the Hamas and Al-Aqsa Martyrs' Brigade organizations launched four rockets into an Israeli village, killing one civilian. On 29 August, Israel reported that the previous day, a suicide bombing carried out by a member of the Islamic Jihad organization wounded 48 civilians in the Israel city of Be'er Sheva. That attack was preceded by militants operating in the Gaza Strip launching rockets against Israel.

The Permanent Observer of Palestine said that on 4 January, Israeli forces killed at least seven Palestinian civilians and wounded eight more in an attack in the town of Beit Lahiya in the Gaza Strip. Between 25 February and 10 April, ten more Palestinian civilians were killed by IDF and dozens more injured.

On 14 April, IDF carried out an extrajudicial killing by assassinating Ibrahim Hashash El-Sumari in a refugee camp in the city of Nablus. Between 10 April and 16 May, 11 more Palestinians were killed by IDF. On 17 August, an Israeli settler killed four Palestinian civilians in the West Bank. In total, from 17 May to 18 August, Israeli forces killed 51 Palestinians.

Security Council consideration (July). On 21 July [meeting 5230], at the request of Kuwait [S/2005/469], in its capacity as Chairman of the Arab Group and on behalf of LAS, the Security Council met to discuss the situation in the Middle East, including the Palestinian question.

The Special Coordinator for the Middle East Peace Process and Personal Representative of the Secretary-General, Alvaro de Soto, said that the forthcoming Israeli withdrawal from Gaza and parts of the northern West Bank continued to overshadow all other issues. The Quartet's Special Envoy for Gaza Disengagement focused his effort on six key issues: border crossings and trade corridors; connecting Gaza with the West Bank; movement within the West Bank; the Gaza airport and seaport; the houses in Israeli settlements; and the greenhouses and dairy industry in the settlements. In addition, the Special Envoy pointed out three essential areas the Palestinians should address, with international community support: the PA's fiscal crisis and development of a fiscal stabilization plan for incorporation into the 2006 budget; the creation of a broad development plan linked to a fiscally sound financial plan for 2006 to 2008; and the design of quick-impact economic programmes to respond to pressures and demands for short-term employment generation. UN agencies operating in the Occupied Palestinian Territory remained committed to supporting Mr. Wolfensohn's rapid action programme.

With respect to violence, there had been a gradual erosion of the informal quasi-ceasefire that had prevailed since the Sharm el-Sheikh summit. Palestinian militants attacked Israeli settlements and urban centres with mortar and Qassam rocket fire. Shooting incidents in the West Bank, in particular, claimed the lives of several Israeli settlers and the level of frequency of such incidents grew significantly. Partially in response to such incidents, Palestinian militants, as well as unarmed Palestinians, were killed by Israeli troops and security forces. On 14 July, in response to a Qassam rocket attack, Israel retaliated by firing missiles against targets in the Gaza Strip; the PA declared a state of emergency in Gaza and Palestinian security forces acted forcefully to prevent the launching of further rockets. In the following days, the violence escalated further, with Israel resuming its practice of targeted killings to prevent terrorist operations. Israel also began amassing military forces outside the Gaza Strip, but vowed to give the PA a last chance to prevent mortar and Qassam rocket fire against Israeli targets inside and outside the Gaza Strip.

The PA had been hard-pressed to establish law and order in both the West Bank and Gaza. President Abbas reiterated his commitment to working towards "one authority, one gun"—a pledge to assert the PA's monopoly on the use of force. Rejecting an offer by President Abbas to join with the PA, Hamas threatened open confrontation with the PA and the continuation of attacks against Israel. The PA demonstrated resolve in confronting challenges to its authority and in pursuing its obligations under the road map. On 23 June, a deal was reached involving the handover of weapons by more than 200 militants in Nablus; similar deals had been previously reached and were partially implemented in Tulkarem and Jericho. On 16 July, in a primetime radio and television address, President Abbas reiterated his commitment to asserting his authority vis-à-vis militants who were threatening to upset the fragile calm that had prevailed during the first months of 2005.

The Permanent Observer of Palestine said that, while the international community was di-

recting its efforts towards the success of Israel's withdrawal from Gaza and some areas in the northern West Bank, Israel was expanding settlements and speeding up the building of the wall. Because of its desire to see the success of Israeli disengagement from Gaza, the international community had been reluctant to exert pressure on the Israeli Government and had been condoning Israel's current settlement activities, its land confiscations, its isolation of Jerusalem and its work to complete the wall. The understandings reached at Sharm el-Sheikh were an encouraging beginning for a return to the negotiating table and for calming conditions on the ground. The PA had taken steps to meet its Sharm el-Sheikh commitments, while the Israeli Government had met none of its commitments, least of all with regard to withdrawal to the lines of September 2000, the freeing of prisoners and ending illegal extrajudicial assassinations, the closures and the siege imposed on the Palestinian people.

Israel said that more than 25,400 terrorist attacks had been launched against Israelis in less than five years. The situation in the Middle East was dire, given that, on the other side of Israel's northern border, the only force that was in control of the territory was a terrorist organization which was being helped, sponsored and guided by two UN Members States. The Israeli Government was preparing to implement an unprecedented initiative: the disengagement of all Israeli civilians and forces from the Gaza Strip and the dismantling of four settlements in the northern West Bank. The implementation of that plan, in the absence of any corresponding acts of good faith from the Palestinian side, had created divisions within Israeli society. The disengagement initiative was not Israel's first plan of choice, as the Government would have preferred a fully negotiated agreement with the PA. However, Israel was not going to waver in its intention to complete the disengagement plan. The PA had failed to fulfil its responsibility to prevent terror emanating from Palestinian areas. As a result, Israel was left with no choice but to find defensive measures to protect itself, such as the security fence. The security fence worked, as there had been a 90 per cent reduction in the number of successful terrorist attacks, 70 per cent in the number of citizens killed and 85 per cent in the number of wounded. Israel was, however, sensitive to the impact of the defensive measures it had been forced to take and was coordinating with PA officials to facilitate humanitarian passage to those areas. Israeli and UN experts were also examining the consequences of those measures on the freedom of movement of Palestinian civilians.

Communications. On 25 July [A/59/884-S/2005/522], Yemen transmitted to the Secretary-General the text of the final communiqué, the Sana'a Declaration and the resolutions adopted by OIC Foreign Ministers at its thirty-second session (Sana'a, Yemen, 28-30 June). The Conference, among other things, affirmed the illegality of Israeli practices in East Jerusalem, aimed at annexing and changing the demographic make-up of the city and condemned Israel for continuing to build the wall on Palestinian territories.

Disengagement

Security Council consideration (August). The Security Council, on 24 August [meeting 5250], discussed the situation in the Middle East, including the Palestinian question.

The Under-Secretary-General for Political Affairs, Ibrahim Gambari, said that the Israeli disengagement from Gaza and northern parts of the West Bank began on 15 August as announced. Despite the dramatic scenes of Israeli military and police personnel removing settlers from their houses in Gaza, the operation mostly proceeded smoothly, aided by the restraint generally observed by militant Palestinian factions. IDF and the Israeli police avoided the use of force and completed the evacuation of the settlements on 22 August, well in advance of the target date. Evacuation of settlers from the settlements in the northern West Bank was carried out on 23 August.

For its part, the PA renewed its commitment to a smooth and peaceful withdrawal and to cooperate and coordinate with the Israeli side towards that end. On 14 August, a large force of Palestinian police began to deploy in several areas of the Gaza Strip adjacent to Jewish settlements to provide buffer cordons and to deter the firing of homemade rockets and mortars.

However, the Under-Secretary-General said that, while Israel's bold first withdrawal from the Occupied Palestinian Territory was welcomed, the situation elsewhere in the occupied territory continued to fester, with many Palestinians fearing that Israel was consolidating its occupation in the West Bank, including East Jerusalem. In addition, non-governmental monitoring groups reported that settlement activity in the West Bank continued during the reporting period. In Jerusalem, on 25 July, the Israeli local planning committee of the Jerusalem municipality approved a Ministry of Housing scheme to construct a new Jewish settlement in the Muslim quarter of Jerusalem's Old City. Also in July, the Knesset approved a three-year aid plan to improve infrastructure, agriculture and settlement expansion in the Jordan Valley area. According to press re-

ports, Prime Minister Sharon confirmed his intention to continue building in the settlement blocs in the West Bank. Settlement expansion was linked to the construction of Israel's security barrier. In August, land expropriation orders for approximately 396 acres were issued in the Jerusalem governorate for the construction of a portion of the barrier around the Ma'ale Adumim settlement which would cut a reported 23 kilometres into the Occupied Palestinian Territory and separate the northern West Bank from the south.

The Under-Secretary-General concluded that Israeli disengagement from Gaza and the northern West Bank marked a watershed in that it constituted the first removal by Israel of settlements on occupied Palestinian territory. Israeli policy demonstrated that it had the requisite maturity to do what was required in order to achieve lasting peace, and IDF the ability to discharge its mission with carefully calibrated restraint. Prime Minister Sharon was to be commended for his determination and courage to carry out the disengagement in the face of forceful and often strident internal opposition.

Communications. On 26 August [S/2005/559], the EU welcomed the historic progress made on Israel's withdrawal from Gaza and parts of the northern West Bank and commended the Israeli Government and the PA for their commitment to overcome the difficult challenges they faced.

On 30 August [A/ES-10/306-S/2005/556], the Chairman of the Committee on the Exercise of the Inalienable Rights of the Palestinian People expressed concern over Israel's decision to expand and consolidate its settlements in the West Bank, despite having removed its settlements in Gaza and parts of the northern West Bank. In particular, Israeli authorities had begun issuing orders to seize Palestinian-owned land for the construction of parts of the separation wall that would eventually surround the Ma'ale Adumim settlement.

The ninety-sixth regular session of the GCC Ministerial Council (Jeddah, Saudi Arabia, 6-7 September) [A/60/388-S/2005/612], among other things, expressed the hope that the evacuation of the Israeli settlements in the Gaza Strip would be followed by steps towards total withdrawal from all occupied Palestinian lands so as to enable the Palestinian people to build an independent State with Al-Quds al-Sharif as its capital.

Statement of Prime Minister Sharon (15 September). Israeli Prime Minister Sharon, speaking before the High-level Plenary Meeting of the General Assembly on 15 September [meeting 5], said that, in withdrawing from the Gaza Strip, Israel had proved that it was ready to make painful concessions to resolve the conflict with the

Palestinians, whose turn it was to prove their desire for peace. The end of Israeli control over the Gaza Strip would allow them to develop their economy and build a peaceful, free, law-abiding and democratic society. Their leadership would be tested to put an end to terror, as well as the terrorist infrastructure, eliminate the regime of armed guards and cease the incitement and indoctrination of hatred towards Israel. Successful implementation of the disengagement plan opened a window of opportunity for advancing peace in accordance with the road map and the Sharm el-Sheik understandings, to which Israel was committed.

Security Council consideration (September). On 23 September [meeting 5270], the Special Coordinator for the Middle East Peace Process and Personal Representative of the Secretary-General reported to the Security Council that Israel withdrew the last of its military personnel and installation from the Gaza Strip on 12 September. Following the completion of the evacuation of civilian army infrastructure, Israeli forces put an end to their permanent presence in the four settlements in the northern West Bank as of 20 September. Facing vociferous opposition, the Israeli Government proved its ability to carry out democratic decisions in the general interest, while knowing that they would cause pain and disruption to a significant number of its citizens. The exemplary consideration shown by the Israeli armed forces towards those affected, on some of whom carefully measured force had to be employed, showed that they could be held to the highest standards in dealing with civilians.

The timing of Israel's disengagement was not the result of an agreement with the Palestinian side but of a unilateral Israeli decision. However, all relevant PA sectors worked constructively to coordinate with their Israeli counterparts and other international actors. Early fears that the operation might have to be conducted under fire were dissipated, for Palestinian armed groups, by and large, held back from violent action against settlers. The Israeli settlers, armed forces and police withdrew in peace.

The Special Coordinator observed that Israel's need for security had led them to install a barrier and set up a system of roadblocks and checkpoints to control the movement of persons and goods into and throughout much of the West Bank. Apart from impeding economic revival, to many Palestinians, the barrier and the closures, and the travails of traversing them, were a source of humiliation and a constant check on their aspiration to one day run their own affairs. The expense incurred in the building of the barrier raised doubts in some minds as to its stated provisionality. Questions had also been posed as to whether the purpose was only to ensure security. While Israelis should understand those considerations and recognize that it was ultimately in their interest to address them, Palestinians, for their part, had to understand, accept and address Israel's need to be assured of the safety and security of its citizens. Countless innocent Israelis had fallen victim to terrorist acts and Israelis had a right to demand and end to those attacks. Those who carried out acts of terror or instigated them should understand that violence had rendered the achievement of the goal of a State in which Palestinians lived in freedom and dignity more distant. The Palestinian people at large also demanded that law and order be established in the streets, which meant not only an efficient police, but also a reliable court system and an end to impunity and corruption. The establishment of a State run by the rule of law, in which the Government held the monopoly over the instruments of violence went hand in hand with the strengthening of Israel's sense of security.

On 29 September [A/60/416-S/2005/619], the Libyan Arab Jamahiriya, on behalf of LAS, transmitted a letter to the Secretary-General from the Arab Group expressing concern at Mr. de Soto's 23 September remarks (see above). In particular, it noted that they referred to Israel's need for security as the reason behind the building of the wall in the Occupied Palestinian Territory, despite the fact that the International Court of Justice (ICJ) in its 2004 advisory opinion [YUN 2004,p.465] had rejected that argument.

On 17 October [A/60/440-S/2005/658/Corr.2], Ministers for Foreign Affairs of the States members of OIC (New York, 23 September), at their annual coordination meeting, noted with regret Israel's defiant response to ICJ's Advisory Opinion, its non-compliance with Assembly resolution ES-10/15 [YUN 2004, p. 465] and its continued construction of the wall in the Occupied Palestinian Territory. The ministers stressed that the Gaza withdrawal and the dismantling of the settlements were promising steps and emphasized that the withdrawal should be complete and irreversible, be accompanied by similar steps in the West bank and consistent with the road map.

Quartet 20 September statement

SECURITY COUNCIL ACTION

On 23 September [meeting 5270], following consultations among Security Council members, the President made statement **S/PRST/2005/44** on behalf of the Council:

The Security Council supports the Statement issued in New York on 20 September 2005 by the Quartet, which is annexed to the present statement.

The Council urges the Government of Israel and the Palestinian Authority to cooperate, along with other parties concerned, with the efforts to achieve the goals set out in the Quartet Statement.

The Council calls for renewed action in parallel by the Government of Israel and the Palestinian Authority on their obligations in accordance with the road map, to ensure continued progress towards the creation of an independent, sovereign, democratic and viable State of Palestine living side by side with Israel in peace and security.

The Council stresses the importance of, and the need to achieve, a just, comprehensive and lasting peace in the Middle East, based on all its relevant resolutions, including resolutions 242(1967), 338(1973), 1397(2002) and 1515(2003), the Madrid terms of reference and the principle of land for peace.

Annex

Quartet Statement

New York, 20 September 2005

Representatives of the Quartet—the Secretary General of the United Nations, Mr. Kofi Annan, the Minister for Foreign Affairs of the Russian Federation, Mr. Sergey Lavrov, the Secretary of State of the United States of America, Ms. Condoleezza Rice, the Secretary of State for Foreign and Commonwealth Affairs of the United Kingdom of Great Britain and Northern Ireland, Mr. Jack Straw, the High Representative for the Common Foreign and Security Policy of the European Union, Mr. Javier Solana, and the European Commissioner for External Relations, Ms. Benita Ferrero-Waldner—met today in New York to discuss the Gaza disengagement and the prospects for movement towards peace in the Middle East.

The Quartet recognizes and welcomes the successful conclusion of the Israeli withdrawal from Gaza and parts of the northern West Bank and the moment of opportunity that it brings to renew efforts on the road map. The Quartet reiterates its belief that this brave and historic decision should open a new chapter on the path to peace in the region. It paid tribute to the political courage of Prime Minister Sharon and commends the Government of Israel, its armed forces and its police for the smooth and professional execution of the operation. It also expresses its appreciation for the responsible behaviour of the Palestinian Authority and people for helping to maintain a peaceful environment during the evacuation. The Quartet applauds the close coordination between the Israeli and Palestinian security services during the process. These significant developments create new opportunities and call for renewed focus on the responsibilities of all parties. The conclusion of disengagement represents an important step toward achieving the vision of two democratic States, Israel and Palestine, living side by side in peace and security.

The Quartet commends continued cooperation between both parties and the United States Security Coordinator, General William Ward, on security issues related to the disengagement. The Quartet calls for an end to all violence and terror. While the leadership of the Palestinian Authority has condemned violence and has sought to encourage Palestinian groups who have engaged in terrorism to abandon this course and engage in the democratic process, the Quartet further urges the Palestinian Authority to maintain law and order and dismantle terrorist capabilities and infrastructure. The Quartet reaffirms the continued importance of comprehensive reform of the Palestinian security services. The rule of law through authorized security institutions is fundamental to democratic practice. The Quartet expresses appreciation to those parties which have made contributions to the security reform effort, particularly Egypt, the European Union and the United States. Finally, the Quartet welcomes the agreement between the Governments of Israel and Egypt on security arrangements along the Gaza-Egypt border.

At today's meeting, Quartet Special Envoy Wolfensohn's report on his current efforts and initiatives was discussed. The Quartet encourages his further work to facilitate continued discussion between the parties to build on the success of disengagement. The Palestinian Authority should demonstrate its ability to govern, and all members of the international community should look for ways to support these efforts. The Quartet will continue to lead international efforts to support sustainable growth of the Palestinian economy and to strengthen the overall capacity of the Palestinian Authority to assume its responsibilities through an aggressive pursuit of state-building and democratic reform efforts. Given the critical importance of free movement in the West Bank to the viability of the Palestinian economy, the Quartet urges an easing of the system of movement restrictions, consistent with Israel's security needs. The Quartet reaffirms that coordinated action by the international donor community is crucial for the success of the Quartet Special Envoy's Quick-Impact Economic Programme, as well as for the longer-term three-year plan for Palestinian development. In this regard, it notes the importance of the $750 million in assistance which will be disbursed to the Palestinian Authority during the remainder of this year. The Quartet urges Arab States to implement existing commitments and to engage fully and positively in response to the Special Envoy's initiatives. To ensure the success of this effort, the Quartet views continued progress on institutional reform of the Palestinian Authority, as well as progress in combating corruption, as essential. The Quartet also welcomes the announcement of Palestinian Legislative Council elections and upcoming municipal elections.

Looking beyond disengagement, the Quartet reviewed progress on implementation of the road map. The Quartet calls for renewed action in parallel by both parties on their obligations in accordance with the sequence of the Road map. As part of the confidence-building process the Quartet urged both sides to return to the cooperative agenda reached at Sharm el-Sheikh, Egypt. Contacts between the parties should be intensified at all levels. The Quartet charges the Envoys to keep progress under review.

Both parties are reminded of their obligations under the road map to avoid unilateral actions which prejudice final status issues. The Quartet reaffirms that any final agreement must be reached through negotiation between the parties and that a new Palestinian State must be truly viable with contiguity in the West Bank and connectivity to Gaza. On settlements, the Quartet welcomed the fact that, in areas covered by disengagement, Israel has gone beyond its obligations under the first phase of the Road map. The Quartet expresses its concern that settlement expansion elsewhere must stop, and Israel must remove unauthorized outposts. The Quartet continues to note with concern the route of the Israeli separation barrier, particularly as it results in the confiscation of Palestinian land, cuts off the movement of people and goods, and undermines Palestinians' trust in the road map process as it appears to prejudge the final borders of a Palestinian State.

The Quartet members exchanged views on the Russian proposal to hold an international meeting of experts in Moscow. Contacts on this matter will continue, taking into consideration the need to give attention to the various aspects of the Middle East situation, including multilateral matters.

The Quartet reiterates its commitment to the principles outlined in previous statements, including those of 4 May 2004, and 9 May and 23 June 2005, and reaffirms its commitment to a just, comprehensive and lasting settlement to the Arab-Israeli conflict based upon Security Council resolutions 242(1967) and 338(1973).

Post-disengagement period

Communications. On 26 September [A/ES-10/307-S/2005/608], the Permanent Observer of Palestine said that Israel had intensified its military campaign in the Occupied Palestinian Territory, escalating overnight air raids and attacks in the Gaza Strip, which resulted in the extrajudicial killing of four Palestinians. At least 15 more Palestinian civilians were wounded during Israeli air raids and more than 200 arrested and detained.

On the same day [A/60/382-S/2005/609], Israel said that, from 23 to 25 September, Hamas had launched more than 40 artillery rockets onto the Israeli town of Sderot, wounding five persons and causing extensive damage. In response to those attacks, Israel deployed forces around the Gaza Strip to prevent further assaults, targeted the terrorist infrastructure in Gaza and arrested wanted terrorists. Subsequently, Hamas issued a ceasefire, which it later abrogated by firing additional rockets onto Israeli towns. In a separate incident, some 20 Palestinians were killed on 23 September because of a Hamas explosion in a neighbourhood in Gaza, for which Hamas blamed Israel. Israel also reported that, on 21 September [A/60/385-S/2005/610], Hamas admitted abducting and killing an Israeli civilian.

Security incidents

On 29 September [A/ES-10/308-S/2005/617], the Permanent Observer of Palestine stated that, between 24 August and 28 September, Israeli military forces killed 24 Palestinians. IDF carried out air and artillery raids and attacks in Gaza leading to extensive infrastructure damage.

On 10 October [A/ES-10/309-S/2005/640], the Permanent Observer of Palestine said that, between 3 and 9 October, IDF killed six Palestinians and wounded dozens of others.

On 17 October [A/60/435-S/2005/655], Israel reported that, on 16 October, Palestinian terrorists associated with the Al-Aqsa Martyrs' Brigade killed three Israeli civilians and wounded another one in two separate drive-by shootings.

On 25 October [A/ES-10/310 S/2005/671], the Permanent Observer of Palestine said that, between 16 and 23 October, IDF killed four Palestinians. Israeli forces also continued with their campaign of arresting and detaining Palestinian civilians.

Israel said that, on 26 October [A/60/448-S/2005/680], a terrorist affiliated with the Islamic Jihad organization carried out a suicide-bombing attack in the city of Hadera, killing five people and wounding 55 others. Despite the increased activity of Islamic Jihad and other terrorist organizations, Palestinian security officers remained inert in the face of that growing threat.

Representatives of the Quartet, in a 28 October statement, condemned the 26 October terrorist attack in Haderat, responsibility for which was claimed by Palestinian Islamic Jihad headquarters in Damascus, Syria. The Quartet urged the Syrian Government to close the offices of the Islamic Jihad and to prevent the use of its territory by armed groups engaged in terrorist acts, The Quartet also encouraged and supported the PA in its effort to prevent armed groups from acting against law and order and the policy of the Authority itself.

Also on 26 October, [A/60/449-S/2005/681], Israel said that the President of Iran, Mahmoud Ahmadinejad, had called for the destruction of the State of Israel. The EU condemned the statement attributed to President Ahmadinejad [S/2005/683] and noted that calls for the destruction of any State were inconsistent with any claim to be a mature and responsible member of the international community.

The Permanent Observer of Palestine said that, on 28 October [A/ES-10/311-S/2005/685], seven Palestinians were killed after an Israeli warplane fired three missiles at a car near a refugee camp in Gaza.

Security Council consideration (October). On 20 October [meeting 5287], the Under-Secretary-

General for Political Affairs said that disengagement had yet to revive the peace process, due to a resurgence of violence on the ground. The security situation had deteriorated significantly during the last week of September and the first week of October. The situation improved somewhat during the second week of October, but on 16 October, militants from the Al-Aqsa Martyrs' Brigade shot dead three Israelis as they travelled to settlements in the West Bank. Israel responded by imposing tight restrictions on Palestinian movement in the West Bank. The Palestinian leadership announced a decision to confiscate illegally held weapons and nominated three officials who would bear overall responsibility for security sector reform. Such steps could contribute significantly to the control of internal violence and to progress towards the fulfilment of Palestinian security related road map commitments. Further progress in that area was absolutely critical during the coming weeks and months.

The Quartet's Special Envoy returned to the region on 7 October to push forward the Quartet's agenda in relation to disengagement. Mr. Wolfensohn sought to conclude agreements on the six-plus-three issues relating to movement, security and reform, which formed the basis of his work since June. The first of the six issues were border crossings and trade corridors. Reopening the Rafah border crossing between Egypt and Gaza was of immediate social and political importance, because it would restore a measure of Palestinian access to the world outside Gaza and pave the way for agreements on border crossing with Israel, the link between Gaza and the West Bank and the reopening of Gaza's air and sea ports. Since 17 September, the Rafah crossing was open for only five days, pending agreement between the parties on the administration of the crossing. According to the Special Envoy, agreement on the crossing regime was close: the parties had reached consensus on the main technical elements of its administration and on a third-party presence along the border with Egypt. The EU had offered to consider such a role in that connection, although a formal invitation had not yet been issued. The flow of people and goods between Israel and Gaza and between Israel and the West Bank needed to be improved. It was the judgement of the Special Envoy that the parties were close to an agreement on a management system for those borders but Israel had, since 5 September, declined to meet with the PA in order to take the negotiations forward. Meanwhile, the Quartet was implementing a major programme of assistance aimed at creating jobs and at boosting Palestinian recovery after the disengagement. The EU proposed in-

creasing assistance to the Palestinians by 250 million euros, on the condition that security and the situation regarding the movement of people improved. Other donors had provided additional assistance, and according to an early estimate, overall disbursements for 2005 would reach between $1.1 billion to $1.3 billion, a 25 to 35 per cent increase over the annual average of the past four years. At least 35 per cent of that international assistance to the Palestinians would be channelled through UN agencies.

The increase in violence played a role in derailing the plans for bilateral talks between the Israeli and Palestinian leaders and also made their domestic positions even more difficult. Prime Minister Sharon carried out disengagement in the face of vocal domestic pressure; that pressure revived following the 24 September rocket attacks on the town of Sderot. On the Palestinian side, on 3 October, the Palestinian Legislative Council called on the President to dissolve the Government and to form another within two weeks. That call was precipitated by heavy armed clashes in Gaza between Palestinian police and militants.

The Palestinians held a third round of municipal elections in the West Bank on 29 September. Elections in Gaza were postponed due to security concerns. Participation in the poll was high and Fatah won over 53 per cent of seats in the municipal councils, compared to 26 per cent won by Hamas. Technical preparations were under way for the forthcoming Palestinian legislative elections, which were scheduled for 25 January 2006.

Communication (15 November). On 15 November [A/ES-10/312-S/2005/720], the Permanent Observer of Palestine said that Israel had escalated its military aggression against the Palestinian people, in particular its campaign of extrajudicial killings. Between 27 October and 14 November, IDF killed 18 Palestinians. Israeli officials had also been making highly inflammatory statements against the Palestinian leadership and the future of peace prospects that had only served to undermine the efforts made by the PA to secure and maintain the ceasefire.

Security Council consideration (November). The Security Council, at a meeting on 30 November [meeting 5312], heard a statement by the Under-Secretary-General for Political Affairs, Mr. Gambari, who had just returned from a visit to the Middle East. He reported that, in mid-November, the Israeli Government and the PA concluded an Agreement on Movement and Access, Agreed Principles for the Rafah Crossing, which envisaged an unprecedented third-party role for the EU, an enhanced contribution by the United States Security Coordinator, support from the Quartet Special Envoy and the continued close involvement of the United Nations and the World Bank. The EU's 90-man-strong Border Assistance Mission would be responsible for resolving any disputes between Israel and the PA arising from the Agreement. The parties agreed that the crossings between Gaza and Israel would operate continuously, which would allow 150 export trucks to be processed daily by the end of 2005 and 400 by the end of 2006. Goods would enter Gaza through Kerem Shalom, where Israel, Egypt and Gaza met. The EU would monitor customs arrangements, with its mission being reviewed in a year's time. Bus convoys between Gaza and the West Bank would start on 15 December and truck convoys on 15 January 2006. The Government of Israel would review the system of movement restrictions in the West Bank and reduce them to the maximum extent possible by the end of 2005. The construction of the seaport was to begin immediately and discussions on the construction of a Palestinian airport would continue. The Agreement resolved a number of pending issues related to Israel's withdrawal of settlements and military infrastructure from Gaza, or set up frameworks for doing so. The United States would work closely with the parties to implement the Agreement and the United Nations would play its part in that regard, particularly with regard to the easing of movement restrictions in the West Bank. The first aspect of the Agreement was implemented on 27 November, when the Rafah crossing reopened under Palestinian control for travelers in both directions and for the outgoing passage of goods under supervision by the EU.

The full implementation of all aspects of the Agreement was a vital step towards Palestinian economic recovery but it would require the strengthening of Palestinian institutions and economic management and the effective distribution of international aid, issues that would be discussed at the mid-December meeting of the Ad Hoc Liaison Committee, the primary policy-making meeting of donors, the PA and the Israeli Government (see p. 521).

The fragile security situation and the need for more decisive action in accordance with the road map were underlined by continued violence. Throughout November, the Israeli army targeted alleged militants in the West Bank and Gaza and undertook major arrest campaigns in the West Bank. The Palestinian security services took some action, including arrests, against those who persisted in carrying out terrorist attacks, to keep weapons off the streets and to assert the rule of law in areas under Palestinian control, though more work needed to be done in that regard. Efforts were also made to rehabilitate for-

mer militia members by employing them in the security services. President Abbas established a leadership committee on security reform, which, in turn, mandated a technical team to develop a white paper on safety and security for Palestinians. That process, which would involve public dialogue in an effort to build national consensus, had the strong support of the United States Security Coordinator, Lieutenant General William Ward, who was to be succeeded by Lieutenant General Keith Dayton.

Technical preparations for the 25 January 2006 legislative elections continued. The United Nations would assist the Palestinian Central Election Commission through a liaison and support unit to coordinate international observers. Meanwhile, in Israel, the Labour Party elected a new leader, Amir Peretz, who informed Prime Minister Sharon that Labour would leave the coalition Government. New elections were expected by the end of March 2006. Prime Minister Sharon announced his intention to leave the Likud party and seek reelection as Prime Minister and head of the new Kadima—or Forward—Party.

The Under-Secretary-General said that he had returned from the region with the strong belief that the only way forward for Israelis and Palestinians alike was for the parties to ensure the success of disengagement by fully implementing the Agreement on Movement and Access and to take renewed action, in parallel, to fulfil their obligations under the road map.

SECURITY COUNCIL ACTION (30 November)

On 30 November [meeting 5313], following consultations among Security Council members, the President made statement **S/PRST/2005/57** on behalf of the Council:

The Security Council welcomes the Agreement on Movement and Access and the Agreed Principles for the Rafah Crossing reached between the Government of Israel and the Palestinian Authority on 15 November 2005. The successful opening of the Rafah crossing on 25 November 2005 represents an important step forward.

The Council commends the efforts of the Quartet, the Quartet Special Envoy and his team, as well as the positive contributions of the Government of Egypt, and expresses its strong appreciation to the European Union for assuming the role of third-party monitor.

The Council calls upon the parties to take immediate action to implement the terms of both agreements according to the timelines established therein.

The Council calls for renewed action in parallel by the Government of Israel and the Palestinian Authority on their obligations in accordance with the Road map, to ensure continued progress towards the creation of a viable, democratic, sovereign and contiguous Palestine living side by side with Israel in peace and security. The Council stresses the importance of, and the need to achieve, a just, comprehensive and lasting peace in the Middle East, based on all its relevant resolutions, including resolutions 242(1967), 338 (1973), 1397(2002) and 1515(2003), the Madrid terms of reference and the principle of land for peace.

Communications (5 December). On 5 December [A/60/580-S/2005/756], Israel said that, on 3 and 4 December, the Al-Aqsa Martyrs' Brigade, a terrorist organization affiliated with PA President Abbas Fatah movement, launched rockets against the town of Nativ Ha'asara causing damage to community property. On the same day [A/60/581-S/2005/757], Israel said that at least five people were killed and more than 55 wounded when a Palestinian terrorist associated with the Islamic Jihad organization detonated himself in the city of Netanya.

Quartet statement (5 December). Representatives of the Quartet, issued a statement on 5 December [SG/2102] on the situation in the Middle East, in which it condemned the terrorist attack in Netanya in the strongest possible terms. The Quartet repeated its demand that the Syrian Government take immediate action to close the offices of the Islamic Jihad and to prevent the use of its territory by armed groups engaged in terrorist acts. The Quartet denounced all acts of terrorism and urged all parties to exercise restraint, avoid escalation of violence and keep channels of communication open.

Communications (8-16 December). On 8 December [A/ES-10/313-S/2005/771], the Permanent Observer of Palestine said that, on 5 December, the Israeli Defense Minister had ordered IDF to launch wide-scale military operations in the Gaza Strip and in the north and northeast parts of the West Bank. On that day, Israeli war planes fired missiles at a house in Gaza, killing two Palestinians and injuring six others. On 7 December, IDF carried out another extrajudicial killing, in which one Palestinian was killed and several others wounded. IDF had tightened its siege of the Occupied Palestinian Territory, isolating the Palestinian population in their towns, further compounding their socio-economic hardships.

On 16 December [A/60/633-S/2005/826], Saudi Arabia transmitted the text of the Makkah Declaration adopted at the Third Extraordinary Session of the Islamic Summit Conference (Makkah Al-Mukarramah, Saudi Arabia, 7-8 December), in which the Conference called for the dismantling of settlements in the Occupied Palestinian Territory, as well as the demolition of the separation wall.

Security Council consideration (December). The Security Council, on 20 December [meeting 5337], discussed the situation in the Middle East, including the Palestinian question.

The Under-Secretary-General for Political Affairs, Mr. Gambari, said that since the end of November, despite the fact that some progress was made toward the implementation of the Access and Movement Agreement between Israel and the PA, violence continued in the region. Following the 5 December suicide bombing in Netanya, (see above) the PA had arrested some 60 suspects, while Israel responded to the attack and to the firing of Qassam rockets against Israeli territory by tightening the closure regime and by implementing a previously announced resumption of targeted killings. Meanwhile, the Palestinian internal security situation had worsened, with attacks on electoral offices, armed clashes between Fatah factions at the party headquarters and between the Palestinian security forces and armed elements.

At the Ad Hoc Liaison Committee meeting (London, 14 December), donors, the PA and the Israeli Government discussed the economic, fiscal and humanitarian situation in the Occupied Palestinian Territory and assessed progress in Palestinian reform. The need for the PA to adhere to the reform agenda and to re-establish fiscal discipline was a central theme of the meeting. The PA presented an update on its precarious financial situation and shared with donors the main elements of its medium-term development plan for the next three years. The meeting adopted a revised donor structure that strengthened the PA's role. Donors agreed on the need for the PA to implement, as a matter of priority, a medium-term fiscal stabilization plan and stressed that reform had to continue in the coming months, even though the election period could make that more difficult. The PA's fiscal situation was so acute that there was real concern that the December salaries of government-employees might not be paid. The Committee also discussed the convening in 2006, of a pledging conference to mobilize the target sum of $3 billion.

Implementation was proceeding on some parts of the Agreement on Movement and Access (see p. 520). The Rafah crossing between Gaza and Egypt, was open for five hours each day since 26 November. The Karni crossing, through which produce entered Israel from Gaza, also remained open since 15 November, allowing the first post-disengagement Palestinian harvest to reach Israeli markets. Despite the concerted efforts of the United States and the Quartet's Special Envoy to resolve outstanding differences and to ensure that Israel's security concerns were met, the commencement of the bus convoys between Gaza and the West Bank, which should have started on 15 December remained suspended.

On 15 December, the fourth round of municipal elections took place in the West Bank, including in larger municipalities such as Nablus, Jenin and AlBireh, where Hamas won an overwhelming majority of seats, and Ramallah, where Fatah won. The fifth, and final round, which would include major constituencies in Gaza, would be held in early 2006, after the legislative elections.

The Under-Secretary-General said that the road map's target date for a final and comprehensive settlement of the Israeli-Palestinian conflict was set for 31 December 2005. It was obvious that, while progress had been made, no comprehensive peace would be achieved by then. That did not detract from the centrality of the road map, which remained the agreed framework for achieving a just and lasting peace in the Middle East. The deadline represented an occasion for all parties to reflect on what more they could do to ensure that road map obligations were met.

Quartet statement (28 December). On 28 December, the Quartet issued a statement welcoming the upcoming Palestinian Legislative Council elections as a positive step toward consolidation of Palestinian democracy and the goal of a two-state solution to the Israeli-Palestinian conflict. It called on the PA and the Central Election Commission to ensure a free, fair and open process in accordance with Palestinian law. The PA had to ensure the security of polling stations and of election personnel, enforce existing law, regulations and decrees, particularly those prohibiting the public display of weapons, external financing of campaigns and the use of religious facilities for campaign purposes. The Quartet reaffirmed that those who wanted to be a part of the political process should not engage in armed group or militia activities, and called on all participants to renounce violence, recognize Israel's right to exist, and to disarm. The Quartet was encouraged by the negotiation of an electoral code of conduct and welcomed the PA's invitation to international election observers. In particular, the Quartet expressed its view that a future PA Cabinet should include no member who had not committed to the principles of Israel's right to exist in peace and security and to an unequivocal end to violence and terrorism. The Quartet believed it was essential that direct dialogue begin immediately between the Israeli Government and the PA to coordinate preparation for the legislative elections. Both parties should work to put in place a mechanism to allow Palestinians residents in Jerusalem to exercise their legitimate democratic rights.

Further communications. In a later communication [A/ES-10/314-S/2006/11], the Permanent Observer of Palestine said that between 14 November and 31 December, IDF killed 27 Palestinians. In addition, Israel had begun implementing a unilateral plan to create a so-called "buffer zone" in the northern Gaza Strip through the shelling and bombing of that area. Israel also refused to implement the Agreement on Movement and Access, as Israeli authorities had yet to allow bus convoy traffic between Gaza and the West Bank, originally scheduled to commence on 15 December.

The Supreme Council of the Gulf Cooperation Council, at its twenty-sixth session (Abu Dhabi, United Arab Emirates, 18-19 December) [A/60/680-S/2006/108], called on Israel to desist from its arbitrary practices against Palestinians, including, among other things, ending targeted assassinations, stopping settlement activity and ceasing construction of the separation wall.

Jerusalem

East Jerusalem, where most of the city's Arab inhabitants lived, remained one of the most sensitive issues in the Middle East peace process and a focal point of concern for the United Nations in 2005.

Committee on Palestinian Rights. In its annual report [A/60/35], the Committee on the Exercise of the Inalienable Rights of the Palestinian People (Committee on Palestinian Rights) expressed concern over the intensified expansion of Israeli settlements in the West Bank, including East Jerusalem, as well as by public pronouncements by Israeli officials in September concerning the future of Jerusalem and its borders, the two issues that were to be resolved through permanent status negotiations between the parties. The Committee also noted that Israel continued the construction of the wall in the occupied territories. In the Jerusalem area, the wall's route remained the same, with 40 more kilometres that would surround the Ma'ale Adumim settlement, as well as four others nearby. The wall, when completed, would place Ma'ale Adumim, its industrial zone, Rachel's Tomb in Bethlehem, and most of East Jerusalem on the Israeli side. A new road being planned to connect Ramallah, north of Jerusalem, with Bethlehem in the south, would deny access for Palestinians to East Jerusalem, because the road would bypass the city. Some 60,000 Palestinians with Jerusalem identity documents would be on the east side of the wall, while some 30,000 Ma'ale Adumim settlers would be in Jerusalem.

Transfer of diplomatic missions

Report of Secretary-General. On 16 August [A/60/258], the Secretary-General reported that four Member States had replied to his request for information on steps taken or envisaged to implement General Assembly resolution 59/32 [YUN 2004, p. 473], which addressed the transfer by some States of their diplomatic missions to Jerusalem, in violation of Security Council resolution 478 (1980) [YUN 1980, p. 426]. Israel had not replied to the Secretary-General's request.

GENERAL ASSEMBLY ACTION

On 1 December [meeting 60], the General Assembly adopted **resolution 60/41** [draft: A/60/L.33 & Add.1] by recorded vote (153-7-12) [agenda item 14].

Jerusalem

The General Assembly,

Recalling its resolution 181(II) of 29 November 1947, in particular its provisions regarding the City of Jerusalem,

Recalling also its resolution 36/120 E of 10 December 1981 and all subsequent resolutions, including resolution 56/31 of 3 December 2001, in which it, inter alia, determined that all legislative and administrative measures and actions taken by Israel, the occupying Power, which have altered or purported to alter the character and status of the Holy City of Jerusalem, in particular the so-called "Basic Law" on Jerusalem and the proclamation of Jerusalem as the capital of Israel, were null and void and must be rescinded forthwith,

Recalling further Security Council resolutions relevant to Jerusalem, including resolution 478(1980) of 20 August 1980, in which the Council, inter alia, decided not to recognize the "Basic Law" and called upon those States which had established diplomatic missions in Jerusalem to withdraw such missions from the Holy City,

Recalling the advisory opinion rendered on 9 July 2004 by the International Court of Justice on the *Legal Consequences of the Construction of a Wall in the Occupied Palestinian Territory,* and recalling resolution ES-10/15 of 20 July 2004,

Expressing its grave concern at any action taken by any body, governmental or non-governmental, in violation of the above-mentioned resolutions,

Expressing its grave concern in particular about the continuation by Israel, the occupying Power, of illegal settlement activities and its construction of the wall in and around East Jerusalem, and the further isolation of the city from the rest of the Occupied Palestinian Territory, which is having a detrimental effect on the lives of Palestinians and could prejudge a final status agreement on Jerusalem,

Reaffirming that the international community, through the United Nations, has a legitimate interest in the question of the City of Jerusalem and the protection of the unique spiritual, religious and cultural dimensions of the city, as foreseen in relevant United Nations resolutions on this matter,

Having considered the report of the Secretary-General,

1. *Reiterates its determination* that any actions taken by Israel to impose its laws, jurisdiction and adminis-

tration on the Holy City of Jerusalem are illegal and therefore null and void and have no validity whatsoever;

2. *Deplores* the transfer by some States of their diplomatic missions to Jerusalem in violation of Security Council resolution 478(1980), and calls once more upon those States to abide by the provisions of the relevant United Nations resolutions, in conformity with the Charter of the United Nations;

3. *Stresses* that a comprehensive, just and lasting solution to the question of the City of Jerusalem should take into account the legitimate concerns of both the Palestinian and Israeli sides and should include internationally guaranteed provisions to ensure the freedom of religion and of conscience of its inhabitants, as well as permanent, free and unhindered access to the holy places by the people of all religions and nationalities;

4. *Requests* the Secretary-General to report to the General Assembly at its sixty-first session on the implementation of the present resolution.

RECORDED VOTE ON RESOLUTION 60/41:

In favour: Afghanistan, Algeria, Andorra, Antigua and Barbuda, Argentina, Armenia, Austria, Azerbaijan, Bahamas, Bahrain, Bangladesh, Barbados, Belarus, Belgium, Belize, Benin, Bhutan, Bolivia, Bosnia and Herzegovina, Botswana, Brazil, Brunei Darussalam, Bulgaria, Burkina Faso, Cambodia, Canada, Cape Verde, Central African Republic, Chile, China, Colombia, Comoros, Croatia, Cuba, Cyprus, Czech Republic, Democratic People's Republic of Korea, Denmark, Djibouti, Dominica, Dominican Republic, Ecuador, Egypt, Eritrea, Estonia, Ethiopia, Finland, France, Gabon, Gambia, Georgia, Germany, Ghana, Greece, Guinea, Guinea-Bissau, Guyana, Hungary, Iceland, India, Indonesia, Iran, Iraq, Ireland, Italy, Jamaica, Japan, Jordan, Kazakhstan, Kenya, Kuwait, Kyrgyzstan, Lao People's Democratic Republic, Latvia, Lebanon, Lesotho, Liberia, Libyan Arab Jamahiriya, Liechtenstein, Lithuania, Luxembourg, Madagascar, Malaysia, Maldives, Mali, Malta, Mauritania, Mauritius, Mexico, Monaco, Mongolia, Morocco, Mozambique, Myanmar, Namibia, Nepal, Netherlands, New Zealand, Nicaragua, Nigeria, Norway, Oman, Pakistan, Panama, Paraguay, Peru, Philippines, Poland, Portugal, Qatar, Republic of Korea, Republic of Moldova, Romania, Russian Federation, Saint Lucia, Saint Vincent and the Grenadines, San Marino, Saudi Arabia, Senegal, Serbia and Montenegro, Singapore, Slovakia, Slovenia, Solomon Islands, Somalia, South Africa, Spain, Sri Lanka, Sudan, Suriname, Swaziland, Sweden, Switzerland, Syrian Arab Republic, Tajikistan, Thailand, The former Yugoslav Republic of Macedonia, Togo, Trinidad and Tobago, Tunisia, Turkey, Turkmenistan, Ukraine, United Arab Emirates, United Kingdom, United Republic of Tanzania, Uruguay, Uzbekistan, Venezuela, Viet Nam, Yemen, Zambia, Zimbabwe.

Against: Costa Rica, Israel, Marshall Islands, Micronesia, Nauru, Palau, United States.

Abstaining: Albania, Australia, Cameroon, El Salvador, Fiji, Guatemala, Haiti, Papua New Guinea, Samoa, Tuvalu, Uganda, Vanuatu.

Economic and social situation

A May report on the economic and social repercussions of the Israeli occupation on the living conditions of Palestinians in the Occupied Palestinian Territory, including East Jerusalem, and of the Arab population in the occupied Syrian Golan [A/60/65-E/2005/13] was prepared by the Economic and Social Commission for Western Asia (ESCWA), in accordance with Economic and Social Council resolution 2004/54 [YUN 2004, p. 474] and General Assembly resolution 59/251 [ibid., p. 475]; it covered developments since the last ESCWA report [ibid., p. 474].

The report noted that the Israeli occupation continued to deepen the economic and social hardship for Palestinians. Economic indicators continued to show negative trends: high unemployment; greater dependency on food aid; and untold losses from the physical destruction of Palestinian homes, public buildings, agricultural assets, infrastructure and private property. Israel's confiscation of Palestinian land and water resources for settlements and the erection of the West Bank barrier accelerated during the period under review. Refugees, women and children bore a significant brunt of those measures. Malnutrition and other health problems afflicted a growing number of Palestinians at a time of curtailed access to needed services. Over 60 per cent of children below 2 years of age, 36 per cent of pregnant women, and over 43 per cent of nursing mothers in the Gaza Strip were anaemic. An estimated 38 per cent of the Palestinian population was subject to food insecurity. Israeli restrictions regularly impeded humanitarian services to the Occupied Palestinian Territory. Israeli settlements, land confiscation and the construction of the barrier in the occupied territory, isolated occupied East Jerusalem, bisected the West Bank, curtailed normal economic and social life, and continued to fuel the conflict. In 2004, the number of Israeli settlers in the West Bank and Gaza Strip grew to 250,179, a 6 per cent increase from 2003. Israeli settlements in the occupied Syrian Golan Heights, housing an estimated 20,000 Israeli settlers, continued to expand unabated. Access to natural resources and social services remained inadequate for the Arab population in the Syrian Golan Heights.

ECONOMIC AND SOCIAL COUNCIL ACTION

On 27 July [meeting 40], the Economic and Social Council adopted **resolution 2005/51** [draft: E/2005/L.24/Rev.1] by recorded vote (49-2-1) [agenda item 11].

Economic and social repercussions of the Israeli occupation on the living conditions of the Palestinian people in the Occupied Palestinian Territory, including Jerusalem, and the Arab population in the occupied Syrian Golan

The Economic and Social Council,

Recalling General Assembly resolution 59/251 of 22 December 2004,

Also recalling its resolution 2004/54 of 23 July 2004,

Guided by the principles of the Charter of the United Nations affirming the inadmissibility of the acquisition of territory by force, and recalling relevant Security Council resolutions, including resolutions 242(1967) of 22 November 1967, 338(1973) of 22 October 1973, 446(1979) of 22 March 1979, 452(1979) of 20 July 1979, 465(1980) of 1 March 1980, 476(1980) of 30 June 1980, 478(1980) of 20 August 1980, 497(1981) of 17 December 1981, 904(1994) of 18 March 1994, 1073 (1996) of 28 September 1996, 1397(2002) of 12 March 2002, 1515(2003) of 19 November 2003 and 1544(2004) of 19 May 2004,

Recalling the resolutions of the tenth emergency special session of the General Assembly, including ES-10/13 of 21 October 2003, ES-10/14 of 8 December 2003 and ES-10/15 of 20 July 2004,

Reaffirming the applicability of the Geneva Convention relative to the Protection of Civilian Persons in Time of War, of 12 August 1949 to the Occupied Palestinian Territory, including East Jerusalem, and other Arab territories occupied by Israel since 1967,

Stressing the importance of the revival of the Middle East peace process on the basis of Security Council resolutions 242(1967), 338(1973), 425(1978) of 19 March 1978, 1397(2002), 1515(2003) and 1544(2004) and the principle of land for peace as well as compliance with the agreements reached between the Government of Israel and the Palestine Liberation Organization, the representative of the Palestinian people,

Reaffirming the principle of the permanent sovereignty of peoples under foreign occupation over their natural resources,

Convinced that the Israeli occupation has gravely impeded the efforts to achieve sustainable development and a sound economic environment in the Occupied Palestinian Territory, including East Jerusalem, and the occupied Syrian Golan,

Gravely concerned about the deterioration of the economic and living conditions of the Palestinian people in the Occupied Palestinian Territory, including East Jerusalem, and of the Arab population of the occupied Syrian Golan and the exploitation by Israel, the occupying Power, of their natural resources,

Gravely concerned also by the grave impact on the economic and social conditions of the Palestinian people caused by Israel's construction of the wall and its associated regime inside the Occupied Palestinian Territory, including in and around East Jerusalem, and the resulting violation of their economic and social rights, including the right to work, to health, to education and to an adequate standard of living,

Recalling, in this regard, the International Covenant on Civil and Political Rights, the International Covenant on Economic, Social and Cultural Rights and the Convention on the Rights of the Child, and affirming that these human rights instruments must be respected in the Occupied Palestinian Territory, including East Jerusalem, as well as in the occupied Syrian Golan,

Gravely concerned at the extensive destruction by Israel, the occupying Power, of agricultural land and orchards in the Occupied Palestinian Territory, including East Jerusalem, during the recent period, including, and in particular, as a result of its unlawful construction of the wall in the Occupied Palestinian Territory, including in and around East Jerusalem,

Recalling the advisory opinion rendered on 9 July 2004 by the International Court of Justice on the *Legal Consequences of the Construction of a Wall in the Occupied Palestinian Territory*, recalling also Assembly resolution ES-10/15, and stressing the need to comply with the obligations mentioned therein,

Expressing concern at the recent escalation of violence that has been characteristic of recent years following a period of relative calm, and, in this context, expressing its concern about the tragic and violent events that have taken place since September 2000, which have led to many deaths and injuries,

Aware of the important work being done by the United Nations and the specialized agencies in support of the economic and social development of the Palestinian people, as well as the assistance being provided in the humanitarian field,

Conscious of the urgent need for the reconstruction and development of the economic and social infrastructure of the Occupied Palestinian Territory, including East Jerusalem, as well as the urgent need to address the dire humanitarian crisis facing the Palestinian people,

Calling upon both parties to fulfil their obligations under the road map in cooperation with the Quartet,

1. *Stresses* the need to preserve the national unity and the territorial integrity of the Occupied Palestinian Territory, including East Jerusalem, and to guarantee the freedom of movement of persons and goods in the Territory, including the removal of restrictions on going into and from East Jerusalem, and the freedom of movement to and from the outside world;

2. *Also stresses* the vital importance of the construction and operation of the airport and the seaport in Gaza and the establishment of the safe passage between the West Bank and Gaza for the economic and social development of the Palestinian people;

3. *Demands* the complete cessation of all acts of violence, including all acts of terror, provocation, incitement and destruction;

4. *Calls upon* Israel, the occupying Power, to end its occupation of Palestinian cities, towns and other populated centres, to cease its destruction of homes and properties, economic institutions and agricultural fields and to end the imposition of all forms of closure and curfew, which impede efforts aimed at the amelioration of the economic and social conditions and the development of the Palestinian people;

5. *Reaffirms* the inalienable right of the Palestinian people and the Arab population of the occupied Syrian Golan to all their natural and economic resources, and calls upon Israel, the occupying Power, not to exploit, endanger or cause loss or depletion of those resources;

6. *Also reaffirms* that Israeli settlements in the Occupied Palestinian Territory, including East Jerusalem, and the occupied Syrian Golan, are illegal and an obstacle to economic and social development, and calls for the full implementation of the relevant Security Council resolutions;

7. *Stresses* that the wall being constructed by Israel in the Occupied Palestinian Territory, including in and around East Jerusalem, is contrary to international law and is seriously debilitating to the economic and social development of the Palestinian people, and calls in this regard for full compliance with the legal obligations mentioned in the 9 July 2004 advisory opinion of the International Court of Justice and in Assembly resolution ES-10/15;

8. *Emphasizes* the importance of the work of the organizations and agencies of the United Nations and of the United Nations Special Coordinator for the Middle East Peace Process and Personal Representative of the Secretary-General to the Palestine Liberation Organization and the Palestinian Authority;

9. *Urges* Member States to encourage private foreign investment in the Occupied Palestinian Territory, including East Jerusalem, in infrastructure, job-creation projects and social development in order to alleviate the hardships being faced by the Palestinian people and improve their living conditions;

10. *Requests* the Secretary-General to submit to the General Assembly at its sixtieth session, through the Economic and Social Council, a report on the implementation of the present resolution and to continue to include in the report of the United Nations Special Coordinator an update on the living conditions of the Palestinian people, in collaboration with relevant United Nations agencies;

11. *Decides* to include the item entitled "Economic and social repercussions of the Israeli occupation on the living conditions of the Palestinian people in the Occupied Palestinian Territory, including East Jerusalem, and the Arab population in the occupied Syrian Golan" in the agenda of its substantive session of 2006.

RECORDED VOTE ON RESOLUTION 2005/51:

In favour: Albania, Armenia, Azerbaijan, Bangladesh, Belgium, Belize, Benin, Brazil, Canada, China, Colombia, Congo, Cuba, Denmark, Ecuador, France, Germany, Guinea, Iceland, India, Indonesia, Ireland, Italy, Jamaica, Japan, Kenya, Lithuania, Malaysia, Mauritius, Mexico, Mozambique, Namibia, Nicaragua, Nigeria, Pakistan, Panama, Poland, Republic of Korea, Russian Federation, Saudi Arabia, Senegal, South Africa, Spain, Thailand, Tunisia, Turkey, United Arab Emirates, United Kingdom, United Republic of Tanzania.

Against: Australia, United States.

Abstaining: Costa Rica.

On the same date (**decision 2005/304**), the Council took note of the note of the Secretary-General transmitting the report prepared by ESCWA (see p. 523).

GENERAL ASSEMBLY ACTION

On 22 December [meeting 68], the General Assembly, on the recommendation of the Second (Economic and Financial) Committee [A/60/484], adopted **resolution 60/183** by recorded vote (156-6-8) [agenda item 38].

Permanent sovereignty of the Palestinian people in the Occupied Palestinian Territory, including East Jerusalem, and of the Arab population in the occupied Syrian Golan over their natural resources

The General Assembly,

Recalling its resolution 59/251 of 22 December 2004, and taking note of Economic and Social Council resolution 2005/51 of 27 July 2005,

Recalling also its resolution 58/292 of 6 May 2004,

Reaffirming the principle of the permanent sovereignty of peoples under foreign occupation over their natural resources,

Guided by the principles of the Charter of the United Nations, affirming the inadmissibility of the acquisition of territory by force, and recalling relevant Security Council resolutions, including resolutions 242(1967) of 22 November 1967, 465(1980) of 1 March 1980 and 497(1981) of 17 December 1981,

Recalling its resolution 2625(XXV) of 24 October 1970,

Reaffirming the applicability of the Geneva Convention relative to the Protection of Civilian Persons in Time of War, of 12 August 1949, to the Occupied Palestinian Territory, including East Jerusalem, and other Arab territories occupied by Israel since 1967,

Recalling, in this regard, the International Covenant on Civil and Political Rights and the International Covenant on Economic, Social and Cultural Rights and affirming that these human rights instruments must be respected in the Occupied Palestinian Territory, including East Jerusalem, as well as in the occupied Syrian Golan,

Recalling also the advisory opinion rendered on 9 July 2004 by the International Court of Justice on the *Legal Consequences of the Construction of a Wall in the Occupied Palestinian Territory*, and recalling further its resolution ES-10/15 of 20 July 2004,

Expressing its concern at the exploitation by Israel, the occupying Power, of the natural resources of the Occupied Palestinian Territory, including East Jerusalem, and other Arab territories occupied by Israel since 1967,

Expressing its concern also at the extensive destruction by Israel, the occupying Power, of agricultural land and orchards in the Occupied Palestinian Territory, including the uprooting of a vast number of fruit-bearing trees,

Aware of the detrimental impact of the Israeli settlements on Palestinian and other Arab natural resources, especially as a result of the confiscation of land and the forced diversion of water resources, and of the dire economic and social consequences in this regard,

Aware also of the detrimental impact on Palestinian natural resources being caused by the unlawful construction of the wall by Israel, the occupying Power, in the Occupied Palestinian Territory, including in and around East Jerusalem, and of its grave effect on the natural resources and economic and social conditions of the Palestinian people,

Reaffirming the need for the immediate resumption of negotiations within the Middle East peace process, on the basis of Security Council resolutions 242(1967), 338(1973) of 22 October 1973, 425(1978) of 19 March 1978 and 1397(2002) of 12 March 2002, the principle of land for peace and the Quartet performance-based road map to a permanent two-State solution to the Israeli-Palestinian conflict, as endorsed by the Security Council in its resolution 1515(2003) of 19 November 2003, and for the achievement of a final settlement on all tracks,

Acknowledging the importance of the Israeli withdrawal from within the Gaza Strip and parts of the northern West Bank and of the dismantlement of settlements therein as a step towards the implementation of the road map,

Recalling the need to end all acts of violence, including acts of terror, provocation, incitement and destruction,

Taking note with appreciation of the note by the Secretary-General transmitting the report prepared by the Economic and Social Commission for Western Asia on the economic and social repercussions of the Israeli occupation on the living conditions of the Palestinian people in the Occupied Palestinian Territory, including Jerusalem, and of the Arab population in the occupied Syrian Golan,

1. *Reaffirms* the inalienable rights of the Palestinian people and the population of the occupied Syrian Golan over their natural resources, including land and water;

2. *Calls upon* Israel, the occupying Power, not to exploit, damage, cause loss or depletion of, or endanger the natural resources in the Occupied Palestinian Territory, including East Jerusalem, and in the occupied Syrian Golan;

3. *Recognizes* the right of the Palestinian people to claim restitution as a result of any exploitation, damage, loss or depletion, or endangerment of their natural resources resulting from illegal measures taken by Israel, the occupying Power, in the Occupied Palestinian Territory, including East Jerusalem, and expresses the hope that this issue will be dealt with in the framework of the final status negotiations between the Palestinian and Israeli sides;

4. *Stresses* that the wall being constructed by Israel in the Occupied Palestinian Territory, including in and around East Jerusalem, is contrary to international law and is seriously depriving the Palestinian people of their natural resources, and calls in this regard for full compliance with the legal obligations mentioned in the 9 July 2004 advisory opinion of the International Court of Justice and in resolution ES-10/15;

5. *Welcomes* the Israeli withdrawal from within the Gaza Strip and parts of the northern West Bank and the dismantlement of the settlements therein as a step towards the implementation of the road map;

6. *Calls upon* Israel, the occupying Power, in this regard, to comply strictly with its obligations under international law, including international humanitarian law, with respect to the alteration of the character and status of the Occupied Palestinian Territory, including East Jerusalem;

7. *Also calls upon* Israel, the occupying Power, to cease the dumping of all kinds of waste materials in the Occupied Palestinian Territory, including East Jerusalem, and in the occupied Syrian Golan, which gravely threaten their natural resources, namely the water and land resources, and pose an environmental hazard and health threat to the civilian populations;

8. *Requests* the Secretary-General to report to it at its sixty-first session on the implementation of the present resolution, and decides to include in the provisional agenda of its sixty-first session the item entitled "Permanent sovereignty of the Palestinian people in the Occupied Palestinian Territory, including East Jerusalem, and of the Arab population in the occupied Syrian Golan over their natural resources".

RECORDED VOTE ON RESOLUTION 60/183:

In favour: Afghanistan, Algeria, Andorra, Angola, Antigua and Barbuda, Argentina, Armenia, Austria, Azerbaijan, Bahamas, Bahrain, Bangladesh, Barbados, Belarus, Belgium, Belize, Benin, Bhutan, Bolivia, Botswana, Brazil, Brunei Darussalam, Bulgaria, Burkina Faso, Burundi, Cambodia, Canada, Cape Verde, Central African Republic, Chad, Chile, China, Colombia, Comoros, Congo, Croatia, Cuba, Cyprus, Czech Republic, Democratic People's Republic of Korea, Denmark, Djibouti, Dominica, Ecuador, Egypt, Eritrea, Estonia, Ethiopia, Fiji, Finland, France, Georgia, Germany, Ghana, Greece, Guatemala, Guinea, Guinea-Bissau, Guyana, Haiti, Hungary, Iceland, India, Indonesia, Iran, Iraq, Ireland, Italy, Jamaica, Japan, Jordan, Kazakhstan, Kenya, Kuwait, Kyrgyzstan, Lao People's Democratic Republic, Latvia, Lebanon, Lesotho, Liberia, Libyan Arab Jamahiriya, Liechtenstein, Lithuania, Luxembourg, Madagascar, Malaysia, Maldives, Mali, Malta, Mauritania, Mauritius, Mexico, Monaco, Mongolia, Morocco, Mozambique, Myanmar, Namibia, Nepal, Netherlands, New Zealand, Nicaragua, Nigeria, Norway, Oman, Pakistan, Panama, Paraguay, Peru, Philippines, Poland, Portugal, Qatar, Republic of Korea, Republic of Moldova, Romania, Russian Federation, Saint Lucia, Saint Vincent and the Grenadines, Samoa, San Marino, Saudi Arabia, Senegal, Serbia and Montenegro, Sierra Leone, Singapore, Slovakia, Slovenia, Somalia, South Africa, Spain, Sri Lanka, Sudan, Suriname, Swaziland, Sweden, Switzerland, Syrian Arab Republic, Tajikistan, Thailand, The former Yugoslav Republic of Macedonia, Togo, Tunisia, Turkey, Uganda, Ukraine, United Arab Emirates, United Kingdom, United Republic of Tanzania, Uruguay, Uzbekistan, Venezuela, Viet Nam, Yemen, Zambia, Zimbabwe.

Against: Australia, Israel, Marshall Islands, Micronesia, Palau, United States.

Abstaining: Albania, Cameroon, Côte d'Ivoire, Dominican Republic, El Salvador, Nauru, Papua New Guinea, Tuvalu.

Other aspects

Special Committee on Israeli Practices. In response to General Assembly resolution 59/121 [YUN 2004, p. 480], the Special Committee to Investigate Israeli Practices Affecting the Human Rights of the Palestinian People and Other Arabs of the Occupied Territories, in September, reported for the thirty-seventh time to the General Assembly on events and the human rights situation in the territories it considered occupied—the Golan Heights, the West Bank, including East Jerusalem, and the Gaza Strip [A/60/380]. The report reflected information gathered during the Committee's mission to Egypt, Jordan and the Syrian Arab Republic from 25 June to 9 July. In those three countries, the Committee met with 46 witnesses representing Palestinian non-governmental organizations (NGOs), as well as individuals from Syria. The report reviewed the human rights situation in the Occupied Palestinian Territory and the Syrian Golan.

As in the past, the Committee was not authorized by Israel to visit the occupied territories, which had been the case since 1968, when the Committee was established [YUN 1968, p. 556]. After 37 years of being denied access to the occupied territories by Israel, the Special Committee wondered whether Israel should not revisit the reasons behind such refusal. The world had changed since the inception of the Special Committee's mandate, with younger generations taking over. Disagreement should not be a hindrance to meeting and interacting; discussing issues of common concern would not affect the legal state of affairs.

The Special Committee, during its field trips to the Middle East, in 2005, was challenged by various interlocutors, including a number of Palestinian witnesses, as to what actions it envisaged to implement its mandate. The Committee, while indicating that its main role and responsibility were to report to the General Assembly, suggested that the time might have come for the Assembly to consider innovative ways of assisting it in fulfilling its mandate.

The Special Committee noted that hopes for progress in the occupied territories tended to vanish in the face of persistent negative factors, such as the loss of control by the Palestinians over strategic resources like water and energy; the loss of contiguity of their lands due to the wall, road closures and checkpoints, as well as to growing settlers' communities and the network of roads built for their benefit. The Committee also noted the serious deterioration of the situation of Palestinian children and youth whose lives were at risk, whose freedom of movement was severely curtailed by long hours of waiting at entry points to the wall or at checkpoints and other restrictions, and whose level of education and academic achievements were negatively affected by the numerous impediments imposed by the occupying authorities.

Report of Special Rapporteur. The Special Rapporteur on the situation of human rights in the Palestinian territories occupied by Israel since 1967, John Dugard, submitted to the Commission on Human Rights at its 2005 session reports describing the situation of human rights in the Occupied Palestinian Territory. [E/CN.4/2005/29 & Add.1, A/60/271], (see pp. 904 & 905).

GENERAL ASSEMBLY ACTION

On 8 December [meeting 62], the General Assembly, on the recommendation of the Fourth (Special Political and Decolonization) Committee [A/60/477], adopted **resolution 60/107** by recorded vote (148-7-17) [agenda item 31].

Israeli practices affecting the human rights of the Palestinian people in the Occupied Palestinian Territory, including East Jerusalem

The General Assembly,

Recalling its relevant resolutions, including resolution 59/124 of 10 December 2004, as well as those adopted at its tenth emergency special session,

Recalling also the relevant resolutions of the Commission on Human Rights,

Bearing in mind the relevant resolutions of the Security Council,

Having considered the report of the Special Committee to Investigate Israeli Practices Affecting the Human Rights of the Palestinian People and Other Arabs of the Occupied Territories and the report of the Secretary-General,

Taking note of the report of the Human Rights Inquiry Commission established by the Commission on Human Rights and the recent reports of the Special Rapporteur of the Commission on Human Rights on the situation of human rights in the Palestinian territories occupied by Israel since 1967,

Recalling the advisory opinion rendered on 9 July 2004 by the International Court of Justice, and recalling also General Assembly resolution ES-10/15 of 20 July 2004,

Noting in particular the Court's reply, including that the construction of the wall being built by Israel, the occupying Power, in the Occupied Palestinian Territory, including in and around East Jerusalem, and its associated regime are contrary to international law,

Recalling the International Covenant on Civil and Political Rights, the International Covenant on Economic, Social and Cultural Rights and the Convention on the Rights of the Child and affirming that these human rights instruments must be respected in the Occupied Palestinian Territory, including East Jerusalem,

Aware of the responsibility of the international community to promote human rights and ensure respect for international law, and recalling in this regard its resolution 2625(XXV) of 24 October 1970,

Reaffirming the principle of the inadmissibility of the acquisition of territory by force,

Reaffirming also the applicability of the Geneva Convention relative to the Protection of Civilian Persons in Time of War, of 12 August 1949, to the Occupied Palestinian Territory, including East Jerusalem, and other Arab territories occupied by Israel since 1967,

Reaffirming further the obligation of the States parties to the Fourth Geneva Convention under articles 146, 147 and 148 with regard to penal sanctions, grave breaches and responsibilities of the High Contracting Parties,

Reaffirming that all States have the right and the duty to take actions in conformity with international law and international humanitarian law to counter deadly acts of violence against their civilian population in order to protect the lives of their citizens,

Stressing the need for full compliance with the Israeli-Palestinian agreements reached within the context of the Middle East peace process, including the Sharm el-Sheikh understandings, and the implementation of the Quartet road map to a permanent two-State solution to the Israeli-Palestinian conflict,

Acknowledging the importance of the Israeli withdrawal from within the Gaza Strip and parts of the northern West Bank and of the dismantlement of settlements therein as a step towards the implementation of the road map,

Expressing grave concern about the continuing systematic violation of the human rights of the Palestinian people by Israel, the occupying Power, including that arising from the excessive use of force, the use of collective punishment, the reoccupation and closure of areas, the confiscation of land, the establishment and expansion of settlements, the construction of the wall inside the Occupied Palestinian Territory in departure from the Armistice Line of 1949, the destruction of property and all other actions by it designed to change the legal status, geographical nature and demographic composition of the Occupied Palestinian Territory, including East Jerusalem,

Gravely concerned about the military actions that have been carried out since 28 September 2000 and that have led to thousands of deaths among Palestinian civilians, including hundreds of children, and tens of thousands of injuries,

Expressing deep concern about the continuing detrimental impact of the extensive destruction caused by the Israeli occupying forces, including of religious, cultural and historical sites, of vital infrastructure and institutions of the Palestinian Authority, and of agricultural land throughout Palestinian cities, towns, villages and refugee camps,

Expressing deep concern also about the Israeli policy of closure and the severe restrictions, including curfews, that continue to be imposed on the movement of persons and goods, including medical and humanitarian personnel and goods, throughout the Occupied Pales-

tinian Territory, including East Jerusalem, and the consequent negative impact on the socio-economic situation of the Palestinian people, which remains that of a dire humanitarian crisis,

Concerned about the continued establishment of checkpoints in the Occupied Palestinian Territory, including East Jerusalem, and the transformation of several of these checkpoints into structures akin to permanent border crossings inside the Occupied Palestinian Territory,

Expressing concern that thousands of Palestinians continue to be held in Israeli prisons or detention centres under harsh conditions that impair their well-being, and also expressing concern about the ill-treatment and harassment of any Palestinian prisoners and all reports of torture,

Convinced of the need for an international presence to monitor the situation, to contribute to ending the violence and protecting the Palestinian civilians and to help the parties to implement agreements reached, and, in this regard, recalls the positive contribution of the Temporary International Presence in Hebron,

Stressing the necessity for the full implementation of all relevant Security Council resolutions,

1. *Reiterates* that all measures and actions taken by Israel, the occupying Power, in the Occupied Palestinian Territory, including East Jerusalem, in violation of the relevant provisions of the Geneva Convention relative to the Protection of Civilian Persons in Time of War, of 12 August 1949, and contrary to the relevant resolutions of the Security Council, are illegal and have no validity;

2. *Demands* that Israel, the occupying Power, comply fully with the provisions of the Fourth Geneva Convention of 1949 and cease immediately all measures and actions taken in violation and in breach of the Convention, including all of its settlement activities and the construction of the wall in the Occupied Palestinian Territory, including in and around East Jerusalem, as well as the extrajudicial executions;

3. *Condemns* all acts of violence, including all acts of terror, provocation, incitement and destruction, especially the excessive use of force by the Israeli occupying forces against Palestinian civilians, resulting in extensive loss of life, vast numbers of injuries and massive destruction of homes, properties, agricultural lands and vital infrastructure;

4. *Expresses grave concern* at the use of suicide bombing attacks against Israeli civilians resulting in extensive loss of life and injury;

5. *Welcomes* the Israeli withdrawal from within the Gaza Strip and parts of the northern West Bank and the dismantlement of the settlements therein as a step towards the implementation of the road map;

6. *Calls upon* Israel, the occupying Power, in this regard, to comply strictly with its obligations under international law, including international humanitarian law, with respect to the alteration of the character and status of the Occupied Palestinian Territory, including East Jerusalem;

7. *Demands* that Israel, the occupying Power, cease all practices and actions which violate the human rights of the Palestinian people, and that it respect human rights law and comply with its legal obligations in this regard;

8. *Demands also* that Israel, the occupying Power, comply with its legal obligations under international law, as mentioned in the advisory opinion rendered on 9 July 2004 by the International Court of Justice and as demanded in resolution ES-10/15 and resolution ES-10/13 of 21 October 2003, and that it immediately cease the construction of the wall in the Occupied Palestinian Territory, including in and around East Jerusalem, dismantle forthwith the structure situated therein, repeal or render ineffective all legislative and regulatory acts relating thereto, and make reparation for all damage caused by the construction of the wall;

9. *Stresses* the need for unity and territorial integrity of all the Occupied Palestinian Territory and to guarantee the freedom of movement of persons and goods within the Palestinian territory, including the removal of restrictions on movement into and from East Jerusalem, and the freedom of movement to and from the outside world;

10. *Stresses also* the need for the full implementation of the Sharm el-Sheikh understandings;

11. *Requests* the Secretary-General to report to the General Assembly at its sixty-first session on the implementation of the present resolution.

RECORDED VOTE ON RESOLUTION 60/107:

In favour: Afghanistan, Algeria, Andorra, Antigua and Barbuda, Argentina, Armenia, Austria, Azerbaijan, Bahamas, Bahrain, Bangladesh, Barbados, Belarus, Belgium, Belize, Benin, Bhutan, Bolivia, Botswana, Brazil, Brunei Darussalam, Bulgaria, Burkina Faso, Burundi, Cambodia, Cape Verde, Central African Republic, Chile, China, Colombia, Croatia, Cuba, Cyprus, Czech Republic, Democratic People's Republic of Korea, Denmark, Djibouti, Dominica, Ecuador, Egypt, Eritrea, Estonia, Ethiopia, Fiji, Finland, France, Gabon, Georgia, Germany, Ghana, Greece, Guinea, Guinea-Bissau, Guyana, Hungary, India, Indonesia, Iran, Iraq, Ireland, Italy, Jamaica, Japan, Jordan, Kazakhstan, Kenya, Kuwait, Kyrgyzstan, Lao People's Democratic Republic, Latvia, Lebanon, Lesotho, Liberia, Libyan Arab Jamahiriya, Liechtenstein, Lithuania, Luxembourg, Malaysia, Maldives, Mali, Malta, Mauritania, Mauritius, Mexico, Monaco, Mongolia, Morocco, Mozambique, Myanmar, Namibia, Nepal, Netherlands, New Zealand, Niger, Nigeria, Norway, Oman, Pakistan, Panama, Paraguay, Peru, Philippines, Poland, Portugal, Qatar, Republic of Korea, Republic of Moldova, Romania, Russian Federation, Saint Lucia, Saint Vincent and the Grenadines, Samoa, San Marino, Saudi Arabia, Senegal, Serbia and Montenegro, Singapore, Slovakia, Slovenia, Somalia, South Africa, Spain, Sri Lanka, Sudan, Suriname, Sweden, Switzerland, Syrian Arab Republic, Tajikistan, Thailand, The former Yugoslav Republic of Macedonia, Timor-Leste, Togo, Trinidad and Tobago, Tunisia, Turkey, Turkmenistan, Ukraine, United Arab Emirates, United Kingdom, United Republic of Tanzania, Uruguay, Uzbekistan, Venezuela, Viet Nam, Yemen, Zambia, Zimbabwe.

Against: Australia, Grenada, Israel, Marshall Islands, Micronesia, Palau, United States.

Abstaining: Albania, Cameroon, Canada, Costa Rica, Dominican Republic, El Salvador, Guatemala, Haiti, Honduras, Iceland, Nicaragua, Papua New Guinea, Solomon Islands, Tonga, Tuvalu, Uganda, Vanuatu.

By **resolution 60/39** of 1 December, the Assembly reaffirmed the right of the Palestinian people to self-determination, including the right to their State, and urged all States and UN specialized agencies and organizations to support the Palestinian people in their quest for self-determination (see p. 536).

Work of Special Committee

In an August report [A/60/294], the Secretary-General stated that all necessary facilities were provided to the Special Committee on Israeli Practices, as requested in General Assembly resolution 59/121 [YUN 2004, p. 480]. Arrangements were made for it to meet in March and June in Geneva, and a field mission was carried out to Egypt, Jordan and the Syrian Arab Republic from 25 June to 9 July. The UN Department of Public Information continued to disseminate information on the Committee's activities.

GENERAL ASSEMBLY ACTION

On 8 December [meeting 62], the General Assembly, on the recommendation of the Fourth Committee [A/60/477], adopted **resolution 60/104** by recorded vote (86-10-74) [agenda item 31].

Work of the Special Committee to Investigate Israeli Practices Affecting the Human Rights of the Palestinian People and Other Arabs of the Occupied Territories

The General Assembly,

Guided by the purposes and principles of the Charter of the United Nations,

Guided also by international humanitarian law, in particular the Geneva Convention relative to the Protection of Civilian Persons in Time of War, of 12 August 1949, as well as international standards of human rights, in particular the Universal Declaration of Human Rights and the International Covenants on Human Rights,

Recalling its relevant resolutions, including resolutions 2443(XXIII) of 19 December 1968 and 59/121 of 10 December 2004, and the relevant resolutions of the Commission on Human Rights,

Recalling also the relevant resolutions of the Security Council,

Taking into account the advisory opinion rendered on 9 July 2004 by the International Court of Justice on the *Legal Consequences of the Construction of a Wall in the Occupied Palestinian Territory*, and recalling in this regard General Assembly resolution ES-10/15 of 20 July 2004,

Convinced that occupation itself represents a gross and grave violation of human rights,

Gravely concerned about the continuing detrimental impact of the events that have taken place since 28 September 2000, including the excessive use of force by the Israeli occupying forces against Palestinian civilians, resulting in thousands of deaths and injuries, and the widespread destruction of property,

Having considered the report of the Special Committee to Investigate Israeli Practices Affecting the Human Rights of the Palestinian People and Other Arabs of the Occupied Territories and the relevant reports of the Secretary-General,

Recalling the Declaration of Principles on Interim Self-Government Arrangements of 13 September 1993 and the subsequent implementation agreements between the Palestinian and Israeli sides,

Expressing the hope that the Israeli occupation will be brought to an early end and that therefore the violation of the human rights of the Palestinian people will cease, and recalling in this regard its resolution 58/292 of 6 May 2004,

1. *Commends* the Special Committee to Investigate Israeli Practices Affecting the Human Rights of the Palestinian People and Other Arabs of the Occupied Territories for its efforts in performing the tasks as-

signed to it by the General Assembly and for its impartiality;

2. *Reiterates its demand* that Israel, the occupying Power, cooperate with the Special Committee in implementing its mandate;

3. *Deplores* those policies and practices of Israel that violate the human rights of the Palestinian people and other Arabs of the occupied territories, as reflected in the report of the Special Committee covering the reporting period;

4. *Expresses grave concern* about the critical situation in the Occupied Palestinian Territory, including East Jerusalem, since 28 September 2000, as a result of unlawful Israeli practices and measures, and especially condemns all Israeli settlement activities and the construction of the wall, as well as the excessive and indiscriminate use of force against the civilian population, including extrajudicial executions;

5. *Requests* the Special Committee, pending complete termination of the Israeli occupation, to continue to investigate Israeli policies and practices in the Occupied Palestinian Territory, including East Jerusalem, and other Arab territories occupied by Israel since 1967, especially Israeli violations of the Geneva Convention relative to the Protection of Civilian Persons in Time of War, of 12 August 1949, and to consult, as appropriate, with the International Committee of the Red Cross according to its regulations in order to ensure that the welfare and human rights of the peoples of the occupied territories are safeguarded and to report to the Secretary-General as soon as possible and whenever the need arises thereafter;

6. *Also requests* the Special Committee to submit regularly to the Secretary-General periodic reports on the current situation in the Occupied Palestinian Territory, including East Jerusalem;

7. *Further requests* the Special Committee to continue to investigate the treatment of prisoners and detainees in the Occupied Palestinian Territory, including East Jerusalem, and other Arab territories occupied by Israel since 1967;

8. *Requests* the Secretary-General:

(a) To provide the Special Committee with all necessary facilities, including those required for its visits to the occupied territories, so that it may investigate Israeli policies and practices referred to in the present resolution;

(b) To continue to make available such staff as may be necessary to assist the Special Committee in the performance of its tasks;

(c) To circulate regularly to Member States the periodic reports mentioned in paragraph 6 above;

(d) To ensure the widest circulation of the reports of the Special Committee and of information regarding its activities and findings, by all means available, through the Department of Public Information of the Secretariat and, where necessary, to reprint those reports of the Special Committee that are no longer available;

(e) To report to the General Assembly at its sixty-first session on the tasks entrusted to him in the present resolution;

9. *Decides* to include in the provisional agenda of its sixty-first session the item entitled "Report of the Special Committee to Investigate Israeli Practices Affecting the Human Rights of the Palestinian People and Other Arabs of the Occupied Territories".

RECORDED VOTE ON RESOLUTION 60/104:

In favour: Afghanistan, Algeria, Antigua and Barbuda, Armenia, Azerbaijan, Bahrain, Bangladesh, Barbados, Belarus, Belize, Benin, Bhutan, Bolivia, Botswana, Brazil, Brunei Darussalam, Burundi, Cambodia, Cape Verde, Chile, China, Colombia, Cuba, Democratic People's Republic of Korea, Djibouti, Dominica, Ecuador, Egypt, Eritrea, Gabon, Ghana, Guinea, Guinea-Bissau, Guyana, India, Indonesia, Iran, Iraq, Jamaica, Jordan, Kenya, Kuwait, Lao People's Democratic Republic, Lebanon, Lesotho, Libyan Arab Jamahiriya, Malaysia, Maldives, Mali, Mauritania, Mauritius, Morocco, Mozambique, Myanmar, Namibia, Nepal, Niger, Nigeria, Oman, Pakistan, Paraguay, Qatar, Saint Lucia, Saint Vincent and the Grenadines, Saudi Arabia, Senegal, Singapore, Somalia, South Africa, Sri Lanka, Sudan, Suriname, Syrian Arab Republic, Togo, Trinidad and Tobago, Tunisia, Turkey, Turkmenistan, United Arab Emirates, United Republic of Tanzania, Uzbekistan, Venezuela, Viet Nam, Yemen, Zambia, Zimbabwe.

Against: Australia, Canada, Grenada, Israel, Marshall Islands, Micronesia, Nauru, Palau, Tuvalu, United States.

Abstaining: Albania, Andorra, Argentina, Austria, Bahamas, Belgium, Bulgaria, Burkina Faso, Cameroon, Costa Rica, Croatia, Cyprus, Czech Republic, Denmark, Dominican Republic, El Salvador, Estonia, Ethiopia, Fiji, Finland, France, Georgia, Germany, Greece, Guatemala, Haiti, Honduras, Hungary, Iceland, Ireland, Italy, Japan, Kazakhstan, Kyrgyzstan, Latvia, Liechtenstein, Lithuania, Luxembourg, Malta, Mexico, Monaco, Mongolia, Netherlands, New Zealand, Nicaragua, Norway, Panama, Papua New Guinea, Peru, Philippines, Poland, Portugal, Republic of Korea, Republic of Moldova, Romania, Russian Federation, Samoa, San Marino, Serbia and Montenegro, Slovakia, Slovenia, Solomon Islands, Spain, Sweden, Switzerland, Tajikistan, Thailand, The former Yugoslav Republic of Macedonia, Tonga, Uganda, Ukraine, United Kingdom, Uruguay, Vanuatu.

Fourth Geneva Convention

Report of Secretary-General. In an August report [A/60/296], the Secretary-General informed the General Assembly that Israel had not replied to his July request for information on steps taken or envisaged to implement Assembly resolution 59/122 [YUN 2004, p. 481] demanding that Israel accept the *de jure* applicability of the Fourth Geneva Convention in the Occupied Palestinian Territory, including East Jerusalem, and that it comply scrupulously with its provisions. The Secretary-General noted that he had drawn the attention of all States parties to the Convention to paragraph 3 of resolution 59/122 calling on them to exert all efforts to ensure respect by Israel for the Convention's provisions, and to paragraph 6 of resolution 59/125 [ibid., p. 516] calling on States not to recognize any legislative or administrative measures and actions taken by Israel in the occupied Syrian Golan.

The High Contracting Parties to the Fourth Geneva Convention had ratified the applicability of the Convention to the Occupied Palestinian Territory at meetings in 1999 [YUN 1999, p. 415] and in 2001 [YUN 2001, p. 425].

GENERAL ASSEMBLY ACTION

On 8 December [meeting 62], the General Assembly, on the recommendation of the Fourth Committee [A/60/477], adopted **resolution 60/105** by recorded vote (158-6-7) [agenda item 31].

Applicability of the Geneva Convention relative to the Protection of Civilian Persons in Time of War, of 12 August 1949, to the Occupied Palestinian Territory, including East Jerusalem, and the other occupied Arab territories

The General Assembly,

Recalling its relevant resolutions, including its resolution 59/122 of 10 December 2004,

Recalling also its resolution ES-10/15 of 20 July 2004,

Bearing in mind the relevant resolutions of the Security Council,

Recalling the Regulations annexed to the Hague Convention IV of 1907, the Geneva Convention relative to the Protection of Civilian Persons in Time of War, of 12 August 1949, and relevant provisions of customary law, including those codified in Additional Protocol I to the four Geneva Conventions,

Having considered the report of the Special Committee to Investigate Israeli Practices Affecting the Human Rights of the Palestinian People and Other Arabs of the Occupied Territories and the relevant reports of the Secretary-General,

Considering that the promotion of respect for the obligations arising from the Charter of the United Nations and other instruments and rules of international law is among the basic purposes and principles of the United Nations,

Recalling the advisory opinion rendered on 9 July 2004 by the International Court of Justice, and also recalling General Assembly resolution ES-10/15,

Noting in particular the Court's reply, including that the Fourth Geneva Convention is applicable in the Occupied Palestinian Territory, including East Jerusalem, and that Israel is in breach of several of the provisions of the Convention,

Noting the convening for the first time, on 15 July 1999, of a Conference of High Contracting Parties to the Fourth Geneva Convention, as recommended by the General Assembly in its resolution ES-10/6 of 9 February 1999, on measures to enforce the Convention in the Occupied Palestinian Territory, including East Jerusalem, and to ensure respect thereof in accordance with article 1 common to the four Geneva Conventions, and aware of the statement adopted by the Conference,

Welcoming the reconvening of the Conference of High Contracting Parties to the Fourth Geneva Convention on 5 December 2001 in Geneva and stressing the importance of the Declaration adopted by the Conference, and underlining the need for the parties to follow up the implementation of the Declaration,

Welcoming and encouraging the initiatives by States parties to the Convention, both individually and collectively, according to article 1 common to the four Geneva Conventions, aimed at ensuring respect for the Convention,

Stressing that Israel, the occupying Power, should comply strictly with its obligations under international law, including international humanitarian law,

1. *Reaffirms* that the Geneva Convention relative to the Protection of Civilian Persons in Time of War, of 12 August 1949, is applicable to the Occupied Palestinian Territory, including East Jerusalem, and other Arab territories occupied by Israel since 1967;

2. *Demands* that Israel accept the de jure applicability of the Convention in the Occupied Palestinian Territory, including East Jerusalem, and other Arab territories occupied by Israel since 1967, and that it comply scrupulously with the provisions of the Convention;

3. *Calls upon* all High Contracting Parties to the Convention, in accordance with article 1 common to the four Geneva Conventions and as mentioned in the advisory opinion of the International Court of Justice of 9 July 2004, to continue to exert all efforts to ensure respect for its provisions by Israel, the occupying Power, in the Occupied Palestinian Territory, including East Jerusalem, and other Arab territories occupied by Israel since 1967,

4. *Reiterates* the need for speedy implementation of the relevant recommendations contained in the resolutions adopted by the General Assembly at its tenth emergency special session, including resolution ES-10/15, with regard to ensuring respect by Israel, the occupying Power, for the provisions of the Convention;

5. *Requests* the Secretary-General to report to the General Assembly at its sixty-first session on the implementation of the present resolution.

RECORDED VOTE ON RESOLUTION 60/105:

In favour: Afghanistan, Algeria, Andorra, Antigua and Barbuda, Argentina, Armenia, Austria, Azerbaijan, Bahamas, Bahrain, Bangladesh, Barbados, Belarus, Belgium, Belize, Benin, Bhutan, Bolivia, Botswana, Brazil, Brunei Darussalam, Bulgaria, Burkina Faso, Burundi, Cambodia, Canada, Cape Verde, Central African Republic, Chile, China, Colombia, Congo, Costa Rica, Croatia, Cuba, Cyprus, Czech Republic, Democratic People's Republic of Korea, Denmark, Djibouti, Dominica, Ecuador, Egypt, El Salvador, Eritrea, Estonia, Fiji, Finland, France, Gabon, Georgia, Germany, Ghana, Greece, Guatemala, Guinea, Guinea-Bissau, Guyana, Honduras, Hungary, Iceland, India, Indonesia, Iran, Iraq, Ireland, Italy, Jamaica, Japan, Jordan, Kazakhstan, Kenya, Kuwait, Kyrgyzstan, Lao People's Democratic Republic, Latvia, Lebanon, Lesotho, Liberia, Libyan Arab Jamahiriya, Liechtenstein, Lithuania, Luxembourg, Malaysia, Maldives, Mali, Malta, Mauritania, Mauritius, Mexico, Monaco, Mongolia, Morocco, Mozambique, Myanmar, Namibia, Nepal, Netherlands, New Zealand, Nicaragua, Niger, Nigeria, Norway, Oman, Pakistan, Panama, Papua New Guinea, Paraguay, Peru, Philippines, Poland, Portugal, Qatar, Republic of Korea, Republic of Moldova, Romania, Russian Federation, Saint Lucia, Saint Vincent and the Grenadines, Samoa, San Marino, Saudi Arabia, Senegal, Serbia and Montenegro, Singapore, Slovakia, Slovenia, Solomon Islands, Somalia, South Africa, Spain, Sri Lanka, Sudan, Suriname, Sweden, Switzerland, Syrian Arab Republic, Tajikistan, Thailand, The former Yugoslav Republic of Macedonia, Timor-Leste, Togo, Tonga, Trinidad and Tobago, Tunisia, Turkey, Turkmenistan, Ukraine, United Arab Emirates, United Kingdom, United Republic of Tanzania, Uruguay, Uzbekistan, Venezuela, Viet Nam, Yemen, Zambia, Zimbabwe.

Against: Grenada, Israel, Marshall Islands, Micronesia, Palau, United States.

Abstaining: Albania, Australia, Cameroon, Dominican Republic, Ethiopia, Haiti, Uganda.

Israeli settlements

Report of Secretary-General. On 24 August [A/60/297], the Secretary-General informed the General Assembly that Israel had not replied to his July request for information on steps taken or envisaged to implement the relevant provisions of resolution 59/123 [YUN 2004, p. 482] demanding that Israel, among other things, cease all construction of the wall and new settlements in the Occupied Palestinian Territory, including East Jerusalem.

GENERAL ASSEMBLY ACTION

On 8 December [meeting 62], the General Assembly, on the recommendation of the Fourth Committee [A/60/477], adopted **resolution 60/106** by recorded vote (153-7-10) [agenda item 31].

Israeli settlements in the Occupied Palestinian Territory, including East Jerusalem, and the occupied Syrian Golan

The General Assembly,

Guided by the principles of the Charter of the United Nations, and affirming the inadmissibility of the acquisition of territory by force,

Recalling its relevant resolutions, including resolution 59/123 of 10 December 2004, as well as those resolutions adopted at its tenth emergency special session,

Recalling also relevant Security Council resolutions, including resolutions 242(1967) of 22 November 1967, 446(1979) of 22 March 1979, 465(1980) of 1 March 1980, 476(1980) of 30 June 1980, 478(1980) of 20 August 1980, 497(1981) of 17 December 1981 and 904 (1994) of 18 March 1994,

Reaffirming the applicability of the Geneva Convention relative to the Protection of Civilian Persons in Time of War, of 12 August 1949, to the Occupied Palestinian Territory, including East Jerusalem, and to the occupied Syrian Golan,

Considering that the transfer by the occupying Power of parts of its own civilian population into the territory it occupies constitutes a breach of the Fourth Geneva Convention and relevant provisions of customary law, including those codified in Additional Protocol I to the Geneva Conventions,

Recalling the advisory opinion rendered on 9 July 2004 by the International Court of Justice on the *Legal Consequences of the Construction of a Wall in the Occupied Palestinian Territory*, and recalling also General Assembly resolution ES-10/15 of 20 July 2004,

Noting that the International Court of Justice concluded that "the Israeli settlements in the Occupied Palestinian Territory (including East Jerusalem) have been established in breach of international law",

Taking note of the recent report of the Special Rapporteur of the Commission on Human Rights on the situation of human rights in the Palestinian territories occupied by Israel since 1967,

Recalling the Declaration of Principles on Interim Self-Government Arrangements of 13 September 1993 and the subsequent implementation agreements between the Palestinian and Israeli sides,

Recalling also the Quartet road map to a permanent two-State solution to the Israeli-Palestinian conflict, and noting specifically its call for a freeze on all settlement activity,

Aware that Israeli settlement activities have involved, inter alia, the transfer of nationals of the occupying Power into the occupied territories, the confiscation of land, the exploitation of natural resources and other illegal actions against the Palestinian civilian population,

Bearing in mind the detrimental impact of Israeli settlement policies, decisions and activities on efforts to achieve peace in the Middle East,

Expressing grave concern about the continuation by Israel, the occupying Power, of settlement activities, in violation of international humanitarian law, relevant United Nations resolutions and the agreements reached between the parties, including the construction and expansion of the settlements in Jabal Abu-Ghneim and Ras Al-Amud in and around Occupied East Jerusalem and the so-called E-1 plan, aimed at connecting its illegal settlements around and further isolating Occupied East Jerusalem,

Expressing grave concern also about the continuing unlawful construction by Israel of the wall inside the Occupied Palestinian Territory, including in and around East Jerusalem, and expressing its concern in particular about the route of the wall in departure from the Armistice Line of 1949, which could prejudge future negotiations and make the two-State solution physically impossible to implement and which is causing the Palestinian people further humanitarian hardship,

Deeply concerned that the wall's route has been traced in such a way as to include the great majority of the Israeli settlements in the Occupied Palestinian Territory, including East Jerusalem,

Reiterating its opposition to settlement activities in the Occupied Palestinian Territory, including East Jerusalem, and to any activities involving the confiscation of land, the disruption of the livelihood of protected persons and the de facto annexation of land,

Recalling the need to end all acts of violence, including acts of terror, provocation, incitement and destruction,

Gravely concerned about the dangerous situation resulting from actions taken by the illegal armed Israeli settlers in the occupied territory,

Acknowledging the importance of the Israeli withdrawal from within the Gaza Strip and parts of the northern West Bank and of the dismantlement of the settlements therein as a step towards the implementation of the road map,

Taking note of the relevant reports of the Secretary-General,

1. *Reaffirms* that Israeli settlements in the Palestinian territory, including East Jerusalem, and in the occupied Syrian Golan are illegal and an obstacle to peace and economic and social development;

2. *Calls upon* Israel to accept the de jure applicability of the Geneva Convention relative to the Protection of Civilian Persons in Time of War, of 12 August 1949, to the Occupied Palestinian Territory, including East Jerusalem, and to the occupied Syrian Golan and to abide scrupulously by the provisions of the Convention, in particular article 49;

3. *Welcomes* the Israeli withdrawal from within the Gaza Strip and parts of the northern West Bank and the dismantlement of the settlements therein as a step towards the implementation of the road map;

4. *Calls upon* Israel, the occupying Power, in this regard, to comply strictly with its obligations under international law, including international humanitarian law, with respect to the alteration of the character and status of the Occupied Palestinian Territory, including East Jerusalem;

5. *Emphasizes* the need for the parties to speedily resolve all remaining issues in the Gaza Strip, including the removal of rubble;

6. *Reiterates its demand* for the immediate and complete cessation of all Israeli settlement activities in all of the Occupied Palestinian Territory, including East Jerusalem, and in the occupied Syrian Golan, and calls for the full implementation of the relevant resolutions of the Security Council;

7. *Demands* that Israel, the occupying Power, comply with its legal obligations, as mentioned in the advisory opinion rendered on 9 July 2004 by the International Court of Justice;

8. *Stresses* the need for full implementation of Security Council resolution 904(1994), in which, among other things, the Council called upon Israel, the occupying Power, to continue to take and implement measures, including confiscation of arms, with the aim of preventing illegal acts of violence by Israeli settlers, and called for measures to be taken to guarantee the safety and protection of the Palestinian civilians in the occupied territory;

9. *Reiterates its calls* for the prevention of all acts of violence by Israeli settlers, especially against Palestinian civilians and properties, particularly in the light of recent developments;

10. *Requests* the Secretary-General to report to the General Assembly at its sixty-first session on the implementation of the present resolution.

RECORDED VOTE ON RESOLUTION 60/106:

In favour: Afghanistan, Algeria, Andorra, Antigua and Barbuda, Argentina, Armenia, Austria, Azerbaijan, Bahamas, Bahrain, Bangladesh, Barbados, Belarus, Belgium, Belize, Benin, Bhutan, Bolivia, Botswana, Brazil, Brunei Darussalam, Bulgaria, Burkina Faso, Burundi, Cambodia, Canada, Cape Verde, Central African Republic, Chile, China, Colombia, Croatia, Cuba, Cyprus, Czech Republic, Democratic People's Republic of Korea, Denmark, Djibouti, Dominica, Ecuador, Egypt, Eritrea, Estonia, Ethiopia, Fiji, Finland, France, Gabon, Georgia, Germany, Ghana, Greece, Guatemala, Guinea, Guinea-Bissau, Guyana, Honduras, Hungary, Iceland, India, Indonesia, Iran, Iraq, Ireland, Italy, Jamaica, Japan, Jordan, Kazakhstan, Kenya, Kuwait, Kyrgyzstan, Lao People's Democratic Republic, Latvia, Lebanon, Lesotho, Liberia, Libyan Arab Jamahiriya, Liechtenstein, Lithuania, Luxembourg, Malaysia, Maldives, Mali, Malta, Mauritania, Mauritius, Mexico, Monaco, Mongolia, Morocco, Mozambique, Myanmar, Namibia, Nepal, Netherlands, New Zealand, Nicaragua, Niger, Nigeria, Norway, Oman, Pakistan, Panama, Paraguay, Peru, Philippines, Poland, Portugal, Qatar, Republic of Korea, Republic of Moldova, Romania, Russian Federation, Saint Lucia, Saint Vincent and the Grenadines, Samoa, San Marino, Saudi Arabia, Senegal, Serbia and Montenegro, Singapore, Slovakia, Slovenia, Somalia, South Africa, Spain, Sri Lanka, Sudan, Suriname, Sweden, Switzerland, Syrian Arab Republic, Tajikistan, Thailand, The former Yugoslav Republic of Macedonia, Timor-Leste, Togo, Trinidad and Tobago, Tunisia, Turkey, Turkmenistan, Ukraine, United Arab Emirates, United Kingdom, United Republic of Tanzania, Uruguay, Uzbekistan, Venezuela, Viet Nam, Yemen, Zambia, Zimbabwe.

Against: Australia, Grenada, Israel, Marshall Islands, Micronesia, Palau, United States.

Abstaining: Albania, Cameroon, Costa Rica, Dominican Republic, El Salvador, Haiti, Papua New Guinea, Solomon Islands, Tonga, Uganda.

Palestinian women

The Secretary-General, in a report [E/CN.6/ 2005/4] to the Commission on the Status of Women, as requested by the Economic and Social Council in resolution 2004/56 [YUN 2004, p. 484], reviewed the situation of Palestinian women and assistance provided by UN organizations from October 2003 to September 2004. He said that during that period, the occupation of Palestinian territory by Israel continued to have a detrimental effect on the lives of Palestinian women and children. The hardship of daily life was felt most acutely by Palestinian women who carried the burden of responsibility within the household because of the death, imprisonment, or unemployment of male members. Between September

2000 and September 2004, some 250 Palestinians had died.

The social, economic and cultural context of women's health remained challenging. In particular, malnutrition continued to have a major impact on the lives of Palestinian women and children. Land confiscation and the destruction of cultivated fields and houses divided families and communities, denied farmers access to their land, workers to their jobs, children and youth to schools, colleges and universities and women and children basic health and social services. In addition, Palestinian women in prison were reported to have been subjected to torture or inhuman and degrading treatment. The severe economic depression of the Palestinian economy since September 2000 continued unabated during the reporting period. Low levels of employment resulted in high levels of poverty among Palestinians, particularly women. Women's labour force participation remained low, in spite of their high and successful secondary school enrolment (only 11 per cent of women of employment age participated in the labour force). In cases where they did participate in the labour market, they were mostly located in the agriculture and service sectors. A number of objectives had been identified to address the low participation of women in the labour force, including upgrading governmental political commitment to include gender, democracy and human rights issues in the policies and plans of the various ministries and relevant legislation and regulations; linking lobbying and advocacy activities with the development of policies and laws; and building a network of links with women governmental institutions and NGOs and human rights organizations at the regional and international levels, and exchanging experience with them on the implementation and support of international conventions on women and human rights. Efforts were made to address discrimination against women and the concerns of Palestinian women through the newly established PA Ministry of Women's Affairs.

The UN system continued to provide direct assistance to Palestinian women. The World Bank implemented the second Palestinian NGO project, under which a counselling centre for women in difficult circumstances was designed. The International Labour Organization established a Palestinian fund for employment and social protection. The United Nations Development Programme (UNDP) initiated a number of projects aimed at women's economic empowerment. In June 2004, UNDP entered into an agreement with the Ministry of Women's Affairs to support the development of a three-year action plan aimed at promoting gender-sensitive structures, programmes and policies. The United Nations Relief and Works Agency for Palestine Refugees in the Near East (UNRWA) granted $2.47 million to women through its microfinance and micro-enterprise programme. (For more information on UNRWA's activities, see p. 544.) The United Nations Development Fund for Women opened a programme office in Jerusalem in April 2004.

The Secretary-General stated that many of the initiatives undertaken by UN system entities were aimed at long-term sustainable development for Palestinian people, including women. Palestinian women continued to require assistance with income-generating projects aimed at poverty alleviation, education and training, access to health care and health-care services, and with ongoing advocacy to combat violence against women and protect their fundamental human rights. While the reports by relevant bodies provided considerable information on the overall situation in the Occupied Palestinian Territory and made reference to women, limited information was provided on the specific situation of women and girls. The specific impact of the crisis on women, as compared to men, should be highlighted so that targeted actions could be taken to mitigate gender-specific negative ones. Gender perspectives should be more fully integrated into international assistance programmes through, among other things, in-depth gender analysis and the collection of data disaggregated by sex, and be fully incorporated into all UN studies and reports on the Palestinian people in order to effectively assess the impact of the situation of Palestinian women. Since the status and living conditions of Palestinian women were linked to achieving a peaceful resolution of the conflict, additional efforts needed to be made by the international community to end the violent confrontations in the Occupied Palestinian Territory.

ECONOMIC AND SOCIAL COUNCIL ACTION

On 26 July [meeting 39], the Economic and Social Council, on the recommendation of the Commission on the Status of Women [E/2005/27 & Corr.1], adopted **resolution 2005/43** by recorded vote (46-2-4) [agenda item 14 *(a)*].

Situation of and assistance to Palestinian women

The Economic and Social Council,

Having considered with appreciation the report of the Secretary-General,

Recalling the Nairobi Forward-looking Strategies for the Advancement of Women, in particular paragraph 260 concerning Palestinian women and children, the Beijing Platform for Action adopted at the Fourth World Conference on Women and the outcome of the twenty-third special session of the General Assembly,

entitled "Women 2000: gender equality, development and peace for the twenty-first century",

Recalling also its resolution 2004/56 of 23 July 2004 and other relevant United Nations resolutions,

Recalling further the Declaration on the Elimination of Violence against Women as it concerns the protection of civilian populations,

Expressing the urgent need for the full resumption of negotiations within the Middle East peace process on its agreed basis and towards the speedy achievement of a final settlement between the Palestinian and Israeli sides,

Concerned about the grave situation of Palestinian women in the Occupied Palestinian Territory, including East Jerusalem, resulting from the severe impact of ongoing illegal Israeli settlement activities and the unlawful construction of the wall, as well as the severe consequences arising from Israeli military operations on and sieges of civilian areas, which have detrimentally impacted their social and economic conditions and deepened the humanitarian crisis faced by Palestinian women and their families,

Recalling the advisory opinion rendered on 9 July 2004 by the International Court of Justice on the *Legal Consequences of the Construction of a Wall in the Occupied Palestinian Territory*, and recalling also General Assembly resolution ES-10/15 of 20 July 2004,

Recalling also the International Covenant on Civil and Political Rights, the International Covenant of Economic, Social and Cultural Rights and the Convention on the Rights of the Child, and affirming that these human rights instruments must be respected in the Occupied Palestinian Territory, including East Jerusalem,

Expressing its condemnation of all acts of violence, including all acts of terror, provocation, incitement and destruction, especially the excessive use of force against Palestinian civilians, many of them women and children, resulting in injury and loss of human life,

1. *Calls upon* the concerned parties, as well as the international community, to exert all the efforts necessary to ensure the full resumption of the peace process on its agreed basis, taking into account the common ground already gained, and calls for measures for tangible improvement of the difficult situation on the ground and the living conditions faced by Palestinian women and their families;

2. *Reaffirms* that the Israeli occupation remains a major obstacle for Palestinian women with regard to their advancement, self-reliance and integration in the development planning of their society;

3. *Demands* that Israel, the occupying Power, comply fully with the provisions and principles of the Universal Declaration of Human Rights, the Regulations annexed to the Hague Convention respecting the Laws and Custom of War on Land of 18 October 1907 (Convention IV), and the Geneva Convention relative to the Protection of Civilian Persons in Time of War, of 12 August 1949, in order to protect the rights of Palestinian women and their families;

4. *Calls upon* Israel to facilitate the return of all refugees and displaced Palestinian women and children to their homes and properties, in compliance with the relevant United Nations resolutions;

5. *Calls upon* the international community to continue to provide urgently needed assistance and serv-

ices in an effort to alleviate the dire humanitarian crisis being faced by Palestinian women and their families and to help in the reconstruction of relevant Palestinian institutions;

6. *Requests* the Commission on the Status of Women to continue to monitor and take action with regard to the implementation of the Nairobi Forward-looking Strategies for the Advancement of Women, in particular paragraph 260 concerning Palestinian women and children, the Beijing Platform for Action and the outcome of the twenty-third special session of the General Assembly, entitled "Women 2000: gender equality, development and peace for the twenty-first century";

7. *Requests* the Secretary-General to continue to review the situation, to assist Palestinian women by all available means, including those set out in his report, and to submit to the Commission on the Status of Women at its fiftieth session a report, including information provided by the Economic and Social Commission for Western Asia, on the progress made in the implementation of the present resolution.

RECORDED VOTE ON RESOLUTION 2005/43:

In favour: Albania, Armenia, Australia, Azerbaijan, Bangladesh, Belgium, Belize, Benin, Brazil, Canada, China, Colombia, Congo, Cuba, Denmark, Ecuador, France, Germany, India, Indonesia, Ireland, Italy, Jamaica, Japan, Kenya, Lithuania, Malaysia, Mauritius, Mexico, Mozambique, Namibia, Nigeria, Pakistan, Panama, Poland, Republic of Korea, Russian Federation, Saudi Arabia, Senegal, South Africa, Spain, Thailand, Turkey, United Arab Emirates, United Kingdom, United Republic of Tanzania.

Against: Australia, United States.

Abstaining: Canada, Democratic Republic of the Congo, Iceland, Nicaragua.

Issues related to Palestine

General aspects

The General Assembly again considered the question of Palestine in 2005. Having discussed the annual report of the Committee on the Exercise of the Inalienable Rights of the Palestinian People (Committee on Palestinian Rights) [A/60/35], the Assembly adopted four resolutions, reaffirming, among other things, the necessity of achieving a peaceful settlement of the Palestine question—the core of Arab-Israeli conflict—and stressing the need for the realization of the inalienable rights of the Palestinians, primarily the right to self-determination, for Israeli withdrawal from the Palestinian territory occupied since 1967 and for resolving the problem of the Palestine refugees. It called on the Secretariat to continue its activities to promote and raise awareness of Palestinian rights.

The most significant political development in the Occupied Palestinian Territory was the build-up to, and implementation of, Israel's evacuation of its settlements in the Gaza Strip and parts of the northern West Bank. The Quartet responded by establishing the Office of the Special Envoy of the Quartet for Gaza Disengagement. In

observance of the International Day of Solidarity with the Palestinian People, celebrated annually on 29 November in accordance with Assembly resolution 32/40 B [YUN 1977, p. 304], the Committee held a solemn meeting.

Report of Secretary-General. In a November report on the peaceful settlement of the question of Palestine [A/60/539-S/2005/701], submitted in response to Assembly resolution 59/31 [YUN 2004, p. 487], the Secretary-General made observations on the status of the Israeli-Palestinian conflict and on international efforts to move the Middle East peace process forward (see also p. 503). On 31 May, the Secretary-General sought the positions of Egypt, Israel, Jordan, Lebanon, the Syrian Arab Republic and the Palestine Liberation Organization regarding steps taken to implement the resolution. As at 20 September, Israel and the Permanent Observer of Palestine had responded.

In a 4 August note verbale, Israel said that it viewed the resolution as unbalanced and politically motivated, and interference in matters that the parties had agreed to resolve within the context of direct bilateral negotiations. The violence in the region was a result of a Palestinian decision to abandon peace negotiations and pursue their goals through violence and terrorism. The one-sided approach of the resolution, which sought to dictate the outcome of the negotiating process, effectively rewarded violence at a time when the Palestinian side should discontinue such acts and boldly pursue peaceful dialogue.

The Permanent Observer, in a 2 August note verbale, said that Israel's withdrawal from Palestinian territory was a fundamental requisite for solving the question of Palestine and achieving a peaceful settlement of the Israeli-Palestinian conflict, based on the two-State solution.

The Secretary-General observed that the window of opportunity to revitalize the Middle East peace process that had emerged during the year, despite setbacks, remained open. The increased coordination between the parties as a result of the smooth and peaceful operation of Israel's disengagement from the Gaza Strip and part of the northern West Bank was a positive step, which should be built upon in the future. The Secretary-General stated that the PA had to push ahead with the reform of its security services. Decisive action in that regard should help to restore law and order. He noted the information in the independent report by the Strategic Assessment Initiative that the Palestinian security services remained weak, overstaffed, badly motivated and under-armed, and were affected by corruption, institutional hierarchies, cults of personality and lack of cohesive training.

He said that Israel had failed to make progress on the implementation of its core commitments under the road map. Settlement expansion and lack of action on removing illegal settlement outposts severely undermined trust. The Secretary-General said that he also remained concerned about the continued construction of the barrier in the West bank, which encroached on Palestinian land. He urged Israel to address its security concerns in a manner that would not increase suffering among Palestinians, prejudge final status or threaten longer-term prospects for peace by making the creation of a viable, contiguous Palestinian State more difficult. Noticing that the humanitarian situation of the Palestinians remained grave, the Secretary-General called upon the international community to provide adequate funding for UNRWA so that it could continue to deliver the necessary services to Palestinian refugees.

GENERAL ASSEMBLY ACTION

On 1 December [meeting 60], the General Assembly adopted **resolution 60/39** [draft A/60/L.31 & Add.1] by recorded vote (156-6-9) [agenda item 15].

Peaceful settlement of the question of Palestine

The General Assembly,

Recalling its relevant resolutions, including those adopted at the tenth emergency special session,

Recalling also its resolution 58/292 of 6 May 2004,

Recalling further relevant Security Council resolutions, including resolutions 242(1967) of 22 November 1967, 338(1973) of 22 October 1973, 1397(2002) of 12 March 2002, 1515(2003) of 19 November 2003 and 1544(2004) of 19 May 2004,

Welcoming the affirmation by the Security Council of the vision of a region where two States, Israel and Palestine, live side by side within secure and recognized borders,

Noting with concern that it has been fifty-eight years since the adoption of resolution 181(II) of 29 November 1947 and thirty-eight years since the occupation of Palestinian territory, including East Jerusalem, in 1967,

Having considered the report of the Secretary-General submitted pursuant to the request made in its resolution 59/31 of 1 December 2004,

Reaffirming the permanent responsibility of the United Nations with regard to the question of Palestine until the question is resolved in all its aspects in accordance with international law,

Recalling the advisory opinion rendered on 9 July 2004 by the International Court of Justice on the *Legal Consequences of the Construction of a Wall in the Occupied Palestinian Territory*, and recalling also its resolution ES-10/15 of 20 July 2004,

Convinced that achieving a final and peaceful settlement of the question of Palestine, the core of the Arab-Israeli conflict, is imperative for the attainment of comprehensive and lasting peace and stability in the Middle East,

Aware that the principle of equal rights and self-determination of peoples is among the purposes and principles enshrined in the Charter of the United Nations,

Affirming the principle of the inadmissibility of the acquisition of territory by war,

Recalling its resolution 2625(XXV) of 24 October 1970,

Reaffirming the illegality of the Israeli settlements in the territory occupied since 1967 and of Israeli actions aimed at changing the status of Jerusalem,

Reaffirming also that the construction by Israel, the occupying Power, of a wall in the Occupied Palestinian Territory, including in and around East Jerusalem, and its associated regime, are contrary to international law,

Affirming once again the right of all States in the region to live in peace within secure and internationally recognized borders,

Recalling the mutual recognition between the Government of the State of Israel and the Palestine Liberation Organization, the representative of the Palestinian people, and the agreements concluded between the two sides and the need for full compliance with those agreements,

Recalling also the endorsement by the Security Council, in resolution 1515(2003), of the Quartet road map to a permanent two-State solution to the Israeli-Palestinian conflict, and stressing the urgent need for its implementation and compliance with its provisions,

Recognizing the efforts being undertaken by the Palestinian Authority, with international support, to rebuild, reform and strengthen its damaged institutions,

Welcoming the important contribution to the peace process of the United Nations Special Coordinator for the Middle East Peace Process and Personal Representative of the Secretary-General to the Palestine Liberation Organization and the Palestinian Authority, including in the framework of the activities of the Quartet,

Welcoming also the convening of international donor meetings, as well as the establishment of international mechanisms to provide assistance to the Palestinian people,

Expressing its concern over the tragic events that have occurred in the Occupied Palestinian Territory, including East Jerusalem, since 28 September 2000, including the large number of deaths and injuries, mostly among Palestinian civilians, the deterioration of the socio-economic and humanitarian conditions of the Palestinian people and the widespread destruction of public and private Palestinian property and infrastructure,

Expressing its grave concern over the repeated military actions in the Occupied Palestinian Territory and the reoccupation of Palestinian population centres by the Israeli occupying forces, and emphasizing in this regard the need for the implementation of the Sharm el-Sheikh understandings,

Emphasizing the importance of the safety and well-being of all civilians in the whole Middle East region, and condemning all acts of violence and terror against civilians on both sides, including the suicide bombings, the extrajudicial executions and the excessive use of force,

Acknowledging the importance of the Israeli withdrawal from within the Gaza Strip and parts of the northern West Bank and of the dismantlement of the settlements therein as a step towards the implementation of the road map,

Stressing the urgent need for sustained and active international involvement, including by the Quartet, to support both parties in revitalizing the peace process towards the resumption and acceleration of direct negotiations between the parties for the achievement of a final peace settlement, in accordance with the road map,

Welcoming the initiatives and efforts undertaken by civil society in pursuit of a peaceful settlement of the question of Palestine,

Taking note of the findings by the International Court of Justice, in its advisory opinion, including on the urgent necessity for the United Nations as a whole to redouble its efforts to bring the Israeli-Palestinian conflict, which continues to pose a threat to international peace and security, to a speedy conclusion, thereby establishing a just and lasting peace in the region,

1. *Reaffirms* the necessity of achieving a peaceful settlement of the question of Palestine, the core of the Arab-Israeli conflict, in all its aspects, and of intensifying all efforts towards that end;

2. *Also reaffirms* its full support for the Middle East peace process, which began in Madrid, and the existing agreements between the Israeli and Palestinian sides, stresses the necessity for the establishment of a comprehensive, just and lasting peace in the Middle East, and welcomes in this regard the ongoing efforts of the Quartet;

3. *Welcomes* the Arab Peace Initiative adopted by the Council of the League of Arab States at its fourteenth session, held in Beirut on 27 and 28 March 2002;

4. *Calls upon* both parties to fulfil their obligations in implementation of the road map by taking parallel and reciprocal steps in this regard, and stresses the importance and urgency of establishing a credible and effective third-party monitoring mechanism including all members of the Quartet;

5. *Welcomes* the Israeli withdrawal from within the Gaza Strip and parts of the northern West Bank and the dismantlement of the settlements therein as a step towards the implementation of the road map;

6. *Calls upon* Israel, the occupying Power, in this regard, to comply strictly with its obligations under international law, including international humanitarian law, with respect to the alteration of the character and status of the Occupied Palestinian Territory, including East Jerusalem;

7. *Emphasizes* the need for the parties, with the help of the international community, speedily and fully to resolve all remaining issues in the Gaza Strip, including a durable arrangement for the border crossings, the airport, the construction of the seaport, the removal of the rubble and the establishment of a permanent physical link between the Gaza Strip and the West Bank, and welcomes the positive role being played in this regard by the Quartet Special Envoy for Disengagement;

8. *Stresses* the need for a speedy end to the reoccupation of Palestinian population centres and for the complete cessation of all acts of violence, including military attacks, destruction and acts of terror;

9. *Also stresses* the need for the immediate implementation of the Sharm el-Sheikh understandings;

10. *Calls upon* the parties, with the support of the Quartet and other interested parties, to exert all efforts necessary to halt the deterioration of the situation, to reverse all measures taken on the ground since 28 September 2000 and to facilitate a speedy resumption of the peace process and the conclusion of a final peaceful settlement;

11. *Demands* that Israel, the occupying Power, comply with its legal obligations under international law, as mentioned in the advisory opinion and as demanded in resolutions ES-10/13 of 21 October 2003 and ES-10/15 of 20 July 2004 and, inter alia, that it immediately cease its construction of the wall in the Occupied Palestinian Territory, including East Jerusalem, and calls upon all States Members of the United Nations to comply with their legal obligations, as mentioned in the advisory opinion;

12. *Reaffirms its commitment*, in accordance with international law, to the two-State solution of Israel and Palestine, living side by side in peace and security within recognized borders, based on the pre-1967 borders;

13. *Reiterates its demand* for the complete cessation of all Israeli settlement activities in the Occupied Palestinian Territory, including East Jerusalem, and in the occupied Syrian Golan, and calls for the full implementation of the relevant Security Council resolutions;

14. *Stresses* the need for:

(a) The withdrawal of Israel from the Palestinian territory occupied since 1967;

(b) The realization of the inalienable rights of the Palestinian people, primarily the right to self-determination and the right to their independent State;

15. *Also stresses* the need for resolving the problem of Palestine refugees in conformity with its resolution 194(III) of 11 December 1948;

16. *Welcomes* the recent agreement on movement and access between the two sides, and stresses the need to ensure that the commitments made therein are fully implemented in accordance with the timeline set out in the agreement;

17. *Urges* Member States to expedite the provision of economic, humanitarian and technical assistance to the Palestinian people and the Palestinian Authority during this critical period to help to alleviate the humanitarian crisis being faced by the Palestinian people, rebuild the Palestinian economy and infrastructure and support the restructuring and reform of Palestinian institutions;

18. *Requests* the Secretary-General to continue his efforts with the parties concerned, and in consultation with the Security Council, towards the attainment of a peaceful settlement of the question of Palestine and the promotion of peace in the region and to submit to the General Assembly at its sixty-first session a report on these efforts and on developments on this matter.

RECORDED VOTE ON RESOLUTION 60/39:

In favour: Afghanistan, Albania, Algeria, Andorra, Antigua and Barbuda, Argentina, Armenia, Austria, Azerbaijan, Bahamas, Bahrain, Bangladesh, Barbados, Belarus, Belgium, Belize, Benin, Bhutan, Bolivia,

Bosnia and Herzegovina, Botswana, Brazil, Brunei Darussalam, Bulgaria, Burkina Faso, Cambodia, Cape Verde, Central African Republic, Chile, China, Colombia, Comoros, Croatia, Cuba, Cyprus, Czech Republic, Democratic People's Republic of Korea, Denmark, Djibouti, Dominica, Dominican Republic, Ecuador, Egypt, El Salvador, Eritrea, Estonia, Ethiopia, Fiji, Finland, France, Gabon, Gambia, Georgia, Germany, Ghana, Greece, Guatemala, Guinea, Guinea-Bissau, Guyana, Haiti, Honduras, Hungary, Iceland, India, Indonesia, Iran, Iraq, Ireland, Italy, Jamaica, Japan, Jordan, Kazakhstan, Kenya, Kuwait, Kyrgyzstan, Lao People's Democratic Republic, Latvia, Lebanon, Lesotho, Liberia, Libyan Arab Jamahiriya, Liechtenstein, Lithuania, Luxembourg, Malaysia, Maldives, Mali, Malta, Mauritania, Mauritius, Monaco, Mongolia, Morocco, Mozambique, Myanmar, Namibia, Nepal, Netherlands, New Zealand, Nicaragua, Nigeria, Norway, Oman, Pakistan, Panama, Paraguay, Peru, Philippines, Poland, Portugal, Qatar, Republic of Korea, Republic of Moldova, Romania, Russian Federation, Saint Lucia, Saint Vincent and the Grenadines, San Marino, Saudi Arabia, Senegal, Serbia and Montenegro, Singapore, Slovakia, Slovenia, Solomon Islands, Somalia, South Africa, Spain, Sri Lanka, Sudan, Suriname, Swaziland, Sweden, Switzerland, Syrian Arab Republic, Tajikistan, Thailand, The former Yugoslav Republic of Macedonia, Togo, Trinidad and Tobago, Tunisia, Turkey, Turkmenistan, Ukraine, United Arab Emirates, United Kingdom, United Republic of Tanzania, Uruguay, Uzbekistan, Venezuela, Viet Nam, Yemen, Zambia, Zimbabwe.

Against: Australia, Israel, Marshall Islands, Micronesia, Palau, United States.

Abstaining: Cameroon, Canada, Costa Rica, Nauru, Papua New Guinea, Samoa, Tuvalu, Uganda, Vanuatu.

Committee on Palestinian Rights

As mandated by General Assembly resolution 59/28 [YUN 2004, p. 491], the Committee on the Exercise of the Inalienable Rights of the Palestinian People reviewed the Palestine question, reported on it and made suggestions to the Assembly and the Security Council.

The Committee followed the Palestine-related activities of intergovernmental bodies, such as, the African Union, the Non-Aligned Movement, and the Organization of the Islamic Conference, and through its Chairman, participation in meetings of those bodies. In March, the Committee's Bureau held consultations with EU representatives as part of the effort to build a constructive relationship on issues of common concern. Throughout the year, the Committee held a number of international events, including the United Nations International Meeting on the Question of Palestine (Geneva, 8-9 March) and the United Nations International Conference of Civil Society in Support of Middle East Peace (Paris, 12-13 July).

The Committee's annual report to the Assembly [A/60/35] covered the period from 7 October 2004 to 5 October 2005. The Committee closely monitored the situation on the ground and was concerned by the continuing violence in the Occupied Palestinian Territory. It condemned the policy of extrajudicial executions, as well as terrorist attacks against Israeli civilians in Israel. It was concerned at the continuation of housing demolitions, particularly in East Jerusalem. The Committee emphasized that the withdrawal of Israel from the Gaza Strip and parts of the northern West Bank should be followed by firm action to implement the Sharm el-Sheik understand-

ings, including the withdrawal from cities in the West Bank, the release of more prisoners and the cessation of all acts of violence. It considered that early agreement was needed on a number of actions that would allow the PA to exercise control over its borders, crossing points, territorial sea and airspace and the establishment of a permanent and direct link to the West Bank.

The Committee noted that the construction of the wall continued in defiance of the ICJ opinion and the position of the international community. It believed that it was imperative that the Secretary-General expedite the establishment of the register of damage caused by the building of the wall and begin the important work in that regard.

The Committee noted that settlement construction and expansion in the West Bank continued apace. In letters to the Secretary-General [A/ES-10/301-S/2005/262, A/ES-10/306-S/2005/556], it expressed serious concern over Israel's decision to expand and consolidate its settlements in the West Bank. It also expressed concern at the deterioration of the health and nutritional status of the Palestinian population, particularly women and children.

It reiterated that the road map remained the best way to achieve the goal of a comprehensive, just and lasting solution to the question of Palestine through the establishment of two States. It intended to address issues such as the need to end the occupation of all Palestinian land; support of the efforts by the PA to rehabilitate the economy, especially that of Gaza; the responsibility of all Governments to apply international law to all aspects of the question of Palestine, in accordance with the ICJ advisory opinion; the humanitarian and socio-economic situation; and the role of civil society.

GENERAL ASSEMBLY ACTION

On 1 December [meeting 60], the General Assembly adopted **resolution 60/36** [A/60/L.28 & Add.1] by recorded vote (106-8-59) [agenda item 15].

Committee on the Exercise of the Inalienable Rights of the Palestinian People

The General Assembly,

Recalling its resolutions 181(II) of 29 November 1947, 194(III) of 11 December 1948, 3236(XXIX) of 22 November 1974, 3375(XXX) and 3376(XXX) of 10 November 1975, 31/20 of 24 November 1976 and all subsequent relevant resolutions, including those adopted by the General Assembly at its emergency special sessions and resolution 59/28 of 1 December 2004,

Recalling also its resolution 58/292 of 6 May 2004,

Having considered the report of the Committee on the Exercise of the Inalienable Rights of the Palestinian People,

Recalling the mutual recognition between the Government of the State of Israel and the Palestine Liberation Organization, the representative of the Palestinian people, as well as the existing agreements between the two sides and the need for full compliance with those agreements,

Recalling also the Quartet road map to a permanent two-State solution to the Israeli-Palestinian conflict,

Recalling further the advisory opinion rendered on 9 July 2004 by the International Court of Justice on the *Legal Consequences of the Construction of a Wall in the Occupied Palestinian Territory*, and recalling also its resolution ES-10/15 of 20 July 2004,

Reaffirming that the United Nations has a permanent responsibility towards the question of Palestine until the question is resolved in all its aspects in a satisfactory manner in accordance with international legitimacy,

1. *Expresses its appreciation* to the Committee on the Exercise of the Inalienable Rights of the Palestinian People for its efforts in performing the tasks assigned to it by the General Assembly, and takes note of its annual report, including the conclusions and recommendations contained in chapter VII thereof;

2. *Requests* the Committee to continue to exert all efforts to promote the realization of the inalienable rights of the Palestinian people, to support the Middle East peace process and to mobilize international support for and assistance to the Palestinian people, and authorizes the Committee to make such adjustments in its approved programme of work as it may consider appropriate and necessary in the light of developments and to report thereon to the General Assembly at its sixty-first session and thereafter;

3. *Also requests* the Committee to continue to keep under review the situation relating to the question of Palestine and to report and make suggestions to the General Assembly, the Security Council or the Secretary-General, as appropriate;

4. *Further requests* the Committee to continue to extend its cooperation and support to Palestinian and other civil society organizations in order to mobilize international solidarity and support for the achievement by the Palestinian people of its inalienable rights and for a peaceful settlement of the question of Palestine, and to involve additional civil society organizations in its work;

5. *Requests* the United Nations Conciliation Commission for Palestine, established under General Assembly resolution 194(III), and other United Nations bodies associated with the question of Palestine to continue to cooperate fully with the Committee and to make available to it, at its request, the relevant information and documentation which they have at their disposal;

6. *Invites* all Governments and organizations to extend their cooperation to the Committee in the performance of its tasks;

7. *Requests* the Secretary-General to circulate the report of the Committee to all the competent bodies of the United Nations, and urges them to take the necessary action, as appropriate;

8. *Also requests* the Secretary-General to continue to provide the Committee with all the necessary facilities for the performance of its tasks.

RECORDED VOTE ON RESOLUTION 60/36:

In favour: Afghanistan, Algeria, Angola, Antigua and Barbuda, Argentina, Armenia, Azerbaijan, Bahamas, Bahrain, Bangladesh, Barbados, Belarus, Belize, Benin, Bhutan, Bolivia, Botswana, Brazil, Brunei Darussalam, Burkina Faso, Cambodia, Cape Verde, Chile, China, Colombia, Comoros, Congo, Costa Rica, Cuba, Cyprus, Democratic People's Republic of Korea, Djibouti, Dominica, Ecuador, Egypt, El Salvador, Eritrea, Ethiopia, Fiji, Gabon, Gambia, Ghana, Guinea, Guinea-Bissau, Guyana, Haiti, India, Indonesia, Iran, Iraq, Jamaica, Jordan, Kazakhstan, Kenya, Kuwait, Kyrgyzstan, Lao People's Democratic Republic, Lebanon, Lesotho, Liberia, Libyan Arab Jamahiriya, Malaysia, Maldives, Mali, Malta, Mauritania, Mauritius, Mexico, Morocco, Mozambique, Myanmar, Namibia, Nepal, Nigeria, Oman, Pakistan, Panama, Paraguay, Philippines, Qatar, Saint Lucia, Saint Vincent and the Grenadines, Saudi Arabia, Senegal, Singapore, Somalia, South Africa, Sri Lanka, Sudan, Suriname, Swaziland, Syrian Arab Republic, Tajikistan, Togo, Trinidad and Tobago, Tunisia, Turkey, Turkmenistan, United Arab Emirates, United Republic of Tanzania, Uzbekistan, Venezuela, Viet Nam, Yemen, Zambia, Zimbabwe.

Against: Australia, Canada, Israel, Marshall Islands, Micronesia, Nauru, Palau, United States.

Abstaining: Albania, Andorra, Austria, Belgium, Bosnia and Herzegovina, Bulgaria, Cameroon, Central African Republic, Croatia, Czech Republic, Denmark, Dominican Republic, Estonia, Finland, France, Georgia, Germany, Greece, Guatemala, Honduras, Hungary, Iceland, Ireland, Italy, Japan, Latvia, Liechtenstein, Lithuania, Luxembourg, Monaco, Netherlands, New Zealand, Nicaragua, Norway, Papua New Guinea, Peru, Poland, Portugal, Republic of Korea, Republic of Moldova, Romania, Russian Federation, Samoa, San Marino, Serbia and Montenegro, Slovakia, Slovenia, Solomon Islands, Spain, Sweden, Switzerland, Thailand, The former Yugoslav Republic of Macedonia, Tuvalu, Uganda, Ukraine, United Kingdom, Uruguay, Vanuatu.

Division for Palestinian Rights

Under the guidance of the Committee on Palestinian Rights, the Division for Palestinian Rights of the UN Secretariat continued to research, monitor, prepare studies, collect and disseminate information on all issues related to the Palestine question. The Division responded to requests for information and issued the following publications: a monthly bulletin covering action taken by the United Nations and intergovernmental organizations on the issue of Palestine; monthly chronology of developments relating to the question of Palestine, based on media reports and other sources; special bulletins and notes on the observance of the International Day of Solidarity with the Palestinian People (29 November); periodic reviews of developments relating to Middle East peace efforts; the annual compilation of resolutions and decisions of the General Assembly and the Security Council relating to the question of Palestine.

The Committee, in its annual report [A/60/35], requested the Division to continue its programme of publications and other informational activities, including the electronic United Nations Information System on the Question of Palestine and the graphic enhancement of the Question of Palestine website. It requested that the annual training programme of PA staff be continued.

GENERAL ASSEMBLY ACTION

On 1 December [meeting 60], the General Assembly adopted **resolution 60/37** [draft A/60/L.29 & Add.1] by recorded vote (105-8-59) [agenda item 15].

Division for Palestinian Rights of the Secretariat

The General Assembly,

Having considered the report of the Committee on the Exercise of the Inalienable Rights of the Palestinian People,

Taking note in particular of the relevant information contained in chapter V.B of that report,

Recalling its resolution 32/40 B of 2 December 1977 and all subsequent relevant resolutions, including resolution 59/29 of 1 December 2004,

1. *Notes with appreciation* the action taken by the Secretary-General in compliance with its resolution 59/29;

2. *Considers* that the Division for Palestinian Rights of the Secretariat continues to make a useful and constructive contribution;

3. *Requests* the Secretary-General to continue to provide the Division with the necessary resources and to ensure that it continues to carry out its programme of work as detailed in the relevant earlier resolutions, in consultation with the Committee on the Exercise of the Inalienable Rights of the Palestinian People and under its guidance, including, in particular, the organization of meetings and conferences in various regions with the participation of all sectors of the international community, the further development and expansion of the documents collection of the United Nations Information System on the Question of Palestine, the preparation and widest possible dissemination of publications and information materials on various aspects of the question of Palestine and the provision of the annual training programme for staff of the Palestinian Authority;

4. *Also requests* the Secretary-General to ensure the continued cooperation of the Department of Public Information and other units of the Secretariat in enabling the Division to perform its tasks and in covering adequately the various aspects of the question of Palestine;

5. *Invites* all Governments and organizations to extend their cooperation to the Division in the performance of its tasks;

6. *Requests* the Committee and the Division, as part of the observance of the International Day of Solidarity with the Palestinian People on 29 November, to continue to organize an annual exhibit on Palestinian rights or a cultural event in cooperation with the Permanent Observer Mission of Palestine to the United Nations, and encourages Member States to continue to give the widest support and publicity to the observance of the Day of Solidarity.

RECORDED VOTE ON RESOLUTION 60/37:

In favour: Afghanistan, Algeria, Angola, Antigua and Barbuda, Argentina, Azerbaijan, Bahamas, Bahrain, Bangladesh, Barbados, Belarus, Belize, Benin, Bhutan, Bolivia, Botswana, Brazil, Brunei Darussalam, Burkina Faso, Cambodia, Cape Verde, Chile, China, Colombia, Comoros, Costa Rica, Cuba, Cyprus, Democratic People's Republic of Korea, Djibouti, Dominica, Dominican Republic, Ecuador, Egypt, El Salvador, Eritrea, Ethiopia, Gabon, Gambia, Ghana, Guinea, Guinea-Bissau, Guyana, Haiti, India, Indonesia, Iran, Iraq, Jamaica, Jordan, Kazakhstan, Kenya, Kuwait, Kyrgyzstan, Lao People's Democratic Republic, Lebanon, Lesotho, Liberia, Libyan Arab Jamahiriya, Malaysia, Maldives, Mali, Malta, Mauritania, Mauritius, Mexico, Morocco, Mozambique, Myanmar, Namibia, Nepal, Nigeria, Oman, Pakistan, Panama, Paraguay, Philippines, Qatar, Saint Lucia, Saint Vincent and the Grenadines, Saudi Arabia, Senegal, Singapore, Somalia, South Africa, Sri Lanka, Sudan, Suriname, Swaziland, Syrian Arab Republic, Tajikistan, Togo, Trinidad and Tobago, Tunisia, Turkey, Turkmenistan, United Arab Emirates, United Republic of Tanzania, Uruguay, Uzbekistan, Venezuela, Viet Nam, Yemen, Zambia, Zimbabwe.

Against: Australia, Canada, Israel, Marshall Islands, Micronesia, Nauru, Palau, United States.

Abstaining: Albania, Andorra, Armenia, Austria, Belgium, Bosnia and Herzegovina, Bulgaria, Cameroon, Central African Republic, Croatia, Czech Republic, Denmark, Estonia, Fiji, Finland, France, Georgia, Germany, Greece, Guatemala, Honduras, Hungary, Iceland, Ireland, Italy, Japan, Latvia, Liechtenstein, Lithuania, Luxembourg, Monaco, Netherlands, New Zealand, Nicaragua, Norway, Papua New Guinea, Peru, Poland, Portugal, Republic of Korea, Republic of Moldova, Romania, Russian Federation, Samoa, San Marino, Serbia and Montenegro, Slovakia, Slovenia, Solomon Islands, Spain, Sweden, Switzerland, Thailand, The former Yugoslav Republic of Macedonia, Tuvalu, Uganda, Ukraine, United Kingdom, Vanuatu.

Special Information programme

As requested in General Assembly resolution 59/30 [YUN 2004, p. 493], the UN Department of Public Information (DPI) continued its special information programme on the question of Palestine, which included the maintenance of the web page on the question of Palestine under Global issues and other pages of the UN website, the issuing of press releases and preparation for the annual training programme for Palestinian broadcasters and journalists. The Radio Section provided coverage of various aspects of the question of Palestine in its broadcasts in all six official languages. The quarterly *UN Chronicle and UN Chronicle Online* reported on relevant issues and action taken by the Assembly and the Security Council. DPI, in cooperation with the Foreign Ministry of Egypt, organized an international media seminar on peace in the Middle East (Cairo, 13-14 June).

As in previous years, the network of the United Nations information centres (UNICs) and other UN offices carried out activities in connection with the International Day of Solidarity with the Palestinian People. Throughout the year, many UNICs dealt with the Palestine question and organized related outreach activities.

GENERAL ASSEMBLY ACTION

On 1 December [meeting 60], the General Assembly adopted **resolution 60/38** [A/60/L.30 & Add.1] by recorded vote (160-7-6) [agenda item 15].

Special information programme on the question of Palestine of the Department of Public Information of the Secretariat

The General Assembly,

Having considered the report of the Committee on the Exercise of the Inalienable Rights of the Palestinian People,

Taking note in particular of the information contained in chapter VI of that report,

Recalling its resolution 59/30 of 1 December 2004,

Convinced that the worldwide dissemination of accurate and comprehensive information and the role of civil society organizations and institutions remain of vital importance in heightening awareness of and support for the inalienable rights of the Palestinian people,

Recalling the mutual recognition between the Government of the State of Israel and the Palestine Liberation Organization, the representative of the Palestinian people, as well as the existing agreements between the two sides and the need for full compliance with those agreements,

Recalling also the Quartet road map to a permanent two-State solution to the Israeli-Palestinian conflict,

Taking note of the advisory opinion rendered on 9 July 2004 by the International Court of Justice on the *Legal Consequences of the Construction of a Wall in the Occupied Palestinian Territory*,

1. *Notes with appreciation* the action taken by the Department of Public Information of the Secretariat in compliance with resolution 59/30;

2. *Considers* that the special information programme on the question of Palestine of the Department is very useful in raising the awareness of the international community concerning the question of Palestine and the situation in the Middle East and that the programme is contributing effectively to an atmosphere conducive to dialogue and supportive of the peace process;

3. *Requests* the Department, in full cooperation and coordination with the Committee on the Exercise of the Inalienable Rights of the Palestinian People, to continue, with the necessary flexibility as may be required by developments affecting the question of Palestine, its special information programme for the biennium 2006-2007, in particular:

(a) To disseminate information on all the activities of the United Nations system relating to the question of Palestine, including reports on the work carried out by the relevant United Nations organizations;

(b) To continue to issue and update publications on the various aspects of the question of Palestine in all fields, including materials concerning the recent developments in that regard, in particular the prospects for peace;

(c) To expand its collection of audio-visual material on the question of Palestine and to continue the production and preservation of such material and the updating of the exhibit in the Secretariat;

(d) To organize and promote fact-finding news missions for journalists to the Occupied Palestinian Territory, including East Jerusalem;

(e) To organize international, regional and national seminars or encounters for journalists, aiming in particular at sensitizing public opinion to the question of Palestine;

(f) To continue to provide assistance to the Palestinian people in the field of media development, in particular to strengthen the training programme for Palestinian broadcasters and journalists initiated in 1995.

RECORDED VOTE ON RESOLUTION 60/38:

In favour: Afghanistan, Albania, Algeria, Andorra, Angola, Antigua and Barbuda, Argentina, Armenia, Austria, Azerbaijan, Bahamas, Bahrain, Bangladesh, Barbados, Belarus, Belgium, Belize, Benin, Bhutan, Bolivia, Bosnia and Herzegovina, Botswana, Brazil, Brunei Darussalam, Bulgaria, Burkina Faso, Cambodia, Canada, Cape Verde, Central African Republic, Chile, China, Colombia, Comoros, Costa Rica, Croatia, Cuba, Cyprus, Czech Republic, Democratic People's Republic of Korea, Denmark, Djibouti, Dominica, Dominican Republic, Ecuador, Egypt, El Salvador, Eritrea, Estonia, Ethiopia, Fiji, Finland, France, Gabon, Gambia, Georgia, Germany, Ghana, Greece, Guatemala, Guinea, Guinea-Bissau, Guyana, Haiti, Honduras, Hungary, Iceland, India, Indonesia, Iran, Iraq, Ireland, Italy, Jamaica, Japan, Jordan, Kazakhstan, Kenya, Kuwait, Kyrgyzstan, Lao People's Democratic Republic, Latvia, Lebanon, Lesotho, Liberia, Libyan Arab Jamahiriya, Liechtenstein, Lithuania, Luxembourg, Malaysia, Maldives, Mali, Malta, Mauritania, Mauritius, Mexico, Monaco, Mongolia, Morocco, Mozambique, Myanmar, Namibia, Nepal, Netherlands, New Zealand, Nicaragua, Nigeria, Norway, Oman, Pakistan, Panama, Paraguay, Peru, Philippines, Poland, Portugal, Qatar, Republic of Korea,

Republic of Moldova, Romania, Russian Federation, Saint Lucia, Saint Vincent and the Grenadines, San Marino, Saudi Arabia, Senegal, Serbia and Montenegro, Singapore, Slovakia, Slovenia, Solomon Islands, Somalia, South Africa, Spain, Sri Lanka, Sudan, Suriname, Swaziland, Sweden, Switzerland, Syrian Arab Republic, Tajikistan, Thailand, The former Yugoslav Republic of Macedonia, Togo, Trinidad and Tobago, Tunisia, Turkey, Turkmenistan, Ukraine, United Arab Emirates, United Kingdom, United Republic of Tanzania, Uruguay, Uzbekistan, Venezuela, Viet Nam, Yemen, Zambia, Zimbabwe.

Against: Australia, Israel, Marshall Islands, Micronesia, Nauru, Palau, United States.

Abstaining: Cameroon, Papua New Guinea, Samoa, Tuvalu, Uganda, Vanuatu.

Assistance to Palestinians

UN activities

In response to General Assembly resolution 59/56 [YUN 2004, p. 495], the Secretary-General submitted a June report [A/60/90-E/2005/80] describing UN and other assistance to the Palestinian people from May 2004 to April 2005.

During the reporting period, the international community continued to work with both parties to ensure that Israel's withdrawal from the Gaza Strip and parts of the northern West Bank proceeded in a manner that contributed to the revival of the Palestinian economy and bolstered the peace process. The macroeconomic indicators for the Occupied Palestinian Territory showed that the economy was resilient, despite the pressures of ongoing conflict and closure. Gross domestic product growth, estimated at three per cent, remained positive. However Israeli restrictions on movement were a proximate cause of economic hardship among ordinary Palestinians. The total number of workers entering Israel and crossing into the Erez industrial zone dropped significantly in 2004 but picked up again as of mid-February 2005.

A critical aspect of institutional support during the reporting period was the emergency financing of the PA's recurrent budget. Salary support was a particularly high priority, given the importance of public sector salaries for individual Palestinian livelihoods and for the economy as a whole. The World Bank served as administrator for the multi-donor public financial management-reform trust fund, which as at May had disbursed over $198 million in budget support to the PA. Given the ongoing political instability and economic hardship, a large proportion of UN assistance to the Occupied Palestinian Territory was directed towards short-term, emergency responses, but operations were frequently affected by restrictions on the movement of goods and personnel. As the political situation appeared to improve in the first months of 2005, the increasing attention of donors to medium-term assistance agendas resulted in a relative decline in support for emergency programmes.

The Office of the Special Coordinator for the Middle East Peace Process and Personal Representative of the Secretary-General to the Palestine Liberation Organization and the PA continued to coordinate UN assistance to the Palestinian people and represent the UN system at donor forums. In April, the Office began serving as the focal point for coordination between the UN system and the new Office of the Quartet's Special Envoy for Disengagement.

The Secretary-General noted that, despite an apparent stabilization of the economy and growth in private sector activities since 2003, progress towards economic recovery was unlikely to benefit all Palestinians equitably. Many refugee and non-refugee Palestinians who lost assets and livelihoods during the years of the second intifada were likely to increase the numbers of the chronically poor and would require targeted social assistance over the medium term. Public institutions were likely to remain only partially able to finance and implement large-scale social assistance programmes in the near term.

He observed that, while international assistance could alleviate the suffering of the Palestinian people, only a peace process and a full and final settlement of the conflict would enable a shift from crisis management and recovery to sustained and sustainable development and prosperity. Such a settlement could be achieved through the full implementation of the Quartet's road map, designed to resolve the Israel-Palestinian conflict and end the occupation.

UNCTAD assistance to Palestinians

At its fifty-second session (Geneva, 3-14 October) [A/60/15], the Trade and Development Board of the United Nations Conference on Trade and Development (UNCTAD) considered the report on UNCTAD assistance to the Palestinian people [TD/B/52/2]. The report stated that UNCTAD's technical cooperation with the Palestinian people continued to provide support in building capacities for effective economic policymaking and management and strengthening the enabling environment for the private sector. The UNCTAD secretariat achieved notable progress in project implementation and its technical assistance had become increasingly relevant to the Palestinian Occupied Territory after the Israeli disengagement from the Gaza Strip. As at mid-2005, UNCTAD had disbursed a total of $2,620,000 in extrabudgetary resources for technical cooperation activities, most of it, some 83 per cent, during the period 2001 to 2004. By the end of 2005, the secretariat expected to conclude three new agreements with donors for project implementation in 2005-2007 totalling over $3 million. An

additional $1 million was still being sought for three other projects to enable implementation in 2006-2007. During the 2004-2005 biennium, technical assistance to the Palestinian people continued to receive extrabudgetary support from Norway, the EU, the International Development Research Centre (Canada) and the International Labour Organization. The United Nations Development Programme continued to extend logistical and liaison field support to UNCTAD. Among the projects implemented were: the establishment of the Palestinian Shippers Council; support for small and medium-sized enterprise development and preparation for Palestine's application for membership in the World Trade Organization (WTO).

GENERAL ASSEMBLY ACTION

On 15 December [meeting 63], the General Assembly adopted **resolution 60/126** [draft: A/60/L.36 & Add.1] without vote [agenda item 73 (d)].

Assistance to the Palestinian people

The General Assembly,

Recalling its resolution 59/56 of 2 December 2004, as well as previous resolutions on the question,

Recalling also the signing of the Declaration of Principles on Interim Self-Government Arrangements in Washington, D.C., on 13 September 1993, by the Government of the State of Israel and the Palestine Liberation Organization, the representative of the Palestinian people, and the subsequent implementation agreements concluded by the two sides,

Recalling further the International Covenant on Civil and Political Rights, the International Covenant on Economic, Social and Cultural Rights and the Convention on the Rights of the Child,

Gravely concerned at the deterioration in the living conditions of the Palestinian people, in particular children, throughout the occupied territory, which constitutes a mounting humanitarian crisis,

Conscious of the urgent need for improvement in the economic and social infrastructure of the occupied territory,

Aware that development is difficult under occupation and is best promoted in circumstances of peace and stability,

Noting the great economic and social challenges facing the Palestinian people and their leadership,

Emphasizing the importance of the safety and well-being of all children in the whole Middle East region,

Deeply concerned about the negative impact, including the health and psychological consequences, of violence on the present and future well-being of children in the region,

Conscious of the urgent necessity for international assistance to the Palestinian people, taking into account the Palestinian priorities,

Welcoming the results of the Conference to Support Middle East Peace, convened in Washington, D.C., on 1 October 1993, the establishment of the Ad Hoc Liaison Committee and the work being done by the World Bank as its secretariat and the establishment of the

Consultative Group, as well as all follow-up meetings and international mechanisms established to provide assistance to the Palestinian people,

Welcoming also the work of the Joint Liaison Committee, which provides a forum in which economic policy and practical matters related to donor assistance are discussed with the Palestinian Authority,

Stressing the continued importance of the work of the Ad Hoc Liaison Committee in the coordination of assistance to the Palestinian people,

Noting the upcoming meeting of the Ad Hoc Liaison Committee to review the state of the Palestinian economy, and progress in drawing up a medium-term development plan for the Palestinian economy,

Stressing the need for the full engagement of the United Nations in the process of building Palestinian institutions and in providing broad assistance to the Palestinian people, and welcoming in this regard the support provided to the Palestinian Authority by the Task Force on Palestinian Reform, established by the Quartet in 2002,

Noting, in this regard, the active participation of the United Nations Special Coordinator for the Middle East Peace Process and Personal Representative of the Secretary-General to the Palestine Liberation Organization and the Palestinian Authority in the activities of the Special Envoys of the Quartet,

Welcoming the endorsement by the Security Council, in its resolution 1515(2003) of 19 November 2003, of the performance-based road map to a permanent two-State solution to the Israeli-Palestinian conflict, and stressing the need for its implementation and compliance with its provisions,

Welcoming also the Israeli withdrawal from the Gaza Strip and parts of the northern West Bank as a step towards implementation of the road map,

Having considered the report of the Secretary-General,

Expressing grave concern at the continuation of the recent tragic and violent events that have led to many deaths and injuries, including among children,

1. *Takes note* of the report of the Secretary-General;

2. *Also takes note* of the report of the Personal Humanitarian Envoy of the Secretary-General on the humanitarian conditions and needs of the Palestinian people;

3. *Expresses its appreciation* to the Secretary-General for his rapid response and efforts regarding assistance to the Palestinian people;

4. *Also expresses its appreciation* to the Member States, United Nations bodies and intergovernmental, regional and non-governmental organizations that have provided and continue to provide assistance to the Palestinian people;

5. *Stresses* the importance of the work of the United Nations Special Coordinator for the Middle East Peace Process and Personal Representative of the Secretary-General to the Palestine Liberation Organization and the Palestinian Authority and of the steps taken under the auspices of the Secretary-General to ensure the achievement of a coordinated mechanism for United Nations activities throughout the occupied territories;

6. *Urges* Member States, international financial institutions of the United Nations system, intergovernmental and non-governmental organizations and regional and interregional organizations to extend, as rapidly and as generously as possible, economic and social assistance to the Palestinian people, in close cooperation with the Palestine Liberation Organization and through official Palestinian institutions;

7. *Calls upon* relevant organizations and agencies of the United Nations system to intensify their assistance in response to the urgent needs of the Palestinian people in accordance with Palestinian priorities set forth by the Palestinian Authority;

8. *Calls upon* the international community to provide urgently needed assistance and services in an effort to alleviate the dire humanitarian crisis being faced by Palestinian children and their families and to help in the reconstruction of relevant Palestinian institutions;

9. *Urges* Member States to open their markets to exports of Palestinian products on the most favourable terms, consistent with appropriate trading rules, and to implement fully existing trade and cooperation agreements;

10. *Calls upon* the international donor community to expedite the delivery of pledged assistance to the Palestinian people to meet their urgent needs;

11. *Stresses*, in this context, the importance of ensuring the free passage of aid to the Palestinian people and the free movement of persons and goods;

12. *Welcomes* the recent agreement on movement and access between the two sides and the subsequent opening of the Rafah border on 25 November 2005, and stresses the need to ensure that the commitments made in the agreement are fully implemented in accordance with the timeline set out in the agreement;

13. *Stresses* the need for all concerned parties to work together for the speedy resolution of all outstanding issues relating to disengagement, and welcomes in this regard the work of the Quartet Special Envoy for Disengagement;

14. *Urges* the international donor community, United Nations agencies and organizations and non-governmental organizations to extend as rapidly as possible emergency economic and humanitarian assistance to the Palestinian people to counter the impact of the current crisis;

15. *Stresses* the need to implement the Paris Protocol on Economic Relations of 29 April 1994, fifth annex to the Israeli-Palestinian Interim Agreement on the West Bank and the Gaza Strip, signed in Washington, D.C., on 28 September 1995, in particular with regard to the full and prompt clearance of Palestinian indirect tax revenues, and welcomes the progress made in this regard;

16. *Suggests* the convening in 2006 of a United Nations-sponsored seminar on assistance to the Palestinian people;

17. *Requests* the Secretary-General to submit a report to the General Assembly at its sixty-first session, through the Economic and Social Council, on the implementation of the present resolution, containing:

(a) An assessment of the assistance actually received by the Palestinian people;

(b) An assessment of the needs still unmet and specific proposals for responding effectively to them;

18. *Decides* to include in the provisional agenda of its sixty-first session the sub-item entitled "Assistance to the Palestinian people".

UNRWA

As at 30 June, some 4.3 million refugees were registered with UNRWA, an increase of 2.3 per cent over the 2004 figure of 4 million. Approximately 70.5 per cent of the registered refugees resided outside the 58 recognized refugee camps. The largest refugee population was registered in Jordan (41.9 per cent), followed by the Gaza Strip (22.6 per cent), the West Bank (16.1 per cent), the Syrian Arab Republic (10 per cent) and Lebanon (9.4 per cent).

In 2005, the United Nations Relief and Works Agency for Palestine Refugees in the Near East continued to provide vital education, health and relief and social services to an ever growing refugee population in the Gaza Strip, the West Bank, Jordan, Lebanon and the Syrian Arab Republic.

In his reports on the work of the Agency from 1 July 2004 to 30 June 2005 [A/60/13] and 1 January 2005 to 31 December 2005 [A/61/13], the UNRWA Commissioner-General said that UNRWA worked closely with the Special Envoy of the Quartet for Gaza Disengagement in determining microfinance and microenterprise programmes to facilitate increased lending and accelerate reconstruction of Palestinian homes demolished during the intifada.

The signing, on 15 November 2005, of the Agreement on Movement and Access and the Agreed Principles for the Rafah Crossing led to hopes of a major improvement in the ability to allow people, but not goods, to move between Gaza and Egypt through the Rafah crossing. However, Palestinian labourers wanting to work in Israel and Palestinian exporters using the commercial crossings out of Gaza into Israel faced increasing difficulties, further exacerbating the dire economic situation.

In February, UNRWA launched its medium-term plan for 2005-2009, which had four main objectives: achieving parity of UNRWA services with host authority and international standards; addressing the needs of the most vulnerable refugees; maximizing the economic potential of refugees; and building capacity within UNRWA. In other internal developments, the Secretary-General appointed Karen Koning AbuZayd as the new Commissioner-General of UNRWA for a three-year term beginning on 28 June 2005, to succeed Peter Hansen, who retired from his post in March.

Advisory Commission. By a 26 September letter to the Commissioner-General, which was included in his annual report [A/60/13], the Chairperson of the Advisory Commission of UNRWA expressed concern at the deteriorating situation in Gaza, the West Bank and Lebanon. The unilateral disengagement by Israel from Gaza and parts of the northern West Bank did not bring the hope for stabilization and subsequent phasing out of UNRWA emergency operations. The deteriorating economic situation and increased poverty in the West Bank and Gaza had created additional demand on the Agency's services.

The Commission opposed Israel's continued efforts to impose a direct charge on Agency containers passing through Karni, as it violated the exemption granted to UNRWA under the 1946 Convention on the Privileges and Immunities of the United Nations [YUN 1946-47, p. 100]. It commended the Lebanese Government on its June announcement to ease restrictions on granting work permits to Palestine refugees in Lebanon so as to make better the conditions of those refugees living in camps.

UNRWA's regular budget for 2005 was set at $396.4 million, against which the Agency received $378.6 million.

On 8 December, the General Assembly decided to continue the membership of those States serving as members of the Advisory Commission to UNRWA. It invited Australia, Canada, Denmark, Germany, Italy, the Netherlands, Norway, Saudi Arabia, Spain, Sweden and Switzerland, whose contributions to UNRWA's activities had exceeded an annual average of $5 million over the past three years, to become members of the Advisory Commission; Palestine to attend and fully participate in the Commission's meetings as an observer; the EU to attend the Commission's meetings; and the League of Arab States to attend also as an observer (**decision 60/522**).

Report of Conciliation Commission. The United Nations Conciliation Commission for Palestine, in its fifty-ninth report covering the period from 1 September 2004 to 31 August 2005 [A/60/277], submitted in response to General Assembly resolution 59/117 [YUN 2004, p. 499], noted its August 2004 report [ibid., p. 497] and observed that it had nothing to report since its submission.

Projects and major service areas

UNRWA continued to implement its regular programmes, providing education, health, social services and microcredit assistance to Palestinian refugees in its five field operations. The education programme remained the largest activity, operating 647 schools, which provided basic and preparatory education to 490,000 pupils, as well as 5 secondary schools in Lebanon, 8 vocational training centres and 3 teacher training colleges. It continued to benefit from close cooperation with UNESCO. The programme also provided staff training, community involvement and strategic development plan, also known as the

"School as a focus for development" project. The Agency launched a psychosocial support programme, designed to reach some 90,000 pupils in the Occupied Palestinian Territory. Through some of its information technology projects, internet access was provided for all Agency schools in Gaza.

The health programme, supervised by the World Health Organization, focused on sustaining adequate levels of investment in primary health care, enhancing institutional capacity-building and developing human resources. Management reforms implemented during the reporting period led to the introduction of new systems for health information, hospital and drug-supply management. The Agency maintained its environmental health services in refugee camps, introducing and/or improving sewage disposal, storm water drainage, and providing drinking water and refuse collection. Major water and sewage system projects were underway in the Syrian Arab Republic and Lebanon in various refugee camps. It conducted three major health research projects to assess the health status of Palestinian refugees, which included prevalence of anaemia among schoolchildren; current contraceptive practices among mothers with children up to 3 years; and oral health status among school children.

The Agency's microfinance and microenterprise programme, aimed at improving the quality of life of small business owners, sustain jobs, and create household assets, grew significantly in 2005. The programme produced record outreach, financing 22,000 loans totalling $20.4 million. Half of that financing was in the Gaza Strip, 31 per cent in the West Bank, 12 per cent in Jordan and 7 per cent in the Syrian Arab Republic.

Through the relief and social services programme, UNRWA continued to provide a social safety net and promote self-reliance for Palestinian refugees, especially women, the elderly, youth and persons with disabilities. Its relief and social services included food support; shelter rehabilitation and cash assistance to families living in conditions of special hardship. Specific services included microenterprise credit, solidarity-group lending, small-scale enterprise, consumer lending, housing loans and small microenterprise training.

The Agency expended $484.2 million during 2005, against a budget of $537.7 million on its regular, project and emergency appeal activities. The largest component was an expenditure of $377.2 million under the regular budget, accounting for nearly 78 per cent of total expenditures. Emergency appeal activities and projects accounted for 18 per cent and 4 per cent, respectively.

Emergency appeals

UNRWA continued its programme of emergency assistance, focusing on food aid, emergency employment creation, shelter repair, rebuilding and health and education. In 2005, the Agency launched an emergency appeal for the West Bank and Gaza for $185.81 million. As at 31 December, $110.7 million had been pledged and $70.15 million received. Its largest-scale emergency activities were the provision of food aid to cover 1.3 million refugees and the creation of 2.3 million workdays for 33,000 unemployed breadwinners. Emergency operations also included the provision of mobile medical clinics in the West Bank and cash assistance and replacement accommodation for those whose shelters had been demolished during Israeli military operations. By the end of 2005, UNRWA had completed 925 new shelters for homeless refugees in the Gaza Strip and had over 1,000 under construction.

GENERAL ASSEMBLY ACTION

On 8 December [meeting 62], the General Assembly, on the recommendations of the Fourth Committee [A/60/476], adopted **resolution 60/100** by recorded vote (161-1-11) [agenda item 30].

Assistance to Palestine refugees

The General Assembly,

Recalling its resolution 194(III) of 11 December 1948 and all its subsequent resolutions on the question, including resolution 59/117 of 10 December 2004,

Recalling also its resolution 302(IV) of 8 December 1949, by which, inter alia, it established the United Nations Relief and Works Agency for Palestine Refugees in the Near East,

Recalling further relevant Security Council resolutions,

Aware of the fact that, for more than five decades, the Palestine refugees have suffered from the loss of their homes, lands and means of livelihood,

Affirming the imperative of resolving the problem of the Palestine refugees for the achievement of justice and for the achievement of lasting peace in the region,

Acknowledging the essential role that the United Nations Relief and Works Agency for Palestine Refugees in the Near East has played for more than fifty-five years since its establishment in ameliorating the plight of the Palestine refugees in the fields of education, health and relief and social services,

Taking note of the report of the Commissioner-General of the United Nations Relief and Works Agency for Palestine Refugees in the Near East covering the period from 1 July 2004 to 30 June 2005,

Aware of the continuing needs of the Palestine refugees throughout all the fields of operation, namely Jordan, Lebanon, the Syrian Arab Republic and the Occupied Palestinian Territory,

Expressing grave concern at the especially difficult situation of the Palestine refugees under occupation, including with regard to their safety, well-being and living conditions,

Noting the signing of the Declaration of Principles on Interim Self-Government Arrangements on 13 September 1993 by the Government of Israel and the Palestine Liberation Organization and the subsequent implementation agreements,

Aware of the important role to be played in the peace process by the Multilateral Working Group on Refugees of the Middle East peace process,

1. *Notes with regret* that repatriation or compensation of the refugees, as provided for in paragraph 11 of General Assembly resolution 194(III), has not yet been effected and that, therefore, the situation of the Palestine refugees continues to be a matter of grave concern;

2. *Also notes with regret* that the United Nations Conciliation Commission for Palestine has been unable to find a means of achieving progress in the implementation of paragraph 11 of General Assembly resolution 194(III), and reiterates its request to the Conciliation Commission to exert continued efforts towards the implementation of that paragraph and to report to the Assembly as appropriate, but no later than 1 September 2006;

3. *Affirms* the necessity for the continuation of the work of the United Nations Relief and Works Agency for Palestine Refugees in the Near East and the importance of its operation and its services for the well-being of the Palestine refugees and for the stability of the region, pending the resolution of the question of the Palestine refugees;

4. *Calls upon* all donors to continue to make the most generous efforts possible to meet the anticipated needs of the Agency, including those mentioned in recent emergency appeals.

RECORDED VOTE ON RESOLUTION 60/100:

In favour: Afghanistan, Algeria, Andorra, Antigua and Barbuda, Argentina, Armenia, Australia, Austria, Azerbaijan, Bahamas, Bahrain, Bangladesh, Barbados, Belarus, Belgium, Belize, Benin, Bhutan, Bolivia, Botswana, Brazil, Brunei Darussalam, Bulgaria, Burkina Faso, Burundi, Cambodia, Canada, Cape Verde, Central African Republic, Chile, China, Colombia, Costa Rica, Croatia, Cuba, Cyprus, Czech Republic, Democratic People's Republic of Korea, Denmark, Djibouti, Dominica, Dominican Republic, Ecuador, Egypt, El Salvador, Eritrea, Estonia, Ethiopia, Fiji, Finland, France, Gabon, Georgia, Germany, Ghana, Greece, Guatemala, Guinea, Guinea-Bissau, Guyana, Honduras, Hungary, Iceland, India, Indonesia, Iran, Iraq, Ireland, Italy, Jamaica, Japan, Jordan, Kazakhstan, Kenya, Kuwait, Kyrgyzstan, Lao People's Democratic Republic, Latvia, Lebanon, Lesotho, Liberia, Libyan Arab Jamahiriya, Liechtenstein, Lithuania, Luxembourg, Malawi, Malaysia, Maldives, Mali, Malta, Mauritania, Mauritius, Mexico, Monaco, Mongolia, Morocco, Mozambique, Myanmar, Namibia, Nepal, Netherlands, New Zealand, Nicaragua, Niger, Nigeria, Norway, Oman, Pakistan, Panama, Papua New Guinea, Paraguay, Peru, Philippines, Poland, Portugal, Qatar, Republic of Korea, Republic of Moldova, Romania, Russian Federation, Rwanda, Saint Lucia, Saint Vincent and the Grenadines, Samoa, San Marino, Saudi Arabia, Senegal, Serbia and Montenegro, Singapore, Slovakia, Slovenia, Solomon Islands, Somalia, South Africa, Spain, Sri Lanka, Sudan, Suriname, Sweden, Switzerland, Syrian Arab Republic, Tajikistan, Thailand, The former Yugoslav Republic of Macedonia, Timor-Leste, Togo, Tonga, Trinidad and Tobago, Tunisia, Turkey, Turkmenistan, Ukraine, United Arab Emirates, United Kingdom, United Republic of Tanzania, Uzbekistan, Venezuela, Viet Nam, Yemen, Zambia, Zimbabwe.

Against: Israel.

Abstaining: Albania, Cameroon, Grenada, Haiti, Marshall Islands, Micronesia, Palau, Tuvalu, Uganda, United States, Vanuatu.

The Assembly, also on 8 December [meeting 62] and on the Fourth Committee's recommendation

[A/60/476], adopted **resolution 60/102** by recorded vote (159-6-3) [agenda item 30].

Operations of the United Nations Relief and Works Agency for Palestine Refugees in the Near East

The General Assembly,

Recalling its resolutions 194(III) of 11 December 1948, 212(III) of 19 November 1948, 302(IV) of 8 December 1949 and all subsequent related resolutions, including its resolution 59/119 of 10 December 2004,

Recalling also the relevant Security Council resolutions,

Having considered the report of the Commissioner-General of the United Nations Relief and Works Agency for Palestine Refugees in the Near East covering the period from 1 July 2004 to 30 June 2005,

Taking note of the letter dated 26 September 2005 from the Chairperson of the Advisory Commission of the United Nations Relief and Works Agency for Palestine Refugees in the Near East addressed to the Commissioner-General,

Deeply concerned about the critical financial situation of the Agency and its effect on the provision of necessary Agency services to the Palestine refugees, including its emergency-related and development programmes,

Recalling Articles 100, 104 and 105 of the Charter of the United Nations and the Convention on the Privileges and Immunities of the United Nations,

Recalling also the Convention on the Safety of United Nations and Associated Personnel,

Affirming the applicability of the Geneva Convention relative to the Protection of Civilian Persons in Time of War, of 12 August 1949, to the Palestinian territory occupied since 1967, including East Jerusalem,

Aware of the continuing needs of the Palestine refugees throughout the Occupied Palestinian Territory and in the other fields of operation, namely Jordan, Lebanon and the Syrian Arab Republic,

Gravely concerned about the extremely difficult living conditions being faced by the Palestine refugees in the Occupied Palestinian Territory, including East Jerusalem, including in the Rafah and Jabaliya refugee camps, resulting, inter alia, from loss of life and injury, extensive destruction and damage to their shelters and properties, and displacement,

Aware of the extraordinary efforts being undertaken by the Agency for the repair or rebuilding of thousands of damaged or destroyed refugee shelters,

Aware also of the valuable work done by the refugee affairs officers of the Agency in providing protection to the Palestinian people, in particular Palestine refugees,

Gravely concerned about the endangerment of the safety of the Agency's staff and about the damage caused to the facilities of the Agency as a result of Israeli military operations during the reporting period,

Deploring the killing of twelve Agency staff members by the Israeli occupying forces since September 2000,

Deploring also the killing and wounding of children in the Agency's schools by the Israeli occupying forces,

Expressing deep concern about the policies of closure and severe restrictions, including the curfews, that continue to be imposed on the movement of persons and goods throughout the Occupied Palestinian Territory, including East Jerusalem, which have had a grave impact on the socio-economic situation of the Palestine refugees and have greatly contributed to the dire humanitarian crisis facing the Palestinian people,

Deeply concerned about the continuing imposition of restrictions on the freedom of movement of the Agency's staff, vehicles and goods, and the harassment and intimidation of the Agency's staff, which undermine and obstruct the work of the Agency, including its ability to provide its essential services, notably its education, health and relief and social services,

Recalling the signing, on 13 September 1993, of the Declaration of Principles on Interim Self-Government Arrangements by the Government of Israel and the Palestine Liberation Organization and the subsequent implementation agreements,

Aware of the agreement between the Agency and the Government of Israel,

Taking note of the agreement reached on 24 June 1994, embodied in an exchange of letters between the Agency and the Palestine Liberation Organization,

Recalling the Geneva Conference convened by the United Nations Relief and Works Agency for Palestine Refugees in the Near East and the Swiss Agency for Development and Cooperation on 7 and 8 June 2004 to increase support for the United Nations Relief and Works Agency,

1. *Expresses its appreciation* to the Commissioner-General of the United Nations Relief and Works Agency for Palestine Refugees in the Near East, as well as to all of the staff of the Agency, for their tireless efforts and valuable work, particularly in the light of the difficult conditions during the past year;

2. *Also expresses its appreciation* to the Advisory Commission of the Agency, and requests it to continue its efforts and to keep the General Assembly informed of its activities;

3. *Takes note with appreciation* of the report of the Working Group on the Financing of the United Nations Relief and Works Agency for Palestine Refugees in the Near East, and the efforts of the Working Group to assist in ensuring the financial security of the Agency, and requests the Secretary-General to provide the necessary services and assistance to the Working Group for the conduct of its work;

4. *Commends* the continuing efforts of the Commissioner-General to increase the budgetary transparency and efficiency of the Agency, as reflected in the Agency's programme budget for the biennium 2006-2007;

5. *Acknowledges* the important support provided by the host Governments to the Agency in the discharge of its duties;

6. *Encourages* the Agency's further consideration of the needs and rights of children in its operations in accordance with the Convention on the Rights of the Child;

7. *Expresses concern* about the temporary relocation of the headquarters international staff of the Agency from Gaza City and the disruption of operations at the headquarters;

8. *Calls upon* Israel, the occupying Power, to comply fully with the provisions of the Geneva Convention relative to the Protection of Civilian Persons in Time of War, of 12 August 1949;

9. *Also calls upon* Israel to abide by Articles 100, 104 and 105 of the Charter of the United Nations and the Convention on the Privileges and Immunities of the United Nations in order to ensure the safety of the personnel of the Agency, the protection of its institutions and the safeguarding of the security of its facilities in the Occupied Palestinian Territory, including East Jerusalem;

10. *Urges* the Government of Israel to speedily compensate the Agency for damage to its property and facilities resulting from actions by the Israeli side;

11. *Calls upon* Israel particularly to cease obstructing the movement of the staff, vehicles and supplies of the Agency and to cease the levying of extra fees and charges, which affect the Agency's operations detrimentally;

12. *Requests* the Commissioner-General to proceed with the issuance of identification cards for Palestine refugees and their descendants in the Occupied Palestinian Territory;

13. *Affirms* that the functioning of the Agency remains essential in all the fields of operation;

14. *Notes* the success of the Agency's microfinance and microenterprise programmes, and calls upon the Agency, in close cooperation with the relevant agencies, to continue to contribute to the development of the economic and social stability of the Palestine refugees in all the fields of operation;

15. *Reiterates its request* to the Commissioner-General to proceed with the modernization of the archives of the Agency through the Palestine Refugee Records Project, and to indicate progress in her report to the General Assembly at its sixty-first session;

16. *Reiterates its previous appeals* to all States, specialized agencies and non-governmental organizations to continue and to augment the special allocations for grants and scholarships for higher education to Palestine refugees in addition to their contributions to the regular budget of the Agency and to contribute to the establishment of vocational training centres for Palestine refugees, and requests the Agency to act as the recipient and trustee for the special allocations for grants and scholarships;

17. *Urges* all States, specialized agencies and non-governmental organizations to continue and to increase their contributions to the Agency so as to ease the ongoing financial constraints, exacerbated by the current humanitarian situation on the ground, and to support the Agency's valuable work in assisting the Palestine refugees.

RECORDED VOTE ON RESOLUTION 60/102:

In favour: Afghanistan, Algeria, Andorra, Antigua and Barbuda, Argentina, Armenia, Australia, Austria, Azerbaijan, Bahamas, Bangladesh, Barbados, Belarus, Belgium, Belize, Benin, Bhutan, Bolivia, Botswana, Brazil, Brunei Darussalam, Bulgaria, Burkina Faso, Burundi, Cambodia, Canada, Cape Verde, Chile, China, Colombia, Costa Rica, Croatia, Cuba, Cyprus, Czech Republic, Democratic People's Republic of Korea, Denmark, Djibouti, Dominica, Dominican Republic, Ecuador, Egypt, El Salvador, Eritrea, Estonia, Ethiopia, Fiji, Finland, France, Gabon, Georgia, Germany, Ghana, Greece, Guatemala, Guinea, Guinea-Bissau, Guyana, Honduras, Hungary, Iceland, India, Indonesia, Iran, Iraq, Ireland, Italy, Jamaica, Japan, Jordan, Kazakhstan, Kenya, Kuwait, Kyrgyzstan, Lao People's Democratic Republic, Latvia, Lebanon, Lesotho, Liberia, Libyan Arab Jamahiriya, Liechtenstein, Lithuania, Luxembourg, Malawi, Malaysia, Maldives, Mali, Malta, Mauritania, Mauritius, Mexico, Monaco, Mongolia, Morocco, Mozambique, Myanmar, Namibia, Nepal, Netherlands, New Zealand, Nicaragua, Niger, Nigeria, Norway, Oman, Pakistan, Panama, Papua New Guinea, Paraguay, Peru, Philippines, Poland, Portugal, Qatar, Republic of Korea, Republic of Moldova, Romania, Russian Federation, Saint Lucia, Saint Vincent and the Grenadines, Samoa, San Marino, Saudi Arabia, Senegal, Serbia and Montenegro, Singapore, Slovakia, Slovenia, Solomon Islands, Somalia, South Africa, Spain, Sri Lanka, Sudan, Suriname, Sweden, Switzerland, Syrian Arab Republic, Tajikistan, Thailand, The former Yugoslav Republic of Macedonia, Timor-Leste, Togo, Tonga, Trinidad and Tobago, Tunisia, Turkey, Turkmenistan, Ukraine, United Arab Emirates, United Kingdom, United Republic of Tanzania, Uruguay, Uzbekistan, Venezuela, Viet Nam, Yemen, Zambia, Zimbabwe.

Against: Grenada, Israel, Marshall Islands, Micronesia, Palau, United States.

Abstaining: Albania, Cameroon, Uganda.

UNRWA financing

At the end of 2004, UNRWA experienced a funding gap for the regular budget of $8.7 million, including exchange rate gains and interest income, and a project budget shortfall of $23 million. Emergency appeals were underfunded by 98.4 million. The overall Agency-wide impact of underfunding meant that UNRWA was unable to implement crucial activities to the value of $130.1 million. The projected funding gap for the 2005 regular budget was estimated to be $11.1 million.

The proposed programme budget for the 2006-2007 biennium [A/60/13/Add.1] amounted to $1,280,560, including $994,329 for the regular budget and $286,321 for projects.

Working Group. The Working Group on the Financing of UNRWA held two meetings in 2005, on 8 September and 18 October. In its report to the General Assembly [A/60/439], the Working Group said that it was concerned about reduced coverage in food and cash assistance in the Occupied Palestinian Territory. As at 30 September, the Agency had received only $92.9 million in confirmed pledges from a total request of $185.8 million for the 2005 emergency appeal, which seriously curtailed its humanitarian activities. In addition, some $6 million remained outstanding for pre-year emergency appeals. The group encouraged donors to increase their contributions to the Agency's 2005 appeal and to pay outstanding contributions. The Working Group also remained concerned about the port and related charges, exacerbated by security procedures, that had been imposed on humanitarian goods imported through Israel by UNRWA. Those charges totalled $27.6 million, as at 31 December 2004.

The Group noted the declining funding gap for the Agency's regular budget, but remained concerned that the trend would not be maintained in 2005. It called for the early and complete fulfilment of pledges and urged the international community to fund fully the 2006-2007 budget, which had been prepared on a needs basis, so as to reverse the effects of successive years of underfunding and bring services up to most government standards and to build capacity.

Displaced persons

In an August report [A/60/212] on compliance with General Assembly resolution 59/118 [YUN 2004, p. 503], which called for the accelerated return of all persons displaced as a result of the June 1967 and subsequent hostilities to their homes in the territories occupied by Israel since 1967, the Secretary-General said that the Agency's information was based on requests by returning registered refugees for the transfer of their entitlements to their areas of return. UNRWA was not involved in arrangements for the return of either refugees or displaced persons not registered with it. Currently, displaced refugees known by UNRWA to have returned to the West Bank and Gaza Strip since 1967 totalled about 25,160. From 1 July 2004 to 30 June 2005, 489 refugees registered by UNRWA had returned to the West Bank and 74 to the Gaza Strip from places outside the Occupied Palestinian Territory. Some of those refugees might not have been displaced since 1967, but were possibly family members of a displaced registered refugee.

GENERAL ASSEMBLY ACTION

On 8 December [meeting 62], the General Assembly, on the recommendation of the Fourth Committee [A/60/476], adopted **resolution 60/101** by recorded vote (161-6-5) [agenda item 30].

Persons displaced as a result of the June 1967 and subsequent hostilities

The General Assembly,

Recalling its resolutions 2252 (ES-V) of 4 July 1967, 2341 B(XXII) of 19 December 1967 and all subsequent related resolutions,

Recalling also Security Council resolutions 237(1967) of 14 June 1967 and 259(1968) of 27 September 1968,

Taking note of the report of the Secretary-General submitted in pursuance of its resolution 59/118 of 10 December 2004,

Taking note also of the report of the Commissioner-General of the United Nations Relief and Works Agency for Palestine Refugees in the Near East covering the period from 1 July 2004 to 30 June 2005,

Concerned about the continuing human suffering resulting from the June 1967 and subsequent hostilities,

Taking note of the relevant provisions of the Declaration of Principles on Interim Self-Government Arrangements of 1993 with regard to the modalities for the admission of persons displaced in 1967, and concerned that the process agreed upon has not yet been effected,

1. *Reaffirms* the right of all persons displaced as a result of the June 1967 and subsequent hostilities to return to their homes or former places of residence in the territories occupied by Israel since 1967;

2. *Expresses deep concern* that the mechanism agreed upon by the parties in article XII of the Declaration of Principles on Interim Self-Government Arrangements of 1993 on the return of displaced persons has not

been complied with, and stresses the necessity for an accelerated return of displaced persons;

3. *Endorses*, in the meantime, the efforts of the Commissioner-General of the United Nations Relief and Works Agency for Palestine Refugees in the Near East to continue to provide humanitarian assistance, as far as practicable, on an emergency basis, and as a temporary measure, to persons in the area who are currently displaced and in serious need of continued assistance as a result of the June 1967 and subsequent hostilities;

4. *Strongly appeals* to all Governments and to organizations and individuals to contribute generously to the Agency and to the other intergovernmental and non-governmental organizations concerned for the above-mentioned purposes;

5. *Requests* the Secretary-General, after consulting with the Commissioner-General, to report to the General Assembly before its sixty-first session on the progress made with regard to the implementation of the present resolution.

RECORDED VOTE ON RESOLUTION 60/101:

In favour: Afghanistan, Algeria, Andorra, Antigua and Barbuda, Argentina, Armenia, Australia, Austria, Azerbaijan, Bahamas, Bahrain, Bangladesh, Barbados, Belarus, Belgium, Belize, Benin, Bhutan, Bolivia, Botswana, Brazil, Brunei Darussalam, Bulgaria, Burkina Faso, Burundi, Cambodia, Cameroon, Canada, Cape Verde, Central African Republic, Chile, China, Colombia, Congo, Costa Rica, Croatia, Cuba, Cyprus, Czech Republic, Democratic People's Republic of Korea, Denmark, Djibouti, Dominica, Ecuador, Egypt, El Salvador, Eritrea, Estonia, Ethiopia, Fiji, Finland, France, Gabon, Georgia, Germany, Ghana, Greece, Guatemala, Guinea, Guinea-Bissau, Guyana, Honduras, Hungary, Iceland, India, Indonesia, Iran,, Iraq, Ireland, Italy, Jamaica, Japan, Jordan, Kazakhstan, Kenya, Kuwait, Kyrgyzstan, Lao People's Democratic Republic, Latvia, Lebanon, Lesotho, Liberia, Libyan Arab Jamahiriya, Liechtenstein, Lithuania, Luxembourg, Malaysia, Maldives, Mali, Malta, Mauritania, Mauritius, Mexico, Monaco, Mongolia, Morocco, Mozambique, Myanmar, Namibia, Nepal, Netherlands, New Zealand, Nicaragua, Niger, Nigeria, Norway, Oman, Pakistan, Panama, Papua New Guinea, Paraguay, Peru, Philippines, Poland, Portugal, Qatar, Republic of Korea, Republic of Moldova, Romania, Russian Federation, Saint Lucia, Saint Vincent and the Grenadines, Samoa, San Marino, Saudi Arabia, Senegal, Serbia and Montenegro, Singapore, Slovakia, Slovenia, Solomon Islands, Somalia, South Africa, Spain, Sri Lanka, Sudan, Suriname, Sweden, Switzerland, Syrian Arab Republic, Tajikistan, Thailand, The former Yugoslav Republic of Macedonia, Timor-Leste, Togo, Tonga, Trinidad and Tobago, Tunisia, Turkey, Turkmenistan, Ukraine, United Arab Emirates, United Kingdom, United Republic of Tanzania, Uruguay, Uzbekistan, Venezuela, Viet Nam, Yemen, Zambia, Zimbabwe.

Against: Grenada, Israel, Marshall Islands, Micronesia, Palau, United States.

Abstaining: Albania, Dominican Republic, Tuvalu, Uganda, Vanuatu.

Property rights

In response to General Assembly resolution 59/120 [YUN 2004, p. 504], the Secretary-General submitted an August report [A/60/256] on steps taken to protect and administer Arab property, assets and property rights in Israel, and establish a fund for income derived therefrom, on behalf of the rightful owners. He indicated that he had transmitted the resolution to Israel and all other Member States, requesting information on any steps taken or envisaged to implement it. The report detailed replies from Israel and the Syrian Arab Republic, covering various aspects of Assembly resolutions 59/117 [YUN 2004, p. 499] and 59/120 pertaining to assistance to Palestine refugees. Israel, in its reply, said that it supported

UNRWA's humanitarian mission and recognized its contribution to the welfare of Palestinian refugee. It was concerned, however, about the politicization of UNRWA operations and the need to take account of the campaign of terror being waged against Israel's citizens. Israel urged UNRWA to draw attention to the misuse of refugee camps by armed elements, in violation of Security Council resolutions and international law.

GENERAL ASSEMBLY ACTION

On 8 December [meeting 62], the General Assembly, on the recommendation of the Fourth Committee [A/60/476], adopted **resolution 60/103** by recorded vote (160-6-3) [agenda item 30].

Palestine refugees' properties and their revenues

The General Assembly,

Recalling its resolutions 194(III) of 11 December 1948, 36/146 C of 16 December 1981 and all its subsequent resolutions on the question,

Taking note of the report of the Secretary-General submitted in pursuance of resolution 59/120 of 10 December 2004,

Taking note also of the report of the United Nations Conciliation Commission for Palestine for the period from 1 September 2004 to 31 August 2005,

Recalling that the Universal Declaration of Human Rights and the principles of international law uphold the principle that no one shall be arbitrarily deprived of his or her property,

Recalling in particular its resolution 394(V) of 14 December 1950, in which it directed the Conciliation Commission, in consultation with the parties concerned, to prescribe measures for the protection of the rights, property and interests of the Palestine refugees,

Noting the completion of the programme of identification and evaluation of Arab property, as announced by the Conciliation Commission in its twenty-second progress report, and the fact that the Land Office had a schedule of Arab owners and file of documents defining the location, area and other particulars of Arab property,

Expressing its appreciation for the work done to preserve and modernize the existing records, including the land records, of the Conciliation Commission and the importance of such records for a just resolution of the plight of the Palestine refugees in conformity with resolution 194(III),

Recalling that, in the framework of the Middle East peace process, the Palestine Liberation Organization and the Government of Israel agreed, in the Declaration of Principles on Interim Self-Government Arrangements of 13 September 1993, to commence negotiations on permanent status issues, including the important issue of the refugees,

1. *Reaffirms* that the Palestine refugees are entitled to their property and to the income derived therefrom, in conformity with the principles of equity and justice;

2. *Requests* the Secretary-General to take all appropriate steps, in consultation with the United Nations Conciliation Commission for Palestine, for the protec-

tion of Arab property, assets and property rights in Israel;

3. *Calls once again* upon Israel to render all facilities and assistance to the Secretary-General in the implementation of the present resolution;

4. *Calls upon* all the parties concerned to provide the Secretary-General with any pertinent information in their possession concerning Arab property, assets and property rights in Israel that would assist him in the implementation of the present resolution;

5. *Urges* the Palestinian and Israeli sides, as agreed between them, to deal with the important issue of Palestine refugees' properties and their revenues within the framework of the final status negotiations of the Middle East peace process;

6. *Requests* the Secretary-General to report to the General Assembly at its sixty-first session on the implementation of the present resolution.

RECORDED VOTE ON RESOLUTION 60/103:

In favour: Afghanistan, Algeria, Andorra, Antigua and Barbuda, Argentina, Armenia, Australia, Austria, Azerbaijan, Bahamas, Bahrain, Bangladesh, Barbados, Belarus, Belgium, Belize, Benin, Bhutan, Bolivia, Botswana, Brazil, Brunei Darussalam, Bulgaria, Burkina Faso, Burundi, Cambodia, Canada, Cape Verde, Central African Republic, Chile, China, Colombia, Costa Rica, Croatia, Cuba, Cyprus, Czech Republic, Democratic People's Republic of Korea, Denmark, Djibouti, Dominica, Dominican Republic, Ecuador, Egypt, El Salvador, Eritrea, Estonia, Ethiopia, Fiji, Finland, France, Gabon, Georgia, Germany, Ghana, Greece, Guatemala, Guinea, Guinea-Bissau, Guyana, Honduras, Hungary, Iceland, India, Indonesia, Iran, Iraq, Ireland, Italy, Jamaica, Japan, Jordan, Kazakhstan, Kenya, Kuwait, Kyrgyzstan, Lao People's Democratic Republic, Latvia, Lebanon, Lesotho, Liberia, Libyan Arab Jamahiriya, Liechtenstein, Lithuania, Luxembourg, Malaysia, Maldives, Mali, Malta, Mauritania, Mauritius, Mexico, Monaco, Mongolia, Morocco, Mozambique, Myanmar, Namibia, Nepal, Netherlands, New Zealand, Nicaragua, Niger, Nigeria, Norway, Oman, Pakistan, Panama, Papua New Guinea, Paraguay, Peru, Philippines, Poland, Portugal, Qatar, Republic of Korea, Republic of Moldova, Romania, Russian Federation, Saint Lucia, Saint Vincent and the Grenadines, Samoa, San Marino, Saudi Arabia, Senegal, Serbia and Montenegro, Singapore, Slovakia, Slovenia, Solomon Islands, Somalia, South Africa, Spain, Sri Lanka, Sudan, Suriname, Sweden, Switzerland, Syrian Arab Republic, Tajikistan, Thailand, The former Yugoslav Republic of Macedonia, Timor-Leste, Togo, Tonga, Trinidad and Tobago, Tunisia, Turkey, Turkmenistan, Ukraine, United Arab Emirates, United Kingdom, United Republic of Tanzania, Uruguay, Uzbekistan, Venezuela, Viet Nam, Yemen, Zambia, Zimbabwe.

Against: Grenada, Israel, Marshall Islands, Micronesia, Palau, United States.

Abstaining: Albania, Cameroon, Uganda.

Peacekeeping operations

In 2005, the United Nations Truce Supervision Organization (UNTSO), originally set up to monitor the ceasefire called for by the Security Council in resolution S/801 of 29 May 1948 [YUN 1947-48, p. 427] in newly partitioned Palestine, continued its work. UNTSO unarmed military observers fulfilled evolving mandates—from supervising the original four armistice agreements between Israel and its neighbours (Egypt, Jordan, Lebanon, Syrian Arab Republic) to observing and monitoring other ceasefires, as well as performing a number of additional tasks. During the year, UNTSO personnel worked with the two remaining UN peacekeeping forces in the Middle East—the United Nations Disengagement Observer Force (UNDOF) in the Golan Heights and the United Nations Interim Force in Lebanon (UNIFIL).

Lebanon

Lebanon became a focus of international attention in February, following the bomb attack that killed former Prime Minister Rafik Hariri and an estimated 20 others in Beirut. More bombings occurred throughout the year, in some cases targeting prominent Lebanese figures, several of whom were killed. Following the assassination of Mr. Hariri, the Secretary-General, at the request of the Security Council, dispatched a mission of inquiry to report on the circumstances of the attack. The mission recommended the establishment of an international commission to investigate the crime, and by June, the United Nations International Independent Investigation Commission (UNIIIC) was operational. The findings of UNIIIC implicated both the Syrian Arab Republic and Lebanon in the assassination. Other UN involvement in Lebanon included the investigation of the technical military team sent to verify the withdrawal of all Syrian military and intelligence presence from Lebanon, pursuant to resolution 1559(2004) [YUN 2004, p. 506]. The team concluded, to the best of its ability, that Syrian military assets, except in one disputed border area, had been withdrawn fully from Lebanon. While it was more difficult to verify the withdrawal of intelligence operatives, in a second trip to Lebanon, the team corroborated its earlier conclusion that there was no remaining visible or significant Syrian intelligence presence in Lebanon. The UN also provided assistance in preparing for the parliamentary elections that ended in June. The completion of those elections on time and in a credible manner was a key element in a transition, in which the Lebanese people expressed their determination to shape their own future, strengthen political institutions and restore their full sovereignty.

Monthly briefings on the Palestine question were given to the Security Council by Alvaro de Soto, Special Coordinator for the Middle East Peace Process and Personal Representative of the Secretary-General, Kieran Prendergast, Under-Secretary-General for Political Affairs, and his replacement, Mr. Gambari. Those briefings also covered developments in southern Lebanon. Terje Roed-Larsen, Special Envoy of the Secretary-General for the implementation of resolution 1559(2004), briefed the Council on the first semi-annual report of the Secretary-General on the implementation of resolution 1559(2004).

The paramilitary group Hizbullah continued to carry out attacks against positions of the Israel Defence Forces (IDF) inside Israel, while IDF continued to carry out attacks within Lebanon. The Shab'a farmlands had been an area of contention since the withdrawal of Israeli forces from Lebanon in June 2000 [YUN 2000, p. 465]. According to the Lebanese Government, Israel's withdrawal from southern Lebanon was incomplete, as Israeli forces continued to occupy the Shab'a farms, while Israel held the view that the area was occupied Syrian territory and thus within the purview of Council resolution 242(1967) [YUN 1967, p. 257] on the Israeli-Syrian conflict, and not resolution 425(1978) [YUN 1978, p. 312], which dealt with Israel's withdrawal from Lebanon. However, Lebanon and the Syrian Arab Republic maintained that the Shab'a farmlands were inside Lebanese territory.

In March 2005, the Secretary-General appointed Geir O. Pedersen as his Personal Representative for Southern Lebanon, responsible for coordinating UN activities in the area. In view of the increased scope of such activities, in November, the Secretary-General expanded Mr. Pedersen's mandate to include coordination of UN political activities for the whole of Lebanon. Accordingly, the title of the post was changed to Personal Representative of the Secretary-General for Lebanon.

Communications. On 12 January [A/59/670-S/2005/23], Lebanon made clarifications regarding the 10 January press release of the Secretary-General and the 11 January press statement of the Security Council President, issued in response to a lethal attack by Hizbullah against an Israeli patrol and the subsequent Israeli military response, which resulted in the injury and death of UN military observers on 9 January.

In communications received throughout the year [A/59/671-S/2005/24, A/59/672-S/2005/25, A/59/673-S/2005/26, A/59/686-S/2005/58, A/59/711-S/2005/105, A/59/712-S/2005/106, A/59/737-S/2005/168, A/59/778-S/2005/242, A/59/799-S/2005/304, A/59/810-S/2005/339, A/59/827-S/2005/369, A/59/859-S/2005/424, A/59/865-S/2005/435, A/59/893-S/2005/526, A/59/911-S/2005/568, A/60/423-S/2005/641, A/60/555-S/2005/715, A/60/569-S/2005/746, A/60/570-S/2005/747, A/60/579-S/2005/755, A/60/638-S/2005/836], Lebanon detailed Israeli acts of aggression and violations of the Blue Line, the provisional border drawn by the United Nations following the withdrawal of Israeli troops from southern Lebanon in 2000, and consequently of Lebanese sovereignty and territorial integrity.

In a series of letters [A/59/667-S/2005/14, A/59/802-S/2005/312, A/59/819-S/2005/352, A/59/858-S/2005/423, A/59/902-S/2005/546, A/60/563-S/2005/731, A/60/639-S/2005/837], Israel reported attacks carried out across the Blue Line by Hizbullah and other militias against Israeli civilian and military targets. Israel also alleged that those attacks were enabled by the complicity of the Government of Lebanon and the support of the Iranian and Syrian regimes.

In two separate responses [A/59/739-S/2005/170, A/59/848-S/2005/389], Iran refuted Israel's allegations, calling them an attempt to distract the international community from the numerous crimes committed by Israel in the region.

Assassination of former Prime Minister Rafik Hariri

On 14 February, an explosion in downtown Beirut killed 20 persons, among them former Lebanese Prime Minister, Rafik Hariri, and injured 220 others; one person was also missing and believed to be among the victims. The killing of Mr. Hariri drew widespread international condemnation. The Security Council President issued a statement the following day (see below).

SECURITY COUNCIL ACTION (February)

On 15 February [meeting 5122], following consultations among Security Council members, the President made statement **S/PRST/2005/4** on behalf of the Council:

> The Security Council received a briefing from the Secretariat on the situation in Lebanon on 15 February 2005.
>
> The Council unequivocally condemns the terrorist bombing in Beirut on 14 February 2005 that killed former Prime Minister of Lebanon Rafik Hariri and others, and caused serious injury to dozens of people, including former Minister Basil Fleihan.
>
> The Council expresses its deepest sympathy and condolences to the people and Government of Lebanon and to the victims and their families.
>
> The Council calls upon the Government of Lebanon to bring to justice the perpetrators, organizers and sponsors of this heinous terrorist act, and notes the Government's commitments in this regard. The Council urges all States, in accordance with its resolutions 1373(2001) and 1566(2004), to cooperate fully in the fight against terrorism.
>
> The Council is gravely concerned by the murder of the former Prime Minister of Lebanon and its possible impact on ongoing efforts by the people of Lebanon to solidify Lebanon's democracy, including during the upcoming parliamentary elections. Such a terrorist act should not jeopardize the holding of those elections in transparent, free and democratic conditions.
>
> The Council is concerned by the potential for further destabilization of Lebanon, and expresses the hope that the Lebanese people will be able to emerge from this terrible event united, and to use peaceful means in support of their long-standing national aspiration to full sovereignty, independence and territorial integrity.

The Council reaffirms its previous calls upon all parties concerned to cooperate fully and urgently with the Council for the full implementation of all relevant resolutions concerning the restoration of the territorial integrity, full sovereignty and political independence of Lebanon.

The Council requests the Secretary-General to follow closely the situation in Lebanon and to report urgently on the circumstances, causes and consequences of this terrorist act.

Consequent upon the Council's request to him in statement S/PRST/2005/4 (above), the Secretary-General announced, on 18 February, that he was sending a fact-finding mission to Beirut to gather such information as was necessary for him to report to the Council in a timely manner. The Mission, to be headed by Peter Fitzgerald (Ireland), included two police investigators, a legal adviser and a political adviser; later additional experts in explosives, ballistics, DNA and crime scene examinations were added. The mission was tasked with examining the crime scene and samples collected from it and to gather facts about the causes, circumstances and consequences of the assassination.

Communication (22 March). In March [A/59/761-S/2005/215], the ninety-fourth session of the Ministerial Council of the Gulf Cooperation Council (GCC) (Riyadh, Saudi Arabia, 13 March), in a press statement, expressed its strong condemnation of the 14 February bombing in Beirut, which killed the former Prime Minister Hariri along with several of his escorts and called for a swift and transparent investigation into the assassination. GCC also applauded Syria's decision to withdraw fully from Lebanon.

Report of mission of inquiry (March). On 24 March [S/2005/203], the Secretary-General transmitted to the Council President the report of the fact-finding mission to Lebanon inquiring into the circumstances, causes and consequences of the assassination of former Prime Minister Rafik Hariri, prepared pursuant to S/PRST/2005/4 (see above). The mission, which conducted its inquiry between 25 February and 16 March, met with a large number of Lebanese officials and representatives of different political groups. It performed a thorough review of the Lebanese investigation and legal proceedings, examined the crime scene and the evidence collected by the local police, collected and analysed samples from the crime scene and interviewed witnesses in relation to the crime.

The mission observed that the specific causes of the assassination of Mr. Hariri could not be reliably asserted until after the perpetrators of the crime were brought to justice. However, it was clear that the assassination took place in a political and security context marked by acute polarization around the Syrian influence in Lebanon and the failure of the Lebanese State to provide adequate protection for its citizens. The mission concluded that the Lebanese security services and the Syrian Military Intelligence bore the primary responsibility for the lack of security, protection, and law and order in Lebanon, thereby contributing to the propagation of a culture of intimidation and impunity. In addition, the Government of the Syrian Arab Republic bore primary responsibility for the political tension that preceded the assassination. It clearly exerted influence beyond the reasonable exercise of cooperative relations, and its interference with the details of governance in Lebanon was the primary reason for the political polarization that ensued, providing the backdrop for Mr. Hariri's assassination.

The review of the Lebanese investigation into the bombing indicated a distinct lack of commitment on the part of the Lebanese authorities to investigating the crime effectively. Their investigation was not carried out in accordance with acceptable international standards, and lacked the confidence of the population necessary for its results to be accepted. To uncover the truth, it would be necessary to entrust the investigation to an international independent commission. Furthermore, it was very doubtful that such an international commission could carry out its tasks satisfactorily—and receive the necessary active cooperation from local authorities—while the current leadership of the Lebanese security services remained in office. It was the mission's view that the restoration of the integrity and credibility of the Lebanese security apparatus was of vital importance to the security and stability of the country. A sustained effort to restructure, reform and retrain the Lebanese security services would be necessary to achieve that end, and would require international assistance and active engagement. The mission was also of the view that international and regional political support would be necessary to safeguard Lebanon's national unity and to shield its fragile polity from unwarranted pressure. Improving the prospects of peace and security in the region would offer a more solid ground for restoring normality in Lebanon.

The Secretary-General, in his letter transmitting the report, noted the mission's observation that an independent international investigation was needed, and endorsed its recommendation that such an investigation be conducted.

Communications (29 March). In identical letters of 29 March to the Secretary-General and the Council President [S/2005/209], the Syrian Arab Republic qualified the mission's report as lacking objectivity, giving only one point of view. It also asked that a reference to an alleged conversation between Rafik Hariri and Syrian President Bashar Al-Assad be removed from the report. Syria stressed the importance of quickly finding the perpetrators of the crime, and said that it would support the position of Lebanon in any investigation. On the same day [A/59/757-S/2005/208], Lebanon informed the Secretary-General that it approved the decision of the Security Council concerning the establishment of an international commission of inquiry into the assassination of former Prime Minister Rafik Hariri and was ready to cooperate with such a commission.

SECURITY COUNCIL ACTION (April)

On 7 April [meeting 5160], the Security Council unanimously adopted **resolution 1595(2005)**. The draft [S/2005/227] was submitted by Denmark, France, Greece, Japan, the Philippines, Romania, the United Kingdom and the United States.

The Security Council,

Reiterating its call for the strict respect of the sovereignty, territorial integrity, unity and political independence of Lebanon under the sole and exclusive authority of the Government of Lebanon,

Endorsing the opinion of the Secretary-General, as expressed in his letter dated 24 March 2005 to the President of the Security Council, that Lebanon is passing through a difficult and sensitive period, that all concerned should imperatively behave with the utmost restraint and that the future of Lebanon should be decided strictly through peaceful means,

Reaffirming its unequivocal condemnation of the terrorist bombing in Beirut on 14 February 2005 that killed former Prime Minister of Lebanon Rafiq Hariri and others, and caused injury to dozens of people, and condemning the subsequent attacks in Lebanon,

Having examined the report of the fact-finding mission to Lebanon inquiring into the circumstances, causes and consequences of this terrorist act, transmitted to the Security Council by the Secretary-General following the statement by the President of the Security Council of 15 February 2005,

Noting with concern the conclusion of the fact-finding mission that the Lebanese investigation process suffers from serious flaws and has neither the capacity nor the commitment to reach a satisfactory and credible conclusion,

Noting, in this context, the opinion of the fact-finding mission that an international independent investigation with executive authority and self-sufficient resources in all relevant fields of expertise would be necessary to elucidate all aspects of this heinous crime,

Mindful of the unanimous demand of the Lebanese people that those responsible be identified and held accountable, and willing to assist Lebanon in the search for the truth,

Welcoming the Government of Lebanon's approval of the decision to be taken by the Council concerning the establishment of an international independent investigation commission, and welcoming also its readiness to cooperate fully with such a commission within the framework of Lebanese sovereignty and of its legal system, as expressed in the letter dated 29 March 2005 from the Chargé d'affaires a.i. of the Permanent Mission of Lebanon to the United Nations addressed to the Secretary-General,

1. *Decides,* consistent with the letter dated 29 March 2005 from the Chargé d'affaires a.i. of the Permanent Mission of Lebanon to the United Nations addressed to the Secretary-General, to establish an international independent investigation commission ("the Commission") based in Lebanon to assist the Lebanese authorities in their investigation of all aspects of this terrorist act, including to help to identify its perpetrators, sponsors and organizers and their accomplices;

2. *Reiterates its call upon* the Government of Lebanon to bring to justice the perpetrators, organizers and sponsors of the 14 February 2005 terrorist bombing, and calls upon the Government of Lebanon to ensure that the findings and conclusions of the investigation by the Commission are taken into account fully;

3. *Decides* that, to ensure the effectiveness of the Commission in the discharge of its duties, the Commission shall:

(a) Enjoy the full cooperation of the Lebanese authorities, including full access to all documentary, testimonial and physical information and evidence in their possession that the Commission deems relevant to the inquiry;

(b) Have the authority to collect any additional information and evidence, both documentary and physical, pertaining to this terrorist act, as well as to interview all officials and other persons in Lebanon that the Commission deems relevant to the inquiry;

(c) Enjoy freedom of movement throughout the Lebanese territory, including access to all sites and facilities that the Commission deems relevant to the inquiry;

(d) Be provided with the facilities necessary to perform its functions, and be granted, with its premises, staff and equipment, the privileges and immunities to which they are entitled under the Convention on the Privileges and Immunities of the United Nations;

4. *Requests* the Secretary-General to consult urgently with the Government of Lebanon with a view to facilitating the establishment and operation of the Commission pursuant to its mandate and terms of reference as mentioned in paragraphs 2 and 3 above, and requests also that he report to the Security Council accordingly and notify it of the date on which the Commission begins its full operations;

5. *Also requests* the Secretary-General, notwithstanding paragraph 4 above, to undertake without delay the steps, measures and arrangements necessary for the speedy establishment and full functioning of the Commission, including recruiting impartial and experienced staff with relevant skills and expertise;

6. *Directs* the Commission to determine procedures for carrying out its investigation, taking into account Lebanese law and judicial procedures;

7. *Calls upon* all States and all parties to cooperate fully with the Commission, and in particular to provide it with any relevant information they may possess pertaining to the above-mentioned terrorist act;

8. *Requests* the Commission to complete its work within three months of the date on which it com-

mences its full operations, as notified by the Secretary-General, and authorizes the Secretary-General to extend the operation of the Commission for a further period not exceeding three months, if he deems it necessary to enable the Commission to complete its investigation, and requests that he inform the Council accordingly;

9. *Also requests* the Commission to report to the Council on the conclusions of its investigation, and requests the Secretary-General to update the Council orally on the progress of the Commission every two months during the operations of the Commission or more frequently as needed.

Communications (May/June). On 13 May [S/2005/317], the Secretary-General informed the Security Council of his intention, in accordance with resolution 1595(2005), to appoint Detlev Mehlis (Germany) as the Commissioner of the United Nations International Independent Investigation Commission (UNIIIC), which the Council noted on 17 May [S/2005/318]. He also informed the Council that the Commission became operational on 16 June based on the memorandum of understanding between the Government of Lebanon and the Commission, concluded by the Commissioner on the same day [S/2005/393]. The Secretary-General intended to report to the Council every two months on the progress of the Commission's work.

Briefings by Under-Secretary-General. The Council President, in his assessment of the Council's work for the month of August [S/2005/367], said that, on 25 August, the Under-Secretary-General for Political Affairs briefed the Council on the UNIIIC investigation during informal consultations. After the briefing, the Council noted that the Commission had made significant progress in its investigation and reiterated support to its efforts to help identify those responsible for the crime. Council members reiterated their call on all States and parties, especially those who had yet to respond adequately, to cooperate fully in order to expedite the Commission's work.

The Under-Secretary-General provided the Council with a further update on 30 August, including information on the detention of four suspects on that day. The Council, in a press statement, took note of the information on the detention of the four suspects, welcomed the progress made in the investigation and expressed the hope that the final report would fully establish the facts and provide solid evidence in support of its findings.

Communications (September/October). On 9 September [S/2005/587], based on the request of the Commissioner, the Secretary-General informed the Council that he intended to extend UNIIIC's mandate for 40 days until 25 October to allow it to complete its investigation, which the Council noted on 15 September [S/2005/588]. During the additional period, UNIIIC staff would be downsized. On 14 October [S/2005/651], Lebanon requested the Secretary-General to extend the mandate further until mid-December to allow UNIIIC to assist in any further investigation of the 14 February bombing and explore possible follow-up measures to the findings and recommendations of its forthcoming report (see below).

Report of International Independent Investigative Committee

On 20 October [S/2005/662], the Secretary-General transmitted to the Security Council President the report of UNIIIC detailing progress made in the investigation of the 14 February Beirut bombing and the conclusions of the Commission up to that point. As a result of the Commission's investigation, a number of people had been arrested and charged with conspiracy to murder and for related crimes in connection with the assassination of Mr. Hariri and 22 others. The Secretary-General expressed his intention to extend UNIIIC's mandate until 15 December.

It was the Commission's view that the assassination was carried out by a group with an extensive organization and considerable resources and capabilities. The crime had been prepared over the course of several months, and for that purpose, the timing and location of Mr. Hariri's movements had been monitored and the itineraries of his convoy recorded in detail. Converging evidence pointed at both Lebanese and Syrian involvement in the terrorist act. It was a well known fact that Syrian military intelligence had a pervasive presence in Lebanon, at least up to the withdrawal of Syrian forces pursuant to resolution 1559(2004) [YUN 2004, p. 506], and former senior security officials of Lebanon were their appointees. Given the infiltration of Lebanese institutions and society by the Syrian and Lebanese intelligence services, it was difficult to imagine that such a complex assassination plot could have been carried out without their knowledge. The Committee was of the view that the likely motive of the assassination was political, but did not rule out fraud, corruption and money-laundering.

During the course of its investigation, the Commission received extensive support from the Government of Lebanon and benefitted from expert input from a number of national and international entities. The Commission concluded that the investigation should be continued by the appropriate Lebanese judicial and security authorities, who had proven during the investigation that, with international assistance and support, they could move ahead and take the lead in an effective and professional manner. A sustained effort on the part of the international community to establish an assistance and cooperation platform together with the Lebanese authorities in the field of security and justice was considered essential.

Having established that many leads pointed directly to the involvement of Syrian security officials in the assassination, it was incumbent upon the Syrian Arab Republic to clarify a considerable part of the unresolved questions. While the Syrian authorities had cooperated to a limited degree with the Commission, several interviewees tried to mislead the investigation by providing false information. A full picture of the assassination could only be obtained through an extensive and credible investigation conducted in an open and transparent manner.

Security Council consideration (October). On 25 October [meeting 5292], the Security Council heard a briefing by the UNIIIC Commissioner, Detlev Mehlis, on the Commission's first report (see above). The Secretary-General was in attendance at the briefing. The Commissioner said that, for such a multidimensional and complex case, the investigation could not be considered complete. More time should be allotted to further investigate the findings and look into emerging leads. During the extended period of its mandate, the Commission would re-interview a number of witnesses and interview new ones and complete its examination of material evidence obtained recently. That would give the Syrian authorities another opportunity to show greater and meaningful cooperation and to provide any relevant substantial evidence. In that regard, they might wish to carry out their own investigation in an open and transparent manner so as to help the Commission fill the gaps and have a clear picture of the organizers and perpetrators. On the completion of the overall investigation, it would be up to the Lebanese authorities to determine the nature and location of any judicial mechanism to be set up.

The Syrian Arab Republic found it regrettable that the report could be seen as accusing Syria of the crime, and said that it had cooperated faithfully and sincerely with UNIIIC.

SECURITY COUNCIL ACTION (October)

On 31 October [meeting 5297], the Security Council unanimously adopted **resolution 1636 (2005)**. The draft [S/2005/684] was submitted by France, the United Kingdom and the United States.

The Security Council,

Reaffirming all its previous relevant resolutions, in particular resolutions 1595(2005) of 7 April 2005,

1373(2001) of 28 September 2001 and 1566(2004) of 8 October 2004,

Reiterating its call for the strict respect of the sovereignty, territorial integrity, unity and political independence of Lebanon under the sole and exclusive authority of the Government of Lebanon,

Reaffirming that terrorism in all its forms and manifestations constitutes one of the most serious threats to peace and security,

Having examined carefully the report of the United Nations International Independent Investigation Commission ("the Commission") concerning its investigation into the terrorist bombing in Beirut on 14 February 2005 that killed former Prime Minister of Lebanon Rafiq Hariri and twenty-two others, and caused injury to dozens of people,

Commending the Commission for the outstanding professional work it has accomplished under difficult circumstances in assisting the Lebanese authorities in their investigation of all aspects of this terrorist act, and taking note of the conclusion of the Commission that the investigation is not yet complete,

Commending States which have provided assistance to the Commission in the discharge of its duties,

Commending the Lebanese authorities for the full cooperation they have provided to the Commission in the discharge of its duties, in accordance with paragraph 3 of resolution 1595(2005),

Recalling that, pursuant to its relevant resolutions, all States are required to afford one another the greatest measure of assistance in connection with criminal investigations or criminal proceedings relating to terrorist acts, and recalling in particular that in resolution 1595(2005) it had requested all States and all parties to cooperate fully with the Commission,

Taking note of the findings of the Commission that although the inquiry has already made considerable progress and achieved significant results, it is of the utmost importance to continue the trail both within and outside Lebanon in order to elucidate fully all aspects of this terrorist act, and in particular to identify and hold accountable all those who bear responsibility in its planning, sponsoring, organization and perpetration,

Mindful of the demand of the Lebanese people that all those responsible for the terrorist bombing that killed former Prime Minister of Lebanon Rafiq Hariri and others be identified and held accountable,

Acknowledging, in this connection, the letter dated 13 October 2005 from the Prime Minister of Lebanon to the Secretary-General requesting that the mandate of the Commission be extended to enable the Commission to continue to assist the competent Lebanese authorities in any further investigation of the various dimensions of the terrorist crime,

Acknowledging also the concurrent recommendation of the Commission that continued international assistance is needed to help the Lebanese authorities to get right to the bottom of this terrorist act and that a sustained effort on the part of the international community to establish an assistance and cooperation platform together with the Lebanese authorities in the field of security and justice is essential,

Willing to continue to assist Lebanon in the search for the truth and in holding those responsible for this terrorist act accountable for their crime,

Calling upon all States to extend to the Lebanese authorities and to the Commission the assistance they may need and request in connection with the inquiry, and in particular to provide them with all relevant information they may possess pertaining to this terrorist attack,

Reaffirming its profound commitment to the national unity and stability of Lebanon, emphasizing that the future of Lebanon should be decided through peaceful means by the Lebanese themselves, free of intimidation and foreign interference, and warning in this regard that attempts to undermine the stability of Lebanon will not be tolerated,

Taking note of the conclusions of the Commission that, given the infiltration of Lebanese institutions and society by the Syrian and Lebanese intelligence services working in tandem, it would be difficult to envisage a scenario whereby such a complex assassination plot could have been carried out without their knowledge, and that there is probable cause to believe that the decision to assassinate former Prime Minister Rafiq Hariri could not have been taken without the approval of top-ranked Syrian security officials,

Mindful of the conclusion of the Commission that while the Syrian authorities, after initial hesitation, have cooperated to a limited degree with the Commission, several Syrian officials have tried to mislead the investigation by giving false or inaccurate statements,

Convinced that it is unacceptable in principle that anyone anywhere should escape accountability for an act of terrorism for any reason, including because of his own obstruction of the investigation or failure to cooperate in good faith,

Determining that this terrorist act and its implications constitute a threat to international peace and security,

Emphasizing the importance of peace and stability in the region, and the need for peaceful solutions,

Acting under Chapter VII of the Charter of the United Nations,

I

1. *Welcomes* the report of the Commission;

2. *Takes note with extreme concern* of the conclusion of the Commission that there is converging evidence pointing at the involvement of both Lebanese and Syrian officials in this terrorist act and that it is difficult to envisage a scenario whereby such a complex assassination could have been carried out without their knowledge;

3. *Decides*, as a step to assist in the investigation of this crime and without prejudice to the ultimate judicial determination of the guilt or innocence of any individual:

(*a*) That all individuals designated by the Commission or the Government of Lebanon as suspected of involvement in the planning, sponsoring, organizing or perpetrating of this terrorist act, upon notification of such designation to and agreement of the Committee established in subparagraph (*b*) below, shall be subject to the following measures:

   – All States shall take the measures necessary to prevent entry into or transit through their territories of such individuals, provided that nothing in the present paragraph shall obligate a State to refuse entry into its territory to its own nationals, or, if such individuals are found with-

in their territory, shall ensure in accordance with applicable law that they are available for interview by the Commission if it so requests;

   – All States shall freeze all funds, financial assets and economic resources that are on their territories that are owned or controlled, directly or indirectly, by such individuals, or that are held by entities owned or controlled, directly or indirectly, by such individuals or by persons acting on their behalf or at their direction; ensure that no funds, financial assets or economic resources are made available by their nationals or by any persons within their territories to or for the benefit of such individuals or entities; and cooperate fully in accordance with applicable law with any international investigations related to the assets or financial transactions of such individuals, entities or persons acting on their behalf, including through the sharing of financial information;

(*b*) To establish, in accordance with rule 28 of its provisional rules of procedure, a Committee of the Security Council consisting of all the members of the Council to undertake the tasks described in the annex to the present resolution;

(*c*) That the Committee and any measures still in force under subparagraph (*a*) will terminate when the Committee reports to the Council that all investigative and judicial proceedings relating to this terrorist attack have been completed, unless otherwise decided by the Council;

4. *Determines* that the involvement of any State in this terrorist act would constitute a serious violation by that State of its obligations to work to prevent and refrain from supporting terrorism, in accordance, in particular, with resolutions 1373(2001) and 1566 (2004), and that it would amount also to a serious violation of its obligation to respect the sovereignty and political independence of Lebanon;

5. *Takes note with extreme concern* of the conclusion of the Commission that, while the Syrian authorities have cooperated in form but not in substance with the Commission, several Syrian officials have tried to mislead the Commission by giving false or inaccurate information, and determines that continued lack of cooperation by the Syrian Arab Republic with the inquiry would constitute a serious violation of its obligations under relevant resolutions, including resolutions 1373(2001), 1566(2004) and 1595(2005);

6. *Takes note* of the recent statement by the Syrian Arab Republic regarding its intention now to cooperate with the Commission, and expects the Government of the Syrian Arab Republic to implement in full the commitments it is now making;

II

7. *Acknowledges* that continued assistance from the Commission to Lebanon, as requested by its Government in the letter dated 13 October 2005 to the Secretary-General and recommended by the Commission in its report, remains necessary to elucidate fully all aspects of this heinous crime, thus enabling all those involved in the planning, sponsoring, organizing and perpetrating of this terrorist act, as well as their accomplices, to be identified and brought to justice;

8. *Welcomes*, in this regard, the decision of the Secretary-General to extend the mandate of the Commission until 15 December 2005, as authorized by the Council in its resolution 1595(2005), and decides that it will extend the mandate further if recommended by the Commission and requested by the Government of Lebanon;

9. *Commends* the Lebanese authorities for the courageous decisions they have already taken in relation to the inquiry, including upon recommendation of the Commission, in particular the arrest and indictment of former Lebanese security officials suspected of involvement in this terrorist act, and encourages the Lebanese authorities to persist in their efforts with the same determination in order to get right to the bottom of this crime;

III

10. *Endorses* the conclusion of the Commission that it is incumbent upon the Syrian authorities to clarify a considerable part of the questions which remain unresolved;

11. *Decides*, in this context, that:

(a) The Syrian Arab Republic must detain those Syrian officials or individuals whom the Commission considers as suspected of involvement in the planning, sponsoring, organizing or perpetrating of this terrorist act, and make them fully available to the Commission;

(b) The Commission shall have vis-à-vis the Syrian Arab Republic the same rights and authorities as mentioned in paragraph 3 of resolution 1595(2005), and the Syrian Arab Republic must cooperate with the Commission fully and unconditionally on that basis;

(c) The Commission shall have the authority to determine the location and modalities for interview of Syrian officials and individuals it deems relevant to the inquiry;

12. *Insists* that the Syrian Arab Republic not interfere in Lebanese domestic affairs, either directly or indirectly, refrain from any attempt aimed at destabilizing Lebanon, and respect scrupulously the sovereignty, territorial integrity, unity and political independence of that country;

IV

13. *Requests* the Commission to report to the Council on the progress of the inquiry by 15 December 2005, including on the cooperation received by the Commission from the Syrian authorities, or anytime before that date if the Commission deems that such cooperation does not meet the requirements of the present resolution, so that the Council, if necessary, can consider further action;

14. *Expresses its readiness* to consider any additional request for assistance from the Government of Lebanon to ensure that all those responsible for this crime are held accountable;

15. *Decides* to remain seized of the matter.

Annex

The following are the functions of the Committee established pursuant to paragraph 3 of this resolution:

1. To register as subject to the measures in paragraph 3 (a) of this resolution an individual designated by the Commission or the Government of Lebanon, provided that within two working days of receipt of such designation no member of the Committee objects, in which case the Committee shall meet within fifteen days to determine the applicability of the measures in paragraph 3 (a).

2. To approve exceptions to the measures established in paragraph 3 (a) on a case-by-case basis:

(i) With respect to the travel restrictions, where the Committee determines that such travel is justified on the ground of humanitarian need, including religious obligation, or where the Committee concludes that an exemption would otherwise further the objectives of this resolution;

(ii) With respect to the freezing of funds and other economic resources, where the Committee determines that such exceptions are necessary for basic expenses, including payments for foodstuffs, rent or mortgage, medicines and medical treatment, taxes, insurance premiums, and public utility charges, or exclusively for payment of reasonable professional fees and reimbursement of incurred expenses associated with the provision of legal services, or fees or service charges for routine holding or maintenance of frozen funds or other financial assets or economic resources.

3. To register the removal of an individual from the scope of the measures in paragraph 3 (a) upon notification from the Commission or the Government of Lebanon that the individual is no longer suspected of involvement in this terrorist act, provided that within two working days of receipt of such designation no member of the Committee objects, in which case the Committee shall meet within fifteen days to determine the removal of an individual from the scope of the measures in paragraph 3 (a).

4. To inform all Member States as to which individuals are subject to the measures in paragraph 3 (a).

Speaking after the vote, the United States said that Syria had chosen to dismiss the UNIIIC report as politically motivated, and had sought to impede the investigation by intentionally misleading UNIIIC. With the unanimous adoption of resolution 1636(2005), the United Nations had taken a step to hold Syria accountable for any further failure to cooperate with UNIIIC's investigations and to consider further action if necessary. The Chapter VII resolution adopted was the only way to compel the Syrian Government to accept the just demands of the United Nations and to cooperate fully with the investigation.

Syria criticized the report as proceeding from the presumption that it was guilty of committing the crime, rather than presuming its innocence. It further stated that the report did not seek the facts and evidence that would lead to the real perpetrator.

Communications (1 November–5 December). By a 1 November letter addressed to the Secretary-General and the President of the Security Council [S/2005/693], Syria transmitted a legislative decree issued on 29 October by Syrian President Bashar Al-Assad. The decree established a Syrian special judicial commission to deal with all matters relating to the UNIIIC mission.

On 14 November [S/2005/717], Syria informed the Secretary-General and the President of the Security Council about the progress of the Syrian judicial commission (see above) established with reference to UNIIIC. The judicial commission had studied the UNIIIC report, expressed its wish to fully cooperate with it, and extended an invitation to the UNIIIC Commissioner to visit Syria in order to implement the cooperation required pursuant to resolution 1636(2005).

In a 28 November note by the Security Council President [S/2005/734], Ambassador Kenzo Oshima (Japan) was identified as Chairman of the Security Council Committee established pursuant to resolution 1636(2005) (see above) concerning the suspects implicated in the assassination of Rafik Hariri. The Committee would have the role of registering those suspects, as well as approving exceptions to the measures imposed on them from a humanitarian standpoint.

By a 5 December letter to the Secretary-General [S/2005/762], Lebanon requested the extension of UNIIIC's mandate for a period of six months from 15 December, with the possibility of an additional extension in the light of progress made in the investigation. Lebanon further urged that no gap be allowed to occur in UNIIIC's work.

Report of UNIIIC (December). In a 10 December report [S/2005/775], UNIIIC outlined in detail substantive progress made on a number of aspects of the investigation into the 14 February bombing that killed Rafik Hariri and 22 others. It was found that the conclusions in its previous report (see p. 554) remained valid and had been reinforced by further investigation. The report demonstrated a growing partnership between UNIIIC and the Lebanese authorities, who were seen as having the will and capacity to carry forward the investigation in Lebanon. The report also described the Commission's efforts to gain the cooperation of the Syrian authorities. While an official channel of communication was operating between UNIIIC and the Syrian authorities regarding cooperation, statements issued by Syria calling upon UNIIIC to reconsider past mistakes and to revise its report made it clear that the Syrian authorities and judicial commission were aiming to cast doubt on the content of the UNIIIC report. That was an attempt to hinder the investigation internally and procedurally. However, the Syrian authorities did make available for questioning the five Syrian officials that UNIIIC had summoned. It was up to the Syrian authorities to be more forthcoming in order to make headway

in what looked to be a long process. Given that its substantive lines of enquiry were far from completed and Syrian participation was slow, UNIIIC recommended that its mandate be extended for another six months.

Security Council consideration (December). On 13 December [meeting 5323], the Security Council was briefed on the second report of UNIIIC (see above) by Detlev Mehlis, Commissioner of UNIIIC. The Secretary-General attended the briefing. According to Mr. Mehlis, UNIIIC was working mainly on two tracks: one Lebanese and one Syrian. On the Lebanese track, UNIIIC had been able to resolve most impediments, thanks to the cooperation of the Lebanese authorities. In parallel to the Lebanese track, UNIIIC had been trying to make headway on the Syrian track, but its relations with the Syrian authorities had been marked by conflicting signals. It was not clear at all times who from the Syrian side was the privileged interlocutor of UNIIIC, causing confusion and delays.

Syria disagreed with the imprecise statements contained in UNIIIC's report, referring to Syria's reluctance to fully cooperate with UNIIIC and its work. On the contrary, Syria had consistently and continuously communicated with UNIIIC.

Communication (13 December). Lebanon, in a 13 December letter to the Secretary-General [S/2005/783], requested the establishment of an international tribunal to try all those found responsible for the murder of Mr. Hariri. It also asked that UNIIIC's mandate be expanded, or an independent international investigation commission be created, to investigate the assassination attempts, assassinations and explosions that took place in Lebanon, starting with the attempt on the life of Minister Marwan Hamade on 1 October 2004.

SECURITY COUNCIL ACTION (December)

On 15 December [meeting 5329], the Security Council unanimously adopted **resolution 1644 (2005)**. The draft [S/2005/788] was submitted by France, the United Kingdom and the United States.

The Security Council,

Reaffirming all its previous relevant resolutions, including resolutions 1595(2005) of 7 April 2005, 1373 (2001) of 28 September 2001, and 1566(2004) of 8 October 2004, and reaffirming in particular resolution 1636(2005) of 31 October 2005,

Reaffirming its strongest condemnation of the terrorist bombing of 14 February 2005, as well as of all other terrorist attacks in Lebanon since October 2004, and reaffirming also that all those involved in these attacks must be held accountable for their crimes,

Having examined carefully the report of the United Nations International Independent Investigation

Commission ("the Commission") concerning its investigation into the terrorist bombing in Beirut on 14 February 2005 that killed former Prime Minister of Lebanon Rafiq Hariri and twenty-two others, and caused injury to dozens of people,

Commending the Commission for the outstanding professional work it has accomplished under difficult circumstances in assisting the Lebanese authorities in their investigation of this terrorist act, and commending in particular Mr. Detlev Mehlis for his leadership in the discharge of his duties as the Head of the Commission and for his dedication to the cause of justice,

Reiterating its call upon all States to extend to the Lebanese authorities and to the Commission the assistance they may need and request in connection with the inquiry, and in particular to provide them with all relevant information they may possess pertaining to this terrorist attack,

Acknowledging the letter dated 5 December 2005 from the Prime Minister of Lebanon to the Secretary-General requesting that the mandate of the Commission be extended for a further period of six months, with a possibility of an additional extension as necessary, to enable the Commission to continue to assist the competent Lebanese authorities in the ongoing investigations of the crime, and to explore possible follow-up measures in order to bring the perpetrators of the said crime to justice, and acknowledging also the concurrent recommendation of the Commission in that regard,

Acknowledging also the letter dated 13 December 2005 from the Prime Minister of Lebanon to the Secretary-General requesting the establishment of a tribunal of an international character to try all those who are found responsible for this terrorist crime and requesting also that the mandate of the Commission be expanded or that another international investigation commission be created, to investigate the terrorist attacks that have taken place in Lebanon since 1 October 2004,

Noting that Syrian authorities have made available Syrian officials for questioning, but deeply concerned at the Commission's assessment of Syrian performance to date, and noting that the Commission is still awaiting the provision of other requested materials from Syrian authorities,

Reaffirming its determination that this terrorist act and its implications constitute a threat to international peace and security,

Acting under Chapter VII of the Charter of the United Nations,

1. *Welcomes* the report of the Commission;

2. *Decides*, as recommended by the Commission and requested by the Government of Lebanon, to extend the mandate of the Commission, as set forth in resolutions 1595(2005) and 1636(2005), initially until 15 June 2006;

3. *Takes note with satisfaction* of the progress of the inquiry achieved since the last report of the Commission to the Security Council, and notes with extreme concern that, while the inquiry is not yet complete, it confirms its previous conclusions and that the Government of the Syrian Arab Republic has yet to provide the Commission with the full and unconditional cooperation demanded in resolution 1636(2005);

4. *Underscores* the obligation and commitment of the Syrian Arab Republic to cooperate fully and unconditionally with the Commission, and specifically demands that the Syrian Arab Republic respond unambiguously and immediately in those areas adduced by the Commissioner and also that it implement without delay any future request of the Commission;

5. *Requests* the Commission to report to the Council on the progress of the inquiry every three months from the adoption of the present resolution, including on the cooperation received from the Syrian authorities, or anytime before that date if the Commission deems that such cooperation does not meet the requirements of the present resolution and of resolutions 1595(2005) and 1636(2005);

6. *Acknowledges* the request of the Government of Lebanon that those eventually charged with involvement in this terrorist attack be tried by a tribunal of an international character, requests the Secretary-General to help the Government of Lebanon to identify the nature and scope of the international assistance needed in this regard, and also requests the Secretary-General to report to the Council in a timely manner;

7. *Authorizes* the Commission, following the request of the Government of Lebanon, to extend its technical assistance, as appropriate, to the Lebanese authorities with regard to their investigations of the terrorist attacks perpetrated in Lebanon since 1 October 2004, and requests the Secretary-General, in consultation with the Commission and the Government of Lebanon, to present recommendations to expand the mandate of the Commission to include investigations of those other attacks;

8. *Requests* the Secretary-General to continue to provide the Commission with the support and resources necessary for the discharge of its duties;

9. *Decides* to remain seized of the matter.

Speaking after the vote, Lebanon thanked the Council for unanimously adopting the resolution.

Syria expressed full appreciation for the efforts made by many Member States to prevent the adoption of a resolution contravening international law and the United Nations Charter. It was regrettable that, although contacts between Syria and UNIIIC were under way and efforts were being made by both sides to reach mutual agreement on issues relating to the questioning of Syrian citizens, certain States had reached selective conclusions based on the Commission's report and had used them in a distorted way against Syria.

Terrorist bombings

In 2005, in addition to the 14 February bombing that killed former Prime Minister Hariri, a series of other bombings in Lebanon killed and injured scores of people, including several prominent Lebanese journalists and political figures.

In various meetings throughout the year, the Security Council denounced those violent acts.

SECURITY COUNCIL ACTION (June/ December)

On 7 June [meeting 5197], following consultations among Security Council members, the President made statement **S/PRST/2005/22** on behalf of the Council:

> The Security Council condemns in the strongest terms the terrorist bombing on 2 June 2005 in Beirut that killed a Lebanese journalist, Samir Qassir, who was a symbol of political independence and freedom, and expresses its deepest sympathy and condolences to the family of the victim and to the people of Lebanon.
>
> The Council welcomes the determination and commitment of the Government of Lebanon to bring to justice the perpetrators, organizers and sponsors of this assassination and determines that this assassination, like others before it, constitutes a pernicious effort to undermine security, stability, sovereignty, political independence and efforts aimed at preserving civil accord in the country.
>
> The Council expresses its concern about the destabilizing impact of political assassinations and other terrorist acts in Lebanon, and warns that the sponsors of recent terrorist acts against political leaders and leading members of civil society in Lebanon should not be permitted to jeopardize the holding of parliamentary elections in transparent, free and democratic conditions.
>
> The Council calls upon all parties to show restraint and a sense of responsibility with a view to the successful completion of the electoral process and government formation in the country.
>
> The Council reaffirms its resolution 1559(2004), and reiterates its call for the strict respect of the sovereignty, territorial integrity, unity and political independence of Lebanon. The Council urges all States, in accordance with its resolutions 1373(2001) and 1566(2004), to cooperate fully in the fight against terrorism.

On 12 December [meeting 5320], following consultations among Security Council members, the President made statement **S/PRST/2005/61** on behalf of the Council:

> The Security Council condemns in the strongest terms the terrorist bombing on 12 December 2005 in the suburbs of Beirut that killed Lebanese member of Parliament, editor and journalist Gebrane Tueni, a patriot who was an outspoken symbol of freedom and the sovereignty and political independence of Lebanon, as well as three others. It expresses its deepest sympathy to the families of those killed and injured.
>
> The Council reiterates its deepest concern about the destabilizing impact of political assassinations and other terrorist acts in Lebanon. It reiterates also its warning that the sponsors of today's and previous terrorist attacks against political leaders and leading members of civil society in Lebanon, whose obvious aim is to undermine Lebanon's security, stability,

> sovereignty, national unity, political independence and press freedom, will not be permitted to succeed and will finally be held accountable for their crimes.
>
> The Council welcomes the determination and commitment of the Government of Lebanon to bring to justice all those responsible for this assassination and others before, and expresses its readiness to consider positively any request for assistance in this regard from the Government of Lebanon.
>
> The Council reaffirms its resolution 1559(2004), and reiterates once again its call for the strict respect of the sovereignty, territorial integrity, unity and political independence of Lebanon. The Council urges all States, in accordance with its resolutions 1373(2001) and 1566(2004), to cooperate fully in the fight against terrorism.

Implementation of Security Council resolution 1559(2004)

Withdrawal of Syrian armed forces

Communication (23 March). On 23 March [S/2005/219], Lebanon and the Syrian Arab Republic transmitted to the President of the Security Council the closing statement of the meeting of the Syrian-Lebanese Higher Council (Damascus, 7 March).

The Council decided to withdraw the Syrian Arab forces stationed in Lebanon to the Bekaa region and the entrance to the Western Bekaa at Dahr al-Baydar up to the Hammana-Mudayrij-Ayn Dara line before the end of March; and to assign to the Joint Military Committee the task of determining the size and period of stay of the Syrian forces in that region and their relationship with the Lebanese State authorities. At the end of the agreed period of stay, both Governments should agree on completion of the withdrawal of the remaining Arab forces.

Report of Secretary-General (April). In April [S/2005/272], the Secretary-General submitted a report on progress made in the implementation of Council resolution 1559(2004), which called for the withdrawal of all remaining foreign forces from Lebanon.

On 12 and 21 March, Syrian President Bashar Al-Assad affirmed to the Secretary-General his March pledge to withdraw Syrian troops and intelligence personnel from Lebanon in fulfillment of resolution 1559(2004). The withdrawal would be done in two stages: the first would relocate about one third of all Syrian troops and intelligence personnel in Lebanon into the Bekaa Valley by the end of March; the second stage would lead to a complete and full withdrawal of all Syrian military personnel, assets and intelligence apparatus. Following the endorsement of the withdrawal plan between President Al-Assad and Lebanese President Lahoud, the first stage of the Syrian withdrawal began on 8 March.

To verify the withdrawal, the Secretary-General dispatched a UN technical mission to the area in April and requested the two Governments to provide it with all relevant documentation concerning the former deployment of all Syrian troops, military assets and intelligence apparatus in Lebanon. The United Nations had been able thus far to verify that the Syrian military intelligence had vacated sites previously occupied in Lebanon under the first stage of the withdrawal plan and confirmed that there was ongoing movement to withdraw Syrian troops from the Bekaa Valley into the Syrian Arab Republic as part of the second stage of the withdrawal. However, some Member States and the Lebanese opposition had asserted that Syrian military intelligence had taken up new positions to the south of Beirut and elsewhere and had been using the headquarters of parties affiliated with the Syrian Government. Both Lebanon and the Syrian Arab Republic denied the assertions.

Although it had stated that it was not constrained in doing so, several incidents over the previous six months had illustrated the fact that the Government of Lebanon did not fully exert control over all of its territory. There had been no noticeable change in the deployment of Lebanese armed forces along the Blue Line, and Government representatives had acknowledged that it had not yet deployed forces to the far south of the country. The Secretary-General stated that more needed to be done to ensure the return of effective governmental authority throughout the south of Lebanon, including the deployment of additional Lebanese armed forces. Despite concerns expressed by both Lebanon and the Syrian Arab Republic regarding the stability of Lebanon after a full Syrian withdrawal, Lebanese officials assured the Secretary-General that the Lebanese armed forces had the capacity to guarantee security and stability. They said that the Lebanese forces were gradually assuming responsibility for the vacated areas.

Throughout the reporting period, the United Nations discussed with various relevant parties the issue of the disbanding and disarmament of Lebanese and non-Lebanese militias, consistent with 1989 Taif Agreement, but had not yet reached operational conclusions on the matter. There was no noticeable change in the status of Palestinian armed groups in Lebanon since the October 2004 report of the Secretary-General [YUN 2004, p. 507], nor in the status of Hizbullah, seen as the most significant remaining armed group. Its activities along the Blue Line highlighted the need for the Government of Lebanon to extend exclusive control over all its territory. The increasingly tense political situation in Lebanon had led to the establishment and operation of so-called armed vigilante groups, which, while not formal militias, could signify the beginning of a return to the days when armed groups and militias were prevalent in Lebanon. That development was discussed with representatives of the Government of Lebanon, who stated that preventive action would be taken.

The Secretary-General observed that, although the parties had made significant progress towards the fulfilment of resolution 1559(2004), all the requirements of that resolution had not been met as at 26 April. The full and complete withdrawal of Syrian troops and military assets would represent a significant step towards ending heavy-handed foreign interference that had characterized Lebanese politics for decades. That withdrawal would require the Syrian and Lebanese Governments to redefine the special relationship between them. In that regard, the Secretary-General expected the two countries to make progress towards establishing mutual diplomatic representation and formalizing their special relationship prior to his next report on the implementation of resolution 1559 (2004).

The Secretary-General noted that the six-week political stalemate in Lebanon raised the spectre of a delay of the parliamentary election scheduled for May. Such a delay would contribute to further exacerbating the political divisions in Lebanon and threaten the country's security, stability and prosperity. He encouraged the idea of inviting international observers to monitor the elections.

Security Council consideration (April). On 29 April [meeting 5172], the Security Council was briefed by the Special Envoy of the Secretary-General for the Implementation of Security Council resolution 1559(2004), Terje Roed-Larsen, on the implementation of that resolution. The briefing was attended by the Secretary-General. Mr. Roed-Larsen commended the decision of Lebanese Prime Minister Mikati's Government to hold elections as scheduled, beginning on 29 May. He welcomed the unequivocal confirmation that Mr. Mikati's new Government had received in the Lebanese Parliament, where on 27 April it passed a vote of confidence, with 109 votes to one, plus three abstentions. That was seen as a strong manifestation of the will of the Lebanese people and an endorsement of Mr. Mikati's pledge to hold parliamentary elections on time.

SECURITY COUNCIL ACTION (May)

On 4 May [meeting 5175], following consultations among Security Council members, the President made statement **S/PRST/2005/17** on behalf of the Council:

> The Security Council recalls all its previous resolutions on Lebanon, in particular resolutions 1559 (2004), 425(1978), 426(1978), 520(1982) and 1583 (2005), as well as the statements by its President on the situation in Lebanon, in particular the statements of 18 June 2000 and 19 October 2004.
>
> The Council reiterates its strong support for the territorial integrity, sovereignty and political independence of Lebanon within its internationally recognized borders and under the sole and exclusive authority of the Government of Lebanon.
>
> The Council welcomes the first semi-annual report of the Secretary-General to the Security Council of 26 April 2005 on the implementation of Council resolution 1559(2004).
>
> The Council welcomes also the fact that the parties concerned have made significant and noticeable progress towards implementing some of the provisions contained in resolution 1559(2004), while expressing concern at the determination of the Secretary-General that there has been no progress in the implementation of other provisions of the resolution, in particular the disarmament of Lebanese and non-Lebanese militias and the extension of the control of the Government of Lebanon over all Lebanese territory, and that the requirements of the resolution have not yet been met.
>
> The Council reiterates its call for the full implementation of all requirements of resolution 1559(2004), and calls upon all concerned parties to cooperate fully with the Council and the Secretary-General to achieve this goal.
>
> The Council acknowledges the letter dated 26 April 2005 from the Minister for Foreign Affairs of the Syrian Arab Republic to the Secretary-General stating that the Syrian Arab Republic has completed the full withdrawal of its forces, military assets and the intelligence apparatus from Lebanon.
>
> The Council calls upon the Government of the Syrian Arab Republic and the Government of Lebanon to extend their full cooperation to the United Nations verification team dispatched by the Secretary-General with their agreement to verify whether there has been full and complete withdrawal, and looks forward to his report.
>
> The Council acknowledges that the full and complete Syrian withdrawal would represent a significant and important step towards Lebanon's full political independence and full exercise of its sovereignty that is the ultimate goal of resolution 1559(2004), thus opening a new chapter in Lebanese history.
>
> The Council welcomes the deployment of Lebanese armed forces to positions vacated by Syrian forces and the assumption of responsibility by the Government of Lebanon for these areas and calls for the deployment of additional Lebanese armed forces throughout the south of the country.
>
> The Council urges all concerned parties to do their utmost to safeguard the stability and national unity of Lebanon and underlines the importance of national dialogue among all Lebanese political forces in this regard.
>
> The Council commends the Lebanese people for the dignified manner in which they have expressed their views and for their commitment to a peaceful and democratic process, and stresses that the Lebanese people must be allowed to decide the future of their country free of violence and intimidation. It condemns, in this context, the recent terrorist acts in Lebanon that have resulted in several deaths and injuries, and calls for their perpetrators to be brought to justice.
>
> The Council welcomes the decision of the Government of Lebanon to conduct elections beginning on 29 May 2005, and underlines the importance that such elections be held according to schedule. The Council shares the opinion of the Secretary-General that a delay in holding the parliamentary elections would contribute to exacerbating further the political divisions in Lebanon and threaten the security, stability and prosperity of the country. The Council underlines the fact that free and credible elections held without foreign interference or influence would be another central indication of the political independence and sovereignty of Lebanon.
>
> The Council encourages the Secretary-General and the Government of Lebanon to reach arrangements for international assistance, including United Nations assistance, to ensure that such elections are conducted in a free and credible manner, in particular by inviting international governmental and/or non-governmental electoral observers to monitor the electoral process. The Council urges Member States to extend assistance accordingly.
>
> The Council commends the Secretary-General and his Special Envoy for their relentless efforts and dedication to facilitate and assist the parties in the implementation of all provisions of resolution 1559 (2004), and requests that they continue their work in this regard.
>
> The Council shares the view that the full implementation of resolution 1559(2004) would contribute positively to the situation in the Middle East in general.

Report of verification team (May). On 23 May [S/2005/331], the Secretary-General transmitted to the Security Council President the report of the technical military team dispatched to Lebanon to verify the full and complete withdrawal of all Syrian troops, military assets and intelligence apparatus.

After travelling more than 1,500 kilometres in Lebanon and visiting 133 former Syrian troop and military intelligence positions, the team found no Syrian military forces, assets or intelligence apparatus in Lebanese territory, with the exception of one Syrian battalion deployed near Deir Al-Ashayr. Eleven former Syrian positions had already been taken over by the Lebanese army. The mission therefore concluded, to the best of its ability, that Syrian troops and military assets had been fully and completely withdrawn from Lebanese territory, with the possible exception of Deir Al-Ashayr, the status of which remained unclear. Due to the absence of a border agreement between the Governments of the

Syrian Arab Republic and Lebanon, and the lack of a clear line of demarcation on the ground, the team was unable to verify whether the Syrian military unit in the Deir Al-Ashayr area was in Syrian or Lebanese territory. The status of that unit would be clarified once the two Governments had concluded a border agreement. The withdrawal of the Syrian intelligence apparatus had been harder to verify. The team could only conclude, to the best of its ability, that no Syrian military intelligence personnel remained in Lebanon in known locations or in military uniform, and was unable to conclude with certainty that all the intelligence apparatus had been withdrawn. In some of the locations previously occupied by the Syrian military intelligence, cells were found which indicated that prisoners had been held.

The team concluded that a further verification mission was not necessary, as it would still be unable to verify the complete withdrawal of clandestine intelligence apparatus.

Communication (11 June). On 11 June [S/2005/388], Syria said that statements made by certain officials in the United States Administration regarding Syrian interference in Lebanese affairs through the action of intelligence agents were unfounded. Syria stated that it had completed the full return of its forces and intelligence apparatus on 26 April.

Elections

In his second report of the implementation of Security Council resolution 1559 (2004) [S/2005/673], the Secretary-General stated that the Lebanese parliamentary elections took place in four rounds, beginning on 29 May, two days before the expiration of the legal term of the sitting Parliament, and concluded on 19 June. The elections were successful, credible and well-conducted technically in a free and non-violent environment. They were monitored by more than 100 international electoral observers. The United Nations provided technical assistance and coordinated the electoral observers. The elections resulted in a clear victory for a coalition, comprising the Future Movement, led by Saad Harri and the Progressive Socialist Party, led by Walid Jumblatt, which gained 72 seats, followed by an alliance of the Amal Party and Hizbullah, 35 seats, and the Free Patriotic Movement led by Michel Aoun who had returned to Lebanon after 14 years in exile, 21 seats.

SECURITY COUNCIL ACTION (June)

On 22 June [meeting 5212], following consultations among Security Council members, the President made statement **S/PRST/2005/26** on behalf of the Council:

The Security Council welcomes the Lebanese parliamentary elections held between 29 May and 19 June 2005. It commends the fair and credible character of the vote and pays tribute to the Lebanese people who demonstrated, throughout the process, their strong commitment to democracy, freedom and independence.

The Council congratulates the newly elected members of the Lebanese Parliament.

The Council commends the Government of Lebanon for the successful conduct of the elections, in accordance with the Constitution and the planned schedule. It expresses its appreciation for the advice and technical support given to the Lebanese authorities by the United Nations Electoral Assistance Division. The Council also pays tribute to the crucial contribution of the international observers, notably from the European Union. In this regard, it welcomes the report of the European Union observer mission and its conclusions regarding the satisfactory conduct of the four electoral stages.

The Council looks forward to the formation of a new government in the near future. It stresses that the establishment of this government in accordance with the constitutional rules and without any foreign interference would be another sign of the political independence and sovereignty of Lebanon.

The Council reaffirms that the Lebanese people must be allowed to decide the future of their country free of violence and intimidation. It strongly condemns, in this context, the recent terrorist acts in Lebanon, in particular the heinous assassination of former leader of the Communist Party George Hawi, and calls for their perpetrators to be brought to justice.

The Council reaffirms its profound commitment to a stable, secure and prosperous Lebanon. It underlines accordingly the need for the newly elected Lebanese authorities to exercise their full sovereignty over the entire territory, to preserve unity through national dialogue, to strengthen the nation's institutions and to respect the principles of good governance, in the sole interest of the Lebanese people.

The Council calls upon the international community to stand ready to examine possible requests from the newly elected Lebanese authorities for enhanced assistance and cooperation, in support of a credible governmental programme of political and economic reform.

The Council reiterates its call for the full implementation of all requirements of resolution 1559 (2004) and urges all concerned parties to cooperate fully with the Council and the Secretary-General to achieve this goal.

The Council also calls for the full implementation of resolution 1595(2005) and looks forward to the cooperation of the newly elected Lebanese authorities in this regard.

The Council reaffirms its strong support for the sovereignty, territorial integrity, unity and political independence of Lebanon within its internationally recognized borders and under the sole and exclusive authority of the Government of Lebanon.

Report of Secretary-General (October). On 26 October [S/2005/673], the Secretary-General submitted his second semi-annual report on the implementation of resolution 1559(2004). He stated that, after intense discussions, a new Government was formed on 19 July, led by Prime Minister Fouad Siniora of the Future Movement. The Government included, for the first time, a member of Hizbullah. Following reports suggesting that Syrian intelligence continued to operate in Lebanon and influence events there, in June, the Secretary-General directed the verification team to return to Lebanon to clarify issues regarding the withdrawal of the Syrian intelligence apparatus. The team reported that numerous sources, including ministers, former ministers and security officials, were of the view that Syrian intelligence activity was taking place in Lebanon. There were credible reports of Syrian intelligence activity, but most were exaggerated. The team also believed it possible that some Syrian intelligence officers had briefly visited Lebanon after their withdrawal and that they maintained networks of contacts. However, the extent and purpose of any such activity were difficult to assess. The verification team corroborated its earlier conclusion that there was no remaining visible or significant Syrian intelligence presence in Lebanon, though the distinctly close historical and other ties between the Syrian Arab Republic and Lebanon also had to be taken into account when assessing a possibly ongoing influence of Syrian intelligence in Lebanon.

Following the May parliamentary elections (see p. 563), the electoral observers emphasized a need for urgent reform of the legal and election framework, as provisions on electoral campaigning were lacking, and shortcomings were found in the areas of election administration, campaign and financial disclosure and voter registration. At the request of the Lebanese authorities, the Secretary-General was maintaining his efforts to assist with the establishment of an appropriate and enduring legal and institutional framework to ensure free and fair electoral processes in Lebanon. The United Nations continued to support the Lebanese National Commission, a special panel of preeminent personalities appointed by the Government of new Prime Minister Fouad Siniora immediately after the parliamentary elections to draft a new and permanent electoral law.

Regarding the disbanding and disarmament of all Lebanese and non-Lebanese militias, there was no fundamental change in the status of such groups, and information suggested that there had been an increasing influx of weaponry and personnel from Syria to some of those groups.

The Government of Lebanon informed the Secretary-General that it had undertaken significant measures towards restricting movement to and from the Palestinian refugee camps in Lebanon. To that end, the Lebanese Armed Forces had enhanced their deployment along the border with the Syrian Arab Republic and increased patrols. They had also increased their presence, erected new checkpoints and tightened controls around the positions of Palestinian armed groups headquartered in the Syrian Arab Republic to the south of Beirut and in the Bekaa Valley. The Secretary-General noted Prime Minister Siniora's call on the Syrian leadership to practice self-restraint in its ties with Palestinian factions, and the Prime Minister's commitment that the Lebanese State and its security institutions had the duty to guarantee the security of the people, citizens and guests, including the Palestinians. The Prime Minister emphasized his resolve to continue the internal dialogue to achieve the disarmament of Palestinian armed groups peacefully, without resorting to confrontation. He would seek, as a first step, to establish order and control among armed Palestinian groups inside the camps. On 8 October, Prime Minister Siniora reached an agreement with PLO factions to organize the armed Palestinian presence in the camps to guarantee security, and with armed Palestinian groups headquartered in Damascus to create a follow-up committee to discuss all issues, including the issue of arms. There was no noticeable change in the operational status and capabilities of Hizbullah, which according to its own leadership, had more than 12,000 missiles at its disposal. Hizbullah, which also operated as a political party, was given a ministerial portfolio in the Government, and the group's leaders indicated their readiness for discussion.

The Government of Lebanon had not yet fully exerted control over all of its territory. In early June, the Lebanese army appeared to be reducing its presence and control in the south of the country as part of an overall redeployment and reduction of troops, as Hizbullah strengthened its own presence in response. After the United Nations had expressed its concern, on 1 July, the Lebanese army reestablished its original presence. Along the Blue Line, a fragile calm continued to prevail during most of the period, though violations had, in one instance, led to deaths and injuries.

The Secretary-General observed that the parties concerned had made considerable progress towards the implementation of resolution 1559(2004). The requirements of the withdrawal of Syrian troops and military assets, as well as of the conduct of free and credible legislative elections had been met. Progress had also been made on broader electoral reforms, with UN assistance. The disbanding and disarming of all Lebanese and non-Lebanese militias were under discussion among the Lebanese and between the Lebanese and the Palestinians. The Secretary-General was also encouraged by his dialogue with the Government of Lebanon on the extension of its control over all of Lebanon's territory. However, tangible results were yet to be achieved in those two areas, and he would continue his efforts in that regard. The complications that had arisen from the lack of a clearly agreed upon and demarcated border between Lebanon and the Syrian Arab Republic also highlighted the need for a formal border agreement and demarcation of that border between the two countries. The Secretary-General noted that, in the aftermath of the withdrawal of the Syrian military and intelligence presence, the Lebanese security and intelligence services needed to regain public confidence. A start had been made in that regard as the Lebanese authorities had undertaken steps to appoint new permanent, professional directors-general who could enjoy the trust of the public and to change personnel, culture, training and equipment.

UNIFIL

In 2005, the United Nations Interim Force in Lebanon (UNIFIL) continued to discharge its mandate by observing, monitoring and reporting on developments in its area of operation. The Security Council twice extended UNIFIL's mandate in 2005, in January and in July, each time for a period of six months.

UNIFIL, established by Council resolution 425(1978) following Israel's invasion of Lebanon [YUN 1978, p. 312], was originally entrusted with confirming the withdrawal of Israeli forces, restoring international peace and security, and assisting Lebanon in regaining authority in southern Lebanon. Following a second invasion in 1982 [YUN 1982, p. 428], the Council, in resolution 511(1982) [ibid., p. 450], authorized the Force to carry out the additional task of providing protection and humanitarian assistance to the local population. Following the withdrawal of Israeli forces from Lebanon in June 2000 [YUN 2000, p. 465], UNIFIL was reinforced to be able to monitor those territories previously occupied by Israeli forces [ibid.] to prevent the recurrence of fighting and create conditions for the restoration of Lebanese authority in the area.

The Force headquarters, based in Naqoura, provided command and control, and liaison with Lebanon and Israel, UNDOF, UNTSO and a number of NGOs.

Since UNIFIL's establishment, 246 members had lost their lives: 79 as a result of firings or bomb explosions, 105 as a result of accidents and 62 from other causes.

Activities

Report of Secretary-General (January). In a January [S/2005/26] report on developments in the UNIFIL area of operations since his previous report [YUN 2004, p. 510], the Secretary-General said that the relatively quiet but tense situation that had prevailed through much of the reporting period was shattered by a Hizbullah roadside bomb attack on an Israeli Defence Forces (IDF) convoy in the Shab'a farms area on 9 January. The attack killed an IDF soldier and the ensuing military reaction by IDF resulted in the death of a UN military observer. UNIFIL operations were concentrated along the Blue Line, and the Force remained focused on maintaining the ceasefire through ground and air patrols of its area of operation, observation from fixed positions and close contact with the parties.

The Secretary-General was disturbed by the resumption of military measures, for which Hizbullah took credit, claiming the prerogative to forcefully resist Israeli occupation of Lebanese territory. He emphasized that no violations of the Blue Line were acceptable and that Lebanon's continually asserted position that the Blue Line was not valid in the Shab'a Farms area was not compatible with Security Council resolutions. Air violations also continued to be a matter of concern, as Israel's policy of overflying Lebanon whenever it saw fit risked provoking retaliation from the Lebanese side. Rocket-firing incidents perpetrated by individuals allegedly affiliated with Palestinian militant factions further demonstrated the volatility of the sector, but to the credit of the parties and UNIFIL, none of those incidents resulted in a military escalation. The Government of Lebanon continued to demonstrate the capacity to exert its security authority through various activities of the Joint Security Force, including prompt responses to specific incidents, but the Secretary-General called for more to be done to ensure the return of effective governmental authority throughout the south. He recommended that UNIFIL's mandate be extended for another six months, until 31 July 2005.

Communication (10 January). On 10 January [S/2005/13], Lebanon requested that UNIFIL's mandate, due to expire at the end of the month, be extended for six months. That would provide a reaffirmation of the international community's commitment to the restoration of Lebanon's sovereignty over its entire territory.

On 28 January [meeting 5117], the Security Council unanimously adopted **resolution 1583(2005)**. The draft [S/2005/53] was submitted by Denmark, France, Greece, Romania, the United Kingdom and the United States.

The Security Council,

Recalling all its previous resolutions on Lebanon, including resolutions 425(1978) and 426(1978) of 19 March 1978 and resolution 1553(2004) of 29 July 2004, as well as the statements by its President on the situation in Lebanon, in particular the statement of 18 June 2000,

Recalling also the letter dated 18 May 2001 from its President to the Secretary-General,

Recalling further the conclusion of the Secretary-General that, as of 16 June 2000, Israel had withdrawn its forces from Lebanon in accordance with resolution 425(1978) and met the requirements defined in the report of the Secretary-General of 22 May 2000, as well as the conclusion of the Secretary-General that the United Nations Interim Force in Lebanon had essentially completed two of the three parts of its mandate, focusing now on the remaining task of restoring international peace and security,

Gravely concerned at the persistence of tension and violence along the Blue Line,

Emphasizing once again the interim nature of the Force,

Recalling its resolution 1308(2000) of 17 July 2000,

Recalling also its resolution 1325(2000) of 31 October 2000,

Recalling further the relevant principles contained in the Convention on the Safety of United Nations and Associated Personnel of 9 December 1994,

Responding to the request of the Government of Lebanon to extend the mandate of the Force for a new period of six months, presented in the letter dated 10 January 2005 from the Permanent Representative of Lebanon to the United Nations addressed to the Secretary-General, while reaffirming that the Security Council has recognized the Blue Line as valid for the purpose of confirming the withdrawal of Israel pursuant to resolution 425(1978) and that the Blue Line must be respected in its entirety,

Expressing its concern over the tensions and potential for escalation as noted in the report of the Secretary-General of 20 January 2005,

1. *Endorses* the report of the Secretary-General of 20 January 2005 on the United Nations Interim Force in Lebanon;

2. *Decides* to extend the present mandate until 31 July 2005;

3. *Reiterates its strong support* for the territorial integrity, sovereignty and political independence of Lebanon within its internationally recognized boundaries and under the sole and exclusive authority of the Government of Lebanon;

4. *Calls upon* the Government of Lebanon to fully extend and exercise its sole and effective authority throughout the south, including through the deployment of sufficient numbers of Lebanese armed and security forces, to ensure a calm environment throughout the area, including along the Blue Line, and to exert control over the use of force on its territory and from it;

5. *Calls upon* the parties to ensure that the Force is accorded full freedom of movement throughout its area of operation as outlined in the report of the Secretary-General, and requests the Force to report any obstruction it may face in the discharge of its mandate;

6. *Reiterates its call upon* the parties to continue to fulfil the commitments they have given to respect fully the entire withdrawal line identified by the United Nations, as set out in the report of the Secretary-General of 16 June 2000, to exercise utmost restraint and to cooperate fully with the United Nations and the Force;

7. *Condemns* all acts of violence, including the recent incidents across the Blue Line that have resulted in the killing and wounding of United Nations military observers, expresses great concern about the serious breaches and the sea, land and continuing air violations of the withdrawal line, and urges the parties to put an end to these violations, to refrain from any act or provocation that could further escalate the tension and to abide scrupulously by their obligation to respect the safety of the Force and other United Nations personnel;

8. *Supports* the continued efforts of the Force to maintain the ceasefire along the withdrawal line through mobile patrols and observation from fixed positions and through close contacts with the parties to correct violations, resolve incidents and prevent their escalation, while stressing the primary responsibility of the parties in this regard;

9. *Welcomes* the continued contribution of the Force to operational mine clearance, encourages further assistance in mine action by the United Nations to the Government of Lebanon in support of both the continued development of its national mine action capacity and clearance of the remaining mine/unexploded ordnance threat in the south, commends donor countries for supporting those efforts through financial and in-kind contributions and encourages further international contributions, and stresses the necessity for the provision to the Government of Lebanon and the Force of any additional existing maps and minefield records;

10. *Requests* the Secretary-General to continue consultations with the Government of Lebanon and other parties directly concerned on the implementation of the present resolution and to report thereon to the Security Council before the end of the present mandate as well as on the activities of the Force and the tasks presently carried out by the United Nations Truce Supervision Organization;

11. *Expresses its intention* to review the mandate and structures of the Force at the end of the present mandate, and requests the Secretary-General, following appropriate consultations, including with the Government of Lebanon, to include in his report recommendations in this regard, taking into account the prevailing situation on the ground, the activities actually performed by the Force in its area of operation and its contribution towards the remaining task of restoring international peace and security;

12. *Looks forward* to the early fulfilment of the mandate of the Force;

13. *Stresses* the importance of, and the need to achieve, a comprehensive, just and lasting peace in the Middle East, based on all its relevant resolutions, including resolutions 242(1967) of 22 November 1967 and 338(1973) of 22 October 1973.

Report of Secretary-General (July). In response to resolution 1583(2005) (see above) the Secretary-General submitted a July report on UNIFIL covering the period from January to July [S/2005/460]. He said that violations of the Blue Line continued throughout the period, most often in the form of recurring air violations by Israeli jets, helicopters and drones, as well as ground violations from the Lebanese side, primarily by Lebanese shepherds. Additionally, there was one Lebanese air violation by a Hizbullah drone. Hostilities in the area escalated in May with armed exchanges between Hizbullah and IDF and with rocket firing by unidentified armed elements. The situation deteriorated significantly on 29 June, when Hizbullah and IDF engaged in a heavy exchange of fire in the Shab'a farms area, resulting in the death of one IDF soldier and two Hizbullah fighters.

The Lebanese Joint Security Force and the Lebanese Army continued to operate in the areas vacated by Israel in 2000. The strength and activity of the Joint Security Force remained the same and their routine activities continued. At the request of UNIFIL, the Joint Security Force intervened on a few occasions to control demonstrations and prevent protestors from approaching the Blue Line facing IDF positions. Nevertheless, the Government of Lebanon continued to maintain the position that, as long as there was no comprehensive peace with Israel, Lebanese armed forces would not be deployed along the Blue Line. With its permanent observation posts, temporary checkpoints and patrols, Hizbullah maintained a visible presence at the Blue Line, occasionally threatening or denying access to UN patrols. However, UNIFIL was able to regain and assert its freedom of movement within a very short period of time.

UNIFIL provided humanitarian assistance to the Lebanese civilian population in the form of medical care, water projects, equipment and services for schools and orphanages and social services for the needy, cooperating closely with the Lebanese authorities, UN agencies, several embassies and other organizations and agencies operating in the country. Following an increase in civilian land-mine casualties in the area along the Blue Line, a joint UN and Lebanese Army team conducted an assessment and subsequently initiated a programme to repair damaged or missing minefield fencing and erect new fencing where required. UNIFIL carried out regular mine-risk education for schoolchildren and continued its operational mine clearance activities, demolishing some 300 mines and pieces of unexploded ordnance.

In accordance with the review of UNIFIL's mandate and structures called for in Security Council resolution 1583(2005) (see p. 566), the Department of Peacekeeping Operations (DPKO) sent an assessment mission to Lebanon from 8 to 14 May. The mission reviewed the deployment concept of UNIFIL troop strength, evaluated its role in fulfilling its current mandate, assessed the political environment and its implications for UNIFIL, evaluated the situation along the Blue Line, and analysed the consequences for UNIFIL's mandate of any possible adjustments to the Force. The team found that the military situation in southern Lebanon and in the vicinity of the Blue Line between Lebanon and Israel had not changed significantly since December 2002, when the size and role of UNIFIL were last reconfigured. Supported by the Observer Group Lebanon, UNIFIL had the authority to investigate and verify operationally sensitive issues, establish liaison with the parties to the conflict and thereby reduce tensions and incidents on the Blue Line. As there were no formal links between the Governments or defence forces of Israel and Lebanon, UNIFIL was the principal source of liaison on military matters between the countries. It was the view of the assessment team that UNIFIL, in conjunction with the Observer Group, had the appropriate size, capabilities, structure and deployment to undertake its tasks in a professional and efficient manner, in accordance with its mandate and regional conditions.

The Secretary-General observed that, during a period characterized by heightened political instability in the country, southern Lebanon enjoyed relative calm. Nevertheless, the hostilities that occurred in May and the grave incident on 29 June demonstrated once more that the situation remained volatile and fragile, with the potential for conditions to deteriorate. He encouraged the parties to do their utmost to avoid all violations of the Blue Line and called upon them to abide by their obligations under the relevant Security Council resolutions, and to cooperate fully with the United Nations and UNIFIL. Since the assassination of former Prime Minister Rafik Hariri on 14 February (see p. 551), Lebanon had undergone a period of increased political uncertainty. The Secretary-General hoped that the newly formed Government of Lebanon would seize the opportunities presented by the changed political situation and make strong efforts to return its full and effective authority throughout the south, including the deployment of Lebanese armed forces, and to do its utmost to prevent attacks from Lebanon across the Blue Line. He agreed with the DPKO assessment that the current level of the force was required to maintain the critical positions to monitor the Blue Line and its approaches and to protect UNIFIL's personnel and assets and the Observer Group Lebanon. The Secretary-General therefore recommended that UNIFIL's mandate be extended until 31 January 2006, with no changes to the strength and composition of the Force.

Communication. On 11 July [S/2005/444], Lebanon requested the extension of UNIFIL's mandate for a further six months, through 31 January 2006.

SECURITY COUNCIL ACTION (July)

On 29 July [meeting 5241], the Security Council unanimously adopted **resolution 1614(2005)**. The draft [S/2005/491] was submitted by France, Greece, the United Kingdom and the United States.

The Security Council,

Recalling all its previous resolutions on Lebanon, including resolutions 425(1978) and 426(1978) of 19 March 1978 and 1583(2005) of 28 January 2005, as well as the statements by its President on the situation in Lebanon, in particular the statement of 18 June 2000,

Recalling also the letter dated 18 May 2001 from its President to the Secretary-General,

Recalling further the conclusion of the Secretary-General that, as of 16 June 2000, Israel had withdrawn its forces from Lebanon in accordance with resolution 425(1978) and met the requirements defined in the report of the Secretary-General of 22 May 2000, as well as the conclusion of the Secretary-General that the United Nations Interim Force in Lebanon had essentially completed two of the three parts of its mandate, focusing now on the remaining task of restoring international peace and security,

Reaffirming that the Security Council has recognized the Blue Line as valid for the purpose of confirming the withdrawal of Israel pursuant to resolution 425 (1978) and that the Blue Line must be respected in its entirety,

Gravely concerned at the persistence of tension and violence along the Blue Line, in particular the hostilities that took place in May 2005 and the grave incident of 29 June 2005, which demonstrated once more that the situation remains volatile and fragile, as outlined in the report of the Secretary-General of 21 July 2005,

Emphasizing once again the interim nature of the Force,

Recalling its resolution 1308(2000) of 17 July 2000,

Recalling also its resolution 1325(2000) of 31 October 2000,

Recalling further the relevant principles contained in the Convention on the Safety of United Nations and Associated Personnel of 9 December 1994,

Responding to the request of the Government of Lebanon to extend the mandate of the Force for a new period of six months presented in the letter dated 11 July 2005 from the Chargé d'affaires a.i. of the Permanent Mission of Lebanon to the United Nations addressed to the Secretary-General,

Taking note of the opinion of the Secretary-General that the situation does not support a change in the mandate of the Force or another reconfiguration of the Force at this stage, and his recommendation that the mandate be extended with no changes to the strength and composition of the Force,

1. *Endorses* the report of the Secretary-General of 21 July 2005 on the United Nations Interim Force in Lebanon;

2. *Decides* to extend the present mandate until 31 January 2006;

3. *Reiterates its strong support* for the territorial integrity, sovereignty and political independence of Lebanon within its internationally recognized boundaries and under the sole and exclusive authority of the Government of Lebanon;

4. *Condemns* all acts of violence, including the recent incidents across the Blue Line that have resulted in deaths and injuries on both sides, expresses great concern about the serious breaches and the sea, land and continuing air violations of the withdrawal line, and urges the parties to put an end to these violations, to refrain from any act or provocation that could further escalate the tension and to abide scrupulously by their obligation to respect the safety of the Force and other United Nations personnel, including by avoiding any course of action which endangers United Nations personnel;

5. *Reiterates its call upon* the parties to continue to fulfil the commitments they have given to respect fully the entire withdrawal line identified by the United Nations, as set out in the report of the Secretary-General of 16 June 2000, and to exercise utmost restraint;

6. *Calls upon* the Government of Lebanon to fully extend and exercise its sole and effective authority throughout the south, including through the deployment of sufficient numbers of Lebanese armed and security forces, to ensure a calm environment throughout the area, including along the Blue Line, and to exert control and monopoly over the use of force on its entire territory and to prevent attacks from Lebanon across the Blue Line;

7. *Welcomes* the intention of the Secretary-General to discuss with the Government of Lebanon the next steps in preparing for an expansion of its authority in the south;

8. *Supports* the continued efforts of the Force to maintain the ceasefire along the withdrawal line through mobile land and air patrols and observation from fixed positions and through close contacts with the parties to correct violations, resolve incidents and prevent their escalation, while stressing the primary responsibility of the parties in this regard;

9. *Welcomes* the continued contribution of the Force to operational mine clearance, encourages further assistance in mine action by the United Nations to the Government of Lebanon in support of both the continued development of its national mine action capacity and clearance of the remaining mine/unexploded ordnance threat in the south, commends donor countries for supporting those efforts through financial and in-kind contributions and encourages further interna-

tional contributions, and stresses the necessity for the provision to the Government of Lebanon and the Force of any additional existing maps and minefield records;

10. *Calls upon* the parties to ensure that the Force is accorded full freedom of movement throughout its area of operation as outlined in the report of the Secretary-General, requests the Force to report any obstruction it may face in the discharge of its mandate, and reiterates its call upon the parties to cooperate fully with the United Nations and the Force;

11. *Welcomes* the efforts being undertaken by the Force to implement the Secretary-General's zero tolerance policy on sexual exploitation and abuse and to ensure full compliance of its personnel with the United Nations code of conduct, requests the Secretary-General to continue to take all necessary action in this regard and to keep the Security Council informed, and urges troop-contributing countries to take appropriate preventive action, including conducting pre-deployment awareness training, and to take disciplinary action and other action to ensure full accountability in cases of such conduct involving their personnel;

12. *Requests* the Secretary-General to continue consultations with the Government of Lebanon and other parties directly concerned on the implementation of the present resolution and to report thereon to the Council before the end of the present mandate as well as on the activities of the Force and the tasks presently carried out by the United Nations Truce Supervision Organization;

13. *Expresses its intention* to keep the mandate and structures of the Force under regular review, taking into account the prevailing situation on the ground, the activities actually performed by the Force in its area of operation, its contribution towards the remaining task of restoring international peace and security, the views of the Government of Lebanon and the implications for the Force of an increased presence of the Lebanese army in the south;

14. *Looks forward* to the early fulfilment of the mandate of the Force;

15. *Stresses* the importance of, and the need to achieve, a comprehensive, just and lasting peace in the Middle East, based on all its relevant resolutions, including resolutions 242(1967) of 22 November 1967 and 338(1973) of 22 October 1973.

Further developments

In a report on developments during the second half of 2005 [S/2006/26], the Secretary-General said that a tense and fragile quiet generally prevailed in the UNIFIL area of operation, interrupted by a few serious clashes across the Blue Line. In the most serious incident, a heavy exchange of fire between Hizbullah and IDF across the Blue Line took place on 21 November, surpassing any activity level since Israel's withdrawal from Lebanon in May 2000. That serious breach of the ceasefire began with heavy Hizbullah mortar and rocket fire against several IDF positions close to the Blue Line. Simultaneously, a large group of Hizbullah fighters infiltrated Ghajar village and launched an assault on the Mayor's of-

fice and the IDF position inside the village, causing significant damage to civilian property. The ensuing Israeli retaliation was heavy and included aerial bombing. The exchange of fire subsequently spread all along the Blue Line and lasted for over nine hours. A number of Hizbullah positions close to the Blue Line were destroyed or heavily damaged and there was significant damage to some IDF positions and equipment. UNIFIL and the Secretary-General's senior representatives in the region were in close contact with the parties throughout the hostilities, urging them to exercise maximum restraint. Their intervention contributed to avoiding a further deterioration of the situation and prevented the incident from escalating out of control. UNIFIL eventually succeeded in brokering a ceasefire. Owing to the volatile situation in the area, UNIFIL maintained a static patrol presence along the northern side of Ghajar village. In November, there was more exchange of fire between IDF and Hizbullah, and on several occasions, unidentified armed elements fired rockets from Lebanese territory towards Israel. Recurrent Israeli air violations were a continuous source of tension, and there were almost daily violations of the line of withdrawal by Lebanese shepherds and frequent incidents of stone throwing from the Lebanese side. Control of the Blue Line and its vicinity seemed to remain for the most part with Hizbullah.

The Secretary-General noted that the rocket firing incidents in August and December carried the potential for military escalation. He also noted IDF restraint, in August, in not responding to such attacks. He was encouraged by the determination and commitment of the Lebanese authorities, in a letter transmitted to him on 28 November, to hold the perpetrators of such attacks responsible so as to avoid a recurrence of such incidents in the future.

Financing

In June, the General Assembly considered the performance report on UNIFIL's budget from 1 July 2003 to 30 June 2004 [A/59/626]. Total expenditure for the period amounted to $89,896,000, compared with a total apportionment of $90,000,000, resulting in an unencumbered balance of $104,000.

The Assembly also had before it the proposed UNIFIL budget for 1 July 2005 to 20 June 2006 [A/59/654], in the amount of $94,277,700, and the related comments and recommendations of the ACABQ [A/59/736/Add.3].

On 22 June [meeting 104], the General Assembly, on the recommendation of the Fifth (Administrative and Budgetary) Committee [A/59/838], adopted **resolution 59/307** by recorded vote (126-2-1) [agenda item 135 (b)].

Financing of the United Nations Interim Force in Lebanon

The General Assembly,

Having considered the reports of the Secretary-General on the financing of the United Nations Interim Force in Lebanon and the related reports of the Advisory Committee on Administrative and Budgetary Questions,

Recalling Security Council resolution 425(1978) of 10 March 1978 regarding the establishment of the United Nations Interim Force in Lebanon and the subsequent resolutions by which the Council extended the mandate of the Force, the latest of which was resolution 1583(2005) of 28 January 2005,

Recalling also its resolution S-8/2 of 21 April 1978 on the financing of the Force and its subsequent resolutions thereon, the latest of which was resolution 58/307 of 18 June 2004,

Reaffirming its resolutions 51/233 of 13 June 1997, 52/237 of 26 June 1998, 53/227 of 8 June 1999, 54/267 of 15 June 2000, 55/180 A of 19 December 2000, 55/180 B of 14 June 2001, 56/214 A of 21 December 2001, 56/214 B of 27 June 2002, 57/325 of 18 June 2003 and 58/307 of 18 June 2004,

Reaffirming also the general principles underlying the financing of United Nations peacekeeping operations, as stated in General Assembly resolutions 1874(S-IV) of 27 June 1963, 3101(XXVIII) of 11 December 1973 and 55/235 of 23 December 2000,

Noting with appreciation that voluntary contributions have been made to the Force,

Mindful of the fact that it is essential to provide the Force with the necessary financial resources to enable it to fulfil its responsibilities under the relevant resolutions of the Security Council,

1. *Takes note* of the status of contributions to the United Nations Interim Force in Lebanon as at 15 April 2005, including the contributions outstanding in the amount of 60.9 million United States dollars, representing some 2 per cent of the total assessed contributions, notes with concern that only seventy-three Member States have paid their assessed contributions in full, and urges all other Member States, in particular those in arrears, to ensure payment of their outstanding assessed contributions;

2. *Expresses its appreciation* to those Member States that have paid their assessed contributions in full, and urges all other Member States to make every possible effort to ensure payment of their assessed contributions to the Force in full;

3. *Expresses deep concern* that Israel did not comply with General Assembly resolutions 51/233, 52/237, 53/227, 54/267, 55/180 A, 55/180 B, 56/214 A, 56/214 B, 57/325 and 58/307;

4. *Stresses once again* that Israel should strictly abide by General Assembly resolutions 51/233, 52/237, 53/227, 54/267, 55/180 A, 55/180 B, 56/214 A, 56/214 B, 57/325 and 58/307;

5. *Expresses concern* at the financial situation with regard to peacekeeping activities, in particular as regards the reimbursements to troop contributors that bear additional burdens owing to overdue payments by Member States of their assessments;

6. *Also expresses concern* at the delay experienced by the Secretary-General in deploying and providing adequate resources to some recent peacekeeping missions, in particular those in Africa;

7. *Emphasizes* that all future and existing peacekeeping missions shall be given equal and non-discriminatory treatment in respect of financial and administrative arrangements;

8. *Also emphasizes* that all peacekeeping missions shall be provided with adequate resources for the effective and efficient discharge of their respective mandates;

9. *Reiterates its request* to the Secretary-General to make the fullest possible use of facilities and equipment at the United Nations Logistics Base at Brindisi, Italy, in order to minimize the costs of procurement for the Force;

10. *Endorses* the conclusions and recommendations contained in the report of the Advisory Committee on Administrative and Budgetary Questions, and requests the Secretary-General to ensure their full implementation;

11. *Requests* the Secretary-General to take all necessary action to ensure that the Force is administered with a maximum of efficiency and economy;

12. *Also requests* the Secretary-General, in order to reduce the cost of employing General Service staff, to continue efforts to recruit local staff for the Force against General Service posts, commensurate with the requirements of the Force;

13. *Reiterates its request* to the Secretary-General to take the necessary measures to ensure the full implementation of paragraph 8 of its resolution 51/233, paragraph 5 of its resolution 52/237, paragraph 11 of its resolution 53/227, paragraph 14 of its resolution 54/267, paragraph 14 of its resolution 55/180 A, paragraph 15 of its resolution 55/180 B, paragraph 13 of its resolution 56/214 A, paragraph 13 of its resolution 56/214 B, paragraph 14 of its resolution 57/325 and paragraph 13 of its resolution 58/307, stresses once again that Israel shall pay the amount of 1,117,005 dollars resulting from the incident at Qana on 18 April 1996, and requests the Secretary-General to report on this matter to the General Assembly at its sixtieth session;

Financial performance report for the period from 1 July 2003 to 30 June 2004

14. *Takes note* of the report of the Secretary-General on the financial performance of the Force for the period from 1 July 2003 to 30 June 2004;

Budget estimates for the period from 1 July 2005 to 30 June 2006

15. *Decides* to appropriate to the Special Account for the United Nations Interim Force in Lebanon the amount of 99,228,300 dollars for the period from 1 July 2005 to 30 June 2006, inclusive of 94,252,900 dollars for the maintenance of the Force, 4,068,400 dollars for the support account for peacekeeping operations and 907,000 dollars for the United Nations Logistics Base;

Financing of the appropriation

16. *Decides also* to apportion among Member States the amount of 8,269,025 dollars for the period from 1 to 31 July 2005, in accordance with the levels updated in General Assembly resolution 58/256 of 23 December 2003, and taking into account the scale of assessments for 2005, as set out in its resolution 58/1 B of 23 December 2003;

17. *Decides further* that, in accordance with the provisions of its resolution 973(X) of 15 December 1955, there shall be set off against the apportionment among Member States, as provided for in paragraph 16 above, their respective share in the Tax Equalization Fund of 447,008 dollars, comprising the estimated staff assessment income of 392,975 dollars approved for the Force, the prorated share of 47,925 dollars of the estimated staff assessment income approved for the support account and the prorated share of 6,108 dollars of the estimated staff assessment income approved for the United Nations Logistics Base;

18. *Decides* to apportion among Member States the amount of 90,959,275 dollars for the period from 1 August 2005 to 30 June 2006 at a monthly rate of 8,269,025 dollars, in accordance with the levels updated in General Assembly resolution 58/256, and taking into account the scale of assessments for 2005 and 2006, as set out in its resolution 58/1 B, subject to a decision of the Security Council to extend the mandate of the Force;

19. *Decides also* that, in accordance with the provisions of its resolution 973(X), there shall be set off against the apportionment among Member States, as provided for in paragraph 18 above, their respective share in the Tax Equalization Fund of 4,917,092 dollars, comprising the estimated staff assessment income of 4,322,725 dollars approved for the Force, the prorated share of 527,175 dollars of the estimated staff assessment income approved for the support account and the prorated share of 67,192 dollars of the estimated staff assessment income approved for the United Nations Logistics Base;

20. *Decides further* that, for Member States that have fulfilled their financial obligations to the Force, there shall be set off against their apportionment, as provided for in paragraphs 16 and 18 above, their respective share of the unencumbered balance and other income in the amount of 8,463,000 dollars in respect of the financial period ended 30 June 2004, in accordance with the levels updated in its resolution 58/256, and taking into account the scale of assessments for 2004, as set out in its resolution 58/1 B;

21. *Decides* that, for Member States that have not fulfilled their financial obligations to the Force, there shall be set off against their outstanding obligations their respective share of the unencumbered balance and other income in the amount of 8,463,000 dollars in respect of the financial period ended 30 June 2004, in accordance with the scheme set out in paragraph 20 above;

22. *Decides also* that the increase of 541,200 dollars in the estimated staff assessment income in respect of the financial period ended 30 June 2004 shall be added to the credits from the amount of 8,463,000 dollars referred to in paragraphs 20 and 21 above;

23. *Emphasizes* that no peacekeeping mission shall be financed by borrowing funds from other active peacekeeping missions;

24. *Encourages* the Secretary-General to continue to take additional measures to ensure the safety and security of all personnel under the auspices of the United Nations participating in the Force;

25. *Invites* voluntary contributions to the Force in cash and in the form of services and supplies acceptable to the Secretary-General, to be administered, as appropriate, in accordance with the procedure and practices established by the General Assembly;

26. *Decides* to include in the provisional agenda of its sixtieth session, under the item entitled "Financing of the United Nations peacekeeping forces in the Middle East", the sub-item entitled "United Nations Interim Force in Lebanon".

RECORDED VOTE ON RESOLUTION 59/307:

In favour: Afghanistan, Algeria, Andorra, Antigua and Barbuda, Argentina, Armenia, Austria, Azerbaijan, Bahamas, Bahrain, Bangladesh, Barbados, Belarus, Belgium, Belize, Botswana, Brazil, Brunei Darussalam, Bulgaria, Burkina Faso, Cambodia, Canada, Cape Verde, Chile, China, Colombia, Congo, Costa Rica, Croatia, Cuba, Cyprus, Czech Republic, Denmark, Djibouti, Dominican Republic, Ecuador, Egypt, Estonia, Finland, France, Gabon, Germany, Ghana, Greece, Guatemala, Guinea, Guyana, Hungary, Iceland, India, Indonesia, Ireland, Italy, Japan, Jordan, Kazakhstan, Kuwait, Latvia, Lebanon, Lesotho, Libyan Arab Jamahiriya, Lithuania, Luxembourg, Madagascar, Malawi, Malaysia, Maldives, Mali, Malta, Mauritania, Mexico, Monaco, Morocco, Namibia, Nepal, Netherlands, New Zealand, Nicaragua, Niger, Nigeria, Norway, Oman, Pakistan, Panama, Paraguay, Peru, Portugal, Qatar, Republic of Korea, Republic of Moldova, Romania, Russian Federation, Rwanda, San Marino, Saudi Arabia, Senegal, Serbia and Montenegro, Sierra Leone, Singapore, Slovakia, Slovenia, Somalia, South Africa, Spain, Sri Lanka, Sudan, Sweden, Switzerland, Syrian Arab Republic, Tajikistan, Thailand, Timor-Leste, Trinidad and Tobago, Tunisia, Turkey, Uganda, Ukraine, United Arab Emirates, United Kingdom, United Republic of Tanzania, Uruguay, Venezuela, Viet Nam, Yemen, Zambia, Zimbabwe.

Against: Israel, United States.

Abstaining: Tonga.

The Assembly adopted the fourth preambular paragraph and operative paragraphs 3, 4 and 13 by a single recorded vote of 77 to 2, with 47 abstentions. The Committee adopted those paragraphs by a recorded vote of 79 to 3, with 50 abstentions.

Syrian Arab Republic

In 2005, the General Assembly again called for Israel's withdrawal from the Golan Heights in the Syrian Arab Republic, which it had occupied since 1967. The area was effectively annexed by Israel when it extended its laws, jurisdiction and administration to the territory towards the end of 1981 [YUN 1981, p. 309].

The United Nations International Independent Investigation Commission (UNIIIC), established following the 14 February assassination of former Lebanese Prime Minister Rafik Hariri (see p. 551), found evidence to suggest Syrian involvement in the incident. UNIIIC concluded that the Syrian authorities had cooperated in form but not in substance with its investigation, and several Syrian officials had tried to mislead UNIIIC by giving false or inaccurate information.

It determined that Syria's continued lack of co-operation in the inquiry would constitute a serious violation of its obligations under relevant resolutions, including 1373(2001), 1566(2004) and 1595(2005). Pursuant to Security Council resolution 1559 (2004), by 26 April, Syria had withdrawn its armed forces and intelligence apparatus from Lebanon (see p. 561). The withdrawal was verified by a UN technical military team. Israeli policies and measures affecting the human rights of the population in the Golan Heights and other occupied territories were monitored by the Special Committee to Investigate Israeli Practices Affecting the Human Rights of the Palestinian People and Other Arabs of the Occupied Territories (Committee on Israeli Practices) and were the subject of resolutions adopted by the Commission on Human Rights (see PART TWO, Chapter III) and the Assembly.

Communications. The Syrian Arab Republic, on 19 January [A/59/677-S/2005/39], responded to Israeli allegations that its Government had sponsored, trained and financed terrorist groups. It called the accusations unfounded, saying that its goal was regional peace and that Israel had been the primary threat to that peace.

On 7 March [A/59/726-S/2005/143], Syria responded to accusations made by Israel to the effect that the Syrian Government supported Islamic Jihad, which Israel held responsible for a 25 February Tel Aviv suicide bombing [A/59/717-S/2005/130] (see p. 513). Syria said that it condemned the bombing, that its competent authorities had denied any Syrian connection to the incident, and that the Israeli Government had a policy of making false accusations.

On 15 April [A/59/781-S/2005/250], Israel held Syria responsible for an incident in which a gunman wearing a shirt with the Palestinian flag crossed the Israeli-Syrian border, infiltrated an Israel Defence Forces (IDF) outpost, and opened fire. It said that Syria was morally and legally obligated to prevent similar incidents in future.

Syria responded on 25 April [A/59/792-S/2005/271], stating that the infiltration referred to by Israel was an isolated incident.

In identical letters of 30 September addressed to the Secretary-General and the Security Council President [A/60/409-S/2005/627], Syria objected to statements made by members of the Israeli administration regarding its intentions to continue settlement operations in the Syrian Golan, as well as statements to the effect that Israel would not return the Golan. Syria asserted that the occupied Golan was Syrian territory that had to be relinquished and that Israel was required under international resolutions to withdraw to the line of 4 June 1967.

The Supreme Council of the Gulf Cooperation Council (GCC), in the Abu Dhabi Declaration adopted at its twenty-sixth session (Abu Dhabi, United Arab Emirates, 18-19 December) [A/60/680-S/2006/108], stressed the need for an Israeli withdrawal from the occupied Syrian Arab Golan to the line of 4 June 1967 and from the Shab'a farmlands in southern Lebanon. It condemned the assassination of former Lebanese Prime Minister Rafik Hariri and other leaders and stressed the desire of GCC States to support political, security and economic stability for the Lebanese people. The Council expressed its satisfaction with the Syrian Arab Republic's receptiveness to Security Council resolution 1644 (2005) (see p. 558) regarding UNIIIC, emphasizing the concern of GCC States for the sovereignty, independence, unity and security of both Syria and Lebanon.

Committee on Israeli Practices. In its annual report [A/60/380], the Committee on Israeli Practices stated that it had visited Damascus, Syria, and Quneitra province, bordering the occupied area, where it met with Syrian authorities and received information from witnesses with personal knowledge of the human rights situation in the occupied Syrian Golan. Syrian Government officials emphasized that the situation continued to deteriorate and that Israel was still pursuing its policy of settlement expansion and land expropriation. New settlements were being planned on the sites of Arab villages destroyed by the occupation forces, and 21 of the 44 existing Israeli settlements were to be expanded. Additionally, 300 Jewish families would be encouraged to settle in the occupied Golan, besides the 700 families already established there during the previous four years. The Syrian population of the occupied Golan was still under threat from landmines, laid close to villages and fields, and in the vicinity of military camps. Israeli authorities continued to bury their nuclear waste about 100 meters from the summit of Jabal al-Sheikh, close to the Syrian border, presenting the threat of catastrophic ecological consequences. Another concern voiced by the Governor of Quneitra was the installation of large air fans on the western side of the Jabal al-Sheikh summit, which in case of leaks, would blow nuclear waste radiation into Syria. The problem of access to education, health care and employment persisted. Schools were overcrowded and in poor condition, and there was a shortage of health centres. Syrian workers in the occupied Golan continuously faced harassment, lack of employment opportunities, dismissal, discrimination during recruitment, low wages and high taxes. Most of them were employed in temporary jobs, unable to work in public sector institutions, where the jobs were reserved for Jewish settlers. They had no trade unions that could represent them and defend their rights.

Reports of Secretary-General (August). In an August report [A/60/258], the Secretary-General transmitted replies from four Member States, in response to his request for information on steps taken or envisaged to implement General Assembly resolution 59/33 [YUN 2004, p. 516], which dealt with Israeli policies in the Syrian territory since 1967, and resolution 59/32 [ibid., p. 473] on the transfer by some States of their diplomatic missions to Jerusalem (see p. 523).

On 24 August [A/60/298], the Secretary-General reported that no reply had been received from Israel to his August request for information on steps taken or envisaged to implement Assembly resolution 59/125 [YUN 2004, p. 516], which called on Israel to desist from changing the physical character, demographic composition, institutional structure and legal status of the Syrian Golan, and from its repressive measures against the population.

GENERAL ASSEMBLY ACTION (December)

On 1 December [meeting 60], the General Assembly adopted **resolution 60/40** [draft: A/60/L.32 & Add.1] by recorded vote (106-6-62) [agenda item 14].

The Syrian Golan

The General Assembly,

Having considered the item entitled "The situation in the Middle East",

Taking note of the report of the Secretary-General,

Recalling Security Council resolution 497(1981) of 17 December 1981,

Reaffirming the fundamental principle of the inadmissibility of the acquisition of territory by force, in accordance with international law and the Charter of the United Nations,

Reaffirming once more the applicability of the Geneva Convention relative to the Protection of Civilian Persons in Time of War, of 12 August 1949, to the occupied Syrian Golan,

Deeply concerned that Israel has not withdrawn from the Syrian Golan, which has been under occupation since 1967, contrary to the relevant Security Council and General Assembly resolutions,

Stressing the illegality of the Israeli settlement construction and other activities in the occupied Syrian Golan since 1967,

Noting with satisfaction the convening in Madrid on 30 October 1991 of the Peace Conference on the Middle East, on the basis of Security Council resolutions 242(1967) of 22 November 1967, 338(1973) of 22 October 1973 and 425(1978) of 19 March 1978 and the formula of land for peace,

Expressing grave concern over the halt in the peace process on the Syrian track, and expressing the hope that peace talks will soon resume from the point they had reached,

1. *Declares* that Israel has failed so far to comply with Security Council resolution 497(1981);

2. *Also declares* that the Israeli decision of 14 December 1981 to impose its laws, jurisdiction and administration on the occupied Syrian Golan is null and void and has no validity whatsoever, as confirmed by the Security Council in its resolution 497(1981), and calls upon Israel to rescind it;

3. *Reaffirms its determination* that all relevant provisions of the Regulations annexed to the Hague Convention of 1907, and the Geneva Convention relative to the Protection of Civilian Persons in Time of War, continue to apply to the Syrian territory occupied by Israel since 1967, and calls upon the parties thereto to respect and ensure respect for their obligations under those instruments in all circumstances;

4. *Determines once more* that the continued occupation of the Syrian Golan and its de facto annexation constitute a stumbling block in the way of achieving a just, comprehensive and lasting peace in the region;

5. *Calls upon* Israel to resume the talks on the Syrian and Lebanese tracks and to respect the commitments and undertakings reached during the previous talks;

6. *Demands once more* that Israel withdraw from all the occupied Syrian Golan to the line of 4 June 1967 in implementation of the relevant Security Council resolutions;

7. *Calls upon* all the parties concerned, the co-sponsors of the peace process and the entire international community to exert all the necessary efforts to ensure the resumption of the peace process and its success by implementing Security Council resolutions 242(1967) and 338(1973);

8. *Requests* the Secretary-General to report to the General Assembly at its sixty-first session on the implementation of the present resolution.

RECORDED VOTE ON RESOLUTION 60/40

In favour: Afghanistan, Algeria, Antigua and Barbuda, Argentina, Armenia, Azerbaijan, Bahamas, Bahrain, Bangladesh, Barbados, Belarus, Belize, Benin, Bhutan, Bolivia, Botswana, Brazil, Brunei Darussalam, Burkina Faso, Cambodia, Cape Verde, Central African Republic, Chile, China, Colombia, Comoros, Congo, Cuba, Democratic People's Republic of Korea, Djibouti, Dominica, Ecuador, Egypt, El Salvador, Eritrea, Ethiopia, Gabon, Gambia, Ghana, Guinea, Guinea-Bissau, Guyana, India, Indonesia, Iran, Iraq, Jamaica, Jordan, Kazakhstan, Kenya, Kuwait, Kyrgyzstan, Lao People's Democratic Republic, Lebanon, Lesotho, Liberia, Libyan Arab Jamahiriya, Madagascar, Malaysia, Maldives, Mali, Mauritania, Mauritius, Mexico, Mongolia, Morocco, Mozambique, Myanmar, Namibia, Nepal, Nicaragua, Nigeria, Oman, Pakistan, Panama, Paraguay, Philippines, Qatar, Russian Federation, Saint Lucia, Saint Vincent and the Grenadines, Saudi Arabia, Senegal, Singapore, Somalia, South Africa, Sri Lanka, Sudan, Suriname, Swaziland, Syrian Arab Republic, Tajikistan, Thailand, Togo, Trinidad and Tobago, Tunisia, Turkey, Turkmenistan, United Arab Emirates, United Republic of Tanzania, Uzbekistan, Venezuela, Viet Nam, Yemen, Zambia, Zimbabwe.

Against: Canada, Israel, Marshall Islands, Micronesia, Palau, United States.

Abstaining: Albania, Andorra, Australia, Austria, Belgium, Bosnia and Herzegovina, Bulgaria, Cameroon, Costa Rica, Croatia, Cyprus, Czech Republic, Denmark, Dominican Republic, Estonia, Fiji, Finland, France, Georgia, Germany, Greece, Guatemala, Haiti, Honduras, Hungary, Iceland, Ireland, Italy, Japan, Latvia, Liechtenstein, Lithuania, Luxembourg, Malta, Monaco, Nauru, Netherlands, New Zealand, Norway, Papua New Guinea, Peru, Poland, Portugal, Republic of Korea, Republic of Moldova, Romania, Samoa, San Marino, Serbia and Montenegro, Slovakia, Slovenia, Solomon Islands, Spain, Sweden, Switzerland, The former Yugoslav Republic of Macedonia, Tuvalu, Uganda, Ukraine, United Kingdom, Uruguay, Vanuatu.

On 8 December [meeting 62], the Assembly, under the agenda item on the report of the Committee on Israeli Practices and on the Fourth Committee's recommendation [A/60/477], adopted **resolution 60/108** by recorded vote (156-1-15) [agenda item 31].

The occupied Syrian Golan

The General Assembly,

Having considered the report of the Special Committee to Investigate Israeli Practices Affecting the Human Rights of the Palestinian People and Other Arabs of the Occupied Territories,

Deeply concerned that the Syrian Golan, occupied since 1967, has been under continued Israeli military occupation,

Recalling Security Council resolution 497(1981) of 17 December 1981,

Recalling also its previous relevant resolutions, the most recent of which was resolution 59/125 of 10 December 2004,

Having considered the report of the Secretary-General submitted in pursuance of resolution 59/125,

Recalling its previous relevant resolutions in which, inter alia, it called upon Israel to put an end to its occupation of the Arab territories,

Reaffirming once more the illegality of the decision of 14 December 1981 taken by Israel to impose its laws, jurisdiction and administration on the occupied Syrian Golan, which has resulted in the effective annexation of that territory,

Reaffirming that the acquisition of territory by force is inadmissible under international law, including the Charter of the United Nations,

Reaffirming also the applicability of the Geneva Convention relative to the Protection of Civilian Persons in Time of War, of 12 August 1949, to the occupied Syrian Golan,

Bearing in mind Security Council resolution 237 (1967) of 14 June 1967,

Welcoming the convening at Madrid of the Peace Conference on the Middle East on the basis of Security Council resolutions 242(1967) of 22 November 1967 and 338(1973) of 22 October 1973 aimed at the realization of a just, comprehensive and lasting peace, and expressing grave concern about the stalling of the peace process on all tracks,

1. *Calls upon* Israel, the occupying Power, to comply with the relevant resolutions on the occupied Syrian Golan, in particular Security Council resolution 497(1981), in which the Council, inter alia, decided that the Israeli decision to impose its laws, jurisdiction and administration on the occupied Syrian Golan was null and void and without international legal effect, and demanded that Israel, the occupying Power, rescind forthwith its decision;

2. *Also calls upon* Israel to desist from changing the physical character, demographic composition, institutional structure and legal status of the occupied Syrian Golan and in particular to desist from the establishment of settlements;

3. *Determines* that all legislative and administrative measures and actions taken or to be taken by Israel, the occupying Power, that purport to alter the character and legal status of the occupied Syrian Golan are null and void, constitute a flagrant violation of international law and of the Geneva Convention relative to the Protection of Civilian Persons in Time of War, of 12 August 1949, and have no legal effect;

4. *Calls upon* Israel to desist from imposing Israeli citizenship and Israeli identity cards on the Syrian citizens in the occupied Syrian Golan, and from its repressive measures against the population of the occupied Syrian Golan;

5. *Deplores* the violations by Israel of the Geneva Convention relative to the Protection of Civilian Persons in Time of War, of 12 August 1949;

6. *Calls once again upon* Member States not to recognize any of the legislative or administrative measures and actions referred to above;

7. *Requests* the Secretary-General to report to the General Assembly at its sixty-first session on the implementation of the present resolution.

RECORDED VOTE ON RESOLUTION 60/108:

In favour: Afghanistan, Algeria, Andorra, Antigua and Barbuda, Argentina, Armenia, Austria, Azerbaijan, Bahamas, Bahrain, Bangladesh, Barbados, Belarus, Belgium, Belize, Benin, Bhutan, Bolivia, Botswana, Brazil, Brunei Darussalam, Bulgaria, Burkina Faso, Burundi, Cambodia, Canada, Cape Verde, Central African Republic, Chile, China, Colombia, Costa Rica, Croatia, Cuba, Cyprus, Czech Republic, Democratic People's Republic of Korea, Denmark, Djibouti, Dominica, Ecuador, Egypt, El Salvador, Eritrea, Estonia, Ethiopia, Fiji, Finland, France, Gabon, Georgia, Germany, Ghana, Greece, Guatemala, Guinea, Guinea-Bissau, Guyana, Honduras, Hungary, Iceland, India, Indonesia, Iran, Iraq, Ireland, Italy, Jamaica, Japan, Jordan, Kazakhstan, Kenya, Kuwait, Kyrgyzstan, Lao People's Democratic Republic, Latvia, Lebanon, Lesotho, Liberia, Libyan Arab Jamahiriya, Liechtenstein, Lithuania, Luxembourg, Malaysia, Maldives, Mali, Malta, Mauritania, Mauritius, Mexico, Monaco, Mongolia, Morocco, Mozambique, Myanmar, Namibia, Nepal, Netherlands, New Zealand, Nicaragua, Niger, Nigeria, Norway, Oman, Pakistan, Panama, Paraguay, Peru, Philippines, Poland, Portugal, Qatar, Republic of Korea, Republic of Moldova, Romania, Russian Federation, Saint Lucia, Saint Vincent and the Grenadines, Samoa, San Marino, Saudi Arabia, Senegal, Serbia and Montenegro, Singapore, Slovakia, Slovenia, Solomon Islands, Somalia, South Africa, Spain, Sri Lanka, Sudan, Suriname, Sweden, Switzerland, Syrian Arab Republic, Tajikistan, Thailand, The former Yugoslav Republic of Macedonia, Timor-Leste, Togo, Trinidad and Tobago, Tunisia, Turkey, Turkmenistan, Ukraine, United Arab Emirates, United Kingdom, United Republic of Tanzania, Uruguay, Uzbekistan, Venezuela, Viet Nam, Yemen, Zambia, Zimbabwe.

Against: Israel.

Abstaining: Albania, Australia, Cameroon, Dominican Republic, Grenada, Haiti, Marshall Islands, Micronesia, Palau, Papua New Guinea, Tonga, Tuvalu, Uganda, United States, Vanuatu.

UNDOF

The mandate of the United Nations Disengagement Observer Force (UNDOF), established by Security Council resolution 350(1974) [YUN 1974, p. 205] to supervise the observance of the ceasefire between Israel and the Syrian Arab Republic in the Golan Heights and ensure the separation of their forces, was renewed twice in 2005, in June and December, each time for a six-month period.

UNDOF maintained an area of separation, which was some 75 kilometres long and varied in width between approximately 12.5 kilometres in the centre to less than 200 metres in the extreme south. The area of separation was inhabited and policed by the Syrian authorities, and no military forces other than UNDOF were permitted within it.

As at 5 December, UNDOF comprised 1,047 troops from Austria (380), Canada (185), Japan (30), Nepal (2), Poland (355) and Slovakia (95). It was assisted by 79 UNTSO military observers.

Lieutenant General Bala Nanda Sharma (Nepal) continued as Force Commander.

Reports of Secretary-General. The Secretary-General reported to the Security Council on UNDOF activities between 8 December 2004 and 10 June 2005 [S/2005/379] and between 10 June and 9 December 2005 [S/2005/767]. Both reports noted that the UNDOF area of operation remained calm, except in the Shab'a farms area. During the year, there were two incidents involving crossings of the ceasefire line. On 15 April, a male civilian crossed the line from the Syrian side and fired at an Israeli military post, and on 8 May, Israeli soldiers crossed into the area of separation and captured a Syrian civilian, who was taken to the Israeli side for interrogation and subsequently released.

UNDOF continued in 2005 to supervise the area of separation between Israeli and Syrian troops in the Golan Heights, ensuring by means of fixed positions and patrols that no military forces of either party were deployed there. The Force, accompanied by liaison officers from the parties concerned, carried out fortnightly inspections of equipment and force levels in the area of limitation. As in the past, both sides denied inspection teams access to some of their positions and imposed restrictions on the Force's freedom of movement. Mines, especially in the area of separation, continued to pose a threat to UNDOF personnel and local inhabitants, and the Force carried out operational mine clearance, supporting the United Nations Children's Fund in mine-awareness activities. The Force assisted the International Committee of the Red Cross with the passage of persons through the area of separation, and provided medical treatment to the local population upon request.

The Secretary-General observed that the situation in the Middle East continued to be very tense and was likely to remain so, unless and until a comprehensive settlement covering all aspects of the problem could be reached. He hoped that determined efforts would be made by all concerned to tackle the problem in all its aspects, with a view to arriving at a just and durable peace settlement, as called for by Council resolution 338(1973) [YUN 1973, p. 213]. Stating that he considered the Force's continued presence in the area to be essential, the Secretary-General, with the agreement of both Israel and Syria, recommended, in June, that UNDOF's mandate be extended until 31 December 2005 and, in December, until 30 June 2006.

SECURITY COUNCIL ACTION (June)

On 17 June [meeting 5205], the Council unanimously adopted **resolution 1605(2005)**. The

draft [S/2005/383] was prepared in consultations among Council members.

The Security Council,

Having considered the report of the Secretary-General of 10 June 2005 on the United Nations Disengagement Observer Force, and reaffirming its resolution 1308(2000) of 17 July 2000,

1. *Calls upon* the parties concerned to implement immediately its resolution 338(1973) of 22 October 1973;

2. *Welcomes* the efforts being undertaken by the United Nations Disengagement Observer Force to implement the Secretary-General's zero tolerance policy on sexual exploitation and abuse and to ensure full compliance of its personnel with the United Nations code of conduct, requests the Secretary-General to continue to take all necessary action in this regard and to keep the Security Council informed, and urges troop-contributing countries to take preventive and disciplinary action to ensure that such acts are properly investigated and punished in cases involving their personnel;

3. *Decides* to renew the mandate of the Force for a period of six months, that is, until 31 December 2005;

4. *Requests* the Secretary-General to submit, at the end of this period, a report on developments in the situation and the measures taken to implement resolution 338(1973).

On 21 December [meeting 5339], the Council unanimously adopted **resolution 1648(2005)**. The draft [S/2005/801] was prepared during consultations among Council members.

The Security Council,

Having considered the report of the Secretary-General of 7 December 2005 on the United Nations Disengagement Observer Force, and reaffirming its resolution 1308(2000) of 17 July 2000,

1. *Calls upon* the parties concerned to implement immediately its resolution 338(1973) of 22 October 1973;

2. *Welcomes* the efforts being undertaken by the United Nations Disengagement Observer Force to implement the Secretary-General's zero-tolerance policy on sexual exploitation and abuse and to ensure full compliance of its personnel with the United Nations code of conduct, requests the Secretary-General to continue to take all necessary action in this regard and to keep the Security Council informed, and urges troop-contributing countries to take preventive and disciplinary action to ensure that such acts are properly investigated and punished in cases involving their personnel;

3. *Decides* to renew the mandate of the Force for a period of six months, that is, until 30 June 2006;

4. *Requests* the Secretary-General to submit, at the end of this period, a report on developments in the situation and the measures taken to implement resolution 338(1973).

After the adoption of each resolution, the President, following consultations among Council members, made identical statements **S/PRST/ 2005/24** [meeting 5205] on 17 June and **S/PRST/**

2005/65 [meeting 5339] on 21 December, on behalf of the Council:

"In connection with the resolution just adopted on the renewal of the mandate of the United Nations Disengagement Observer Force, I have been authorized to make the following complementary statement on behalf of the Security Council:

'As is known, the report of the Secretary-General on the United Nations Disengagement Observer Force states in paragraph 12: "... the situation in the Middle East is very tense and is likely to remain so, unless and until a comprehensive settlement covering all aspects of the Middle East problem can be reached." That statement of the Secretary-General reflects the view of the Security Council.'"

Financing

The General Assembly had before it the performance report on UNDOF's budget for 1 July 2003 to 30 June 2004 [A/59/625]. Expenditures totalled $39,743,800 against an apportionment of $40,009,200, resulting in an unencumbered balance of $265,400. It also had before it the UNDOF budget for 1 July 2005 to 30 June 2006 [A/59/653 & Corr. 1, 2], totalling $41,581,200 and ACABQ's comments and recommendations thereon [A/59/736/Add.4].

GENERAL ASSEMBLY ACTION (June)

On 22 June [meeting 104], the General Assembly, on the recommendation of the Fifth Committee [A/59/837], adopted **resolution 59/306** without vote [agenda item 135 *(a)*].

Financing of the United Nations Disengagement Observer Force

The General Assembly,

Having considered the reports of the Secretary-General on the financing of the United Nations Disengagement Observer Force and the related reports of the Advisory Committee on Administrative and Budgetary Questions,

Recalling Security Council resolution 350(1974) of 31 May 1974 regarding the establishment of the United Nations Disengagement Observer Force and the subsequent resolutions by which the Council extended the mandate of the Force, the latest of which was resolution 1578(2004) of 15 December 2004,

Recalling also its resolution 3211 B(XXIX) of 29 November 1974 on the financing of the United Nations Emergency Force and of the United Nations Disengagement Observer Force and its subsequent resolutions thereon, the latest of which was resolution 58/306 of 18 June 2004,

Reaffirming the general principles underlying the financing of United Nations peacekeeping operations, as stated in General Assembly resolutions 1874(S-IV) of 27 June 1963, 3101(XXVIII) of 11 December 1973 and 55/235 of 23 December 2000,

Mindful of the fact that it is essential to provide the Force with the necessary financial resources to enable it to fulfil its responsibilities under the relevant resolutions of the Security Council,

1. *Requests* the Secretary-General to entrust the Head of Mission with the task of formulating future budget proposals in full accordance with the provisions of General Assembly resolution 59/296 of 22 June 2005, as well as other relevant resolutions;

2. *Takes note* of the status of contributions to the United Nations Disengagement Observer Force as at 15 April 2005, including the contributions outstanding in the amount of 16.2 million United States dollars, representing some 1 per cent of the total assessed contributions, notes with concern that only forty-nine Member States have paid their assessed contributions in full, and urges all other Member States, in particular those in arrears, to ensure the payment of their outstanding assessed contributions;

3. *Expresses its appreciation* to those Member States which have paid their assessed contributions in full, and urges all other Member States to make every possible effort to ensure payment of their assessed contributions to the Force in full;

4. *Expresses concern* at the financial situation with regard to peacekeeping activities, in particular as regards the reimbursements to troop contributors that bear additional burdens owing to overdue payments by Member States of their assessments;

5. *Also expresses concern* at the delay experienced by the Secretary-General in deploying and providing adequate resources to some recent peacekeeping missions, in particular those in Africa;

6. *Emphasizes* that all future and existing peacekeeping missions shall be given equal and non-discriminatory treatment in respect of financial and administrative arrangements;

7. *Also emphasizes* that all peacekeeping missions shall be provided with adequate resources for the effective and efficient discharge of their respective mandates;

8. *Reiterates its request* to the Secretary-General to make the fullest possible use of facilities and equipment at the United Nations Logistics Base at Brindisi, Italy, in order to minimize the costs of procurement for the Force;

9. *Endorses* the conclusions and recommendations contained in the report of the Advisory Committee on Administrative and Budgetary Questions, and requests the Secretary-General to ensure their full implementation;

10. *Requests* the Secretary-General to ensure the full implementation of the relevant provisions of its resolution 59/296;

11. *Also requests* the Secretary-General to take all necessary action to ensure that the Force is administered with a maximum of efficiency and economy;

12. *Further requests* the Secretary-General, in order to reduce the cost of employing General Service staff, to continue efforts to recruit local staff for the Force against General Service posts, commensurate with the requirements of the Force;

Financial performance report for the period from 1 July 2003 to 30 June 2004

13. *Takes note* of the report of the Secretary-General on the financial performance of the Force for the period from 1 July 2003 to 30 June 2004;

**Budget estimates for the period
from 1 July 2005 to 30 June 2006**

14. *Decides* to appropriate to the Special Account for the United Nations Disengagement Observer Force the amount of 43,706,100 dollars for the period from 1 July 2005 to 30 June 2006, inclusive of 41,521,400 dollars for the maintenance of the Force, 1,786,400 dollars for the support account for peacekeeping operations and 398,300 dollars for the United Nations Logistics Base;

Financing of the appropriation

15. *Decides also* to apportion among Member States the amount of 43,706,100 dollars at a monthly rate of 3,642,175 dollars, in accordance with the levels updated in General Assembly resolution 58/256 of 23 December 2003, and taking into account the scale of assessments for 2005 and 2006, as set out in its resolution 58/1 B of 23 December 2003, subject to a decision of the Security Council to extend the mandate of the Force;

16. *Decides further* that, in accordance with the provisions of its resolution 973(X) of 15 December 1955, there shall be set off against the apportionment among Member States, as provided for in paragraph 15 above, their respective share in the Tax Equalization Fund of 1,427,100 dollars, comprising the estimated staff assessment income of 1,142,400 dollars approved for the Force for the period from 1 July 2005 to 30 June 2006, the prorated share of 252,500 dollars of the estimated staff assessment income approved for the support account and the prorated share of 32,200 dollars of the estimated staff assessment income approved for the United Nations Logistics Base;

17. *Decides* that, for Member States that have fulfilled their financial obligations to the Force, there shall be set off against their apportionment, as provided for in paragraph 15 above, their respective share of the unencumbered balance and other income in the amount of 1,593,400 dollars in respect of the financial period ended 30 June 2004, in accordance with the levels updated in its resolution 58/256, and taking into account the scale of assessments for 2004, as set out in its resolutions 58/1 B;

18. *Decides also* that, for Member States that have not fulfilled their financial obligations to the Force, there shall be set off against their outstanding obligations their respective share of the unencumbered balance and other income in the amount of 1,593,400 dollars in respect of the financial period ended 30 June 2004, in accordance with the scheme set out in paragraph 17 above;

19. *Decides further* that the increase of 105,100 dollars in the estimated staff assessment income in respect of the financial period ended 30 June 2004 shall be added to the credits from the amount of 1,593,400 dollars referred to in paragraphs 17 and 18 above;

20. *Emphasizes* that no peacekeeping mission shall be financed by borrowing funds from other active peacekeeping missions;

21. *Encourages* the Secretary-General to continue to take additional measures to ensure the safety and security of all personnel under the auspices of the United Nations participating in the Force, bearing in mind paragraphs 5 and 6 of Security Council resolution 1502(2003) of 26 August 2003;

22. *Invites* voluntary contributions to the Force in cash and in the form of services and supplies acceptable to the Secretary-General, to be administered, as appropriate, in accordance with the procedure and practices established by the General Assembly;

23. *Decides* to include in the provisional agenda of its sixtieth session, under the item entitled "Financing of the United Nations peacekeeping forces in the Middle East", the sub-item entitled "United Nations Disengagement Observer Force".

Chapter VII

Disarmament

In 2005, the United Nations continued efforts to advance the cause of disarmament, especially in combating the proliferation of weapons of mass destruction and conventional armaments. However, those opportunities were undermined by deepening differences among Member States on a number of security issues of global concern, resulting in, according to the Secretary-General, a crisis of relevance for the multilateral disarmament negotiating framework. Those differences, which mostly arose over procedural and organizational questions, prevented the Conference on Disarmament and the Disarmament Commission from undertaking any substantive work for the seventh and fourth consecutive years, respectively. For the same reason, the 2005 Review Conference of the Parties to the Treaty on the Non-Proliferation of Nuclear Weapons (NPT), which took place in May, ended without a consensus outcome on any substantive issue on its agenda and the High-Level Plenary Meeting of the General Assembly (2005 World Summit), held in September, excluded from its Outcome Document any substantive pronouncement on disarmament and non-proliferation.

International anxiety arose over particular situations of concern, especially the nuclear programmes of the Democratic People's Republic of Korea, which announced early in the year that it had manufactured nuclear weapons, and of Iran, which decided to resume uranium conversion it had voluntarily suspended previously. Against that background, the Secretary-General called for measures to revitalize NPT as the cornerstone of the global non-proliferation regime, while the Assembly called on States to comply with their nuclear disarmament and non-proliferation commitments and to avoid action that might be detrimental to either cause.

In continuing efforts to address perceived threats to global peace and stability stemming from the potential proliferation of weapons of mass destruction, the Secretary-General outlined a strategy to prevent terrorists from gaining access to those weapons, while the Security Council emphasized the need for the effective implementation of the sanctions imposed against such terrorist organizations as Al-Qaida and the Taliban. To safeguard the operation of nuclear installations, the International Atomic Energy Agency convened a conference of the States parties to the Convention on the Physical Protection of Nuclear Materials, which adopted amendments extending the Convention's scope to cover nuclear facilities. In November, the tenth session of the States parties to the Convention on the Prohibition of the Development, Stockpiling and Use of Chemical Weapons and on Their Destruction (Chemical Weapons Convention) decided that 29 April—the date in 1997 of the Convention's entry into force—would be observed yearly as the day of remembrance for chemical warfare victims.

There were also positive developments regarding the movement to make whole geographic regions nuclear-weapon-free zones, following the finalization of the draft text on a Central Asian nuclear-weapon-free zone treaty, negotiated over seven years. The first Conference of States parties and signatories to the four existing treaties establishing such zones in Africa, Latin America and the Caribbean, South-East Asia and the South Pacific took place in Mexico City and considered cooperative ways of strengthening those zones, thereby raising the momentum for the idea of a nuclear-weapon-free southern hemisphere and adjacent areas.

In the field of conventional disarmament, Member States maintained focus in dealing with security problems relating to the spread of small arms and light weapons at national and regional levels and within the framework of the Programme of Action adopted by the 2001 UN Conference on the Illicit Trade in Small Arms and Light Weapons in All Its Aspects. The most auspicious development in that regard was the Assembly's adoption of a politically binding international instrument to enable States to identify and trace those weapons effectively. It also established a group of governmental experts to consider further steps to enhance international cooperation in tackling illicit brokering in those weapons. In other action, the Assembly continued to promote the relationship between disarmament and development, encouraging the international community to accord attention to the contribution that disarmament could make towards the achievement of the Millennium Development Goals.

On the bilateral level, the United States and the Russian Federation continued to implement their 2002 Strategic Offensive Reduction Treaty (Moscow Treaty), under which they had agreed to cut the level of their deployed strategic nuclear warheads to between 3,000 and 3,500 by 31 December 2012.

UN role in disarmament

UN machinery

In 2005, as in previous years, disarmament issues before the United Nations were considered mainly through the Security Council, the General Assembly and its First (Disarmament and International Security) Committee, the Disarmament Commission (a deliberative body) and the Conference on Disarmament (a multilateral negotiating forum, which met in Geneva). In addition, the Organization increasingly engaged civil society organizations concerned with disarmament issues.

The UN Department for Disarmament Affairs (DDA) continued to support the work of Member States and treaty bodies, to service the Advisory Board on Disarmament Matters and to administer the UN Disarmament Fellowship Programme.

Fourth special session devoted to disarmament

The General Assembly had decided, by resolution 51/45 C [YUN 1996, p. 447], to convene the fourth special session of the Assembly devoted to disarmament in 1999, subject to the emergence of consensus on its agenda and objectives, which had not been achieved. To facilitate agreement on the issue, the Assembly, by resolution 57/61, established an open-ended working group in 2002 [YUN 2002, p. 487] to consider a basis for consensus, but its efforts were to no avail. By resolution 59/71 [YUN 2004, p. 522], the Assembly re-established the group and mandated it to hold an organizational session in order to set the dates for its substantive session in 2006.

On 8 December, the Assembly decided to include in the provisional agenda of its sixty-first (2006) session the item entitled "Convening of the fourth special session of the General Assembly devoted to disarmament" (**decision 60/518**).

Disarmament Commission

In 2005, the Disarmament Commission, composed of all UN Member States, again did not hold any substantive meetings as no agreement could be reached on an agenda for discussing two preliminary items pertaining to nuclear and conventional weapons.

The Commission held five informal meetings (New York, June-July) [A/60/42] and a number of organizational meetings in July, November and December, to discuss possible topics for inclusion in its provisional agenda, based on the Chairman's proposals. On 18 and 19 July, the Commission agreed, ad referendum, to the inclusion of two items: recommendations for nuclear disarmament and non-proliferation of nuclear weapons in all its aspects, in particular for achieving the objective of nuclear disarmament; and practical confidence-building measures in the field of conventional weapons. On 20 July, the Commission further agreed, provisionally, to include in its report the issue of measures for improving the effectiveness of the Commission's methods of work, for consideration during its 2006 substantive session. However, agreement could not be reached on the proposed agenda items, following a 22 July motion by one delegation for an oral amendment to the item on nuclear disarmament. Consequently, the Commission decided, on 26 July, to close its 2005 organizational session.

On 8 December [meeting 62], the General Assembly, on the recommendation of the First Committee [A/60/465], adopted **resolution 60/91** without vote [agenda item 99 (d)].

Report of the Disarmament Commission

The General Assembly,

Having considered the report of the Disarmament Commission,

Recalling its resolutions 47/54 A of 9 December 1992, 47/54 G of 8 April 1993, 48/77 A of 16 December 1993, 49/77 A of 15 December 1994, 50/72 D of 12 December 1995, 51/47 B of 10 December 1996, 52/40 B of 9 December 1997, 53/79 A of 4 December 1998, 54/56 A of 1 December 1999, 55/35 C of 20 November 2000, 56/26 A of 29 November 2001, 57/95 of 22 November 2002, 58/67 of 8 December 2003 and 59/105 of 3 December 2004,

Considering the role that the Disarmament Commission has been called upon to play and the contribution that it should make in examining and submitting recommendations on various problems in the field of disarmament and in the promotion of the implementation of the relevant decisions adopted by the General Assembly at its tenth special session,

Bearing in mind its decision 52/492 of 8 September 1998,

1. *Takes note* of the report of the Disarmament Commission;

2. *Reaffirms* the mandate of the Disarmament Commission as the specialized, deliberative body within the United Nations multilateral disarmament machinery that allows for in-depth deliberations on specific disarmament issues, leading to the submission of concrete recommendations on those issues;

3. *Reaffirms also* the importance of further enhancing the dialogue and cooperation among the First Committee of the General Assembly, the Disarmament Commission and the Conference on Disarmament;

4. *Requests* the Disarmament Commission to continue its work in accordance with its mandate, as set forth in paragraph 118 of the Final Document of the Tenth Special Session of the General Assembly, and with paragraph 3 of Assembly resolution 37/78 H of 9 December 1982, and to that end to make every effort to achieve specific recommendations on the items on its agenda, taking into account the adopted "Ways and means to enhance the functioning of the Disarmament Commission";

5. *Welcomes* the efforts made by the Disarmament Commission during its organizational meeting in July 2005 towards achieving its objectives, and recommends that the Commission intensify consultations on those efforts with a view to reaching definitive agreements before the start of its substantive session in 2006;

6. *Requests* the Disarmament Commission to meet for a period not exceeding three weeks during 2006, from 10 to 28 April, and to submit a substantive report to the General Assembly at its sixty-first session;

7. *Requests* the Secretary-General to transmit to the Disarmament Commission the annual report of the Conference on Disarmament, together with all the official records of the sixtieth session of the General Assembly relating to disarmament matters, and to render all assistance that the Commission may require for implementing the present resolution;

8. *Also requests* the Secretary-General to ensure full provision to the Disarmament Commission and its subsidiary bodies of interpretation and translation facilities in the official languages and to assign, as a matter of priority, all the necessary resources and services, including verbatim records, to that end;

9. *Decides* to include in the provisional agenda of its sixty-first session the item entitled "Report of the Disarmament Commission".

Conference on Disarmament

The Conference on Disarmament, the multilateral negotiating body, held a three-part session in Geneva (24 January–1 April, 30 May–15 July and 8 August–23 September) [A/60/27].

The Conference, in 29 formal and 6 informal plenary meetings, continued to consider the cessation of the nuclear arms race and nuclear disarmament; prevention of nuclear war; prevention of an arms race in outer space; effective international arrangements to assure non-nuclear-weapon States against the use or threat of use of nuclear weapons; new types of weapons of mass destruction (WMDs) and new systems of delivery of such weapons (see p. 600); radiological weapons; a comprehensive programme of disarmament; and transparency in armaments.

Before adopting the agenda, the Conference discussed a proposal by France for a new item entitled "New and additional issues". While those favouring the idea argued that the traditional agenda of the Conference did not fully reflect the current threats and challenges to non-proliferation and disarmament, others felt that the meaning of the new item was not clear. The Conference reached an understanding, enabling it to deal with any new issue within the existing agenda, including terrorism and WMDs, as well as strengthening compliance with arms control and disarmament agreements, provided that consensus existed.

To overcome the persisting impasse among delegates over a programme of work for the Conference, successive Presidents conducted intensive consultations, in the course of which a number of informal proposals were put forward. Despite those efforts, no agreement could be reached, as delegates maintained their previously pronounced positions. The Non-Aligned Movement, in particular, continued to oppose any marginalization of the issue of negative security assurances and renewed support for the 2003 cross-group proposal on the work programme presented by five former Presidents ("A-5 proposal") [YUN 2003, p. 531], which was also endorsed by a number of other States, including China and the Russian Federation. Western States, on the other hand, were more inclined towards breaking existing linkages between agenda items and establishing subsidiary bodies on the basis of their own merits.

During the second part of the session, the President of the Conference (Norway) organized a series of plenary meetings on the four core topics on the agenda (nuclear disarmament, the prohibition of the production of fissile material for weapon purposes, the prevention of an arms race in outer space, and negative security assurances) and on other issues relevant to the international security environment. Views were exchanged on such issues as the functioning of the disarmament machinery and the way ahead in multilateral disarmament and non-proliferation, in the light of the failure of the 2005 Review Conference (see p. 597) on the 1968 Treaty on the Non-Proliferation of Nuclear Weapons (NPT) [YUN 1968, p. 17]. Although the initiative was supported by some delegations, others expressed doubts about the utility of those discussions, which came to a halt with the end of the Norwegian Presidency of the Conference. Regarding the adoption of a programme of work, the last President of the 2005 session (Peru) submitted a new proposal merging earlier ideas. Unfortunately, the Conference took no decision on the proposal and concluded its 2005 session without resolving the issue. Consequently, for the seventh consecutive year, the Conference did not establish any mechanism to address any of its agenda items.

Concerned over the impasse, Foreign Ministers from nine countries (Canada, Finland, Kazakhstan, the Netherlands, Peru, Poland, Slovakia, Sweden, Ukraine) and one Parliamentary Secretary for Foreign Affairs (Japan) attending a high-level segment of the Conference, provided ideas on how to rebuild its political role in arms control and disarmament. While noting that the responsibility for the impasse should not be attributed to any single State or group, they emphasized the need to develop new political consensus that would make it possible to go beyond national security interests. The Conference decided to hold its 2006 session between January and September and asked its current and incoming Presidents to conduct consultations during the intersessional period and make recommendations, taking into account all relevant proposals.

GENERAL ASSEMBLY ACTION

On 8 December [meeting 62], the General Assembly, on the recommendation of the First Committee [A/60/465], adopted **resolution 60/90** without vote [agenda item 99 (c)].

Report of the Conference on Disarmament

The General Assembly,

Having considered the report of the Conference on Disarmament,

Convinced that the Conference on Disarmament, as the sole multilateral disarmament negotiating forum of the international community, has the primary role in substantive negotiations on priority questions of disarmament,

Recognizing the need to conduct multilateral negotiations with the aim of reaching agreement on concrete issues,

Recalling, in this respect, that the Conference has a number of urgent and important issues for negotiation,

Taking note of active discussions held on the programme of work during the 2005 session of the Conference, as duly reflected in the report and the records of the plenary meetings,

Taking note also of significant contributions made during the 2005 session to promote substantive discussions on issues on the agenda, as well as of discussions held on other issues that could also be relevant to the current international security environment,

Stressing the urgent need for the Conference to commence its substantive work at the beginning of its 2006 session,

Recognizing the addresses of Ministers for Foreign Affairs as expressions of support for the endeavours of the Conference and its role as the sole multilateral disarmament negotiating forum,

1. *Reaffirms* the role of the Conference on Disarmament as the sole multilateral disarmament negotiating forum of the international community;

2. *Calls upon* the Conference to intensify consultations and explore possibilities with a view to reaching an agreement on a programme of work;

3. *Takes note* of the strong collective interest of the Conference in commencing substantive work as soon as possible during its 2006 session;

4. *Welcomes* the decision of the Conference to request its current President and the incoming President to conduct consultations during the intersessional period and, if possible, to make recommendations, taking into account all relevant proposals, including those submitted as the documents of the Conference, views presented and discussions held, and to endeavour to keep the membership of the Conference informed, as appropriate, of their consultations, as expressed in paragraph 38 of its report;

5. *Requests* all States members of the Conference to cooperate with the current President and successive Presidents in their efforts to guide the Conference to the early commencement of substantive work in its 2006 session;

6. *Requests* the Secretary-General to continue to ensure the provision to the Conference of adequate administrative, substantive and conference support services;

7. *Requests* the Conference to submit a report on its work to the General Assembly at its sixty-first session;

8. *Decides* to include in the provisional agenda of its sixty-first session the item entitled "Report of the Conference on Disarmament".

Multilateral disarmament agreements

As at 31 December 2005, the following number of States had become parties to the multilateral agreements listed below (in chronological order, with the years in which they were initially signed or opened for signature).

(Geneva) Protocol for the Prohibition of the Use in War of Asphyxiating, Poisonous or Other Gases, and of Bacteriological Methods of Warfare (1925): 133 parties

The Antarctic Treaty (1959): 45 parties

Treaty Banning Nuclear Weapon Tests in the Atmosphere, in Outer Space and under Water (1963): 124 parties

Treaty on Principles Governing the Activities of States in the Exploration and Use of Outer Space, including the Moon and Other Celestial Bodies (1967) [YUN 1966, p. 41, GA res. 2222(XXI), annex]: 98 parties

Treaty for the Prohibition of Nuclear Weapons in Latin America and the Caribbean (Treaty of Tlatelolco) (1967): 39 parties

Treaty on the Non-Proliferation of Nuclear Weapons (1968) [YUN 1968, p. 17, GA res. 2373(XXII), annex]: 189 parties

Treaty on the Prohibition of the Emplacement of Nuclear Weapons and Other Weapons of Mass Destruction on the Seabed and the Ocean Floor and in the Subsoil Thereof (1971) [YUN 1970, p. 18, GA res. 2660(XXV), annex]: 92 parties

Convention on the Prohibition of the Development, Production and Stockpiling of Bacteriological (Biological) and Toxin Weapons and on Their

Destruction (1972) [YUN 1971, p. 19, GA res. 2826 (XXVI), annex]: 154 parties

Convention on the Prohibition of Military or Any Other Hostile Use of Environmental Modification Techniques (1977) [YUN 1976, p. 45, GA res. 31/72, annex]: 72 parties

Agreement Governing the Activities of States on the Moon and Other Celestial Bodies (1979) [YUN 1979, p. 111, GA res. 34/68, annex]: 12 parties

Convention on Prohibitions or Restrictions on the Use of Certain Conventional Weapons Which May Be Deemed to Be Excessively Injurious or to Have Indiscriminate Effects (1981): 100 parties

South Pacific Nuclear-Free Zone Treaty (Treaty of Rarotonga) (1985): 17 parties

Treaty on Conventional Armed Forces in Europe (CFE Treaty) (1990): 30 parties

Treaty on Open Skies (1992): 33 parties

Convention on the Prohibition of the Development, Production, Stockpiling and Use of Chemical Weapons and on Their Destruction (1993): 175 parties

Treaty on the South-East Asia Nuclear Weapon-Free Zone (Bangkok Treaty) (1995): 10 parties

African Nuclear-Weapon-Free Zone Treaty (Pelindaba Treaty) (1996): 23 parties

Comprehensive Nuclear-Test-Ban Treaty (1996): 126 parties

Inter-American Convention against the Illicit Manufacturing of and Trafficking in Firearms, Ammunition, Explosives, and Other Related Materials (1997): 26 parties

Convention on the Prohibition of the Use, Stockpiling, Production and Transfer of Anti-Personnel Mines and on Their Destruction (Mine-Ban Convention, formerly known as Ottawa Convention) (1997): 148 parties

Inter-American Convention on Transparency in Conventional Weapons Acquisitions (1999): 11 parties

Agreement on Adaptation of the CFE Treaty (1999): 4 parties

[*United Nations Disarmament Yearbook*, vol. 29: *2005*, Sales No. E.06.IX.1]

Nuclear disarmament

Report of Secretary-General. In response to General Assembly resolutions 59/77 [YUN 2004, p. 532] and 59/79 [ibid., p. 534], the Secretary-General submitted a July report [A/60/122] assessing efforts to address nuclear disarmament issues. He observed that dangers resulting from the acquisition, possession and possible use of WMDs, including nuclear weapons and radiological dispersal devices, or "dirty bombs", were challenges the international community continued to confront. To effectively reduce related threats, efforts were needed at the unilateral, bilateral and multilateral levels, and nuclear-weapon States bore the responsibility to reduce existing arsenals. The Secretary-General acknowledged that some progress had been made in that regard, as the implementation of the 2002 Moscow Treaty [YUN 2002, p. 493], signed by the Russian Federation and the United States, had helped strengthen international peace and security. However, applying the principles of transparency, irreversibility and verification to the Treaty would greatly enhance the international nuclear non-proliferation regime. Another positive development was a five-year research programme undertaken by the United Kingdom to study techniques and technologies with the potential for use in verifying future arrangements for the control, reduction and elimination of nuclear weapon stockpiles. The summary findings of the study were outlined in a working paper presented to the 2005 NPT Review Conference (see p. 597). Also important were continuing international efforts to achieve universal adherence to, and effective implementation of existing arms control and disarmament agreements. Unfortunately, owing to persisting divergence of views, the NPT Review Conference concluded without agreement on substantive issues, thereby missing the opportunity to address important threats and challenges to the international non-proliferation regime. As the cornerstone of that regime, action was needed on many fronts to revitalize the NPT, including strengthening confidence in the Treaty's integrity; achieving further irreversible cuts in nuclear arsenals; ensuring that compliance measures were more effective; taking action to reduce the threat of proliferation to States and non-State actors; and finding durable ways to reconcile the right to peaceful uses with the imperative of non-proliferation. Reflecting on the fact that the Comprehensive Nuclear-Test-Ban Treaty (CTBT) (see p. 593) still lacked the ratifications required for its entry into force, the Secretary-General called on States that had not yet done so to sign and ratify it as soon as possible, especially those whose ratification was needed to enable it to take effect. Regarding the impasse preventing the Conference on Disarmament from resuming substantive work, he encouraged States members of the Conference to overcome their differences and agree on a programme of work that would facilitate the resumption of negotiations without further delay. It was critical for the Conference to succeed in doing so, as the relevance of multilateral disarmament machinery had been called into question. Noting that the full implementation of the seven recommendations put forth by his Advisory Board on Disarmament Matters in 2001 [YUN 2001, p. 474] for reducing nuclear dangers required further efforts, the Secretary-General said he was continuing to support initiatives and actions taken to that effect, as requested in Assembly resolution 59/79. With regard to the proposal contained in the 2000 Millennium Declaration [YUN 2000, p. 49] for convening an international conference to identify ways of eliminating nuclear dangers, consultations with Member States demonstrated that international consensus for holding such a conference remained elusive.

Conference on Disarmament

In 2005, the continuing lack of consensus over a programme of work (see p. 580) prevented the Conference on Disarmament, for the seventh consecutive year, from establishing any subsidiary body to deal with nuclear disarmament, leaving the issue to be addressed during plenary meetings where delegates reaffirmed or further elaborated their respective positions. The disappointing outcome of the 2005 NPT Review Conference (see p. 597), as well as the outcome of the 2005 World Summit (see p. 47) had further entrenched the divergent views among delegations. Against that background, the Non-Aligned Movement continued to accord the highest priority to the elimination of nuclear weapons within a specified time frame; the Western group underscored the high importance attached to negotiations on a fissile material cut-off treaty as a contribution to nuclear disarmament; China and the Russian Federation maintained emphasis on the prevention of an arms race in outer space (PAROS); and many other delegations reasserted the link between nuclear disarmament and non-proliferation.

Fissile material

In 2005, the Conference on Disarmament made no progress on the question of negotiating a fissile material cut-off treaty (FMCT) to prohibit the production of fissile material for nuclear weapons and other nuclear explosive devices, because disagreements over a programme of work prevented the Conference from establishing any mechanism to consider the items on its agenda. During plenary meetings, however, delegates reaffirmed their respective positions on the issue. As opposed to those who favoured negotiations on the FMCT, the Group of 21 (G-21) emphasized the priority it attached to creating an ad hoc committee to deal with nuclear disarmament instead. Delegations also addressed the issue of verification as a possible element of FMCT, with many States arguing that it should be an integral part of the negotiations, while others, notably the United States, believed that proposals for FMCT could be achieved without a verification mechanism. Positions also continued to differ on whether the proposed negotiations should cover existing stockpiles of fissile materials and on the desirability of declaring a moratorium on the production of those materials for nuclear weapons or other nuclear explosive devices before the conclusion of a treaty.

The General Assembly, in **resolution 60/70** (see p. 588) urged the Conference on Disarmament to agree on a programme of work, which would include the immediate commencement of negotiations on an FMCT, to be concluded within five years.

Security assurances

The Conference on Disarmament was also unable to establish a subsidiary body to address the question of effective international arrangements to assure non-nuclear-weapon States against the use or threat of use of nuclear weapons, leaving the topic to be discussed primarily at a 7 July thematic debate that also considered other items. Many delegates made references to Security Council resolution 984(1995) [YUN 1995, p. 192] on the issue and linked the need for security assurances with the provisions of article VI of NPT relating to States parties' obligation to pursue negotiations in good faith on the cessation of the nuclear arms race and on nuclear disarmament. They also invoked the 1996 advisory opinion of the International Court of Justice (ICJ) [YUN 1996, p. 461], which held that the threat or use of nuclear weapons would generally be contrary to the rules of international law applicable in armed conflict. Members of the Non-Aligned Movement, concerned about the development of new types of nuclear weapons and new doctrines expounding their possible use, underlined that, pending the total elimination of nuclear weapons, there was a need to conclude a universal, unconditional and legally binding instrument on security assurances to non-nuclear-weapon States.

GENERAL ASSEMBLY ACTION

On 8 December [meeting 62], the General Assembly, on the recommendation of the First Committee [A/60/461], adopted **resolution 60/53** by recorded vote (120-0-59) [agenda item 95].

Conclusion of effective international arrangements to assure non-nuclear-weapon States against the use or threat of use of nuclear weapons

The General Assembly,

Bearing in mind the need to allay the legitimate concern of the States of the world with regard to ensuring lasting security for their peoples,

Convinced that nuclear weapons pose the greatest threat to mankind and to the survival of civilization,

Welcoming the progress achieved in recent years in both nuclear and conventional disarmament,

Noting that, despite recent progress in the field of nuclear disarmament, further efforts are necessary towards the achievement of general and complete disarmament under effective international control,

Convinced that nuclear disarmament and the complete elimination of nuclear weapons are essential to remove the danger of nuclear war,

Determined to abide strictly by the relevant provisions of the Charter of the United Nations on the non-use of force or threat of force,

Recognizing that the independence, territorial integrity and sovereignty of non-nuclear-weapon States need to be safeguarded against the use or threat of use of force, including the use or threat of use of nuclear weapons,

Considering that, until nuclear disarmament is achieved on a universal basis, it is imperative for the international community to develop effective measures and arrangements to ensure the security of non-nuclear-weapon States against the use or threat of use of nuclear weapons from any quarter,

Recognizing that effective measures and arrangements to assure non-nuclear-weapon States against the use or threat of use of nuclear weapons can contribute positively to the prevention of the spread of nuclear weapons,

Bearing in mind paragraph 59 of the Final Document of the Tenth Special Session of the General Assembly, the first special session devoted to disarmament, in which it urged the nuclear-weapon States to pursue efforts to conclude, as appropriate, effective arrangements to assure non-nuclear-weapon States against the use or threat of use of nuclear weapons, and desirous of promoting the implementation of the relevant provisions of the Final Document,

Recalling the relevant parts of the special report of the Committee on Disarmament submitted to the General Assembly at its twelfth special session, the second special session devoted to disarmament, and of the special report of the Conference on Disarmament submitted to the Assembly at its fifteenth special session, the third special session devoted to disarmament, as well as the report of the Conference on its 1992 session,

Recalling also paragraph 12 of the Declaration of the 1980s as the Second Disarmament Decade, contained in the annex to its resolution 35/46 of 3 December 1980, which states, inter alia, that all efforts should be exerted by the Committee on Disarmament urgently to negotiate with a view to reaching agreement on effective international arrangements to assure non-nuclear-weapon States against the use or threat of use of nuclear weapons,

Noting the in-depth negotiations undertaken in the Conference on Disarmament and its Ad Hoc Committee on Effective International Arrangements to Assure Non-Nuclear-Weapon States against the Use or Threat of Use of Nuclear Weapons, with a view to reaching agreement on this question,

Taking note of the proposals submitted under the item in the Conference on Disarmament, including the drafts of an international convention,

Taking note also of the relevant decision of the Thirteenth Conference of Heads of State or Government of Non-Aligned Countries, held in Kuala Lumpur from 20 to 25 February 2003, as well as the relevant recommendations of the Organization of the Islamic Conference,

Taking note further of the unilateral declarations made by all the nuclear-weapon States on their policies of non-use or non-threat of use of nuclear weapons against the non-nuclear-weapon States,

Noting the support expressed in the Conference on Disarmament and in the General Assembly for the elaboration of an international convention to assure non-nuclear-weapon States against the use or threat of use of nuclear weapons, as well as the difficulties pointed out in evolving a common approach acceptable to all,

Taking note of Security Council resolution 984(1995) of 11 April 1995 and the views expressed on it,

Recalling its relevant resolutions adopted in previous years, in particular resolutions 45/54 of 4 December 1990, 46/32 of 6 December 1991, 47/50 of 9 December 1992, 48/73 of 16 December 1993, 49/73 of 15 December 1994, 50/68 of 12 December 1995, 51/43 of 10 December 1996, 52/36 of 9 December 1997, 53/75 of 4 December 1998, 54/52 of 1 December 1999, 55/31 of 20 November 2000, 56/22 of 29 November 2001, 57/56 of 22 November 2002, 58/35 of 8 December 2003 and 59/64 of 3 December 2004,

1. *Reaffirms* the urgent need to reach an early agreement on effective international arrangements to assure non-nuclear-weapon States against the use or threat of use of nuclear weapons;

2. *Notes with satisfaction* that in the Conference on Disarmament there is no objection, in principle, to the idea of an international convention to assure non-nuclear-weapon States against the use or threat of use of nuclear weapons, although the difficulties with regard to evolving a common approach acceptable to all have also been pointed out;

3. *Appeals* to all States, especially the nuclear-weapon States, to work actively towards an early agreement on a common approach and, in particular, on a common formula that could be included in an international instrument of a legally binding character;

4. *Recommends* that further intensive efforts be devoted to the search for such a common approach or common formula and that the various alternative approaches, including, in particular, those considered in the Conference on Disarmament, be explored further in order to overcome the difficulties;

5. *Also recommends* that the Conference on Disarmament actively continue intensive negotiations with a view to reaching early agreement and concluding effective international arrangements to assure the non-nuclear-weapon States against the use or threat of use of nuclear weapons, taking into account the widespread support for the conclusion of an international convention and giving consideration to any other proposals designed to secure the same objective;

6. *Decides* to include in the provisional agenda of its sixty-first session the item entitled "Conclusion of effective international arrangements to assure non-nuclear-weapon States against the use or threat of use of nuclear weapons".

RECORDED VOTE ON RESOLUTION 60/53:

In favour: Afghanistan, Algeria, Antigua and Barbuda, Azerbaijan, Bahamas, Bahrain, Bangladesh, Barbados, Belize, Benin, Bhutan, Botswana, Brunei Darussalam, Burkina Faso, Burundi, Cambodia, Cameroon, Cape Verde, Central African Republic, Chile, China, Colombia, Comoros, Congo, Costa Rica, Côte d'Ivoire, Cuba, Democratic People's Republic of Korea, Democratic Republic of the Congo, Djibouti, Dominica, Dominican Republic, Ecuador, Egypt, El Salvador, Eritrea, Ethiopia, Fiji, Gabon, Ghana, Grenada, Guatemala, Guinea, Guinea-Bissau, Guyana, Haiti, Honduras, India, Indonesia, Iran, Iraq, Jamaica, Japan, Jordan, Kazakhstan, Kenya, Kuwait, Kyrgyzstan, Lao People's Democratic Republic, Lebanon, Lesotho, Liberia, Libyan Arab Jamahiriya, Madagascar, Malawi, Malaysia, Maldives, Mali, Mauritania, Mauritius, Mexico, Mongolia, Morocco, Mozambique, Myanmar, Namibia, Nepal, Nicaragua, Niger, Nigeria, Oman, Pakistan, Panama, Paraguay, Peru, Philippines, Qatar, Saint Lucia, Saint Vincent and the Grenadines, Samoa, Sao Tome and Principe, Saudi Arabia, Senegal, Sierra Leone, Singapore, Somalia, Sri Lanka, Sudan, Suriname, Syrian Arab Republic, Tajikistan, Thailand, Timor-Leste, Togo, Trinidad and Tobago, Tunisia, Turkmenistan, Tuvalu, Uganda, Ukraine, United Arab Emirates, United Republic of Tanzania, Uruguay, Uzbekistan, Vanuatu, Venezuela, Viet Nam, Yemen, Zambia, Zimbabwe.

Against: None.

Abstaining: Albania, Andorra, Argentina, Armenia, Australia, Austria, Belarus, Belgium, Bolivia, Bosnia and Herzegovina, Brazil, Bulgaria, Canada, Croatia, Cyprus, Czech Republic, Denmark, Estonia, Finland, France, Georgia, Germany, Greece, Hungary, Iceland, Ireland, Israel, Italy, Latvia, Liechtenstein, Lithuania, Luxembourg, Malta, Marshall Islands, Micronesia, Monaco, Netherlands, New Zealand, Norway, Palau, Papua New Guinea, Poland, Portugal, Republic of Korea, Republic of Moldova, Romania, Russian Federation, San Marino, Serbia and Montenegro, Slovakia, Slovenia, South Africa, Spain, Sweden, Switzerland, The former Yugoslav Republic of Macedonia, Turkey, United Kingdom, United States.

Disarmament Commission

The Disarmament Commission considered a proposal by its Chairman to include in the substantive agenda for its 2005 session an item entitled "Recommendations for nuclear disarmament and non-proliferation of nuclear weapons in all its aspects, in particular for achieving the objective of nuclear disarmament". However, unresolved differences among delegates regarding the agenda prevented the Commission from deliberating on any substantive issue, including those pertaining to nuclear disarmament (see p. 579).

START and other bilateral agreements and unilateral measures

In 2005, the United States and the Russian Federation continued to implement the 2002 Strategic Offensive Reductions Treaty (SORT), also known as the Moscow Treaty [YUN 2002, p. 493], under which they had agreed to reduce the level of their deployed strategic nuclear warheads to between 3,000 and 3,500 by 31 December 2012. To achieve the reductions, the United States planned to reduce its operationally deployed strategic nuclear warheads to between 3,500-4,000 by 2007. It anticipated that reductions thereafter would involve decreasing the number of operationally deployed strategic nuclear warheads on ballistic missiles and at heavy bomber bases. Against that background, the United States envisioned no obstacles to its capacity to

meet its commitments under SORT, and neither party had expressed concerns about the intent or ability of the other to do so. The verification of both sides' compliance was expected to be facilitated by increasing openness in their strategic relationship under SORT and by the knowledge gained from their implementation of their 1991 Treaty on the Reduction and Limitation of Strategic Offensive Arms (START I) [YUN 1991, p. 34], scheduled to expire in 2009.

In April, the European Community and the Gulf Cooperation Council, at the fifteenth session of their Joint Council (Manama, Bahrain, 5 April), underlined the importance of compliance with and implementation of existing disarmament and non-proliferation agreements and other relevant international obligations. Both sides stressed the importance to the universalization of international instruments against the proliferation of WMDs and their means of delivery through signature, accession or ratification of all relevant instruments.

At the seventh Asia-Europe Meeting (Kyoto, Japan, 6-7 May), 48 Foreign Ministers from Asian countries and the European Union (EU) emphasized the importance of reinforcing efforts in addressing disarmament and the non-proliferation of WMDs and their means of delivery, and the need to promote universalisation in implementing related treaties and norms, including in the area of counter-terrorism.

The fifteenth EU-Russia Summit (Moscow, 10 May) adopted road maps for tackling mutual challenges, including strengthening cooperation on security and crisis management to address such global and regional challenges as those relating to WMD proliferation, export controls and disarmament, with a view to harmonizing positions and coordinating actions on the international stage. In order to pursue that objective, both sides outlined priority areas for enhanced cooperation on disarmament, arms control and non-proliferation issues.

In preparation for the High-Level Plenary Meeting of the General Assembly (2005 World Summit) (see p. 47), Ministers for Foreign Affairs of the Non-Aligned Movement, at a special meeting (Doha, Qatar, 13 June) [A/59/880], issued a declaration reaffirming the importance of achieving the total elimination of WMDs, particularly nuclear weapons. Recalling that Member States had resolved in the 2000 Millennium Declaration [YUN 2000, p. 49] to strive for the elimination of those weapons and to keep all options open, they reaffirmed the need for States to fulfil their arms control and disarmament obligations, maintaining that the ultimate objective of all efforts in that regard was general and complete disarmament.

On 18 July, Indian Prime Minister Manmohan Singh and United States President George W. Bush, in a joint statement, resolved to establish a global partnership to provide leadership in areas of mutual concern and interest, including in the field of non-proliferation and security. They committed themselves to playing a leading role in international efforts to prevent the proliferation of WMDs, including nuclear, chemical, biological and radiological weapons, and to working together for such other nuclear non-proliferation initiatives as the conclusion of a multilateral fissile material cut-off treaty and securing nuclear materials and technology.

On 16 September in Washington, D.C., Russian President Vladimir Putin and United States President George W. Bush, at a joint press conference, expressed their understanding about the need to stop the spread of WMDs, with emphasis on ensuring that terrorists not obtain those weapons. They also identified with the common goal of preventing non-nuclear-weapon States from acquiring nuclear weapons, most notably Iran and the Democratic People's Republic of Korea (DPRK). Addressing the need to improve nuclear security, they indicated that they had reached a milestone during the year in non-proliferation cooperation by completing the conversion of 10,000 Russian nuclear warheads into peaceful fuel for United States power reactors.

GENERAL ASSEMBLY ACTION

On 8 December [meeting 61], the General Assembly, on the recommendation of the First Committee [A/60/463], adopted four resolutions and one decision related to nuclear disarmament. The Assembly adopted **resolution 60/56** by recorded vote (153-5-20) [agenda item 97 (*l*)].

Towards a nuclear-weapon-free world: accelerating the implementation of nuclear disarmament commitments

The General Assembly,

Recalling its resolutions 58/51 of 8 December 2003 and 59/75 of 3 December 2004,

Also recalling the decisions and resolution on the Middle East of the 1995 Review and Extension Conference of the Parties to the Treaty on the Non-Proliferation of Nuclear Weapons and the Final Document of the 2000 Review Conference of the Parties to the Treaty on the Non-Proliferation of Nuclear Weapons,

Regretting the lack of any substantive outcome of the 2005 Review Conference of the Parties to the Treaty on the Non-Proliferation of Nuclear Weapons, as well as the inability of the General Assembly, at its 2005 World Summit, to reach agreement on matters relating to nuclear disarmament and nuclear non-proliferation,

Bearing in mind that 2005 marks the sixtieth anniversary of the dropping of atomic bombs on Hiroshima and Nagasaki, Japan, and that humankind should never again be exposed to such horrific devastation,

Expressing its grave concern at the danger to humanity posed by the possibility that nuclear weapons could be used,

Noting the growing concern at the lack of implementation of binding obligations and agreed steps towards nuclear disarmament,

Reaffirming that nuclear disarmament and nuclear non-proliferation are mutually reinforcing processes requiring urgent irreversible progress on both fronts,

Recalling the unequivocal undertaking by the nuclear-weapon States to accomplish the total elimination of their nuclear arsenals, leading to nuclear disarmament, in accordance with commitments made under article VI of the Treaty on the Non-Proliferation of Nuclear Weapons,

Underlining the importance of the Treaty and its universality to achieving nuclear disarmament and nuclear non-proliferation,

1. *Reaffirms* that the outcome of the 2000 Review Conference of the Parties to the Treaty on the Non-Proliferation of Nuclear Weapons sets out the framework for systematic and progressive efforts towards nuclear disarmament;

2. *Calls upon* the nuclear-weapon States to accelerate the implementation of the practical steps towards nuclear disarmament that were agreed upon at the 2000 Review Conference, thereby contributing to a safer world for all;

3. *Calls upon* all States to comply fully with commitments made regarding nuclear disarmament and nuclear non-proliferation and not to act in any way that may be detrimental to either cause or that may lead to a new nuclear arms race;

4. *Calls upon* all States parties to spare no efforts to achieve the universality of the Treaty on the Non-Proliferation of Nuclear Weapons, and urges India, Israel and Pakistan, which are not yet parties to the Treaty, to accede to it as non-nuclear-weapon States promptly and without conditions;

5. *Decides* to include in the provisional agenda of its sixty-first session the item entitled "Towards a nuclear-weapon-free world: accelerating the implementation of nuclear disarmament commitments" and to review the implementation of the present resolution at that session.

RECORDED VOTE ON RESOLUTION 60/56:

In favour: Afghanistan, Algeria, Andorra, Argentina, Armenia, Austria, Azerbaijan, Bahamas, Bahrain, Bangladesh, Barbados, Belgium, Belize, Benin, Bolivia, Bosnia and Herzegovina, Botswana, Brazil, Brunei Darussalam, Bulgaria, Burkina Faso, Burundi, Cambodia, Cameroon, Canada, Cape Verde, Central African Republic, Chile, China, Colombia, Comoros, Congo, Costa Rica, Côte d'Ivoire, Croatia, Cuba, Cyprus, Czech Republic, Democratic People's Republic of Korea, Democratic Republic of the Congo, Denmark, Djibouti, Dominica, Dominican Republic, Ecuador, Egypt, El Salvador, Eritrea, Ethiopia, Fiji, Finland, Gabon, Germany, Ghana, Grenada, Guatemala, Guinea, Guinea-Bissau, Guyana, Haiti, Honduras, Iceland, Indonesia, Iran, Iraq, Ireland, Italy, Jamaica, Japan, Jordan, Kazakhstan, Kenya, Kuwait, Kyrgyzstan, Lao People's Democratic Republic, Lebanon, Lesotho, Liberia, Libyan Arab Jamahiriya, Liechtenstein, Lithuania, Luxembourg, Madagascar, Malawi, Malaysia, Maldives, Mali, Malta, Marshall Islands, Mauritania, Mauritius, Mexico, Mongolia, Morocco, Mozambique, Myanmar, Namibia, Nepal, Netherlands, New Zealand, Nicaragua, Niger, Nigeria, Norway, Oman, Panama, Papua New Guinea, Paraguay, Peru, Philippines, Qatar, Republic of Korea, Republic of Moldova, Saint Lucia, Saint Vincent and the Grenadines,

Samoa, San Marino, Sao Tome and Principe, Saudi Arabia, Senegal, Serbia and Montenegro, Sierra Leone, Singapore, Slovakia, Solomon Islands, Somalia, South Africa, Sri Lanka, Sudan, Suriname, Sweden, Switzerland, Syrian Arab Republic, Tajikistan, Thailand, Timor-Leste, Togo, Tonga, Trinidad and Tobago, Tunisia, Turkey, Tuvalu, Uganda, Ukraine, United Arab Emirates, United Republic of Tanzania, Uruguay, Uzbekistan, Venezuela, Viet Nam, Yemen, Zambia, Zimbabwe.

Against: France, India, Israel, United Kingdom, United States.

Abstaining: Albania, Australia, Belarus, Bhutan, Estonia, Georgia, Greece, Hungary, Latvia, Micronesia, Pakistan, Palau, Poland, Portugal, Romania, Russian Federation, Saint Kitts and Nevis, Slovenia, Spain, The former Yugoslav Republic of Macedonia.

The First Committee adopted paragraph 4 by a separate recorded vote of 148 to 3, with 9 abstentions. The Assembly retained the paragraph by a recorded vote of 158 to 2, with 11 abstentions.

The Assembly adopted **resolution 60/65** by recorded vote (168-2-7) [agenda item 97].

Renewed determination towards the total elimination of nuclear weapons

The General Assembly,

Recalling, on the sixtieth anniversary of the atomic bombings in Hiroshima and Nagasaki, Japan, the need for all States to take further practical steps and effective measures towards the total elimination of nuclear weapons, with a view to achieving a peaceful and safe world free of nuclear weapons, and renewing the determination to do so,

Noting that the ultimate objective of the efforts of States in the disarmament process is general and complete disarmament under strict and effective international control,

Recalling its resolution 59/76 of 3 December 2004,

Convinced that every effort should be made to avoid nuclear war and nuclear terrorism,

Reaffirming the crucial importance of the Treaty on the Non-Proliferation of Nuclear Weapons as the cornerstone of the international nuclear disarmament and non-proliferation regime, and expressing regret over the lack of agreement on substantive issues at the 2005 Review Conference of the Parties to the Treaty on the Non-Proliferation of Nuclear Weapons, as well as over the elimination of references to nuclear disarmament and non-proliferation in the 2005 World Summit Outcome,

Recalling the decisions and the resolution of the 1995 Review and Extension Conference of the Parties to the Treaty on the Non-Proliferation of Nuclear Weapons and the Final Document of the 2000 Review Conference of the Parties to the Treaty,

Recognizing that the enhancement of international peace and security and the promotion of nuclear disarmament are mutually reinforcing,

Reaffirming that further advancement in nuclear disarmament will contribute to consolidating the international regime for nuclear non-proliferation and thereby ensuring international peace and security,

Expressing deep concern regarding the growing dangers posed by the proliferation of weapons of mass destruction, inter alia, nuclear weapons, including that caused by proliferation networks,

Welcoming the Final Declaration of the fourth Conference on Facilitating the Entry into Force of the Comprehensive Nuclear-Test-Ban Treaty, convened in New York in September 2005,

1. *Reaffirms* the importance of all States parties to the Treaty on the Non-Proliferation of Nuclear Weapons complying with their obligations under all the articles of the Treaty, and stresses the importance of an effective Treaty review process;

2. *Also reaffirms* the importance of the universality of the Treaty, and calls upon States not parties to the Treaty to accede to it as non-nuclear-weapon States without delay and without conditions, and pending their accession to refrain from acts that would defeat the objective and purpose of the Treaty as well as to take practical steps in support of the Treaty;

3. *Encourages* further steps leading to nuclear disarmament, to which all States parties to the Treaty are committed under article VI of the Treaty, including deeper reductions in all types of nuclear weapons, and emphasizes the importance of applying irreversibility and verifiability, as well as increased transparency in a way that promotes international stability and undiminished security for all, in the process of working towards the elimination of nuclear weapons;

4. *Encourages* the Russian Federation and the United States of America to implement fully the Treaty on Strategic Offensive Reductions, which should serve as a step for further nuclear disarmament, and to undertake nuclear arms reductions beyond those provided for by the Treaty, while welcoming the progress made by nuclear-weapon States, including the Russian Federation and the United States, on nuclear arms reductions;

5. *Encourages* States to continue to pursue efforts, within the framework of international cooperation, contributing to the reduction of nuclear-weapons-related materials;

6. *Calls for* the nuclear-weapon States to further reduce the operational status of nuclear weapons systems in ways that promote international stability and security;

7. *Stresses* the necessity of a diminishing role for nuclear weapons in security policies to minimize the risk that these weapons will ever be used and to facilitate the process of their total elimination, in a way that promotes international stability and based on the principle of undiminished security for all;

8. *Urges* all States that have not yet done so to sign and ratify the Comprehensive Nuclear-Test-Ban Treaty at the earliest opportunity with a view to its early entry into force, stresses the importance of maintaining existing moratoriums on nuclear-weapon test explosions pending the entry into force of the Treaty, and reaffirms the importance of the continued development of the Comprehensive Nuclear-Test-Ban Treaty verification regime, including the international monitoring system, which will be required to provide assurance of compliance with the Treaty;

9. *Emphasizes* the importance of the immediate commencement of negotiations on a fissile material cut-off treaty and its early conclusion, and calls upon all nuclear-weapon States and States not parties to the Treaty on the Non-Proliferation of Nuclear Weapons to declare moratoriums on the production of fissile material for any nuclear weapons pending the entry into force of the Treaty;

10. *Calls upon* all States to redouble their efforts to prevent and curb the proliferation of nuclear and other

weapons of mass destruction and their means of delivery;

11. *Stresses* the importance of further efforts for non-proliferation, including the universalization of the International Atomic Energy Agency comprehensive safeguards agreements and Model Protocol Additional to the Agreement(s) between State(s) and the International Atomic Energy Agency for the Application of Safeguards approved by the Board of Governors of the International Atomic Energy Agency on 15 May 1997, and the full implementation of Security Council resolution 1540(2004) of 28 April 2004;

12. *Encourages* all States to undertake concrete activities to implement, as appropriate, the recommendations contained in the report of the Secretary-General on the United Nations study on disarmament and non-proliferation education, submitted to the General Assembly at its fifty-seventh session, and to voluntarily share information on efforts they have been undertaking to that end;

13. *Encourages* the constructive role played by civil society in promoting nuclear non-proliferation and nuclear disarmament.

RECORDED VOTE RESOLUTION 60/65:

In favour: Afghanistan, Albania, Algeria, Andorra, Antigua and Barbuda, Argentina, Armenia, Australia, Austria, Azerbaijan, Bahamas, Bahrain, Bangladesh, Barbados, Belarus, Belgium, Belize, Bolivia, Bosnia and Herzegovina, Botswana, Brazil, Brunei Darussalam, Bulgaria, Burkina Faso, Burundi, Cambodia, Cameroon, Canada, Cape Verde, Central African Republic, Chile, Colombia, Comoros, Congo, Costa Rica, Côte d'Ivoire, Croatia, Cyprus, Czech Republic, Democratic Republic of the Congo, Denmark, Djibouti, Dominica, Dominican Republic, Ecuador, Egypt, El Salvador, Eritrea, Estonia, Ethiopia, Fiji, Finland, France, Gabon, Georgia, Germany, Ghana, Greece, Grenada, Guatemala, Guinea, Guinea-Bissau, Guyana, Haiti, Honduras, Hungary, Iceland, Indonesia, Iran, Iraq, Ireland, Italy, Jamaica, Japan, Jordan, Kazakhstan, Kenya, Kuwait, Kyrgyzstan, Lao People's Democratic Republic, Latvia, Lebanon, Lesotho, Liberia, Libyan Arab Jamahiriya, Liechtenstein, Lithuania, Luxembourg, Madagascar, Malawi, Malaysia, Maldives, Mali, Malta, Marshall Islands, Mauritania, Mauritius, Mexico, Micronesia, Monaco, Mongolia, Morocco, Mozambique, Namibia, Nepal, Netherlands, New Zealand, Nicaragua, Niger, Nigeria, Norway, Oman, Palau, Panama, Papua New Guinea, Paraguay, Peru, Philippines, Poland, Portugal, Qatar, Republic of Korea, Republic of Moldova, Romania, Saint Lucia, Saint Vincent and the Grenadines, Samoa, San Marino, Sao Tome and Principe, Saudi Arabia, Senegal, Serbia and Montenegro, Singapore, Slovakia, Slovenia, Solomon Islands, Somalia, South Africa, Spain, Sri Lanka, Sudan, Suriname, Sweden, Switzerland, Syrian Arab Republic, Tajikistan, Thailand, The former Yugoslav Republic of Macedonia, Timor-Leste, Togo, Tonga, Tunisia, Turkey, Turkmenistan, Tuvalu, Uganda, Ukraine, United Arab Emirates, United Kingdom, United Republic of Tanzania, Uruguay, Uzbekistan, Vanuatu, Venezuela, Viet Nam, Yemen, Zambia, Zimbabwe.

Against: India, United States.

Abstaining: Bhutan, China, Cuba, Democratic People's Republic of Korea, Israel, Myanmar, Pakistan.

The Assembly adopted **resolution 60/70** by recorded vote (113-45-20) [agenda item 97 *(m)*].

Nuclear disarmament

The General Assembly,

Recalling its resolution 49/75 E of 15 December 1994 on a step-by-step reduction of the nuclear threat, and its resolutions 50/70 P of 12 December 1995, 51/45 O of 10 December 1996, 52/38 L of 9 December 1997, 53/77 X of 4 December 1998, 54/54 P of 1 December 1999, 55/33 T of 20 November 2000, 56/24 R of 29 November 2001, 57/79 of 22 November 2002, 58/56 of 8 December 2003 and 59/77 of 3 December 2004 on nuclear disarmament,

Reaffirming the commitment of the international community to the goal of the total elimination of nuclear weapons and the establishment of a nuclear-weapon-free world,

Bearing in mind that the Convention on the Prohibition of the Development, Production and Stockpiling of Bacteriological (Biological) and Toxin Weapons and on Their Destruction of 1972 and the Convention on the Prohibition of the Development, Production, Stockpiling and Use of Chemical Weapons and on Their Destruction of 1993 have already established legal regimes on the complete prohibition of biological and chemical weapons, respectively, and determined to achieve a nuclear weapons convention on the prohibition of the development, testing, production, stockpiling, loan, transfer, use and threat of use of nuclear weapons and on their destruction, and to conclude such an international convention at an early date,

Recognizing that there now exist conditions for the establishment of a world free of nuclear weapons, and stressing the need to take concrete practical steps towards achieving this goal,

Bearing in mind paragraph 50 of the Final Document of the Tenth Special Session of the General Assembly, the first special session devoted to disarmament, calling for the urgent negotiation of agreements for the cessation of the qualitative improvement and development of nuclear-weapon systems, and for a comprehensive and phased programme with agreed time frames, wherever feasible, for the progressive and balanced reduction of nuclear weapons and their means of delivery, leading to their ultimate and complete elimination at the earliest possible time,

Reaffirming the conviction of the States parties to the Treaty on the Non-Proliferation of Nuclear Weapons that the Treaty is a cornerstone of nuclear non-proliferation and nuclear disarmament and the importance of the decision on strengthening the review process for the Treaty, the decision on principles and objectives for nuclear non-proliferation and disarmament, the decision on the extension of the Treaty and the resolution on the Middle East, adopted by the 1995 Review and Extension Conference of the Parties to the Treaty on the Non-Proliferation of Nuclear Weapons,

Stressing the importance of the thirteen steps for the systematic and progressive efforts to achieve the objective of nuclear disarmament leading to the total elimination of nuclear weapons, as agreed to by the States parties in the Final Document of the 2000 Review Conference of the Parties to the Treaty on the Non-Proliferation of Nuclear Weapons, held in New York from 24 April to 19 May 2000,

Reiterating the highest priority accorded to nuclear disarmament in the Final Document of the Tenth Special Session of the General Assembly and by the international community,

Reiterating its call for an early entry into force of the Comprehensive Nuclear-Test-Ban Treaty,

Noting with appreciation the entry into force of the Treaty on the Reduction and Limitation of Strategic Offensive Arms (START I), to which Belarus, Kazakhstan, the Russian Federation, Ukraine and the United States of America are States parties,

Also noting with appreciation the entry into force of the Treaty between the United States of America and the Russian Federation on Strategic Offensive Reductions ("the Moscow Treaty") as a significant step towards reducing their deployed strategic nuclear weapons, while calling for further irreversible deep cuts in their nuclear arsenals,

Further noting with appreciation the unilateral measures taken by the nuclear-weapon States for nuclear arms limitation, and encouraging them to take further such measures,

Recognizing the complementarity of bilateral, plurilateral and multilateral negotiations on nuclear disarmament, and that bilateral negotiations can never replace multilateral negotiations in this respect,

Noting the support expressed in the Conference on Disarmament and in the General Assembly for the elaboration of an international convention to assure non-nuclear-weapon States against the use or threat of use of nuclear weapons, and the multilateral efforts in the Conference on Disarmament to reach agreement on such an international convention at an early date,

Recalling the advisory opinion of the International Court of Justice on the *Legality of the Threat or Use of Nuclear Weapons,* issued on 8 July 1996, and welcoming the unanimous reaffirmation by all Judges of the Court that there exists an obligation for all States to pursue in good faith and bring to a conclusion negotiations leading to nuclear disarmament in all its aspects under strict and effective international control,

Mindful of paragraph 74 and other relevant recommendations in the Final Document of the Thirteenth Conference of Heads of State or Government of Non-Aligned Countries, held at Kuala Lumpur from 20 to 25 February 2003, calling upon the Conference on Disarmament to establish, as soon as possible and as the highest priority, an ad hoc committee on nuclear disarmament and to commence negotiations on a phased programme for the complete elimination of nuclear weapons with a specified framework of time,

Recalling paragraph 61 of the Final Document of the Fourteenth Ministerial Conference of the Movement of Non-Aligned Countries, held in Durban, South Africa, from 17 to 19 August 2004,

Also recalling paragraph 19 of the declaration of the special meeting of the Ministers for Foreign Affairs of the Non-Aligned Movement, held in Doha on 13 June 2005,

Reaffirming the specific mandate conferred by the General Assembly in its decision 52/492 of 8 September 1998 upon the Disarmament Commission to discuss the subject of nuclear disarmament as one of its main substantive agenda items,

Recalling the United Nations Millennium Declaration, in which Heads of State and Government resolve to strive for the elimination of weapons of mass destruction, in particular nuclear weapons, and to keep all options open for achieving this aim, including the possibility of convening an international conference to identify ways of eliminating nuclear dangers,

Reaffirming that, in accordance with the Charter of the United Nations, States should refrain from the use or the threat of use of nuclear weapons in settling their disputes in international relations,

Seized of the danger of the use of weapons of mass destruction, particularly nuclear weapons, in terrorist acts and the urgent need for concerted international efforts to control and overcome it,

1. *Recognizes* that, in view of recent political developments, the time is now opportune for all the nuclear-weapon States to take effective disarmament measures with a view to achieving the elimination of these weapons;

2. *Reaffirms* that nuclear disarmament and nuclear non-proliferation are substantively interrelated and mutually reinforcing, that the two processes must go hand in hand and that there is a genuine need for a systematic and progressive process of nuclear disarmament;

3. *Welcomes and encourages* the efforts to establish new nuclear-weapon-free zones in different parts of the world on the basis of agreements or arrangements freely arrived at among the States of the regions concerned, which is an effective measure for limiting the further spread of nuclear weapons geographically and contributes to the cause of nuclear disarmament;

4. *Recognizes* that there is a genuine need to diminish the role of nuclear weapons in strategic doctrines and security policies to minimize the risk that these weapons will ever be used and to facilitate the process of their total elimination;

5. *Urges* the nuclear-weapon States to stop immediately the qualitative improvement, development, production and stockpiling of nuclear warheads and their delivery systems;

6. *Also urges* the nuclear-weapon States, as an interim measure, to de-alert and deactivate immediately their nuclear weapons and to take other concrete measures to reduce further the operational status of their nuclear-weapon systems;

7. *Reiterates its call upon* the nuclear-weapon States to undertake the step-by-step reduction of the nuclear threat and to carry out effective nuclear disarmament measures with a view to achieving the total elimination of these weapons;

8. *Calls upon* the nuclear-weapon States, pending the achievement of the total elimination of nuclear weapons, to agree on an internationally and legally binding instrument on a joint undertaking not to be the first to use nuclear weapons, and calls upon all States to conclude an internationally and legally binding instrument on security assurances of non-use and non-threat of use of nuclear weapons against non-nuclear-weapon States;

9. *Urges* the nuclear-weapon States to commence plurilateral negotiations among themselves at an appropriate stage on further deep reductions of nuclear weapons as an effective measure of nuclear disarmament;

10. *Underlines* the importance of applying the principle of irreversibility to the process of nuclear disarmament, nuclear and other related arms control and reduction measures;

11. *Underscores* the importance of the unequivocal undertaking by the nuclear-weapon States in the Final Document of the 2000 Review Conference of the Parties to the Treaty on the Non-Proliferation of Nuclear Weapons to accomplish the total elimination of their nuclear arsenals leading to nuclear disarmament, to which all States parties are committed under article VI of the Treaty, and the reaffirmation by the States parties that the total elimination of nuclear weapons is the only absolute guarantee against the use or threat of use of nuclear weapons;

12. *Calls for* the full and effective implementation of the thirteen steps for nuclear disarmament con-

tained in the Final Document of the 2000 Review Conference;

13. *Urges* the nuclear-weapon States to carry out further reductions of non-strategic nuclear weapons, based on unilateral initiatives and as an integral part of the nuclear arms reduction and disarmament process;

14. *Calls for* the immediate commencement of negotiations in the Conference on Disarmament on a non-discriminatory, multilateral and internationally and effectively verifiable treaty banning the production of fissile material for nuclear weapons or other nuclear explosive devices on the basis of the report of the Special Coordinator and the mandate contained therein;

15. *Urges* the Conference on Disarmament to agree on a programme of work which includes the immediate commencement of negotiations on such a treaty with a view to their conclusion within five years;

16. *Calls for* the conclusion of an international legal instrument or instruments on adequate security assurances to non-nuclear-weapon States;

17. *Also calls for* the early entry into force and strict observance of the Comprehensive Nuclear-Test-Ban Treaty;

18. *Expresses its regret* that the 2005 Review Conference of the Parties to the Treaty on the Non-Proliferation of Nuclear Weapons was unable to achieve any substantive result and that the 2005 World Summit Outcome failed to make any reference to nuclear disarmament and nuclear non-proliferation;

19. *Also expresses its regret* that the Conference on Disarmament was unable to establish an ad hoc committee on nuclear disarmament at its 2005 session, as called for in resolution 59/104 of 3 December 2004;

20. *Reiterates its call upon* the Conference on Disarmament to establish, on a priority basis, an ad hoc committee to deal with nuclear disarmament early in 2006 and to commence negotiations on a phased programme of nuclear disarmament leading to the eventual total elimination of nuclear weapons;

21. *Calls for* the convening of an international conference on nuclear disarmament in all its aspects at an early date to identify and deal with concrete measures of nuclear disarmament;

22. *Requests* the Secretary-General to submit to the General Assembly at its sixty-first session a report on the implementation of the present resolution;

23. *Decides* to include in the provisional agenda of its sixty-first session the item entitled "Nuclear disarmament".

RECORDED VOTE ON RESOLUTION 60/70:

In favour: Afghanistan, Algeria, Antigua and Barbuda, Bahamas, Bahrain, Bangladesh, Barbados, Belize, Benin, Bhutan, Bolivia, Botswana, Brazil, Brunei Darussalam, Burkina Faso, Burundi, Cambodia, Cameroon, Cape Verde, Central African Republic, Chile, China, Colombia, Congo, Costa Rica, Côte d'Ivoire, Cuba, Democratic People's Republic of Korea, Democratic Republic of the Congo, Djibouti, Dominica, Dominican Republic, Ecuador, Egypt, El Salvador, Eritrea, Ethiopia, Fiji, Gabon, Ghana, Grenada, Guatemala, Guinea, Guinea-Bissau, Guyana, Haiti, Honduras, Iran, Iraq, Jamaica, Jordan, Kenya, Kuwait, Lao People's Democratic Republic, Lebanon, Lesotho, Liberia, Libyan Arab Jamahiriya, Madagascar, Malawi, Malaysia, Maldives, Mali, Mauritania, Mexico, Mongolia, Morocco, Mozambique, Myanmar, Namibia, Nepal, New Zealand, Nicaragua, Niger, Nigeria, Oman, Panama, Paraguay, Peru, Philippines, Qatar, Saint Lucia, Saint Vincent and the Grenadines, Samoa, Sao Tome and Principe, Saudi Arabia, Senegal, Sierra Leone, Singapore, Solomon Islands, Somalia, South Africa, Sri Lanka, Sudan, Suriname, Syrian Arab Republic, Thailand, Timor-Leste, Togo, Tonga, Trinidad and Tobago, Tunisia, Tuvalu, Uganda, United Arab Emirates, United Republic of Tanzania, Uruguay, Vanuatu, Venezuela, Viet Nam, Yemen, Zambia, Zimbabwe.

Against: Albania, Andorra, Australia, Austria, Belgium, Bosnia and Herzegovina, Bulgaria, Canada, Croatia, Cyprus, Czech Republic, Denmark, Estonia, Finland, France, Georgia, Germany, Greece, Hungary, Iceland, Israel, Italy, Latvia, Liechtenstein, Lithuania, Luxembourg, Marshall Islands, Micronesia, Monaco, Netherlands, Norway, Palau, Poland, Portugal, Romania, San Marino, Serbia and Montenegro, Slovakia, Slovenia, Spain, Switzerland, The former Yugoslav Republic of Macedonia, Turkey, United Kingdom, United States.

Abstaining: Argentina, Armenia, Azerbaijan, Belarus, India, Ireland, Japan, Kazakhstan, Kyrgyzstan, Malta, Mauritius, Pakistan, Papua New Guinea, Republic of Korea, Republic of Moldova, Russian Federation, Sweden, Tajikistan, Ukraine, Uzbekistan.

The Assembly adopted **resolution 60/79** by recorded vote (115-49-15) [agenda item 97 *(o)*].

Reducing nuclear danger

The General Assembly,

Bearing in mind that the use of nuclear weapons poses the most serious threat to mankind and to the survival of civilization,

Reaffirming that any use or threat of use of nuclear weapons would constitute a violation of the Charter of the United Nations,

Convinced that the proliferation of nuclear weapons in all its aspects would seriously enhance the danger of nuclear war,

Convinced also that nuclear disarmament and the complete elimination of nuclear weapons are essential to remove the danger of nuclear war,

Considering that, until nuclear weapons cease to exist, it is imperative on the part of the nuclear-weapon States to adopt measures that assure non-nuclear-weapon States against the use or threat of use of nuclear weapons,

Considering also that the hair-trigger alert of nuclear weapons carries unacceptable risks of unintentional or accidental use of nuclear weapons, which would have catastrophic consequences for all mankind,

Emphasizing the imperative need to adopt measures to avoid accidental, unauthorized or unexplained incidents arising from computer anomaly or other technical malfunctions,

Conscious that limited steps relating to detargeting have been taken by the nuclear-weapon States and that further practical, realistic and mutually reinforcing steps are necessary to contribute to the improvement in the international climate for negotiations leading to the elimination of nuclear weapons,

Mindful that the reduction of tensions brought about by a change in nuclear doctrines would positively impact on international peace and security and improve the conditions for the further reduction and the elimination of nuclear weapons,

Reiterating the highest priority accorded to nuclear disarmament in the Final Document of the Tenth Special Session of the General Assembly and by the international community,

Recalling that in the advisory opinion of the International Court of Justice on the *Legality of the Threat or Use of Nuclear Weapons* it is stated that there exists an obligation for all States to pursue in good faith and bring to a conclusion negotiations leading to nuclear disarmament in all its aspects under strict and effective international control,

Recalling also the call in the United Nations Millennium Declaration to seek to eliminate the dangers posed by weapons of mass destruction and the resolve to strive for the elimination of weapons of mass destruction, particularly nuclear weapons, including the possibility of convening an international conference to identify ways of eliminating nuclear dangers,

1. *Calls for* a review of nuclear doctrines and, in this context, immediate and urgent steps to reduce the risks of unintentional and accidental use of nuclear weapons;

2. *Requests* the five nuclear-weapon States to take measures towards the implementation of paragraph 1 above;

3. *Calls upon* Member States to take the necessary measures to prevent the proliferation of nuclear weapons in all its aspects and to promote nuclear disarmament, with the objective of eliminating nuclear weapons;

4. *Takes note* of the report of the Secretary-General submitted pursuant to paragraph 5 of General Assembly resolution 59/79 of 3 December 2004;

5. *Requests* the Secretary-General to intensify efforts and support initiatives that would contribute towards the full implementation of the seven recommendations identified in the report of the Advisory Board on Disarmament Matters that would significantly reduce the risk of nuclear war, and also to continue to encourage Member States to endeavour to create conditions that would allow the emergence of an international consensus to hold an international conference as proposed in the United Nations Millennium Declaration, to identify ways of eliminating nuclear dangers, and to report thereon to the General Assembly at its sixty-first session;

6. *Decides* to include in the provisional agenda of its sixty-first session the item entitled "Reducing nuclear danger".

RECORDED VOTE ON RESOLUTION 60/79:

In favour: Afghanistan, Algeria, Antigua and Barbuda, Bahamas, Bahrain, Bangladesh, Barbados, Belize, Benin, Bhutan, Bolivia, Botswana, Brazil, Brunei Darussalam, Burkina Faso, Burundi, Cambodia, Cameroon, Cape Verde, Central African Republic, Chile, Colombia, Congo, Costa Rica, Côte d'Ivoire, Cuba, Democratic People's Republic of Korea, Democratic Republic of the Congo, Djibouti, Dominica, Dominican Republic, Ecuador, Egypt, El Salvador, Eritrea, Ethiopia, Fiji, Gabon, Ghana, Grenada, Guatemala, Guinea, Guinea-Bissau, Guyana, Haiti, Honduras, India, Indonesia, Iran, Iraq, Jamaica, Jordan, Kenya, Kuwait, Lao People's Democratic Republic, Lebanon, Lesotho, Liberia, Libyan Arab Jamahiriya, Madagascar, Malawi, Malaysia, Maldives, Mali, Mauritania, Mauritius, Mexico, Mongolia, Morocco, Mozambique, Myanmar, Namibia, Nepal, Nicaragua, Niger, Nigeria, Oman, Pakistan, Panama, Peru, Philippines, Qatar, Saint Lucia, Saint Vincent and the Grenadines, Samoa, Sao Tome and Principe, Saudi Arabia, Senegal, Sierra Leone, Singapore, Solomon Islands, Somalia, South Africa, Sri Lanka, Sudan, Suriname, Syrian Arab Republic, Thailand, Timor-Leste, Togo, Tonga, Trinidad and Tobago, Tunisia, Turkmenistan, Tuvalu, Uganda, United Arab Emirates, United Republic of Tanzania, Uruguay, Vanuatu, Venezuela, Viet Nam, Yemen, Zambia, Zimbabwe.

Against: Albania, Andorra, Australia, Austria, Belgium, Bosnia and Herzegovina, Bulgaria, Canada, Croatia, Cyprus, Czech Republic, Denmark, Estonia, Finland, France, Georgia, Germany, Greece, Hungary, Iceland, Ireland, Israel, Italy, Latvia, Liechtenstein, Lithuania, Luxembourg, Malta, Marshall Islands, Micronesia, Monaco, Netherlands, New Zealand, Norway, Palau, Poland, Portugal, Romania, San Marino, Serbia and Montenegro, Slovakia, Slovenia, Spain, Sweden, Switzerland, The former Yugoslav Republic of Macedonia, Turkey, United Kingdom, United States.

Abstaining: Argentina, Armenia, Azerbaijan, Belarus, China, Japan, Kazakhstan, Kyrgyzstan, Paraguay, Republic of Korea, Republic of Moldova, Russian Federation, Tajikistan, Ukraine, Uzbekistan.

The Assembly adopted **decision 60/517** by recorded vote (128-5-40) [agenda item 97 *(cc)*].

United Nations conference to identify ways of eliminating nuclear dangers in the context of nuclear disarmament

At its 61st plenary meeting, on 8 December 2005, the General Assembly, by a recorded vote of 128 to 5, with 40 abstentions, and on the recommendation of the First Committee, decided to include in the provisional agenda of its sixty-first session the item entitled "United Nations conference to identify ways of eliminating nuclear dangers in the context of nuclear disarmament".

RECORDED VOTE ON DECISION 60/517:

In favour: Afghanistan, Algeria, Antigua and Barbuda, Argentina, Armenia, Bahamas, Bahrain, Bangladesh, Barbados, Belarus, Belize, Benin, Bhutan, Bolivia, Botswana, Brazil, Brunei Darussalam, Burkina Faso, Burundi, Cambodia, Cameroon, Cape Verde, Chile, China, Democratic People's Republic of Korea, Democratic Republic of the Congo, Djibouti, Dominica, Dominican Republic, Ecuador, Egypt, El Salvador, Eritrea, Ethiopia, Fiji, Gabon, Ghana, Grenada, Guatemala, Guinea, Guinea-Bissau, Guyana, Haiti, Honduras, India, Indonesia, Iran, Iraq, Ireland, Jamaica, Japan, Jordan, Kazakhstan, Kenya, Kuwait, Kyrgyzstan, Lao People's Democratic Republic, Lebanon, Lesotho, Liberia, Libyan Arab Jamahiriya, Madagascar, Malawi, Malaysia, Maldives, Mali, Malta, Marshall Islands, Mauritania, Mauritius, Mexico, Mongolia, Morocco, Mozambique, Myanmar, Namibia, Nepal, New Zealand, Nicaragua, Niger, Nigeria, Oman, Pakistan, Panama, Papua New Guinea, Paraguay, Peru, Philippines, Qatar, Saint Lucia, Saint Vincent and the Grenadines, Samoa, Saudi Arabia, Senegal, Sierra Leone, Singapore, Solomon Islands, Somalia, South Africa, Sri Lanka, Sudan, Suriname, Sweden, Syrian Arab Republic, Tajikistan, Thailand, Timor Leste, Togo, Trinidad and Tobago, Tunisia, Uganda, Ukraine, United Arab Emirates, United Republic of Tanzania, Uruguay, Uzbekistan, Vanuatu, Venezuela, Viet Nam, Yemen, Zambia, Zimbabwe.

Against: France, Israel, Poland, United Kingdom, United States.

Abstaining: Albania, Andorra, Australia, Austria, Azerbaijan, Belgium, Bosnia and Herzegovina, Bulgaria, Canada, Croatia, Czech Republic, Denmark, Estonia, Finland, Georgia, Germany, Greece, Hungary, Iceland, Italy, Latvia, Liechtenstein, Lithuania, Luxembourg, Netherlands, Norway, Palau, Portugal, Republic of Korea, Republic of Moldova, Romania, Russian Federation, San Marino, Serbia and Montenegro, Slovakia, Slovenia, Spain, Switzerland, The former Yugoslav Republic of Macedonia, Turkey.

Missile defence issues

In 2005, the international community continued to address global security challenges stemming from missile defence issues, particularly the related proliferation of long-range ballistic missiles. The United States, whose plans to build a missile defence system [YUN 1999, p. 469] aroused much concern in that regard, continued to develop the system, primarily through its Missile Defense Agency. During the year, the Agency successfully completed two additional interceptor emplacements. By the end of the year, it would achieve a total of 10 Ground-Based Interceptors, with two at the United States Air Force base in Vandenberg, California and at its Army base in Fort Greely, Alaska. The Agency conducted numerous related missile tests in the course of the year and also upgraded integral radar and surveillance systems.

The fifteenth EU-Russia Summit (Moscow, 10 May) pledged to conduct dialogue on developing a legally binding arrangement for a global system of control for the non-proliferation of missiles and their related technology, taking into account the wide subscription to the non-legally binding international code of conduct against ballistic missile proliferation, also known as the Hague Code of Conduct [YUN 2002, p. 504]. The following month, the EU-United States meeting on the joint programme of work on the non-proliferation of WMDs (Washington, 20 June) pledged to increase efforts to promote adherence to the Hague Code of Conduct among other disarmament and non-proliferation arrangements. Expressing similar sentiments in a statement on non-proliferation, the Group of major industrialized countries (G-8) (Scotland, United Kingdom, 6-8 July) called on States accede to the Code, and on DPRK in particular not to contribute to missile proliferation and to maintain indefinitely its moratorium on the launching of missiles.

In June, the subscribing States to the Hague Code of Conduct, at their fourth regular meeting (Vienna, 2-3 June), discussed, among other subjects, confidence-building measures, such as pre-launch notifications and annual declarations. As part of future outreach activities, they considered the need to promote the universalization of the Code in specific regions and also agreed on the text of a draft resolution for consideration by the General Assembly at its sixtieth (2005) session. The fifth regular meeting of the subscribing States was scheduled to be held in Vienna in June 2006 to continue discussions on confidence-building measures and the universalization of the Code. At year's end, subscribing States to the Code numbered 123.

In September, the Missile Technology Control Regime (MTCR)—an informal and voluntary association of countries sharing the goals of non-proliferation of unmanned delivery systems capable of delivering WMDs—at its twentieth plenary meeting (Madrid, Spain, 12-16 September), evaluated trends in missile proliferation, particularly regarding tests and activities of concern in the Middle East and South and East Asia, among other regions. Recognizing that export controls remained an essential tool in addressing missile proliferation, the Plenary renewed its commitment to the strict implementation and enforcement of such controls, including the strengthening of existing rules to respond to technological development and the evolving security environment.

GENERAL ASSEMBLY ACTION

On 8 December [meeting 61], the General Assembly, on the recommendation of the First Committee [A/60/463], adopted **resolution 60/62** by recorded vote (158-1-11) [agenda item 97 (y)].

The Hague Code of Conduct against Ballistic Missile Proliferation

The General Assembly,

Concerned about the increasing regional and global security challenges caused, inter alia, by the ongoing proliferation of ballistic missiles capable of delivering weapons of mass destruction,

Bearing in mind the purposes and principles of the United Nations and its role and responsibility in the field of international peace and security in accordance with the Charter of the United Nations,

Emphasizing the significance of regional and international efforts to prevent and curb comprehensively the proliferation of ballistic missile systems capable of delivering weapons of mass destruction, as a contribution to international peace and security,

Welcoming the adoption of the Hague Code of Conduct against Ballistic Missile Proliferation on 25 November 2002 at The Hague, and convinced that the Code of Conduct will contribute to enhancing transparency and confidence among States,

Recalling its resolution 59/91 of 3 December 2004 entitled "The Hague Code of Conduct against Ballistic Missile Proliferation",

Confirming its commitment to the Declaration on International Cooperation in the Exploration and Use of Outer Space for the Benefit and in the Interest of All States, Taking into Particular Account the Needs of Developing Countries, as contained in the annex to its resolution 51/122 of 13 December 1996,

Recognizing that States should not be excluded from utilizing the benefits of space for peaceful purposes, but that in reaping such benefits and in conducting related cooperation they must not contribute to the proliferation of ballistic missiles capable of carrying weapons of mass destruction,

Mindful of the need to combat the proliferation of weapons of mass destruction and their means of delivery,

1. *Notes with satisfaction* that one hundred and twenty-three States have already subscribed to the Hague Code of Conduct against Ballistic Missile Proliferation as a practical step against the proliferation of weapons of mass destruction and their means of delivery;

2. *Invites* all States that have not yet subscribed to the Code of Conduct to do so;

3. *Encourages* the exploration of further ways and means to deal effectively with the problem of the proliferation of ballistic missiles capable of delivering weapons of mass destruction;

4. *Decides* to include in the provisional agenda of its sixty-first session the item entitled "The Hague Code of Conduct against Ballistic Missile Proliferation".

RECORDED VOTE ON RESOLUTION 60/62:

In favour: Afghanistan, Albania, Andorra, Argentina, Armenia, Australia, Austria, Azerbaijan, Bahamas, Bangladesh, Barbados, Belarus, Belgium, Belize, Benin, Bhutan, Bolivia, Bosnia and Herzegovina, Botswana, Brazil, Brunei Darussalam, Bulgaria, Burkina Faso, Burundi, Cambodia, Cameroon, Canada, Cape Verde, Central African Republic, Chile, China, Colombia, Costa Rica, Côte d'Ivoire, Croatia, Cyprus, Czech Republic, Democratic Republic of the Congo, Denmark, Djibouti, Dominica, Dominican Republic, Ecuador, El Salvador, Eritrea, Estonia, Ethiopia, Fiji, Finland, France, Gabon, Georgia, Germany, Ghana, Greece, Grenada, Guatemala, Guinea, Guinea-Bissau, Guyana, Haiti, Honduras, Hungary, Iceland, Ireland, Israel, Italy, Jamaica, Japan, Jordan, Kazakhstan, Kenya, Kuwait, Kyrgyzstan, Latvia, Lesotho, Liberia, Libyan Arab Jamahiriya, Liechtenstein, Lithuania, Luxembourg, Madagascar, Malawi, Maldives, Mali, Malta, Marshall Islands, Micronesia, Monaco, Mongolia, Morocco, Mozambique, Myanmar, Namibia, Nepal, Netherlands, New Zealand, Nicaragua, Niger, Nigeria, Norway, Oman, Palau, Panama, Papua New Guinea, Paraguay, Peru, Philippines, Poland, Portugal, Qatar, Republic of Korea, Republic of Moldova, Romania, Russian Federation, Saint Lucia, Saint Vincent and the Grenadines, Samoa, San Marino, Sao Tome and Principe, Senegal, Serbia and Montenegro, Sierra Leone, Singapore,

Slovakia, Slovenia, Solomon Islands, Somalia, South Africa, Spain, Sri Lanka, Sudan, Suriname, Sweden, Switzerland, Tajikistan, Thailand, The former Yugoslav Republic of Macedonia, Timor-Leste, Togo, Tonga, Trinidad and Tobago, Tunisia, Turkey, Turkmenistan, Tuvalu, Uganda, Ukraine, United Kingdom, United Republic of Tanzania, United States, Uruguay, Uzbekistan, Vanuatu, Venezuela, Yemen, Zambia, Zimbabwe.

Against: Iran.

Abstaining: Algeria, Cuba, Egypt, India, Indonesia, Lebanon, Malaysia, Mauritius, Mexico, Pakistan, Syrian Arab Republic.

Also on 8 December [meeting 61], the Assembly, on the recommendation of the First Committee [A/60/463], adopted **decision 60/515** by recorded vote (120-2-53) [agenda item 97 *(f)*].

Missiles

At its 61st plenary meeting, on 8 December 2005, the General Assembly, by a recorded vote of 120 to 2, with 53 abstentions, and on the recommendation of the First Committee, recalling its resolutions 54/54 F of 1 December 1999, 55/33 A of 20 November 2000, 56/24 B of 29 November 2001, 57/71 of 22 November 2002, 58/37 of 8 December 2003 and 59/67 of 3 December 2004, decided to include in the provisional agenda of its sixty-first session the item entitled "Missiles".

RECORDED VOTE ON DECISION 60/515

In favour: Afghanistan, Algeria, Antigua and Barbuda, Argentina, Armenia, Bahamas, Bahrain, Bangladesh, Barbados, Belarus, Belize, Benin, Bhutan, Botswana, Brazil, Brunei Darussalam, Burkina Faso, Burundi, Cambodia, Cameroon, Cape Verde, Chile, China, Colombia, Congo, Costa Rica, Côte d'Ivoire, Cuba, Democratic People's Republic of Korea, Democratic Republic of the Congo, Djibouti, Dominica, Dominican Republic, Ecuador, Egypt, El Salvador, Eritrea, Ethiopia, Fiji, Gabon, Ghana, Grenada, Guatemala, Guinea, Guinea-Bissau, Guyana, Haiti, Honduras, India, Indonesia, Iran, Iraq, Jamaica, Jordan, Kazakhstan, Kenya, Kuwait, Kyrgyzstan, Lao People's Democratic Republic, Lebanon, Lesotho, Liberia, Libyan Arab Jamahiriya, Malawi, Malaysia, Maldives, Mali, Mauritania, Mauritius, Mexico, Mongolia, Morocco, Mozambique, Myanmar, Namibia, Nepal, Nicaragua, Nigeria, Oman, Pakistan, Panama, Paraguay, Peru, Philippines, Qatar, Republic of Korea, Russian Federation, Saint Lucia, Saint Vincent and the Grenadines, Saudi Arabia, Senegal, Sierra Leone, Singapore, Solomon Islands, Somalia, South Africa, Sri Lanka, Sudan, Suriname, Syrian Arab Republic, Tajikistan, Thailand, Timor-Leste, Togo, Tonga, Trinidad and Tobago, Tunisia, Turkmenistan, Tuvalu, Uganda, Ukraine, United Arab Emirates, United Republic of Tanzania, Uruguay, Uzbekistan, Venezuela, Viet Nam, Yemen, Zambia, Zimbabwe.

Against: Israel, United States.

Abstaining: Albania, Andorra, Australia, Austria, Azerbaijan, Belgium, Bolivia, Bosnia and Herzegovina, Bulgaria, Canada, Croatia, Cyprus, Czech Republic, Denmark, Estonia, Finland, France, Georgia, Germany, Greece, Hungary, Iceland, Ireland, Italy, Japan, Latvia, Liechtenstein, Lithuania, Luxembourg, Malta, Marshall Islands, Monaco, Netherlands, New Zealand, Norway, Palau, Papua New Guinea, Poland, Portugal, Republic of Moldova, Romania, Samoa, San Marino, Serbia and Montenegro, Slovakia, Slovenia, Spain, Sweden, Switzerland, The former Yugoslav Republic of Macedonia, Turkey, United Kingdom, Vanuatu.

Comprehensive Nuclear-Test-Ban Treaty

Status

As at 31 December, 176 States had signed the 1996 Comprehensive Nuclear-Test-Ban Treaty (CTBT) adopted by General Assembly resolution 50/245 [YUN 1996, p. 454], and 126 had ratified it. During the year, instruments of ratification were deposited by Cook Islands, Djibouti, Haiti, Madagascar, Saint Kitts and Nevis and Vanuatu. In accordance with article XIV, CTBT would enter into force 180 days after the 44 States possessing nuclear reactors, listed in annex 2 of the Treaty,

had deposited their instruments of ratification. By year's end, 33 of those States had ratified the Treaty.

Reports of Secretary-General. In response to General Assembly resolution 59/109 [YUN 2004, p. 539], the Secretary-General submitted a July report [A/60/127] containing information prepared by the Preparatory Commission for the Comprehensive Nuclear-Test-Ban Treaty Organization (CTBTO) (see p. 594) on the efforts of ratifying States towards the Treaty's universalization and possibilities for providing assistance on ratification procedures to States requesting it.

By a 20 July note [A/60/136], the Secretary-General informed the Assembly of the availability of the report of the Commission's Executive Secretary covering its activities in 2004.

Conference on facilitating entry into force

The fourth Conference on Facilitating the Entry into Force of CTBT (New York, 21-23 September) [CTBT-Art.XIV/2005/6] was convened in accordance with article XIV of the Treaty, which stipulated that if the Treaty had not entered into force three years from the date it opened for signature [YUN 1996, p. 452], the depositary should convene a conference at the request of a majority of ratifying States to consider and decide by consensus measures to facilitate an early entry into force. The first such Conference took place in 1999 [YUN 1999, p. 471], the second in 2001 [YUN 2001, p. 482] and the third in 2003 [YUN 2003, p. 547].

The Conference had before it a draft final declaration [CTBT-Art.XIV/2005/WP.1] and a document outlining the activities undertaken by signatory and ratifying States aimed at helping the Treaty take effect [CTBT-Art.XIV/2005/4]. On 23 September, the Conference adopted a Final Declaration and measures to promote the Treaty's entry into force, in which participants called upon States that had not done so to sign and ratify the Treaty promptly, particularly those whose ratification was needed for the Treaty to take effect. As an interim measure, they emphasized the need to maintain voluntary adherence to a moratorium on nuclear weapon test explosions and any other nuclear explosion and called on States to desist from such activities. Acknowledging the scientific and civil benefits of the CTBT verification system being established, participants pledged to consider ways to ensure that those benefits could be broadly shared by the international community, in conformity with the Treaty. They agreed to maintain the practice of selecting one of the ratifying States as a coordinator to promote cooperation through informal consultations with all interested countries aimed at promoting further signatures and ratifications, and that the special representative appointed following the 2003 Conference [YUN 2003, p. 547] would continue to assist the coordinating State in that regard. The Conference recommended that ratifying States consider establishing a trust fund, financed through voluntary contributions, to support an outreach programme for promoting the Treaty, and that the Provisional Technical Secretariat continue to provide States with legal assistance with respect to the ratification process and implementation measures.

GENERAL ASSEMBLY ACTION

On 8 December [meeting 62], the General Assembly, on the recommendation of the First Committee [A/60/469], adopted **resolution 60/95** by recorded vote (172-1-4) [agenda item 103].

Comprehensive Nuclear-Test-Ban Treaty

The General Assembly,

Reiterating that the cessation of nuclear-weapon test explosions or any other nuclear explosions constitutes an effective nuclear disarmament and non-proliferation measure, and convinced that this is a meaningful step in the realization of a systematic process to achieve nuclear disarmament,

Recalling that the Comprehensive Nuclear-Test-Ban Treaty, adopted by its resolution 50/245 of 10 September 1996, was opened for signature on 24 September 1996,

Stressing that a universal and effectively verifiable Comprehensive Nuclear-Test-Ban Treaty constitutes a fundamental instrument in the field of nuclear disarmament and non-proliferation,

Encouraged by the signing of the Treaty by one hundred and seventy-six States, including forty-one of the forty-four needed for its entry into force, and welcoming the ratification of one hundred and twenty-five States, including thirty-three of the forty-four needed for its entry into force, among which there are three nuclear-weapon States,

Recalling its resolution 59/109 of 3 December 2004,

Welcoming the Final Declaration of the fourth Conference on Facilitating the Entry into Force of the Comprehensive Nuclear-Test-Ban Treaty, held in New York from 21 to 23 September 2005, pursuant to article XIV of the Treaty,

1. *Stresses* the importance and urgency of signature and ratification, without delay and without conditions, to achieve the earliest entry into force of the Comprehensive Nuclear-Test-Ban Treaty;

2. *Welcomes* the contributions by the States signatories to the work of the Preparatory Commission for the Comprehensive Nuclear-Test-Ban Treaty Organization, in particular its efforts to ensure that the Treaty's verification regime will be capable of meeting the verification requirements of the Treaty upon its entry into force, in accordance with article IV of the Treaty;

3. *Underlines* the need to maintain momentum towards completion of the verification regime;

4. *Urges* all States to maintain their moratoriums on nuclear-weapon test explosions or any other nuclear explosions and to refrain from acts that would defeat the object and purpose of the Treaty;

5. *Urges* all States that have not yet signed the Treaty to sign and ratify it as soon as possible;

6. *Urges* all States that have signed but not yet ratified the Treaty, in particular those whose ratification is needed for its entry into force, to accelerate their ratification processes with a view to their earliest successful conclusion;

7. *Urges* all States to remain seized of the issue at the highest political level;

8. *Requests* the Secretary-General, in consultation with the Preparatory Commission for the Comprehensive Nuclear-Test-Ban Treaty Organization, to prepare a report on the efforts of States that have ratified the Treaty towards its universalization and possibilities for providing assistance on ratification procedures to States that so request it, and to submit such a report to the General Assembly at its sixty-first session;

9. *Decides* to include in the provisional agenda of its sixty-first session the item entitled "Comprehensive Nuclear-Test-Ban Treaty".

RECORDED VOTE ON RESOLUTION 60/95:

In favour: Afghanistan, Albania, Algeria, Andorra, Angola, Antigua and Barbuda, Argentina, Armenia, Australia, Austria, Azerbaijan, Bahamas, Bahrain, Bangladesh, Barbados, Belarus, Belgium, Belize, Benin, Bhutan, Bolivia, Bosnia and Herzegovina, Botswana, Brazil, Brunei Darussalam, Bulgaria, Burkina Faso, Burundi, Cambodia, Cameroon, Canada, Cape Verde, Central African Republic, Chile, China, Congo, Costa Rica, Côte d'Ivoire, Croatia, Cuba, Cyprus, Czech Republic, Denmark, Djibouti, Dominica, Dominican Republic, Ecuador, Egypt, El Salvador, Eritrea, Estonia, Ethiopia, Fiji, Finland, France, Gabon, Georgia, Germany, Ghana, Greece, Grenada, Guatemala, Guinea, Guinea-Bissau, Guyana, Haiti, Honduras, Hungary, Iceland, Indonesia, Iran, Iraq, Ireland, Israel, Italy, Jamaica, Japan, Jordan, Kazakhstan, Kenya, Kuwait, Kyrgyzstan, Lao People's Democratic Republic, Latvia, Lebanon, Lesotho, Liberia, Libyan Arab Jamahiriya, Liechtenstein, Lithuania, Luxembourg, Madagascar, Malawi, Malaysia, Maldives, Mali, Malta, Marshall Islands, Mauritania, Mexico, Micronesia, Monaco, Mongolia, Morocco, Mozambique, Myanmar, Namibia, Nepal, Netherlands, New Zealand, Nicaragua, Niger, Nigeria, Norway, Oman, Pakistan, Palau, Panama, Papua New Guinea, Paraguay, Peru, Philippines, Poland, Portugal, Qatar, Republic of Korea, Republic of Moldova, Romania, Russian Federation, Saint Lucia, Saint Vincent and the Grenadines, Samoa, San Marino, Saudi Arabia, Senegal, Serbia and Montenegro, Sierra Leone, Singapore, Slovakia, Slovenia, Solomon Islands, Somalia, South Africa, Spain, Sri Lanka, Sudan, Suriname, Sweden, Switzerland, Tajikistan, Thailand, The former Yugoslav Republic of Macedonia, Timor-Leste, Togo, Tonga, Trinidad and Tobago, Tunisia, Turkey, Turkmenistan, Tuvalu, Ukraine, United Arab Emirates, United Kingdom, United Republic of Tanzania, Uruguay, Uzbekistan, Vanuatu, Venezuela, Viet Nam, Yemen, Zambia, Zimbabwe.

Against: United States.

Abstaining: Colombia, India, Mauritius, Syrian Arab Republic.

Preparatory Commission for the CTBT Organization

During the year, the Preparatory Commission for the Comprehensive Nuclear-Test-Ban Treaty Organization (CTBTO), established in 1996 [YUN 1996, p. 452], continued to develop the Treaty's verification regime for monitoring Treaty compliance. Further progress was made in setting up the International Monitoring System (IMS) [YUN 1999, p. 472], the global network of 337 facilities (comprising 321 monitoring stations and 16 related laboratories) in 90 countries designed to detect nuclear explosions prohibited by CTBT via a global satellite communication system. The relevant information would then be transmitted to the International Data Centre (IDC) in Vienna for processing. At year's end, the installation of 219 of those stations (68 per cent) had been completed, 156 of which were certified as meeting the requisite technical requirements. In addition, six laboratories were certified. The development of provisional operation and maintenance processes and procedures continued during the year, and significant progress was made in configuration and information management through the establishment of baseline configuration of certified stations in the database of the technical secretariat. In the course of the year, the number of those stations in IDC operations reached the 50 per cent mark, substantially enhancing the geographic coverage of data being received. Also, some 89 national data centres increased their data processing capacity, resulting in over three million data segments and products being distributed to authorized users. Following the Indian Ocean tsunami disaster of December 2004 [YUN 2004, p. 952], the Preparatory Commission began testing the usefulness of IMS data in the context of a tsunami alert.

During the first part of its twenty-fourth session, the Preparatory Commission held a special session (Vienna, 4 March) [CTBT/PC-24/1] to consider its possible contribution to tsunami warning and other alert systems. It tasked its provisional technical secretariat to explore with national and international tsunami warning organizations recognized by the United Nations Educational, Scientific and Cultural Organization (UNESCO) data and products that could be provided by the secretariat for tsunami warning. The Commission held the main part of its twenty-fourth (27-28 June) [CTBT/PC-24/3] and its twenty-fifth (14 September, 17 October, 14-18 November) [CTBT/PC-25/1, CTBT/PC-25/2, CTBT/PC-25/3] sessions, both in Vienna, to consider the reports of its working groups and to discuss organizational, budgetary and other matters. The Commission adopted its 2006 programme budget in the combined amounts of $50,894,000 and 44,437,900 euros, of which approximately $30 million and 12 million euros were earmarked for the IMS network.

Prohibition of the use of nuclear weapons

In 2005, the Conference on Disarmament remained unable to undertake negotiations on a convention on the prohibition of the use of nuclear weapons, as called for in General Assembly resolution 59/102 [YUN 2004, p. 540], owing to the impasse among delegates over a programme of work.

The Assembly, in **resolution 60/88** (see below), reiterated its request to the Conference to commence negotiations in order to reach agreement on such a convention, and to report thereon.

GENERAL ASSEMBLY ACTION

On 8 December [meeting 62], the General Assembly, on the recommendation of the First Committee [A/60/464], adopted **resolution 60/88** by recorded vote (111-49-13) [agenda item 98 (*f*)].

Convention on the Prohibition of the Use of Nuclear Weapons

The General Assembly,

Convinced that the use of nuclear weapons poses the most serious threat to the survival of mankind,

Bearing in mind the advisory opinion of the International Court of Justice of 8 July 1996 on the *Legality of the Threat or Use of Nuclear Weapons,*

Convinced that a multilateral, universal and binding agreement prohibiting the use or threat of use of nuclear weapons would contribute to the elimination of the nuclear threat and to the climate for negotiations leading to the ultimate elimination of nuclear weapons, thereby strengthening international peace and security,

Conscious that some steps taken by the Russian Federation and the United States of America towards a reduction of their nuclear weapons and the improvement in the international climate can contribute towards the goal of the complete elimination of nuclear weapons,

Recalling that, in paragraph 58 of the Final Document of the Tenth Special Session of the General Assembly, it is stated that all States should actively participate in efforts to bring about conditions in international relations among States in which a code of peaceful conduct of nations in international affairs could be agreed upon and that would preclude the use or threat of use of nuclear weapons,

Reaffirming that any use of nuclear weapons would be a violation of the Charter of the United Nations and a crime against humanity, as declared in its resolutions 1653(XVI) of 24 November 1961, 33/71 B of 14 December 1978, 34/83 G of 11 December 1979, 35/152 E of 12 December 1980 and 36/92 I of 9 December 1981,

Determined to achieve an international convention prohibiting the development, production, stockpiling and use of nuclear weapons, leading to their ultimate destruction,

Stressing that an international convention on the prohibition of the use of nuclear weapons would be an important step in a phased programme towards the complete elimination of nuclear weapons, with a specified framework of time,

Noting with regret that the Conference on Disarmament, during its 2005 session, was unable to undertake negotiations on this subject as called for in General Assembly resolution 59/102 of 3 December 2004,

1. *Reiterates its request* to the Conference on Disarmament to commence negotiations in order to reach agreement on an international convention prohibiting the use or threat of use of nuclear weapons under any circumstances;

2. *Requests* the Conference on Disarmament to report to the General Assembly on the results of those negotiations.

In favour: Afghanistan, Algeria, Angola, Antigua and Barbuda, Bahamas, Bahrain, Bangladesh, Barbados, Belize, Benin, Bhutan, Bolivia, Botswana, Brazil, Brunei Darussalam, Burkina Faso, Burundi, Cambodia, Cameroon, Cape Verde, Central African Republic, Chile, China, Colombia, Congo, Costa Rica, Côte d'Ivoire, Cuba, Democratic People's Republic of Korea, Djibouti, Dominica, Dominican Republic, Ecuador, Egypt, El Salvador, Eritrea, Ethiopia, Fiji, Gabon, Ghana, Grenada, Guatemala, Guinea, Guyana, Haiti, Honduras, India, Indonesia, Iran, Iraq, Jamaica, Jordan, Kenya, Kuwait, Lao People's Democratic Republic, Lebanon, Lesotho, Liberia, Libyan Arab Jamahiriya, Madagascar, Malawi, Malaysia, Maldives, Mali, Mauritania, Mauritius, Mexico, Mongolia, Morocco, Mozambique, Myanmar, Namibia, Nepal, Nicaragua, Niger, Nigeria, Oman, Pakistan, Panama, Paraguay, Peru, Philippines, Qatar, Saint Lucia, Saint Vincent and the Grenadines, Samoa, Saudi Arabia, Senegal, Singapore, Somalia, South Africa, Sri Lanka, Sudan, Suriname, Syrian Arab Republic, Thailand, Timor-Leste, Togo, Tonga, Trinidad and Tobago, Tunisia, Turkmenistan, United Arab Emirates, United Republic of Tanzania, Uruguay, Vanuatu, Venezuela, Viet Nam, Yemen, Zambia, Zimbabwe.

Against: Albania, Andorra, Australia, Austria, Belgium, Bosnia and Herzegovina, Bulgaria, Canada, Croatia, Cyprus, Czech Republic, Denmark, Estonia, Finland, France, Georgia, Germany, Greece, Hungary, Iceland, Ireland, Israel, Italy, Latvia, Liechtenstein, Lithuania, Luxembourg, Malta, Marshall Islands, Micronesia, Monaco, Netherlands, New Zealand, Norway, Palau, Poland, Portugal, Romania, San Marino, Serbia and Montenegro, Slovakia, Slovenia, Spain, Sweden, Switzerland, The former Yugoslav Republic of Macedonia, Turkey, United Kingdom, United States.

Abstaining: Argentina, Armenia, Azerbaijan, Belarus, Japan, Kazakhstan, Kyrgyzstan, Republic of Korea, Republic of Moldova, Russian Federation, Tajikistan, Ukraine, Uzbekistan.

Advisory opinion of the International Court of Justice

Pursuant to General Assembly resolution 59/83 [YUN 2004, p. 541] on the advisory opinion of the International Court of Justice (ICJ) that the threat or use of nuclear weapons was contrary to the UN Charter [YUN 1996, p. 461], the Secretary-General presented information received from six States (Chile, Guatemala, Japan, Mexico, Panama, Syrian Arab Republic) on measures they had taken to implement the resolution and towards nuclear disarmament [A/60/122].

GENERAL ASSEMBLY ACTION

On 8 December [meeting 61], the General Assembly, on the recommendation of the First Committee [A/60/463], adopted **resolution 60/76** by recorded vote (126-29-24) [agenda item 97 *(q)*].

Follow-up to the advisory opinion of the International Court of Justice on the
Legality of the Threat or Use of Nuclear Weapons

The General Assembly,

Recalling its resolutions 49/75 K of 15 December 1994, 51/45 M of 10 December 1996, 52/38 O of 9 December 1997, 53/77 W of 4 December 1998, 54/54 Q of 1 December 1999, 55/33 X of 20 November 2000, 56/24 S of 29 November 2001, 57/85 of 22 November 2002, 58/46 of 8 December 2003 and 59/83 of 3 December 2004,

Convinced that the continuing existence of nuclear weapons poses a threat to all humanity and that their use would have catastrophic consequences for all life on Earth, and recognizing that the only defence against a nuclear catastrophe is the total elimination of nuclear weapons and the certainty that they will never be produced again,

Reaffirming the commitment of the international community to the goal of the total elimination of nuclear weapons and the creation of a nuclear-weapon-free world,

Mindful of the solemn obligations of States parties, undertaken in article VI of the Treaty on the Non-Proliferation of Nuclear Weapons, particularly to pursue negotiations in good faith on effective measures relating to cessation of the nuclear-arms race at an early date and to nuclear disarmament,

Recalling the principles and objectives for nuclear non-proliferation and disarmament adopted at the 1995 Review and Extension Conference of the Parties to the Treaty on the Non-Proliferation of Nuclear Weapons,

Emphasizing the unequivocal undertaking by the nuclear-weapon States to accomplish the total elimination of their nuclear arsenals leading to nuclear disarmament, adopted at the 2000 Review Conference of the Parties to the Treaty on the Non Proliferation of Nuclear Weapons,

Recalling the adoption of the Comprehensive Nuclear-Test-Ban Treaty in its resolution 50/245 of 10 September 1996, and expressing its satisfaction at the increasing number of States that have signed and ratified the Treaty,

Recognizing with satisfaction that the Antarctic Treaty and the treaties of Tlatelolco, Rarotonga, Bangkok and Pelindaba are gradually freeing the entire southern hemisphere and adjacent areas covered by those treaties from nuclear weapons,

Stressing the importance of strengthening all existing nuclear-related disarmament and arms control and reduction measures,

Recognizing the need for a multilaterally negotiated and legally binding instrument to assure non nuclear-weapon States against the threat or use of nuclear weapons,

Reaffirming the central role of the Conference on Disarmament as the sole multilateral disarmament negotiating forum, and regretting the lack of progress in disarmament negotiations, particularly nuclear disarmament, in the Conference during its 2005 session,

Emphasizing the need for the Conference on Disarmament to commence negotiations on a phased programme for the complete elimination of nuclear weapons with a specified framework of time,

Expressing its regret over the failure of the 2005 Review Conference of the Parties to the Treaty on the Non-Proliferation of Nuclear Weapons to reach agreement on any substantive issues,

Expressing its deep concern at the lack of progress in the implementation of the thirteen steps to implement article VI of the Treaty on the Non-Proliferation of Nuclear Weapons agreed to at the 2000 Review Conference of the Parties to the Treaty on the Non-Proliferation of Nuclear Weapons,

Desiring to achieve the objective of a legally binding prohibition of the development, production, testing, deployment, stockpiling, threat or use of nuclear weapons and their destruction under effective international control,

Recalling the advisory opinion of the International Court of Justice on the *Legality of the Threat or Use of Nuclear Weapons,* issued on 8 July 1996,

Taking note of the relevant portions of the report of the Secretary-General relating to the implementation of resolution 59/83,

1. *Underlines once again* the unanimous conclusion of the International Court of Justice that there exists an obligation to pursue in good faith and bring to a conclusion negotiations leading to nuclear disarmament in all its aspects under strict and effective international control;

2. *Calls once again upon* all States immediately to fulfil that obligation by commencing multilateral negotiations leading to an early conclusion of a nuclear weapons convention prohibiting the development, production, testing, deployment, stockpiling, transfer, threat or use of nuclear weapons and providing for their elimination;

3. *Requests* all States to inform the Secretary-General of the efforts and measures they have taken on the implementation of the present resolution and nuclear disarmament, and requests the Secretary-General to apprise the General Assembly of that information at its sixty-first session;

4. *Decides* to include in the provisional agenda of its sixty-first session the item entitled "Follow-up to the advisory opinion of the International Court of Justice on the *Legality of the Threat or Use of Nuclear Weapons*".

RECORDED VOTE ON RESOLUTION 60/76:

In favour: Afghanistan, Algeria, Antigua and Barbuda, Argentina, Bahamas, Bahrain, Bangladesh, Barbados, Belize, Bhutan, Bolivia, Botswana, Brazil, Brunei Darussalam, Burkina Faso, Burundi, Cambodia, Cameroon, Cape Verde, Central African Republic, Chile, China, Colombia, Congo, Costa Rica, Côte d'Ivoire, Cuba, Democratic People's Republic of Korea, Democratic Republic of the Congo, Djibouti, Dominica, Dominican Republic, Ecuador, Egypt, El Salvador, Eritrea, Ethiopia, Fiji, Gabon, Germany, Ghana, Grenada, Guatemala, Guinea, Guinea-Bissau, Guyana, Haiti, Honduras, India, Indonesia, Iran, Iraq, Ireland, Jamaica, Jordan, Kenya, Kuwait, Lao People's Democratic Republic, Lebanon, Lesotho, Liberia, Libyan Arab Jamahiriya, Madagascar, Malawi, Malaysia, Maldives, Mali, Malta, Mauritania, Mauritius, Mexico, Mongolia, Morocco, Mozambique, Myanmar, Namibia, Nepal, New Zealand, Nicaragua, Niger, Nigeria, Oman, Pakistan, Panama, Papua New Guinea, Paraguay, Peru, Philippines, Qatar, Saint Lucia, Saint Vincent and the Grenadines, Samoa, San Marino, Sao Tome and Principe, Saudi Arabia, Senegal, Sierra Leone, Singapore, Solomon Islands, Somalia, South Africa, Sri Lanka, Sudan, Suriname, Sweden, Syrian Arab Republic, Tajikistan, Thailand, Timor-Leste, Togo, Tonga, Trinidad and Tobago, Tunisia, Turkmenistan, Tuvalu, Uganda, Ukraine, United Arab Emirates, United Republic of Tanzania, Uruguay, Vanuatu, Venezuela, Viet Nam, Yemen, Zambia, Zimbabwe.

Against: Albania, Belgium, Bulgaria, Czech Republic, Denmark, France, Georgia, Greece, Hungary, Iceland, Israel, Italy, Latvia, Lithuania, Luxembourg, Monaco, Netherlands, Norway, Palau, Poland, Portugal, Romania, Russian Federation, Slovakia, Slovenia, Spain, Turkey, United Kingdom, United States.

Abstaining: Andorra, Armenia, Australia, Austria, Azerbaijan, Belarus, Bosnia and Herzegovina, Canada, Croatia, Cyprus, Estonia, Finland, Japan, Kazakhstan, Kyrgyzstan, Liechtenstein, Marshall Islands, Micronesia, Republic of Korea, Republic of Moldova, Serbia and Montenegro, Switzerland, The former Yugoslav Republic of Macedonia, Uzbekistan.

The First Committee adopted paragraph 1 by a recorded vote of 142 to 3, with 5 abstentions. The Assembly retained the paragraph by a recorded vote of 165 to 3, with 4 abstentions.

Non-proliferation issues

Non-Proliferation Treaty

Status

In 2005, the number of States party to the 1968 Treaty on the Non-Proliferation of Nuclear Weapons (NPT), adopted by the General Assembly in resolution 2373(XXII) [YUN 1968, p. 17], remained at 189. NPT entered into force on 5 March 1970.

NPT Review Conference

The 2005 Review Conference of the Parties to the Treaty on the Non-Proliferation of Nuclear Weapons (New York, 2-27 May) [NPT/CONF.2005/57] was held to review the Treaty's operation, as provided for in article VIII, paragraph 3, and in accordance with General Assembly resolution 56/24 O [YUN 2001, p. 483] and with the decisions of the 1995 Review Conference [YUN 1995, p. 189], which extended NPT indefinitely and provided for further review conferences at five-year intervals. Previous quinquennial review conferences took place in 1975 [YUN 1975, p. 27], 1980 [YUN 1980, p. 51], 1985 [YUN 1985, p. 56], 1990 [YUN 1990, p. 50], 1995 [YUN 1995, p. 189] and 2000 [YUN 2000, p. 487].

The Preparatory Committee for the 2005 Conference had met in 2002 [YUN 2002, p. 507], 2003 [YUN 2003, p. 549] and 2004 [YUN 2004, p. 542].

Participants at the Conference included 153 States parties and Palestine as an observer, representatives of the United Nations, the International Atomic Energy Agency (IAEA), regional and intergovernmental organizations, research institutes and non-governmental organizations (NGOs). The Conference established three Main Committees and corresponding subsidiary bodies, a Drafting Committee and a Credentials Committee. Substantive issues were to be discussed by the Main Committees, including a review of the implementation of the Treaty's provisions relating to the non-proliferation of nuclear weapons, disarmament and international peace and security; security assurances; and the Treaty's role in promoting the non-proliferation of nuclear weapons, nuclear disarmament in strengthening international peace and security and measures aimed at strengthening the implementation of the Treaty and achieving its universality. The issue of Treaty withdrawal was also accorded special consideration, in the light of DPRK's withdrawal from the Treaty, its previous non-compliance with its non-proliferation obligations and most importantly, its announcement earlier in the year that it had manufactured nuclear weapons. Unfortunately, deliberations within the Main Committees, based on working papers presented by the Chairman, were undermined by pronounced disagreements among the parties on procedural issues and over all the substantive agenda items on nuclear non-proliferation and disarmament-related questions, particularly the language in which to address key aspects of the issues under review. Consequently, the Conference was not able to achieve a consensus outcome on any of the substantive issues on its agenda concerning the review of the implementation of the Treaty's provisions. On 27 May, the Conference adopted a Final Document, which merely outlined its organizational and procedural arrangements and a summary record of its proceedings.

Several States parties, disappointed at the outcome of the Conference, stressed the need to strengthen the Treaty and to address the challenges facing it. Nonetheless, the President of the Conference concluded that the proceedings strengthened his conviction that NPT still enjoyed the strong support of all States parties.

Related events held during the Conference included a meeting on verification pursuant to the NPT: concluding safeguards agreements and additional protocols, sponsored by the IAEA (5 May); a workshop which considered the question "why do States abandon nuclear weapons ambitions?", sponsored by Finland on behalf of the Weapons of Mass Destruction Commission (9 May); a workshop on United Nations capacity for monitoring weapons of mass destruction, sponsored by New Zealand (10 May); a presentation on verification by the United Kingdom (10 May); and a meeting on transparency and accountability in nuclear arms, sponsored by Germany (17 May).

Communications. Ministers for Foreign Affairs of the Non-Aligned Movement, at a special meeting (Doha, Qatar, 13 June) [A/59/880], expressed disappointment over the inability of the Review Conference to reach consensus on the substantive questions relating to NPT. Noting that its members had acted in good faith to advance positions towards strengthening the Treaty, the Ministers pointed to the unwillingness of some States, including certain nuclear-weapon States, to honour their previous obligations and commitments in nuclear disarmament and non-proliferation.

On 26 July [A/60/415], the Foreign Ministers of Australia, Chile, Indonesia, Norway, Romania, South Africa and the United Kingdom issued a joint declaration on disarmament and non-proliferation expressing their disappointment at the outcome of the 2005 Review Conference and calling on all States to take a strong stand on disarmament and non-proliferation at the High-Level Plenary Meeting of the General Assembly (2005 World Summit) (see p. 47). A large number of countries from all regions expressed support for the initiative.

GENERAL ASSEMBLY ACTION

On 8 December [meeting 61], the General Assembly, on the recommendation of the First Com-

mittee [A/60/463], adopted **resolution 60/72** by recorded vote (87-56-26) [agenda item 97].

Follow-up to nuclear disarmament obligations agreed to at the 1995 and 2000 Review Conferences of the Parties to the Treaty on the Non-Proliferation of Nuclear Weapons

The General Assembly,

Recalling its various resolutions in the field of nuclear disarmament, including its most recent, resolutions 59/77, 59/83 and 59/102 of 3 December 2004,

Bearing in mind its resolution 2373(XXII) of 12 June 1968, the annex to which contains the Treaty on the Non-Proliferation of Nuclear Weapons,

Noting the provisions of article VIII, paragraph 3, of the Treaty regarding the convening of review conferences at five-year intervals,

Recalling its resolution 50/70 Q of 12 December 1995, in which the General Assembly noted that the States parties to the Treaty affirmed the need to continue to move with determination towards the full realization and effective implementation of the provisions of the Treaty, and accordingly adopted a set of principles and objectives,

Recalling also that, on 11 May 1995, the 1995 Review and Extension Conference of the Parties to the Treaty on the Non-Proliferation of Nuclear Weapons adopted three decisions on strengthening the review process for the Treaty, principles and objectives for nuclear non-proliferation and disarmament, and extension of the Treaty,

Reaffirming the resolution on the Middle East adopted on 11 May 1995 by the 1995 Review and Extension Conference of the Parties to the Treaty, in which the Conference reaffirmed the importance of the early realization of universal adherence to the Treaty and placement of nuclear facilities under full-scope International Atomic Energy Agency safeguards,

Reaffirming also its resolution 55/33 D of 20 November 2000, in which the General Assembly welcomed the adoption by consensus on 19 May 2000 of the Final Document of the 2000 Review Conference of the Parties to the Treaty on the Non-Proliferation of Nuclear Weapons, including, in particular, the documents entitled "Review of the operation of the Treaty, taking into account the decisions and the resolution adopted by the 1995 Review and Extension Conference" and "Improving the effectiveness of the strengthened review process for the Treaty",

Taking into consideration the unequivocal undertaking by the nuclear-weapon States, in the Final Document of the 2000 Review Conference of the Parties to the Treaty, to accomplish the total elimination of their nuclear arsenals leading to nuclear disarmament, to which all States parties to the Treaty are committed under article VI of the Treaty,

Gravely concerned over the failure of the 2005 Review Conference of the Parties to the Treaty to reach any substantive agreement on the follow-up to the nuclear disarmament obligations,

1. *Determines* to pursue practical steps for systematic and progressive efforts to implement article VI of the Treaty on the Non-Proliferation of Nuclear Weapons and paragraphs 3 and 4 *(c)* of the decision on principles and objectives for nuclear non-proliferation and

disarmament of the 1995 Review and Extension Conference of the Parties to the Treaty;

2. *Calls for* practical steps, as agreed to at the 2000 Review Conference of the Parties to the Treaty, to be taken by all nuclear-weapon States that would lead to nuclear disarmament in a way that promotes international stability and, based upon the principle of undiminished security for all, for:

(a) Further efforts to be made by the nuclear-weapon States to reduce their nuclear arsenals unilaterally;

(b) Increased transparency by the nuclear-weapon States with regard to nuclear weapons capabilities and the implementation of agreements pursuant to article VI of the Treaty and as a voluntary confidence-building measure to support further progress in nuclear disarmament;

(c) The further reduction of non-strategic nuclear weapons, based on unilateral initiatives and as an integral part of the nuclear arms reduction and disarmament process;

(d) Concrete agreed measures to reduce further the operational status of nuclear weapons systems;

(e) A diminishing role for nuclear weapons in security policies so as to minimize the risk that these weapons will ever be used and to facilitate the process of their total elimination;

(f) The engagement, as soon as appropriate, of all the nuclear-weapon States in the process leading to the total elimination of their nuclear weapons;

3. *Notes* that the 2000 Review Conference of the Parties to the Treaty agreed that legally binding security assurances by the five nuclear-weapon States to the non-nuclear-weapon States parties to the Treaty strengthen the nuclear non-proliferation regime;

4. *Urges* the States parties to the Treaty to follow up on the implementation of the nuclear disarmament obligations under the Treaty agreed to at the 1995 and 2000 Review Conferences of the Parties to the Treaty within the framework of the 2010 Review Conference of the Parties to the Treaty and its preparatory committee;

5. *Decides* to include in the provisional agenda of its sixty-second session an item entitled "Follow-up to nuclear disarmament obligations agreed to at the 1995 and 2000 Review Conferences of the Parties to the Treaty on the Non-Proliferation of Nuclear Weapons".

RECORDED VOTE ON RESOLUTION 60/72:

In favour: Algeria, Antigua and Barbuda, Bahamas, Bahrain, Bangladesh, Barbados, Belize, Benin, Bhutan, Botswana, Brazil, Brunei Darussalam, Burkina Faso, Cambodia, Cuba, Democratic People's Republic of Korea, Democratic Republic of the Congo, Djibouti, Dominica, Egypt, Eritrea, Fiji, Gabon, Ghana, Grenada, Guinea, Guyana, Haiti, Indonesia, Iran, Iraq, Jamaica, Jordan, Kazakhstan, Kenya, Kuwait, Kyrgyzstan, Lao People's Democratic Republic, Lebanon, Lesotho, Libyan Arab Jamahiriya, Malawi, Malaysia, Maldives, Mali, Mauritania, Mauritius, Mongolia, Morocco, Mozambique, Myanmar, Namibia, Nepal, Nigeria, Oman, Philippines, Qatar, Saint Lucia, Saint Vincent and the Grenadines, Sao Tome and Principe, Saudi Arabia, Senegal, Sierra Leone, Singapore, Solomon Islands, Somalia, South Africa, Sri Lanka, Sudan, Suriname, Syrian Arab Republic, Tajikistan, Thailand, Togo, Trinidad and Tobago, Tunisia, Turkmenistan, Uganda, United Arab Emirates, United Republic of Tanzania, Uruguay, Uzbekistan, Venezuela, Viet Nam, Yemen, Zambia, Zimbabwe.

Against: Albania, Andorra, Australia, Austria, Belgium, Bosnia and Herzegovina, Bulgaria, Canada, Croatia, Cyprus, Czech Republic, Denmark, Estonia, Finland, France, Georgia, Germany, Greece, Hungary, Iceland, Ireland, Israel, Italy, Japan, Latvia, Liechtenstein, Lithuania, Luxembourg, Malta, Marshall Islands, Micronesia, Monaco, Netherlands, New Zealand, Norway, Palau, Poland, Portugal, Republic of Korea, Republic of Moldova, Romania, Russian Federation, Samoa, San Marino, Serbia and Montenegro, Slovakia, Slovenia, Spain, Sweden, Switzerland, The former Yugoslav Republic of Macedonia, Turkey, Ukraine, United Kingdom, United States, Vanuatu.

Abstaining: Argentina, Armenia, Belarus, Bolivia, Burundi, Chile, China, Colombia, Costa Rica, Côte d'Ivoire, Dominican Republic, Ecuador, El Salvador, Ethiopia, Guatemala, Honduras, India, Liberia, Mexico, Nicaragua, Niger, Pakistan, Panama, Papua New Guinea, Paraguay, Peru.

Non-proliferation of weapons of mass destruction

In his March report to the 2005 World Summit entitled "In larger freedom: towards development, security and human rights for all" [A/59/2005 & Add.1] (see p. 67), the Secretary-General highlighted the security challenges relating to nuclear, chemical and biological weapons and multilateral efforts to tackle them. He noted in particular that while NPT currently faced a crisis of confidence and compliance owing to increasing strain on verification and enforcement, the Conference on Disarmament faced a similar crisis of relevance, resulting partly from dysfunctional decision-making procedures and consequent paralysis. He stressed that progress in disarmament and non-proliferation was essential and that neither should be held hostage. While recognizing the disarmament efforts of nuclear-weapon States, the Secretary-General said the unique status of those States also entailed a unique responsibility to do more, including but not limited to further reductions in their arsenals of non-strategic nuclear weapons and pursuing arms control agreements that entailed both dismantlement and irreversibility. In addition, they should reaffirm their commitment to negative security assurances. Swift negotiation of a fissile material cut-off treaty was essential and the moratorium on nuclear test explosions should be upheld until the entry into force of CTBT (see p. 593).

Noting the fact that the technology required for civilian nuclear fuel could also be used to develop nuclear weapons, the Secretary-General said that, while the access of non-nuclear-weapon States to the benefits of nuclear technology for peaceful purposes should not be curtailed, there was a need to focus on creating incentives for States to forgo voluntarily the development of domestic uranium enrichment and plutonium separation capacities. Recent efforts to supplement NPT as the foundation of the non-proliferation regime should be welcomed, including Security Council resolution 1540(2004) [YUN 2004, p. 544], which was designed to prevent non-State actors from acquiring WMDs and their means of delivery, and the Proliferation Security Initiative [YUN 2003, p. 536], under which States were cooperating to prevent illicit trafficking in WMDs. Also, Member States should adopt effective national export controls covering missiles and other means of WMD delivery, rockets and shoulder-fired missiles, as well as banning their transfer to non-State actors. The Secretary-General stated that his capacity to investigate the suspected use of biological agents, as authorized by the General Assembly, should also be strengthened to incorporate the latest technology and expertise. Adding that the Security Council should be better informed on all matters relevant to nuclear, chemical and biological threats, the Secretary-General encouraged the Council to invite regularly the Directors-General of IAEA and of the Organization for the Prohibition of Chemical Weapons (OPCW) to brief it on the status of safeguards and verification processes. The Secretary-General declared his readiness, in consultation with the Director-General of the World Health Organization (WHO), to use his powers under Article 99 of the UN Charter to call the Council's attention to any overwhelming outbreak of infectious diseases that threatened international peace and security.

Security Council Committee on WMDs. On 7 January [S/2005/11], the Security Council President informed the Secretary-General that the Council had taken note of his intention, announced in 2004 [YUN 2004, p. 545], to appoint four experts to assist the Council Committee established pursuant to resolution 1540(2004) [ibid., p. 544] to monitor the implementation of measures set out in that resolution to combat the proliferation of WMDs and their means of delivery. On 6 May [S/2005/299], the Secretary-General informed the Council of his appointment of an additional four experts to facilitate the Committee's work.

During the year, the Committee became fully operational and began the substantive part of its work. In April [S/PV.5168], July [S/PV.5229] and October [S/PV.5293 & Corr.1], the Committee Chairman briefed the Council on the Committee's programme of work for the year, a key aspect of which related to the examination of national reports, as called for in resolution 1540(2004).

On 25 April [meeting 5168], the Council, in Presidential statement **S/PRST/2005/16** (see p. 109), invited the Committee to pursue its undertakings in accordance with its approved programme of work and called on States that had not done so to submit national reports as soon as possible. In subsequent action on 20 July [meeting 5229], the Council, in Presidential statement **S/PRST/2005/34** (see p. 110), encouraged the Committee to enhance cooperation with related Council bodies and other organizations, with a view to developing best practices to provide clarity and guidance to States on the implementation of relevant resolutions.

On 19 December [S/2005/799], the Committee Chairman submitted a consolidated report on the Committee's activities and the results achieved during the period from 1 January to 16 December. The report indicated that 124 States had submitted national reports, 42 of which were subsequently updated in response to the Chairman's request for additional information. Having determined in that regard that some States might require technical assistance from international organizations with the requisite expertise, particularly IAEA and OPCW, the Committee facilitated the process for providing such assistance through cooperation with competent organizations. To further improve its work, it accorded priority to transparency by maintaining regular contacts with Member States and undertaking joint briefings with other Council bodies. It also undertook awareness-raising activities, the most notable being the first regional seminar for countries of Latin America and the Caribbean entitled "Advancing the implementation of Security Council resolution 1540(2004)", which was organized jointly by Argentina and the United Kingdom (Buenos Aires, Argentina, 26-28 September) and designed to promote better understanding of the objectives of that resolution and of the steps to be taken in implementing it. The Committee also promoted its outreach programme in Africa and Eurasia and participated in a number of related international meetings, including the second World Conference of Speakers of Parliaments (New York, 7-9 September) the workshop entitled "The Global Bargain for Biosecurity and Health" (Kampala, Uganda, 28 September–1 October), and the Seventh International Export Control Conference organized jointly by the United States and Sweden (Stockholm, Sweden, 20-22 September), which considered recent export control initiatives and ways to strengthen non-proliferation efforts globally.

The Committee Chairman noted that, although the Committee had achieved the targets set out in its 2005 work programmes, full implementation of resolution 1540(2004) by all States through national legislation and measures to enforce such legislation was a long-term objective that went beyond the Committee's current mandate. Continuous efforts would be required at the national, regional and international levels to provide capacity-building and assistance.

New types of weapons of mass destruction

In 2005, the persisting disagreement among delegates over a programme of work again prevented the Conference on Disarmament [A/60/27] from establishing any mechanism to consider any of its agenda items, including the item on "New types of weapons of mass destruction and new systems of such weapons; radiological weapons". As a result, the topic was addressed only during plenary meetings when delegations reaffirmed their respective positions on the item.

The General Assembly, in resolution 60/46 (see below), reaffirmed the need to prevent the emergence of new types of weapons of mass destruction and asked the Conference on Disarmament to keep the matter under review.

GENERAL ASSEMBLY ACTION

On 8 December [meeting 61], the Assembly, on the recommendation of the First Committee [A/60/453], adopted **resolution 60/46** by recorded vote (180-1-1) [agenda item 87].

Prohibition of the development and manufacture of new types of weapons of mass destruction and new systems of such weapons: report of the Conference on Disarmament

The General Assembly,

Recalling its previous resolutions on the prohibition of the development and manufacture of new types of weapons of mass destruction and new systems of such weapons,

Recalling also its resolutions 51/37 of 10 December 1996, 54/44 of 1 December 1999 and 57/50 of 22 November 2002 relating to the prohibition of the development and manufacture of new types of weapons of mass destruction and new systems of such weapons,

Recalling further paragraph 77 of the Final Document of the Tenth Special Session of the General Assembly,

Determined to prevent the emergence of new types of weapons of mass destruction that have characteristics comparable in destructive effect to those of weapons of mass destruction identified in the definition of weapons of mass destruction adopted by the United Nations in 1948,

Noting the desirability of keeping the matter under review, as appropriate,

1. *Reaffirms* that effective measures should be taken to prevent the emergence of new types of weapons of mass destruction;

2. *Requests* the Conference on Disarmament, without prejudice to further overview of its agenda, to keep the matter under review, as appropriate, with a view to making, when necessary, recommendations on undertaking specific negotiations on identified types of such weapons;

3. *Calls upon* all States, immediately following any recommendations of the Conference on Disarmament, to give favourable consideration to those recommendations;

4. *Requests* the Secretary-General to transmit to the Conference on Disarmament all documents relating to the consideration of this item by the General Assembly at its sixtieth session;

5. *Requests* the Conference on Disarmament to report the results of any consideration of the matter in its annual reports to the General Assembly;

6. *Decides* to include in the provisional agenda of its sixty-third session the item entitled "Prohibition of the

development and manufacture of new types of weapons of mass destruction and new systems of such weapons: report of the Conference on Disarmament".

RECORDED VOTE ON RESOLUTION 60/46:

In favour: Afghanistan, Albania, Algeria, Andorra, Antigua and Barbuda, Argentina, Armenia, Australia, Austria, Azerbaijan, Bahamas, Bahrain, Bangladesh, Barbados, Belarus, Belgium, Belize, Benin, Bhutan, Bolivia, Bosnia and Herzegovina, Botswana, Brazil, Brunei Darussalam, Bulgaria, Burkina Faso, Burundi, Cambodia, Cameroon, Canada, Cape Verde, Central African Republic, Chad, Chile, China, Colombia, Comoros, Congo, Costa Rica, Côte d'Ivoire, Croatia, Cuba, Cyprus, Czech Republic, Democratic People's Republic of Korea, Democratic Republic of the Congo, Denmark, Djibouti, Dominica, Dominican Republic, Ecuador, Egypt, El Salvador, Eritrea, Estonia, Ethiopia, Fiji, Finland, France, Gabon, Georgia, Germany, Ghana, Greece, Grenada, Guatemala, Guinea, Guinea-Bissau, Guyana, Haiti, Honduras, Hungary, Iceland, India, Indonesia, Iran, Iraq, Ireland, Italy, Jamaica, Japan, Jordan, Kazakhstan, Kenya, Kuwait, Kyrgyzstan, Lao People's Democratic Republic, Latvia, Lebanon, Lesotho, Liberia, Libyan Arab Jamahiriya, Liechtenstein, Lithuania, Luxembourg, Madagascar, Malawi, Malaysia, Maldives, Mali, Malta, Marshall Islands, Mauritania, Mauritius, Mexico, Micronesia, Monaco, Mongolia, Morocco, Mozambique, Myanmar, Namibia, Nepal, Netherlands, New Zealand, Nicaragua, Niger, Nigeria, Norway, Oman, Pakistan, Palau, Panama, Papua New Guinea, Paraguay, Peru, Philippines, Poland, Portugal, Qatar, Republic of Korea, Republic of Moldova, Romania, Russian Federation, Saint Lucia, Saint Vincent and the Grenadines, Samoa, San Marino, Sao Tome and Principe, Saudi Arabia, Senegal, Serbia and Montenegro, Sierra Leone, Singapore, Slovakia, Slovenia, Solomon Islands, Somalia, South Africa, Spain, Sri Lanka, Sudan, Suriname, Sweden, Switzerland, Syrian Arab Republic, Tajikistan, Thailand, The former Yugoslav Republic of Macedonia, Timor-Leste, Togo, Tonga, Trinidad and Tobago, Tunisia, Turkey, Turkmenistan, Tuvalu, Uganda, Ukraine, United Arab Emirates, United Kingdom, United Republic of Tanzania, Uruguay, Uzbekistan, Vanuatu, Venezuela, Viet Nam, Yemen, Zambia, Zimbabwe.

Against: United States.

Abstaining: Israel.

Terrorism and WMDs

In 2005, the United Nations maintained efforts to address the growing threat to global peace and stability posed by international terrorism, particularly the risk of acquisition and use by terrorists of WMDs. In January, the Counter-Terrorism Committee, established pursuant to Security Council resolution 1373(2001) [YUN 2001, p. 61] (see p. 107), continued to implement its mandate to monitor Member States' efforts to combat terrorism.

In his March report to the 2005 World Summit (see p. 67), the Secretary-General determined that terrorism and weapons of mass destruction were among the threats to peace and security in the twenty-first century and threatened all that the United Nations stood for. As such, he outlined a strategy for dealing with it, based on five pillars: dissuading people from resorting to terrorism or supporting it; denying terrorists access to funds and materials; deterring States from sponsoring terrorism; developing State capacity to defeat terrorism; and defending human rights.

In April, the General Assembly adopted by consensus, in resolution 59/290 (see p. 1411), the International Convention for the Suppression of Acts of Nuclear Terrorism. By the terms of the Convention, Member States were called upon to develop legal frameworks criminalizing nuclear terrorism-related offenses and to promote international cooperation in investigating and prosecuting offenders. In other action, the Assembly, in resolution 60/78 (see below) requested the Secretary-General to report on measures already taken by international organizations regarding the linkage between the fight against terrorism and WMD proliferation, and to seek Member States' views on additional measures for tackling the threat. Focusing on radiological terrorism, the Assembly, in resolution 60/73 (see p. 603), called on Member States to support international efforts to prevent the acquisition and use by terrorists of radioactive materials and sources. In July, the Security Council, in resolution 1617(2005) on threats to international peace and security caused by terrorist acts (see p. 410) expressed concern over the possible use by Al-Qaida or the Taliban and their associates of chemical, biological, radiation or nuclear weapons and material and emphasized the need for the effective implementation of the sanctions imposed against them. In an August report [A/60/285] to the Assembly, the Advisory Board on Disarmament Matters highlighted the urgency of addressing proliferation challenges stemming from States' possible acquisition of nuclear weapons under the cover of peaceful nuclear activities and related terrorists threats.

IAEA, in an effort to strengthen the Convention on the Physical Protection of Nuclear Material [YUN 1980, p. 161], convened a conference of the States parties (Vienna, 4-8 July) [GOV/INF/2005/10-GC(49)/INF/6], which adopted by consensus a number of amendments to the Convention. The first changed its title to "Convention on the Physical Protection of Nuclear Material and Nuclear Facilities", thereby extending its scope to cover the protection of nuclear facilities and the domestic transport, storage and use of nuclear material. Other amendments revised and fortified many of the Convention's principles and provisions. On 30 September, the IAEA General Conference, in a resolution [GC(49)/RES/10] on nuclear security: measures to protect against nuclear terrorism, welcomed those amendments, encouraged the States parties to ratify them and appealed to States that had not done so to adhere to the Convention. In the same resolution [GC(49)/RES/10], the Conference called on Member States to provide political, financial and technical support to improve nuclear and radiological security and prevent related terrorism. Also in September [GC(49)17], the IAEA Board of Governors approved a new nuclear security plan for 2006-2009, which outlined measures and activities planned to help prevent nuclear and radiological terrorism.

Report of Secretary-General. In accordance with General Assembly resolution 59/80 [YUN 2004, p. 577], the Secretary-General, in an August report, with a later addendum [A/60/185 & Add.1], presented the views of 10 Member States and 11 international organizations, including UN agencies, on measures they had taken to prevent terrorists from acquiring WMDs.

GENERAL ASSEMBLY ACTION

On 8 December [meeting 61], the General Assembly, on the recommendation of the First Committee [A/60/463], adopted **resolution 60/78** without vote [agenda item 97 *(p)*].

Measures to prevent terrorists from acquiring weapons of mass destruction

The General Assembly,

Recalling its resolution 59/80 of 3 December 2004,

Recognizing the determination of the international community to combat terrorism, as evidenced in relevant General Assembly and Security Council resolutions,

Deeply concerned by the growing risk of linkages between terrorism and weapons of mass destruction, and in particular by the fact that terrorists may seek to acquire weapons of mass destruction,

Cognizant of the steps taken by States to implement Security Council resolution 1540(2004) on the non-proliferation of weapons of mass destruction, adopted on 28 April 2004,

Welcoming the adoption, by consensus, of the International Convention for the Suppression of Acts of Nuclear Terrorism on 13 April 2005,

Welcoming also the adoption, by consensus, of amendments to strengthen the Convention on the Physical Protection of Nuclear Material by the International Atomic Energy Agency on 8 July 2005,

Noting the support expressed in the Final Document of the Thirteenth Conference of Heads of State or Government of Non-Aligned Countries, which was held in Kuala Lumpur from 20 to 25 February 2003, and in the Final Document of the Fourteenth Ministerial Conference of the Movement of Non-Aligned Countries, which was held in Durban, South Africa, from 17 to 19 August 2004, for measures to prevent terrorists from acquiring weapons of mass destruction,

Noting also that the Group of Eight, the European Union, the Regional Forum of the Association of Southeast Asian Nations and others have taken into account in their deliberations the dangers posed by the acquisition by terrorists of weapons of mass destruction, and the need for international cooperation in combating it,

Acknowledging the consideration of issues relating to terrorism and weapons of mass destruction by the Advisory Board on Disarmament Matters,

Taking note of resolution GC(49)/RES/10, adopted on 30 September 2005 by the General Conference of the International Atomic Energy Agency at its forty-ninth regular session,

Taking note also of the report of the Policy Working Group on the United Nations and Terrorism,

Taking note further of the report of the Secretary-General, submitted pursuant to paragraphs 2 and 4 of resolution 59/80,

Mindful of the urgent need for addressing, within the United Nations framework and through international cooperation, this threat to humanity,

Emphasizing that progress is urgently needed in the area of disarmament and non-proliferation in order to help to maintain international peace and security and to contribute to global efforts against terrorism,

1. *Calls upon* all Member States to support international efforts to prevent terrorists from acquiring weapons of mass destruction and their means of delivery;

2. *Invites* all Member States to consider signing and ratifying the International Convention for the Suppression of Acts of Nuclear Terrorism in order to bring about its early entry into force;

3. *Urges* all Member States to take and strengthen national measures, as appropriate, to prevent terrorists from acquiring weapons of mass destruction, their means of delivery and materials and technologies related to their manufacture, and invites them to inform the Secretary-General, on a voluntary basis, of the measures taken in this regard;

4. *Encourages* cooperation among and between Member States and relevant regional and international organizations for strengthening national capacities in this regard;

5. *Requests* the Secretary-General to compile a report on measures already taken by international organizations on issues relating to the linkage between the fight against terrorism and the proliferation of weapons of mass destruction, to seek the views of Member States on additional relevant measures for tackling the global threat posed by the acquisition by terrorists of weapons of mass destruction and to report to the General Assembly at its sixty-first session;

6. *Decides* to include in the provisional agenda of its sixty-first session the item entitled "Measures to prevent terrorists from acquiring weapons of mass destruction".

On the same date [meeting 61], the Assembly, on the recommendation of the First Committee [A/60/463], adopted **resolution 60/73** without vote [agenda item 97].

Preventing the risk of radiological terrorism

The General Assembly,

Recognizing the essential contribution of radioactive materials and sources to social and economic development, and the benefits drawn from their use for all States,

Recognizing also the determination of the international community to combat terrorism, as evident in relevant General Assembly and Security Council resolutions,

Deeply concerned by the threat of terrorism and the risk that terrorists may acquire, traffic in or use radioactive materials or sources in radiological dispersion devices,

Recalling the importance of international conventions aimed at preventing and suppressing such a risk, in particular the International Convention for the Sup-

pression of Acts of Nuclear Terrorism, adopted on 13 April 2005,

Noting that actions of the international community to combat the proliferation of weapons of mass destruction and prevent access by non-State actors to weapons of mass destruction and related material, notably Security Council resolution 1540(2004) of 28 April 2004, constitute contributions to the protection against nuclear and radiological terrorism,

Stressing the importance of the role of the International Atomic Energy Agency in promoting and reinforcing the safety and security of radioactive materials and sources, in particular by supporting the improvement of national legal and regulatory infrastructure,

Taking note of the importance of the Joint Convention on the Safety of Spent Fuel Management and on the Safety of Radioactive Waste Management with respect to the safety of the end of life of radioactive sources,

Taking note also of the importance of the Code of Conduct on the Safety and Security of Radioactive Sources as a valuable instrument for enhancing the safety and security of radioactive sources, while recognizing that the Code is not a legally binding instrument, and of the International Atomic Energy Agency Revised Action Plan for the Safety and Security of Radioactive Sources and its Nuclear Security Plan for 2006-2009,

Taking note further of resolutions GC(49)/RES/9 and GC(49)/RES/10, adopted by the General Conference of the International Atomic Energy Agency at its forty-ninth regular session, which address measures to strengthen international cooperation in nuclear, radiation and transport safety and waste management and measures to protect against nuclear and radiological terrorism,

Welcoming the ongoing individual and collective efforts of Member States to take into account in their deliberations the dangers posed by the lack or insufficiency of control over radioactive materials and sources, and recognizing the need for States to take more effective measures to strengthen those controls in accordance with their national legal authorities and legislation and consistent with international law,

Welcoming also the fact that Member States have undertaken multilateral actions to address this issue, as reflected in General Assembly resolution 57/9 of 11 November 2002,

Welcoming further the contribution of the International Atomic Energy Agency International Conference on the Safety and Security of Radioactive Sources: Towards a Global System for the Continuous Control of Sources throughout Their Life Cycle, held in Bordeaux, France, from 27 June to 1 July 2005, to the activities of the Agency on these issues,

Mindful of the need for addressing, within the United Nations framework and through international cooperation, this rising concern for international security,

1. *Calls upon* Member States to support international efforts to prevent the acquisition and use by terrorists of radioactive materials and sources, and, if necessary, suppress such acts, in accordance with their national legal authorities and legislation and consistent with international law;

2. *Urges* Member States to take and strengthen national measures, as appropriate, to prevent the acquisition and use by terrorists of radioactive materials and sources as well as terrorist attacks on nuclear plants and facilities which would result in radioactive releases, and, if necessary, suppress such acts, in particular by taking effective measures to account for, secure and physically protect such high-risk materials in accordance with their international obligations;

3. *Invites* all Member States that have not yet done so to sign and ratify the International Convention for the Suppression of Acts of Nuclear Terrorism;

4. *Invites* Member States to support and endorse the efforts of the International Atomic Energy Agency to enhance the safety and security of radioactive sources, as described in the Agency's Nuclear Security Plan for 2006-2009, urges all States to work towards following the guidance contained in the Agency Code of Conduct on the Safety and Security of Radioactive Sources, including, as appropriate, the guidance on the import and export of radioactive sources, noting that the guidance is complementary to the Code, and encourages Member States to notify the Director General of the Agency of their intention to do so pursuant to resolution GC(48)/RES/10 of the General Conference of the Agency, recognizes the value of information exchange on national approaches to controlling radioactive sources, and encourages consultations by the secretariat of the Agency with its member States with a view to establishing a formalized process for a periodic exchange of information and lessons learned and for the evaluation of progress made by States towards implementing the provisions of the Code;

5. *Encourages* cooperation among and between Member States and through relevant international and, where appropriate, regional organizations for strengthening national capacities in this regard;

6. *Decides* to include in the provisional agenda of its sixty-second session an item entitled "Preventing the risk of radiological terrorism".

Multilateralism in disarmament and non-proliferation

Report of Secretary-General. In response to General Assembly resolution 59/69 [YUN 2004, p. 546], the Secretary-General, in a July report, with a later addendum [A/60/98 & Add.1], presented replies received from 10 Governments regarding the promotion of multilateralism in the area of disarmament and non-proliferation.

Other developments. On 13 May [S/2005/521], the Indian Parliament passed the Weapons of Mass Destruction and their Delivery System (Prohibition of Unlawful Activities) Bill, prohibiting unlawful activities in relation to WMDs and fulfilling India's obligations pursuant to Security Council resolution 1540(2004) [YUN 2004, p. 544].

In a 2 June statement [CD/1750], Poland summarized the 2005 activities undertaken to promote the Proliferation Security Initiative (PSI), including a number of naval, air and ground interdiction exercises and other measures to improve information exchange and cooperation between the participating countries' special services, border and customs officers. Launched in Krakow, Poland, in 2003 [YUN 2003, p. 536], PSI was intended to combat the proliferation of WMDs by searching suspicious land, air and sea vessels and to confiscate any illegal weapons on board. Over 60 countries were involved. In commemoration of the second anniversary of the founding of PSI, United States President George W. Bush urged all States to join the global campaign by endorsing the Initiative's principle of interdiction and by committing to working to end the security threat posed by WMD proliferation.

The EU and the United States, at their 2005 summit (Washington, D.C., 20 June), adopted a declaration on enhancing cooperation in the field of non-proliferation and the fight against terrorism, by which they pledged to further strengthen measures against the spread of WMDs by State and non-State actors; and to respond more effectively to related threats, particularly with regard to the policies and activities of Iran and DPRK. They also adopted an EU–United States joint programme of work on the non-proliferation of WMDs.

At the fifteenth plenary meeting of the Nuclear Suppliers Group (Oslo, Norway, 23-24 June), the 45 participating States analysed current proliferation challenges, particularly those posed by DPRK and Iran, and declared their readiness to cooperate in implementing Security Council resolution 1540(2004) [YUN 2004, p. 544]. They also adopted measures to further strengthen their national export controls.

The Group of major industrialized countries G-8 (Scotland, United Kingdom, 6-8 July) adopted a statement on non-proliferation emphasizing their determination to meet related challenges decisively, through national efforts and effective multilateralism. They reaffirmed their commitment to their 2002 Global Partnership against the Proliferation of Weapons and Materials of Mass Destruction [YUN 2002, p. 494], under which they had pledged to support cooperative projects addressing non-proliferation, disarmament, counter-terrorism and nuclear safety issues, and renewed their pledge to raise up to $20 billion towards that end by 2012.

On 18 July, United States President George W. Bush and Indian Prime Minister Manmohan Singh, in a joint statement, announced the establishment of a global partnership to promote stability, democracy, prosperity and peace in the world, and to provide global leadership in areas of mutual concern and interest, including on non-proliferation and security questions.

On 24 October [A/60/549], the People's Council of Turkmenistan adopted a statement of support of international initiatives to combat the proliferation of WMDs, in which, among other things, it announced the country's prohibition of the use of its sovereign airspace for the transportation of those weapons and related materials, as well as missiles and missile technology.

On 17 November, the European Parliament adopted a resolution on the non-proliferation of WMDs, by which it called for, among other things, preventing the proliferation of ballistic missiles with extended range and greater accuracy; developing and enforcing effective export and transit controls and reinforcing border security to limit the risk of sensitive WMD-related materials falling into the wrong hands; fostering the role of the UN Security Council and enhancing expertise in meeting the challenge of proliferation; and strengthening effective multilateralism in addressing non-proliferation questions.

GENERAL ASSEMBLY ACTION

On 8 December [meeting 61], the General Assembly, on the recommendation of the First Committee [A/60/463], adopted **resolution 60/59** by recorded vote (122-8-50) [agenda item 97 (h)].

Promotion of multilateralism in the area of disarmament and non-proliferation

The General Assembly,

Determined to foster strict respect for the purposes and principles enshrined in the Charter of the United Nations,

Recalling its resolution 56/24 T of 29 November 2001 on multilateral cooperation in the area of disarmament and non-proliferation and global efforts against terrorism and other relevant resolutions, as well as its resolutions 57/63 of 22 November 2002, 58/44 of 8 December 2003 and 59/69 of 3 December 2004 on promotion of multilateralism in the area of disarmament and non-proliferation,

Recalling also the purpose of the United Nations to maintain international peace and security and, to that end, to take effective collective measures for the prevention and removal of threats to the peace and for the suppression of acts of aggression or other breaches of the peace, and to bring about by peaceful means, and in conformity with the principles of justice and international law, adjustment or settlement of international disputes or situations which might lead to a breach of the peace, as enshrined in the Charter,

Recalling further the United Nations Millennium Declaration, which states, inter alia, that the responsibility for managing worldwide economic and social development, as well as threats to international peace and security, must be shared among the nations of the world and should be exercised multilaterally and that, as the most universal and most representative organization in the world, the United Nations must play the central role,

Convinced that, in the globalization era and with the information revolution, arms regulation, non-proliferation and disarmament problems are more than ever the concern of all countries in the world, which are affected in one way or another by these problems and, therefore, should have the possibility to participate in the negotiations that arise to tackle them,

Bearing in mind the existence of a broad structure of disarmament and arms regulation agreements resulting from non-discriminatory and transparent multilateral negotiations with the participation of a large number of countries, regardless of their size and power,

Aware of the need to advance further in the field of arms regulation, non-proliferation and disarmament on the basis of universal, multilateral, non-discriminatory and transparent negotiations with the goal of reaching general and complete disarmament under strict international control,

Recognizing the complementarity of bilateral, plurilateral and multilateral negotiations on disarmament,

Recognizing also that the proliferation and development of weapons of mass destruction, including nuclear weapons, are among the most immediate threats to international peace and security which need to be dealt with, with the highest priority,

Considering that the multilateral disarmament agreements provide the mechanism for States parties to consult one another and to cooperate in solving any problems which may arise in relation to the objective of, or in the application of, the provisions of the agreements and that such consultations and cooperation may also be undertaken through appropriate international procedures within the framework of the United Nations and in accordance with the Charter,

Stressing that international cooperation, the peaceful settlement of disputes, dialogue and confidence-building measures would contribute essentially to the creation of multilateral and bilateral friendly relations among peoples and nations,

Being concerned at the continuous erosion of multilateralism in the field of arms regulation, non-proliferation and disarmament, and recognizing that a resort to unilateral actions by Member States in resolving their security concerns would jeopardize international peace and security and undermine confidence in the international security system as well as the foundations of the United Nations itself,

Reaffirming the absolute validity of multilateral diplomacy in the field of disarmament and non-proliferation, and determined to promote multilateralism as an essential way to develop arms regulation and disarmament negotiations,

1. *Reaffirms* multilateralism as the core principle in negotiations in the area of disarmament and non-proliferation with a view to maintaining and strengthening universal norms and enlarging their scope;

2. *Also reaffirms* multilateralism as the core principle in resolving disarmament and non-proliferation concerns;

3. *Urges* the participation of all interested States in multilateral negotiations on arms regulation, non-proliferation and disarmament in a non-discriminatory and transparent manner;

4. *Underlines* the importance of preserving the existing agreements on arms regulation and disarmament, which constitute an expression of the results of international cooperation and multilateral negotiations in response to the challenges facing mankind;

5. *Calls once again upon* all Member States to renew and fulfil their individual and collective commitments to multilateral cooperation as an important means of pursuing and achieving their common objectives in the area of disarmament and non-proliferation;

6. *Requests* the States parties to the relevant instruments on weapons of mass destruction to consult and cooperate among themselves in resolving their concerns with regard to cases of non-compliance as well as on implementation, in accordance with the procedures defined in those instruments, and to refrain from resorting or threatening to resort to unilateral actions or directing unverified non-compliance accusations against one another to resolve their concerns;

7. *Takes note* of the report of the Secretary-General containing the replies of Member States on the promotion of multilateralism in the area of disarmament and non-proliferation, submitted pursuant to resolution 59/69;

8. *Requests* the Secretary-General to seek the views of Member States on the issue of the promotion of multilateralism in the area of disarmament and non-proliferation and to submit a report thereon to the General Assembly at its sixty-first session;

9. *Decides* to include in the provisional agenda of its sixty-first session the item entitled "Promotion of multilateralism in the area of disarmament and non-proliferation".

RECORDED VOTE ON RESOLUTION 60/59:

In favour: Afghanistan, Algeria, Antigua and Barbuda, Azerbaijan, Bahamas, Bahrain, Bangladesh, Barbados, Belarus, Belize, Benin, Bhutan, Bolivia, Botswana, Brazil, Brunei Darussalam, Burkina Faso, Burundi, Cambodia, Cameroon, Cape Verde, Central African Republic, Chile, China, Colombia, Comoros, Congo, Costa Rica, Côte d'Ivoire, Cuba, Democratic People's Republic of Korea, Democratic Republic of the Congo, Djibouti, Dominica, Dominican Republic, Ecuador, Egypt, El Salvador, Eritrea, Ethiopia, Fiji, Gabon, Ghana, Grenada, Guatemala, Guinea, Guinea-Bissau, Guyana, Haiti, Honduras, India, Indonesia, Iran, Iraq, Jamaica, Jordan, Kazakhstan, Kenya, Kuwait, Kyrgyzstan, Lao People's Democratic Republic, Lebanon, Lesotho, Liberia, Libyan Arab Jamahiriya, Madagascar, Malawi, Malaysia, Maldives, Mali, Mauritania, Mauritius, Mexico, Mongolia, Morocco, Mozambique, Myanmar, Namibia, Nepal, Nicaragua, Niger, Nigeria, Oman, Pakistan, Panama, Paraguay, Peru, Philippines, Qatar, Russian Federation, Saint Lucia, Saint Vincent and the Grenadines, Sao Tome and Principe, Saudi Arabia, Senegal, Sierra Leone, Singapore, Solomon Islands, Somalia, South Africa, Sri Lanka, Sudan, Suriname, Syrian Arab Republic, Tajikistan, Thailand, Timor-Leste, Togo, Trinidad and Tobago, Tunisia, Turkmenistan, Tuvalu, Uganda, United Arab Emirates, United Republic of Tanzania, Uruguay, Uzbekistan, Venezuela, Viet Nam, Yemen, Zambia, Zimbabwe.

Against: Albania, France, Israel, Latvia, Marshall Islands, Micronesia, United Kingdom, United States.

Abstaining: Andorra, Argentina, Armenia, Australia, Austria, Belgium, Bosnia and Herzegovina, Bulgaria, Canada, Croatia, Cyprus, Czech Republic, Denmark, Estonia, Finland, Georgia, Germany, Greece, Hungary, Iceland, Ireland, Italy, Japan, Liechtenstein, Lithuania, Luxembourg, Malta, Monaco, Netherlands, New Zealand, Norway, Palau, Papua New Guinea, Poland, Portugal, Republic of Korea, Republic of Moldova, Romania, Samoa, San Marino, Serbia and Montenegro, Slovakia, Slovenia, Spain, Sweden, Switzerland, The former Yugoslav Republic of Macedonia, Turkey, Ukraine, Vanuatu.

IAEA safeguards

As at 31 December, the Model Protocol Additional to Safeguards Agreements strengthening the safeguards regime of IAEA, approved by the Agency's Board of Governors in 1997 [YUN 1997, p. 486], had been signed and/or approved by 113 States, including the five nuclear-weapon States, and was in force or being provisionally applied in 73 States.

As in previous years, the IAEA General Conference [GC(49)/RES/13] requested concerned States and other parties to safeguard agreements, including nuclear-weapon States, that had not done so to sign additional protocols promptly and bring them into force as soon as possible, in conformity with their national legislation. The Conference called for innovative technological solutions to strengthen the effectiveness of safeguards and for cooperation among member States to facilitate the exchange of equipment, material and scientific and technological information for implementing those protocols. It commended member States, notably Japan, that had implemented elements of a plan of action first outlined in a 2000 resolution of the Conference [YUN 2000, p. 505] and updated in February 2005, and recommended that other member States consider such action to facilitate the entry into force of comprehensive safeguards agreements and additional protocols.

In 2005, international anxiety over DPRK's nuclear status rose markedly in the wake of its 10 February announcement that it had manufactured nuclear weapons and its continued denial of access to IAEA to verify that it had declared all nuclear material subject to Agency safeguards. Consequently, the Agency remained unable to draw any conclusions or provide assurances about nuclear material or activities in the country. In a 4 August report to the General Conference [GC(49)/13], the Director General noted that DPRK's nuclear activities outside international verification were a serious challenge to the nuclear non-proliferation regime and its admission; that it possessed nuclear weapons was a matter of the utmost concern, with serious security implications. On 30 September [GC(49)/RES/14], the General Conference, while expressing concern over the DPRK's official statement that it had nuclear weapons, welcomed progress at the six-party talks (see p. 450) toward the goal of the verifiable denucleariation of the Korean Peninsula and called on the DPRK to cooperate with the Agency in the full and effective implementation of comprehensive IAEA safeguards.

On 1 August [INFCIRC/648], Iran notified IAEA that it had decided to resume uranium conversion, which it had suspended voluntarily in 2003 as a confidence-building measure and as part of an agreement with France, Germany and the United Kingdom to promote transparency, cooperation and access to nuclear and other advanced technology. It had taken that action because it had received little in return for the expansion of its voluntary confidence-building measures and had not gained the expected benefit of unrestricted access to advanced nuclear technology. Nonetheless, it would continue to abide by its obligations under the NPT. In a 9 August statement to the IAEA Board of Governors, issued on behalf of the EU, the United Kingdom expressed regret about Iran's actions at a time when outstanding questions about its nuclear programme had yet to be resolved and new questions about its plutonium-related activities had arisen. It asked the Board to react firmly. On 11 August [GOV/2005/64], the Board urged Iran to reestablish full suspension of all enrichment-related activities on the same voluntary and non-legally binding basis as requested in previous Board resolutions and to permit the Director General to reinstate seals that had been removed at its Uranium Conversion Facility in Esfahan. On 24 September [GOV/2005/77], the Board, having considered a situation report by the Director General [GOV/2005/67], found that Iran's history of concealment of its nuclear activities and related issues and the resulting lack of confidence in its nuclear programme being exclusively for peaceful purposes, had raised questions that were within the competence of the Security Council. It urged Iran to suspend all enrichment-related and reprocessing activity in order to help the Director General resolve outstanding questions and provide necessary assurances and to return to the negotiating process. On 18 November [GOV/2005/87], the Director General reported that, although Iran had provided access to necessary documentation and other information relating to its procurement network, it needed to become more transparent in providing data on the procurement of dual use equipment and in permitting visits to relevant military facilities and research and development locations.

Concerning Iraq, the Director General, in a 26 September statement to the General Conference, said that IAEA's mandate under various Security Council resolutions to maintain inspections of Iraq's nuclear programme remained in effect in 2005 and the Agency's future work in that regard was expected to be guided by the Council's planned review of the mandate, as indicated in resolution 1546(2004) [YUN 2004, p. 548]. Pending that review, the Agency had reduced to a minimum the staff of its Iraq Nuclear Verification Office (INVO). He hoped the review would be undertaken as soon as possible.

Note by Secretary-General. In August [A/60/204], the Secretary-General informed the General Assembly of the availability of the forty-ninth report of IAEA [GC(49)/5] covering its 2004 activities.

Communication. On 1 November [A/C.1/60/5], the DPRK alleged that the United States and the United Kingdom, in arguments made in the First Committee of the General Assembly regarding the nuclear issue on the Korean Peninsula, had attempted to mislead world opinion by urging the DPRK to dismantle its nuclear weapons programme unconditionally, in accordance with the Beijing joint statement under the six-party talks (see p. 450), as though it carried the obligation of only the DPRK. The denuclearization of the Peninsula could not be achieved only through the unilateral abandonment by the DPRK of its nuclear programmes.

Middle East

In 2005, the General Assembly (see below) and the IAEA General Conference [GC(49)/RES/15] took action regarding the risk of nuclear proliferation in the Middle East. While the Assembly continued to call on the non-party in the region to place all its nuclear facilities under IAEA safeguards, IAEA reaffirmed the need for States in the region to accept the application of full-scope Agency safeguards to all their nuclear activities.

In response to Assembly resolution 59/106 [YUN 2004, p. 549], the Secretary-General reported in October [A/60/126 (Part II)] that, apart from the IAEA resolution on the application of IAEA safeguards in the Middle East, which was annexed to his report, he had not received any additional information since his 2004 report [YUN 2004, p. 549].

On 8 December [meeting 62], the General Assembly, on the recommendation of the First Committee [A/60/466], adopted **resolution 60/92** by recorded vote (164-5-5) [agenda item 100].

The risk of nuclear proliferation in the Middle East

The General Assembly,

Bearing in mind its relevant resolutions,

Taking note of the relevant resolutions adopted by the General Conference of the International Atomic Energy Agency, the latest of which is resolution GC(49)/RES/15 adopted on 30 September 2005,

Cognizant that the proliferation of nuclear weapons in the region of the Middle East would pose a serious threat to international peace and security,

Mindful of the immediate need for placing all nuclear facilities in the region of the Middle East under full-scope safeguards of the Agency,

Recalling the decision on principles and objectives for nuclear non-proliferation and disarmament adopted by the 1995 Review and Extension Conference of the Parties to the Treaty on the Non-Proliferation of Nuclear Weapons on 11 May 1995, in which the Conference urged universal adherence to the Treaty as an urgent priority and called upon all States not yet parties to the Treaty to accede to it at the earliest date, particularly those States that operate unsafeguarded nuclear facilities,

Recognizing with satisfaction that, in the Final Document of the 2000 Review Conference of the Parties to the Treaty on the Non-Proliferation of Nuclear Weapons, the Conference undertook to make determined efforts towards the achievement of the goal of universality of the Treaty, called upon those remaining States not parties to the Treaty to accede to it, thereby accepting an international legally binding commitment not to acquire nuclear weapons or nuclear explosive devices and to accept Agency safeguards on all their nuclear activities, and underlined the necessity of universal adherence to the Treaty and of strict compliance by all parties with their obligations under the Treaty,

Recalling the resolution on the Middle East adopted by the 1995 Review and Extension Conference on 11 May 1995, in which the Conference noted with concern the continued existence in the Middle East of unsafeguarded nuclear facilities, reaffirmed the importance of the early realization of universal adherence to the Treaty and called upon all States in the Middle East that had not yet done so, without exception, to accede to the Treaty as soon as possible and to place all their nuclear facilities under full-scope Agency safeguards,

Noting that Israel remains the only State in the Middle East that has not yet become party to the Treaty,

Concerned about the threats posed by the proliferation of nuclear weapons to the security and stability of the Middle East region,

Stressing the importance of taking confidence-building measures, in particular the establishment of a nuclear-weapon-free zone in the Middle East, in order to enhance peace and security in the region and to consolidate the global non-proliferation regime,

Emphasizing the need for all parties directly concerned to consider seriously taking the practical and urgent steps required for the implementation of the proposal to establish a nuclear-weapon-free zone in the region of the Middle East in accordance with the relevant resolutions of the General Assembly and, as a means of promoting this objective, inviting the countries concerned to adhere to the Treaty and, pending the establishment of the zone, to agree to place all their nuclear activities under Agency safeguards,

Noting that one hundred and seventy-six States have signed the Comprehensive Nuclear-Test-Ban Treaty, including a number of States in the region,

1. *Welcomes* the conclusions on the Middle East of the 2000 Review Conference of the Parties to the Treaty on the Non-Proliferation of Nuclear Weapons;

2. *Reaffirms* the importance of Israel's accession to the Treaty on the Non-Proliferation of Nuclear Weapons and placement of all its nuclear facilities under comprehensive International Atomic Energy Agency safeguards, in realizing the goal of universal adherence to the Treaty in the Middle East;

3. *Calls upon* that State to accede to the Treaty without further delay and not to develop, produce, test or otherwise acquire nuclear weapons, and to renounce possession of nuclear weapons, and to place all its unsafeguarded nuclear facilities under full-scope Agency safeguards as an important confidence-building measure among all States of the region and as a step towards enhancing peace and security;

4. *Requests* the Secretary-General to report to the General Assembly at its sixty-first session on the implementation of the present resolution;

5. *Decides* to include in the provisional agenda of its sixty-first session the item entitled "The risk of nuclear proliferation in the Middle East".

RECORDED VOTE ON RESOLUTION 60/92:

In favour: Afghanistan, Albania, Algeria, Andorra, Angola, Antigua and Barbuda, Argentina, Armenia, Austria, Azerbaijan, Bahamas, Bahrain, Bangladesh, Barbados, Belarus, Belgium, Belize, Benin, Bhutan, Bolivia, Bosnia and Herzegovina, Botswana, Brazil, Brunei Darussalam, Bulgaria, Burkina Faso, Cambodia, Canada, Cape Verde, Central African Republic, Chile, China, Colombia, Congo, Costa Rica, Côte d'Ivoire, Croatia, Cuba, Cyprus, Czech Republic, Democratic People's Republic of Korea, Denmark, Djibouti, Dominica, Dominican Republic, Ecuador, Egypt, El Salvador, Eritrea, Estonia, Fiji, Finland, France, Gabon, Georgia, Germany, Ghana, Greece, Grenada, Guatemala, Guinea, Guyana, Haiti, Honduras, Hungary, Iceland, Indonesia, Iran, Iraq, Ireland, Italy, Jamaica, Japan, Jordan, Kazakhstan, Kenya, Kuwait, Kyrgyzstan, Lao People's Democratic Republic, Latvia, Lebanon, Lesotho, Liberia, Libyan Arab Jamahiriya, Liechtenstein, Lithuánia, Luxembourg, Madagascar, Malawi, Malaysia, Maldives, Mali, Malta, Mauritania, Mauritius, Mexico, Monaco, Mongolia, Morocco, Mozambique, Myanmar, Namibia, Nepal, Netherlands, New Zealand, Nicaragua, Niger, Nigeria, Norway, Oman, Pakistan, Panama, Paraguay, Peru, Philippines, Poland, Portugal, Qatar, Republic of Korea, Republic of Moldova, Romania, Russian Federation, Saint Lucia, Saint Vincent and the Grenadines, Samoa, San Marino, Saudi Arabia, Senegal, Serbia and Montenegro, Sierra Leone, Singapore, Slovakia, Slovenia, Somalia, South Africa, Spain, Sri Lanka, Sudan, Suriname, Sweden, Switzerland, Syrian Arab Republic, Tajikistan, Thailand, The former Yugoslav Republic of Macedonia, Timor-Leste, Togo, Trinidad and Tobago, Tunisia, Turkey, Turkmenistan, Tuvalu, Ukraine, United Arab Emirates, United Kingdom, United Republic of Tanzania, Uruguay, Uzbekistan, Vanuatu, Venezuela, Viet Nam, Yemen, Zambia, Zimbabwe.

Against: Israel, Marshall Islands, Micronesia, Palau, United States.

Abstaining: Australia, Cameroon, Ethiopia, India, Tonga.

The First Committee adopted the sixth preambular paragraph by a separate recorded vote of 145 to 2, with 5 abstentions. The Assembly retained the paragraph by a recorded vote of 162 to 2, with 6 abstentions.

Radioactive waste

To enhance the safe transport of radioactive material, IAEA updated its comprehensive training manual on transport safety to include the latest requirements of the Agency's Transport Regulations. In June, the IAEA Board of Governors approved a new policy for reviewing and revising those Regulations every two years to strengthen their effectiveness and enable member States to more easily harmonize national regulations with them. In September [GC/49/RES/9], the IAEA General Conference encouraged a wider participation in the review process by concerned member States. Recognizing concerns about the potential for damage in the event of an accident while transporting radioactive materials by sea, including pollution of the marine environment, the Conference urged member States that did not have national regulatory documents governing the transport of those materials to adopt them and ensure that they conformed with the amended edition of the IAEA Transport Regulations. During the year, a number of international organizations and carriers, including the International Maritime Organization (IMO), the International Civil Aviation Organization (ICAO) and the International Federation of Air Line Pilots Associations addressed the issue of denial of shipments of radioactive materials intended for use in medical diagnosis and treatment.

Conferences. In 2005, IAEA organized two international conferences on the safety of radioactive materials: the international conference on the safety and security of radioactive sources: towards a global system for the continuous control over sources throughout their life cycle (Bordeaux, France, 27 June–1 July), which promoted information exchange on key issues relating to the safety and security of radioactive sources and adopted a number of findings and recommendations; and the international conference on the safety of radioactive waste disposal (Tokyo, Japan, 3-7 October), which considered, among other things, possible disposal options available.

GENERAL ASSEMBLY ACTION

On 8 December [meeting 61], the General Assembly, on the recommendation of the First Committee [A/60/463], adopted **resolution 60/57** without vote [agenda item 97 (*b*)].

Prohibition of the dumping of radioactive wastes

The General Assembly,

Bearing in mind resolutions CM/Res.1153(XLVIII) of 1988 and CM/Res.1225(L) of 1989, adopted by the Council of Ministers of the Organization of African Unity, concerning the dumping of nuclear and industrial wastes in Africa,

Welcoming resolution GC(XXXIV)/RES/530 establishing a Code of Practice on the International Transboundary Movement of Radioactive Waste, adopted on 21 September 1990 by the General Conference of the International Atomic Energy Agency at its thirty-fourth regular session,

Taking note of the commitment by the participants in the Summit on Nuclear Safety and Security, held in Moscow on 19 and 20 April 1996, to ban the dumping at sea of radioactive wastes,

Considering its resolution 2602 C(XXIV) of 16 December 1969, in which it requested the Conference of the Committee on Disarmament, inter alia, to consider effective methods of control against the use of radiological methods of warfare,

Aware of the potential hazards underlying any use of radioactive wastes that would constitute radiological warfare and its implications for regional and international security, in particular for the security of developing countries,

Recalling all its resolutions on the matter since its forty-third session in 1988, including its resolution 51/45 J of 10 December 1996,

Also recalling resolution GC(45)/RES/10 adopted by consensus on 21 September 2001 by the General Conference of the International Atomic Energy Agency at its forty-fifth regular session, in which States shipping radioactive materials are invited to provide, as appropriate, assurances to concerned States, upon their request, that the national regulations of the shipping State take into account the Agency's transport regulations and to provide them with relevant information relating to the shipment of such materials; the information provided should in no case be contradictory to the measures of physical security and safety,

Welcoming the adoption at Vienna, on 5 September 1997, of the Joint Convention on the Safety of Spent Fuel Management and on the Safety of Radioactive Waste Management, as recommended by the participants at the Summit on Nuclear Safety and Security,

Noting with satisfaction that the Joint Convention entered into force on 18 June 2001,

Noting that the first Review Meeting of the Contracting Parties to the Joint Convention on the Safety of Spent Fuel Management and on the Safety of Radioactive Waste Management was convened in Vienna from 3 to 14 November 2003,

Desirous of promoting the implementation of paragraph 76 of the Final Document of the Tenth Special Session of the General Assembly, the first special session devoted to disarmament,

1. *Takes note* of the part of the report of the Conference on Disarmament relating to a future convention on the prohibition of radiological weapons;

2. *Expresses grave concern* regarding any use of nuclear wastes that would constitute radiological warfare and have grave implications for the national security of all States;

3. *Calls upon* all States to take appropriate measures with a view to preventing any dumping of nuclear or radioactive wastes that would infringe upon the sovereignty of States;

4. *Requests* the Conference on Disarmament to take into account, in the negotiations for a convention on the prohibition of radiological weapons, radioactive wastes as part of the scope of such a convention;

5. *Also requests* the Conference on Disarmament to intensify efforts towards an early conclusion of such a convention and to include in its report to the General Assembly at its sixty-second session the progress recorded in the negotiations on this subject;

6. *Takes note* of resolution CM/Res.1356(LIV) of 1991, adopted by the Council of Ministers of the Organization of African Unity, on the Bamako Convention on the Ban on the Import of Hazardous Wastes into Africa and on the Control of Their Transboundary Movements within Africa;

7. *Expresses the hope* that the effective implementation of the International Atomic Energy Agency Code of Practice on the International Transboundary Movement of Radioactive Waste will enhance the protection of all States from the dumping of radioactive wastes on their territories;

8. *Appeals* to all Member States that have not yet taken the necessary steps to become party to the Joint Convention on the Safety of Spent Fuel Management and on the Safety of Radioactive Waste Management to do so as soon as possible;

9. *Decides* to include in the provisional agenda of its sixty-second session the item entitled "Prohibition of the dumping of radioactive wastes".

Also on 8 December, the Assembly adopted resolution 60/73 on preventing the risk of radiological terrorism (see p. 603).

Nuclear-weapon-free zones

Africa

As at 31 December, 23 States had ratified the African Nuclear-Weapon-Free Zone Treaty (Treaty of Pelindaba) [YUN 1995, p. 203], which was opened for signature in 1996 [YUN 1996, p. 486]. China, France and the United Kingdom had ratified Protocols I and II thereto, and France had also ratified Protocol III. The Russian Federation and the United States had signed Protocols I and II. The Treaty had 55 signatories. By the terms of the Treaty, ratification by 28 States was required for its entry into force.

GENERAL ASSEMBLY ACTION

On 8 December [meeting 61], the General Assembly, on the recommendation of the First Committee [A/60/456], adopted **resolution 60/49** without vote [agenda item 90].

African Nuclear-Weapon-Free Zone Treaty

The General Assembly,

Recalling its resolutions 51/53 of 10 December 1996 and 56/17 of 29 November 2001 and all its other relevant resolutions, as well as those of the Organization of African Unity,

Recalling also the signing of the African Nuclear-Weapon-Free Zone Treaty (Treaty of Pelindaba) at Cairo on 11 April 1996,

Recalling further the Cairo Declaration adopted on that occasion, which emphasized that nuclear-weapon-free zones, especially in regions of tension, such as the Middle East, enhance global and regional peace and security,

Taking note of the statement made by the President of the Security Council on behalf of the members of the Council on 12 April 1996, affirming that the signature of the African Nuclear-Weapon-Free Zone Treaty constituted an important contribution by the African countries to the maintenance of international peace and security,

Considering that the establishment of nuclear-weapon-free zones, especially in the Middle East, would enhance the security of Africa and the viability of the African nuclear-weapon-free zone,

1. *Calls upon* African States that have not yet done so to sign and ratify the African Nuclear-Weapon-Free Zone Treaty (Treaty of Pelindaba) as soon as possible so that it may enter into force without delay;

2. *Expresses its appreciation* to the nuclear-weapon States that have signed the Protocols that concern them, and calls upon those that have not yet ratified the Protocols concerning them to do so as soon as possible;

3. *Calls upon* the States contemplated in Protocol III to the Treaty that have not yet done so to take all necessary measures to ensure the speedy application of the Treaty to territories for which they are, de jure or de facto, internationally responsible and that lie within the limits of the geographical zone established in the Treaty;

4. *Calls upon* the African States parties to the Treaty on the Non-Proliferation of Nuclear Weapons that have not yet done so to conclude comprehensive safeguards agreements with the International Atomic Energy Agency pursuant to the Treaty, thereby satisfying the requirements of article 9 *(b)* of and annex II to the Treaty of Pelindaba when it enters into force, and to conclude additional protocols to their safeguards agreements on the basis of the Model Protocol approved by the Board of Governors of the Agency on 15 May 1997;

5. *Expresses its gratitude* to the Secretary-General, the Chairman of the Commission of the African Union and the Director General of the International Atomic Energy Agency for the diligence with which they have rendered effective assistance to the signatories to the Treaty;

6. *Decides* to include in the provisional agenda of its sixty-second session the item entitled "African Nuclear-Weapon-Free Zone Treaty".

Asia

Central Asia

During the year, the Department for Disarmament Affairs (DDA), through its Regional Centre for Peace and Disarmament in Asia and the Pacific (see p. 648), facilitated the conclusion of seven years of negotiations to finalize the text on a Central Asian nuclear-weapon-free zone treaty. The draft text, which was considered at a meeting (Tashkent, Uzbekistan, 7-9 February) attended by the five Central Asian States (Kazakhstan, Kyrgyzstan, Tajikistan, Turkmenistan, Uzbekistan), reflected developments in the field of nuclear disarmament and non-proliferation, including those relating to the CTBT (see p. 593) and the IAEA Additional Protocol (see p. 606).

On 8 December, the General Assembly decided to include in the provisional agenda of its sixty-first (2006) session the item entitled "Establishment of a nuclear-weapon-free zone in Central Asia" (**decision 60/516**).

Mongolia

The Organization continued efforts in 2005 to consolidate Mongolia's nuclear-weapon-free status, mainly through DDA's Regional Centre for Peace and Disarmament in Asia and the Pacific (see p. 648), which organized a series of consultations with relevant UN agencies to follow up on the recommendations made in the two studies on economic and ecological vulnerabilities as they related to human security in Mongolia.

South-East Asia

In 2005, the States parties to the Treaty on the South-East Asia Nuclear-Weapon-Free Zone (Bangkok Treaty), which opened for signature in

1995 [YUN 1995, p. 207] and entered into force in 1997 [YUN 1997, p. 495], maintained efforts to establish an institutional framework to implement the Treaty. To that end, Ministers from members of the Association of South-East Asian Nations (ASEAN), at the twelfth meeting of the ASEAN Regional Forum (Vientiane, Lao People's Democratic Republic, 29 July), reaffirmed the importance of continuing consultation on the Treaty's Protocol between the States parties and nuclear-weapon States.

Latin America and the Caribbean

During the year, the nineteenth regular session of the General Conference of the Agency for the Prohibition of Nuclear Weapons in Latin America and the Caribbean (OPANAL) (Santiago, Chile, 7-8 November) [GC/res.487], adopted the Declaration of Santiago de Chile, by which countries in the region resolved to intensify cooperation and coordination mechanisms with other nuclear-weapon-free zones and with those that might be established in the future, in order to speed up the achievement of common objectives and promote the consolidation of the legal regimes established by the zones. They reaffirmed support for the total elimination of nuclear weapons, and reiterated to the nuclear powers that had signed or ratified Additional Protocols I and II to the Treaty for the Prohibition of Nuclear Weapons in Latin America and the Caribbean (Treaty of Tlatelolco) [YUN 1967, p. 13] with reservations or unilateral interpretations affecting the denuclearized status of the zone, to modify or withdraw such reservations.

GENERAL ASSEMBLY ACTION

On 8 December [meeting 61], the General Assembly, on the recommendation of the First Committee [A/60/457], adopted **resolution 60/50** without vote [agenda item 91].

Consolidation of the regime established by the Treaty for the Prohibition of Nuclear Weapons in Latin America and the Caribbean (Treaty of Tlatelolco)

The General Assembly,

Recalling that the Treaty for the Prohibition of Nuclear Weapons in Latin America and the Caribbean (Treaty of Tlatelolco) was opened for signature at Mexico City on 14 February 1967,

Recalling also that, in its preamble, the Treaty of Tlatelolco states that military denuclearized zones are not an end in themselves but rather a means for achieving general and complete disarmament at a later stage,

Recalling further that, in its resolution 2286(XXII) of 5 December 1967, it welcomed with special satisfaction the Treaty of Tlatelolco as an event of historic significance in the efforts to prevent the proliferation of nuclear weapons and to promote international peace and security,

Recalling that in 1990, 1991 and 1992 the General Conference of the Agency for the Prohibition of Nuclear Weapons in Latin America and the Caribbean approved and opened for signature a set of amendments to the Treaty of Tlatelolco, with the aim of enabling the full entry into force of that instrument,

Highlighting that the Treaty of Tlatelolco is now in force for thirty-three sovereign States of the region, thereby consolidating the first nuclear-weapon-free zone established in a densely populated region,

Noting with satisfaction the leadership of the Agency for the Prohibition of Nuclear Weapons in Latin America and the Caribbean in the convening of the first Conference of States Parties and Signatories to Treaties that Establish Nuclear-Weapon-Free Zones, held in Tlatelolco, Mexico, from 26 to 28 April 2005,

Reaffirming the importance of strengthening the Agency as the appropriate legal and political forum for ensuring cooperation with the agencies of other nuclear-weapon-free zones,

1. *Welcomes* the fact that the Treaty for the Prohibition of Nuclear Weapons in Latin America and the Caribbean (Treaty of Tlatelolco) is now in force for the sovereign States of the region, and that this fact was officially acknowledged by the General Conference of the Agency for the Prohibition of Nuclear Weapons in Latin America and the Caribbean at its eighteenth session, held at Havana on 5 and 6 November 2003, and takes note of the results of the aforementioned session of the General Conference, including the adoption of the Havana Declaration;

2. *Urges* the countries of the region that have not yet done so to deposit their instruments of ratification of the amendments to the Treaty of Tlatelolco approved by the General Conference of the Agency in its resolutions 267 (E-V), 268(XII) and 290 (E-VII);

3. *Decides* to include in the provisional agenda of its sixty-second session the item entitled "Consolidation of the regime established by the Treaty for the Prohibition of Nuclear Weapons in Latin America and the Caribbean (Treaty of Tlatelolco)".

Middle East

In response to General Assembly resolution 59/63 on the establishment of a nuclear-weapon-free zone in the Middle East [YUN 2004, p. 552], the Secretary-General, in a July report, with later addenda [A/60/126 (Part I) & Add.1, 2], provided information on the resolution's implementation. He stated that he had maintained consultation with concerned parties within and beyond the region to explore further ways of promoting the establishment of the zone, but was concerned that developments in the region since his 2004 report [YUN 2004, p. 552] might affect efforts towards that goal. Welcoming recent attempts to give new impetus to the road map for peace in the region developed by the Quartet of the European Union, the Russian Federation, the United States and the United Nations (see p. 502), the Secretary-General called on all parties concerned to resume dialogue, with a view to creating stable security conditions and an eventual settlement that would facilitate the process of establishing the zone. The report included the views of Bolivia, Canada, Chile, Egypt, Iran, Israel, Japan, Mexico, the Russian Federation and the Syrian Arab Republic.

In September, the IAEA General Conference adopted a resolution on the Middle East [GC(49)/RES/15] calling on all parties directly concerned to take the steps required to implement the proposal for a mutually and effectively verifiable nuclear-weapon-free zone in the region.

GENERAL ASSEMBLY ACTION

On 8 December [meeting 61], the General Assembly, on the recommendation of the First Committee [A/60/460], adopted **resolution 60/52** without vote [agenda item 94].

Establishment of a nuclear-weapon-free zone in the region of the Middle East

The General Assembly,

Recalling its resolutions 3263(XXIX) of 9 December 1974, 3474(XXX) of 11 December 1975, 31/71 of 10 December 1976, 32/82 of 12 December 1977, 33/64 of 14 December 1978, 34/77 of 11 December 1979, 35/147 of 12 December 1980, 36/87 A and B of 9 December 1981, 37/75 of 9 December 1982, 38/64 of 15 December 1983, 39/54 of 12 December 1984, 40/82 of 12 December 1985, 41/48 of 3 December 1986, 42/28 of 30 November 1987, 43/65 of 7 December 1988, 44/108 of 15 December 1989, 45/52 of 4 December 1990, 46/30 of 6 December 1991, 47/48 of 9 December 1992, 48/71 of 16 December 1993, 49/71 of 15 December 1994, 50/66 of 12 December 1995, 51/41 of 10 December 1996, 52/34 of 9 December 1997, 53/74 of 4 December 1998, 54/51 of 1 December 1999, 55/30 of 20 November 2000, 56/21 of 29 November 2001, 57/55 of 22 November 2002, 58/34 of 8 December 2003 and 59/63 of 3 December 2004 on the establishment of a nuclear-weapon-free zone in the region of the Middle East,

Recalling also the recommendations for the establishment of such a zone in the Middle East consistent with paragraphs 60 to 63, and in particular paragraph 63 *(d)*, of the Final Document of the Tenth Special Session of the General Assembly,

Emphasizing the basic provisions of the above-mentioned resolutions, which call upon all parties directly concerned to consider taking the practical and urgent steps required for the implementation of the proposal to establish a nuclear-weapon-free zone in the region of the Middle East and, pending and during the establishment of such a zone, to declare solemnly that they will refrain, on a reciprocal basis, from producing, acquiring or in any other way possessing nuclear weapons and nuclear explosive devices and from permitting the stationing of nuclear weapons on their territory by any third party, to agree to place their nuclear facilities under International Atomic Energy Agency safeguards and to declare their support for the establishment of the zone and to deposit such declarations with the Security Council for consideration, as appropriate,

Reaffirming the inalienable right of all States to acquire and develop nuclear energy for peaceful purposes,

Emphasizing the need for appropriate measures on the question of the prohibition of military attacks on nuclear facilities,

Bearing in mind the consensus reached by the General Assembly since its thirty-fifth session that the establishment of a nuclear-weapon-free zone in the Middle East would greatly enhance international peace and security,

Desirous of building on that consensus so that substantial progress can be made towards establishing a nuclear-weapon-free zone in the Middle East,

Welcoming all initiatives leading to general and complete disarmament, including in the region of the Middle East, and in particular on the establishment therein of a zone free of weapons of mass destruction, including nuclear weapons,

Noting the peace negotiations in the Middle East, which should be of a comprehensive nature and represent an appropriate framework for the peaceful settlement of contentious issues in the region,

Recognizing the importance of credible regional security, including the establishment of a mutually verifiable nuclear-weapon-free zone,

Emphasizing the essential role of the United Nations in the establishment of a mutually verifiable nuclear-weapon-free zone,

Having examined the report of the Secretary-General on the implementation of resolution 59/63,

1. *Urges* all parties directly concerned to consider seriously taking the practical and urgent steps required for the implementation of the proposal to establish a nuclear-weapon-free zone in the region of the Middle East in accordance with the relevant resolutions of the General Assembly, and, as a means of promoting this objective, invites the countries concerned to adhere to the Treaty on the Non-Proliferation of Nuclear Weapons;

2. *Calls upon* all countries of the region that have not done so, pending the establishment of the zone, to agree to place all their nuclear activities under International Atomic Energy Agency safeguards;

3. *Takes note* of resolution GC(49)/RES/15, adopted on 30 September 2005 by the General Conference of the International Atomic Energy Agency at its forty-ninth regular session, concerning the application of Agency safeguards in the Middle East;

4. *Notes* the importance of the ongoing bilateral Middle East peace negotiations and the activities of the multilateral Working Group on Arms Control and Regional Security in promoting mutual confidence and security in the Middle East, including the establishment of a nuclear-weapon-free zone;

5. *Invites* all countries of the region, pending the establishment of a nuclear-weapon-free zone in the region of the Middle East, to declare their support for establishing such a zone, consistent with paragraph 63 *(d)* of the Final Document of the Tenth Special Session of the General Assembly, and to deposit those declarations with the Security Council;

6. *Also invites* those countries, pending the establishment of the zone, not to develop, produce, test or otherwise acquire nuclear weapons or permit the stationing on their territories, or territories under their

control, of nuclear weapons or nuclear explosive devices;

7. *Invites* the nuclear-weapon States and all other States to render their assistance in the establishment of the zone and at the same time to refrain from any action that runs counter to both the letter and the spirit of the present resolution;

8. *Takes note* of the report of the Secretary-General;

9. *Invites* all parties to consider the appropriate means that may contribute towards the goal of general and complete disarmament and the establishment of a zone free of weapons of mass destruction in the region of the Middle East;

10. *Requests* the Secretary-General to continue to pursue consultations with the States of the region and other concerned States, in accordance with paragraph 7 of resolution 46/30 and taking into account the evolving situation in the region, and to seek from those States their views on the measures outlined in chapters III and IV of the study annexed to his report of 10 October 1990 or other relevant measures, in order to move towards the establishment of a nuclear-weapon-free zone in the Middle East;

11. *Also requests* the Secretary-General to submit to the General Assembly at its sixty-first session a report on the implementation of the present resolution;

12. *Decides* to include in the provisional agenda of its sixty-first session the item entitled "Establishment of a nuclear-weapon-free zone in the region of the Middle East".

South Pacific

In 2005, the number of States that had ratified the 1985 South Pacific Nuclear-Free Zone Treaty (Treaty of Rarotonga) [YUN 1985, p. 58], remained at 17. China and the Russian Federation had ratified Protocols 2 and 3, and France, the United Kingdom and the United States had ratified all three Protocols.

Under Protocol 1, the States internationally responsible for territories situated within the zone would undertake to apply the relevant prohibitions of the Treaty to those territories; under Protocol 2, the five nuclear-weapon States would provide security assurances to parties or territories within the same zone; and under Protocol 3, the five would not carry out nuclear tests in the zone.

Southern hemisphere and adjacent areas

The first Conference of States Parties and Signatories to Treaties that Establish Nuclear-Weapon-Free Zones (Tlatelolco, Mexico, 26-28 April) [A/60/121] considered cooperative ways of strengthening the nuclear-weapon-free zone regime, thereby contributing to the disarmament and nuclear non-proliferation processes and advancing the achievement of the universal goal of a nuclear-weapon-free world. The Conference, attended by the States parties and signatories to the Treaties of Bangkok, Pelindaba, Rarotonga and Tlatelolco establishing the four zones cur-

rently in existence, and by Mongolia, which maintained an international nuclear-weapon-free status, adopted the Declaration of the Conference of Nuclear-Weapon-Free Zones (the Declaration of Tlatelolco), in which they reaffirmed that the continued existence of nuclear weapons constituted a threat to all humanity. They expressed the conviction that the establishment of internationally-recognized nuclear-weapon-free zones strengthened global and regional peace and security, reinforced the nuclear non-proliferation regime and contributed to nuclear disarmament. They emphasized that the status of those zones should be respected by all States within and outside the regions covered, most notably the nuclear-weapon States whose cooperation was essential for the maximum effectiveness of the zones. The participants also reaffirmed their commitment to reaching the common objectives set forth in the treaties of the four existing zones.

GENERAL ASSEMBLY ACTION

On 8 December [meeting 61], the General Assembly, on the recommendation of the First Committee [A/60/463], adopted **resolution 60/58** by recorded vote (167-3-8) [agenda item 97 *(s)*].

Nuclear-weapon-free southern hemisphere and adjacent areas

The General Assembly,

Recalling its resolutions 51/45 B of 10 December 1996, 52/38 N of 9 December 1997, 53/77 Q of 4 December 1998, 54/54 L of 1 December 1999, 55/33 I of 20 November 2000, 56/24 G of 29 November 2001, 57/73 of 22 November 2002, 58/49 of 8 December 2003 and 59/85 of 3 December 2004,

Recalling also the adoption by the Disarmament Commission at its 1999 substantive session of a text entitled "Establishment of nuclear-weapon-free zones on the basis of arrangements freely arrived at among the States of the region concerned",

Determined to pursue the total elimination of nuclear weapons,

Determined also to continue to contribute to the prevention of the proliferation of nuclear weapons in all its aspects and to the process of general and complete disarmament under strict and effective international control, in particular in the field of nuclear weapons and other weapons of mass destruction, with a view to strengthening international peace and security, in accordance with the purposes and principles of the Charter of the United Nations,

Recalling the provisions on nuclear-weapon-free zones of the Final Document of the Tenth Special Session of the General Assembly, the first special session devoted to disarmament,

Stressing the importance of the treaties of Tlatelolco, Rarotonga, Bangkok and Pelindaba establishing nuclear-weapon-free zones, as well as the Antarctic Treaty, to, inter alia, achieve a world entirely free of nuclear weapons,

Underlining the value of enhancing cooperation among the nuclear-weapon-free-zone treaty members by means of mechanisms such as joint meetings of States parties, signatories and observers to those treaties,

Noting, in this context, that the first Conference of States Parties and Signatories to Treaties that Establish Nuclear-Weapon-Free Zones was held in Tlatelolco, Mexico, from 26 to 28 April 2005, on the eve of the 2005 Review Conference of the Parties to the Treaty on the Non-Proliferation of Nuclear Weapons,

Recalling the applicable principles and rules of international law relating to the freedom of the high seas and the rights of passage through maritime space, including those of the United Nations Convention on the Law of the Sea,

1. *Welcomes* the continued contribution that the Antarctic Treaty and the treaties of Tlatelolco, Rarotonga, Bangkok and Pelindaba are making towards freeing the southern hemisphere and adjacent areas covered by those treaties from nuclear weapons;

2. *Also welcomes* the ratification by all original parties of the Treaty of Rarotonga, and calls upon eligible States to adhere to the treaty and the protocols thereto;

3. *Further welcomes* the efforts towards the completion of the ratification process of the Treaty of Pelindaba, and calls upon the States of the region that have not yet done so to sign and ratify the treaty, with the aim of its early entry into force;

4. *Calls upon* all concerned States to continue to work together in order to facilitate adherence to the protocols to nuclear-weapon-free-zone treaties by all relevant States that have not yet done so;

5. *Welcomes* the steps taken to conclude further nuclear-weapon-free-zone treaties on the basis of arrangements freely arrived at among the States of the region concerned, and calls upon all States to consider all relevant proposals, including those reflected in its resolutions on the establishment of nuclear-weapon-free zones in the Middle East and South Asia;

6. *Also welcomes* the ongoing efforts to establish a nuclear-weapon-free zone in Central Asia;

7. *Affirms its conviction* of the important role of nuclear-weapon-free zones in strengthening the nuclear non-proliferation regime and in extending the areas of the world that are nuclear-weapon-free, and, with particular reference to the responsibilities of the nuclear-weapon States, calls upon all States to support the process of nuclear disarmament and to work for the total elimination of all nuclear weapons;

8. *Welcomes* the progress made on increased collaboration within and between zones at the first Conference of States Parties and Signatories to Treaties that Establish Nuclear-Weapon-Free Zones, at which States reaffirmed their need to cooperate in order to achieve their common objectives;

9. *Congratulates* the States parties and signatories to the treaties of Tlatelolco, Rarotonga, Bangkok and Pelindaba, as well as Mongolia, for their efforts to pursue the common goals envisaged in those treaties and to promote the nuclear-weapon-free status of the southern hemisphere and adjacent areas, and calls upon them to explore and implement further ways and means of cooperation among themselves and their treaty agencies;

10. *Encourages* the competent authorities of the nuclear-weapon-free-zone treaties to provide assistance to the States parties and signatories to those treaties so as to facilitate the accomplishment of these goals;

11. *Decides* to include in the provisional agenda of its sixty-first session the item entitled "Nuclear-weapon-free southern hemisphere and adjacent areas".

RECORDED VOTE ON RESOLUTION 60/58:

In favour: Afghanistan, Albania, Algeria, Andorra, Antigua and Barbuda, Argentina, Armenia, Australia, Austria, Azerbaijan, Bahamas, Bahrain, Bangladesh, Barbados, Belarus, Belgium, Belize, Benin, Bolivia, Bosnia and Herzegovina, Botswana, Brazil, Brunei Darussalam, Bulgaria, Burkina Faso, Burundi, Cambodia, Cameroon, Canada, Cape Verde, Central African Republic, Chile, China, Colombia, Comoros, Congo, Costa Rica, Côte d'Ivoire, Croatia, Cuba, Cyprus, Czech Republic, Democratic People's Republic of Korea, Democratic Republic of the Congo, Denmark, Djibouti, Dominica, Dominican Republic, Ecuador, Egypt, El Salvador, Eritrea, Estonia, Ethiopia, Fiji, Finland, Gabon, Georgia, Germany, Ghana, Greece, Grenada, Guatemala, Guinea, Guinea-Bissau, Guyana, Haiti, Honduras, Hungary, Iceland, Indonesia, Iran, Iraq, Ireland, Italy, Jamaica, Japan, Jordan, Kazakhstan, Kenya, Kuwait, Kyrgyzstan, Lao People's Democratic Republic, Latvia, Lebanon, Lesotho, Liberia, Libyan Arab Jamahiriya, Liechtenstein, Lithuania, Luxembourg, Madagascar, Malawi, Malaysia, Maldives, Mali, Malta, Mauritania, Mauritius, Mexico, Mongolia, Morocco, Mozambique, Myanmar, Namibia, Nepal, Netherlands, New Zealand, Nicaragua, Niger, Nigeria, Norway, Oman, Panama, Papua New Guinea, Paraguay, Peru, Philippines, Poland, Portugal, Qatar, Republic of Korea, Republic of Moldova, Romania, Saint Lucia, Saint Vincent and the Grenadines, Samoa, San Marino, Sao Tome and Principe, Saudi Arabia, Senegal, Serbia and Montenegro, Singapore, Slovakia, Slovenia, Solomon Islands, Somalia, South Africa, Sri Lanka, Sudan, Suriname, Sweden, Switzerland, Syrian Arab Republic, Tajikistan, Thailand, The former Yugoslav Republic of Macedonia, Timor-Leste, Togo, Tonga, Trinidad and Tobago, Tunisia, Turkey, Turkmenistan, Tuvalu, Uganda, Ukraine, United Arab Emirates, United Republic of Tanzania, Uruguay, Uzbekistan, Vanuatu, Venezuela, Viet Nam, Yemen, Zambia, Zimbabwe.

Against: France, United Kingdom, United States.

Abstaining: Bhutan, India, Israel, Marshall Islands, Pakistan, Palau, Russian Federation, Spain.

The First Committee adopted paragraph 5 and its last three words, "and South Asia", by two separate recorded votes of 140 to 2, with 7 abstentions and 141 to 1, with 9 abstentions, respectively. The Assembly retained that paragraph and its last three words, by recorded votes of 162 to 2, with 7 abstentions and 162 to 1, with 9 abstentions, respectively.

Bacteriological (biological) and chemical weapons

In 2005, the continuing threat posed by biological and chemical weapons, particularly the possibility of their acquisition by terrorists, remained of pressing concern to the international community, fuelling further calls for strengthening the Convention on the Prohibition of the Development, Production and Stockpiling of Bacteriological (biological) and Toxin Weapons and on Their Destruction (BWC) (see p. 615) and the Convention on the Prohibition of the Development, Stockpiling and Use of Chemical Weapons and on Their Destruction (CWC) (see p. 616). States parties to both instruments continued to implement national measures addressing those concerns, while the Security Council Committee established pursuant to Council resolution 1540(2004) [YUN 2004, p. 544] to monitor Member States' implementation of measures to combat the proliferation of WMDs, including chemical and biological weapons, became fully operational and began the substantive part of its work (see p. 600).

Bacteriological (biological) weapons

Meeting of States parties

As decided by the States parties to BWC in 2003 [YUN 2003, p. 559], the third and final scheduled annual meeting of those States was convened (Geneva, 5-9 December) [BWC/MSP/2005/3] to discuss and promote common understanding and effective action on the content, promulgation and adoption of codes of conduct for scientists. While recognizing that they themselves had the primary responsibility for implementing the Convention, States parties acknowledged that codes of conduct voluntarily adopted for scientists in relevant fields could support the object and purpose of the Convention. Considering the differences in national requirements and circumstances, a range of different approaches existed for developing such codes, which should reflect the Convention's provisions and contribute to national implementation measures, while not impeding scientific discovery, placing undue constraints on research or international cooperation and exchange for peaceful purposes. Since science had the potential to be misused in ways prohibited by the Convention, codes of conduct should require and enable relevant actors to reasonably foresee the consequences of their activities.

The States parties agreed that those codes should not just apply to scientists but to everyone involved in scientific activity, including managers and technical and ancillary staff. The codes should be compatible with national legislation and regulatory controls and contribute to national implementation measures. They should be simple, clear and easily understandable to scientists and the wider civil society; helpful and effective for guiding relevant actors in making decisions and taking action in accordance with the Convention's purposes and objectives; sufficiently broad in scope; and regularly reviewed, evaluated for effectiveness and revised as necessary.

Regarding the adoption of codes of conduct, States parties also agreed on demonstrating the benefits of codes and encouraging relevant actors to develop them themselves; using existing codes, mechanisms, frameworks and bodies as far as possible; and tailoring adoption strategies to individual needs. States parties further agreed on the value of continuous efforts on promulgation of the codes through appropriate channels, and that the lessons, perspectives, recommendations and conclusions drawn from the statements and working papers presented at the experts' meeting (see below), as well as a synthesis of the issues considered and views expressed, prepared by the Chairman and annexed to the meeting's report, should be considered. Participants were encouraged to inform the Sixth Review Conference of any actions, measures or steps they had taken based on discussions at the 2005 meeting of States parties and experts' meeting, in order to facilitate the work of the Conference. The States parties decided that the Preparatory Committee for the Sixth Review Conference would be held in Geneva, in April 2006, with the Conference scheduled for November and December of the same year.

Experts' meeting

In accordance with the outcome of the Fifth Review Conference [YUN 2002, p. 516], the 2005 meeting of States parties (see above) was preceded by a preparatory expert meeting (Geneva, 13-24 June) [BWC/MSP/2005/MX/3], which addressed issues relating to the topics discussed by the meeting of States parties. The experts also considered government science and other relevant matters concerning universities, funders, research, publishers, industry and professional bodies. The meeting had before it a number of working papers and heard statements and thematic presentations from States parties and observer organizations. On 24 June, the meeting adopted its report, to which was annexed a compilation of the lessons, perspectives, recommendations, conclusions and proposals drawn from the presentations, statements and working papers considered.

GENERAL ASSEMBLY ACTION

On 8 December [meeting 62], the General Assembly, on the recommendation of the First Committee [A/60/470], adopted **resolution 60/96** without vote [agenda item 104].

Convention on the Prohibition of the Development, Production and Stockpiling of Bacteriological (Biological) and Toxin Weapons and on Their Destruction

The General Assembly,

Recalling its previous resolutions relating to the complete and effective prohibition of bacteriological (biological) and toxin weapons and to their destruction,

Noting with satisfaction that there are one hundred and fifty-five States parties to the Convention on the Prohibition of the Development, Production and Stockpiling of Bacteriological (Biological) and Toxin Weapons and on Their Destruction, including all of the permanent members of the Security Council,

Bearing in mind its call upon all States parties to the Convention to participate in the implementation of the recommendations of the Review Conferences, including the exchange of information and data agreed to in the Final Declaration of the Third Review Conference of the Parties to the Convention on the Prohibition of the Development, Production and Stockpiling of Bacteriological (Biological) and Toxin Weapons and on Their Destruction, and to provide such information and data in conformity with standardized procedure to the Secretary-General on an annual basis and no later than 15 April,

Welcoming the reaffirmation made in the Final Declaration of the Fourth Review Conference that under all circumstances the use of bacteriological (biological) and toxin weapons and their development, production and stockpiling are effectively prohibited under article I of the Convention,

Recalling the decision reached at the Fifth Review Conference to hold three annual meetings of the States parties of one week's duration each year commencing in 2003 until the Sixth Review Conference and to hold a two-week meeting of experts to prepare for each meeting of the States parties,

Recalling also the decision reached at the Fifth Review Conference that the Sixth Review Conference would be held in Geneva in 2006 and would be preceded by a preparatory committee,

1. *Notes with satisfaction* the increase in the number of States parties to the Convention on the Prohibition of the Development, Production and Stockpiling of Bacteriological (Biological) and Toxin Weapons and on Their Destruction, reaffirms the call upon all signatory States that have not yet ratified the Convention to do so without delay, and calls upon those States that have not signed the Convention to become parties thereto at an early date, thus contributing to the achievement of universal adherence to the Convention;

2. *Welcomes* the information and data provided to date, and reiterates its call upon all States parties to the Convention to participate in the exchange of information and data agreed to in the Final Declaration of the Third Review Conference of the Parties to the Convention;

3. *Recalls* the decision reached at the Fifth Review Conference to discuss and promote common understanding and effective action in 2003 on the two topics of the adoption of necessary national measures to implement the prohibitions set forth in the Convention, including the enactment of penal legislation, and national mechanisms to establish and maintain the security and oversight of pathogenic micro-organisms and toxins; in 2004 on the two topics of enhancing international capabilities for responding to, investigating and mitigating the effects of cases of alleged use of biological or toxin weapons or suspicious outbreaks of disease, and strengthening and broadening national and international institutional efforts and existing mechanisms for the surveillance, detection, diagnosis and combating of infectious diseases affecting humans, animals and plants; and in 2005 on the topic of the content, promulgation and adoption of codes of conduct for scientists; and calls upon the States parties to the Convention to participate in its implementation;

4. *Welcomes* the significant participation of the States parties at the meetings of States parties and meetings of experts to date and the constructive and useful exchange of information achieved, and welcomes also the discussion and the promotion of common understanding and effective action on agreed topics;

5. *Notes* that, in accordance with the decision reached at the Fifth Review Conference, the Sixth Review Conference will be held in Geneva in 2006 and the dates will be formally agreed by the preparatory committee for that Conference, which will be open to all States parties to the Convention and which will meet in Geneva during the week beginning 24 April 2006;

6. *Requests* the Secretary-General to continue to render the necessary assistance to the depositary Governments of the Convention and to provide such services as may be required for the implementation of the decisions and recommendations of the Review Conferences, including all necessary assistance to the annual meetings of the States parties and the meetings of experts, and to render the necessary assistance and provide such services as may be required for the Sixth Review Conference and the preparations for it;

7. *Decides* to include in the provisional agenda of its sixty-first session the item entitled "Convention on the Prohibition of the Development, Production and Stockpiling of Bacteriological (Biological) and Toxin Weapons and on Their Destruction".

Chemical weapons

Chemical weapons convention

In 2005, Antigua and Barbuda, Bhutan, Cambodia, the Democratic Republic of the Congo (DRC), Grenada, Honduras, Niue and Vanuatu ratified or acceded to the Convention on the Prohibition of the Development, Stockpiling and Use of Chemical Weapons and on Their Destruction (CWC), bringing the total number of States parties to 175. The number of signatories stood at 165. The Convention, adopted by the Conference on Disarmament in 1992 [YUN 1992, p. 65], entered into force in 1997 [YUN 1997, p. 499].

The tenth session of the Conference of the States parties (The Hague, Netherlands, 7-11 November) [C-10/5] considered, among other issues, the status of the Convention's implementation, fostering international cooperation for peaceful purposes in the field of chemical activities, ensuring the Convention's universality and administrative and budgetary matters. The Conference adopted decisions on follow-up to the plan of action regarding the implementation of article VII of the Convention addressing national implementation measures; a format for the formulation, specification or renewal of offers of assistance under article X on assistance and protection from chemical weapons; amendments to the confidentiality policy of the Organization for the Prohibition of Chemical Weapons (OPCW); the full implementation of article XI on economic and technological development; the implementation of the plan of action concerning the Convention's universality; the establishment of an OPCW Office in Africa; the captive use of Schedule 1 chemicals; and administrative, financial and oversight matters, including OPCW's 2006 programme and budget. The Conference approved the Libyan Arab Jamahiriya's request for an extension of the intermediate deadlines for the destruction of its categories 1, 2 and 3 chemical weapons stockpiles. It decided that 29 April—the date in 1997 of the Convention's entry into force—would be observed yearly as the day of remembrance for all victims of chemical warfare. It also decided to hold its eleventh session in December 2006.

GENERAL ASSEMBLY ACTION

On 8 December [meeting 61], the General Assembly, on the recommendation of the First Committee [A/60/463], adopted **resolution 60/67** without vote [agenda item 97 (j)].

Implementation of the Convention on the Prohibition of the Development, Production, Stockpiling and Use of Chemical Weapons and on Their Destruction

The General Assembly,

Recalling its previous resolutions on the subject of chemical weapons, in particular resolution 59/72 of 3 December 2004, adopted without a vote, in which it noted with appreciation the ongoing work to achieve the objective and purpose of the Convention on the Prohibition of the Development, Production, Stockpiling and Use of Chemical Weapons and on Their Destruction,

Determined to achieve the effective prohibition of the development, production, acquisition, transfer, stockpiling and use of chemical weapons and their destruction,

Noting with satisfaction that, since the adoption of resolution 59/72, seven additional States have ratified the Convention or acceded to it, bringing the total number of States parties to the Convention to one hundred and seventy-four,

Reaffirming the importance of the outcome of the First Special Session of the Conference of the States Parties to Review the Operation of the Chemical Weapons Convention, including the Political Declaration, in which the States parties reaffirmed their commitment to achieving the objective and purpose of the Convention, and the final report, which addressed all aspects of the Convention and made important recommendations on its continued implementation,

1. *Emphasizes* that the universality of the Convention on the Prohibition of the Development, Production, Stockpiling and Use of Chemical Weapons and

on Their Destruction is fundamental to the achievement of its objective and purpose and acknowledges progress made in the implementation of the action plan for the universality of the Convention, and calls upon all States that have not yet done so to become parties to the Convention without delay;

2. *Underlines* that the Convention and its implementation contribute to enhancing international peace and security, and emphasizes that its full, universal and effective implementation will contribute further to that purpose by excluding completely, for the sake of all humankind, the possibility of the use of chemical weapons;

3. *Stresses* that the full and effective implementation of all provisions of the Convention, including those on national implementation (article VII) and assistance and protection against chemical weapons (article X), constitutes an important contribution to the efforts of the United Nations in the global fight against terrorism in all its forms and manifestations;

4. *Also stresses* the importance to the Convention that all possessors of chemical weapons, chemical weapons production facilities or chemical weapons development facilities, including previously declared possessor States, should be among the States parties to the Convention, and welcomes progress to that end;

5. *Notes* that the effective application of the verification system builds confidence in compliance with the Convention by States parties;

6. *Stresses* the importance of the Organization for the Prohibition of Chemical Weapons in verifying compliance with the provisions of the Convention as well as in promoting the timely and efficient accomplishment of all its objectives;

7. *Urges* all States parties to the Convention to meet in full and on time their obligations under the Convention and to support the Organization for the Prohibition of Chemical Weapons in its implementation activities;

8. *Welcomes* progress made in the implementation of the action plan on the implementation of article VII obligations and commends the States parties and the Technical Secretariat for assisting other States parties, on request, with the implementation of their article VII obligations, and urges States parties that have not fulfilled their obligations under article VII to do so without further delay, in accordance with their constitutional processes;

9. *Reaffirms* the importance of article XI provisions relating to the economic and technological development of States parties and recalls that the full, effective and non-discriminatory implementation of those provisions contributes to universality, and also reaffirms the undertaking of the States parties to foster international cooperation for peaceful purposes in the field of chemical activities of the States parties and the importance of that cooperation and its contribution to the promotion of the Convention as a whole;

10. *Notes with appreciation* the ongoing work of the Organization for the Prohibition of Chemical Weapons to achieve the objective and purpose of the Convention, to ensure the full implementation of its provisions, including those for international verification of compliance with it, and to provide a forum for consultation and cooperation among States parties, and also notes with appreciation the substantial contribution of

the Technical Secretariat and the Director-General to the continued development and success of the Organization;

11. *Welcomes* the cooperation between the United Nations and the Organization for the Prohibition of Chemical Weapons within the framework of the Relationship Agreement between the United Nations and the Organization, in accordance with the provisions of the Convention;

12. *Decides* to include in the provisional agenda of its sixty-first session the item entitled "Implementation of the Convention on the Prohibition of the Development, Production, Stockpiling and Use of Chemical Weapons and on Their Destruction".

Organization for the Prohibition of Chemical Weapons

In 2005, OPCW continued to undertake wide-ranging chemical disarmament, non-proliferation and assistance and protection activities, towards the complete elimination of chemical weapons.

Since the Convention's entry into force in 1997 [YUN 1997, p. 499], OPCW had verified the destruction of approximately 12,435 tons of chemical warfare agents declared by five of the six identified chemical weapons possessor States, accounting for over 17 per cent of the total stockpiles declared. To ensure the complete destruction of those weapons and their non-proliferation, OPCW undertook up to 2,200 inspection exercises at over 800 sites in 72 countries. In the area of international cooperation and assistance, OPCW collaborated with Ukraine and the Euro-Atlantic Disaster Response Coordination Centre of the North Atlantic Treaty Organization (NATO) in the organization of an exercise on the delivery of assistance entitled "Joint Assistance 2005" conducted at the Yavoriv training area (Lviv, Ukraine, 9-13 October), aimed at testing the requisite skills and capacities in investigating alleged use of chemical warfare agents. The exercise, which involved some 1,000 participants from OPCW member States, defined international cooperation procedures for delivering emergency assistance following a simulated terrorist attack with chemical warfare agents. OPCW also undertook capacity-building projects, notably in the Middle East and Central Asia, while implementation efforts were enhanced by a number of national and regional meetings in Latin America and the Caribbean.

The OPCW Executive Council held its fortieth (15-18 March), forty-first (28 June–1 July) forty-second (27-30 September) and forty-third (6-9 December) sessions. It adopted decisions on the destruction of chemical weapons and/or the conversion of chemical weapons production facilities (CWPFs) and on issues relating to the chemical industry and financial matters. It made recommen-

dations regarding the plan of action for implementing article VII obligations on national implementation measures, reviewed the effectiveness of verification activities, monitored the implementation of the action plan for the Convention's universality, approved facility agreements between OPCW and a number of States parties and established an open-ended working group on the establishment of an OPCW office in Africa.

Conventional weapons

Programme of Action on illicit trade in small arms

In 2005, the international community continued to address security challenges relating to the spread of small arms within the framework of the Programme of Action to Prevent, Combat and Eradicate the Illicit Trade in Small Arms and Light Weapons in All Its Aspects [YUN 2001, p. 499]. The Security Council, in statement S/PRST/2005/7 (see p. 619), encouraged international and regional cooperation in identifying the origin and transfer of those weapons in order to prevent their diversion, particularly to terrorist groups, and to restrict their supply to areas of instability. The General Assembly, in decision 60/519 (see p. 621), adopted an international instrument to enable States to identify and trace small arms and light weapons effectively, and in resolution 60/81 (see p. 625) established a Group of Governmental Experts to consider further steps to enhance international cooperation in tackling illicit brokering in those weapons. In resolution 60/68 (see p. 621), it called on States to better address the negative humanitarian and development impact of illicit small arms and light weapons and their excessive accumulation, including by integrating comprehensive armed violence prevention programmes into their national development strategies.

The second biennial meeting of States to consider the implementation of the Programme of Action (New York, 11-15 July), as well as ongoing consultations on the illicit brokering of those weapons, reached a broad consensus on the need for further international action to address the small arms problem. Member States continued to make progress in strengthening the Convention on excessively injurious conventional weapons and related Protocols and to promote transparency in armaments. In July, the Protocol against the Illicit Manufacturing of and Trafficking in Firearms, Their Parts and Components and Ammunition, supplementing the United Nations Convention against Transnational Organized Crime [YUN 2001, p. 1036], entered into force.

Report of Secretary-General. Responding to Security Council presidential statement S/PRST/ 2004/1 [YUN 2004, p. 559], the Secretary-General submitted a February report [S/2005/69] updating the Council on the initiatives undertaken to implement the recommendations contained in his 2002 report [YUN 2002, p. 521] on ways the Council could contribute to dealing with the illicit trade in small arms and light weapons. The Secretary-General reported that much progress had been achieved in some key areas, including under the recommendation on tracing illicit arms flow, through the work of the Open-ended Working Group (see below) which negotiated the draft international instrument for the timely and reliable identification and tracing of small arms and light weapons, adopted subsequently by the Assembly in decision 60/519 (see p. 621). Progress was also being made on the issue of the illicit brokering in those weapons, which had been a source of concern, particularly in connection with the activities of terrorist groups. Notable progress had also been made regarding the systematic establishment of monitoring mechanisms to support the implementation of sanctions, the adoption of more vigorous measures against violations of arms embargoes and efforts to increase participation in the Organization's reporting instruments on arms transparency. However, more needed to be done in other areas, particularly regarding interaction between the Council and the Assembly, for which no structure had been established. In order to develop a coherent and comprehensive UN policy on small arms and light weapons, he recommended that both organs establish a committee to examine how they might work together in that regard. Much also remained to be done to implement his other recommendations regarding support for the Small Arms Advisory Service and for the reintegration of former combatants into their communities.

SECURITY COUNCIL ACTION

On 17 February [meeting 5127], following consultations among Security Council members, the President made statement report **S/PRST/2005/7** on behalf of the Council:

The Security Council welcomes the report of the Secretary-General of 7 February 2005 on the implementation of his recommendations to the Council on small arms, and reaffirms the statements by its President of 24 September 1999, 31 August 2001, 31 October 2002 and 19 January 2004.

The Council recalls its primary responsibility under the Charter of the United Nations for the maintenance of international peace and security. In this regard, the Council recognizes that the dissemination of illicit small arms and light weapons has hampered the peaceful settlement of disputes, fuelled such disputes into armed conflicts and contributed to the prolongation of such armed conflicts. The Council reaffirms the inherent right of individual or collective self-defence in accordance with Article 51 of the Charter and, subject to the Charter, the right of each State to import, produce and retain small arms and light weapons for its self-defence and security needs.

The Council encourages the arms-exporting countries to exercise the highest degree of responsibility in small arms and light weapons transactions according to their existing responsibilities under relevant international law. It also encourages international and regional cooperation in identifying the origin and transfer of small arms and light weapons in order to prevent their diversion, in particular, to Al-Qaida and other terrorist groups. The Council welcomes the significant steps that have been taken by Member States and international and regional organizations in this regard. The obligation of Member States to enforce the arms embargo should be coupled with enhanced international and regional cooperation concerning arms exports. The Council encourages Members to undertake vigorous actions aimed at restricting the supply of small arms, light weapons and ammunitions to areas of instability.

The Council takes note that the United Nations Second Biennial Meeting of States to Consider the Implementation of the Programme of Action to Prevent, Combat and Eradicate the Illicit Trade in Small Arms and Light Weapons in All Its Aspects will be held from 11 to 15 July 2005, and encourages Member States to fully cooperate with the Chair of the Meeting to have a successful outcome.

The Council notes with appreciation that regional actions on illicit trade in small arms and light weapons in all its aspects have been strengthened in recent years, and encourages the continuation of assistance at the national, regional and international levels that would fit the needs of Member States to implement the recommendations contained in the Programme of Action to Prevent, Combat and Eradicate the Illicit Trade in Small Arms and Light Weapons in All Its Aspects, adopted on 20 July 2001 by the United Nations Conference on the Illicit Trade in Small Arms and Light Weapons in All Its Aspects.

The Council welcomes the ongoing efforts by the open-ended working group established by the General Assembly in resolution 58/241 of 23 December 2003 to negotiate an international instrument to enable States to identify and trace, in a timely and reliable manner, illicit small arms and light weapons, and calls upon all Member States to support all efforts aimed at this purpose. It expresses the wish that the ongoing work within the group will lead to a positive conclusion at its third session as scheduled.

The Council welcomes the adoption by the General Assembly of resolution 59/86 of 3 December 2004 in which, among other things, it requested the Secretary-General to continue broad-based consultations on further steps to enhance international cooperation in preventing, combating and eradicating illicit brokering in small arms and light weapons, with a view to establishing a group of governmental experts to consider the issue.

The Council welcomes the inclusion of man-portable air defence systems, on an exceptional basis, in the United Nations Register on Conventional Arms.

The Council further encourages Member States that have not already done so to establish the necessary legislative or other measures, including the use of authenticated end-user certificates, to ensure effective control over the export and transit of small arms and light weapons.

The Council renews the support given to the plan of the Economic Community of West African States to strengthen the moratorium signed in Abuja on 31 October 1998 on the import, export and manufacture of small arms and light weapons, and to replace it with a mandatory convention. It welcomes the decision by the European Council on 2 December 2004 to significantly support this initiative, and calls upon all States and organizations in a position to do so to support this endeavour.

The Council calls upon all Member States to enforce all Council resolutions on sanctions, including those imposing arms embargoes, in accordance with the Charter, and to bring their own domestic implementation into compliance with the Council's measures on sanctions. The Council calls upon all Member States to continue to make available to the sanctions committees all pertinent information on any alleged violations of arms embargoes and to take appropriate measures to investigate such allegations. The Council urges Member States in a position to do so to provide assistance to interested States in strengthening their capacity to fulfil their obligations in this regard.

The Council underlines the fact that the issue of the illicit trade in small arms and light weapons must be addressed together with the disarmament, demobilization and reintegration process in the post-conflict phases. The Council recognizes that disarmament, demobilization and reintegration is closely linked with long-term peace and security in a post-conflict situation, and recalls that a growing number of peacekeeping missions contain the disarmament, demobilization and reintegration element as part of their mandate. In this regard, the Council stresses the importance of a comprehensive international and regional approach to disarmament, demobilization and reintegration that is not limited to the political and security aspects of disarmament, demobilization and reintegration of former combatants, but addresses also its social and economic aspects, including special needs of child soldiers and women.

The Council, while bearing in mind that the issue of the illicit small arms and light weapons has a multidisciplinary nature, encourages Member States, in a position to do so, to provide assistance and support to the United Nations Coordinating Action on Small Arms mechanism.

The Council continues to recognize the need to engage the relevant international organizations, non-governmental organizations, business and financial institutions and other actors at the international, regional and local levels to contribute to the implementation of arms embargoes and to the wider objective of preventing illicit trafficking of small arms and light weapons.

The Council requests the Secretary-General to update the Council on 28 February 2006 for its earliest possible consideration of the implementation of all the recommendations contained in his report of 20 September 2002 on small arms.

Working Group activities. The Open-ended Working Group to Negotiate an International Instrument to Enable States to Identify and Trace, in a Timely and Reliable Manner, Illicit Small Arms and Light Weapons, established by General Assembly resolution 58/241 [YUN 2003, p. 564], held its second (24 January–4 February) and third (6-17 June) substantive sessions [A/60/88 & Corr.1, 2], in New York. The Group, in a total of 58 meetings, negotiated the instrument, based on the Chairman's draft text. Following several readings of the draft text, the Group considered, on 17 June, the Chairman's compromise proposals and adopted by consensus a draft international instrument of a political character, which it recommended for adoption by the General Assembly. The Group also recommended that, the issue of small arms and light weapons ammunition be addressed in a comprehensive manner as part of a separate process and that the applicability of the provisions of the draft instrument to UN peacekeeping operations be considered further. The draft instrument was annexed to the Group's report.

Biennial meeting of States. In response to General Assembly resolution 59/86 [YUN 2004, p. 561], the Second Biennial Meeting of States to Consider the Implementation of the Programme of Action to Prevent, Combat and Eradicate the Illicit Trade in Small Arms and Light Weapons in All Its Aspects [YUN 2001, p. 499] was convened (New York, 11-15 July) [A/CONF.192/BMS/2005/1]. It had before it the report of the Open-ended Working Group to negotiate an international instrument (see above) and national reports on the implementation of the 2001 Programme of Action submitted by 100 States. The Meeting considered the implementation of the Programme under the following themes: weapons collection and destruction; stockpile management; disarmament, demobilization and reintegration of former combatants; capacity-building; resource mobilization; institution-building; marking and tracing; linkages (terrorism, organized crime, trafficking in drugs and precious minerals); import/export control; illicit brokering; human development; public awareness and culture of peace; and children, women and the elderly. International cooperation and assistance were discussed as a cross-cutting theme. Some issues relevant to the illicit trade in small arms and light weapons but not covered by the Programme were also addressed.

Member States reaffirmed their strong commitment to the implementation of the Programme of Action, and while welcoming the significant progress made in that regard at the national, regional and global levels, they recognized that further action was needed to fulfil the commitments contained in the Programme. The Meeting, with a view to strengthening the implementation of the Programme and contributing to a successful review conference in 2006, noted that further follow-up to the implementation process could benefit from being consolidated around future biennial meetings of States.

Report of Secretary-General. As requested in General Assembly resolutions 59/74 [YUN 2004, p. 560] and 59/86 [ibid., p. 561], the Secretary-General submitted a July report [A/60/161] covering the period from July 2004 to July 2005, which summarized national, subregional and regional activities undertaken in Africa to assist States in curbing the illicit trade in small arms and in collecting and disposing of them. The report also provided an overview of activities undertaken by the UN system and by States to combat the illicit trade in those weapons and to implement the 2001 Programme of Action.

The Secretary-General noted that continuing efforts were being made to assist countries in addressing the proliferation of illicit weapons in their territories in implementing the provisions of the 2001 Programme of Action. Efforts at the regional level were also very encouraging and there was a noticeable improvement in the collaboration and cooperation of members of the Coordinating Action on Small Arms (CASA) mechanism [YUN 1998, p. 525]. Initiatives undertaken by the UN system under the auspices of CASA attested to the fact that assistance to States and the development of capacity to implement the 2001 Programme of Action remained a central priority of the United Nations. At the global level, the outcome of the work of the Open-ended Working Group to negotiate an international instrument on tracing such weapons constituted a significant step towards the realization of the commitments under the 2001 Programme of Action. That politically binding international instrument, agreed upon by the Group, would provide States with an important tool to enhance cooperation in tracing the sources of leakage of small arms and light weapons into the illicit trade.

Communications. On 13 June [A/59/844], the United Kingdom transmitted the conclusions of an international experts' meeting (London, 26 May), which explored how an arms trade treaty could help to set common global principles for the trade in conventional arms.

On 23 September [A/60/379-S/2005/606], Georgia transmitted a statement by its Foreign Ministry on recent developments in the conflict zone of its Tskhinvali region, including the alleged display by separatist forces of heavy conventional weapons and of the existence of illicit arms in the zone.

GENERAL ASSEMBLY ACTION

The General Assembly adopted **decision 60/519** by recorded vote (151-0-25) [agenda item 97].

International instrument to enable States to identify and trace, in a timely and reliable manner, illicit small arms and light weapons

At its 61st plenary meeting, on 8 December 2005, the General Assembly, by a recorded vote of 151 to none, with 25 abstentions, and on the recommendation of the First Committee, decided to adopt the International Instrument to Enable States to Identify and Trace, in a Timely and Reliable Manner, Illicit Small Arms and Light Weapons, contained in the annex to the report of the Open-ended Working Group to Negotiate an International Instrument to Enable States to Identify and Trace, in a Timely and Reliable Manner, Illicit Small Arms and Light Weapons.

RECORDED VOTE ON DECISION 60/519:

In favour: Afghanistan, Albania, Algeria, Andorra, Armenia, Australia, Austria, Azerbaijan, Bahamas, Bahrain, Bangladesh, Belarus, Belgium, Belize, Benin, Bhutan, Bosnia and Herzegovina, Botswana, Brunei Darussalam, Bulgaria, Burkina Faso, Burundi, Cambodia, Cameroon, Canada, Cape Verde, Central African Republic, China, Congo, Côte d'Ivoire, Croatia, Cuba, Cyprus, Czech Republic, Democratic Republic of the Congo, Denmark, Djibouti, Dominica, Egypt, Eritrea, Estonia, Ethiopia, Fiji, Finland, France, Gabon, Georgia, Germany, Ghana, Greece, Guinea, Guinea-Bissau, Guyana, Haiti, Hungary, Iceland, India, Indonesia, Iran, Iraq, Ireland, Israel, Italy, Japan, Jordan, Kazakhstan, Kenya, Kuwait, Kyrgyzstan, Latvia, Lebanon, Lesotho, Liberia, Libyan Arab Jamahiriya, Liechtenstein, Lithuania, Luxembourg, Madagascar, Malawi, Malaysia, Maldives, Mali, Malta, Marshall Islands, Mauritania, Mauritius, Micronesia, Monaco, Mongolia, Morocco, Mozambique, Myanmar, Namibia, Nepal, Netherlands, New Zealand, Niger, Nigeria, Norway, Oman, Pakistan, Palau, Papua New Guinea, Philippines, Poland, Portugal, Qatar, Republic of Korea, Republic of Moldova, Romania, Russian Federation, Samoa, San Marino, Sao Tome and Principe, Saudi Arabia, Senegal, Serbia and Montenegro, Sierra Leone, Singapore, Slovakia, Slovenia, Solomon Islands, Somalia, South Africa, Spain, Sri Lanka, Sudan, Suriname, Sweden, Switzerland, Syrian Arab Republic, Tajikistan, Thailand, The former Yugoslav Republic of Macedonia, Timor-Leste, Togo, Tunisia, Turkey, Tuvalu, Uganda, Ukraine, United Arab Emirates, United Kingdom, United Republic of Tanzania, United States, Uzbekistan, Vanuatu, Viet Nam, Yemen, Zambia, Zimbabwe.

Against: None.

Abstaining: Antigua and Barbuda, Argentina, Barbados, Bolivia, Brazil, Chile, Colombia, Costa Rica, Dominican Republic, Ecuador, El Salvador, Grenada, Guatemala, Honduras, Jamaica, Mexico, Nicaragua, Panama, Paraguay, Peru, Saint Lucia, Saint Vincent and the Grenadines, Trinidad and Tobago, Uruguay, Venezuela.

Also, on 8 December [meeting 61], the General Assembly, on the recommendation of the First Committee [A/60/463], adopted five resolutions relating to conventional weapons and the illicit traffic in small arms and light weapons. The Assembly adopted **resolution 60/68** by recorded vote (177-1-0) [agenda item 97].

Addressing the negative humanitarian and development impact of the illicit manufacture, transfer and circulation of small arms and light weapons and their excessive accumulation

The General Assembly,

Reaffirming its respect for and commitment to international law and the purposes and principles enshrined in the Charter of the United Nations,

Recognizing that, as stated in the Programme of Action to Prevent, Combat and Eradicate the Illicit Trade in Small Arms and Light Weapons in All Its Aspects, the illicit manufacture, transfer and circulation of small arms and light weapons and their excessive accumulation have a wide range of humanitarian and socio-economic consequences and pose a serious threat to peace, reconciliation, safety, security, stability and sustainable development at the individual, local, national, regional and international levels,

Concerned by the implications that poverty and underdevelopment may have for the illicit trade in small arms and light weapons in all its aspects, and determined to reduce the human suffering caused by the illicit trade in small arms and light weapons in all its aspects and to enhance the respect for life and the dignity of the human person through the promotion of a culture of peace,

Reaffirming the urgent necessity for international cooperation and assistance, including financial and technical assistance, as appropriate, to support and facilitate efforts at the local, national, regional and global levels to prevent, combat and eradicate the illicit trade in small arms and light weapons in all its aspects,

Recalling the second biennial meeting of States to consider the implementation of the Programme of Action at which States, while welcoming the significant progress made in that regard, recognized that further action was required to fulfil the commitments undertaken in the Programme of Action,

Recognizing that, in 2005, world leaders expressed grave concern at the negative effects on development, peace and security, and human rights posed by, inter alia, the illicit trade of small arms and light weapons, and that they committed themselves to supporting the implementation of the Programme of Action,

Noting, in that regard, that the 2006 review conference on the Programme of Action represents an opportunity to address interconnected peace and security and development challenges, which are relevant to the agenda of the conference,

Placing particular emphasis on the regions of the world where conflicts have come to an end and where serious problems with the excessive and destabilizing accumulation of small arms and light weapons have to be dealt with urgently,

Calls upon States, when addressing the issue of the illicit trade in small arms and light weapons in all its aspects, explore ways, as appropriate, to more effectively address the humanitarian and development impact of the illicit manufacture, transfer and circulation of small arms and light weapons and their excessive accumulation, in particular in conflict or post-conflict situations, including by:

(a) Developing, where appropriate, comprehensive armed violence prevention programmes integrated into national development strategies, including poverty reduction strategies;

(b) Building on the commitment by States and appropriate international and regional organizations in a position to do so to, upon the request of the relevant authorities, seriously consider rendering assistance, including technical and financial assistance where needed, such as small arms funds, in order to support the implementation of measures to prevent, combat and eradicate the illicit trade in small arms and light weapons in all its aspects, as contained in the Programme of Action to Prevent, Combat and Eradicate the Illicit Trade in Small Arms and Light Weapons in All Its Aspects;

(c) Encouraging United Nations peacekeeping operations to address the safe storage and disposal of small arms and light weapons as an integral part of disarmament, demobilization and reintegration programmes;

(d) Systematically including national measures to regulate small arms and light weapons in longer term post-conflict peacebuilding strategies and programmes;

(e) Ensuring, where appropriate, that the activities mentioned in subparagraphs *(c)* and *(d)* above take full account of the roles that women and women's organizations could play in small arms disarmament, demobilization and reintegration processes; the requirement that the needs of women and girl combatants and dependants be addressed in disarmament, demobilization and reintegration programmes; and the commitment to promote and protect the rights and welfare of children in armed conflicts.

RECORDED VOTE ON RESOLUTION 60/68:

In favour: Afghanistan, Albania, Algeria, Andorra, Antigua and Barbuda, Argentina, Armenia, Australia, Austria, Azerbaijan, Bahamas, Bahrain, Bangladesh, Barbados, Belarus, Belgium, Belize, Benin, Bhutan, Bolivia, Bosnia and Herzegovina, Botswana, Brazil, Brunei Darussalam, Bulgaria, Burkina Faso, Burundi, Cambodia, Cameroon, Canada, Cape Verde, Central African Republic, Chile, China, Colombia, Comoros, Congo, Costa Rica, Côte d'Ivoire, Croatia, Cuba, Cyprus, Czech Republic, Democratic People's Republic of Korea, Democratic Republic of the Congo, Denmark, Djibouti, Dominica, Dominican Republic, Ecuador, Egypt, El Salvador, Eritrea, Estonia, Ethiopia, Fiji, Finland, France, Gabon, Georgia, Germany, Ghana, Greece, Grenada, Guatemala, Guinea, Guinea-Bissau, Guyana, Haiti, Honduras, Hungary, Iceland, India, Indonesia, Iran, Iraq, Ireland, Israel, Italy, Jamaica, Japan, Jordan, Kazakhstan, Kenya, Kuwait, Kyrgyzstan, Latvia, Lebanon, Lesotho, Liberia, Libyan Arab Jamahiriya, Liechtenstein, Lithuania, Luxembourg, Madagascar, Malawi, Malaysia, Maldives, Mali, Malta, Marshall Islands, Mauritania, Mauritius, Mexico, Micronesia, Monaco, Mongolia, Morocco, Mozambique, Myanmar, Namibia, Nepal, Netherlands, New Zealand, Nicaragua, Niger, Nigeria, Norway, Oman, Pakistan, Palau, Panama, Papua New Guinea, Paraguay, Peru, Philippines, Poland, Portugal, Qatar, Republic of Korea, Republic of Moldova, Romania, Russian Federation, Saint Lucia, Saint Vincent and the Grenadines, Samoa, San Marino, Sao Tome and Principe, Saudi Arabia, Senegal, Serbia and Montenegro, Sierra Leone, Singapore, Slovakia, Slovenia, Solomon Islands, Somalia, South Africa, Spain, Sri Lanka, Sudan, Suriname, Sweden, Switzerland, Syrian Arab Republic, Tajikistan, Thailand, The former Yugoslav Republic of Macedonia, Timor-Leste, Togo, Trinidad and Tobago, Tunisia, Turkey, Tuvalu, Uganda, Ukraine, United Arab Emirates, United Kingdom, United Republic of Tanzania, Uruguay, Uzbekistan, Vanuatu, Venezuela, Viet Nam, Yemen, Zambia, Zimbabwe.

Against: United States.

Abstaining: None.

The Assembly adopted **resolution 60/71** without vote [agenda item 97 *(k)*].

Assistance to States for curbing the illicit traffic in small arms and light weapons and collecting them

The General Assembly,

Recalling its resolution 59/74 of 3 December 2004 on assistance to States for curbing the illicit traffic in small arms and collecting them,

Deeply concerned by the magnitude of human casualty and suffering, especially among children, caused by the illicit proliferation and use of small arms and light weapons,

Concerned by the negative impact that the illicit proliferation and use of those weapons continue to have on the efforts of States in the Sahelo-Saharan subregion in the areas of poverty eradication, sustainable development and the maintenance of peace, security and stability,

Taking note of the latest report of the Secretary-General on assistance to States for curbing illicit traffic in small arms and collecting them and the illicit trade in small arms and light weapons in all its aspects, in which he states, inter alia, that continued efforts are being made to provide assistance to countries in need of addressing the proliferation of illicit weapons in their territories,

Welcoming the decision taken by the Economic Community of West African States to strengthen the moratorium on the importation, exportation and manufacture of small arms and light weapons in West Africa, adopted by the Heads of State and Government of the Economic Community at Abuja on 31 October 1998, by upgrading it to a legally binding instrument,

Welcoming also, in that regard, the decision of the European Union to significantly support the initiative of the Economic Community to strengthen the moratorium,

Welcoming further the decision taken by the Economic Community to establish a Small Arms Unit and to adopt a new Small Arms Control Programme,

Bearing in mind the Bamako Declaration on an African Common Position on the Illicit Proliferation, Circulation and Trafficking of Small Arms and Light Weapons, adopted at Bamako on 1 December 2000,

Recalling the report of the Secretary-General entitled "In larger freedom: towards development, security and human rights for all", in which he emphasized that States must strive just as hard to eliminate the threat of illicit small arms and light weapons as they do to eliminate the threat of weapons of mass destruction,

Taking note of the report of the second biennial meeting of States to consider the implementation of the Programme of Action to Prevent, Combat and Eradicate the Illicit Trade in Small Arms and Light Weapons in All Its Aspects at the national, regional and global levels, held in New York from 11 to 15 July 2005,

Welcoming the expression of support in the 2005 World Summit Outcome for the implementation of the Programme of Action,

Taking note of the draft International Instrument to Enable States to Identify and Trace, in a Timely and Reliable Manner, Illicit Small Arms and Light Weapons, concluded in June 2005,

Recognizing the important role that the organizations of civil society play in raising public awareness in efforts to curb the illicit traffic in small arms and light weapons,

1. *Commends* the United Nations, international, regional and other organizations for their assistance to States for curbing the illicit traffic in small arms and light weapons and collecting them;

2. *Encourages* the Secretary-General to pursue his efforts in the context of the implementation of General Assembly resolution 49/75 G of 15 December 1994

and the recommendations of the United Nations advisory missions, aimed at curbing the illicit circulation of small arms and light weapons and collecting them in the affected States that so request, with the support of the United Nations Regional Centre for Peace and Disarmament in Africa and in close cooperation with the African Union;

3. *Encourages* the international community to support the implementation of the moratorium on the importation, exportation and manufacture of small arms and light weapons in West Africa, and to extend further assistance in transforming the moratorium into a legally binding instrument;

4. *Encourages* the countries of the Sahelo-Saharan subregion to facilitate the effective functioning of national commissions to combat the illicit proliferation of small arms and light weapons, and, in that regard, invites the international community to lend its support wherever possible;

5. *Encourages* the collaboration of organizations and associations of civil society in the efforts of the national commissions to combat the illicit traffic in small arms and light weapons and in the implementation of the Programme of Action to Prevent, Combat and Eradicate the Illicit Trade in Small Arms and Light Weapons in All Its Aspects;

6. *Also encourages* cooperation among State organs, international organizations and civil society in supporting programmes and projects aimed at combating the illicit traffic in small arms and light weapons and collecting them;

7. *Calls upon* the international community to provide technical and financial support to strengthen the capacity of civil society organizations to take action to combat the illicit trade in small arms and light weapons;

8. *Invites* the Secretary-General and those States and organizations that are in a position to do so to continue to provide assistance to States for curbing the illicit traffic in small arms and light weapons and collecting them;

9. *Requests* the Secretary-General to continue to consider the matter and to report to the General Assembly at its sixty-first session on the implementation of the present resolution;

10. *Decides* to include in the provisional agenda of its sixty-first session an item entitled "Assistance to States for curbing the illicit traffic in small arms and light weapons and collecting them"

The Assembly adopted **resolution 60/74** without vote [agenda item 97 *(dd)*].

Problems arising from the accumulation of conventional ammunition stockpiles in surplus

The General Assembly,

Mindful of contributing to the process initiated within the framework of the United Nations reform to make the Organization more effective in maintaining peace and security by giving it the resources and tools it needs for conflict prevention, peaceful resolution of disputes, peacekeeping, post-conflict peacebuilding and reconstruction,

Underlining the importance of a comprehensive and integrated approach to disarmament through the development of practical measures,

Taking note of the report of the Group of Experts on the problem of ammunition and explosives,

Recalling the recommendation contained in paragraph 27 of the report submitted by the Chairman of the Open-ended Working Group to Negotiate an International Instrument to Enable States to Identify and Trace, in a Timely and Reliable Manner, Illicit Small Arms and Light Weapons, namely, to address the issue of small arms and light weapons ammunition in a comprehensive manner as part of a separate process conducted within the framework of the United Nations,

Noting with satisfaction the work and measures pursued at the regional and subregional levels with regard to the issue of conventional ammunition,

Recalling its decision 59/515 of 3 December 2004, by which it decided to include the question of conventional ammunition stockpiles in surplus in the agenda of its sixtieth session,

1. *Encourages* all interested States to assess, on a voluntary basis, whether, in conformity with their legitimate security needs, parts of their stockpiles of conventional ammunition should be considered to be in surplus, and recognizes that the security of such stockpiles must be taken into consideration and that appropriate controls with regard to the security and safety of stockpiles of conventional ammunition are indispensable at the national level in order to eliminate the risk of explosion, pollution or diversion;

2. *Appeals* to all interested States to determine the size and nature of their surplus stockpiles of conventional ammunition, whether they represent a security risk, if appropriate, their means of destruction, and whether external assistance is needed to eliminate this risk;

3. *Encourages* States in a position to do so to assist interested States within a bilateral framework or through international or regional organizations, on a voluntary and transparent basis, in elaborating and implementing programmes to eliminate surplus stockpiles or to improve their management;

4. *Encourages* all Member States to examine the possibility of developing and implementing, within a national, regional or subregional framework, measures to address accordingly the illicit trafficking related to the accumulation of such stockpiles;

5. *Requests* the Secretary-General to seek the views of Member States regarding the risks arising from the accumulation of conventional ammunition stockpiles in surplus and regarding national ways of strengthening controls on conventional ammunition, and to submit a report to the General Assembly at its sixty-first session;

6. *Decides* to include this issue in the provisional agenda of its sixty-first session.

The Assembly adopted **resolution 60/77** without vote [agenda item 97 (x)].

Prevention of the illicit transfer and unauthorized access to and use of man-portable air defence systems

The General Assembly,

Recalling its resolutions 58/42 and 58/54 of 8 December 2003, 58/241 of 23 December 2003 and 59/90 of 3 December 2004,

Recognizing that disarmament, arms control and non-proliferation are essential for the maintenance of international peace and security,

Acknowledging the authorized trade in man-portable air defence systems between Governments and the legitimate right of Governments to possess such weapons in the interests of their national security,

Recognizing the threat to civil aviation, peace-keeping, crisis management and security posed by the illicit transfer and unauthorized access to and use of man-portable air defence systems,

Taking into account the fact that man-portable air defence systems are easily carried, concealed, fired and, in certain circumstances, obtained,

Recognizing that effective control over man-portable air defence systems acquires special importance in the context of the intensified international fight against global terrorism,

Convinced of the importance of effective national control of transfers of man-portable air defence systems and their training and instruction materials and of the safe and effective management of stockpiles of such weapons,

Acknowledging the role of the unauthorized transfer of relevant materials and information in assisting the unauthorized manufacture and illicit transfer of man-portable air defence systems and related components,

Welcoming the ongoing efforts of, and noting declarations by, various international and regional forums to enhance transport security and to strengthen management of man-portable air defence systems stockpiles in order to prevent the illicit transfer and unauthorized access to and use of such weapons,

Noting the importance of information exchange and transparency in the trade in man-portable air defence systems to build confidence and security among States and to prevent the illicit trade in and unauthorized access to such weapons,

Acknowledging the considerable efforts of some Member States to collect, secure and destroy voluntarily those man-portable air defence systems declared to be surplus by the competent national authority,

1. *Emphasizes* the importance of the full implementation of the Programme of Action to Prevent, Combat and Eradicate the Illicit Trade in Small Arms and Light Weapons in All Its Aspects, adopted by the United Nations Conference on the Illicit Trade in Small Arms and Light Weapons in All Its Aspects;

2. *Urges* Member States to support current international, regional and national efforts to combat and prevent the illicit transfer of man-portable air defence systems and unauthorized access to and use of such weapons;

3. *Stresses* the importance of effective and comprehensive national controls on the production, stockpiling, transfer and brokering of man-portable air defence systems to prevent the illicit trade in and unauthorized access to and use of such weapons, their components and training and instruction materials;

4. *Encourages* Member States to enact or improve legislation, regulations, procedures and stockpile management practices and to assist other States, at their request, to exercise effective control over access to and transfer of man-portable air defence systems so as to prevent the illicit brokering and transfer of and unauthorized access to and use of such weapons;

5. *Also encourages* Member States to enact or improve legislation, regulations and procedures to ban the transfer of man-portable air defence systems to non-State end-users and to ensure that such weapons are exported only to Governments or agents authorized by a Government;

6. *Encourages* initiatives to exchange information and to mobilize resources and technical expertise to assist States, at their request, in enhancing national controls and stockpile management practices to prevent unauthorized access to and use and transfer of man-portable air defence systems and to destroy excess or obsolete stockpiles of such weapons, as appropriate;

7. *Decides* to remain seized of the matter.

The Assembly adopted **resolution 60/81** without vote [agenda item 97 *(t)*].

The illicit trade in small arms and light weapons in all its aspects

The General Assembly,

Recalling its resolutions 56/24 V of 24 December 2001, 57/72 of 22 November 2002, 58/241 of 23 December 2003 and 59/86 of 3 December 2004,

Emphasizing the importance of the early and full implementation of the Programme of Action to Prevent, Combat and Eradicate the Illicit Trade in Small Arms and Light Weapons in All Its Aspects, adopted by the United Nations Conference on the Illicit Trade in Small Arms and Light Weapons in All Its Aspects,

Welcoming the efforts by Member States to submit, on a voluntary basis, national reports on their implementation of the Programme of Action,

Noting with satisfaction regional and subregional efforts being undertaken in support of the implementation of the Programme of Action, and commending the progress that has already been made in this regard, including tackling both supply and demand factors that are relevant to addressing the illicit trade in small arms and light weapons,

Recognizing the efforts undertaken by non-governmental organizations in the provision of assistance to States for the implementation of the Programme of Action,

Taking into account the relevant paragraphs on the illicit trade in small arms and light weapons in the 2005 World Summit Outcome,

Welcoming the report of the Second Biennial Meeting of States to Consider the Implementation of the Programme of Action to Prevent, Combat and Eradicate the Illicit Trade in Small Arms and Light Weapons in All Its Aspects, held in New York from 11 to 15 July 2005, and expressing its appreciation for the efforts undertaken by the Chair of the Meeting,

Taking note of the report of the Open-ended Working Group to Negotiate an International Instrument to Enable States to Identify and Trace, in a Timely and Reliable Manner, Illicit Small Arms and Light Weapons,

Recognizing that illicit brokering in small arms and light weapons is a serious problem that the international community should address urgently, and, in this regard, welcoming the broad-based consultations held by the Secretary-General with all Member States and interested regional and subregional organizations on further steps to enhance international cooperation in preventing, combating and eradicating illicit brokering in small arms and light weapons,

Taking note of the report of the Secretary-General on the implementation of resolution 59/86,

Conscious of its decision to convene in New York the United Nations conference to review progress made in the implementation of the Programme of Action to Prevent, Combat and Eradicate the Illicit Trade in Small Arms and Light Weapons in All Its Aspects for a period of two weeks, from 26 June to 7 July 2006, and its preparatory committee for two weeks, from 9 to 20 January 2006, followed, if necessary, by a subsequent session of up to two weeks in duration, which is especially relevant in order to set the agenda for activities of the international community for continuing to tackle problems in this field beyond 2006,

1. *Encourages* all initiatives, including those of the United Nations, other international organizations, regional and subregional organizations, non-governmental organizations and civil society, for the successful conclusion of the United Nations conference to review progress made in the implementation of the Programme of Action to Prevent, Combat and Eradicate the Illicit Trade in Small Arms and Light Weapons in All Its Aspects in order to set the agenda for tackling problems in the illicit trade in small arms and light weapons by the international community beyond 2006, and calls upon all Member States to continue to contribute towards the preparation of the conference and to make every effort to fully implement the Programme of Action;

2. *Calls upon* all States to implement the International Instrument to Enable States to Identify and Trace, in a Timely and Reliable Manner, Illicit Small Arms and Light Weapons;

3. *Decides* to establish a group of governmental experts, appointed by the Secretary-General on the basis of equitable geographical representation, commencing after the review conference and no later than 2007, to consider further steps to enhance international cooperation in preventing, combating and eradicating illicit brokering in small arms and light weapons in three sessions of one week's duration each, and to submit the report on the outcome of its study to the General Assembly at its sixty-second session;

4. *Requests* the Secretary-General to provide the group of governmental experts with any assistance and services that may be required for the discharge of its tasks;

5. *Continues* to encourage all initiatives, including regional and subregional ones, to mobilize resources and expertise to promote the implementation of the Programme of Action and to provide assistance to States in its implementation;

6. *Requests* the Secretary-General to continue to collate and circulate data and information provided by States on a voluntary basis, including national reports, on their implementation of the Programme of Action, and encourages Member States to submit such reports;

7. *Also requests* the Secretary-General to report to the General Assembly at its sixty-first session on the implementation of the present resolution;

8. *Decides* to include in the provisional agenda of its sixty-first session the item entitled "The illicit trade in small arms and light weapons in all its aspects".

(For regional initiatives regarding implementation of the Programme of Action, see pp. 641-652.)

Convention on excessively injurious conventional weapons and Protocols

As at 31 December, the accessions of Liberia and Venezuela and the ratification of Turkey brought to 100 the number of States parties to the 1980 Convention on Prohibitions or Restrictions on the Use of Certain Conventional Weapons Which May Be Deemed to Be Excessively Injurious or to Have Indiscriminate Effects [YUN 1980, p. 76] and its annexed Protocols on Non-Detectable Fragments (Protocol I); on Prohibitions or Restrictions on the Use of Mines, Booby Traps and Other Devices, as amended on 3 May 1996 (Protocol II) [YUN 1996, p. 484]; and on Prohibitions or Restrictions on the Use of Incendiary Weapons (Protocol III). The 1995 Additional Protocol on Blinding Laser Weapons (Protocol IV) [YUN 1995, p. 221], which took effect on 30 July 1998 [YUN 1998, p. 530], had 81 parties following the consent of Liberia and Turkey in 2005 to be bound by the Protocol's terms.

Group of Governmental Experts

The Group of Governmental Experts established by the Second Review Conference of the States parties to the Convention [YUN 2001, p. 504] to consider the issues of explosive remnants of war, mines other than anti-personnel mines, small-calibre weapons and ammunition, and promotion of compliance with the Convention and its annexed Protocols, held its tenth (7-11 March) [CCW/GGE/X/5], eleventh (2-12 August) [CCW/GGE/XI/4] and twelfth (14-22 November) [CCW/GGE/XII/4] sessions, all in Geneva. The Group discussed issues relating to the weapons under consideration and preparations for the Third Review Conference of the States parties, and considered working papers and presentations from delegations, international organizations and other participants, including military experts. The Group also had before it the reports of its working groups on explosive remnants of war and on mines other than anti-personnel mines. The latter did not reach agreement on recommendations and consequently forwarded the issue to the Meeting of the States parties (see below). On 22 November, the Group adopted its report and recommended that the Third Review Conference be held in November 2006 and that the Meeting of States parties nominate the President-designate for the Conference, who should undertake consultations during the intersessional period on possible options to promote compliance with the Convention and its annexed Protocols and submit a consensus report to the States parties. The President-designate should undertake consultations on the establishment of a sponsorship programme under the Convention and report thereon. The Group further recommended that follow-up work arising from the States parties' meeting be held under the oversight of the President-designate and that intersessional work be undertaken in three sessions during 2006.

Annual Conference of States Parties to Amended Protocol II

The Seventh Annual Conference of the States Parties to Amended Protocol II (Geneva, 23 November) [CCW/AP.II/CONF.7/2] reviewed the operation and status of that Protocol, considered related issues and examined national reports received from 59 States parties. The Conference adopted a final document containing conclusions and recommendations and an appeal to States to accede to Amended Protocol II. It recommended that the Secretary-General, as depositary, and the President of the Conference exercise their authority to achieve the goal of universality of the Protocol and called on the States parties to promote wider adherence.

Meeting of States parties

The 2005 Meeting of the States parties (Geneva, 24-25 November) [CCW/MSP/2005/2 & Corr.1] considered the work of the Group of Governmental Experts (see above) and decided that the Group should continue its work in 2006 in three sessions. It mandated the Working Group on Explosive Remnants of War to continue to consider the implementation of existing principles of international humanitarian law and possible preventive measures, aimed at improving the design of certain types of munitions, including sub-munitions, with a view to minimizing their risk of becoming explosive remnants of war. The working group on mines other than anti-personnel mines was asked to consider all proposals in that category of mines and to make recommendations for consideration by the Third Review Conference of the Convention in 2006. The meeting endorsed the recommendations of the Group of Experts regarding preparations for the Conference and the intersessional duties of the President-designate (see above). It decided that the Eighth Annual Conference of the States parties to Amended Protocol II would be held in November 2006 in Geneva and called on States parties to the Convention to promote wider adherence to the instrument and its annexed Protocols in their respective regions, and to organize national or regional workshops and conferences towards that end.

GENERAL ASSEMBLY ACTION

On 8 December [meeting 62], the General Assembly, on the recommendation of the First Committee [A/60/467], adopted **resolution 60/93** without vote [agenda item 101].

Convention on Prohibitions or Restrictions on the Use of Certain Conventional Weapons Which May Be Deemed to Be Excessively Injurious or to Have Indiscriminate Effects

The General Assembly,

Recalling its resolution 59/107 of 3 December 2004,

Recalling with satisfaction the adoption and the entry into force of the Convention on Prohibitions or Restrictions on the Use of Certain Conventional Weapons Which May Be Deemed to Be Excessively Injurious or to Have Indiscriminate Effects, and its amended article 1, and the Protocol on Non-Detectable Fragments (Protocol I), the Protocol on Prohibitions or Restrictions on the Use of Mines, Booby Traps and Other Devices (Protocol II) and its amended version, the Protocol on Prohibitions or Restrictions on the Use of Incendiary Weapons (Protocol III) and the Protocol on Blinding Laser Weapons (Protocol IV),

Recalling the decision of the Second Review Conference of the States Parties to the Convention on Prohibitions or Restrictions on the Use of Certain Conventional Weapons Which May Be Deemed to Be Excessively Injurious or to Have Indiscriminate Effects to establish an open-ended group of governmental experts with two separate coordinators on explosive remnants of war and on mines other than anti-personnel mines,

Recalling also the role played by the International Committee of the Red Cross in the elaboration of the Convention and the Protocols thereto, and welcoming the particular efforts of various international, nongovernmental and other organizations in raising awareness of the humanitarian consequences of explosive remnants of war,

1. *Calls upon* all States that have not yet done so to take all measures to become parties, as soon as possible, to the Convention on Prohibitions or Restrictions on the Use of Certain Conventional Weapons Which May Be Deemed to Be Excessively Injurious or to Have Indiscriminate Effects and the Protocols thereto, as amended, with a view to achieving the widest possible adherence to these instruments at an early date, and so as to ultimately achieve their universality;

2. *Calls upon* all States parties to the Convention that have not yet done so to express their consent to be bound by the Protocols to the Convention and the amendment extending the scope of the Convention and the Protocols thereto to include armed conflicts of a non-international character;

3. *Welcomes with satisfaction* the adoption of the Protocol on Explosive Remnants of War (Protocol V) at the Meeting of the States Parties to the Convention held in Geneva on 27 and 28 November 2003, and calls upon the States parties to express their consent to be bound by the Protocol and to notify the depositary at an early date of their consent;

4. *Notes* the decision of the Meeting of the States Parties that the Working Group on Mines Other Than Anti-Personnel Mines would continue its work in 2005 with the mandate to consider all proposals on mines other than anti-personnel mines put forward since the establishment of the Group of Governmental Experts, and to conduct meetings of military experts to provide advice, with the aim of elaborating appropriate recommendations on this issue for submission to the next Meeting of the States Parties;

5. *Also notes* the decision of the Meeting of the States Parties that the Working Group on Explosive Remnants of War would continue its work in 2005 with the mandate to continue to consider, including through participation of legal experts, the implementation of existing principles of international humanitarian law and to further study, on an open-ended basis, with particular emphasis on meetings of military and technical experts, possible preventive measures aimed at improving the design of certain specific types of munitions, including sub-munitions, with a view to minimizing the humanitarian risk of these munitions becoming explosive remnants of war;

6. *Further notes* the decision of the Meeting of the States Parties that the Chairperson-designate should continue to undertake consultations during the intersessional period on possible options with respect to promoting compliance with the Convention and the Protocols thereto, taking into account proposals put forward;

7. *Expresses support* for the work conducted by the Group of Governmental Experts, and encourages the Chairperson-designate and the Group to conduct work, in accordance with the mandate for 2005, with the aim of elaborating appropriate recommendations on mines other than anti-personnel mines, for submission to the Meeting of the States Parties on 24 and 25 November 2005, and to report on the work done on compliance, as well as on the implementation of existing principles of international humanitarian law and on possible preventive technical measures to minimize the risk of munitions becoming explosive remnants of war;

8. *Recalls* the decision of the Second Review Conference of the States Parties to the Convention on Prohibitions or Restrictions on the Use of Certain Conventional Weapons Which May Be Deemed to Be Excessively Injurious or to Have Indiscriminate Effects to convene a further conference not later than 2006, requests that the conference be held in November 2006 in Geneva and be preceded by as many preparatory meetings as deemed necessary by the States parties, and also requests the Meeting of the States Parties on 24 and 25 November 2005 to take a final decision on these matters;

9. *Notes* that, in conformity with article 8 of the Convention, the Third Review Conference may consider any proposal for amendments to the Convention or the Protocols thereto as well as any proposal for additional protocols relating to other categories of conventional weapons not covered by existing protocols to the Convention;

10. *Requests* that the Third Review Conference and its preparatory meetings exert maximum effort to promote universalization of the Convention, as amended,

and of all Protocols thereto, including through the holding of regional conferences and seminars;

11. *Requests* the Secretary-General to render the necessary assistance and to provide such services, including summary records, as may be required for the Meeting of the States Parties on 24 and 25 November 2005, as well as for any possible continuation of work after the Meeting, should the States parties deem it appropriate, and for the Third Review Conference and its preparatory meetings;

12. *Also requests* the Secretary-General, in his capacity as depositary of the Convention and the Protocols thereto, to continue to inform the General Assembly periodically, by electronic means, of ratifications and acceptances of and accessions to the Convention, its amended article 1, and the Protocols thereto;

13. *Decides* to include in the provisional agenda of its sixty-first session the item entitled "Convention on Prohibitions or Restrictions on the Use of Certain Conventional Weapons Which May Be Deemed to Be Excessively Injurious or to Have Indiscriminate Effects".

Practical disarmament

The Group of Interested States, established in 1998 [YUN 1998, p. 531] to examine and support concrete practical disarmament initiatives, met four times during 2005 to assess project proposals and review requests for assistance by Governments. Projects funded through the Group included a joint UN fact-finding mission to Burundi involving the UN Department for Disarmament Affairs (DDA) and the UNDP Bureau for Crisis Prevention, and the funding of travel expenses for an expert from Kenya who briefed the Group on the small arms and light weapons situation and related activities in the Sudan and Uganda. The Group also supported a project on the implementation of measures to control those weapons in southern Sudan, being implemented by the Bonn International Centre for Conversion.

Disarmament Commission action. In 2005 [A/60/42], the Disarmament Commission considered, as one of its proposed agenda items, practical confidence-building measures in the field of conventional weapons, but owing to unresolved disagreements among delegations regarding the item, the Commission was not able to reach consensus on its substantive agenda and decided to continue deliberations in 2006.

Transparency

Conference on Disarmament. In 2005, the continuing deadlock among delegates over a substantive programme of work again prevented the Conference on Disarmament [A/60/27] from establishing or re-establishing any mechanism to deal with transparency in armaments, leaving the item to be addressed at plenary meetings, where delegates reaffirmed their respective positions.

GENERAL ASSEMBLY ACTION

On 8 December [meeting 61], the General Assembly, on the recommendation of the First Committee [A/59/463], adopted two resolutions relating to transparency in conventional arms transfers. The Assembly adopted **resolution 60/69** without vote [agenda item 97 *(e)*].

National legislation on transfer of arms, military equipment and dual-use goods and technology

The General Assembly,

Recognizing that disarmament, arms control and non-proliferation are essential for the maintenance of international peace and security,

Recalling that effective national control of the transfer of arms, military equipment and dual-use goods and technology, including those transfers that could contribute to proliferation activities, is an important tool for achieving those objectives,

Recalling also that the States parties to the international disarmament and non-proliferation treaties have undertaken to facilitate the fullest possible exchange of materials, equipment and technological information for peaceful purposes, in accordance with the provisions of those treaties,

Considering that the exchange of national legislation, regulations and procedures on the transfer of arms, military equipment and dual-use goods and technology contributes to mutual understanding and confidence among Member States,

Convinced that such an exchange would be beneficial to Member States that are in the process of developing such legislation,

Reaffirming the inherent right of individual or collective self-defence in accordance with Article 51 of the Charter of the United Nations,

1. *Invites* Member States that are in a position to do so, without prejudice to the provisions contained in Security Council resolution 1540(2004) of 28 April 2004, to enact or improve national legislation, regulations and procedures to exercise effective control over the transfer of arms, military equipment and dual-use goods and technology, while ensuring that such legislation, regulations and procedures are consistent with the obligations of States parties under international treaties;

2. *Encourages* Member States to provide, on a voluntary basis, information to the Secretary-General on their national legislation, regulations and procedures on the transfer of arms, military equipment and dual-use goods and technology, as well as the changes therein, and requests the Secretary-General to make this information accessible to Member States;

3. *Decides* to remain attentive to the matter.

The Assembly adopted **resolution 60/82** without vote [agenda item 97 *(z)*].

Information on confidence-building measures in the field of conventional arms

The General Assembly,

Guided by the purposes and principles enshrined in the Charter of the United Nations,

Bearing in mind the contribution of confidence-building measures in the field of conventional arms, adopted on the initiative and with the agreement of the States concerned, to the improvement of the overall international peace and security situation,

Convinced that the relationship between the development of confidence-building measures in the field of conventional arms and the international security environment can also be mutually reinforcing,

Considering the important role that confidence-building measures in the field of conventional arms can also play in creating favourable conditions for progress in the field of disarmament,

Recognizing that the exchange of information on confidence-building measures in the field of conventional arms contributes to mutual understanding and confidence among Member States,

1. *Welcomes* all confidence-building measures in the field of conventional arms already undertaken by Member States as well as the information on such measures voluntarily provided;

2. *Encourages* Member States to continue to adopt confidence-building measures in the field of conventional arms and to provide information in that regard;

3. *Also encourages* Member States to continue the dialogue on confidence-building measures in the field of conventional arms;

4. *Requests* the Secretary-General to establish, with the financial support of States in a position to do so, an electronic database containing information provided by Member States and to assist them, at their request, in the organization of seminars, courses and workshops aimed at enhancing the knowledge of new developments in this field;

5. *Decides* to include in the provisional agenda of its sixty-first session the item entitled "Information on confidence-building measures in the field of conventional arms".

UN Register of Conventional Arms

In response to General Assembly resolution 58/54 [YUN 2003, p. 568], the Secretary-General submitted the thirteenth annual report on the United Nations Register of Conventional Arms [A/60/160 & Corr.1 & Add.1, 2], established in 1992 [YUN 1992, p. 75] to promote enhanced levels of transparency on arms transfers. The report presented information provided by 115 Governments on imports and exports in 2004 in the seven categories of conventional arms covered (battle tanks, armoured combat vehicles, large-calibre artillery systems, attack helicopters, combat aircraft, warships and missiles and missile launchers). Governments also provided information on military holdings and procurement through national production and on small arms and light weapons and national policies. The report indicated a slight increase in the number of submissions from 114 in 2003.

In response to the Assembly's request that the Secretary-General implement the recommendations contained in the 2003 report of the Group

of Governmental Experts on the continuing operation and further development of the Register [YUN 2003, p. 568], the report highlighted numerous activities undertaken by the Secretariat during the year, through DDA and in collaboration with Governments and regional organizations, in order to enhance awareness of the Register and to encourage greater participation in it.

GENERAL ASSEMBLY ACTION

On 23 December [meeting 69], the General Assembly, on the recommendation of the First Committee [A/59/463], adopted **resolution 60/226** by recorded vote (99-0-22) [agenda item 97 (d)].

Transparency in armaments

The General Assembly,

Recalling its resolutions 46/36 L of 9 December 1991, 47/52 L of 15 December 1992, 48/75 E of 16 December 1993, 49/75 C of 15 December 1994, 50/70 D of 12 December 1995, 51/45 H of 10 December 1996, 52/38 R of 9 December 1997, 53/77 V of 4 December 1998, 54/54 O of 1 December 1999, 55/33 U of 20 November 2000, 56/24 Q of 29 November 2001, 57/75 of 22 November 2002 and 58/54 of 8 December 2003 entitled "Transparency in armaments",

Continuing to take the view that an enhanced level of transparency in armaments contributes greatly to confidence-building and security among States and that the establishment of the United Nations Register of Conventional Arms constitutes an important step forward in the promotion of transparency in military matters,

Welcoming the consolidated report of the Secretary-General on the Register, which includes the returns of Member States for 2004,

Welcoming also the response of Member States to the request contained in paragraphs 9 and 10 of resolution 46/36 L to provide data on their imports and exports of arms, as well as available background information regarding their military holdings, procurement through national production and relevant policies,

Welcoming further the inclusion by some Member States of their transfers of small arms and light weapons in their annual report to the Register as part of their additional background information,

Stressing that the continuing operation of the Register and its further development should be reviewed in order to secure a Register that is capable of attracting the widest possible participation,

1. *Reaffirms its determination* to ensure the effective operation of the United Nations Register of Conventional Arms, as provided for in paragraphs 7 to 10 of resolution 46/36 L;

2. *Calls upon* Member States, with a view to achieving universal participation, to provide the Secretary-General, by 31 May annually, with the requested data and information for the Register, including nil reports if appropriate, on the basis of resolutions 46/36 L and 47/52 L, the recommendations contained in paragraph 64 of the 1997 report of the Secretary-General on the continuing operation of the Register and its further development, the recommendations contained in paragraph 94 of the 2000 report of the Secretary-

General and the appendices and annexes thereto and the recommendations contained in paragraphs 112 to 114 of the 2003 report of the Secretary-General;

3. *Invites* Member States in a position to do so, pending further development of the Register, to provide additional information on procurement through national production and military holdings and to make use of the "Remarks" column in the standardized reporting form to provide additional information such as types or models and to include transfers of small arms and light weapons, using definitions and reporting measures they deem appropriate, as part of their additional background information;

4. *Reaffirms its decision*, with a view to further development of the Register, to keep the scope of and participation in the Register under review and, to that end:

(*a*) Recalls its request to Member States to provide the Secretary-General with their views on the continuing operation of the Register and its further development and on transparency measures related to weapons of mass destruction;

(*b*) Requests the Secretary-General, with the assistance of a group of governmental experts to be convened in 2006, within available resources, on the basis of equitable geographical representation, to prepare a report on the continuing operation of the Register and its further development, taking into account the work of the Conference on Disarmament, the views expressed by Member States and the reports of the Secretary-General on the continuing operation of the Register and its further development, with a view to taking a decision at its sixty-first session;

5. *Requests* the Secretary-General to implement the recommendations contained in his 2000 and 2003 reports on the continuing operation of the Register and its further development and to ensure that sufficient resources are made available for the Secretariat to operate and maintain the Register;

6. *Invites* the Conference on Disarmament to consider continuing its work undertaken in the field of transparency in armaments;

7. *Reiterates its call upon* all Member States to cooperate at the regional and subregional levels, taking fully into account the specific conditions prevailing in the region or subregion, with a view to enhancing and coordinating international efforts aimed at increased openness and transparency in armaments;

8. *Requests* the Secretary-General to report to the General Assembly at its sixty-first session on progress made in implementing the present resolution;

9. *Decides* to include in the provisional agenda of its sixty-first session the item entitled "Transparency in armaments".

RECORDED VOTE ON RESOLUTION 60/226:

In favour: Andorra, Antigua and Barbuda, Argentina, Armenia, Australia, Austria, Azerbaijan, Bangladesh, Barbados, Belarus, Belgium, Benin, Brazil, Brunei Darussalam, Bulgaria, Cambodia, Canada, Chile, Costa Rica, Croatia, Cyprus, Czech Republic, Denmark, Dominican Republic, Ecuador, El Salvador, Eritrea, Estonia, Finland, France, Georgia, Germany, Ghana, Greece, Guatemala, Guyana, Hungary, Iceland, India, Indonesia, Ireland, Italy, Jamaica, Japan, Kazakhstan, Kyrgyzstan, Lao People's Democratic Republic, Latvia, Lesotho, Liechtenstein, Lithuania, Luxembourg, Malaysia, Maldives, Mali, Malta, Mauritius, Mexico, Monaco, Myanmar, Namibia, Nepal, Netherlands, New Zealand, Niger, Nigeria, Norway, Panama, Peru, Philippines, Poland, Portugal, Republic of Korea, Romania, Russian Federation, San Marino, Serbia and Montenegro, Singapore, Slovakia, Slovenia, South Africa, Spain, Sri Lanka, Sweden, Switzerland, Thailand, The former Yugoslav Republic of

Macedonia, Timor-Leste, Togo, Trinidad and Tobago, Turkey, Ukraine, United Kingdom, United Republic of Tanzania, United States, Uruguay, Uzbekistan, Venezuela, Zambia.

Against: None.

Abstaining: Algeria, Bahrain, China, Comoros, Cuba, Djibouti, Egypt, Iran, Iraq, Jordan, Kuwait, Libyan Arab Jamahiriya, Mauritania, Morocco, Oman, Pakistan, Qatar, Saudi Arabia, Syrian Arab Republic, Tunisia, United Arab Emirates, Yemen.

The First Committee adopted by separate recorded votes the words "and the recommendations contained in paragraphs 112 to 114 of the 2003 report of the Secretary-General" in paragraph 2 of the resolution (108 to 1, with 16 abstentions); paragraph 3 (115 to 0, with 18 abstentions); paragraph 4 (*b*) (118 to 0, with 16 abstentions); and paragraph 6 (116 to 0, with 19 abstentions). The Assembly retained those paragraphs by separate recorded votes of 97 to none, with 20 abstentions; 94 to none, with 22 abstentions; 97 to none, with 19 abstentions; and 93 to none, with 22 abstentions, respectively.

Transparency of military expenditures

In response to General Assembly resolution 58/28 [YUN 2003, p. 570], the Secretary-General, in a July report with later addenda [A/60/159 & Add.1, 2, 3], presented reports from 77 Member States on military expenditures for the latest fiscal year for which data were available. The reporting instrument was that recommended by the Assembly in resolution 35/142 B [YUN 1980, p. 88].

The report also described activities undertaken by the Secretariat, through DDA, to enhance familiarity with and encourage greater participation in the standardized reporting instrument. Those included a DDA presentation to the Committee on Hemispheric Security of the Organization of American States (OAS) (Washington, D.C., 25 April) and a regional workshop focusing on the Horn of Africa, the Great Lakes region and Southern Africa (Nairobi, Kenya, 31 May–2 June), organized by DDA, with support from a number of Member States. Also in May, DDA published technical guidelines to assist Member States in preparing their submissions on military expenditures, in accordance with the UN reporting matrix.

GENERAL ASSEMBLY ACTION

On 8 December [meeting 61], the General Assembly, on the recommendation of the First Committee [A/59/451], adopted **resolution 60/44** without vote [agenda item 85 (*b*)].

Objective information on military matters, including transparency of military expenditures

The General Assembly,

Recalling its resolutions 53/72 of 4 December 1998, 54/43 of 1 December 1999, 56/14 of 29 November 2001 and 58/28 of 8 December 2003 on objective information on military matters, including transparency of military expenditures,

Also recalling its resolution 35/142 B of 12 December 1980, which introduced the United Nations system for the standardized reporting of military expenditures, and its resolutions 48/62 of 16 December 1993, 49/66 of 15 December 1994, 51/38 of 10 December 1996 and 52/32 of 9 December 1997, calling upon all Member States to participate in it, and its resolution 47/54 B of 9 December 1992, endorsing the guidelines and recommendations for objective information on military matters and inviting Member States to provide the Secretary-General with relevant information regarding their implementation,

Noting that since then, national reports on military expenditures and on the guidelines and recommendations for objective information on military matters have been submitted by a number of Member States belonging to different geographic regions,

Convinced that the improvement of international relations forms a sound basis for promoting further openness and transparency in all military matters,

Also convinced that transparency in military matters is an essential element for building a climate of trust and confidence between States worldwide and that a better flow of objective information on military matters can help to relieve international tension and is therefore an important contribution to conflict prevention,

Noting the role of the standardized reporting system, as instituted through its resolution 35/142 B, as an important instrument to enhance transparency in military matters,

Conscious that the value of the standardized reporting system would be enhanced by a broader participation of Member States,

Welcoming, therefore, the report of the Secretary-General on ways and means to implement the guidelines and recommendations for objective information on military matters, including, in particular, how to strengthen and broaden participation in the standardized reporting system,

Recalling that the guidelines and recommendations for objective information on military matters recommended certain areas for further consideration, such as the improvement of the standardized reporting system,

Noting the efforts of several regional organizations to promote transparency of military expenditures, including standardized annual exchanges of relevant information among their member States,

1. *Calls upon* Member States to report annually, by 30 April, to the Secretary-General their military expenditures for the latest fiscal year for which data are available, using, preferably and to the extent possible, the reporting instrument as recommended in its resolution 35/142 B or, as appropriate, any other format developed in conjunction with similar reporting on military expenditures to other international or regional organizations, and, in the same context, encourages Member States to submit nil returns, if appropriate;

2. *Recommends* the guidelines and recommendations for objective information on military matters to all Member States for implementation, fully taking into account specific political, military and other conditions prevailing in a region, on the basis of initiatives and with the agreement of the States of the region concerned;

3. *Encourages* relevant international bodies and regional organizations to promote transparency of military expenditures and to enhance complementarity among reporting systems, taking into account the particular characteristics of each region, and to consider the possibility of an exchange of information with the United Nations;

4. *Takes note* of the reports of the Secretary-General on objective information on military matters, including transparency of military expenditures;

5. *Requests* the Secretary-General, within available resources:

(a) To continue the practice of sending an annual note verbale to Member States requesting the submission of data to the United Nations system for the standardized reporting of military expenditures, together with the reporting format and related instructions, and to publish in a timely fashion in appropriate United Nations media the due date for transmitting data on military expenditures;

(b) To circulate annually the reports on military expenditures as received from Member States;

(c) To continue consultations with relevant international bodies, with a view to ascertaining requirements for adjusting the present instrument, with a view to encouraging wider participation, and to make recommendations, based on the outcome of those consultations and taking into account the views of Member States, on necessary changes to the content and structure of the standardized reporting system;

(d) To encourage relevant international bodies and organizations to promote transparency of military expenditures and to consult with those bodies and organizations with emphasis on examining possibilities for enhancing complementarity among international and regional reporting systems and for exchanging related information between those bodies and the United Nations;

(e) To encourage the United Nations regional centres for peace and disarmament in Africa, in Asia and the Pacific, and in Latin America and the Caribbean to assist Member States in their regions in enhancing their knowledge of the standardized reporting system;

(f) To promote international and regional/subregional symposiums and training seminars to explain the purpose of the standardized reporting system and to give relevant technical instructions;

(g) To report on experiences gained during such symposiums and training seminars;

6. *Encourages* Member States:

(a) To inform the Secretary-General about possible problems with the standardized reporting system and their reasons for not submitting the requested data;

(b) To continue to provide the Secretary-General, in time for deliberation by the General Assembly at its sixty-second session, with their views and suggestions on ways and means to strengthen and broaden participation in the standardized reporting system, including necessary changes to its content and structure;

7. *Decides* to include in the provisional agenda of its sixty-second session the item entitled "Objective information on military matters, including transparency of military expenditures".

Verification

In response to General Assembly resolution 59/60 [YUN 2004, p. 568], the Secretary-General submitted a July report with later addendum [A/60/96 & Add.1] containing the views of eight Member States (Canada, Chile, Guatemala, Iran, Japan, Mexico, Russian Federation, Sweden) on the importance of effective verification measures in disarmament agreements.

In October [A/60/458], the First Committee considered the issue of verification in all its aspects, including the role of the United Nations in the field of verification. It had before it the above-mentioned report of the Secretary-General.

On 8 December, the Assembly took note of the First Committee's report on the item (**decision 60/514**).

Anti-personnel mines

1997 Convention

The number of States parties to the Convention on the Prohibition of the Use, Stockpiling, Production and Transfer of Anti-personnel Mines and on Their Destruction (Mine-Ban Convention), adopted in 1997 [YUN 1997, p. 503], and which entered into force in 1999 [YUN 1999, p. 498], reached 148 as at 31 December. During the year, four States adhered to the Convention.

Meeting of States parties

As decided by the 2004 Review Conference of the Convention [YUN 2004, p. 568], the Sixth Meeting of the States parties was convened (Zagreb, Croatia, 28 November–2 December) [APLC/MSP.6/2005/5] to consider the Convention's general status and operation. It reviewed progress made and remaining challenges in the pursuit of the Convention's aims and in the application of the Nairobi Action Plan 2005-2009, adopted at the 2004 Review Conference. Particular provisions of the Convention discussed included the submission of requests under article 5 on the destruction of anti-personnel mines in mined areas, under article 8 on facilitation and clarification of compliance, and under article 7 on transparency measures.

The Meeting had before it a background document, contained in part II of its report, entitled "Achieving the aims of the Nairobi Plan of Action: the Zagreb progress report", presented by Austria and Croatia and designed to support the application of the Nairobi Plan by measuring progress made between 3 December 2004 and 2 December 2005. The Zagreb progress report highlighted priority areas of work relating to the Action Plan and was considered the first in a series of annual progress reports to be prepared by States parties in advance of the Second Review Conference in 2009.

On 2 December, the Meeting agreed to amend the article 7 reporting format based on a proposal by Argentina and Chile, which was annexed to its report. It adopted the Zagreb Declaration, contained in part III of its report, reaffirming the commitments made by the States parties in the Nairobi Action Plan, particularly the determination to meet outstanding challenges in realizing the universalization of the Convention, ending the use of anti-personnel mines globally, destroying stockpiled mines, clearing mined areas, providing mine risk education and assisting the victims. The Meeting acknowledged the work of the Standing Committees and agreed that they would meet from 8 to 12 May 2006. It scheduled the Seventh Meeting of the States parties for September 2006 in Geneva, and the Eighth in 2007 in Jordan.

GENERAL ASSEMBLY ACTION

On 8 December [meeting 61], the General Assembly, on the recommendation of the First Committee [A/60/463], adopted **resolution 60/80** by recorded vote (158-0-17) [agenda item 97 (r)].

Implementation of the Convention on the Prohibition of the Use, Stockpiling, Production and Transfer of Anti-personnel Mines and on Their Destruction

The General Assembly,

Recalling its resolutions 54/54 B of 1 December 1999, 55/33 V of 20 November 2000, 56/24 M of 29 November 2001, 57/74 of 22 November 2002, 58/53 of 8 December 2003 and 59/84 of 3 December 2004,

Reaffirming its determination to put an end to the suffering and casualties caused by anti-personnel mines, which kill or maim hundreds of people every week, mostly innocent and defenceless civilians and especially children, obstruct economic development and reconstruction, inhibit the repatriation of refugees and internally displaced persons and have other severe consequences for years after emplacement,

Believing it necessary to do the utmost to contribute in an efficient and coordinated manner to facing the challenge of removing anti-personnel mines placed throughout the world and to assure their destruction,

Wishing to do the utmost in ensuring assistance for the care and rehabilitation, including the social and economic reintegration, of mine victims,

Welcoming the entry into force, on 1 March 1999, of the Convention on the Prohibition of the Use, Stockpiling, Production and Transfer of Anti-personnel Mines and on Their Destruction, and noting with satisfaction the work undertaken to implement the Convention and the substantial progress made towards addressing the global landmine problem,

Recalling the first to fifth meetings of the States parties to the Convention held in Maputo (1999), Geneva

(2000), Managua (2001), Geneva (2002) and Bangkok (2003),

Recalling also the First Review Conference of the States Parties to the Convention on the Prohibition of the Use, Stockpiling, Production and Transfer of Anti-personnel Mines and on Their Destruction, held in Nairobi from 29 November to 3 December 2004, at which the international community renewed its unwavering commitment to achieving the goal of a world free of anti-personnel mines and witnessed the adoption by the States parties to the Convention of the Nairobi Action Plan 2005-2009 to achieve major progress towards ending, for all people and for all time, the suffering caused by anti-personnel mines,

Recalling further the 2005 World Summit Outcome, wherein Heads of State and Government, inter alia, urged the States parties to the Convention to fully implement their obligations,

Noting with satisfaction that additional States have ratified or acceded to the Convention, bringing the total number of States that have formally accepted the obligations of the Convention to one hundred and forty-seven,

Emphasizing the desirability of attracting the adherence of all States to the Convention, and determined to work strenuously towards the promotion of its universalization,

Noting with regret that anti-personnel mines continue to be used in conflicts around the world, causing human suffering and impeding post-conflict development,

1. *Invites* all States that have not signed the Convention on the Prohibition of the Use, Stockpiling, Production and Transfer of Anti-personnel Mines and on Their Destruction to accede to it without delay;

2. *Urges* all States that have signed but have not ratified the Convention to ratify it without delay;

3. *Stresses* the importance of the full and effective implementation of and compliance with the Convention, including through the swift implementation of the Nairobi Action Plan 2005-2009;

4. *Urges* all States parties to provide the Secretary-General with complete and timely information as required under article 7 of the Convention in order to promote transparency and compliance with the Convention;

5. *Invites* all States that have not ratified the Convention or acceded to it to provide, on a voluntary basis, information to make global mine action efforts more effective;

6. *Renews its call upon* all States and other relevant parties to work together to promote, support and advance the care, rehabilitation and social and economic reintegration of mine victims, mine risk education programmes and the removal and destruction of anti-personnel mines placed or stockpiled throughout the world;

7. *Invites and encourages* all interested States, the United Nations, other relevant international organizations or institutions, regional organizations, the International Committee of the Red Cross and relevant non-governmental organizations to participate in the sixth meeting of the States parties to the Convention, to be held in Zagreb from 28 November to 2 December 2005, and in the intersessional work programme established at the first meeting of the States parties, and

further developed at subsequent meetings of the States parties;

8. *Requests* the Secretary-General, in accordance with article 11, paragraph 2, of the Convention, to undertake the preparations necessary to convene the next meeting of the States parties, pending a decision to be taken at the sixth meeting of the States parties, and on behalf of the States parties and in accordance with article 11, paragraph 4, of the Convention, to invite States not parties to the Convention, as well as the United Nations, other relevant international organizations or institutions, regional organizations, the International Committee of the Red Cross and relevant non-governmental organizations to attend the seventh meeting of the States parties as observers;

9. *Decides* to include in the provisional agenda of its sixty-first session the item entitled "Implementation of the Convention on the Prohibition of the Use, Stockpiling, Production and Transfer of Anti-personnel Mines and on Their Destruction".

RECORDED VOTE ON RESOLUTION 60/80:

In favour: Afghanistan, Albania, Algeria, Andorra, Antigua and Barbuda, Argentina, Armenia, Australia, Austria, Azerbaijan, Bahamas, Bahrain, Bangladesh, Barbados, Belarus, Belgium, Belize, Benin, Bhutan, Bolivia, Bosnia and Herzegovina, Botswana, Brazil, Brunei Darussalam, Bulgaria, Burkina Faso, Burundi, Cambodia, Cameroon, Canada, Cape Verde, Central African Republic, Chile, China, Colombia, Congo, Costa Rica, Côte d'Ivoire, Croatia, Cyprus, Czech Republic, Democratic Republic of the Congo, Denmark, Djibouti, Dominica, Dominican Republic, Ecuador, El Salvador, Eritrea, Estonia, Ethiopia, Fiji, Finland, France, Gabon, Georgia, Germany, Ghana, Greece, Grenada, Guatemala, Guinea, Guinea-Bissau, Guyana, Haiti, Honduras, Hungary, Iceland, Indonesia, Iraq, Ireland, Italy, Jamaica, Japan, Jordan, Kenya, Kuwait, Latvia, Lesotho, Liberia, Liechtenstein, Lithuania, Luxembourg, Madagascar, Malawi, Malaysia, Maldives, Mali, Malta, Marshall Islands, Mauritania, Mauritius, Mexico, Micronesia, Monaco, Morocco, Mozambique, Namibia, Nepal, Netherlands, New Zealand, Nicaragua, Niger, Nigeria, Norway, Oman, Panama, Papua New Guinea, Paraguay, Peru, Philippines, Poland, Portugal, Qatar, Republic of Moldova, Romania, Saint Lucia, Saint Vincent and the Grenadines, Samoa, San Marino, Sao Tome and Principe, Senegal, Serbia and Montenegro, Sierra Leone, Singapore, Slovakia, Slovenia, Solomon Islands, Somalia, South Africa, Spain, Sri Lanka, Sudan, Suriname, Sweden, Switzerland, Tajikistan, Thailand, The former Yugoslav Republic of Macedonia, Timor-Leste, Togo, Tonga, Trinidad and Tobago, Tunisia, Turkey, Turkmenistan, Tuvalu, Uganda, Ukraine, United Arab Emirates, United Kingdom, United Republic of Tanzania, Uruguay, Vanuatu, Venezuela, Yemen, Zambia, Zimbabwe.

Against: None.

Abstaining: Cuba, Egypt, India, Iran, Israel, Kazakhstan, Kyrgyzstan, Libyan Arab Jamahiriya, Myanmar, Pakistan, Palau, Republic of Korea, Russian Federation, Syrian Arab Republic, United States, Uzbekistan, Viet Nam.

Other disarmament issues

Prevention of an arms race in outer space

As the Conference on Disarmament [A/60/27] remained deadlocked on a work programme during the year, it was not able to establish a subsidiary body to deal with its substantive agenda items, including the question of the prevention of an arms race in outer space. Nonetheless, delegates devoted one plenary meeting to discussion of related matters. China and the Russian Federation, the primary advocates of the need for a legal instrument on the issue, maintained their collaboration in that regard. While many delegates identified with their position and reaffirmed support for the establishment of an ad hoc committee to address the item, others remained opposed to the idea, making consensus impossible. In March, China and the Russian Federation collaborated with the United Nations Institute for Disarmament Research (UNIDIR) and Canada's Simons Centre for Disarmament and Nonproliferation Research to host an international conference on safeguarding space security: prevention of an arms race in outer space (Geneva, 21-22 March) [CD/1753], which brought the issue of space security to a new level of political urgency and declared it a priority for the international community to develop a work programme on the topic.

An open-ended informal meeting organized by the Russian Federation (Geneva, 16 August) [CD/1756] considered the possible elements for a future international legal agreement on the prevention of the deployment of weapons in outer space and the threat or use of force against outer space objects.

The General Assembly, in resolution 60/54 (see below), asked the Conference on Disarmament to complete the examination and updating of the mandate contained in its 1992 decision [YUN 1992, p. 97] and to establish an ad hoc committee as early as possible during its 2006 session.

GENERAL ASSEMBLY ACTION

On 8 December [meeting 61], the General Assembly, on the recommendation of the First Committee [A/60/462], adopted **resolution 60/54** by recorded vote (180-2-0) [agenda item 96].

Prevention of an arms race in outer space

The General Assembly,

Recognizing the common interest of all mankind in the exploration and use of outer space for peaceful purposes,

Reaffirming the will of all States that the exploration and use of outer space, including the Moon and other celestial bodies, shall be for peaceful purposes and shall be carried out for the benefit and in the interest of all countries, irrespective of their degree of economic or scientific development,

Reaffirming also the provisions of articles III and IV of the Treaty on Principles Governing the Activities of States in the Exploration and Use of Outer Space, including the Moon and Other Celestial Bodies,

Recalling the obligation of all States to observe the provisions of the Charter of the United Nations regarding the use or threat of use of force in their international relations, including in their space activities,

Reaffirming paragraph 80 of the Final Document of the Tenth Special Session of the General Assembly, in which it is stated that in order to prevent an arms race in outer space, further measures should be taken and appropriate international negotiations held in accordance with the spirit of the Treaty,

Recalling its previous resolutions on this issue, and taking note of the proposals submitted to the General Assembly at its tenth special session and at its regular sessions, and of the recommendations made to the competent organs of the United Nations and to the Conference on Disarmament,

Recognizing that prevention of an arms race in outer space would avert a grave danger for international peace and security,

Emphasizing the paramount importance of strict compliance with existing arms limitation and disarmament agreements relevant to outer space, including bilateral agreements, and with the existing legal regime concerning the use of outer space,

Considering that wide participation in the legal regime applicable to outer space could contribute to enhancing its effectiveness,

Noting that the Ad Hoc Committee on the Prevention of an Arms Race in Outer Space, taking into account its previous efforts since its establishment in 1985 and seeking to enhance its functioning in qualitative terms, continued the examination and identification of various issues, existing agreements and existing proposals, as well as future initiatives relevant to the prevention of an arms race in outer space, and that this contributed to a better understanding of a number of problems and to a clearer perception of the various positions,

Noting also that there were no objections in principle in the Conference on Disarmament to the re-establishment of the Ad Hoc Committee, subject to re-examination of the mandate contained in the decision of the Conference on Disarmament of 13 February 1992,

Emphasizing the mutually complementary nature of bilateral and multilateral efforts in the field of preventing an arms race in outer space, and hoping that concrete results will emerge from those efforts as soon as possible,

Convinced that further measures should be examined in the search for effective and verifiable bilateral and multilateral agreements in order to prevent an arms race in outer space, including the weaponization of outer space,

Stressing that the growing use of outer space increases the need for greater transparency and better information on the part of the international community,

Recalling, in this context, its previous resolutions, in particular resolutions 45/55 B of 4 December 1990, 47/51 of 9 December 1992 and 48/74 A of 16 December 1993, in which, inter alia, it reaffirmed the importance of confidence-building measures as a means conducive to ensuring the attainment of the objective of the prevention of an arms race in outer space,

Conscious of the benefits of confidence- and security-building measures in the military field,

Recognizing that negotiations for the conclusion of an international agreement or agreements to prevent an arms race in outer space remain a priority task of the Ad Hoc Committee and that the concrete proposals on confidence-building measures could form an integral part of such agreements,

1. *Reaffirms* the importance and urgency of preventing an arms race in outer space and the readiness of all States to contribute to that common objective, in

conformity with the provisions of the Treaty on Principles Governing the Activities of States in the Exploration and Use of Outer Space, including the Moon and Other Celestial Bodies;

2. *Reaffirms its recognition*, as stated in the report of the Ad Hoc Committee on the Prevention of an Arms Race in Outer Space, that the legal regime applicable to outer space does not in and of itself guarantee the prevention of an arms race in outer space, that the regime plays a significant role in the prevention of an arms race in that environment, that there is a need to consolidate and reinforce that regime and enhance its effectiveness and that it is important to comply strictly with existing agreements, both bilateral and multilateral;

3. *Emphasizes* the necessity of further measures with appropriate and effective provisions for verification to prevent an arms race in outer space;

4. *Calls upon* all States, in particular those with major space capabilities, to contribute actively to the objective of the peaceful use of outer space and of the prevention of an arms race in outer space and to refrain from actions contrary to that objective and to the relevant existing treaties in the interest of maintaining international peace and security and promoting international cooperation;

5. *Reiterates* that the Conference on Disarmament, as the sole multilateral disarmament negotiating forum, has the primary role in the negotiation of a multilateral agreement or agreements, as appropriate, on the prevention of an arms race in outer space in all its aspects;

6. *Invites* the Conference on Disarmament to complete the examination and updating of the mandate contained in its decision of 13 February 1992 and to establish an ad hoc committee as early as possible during its 2006 session;

7. *Recognizes*, in this respect, the growing convergence of views on the elaboration of measures designed to strengthen transparency, confidence and security in the peaceful uses of outer space;

8. *Urges* States conducting activities in outer space, as well as States interested in conducting such activities, to keep the Conference on Disarmament informed of the progress of bilateral and multilateral negotiations on the matter, if any, so as to facilitate its work;

9. *Decides* to include in the provisional agenda of its sixty-first session the item entitled "Prevention of an arms race in outer space".

RECORDED VOTE ON RESOLUTION 60/54:

In favour: Afghanistan, Albania, Algeria, Andorra, Antigua and Barbuda, Argentina, Armenia, Australia, Austria, Azerbaijan, Bahamas, B⁻ⁱⁿⁱⁿ, Bangladesh, Barbados, Belarus, Belgium, Belize, Benin, Bhutan, Bolivia, Bosnia and Herzegovina, Botswana, Brazil, Brunei Darussalam, Bulgaria, Burkina Faso, Burundi, Cambodia, Cameroon, Canada, Cape Verde, Central African Republic, Chad, Chile, China, Colombia, Comoros, Congo, Costa Rica, Côte d'Ivoire, Croatia, Cuba, Cyprus, Czech Republic, Democratic People's Republic of Korea, Democratic Republic of the Congo, Denmark, Djibouti, Dominica, Dominican Republic, Ecuador, Egypt, El Salvador, Eritrea, Estonia, Ethiopia, Fiji, Finland, France, Gabon, Georgia, Germany, Ghana, Greece, Grenada, Guatemala, Guinea, Guinea-Bissau, Guyana, Haiti, Honduras, Hungary, Iceland, India, Indonesia, Iran, Iraq, Ireland, Italy, Jamaica, Japan, Jordan, Kazakhstan, Kenya, Kuwait, Kyrgyzstan, Lao People's Democratic Republic, Latvia, Lebanon, Lesotho, Liberia, Libyan Arab Jamahiriya, Liechtenstein, Lithuania, Luxembourg, Madagascar, Malawi, Malaysia, Maldives, Mali, Malta, Marshall Islands, Mauritania, Mauritius, Mexico, Micronesia, Monaco, Mongolia, Morocco, Mozambique, Myanmar, Namibia, Nepal, Netherlands, New Zealand, Nicaragua, Niger, Nigeria, Norway,

Oman, Pakistan, Palau, Panama, Papua New Guinea, Paraguay, Peru, Philippines, Poland, Portugal, Qatar, Republic of Korea, Republic of Moldova, Romania, Russian Federation, Saint Lucia, Saint Vincent and the Grenadines, Samoa, San Marino, Sao Tome and Principe, Saudi Arabia, Senegal, Serbia and Montenegro, Sierra Leone, Singapore, Slovakia, Slovenia, Solomon Islands, Somalia, South Africa, Spain, Sri Lanka, Sudan, Suriname, Sweden, Switzerland, Syrian Arab Republic, Tajikistan, Thailand, The former Yugoslav Republic of Macedonia, Timor-Leste, Togo, Tonga, Trinidad and Tobago, Tunisia, Turkey, Turkmenistan, Tuvalu, Uganda, Ukraine, United Arab Emirates, United Kingdom, United Republic of Tanzania, Uruguay, Uzbekistan, Vanuatu, Venezuela, Viet Nam, Yemen, Zambia, Zimbabwe.

Against: Israel, United States.

Abstaining: None.

On the same date [meeting 61], the Assembly, on the recommendation of the First Committee [A/60/463], adopted **resolution 60/66** by recorded vote (178-1-1) [agenda item 97].

Transparency and confidence-building measures in outer space activities

The General Assembly,

Reaffirming that the prevention of an arms race in outer space would avert a grave danger to international peace and security,

Conscious that further measures should be examined in the search for agreements to prevent an arms race in outer space, including the weaponization of outer space,

Recalling, in this context, its previous resolutions which, inter alia, emphasize the need for increased transparency and confirm the importance of confidence-building measures as a conducive means of ensuring the attainment of the objective of the prevention of an arms race in outer space,

Recalling also the report of the Secretary-General to its forty-eighth session, the annex to which contains the study by governmental experts on the application of confidence-building measures in outer space,

1. *Invites* all Member States to inform the Secretary-General before its sixty-first session of their views on the advisability of further developing international outer space transparency and confidence-building measures in the interest of maintaining international peace and security and promoting international cooperation and the prevention of an arms race in outer space;

2. *Decides* to include in the provisional agenda of its sixty-first session an item entitled "Transparency and confidence-building measures in outer space activities".

RECORDED VOTE ON RESOLUTION 60/66:

In favour: Afghanistan, Albania, Algeria, Andorra, Antigua and Barbuda, Argentina, Armenia, Australia, Austria, Azerbaijan, Bahamas, Bahrain, Bangladesh, Barbados, Belarus, Belgium, Belize, Benin, Bhutan, Bolivia, Bosnia and Herzegovina, Botswana, Brazil, Brunei Darussalam, Bulgaria, Burkina Faso, Burundi, Cambodia, Cameroon, Canada, Cape Verde, Central African Republic, Chile, China, Colombia, Comoros, Congo, Costa Rica, Côte d'Ivoire, Croatia, Cuba, Cyprus, Czech Republic, Democratic People's Republic of Korea, Democratic Republic of the Congo, Denmark, Djibouti, Dominica, Dominican Republic, Ecuador, Egypt, El Salvador, Eritrea, Estonia, Ethiopia, Fiji, Finland, France, Gabon, Georgia, Germany, Ghana, Greece, Grenada, Guatemala, Guinea, Guinea-Bissau, Guyana, Haiti, Honduras, Hungary, Iceland, India, Indonesia, Iran, Iraq, Ireland, Italy, Jamaica, Japan, Jordan, Kazakhstan, Kenya, Kuwait, Kyrgyzstan, Lao People's Democratic Republic, Latvia, Lebanon, Lesotho, Liberia, Libyan Arab Jamahiriya, Liechtenstein, Lithuania, Luxembourg, Madagascar, Malawi, Malaysia, Maldives, Mali, Malta, Marshall Islands, Mauritania, Mauritius, Mexico, Micronesia, Monaco, Mongolia, Morocco, Mozambique, Myanmar, Namibia, Nepal, Netherlands, New Zealand, Nicaragua, Niger, Nigeria, Norway, Oman, Pakistan, Palau, Panama, Papua New Guinea, Paraguay, Peru, Philippines, Poland, Portugal, Qatar, Republic of Korea, Republic of Moldova, Romania, Russian Federation, Saint Lucia, Saint Vincent and the Grenadines, Samoa, San Marino, Sao Tome and Principe, Saudi Arabia, Senegal, Serbia and Montenegro, Sierra Leone, Singapore, Slovakia, Slovenia, Solomon Islands, Somalia, South Africa, Spain, Sri Lanka, Sudan, Suriname, Sweden, Switzerland, Syrian Arab Republic, Tajikistan, Thailand, The former Yugoslav Republic of Macedonia, Timor-Leste, Togo, Trinidad and Tobago, Tunisia, Turkey, Turkmenistan, Tuvalu, Uganda, Ukraine, United Arab Emirates, United Kingdom, United Republic of Tanzania, Uruguay, Uzbekistan, Vanuatu, Venezuela, Viet Nam, Yemen, Zambia, Zimbabwe.

Against: United States.

Abstaining: Israel.

Disarmament and development

In 2005, the relationship between disarmament and development remained a controversial issue in the international community. While the majority of Member States, mostly members of the Non-Aligned Movement, continued to call for the implementation of the action programme adopted by the 1987 International Conference, which examined the relationship in all its aspects [YUN 1987, p. 82], other States, particularly EU member States and the United States, emphasized that an automatic link did not exist between both concepts.

High-level Steering Group. Pursuant to General Assembly resolution 59/78 [YUN 2004, p. 580], the Secretary-General submitted a July report [A/60/94] containing the observations of the high-level Steering Group on Disarmament and Development established in 1999 [YUN 1999, p. 506], regarding the 2004 report of the Group of Governmental Experts on the relationship [YUN 2004, p. 579]. The Steering Group acknowledged the importance of the recommendation of the Expert Group that the UN and other intergovernmental organizations make greater efforts to integrate their disarmament, humanitarian and development activities. The Group announced that it had designated focal points at the working level and was examining how disarmament-related issues and development could be better integrated into the activities of appropriate components of the UN system. It was also considering modalities for raising greater awareness of the subject. The Group summarized activities relevant to disarmament and development undertaken by its partner departments and agency and highlighted similar initiatives being undertaken by various components of the UN system. Unfortunately, financial constraints continued to hamper efforts to implement activities promoting disarmament and development.

GENERAL ASSEMBLY ACTION

On 8 December [meeting 61], the General Assembly, on the recommendation of the First Committee [A/60/463], adopted **resolution 60/61** by recorded vote (177-1-2) [agenda item 97 *(n)*].

Relationship between disarmament and development

The General Assembly,

Recalling that the Charter of the United Nations envisages the establishment and maintenance of international peace and security with the least diversion for armaments of the world's human and economic resources,

Recalling also the provisions of the Final Document of the Tenth Special Session of the General Assembly concerning the relationship between disarmament and development, as well as the adoption on 11 September 1987 of the Final Document of the International Conference on the Relationship between Disarmament and Development,

Recalling further its resolutions 49/75 J of 15 December 1994, 50/70 G of 12 December 1995, 51/45 D of 10 December 1996, 52/38 D of 9 December 1997, 53/77 K of 4 December 1998, 54/54 T of 1 December 1999, 55/33 L of 20 November 2000, 56/24 E of 29 November 2001, 57/65 of 22 November 2002 and 59/78 of 3 December 2004, and its decision 58/520 of 8 December 2003,

Bearing in mind the Final Document of the Twelfth Conference of Heads of State or Government of Non-Aligned Countries, held in Durban, South Africa, from 29 August to 3 September 1998, and the Final Document of the Thirteenth Ministerial Conference of the Movement of Non-Aligned Countries, held in Cartagena, Colombia, on 8 and 9 April 2000,

Mindful of the changes in international relations that have taken place since the adoption on 11 September 1987 of the Final Document of the International Conference on the Relationship between Disarmament and Development, including the development agenda that has emerged over the past decade,

Bearing in mind the new challenges for the international community in the field of development, poverty eradication and the elimination of the diseases that afflict humanity,

Stressing the importance of the symbiotic relationship between disarmament and development and the important role of security in this connection, and concerned at increasing global military expenditure, which could otherwise be spent on development needs,

1. *Welcomes* the report of the Group of Governmental Experts on the relationship between disarmament and development and its reappraisal of this significant issue in the current international context;

2. *Stresses* the central role of the United Nations in the disarmament-development relationship, and requests the Secretary-General to strengthen further the role of the Organization in this field, in particular the high-level Steering Group on Disarmament and Development, in order to assure continued and effective coordination and close cooperation between the relevant United Nations departments, agencies and sub-agencies;

3. *Requests* the Secretary-General to continue to take action, through appropriate organs and within available resources, for the implementation of the action programme adopted at the 1987 International Conference on the Relationship between Disarmament and Development;

4. *Urges* the international community to devote part of the resources made available by the implemen-

tation of disarmament and arms limitation agreements to economic and social development, with a view to reducing the ever-widening gap between developed and developing countries;

5. *Encourages* the international community to achieve the Millennium Development Goals and to make reference to the contribution that disarmament could provide in meeting them when it reviews its progress towards this purpose in 2006, as well as to make greater efforts to integrate disarmament, humanitarian and development activities;

6. *Encourages* the relevant regional and subregional organizations and institutions, non-governmental organizations and research institutes to incorporate issues related to the relationship between disarmament and development in their agendas and, in this regard, to take into account the report of the Group of Governmental Experts;

7. *Requests* the Secretary-General to report to the General Assembly at its sixty-first session on the implementation of the present resolution;

8. *Decides* to include in the provisional agenda of its sixty-first session the item entitled "Relationship between disarmament and development".

RECORDED VOTE ON RESOLUTION 60/61:

In favour: Afghanistan, Albania, Algeria, Andorra, Antigua and Barbuda, Argentina, Armenia, Australia, Austria, Azerbaijan, Bahamas, Bahrain, Bangladesh, Barbados, Belarus, Belgium, Belize, Benin, Bhutan, Bolivia, Bosnia and Herzegovina, Botswana, Brazil, Brunei Darussalam, Bulgaria, Burkina Faso, Burundi, Cambodia, Cameroon, Canada, Cape Verde, Central African Republic, Chile, China, Colombia, Comoros, Congo, Costa Rica, Côte d'Ivoire, Croatia, Cuba, Cyprus, Czech Republic, Democratic People's Republic of Korea, Democratic Republic of the Congo, Denmark, Djibouti, Dominica, Dominican Republic, Ecuador, Egypt, El Salvador, Eritrea, Estonia, Ethiopia, Fiji, Finland, Gabon, Georgia, Germany, Ghana, Greece, Grenada, Guatemala, Guinea, Guinea-Bissau, Guyana, Haiti, Honduras, Hungary, Iceland, India, Indonesia, Iran, Iraq, Ireland, Italy, Jamaica, Japan, Jordan, Kazakhstan, Kenya, Kuwait, Kyrgyzstan, Lao People's Democratic Republic, Latvia, Lebanon, Lesotho, Liberia, Libyan Arab Jamahiriya, Liechtenstein, Lithuania, Luxembourg, Madagascar, Malawi, Malaysia, Maldives, Mali, Malta, Marshall Islands, Mauritania, Mauritius, Mexico, Micronesia, Monaco, Mongolia, Morocco, Mozambique, Myanmar, Namibia, Nepal, Netherlands, New Zealand, Nicaragua, Niger, Nigeria, Norway, Oman, Palau, Panama, Papua New Guinea, Paraguay, Peru, Philippines, Poland, Portugal, Qatar, Republic of Korea, Republic of Moldova, Romania, Russian Federation, Saint Lucia, Saint Vincent and the Grenadines, Samoa, San Marino, Sao Tome and Principe, Saudi Arabia, Senegal, Serbia and Montenegro, Sierra Leone, Singapore, Slovakia, Slovenia, Solomon Islands, Somalia, South Africa, Spain, Sri Lanka, Sudan, Suriname, Sweden, Switzerland, Syrian Arab Republic, Tajikistan, Thailand, The former Yugoslav Republic of Macedonia, Timor-Leste, Togo, Tonga, Trinidad and Tobago, Tunisia, Turkey, Turkmenistan, Tuvalu, Uganda, Ukraine, United Arab Emirates, United Kingdom, United Republic of Tanzania, Uruguay, Uzbekistan, Vanuatu, Venezuela, Viet Nam, Yemen, Zambia, Zimbabwe.

Against: United States.

Abstaining: France, Israel.

Human rights, human security and disarmament

As part of growing international efforts to protect civilians' human rights in situations of armed conflict, the Subcommission on the Promotion and Protection of Human Rights (see p. 713) considered in 2005 the threat posed to those rights by weapons accumulation and proliferation. It considered a set of revised draft principles on the prevention of human rights violations committed with small arms, prepared by Barbara Frey (United States), the Special Rapporteur man-

dated in 2002 [YUN 2002, p. 720] to conduct a study on the topic.

The question of the relationship between disarmament and human security was taken up during the year by UNIDIR (see p. 640). Its activities on the issue related primarily to the small arms scourge and the danger posed by explosive remnants of war and landmines, as those weapons continued to be widely used, crippling human activities and hampering peace and the reconstruction of post-conflict societies. In collaboration with DDA and other partners, UNIDIR made efforts to identify ways to control those weapons and seek adequate solutions to the security concerns of affected populations.

Arms limitation and disarmament agreements

Responding to General Assembly resolution 59/68 [YUN 2004, p. 581], the Secretary-General submitted a July report with later addendum [A/60/97 & Add.1], containing information from six Member States on measures they had taken to ensure the application of scientific and technological progress in the context of international security, disarmament and related areas, without detriment to the environment or to its effective contribution to attaining sustainable development.

GENERAL ASSEMBLY ACTION

On 8 December [meeting 61], the General Assembly, on the recommendation of the First Committee [A/60/463], adopted **resolution 60/60** by recorded vote (176-1-4) [agenda item 97 *(g)*].

Observance of environmental norms in the drafting and implementation of agreements on disarmament and arms control

The General Assembly,

Recalling its resolutions 50/70 M of 12 December 1995, 51/45 E of 10 December 1996, 52/38 E of 9 December 1997, 53/77 J of 4 December 1998, 54/54 S of 1 December 1999, 55/33 K of 20 November 2000, 56/24 F of 29 November 2001, 57/64 of 22 November 2002, 58/45 of 8 December 2003 and 59/68 of 3 December 2004,

Emphasizing the importance of the observance of environmental norms in the preparation and implementation of disarmament and arms limitation agreements,

Recognizing that it is necessary to take duly into account the agreements adopted at the United Nations Conference on Environment and Development, as well as prior relevant agreements, in the drafting and implementation of agreements on disarmament and arms limitation,

Taking note of the report of the Secretary-General,

Mindful of the detrimental environmental effects of the use of nuclear weapons,

1. *Reaffirms* that international disarmament forums should take fully into account the relevant environmental norms in negotiating treaties and agreements on disarmament and arms limitation and that all States, through their actions, should contribute fully to ensuring compliance with the aforementioned norms in the implementation of treaties and conventions to which they are parties;

2. *Calls upon* States to adopt unilateral, bilateral, regional and multilateral measures so as to contribute to ensuring the application of scientific and technological progress within the framework of international security, disarmament and other related spheres, without detriment to the environment or to its effective contribution to attaining sustainable development;

3. *Welcomes* the information provided by Member States on the implementation of the measures they have adopted to promote the objectives envisaged in the present resolution;

4. *Invites* all Member States to communicate to the Secretary-General information on the measures they have adopted to promote the objectives envisaged in the present resolution, and requests the Secretary-General to submit a report containing this information to the General Assembly at its sixty-first session;

5. *Decides* to include in the provisional agenda of its sixty-first session the item entitled "Observance of environmental norms in the drafting and implementation of agreements on disarmament and arms control".

RECORDED VOTE RESOLUTION 60/60:

In favour: Afghanistan, Albania, Algeria, Andorra, Antigua and Barbuda, Argentina, Armenia, Australia, Austria, Azerbaijan, Bahamas, Bahrain, Bangladesh, Barbados, Belarus, Belgium, Belize, Benin, Bhutan, Bolivia, Bosnia and Herzegovina, Botswana, Brazil, Brunei Darussalam, Bulgaria, Burkina Faso, Burundi, Cambodia, Cameroon, Canada, Cape Verde, Central African Republic, Chile, China, Colombia, Comoros, Congo, Costa Rica, Côte d'Ivoire, Croatia, Cuba, Cyprus, Czech Republic, Democratic People's Republic of Korea, Democratic Republic of the Congo, Denmark, Djibouti, Dominica, Dominican Republic, Ecuador, Egypt, El Salvador, Eritrea, Estonia, Ethiopia, Fiji, Finland, Gabon, Georgia, Germany, Ghana, Greece, Grenada, Guatemala, Guinea, Guinea-Bissau, Guyana, Haiti, Honduras, Hungary, Iceland, India, Indonesia, Iran, Iraq, Ireland, Italy, Jamaica, Japan, Jordan, Kazakhstan, Kenya, Kuwait, Kyrgyzstan, Lao People's Democratic Republic, Latvia, Lebanon, Lesotho, Liberia, Libyan Arab Jamahiriya, Liechtenstein, Lithuania, Luxembourg, Madagascar, Malawi, Malaysia, Maldives, Mali, Malta, Marshall Islands, Mauritania, Mauritius, Mexico, Micronesia, Monaco, Mongolia, Morocco, Mozambique, Myanmar, Namibia, Nepal, Netherlands, New Zealand, Nicaragua, Niger, Nigeria, Norway, Oman, Pakistan, Panama, Papua New Guinea, Paraguay, Peru, Philippines, Poland, Portugal, Qatar, Republic of Korea, Republic of Moldova, Romania, Russian Federation, Saint Lucia, Saint Vincent and the Grenadines, Samoa, San Marino, Sao Tome and Principe, Saudi Arabia, Senegal, Serbia and Montenegro, Sierra Leone, Singapore, Slovakia, Slovenia, Solomon Islands, Somalia, South Africa, Spain, Sri Lanka, Sudan, Suriname, Sweden, Switzerland, Syrian Arab Republic, Tajikistan, Thailand, The former Yugoslav Republic of Macedonia, Timor-Leste, Togo, Tonga, Trinidad and Tobago, Tunisia, Turkey, Turkmenistan, Tuvalu, Uganda, Ukraine, United Arab Emirates, United Republic of Tanzania, Uruguay, Uzbekistan, Vanuatu, Venezuela, Viet Nam, Yemen, Zambia, Zimbabwe.

Against: United States.

Abstaining: France, Israel, Palau, United Kingdom.

Also on 8 December [meeting 61], the Assembly, on the recommendation of the First Committee [A/60/463], adopted **resolution 60/55** by recorded vote (163-0-10) [agenda item 97].

Compliance with non-proliferation, arms limitation and disarmament agreements

The General Assembly,

Recalling its resolution 57/86 of 22 November 2002 and other relevant resolutions on the question,

Recognizing the abiding concern of all Member States for maintaining respect for the rights and obligations arising from treaties to which they are parties and other sources of international law,

Convinced that observance by Member States of the Charter of the United Nations and compliance with non-proliferation, arms limitation and disarmament agreements to which they are parties and with other agreed obligations are essential for regional and global peace, security and stability,

Stressing that failure by States parties to comply with such agreements and other agreed obligations not only adversely affects the security of States parties but can also create security risks for other States relying on the constraints and commitments stipulated in those agreements,

Stressing also that the viability and effectiveness of non-proliferation, arms limitation and disarmament agreements and other agreed obligations require that those agreements be fully complied with,

Concerned by non-compliance by some States with their respective obligations,

Noting that verification and compliance, and enforcement in a manner consistent with the Charter, are integrally related,

Recognizing that full compliance by States with their respective non-proliferation, arms limitation and disarmament agreements and other agreed obligations contributes to efforts to prevent the development and proliferation of weapons of mass destruction and their technologies and means of delivery contrary to international obligations, and to efforts to deny non-State actors access to such capabilities,

1. *Underscores* the contribution that compliance with non-proliferation, arms limitation and disarmament agreements and other agreed obligations makes to enhancing confidence and strengthening security and stability;

2. *Urges* all States to implement and to comply fully with their respective obligations;

3. *Urges* those States not currently in compliance with their respective obligations to make the strategic decision to come back into compliance with those obligations;

4. *Calls upon* all Member States to take concerted action in a manner consistent with relevant international law to encourage, through bilateral and multilateral means, the compliance by all States with their respective non-proliferation, arms limitation and disarmament agreements and other agreed obligations and to hold those not in compliance with such agreements accountable for their non-compliance in a manner consistent with the Charter of the United Nations;

5. *Encourages* efforts by all States parties, the United Nations and other international organizations, pursuant to their mandates, to take action, consistent with the Charter, to prevent serious damage to international security and stability arising from non-compliance by States with their existing non-proliferation, arms limitation and disarmament obligations;

6. *Decides* to remain seized of the matter.

RECORDED VOTE ON RESOLUTION 60/55:

In favour: Afghanistan, Albania, Algeria, Andorra, Antigua and Barbuda, Argentina, Armenia, Australia, Austria, Azerbaijan, Bahamas, Bahrain, Bangladesh, Belgium, Belize, Benin, Bhutan, Bolivia, Bosnia and Herzegovina, Botswana, Brazil, Brunei Darussalam, Bulgaria, Burkina Faso, Burundi, Cambodia, Cameroon, Canada, Cape Verde, Central African Republic, Chile, Colombia, Comoros, Congo, Costa Rica, Côte d'Ivoire, Croatia, Cyprus, Czech Republic, Democratic Republic of the Congo, Denmark, Djibouti, Dominica, Dominican Republic, Ecuador, El Salvador, Eritrea, Estonia, Ethiopia, Fiji, Finland, France, Gabon, Georgia, Germany, Ghana, Greece, Grenada, Guatemala, Guinea, Guinea-Bissau, Guyana, Haiti, Honduras, Hungary, Iceland, India, Iraq, Ireland, Israel, Italy, Japan, Jordan, Kazakhstan, Kenya, Kuwait, Kyrgyzstan, Latvia, Lebanon, Lesotho, Liberia, Libyan Arab Jamahiriya, Liechtenstein, Lithuania, Luxembourg, Madagascar, Malawi, Malaysia, Maldives, Mali, Malta, Marshall Islands, Mauritania, Mauritius, Mexico, Micronesia, Monaco, Mongolia, Morocco, Mozambique, Myanmar, Namibia, Nepal, Netherlands, New Zealand, Nicaragua, Niger, Nigeria, Norway, Oman, Palau, Panama, Papua New Guinea, Paraguay, Peru, Philippines, Poland, Portugal, Qatar, Republic of Korea, Republic of Moldova, Romania, Saint Lucia, Saint Vincent and the Grenadines, Samoa, San Marino, Sao Tome and Principe, Saudi Arabia, Senegal, Serbia and Montenegro, Sierra Leone, Singapore, Slovakia, Slovenia, Solomon Islands, Somalia, Spain, Sri Lanka, Sudan, Suriname, Sweden, Switzerland, Syrian Arab Republic, Tajikistan, Thailand, The former Yugoslav Republic of Macedonia, Timor-Leste, Togo, Trinidad and Tobago, Tunisia, Turkey, Turkmenistan, Uganda, Ukraine, United Arab Emirates, United Kingdom, United Republic of Tanzania, United States, Uruguay, Vanuatu, Yemen, Zambia, Zimbabwe.

Against: None.

Abstaining: Barbados, Belarus, Cuba, Egypt, Indonesia, Iran, Jamaica, Russian Federation, South Africa, Venezuela.

Studies, information and training

Disarmament studies programme

During the year, DDA and Canada organized a panel discussion (New York, 20 October) on verifying disarmament and non-proliferation agreements, which explored issues relating to the work of the Panel of Governmental Experts on verification, to be established in 2006, pursuant to General Assembly resolution 59/60 [YUN 2004, p. 568]. In other developments, Governments, UN organizations, and civil society groups began implementation of the recommendations contained in the UN study on disarmament and non-proliferation education, as called for in Assembly resolution 59/93 [ibid., p. 582].

In 2005, the Assembly, in resolution 60/81 (see p. 625), decided to establish a group of governmental experts to consider further steps to enhance international cooperation in preventing, combating and eradicating illicit brokering in small arms and light weapons and to report to the Assembly in 2007. By resolution 60/226 (see p. 629), the Assembly requested the Secretary-General, with the assistance of a group of governmental experts to be convened in 2006, to prepare a report on the continuing operation of the UN Register of Conventional Arms and its further development, with a view to making a decision at its sixty-first (2006) session.

Disarmament Information Programme

During the year, priority issues for the Disarmament Information Programme were WMDs and conventional weapons, especially small arms and light weapons. Other areas covered included the publications programme; website access, exhibits and the activities of the Secretary-General's Messenger of Peace programme; cooperation with civil society, NGOs in particular; and the activities of the UN Department of Public Information (DPI) (see p. 691), which administered the Programme in close collaboration with DDA, on information campaigns supporting major disarmament-related events and conferences. DDA continued to work closely with such NGOs as Reaching Critical Will and the International Action Network on Small Arms to facilitate the participation of civil society organizations at meetings, including the 2005 NPT Review Conference (see p. 597) and the second biennial meeting of States to consider the implementation of the 2001 Programme of Action on Small Arms [YUN 2001, p. 499]. DPI focused on the promotion and coverage of major disarmament-related conferences. Its activities included public information campaigns, radio and television broadcasts, webcasts and printed material.

Advisory Board on Disarmament Matters

The Advisory Board on Disarmament Matters, which advised the Secretary-General on the disarmament studies programme and implementation of the Disarmament Information Programme and served as the Board of Trustees of the United Nations Institute for Disarmament Research (UNIDIR) (see below), held its forty-fourth and forty-fifth sessions (New York, 23-25 February; Geneva, 29 June-1 July) [A/60/285]. The Board deliberated on nuclear fuel cycle and fissile material control; regional security and global norms; small arms and light weapons; challenges and opportunities at the regional level regarding WMDs and conventional arms; and a review of the disarmament machinery. On the issue of nuclear fuel cycle and fissile material control, the Board recommended that nearer-term opportunities for multilateral nuclear approaches, based on voluntary participation, be considered, and that the recommendation of the High-level Panel on Threats, Challenges and Change [YUN 2004, p. 54] for a voluntary moratorium on the development of more facilities, matched by the guaranteed supply of fissile material, be further elaborated. Existing approaches and instruments should be utilized fully to strengthen the security of fissile material and all States with advanced nuclear programmes, whether or not they were parties to NPT, should participate actively in international efforts to prevent the proliferation of nuclear weapons. Concerning small arms and light weapons, the Board proposed that the High-level Plenary Meeting of the sixtieth session of the General Assembly (see p. 47) accord high priority to the challenge posed by those weapons. The second Biennial Meeting of States to Consider the Implementation of the Programme of Action adopted by the 2001 UN Conference on small arms [YUN 2001, p. 499] and the first review conference on the Programme's Implementation, to be held in 2006, should aim to expand and deepen global norms governing that category of weapons. The United Nations should take the lead in enhancing the inclusive process at the global, regional, national and civil society levels, in order to better address the threat posed by those weapons. In addition, international coordination and cooperation should be strengthened, including between the General Assembly and the Security Council, and between the United Nations and relevant financial institutions, so as to facilitate effective action in a comprehensive and integrated manner.

On the issue of challenges and opportunities at the regional level regarding WMDs and conventional arms, the Board recommended, among other things, interregional dialogue to share information, successful experiences and lessons learned, and strengthening cooperation between regional organizations or mechanisms to promote disarmament and non-proliferation. As to the disarmament machinery, the Board proposed that the Conference on Disarmament be strengthened, without prejudice to adjustments in its procedural arrangements that could facilitate progress in the consideration of disarmament measures. Also, the functioning of the First Committee should be improved to enable it to address better traditional and current security challenges facing the international community, particularly those regarding disarmament and non-proliferation.

In its capacity as UNIDIR's Board of Trustees (see below), the Board made recommendations concerning the Institute's 2005 work programme and budget. After considering an audit report on UNIDIR's activities by the Office of Internal Oversight Services (see below), which identified difficulties relating to its staffing and funding status, the Board recommended that UNIDIR's core staff be funded from the UN regular budget and that the Institute explore ways to apply UN staff regulations and rules to all its personnel.

UN Institute for Disarmament Research

OIOS audit report. Between November 2004 and January 2005, the Office of Internal Oversight Services (OIOS) conducted its first audit of UNIDIR's programmes and activities, with a total

expenditure of $4.2 million undertaken in the period from January 2002 to October 2004. The audit intended to determine, among other things, the effectiveness of UNIDIR's management structure and practices in achieving its programmes and of internal controls to ensure the efficient use of resources and compliance with UN regulations and rules, focused on the Institute's statute, funding research projects, outputs and outreach activities. OIOS established that UNIDIR's research and other activities were making a positive impact, but found that some areas needed attention. In particular, it had concerns regarding the in which the Institute managed its staff and about its funding status and made a number of recommendations for improvement.

During the year, UNIDIR marked the twenty-fifth anniversary of its establishment.

Report of Secretary-General. The Secretary-General transmitted to the General Assembly the report of the UNIDIR Director covering the period from August 2004 to July 2005 [A/60/135], as well as the report of the UNIDIR Board of Trustees on the proposed 2005-2006 programme of work and budget [YUN 2004, p. 548]. The Institute's research activities continued to focus on global security, regional security and human security, addressing the full range of substantive disarmament issues, from small arms to weapons in space. As in previous years, the report highlighted the scope of UNIDIR's research activities worldwide, including through conferences, seminars and discussion meetings, as well as its networking initiatives with UN system specialized agencies, organizations and institutions. The report also contained a list of UNIDIR publications issued during the reporting period.

The General Assembly, in section IV of **resolution 60/248** (see p. 1494), having considered the Secretary-General's request for a subvention to UNIDIR [A/C.5/60/3], as recommended by the Board of Trustees, and the related report of the Advisory Committee on Administrative and Budgetary Questions [A/60/7/Add.8], approved a subvention for the Institute in the amount of $468,100 from the UN regular budget for the 2006-2007 biennium.

GENERAL ASSEMBLY ACTION

On 8 December [meeting 62], the General Assembly, on the recommendation of the First Committee [A/60/465], adopted **resolution 60/89** without vote [agenda item 99 *(b)*].

Twenty-fifth anniversary of the United Nations Institute for Disarmament Research

The General Assembly,

Recalling its resolution 34/83 M of 11 December 1979, in which it requested the Secretary-General to establish the United Nations Institute for Disarmament Research on the basis of the recommendations contained in the report of the Secretary-General,

Reaffirming its resolution 39/148 H of 17 December 1984, in which it approved the statute of the Institute, renewed the invitation to Governments to consider making voluntary contributions to the Institute and requested the Secretary-General to continue to give the Institute administrative and other support,

Recalling its resolution 45/62 G of 4 December 1990 on the tenth anniversary of the Institute and its resolution 55/35 A of 20 November 2000 on the twentieth anniversary of the Institute,

Considering the continuing need for the international community to have access to independent and in-depth research on security issues and prospects for disarmament and non-proliferation,

Underlining the particularly relevant contribution of the Institute to thinking and analysis on international security issues in the current context,

Taking note of the audit report of the Office of Internal Oversight Services on the Institute, which makes a positive assessment of the impact of the work of the Institute and recommends that the Institute should seek adequate funding from the regular budget to better meet the costs of its core staff and that the Institute, in consultation with its Board of Trustees, should establish specific posts for the core functions of the Institute,

Taking note also of the report of the Secretary-General on the work of the Advisory Board on Disarmament Matters, in which, after considering the audit report of the Office of Internal Oversight Services, the Board recommended that the costs of the core staff of the Institute should be funded from the regular budget of the United Nations,

1. *Welcomes* the twenty-fifth anniversary of the establishment of the United Nations Institute for Disarmament Research;

2. *Recognizes* the importance, the timeliness and the high quality of the work of the Institute;

3. *Reiterates its conviction* that the Institute should continue to conduct independent research on problems relating to disarmament and security and to undertake specialized research requiring a high degree of expertise;

4. *Appeals* to all Member States to continue to make financial contributions to the Institute in order to ensure its viability and the quality of its work over the long term;

5. *Recommends* that the Secretary-General implement the relevant recommendations of the Office of Internal Oversight Services and the decisions of the Board of Trustees of the Institute and continue to seek ways to increase the funding of the Institute, within existing resources.

Disarmament fellowship, training and advisory services

In 2005, 30 fellows participated in the UN disarmament fellowship, training and advisory services programme, which began in Geneva on 29 August and terminated in New York on 2 November. The programme comprised study sessions in Geneva and New York and study visits to intergovernmental organizations working in the field of disarmament, and to Member States, including Germany and Japan.

Regional disarmament

In 2005, the United Nations continued to promote regional approaches to disarmament and security and to complement relevant activities by strengthening predictable partnerships and arrangements with regional organizations. In February, the Security Council acknowledged in presidential statement S/PRST/2005/7 (see p. 619) the significant contribution of regional organizations in combating the proliferation of those weapons and encouraged continuing assistance to Member States to implement the Programme of Action adopted by the UN Conference on the Illicit Trade in Small Arms and Light Weapons in All Its Aspects[YUN 2001, p. 499].

Reports of Secretary-General. Pursuant to General Assembly resolution 59/88 [YUN 2004, p. 574], the Secretary-General, in July [A/60/92], presented the views of three States (Bolivia, Bosnia and Herzegovina, Georgia) regarding conventional arms control at the regional and subregional levels.

In response to Assembly resolution 59/87 [YUN 2004, p. 575], he also submitted a July report with later addendum [A/60/119 & Add.1] containing the views of 12 States (Albania, Bolivia, Burkina Faso, Grenada, Guatemala, Japan, Mexico, Poland, Senegal, Sierra Leone, Thailand, Turkey) on confidence-building measures in the regional and subregional context.

GENERAL ASSEMBLY ACTION

On 8 December [meeting 61], the General Assembly, on the recommendation of the First Committee [A/60/463], adopted three resolutions relating to regional disarmament. The Assembly adopted **resolution 60/63** without vote [agenda item 97 (w)].

Regional disarmament

The General Assembly,

Recalling its resolutions 45/58 P of 4 December 1990, 46/36 I of 6 December 1991, 47/52 J of 9 December 1992, 48/75 I of 16 December 1993, 49/75 N of 15 December 1994, 50/70 K of 12 December 1995, 51/45 K of 10 December 1996, 52/38 P of 9 December 1997, 53/77 O of 4 December 1998, 54/54 N of 1 December 1999, 55/33 O of 20 November 2000, 56/24 H of 29 November 2001, 57/76 of 22 November 2002, 58/38 of 8 December 2003 and 59/89 of 3 December 2004 on regional disarmament,

Believing that the efforts of the international community to move towards the ideal of general and complete disarmament are guided by the inherent human desire for genuine peace and security, the elimination of the danger of war and the release of economic, intellectual and other resources for peaceful pursuits,

Affirming the abiding commitment of all States to the purposes and principles enshrined in the Charter of the United Nations in the conduct of their international relations,

Noting that essential guidelines for progress towards general and complete disarmament were adopted at the tenth special session of the General Assembly,

Taking note of the guidelines and recommendations for regional approaches to disarmament within the context of global security adopted by the Disarmament Commission at its 1993 substantive session,

Welcoming the prospects of genuine progress in the field of disarmament engendered in recent years as a result of negotiations between the two super-Powers,

Taking note of the recent proposals for disarmament at the regional and subregional levels,

Recognizing the importance of confidence-building measures for regional and international peace and security,

Convinced that endeavours by countries to promote regional disarmament, taking into account the specific characteristics of each region and in accordance with the principle of undiminished security at the lowest level of armaments, would enhance the security of all States and would thus contribute to international peace and security by reducing the risk of regional conflicts,

1. *Stresses* that sustained efforts are needed, within the framework of the Conference on Disarmament and under the umbrella of the United Nations, to make progress on the entire range of disarmament issues;

2. *Affirms* that global and regional approaches to disarmament complement each other and should therefore be pursued simultaneously to promote regional and international peace and security;

3. *Calls upon* States to conclude agreements, wherever possible, for nuclear non-proliferation, disarmament and confidence-building measures at the regional and subregional levels;

4. *Welcomes* the initiatives towards disarmament, nuclear non-proliferation and security undertaken by some countries at the regional and subregional levels;

5. *Supports and encourages* efforts aimed at promoting confidence-building measures at the regional and subregional levels to ease regional tensions and to further disarmament and nuclear non-proliferation measures at the regional and subregional levels;

6. *Decides* to include in the provisional agenda of its sixty-first session the item entitled "Regional disarmament".

The Assembly adopted **resolution 60/64** without vote [agenda item 97 *(u)*].

Confidence-building measures in the regional and subregional context

The General Assembly,

Guided by the purposes and principles enshrined in the Charter of the United Nations,

Recalling its resolution 59/87 of 3 December 2004,

Recalling also its resolution 57/337 of 3 July 2003, entitled "Prevention of armed conflict", in which it called upon Member States to settle their disputes by peaceful means, as set out in Chapter VI of the Charter, inter alia, by any procedures adopted by the parties,

Recalling further the resolutions and guidelines adopted by consensus by the General Assembly and the Disarmament Commission relating to confidence-building measures and their implementation at the global, regional and subregional levels,

Considering the importance and effectiveness of confidence-building measures taken at the initiative and with the agreement of all States concerned and taking into account the specific characteristics of each region, since such measures can contribute to regional stability,

Convinced that resources released by disarmament, including regional disarmament, can be devoted to economic and social development and to the protection of the environment for the benefit of all peoples, in particular those of the developing countries,

Recognizing the need for meaningful dialogue among States concerned to avert conflict,

Welcoming the peace processes already initiated by States concerned to resolve their disputes through peaceful means bilaterally or through mediation, inter alia, by third parties, regional organizations or the United Nations,

Recognizing that States in some regions have already taken steps towards confidence-building measures at the bilateral, subregional and regional levels in the political and military fields, including arms control and disarmament, and noting that such confidence-building measures have improved peace and security in those regions and contributed to progress in the socio-economic conditions of their people,

Concerned that the continuation of disputes among States, particularly in the absence of an effective mechanism to resolve them through peaceful means, may contribute to the arms race and endanger the maintenance of international peace and security and the efforts of the international community to promote arms control and disarmament,

1. *Calls upon* Member States to refrain from the use or threat of use of force, in accordance with the purposes and principles of the Charter of the United Nations;

2. *Reaffirms its commitment* to the peaceful settlement of disputes under Chapter VI of the Charter, in particular Article 33, which provides for a solution by negotiation, enquiry, mediation, conciliation, arbitration, judicial settlement, resort to regional agencies or arrangements or other peaceful means chosen by the parties;

3. *Reaffirms* the ways and means regarding confidence- and security-building measures set out in the report of the Disarmament Commission on its 1993 session;

4. *Calls upon* Member States to pursue those ways and means through sustained consultations and dialogue, while at the same time avoiding actions which may hinder or impair such a dialogue;

5. *Urges* States to comply strictly with all bilateral, regional and international agreements, including

arms control and disarmament agreements, to which they are party;

6. *Emphasizes* that the objective of confidence-building measures should be to help to strengthen international peace and security and be consistent with the principle of undiminished security at the lowest level of armament;

7. *Encourages* the promotion of bilateral and regional confidence-building measures, with the consent and participation of the parties concerned, to avoid conflict and prevent the unintended and accidental outbreak of hostilities;

8. *Requests* the Secretary-General to submit a report to the General Assembly at its sixty-first session containing the views of Member States on confidence-building measures in the regional and subregional context;

9. *Decides* to include in the provisional agenda of its sixty-first session the item entitled "Confidence-building measures in the regional and subregional context".

The Assembly adopted **resolution 60/75** by recorded vote (174-1-1) [agenda item 97 *(v)*].

Conventional arms control at the regional and subregional levels

The General Assembly,

Recalling its resolutions 48/75 J of 16 December 1993, 49/75 O of 15 December 1994, 50/70 L of 12 December 1995, 51/45 Q of 10 December 1996, 52/38 Q of 9 December 1997, 53/77 P of 4 December 1998, 54/54 M of 1 December 1999, 55/33 P of 20 November 2000, 56/24 I of 29 November 2001, 57/77 of 22 November 2002, 58/39 of 8 December 2003 and 59/88 of 3 December 2004,

Recognizing the crucial role of conventional arms control in promoting regional and international peace and security,

Convinced that conventional arms control needs to be pursued primarily in the regional and subregional contexts, since most threats to peace and security in the post-cold-war era arise mainly among States located in the same region or subregion,

Aware that the preservation of a balance in the defence capabilities of States at the lowest level of armaments would contribute to peace and stability and should be a prime objective of conventional arms control,

Desirous of promoting agreements to strengthen regional peace and security at the lowest possible level of armaments and military forces,

Noting with particular interest the initiatives taken in this regard in different regions of the world, in particular the commencement of consultations among a number of Latin American countries and the proposals for conventional arms control made in the context of South Asia, and recognizing, in the context of this subject, the relevance and value of the Treaty on Conventional Armed Forces in Europe, which is a cornerstone of European security,

Believing that militarily significant States and States with larger military capabilities have a special responsibility in promoting such agreements for regional security,

Believing also that an important objective of conventional arms control in regions of tension should be to prevent the possibility of military attack launched by surprise and to avoid aggression,

1. *Decides* to give urgent consideration to the issues involved in conventional arms control at the regional and subregional levels;

2. *Requests* the Conference on Disarmament to consider the formulation of principles that can serve as a framework for regional agreements on conventional arms control, and looks forward to a report of the Conference on this subject;

3. *Requests* the Secretary-General, in the meantime, to seek the views of Member States on the subject and to submit a report to the General Assembly at its sixty-first session;

4. *Decides* to include in the provisional agenda of its sixty-first session the item entitled "Conventional arms control at the regional and subregional levels".

RECORDED VOTE ON RESOLUTION 60/75:

In favour: Afghanistan, Albania, Algeria, Andorra, Antigua and Barbuda, Argentina, Armenia, Australia, Austria, Azerbaijan, Bahamas, Bahrain, Bangladesh, Barbados, Belarus, Belgium, Belize, Benin, Bolivia, Bosnia and Herzegovina, Botswana, Brazil, Brunei Darussalam, Bulgaria, Burkina Faso, Burundi, Cambodia, Cameroon, Canada, Cape Verde, Central African Republic, Chile, China, Colombia, Congo, Costa Rica, Côte d'Ivoire, Croatia, Cyprus, Czech Republic, Democratic Republic of the Congo, Denmark, Djibouti, Dominica, Dominican Republic, Ecuador, Egypt, El Salvador, Eritrea, Estonia, Ethiopia, Fiji, Finland, France, Gabon, Georgia, Germany, Ghana, Greece, Grenada, Guatemala, Guinea, Guinea-Bissau, Guyana, Haiti, Honduras, Hungary, Iceland, Indonesia, Iran, Iraq, Ireland, Israel, Italy, Jamaica, Japan, Jordan, Kazakhstan, Kenya, Kuwait, Kyrgyzstan, Latvia, Lebanon, Lesotho, Liberia, Libyan Arab Jamahiriya, Liechtenstein, Lithuania, Luxembourg, Madagascar, Malawi, Malaysia, Maldives, Mali, Malta, Marshall Islands, Mauritania, Mauritius, Mexico, Micronesia, Monaco, Mongolia, Morocco, Mozambique, Myanmar, Namibia, Nepal, Netherlands, New Zealand, Nicaragua, Niger, Nigeria, Norway, Oman, Pakistan, Palau, Panama, Papua New Guinea, Paraguay, Peru, Philippines, Poland, Portugal, Qatar, Republic of Korea, Republic of Moldova, Romania, Russian Federation, Saint Lucia, Saint Vincent and the Grenadines, Samoa, San Marino, Sao Tome and Principe, Saudi Arabia, Senegal, Serbia and Montenegro, Sierra Leone, Singapore, Slovakia, Slovenia, Solomon Islands, Somalia, South Africa, Spain, Sri Lanka, Sudan, Suriname, Sweden, Switzerland, Syrian Arab Republic, Tajikistan, Thailand, The former Yugoslav Republic of Macedonia, Timor-Leste, Togo, Tonga, Trinidad and Tobago, Tunisia, Turkey, Turkmenistan, Tuvalu, Uganda, Ukraine, United Arab Emirates, United Kingdom, United Republic of Tanzania, United States, Uruguay, Uzbekistan, Vanuatu, Venezuela, Yemen, Zambia, Zimbabwe.

Against: India.

Abstaining: Bhutan.

Africa

In 2005, African States maintained efforts to address challenges stemming from the proliferation of small arms and light weapons on the continent. The Regional Consultation of Governmental Experts on Small Arms and Light Weapons and the Biennial Meeting of States Reporting in West Africa (Bamako, Mali, 28-29 April) reviewed regional and international commitments and initiatives and mechanisms regarding those weapons. They discussed, among other things, common concerns and needs relating to three broad themes: country reporting to the Biennial Meeting of States to Consider the Implementation of the 2001 Programme of Action on small arms (see p. 618); ways to support a newly created small arms unit of the Economic Community of

West African States (ECOWAS) in fulfilling its tasks; and the complementarity and/or compatibility of existing regional commitments to the control of illicit arms.

The Third Ministerial Review Conference of the Nairobi Declaration on the Problem of the Proliferation of Illicit Small Arms and Light Weapons in the Great Lakes Region and Horn of Africa [YUN 2000, p. 518] (Nairobi, 20-21 June) declared its commitment to continue efforts in tackling the problem. To that end, it established a Regional Centre for Small Arms and Light Weapons (RECSA) to oversee the full implementation of the Nairobi Declaration and related Protocol in the Great Lakes Region and the Horn of Africa.

The Second Continental Conference of African Governmental Experts and Regional Economic Communities on the Illicit Small Arms Trade (Windhoek, Namibia, 14-16 December) agreed on measures at the national, regional and international levels for implementing the Programme of Action adopted by the 2001 UN Conference on small arms [YUN 2001, p. 499] and to present a common African position at the planned 2006 Conference to review progress in the implementation process. It requested the African Union to take follow-up action, including organizing biennial high-level governmental meetings in 2008, 2010 and 2012, to review progress. To reinforce efforts in combating the illicit trafficking in small arms and light weapons, particularly illicit brokering, Interpol and the International Criminal Court (ICC) Prosecutor collaborated on a project to collect and analyse information on key figures involved in those activities and on their mode of operation in the Great Lakes region. The project was expected to provide the international law enforcement community with an additional tool for tackling those criminal activities. UNDP's Bureau for Crisis Prevention and Recovery and Small Arms and Demobilization Unit organized a meeting, which considered lessons learned from the Small Arms Reduction Programme in the Great Lakes Region and ways to increase support for enhancing the regional agenda in that context.

Standing Advisory Committee

At its twenty-second ministerial meeting (Brazzaville, Republic of the Congo, 14-18 March) [A/59/769-S/2005/212], the Standing Advisory Committee on Security Questions in Central Africa reviewed the geopolitical and security situation in its member States, the mercenary threat in Central Africa, its own role in promoting peace and development in the Great Lakes region, preparations for a military exercise in the Sudanese region of Bahr-El-Ghazal and regional contribution to the work of the Second Biennial Meeting of States on the implementation of the Programme of Action adopted by the 2001 UN Conference [YUN 2001, p. 499]. While welcoming the positive developments in the Central African Republic (see p. 217), including the holding of legislative and presidential elections and the establishment of the national Disarmament, Demobilization and Reintegration Commission for ex-combatants, the Committee expressed concern at continuing insecurity in that country, characterized by abuses and summary executions by agents of law and order and noted the commitment of the authorities to bring the perpetrators to justice. The Committee also expressed concern at persisting tensions on the border between the Democratic Republic of the Congo (DRC) and Rwanda and welcomed their mutual efforts to improve the situation. It adopted two declarations on the mercenary threat in Central Africa and on peace, security, democracy and development in the Great Lakes region, respectively, both of which were annexed to its report.

In response to General Assembly resolution 59/96 [YUN 2004, p. 571], the Secretary-General, in July [A/60/166], described the activities of the Committee. He observed that the Committee, which remained the only forum for States members of the Economic Community of Central African States (ECCAS) to meet regularly to examine political and security developments in the region, demonstrated its valuable role by adopting two declarations during the year. He observed that the declaration on mercenary activity in Central Africa addressed the obstacle which such activity posed to peace, stability and development in the region. The declaration on peace, security, democracy and development in the Great Lakes region recognized the link between peace in that region and in the Central African subregion. Despite those commendable initiatives, however, concrete actions were imperative in order for the Central African subregion to attain sustainable peace, stability and development. It was critical, therefore, that the Council for Peace and Security in Central Africa, established in 1999 [YUN 1999, p. 500], became operational, particularly its early warning mechanisms. It was also vital that the capacity of the ECCAS secretariat be strengthened to enable it to spearhead the implementation of the various declarations, decisions and recommendations of the Committee.

In September, the Congo transmitted the report of the Committee's twenty-third ministerial meeting (Brazzaville, Congo, 29 August–2 September) [A/60/393-S/2005/616]. The Committee continued to consider issues relating to its member States' geopolitical and security situation, security cooperation among them, and the review of related declarations and other initiatives. It also adopted its 2005-2006 programme of work.

GENERAL ASSEMBLY ACTION

On 8 December [meeting 62], the General Assembly, on the recommendation of the First Committee [A/60/464], adopted **resolution 60/87** without vote [agenda item 98 (a)].

Regional confidence-building measures: activities of the United Nations Standing Advisory Committee on Security Questions in Central Africa

The General Assembly,

Bearing in mind the purposes and principles of the United Nations and its primary responsibility for the maintenance of international peace and security in accordance with the Charter of the United Nations,

Recalling its resolutions 43/78 H and 43/85 of 7 December 1988, 44/21 of 15 November 1989, 45/58 M of 4 December 1990, 46/37 B of 6 December 1991, 47/53 F of 15 December 1992, 48/76 A of 16 December 1993, 49/76 C of 15 December 1994, 50/71 B of 12 December 1995, 51/46 C of 10 December 1996, 52/39 B of 9 December 1997, 53/78 A of 4 December 1998, 54/55 A of 1 December 1999, 55/34 B of 20 November 2000, 56/25 A of 29 November 2001, 57/88 of 22 November 2002, 58/65 of 8 December 2003 and 59/96 of 3 December 2004,

Considering the importance and effectiveness of confidence-building measures taken at the initiative and with the participation of all States concerned and taking into account the specific characteristics of each region, since such measures can contribute to regional stability and to international peace and security,

Convinced that the resources released by disarmament, including regional disarmament, can be devoted to economic and social development and to the protection of the environment for the benefit of all peoples, in particular those of the developing countries,

Recalling the guidelines for general and complete disarmament adopted at its tenth special session, the first special session devoted to disarmament,

Convinced that development can be achieved only in a climate of peace, security and mutual confidence both within and among States,

Bearing in mind the establishment by the Secretary-General on 28 May 1992 of the United Nations Standing Advisory Committee on Security Questions in Central Africa, the purpose of which is to encourage arms limitation, disarmament, non-proliferation and development in the subregion,

Recalling the Brazzaville Declaration on Cooperation for Peace and Security in Central Africa, the Bata Declaration for the Promotion of Lasting Democracy, Peace and Development in Central Africa and the Yaoundé Declaration on Peace, Security and Stability in Central Africa,

Bearing in mind resolutions 1196(1998) and 1197 (1998), adopted by the Security Council on 16 and 18 September 1998 respectively, following its consideration of the report of the Secretary-General on the causes of conflict and the promotion of durable peace and sustainable development in Africa,

Emphasizing the need to strengthen the capacity for conflict prevention and peacekeeping in Africa,

Recalling the decision of the fourth ministerial meeting of the Standing Advisory Committee in favour of establishing, under the auspices of the Office of the United Nations High Commissioner for Human Rights, a subregional centre for human rights and democracy in Central Africa at Yaoundé,

Noting with satisfaction the efforts being made by the countries members of the Economic Community of Central African States to promote peace and security in their subregion, including the visit to Kinshasa, on 24 June 2005, of the President of the Republic of the Congo and current Chairman of the Economic Community of Central African States, as well as the convening in Kinshasa, on 16 July 2005, of a quadripartite summit of the Heads of State of Angola, the Congo, the Democratic Republic of the Congo and Gabon, held within the framework of the mandate entrusted to the current Chairman at the twelfth session of the Conference of Heads of State and Government of the Economic Community of Central African States,

Noting with satisfaction also the improvement in the situation between the Democratic Republic of the Congo and Rwanda, particularly the encouraging results of the meetings of the Democratic Republic of the Congo-Rwanda-Uganda Tripartite Commission on security in that part of the Great Lakes region,

Taking note of the successful completion of electoral processes in the Central African Republic and Burundi,

Recognizing the importance of disarmament, demobilization and reintegration programmes in strengthening peace, political stability and reconstruction, especially in post-conflict situations,

1. *Takes note* of the report of the Secretary-General on regional confidence-building measures, which deals with the activities of the United Nations Standing Advisory Committee on Security Questions in Central Africa in the period since the adoption by the General Assembly of its resolution 59/96;

2. *Reaffirms its support* for efforts aimed at promoting confidence-building measures at the regional and subregional levels in order to ease tensions and conflicts in Central Africa and to further sustainable peace, stability and development in the subregion;

3. *Encourages* the States members of the Economic Community of Central African States to pursue their efforts to promote peace and security in their subregion;

4. *Encourages* the Democratic Republic of the Congo and Rwanda to pursue their efforts to strengthen their bilateral relations;

5. *Strongly appeals* to the international community to provide all necessary support for the smooth functioning of the electoral process currently under way in the Democratic Republic of the Congo;

6. *Appeals* to the international community to support the efforts undertaken by the States concerned to implement disarmament, demobilization and reintegration programmes;

7. *Reaffirms its support* for the programme of work of the Standing Advisory Committee adopted at the organizational meeting of the Committee, held at Yaoundé from 27 to 31 July 1992;

8. *Notes with satisfaction* the progress made by the Standing Advisory Committee in implementing its programme of work for the period 2004-2005;

9. *Emphasizes* the importance of providing the States members of the Standing Advisory Committee with the essential support they need to carry out the full programme of activities which they adopted at their ministerial meetings;

10. *Welcomes* the creation of a mechanism for the promotion, maintenance and consolidation of peace and security in Central Africa, known as the Council for Peace and Security in Central Africa, by the Conference of Heads of State and Government of the countries members of the Economic Community of Central African States, held at Yaoundé on 25 February 1999, and requests the Secretary-General to give his full support to the effective realization of that important mechanism;

11. *Emphasizes* the need to make the early warning mechanism in Central Africa operational so that it will serve, on the one hand, as an instrument for analysing and monitoring political situations in the States members of the Standing Advisory Committee with a view to preventing the outbreak of future armed conflicts and, on the other hand, as a technical body through which the member States will carry out the programme of work of the Committee, adopted at its organizational meeting held at Yaoundé in 1992, and requests the Secretary-General to provide it with the assistance necessary for it to function properly;

12. *Requests* the Secretary-General and the United Nations High Commissioner for Human Rights to continue to provide their full assistance for the proper functioning of the Subregional Centre for Human Rights and Democracy in Central Africa;

13. *Requests* the Secretary-General, pursuant to Security Council resolution 1197(1998), to provide the States members of the Standing Advisory Committee with the necessary support for the implementation and smooth functioning of the Council for Peace and Security in Central Africa and the early warning mechanism;

14. *Also requests* the Secretary-General to support the establishment of a network of parliamentarians with a view to the creation of a subregional parliament in Central Africa;

15. *Requests* the Secretary-General and the United Nations High Commissioner for Refugees to continue to provide increased assistance to the countries of Central Africa for coping with the problems of refugees and displaced persons in their territories;

16. *Thanks* the Secretary-General for having established the Trust Fund for the United Nations Standing Advisory Committee on Security Questions in Central Africa;

17. *Appeals* to Member States and to governmental and non-governmental organizations to make additional voluntary contributions to the Trust Fund for the implementation of the programme of work of the Standing Advisory Committee;

18. *Thanks* the Secretary-General for sending a multidisciplinary mission from 8 to 22 June 2003 for the purpose of undertaking an assessment of the priority needs of the region and challenges confronting it in the areas of peace, security, economic development,

human rights and HIV/AIDS, and in the humanitarian field;

19. *Requests* the Secretary-General to continue to provide the States members of the Standing Advisory Committee with assistance to ensure that they are able to carry on their efforts;

20. *Calls upon* the Secretary-General to submit to the General Assembly at its sixty-first session a report on the implementation of the present resolution;

21. *Decides* to include in the provisional agenda of its sixty-first session the item entitled "Regional confidence-building measures: activities of the United Nations Standing Advisory Committee on Security Questions in Central Africa".

Regional Centre for Peace and Disarmament in Africa

In response to General Assembly resolution 59/101 [YUN 2004, p. 586], the Secretary-General described the activities of the United Nations Regional Centre for Peace and Disarmament in Africa [A/60/153], covering the period from July 2004 to June 2005. The Centre was established in Lomé, Togo, in 1986 [YUN 1986, p. 85].

During the reporting period, the Centre maintained focus on the priority areas of peace and security, which remained at the core of its work; arms control and disarmament; research, information and publication; and cooperation with regional organizations and civil society. The Centre participated in the Conference of Heads of State and Government of ECOWAS (Accra, Ghana, 25 January) on the crisis in Côte d'Ivoire, which provided it with an opportunity to explore the possible role it could play in the disarmament aspects of the peace process. In the Great Lakes region, the Centre, in collaboration with UNDP, deployed a one-month mission in the DRC to review the disarmament, demobilization and reintegration process launched in the context of the peace process in that country. In continuing efforts to promote civil-military relations in Africa, the Centre produced a draft code of conduct for armed and security forces on the continent, for consideration by the AU Commission. In related action, it launched pilot surveys, the first ones in Togo, which would serve as a basis for formulating action-oriented programmes to address areas of tension between the civilian population and the military, especially in emerging democracies in Africa. The Centre completed work on the parliamentary defence committees training course for West Africa and contributed to civil society efforts in Togo to mainstream gender in peace and disarmament processes. It also promoted adherence to and implementation of multilateral disarmament agreements on WMDs and supported regional efforts to tackle the small arms scourge.

In cooperation with its partners, including the AU and UNIDIR, the Centre elaborated the terms of reference and operational framework and guidelines for conducting national inventories of local capacities for the production of small arms and light weapons in the participating States of the Small Arms Transparency and Control Regime in Africa, launched in 2003 [YUN 2003, p. 587]. Between March and June, field missions were deployed to participating countries to launch the inventory process. In April, the Centre, together with UNDP's Bureau for Crisis Prevention and Recovery and UNIDIR, participated in a mission to six southern African countries (Lesotho, Malawi, Mozambique, Swaziland, Zambia, Zimbabwe) to raise awareness about the problem of small arms and light weapons and to build national capacity for tackling it. Other activities of the Centre promoted research in the areas of peace and disarmament on the continent, and cooperation with regional organizations and NGOs in advancing related courses, through exchange programmes and the provision of technical advice and expertise, particularly regarding the drafting of concept papers, project documents and conference reports.

GENERAL ASSEMBLY ACTION

On 8 December [meeting 62], the General Assembly, on the recommendation of the First Committee [A/60/464], adopted **resolution 60/86** without vote [agenda item 98 (e)].

United Nations Regional Centre for Peace and Disarmament in Africa

The General Assembly,

Mindful of the provisions of Article 11, paragraph 1, of the Charter of the United Nations stipulating that a function of the General Assembly is to consider the general principles of cooperation in the maintenance of international peace and security, including the principles governing disarmament and arms limitation,

Recalling its resolutions 40/151 G of 16 December 1985, 41/60 D of 3 December 1986, 42/39 J of 30 November 1987 and 43/76 D of 7 December 1988 on the United Nations Regional Centre for Peace and Disarmament in Africa, and its resolutions 46/36 F of 6 December 1991 and 47/52 G of 9 December 1992 on regional disarmament, including confidence-building measures,

Recalling also its resolutions 48/76 E of 16 December 1993, 49/76 D of 15 December 1994, 50/71 C of 12 December 1995, 51/46 E of 10 December 1996, 52/220 of 22 December 1997, 53/78 C of 4 December 1998, 54/55 B of 1 December 1999, 55/34 D of 20 November 2000, 56/25 D of 29 November 2001, 57/91 of 22 November 2002, 58/61 of 8 December 2003 and 59/101 of 3 December 2004,

Aware of the important role that the Regional Centre can play in promoting confidence-building and arms-limitation measures at the regional level, thereby promoting progress in the area of sustainable development,

Taking note of the report of the Secretary-General, in which it was stated that the Regional Centre continued to carry out its mandate under very strenuous financial and operational difficulties,

Concerned that the activities and staffing of the Regional Centre have been reduced in view of the limited resources at its disposal,

Deeply concerned that, as noted in the report of the Secretary-General, the future of the Regional Centre looks bleak owing to the lack of a reliable source of funding that would ensure the sustainability of its operations,

Bearing in mind the efforts undertaken to mobilize the necessary resources for the operational costs of the Regional Centre,

Conscious of the need to review the mandate and programmes of the Regional Centre in the light of developments in the field of peace and security in Africa since its establishment,

Taking into account the need to establish close cooperation between the Regional Centre and the Peace and Security Council of the African Union, in particular its institutions in the field of peace, disarmament and security, as well as with relevant United Nations bodies and programmes in Africa for greater effectiveness,

1. *Requests* the Secretary-General to establish, within existing resources, a consultative mechanism of interested States, in particular African States, for the reorganization of the United Nations Regional Centre for Peace and Disarmament in Africa, and to report thereon to the General Assembly at its sixty-first session;

2. *Appeals once again* to all States, as well as to international governmental and non-governmental organizations and foundations, to make voluntary contributions in order to strengthen the programmes and activities of the Regional Centre and facilitate their implementation;

3. *Requests* the Secretary-General to continue to provide the necessary support to the Regional Centre for better achievements and results;

4. *Also requests* the Secretary-General to facilitate close cooperation between the Regional Centre and the African Union, in particular in the areas of peace, security and development, and to continue to provide assistance towards stabilizing the financial situation of the Centre;

5. *Appeals in particular* to the Regional Centre, in cooperation with the African Union, regional and sub-regional organizations and the African States, to take steps to promote the consistent implementation of the Programme of Action to Prevent, Combat and Eradicate the Illicit Trade in Small Arms and Light Weapons in All Its Aspects;

6. *Requests* the Secretary-General to report to the General Assembly at its sixty-first session on the implementation of the present resolution;

7. *Decides* to include in the provisional agenda of its sixty-first session the item entitled "United Nations Regional Centre for Peace and Disarmament in Africa".

Asia and the Pacific

In 2005, disarmament and non-proliferation issues in Asia and the Pacific continued to be addressed by the regional States within the framework of the Association of Southeast Asian Nations (ASEAN), its Regional Forum (ARF) and the six-member Shanghai Cooperation Organization (SCO) (China, Kazakhstan, Kyrgystan, Russian Federation, Tajikistan, Uzbekistan). SCO, founded in 2001 as a multilateral platform for strengthening regional peace, security and stability, at its fifth summit (Astana, Kazakhstan, 5 July), adopted a declaration expressing member States' determination to contribute to efforts to strengthen international security at sea and in the air, especially with regard to combating terrorism and other challenges and threats. The twelfth ARF ministerial meeting (Vientiane, Lao People's Democratic Republic, 29 July), pointing to the continuing security challenge posed by the proliferation of WMDs and their delivery vehicles, particularly regarding the risk of those weapons falling into the hands of terrorists, underlined the need to maintain efforts to strengthen the international legal foundation for combating terrorism. The Ministers expressed support for the work of the Security Council Committee established pursuant to resolution 1540(2004) [YUN 2004, p. 544] to monitor national efforts to combat WMD proliferation, the importance of the NPT in promoting nuclear disarmament and the need for all regional States to combat illicit trafficking in small arms and light weapons. At the first East Asia summit (Kuala Lumpur, Malaysia, 14 December), ASEAN leaders endorsed the idea of denuclearizing the Korean Peninsula in a peaceful and verifiable manner within the framework of the six-party talks (see p. 450) as something that could contribute to the peace, stability and prosperity of the region.

Regional Centre for Peace and Disarmament in Asia and the Pacific

As requested by the General Assembly in resolution 59/100 [YUN 2004, p. 587], the Secretary-General reported in July on the activities of the United Nations Regional Centre for Peace and Disarmament in Asia and the Pacific from July 2004 to July 2005 [A/60/152]. The Centre was inaugurated in Kathmandu, Nepal, in 1989 [YUN 1989, p. 88].

During the reporting period, the Centre continued to promote disarmament and security through the organization of meetings and conferences, including a regional workshop to address issues relating to small arms (Beijing, China, 19-21 April), which enabled the regional States to exchange experiences on efforts to combat those weapons, identify related problems and challenges and explore ways to implement the 2001 Programme of Action adopted by the UN Conference on small arms [YUN 2001, p. 499]. The Centre contributed to the work of a study group on countering the proliferation of WMDs (Singapore, 27-28 May), under the auspices of the Council for Security Cooperation in Asia and the Pacific, and to ongoing efforts to advance cooperation with regional States and organizations in addressing security issues of concern. The Centre initiated consultations with some ASEAN members on disarmament and non-proliferation education. It also continued to develop working relations with disarmament-related intergovernmental organizations, including IAEA, OPCW, and CTBTO.

In efforts to maintain support to the five Central Asian States in finalizing the draft text of a treaty to make the region a nuclear-weapon-free zone, the Centre organized a series of expert group meetings, which facilitated the conclusion of negotiations on the text and the adoption of the Central Asian Nuclear-Weapon-Free-Zone Treaty and Protocol (see p. 610). In June, the Centre helped the United Nations Association of Japan to organize an international symposium on peace and environmental issues in Ishikawa (Kanazawa, Japan, 13-14 June), which addressed current peace and environmental issues in the region, as well as other security concerns. It also provided assistance in consolidating and strengthening Mongolia's nuclear-weapon-free status and, to that end, organized a meeting of a consultative group of UN departments, programmes, funds and agencies (New York, 7 July), which focused on follow-up to the studies conducted by the United Nations Department of Economic and Social Affairs (DESA) and UNDP on ecological vulnerabilities and human security in the country. In cooperation with Japan, the Centre organized a conference (Kyoto, Japan, 17-19 August) on the subject "The United Nations: after six decades and renewed efforts for the promotion of disarmament", which addressed the wide range of issues raised at the 2005 NPT Review Conference (see p. 597). The Centre also collaborated with the Republic of Korea to organize the fourth "UN–Republic of Korea Joint Conference on Disarmament and Non-Proliferation (Busan, 1-3 December), which considered challenges to the nuclear non-proliferation regime and ways to strengthen it. Other regional workshops organized by the Centre promoted the UN study on non-proliferation education.

Consultations continued during the year with the host country on the Centre's relocation from

UN Headquarters in New York, including the draft host country agreement and the draft memorandum of understanding on operational costs. Given the Centre's financial and logistical difficulties, the Secretary-General was considering the possibility of co-locating it with the Economic Commission for Asia and the Pacific in Bangkok, as a way of ensuring its operational viability.

Communications. On 2 August [A/60/230], the host country of the Centre, Nepal, reaffirmed its commitment to the Centre's relocation and its eagerness to sign the related host country agreement with the United Nations at the earliest possible date. It indicated its intention to bear the operating costs of the Centre, including additional security-related expenses, and requested a revised text of the host country agreement.

In a related 14 September communication [A/60/369], Nepal emphasized its willingness to sort out outstanding issues relating to the Centre's relocation and stated, in that connection, that privileges and immunities for the Centre's locally recruited staff would be granted in accordance with the provisions of the Convention on the Privileges and Immunities of the United Nations [YUN 1946-47, p. 100, GA res. 22 A (I)].

GENERAL ASSEMBLY ACTION

On 8 December [meeting 62], the General Assembly, on the recommendation of the First Committee [A/60/464], adopted **resolution 60/85** without vote [agenda item 98 (d)].

United Nations Regional Centre for Peace and Disarmament in Asia and the Pacific

The General Assembly,

Recalling its resolutions 42/39 D of 30 November 1987 and 44/117 F of 15 December 1989, by which it established the United Nations Regional Centre for Peace and Disarmament in Asia and renamed it the United Nations Regional Centre for Peace and Disarmament in Asia and the Pacific, with headquarters in Kathmandu and with the mandate of providing, on request, substantive support for the initiatives and other activities mutually agreed upon by the Member States of the Asia-Pacific region for the implementation of measures for peace and disarmament, through appropriate utilization of available resources,

Taking note of the report of the Secretary-General, in which he expresses his belief that the mandate of the Regional Centre remains valid and that the Centre has been a useful instrument for fostering a climate of cooperation for peace and disarmament in the region,

Noting that trends in the post-cold-war era have emphasized the function of the Regional Centre in assisting Member States as they deal with new security concerns and disarmament issues emerging in the region,

Commending the useful activities carried out by the Regional Centre in encouraging regional and subregional dialogue for the enhancement of openness, transparency and confidence-building, as well as the promotion of disarmament and security through the organization of regional meetings, which has come to be widely known within the Asia-Pacific region as "the Kathmandu process",

Expressing its appreciation to the Regional Centre for its organization of meetings and conferences in the region, held in Sapporo, Japan, from 26 to 29 July 2004, in Nadi, Fiji, from 18 to 20 August 2004, on Jeju Island, Republic of Korea, from 6 to 8 December 2004, in Beijing from 19 to 21 April 2005 and in Kanazawa, Japan, on 13 and 14 June 2005,

Welcoming the idea of the possible creation of an educational and training programme for peace and disarmament in Asia and the Pacific for young people with different backgrounds, to be financed from voluntary contributions,

Noting the important role of the Regional Centre in assisting region-specific initiatives of Member States, including its continued assistance in finalizing a treaty related to the establishment of a nuclear-weapon-free zone in Central Asia, as well as to Mongolia's international security and nuclear-weapon-free status,

Appreciating highly the overall support that Nepal has extended as the host nation of the headquarters of the Regional Centre,

1. *Reaffirms its strong support* for the forthcoming operation and further strengthening of the United Nations Regional Centre for Peace and Disarmament in Asia and the Pacific;

2. *Underlines* the importance of the Kathmandu process as a powerful vehicle for the development of the practice of region-wide security and disarmament dialogue;

3. *Expresses its appreciation* for the continuing political support and voluntary financial contributions to the Regional Centre, which are essential for its continued operation;

4. *Appeals* to Member States, in particular those within the Asia-Pacific region, as well as to international governmental and non-governmental organizations and foundations, to make voluntary contributions, the only resources of the Regional Centre, to strengthen the programme of activities of the Centre and the implementation thereof;

5. *Requests* the Secretary-General, taking note of paragraph 6 of General Assembly resolution 49/76 D of 15 December 1994, to provide the Regional Centre with the necessary support, within existing resources, in carrying out its programme of activities;

6. *Urges* the Secretary-General to ensure the physical operation of the Regional Centre from Kathmandu within six months of the date of signature of the host country agreement and to enable the Centre to function effectively;

7. *Requests* the Secretary-General to report to the General Assembly at its sixty-first session on the implementation of the present resolution;

8. *Decides* to include in the provisional agenda of its sixty-first session the item entitled "United Nations Regional Centre for Peace and Disarmament in Asia and the Pacific".

Europe

During the year, European countries continued to address security and disarmament issues within the framework of regional institutions. The EU, which had considerably increased its activities on matters relating to WMDs and small arms and light weapons, implemented during the year a significant number of concrete actions foreseen in its 2003 security strategy [YUN 2003, p. 576] for addressing global security threats and challenges. In a bid to help strengthen nuclear security, the EU adopted a Joint Action in July [2005/574/CFSP] pledging support for IAEA activities in the areas of nuclear security and verification. To that end, it undertook to implement projects that would help strengthen the physical protection of nuclear and other radioactive materials in use, storage and transport of nuclear facilities; secure radioactive materials in non-nuclear applications; strengthen States' capabilities for detection and response to illicit trafficking in those materials; and provide legislative assistance for the implementation of States' obligations under IAEA safeguards agreements and additional protocols.

During the year, the EU also made efforts to support the activities of OPCW (see p. 618), aimed at promoting the universalization of the Chemical Weapons Convention and at supporting its implementation by States. It continued its work on conventional arms control through the 1998 EU Code of Conduct for Arms Export [YUN 1998, p. 540]. Priorities for the future included outreach to promote the Code's principles and criteria, and providing practical and technical assistance to States in that context. The EU endorsed the principle of an international arms trade treaty and made a commitment in October to work towards its negotiation. In December, the European Council adopted the EU Strategy to combat illicit accumulation and trafficking in small arms and light weapons and their ammunition. The Organization for Security and Cooperation in Europe (OSCE) also accorded particular attention to security-related concerns posed by the illicit trafficking of small arms and light weapons. The thirteenth meeting of the OSCE Ministerial Council (Ljubljana, Slovenia, 5-6 December) adopted a decision on further efforts to implement previous OSCE documents on those weapons, aspects of which covered ammunition stockpiles. OSCE also assisted many of its participating States to reduce conventional arms stocks, improve stockpile security or destroy excess or unwelcome armaments. Those States began drafting a "best practice guide" on stockpiles of conventional ammunition. OSCE also accorded considerable attention to WMD proliferation and the threat of their acquisition by non-State actors, focusing on ways of assisting in the implementation of Security Council resolution 1540(2004)

[YUN 2004, p. 544] on measures to combat the problem.

Communications. On 19 August [A/60/292], the Russian Federation transmitted the text of a 22 June declaration of the States members of the Collective Security Treaty Organization, by which they pledged to take measures to encourage national procedures for the ratification of the Agreement on Adaptation of the Treaty on Conventional Armed Forces in Europe.

Latin America

In 2005, the Organization of American States (OAS) continued to promote regional disarmament and non-proliferation initiatives. The OAS General Assembly, at its thirty-fifth regular session (Florida, United States, 5-7 June), adopted resolutions underscoring the disarmament elements of the Inter-American Convention against the Illicit Manufacturing of and Trafficking in Firearms, Ammunition, Explosives, and Other Related Materials (CIFTA); consolidation of the regime established in the Treaty for the Prohibition of Nuclear Weapons in Latin America and the Caribbean (Treaty of Tlatelolco) (see p. 611); the Americas as a biological- and chemical-weapons-free region; the proliferation of and the illicit trade in small arms and light weapons in all its aspects; disarmament and non-proliferation education; the Inter-American Convention on Transparency in Conventional Weapons Acquisitions; inter-American support for the CTBT; and the Americas as an anti-personnel land-mine-free zone. Within the framework of CIFTA, the first meeting of national authorities directly responsible for granting the export, import and international transit licences or authorizations for transfers of firearms, ammunition, explosives and other related materials (Washington, D.C., 6-7 October) discussed mechanisms to help prevent the illegal manufacturing and trafficking in firearms. The Fourth Summit of the Americas (Mar del Plata, Argentina, 4-5 November) adopted the Declaration of Mar Del Plata reaffirming commitment to the objectives and purposes of the 2003 Declaration on Security in the Americas [YUN 2003, p. 577], based on a multidimensional concept of security and cooperation among the regional States. The Central American Integration System, with support from UNDP's Bureau for Crisis Prevention and Recovery/ Small Arms and Demobilization Unit, developed a regional small arms control project expected to begin operation in 2006. The Unit, together with the United Kingdom, also supported Nicaragua in developing and implementing a project relating to the control of those weapons.

Regional Centre

Pursuant to General Assembly resolution 59/99 [YUN 2004, p. 589], the Secretary-General submitted a July report [A/60/132] describing the activities of the United Nations Regional Centre for Peace, Disarmament and Development in Latin America and the Caribbean from July 2004 to June 2005. The Centre was inaugurated in Lima, Peru, in 1987 [YUN 1987, p. 88].

The Centre focused attention on WMDs and stockpile management; training courses for the law enforcement community, members of Parliament and NGO representatives; guidance on reporting in connection with weapons-related instruments; and development of methodologies for future confidence-building measures between States. Concerning the promotion of subregional and regional security, the Centre devoted increased attention to defining, better understanding and supporting projects that affected the security and lives of people on a daily basis. It also helped coordinate the efforts of related entities and undertook capacity-building initiatives on the link between security and sustainable development.

In the field of good governance and security sector reform, the Centre supported a project in Costa Rica aimed at researching ways to reduce the impact of firearms-related violence on human development, improve firearms legislation and conduct capacity-building activities, decentralize firearms-related policy and develop awareness on firearms control. A similar initiative in Guatemala involved studies on the impact of firearms proliferation on development. The Centre also fostered the development and implementation of firearms-related instruments, the strengthening of firearms legislation, the development of training courses. It focused on assisting with weapons destruction and stockpile management, increasing database tools to enhance coordination and the exchange of information, enhancing participation of the firearms, ammunition and explosives industry and fostering UN coordination. In that context, it helped organize various conferences and workshops to assist the regional States in implementing their obligations regarding such issues as the design of firearms legislation and the development of capacity-building courses and reporting procedures.

During the reporting period, the Centre, in cooperation with several partners, developed and organized training courses on the control of the legal arms trade and the illicit trafficking in firearms, ammunition and explosives, in which some 329 individuals in the region participated, including law enforcement officials, members of Parliament and NGO representatives. Regarding

weapons destruction and stockpile management, the Centre assisted with the destruction or removal of 52,000 firearms in Brazil, Costa Rica and Paraguay, as well as the destruction of over 96 tons of ammunition and explosives in Paraguay. Plans were currently under way for additional weapons destruction in those countries. The Centre assisted regional States to enhance confidence- and security-building measures by helping to develop a standardized methodology on the comparison of military expenditures, which provided the basis for the discussion of the mission, objectives and policies of national defence. It also assisted in developing defence white papers addressing issues relating to the strengthening of democratic values, practices and human security in the region. The Centre undertook a variety of other activities designed to enhance cooperation for a safer region by promoting dialogue and information exchange among the regional States and supporting efforts in the field of regional security.

GENERAL ASSEMBLY ACTION

On 8 December [meeting 62], the General Assembly, on the recommendation of the First Committee [A/60/464], adopted **resolution 60/84** without vote [agenda item 98 (c)].

United Nations Regional Centre for Peace, Disarmament and Development in Latin America and the Caribbean

The General Assembly,

Recalling its resolutions 41/60 J of 3 December 1986, 42/39 K of 30 November 1987 and 43/76 H of 7 December 1988 on the United Nations Regional Centre for Peace, Disarmament and Development in Latin America and the Caribbean, with headquarters in Lima,

Recalling also its resolutions 46/37 F of 9 December 1991, 48/76 E of 16 December 1993, 49/76 D of 15 December 1994, 50/71 C of 12 December 1995, 52/220 of 22 December 1997, 53/78 F of 4 December 1998, 54/55 F of 1 December 1999, 55/34 E of 20 November 2000, 56/25 E of 29 November 2001, 57/89 of 22 November 2002, 58/60 of 8 December 2003 and 59/99 of 3 December 2004,

Underlining the revitalization of the Regional Centre, the efforts made by the Government of Peru and other countries to that end, as well as the important work done by the Director of the Centre,

Recognizing that the Regional Centre has continued to act as an instrument for the implementation of regional initiatives and has intensified its contribution to the coordination of United Nations efforts towards peace and security,

Welcoming the report of the Secretary-General, which concludes that the Regional Centre has continued to provide assistance to States in the Latin American and Caribbean region in the implementation of regional initiatives in the areas of peace, disarmament and development and that during the period under review, such assistance was provided in the form of, inter alia, weapons destruction and stockpile management, training courses for the law enforcement community, members of Parliament and their advisers and representatives of non-governmental organizations, guidance on reporting in connection with weapons-related instruments and the development of methodologies for future confidence-building measures among States,

Recalling the report of the Group of Governmental Experts on the relationship between disarmament and development, referred to in General Assembly resolution 59/78 of 3 December 2004, which is of utmost interest with regard to the role that the Regional Centre plays in promoting the issue in the region in pursuit of its mandate to promote economic and social development related to peace and disarmament,

Noting that security and disarmament issues have always been recognized as significant topics in Latin America and the Caribbean, the first inhabited region in the world to be declared a nuclear-weapon-free zone,

Welcoming the support provided by the Regional Centre to strengthening the nuclear-weapon-free zone established by the Treaty for the Prohibition of Nuclear Weapons in Latin America and the Caribbean (Treaty of Tlatelolco), as well as to promoting and assisting the ratification and implementation of existing multilateral agreements related to weapons of mass destruction and to promoting peace and disarmament education projects during the period under review,

Bearing in mind the important role that the Regional Centre can play in promoting confidence-building measures, arms control and limitation, disarmament and development at the regional level,

Bearing in mind also the importance of information, research, education and training for peace, disarmament and development in order to achieve understanding and cooperation among States,

Recognizing the need to provide the three United Nations regional centres for peace and disarmament with sufficient financial resources and cooperation for the planning and implementation of their programmes of activities,

1. *Reiterates its strong support* for the role of the United Nations Regional Centre for Peace, Disarmament and Development in Latin America and the Caribbean in the promotion of United Nations activities at the regional level to strengthen peace, stability, security and development among its member States;

2. *Expresses its satisfaction and congratulates* the Regional Centre for the expansion of the vast range of activities carried out in the last year in the fields of peace, disarmament and development, and requests the Centre to take into account the proposals to be submitted by the countries of the region in promoting confidence-building measures, arms control and limitation, transparency, disarmament and development at the regional level;

3. *Expresses its appreciation* for the political support and financial contributions to the Regional Centre, which are essential for its continued operation;

4. *Invites* all States of the region to continue to take part in the activities of the Regional Centre, proposing items for inclusion in its programme and making greater and better use of the potential of the Centre to

meet the current challenges facing the international community with a view to fulfilling the aims of the Charter of the United Nations in the fields of peace, disarmament and development;

5. *Recognizes* that the Regional Centre has an important role in the promotion and development of regional initiatives agreed upon by the countries of Latin America and the Caribbean in the field of weapons of mass destruction, in particular nuclear weapons, conventional arms, including small arms and light weapons, as well as the relationship between disarmament and development;

6. *Encourages* the Regional Centre to further develop activities in the important area of disarmament and development;

7. *Highlights* the conclusion contained in the report of the Secretary-General that, through its activities, the Regional Centre has demonstrated its role as a viable regional actor in assisting States in the region to advance the cause of peace, disarmament and development in Latin America and the Caribbean;

8. *Appeals* to Member States, in particular those within the Latin American and Caribbean region, as well as to international governmental and non-governmental organizations and foundations, to make and to increase voluntary contributions to strengthen the Regional Centre, its programme of activities and the implementation thereof;

9. *Requests* the Secretary-General to provide the Regional Centre with all necessary support, within existing resources, so that it may carry out its programme of activities in accordance with its mandate;

10. *Also requests* the Secretary-General to report to the General Assembly at its sixty-first session on the implementation of the present resolution;

11. *Decides* to include in the provisional agenda of its sixty-first session the item entitled "United Nations Regional Centre for Peace, Disarmament and Development in Latin America and the Caribbean".

On 8 December [meeting 62], the General Assembly, on the recommendation of the First Committee [A/60/464], adopted **resolution 60/83** without vote [agenda item 98 *(b)*].

United Nations regional centres for peace and disarmament

The General Assembly,

Recalling its resolution 59/98 of 3 December 2004 regarding the maintenance and revitalization of the three United Nations regional centres for peace and disarmament,

Recalling also the reports of the Secretary-General on the United Nations Regional Centre for Peace and Disarmament in Africa, the United Nations Regional Centre for Peace and Disarmament in Asia and the Pacific and the United Nations Regional Centre for Peace, Disarmament and Development in Latin America and the Caribbean,

Reaffirming its decision, taken in 1982 at its twelfth special session, to establish the United Nations Disarmament Information Programme, the purpose of which is to inform, educate and generate public understanding and support for the objectives of the United Nations in the field of arms control and disarmament,

Bearing in mind its resolutions 40/151 G of 16 December 1985, 41/60 J of 3 December 1986, 42/39 D of 30 November 1987 and 44/117 F of 15 December 1989 on the regional centres for peace and disarmament in Nepal, Peru and Togo,

Recognizing that the changes that have taken place in the world have created new opportunities as well as posed new challenges for the pursuit of disarmament, and, in this regard, bearing in mind that the regional centres for peace and disarmament can contribute substantially to understanding and cooperation among States in each particular region in the areas of peace, disarmament and development,

Noting that in paragraph 146 of the Final Document of the Twelfth Conference of Heads of State or Government of the Non-Aligned Countries, held at Durban, South Africa, from 29 August to 3 September 1998, the Heads of State or Government welcomed the decision adopted by the General Assembly on maintaining and revitalizing the three regional centres for peace and disarmament in Nepal, Peru and Togo,

1. *Reiterates* the importance of the United Nations activities at the regional level to increase the stability and security of its Member States, which could be promoted in a substantive manner by the maintenance and revitalization of the three regional centres for peace and disarmament;

2. *Reaffirms* that, in order to achieve positive results, it is useful for the three regional centres to carry out dissemination and educational programmes that promote regional peace and security and that are aimed at changing basic attitudes with respect to peace and security and disarmament so as to support the achievement of the purposes and principles of the United Nations;

3. *Appeals* to Member States in each region and those that are able to do so, as well as to international governmental and non-governmental organizations and foundations, to make voluntary contributions to the regional centres in their respective regions to strengthen their activities and initiatives;

4. *Emphasizes* the importance of the activities of the regional branch of the Department for Disarmament Affairs of the Secretariat;

5. *Requests* the Secretary-General to provide all necessary support, within existing resources, to the regional centres in carrying out their programmes of activities;

6. *Decides* to include in the provisional agenda of its sixty-first session the item entitled "United Nations regional centres for peace and disarmament".

Chapter VIII

Other political and security questions

In 2005, the United Nations continued to consider political and security questions relating to its efforts to support democratization worldwide, the promotion of decolonization, the Organization's public information activities and the peaceful uses of outer space.

The Organization continued to promote and strengthen democratic practices and principles around the world and to better coordinate and strengthen UN activities to support that objective. In July, the Secretary-General announced the establishment of the United Nations Democracy Fund, a voluntary trust fund to promote democracy worldwide. Efforts also continued to promote measures to ensure regional peace, security and stability, especially in Antarctica, the South Atlantic and the Indian Ocean, through the General Assembly's ad hoc committees established for those purposes. The Special Committee on the Situation with regard to the Implementation of the Declaration on the Granting of Independence to Colonial Countries and Peoples reviewed progress in the implementation of the 1960 Declaration, particularly the exercise of self-determination by the remaining Non-Self-Governing Territories.

During the year, the national representative body of Tokelau, a New Zealand administered Territory, approved a draft treaty of free association between Tokelau and New Zealand, and the holding of a referendum on the change in the Territory's status in 2006. The Special Committee, at the invitation of the Bermuda Independence Commission, visited Bermuda during the year to assess the type of assistance the UN system could provide to help that Territory define its future status. Progress was also made in the new Tripartite Forum for Dialogue on Gibraltar.

In the area of information, the Secretary-General reported that the process of reorientation of the Department of Public Information (DPI), launched in 2002, was completed, and that DPI had implemented those aspects of the 2002 comprehensive review of its work that were within his authority. While the Regional United Nations Information Centre (UNIC) in Brussels, Belgium, made steady progress as an information hub for Western Europe, the Secretary-General revised his plan for the further rationalization of information centres around hubs in other regions and proposed instead a strategic recalibration of the existing network of UNICs, by which key centres in each region would be strengthened to support other centres. The Secretary-General also set out new strategic directions for UN libraries to align library policy with the recommendations put forward in his 2002 report on strengthening the United Nations: an agenda for further change.

In a December resolution on developments in information and telecommunications, the Assembly called on Member States to consider existing and potential threats in the field of information security. Regarding the role of science and technology in the context of international security, the Assembly, in another December resolution, encouraged UN bodies, within existing mandates, to promote the application of science and technology for peaceful purposes.

The Committee on the Peaceful Uses of Outer Space considered the implementation of the recommendations of the Third (1999) United Nations Conference on the Exploration and Peaceful Uses of Outer Space. Implementation of the recommendations by Member States continued through regional and international efforts and the work of some of the action teams established for that purpose.

The United Nations Scientific Committee on the Effects of Atomic Radiation held its fifty-third session.

General aspects of international security

Support for democracies

UN system activities

Reports of Secretary-General. The Secretary-General, in his report to the 2005 World Summit (see p. 67), entitled "In larger freedom: towards development, security and human rights for all" [A/59/2005], said that the United Nations had done more than any other single organization to promote and strengthen democratic institutions and practices around the world by supporting emerging democracies with legal, technical and financial assistance and advice. However, the impact of that work was reduced by the way it was dispersed among the different parts of the UN bureaucracy. Significant gaps still existed in the UN's capacity in several critical areas. The Organization as a whole needed to be better coordinated and resources mobilized more effectively. It should not restrict its role to norm-setting but expand it to help broaden and deepen democratic trends throughout the world. He supported the establishment of a democracy fund (see below).

In a November report [A/60/556], submitted in response to General Assembly resolutions 58/13 [YUN 2003, p. 594] and 58/281 [YUN 2004, p. 592], the Secretary-General discussed the follow-up to the Fifth (2003) International Conference of New or Restored Democracies [YUN 2003, p. 593]; preparations for the Sixth International Conference, to be held in Doha, Qatar, from 30 October to 1 November 2006; and proposals for strengthening UN support for democratic governance.

The Secretary-General believed that strengthening new and restored democracies, as well as respect for human rights and the rule of law, was essential for preventing the emergence of new security threats and combating existing ones. Significant progress had been made by the Chair of the Fifth International Conference in strengthening and institutionalizing the new or restored democracies movement, but the implementation of the decisions taken at each conference needed to be strengthened and broadened. He planned to ask relevant UN entities to study the comparative advantages, complementarity and distribution of labour of various intergovernmental democracy movements, organizations and institutes, and how the UN system had worked and could work further to support them. The Secretary-General called on the Assembly to decide, taking into account the financial implications, on ways to strengthen UN support to the Chair of the International Conference and UN cooperation with relevant movements and organizations to make their work in that area more effective and complementary.

In Assembly **resolution 60/1** (see p. 48), world leaders renewed their commitment to support democracy by strengthening countries' capacity to implement democratic principles and practices and resolved to strengthen UN capacity to assist Member States. They also welcomed the establishment of the Democracy Fund in July (see below).

Democracy Fund

The Secretary-General, in his March report entitled "In larger freedom: towards development, security and human rights for all" [A/59/2005] (see p. 67), said that he supported the creation of a UN democracy fund, first proposed by United States President George W. Bush in 2004 [YUN 2004, p. 66] to provide assistance to countries seeking to establish or strengthen their democracy. He intended to ensure closer coordination of UN activities in that regard by establishing a more explicit link between the democratic governance work of the United Nations Development Programme (UNDP) and the Electoral Assistance Division of the UN Department of Political Affairs.

Addressing the fifth African Union Summit (Sirte, Libyan Arab Jamahiriya, 4 July), the Secretary-General announced the establishment of the United Nations Democracy Fund (UNDEF), the primary purpose of which would be to promote democracy throughout the world by providing assistance for projects that consolidated and strengthened democratic institutions and facilitated democratic governance in new or restored democracies, as was called for by the General Assembly in resolution 58/13 [YUN 2003, p. 594]. UNDEF would complement current UN efforts and ensure an integrated, holistic, capacity-building and demand-driven approach. It would be a voluntary trust fund, located within the UN Fund for International Partnerships and overseen by an Advisory Board.

In his October report [A/60/430] on the implementation of the decisions of the 2005 World Summit Outcome (see p. 77), the Secretary-General stated that 15 countries had so far made pledges to the Fund, amounting to $42.2 million.

Regional aspects of international peace and security

Antarctica

In response to General Assembly resolution 57/51 [YUN 2002, p. 555], the Secretary-General submitted an August report [A/60/222], prepared by the United Nations Environment Programme (UNEP), on the activities of the Antarctic Treaty system and international bodies and recent developments pertaining to the Antarctic environment. The information was drawn from the final reports of the Twenty-fifth through Twenty-eighth Antarctic Treaty Consultative Meetings (ATCMs) (Warsaw, Poland, 10-20 September 2002;

Madrid, Spain, 9-20 June 2003; Cape Town, South Africa, 24 May–4 June 2004; and Stockholm, Sweden, 6-17 June 2005), and from information provided by the parties to the Antarctic Treaty, which was adopted in 1959 and entered into force on 23 June 1961.

The three inspections carried out in Antarctica since 2002 to ensure observance of the Treaty's provisions found that all stations and facilities were in compliance with those provisions. The inspections also checked the implementation of the 1991 Protocol on Environmental Protection to the Antarctic Treaty (Madrid Protocol), and noted a high degree of understanding of the Protocol and of developments regarding the use of alternative energy systems, including wind and solar. However, a number of areas were identified for improvement, including fuel transfer and storage containment; oil spill contingency plans; the environmental impact assessment of current activities; air emission filtering and monitoring; and sewage treatment systems. One inspection found a significant number of stations unoccupied and little coordination in scientific research in the Antarctic Peninsula, even among neighbouring stations. As at June 2005, there were 32 parties to the Protocol.

Fishing, sealing and whaling were regulated by the 1980 Convention on the Conservation of Antarctic Marine Living Resources. Towards the implementation of its conservation measures, the Commission for the Conservation of Antarctic Marine Living Resources was increasingly cooperating with non-contracting parties, and had further strengthened cooperation with the Antarctic Treaty parties.

The report also described recent developments pertaining to the Antarctic environment, including those relating to science and support activities; environmental monitoring; the publication of a "state of the Antarctic environment" report; the development of environmental impact assessment procedures; safety of operations, emergency response and contingency planning; waste disposal and management; prevention of marine pollution; ozone depletion; conservation of Antarctic fauna and flora; area protection and management; the question of liability arising from activities covered by the Madrid Protocol; Antarctic tourism and other non-governmental operations; biological prospecting; and preparations for the third International Polar Year 2007-2008, for which a joint planning committee had been established by the International Council for Science and the World Meteorological Organization in 2004 [YUN 2004, p. 1504].

The Secretary-General stated that Antarctica had witnessed successful international coopera-

tion in research, particularly in connection with the study of global changes. However, illegal, unregulated and unreported fishing for toothfish in the Southern Ocean still exceeded reported catches, despite major efforts to address those activities. Further enforcement and cooperation were required from all States involved to end them and efforts should continue to ensure that expanding commercial activities in the region would not affect the successes of the Treaty system, in particular in securing Antarctica as a natural reserve, devoted to peace and science. Global changes, in particular climate change and the depletion of the ozone layer, remained major threats to the integrity of the Antarctic environment.

GENERAL ASSEMBLY ACTION

On 8 December [meeting 61], the General Assembly, on the recommendation of the First (Disarmament and International Security) Committee [A/60/454], adopted **resolution 60/47** without vote [agenda item 88].

Question of Antarctica

The General Assembly,

Recalling its resolution 57/51 of 22 November 2002, in which it requested the Secretary-General to submit a report consisting of the information provided by the Antarctic Treaty Consultative Parties on their consultative meetings, on their activities in Antarctica and on developments in relation to Antarctica,

Taking into account the debates on the question of Antarctica held since its thirty-eighth session,

Conscious of the particular significance of Antarctica to the international community, including for international peace and security, the global and regional environment, its effects on global and regional climate conditions, and scientific research,

Reaffirming that the management and use of Antarctica should be conducted in accordance with the purposes and principles of the Charter of the United Nations and in the interest of maintaining international peace and security and of promoting international cooperation for the benefit of mankind as a whole,

Recognizing that the Antarctic Treaty, which provides, inter alia, for the demilitarization of the continent, the prohibition of nuclear explosions and the disposal of nuclear wastes, the freedom of scientific research and the free exchange of scientific information, is in furtherance of the purposes and principles of the Charter,

Noting with satisfaction the entry into force of the Protocol on Environmental Protection to the Antarctic Treaty on 14 January 1998, under which Antarctica has been designated as a natural reserve, devoted to peace and science, and the provisions contained in the Protocol regarding the protection of the Antarctic environment and dependent and associated ecosystems, including the need for environmental impact assessment in the planning and conduct of all relevant activities in Antarctica,

Welcoming the continuing cooperation among countries undertaking scientific research activities in Antarctica, which may help to minimize human impact on the Antarctic environment,

Welcoming also the increasing awareness of and interest in Antarctica shown by the international community, and convinced of the advantages to the whole of mankind of a better knowledge of Antarctica,

Welcoming further the secretariat of the Antarctic Treaty, established in Buenos Aires, which became operational as of 1 September 2004,

Reaffirming its conviction that, in the interest of all mankind, Antarctica should continue forever to be used exclusively for peaceful purposes and that it should not become the scene or object of international discord,

1. *Takes note* of the report of the Secretary-General on the question of Antarctica and the role accorded by the Secretary-General to the United Nations Environment Programme in preparing his report, and also of the Twenty-sixth Antarctic Treaty Consultative Meeting, held in Madrid from 9 to 20 June 2003, the Twenty-seventh Antarctic Treaty Consultative Meeting, held in Cape Town, South Africa, from 24 May to 4 June 2004, and the Twenty-eighth Antarctic Treaty Consultative Meeting, held in Stockholm from 6 to 17 June 2005;

2. *Recalls* the statement under chapter 17 of Agenda 21, adopted by the United Nations Conference on Environment and Development, that States carrying out research activities in Antarctica should, as provided for in article III of the Antarctic Treaty, continue:

(*a*) To ensure that data and information resulting from such research are freely available to the international community;

(*b*) To enhance the access of the international scientific community and the specialized agencies of the United Nations system to such data and information, including the encouragement of periodic seminars and symposiums;

3. *Welcomes* the invitations to the Executive Director of the United Nations Environment Programme to attend Antarctic Treaty Consultative Meetings in order to assist such meetings in their substantive work, and urges the parties to continue to do so for future consultative meetings;

4. *Welcomes also* the practice whereby the Antarctic Treaty Consultative Parties regularly provide the Secretary-General with information on their consultative meetings and on their activities in Antarctica, and encourages the parties to continue to provide the Secretary-General and interested States with information on those meetings, activities and developments in relation to Antarctica;

5. *Decides* to remain seized of the matter.

South Atlantic

As requested in General Assembly resolution 58/10 [YUN 2003, p. 596], the Secretary-General submitted an August report on the zone of peace and cooperation of the South Atlantic [A/60/253], declared in 1986 to promote cooperation among States of the region in the political, economic, sci-

entific, technical, cultural and other fields [YUN 1986, p. 369]. The Secretary-General stated that, as at 8 August, five States (Argentina, Bolivia, Iraq, Kenya, Panama) and one UN body (United Nations Office on Drugs and Crime) had responded to his request for views on the implementation of the declaration.

On 31 October (**decision 60/509**), the Assembly decided to defer consideration of the item on the zone of peace and cooperation of the South Atlantic and the Secretary-General's report thereon, include it in the provisional agenda of its sixty-first (2006) session and maintain biennial consideration of the item thereafter.

Indian Ocean

In 2005, the Ad Hoc Committee on the Indian Ocean (New York, 26 July) [A/60/29] continued to consider approaches for achieving the goals of the 1971 Declaration of the Indian Ocean as a Zone of Peace, adopted by the General Assembly in resolution 2832(XXVI) [YUN 1971, p. 34].

Pursuant to Assembly resolution 58/29 [YUN 2003, p. 597], the Chairman of the Committee, following informal consultations with Committee members, stated that regional groupings had undertaken a number of cooperative initiatives to bring about socio-economic development in the Indian Ocean region. However, new threats, such as terrorism, were affecting regional stability and security, and disarmament and arms control efforts lagged. The Committee was the only UN body of its kind with a capacity to address security issues in a broader sense, involving all interrelated aspects and new approaches to the scope of its work could be explored in the context of the ongoing UN reform process, which sought to promote larger freedom, while encompassing security, human rights and development. In that effort, it might be necessary to revise the Declaration to bring it in line with current realities, and give the Committee a new focus so as to become useful to the UN system. While there appeared to be a general sense among members that the Declaration's objectives remained relevant, a number of complexities and constraints stood in the way of its implementation. It was felt that more time would be needed before any discussion could take place on practical measures to ensure peace and stability in the Indian Ocean in line with the Declaration.

France, the United Kingdom and the United States had not yet changed their position on non-participation in the Committee. The Committee remained convinced that the participation of all permanent members of the Security Council and major maritime users in its work was important and would assist in a mutually beneficial dialogue aimed at peace, security and stability in the region. It decided that the Bureau would meet before the Committee's 2007 session to examine ways to revitalize its work.

The Committee reaffirmed the conclusions of its 1994 [YUN 1994, p. 155], 1995 [YUN 1995, p. 182] and 1996 [YUN 1996, p. 512] sessions and requested the Chairman to continue informal consultations with the Committee members and to report to the Assembly's sixty-second (2007) session.

GENERAL ASSEMBLY ACTION

On 8 December [meeting 61], the General Assembly, on the recommendation of the First Committee [A/60/455], adopted **resolution 60/48** by recorded vote (132-3-46) [agenda item 89].

Implementation of the Declaration of the Indian Ocean as a Zone of Peace

The General Assembly,

Recalling the Declaration of the Indian Ocean as a Zone of Peace, contained in its resolution 2832(XXVI) of 16 December 1971, and recalling also its resolutions 54/47 of 1 December 1999, 56/16 of 29 November 2001 and 58/29 of 8 December 2003 and other relevant resolutions,

Recalling also the report of the Meeting of the Littoral and Hinterland States of the Indian Ocean held in July 1979,

Recalling further paragraph 102 of the Final Document of the Thirteenth Conference of Heads of State or Government of Non-Aligned Countries, held at Kuala Lumpur, from 20 to 25 February 2003, in which it was noted, inter alia, that the Chairperson of the Ad Hoc Committee on the Indian Ocean would continue his informal consultations on the future work of the Committee,

Emphasizing the need to foster consensual approaches that are conducive to the pursuit of such endeavours,

Noting the initiatives taken by countries of the region to promote cooperation, in particular economic cooperation, in the Indian Ocean area and the possible contribution of such initiatives to overall objectives of a zone of peace,

Convinced that the participation of all permanent members of the Security Council and the major maritime users of the Indian Ocean in the work of the Ad Hoc Committee is important and would assist the progress of a mutually beneficial dialogue to develop conditions of peace, security and stability in the Indian Ocean region,

Considering that greater efforts and more time are required to develop a focused discussion on practical measures to ensure conditions of peace, security and stability in the Indian Ocean region,

Having considered the report of the Ad Hoc Committee on the Indian Ocean,

1. *Takes note* of the report of the Ad Hoc Committee on the Indian Ocean;

2. *Reiterates its conviction* that the participation of all permanent members of the Security Council and the major maritime users of the Indian Ocean in the work

of the Ad Hoc Committee is important and would greatly facilitate the development of a mutually beneficial dialogue to advance peace, security and stability in the Indian Ocean region;

3. *Requests* the Chairman of the Ad Hoc Committee to continue his informal consultations with the members of the Committee and to report through the Committee to the General Assembly at its sixty-second session;

4. *Requests* the Secretary-General to continue to render, within existing resources, all necessary assistance to the Ad Hoc Committee, including the provision of summary records;

5. *Decides* to include in the provisional agenda of its sixty-second session the item entitled "Implementation of the Declaration of the Indian Ocean as a Zone of Peace".

RECORDED VOTE ON RESOLUTION 60/48:

In favour: Afghanistan, Algeria, Antigua and Barbuda, Argentina, Armenia, Australia, Azerbaijan, Bahamas, Bahrain, Bangladesh, Barbados, Belarus, Belize, Benin, Bhutan, Bolivia, Botswana, Brazil, Brunei Darussalam, Burkina Faso, Burundi, Cambodia, Cameroon, Cape Verde, Central African Republic, Chile, China, Colombia, Comoros, Congo, Costa Rica, Côte d'Ivoire, Cuba, Democratic People's Republic of Korea, Democratic Republic of the Congo, Djibouti, Dominica, Dominican Republic, Ecuador, Egypt, El Salvador, Eritrea, Ethiopia, Fiji, Gabon, Ghana, Grenada, Guatemala, Guinea, Guinea-Bissau, Guyana, Haiti, Honduras, India, Indonesia, Iran, Iraq, Jamaica, Japan, Jordan, Kazakhstan, Kenya, Kuwait, Kyrgyzstan, Lao People's Democratic Republic, Lebanon, Lesotho, Liberia, Libyan Arab Jamahiriya, Madagascar, Malawi, Malaysia, Maldives, Mali, Mauritania, Mauritius, Mexico, Mongolia, Morocco, Mozambique, Myanmar, Namibia, Nepal, New Zealand, Nicaragua, Niger, Nigeria, Oman, Pakistan, Panama, Paraguay, Peru, Philippines, Qatar, Republic of Korea, Russian Federation, Saint Lucia, Saint Vincent and the Grenadines, Samoa, Sao Tome and Principe, Saudi Arabia, Senegal, Sierra Leone, Singapore, Solomon Islands, Somalia, South Africa, Sri Lanka, Sudan, Suriname, Syrian Arab Republic, Tajikistan, Thailand, Timor-Leste, Togo, Tonga, Trinidad and Tobago, Tunisia, Turkmenistan, Tuvalu, Uganda, Ukraine, United Arab Emirates, United Republic of Tanzania, Uruguay, Uzbekistan, Vanuatu, Venezuela, Viet Nam, Yemen, Zambia, Zimbabwe.

Against: France, United Kingdom, United States.

Abstaining: Albania, Andorra, Austria, Belgium, Bosnia and Herzegovina, Bulgaria, Canada, Croatia, Cyprus, Czech Republic, Denmark, Estonia, Finland, Georgia, Germany, Greece, Hungary, Iceland, Ireland, Israel, Italy, Latvia, Liechtenstein, Lithuania, Luxembourg, Malta, Marshall Islands, Micronesia, Monaco, Netherlands, Norway, Palau, Papua New Guinea, Poland, Portugal, Republic of Moldova, Romania, San Marino, Serbia and Montenegro, Slovakia, Slovenia, Spain, Sweden, Switzerland, The former Yugoslav Republic of Macedonia, Turkey.

Decolonization

The General Assembly's Special Committee on the Situation with regard to the Implementation of the Declaration on the Granting of Independence to Colonial Countries and Peoples (Special Committee on decolonization) held its annual session in New York in two parts—17 February and 11 March (first part); and 6-8, 13, 15-16 and 20-24 June (second part). It considered various aspects of the implementation of the 1960 Declaration, adopted by the Assembly in resolution 1514(XV) [YUN 1960, p. 49], including general decolonization issues and the situation of individual Non-Self-Governing Territories (NSGTs). In accordance with Assembly resolution 59/129

[YUN 2004, p. 598], the Special Committee transmitted to the Assembly the report on its 2005 activities [A/60/23].

Decade for the Eradication of Colonialism

As required under the plan of action for the Second International Decade for the Eradication of Colonialism (2001-2010) [YUN 2001, p. 530], declared by the General Assembly in resolution 55/146 [YUN 2000, p. 548], the Secretary-General submitted a midpoint report in April [A/60/71 & Add.1] on action taken to date to implement the Plan of Action by UN organs and Member States. Action taken by UN specialized agencies was covered in a separate report of the Economic and Social Council President [E/2005/47 & Corr.1] (see p. 662).

The Secretary-General concluded that the task of eradicating colonialism remained unfinished, requiring the sustained and determined efforts of all concerned. Some specialized agencies and regional commissions continued to facilitate the participation of many NSGTs in their bodies as observers or associate members, enabling their participation in world conferences on economic and social issues. The Special Committee on decolonization continued to strengthen consultation mechanisms and dialogue with the administering powers and improvements in some NSGTs offered a unique opportunity to develop decolonization plans on a case-by-case basis with their participation. That opportunity should be seized to accelerate the decolonization process and ensure the implementation of UN resolutions on the subject.

(For more information on developments in specific NSGTs, see the relevant sections below.)

GENERAL ASSEMBLY ACTION

On 8 December [meeting 62], the General Assembly, on the recommendation of the Fourth (Special Political and Decolonization) Committee [A/60/472], adopted **resolution 60/120** by recorded vote (133-3-36) [agenda item 26].

Second International Decade for the Eradication of Colonialism

The General Assembly,

Recalling its resolution 55/146 of 8 December 2000, by which it declared the period 2001-2010 the Second International Decade for the Eradication of Colonialism,

Recalling also that 2005 marks the mid-point of the Decade,

Recalling further that the plan of action for the Decade requested the Secretary-General to submit a report on action taken to implement the plan of action,

Having examined the report of the Secretary-General on the implementation of the plan of action,

Taking into account the important contribution of the United Nations in the field of decolonization, in particular through the Special Committee on the Situation with regard to the Implementation of the Declaration on the Granting of Independence to Colonial Countries and Peoples,

1. *Takes note* of the report of the Secretary-General;
2. *Calls upon* Member States to redouble their efforts to implement the plan of action for the Second International Decade for the Eradication of Colonialism;
3. *Calls upon* the administering Powers to cooperate fully with the Special Committee on the Situation with regard to the Implementation of the Declaration on the Granting of Independence to Colonial Countries and Peoples to develop constructive programmes of work on a case-by-case basis for the Non-Self-Governing Territories to facilitate the implementation of the mandate of the Special Committee and the relevant resolutions of the United Nations on decolonization;
4. *Requests* Member States, the specialized agencies and other organizations of the United Nations system, and other governmental and non-governmental organizations actively to support and participate in the implementation of the plan of action during the Decade;
5. *Requests* the Secretary-General to continue to provide the necessary resources for the successful implementation of the plan of action;
6. *Also requests* the Secretary-General to report to the General Assembly at its sixty-fifth session on the implementation of the present resolution.

RECORDED VOTE ON RESOLUTION 60/120:

In favour: Afghanistan, Algeria, Andorra, Antigua and Barbuda, Argentina, Armenia, Australia, Azerbaijan, Bahamas, Bahrain, Bangladesh, Barbados, Belarus, Belize, Benin, Bhutan, Bolivia, Botswana, Brazil, Brunei Darussalam, Burkina Faso, Burundi, Cambodia, Cameroon, Canada, Cape Verde, Central African Republic, Chile, China, Colombia, Congo, Costa Rica, Cuba, Cyprus, Democratic People's Republic of Korea, Democratic Republic of the Congo, Djibouti, Dominica, Dominican Republic, Ecuador, Egypt, El Salvador, Eritrea, Ethiopia, Fiji, Gabon, Ghana, Grenada, Guatemala, Guinea, Guinea-Bissau, Guyana, Haiti, Honduras, India, Indonesia, Iran, Iraq, Ireland, Jamaica, Japan, Jordan, Kazakhstan, Kenya, Kuwait, Kyrgyzstan, Lao People's Democratic Republic, Lebanon, Lesotho, Liberia, Libyan Arab Jamahiriya, Madagascar, Malawi, Malaysia, Maldives, Mali, Malta, Mauritania, Mauritius, Mexico, Mongolia, Morocco, Mozambique, Myanmar, Namibia, Nepal, New Zealand, Nicaragua, Niger, Nigeria, Oman, Pakistan, Panama, Papua New Guinea, Paraguay, Peru, Philippines, Portugal, Qatar, Republic of Korea, Romania, Russian Federation, Saint Lucia, Saint Vincent and the Grenadines, Samoa, San Marino, Saudi Arabia, Senegal, Singapore, Solomon Islands, South Africa, Spain, Sri Lanka, Sudan, Suriname, Syrian Arab Republic, Tajikistan, Thailand, Timor-Leste, Togo, Trinidad and Tobago, Tunisia, Tuvalu, Uganda, United Arab Emirates, United Republic of Tanzania, Uruguay, Vanuatu, Venezuela, Viet Nam, Yemen, Zambia, Zimbabwe.

Against: Israel, United Kingdom, United States.

Abstaining: Albania, Austria, Belgium, Bulgaria, Croatia, Czech Republic, Denmark, Estonia, Finland, France, Georgia, Germany, Greece, Hungary, Iceland, Italy, Latvia, Liechtenstein, Lithuania, Luxembourg, Marshall Islands, Micronesia, Monaco, Netherlands, Norway, Palau, Poland, Republic of Moldova, Serbia and Montenegro, Slovakia, Slovenia, Sweden, Switzerland, The former Yugoslav Republic of Macedonia, Turkey, Ukraine.

Caribbean regional seminar

As part of its efforts to implement the plan of action for the Second International Decade for the Eradication of Colonialism (2001-2010), the Special Committee on decolonization [A/60/23] organized a Caribbean regional seminar (Canouan, Saint Vincent and the Grenadines, 17-19 May) to assess the situation in NSGTs.

After conducting a midterm review of the implementation of the plan of action, the seminar recommended that the Special Committee, the administering Powers and NSGTs discuss innovative ways to expedite the implementation of the goals of the Second International Decade and that the Special Committee continue to monitor the evolution of NSGTs towards self-determination. The Special Committee should include NSGT representatives, on a case-by-case basis in the consultations between the Special Committee and the administering Powers and continue to develop a mechanism to review, annually, the implementation of the specific recommendations on decolonization.

The seminar also recommended that the Special Committee, along with the UN Department of Public Information (DPI) and other UN bodies, develop a programme to disseminate information and raise public awareness in NSGTs of the legitimate political status options available to them. UN information centres (UNICs) should be directed to disseminate information on decolonization to NSGTs and the administering Powers and the Electoral Assistance Division of the UN Department of Political Affairs (DPA) should be asked to support and assist any consultation process held in an NSGT regarding any act of self-determination.

Participants supported closer cooperation between the Special Committee and the Economic and Social Council in order to promote increased UN assistance in the economic and social sphere to NSGTs. They also urged the Special Committee to solicit the Council's assistance regarding the implementation of Council resolution 2004/53 [YUN 2004, p. 596] on the implementation of the 1960 Declaration by the UN specialized agencies and international institutions associated with the United Nations. The seminar stressed that the UN system should continue to strengthen measures of support and formulate programmes of assistance to the remaining NSGTs, and make proposals for the full implementation of relevant UN resolutions by the specialized agencies, as detailed in Assembly resolution 56/67 [YUN 2001, p. 534]. Participants requested those Special Committee members that were members of the Economic and Social Council to support the inclusion of those NSGTs that were associate members of UN regional commissions as observers in the Council. They recommended that the Special Committee establish closer ties with the Caribbean Community and Common Market and the Organisation of Eastern Caribbean States, and encouraged Caribbean NSGTs to develop closer contacts with those two organizations.

Participants welcomed the presence at the seminar of a representative of France and regretted the lack of representation of the United Kingdom, which had participated in previous seminars. They recommended that the Special Committee integrate, to the extent possible, the seminar's recommendations into its resolutions on decolonization, as they were important expressions of the people of the NSGTs.

GENERAL ASSEMBLY ACTION

On 8 December [meeting 62], the General Assembly, on the recommendation of the Fourth Committee [A/60/472], adopted **resolution 60/119** by recorded vote (166-3-4) [agenda item 26].

Implementation of the Declaration on the Granting of Independence to Colonial Countries and Peoples

The General Assembly,

Having examined the report of the Special Committee on the Situation with regard to the Implementation of the Declaration on the Granting of Independence to Colonial Countries and Peoples,

Recalling its resolution 1514(XV) of 14 December 1960, containing the Declaration on the Granting of Independence to Colonial Countries and Peoples, and all its subsequent resolutions concerning the implementation of the Declaration, the most recent of which was resolution 59/136 of 10 December 2004, as well as the relevant resolutions of the Security Council,

Bearing in mind its resolution 55/146 of 8 December 2000, by which it declared the period 2001-2010 the Second International Decade for the Eradication of Colonialism, and the need to examine ways to ascertain the wishes of the peoples of the Non-Self-Governing Territories on the basis of resolution 1514 (XV) and other relevant resolutions on decolonization,

Recognizing that the eradication of colonialism has been one of the priorities of the United Nations and continues to be one of its priorities for the decade that began in 2001,

Reconfirming the need to take measures to eliminate colonialism by 2010, as called for in its resolution 55/146,

Reiterating its conviction of the need for the eradication of colonialism, as well as racial discrimination and violations of basic human rights,

Noting with satisfaction the achievements of the Special Committee in contributing to the effective and complete implementation of the Declaration and other relevant resolutions of the United Nations on decolonization,

Stressing the importance of the formal participation of the administering Powers in the work of the Special Committee,

Noting with interest the cooperation and active participation of some administering Powers in the work of the Special Committee, and encouraging the others also to do so,

Taking note of the fact that the Special Committee held a Caribbean regional seminar on the mid-term review, follow-up and priorities for action of the Second International Decade for the Eradication of Colonialism at Canouan, Saint Vincent and the Grenadines, from 17 to 19 May 2005,

1. *Reaffirms* its resolution 1514(XV) and all other resolutions and decisions on decolonization, including its resolution 55/146, by which it declared the period 2001-2010 the Second International Decade for the Eradication of Colonialism, and calls upon the administering Powers, in accordance with those resolutions, to take all necessary steps to enable the peoples of the Non-Self-Governing Territories concerned to exercise fully as soon as possible their right to self-determination, including independence;

2. *Reaffirms once again* that the existence of colonialism in any form or manifestation, including economic exploitation, is incompatible with the Charter of the United Nations, the Declaration on the Granting of Independence to Colonial Countries and Peoples and the Universal Declaration of Human Rights;

3. *Reaffirms its determination* to continue to take all steps necessary to bring about the complete and speedy eradication of colonialism and the faithful observance by all States of the relevant provisions of the Charter, the Declaration on the Granting of Independence to Colonial Countries and Peoples and the Universal Declaration of Human Rights;

4. *Affirms once again its support* for the aspirations of the peoples under colonial rule to exercise their right to self-determination, including independence, in accordance with relevant resolutions of the United Nations on decolonization;

5. *Calls upon* the administering Powers to cooperate fully with the Special Committee to finalize before the end of 2005 a constructive programme of work on a case-by-case basis for the Non-Self-Governing Territories to facilitate the implementation of the mandate of the Special Committee and the relevant resolutions on decolonization, including resolutions on specific Territories;

6. *Welcomes* the progress made in the ongoing consultations between the Special Committee and New Zealand, as administering Power for Tokelau, with the participation of representatives of the people of Tokelau, as evidenced by the decision of the General Fono of Tokelau in November 2003 to actively explore with New Zealand the option of self-government in free association;

7. *Also welcomes* the dispatch of the United Nations special mission to Bermuda, at the request of the territorial Government and with the concurrence of the administering Power, which provided information to the people of the Territory on the role of the United Nations in the process of self-determination, on the legitimate political status options, as clearly defined in General Assembly resolution 1541(XV) of 15 December 1960, and on the experiences of other small States which have achieved a full measure of self-government;

8. *Requests* the Special Committee to continue to seek suitable means for the immediate and full implementation of the Declaration and to carry out the actions approved by the General Assembly regarding the International Decade for the Eradication of Colonialism and the Second International Decade for the Eradication of Colonialism in all Territories that have not

yet exercised their right to self-determination, including independence, and in particular:

(a) To formulate specific proposals to bring about an end to colonialism and to report thereon to the General Assembly at its sixty-first session;

(b) To continue to examine the implementation by Member States of resolution 1514(XV) and other relevant resolutions on decolonization;

(c) To continue to examine the political, economic and social situation in the Non-Self-Governing Territories, and to recommend, as appropriate, to the General Assembly the most suitable steps to be taken to enable the populations of those Territories to exercise their right to self-determination, including independence, in accordance with relevant resolutions on decolonization, including resolutions on specific Territories;

(d) To finalize before the end of 2006 a constructive programme of work on a case-by-case basis for the Non-Self-Governing Territories to facilitate the implementation of the mandate of the Special Committee and the relevant resolutions on decolonization, including resolutions on specific Territories;

(e) To continue to dispatch visiting missions to the Non-Self-Governing Territories in accordance with relevant resolutions on decolonization, including resolutions on specific Territories;

(f) To conduct seminars, as appropriate, for the purpose of receiving and disseminating information on the work of the Special Committee, and to facilitate participation by the peoples of the Non-Self-Governing Territories in those seminars;

(g) To take all necessary steps to enlist worldwide support among Governments, as well as national and international organizations, for the achievement of the objectives of the Declaration and the implementation of the relevant resolutions of the United Nations;

(h) To observe annually the Week of Solidarity with the Peoples of Non-Self-Governing Territories;

9. *Calls upon* all States, in particular the administering Powers, as well as the specialized agencies and other organizations of the United Nations system, to give effect within their respective spheres of competence to the recommendations of the Special Committee for the implementation of the Declaration and other relevant resolutions of the United Nations;

10. *Calls upon* the administering Powers to ensure that the economic activities in the Non-Self-Governing Territories under their administration do not adversely affect the interests of the peoples but instead promote development, and to assist them in the exercise of their right to self-determination;

11. *Urges* the administering Powers concerned to take effective measures to safeguard and guarantee the inalienable rights of the peoples of the Non-Self-Governing Territories to their natural resources, including land, and to establish and maintain control over the future development of those resources, and requests the administering Powers to take all necessary steps to protect the property rights of the peoples of those Territories;

12. *Urges* all States, directly and through their action in the specialized agencies and other organizations of the United Nations system, to provide moral and material assistance to the peoples of the Non-Self-Governing Territories, and requests the administering

Powers to take steps to enlist and make effective use of all possible assistance, on both a bilateral and a multilateral basis, in the strengthening of the economies of those Territories;

13. *Reaffirms* that the United Nations visiting missions to the Territories are an effective means of ascertaining the situation in the Territories, as well as the wishes and aspirations of their inhabitants, and calls upon the administering Powers to continue to cooperate with the Special Committee in the discharge of its mandate and to facilitate visiting missions to the Territories;

14. *Calls upon* the administering Powers that have not participated formally in the work of the Special Committee to do so at its session in 2006;

15. *Requests* the Secretary-General, the specialized agencies and other organizations of the United Nations system to provide economic, social and other assistance to the Non-Self-Governing Territories and to continue to do so, as appropriate, after they exercise their right to self-determination, including independence;

16. *Approves* the report of the Special Committee on the Situation with regard to the Implementation of the Declaration on the Granting of Independence to Colonial Countries and Peoples covering its work during 2005, including the programme of work envisaged for 2006;

17. *Requests* the Secretary-General to provide the Special Committee with the facilities and services required for the implementation of the present resolution, as well as the other resolutions and decisions on decolonization adopted by the General Assembly and the Special Committee.

RECORDED VOTE ON RESOLUTION 60/119:

In favour: Afghanistan, Algeria, Andorra, Angola, Antigua and Barbuda, Argentina, Armenia, Australia, Austria, Azerbaijan, Bahamas, Bahrain, Bangladesh, Barbados, Belarus, Belize, Benin, Bhutan, Bolivia, Botswana, Brazil, Brunei Darussalam, Bulgaria, Burkina Faso, Burundi, Cambodia, Cameroon, Canada, Cape Verde, Central African Republic, Chile, China, Colombia, Congo, Costa Rica, Côte d'Ivoire, Croatia, Cuba, Cyprus, Czech Republic, Democratic People's Republic of Korea, Denmark, Djibouti, Dominica, Dominican Republic, Ecuador, Egypt, El Salvador, Eritrea, Estonia, Ethiopia, Fiji, Finland, Gabon, Georgia, Ghana, Greece, Grenada, Guatemala, Guinea, Guinea-Bissau, Guyana, Haiti, Honduras, Hungary, Iceland, India, Indonesia, Iran, Iraq, Ireland, Italy, Jamaica, Japan, Jordan, Kazakhstan, Kenya, Kuwait, Kyrgyzstan, Lao People's Democratic Republic, Latvia, Lebanon, Lesotho, Liberia, Libyan Arab Jamahiriya, Liechtenstein, Lithuania, Luxembourg, Madagascar, Malawi, Malaysia, Maldives, Mali, Malta, Marshall Islands, Mauritania, Mauritius, Mexico, Monaco, Mongolia, Morocco, Mozambique, Myanmar, Namibia, Nepal, Netherlands, New Zealand, Nicaragua, Niger, Nigeria, Norway, Oman, Pakistan, Palau, Panama, Papua New Guinea, Paraguay, Peru, Philippines, Poland, Portugal, Qatar, Republic of Korea, Republic of Moldova, Romania, Russian Federation, Saint Lucia, Saint Vincent and the Grenadines, Samoa, San Marino, Saudi Arabia, Senegal, Serbia and Montenegro, Singapore, Slovakia, Slovenia, Solomon Islands, South Africa, Spain, Sri Lanka, Sudan, Suriname, Sweden, Switzerland, Syrian Arab Republic, Tajikistan, Thailand, The former Yugoslav Republic of Macedonia, Timor-Leste, Togo, Tonga, Trinidad and Tobago, Tunisia, Turkey, Tuvalu, Uganda, Ukraine, United Arab Emirates, United Republic of Tanzania, Uruguay, Vanuatu, Venezuela, Viet Nam, Yemen, Zambia, Zimbabwe.

Against: Israel, United Kingdom, United States.

Abstaining: Albania, Belgium, France, Germany.

Implementation by international organizations

In a March report [A/60/64], the Secretary-General stated that he had brought General Assembly resolution 59/129 [YUN 2004, p. 598] to the attention of UN specialized agencies and other international institutions associated with the United Nations and invited them to submit information regarding their implementation activities in support of NSGTs. Replies received from three agencies or institutions were summarized in a May report of the Economic and Social Council President on consultations held with the Chairman of the Special Committee on decolonization [E/2005/47 & Corr.1]. According to the information provided, a number of specialized agencies and organizations continued to extend assistance programmes to NSGTs from their own budgetary resources, in addition to their respective contributions as executing agencies of projects funded by UNDP. Seven specialized agencies indicated that they were not currently carrying out any assistance programmes in NSGTs.

ECONOMIC AND SOCIAL COUNCIL ACTION

On 27 July [meeting 40], the Economic and Social Council adopted **resolution 2005/49** [draft: E/2005/L.22, orally revised] by recorded vote (32-0-20) [agenda item 9].

Support to Non-Self-Governing Territories by the specialized agencies and international institutions associated with the United Nations

The Economic and Social Council,

Having examined the report of the Secretary-General and the report of the President of the Economic and Social Council containing the information submitted by the specialized agencies and the international institutions associated with the United Nations on their activities with regard to the implementation of the Declaration on the Granting of Independence to Colonial Countries and Peoples,

Having heard the statement by the representative of the Special Committee on the Situation with regard to the Implementation of the Declaration on the Granting of Independence to Colonial Countries and Peoples,

Recalling General Assembly resolutions 1514(XV) of 14 December 1960 and 1541(XV) of 15 December 1960, the resolutions of the Special Committee and other relevant resolutions and decisions, including, in particular, Economic and Social Council resolution 2004/53 of 23 July 2004,

Bearing in mind the relevant provisions of the final documents of the successive Conferences of Heads of State or Government of Non-Aligned Countries and of the resolutions adopted by the Assembly of Heads of State and Government of the African Union, the Pacific Islands Forum and the Caribbean Community,

Conscious of the need to facilitate the implementation of the Declaration,

Welcoming the participation, in the capacity of observer, of those Non-Self-Governing Territories that are associate members of the regional commissions in world conferences in the economic and social sphere, subject to the rules of procedure of the General Assembly and in accordance with relevant United Nations resolutions and decisions, including resolutions and decisions of the General Assembly and the Special Committee on specific Territories,

Noting that only some specialized agencies and organizations of the United Nations system have been involved in providing assistance to Non-Self-Governing Territories,

Welcoming the assistance extended to Non-Self-Governing Territories by certain specialized agencies and other organizations of the United Nations system, in particular the United Nations Development Programme,

Stressing that, because the development options of the small island Non-Self-Governing Territories are limited, there are special challenges to planning for and implementing sustainable development and that those Territories will be constrained in meeting the challenges without the continued cooperation and assistance of the specialized agencies and other organizations of the United Nations system,

Stressing also the importance of securing the resources necessary to fund expanded programmes of assistance for the peoples concerned and the need to enlist the support of all the major funding institutions within the United Nations system in that regard,

Reaffirming the mandate of the specialized agencies and other organizations of the United Nations system to take all appropriate measures, within their respective spheres of competence, to ensure the full implementation of Assembly resolution 1514(XV) and other relevant resolutions,

Expressing its appreciation to the African Union, the Pacific Islands Forum, the Caribbean Community and other regional organizations for the continued cooperation and assistance they have extended to the specialized agencies and other organizations of the United Nations system in this regard,

Expressing its conviction that closer contacts and consultations between and among the specialized agencies and other organizations of the United Nations system and regional organizations help to facilitate the effective formulation of programmes of assistance for the peoples concerned,

Mindful of the imperative need to keep under continuous review the activities of the specialized agencies and other organizations of the United Nations system in the implementation of the various United Nations decisions related to decolonization,

Bearing in mind the extremely fragile economies of the small island Non-Self-Governing Territories and their vulnerability to natural disasters, such as hurricanes, cyclones and sea-level rise, and recalling the relevant resolutions of the General Assembly,

Recalling General Assembly resolution 59/129 of 10 December 2004, entitled "Implementation of the Declaration on the Granting of Independence to Colonial Countries and Peoples by the specialized agencies and the international institutions associated with the United Nations",

1. *Takes note* of the report of the President of the Economic and Social Council, and endorses the observations and suggestions arising therefrom;

2. *Also takes note* of the report of the Secretary-General;

3. *Recommends* that all States intensify their efforts in the specialized agencies and other organizations of the United Nations system to ensure the full and effective implementation of the Declaration on the Granting of Independence to Colonial Countries and Peoples contained in Assembly resolution 1514(XV), and other relevant resolutions of the United Nations;

4. *Reaffirms* that the specialized agencies and other organizations and institutions of the United Nations system should continue to be guided by the relevant resolutions of the United Nations in their efforts to contribute to the implementation of the Declaration and all other relevant General Assembly resolutions;

5. *Also reaffirms* that the recognition by the General Assembly, the Security Council and other United Nations organs of the legitimacy of the aspirations of the peoples of the Non-Self-Governing Territories to exercise their right to self-determination entails, as a corollary, the extension of all appropriate assistance to those peoples;

6. *Expresses its appreciation* to those specialized agencies and other organizations of the United Nations system that have continued to cooperate with the United Nations and the regional and subregional organizations in the implementation of Assembly resolution 1514(XV) and other relevant resolutions of the United Nations, and requests all the specialized agencies and other organizations of the United Nations system to implement the relevant provisions of those resolutions;

7. *Requests* the specialized agencies and other organizations of the United Nations system and international and regional organizations to examine and review conditions in each Territory so as to take appropriate measures to accelerate progress in the economic and social sectors of the Territories;

8. *Requests* the specialized agencies and other organizations and bodies of the United Nations system and regional organizations to strengthen existing measures of support and to formulate appropriate programmes of assistance to the remaining Non-Self-Governing Territories, within the framework of their respective mandates, in order to accelerate progress in the economic and social sectors of those Territories;

9. *Recommends* that the executive heads of the specialized agencies and other organizations of the United Nations system formulate, with the active cooperation of the regional organizations concerned, concrete proposals for the full implementation of the relevant resolutions of the United Nations and submit the proposals to their governing and legislative organs;

10. *Also recommends* that the specialized agencies and other organizations of the United Nations system continue to review, at the regular meetings of their governing bodies, the implementation of Assembly resolution 1514(XV) and other relevant resolutions of the United Nations;

11. *Welcomes* the continuing initiative exercised by the United Nations Development Programme in maintaining close liaison among the specialized agencies and other organizations of the United Nations system, including the Economic Commission for Latin America and the Caribbean and the Economic and Social Commission for Asia and the Pacific, and in providing assistance to the peoples of the Non-Self-Governing Territories;

12. *Requests* the Department of Public Information of the Secretariat, in consultation with the United Nations Development Programme, the specialized

agencies and the Special Committee on the Situation with regard to the Implementation of the Declaration on the Granting of Independence to Colonial Countries and Peoples, to prepare an information leaflet on assistance programmes available to the Non-Self-Governing Territories and to disseminate it widely among them;

13. *Encourages* Non-Self-Governing Territories to take steps to establish and/or strengthen disaster preparedness and management institutions and policies;

14. *Requests* the administering Powers concerned to facilitate, when appropriate, the participation of appointed and elected representatives of Non-Self-Governing Territories in the meetings and conferences of the specialized agencies and other organizations of the United Nations system, in accordance with relevant United Nations resolutions and decisions, including resolutions and decisions of the General Assembly and the Special Committee related to specific Territories, so that the Territories may benefit from the related activities of those agencies and organizations;

15. *Recommends* that all Governments intensify their efforts in the specialized agencies and other organizations of the United Nations system of which they are members to accord priority to the question of providing assistance to the peoples of the Non-Self-Governing Territories;

16. *Draws the attention* of the Special Committee to the present resolution and to the discussion held on the subject at the substantive session of 2005 of the Economic and Social Council;

17. *Welcomes* the adoption by the Economic Commission for Latin America and the Caribbean of its resolution 574(XXVII) of 16 May 1998 calling for the mechanisms necessary for its associate members, including small island Non-Self-Governing Territories, to participate in the special sessions of the General Assembly, subject to the rules of procedure of the Assembly, to review and assess the implementation of the plans of action of those United Nations world conferences in which the Territories originally participated in the capacity of observer, and in the work of the Economic and Social Council and its subsidiary bodies;

18. *Requests* the President of the Council to continue to maintain close contact on these matters with the Chairman of the Special Committee and to report thereon to the Council;

19. *Requests* the Secretary-General to follow the implementation of the present resolution, paying particular attention to cooperation and integration arrangements for maximizing the efficiency of the assistance activities undertaken by various organizations of the United Nations system, and to report thereon to the Council at its substantive session of 2006;

20. *Decides* to keep these questions under continuous review.

RECORDED VOTE ON RESOLUTION 2005/49:

In favour: Azerbaijan, Bangladesh, Belize, Benin, Brazil, China, Colombia, Congo, Costa Rica, Cuba, Ecuador, Guinea, India, Indonesia, Jamaica, Kenya, Malaysia, Mauritius, Mexico, Mozambique, Namibia, Nicaragua, Nigeria, Pakistan, Panama, Saudi Arabia, Senegal, South Africa, Thailand, Tunisia, United Arab Emirates, United Republic of Tanzania.

Against: None.

Abstaining: Albania, Armenia, Australia, Belgium, Canada, Denmark, France, Germany, Iceland, Ireland, Italy, Japan, Lithuania, Poland, Republic of Korea, Russian Federation, Spain, Turkey, United Kingdom, United States.

GENERAL ASSEMBLY ACTION

On 8 December [meeting 62], the General Assembly, on the recommendation of the Fourth Committee [A/60/482, orally amended], adopted **resolution 60/112** by recorded vote (123-0-50) [agenda item 36].

Implementation of the Declaration on the Granting of Independence to Colonial Countries and Peoples by the specialized agencies and the international institutions associated with the United Nations

The General Assembly,

Having considered the item entitled "Implementation of the Declaration on the Granting of Independence to Colonial Countries and Peoples by the specialized agencies and the international institutions associated with the United Nations",

Having also considered the report of the Secretary-General and the report of the Economic and Social Council on the item,

Having examined the chapter of the report of the Special Committee on the Situation with regard to the Implementation of the Declaration on the Granting of Independence to Colonial Countries and Peoples relating to the item,

Recalling General Assembly resolutions 1514(XV) of 14 December 1960 and 1541(XV) of 15 December 1960 and the resolutions of the Special Committee, as well as other relevant resolutions and decisions, including in particular Economic and Social Council resolution 2004/53 of 23 July 2004,

Bearing in mind the relevant provisions of the final documents of the successive Conferences of Heads of State or Government of Non-Aligned Countries and of the resolutions adopted by the Assembly of Heads of State and Government of the African Union, the Pacific Islands Forum and the Caribbean Community,

Conscious of the need to facilitate the implementation of the Declaration on the Granting of Independence to Colonial Countries and Peoples, contained in resolution 1514(XV),

Noting that the large majority of the remaining Non-Self-Governing Territories are small island Territories,

Welcoming the assistance extended to Non-Self-Governing Territories by certain specialized agencies and other organizations of the United Nations system, in particular the United Nations Development Programme,

Also welcoming the current participation in the capacity of observers of those Non-Self-Governing Territories that are associate members of regional commissions in the world conferences in the economic and social sphere, subject to the rules of procedure of the General Assembly and in accordance with relevant United Nations resolutions and decisions, including resolutions and decisions of the Assembly and the Special Committee on specific Territories,

Noting that only some specialized agencies and other organizations of the United Nations system have been involved in providing assistance to Non-Self-Governing Territories,

Stressing that, because the development options of the small island Non-Self-Governing Territories are limited, there are special challenges to planning for and implementing sustainable development and that those Territories will be constrained in meeting the challenges without the continuing cooperation and assistance of the specialized agencies and other organizations of the United Nations system,

Stressing also the importance of securing the necessary resources for funding expanded programmes of assistance for the peoples concerned and the need to enlist the support of all major funding institutions within the United Nations system in that regard,

Reaffirming the mandates of the specialized agencies and other organizations of the United Nations system to take all appropriate measures, within their respective spheres of competence, to ensure the full implementation of General Assembly resolution 1514(XV) and other relevant resolutions,

Expressing its appreciation to the African Union, the Pacific Islands Forum, the Caribbean Community and other regional organizations for the continued cooperation and assistance they have extended to the specialized agencies and other organizations of the United Nations system in this regard,

Expressing its conviction that closer contacts and consultations between and among the specialized agencies and other organizations of the United Nations system and regional organizations help to facilitate the effective formulation of programmes of assistance to the peoples concerned,

Mindful of the imperative need to keep under continuous review the activities of the specialized agencies and other organizations of the United Nations system in the implementation of the various United Nations resolutions and decisions relating to decolonization,

Bearing in mind the extremely fragile economies of the small island Non-Self-Governing Territories and their vulnerability to natural disasters, such as hurricanes, cyclones and sea-level rise, and recalling the relevant resolutions of the General Assembly,

Recalling General Assembly resolution 59/129 of 10 December 2004 on the implementation of the Declaration by the specialized agencies and the international institutions associated with the United Nations,

1. *Takes note* of the report of the Secretary-General;

2. *Recommends* that all States intensify their efforts in the specialized agencies and other organizations of the United Nations system in which they are members to ensure the full and effective implementation of the Declaration on the Granting of Independence to Colonial Countries and Peoples, contained in General Assembly resolution 1514(XV), and other relevant resolutions of the United Nations;

3. *Reaffirms* that the specialized agencies and other organizations and institutions of the United Nations system should continue to be guided by the relevant resolutions of the United Nations in their efforts to contribute to the implementation of the Declaration and all other relevant General Assembly resolutions;

4. *Reaffirms also* that the recognition by the General Assembly, the Security Council and other United Nations organs of the legitimacy of the aspirations of the peoples of the Non-Self-Governing Territories to exercise their right to self-determination entails, as a corollary, the extension of all appropriate assistance to those peoples;

5. *Expresses its appreciation* to those specialized agencies and other organizations of the United Nations system that have continued to cooperate with the United Nations and the regional and subregional organizations in the implementation of General Assembly resolution 1514(XV) and other relevant resolutions of the United Nations, and requests all the specialized agencies and other organizations of the United Nations system to implement the relevant provisions of those resolutions;

6. *Requests* the specialized agencies and other organizations of the United Nations system and international and regional organizations to examine and review conditions in each Territory so as to take appropriate measures to accelerate progress in the economic and social sectors of the Territories;

7. *Urges* those specialized agencies and organizations of the United Nations system that have not yet provided assistance to Non-Self-Governing Territories to do so as soon as possible;

8. *Requests* the specialized agencies and other organizations and institutions of the United Nations system and regional organizations to strengthen existing measures of support and formulate appropriate programmes of assistance to the remaining Non-Self-Governing Territories, within the framework of their respective mandates, in order to accelerate progress in the economic and social sectors of those Territories;

9. *Requests* the specialized agencies and other organizations of the United Nations system concerned to provide information on:

(*a*) Environmental problems facing the Non-Self-Governing Territories;

(*b*) The impact of natural disasters, such as hurricanes and volcanic eruptions, and other environmental problems, such as beach and coastal erosion and droughts, on those Territories;

(*c*) Ways and means to assist the Territories to fight drug trafficking, money-laundering and other illegal and criminal activities;

(*d*) The illegal exploitation of the marine resources of the Territories and the need to utilize those resources for the benefit of the peoples of the Territories;

10. *Recommends* that the executive heads of the specialized agencies and other organizations of the United Nations system formulate, with the active cooperation of the regional organizations concerned, concrete proposals for the full implementation of the relevant resolutions of the United Nations and submit the proposals to their governing and legislative organs;

11. *Also recommends* that the specialized agencies and other organizations of the United Nations system continue to review at the regular meetings of their governing bodies the implementation of General Assembly resolution 1514(XV) and other relevant resolutions of the United Nations;

12. *Welcomes* the adoption by the Economic Commission for Latin America and the Caribbean of its resolution 574(XXVII) of 16 May 1998 calling for the necessary mechanisms for its associate members, including small island Non-Self-Governing Territories, to participate in the special sessions of the General As-

sembly, subject to the rules of procedure of the Assembly, to review and assess the implementation of the plans of action of those United Nations world conferences in which the Territories originally participated in the capacity of observer, and in the work of the Economic and Social Council and its subsidiary bodies;

13. *Requests* the Chairman of the Special Committee on the Situation with regard to the Implementation of the Declaration on the Granting of Independence to Colonial Countries and Peoples to continue to maintain close contact on these matters with the President of the Economic and Social Council;

14. *Requests* the Department of Public Information of the Secretariat, in consultation with the United Nations Development Programme, the specialized agencies and the Special Committee, to prepare an information leaflet on assistance programmes available to the Non-Self-Governing Territories and to disseminate it widely in them;

15. *Welcomes* the continuing initiative exercised by the United Nations Development Programme in maintaining close liaison among the specialized agencies and other organizations of the United Nations system, including the Economic Commission for Latin America and the Caribbean and the Economic and Social Commission for Asia and the Pacific, and in providing assistance to the peoples of the Non-Self-Governing Territories;

16. *Encourages* the Non-Self-Governing Territories to take steps to establish and/or strengthen disaster preparedness and management institutions and policies;

17. *Requests* the administering Powers concerned to facilitate, when appropriate, the participation of appointed and elected representatives of Non-Self-Governing Territories in the relevant meetings and conferences of the specialized agencies and other organizations of the United Nations system, in accordance with relevant United Nations resolutions and decisions, including resolutions and decisions of the General Assembly and the Special Committee on specific Territories, so that the Territories may benefit from the related activities of those agencies and organizations;

18. *Recommends* that all Governments intensify their efforts in the specialized agencies and other organizations of the United Nations system of which they are members to accord priority to the question of providing assistance to the peoples of the Non-Self-Governing Territories;

19. *Requests* the Secretary-General to continue to assist the specialized agencies and other organizations of the United Nations system in working out appropriate measures for implementing the relevant resolutions of the United Nations and to prepare for submission to the relevant bodies, with the assistance of those agencies and organizations, a report on the action taken in implementation of the relevant resolutions, including the present resolution, since the circulation of his previous report;

20. *Commends* the Economic and Social Council for its debate and resolution on this question, and requests it to continue to consider, in consultation with the Special Committee, appropriate measures for the coordination of the policies and activities of the specialized agencies and other organizations of the United Nations system in implementing the relevant resolutions of the General Assembly;

21. *Requests* the specialized agencies to report periodically to the Secretary-General on the implementation of the present resolution;

22. *Requests* the Secretary-General to transmit the present resolution to the governing bodies of the appropriate specialized agencies and international institutions associated with the United Nations so that those bodies may take the necessary measures to implement the resolution, and also requests the Secretary-General to report to the General Assembly at its sixty-first session on the implementation of the present resolution;

23. *Requests* the Special Committee to continue to examine the question and to report thereon to the General Assembly at its sixty-first session.

RECORDED VOTE ON RESOLUTION 60/112:

In favour: Afghanistan, Algeria, Angola, Antigua and Barbuda, Argentina, Australia, Bahamas, Bahrain, Bangladesh, Barbados, Belarus, Belize, Benin, Bhutan, Bolivia, Botswana, Brazil, Brunei Darussalam, Bulgaria, Burkina Faso, Burundi, Cambodia, Cameroon, Cape Verde, Central African Republic, Chile, China, Colombia, Congo, Costa Rica, Côte d'Ivoire, Cuba, Democratic People's Republic of Korea, Djibouti, Dominica, Dominican Republic, Ecuador, Egypt, El Salvador, Eritrea, Ethiopia, Fiji, Gabon, Ghana, Grenada, Guatemala, Guinea, Guinea-Bissau, Guyana, Haiti, Honduras, India, Indonesia, Iran, Iraq, Jamaica, Jordan, Kenya, Kuwait, Kyrgyzstan, Lao People's Democratic Republic, Lebanon, Lesotho, Liberia, Libyan Arab Jamahiriya, Madagascar, Malawi, Malaysia, Maldives, Mali, Marshall Islands, Mauritania, Mauritius, Mexico, Mongolia, Morocco, Mozambique, Myanmar, Namibia, Nepal, New Zealand, Nicaragua, Niger, Nigeria, Oman, Pakistan, Palau, Panama, Papua New Guinea, Paraguay, Peru, Philippines, Qatar, Rwanda, Saint Lucia, Saint Vincent and the Grenadines, Samoa, Saudi Arabia, Senegal, Singapore, Solomon Islands, South Africa, Sri Lanka, Sudan, Suriname, Syrian Arab Republic, Thailand, Timor-Leste, Togo, Tonga, Trinidad and Tobago, Tunisia, Tuvalu, Uganda, United Arab Emirates, United Republic of Tanzania, Uruguay, Vanuatu, Venezuela, Viet Nam, Yemen, Zambia, Zimbabwe.

Against: None.

Abstaining: Albania, Andorra, Armenia, Austria, Azerbaijan, Belgium, Canada, Croatia, Cyprus, Czech Republic, Denmark, Estonia, Finland, France, Georgia, Germany, Greece, Hungary, Iceland, Ireland, Israel, Italy, Japan, Kazakhstan, Latvia, Liechtenstein, Lithuania, Luxembourg, Malta, Monaco, Netherlands, Norway, Poland, Portugal, Republic of Korea, Republic of Moldova, Romania, Russian Federation, San Marino, Serbia and Montenegro, Slovakia, Slovenia, Spain, Sweden, Switzerland, Tajikistan, The former Yugoslav Republic of Macedonia, Turkey, Ukraine, United Kingdom.

Military activities and arrangements in colonial countries

Secretariat working papers on Bermuda [A/AC.109/2005/5], Guam [A/AC.109/2005/7] and the United States Virgin Islands [A/AC.109/2005/9] contained information on, among other subjects, military activities and arrangements by the administering Powers in those Territories.

Economic and other activities affecting the interests of NSGTs

The Special Committee on decolonization continued consideration of economic and other activities affecting the interests of the peoples of NSGTs. It had before it Secretariat working papers containing information on, among other subjects, economic conditions, with particular reference to foreign economic activities, in Anguilla [A/AC.109/2005/4], Bermuda [A/AC.109/2005/5], the

British Virgin Islands [A/AC.109/2005/12], the Cayman Islands [A/AC.109/2005/6], Montserrat [A/AC.109/2005/16], New Caledonia [A/AC.109/2005/13], the Turks and Caicos Islands [A/AC.109/2005/8] and the United States Virgin Islands [A/AC.109/2005/9].

GENERAL ASSEMBLY ACTION

On 8 December [meeting 62], the General Assembly, on the recommendation of the Fourth Committee [A/60/481], adopted **resolution 60/111** by recorded vote (169-1-3) [agenda item 35].

Economic and other activities which affect the interests of the peoples of the Non-Self-Governing Territories

The General Assembly,

Having considered the item entitled "Economic and other activities which affect the interests of the peoples of the Non-Self-Governing Territories",

Having examined the chapter of the report of the Special Committee on the Situation with regard to the Implementation of the Declaration on the Granting of Independence to Colonial Countries and Peoples relating to the item,

Recalling General Assembly resolution 1514(XV) of 14 December 1960, as well as all other relevant resolutions of the Assembly, including, in particular, resolutions 46/181 of 19 December 1991 and 55/146 of 8 December 2000,

Reaffirming the solemn obligation of the administering Powers under the Charter of the United Nations to promote the political, economic, social and educational advancement of the inhabitants of the Territories under their administration and to protect the human and natural resources of those Territories against abuses,

Reaffirming also that any economic or other activity that has a negative impact on the interests of the peoples of the Non-Self-Governing Territories and on the exercise of their right to self-determination in conformity with the Charter and General Assembly resolution 1514(XV) is contrary to the purposes and principles of the Charter,

Reaffirming further that the natural resources are the heritage of the peoples of the Non-Self-Governing Territories, including the indigenous populations,

Aware of the special circumstances of the geographical location, size and economic conditions of each Territory, and bearing in mind the need to promote the economic stability, diversification and strengthening of the economy of each Territory,

Conscious of the particular vulnerability of the small Territories to natural disasters and environmental degradation,

Conscious also that foreign economic investment, when undertaken in collaboration with the peoples of the Non-Self-Governing Territories and in accordance with their wishes, could make a valid contribution to the socio-economic development of the Territories and also to the exercise of their right to self-determination,

Concerned about any activities aimed at exploiting the natural and human resources of the Non-Self-Governing Territories to the detriment of the interests of the inhabitants of those Territories,

Bearing in mind the relevant provisions of the final documents of the successive Conferences of Heads of State or Government of Non-Aligned Countries and of the resolutions adopted by the Assembly of Heads of State and Government of the African Union, the Pacific Islands Forum and the Caribbean Community,

1. *Reaffirms* the right of peoples of Non-Self-Governing Territories to self-determination in conformity with the Charter of the United Nations and with General Assembly resolution 1514(XV), containing the Declaration on the Granting of Independence to Colonial Countries and Peoples, as well as their right to the enjoyment of their natural resources and their right to dispose of those resources in their best interest;

2. *Affirms* the value of foreign economic investment undertaken in collaboration with the peoples of the Non-Self-Governing Territories and in accordance with their wishes in order to make a valid contribution to the socio-economic development of the Territories;

3. *Reaffirms* the responsibility of the administering Powers under the Charter to promote the political, economic, social and educational advancement of the Non-Self-Governing Territories, and reaffirms the legitimate rights of their peoples over their natural resources;

4. *Reaffirms its concern* about any activities aimed at the exploitation of the natural resources that are the heritage of the peoples of the Non-Self-Governing Territories, including the indigenous populations, in the Caribbean, the Pacific and other regions, and of their human resources, to the detriment of their interests, and in such a way as to deprive them of their right to dispose of those resources;

5. *Reaffirms* the need to avoid any economic and other activities that adversely affect the interests of the peoples of the Non-Self-Governing Territories;

6. *Calls once again upon* all Governments that have not yet done so to take, in accordance with the relevant provisions of General Assembly resolution 2621(XXV) of 12 October 1970, legislative, administrative or other measures in respect of their nationals and the bodies corporate under their jurisdiction that own and operate enterprises in the Non-Self-Governing Territories that are detrimental to the interests of the inhabitants of those Territories, in order to put an end to such enterprises;

7. *Reiterates* that the damaging exploitation and plundering of the marine and other natural resources of the Non-Self-Governing Territories, in violation of the relevant resolutions of the United Nations, are a threat to the integrity and prosperity of those Territories;

8. *Invites* all Governments and organizations of the United Nations system to take all possible measures to ensure that the permanent sovereignty of the peoples of the Non-Self-Governing Territories over their natural resources is fully respected and safeguarded in accordance with the relevant resolutions of the United Nations on decolonization;

9. *Urges* the administering Powers concerned to take effective measures to safeguard and guarantee the inalienable right of the peoples of the Non-Self-Governing Territories to their natural resources and to establish and maintain control over the future devel-

opment of those resources, and requests the administering Powers to take all necessary steps to protect the property rights of the peoples of those Territories in accordance with the relevant resolutions of the United Nations on decolonization;

10. *Calls upon* the administering Powers concerned to ensure that no discriminatory working conditions prevail in the Territories under their administration and to promote in each Territory a fair system of wages applicable to all the inhabitants without any discrimination;

11. *Requests* the Secretary-General to continue, through all means at his disposal, to inform world public opinion of any activity that affects the exercise of the right of the peoples of the Non-Self-Governing Territories to self-determination in conformity with the Charter and General Assembly resolution 1514(XV);

12. *Appeals* to trade unions and non-governmental organizations, as well as individuals, to continue their efforts to promote the economic well-being of the peoples of the Non-Self-Governing Territories and also appeals to the media to disseminate information about the developments in this regard;

13. *Decides* to follow the situation in the Non-Self-Governing Territories so as to ensure that all economic activities in those Territories are aimed at strengthening and diversifying their economies in the interest of their peoples, including the indigenous populations, and at promoting the economic and financial viability of those Territories;

14. *Requests* the Special Committee on the Situation with regard to the Implementation of the Declaration on the Granting of Independence to Colonial Countries and Peoples to continue to examine this question and to report thereon to the General Assembly at its sixty-first session.

RECORDED VOTE ON RESOLUTION 60/111:

In favour: Afghanistan, Algeria, Andorra, Angola, Antigua and Barbuda, Argentina, Armenia, Australia, Austria, Azerbaijan, Bahamas, Bahrain, Bangladesh, Barbados, Belarus, Belgium, Belize, Benin, Bhutan, Bolivia, Botswana, Brazil, Brunei Darussalam, Bulgaria, Burkina Faso, Burundi, Cambodia, Cameroon, Canada, Cape Verde, Central African Republic, Chile, China, Colombia, Congo, Costa Rica, Côte d'Ivoire, Croatia, Cuba, Cyprus, Czech Republic, Democratic People's Republic of Korea, Denmark, Djibouti, Dominica, Dominican Republic, Ecuador, Egypt, El Salvador, Eritrea, Estonia, Ethiopia, Fiji, Finland, Gabon, Georgia, Germany, Ghana, Greece, Grenada, Guatemala, Guinea, Guinea-Bissau, Guyana, Haiti, Honduras, Hungary, Iceland, India, Indonesia, Iran, Iraq, Ireland, Italy, Jamaica, Japan, Jordan, Kazakhstan, Kenya, Kuwait, Kyrgyzstan, Lao People's Democratic Republic, Latvia, Lebanon, Lesotho, Liberia, Libyan Arab Jamahiriya, Liechtenstein, Lithuania, Luxembourg, Madagascar, Malawi, Malaysia, Maldives, Mali, Malta, Marshall Islands, Mauritania, Mauritius, Mexico, Mongolia, Morocco, Mozambique, Myanmar, Namibia, Nepal, Netherlands, New Zealand, Nicaragua, Niger, Nigeria, Norway, Oman, Pakistan, Palau, Panama, Papua New Guinea, Paraguay, Peru, Philippines, Poland, Portugal, Qatar, Republic of Korea, Republic of Moldova, Romania, Russian Federation, Rwanda, Saint Lucia, Saint Vincent and the Grenadines, Samoa, San Marino, Saudi Arabia, Senegal, Serbia and Montenegro, Singapore, Slovakia, Slovenia, Solomon Islands, South Africa, Spain, Sri Lanka, Sudan, Suriname, Sweden, Switzerland, Syrian Arab Republic, Tajikistan, Thailand, The former Yugoslav Republic of Macedonia, Timor-Leste, Togo, Tonga, Trinidad and Tobago, Tunisia, Turkey, Turkmenistan, Tuvalu, Uganda, Ukraine, United Arab Emirates, United Republic of Tanzania, Uruguay, Vanuatu, Venezuela, Viet Nam, Yemen, Zambia, Zimbabwe.

Against: United States.

Abstaining: Albania, France, United Kingdom.

Dissemination of information

The Special Committee on decolonization held consultations in June with representatives of DPA and DPI on the dissemination of information on decolonization. It also considered a report of the Secretary-General on DPI activities on the topic from June 2004 to March 2005 [A/AC.109/2005/18].

GENERAL ASSEMBLY ACTION

On 8 December [meeting 62], the General Assembly, on the recommendation of the Fourth Committee [A/60/472], adopted **resolution 60/118** by recorded vote (167-3-2) [agenda item 26].

Dissemination of information on decolonization

The General Assembly,

Having examined the chapter of the report of the Special Committee on the Situation with regard to the Implementation of the Declaration on the Granting of Independence to Colonial Countries and Peoples relating to the dissemination of information on decolonization and publicity for the work of the United Nations in the field of decolonization,

Recalling General Assembly resolution 1514(XV) of 14 December 1960, containing the Declaration on the Granting of Independence to Colonial Countries and Peoples, and other resolutions and decisions of the United Nations concerning the dissemination of information on decolonization, in particular Assembly resolution 59/135 of 10 December 2004,

Recognizing the need for flexible, practical and innovative approaches towards reviewing the options of self-determination for the peoples of Non-Self-Governing Territories with a view to implementing the plan of action for the Second International Decade for the Eradication of Colonialism,

Reiterating the importance of dissemination of information as an instrument for furthering the aims of the Declaration, and mindful of the role of world public opinion in effectively assisting the peoples of Non-Self-Governing Territories to achieve self-determination,

Recognizing the role played by the administering Powers in transmitting information to the Secretary-General in accordance with the terms of Article 73 *e* of the Charter of the United Nations,

Aware of the role of non-governmental organizations in the dissemination of information on decolonization,

1. *Approves* the activities in the field of dissemination of information on decolonization undertaken by the Department of Public Information and the Department of Political Affairs of the Secretariat, in accordance with the relevant resolutions of the United Nations on decolonization;

2. *Considers it important* to continue and expand its efforts to ensure the widest possible dissemination of information on decolonization, with particular emphasis on the options of self-determination available for the peoples of Non-Self-Governing Territories;

3. *Requests* the Department of Political Affairs and the Department of Public Information to implement the recommendations of the Special Committee on the Situation with regard to the Implementation of the Declaration on the Granting of Independence to Colonial Countries and Peoples to continue their efforts to take measures through all the media available, including publications, radio and television, as well as the

Internet, to give publicity to the work of the United Nations in the field of decolonization and, inter alia:

(a) To develop procedures to collect, prepare and disseminate, particularly to the Territories, basic material on the issue of self-determination of the peoples of Non-Self-Governing Territories;

(b) To seek the full cooperation of the administering Powers in the discharge of the tasks referred to above;

(c) To develop a working relationship with the appropriate regional and intergovernmental organizations, particularly in the Pacific and Caribbean regions, by holding periodic consultations and exchanging information;

(d) To encourage the involvement of non-governmental organizations in the dissemination of information on decolonization;

(e) To encourage the involvement of Non-Self-Governing Territories in the dissemination of information on decolonization;

(f) To report to the Special Committee on measures taken in the implementation of the present resolution.

4. *Requests* all States, including the administering Powers, to accelerate the dissemination of information referred to in paragraph 2 above;

5. *Requests* the Special Committee to continue to examine this question and to report to the General Assembly at its sixty-first session on the implementation of the present resolution.

RECORDED VOTE ON RESOLUTION 60/118:

In favour: Afghanistan, Algeria, Andorra, Angola, Antigua and Barbuda, Argentina, Armenia, Australia, Austria, Azerbaijan, Bahamas, Bahrain, Bangladesh, Barbados, Belarus, Belgium, Belize, Benin, Bhutan, Bolivia, Botswana, Brazil, Brunei Darussalam, Bulgaria, Burkina Faso, Burundi, Cambodia, Cameroon, Cape Verde, Central African Republic, Chile, China, Colombia, Congo, Costa Rica, Côte d'Ivoire, Croatia, Cuba, Cyprus, Czech Republic, Democratic People's Republic of Korea, Denmark, Djibouti, Dominica, Dominican Republic, Ecuador, Egypt, El Salvador, Eritrea, Estonia, Ethiopia, Fiji, Finland, Gabon, Georgia, Germany, Ghana, Greece, Grenada, Guatemala, Guinea, Guinea-Bissau, Guyana, Haiti, Honduras, Hungary, Iceland, India, Indonesia, Iran, Iraq, Ireland, Italy, Jamaica, Japan, Jordan, Kazakhstan, Kenya, Kuwait, Kyrgyzstan, Lao People's Democratic Republic, Latvia, Lebanon, Lesotho, Liberia, Libyan Arab Jamahiriya, Liechtenstein, Lithuania, Luxembourg, Madagascar, Malawi, Malaysia, Maldives, Mali, Malta, Marshall Islands, Mauritania, Mauritius, Mexico, Monaco, Mongolia, Morocco, Mozambique, Myanmar, Namibia, Nepal, Netherlands, New Zealand, Nicaragua, Niger, Nigeria, Norway, Oman, Pakistan, Palau, Panama, Papua New Guinea, Paraguay, Peru, Philippines, Poland, Portugal, Qatar, Republic of Korea, Republic of Moldova, Romania, Russian Federation, Saint Lucia, Saint Vincent and the Grenadines, Samoa, San Marino, Saudi Arabia, Senegal, Serbia and Montenegro, Singapore, Slovakia, Slovenia, Solomon Islands, South Africa, Spain, Sri Lanka, Sudan, Suriname, Sweden, Switzerland, Syrian Arab Republic, Tajikistan, Thailand, The former Yugoslav Republic of Macedonia, Timor-Leste, Togo, Trinidad and Tobago, Tunisia, Turkey, Tuvalu, Uganda, Ukraine, United Arab Emirates, United Republic of Tanzania, Uruguay, Vanuatu, Venezuela, Viet Nam, Yemen, Zambia, Zimbabwe.

Against: Israel, United Kingdom, United States.

Abstaining: Albania, France.

Information on Territories

In response to General Assembly resolution 59/127 [YUN 2004, p. 603], the Secretary-General submitted an April report [A/60/69 & Corr.1] showing the dates of transmittal of information on economic, social and educational conditions in NSGTs for the years 2002-2004, under Article 73 *e* of the Charter of the United Nations.

On 8 December [meeting 62], the General Assembly, on the recommendation of the Fourth Committee [A/60/480], adopted **resolution 60/110** by recorded vote (169-0-5) [agenda item 34].

Information from Non-Self-Governing Territories transmitted under Article 73 *e* of the Charter of the United Nations

The General Assembly,

Recalling its resolution 1970(XVIII) of 16 December 1963, in which it requested the Special Committee on the Situation with regard to the Implementation of the Declaration on the Granting of Independence to Colonial Countries and Peoples to study the information transmitted to the Secretary-General in accordance with Article 73 *e* of the Charter of the United Nations and to take such information fully into account in examining the situation with regard to the implementation of the Declaration, contained in General Assembly resolution 1514(XV) of 14 December 1960,

Recalling also its resolution 59/127 of 10 December 2004, in which it requested the Special Committee to continue to discharge the functions entrusted to it under resolution 1970(XVIII),

Stressing the importance of timely transmission by the administering Powers of adequate information under Article 73 *e* of the Charter, in particular in relation to the preparation by the Secretariat of the working papers on the Territories concerned,

Having examined the report of the Secretary-General,

1. *Reaffirms* that, in the absence of a decision by the General Assembly itself that a Non-Self-Governing Territory has attained a full measure of self-government in terms of Chapter XI of the Charter of the United Nations, the administering Power concerned should continue to transmit information under Article 73 *e* of the Charter with respect to that Territory;

2. *Requests* the administering Powers concerned to transmit or continue to transmit to the Secretary-General the information prescribed in Article 73 *e* of the Charter, as well as the fullest possible information on political and constitutional developments in the Territories concerned, within a maximum period of six months following the expiration of the administrative year in those Territories;

3. *Requests* the Secretary-General to continue to ensure that adequate information is drawn from all available published sources in connection with the preparation of the working papers relating to the Territories concerned;

4. *Requests* the Special Committee on the Situation with regard to the Implementation of the Declaration on the Granting of Independence to Colonial Countries and Peoples to continue to discharge the functions entrusted to it under General Assembly resolution 1970(XVIII), in accordance with established procedures.

RECORDED VOTE ON RESOLUTION 60/110:

In favour: Afghanistan, Algeria, Andorra, Angola, Antigua and Barbuda, Argentina, Armenia, Australia, Austria, Azerbaijan, Bahamas, Bahrain, Bangladesh, Barbados, Belarus, Belgium, Belize, Benin, Bhutan, Bolivia, Botswana, Brazil, Brunei Darussalam, Bulgaria, Burkina Faso, Burundi, Cambodia, Cameroon, Canada, Cape Verde, Central African Republic, Chile, China, Colombia, Congo, Costa Rica, Côte d'Ivoire, Croatia, Cuba, Cyprus, Czech Republic, Democratic People's Republic of

Korea, Denmark, Djibouti, Dominica, Dominican Republic, Ecuador, Egypt, El Salvador, Eritrea, Estonia, Ethiopia, Fiji, Finland, Gabon, Georgia, Germany, Ghana, Greece, Grenada, Guatemala, Guinea, Guinea-Bissau, Guyana, Haiti, Honduras, Hungary, Iceland, India, Indonesia, Iran, Iraq, Ireland, Italy, Jamaica, Japan, Jordan, Kazakhstan, Kenya, Kuwait, Kyrgyzstan, Lao People's Democratic Republic, Latvia, Lebanon, Lesotho, Liberia, Libyan Arab Jamahiriya, Liechtenstein, Lithuania, Luxembourg, Madagascar, Malawi, Malaysia, Maldives, Mali, Malta, Marshall Islands, Mauritania, Mauritius, Mexico, Micronesia, Mongolia, Morocco, Mozambique, Myanmar, Namibia, Nepal, Netherlands, New Zealand, Nicaragua, Niger, Nigeria, Norway, Oman, Pakistan, Palau, Panama, Papua New Guinea, Paraguay, Peru, Philippines, Poland, Portugal, Qatar, Republic of Korea, Republic of Moldova, Romania, Russian Federation, Saint Lucia, Saint Vincent and the Grenadines, Samoa, San Marino, Saudi Arabia, Senegal, Serbia and Montenegro, Singapore, Slovakia, Slovenia, Solomon Islands, South Africa, Spain, Sri Lanka, Sudan, Suriname, Sweden, Switzerland, Syrian Arab Republic, Tajikistan, Thailand, The former Yugoslav Republic of Macedonia, Timor-Leste, Togo, Tonga, Trinidad and Tobago, Tunisia, Turkey, Turkmenistan, Tuvalu, Uganda, Ukraine, United Arab Emirates, United Republic of Tanzania, Uruguay, Vanuatu, Venezuela, Viet Nam, Yemen, Zambia, Zimbabwe.
Against: None.
Abstaining: Albania, France, Israel, United Kingdom, United States.

Study and training

In response to General Assembly resolution 59/130 [YUN 2004, p. 604], the Secretary-General reported [A/60/67] on offers of study and training scholarships for inhabitants of NSGTs during the period 16 April 2004 to 25 March 2005 by five Member States (Australia, Malaysia, Portugal, Thailand, United Kingdom) and one non-member State (Holy See). Fifty-eight Member States and one non-member State had made such offers over the years.

GENERAL ASSEMBLY ACTION

On 8 December [meeting 62], the General Assembly, on the recommendation of the Fourth Committee [A/60/483], adopted **resolution 60/113** without vote [agenda item 37].

Offers by Member States of study and training facilities for inhabitants of Non-Self-Governing Territories

The General Assembly,

Recalling its resolution 59/130 of 10 December 2004,

Having examined the report of the Secretary-General on offers by Member States of study and training facilities for inhabitants of Non-Self-Governing Territories, prepared pursuant to its resolution 845(IX) of 22 November 1954,

Conscious of the importance of promoting the educational advancement of the inhabitants of Non-Self-Governing Territories,

Strongly convinced that the continuation and expansion of offers of scholarships is essential in order to meet the increasing need of students from Non-Self-Governing Territories for educational and training assistance, and considering that students in those Territories should be encouraged to avail themselves of such offers,

1. *Takes note* of the report of the Secretary-General;

2. *Expresses its appreciation* to those Member States that have made scholarships available to the inhabitants of Non-Self-Governing Territories;

3. *Invites* all States to make or to continue to make generous offers of study and training facilities to the inhabitants of those Territories that have not yet attained self-government or independence and, wherever possible, to provide travel funds to prospective students;

4. *Urges* the administering Powers to take effective measures to ensure the widespread and continuous dissemination in the Territories under their administration of information relating to offers of study and training facilities made by States and to provide all the necessary facilities to enable students to avail themselves of such offers;

5. *Requests* the Secretary-General to report to the General Assembly at its sixty-first session on the implementation of the present resolution;

6. *Draws the attention* of the Special Committee on the Situation with regard to the Implementation of the Declaration on the Granting of Independence to Colonial Countries and Peoples to the present resolution.

Visiting missions

In June, the Special Committee on decolonization considered the question of sending visiting missions to NSGTs [A/60/23]. It adopted a resolution stressing the need to dispatch periodic visiting missions to facilitate the full implementation of the 1960 Declaration on decolonization and called on the administering Powers to receive those missions in the Territories under their administration.

The Committee recommended to the General Assembly for adoption draft resolutions on 11 small NSGTs (see p. 677) and on Tokelau (see p. 675), endorsing a number of conclusions and recommendations concerning the sending of visiting missions to those Territories.

Bermuda mission

In March, the Special Committee on decolonization accepted an 18 February invitation from the Bermuda Independence Commission to send a UN Special Mission to Bermuda in two phases (March and May), subject to the concurrence of the United Kingdom (the administering Power). The Mission's objective was to gather first-hand information on the situation in Bermuda and assess the type of assistance the UN system could provide to the self-determination process in that Territory, with a view to defining its future status. It should also inform Bermudians about the process of self-determination and subsequent decolonization under the UN Charter and about the Special Committee's mandate, as well as the wider UN system in that regard.

The Special Mission visited Bermuda from 26 to 31 March and from 30 May to 3 June. In its June report [A/AC.109/2005/19], the Mission concluded that there was insufficient knowledge and awareness among the people of Bermuda and its political leadership of the role of international law in the process of political and constitutional development, including the role the UN system could play in supporting the self-determination and subsequent decolonization of the Territory. The message heard by Bermudians on the question was mixed, since the available political options presented by the administering Power differed substantively from the consensus position in UN resolutions, which confirmed a broader range of legitimate political alternatives. The issue of whether Bermuda's current status was self-governing or not was also raised and the Mission provided information on the minimum standards for what constituted self-government. It was evident that the lack of previous communication with the United Nations had resulted in a number of misconceptions in Bermuda regarding the Organization's role in the self-determination process and the parameters of self-government. The Mission therefore provided a mechanism of communication between the people of Bermuda and their leadership, on one hand, and the United Nations, on the other.

Puerto Rico

In accordance with the Special Committee's 2004 resolution concerning the self-determination and independence of Puerto Rico [YUN 2004, p. 604], the Committee's Rapporteur, in an April report [A/AC.109/2005/L.3], provided information on Puerto Rico, including recent political, military and economic developments and UN action.

Following its usual practice, the Special Committee acceded to requests for hearings from representatives of a number of organizations, who presented their views on 13 June [A/60/23]. The Committee adopted a resolution, without vote, by which it reaffirmed the inalienable right of the people of Puerto Rico to self-determination and independence; called upon the United States to assume its responsibility of expediting a process to allow the Puerto Rican people to exercise that right; urged the United States to return the occupied land and installations on Vieques Island and in Ceiba to the people of Puerto Rico; and requested the Rapporteur to report in 2006 on the resolution's implementation.

Territories under review

Falkland Islands (Malvinas)

The Special Committee on decolonization, in considering the question of the Falkland Islands (Malvinas) on 15 June [A/60/23], examined a Secretariat working paper on constitutional and political developments, mine clearance and eco-

nomic and social conditions in that Territory [A/AC.109/2005/17]. It adopted a resolution requesting Argentina and the United Kingdom to consolidate the current dialogue and cooperation by resuming negotiations to find a peaceful solution to the sovereignty dispute.

Argentina, in a 3 January statement [A/59/662], recalled its objective to recover full sovereignty over the Malvinas, South Georgia and South Sandwich Islands and surrounding maritime areas through peaceful means. It reaffirmed the need to carry out UN resolutions and the Organization of American States declarations urging the resumption of bilateral negotiations in order to find a just, peaceful and lasting solution to the sovereignty dispute. It also recalled its readiness to resume such negotiations immediately and exhorted the United Kingdom to do likewise.

The United Kingdom responded on 31 January [A/59/687] that it had no doubts about its sovereignty over the Falkland Islands, South Georgia and South Sandwich Islands, and rejected Argentina's claim to sovereignty.

Annexed to a 10 May letter [A/60/76] from Argentina to the Secretary-General were identical notes dated 20 April from Argentina, addressed to Luxembourg in its capacity as President of the EU Council and President of the European Commission, and 6 May to the British Embassy in Buenos Aires. In those notes, Argentina drew attention to part III, title IV, annex II of the 2004 Constitutional Treaty of the EU, which referred to the Malvinas Islands, South Georgia, South Sandwich Islands and the "British Antarctic Territory", and reiterated its previous rejection of such references in the 1957 Constitutional Treaty (Treaty of Rome) establishing the European Economic Community. It recalled that the islands in question and the surrounding maritime areas were an integral part of its territory, and were illegally occupied by the United Kingdom and were the subject of a sovereignty dispute. The inclusion of those territories in the annex on the association of the overseas countries and territories, in no way affected Argentina's sovereignty and jurisdiction. Argentina also noted that the inclusion of the "British Antarctic Territory" in annex II did not affect Argentina's rights in the Argentine Antarctic Sector.

On 7 June [A/59/843], the United Kingdom rejected the protest contained in Argentina's 6 May letter, stating that the inclusion of the islands in question and the British Antarctic Territory in the Treaty establishing a Constitution for Europe confirmed the current position with regard to the status of those British Overseas Territories, which had been included in the Rome Treaty since the accession of the United Kingdom on 1 January 1973.

In a 6 July letter to the Economic and Social Council President [E/2005/84], Argentina referred to the Council President's May report [E/2004/47] on consultations held with the Chairman of the Special Committee on decolonization and its reference to the United Kingdom's declaration that international labour conventions were applicable under article 35 of the constitution of the International Labour Organization (ILO) to the Falkland Islands (Malvinas). Argentina requested that all references to the Malvinas Islands in the Council's official documentation should conform to the provisions on bilingual terminology contained in the UN Secretariat's 1999 editorial directive, and that special reference be made, in a footnote, to the existence of a sovereignty dispute between Argentina and the United Kingdom over the Malvinas Islands. A June corrigendum to the report [E/2005/47/Corr.1] contained such a footnote.

On 25 July [E/2005/87], the United Kingdom, responding to Argentina's 6 July letter, stated that it had no doubts about its sovereignty over the Falkland Islands, South Georgia and South Sandwich Islands, as well as the surrounding maritime areas, and rejected Argentina's claims to sovereignty over those islands and areas and its assertion that they were under illegal occupation by the United Kingdom.

Addressing the General Assembly during the general debate on 14 September [A/60/PV.4], Argentina's President, Néstor Kirchner, reaffirmed his country's readiness to reach a final, fair and peaceful solution to the sovereignty dispute and urged the United Kingdom to resume negotiations. In exercise of its right of reply, the United Kingdom, in a 16 September letter to the Assembly President [A/60/361], responded that the elected representatives of the Falkland Islands had again asked the Special Committee on decolonization to recognize that they, like any other people, were entitled to exercise their right of self-determination, and reiterated that the people of the Falkland Islands did not wish for any change in the status of the Islands. The United Kingdom stated that there could be no negotiations on sovereignty unless and until such time as the islanders so wished.

On 28 October [A/60/527], Argentina expressed strong rejection of and formal protest at a new measure whereby the United Kingdom claimed to assign ownership rights to the fisheries resources in the maritime areas surrounding the Malvinas Islands. Argentina said that the South Atlantic Fisheries Commission made no provision for an agreed fisheries administration be-tween the two countries and the United Kingdom's unilateral measure was incompatible with the bilateral arrangements on cooperation for the conservation of fisheries resources. Moreover, the new measure was not compatible with the General Assembly's call in resolution 31/49 [YUN 1976, p. 747] that the two parties refrain from taking decisions that would imply the introduction of unilateral modifications in the situation, while negotiations on the sovereignty dispute were ongoing.

On 1 December [A/60/583], the United Kingdom rejected Argentina's protest and reiterated that the Falkland Islands Government was entitled to adopt whatever measure it considered necessary to conserve, manage, and exploit fish stocks within its waters. It was disappointed that the matter was affecting the level of Argentina's cooperation on the conservation of fisheries resources under the South Atlantic Fisheries Commission.

On 12 December [A/60/594], Argentina stated that the British unilateral measures seriously impaired cooperation in the South Atlantic Fisheries Commission and that it would take legal actions available to it regarding enterprises that exploited fisheries resources in the Argentine exclusive economic zone without appropriate authorization.

Gibraltar

The Special Committee on decolonization considered the question of Gibraltar on 7 June [A/60/23]. Before it was a Secretariat working paper describing political developments and economic and social conditions in that Territory, and setting forth the positions of the United Kingdom (the administering Power), Gibraltar and Spain concerning Gibraltar's future status [A/AC.109/2005/11].

Gibraltar's Chief Minister, Peter Caruana, in his New Year message, said that the December 2004 agreement between the United Kingdom, Spain and Gibraltar [YUN 2004, p. 606] to set up a new trilateral process of dialogue outside the Brussels Process [YUN 1984, p. 1075] was a major political development. As far as Gibraltar was concerned, the Brussels agreement [ibid.] had become totally irrelevant and should be formally abandoned by the United Kingdom and Spain. There was no prospect of Gibraltar's participation in it, nor could there be any question of parallel bilateral sovereignty talks between the United Kingdom and Spain.

The new Trilateral Forum for Dialogue held three meetings (Malaga, Spain, 10-11 February; Faro, Portugal, 8-9 July; Mallorca, Spain, 10-11 October), to discuss, among other subjects, the possibility of an expanded use of Gibraltar's airport, pension entitlements of Spanish workers who had worked in Gibraltar until 1969 and improvements in telephone communication between Gibraltar and Spain. According to joint statements made after the meetings, significant progress was made and all three participants hoped to convene a full ministerial meeting in the near future to transform the results of the negotiations into political decisions.

A later Secretariat working paper [A/AC.109/2006/9] reported that on 5 October, the United Kingdom representative had told the Fourth Committee, that his country welcomed the progress being made in the constitutional review process which begun in 2004 [YUN 2004, p. 605] between the United Kingdom and the 10 NSGTs, including Gibraltar, under its administration.

Gibraltar's Chief Minister, speaking before the Fourth Committee on 6 October, said that the position of the people of Gibraltar was that their homeland could be decolonized only through the exercise of their inalienable right to freely decide their own political future. The Committee, or Spain and the United Kingdom, could refer the matter to the International Court of Justice for an advisory opinion if they disagreed with that position. It was expected that Gibraltar's negotiations with the United Kingdom on a non-colonial constitution, endowing the people of Gibraltar with the greatest possible measure of self-government, would be concluded satisfactorily in early 2006. Gibraltar would continue to participate in the Trilateral Forum for Dialogue.

At that same meeting, Spain's representative said that, in the case of decisions properly taken bilaterally between Spain and the United Kingdom, it was understood that the latter country would not reach agreement without Gibraltar's consent, and with regard to the issue of Gibraltar's sovereignty, the aspirations and interest of the people of Gibraltar would be taken into account. The atmosphere of mutual confidence and cooperation that had been instituted meant that, as the Forum proceeded with its work, it would be possible to begin at the appropriate moment, to consider a definitive solution to the question of Gibraltar. The United Kingdom representative welcomed Spain's remarks, saying that issues related to Gibraltar could only be resolved in a climate of trust.

On 8 December (**decision 60/525**), the Assembly urged Spain and the United Kingdom, while listening to the interests and aspirations of Gibraltar, to reach, in the spirit of the 1984 statement on Gibraltar agreed to by both countries [YUN 1984, p. 1075], a definitive solution to the question of Gibraltar, in the light of relevant Assembly resolutions and applicable principles, and in the spirit of the UN Charter. It also welcomed the establishment of the new Tripartite Forum for Dialogue on Gibraltar, under the December 2004 statement [YUN 2004, p. 606], separate from the Brussels process.

New Caledonia

The Special Committee on decolonization considered the question of New Caledonia on 16 June [A/60/23]. Before it was a Secretariat working paper [A/AC.109/2005/13] describing the political situation and economic data and developments in the Territory.

A later Secretariat working paper [A/AC.109/2006/14] reported that, in January, following the 2004 elections [YUN 2004, p. 606], which ended the 25-year domination of the Caledonian Government by the Rassemblement pour la Calédonie dans la République (RPCR), which favoured integration with France (the administering Power), Jacques Lafleur resigned as RPCR President and was replaced by Pierre Frogier. A report by the French National Assembly indicated that the election results led to growing political divisions between a pro-independence North and an anti-independence South.

The Committee of signatories of the 1998 Nouméa Accord on New Caledonia's future status [YUN 1998, p. 574] met in Paris in January and discussed: the composition of the electorate for New Caledonian elections; the introduction of the euro; the 2006-2009 development arrangements; and the implications of the new census related to financial support for New Caledonia. In November, the pro-independence Union Calédonienne (UC) confirmed as its President, Pascal Naouna, a strong supporter of the fixed electoral body whereby only people born in New Caledonia could vote in the Territory. In contrast, the RPCR President, in October, had defended the "sliding" electoral body's provisions, whereby 10 years of residence would be sufficient for eligibility to vote in the independence referendum to be held between 2014 and 2019. In the same month, the Libération Kanak Socialiste party reaffirmed its opposition to those provisions, even for non-natives who would have resided in New Caledonia for 20 years on the date of the vote. Inter-ethnic strain between the Kanaks and settlers from the French territory of Wallis and Futuna continued to cause tension in New Caledonia.

Addressing the Fourth Committee on 10 October, Mr. Roch Wamytan, the Front de libération nationale kanak socialiste (FLNKS) representative, said that independence was his country's non-negotiable aim and FLNKS had signed the Nouméa

Accord with a view to ending colonial rule. He claimed that France continued to fund European settlement and metallurgical projects, while tax breaks stimulated immigration to the Territory's South Province, which could ultimately lead to the partition of New Caledonia. He said that the vote on the issue of voter eligibility in a future referendum on self-determination, which had been postponed to 2006, would likely be postponed indefinitely, owing to the upcoming French Presidential elections in 2007. During his visit in 2003 [YUN 2003, p. 612], French President Jacques Chirac promised to resolve the question of voter registration before the end of his term of office.

During the period under review, five country laws (lois du pays), which had the full force of law and could be contested only before the Constitutional Council, were adopted, the most recent relating to social, finance and customs issues and various tax laws.

GENERAL ASSEMBLY ACTION

On 8 December [meeting 62], the General Assembly, on the recommendation of the Fourth Committee [A/60/472], adopted **resolution 60/115** without vote [agenda item 26].

Question of New Caledonia

The General Assembly,

Having considered the question of New Caledonia,

Having examined the chapter of the report of the Special Committee on the Situation with regard to the Implementation of the Declaration on the Granting of Independence to Colonial Countries and Peoples relating to New Caledonia,

Reaffirming the right of peoples to self-determination as enshrined in the Charter of the United Nations,

Recalling General Assembly resolutions 1514(XV) of 14 December 1960 and 1541(XV) of 15 December 1960,

Noting the importance of the positive measures being pursued in New Caledonia by the French authorities, in cooperation with all sectors of the population, to promote political, economic and social development in the Territory, including measures in the area of environmental protection and action with respect to drug abuse and trafficking, in order to provide a framework for its peaceful progress to self-determination,

Noting also, in this context, the importance of equitable economic and social development, as well as continued dialogue among the parties involved in New Caledonia in the preparation of the act of self-determination of New Caledonia,

Noting with satisfaction the intensification of contacts between New Caledonia and neighbouring countries of the South Pacific region,

1. *Welcomes* the significant developments that have taken place in New Caledonia as exemplified by the signing of the Nouméa Accord of 5 May 1998 by the representatives of New Caledonia and the Government of France;

2. *Urges* all the parties involved, in the interest of all the people of New Caledonia, to maintain, in the framework of the Nouméa Accord, their dialogue in a spirit of harmony;

3. *Notes* the relevant provisions of the Nouméa Accord aimed at taking more broadly into account the Kanak identity in the political and social organization of New Caledonia, and also those provisions of the Accord relating to control of immigration and protection of local employment;

4. *Also notes* the relevant provisions of the Nouméa Accord to the effect that New Caledonia may become a member or associate member of certain international organizations, such as international organizations in the Pacific region, the United Nations, the United Nations Educational, Scientific and Cultural Organization and the International Labour Organization, according to their regulations;

5. *Further notes* the agreement between the signatories of the Nouméa Accord that the progress made in the emancipation process shall be brought to the attention of the United Nations;

6. *Welcomes* the fact that the administering Power invited to New Caledonia, at the time the new institutions were established, a mission of information which comprised representatives of countries of the Pacific region;

7. *Calls upon* the administering Power to continue to transmit to the Secretary-General information as required under Article 73 *e* of the Charter;

8. *Invites* all the parties involved to continue promoting a framework for the peaceful progress of the Territory towards an act of self-determination in which all options are open and which would safeguard the rights of all sectors of the population, according to the letter and the spirit of the Nouméa Accord, which is based on the principle that it is for the populations of New Caledonia to choose how to control their destiny;

9. *Welcomes* the measures that have been taken to strengthen and diversify the New Caledonian economy in all fields, and encourages further such measures in accordance with the spirit of the Matignon and Nouméa Accords;

10. *Also welcomes* the importance attached by the parties to the Matignon and Nouméa Accords to greater progress in housing, employment, training, education and health care in New Caledonia;

11. *Acknowledges* the contribution of the Melanesian Cultural Centre to the protection of the indigenous Kanak culture of New Caledonia;

12. *Notes* the positive initiatives aimed at protecting the natural environment of New Caledonia, notably the "Zonéco" operation designed to map and evaluate marine resources within the economic zone of New Caledonia;

13. *Acknowledges* the close links between New Caledonia and the peoples of the South Pacific and the positive actions being taken by the French and territorial authorities to facilitate the further development of those links, including the development of closer relations with the countries members of the Pacific Islands Forum;

14. *Welcomes,* in this regard, the accession by New Caledonia to the status of observer in the Pacific Islands Forum, continuing high-level visits to New Caledonia by delegations from countries of the Pacific region and high-level visits by delegations from New

Caledonia to countries members of the Pacific Islands Forum;

15. *Welcomes also* the cooperative attitude of other States and Territories in the region towards New Caledonia, its economic and political aspirations and its increasing participation in regional and international affairs and its intention to host the 2005 meeting of the Ministerial Committee of the Pacific Islands Forum;

16. *Decides* to keep under continuous review the process unfolding in New Caledonia as a result of the signing of the Nouméa Accord;

17. *Requests* the Special Committee on the Situation with regard to the Implementation of the Declaration on the Granting of Independence to Colonial Countries and Peoples to continue the examination of the question of the Non-Self-Governing Territory of New Caledonia and to report thereon to the General Assembly at its sixty-first session.

Tokelau

On 24 June, the Special Committee on decolonization considered the question of Tokelau (the three small atolls of Nukunonu, Fakaofo and Atafu in the South Pacific), administered by New Zealand [A/60/23]. Before it was a Secretariat working paper covering constitutional and political developments, and economic and social conditions in the Territory, and setting out the positions of New Zealand and Tokelau on the Territory's future status [A/AC.109/2005/3].

A later Secretariat working paper [A/AC.109/2006/10] reported that elections for Faipule (the representative of each village/atoll), Pulenuku (the mayor of each village/atoll) and General Fono (Tokelau's national representative body) were held in January. Pio Tuia was re-elected Faipule of Nukunonu and was installed as Ulu-o-Tokelau for the year (titular head of the Territory, a position that was rotated annually among the three Faipule). Kolouei O'Brien and Kuresa Nasau were also re-elected Faipule of Fakaofo and Atafu, respectively.

In August, the General Fono endorsed Tokelau's draft constitution; approved the text of a draft treaty of free association between Tokelau and New Zealand as a basis for an act of self-determination; and appointed a translation committee and a referendum commission. In November, it approved the translations of the draft constitution and draft treaty, as well as the draft referendum rules, including a closing date of 23 December for voter registration. It set 11 to 15 February 2006 as the dates for the referendum; agreed that an overall majority of two thirds of the valid votes cast would be required for a change of Tokelau's status; and decided that the voting should take place sequentially in Apia, and on the three atolls.

New Zealand, on behalf of itself and Tokelau, formally invited the United Nations to monitor the act of self-determination and indicated that the presence of representatives of the Special Committee would also be welcome.

Speaking before the Special Committee on decolonization on 24 June, the Administrator of New Zealand noted that the previous 12 months had seen an intensification of work on all fronts, including a series of regional and international meetings and the signing of a new three-year agreement between Tokelau and New Zealand on economic support for the Territory. Work was well advanced on legislative amendments that would be required in New Zealand to give effect to Tokelau's decision to become self-governing. Tokelau, which retained the option of revisiting the question of its status in the future, faced extreme challenges owing to its small size, isolation and lack of natural resources, and would need support from the international community. New Zealand hoped that Member States would help build the Tokelau International Trust Fund, established in 2004 [YUN 2004, p. 608], to a level where it could provide an independent source of revenue to future generations. To that end, the United Nations Development Programme (UNDP) would facilitate a donors' round-table meeting for the Trust Fund in New York after the act of self-determination. The Administrator also announced a further contribution by New Zealand of 7.5 million New Zealand dollars to the Fund, which was welcomed by the Ulu-o-Tokelau, who also hoped that the international community would be equally generous.

GENERAL ASSEMBLY ACTION

On 8 December [meeting 62], the General Assembly, on the recommendation of the Fourth Committee [A/60/472], adopted **resolution 60/116** without vote [agenda item 26].

Question of Tokelau

The General Assembly,

Having considered the question of Tokelau,

Having examined the chapter of the report of the Special Committee on the Situation with regard to the Implementation of the Declaration on the Granting of Independence to Colonial Countries and Peoples relating to Tokelau,

Recalling General Assembly resolution 1514(XV) of 14 December 1960, containing the Declaration on the Granting of Independence to Colonial Countries and Peoples, and all resolutions and decisions of the United Nations relating to Non-Self-Governing Territories, in particular Assembly resolution 59/133 of 10 December 2004,

Noting with appreciation the continuing exemplary cooperation of New Zealand as the administering Power with regard to the work of the Special Committee relating to Tokelau and its readiness to permit access by United Nations visiting missions to the Territory,

Noting also with appreciation the collaborative contribution to the development of Tokelau by New Zealand and the specialized agencies and other organizations of the United Nations system, in particular the United Nations Development Programme,

Recalling the inauguration in 1999 of a national legislative body, the General Fono, based on village elections by universal adult suffrage and the assumption by that body in June 2003 of full responsibility for the Tokelau budget,

Recalling also the report of the United Nations mission dispatched in August 2002 to Tokelau at the invitation of the Government of New Zealand and the representatives of Tokelau,

Noting that, as a small island Territory, Tokelau exemplifies the situation of most remaining Non-Self-Governing Territories and that, as a case study pointing to successful cooperation for decolonization, Tokelau has wider significance for the United Nations as it seeks to complete its work in decolonization,

Recalling that New Zealand and Tokelau signed in November 2003 a document entitled "Joint statement of the principles of partnership", which sets out in writing, for the first time, the rights and obligations of the two partner countries,

Bearing in mind the decision of the General Fono at its meeting in November 2003, following extensive consultations undertaken in all three villages, to explore formally with New Zealand the option of self-government in free association, and its decision in August 2005 to hold a referendum on self-government on the basis of a draft constitution for Tokelau and a treaty of free association with New Zealand,

1. *Notes* that Tokelau remains firmly committed to the development of self-government and to an act of self-determination that would result in Tokelau assuming a status in accordance with the options on future status for Non-Self-Governing Territories contained in principle VI of the annex to General Assembly resolution 1541(XV) of 15 December 1960;

2. *Welcomes* the substantial progress made towards the devolution of power to the three taupulega (village councils), in particular the delegation of the Administrator's powers to the three taupulega with effect from 1 July 2004 and the assumption by each taupulega from that date of full responsibility for the management of all its public services;

3. *Recalls* the decision of the General Fono in November 2003, following extensive consultations in all three villages and a meeting of the Special Committee on the Constitution of Tokelau, to explore formally with New Zealand the option of self-government in free association, and the discussions between Tokelau and New Zealand pursuant to the General Fono decision;

4. *Welcomes* the decision of the General Fono in August 2005 to hold a referendum on self-government on the basis of a draft constitution for Tokelau and a treaty of free association with New Zealand, and notes the General Fono's enactment of rules for the referendum;

5. *Notes* that it is the wish of Tokelau, supported by New Zealand, that the United Nations monitor the referendum;

6. *Acknowledges* Tokelau's initiative in devising a strategic economic development plan for the period 2002-2004 to advance its capacity for self-government,

and notes that a plan for the period 2005-2007 has been finalized;

7. *Also acknowledges* the continuing assistance that New Zealand has committed to promoting Tokelau's welfare, as well as the cooperation of the United Nations Development Programme, including the relief and recovery assistance provided in the aftermath of Cyclone Percy earlier this year;

8. *Further acknowledges* Tokelau's need for continued reassurance, given the cultural adjustments that are taking place with the strengthening of its capacity for self-government and, since local resources cannot adequately cover the material side of self-determination, the ongoing responsibility of Tokelau's external partners to assist Tokelau in balancing its desire to be self-reliant to the greatest extent possible with its need for external assistance;

9. *Welcomes* the establishment of the Tokelau International Trust Fund to support the future development needs of Tokelau and the facilitation of this process through a donor round table to be convened by the United Nations Development Programme following an act of self-determination by Tokelau, and calls upon Member States and international and regional agencies to announce contributions to the Fund and thereby lend practical support to assist this emerging country in overcoming the problems of smallness, isolation and lack of resources;

10. *Also welcomes* the assurance of the Government of New Zealand that it will meet its obligations to the United Nations with respect to Tokelau and abide by the freely expressed wishes of the people of Tokelau with regard to their future status;

11. *Further welcomes* the cooperative attitude of the other States and territories in the region towards Tokelau, its economic and political aspirations and its increasing participation in regional and international affairs;

12. *Welcomes* the associate membership of Tokelau in the United Nations Educational, Scientific and Cultural Organization, its recent accession to membership in the Forum Fisheries Agency and its application for observer status at the Pacific Islands Forum and associate membership in the South Pacific Applied Geoscience Commission;

13. *Calls upon* the administering Power and United Nations agencies to continue to provide assistance to Tokelau as it further develops its economy and governance structures in the context of its ongoing constitutional evolution;

14. *Welcomes* the actions taken by the administering Power to transmit information regarding the political, economic and social situation of Tokelau to the Secretary-General;

15. *Notes with satisfaction* the successful visit to Tokelau in October 2004 by the Chairman of the Special Committee on the Situation with regard to the Implementation of the Declaration on the Granting of Independence to Colonial Countries and Peoples to attend the workshop of the Tokelauan Special Committee on the Constitution;

16. *Notes* the considerable progress made towards the adoption of a Constitution and of national symbols by Tokelau, the steps taken by Tokelau and New Zealand to agree to a draft treaty of free association as a basis for an act of self-determination and the strong

support expressed by Tokelauan communities in New Zealand for the move by Tokelau towards self-determination;

17. *Welcomes* the invitation extended by the representatives of Tokelau and the administering Power to the United Nations to monitor an act of self-determination by Tokelau;

18. *Requests* the Special Committee to continue to examine the question of the Non-Self-Governing Territory of Tokelau and to report thereon to the General Assembly at its sixty-first session.

Western Sahara

The Special Committee on decolonization considered the question of Western Sahara on 8 June [A/60/23]. A Secretariat working paper [A/AC.109/2005/2] detailed the Secretary-General's good offices with the parties concerned and actions taken by the General Assembly and Security Council (see p. 363). The Special Committee transmitted the relevant documentation to the Assembly's sixtieth (2005) session to facilitate the Fourth Committee's consideration of the question. The Secretary-General's report was submitted to the Assembly in July [A/60/116].

Island Territories

In June, the Special Committee on decolonization [A/60/23] considered working papers on American Samoa [A/AC.109/2005/15], Anguilla [A/AC.109/2005/4], Bermuda [A/AC.109/2005/5], the British Virgin Islands [A/AC.109/2005/12], the Cayman Islands [A/AC.109/2005/6], Guam [A/AC.109/2005/7], Montserrat [A/AC.109/2005/16], Pitcairn [A/AC.109/2005/10], Saint Helena [A/AC.109/2005/14], the Turks and Caicos Islands [A/AC.109/2005/8] and the United States Virgin Islands [A/AC.109/2005/9], describing political developments and economic and social conditions in each of those 11 island Territories. On 20 June, the Committee approved a two-part consolidated draft resolution for adoption by the General Assembly (see below).

GENERAL ASSEMBLY ACTION

On 8 December [meeting 62], the General Assembly, on the recommendation of the Fourth Committee [A/60/472], adopted **resolutions 60/117 A** and **B** without vote [agenda item 26].

Questions of American Samoa, Anguilla, Bermuda, the British Virgin Islands, the Cayman Islands, Guam, Montserrat, Pitcairn, Saint Helena, the Turks and Caicos Islands and the United States Virgin Islands

A

General

The General Assembly,

Having considered the questions of the Non-Self-Governing Territories of American Samoa, Anguilla, Bermuda, the British Virgin Islands, the Cayman Islands, Guam, Montserrat, Pitcairn, Saint Helena, the Turks and Caicos Islands and the United States Virgin Islands, hereinafter referred to as "the Territories",

Having examined the relevant chapter of the report of the Special Committee on the Situation with regard to the Implementation of the Declaration on the Granting of Independence to Colonial Countries and Peoples,

Recalling all resolutions and decisions of the United Nations relating to those Territories, including, in particular, the resolutions adopted by the General Assembly at its fifty-ninth session on the individual Territories covered by the present resolution,

Recognizing that all available options for self-determination of the Territories are valid as long as they are in accordance with the freely expressed wishes of the peoples concerned and in conformity with the clearly defined principles contained in resolutions 1514(XV) of 14 December 1960, 1541(XV) of 15 December 1960 and other resolutions of the Assembly,

Recalling General Assembly resolution 1541(XV), containing the principles that should guide Member States in determining whether or not an obligation exists to transmit the information called for under Article 73 *e* of the Charter of the United Nations,

Expressing its concern that more than forty-four years after the adoption of the Declaration there still remain a number of Non-Self-Governing Territories,

Conscious of the importance of continuing effective implementation of the Declaration, taking into account the target set by the United Nations to eradicate colonialism by 2010 and the plan of action for the Second International Decade for the Eradication of Colonialism,

Recognizing that the specific characteristics and the sentiments of the peoples of the Territories require flexible, practical and innovative approaches to the options of self-determination, without any prejudice to territorial size, geographical location, size of population or natural resources,

Taking note of the stated position of the Government of the United Kingdom of Great Britain and Northern Ireland on the Non-Self-Governing Territories under its administration,

Taking note also of the stated position of the Government of the United States of America on the Non-Self-Governing Territories under its administration,

Taking note further of the stated positions of the representatives of the Non-Self-Governing Territories before the Special Committee and in its regional seminars,

Noting the constitutional developments in some Non-Self-Governing Territories about which the Special Committee has received information,

Aware of the importance both to the Territories and to the Special Committee of the participation of elected and appointed representatives of the Territories in the work of the Special Committee,

Convinced that the wishes and aspirations of the peoples of the Territories should continue to guide the development of their future political status and that referendums, free and fair elections and other forms of popular consultation play an important role in ascertaining the wishes and aspirations of the people,

Convinced also that any negotiations to determine the status of a Territory must take place with the active involvement and participation of the people of that Territory, under the supervision of the United Nations, on a case-by-case basis, and that the views of the peoples of the Non-Self-Governing Territories in respect of their right to self-determination should be ascertained,

Aware of the importance of international financial services for the economies of some of the Non-Self-Governing Territories,

Noting the continued cooperation of the Non-Self-Governing Territories at the local and regional levels, including their participation in the work of regional organizations,

Mindful that United Nations visiting missions provide an effective means of ascertaining the situation in the Territories, that some Territories have not received a United Nations visiting mission for a long time and that no visiting missions have been sent to some of the Territories, and considering the possibility of sending further visiting missions to the Territories at an appropriate time and in consultation with the administering Powers,

Mindful also that, in order for the Special Committee to enhance its understanding of the political status of the peoples of the Territories and to fulfil its mandate effectively, it is important for it to be apprised by the administering Powers and to receive information from other appropriate sources, including the representatives of the Territories, concerning the wishes and aspirations of the peoples of the Territories,

Recognizing the need for the Special Committee to embark actively on a public awareness campaign aimed at assisting the peoples of the Territories in gaining an understanding of the options of self-determination,

Mindful, in this connection, that the holding of regional seminars in the Caribbean and Pacific regions and at Headquarters and other venues, with the active participation of representatives of the Non-Self-Governing Territories, provides a helpful means for the Special Committee to fulfil its mandate, and that the regional nature of the seminars, which alternate between the Caribbean and the Pacific, is a crucial element in their success, while recognizing the need for reviewing the role of those seminars in the context of a United Nations programme for ascertaining the political status of the Territories,

Mindful also that, by holding a Caribbean regional seminar in Canouan, Saint Vincent and the Grenadines, from 17 to 19 May 2005, the Special Committee was able to hear the views of the representatives of the Territories and Member States as well as organizations and experts in the region, in order to review the political, economic and social conditions in the Territories,

Conscious of the particular vulnerability of the Territories to natural disasters and environmental degradation and, in this connection, bearing in mind the applicability to the territories of the programmes of action of the United Nations Conference on Environment and Development, the World Conference on Natural Disaster Reduction, the Global Conference on the Sustainable Development of Small Island Developing States, the International Conference on Population and Development, the United Nations Conference on Human Settlements (Habitat II), the World Summit on Sustainable Development, the World Conference against Racism, Racial Discrimination, Xenophobia and Related Intolerance and other relevant United Nations world conferences and summits,

Noting with appreciation the contribution to the development of some Territories by specialized agencies and other organizations of the United Nations system, in particular the United Nations Development Programme, the Economic Commission for Latin America and the Caribbean and the Economic and Social Commission for Asia and the Pacific, as well as regional institutions such as the Caribbean Development Bank, the Caribbean Community, the Organization of Eastern Caribbean States, the Pacific Islands Forum and the agencies of the Council of Regional Organizations in the Pacific,

Aware that the Human Rights Committee, as part of its mandate under the International Covenant on Civil and Political Rights, reviews the status of the self-determination process of small island Territories under examination by the Special Committee,

Recalling the ongoing efforts of the Special Committee in carrying out a critical review of its work with the aim of making appropriate and constructive recommendations and decisions to attain its objectives in accordance with its mandate,

1. *Reaffirms* the inalienable right of the peoples of the Territories to self-determination, in conformity with the Charter of the United Nations and with General Assembly resolution 1514(XV), containing the Declaration on the Granting of Independence to Colonial Countries and Peoples;

2. *Reaffirms also* that, in the process of decolonization, there is no alternative to the principle of self-determination, which is also a fundamental human right, as recognized under the relevant human rights conventions;

3. *Reaffirms further* that it is ultimately for the peoples of the Territories themselves to determine freely their future political status in accordance with the relevant provisions of the Charter, the Declaration and the relevant resolutions of the General Assembly, and in that connection reiterates its long-standing call for the administering Powers, in cooperation with the territorial Governments, to promote political education in the Territories in order to foster an awareness among the people of their right to self-determination in conformity with the legitimate political status options, based on the principles clearly defined in General Assembly resolution 1541(XV);

4. *Requests* the administering Powers to transmit regularly to the Secretary-General information called for under Article 73 *e* of the Charter;

5. *Stresses* the importance of the Special Committee on the Situation with regard to the Implementation of the Declaration on the Granting of Independence to Colonial Countries and Peoples being apprised of the views and wishes of the peoples of the Territories and enhancing its understanding of their conditions, including the nature and scope of the existing political and constitutional arrangements between the Non-Self-Governing Territories and their respective administering Powers;

6. *Reaffirms* the responsibility of the administering Powers under the Charter to promote the economic

and social development and to preserve the cultural identity of the Territories, and recommends that priority continue to be given, in consultation with the territorial Governments concerned, to the strengthening and diversification of their respective economies;

7. *Requests* the Special Committee to continue to follow closely the developments in legislation in the area of international financial services and their impact on the economy in some of the Territories;

8. *Requests* the Territories and the administering Powers to take all necessary measures to protect and conserve the environment of the Territories under their administration against any environmental degradation, and once again requests the specialized agencies concerned to continue to monitor environmental conditions in those Territories;

9. *Welcomes* the participation of the Non-Self-Governing Territories in regional activities, including the work of regional organizations;

10. *Stresses* the importance of implementing the plan of action for the Second International Decade for the Eradication of Colonialism, in particular by expediting the application of the work programme for the decolonization of each Non-Self-Governing Territory, on a case-by-case basis and by completing the periodic analyses of the progress and extent of the implementation of the Declaration in each Territory;

11. *Invites* the administering Powers to participate fully in the work of the Special Committee in order to implement the provisions of Article 73 *e* of the Charter and the Declaration and in order to advise the Special Committee on the implementation of provisions under Article 73 *b* of the Charter on efforts to promote self-government in the Territories;

12. *Urges* Member States to contribute to the efforts of the United Nations to usher in a world free of colonialism within the Second International Decade for the Eradication of Colonialism, and calls upon them to continue to give their full support to the Special Committee in its endeavours towards that noble goal;

13. *Notes* that some Non-Self-Governing Territories have expressed concern at the procedure followed by one administering Power, contrary to the wishes of the Territories themselves, namely, of amending or enacting legislation for the Territories through Orders in Council, in order to apply to the Territories the international treaty obligations of the administering Power;

14. *Takes note* of the constitutional reviews in the Territories administered by the United Kingdom of Great Britain and Northern Ireland, led by the territorial Governments and designed to address the internal constitutional structure within the present territorial arrangement;

15. *Also takes note* of the report of the Secretary-General on the midterm review of the Second International Decade for the Eradication of Colonialism, and requests the Secretary-General to report to the General Assembly at its sixty-first session on the implementation of decolonization resolutions adopted since the declaration of the Second International Decade;

16. *Requests* the Special Committee to collaborate with the Human Rights Committee within the framework of its mandate on the right to self-determination as contained in the International Covenant on Civil and Political Rights with the aim of exchanging information, given that the Committee reviews political and constitutional developments in many of the Non-Self-Governing Territories that are under review by the Special Committee;

17. *Also requests* the Special Committee to continue to examine the question of the Non-Self-Governing Territories and to report thereon to the General Assembly at its sixty-first session.

B

Individual Territories

The General Assembly,

Referring to resolution A above,

I

American Samoa

Taking note of the position of the administering Power and the statements of representatives of American Samoa made in the regional seminars expressing satisfaction with the Territory's present relationship with the United States of America,

Noting that the Government of the Territory continues to take steps to increase revenues and decrease government expenditures,

Noting also that the Territory, similar to isolated communities with limited funds, continues to experience a lack of adequate medical and other infrastructural facilities,

1. *Notes* that the Department of the Interior of the United States of America provides that the Secretary of the Interior has administrative jurisdiction over American Samoa;

2. *Calls upon* the administering Power to continue to assist the territorial Government in the economic and social development of the Territory, including measures to rebuild financial management capabilities and strengthen other governmental functions of the Government of the Territory, and welcomes the assistance from the administering Power to the Territory in its recovery efforts following the recent floods;

3. *Welcomes* the invitation extended to the Special Committee on the Situation with regard to the Implementation of the Declaration on the Granting of Independence to Colonial Countries and Peoples by the Governor of American Samoa and reiterated, most recently at the Caribbean regional seminar held in Canouan, Saint Vincent and the Grenadines, from 17 to 19 May 2005, to send a visiting mission to the Territory, calls upon the administering Power to facilitate such a mission, and requests the Chairman of the Special Committee to take all the necessary steps to that end;

4. *Takes note* of the statement of the representative of the Governor of the Territory at the Caribbean regional seminar requesting the Special Committee to provide information on the process of self-governance;

II

Anguilla

Taking note of the constitutional review process led by the territorial Government,

Recalling the holding of the 2003 Caribbean regional seminar in Anguilla, the first time that the seminar has been held in a Non-Self-Governing Territory,

Noting the desire of the territorial Government and the people of Anguilla for a visiting mission by the Special Committee,

Aware of the efforts of the Government of Anguilla to continue to develop the Territory as a viable offshore centre and well-regulated financial centre for investors by enacting modern company and trust laws, as well as partnership and insurance legislation, and computerizing the company registry system,

1. *Welcomes* the constitutional review process led by the Government of Anguilla in cooperation with the administering Power;

2. *Recalls* the cooperation of the territorial Government of Anguilla and the United Kingdom of Great Britain and Northern Ireland in holding the 2003 Caribbean regional seminar in Anguilla, and notes that the staging of the seminar in a Non-Self-Governing Territory for the first time, as well as a town hall meeting between the people of Anguilla and the Special Committee during the seminar, contributed to its success;

III

Bermuda

Noting the results of the independence referendum held on 16 August 1995, conscious of the different viewpoints of the political parties of the Territory on the future status of the Territory, and aware of the active boycott of the referendum by the then-opposition party,

Noting also the statement of the Premier of Bermuda in his Founder's Day address that there could never be a true democracy as long as the country remains a colony or an overseas dependent Territory, and that only with independence can national unity be forged and pride in being Bermudian fully developed,

1. *Welcomes* the agreement reached in June 2002 between the United States of America, the United Kingdom of Great Britain and Northern Ireland and the Territory formally transferring the former military base lands to the territorial Government, and the provision of financial resources to address some of the environmental problems;

2. *Also welcomes* the dispatch of the United Nations special mission to Bermuda at the request of the territorial Government and with the concurrence of the administering Power, which provided information to the people of the Territory on the role of the United Nations in the process of self-determination, on the legitimate political status options as clearly defined in General Assembly resolution 1541(XV) and on the experiences of other small States that have achieved a full measure of self-government;

3. *Decides* to follow closely the public consultations on the future political status of Bermuda under way in the Territory, and requests the relevant United Nations organizations to provide assistance to the Territory, if requested, in the context of its public education programme;

IV

British Virgin Islands

Taking note of the constitutional review process led by the territorial Government,

Noting that the Territory continues to emerge as one of the world's leading offshore financial centres,

1. *Welcomes* the constitutional review process led by the Government of the British Virgin Islands in cooperation with the administering Power;

2. *Takes note* of the statement made by the representative of the Legislative Council of the Territory at the Caribbean regional seminar held in Canouan, Saint Vincent and the Grenadines, from 17 to 19 May 2005, who presented an analysis of the internal constitutional review process;

3. *Welcomes* the establishment of the Inter-Virgin Islands Council between the elected Governments of the British Virgin Islands and the United States Virgin Islands as a mechanism for functional cooperation between the two neighbouring Territories and the subsequent creation of eleven standing committees on natural resources management, mutual disaster preparedness and assistance and constitutional development, among other areas;

V

Cayman Islands

Taking note of the constitutional review process led by the territorial Government,

Noting the approval by the Cayman Islands Legislative Assembly of the Territory's Vision 2008 Development Plan, which aims to promote development that is consistent with the aims and values of Caymanian society,

1. *Welcomes* the continuing constitutional review process led by the Government of the Cayman Islands in cooperation with the administering Power;

2. *Takes note* of the statement made by the representative of the Non-Governmental Organizations Constitutional Working Group of the Cayman Islands Chamber of Commerce at the Caribbean regional seminar held in Canouan, Saint Vincent and the Grenadines, from 17 to 19 May 2005, which called for a comprehensive educational programme, to be defined by the Special Committee, on the issue of self-determination, as well as a visiting mission to the Territory;

VI

Guam

Recalling that, in a referendum held in 1987, the registered and eligible voters of Guam endorsed a draft Guam Commonwealth Act that would establish a new framework for relations between the Territory and the administering Power, providing for a greater measure of internal self-government for Guam and recognition of the right of the Chamorro people of Guam to self-determination for the Territory,

Recalling also the requests by the elected representatives and non-governmental organizations of the Territory that Guam not be removed from the list of the Non-Self-Governing Territories with which the Special Committee is concerned, pending the self-determination of the Chamorro people and taking into account their legitimate rights and interests,

Aware that negotiations between the administering Power and the territorial Government on the draft Guam Commonwealth Act are no longer continuing and that Guam has established the process for a self-determination vote by the eligible Chamorro voters,

Cognizant that the administering Power continues to implement its programme of transferring surplus federal land to the Government of Guam,

Noting that the people of the Territory have called for reform in the programme of the administering Power with respect to the thorough, unconditional and expeditious transfer of land property to the people of Guam,

Conscious that immigration into Guam has resulted in the indigenous Chamorros becoming a minority in their homeland,

Aware of the potential for diversifying and developing the economy of Guam through commercial fishing and agriculture and other viable activities,

Recalling the dispatch in 1979 of a United Nations visiting mission to the Territory, and noting the recommendation of the 1996 Pacific regional seminar for sending a visiting mission to Guam,

1. *Calls upon* the administering Power to take into consideration the expressed will of the Chamorro people as supported by Guam voters in the plebiscite of 1987 and as provided for in Guam law, encourages the administering Power and the territorial Government of Guam to enter into negotiations on the matter, and requests the administering Power to inform the Secretary-General of progress to that end;

2. *Requests* the administering Power to continue to assist the elected territorial Government in achieving its political, economic and social goals;

3. *Also requests* the administering Power, in cooperation with the territorial Government, to continue to transfer land to the original landowners of the Territory;

4. *Further requests* the administering Power to continue to recognize and respect the political rights and the cultural and ethnic identity of the Chamorro people of Guam, and to take all necessary measures to respond to the concerns of the territorial Government with regard to the question of immigration;

5. *Requests* the administering Power to cooperate in establishing programmes specifically intended to promote the sustainable development of economic activities and enterprises, noting the special role of the Chamorro people in the development of Guam;

6. *Also requests* the administering Power to continue to support appropriate measures by the territorial Government aimed at promoting growth in commercial fishing and agricultural and other viable activities;

VII

Montserrat

Taking note with interest of the statements made and the information on the political and economic situation in Montserrat provided by the Chief Minister of the Territory to the Caribbean regional seminar, held at The Valley, Anguilla, from 20 to 22 May 2003,

Noting with concern the dire consequences of a volcanic eruption, which led to the evacuation of three quarters of the Territory's population to safe areas of the island and to areas outside the Territory, in particular Antigua and Barbuda and the United Kingdom of Great Britain and Northern Ireland, and which continues to have enduring consequences for the economy of the island,

Welcoming the continued assistance provided to the Territory by States members of the Caribbean Community, in particular Antigua and Barbuda, which has offered safe refuge and access to educational and

health facilities, as well as employment for thousands who have left the Territory,

Noting the continuing efforts of the administering Power to deal with the consequences of the volcanic eruption,

Noting with concern that a number of the inhabitants of the Territory continue to live in shelters because of volcanic activity,

Taking note of the constitutional review process led by the territorial Government,

1. *Calls upon* the administering Power, the specialized agencies and other organizations of the United Nations system, as well as regional and other organizations, to continue to provide assistance to the Territory in alleviating the consequences of the volcanic eruption;

2. *Welcomes* the continuing constitutional review process led by the Government of Montserrat in cooperation with the administering Power;

VIII

Pitcairn

Taking into account the unique nature of Pitcairn in terms of population and area,

Requests the administering Power to continue its assistance for the improvement of the economic, social, educational and other conditions of the population of the Territory and to continue its discussions with the representatives of Pitcairn on how best to support their economic security;

IX

Saint Helena

Taking into account the unique character of Saint Helena, its population and its natural resources,

Taking note of the constitutional review process led by the territorial Government and the consultative poll with regard to a new Constitution held in Saint Helena on 25 May 2005,

Aware of the efforts of the administering Power and the territorial authorities to improve the socio-economic conditions of the population of Saint Helena, in particular in the sphere of food production, continuing high unemployment and limited transport and communications,

Noting the importance of improving the infrastructure and accessibility of Saint Helena,

Noting also the importance of the right to nationality for Saint Helenians and their request that it, in principle, be included in the new Constitution,

Noting with concern the problem of unemployment on the island and the joint action of the administering Power and the territorial Government to deal with it,

1. *Welcomes* the continuing constitutional review process and the recent consultative poll led by the Government of Saint Helena in cooperation with the administering Power;

2. *Also welcomes* the decision by the administering Power to provide funding for the construction of an international airport on Saint Helena to become operational in 2010, including all required infrastructure;

3. *Requests* the administering Power and relevant international organizations to continue to support the efforts of the territorial Government to address the socio-economic development challenges, including the high unemployment and the limited transport and commu-

nications problems, as well as to support the additional infrastructure required for the airport project;

4. *Calls upon* the administering Power to take into account the concerns of Saint Helenians with regard to the right to nationality;

X

Turks and Caicos Islands

Noting the results of the general election held in April 2003,

Noting with concern the vulnerability of the Territory to drug trafficking and related activities, as well as its problems caused by illegal immigration and the need for continued cooperation between the administering Power and the territorial Government in countering drug trafficking and money-laundering,

Taking note of the constitutional review process led by the territorial Government,

1. *Welcomes* the continuing constitutional review process led by the Government of the Turks and Caicos Islands in cooperation with the administering Power;

2. *Takes note* of the statement made by the Chief Minister of the Territory at the Caribbean regional seminar held in Canouan, Saint Vincent and the Grenadines, from 17 to 19 May 2005, that his Government was in favour of a reasonable period of full internal self-government before moving to independence;

XI

United States Virgin Islands

Taking note with interest of the statements made and the information provided by the representative of the Governor of the Territory at the Caribbean regional seminar held in Canouan, Saint Vincent and the Grenadines, from 17 to 19 May 2005,

Noting the continuing interest of the territorial Government in seeking associate membership in the Organization of Eastern Caribbean States and observer status in the Caribbean Community and the pending request by the Territory to the administering Power for the delegation of authority to proceed, as well as the 2003 resolution of the territorial legislature in support of that request,

Noting also the expressed interest of the territorial Government to be included in regional programmes of the United Nations Development Programme,

Noting further the necessity of further diversifying the economy of the Territory and the efforts of the Government of the Territory to promote the Territory as an offshore financial services centre,

Recalling that the Territory has not received a United Nations visiting mission since 1977, and bearing in mind the formal request of the Territory for such a mission in 1993 to assist the Territory in its political education process and to observe the Territory's only referendum on political status options in its history,

Noting the stated position of the elected Government of the Territory in opposition to legislation presently before the Congress of the administering Power to appoint a chief financial officer against the wishes of the elected Government of the Territory, and bearing in mind resolution 1664 of 17 December 2003 adopted by the Legislature of the Territory at its twenty-fifth session, in which the Legislature opposed the proposal and indicated that it would retard political and civil progress,

Noting also the ongoing cooperation between the territorial Government and Denmark on the exchange of artefacts and archives,

1. *Requests* the administering Power to continue to assist the territorial Government in achieving its political, economic and social goals;

2. *Once again requests* the administering Power to facilitate the participation of the Territory, as appropriate, in various organizations, in particular the Organization of Eastern Caribbean States, the Caribbean Community and the Association of Caribbean States;

3. *Calls for* the inclusion of the Territory in regional programmes of the United Nations Development Programme, consistent with the participation of other Non-Self-Governing Territories;

4. *Welcomes* the establishment of the Inter–Virgin Islands Council between the elected Governments of the United States Virgin Islands and the British Virgin Islands and as a mechanism of functional cooperation between the two neighbouring Territories, and the subsequent creation of eleven standing committees on natural resources management, mutual disaster preparedness and assistance, constitutional development, among other areas;

5. *Calls upon* the administering Power to refrain from enacting any legislative or other measures that would reduce the authority of the elected Government of the Territory to control its own financial affairs;

6. *Notes* the position of the territorial Government, including its articulation in resolution 1609 of 9 April 2001, adopted by the Legislature of the Territory at its twenty-fourth session, of its opposition to the assumption by the administering Power of submerged land in territorial waters, having regard to relevant resolutions of the General Assembly on the ownership and control of natural resources, including marine resources, by the people of the Non-Self-Governing Territories, and its calls for the return of those marine resources within its jurisdiction;

7. *Notes with appreciation* the cooperation agreements existing between the Territory and Denmark, the former colonial Power of the Territory, on the exchange of artefacts and the repatriation of archival material, consistent with the Durban Declaration and Programme of Action adopted by the World Conference against Racism, Racial Discrimination, Xenophobia and Related Intolerance on 8 September 2001, and once again requests the United Nations Educational, Scientific and Cultural Organization, under its records and archives management programme, to assist the Territory in carrying out its artefacts and archival initiative.

Information

UN public information

The General Assembly's Committee on Information, at its twenty-seventh session (New York, 18 April–3 May) [A/60/21], continued to consider UN information policies and activities and to evaluate and follow up efforts made and progress achieved in information and communications.

The major report before the Committee dealt with the reorientation of UN activities in public information and communications. The Committee also considered reports on the rationalization of the network of UN information centres (UNICs); modernization and integrated management of UN libraries, including the 2004 Office of Internal Oversight Services (OIOS) report on the topic [YUN 2004, p. 627]; the 2004 activities of the United Nations Communications Group (UNCG) [YUN 2004, p. 629]; and progress towards parity among the official languages on the UN website.

Those issues and the Secretary-General's report on questions relating to information [A/60/173] are discussed in the relevant sections below.

By **decision 60/524** of 8 December, the Assembly increased the Committee's membership from 107 to 108.

GENERAL ASSEMBLY ACTION

On 8 December [meeting 62], the General Assembly, on the recommendation of the Fourth Committee [A/60/479], adopted **resolutions 60/109 A** and **B** without vote [agenda item 33].

Questions relating to information

A

Information in the service of humanity

The General Assembly,

Taking note of the comprehensive and important report of the Committee on Information,

Also taking note of the report of the Secretary-General on questions relating to information,

Urges all countries, organizations of the United Nations system as a whole and all others concerned, reaffirming their commitment to the principles of the Charter of the United Nations and to the principles of freedom of the press and freedom of information, as well as to those of the independence, pluralism and diversity of the media, deeply concerned by the disparities existing between developed and developing countries and the consequences of every kind arising from those disparities that affect the capability of the public, private or other media and individuals in developing countries to disseminate information and communicate their views and their cultural and ethical values through endogenous cultural production, as well as to ensure the diversity of sources and their free access to information, and recognizing the call in this context for what in the United Nations and at various international forums has been termed "a new world information and communication order, seen as an evolving and continuous process":

(a) To cooperate and interact with a view to reducing existing disparities in information flows at all levels by increasing assistance for the development of communication infrastructures and capabilities in developing countries, with due regard for their needs and the priorities attached to such areas by those countries, and in order to enable them and the public,

private or other media in developing countries to develop their own information and communication policies freely and independently and increase the participation of media and individuals in the communication process, and to ensure a free flow of information at all levels;

(b) To ensure for journalists the free and effective performance of their professional tasks and condemn resolutely all attacks against them;

(c) To provide support for the continuation and strengthening of practical training programmes for broadcasters and journalists from public, private and other media in developing countries;

(d) To enhance regional efforts and cooperation among developing countries, as well as cooperation between developed and developing countries, to strengthen communication capacities and to improve the media infrastructure and communication technology in the developing countries, especially in the areas of training and dissemination of information;

(e) To aim at, in addition to bilateral cooperation, providing all possible support and assistance to the developing countries and their media, public, private or other, with due regard to their interests and needs in the field of information and to action already adopted within the United Nations system, including:

  (i) The development of the human and technical resources that are indispensable for the improvement of information and communication systems in developing countries and support for the continuation and strengthening of practical training programmes, such as those already operating under both public and private auspices throughout the developing world;

  (ii) The creation of conditions that will enable developing countries and their media, public, private or other, to have, by using their national and regional resources, the communication technology suited to their national needs, as well as the necessary programme material, especially for radio and television broadcasting;

  (iii) Assistance in establishing and promoting telecommunication links at the subregional, regional and interregional levels, especially among developing countries;

  (iv) The facilitation, as appropriate, of access by the developing countries to advanced communication technology available on the open market;

(f) To provide full support for the International Programme for the Development of Communication of the United Nations Educational, Scientific and Cultural Organization, which should support both public and private media.

B

United Nations public information policies and activities

The General Assembly,

Emphasizing the role of the Committee on Information as its main subsidiary body mandated to make recommendations to it relating to the work of the Department of Public Information of the Secretariat,

Reaffirming its resolution 13(I) of 13 February 1946, establishing the Department, which states in paragraph 2 of annex I that "the activities of the Department should be so organized and directed as to promote to the greatest possible extent an informed understanding of the work and purposes of the United Nations among the peoples of the world",

Concurring with the view of the Secretary-General that the contents of public information and communications should be placed at the heart of the strategic management of the United Nations and that a culture of communications should permeate all levels of the Organization, as a means of fully informing the peoples of the world of the aims and activities of the United Nations, in accordance with the purposes and principles enshrined in the Charter of the United Nations, in order to create broad-based global support for the United Nations,

Stressing that the primary mission of the Department of Public Information is to provide, through its outreach activities, accurate, impartial, comprehensive and timely information to the public on the tasks and responsibilities of the United Nations in order to strengthen international support for the activities of the Organization with the greatest transparency,

Recalling that the comprehensive review of the work of the Department of Public Information, requested by the General Assembly in its resolution 56/253 of 24 December 2001, and the implementation of its second phase, described in the report of the Secretary-General on reorientation of United Nations activities in the field of public information and communications to the Committee on Information at its twenty-fifth session, as well as the report of the Secretary-General entitled "Strengthening of the United Nations: an agenda for further change", and Assembly resolutions 57/300 of 20 December 2002 and 59/126 B of 10 December 2004, as they apply to the Department, providing an opportunity to take due steps to enhance the efficiency and effectiveness of the Department and to maximize the use of its resources,

Expressing concern that the gap in the information and communication technologies between the developed and the developing countries has continued to widen and that vast segments of the population in developing countries are not benefiting from the present information and technology revolution, and, in this regard, underlining the necessity of rectifying the imbalances of the global information and technology revolution in order to make it more just, equitable and effective,

Recognizing that developments in the information and communication technology revolution open vast new opportunities for economic growth and social development and can play an important role in the eradication of poverty in developing countries, and, at the same time, emphasizing that the revolution also poses challenges and risks and could lead to the further widening of disparities between and within countries,

Recalling its resolution 59/309 of 22 June 2005 on multilingualism, and emphasizing the importance of making appropriate use of the official languages of the United Nations in the activities of the Department of Public Information, aiming to eliminate the disparity between the use of English and the five other official languages,

Welcoming Cape Verde, Iceland, Luxembourg, Madagascar and Qatar to membership in the Committee on Information,

I

Introduction

1. *Reaffirms* its resolution 13(I), in which it established the Department of Public Information, and all other relevant General Assembly resolutions related to the activities of the Department, and requests the Secretary-General, in respect of the public information policies and activities of the United Nations, to continue to implement fully the recommendations contained in paragraph 2 of its resolution 48/44 B of 10 December 1993 and other mandates as established by the General Assembly;

2. *Also reaffirms* that the United Nations remains the indispensable foundation of a peaceful and just world and that its voice must be heard in a clear and effective manner, and emphasizes the essential role of the Department of Public Information in this context, the activities of which should be so organized and directed as to promote to the greatest possible extent an informed understanding of the work and purposes of the United Nations among the peoples of the world;

3. *Stresses* the importance of the clear and timely provision of information by the Secretariat to Member States, upon their request, within the framework of existing mandates and procedures;

4. *Reaffirms* the central role of the Committee on Information in United Nations public information policies and activities, including the prioritization of those activities, and decides that recommendations relating to the programme of the Department of Public Information shall originate, to the extent possible, in the Committee and shall be considered by the Committee;

5. *Requests* the Department of Public Information, following the priorities laid down by the General Assembly in its resolution 59/275 of 23 December 2004, and guided by the United Nations Millennium Declaration, to pay particular attention to such major issues as the eradication of poverty, conflict prevention, sustainable development, human rights, the HIV/AIDS epidemic, combating terrorism in all its forms and manifestations and the needs of the African continent;

6. *Also requests* the Department of Public Information to pay particular attention to progress in implementing the internationally agreed development goals, including those contained in the Millennium Declaration, and the outcomes of the major related United Nations summits and conferences in carrying out its activities;

7. *Reaffirms* the need to enhance the technological infrastructure of the Department of Public Information on a continuous basis in order to widen its outreach and improve the United Nations website;

8. *Recognizes* the important work carried out by the United Nations Educational, Scientific and Cultural Organization and its collaboration with news agencies and broadcasting organizations in developing countries in disseminating information on priority issues, and encourages a continued collaboration between the Department of Public Information and the United Nations Educational, Scientific and Cultural Organization in the promotion of culture and in the fields of education and communication;

II

General activities of the Department of Public Information

9. *Notes* the proposals of the Secretary-General to improve the effective and targeted delivery of public information activities, emphasizes that these proposals should be in accordance with the relevant resolutions and decisions of the General Assembly, and requests the Secretary-General to report thereon to the Committee on Information at its twenty-eighth session;

10. *Acknowledges* that the Department of Public Information has entered the third and final year of its collaborative project with the Office of Internal Oversight Services to systematically evaluate public information products and activities, and requests the Secretary-General to report on the final outcome of the project to the Committee on Information at its twenty-eighth session;

11. *Requests* the Department of Public Information, in this regard, to continue to evaluate its products and activities with the objective of improving their effectiveness, including through interdepartmental consultations;

12. *Reaffirms* that the Department of Public Information is the focal point for information policies of the United Nations and the primary news centre for information about the United Nations, its activities and those of the Secretary-General;

13. *Also reaffirms* the importance of better coordination between the Department of Public Information and the Office of the Spokesman for the Secretary-General, and requests the Secretary-General to ensure consistency in the messages of the Organization;

14. *Further reaffirms* that the Department of Public Information must prioritize its work programme while respecting existing mandates and in line with regulation 5.6 of the Regulations and Rules Governing Programme Planning, the Programme Aspects of the Budget, the Monitoring of Implementation and the Methods of Evaluation, to focus its message and concentrate its efforts better and, as a function of performance management, to match its programmes with the needs of its target audiences, on the basis of improved feedback and evaluation mechanisms;

15. *Notes with appreciation* the efforts of the Department of Public Information to publicize the work and decisions of the General Assembly, encourages the Department to further strengthen its working relationship with the Office of the President of the General Assembly, and requests the Secretary-General to report thereon to the Committee on Information at its twenty-eighth session;

16. *Requests* the Secretary-General to continue to exert all efforts to ensure that publications and other information services of the Secretariat, including the United Nations website and the United Nations News Service, contain comprehensive, objective and equitable information about the issues before the Organization and that they maintain editorial independence, impartiality, accuracy and full consistency with resolutions and decisions of the General Assembly;

17. *Encourages* the Department of Public Information to continue to coordinate closely with all other departments of the Secretariat, to avoid duplication in the issuance of United Nations publications and to ensure that they are produced in a cost-effective manner;

18. *Emphasizes* that the Department of Public Information should maintain and improve its activities in the areas of special interest to developing countries and, where appropriate, other countries with special needs, and that the Department's activities should contribute to bridging the existing gap between the developing and the developed countries in the crucial field of public information and communications;

19. *Encourages* the Secretary-General to continue to strengthen the coordination between the Department of Public Information and other departments of the Secretariat in the context of its client-oriented approach and to identify target audiences and develop information programmes and media strategies for priority issues, and emphasizes that public information capacities and activities in other departments should function under the guidance of the Department;

20. *Welcomes* the initiatives that have been taken by the Department of Public Information to strengthen the public information system of the United Nations, and, in this regard, stresses the importance of the coherent and results-oriented approach being taken by the United Nations, the specialized agencies and the programmes and funds of the United Nations system involved in public information activities and the provision of resources for their implementation, and that feedback from Member States on the relevance and effectiveness of programme delivery should be taken into account;

21. *Notes with appreciation* the continued efforts of the Department of Public Information in issuing daily press releases, and requests the Department to continue providing this invaluable service to both Member States and representatives of the media, while considering possible means of improving their production process and streamlining their format, structure and length, keeping in mind the views of Member States;

22. *Also notes with appreciation* the efforts of the Department of Public Information to work at the local level with other organizations and bodies of the United Nations system to enhance the coordination of their communication activities, and requests the Secretary-General to report to the Committee on Information at its twenty-eighth session on progress achieved in this regard and on the activities of the United Nations Communications Group;

23. *Calls upon* the Department of Public Information to continue to examine its policies and activities regarding the durable preservation of its radio, television and photographic archives, to take action, within existing resources, to ensure that such archives are preserved and are accessible and to report to the Committee on Information at its twenty-eighth session;

Multilingualism and public information

24. *Emphasizes* the importance of making appropriate use of all the official languages of the United Nations in all the activities of the Department of Public Information, with the aim of eliminating the disparity between the use of English and the five other official languages;

25. *Welcomes* the ongoing efforts of the Department of Public Information to enhance multilingualism in

its activities, and encourages the Department to continue its endeavours in this regard;

26. *Emphasizes* the importance of ensuring the full, equitable treatment of all the official languages of the United Nations in all activities of the Department of Public Information, and, in this regard, reaffirms its request to the Secretary-General to ensure that the Department has appropriate staffing capacity in all official languages of the United Nations to undertake all its activities;

27. *Stresses* the importance of fully implementing its resolution 52/214 of 22 December 1997, in section C of which it requested the Secretary-General to ensure that the texts of all new public documents in all six official languages and information materials of the United Nations are made available daily through the United Nations website and are accessible to Member States without delay;

28. *Reiterates* paragraph 4 of section C of its resolution 52/214, and requests the Secretary-General to continue towards completion of the task of uploading all important older United Nations documents on the United Nations website in all six official languages on a priority basis, so that these archives are also available to Member States through that medium;

29. *Reaffirms* that it is important that the Secretary-General include in future programme budget proposals for the Department of Public Information the importance of using all six official languages in its activities;

30. *Takes note with appreciation* of the work done by the network of United Nations information centres in favour of the publication of United Nations information materials and the translation of important documents in languages other than United Nations official languages, with a view to reaching the widest possible spectrum of audiences and extending the United Nations message to all the corners of the world in order to strengthen international support for the activities of the Organization;

Bridging the digital divide

31. *Notes with satisfaction* the adoption of the Declaration of Principles and the Plan of Action at the first phase of the World Summit on the Information Society, held in Geneva from 10 to 12 December 2003, and welcomes the holding of the second phase of the Summit from 16 to 18 November 2005 in Tunis;

32. *Calls upon* the Department of Public Information to contribute to raising the awareness of the international community of the importance of the World Summit on the Information Society and the need to join efforts to make it a success;

33. *Recalls* paragraph 32 of its resolution 59/126 B, and welcomes the contribution of the Department of Public Information in publicizing the efforts of the Secretary-General to close the digital divide as a means of spurring economic growth and as a response to the continuing gap between developed and developing countries, and, in this context, requests the Department to further enhance its role;

Network of United Nations information centres

34. *Emphasizes* the importance of the network of United Nations information centres in enhancing the public image of the United Nations and in disseminating messages on the United Nations to local populations, especially in developing countries;

35. *Takes note* of the report of the Secretary-General on further rationalization of the network of United Nations information centres, and, in this regard, recognizes the constraints of further regionalization as described in paragraph 25 of the report;

36. *Stresses* the importance of rationalizing the network of United Nations information centres, and, in this regard, requests the Secretary-General to continue to make proposals in this direction, including through the redeployment of resources where necessary, and to report to the Committee on Information at its twenty-eighth session;

37. *Reaffirms* that rationalization of United Nations information centres must be carried out on a case-by-case basis in consultation with all concerned Member States in which existing information centres are located, the countries served by those information centres and other interested countries in the region, taking into consideration the distinctive characteristics of each region;

38. *Recognizes* that the network of United Nations information centres, especially in developing countries, should continue to enhance its impact and activities, including through strategic communications support, and calls upon the Secretary-General to submit a report on the implementation of this approach to the Committee on Information at its twenty-eighth session;

39. *Stresses* the importance of taking into account the special needs and requirements of developing countries in the field of information and communications technology for the effective flow of information in those countries;

40. *Also stresses* that the Department of Public Information, through its network of United Nations information centres, should continue to promote public awareness of and mobilize support for the work of the United Nations at the local level, bearing in mind that information in local languages has the strongest impact on local populations;

41. *Further stresses* the importance of efforts to strengthen the outreach activities of the United Nations to those Member States remaining outside the network of United Nations information centres, and encourages the Secretary-General, within the context of rationalization, to extend the services of the network of United Nations information centres to those Member States;

42. *Stresses* that the Department of Public Information should continue to review the allocation of both staff and financial resources to the United Nations information centres in developing countries, emphasizing the needs of the least developed countries;

43. *Encourages* the network of United Nations information centres to continue to develop web pages in local languages, also encourages the Department of Public Information to provide resources and technical facilities, in particular to those information centres whose web pages are not yet operational, and further encourages host countries to respond to the needs of the information centres;

44. *Takes note* of the proposal by the Secretary-General to work closely with the Governments concerned to explore the possibility of identifying rent-

free premises, while taking into account the economic condition of the host countries and bearing in mind that such support should not be a substitute for the full allocation of financial resources for the information centres in the context of the programme budget of the United Nations;

45. *Also takes note* of the report of the Secretary-General containing the discussion regarding the creation of a United Nations information centre in Luanda to address the special needs of Portuguese-speaking African countries, welcomes the offer made by the Government of Angola to host the centre as part of the network of United Nations information centres by providing rent-free premises, and encourages the Secretary-General, within the context of rationalization, to take all necessary measures to accommodate those needs;

III

Strategic communications services

46. *Takes note* of paragraph 19 of the report of the Secretary-General on the continuing reorientation of United Nations activities in the field of public information and communications, and, in this context, reaffirms that the Department of Public Information is the principal department responsible for the implementation of information strategies, as mandated;

47. *Reaffirms* the role of the strategic communications services in devising and disseminating United Nations messages by developing communications strategies, in close collaboration with the substantive departments, United Nations funds and programmes and the specialized agencies, in full compliance with the legislative mandates;

Promotional campaigns

48. *Recognizes* that promotional campaigns aimed at supporting special sessions and international conferences of the United Nations are part of the core responsibility of the Department of Public Information, welcomes the efforts of the Department to examine creative ways in which it can organize and implement these campaigns in partnership with the substantive departments concerned, using the United Nations Millennium Declaration as its guide, and requests the Department to pay particular attention to progress in implementing the internationally agreed development goals, including those contained in the Millennium Declaration, and the outcomes of the major related United Nations summits and conferences in carrying out its activities;

49. *Appreciates* the work of the Department of Public Information in promoting, through its campaigns, issues of importance to the international community, such as sustainable development, strategic coordination in humanitarian relief, especially in natural disasters and other crises, children, HIV/AIDS, malaria and other diseases and decolonization, as well as the dialogue among civilizations, culture of peace and tolerance and the consequences of the Chernobyl disaster, and encourages the Department, in cooperation with the countries concerned and with the relevant organizations and bodies of the United Nations system, to continue to take appropriate measures to enhance world public awareness of these and other important global issues;

50. *Welcomes* the new initiative of the Department of Public Information entitled "Ten Stories the World Should Hear More About";

51. *Encourages* the Department of Public Information to continue to work within the United Nations Communications Group to coordinate the preparation and implementation of communication strategies with the heads of information of the agencies, funds and programmes of the United Nations system, and requests the Secretary-General to report to the Committee on Information at successive sessions on the activities of the Group;

52. *Stresses* the need for the renewed emphasis in support of Africa's development, in particular by the Department of Public Information, in order to promote awareness in the international community of the nature of the critical economic and social situation in Africa and of the priorities of the New Partnership for Africa's Development;

Role of the Department of Public Information in United Nations peacekeeping

53. *Commends* the efforts of the Secretary-General to strengthen the public information capacity of the Department of Public Information for the establishment and functioning of the information components of United Nations peacekeeping operations and of political and peacebuilding missions, including its promotional efforts and other information support activities, and requests the Secretariat to continue to ensure the involvement of the Department from the planning stage of future operations through interdepartmental consultations and coordination with other departments of the Secretariat, in particular with the Department of Peacekeeping Operations;

54. *Stresses* the importance of enhancing the public information capacity of the Department of Public Information in the field of peacekeeping operations and its role in the selection process of spokespersons for United Nations peacekeeping operations or missions, and, in this regard, encourages the Department to second spokespersons who have the necessary skills to fulfil the tasks of the operations or missions, taking into account the principle of equitable geographical distribution in accordance with Chapter XV, Article 101, paragraph 3, of the Charter of the United Nations, and to consider views expressed, especially by host countries, when appropriate, in this regard;

55. *Welcomes* the actions taken by the Department of Public Information to increase its involvement in the planning stage of new or expanding peacekeeping operations, as well as the deployment of public information components in new missions, also welcomes the improvements made to the peacekeeping portal on the United Nations website, and encourages the Department of Public Information to continue its efforts in supporting the peacekeeping missions to further develop their websites;

56. *Encourages* the Department of Public Information and the Department of Peacekeeping Operations to continue their cooperation in raising awareness of the new realities, successes and challenges faced by peacekeeping operations, especially multidimensional and complex ones, and of the recent surge in United Nations peacekeeping activities, and welcomes efforts by the two Departments to develop and implement a

comprehensive communications strategy on current challenges facing United Nations peacekeeping;

57. *Also encourages* the Department of Public Information and the Department of Peacekeeping Operations to cooperate in establishing an effective outreach programme to explain the policy of the Organization against sexual exploitation and abuse;

58. *Requests* the Secretary-General to continue to report to the Committee on Information at its successive sessions on the role of the Department of Public Information in United Nations peacekeeping operations;

Role of the Department of Public Information in strengthening dialogue among civilizations and the culture of peace as means of enhancing understanding among nations

59. *Recalls* its resolutions 53/22 of 4 November 1998 and 55/23 of 13 November 2000 on the United Nations Year of Dialogue among Civilizations, 52/15 of 20 November 1997, by which it proclaimed 2000 the International Year for the Culture of Peace, 53/25 of 10 November 1998, by which it proclaimed the period 2001-2010 the International Decade for a Culture of Peace and Non-Violence for the Children of the World, 56/6 of 9 November 2001 on the Global Agenda for Dialogue among Civilizations, and 59/142 of 15 December 2004 on the promotion of religious and cultural understanding, harmony and cooperation, encourages the Department of Public Information to continue to provide the necessary support for the dissemination of information pertaining to dialogue among civilizations and the culture of peace and to take due steps in fostering the culture of dialogue among civilizations via all mass media, such as the Internet, print, radio and television, and requests the Secretary-General to submit a report in this regard to the Committee on Information at its successive sessions;

IV

News services

60. *Stresses* that the central objective of the news services implemented by the Department of Public Information is the timely delivery of accurate, objective and balanced news and information emanating from the United Nations system in all four mass media—print, radio, television and Internet—to the media and other audiences worldwide, with the overall emphasis on multilingualism, and reiterates its request to the Department to ensure that all news-breaking stories and news alerts are accurate, impartial and free of bias;

Traditional means of communication

61. *Also stresses* that radio remains one of the most cost-effective and far-reaching traditional media available to the Department of Public Information and an important instrument in United Nations activities, including development and peacekeeping, with a view to achieving a broad client base around the world;

62. *Notes* that the international radio broadcasting capacity for the United Nations is an integral part of the activities of the Department of Public Information, and requests the Secretary-General to make every effort to ensure its success and to report on its activities to the Committee on Information at its twenty-eighth session;

63. *Encourages* the Secretary-General to achieve parity in the six official languages in United Nations radio production;

64. *Notes* the efforts being made by the Department of Public Information to disseminate programmes directly to broadcasting stations all over the world in the six official languages, with the addition of Portuguese, as well as in other languages where possible, and, in this regard, stresses the need for impartiality and objectivity concerning information activities of the United Nations;

65. *Encourages* the Department of Public Information to continue building partnerships with local, national and regional broadcasters to extend the United Nations message to all the corners of the world in an accurate and impartial way, and also encourages the Radio and Television Service of the Department to continue to take full advantage of the technological infrastructure made available in recent years;

United Nations website

66. *Reaffirms* that the United Nations website remains a very useful tool for the media, non-governmental organizations, educational institutions, Member States and the general public, and, in this regard, reiterates its appreciation for the efforts of the Department of Public Information in creating and maintaining it;

67. *Recognizes* the efforts made by the Department of Public Information to implement the basic accessibility requirements for persons with disabilities to the United Nations website, calls upon the Department to continue to work towards compliance with all levels of accessibility requirements on all pages of the website with the aim of ensuring its accessibility by persons with different kinds of disabilities, and requests the Secretary-General to report to the Committee on Information at its twenty-eighth session on progress made in this regard;

68. *Reaffirms* the need to achieve full parity among the six official languages on United Nations websites while noting with concern the increasing gap among different official languages on United Nations websites;

69. *Takes note* of the fact that the multilingual development and enrichment of the United Nations website has improved, although at a slower rate than expected owing to several constraints that need to be addressed, and, in this regard, requests the Department of Public Information, in coordination with content-providing offices, to improve the actions undertaken to achieve parity among the six official languages on the United Nations website;

70. *Welcomes* the cooperative arrangements undertaken by the Department of Public Information with academic institutions to increase the number of web pages available in some official languages, and encourages the Secretary-General to explore additional ways to further extend these cooperative arrangements to include all the official languages of the United Nations;

71. *Stresses* the need to adopt a decision on the multilingual development, maintenance and enrichment of the United Nations website, and requests the Secretary-General to submit proposals to establish separate language units for each of the six official lan-

guages within the Department of Public Information, in order to achieve full parity among the official languages of the United Nations;

72. *Reaffirms* paragraph 2 of part IX of its resolution 59/276 of 23 December 2004 on proposals to strengthen the United Nations website;

73. *Reaffirms its request* to the Secretary-General to ensure, until such a decision has been taken and implemented and while maintaining an up-to-date and accurate website, the adequate distribution of financial and human resources within the Department of Public Information allocated to the United Nations website among all official languages, taking into consideration the specificity of each official language on a continuous basis;

74. *Takes note* of the proposal of the Secretary-General to translate all English language materials and databases posted on the United Nations websites by the respective content-providing offices of the Secretariat into all official languages, and reiterates its request to the Secretary-General to report to the Committee on Information at its twenty-eighth session on the most practical, efficient and cost-effective means of implementing this proposal;

75. *Encourages* the Secretary-General to continue to take full advantage of recent developments in information technology in order to improve, in a cost-effective manner, the expeditious dissemination of information on the United Nations, in accordance with the priorities established by General Assembly resolutions and taking into account the linguistic diversity of the Organization;

76. *Recognizes* that some official languages use non-Latin and bidirectional scripts and that technological infrastructures and supportive applications in the United Nations are based on Latin script, which leads to difficulties in processing non-Latin and bidirectional scripts, and requests the Department of Public Information, in cooperation with the Information Technology Services Division of the Department of Management, to continue its efforts to ensure that technological infrastructures and supportive applications in the United Nations fully support Latin, non-Latin and bidirectional scripts in order to enhance the equality of all official languages on the United Nations website;

77. *Notes with satisfaction* that access to the Official Document System of the United Nations, which is now being provided free to the public through its integration with the United Nations website, has resulted in a significant enhancement of the multilingual nature of the website owing to the availability of United Nations parliamentary documentation in the six official languages;

78. *Also notes with satisfaction* that United Nations webcast services provide live video of United Nations meetings and events, and encourages the Department of Public Information to also make the webcast available in the original language in which it is delivered;

79. *Welcomes* the electronic mail-based United Nations News Service, distributed worldwide in the English and French languages through e-mail by the Department of Public Information, and requests the Department as a matter of priority to continue to examine ways to provide this service in all official languages;

80. *Requests* the Secretary-General to continue to work within the United Nations System Chief Executives Board for Coordination and other appropriate inter-agency bodies to establish a United Nations gateway, an inter-agency search facility in which all entities of the United Nations system should be encouraged to participate, and requests the Secretary-General to report to the Committee on Information at its successive sessions on the activities of the High-level Committee on Management in this regard;

V

Library services

81. *Takes note with appreciation* of the report of the Secretary-General entitled "Modernization and integrated management of United Nations libraries: new strategic directions";

82. *Calls upon* the Department of Public Information to continue to lead the Steering Committee for the Modernization and Integrated Management of United Nations Libraries, and encourages the member libraries of the Steering Committee to coordinate closely and to establish time frames for the fulfilment of its programme of work;

83. *Takes note* of the report of the Office of Internal Oversight Services on the review of the operations and management of United Nations libraries, requests the Steering Committee to pursue new strategies for the work of United Nations libraries, which should aim at enhancing the effectiveness of libraries within existing legislative mandates, and requests the Secretary-General to report to the Committee on Information at its twenty-eighth session;

84. *Also takes note* of the steps taken by the Dag Hammarskjöld Library and the other member libraries of the Steering Committee to align their activities, services and outputs more closely with the goals, objectives and operational priorities of the Organization;

85. *Reiterates* the need to enable the provision of hard copies of library materials to Member States, and notes the efforts of the Secretary-General to enrich, on a multilingual basis, the stock of books and journals in the Dag Hammarskjöld Library, including publications on peace and security and development-related issues, in order to ensure that the Library is enriched and continues to be a broadly accessible resource for information about the United Nations and its activities;

86. *Recognizes* the importance of the depository libraries in disseminating information and knowledge about United Nations activities, and, in this connection, urges the Dag Hammarskjöld Library, in its capacity as the focal point, to continue to take the initiatives necessary to strengthen such libraries by providing regional training and other assistance and by improving their role with the aim of strengthening their support to users in developing countries;

87. *Requests* the Secretary-General to report to the Committee on Information at its twenty-eighth session on the activities of the Steering Committee and the work of the Dag Hammarskjöld Library, including on the application of measures to enhance the effectiveness of the libraries within existing legislative mandates;

88. *Acknowledges* that the Dag Hammarskjöld Library, as part of the Outreach Division of the Depart-

ment of Public Information, endeavours to facilitate access to timely and up-to-date library products and services for use by delegates, permanent missions of Member States, the Secretariat, researchers and depository libraries worldwide;

89. *Notes* the holding of training courses conducted by the Dag Hammarskjöld Library for the representatives of Member States and Secretariat staff on the use of Cyberseek, web search, the Intranet, United Nations documentation, United Nations Info Quest and the Official Document System of the United Nations;

90. *Recalls* paragraph 44 of its resolution 56/64 B of 24 December 2001, in which it welcomed the role of the Department of Public Information in fostering increased collaboration among libraries of the United Nations system;

VI

Outreach services

91. *Acknowledges* that the outreach services implemented by the Department of Public Information continue to work towards promoting awareness of the role and work of the United Nations on priority issues;

92. *Notes* the importance of the continued implementation by the Department of Public Information of the ongoing programme for broadcasters and journalists from developing countries and countries with economies in transition, as mandated by the General Assembly, and encourages the Department to consider how best to maximize the benefits derived from the programme by reviewing, inter alia, its duration and the number of its participants;

93. *Welcomes* the movement towards educational outreach and the orientation of the *UN Chronicle*, both print and online editions, and, to this end, encourages the *UN Chronicle* to continue to develop co-publishing partnerships, collaborative educational activities and events, including the "Unlearning Intolerance" seminar series, with civil society organizations and institutions of higher learning;

94. *Reaffirms* the important role that guided tours play as a means of reaching out to the general public, including children and students at all levels;

95. *Welcomes* the efforts undertaken by the Department of Public Information in organizing exhibitions on important United Nations-related issues within existing mandates at United Nations Headquarters and at other United Nations offices as a useful tool for reaching out to the general public;

96. *Requests* the Department of Public Information to strengthen its role as a focal point for two-way interaction with civil society relating to the priorities and concerns of the Organization;

97. *Commends* the United Nations Correspondents Association on its Dag Hammarskjöld Memorial Scholarship Fund, which sponsors journalists from developing countries to come to the United Nations Headquarters and report on the activities during the General Assembly, and urges donors to extend financial support to the Fund so that it may increase the number of such scholarships to journalists in this context;

98. *Expresses its appreciation* for the efforts and contribution of United Nations Messengers of Peace, Goodwill Ambassadors and other advocates to promote the work of the United Nations and to enhance international public awareness of its priorities and concerns, and calls upon the Department of Public Information to continue to involve them in its communications and media strategies and outreach activities;

99. *Requests* the Secretary-General to report to the Committee on Information at its next session on the activities being carried out by the Department of Public Information to enhance the public image of the Organization, especially where there is a component of the network of United Nation information centres;

VII

Final remarks

100. *Requests* the Secretary-General to ensure that all reports requested by the Committee on Information are submitted and issued in accordance with the legislative mandate;

101. *Also requests* the Secretary-General to report to the Committee on Information at its twenty-eighth session and to the General Assembly at its sixty-first session on the activities of the Department of Public Information and on the implementation of the recommendations contained in the present resolution;

102. *Requests* the Committee on Information to report to the General Assembly at its sixty-first session;

103. *Decides* to include in the provisional agenda of its sixty-first session the item entitled "Questions relating to information".

Reorientation of information and communications activities

In response to General Assembly resolution 59/126 B [YUN 2004, p. 616], the Secretary-General, in a February report to the Committee on Information [A/AC.198/2005/2 & Corr.1], detailed progress in the continuing reorientation of the Department of Public Information (DPI), launched in 2002 [YUN 2002, p. 585].

Responding to the needs of its global audience, DPI maintained a balance between new communications technologies, especially the Internet, and traditional media, including radio and print materials. At the same time, it widened its pool of communications partners in the private, public and corporate sectors. In response to allegations of corruption, mismanagement and lack of transparency and accountability within the Organization, DPI strengthened its monitoring of media around the world to provide senior officials with press materials and regular analyses. It also strengthened its media outreach capacity to ensure a coordinated and rapid response to misinformation, as well as the formulation of substantive information for the use of UN officials when speaking to the press on specific issues. In addition, DPI assisted in the drafting of opinion articles by senior officials for publication in newspapers around the world to further project the Organization's perspective on crucial issues. It undertook proactive outreach efforts aimed at showing the media and the public at large the many ways in which the Organization was responding to global challenges on a daily basis. Throughout the second half of 2004 and early 2005, DPI concentrated on drawing the world's attention to the UN revitalization and reform process promoted by the Secretary-General. At the center of its campaign were preparations for the high-level plenary meeting of the General Assembly in September (see p. 47). Rallying greater support for the Millennium Development Goals (MDGs) [YUN 2000, p. 51], especially at the national level, was also a central focus for DPI.

A cornerstone of DPI's reorientation process was the creation of a culture of evaluation. The collaborative project with OIOS to evaluate all DPI activities was in its final year. The systematic review of the impact of public information activities had encouraged managers at all levels to focus on the evaluation of programme outcomes. Survey activities had more than doubled with the introduction of the annual programme impact review. Overall, surveys conducted since 2002 demonstrated that DPI had managed to meet the demands of 80 per cent of its target audiences in terms of usefulness, relevance and quality of products, activities and services. DPI was building its technical infrastructure and internal capacities to conduct systematic media monitoring and analysis of its communications campaigns and press coverage of UN activities. The client planning process initiated in 2003 [YUN 2003, p. 631] as part of DPI's reform was further strengthened.

Guided by the United Nations Millennium Declaration adopted by the Assembly in resolution 55/2 [YUN 2000, p. 49] and resolutions 58/101 B [YUN 2003, p. 623] and 59/126 B [YUN 2004, p. 616], DPI continued to pay particular attention to the major issues of poverty, conflict prevention, sustainable development, human rights, the HIV/AIDS epidemic, combating terrorism, the needs of Africa, and dialogue among civilizations and cultures of peace.

In the light of the surge in demand for UN peacekeeping, DPI raised awareness about UN peacekeeping operations, particularly the challenges posed in deploying new and expanded missions, and prepared public information components of peacekeeping operations for rapid and effective deployment. DPI continued its close cooperation with the UN Department of Peacekeeping Operations (DPKO), intensifying planning and coordination in the preparation and dissemination of public information materials to the media and UNICs, and provided backstopping support to the public information components of ongoing peace missions.

The Regional United Nations Information Centre in Brussels, Belgium, established in 2004 [YUN 2004, p. 628], made steady progress as a regional information hub for Western Europe, establishing and expanding its dissemination, media-monitoring and promotional activities in an increasing number of languages to all 22 countries of the region it served. It also emerged as a venue for major UN events, including the launching of key reports, press briefings and other media-aimed activities. (For further information on UNIC rationalization, see p. 694.)

The Secretary-General also described DPI's efforts to connect with the media, focusing on strengthening partnerships with radio and television broadcasters and with civil society to enhance outreach, and to implement knowledge services through the Dag Hammarskjöld Library. (For information on UN libraries, see p. 692.)

The report concluded that the reorientation process was completed. DPI had implemented those aspects of the comprehensive review of its work within the Secretary-General's authority, based on Assembly resolutions and guidance provided by the Committee on Information. DPI was well prepared to take on the challenge of telling the story of a renewed and revitalized United Nations, but needed the support of Member States and the Committee to do so effectively.

DPI activities

In response to General Assembly resolution 59/126 B [YUN 2004, p. 616], the Secretary-General submitted an August report [A/60/173] covering DPI's activities since his previous report [ibid., p. 624], which were organized within its four sub-programmes: strategic communications services, news services, library services and outreach services. The report also included an overview of DPI's continuing efforts to promote and refine a culture of evaluation.

DPI continued to communicate to the world the process of UN revitalization and reform envisaged by the Secretary-General. It also played a key role in planning and carrying out a worldwide communications strategy for the launch of the Secretary-General's report entitled "In larger freedom: towards development, security and human rights for all" [A/59/2005] (see p. 67), which was presented to the High-level Plenary Meeting of the General Assembly in September (see p. 47). To promote the development agenda of that meeting, the Department organized a multi-site launch of the *Millennium Development Goals Report 2005* in a reader-friendly format describing progress on the implementation of the UN MDGs [YUN 2000, p. 51]. DPI also completed an intensive promotional campaign for the 2005 review of the implementation of the 1995 Beijing Platform for Action [YUN 1995, p. 1170] and the outcome documents of the twenty-third (2000) special session of the General Assembly on women [YUN 2000, p. 1082] by the Commission on the Status of Women. The Department made the protection and promotion of human rights a priority issue, and collaborated with the UN Department of Political Affairs and the Committee of 24 to disseminate information on decolonization.

DPI worked closely with DPKO to further develop and adjust its global communications strategy in support of UN peace operations, particularly in assisting newly established operations in launching effective, well-prepared and properly equipped public information components. It helped train 25 public information field officers in rapid response and peacekeeping planning and doctrine; worked with DPKO to develop a public information module for its framework plan on disarmament, demobilization and reintegration programmes; developed communications strategies, guidance and training on the issue of sexual exploitation and abuse; elaborated a communication strategy for raising the Secretary-General's profile on the situation in Darfur, the Sudan, in May; and drafted a strategy to promote the Secretary-General's approach to counter-terrorism as well as provided public information support to the Counter-Terrorism Executive Directorate, other counter-terrorism bodies and the Secretariat.

The UN website, which was in its tenth year of operation, had become a premier site for providing a wide range of information in multiple languages to users around the world. Enhancing the site's multilingual capacity was a key goal for DPI, which had used in-house technical and linguistic expertise to introduce programming and graphic design as a common service for all official languages. The UN News Centre portal continued to gain importance as a focal point for the latest news and related resources on UN global activities.

DPI continued to strengthen its radio programming and expand partnerships with international broadcasters, and, in the light of the broadband and mobile revolutions, was exploring ways to offer more varied content from the entire UN family, ensuring that its products, delivered through multiple means and platforms, appealed specifically to various target audiences. A pilot survey, conducted in November 2004, as part of DPI's self-evaluation efforts, indicated that overall, clients had a positive view of UN radio and video programmes. A larger-scale survey was to be conducted in the third quarter of 2005.

The *UN Chronicle* further strengthened the targeting of educators and institutions of higher education through the use of thematic clusters that could be used as part of their curricula. Its Feature Service re-disseminated some 40 articles from eminent contributors through UNICs to newspapers and magazines worldwide.

DPI continued to build partnerships with non-governmental organizations (NGOs) through weekly briefings, the annual orientation programme for newly associated NGO representatives, communication workshops, the NGO website and the NGO Resource Centre. As at June 2005, the total number of associated NGOs stood at 1,517.

Library services

As at June 2005, there were 405 active depository libraries and electronic deposit recipients increased from 127 to 138. During the reporting period, the Dag Hammarskjöld Library conducted more than 150 training sessions for some 1,300 trainees, including Secretariat staff and mission personnel. Its web page continued to expand services in the six official languages within the limits of available resources.

The Library would coordinate the revamping of the UN Intranet, known as iSeek, and to that end, had conducted a needs assessment in April and formed a dedicated unit in the Library's Knowledge Sharing Section during the third quarter of the year. The Library continued to bring high-quality information resources to official users by purchasing online information services at considerably reduced prices through the United Nations System Electronic Information Acquisitions Consortium.

The Steering Committee for the Modernization and Integrated Management of United Nations Libraries, established in 2003 [YUN 2003, p. 635], held three meetings between September 2004 and July 2005. The September 2004 meeting focused on the development of a strategy for UN libraries and information services for the future. In March 2005, the Steering Committee endorsed the report on new strategic directions for UN libraries, which was submitted by its Subcommittee on Strategic Directions for UN Libraries. The report [A/AC.198/2005/4] (see p. 693) was also submitted to the Committee on Information at its twenty-seventh (2005) session. The Steering Committee decided to reorganize its work programme by focusing on the management of UN documentation, information skills and learning, electronic and web resources and knowledge-sharing.

The Dag Hammarskjöld Library reorganized its services at the end of 2004, placing greater focus on fostering knowledge management. Steps taken in that regard included the establishment of a weekly reading and discussion group to foster the exchange of ideas among Library staff; an online forum for staff members to improve internal communication within the Library; a personal knowledge management programme that incorporated client needs assessment, one-on-one coaching and small team training programmes; and capacity-building activities aimed at enhancing the skills and knowledge of Library staff.

Management of UN libraries

Pursuant to resolution 59/126 B [YUN 2004, p. 616], the Secretary-General submitted a February report [A/AC.198/2005/4] defining strategic directions for the libraries that served the UN Secretariat, UN bodies, Member States and its broader constituency. The report also provided information on libraries throughout the UN system that would be affected by the changes envisaged.

The report stated that technological advances and organizational change had allowed for UN libraries to move from being independent repositories to a network of knowledge-sharing communities (from collections to connections). With those changes, the potential of value added by the library would increase, providing the opportunity for new, more relevant services. UN documents would remain at the core of library collections and more attention and resources would be devoted both to preserving those materials and making them more accessible and available. The Dag Hammarskjöld Library would focus staff resources on ensuring that the unique content of the UN document collections was put to best use. Libraries would produce electronic collections of external materials on demand through systems that provided access to multiple types of information resources held in different locations. Although print collections would not disappear, they would become smaller and more focused. As vendors of electronic journals and news sources developed systems to allow more direct, on-demand delivery of their materials directly to individual users, UN libraries would redirect their specialized expertise to helping users select optimal delivery mechanisms. Such changes, facilitated by a higher level of resource sharing, would reduce the costly duplication of acquisitions. The libraries would increasingly turn to electronic sources for new information products to summarize, filter and select relevant and timely information for users. The greatest change in the work of UN libraries would be the realignment of their services towards operational priorities. The role

of UN libraries as preservers and disseminators of cultural information would be enhanced and new services would support the creation of a knowledge-enabling environment in and among the UN library system. The needs of individual users and small teams would be met through the introduction at the Dag Hammarskjöld Library of a Personal Knowledge Management programme, which would include team training and individual coaching in the tools and techniques provided by the Organization. Personal Knowledge Management teams would work with support service units to ensure that users had the most appropriate tools to meet their needs and that they knew how to use them. With UN documentation available free of charge over the Internet through the Official Document System (ODS), the role of depository libraries would have to be re-examined. As part of their contribution to bridging the digital divide and supporting education in developing countries, UN libraries would work through the depository libraries to support users in those countries. The buildings and physical environment that had characterized UN libraries were being re-examined in the light of new ways of working. Paper-based collections of externally published books and periodicals would remain essential for the UN libraries for some time, but would be reduced if those materials became more readily available outside UN libraries.

UN library staff would strengthen their skills in communications, software performance, interviewing, coaching and training, information systems design and electronic publishing, and would align their work more closely with the goals, objectives and operational priorities of the Organization. The ability of library staff to analyse and evaluate information environments and sources would be enhanced to produce value-added products and services targeted to the needs of UN users. The staff would move towards a more interactive role, acting as a catalyst in and across organizations. The programme of change within UN libraries would be carried out through collaboration between the libraries and the constituencies they served.

The goal of transforming the skills, methods and knowledge bases of UN libraries into a powerful resource for the Organization in the twenty-first century would require training and technological resources, and a careful evaluation of information policy issues and staffing procedures in the planning process. Implementation of those new directions would ensure that UN libraries aligned their policy with the recommendations put forward by the Secretary-General in his 2002 report on strengthening the United Nations: an agenda for further change [YUN 2002, p. 585].

By **decision 59/557** of 13 April, the General Assembly deferred until its sixtieth (2005) session consideration of the 2004 OIOS report on the review of the operations and management of UN libraries [YUN 2004, p. 627].

United Nations information centres

Pursuant to General Assembly resolutions 57/300 [YUN 2002, p. 1353], 58/101 B [YUN 2003, p. 623] and 59/126 B [YUN 2004, p. 616], the Secretary-General submitted a February report [A/AC.198/2005/3] on the further rationalization of the United Nations information centres (UNICs) network. It provided information on the implementation of the regionalization initiative in Western Europe that began with the opening of the regional UNIC in Brussels in 2004 [YUN 2004, p. 628], and in other high-cost developed countries, and set out a proposed implementation strategy for other regions.

The Secretary-General stated that underlying further rationalization of the network of UNICs was DPI's strategic approach to communications, emphasizing the use of new technologies, expanded partnerships, and a reallocation of resources to achieve greater overall impact, and taking into account the practical concerns and geographic realities facing such a network. However, DPI's analysis of the current situation in the field and of the various proposals for further rationalization revealed that further progress towards regionalization would require a level of funding not currently available to the Department. The unanticipated reduction of $2 million from the 2004-2005 biennium allocation for UNICs [ibid.] drained resources that were intended for strengthening those in developing countries and facilitating the creation of regional hubs. In addition, rising operational expenditures had further strained UNICs' budgets.

Faced with those concerns, DPI recommended a strategic recalibration of the existing network of UNICs by systematically extending a regional approach to communications to the rest of the network. Key information centres in each region would be strengthened to enable them to play a greater role in providing broad strategic communications guidance, coordination and support to centres in that region. That would be accommodated within current budgetary allocations and entail a strategic alignment of existing staff resources. The recalibration would help focus UNICs' work on priority thematic issues and concerns of particular relevance in each region, and enable DPI to fulfil its mission statement [YUN 2003, p. 630] by communicating more strategically to achieve the greatest impact in the field. The report concluded that an adequate level of operational resources was essential for progress towards a broader realignment of the network of UNICs, in consultation with regional groups and individual States concerned.

Development of UN website

In response to General Assembly resolution 59/126 B [YUN 2004, p. 616], the Secretary-General submitted to the Committee on Information a February report on the multilingual development, maintenance and enrichment of the UN website [A/AC.198/2005/6]. The report provided updates in that regard and outlined proposals for achieving the goal of parity among UN official languages on the website.

The report stated that the UN website was a decentralized system on which various departments were entitled to post their materials. As manager of the website, DPI emphasized that, to ensure coherence, avoid duplication and rationalize its management, coordination should be enhanced in terms of language and technical expertise. To that end, the Working Group on Internet Matters of the UN Publications Board was working to improve guidelines to promote a more coordinated and centralized approach to website development in languages other than English.

Accesses to the UN website grew from 2.1 billion in 2003 to 2.3 billion in 2004 and page views rose by nearly 26 per cent, indicating continued growth of interest in and use of UN materials via the website. However, while the upward trend in website use was consistent among the language sites, the level of increase varied widely. The Web Services Section, which handled the bulk of the language pages, posted more new or updated pages in languages other than English or French, signifying a positive move towards incorporating more materials in the languages, but other content-providing UN offices posted new pages or updated existing ones overwhelmingly in English.

To further advance parity on the website, DPI was taking steps to supplement regular staffing resources and had increased the number of pages available in some languages through pro bono translations provided by academic institutions, signing agreements to that end with universities in Belarus, China and Spain. However, the need for editorial control, programming and processing had put an additional workload on existing staff resources. The site-wide search engine for all UN official languages was implemented in September 2004, but its further development would be sporadic, as adequate resources had not been identified. Using in-house technical and linguistic expertise, the Web Services Section introduced programming and graphic design as a common service for all languages. The use of UNICODE software had drastically reduced the need to create the underlying programming for each language separately. A UN radio site was launched in English and was also being made available in other languages. Information on UN activities was also available on the web to local audiences in 27 other languages, thanks largely to the work of UNICs.

DPI continued to improve linguistic parity without sacrificing the comprehensive and up-to-date nature of the site. Parity had already been achieved in the General Assembly, the Security Council, news and radio portions of the site. UN Webcast planned to expand its Internet services in the six official languages and was building partnerships with other departments and offices to produce training and other informational webcast videos for distance learning.

Resources were also being allocated to ensure accessibility to the UN website by persons with disabilities. The basic accessibility requirements for the top layers of the site had been implemented, and plans were being made to redesign it to ensure better navigation, presentation, search and accessibility, in compliance with the requirements for persons with disabilities.

The report concluded that DPI would be unable to redeploy additional resources towards linguistic parity on the UN website without adversely affecting other mandated activities. Proposals to strengthen the UN website would be submitted within the context of the 2006-2007 proposed programme budget to further enable DPI to accelerate the move toward parity in the maintenance and development of key areas of the site.

UN Communications Group

The Secretary-General's August report on questions relating to information [A/60/173] included information on the 2005 activities of the United Nations Communications Group (UNCG), established in 2002 [YUN 2002, p. 589]. The Group, which had evolved into a communications platform for the entire UN system, held its fourth annual meeting in Geneva on 23-24 May. The Group took steps to further enhance cooperation and coordination among UN communicators, which included: the April launch of a media calendar of events; the establishment of a new operating model for UNCG that would consolidate UN system communications resources at the country level and eliminate duplication and/or overlap; and the adoption of a business plan for the promotion of the International Year of Sport and

Physical Education 2005 (see p. 1206) to be implemented system-wide. UNifeed, a satellite newsfeed allowing broadcasters immediate access to the audio and visual material of DPI and UN agencies, was launched in March, bringing UNCG members into an unprecedented partnership with international broadcast networks.

Information and communications in the context of international security

In response to General Assembly resolution 59/61 [YUN 2004, p. 630], the Secretary-General, in a July report and later addendum [A/60/95 & Add.1], transmitted the views of four Member States on the general appreciation of the issues of information security; the definition of basic notions related to information security, including unauthorized interference with or misuse of information and telecommunication systems and information resources; and the context of relevant international concepts aimed at strengthening the security of global information and telecommunication systems.

Group of Governmental Experts. The Group of Governmental Experts on Developments in the Field of Information and Telecommunications in the Context of International Security, appointed by the Secretary-General in 2004 [YUN 2004, p. 630], held its second (Geneva, 28 March–1 April) and third (New York, 11-22 July) sessions. The Secretary-General submitted a report on their activities in August [A/60/202]. The Group held a comprehensive, in-depth exchange of views on developments in information and telecommunications in the context of international security, taking into account replies received from Member States in response to Assembly resolution 59/61 [YUN 2004, p. 630] and earlier resolutions on the topic, as well as contributions and background papers from individual members of the Group. However, given the complexity of the issues involved, no consensus was reached on the preparation of a final report.

GENERAL ASSEMBLY ACTION

On 8 December [meeting 61], the General Assembly, on the recommendation of the First Committee [A/60/452], adopted **resolution 60/45** by recorded vote (177-1-0) [agenda item 86].

Developments in the field of information and telecommunications in the context of international security

The General Assembly,

Recalling its resolutions 53/70 of 4 December 1998, 54/49 of 1 December 1999, 55/28 of 20 November 2000, 56/19 of 29 November 2001, 57/53 of 22 November 2002, 58/32 of 8 December 2003, and 59/61 of 3 December 2004,

Recalling also its resolutions on the role of science and technology in the context of international security, in which, inter alia, it recognized that scientific and technological developments could have both civilian and military applications and that progress in science and technology for civilian applications needed to be maintained and encouraged,

Noting that considerable progress has been achieved in developing and applying the latest information technologies and means of telecommunication,

Affirming that it sees in this process the broadest positive opportunities for the further development of civilization, the expansion of opportunities for co-operation for the common good of all States, the en-hancement of the creative potential of humankind and additional improvements in the circulation of infor-mation in the global community,

Recalling, in this connection, the approaches and principles outlined at the Information Society and Development Conference, held in Midrand, South Africa, from 13 to 15 May 1996,

Bearing in mind the results of the Ministerial Confer-ence on Terrorism, held in Paris on 30 July 1996, and the recommendations that it made,

Bearing in mind also the results of the first phase of the World Summit on the Information Society, held in Geneva from 10 to 12 December 2003,

Noting that the dissemination and use of informa-tion technologies and means affect the interests of the entire international community and that optimum effectiveness is enhanced by broad international co-operation,

Expressing its concern that these technologies and means can potentially be used for purposes that are in-consistent with the objectives of maintaining interna-tional stability and security and may adversely affect the integrity of the infrastructure of States to the detri-ment of their security in both civil and military fields,

Considering that it is necessary to prevent the use of information resources or technologies for criminal or terrorist purposes,

Noting the contribution of those Member States that have submitted their assessments on issues of informa-tion security to the Secretary-General pursuant to paragraphs 1 to 3 of resolutions 53/70, 54/49, 55/28, 56/19, 57/53, 58/32 and 59/61,

Taking note of the reports of the Secretary-General containing those assessments,

Welcoming the initiative taken by the Secretariat and the United Nations Institute for Disarmament Re-search in convening an international meeting of ex-perts in Geneva in August 1999 on developments in the field of information and telecommunications in the context of international security, as well as its results,

Considering that the assessments of the Member States contained in the reports of the Secretary-General and the international meeting of experts have contributed to a better understanding of the substance of issues of international information security and re-lated notions,

Bearing in mind that the Secretary-General, in fulfil-ment of resolution 58/32, established in 2004 a group of governmental experts, which, in accordance with its mandate, considered existing and potential threats in

the sphere of information security and possible coop-erative measures to address them and conducted a study on relevant international concepts aimed at strengthening the security of global information and telecommunications systems,

Taking note of the report of the Secretary-General on the Group of Governmental Experts on Developments in the Field of Information and Telecommunications in the Context of International Security, prepared on the basis of the results of the Group's work,

1. *Calls upon* Member States to promote further at multilateral levels the consideration of existing and po-tential threats in the field of information security, as well as possible measures to limit the threats emerging in this field, consistent with the need to preserve the free flow of information;

2. *Considers* that the purpose of such measures could be served through the examination of relevant international concepts aimed at strengthening the security of global information and telecommunica-tions systems;

3. *Invites* all Member States to continue to inform the Secretary-General of their views and assessments on the following questions:

(a) General appreciation of the issues of information security;

(b) Efforts taken at the national level to strengthen in-formation security and promote international coopera-tion in this field;

(c) The content of the concepts mentioned in para-graph 2 above;

(d) Possible measures that could be taken by the inter-national community to strengthen information security at the global level;

4. *Requests* the Secretary-General, with the assist-ance of a group of governmental experts, to be estab-lished in 2009 on the basis of equitable geographical distribution, to continue to study existing and poten-tial threats in the sphere of information security and possible cooperative measures to address them, as well as the concepts referred to in paragraph 2 above, and to submit a report on the results of this study to the General Assembly at its sixty-fifth session;

5. *Decides* to include in the provisional agenda of its sixty-first session the item entitled "Developments in the field of information and telecommunications in the context of international security".

RECORDED VOTE ON RESOLUTION 60/45:

In favour: Afghanistan, Albania, Algeria, Andorra, Antigua and Barbuda, Argentina, Armenia, Australia, Austria, Azerbaijan, Bahamas, Bahrain, Bangladesh, Barbados, Belarus, Belgium, Belize, Benin, Bhu-tan, Bolivia, Bosnia and Herzegovina, Botswana, Brazil, Brunei Darussalam, Bulgaria, Burkina Faso, Burundi, Cambodia, Cameroon, Canada, Cape Verde, Central African Republic, Chad, Chile, China, Colombia, Comoros, Congo, Costa Rica, Côte d'Ivoire, Croatia, Cuba, Cyprus, Czech Republic, Democratic People's Republic of Korea, Den-mark, Djibouti, Dominica, Dominican Republic, Ecuador, Egypt, El Salva-dor, Eritrea, Estonia, Ethiopia, Fiji, Finland, France, Gabon, Georgia, Ger-many, Ghana, Greece, Grenada, Guatemala, Guinea, Guinea-Bissau, Guyana, Haiti, Honduras, Hungary, Iceland, India, Indonesia, Iran, Iraq, Ireland, Israel, Italy, Jamaica, Japan, Jordan, Kazakhstan, Kenya, Kuwait, Kyrgyzstan, Lao People's Democratic Republic, Latvia, Lebanon, Le-sotho, Liberia, Libyan Arab Jamahiriya, Liechtenstein, Lithuania, Luxem-bourg, Madagascar, Malawi, Malaysia, Maldives, Mali, Malta, Marshall Islands, Mauritania, Mauritius, Mexico, Micronesia, Monaco, Mongolia, Morocco, Myanmar, Namibia, Nepal, Netherlands, New Zealand, Nicara-gua, Niger, Nigeria, Norway, Oman, Pakistan, Palau, Panama, Paraguay, Peru, Philippines, Poland, Portugal, Qatar, Republic of Korea, Republic of Moldova, Romania, Russian Federation, Saint Lucia, Saint Vincent and the Grenadines, Samoa, San Marino, Sao Tome and Principe, Saudi Arabia, Senegal, Serbia and Montenegro, Sierra Leone, Singapore,

Slovakia, Slovenia, Solomon Islands, Somalia, South Africa, Spain, Sri Lanka, Sudan, Suriname, Sweden, Switzerland, Syrian Arab Republic, Tajikistan, Thailand, The former Yugoslav Republic of Macedonia, Timor-Leste, Togo, Trinidad and Tobago, Tunisia, Turkey, Turkmenistan, Tuvalu, Uganda, Ukraine, United Arab Emirates, United Kingdom, United Republic of Tanzania, Uruguay, Uzbekistan, Vanuatu, Venezuela, Viet Nam, Yemen, Zambia, Zimbabwe.
Against: United States.
Abstaining: None.

Science and technology in international security and disarmament

On 8 December [meeting 61], the General Assembly, on the recommendation of the First Committee [A/60/459], adopted **resolution 60/51** by recorded vote (110-53-17) [agenda item 93].

Role of science and technology in the context of international security and disarmament

The General Assembly,

Recognizing that scientific and technological developments can have both civilian and military applications and that progress in science and technology for civilian applications needs to be maintained and encouraged,

Concerned that military applications of scientific and technological developments can contribute significantly to the improvement and upgrading of advanced weapons systems and, in particular, weapons of mass destruction,

Aware of the need to follow closely the scientific and technological developments that may have a negative impact on international security and disarmament, and to channel scientific and technological developments for beneficial purposes,

Cognizant that international transfers of dual-use as well as high-technology products, services and know-how for peaceful purposes are important for the economic and social development of States,

Also cognizant of the need to regulate such transfers of dual-use goods and technologies and high technology with military applications through multilaterally negotiated, universally applicable, non-discriminatory guidelines,

Expressing its concern about the growing proliferation of ad hoc and exclusive export control regimes and arrangements for dual-use goods and technologies, which tend to impede the economic and social development of developing countries,

Recalling that in the Final Document of the Thirteenth Conference of Heads of State or Government of Non-Aligned Countries, held in Kuala Lumpur from 20 to 25 February 2003, it was again noted with concern that undue restrictions on exports to developing countries of material, equipment and technology for peaceful purposes persisted,

Emphasizing that internationally negotiated guidelines for the transfer of high technology with military applications should take into account the legitimate defence requirements of all States and the requirements for the maintenance of international peace and security, while ensuring that access to high-technology products and services and know-how for peaceful purposes is not denied,

1. *Affirms* that scientific and technological progress should be used for the benefit of all mankind to promote the sustainable economic and social development of all States and to safeguard international security, and that international cooperation in the use of science and technology through the transfer and exchange of technological know-how for peaceful purposes should be promoted;

2. *Invites* Member States to undertake additional efforts to apply science and technology for disarmament-related purposes and to make disarmament-related technologies available to interested States;

3. *Urges* Member States to undertake multilateral negotiations with the participation of all interested States in order to establish universally acceptable, non-discriminatory guidelines for international transfers of dual-use goods and technologies and high technology with military applications;

4. *Encourages* United Nations bodies to contribute, within existing mandates, to promoting the application of science and technology for peaceful purposes;

5. *Decides* to include in the provisional agenda of its sixty-first session the item entitled "Role of science and technology in the context of international security and disarmament".

RECORDED VOTE ON RESOLUTION 60/51:

In favour: Afghanistan, Algeria, Antigua and Barbuda, Bahamas, Bahrain, Bangladesh, Barbados, Belize, Benin, Bhutan, Bolivia, Botswana, Brunei Darussalam, Burkina Faso, Burundi, Cambodia, Cameroon, Cape Verde, Central African Republic, Chile, China, Colombia, Comoros, Congo, Costa Rica, Côte d'Ivoire, Cuba, Democratic People's Republic of Korea, Democratic Republic of the Congo, Djibouti, Dominica, Dominican Republic, Ecuador, Egypt, El Salvador, Eritrea, Ethiopia, Fiji, Gabon, Ghana, Grenada, Guatemala, Guinea, Guinea-Bissau, Guyana, Haiti, Honduras, India, Indonesia, Iran, Iraq, Jamaica, Jordan, Kenya, Kuwait, Lao People's Democratic Republic, Lebanon, Lesotho, Liberia, Libyan Arab Jamahiriya, Madagascar, Malawi, Malaysia, Maldives, Mali, Mauritania, Mauritius, Mexico, Mongolia, Morocco, Mozambique, Myanmar, Namibia, Nepal, Nicaragua, Niger, Nigeria, Oman, Pakistan, Panama, Peru, Philippines, Qatar, Saint Lucia, Saint Vincent and the Grenadines, Sao Tome and Principe, Saudi Arabia, Senegal, Sierra Leone, Singapore, Somalia, Sri Lanka, Sudan, Suriname, Syrian Arab Republic, Thailand, Timor-Leste, Togo, Trinidad and Tobago, Tunisia, Turkmenistan, Tuvalu, Uganda, United Arab Emirates, United Republic of Tanzania, Venezuela, Viet Nam, Yemen, Zambia, Zimbabwe.
Against: Albania, Andorra, Australia, Austria, Belgium, Bosnia and Herzegovina, Bulgaria, Canada, Croatia, Cyprus, Czech Republic, Denmark, Estonia, Finland, France, Georgia, Germany, Greece, Hungary, Iceland, Ireland, Israel, Italy, Japan, Latvia, Liechtenstein, Lithuania, Luxembourg, Malta, Marshall Islands, Micronesia, Monaco, Netherlands, New Zealand, Norway, Palau, Papua New Guinea, Poland, Portugal, Republic of Korea, Republic of Moldova, Romania, San Marino, Serbia and Montenegro, Slovakia, Slovenia, Spain, Sweden, Switzerland, The former Yugoslav Republic of Macedonia, Turkey, United Kingdom, United States.
Abstaining: Argentina, Armenia, Azerbaijan, Belarus, Brazil, Kazakhstan, Kyrgyzstan, Paraguay, Russian Federation, Samoa, South Africa, Tajikistan, Tonga, Ukraine, Uruguay, Uzbekistan, Vanuatu.

Peaceful uses of outer space

The Committee on the Peaceful Uses of Outer Space (Committee on Outer Space), at its forty-eighth session (Vienna, 8-17 June) [A/60/20 & Corr.1], discussed ways to maintain outer space for peaceful purposes, the spin-off benefits of space technology, space and society, and space and water. It examined the implementation of the recommendations of the Third (1999) United Nations Conference on the Exploration and Peaceful Uses of Outer Space (UNISPACE III) [YUN 1999, p. 556], and reviewed the work of its two subcommittees, one dealing with scientific and technical issues and the other with legal questions.

In accordance with General Assembly resolution 59/116 [YUN 2004, p. 632], Colombia, in its capacity as pro tempore secretariat of the Fourth (2002) Space Conference of the Americas [YUN 2002, p. 598], submitted a July report to the Committee [A/AC.105/L.261] on the implementation of the Conference's mandates.

GENERAL ASSEMBLY ACTION

On 8 December [meeting 62], the General Assembly, on the recommendation of the Fourth Committee [A/60/475], adopted **resolution 60/99** without vote [agenda item 29].

International cooperation in the peaceful uses of outer space

The General Assembly,

Recalling its resolutions 51/122 of 13 December 1996, 54/68 of 6 December 1999, 59/2 of 20 October 2004 and 59/116 of 10 December 2004,

Deeply convinced of the common interest of mankind in promoting and expanding the exploration and use of outer space, as the province of all mankind, for peaceful purposes and in continuing efforts to extend to all States the benefits derived therefrom, and also of the importance of international cooperation in this field, for which the United Nations should continue to provide a focal point,

Reaffirming the importance of international cooperation in developing the rule of law, including the relevant norms of space law and their important role in international cooperation for the exploration and use of outer space for peaceful purposes, and of the widest possible adherence to international treaties that promote the peaceful uses of outer space in order to meet emerging new challenges, especially for developing countries,

Seriously concerned about the possibility of an arms race in outer space, and bearing in mind the importance of article IV of the Treaty on Principles Governing the Activities of States in the Exploration and Use of Outer Space, including the Moon and Other Celestial Bodies,

Recognizing that all States, in particular those with major space capabilities, should contribute actively to the goal of preventing an arms race in outer space as an essential condition for the promotion and strengthening of international cooperation in the exploration and use of outer space for peaceful purposes,

Considering that space debris is an issue of concern to all nations,

Noting the progress achieved in the further development of peaceful space exploration and applications as well as in various national and cooperative space projects, which contributes to international cooperation, and the importance of further developing the legal framework to strengthen international cooperation in this field,

Convinced of the importance of the recommendations in the resolution entitled "The Space Millennium: Vienna Declaration on Space and Human Development", adopted by the Third United Nations Conference on the Exploration and Peaceful Uses of Outer Space (UNISPACE III), held at Vienna from 19 to 30 July 1999, and the need to promote the use of space technology towards implementing the United Nations Millennium Declaration,

Taking note of the actions already taken as well as those to be embarked upon to further implement the recommendations of UNISPACE III, as reflected in resolution 59/2 and the Plan of Action of the Committee on the Peaceful Uses of Outer Space,

Convinced that the use of space science and technology and their applications in such areas as telemedicine, tele-education, disaster management and environmental protection as well as other Earth observation applications contribute to achieving the objectives of the global conferences of the United Nations that address various aspects of economic, social and cultural development, inter alia, poverty eradication,

Having considered the report of the Committee on the Peaceful Uses of Outer Space on the work of its forty-eighth session,

1. *Endorses* the report of the Committee on the Peaceful Uses of Outer Space on the work of its forty-eighth session;

2. *Urges* States that have not yet become parties to the international treaties governing the uses of outer space to give consideration to ratifying or acceding to those treaties as well as incorporating them in their national legislation;

3. *Notes* that, at its forty-fourth session, the Legal Subcommittee of the Committee on the Peaceful Uses of Outer Space continued its work, as mandated by the General Assembly in its resolution 59/116;

4. *Endorses* the recommendation of the Committee that the Legal Subcommittee, at its forty-fifth session, taking into account the concerns of all countries, in particular those of developing countries:

(a) Consider the following as regular agenda items:
(i) General exchange of views;
(ii) Status and application of the five United Nations treaties on outer space;
(iii) Information on the activities of international organizations relating to space law;
(iv) Matters relating to:
  a. The definition and delimitation of outer space;
  b. The character and utilization of the geostationary orbit, including consideration of ways and means to ensure the rational and equitable use of the geostationary orbit without prejudice to the role of the International Telecommunication Union;

(b) Consider the following single issues/items for discussion:
(i) Review and possible revision of the Principles Relevant to the Use of Nuclear Power Sources in Outer Space;

(ii) Examination and review of the developments concerning the draft protocol on matters specific to space assets to the Convention on International Interests in Mobile Equipment;

(c) Consider the practice of States and international organizations in registering space objects in accordance with the workplan adopted by the Committee;

5. *Notes* that the Legal Subcommittee, at its forty-fifth session, will submit its proposals to the Committee for new items to be considered by the Subcommittee at its forty-sixth session, in 2007;

6. *Also notes* that, in the context of paragraph 4 (a) (ii) above, the Legal Subcommittee, at its forty-fifth session, will reconvene its Working Group and review the need to extend the mandate of the Working Group beyond that session of the Subcommittee;

7. *Further notes* that, in the context of paragraph 4 (a) (iv) a. above, the Legal Subcommittee will reconvene its Working Group on the item only to consider matters relating to the definition and delimitation of outer space;

8. *Agrees* that, in the context of paragraph 4 (c) above, the Legal Subcommittee should reconvene its Working Group in accordance with the workplan adopted by the Committee;

9. *Notes* that the Scientific and Technical Subcommittee, at its forty-second session, continued its work as mandated by the General Assembly in its resolution 59/116;

10. *Endorses* the recommendation of the Committee that the Scientific and Technical Subcommittee, at its forty-third session, taking into account the concerns of all countries, in particular those of developing countries:

(a) Consider the following items:

(i) General exchange of views and introduction to reports submitted on national activities;

(ii) United Nations Programme on Space Applications;

(iii) Implementation of the recommendations of the Third United Nations Conference on the Exploration and Peaceful Uses of Outer Space (UNISPACE III);

(iv) Matters relating to remote sensing of the Earth by satellite, including applications for developing countries and monitoring of the Earth's environment;

(b) Consider the following items in accordance with the workplans adopted by the Committee:

(i) Space debris;
(ii) Use of nuclear power sources in outer space;
(iii) Space-system-based telemedicine;
(iv) Near-Earth objects;
(v) Space-system-based disaster management support;
(vi) International Heliophysical Year 2007;

(c) Consider the following single issue/item for discussion: examination of the physical nature and technical attributes of the geostationary orbit and its utilization and applications, including in the field of space communications, as well as other questions relating to developments in space communications, taking particular account of the needs and interests of developing countries;

11. *Notes* that the Scientific and Technical Subcommittee, at its forty-third session, will submit its propo-

sal to the Committee for a draft provisional agenda for the forty-fourth session of the Subcommittee, in 2007;

12. *Endorses* the recommendation of the Committee that the symposium to strengthen the partnership with industry should be organized during the first week of the forty-third session of the Scientific and Technical Subcommittee and should address synthetic aperture radar missions and their applications;

13. *Agrees* that, in the context of paragraphs 10 (a) (ii) and (iii) and 11 above, the Scientific and Technical Sub-committee, at its forty-third session, should reconvene the Working Group of the Whole;

14. *Also agrees* that, in the context of paragraph 10 (b) (i) above, the Scientific and Technical Subcommittee, at its forty-third session, should reconvene its Working Group on Space Debris to consider issues arising from its workplan and, in particular, the draft of the space debris mitigation document of the Subcommittee and that the Working Group should continue its intersessional work as required to expedite agreement on the document;

15. *Further agrees* that, in the context of paragraph 10 (b) (ii) above, the Scientific and Technical Subcommittee, at its forty-third session, should reconvene its Working Group on the Use of Nuclear Power Sources in Outer Space and that the Working Group should continue its intersessional work on the topics described in the multi-year workplan as amended by the Subcommittee at its forty-second session;

16. *Agrees* that a joint technical workshop on the objectives, scope and general attributes of a potential technical safety standard for nuclear power sources in outer space should be organized together with the International Atomic Energy Agency and held during the forty-third session of the Scientific and Technical Subcommittee;

17. *Endorses* the United Nations Programme on Space Applications for 2006, as proposed to the Committee by the Expert on Space Applications and endorsed by the Committee;

18. *Notes with satisfaction* that, in accordance with paragraph 30 of General Assembly resolution 50/27 of 6 December 1995, the African regional centres for space science and technology education, in the French language and in the English language, located in Morocco and Nigeria, respectively, as well as the Centre for Space Science and Technology Education in Asia and the Pacific and the Regional Centre for Space Science and Technology Education for Latin America and the Caribbean, entered into an affiliation agreement with the Office for Outer Space Affairs of the Secretariat and have continued their education programmes in 2005;

19. *Agrees* that the regional centres referred to in paragraph 18 above should continue to report to the Committee on their activities on an annual basis;

20. *Notes with satisfaction* that the Centre for Space Science and Technology Education in Asia and the Pacific celebrated its tenth anniversary in 2005;

21. *Also notes with satisfaction* the contribution being made by the Scientific and Technical Subcommittee and the efforts of Member States and the Office for Outer Space Affairs to promote and support the activities being organized within the framework of the International Heliophysical Year 2007;

22. *Further notes with satisfaction* that the Government of Ecuador will be hosting the Fifth Space Conference of the Americas in Quito in July 2006 and that the Government of Chile will organize a preparatory meeting for the Conference, with the support of the Government of Colombia, the United Nations Educational, Scientific and Cultural Organization and the United Nations Office for Outer Space Affairs, during the International Air and Space Fair, to be held in Santiago in March 2006;

23. *Notes with satisfaction* that the Pro Tempore Secretariat of the Fourth Space Conference of the Americas, in accordance with paragraph 21 of resolution 59/116, informed the Committee of its activities to implement the Declaration of Cartagena de Indias and the Plan of Action of the Conference;

24. *Also notes with satisfaction* that the Federal Government of Nigeria, in collaboration with the Governments of Algeria and South Africa, hosted the first African Leadership Conference on Space Science and Technology for Sustainable Development from 23 to 25 November 2005 and that the Conference provided, under the theme "Space: an indispensable tool for Africa's development", a forum to exchange information on global space activities for societal development and African needs, including capacity-building, to benefit from the applications of space science and technology and to consider how to strengthen the participation of Africa in the work of the Committee and its Subcommittees;

25. *Further notes with satisfaction* that the Islamic Republic of Iran, in cooperation with the Economic and Social Commission for Asia and the Pacific, hosted the eleventh session of the Intergovernmental Consultative Committee on the Regional Space Applications Programme for Sustainable Development in September 2005;

26. *Recommends* that more attention be paid and political support be provided to all matters relating to the protection and the preservation of the outer space environment, especially those potentially affecting the Earth's environment;

27. *Considers* that it is essential that Member States pay more attention to the problem of collisions of space objects, including those with nuclear power sources, with space debris, and other aspects of space debris, calls for the continuation of national research on this question, for the development of improved technology for the monitoring of space debris and for the compilation and dissemination of data on space debris, also considers that, to the extent possible, information thereon should be provided to the Scientific and Technical Subcommittee and agrees that international cooperation is needed to expand appropriate and affordable strategies to minimize the impact of space debris on future space missions;

28. *Urges* all States, in particular those with major space capabilities, to contribute actively to the goal of preventing an arms race in outer space as an essential condition for the promotion of international cooperation in the exploration and use of outer space for peaceful purposes;

29. *Emphasizes* the need to increase the benefits of space technology and its applications and to contribute to an orderly growth of space activities favourable to sustained economic growth and sustainable develop-

ment in all countries, including mitigation of the consequences of disasters, in particular in the developing countries;

30. *Notes* that space science and technology and their applications could make important contributions to economic, social and cultural development and welfare, as indicated in the resolution entitled "The Space Millennium: Vienna Declaration on Space and Human Development";

31. *Reiterates* that the benefits of space technology and its applications should be prominently brought to the attention, in particular, of the major United Nations conferences and summits for economic, social and cultural development and related fields and that the use of space technology should be promoted towards achieving the objectives of those conferences and summits and for implementing the United Nations Millennium Declaration;

32. *Requests* the Secretary-General to submit to the General Assembly at its sixty-first session, through the Committee on the Peaceful Uses of Outer Space, a report on the inclusion of the issue of the use of space technology in the reports submitted by the Secretary-General to those conferences and summits, and its inclusion in the outcomes and commitments of those conferences and summits;

33. *Notes with satisfaction* the increased efforts of the Committee and its Scientific and Technical Subcommittee as well as the Office for Outer Space Affairs and the Inter-Agency Meeting on Outer Space Activities to promote the use of space science and technology and their applications in carrying out actions recommended in the Plan of Implementation of the World Summit on Sustainable Development ("Johannesburg Plan of Implementation");

34. *Urges* entities of the United Nations system, particularly those participating in the Inter-Agency Meeting on Outer Space Activities, to examine, in cooperation with the Committee, how space science and technology and their applications could contribute to implementing the United Nations Millennium Declaration, particularly in the areas relating to, inter alia, food security and increasing opportunities for education;

35. *Invites* the Inter-Agency Meeting on Outer Space Activities to continue to contribute to the work of the Committee and to report to the Committee and its Scientific and Technical Subcommittee on the work conducted at its annual sessions;

36. *Notes with satisfaction* that the open informal meetings, held in conjunction with the annual sessions of the Inter-Agency Meeting on Outer Space Activities and in which representatives of member States and observers in the Committee participate, provide a constructive mechanism for an active dialogue between the entities of the United Nations system and member States and observers in the Committee;

37. *Encourages* entities of the United Nations system to participate fully in the work of the Inter-Agency Meeting on Outer Space Activities;

38. *Notes* that space technology could play a central role in disaster reduction and that both the Committee and its Scientific and Technical Subcommittee could contribute to the implementation of the Hyogo Declaration and the Hyogo Framework for Action 2005-2015, adopted by the World Conference on Disaster Reduc-

tion, held at Kobe, Hyogo, Japan, from 18 to 22 January 2005;

39. *Requests* the Committee to continue to consider, as a matter of priority, ways and means of maintaining outer space for peaceful purposes and to report thereon to the General Assembly at its sixty-first session, and agrees that during its consideration of the matter, the Committee could continue to consider ways to promote regional and interregional cooperation based on experiences stemming from the Space Conference of the Americas and the role space technology could play in the implementation of recommendations of the World Summit on Sustainable Development;

40. *Notes with satisfaction* that the Committee would be establishing a closer link between its work to implement the recommendations of UNISPACE III and the work of the Commission on Sustainable Development by contributing to the thematic areas that will be addressed by the Commission;

41. *Agrees* that the Director of the Division for Sustainable Development of the Department of Economic and Social Affairs of the Secretariat should be invited to participate in the sessions of the Committee to inform it how it could best contribute to the work of the Commission;

42. *Also agrees* that the Director of the Office for Outer Space Affairs should participate in the sessions of the Commission on Sustainable Development to raise awareness and promote the benefits of space science and technology for sustainable development;

43. *Notes with satisfaction* the progress made, in accordance with General Assembly resolution 59/2, by Global Navigation Satellite Systems (GNSS) and augmentation system providers to establish an international committee on GNSS and by the ad hoc expert group established to study the possibility of creating an international entity to provide for coordination and the means of realistically optimizing the effectiveness of space-based services for use in disaster management;

44. *Welcomes* the fact that the Office for Outer Space Affairs could integrate into its programme of work a number of actions identified for implementation by the Office in the Plan of Action of the Committee for the further implementation of the recommendations of UNISPACE III;

45. *Notes* that some actions identified for implementation by the Office in the Plan of Action could only be integrated into its programme of work if additional staff and financial resources were provided;

46. *Urges* all Member States to contribute to the Trust Fund for the United Nations Programme on Space Applications to enhance the capacity of the Office to provide technical and legal advisory services and initiate pilot projects in accordance with the Plan of Action of the Committee, while maintaining the priority thematic areas agreed by the Committee;

47. *Agrees* that the Committee should continue to consider a report on the activities of the International Satellite System for Search and Rescue as a part of its consideration of the United Nations Programme on Space Applications under the agenda item entitled "Report of the Scientific and Technical Subcommittee", and invites Member States to report on their activities regarding the System;

48. *Requests* the Committee to continue to consider, at its forty-ninth session, its agenda item entitled "Spin-off benefits of space technology: review of current status";

49. *Also requests* the Committee to continue to consider, at its forty-ninth session, under its agenda item entitled "Space and society", the special theme for the focus of discussions for the period 2004-2006 "Space and education", in accordance with the workplan adopted by the Committee;

50. *Agrees* that the Committee should continue to consider, at its forty-ninth session, its agenda item entitled "Space and water";

51. *Also agrees* that a new item entitled "Recommendations of the World Summit on the Information Society" should be included in the agenda of the Committee at its forty-ninth session, with a view to contributing to their implementation;

52. *Further agrees* that a symposium on space and forests should be held during the forty-ninth session of the Committee;

53. *Notes with satisfaction* that the Committee agreed to consider, at its forty-ninth session, under its agenda item "Other matters", the evolution of space activities and how to develop a long-term plan to strengthen the role of the Committee in international cooperation in the peaceful uses of outer space;

54. *Notes* that in accordance with the agreement reached by the Committee at its forty-sixth session on the measures relating to the future composition of the bureaux of the Committee and its subsidiary bodies, on the basis of the measures relating to the working methods of the Committee and its subsidiary bodies, the Group of African States, the Group of Eastern European States, the Group of Latin American and Caribbean States and the Group of Western European and Other States nominated their candidates for the offices of Second Vice-Chair/Rapporteur of the Committee, First Vice-Chair of the Committee, Chair of the Legal Subcommittee and Chair of the Committee, respectively, for the period 2006-2007;

55. *Urges* the Group of Asian States to nominate its candidate for the office of Chair of the Scientific and Technical Subcommittee for the period 2006-2007 in time for the Subcommittee to begin its work at its forty-third session as scheduled;

56. *Agrees* that, upon the nomination of the candidate of the Group of Asian States for the Chair of the Scientific and Technical Subcommittee, the two Subcommittees should elect their officers;

57. *Notes* that the Committee, at its forty-ninth session, would endorse the election of the officers of its Subcommittees and would elect its officers for the period 2006-2007;

58. *Also notes* that the Group of Western European and Other States nominated its candidate for the office of Second Vice-Chair/Rapporteur of the Committee, for the period 2008-2009, at the forty-eighth session of the Committee, for its consideration;

59. *Further notes* that each of the regional groups has the responsibility to actively promote the participation in the work of the Committee and its subsidiary bodies of the member States of the Committee that are also members of the respective regional groups, and agrees that the regional groups should consider this Committee-related matter among their members;

60. *Endorses* the decision of the Committee to grant permanent observer status to the European Space Policy Institute;

61. *Urges* the Committee to expand the scope of international cooperation relating to the social, economic, ethical and human dimensions in space science and technology applications;

62. *Requests* entities of the United Nations system and other international organizations to continue and, where appropriate, to enhance their cooperation with the Committee and to provide it with reports on the issues dealt with in the work of the Committee and its subsidiary bodies.

Implementation of UNISPACE III recommendations

In accordance with General Assembly resolution 59/2 [YUN 2004, p. 637], the Committee on Outer Space considered the implementation of the UNISPACE III recommendations. Before it were the Secretary-General's 2004 note transmitting the Committee's report on the implementation of the recommendations [YUN 2004, p. 636] and a series of conference room papers on issues related to that topic. The Committee emphasized the importance of implementing the plan of action for operationalizing the UNISPACE III recommendations. It noted the continuing implementation of the recommendations by Member States through national, regional and international efforts, and the work of some of the action teams established in 2001 [YUN 2001, p. 568] and 2003 [YUN 2003, p. 641].

The Committee agreed that, in order to establish a closer link between its efforts to implement the UNISPACE III recommendations and the work of the Commission on Sustainable Development, the Director of the Division for Sustainable Development of the UN Department of Economic and Social Affairs should be invited to participate in the Committee's sessions, and the Director of the Office for Outer Space Affairs should attend the Commission's sessions, with a view to raising awareness and promoting the benefits of space science and technology. It agreed that Member States should provide inputs for the development of a concise document for the policy year of the Commission's 2006-2007 thematic policy areas, which the Scientific and Technical Subcommittee should review and finalize in 2006, with the support of the Action Team on Sustainable Development, and transmit to the Commission on the Committee's behalf. In addition, they should provide inputs for the Committee's annual contribution to the work of the Commission one year before the Commission addressed the thematic areas. The Subcommittee should review and finalize it. In that regard, the Committee agreed that the Subcommittee should finalize, in 2006, the Committee's contribution for that year and the first draft for 2007.

The Committee reviewed a draft of the study agreed to by the Assembly in resolution 59/2, conducted by the ad hoc expert group, on the possibility of creating an international entity to provide for coordination and the means of realistically optimizing the effectiveness of space-based services for use in disaster management. It requested the ad hoc expert group to finalize the study, which should be reviewed by Member States and the Fourth Committee's Working Group of the Whole and submitted to the Subcommittee in 2006 for review and recommendation to the Committee.

The Committee also considered the strategy, presented by the Office for Outer Space Affairs [A/AC.105/L.262], in accordance with resolution 59/2, for incorporating into its programme of work the actions identified for implementation by the Office in the Committee's 2004 plan of action. The Committee welcomed the fact that the Office could integrate, within existing resources, many of the actions contained in the plan. However, to accommodate new actions, the Office would need to adjust its operational priorities and increase its extrabudgetary resources in order to provide technical and legal services and initiate pilot projects.

The Committee agreed that the Office should promote cooperation with and support for the regional centres for space science at the regional and international levels, and should launch a support campaign for the centres among space-related institutions and relevant companies. The Committee considered the activities of the UN Programme on Space Applications and agreed that the Programme should continue to focus on thematic areas identified by the Expert on Space Applications in her briefing to the Committee and include water among its thematic priority areas, as a contribution to the work of the Commission on Sustainable Development.

In accordance with Assembly resolution 59/116 [YUN 2004, p. 632], the Scientific and Technical Subcommittee convened the Working Group of the Whole to consider the implementation of the UNISPACE III recommendations.

Scientific and Technical Subcommittee

The Scientific and Technical Subcommittee of the Committee on Outer Space, at its forty-second session (Vienna, 21 February–4 March) [A/AC.105/848], considered the United Nations Programme on Space Applications and the implementation of the UNISPACE III recommendations. It also dealt with matters relating to the remote sensing of the Earth by satellite, including applications for developing countries and monitoring of the Earth's environment; space debris; the use of nuclear power sources in space; space-system-based telemedicine and disaster management support; near-Earth objects; the examination of the physical nature and technical attributes of the geostationary orbit and its utilization and applications; and support to proclaim 2007 as the International Geophysical and Heliophysical Year.

UN Programme on Space Applications

The United Nations Programme on Space Applications, as mandated by General Assembly resolution 37/90 [YUN 1982, p. 163], continued to assist developing countries and countries with economies in transition to establish or strengthen their capacity in space science and technology through long-term training fellowships, technical advisory services, regional and international training courses and conferences, and to promote cooperation between developed and developing countries.

The United Nations Expert on Space Applications [A/AC.105/861] said that the Programme continued to emphasize cooperation with Member States at the regional and international levels in support of the UN-affiliated regional centres for space science and technology education. Within the framework of the Programme, and with the cooperation of the Australian Maritime Safety Authority, the United Nations/Australia Training Course on Satellite-Aided Search and Rescue was organized (Canberra, Australia, 14-18 March) [A/AC.105/851] to benefit countries in the Pacific region. Under the Programme's priority area of space technology for disaster management, which aimed at supporting developing countries' use of space technology to deal with natural disasters, the Programme organized jointly with the Algerian Space Agency, the United Nations/Algeria/European Space Agency (ESA) International Seminar on the Use of Space Technology for Disaster Management: Prevention and Management of Natural Disasters (Algiers, Algeria, 22-26 May) [A/AC.105/852]. The Programme initiated the United Nations/ESA/Argentina Workshop on the Use of Space Technology for Human Health for the benefit of Latin American countries (Córdoba, Argentina, 19-23 September) and the Office for Outer Space Affairs/Economic and Social Commission for Asia and the Pacific/China Workshop on Tele-Health Development in Asia and the Pacific (Guangzhou, China, 5-9 December). The United Nations International Meeting for the Establishment of the International Committee on Global

Navigation Satellite Systems (ICG) (Vienna, 1-2 December) established the Committee on a voluntary basis. Other workshops held during the year included the fifteenth United Nations/International Astronautical Federation Workshop on Space Education and Capacity-Building for Sustainable Development (Kitakyushu, Japan, 14-15 October) [A/AC.105/854]; the United Nations/ESA/United States National Aeronautics and Space Administration Workshop on the International Heliophysical Year 2007 (Abu Dhabi and Al-Ain, United Arab Emirates, 20-23 November) [A/AC.105/856]; and the fourth United Nations Workshop on Space Law (Abuja, Nigeria, 21-24 November). In all, the Programme held 10 workshops, training courses and conferences in 2005 and provided technical advisory services to activities promoting regional cooperation.

Following consideration of the report of the Expert on Space Applications [A/AC.105/840], describing 2004 programme activities, those scheduled for 2005, and activities of UN-affiliated regional centres for space science and technology education for 2004, 2005 and 2006, the Subcommittee reiterated its concern over the Programme's limited financial resources and appealed to Member States for voluntary contributions.

The General Assembly, in **resolution 60/99** (see p. 698), endorsed the Programme on Space Applications for 2006, as proposed by the Expert.

Cooperation

The Inter-Agency Meeting on Outer Space Activities, at its twenty-fifth session (Vienna, 31 January–2 February) [A/AC.105/842], discussed the coordination of plans and programmes in the practical application of space technology and related areas; ways of establishing inventories of space-related resources, especially data sets, space-related devices and educational and training materials; involvement of UN entities in the International Charter on Space and Major Disasters, to which the UN Office for Outer Space Affairs became a cooperating body in 2003 [YUN 2003, p. 643]; space-related outcomes of the 2002 World Summit on Sustainable Development [YUN 2002, p. 821]; electronic information-networking in the UN system; implementation of the UNISPACE III recommendations; and a revised brochure on the use of space technology by the UN system for sustainable development.

Noting the reduced participation of some UN entities that played key roles in various coordinated space-related activities, the Meeting agreed that letters emphasizing the benefits of participating in its meetings should be sent by the Director of the Office for Outer Space Affairs to the heads of those entities. The Committee on Outer Space should also encourage UN system entities to participate in the Meeting's work. Those entities could enhance their participation in the meetings of the Committee and the Scientific and Technical Subcommittee by submitting written reports instead of making oral presentations, as well as information and reports on their activities related to the work of the Committee and its Subcommittee. The Meeting invited UN entities to contribute to a unified list of space-related training events for 2005 maintained by the Office for Outer Space Affairs. The Meeting reviewed and amended the Secretary-General's draft report on the coordination of space-related activities within the UN system: directions and anticipated results for the period 2005-2006 [A/AC.105/841].

The Meeting noted that the World Health Organization (WHO) would be taking a leading role in telemedicine and would welcome cooperation with other UN system entities and that the Office for Outer Space Affairs had invited interested entities to join in the development of pilot projects for water resource management that included the use of space technologies.

The Meeting agreed that the Office of Outer Space Affairs should coordinate with UN system entities in setting up a web page that would make available links to inventories of space-related resources that could be shared. The web page should be reviewed in 2006.

Having examined the list of space-related initiatives and programmes of Member States of the Committee on Outer Space and within the UN system that responded to recommendations contained in the Plan of Implementation of the 2002 World Summit on Sustainable Development [YUN 2002, p. 821], it agreed that UN system entities should be invited to provide, by 16 February, updated information and comments for inclusion in the list, an updated version of which should be submitted to the Scientific and Technical Subcommittee at its forty-second (2005) session.

The Meeting agreed that UN system entities should examine the 2004 Committee on Outer Space plan of action for the implementation of the UNISPACE III recommendations [YUN 2004, p. 637], with a view to identifying those actions that they could address or to which they could contribute. Noting that the brochure on the use of space technology by the UN system for sustainable development had proven to be useful in disseminating information on how UN system entities were using space technology for sustainable development, the meeting directed the Office of Outer Space Affairs to explore the possibility of making it available in the six UN official languages. It invited interested UN entities to provide funding and in-kind support for printing the brochure.

The Meeting also agreed that its informal open session, held in conjunction with its annual sessions, was a constructive mechanism for ensuring active dialogue between UN entities and member States of the Committee on Outer Space.

In response to the Meeting's 2003 request [YUN 2003, p. 643] that the Scientific and Technical Subcommittee invite UN entities to submit annual reports on specific themes, the Meeting submitted a February report [A/AC.105/843] to the Committee on Outer Space on new and emerging technologies and applications and initiatives for space-related inter-agency cooperation.

Scientific and technical issues

In 2005, the Scientific and Technical Subcommittee [A/AC.105/848] continued to emphasize the importance of providing non-discriminatory access to remote sensing data and to derive information at reasonable cost and in a timely manner, and capacity-building for the adoption and use of remote sensing technology, in particular to meet the needs of developing countries. It encouraged further international cooperation in the use of remote sensing satellites, in particular by sharing experiences and technologies through bilateral, regional and international collaborative projects.

The Subcommittee agreed that Member States, in particular space-faring countries, should pay more attention to the problem of the collision of space objects, including those with nuclear power sources on board, with space debris, and to other aspects of space debris, and make available the results of national research on space debris, including information on minimizing its creation. The Subcommittee noted that the Inter-Agency Space Debris Coordination Committee (IADC) continued to achieve progress in understanding the technical issues related to space debris. Pursuant to General Assembly resolution 59/116 [YUN 2004, p. 632], the Subcommittee reconvened its Working Group on Space Debris to consider the 2003 IADC proposals on space debris mitigation [YUN 2003, p. 644], and endorsed the working group's report, which was annexed to the Subcommittee's report.

Also, in accordance with resolution 59/116, the Subcommittee reconvened its Working Group on the Use of Nuclear Power Sources (NPS) in Outer Space and noted the progress made during the intersessional period by the Working Group on the development of potential implementation options for establishing an international technically based framework of goals and recommendations for the safety of planned and currently foreseeable space NPS applications. The Subcommittee also noted that the Working Group had agreed to hold a joint technical workshop with the International Atomic Energy Agency (IAEA), in 2006, on a potential technical safety standard for NPS in outer space, as proposed in the Group's working paper [A/AC.105/C.1/L.278]. The Subcommittee endorsed the Working Group's report, which was annexed to the Subcommittee's report and the recommendation that the Group continue its intersessional work on the topics described in the multi-year programme on the use of NPS adopted in 2003 [YUN 2003, p. 644], as amended. The Subcommittee noted that relief efforts conducted in response to the Indian Ocean tsunami disaster of 26 December 2004 [YUN 2004, p. 952] had shown that emergency satellite-based communications were crucial in saving lives and reducing human suffering.

The Committee on Outer Space [A/60/20 & Corr.1] agreed that the Working Group on the Use of Nuclear Power Sources in Outer Space should continue its intersessional work, by electronic means, in close cooperation with IAEA and the Office of Outer Space Affairs to finalize the technical workshop to be held jointly in 2006 on the objective, scope and general attributes of a potential technical safety standard for nuclear power sources in outer space. During the intersessional meeting (Vienna, 13-15 June) [A/AC.105/L.260], the Working Group finalized a list of workshop objectives and topics and prepared an indicative schedule of work. In response to the Subcommittee's request that Member States and regional space agencies continue to report on national research concerning the safety of space objects with NPS, the Secretariat submitted, in a January addendum [A/AC.105/838/Add.1] to a 2004 note [YUN 2004, p. 641], the reply received from one Member State.

Also submitted to the Subcommittee were a Secretariat note [A/AC.105/857] and a series of addenda [A/AC.105/832/Add.1-4] to a 2004 note [YUN 2004, p. 641] containing information received from 11 Member States on their space activities.

Legal Subcommittee

The Legal Subcommittee, at its forty-fourth session (Vienna, 4-15 April) [A/AC.105/850], reconvened its working group on the examination of the preliminary draft protocol on matters specific to space assets to the Convention on International Interests in Mobile Equipment, which was opened for signature in 2001 [YUN 2001, p. 570]. The working group considered separately the possi-

bility of the United Nations serving as supervisory body under the future protocol and the relationship between the terms of the future protocol and the rights and obligations of States under the legal regime applicable to outer space.

In response to the group's 2003 recommendation [YUN 2004, p. 641], endorsed by the General Assembly in resolution 59/116 [ibid., p. 633], an open-ended ad hoc working group was established to continue consideration of the appropriateness of the United Nations serving as supervisory authority, in the period between its Subcommittee's 2004 and 2005 sessions. The ad hoc working group's final report [A/AC.105/C.2/L.256] was appended to that of the Subcommittee's, as well as a draft resolution on the subject submitted by Canada, the Czech Republic, France, Germany, Hungary, Italy, the Netherlands, Spain, Sweden and the United States for possible future consideration and adoption by the Assembly. The Subcommittee reported that consensus was not reached on the question of the appropriateness of the United Nations serving as supervisory authority.

The Subcommittee also reconvened its working group on the definition and delimitation of outer space, which considered an analytical summary of the replies to a questionnaire on possible legal issues with regard to aerospace objects [A/AC.105/C.2/L.249/Add.1] and on the preferences of Member States in that regard [A/AC.105/849]. The working group agreed to: continue to invite Member States to reply to the questionnaire and submit their preferences regarding those replies, as well as proposals on a methodology for reviewing them, with a view to developing an acceptable common understanding regarding the definition and delimitation of outer space, along with information on national legislation or practices relating to the subject. The working group recommended that the Committee on Outer Space invite the Subcommittee to prepare a report on the technical characteristics of aerospace objects in the light of the current level of technological advancement and possible developments in the foreseeable future.

Also, in accordance with Assembly resolution 59/116, the Subcommittee established, in April, a working group on the practice of States and international organizations in registering space objects. The working group had before it a Secretariat background paper on the subject [A/AC.105/C.2/L.255 & Corr.1, 2] and a conference room paper containing statistical information on the number of space objects launched and registered or unregistered between 1957 and 2004.

The working group encouraged States parties to the 1974 Convention on Registration of Objects

Launched into Outer Space (the Registration Convention), contained in Assembly resolution 3235(XXIX) [YUN 1974, p. 63], to provide information to the Secretary-General in accordance with the Convention and establish a national registry and inform the Secretary-General accordingly. UN Member States that had not yet done so were encouraged to become party to the Convention and to furnish, until such time, information in accordance with Assembly resolution 1721 B (XVI) [YUN 1961, p. 35]. States should study the background paper and submit information and views on the issues of harmonization of practices (administrative and practical), non-registration of space objects, and practice with regard to the transfer of ownership of space objects in orbit and registration/non-registration of "foreign" space objects. The working group also agreed that international intergovernmental organizations should again be invited to submit information on their practices in registering space objects and the Secretariat should prepare a list of all States that had launched objects into outer space.

To facilitate its consideration of the benefits of being party to the Registration Convention, the working group agreed that the Secretariat should prepare a paper on the subject, based on the indicative list of benefits to, and rights and obligations of, parties to the five UN treaties on outer space [YUN 2001, p. 571], and compile relevant elements from the proceedings of the UN workshops on space law.

The Subcommittee agreed that it would be premature for the working group on the status and application of the five UN treaties on outer space, to meet during the current session, as Member States and international organizations needed time to respond to the letters sent to them concerning those treaties and to the Assembly's recommendation in resolution 59/115 [YUN 2004, p. 642] on the voluntary submission by Member States of information on their current practices regarding on-orbit transfer of ownership of space objects. It agreed to reconvene the working group in 2006. The Subcommittee also agreed that Member States should regularly provide the Office of Outer Space Affairs with information on their national space legislation and policy in order for the Office to maintain an up-to-date database on that subject.

The Subcommittee also considered a Secretariat note [A/AC.105/C.2/L.254 & Corr.1 & Add.1] and a conference room paper containing information on activities related to space law received from five international organizations.

The Committee on Outer Space [A/60/20 & Corr.1] endorsed the recommendations of the Subcommittee and its working groups on the def-

inition and delimitation of outer space and on the practice of States and international organizations in registering space objects.

Effects of atomic radiation

At its fifty-third session (Vienna, 26-30 September) [A/60/46], the United Nations Scientific Committee on the Effects of Atomic Radiation continued the development of new documents on the sources and effects of ionizing radiation, last reviewed by the Committee in 2004 [YUN 2004, p. 642]. It held detailed technical discussions that resulted in clear instructions to the Secretariat on the content and form of future scientific annexes. It was envisaged that a report with scientific annexes would be submitted to the General Assembly for consideration in 2006, and additional annexes in 2007. The Committee reviewed advanced draft documents on the exposure of workers and the public to various sources of radiation; re-evaluated the risks from radon in homes and workplaces; reviewed the risk and effects of radiation on non-human biota; considered new evidence for the mechanisms by which ionizing radiation could induce health effects; evaluated new epidemiological studies of radiation and cancer; reviewed evidence for diseases other than cancer that might be related to radiation exposure; and analysed the wide variability globally in medical radiation exposures and the health impact due to radiation from the 1986 Chernobyl accident [YUN 1986, p. 584], for which the Committee had established official collaboration with scientists in Belarus, the Russian Federation and Ukraine in 2003 [YUN 2003, p. 650], later known as the Chernobyl Forum. The Committee noted that the Forum's recent findings affirmed the scientific conclusions on the health consequences due to radiation from the accident, which the Committee had reported to the Assembly in 2000 [YUN 2000, p. 590], and expressed its readiness to continue to provide the scientific basis for a better understanding of those consequences. It called on Member States, UN system specialized agencies and other scientific international and national bodies to provide information for its reviews.

The need for the restoration of an adequate operating budget to allow the Committee to fulfil its mandate, most recently expressed in Assembly resolutions 58/88 [YUN 2003, p. 650] and 59/114 [YUN 2004, p. 643], remained a concern. Although increased funds had been provided for recruiting consultants, only partial restitution had occurred. The Committee anticipated that, pursuant to resolution 59/114, funding in the 2008-2009 biennium would be strengthened, and the United Nations Environment Programme would provide additional resources in 2006-2007 to allow for the effective implementation of the plans endorsed by the Assembly.

The Committee decided to hold its fifty-fourth session in Vienna from 29 May to 2 June 2006.

GENERAL ASSEMBLY ACTION

On 8 December [meeting 62], the General Assembly, on the recommendation of the Fourth Committee [A/60/474], adopted **resolution 60/98** without vote [agenda item 28].

Effects of atomic radiation

The General Assembly,

Recalling its resolution 913(X) of 3 December 1955, by which it established the United Nations Scientific Committee on the Effects of Atomic Radiation, and its subsequent resolutions on the subject, including resolution 59/114 of 10 December 2004, in which, inter alia, it requested the Scientific Committee to continue its work,

Taking note with appreciation of the work of the Scientific Committee,

Reaffirming the desirability of the Scientific Committee continuing its work,

Concerned about the potentially harmful effects on present and future generations resulting from the levels of radiation to which mankind and the environment are exposed,

Noting the views expressed by Member States at its sixtieth session with regard to the work of the Scientific Committee,

Noting with satisfaction that some Member States have expressed particular interest in becoming members of the Scientific Committee, and expressing its intention to consider the issue further at its next session,

Conscious of the continuing need to examine and compile information about atomic and ionizing radiation and to analyse its effects on mankind and the environment,

1. *Commends* the United Nations Scientific Committee on the Effects of Atomic Radiation for the valuable contribution it has been making in the course of the past fifty years, since its inception, to wider knowledge and understanding of the levels, effects and risks of ionizing radiation, and for fulfilling its original mandate with scientific authority and independence of judgement;

2. *Reaffirms* the decision to maintain the present functions and independent role of the Scientific Committee;

3. *Requests* the Scientific Committee to continue its work, including its important activities to increase knowledge of the levels, effects and risks of ionizing radiation from all sources, and invites the Scientific Committee to submit its programme of work to the General Assembly;

4. *Endorses* the intentions and plans of the Scientific Committee for its future activities of scientific review and assessment on behalf of the General Assembly;

5. *Requests* the Scientific Committee to continue at its next session the review of the important problems in the field of ionizing radiation and to report thereon to the General Assembly at its sixty-first session;

6. *Emphasizes* the need for the Scientific Committee to hold regular sessions on an annual basis so that its report can reflect the latest developments and findings in the field of ionizing radiation and thereby provide updated information for dissemination among all States;

7. *Expresses its appreciation* for the assistance rendered to the Scientific Committee by Member States, the specialized agencies, the International Atomic Energy Agency and non-governmental organizations, and invites them to increase their cooperation in this field;

8. *Invites* the Scientific Committee to continue its consultations with scientists and experts from interested Member States in the process of preparing its future scientific reports, and requests the Secretariat to facilitate such consultations;

9. *Welcomes*, in this context, the readiness of Member States to provide the Scientific Committee with relevant information on the effects of ionizing radiation in affected areas, and invites the Scientific Committee to analyse and give due consideration to such information, particularly in the light of its own findings;

10. *Invites* Member States, the organizations of the United Nations system and non-governmental organizations concerned to provide further relevant data about doses, effects and risks from various sources of radiation, which would greatly help in the preparation of future reports of the Scientific Committee to the General Assembly;

11. *Requests* the United Nations Environment Programme to continue providing support for the effective conduct of the work of the Scientific Committee and for the dissemination of its findings to the General Assembly, the scientific community and the public;

12. *Urges* the United Nations Environment Programme to review and strengthen the present funding of the Scientific Committee, pursuant to paragraph 6 of resolution 59/114, so that the Committee can discharge the responsibilities and mandate entrusted to it by the General Assembly.

PART TWO

Human rights

Chapter I

Promotion of human rights

In 2005, human rights were promoted through initiatives undertaken by legally binding instruments and the Commission on Human Rights and its subsidiary body, the Subcommission on the Promotion and Protection of Human Rights. The Office of the United Nations High Commissioner for Human Rights continued its coordination and implementation activities, and provided advisory services and assistance through its technical cooperation programme.

As a follow-up to the conclusion of the United Nations Decade for Human Rights Education (1995-2004), the World Programme for Human Rights Education, proclaimed in 2004 by the General Assembly, began on 1 January 2005. Subsequently, the Assembly adopted the revised plan of action for the Programme's first phase (2005-2007), which focused on primary and secondary school systems. Within the framework of his reform agenda to further improve the work of the United Nations and its common system, the Secretary-General proposed that the Commission on Human Rights be replaced with a smaller standing body to enable the Organization to take the cause of human rights as seriously as those of security and development. In September, the Assembly, acting on the Secretary-General's proposal, created the Human Rights Council and charged it with promoting universal respect for human rights and fundamental freedoms for all, addressing violations and mainstreaming human rights within the UN system. In the same context, the Office of the United Nations High Commissioner for Human Rights drew up a Plan of Action outlining a strategic vision for its future work. Other human rights monitoring bodies continued to promote civil, political, economic, social and cultural rights, and took action to eliminate racial discrimination and discrimination against women, to protect the rights of children and migrant workers and their families, and to end the practice of torture and other cruel, inhuman or degrading treatment or punishment.

The year also marked the midterm review of the International Decade for a Culture of Peace and Non-Violence for the Children of the World (2001-2010), proclaimed in 1998. The Director-General of the United Nations Educational, Scientific and Cultural Organization, which led efforts to implement the Decade, recommended measures to maintain visibility between the midpoint and the completion of the Decade. In December, the Assembly reaffirmed that the objective of the Decade was to strengthen further the global movement for a culture of peace and invited Member States to observe 21 September yearly as the International Day of Peace, and as a day of global ceasefire and non-violence.

UN machinery

Commission on Human Rights

The Commission on Human Rights held its sixty-first session in Geneva from 14 March to 22 April [E/2005/23 & Corr.1], during which it adopted 85 resolutions and 18 decisions. It recommended 43 draft decisions and one draft resolution for adoption by the Economic and Social Council. The Council took note of the Commission's report on 25 and 27 July (**decision 2005/296**).

In response to a 2000 Commission decision on enhancing the effectiveness of its mechanisms [YUN 2000, p. 595], the Commission Chairperson convened a one-day informal meeting on 27 September to facilitate the exchange of information in preparation for the General Assembly's sixtieth (2005) session [E/CN.4/IM/2005/1]. In a September note [E/CN.4/IM/2005/2], the Secretariat summarized the post-sessional meetings and activities of the Commission's Expanded Bureau.

The Commission had before it a discussion paper on enhancing and strengthening the effectiveness of its mechanisms and responses thereto, prepared by Asian human rights experts. On 21 April [dec. 2005/113], the Commission requested the High Commissioner to transmit the discussion paper to the special procedures and to solicit their views; organize an informal consultation between the special procedures and States devoted to an exchange of views on the item at the annual meeting of those procedures in 2005; study the issues raised in the discussion paper and contributions thereto and identify the practical steps taken by her Office to address them; organize an open-ended seminar in 2005 as part of efforts to enhance and strengthen the effectiveness of the special procedures; and report in

2006 on the implementation of the Commission's current decision. On 25 July, the Economic and Social Council endorsed the Commission's requests to the High Commissioner (**decision 2005/290**).

In response to the Commission's request (see above), the Office of the United Nations High Commissioner for Human Rights (OHCHR) organized a seminar on strengthening the effectiveness of the special procedures (Geneva, 12-13 October) [E/CN.4/2006/116], during which participants agreed that those procedures should be an integral part of the proposed human rights council (see below). It was also agreed that the human rights system could be further enhanced by fostering a greater sense of collegiality among mandate holders.

Organization of work

Note by Secretariat. The Commission had before it a note by the Secretariat [E/CN.4/2005/9] containing statistical data on its 2004 session, which was intended to assist with the organization of the Commission's work in 2005.

On 14 March [dec. 2005/101], the Commission invited special representatives, special rapporteurs, chairpersons and chairpersons/rapporteurs of various working groups and experts to participate in its meetings.

On 21 April [dec. 2005/114], the Commission decided that the first meeting of its sixty-second (2006) session would take place in January to elect its officers and that the session would be held from 13 March to 21 April. The Economic and Social Council approved the Commission's decision on 25 July (**decision 2005/291**).

Also on 21 April [dec. 2005/115], the Commission recommended that the Council authorize six additional meetings for its sixty-second session and requested the Chairperson of that session to organize the session's work within the time normally allotted so that the additional meetings would be utilized only if necessary.

On 25 July, the Council approved that measure (**decision 2005/292**).

Thematic procedures

In January, the Secretary-General provided a list of thematic and country-specific procedures and other Commission mechanisms for 2005 [E/CN.4/2005/1/Add.1]. Pursuant to a 2004 Commission resolution [YUN 2004, p. 648], he submitted a March report [E/CN.4/2005/108] containing references to the conclusions and recommendations of thematic special rapporteurs and working groups. The twelfth meeting of special rapporteurs/ representatives, independent experts and chair-

persons of working groups of the special procedures of the Commission and of the advisory services programme was held in June [E/CN.4/ 2006/4] (see p. 732).

Proposal for a human rights council

Report of Secretary-General (March). In the main part of his March report entitled "In larger freedom: towards development, security and human rights for all" [A/59/2005] (see p. 67), submitted to the 2005 World Summit, the Secretary-General suggested that the Commission on Human Rights be replaced with a smaller human rights council, to enable the Organization to take the cause of human rights as seriously as those of security and development. While acknowledging that the Commission had provided the international community with a universal framework for addressing human rights issues and a unique opportunity for working with civil society, the Secretary-General noted that the Commission's capacity to perform its tasks had been undermined by its declining credibility and professionalism. States sought Commission membership not to help strengthen human rights but to protect themselves from criticism or to criticize others, the Secretary-General observed. Consequently, a credibility deficit had developed, casting a shadow on the reputation of the UN system as a whole. Against that background, the creation of a human rights council would accord human rights a more authoritative position, corresponding to the primacy of human rights in the UN Charter.

While addressing the Commission on 7 April [E/CN.4/2005/SR.37], the Secretary-General outlined a key peer review function for the proposed human rights council, which was to evaluate States' fulfilment of their human rights obligations.

Commission action. On 22 April [E/2005/23 (dec. 2005/116)], the Commission, by a recorded vote of 34 to 15, with 4 abstentions, decided to establish an open-ended working group, to be chaired by its current Chairperson, and to convene a five-day intersessional meeting in June to reflect on the recommendations contained in the Secretary-General's March report (see above), with a view to contributing to the intergovernmental deliberations in the General Assembly on the proposed reform of the United Nations. To that end, the Commission also decided to convene a one-day special session to adopt formally the outcome of the working group.

On 9 June, the Economic and Social Council, taking note of the Commission's decision, requested its Chairperson to organize during the Commission's 2005 session an open-ended informal consultation of up to two days to reflect on the human rights recommendations contained in the Secretary-General's report (see above), and to prepare a summary thereof by 15 June, to be transmitted to the Assembly through the Council (**decision 2005/217**).

Those consultations took place on 20 June [A/59/847-E/2005/73], during which participants considered the role, functions, status and composition of the proposed new human rights body and related issues, as well as treaty body reform and the work of OHCHR.

Report of Secretary-General (May). In a 23 May addendum to his March report [A/59/2005/Add.1], the Secretary-General further explained that the establishment of a human rights council would reflect in concrete terms the increasing importance of human rights in the collective work of the Organization. It would offer structural clarity, given that the Organization already had Councils dealing with two other main issues—security and development. The proposed council would be a standing body, able to meet regularly and at any time to address imminent crises and enable timely and in-depth consideration of human rights issues. Its members would be elected directly by the General Assembly—the United Nations principal legislative body—which should make them more accountable and give the council greater authority than the Commission, which was a subsidiary body of the Economic and Social Council. Furthermore, a relatively smaller membership would enable the proposed council to hold more focused debates and discussions. The Secretary-General suggested that Member States agree on a number of issues in advance of the 2005 World Summit (see p. 47), including the proposed council's mandate and function, composition and size and whether it should be a principal organ of the Organization or subsidiary body of the Assembly. Thereafter, Member States could agree to endorse, in principle, the establishment of a human rights council in the Summit's Final Declaration. Further work on how the council would fulfil its functions and other details would be addressed in the post-summit phase.

General Assembly action. The General Assembly, in resolution 60/1 of 16 September entitled the 2005 World Summit Outcome (see p. 48), resolved to create a Human Rights Council, which would be responsible for promoting universal respect for the protection of human rights and fundamental freedoms for all. The Council should address human rights violations and make recommendations thereon, and should also promote effective coordination and mainstreaming of human rights within the UN system.

The Assembly President was requested to conduct negotiations during the Assembly's sixtieth (2005) session, aimed at establishing the Council's mandate, modalities, functions, size, composition, membership, working method and procedures.

Subcommission on the Promotion and Protection of Human Rights

The Subcommission on the Promotion and Protection of Human Rights, at its fifty-seventh session (Geneva, 25 July–12 August) [E/CN.4/2006/2], adopted 32 resolutions and 15 decisions, and recommended 7 draft decisions for adoption by the Commission.

On 10 August [dec. 2005/107], the Subcommission, by a roll-call vote of 19 to none, with 2 abstentions, requested OHCHR to provide the Subcommission annually and before the beginning of its sessions with a list of countries that had proclaimed a state of emergency; States that had issued a standing invitation to the special procedures; States that had rejected a request by a special procedure; States that were members of the Commission, including those that had issued standing invitations; States on the Commission's agenda; States being considered under the Commission's agenda item 9 on the question of the violation of human rights and fundamental freedoms in any part of the world that had denied access to the special procedures; and States where those procedures had indicated inadequate or nonexistent follow-up to their recommendations.

On 11 August [dec. 2005/113], the Subcommission approved the composition of its working groups for 2006.

On the same date [dec. 2005/114], the Subcommission, following an exchange of views on issues relating to the proposed reform of the United Nations, including of its human rights mechanisms (see p. 712), asked its Chairperson to transmit to the Commission's Chairperson and to OHCHR a document, annexed to its current decision, on the role of an independent expert body within the context of the reform of the UN human rights machinery, and to request that it be distributed widely, particularly to Member States. The document, intended to contribute to the debate on reform initiatives, concluded that, for 58 years, the political standard-setting organs had felt the need for an independent expert body. That need had not disappeared and would increase in the future.

Working papers. The Subcommission had before it a working paper [E/CN.4/Sub.2/2005/4] on the organization, content and outcome of its work under agenda item 2 on the question of human rights and fundamental freedoms, prepared by Françoise Hampson (United Kingdom), in response to a 2004 Subcommission request [YUN 2004, p. 648]. The paper set out the background to concerns regarding the manner in which the Subcommission addressed the item, examined the role and importance of the subject and made suggestions for improving its deliberations on the item, with a view to enabling the Subcommission to retain its mandate, contribute distinctively to the examination of human rights violations and avoid the duplication of work with other bodies.

The Subcommission also considered a June working paper [E/CN.4/Sub.2/2005/5] on its methods of work relating to reports, submitted by Emmanuel Decaux (France), in response to a 2004 Subcommission request [YUN 2004, p. 648]. The paper, which aimed to provide a framework to facilitate in-depth debate among Subcommission members, focused on the guidelines annexed to a 1999 Subcommission decision [YUN 1999, p. 569] and examined, among other things, the origins of studies considered by the Subcommission, the factors governing the selection of those studies, and their organization and scope. Reflecting on the Subcommission's 2003 [YUN 2003, p. 656] and 2004 [YUN 2004, p. 648] deliberations, it raised questions and made suggestions, with a view to stimulating joint discussion. The paper stated that the Subcommission should decide whether a working group needed to be set up, as had been done previously, given the uncertainty arising from ongoing negotiations at the High-level Plenary Meeting of the General Assembly (2005 World Summit).

Report of Subcommission Chairperson. The Commission had before it a report [E/CN.4/2005/90] of the Subcommission's 2004 Chairperson, Soli Jehangir Sorabjee (India), which summarized the Subcommission's work in 2004.

Commission action. On 20 April [res. 2005/53], the Commission decided that the Subcommission should continue to debate country situations not being addressed by the Commission, but should not adopt country-specific resolutions, decisions or chairperson's statements. It further decided that the Subcommission could best assist it by providing it with independent expert studies and working papers; recommendations based on their studies; and studies, research and expert advice at the Commission's request. It recommended that the Subcommission should continue holding annual closed meetings with the Commission's Expanded Bureau; streamlining its agenda; holding closed meetings on its working rules, procedures and timetables; drafting as many of its resolutions as possible in closed ses-

sion; and using a question-and-answer format and expert panel discussions. The Commission also recommended that the Subcommission improve its methods of work by focusing on its primary role as the Commission's advisory body; giving particular attention to studies recommended or confirmed by the Commission; respecting the highest standards of impartiality and expertise, and avoiding acts which would undermine the independence of its members; facilitating participation by non-governmental organizations (NGOs); considering studies and working papers by special rapporteurs and its members before sending them to the Commission; taking further steps to accomplish its work within a three-week session; proposing to the Commission ways to assist it in improving its work and vice versa; focusing on human rights questions relating to its mandate; avoiding duplication of its work with that of other bodies and mechanisms; and giving appropriate regard to legal opinions addressed to it. The Commission outlined criteria for States when nominating and electing Subcommission members and alternates.

OHCHR was asked to ensure that all initiatives of the Subcommission with financial implications for the UN budget, including from voluntary sources, were brought before the Commission for consideration. It should submit to the Commission in 2006 a comprehensive report on the administrative and programme budget of the Subcommission and recommendations for strengthening and enhancing its budgetary planning and management. The Secretary-General was asked to support the Subcommission by making available documentation in good time before each session in UN official languages and assisting it with requests for information from Governments, intergovernmental organizations and NGOs. The Commission recommended that the Subcommission Chairperson or his/her representative attend the meeting of special rapporteurs/representatives, experts and chairpersons of working groups of the special procedures of the Commission (see p. 732) and the meeting of chairpersons of treaty bodies (see p. 723) to facilitate coordination between the Subcommission and other relevant UN bodies and procedures. The Chairperson of the Subcommission's 2005 session was asked to report in 2006 on how recent enhancements of the Subcommission's procedures had worked in practice.

Subcommission action. On 8 August [dec. 2005/104], the Subcommission requested its Chairperson to forward the summary records of its 2005 deliberations on agenda item 2 to the Commission, as requested in Commission resolution 2005/53 (see above).

Notes by Secretary-General. A note of the Secretary-General, with a later addendum [E/CN.4/2006/80 & Add.1], contained the nominations and biographical data of candidates for election to the 26-member Subcommission and the corresponding alternates, as the term of office of half the membership was due to expire.

A May note of the Secretary-General [E/CN.4/Sub.2/2005/32] reviewed developments between 1 June 2004 and 1 June 2005 in areas with which the Subcommission had been concerned.

Office of the High Commissioner for Human Rights

Reports of High Commissioner. The UN High Commissioner for Human Rights, Louise Arbour (Canada), in a 17 May report [E/2005/65] to the Economic and Social Council, addressed the human rights dimension of the Millennium Declaration [YUN 2000, p. 49], particularly regarding the link between human rights and the Millennium Development Goals (MDGs) [ibid., p. 51]. Stressing that it was only in ensuring respect for human rights that MDGs could be achieved in a sustainable way, the High Commissioner identified a number of human rights concerns in that regard, concerning respect for the principle of non-discrimination, meaningful participation and adequate monitoring and accountability mechanisms. Regarding the implications of adopting a rights-based approach for specific goals, the report drew attention to the work undertaken by UN human rights mechanisms on rights-based approaches to development issues, including related guidelines published by OHCHR. It concluded that the current review of the Millennium Declaration should recognize States' human rights obligations to the strategies for achieving the MDGs.

The Council took note of the High Commissioner's report on 25 and 27 July (**decision 2005/296**).

By a 26 May report to the General Assembly [A/59/2005/Add.3], the Secretary-General transmitted the Plan of Action submitted by the High Commissioner, as called for in the main part of his March report to the 2005 World Summit (see p. 67). The Plan was drawn up against the backdrop of discussions on the future of the Commission, within the context of the Secretary-General's proposal for replacing it with an upgraded human rights council (see p. 712). As such, the Plan focused on the work of OHCHR and presented a strategic vision for the future direction of the Office, building on the Secretary-General's view that much more needed to be done by the international community to address

current human rights threats and that OHCHR should be better resourced to play its central role in meeting that challenge. Given that combating human rights problems stemming from poverty, discrimination, conflict, impunity, democratic deficits and institutional weaknesses necessitated greater focus on the implementation of human rights norms and standards developed in the past 60 years, the Plan envisaged action to address to a range of "implementation gaps", including those relating to knowledge, capacity, commitment and security. Based on the premise that OHCHR's mission was to help close those gaps and thereby empower people to realize their rights, the Plan set forth action points in five areas relating to country engagement, leadership, partnership, the UN human rights bodies and management, staffing and planning. The Plan's implementation was intended to begin within the year.

The High Commissioner's report to the Assembly [A/60/36] further described the Plan of Action, highlighting its two dimensions: programming human rights work, in accordance with the Secretary-General's reform agenda; and optimizing the use of resources, capacities and strengths of the UN human rights programme. The report noted that the goals of the Plan—protection and empowerment—reflected a more holistic view of the activities of the human rights programme and a recognition that human rights protection and the empowerment of individual right holders and duty bearers were decisive for bridging the gap between human rights rhetoric and reality. The Plan set out a strategy to address key human rights challenges, indicating that OHCHR needed to assume responsibility for identifying those challenges and obstacles, shaping international dialogues around them and proposing common strategies for addressing them effectively. To that end, the Plan outlined a series of initiatives, including, among others, periodic UN system-wide consultations and a global campaign for human rights. Pointing out that the reform of the human rights machinery would be an essential step in ensuring the effective implementation of human rights norms and standards at the national level, the High Commissioner reaffirmed support for a new human rights body (Human Rights Council), as proposed by the Secretary-General (see p. 712) and subsequently established by the Assembly in resolution 60/1 (see p. 48). The report also highlighted various activities undertaken during the year by the High Commissioner and OHCHR to implement the Plan of Action, concluding, however, that its full realization and success depended on Member States' support. The High Commissioner urged

Assembly members to join in future efforts to ensure a stronger and better-equipped OHCHR to meet the human rights needs of States, institutional partners, civil society and, most importantly, victims of human rights violations everywhere.

On 16 December, the General Assembly took note of a report of the Third (Social, Humanitarian and Cultural) Committee [A/60/509/Add.5] regarding the High Commissioner's report (**decision 60/535**).

Strengthening the function of OHCHR

Report of High Commissioner. In her first annual report to the Commission [E/CN.4/2005/12], the High Commissioner highlighted OHCHR activities designed to strengthen its capacity to promote and protect human rights at the country level, including through the provision of technical cooperation, support to national institutions, monitoring and protection work, and support to country rapporteurs and independent experts of the Commission. An important means of strengthening national systems of human rights protection was through cooperation with, and capacity-building for, UN country teams.

Composition of staff

Report of High Commissioner. In response to a 2004 Commission request [YUN 2004, p. 651], the High Commissioner submitted a report on the composition of OHCHR staff by nationality, grade and gender, as at 31 December 2004 [E/CN.4/2005/109].

Commission action. On 20 April [res. 2005/72], by a recorded vote of 36 to 15, with 2 abstentions, the Commission reaffirmed that it was necessary to change the prevailing geographical distribution of OHCHR staff, and requested the Secretary-General to ensure that particular attention was paid to recruiting staff from unrepresented and underrepresented Member States, particularly from developing countries and countries with economies in transition. The High Commissioner was asked to ensure that the one-time post regularization of all core posts at headquarters and in the field resulted in a new and balanced geographical distribution of OHCHR staff; prepare an action plan aimed at reducing the current staff imbalance, indicating specific targets and deadlines to be achieved; avoid duplication of functions and work toward the goal of improved effectiveness and management; use the Junior Professional Officers programme as a tool for training national technical personnel in developing countries and countries with economies in transition; and report in 2006. The General

Assembly and its appropriate subsidiary bodies were invited to give due consideration to the Commission's current resolution and to the 2004 report of the Joint Inspection Unit (JIU) [YUN 2004, p. 650] on a management review of OHCHR and the recommendations contained therein. JIU was asked to assist the Commission in monitoring the implementation of its current resolution and to submit to the Assembly in 2006 and to the Commission in 2007 a follow-up review of the implementation of the decisions of the Commission and other UN intergovernmental bodies regarding the management, programmes and administration of OHCHR, particularly their impact on the recruitment policy and staff composition. Annexed to the Commission's resolution was tabular information on the geographical distribution of OHCHR's staff between 2001 and 2005.

On 25 July, the Economic and Social Council endorsed the Commission's request to the Assembly and its subsidiary bodies, and to JIU (**decision 2005/274**).

Annual Appeal 2005

During the year, OHCHR received $73.9 million in voluntary contributions from donors towards activities outlined in the 2005 Annual Appeal, representing an increase of $13.9 million over 2004. The UN regular budget provided $34.8 million in 2005.

Strengthening action to promote human rights

In response to General Assembly resolutions 56/153 [YUN 2001, p. 582], 57/203 [YUN 2002, p. 616], 58/168 [YUN 2003, p. 660] and 59/190 [YUN 2004, p. 652], the Secretary-General, in a July report [A/60/134], submitted the proposals of one Member State (Georgia) for strengthening UN action in human rights through the promotion of international cooperation based on the principles of non-selectivity, impartiality and objectivity.

On 16 December, the Assembly took note of the Secretary-General's report (**decision 60/533**).

International cooperation in the field of human rights

On 20 April [res. 2005/54], the Commission called on Member States, specialized agencies and intergovernmental organizations to continue constructive dialogue and consultations to enhance the understanding of human rights promotion and protection and fundamental freedoms. States and relevant UN human rights mechanisms and procedures were asked to continue to pay attention to the importance of mutual cooperation in ensuring human rights promotion and protection.

GENERAL ASSEMBLY ACTION

On 16 December [meeting 64], the General Assembly, on the recommendation of the Third Committee [A/60/509/Add.2], adopted **resolution 60/156** without vote [agenda item 71 (b)].

Enhancement of international cooperation in the field of human rights

The General Assembly,

Reaffirming its commitment to promoting international cooperation, as set forth in the Charter of the United Nations, in particular Article 1, paragraph 3, as well as relevant provisions of the Vienna Declaration and Programme of Action adopted by the World Conference on Human Rights on 25 June 1993, for enhancing genuine cooperation among Member States in the field of human rights,

Recalling its adoption of the United Nations Millennium Declaration on 8 September 2000 and its resolution 59/187 of 20 December 2004, and taking note of Commission on Human Rights resolution 2005/54 of 20 April 2005 on the enhancement of international cooperation in the field of human rights,

Recalling also the World Conference against Racism, Racial Discrimination, Xenophobia and Related Intolerance, held at Durban, South Africa, from 31 August to 8 September 2001, and its role in the enhancement of international cooperation in the field of human rights,

Recognizing that the enhancement of international cooperation in the field of human rights is essential for the full achievement of the purposes of the United Nations, including the effective promotion and protection of all human rights,

Reaffirming that dialogue among religions, cultures and civilizations in the field of human rights could contribute greatly to the enhancement of international cooperation in this field,

Emphasizing the need for further progress in the promotion and encouragement of respect for human rights and fundamental freedoms through, inter alia, international cooperation,

Underlining the fact that mutual understanding, dialogue, cooperation, transparency and confidence-building are important elements in all the activities for the promotion and protection of human rights,

Recalling the adoption of resolution 2000/22 of 18 August 2000, on the promotion of dialogue on human rights issues, by the Subcommission on the Promotion and Protection of Human Rights at its fifty-second session,

1. *Reaffirms* that it is one of the purposes of the United Nations and the responsibility of all Member States to promote, protect and encourage respect for human rights and fundamental freedoms through, inter alia, international cooperation;

2. *Recognizes* that, in addition to their separate responsibilities to their individual societies, States have a collective responsibility to uphold the principles of human dignity, equality and equity at the global level;

3. *Reaffirms* that dialogue among cultures and civilizations facilitates the promotion of a culture of tolerance and respect for diversity, and welcomes in this regard the holding of conferences and meetings at the national, regional and international levels on dialogue among civilizations;

4. *Urges* all actors on the international scene to build an international order based on inclusion, justice, equality and equity, human dignity, mutual understanding and promotion of and respect for cultural diversity and universal human rights, and to reject all doctrines of exclusion based on racism, racial discrimination, xenophobia and related intolerance;

5. *Reaffirms* the importance of the enhancement of international cooperation for the promotion and protection of human rights and for the achievement of the objectives of the fight against racism, racial discrimination, xenophobia and related intolerance;

6. *Considers* that international cooperation in the field of human rights, in conformity with the purposes and principles set out in the Charter of the United Nations and international law, should make an effective and practical contribution to the urgent task of preventing violations of human rights and fundamental freedoms;

7. *Reaffirms* that the promotion, protection and full realization of all human rights and fundamental freedoms should be guided by the principles of universality, non-selectivity, objectivity and transparency, in a manner consistent with the purposes and principles set out in the Charter;

8. *Calls upon* Member States, specialized agencies and intergovernmental organizations to continue to carry out a constructive dialogue and consultations for the enhancement of understanding and the promotion and protection of all human rights and fundamental freedoms, and encourages non-governmental organizations to contribute actively to this endeavour;

9. *Invites* States and relevant United Nations human rights mechanisms and procedures to continue to pay attention to the importance of mutual cooperation, understanding and dialogue in ensuring the promotion and protection of all human rights;

10. *Decides* to continue its consideration of the question at its sixty-first session.

Right to promote and protect human rights

Human rights defenders

Reports of Special Representative. In his annual report to the Commission [E/CN.4/2005/101], the Secretary-General's Special Representative on human rights defenders, Hina Jilani (Pakistan), described her activities, analysed trends in Governments' responses to her communications, examined the situation and role of human rights defenders in the context of international peace and security, including numerous allegations of violations of their rights, and made recommendations for recognizing and promoting their work. The Special Representative had sent 316 communications, of which 251 were sent jointly with other mechanisms, concerning over 330 cases of alleged violations against some 895 defenders and 165 NGOs. Defenders were targeted in their professional capacities as journalists, lawyers and doctors, with trade unionists, victims' relatives and civil servants also suffering hostility in their work. The Special Representative was concerned that violations were increasingly shifting from low-level targeting, such as intimidation and harassment, to more serious attacks that resulted to the death of some 47 defenders in the reporting period, with much of the atrocities allegedly committed by the police and security forces. The Special Representative urged States to respect the peaceful expression of demands for human rights; refrain from stigmatizing and discrediting the work of human rights defenders; review their legislation and ensure it conformed with the 1998 Declaration on the Right and Responsibility of Individuals, Groups and Organs of Society to Promote and Protect Universally Recognized Human Rights and Fundamental Freedoms (Declaration on human rights defenders) adopted by the General Assembly in resolution 53/144 [YUN 1998, p. 608]; guarantee a positive environment for the defence of internationally recognized human rights; and train the judiciary, law enforcement agencies and other branches of Government accordingly. Governments and other warring parties in situations of armed conflicts were urged to refrain from targeting defenders, while UN organs and agencies were asked to pay particular attention to their protection. A March addendum to the report [E/CN.4/2005/101/Add.1] summarized communications sent to and received from Governments.

The Special Representative visited Nigeria (3-12 May) to assess the situation and role of human rights defenders in the country [E/CN.4/2006/95/Add.2]. She described the country's vibrant civil society, where defenders addressed a vast array of issues relating to civil and political rights, including freedom of expression, illegal detention, summary executions, police abuse, women's rights and a variety of economic, social and cultural rights. The oppressive military regimes of the 1990s had systematically targeted defenders, many of whom suffered egregious violations, including extrajudicial killings, aimed at suppressing their activities and silencing them. The transition to civilian rule in 1999 brought hope for a new era of respect for fundamental rights and democracy, as the Government, in efforts to promote human rights, adopted laws, developed policies and strengthened relevant institutions, which helped establish a more constructive environment for defenders to work in. The Government's initiatives in that regard included the ratification of key international human rights instruments; increased support for the National Human Rights Commission mandated to collaborate with defenders; and the development of a national plan of action designed to serve as a framework for sustained and coordinated country-wide measures to promote and protect human rights. The transition to democracy, however, also brought new challenges, especially regarding the transformation of State structures and the political, economic and social conditions that affected the enjoyment of human rights. In particular, while defenders reported an overall improvement in their situation following the advent of civilian rule, they maintained that some federal laws continued to undermine their work and safety, including those relating to the freedom of association, of assembly and of information. The Government also remained intolerant of defenders working on issues perceived as sensitive and relating mostly to democratic governance, elections, corruption, economic, social and environmental rights, as well as women's rights.

The Special Representative, expressing concern at those remaining shortcomings, called on the Government to further strengthen the National Human Rights Commission by providing for its independence and autonomy and to establish directorates for citizen's rights and ensure that they were sufficiently funded to fulfil their mandate. She also recommended that the Government reconsider any plans for adopting regulations that infringed on the freedom of association of human rights organizations or that limited their independence; review the provisions of the Public Order Act to ensure respect for the freedom of assembly; expedite the process of adopting an adequate legislative framework for freedom of information; and take measures to address impunity and to adequately protect election monitors and journalists within the context of the elections planned for 2007.

In Israel and the Occupied Palestinian Territory (5-11 October) [E/CN.4/2006/95/Add.3], where defenders operated against a backdrop of 38 years of occupation and conflict, the Special Representative found that security-driven laws and practices had resulted in the repression of activities for defending human rights. The main concern of defenders in both Israel and the Occupied Palestinian Territory was the violation of the rights of the Palestinian population under Israeli occupation, as they were being deprived of even the basic right to human dignity. Although the Israeli Government generally respected the rights of Israeli defenders and did not seem to restrain their activities within Israel, the same defenders faced difficulties in promoting and protecting the rights of minorities, including the Arab and Palestinian communities in Israel and in the Occupied Palestinian Territory. In that regard, violations by Israeli authorities against defenders included, among other things, unlawful killings, harassment or threats to physical integrity; administrative detention and ill-treatment; restrictions on the freedom of movement; denial of humanitarian access; infringements on the right to freedom of assembly and to protest; and settler violence. The Special Representative was particularly concerned that, in the wake of Israel's unilateral withdrawal from the Gaza Strip (see p. 535), defenders in Gaza might become more vulnerable to obstruction and risks, owing to their isolation from other parts of the Palestinian territory and the outside world. The difficulties facing defenders were compounded by the failure of the Palestinian authority itself to respect human rights and the rule of law in areas under its control. Consequently, the security of defenders, particularly those who exposed violations by security agents, was affected by lawlessness and impunity for human rights abusers. Affirming that resistance to the occupation was a legitimate right of the Palestinian people, the Special Representative recommended that Israel end the administrative detention of defenders and allow peaceful activities in defence of human rights to be conducted free of fear and risk. She further recommended that the Palestinian Authority respect the rule of law, ensure that the fundamental rights and freedoms of the Palestinian population were fully restored and protected in areas under its control, end impunity for human rights violations and investigate complaints against officials, who threatened defenders. The Special Representative asked the United Nations to prioritize support for defenders and to adopt measures for their protection, suggesting that the Organization's international monitoring and reporting mechanisms and those documenting violations with the objective of compensating victims be given a wider mandate to help protect them. The United Nations also needed to take concrete action, in accordance with its Charter, to enforce compliance with international law in the Occupied Palestinian Territory.

In Brazil (5-21 December) [E/CN.4/2006/95/Add.4], the Special Representative acknowledged the existence, despite difficult circumstances, of a vibrant human rights movement and examined the situation of defenders concerned with the rights of landless rural workers, peasants, indigenous communities, people of African descent and other minorities. She highlighted positive efforts by the Government to ensure that defenders operated unimpeded and in safety, noting that the Government respected defenders' work

and had adopted policies and initiatives to facilitate the implementation of a legal framework for human rights protection. Despite those initiatives, serious concerns persisted, owing to a wide gap between policy declaration and implementation and the creation of mechanisms and their effectiveness. Of particular concern, were reports of violent incidents and threats that hampered defenders' security and compelled many of them to flee their homes for long periods, perpetuating distrust and lack of faith in existing human rights mechanisms and initiatives. In their efforts to expose human rights violations and end impunity for the perpetrators, defenders suffered numerous assassination attempts, killings and threats by "extermination groups" linked to security forces, unfair and malicious prosecution, and numerous other crimes. The Special Representative believed that more uniformity of commitment to the implementation of human rights policies by federal and states authorities could mitigate those concerns and highlighted the need for the legislature to become more sensitive to human rights issues and assign more priority to protecting activities for defending them. The Government needed to adopt more comprehensive strategies for protecting defenders and ending impunity for violations against them. There was also a need for the State to be more proactive in addressing social conflict and legitimizing defenders' intervention on behalf of local movements. It was the State's responsibility to ensure that defenders were not isolated in that struggle for social justice.

A September note of the Secretary-General [A/60/339] transmitted the Special Representative's annual report, in accordance with General Assembly resolution 59/192 [YUN 2004, p. 657] and Commission resolution 2005/67 (see p. 720). The Special Representative described the contribution of human rights defenders to the efforts of UN system bodies, particularly the Security Council and the Commission, to preserve and restore international peace and security. She determined that defenders had been mostly active regarding early warning about threats and challenges, human rights preservation in situations of armed conflict and in addressing human rights issues in peacebuilding operations. Defenders provided early warning of emerging problems, including gross human rights violations, and helped prevent their deterioration. Where peace and security had already collapsed, they protected the civilians affected and their constant monitoring helped expose deviations from international human rights and humanitarian law by parties to conflicts, allowing the international community to take action. Defenders also contributed significantly to post-conflict peacebuilding by helping to strengthen the rule of law in the countries concerned, addressing the human rights factors that caused the conflict and supporting the establishment of democratic principles. Case studies illustrating such efforts by defenders included the armed conflicts in the Sudan (particularly in the Darfur region), and in Nepal and Guatemala, where they helped alert the Security Council and the Commission to the violations against civilians and the need to take action. Despite their fundamental role, and sometimes because of it, defenders were themselves victims of killings, disappearances, torture, arbitrary arrest and detention, harassment and intimidation. The Special Representative recommended that the Security Council and the Commission accord greater attention to protecting defenders. Noting that both the Council and the Commission had expressed interest in developing early warning mechanisms to alert them to emerging peace and human rights problems, the Special Representative stated that defenders, through their work, already served as such a mechanism. Pointing out that previous failure by both bodies to respond sufficiently early to defenders' warnings had caused peace and human rights concerns to deteriorate, the Special Representative recommended that the Security Council and the Commission react more expeditiously to information from defenders on evolving issues and consider how such information could reach them in a timely manner. She further recommended that the essential role of defenders be recognized within the context of a reformed Commission on Human Rights (Human Rights Council) (see p. 712), to which they should be given adequate access to report on relevant issues and have those reports be duly considered. Other recommendations on the need to protect defenders and to facilitate their work were addressed to States, the UN Secretariat and specialized agencies.

On 16 December, the Assembly took note of the Secretary-General's note (**decision 60/533**).

Commission action. On 20 April [res. 2005/67], the Commission, condemning all human rights violations committed against persons promoting and defending human rights and fundamental freedoms, called on States to protect human rights defenders and asked the Special Representative to report on her activities to the General Assembly and to the Commission. The Secretary-General and concerned UN agencies and organizations were requested to assist her, while OHCHR was asked to draw the attention of UN bodies to her reports.

Communication. On 24 March [E/CN.4/2005/ G/25], Turkey transmitted its observations on the Special Representative's report on her visit to the country. While pointing to encouraging findings in the report, it disagreed with references to the activities of the Kurdistan Workers' Party (PKK), which it alleged was a terrorist organization. As such, Turkey's struggle against that organization should not have been portrayed as an armed conflict but as a "fight against terrorism". It was also unfair that a new law it had adopted to improve the conditions under which human rights defenders operated in the country were not well covered in the Special Representative's report. Furthermore, a majority of the recommendations contained in the report had been implemented well before the Special Representative's visit.

GENERAL ASSEMBLY ACTION

On 16 December [meeting 64], the General Assembly, on the recommendation of the Third Committee [A/60/509/Add.2], adopted **resolution 60/161** without vote [agenda item 71 (*b*)].

Declaration on the Right and Responsibility of Individuals, Groups and Organs of Society to Promote and Protect Universally Recognized Human Rights and Fundamental Freedoms

The General Assembly,

Recalling its resolution 53/144 of 9 December 1998, by which it adopted by consensus the Declaration on the Right and Responsibility of Individuals, Groups and Organs of Society to Promote and Protect Universally Recognized Human Rights and Fundamental Freedoms annexed to that resolution, and reiterating the importance of the Declaration and its wide dissemination,

Recalling also all previous resolutions on this subject, in particular its resolution 59/192 of 20 December 2004 and Commission on Human Rights resolution 2005/67 of 20 April 2005,

Noting with deep concern that, in many countries, persons and organizations engaged in promoting and defending human rights and fundamental freedoms are facing threats, harassment and insecurity as a result of those activities,

Gravely concerned by the continuing high level of human rights violations committed against persons engaged in promoting and defending human rights and fundamental freedoms around the world and by the fact that, in a number of countries in all regions of the world, impunity for threats, attacks and acts of intimidation against human rights defenders persists and that this has a negative impact on their work and safety,

Recalling that human rights defenders are entitled to equal protection of the law, and deeply concerned about the increase in new restrictive legislation regulating the creation and operation of non-governmental organizations and any abuse of civil or criminal proceedings against them because of their activities for the promotion and protection of human rights and fundamental freedoms,

Concerned by the considerable number of communications received by the Special Representative of the Secretary-General on the situation of human rights defenders that, together with the reports submitted by some of the special procedure mechanisms, indicate the serious nature of the risks faced by human rights defenders, including women human rights defenders,

Emphasizing the important role that individuals, non-governmental organizations and groups play in the promotion and protection of human rights and fundamental freedoms, including in combating impunity, promoting access to justice, information and public participation in decision-making and promoting, strengthening and preserving democracy,

Recognizing the substantial role that human rights defenders can play in supporting peace through dialogue, openness, participation and justice, including by monitoring and reporting on human rights,

Recalling that, in accordance with article 4 of the International Covenant on Civil and Political Rights, certain rights are recognized as non-derogable in any circumstances and that any measures derogating from other provisions of the Covenant must be in accordance with that article in all cases, and underlining the exceptional and temporary nature of any such derogations, as stated in General Comment No. 29, on states of emergency, adopted by the Human Rights Committee on 24 July 2001,

Gravely concerned that, in some instances, national security and counter-terrorism legislation and other measures have been misused to target human rights defenders or have hindered their work and safety in a manner contrary to international law,

Welcoming the significant work conducted by the Special Representative, and encouraging strengthened cooperation between the Special Representative and other special procedures of the Commission on Human Rights as well as other relevant United Nations bodies, offices, departments and specialized agencies and personnel, both at headquarters and at the country level,

Welcoming also regional initiatives for the promotion and protection of human rights and the cooperation between international and regional mechanisms for the protection of human rights defenders, and encouraging further development in this regard,

Welcoming further the steps taken by some States towards adopting national policies or legislation for the protection of human rights defenders,

Recalling that the primary responsibility for promoting and protecting human rights rests with the State, and reaffirming that national legislation consistent with the Charter of the United Nations and other international obligations of the State in the field of human rights and fundamental freedoms is the juridical framework within which human rights defenders conduct their activities, and noting with deep concern that the activities of some non-State actors pose a major threat to the security of human rights defenders,

Emphasizing the need for strong and effective measures for the protection of human rights defenders,

1. *Calls upon* all States to promote and give full effect to the Declaration on the Right and Responsibility of Individuals, Groups and Organs of Society to Promote and Protect Universally Recognized Human Rights and Fundamental Freedoms, including by taking, as appropriate, practical steps to that end;

2. *Welcomes* the reports of the Special Representative of the Secretary-General on the situation of human rights defenders and her contribution to the effective promotion of the Declaration and the improvement of the protection of human rights defenders worldwide;

3. *Condemns* all human rights violations committed against persons engaged in promoting and defending human rights and fundamental freedoms around the world, and urges States to take all appropriate action, consistent with the Declaration and all other relevant human rights instruments, to eliminate such human rights violations;

4. *Calls upon* all States to take all necessary measures to ensure the protection of human rights defenders, at both the local and the national levels, including in times of conflict and peacebuilding;

5. *Also calls upon* all States to ensure, protect and respect the freedom of expression and association of human rights defenders and, where registration is required, to facilitate registration, including through the establishment of effective and transparent criteria and non-discriminatory, expeditious and inexpensive procedures in accordance with national legislation;

6. *Urges* States to ensure that any measures to combat terrorism and preserve national security comply with their obligations under international law, in particular under international human rights law, and do not hinder the work and safety of human rights defenders;

7. *Also urges* States to take appropriate measures to address the question of impunity for attacks, threats and acts of intimidation against human rights defenders and their relatives, including by ensuring that complaints from human rights defenders are promptly investigated and addressed in a transparent, independent and accountable manner;

8. *Urges* all States to cooperate with and assist the Special Representative in the performance of her tasks and to furnish, upon request, all information for the fulfilment of her mandate;

9. *Calls upon* States to give serious consideration to responding favourably to the requests of the Special Representative to visit their countries, and urges them to enter into a constructive dialogue with the Special Representative with respect to the follow-up to and implementation of her recommendations so as to enable her to fulfil her mandate even more effectively;

10. *Urges* those States that have not yet responded to the communications transmitted to them to do so without delay and to investigate expeditiously urgent appeals and allegations brought to their attention by the Special Representative;

11. *Invites* States to translate the Declaration into national languages and to take measures to improve its dissemination;

12. *Encourages* States to promote awareness and training in regard to the Declaration in order to enable officials, agencies, authorities and the judiciary to observe the provisions of the Declaration and thus to promote better understanding and respect for human rights defenders;

13. *Invites* relevant United Nations bodies, including at the country level, within their respective mandates and working in cooperation with States, to give

due consideration to the Declaration and to the reports of the Special Representative, and in this context requests the Office of the United Nations High Commissioner for Human Rights to draw the attention of all relevant United Nations bodies, including at the country level, to the reports of the Special Representative;

14. *Requests* that the Office of the High Commissioner as well as other relevant United Nations bodies, offices, departments and specialized agencies consider ways in which they can assist States to strengthen the role and security of human rights defenders, including in conflict situations and peacebuilding;

15. *Requests* the Secretary-General to provide the Special Representative with human, material and financial resources in order to enable her to continue to carry out her mandate effectively, including through country visits;

16. *Requests* all concerned United Nations agencies and organizations, within their mandates, to provide all possible assistance and support to the Special Representative in the implementation of her programme of activities;

17. *Requests* the Special Representative to continue to report annually on her activities to the General Assembly and to the Commission on Human Rights in accordance with her mandate;

18. *Decides* to consider the question at its sixty-second session under the item entitled "Human rights questions".

Human rights and human responsibilities

Report of High Commissioner. In response to a 2004 Commission request [YUN 2004, p. 658], the High Commissioner submitted a February report [E/CN.4/2005/99] containing the views of 27 Member States, two intergovernmental organizations and one NGO on the pre-draft declaration on human social responsibilities.

Commission action. On 20 April [dec. 2005/111], by a recorded vote of 26 to 25, with 1 abstention, the Commission asked Miguel Alfonso Martínez (Cuba) to prepare, without financial implications and for submission in 2006, a new version of his 2003 report on human responsibilities [E/CN.4/2003/105, annex 1], taking into account the comments made by Member States, intergovernmental organizations and NGOs.

Other aspects

Good governance

Commission action. On 20 April [res. 2005/68], the Commission, welcoming the report on the 2004 seminar on good governance practices for the promotion of human rights [YUN 2004, p. 658], requested the High Commissioner to ensure that relevant UN agencies and other bodies with governance programmes were aware of the seminar's outcome and to encourage them to examine whether their approaches to good governance

promoted human rights. The High Commissioner was further asked to publish for consultation by States a selection of practices arising from the seminar, and to convene another seminar in 2006 on the role of anti-corruption measures at the national and international levels in good practices for promoting and protecting human rights.

Human rights instruments

General aspects

In 2005, seven UN human rights instruments were in force, whose implementation were monitored by expert bodies. The instruments and their treaty bodies were: the 1965 International Convention on the Elimination of All Forms of Racial Discrimination [YUN 1965, p. 440, GA res. 2106 A (XX)] (Committee on the Elimination of Racial Discrimination); the 1966 International Covenant on Civil and Political Rights and the Optional Protocol thereto [YUN 1966, p. 423, GA res. 2200 A (XXI)] and the Second Optional Protocol aiming at the abolition of the death penalty [YUN 1989, p. 484, GA res. 44/128] (Human Rights Committee); the 1966 International Covenant on Economic, Social and Cultural Rights [YUN 1966, p. 419, GA res. 2200 A (XXI)] (Committee on Economic, Social and Cultural Rights); the 1979 Convention on the Elimination of All Forms of Discrimination against Women [YUN 1979, p. 895, GA res. 54/4] (Committee on the Elimination of Discrimination against Women); the 1984 Convention against Torture and Other Cruel, Inhuman or Degrading Punishment [YUN 1984, p. 813, GA res. 39/46] and related 2002 Optional Protocol [YUN 2002, p. 631, GA res. 57/199] (Committee against Torture); the 1989 Convention on the Rights of the Child [YUN 1989, p. 560, GA res. 44/25] and Optional Protocols on the involvement of children in armed conflict and on the sale of children, child prostitution and child pornography [YUN 2000, pp. 616 & 618, GA res. 54/263] (Committee on the Rights of the Child); and the 1990 International Convention on the Protection of the Rights of All Migrant Workers and Members of Their Families [YUN 1990, p. 594, GA res. 45/158] (Committee on the Protection of the Rights of All Migrant Workers and Migrants and Their Families).

Interim report of Special Rapporteur. In a June interim report [E/CN.4/Sub.2/2005/8] submitted in response to a 2004 Commission request [YUN 2004, p. 659], the Special Rapporteur on the study of the universal implementation of international human rights treaties, Emmanuel Decaux

(France), provided a brief overview of the current situation and updated information contained in his previous report [ibid.]. The current report, which focused on developing the first set of working hypotheses proposed by the Special Rapporteur in 2004 [ibid.], reviewed UN annual initiatives to encourage universal participation in relevant treaties, discussed good practice in that context and suggested measures to revive a movement towards universal ratification of international human rights instruments. The Special Rapporteur was expected to submit a final report on the study in 2006, as requested by the Commission [ibid.].

Subcommission action. On 8 August [res. 2005/4], the Subcommission asked the Secretary-General to continue to assist the Special Rapporteur, who would submit a final report in 2006.

Human rights treaty body system

Meeting of chairpersons. A May note by the Secretary-General [HRI/MC/2005/1 & Corr.1] contained the provisional agenda and annotations for the seventeenth meeting of chairpersons of human rights treaty bodies (see below). In an August note [A/60/278], he submitted the report of the meeting (Geneva, 23 and 24 June). The meeting considered the follow-up recommendations of the sixteenth meeting [YUN 2004, p. 660] and reviewed developments relating to the work of the treaty bodies. In that context, the chairpersons considered the issues of strengthening support to the treaty bodies, enhancing their effectiveness and streamlining their reporting procedures and requirements.

The meeting had before it Secretariat reports providing an overview of the current working methods of treaty bodies relating to the State party reporting process [HRI/MC/2005/4]; a comparative analysis of reservations [HRI/MC/2005/5]; a report [HRI/MC/2005/6 & Add.1] on the discussions of the treaty bodies in the past year regarding provisional guidelines for reporting with an expanded core document, prepared by the Rapporteur of the Third Inter-Committee Meeting, Kamel Filali (Algeria); and the revised draft of the guidelines [HRI/MC/2005/3], prepared by the Secretariat. Also held, was the seventh joint meeting of treaty body chairpersons, special rapporteurs/representatives, independent experts and chairpersons of working groups of the Commission's special procedures. The meeting adopted recommendations relating to interaction with the Commission; technical cooperation; cooperation with special procedures; statistical information relating to human rights; and meetings with mandate-holders. The chairpersons requested the Secretariat to organize consultations between the treaty bodies, States parties, OHCHR, UN entities and other stakeholders to discuss the Secretary-General's proposals for reforming the UN human rights system, as contained in his report to the 2005 World Summit (see p. 67), as well as the related proposals contained in the Plan of Action presented by the High Commissioner for the reform of the treaty body system (see p. 715). Annexed to the report was the report of the Fourth Inter-Committee Meeting of human rights treaty bodies (Geneva, 20-22 June), which adopted recommendations on reporting guidelines, reservations, technical terminology, NGO participation and engagement with national human rights institutions.

On 16 December, the General Assembly took note of the report of the chairpersons' meeting (**decision 60/533**).

Report of Secretary-General. An August report of the Secretary-General [A/60/278] described efforts to implement General Assembly resolution 57/202 [YUN 2002, p. 623] on the effective implementation of international human rights instruments, including reporting obligations under those instruments. The report focused on the outcomes of the chairpersons' meetings (see above) and on the work of treaty bodies relating to cooperation and harmonization of work.

Equitable geographical distribution in the membership of the human rights treaty bodies

Report of High Commissioner. In response to General Assembly resolution 59/181 [YUN 2004, p. 661], the High Commissioner submitted a September report [A/60/351 & Corr.1] on the equitable geographical distribution in the membership of the human rights treaty bodies. The report provided information on the system of electing treaty body members, analysed the past and current membership of each treaty body by geographical region and concluded that the election modalities was a matter for the States parties.

On 16 December, the General Assembly took note of the High Commissioner's report (**decision 60/533**).

Reservations to human rights treaties

Report of Secretariat. As requested by the Third Inter-Committee Meeting of human rights treaty bodies [YUN 2004, p. 660], a June Secretariat report [HRI/MC/2005/5] provided information on the practice of human rights treaty bodies regarding reservations to the treaties they monitored. The report described the provisions in relevant treaties relating to reservations and those in the 1969 Convention on the Law of Treaties [YUN 1969, p. 784] and also surveyed the treaty bodies' approaches to reservations and the response of other UN bodies to the issue.

The report found that, although the issue of reservations had been of significant concern to treaty bodies, the way in which they expressed that concern and the remedial measures they recommended varied. While they had all been motivated to restrict the scope of existing reservations and had encouraged their removal by States parties, they offered little guidance on the criteria by which a reservation should be determined impermissible and in breach of a treaty's object and purpose and on the consequences of such a determination. As such, there was a need for treaty bodies to take a more harmonized approach to the issue, which might be guided by a joint general comment. Annexed to the report were an outline of the practice of the treaty bodies with respect to reservations, including concluding observations/comments and miscellaneous issues, as well as tables of reservations, objections and withdrawals.

GENERAL ASSEMBLY ACTION

On 16 December [meeting 64], the General Assembly, on the recommendation of the Third Committee [A/60/509/Add.1], adopted **resolution 60/149** without vote [agenda item 71 *(a)*].

International Covenants on Human Rights

The General Assembly,

Recalling its resolution 58/165 of 22 December 2003 and Commission on Human Rights resolution 2004/69 of 21 April 2004,

Mindful that the International Covenants on Human Rights constitute the first all-embracing and legally binding international treaties in the field of human rights and, together with the Universal Declaration of Human Rights, form the core of the International Bill of Human Rights,

Taking note of the report of the Secretary-General on the status of the International Covenant on Economic, Social and Cultural Rights, the International Covenant on Civil and Political Rights and the Optional Protocols to the International Covenant on Civil and Political Rights,

Recalling the International Covenant on Economic, Social and Cultural Rights and the International Covenant on Civil and Political Rights, and reaffirming that all human rights and fundamental freedoms are universal, indivisible, interdependent and interrelated and that the promotion and protection of one category of rights should never exempt or excuse States from the promotion and protection of the other rights,

Recognizing the important role of the Human Rights Committee and the Committee on Economic, Social and Cultural Rights in examining the progress made by States parties in fulfilling the obligations undertaken in the International Covenants on Human Rights and the Optional Protocols to the International Covenant on Civil and Political Rights and in providing recommendations to States parties on their implementation,

Considering that the effective functioning of the Human Rights Committee and the Committee on Economic, Social and Cultural Rights is indispensable for the full and effective implementation of the International Covenants on Human Rights,

Recognizing the importance of regional human rights instruments and monitoring mechanisms in complementing the universal system of promotion and protection of human rights,

1. *Reaffirms* the importance of the International Covenants on Human Rights as major components of international efforts to promote universal respect for and observance of human rights and fundamental freedoms;

2. *Strongly appeals* to all States that have not yet done so to become parties to the International Covenant on Economic, Social and Cultural Rights and the International Covenant on Civil and Political Rights, and to consider as a matter of priority acceding to the Optional Protocols to the International Covenant on Civil and Political Rights and making the declaration provided for in article 41 of the International Covenant on Civil and Political Rights, and, while acknowledging that additional States have recently become parties to these instruments, requests the Secretary-General to continue to support the annual treaty event to this end;

3. *Invites* the United Nations High Commissioner for Human Rights to intensify systematic efforts to encourage States to become parties to the International Covenants on Human Rights and, through the programme of advisory services in the field of human rights, to assist such States, at their request, in ratifying or acceding to the Covenants and to the Optional Protocols to the International Covenant on Civil and Political Rights with a view to achieving universal adherence;

4. *Calls for* the strictest compliance by States parties with their obligations under the International Covenant on Economic, Social and Cultural Rights and the International Covenant on Civil and Political Rights and, where applicable, the Optional Protocols to the International Covenant on Civil and Political Rights;

5. *Emphasizes* that States must ensure that any measure to combat terrorism complies with their obligations under relevant international law, including their obligations under the International Covenants on Human Rights, and welcomes the establishment by the Commission on Human Rights of the mandate of a Special Rapporteur on the promotion and protection of human rights and fundamental freedoms while countering terrorism;

6. *Stresses* the importance of avoiding the erosion of human rights by derogation, and recalls that, in accordance with article 4 of the International Covenant on Civil and Political Rights, certain rights are recognized as non-derogable in any circumstances and that any measures derogating from the provisions of the Covenant must be in accordance with that article in all cases, bearing in mind the need for States parties to provide the fullest possible information during states of emergency so that the justification for the appropriateness of measures taken in those circumstances can be assessed, and underlining the exceptional and temporary nature of any such derogations;

7. *Encourages* States parties to consider limiting the extent of any reservations that they lodge to the International Covenants on Human Rights and the Optional Protocols to the International Covenant on Civil and Political Rights, to formulate any reservations as precisely and narrowly as possible, and to regularly review such reservations with a view to withdrawing them so as to ensure that no reservation is incompatible with the object and purpose of the relevant treaty;

8. *Welcomes* the annual reports of the Human Rights Committee submitted to the General Assembly at its fifty-ninth and sixtieth sessions, and takes note of the General Comments adopted by the Committee, including the most recent, General Comment No. 31 on the nature of the general legal obligation imposed on States parties to the International Covenant on Civil and Political Rights;

9. *Also welcomes* the reports of the Committee on Economic, Social and Cultural Rights on its thirtieth and thirty-first sessions and on its thirty-second and thirty-third sessions, and takes note of the General Comments adopted by the Committee, including the most recent, General Comment No. 16 on the equal right of men and women to the enjoyment of all economic, social and cultural rights, adopted by the Committee at its thirty-fourth session;

10. *Expresses regret* at the number of States parties that have failed to fulfil their reporting obligations under the International Covenants on Human Rights, and urges States parties to fulfil their reporting obligations on time and to attend and participate in the consideration of the reports by the Human Rights Committee and the Committee on Economic, Social and Cultural Rights when so requested;

11. *Urges* States parties to make use in their reports of sex-disaggregated data, and stresses the importance of integrating a gender perspective in the implementation of the International Covenants on Human Rights at the national level, including in the national reports of States parties and in the work of the Human Rights Committee and of the Committee on Economic, Social and Cultural Rights;

12. *Strongly encourages* States parties that have not yet submitted core documents to the Office of the United Nations High Commissioner for Human Rights to do so, and invites all States parties regularly to review and update their core documents while bearing in mind the current discussion on the elaboration of an expanded core document;

13. *Urges* States parties to take duly into account, in implementing the provisions of the International Covenants on Human Rights, the recommendations and observations made during the consideration of their reports by the Human Rights Committee and by the Committee on Economic, Social and Cultural Rights, and the views adopted by the Human Rights Committee under the first Optional Protocol to the International Covenant on Civil and Political Rights;

14. *Urges* all States to publish the texts of the International Covenant on Economic, Social and Cultural Rights, the International Covenant on Civil and Political Rights and the Optional Protocols to the International Covenant on Civil and Political Rights in as many local languages as possible and to distribute them and make them known as widely as possible to all individuals within their territory and subject to their jurisdiction;

15. *Urges* each State party to give particular attention to the dissemination at the national level of their reports submitted to the Human Rights Committee and the Committee on Economic, Social and Cultural Rights and, further, to translate, publish and make available as widely as possible to all individuals within its territory and subject to its jurisdiction by appropriate means the full text of the recommendations and observations made by the Committees after the examination of those reports;

16. *Reiterates* that States parties should take into account, in their nomination of members to the Human Rights Committee and the Committee on Economic, Social and Cultural Rights, that the Committees shall be composed of persons of high moral character and recognized competence in the field of human rights, consideration being given to the usefulness of the participation of some persons having legal experience, and to equal representation of women and men, and that members serve in their personal capacity, and also reiterates that, in the elections of the Committees, consideration shall be given to equitable geographical distribution of membership and to the representation of the different forms of civilization and of the principal legal systems;

17. *Invites* the Human Rights Committee and the Committee on Economic, Social and Cultural Rights, when considering the reports of States parties, to continue to identify specific needs that might be addressed by United Nations departments, funds and programmes and the specialized agencies, including through the advisory services and technical assistance programme of the Office of the United Nations High Commissioner for Human Rights;

18. *Stresses* the need for improved coordination among relevant United Nations mechanisms and bodies in supporting States parties, upon their request, in implementing the International Covenants on Human Rights and the Optional Protocols to the International Covenant on Civil and Political Rights, and encourages continued efforts in this direction;

19. *Expresses its appreciation* for the efforts made so far by the Human Rights Committee and the Committee on Economic, Social and Cultural Rights to improve the efficiency of their working methods and encourages the Committees to pursue their efforts, welcomes in this regard the meetings held by the Committees and States parties to exchange ideas on how to render the working methods of the Committees more efficient, and encourages all States parties to continue to contribute to the dialogue with practical and concrete proposals and ideas on ways to improve the effective functioning of the Committees;

20. *Takes note* of the proposals of the Secretary-General and the United Nations High Commissioner for Human Rights as well as other proposals on human rights treaty body reform, inter alia, to harmonize reporting requirements and to create a unified standing treaty body, and looks forward to further deliberations on this subject;

21. *Welcomes* the continuing efforts of the Human Rights Committee and the Committee on Economic, Social and Cultural Rights to strive for uniform stand-

ards in the implementation of the provisions of the International Covenants on Human Rights;

22. *Notes* the need for further consideration of the issue of justiciability of the rights set forth in the International Covenant on Economic, Social and Cultural Rights and for further efforts towards developing indicators and benchmarks to measure progress in the national implementation by States parties of the rights protected by the Covenant;

23. *Takes note with appreciation* of the report of the open-ended working group of the Commission on Human Rights established with a view to considering options regarding the elaboration of an optional protocol to the International Covenant on Economic, Social and Cultural Rights on its second session, and encourages all parties to participate actively in the third session, at which the working group will consider a paper with elements for an optional protocol presenting a non-judgemental analysis of all the various options for an optional protocol, to be submitted by the Chairperson of the working group in order to facilitate a more focused discussion at the third session;

24. *Encourages* the specialized agencies that have not yet done so to submit their reports on the progress made in achieving the observance of the provisions of the International Covenant on Economic, Social and Cultural Rights, in accordance with article 18 of the Covenant, and expresses its appreciation to those that have done so;

25. *Encourages* the Secretary-General to continue to assist States parties to the International Covenants on Human Rights in the preparation of their reports, including by convening seminars or workshops at the national level for the training of government officials engaged in the preparation of such reports and by exploring other possibilities available under the programme of advisory services in the field of human rights;

26. *Requests* the Secretary-General to ensure that the Office of the United Nations High Commissioner for Human Rights effectively assists the Human Rights Committee and the Committee on Economic, Social and Cultural Rights in the implementation of their respective mandates by providing, inter alia, adequate Secretariat staff resources and conference and other relevant support services;

27. *Also requests* the Secretary-General to keep the General Assembly informed of the status of the International Covenants on Human Rights and the Optional Protocols to the International Covenant on Civil and Political Rights, including all reservations and declarations, through the United Nations websites.

Covenant on Civil and Political Rights and Optional Protocols

Accessions and ratifications

As at 31 December, parties to the International Covenant on Civil and Political Rights and the Optional Protocol thereto, adopted by the General Assembly in resolution 2200 A (XXI) [YUN 1966, p. 423], numbered 154 and 105, respectively.

During the year, Honduras became a party to the Optional Protocol to the Covenant.

The Second Optional Protocol, aimed at the abolition of the death penalty, adopted by the Assembly in resolution 44/128 [YUN 1989, p. 484], was acceded to by Canada and Liberia, bringing the total number of States parties to 56 as at 31 December.

Note by Secretariat. In response to a 2004 Commission request [YUN 2004, p. 633] that the Secretary-General report on the status of the International Covenant on Civil and Political Rights and its Optional Protocols, and of the International Covenant on Economic, Social and Cultural Rights, a Secretariat note [E/CN.4/2005/95] informed the Commission that the Secretary-General would submit the requested report in 2006. Meanwhile, relevant information on the subject might be found on the websites of the United Nations Office of Legal Affairs Treaty Section and of OHCHR (http://untreaty.un.org; http://www.unhchr.ch).

Implementation

Monitoring body. The Human Rights Committee, established under article 28 of the Covenant, held three sessions in 2005: its eighty-third from 14 March to 1 April (New York), its eighty-fourth from 11 to 29 July (Geneva) [A/60/40, vol. I] and its eighty-fifth from 17 October to 3 November (Geneva) [A/61/41, vol. I]. In 2005, the Committee considered reports from 13 States—Brazil, Canada, Greece, Iceland, Italy, Kenya, Mauritius, Paraguay, Slovenia, the Syrian Arab Republic, Thailand, Uzbekistan and Yemen—under article 40. It adopted views on communications from some individuals alleging violations of their rights under the Covenant, and decided that other such communications were inadmissible. Those views and decisions were annexed to the Committee's reports [A/60/40, vol. II; A/61/40, vol. II].

By notifications of 25 January, 31 March, 8 April, 24 May and 20 July, Peru stated that it had extended the state of emergency in different provinces and parts of the country, declared initially in 2003 [YUN 2003, p. 670]. On 20 September, it notified other States through the intermediary of the Secretary-General of the further extension of the state of emergency for 60 days, and by further notifications of 1 and 23 December, it again extended the State of emergency. On 1 February, Nepal proclaimed a state of emergency in the entire kingdom, which it revoked on 5 May. On 18 August, Ecuador notified other States, through the intermediary of the Secretary-General, of the declaration of a state of emergency in different provinces of the country, which was extended to other parts on 22 August. On 14 October, Guatemala informed the Secretary-General that its Congress had adopted a legislative decree recognizing a state of national disaster in parts of the country for 30 days. On 15 November, France informed the Secretary-General that it had declared a state of emergency throughout the metropolitan territory.

On 16 December, the General Assembly took note of the report of the Human Rights Committee on its eighty-second to eighty-fourth sessions (**decision 60/533**).

Covenant on Economic, Social and Cultural Rights

Accessions and ratifications

As at 31 December, the number of parties to the International Covenant on Economic, Social and Cultural Rights, adopted by the General Assembly in resolution 2200 A (XXI) [YUN 1966, p. 419], remained at 151.

Note by Secretariat. The Commission had before it a Secretariat note [E/CN.4/2005/95] informing it that the Secretary-General would report in 2006 on the status of the Covenant, in accordance with the Commission's 2004 request [YUN 2004, p. 663].

Draft optional protocol

In response to a 2004 Commission request [YUN 2004, p. 663], the open-ended Working Group to consider options regarding the elaboration of an optional protocol to the Covenant held its second session (Geneva, 10-20 January) [E/CN.4/2005/52]. The optional protocol would be designed to establish a complaints procedure format for individuals or groups who felt that their rights under the Covenant had been violated. Background information for the Group's discussions was provided in a report of the Secretary-General [E/CN.4/2005/WG.23/2] containing a comparative summary of existing communications and inquiry procedures and practices under international human rights instruments and the UN system, submitted in response to a 2004 Commission request [YUN 2004, p. 663].

After considering preliminary views on options by States, delegations and representatives of intergovernmental organizations and NGOs, the Working Group held an interactive dialogue with the Commission's special rapporteurs whose mandates addressed economic, social and cultural rights, and with experts of the International Labour Organization (ILO), the United Nations Educational, Scientific and Cultural Organization (UNESCO), the Committee on Economic, Social and Cultural Rights, the Committee against

Torture (CAT) and the Committee on the Elimination of Discrimination against Women (CEDAW). The Group also met with regional experts, including the Commissioner of the African Commission on Human and Peoples' Rights and the Deputy Executive Secretary of the Committee of Independent Experts (European Committee of Social Rights).

The Group requested its Chairperson-Rapporteur to submit to its third session a document listing elements that could be contained in an optional protocol, including, among other things, an explanation of its nature and scope; ways to ensure the effective functioning of a communications procedure; the criteria for admissibility of complaints; the standing of individuals or groups under an optional protocol; the nature of economic, social and cultural rights, particularly regarding the risk of interference in domestic political discussions about resource allocation; the cost implications of an optional protocol with a complaints mechanism; the relationship between an optional protocol and existing mechanisms; an analysis and assessment of the potential impact of an optional protocol on improving the implementation of economic, social and cultural rights at the national level; and the option of having no optional protocol.

Commission action. On 15 April [res. 2005/22], the Commission, by a recorded vote of 50 to none, with 3 abstentions, called on States to give full effect to economic, social and cultural rights and guarantee that they would be exercised without discrimination; consider signing and ratifying the International Covenant on Economic, Social and Cultural Rights and take it into account in relevant national and international policy-making processes; and ensure the participation of civil society representatives in preparing periodic reports to the Committee on Economic, Social and Cultural Rights and in implementing its recommendations. The Commission requested the open-ended Working Group to consider options regarding the elaboration of an optional protocol to the Covenant (see above) and to report in 2006, and the Secretary-General, to report also in 2006 on the implementation of the current resolution.

Implementation

Monitoring body. The Committee on Economic, Social and Cultural Rights held its thirty-fourth (25 April–13 May) and thirty-fifth (7-25 November) sessions, both in Geneva [E/2006/22]. Its pre-sessional working group also met in Geneva from 16 to 20 May and from 28 November to 2 December to identify issues to be discussed with reporting States.

On 25 and 27 July, the Economic and Social Council took note of the Committee's reports on its thirty-second and thirty-third sessions, held in 2004 [YUN 2004, p. 644] (**decision 2005/296**).

In 2005, the Committee examined reports under articles 16 and 17 of the Covenant submitted by Austria, Bosnia and Herzegovina, China (including Hong Kong SAR and Macao SAR), Libyan Arab Jamahiriya, Norway, Serbia and Montenegro, Slovenia, Uzbekistan and Zambia.

The Committee adopted three general comments, including, on 10 May, general comment No. 16 (2005) on the equal right of men and women to the enjoyment of economic, social and cultural rights, covered in article 3 of the Covenant; on 21 November, general comment No. 17 (2005) on the right of everyone to benefit from the protection of the moral and material interests resulting from any scientific and literary artistic production of which he was the author, covered in article 15 (1) *(c)*; and on 24 November, general comment No. 18 (2005) on the right to work, covered in article 6.

OHCHR was invited to consider the possibility of organizing, in 2006, a workshop on follow-up action to its concluding observations for States parties to the Covenant from the East European region whose reports had recently been considered by the Committee.

Reports of Secretary-General. In accordance with a 2004 Commission request [YUN 2004, p. 663], the Secretary-General submitted a report [E/CN.4/2005/39] highlighting the activities undertaken and other developments within the international human rights system to promote the realization of economic, social and cultural rights. The report found that progress had been made to increase focus and understanding on those rights, marked by higher levels of cooperation with UN agencies, particularly in the context of the Food and Agriculture Organization of the United Nations (FAO) Voluntary Guidelines on the Right to Food. There was also greater focus on technical cooperation and further progress in raising awareness through the work of treaty bodies about the nature of the rights concerned. In particular, the Committee on Economic, Social and Cultural Rights had continued to draft a general comment on article 3 of the Covenant on Economic, Social and Cultural Rights (right to the enjoyment of those rights), and on article 6 (right to work) and article 15 (1) *(c)* (right to benefit from the protection of the moral and material interests resulting from scientific, literary or artistic production). The Commission's special procedures continued to play a key role in promoting a more effective realization of the rights in ques-

tion and OHCHR had maintained cooperation with other UN agencies to integrate them into the UN system.

Pursuant to General Assembly resolution 58/165 [YUN 2003, p. 671], the Secretary-General, on 19 August [A/60/284], reported on the status of the International Covenant on Civil and Political Rights and its Optional Protocols (see p. 726), and of the International Covenant on Economic, Social and Cultural Rights (see p. 727).

On 16 December, the Assembly took note of the Secretary-General's report (**decision 60/533**).

Convention against racial discrimination

Accessions and ratifications

As at 31 December, the number of parties to the International Convention on the Elimination of All Forms of Racial Discrimination, adopted by the General Assembly in resolution 2106 A (XX) [YUN 1965, p. 440], remained at 170.

On 20 April [res. 2005/64], by a recorded vote of 38 to 1, with 14 abstentions, the Commission reiterated the call made in the Durban Plan of Action, adopted at the World Conference against Racism, Racial Discrimination, Xenophobia and Related Intolerance [YUN 2001, p. 615], to achieve universal ratification of the Convention by 2005 and for all States to consider making the declaration provided for in article 14 (see below). It asked OHCHR to publish a list of countries yet to ratify the Convention, reinvigorate the campaign for universal ratification and report thereon in 2006. The Commission welcomed the adoption by the Committee on Racial Discrimination of general comment XXX on discrimination against non-citizens [YUN 2004, p. 665] and stressed the need to implement it.

On 25 July, the Economic and Social Council took note of the Commission's resolution (**decision 2005/272**).

Implementation

Monitoring body. The Committee on the Elimination of Racial Discrimination (CERD), established under article 8 of the Convention, held its sixty-sixth (21 February–11 March) and sixty-seventh (2-19 August) sessions [A/60/18], both in Geneva.

The Committee considered reports submitted by Australia, Azerbaijan, Bahrain, Barbados, France, Georgia, Iceland, Ireland, the Lao People's Democratic Republic, Nigeria, Turkmenistan, the United Republic of Tanzania, Venezuela and Zambia. Under article 9 relating to measures to give effect to the Convention's provisions, the Committee considered Botswana's response to its 2002 observations [YUN 2002, p. 628] and informed it on 10 March that several aspects of its relevant legislation, including the Tribal Territories Act and its Constitution, had a discriminatory effect on some ethnic groups, particularly those subordinate to a dominant tribe on a Tribal Territory. The Committee asked to be kept informed of Botswana's ongoing reform process.

On 11 March, the Committee adopted a decision on Surinam, recommending the country's legal acknowledgment of indigenous peoples' right to possess, develop, control and use their communal lands and to participate in the exploitation and management of the associated natural resources. Suriname was invited to comment by 15 April on the Committee's assessment of its draft Mining Act as it affected indigenous and tribal peoples' right to be consulted and fairly compensated for any damage by mining activities.

With regard to the Convention's implementation in States parties whose reports were seriously overdue, the Committee adopted a decision on Papua New Guinea, regretting that, despite repeated requests, it had not fulfilled its obligations under the Convention. CERD adopted decisions also regretting the situations of Malawi, Seychelles and Saint Lucia and informing them that it intended to proceed with the adoption of concluding observations under its review procedure in the absence of their response by 31 January 2006 to relevant questions designed to facilitate the resumption of dialogue.

Under article 14 of the Convention, CERD considered communications from individuals or groups claiming violation of their rights enumerated in the Convention by a State party. Forty-six States parties had recognized CERD's competence to do so (Algeria, Australia, Austria, Azerbaijan, Belgium, Brazil, Bulgaria, Chile, Costa Rica, Cyprus, Czech Republic, Denmark, Ecuador, Finland, France, Georgia, Germany, Hungary, Iceland, Ireland, Italy, Liechtenstein, Luxembourg, Malta, Mexico, Monaco, Netherlands, Norway, Peru, Poland, Portugal, Republic of Korea, Romania, Russian Federation, Senegal, Serbia and Montenegro, Slovakia, Slovenia, South Africa, Spain, Sweden, Switzerland, The former Yugoslav Republic of Macedonia, Ukraine, Uruguay, Venezuela).

Pursuant to article 15 of the Convention, the Committee was empowered to consider petitions, reports and other information relating to Trust and Non-Self-Governing Territories. The Committee noted, as it had in the past, the difficulty in fulfilling its functions in that regard, owing to the lack of copies of relevant petitions and to the fact that reports contained scant information

relating directly to the Convention's principles and objectives.

CERD also considered follow-up to the 2001 World Conference against Racism, Racial Discrimination, Xenophobia and Related Intolerance [YUN 2001, p. 615] and to the Third Decade to Combat Racism and Racial Discrimination (1993-2003), proclaimed by the General Assembly in resolution 48/91 [YUN 1993, p. 853] (see p. 757).

The Committee adopted decisions under its early warning and urgent action procedures regarding the situation in New Zealand [dec. 1 (66)], Darfur, Sudan [dec. 2 (66)], and Suriname [dec. 1 (67)]. It also addressed the situations of the Western Shoshone indigenous people in the United States and the Tatars in Crimea, Ukraine, drew both parties' attention to a list of questions to clarify the situation of the communities concerned and asked them to respond by 31 December, for discussion at its 2006 session. CERD also adopted a decision on follow-up to the declaration on the prevention of genocide: indicators of patterns of systematic and massive racial discrimination, and general recommendation XXXI on the prevention of racial discrimination in the administration and functioning of the criminal justice system.

As at 31 December, 41 States parties had accepted an amendment to article 8 of the Convention regarding the financing of CERD [YUN 1992, p. 714]. The amendment was to enter into force when accepted by a two-thirds majority of States parties, comprising approximately 113 of the 170 States parties to the Convention. A meeting of the States parties, planned for 12 January 2006, would elect nine candidates to replace Committee members whose terms of office were to expire shortly thereafter [CERD/SP/68 & Add.1].

Subregional workshop. A subregional workshop (Cairo, Egypt, 19-22 December) [HRI/EGY/SEM/2006/1], attended by over 50 participants from six North African countries (Algeria, Egypt, Libyan Arab Jamahiriya, Mauritania, Morocco, Tunisia), adopted a series of recommendations to support and enhance States' capacity to implement the concluding comments/observations of CEDAW and CERD and to strengthen cooperation with other relevant stakeholders for that purpose.

Convention against torture

Accessions and ratifications

As at 31 December, 141 States were parties to the 1984 Convention against Torture and Other Cruel, Inhuman or Degrading Treatment or Punishment, adopted by the General Assembly in resolution 39/46 [YUN 1984, p. 813]. Madagascar and Nicaragua ratified the Convention during the year. The Optional Protocol to the Convention, which was adopted in resolution 57/199 [YUN 2002, p. 631] and opened for signature on 4 February 2003, had 49 signatories and 16 States parties (Albania, Argentina, Costa Rica, Croatia, Denmark, Georgia, Liberia, Mali, Malta, Mauritius, Mexico, Paraguay, Poland, Sweden, United Kingdom, Uruguay). The Protocol would enter into force 30 days following the deposit of the twentieth instrument of ratification or accession. As at 1 July, 51 parties had made the required declarations under articles 21 and 22 (under which a party recognized the competence of the Committee against Torture to receive and consider communications by which a party claimed that another was not fulfilling its obligations under the Convention, and from or on behalf of individuals who claimed to be victims of a violation of the Convention by a State party). Four parties had made the declaration only under article 21, bringing the total number of declarations under that article to 55, while five had made the declaration only under article 22, bringing the total of declarations under that article to 56. Amendments to articles 17 and 18, adopted in 1992 [YUN 1992, p. 735], had been accepted by 27 parties as at year's end.

Commission action. On 19 April [res. 2005/39], the Commission urged States to become parties to the Convention and to limit the extent of their reservations. Ratifying or acceding States were invited to make the declarations provided for in articles 21 and 22 and to comply with their obligations pursuant to article 19, including reporting obligations.

Report of Secretary-General. The Secretary-General reported on the status of the Convention, its Optional Protocol and the declarations provided for in articles 21 and 22 as at 1 July [A/60/220]. On 16 December, the General Assembly took note of the report (**decision 60/533**).

Election of Committee members. The Tenth Meeting of States Parties to the Convention (Geneva, 31 November) elected five members to the Committee against Torture, for a four-year term, effective 1 January 2006, to replace those whose terms were due to expire on 31 December.

Implementation

Monitoring body. The Committee against Torture, established as a monitoring body under the Convention, held its thirty-fourth and thirty-fifth sessions in Geneva from 2 to 20 May [A/60/44] and 14 to 25 November [A/61/44], respectively. Under article 19, it considered reports submitted by Albania, Austria, Bahrain, Bosnia and Herzegovina, Canada, the Democratic Republic of the Congo, Ecuador, Finland, France, Nepal, Sri Lanka, Switzerland and Uganda. During the year, the Committee continued its work in accordance with article 20, under which it studied reliable information that appeared to contain well-founded indications that torture was systematically practised in a State party. Within the framework of its follow-up activities, the Rapporteur of article 20 continued to encourage those States parties on which enquiries had been conducted to implement the related recommendations of the Committee. Under article 22, the Committee considered communications submitted by individuals who claimed that their rights under the Convention had been violated by a State party and who had exhausted all available domestic remedies.

Convention on elimination of discrimination against women and Optional Protocol

(For details on the status of the Convention and on the Optional Protocol, see p. 1271.)

Convention on the Rights of the Child

Accessions and ratifications

As at 31 December, the number of States parties to the 1989 Convention on the Rights of the Child, adopted by the General Assembly in resolution 44/25 [YUN 1989, p. 560], remained at 192. States parties to the Optional Protocol to the Convention on the involvement of children in armed conflict, adopted by the Assembly in resolution 54/263 [YUN 2000, p. 615], rose to 105, with ratification during the year by Armenia, Benin, Colombia, India, Israel, Latvia, Liechtenstein, Poland, the Sudan, Togo and Ukraine, and accession by Eritrea, Nicaragua and Turkmenistan. The Optional Protocol to the Convention on the sale of children, child prostitution and child pornography, also adopted by resolution 54/263, had 101 States parties, with ratification in 2005 by Armenia, Benin, Canada, India, Japan, the Netherlands and Poland, and accession by Angola, Eritrea, Georgia, Saint Vincent and the Grenadines and Turkmenistan.

Commission action. On 19 April [res. 2005/44], by a recorded vote of 52 to 1, the Commission urged States to sign and ratify or accede to the Convention and its Optional Protocols, implement them fully and end impunity for perpetrators of crimes against children. The Secretary-General should assist the Committee on the

Rights of the Child, while OHCHR, UN mechanisms and relevant UN system organs were asked to incorporate a strong child-rights perspective in all their activities, and to train their staff in child protection matters.

The Secretary-General reported on the status of the Convention and Optional Protocols as at 30 June [A/60/175 & Corr.1] and 6 December [E/CN.4/2006/64].

On 23 December, the Assembly urged States that had not done so to become parties to the Convention and the Optional Protocols thereto, and to strengthen cooperation with CRC (**resolution 60/231**) (see p. 855).

Implementation

Monitoring body. In 2005, the Committee on the Rights of the Child (CRC) held its thirty-eighth (10-28 January) [CRC/C/146], thirty-ninth (17 May-3 June) [CRC/C/150] and fortieth (12-30 September) [CRC/C/153] sessions, all in Geneva. Its working group met to review State party reports and identify the main questions to be discussed with representatives of the reporting States.

Under article 44 of the Convention, CRC considered initial or periodic reports submitted by Albania, Algeria, Australia, Austria, the Bahamas, Belize, Bolivia, Bosnia and Herzegovina, China (including Hong Kong SAR and Macao SAR), Costa Rica, Denmark, Ecuador, Finland, Iran, Luxembourg, Mongolia, Nepal, Nicaragua, Nigeria, Norway, the Philippines, the Russian Federation, Saint Lucia, Sweden, Togo, Trinidad and Tobago, Uganda and Yemen.

In September, the Committee held a day of general discussion on the subject of children without parental care and adopted recommendations and general comment No. 7 on Implementing Child Rights in Early Childhood. It also discussed the drafts of other general comments on unaccompanied and asylum-seeking children, fundamental principles in the juvenile justice system, and the rights of indigenous children and of children with disabilities.

Subregional workshop. A subregional workshop (Buenos Aires, Argentina) [HRI/ARG/SEM/2006/1], attended by participants from 10 Latin American States (Argentina, Bolivia, Brazil, Chile, Colombia, Ecuador, Paraguay, Peru, Uruguay, Venezuela), discussed issues relating to the rights of the child and adopted recommendations to enhance the implementation of the Committee's concluding observations in the subregion.

Convention on migrant workers

Accessions and ratifications

As at 31 December, the number of States parties to the International Convention on the Protection of the Rights of All Migrant Workers and Members of Their Families, adopted by the General Assembly in resolution 45/158 [YUN 1990, p. 594] and which entered into force in 2003 [YUN 2003, p. 676], totalled 34. During the year, Chile, Lesotho and Peru ratified the Convention, while Algeria, Honduras, Nicaragua and the Syrian Arab Republic acceded to it.

The Secretary-General reported on the status of the Convention as at 1 August [A/60/272].

Commission action. On 19 April [res. 2005/47], the Commission requested States to promote and protect the human rights and fundamental freedoms of all migrants, especially those of women and children, regardless of their immigration status, in conformity with the Convention and other relevant international human rights instruments, norms and standards.

In July, the Economic and Social Council took note of the Commission's action (**decision 2005/267**).

Implementation

Monitoring body. In 2005, the Committee on the Protection of the Rights of All Migrant Workers and Members of Their Families held its second (25-29 April) [A/60/48] and third (12-16 December) [A/61/48] sessions, both in Geneva, at which it adopted provisional guidelines for the submission of initial reports by States and agreed to follow the practices of other treaty bodies in considering those reports.

It also discussed, among other things, ways to simplify and harmonize reporting, cooperation with States parties and other concerned bodies, and treaty body reform. The Committee held days of general discussion on 28 April and 15 December on "protecting the rights of all migrant workers as a tool to enhance development", to enable it to contribute to the high-level dialogue of the General Assembly devoted to international migration and development, to be held in 2006, pursuant to Assembly resolution 58/208 [YUN 2003, p. 1087].

Concerned that it had not yet received any reports from State parties under article 73 of the Convention relating to States parties' obligation to report on measures they had taken to give effect to the Convention's provisions, the Committee urged States to fulfil their reporting obligation in accordance with the provisional reporting guidelines it had adopted. In December, it elected five members to replace those whose terms were due to expire on 31 December and requested the Secretary-General to arrange two sessions in 2006.

On 16 December, the Assembly took note of the Committee's report on its second session (**decision 60/533**).

Convention on genocide

As at 31 December, 138 States were parties to the 1948 Convention on the Prevention and Punishment of the Crime of Genocide, adopted by the General Assembly in resolution 260 A (III) [YUN 1948-49, p. 959]. During the year, Bolivia ratified the Convention and the United Arab Emirates acceded to it.

Commission action. On 20 April [res. 2005/62], the Commission called on States that had not ratified or acceded to the Convention to do so and, where necessary, to enact national legislation in conformity with its provisions. It stressed the importance of enhanced international cooperation in fostering the principles enshrined in the Convention and invited the Secretariat and relevant UN system bodies and agencies to disseminate it widely, in order to ensure its universality.

It requested the Secretary-General to make available to the Commission in 2006 a report on the implementation of his five-point action plan for preventing genocide and on the activities of the special Adviser on the Prevention of Genocide, who should, in 2006 and 2007, report on progress made in discharging his mandate.

The Economic and Social Council, by **decision 2005/295**, endorsed that request.

Other activities

Follow-up to the 1993 World Conference

Report of High Commissioner. In a March report [E/CN.4/2005/12] on follow-up to the World Conference on Human Rights [YUN 1993, p. 908], the High Commissioner described OHCHR activities to help promote and protect human rights at the national level, strengthen the rule of law, transitional justice and democracy, support and strengthen the establishment of national human rights institutions and counter impunity for perpetrators of human rights violations. The report also discussed the situation of groups vulnerable to discrimination in various regions, including especially indigenous peoples, migrants and women, as well as issues relating to human trafficking and human rights and development.

Highlighting a number of challenges in the task of protecting human rights for all, most notably terrorism, peace and development questions and the resurgence of torture, the report observed that the human rights community could best respond to those challenges from a human rights perspective and within the framework of existing instruments and the related legal obligations of States.

Annual meeting. In August, the High Commissioner transmitted the report of the twelfth meeting of special rapporteurs/representatives, independent experts and chairpersons of working groups of the Commission's special procedures and advisory services programme (Geneva, 20-24 June) [E/CN.4/2006/4]. Participants discussed issues relating to the effectiveness of the special procedures system, both in terms of the functioning of each mandate and of the system as a whole. Discussions focused on identifying specific measures to be taken within the context of current efforts to reform the Commission and measures to enhance coordination among the procedures, in order to better follow up on their findings and recommendations and to communicate more effectively.

The meeting agreed to establish a coordination committee, whose principal role would be to assist individual experts to carry out their mandates effectively and promote the standing of the special procedures system within the broader framework of the UN and its human rights programmes. The committee's main function was to facilitate coordination among mandate-holders and act as a bridge between them and OHCHR, other UN human rights components and civil society. However, its role would be limited to making recommendations in order to ensure the independence and autonomy of mandate-holders, and would be reviewed by the 2006 meeting of special procedures. Participants also considered follow-up measures to encourage, facilitate and monitor the implementation of the recommendations of special procedures, requesting OHCHR, in that regard, to present a separate annual report to the Commission containing statistics reflecting responses to requests by those procedures for visits and communications arising therefrom. To facilitate a more effective strategy for communications, they agreed that OHCHR should consider appointing a communication specialist to work closely with the coordination committee and individual mandate-holders.

On 16 December, the Assembly took note of the Third Committee's report [A/50/509/Add.4] on the implementation of and follow-up to the Vienna Declaration and Programme of Actions, adopted at the 1993 World Conference (**decision 60/534**).

Advisory services and technical cooperation

Report of Secretary-General. In accordance with Commission resolution 2004/81 [YUN 2004, p. 670], the Secretary-General submitted his annual report [E/CN.4/2006/104] describing OHCHR technical cooperation programme, which provided assistance for building national and regional human rights infrastructure. Highlighting the programme's continuing growth, the report noted that OHCHR had refined the policy orientation of the programme, in the light of the Secretary-General's reform initiatives. The OHCHR Plan of Action, in particular, developed within the context of discussions to reform the Commission (see p. 715), of which a summary was annexed to the report, was changing the way the Office carried out its work, including the Technical Cooperation Programme. At a time of such fundamental changes, clear operational and policy guidance was important to ensure consistency and common understanding and OHCHR had taken steps to develop a suitable policy framework for the Programme, through consolidating, updating and streamlining past discussions and positions.

In 2005, the Voluntary Fund for Technical Cooperation in the Field of Human Rights funded 42 projects, of which 14 were completed during the year, while the implementation of 28 others was in progress. There were 23 new requests. As at 31 December, the Fund had received approximately $18.7 million for the 2004-2005 biennium, against expenditure of over $19 million. The Fund's Board of Trustees, at its twenty-third session (7-10 June), reviewed the programme's status and discussed technical cooperation in the context of the Secretary-General's reform agenda, regional activities, strategies and plans in the Asia-Pacific and Arab regions, cooperation between UNICEF and OHCHR in the follow-up to treaty body recommendations and a human rights approach to programming. It advised OHCHR on policy orientation, global vision and strategy on a broader level. Its twenty-fourth session, initially scheduled for November, was postponed to January 2006. As at year's end, the Fund's income amounted to $27.7 million, including carry over from the previous year. Expenditure totalled $19.2 million for the 2004-2005 biennium.

Working paper. In response to a 2004 Subcommission request [YUN 2004, p. 670], Gudmundur Alfredsson (Iceland) and Ibrahim Salama (Egypt) presented a June working paper [E/CN.4/Sub.2/2005/41], which examined the content and delivery of technical cooperation in the field of human rights. The paper discussed related institutional issues within the UN system, including the mainstreaming of human rights and rights-based activities; the substantive basis for technical cooperation in human rights instruments adopted by the United Nations and accepted by States; dialogue and exchange of positive experiences; national ownership as a crucial element for sustainability; and technical aspects concerning delivery, such as national and international actors, local expertise and independent evaluations.

Subcommission action. On 11 August [res. 2005/25], the Subcommission, taking into account the working paper on technical cooperation (see above), decided to appoint Mr. Alfredsson and Mr. Salama as Special Rapporteurs with the task of preparing a comprehensive study focusing on the best ways to include economic, social and cultural rights in international, regional and bilateral technical cooperation in the field of human rights. It asked the Secretary-General to assist them, and UN offices and agencies to respond favourably to their queries.

Afghanistan

Note by Secretary-General. A January note of the Secretary-General [E/CN.4/2005/112], submitted in response to a 2004 Commission request [YUN 2004, p. 671], highlighted the work of the independent expert on technical cooperation in the field of human rights in Afghanistan, including a planned mission to the country during the year, as well as the efforts of the UN Assistance Mission in Afghanistan (UNAMA) (see p. 408) to enhance the role of its gender adviser.

Report of independent expert. During his second mission to Afghanistan (30 January–7 February) [E/CN.4/2005/122], the independent expert, following extensive research and broad-based consultations with senior Government officials, the country's human rights institutions and UN bodies and NGOs operating there, acknowledged that some progress had been made to promote and protect human rights. Notable positive developments included advances in the country's democratic process, the release, based on his appeal, of some 730 individuals illegally held in inhuman conditions for over 30 months and developments relating to a national transitional justice strategy. However, pressing human rights issues remained, and those demanding the immediate attention of the Government and the international community included: the activities of factional commanders involved in illegal land seizures, extortion and intimidation; arbitrary arrest and routine violations of the administration of justice by the Afghan National Police; the lack of due process and the use of torture by State security and intelligence operatives; threats to the country's security and human rights promotion and protection by the illegal drug industry; poor prison conditions, particularly with regard to women and children and other egregious violations of women's rights; child trafficking and other abusive treatment of children; inadequate rights for the disabled and the displaced; and the actions of the United States–led coalition forces that appeared to be unregulated, and to have allegedly violated international human rights and humanitarian law. The expert emphasized that the country's future depended on strengthening the rule of law, improving the administration of justice and promoting and protecting human rights, and to that end, recommended a comprehensive strategic plan. Other recommendations related to oversight for State security institutions; action against poppy cultivation and drug trafficking; and the need to address social and economic issues, secure women's and children's rights, resolve pressing land and housing questions, improve access to education, strengthen civil society and transitional or post-conflict justice, ensure the successful conduct of elections, and ensure that the activities of coalition forces accorded with international human rights and humanitarian law.

Commission action. The Commission Chairperson, in a 21 April statement on technical cooperation in the field of human rights in Afghanistan [E/2005/23], which the Commission adopted by consensus, said that the Commission welcomed the new Afghan Constitution adopted in 2004 [YUN 2004, p. 761], which stated that the citizens, whether men or women, were equal before the law and also provided for adequate representation of women in the Wolesi Jirga (House of the People) and Meshrano Jirga (House of Elders). Noting that the protection and promotion of women's and children's rights were of paramount importance, particularly regarding access to education, health care and full participation in all aspects of Afghan life, the Commission expressed concern about the continuing violence and abuse against women and girls, including honour crimes, early and forced marriages, and human trafficking, which still occurred in certain parts of the country. The security situation also remained fragile owing to extremist violence and related criminality. To address those problems, the Commission called for the adoption of comprehensive anti-trafficking legislation and emphasized that an environment free from vio-

lence, discrimination and abuse for all Afghans was essential for a viable and sustainable recovery and reconstruction process. It also addressed the need to expose human rights violations, hold the perpetrators accountable and obtain justice and reparations for the victims, and encouraged the Government to assist the Afghan Independent Human Rights Commission to enable it to fulfil its mandate. The High Commissioner was asked to monitor the human rights situation in Afghanistan, expand the programme of advisory services and technical cooperation there and report to the General Assembly in 2005, and to the Commission in 2006. The Secretary-General was asked to ensure the appointment of a senior gender adviser within the newly established Gender Unit of UNAMA.

On 25 July, the Economic and Social Council endorsed the Commission's requests to the High Commissioner (**decision 2005/293**).

Report of High Commissioner. A September note of the Secretary-General [A/60/343] transmitted the report of the High Commissioner on the situation of human rights in Afghanistan and on the achievements of the technical assistance in the field of human rights, prepared in accordance with the Commission's requests, contained in its Chairperson's statement (see above). The High Commissioner noted that, despite the achievement of many of the benchmarks in the 2001 Bonn Agreement [YUN 2001, p. 311], the human rights situation in Afghanistan remained of great concern, with much of the problem attributable to the security situation and weakness in governance. Factional commanders and former warlords remained major power brokers, and conflict between anti-Government entities and Government and international forces combating them had taken a toll on civilians. The rule of law was emerging only slowly, and reform in the justice system was patchy, with impunity often prevailing. She concluded that the political achievements made, including the holding of Parliamentary elections, while crucial, were not a full measure of progress towards a society where human rights were respected and protected. As such, there was a need for the Government and the international community to continue making bold strides in human rights. All the Afghan people needed to be empowered, including men, women, persons with disabilities and members of all ethnic groups, to enable them to assert and claim their rights. Only then could human rights be more readily respected, protected and fulfilled. The High Commissioner recommended that the Government and the international community protect the right of the civilians affected by the continuing armed conflict in parts of the country, in accordance with international human rights and humanitarian law. She also proposed measures concerning the rule of law and administration of justice, transitional justice, the situation of women and children, economic, social and cultural rights, and capacity-building to enhance the role of the Afghan Independent Human Rights Commission and NGOs.

The General Assembly took note of the note by the Secretary-General on 16 December (**decision 60/533**).

Burundi

Commission action. On 20 April [res. 2005/75], the Commission, condemning all acts of violence and violations of human rights and international humanitarian law in Burundi, urged the Transitional Government to establish an independent national human rights commission to promote and protect human rights. The independent expert on the human rights situation in the country was asked to continue his work and to submit an interim report to the General Assembly in 2005 and report to the Commission in 2006.

On 25 July, the Economic and Social Council endorsed the Commission's requests (**decision 2005/275**).

Reports of independent expert. A September note of the Secretary-General [A/60/354] transmitted to the General Assembly the expert's interim report on the human rights situation in Burundi during the period from January to 15 August, pursuant to Commission resolution 2005/75 (see above). The report provided information on the expert's third visit to Burundi (2-10 July), which coincided with the legislative elections of 4 July. The expert found that peace in the country was advancing steadily and that there had been progress in the legislative process and improvements in the security and human rights situations. The country had promulgated its new Constitution on 22 March, following a referendum, which drew a voter turnout of 92 per cent, many of them women. Other positive developments included efforts to establish a Truth and Reconciliation Commission and the initiation of the demobilization process for over 12,000 ex-combatants, including 2,939 children. Despite those advances, human rights violations occurred on a daily basis, largely due to the continued armed conflict in the country and to sub-regional factors, such as mass migrations and the proliferation of small arms. Armed elements, including the military, allegedly violated the right to life and committed torture, arbitrary detention, sexual violence and mass displacement of people. Poverty compounded the country's human rights problems, as it restricted access to health care and encouraged the transmission of HIV/AIDS. The impact of reform in the judicial sector had been limited. Prisons were overcrowded and no consensus had been reached on who should be categorized as a "political prisoner". The expert reiterated the recommendations set out in his 2004 report [YUN 2004, p. 671] that had not yet been implemented, and proposed new measures to the parties to the conflict, whom he urged to respect the rights of civilians; to the Burundian authorities, whom he requested to combat impunity, end arbitrary detention and torture, and continue with the reforms provided for by the Arusha Agreement [YUN 2000, p. 146]; and to the international community, which he urged to maintain humanitarian and development assistance to Burundi. The Assembly took note of the expert's report on 16 December (**decision 60/533**).

A later report of the expert [E/CN.4/2006/109] provided information on his fourth visit to Burundi (4-5 October). While he continued to acknowledge positive developments in the political process, most notably the successful completion of elections, the expert reported a deplorable deterioration of the human rights situation, owing to the continuation of the armed conflict and related violence, of which civilians remained the main victims. The overall security situation remained fragile, and a weak judiciary and perceived climate of impunity continued to give rise to human rights violations, including of the rights to life; to liberty, security and inviolability of the person; and to freedom of movement and of the choice of one's residence. In particular, alleged violations of the rights of women, children and other vulnerable groups continued. The expert urged the Government to implement urgent measures to strengthen the judicial system, combat impunity and bring perpetrators of human rights violations to justice. Troubled by reports of persisting sexual violence in the country, he called for swift and concrete government measures to combat the phenomenon. He also recommended action on issues relating to prisoners and encouraged the authorities to maintain efforts to establish institutions provided for in the Arusha Agreement, particularly those relating to human rights. Other recommendations were addressed to the international community to ensure better human rights protection and promotion in the country.

Cambodia

Commission action. On 20 April [res. 2005/77], the Commission welcomed Cambodia's improvements in its human rights situation, while still expressing concern about continuing violations relating to the rule of law, the judiciary, human trafficking, violence against activists, impunity and corruption. Also welcoming the signing of a new memorandum of understanding between the Government and OHCHR on the implementation of a technical cooperation programme on human rights, the Commission encouraged efforts to improve further the country's human rights situation, especially through the establishment of the rule of law and judicial reform. It invited the Secretary-General and the international community to continue to assist the Government in improving democracy and protecting human rights, and requested the Secretary-General to report in 2006.

Report of Special Representative. Following the resignations of the former Special Representatives, Yash Ghai (Kenya) was appointed the new Special Representative of the Secretary-General for human rights in Cambodia. During his first visit to the country (28 November–5 December) [E/CN.4/2006/110], he accorded particular attention to its Constitution, the justice sector and the rule of law, and the status of fundamental freedoms. He found unfavourable circumstances for democratic participation in State affairs, as the Government's frequent use of lawsuits to counter dissent and opposition made it hard for opposition-party politicians, trade unions, journalists, civil society and human rights organizations to express their views. Consequently, well known public figures had been unable to return to the country or were in jail awaiting trial for such charges as defamation, disinformation and incitement. Although Cambodia's Constitution incorporated international human rights instruments to which the country was a party, its provisions had been mostly disregarded and its safeguards weakened. The legal framework for effective rule of law was inadequate, as the country maintained the transitional code of criminal law and procedure adopted, for temporary purposes only, by the United Nations Transitional Authority in Cambodia, which operated between February 1992 [YUN 1992, p. 243] and September 1993 [YUN 1993, p. 371]. Against that background, there were indications of abuse of the law and pervasive impunity for politically or economically prominent persons. The way that Cambodia's land and natural resources were managed also created a major problem, with the Government withholding information on those resources conceded to private companies and the military in the name of development. Such practices and other resource abuse had affected the livelihood of the rural poor harshly, particularly indigenous communities. The Representative

addressed recommendations to the authorities, urging that priority be given to strengthening institutions central to upholding and implementing the Constitution and to strengthening the independence and functioning of the legal and judicial process. Other recommendations related to the need to: restore an environment conducive to public debate and the exercise of democratic rights, particularly regarding freedoms of expression, of association and of peaceful assembly; update the legal framework for the effective rule of law and repeal of provisions contradicting human rights; reinstate parliamentary immunity to opposition members and drop the charges against them; end impunity; and implement the land law and resolve land disputes fairly and in accordance with domestic and international laws.

OHCHR/Cambodia

Report of Secretary-General. A report of the Secretary-General [E/CN.4/2006/105] described the role and achievements of OHCHR/Cambodia in 2005 in assisting the Cambodian Government and people to promote and protect human rights. During the year, the Office continued to monitor the overall human rights situation, and responded to violations, giving first priority to the problems confronted by NGOs and human rights defenders in their work. The Office brought its concerns to the attention of the authorities and requested their intervention. It also continued to advocate for structural reform of key institutions to guarantee an independent and professional judiciary, and worked with the courts to help address deficiencies in justice delivery. It followed up on the 2004 recommendations of the Special Representative [YUN 2004, p. 673] on land concessions for economic purposes, responded to the problems arising in some concessions, and monitored the continuing award of land and other concessions of Cambodia's natural resources. During the reporting period, OHCHR gave particular attention to the right to adequate housing (see p. 843), and to preventing forced evictions, especially in Phnom Penh. It also made efforts to help integrate and implement human rights standards in development policies and programmes.

Chad

Commission action. On 22 April [dec. 2005/118], the Commission asked OHCHR to expand its cooperation with the Government of Chad regarding the promotion and protection of human rights.

Democratic Republic of the Congo

Commission action. On 21 April [res. 2005/85], the Commission, expressing concern at persistent reports of violations of human rights and international humanitarian law in the eastern part of the Democratic Republic of the Congo (DRC), particularly in North Kivu and South Kivu, northern Katanga and Ituri, condemned the impunity enjoyed by those responsible and decided to extend the mandate of the independent expert for one year. The expert was requested to submit a progress report to the General Assembly in 2005 and to report to the Commission in 2006. The Secretary-General was asked to provide advisory services to the DRC in the field of human rights.

On 25 July, the Economic and Social Council endorsed the Commission's requests to the independent expert and the Secretary-General (**decision 2005/282**).

Reports of independent expert. By a 29 September note [A/60/395], the Secretary-General transmitted the expert's report to the General Assembly, pursuant to Assembly resolution 59/207 [YUN 2004, p. 674] and Commission resolution 2005/85 (see p. 736). The report contained information on the expert's visit to the DRC (16-27 August), particularly the capital city of Kinshasa, the sensitive region of Ituri and the region of Bunia, where he inspected the central prison and its holding cell. He consulted widely with Government officials, UN entities there and civil society organizations, focusing on alleged human rights violations and issues relating to justice, impunity and the electoral process. Thereafter, he observed that the human rights situation throughout the country remained a matter of concern, especially in some eastern regions and in northern Katanga, where militias and other armed groups were committing massive human rights violations with impunity. Massacres of civilians, pillage, mass rape of women and girls and summary executions, among other things, seriously undermined the Transitional Government's efforts to improve the situation. The suppression of peaceful demonstrations in many parts of the country, the precarious situation of unpaid or underpaid public officials and the threats and harassment suffered by journalists and human rights defenders fomented unrest and jeopardized the prospects for peace in the country. Other major sources of concern included the lack of consensus in the joint management of the transition period, the steady deterioration of law and order in the Orientale province of Ituri following repeated attacks by armed militias, the lack of an independent judiciary, general insecurity and the trafficking and illegal exploitation of natural resources. The expert recommended that all the Congolese parties promote a culture of peace, tolerance and reconciliation among the population, and recognize the need also to foster a culture of dialogue and to reject violence and ethnic hatred. He addressed a number of other measures to the Government and the international community, and proposed to the Commission, the General Assembly, the Security Council and the Economic and Social Council, the establishment, by decision of the Security Council, of an international criminal tribunal for the DRC. Failing that, consideration should be given to setting up mixed criminal chambers within existing Congolese courts to hear cases of the crimes that had been committed.

A later report of the expert to the Commission [E/CN.4/2006/113] contained the same account of his visit to the DRC during the year.

GENERAL ASSEMBLY ACTION

On 16 December [meeting 64], the General Assembly, on the recommendation of the Third Committee [A/60/509/Add.3], adopted **resolution 60/170** by recorded vote (102-3-67) [agenda item 71 (c)].

Situation of human rights in the Democratic Republic of the Congo

The General Assembly,

Reaffirming that all States Members of the United Nations have an obligation to promote and protect human rights and fundamental freedoms, and the duty to fulfil the obligations they have undertaken under the various instruments in this field,

Noting that the Democratic Republic of the Congo is a party to several international and regional human rights instruments and to several instruments pertaining to international humanitarian law,

Underlining the importance of elections as the foundation for the longer-term restoration of peace and stability, national reconciliation, the rule of law and lasting promotion and protection of human rights in the Democratic Republic of the Congo,

Recalling its previous resolutions, as well as those of the Commission on Human Rights and the Security Council, on the situation in the Democratic Republic of the Congo,

1. *Welcomes:*

(a) The report of the independent expert on the situation of human rights in the Democratic Republic of the Congo of 29 September 2005, as well as his visit to the Democratic Republic of the Congo in August 2005;

(b) The strengthened mandate of the United Nations Organization Mission in the Democratic Republic of the Congo regarding the protection of civilians in accordance with Security Council resolution 1592(2005) of 30 March 2005, and expresses its support for the continued work of the Mission and the Special Representative of the Secretary-General for the Democratic Republic of the Congo;

(c) The work accomplished by the human rights field office in the Democratic Republic of the Congo, and encourages the office to pursue and enhance its cooperation with the relevant agencies of the United Nations and the United Nations Organization Mission in the Democratic Republic of the Congo in the fulfilment of its mandate;

(*d*) The measures taken in 2005 by the authorities of the Democratic Republic of the Congo to arrest and detain leaders of militia groups suspected of committing killings and other serious crimes against civilians;

(*e*) The substantial progress made by the transitional national Government and the Independent Electoral Commission, with the welcome assistance of the United Nations Organization Mission in the Democratic Republic of the Congo, towards the holding of elections before June 2006 as specified in the Global and All-Inclusive Agreement, in particular the registration of voters and the enthusiasm shown by the Congolese people to embrace a democratic future;

2. *Takes note* of the continuing investigation by the Office of the Prosecutor of the International Criminal Court, based upon the referral of the Democratic Republic of the Congo, into crimes allegedly committed in the territory of the Democratic Republic of the Congo since the entry into force of the Rome Statute of the International Criminal Court on 1 July 2002;

3. *Requests* the United Nations High Commissioner for Human Rights to ensure that consultations continue between the field office of the Office of the High Commissioner in the Democratic Republic of the Congo and the Secretary-General concerning the ways in which to assist the transitional Government of the Democratic Republic of the Congo in tackling the problem of impunity, and looks forward to the report of the High Commissioner to the Commission on Human Rights at its sixty-second session on those consultations and on possible options for putting an end to the impunity of the perpetrators of crimes committed before 1 July 2002;

4. *Condemns:*

(*a*) The ongoing violations of human rights and international humanitarian law, particularly in North Kivu and South Kivu, northern Katanga and other areas in the eastern part of the Democratic Republic of the Congo, including armed violence and reprisals against the civilian population and the recourse to sexual violence against women and children, including in situations where such practices are being used as a weapon of war;

(*b*) The killing of United Nations peacekeeping troops by militia groups in Ituri Province, eastern Democratic Republic of the Congo, in February 2005 and in June 2005;

(*c*) The killing of Pascal Kabungulu Kibembi, Executive Secretary of the human rights non-governmental organization Héritiers de la Justice on 31 July 2005 and the harassment of human rights defenders across the country, but particularly in the eastern Democratic Republic of the Congo;

(*d*) The continued illegal exploitation of natural resources in the eastern Democratic Republic of the Congo and killings and other serious crimes against civilians committed by groups linked to the mining and trading of those resources, as well as the linkage between the illegal exploitation of natural resources, illicit trade in such resources and the proliferation and trafficking of arms as one of the factors fuelling and exacerbating conflicts in the Democratic Republic of the Congo;

5. *Urges* all the parties, including non-signatories of the Global and All-Inclusive Agreement on the Transition, in the Democratic Republic of the Congo:

(*a*) To respect and further implement the Global and All-Inclusive Agreement and to cease immediately any action which impedes the consolidation of the sovereignty, unity and territorial integrity of the Democratic Republic of the Congo;

(*b*) To support the transitional Government and its institutions in order to allow for the re-establishment of political and economic stability and for the gradual reinforcement of State structures over the entire territory of the Democratic Republic of the Congo, in accordance with their obligations under the transitional Constitution and as per the text of the Constitution submitted for referendum in December 2005;

(*c*) To put an immediate end to the recruitment and use of child soldiers, which is contrary to international law and to the African Charter on the Rights and Welfare of the Child, with the understanding that, under the Convention on the Rights of the Child and the Optional Protocol thereto on the involvement of children in armed conflict, and in accordance with Security Council resolutions 1539(2004) of 22 April 2004 and 1612(2005) of 26 July 2005 on children and armed conflict, persons under the age of 18 are entitled to special protection, and to develop and implement without delay the action plans called for in Council resolutions 1539(2004) and 1612(2005);

(*d*) To take special measures to protect women and children from the appalling violence, including sexual violence, which continues to be prevalent throughout the country, in particular in the eastern part of the country, and to bring the perpetrators of such crimes to justice as soon as possible, and condemns in particular the widespread use of sexual violence as a means of warfare;

(*e*) To respect international humanitarian law, in particular on the protection of civilians, and to ensure the safety, security and freedom of movement of all civilians and United Nations and associated personnel, and the unhindered access of humanitarian personnel to all of the affected population throughout the territory of the Democratic Republic of the Congo in accordance with Security Council resolutions 1265 (1999) of 17 September 1999 and 1296(2000) of 19 April 2000;

(*f*) To promote the full enjoyment of all human rights and to protect the safety, security and freedom of movement of all human rights defenders;

6. *Calls upon* the Government of National Unity and Transition to take specific measures:

(*a*) To complete the objectives of the transitional period as laid down in the Global and All-Inclusive Agreement, in particular the holding of free and transparent elections at all levels within the specified timetable, enabling the establishment of a democratic constitutional regime, and the formation of a restructured and fully integrated national army, and also the formation of an integrated and adequately resourced national police force, while ensuring that government institutions, including the army and police, are trained in human rights aspects of their work; and ensuring that both light and heavy weapons are being surrendered in the disarmament process;

(*b*) To strengthen the transitional institutions, in particular to set up effectively the Independent Electoral Commission, and to make more effective the institutions for the strengthening of democracy, namely, the Truth and Reconciliation Commission, the Human Rights Monitoring Centre and the Haute Autorité des Médias, and to re-establish stability and the rule of law over the entire territory of the Democratic Republic of the Congo, thereby returning peace and progress to its people;

(*c*) To comply fully with its obligations under international human rights instruments and, accordingly, to continue to cooperate with United Nations mechanisms for the protection of human rights and further strengthen its cooperation with the Office of the United Nations High Commissioner for Human Rights and the Human Rights Section of the United Nations Organization Mission in the Democratic Republic of the Congo;

(*d*) To put an end to impunity and to ensure, as it is duty-bound to do, that those responsible for human rights violations and grave breaches of international humanitarian law are brought to justice in accordance with applicable international procedural standards, and to carry out urgently a comprehensive reform of the judicial and prison system;

(*e*) To promote the full enjoyment of all human rights by women and children and to meet the special needs of women and girls in post-conflict reconstruction, as well as to ensure the full participation of women in all aspects of conflict resolution and peace processes, including peacekeeping, conflict management and peacebuilding, as a matter of priority, in accordance with Security Council resolution 1325 (2000) of 31 October 2000 on women and peace and security;

(*f*) To continue to cooperate fully with the International Criminal Court and with the International Criminal Tribunal for Rwanda, by ensuring that they have all necessary means with which to accomplish their tasks;

(*g*) To continue to uphold its commitment to abolishing the death penalty and not to impose it on juvenile offenders in line with its obligations assumed under the relevant provisions of the International Covenant on Civil and Political Rights and other human rights instruments;

(*h*) To prevent the use of the media to incite hatred or tensions among communities, while respecting freedom of expression and of the press, particularly during the electoral campaign;

(*i*) To ensure that human rights defenders are protected from abuses, threats and harassment;

(*j*) To accelerate its programme to demobilize, disarm and reintegrate former combatants, taking into account the special needs of women and children, including girls, associated with those combatants;

(*k*) To ensure the rights and well-being of internally displaced persons;

(*l*) To increase its efforts to eliminate corruption in the Democratic Republic of the Congo, which contributes to a general climate of impunity, and to take steps towards the setting up of an arrangement to strengthen support for good governance and transparent economic management, with the support of the International Committee in Support of the Transition,

the United Nations Organization Mission in the Democratic Republic of the Congo, international financial institutions and donors;

7. *Calls upon* the Governments of countries in the region, including the Democratic Republic of the Congo:

(*a*) To contribute to preventing armed groups operating in the eastern Democratic Republic of the Congo from perpetrating killings and other serious crimes by tackling the illicit trade by those armed groups in illegally extracted natural resources as well as the linkage between the illegal exploitation of natural resources, illicit trade in such resources and the proliferation and trafficking of arms, including by preventing support for such armed groups, while fully respecting the sovereignty, unity and territorial integrity of the Democratic Republic of the Congo;

(*b*) To work with the United Nations Organization Mission in the Democratic Republic of the Congo to take urgent steps towards the disarmament and resettlement or repatriation of foreign armed groups, which remain a threat to regional peace and perpetrate killings and serious crimes against the civilian population of the Democratic Republic of the Congo;

(*c*) To support the transitional process in the Democratic Republic of the Congo and adhere fully to the Principles on Good-neighbourly Relations and Cooperation between the Democratic Republic of the Congo and Burundi, Rwanda and Uganda, signed in New York on 25 September 2003, to continue to work towards the successful implementation of the Joint Verification Mechanism, to work through the Tripartite Commission Plus One and to respect the principles of the Dar es Salaam Declaration of 20 November 2004, and welcomes steps taken in this regard to date;

(*d*) To peacefully repatriate members of the Forces démocratiques de libération du Rwanda returning to Rwanda, in accordance with the applicable norms of international law and with respect for human rights and fundamental freedoms, and to ensure the rights and well-being of returnees and refugee populations;

(*e*) To continue to cooperate with the International Criminal Court and with the International Criminal Tribunal for Rwanda, and, specifically in the case of the Democratic Republic of the Congo, to make swift progress towards passing legislation necessary for the International Criminal Court's investigations in the Democratic Republic of the Congo to proceed smoothly;

8. *Urges* the Secretary-General to continue his work aimed at eliminating sexual exploitation and abuse committed by personnel serving the United Nations Organization Mission in the Democratic Republic of the Congo;

9. *Encourages* the international community:

(*a*) To continue to support the transitional process in the Democratic Republic of the Congo and its institutions and, in particular, to support the electoral process and to provide further assistance for the reform of the justice system;

(*b*) To observe the arms embargo on the Democratic Republic of the Congo established by Security Council resolution 1493(2003) of 28 July 2003 and expanded by Council resolution 1596(2005) of 18 April 2005, and to enforce the sanctions measures against individuals identified by the Council in line with its resolution 1596(2005) and its resolution 1616(2005) of 29 July 2005;

(c) To continue to exert political pressure on concerned States and members of armed groups based in the eastern Democratic Republic of the Congo in order to limit their capacity for continued fund-raising, which contributes to ongoing killings and other serious crimes;

10. *Decides* to continue to examine the situation of human rights in the Democratic Republic of the Congo, and requests the independent expert on the situation of human rights in the Democratic Republic of the Congo to report to the General Assembly at its sixty-first session.

Haiti

Commission action. On 21 April [E/2005/23], the Commission Chairperson, in a statement concerning technical cooperation and the situation of human rights in Haiti, stated that the Commission welcomed the efforts of the Haitian transitional authorities to protect and promote human rights and encouraged continued international support for those efforts. It noted with concern the difficulties in the functioning of the judicial system arising from pretrial detention and encouraged the authorities to continue efforts to expedite justice. The Commission welcomed the authorities' agreement to the opening of an OHCHR office in the country, and invited the independent expert to continue his mission and report thereon in 2006.

On 25 July, the Economic and Social Council approved the Commission's request to the independent expert (**decision 2005/294**).

Report of independent expert. Independent expert Louis Joinet (France) visited Haiti three times in 2005 [E/CN.4/2006/115], where he focused on the issues of insecurity and vulnerable groups, human rights violations and the failure of justice. He found that, despite gradual improvement in the provinces, the situation in the capital was increasingly disturbing, owing in particular to a daily increase in kidnaping incidents. The situation concerning children's rights had deteriorated due to growing poverty and violence, illustrated by the fact that some 2,500 children lived on the streets in the capital and that the country's armed factions recruited children. In addition, up to 47 per cent of sexual assaults involved minors, school enrolment rate was low in the most disadvantaged districts and some 200,000 children, including orphans, were infected by the HIV virus. The situation of women was also worrisome, with up to 85 per cent of cases of interpersonal violence involving them, particularly regarding increasing reports of rape. Efforts to secure women's rights had involved the launching of a national plan to combat violence against them, which resulted in an obligation for doctors to issue medical certificates in cases of injuries that might be linked to sexual assault, the criminalization of rape and the progressive lifting of the taboo on the voluntary termination of pregnancy.

Also of concern were mass expulsions of people of Haitian origin from the Dominican Republic under conditions that violated their rights, as well as the mass deportation through processes that lacked a legal basis, particularly from the United States, of convicted Haitians who had served their sentences. The justice system was undermined by a number of other problems, including damage to judicial facilities, recurrent abuse of extended pretrial detention and interference with the judiciary by the executive arm of government, illustrated by the alleged dismissal (reportedly misrepresented as retirements) of five judges from the Court of Cassation. The expert recommended that priority be given to efforts to combat insecurity and poverty, which had been the major cause of the violence experienced by the poorest. He also proposed measures to improve the justice system, advance women's rights, improve such electoral processes as voter registration, reform the land register, and develop stand-alone, small-scale water supply projects.

Liberia

Commission action. On 22 April [dec. 2005/117], the Commission took note of the 2004 report of the independent expert [YUN 2004, p. 676] on the situation of human rights in Liberia and decided to consider the question in 2006.

Report of independent expert. The independent expert on the human rights situation in Liberia, Charlotte Abaka (Ghana), visited the country (25 September–6 October) [E/CN.4/2006/114] and found that progress had been made, including improvements in the security situation, which enhanced the freedom of movement and facilitated the conduct of national elections. Other positive developments included the enhancement of laws to improve the functioning of national institutions concerned with human rights, such as the Truth and Reconciliation Commission Act and the Act establishing the Independent National Commission on Human Rights; Liberia's recent ratification of several international human rights treaties; the resettlement of 39,851 refugees and over 221,828 internally displaced persons (IDPs); and efforts to improve the justice system, particularly as a result of the creation of a Case Flow Management Committee, which helped reduce prison congestion in some counties. Despite those encouraging developments, the expert noted that human rights violations had continued, and a major concern was that two of the country's five main rubber plantations were being controlled by former combatants, and the line between State and corporate responsibility for the human rights concerns on those plantations was blurred. Although the Transitional Government was making efforts to secure women's rights, including the development of a draft law on rape, women continued to suffer increasing incidents of rape, domestic violence, harmful traditional practices, ritual killings and trial by ordeal. Also of major concern were egregious violations of children's rights owing to variations in the legal definition of a child and the consequent lack of formal recognition of children's special needs, a high incidence of sexual assault against them, and the prevalence of illegal, privately run orphanages, among other reasons. The problem was compounded by the fact that those violations attracted only slight attention from the justice system, which was hampered by poor court management and corruption. The expert also noted shortcomings regarding the realization of the rights to an adequate standard of living, fair remuneration and regular payment of wages, to physical and mental health, and to education. She addressed recommendations to the Liberian authorities to better address human rights, including the establishment of such national institutions as the Truth and Reconciliation Committee, a National Human Rights Council, a judicial council and a law reform commission, as well as measures against corruption and on the need to review salaries for government officials and expedite action in giving effect to the international treaties it had ratified. She recommended that the Security Council strengthen and extend the current human rights mandate of the United Nations Mission in Liberia (UNMIL) (see p. 256) and that OHCHR, Governments and the international community support UNMIL and reform efforts in Liberia.

Nepal

Reports of OHCHR. In response to a request contained in the 2004 statement of the Commission's Chairperson [YUN 2004, p. 676], OHCHR submitted a January report [E/CN.4/2005/114] on the question of human rights assistance to Nepal. The report provided an overview of the deteriorating human rights situation in the country, characterized by widespread systematic violations, particularly among the civilian population and resulting from increased military activity on both sides of the ongoing conflict between the Communist Party Nepal–Maoist (CPN) and the Government. Grave violations allegedly committed by the former included mass abductions, particularly of children, executions, torture and disappearances. In addition, there were reports

of frequent blockades, enforced through terror, including the use of landmines, which created considerable social and economic hardship among the poor population. Government forces reportedly committed similar violations, and in the past year, there had been increasing reports of threats and reprisals against human rights defenders from both sides. The report also highlighted OHCHR activities in the country, which included advice and assistance to the National Human Rights Commission and to the Government on human rights commitments, support to the UN Resident Coordinator and the Country Team, the development of regular exchanges of information and views with civil society and cooperation with regional and international partners. The Office proposed measures for ending the cycle of violence and impunity and to ensure the efficiency of the National Human Rights Commission, a strong and active civil society, and a more active engagement in Nepal by the United Nations and the international community.

Commission action. On 20 April [res. 2005/78], the Commission, condemning the human rights violations of the Communist Party Nepal–Maoist (CPN), urged the Government to take measures to prevent and end those violations; begin a national political dialogue to restore peace; assist IDPs; safeguard judicial remedies; support the National Human Rights Commission of Nepal; and request the technical assistance of the United Nations and the international community in planning local elections. It requested the High Commissioner to establish an office in Nepal, in accordance with an 11 April Agreement with the Government, in order to assist the authorities in developing policies to promote and protect human rights, to monitor the situation of human rights in the country and report to the General Assembly in 2005, and to the Commission in 2006.

On 25 July, the Economic and Social Council endorsed the Commission's requests to the High Commissioner (**decision 2005/277**).

Report of High Commissioner. By a September note [A/60/359], the Secretary-General transmitted a report of the High Commissioner regarding the human rights situation and OHCHR activities in Nepal, including technical cooperation, submitted in response to Commission resolution 2005/78 (see above). The report described the political, legal and human rights situation in the country and examined the trend regarding respect for international human rights and humanitarian law, including by State authorities, the Communist Party Nepal–Maoist (CPN), vigilante elements and other groups. It considered, in particular, the status of democratic rights relative to arbitrary detention, freedom of movement and fair trial, and to the freedom of assembly, of expression and of association. The report determined that long-standing human rights concerns, including economic impoverishment, social inequities and discrimination, were among the root causes of the crisis in the country, and under the circumstances, the rights to food and to adequate water and other economic, social and cultural rights were all at risk. Particular issues of concern included the practice of caste and ethnic discrimination, mainly against the Dalits, who were relegated to the lowest caste, and which was also inflicted on the over 60 different indigenous communities in the country. Gender discrimination and human trafficking, affecting mostly women and girls, were also critical problems. Other groups of concern were IDPs compelled by human rights problems to flee their homes; children, who were abducted by the Communist Party Nepal–Maoist (CPN) as combatants, human shields or servants; and human rights defenders vulnerable to arrests and travel restrictions.

OHCHR, which had been active in Nepal since 2003 to assist with human rights issues, enhanced its presence in the country during the year with the establishment of an office there, following an April agreement with the Government. Thereafter, it presented Member States with a plan for the new office, comprising some 50 international staff, including UN volunteers and national professional and support staff. The office was mandated to advise the Resident Coordinator and the Country Team on human rights protection and capacity-building, and to coordinate human rights activities. To that end, an inter-agency human rights protection working group had been established, and would, in turn, establish subgroups on the protection of children and IDPs and on other priority human rights protection issues. During the year, the office received and investigated reports of ongoing violations by both parties to the conflict, particularly regarding extrajudicial executions, disappearances, arbitrary arrest and detention, and torture, and also addressed the question of accountability for violations by military personnel and of responsibility for the protection of the civilian population. In other developments, OHCHR reviewed the appointment of new commissioners to the National Human Rights Council after a controversial amendment to the procedure for such appointments, assessed how the development might impact the work of that body, and made recommendations for future assistance.

On 16 December, the General Assembly took note of the High Commissioner's report (**decision 60/533**).

Sierra Leone

Reports of High Commissioner. In response to a 2004 Commission request [YUN 2004, p. 676], the High Commissioner submitted a February report [E/CN.4/2005/113] on the situation of human rights in Sierra Leone. The report examined human rights challenges relating to the right to life and security of the person, amputees and war-wounded, children's welfare, gender-based violence and women's rights, refugees, returnees and IDPs. It also analysed the human rights activities of the United Nations Mission in Sierra Leone (UNAMSIL) (see p. 276) and other UN entities in the country, including OHCHR, and considered developments concerning transitional justice. The High Commissioner observed that there had been a continuing consolidation of progress in the field of human rights in Sierra Leone, and developments in that regard included the submission by the Truth and Reconciliation Commission of recommendations, some of which, by statute, were binding on the Government; trials in process by the Special Court for Sierra Leone; increased compliance by law enforcement officers with the rule of law; and relative improvements in detention conditions. Despite that progress, violations persisted, including of the right to life. In that regard, reports of unresolved killings involved women, who also suffered unfavourable traditional and cultural practices and sexual exploitation, as well as children, many of whom had been abducted as child soldiers, maimed, and subjected to forced labour, sexual slavery and child trafficking. The situation of amputees and war-wounded also highlighted human rights challenges in Sierra Leone, as many of them had been compelled to become city beggars owing to the Government's failure to address their needs, particularly regarding adequate housing, among other things. Additional shortcomings in the field of economic, social and cultural rights threatening the hard-won peace included a high level of youth unemployment, limited possibility for education and skills training, poor health facilities, high levels of corruption, and continuing discrimination against women. Those issues needed to be addressed to ensure the long-term sustainability of the progress made. In particular, greater efforts should be made to achieve the Millennium Development Goals (MDGs) [YUN 2000, p. 51].

In an August note [A/60/349], the Secretary-General transmitted the High Commissioner's report on assistance to Sierra Leone in the field of human rights, submitted in response to Commission resolution 2005/76 (see p. 743). After examining the human rights situation in the country, the High Commissioner, noting progress towards achieving the benchmarks set for UNAMSIL by year's end, stated that the peace remained fragile owing to a number of human rights concerns. She observed that the critical issues of marginalization and exclusion at the root of the conflict were yet to be addressed and that sufficient efforts were not being made to protect women and children from violations. Other problems included widespread corruption, a weak judiciary and impunity. Overall, however, the poor state of the economy constituted the largest potential threat to peace, stability and the continuous enjoyment of human rights and fundamental freedoms under the rule of law. The High Commissioner recommended that the human rights situation in the country continue to be closely monitored, investigated and documented, with the human rights components of UNAMSIL and the United Nations Mission in Liberia (UNMIL) undertaking more public reporting on individual responsibilities for violations and other issues of concern. Further recommendations concerned the need for continuing training and capacity-building in the area of human rights; the establishment of a national human rights commission; reform of the justice system and of relevant laws, as well as the ratification and implementation of international instruments, in order to ensure respect for human rights and fundamental freedoms, particularly regarding women's and children's rights. It was also vital to maintain a strong human rights presence in Sierra Leone after the termination of UNAMSIL, to support the national authorities in addressing human rights issues.

On 16 December, the General Assembly took note of the High Commissioner's report (**decision 60/533**).

Commission action. On 20 April [res. 2005/76], the Commission, welcoming progress achieved in the field of human rights in Sierra Leone, expressed concern at developments that could threaten that progress, including the return of ex-combatants, increasing reports of child trafficking and the plight of amputees and mutilated victims of the conflict in the country. It urged the Government to continue to promote and protect human rights, accord priority attention to the needs of mutilated victims and further strengthen its judicial system. The Commission asked the High Commissioner and the international community to assist the Government in strengthening its capacity to review and update national legislation, particularly relating to women, children and vulnerable groups. The High Commissioner was further asked to report to the General Assembly in 2005, and to the Commission in 2006.

On 25 July, the Economic and Social Council endorsed the Commission's request to the High Commissioner (**decision 2005/276**).

Somalia

Commission action. On 21 April [res. 2005/83], the Commission, welcoming the newly established transitional institutions in Somalia among important steps towards a durable solution to the conflict there, condemned the ongoing and widespread human rights violations, the forced recruitment of children for use in the armed conflict and those who obstructed the peace process by persisting with confrontation and violence, including hostage-taking, abduction and murder. It called on the Transitional Federal Government to establish a national commission on human rights to promote and protect rights, combat impunity, bring perpetrators to justice, and integrate human rights standards into national institutions. The High Commissioner was asked to provide for the translation into Somali language and subsequent dissemination within the country of international human rights treaties and the Commission's current resolution, while the transnational federal institutions were requested to cooperate with the Commission's mechanisms, particularly its special procedures. The Commission decided to extend the mandate of the independent expert on the situation of human rights in Somalia for a further year and requested him to report to the Commission in 2006.

On 25 July, the Economic and Social Council endorsed the Commission's requests to the independent expert (**decision 2005/281**).

Report of independent expert. In response to a 2004 Commission request [YUN 2004, p. 677], the independent expert on the situation of human rights in Somalia, Ghanim Alnajjar (Kuwait), submitted a March report [E/CN.4/2005/117] covering the period from December 2004 to February 2005, during which he undertook a mission to the country, including visits to Puntland (31 January–2 February) and Somaliland (3-5 February). He observed some optimism towards resolving the border conflict between those two regions, with the authorities undertaking infrastructure projects and NGOs maintaining efforts to address local human rights issues. In Somaliland, where he helped negotiate the release of a 17 year-old girl sentenced to five years' incarceration for alleged espionage and lying about her clan identity, the expert found a number of other causes for concern, including an increase in police brutality, an alarming trend in juvenile suicides, the forced return of refugees and reports of threats to human rights defenders and journalists, to freedom of association and opinion. In Puntland, large-scale illegal fishing by foreign trawlers, complicated by recent droughts, floods and the long-term effects of a ban on livestock infringed on the economic and social rights of the population. In other parts of Somalia, the right to life continued to be violated extensively, owing to continuing insecurity and violence, particularly in the south and most notably in the capital city Mogadishu, where unrelenting inter-clan fighting resulted in many dead and wounded civilians. The expert noted that the greatest threat to security in Somalia was weapons proliferation, owing mainly to large-scale violations of the arms embargo. Notable violations related to increasing incidents of hostage-taking, which affected the freedom of the press; economic, social and cultural rights; prison conditions; the rights of minorities, including women and children; the rule of law; and the rights of refugees and IDPs. The expert recommended that the Somali authorities accord particular attention to children's and women's rights and establish independent institutions to promote and protect human rights. He also proposed that UN bodies study the possibility of establishing an independent organization to protect the endangered Somali coastline and that the Secretary-General and the Security Council establish a committee of independent experts to examine allegations of past violations and related crimes against humanity committed in Somalia. OHCHR should deploy a senior human rights officer to Nairobi, with the possibility of moving to Mogadishu at a later stage, charged with traveling frequently to Somalia to document violations, undertaking human rights advocacy duties and providing expertise when requested.

Timor-Leste

Report of High Commissioner. In response to a request contained in a 2004 statement of the Commission's Chairperson [YUN 2004, p. 677], the High Commissioner reported on technical cooperation in the field of human rights in Timor-Leste [E/CN.4/2005/115]. The report summarized the activities of OHCHR and of the Human Rights Unit of the United Nations Mission of Support in East Timor (UNMISET) (see p. 439), which were working together to implement a two-year technical cooperation project with the Government of Timor-Leste. It also discussed other technical assistance activities in the field of capacity-building regarding the justice system, the prisons, strengthening the legislative framework for police operations, monitoring alleged human rights violations by the defence forces of Timor-Leste, the role of a Provedor (ombudsperson with administrative oversight and the task of promoting and protecting human rights), intolerance, accession to international human rights instruments, and support to NGOs and other civil society organizations in promoting human rights. In addition, the report examined issues relevant to transitional justice in the country, as well as the human rights situation of vulnerable groups, including women, children, refugees, illegal immigrants and religious minorities. The report noted that, although considerable progress had been made in addressing the human rights situation in Timor-Leste, significant challenges remained. Notable achievements included the fact that the Commission for Reception, Truth and Reconciliation, charged with conducting community reconciliation hearings, successfully completed its work, and that the law establishing a national human rights institution and the office of the Provedor and Justice had been promulgated. On the negative side, however, the post of Prevedor was yet to be filled and alleged human rights violations had increased, particularly against women, children and refugees. Also, accountability mechanisms were unclear and inadequate, and the justice system remained weak. In efforts to address some of those problems, OHCHR and the Human Rights Unit of UNMISET had provided human rights training to law enforcement and prison officials, and to civil society and NGOs. Continuing technical assistance was being provided to the Commission for Reception, Truth and Reconciliation, and a technical advisor on human rights treaty reporting had been appointed to assist the Government in preparing its reports under international human rights instruments to which the country was a party. Nonetheless, there was a need for further technical assistance and advisory services to strengthen State institutions and civil society capacities for promoting and protecting human rights, and to ensure their sustainability after the scheduled withdrawal of UNMISET within the year. To that end, the High Commissioner recommended that the international community provide adequate resources to fund the continuation of a technical cooperation programme between OHCHR and the Government. She also addressed a series of recommendations to the Government for improving the human rights situation in the country, including through the expeditious appointment of the Provedor, effective independent monitoring of detention conditions, tackling police misconduct and violations, providing more legal assistance to women and strengthening their access to justice, and expediting the process of reuniting separated children with their families.

Human rights education

World Programme for Human Rights Education

Report of High Commissioner. In accordance with a 2004 Commission request [YUN 2004, p. 678], the High Commissioner submitted a report [E/CN.4/2005/98] on progress made regarding follow-up to the United Nations Decade for Human Rights Education, proclaimed by the General Assembly in resolution 49/184 [YUN 1994, p. 1039] and which ended in 2004. The report provided information on related events in the past year, particularly the Assembly's proclamation of the World Programme for Human Rights Education, conceived to advance the implementation of human rights education programmes in all sectors [YUN 2004, p. 678], with effect from 1 January 2005. It also reflected on the contents of the draft plan of action for the first phase (2005-2007) of the World Programme, prepared jointly by OHCHR and UNESCO [ibid.] and considered by the Assembly.

Note by Secretary-General. By a 2 March note [A/59/525/Rev.1], the Secretary-General transmitted, for adoption by the General Assembly, a revised draft plan of action for the first phase (2005-2007) of the World Programme, prepared by OHCHR, in consultation with UNESCO and based on comments received from Member States, in accordance with General Assembly resolution 59/113 [YUN 2004, p. 678]. The revised draft, annexed to the note, addressed issues relating to the context and definition of human rights education. It also considered specific issues concerning the first phase, the implementation strategy at the national level, coordination of implementation efforts, international cooperation and support, and evaluation.

Commission action. On 20 April [res. 2005/61], the Commission, welcoming the High Commissioner's report (see above), encouraged the Assembly to adopt the revised plan of action for the first phase (2005-2007) of the Programme. It asked OHCHR and UNESCO to disseminate it widely once adopted, and States to implement it. The High Commissioner and UN system bodies were asked to promote and assist in the national implementation of the plan, and the High Commissioner was further asked to report in 2006.

GENERAL ASSEMBLY ACTION

On 14 July [meeting 113], the General Assembly adopted **resolution 59/113 B** [draft A/59/L.65 & Add.1] without vote [agenda item 105 (b)].

World Programme for Human Rights Education

The General Assembly,

Recalling the relevant resolutions adopted by the General Assembly and the Commission on Human Rights concerning the United Nations Decade for Human Rights Education, 1995-2004,

Convinced that human rights education is a long-term and lifelong process through which everyone learns tolerance and respect for the dignity of others and the means and methods of ensuring that respect in all societies,

Believing that human rights education is essential to the realization of human rights and fundamental freedoms and contributes significantly to promoting equality, preventing conflict and human rights violations and enhancing participation and democratic processes, with a view to developing societies in which all human beings are valued and respected,

Welcoming the proclamation by the General Assembly on 10 December 2004 of the World Programme for Human Rights Education, structured in consecutive phases, which began on 1 January 2005,

1. *Adopts* the revised draft plan of action for the first phase (2005-2007) of the World Programme for Human Rights Education, which focuses on primary and secondary school systems;

2. *Encourages* all States to develop initiatives within the World Programme and, in particular, to implement, within their capabilities, the plan of action;

3. *Requests* the Office of the United Nations High Commissioner for Human Rights, in close cooperation with the United Nations Educational, Scientific and Cultural Organization, to promote the national implementation of the plan of action, provide relevant technical assistance when requested and coordinate related international efforts;

4. *Appeals* to relevant organs, bodies or agencies of the United Nations system, as well as all other international and regional intergovernmental and non-governmental organizations, within their respective mandates, to promote and technically assist, when requested, the national implementation of the plan of action;

5. *Calls upon* all existing national human rights institutions to assist in the implementation of human rights education programmes consistent with the plan of action;

6. *Requests* the Office of the United Nations High Commissioner for Human Rights and the United Nations Educational, Scientific and Cultural Organization to widely disseminate the plan of action among States and inter-governmental and non-governmental organizations.

Subcommission action. On 11 August [res. 2005/26], the Subcommission recommended that human rights treaty bodies, when examining reports of States parties, devote attention to human rights education, particularly in the framework of the World Programme for Human Rights Education, and that the item be included in the agenda of the annual meeting of the persons chairing the treaty bodies, to enable them to make recommendations on how human rights education could contribute to national capacity-building, aimed at strengthening national human rights protection mechanisms.

Children and a culture of peace

Report of UNESCO Director-General. In response to General Assembly resolutions 59/142 [YUN 2004, p. 1102] and 59/143 [ibid., p. 679] on the promotion of religious and cultural understanding, harmony and cooperation, and on the International Decade for a Culture of Peace and Non-violence for the Children of the World (2001-2010), proclaimed in 1998 [YUN 1998, p. 639], the Secretary-General transmitted a report [A/60/279] of the UNESCO Director-General on a midterm review of the Decade. The report analysed work undertaken by the UN system, civil society organizations and UNESCO during the past five years. At the national level, UNESCO National Commissions had coordinated culture of peace activities, and 26 of them, representing all regions, had responded to questionnaires on actions taken, progress achieved and remaining challenges. Action in fostering the culture was taken mainly through education programmes, the promotion of sustainable economic and social development, the promotion of respect for human rights and equality between men and women, support for democratic participation, advancement of understanding, tolerance and solidarity, support for participatory communication and free flow of information and knowledge, and promotion of international peace and solidarity. Respondents reported progress in terms of increased children's access to schools, owing to the improved awareness of parents of the need for basic education; improved health-care services and infrastructure; enhanced involvement of governmental institutions in relevant activities; better participation of citizens in electoral processes; and increased participation of women in decision-making at the local and national levels. A change in mentalities and behaviour was observed in some countries in post-conflict situations, where violence decreased markedly and ex-combatants experienced better integration into civilian society. At the global level, progress included increased civil society awareness of issues relating to a culture of peace and of peaceful conflict resolution. Major obstacles to further progress were political instability and the complexity of violence, exacerbated by a lack of interest and of political support from national and international authorities and the mass media. Other obstacles included the lack of human and financial resources, poverty, male-female inequality in access to education, HIV/AIDS, unemployment, illiteracy, traditional religious beliefs and the lack of political will. Additional reports on the activities undertaken, the progress made and integral problems in promoting the culture were provided by 36 NGOs that had also responded to the questionnaires. In the light of the obstacles highlighted, respondents advocated the development of national and regional plans of action, the creation of national and international coordination mechanisms, better monitoring of the activities carried out by various actors and better information-sharing and communication on issues pertaining to the Decade at all levels. Also needed were better training in conflict resolution and the development of appropriate methodologies of intervention on issues relating to a culture of peace and human rights and better communication and information mechanisms at the national level.

To maintain visibility and momentum between the midpoint and the completion of the Decade, the report proposed that a global framework be promoted to integrate the various objectives of the Declaration and Programme of Action on a Culture of Peace, which should launch national, regional or international events to demonstrate the Decade's objectives, and, among other things, mobilize the requisite resources for those activities. Annexed to the report was a summary of the views of some 700 civil society organizations from over 100 countries, which had responded to the questionnaires regarding the progress made and obstacles towards a culture of peace and non-violence during the first half of the Decade.

GENERAL ASSEMBLY ACTION

On 20 October [meeting 36], the General Assembly adopted **resolution 60/3** [draft A/60/L.5 & Add.1] without vote [agenda item 43].

International Decade for a Culture of Peace and Non-Violence for the Children of the World, 2001-2010

The General Assembly,

Bearing in mind the Charter of the United Nations, including the purposes and principles contained therein, and especially the dedication to saving succeeding generations from the scourge of war,

Recalling the Constitution of the United Nations Educational, Scientific and Cultural Organization, which states that, "since wars begin in the minds of men, it is in the minds of men that the defences of peace must be constructed",

Recalling also its previous resolutions on a culture of peace, in particular resolution 52/15 of 20 November 1997 proclaiming 2000 the International Year for the Culture of Peace, resolution 53/25 of 10 November 1998 proclaiming the period 2001-2010 the International Decade for a Culture of Peace and Non-Violence for the Children of the World, and resolutions 56/5 of 5 November 2001, 57/6 of 4 November 2002, 58/11 of 10 November 2003 and 59/143 of 15 December 2004,

Reaffirming the Declaration and Programme of Action on a Culture of Peace, recognizing that they serve, inter alia, as the basis for the observance of the Decade, and convinced that the effective and successful observance of the Decade throughout the world will promote a culture of peace and non-violence that benefits humanity, in particular future generations,

Recalling the United Nations Millennium Declaration, which calls for the active promotion of a culture of peace,

Taking note of Commission on Human Rights resolution 2000/66 of 26 April 2000, entitled "Towards a culture of peace",

Taking note also of the report of the Secretary-General on the International Decade for a Culture of Peace and Non-Violence for the Children of the World, including paragraph 28 thereof, which indicates that each of the ten years of the Decade will be marked with a different priority theme related to the Programme of Action,

Noting the relevance of the World Summit on Sustainable Development, held in Johannesburg, South Africa, from 26 August to 4 September 2002, the International Conference on Financing for Development, held in Monterrey, Mexico, from 18 to 22 March 2002, the special session of the General Assembly on children, held in New York from 8 to 10 May 2002, the World Conference against Racism, Racial Discrimination, Xenophobia and Related Intolerance, held in Durban, South Africa, from 31 August to 8 September 2001, and the United Nations Decade for Human Rights Education, 1995-2004, for the International Decade for a Culture of Peace and Non-Violence for the Children of the World, 2001-2010, as well as the need to implement, as appropriate, the relevant decisions agreed upon therein,

Recognizing that all efforts made by the United Nations system in general and the international community at large for peacekeeping, peacebuilding, the prevention of conflicts, disarmament, sustainable development, the promotion of human dignity and human rights, democracy, the rule of law, good governance and gender equality at the national and international levels contribute greatly to the culture of peace,

Noting that its resolution 57/337 of 3 July 2003 on the prevention of armed conflict could contribute to the further promotion of a culture of peace,

Taking into account the "Manifesto 2000" initiative of the United Nations Educational, Scientific and Cultural Organization promoting a culture of peace, which has so far received over seventy-five million signatures of endorsement throughout the world,

Taking note with appreciation of the report of the Director-General of the United Nations Educational, Scientific and Cultural Organization on the implementation of resolution 59/143,

Taking note of the 2005 World Summit Outcome adopted at the High-level Plenary Meeting of the General Assembly,

1. *Reiterates* that the objective of the International Decade for a Culture of Peace and Non-Violence for the Children of the World, 2001-2010, is to strengthen further the global movement for a culture of peace following the observance of the International Year for the Culture of Peace in 2000;

2. *Invites* Member States to continue to place greater emphasis on and expand their activities promoting a culture of peace and non-violence, in particular during the Decade, at the national, regional and international levels and to ensure that peace and non-violence are fostered at all levels;

3. *Commends* the United Nations Educational, Scientific and Cultural Organization for recognizing the promotion of a culture of peace as the expression of its fundamental mandate, and encourages it, as the lead agency for the Decade, to strengthen further the activities it has undertaken for promoting a culture of peace, including the dissemination of the Declaration and Programme of Action on a Culture of Peace and related materials in various languages across the world;

4. *Also commends* the relevant United Nations bodies, in particular the United Nations Children's Fund, the United Nations Development Fund for Women and the University for Peace, for their activities in further promoting a culture of peace and non-violence, including the promotion of peace education and activities related to specific areas identified in the Programme of Action on a Culture of Peace, and encourages them to continue and further strengthen and expand their efforts;

5. *Encourages* the appropriate authorities to provide education, in children's schools, that includes lessons in mutual understanding, tolerance, active citizenship, human rights and the promotion of a culture of peace;

6. *Commends* civil society, including non-governmental organizations and young people, for their activities in further promoting a culture of peace and non-violence, including through their campaign to raise awareness on a culture of peace, and takes note of the progress achieved by more than seven hundred organizations in more than one hundred countries;

7. *Encourages* civil society, including non-governmental organizations, to further strengthen its efforts in furtherance of the objectives of the Decade, inter alia, by adopting its own programme of activities to complement the initiatives of Member States, the organizations of the United Nations system and other international and regional organizations;

8. *Encourages* the involvement of the mass media in education for a culture of peace and non-violence, with particular regard to children and young people, including through the planned expansion of the Culture of Peace News Network as a global network of Internet sites in many languages;

9. *Welcomes* the efforts made by the United Nations Educational, Scientific and Cultural Organization to continue the communication and networking arrangements established during the International Year for providing an instant update of developments related to the observance of the Decade;

10. *Invites* Member States to observe 21 September each year as the International Day of Peace, as a day of global ceasefire and non-violence, in accordance with resolution 55/282 of 7 September 2001;

11. *Invites* Member States, as well as civil society, including non-governmental organizations, to continue providing information to the Secretary-General on the observance of the Decade and the activities undertaken to promote a culture of peace and non-violence;

12. *Appreciates* the participation of Member States in the day of plenary meetings to review progress made in the implementation of the Declaration and Programme of Action on a Culture of Peace and the observance of the Decade at its midpoint;

13. *Requests* the Secretary-General to explore enhancing mechanisms for the implementation of the

Declaration and Programme of Action on a Culture of Peace;

14. *Also requests* the Secretary-General to submit to the General Assembly at its sixty-first session a report on the implementation of the present resolution;

15. *Decides* to include in the provisional agenda of its sixty-first session the item entitled "Culture of peace".

National institutions and regional arrangements

National institutions for human rights promotion and protection

Commission action. On 20 April [res. 2005/74], the Commission, affirming the important role of national human rights institutions to protect and promote the rights of particularly vulnerable groups, welcomed the decision of a growing number of States to establish such institutions, consistent with the Paris Principles relating to the status of national institutions for the promotion and protection of human rights (Paris Principles), adopted in General Assembly resolution 48/134 [YUN 1993, p. 899]. Further welcoming the strengthening of cooperation among those institutions, including through the International Coordinating Committee of National Institutions for the promotion and protection of human rights (for which OHCHR served as secretariat), the Commission asked the Secretary-General to assist the Committee's meetings and to report in 2006 on the process it used to accredit national institutions in compliance with the Paris Principles, and to ensure that the process was strengthened with periodic review. The Secretary-General was further asked to report, also in 2006, on the implementation of the Commission's resolution. In accordance with the recommendations contained in the Secretary-General's 2004 report [YUN 2004, p. 681], the Commission asked its Chairperson to finalize by 2006, the modalities for national institutions to participate in the work of the Commission and its subsidiary bodies, and for continuing the practice of issuing documents from those institutions under their own symbol numbers.

Reports of Secretary-General. In response to a 2004 Commission request [YUN 2004, p. 680], the Secretary-General, in a January report [E/CN.4/2005/107], discussed ways to enhance the participation of national human rights institutions in the Commission's work, with the objective of outlining a possible means of strengthening the status of those institutions in international forums, in order to feed national human rights challenges and experiences into the international agenda and to provide for effective follow-up at the national level of related recommendations. Against that background, the report provided a historical overview of calls within the Commission for enhancing the participation of national institutions and described their work, noting that their involvement in the Commission's work had grown over the years. Nonetheless, their status and the nature of their participation had yet to be formally defined. Issues of particular concern related to their accreditation by the International Coordinating Committee and their compliance with the Paris Principles. The Secretary-General recommended that strengthening the accreditation procedures of the Committee be accorded priority, and the Commission might wish to request that a report be submitted to it on action taken to that effect by the Committee. He also recommended that national institutions be permitted to address substantive issues under various items on the Commission's agenda other than the item relating to national institutions and regional arrangements, as that would enrich the information provided to the Commission and assist it in making informed decisions. There was also scope for a continued engagement with national institutions through the Subcommission, working groups and various Commission mechanisms, which could help strengthen the Commission's work. The Commission might wish to put in place a consultative process with OHCHR and the International Coordinating Committee to further explore ways in enhancing the participation of national institutions in that regard.

A later report of the Secretary-General [E/CN.4/2006/101], covering January to December 2005, contained information on the activities undertaken by OHCHR to establish and strengthen national institutions, measures taken by Governments and national institutions in that regard, and cooperation between those institutions and international mechanisms to promote and protect human rights.

During the reporting period, at the request of Governments, OHCHR provided advice and information on activities and issues which might assist national institutions in Afghanistan, Angola, Belgium, Burkina Faso, Burundi, Cameroon, Chile, China, Colombia, the Comoros, the Congo, Côte d'Ivoire, the Democratic Republic of the Congo, Djibouti, El Salvador, Finland, Iraq, Italy, Jordan, the province of Kosovo (Serbia and Montenegro), Lesotho, Liberia, Maldives, Mauritania, Nepal, the Niger, Norway, Pakistan, Qatar, Saudi Arabia, Serbia and Montenegro, Sierra Leone, Sri Lanka, the Sudan, the former Yugoslav Republic of Macedonia, Timor-Leste, Turkey, the United Kingdom and Uruguay. The national institutions of Afghanistan, Mongolia, Nepal, the Occupied Palestinian Territory, including East Jerusalem, Rwanda and Zambia benefited from the support programmes provided by the National Institutions Unit of OHCHR's Capacity-Building and Field Operations Branch, often in collaboration with the United Nations Development Programme (UNDP) and UN missions. During its 2005 session (Geneva, 14-15 April), the International Coordinating Committee discussed a paper on early warning mechanisms and agreed to establish a working group with at least one representative from each region to follow up on the commitments made at the Seventh International Conference of National Human Rights Institutions [YUN 2004, p. 681], based on feedback from a questionnaire provided by OHCHR. Support was given to regional initiatives, including the International Conference on National Institutions in the Arab Region (Cairo, Egypt, 6-8 March) (see p. 752), the international seminar on illicit trafficking of migrants and smuggling (Campeche, Mexico, 10-11 March), the fourth annual meeting of the Network of National Institutions of the Americas (12 April), the Asia Pacific Regional Training Programme on Human Rights Investigations (Tagaytay City, the Philippines, 18-22 April), a meeting of the Coordinating Committee of African National Institutions (12 April), the Tenth annual meeting of the Asia Pacific Forum (Ulaanbaatar, Mongolia, 24-26 August), the thirteenth Workshop on Regional Cooperation for the Promotion and Protection of Human Rights in the Asia-Pacific Region (Beijing, China, 30 August–2 September), a regional workshop on national human rights institutions and the right to education (Copán, Honduras, 21-23 September), the first congress of the *Association francophone des commissions nationales des droits de l'homme* on economic, social and cultural rights (Montreal, Canada, 29 September–1 October) and the fifth Conference of African National Institutions (Abuja, Nigeria, 8-10 December). In Europe, OHCHR participated in meetings of the European Coordinating Group of National Human Rights Institutions (Paris, 16 February; Geneva, 12 April) and met with the *Commission nationale consultative des droits de l'homme* (Paris 6-7 June) to help define a common strategy in establishing and strengthening national human rights institutions in Europe and Central Asia. OHCHR also assisted UN operations in Burundi, Kosovo (Serbia and Montenegro), Liberia, Sierra Leone and the Sudan in addressing issues relating to national human rights institutions and undertook or participated in several national and regional activities to support related initiatives. In November, OHCHR

launched the *Economic, Social and Cultural Rights: Handbook for National Human Rights Institutions*, No. 12 in the *Professional Training Series*, focusing on the role of those institutions in promoting and protecting economic, social and cultural rights. It also provided support for the International Round Table on National Institutions and the Implementation of Economic, Social and Cultural Rights (New Delhi, India, 29 November–1 December), which adopted the New Delhi Concluding Statement, annexed to the report. Various other initiatives of national institutions supported during the year by OHCHR related to migration, gender, rights of persons with disabilities, indigenous peoples, minorities, HIV/ AIDS prevention and related discrimination, the prevention of conflict and of torture, and the Paris Principles.

GENERAL ASSEMBLY ACTION

On 16 December [meeting 64], the General Assembly, on the recommendation of the Third Committee [A/60/509/Add.2], adopted **resolution 60/154** without vote [agenda item 71 *(b)*].

National institutions for the promotion and protection of human rights

The General Assembly,

Recalling its resolutions and those of the Commission on Human Rights concerning national institutions for the promotion and protection of human rights,

Welcoming the rapidly growing interest throughout the world in the creation and strengthening of independent, pluralistic national institutions for the promotion and protection of human rights,

Convinced of the important role that such national institutions play and will continue to play in promoting and protecting human rights and fundamental freedoms and in developing and enhancing public awareness of those rights and freedoms,

Recognizing that the United Nations has played an important role and should continue to play a more important role in assisting the development of national institutions,

Recalling the Vienna Declaration and Programme of Action adopted by the World Conference on Human Rights on 25 June 1993, which reaffirmed the important and constructive role played by national human rights institutions, in particular in their advisory capacity to the competent authorities and their role in remedying human rights violations, in disseminating information on human rights and in education in human rights,

Recalling also the Beijing Declaration and Platform for Action, in which Governments were urged to create or strengthen independent national institutions for the promotion and protection of human rights, including the human rights of women,

Reaffirming that all human rights are universal, indivisible, interrelated, interdependent and mutually reinforcing, and that all human rights must be treated in a fair and equal manner, on the same footing and with same emphasis,

Bearing in mind the significance of national and regional particularities and various historical, cultural and religious backgrounds, and that all States, regardless of their political, economic and cultural systems, have the duty to promote and protect all human rights and fundamental freedoms, ·

Recalling the programme of action adopted by national institutions, at their meeting held in Vienna in June 1993 during the World Conference on Human Rights, for the promotion and protection of human rights, in which it was recommended that United Nations activities and programmes should be reinforced to meet the requests for assistance from States wishing to establish or strengthen their national institutions for the promotion and protection of human rights,

Noting the valuable role played and contributions made by national institutions in United Nations meetings dealing with human rights and the importance of their continued appropriate participation,

Welcoming the strengthening in all regions of regional cooperation among national human rights institutions and between national human rights institutions and other regional human rights forums,

Noting with appreciation the existence of the regional human rights networks in Europe, and the continuing work of the Network of National Institutions for the Promotion and Protection of Human Rights in the Americas, the Asia Pacific Forum of National Human Rights Institutions and the Coordinating Committee of African National Human Rights Institutions,

Welcoming the strengthening of international cooperation among national human rights institutions, including through the International Coordinating Committee of National Institutions,

1. *Welcomes* the report of the Secretary-General;

2. *Reaffirms* the importance of the development of effective, independent and pluralistic national institutions for the promotion and protection of human rights, in keeping with the principles relating to the status of national institutions for the promotion and protection of human rights ("the Paris Principles"), contained in the annex to resolution 48/134 of 20 December 1993;

3. *Reiterates* the continued importance of the Paris Principles, recognizes the value of further strengthening their application, where appropriate, and encourages States, national institutions and other interested parties to consider ways to achieve this;

4. *Recognizes* that, in accordance with the Vienna Declaration and Programme of Action, it is the right of each State to choose the framework for national institutions that is best suited to its particular needs at the national level in order to promote human rights in accordance with international human rights standards;

5. *Also recognizes* that national institutions have a crucial role to play in promoting and ensuring the indivisibility and interdependence of all human rights, and calls upon States to ensure that all human rights are appropriately reflected in the mandate of their national human rights institutions when established;

6. *Encourages* Member States to establish effective, independent and pluralistic national institutions or, where they already exist, to strengthen them for the promotion and protection of human rights, as outlined in the Vienna Declaration and Programme of Action;

7. *Welcomes* the growing number of States establishing or considering the establishment of national institutions for the promotion and protection of human rights;

8. *Encourages* national institutions for the promotion and protection of human rights established by Member States to continue to play an active role in preventing and combating all violations of human rights as enumerated in the Vienna Declaration and Programme of Action and relevant international instruments;

9. *Notes with satisfaction* the efforts of those States that have provided their national institutions with more autonomy and independence, including by giving them an investigative role or enhancing such a role, and encourages other Governments to consider taking similar steps;

10. *Reaffirms* the role of national institutions, where they exist, as appropriate agencies, inter alia, for the dissemination of human rights materials and other public information activities, including those of the United Nations;

11. *Urges* the Secretary-General to continue to give high priority to requests from Member States for assistance in the establishment and strengthening of national human rights institutions as part of the United Nations Programme of Advisory Services and Technical Assistance in the Field of Human Rights;

12. *Commends* the high priority given by the Office of the United Nations High Commissioner for Human Rights to work on national institutions, encourages the High Commissioner, in view of the expanded activities relating to national institutions, to ensure that appropriate arrangements are made and budgetary resources provided to continue and further extend activities in support of national human rights institutions, and invites Governments to contribute additional funds to the United Nations Voluntary Fund for Technical Cooperation in the Field of Human Rights for that purpose;

13. *Welcomes* the establishment of a national institutions website as an important vehicle for the delivery of information to national institutions and also the launch of a database of comparative analysis of procedures and methods of complaint-handling by national human rights institutions;

14. *Notes with appreciation* the increasingly active and important role of the International Coordinating Committee of National Institutions, in close cooperation with the Office of the United Nations High Commissioner for Human Rights, in assisting Governments and national institutions, when requested, to follow up on relevant resolutions and recommendations concerning the strengthening of national institutions;

15. *Also notes with appreciation* the holding of regular meetings of the International Coordinating Committee of National Institutions and the arrangements for the participation of national human rights institutions in the annual sessions of the Commission on Human Rights;

16. *Requests* the Secretary-General to continue to provide the necessary assistance for holding meetings of the International Coordinating Committee of National Institutions during the sessions of the Commission on Human Rights, in cooperation with the Office of the United Nations High Commissioner for Human Rights;

17. *Welcomes* the continuation of the practice of national institutions convening regional meetings in some

regions, and its initiation in others, and encourages national institutions, in cooperation with the United Nations High Commissioner for Human Rights, to organize similar events with Governments and nongovernmental organizations in their own regions;

18. *Requests* the Secretary-General to continue to provide, including from the United Nations Voluntary Fund for Technical Cooperation in the Field of Human Rights, the necessary assistance for holding international and regional meetings of national institutions;

19. *Recognizes* the important and constructive role that civil society can play, in cooperation with national institutions, for better promotion and protection of human rights;

20. *Expresses its appreciation* to those Governments that have contributed additional resources for the purpose of the establishment and strengthening of national human rights institutions;

21. *Encourages* all Member States to take appropriate steps to promote the exchange of information and experience concerning the establishment and effective operation of national institutions;

22. *Encourages* all United Nations entities, funds and agencies to work in close cooperation with national institutions in the promotion and protection of human rights, and in this regard welcomes efforts made through the action 2 initiative of the Secretary-General;

23. *Requests* the Secretary-General to report to the General Assembly at its sixty-second session on the implementation of the present resolution.

Regional arrangements

Commission action. On 20 April [res. 2005/73], the Commission, welcoming the progress made in establishing regional and subregional arrangements for promoting and protecting human rights, requested OHCHR to pay special attention to the most appropriate ways of assisting countries. The Secretary-General was asked to include in his 2006 report to the General Assembly information on progress made in reinforcing information sharing and collaboration between UN organs and regional organizations since the adoption of the Vienna Declaration and Programme of Action by the 1993 World Conference [YUN 1993, p. 908]. The Secretary-General was further asked to report to the Commission in 2007.

Report of Secretary-General. In response to a 2003 Commission request [YUN 2003, p. 693], the Secretary-General submitted a report [E/CN.4/2005/104] focusing on the regional strategies of OHCHR and the most significant developments since 2003. During the reporting period, OHCHR systematically pursued regional and subregional approaches to human rights promotion, through a variety of complementary means and methods, including by concluding cooperative agreements with UN agencies and regional institutions, undertaking joint regional projects, sponsoring or organizing consultations and dialogues, and outposting regional and subregional representatives.

In Africa, OHCHR focused on a subregional approach in East, Central, Southern and West Africa, where consultations and dialogues on priority issues had continued with various sectors of African society producing tangible results and providing guidance to Governments, regional organizations and NGOs, and better links to the New Partnership for Africa's Development (NEPAD) (see p. 1003), the African Union and other subregional groups. In particular, OHCHR continued to support the African Union's efforts to strengthen its human rights system and to ensure subregional representation to enhance national and subregional human rights capacities. In the Arab region, OHCHR had developed cooperative projects with several countries in the area and had identified key issues of common concern, including human rights awareness-raising, civil society networking and training, and the need to translate human rights materials into Arabic. A joint regional project with UNDP on those issues was under way. In cooperation with regional organizations and UN Country Teams, the OHCHR Beirut-based Regional Office for the Arab Region continued to undertake activities to enable OHCHR to strengthen partnerships outside the UN system and to respond better to the human rights needs and priorities of the regional States, particularly with regard to the issues of mainstreaming human rights in development programmes and strengthening civil society organizations through capacity-building, training and participation in national and regional activities. In follow-up to the adoption of the Arab Charter on Human Rights [YUN 2004, p. 681], OHCHR planned to develop a broader technical cooperation programme, in collaboration with the League of Arab States, and intended to enhance its human rights capacities. In Asia and the Pacific, OHCHR had undertaken numerous activities that helped reinforce regional cooperation for promoting and protecting human rights in four priority areas, including national human rights action plans; national human rights institutions; human rights education; and strategies for the realization of economic, social and cultural rights and the right to development. Consultations continued with Governments, aimed at the possible establishment of regional human rights arrangements. The Bangkok-based OHCHR Regional Representative, primarily charged to facilitate exchange of information and experiences in the region, maintained efforts to help the UN system and civil society assist Governments to better protect human rights. A project on "Human rights approach to development—lessons learned", initiated by the Representative's Office, was expected to be concluded during the year. In the context of the Asia-Pacific framework, consultations were also held with Governments, supported by national human rights institutions and civil society organizations, which were aimed at the possible establishment of regional arrangements.

In Europe, Central Asia and the Caucasus, OHCHR further intensified its cooperation with regional organizations, including the Council of Europe, the Organization for Security and Cooperation in Europe (OSCE) and the European Union. Its activities in that regard reflected the contents of the UN human rights programme, as highlighted in the Vienna Declaration and Programme of Action, adopted by the World Conference on Human Rights [YUN 1993, p. 908]. OHCHR maintained efforts to consolidate subregional approaches by establishing programmes for Central Asia and South-East Europe, and by conducting planning activities for the Caucasus. That approach, intended to complement the work of UN agencies, regional organizations and other international actors in the region, focused on key human rights gaps not covered by the mandates of those organizations. The implementation of a four-year regional human rights project, which OHCHR had initiated in Central Asian States (Kazakhstan, Kyrgyzstan, Tajikistan, Uzbekistan) in 2004 [YUN 2004, p. 682], continued, aimed at raising public understanding of human rights.

In Latin America and the Caribbean, OHCHR continued to support the establishment and strengthening of the Network of National Human Rights Institutions of the Americas, particularly its meetings and seminars on specific issues, including the rights of indigenous peoples, the rights of persons with disabilities and the prevention of torture. Such meetings enabled the exchange of experiences and best practices among national human rights institutions in the region, and also helped strengthen cooperation among them.

Conference. During the year, OHCHR, in cooperation with Egypt's National Council for Human Rights, UNDP and the League of Arab States, organized a regional conference on human rights institutions in the Arab world (Cairo, Egypt, 6-8 March) (see p. 749) [E/CN.4/2005/G/34], which discussed, among other things, ways of promoting respect for human rights in the region. The conference adopted the Cairo Declaration, by which the participants, including delegations from 17 Arab States, emphasized the importance of promoting and protecting human rights. They affirmed the special value of the role of national human rights institutions and encouraged re-

gional States that had not done so to establish such institutions. They also stressed the need for inter-Arab cooperation on human rights and called on Arab Governments to speed up the process for ratifying and implementing the Arab Charter on Human Rights and other international human rights instruments. The Conference also adopted a number of recommendations designed to strengthen human rights in the region.

Africa

In September [A/60/353], the Secretary-General submitted a report on the Subregional Centre for Human Rights and Democracy in Central Africa, based in Yaoundé, Cameroon. On 27 January, the Centre, in collaboration with civil society organizations, launched in Cameroon's police stations the United Nations campaign for the dissemination of the 1984 Convention against Torture and Other Cruel, Inhuman or Degrading Treatment or Punishment [YUN 1984, p. 813, GA res. 39/46]. As part of its training activities, the Centre helped organize seminars on human rights and indigenous women in Central Africa (Yaoundé, Cameroon, 3 February) and on the role of civil society in the implementation of the Durban Declaration and Programme of Action adopted at the 2001 World Conference on racism [YUN 2001, p. 615] (Yaoundé, Cameroon, July). It collaborated with the Joint United Nations Programme on HIV/AIDS (UNAIDS) and the Rwandan Government to organize for civil society representatives from the Economic Community of Central African States (ECCAS) a capacity-building workshop (Rwanda, 27-29 June) on the role of civil society in the fight against discrimination and stigmatization of people living with HIV/AIDS, which ended with the adoption of a declaration and code of conduct and the establishment of a network of activists on the disease in that subregion. It also partnered with the UN Resident Coordinator in Equatorial Guinea to organize a two-day working session (Malabo, Equatorial Guinea, June) on follow-up to human rights training projects it had designed for the country, scheduled to be implemented during 2005 and 2006. Under the Centre's internship programme, the fourteenth group of interns comprising lawyers and human rights activists with outstanding records, drawn from Burundi, the Congo, the Democratic Republic of the Congo, Kenya, Germany and the United States, completed their training, bringing to 42 the total number of such interns trained by the Centre. The Centre also undertook a variety of other activities in support of peace processes, conflict prevention and early warning projects, and electoral processes. In addition, it disseminated information on human rights through its publications, continued to provide advice and technical assistance to ECCAS and collaborated with UN agencies to support efforts to promote and protect human rights in the Central African subregion. The report concluded that OHCHR, through the Centre, had helped increase recognition of the need to uphold and promote human rights and democratic principles by various stakeholders in the subregion. Given increasing requests to the Centre for technical assistance, additional funds should be envisaged to enable it to respond effectively.

GENERAL ASSEMBLY ACTION

On 16 December [meeting 64], the General Assembly, on the recommendation of the Third Committee [A/60/509/Add.2], adopted **resolution 60/151** without vote [agenda item 71 (b)].

Subregional Centre for Human Rights and Democracy in Central Africa

The General Assembly,

Recalling its resolution 55/105 of 4 December 2000 concerning regional arrangements for the promotion and protection of human rights,

Recalling also its resolution 59/183 of 20 December 2004 on the Subregional Centre for Human Rights and Democracy in Central Africa,

Recalling further its resolutions 55/34 B of 20 November 2000 and 55/233 of 23 December 2000, section III of resolution 55/234 of 23 December 2000, and resolution 58/176 of 22 December 2003,

Recalling that the World Conference on Human Rights recommended that more resources be made available for the strengthening of regional arrangements for the promotion and protection of human rights under the programme of technical cooperation in the field of human rights of the Office of the United Nations High Commissioner for Human Rights,

Recalling also the report of the High Commissioner,

Taking note of the holding of the twenty-second ministerial meeting of the United Nations Standing Advisory Committee on Security Questions in Central Africa in Brazzaville from 14 to 18 March 2005,

Taking note also of the report of the Secretary-General,

Welcoming the 2005 World Summit Outcome, in particular the decision confirmed therein to double the regular budget of the Office of the High Commissioner over the next five years,

1. *Welcomes* the activities of the Subregional Centre for Human Rights and Democracy in Central Africa at Yaoundé;

2. *Notes with satisfaction* the support provided for the establishment of the Centre by the host country;

3. *Requests* the Secretary-General and the United Nations High Commissioner for Human Rights to provide additional funds and human resources to enable the Centre to respond positively and effectively to the growing needs in the promotion and protection of human rights and in developing a culture of democracy in the Central African subregion;

4. *Requests* the Secretary-General to submit to the General Assembly at its sixty-first session a report on the implementation of the present resolution.

Asia and the Pacific

Note by Secretariat. A January note of the Secretariat [E/CN.4/2005/105] informed the Commission that the thirteenth Annual Workshop on Regional Cooperation for the Promotion and Protection of Human Rights in the Asian and Pacific Region, initially scheduled to take place in February, had been postponed due to the effects of the December 2004 tsunami on many of the participating countries. The Secretary-General, who had been requested in a 2004 Commission resolution [YUN 2004, p. 684] to report in 2005 on the workshop's outcome, would submit the requested report at the conclusion of the workshop.

Commission action. On 20 April [res. 2005/71], the Commission requested the Secretary-General to submit a report in 2006 containing the conclusions of the thirteenth Workshop on Regional Cooperation for the Promotion and Protection of Human Rights in the Asian and Pacific Region and information on the progress made in implementing its current resolution.

Report of Secretary-General. In December [E/CN.4/2006/100], the Secretary-General reported on the outcomes of the thirteenth Annual Workshop on Regional Cooperation in the Asian and Pacific Region (Beijing, China, 30 August–2 September), which reviewed the four pillars under the Framework of Regional Technical Cooperation Programme for Asia and the Pacific (Tehran Framework), adopted in 1998 [YUN 1998, p. 641], future directions for the Framework and recent regional and subregional human rights initiatives. In addition, the Workshop held an in-depth thematic discussion on human rights and human trafficking, in accordance with the conclusions of the twelfth Workshop [YUN 2004, p. 684] and also discussed progress achieved since then, reviewed three intersessional regional and subregional workshops, and examined the report of the ninth annual meeting of the Asia-Pacific Forum (Seoul, Republic of Korea, 14-17 September). The Workshop adopted conclusions addressing needs and challenges relating to the implementation of national human rights plans of action and capacity-building; human rights education; national human rights institutions; the realization of the right to development and of economic, social and cultural rights; and human rights and human trafficking.

In a later addendum [E/CN.4/2006/100/Add.1], the Secretary-General reported on the conclusions and recommendations of the Expert Meeting on National Human Rights Plans of Action and Human Rights Education in the Asia-Pacific Region (Bangkok, Thailand, 20-22 October). The Meeting focused on processes and components relevant to national action plans, including the responsibilities of various actors; strategies for effective implementation and monitoring; linkage with other planning processes; and human rights education as a potential priority area. It adopted conclusions on the value of such action plans, the related preparatory process and challenge of implementation, as well as the involvement of national human rights institutions and civil society, and addressed a series of recommendations to Governments and the United Nations. The report also outlined the conclusions of the 2004 subregional workshop for judges and lawyers on the justiciability of economic, social and cultural rights in South-East Asia [YUN 2004, p. 682].

South West Asia and the Arab region

On 16 December [meeting 64], the General Assembly, on the recommendation of the Third Committee [A/60/509/Add.2], adopted resolution **60/153** without vote [agenda item 71 *(b)*].

Establishment of a United Nations human rights training and documentation centre for South-West Asia and the Arab region

The General Assembly,

Guided by the fundamental and universal principles enshrined in the Charter of the United Nations and the Universal Declaration of Human Rights,

Recalling the Vienna Declaration and Programme of Action of 1993, which reiterated the need to consider the possibility of establishing regional and subregional arrangements for the promotion and protection of human rights where they do not already exist,

Recalling also its resolutions 32/127 of 16 December 1977, 51/102 of 12 December 1996 and all its subsequent resolutions concerning regional arrangements for the promotion and protection of human rights,

Recalling further Commission on Human Rights resolution 1993/51 of 9 March 1993 and all its subsequent resolutions concerning regional arrangements for the promotion and protection of human rights,

Recalling the report of the Secretary-General on regional arrangements for the promotion and protection of human rights,

Reaffirming its endorsement of the Vienna Declaration and Programme of Action of 1993, and the universality, indivisibility, interdependence and interrelatedness of all human rights, economic, civil, cultural, political and social, including the right to development,

Reaffirming also that regional cooperation plays a fundamental role in promoting and protecting human rights and should reinforce universal human rights, as contained in international human rights instruments, and their protection,

Committed to enhancing subregional, regional and international cooperation to promote universal respect

for and observance of human rights and fundamental freedoms, in conformity with international obligations,

Convinced that cooperation between the United Nations and regional initiatives in the field of human rights continues to be both substantive and supportive and that possibilities exist for increased cooperation,

Recalling its resolution 49/184 of 23 December 1994 proclaiming the United Nations Decade for Human Rights Education, 1995-2004, and its resolution 59/113 of 10 December 2004 proclaiming the World Programme for Human Rights Education, to begin on 1 January 2005, and Commission on Human Rights resolution 1993/56 of 9 March 1993 on education and human rights and Commission resolution 2003/70 of 25 April 2003 on the United Nations Decade for Human Rights Education,

Recognizing that human rights education can play a crucial role in enhancing respect for human rights and fundamental freedoms and can contribute to the promotion of human rights, the achievement of a culture of peace, in particular the teaching of the practice of non-violence, and respect for the rule of law,

Noting the endorsement and the support expressed by the Council of the League of Arab States and the member States of the Gulf Cooperation Council and in the Brasilia Declaration adopted at the South American and Arab Countries Summit for the initiative of the State of Qatar to host a United Nations centre for human rights for South-West Asia and the Arab region,

Noting also Commission on Human Rights resolutions 2005/71 and 2005/73 of 20 April 2005 welcoming the offer by the Government of Qatar to host a United Nations centre for human rights for South-West Asia and the Arab region,

Noting further the support expressed at the thirteenth Workshop on Regional Cooperation for the Promotion and Protection of Human Rights in the Asia-Pacific Region, held in Beijing from 30 August to 2 September 2005, for the initiative of the State of Qatar to host a United Nations centre for human rights for South-West Asia and the Arab region,

Mindful of the vastness of and the diversity within South-West Asia and the Arab region,

1. *Takes note with satisfaction* of the continuing cooperation and assistance of the Office of the United Nations High Commissioner for Human Rights in the further strengthening of the existing regional arrangements and regional machineries for the promotion and protection of human rights, in particular through technical cooperation which is aimed at national capacity-building, public information and education, with a view to exchanging information and experience in the field of human rights;

2. *Welcomes* the initiative of the Government of Qatar to host a United Nations human rights training and documentation centre for South-West Asia and the Arab region, which will be under the supervision of the Office of the High Commissioner, with the mandate to undertake training and documentation activities according to international human rights standards and to support such efforts within the region by Governments, United Nations agencies and pro-

grammes, national human rights institutions and non-governmental organizations;

3. *Requests* the Secretary-General and the Office of the High Commissioner to give their support to the establishment of a United Nations human rights training and documentation centre for South-West Asia and the Arab region, to conclude an agreement with the host country regarding its establishment and to make available resources for the establishment of the centre;

4. *Requests* the Secretary-General to submit to the General Assembly at its sixty-first session a report on the implementation of the present resolution;

5. *Decides* to consider the question further at its sixty-first session.

Cooperation with human rights bodies

Report of Secretary-General. A report of the Secretary-General [E/CN.4/2005/31] described situations in which persons or NGO members had allegedly suffered intimidation or reprisals for having cooperated with UN human rights bodies regarding human rights violations.

Commission action. On 14 April [res. 2005/9], the Commission urged Governments to refrain from intimidating persons who sought to cooperate or had cooperated with representatives of UN human rights bodies; persons who availed themselves of UN procedures and who had provided legal assistance to them for that purpose; those who submitted communications under procedures established by human rights instruments; and relatives of victims of human rights violations. It requested representatives of UN human rights bodies to help prevent such intimidation and to include in their reports allegations of intimidation or reprisals and of hampering access to UN human rights procedures, and an account of the action they had taken. The Secretary-General was asked to draw the attention of UN human rights treaty bodies to the Commission's resolution and to report in 2006.

Chapter II

Protection of human rights

In 2005, the United Nations continued to focus attention on the protection of human rights in civil and political terms and in the economic, social and cultural fields. Ongoing efforts to further secure indigenous peoples' rights were advanced with the adoption by the General Assembly of the Programme of Action for the Second International Decade of the World's Indigenous People, which took effect on 1 January, under the theme "Partnership for action and dignity". Progress also continued with follow-up activities to implement the Durban Declaration and Programme of Action, adopted at the 2001 World Conference against Racism, Racial Discrimination, Xenophobia and Related Intolerance. In February, the independent experts appointed to monitor follow-up activities underlined the tangible impact of related actions by Governments and civil society on peoples' lives and called for a plan for the five-year review of the implementation of the Declaration. In commemoration of the sixtieth anniversary of the liberation of the Nazi concentration camps, the Assembly reaffirmed that the Holocaust, which resulted in the murder of one third of the Jewish people, along with countless members of other minorities, remained a warning of the dangers of hatred, bigotry and racism, and designated 27 January as an international day of commemoration in memory of holocaust victims. Demonstrating the Organization's increasing concern about the welfare of children caught in situations of armed conflict, the Secretary-General presented to the Security Council an action plan for the effective application of international norms and standards for protecting the rights of the child in that regard. Towards the same end, the Council, in a February Presidential statement, strongly condemned the recruitment and use of child soldiers by parties to armed conflict and urged that such intolerable practice be halted promptly. Marking a turning point in ensuring compensation for victims of human rights violations, the Economic and Social Council adopted, in July, the Basic Principles and Guidelines on the Right to a Remedy and Reparations for Victims of Gross Violations of International Human Rights Law and Serious Violations of International Humanitarian Law, which established a legal framework for States' obligations and victims' rights in the adminis-

tration of justice. In related action, the Commission on Human Rights adopted an updated Set of Principles for the protection and promotion of human rights through action to combat impunity.

In 2005, the Commission and its subsidiary body, the Subcommission on the Promotion and Protection of Human Rights, established new mandates for independent experts on minority issues and on the right of peoples to international solidarity. Additional mandates were also created for special rapporteurs to monitor the promotion and protection of human rights during countering terrorism actions, and to undertake studies on discrimination against leprosy victims and members of their families, on the accountability of international personnel taking part in peace operations and on the legal implications of the disappearance of States and other territories for environmental reasons. Also created was a new mandate for a working group on the use of mercenaries as a means of violating human rights. Special rapporteurs, special representatives and independent experts of the Commission and the Subcommission examined, among other issues, contemporary forms of racism; the rights of migrants, freedom of religion or belief; mercenary activity; the independence of the judiciary; extralegal executions; allegations of torture; freedom of expression; human rights and terrorism; the prevention of human rights violations committed with small arms and light weapons; the right to development; the effects of structural adjustment programmes and foreign debt on human rights; corruption and its impact on the enjoyment of human rights; human rights and extreme poverty; the right to food; the right to adequate housing; the right to education; illicit practices related to toxic and dangerous products and wastes; the right to physical and mental health; human rights and the human genome; violence against women; violence against children; the sale of children, child prostitution and child pornography; children affected by armed conflict; internally displaced persons; and the human rights and fundamental freedoms of indigenous people.

Working groups considered the problems of racial discrimination affecting people of African descent, discrimination against minorities, arbitrary detention, enforced or involuntary disappearances, the right to development, working methods and activities of transnational corporations, contemporary forms of slavery and the rights of indigenous peoples.

Racism and racial discrimination

Follow-up to 2001 World Conference

Reports of the High Commissioner. In accordance with a 2004 Commission request [YUN 2004, p. 687], the High Commissioner submitted a report [E/CN.4/2005/16] describing the activities undertaken by her Office to implement the recommendations adopted at the second session of the Intergovernmental Working Group, established in 2002 [YUN 2002, p. 661] to recommend measures for the effective implementation of the Durban Declaration and Programme of Action (DDPA). DDPA was adopted by the 2001 World Conference against Racism, Racial Discrimination, Xenophobia and Related Intolerance [YUN 2001, p. 615]. During that session, the Working Group focused on the themes of education, poverty, and complementary standards. The report highlighted the various activities relating to those themes, including meetings, projects, studies, and publications, which the Office of the High Commissioner for Human Rights (OHCHR) had helped implement, often in collaboration with other UN system agencies. Under education, which the report described as an effective tool for empowering people to understand and exercise their human rights, OHCHR promoted tolerance, religious diversity and debate on dialogue among cultures. Regarding poverty, OHCHR continued to explore and promote explicit recognition of the linkages between human rights and poverty, including through support to the work of the independent expert on human rights and extreme poverty and of experts of the Subcommission on the question of developing guiding principles on implementing human rights norms and standards for combating extreme poverty. In addition, OHCHR supported Governments' efforts to improve race relations and undertook a number of activities to mainstream DDPA into the mandates and programmes of the United Nations and its specialized agencies, and of other international organizations and non-governmental organizations (NGOs). The report concluded that significant progress had been achieved in implementing relevant recommendations of the Working Group.

In response to a further 2004 Commission request [YUN 2004, p. 687], the High Commissioner reported on OHCHR efforts to explore the possibility of developing a racial equality index [E/CN.4/2005/17], as proposed by the independent eminent experts appointed to follow up the implementation of DDPA provisions [YUN 2003, p. 698]. The Office undertook preliminary research on the problems of discrimination in general, and racial discrimination in particular. It gathered information on socio-economic indicators, justice and criminality, and disaggregated the data by race, colour and ethnic origin. The Office further found that, although a racial equality index appeared to be a potentially important tool for substantive research in identifying the causes and manifestations of racial discrimination in a society, its complexity warranted serious consideration of its usefulness for decision makers. It was also necessary to establish the methodological soundness of such a tool if the outcome of the exercise was to be credible. As such, the Commission needed to further consider the issue.

Report of independent experts. At its second meeting (21-23 February) [E/CN.4/2005/125 & Corr.1], the independent eminent experts appointed in 2003 [YUN 2003, p. 698] to follow-up the implementation of DDPA provisions addressed the scope of their mandate and how best to implement it. They considered the reports of the High Commissioner and the Secretary-General on Member States' efforts to implement DDPA and expressed concern that limited responses had been received following requests for information on related initiatives and activities, making it difficult to identify relevant trends. Additional problems were posed by the diverse nature of the information received, which prevented the systematic evaluation of the progress made since the 2001 World Conference on Racism [YUN 2001, p. 615]. The experts assessed international standards and instruments to combat racial discrimination, with a view to preparing complementary standards, deliberated on implementation strategies and possible modalities for action, consulted with regional representatives and explored ways to follow-up on their first meeting [YUN 2003, p. 698]. They concluded that the implementation of DDPA had taken a variety of forms worldwide and that the tangible impact could be felt in the lives of people through actions by Governments and civil society. Nonetheless, the international community had not achieved any real breakthrough in countering the scourges of racial discrimination, which constituted the root causes of many contemporary conflicts. The experts stressed the importance of education and awareness-raising as tools for combating discrimination and proposed that the relationship between racism, racial discrimination, xenophobia and related intolerance and new information technologies be given attention at the second phase of the World Summit on the Information Society, scheduled for November (see p. 933). They appealed to the Commission and the General Assembly to adopt a plan for the five-year review of DDPA implementation and called on Member States to take into account the content of DDPA during the High-level Plenary Meeting of the Assembly (2005 World Summit) (see p. 47) to review the implementation of the Millennium Declaration, adopted at the 2000 Millennium Summit [YUN 2000, p. 49]. The experts also reiterated the recommendation adopted at their first meeting on the need for a racial equality index aimed at measuring existing racial inequalities, and encouraged the High Commissioner to pursue efforts in addressing the issue.

Commission action. On 20 April [res. 2005/64], the Commission, by a recorded vote of 38 to 1, with 14 abstentions, called on States and OHCHR to implement the recommendations of the Intergovernmental Working Group at its third session [YUN 2004, p. 686], and asked OHCHR to report thereon in 2006. The Commission decided to convene the Group's fourth session in 2006 to consider the thematic issue of globalization and racism. OHCHR was requested to convene, during that session, and in consultation with Member States, a high-level seminar focusing on racism and the Internet, and on producing a list of areas where gaps existed and for which complementary standards were necessary. Taking note of the High Commissioner's report on the possibility of developing a racial equality index (see above), the Commission requested her to expedite the consultative process on the issue in 2005 and to submit a draft basic document on the proposed index for consideration in 2006. In an effort to promote a world of sports free from racism and within the context of the 2006 World Cup tournament, the Commission invited the Fédération Internationale de Football Association (FIFA) to consider introducing a visible theme promoting non-racism in football.

Report of Secretary-General. In accordance with General Assembly resolution 59/177 [YUN 2004, p. 688], the Secretary-General submitted an August report [A/60/307 & Corr.1, 2] summarizing the activities undertaken by States, UN bodies, OHCHR, specialized agencies, international and regional organizations, national human rights institutions, NGOs and youth groups to implement DDPA. He observed that those activities demonstrated continuing momentum against racial discrimination and growing cooperation and mu-

tual assistance between stakeholders. Governments were reacting more often to such new forms of racism as cybercrime and the dissemination of racist ideologies through the Internet, and a trend was also developing towards improved monitoring and reporting of racist crimes and incidents.

On 16 December, the Assembly took note of the Secretary-General's report (**decision 60/531**).

CERD action. In 2005 [A/60/18], the Committee on the Elimination of Racial Discrimination (see p. 728) considered follow-up to the World Conference against Racism [YUN 2001, p. 615], focusing on the 2004 report of the Intergovernmental Working Group [YUN 2004, p. 686], in relation to the development of complementary standards to strengthen and update international instruments against racism, racial discrimination, xenophobia and related intolerance in all its aspects.

Working Group on people of African descent. The Working Group of Experts on People of African Descent, established in accordance with the 2002 Durban Declaration and Programme of Action [YUN 2002, p. 661] to consider problems of racial discrimination affecting people of African descent, held its fifth session (Geneva, 29 August–2 September) [E/CN.4/2006/19]. The Working Group examined the themes of mainstreaming the situation of people of African descent in plans for achieving the UN Millennium Development Goals (MDGs) [YUN 2000, p. 51], the empowerment of women of African descent and the role of political parties in the integration of people of African descent into political life and decision-making processes. The experts agreed that, due to conceptual limitations and data collection inadequacies, it was difficult to evaluate the extent of racial discrimination. Positive measures aimed at accelerating the substantive equality of people of African descent were needed, as were strong monitoring and evaluation mechanisms at the national level, in order to assess progress made and the effectiveness of those measures, and to identify good practices. The experts recommended that a "Durban + 5" activity be organized, with OHCHR assistance, to evaluate the implementation of DDPA provisions, particularly by examining national action plans and regional progress. They also adopted numerous conclusions and recommendations under each of the themes considered, as well as a three-year programme of work.

The experts visited Belgium (13-17 June) [E/CN.4/2006/19/Add.1] at the invitation of the Government, where they raised concerns relating to the disempowered situation of people of African descent. The problem stemmed from discriminatory practices at the work place, which hampered their enjoyment of equal employment opportunities and access to education and adequate housing. While recognizing the efforts of the authorities to improve the situation, notably by translating DDPA provisions into the national legislative framework for remedial action, the experts recommended a series of measures highlighting the necessity for further awareness-raising for private enterprises on the issue of discrimination and the need for the work environment to reflect the diversity of society. They also advocated measures to counter inequalities in educational outcome for children of foreign origin, for combating racism and discrimination and for promoting African culture and traditions in Belgium. The experts invited associations of people of African descent to devise strategies to cooperate and establish a common platform to interface with government authorities.

Regional seminars. OHCHR, in collaboration with Gabon, organized a seminar (Libreville, Gabon, 27-29 July) [E/CN.4/2006/21] for member States of the Economic Community of Central African States (ECCAS) on the role of civil society in implementing DDPA, which aimed to provide a platform for an exchange of views and experiences on how to bring all population groups into the political process and to discuss best practices. The seminar addressed 21 recommendations to ECCAS member States and OHCHR.

OHCHR also organized a regional seminar for South and South-East Asia (Bangkok, Thailand, 19-21 September) [E/CN.4/2006/22] to identify obstacles and challenges impeding the implementation of DDPA in education, and promote discussions of human rights-based strategies for overcoming exclusion and achieving wider access to primary and secondary education. The seminar adopted several conclusions and recommendations, which confirmed challenges in the implementation of internal standards, and also identified good practices at the national, regional and local levels with respect to effective implementation.

In collaboration with the United Nations Development Programme (UNDP), OHCHR organized a regional workshop (Chincha, Peru, 2-4 November) [E/CN.4/2006/23] for the Americas on strategies for the inclusion of people of African descent in programmes to reduce poverty and achieve the MDG on eradicating extreme poverty [YUN 2000, p. 51]. The workshop's main objective was to develop strategies for involving people of African descent in the development, implementation, monitoring and assessment of poverty-reduction programmes, as well as the preparation of related strategy papers. The workshop

adopted a declaration on ending poverty among people of African descent and indigenous peoples, and made recommendations to States, UN bodies and civil society actors regarding education, employment, affirmative action policies, data collection and gender. The workshop invited the General Assembly to consider proclaiming an international decade for people of African descent, with the aim of strengthening international cooperation in resolving their human rights and socio-economic problems, and to establish a voluntary fund for them, which would provide technical assistance in implementing development projects and promoting affirmative action.

GENERAL ASSEMBLY ACTION

On 16 December [meeting 64], the General Assembly, on the recommendation of the Third (Social, Humanitarian and Cultural) Committee [A/60/507], adopted **resolution 60/144** by recorded vote (172-3-4) [agenda item 69].

Global efforts for the total elimination of racism, racial discrimination, xenophobia and related intolerance and the comprehensive implementation of and follow-up to the Durban Declaration and Programme of Action

The General Assembly,

Recalling its resolution 59/177 of 20 December 2004, in which it firmly consolidated the global drive for the total elimination of racism, racial discrimination, xenophobia and related intolerance and recognized the absolute necessity and the imperative nature of the political will for the achievement of the commitments undertaken in the Durban Declaration and Programme of Action adopted by the World Conference against Racism, Racial Discrimination, Xenophobia and Related Intolerance, held in Durban, South Africa, from 31 August to 8 September 2001,

Recalling also its resolution 58/160 of 22 December 2003, in which it decided to place emphasis on the concrete implementation of the Durban Declaration and Programme of Action as a solid foundation for a broad-based consensus for further actions and initiatives towards the total elimination of the scourge of racism,

Recalling further its resolution 57/195 of 18 December 2002, in which it outlined the important roles and responsibilities of the various organs of the United Nations and other stakeholders at the international, regional and national levels, including, in particular, the Commission on Human Rights, and its resolution 56/266 of 27 March 2002, in which it endorsed the Durban Declaration and Programme of Action as constituting a solid foundation for further action and initiatives towards the total elimination of the scourge of racism,

Reiterating that all human beings are born free and equal in dignity and rights and have the potential to contribute constructively to the development and well-being of their societies, and that any doctrine of racial superiority is scientifically false, morally condemnable, socially unjust and dangerous and must be rejected, together with theories that attempt to determine the existence of separate human races,

Convinced that racism, racial discrimination, xenophobia and related intolerance manifest themselves in a differentiated manner for women and girls and may be among the factors leading to a deterioration in their living conditions, poverty, violence, multiple forms of discrimination and the limitation or denial of their human rights, and recognizing the need to integrate a gender perspective into relevant policies, strategies and programmes of action against racism, racial discrimination, xenophobia and related intolerance in order to address multiple forms of discrimination,

Taking note of Commission on Human Rights resolutions 2002/68 of 25 April 2002, 2003/30 of 23 April 2003, 2004/88 of 22 April 2004 and 2005/64 of 20 April 2005, by which the international community put into effect mechanisms for the effective implementation of the Durban Declaration and Programme of Action,

Underlining the primacy of political will, international cooperation and adequate funding at the national, regional and international levels for the successful implementation of the Durban Programme of Action,

Alarmed at the increase in racist violence and xenophobic ideas in many parts of the world, in political circles, in the sphere of public opinion and in society at large, inter alia, as a result of the resurgent activities of associations established on the basis of racist and xenophobic platforms and charters, and the persistent use of those platforms and charters to promote or incite racist ideologies,

Underlining the importance of urgently eliminating continuing and violent trends involving racism and racial discrimination, and conscious that any form of impunity for crimes motivated by racist and xenophobic attitudes plays a role in weakening the rule of law and democracy, tends to encourage the recurrence of such crimes and requires resolute action and cooperation for its eradication,

Welcoming the determination of the United Nations High Commissioner for Human Rights to profile and increase the visibility of the struggle against racism, racial discrimination, xenophobia and related intolerance and her intention to make this a cross-cutting issue in the activities and programmes of her Office,

Taking note of the interim report of the Special Rapporteur of the Commission on Human Rights on contemporary forms of racism, racial discrimination, xenophobia and related intolerance,

I
Basic general principles

1. *Acknowledges* that no derogation from the prohibition of racial discrimination, genocide, the crime of apartheid or slavery is permitted, as defined in the obligations under the relevant human rights instruments;

2. *Expresses its profound concern about and its unequivocal condemnation* of all forms of racism and racial discrimination, including related acts of racially motivated violence, xenophobia and intolerance, as well as propaganda activities and organizations that attempt

to justify or promote racism, racial discrimination, xenophobia and related intolerance in any form;

3. *Expresses deep concern* at recent attempts to establish hierarchies among emerging and resurgent forms of racism, racial discrimination, xenophobia and related intolerance, and urges States to adopt measures to address these scourges with the same emphasis and vigour with a view to preventing this practice and protecting victims;

4. *Stresses* that States and international organizations have a responsibility to ensure that measures taken in the struggle against terrorism do not discriminate in purpose or effect on grounds of race, colour, descent or national or ethnic origin, and urges all States to rescind or refrain from all forms of racial profiling;

5. *Recognizes* that States should implement and enforce appropriate and effective legislative, judicial, regulatory and administrative measures to prevent and protect against acts of racism, racial discrimination, xenophobia and related intolerance, thereby contributing to the prevention of human rights violations;

6. *Emphasizes* that it is the responsibility of States to adopt effective measures to combat criminal acts motivated by racism, racial discrimination, xenophobia and related intolerance, including measures to ensure that such motivations are considered an aggravating factor for the purposes of sentencing, to prevent those crimes from going unpunished and to ensure the rule of law;

7. *Urges* all States to review and, where necessary, revise their immigration laws, policies and practices so that they are free of racial discrimination and compatible with their obligations under international human rights instruments;

8. *Condemns* the misuse of print, audio-visual and electronic media and new communication technologies, including the Internet, to incite violence motivated by racial hatred, and calls upon States to take all necessary measures to combat this form of racism in accordance with the commitments that they have undertaken under the Durban Declaration and Programme of Action, in particular paragraph 147 of the Programme of Action, in accordance with existing international and regional standards of freedom of expression and taking all necessary measures to guarantee the right to freedom of opinion and expression;

9. *Encourages* all States to include in their educational curricula and social programmes at all levels, as appropriate, knowledge of and tolerance and respect for foreign cultures, peoples and countries;

10. *Stresses* the responsibility of States to mainstream a gender perspective in the design and development of prevention, education and protection measures aimed at the eradication of racism, racial discrimination, xenophobia and related intolerance at all levels, to ensure that they effectively target the distinct situations of women and men;

II
International Convention on the Elimination of All Forms of Racial Discrimination

11. *Reaffirms* that universal adherence to and full implementation of the International Convention on the Elimination of All Forms of Racial Discrimination

are of paramount importance for the promotion of equality and non-discrimination in the world;

12. *Reiterates* the call made by the World Conference against Racism, Racial Discrimination, Xenophobia and Related Intolerance, in paragraph 75 of the Durban Programme of Action, to achieve universal ratification of the Convention by 2005 and for all States to consider making the declaration envisaged under article 14 of the Convention, and endorses the grave concern expressed by the Commission on Human Rights in its resolution 2005/64 to the effect that, with one hundred and seventy ratifications and only forty-six declarations, the deadline for universal ratification decided by the Conference has, regrettably, not been realized;

13. *Urges*, in the above context, the Office of the United Nations High Commissioner for Human Rights to maintain and issue regular updates on its website of a list of countries that have not yet ratified the Convention and to encourage such countries to demonstrate their practical commitment to meet the goal of universal ratification as decided upon by the World Conference;

14. *Expresses concern* at the serious delays in the submission of overdue reports to the Committee on the Elimination of Racial Discrimination, which impedes the effectiveness of the Committee, and makes a strong appeal to all States parties to the Convention to comply with their treaty obligations;

15. *Invites* States parties to the Convention to ratify the amendment to article 8 of the Convention, on the financing of the Committee, and calls for adequate additional resources from the regular budget of the United Nations to enable the Committee to discharge its mandate fully;

16. *Welcomes* the work of the Committee in applying the Convention to the new and contemporary forms of racism and racial discrimination, bearing in mind the need to identify the gaps in the existing international human rights instruments, notably the International Convention on the Elimination of All Forms of Racial Discrimination, for which complementary standards are necessary;

17. *Recognizes* the contribution to be made to the above process by conducting an in-depth assessment and evaluation of the implementation of existing international human rights instruments by States parties;

18. *Urges* all States parties to the Convention to intensify their efforts to implement the obligations that they have accepted under article 4 of the Convention, with due regard to the principles of the Universal Declaration of Human Rights and article 5 of the Convention;

19. *Notes* that the Committee holds that the prohibition of the dissemination of ideas based on racial superiority or racial hatred is compatible with the right to freedom of opinion and expression as outlined in article 19 of the Universal Declaration of Human Rights and in article 5 of the Convention;

20. *Welcomes* the emphasis placed by the Committee on the importance of follow-up to the World Conference and the measures recommended to strengthen the implementation of the Convention as well as the functioning of the Committee;

III
Comprehensive implementation of and follow-up to the Durban Declaration and Programme of Action

21. *Acknowledges* that the outcome of the World Conference against Racism, Racial Discrimination, Xenophobia and Related Intolerance is on an equal footing with the outcomes of all the major United Nations conferences, summits and special sessions in the human rights and social fields;

22. *Also acknowledges* that the World Conference, which was the third world conference against racism, was significantly different from the previous two conferences, as evidenced by the inclusion in its title of two important components relating to contemporary forms of racism, namely, xenophobia and related intolerance;

23. *Emphasizes* that the basic responsibility for effectively combating racism, racial discrimination, xenophobia and related intolerance lies with States, and to this end stresses that States have the primary responsibility to ensure full and effective implementation of all commitments and recommendations contained in the Durban Declaration and Programme of Action;

24. *Also emphasizes* the fundamental and complementary role of national human rights institutions, regional bodies or centres and civil society, working jointly with States towards the achievement of the objectives of the Durban Declaration and Programme of Action;

25. *Welcomes* the steps taken by numerous Governments, in particular the elaboration and implementation of national action plans to combat racism, racial discrimination, xenophobia and related intolerance, and steps taken by national human rights institutions and non-governmental organizations, towards the full implementation of the Durban Declaration and Programme of Action, and affirms this trend as a demonstration of commitment for the elimination of all scourges of racism at the national level;

26. *Calls upon* all States that have not yet elaborated their national action plans on the combating of racism, racial discrimination, xenophobia and related intolerance to comply with their commitments undertaken at the World Conference;

27. *Calls upon* all States to formulate and implement without delay, at the national, regional and international levels, policies and plans of action to combat racism, racial discrimination, xenophobia and related intolerance, including their gender-based manifestations;

28. *Urges* States to support the activities of existing regional bodies or centres that combat racism, racial discrimination, xenophobia and related intolerance in their respective regions, and recommends the establishment of such bodies in all regions where they do not exist;

29. *Recognizes* the fundamental role of civil society in the fight against racism, racial discrimination, xenophobia and related intolerance, in particular in assisting States to develop regulations and strategies, in taking measures and action against such forms of discrimination and through follow-up implementation;

30. *Decides* that the General Assembly, through its role in policy formulation, the Economic and Social Council, through its role in overall guidance and coordination, in accordance with their respective roles

under the Charter of the United Nations and Assembly resolution 50/227 of 24 May 1996, and the Commission on Human Rights shall constitute a three-tiered intergovernmental process for the comprehensive implementation of and follow-up to the Durban Declaration and Programme of Action;

31. *Stresses and reaffirms* its role as the highest intergovernmental mechanism for the formulation and appraisal of policy on matters related to the economic, social and related fields, in accordance with Chapter IX of the Charter, including in the comprehensive implementation of and follow-up to the goals and targets set at all the major United Nations conferences, summits and special sessions;

32. *Welcomes* the second meeting of the group of independent eminent experts, held in Geneva from 21 to 23 February 2005, in particular its programme of work, notes its appeal for convening a five-year review of the implementation of the Durban Declaration and Programme of Action, and in this context urges Member States and relevant stakeholders to give due consideration to its appeal with a view to its examination at the sixty-first session;

33. *Reaffirms* that the Commission on Human Rights, as a functional commission of the Economic and Social Council, shall have a central role in the monitoring of the implementation of the Durban Declaration and Programme of Action within the United Nations system and in advising the Council thereon;

34. *Expresses its appreciation* for the continuing work in follow-up to the World Conference, and in this regard endorses the outcome of the third session of the Intergovernmental Working Group on the Effective Implementation of the Durban Declaration and Programme of Action, while taking note of the outcome of the fourth session of the Working Group of Experts on People of African Descent, and calls for their implementation by all stakeholders;

35. *Welcomes* the convening of the high-level seminar in January 2006 under the auspices of the Office of the United Nations High Commissioner for Human Rights as set out in Commission on Human Rights resolution 2005/64, and encourages all States to participate in this seminar at the appropriate level;

36. *Acknowledges* the centrality of resource mobilization, effective global partnership and international cooperation in the context of paragraphs 157 and 158 of the Durban Programme of Action for the successful realization of commitments undertaken at the World Conference, and to this end emphasizes the central role to be played by the group of independent eminent experts on the implementation of the Durban Declaration and Programme of Action in mobilizing the necessary political will required for the successful implementation of the Declaration and Programme of Action;

37. *Requests* the Secretary-General to provide the necessary resources for the effective fulfilment of the mandates of the Intergovernmental Working Group on the Effective Implementation of the Durban Declaration and Programme of Action, the Working Group of Experts on People of African Descent and the group of independent eminent experts on the implementation of the Durban Declaration and Programme of Action;

38. *Expresses its concern* at the increasing incidence of racism in various sporting events, while noting with appreciation the efforts made by some governing bodies of the various sporting codes to combat racism, and in this regard invites all international sporting bodies to promote, through their national, regional and international federations, a world of sport free from racism and racial discrimination;

39. *Invites*, in this context, the Fédération internationale de football association, in connection with the 2006 and 2010 soccer World Cup tournaments to be held in Germany and in South Africa, respectively, to consider introducing a visible theme on non-racism in football, and requests the Secretary-General to bring this invitation to the attention of the Fédération and to bring the issue of racism in sport to the attention of other relevant international sporting bodies;

IV
Special Rapporteur of the Commission on Human Rights on contemporary forms of racism, racial discrimination, xenophobia and related intolerance and follow-up to his visits

40. *Expresses its full support and appreciation* for the work of the Special Rapporteur of the Commission on Human Rights on contemporary forms of racism, racial discrimination, xenophobia and related intolerance, and encourages its continuation;

41. *Reiterates its call* to all Member States, intergovernmental organizations, relevant organizations of the United Nations system and non-governmental organizations to cooperate fully with the Special Rapporteur, and calls upon States to consider responding favourably to his requests for visits so as to enable him to fulfil his mandate fully and effectively;

42. *Recognizes with deep concern* the increase in anti-Semitism, Christianophobia and Islamophobia in various parts of the world, as well as the emergence of racial and violent movements based on racism and discriminatory ideas directed against Arab, Christian, Jewish and Muslim communities, communities of people of African descent, communities of people of Asian descent and other communities;

43. *Encourages* closer collaboration between the Special Rapporteur and the Office of the United Nations High Commissioner for Human Rights, in particular the Anti-Discrimination Unit;

44. *Urges* the United Nations High Commissioner for Human Rights to provide States, at their request, with advisory services and technical assistance to enable them to implement fully the recommendations of the Special Rapporteur;

45. *Requests* the Secretary-General to provide the Special Rapporteur with all the necessary human and financial assistance to carry out his mandate efficiently, effectively and expeditiously and to enable him to submit an interim report to the General Assembly at its sixty-first session;

46. *Takes note* of the recommendations contained in the interim report of the Special Rapporteur, and urges Member States and other relevant stakeholders to consider implementing those recommendations;

47. *Requests* the Special Rapporteur to continue giving particular attention to the negative impact of racism, racial discrimination, xenophobia and related intolerance on the full enjoyment of civil, cultural,

economic, political and social rights by national or ethnic, religious and linguistic minorities, immigrant populations, asylum-seekers and refugees;

48. *Invites* Member States to demonstrate greater commitment to fighting racism in sport by conducting educational and awareness-raising activities and by strongly condemning the perpetrators of racist incidents, in cooperation with national and international sports organizations;

V
General

49. *Requests* the Secretary-General to submit a report on the implementation of the present resolution to the General Assembly at its sixty-first session;

50. *Decides* to remain seized of this important matter at its sixty-first session under the item entitled "Elimination of racism and racial discrimination".

RECORDED VOTE ON RESOLUTION 60/144:

In favour: Afghanistan, Albania, Algeria, Andorra, Angola, Antigua and Barbuda, Argentina, Armenia, Austria, Azerbaijan, Bahamas, Bahrain, Bangladesh, Barbados, Belarus, Belgium, Belize, Benin, Bhutan, Bolivia, Bosnia and Herzegovina, Botswana, Brazil, Brunei Darussalam, Bulgaria, Burkina Faso, Burundi, Cambodia, Cameroon, Cape Verde, Chile, China, Colombia, Comoros, Costa Rica, Côte d'Ivoire, Croatia, Cuba, Cyprus, Czech Republic, Democratic People's Republic of Korea, Democratic Republic of the Congo, Denmark, Djibouti, Dominica, Dominican Republic, Ecuador, Egypt, El Salvador, Eritrea, Estonia, Ethiopia, Fiji, Finland, France, Gabon, Gambia, Georgia, Germany, Ghana, Greece, Grenada, Guatemala, Guinea, Guinea-Bissau, Guyana, Haiti, Honduras, Hungary, Iceland, India, Indonesia, Iran, Iraq, Ireland, Italy, Jamaica, Japan, Jordan, Kazakhstan, Kenya, Kuwait, Kyrgyzstan, Lao People's Democratic Republic, Latvia, Lebanon, Lesotho, Libyan Arab Jamahiriya, Liechtenstein, Lithuania, Luxembourg, Madagascar, Malawi, Malaysia, Maldives, Mali, Malta, Mauritania, Mauritius, Mexico, Micronesia, Monaco, Mongolia, Morocco, Mozambique, Myanmar, Namibia, Nepal, Netherlands, New Zealand, Nicaragua, Niger, Nigeria, Norway, Oman, Pakistan, Panama, Papua New Guinea, Paraguay, Peru, Philippines, Poland, Portugal, Qatar, Republic of Korea, Republic of Moldova, Romania, Russian Federation, Rwanda, Saint Lucia, Saint Vincent and the Grenadines, Samoa, San Marino, Saudi Arabia, Senegal, Serbia and Montenegro, Singapore, Slovakia, Slovenia, Solomon Islands, Somalia, South Africa, Spain, Sri Lanka, Sudan, Suriname, Sweden, Switzerland, Syrian Arab Republic, Tajikistan, Thailand, The former Yugoslav Republic of Macedonia, Timor-Leste, Togo, Tonga, Trinidad and Tobago, Tunisia, Turkey, Turkmenistan, Uganda, Ukraine, United Arab Emirates, United Kingdom , United Republic of Tanzania, Uruguay, Uzbekistan, Vanuatu, Venezuela, Viet Nam, Yemen, Zambia, Zimbabwe.

Against: Israel, Marshall Islands, United States.

Abstaining: Australia, Canada, Palau, Tuvalu.

Contemporary forms of racism

Reports of Special Rapporteur. In his annual report to the Commission [E/CN.4/2005/18], the Special Rapporteur on contemporary forms of racism, racial discrimination, xenophobia and related intolerance, Doudou Diène (Senegal), described activities he had undertaken since his 2004 report [YUN 2004, p. 692]. Those activities focused on fieldwork and on strengthening cooperation with regional and institutional partners, particularly regarding general and specific forms of racism, such as anti-Semitism and Islamophobia. He also stepped up consultations and cooperation with relevant bodies on the issue of racism in sports and considered contemporary manifestations of the phenomenon in terms of the impact of identity constructs on racism, discrimination and xenophobia, hierarchy of forms of discrimination and intellectual justification of racism and xenophobia, the rise of parties and movements with racist and xenophobic platforms and the situation of the Roma and other groups vulnerable to racial discrimination. In considering those issues, the Special Rapporteur pursued a dual strategy, which, on the one hand, aimed at extending and strengthening the legal and political responses to intolerance, and on the other hand, sought an intellectual and ethical approach, aimed at better understanding the roots of intolerance. On the basis of the information gathered, the Special Rapporteur noted the following prominent tendencies: the growing importance of the identity factor in recent manifestations of racism, racial discrimination and xenophobia; the inclination to hierarchize different forms of racial discrimination; a more pronounced interest to provide an intellectual justification for racism and intolerance; the rise and growing influence of parties and movements with racist and xenophobic platforms; and the exacerbation of the phenomenon of racism in sport. The Special Rapporteur addressed recommendations to the Commission, Member States, regional organizations and civil society actors on how best to address those tendencies. He proposed, in particular, that the Commission devise an intellectual strategy for combating racism in the domain of ideas, concepts, images, perceptions and value systems, and that all forms of such discrimination be treated equally, as any hierarchization of the problem would undermine universal efforts to tackle it. The Commission should alert Member States to ways in which racism and racial discrimination could enter the mainstream of society through political platforms, and Member States needed to demonstrate greater commitment to fighting racism in sports.

In a February addendum to the report [E/CN.4/2005/Add.1 & Corr.1], the Special Rapporteur summarized communications transmitted to Governments regarding cases of racism, racial discrimination, xenophobia and related intolerance, and replies received.

In response to a 2004 Commission request [YUN 2004, p. 706] that he examine the situation of Muslim and Arab peoples in various parts of the world in the aftermath of the terrorist attacks of 11 September 2001 in the United States [YUN 2001, p. 60], the Special Rapporteur submitted a report [E/CN.4/2005/18/Add.4] on the defamation of religions, particularly anti-Semitism, Christianophobia and Islamophobia. The report analysed each of those forms of discrimination, considered universal efforts to combat them, and found that the religious and socio-political factors that led to intolerance in each case were increasing. The Special Rapporteur made recommendations to the Commission and Member States on the need to combat the specific cultural and historical roots of each type of intolerance while treating all religious phobias equally and promoting religious and spiritual pluralism. In measures to combat racism and racial discrimination, the Commission should take greater account of the increasing intertwining of race, ethnicity, culture and religion, and of the rise of anti-Semitism, Christianophobia and Islamophobia, and in that regard, it was important to draw Member States' attention to the clash of cultures, civilizations and religions, particularly in the current context of efforts to combat terrorism.

The Special Rapporteur visited Japan (3-11 July) [E/CN.4/2006/16/Add.2 & Corr.1], where he assessed the impact of discrimination on minorities, including victims of the caste-like system; indigenous people (mostly the Ainu, estimated at between 30,000 and 50,000 people) and the Buraku and Okinawa peoples; descendants of former Japanese colonies (Koreans and Chinese); and foreigners and migrants from other Asian nations and elsewhere. Discrimination against those minorities was evident in social and economic life, as surveys of the situation highlighted their marginalization regarding access to education, employment, health and housing. Politically, they were poorly represented in State institutions, and culturally, they were affected by poor recognition and transmission of their history and the perpetuation of an unfavourable image. While acknowledging policies and measures adopted by the authorities to address the problem, including laws that promoted minority rights, the Special Rapporteur was concerned that there was no national legislation that specifically outlawed racial discrimination or provided a judicial remedy for the victims. He recommended that the Government officially recognize the existence of racial discrimination in the country, and express the will to combat it; adopt a national law against the problem; establish a national commission for equality and human rights; and rewrite the teaching history to better reflect the history of minorities and Japan's relations with neighbouring countries.

Commission action. On 12 April [res. 2005/3], the Commission, by a recorded vote of 31 to 16, with 5 abstentions, asked the Special Rapporteur to continue to examine the situation of Muslims and Arab peoples in various parts of the world in the aftermath of the September 2001 terrorist attacks in the United States [YUN 2001, p. 60], and to report thereon in 2006.

By a recorded vote of 46 to none, with 4 abstentions, the Commission, on 14 April [res. 2005/5], alarmed at the spread in many parts of the world of various extremist political parties, movements and groups, including neo-Nazis and skinheads, stressed that the practices of such organizations fueled contemporary forms of racism and were incompatible with Member States' obligations under the UN Charter and detrimental to the Organization's goals and principles. The Commission asked the Special Rapporteur to reflect on the issue, make relevant recommendations and report in 2006, taking into account the views of Governments and NGOs.

On 20 April [res. 2005/64], the Commission, by a recorded vote of 38 to 1, with 14 abstentions, extended the Special Rapporteur's mandate for a period of three years and asked him to submit an interim report to the General Assembly in 2005 and to report to the Commission in 2006. The Secretary-General was asked to assist him.

By **decision 2005/272** of 25 July, the Economic and Social Council endorsed the Commission's decision to extend the Special Rapporteur's mandate and its request to the Secretary-General to assist him.

Further reports of Special Rapporteur. The Special Rapporteur visited Brazil (17-26 October) [E/CN.4/2006/16/Add.3] to assess the situation of racial discrimination and the Government's efforts to combat it. After analysing the views of the authorities and representatives of civil society organizations and ethnic groups in the country, the Special Rapporteur found that racial discrimination had influenced the structure of the entire Brazilian society for the past five centuries. The phenomenon was rooted in the system of slavery, founded on racist intellectual and ideological sentiments, which affected the mentalities and societal structures of States like Brazil that had participated in that system. The most striking manifestation of the problem was social, economic and political marginalization, as well as cultural repression. Those most affected were people of African descent, who accounted for 46 per cent of the Brazilian population and the majority among its ethnic groups. Also affected was the country's Amerindian community, comprising 0.4 per cent of the population, and other vulnerable groups, such as migrant workers, refugees and asylum-seekers. The Special Rapporteur noted in that regard that "traveling in Brazil was like moving simultaneously between two different planets, from that of the lively, coloured and mixed races of the streets to that of the almost all-white corridors of political, social, economic and media power". There was almost a complete lack of representation of blacks and Indians in State institutions. Although the authorities had recognized the existence and depth of racism and had adopted a number of laws to combat it, resistance to those policies remained, even among some federal and local authorities. The Special Rapporteur recommended measures aimed at translating the Government's political will into a legal and cultural strategy to eradicate the deeply rooted causes and consequences of racism and racial discrimination in Brazilian society. He proposed, in particular, that the Government establish a comprehensive national programme for the eradication of racism, based on DDPA provisions, a national commission on truth and reconciliation on racism and racial discrimination and a national commission for equality and human rights. The Government should accord priority to the prevention of violence against Indians and Afro-Brazilians, and make efforts to protect and support the indigenous and quilombo communities.

In accordance with General Assembly resolution 59/177 [YUN 2004, p. 688], the Secretary-General, in August [A/60/283], transmitted the Special Rapporteur's interim report, which summarized his activities during the year. The report drew the Assembly's attention to developments of particular concern, including a rise in racism and xenophobia as a result of identity constructs, and the mistreatment, contrary to international standards, of aliens, asylum-seekers, refugees and immigrants by the official administrative services of many States. The growing number of counter-terrorism policies and programmes by Member States were generating new forms of discrimination against groups and entire communities, religious and spiritual traditions, and in that context, the resurgence of Islamophobia had to be given particular attention. The Assembly should invite Member States to be more vigilant to all forms of religious defamation; to address the resurgence of racism, manifested through the erosion of the economic and social rights of national, ethnic, cultural and religious minorities, and of immigrants, asylum-seekers and refugees; and to take measures to prevent the discriminatory treatment of people in waiting and holding areas at airports and borders. The Special Rapporteur also discussed the upsurge of racism in sports, and invited Member States and national and international sporting bodies to address it.

Communication. In March [E/CN.4/2005/G/22], Thailand, referring to the Special Rapporteur's report (see above), provided information on the situation and incidents in southern Thailand.

GENERAL ASSEMBLY ACTION

On 16 December [meeting 64], the General Assembly, on the recommendation of the Third Committee [A/60/507], adopted **resolution 60/143** by recorded vote (114-4-57) [agenda item 69].

Inadmissibility of certain practices that contribute to fuelling contemporary forms of racism, racial discrimination, xenophobia and related intolerance

The General Assembly,

Guided by the Charter of the United Nations, the Universal Declaration of Human Rights, the International Covenant on Civil and Political Rights, the International Convention on the Elimination of All Forms of Racial Discrimination and other relevant human rights instruments,

Recalling the provisions of Commission on Human Rights resolutions 2004/16 of 16 April 2004 and 2005/5 of 14 April 2005,

Recalling also the Charter of the Nuremberg Tribunal and the Judgement of the Tribunal, which recognized the Waffen SS organization and all its integral parts as criminal and declared it responsible for many war crimes and crimes against humanity,

Recalling further the relevant provisions of the Durban Declaration and Programme of Action adopted by the World Conference against Racism, Racial Discrimination, Xenophobia and Related Intolerance on 8 September 2001, in particular paragraph 2 of the Declaration and paragraph 86 of the Programme of Action,

Recalling equally the study undertaken by the Special Rapporteur of the Commission on Human Rights on contemporary forms of racism, racial discrimination, xenophobia and related intolerance, and taking note of his report,

Alarmed, in this regard, at the spread in many parts of the world of various extremist political parties, movements and groups, including neo-Nazis and skinhead groups,

1. *Reaffirms* the provision of the Durban Declaration in which States condemned the persistence and resurgence of neo-Nazism, neo-Fascism and violent nationalist prejudice and stated that those phenomena could never be justified in any instance or in any circumstances;

2. *Expresses deep concern* over the glorification of the Nazi movement and former members of the Waffen SS organization, including by erecting monuments and memorials as well as holding public demonstrations in the name of the glorification of the Nazi past, the Nazi movement and neo-Nazism;

3. *Notes with concern* the increase in the number of racist incidents in several countries and the rise of skinhead groups, which have been responsible for many of these incidents, as observed by the Special Rapporteur of the Commission on Human Rights on contemporary forms of racism, racial discrimination, xenophobia and related intolerance;

4. *Reaffirms* that such acts may be qualified to fall within the scope of activities described in article 4 of the International Convention on the Elimination of All Forms of Racial Discrimination, and that they represent a clear and manifest abuse of the rights to freedom of peaceful assembly and of association as well as the rights to freedom of opinion and expression within the meaning of those rights as guaranteed by the Universal Declaration of Human Rights, the International

Covenant on Civil and Political Rights and the International Convention on the Elimination of All Forms of Racial Discrimination;

5. *Stresses* that the practices described above do injustice to the memory of the countless victims of crimes against humanity committed in the Second World War, in particular those committed by the SS organization, and poison the minds of young people, in particular in the year of the sixtieth anniversary of victory in the Second World War and the liberation of Auschwitz and other concentration camps, and that those practices are incompatible with the obligations of States Members of the United Nations under its Charter and are incompatible with the goals and principles of the Organization;

6. *Also stresses* that such practices fuel contemporary forms of racism, racial discrimination, xenophobia and related intolerance and contribute to the spread and multiplication of various extremist political parties, movements and groups, including neo-Nazis and skinhead groups;

7. *Emphasizes* the need to take the necessary measures to put an end to the practices described above, and calls upon States to take more effective measures to combat those phenomena and the extremist movements, which pose a real threat to democratic values;

8. *Reaffirms* that, according to article 4 of the International Convention on the Elimination of All Forms of Racial Discrimination, States parties to that instrument are, inter alia, under the obligation:

(a) To condemn all propaganda and all organizations that are based on ideas of racial superiority or that attempt to justify or promote racial hatred and discrimination in any form;

(b) To undertake to adopt immediate and positive measures designed to eradicate all incitement to, or acts of, such discrimination with due regard to the principles embodied in the Universal Declaration of Human Rights and the rights expressly set forth in article 5 of the Convention;

(c) To declare as an offence punishable by law all dissemination of ideas based on racial superiority or hatred, incitement to racial discrimination, as well as all acts of violence or incitement to such acts against any race or group of persons of another colour or ethnic origin, and also the provision of any assistance to racist activities, including the financing thereof;

(d) To declare illegal and prohibit organizations and organized and all other propaganda activities that promote and incite racial discrimination and to recognize participation in such organizations or activities as an offence punishable by law;

(e) To prohibit public authorities or public institutions, national or local, from promoting or inciting racial discrimination;

9. *Recalls* the request of the Commission on Human Rights in its resolution 2005/5 that the Special Rapporteur continue to reflect on this issue, make relevant recommendations in his report to the Commission at its sixty-second session and seek and take into account in this regard the views of Governments and non-governmental organizations;

10. *Invites* Governments and non-governmental organizations to cooperate fully with the Special Rapporteur in the exercise of the aforementioned task;

11. *Decides* to remain seized of the issue.

RECORDED VOTE ON RESOLUTION 60/143:

In favour: Afghanistan, Algeria, Angola, Antigua and Barbuda, Argentina, Armenia, Azerbaijan, Bahamas, Bahrain, Bangladesh, Barbados, Belarus, Belize, Benin, Bhutan, Bolivia, Botswana, Brazil, Brunei Darussalam, Burundi, Cambodia, Cameroon, Cape Verde, Chile, China, Colombia, Comoros, Costa Rica, Côte d'Ivoire, Cuba, Democratic People's Republic of Korea, Democratic Republic of the Congo, Djibouti, Dominica, Dominican Republic, Ecuador, Egypt, El Salvador, Eritrea, Ethiopia, Gabon, Gambia, Ghana, Grenada, Guatemala, Guinea, Guyana, Haiti, Honduras, India, Indonesia, Iran, Iraq, Israel, Jamaica, Jordan, Kazakhstan, Kenya, Kuwait, Kyrgyzstan, Lao People's Democratic Republic, Lesotho, Libyan Arab Jamahiriya, Madagascar, Malawi, Malaysia, Maldives, Mauritania, Mauritius, Mexico, Mongolia, Morocco, Mozambique, Myanmar, Namibia, Nicaragua, Niger, Nigeria, Oman, Pakistan, Paraguay, Peru, Philippines, Qatar, Russian Federation, Rwanda, Saint Lucia, Saint Vincent and the Grenadines, Saudi Arabia, Senegal, Singapore, Somalia, South Africa, Sudan, Suriname, Syrian Arab Republic, Tajikistan, Thailand, Timor-Leste, Togo, Trinidad and Tobago, Tunisia, Turkmenistan, Tuvalu, Uganda, United Arab Emirates, United Republic of Tanzania, Uruguay, Uzbekistan, Venezuela, Viet Nam, Yemen, Zambia, Zimbabwe.

Against: Japan, Marshall Islands, Micronesia, United States.

Abstaining: Albania, Andorra, Australia, Austria, Belgium, Bosnia and Herzegovina, Bulgaria, Burkina Faso, Canada, Croatia, Cyprus, Czech Republic, Denmark, Estonia, Fiji, Finland, France, Georgia, Germany, Greece, Hungary, Iceland, Ireland, Italy, Latvia, Liechtenstein, Lithuania, Luxembourg, Malta, Monaco, Nepal, Netherlands, New Zealand, Norway, Palau, Panama, Papua New Guinea, Poland, Portugal, Republic of Korea, Republic of Moldova, Romania, Samoa, San Marino, Serbia and Montenegro, Slovakia, Slovenia, Solomon Islands, Spain, Sri Lanka, Sweden, Switzerland, The former Yugoslav Republic of Macedonia, Turkey, Ukraine, United Kingdom , Vanuatu.

Study of political platforms

On 19 April [res. 2005/36], the Commission, condemning political platforms and organizations based on racism, xenophobia or doctrines of racial superiority and related discrimination, recommended the creation, where they did not exist, of monitoring, reporting, documentation and information-processing institutions and procedures in order to prevent and reduce racial, ethnic or religious tensions. OHCHR was invited to continue efforts, in collaboration with the Special Rapporteur, to further analyse the issue of incitement and promotion of racism, racial discrimination, xenophobia and related intolerance in political debate. The Special Rapporteur was asked to review and further expand his 2004 study on the question of political platforms that promoted or incited racial discrimination [YUN 2004, p. 695], and to report in 2006.

Right to nationality

On 19 April [res. 2005/45], the Commission, recognizing that arbitrary deprivation of nationality on racial, national, ethnic, religious, political or gender grounds violated human rights and fundamental freedoms, called on States to refrain from taking discriminatory measures and enacting legislation that would result in such deprivation and to prevent and reduce statelessness. States that had not yet done so were asked to consider acceding to the 1961 Convention on the Reduction of Statelessness [YUN 1961, p. 533] and the 1954 Convention relating to the Status of Stateless Persons [YUN 1954, p. 416]. The Secretary-General was asked to collect information on the issue from relevant sources for the Commission's consideration in 2006.

Protection of migrants

Report of Special Rapporteur. The Special Rapporteur on the human rights of migrants, Gabriela Rodríguez Pizarro (Costa Rica), in a report covering her 2004 activities [E/CN.4/2005/85], described the situation regarding her two research priority areas, namely racism, racial discrimination and xenophobia against immigrants and the situation of migrant women and unaccompanied minors. Judging from the alleged violations she had received, the Special Rapporteur determined that the most frequent abuses against migrants were discriminatory, xenophobic and racist practices that occurred during the administrative detention of undocumented migrants and the exploitation of migrant workers in various ways. Administrative detention amounted to discrimination against the exercise of migrants' basic right to freedom and legal security and the arbitrary denial of their right to an effective recourse against police detention, a situation that had become widespread owing to States' application of special legislation to combat terrorism. There were also instances of discrimination against migrants regarding access to the labour market, home purchase or rental, and in education opportunities. Women migrants were at greater risk of discrimination and abuse than men, owing to the tendency for them to be employed in the shadow economy and relatively less skilled work, and to become more dependent on their employers, making them more vulnerable to exploitation. Unaccompanied minors were also at great risk of violence, exploitation, child trafficking and discrimination, and were more vulnerable to sexual abuse and being coerced into begging, drug dealing or prostitution by criminals. States seemed slow to take account of the best interests of such minors regarding the issues of detention, repatriation procedures and family reunification. Consequently, alleged summary deportations of those affected persisted, as well as their ill-treatment at reception centres and detention. In terms of progress made in protecting migrants' rights, the Special Rapporteur said that a number of trade unions in host countries were making efforts to address the labour situation of migrant workers and some countries had adopted national plans of action, in line with the recommendations contained in the Durban Declaration and Programme of Action (DDPA) adopted at the World Conference against Racism, Racial Discrimination, Xenophobia and Related Intolerance [YUN 2001, p. 615], particularly regard-

ing the provisions on migrants. Yet, alarming manifestations of discrimination against them persisted, characterized by resurgent traditional forms of discrimination, rooted in colour-based racism, and the appearance of new forms targeting non-citizens, refugees and immigrants. The Special Rapporteur recommended that States be held responsible and punished for abuses and violations of migrants' rights and urged that the Commission continue its work on the "Basic Principles and Guidelines on the Right to a Remedy and Reparation for Victims of Violations of International Human Rights and Humanitarian Law" (see p. 792) and that the General Assembly do likewise regarding the codification of the draft articles on responsibility of States for internationally wrongful acts submitted by the International Law Commission [YUN 2001, p. 1218]. OHCHR should participate more actively in migration-management forums and help run specific programmes on migrants' human rights. UNDP needed to be aware of the migration-development nexus and promote local level programmes in the countries where migration began. The Special Rapporteur was confident that the Assembly's high-level dialogues on international migration and development, scheduled for 2006 (see p. 1176), would provide a fresh opportunity to consider strategies and mechanisms for addressing the myriad aspects of migration.

An addendum to the report [E/CN.4/2005/85/Add.1 & Corr. 1] summarized the communications the Special Rapporteur had sent to 51 Governments and responses thereto regarding individual cases of alleged violations of migrants' human rights and general situations concerning their rights in specific countries.

Commission action. On 19 April [res. 2005/47], the Commission strongly condemned racism, racial discrimination, xenophobia and related intolerance against migrants and asked States to promote and protect their rights. The Commission extended the Special Rapporteur's mandate for three years, encouraged her to continue to examine ways of overcoming obstacles in that regard, and requested that she report to the Assembly in 2005 and to the Commission in 2006. The Secretary-General was requested to assist her.

On 25 July, the Economic and Social Council approved the Commission's decision to extend the Special Rapporteur's mandate and endorsed its request to the Secretary-General to assist her (**decision 2005/267**).

Further reports of Special Rapporteur. At the invitation of the Government, the Special Rapporteur visited Burkina Faso (2-9 February) [E/CN.4/2006/73/Add.2] to assess the situation of migrants, including some 350,000 of its nationals repatriated from neighbouring Côte d'Ivoire, which had been in the throes of conflict since a 2002 failed attempt by armed rebels to overthrow the Government [YUN 2002, p. 180]. The plight of those returnees, who faced extreme poverty, particularly women and children, highlighted problems regarding the fundamental rights of migrants, most notably socio-economic rights relating to poor access to employment, social security, health, housing, food and education. Child trafficking was of particular concern in Burkina Faso, affecting the large percentage of children who left home in search of a better life, most of whom found work on plantations as domestic workers or were left in the care of Koranic teachers. To address those problems, the Special Rapporteur recommended more determined structural action against child trafficking and the development and implementation of a clearly defined migration policy, as a means of dealing effectively with irregular migration flows and optimizing the potential benefits of international migration to Burkina Faso's development. In that context, priority should be given to the conclusion of bilateral agreements with countries expelling Burkinabe nationals, especially the Libyan Arab Jamahiriya, in order to safeguard the dignity of irregular migrants at the time of repatriation. She also advocated that Burkina Faso participate actively in regional migration processes; seek ways of optimizing the benefits of international migration; and introduce stricter controls of civil status documents used in the preparation of national passports and transparent procedures respectful of human rights in the area of irregular migration. Other recommendations concerned measures to facilitate the socio-economic resettlement of returnees and the need for the international community to support the resettlement process.

In July, the Commission appointed Jorge Bustamante (Mexico) as the new Special Rapporteur on the human rights of migrants.

Interim report of Special Rapporteur. In response to General Assembly resolution 59/194 [YUN 2004, p. 699] and Commission resolution 2005/47 (see p. 767), the Secretary-General, by a September note [A/60/357], transmitted the interim report of the Special Rapporteur, which made preliminary observations regarding migration and described the working methods he intended to adopt in fulfilling his mandate.

Report of Secretary-General. In accordance with General Assembly resolution 59/194 [YUN 2004, p. 699], the Secretary-General, in an August report [A/60/272], summarized communications received from 11 States providing information on legal provisions, programmes, campaigns and policies established to protect migrants. The Secretary-General was encouraged by the increasing number of bilateral, regional and international consultations on migration and the protection of migrants, and by States' efforts in that regard. He welcomed the work of the Committee on Migrant Workers (see p. 731), which monitored the compliance of States parties with the provisions of the 1990 International Convention on the Protection of the Rights of All Migrant Workers and Members of Their Families [YUN 1990, p. 594] and urged Member States who had not done so to ratify and adhere to that instrument. The Special Rapporteur was encouraged to continue working for the protection of migrants, particularly women and children, maintain the programme of visits and continue promoting dialogue and cooperation on the issue of migration.

Communications. On 16 March [E/CN.4/2005/G/19], Italy provided its observations on the report of the former Special Rapporteur following her 2004 visit to the country [YUN 2004, p. 697]. It emphasized that it had enacted legislation that focused on integration, reception and full protection of migrants' rights and disagreed with the Special Rapporteur's suggestion that the provisions of that legislation were potentially restrictive of migrants' rights.

On 18 March [E/CN.4/2005/G/31], Peru clarified aspects of the former Special Rapporteur's report on her 2004 visit to the country [YUN 2004, p. 698].

GENERAL ASSEMBLY ACTION

On 16 December [meeting 64], the General Assembly, on the recommendation of the Third Committee [A/60/507], adopted **resolution 60/169** without vote [agenda item 71 (b)].

Protection of migrants

The General Assembly,

Reaffirming the Universal Declaration of Human Rights, which proclaims that all human beings are born free and equal in dignity and rights and that everyone is entitled to all the rights and freedoms set out therein, without distinction of any kind, in particular as to race, colour or national origin,

Recalling its resolution 59/194 of 20 December 2004, taking note of Commission on Human Rights resolution 2005/47 of 19 April 2005, and recalling its resolution 40/144 of 13 December 1985, by which it adopted the Declaration on the Human Rights of Individuals Who are not Nationals of the Country in which They Live,

Considering that every State party to the International Covenant on Civil and Political Rights must ensure to all individuals within its territory and subject to its jurisdiction the rights recognized in the Covenant, and that every State party to the International Covenant on Economic, Social and Cultural Rights has undertaken to guarantee the exercise of all rights enunciated in that Covenant without discrimination of any kind, including, in particular, on the basis of national origin,

Reaffirming the provisions concerning migrants adopted by the World Conference on Human Rights, the International Conference on Population and Development, the World Summit for Social Development and the Fourth World Conference on Women,

Reaffirming also the provisions on the human rights of migrants contained in the Durban Declaration and Programme of Action adopted by the World Conference against Racism, Racial Discrimination, Xenophobia and Related Intolerance on 8 September 2001, and expressing its satisfaction at the important recommendations made for the development of international and national strategies for the protection of migrants and for the design of migration policies that fully respect the human rights of migrants,

Recalling the renewed commitment made in the United Nations Millennium Declaration and at the 2005 World Summit to take measures to ensure respect for and protection of the human rights of migrants, migrant workers and their families, to eliminate the increasing acts of racism and xenophobia in many societies and to promote greater harmony, tolerance and respect in all societies,

Taking note of advisory opinion OC-16/99 of 1 October 1999 on the Right to Information on Consular Assistance in the Framework of the Guarantees of the Due Process of Law and advisory opinion OC-18/03 of 17 September 2003 on the Juridical Condition and Rights of the Undocumented Migrants, issued by the Inter-American Court of Human Rights,

Taking note also of the Judgment of the International Court of Justice of 31 March 2004 in the case concerning *Avena and Other Mexican Nationals,* and recalling the obligations of States reaffirmed therein,

Encouraged by the increasing interest of the international community in the effective and full protection of the human rights of all migrants, and underlining the need to make further efforts to ensure respect for the human rights and fundamental freedoms of all migrants,

Aware of the increasing number of migrants worldwide, and bearing in mind the situation of vulnerability in which migrants and their accompanying families can find themselves when outside their States of origin owing, inter alia, to the difficulties they encounter because of discrimination in society, differences of language, custom and culture, as well as the economic and social difficulties and obstacles to the return of migrants to their States of origin, especially those who are undocumented or in an irregular migratory situation,

Emphasizing the global character of the migratory phenomenon, the importance of international, regional and bilateral cooperation and dialogue in this regard, as appropriate, and the need to protect the human rights of migrants, particularly at a time in which migration flows have increased in the globalized economy and take place in a context of new security concerns,

Bearing in mind that policies and initiatives on the issue of migration, including those that refer to the orderly management of migration, should promote holistic approaches that take into account the causes and consequences of the phenomenon, as well as the full respect of the human rights and fundamental freedoms of migrants,

Concerned at the large and growing number of migrants, especially women and children, who place themselves in a vulnerable situation by attempting to cross international borders without the required travel documents, and underlining the obligation of States to respect the human rights of those migrants,

Deeply concerned at the manifestations of violence, racism, racial discrimination, xenophobia and other forms of intolerance and inhuman and degrading treatment against migrants, especially women and children, in different parts of the world,

Concerned that the Special Rapporteur of the Commission on Human Rights on contemporary forms of racism, racial discrimination, xenophobia and related intolerance has indicated the appearance of new forms of discrimination targeting migrants, among other groups,

Noting the strong concern expressed by the special rapporteurs, special representatives, independent experts and chairpersons of working groups of the special procedures of the Commission on Human Rights and of the advisory services programme regarding the continued deterioration in the situation and the denial of the human rights of migrants, in particular current attempts to institutionalize discrimination against and exclusion of migrants, in the joint statement made at their eleventh annual meeting,

Highlighting the importance of creating conditions that favour greater harmony, tolerance and respect between migrants and the rest of society in countries of transit or destination in order to eliminate manifestations of racism and xenophobia against migrants, including members of their families,

Recognizing the positive and diverse contributions that migrants make to host societies and societies of origin and the efforts that some host countries and countries of origin undertake to integrate and reintegrate migrants,

Recognizing also the increasing participation of women in international migration movements,

Acknowledging the work of the Committee on the Protection of the Rights of All Migrant Workers and Members of Their Families,

Acknowledging also the work done by the International Labour Organization and the International Organization for Migration in addressing migration issues,

Resolved to ensure respect for the human rights and fundamental freedoms of all migrants,

1. *Strongly condemns* the manifestations and acts of racism, racial discrimination, xenophobia and related intolerance against migrants and the stereotypes often applied to them, and urges States to apply the existing laws when xenophobic or intolerant acts, manifestations or expressions against migrants occur, in order to eradicate impunity for those who commit xenophobic and racist acts, and calls upon States to implement fully the commitments and recommendations relating to the promotion and protection of the human rights of migrants contained in the Durban Declaration and Programme of Action through, inter alia, the adoption of national plans of action, as recommended by the World Conference against Racism, Racial Discrimination, Xenophobia and Related Intolerance;

2. *Strongly condemns also* all forms of racial discrimination and xenophobia related to access to employment, vocational training, housing, schooling, health services and social services, as well as services intended for use by the public;

3. *Welcomes* the active role played by governmental and non-governmental organizations in combating racism and xenophobia and in assisting victims of racist acts, including migrant victims;

4. *Calls upon* all States to consider reviewing and, where necessary, revising immigration policies with a view to eliminating all discriminatory practices against migrants and their families and adopting effective action to create conditions that foster greater harmony, tolerance and respect within societies, and to provide specialized training for government policymaking, law enforcement, migration and other concerned officials, including in cooperation with non-governmental organizations and civil society;

5. *Requests* States effectively to promote and protect the human rights and fundamental freedoms of all migrants, regardless of their immigration status, especially those of women and children, in conformity with the Universal Declaration of Human Rights and the international instruments to which they are party, which may include the International Covenants on Human Rights, the Convention against Torture and Other Cruel, Inhuman or Degrading Treatment or Punishment, the Convention on the Elimination of All Forms of Discrimination against Women, the Convention on the Rights of the Child, the International Convention on the Elimination of All Forms of Racial Discrimination, the International Convention on the Protection of the Rights of All Migrant Workers and Members of Their Families and other relevant human rights instruments;

6. *Requests* all States, international organizations and relevant stakeholders to take into account in their policies and initiatives on migration issues the global character of the migratory phenomenon and to give due consideration to international, regional and bilateral cooperation in this field, with a view to addressing, in a comprehensive manner, its causes and consequences and granting priority to the protection of the human rights of migrants;

7. *Welcomes* the increasing number of signatures and ratifications or accessions to the International Convention on the Protection of the Rights of All Migrant Workers and Members of Their Families, and calls upon States that have not done so to consider signing and ratifying or acceding to the Convention as a matter of priority;

8. *Urges* States parties to the United Nations Convention against Transnational Organized Crime and supplementing protocols thereto, namely, the Protocol against the Smuggling of Migrants by Land, Sea and Air and the Protocol to Prevent, Suppress and Punish Trafficking in Persons, Especially Women and Children, to implement them fully, and calls upon States that have not done so to consider ratifying them as a matter of priority;

9. *Reaffirms emphatically* the duty of States parties to ensure full respect for and observance of the Vienna Convention on Consular Relations of 1963, in particular with regard to the right of all foreign nationals, regardless of their immigration status, to communicate with a consular official of the sending State in the case of arrest, imprisonment, custody or detention, and the obligation of the receiving State to inform without delay the foreign national of his or her rights under the Convention;

10. *Expresses concern* about the legislation and the measures adopted by some States that restrict the human rights and fundamental freedoms of migrants;

11. *Welcomes* immigration programmes, adopted by some countries, that allow migrants to integrate fully into the host countries, facilitate family reunification and promote a harmonious, tolerant and respectful environment, and encourages States to consider the possibility of adopting these types of programmes;

12. *Calls upon* States to facilitate family reunification in an expeditious and effective manner, with due regard to applicable laws, as such reunification has a positive effect on the integration of migrants;

13. *Encourages* all States to integrate a gender and age perspective in developing and implementing international migration policies and programmes in order to adopt the necessary measures to better protect women and children against possible dangers and abuse associated with migration and to foster opportunities for their contribution to their societies of origin and destination;

14. *Calls upon* States to promote and protect all human rights of migrant children, given their vulnerability, in particular unaccompanied migrant children, ensuring that the best interests of the children are a primary consideration, underlines the importance of reuniting them with their parents, when possible, and encourages the relevant United Nations bodies, within the framework of their respective mandates, to pay special attention to the conditions of migrant children in all States and, where necessary, to put forward recommendations for strengthening their protection, especially against sexual abuse, sexual exploitation, trafficking, the threat or use of force or other forms of coercion, including coercion into begging and drug dealing, in particular by national or transnational organized crime groups;

15. *Encourages* States of origin to promote and protect the human rights of those families of migrant workers that remain in the countries of origin, paying particular attention to children and adolescents whose parents have emigrated, and encourages international organizations to consider supporting States in this regard;

16. *Requests* all States, in conformity with national legislation and applicable international legal instruments to which they are party, to enforce labour law effectively, including by addressing violations of such law, with regard to migrant workers' labour relations and working conditions, inter alia, those related to their remuneration and conditions of health, safety at work and the right to freedom of association;

17. *Encourages* all States to remove obstacles that may prevent the safe, unrestricted and expeditious transfer of earnings, assets and pensions of migrants to their country of origin or to any other countries, in conformity with applicable legislation, and to consider, as appropriate, measures to solve other problems that may impede such transfers;

18. *Calls upon* States to observe national legislation and applicable international legal instruments to

which they are party when enacting national security measures in order to respect the human rights of migrants;

19. *Urges* all States to adopt effective measures to put an end to the arbitrary arrest and detention of migrants and to take action to prevent and punish any form of illegal deprivation of liberty of migrants by individuals or groups;

20. *Also urges* all States to employ duly authorized and trained government officials to enforce their immigration laws and border controls and to take appropriate and effective measures to deter and prevent private persons or groups from violating criminal and immigration laws relating to border enforcement and from wrongfully undertaking actions reserved to government officials, including by prosecuting those violations of the law that may result from such actions;

21. *Requests* States to adopt concrete measures to prevent the violation of the human rights of migrants while in transit, including in ports and airports and at borders and migration checkpoints, to train public officials who work in those facilities and in border areas to treat migrants respectfully and in accordance with the law, and to prosecute, in conformity with applicable law, any act of violation of the human rights of migrants, inter alia, arbitrary detention, torture and violations of the right to life, including extrajudicial executions, during their transit from their country of origin to the country of destination and vice versa, including their transit through national borders;

22. *Calls upon* States that have not yet done so to enact domestic legislation and to take further effective measures to combat and prosecute international trafficking in and smuggling of migrants, recognizing that these crimes may endanger the lives of migrants or subject them to harm, servitude or exploitation, which may include debt bondage, slavery and sexual exploitation or forced labour, and urges States to strengthen international cooperation to combat such trafficking and smuggling and to protect the victims of trafficking;

23. *Encourages* States, in cooperation with non-governmental organizations, to undertake information campaigns aimed at clarifying opportunities, limitations and rights in the event of migration, so as to enable everyone, in particular women, to make informed decisions and to prevent them from becoming victims of trafficking and utilizing dangerous means of access to countries of transit and destination that put their lives and physical integrity at risk;

24. *Also encourages* States to consider participating in international and regional dialogues on migration that include countries of origin and destination, as well as countries of transit, and invites them to consider negotiating bilateral and regional agreements on migrant workers within the framework of applicable human rights law and designing and implementing programmes with States of other regions to protect the rights of migrants;

25. *Requests* Member States, the United Nations system, international organizations, civil society and all relevant stakeholders, especially the United Nations High Commissioner for Human Rights and her Office, as well as the Special Rapporteur of the Commission on Human Rights on the human rights of migrants, to ensure that the perspective of the human rights of migrants is included among the priority issues in the ongoing discussions on migration and development within the United Nations system, including, in particular, at the high-level dialogue on international migration and development that will be held in 2006, pursuant to General Assembly resolution 58/208 of 23 December 2003;

26. *Invites* States, the United Nations system and intergovernmental and non-governmental organizations to observe, on 18 December of each year, International Migrants Day, proclaimed by the General Assembly, through, inter alia, the dissemination of information on the human rights and fundamental freedoms of migrants and on their economic, social and cultural contributions to their host and home countries, the sharing of experience and the adoption of measures to ensure their protection, and to promote greater harmony, tolerance and respect between migrants and the societies in which they live;

27. *Welcomes* the renewal of the mandate of the Special Rapporteur of the Commission on Human Rights on the human rights of migrants for a period of three years and the appointment of the new Special Rapporteur, and takes note with interest of the interim report submitted by him to the General Assembly, including the proposed methods of work for the fulfilment of his mandate;

28. *Requests* all Governments to cooperate fully with the Special Rapporteur in the performance of the tasks and duties mandated, to furnish all information requested and to respond appropriately and expeditiously to his urgent appeals and to give serious consideration to his requests to visit their countries, and welcomes in this regard the standing invitations extended by some Member States to all special procedures, including the Special Rapporteur;

29. *Requests* all relevant mechanisms to cooperate with the Special Rapporteur;

30. *Requests* the Secretary-General to give the Special Rapporteur all the human and financial assistance necessary for the fulfilment of his mandate;

31. *Takes note* of the report of the Committee on the Protection of the Rights of All Migrant Workers and Members of Their Families on its second session, and requests the Secretary-General to arrange, within existing resources, two sessions for the Committee in 2006, in spring and autumn, respectively, each of a duration of one week;

32. *Takes note also* of the report of the Secretary-General on the protection of migrants, and calls upon Member States and all relevant stakeholders to consider the implementation of the recommendations contained therein;

33. *Decides* to examine the question further at its sixty-first session under the item entitled "Human rights questions".

Other forms of intolerance

Impact of intolerance

By a June note [E/CN.4/Sub.2/2005/31], the Secretariat informed the Subcommission that Soli

Sorabjee (India) had indicated that he would not be able to submit the working paper on the impact of intolerance on the enjoyment and exercise of human rights, which the Subcommission had requested in 2004 [YUN 2004, p. 702].

Cultural prejudice

Report of High Commissioner. In response to a 2004 Commission request [YUN 2004, p. 702], the High Commissioner submitted a report [E/CN.4/2005/40] summarizing replies received from one Government, one UN system agency and three NGOs on the appointment of a special rapporteur and on steps they had taken to promote the full enjoyment of cultural rights.

Commission action. By a recorded vote of 39 to 1, with 13 abstentions, the Commission, on 14 April [res. 2005/20], reaffirming that cultural rights were an integral part of human rights, recognized that States had the responsibility to promote the full enjoyment of cultural rights and to enhance respect for different cultural identities. The Commission called on States, intergovernmental organizations and NGOs to implement its resolution and asked the High Commissioner to consult with them on the possibility of establishing a thematic procedure, whose mandate would be the comprehensive implementation of the resolution, and to report in 2006.

Note by Secretary-General. Pursuant to General Assembly resolution 58/167 [YUN 2003, p. 710], the Secretary-General, in an 8 September note [A/60/340], informed the Assembly that no comments had been received from Member States, UN agencies and NGOs on the subject of human rights and cultural diversity. However, a more comprehensive report would be submitted on the issue, and in that connection, the Assembly should note that the Commission, in its resolution 2005/20 (see above), had requested the High Commissioner to consult States and intergovernmental organizations and NGOs on the scope of a mandate for an independent expert on the promotion and enjoyment of cultural rights, and to report thereon.

GENERAL ASSEMBLY ACTION

On 16 December [meeting 64], the General Assembly, on the recommendation of the Third Committee [A/60/509], adopted **resolution 60/167** without vote [agenda item 71 (b)].

Human rights and cultural diversity

The General Assembly,

Recalling the Universal Declaration of Human Rights, the International Covenant on Economic, Social and Cultural Rights and the International Covenant on Civil and Political Rights, as well as other pertinent human rights instruments,

Recalling also its resolutions 54/160 of 17 December 1999, 55/91 of 4 December 2000, 57/204 of 18 December 2002 and 58/167 of 22 December 2003, and recalling further its resolutions 54/113 of 10 December 1999, 55/23 of 13 November 2000 and 60/4 of 20 October 2005 concerning the United Nations Year of Dialogue among Civilizations,

Noting that numerous instruments within the United Nations system promote cultural diversity, as well as the conservation and development of culture, in particular the Declaration of the Principles of International Culture Cooperation proclaimed on 4 November 1966 by the General Conference of the United Nations Educational, Scientific and Cultural Organization at its fourteenth session,

Taking note of the note by the Secretary-General,

Welcoming the adoption of the Global Agenda for Dialogue among Civilizations by its resolution 56/6 of 9 November 2001,

Welcoming also the contribution of the World Conference against Racism, Racial Discrimination, Xenophobia and Related Intolerance, held at Durban, South Africa, from 31 August to 8 September 2001, to the promotion of respect for cultural diversity,

Welcoming further the Universal Declaration on Cultural Diversity of the United Nations Educational, Scientific and Cultural Organization, together with its Action Plan, adopted on 2 November 2001 by the General Conference of the United Nations Educational, Scientific and Cultural Organization at its thirty-first session, in which member States invited the United Nations system and other intergovernmental and nongovernmental organizations concerned to cooperate with the United Nations Educational, Scientific and Cultural Organization in the promotion of the principles set forth in the Declaration and its Action Plan with a view to enhancing the synergy of actions in favour of cultural diversity,

Reaffirming that all human rights are universal, indivisible, interdependent and interrelated and that the international community must treat human rights globally in a fair and equal manner, on the same footing and with the same emphasis, and that, while the significance of national and regional particularities and various historical, cultural and religious backgrounds must be borne in mind, it is the duty of States, regardless of their political, economic and cultural systems, to promote and protect all human rights and fundamental freedoms,

Recognizing that cultural diversity and the pursuit of cultural development by all peoples and nations are a source of mutual enrichment for the cultural life of humankind,

Taking into account that a culture of peace actively fosters non-violence and respect for human rights and strengthens solidarity among peoples and nations and dialogue between cultures,

Recognizing that all cultures and civilizations share a common set of universal values,

Recognizing also that the promotion of the rights of indigenous people and their cultures and traditions will contribute to the respect for and observance of cultural diversity among all peoples and nations,

Considering that tolerance of cultural, ethnic, religious and linguistic diversities, as well as dialogue among and within civilizations, is essential for peace, understanding and friendship among individuals and people of different cultures and nations of the world, while manifestations of cultural prejudice, intolerance and xenophobia towards different cultures and religions generate hatred and violence among peoples and nations throughout the world,

Recognizing in each culture a dignity and value that deserve recognition, respect and preservation, and convinced that, in their rich variety and diversity, and in the reciprocal influences that they exert on one another, all cultures form part of the common heritage belonging to all humankind,

Convinced that the promotion of cultural pluralism and tolerance towards and dialogue among various cultures and civilizations would contribute to the efforts of all peoples and nations to enrich their cultures and traditions by engaging in a mutually beneficial exchange of knowledge and intellectual, moral and material achievements,

Acknowledging the diversity of the world, recognizing that all cultures and civilizations contribute to the enrichment of humankind, acknowledging the importance of respect and understanding for religious and cultural diversity throughout the world, and, in order to promote international peace and security, committing itself to advancing human welfare, freedom and progress everywhere, as well as to encouraging tolerance, respect, dialogue and cooperation among different cultures, civilizations and peoples,

1. *Affirms* the importance for all peoples and nations to hold, develop and preserve their cultural heritage and traditions in a national and international atmosphere of peace, tolerance and mutual respect;

2. *Welcomes* the adoption on 8 September 2000 of the United Nations Millennium Declaration, in which Member States consider, inter alia, that tolerance is one of the fundamental values essential to international relations in the twenty-first century and that it should include the active promotion of a culture of peace and dialogue among civilizations, with human beings respecting one another in all their diversity of belief, culture and language, neither fearing nor repressing differences within and between societies but cherishing them as a precious asset of humanity;

3. *Recognizes* the right of everyone to take part in cultural life and to enjoy the benefits of scientific progress and its applications;

4. *Affirms* that the international community should strive to respond to the challenges and opportunities posed by globalization in a manner that ensures respect for the cultural diversity of all;

5. *Expresses its determination* to prevent and mitigate cultural homogenization in the context of globalization, through increased intercultural exchange guided by the promotion and protection of cultural diversity;

6. *Affirms* that intercultural dialogue essentially enriches the common understanding of human rights and that the benefits to be derived from the encouragement and development of international contacts and cooperation in the cultural fields are important;

7. *Welcomes* the recognition at the World Conference against Racism, Racial Discrimination, Xenophobia and Related Intolerance of the necessity of respecting and maximizing the benefits of diversity within and among all nations in working together to build a harmonious and productive future by putting into practice and promoting values and principles such as justice, equality and non-discrimination, democracy, fairness and friendship, tolerance and respect within and among communities and nations, in particular through public information and educational programmes to raise awareness and understanding of the benefits of cultural diversity, including programmes in which the public authorities work in partnership with international and non-governmental organizations and other sectors of civil society;

8. *Recognizes* that respect for cultural diversity and the cultural rights of all enhances cultural pluralism, contributing to a wider exchange of knowledge and understanding of cultural background, advancing the application and enjoyment of universally accepted human rights throughout the world and fostering stable, friendly relations among peoples and nations worldwide;

9. *Emphasizes* that the promotion of cultural pluralism and tolerance at the national, regional and international levels is important for enhancing respect for cultural rights and cultural diversity;

10. *Also emphasizes* that tolerance and respect for diversity facilitate the universal promotion and protection of human rights, including gender equality and the enjoyment of all human rights by all, and underlines the fact that tolerance and respect for cultural diversity and the universal promotion and protection of human rights are mutually supportive;

11. *Urges* all actors on the international scene to build an international order based on inclusion, justice, equality and equity, human dignity, mutual understanding and promotion of and respect for cultural diversity and universal human rights, and to reject all doctrines of exclusion based on racism, racial discrimination, xenophobia and related intolerance;

12. *Urges* States to ensure that their political and legal systems reflect the multicultural diversity within their societies and, where necessary, to improve democratic institutions so that they are more fully participatory and avoid marginalization and exclusion of, and discrimination against, specific sectors of society;

13. *Calls upon* States, international organizations and United Nations agencies, and invites civil society, including non-governmental organizations, to recognize and promote respect for cultural diversity for the purpose of advancing the objectives of peace, development and universally accepted human rights;

14. *Requests* the Secretary-General, in the light of the present resolution, to prepare a report on human rights and cultural diversity, taking into account the views of Member States, relevant United Nations agencies and non-governmental organizations, as well as the considerations in the present resolution regarding the recognition and importance of cultural diversity among all peoples and nations in the world, and to submit the report to the General Assembly at its sixty-second session;

15. *Requests* the Office of the United Nations High Commissioner for Human Rights to continue to bear in mind fully the issues raised in the present resolution in the course of its activities for the promotion and protection of human rights;

16. *Decides* to continue consideration of the question at its sixty-second session under the sub-item entitled "Human rights questions, including alternative approaches for improving the effective enjoyment of human rights and fundamental freedoms".

Discrimination against minorities

Report of High Commissioner. In response to a 2004 Commission request [YUN 2004, p. 702], the High Commissioner submitted a March report [E/CN.4/2005/81] on the study of options for the timely identification of minority issues and related measures. The report summarized information presented by Governments and NGOs on the subject, the views contained in the High Commissioner's 2004 report to the Commission [YUN 2004, p. 702], recent developments with respect to minority issues and an analysis of the options for the timely identification of minority issues, which involved a review of the work of existing human rights bodies and mechanisms dealing with them. The report noted that minorities faced specific and often grave human rights violations that could lead to political instability and conflict, and that the root causes of their problems were often linked to discrimination against them, the non-recognition of aspects of their identity and the denial of their effective participation in decisions affecting them. Thus, significant gaps existed in the protection of minority rights and the United Nations needed to strengthen its capacity to tackle the problem. Those gaps were particularly visible in the context of timely identification and swift or urgent action, and it was encouraging that States and other actors had expressed interest in considering modalities to address the situation. It was also auspicious that human rights mechanisms currently concerned with minority issues possessed a considerable potential to tackle, in a timely fashion, the problems faced by minorities. However, to fully utilize them required that they be strengthened significantly in terms of time and resources. The report also reflected on the varied proposals made by the Subcommission and its Working Group on Minorities (see below) for strengthening minority protection, including through the establishment of a special procedure and an international year of the world's minorities.

Commission action. On 21 April [res. 2005/79], the Commission urged States to promote and protect the rights of persons belonging to national or ethnic, religious and linguistic minorities, give special attention to protecting their children's rights and take measures to protect their cultural and religious sites. The High Commis-

sioner was requested to appoint an independent expert on minority issues for a period of two years, with the mandate to promote the implementation of the Declaration on the Rights of Persons Belonging to National or Ethnic, Religious and Linguistic Minorities, adopted by the General Assembly in resolution 47/135 [YUN 1992, p. 722]; identify best practices and possibilities for technical cooperation at the request of Governments; apply a gender perspective in his or her work; cooperate closely, while avoiding duplication, with UN bodies, mandates, mechanisms and regional organizations; and to take into account the views of NGOs on matters pertaining to the mandate. The Commission requested that the expert report to it annually on his or her activities, including recommendations for effective strategies for better implementation of minorities' rights. In the light of its current resolution, the Commission decided to amend the mandate of the Working Group on Minorities of the Subcommission (see below) to allow it to hold one annual session of three consecutive working days, focusing its work on interactive dialogue with NGOs and support for the independent expert, who would participate as an observer. The High Commissioner was asked to provide the expert with the necessary resources for the effective fulfilment of the mandate, review the mechanisms' performance and effectiveness after two years and report thereon in 2007.

On 25 July (**decision 2005/278**), the Economic and Social Council endorsed the Commission's requests to the High Commissioner to appoint an independent expert; to the Secretary-General to provide him with the resources for fulfilling the mandate; and to the expert to submit annual reports. The Council further endorsed the Commission's decision to amend the mandate of the Subcommission's Working Group on Minorities.

Also in July, the Commission appointed Gay McDougall (United States) as the independent expert on minority issues.

Working Group activities. The five-member Working Group on Minorities, at its eleventh session (Geneva, 30 May–3 June) [E/CN.4/Sub.2/2005/27], reviewed the promotion of the 1992 Declaration, examined possible solutions to problems involving minorities, including the promotion of mutual understanding between and among minorities and Governments, and recommended further measures to promote and protect minority rights. The Group also discussed its future role.

The Group had before it working papers on minorities and self-determination [E/CN.4/Sub.2/AC.5/2005/WP.1], international and national actions for the protection of the rights of minorities: the role of the Working Group [E/CN.4/ Sub.2/AC.5/2004/WP.3], the Millennium Development Goals: helping or harming minorities [E/CN.4/Sub.2/AC.5/2005/WP.4], and towards a general comment on self-determination and autonomy [E/CN.4/Sub.2/AC.5/2005/WP.5]. It also considered a commentary on the 1992 Declaration, prepared by Asbjrrn Eide (Norway) and presented on behalf of the Group as a whole [E/CN.4/ Sub.2/AC.5/2005/2]; a report of the African Commission on Human and Peoples' Rights Working Group of Experts on Indigenous Populations/ Communities [E/CN.4/Sub.2/AC.5/2005/WP.3]; reports of the 2004 Sub-Regional Seminars on Minority Rights in Central and South Asia [YUN 2004, p. 705]; and a document on minorities and the work of national human rights institutions [E/CN.4/Sub.2/AC.5/2005/3].

In its decisions and recommendations, the Group decided to include in the agenda of its 2006 session an item on the promotion and practical realization of the 1992 Declaration and solutions to problems involving minorities, including conflict prevention and resolution. Thematic issues proposed for discussion in 2006 included the question of mainstreaming minorities' rights into the MDGs, particularly the goal on eradicating extreme poverty by 2015, and cooperation with the independent expert on minority issues and UN organizations. The Group encouraged further regional and subregional meetings, in cooperation with regional mechanisms, and recommended that training on the use of UN human rights mechanisms be held in conjunction with those meetings. It also recommended that a seminar on the Roma be organized, in cooperation with the Council of Europe, to which Roma representatives from non-European countries should be invited. It invited NGOs and academic institutions to present studies on the promotion and protection of the rights of specific minorities, including Pastoralists, Afro-descendants and Fisherfolk. The Group decided to forward the statements made by minority representatives and NGOs at its current session to the Governments concerned and invited them to share their response with the Group, with a view to promoting dialogue between and among minorities and Governments. Minorities and related organizations were invited to prepare further submissions prior to the Group's next session, and to describe their areas of concern, the main problems in meeting those concerns and suggestions on effective remedies. United Nations system bodies were also invited to present information on their contribution to the full realization of the rights and principles set forth in the 1992 Declaration. The Group recommended that the Sub-

commission support a study on the utility and advisability of an international convention on the rights of minorities and addressed recommendations to Governments on the need to protect the rights of minorities residing within their territory, provide effective and easily accessible remedies to redress violations against them, and bring to justice those responsible for such violations. In that context, the Group emphasized the importance of establishing a voluntary fund to support the participation of minority representatives in its meetings, especially those from developing countries, and recommended that OHCHR continue to organize training on universal and regional standards and mechanisms, in order to strengthen minority representatives' cooperation with human rights procedures. It should, in addition, continue the Minority Fellowship Programme, first organized during the Group's current session, as well as the further preparation of a minority profile and matrix and the update and preparation of other pamphlets, for inclusion in the United Nations Guide for Minorities. The Group asked OHCHR to re-issue the publication entitled *Human Rights: A Basic Handbook for UN Staff* and make it available to minority representatives in order to promote awareness among them of the UN human rights programme, and to ensure that minority issues were mainstreamed into the work of its human rights-based approaches to development, particularly through the proposed task force on the MDGs. The Group's other recommendations for safeguarding minorities' rights were addressed to regional, national and international development agencies and UN system bodies, including peacekeeping and peacebuilding operations and humanitarian organizations.

Subcommission action. On 10 August [res. 2005/18], the Subcommission asked the Commission to request the Economic and Social Council to authorize the Working Group to meet for five working days prior to the Subcommission's 2006 session and subsequent sessions. It instructed the Group to continue efforts to identify, study and analyse problems faced by minorities and to encourage dialogue concerning those problems.

Report of Secretary-General. In response to General Assembly resolution 58/182 [YUN 2003, p. 714], the Secretary-General submitted a 6 September report [A/60/333] on the effective promotion of the 1992 Declaration. The report described efforts by the United Nations and its bodies to assist Governments in finding the expertise for addressing minority issues, including through the newly appointed independent expert on minority issues (see p. 774). It also analysed the involvement of relevant international actors and participation of NGOs and persons belonging to minorities in minority-related activities, and identified good practices in the field of education on minority questions, including the issue of instruction in minority languages and the content of the curriculum. The report concluded that there was a growing recognition that the promotion and protection of minorities' rights were integral to the process of strengthening the political and social stability of States and to development within a democratic framework based on the rule of law. It was, therefore, essential for programmes and projects implemented by the United Nations at the country level to include minority-related issues. Mainstreaming minorities' rights into the work of the United Nations in peace and security and development could significantly enrich that task and enhance its impact, and the 1992 Declaration should guide the process. It was vital to involve minorities in the work of the Organization at the international and national levels and OHCHR and other UN agencies and programmes should continue to develop training tools and information materials towards that end. They should also facilitate the participation of minorities in seminars, workshops and training sessions, and assist in building the relative capacities of Governments and civil society. The voluntary fund for minority activities, proposed by the Commission in 2004 [YUN 2004, p. 703], might be an important instrument in that regard.

Workshop. In efforts to help resolve and prevent conflicts affecting minorities, strengthen the human rights perspective of recommendations in related work and support initiatives to increase civil society participation in the work of the United Nations, OHCHR organized a workshop on minorities and conflict prevention and resolution (26-27 May) [E/CN.4/Sub.2/AC.5/2006/2], aimed at providing minority participants an opportunity to make observations on the issue. Participants addressed, among other subjects, the root causes of conflict from the perspective of minorities and identified opportunities for their participation in the work of the United Nations and for action by the Organization and Member States to protect them. They adopted concluding observations on those topics and made recommendations concerning the development of a minority profile and matrix for use by the Working Group on Minorities, the independent expert and other UN bodies and mechanisms in identifying the causes of conflicts and assisting in early warning, prevention and resolution initiatives. A number of other recommendations advocated related conflict prevention initiatives.

GENERAL ASSEMBLY ACTION

On 16 December [meeting 64], the General Assembly, on the recommendation of the Third Committee [A/60/509], adopted **resolution 60/160** without vote [agenda item 71 *(b)*].

Effective promotion of the Declaration on the Rights of Persons Belonging to National or Ethnic, Religious and Linguistic Minorities

The General Assembly,

Recalling its resolution 47/135 of 18 December 1992, as well as its subsequent resolutions on the Declaration on the Rights of Persons Belonging to National or Ethnic, Religious and Linguistic Minorities,

Noting that the promotion and protection of the rights of persons belonging to national or ethnic, religious and linguistic minorities contributes to political and social stability and peace and enriches the cultural diversity and heritage of society, as reaffirmed in the 2005 World Summit Outcome,

Concerned by the frequency and severity of disputes and conflicts concerning minorities and their often tragic consequences, and concerned also that persons belonging to minorities are particularly vulnerable to displacement,

Recognizing that the effective promotion and protection of the rights of persons belonging to minorities is a fundamental part of the promotion and protection of human rights, and acknowledging that measures in this area can also contribute significantly to conflict prevention,

Emphasizing the role that national institutions can play in early warning for problems regarding minority situations,

Emphasizing also the importance of human rights education as an effective tool to promote an inclusive society and understanding of and tolerance towards and among persons belonging to minorities,

Acknowledging that the United Nations has an important role to play regarding the protection of minorities by, inter alia, taking due account of and giving effect to the Declaration,

Noting that the Working Group on Minorities of the Subcommission on the Promotion and Protection of Human Rights held its tenth and eleventh sessions from 1 to 5 March 2004 and from 30 May to 3 June 2005, respectively,

Noting with appreciation the appointment of the independent expert on minority issues by the United Nations High Commissioner for Human Rights on 29 July 2005, as requested by the Commission on Human Rights in its resolution 2005/79 of 21 April 2005,

1. *Takes note* of the report of the Secretary-General;

2. *Recognizes* that respect for human rights and the promotion of understanding and tolerance by Governments as well as between and among minorities are central to the promotion and protection of the rights of persons belonging to minorities;

3. *Reaffirms* the obligation of States to ensure that persons belonging to minorities may exercise fully and effectively all human rights and fundamental freedoms without any discrimination and in full equality before the law, as proclaimed in the Declaration on the Rights of Persons Belonging to National or Ethnic, Religious and Linguistic Minorities, and draws attention to the relevant provisions of the Durban Declaration

and Programme of Action, including the provisions on forms of multiple discrimination;

4. *Encourages* States, in their follow-up to the World Conference against Racism, Racial Discrimination, Xenophobia and Related Intolerance, to include aspects relating to minorities in their national plans of action and, in this context, to take forms of multiple discrimination fully into account;

5. *Urges* States and the international community to promote and protect the rights of persons belonging to national or ethnic, religious and linguistic minorities, as set out in the Declaration, including through the encouragement of conditions for the promotion of their identity, the provision of adequate education and the facilitation of their participation in all aspects of the political, economic, social, religious and cultural life of society and in the economic progress and development of their country, without discrimination, and to apply a gender perspective while doing so;

6. *Calls upon* States to give special attention to the promotion and protection of the human rights of children belonging to minorities, taking into account that girls and boys may face different types of risks;

7. *Urges* States to take, as appropriate, all necessary constitutional, legislative, administrative and other measures to promote and give effect to the Declaration, and appeals to States to cooperate bilaterally and multilaterally, in accordance with the Declaration, in order to promote and protect the rights of persons belonging to national or ethnic, religious and linguistic minorities;

8. *Calls upon* States to take all appropriate measures to protect the cultural and religious sites of national or ethnic, religious and linguistic minorities;

9. *Calls upon* the Secretary-General to make available, at the request of Governments concerned, qualified expertise on minority issues, including the prevention and resolution of disputes, to assist in existing or potential situations involving minorities;

10. *Calls upon* the United Nations High Commissioner for Human Rights to promote, within her mandate, the implementation of the Declaration, to continue to engage in a dialogue with Governments for that purpose and to disseminate widely the *United Nations Guide for Minorities*;

11. *Requests* the High Commissioner to continue her efforts to improve the coordination and cooperation among United Nations programmes and agencies on activities related to the promotion and protection of the rights of persons belonging to minorities and to take the work of relevant regional organizations active in the field of human rights into account in her endeavours;

12. *Welcomes* the inter-agency consultation of the High Commissioner with United Nations programmes and agencies on minority issues, and calls upon those programmes and agencies to contribute actively to this process;

13. *Encourages* intergovernmental and nongovernmental organizations to continue to contribute to the promotion and protection of the rights of persons belonging to national or ethnic, religious and linguistic minorities;

14. *Calls upon* the Working Group on Minorities of the Subcommission on the Promotion and Protection of Human Rights to implement fully its mandate, focusing its work on interactive dialogue with relevant non-governmental organizations and on conceptual support of, and dialogue with, the independent expert on minority issues, by recommending, on the basis of its findings, further measures for the promotion and protection of the rights of persons belonging to national or ethnic, religious and linguistic minorities;

15. *Invites* the High Commissioner to seek voluntary contributions to facilitate the effective participation of representatives of non-governmental organizations and persons belonging to minorities, in particular those from developing countries, in minority-related activities organized by the United Nations, particularly its human rights bodies, and in doing so to give particular attention to ensuring the participation of young people and women;

16. *Decides* to continue consideration of the question at its sixty-second session under the item entitled "Human rights questions".

Leprosy victims

Note by Secretariat. By a 15 July note [E/CN.4/Sub.2/2005/29], the Secretariat informed the Subcommission that, owing to the late submission of the working paper on discrimination against leprosy victims and their families (see below), which it had requested in 2004 [YUN 2004, p. 705], the paper had been issued only in the language of submission.

Working paper. In response to a 2004 Subcommission request [ibid.], Yozo Yokota (Japan) submitted a 14 July preliminary working paper on discrimination against leprosy victims and their families [E/CN.4/Sub.2/2005/WP.1]. The paper considered the nature of the disease and its human rights dimension and presented case studies of countries where significant improvements had been made in treating leprosy patients and in overcoming related discrimination. The paper also gave an overview of important international conferences on leprosy-related discrimination. It concluded that, although leprosy was curable and modern medical science had proven that it was not transmitted to most people in ordinary human contact, discrimination had persisted against patients and their families owing to the lack of knowledge and mistaken ideas about the disease. Against that background, the forced institutionalization of the victims, often adopted by many countries, was a serious violation of basic human rights and fundamental freedoms, as well as the dignity and security of the person. The report recommended that Governments abolish legislation that required such institutionalization and provide instead, effective, prompt and free treatment and appropriate remedies to those affected. Discrimination of any kind against them should be prohibited and leprosy education included in school curricula to give correct information about the disease and the need to prevent discrimination against afflicted persons. The Subcommission should request the Commission to appoint a Special Rapporteur on leprosy and human rights to facilitate information gathering from Governments, UN bodies and NGOs. Regional seminars should be organized to hear the views and experiences of patients and their families, as well as doctors, social workers, experts, NGOs and Government officials. Efforts should also be made to include an element of effective leprosy education in formulating and implementing the first phase of the World Programme for Human Rights Education (see p. 745).

Subcommission action. On 11 August [res. 2005/24], the Subcommission, welcoming the preliminary working paper on discrimination against leprosy victims, endorsed the conclusions and recommendations contained therein, and the proposal to organize regional seminars on the topic. It decided to appoint Mr. Yokota as Special Rapporteur to prepare a comprehensive study on discrimination against leprosy victims and their families and requested him to enter into dialogue with relevant entities and to submit a preliminary report in 2006, a progress report in 2007 and a final report in 2008.

Discrimination based on work and descent

Commission action. On 19 April [dec. 2005/109], the Commission approved a 2004 decision of the Subcommission [YUN 2004, p. 705] to appoint Yozo Yokota (Japan) and Chin-Sung Chung (Republic of Korea) as Special Rapporteurs on discrimination based on work and descent, with the task of preparing a comprehensive study on the subject, on the basis of three working papers submitted to the Subcommission in 2001 [YUN 2001, p. 625], 2003 [YUN 2003, p. 715] and 2004 [YUN 2004, p. 705]. The Commission also approved the Subcommission's request to the Special Rapporteurs to submit a preliminary report in 2005, a progress report in 2006 and a final report in 2007, and to the Secretary-General and High Commissioner to assist them.

On 25 July, the Economic and Social Council endorsed the Commission's decision to appoint the Special Rapporteurs and approved its requests to them to submit reports (**decision 2005/288**).

Report of Special Rapporteurs. In response to a 2004 Subcommission request [YUN 2004, p. 705], the Special Rapporteurs on discrimination based on work and descent, Yozo Yokota and Chin-Sung Chung, submitted a preliminary report [E/CN.4/Sub.2/2005/30] focusing on the elaboration of a questionnaire to Governments, national human rights institutions, NGOs and UN organs and agencies, for the purpose of identifying best practices and to gather comprehensive information regarding constitutional, legislative, judicial, administrative and educational measures taken to address discrimination based on work and descent. The Special Rapporteurs recommended that the Subcommission approve the questionnaire, which was annexed to the report, and that it endorse the proposal to hold in 2006 a general consultation and two regional workshops in Asia and Africa.

Subcommission action. On 11 August [res. 2005/22], the Subcommission approved the Special Rapporteurs' proposal to send the questionnaire to Governments, national human rights institutions, relevant UN bodies and specialized agencies and NGOs, and requested recipients to respond in a timely and constructive manner. It also endorsed their proposal to hold a general consultation in Geneva in 2006 and to organize two regional workshops. The Subcommission asked the Special Rapporteurs to reflect the results of the questionnaire, the consultation and workshops in the progress report to be submitted in 2006, and to continue drafting the principles and guidelines for the effective elimination of discrimination based on work and descent. The Secretary-General and the High Commissioner were requested to assist them.

Non-discrimination

Commission action. On 15 April [dec. 2005/105], the Commission approved a 2004 decision of the Subcommission [YUN 2004, p. 706] to appoint Marc Bossuyt (Belgium) as Special Rapporteur on non-discrimination as enshrined in article 2, paragraph 2, of the International Covenant on Economic, Social and Cultural Rights, adopted by the General Assembly in resolution 2200 A (XXI) [YUN 1966, p. 419]. It also approved the request that he submit a preliminary report in 2005, a progress report in 2006 and a final report in 2007, and the request to the Secretary-General to assist him.

By **decision 2005/284** of 25 July, the Economic and Social Council endorsed the Commission's decision to appoint Marc Bossuyt as the Special Rapporteur and its request that Mr. Bossuyt submit reports. The Council also approved the Commission's request to the Secretary-General to assist him.

Report of Special Rapporteur. The Special Rapporteur on non-discrimination as enshrined in article 2, paragraph 2 of the International Covenant on Economic, Social and Cultural Rights, Marc Bossuyt, submitted a June preliminary report [E/CN.4/Sub.2/2005/19 & Corr.1, 2] on the topic.

The report reviewed academic writings on the nature of economic, social and cultural rights, distinguishing between rights that required no action by the State and those that required active State intervention. The report noted that, although the mechanisms for implementing those rights and obligations differed, both categories of rights were equally important, and that the lack of respect for any right had a detrimental effect on other rights. The rights contained in the International Covenant on Economic, Social and Cultural Rights, such as the right to education and the freedom of education, contained elements of both sets of rights. However, while the prohibition on discrimination was applicable to all human rights, it had more far-reaching effects regarding rights that carried positive obligations. The progress and final reports of the Special Rapporteur would consider the elements that would allow the determination of a violation of the prohibition on discrimination with respect to economic, social and cultural rights.

Subcommission action. On 8 August [res. 2005/7], the Subcommission asked the Special Rapporteur to submit an interim report in 2006 and a final report in 2007, and the Secretary-General to assist him.

Religious intolerance

Report of Special Rapporteur. In her first annual report to the Commission [E/CN.4/2005/61 & Corr.1], the Special Rapporteur on freedom of religion and belief, Asma Jahangir (Pakistan), reviewed her activities, analysed particular situations involving violations of the freedom of religion and provided observations on a number of relevant issues. Noting that the twenty-first century posed new challenges for her mandate, such as the use of religious beliefs for political purposes and the increasing negative stereotyping of some religions, the Special Rapporteur undertook activities pertaining to the principles of protection and prevention, which played a crucial role in challenging religious intolerance. Most of the violations she addressed also infringed on other human rights, including the rights to life, not to be subjected to torture and other inhuman or degrading treatment or punishment, to liberty and security of the person, to freedom of movement and association, and to freedom of opinion and expression. Other violations occurred within the context of interreligious violence, the issue of forced conversion, attacks and restrictions against places of worship, religious buildings and property, and the banning of religious publications. The Special Rapporteur also considered a number of other issues relevant to her mandate,

including the procedure for the registration of religious communities, anti-terrorism legislation, the categorization of religions, religious symbols, and the relationship between the freedoms of religion and of expression. She concluded that a large number of people worldwide suffered limitations to their right to the freedom of religion or belief, and that the September 2001 terrorist attacks in the United States [YUN 2001, p. 60] continued to have a dramatic impact in that regard. Of particular concern was that States continued to adopt legislation and measures establishing a confusing and misleading link between certain religions and terrorism, which affected those whose religion or belief was targeted. Also of major concern was the widely applied practice of forced conversions, mostly by non-State actors, which, the Special Rapporteur observed, breached the most fundamental part of freedom of religion. She stressed, in that context, that States had an obligation to protect and remedy the situation of those who had suffered religious intolerance and to bring perpetrators to justice. Governments needed to pay more attention to protecting religious sites, buildings and shrines from increasing acts of desecration by non-State actors.

In a March addendum [E/CN.4/2005/61/Add.1] to the report, the Special Rapporteur summarized 69 communications she had sent to 42 States and the replies received from 28 of them, regarding violations and governmental action that was inconsistent with the provisions of the 1981 Declaration on the Elimination of All Forms of Intolerance and of Discrimination based on Religion or Belief, adopted in General Assembly resolution 36/55 [YUN 1981, p. 881].

Report of High Commissioner. In response to a 2004 Commission request [YUN 2004, p. 706], the High Commissioner submitted a February report [E/CN.4/2005/15] summarizing the activities undertaken by the United Nations, intergovernmental bodies, human rights mechanisms, specialized agencies and programmes, including OHCHR, to support intercultural dialogue, respect and tolerance. The High Commissioner noted that, although many steps had been taken to counter religious intolerance, which she described as one of the basic evils of history, there were increasing and serious instances of discrimination on the grounds of religion or belief, and defamation of religions was one of its most aggressive manifestations. Further efforts needed to be made to counter the problem by strategizing and harmonizing action at the local, country, regional and international levels, and education systems and awareness-raising should play a decisive role in such strategies. Fostering a culture of respect should also be accompanied by adequate legislative and administrative measures to specifically counter discrimination and intolerance in all spheres of life.

Commission action. On 12 April [res. 2005/3], the Commission, by a recorded vote of 31 to 16, with 5 abstentions, called on the High Commissioner to promote and include human rights aspects in the dialogue among civilizations, by integrating them into topical seminars and special debates on the positive contributions of cultures and religious and cultural diversity, to hold joint conferences with other international organizations to promote understanding of the universality of human rights and their implementation, and to report in 2006.

On 19 April [res. 2005/40], the Commission urged States to guarantee freedom of thought, conscience, religion and belief and to combat hatred, intolerance and acts of violence based on religion or belief, particularly with regard to religious minorities. It stressed the need for international and regional organizations, as well as civil society groups and relevant parts of the UN system, to strengthen dialogue by revitalizing the Global Agenda for Dialogue among Civilizations, proclaimed by the General Assembly in resolution 56/6 [YUN 2001, p. 1014], and asked the Special Rapporteur to report to the General Assembly in 2005 and to the Commission in 2006.

Further reports of Special Rapporteur. At the invitation of the Government, the Special Rapporteur visited Nigeria (27 February–7 March) [E/CN.4/2006/5/Add.2, E/CN.4/2005/61/Add.2], where pre-existing tensions and lack of understanding between the predominant Muslim and Christian populations had flared up yet again. In particular, the adoption in parts of northern Nigeria of criminal law based on sharia codes (Muslim law governing acts of worship and human interaction, which prescribed punishments for offences pronounced therein, including a mandatory death penalty for extra-marital relations and rape, among other crimes) had provoked negative reactions from non-Muslim communities. Although only Muslims were subject to the sharia penal codes, many Christians and Muslims had complained that the interpretation and/or method of implementing those codes were either not acceptable or violated their right to freedom of religion or belief. A major concern in that regard was the climate of fear created by the associated religious tensions and violence, to which thousands of Nigerians had lost their lives in recent years. While economic, political and other factors had contributed to such tension, the consequent polarization often manifested along religious lines. An especially alarming development in the implementation of the sharia system was

the institutionalization of enforcement bodies known as Hisbah, composed of young, untrained Muslim civilians charged with enforcing the principles of Islam and whose activities had resulted in violent and arbitrary human rights violations against non-Muslim women. Other violations were being perpetrated by non-State actors or as a result of the lack of appropriate Government measures to protect the people. Against that background, the Special Rapporteur determined that the level of enjoyment of the right to freedom of religion or belief in Nigeria was not satisfactory and recommended that the Government adopt a more careful approach in supporting any religious community in the country, refrain from interfering with religious matters that did not endanger human rights, act firmly whenever human rights violations were religion-related, and further strengthen inter-religious dialogue. Regarding the sharia penal codes, the Government should respect international human rights instruments to which it was party, end the practice of Hisbah and ensure that the citizens enjoyed freedom of religion and of expression, by allowing them to express dissent within their religion, without fear of retaliation or threat. To better tackle religious tensions and communal violence, the Government should strengthen early warning mechanisms, protect religious groups that might be targeted and ensure that justice was dispensed promptly and properly.

In Sri Lanka (2-12 May) [E/CN.4/2006/5/Add.3], the Special Rapporteur examined the situation of freedom of religion or belief in the light of reports of attacks against certain religious groups, acts of unethical conversions and the introduction of draft laws criminalizing those acts. She found that, although the Government respected freedom of religion or belief, religious tolerance and harmony among religious groups in the country had declined, and the greatest tension existed between the Buddhist community and certain Christian groups there. Of particular concern was the alleged proselytising behaviour of some Christians groups, often referred to as fundamentalists, who appeared in the country in recent decades and whose reportedly unethical attempts to convert other faiths within the country, mostly the Buddhists and members of the Hindu community, had been described as unwelcome interference and a new form of colonialism. Reports reaching the Special Rapporteur alleged that the fundamentalist groups influenced people into changing religions by promising such material benefits as food, medicine, bicycles, housing, or assistance with securing a job, which many Sri Lankans considered an abuse or manipulation of the most vulnerable sections of the population. The phenomenon became more prominent within the context of the humanitarian activities of some foreign NGOs, following the December 2004 tsunami [YUN 2004, p. 952]. The resulting tension and related violence, including the destruction or desecration of religious symbols, encouraged the adoption of a draft legislation criminalizing unethical conversions. Against that background, the Special Rapporteur, while acknowledging periods of a high level of religious harmony in Sri Lanka, concluded that the deterioration in recent years of religious tolerance in the country and the lack of appropriate Government action had brought respect for freedom of religion or belief to an unsatisfactory level. She recommended that the Government effectively combat the persecution of religious minorities by investigating all acts of violence or religious intolerance and ensuring prompt justice and appropriate compensation to the victims. Rather than going ahead with its draft legislation against unethical conversion, which was incompatible with human rights law, the Government should implement existing criminal legal provisions that could appropriately address the behaviour of religious groups and organizations. It should, in addition, consider mechanisms to enable it to better deal with religious tension, including seeking the assistance of UN agencies and civil society in exploring possible models for the creation of an interreligious body that could help diffuse such tension.

In France (18-29 September) [E/CN.4/2006/5/Add.4], the Special Rapporteur focused on a 2004 legislation prohibiting the wearing of conspicuous religious symbols in public schools and on the situation of cult groups and certain religious movements or communities (*sectes*). While noting the country's recognition of the principle of the separation of Church and State and the Government's respect for the right to freedom of religion or belief, a number of concerns remained, including the selective interpretation in some circumstances of that principle, which undermined the freedom of religion. Regarding the law against the wearing of conspicuous religious symbols, which was supported by the authorities and the population, and which was intended to apply to all persons, the Special Rapporteur found that certain religious minorities, notably Muslims, were mainly affected. The law was appropriate insofar as it was intended, in accordance with the principle of the best interest of the child, to protect the autonomy of minors who might be pressured or forced to wear a headscarf or other religious symbols. However, the law denied the right of those minors who had freely chosen to wear a religious symbol to school as part of their religious belief. In a number of cases, the implementation of the law by educational institutions had led to abuses and humiliation of young Muslim women especially. Considering the situation of cult groups, which were allegedly responsible for a variety of serious human rights violations, including the infringement of physical integrity, sequestration, failure to assist a person in danger or exposed to illegal medical practices, defamation and violations of labour or social law, the Special Rapporteur determined that the policy and measures adopted by the authorities to deal with the problem had provoked situations that curtailed the right to freedom of religion or belief of members of those groups. The Special Rapporteur recommended a flexible implementation of the law banning the wearing of conspicuous religious symbols, in order to accommodate school children for whom the display of such symbols constituted an essential part of their faith. The Government should promptly provide redress for victims of discrimination or other act of religious intolerance, owing to their religious symbols, and ensure that its mechanisms for dealing with cult groups and related religious communities delivered a message based on tolerance, freedom of religion or belief and due process. Additional recommendations addressed acts of religious intolerance against the Jewish community in France and the freedom of religion or belief of persons deprived of their liberties.

By a September note [A/60/399], the Secretary-General transmitted to the General Assembly a report of the Special Rapporteur, which highlighted aspects of her mandate, updated information on the status of communications sent to Governments over the past year and drew attention to the importance of cooperation between the Commission's special procedures and of the preventative and early warning aspects of the mandate. Of particular concern to the Special Rapporteur was the unsatisfactory level of cooperation she received from States during in situ visits, and encouraged the creation of a mechanism to deal more systematically with countries that fell within that category. Other issues of concern related to the right to choose, change or maintain a religion and the freedom of religion or belief of persons deprived of their liberty. Stressing that the right to adopt a religion of one's choice was a core element of the freedom of religion and should not be limited in any way, the Special Rapporteur stated that States had an obligation to protect that right, especially when threatened by non-State actors. She also recommended that freedom of religion receive more emphasis in the training of the personnel of detention facilities and other places where people were deprived of their liberty.

On 16 December, the Assembly took note of the Special Rapporteur's report (**decision 60/533**).

GENERAL ASSEMBLY ACTION

On 16 December [meeting 64], the General Assembly, on the recommendation of the Third Committee [A/60/509], adopted **resolution 60/150** by recorded vote (101-53-20) [agenda item 71 (*b*)].

Combating defamation of religions

The General Assembly,

Recalling that all States have pledged themselves, under the Charter of the United Nations, to promote and encourage universal respect for and observance of human rights and fundamental freedoms for all without distinction as to race, sex, language or religion,

Recalling also the relevant resolutions of the Commission on Human Rights in this regard,

Recalling further the United Nations Millennium Declaration adopted by the General Assembly on 8 September 2000, welcoming the resolve expressed in the Millennium Declaration to take measures to eliminate the increasing acts of racism and xenophobia in many societies and to promote greater harmony and tolerance in all societies, and looking forward to its effective implementation at all levels, including in the context of the Durban Declaration and Programme of Action adopted by the World Conference against Racism, Racial Discrimination, Xenophobia and Related Intolerance, held in Durban, South Africa, from 31 August to 8 September 2001,

Recalling the proclamation of the Global Agenda for Dialogue among Civilizations, and inviting States, the organizations and bodies of the United Nations system, within existing resources, other international and regional organizations and civil societies to contribute to the implementation of the Programme of Action contained in the Global Agenda,

Welcoming the progress achieved in the follow-up to the Durban Declaration and Programme of Action,

Noting with regret the cancellation of the meeting on the theme "Civilization and harmony: values and mechanisms of the global order", which was to be held in Istanbul, Turkey, in 2004 as a follow-up to the Organization of the Islamic Conference-European Union joint forum on the theme "Civilization and harmony: the political dimension", held in Istanbul on 12 and 13 February 2002, and underscoring the fact that such initiatives to deepen dialogue and reinforce understanding between the two biggest groups of nations of Eurasia and Africa will be continued,

Reaffirming that discrimination against human beings on the grounds of religion or belief constitutes an affront to human dignity and a disavowal of the principles of the Charter,

Convinced that religious and cultural diversity in a globalizing world needs to be used as a vehicle for creativity, dynamism and the promotion of social justice, tolerance and understanding, as well as international peace and security, and not as a rationale for a new ideological and political confrontation,

Recognizing the valuable contributions of all religions to modern civilization and the contribution that dialogue among civilizations can make to an improved awareness and understanding of the common values shared by all humankind,

Reaffirming that cultural diversity is a cherished asset for the advancement and welfare of humanity at large and should be valued, enjoyed, genuinely accepted and embraced as a permanent feature that enriches our societies,

Emphasizing that States, non-governmental organizations, religious bodies and the media have an important role to play in promoting tolerance and freedom of religion and belief, in particular through education that teaches tolerance and respect for religion and belief,

Alarmed at the continuing negative impact of the events of 11 September 2001 on Muslim minorities and communities in some non-Muslim countries, the negative projection of Islam in the media and the introduction and enforcement of laws that specifically discriminate against and target Muslims,

Alarmed also at the serious instances of intolerance, discrimination and acts of violence based on religion or belief, intimidation and coercion motivated by extremism, religious or otherwise, occurring in many parts of the world and threatening the enjoyment of human rights and fundamental freedoms,

Noting with concern that defamation of religions is among the causes of social disharmony and leads to violations of human rights,

Noting with deep concern the increasing trend in recent years of statements attacking religions, Islam and Muslims in particular, especially in human rights forums,

1. *Expresses deep concern* at the negative stereotyping of religions and manifestations of intolerance and discrimination in matters of religion or belief still in evidence in some regions of the world;

2. *Strongly deplores* physical attacks and assaults on businesses, cultural centres and places of worship of all religions as well as targeting of religious symbols;

3. *Notes with deep concern* the intensification of the campaign of defamation of religions and the ethnic and religious profiling of Muslim minorities in the aftermath of the tragic events of 11 September 2001;

4. *Expresses its deep concern* that Islam is frequently and wrongly associated with human rights violations and terrorism;

5. *Also expresses its deep concern* at programmes and agendas pursued by extremist organizations and groups aimed at the defamation of religions, in particular when supported by Governments;

6. *Deplores* the use of the print, audio-visual and electronic media, including the Internet, and any other means to incite acts of violence, xenophobia or related intolerance and discrimination against Islam or any other religion;

7. *Recognizes* that, in the context of the fight against terrorism and the reaction to counter-terrorism measures, defamation of religions becomes an aggravating factor that contributes to the denial of fundamental rights and freedoms of target groups, as well as their economic and social exclusion;

8. *Stresses* the need to effectively combat defamation of all religions, Islam and Muslims in particular, especially in human rights forums;

9. *Urges* States to take resolute action to prohibit the dissemination through political institutions and organizations of racist and xenophobic ideas and material aimed at any religion or its followers that constitute incitement to discrimination, hostility or violence;

10. *Also urges* States to provide, within their respective legal and constitutional systems, adequate protection against acts of hatred, discrimination, intimidation and coercion resulting from defamation of religions, to take all possible measures to promote tolerance and respect for all religions and their value systems and to complement legal systems with intellectual and moral strategies to combat religious hatred and intolerance;

11. *Urges* all States to ensure that all public officials, including members of law enforcement bodies, the military, civil servants and educators, in the course of their official duties, respect different religions and beliefs and do not discriminate on the grounds of religion or belief, and that necessary and appropriate education or training is provided;

12. *Underscores* the need to combat defamation of religions by strategizing and harmonizing actions at the local, national, regional and international levels through education and awareness-raising;

13. *Urges* States to ensure equal access to education for all, in law and in practice, including access to free primary education for all children, both girls and boys, and access for adults to lifelong learning and education based on respect for human rights, diversity and tolerance, without discrimination of any kind, and to refrain from any legal or other measures leading to racial segregation in access to schooling;

14. *Calls upon* the international community to initiate a global dialogue to promote a culture of tolerance and peace based on respect for human rights and religious diversity, and urges States, non-governmental organizations, religious bodies and the print and electronic media to support and promote such a dialogue;

15. *Calls upon* the United Nations High Commissioner for Human Rights to promote and include human rights aspects in the dialogue among civilizations, inter alia, through:

(a) Integrating them into topical seminars and special debates on the positive contributions of cultures, as well as religious and cultural diversity, including through educational programmes, particularly the World Programme for Human Rights Education proclaimed on 10 December 2004;

(b) Collaboration by the Office of the United Nations High Commissioner for Human Rights with other relevant international organizations in holding joint conferences designed to encourage this dialogue and promote understanding of the universality of human rights and their implementation at various levels;

16. *Requests* the Secretary-General to submit a report on the implementation of the present resolution to the General Assembly at its sixty-first session.

RECORDED VOTE ON RESOLUTION 60/150:

In favour: Afghanistan, Algeria, Angola, Antigua and Barbuda, Argentina, Azerbaijan, Bahamas, Bahrain, Bangladesh, Barbados, Belarus, Belize, Benin, Bhutan, Bolivia, Brazil, Brunei Darussalam, Burkina Faso, Cambodia, Cameroon, Chile, China, Colombia, Comoros, Costa Rica, Côte d'Ivoire, Cuba, Democratic People's Republic of Korea, Djibouti,

Dominica, Dominican Republic, Ecuador, Egypt, El Salvador, Eritrea, Ethiopia, Fiji, Gabon, Gambia, Grenada, Guatemala, Guinea, Guinea-Bissau, Guyana, Haiti, Indonesia, Iran, Iraq, Jamaica, Jordan, Kazakhstan, Kuwait, Kyrgyzstan, Lao People's Democratic Republic, Lebanon, Lesotho, Libyan Arab Jamahiriya, Malaysia, Maldives, Mali, Mauritius, Mexico, Morocco, Mozambique, Myanmar, Nicaragua, Niger, Oman, Pakistan, Paraguay, Peru, Philippines, Qatar, Russian Federation, Rwanda, Saint Lucia, Saint Vincent and the Grenadines, Saudi Arabia, Senegal, Singapore, Somalia, South Africa, Sudan, Suriname, Syrian Arab Republic, Tajikistan, Thailand, Timor-Leste, Togo, Trinidad and Tobago, Tunisia, Turkey, Turkmenistan, Uganda, United Arab Emirates, Uruguay, Uzbekistan, Venezuela, Viet Nam, Yemen, Zimbabwe.

Against: Albania, Andorra, Australia, Austria, Belgium, Bosnia and Herzegovina, Bulgaria, Canada, Croatia, Cyprus, Czech Republic, Denmark, Estonia, Finland, France, Georgia, Germany, Greece, Hungary, Iceland, Ireland, Israel, Italy, Japan, Latvia, Liechtenstein, Lithuania, Luxembourg, Malta, Marshall Islands, Mauritania, Micronesia, Monaco, Netherlands, New Zealand, Norway, Palau, Poland, Portugal, Republic of Moldova, Romania, Samoa, San Marino, Serbia and Montenegro, Slovakia, Slovenia, Spain, Sweden, Switzerland, The former Yugoslav Republic of Macedonia, Ukraine, United Kingdom, United States.

Abstaining: Armenia, Botswana, Cape Verde, Democratic Republic of the Congo, Ghana, Honduras, India, Kenya, Madagascar, Malawi, Namibia, Nepal, Nigeria, Panama, Papua New Guinea, Republic of Korea, Solomon Islands, Sri Lanka, United Republic of Tanzania, Zambia.

Also on 16 December [meeting 64], the General Assembly, on the recommendation of the Third Committee [A/60/509], adopted **resolution 60/166** without vote [agenda item 71 (b)].

Elimination of all forms of intolerance and of discrimination based on religion or belief

The General Assembly,

Recalling its resolution 36/55 of 25 November 1981, by which it proclaimed the Declaration on the Elimination of All Forms of Intolerance and of Discrimination Based on Religion or Belief,

Recalling also article 18 of the International Covenant on Civil and Political Rights, article 18 of the Universal Declaration of Human Rights and other relevant human rights provisions,

Reaffirming the call of the World Conference on Human Rights upon all Governments to take all appropriate measures in compliance with their international obligations and with due regard to their respective legal systems to counter intolerance and related violence based on religion or belief, including practices of discrimination against women and the desecration of religious sites, recognizing that every individual has the right to freedom of thought, conscience, expression and religion,

Reaffirming also the recognition by the World Conference on Human Rights that all human rights are universal, indivisible, interdependent and interrelated,

Recalling General Assembly resolution 56/6 of 9 November 2001 on the Global Agenda for Dialogue among Civilizations, in which the Assembly recognized the valuable contribution that dialogue among civilizations could make to an improved awareness and understanding of the common values shared by all humankind,

Acknowledging that in order to be effective, such a dialogue should be based on respect for the dignity of adherents of religions and beliefs, as well as respect for diversity and the universal promotion and protection of human rights,

Considering that religion or belief, for those who profess either, is one of the fundamental elements in their conception of life and that freedom of religion or belief should be fully respected and guaranteed,

Considering also that the disregard for and infringement of human rights and fundamental freedoms, in particular the right to freedom of thought, conscience, religion or belief, have brought, directly or indirectly, wars and great suffering to humankind,

Recognizing the importance of promoting dialogue among civilizations in order to enhance mutual understanding and knowledge among different social groups, cultures and civilizations in various areas, including culture, religion, education, information, science and technology, and in order to contribute to the promotion and protection of human rights and fundamental freedoms,

Recalling Commission on Human Rights resolution 2005/40 of 19 April 2005 on the elimination of all forms of intolerance and of discrimination based on religion or belief,

Seriously concerned at all attacks upon religious places, sites and shrines, including any deliberate destruction of relics and monuments,

Seriously concerned also at the misuse of registration procedures as a means to limit the right to freedom of religion or belief of members of certain religious communities and at the limitations placed on religious publications,

Recognizing the important work carried out by the Human Rights Committee in providing guidance with respect to the scope of the freedom of religion or belief,

Convinced of the need to address, for instance, in the context of the Global Agenda for Dialogue among Civilizations the rise in all parts of the world of religious extremism affecting the rights of individuals and groups based on religion or belief, the situations of violence and discrimination that affect many women as a result of religion or belief and the abuse of religion or belief for ends inconsistent with the Charter of the United Nations and other relevant instruments of the United Nations,

Resolved to adopt all necessary and appropriate measures for the speedy elimination of such intolerance based on religion or belief in all its forms and manifestations and to prevent and combat discrimination based on religion or belief,

Noting that a formal or legal distinction at the national level between different kinds of religions or faith-based communities may, in some cases, constitute discrimination and may impinge on the enjoyment of the freedom of religion or belief,

Underlining the importance of education in the promotion of tolerance which involves the acceptance by the public of, and its respect for, diversity, including with regard to religious expressions, and underlining also the fact that education, in particular at school, should contribute in a meaningful way to promoting tolerance and the elimination of discrimination based on religion or belief,

Recalling the importance of the International Consultative Conference on School Education in relation to Freedom of Religion or Belief, Tolerance and Non-Discrimination, held in Madrid from 23 to 25 November 2001, and continuing to invite Governments to give consideration to the Final Document adopted at the Conference,

Emphasizing that States, regional organizations, non-governmental organizations, religious bodies and the media have an important role to play in promoting tolerance, respect and freedom of religion or belief,

Recognizing the importance of interreligious and intrareligious dialogue and the role of religious and other non-governmental organizations in promoting tolerance in matters relating to religion or belief,

Believing that further intensified efforts are therefore required to promote and protect the right to freedom of thought, conscience, religion or belief and to eliminate all forms of hatred, intolerance and discrimination based on religion or belief, as also noted at the World Conference against Racism, Racial Discrimination, Xenophobia and Related Intolerance,

1. *Takes note with appreciation* of the work and the report of the Special Rapporteur of the Commission on Human Rights on freedom of religion or belief;

2. *Condemns* all forms of intolerance and of discrimination based on religion or belief;

3. *Encourages* the efforts made by the United Nations High Commissioner for Human Rights to coordinate in the field of human rights the activities of relevant United Nations organs, bodies and mechanisms dealing with all forms of intolerance and of discrimination based on religion or belief;

4. *Urges* States:

(a) To ensure that their constitutional and legislative systems provide adequate and effective guarantees of freedom of thought, conscience, religion and belief to all without distinction, inter alia, by the provision of effective remedies in cases where the right to freedom of thought, conscience, religion or belief, or the right to practise freely one's religion, including the right to change one's religion or belief, is violated;

(b) To exert the utmost efforts, in accordance with their national legislation and in conformity with international human rights law, to ensure that religious places, sites, shrines and religious symbols are fully respected and protected and to take additional measures in cases where they are vulnerable to desecration or destruction;

(c) To review, whenever relevant, existing registration practices in order to ensure the right of all persons to manifest their religion or belief, alone or in community with others and in public or in private;

(d) To ensure, in particular, the right of all persons to worship or assemble in connection with a religion or belief and to establish and maintain places for these purposes and the right of all persons to write, issue and disseminate relevant publications in these areas;

(e) To ensure that, in accordance with appropriate national legislation and in conformity with international human rights law, the freedom of all persons and members of groups to establish and maintain religious, charitable or humanitarian institutions is fully respected and protected;

(f) To ensure that no one within their jurisdiction is deprived of the right to life, liberty or security of person because of religion or belief and that no one is subjected to torture or arbitrary arrest or detention on that account and to bring to justice all perpetrators of violations of these rights;

(g) To ensure that all public officials and civil servants, including members of law enforcement bodies, the military and educators, in the course of their official duties, respect different religions and beliefs and do not discriminate on the grounds of religion or belief, and that all necessary and appropriate education or training is provided;

5. *Recognizes with deep concern* the overall rise in instances of intolerance and violence directed against members of many religious and other communities in various parts of the world, including cases motivated by Islamophobia, anti-Semitism and Christianophobia;

6. *Expresses concern* over the persistence of institutionalized social intolerance and discrimination practised against many in the name of religion or belief;

7. *Condemns* any advocacy of religious hatred that constitutes incitement to discrimination, hostility or violence, whether it involves the use of print, audiovisual and electronic media or any other means;

8. *Stresses* the need to strengthen dialogue, inter alia, by revitalizing the Global Agenda for Dialogue among Civilizations;

9. *Invites* States, the Special Rapporteur, the Office of the United Nations High Commissioner for Human Rights and other relevant entities of the United Nations system, such as the United Nations Educational, Scientific and Cultural Organization, and other international and regional organizations and civil society to consider promoting dialogue among civilizations in order to contribute to the elimination of intolerance and discrimination based on religion or belief, inter alia, by addressing the following issues within the framework of international standards of human rights:

(*a*) The rise of religious extremism affecting religions in all parts of the world;

(*b*) The situations of violence and discrimination that affect many women as a result of religion or belief;

(*c*) The use of religion or belief for ends inconsistent with the Charter of the United Nations and other relevant instruments of the United Nations;

10. *Urges* States to step up their efforts to eliminate intolerance and discrimination based on religion or belief, notably by:

(*a*) Taking all necessary and appropriate action, in conformity with international standards of human rights, to combat hatred, intolerance and acts of violence, intimidation and coercion motivated by intolerance based on religion or belief, as well as incitement to hostility and violence, with particular regard to religious minorities, and devoting particular attention to practices that violate the human rights of women and discriminate against women, including in the exercise of their right to freedom of thought, conscience, religion or belief;

(*b*) Promoting and encouraging, through education and other means, understanding, tolerance and respect in all matters relating to freedom of religion or belief;

(*c*) Undertaking all appropriate efforts to encourage those engaged in teaching to cultivate respect for all religions or beliefs, thereby promoting mutual understanding and tolerance;

11. *Invites* Governments, religious bodies and civil society to continue to undertake dialogue at all levels to promote greater tolerance, respect and understanding;

12. *Emphasizes* the importance of a continued and strengthened dialogue among and within religions or beliefs, including as encompassed in the dialogue among civilizations, to promote greater tolerance, respect and mutual understanding;

13. *Also emphasizes* that equating any religion with terrorism should be avoided, as this may have adverse consequences on the enjoyment of the right to freedom of religion or belief of all members of the religious communities concerned;

14. *Further emphasizes* that, as underlined by the Human Rights Committee, restrictions on the freedom to manifest religion or belief are permitted only if limitations are prescribed by law, are necessary to protect public safety, order, health or morals, or the fundamental rights and freedoms of others, and are applied in a manner that does not vitiate the right to freedom of thought, conscience and religion;

15. *Encourages* the continuing efforts in all parts of the world of the Special Rapporteur to examine incidents and governmental actions that are incompatible with the provisions of the Declaration on the Elimination of All Forms of Intolerance and of Discrimination Based on Religion or Belief and to recommend remedial measures, as appropriate;

16. *Stresses* the need for the Special Rapporteur to continue to apply a gender perspective, inter alia, through the identification of gender-specific abuses, in the reporting process, including in information collection and in recommendations;

17. *Welcomes and encourages* the continuing efforts of all actors in society, including non-governmental organizations and bodies and groups based on religion or belief, to promote the implementation of the Declaration, and further encourages their work in promoting freedom of religion or belief and in highlighting cases of religious intolerance, discrimination and persecution;

18. *Recommends* that the United Nations and other actors, in their efforts to promote freedom of religion or belief, ensure the widest possible dissemination of the text of the Declaration in as many different languages as possible by United Nations information centres and by other interested bodies;

19. *Decides* to continue its consideration of measures to implement the Declaration;

20. *Welcomes* the work of the Special Rapporteur and urges all Governments to cooperate fully with the Special Rapporteur and to respond favourably to her requests to visit their countries and to provide her with all necessary information so as to enable her to fulfil her mandate even more effectively;

21. *Requests* the Secretary-General to ensure that the Special Rapporteur receives the necessary resources to enable her to discharge her mandate fully;

22. *Requests* the Special Rapporteur to submit an interim report to the General Assembly at its sixty-first session;

23. *Decides* to consider the question of the elimination of all forms of religious intolerance at its sixty-first session under the item entitled "Human rights questions".

Civil and political rights

Right to self-determination

Report of the Secretary-General. In response to General Assembly resolution 59/180 [YUN 2004,

p. 709], the Secretary-General submitted an August report [A/60/268] summarizing Commission discussions on human rights violations, particularly regarding the right to self-determination, as well as relevant principles from the jurisprudence of the Human Rights Committee (see p. 726), the expert body monitoring the implementation of the International Covenant on Civil and Political Rights by the States parties.

Communication. On 21 May [E/CN.4/2005/G/23], Armenia alleged that Azerbaijan had violated the right to self-determination of the Nagorny Karabakh territory in the Caucus region (see p. 490), by annulling its autonomous status without its peoples' consent and by refusing to yield the territory. That action violated article 1 of the UN Charter, which recognized the equal rights and self-determination of peoples.

GENERAL ASSEMBLY ACTION

On 16 December [meeting 64], the General Assembly, on the recommendation of the Third Committee [A/60/508], adopted **resolution 60/145** without vote [agenda item 70].

Universal realization of the right of peoples to self-determination

The General Assembly,

Reaffirming the importance, for the effective guarantee and observance of human rights, of the universal realization of the right of peoples to self-determination enshrined in the Charter of the United Nations and embodied in the International Covenants on Human Rights, as well as in the Declaration on the Granting of Independence to Colonial Countries and Peoples contained in General Assembly resolution 1514(XV) of 14 December 1960,

Welcoming the progressive exercise of the right to self-determination by peoples under colonial, foreign or alien occupation and their emergence into sovereign statehood and independence,

Deeply concerned at the continuation of acts or threats of foreign military intervention and occupation that are threatening to suppress, or have already suppressed, the right to self-determination of peoples and nations,

Expressing grave concern that, as a consequence of the persistence of such actions, millions of people have been and are being uprooted from their homes as refugees and displaced persons, and emphasizing the urgent need for concerted international action to alleviate their condition,

Recalling the relevant resolutions regarding the violation of the right of peoples to self-determination and other human rights as a result of foreign military intervention, aggression and occupation, adopted by the Commission on Human Rights at its sixty-first and previous sessions,

Reaffirming its previous resolutions on the universal realization of the right of peoples to self-determination, including resolution 59/180 of 20 December 2004,

Reaffirming also its resolution 55/2 of 8 September 2000, containing the United Nations Millennium

Declaration, and recalling its resolution 60/1 of 16 September 2005, containing the 2005 World Summit Outcome, which, inter alia, upheld the right to self-determination of peoples under colonial domination and foreign occupation,

Taking note of the report of the Secretary-General on the right of peoples to self-determination,

1. *Reaffirms* that the universal realization of the right of all peoples, including those under colonial, foreign and alien domination, to self-determination is a fundamental condition for the effective guarantee and observance of human rights and for the preservation and promotion of such rights;

2. *Declares its firm opposition* to acts of foreign military intervention, aggression and occupation, since these have resulted in the suppression of the right of peoples to self-determination and other human rights in certain parts of the world;

3. *Calls upon* those States responsible to cease immediately their military intervention in and occupation of foreign countries and territories and all acts of repression, discrimination, exploitation and maltreatment, in particular the brutal and inhuman methods reportedly employed for the execution of those acts against the peoples concerned;

4. *Deplores* the plight of millions of refugees and displaced persons who have been uprooted as a result of the aforementioned acts, and reaffirms their right to return to their homes voluntarily in safety and honour;

5. *Requests* the Commission on Human Rights to continue to give special attention to the violation of human rights, especially the right to self-determination, resulting from foreign military intervention, aggression or occupation;

6. *Requests* the Secretary-General to report on the question to the General Assembly at its sixty-first session under the item entitled "Right of peoples to self-determination".

Right of Palestinians

By a recorded vote of 49 to 1, with 2 abstentions, the Commission, on 7 April [res. 2005/1], reaffirming the inalienable right of the Palestinian people to self-determination, urged Member States and relevant UN system bodies to support and assist them in the early realization of that right.

GENERAL ASSEMBLY ACTION

On 16 December [meeting 64], the General Assembly, on the recommendation of the Third Committee [A/60/508], adopted **resolution 60/146** by recorded vote (170-5-1) [agenda item 70].

The right of the Palestinian people to self-determination

The General Assembly,

Aware that the development of friendly relations among nations, based on respect for the principle of equal rights and self-determination of peoples, is among the purposes and principles of the United Nations, as defined in the Charter,

Recalling, in this regard, its resolution 2625(XXV) of 24 October 1970 entitled "Declaration on Principles of International Law concerning Friendly Relations and Cooperation among States in accordance with the Charter of the United Nations",

Bearing in mind the International Covenants on Human Rights, the Universal Declaration of Human Rights, the Declaration on the Granting of Independence to Colonial Countries and Peoples and the Vienna Declaration and Programme of Action adopted at the World Conference on Human Rights on 25 June 1993,

Recalling the Declaration on the Occasion of the Fiftieth Anniversary of the United Nations,

Recalling also the United Nations Millennium Declaration,

Recalling further the advisory opinion rendered on 9 July 2004 by the International Court of Justice on the *Legal Consequences of the Construction of a Wall in the Occupied Palestinian Territory*, and noting in particular the reply of the Court, including on the right of peoples to self-determination, which is a right *erga omnes*,

Recalling the conclusion of the Court, in its advisory opinion of 9 July 2004, that the construction of the wall by Israel, the occupying Power, in the Occupied Palestinian Territory, including East Jerusalem, along with measures previously taken, severely impedes the right of the Palestinian people to self-determination,

Expressing the urgent need for the resumption of negotiations within the Middle East peace process on its agreed basis and for the speedy achievement of a final settlement between the Palestinian and Israeli sides,

Recalling its resolution 59/179 of 20 December 2004,

Affirming the right of all States in the region to live in peace within secure and internationally recognized borders,

1. *Reaffirms* the right of the Palestinian people to self-determination, including the right to their independent State of Palestine;

2. *Urges* all States and the specialized agencies and organizations of the United Nations system to continue to support and assist the Palestinian people in the early realization of their right to self-determination.

RECORDED VOTE ON RESOLUTION 60/146:

In favour: Afghanistan, Albania, Algeria, Andorra, Angola, Antigua and Barbuda, Argentina, Armenia, Austria, Azerbaijan, Bahamas, Bahrain, Bangladesh, Barbados, Belarus, Belgium, Belize, Benin, Bhutan, Bolivia, Bosnia and Herzegovina, Botswana, Brazil, Brunei Darussalam, Bulgaria, Burkina Faso, Burundi, Cambodia, Cameroon, Canada, Cape Verde, Chile, China, Colombia, Comoros, Costa Rica, Côte d'Ivoire, Croatia, Cuba, Cyprus, Czech Republic, Democratic People's Republic of Korea, Democratic Republic of the Congo, Denmark, Djibouti, Dominica, Dominican Republic, Ecuador, Egypt, El Salvador, Eritrea, Estonia, Ethiopia, Fiji, Finland, France, Gabon, Gambia, Georgia, Germany, Ghana, Greece, Guatemala, Guinea, Guinea-Bissau, Guyana, Haiti, Honduras, Hungary, Iceland, India, Indonesia, Iran, Iraq, Ireland, Italy, Jamaica, Japan, Jordan, Kazakhstan, Kenya, Kuwait, Kyrgyzstan, Lao People's Democratic Republic, Latvia, Lebanon, Lesotho, Libyan Arab Jamahiriya, Liechtenstein, Lithuania, Luxembourg, Madagascar, Malawi, Malaysia, Maldives, Mali, Malta, Mauritania, Mauritius, Mexico, Monaco, Mongolia, Morocco, Mozambique, Myanmar, Namibia, Nepal, Netherlands, New Zealand, Nicaragua, Niger, Nigeria, Norway, Oman, Pakistan, Panama, Papua New Guinea, Paraguay, Peru, Philippines, Poland, Portugal, Qatar, Republic of Korea, Republic of Moldova, Romania, Russian Federation, Rwanda, Saint Lucia, Saint Vincent and the Grenadines, Samoa, San Marino, Saudi Arabia, Senegal, Serbia and Montenegro, Singapore, Slovakia, Slovenia, Solomon Islands, Somalia, South Africa, Spain, Sri Lanka, Sudan, Suriname, Sweden, Switzerland, Syrian Arab Republic, Tajikistan, Thailand, The former Yugoslav Republic of Macedonia, Timor-Leste, Togo, Trinidad and Tobago, Tunisia, Turkey, Turkmenistan, Uganda, Ukraine, United Arab Emirates, United Kingdom, United Repub-

lic of Tanzania, Uruguay, Uzbekistan, Vanuatu, Venezuela, Viet Nam, Yemen, Zambia, Zimbabwe.

Against: Israel, Marshall Islands, Micronesia, Palau, United States.

Abstaining: Australia.

Western Sahara

On 7 April [E/2005/23], the Commission agreed by consensus to defer its consideration of the question of Western Sahara to its sixty-second (2006) session.

Mercenaries

Report of Special Rapporteur. In response to a 2004 Commission request [YUN 2004, p. 711], the Special Rapporteur on the question of the use of mercenaries, Shaista Shameem (Fiji), in her first report [E/CN.4/2005/14] to the Commission, summarized replies from Governments regarding a proposal for the legal definition of mercenaries contained in the final report of her predecessor in 2004 [YUN 2004, p. 711], described developments in mercenary activities in Africa and discussed the impact of the activities of private companies offering military assistance, consultancy and security services on the international market. The report also highlighted the distinction between mercenary and terrorist activities, examined the current status of the Convention Against the Recruitment, Use, Financing and Training of Mercenaries (see p. 789), and considered the outcome of the third expert meeting on mercenaries [ibid., p. 712]. Reflecting on the arrest and trial of many of the suspected mercenaries implicated in the alleged attempt to overthrow the democratically elected Government of Equatorial Guinea [ibid., p. 232], the Special Rapporteur, while noting concerns over claims of violations of the defendants' rights, advocated that the legal proceedings be pursued in a manner consistent with legal and human rights standards. Noting regional initiatives for the repatriation of former combatants in Liberia and Sierra Leone, she pointed out that in post-conflict situations, such initiatives and related training efforts would help reduce the pool of foreign ex-combatants from which mercenaries were often recruited for armed conflicts in other countries. The Special Rapporteur also noted that the proliferation in the last decade of international private military companies associated with mercenary activity, which were operating in over 50 countries around the world, had outstripped the effectiveness of existing legal framework and enforcement mechanisms for addressing the problem. The Special Rapporteur emphasized that the nature and the degree of accountability of those organizations and their employees were uncertain. She cited the involvement of private military contractors in the alleged abuse of Iraqi prisoners at the United

States-run Abu Ghraib prison [ibid., p. 346], pointing out that neither the United States jurisdiction of military law nor Iraqi law could be applied in investigating those incidents. In her recommendations, the Special Rapporteur said there was a need to examine whether the proposed new legal definition of mercenaries would encourage States that had not done so to ratify the International Convention against the Recruitment, Use, Financing and Training of Mercenaries. It was also important to explore whether licensing and regulating genuine private security companies through national legislation or international mechanisms could help establish clear lines of accountability for bona fide companies and identify other organizations engaging in mercenary activity to the detriment of human rights and peoples' right to self-determination.

Commission action. On 7 April [res. 2005/2], the Commission, by a recorded vote of 35 to 15, with 2 abstentions, while acknowledging the Special Rapporteur's work, decided to end the mandate and to establish a working group on the use of mercenaries as a means of violating human rights and impeding the exercise of the right of peoples to self-determination. The working group, which would comprise five independent experts, was asked to continue the work begun by previous Commission mechanisms on mercenaries, taking into account the proposal for a new legal definition of a mercenary drafted by the Special Rapporteur in 2004 [YUN 2004, p. 711] and the new forms, manifestations and modalities of mercenary activities occurring around the world, to consult with States, intergovernmental organizations and NGOs in the fulfillment of its mandate and to report in 2006. The Commission asked OHCHR to publicize the adverse effects of mercenary activities on the right to self-determination, provide advisory services to affected States when requested and support the working group in implementing its mandate, as elaborated by the Commission and endorsed by the Economic and Social Council (see below).

ECONOMIC AND SOCIAL COUNCIL ACTION

In July, the Economic and Social Council, on the recommendation of the Commission on Human Rights [E/2005/23], adopted **decision 2005/255** by recorded vote (29-18-0) [agenda item 14 (g)].

The use of mercenaries as a means of violating human rights and impeding the exercise of the right of peoples to self-determination

At its 38th plenary meeting, on 25 July 2005, the Economic and Social Council took note of Commission on Human Rights resolution 2005/2 of 7 April 2005, and endorsed the Commission's decision to establish a working group on the use of mercenaries as a

means of violating human rights and impeding the exercise of the right of peoples to self-determination, to be composed of five independent experts, one from each regional group, to meet intersessionally for a period of three years, with the following mandate:

(*a*) To elaborate and present concrete proposals on possible new standards, general guidelines or basic principles encouraging the further protection of human rights, in particular the right of peoples to self-determination, while facing current and emergent threats posed by mercenaries or mercenary-related activities;

(*b*) To seek opinions and contributions from Governments, intergovernmental and non-governmental organizations on questions relating to its mandate;

(*c*) To monitor mercenaries and mercenary-related activities in all their forms and manifestations in different parts of the world;

(*d*) To study and identify emerging issues, manifestations and trends regarding mercenaries or mercenary-related activities and their impact on human rights, particularly on the right of peoples to self-determination;

(*e*) To monitor and study the effects of the activities of private companies offering military assistance, consultancy and security services on the international market on the enjoyment of human rights, particularly the right of peoples to self-determination, and to prepare draft international basic principles that encourage respect for human rights on the part of those companies in their activities.

The Council also endorsed the request of the Commission to the Working Group to report annually to the Commission and the General Assembly.

RECORDED VOTE ON DECISION 2005/255:

In favour: Armenia, Azerbaijan, Bangladesh, Belize, Brazil, China, Colombia, Congo, Cuba, Ecuador, Guinea, India, Indonesia, Jamaica, Kenya, Malaysia, Mauritius, Mexico, Namibia, Nicaragua, Panama, Russian Federation, Senegal, South Africa, Thailand, Tunisia, United Arab Emirates, United Republic of Tanzania.

Against: Albania, Australia, Belgium, Canada, Denmark, France, Germany, Iceland, Ireland, Italy, Japan, Lithuania, Poland, Republic of Korea, Spain, Turkey, United Kingdom, United States.

Abstaining: None.

Note by Secretary-General. In response to General Assembly resolution 59/178 [YUN 2004, p. 712], the Secretary-General, by an August note [A/60/263], transmitted a report of the Special Rapporteur, which provided an overview of her activities, the status of her work and how it could be further developed under the mandate of the working group on the use of mercenaries established in Commission resolution 2005/2 (see above). She determined that there was need for a fundamental reconsideration of issues concerning mercenaries, particularly regarding the responsibility of States and the United Nations in addressing related activities. Notable problems in that context included the fact that the 1989 Convention (see p. 789) had only negligible support, demonstrated by the remarkably small number of signatures and ratifications. In addition, there was ambiguity with regard to the status of the private military and security companies, many of which employed mercenaries. Noting that she had received a limited number of responses from Member States on the proposal for a new legal definition of a mercenary, the Special Rapporteur believed that the process towards adopting some version of the new definition was likely to be prolonged if the current course was followed. She concluded that Member States were demonstrating their own ambiguous positions and understanding with respect to the roles and duties of States in the fast-evolving climate of international security and UN peacekeeping. The Special Rapporteur recommended a substantive and comprehensive review of the legal definition of mercenaries and their activities and that the working group on the use of mercenaries consider taking the process forward within the framework of its mandate. She also advocated that the United Nations should debate the fundamental question of the role of the State with respect to the use of force, so as to reach a common understanding on the respective duties and responsibilities of the different actors in the current context, and their respective obligations for promoting and protecting human rights. Such a debate could result in the revamping or revocation of the 1989 Convention. The Special Rapporteur also reported on the current status of that Convention, her contacts with private military and security companies, and efforts to develop a code of conduct for that sector. Annexed to the report was a communication issued by the International Peace Operations Association at the end of its meeting with the Special Rapporteur (London, 27-28 June), calling on the United Nations to re-examine the term "mercenary" and its derogatory connotations, and indicating its intention to develop an international code of conduct for private sector operations in conflict/post conflict environments.

Note by Secretariat. An August note of the Secretariat [A/60/319] set out the mandate of the newly established working group on the use of mercenaries as a means of violating human rights and impeding the exercise of the right to self-determination, established in Commission resolution 2005/2 and endorsed by the Economic and Social Council in resolution 2005/255 (see p. 788). The note also announced the appointment of the five members of the working group and the scheduling of its first session in October.

On 16 December, the General Assembly took note of the note by the Secretariat and that of the Secretary-General transmitting the report of the Special Rapporteur (**decision 60/532**).

1989 International Convention

As at 31 December, 27 States had become parties to the 1989 International Convention against the Recruitment, Use, Financing and Training of Mercenaries, adopted by the General Assembly in resolution 44/34 [YUN 1989, p. 825], with the accession of Liberia in 2005. The Convention entered into force in 2001 [YUN 2001, p. 632].

Administration of justice

Commission action. On 19 April [dec. 2005/108], the Commission approved the Subcommission's 2004 decision [YUN 2004, p. 715] to appoint Lalaina Rakotoarisoa (Madagascar) as Special Rapporteur entrusted with preparing a detailed study on the difficulties of establishing guilt and/or responsibilities with regard to crimes of sexual violence, its request that she submit a preliminary report in 2005, an interim report in 2006 and a final report in 2007, and its request to the Secretary-General to assist her.

On 25 July, the Economic and Social Council endorsed the Commission's decision and approved its requests to the Special Rapporteur and to the Secretary-General (**decision 2005/287**).

Working group activities. Established by the Subcommission on 25 July [dec. 2005/101], the five-member sessional working group on the administration of justice met on 25 and 29 July and in August [E/CN.4/Sub.2/2005/11]. The group discussed international criminal justice, women and the criminal justice system, the right to an effective remedy and the issue of transitional justice.

Pursuant to a 2004 Subcommission request [YUN 2004, p. 715], the group had before it a June report on the administration of justice through military tribunals [E/CN.4/Sub.2/2005/9], prepared by the Subcommission's Special Rapporteur on that subject, Emmanuel Decaux (France), which updated his 2003 [YUN 2003, p. 725] and 2004 [YUN 2004, p. 714] reports on the issue. The current report presented 19 draft principles governing the administration of justice through military tribunals and called for broad consultations with States, international and national human rights organizations and NGOs to examine those drafts in depth.

The group also had before it a 21 June working paper on the relationship between human rights law and international humanitarian law [E/CN.4/Sub.2/2005/14], prepared by Françoise Hampson (United Kingdom) and Ibrahim Salama (Egypt), in response to a further 2004 Subcommission request [YUN 2004, p. 715]. The paper discussed the potential for institutional complementarity and mutual reinforcement of human rights law and international humanitarian law; terminology, the history of the law of armed conflict; the question of whether human rights law and international humanitarian law could be applicable to the same circumstances; and whether human rights law could be applied outside national territory. It concluded by identifying related areas for further study, and recommended the establishment of a Subcommission working group to consider those issues

In response to a further 2004 Subcommission request [ibid., p. 716], the group considered a 21 June working paper on the right to an effective remedy in criminal proceedings [E/CN.4/Sub.2/2005/13], submitted by Mohamed Habib Cherif (Tunisia). The paper addressed the international, regional and national sources of the right and its specific content, namely the right to an independent, impartial tribunal, to adequate and prompt reparation, and to accurate and relevant information. It determined that the right to a remedy, leading to a fair trial, was the cornerstone of the rule of law and of human rights mechanisms. Under any circumstance, it was one of the most important human rights and every State subject to the rule of law had a duty to establish a judicial system that met the requirements of a fair trial. The paper recommended that the draft third optional protocol to the International Covenant on Civil and Political Rights, which guaranteed the right to an effective remedy and a fair trial, be reviewed and adopted.

The group discussed a 27 June working paper on the implementation in domestic law of the right to an effective remedy [E/CN.4/Sub.2/2005/15], prepared by Ms. Hampson, as requested by the Subcommission [YUN 2004, p. 716]. The paper, which explained the scope and importance of the right, explored its content and areas in which difficulties arose, and suggested practical measures that could be taken by human rights bodies and NGOs to examine it more systematically.

The group further discussed a 14 July progress report on discrimination in the criminal justice system [E/CN.4/Sub.2/2005/7], submitted by Leïla Zerrougui (Algeria), pursuant to a 2004 Subcommission request [YUN 2004, p. 715], which analysed institutional and structural discrimination in the national criminal justice system and highlighted direct or indirect discrimination that seriously impaired the enjoyment of the fundamental rights of the most vulnerable. The final report would consider, among other things, discriminatory treatment in prison administration and a gender-specific approach to discrimination.

Lalaina Rakotoarisoa (Madagascar), appointed Special Rapporteur in 2004 to prepare a study on the difficulties of establishing guilt and/or responsibilities with regard to crimes of sexual violence [YUN 2004, p. 715], made an oral presentation

to the group, in accordance with a 2004 Subcommission request [ibid., p. 715].

Subcommission action. On 10 August [res. 2005/13], the Subcommission, taking note of the discussions of the sessional working group (see above), reaffirmed the importance of the full and effective implementation of all UN standards on human rights in the administration of justice. It welcomed a proposal by NGOs to organize, in consultation with OHCHR, a seminar on transitional justice to prepare papers for submission to the working group's next session and invited States, competent UN bodies, intergovernmental organizations, NGOs and national human rights institutions to provide information to the group at its future sessions.

On the same date [res. 2005/15], the Subcommission decided to transmit to the Commission the updated draft principles on the administration of justice through military tribunals, prepared by Emmanuel Decaux (see p. 789). It requested Mr. Decaux to prepare, without financial implications, a note to facilitate the Commission's examination of the draft, taking into account the comments and observations of the Subcommission, and to revise it.

On 8 August [res. 2005/3], the Subcommission asked Lalaina Rakotoarisoa to submit in 2006 a preliminary report on the difficulties of establishing responsibility or guilt with regard to crimes of sexual violence, and the Secretary-General to assist her in implementing her mandate.

Also on 8 August [res. 2005/5], the Subcommission requested Ms. Zerrougui to submit a final report on discrimination in the criminal justice system, for consideration in 2006, and asked the Secretary-General to assist her.

On the same date [dec. 2005/105], the Subcommission requested Vladimir Kartashkin (Russian Federation) to prepare, without financial implications and for consideration in 2006, a working paper on human rights and State sovereignty; and Ms. Hampson and Mr. Cherif to prepare, without financial implications, an expanded working paper on the implementation of the right to an effective remedy for human rights violations, for submission to the working group in 2006 [dec. 2005/106].

On 10 August [dec. 2005/108], the Subcommission further requested Ms. Hampson to prepare, without financial implications, a working paper on the circumstances in which civilians could lose their immunity from attack under international humanitarian and human rights law; Ibrahim Salama, to prepare, without financial implications, a working paper on measures designed to prevent violations in circumstances in which international humanitarian law and international human rights law were both applicable; and Yozo Yokota (Japan), to prepare, without financial implications, a working paper on the issues of amnesties, impunity and accountability for violations of international humanitarian law and international human rights law. The papers were all to be submitted to the working group in 2006.

In further action on 10 August [dec. 2005/109], the Subcommission asked Janio Iván Tuñón Veilles (Panama) to prepare, without financial implications, a working paper on transitional justice and investigation mechanisms for truth and reconciliation, with an emphasis on the experiences in Latin America, and to submit it to the working group in 2006.

GENERAL ASSEMBLY ACTION

On 16 December [meeting 64], the General Assembly, on the recommendation of Third Committee [A/60/509], adopted **resolution 60/159** without vote [agenda item 71(b)].

Human rights in the administration of justice

The General Assembly,

Bearing in mind the principles embodied in articles 3, 5, 8, 9 and 10 of the Universal Declaration of Human Rights and the relevant provisions of the International Covenant on Civil and Political Rights and the Optional Protocols thereto, in particular article 6 of the Covenant, which states, inter alia, that no one shall be arbitrarily deprived of his life and prohibits the imposition of the death penalty for crimes committed by persons below 18 years of age, and article 10, which provides that all persons deprived of their liberty shall be treated with humanity and with respect for the inherent dignity of the human person,

Bearing in mind also the relevant provisions of the Convention against Torture and Other Cruel, Inhuman or Degrading Treatment or Punishment, the International Convention on the Elimination of All Forms of Racial Discrimination, in particular the right to equal treatment before tribunals and all other organs administering justice, the Convention on the Rights of the Child, in particular article 37, according to which every child deprived of liberty shall be treated in a manner that takes into account the needs of persons of his or her age, and the Convention on the Elimination of All Forms of Discrimination against Women, in particular the obligation to treat men and women equally in all stages of procedures in courts and tribunals,

Calling attention to the numerous international standards in the field of the administration of justice,

Convinced that the independence and impartiality of the judiciary are essential prerequisites for the protection of human rights, good governance and democracy as well as for ensuring that there is no discrimination in the administration of justice, and should therefore be respected in all circumstances,

Noting the adoption by the Committee on the Elimination of Racial Discrimination of general rec-

ommendation XXXI on the prevention of racial discrimination in the administration and functioning of the criminal justice system,

Emphasizing that the right to access to justice, as contained in applicable international human rights instruments, forms an important basis for strengthening the rule of law through the administration of justice,

Mindful of the importance of ensuring respect for the rule of law and human rights in the administration of justice, in particular in post-conflict situations, as a crucial contribution to building peace and justice and ending impunity,

Recalling the Guidelines for Action on Children in the Criminal Justice System and the establishment and subsequent meetings of the Inter-Agency Coordination Panel on Juvenile Justice,

Calling attention to the relevant provisions of the Vienna Declaration on Crime and Justice: Meeting the Challenges of the Twenty-first Century, and of the plans of action for its implementation and follow-up,

Recalling its resolution 58/183 of 22 December 2003, as well as Commission on Human Rights resolution 2004/43 of 19 April 2004, and Economic and Social Council resolution 2004/28 of 21 July 2004 entitled "United Nations standards and norms in crime prevention and criminal justice",

1. *Reaffirms* the importance of the full and effective implementation of all United Nations standards on human rights in the administration of justice;

2. *Reiterates its call* to all Member States to spare no effort in providing for effective legislative and other mechanisms and procedures, as well as adequate resources, to ensure the full implementation of those standards;

3. *Affirms* that States must ensure that any measure taken to combat terrorism, including in the administration of justice, complies with their obligations under international law, in particular international human rights, refugee and humanitarian law;

4. *Invites* Governments to provide for training, including anti-racist, multicultural and gender-sensitive training, in human rights in the administration of justice, including juvenile justice, to all judges, lawyers, prosecutors, social workers, immigration and police officers and other professionals concerned, including personnel deployed in international field presences;

5. *Invites* States to make use of technical assistance offered by the relevant United Nations programmes in order to strengthen national capacities and infrastructures in the field of the administration of justice;

6. *Appeals* to Governments to include in their national development plans the administration of justice as an integral part of the development process and to allocate adequate resources for the provision of legal-aid services with a view to promoting and protecting human rights, and invites the international community to respond favourably to requests for financial and technical assistance for the enhancement and strengthening of the administration of justice;

7. *Encourages* the regional commissions, the specialized agencies, United Nations institutes active in the areas of human rights and crime prevention and criminal justice, and other relevant parts of the United Nations system, as well as intergovernmental and nongovernmental organizations, including national pro-

fessional associations concerned with promoting United Nations standards in this field, and other segments of civil society, including the media, to continue to develop their activities in promoting human rights in the administration of justice;

8. *Invites* the Commission on Human Rights and the Commission on Crime Prevention and Criminal Justice, as well as the Office of the United Nations High Commissioner for Human Rights and the United Nations Office on Drugs and Crime, to closely coordinate their activities relating to the administration of justice;

9. *Calls upon* mechanisms of the Commission on Human Rights and its subsidiary bodies, including special rapporteurs, special representatives and working groups, to continue to give special attention to questions relating to the effective promotion and protection of human rights in the administration of justice, including juvenile justice, and to provide, where appropriate, specific recommendations in this regard, including proposals for advisory services and technical assistance measures;

10. *Calls upon* the Office of the United Nations High Commissioner for Human Rights and the United Nations Office on Drugs and Crime to reinforce, within their respective mandates, their activities relating to national capacity-building in the field of the administration of justice, in particular in post-conflict situations and, in this context, in cooperation with the Department of Peacekeeping Operations of the Secretariat;

11. *Encourages* the Office of the High Commissioner to continue organizing training courses and other relevant activities aimed at enhancing the promotion and protection of human rights in the field of the administration of justice, and welcomes the publication of the *Manual on Human Rights Training for Prison Officials*;

12. *Welcomes* the increased attention paid to the issue of juvenile justice by the High Commissioner and the United Nations Children's Fund, in particular through technical assistance activities, and, taking into account the fact that international cooperation to promote juvenile justice reform has become a priority within the United Nations system, encourages the further activities of the High Commissioner and the United Nations Children's Fund, within their mandates, in this regard;

13. *Encourages* the Inter-Agency Coordination Panel on Juvenile Justice to further increase cooperation among the partners involved, to develop common indicators, tools and manuals, to share information and to pool their capacities and interests in order to increase the effectiveness of programme implementation, and takes note with appreciation of the publication entitled "Protecting the rights of children in conflict with the law";

14. *Welcomes* the adoption by the Economic and Social Council of the Guidelines on Justice in Matters involving Child Victims and Witnesses of Crime, set out in the annex to its resolution 2005/20 of 22 July 2005, and encourages all relevant actors to draw upon the Guidelines where appropriate;

15. *Encourages* the independent expert for the United Nations study on violence against children to address in his final report the prevalence of violence in the juvenile justice system;

16. *Invites* Governments, relevant international and regional bodies, national human rights institutions and non-governmental organizations to devote increased attention to the issue of women in prison, including the children of women in prison, with a view to identifying and addressing the key problems;

17. *Underlines* the importance of rebuilding and strengthening structures for the administration of justice and respect for the rule of law and human rights in post-conflict situations, and requests the Secretary-General to ensure system-wide coordination and coherence of programmes and activities of the relevant parts of the United Nations system, including through the proposed Peacebuilding Commission and the Rule of Law Assistance Unit, in the field of the administration of justice in post-conflict situations, including assistance provided through United Nations field presences;

18. *Stresses* the special need for national capacity-building in the field of the administration of justice, in particular through reform of the judiciary, the police and the penal system, as well as juvenile justice reform, in order to establish and maintain stable societies and the rule of law in post-conflict situations, and in this context welcomes the role of the Office of the High Commissioner in supporting the establishment and functioning of transitional justice mechanisms in post-conflict situations;

19. *Decides* to consider the question of human rights in the administration of justice at its sixty-second session under the item entitled "Human rights questions".

Compensation for victims

Commission action. By a recorded vote of 40 to none, with 13 abstentions, the Commission, on 19 April [res. 2005/35], welcomed the report of Mr. Alejandro Salinas, the Chairperson-Rapporteur of the third consultative meeting on the basic principles and guidelines on the right to a remedy and reparation for victims of violations of international human rights and humanitarian law [YUN 2004, p. 716], which indicated that the draft basic principles and guidelines had been finalized, in response to a 2004 Commission request [ibid.]. The Commission adopted the draft, which was annexed to its current resolution, and recommended that States promote respect for the basic principles and guidelines and bring them to the attention of members of the executive bodies of Government, particularly law enforcement officials and military and security forces, legislative bodies and the judiciary, as well as victims and their representatives, human rights defenders, lawyers, the media and the public in general.

ECONOMIC AND SOCIAL COUNCIL ACTION

On 25 July, the Economic and Social Council, on the recommendation of the Commission on Human Rights [E/2005/23], adopted **resolution**

2005/30 by recorded vote (43-0-5) [agenda item 14 (g)].

Basic Principles and Guidelines on the Right to a Remedy and Reparation for Victims of Gross Violations of International Human Rights Law and Serious Violations of International Humanitarian Law

The Economic and Social Council,

Taking note of Commission on Human Rights resolution 2005/35 of 19 April 2005, in which the Commission adopted the text of the Basic Principles and Guidelines on the Right to a Remedy and Reparation for Victims of Gross Violations of International Human Rights Law and Serious Violations of International Humanitarian Law,

1. *Expresses its appreciation* to the Commission on Human Rights for the adoption of the Basic Principles and Guidelines on the Right to a Remedy and Reparation for Victims of Gross Violations of International Human Rights Law and Serious Violations of International Humanitarian Law;

2. *Adopts* the Basic Principles and Guidelines as contained in the annex to the present resolution;

3. *Recommends* to the General Assembly that it adopt the Basic Principles and Guidelines.

(See General Assembly resolution 60/147 below for full text of Principles and Guidelines.)

RECORDED VOTE ON RESOLUTION 2005/30:

In favour: Armenia, Azerbaijan, Bangladesh, Belgium, Belize, Brazil, Canada, Denmark, Ecuador, France, Guinea, Iceland, Indonesia, Ireland, Italy, Jamaica, Japan, Kenya, Lithuania, Malaysia, Mauritius, Mexico, Namibia, Nicaragua, Panama, Poland, Republic of Korea, Russian Federation, Saudi Arabia, Senegal, South Africa, Spain, Thailand, Tunisia, Turkey, United Arab Emirates, United Kingdom, United Republic of Tanzania.
Against: None.
Abstaining: Australia, Germany, India, Nigeria, United States.

GENERAL ASSEMBLY ACTION

On 16 December [meeting 64], the General Assembly, on the recommendation of the Third Committee [A/60/509], adopted **resolution 60/147** without vote [agenda item 71 (a)].

Basic Principles and Guidelines on the Right to a Remedy and Reparation for Victims of Gross Violations of International Human Rights Law and Serious Violations of International Humanitarian Law

The General Assembly,

Guided by the Charter of the United Nations, the Universal Declaration of Human Rights, the International Covenants on Human Rights, other relevant human rights instruments and the Vienna Declaration and Programme of Action,

Affirming the importance of addressing the question of remedies and reparation for victims of gross violations of international human rights law and serious violations of international humanitarian law in a systematic and thorough way at the national and international levels,

Recognizing that, in honouring the victims' right to benefit from remedies and reparation, the international community keeps faith with the plight of victims, survivors and future human generations and reaffirms international law in the field,

Recalling the adoption of the Basic Principles and Guidelines on the Right to a Remedy and Reparation

for Victims of Gross Violations of International Human Rights Law and Serious Violations of International Humanitarian Law by the Commission on Human Rights in its resolution 2005/35 of 19 April 2005 and by the Economic and Social Council in its resolution 2005/30 of 25 July 2005, in which the Council recommended to the General Assembly that it adopt the Basic Principles and Guidelines,

1. *Adopts* the Basic Principles and Guidelines on the Right to a Remedy and Reparation for Victims of Gross Violations of International Human Rights Law and Serious Violations of International Humanitarian Law annexed to the present resolution;

2. *Recommends* that States take the Basic Principles and Guidelines into account, promote respect thereof and bring them to the attention of members of the executive bodies of government, in particular law enforcement officials and military and security forces, legislative bodies, the judiciary, victims and their representatives, human rights defenders and lawyers, the media and the public in general;

3. *Requests* the Secretary-General to take steps to ensure the widest possible dissemination of the Basic Principles and Guidelines in all the official languages of the United Nations, including by transmitting them to Governments and intergovernmental and nongovernmental organizations and by including the Basic Principles and Guidelines in the United Nations publication entitled *Human Rights: A Compilation of International Instruments.*

Annex

Basic Principles and Guidelines on the Right to a Remedy and Reparation for Victims of Gross Violations of International Human Rights Law and Serious Violations of International Humanitarian Law

Preamble

The General Assembly,

Recalling the provisions providing a right to a remedy for victims of violations of international human rights law found in numerous international instruments, in particular article 8 of the Universal Declaration of Human Rights, article 2 of the International Covenant on Civil and Political Rights, article 6 of the International Convention on the Elimination of All Forms of Racial Discrimination, article 14 of the Convention against Torture and Other Cruel, Inhuman or Degrading Treatment or Punishment, and article 39 of the Convention on the Rights of the Child, and of international humanitarian law as found in article 3 of the Hague Convention respecting the Laws and Customs of War on Land of 18 October 1907 (Convention IV), article 91 of the Protocol Additional to the Geneva Conventions of 12 August 1949, and relating to the Protection of Victims of International Armed Conflicts (Protocol I) of 8 June 1977, and articles 68 and 75 of the Rome Statute of the International Criminal Court,

Recalling the provisions providing a right to a remedy for victims of violations of international human rights found in regional conventions, in particular article 7 of the African Charter on Human and Peoples' Rights, article 25 of the American Convention on Human Rights, and article 13 of the Convention for the Protection of Human Rights and Fundamental Freedoms,

Recalling the Declaration of Basic Principles of Justice for Victims of Crime and Abuse of Power emanating from the deliberations of the Seventh United Nations Congress on the Prevention of Crime and the Treatment of Offenders and General Assembly resolution 40/34 of 29 November 1985 by which the Assembly adopted the text recommended by the Congress,

Reaffirming the principles enunciated in the Declaration of Basic Principles of Justice for Victims of Crime and Abuse of Power, including that victims should be treated with compassion and respect for their dignity, have their right to access to justice and redress mechanisms fully respected, and that the establishment, strengthening and expansion of national funds for compensation to victims should be encouraged, together with the expeditious development of appropriate rights and remedies for victims,

Noting that the Rome Statute of the International Criminal Court requires the establishment of "principles relating to reparations to, or in respect of, victims, including restitution, compensation and rehabilitation", requires the Assembly of States Parties to establish a trust fund for the benefit of victims of crimes within the jurisdiction of the Court, and of the families of such victims, and mandates the Court "to protect the safety, physical and psychological well-being, dignity and privacy of victims" and to permit the participation of victims at all "stages of the proceedings determined to be appropriate by the Court",

Affirming that the Basic Principles and Guidelines contained herein are directed at gross violations of international human rights law and serious violations of international humanitarian law which, by their very grave nature, constitute an affront to human dignity,

Emphasizing that the Basic Principles and Guidelines contained herein do not entail new international or domestic legal obligations but identify mechanisms, modalities, procedures and methods for the implementation of existing legal obligations under international human rights law and international humanitarian law which are complementary though different as to their norms,

Recalling that international law contains the obligation to prosecute perpetrators of certain international crimes in accordance with international obligations of States and the requirements of national law or as provided for in the applicable statutes of international judicial organs, and that the duty to prosecute reinforces the international legal obligations to be carried out in accordance with national legal requirements and procedures and supports the concept of complementarity,

Noting that contemporary forms of victimization, while essentially directed against persons, may nevertheless also be directed against groups of persons who are targeted collectively,

Recognizing that, in honouring the victims' right to benefit from remedies and reparation, the international community keeps faith with the plight of victims, survivors and future human generations and reaffirms the international legal principles of accountability, justice and the rule of law,

Convinced that, in adopting a victim-oriented perspective, the international community affirms its human solidarity with victims of violations of international law, including violations of international human rights law and international humanitarian law, as well as with humanity at large, in accordance with the following Basic Principles and Guidelines,

Adopts the following Basic Principles and Guidelines:

I. Obligation to respect, ensure respect for and implement international human rights law and international humanitarian law

1. The obligation to respect, ensure respect for and implement international human rights law and international humanitarian law as provided for under the respective bodies of law emanates from:

(*a*) Treaties to which a State is a party;

(*b*) Customary international law;

(*c*) The domestic law of each State.

2. If they have not already done so, States shall, as required under international law, ensure that their domestic law is consistent with their international legal obligations by:

(*a*) Incorporating norms of international human rights law and international humanitarian law into their domestic law, or otherwise implementing them in their domestic legal system;

(*b*) Adopting appropriate and effective legislative and administrative procedures and other appropriate measures that provide fair, effective and prompt access to justice;

(*c*) Making available adequate, effective, prompt and appropriate remedies, including reparation, as defined below;

(*d*) Ensuring that their domestic law provides at least the same level of protection for victims as that required by their international obligations.

II. Scope of the obligation

3. The obligation to respect, ensure respect for and implement international human rights law and international humanitarian law as provided for under the respective bodies of law, includes, inter alia, the duty to:

(*a*) Take appropriate legislative and administrative and other appropriate measures to prevent violations;

(*b*) Investigate violations effectively, promptly, thoroughly and impartially and, where appropriate, take action against those allegedly responsible in accordance with domestic and international law;

(*c*) Provide those who claim to be victims of a human rights or humanitarian law violation with equal and effective access to justice, as described below, irrespective of who may ultimately be the bearer of responsibility for the violation; and

(*d*) Provide effective remedies to victims, including reparation, as described below.

III. Gross violations of international human rights law and serious violations of international humanitarian law that constitute crimes under international law

4. In cases of gross violations of international human rights law and serious violations of international humanitarian law constituting crimes under international law, States have the duty to investigate and, if there is sufficient evidence, the duty to submit to prosecution the person allegedly responsible for the violations and, if found guilty, the duty to punish her or him. Moreover, in these cases, States should, in accordance with international law, cooperate with one another and assist international judicial organs compe-

tent in the investigation and prosecution of these violations.

5. To that end, where so provided in an applicable treaty or under other international law obligations, States shall incorporate or otherwise implement within their domestic law appropriate provisions for universal jurisdiction. Moreover, where it is so provided for in an applicable treaty or other international legal obligations, States should facilitate extradition or surrender offenders to other States and to appropriate international judicial bodies and provide judicial assistance and other forms of cooperation in the pursuit of international justice, including assistance to, and protection of, victims and witnesses, consistent with international human rights legal standards and subject to international legal requirements such as those relating to the prohibition of torture and other forms of cruel, inhuman or degrading treatment or punishment.

IV. Statutes of limitations

6. Where so provided for in an applicable treaty or contained in other international legal obligations, statutes of limitations shall not apply to gross violations of international human rights law and serious violations of international humanitarian law which constitute crimes under international law.

7. Domestic statutes of limitations for other types of violations that do not constitute crimes under international law, including those time limitations applicable to civil claims and other procedures, should not be unduly restrictive.

V. Victims of gross violations of international human rights law and serious violations of international humanitarian law

8. For purposes of the present document, victims are persons who individually or collectively suffered harm, including physical or mental injury, emotional suffering, economic loss or substantial impairment of their fundamental rights, through acts or omissions that constitute gross violations of international human rights law, or serious violations of international humanitarian law. Where appropriate, and in accordance with domestic law, the term "victim" also includes the immediate family or dependants of the direct victim and persons who have suffered harm in intervening to assist victims in distress or to prevent victimization.

9. A person shall be considered a victim regardless of whether the perpetrator of the violation is identified, apprehended, prosecuted, or convicted and regardless of the familial relationship between the perpetrator and the victim.

VI. Treatment of victims

10. Victims should be treated with humanity and respect for their dignity and human rights, and appropriate measures should be taken to ensure their safety, physical and psychological well-being and privacy, as well as those of their families. The State should ensure that its domestic laws, to the extent possible, provide that a victim who has suffered violence or trauma should benefit from special consideration and care to avoid his or her re-traumatization in the course of legal and administrative procedures designed to provide justice and reparation.

VII. Victims' right to remedies

11. Remedies for gross violations of international human rights law and serious violations of international humanitarian law include the victim's right to the following as provided for under international law:

(a) Equal and effective access to justice;

(b) Adequate, effective and prompt reparation for harm suffered;

(c) Access to relevant information concerning violations and reparation mechanisms.

VIII. Access to justice

12. A victim of a gross violation of international human rights law or of a serious violation of international humanitarian law shall have equal access to an effective judicial remedy as provided for under international law. Other remedies available to the victim include access to administrative and other bodies, as well as mechanisms, modalities and proceedings conducted in accordance with domestic law. Obligations arising under international law to secure the right to access justice and fair and impartial proceedings shall be reflected in domestic laws. To that end, States should:

(a) Disseminate, through public and private mechanisms, information about all available remedies for gross violations of international human rights law and serious violations of international humanitarian law;

(b) Take measures to minimize the inconvenience to victims and their representatives, protect against unlawful interference with their privacy as appropriate and ensure their safety from intimidation and retaliation, as well as that of their families and witnesses, before, during and after judicial, administrative, or other proceedings that affect the interests of victims;

(c) Provide proper assistance to victims seeking access to justice;

(d) Make available all appropriate legal, diplomatic and consular means to ensure that victims can exercise their rights to remedy for gross violations of international human rights law or serious violations of international humanitarian law.

13. In addition to individual access to justice, States should endeavour to develop procedures to allow groups of victims to present claims for reparation and to receive reparation, as appropriate.

14. An adequate, effective and prompt remedy for gross violations of international human rights law or serious violations of international humanitarian law should include all available and appropriate international processes in which a person may have legal standing and should be without prejudice to any other domestic remedies.

IX. Reparation for harm suffered

15. Adequate, effective and prompt reparation is intended to promote justice by redressing gross violations of international human rights law or serious violations of international humanitarian law. Reparation should be proportional to the gravity of the violations and the harm suffered. In accordance with its domestic laws and international legal obligations, a State shall provide reparation to victims for acts or omissions which can be attributed to the State and constitute gross violations of international human rights law or serious violations of international humanitarian law. In cases where a person, a legal person, or other entity is found liable for reparation to a victim, such party

should provide reparation to the victim or compensate the State if the State has already provided reparation to the victim.

16.   States should endeavour to establish national programmes for reparation and other assistance to victims in the event that the parties liable for the harm suffered are unable or unwilling to meet their obligations.

17.   States shall, with respect to claims by victims, enforce domestic judgements for reparation against individuals or entities liable for the harm suffered and endeavour to enforce valid foreign legal judgements for reparation in accordance with domestic law and international legal obligations. To that end, States should provide under their domestic laws effective mechanisms for the enforcement of reparation judgements.

18.   In accordance with domestic law and international law, and taking account of individual circumstances, victims of gross violations of international human rights law and serious violations of international humanitarian law should, as appropriate and proportional to the gravity of the violation and the circumstances of each case, be provided with full and effective reparation, as laid out in principles 19 to 23, which include the following forms: restitution, compensation, rehabilitation, satisfaction and guarantees of non-repetition.

19.   *Restitution* should, whenever possible, restore the victim to the original situation before the gross violations of international human rights law or serious violations of international humanitarian law occurred. Restitution includes, as appropriate: restoration of liberty, enjoyment of human rights, identity, family life and citizenship, return to one's place of residence, restoration of employment and return of property.

20.   *Compensation* should be provided for any economically assessable damage, as appropriate and proportional to the gravity of the violation and the circumstances of each case, resulting from gross violations of international human rights law and serious violations of international humanitarian law, such as:

(a)   Physical or mental harm;

(b)   Lost opportunities, including employment, education and social benefits;

(c)   Material damages and loss of earnings, including loss of earning potential;

(d)   Moral damage;

(e)   Costs required for legal or expert assistance, medicine and medical services, and psychological and social services.

21.   *Rehabilitation* should include medical and psychological care as well as legal and social services.

22.   *Satisfaction* should include, where applicable, any or all of the following:

(a)   Effective measures aimed at the cessation of continuing violations;

(b)   Verification of the facts and full and public disclosure of the truth to the extent that such disclosure does not cause further harm or threaten the safety and interests of the victim, the victim's relatives, witnesses, or persons who have intervened to assist the victim or prevent the occurrence of further violations;

(c)   The search for the whereabouts of the disappeared, for the identities of the children abducted, and for the bodies of those killed, and assistance in the recovery, identification and reburial of the bodies in accordance with the expressed or presumed wish of the victims, or the cultural practices of the families and communities;

(d)   An official declaration or a judicial decision restoring the dignity, the reputation and the rights of the victim and of persons closely connected with the victim;

(e)   Public apology, including acknowledgement of the facts and acceptance of responsibility;

(f)   Judicial and administrative sanctions against persons liable for the violations;

(g)   Commemorations and tributes to the victims;

(h)   Inclusion of an accurate account of the violations that occurred in international human rights law and international humanitarian law training and in educational material at all levels.

23.   *Guarantees of non-repetition* should include, where applicable, any or all of the following measures, which will also contribute to prevention:

(a)   Ensuring effective civilian control of military and security forces;

(b)   Ensuring that all civilian and military proceedings abide by international standards of due process, fairness and impartiality;

(c)   Strengthening the independence of the judiciary;

(d)   Protecting persons in the legal, medical and health-care professions, the media and other related professions, and human rights defenders;

(e)   Providing, on a priority and continued basis, human rights and international humanitarian law education to all sectors of society and training for law enforcement officials as well as military and security forces;

(f)   Promoting the observance of codes of conduct and ethical norms, in particular international standards, by public servants, including law enforcement, correctional, media, medical, psychological, social service and military personnel, as well as by economic enterprises;

(g)   Promoting mechanisms for preventing and monitoring social conflicts and their resolution;

(h)   Reviewing and reforming laws contributing to or allowing gross violations of international human rights law and serious violations of international humanitarian law.

X.   Access to relevant information concerning violations and reparation mechanisms

24.   States should develop means of informing the general public and, in particular, victims of gross violations of international human rights law and serious violations of international humanitarian law of the rights and remedies addressed by these Basic Principles and Guidelines and of all available legal, medical, psychological, social, administrative and all other services to which victims may have a right of access. Moreover, victims and their representatives should be entitled to seek and obtain information on the causes leading to their victimization and on the causes and conditions pertaining to the gross violations of international human rights law and serious violations of international humanitarian law and to learn the truth in regard to these violations.

XI.   Non-discrimination

25.   The application and interpretation of these Basic Principles and Guidelines must be consistent with

international human rights law and international humanitarian law and be without any discrimination of any kind or on any ground, without exception.

XII. Non-derogation

26. Nothing in these Basic Principles and Guidelines shall be construed as restricting or derogating from any rights or obligations arising under domestic and international law. In particular, it is understood that the present Basic Principles and Guidelines are without prejudice to the right to a remedy and reparation for victims of all violations of international human rights law and international humanitarian law. It is further understood that these Basic Principles and Guidelines are without prejudice to special rules of international law.

XIII. Rights of others

27. Nothing in this document is to be construed as derogating from internationally or nationally protected rights of others, in particular the right of an accused person to benefit from applicable standards of due process.

Rule of law

Non-State actors

In response to a 2004 Subcommission request [YUN 2004, p. 717], Gáspár Bíró (Hungary) and Antoanella-Iulia Motoc (Romania) submitted a working paper on human rights and non-State actors [E/CN.4/Sub.2/2005/40], in order to approach systematically the question of accountability under international human rights law. The paper aimed to provide an overview of the most characteristic views expressed on the subject, including those relating to the definition of non-State actors; a possible typology, in terms of a distinction between political actors and other actors in international relations; the non-State element relative to the internal authorization of sub-State treaty-making and the individual accountable for human rights violations; an understanding of relevant international organizations in addressing the subject; and the role of NGOs and other non-State actors, such as Commission mechanisms. It also discussed the contemporary crises of nation-States following the rise of non-State actors and networks, and the status of transnational corporations that also operated as such actors. The paper concluded by identifying issues for further clarification, which related to political and non-political actors, the alternative designation of non-State actors as transnational actors, freely assumed and/or intentionally assigned responsibilities, and those who were benefiting or losing from the international order.

Subcommission action. On 11 August [dec. 2005/112], the Subcommission requested Mr. Bíró, Ms. Motoc, David Rivkin (United States) and Ibrahim Salama (Egypt) to prepare, without financial implications, an expanded working paper on human rights and non-State actors, taking into account the discussions of the Subcommission, for consideration in 2006.

Civilians in armed conflict

Commission action. On 20 April [res. 2005/63], the Commission, by a recorded vote of 51 to 1, with 1 abstention, urged parties to armed conflict to comply with their obligations under international humanitarian law regarding the protection of the civilian population. To that end, it asked States to comply with their human rights obligations and invited the international community to support regional efforts.

Subcommission action. On 8 August [res. 2005/2], the Subcommission expressed concern about military operations directed against medical facilities, transport and personnel and invited the Special Rapporteur on the right to the highest attainable standard of physical and mental health to address urgently the issue of the protection of such facilities in situations of armed conflict.

On 10 August [res. 2005/10], the Subcommission, emphasizing that no alleged political, philosophical, religious or military ground justified attacks against persons entitled to protection as civilians, affirmed that anyone who knowingly financed such attacks, prohibited by customary international criminal law, was guilty of an international crime.

On the same date [res. 2005/14], the Subcommission, concerned about alleged criminal behaviour and other misconduct by military and civilian personnel in peace support operations, appointed Françoise Hampson (United Kingdom) as Special Rapporteur with the task of preparing a comprehensive study on the accountability of international personnel taking part in peace support operations. She was asked to submit a preliminary report in 2006, a progress report in 2007 and a final report in 2008. The Secretary-General was requested to assist her, including by facilitating a possible visit to the UN Secretariat to distribute a questionnaire to States contributing troops to peace support operations. The Subcommission decided that, should its appointment of Ms. Hampson as Special Rapporteur not be approved by the Commission or the Economic and Social Council, she should prepare a working paper on the assigned topic, for consideration in 2006.

Report of Secretary-General. A November report [S/2005/740] of the Secretary-General on the protection of civilians in armed conflict reviewed emerging trends, related issues of concern to the Security Council, the framework for discussing the complex range of issues relevant for ensuring respect for civilian status and the next steps that should be taken regarding the questions of protection, the provision of humanitarian assistance, peacemaking and monitoring and reporting. Highlighting the main events of the past five years that had shaped the protection environment, the Secretary-General observed that, during that period, civilians were caught up in armed conflict or acts of terrorism in diverse situations, including in Afghanistan, Burundi, Colombia, the Democratic Republic of the Congo, Iraq, the Occupied Palestinian Territory, Nepal, the Sudan, Uganda, as well as in the West Africa region and elsewhere. The impact of armed conflict on civilians went far beyond the notion of collateral damage, as targeted attacks, forced displacement and conscription, sexual violence, indiscriminate killings, malnutrition, hunger, disease and loss of livelihoods collectively painted an extremely grim picture of its human costs. Although the number of such conflicts decreased from 50 in 1992 to 30 in 2004, the current trend toward low-intensity conflicts fought by smaller and less well-trained armed groups and with small arms and light weapons in urban and rural areas placed civilians at greater risk of being caught in cross fires and used as human shields, and forced to surrender their food and money or forcibly recruited into armed groups, many of them, as child soldiers.

Select areas of concern to the Security Council related to the nature of violence against civilians, the security of displaced persons and host communities, special issues relating to women and children, and access to vulnerable population. Despite the fact that the UN agenda for protecting civilians in armed conflict continued to provide an important framework for safeguarding civilian status in conflict situations, including Council resolutions 1265(1999) [YUN 1999, p. 649] and 1296(2000) [YUN 2000, p. 667], which provided a solid basis for response, and relative progress had been made in implementing the framework, gaps remained, which needed to be addressed in order to consolidate progress in meeting protection needs. Notably, new challenges to the safety and well-being of civilian populations had emerged, and tools at the disposal of the international community to address them needed to be developed accordingly. Protection from physical and sexual violence was one of the major challenges in that regard, and the framework by which the Council could support civilian protection needed to be updated to better reflect UN capacity to respond. To ensure a clear focus on protection that could be reflected in the Council's work, it was essential to establish the capacity

to collate necessary information, including that relating to protection incidents in countries of concern to the Council. In addition, improvements in the design of peacekeeping missions, supported by mandates that addressed the specific protection needs of a conflict or the post-conflict environment would contribute to the protection of civilians. Enhancing the capacity and readiness of regional organizations to respond to protection concerns would also contribute significantly to the effectiveness with which the protection needs of civilians were addressed.

SECURITY COUNCIL ACTION

On 21 June 2005 [meeting 5209], the Security Council discussed the protection of civilians in armed conflict. Its President, following consultations among Council members, made statement **S/PRST/2005/25** on behalf of the Council:

The Security Council, recalling its resolutions 1265(1999) and 1296(2000) as well as statements made by its Presidents on the protection of civilians in armed conflict, reiterates its commitment to address the widespread impact of armed conflict on civilian populations.

The Council reaffirms its strong condemnation of the deliberate targeting of civilians or other protected persons in situations of armed conflict, and calls upon all parties to put an end to such practices. It expresses, in particular, its deep concern at the use of sexual violence as a weapon of war. It calls upon all States to put an end to impunity also in this regard.

The Council is gravely concerned about limited progress on the ground to ensure the effective protection of civilians in situations of armed conflict. It stresses, in particular, the urgent need for providing better physical protection for displaced populations as well as for other vulnerable groups, in particular women and children. Efforts should be focused in areas where these populations and groups are most at risk. At the same time, it considers that contributing to the establishment of a secure environment for all vulnerable populations should be a key objective of peacekeeping operations.

The Council invites, accordingly, the Secretary-General to include in his next report recommendations on ways to better address the persisting and emerging protection challenges in the evolving peacekeeping environment. Upon receipt of this report, it expresses its intention to take further action to strengthen and to enhance the protection of civilians in armed conflict, including, if necessary, the possible adoption of a resolution in this regard.

Missing persons

Report of Secretary-General. In accordance with a 2002 Commission request [YUN 2002, p. 696], the Secretary-General, in February [E/CN.4/2005/83], summarized replies received from three Governments and one international humanitarian organization on the issue of missing persons.

Arbitrary detention

Commission action. On 19 April [res. 2005/28], the Commission encouraged States to consider the recommendations of the Working Group on Arbitrary Detention (see below) to cooperate with it, consider its requests for visits and to ensure that their legislation, regulations and practices conformed with international standards and instruments. The Secretary-General was asked to assist Governments, special rappporteurs and working groups to ensure the promotion and observance of guarantees relating to the prevention of arbitrary detention laid down in relevant international instruments, and to assist the Group. The Group was asked to report in 2006.

Working Group activities. The Working Group on Arbitrary Detention held its forty-second (23-27 May), forty-third (29 August–2 September) and forty-fourth (21-30 November) sessions, all in Geneva [E/CN.4/2006/7]. During the year, the Group adopted 48 opinions concerning 115 persons in 30 countries; the texts of those opinions were contained in a separate report [E/CN.4/2006/7/Add.1]. The Group also transmitted 181 urgent appeals concerning 565 individuals to 56 Governments, of which 168 were issued jointly with other thematic or country-oriented mandates of the Commission. In 32 cases, the Governments concerned informed the Group that they had taken measures to remedy the situation of detainees.

In 2005, the Group considered issues relating to the use of the Internet; such issues of concern as the use of secret prisons and over-incarceration; and its own competence regarding cases of detention that were linked to an armed conflict. In November, the Group adopted its deliberation No. 8 concerning the deprivation of liberty linked to/resulting from the use of the Internet, against the background of an increasing number of communications on behalf of affected individuals. The Group held, in that context, that the freedom to impart, receive or seek information through the Internet was protected under international law in the same way as any other form of expression of opinions, ideas or convictions. In effect, the peaceful, non-violent expression or manifestation of one's opinion, or dissemination and reception of information, including through the Internet, if it did not constitute incitement to national, racial or religious hatred or violence, remained within the boundaries of freedom of expression. However, the use of the Internet might be restricted if it unduly interfered with the rights of others or aimed to promote terrorist purposes. The Group recommended that States take its deliberation No. 8 into account when addressing the legislative or law enforcement aspects of the use of the Internet. In other recommendations, it urged States to stop operating secret prisons and detention facilities, and when cooperating with other States in their lawful fights against terrorism, to ensure that the transfer of suspected individuals rested on a sound legal basis. States should also avoid over-incarceration and mitigate the over-representation of minorities and other vulnerable groups among the prison population. In addition, they should also guarantee to detained foreign nationals the right to challenge the lawfulness of their detention.

At the invitation of the Government, three Working Group members visited Canada (1-15 June) [E/CN.4/2006/7/Add.2], where they reviewed the institutional and legal frameworks for detention. The Group identified several positive aspects of the country's justice system relating to the independence of the judiciary and checks on the criminal justice system; a reduction in the incarceration rate; efforts to reduce pretrial detention, particularly of persons belonging to vulnerable and marginalized groups; and the limited duration of immigration custody. It found in particular, that the country possessed a strong, independent judiciary, which strove to ensure that trials were fair and that the deprivation of liberty was lawful. The control exercised by the judiciary was complemented by the active role of lawyers in private practice, NGOs and commission of inquiry for the administration of justice. It was also encouraging that the incarceration rate in the country had reduced significantly, owing largely to legislation that provided for the enhanced use of sanctions other than incarceration. Despite those encouraging factors, problems remained, including the continuing over-representation of aboriginals in the corrections system, and increased recourse to pretrial detention, which mostly affected vulnerable social groups, including minorities, the poor and persons with mental health problems. Furthermore, although Canada had a well-developed criminal legal aid system to secure the constitutionally guaranteed right to counsel, in practice, the system left many needs uncovered. Other sources of concern included the existence of several provisions of the immigration law governing detention of asylum-seekers and migrants, which had resulted in the unjustifiable detention of aliens who were not able to challenge their detention, and a security certificate process, which authorized the detention of aliens for years on the suspicion that they posed a security threat, without raising criminal charges. The Group addressed recommendations to the Government regarding the issues the over-representation of Aboriginals in prisons, the excessive use of pretrial detention in dealing with accused persons belonging to vulnerable social groups, and unmet needs for legal aid. It proposed changes to immigration law and policy, recommending, in that regard, that terrorism suspects be detained in the criminal process, with the relevant safeguards, rather than under immigration laws.

In South Africa (4-19 September) [E/CN.4/2006/7/Add.3], where the Group acknowledged dramatic changes over the past 15 years and an emerging democratic culture, it found that the protection of human rights, particularly the rights of arrested and detained persons were well established in the Constitution. It also highlighted improvements in the correctional system, which was oriented towards rehabilitation and reinsertion, and the establishment by the Government of a legal aid system available to all detainees in the criminal process. Contrary to those positive elements was a high rate of incarceration in the country, attributed partly to the harsh and long sentences passed by the courts and mandatory minimum sentences that were applicable to a wide range of offences. The situation had resulted in a worrisome number of persons in detention serving long sentences and an alarming rate of overcrowding in detention facilities. Also of concern were the fact that the behaviour of some police officers had led to a negative perception of police activities and that, in some cases, foreigners were deprived of their liberty. The Group encouraged ongoing reforms to improve the treatment of young offenders and to set up a specialized justice system for minors. It recommended that the Government adopt alternative measures to detention and reduce the duration of pretrial detention, avoid holding pretrial detainees in police cells, and in sentencing, take into account time already spent in pre-trial custody. The Government should also take appropriate measures to allow for an effective challenge of the detention of illegal foreigners to enable them exercised the rights guaranteed under the Constitution.

Impunity

Report of independent expert. In response to a 2004 Commission request [YUN 2004, p. 722], the independent expert to update the 1997 [YUN 1997, p. 655] set of principles to combat impunity, Diane Orentlicher (United States), submitted a February report [E/CN.4/2005/102] updating the principles in the light of recent developments in international law and practice, including those noted in her 2004 study [YUN 2004, p. 722]. The current report, which was based on information provided by Governments, revised various parts of the text of the principles, including those relating to the

definition of relevant terms, the right to know, the right to justice, and the right to reparation/guarantees of non-recurrence. In that context, the study chronicled the advances in national and international efforts to combat impunity since the set of principles was submitted in 1997. The expert observed that, since then, seemingly impregnable barriers to prosecution had been dismantled in countries that had endured dictatorship, and States had cooperated to ensure prosecution of officials at the highest levels of government before international tribunals and national courts. A new breed of court, combining national and international elements, had evolved to help render justice for atrocious crimes, and against that background, Government and civil society had benefited from an expanding repertoire of tools for combating impunity. In sum, relevant developments in international law had strongly affirmed the principles, while providing further clarification of the scope of States' established legal obligations.

An addendum to the report [E/CN.4/2005/102/Add.1] presented the expert's revised text of the principles.

Commission action. On 21 April [res. 2005/81], the Commission, taking note of the report of the independent expert and the updated set of principles for the protection and promotion of human rights through action to combat impunity (see above), asked the High Commissioner to disseminate them and make them available in an accessible and user-friendly format, including in the UN publication entitled *Human Rights: A Compilation of International Instruments.* The Secretary-General was asked to invite States, intergovernmental organizations and NGOs to provide information on steps they had taken to combat impunity and on remedies available to victims, and to report in 2006 on developments in international law and practice relevant to combating impunity.

Working paper. In response to a 2002 Subcommission request [YUN 2002, p. 699], Françoise Hampson (United Kingdom) submitted a July working paper [E/CN.4/Sub.2/2005/42] on the accountability of international personnel taking part in peace support operations. The paper defined the scope of those operations, the missions in question and the personnel who might be involved, and examined who was potentially subject to particular jurisdictions, the operation of the system in practice and the impact of impunity. It concluded that, although significant changes had been made in efforts to deal with criminal and disciplinary matters outside the mandate of peace operations, the United Nations did not appear to accept accountability for acts committed within those mandates. That posed particular difficulties in the case of peace support operations where the Organization was, in effect, the Government of the territory, or in the case of personnel other than military personnel. In practical terms, the problems appeared to relate to the prevention of misconduct and to operationalization of the system regarding how complaints were made and received. The paper identified several issues which merited further study and recommended that the Subcommission request the Commission to appoint a special rapporteur to study the subject.

Right to the truth

Commission action. On 20 April [res. 2005/66], the Commission, stressing the imperative for society to recognize the right of victims of gross human rights violations to know the truth, including the identity of the perpetrators and the causes, facts and circumstances in which such violations took place, welcomed the establishment in several States of specific judicial and non-judicial mechanisms, such as truth and reconciliation commissions that complemented the justice system. It encouraged the States concerned to disseminate and implement the recommendations of such mechanisms, and other States, to consider establishing them. OHCHR was asked to prepare, for consideration in 2006, a study on the right to the truth, including information on the basis, scope and content of the right under international law, as well as best practices and recommendations for effective implementation of the right. Special rapporteurs and other Commission mechanisms were invited to take the issue into account in their work.

Independence of the judicial system

Report of Special Rapporteur. The Special Rapporteur on the independence of judges and lawyers, Leandro Despouy (Argentina), submitted a report [E/CN.4/2005/60], which provided an overview of his 2004 activities. He had transmitted 104 urgent appeals, 34 letters of allegation and 15 press releases to 53 Governments, replies to which were received from 38 countries. An addendum to the report [E/CN.4/2005/60/Add.1] contained summaries of the communications sent and the replies thereto. The report focused on issues relating to the thematic questions of the impact of the fight against terrorism on human rights and the administration of justice in a period of transition. In that context, it examined the rise of terrorism and efforts to combat the phenomenon within the law, worrisome developments concerning the status of enemy com-

batants and their effects in practical terms, administrative detention without legal safeguards, the improper use of military courts to try civilians, and the consequences for other human rights of counter-terrorism and measures taken on the grounds of national security. In addition, the report considered the questions of reconstructing the judiciary, fighting against impunity, re-establishing truth and ensuring justice, reparation and compensation for victims, as well as good practices and tools to assist new authorities and the work of the International Criminal Court (ICC) (see p. 1402) within the framework of post-conflict justice. Highlighting the extent to which the right to a fair trial by an independent and impartial court of law might be affected by counter-terrorism measures, the Special Rapporteur proposed that a study be undertaken on the compatibility of action taken by States to combat terrorism and preserve national security with the rules of international law. He also proposed that the Commission further examine the question of justice in a period of transition, so as to provide States in transition with the necessary tools and references to help them respond to challenges concerning justice, impunity and the right of victims to the truth, reparation and compensation. Advocating a complementary approach in UN work on the problem, the Special Rapporteur recommended that the Commission envisage a special procedure for supervising the compatibility of ongoing or planned counter-terrorism or security measures with the current rules of international law. Other recommendations related to justice in post-conflict and transition periods, capital punishment, training of judges and lawyers and mechanisms for cooperation with States.

Commission action. On 19 April [res. 2005/30], by a recorded vote of 52 to none, with 1 abstention, the Commission called on States that used military courts to try criminal offenders to ensure that such courts were an integral part of the general judicial system and that they applied internationally recognized due process procedures. The Special Rapporteur was asked to take the Commission's current resolution into account in discharging his mandate and to report in 2006.

Also on 19 April [res. 2005/33], the Commission called on Governments to respect and uphold the independence of judges and lawyers and asked the High Commissioner to continue to provide technical assistance to train them. The Special Rapporteur was requested to report to the General Assembly in 2005 and to the Commission in 2006, and the Secretary-General was asked to assist him.

On 25 July, the Economic and Social Council endorsed the Commission's requests to the Special Rapporteur and the Secretary-General (**decision 2005/263**).

Further reports of Special Rapporteur. At the invitation of the Government, the Special Rapporteur undertook preliminary (13-18 March) [E/CN.4/2005/60/Add.4] and follow-up (11-15 July) [E/CN.4/2006/52/Add.2] visits to Ecuador, where he studied the situation regarding the country's highest courts, following recent decisions by the National Congress, which resulted in the removal of some judges and appointment of their successors in a manner that might have violated the constitutional order and independence of the country's judiciary. Reflecting on suggestions that the changes were made because the majority parties dominated the court and in order to rectify a constitutional anomaly whereby one member of the court belonged to a party that no longer existed, the Special Rapporteur noted, in March, that the National Congress was not competent to resolve or rectify an unconstitutional situation, since that was the exclusive right of the Constitutional Court. In a series of preliminary recommendations, he observed that, since it was the National Congress that had taken the principal steps that provoked the situation, it was incumbent on it to adopt measures to rectify the situation. The country needed to devise a formula to govern appointments to the Supreme Court in a manner that guaranteed the independence, suitability and probity of judges.

Following further examination of the situation during his July visit, the Special Rapporteur found that the Government had begun to implement some of the recommendations he had made in March, particularly by establishing a Qualifications Committee, which appointed new Supreme Court judges in a transparent manner, with public oversight and under the supervision of international and national bodies, including judges from other regional States. In further recommendations, he advocated urgent reforms of the justice system, including the enactment of a new law on the organization of the judiciary, its standards and safeguards, the practical application of the principle that only judicial bodies might perform judicial functions and the establishment of an effective legal aid system. Priority should be given to the establishment of the Constitutional Court, the adoption of rules for the Supreme Electoral Court and the appointment of a Comptroller General and an Attorney-General.

By an August note [A/60/321], the Secretary-General transmitted a report of the Special Rapporteur, submitted in accordance with Commission resolution 2005/33 (see above). The report outlined the terms of reference for his mandate and developments in that regard, described his main activities and reflected on the progress made in the field of human rights. It also identified issues of concern to the Special Rapporteur, the first of which related to the situation in Ecuador following the unconstitutional dismissal of many members of the judiciary, including Supreme Court judges, which had prompted the Special Rapporteur to visit the country twice within the year. Other issues of concern related to the questions of counter-terrorism and the right to a fair trial, the work of the ICC (see p. 1402), judicial proceedings at the Iraqi Special Tribunal, and transitional justice and the right to the truth. Regarding the situation in Ecuador, the Special Rapporteur noted that actions that undermined justice could have such serious political consequences as those that affected the country in April, culminating in the removal of its President. To redress the situation, he stressed the need for greater transparency and credibility to the process of selecting judges, and recommended that, in accordance with Ecuadorian legislation, international observers, particularly the United Nations, should oversee the process.

Turning to other issues, the Special Rapporteur observed that many States, including the United Kingdom and the United States, were currently discussing or adopting measures for combating suspected terrorists, which could undermine international human rights standards. While condemning terrorist practices, including the bloody attacks in London and Egypt (Sharm El Sheik) within the year (see pp. 103 & 105), he emphasized the need for concerted international action in combating the scourge. He noted nonetheless, that there had been setbacks regarding respect for the rule of law and human rights, owing to counter-terrorism measures. Of particular concern, was a tendency to roll back existing levels of international protection, as was the continuing opposition of some Governments to ICC and the manner in which trials were being conducted by the Iraqi Special Tribunal. He observed, in particular, that the Tribunal's power to impose capital punishment contravened international human rights standards. Reflecting on efforts to reform the Commission through the creation of a standing human rights council (see p. 712), the Special Rapporteur hoped that the restructuring would acknowledge the cross-cutting nature of the issues he had addressed and establish the mechanisms to strengthen his work.

At the invitation of the Government, the Special Rapporteur visited Kyrgyzstan (18-22 September) [E/CN.4/2006/52/Add.3], where he gained an insight into the issues and challenges facing the judiciary and the main actors in the administration of justice. He found that the country's new leadership had undertaken several reforms and initiated developments favourable to the judicial system, including legislative initiatives; constitutional amendments transferring the power to issue arrest warrants to the judiciary; introducing juries and lay assessors and enabling courts to control their budgets; and a proposal to abolish the death penalty. Despite those efforts, the judiciary still did not operate as a fully independent institution capable of administering fair and independent justice and safeguarding and protecting human rights. Widespread corruption among the judiciary continued, owing partly to low salary levels, and there was a lack of trust of the population in the judicial system. The Bar had the potential to play a fundamental role in safeguarding human rights, yet it was weakened by the failure to implement the principle of equality of arms and continuing executive control over admissions and regulatory procedures.

The Special Rapporteur called for the consolidation of constitutional and legislative reforms and made recommendations to the Government on the need for a legal framework better equipped to ensure the full independence of the judges and lawyers and enhanced respect for human rights principles. Other recommendations addressed the need to ensure a fairer balance between the respective roles of the judiciary and defence lawyers. The Special Rapporteur further recommended the strengthening of the judiciary as a fully independent institution capable of protecting human rights and fundamental freedoms, of the Bar to ensure it could play its role in protecting clients' rights, and of the court system and other institutions to enable them to function effectively, and in a transparent manner.

In Tajikistan (23-30 September) [E/CN.4/2006/ 52/Add.4], the Special Rapporteur examined the status of and recent developments regarding the judiciary. He found that the country had introduced significant judicial reforms since the 1997 peace accord that ended its six-year civil war, including a moratorium on the death penalty, the adoption of new civil and criminal codes, the extension of judges' tenures and the ratification of all major international human rights instruments. While acknowledging those measures, the Special Rapporteur found the strengthening of the role of the prosecutor disquieting, as that represented a step backwards and a development towards forms of authoritarianism that were a feature of the past. It was all the more disturbing as Tajikistan was a country exposed to major geopolitical challenges and was struggling with a high percentage of people living in poverty and a high level of endemic corruption that affected al-

most all spheres of life. In addition, the executive branch remained very influential in the selection and appointment procedures for judges, with the vulnerable position of lawyers posing additional problems. To help Tajikistan accelerate the judicial reform process leading to a fully independent judiciary, the Special Rapporteur recommended numerous measures to the Government for bringing the national legal system in compliance with international standards governing the independence of the judiciary; strengthen related institutional structures and mechanisms; address the problem of the weak role of lawyers; strengthen national human rights institutions and mechanisms; provide for training, continuing legal education and the availability of legal information material; and address the problem of corruption.

Capital punishment

Report of Secretary-General. Pursuant to a 2004 Commission request [YUN 2004, p. 724], the Secretary-General, in March [E/2005/3], submitted his seventh quinquennial report on capital punishment and the implementation of safeguards guaranteeing protection of the rights of those facing the death penalty, covering the period 1999 to 2003. The report drew on current criminological data and information from Member States, intergovernmental organizations, UN specialized agencies and NGOs, gathered through a questionnaire. Of the 52 countries that responded, 33 (63 per cent) were abolitionists at the beginning of the reporting period, accounting for 47 per cent of all abolitionist countries. Of 34 de facto abolitionist countries—those that had retained the death penalty for ordinary crimes but had not executed anyone in the last 10 years or more—only five (about 10 per cent) replied, and of the 78 States that retained and enforced capital punishment during the reporting period, only eight (about 11 per cent) responded.

At the beginning of the quinquennial period, 70 countries and territories had embraced total abolition of the death penalty, a considerably higher number than at the beginning of the previous quinquennium [YUN 2000, p. 672]. During the current survey period, two of the de facto abolitionists became abolitionists for all offences, four became abolitionists for ordinary offences and three resumed executions, thereby becoming retentionists. Of the 78 countries that were retentionists in 1999, three became abolitionists for all crimes, 15 became de facto abolitionists, and 59 maintained their status as retentionist countries, although 18 of them did not carry out judicial executions between 1999 and 2003. Over that period, figures available suggested that an estimated 18,200 persons were sentenced to death, and 9,000 judicially executed, marking a reduction from 23,000 persons sentenced to death and 13,500 executed in the last reporting period (1994-1998).

The report also included information on the implementation of the safeguards guaranteeing protection of the rights of those facing the death penalty, adopted by the Economic and Social Council in resolution 1984/50 [YUN 1984, p. 709]. The Secretary-General, while acknowledging an encouraging trend towards abolition and restriction of the use of capital punishment in most countries, observed, nonetheless, that much remained to be done in the implementation of the 1984 safeguards in countries retaining the death penalty.

Commission action. On 20 April [res. 2005/59], by a recorded vote of 26 to 17, with 10 abstentions, the Commission called on States that still maintained the death penalty to abolish it, and, in the meantime, establish a moratorium on executions, to restrict the number of offences for which the death penalty might be imposed; not to impose it for crimes committed by persons below 18 years of age and on a person suffering from mental disorder; to exclude pregnant women and mothers with dependent infants; and to provide the Secretary-General and relevant UN bodies with information relating to the use of capital punishment and the observance of safeguards guaranteeing the rights of those facing it, as contained in Economic and Social Council resolution 1984/50 [YUN 1984, p. 709]. The Secretary-General was asked to submit, in 2006, a supplement to his quinquennial report, paying attention to the imposition of the death penalty on persons younger than 18 years at the time of the offence and on persons suffering from any mental or intellectual disabilities.

By **decision 2005/247** of 22 July, the Economic and Social Council requested the Secretary-General to continue collecting relevant data and information, in consultation with Governments, specialized agencies, intergovernmental organizations and NGOs, on capital punishment and the safeguards guaranteeing protection of the rights of those facing the death penalty and to prepare additional quinquennial reports on the subject for the consideration of the Commission on Crime Prevention and Criminal Justice and, upon request, the Commission on Human Rights.

Forensic science

Note by Secretariat. By a 21 March note [E/CN.4/2005/56], the Secretariat informed the Commission that the High Commissioner was finalizing, for submission in due course, the progress report on human rights and forensic science, pursuant to a 2003 Commission request [YUN 2003, p. 736].

Commission action. On 19 April [res. 2005/26], the Commission, welcoming the increased use of forensic investigations in situations of grave violations of human rights and international humanitarian law, encouraged Governments to establish thorough prompt and impartial investigation, documentation procedures on the practice, and ensure that personal information, including medical and genetic data, was not used in a way that might infringe on human rights, such as the right to privacy. The Secretary-General was asked to provide the requisite resources to fund OHCHR's efforts to implement the Commission's resolution, including a revision of the *Manual on the Effective Prevention and Investigation of Extralegal, Arbitrary and Summary Executions* [Sales No. E.91.IV.1]. The Commission recommended that OHCHR encourage forensic experts to promote the consolidation of relevant guidelines, with a view to harmonizing the procedures in forensic investigation and repatriation, and to encourage the dissemination and use of the principles, best practices and manuals referred to in the resolution. The High Commissioner was asked to update continuously OHCHR's consolidated database of forensic experts and to submit in 2007, an updated version of the report requested by the Commission in 2003 [YUN 2003, p. 736], which related to the examination of living persons.

Right to democracy

Report of High Commissioner. In response to a 2003 Commission request [YUN 2003, p. 736], the High Commissioner submitted a report [E/CN.4/2005/57], which compiled documents and texts used by various intergovernmental, international, regional and subregional organizations aimed at promoting and consolidating democracy. The texts expressed the adherence of those organizations to such principles and objectives as equality of law, freedom of expression and association and participation in the decision-making process. They also contained commitments to the strengthening and implementation of the essential elements of democracy, such as separation of powers, empowerment and enhancement of parliaments, independence of the judiciary, fair and transparent elections, opposition to unconstitutional changes of Government, popular participation, decentralization of power, freedom of the press, freedom of the members of the Bar, and the subsidiary role of the armed forces, the police or the security forces in a democracy.

In response to a 2004 Commission request [YUN 2004, p. 724], the High Commissioner submitted a February report [E/CN.4/2005/127], which summarized the views of one UN department, one UN system organization and two regional organizations on the role they had played in promoting and consolidating democracy.

Commission action. By a recorded vote of 46 to none, with 7 abstentions, the Commission, on 19 April [res. 2005/32], reaffirmed that democracy facilitated the promotion and protection of civil and political rights and called on States to strengthen the rule of law and promote democracy by upholding the separation of powers, guaranteeing that no individual or institution was above the law and respecting equal protection under the law. OHCHR was urged to further develop its technical assistance programmes in the area of administration of justice to include more training on human rights standards and jurisprudence for members of the executive, legislative and judicial branches of Governments, and to cooperate with and assist them at their request.

Expert seminar. In accordance with a 2003 Commission request [YUN 2003, p. 736], OHCHR held an expert seminar (Geneva, 28 February–2 March) to promote an analytical approach towards action-oriented conclusions on democracy and the rule of law, building on the first expert seminar held in 2002 [YUN 2002, p. 702]. From that perspective, participants explored the interaction between democracy, human rights and the rule of law and power dynamics, related challenges and how to address the issues of equality, participation and accountability, and measures to enhance democracy and the rule of law. They agreed that democracy and the rule of law were interdependent and necessary to create an environment in which human rights could be realized. However, while significant gains had been made on every continent in advancing democracy, each society had its own institutional traditions, which should function under universally accepted principles and norms. The seminar made several recommendations to States and the international community on how to promote and strengthen better democracy, the rule of law and human rights, particularly with regard to judicial authorities and Parliaments, and to tackle related challenges.

Electoral processes

Commission action. On 19 April [res. 2005/29], the Commission, by a recorded vote of 28 to 14, with 11 abstentions, urged States to foster democracy that promoted people's welfare and invited its mechanisms and human rights treaty bodies to continue to take into account the discharge of their respective mandates, the question of strengthening popular participation, equity, social justice and non-discrimination as the foundations of democracy.

Report of Secretary-General. In response to General Assembly resolution 58/180 [YUN 2003, p. 737], the Secretary-General, in an October report [A/60/431] covering UN electoral activities undertaken since his 2003 report on the subject [YUN 2003, p. 736], stated that the Organization's role in technical assistance and in post-conflict elections increased quantitatively and in complexity, illustrating the importance of forging a better link between electoral events and parallel processes in such areas as human rights, the rule of law and institution-building. The United Nations had received 326 requests for electoral assistance from 101 Member States, of which 223 led to related projects. That level of requests represented a phenomenal increase of over 600 per cent relative to the 52 requests received in 2003 [ibid.]. The number of UN peacekeeping missions with electoral responsibilities also grew to include Burundi, Côte d'Ivoire, Haiti, Iraq and Liberia, in addition to existing missions in Afghanistan and the Democratic Republic of the Congo. Much Progress was made in consolidating and coordinating electoral assistance capacities within the UN system, with related activities strengthened through arrangements between the Electoral Assistance Division of the UN Department of Political Affairs and the main UN entities providing such assistance. While most technical assistance projects implemented by the Organization continued to be related to specific events, such as voter registration, an election or a change in the electoral law, efforts were also made to increase long-term projects with national electoral authorities to gradually improve electoral processes. Despite those positive developments, serious challenges remained, and in that context, the report made a number of recommendations highlighting the need for the United Nations to develop or recruit additional expertise in such election specialties as voter registration, electronic voting and election administration. It also advocated the development of means to ensure a consistent and sustained follow-up to electoral assistance; further strengthening of the function of the Focal Point for Electoral Assistance Activities; cooperation and coordination within the United Nations and between it and other organizations, including the recruitment of electoral experts to help in negotiations for peace agreements; tackling administrative impediments; and the active support of Member States.

On 16 December [meeting 64], the General Assembly, on the recommendation of the Third Committee [A/60/509/Add.2], adopted **resolution 60/162** by recorded vote (173-0-1) [agenda item 71 (*b*)].

Strengthening the role of the United Nations in enhancing the effectiveness of the principle of periodic and genuine elections and the promotion of democratization

The General Assembly,

Recalling its previous resolutions on the subject, in particular resolution 58/180 of 22 December 2003,

Reaffirming that United Nations electoral assistance and support for the promotion of democratization are provided only at the specific request of the Member State concerned,

Noting with satisfaction that increasing numbers of Member States are using elections as a peaceful means of discerning the will of the people, which builds confidence in representational governance and contributes to greater national peace and stability,

Recalling the Universal Declaration of Human Rights, adopted on 10 December 1948, in particular the principle that the will of the people, as expressed through periodic and genuine elections, shall be the basis of government authority, as well as the right freely to choose representatives through periodic and genuine elections, which shall be by universal and equal suffrage and held by secret vote or by equivalent free voting procedures,

Taking note with interest of Commission on Human Rights resolution 2004/30 of 19 April 2004 on enhancing the role of regional, subregional and other organizations and arrangements in promoting and consolidating democracy and Commission resolution 2005/32 of 19 April 2005 on democracy and the rule of law;

Recognizing the need for strengthening democratic processes, electoral institutions and national capacity-building, including the capacity to administer fair elections, increase citizen participation and provide civic education, in requesting countries in order to consolidate and regularize the achievements of previous elections and support subsequent elections,

Welcoming the support provided by States to the electoral assistance activities of the United Nations, inter alia, through the provision of electoral experts, including electoral commission staff, and observers, as well as through contributions to the United Nations Trust Fund for Electoral Observation,

Welcoming also the contributions made by international and regional organizations and also by non-governmental organizations to enhancing the effectiveness of the principle of periodic and genuine elections and the promotion of democratization,

Having considered the report of the Secretary-General on United Nations activities aimed at enhancing the effectiveness of the principle of periodic and genuine elections and the promotion of democratization,

1. *Welcomes* the report of the Secretary-General;

2. *Commends* the electoral assistance provided upon request to Member States by the United Nations, and requests that such assistance continue on a case-by-case basis in accordance with the evolving needs of requesting countries to develop, improve and refine their electoral institutions and processes, recognizing that the fundamental responsibility of organizing free and fair elections lies with Governments;

3. *Requests* the Electoral Assistance Division of the Department of Political Affairs of the Secretariat, in its role as coordinator of United Nations electoral assistance, to continue to inform Member States regularly about the requests received and the nature of any assistance provided;

4. *Requests* that the United Nations continue its efforts to ensure, before undertaking to provide electoral assistance to a requesting State, that there is adequate time to organize and carry out an effective mission for providing such assistance, including the provision of long-term technical cooperation, that conditions exist to allow a free and fair election and that the results of the mission will be reported comprehensively and consistently;

5. *Recommends* that, throughout the time span of the entire electoral process, including before and after elections, as appropriate, based on needs-assessment missions, the United Nations continue to provide technical advice and other assistance to requesting States and electoral institutions in order to help to strengthen their democratic processes;

6. *Notes with appreciation* additional efforts being made to enhance cooperation with other international, governmental and non-governmental organizations in order to facilitate more comprehensive and needs-specific responses to requests for electoral assistance, and encourages those organizations to share knowledge and experience in order to promote best practices in the assistance they provide and in their reporting on electoral processes, and expresses its appreciation to those Member States, regional organizations and non-governmental organizations that have provided observers or technical experts in support of United Nations electoral assistance efforts;

7. *Recalls* the establishment by the Secretary-General of the United Nations Trust Fund for Electoral Observation, and calls upon Member States to consider contributing to the Fund;

8. *Encourages* the Secretary-General, through the Electoral Assistance Division, to continue responding to the evolving nature of requests for assistance and the growing need for specific types of medium-term expert assistance aimed at supporting and strengthening the existing capacity of the requesting Government, in particular by enhancing the capacity of national electoral institutions;

9. *Requests* the Secretary-General to provide the Electoral Assistance Division with adequate human and financial resources to allow it to carry out its mandate, and to continue to ensure that the Office of the United Nations High Commissioner for Human Rights is able to respond, within its mandate and in close coordination with the Division, to the numerous and increasingly complex and comprehensive requests from Member States for advisory services;

10. *Notes with satisfaction* the comprehensive coordination between the Electoral Assistance Division and the United Nations Development Programme, and encourages further engagement of the Office of the United Nations High Commissioner for Human Rights in this context;

11. *Requests* the United Nations Development Programme to continue its governance assistance programmes in cooperation with other relevant organizations, in particular those that strengthen democratic institutions and linkages between civil society and Governments;

12. *Reiterates* the importance of reinforced coordination within and outside the United Nations system in this regard;

13. *Requests* the Secretary-General to report to the General Assembly at its sixty-second session on the implementation of the present resolution, in particular on the status of requests from Member States for electoral assistance, and on his efforts to enhance support by the Organization for the democratization process in Member States.

RECORDED VOTE ON RESOLUTION 60/162:

In favour: Afghanistan, Albania, Algeria, Andorra, Angola, Antigua and Barbuda, Argentina, Armenia, Australia, Austria, Azerbaijan, Bahamas, Bahrain, Bangladesh, Barbados, Belarus, Belgium, Belize, Benin, Bhutan, Bolivia, Bosnia and Herzegovina, Botswana, Brazil, Brunei Darussalam, Bulgaria, Burkina Faso, Burundi, Cambodia, Cameroon, Canada, Cape Verde, Chile, China, Colombia, Comoros, Costa Rica, Côte d'Ivoire, Croatia, Cyprus, Czech Republic, Democratic People's Republic of Korea, Democratic Republic of the Congo, Denmark, Djibouti, Dominica, Dominican Republic, Ecuador, Egypt, El Salvador, Eritrea, Estonia, Ethiopia, Fiji, Finland, France, Gabon, Gambia, Georgia, Germany, Ghana, Greece, Grenada, Guatemala, Guinea, Guinea-Bissau, Guyana, Haiti, Honduras, Hungary, Iceland, India, Indonesia, Iran, Iraq, Ireland, Israel, Italy, Jamaica, Japan, Jordan, Kazakhstan, Kenya, Kuwait, Kyrgyzstan, Lao People's Democratic Republic, Latvia, Lebanon, Lesotho, Libyan Arab Jamahiriya, Liechtenstein, Lithuania, Luxembourg, Madagascar, Malawi, Malaysia, Maldives, Mali, Malta, Marshall Islands, Mauritania, Mauritius, Mexico, Micronesia, Monaco, Mongolia, Morocco, Mozambique, Myanmar, Namibia, Nepal, Netherlands, New Zealand, Nicaragua, Niger, Nigeria, Norway, Oman, Pakistan, Palau, Panama, Papua New Guinea, Paraguay, Peru, Philippines, Poland, Portugal, Qatar, Republic of Korea, Romania, Russian Federation, Rwanda, Saint Lucia, Saint Vincent and the Grenadines, Samoa, San Marino, Saudi Arabia, Senegal, Serbia and Montenegro, Singapore, Slovakia, Slovenia, Solomon Islands, Somalia, South Africa, Spain, Sri Lanka, Sudan, Suriname, Sweden, Switzerland, Tajikistan, Thailand, The former Yugoslav Republic of Macedonia, Timor-Leste, Togo, Tunisia, Turkey, Turkmenistan, Uganda, Ukraine, United Arab Emirates, United Kingdom, United Republic of Tanzania, United States, Uruguay, Uzbekistan, Vanuatu, Venezuela, Viet Nam, Yemen, Zambia, Zimbabwe.

Against: None.

Abstaining: Tuvalu.

On the same date [meeting 64], the Assembly, on the recommendation of the Third Committee [A/60/509/Add.2], adopted **resolution 60/164** by recorded vote (110-6-61) [agenda item 71 (*b*)].

Respect for the principles of national sovereignty and diversity of democratic systems in electoral processes as an important element for the promotion and protection of human rights

The General Assembly,

Reaffirming the purpose of the United Nations to develop friendly relations among nations based on respect for the principle of equal rights and self-determination of peoples and to take other appropriate measures to strengthen universal peace,

Recalling its resolution 1514(XV) of 14 December 1960, containing the Declaration on the Granting of Independence to Colonial Countries and Peoples,

Recalling also its resolution 2625(XXV) of 24 October 1970, by which it approved the Declaration on Principles of International Law concerning Friendly Relations and Cooperation among States in accordance with the Charter of the United Nations,

Reaffirming the right to self-determination, by virtue of which all peoples can freely determine their political status and freely pursue their economic, social and cultural development,

Recognizing that the principles enshrined in Article 2 of the Charter, in particular respect for national sovereignty, should be respected in the holding of elections,

Recognizing also the richness and diversity of democratic political systems and models of free and fair electoral processes in the world, based on national and regional particularities and various backgrounds,

Stressing the responsibility of States in ensuring ways and means to facilitate full and effective popular participation in their electoral processes,

Recognizing the contribution made by the United Nations of electoral assistance provided to numerous States upon their request,

Reaffirming the solemn commitment of all States to fulfil their obligations to promote universal respect for, and observance and protection of, all human rights and fundamental freedoms for all in accordance with the Charter, other instruments relating to human rights, and international law,

Reaffirming also that democracy, sustainable development and respect for human rights and fundamental freedoms, as well as good governance at all levels, are interdependent and mutually reinforcing, and determined to strengthen respect for the rule of law at the national and international levels,

Welcoming the commitment of all Member States, expressed in the United Nations Millennium Declaration, to work collectively for more inclusive political processes allowing genuine participation by all citizens in all countries,

1. *Reaffirms* that all peoples have the right to self-determination, by virtue of which they freely determine their political status and freely pursue their economic, social and cultural development, and that every State has the duty to respect that right, in accordance with the provisions of the Charter of the United Nations;

2. *Reiterates* that periodic, fair and free elections are important elements for the promotion and protection of human rights;

3. *Reaffirms* the right of peoples to determine methods and to establish institutions regarding electoral processes and, consequently, that there is no single model of democracy or of democratic institutions and that States should ensure all the necessary mechanisms and means to facilitate full and effective popular participation in those processes;

4. *Also reaffirms* that free development of the national electoral process in each State should be fully honoured in a manner that fully respects the principles established in the Charter and in the Declaration on Principles of International Law concerning Friendly Relations and Cooperation among States in accordance with the Charter of the United Nations;

5. *Calls upon* all States to refrain from financing political parties or other organizations in any other State in a way that is contrary to the principles of the Charter and that undermines the legitimacy of its electoral processes;

6. *Condemns* any act of armed aggression or threat or use of force against peoples, their elected Governments or their legitimate leaders;

7. *Reaffirms* that the will of the people shall be the basis of the authority of government and that this will shall be expressed in periodic and genuine elections, which shall be by universal and equal suffrage and shall be held by secret vote or by equivalent free voting procedures;

8. *Decides* to continue its consideration of the question of the respect for the principles of national sovereignty and diversity of democratic systems in electoral processes as an important element for the promotion and protection of human rights at its sixty-second session under the item entitled "Human rights questions".

RECORDED VOTE ON RESOLUTION 60/164:

In favour: Afghanistan, Algeria, Angola, Antigua and Barbuda, Azerbaijan, Bahamas, Bahrain, Bangladesh, Barbados, Belarus, Belize, Benin, Bhutan, Bolivia, Brazil, Brunei Darussalam, Burkina Faso, Burundi, Cambodia, Cameroon, Cape Verde, China, Colombia, Comoros, Côte d'Ivoire, Cuba, Democratic People's Republic of Korea, Democratic Republic of the Congo, Djibouti, Dominica, Dominican Republic, Ecuador, Egypt, El Salvador, Eritrea, Ethiopia, Gabon, Gambia, Ghana, Grenada, Guinea, Guinea-Bissau, Guyana, Haiti, Indonesia, Iran, Jamaica, Japan, Jordan, Kazakhstan, Kenya, Kuwait, Kyrgyzstan, Lao People's Democratic Republic, Lebanon, Lesotho, Libyan Arab Jamahiriya, Madagascar, Malawi, Malaysia, Maldives, Mali, Mauritania, Mauritius, Mongolia, Morocco, Mozambique, Myanmar, Namibia, Nepal, Nicaragua, Niger, Nigeria, Oman, Pakistan, Panama, Papua New Guinea, Paraguay, Peru, Philippines, Qatar, Russian Federation, Rwanda, Saint Lucia, Saint Vincent and the Grenadines, Saudi Arabia, Senegal, Singapore, Somalia, South Africa, Sri Lanka, Sudan, Suriname, Syrian Arab Republic, Tajikistan, Thailand, Timor-Leste, Togo, Trinidad and Tobago, Tunisia, Turkmenistan, Uganda, United Arab Emirates, United Republic of Tanzania, Uzbekistan, Venezuela, Viet Nam, Yemen, Zambia, Zimbabwe.

Against: Australia, Israel, Marshall Islands, Micronesia, Palau, United States.

Abstaining: Albania, Andorra, Argentina, Armenia, Austria, Belgium, Bosnia and Herzegovina, Botswana, Bulgaria, Canada, Chile, Costa Rica, Croatia, Cyprus, Czech Republic, Denmark, Estonia, Fiji, Finland, France, Georgia, Germany, Greece, Guatemala, Honduras, Hungary, Iceland, India, Iraq, Ireland, Italy, Latvia, Liechtenstein, Lithuania, Luxembourg, Malta, Mexico, Monaco, Netherlands, New Zealand, Norway, Poland, Portugal, Republic of Korea, Republic of Moldova, Romania, Samoa, San Marino, Serbia and Montenegro, Slovakia, Slovenia, Solomon Islands, Spain, Sweden, Switzerland, The former Yugoslav Republic of Macedonia, Turkey, Ukraine, United Kingdom, Uruguay, Vanuatu.

Other issues

Extralegal executions

Reports of Special Rapporteur. The Special Rapporteur on extrajudicial, summary or arbitrary executions, Philip Alston (Australia), in his first annual report [E/CN.4/2005/7 & Corr.1], outlined his terms of reference, legal framework and methods of work, and highlighted his communications with Governments, which were contained in an addendum [E/CN.4/2005/7/Add.1]. Between 1 December 2003 and 30 September 2004, the Special Rapporteur transmitted 201 communications to 63 countries, comprising 112 urgent appeals and 89 letters of allegations concerning 1,799 individuals who had reportedly suffered violations of their right to life. The report summarized the cases transmitted, noting that the response rate, which stood at about 54 per cent, meant that almost half of all the communications

sent drew no response from the Governments concerned within a reasonable time period. Other parts of the report focused on genocide and crimes against humanity; violations of the right to life in armed conflict and internal strife; capital punishment; and violations of the right to life by non-State actors.

The Special Rapporteur noted that, despite several encouraging developments regarding UN system initiatives against genocide in the past year, the problem continued to be characterized by outright denial, refusal to address the issue, or undermining of the initiatives designed to respond to the most serious cases of alleged genocide. With a growing number of civilians being killed in situations of armed conflict and internal strife, respect for established and binding international norms was fading, illustrated partly by the proliferation of proposals seeking to justify illegal executions, which undermined the essential foundations of human rights law. Addressing capital punishment and related issues, including the need for transparency, the importance of periodic reviews of its implementation and cases where it was mandatory, the Special Rapporteur noted that killings by non-State actors were among the most complex issues that needed to be dealt with, and raised with Governments related matters with respect to State responsibility in that context. In effect, States could be held accountable for killings by non-State actors. Therefore, it was the obligation of Governments to be diligent in dealing with the problem. The Special Rapporteur recommended that States ratify the Statute of the International Criminal Court, in order to promote its objectives, among which was the prevention of genocide and crimes against humanity. In addition, permanent members of the UN Security Council should pledge not to use their veto power in cases involving genocide; proposals justifying or rationalizing the arbitrary execution of individuals alleged to have committed crimes or linked to terrorism should be condemned without reservations, given that they undermined international human rights law; and national investigation of alleged violations of international law by armed or security forces should be conducted, with their results made public.

The Special Rapporteur visited Nigeria (27 June–8 July) [E/CN.4/2006/53/Add.4], where serious problems existed regarding extrajudicial executions, illustrated by the alleged killing in police custody of armed robbers in the southeastern State of Enugu, in January, and by the framing and killing of six innocent civilians by the police in the Apo local Government area of Benue State in the east central part of the country, in June.

Other worrisome reports were the killing in 2004 by security forces of an innocent bystander who witnessed their misconduct during communal violence in Kano, northern Nigeria, and the death penalty by stoning under sharia (Muslim law) for such acts as adultery and homosexuality in a number of States. The problem largely stemmed from the fact that the Nigerian Police force, which was seriously under-resourced and confronted with a high rate of violent crime, often resorted to corruption, arbitrariness, torture, excessive use of force and executions, of which there were no systematic statistical record. As armed robbery was a capital offence, police often used that label as a pretext for extrajudicial executions or claimed that victims were attempting to escape from custody. Matters were worsened by the fact that the standing rules for use of firearms by the police were deeply flawed, and police officers' enjoyment of impunity facilitated extrajudicial executions. Overall, the problem was closely linked to inadequacies at almost all levels of the Nigerian criminal justice system: forensic investigation, coroner's inquiries, prosecution process, functioning of the judiciary, and detention procedures.

While acknowledging encouraging developments, such as the Government's efforts to combat corruption and public admission of the problem of widespread extrajudicial executions and commitment to ending it, the Special Rapporteur recommended that the Government introduce a standard practice of official inquiry into cases of extrajudicial executions and the publication within six months of the reports of such inquiries; declare the death penalty unconstitutional for such offences as adultery and sodomy, and remove armed robbery as a capital offence; commute the sentence of all prisoners who had spent years on death row; and review the convictions of all persons sentenced to death or life imprisonment under martial law. UNICEF should take up the review of death row prisoners for crimes committed before they were 18 years old. Other recommendations advocated accountability for extrajudicial executions through the establishment of an annual register for recording all such incidents, police reform, the end of the use of vigilante groups and community policing, international development assistance, and legislation to compel the cooperation of military and police officers with official inquiries.

In Sri Lanka (28 November–6 December) [E/CN.4/2006/53/Add.5], the Special Rapporteur found that extrajudicial executions were among the factors exacerbating the conflict between the Government and the rebel Liberation Tigers of Tamil Eelam (LTTE). Many Tamil and Muslim civilians had been killed because they sought to exercise their freedoms of expression, movement, association and participation in ways that were not supportive of one or another of the factions in the conflict, and many others had been killed in retaliation or because they were sympathizers. Unfortunately, almost none of those or other extrajudicial executions had been effectively investigated. In the light of those developments, the Special Rapporteur examined the problem of deaths in custody, the causes of which allegedly included the inadequate training of police in criminal investigation, the widespread use of torture to extract confessions and the failure to impose effective disciplinary measures against police officers guilty of torture. The Special Rapporteur made recommendations on, among other things, the need for a wide-ranging human rights agreement, including an effective monitoring mechanism; the importance of all parties to respect the provisions of the Geneva Convention Relative to the Protection of Civilian Persons in Time of War; arrangements to compensate the families of all non-combatants killed during the conflict; effective police investigation of all extrajudicial killings and a programme to train police reservists in criminal detection and investigation; and the need for the LTTE to adopt concrete steps to demonstrate its commitment to human rights, including the denunciation of killings attributed to it.

Commission action. On 19 April [res. 2005/34], the Commission, by a recorded vote of 36 to none, with 17 abstentions, strongly condemned all extrajudicial, summary or arbitrary executions, and demanded that States end the practice in all its forms. The Commission asked the Secretary-General and the High Commissioner to use their best endeavours in cases where the minimum standard of legal safeguards provided for in the International Covenant on Civil and Political Rights (see p. 726) appeared not to be respected. The Secretary-General was also asked to provide the Special Rapporteur with adequate resources, and to ensure that personnel specialized in human rights and humanitarian law formed part of UN missions, in order to deal with extrajudicial, summary or arbitrary executions.

Disappearance of persons

Draft instrument. Pursuant to a 2004 Commission request [YUN 2004, p. 730], the intersessional open-ended working group established to prepare a draft legally binding instrument for the protection of all persons from enforced disappearance held its fourth (31 January–11 February) [E/CN.4/2005/66] and fifth (12-23 September)

[E/CN.4/2006/57] sessions, both in Geneva. In January, the group continued to discuss the Chairman's working paper, which it first revised in 2004 [YUN 2004, p. 730], taking into account comments made by delegations and informal consultations. Relevant issues considered during the group's current session included the definition of enforced disappearance, the various obligations of States in terms of legislative and other measures to ensure the recognition of enforced disappearance as a criminal offence attracting consequences and penalties under national and international law, the form of the future instrument and functions of a monitoring body, as well as the number of ratifications necessary for its entry into force. In September, the group continued discussions on the draft instrument, focusing primarily on the articles on which agreement in principle was yet to be achieved. Those included draft article 2 on acts similar to enforced disappearances committed by non-State actors, draft article 20 on the refusal to provide information on a detainee, and draft article 32 on the extension of the instrument to all territories for whose international relations a State was responsible. Discussions also continued on the form of the instrument and nature and functions of the monitoring body. Subsequently, the group undertook a complete review of all substantive articles and final provisions of the draft instrument and approved them. A number of delegations made statements expressing satisfaction with the work accomplished by the group and emphasizing the importance of the new convention. In the absence of a provision on reservations, Egypt, supported by Iran, stated that it was understood that States parties had the right to enter reservations to any of the instrument's articles, in accordance with international jurisprudence and the Vienna Convention on the Law of Treaties [YUN 1986, p. 1006]. In response, the Chairperson said States parties would have the right to enter reservations at the time of accession, on the understanding that such reservations had to be in keeping with international law. In particular, if a reservation related to the substance of the instrument, other States parties could challenge it. On 23 September, the group adopted its report, ad referendum, to which was annexed the finalized draft instrument for transmission to the Commission and approval by the General Assembly.

Commission action. On 19 April [res. 2005/27], the Commission urged States to promote and give full effect to the 1992 Declaration on the Protection of All Persons from Enforced Disappearance, adopted by the General Assembly in resolution 47/133 [YUN 1992, p. 744], and to cooperate with the Working Group on Enforced or Involuntary Disappearances (see below). The Working Group was asked to report in 2006 and States to provide it with information on preventative measures and action taken to give effect to the Declaration. The Secretary-General was asked to assist it, to provide the requisite resources to update the database on cases of enforced disappearance and to inform the Commission of steps taken to disseminate and promote the Declaration. The Commission asked the intersessional working group (see above) to meet for 10 days before the end of the year to complete its work and to report in 2006.

On 25 July, the Economic and Social Council approved the Commission's request to the intersessional working group (**decision 2005/262**).

Working Group activities. The five-member Working Group on Involuntary Disappearances held three sessions in 2005: its seventy-fifth (Bangkok, 26 May–3 June), seventy-sixth (an e-meeting to consider only individual cases), and seventy-seventh (Geneva, 21-30 November) [E/CN.4/2006/56]. In addition to its core mandate, which was to act as a channel of communication between families of disappeared persons and the Governments concerned, with a view to ensuring that sufficiently documented individual cases were investigated, the Working Group monitored States' compliance with the 1992 Declaration. Cases under active consideration by the Group totalled 41,128, concerning 79 countries with outstanding cases of alleged disappearance. Up to 30 November, the last day of its seventy-seventh session, the Group had transmitted 535 new cases of disappearance to 22 States, 91 of which allegedly occurred in 2005. It also sent 132 urgent action appeals to 12 countries, filed 15 others jointly with other Commission special procedures and clarified 1,347 cases. The Group's report summarized information concerning disappearances received from 81 countries. The Group, regretting the continuing occurrence of the phenomenon of disappearances in many countries, expressed concern that children had been affected in a number of cases, which was a particularly heinous crime.While in the past the phenomenon was mainly associated with the policies of authoritarian regimes, currently it occurred in more complex situations of internal conflict or tensions that generated violence, humanitarian crises and human rights violations. The Group was especially troubled about alleged linkages of disappearances to the war on terror, as some countries used the need to combat terrorism as a justification to repress opposition groups, which sometimes resulted in disappearances. The Group called on Governments to comply with their obligations under relevant provisions of the 1992 Declaration, reminding them that preventive measures, aimed at democratizing governance and making human rights the cornerstone of public policy, were crucial to combatting disappearances. A further goal of public policy in that regard, was the eradication of the culture of impunity for perpetrators of enforced disappearances. Concerned that the culprits might take advantage of post-conflict amnesty laws to escape justice and that such a situation might result in impunity, the Group, in an effort to contribute to the progressive development of international law on the subject, adopted a general comment on article 18 of the 1992 Declaration, which precluded exemption from criminal proceedings or sanctions for persons involved in all acts of enforced disappearance. The Group also commissioned a comparative study on the criminal law treatment of enforced or involuntary disappearances and invited Governments to provide related information within their national law, for inclusion in the study, scheduled for publication in 2006.

Two Working Group members visited Colombia (5-13 July) [E/CN.4/2006/56/Add.1] to monitor progress made since the Group's first visit [YUN 1988, p. 522] in preventing and resolving the problem of enforced or involuntary disappearances, and to investigate the development of the phenomenon in the country. The Group noted that, since 1988, Colombia, which had been in the throes of internal conflict and related human rights violations, had developed constitutional and legal mechanisms for dealing with enforced disappearances. Against that background, significant changes included constitutional provisions forbidding the phenomenon, incorporation into its criminal code of a definition of enforced disappearance that included all the elements of the 1992 Declaration, the country's ratification of the Inter-American Convention on Forced Disappearance of Persons, and the establishment of a number of State institutions to deal with the phenomenon. Despite the progress illustrated by those developments, the Group observed contradictory views of the situation from NGOs and the Government and between the authorities within and outside the capital. Additional shortcomings included the existence of a gap between the legal progress made and practical implementation of relevant laws and procedures, overlapping functions of institutions and agencies and competing programmes and missions, legal challenges regarding the definition of the criminal offence of enforced disappearance relative to non-State actors, difficulties in tracing the fate and whereabouts of victims, and inadequate reporting of cases. Other matters of concern related to the legal provisions for the demobilization of paramilitaries in relation to enforced disappearances, the protection regime and an environment of fear and terror under which most victims and their families lived, and the Government's lack of political will to root out the problem of disappearances in Colombia. The Group made recommendations for tackling the situation of ongoing disappearances in the country, protecting the families of victims and the NGOs working to locate them, solving the situation of underreported cases due to fear and impunity, and implementing more effectively existing legal mechanisms on disappearances.

Holocaust remembrance

In November, the General Assembly, reaffirming that the Holocaust, which resulted in the murder of one third of the Jewish people, along with countless members of other minorities, would forever be a warning of the dangers of hatred, bigotry, racism, and prejudice, resolved to designate 27 January as an international day of commemoration in memory of the victims of the Holocaust (see below).

GENERAL ASSEMBLY ACTION

On 1 November [meeting 42], the General Assembly adopted **resolution 60/7** [draft: A/60/L.12 & Add.1] without vote [agenda item 72].

Holocaust remembrance

The General Assembly,

Reaffirming the Universal Declaration of Human Rights, which proclaims that everyone is entitled to all the rights and freedoms set forth therein, without distinction of any kind, such as race, religion or other status,

Recalling article 3 of the Universal Declaration of Human Rights, which states that everyone has the right to life, liberty and security of person,

Recalling also article 18 of the Universal Declaration of Human Rights and article 18 of the International Covenant on Civil and Political Rights, which state that everyone has the right to freedom of thought, conscience and religion,

Bearing in mind that the founding principle of the Charter of the United Nations, "to save succeeding generations from the scourge of war", is testimony to the indelible link between the United Nations and the unique tragedy of the Second World War,

Recalling the Convention on the Prevention and Punishment of the Crime of Genocide, which was adopted in order to avoid repetition of genocides such as those committed by the Nazi regime,

Recalling also the preamble of the Universal Declaration of Human Rights, which states that disregard and contempt for human rights have resulted in barbarous acts which have outraged the conscience of mankind,

Taking note of the fact that the sixtieth session of the General Assembly is taking place during the sixtieth year of the defeat of the Nazi regime,

Recalling the twenty-eighth special session of the General Assembly, a unique event, held in commemoration of the sixtieth anniversary of the liberation of the Nazi concentration camps,

Honouring the courage and dedication shown by the soldiers who liberated the concentration camps,

Reaffirming that the Holocaust, which resulted in the murder of one third of the Jewish people, along with countless members of other minorities, will forever be a warning to all people of the dangers of hatred, bigotry, racism and prejudice,

1. *Resolves* that the United Nations will designate 27 January as an annual International Day of Commemoration in memory of the victims of the Holocaust;

2. *Urges* Member States to develop educational programmes that will inculcate future generations with the lessons of the Holocaust in order to help to prevent future acts of genocide, and in this context commends the Task Force for International Cooperation on Holocaust Education, Remembrance and Research;

3. *Rejects* any denial of the Holocaust as an historical event, either in full or part;

4. *Commends* those States which have actively engaged in preserving those sites that served as Nazi death camps, concentration camps, forced labour camps and prisons during the Holocaust;

5. *Condemns without reserve* all manifestations of religious intolerance, incitement, harassment or violence against persons or communities based on ethnic origin or religious belief, wherever they occur;

6. *Requests* the Secretary-General to establish a programme of outreach on the subject of the "Holocaust and the United Nations" as well as measures to mobilize civil society for Holocaust remembrance and education, in order to help to prevent future acts of genocide; to report to the General Assembly on the establishment of this programme within six months from the date of the adoption of the present resolution; and to report thereafter on the implementation of the programme at its sixty-third session.

Communication. On 9 December, in identical letters addressed to the Secretary-General and the President of the Security Council [A/60/586-S/2005/776], Israel called attention to Iran's statements, which reportedly cast doubt on the truth of the Holocaust. Noting that Iran had joined to adopt by consensus General Assembly resolution 60/7 (see above) on Holocaust remembrance, which rejected any denial of the Holocaust as an historical event, Israel urged the international community to take swift and strong action against Iran.

Torture and cruel treatment

Reports of Special Rapporteur. In response to a 2004 Commission request [YUN 2004, p. 733], the Special Rapporteur on torture, Theo van Boven (Netherlands), submitted his final report to the Commission [E/CN.4/2005/62] describing his activities from 16 December 2003 to 30 November 2004. He had sent 223 letters to 77 countries on alleged torture of individuals and 330 urgent appeals to 72 Governments on behalf of individuals who, it was feared, might suffer torture and other forms of ill-treatment. A summary of communications sent by the Special Rapporteur and of replies received were contained in an addendum to the report [E/CN.4/2005/62/Add.1]. Building on the findings of his 2003 preliminary study [YUN 2003, p. 741] on the situation of trade in and production of equipment specifically designed to inflict torture or other cruel, inhuman or degrading treatment, its origin, destination and forms, the Special Rapporteur outlined a policy strategy for preventing effectively the spread of torture technology—instruments and techniques commonly used in law enforcement but implicated in torture and ill-treatment. From that perspective, the report highlighted some of the challenges in measuring the global trade and proliferation of such instruments and techniques; considered the need to monitor developments in security and law enforcement technology that could easily be used for torture, as well as the transfer of interrogation techniques, know-how and hardware; and updated information regarding the European Commission's proposal for trade regulation, referred to in the Special Rapporteur's 2003 preliminary report [ibid.]. Within the existing framework of international standards to prohibit torture and other cruel, inhuman or degrading treatment or punishment, the Special Rapporteur made a series of recommendations to States regarding the manufacture, transfer, use and prohibition of products and techniques designed specifically to inflict torture, and asked his successor and the Committee against Torture (see p. 730) to examine the trade in torture instruments in the course of their work.

Commission action. On 19 April [res. 2005/39], the Commission, condemning all forms of torture, urged States to become parties to the 1984 Convention against Torture and Other Cruel, Inhuman or Degrading Treatment or Punishment (see p. 729). Governments were called up on to prohibit the practice; prevent the production, trade, export and use of equipment specifically designed for it; and not to expel, return, extradite or transfer a person to another State where he or she might be subjected to torture. The Special Rapporteur was asked to submit an interim report to the General Assembly in 2005 on the overall trends and developments regarding his mandate, and a full report to the Commission in 2006.

On 25 July, the Economic and Social Council endorsed the Commission's requests to the Special Rapporteur (**decision 2005/265**).

Subcommission action. On 8 August [res. 2005/1], the Subcommission recommended that all States develop independent and effective mechanisms as concrete means of combating torture and other cruel, inhuman or degrading treatment or punishment.

On 10 August [res. 2005/12], the Subcommission, by a roll-call vote of 21 to 1, with 2 abstentions, concluded that the transfer of a person to a State where that person could face a real risk of being subjected to torture, cruel, inhuman or degrading treatment or extrajudicial killing would be a breach of customary international law. It recommended that in situations where there was such a risk, no transfer should be carried out unless the State effecting the transfer sought and received credible assurances from the State to which the person was to be transferred that he or she would not be subjected to torture.

Further reports of Special Rapporteur. In 2005, the new Special Rapporteur on torture, Manfred Nowak (Austria), appointed in November 2004 [YUN 2004, p. 733], visited Georgia (19-25 February) [E/CN.4/2005/62/Add.3] to assess the prevailing situation of torture, promote preventive mechanisms and initiate cooperation with the Government. While acknowledging the Government's efforts to tackle corruption, uphold the rule of law and reform the criminal justice system, torture and ill-treatment by law enforcement officials still existed in the country. The common characteristics of the cases examined by the Special Rapporteur included the perpetration of torture in the first 72 hours of police custody to extract confessions for alleged offences, and the methods used, such as beatings with fists, butts of guns and truncheons, as well as electric shocks and cigarette burns. In those circumstances, victims suffered broken bones, burns, scars and neuro-psychological effects, among other things. The Special Rapporteur made preliminary recommendations addressing impunity, detention conditions, preventive measures against torture, the need to abolish the death penalty and for international cooperation in assisting the country's implementation of his recommendations.

In Mongolia (6-9 June) [E/CN.4/2006/6/Add.4], the Special Rapporteur also found that torture existed, particularly in police stations and pretrial detention facilities, as evidenced by two recent instances of detainees tortured to death. Impunity for torture and ill-treatment continued unimpeded, owing to the absence in the criminal code of a definition of torture that was consistent with the Convention against Torture and Other Cruel, Inhuman or Degrading Treatment or Punishment (see p. 729), the lack of effective mechanisms to investigate alleged cases, and a basic lack of awareness of prosecutors, lawyers and the judiciary of international standards relating to the prohibition of torture. Consequently, victims had no effective recourse to justice, compensation and rehabilitation. Issues of particular concern included overcrowding in detention facilities, the situation of prisoners subjected to special isolation regimes and compelled to serve several-year terms virtually in total isolation, and the situation of death row inmates, who were also held in complete isolation, handcuffed, shackled and denied adequate food. The Special Rapporteur recommended, among other things, that the authorities declare a policy of non-tolerance for torture and end the culture of impunity; ensure those legally arrested were not held for more than the time required by law, including through an amendment of the Criminal Procedure Code; ensure confessions were obtained appropriately; provide for an independent authority to promptly and thoroughly investigate all allegations of torture; and end the special isolation regime and ensure death row inmates were detained in accordance with the standard minimum rules for the treatment of prisoners.

Pursuant to General Assembly resolution 59/182 [YUN 2004, p. 735] and Commission resolution 2005/39 (see p. 812), the Secretary-General, in August, transmitted the interim report of the Special Rapporteur [A/60/316], which further described his activities and addressed issues of special concern. In addition to the communications contained in his report to the Commission (see above), the Special Rapporteur transmitted 41 letters of alleged torture to 30 Governments and 133 urgent appeals to 47 Governments on behalf of persons who might be at risk of torture or other forms of ill-treatment. He drew the Assembly's attention to the issue of corporal punishment—amputation, stoning, strangulation, eye-gouging, flogging and beating—which was of particular concern and which many States justified as lawfully sanctioned punishment under domestic or religious law falling outside the prohibition against torture. After reviewing relevant jurisprudence of UN human rights treaty bodies and regional human rights mechanisms, the Special Rapporteur concluded that corporal punishment was, to the contrary, inconsistent with international instruments prohibiting torture and other cruel, inhuman or degrading treatment or punishment. He also addressed the principle of non-refoulment and the use of diplomatic assurances or formal guarantees between Governments that a person to be returned would not be subjected to torture, ill-treatment or the death penalty and would be afforded the right to a fair trial. The Special Rapporteur determined, in that regard, that such assurances were unreliable and ineffective in protecting against torture and called on Governments to observe the principle of non-refoulment scrupulously and not to expel any person to frontiers or territories where they might run the risk of human rights violations.

The Special Rapporteur visited Nepal (10-16 September) [E/CN.4/2006/6/Add.5] to examine numerous allegations relating to torture and ill-treatment he had received, primarily within the context of the Government's armed conflict with the Communist Party of Nepal (Maoist). He found that the police and Royal Nepalese Army (RNA) systematically practiced torture, including beatings with bamboo poles and plastic pipes, kicking with boots, pouring water into the nose, electric shocks to the ears, trampling on thighs and legs, and maintaining prisoners in stress positions, among other things. Despite constitutional and legal provisions to safeguard the rights of criminal suspects, many of those rights were not being respected, including timely access to a lawyer, arraignment before a judge within 24 hours of arrest and medical examinations upon arrest or transfer. Detainees registers were poorly kept, if at all, and there was a general lack of confidence in the justice system and rule of law among torture victims and their families. Preventive detention legislation, such as the Public Security Act and the Terrorist and Disruptive Activities Ordinance, provided the police and military with sweeping powers to detain suspects for preventive reasons, sometimes for months. Of particular concern, was a culture of impunity for torture, which emphasized compensation to the victims as an alternative to criminal proceedings against the perpetrator. The Special Rapporteur recommended corrective measures to the Government, including the denouncement of torture and impunity by the highest authorities; the criminalization of incommunicado detention; independent medical examination of how persons in custody were treated; prompt investigations of all allegations of torture and the suspension from duty of public officials indicted for abuse of torture; compensation to victims; and requisite training for security officials, legal professionals and the judiciary. He also called on the Maoists to end torture and recommended that the Government continue to cooperate with relevant international organizations, including OHCHR, in requesting assistance with the follow-up to his recommendations.

According to the Special Rapporteur, Nepal subsequently objected to his findings and maintained that it did not tolerate, condone or permit torture, nor did it allow impunity.

Communication. On 21 March [E/CN.4/2005/G/21], Uzbekistan stated that it had implemented 18 of the 22 recommendations made by the former Special Rapporteur, and provided information relating to the measures it had taken.

Voluntary fund for victims of torture

Commission action. On 19 April [res. 2005/39], the Commission, recognizing the need for international assistance to victims of torture, appealed to Governments, organizations and individuals to contribute annually to the United Nations Voluntary Fund for Victims of Torture and, if possible, to increase their contributions. The Secretary-General was asked to continue to include the Fund among the programmes receiving donations at the annual UN Pledging Conference for Development Activities and to ensure adequate staffing and technical facilities for UN bodies and mechanisms dealing with torture. The Fund's Board of Trustees was asked to report in 2006.

Report of Secretary-General. An August report of the Secretary-General [A/60/215] provided information on the recommendations of the Fund's Board of Trustees at its twenty-fourth session (Geneva, 13-22 April). Contributions received during the year totaled $8,736,785 from 25 countries and three individuals, while pledges stood at $1,444,327 from seven States. Against requests amounting to $14 million, the Board recommended that $8.5 million be allocated to new grants, to fund 186 projects in 68 countries providing medical, legal, social, economic and psychological assistance to victims of torture and members of their families, which were approved on 27 May by the High Commissioner, on behalf of the Secretary-General. Annexed to the Board's report was a list of the organizations and activities financed by the Fund in 2005. The Board maintained the practice of financing requests for training and seminars, and recommended, in that regard, that the amount of $50,000 be allocated for the organization of six workshops. It also allocated $125,000 for emergency assistance to organizations that might encounter unforeseen financial difficulties before its next session. The Board estimated that $15 million would be needed to enable it assist torture victims in 2006. The report also summarized action taken by the Fund's secretariat to implement the recommendations of the Office of Internal Oversight Services during its 2004 review of the Fund's functioning [YUN 2004, p. 734].

On 16 December (**decision 60/533**), the General Assembly took note of the Secretary-General's report.

GENERAL ASSEMBLY ACTION

On 16 December [meeting 64], the General Assembly, on the recommendation of the Third Committee [A/60/509/Add.1], adopted **resolution 60/148** without vote [agenda item 71 (*a*)].

Torture and other cruel, inhuman or degrading treatment or punishment

The General Assembly,

Reaffirming that no one shall be subjected to torture or to other cruel, inhuman or degrading treatment or punishment,

Recalling that freedom from torture and other cruel, inhuman or degrading treatment or punishment is a non-derogable right that must be protected under all circumstances, including in times of international or internal armed conflict or disturbance, and that the absolute prohibition of torture and other cruel, inhuman or degrading treatment or punishment is affirmed in relevant international instruments,

Recalling also that a number of international, regional and domestic courts, including the International Tribunal for the Prosecution of Persons Responsible for Serious Violations of International Humanitarian Law Committed in the Territory of the Former Yugoslavia since 1991, have recognized that the prohibition of torture is a peremptory norm of international law and have held that the prohibition of cruel, inhuman or degrading treatment or punishment is customary international law,

Recalling further the definition of torture contained in article 1 of the Convention against Torture and Other Cruel, Inhuman or Degrading Treatment or Punishment,

Noting that under the Geneva Conventions of 1949 torture and inhuman treatment are a grave breach and that under the statutes of the International Tribunal for the Former Yugoslavia and of the International Criminal Tribunal for the Prosecution of Persons Responsible for Genocide and Other Serious Violations of International Humanitarian Law Committed in the Territory of Rwanda and Rwandan Citizens Responsible for Genocide and Other Such Violations Committed in the Territory of Neighbouring States between 1 January and 31 December 1994, and the Rome Statute of the International Criminal Court acts of torture constitute war crimes and can constitute crimes against humanity,

Commending the persistent efforts by non-governmental organizations, including the considerable network of centres for the rehabilitation of victims of torture, to combat torture and to alleviate the suffering of victims of torture,

1. *Condemns* all forms of torture and other cruel, inhuman or degrading treatment or punishment, including through intimidation, which are and shall remain prohibited at any time and in any place whatsoever and can thus never be justified, and calls upon all States to implement fully the absolute prohibition of torture and other cruel, inhuman or degrading treatment or punishment;

2. *Emphasizes* that States must take persistent, determined and effective measures to prevent and combat torture and other cruel, inhuman or degrading treatment or punishment, including their gender-based manifestations, and also emphasizes the importance of taking fully into account the recommendations and conclusions of the relevant treaty bodies and mechanisms, including the Committee against Torture and the Special Rapporteur of the Commission on Human Rights on torture and other cruel, inhuman or degrading treatment or punishment;

3. *Condemns* any action or attempt by States or public officials to legalize, authorize or acquiesce in torture and other cruel, inhuman or degrading treatment or punishment under any circumstances, including on grounds of national security or through judicial decisions;

4. *Stresses* that all allegations of torture or other cruel, inhuman or degrading treatment or punishment must be promptly and impartially examined by the competent national authority, that those who encourage, order, tolerate or perpetrate acts of torture must be held responsible and severely punished, including the officials in charge of the place of detention where the prohibited act is found to have been committed, and takes note in this respect of the Principles on the Effective Investigation and Documentation of Torture and Other Cruel, Inhuman or Degrading Treatment or Punishment (the Istanbul Principles) as a useful tool in efforts to combat torture;

5. *Stresses also* that all acts of torture must be made offences under domestic criminal law, and emphasizes that acts of torture are serious violations of international humanitarian law and in this regard constitute war crimes and can constitute crimes against humanity, and that the perpetrators of all acts of torture must be prosecuted and punished;

6. *Urges* States to ensure that any statement that is established to have been made as a result of torture shall not be invoked as evidence in any proceedings, except against a person accused of torture as evidence that the statement was made;

7. *Stresses* that States must not punish personnel who are involved in the custody, interrogation or treatment of any individual subjected to any form of arrest, detention or imprisonment for not obeying orders to commit or conceal acts amounting to torture or other cruel, inhuman or degrading treatment or punishment;

8. *Urges* States not to expel, return ("refouler"), extradite or in any other way transfer a person to another State where there are substantial grounds for believing that the person would be in danger of being subjected to torture, and recognizes that diplomatic assurances, where used, do not release States from their obligations under international human rights, humanitarian and refugee law, in particular the principle of non-refoulement;

9. *Stresses* that national legal systems must ensure that victims of torture and other cruel, inhuman or degrading treatment or punishment obtain redress, are awarded fair and adequate compensation and receive appropriate social and medical rehabilitation, urges States to take effective measures to this end, and in this regard encourages the development of rehabilitation centres;

10. *Recalls* its resolution 43/173 of 9 December 1988 on the Body of Principles for the Protection of All Persons under Any Form of Detention or Imprisonment, and in this context stresses that ensuring that any individual arrested or detained is promptly brought before a judge or other independent judicial officer in person and permitting prompt and regular medical care and legal counsel as well as visits by family members and independent monitoring mechanisms can be effective measures for the prevention of torture and other cruel, inhuman or degrading treatment and punishment;

11. *Reminds* all States that prolonged incommunicado detention or detention in secret places may facilitate the perpetration of torture and other cruel, inhuman or degrading treatment or punishment and can in itself constitute a form of such treatment, and urges all States to respect the safeguards concerning the liberty, security and dignity of the person;

12. *Calls upon* all States to take appropriate effective legislative, administrative, judicial and other measures to prevent and prohibit the production, trade, export and use of equipment that is specifically designed to inflict torture or other cruel, inhuman or degrading treatment;

13. *Urges* all States that have not yet done so to become parties to the Convention against Torture and Other Cruel, Inhuman or Degrading Treatment or Punishment as a matter of priority;

14. *Invites* all States parties to the Convention that have not yet done so to make the declarations provided for in articles 21 and 22 of the Convention concerning inter-State and individual communications, to consider the possibility of withdrawing their reservations to article 20 of the Convention and to notify the Secretary-General of their acceptance of the amendments to articles 17 and 18 of the Convention as soon as possible;

15. *Urges* States parties to comply strictly with their obligations under the Convention, including, in view of the high number of reports not submitted in time, their obligation to submit reports in accordance with article 19 of the Convention, and invites States parties to incorporate a gender perspective and information concerning children and juveniles when submitting reports to the Committee against Torture;

16. *Calls upon* States parties to give early consideration to signing and ratifying the Optional Protocol to the Convention against Torture and Other Cruel, Inhuman or Degrading Treatment or Punishment, which provides further measures for use in the fight against and prevention of torture and other cruel, inhuman or degrading treatment or punishment;

17. *Welcomes* the work of the Committee against Torture and the report of the Committee, submitted in accordance with article 24 of the Convention;

18. *Calls upon* the United Nations High Commissioner for Human Rights, in conformity with her mandate established by the General Assembly in its resolution 48/141 of 20 December 1993, to continue to provide, at the request of States, advisory services for the prevention of torture and other cruel, inhuman or degrading treatment or punishment, including for the preparation of national reports to the Committee against Torture and for the establishment and operation of national preventive mechanisms, as well as tech-

nical assistance for the development, production and distribution of teaching material for this purpose;

19. *Notes with appreciation* the interim report of the Special Rapporteur of the Commission on Human Rights on torture and other cruel, inhuman or degrading treatment or punishment, and encourages the Special Rapporteur to continue to include in his recommendations proposals on the prevention and investigation of torture and other cruel, inhuman or degrading treatment or punishment, including its gender-based manifestations;

20. *Requests* the Special Rapporteur to continue to consider including in his report information on the follow-up by States to his recommendations, visits and communications, including progress made and problems encountered, and on other official contacts;

21. *Calls upon* all States to cooperate with and assist the Special Rapporteur in the performance of his task, to supply all necessary information requested by the Special Rapporteur, to fully and expeditiously respond to and follow up his urgent appeals, to give serious consideration to responding favourably to requests by the Special Rapporteur to visit their countries and to enter into a constructive dialogue with the Special Rapporteur on requested visits to their countries as well as with respect to the follow-up to his recommendations;

22. *Stresses* the need for the continued regular exchange of views among the Committee against Torture, the Special Rapporteur and other relevant United Nations mechanisms and bodies, as well as for the pursuance of cooperation with relevant United Nations programmes, notably the United Nations Crime Prevention and Criminal Justice Programme, with a view to enhancing further their effectiveness and cooperation on issues relating to torture, inter alia, by improving their coordination;

23. *Recognizes* the global need for international assistance to victims of torture, stresses the importance of the work of the Board of Trustees of the United Nations Voluntary Fund for Victims of Torture, and appeals to all States and organizations to contribute annually to the Fund, preferably with a substantial increase in the level of contributions;

24. *Requests* the Secretary-General to continue to transmit to all States the appeals of the General Assembly for contributions to the Fund and to include the Fund on an annual basis among the programmes for which funds are pledged at the United Nations Pledging Conference for Development Activities;

25. *Also requests* the Secretary-General to ensure, within the overall budgetary framework of the United Nations, the provision of adequate staff and facilities for the bodies and mechanisms involved in combating torture and assisting victims of torture commensurate with the strong support expressed by Member States for combating torture and assisting victims of torture, noting the upcoming entry into force of the Optional Protocol to the Convention;

26. *Further requests* the Secretary-General to submit to the Commission on Human Rights at its sixty-second session and to the General Assembly at its sixty-first session a report on the status of the Convention and a report on the operations of the Fund;

27. *Calls upon* all States, the Office of the United Nations High Commissioner for Human Rights and

other United Nations bodies and agencies, as well as relevant intergovernmental and non-governmental organizations, to commemorate, on 26 June, the United Nations International Day in Support of Victims of Torture;

28. *Decides* to consider at its sixty-first session the reports of the Secretary-General, including the report on the United Nations Voluntary Fund for Victims of Torture, the report of the Committee against Torture and the interim report of the Special Rapporteur of the Commission on Human Rights on torture and other cruel, inhuman or degrading treatment or punishment.

Right to peaceful assembly

On 19 April [res. 2005/37], the Commission, by a recorded vote of 45 to none, with 8 abstentions, called on Member States to respect and protect the rights of individuals to associate and to assembly peacefully, and to ensure that any restrictions on the free exercise of those rights were in accordance with international law. OHCHR was asked to assist States in that regard, including through technical assistance, and to cooperate in doing so with relevant UN system bodies and other intergovernmental organizations. The Commission encouraged civil society, including NGOs and the private sector, to promote and facilitate the rights, and called upon the Commission's special procedures to consider them in their work.

Freedom of expression

Report of Special Rapporteur. In accordance with a 2002 Commission request [YUN 2002, p. 716], the Special Rapporteur on the promotion and protection of the right to freedom of opinion and expression, Ambeyi Ligabo (Kenya), described his 2004 activities [E/CN.4/2005/64 & Corr. 1]. He had sent 449 urgent appeals and 161 allegation letters on behalf of 1,782 individuals whose rights to freedom of opinion and expression were reportedly threatened or violated. The texts of the communications he had sent and the replies received from Governments were summarized in an addendum [E/CN.4/2005/64/Add.1]. The Special Rapporteur also updated information contained in his previous report [YUN 2004, p. 736], particularly concerning the right of access to information, and in the light of the final session of the World Summit on the Information Society (see p. 933), he reviewed UN action regarding the freedom of opinion and expression, in order to derive new proposals for future direction. He concluded that, despite some progress, the situation remained grim. While a number of countries had adopted positive measures, several others had recently enacted restrictive legislation, particularly against new forms of freedom of expres-

sion and defamation. Many Governments used anti-terrorism and national security legislation to restrict that freedom. The Special Rapporteur found that media security and concentration were major sources of concern, with numerous journalists killed while performing their duties, either by paramilitary groups or undercover law enforcement officials, rebel groups or terrorists. Yet, most of those crimes were not adequately punished. The Special Rapporteur recommended, among other things, that Governments review existing practices and take remedial actions in all fields relating to the promotion and protection of freedom of expression. He encouraged civil society organizations to continue to provide him with information on the realization and violations of the right to that freedom and reiterated his proposal to the Commission for a study on the security of journalists, especially in armed conflict situations. He would give further consideration to the drafting of a set of recommendations supporting a comparative study of measures to better implement the right of access to information.

Commission action. On 19 April [res. 2005/38], the Commission called on States to ensure respect for the right to freedom of opinion and expression; end violations of the right and create conditions to prevent such violations; and ensure that victims of violations had an effective remedy. It extended the Special Rapporteur's mandate for a period of three years and asked him to report in 2006, and the Secretary-General to assist him.

On 25 July, the Economic and Social Council approved the Commission's request to the Special Rapporteur (**decision 2005/264**).

Communication. On 18 March [E/CN.4/2005/G/20], Italy transmitted its observations on the Special Rapporteur's report, following his 2004 visit to the country [YUN 2004, p. 738], particularly regarding legislation on the organization of its broadcasting system and alleged public subsidies and conflicts of interest in the media sector.

Terrorism

Report of High Commissioner. In response to General Assembly resolution 59/191 [YUN 2004, p. 741] and to a 2004 Commission request [ibid., p. 739], the High Commissioner submitted a report [E/CN.4/2005/100] reviewing action taken by her Office and the UN human rights system to further protect human rights and fundamental freedoms while countering terrorism. In addition to its work with the Security Council's Counter-Terrorism Committee (see p. 107) and others in the area of technical assistance, OHCHR maintained cooperation and information exchange on the subject with other partners, including the Council of Europe and the Organization for Security and Cooperation in Europe. Moreover, the Office had assumed a central role in the framework for cooperation in confronting new challenges to international peace and security, including international terrorism. It also provided support to the Commission's independent expert on the protection of human rights while countering terrorism (see below) and to the Subcommission's work on the subject. OHCHR continued to update the *Digest of Jurisprudence of the United Nations and Regional Organizations on the Protection of Human Rights while Countering Terrorism*, first compiled in 2003 [YUN 2003, p. 746], and reviewed in 2004 [YUN 2004, p. 739]. The High Commissioner, noting that UN human rights mechanisms remained concerned over counter-terrorism measures that jeopardized human rights and fundamental freedoms, expressed the hope that strengthened action by the United Nations on the issue would result in more consistent adherence by States to international human rights obligations in their efforts to counter terrorism.

Report of independent expert. By a 7 February note [E/CN.4/2005/103], the High Commissioner transmitted the report of the independent expert on the protection of human rights while countering terrorism, Robert K. Goldman (United States), prepared in response to a 2004 Commission request [YUN 2004, p. 739]. Building on the High Commissioner's 2004 study [ibid., p. 740] relating to the compatibility of national counter-terrorism measures with international human rights obligations, the report identified key issues affecting the enjoyment of human rights in the struggle against terrorism that had not been addressed or extensively developed by other mandate holders. Those issues included the question of upholding the rule of law while countering terrorism, within the context of human rights protection in emergency situations; the role of the civilian judiciary in supervising counter-terrorism measures; the applicability and relevance of international humanitarian law; the relationship between international human rights and humanitarian law during armed conflicts; the principle of *nullum crimen sine lege* (pertaining to the principles of criminal law) and the definitions of terrorism and related offences; the rights to liberty and security of persons, of detained children, to due process and a fair trial and to humane treatment; to property and to privacy; the role of military tribunals; the principle of non-refoulement and the inter-State transfer of persons, including terrorist suspects; diplo-

matic assurances; and the principle of non-discrimination and techniques to screen terrorist suspects. The report also considered ways to strengthen the UN human rights mechanisms for protecting human rights and fundamental freedoms while countering terrorism, and concluded that, despite significant efforts in that regard by the UN human rights system, gaps existed in the coverage of the monitoring systems of the special procedures and the treaty bodies. The expert recommended that the Commission consider the creation of a special procedure with a multidimensional mandate to monitor States' counter-terrorism measures and their compatibility with international human rights law.

Commission action. On 19 April [dec. 2005/107], the Commission, acknowledging the 2004 final report of the Special Rapporteur on terrorism and human rights, Kalliopi Koufa (Greece) [YUN 2004, p. 739], decided, by a recorded vote of 40 to 2, with 11 abstentions, to recommend to the Economic and Social Council that all the reports and documents she had submitted be compiled and published as part of the *Human Rights Study Series*.

On 21 April [res. 2005/80], the Commission, deploring human rights violations in the fight against terrorism, reaffirmed that States needed to ensure that measures to combat terrorism complied with their obligations under international law, particularly regarding human rights, refugee and humanitarian law. States were also encouraged to take into account relevant UN resolutions and decisions on human rights while countering terrorism. The Commission requested the High Commissioner to examine the matter, make recommendations concerning States' obligations, provide assistance and advice to States upon their request, and to report regularly on the implementation of the Commission's current resolution. The Commission decided to appoint, for three years, a special rapporteur on the promotion and protection of human rights and fundamental freedoms while countering terrorism, with a mandate to: make concrete recommendations on the matter; gather, request, receive and exchange information and communications with Governments and other actors regarding alleged violations; identify, exchange and promote best practices on counter-terrorism measures that respected human rights and fundamental freedoms; work in close coordination with other relevant UN bodies and mechanisms; develop regular dialogue between all relevant actors; and report regularly to the Commission and the General Assembly.

On 25 July, the Economic and Social Council approved the Commission's decision to appoint a special rapporteur and its requests to the High Commissioner (**decision 2005/279**).

Also in July, the Commission appointed Martin Scheinin (Finland) as the new Special Rapporteur on the protection and promotion of human rights and fundamental freedoms while countering terrorism.

ECONOMIC AND SOCIAL COUNCIL ACTION

On 25 July, the Economic and Social Council, on the recommendation of the Commission on Human Rights [E/2005/23], adopted **decision 2005/286** by recorded vote (33-2-14) [agenda item 14 (g)].

Terrorism and human rights

At its 38th plenary meeting, on 25 July 2005, the Economic and Social Council took note of Commission on Human Rights decision 2005/107 of 19 April 2005, and endorsed the Commission's recommendation that a compilation into a comprehensive document of all the reports and documents submitted to date by the Special Rapporteur of the Subcommission on the Promotion and Protection of Human Rights on terrorism and human rights be published as a United Nations publication as part of the *Human Rights Study Series.*

RECORDED VOTE ON DECISION 2005/286:

In favour: Armenia, Azerbaijan, Bangladesh, Belize, Brazil, China, Colombia, Costa Rica, Cuba, Ecuador, Guinea, India, Indonesia, Jamaica, Japan, Kenya, Malaysia, Mauritius, Mexico, Mozambique, Namibia, Nicaragua, Pakistan, Panama, Russian Federation, Saudi Arabia, Senegal, South Africa, Thailand, Tunisia, Turkey, United Arab Emirates, United Republic of Tanzania.

Against: Australia, United States.

Abstaining: Albania, Belgium, Canada, Denmark, France, Germany, Iceland, Ireland, Italy, Lithuania, Poland, Republic of Korea, Spain, United Kingdom.

Working Group. The sessional working group established by the Subcommission in 2004 [YUN 2004, p. 740] to elaborate detailed principles and guidelines concerning the promotion and protection of human rights when combating terrorism met during the year (2-3 August) [E/CN.4/Sub.2/2005/43]. The group discussed issues relating to its mandate and heard comments from Subcommission experts, Member States, national human rights institutions and NGOs. The group had before it an expanded working paper containing a preliminary framework draft of principles and guidelines concerning human rights and terrorism, prepared by the Special Rapporteur on terrorism and human rights, Kalliopi K. Koufa (Greece), in response to a 2004 Subcommission request [YUN 2004, p. 740], as well as her preliminary working paper which the Subcommission had considered in 2004 [ibid.]. The group decided to continue its work in 2006 and requested Ms. Koufa, who also served as its Chairperson, to update her draft. In related action, it requested that four papers be prepared for the Subcommission's consideration, and mandated Ms. Koufa to prepare the first, which

would elaborate on the issues outlined in her draft and on exceptions and derogations, based on the Committee on Human Rights general comment No. 29 of 2001 [YUN 2001, p. 590] concerning derogations during a state of emergency. The group mandated Marc Bossuyt (Belgium) and Ibrahim Salama (Egypt) to prepare the second paper on freedom of expression; Françoise Hampson (United Kingdom), the third, on international judicial cooperation; and Emmanuel Decaux (France), the fourth, on the rights of victims of terrorist acts.

Subcommission action. On 25 July [dec. 2005/103], the Subcommission decided to establish a sessional working group to elaborate detailed principles and guidelines concerning the promotion and protection of human rights when combating terrorism.

On 11 August [res. 2005/31], the Subcommission endorsed the recommendations contained in the report of the sessional working group (see above) and requested OHCHR to disseminate them to States, UN system bodies, regional intergovernmental organizations, national human rights institutions, NGOs, UN bodies, agencies and other mechanisms. It invited stakeholders to provide information and data to the working group to assist it in carrying out its mandate.

Reports of Secretary-General. In accordance with General Assembly resolution 59/195 [YUN 2004, p. 742], the Secretary-General submitted a September report [A/60/326] summarizing replies received from seven Governments in response to an OHCHR questionnaire seeking the views of Member States on the implications of terrorism in all its forms and manifestations for the full enjoyment of human rights and fundamental freedoms, and on the possible establishment of a voluntary fund for victims of terrorism and on ways to rehabilitate them.

On 16 December, the Assembly took note of the Secretary-General's report on human rights and terrorism (above) (**decision 60/533**).

Pursuant to Assembly resolution 59/191 [YUN 2004, p. 741], and to Commission resolution 2005/80 (see p. 818), the Secretary-General, on 22 September [A/60/374], provided an overview of developments in the United Nations regarding the protection of human rights while fighting against terrorism. Most notably, he had delivered an address to the International Summit on Democracy, Terrorism and Security (10 March, Madrid, Spain), in which he outlined the five elements of the UN strategy for responding to the terrorist threat, as recommended by the High-level Panel on Threats, Challenges and Change [YUN 2004, p. 54]. Those elements were to: defend human rights in the struggle against terrorism;

dissuade disaffected groups from choosing ter- rorism as a tactic; deny terrorists the means to carry out their attacks; deter States from support- ing terrorist groups; and develop State capacity to prevent terrorism. An implementation task force established for that strategy held its first meeting during the year. The report also re- flected on relevant activities undertaken by the High Commissioner and OHCHR, and by the Commission, human rights treaty bodies and special procedures. A particularly important de- velopment during the year was the Commission's appointment of a Special Rapporteur on the pro- motion and protection of human rights while countering terrorism. The report also summa- rized the deliberations and outcome of an expert seminar (Strasbourg, France, 13-14 June) on hu- man rights, counter-terrorism and states of emergency, organised by OHCHR to explore ways of strengthening human rights protection in counter-terrorism measures at the national level. The seminar had discussed the general princi- ples of human rights in the counter-terrorism context; national experiences with states of emergency; fundamental principles of fair trial; torture; extradition; and non-refoulement. The seminar adopted conclusions aimed at further defending human rights while combating terror and identified issues requiring further attention.

The Secretary-General concluded that, while States had a duty to protect their citizens from terrorism, counter-terrorism measures needed to conform with international human rights, hu- manitarian and refugee law, which was currently not the case in many instances.

Report of Special Rapporteur. By a 21 Sep- tember note [A/60/370], the Secretary-General transmitted the preliminary report of the newly appointed Special Rapporteur on the protection of human rights and fundamental freedoms while countering terrorism, Martin Scheinin (Finland), submitted in accordance with Com- mission resolution 2005/80 (see p. 818). The re- port outlined the conceptual framework of the Special Rapporteur's mandate, emphasizing the following four key features: the importance of complementarity in the work of mandate holders in general, the comprehensiveness of his man- date as a multidimensional mechanism, the pro- active nature of his work, and the thematic ap- proach he would adopt in addressing substantive issues relating to his mandate. Those themes would be further developed in the Special Rap- porteur's future reports.

GENERAL ASSEMBLY ACTION

On 16 December [meeting 64], the General As- sembly, on the recommendation of the Third

Committee [A/60/509/Add.2], adopted **resolution 60/158** without vote [agenda item 71 *(b)*].

Protection of human rights and fundamental freedoms while countering terrorism

The General Assembly,

Reaffirming the purposes and principles of the Char- ter of the United Nations,

Reaffirming also the fundamental importance, in- cluding in response to terrorism and the fear of terror- ism, of respecting all human rights and fundamental freedoms and the rule of law,

Recalling that States are under the obligation to pro- tect all human rights and fundamental freedoms of all persons,

Acknowledging the important contribution of meas- ures taken at all levels against terrorism, consistent with international law, in particular international hu- man rights law and refugee and humanitarian law, to the functioning of democratic institutions and the maintenance of peace and security and thereby to the full enjoyment of human rights, as well as the need to continue this fight, including through international cooperation and the strengthening of the role of the United Nations in this respect,

Deeply deploring the occurrence of violations of hu- man rights and fundamental freedoms in the context of the fight against terrorism, as well as violations of international refugee law and international humanita- rian law,

Recognizing that the respect for human rights, the re- spect for democracy and the respect for the rule of law are interrelated and mutually reinforcing,

Recognizing also that all States must fully respect the non-refoulement obligations under international refugee and human rights law, while at the same time bearing in mind relevant exclusion provisions under international refugee law,

Welcoming the various initiatives to strengthen the promotion and protection of human rights in the con- text of counter-terrorism adopted by the United Nations and regional intergovernmental bodies, as well as by States,

Noting the declarations, statements and recommen- dations of a number of human rights treaty monitor- ing bodies and special procedures on the question of the compatibility of counter-terrorism measures with human rights obligations,

Recalling its resolutions 57/219 of 18 December 2002, 58/187 of 22 December 2003 and 59/191 of 20 December 2004, Commission on Human Rights reso- lutions 2003/68 of 25 April 2003, 2004/87 of 21 April 2004 and 2005/80 of 21 April 2005 and other relevant resolutions of the General Assembly and the Commis- sion on Human Rights,

Recalling also its resolution 48/141 of 20 December 1993 and, inter alia, the responsibility of the United Nations High Commissioner for Human Rights to pro- mote and protect the effective enjoyment of all human rights,

Reaffirming that acts, methods and practices of ter- rorism in all its forms and manifestations are activities aimed at the destruction of human rights, fundamen- tal freedoms and democracy, threatening territorial in- tegrity, security of States and destabilizing legitimately constituted Governments, and that the international community should take the necessary steps to enhance cooperation to prevent and combat terrorism,

Noting the declaration on the issue of combating terrorism contained in the annex to Security Council resolution 1456(2003) of 20 January 2003, in particular the statement that States must ensure that any measures taken to combat terrorism comply with all their obligations under international law and should adopt such measures in accordance with international law, in particular international human rights, refugee and humanitarian law,

Reaffirming its unequivocal condemnation of all acts, methods and practices of terrorism in all its forms and manifestations, wherever and by whomsoever committed, regardless of their motivation, as criminal and unjustifiable, and renewing its commitment to strengthen international cooperation to prevent and combat terrorism,

Stressing that everyone is entitled to all the rights and freedoms recognized in the Universal Declaration of Human Rights without distinction of any kind, including on the grounds of race, colour, sex, language, religion, political or other opinion, national or social origin, property, birth or other status,

1. *Reaffirms* that States must ensure that any measure taken to combat terrorism complies with their obligations under international law, in particular international human rights, refugee and humanitarian law;

2. *Deplores* the suffering caused by terrorism to the victims and their families, and expresses its profound solidarity with them;

3. *Reaffirms* the obligation of States, in accordance with article 4 of the International Covenant on Civil and Political Rights, to respect certain rights as non-derogable in any circumstances, recalls, in regard to all other Covenant rights, that any measures derogating from the provisions of the Covenant must be in accordance with that article in all cases, and underlines the exceptional and temporary nature of any such derogations;

4. *Calls upon* States to raise awareness about the importance of these obligations among national authorities involved in combating terrorism;

5. *Urges* States to fully respect non-refoulement obligations under international refugee and human rights law and, at the same time, to review, with full respect for these obligations and other legal safeguards, the validity of a refugee status decision in an individual case if credible and relevant evidence comes to light that indicates that the person in question has committed any criminal acts, including terrorist acts, falling under the exclusion clauses under international refugee law;

6. *Welcomes* the establishment by the Commission on Human Rights in its resolution 2005/80 of the mandate of the Special Rapporteur on the promotion and protection of human rights and fundamental freedoms while countering terrorism;

7. *Reaffirms* that it is imperative that all States work to uphold and protect the dignity of individuals and their fundamental freedoms, as well as democratic practices and the rule of law, while countering terrorism, as stated in the report of the Secretary-General submitted pursuant to General Assembly resolution 58/187;

8. *Takes note with appreciation* of the study of the United Nations High Commissioner for Human Rights submitted pursuant to resolution 58/187;

9. *Encourages* States to make available to relevant national authorities the "Digest of Jurisprudence of the United Nations and Regional Organizations on the Protection of Human Rights while Countering Terrorism" and to take into account its content, and requests the High Commissioner to update and publish it periodically;

10. *Welcomes* the ongoing dialogue established in the context of the fight against terrorism between the Security Council and its Counter-Terrorism Committee and the relevant bodies for the promotion and protection of human rights, and encourages the Security Council and its Counter-Terrorism Committee to strengthen the links and to continue to develop cooperation with relevant human rights bodies, in particular with the Office of the United Nations High Commissioner for Human Rights, the Special Rapporteur of the Commission on Human Rights on the promotion and protection of human rights and fundamental freedoms while countering terrorism and other relevant special procedures and mechanisms of the Commission, giving due regard to the promotion and protection of human rights in the ongoing work pursuant to relevant Security Council resolutions relating to terrorism;

11. *Stresses* that, while developing, as agreed at the 2005 World Summit, a strategy to promote comprehensive, coordinated and consistent counter-terrorism responses, full consideration should be given throughout the process to the protection of human rights and fundamental freedoms and to the provisions of international humanitarian law and international refugee law;

12. *Requests* all relevant special procedures and mechanisms of the Commission on Human Rights, as well as the United Nations human rights treaty bodies, to cooperate, within their mandates, with the Special Rapporteur on the promotion and protection of human rights and fundamental freedoms while countering terrorism, and encourages the Special Rapporteur to work closely with them to coordinate efforts, where appropriate, in order to promote a consistent approach on this subject;

13. *Encourages* States, while countering terrorism, to take into account relevant United Nations resolutions and decisions on human rights, and encourages them to consider the recommendations of the special procedures and mechanisms of the Commission on Human Rights and the relevant comments and views of United Nations human rights treaty bodies;

14. *Takes note with appreciation* of the report of the independent expert on the protection of human rights and fundamental freedoms while countering terrorism;

15. *Takes note with interest* of the report of the Secretary-General submitted pursuant to General Assembly resolution 59/191;

16. *Takes note with appreciation* of the report of the Special Rapporteur submitted pursuant to Commission on Human Rights resolution 2005/80, and the four features of his mandate emphasized, namely, complementarity, comprehensiveness, its proactive nature and its thematic approach, and requests the Spe-

cial Rapporteur to report regularly to the General Assembly and to the Commission on Human Rights;

17. *Requests* all Governments to cooperate fully with the Special Rapporteur in the performance of the tasks and duties mandated, including by reacting promptly to the urgent appeals of the Special Rapporteur and providing the information requested;

18. *Requests* the High Commissioner, making use of existing mechanisms, to continue:

(a) To examine the question of the protection of human rights and fundamental freedoms while countering terrorism, taking into account reliable information from all sources;

(b) To make general recommendations concerning the obligation of States to promote and protect human rights and fundamental freedoms while taking actions to counter terrorism;

(c) To provide assistance and advice to States, upon their request, on the protection of human rights and fundamental freedoms while countering terrorism, as well as to relevant United Nations bodies;

19. *Requests* the Secretary-General to submit a report on the implementation of the present resolution to the Commission on Human Rights at its sixty-second session and to the General Assembly at its sixty-first session.

Hostage-taking

On 19 April [res. 2005/31], the Commission, condemning all acts of hostage-taking in the world, demanded the immediate and unconditional release of all hostages. It called upon States to prevent, combat and punish hostage-taking, and urged thematic rapporteurs and working groups to address the consequences of such acts in their reports.

Peace and security

Commission action. By a recorded vote of 32 to 15, with 6 abstentions, the Commission, on 20 April [res. 2005/56], affirmed that States should promote international peace and security, and urged them to respect and put into practice the principles and purposes of the UN Charter in their relations with other States. It called on the High Commissioner to carry out a constructive dialogue and consultations with Member States, specialized agencies and intergovernmental organizations on how the Commission could work for the promotion of peace, and encouraged NGOs to contribute to the endeavour.

GENERAL ASSEMBLY ACTION

On 16 December [meeting 64], the General Assembly, on the recommendation of the Third Committee [A/60/509/Add.2], adopted **resolution 60/163** by recorded vote of 116-53-8 [agenda item 71 (b)].

Promotion of peace as a vital requirement for the full enjoyment of all human rights by all

The General Assembly,

Recalling its resolution 58/192 of 22 December 2003,

Recalling also Commission on Human Rights resolution 2005/56 of 20 April 2005 entitled "Promotion of peace as a vital requirement for the full enjoyment of all human rights by all",

Taking note of its resolution 39/11 of 12 November 1984 entitled "Declaration on the Right of Peoples to Peace", and the United Nations Millennium Declaration,

Determined to foster strict respect for the purposes and principles enshrined in the Charter of the United Nations,

Bearing in mind that one of the purposes of the United Nations is to achieve international cooperation in solving international problems of an economic, social, cultural or humanitarian character and in promoting and encouraging respect for human rights and for fundamental freedoms for all without distinction as to race, sex, language or religion,

Underlining, in accordance with the purposes and principles of the United Nations, its full and active support for the United Nations and for the enhancement of its role and effectiveness in strengthening international peace, security and justice and in promoting the solution of international problems, as well as the development of friendly relations and cooperation among States,

Reaffirming the obligation of all States to settle their international disputes by peaceful means in such a manner that international peace and security and justice are not endangered,

Emphasizing its objective of promoting better relations among all States and contributing to setting up conditions in which their people can live in true and lasting peace, free from any threat to or attempt against their security,

Reaffirming the obligation of all States to refrain in their international relations from the threat or use of force against the territorial integrity or political independence of any State, or in any other manner inconsistent with the purposes of the United Nations,

Reaffirming its commitment to peace, security and justice and the continuing development of friendly relations and cooperation among States,

Rejecting the use of violence in pursuit of political aims, and stressing that only peaceful political solutions can ensure a stable and democratic future for all people around the world,

Reaffirming the importance of ensuring respect for the principles of the sovereignty, territorial integrity and political independence of States and non-intervention in matters that are essentially within the domestic jurisdiction of any State, in accordance with the Charter and international law,

Reaffirming also that all peoples have the right to self-determination, by virtue of which they freely determine their political status and freely pursue their economic, social and cultural development,

Reaffirming further the Declaration on Principles of International Law concerning Friendly Relations and Cooperation among States in accordance with the Charter of the United Nations,

Recognizing that peace and development are mutually reinforcing, including in the prevention of armed conflict,

Affirming that human rights include social, economic and cultural rights and the right to peace, a healthy environment and development, and that development is in fact the realization of those rights,

Underlining the fact that the subjection of peoples to alien subjugation, domination and exploitation constitutes a denial of fundamental rights, is contrary to the Charter and is an impediment to the promotion of world peace and cooperation,

Recalling that everyone is entitled to a social and international order in which the rights and freedoms set forth in the Universal Declaration of Human Rights can be fully realized,

Convinced of the aim of creating conditions of stability and well-being, which are necessary for peaceful and friendly relations among nations based on respect for the principles of equal rights and self-determination of peoples,

Convinced also that life without war is the primary international prerequisite for the material well-being, development and progress of countries and for the full implementation of the rights and fundamental human freedoms proclaimed by the United Nations,

Convinced further that international cooperation in the field of human rights contributes to creating an international environment of peace and stability,

1. *Stresses* that peace is a vital requirement for the promotion and protection of all human rights for all;

2. *Also stresses* that the deep fault line that divides human society between the rich and the poor and the ever-increasing gap between the developed and developing worlds pose a major threat to global prosperity, peace and security and stability;

3. *Solemnly declares* that the peoples of our planet have a sacred right to peace and that the preservation and promotion of peace constitutes a fundamental obligation of each State;

4. *Emphasizes* that the preservation and promotion of peace demands that the policies of States be directed towards the elimination of the threat of war, particularly nuclear war, the renunciation of the use or threat of use of force in international relations and the settlement of international disputes by peaceful means on the basis of the Charter of the United Nations;

5. *Affirms* that all States should promote the establishment, maintenance and strengthening of international peace and security and an international system based on respect for the principles enshrined in the Charter and the promotion of all human rights and fundamental freedoms, including the right to development and the right of peoples to self-determination;

6. *Urges* all States to respect and to put into practice the purposes and principles of the Charter in their relations with other States, irrespective of their political, economic or social system and of their size, geographical location or level of economic development;

7. *Reaffirms* the duty of all States, in accordance with the principles of the Charter, to use peaceful means to settle any dispute to which they are parties and the continuance of which is likely to endanger the maintenance of international peace and security, as a vital requirement for the promotion and protection of all human rights of everyone and all peoples;

8. *Calls upon* the United Nations High Commissioner for Human Rights to carry out a constructive dialogue and consultations with Member States, the specialized agencies and intergovernmental organizations on how the Commission on Human Rights could work for the promotion of an international environment conducive to the full realization of the right of peoples to peace, and encourages non-governmental organizations to contribute actively to this endeavour;

9. *Invites* States and relevant United Nations human rights mechanisms and procedures to continue to pay attention to the importance of mutual cooperation, understanding and dialogue in ensuring the promotion and protection of all human rights;

10. *Decides* to continue consideration of the question of the promotion of the right of peoples to peace at its sixty-second session under the item entitled "Human rights questions".

RECORDED VOTE ON RESOLUTION 60/163:

In favour: Afghanistan, Algeria, Angola, Antigua and Barbuda, Azerbaijan, Bahamas, Bahrain, Bangladesh, Barbados, Belarus, Belize, Benin, Bhutan, Bolivia, Botswana, Brazil, Brunei Darussalam, Burkina Faso, Burundi, Cambodia, Cameroon, Cape Verde, China, Colombia, Comoros, Costa Rica, Côte d'Ivoire, Cuba, Democratic People's Republic of Korea, Democratic Republic of the Congo, Djibouti, Dominica, Dominican Republic, Ecuador, Egypt, El Salvador, Eritrea, Ethiopia, Fiji, Gabon, Gambia, Ghana, Grenada, Guatemala, Guinea, Guinea-Bissau, Guyana, Haiti, Honduras, Indonesia, Iran, Jamaica, Jordan, Kazakhstan, Kenya, Kuwait, Kyrgyzstan, Lao People's Democratic Republic, Lebanon, Lesotho, Libyan Arab Jamahiriya, Madagascar, Malawi, Malaysia, Maldives, Mali, Mauritania, Mauritius, Mongolia, Morocco, Mozambique, Myanmar, Namibia, Nepal, Nicaragua, Niger, Nigeria, Oman, Pakistan, Panama, Papua New Guinea, Paraguay, Peru, Philippines, Qatar, Russian Federation, Rwanda, Saint Lucia, Saint Vincent and the Grenadines, Saudi Arabia, Senegal, Solomon Islands, Somalia, South Africa, Sri Lanka, Sudan, Suriname, Syrian Arab Republic, Tajikistan, Thailand, Timor-Leste, Togo, Trinidad and Tobago, Tunisia, Turkmenistan, Tuvalu, Uganda, United Arab Emirates, United Republic of Tanzania, Uruguay, Uzbekistan, Venezuela, Viet Nam, Yemen, Zambia, Zimbabwe.

Against: Albania, Andorra, Australia, Austria, Belgium, Bosnia and Herzegovina, Bulgaria, Canada, Croatia, Cyprus, Czech Republic, Denmark, Estonia, Finland, France, Georgia, Germany, Greece, Hungary, Iceland, Ireland, Israel, Italy, Japan, Latvia, Liechtenstein, Lithuania, Luxembourg, Malta, Marshall Islands, Micronesia, Monaco, Netherlands, New Zealand, Norway, Palau, Poland, Portugal, Republic of Korea, Republic of Moldova, Romania, San Marino, Serbia and Montenegro, Slovakia, Slovenia, Spain, Sweden, Switzerland, The former Yugoslav Republic of Macedonia, Turkey, Ukraine, United Kingdom, United States.

Abstaining: Argentina, Armenia, Chile, India, Mexico, Samoa, Singapore, Vanuatu.

Small arms

Note by Secretariat. By a 16 June note [E/CN.4/Sub.2/2005/35], the Secretariat informed the Subcommission that the Special Rapporteur on the prevention of human rights violations committed with small arms and light weapons, Barbara Frey (United States), would not be able to submit her final report, as requested by the Subcommission in 2004 [YUN 2004, p. 744]. She had indicated that she needed extra time to compile and evaluate the responses of Governments to her questionnaire and requested that she be allowed to submit the report in 2006. Annexed to the note were the draft principles on the prevention of human rights violations committed with small arms and commentary thereto, which the Special Rapporteur had presented to the Subcommission in 2004 [ibid.], and which she had further revised.

Subcommission action. On 11 August [dec. 2005/110], the Subcommission encouraged Governments that had not yet done so to submit responses to the Special Rapporteur's questionnaire, preferably by 1 November, to enable her to complete her work. She was asked to submit her final report in 2006.

Economic, social and cultural rights

Right to development

Reports of Secretary-General. The Commission had before it a report of the Secretary-General [E/CN.4/2005/39], submitted in accordance with a 2004 Commission request [YUN 2004, p. 746], which described the activities undertaken by the Committee on Economic, Social and Cultural Rights, the Committee on the Rights of the Child, special procedures on economic, social and cultural rights and OHCHR to contribute to the articulation and realization of economic, social and cultural rights. The Secretary-General concluded that progress had continued in increasing the understanding of those rights, marked by higher levels of cooperation among UN agencies, particularly within the context of the adoption of voluntary guidelines on the right to food by the Food and Agriculture Organization (FAO) of the United Nations, as well as a greater focus on technical cooperation on related issues.

An August report of the Secretary-General [A/60/286], submitted in accordance with General Assembly resolution 59/185 [YUN 2004, p. 747], updated and complemented information contained in the High Commissioner's report (see below). The report summarized the activities of the open-ended Working Group on the Right to Development (see below) and of its high-level task force on the implementation of the right, as well as related action by OHCHR, the Commission and the Subcommission.

On 16 July, the Assembly took note of the Secretary-General's report (**decision 60/533**).

Report of the High Commissioner. In response to 1998 [YUN 1998, p. 683] and 2004 [YUN 2004, p. 746] Commission requests, the High Commissioner submitted a January report [E/CN.4/2005/24], which summarized OHCHR activities undertaken to implement the right to development and provided information on the implementation of related General Assembly and Commission resolutions, and on UN system interagency cooperation to implement Commission resolutions.

In response to a 1999 Subcommission request [YUN 1999, p. 652] for the annual transmission of information relating to the realization of the right to development, the Secretary-General, in a June Secretariat note [E/CN.4/Sub.2/2005/16], drew attention to the High Commissioner's report (see above).

Working Group activities. The open-ended Working Group on the Right to Development, at its sixth session (Geneva, 14-18 February) [E/CN.4/2005/25], considered the High Commissioner's report (see above) and the report of the high-level task force, which the Group established in 2004 [YUN 2004, p. 746], on the implementation of the right to development (see below), and also heard presentations from two Member States on the way forward. In its conclusions, the Group agreed on the importance of continuing partnerships among the Commission, UN bodies, multilateral financial and development institutions and the World Trade Organization (WTO) for implementing the right to development. It accorded priority to evolving, assessing and disseminating measures for realizing the right, through collaborative efforts by stakeholders at the national and international levels, and recognized that States had a duty to formulate development policies to facilitate the full realization of the right, in accordance with the provisions of the Declaration on the Right to Development, adopted by the General Assembly in resolution 41/128 [YUN 1986, p. 717]. The Group also adopted conclusions advocating the timely attainment of the MDGs [YUN 2000, p. 51], and the necessity for introducing human rights standards and principles in impact assessments of trade and development rules and policies.

Noting that an unsustainable debt burden was obstructing developing countries from achieving the MDGs and progressing with the realization of the right to development, the Group called for more official development assistance (ODA) from donor countries. It also recommended that the Commission extend the mandate of the high-level task force for a further year to examine Millennium Development Goal 8 on the value of global partnership for development. OHCHR was requested to undertake and make available to policy makers a mapping of the MDGs against the provisions of relevant international human rights instruments, as a means of mobilizing, strengthening and sustaining efforts to implement those Goals in a manner compatible with the right to development. It was also asked to assist the high-level task force; provide an outline for the compendium of partnerships for development cooperation and other multilateral and bilateral arrangements contributing to the realization of the right; identify common elements and best practices emerging therefrom, for the Working Group's consideration in 2006; and bring the conclusions and recommendations of the task force and the Group to the attention of relevant international institutions. The Group prepared a list of issues to guide its future work, considered ongoing activities and recommended that the Commission renew the Group's mandate for a further year.

The Group's high-level task force, established by the Commission in 2004 [YUN 2004, p. 746] to consider issues relating to the implementation of the right to development, held its first (13-17 December 2004) [E/CN.4/2005/WG.18/2] and second (14-18 November 2005) [E/CN.4/2005/WG.18/TF/3] sessions, both in Geneva. At its first session, it discussed obstacles and challenges to implementation efforts, social impact assessments in the areas of trade and development at the national and international levels, and within the context of those two topics, it considered the issue of best practices. The task force adopted, for the Working Group's consideration, conclusions and recommendations relating to the topics it had considered. It also considered, among other things, measures to enable developing countries to overcome the obstacle posed by a heavy debt burden in achieving the MDGs and the need for such practical tools as guidelines and indicators to help translate human rights norms and principles into accessible parameters in undertaking social impact assessments. In November, the task force reviewed the evolution of and recent developments in global partnerships for development. It considered regional and national perspectives on the topic, as well as the criteria for evaluating Millennium Development Goal 8 and the value that the right to development would add to global partnerships. The task force adopted conclusions on the issues of aid, trade, debt, technology transfer, Millennium Development Goal 8 questions, the role of the private sector, global governance, migration and regional initiatives. It made recommendations relating to the criteria for assessing global partnerships for realizing the right to development; the activities of treaty bodies; the work of civil society and national institutions; the involvement of States; the monitoring mechanisms and activities of transnational corporations; and the work of UN country teams, OHCHR and international financial institutions.

Note by Secretariat. By a December note [E/CN.4/2006/WG.18/3], the Secretariat transmitted to members of the Working Group the report of the high-level task force on its second meeting (see above).

Commission action. On 12 April [res. 2005/4], by a recorded vote of 48 to 2, with 2 abstentions, the Commission endorsed the conclusions and recommendations of the Working Group at its sixth session (see above) and called for their effective implementation. Noting with concern that the Subcommission had not submitted the concept document on the right to development (see below) requested by the Commission in 2003 [YUN 2003, p. 753], it called for the submission of the document without delay, for the Commission's consideration in 2006. The Commission asked OHCHR to support the Subcommission in its work on the concept document and, the High Commissioner, to undertake activities aimed at strengthening global partnership for development between Member States, development agencies and international development institutions, and to reflect those activities in her 2006 report to the Commission. The Commission decided to renew the mandate of the Working Group for one year and to convene its seventh session before the Commission's 2006 session.

On 15 April [res. 2005/22], by a recorded vote of 50 to none, with 3 abstentions, the Commission called on States to guarantee economic, social and cultural rights without discrimination of any kind; to secure, through national development policies and with international assistance, the full realization of those rights, giving particular attention to the most vulnerable and disadvantaged, most often women and children, and communities living in extreme poverty; and to promote the effective participation of civil society in decision-making processes related to those rights. The Secretary-General was asked to report in 2006 on the implementation of the Commission's resolution.

ECONOMIC AND SOCIAL COUNCIL ACTION

On 25 July, the Economic and Social Council, on the recommendation of the Commission on Human Rights [E/2005/23], adopted **decision 2005/256** by recorded vote (46-2-1) [agenda item 14 *(g)*].

The right to development

At its 38th plenary meeting, on 25 July 2005, the Economic and Social Council took note of Commission on Human Rights resolution 2005/4 of 12 April 2005, and approved the decision of the Commission to renew for one year the mandate of the open-ended working group established to monitor and review progress made in the promotion and implementation of the right to development and to convene its seventh session before the sixty-second session of the Commission for a period of ten working days, five of which shall be allocated to the second meeting of the high-level task force on the right to development to be held well in advance of the session of the working group.

RECORDED VOTE ON DECISION 2005/256:

In favour: Albania, Armenia, Azerbaijan, Bangladesh, Belgium, Belize, Brazil, Canada, China, Colombia, Congo, Costa Rica, Cuba, Denmark, Ec-

uador, France, Germany, Guinea, Iceland, India, Indonesia, Ireland, Italy, Jamaica, Kenya, Lithuania, Malaysia, Mauritius, Mexico, Mozambique, Namibia, Nicaragua, Panama, Poland, Republic of Korea, Russian Federation, Saudi Arabia, Senegal, South Africa, Spain, Thailand, Tunisia, Turkey, United Arab Emirates, United Kingdom, United Republic of Tanzania.
Against: Australia, United States.
Abstaining: Japan.

Working paper. In response to a 2003 Subcommission request [YUN 2003, p. 754], Florizelle O'Connor (Jamaica) submitted a June working paper [E/CN.4/Sub.2/2005/23], designed as a concept document on the right to development. The paper discussed concepts which she considered essential for the improvement and advancement of ongoing work on the right, and the importance of many of the Subcommission's projects in laying the foundation for a human rights approach to that right, including studies on slavery and slave-practices, globalization, the right to drinking water, and extreme poverty. It also addressed the importance of creating human rights indicators and principles for development partnerships. The paper highlighted the need to question the validity of emerging human rights indicators to ensure that they measured the right things, and the importance of focusing on a human rights approach to the right, as well as the value of good governance to the successful implementation of development programmes, and of funding support. It recommended, among other things, that the Subcommission adopt in 2005, a thematic resolution on the right to development, summarizing its work in that field and encouraging dialogue with other UN bodies. It should also request authors of studies or working papers under the agenda item concerning economic, social and cultural rights to make observations and recommendations in their reports pertaining to the right to development and to consider developing draft standards or guidelines to facilitate transparency and the participation of local communities in their own development programmes. In order to facilitate the broadest discussion on the right to development, the Subcommission should recommend that the World Programme for Human Rights Education (see p. 745) should be sued to focus on education on the right.

Subcommission action. On 10 August [res. 2005/17], the Subcommission, welcoming Ms. O'Connor's concept document, decided to submit it to the Commission in 2006. The Subcommission asked her to continue her work and to submit a further working paper for consideration in 2006.

GENERAL ASSEMBLY ACTION

On 16 December [meeting 64], the General Assembly, on the recommendation of the Third Committee [A/60/509/Add.2], adopted **resolution 60/157** by recorded vote (172-2-5) [agenda item 71 (b)].

The right to development

The General Assembly,

Guided by the Charter of the United Nations, which expresses, in particular, the determination to promote social progress and better standards of life in larger freedom, as well as to employ international mechanisms for the promotion of the economic and social advancement of all peoples,

Recalling the Universal Declaration of Human Rights as well as the International Covenant on Civil and Political Rights and the International Covenant on Economic, Social and Cultural Rights,

Recalling also the outcomes of all the major United Nations conferences and summits in the economic and social fields,

Recalling further that the Declaration on the Right to Development, adopted by the General Assembly in its resolution 41/128 of 4 December 1986, confirmed that the right to development is an inalienable human right and that equality of opportunity for development is a prerogative both of nations and of individuals who make up nations, and that the individual is the central subject and beneficiary of development,

Stressing that the Vienna Declaration and Programme of Action reaffirmed the right to development as a universal and inalienable right and an integral part of fundamental human rights, and the individual as the central subject and beneficiary of development,

Reaffirming the objective of making the right to development a reality for everyone, as set out in the United Nations Millennium Declaration, adopted by the General Assembly on 8 September 2000,

Reaffirming also the universality, indivisibility, interrelatedness, interdependence and mutually reinforcing nature of all civil, cultural, economic, political and social rights, including the right to development,

Recalling the framework modalities agreed to at the General Council meeting of the World Trade Organization in Geneva on 1 August 2004 in key areas such as agriculture, market access for non-agricultural products, trade facilitation, development and services,

Recalling also the outcome of the eleventh session of the United Nations Conference on Trade and Development, held at Sno Paulo, Brazil, from 13 to 18 June 2004, on the theme "Enhancing the coherence between national development strategies and global economic processes towards economic growth and development, particularly of developing countries",

Recalling further all its previous resolutions and those of the Commission on Human Rights on the right to development, in particular Commission resolution 1998/72 of 22 April 1998, on the urgent need to make further progress towards the realization of the right to development as set out in the Declaration on the Right to Development,

Recalling the Thirteenth Conference of Heads of State or Government of Non-Aligned Countries, held at Kuala Lumpur from 20 to 25 February 2003, and the Fourteenth Ministerial Conference of the Movement of Non-Aligned Countries, held at Durban, South Africa, from 17 to 19 August 2004,

Reiterating its continuing support for the New Partnership for Africa's Development as a development framework for Africa,

Recognizing that historical injustices have undeniably contributed to the poverty, underdevelopment, marginalization, social exclusion, economic disparity, instability and insecurity that affect many people in different parts of the world, in particular in developing countries,

Stressing that poverty eradication is one of the critical elements in the promotion and realization of the right to development and that poverty is a multifaceted problem that requires a multifaceted and integrated approach in addressing economic, political, social, environmental and institutional dimensions at all levels, especially in the context of the millennium development goal of halving, by 2015, the proportion of the world's people whose income is less than one dollar a day and the proportion of people who suffer from hunger,

1. *Endorses* the agreed conclusions and recommendations adopted by the Working Group on the Right to Development at its sixth session, and calls for their immediate, full and effective implementation by the Office of the United Nations High Commissioner for Human Rights and other relevant actors;

2. *Welcomes* the convening of the first meeting of the high-level task force on the implementation of the right to development, held at Geneva from 13 to 17 December 2004, and expresses its appreciation to the task force for the work it has undertaken;

3. *Notes with appreciation* that the high-level task force, at its second meeting, examined millennium development goal 8 on a global partnership for development and suggested criteria for its periodic evaluation with the aim of improving the effectiveness of global partnership with regard to the realization of the right to development;

4. *Stresses* the importance of the core principles contained in the conclusions of the Working Group at its third session, congruent with the purpose of international human rights instruments, such as equality, non-discrimination, accountability, participation and international cooperation, as critical to mainstreaming the right to development at the national and international levels, and underlines the importance of the principles of equity and transparency;

5. *Notes with appreciation* that the Subcommission on the Promotion and Protection of Human Rights decided at its fifty-seventh session to submit the concept document establishing options and their feasibility for the implementation of the right to development to the Commission on Human Rights at its sixty-second session, in this regard calls upon the Commission to give due consideration to the options contained therein, and requests the Secretary-General to report on progress in this regard to the General Assembly at its sixty-first session;

6. *Takes note* of the convening and outcome of the third Social Forum held at Geneva on 21 and 22 July 2005 on the theme "Poverty and economic growth: challenges to human rights" and the strong support extended to it by the Subcommission on the Promotion and Protection of Human Rights, and invites Member States and all other stakeholders to participate actively in its subsequent sessions;

7. *Reaffirms* the commitment to implement the goals and targets set out in all the outcome documents of the major United Nations conferences and summits and their review processes, in particular those relating to the realization of the right to development, recognizing that the realization of the right to development is critical to achieving the objectives, goals and targets set in those outcome documents;

8. *Also reaffirms* that the realization of the right to development is essential to the implementation of the Vienna Declaration and Programme of Action, which regards all human rights as universal, indivisible, interdependent and interrelated, places the human person at the centre of development and recognizes that, while development facilitates the enjoyment of all human rights, the lack of development may not be invoked to justify the abridgement of internationally recognized human rights;

9. *Stresses* that the primary responsibility for the promotion and protection of all human rights lies with the State, and reaffirms that States have the primary responsibility for their own economic and social development and that the role of national policies and development strategies cannot be overemphasized;

10. *Reaffirms* the primary responsibility of States to create national and international conditions favourable to the realization of the right to development as well as their commitment to cooperate with each other to that end;

11. *Also reaffirms* the need for an international environment that is conducive to the realization of the right to development;

12. *Stresses* the need to strive for greater acceptance, operationalization and realization of the right to development at the international and national levels, and calls upon States to institute the measures required for the implementation of the right to development as a fundamental human right;

13. *Emphasizes* the critical importance of identifying and analysing obstacles impeding the full realization of the right to development at both the national and the international levels;

14. *Affirms* that, while globalization offers both opportunities and challenges, the process of globalization remains deficient in achieving the objectives of integrating all countries into a globalized world, and stresses the need for policies and measures at the national and global levels to respond to the challenges and opportunities of globalization if this process is to be made fully inclusive and equitable;

15. *Recognizes* that, despite continuous efforts on the part of the international community, the gap between developed and developing countries remains unacceptably wide, that developing countries continue to face difficulties in participating in the globalization process and that many risk being marginalized and effectively excluded from its benefits;

16. *Underlines* the fact that the international community is far from meeting the target set in the United Nations Millennium Declaration of halving the number of people living in poverty by 2015, reaffirms the commitment made to meet that target, and emphasizes the principle of international cooperation, including partnership and commitment, between developed and developing countries towards achieving the goal;

17. *Urges* developed countries that have not yet done so to make concrete efforts towards meeting the targets of 0.7 per cent of their gross national product for official development assistance to developing countries and 0.15 to 0.2 per cent of their gross national product to least developed countries, and encourages developing countries to build on the progress achieved in ensuring that official development assistance is used effectively to help to meet development goals and targets;

18. *Recognizes* the need to address market access for developing countries, including in agriculture, services and non-agricultural products, in particular those of interest to developing countries;

19. *Calls for* the implementation of a desirable pace of meaningful trade liberalization, including in areas under negotiation; implementation of commitments on implementation-related issues and concerns; review of special and differential-treatment provisions, with a view to strengthening them and making them more precise, effective and operational; avoidance of new forms of protectionism; and capacity-building and technical assistance for developing countries as important issues in making progress towards the effective implementation of the right to development;

20. *Recognizes* the important link between the international economic, commercial and financial spheres and the realization of the right to development, stresses, in this regard, the need for good governance and broadening the base of decision-making at the international level on issues of development concern and the need to fill organizational gaps, as well as strengthen the United Nations system and other multilateral institutions, and also stresses the need to broaden and strengthen the participation of developing countries and countries with economies in transition in international economic decision-making and norm-setting;

21. *Also recognizes* that good governance and the rule of law at the national level assist all States in the promotion and protection of human rights, including the right to development, and agrees on the value of the ongoing efforts being made by States to identify and strengthen good governance practices, including transparent, responsible, accountable and participatory government, that are responsive and appropriate to their needs and aspirations, including in the context of agreed partnership approaches to development, capacity-building and technical assistance;

22. *Further recognizes* the important role and the rights of women and the application of a gender perspective as a cross-cutting issue in the process of realizing the right to development, and notes in particular the positive relationship between women's education and their equal participation in the civil, cultural, economic, political and social activities of the community and the promotion of the right to development;

23. *Stresses* the need for the integration of the rights of children, girls and boys alike, in all policies and programmes, and for ensuring the promotion and protection of those rights, especially in areas relating to health, education and the full development of their capacities;

24. *Also stresses* that further and additional measures must be taken at the national and international levels to fight HIV/AIDS and other communicable diseases, taking into account ongoing efforts and programmes, and reiterates the need for international assistance in this regard;

25. *Recognizes* the need for strong partnerships with civil society organizations and the private sector in pursuit of poverty eradication and development, as well as for corporate social responsibility;

26. *Emphasizes* the urgent need for taking concrete and effective measures to prevent, combat and criminalize all forms of corruption at all levels, to prevent, detect and deter in a more effective manner international transfers of illicitly acquired assets and to strengthen international cooperation in asset recovery consistent with the principles of the United Nations Convention against Corruption, particularly chapter V thereof, stresses the importance of a genuine political commitment on the part of all Governments through a firm legal framework, and in this context urges States to sign and ratify as soon as possible, and States parties to implement effectively, the Convention;

27. *Also emphasizes* the need to strengthen further the activities of the Office of the United Nations High Commissioner for Human Rights in the promotion and realization of the right to development, including ensuring effective use of the financial and human resources necessary to fulfil its mandate, and calls upon the Secretary-General to provide the Office of the High Commissioner with the necessary resources;

28. *Reaffirms* the request to the High Commissioner, in mainstreaming the right to development, to undertake effectively activities aimed at strengthening the global partnership for development between Member States, development agencies and the international development, financial and trade institutions, and to reflect those activities in detail in her report to the Commission on Human Rights at its sixty-second session;

29. *Calls upon* the United Nations agencies, funds and programmes, as well as the specialized agencies, to mainstream the right to development in their operational programmes and objectives, and stresses the need for the international financial and multilateral trading systems to mainstream the right to development in their policies and objectives;

30. *Requests* the Secretary-General to bring the present resolution to the attention of Member States, United Nations organs and bodies, specialized agencies, funds and programmes, international development and financial institutions, in particular the Bretton Woods institutions, and non-governmental organizations;

31. *Also requests* the Secretary-General to submit a report to the General Assembly at its sixty-first session and an interim report to the Commission on Human Rights at its sixty-second session on the implementation of the present resolution, including efforts undertaken at the national, regional and international levels in the promotion and realization of the right to development, and invites the chairperson of the Working Group on the Right to Development to present a verbal update to the General Assembly at its sixty-first session.

RECORDED VOTE ON RESOLUTION 60/157:

In favour: Afghanistan, Albania, Algeria, Andorra, Angola, Antigua and Barbuda, Argentina, Armenia, Austria, Azerbaijan, Bahamas, Bahrain, Bangladesh, Barbados, Belarus, Belgium, Belize, Benin, Bhutan, Bolivia, Bosnia and Herzegovina, Botswana, Brazil, Brunei Darussalam, Bulgaria, Burkina Faso, Burundi, Cambodia, Cameroon, Cape Verde, Chile, China,

Colombia, Comoros, Costa Rica, Côte d'Ivoire, Croatia, Cuba, Cyprus, Czech Republic, Democratic People's Republic of Korea, Democratic Republic of the Congo, Denmark, Djibouti, Dominica, Dominican Republic, Ecuador, Egypt, El Salvador, Eritrea, Estonia, Ethiopia, Fiji, Finland, France, Gabon, Gambia, Georgia, Germany, Ghana, Greece, Grenada, Guatemala, Guinea, Guinea-Bissau, Guyana, Haiti, Honduras, Hungary, Iceland, India, Indonesia, Iran, Iraq, Ireland, Italy, Jamaica, Jordan, Kazakhstan, Kenya, Kuwait, Kyrgyzstan, Lao People's Democratic Republic, Latvia, Lebanon, Lesotho, Libyan Arab Jamahiriya, Liechtenstein, Lithuania, Luxembourg, Madagascar, Malawi, Malaysia, Maldives, Mali, Malta, Mauritania, Mauritius, Mexico, Micronesia, Monaco, Mongolia, Morocco, Mozambique, Myanmar, Namibia, Nepal, Netherlands, New Zealand, Nicaragua, Niger, Nigeria, Norway, Oman, Pakistan, Panama, Papua New Guinea, Paraguay, Peru, Philippines, Poland, Portugal, Qatar, Republic of Korea, Republic of Moldova, Romania, Russian Federation, Rwanda, Saint Lucia, Saint Vincent and the Grenadines, Samoa, San Marino, Saudi Arabia, Senegal, Serbia and Montenegro, Singapore, Slovakia, Slovenia, Solomon Islands, Somalia, South Africa, Spain, Sri Lanka, Sudan, Suriname, Sweden, Switzerland, Syrian Arab Republic, Tajikistan, Thailand, The former Yugoslav Republic of Macedonia, Timor-Leste, Togo, Tonga, Trinidad and Tobago, Tunisia, Turkey, Turkmenistan, Tuvalu, Uganda, Ukraine, United Arab Emirates, United Kingdom, United Republic of Tanzania, Uruguay, Uzbekistan, Vanuatu, Venezuela, Viet Nam, Yemen, Zambia, Zimbabwe.

Against: Marshall Islands, United States.

Abstaining: Australia, Canada, Israel, Japan, Palau.

Human rights and international solidarity

Commission action. On 20 April [res. 2005/55], the Commission, by a recorded vote of 37 to 15, with 1 abstention, urged the international community to promote and consolidate international assistance to developing countries in their endeavours for development and for the promotion of conditions that could make possible the full realization of human rights. It recognized that the "third generation rights" or "right to solidarity" needed further progressive development within the UN human rights machinery to respond to the increasing challenges to international cooperation in that area. The Commission decided to appoint an independent expert on human rights and international solidarity for a period of three years, to study the issue and prepare a draft declaration on the right of peoples to international solidarity. The expert was also asked to report annually to the Commission, taking into account the outcomes of major UN and other global meetings in the economic and social fields and to seek the views of Governments, UN agencies and other relevant entities.

ECONOMIC AND SOCIAL COUNCIL ACTION

On 25 July, the Economic and Social Council, on the recommendation of the Commission on Human Rights [E/2005/23], adopted **decision 2005/271** by recorded vote (32-18-0) [agenda item 14 *(g)*].

Human rights and international solidarity

At its 38th plenary meeting, on 25 July 2005, the Economic and Social Council took note of Commission on Human Rights resolution 2005/55 of 20 April 2005, and endorsed the decision of the Commission to appoint an independent expert on human rights and international solidarity for a period of three years to study the issue and prepare a draft declaration on the

right of peoples to international solidarity, taking into account the outcomes of all major United Nations and other global summits and ministerial meetings in the economic and social fields and seeking views and contributions from Governments, United Nations agencies, other relevant international organizations and non-governmental organizations.

The Council also approved the request of the Commission to the independent expert to report annually to the Commission on the progress made in the fulfilment of his/her mandate.

RECORDED VOTE ON DECISION 2005/271:

In favour: Armenia, Azerbaijan, Bangladesh, Belize, Brazil, China, Colombia, Congo, Costa Rica, Cuba, Ecuador, Guinea, India, Indonesia, Jamaica, Kenya, Malaysia, Mauritius, Mexico, Mozambique, Namibia, Nicaragua, Nigeria, Pakistan, Panama, Russian Federation, Saudi Arabia, Senegal, South Africa, Thailand, Tunisia, United Republic of Tanzania.

Against: Albania, Australia, Belgium, Canada, Denmark, France, Germany, Iceland, Ireland, Italy, Japan, Lithuania, Poland, Republic of Korea, Spain, Turkey, United Kingdom, United States.

Also in July, Rudi Muhammah Rizki (Indonesia) was appointed as independent expert on the right of peoples to international solidarity.

Note by Secretariat. By a June note [E/CN.4/Sub.2/2005/37], the Secretariat informed the Subcommission that Rui Baltazar Dos Santos Alves (Mozambique) had indicated that he would not be able to submit the expanded working paper, which the Subcommission had requested in 2004 [YUN 2004, p. 750].

Democratic and equitable international order

Commission action. On 20 April [res. 2005/57], the Commission, by a recorded vote of 32 to 15, with 6 abstentions, affirmed that a democratic and equitable international order fostered the full realization of all human rights and urged States to continue efforts to establish such order. The Commission asked human rights treaty bodies, OHCHR, and Commission and Subcommission mechanisms to contribute to the implementation of its resolution, and the Secretary-General, to bring it to the attention of Member States, UN organs and bodies, intergovernmental organizations and NGOs and to disseminate it widely.

Expert seminar. In response to a 2003 Commission request [YUN 2003, p. 736] and to General Assembly resolution 59/193 [YUN 2004, p. 750], OHCHR organized an expert seminar [E/CN.4/2005/58] (Geneva, 28 February–2 March) to explore the linkages between democracy, the rule of law and human rights, which built on the outcome of the first such expert seminar [YUN 2002, p. 702] and adopted conclusions and recommendations.

Globalization

Report of High Commissioner. In response to a 2004 Commission request [YUN 2004, p. 753], the High Commissioner submitted a report [E/CN.4/

2005/41], which considered the relevance to globalization of the enjoyment of the right to participate in the conduct of public affairs and related rights, and suggested ways in which that right could be promoted in the context of globalization. The report outlined the legal basis of participation in the principal human rights treaties and explored the enjoyment of participatory rights in globalization processes in three areas: the promotion of those rights in national level policy-making as it related to globalization; the capacity of States to respect the will of the people in decision-making processes in global institutions, expressed through the enjoyment of participatory rights; and the increasing role of individuals and civil society groups in policy discussion and decision-making at the global level. It made several recommendations relating to, among other things, understanding the international dimensions of the right to take part in the conduct of public affairs; undertaking human rights impact assessments of global rules, policies and projects; strengthening the role of parliaments in global governance; clarifying the human rights responsibilities of non-State actors; increasing the voice of civil society in institutions relating to globalization; and the possibility of further study on methodologies for undertaking human rights impact assessment.

Commission action. By a recorded vote of 38 to 15, the Commission, on 14 April [res. 2005/17], reaffirmed the commitment to create an environment conducive to development and the elimination of poverty through good governance, transparency in the financial, monetary and trading systems and the commitment to an open, equitable, rule-based, predicable and non-discriminatory multilateral trading and financial system. The Commission urged the international community, at the General Assembly's High-Level Plenary Meeting, to be held at the commencement of its sixtieth (2005) session (World Summit) (see p. 47), to take measures, including enhancing official development assistance, and resolving the problems of the external debt, market access, capacity-building, and dissemination of knowledge and technology, in order to integrate developing countries into the global order. The High Commissioner was asked to bring her comprehensive analytical report (see above) to the attention of WTO and other relevant international organizations, with a view to operationalizing its conclusions and recommendations.

GENERAL ASSEMBLY ACTION

On 16 December [meeting 64], the General Assembly, on the recommendation of the Third Committee [A/60/509/Add.2], adopted **resolution**

60/152 by a recorded vote (121-53-4) [agenda item 71 (b)].

Globalization and its impact on the full enjoyment of all human rights

The General Assembly,

Guided by the purposes and principles of the Charter of the United Nations, and expressing, in particular, the need to achieve international cooperation in promoting and encouraging respect for human rights and fundamental freedoms for all without distinction,

Recalling the Universal Declaration of Human Rights, as well as the Vienna Declaration and Programme of Action adopted by the World Conference on Human Rights on 25 June 1993,

Recalling also the International Covenant on Civil and Political Rights and the International Covenant on Economic, Social and Cultural Rights,

Recalling further the Declaration on the Right to Development adopted by the General Assembly in its resolution 41/128 of 4 December 1986,

Recalling the United Nations Millennium Declaration and the outcome documents of the twenty-third and twenty-fourth special sessions of the General Assembly, held in New York from 5 to 10 June 2000 and in Geneva from 26 June to 1 July 2000, respectively,

Recalling also its resolution 59/184 of 20 December 2004,

Recalling further Commission on Human Rights resolution 2005/17 of 14 April 2005 on globalization and its impact on the full enjoyment of all human rights,

Recognizing that all human rights are universal, indivisible, interdependent and interrelated and that the international community must treat human rights globally in a fair and equal manner, on the same footing and with the same emphasis,

Realizing that globalization affects all countries differently and makes them more exposed to external developments, positive as well as negative, inter alia, in the field of human rights,

Realizing also that globalization is not merely an economic process, but that it also has social, political, environmental, cultural and legal dimensions, which have an impact on the full enjoyment of all human rights,

Reaffirming the commitment contained in paragraphs 19 and 47 of the 2005 World Summit Outcome to promote fair globalization and the development of the productive sectors in developing countries to enable them to participate more effectively in and benefit from the process of globalization,

Realizing the need to undertake a thorough, independent and comprehensive assessment of the social, environmental and cultural impact of globalization on societies,

Recognizing in each culture a dignity and value that deserve recognition, respect and preservation, convinced that, in their rich variety and diversity and in the reciprocal influences that they exert on one another, all cultures form part of the common heritage belonging to all humankind, and aware that the risk of a global monoculture poses more of a threat if the developing world remains poor and marginalized,

Recognizing also that multilateral mechanisms have a unique role to play in meeting the challenges and opportunities presented by globalization,

Emphasizing the global character of the migratory phenomenon, the importance of international, regional and bilateral cooperation and the need to protect human rights of migrants, particularly at a time in which migration flows have increased in the globalized economy,

Expressing concern at the negative impact of international financial turbulence on social and economic development and on the full enjoyment of all human rights,

Recognizing that globalization should be guided by the fundamental principles that underpin the corpus of human rights, such as equity, participation, accountability, non-discrimination at both the national and the international levels, respect for diversity, tolerance and international cooperation and solidarity,

Emphasizing that the existence of widespread extreme poverty inhibits the full and effective enjoyment of human rights; its immediate alleviation and eventual elimination must remain a high priority for the international community,

Strongly reiterating the determination to ensure the timely and full realization of the development goals and objectives agreed at the major United Nations conferences and summits, including those agreed at the Millennium Summit that are described as the Millennium Development Goals, which have helped to galvanize efforts towards poverty eradication,

Deeply concerned at the inadequacy of measures to narrow the widening gap between the developed and the developing countries, and within countries, which has contributed, inter alia, to deepening poverty and has adversely affected the full enjoyment of all human rights, in particular in developing countries,

Noting that human beings strive for a world that is respectful of human rights and cultural diversity and that, in this regard, they work to ensure that all activities, including those affected by globalization, are consistent with those aims,

1. *Recognizes* that, while globalization, by its impact on, inter alia, the role of the State, may affect human rights, the promotion and protection of all human rights is first and foremost the responsibility of the State;

2. *Emphasizes* that development should be at the centre of the international economic agenda and that coherence between national development strategies and international obligations and commitments is imperative for an enabling environment for development and an inclusive and equitable globalization;

3. *Reaffirms* that narrowing the gap between rich and poor, both within and between countries, is an explicit goal at the national and international levels, as part of the effort to create an enabling environment for the full enjoyment of all human rights;

4. *Reaffirms also* the commitment to create an environment at both the national and the global levels that is conducive to development and to the elimination of poverty through, inter alia, good governance within each country and at the international level, transparency in the financial, monetary and trading systems and commitment to an open, equitable, rule-based, predictable and non-discriminatory multilateral trading and financial system;

5. *Recognizes* that, while globalization offers great opportunities, the fact that its benefits are very unevenly shared and its costs unevenly distributed represents an aspect of the process that affects the full enjoyment of all human rights, in particular in developing countries;

6. *Welcomes* the report of the United Nations High Commissioner for Human Rights on globalization and its impact on the full enjoyment of human rights, which focuses on the liberalization of agricultural trade and its impact on the realization of the right to development, including the right to food, and takes note of the conclusions and recommendations contained therein;

7. *Calls upon* Member States, relevant agencies of the United Nations system, intergovernmental organizations and civil society to promote equitable and environmentally sustainable economic growth for managing globalization so that poverty is systematically reduced and the international development targets are achieved;

8. *Recognizes* that only through broad and sustained efforts, including policies and measures at the global level to create a shared future based upon our common humanity in all its diversity, can globalization be made fully inclusive and equitable and have a human face, thus contributing to the full enjoyment of all human rights;

9. *Underlines* the urgent need to establish an equitable, transparent and democratic international system to strengthen and broaden the participation of developing countries in international economic decision-making and norm-setting;

10. *Affirms* that globalization is a complex process of structural transformation, with numerous interdisciplinary aspects, which has an impact on the enjoyment of civil, political, economic, social and cultural rights, including the right to development;

11. *Affirms also* that the international community should strive to respond to the challenges and opportunities posed by globalization in a manner that ensures respect for the cultural diversity of all;

12. *Underlines*, therefore, the need to continue to analyse the consequences of globalization for the full enjoyment of all human rights;

13. *Takes note* of the report of the Secretary-General, and requests him to seek further the views of Member States and relevant agencies of the United Nations system and to submit a substantive report on the subject to the General Assembly at its sixty-first session.

RECORDED VOTE ON RESOLUTION 60/152:

In favour: Afghanistan, Algeria, Angola, Antigua and Barbuda, Argentina, Armenia, Azerbaijan, Bahamas, Bahrain, Bangladesh, Barbados, Belarus, Belize, Benin, Bhutan, Bolivia, Botswana, Brunei Darussalam, Burkina Faso, Burundi, Cambodia, Cameroon, Cape Verde, China, Colombia, Comoros, Costa Rica, Côte d'Ivoire, Cuba, Democratic People's Republic of Korea, Democratic Republic of the Congo, Djibouti, Dominica, Dominican Republic, Ecuador, Egypt, El Salvador, Eritrea, Ethiopia, Fiji, Gabon, Gambia, Ghana, Grenada, Guatemala, Guinea, Guinea-Bissau, Guyana, Haiti, Honduras, India, Indonesia, Iran, Jamaica, Jordan, Kazakhstan, Kenya, Kuwait, Kyrgyzstan, Lao People's Democratic Republic, Lebanon, Lesotho, Libyan Arab Jamahiriya, Madagascar, Malawi, Malaysia, Maldives, Mali, Mauritania, Mauritius, Mexico, Mongolia, Morocco, Mozambique, Myanmar, Namibia, Nepal, Nicaragua, Niger, Nigeria, Oman, Pakistan, Panama, Papua New Guinea, Paraguay, Peru, Philippines, Qatar, Russian Federation, Rwanda, Saint Lucia, Saint Vincent and the Grenadines, Samoa, Saudi Arabia, Senegal, Solomon Islands, Somalia, South Africa, Sri Lanka, Sudan, Suriname, Syrian Arab Republic, Tajikistan, Thailand, Timor-Leste, Togo, Tonga, Trinidad and Tobago, Tunisia, Turkmenistan, Uganda, United Arab Emirates, United Republic of

Tanzania, Uruguay, Uzbekistan, Vanuatu, Venezuela, Viet Nam, Yemen, Zambia, Zimbabwe.

Against: Albania, Andorra, Australia, Austria, Belgium, Bosnia and Herzegovina, Bulgaria, Canada, Croatia, Cyprus, Czech Republic, Denmark, Estonia, Finland, France, Georgia, Germany, Greece, Hungary, Iceland, Ireland, Israel, Italy, Japan, Latvia, Liechtenstein, Lithuania, Luxembourg, Malta, Marshall Islands, Micronesia, Monaco, Netherlands, New Zealand, Norway, Palau, Poland, Portugal, Republic of Korea, Republic of Moldova, Romania, San Marino, Serbia and Montenegro, Slovakia, Slovenia, Spain, Sweden, Switzerland, The former Yugoslav Republic of Macedonia, Turkey, Ukraine, United Kingdom, United States.

Abstaining: Brazil, Chile, Iraq, Singapore.

Structural adjustment policies

Reports of independent expert. The Commission considered a January report [E/CN.4/2005/42] of the independent expert on the effects of structural adjustment policies and foreign debt on human rights, Bernards Mudho (Kenya). The report reviewed the previous work undertaken by the Commission and Subcommission that was relevant to the question of draft general guidelines to be followed by States and national and international financial institutions in the decision-making and execution of debt repayments and structural reform programmes. It suggested a framework and some elements for consideration in elaborating the guidelines and also reviewed significant recent developments in debt sustainability issues that were relevant to policies and programmes of international financial institutions. In that context, the report highlighted the origin and scale of external debt and creditors' response; the Heavily Indebted Poor Countries (HIPC) Initiative and its status and impact and the extension of its sunset clause; the new approach under way at the World Bank and International Monetary Fund (IMF) to debt sustainability, which advocated country-specific considerations in developing appropriate external borrowing strategies; the effect of debt on developing countries' efforts to finance the MDGs; and the evolution of the World Bank's approach to adjustment lending. The expert determined that, although HIPC countries faced many difficulties, the initiative had helped them increase poverty-reduction expenditures and that the World Bank/IMF new approach to debt sustainability had vital policy implications for donors, creditors and borrowers and should benefit from important human rights considerations that were being elaborated within the context of the draft guidelines. The report made recommendations for the next steps in further elaborating those guidelines, including the possibility of organizing an expert consultation of international finance institutions to contribute to the process. The expert suggested that the Commission encourage him to continue to cooperate with Commission and Subcommission mechanisms and treaty bodies in furthering efforts towards the

draft general guidelines, develop additional ideas and elements for inclusion in the draft, further explore the interlinkages with trade and other issues, including HIV/AIDS, when examining the impact of structural adjustment policies and foreign debt on the enjoyment of human rights, and contribute to the follow-up process for the 2002 International Conference on Financing for Development (see p. 1060).

Over the past year, the expert visited Kyrgyzstan [E/CN.4/2005/42/Add.1], where he examined, among other things, the effects of the burden of foreign debt and the policies adopted to address them, and recommended measures and actions to alleviate such effects.

Commission action. By a recorded vote of 33 to 14, with 6 abstentions, the Commission, on 14 April [res. 2005/19], asked the independent expert to explore further the interlinkages with trade and other issues, including HIV/AIDS, when examining the impact of structural adjustment policies and foreign debt, and to contribute to the follow-up to the 2002 International Conference on Financing for Development [YUN 2002, p. 953], with a view to bringing to the Commission's attention the effects of structural adjustment and foreign debt on the enjoyment of human rights. The expert was asked to seek the views of States, international organizations, UN agencies, regional commissions, financial institutions and NGOs on the draft, to present a final draft for the Commission's consideration in 2006 and to report to the General Assembly on the effects of economic reform policies and foreign debt on the full enjoyment of human rights. The Secretary-General was asked to assist him. The Commission decided to convene a three-day expert consultation, with participants from UN-system organizations, to contribute to the expert's work in finalizing the draft guidelines, and to replace the phrase "effects of structural adjustment policies" with "effects of economic reform policies" in the title of the special procedure's mandate.

ECONOMIC AND SOCIAL COUNCIL ACTION

On 25 July, the Economic and Social Council, on the recommendation of the Commission on Human Rights [E/2005/23], adopted **decision 2005/260** by recorded vote (29-18-4) [agenda item 14 (g)].

Effects of economic reform policies and foreign debt on the full enjoyment of all human rights

At its 38th plenary meeting, on 25 July 2005, the Economic and Social Council took note of Commission on Human Rights resolution 2005/19 of 14 April 2005, and endorsed the Commission's decision to request the independent expert to report to the General Assembly on the issue of the effects of economic reform policies and foreign debt on the full enjoyment of human rights, particularly economic, social and cultural rights.

The Council also endorsed the Commission's request to the Secretary-General to provide the independent expert with all necessary assistance, in particular the staff and resources required to carry out his functions, as well as to facilitate his participation in and contribution to the follow-up process of the International Conference on Financing for Development, including in the multi-stakeholder consultations to be organized in 2005 on issues relevant to his mandate.

RECORDED VOTE ON DECISION 2005/260

In favour: Bangladesh, Belize, Brazil, China, Colombia, Congo, Cuba, Ecuador, Guinea, India, Indonesia, Jamaica, Kenya, Malaysia, Mauritius, Mozambique, Namibia, Nicaragua, Nigeria, Pakistan, Panama, Russian Federation, Saudi Arabia, Senegal, South Africa, Thailand, Tunisia, United Arab Emirates, United Republic of Tanzania.

Against: Albania, Australia, Belgium, Canada, Denmark, France, Germany, Iceland, Ireland, Italy, Japan, Lithuania, Poland, Republic of Korea, Spain, Turkey, United Kingdom, United States.

Abstaining: Armenia, Azerbaijan, Costa Rica, Mexico.

Adverse effects of debt

By a June note [E/CN.4/Sub.2/2005/24], the Secretariat informed the Subcommission that El-Hadji Guissé (Senegal) had indicated that he would make an oral presentation in lieu of the expanded working paper on the effects of debt on human rights, requested by the Subcommission in 2004 [YUN 2004, p. 755].

Social Forum

Note by OHCHR. In June [E/CN.4/Sub.2/SF/2005/2], OHCHR presented the organizational details of the 2005 Social Forum, held in accordance with Economic and Social Council decisions 2003/264 [YUN 2003, p. 760] and 2004/217 [YUN 2004, p. 755].

Social Forum session. At its third session (Geneva, 21-22 July) [E/CN.4/Sub.2/2005/21], the Social Forum held panel discussions on the perspectives of those living in poverty: voices from around the world; growth with accountability; and methods and instruments of accountability. It adopted conclusions on issues relating to poverty eradication and recommended that consideration be given to enhancing the full and meaningful participation of the poor in the process of formulating policies and strategies to attain the MDGs. As civil society organizations played a key role in the development process, they should support the participation of the poor in related decision-making, and in that regard, institutionalize their means for effective participation; become literate in macroeconomic and international public finance discourses; and ensure transparency and accountability of their internal structures. Emphasizing the need for an effective accountability mechanism, the Forum noted that, since access to formal justice was often non-

existent to those living in extreme poverty, it was necessary to promote within the national poverty reduction strategic innovative means for ensuring that obligations were discharged. As a corollary, there was a need to educate people of their rights to complain and criticize official policy. States should consider the importance for national human rights institutions to have a mandate to monitor the enjoyment of economic, social and cultural rights, as well as the opportunity to provide human rights-based policy recommendations to Governments.

The Forum had before it a June working paper on participation, development and human rights [E/CN.4/Sub.2/SF/2005/3], submitted by José Bengoa (Chile), in response to a 2004 Subcommission request [YUN 2004, p. 756]. The paper examined participation in public affairs and decision-making processes as a human right and a means of empowerment, considered passive and active participation and analysed participation within the context of the MDGs and related efforts to combat extreme poverty. It observed that the lack of participation was the main reason for the failure of poverty alleviation policies, as without high levels of participation by the people, economic growth was usually selective and segmented.

Subcommission action. On 8 August [res. 2005/8], the Subcommission, taking note of the conclusions and recommendations of the Social Forum (see above), called on States, intergovernmental and civil society organizations to take them into account when designing and implementing poverty reduction programmes and strategies. It decided that the next meeting of the Forum would be held in 2006 in Geneva and that the theme would be "The fight against poverty and the right of participation: the role of women", to be addressed within the context of the preparation of the review of the first United Nations Decade for the Eradication of Poverty (1997-2006), proclaimed by the General Assembly in resolution 50/107 [YUN 1995, p. 844]. Chin-Sung Chung (Republic of Korea) was asked to prepare a working paper on the challenges of women's participation in policies and strategies to combat poverty for the Forum's consideration in 2006. The Subcommission requested OHCHR to seek an effective means of ensuring consultation and the broadest possible participation in the Forum, and the Chairperson of the Committee on the Elimination of Discrimination against Women (CEDAW) (see p. 1271), to participate in the Forum's next session and to make a presentation on the chosen theme. The Forum was invited to report to the Subcommission in 2006 regarding its discussions, recommendations and conclusions, while the Secretary-General was requested to adopt appropriate measures to disseminate information about the Forum, invite relevant individuals and organizations to attend it and to take measures for its success.

Transnational corporations

Report of High Commissioner. In response to a 2004 Commission decision [YUN 2004, p. 756], the High Commissioner submitted a February report [E/CN.4/2005/91], which considered the scope and legal status of existing initiatives and standards on the responsibilities of transnational corporations (TNCs) and related business enterprises with regard to human rights, as well as outstanding issues requiring further consideration by the Commission. In considering the responsibilities of business regarding human rights, the report emphasized that States were the primary duty bearers of human rights, and that, although business could affect the enjoyment of those rights significantly, its influence differed from that of States. The responsibilities of States could not, therefore, simply be transferred to business, as the responsibilities of the latter needed to be defined separately, and in proportion to its nature and activities. Observing, however, that there were gaps in understanding the human rights responsibilities of business, the High Commissioner adopted conclusions and made recommendations to help advance dialogue between States and different stakeholders on the issue and to assist the Commission to identify options for strengthening standards on the responsibilities of transnational corporations and related business enterprises with regard to human rights. Noting a growing interest in further discussing the possibility of drafting a UN statement on universal human rights standards applicable to business, she pointed to the need to develop tools, particularly training materials and methodologies, for undertaking human rights impact assessments and to assist businesses in implementing their responsibilities. She also identified issues raised in the report that required further study and clarification.

Commission action. On 20 April [res. 2005/69], by a recorded vote of 49 to 3, with 1 abstention, the Commission requested the Secretary-General to appoint a special representative on the issue of human rights and transnational corporations and other business enterprises, for an initial period of two years to: identify and clarify standards of corporate responsibility and accountability for transnational corporations and other business enterprises with regard to human rights; elaborate on the role of States in regulating and adjudicating the role of such corporations; re-

search and clarify the implications for those corporations of such concepts as "complicity" and "sphere of influence"; develop materials and methodologies for undertaking human rights impact assessments of their activities; and compile a compendium of best practices of States and transnational corporations and other business enterprises. The representative was asked to liaise closely with the Special Adviser to the Secretary-General for the Global Compact; to consult with all stakeholders, including States, relevant UN bodies and civil society organization; and to submit an interim report to the Commission in 2006 and a final report in 2007. The High Commissioner was asked to support those efforts and to cooperate with the expert in convening an annual meeting with senior executives from companies and experts from relevant sectors, in order to raise awareness and share best practice, and to report to the Commission in 2006 on the outcome of the first such meeting.

ECONOMIC AND SOCIAL COUNCIL ACTION

On 25 July, the Economic and Social Council, on the recommendation of the Commission on Human Rights [E/2005/23], adopted **decision 2005/273** by recorded vote (47-3-0) [agenda item 14 (g)].

Human rights and transnational corporations and other business enterprises

At its 38th plenary meeting, on 25 July 2005, the Economic and Social Council took note of Commission on Human Rights resolution 2005/69 of 20 April 2005, and approved the request of the Commission to the Secretary-General to appoint a special representative on the issue of human rights and transnational corporations and other business enterprises, for an initial period of two years, to undertake the activities set out in that resolution.

The Council also endorsed the Commission's request to the United Nations High Commissioner for Human Rights to convene annually, in cooperation with the Special Representative, a meeting with senior executives from companies and experts from a particular sector, such as the pharmaceutical, extractive or chemical industries, to consider, within the mandate of the Special Representative, the specific human rights issues faced by those sectors, to raise awareness and share best practice, and to report on the outcome of the first meeting to the Commission at its sixty-second session.

RECORDED VOTE ON DECISION 2005/273:

In favour: Albania, Armenia, Azerbaijan, Bangladesh, Belgium, Belize, Brazil, Canada, China, Colombia, Congo, Costa Rica, Cuba, Denmark, Ecuador, France, Germany, Guinea, Iceland, India, Indonesia, Ireland, Italy, Jamaica, Japan, Kenya, Lithuania, Malaysia, Mauritius, Mexico, Nicaragua, Pakistan, Panama, Poland, Republic of Korea, Russian Federation, Saudi Arabia, Senegal, Spain, Thailand, Tunisia, Turkey, United Arab Emirates, United Kingdom, United Republic of Tanzania.
Against: Australia, South Africa, United States.

Working group activities. The working group on the working methods and activities of TNCs, at its seventh session (Geneva, 27 and 29 July) [E/CN.4/Sub.2/2005/22], continued its consideration of the draft norms on the responsibilities of TNCs and other business enterprises, towards the elaboration of a binding instrument. The group had before it a number of relevant background documents, including the draft norms approved by the Subcommission in 2003 [YUN 2003, p. 761] and commentary thereto, as well as the report of the High Commissioner (see p. 834). The group considered current standards and standard-setting activities and related comments by its members, Subcommission experts, Member States and NGOs, and adopted recommendations on its future work.

Subcommission action. On 25 July [dec. 2005/102], the Subcommission decided to establish a sessional working group to examine the working methods and activities of TNCs (see above).

On 8 August [res. 2005/6], the Subcommission invited Gáspár Bíró (Hungary) to prepare a working paper on the role of States in the guarantee of human rights, with a reference to the activities of TNCs and other business entities, and Chin-Sung Chung (Republic of Korea) and Florizelle O'Connor (Jamaica), to prepare a working paper on bilateral and multilateral economic agreements and their impact on the human rights of the beneficiaries for submission in 2006. It decided that the group's 2006 agenda would include a review of developments related to the responsibilities of business with regard to human rights; a consideration of possible situations where business might facilitate or generate human rights violations and the identification of appropriate responses thereto; as well as consideration of possible ways of protecting individuals or groups from harm caused by business activities. The group was requested to report in 2006.

Coercive economic measures

Commission action. By a recorded vote of 37 to 14, with 2 abstentions, the Commission, on 14 April [res. 2005/14], decided to consider the negative impact of unilateral coercive measures with regard to implementing the right to development and invited relevant special rapporteurs and thematic mechanisms to pay attention to the issue. It requested the High Commissioner to give urgent consideration to its resolution, and the Secretary-General, to bring it to the attention of Member States, to seek their views on the implications and negative effects of unilateral coercive measures and to report in 2006.

Reports of Secretary-General. In response to a 2004 Commission request [YUN 2004, p. 757], the Secretary-General summarized information received from two States (Cuba, Qatar) on the implications and negative effects of unilateral coercive economic measures [E/CN.4/2005/37].

In response to General Assembly resolution 59/188 [YUN 2004, p. 757], the Secretary-General, in an October report [A/60/305], presented further information from five States (Azerbaijan, Cuba, Georgia, Iraq, Lebanon) regarding such measures.

On 16 December, the Assembly took note of the Secretary-General's report (**decision 60/533**).

On 16 December [meeting 64], the General Assembly, on the recommendation of the Third Committee [A/60/509/Add.2], adopted **resolution 60/155** by recorded vote (125-53-0) [agenda item 71 (b)].

Human rights and unilateral coercive measures

The General Assembly,

Recalling all its previous resolutions on this subject, the most recent of which was resolution 59/188 of 20 December 2004, and Commission on Human Rights resolution 2005/14 of 14 April 2005,

Reaffirming the pertinent principles and provisions contained in the Charter of Economic Rights and Duties of States proclaimed by the General Assembly in its resolution 3281(XXIX) of 12 December 1974, in particular article 32 thereof, in which it declared that no State may use or encourage the use of economic, political or any other type of measures to coerce another State in order to obtain from it the subordination of the exercise of its sovereign rights,

Taking note of the report of the Secretary-General, submitted pursuant to Commission on Human Rights resolution 1999/21 of 23 April 1999, and the reports of the Secretary-General on the implementation of resolutions 52/120 of 12 December 1997 and 55/110 of 4 December 2000,

Recognizing the universal, indivisible, interdependent and interrelated character of all human rights, and, in this regard, reaffirming the right to development as an integral part of all human rights,

Recalling that the World Conference on Human Rights, held at Vienna from 14 to 25 June 1993, called upon States to refrain from any unilateral coercive measure not in accordance with international law and the Charter of the United Nations that creates obstacles to trade relations among States and impedes the full realization of all human rights,

Bearing in mind all the references to this question in the Copenhagen Declaration on Social Development adopted by the World Summit for Social Development on 12 March 1995, the Beijing Declaration and Platform for Action adopted by the Fourth World Conference on Women on 15 September 1995, the Istanbul Declaration on Human Settlements and the Habitat Agenda adopted by the second United Nations Conference on Human Settlements (Habitat II) on 14 June 1996, and their five-year reviews,

Expressing its concern about the negative impact of unilateral coercive measures on international relations, trade, investment and cooperation,

Expressing its grave concern that, in some countries, the situation of children is adversely affected by unilateral coercive measures not in accordance with international law and the Charter that create obstacles to trade relations among States, impede the full realization of social and economic development and hinder the well-being of the population in the affected countries, with particular consequences for women and children, including adolescents,

Deeply concerned that, despite the recommendations adopted on this question by the General Assembly and recent major United Nations conferences, and contrary to general international law and the Charter, unilateral coercive measures continue to be promulgated and implemented with all their negative implications for the social-humanitarian activities and economic and social development of developing countries, including their extraterritorial effects, thereby creating additional obstacles to the full enjoyment of all human rights by peoples and individuals under the jurisdiction of other States,

Bearing in mind all the extraterritorial effects of any unilateral legislative, administrative and economic measures, policies and practices of a coercive nature against the development process and the enhancement of human rights in developing countries, which create obstacles to the full realization of all human rights,

Noting the continuing efforts of the open-ended Working Group on the Right to Development of the Commission on Human Rights, and reaffirming in particular its criteria, according to which unilateral coercive measures are one of the obstacles to the implementation of the Declaration on the Right to Development,

1. *Urges* all States to refrain from adopting or implementing any unilateral measures not in accordance with international law and the Charter of the United Nations, in particular those of a coercive nature with all their extraterritorial effects, which create obstacles to trade relations among States, thus impeding the full realization of the rights set forth in the Universal Declaration of Human Rights and other international human rights instruments, in particular the right of individuals and peoples to development;

2. *Also urges* all States to take steps to avoid and to refrain from adopting any unilateral measures not in accordance with international law and the Charter that impede the full achievement of economic and social development by the population of the affected countries, in particular children and women, that hinder their well-being and that create obstacles to the full enjoyment of their human rights, including the right of everyone to a standard of living adequate for their health and well-being and their right to food, medical care and the necessary social services, as well as to ensure that food and medicine are not used as tools for political pressure;

3. *Invites* all States to consider adopting administrative or legislative measures, as appropriate, to counteract the extraterritorial applications or effects of unilateral coercive measures;

4. *Rejects* unilateral coercive measures with all their extraterritorial effects as tools for political or economic pressure against any country, in particular against developing countries, because of their negative effects on the realization of all the human rights of vast sectors of their populations, in particular children, women and the elderly;

5. *Calls upon* Member States that have initiated such measures to commit themselves to their obligations and responsibilities arising from the international human rights instruments to which they are party by revoking such measures at the earliest possible time;

6. *Reaffirms,* in this context, the right of all peoples to self-determination, by virtue of which they freely determine their political status and freely pursue their economic, social and cultural development;

7. *Urges* the Commission on Human Rights to take fully into account the negative impact of unilateral coercive measures, including the enactment of national laws and their extraterritorial application, in its task concerning the implementation of the right to development;

8. *Requests* the United Nations High Commissioner for Human Rights, in discharging her functions relating to the promotion, realization and protection of the right to development and bearing in mind the continuing impact of unilateral coercive measures on the population of developing countries, to give priority to the present resolution in her annual report to the General Assembly;

9. *Requests* the Secretary-General to bring the present resolution to the attention of all Member States, to continue to collect their views and information on the implications and negative effects of unilateral coercive measures on their populations and to submit an analytical report thereon to the General Assembly at its sixty-first session, highlighting the practical and preventive measures in this respect;

10. *Decides* to examine the question on a priority basis at its sixty-first session under the sub-item entitled "Human rights questions, including alternative approaches for improving the effective enjoyment of human rights and fundamental freedoms".

RECORDED VOTE ON RESOLUTION 60/155:

In favour: Algeria, Angola, Antigua and Barbuda, Argentina, Armenia, Azerbaijan, Bahamas, Bahrain, Bangladesh, Barbados, Belarus, Belize, Benin, Bhutan, Bolivia, Botswana, Brazil, Brunei Darussalam, Burkina Faso, Burundi, Cambodia, Cameroon, Cape Verde, Chile, China, Colombia, Comoros, Costa Rica, Côte d'Ivoire, Cuba, Democratic People's Republic of Korea, Democratic Republic of the Congo, Djibouti, Dominica, Dominican Republic, Ecuador, Egypt, El Salvador, Eritrea, Ethiopia, Fiji, Gabon, Gambia, Ghana, Grenada, Guatemala, Guinea, Guinea-Bissau, Guyana, Haiti, Honduras, India, Indonesia, Iran, Iraq, Jamaica, Jordan, Kazakhstan, Kenya, Kuwait, Kyrgyzstan, Lao People's Democratic Republic, Lebanon, Lesotho, Libyan Arab Jamahiriya, Madagascar, Malawi, Malaysia, Maldives, Mali, Mauritania, Mauritius, Mexico, Mongolia, Morocco, Mozambique, Myanmar, Namibia, Nepal, Nicaragua, Niger, Nigeria, Oman, Pakistan, Panama, Papua New Guinea, Paraguay, Peru, Philippines, Qatar, Russian Federation, Rwanda, Saint Lucia, Saint Vincent and the Grenadines, Samoa, Saudi Arabia, Senegal, Singapore, Solomon Islands, Somalia, South Africa, Sri Lanka, Sudan, Suriname, Syrian Arab Republic, Tajikistan, Thailand, Timor-Leste, Togo, Tonga, Trinidad and Tobago, Tunisia, Turkmenistan, Tuvalu, Uganda, United Arab Emirates, United Republic of Tanzania, Uruguay, Uzbekistan, Vanuatu, Venezuela, Viet Nam, Yemen, Zambia, Zimbabwe.

Against: Albania, Andorra, Australia, Austria, Belgium, Bosnia and Herzegovina, Bulgaria, Canada, Croatia, Cyprus, Czech Republic, Denmark, Estonia, Finland, France, Georgia, Germany, Greece, Hungary, Iceland, Ireland, Israel, Italy, Japan, Latvia, Liechtenstein, Lithuania, Luxembourg, Malta, Marshall Islands, Micronesia, Monaco, Netherlands, New Zealand, Norway, Palau, Poland, Portugal, Republic of Korea, Republic of Moldova, Romania, San Marino, Serbia and Montenegro, Slovakia, Slovenia, Spain, Sweden, Switzerland, The former Yugoslav Republic of Macedonia, Turkey, Ukraine, United Kingdom, United States.

Abstaining: None.

Corruption

Commission action. On 15 April [dec. 2005/104], the Commission endorsed the Subcommission's 2004 request [YUN 2004, p. 759] to the Secretary-General to facilitate the work of the Special Rapporteur in preparing a comprehensive study on corruption and its impact on the full enjoyment of human rights, by enabling her to attend the meeting of the "Friends of the United Nations Convention against Corruption" in Vienna.

On 25 July, the Economic and Social Council endorsed the Commission's decision (**decision 2005/283**).

Report of Special Rapporteur. In accordance with a 2003 Subcommission request [YUN 2003, p. 764], the Special Rapporteur on corruption and its impact on the enjoyment of human rights, Christy Mbonu (Nigeria), submitted a June progress report [E/CN.4/Sub.2/2005/18]. Building on her 2004 preliminary report, the current report focused on institutions considered to be more prone to corruption, including those necessary to sustain democracy, such as political parties and parliaments. In that context, it highlighted the problem posed by party corruption, particularly in developing countries and countries in transition, noting that political parties often abused their positions to extort bribes and provide members and followers with lucrative positions, and that corruption among parliamentarians compromised their legislative, oversight and financial control and representational roles. The report also examined the impact of corruption on the integrity of the judiciary and law enforcement agencies, public sector procurement and procurement at international organizations. It discussed the effect of capital flight through corruption, which was described as one of the main causes of poverty in developing countries, particularly as it related to tax evasion and the illegal export of capital. Highlighting international efforts to combat the problem, including through regional mechanisms and the legal framework provided by the United Nations Convention against Corruption, adopted in General Assembly resolution 58/4 [YUN 2003, p. 1127], the report noted the successes and challenges of civil society groups and States in that regard. Against that background, it outlined conclusions and recommendations underscoring the way in which corruption violated all regimes of rights and the fact that it remained one of the major obstacles to honest and transparent government, the consolidation of democracy and the promotion of sustainable development. The report called for the focusing of international efforts on turning the tide against perpetrators; measures by States to ensure that the vice was eliminated from political parties and parliaments; the strengthening of legislation to tackle the problem in procurement activities; and assistance to States by international financial institutions in designing economic policies that included transparency in procurement. It also highlighted the importance of ratifying and incorporating into domestic laws the UN Convention against Corruption, of international cooperation in repatriating the funds of illicit origin siphoned from developing countries and of the crucial role of civil society and the media in the fight against corruption.

Subcommission action. On 10 August [res. 2005/16], the Subcommission urged States to introduce national mechanisms to prevent and combat corruption and, in that regard, requested the Secretary-General to assist the Special Rapporteur in her work, including study visits to interested countries, to enable her to examine related obstacles and challenges confronting those mechanisms.

Extreme poverty

Report of independent expert. In accordance with a 2004 Commission request [YUN 2004, p. 759], the independent expert on the question of human rights and extreme poverty, Arjun Sengupta (India), submitted his first report [E/CN.4/2005/49], in which he proposed a definition of extreme poverty, explored how that definition could be linked to human rights and suggested concrete actions at the national and international levels that could contribute to a more efficient eradication of poverty. In that context, the expert determined that extreme poverty should be defined as a composite of income poverty, human development poverty and social exclusion, and should encompass the notions of lack of basic security and capability deprivation. Such a definition would aid the development of targeted and integrated policies for dealing with the issue. A resolution or declaration would be necessary to characterize poverty as a violation or denial of human rights, with corresponding obligations for realizing human rights and eradicating poverty. At the national level, actions would aim at fulfilling civil, political, economic, social and cultural rights to eradicate poverty and social exclusion, particularly targeted and sustainable employment-generation strategies to eradicate poverty as part of human rights-based national poverty reduction strategies. At the international level, the expert underlined the role of financial institutions in facilitating human rights-based poverty-reduction efforts and recommended the establishment of a mechanism for coordinating the development cooperation activities of Governments and agencies.

Commission action. On 14 April [res. 2005/16], the Commission asked OHCHR to give high priority to the relationship between extreme poverty and human rights and to pursue further work in that area. It requested OHCHR, the independent expert on extreme poverty (see p. 837) and the Subcommission to ensure coordination and coherence of their work and to continue consultations with the poorest, civil society and interested States. The Commission invited treaty bodies to take into account, when considering the reports of States parties, the question of extreme poverty and human rights, and the independent expert, to maintain focus on the link between human rights and extreme poverty and to report in 2006. The United Nations was called upon to strengthen poverty eradication as a priority throughout the common system.

International declaration

Ad hoc group of experts. In response to a 2004 Subcommission request [YUN 2004, p. 760], Mr. José Bengoa, in his capacity as coordinator of the ad hoc group of experts to prepare a study on the draft international declaration on extreme poverty and human rights, presented a July progress report [E/CN.4/Sub.2/2005/20] on the need to develop guiding principles on the implementation of human rights norms and standards in the context of the fight against extreme poverty. The report considered the challenge of poverty eradication and summarized discussions held on extreme poverty and human rights (see below). Based on those discussions and on the work of the independent expert (see p. 837), the group emphasized the need to develop an instrument on human rights and extreme poverty, and recommended the continuation of its consultations with the poor, so as to bring together relevant elements for the drafting of an international declaratory instrument on human rights and the elimination of extreme poverty for submission to the Subcommission in 2006. The Commission should be requested to authorize the establishment of a working group charged with the drafting of such an instrument, based on the work of the ad hoc group of experts. There was a need to embark on a new phase, which should include the organization of an expert seminar to frame the draft instrument, among other things.

A July addendum [E/CN.4/Sub.2/2005/20/Add.1] summarized the discussions of a seminar on extreme poverty and human rights (São Paulo, Brazil, 2-3 March), sponsored by the Nippon Foundation, a Tokyo-based charity organization, and its affiliate, the Sasakawa Memorial Health Foundation, and of regional consultations (Bangkok, Thailand, 26-27 March), organized by ATD Fourth World, an international NGO dedicated to the eradication of extreme poverty. It also provided information on the development of extreme poverty as a human rights issue within UN human rights mechanisms and a list of resolutions and documentation relating to the work of the ad hoc group of experts.

Subcommission action. On 8 August [res. 2005/9], the Subcommission requested the ad hoc group of experts to continue extensive consultations with regional and international intergovernmental organizations, NGOs, local associations, academics and other competent persons, and through regional seminars, to ensure the involvement of persons living in extreme poverty. The group was further requested to prepare, without financial implications, a final report for submission in 2006. The Subcommission called on the Commission to replace the ad hoc group with a new group, comprising five Subcommission members and with a specific mandate to continue consideration of the subject, taking into account the results already attained.

Right to food

Reports of Special Rapporteur. In response to a 2004 Commission request [YUN 2004, p. 762], the Special Rapporteur on the right to food, Jean Ziegler (Switzerland), in a January report [E/CN.4/2005/47], reviewed his 2004 activities to promote and monitor the right. During the year, he transmitted a number of communications regarding urgent situations or alleged violations concerning the right to seven countries, as well as to the Occupied Palestinian Territory, and received responses from two of them. The report described the Special Rapporteur's efforts to promote a growing awareness of the right to food, including through meetings with numerous civil society organizations, and detailed several positive developments with respect to the right. Despite that progress, situations of special concern persisted in many countries, including the Darfur region of the Sudan, where militia groups had allegedly destroyed or looted crops, agricultural areas, livestock and drinking water installations; the Democratic People's Republic of Korea, where millions of people suffered from a silent famine; Iraq, where many people had died of increasingly difficult living conditions; and the Occupied Palestinian Territory, where the occupying forces continued to violate the right to food; and in regions struck by natural disasters, such as the tsunami in Asia and the locust infestations in western Africa. The Special Rapporteur stressed that the right to food was a human right that had to be respected and enforced around the world. In that connection, he participated in an initiative to develop a set of internationally accepted voluntary guidelines to support the progressive realization of the right. Those Guidelines, adopted by the Council of the Food and Agriculture Organization of the United Nations (FAO) in 2004 [YUN 2004, p. 1486], provided an internationally accepted definition of the right to food, addressed how that right could be incorporated into government strategies and institutions and called on States to set up mechanisms to inform people of their right to food and to increase access to justice in that regard. As part of his mandate to examine emerging issues, the Special Rapporteur examined current discussions regarding the extraterritorial obligations of States to the right, and recommended that Governments recognize those obligations. Other recommendations advocated the commitment of Governments to respect, protect and fulfill the right to food of people living within their territories, as well as the practical implementation of the FAO Voluntary Guidelines (see above) and their incorporation into national development programmes for food security and poverty reduction.

The Special Rapporteur visited Guatemala (26 January–4 February) [E/CN.4/2006/44/Add.1], where acute malnutrition had increased and extreme poverty levels remained high, particularly among indigenous people, owing to a long history of social exclusion and inequality. The Special Rapporteur examined food insecurity issues in the country, such as hunger and social conflict, and considered the legal and policy framework for the right to food there. He found that, despite the progress made in the 1990s to reduce poverty and malnutrition, the gap between the rich and poor was widening and the country was not using its maximum available resources to fight hunger. Over 60 per cent of Guatemalans survived on an income that did not cover their basic food needs, preventing them from exercising their right to food. The main obstacles to the realization of the right included the country's model of exclusionary development that concentrated wealth and power in the hands of a small elite, persistent impunity for human rights violations and the lack of equality before the law for the people, and the model of export-oriented agriculture. The Special Rapporteur recommended the full implementation of Guatemala's legal and policy framework for the realization of the right to food of all Guatemalans, to be implemented within the context of its peace accords [YUN 1996, p. 168; YUN 1997, p. 176]. Specific recommendations to the Government included the rec-

ognition of indigenous communities' land rights; the prompt implementation of the Law on Land Registry and the elaboration of an Agrarian Code to regulate the access, use and tenure of land, which respected the right to food; and the establishment of a special unit within the Office of the Human Rights Ombudsman to monitor the realization of the right and the related obligations of the State.

The Special Rapporteur undertook an urgent mission to the Niger (8-12 July) [A/60/350] to raise awareness about the dramatic food situation in the country, where some 3.6 million people, accounting for almost a third of the population and including 800,000 children, faced acute malnutrition. Infants were reportedly dying of starvation. The acute food crisis had resulted from a combination of unfavourable economic trends and structural shortcomings, caused mainly by the drought and locust invasion that destroyed many crops and impeded pasture and cereal production in 2004. It was a matter of concern that the response of the international community had been extremely slow. Of the $16.2 million requested in an urgent appeal to cover the country's essential needs, only $3.8 million had been received. The Special Rapporteur concluded that the immediate provision of food aid was essential and urged the Government to begin free distribution of such aid to vulnerable groups, especially children, pregnant women and elderly people, and to guarantee free access to health units for undernourished children. Addressing the underlying structural causes of hunger was also essential to limit vulnerability to future famines and to fully realize the right to food of the people of the Niger.

In India (20 August–2 September) [E/CN.4/2006/44/Add.2], the Special Rapporteur found that, despite relative progress in Government efforts to eradicate famine and food shortages, millions of Indians remained undernourished and starvation deaths persisted. With falling agricultural wages, increasing landlessness and rising food prices, food insecurity was growing particularly in rural areas. While recent economic growth generated employment, mostly in high-tech sectors, it was insufficient to absorb the loss of livelihood from agriculture, on which two thirds of the population still depended. Violations of the right to food had involved over 250 cases of starvation deaths, discrimination against the scheduled castes and tribes, displacements or evictions of people by the State without adequate resettlement or rehabilitation, the lack of protection against the activities of private companies and the lack of implementation of food-based schemes in most states in the country.

The Special Rapporteur recommended, among other measures, the effective monitoring of the severity of chronic undernourishment and malnutrition and accountability for related deaths, including by the national and state human rights commissions and local *panchayat* (self-governing) bodies; the establishment of a framework law with a national strategy for the implementation of the right to food; the implementation of land and agrarian reforms to strengthen smallholder agricultural livelihoods; and the strengthening of public food distribution schemes to ensure that food aid reached all those in need. The implementation of all food-based schemes should be improved by incorporating the human rights principles of non-discrimination, participation, transparency and accountability, and food security programmes should ensure nutritional security and better emphasize the protection and promotion of sustainable livelihoods.

Commission action. By a recorded vote of 52 to 1, the Commission, on 13 April [res. 2005/18], considering it intolerable that there were some 852 million undernourished people in the world, asked States, private actors and international organizations to promote the effective realization of the right to food for all. The Special Rapporteur was asked to submit an interim report to the General Assembly in 2005 (see below) and to report to the Commission in 2006, with the assistance of the High Commissioner, while Governments, UN agencies, funds and programmes, treaty bodies and NGOs were invited to cooperate with him by submitting suggestions on ways to realize the right to food.

Further report of Special Rapporteur. In accordance with General Assembly resolution 59/202 [YUN 2004, p. 763], the Secretary-General, in September, transmitted a report of the Special Rapporteur [A/60/350], which addressed the emerging issues of the right to food of indigenous peoples and the responsibilities of international organizations regarding that right. Addressing the former, the report noted that in most countries, hunger and malnutrition were disproportionately higher among indigenous populations, making it urgent to strengthen the protection of their rights in that regard, including by better protecting their land and resources. Considering international organizations, the Special Rapporteur was concerned that projects financed by such organizations as the World Bank could have a negative impact on the right to food of vulnerable populations, sometimes causing them to be displaced from their land and to lose access to their traditional livelihoods. It was also of concern that economic development models promoted and imposed by international orga-

nizations such as the Bank, the IMF and the World Trade Organization (WTO) were threatening the right to food of small farmers worldwide. Although important recent progress had been made in some countries to tackle food security problems, the overall trend was one of regression rather than the progressive realization of the right to food. The Special Rapporteur determined that hunger appeared to have increased every year since the 1996 World Food Summit [YUN 1996, p. 1129], which was dedicated to combating hunger. The situation in Africa was particularly disturbing, given that up to nine countries on the continent suffered from critical food emergencies. The Special Rapporteur recommended that Governments take urgent action to halt global undernourishment, respond rapidly to the food crises currently affecting Africa, and accord special attention to the situation and rights of indigenous peoples, who suffered from disproportionately high levels of hunger and malnutrition. Food security should be ensured as a human right and not left up to the vagaries of the market system, which could not address hunger in times of emergency, and international organizations should recognize that they had binding responsibilities towards human rights, including the right to food.

GENERAL ASSEMBLY ACTION

On 16 December [meeting 64], the General Assembly, on the recommendation of the Third Committee [A/60/509/Add.2], adopted **resolution 60/165** by a recorded vote (176-1-1) [agenda item 71 *(b)*].

The right to food

The General Assembly,

Recalling its resolution 59/202 of 20 December 2004, as well as all Commission on Human Rights resolutions in this regard, in particular resolution 2005/18 of 14 April 2005,

Recalling also the Universal Declaration of Human Rights, which provides that everyone has the right to a standard of living adequate for her or his health and well-being, including food, the Universal Declaration on the Eradication of Hunger and Malnutrition and the United Nations Millennium Declaration,

Recalling further the provisions of the International Covenant on Economic, Social and Cultural Rights, in which the fundamental right of every person to be free from hunger is recognized,

Bearing in mind the Rome Declaration on World Food Security and the World Food Summit Plan of Action and the Declaration of the World Food Summit: five years later, adopted in Rome on 13 June 2002,

Welcoming the concrete recommendations contained in the Voluntary Guidelines to Support the Progressive Realization of the Right to Adequate Food in the Context of National Food Security, adopted by the Council of the Food and Agriculture Organization of the United Nations in November 2004,

Reaffirming that all human rights are universal, indivisible, interdependent and interrelated,

Reaffirming also that a peaceful, stable and enabling political, social and economic environment, at both the national and the international levels, is the essential foundation that will enable States to give adequate priority to food security and poverty eradication,

Reiterating, as in the Rome Declaration on World Food Security and the Declaration of the World Food Summit: five years later, that food should not be used as an instrument of political or economic pressure, and reaffirming in this regard the importance of international cooperation and solidarity, as well as the necessity of refraining from unilateral measures that are not in accordance with international law and the Charter of the United Nations and that endanger food security,

Convinced that each State must adopt a strategy consistent with its resources and capacities to achieve its individual goals in implementing the recommendations contained in the Rome Declaration on World Food Security and the World Food Summit Plan of Action and, at the same time, cooperate regionally and internationally in order to organize collective solutions to global issues of food security in a world of increasingly interlinked institutions, societies and economies where coordinated efforts and shared responsibilities are essential,

Recognizing that the problems of hunger and food insecurity have global dimensions and that they are likely to persist and even to increase dramatically in some regions unless urgent, determined and concerted action is taken, given the anticipated increase in the world's population and the stress on natural resources,

Expressing its deep concern at the number and scale of natural disasters, diseases and pests and their increasing impact in recent years, which have resulted in massive loss of life and livelihood and threatened agricultural production and food security, in particular in developing countries,

Stressing the importance of reversing the continuing decline of official development assistance devoted to agriculture, both in real terms and as a share of total official development assistance,

1. *Reaffirms* that hunger constitutes an outrage and a violation of human dignity and therefore requires the adoption of urgent measures at the national, regional and international levels for its elimination;

2. *Also reaffirms* the right of everyone to have access to safe and nutritious food, consistent with the right to adequate food and the fundamental right of everyone to be free from hunger, so as to be able to fully develop and maintain their physical and mental capacities;

3. *Considers it intolerable* that there are about 852 million undernourished people in the world, that every five seconds a child under the age of 5 dies from hunger or hunger-related diseases somewhere in the world, when, according to the Food and Agriculture Organization of the United Nations, the planet could produce enough food to provide 2,100 kilocalories per person per day to 12 billion people, twice the world's present population;

4. *Expresses its concern* that women are disproportionately affected by hunger, food insecurity and poverty, in part as a result of gender inequality and discrimination, that in many countries, girls are twice as likely as boys to die from malnutrition and preventable childhood diseases, and that it is estimated that almost twice as many women as men suffer from malnutrition;

5. *Encourages* all States to take action to address gender inequality and discrimination against women, in particular where it contributes to the malnutrition of women and girls, including measures to ensure the full and equal realization of the right to food and ensuring that women have equal access to resources, including income, land and water, to enable them to feed themselves and their families;

6. *Encourages* the Special Rapporteur of the Commission on Human Rights on the right to food to continue mainstreaming a gender perspective in the fulfilment of his mandate, and encourages the Food and Agriculture Organization of the United Nations and all other United Nations bodies and mechanisms addressing the right to food and food insecurity to integrate a gender perspective into their relevant policies, programmes and activities;

7. *Encourages* all States to take steps with a view to achieving progressively the full realization of the right to food, including steps to promote the conditions for everyone to be free from hunger and, as soon as possible, to enjoy fully the right to food, and to create and adopt national plans to combat hunger;

8. *Acknowledges* that many indigenous organizations and representatives of indigenous communities have expressed in different forums their deep concerns over the obstacles and challenges for their full enjoyment of the right to food, and calls upon States to take special actions to combat the root causes of the disproportionately high level of hunger and malnutrition among indigenous peoples and the continuous discrimination against them;

9. *Requests* all States and private actors, as well as international organizations within their respective mandates, to take fully into account the need to promote the effective realization of the right to food for all, including in the ongoing negotiations in different fields;

10. *Stresses* the need to make efforts to mobilize and optimize the allocation and utilization of technical and financial resources from all sources, including external debt relief for developing countries, and to reinforce national actions to implement sustainable food security policies;

11. *Recalls* the importance of the New York Declaration on Action against Hunger and Poverty, which has been supported by more than one hundred countries to date, and recommends the continuation of efforts aimed at identifying additional sources of financing for the fight against hunger and poverty;

12. *Recognizes* that the promises made at the World Food Summit in 1996 to halve the number of persons who are undernourished are not being fulfilled, and invites once again all international financial and development institutions, as well as the relevant United Nations agencies and funds, to give priority to and provide the necessary funding to realize the aim of halving by 2015 the proportion of people who suffer from hunger, as well as the right to food as set out in

the Rome Declaration on World Food Security and the United Nations Millennium Declaration;

13. *Urges* States to give adequate priority in their development strategies and expenditures to the realization of the right to food;

14. *Stresses* the importance of international development cooperation and assistance, in particular in emergency situations such as natural and man-made disasters, diseases and pests, for the realization of the right to food and the achievement of sustainable food security, while recognizing that each country has the primary responsibility for ensuring the implementation of national programmes and strategies in this regard;

15. *Calls upon* Member States, the United Nations system and other relevant stakeholders to support national efforts aimed at responding rapidly to the food crises currently occurring across Africa;

16. *Invites* all relevant international organizations, including the World Bank and the International Monetary Fund, to promote policies and projects that have a positive impact on the right to food, to ensure that partners respect the right to food in the implementation of common projects, to support strategies of Member States aimed at the fulfilment of the right to food and to avoid any actions that could have a negative impact on the realization of the right to food;

17. *Takes note* of the interim report of the Special Rapporteur of the Commission on Human Rights on the right to food, and also takes note of his valuable work in the promotion of the right to food;

18. *Supports* the realization of the mandate of the Special Rapporteur as extended by the Commission on Human Rights in its resolution 2003/25 of 22 April 2003;

19. *Requests* the Secretary-General and the United Nations High Commissioner for Human Rights to provide all the necessary human and financial resources for the effective fulfilment of the mandate of the Special Rapporteur;

20. *Welcomes* the work already done by the Committee on Economic, Social and Cultural Rights in promoting the right to adequate food, in particular its General Comment No. 12 (1999) on the right to adequate food (article 11 of the International Covenant on Economic, Social and Cultural Rights), in which the Committee affirmed, inter alia, that the right to adequate food is indivisibly linked to the inherent dignity of the human person and is indispensable for the fulfilment of other human rights enshrined in the International Bill of Human Rights, and is also inseparable from social justice, requiring the adoption of appropriate economic, environmental and social policies, at both the national and the international levels, oriented to the eradication of poverty and the fulfilment of all human rights for all;

21. *Recalls* General Comment No. 15 (2002) of the Committee on the right to water (articles 11 and 12 of the Covenant), in which the Committee noted, inter alia, the importance of ensuring sustainable water resources for human consumption and agriculture in realization of the right to adequate food;

22. *Welcomes* the adoption by the Council of the Food and Agriculture Organization of the United Nations of the Voluntary Guidelines to Support the Progressive Realization of the Right to Adequate Food in the Context of National Food Security, which represent a practical tool to promote the realization of the right to food for all, contribute to the achievement of food security and thus provide an additional instrument in the attainment of internationally agreed development goals, including those contained in the Millennium Declaration;

23. *Also welcomes* the continued cooperation of the High Commissioner, the Committee and the Special Rapporteur, and encourages them to continue their cooperation in this regard;

24. *Calls upon* all Governments to cooperate with and assist the Special Rapporteur in his task, to supply all necessary information requested by him and to give serious consideration to responding favourably to the requests of the Special Rapporteur to visit their countries to enable him to fulfil his mandate more effectively;

25. *Requests* the Special Rapporteur to submit a comprehensive report to the Commission on Human Rights at its sixty-second session and an interim report to the General Assembly at its sixty-first session on the implementation of the present resolution;

26. *Invites* Governments, relevant United Nations agencies, funds and programmes, treaty bodies and civil society actors, including non-governmental organizations, as well as the private sector, to cooperate fully with the Special Rapporteur in the fulfilment of his mandate, inter alia, through the submission of comments and suggestions on ways and means of realizing the right to food;

27. *Decides* to continue the consideration of the question at its sixty-first session under the item entitled "Human rights questions".

RECORDED VOTE ON RESOLUTION 60/165:

In favour: Afghanistan, Albania, Algeria, Andorra, Angola, Antigua and Barbuda, Argentina, Armenia, Australia, Austria, Azerbaijan, Bahamas, Bahrain, Bangladesh, Barbados, Belarus, Belgium, Belize, Benin, Bhutan, Bolivia, Bosnia and Herzegovina, Botswana, Brazil, Brunei Darussalam, Bulgaria, Burkina Faso, Burundi, Cambodia, Cameroon, Canada, Cape Verde, Chile, China, Colombia, Comoros, Costa Rica, Côte d'Ivoire, Croatia, Cuba, Cyprus, Czech Republic, Democratic People's Republic of Korea, Democratic Republic of the Congo, Denmark, Djibouti, Dominica, Dominican Republic, Ecuador, Egypt, El Salvador, Eritrea, Estonia, Ethiopia, Fiji, Finland, France, Gabon, Gambia, Georgia, Germany, Ghana, Greece, Grenada, Guatemala, Guinea, Guinea-Bissau, Haiti, Honduras, Hungary, Iceland, India, Indonesia, Iran, Iraq, Ireland, Italy, Jamaica, Japan, Jordan, Kazakhstan, Kenya, Kuwait, Kyrgyzstan, Lao People's Democratic Republic, Latvia, Lebanon, Lesotho, Libyan Arab Jamahiriya, Liechtenstein, Lithuania, Luxembourg, Madagascar, Malawi, Malaysia, Maldives, Mali, Malta, Marshall Islands, Mauritania, Mauritius, Mexico, Micronesia, Monaco, Mongolia, Morocco, Mozambique, Myanmar, Namibia, Nepal, Netherlands, New Zealand, Nicaragua, Niger, Nigeria, Norway, Oman, Pakistan, Palau, Panama, Papua New Guinea, Paraguay, Peru, Philippines, Poland, Portugal, Qatar, Republic of Korea, Republic of Moldova, Romania, Russian Federation, Rwanda, Saint Lucia, Saint Vincent and the Grenadines, Samoa, San Marino, Saudi Arabia, Senegal, Serbia and Montenegro, Singapore, Slovakia, Slovenia, Solomon Islands, Somalia, South Africa, Spain, Sri Lanka, Sudan, Suriname, Sweden, Switzerland, Syrian Arab oftlineRepublic, Tajikistan, Thailand, The former Yugoslav Republic of Macedonia, Timor-Leste, Togo, Tonga, Trinidad and Tobago, Tunisia, Turkey, Turkmenistan, Tuvalu, Uganda, Ukraine, United Arab Emirates, United Kingdom, United Republic of Tanzania, Uruguay, Uzbekistan, Vanuatu, Venezuela, Viet Nam, Yemen, Zambia, Zimbabwe.

Against: United States.

Abstaining: Israel.

Right to adequate housing

Reports of Special Rapporteur. The Special Rapporteur on the right to adequate housing,

Miloon Kothari (India), in a March report [E/CN.4/2005/48], focused on homelessness, its causes and impacts. Reflecting on the fact that approximately 100 million people worldwide had no place to live and that over one billion were inadequately housed, the report described homelessness as the most visible and severe symptom of the lack of respect for the right to adequate housing. It examined common definitions of homelessness, the legal basis for protection against it, and the driving forces behind the problem, including structural factors, such as poverty, unplanned urban migration and large-scale developmental and infrastructure projects; legislation and policy questions, such as the privatization of civic services; conflict situations; and landlessness. Mostly affected were women, children and youth, indigenous peoples, persons with disabilities, and communities discriminated against on the basis of ethnicity and descent. The Special Rapporteur concluded, among other things, that the right to adequate housing needed to be recognized as being linked to numerous other human rights, including the right to security of the person and of the home. Pointing out that the principle of non-discrimination should guide all aspects of programme design and implementation in policy-making relating to the right to adequate housing, he called for a combination of a humanitarian and human rights approaches in addressing the crises faced by millions living in inadequate and insecure housing. Specific recommendations for furthering the right related to legislation and regulation, programme design and financing, and enforcement, protection and monitoring strategies.

The Special Rapporteur visited Iran (19-31 July) [E/CN.4/2005/41/Add.2], where he examined and reported on the status of the realization of the right to adequate housing, with particular attention to gender equity and non-discrimination. He found that efforts in that regard faced a number of obstacles and challenges relating mainly to the prohibitive costs of housing in the country and policies and programmes that did not seem to improve access to adequate housing for the very poor. That failure resulted from the inaccessibility of Government credit facilities, and leasing and pro-housing savings programmes to the very poor; distortions in Government incentives to large-scale builders of low-price housing units; urban bias in the planning of housing programmes; and the lack of coordination between different Government branches, agencies and organizations responsible for implementation. Additional causes for concern included continuing discrimination against ethnic and religious minorities, nomadic groups and women with re-

spect to adequate housing rights; the high number of alleged cases of land confiscation and forced evictions; and the poor and limited status of related basic services for informal settlements and poor neighbourhoods. The Special Rapporteur addressed a series of recommendations to the Government, including a legal and administrative review of the doctrine of "eminent domain", which prevented individuals and groups from challenging State acquisition of housing and land; the development of further policies to ensure women's equal access to housing, land property and inheritance; the adoption of policies to avoid land and housing speculation; further attention to marginalized provinces; public participation in the elaboration of development plans and the preparation and assessment of housing projects; and the reinforcement, expansion and implementation of policies aimed at groups in vulnerable situations and minorities.

In Cambodia (22 August–3 September) [E/CN.4/2006/41/Add.3], where years of civil conflict and related land acquisition on a massive scale had exacerbated land disputes and distorted land ownership patterns to the disadvantage of the poor, the Special Rapporteur found numerous problems, including the inability of the land management system to address the consequences of the lack of land records destroyed during the Khmer Rouge period. Other problems related to the undeveloped and non-transparent land registration system, the absence of cadastral index maps, inadequate land laws and procedures, unclear delineation of State land and the weakness of the justice system. Particularly worrisome were Government land exchanges, which relocated families to remote areas often lacking adequate infrastructure and access to water and sanitation; forced evictions; intimidation and threats by local authorities and private developers, as well as urban infrastructure development, which often resulted in dubious deals and involuntary relocations or resettlements; arbitrary detention of homeless persons, including children, under the pretext of "beautifying" the city; and a severe lack of public services in rural areas. While the Special Rapporteur was encouraged by some initiatives taken by NGOs and the municipality of Phnom Penh to promote a rights-based approach to urban development and housing rights, he remained concerned about the situation and urged the Government to adopt progressive measures to secure adequate housing for all Cambodians, in accordance with its international human rights obligations. He recommended, in particular, the clear mapping of the housing needs of the country and an interpretation of the data from a human rights perspective, aimed at the development of a comprehensive national housing policy, and urgent attention to those living in distressed housing and living conditions, including slum and relocation site dwellers.

Women's right to property and adequate housing

Report of Special Rapporteur. In response to a 2003 Commission request [YUN 2003, p.770], the Special Rapporteur on the right to adequate housing (see above), submitted a February progress report [E/CN.4/2005/43] on a study of women's equal ownership of, access to and control over land and the equal right to own property and to adequate housing, which built on the 2003 report on the topic [YUN 2003, p. 769]. The current report examined the interrelated issue of land, property and inheritance, and other human rights issues, such as the rights to water and to health, in order to provide a more comprehensive analysis of women's right to adequate housing. Based on questionnaire responses, testimonies and outcomes of regional consultations with civil society, the key themes that emerged as critical issues in the context of that right were violence against women, forced evictions, homelessness, cultural norms and practices, other barriers as poverty, gender discrimination and some countries' lack of national implementation mechanisms for human rights treaties, including national housing laws. Women's right in that regard was especially affected by the lack of secure tenure, information about their human rights, and access to affordable social services, owing to privatization, credit and housing subsidies, as well as adequate housing programmes, owing to bureaucratic barriers. While acknowledging the increasing recognition by international and national laws of women's right to adequate housing, the Special Rapporteur observed that considerable gaps existed between such recognition and the reality of large-scale denial of that right. To improve the situation, he addressed several recommendations to States, the United Nations and civil society actors, regarding the need for, among other actions, the implementation of innovative government housing policies and programmes and the integration of women's human rights into poverty reduction strategies, anti-poverty policies and rural development and land reform programmes. He also emphasized the adoption of an indivisibility-of-rights approach to promoting women's right to adequate housing.

Commission action. On 15 April [res. 2005/25], the Commission encouraged Governments to support the transformation of customs and traditions that discriminated against women and denied them security of tenure and equal owner-ship of, access to, and control over land, and equal rights to own property and to adequate housing. It recommended that international, regional, national and local housing financing institutions and other credit facilities facilitate women's participation and remove discriminatory policies, giving special consideration to single women and households headed by women. The Secretary-General was invited to encourage UN entities to undertake initiatives that promoted women's rights to own property and to adequate housing, while the Special Rapporteur was asked to submit a final report, in 2006, containing the study on women and adequate housing, and States were invited to respond to the questionnaire he had prepared.

Right to education

Report of Special Rapporteur. The Special Rapporteur on the right to education, Vernor Muñoz Villalobos (Costa Rica), in his first report to the Commission [E/CN.4/2005/50], described his planned activities and the issues he intended to consider toward the implementation of his mandate. Following up on his predecessor's work, the Special Rapporteur said he would continue to strengthen the human rights dimension of education by encouraging a shift from policies addressing education as an economic good to those that considered it as a right. He would focus on the financial resources allocated to education and the need for free compulsory primary education, and engage various key partners in a dialogue on the issue. Reflecting on financial and structural constraints and on discrimination, as major impediments to the full enjoyment of the right to education, the Special Rapporteur said he would accord particular attention to the access of girls and adolescents to education, and examine the exercise of the right by migrants, indigenous populations, minorities and persons with different capacities. He would review security in schools and the exercise of the right to education in emergency situations, including those relating to displacement, armed conflicts, military occupation and intra-school violence.

Commission action. On 15 April [res. 2005/21], the Commission urged States to give full effect to the right to education and to guarantee that the right was recognized and exercised without discrimination. It invited the Special Rapporteur to gather, request, receive and exchange information from all relevant sources, to intensify efforts aimed at identifying ways to overcome obstacles and difficulties in realizing the right, to apply a gender perspective to his work and, with the Secretary-General's assistance, to report in 2006.

Environmental and scientific concerns

Toxic wastes

Reports of Special Rapporteur. In response to a 2004 Commission request [YUN 2004, p. 767], the Special Rapporteur on the adverse effects of the illicit movement and dumping of toxic and dangerous products and wastes on the enjoyment of human rights, Okechukwu Ibeanu (Nigeria), submitted a preliminary report [E/CN.4/2005/45], which analysed his mandate and its relationship to existing multilateral environmental agreements, particularly the 1989 Basel Convention on . the Control of Transboundary Movements of Hazardous Wastes and Their Disposal [YUN 1989, p. 420]. It also outlined the scope of his mandate, the methodology he intended to adopt in implementing it and the activities he had undertaken. He also reviewed communications and observations received from Governments and NGOs. To assist him in his work, the Special Rapporteur encouraged Governments to respond to his requests for comments on allegations brought to his attention and for in situ visits.

An addendum to the report [E/CN.4/2005/45/Add.1] updated information on previously reported cases of alleged human rights violations relating to the mandate.

Commission action. By a recorded vote of 37 to 13, with 2 abstentions, the Commission, on 14 April [res. 2005/15], reaffirmed that illicit traffic and dumping of toxic and dangerous products and wastes constituted a serious threat to human rights and urged Governments to prevent it, including through the ratification of related international instruments. Developed countries and international financial institutions were asked to provide financial assistance for implementing the Programme of Action adopted at the First Continental Conference for Africa on the Environmentally Sounds Management of Unwanted Stocks of Hazardous Wastes and Their Prevention [YUN 2001, p. 972]. The Special Rapporteur was asked to study, in consultation with relevant UN bodies, the problems of, and solutions to illicit trafficking and to report in 2006. The Secretary-General was asked to assist him.

Environmental protection and sustainable development

Report of Secretary-General. In response to a 2004 Commission request [YUN 2004, p. 768], the Secretary-General, in January [E/CN.4/2005/96], updated his 2004 report [ibid.] on the relationship between the environment and human rights as part of sustainable development. In that context, the report analysed related developments at the international and regional levels, including the work of human rights treaty bodies, Commission special procedures, multilateral environmental agreements, intergovernmental and civil society organizations, the UN Economic Commission for Europe and the European Court of Human Rights. Regarding developments at the national level, the report considered constitutional and legal provisions for preserving the environment, the status of the right to information on and public participation in environmental matters, relevant jurisprudence and references to environment-related issues in States parties' reports to treaty bodies. The report concluded that the work of many of those entities illustrated a growing recognition of the connection between environmental protection and human rights since the World Summit on Sustainable Development [YUN 2002, p. 821]. At the regional level, in particular, the Aarhus Convention in Europe [YUN 1998, p. 952] and a growing number of decisions by regional courts provided examples of such recognition. Those links were reinforced by developments at the national level, within the framework of the justice system and administrative practices and decisions.

Commission action. On 20 April [res. 2005/60], the Commission asked the High Commissioner and the United Nations Environment Programme (UNEP) to continue to coordinate their efforts in capacity-building activities, in cooperation with other relevant bodies and organizations. The High Commissioner was asked to disseminate widely the reports considered and resolutions adopted by the Commission, as well as the observations and recommendations of human rights treaty bodies on environmental protection issues. The Secretary-General was asked to submit in 2007, a report on how respect for human rights could contribute to sustainable development and to include information that would update his report on human rights and the environment as part of sustainable development.

Disappearance of States for environmental reasons

Commission action. On 20 April [dec. 2005/112], the Commission, by a recorded vote of 51 to 2, welcomed the working paper on the human rights situation of indigenous peoples in States and other territories threatened with extinction for environmental reasons [YUN 2004, p. 768], and endorsed the 2004 request of the Subcommission [ibid.] to Françoise Hampson (United Kingdom) to submit an expanded working paper in 2005 (see p. 846), and its request to the Secretary-General to assist her, by facilitating contacts with

States, including by transmitting a questionnaire she had elaborated soliciting information for her study.

Working paper. In accordance with the Subcommission's request [YUN 2004, p. 768] and Commission decision 2005/112 (see p. 845), Ms. Hampson submitted an expanded working paper on the subject [E/CN.4/Sub.2/2005/28]. The paper updated information contained in her 2004 report [YUN 2004, p. 768] and explained the issues to be addressed by the questionnaire, which would seek to establish the types of environmental threats facing different populations, including from volcanoes, earthquakes, tidal waves and rising sea levels. In that regard, affected States fell into three categories: those that would disappear totally; those, of which a significant part would disappear, leaving only territory that would be unable to support the remaining population; and those, of which a significant part would disappear, with serious implications for the remaining population. The paper examined the legal and human rights implications of the situation, particularly those relating to the citizenship rights of affected populations and rights relating to their forced relocation to other States. Focusing on the States most likely to be affected (Tuvalu, Nauru, Kiribati, Maldives, the Bahamas), the paper considered action currently being taken to address the problem and possible future action.

Subcommission action. On 10 August [res. 2005/20], the Subcommission appointed Ms. Hampson as Special Rapporteur to prepare, based on her expanded working paper and comments thereon, a comprehensive study on the legal implications of the disappearance of States and other territories for environmental reasons, including the human rights implications for the residents of those states, with particular reference to indigenous peoples. The Special Rapporteur was requested to submit a preliminary report in 2006, a progress report in 2007, and a final report in 2008. The Secretary-General was asked to assist her.

Right to physical and mental health

Reports of Special Rapporteur. The Special Rapporteur on the right to the highest attainable standard of physical and mental health, Paul Hunt (New Zealand), in a February report [E/CN.4/2005/51] describing his activities, stated that, between 2 December 2004 and 1 December 2005, he had transmitted 38 communications, including urgent appeals, to 25 Governments on alleged violations of the right to physical and mental health of numerous persons, with similar communications sent to the United Nations In-

terim Administration Mission in Kosovo (UNMIK) and the Global Fund to Fight AIDS, Tuberculosis and Malaria. The communications sent and replies received were summarized in a separate document [E/CN.4/2006/48/Add.1].

In the February report, the Special Rapporteur focused on the situation of persons with mental disabilities, whom he observed, were among the most neglected, marginalized and vulnerable. The report reviewed evolving human rights standards and obligations relating to persons with mental disabilities and highlighted three related issues demanding particular attention: intellectual disability, the right to community integration and consent to treatment. It observed that some 450 million people were affected globally, very few of whom were receiving treatment, care and support. While mental and behavioural disorders were estimated to account for 12 per cent of the global burden of disease, the mental health budget of most countries was less than one per cent of their total health expenditure. Over 40 per cent of countries had no mental health policy and more than 30 per cent had no mental health programme. Against that background, mental health was among the most neglected element of the right to health. International organizations had also given little attention to mental health, although the World Health Organization (WHO) and the Pan American Health Organization (PAHO) were making efforts to redress the situation. Civil society organizations and other stakeholders were also making significant progress in advancing debates on the issue of mental disabilities and human rights and in promoting an understanding of the problem. Nonetheless, the Special Rapporteur recommended that States should enhance legal initiatives in mental disability to ensure the right to health and other human rights. They should devote more of their health budgets to mental health, particularly for prevention and community-based treatment and care, and request technical cooperation from WHO and PAHO and financial assistance from donors.

The Special Rapporteur visited Uganda (17-25 March) [E/CN.4/2006/48/Add.2] to consider, from a human rights perspective, the issue of neglected diseases, also known as "poverty-related" tropical diseases, which had inflicted severe and permanent disabilities and deformities on some one billion people around the world, particularly among the poorest in developing countries. In Uganda, those diseases included lymphatic filariasis (elephantiasis), leprosy and human African trypanosomiasis (sleeping sickness) and soil-transmitted diseases, among others. While the Government had achieved impressive health successes in some areas, most notably in halting and reversing the spread of HIV/AIDS, significant challenges remained, as poor infrastructure curtailed access to health-care facilities, especially in rural areas, where only 49 per cent of households had such access. Communicable diseases, such as malaria, parasitic infection, HIV and tuberculosis, fueled by poor sanitation and water resources, were widespread and contributed to high levels of morbidity and mortality, particularly among women and children. The Special Rapporteur identified the main features of a right-to-health approach to neglected diseases in the Ugandan context. He outlined conclusions on the issues addressed in the report and made recommendations for improving Uganda's capacity to tackle neglected diseases, including the possible alignment of various mass drug administration mechanisms in the country and an increase in their sustainable and predictable contributions to Uganda's health sector by development partners.

Commission action. By a recorded vote of 52 to 1, the Commission, on 15 April [res. 2005/24], called on States to guarantee that the right of everyone to the enjoyment of the highest attainable standard of physical and mental health would be exercised without discrimination, and to recognize the needs of persons with disabilities, by reflecting those needs in national health and social policies. The Commission recommended that States review their legislation, procedural safeguards and practices relating to the treatment of persons with disabilities relating to mental disorders, taking into account, the principle of informed consent. It decided to extend, for a period of three years, the Special Rapporteur's mandate and requested him to submit a report annually to the Commission and an interim report to the General Assembly. The High Commissioner was asked to assist him.

ECONOMIC AND SOCIAL COUNCIL ACTION

On 25 July, the Economic and Social Council, on the recommendation of the Commission on Human Rights [E/2005/23], adopted **decision 2005/261** by recorded vote (50-1-0) [agenda item 14 (g)].

The right of everyone to the enjoyment of the highest attainable standard of physical and mental health

At its 38th plenary meeting, on 25 July 2005, the Economic and Social Council took note of Commission on Human Rights resolution 2005/24 of 15 April 2005, and approved the Commission's decision to extend for a period of three years the mandate of the Special Rapporteur of the Commission on Human Rights on the right of everyone to the enjoyment of the highest attainable standard of physical and mental health.

Further report of Special Rapporteur. In accordance with Commission resolution 2005/24 (see above), the Secretary-General, by a September note [A/60/348], transmitted the Special Rapporteur's interim report, which discussed the work of the Commission on Social Determinants of Health, established by WHO to study the social dimensions of health, the importance of health professionals' education in human rights, and the migration of health professionals from developing to developed countries, otherwise known as the "brain drain". The Special Rapporteur concluded that the integration of human rights into national and international policies affecting the skills drain was likely to make those policies more effective, robust, equitable, inclusive and meaningful to those living in poverty. The report considered three possible policy responses to the brain drain phenomenon in developing countries: the strengthening of health systems in those countries; ethical recruitment by destination counties; and compensation or restitution. It suggested that developed countries establish independent national offices to monitor their international cooperation on health, including those policies relating to the brain drain.

By **decision 60/533** of 16 December, the General Assembly took note of the Special Rapporteur's report.

Communication. On 21 March [E/CN.4/2005/G/32], Peru transmitted its comments on the Special Rapporteur's report, following his 2004 visit to that country [YUN 2004, p. 769]. Peru's Ministry of Health was aware of the need to give priority to the formulation and implementation of a comprehensive rights-based health policy that would benefit its poorest and most vulnerable groups. A national campaign had been launched to enable all Peruvian citizens to enjoy the right to health.

Human rights and HIV/AIDS

On 21 April [res. 2005/84], the Commission invited States, UN entities, international organizations and NGOs to ensure the respect, protection and fulfillment of HIV/AIDS-related human rights, as contained in the guidelines on HIV/AIDS and human rights adopted by the Second International Consultation on HIV/AIDS and Human Rights [YUN 1996, p. 617]. States were further urged to ensure that their laws, policies and practices, including those in the workplace, respected human rights in the context of HIV/AIDS, promoted effective programmes for its treatment, and prohibited HIV-related discrimination. In particular, they should ensure full and equal access for women and children to HIV prevention and related information, voluntary counselling and testing, and education and care. Human rights treaty bodies were invited to give particular attention to HIV-related rights when considering reports submitted by States parties. The Secretary-General was requested to solicit comments from Governments, UN bodies, international organizations and NGOs on steps to promote and implement programmes addressing the HIV-related human rights of women, children and vulnerable groups in the context of prevention, care and access to treatment, and to report thereon in 2006.

Access to medication

Report of Secretary-General. The Commission had before it a report of the Secretary-General [E/CN.4/2005/38], submitted in response to a 2004 Commission request [YUN 2004, p. 770], which summarized information received from eight Governments, four UN bodies, and NGOs on steps they had taken to promote access to medication in the context of pandemics, such as HIV/AIDS, tuberculosis and malaria.

Commission action. On 15 April [res. 2005/23], the Commission recognized that access to medication in the context of pandemics, such as HIV/AIDS, tuberculosis and malaria, was fundamental to achieving the full realization of the right of everyone to the enjoyment of the highest attainable standard of physical and mental health. It called on States to develop and implement national strategies in order to realize access for all to prevention-related goods and services, and to establish or strengthen national health and social infrastructure for the effective delivery of treatment, care and support in responding to such pandemics. The Secretary-General was asked to solicit comments from Governments, UN entities, international organizations and NGOs on steps taken to implement the Commission's resolution, and to report in 2006.

Water and sanitation services

Report of Special Rapporteur. In accordance with a 2004 Subcommission request [YUN 2004, p. 771], the Special Rapporteur on the realization of the right to drinking water and sanitation, El Hadji Guissé (Senegal), submitted draft guide-

lines for the realization of the right to water supply and sanitation [E/CN.4/Sub.2/2005/25], which were intended to assist government policymakers, international agencies and civil society representatives working in the water and sanitation sector to implement the right.

Commission action. On 15 April [dec. 2005/106], the Commission approved the 2004 request [YUN 2004, p. 770] of the Subcommission that the report of the Special Rapporteur be published in the official languages of the United Nations.

ECONOMIC AND SOCIAL COUNCIL ACTION

On 25 July, the Economic and Social Council, on the recommendation of the Commission on Human Rights [E/2005/23], adopted **decision 2005/285** by recorded vote (47-2-0) [agenda item 14 (g)].

Promotion of the realization of the right to drinking water and sanitation

At its 38th plenary meeting, on 25 July 2005, the Economic and Social Council took note of Commission on Human Rights decision 2005/106 of 15 April 2005, and endorsed the Commission's request that the reports of the Special Rapporteur of the Subcommission on the Promotion and Protection of Human Rights on the conduct of a detailed study on the relationship between the enjoyment of economic, social and cultural rights and the promotion of the realization of the right to drinking water supply and sanitation at the national and international levels be published in the official languages of the United Nations.

RECORDED VOTE ON DECISION 2005/285:

In favour: Albania, Armenia, Azerbaijan, Bangladesh, Belgium, Belize, Brazil, Canada, China, Colombia, Congo, Costa Rica, Cuba, Denmark, Ecuador, France, Germany, Guinea, Iceland, India, Indonesia, Ireland, Italy, Jamaica, Kenya, Lithuania, Malaysia, Mauritius, Mexico, Mozambique, Namibia, Nicaragua, Pakistan, Panama, Poland, Republic of Korea, Russian Federation, Saudi Arabia, Senegal, South Africa, Spain, Thailand, Tunisia, Turkey, United Arab Emirates, United Kingdom, United Republic of Tanzania.

Against: Japan, United States.

Bioethics

Report of Secretary-General. In accordance with a 2003 Commission request [YUN 2003, p. 775], the Secretary-General submitted a report [E/CN.4/2005/93] summarizing information provided by 11 Governments, as well as human rights bodies and OHCHR, on the relationship between human rights and bioethics.

Report of Special Rapporteur. In response to a 2004 Commission request [YUN 2004, p. 771], the Special Rapporteur on human rights and the human genome, Antoanella-Iulia Motoc (Romania), submitted a July interim report [E/CN.4/Sub.2/2005/38], which considered issues relating to intellectual property rights in the context of biotechnology and genetic resources. The report reviewed the 1994 Agreement on Trade-Related Aspects of Intellectual Property Rights (TRIPS)

[YUN 1994, p. 1464] and other international instruments, with reference to specific provisions on the application of patents to genetic resources. It also examined relevant national and regional legislation relating to patents. The Special Rapporteur observed that, as a recent phenomenon, international intellectual property lawmaking had permeated international regimes concerning biodiversity, plant genetic resources, and public health and human rights. At the same time, the TRIPS agreement had come under increasing challenge, as two systems existed: one for developed countries, which emphasized patent and privatization and their ability to promote innovation, and the other, which led developing countries to close their systems around the notion of State sovereignty, thereby potentially undermining scientific research. Yet, both systems questioned the notion of "a common human heritage". The Special Rapporteur recommended that efforts be made to reconcile the two systems through the promotion of scientific research.

Subcommission action. On 11 August [dec. 2005/111], the Subcommission asked the Special Rapporteur to submit a final report in 2006, and the Secretary-General to assist her.

Human cloning

On 8 March, the General Assembly adopted the United Nations Declaration on Human Cloning (**resolution 59/280**) (see p. 1454), which called on Member States to prohibit all forms of human cloning that were incompatible with human dignity and the protection of human life.

Slavery and related issues

Working group activities. The five-member Working Group on Contemporary Forms of Slavery, at its thirtieth session (Geneva, 6-10 June) [E/CN.4/Sub.2/2005/34], devoted priority attention to the review and assessment of its activities and working experience since its establishment, as well as the implementation of human rights standards on contemporary forms of slavery, including trafficking in persons, sexual exploitation and the protection of children from exploitation. The Group discussed the need to ensure effective implementation of the slavery conventions, heard testimonies from victims of bonded labour and forced marriage, discussed the working conditions of migrant workers, considered information about the issue of boys trafficked as camel jockeys and of traditional practices as a contributing factor for the perpetuation of slavery. It adopted recommendations for its future work and for the work of the Subcommission, human rights treaty bodies and other relevant actors. The Group recommended that the Subcommission request one of its members to draft a working paper examining the feasibility of a study on the human rights dimensions of prostitution. It decided to sharpen its thematic focus and to devote more time during its sessions to discussions of a specific theme, leading to the adoption of thematic recommendations. It would give priority to the identification of remaining slavery-related issues not appropriately addressed by other human rights mechanisms and focus its activities on those issues. The Group selected as its theme for 2006 the human rights dimensions of prostitution and the need to strengthen international cooperation to suppress international transfers of profits from the exploitation of the prostitution of others and trafficking in persons.

The Group had before it an informal background document on its main activities since its establishment, reports on the status of the 1956 Supplementary Convention on the Abolition of Slavery [YUN 1956, p. 228] and the 1949 Convention for the Suppression of the Traffic in Persons and the Exploitation of the Prostitution of Others [YUN 1948-49, p. 613] [E/CN.4/Sub.2/AC.2/2005/2 & E/CN.4/Sub.2/AC.2/2005/3] and the report of the Secretary-General (see below).

Report of Secretary-General. A June report of the Secretary-General [E/CN.4/Sub.2/AC.2/2005/4], submitted in accordance with a 2004 Subcommission resolution [YUN 2004, p. 773], summarized information on various slavery-related issues received from four Governments and ILO.

Subcommission action. On 11 August [res. 2005/29], the Subcommission recommended States' ratification of treaties on slavery-related issues and that human rights treaty bodies and other entities established under the auspices of specialized agencies take into account the obligations under the conventions on slavery in the discharge of their respective mandates. The Subcommission requested Ibrahim Salama (Egypt) to draft a working paper examining the feasibility of a study on the human rights dimensions of prostitution, taking into account the latest developments on that matter. The High Commissioner was asked to bring the Subcommission's resolution to the attention of States, international organizations and national human rights institutions and to request them to provide information to the Working Group.

Fund on slavery

Note by Secretariat. In a February note [E/CN.4/2005/86/Add.1], the Secretariat informed the Commission that, owing to the postponement of the tenth session of the Board of Trustees of the United Nations Voluntary Trust Fund on Contemporary Forms of Slavery (7-11 March), it would not be possible to submit the session's recommendations to the Commission in 2005. Interested Governments were invited to contact the Board of Trustees for more information.

Report of Secretary-General. In August [A/60/273], the Secretary-General reported that the Fund's Board of Trustees, at its tenth session (7-11 March), recommended 25 new project grants amounting to $215,330 to assist work in 15 countries in Africa, the Americas, Asia and Europe, and seven travel grants amounting to $14,800 to enable NGO representatives to participate in the deliberations of the Working Group on Contemporary Forms of Slavery (see above). The Board estimated that, in order to fulfil its mandate satisfactorily, the Fund would need an additional $600,500 before its eleventh session, scheduled for January 2006. On 16 March, the High Commissioner, on behalf of the Secretary-General, approved the Board's recommendations.

In a later report [E/CN.4/2006/76], the Secretary-General reported that contributions available to the Fund, as at 31 December 2005, stood at $809,010.

Subcommission action. On 11 August [res. 2005/30], the Subcommission urged Governments, NGOs and other private or public entities to contribute to the Fund and to do so by September to allow it to fulfil effectively its mandate in 2006.

On 16 December, the General Assembly took note of the Secretary-General's August report (**decision 60/533**).

Sexual exploitation during armed conflict

Report of High Commissioner. The High Commissioner, in a July report [E/CN.4/Sub.2/2005/33], reviewed the activities of the Commission, treaty monitoring bodies and various human rights mechanisms, as well as developments in international criminal, human rights and humanitarian law on the issue of systematic rape, sexual slavery and slavery-like practices in situations of armed conflict, since 2004. Noting that sexual abuse had become a tactic of war, being used to dominate and humiliate the civilian population, the High Commissioner highlighted two important relevant instruments designed to tackle the problem, which were adopted by the Commission in 2005: the updated Set of Principles for the protection and promotion of human rights through action to combat impunity (see p. 800) and the Basic Principles and Guidelines on the Right to Remedy and Reparation for Vic-

tims of Gross Violations of International Human Rights Law and Serious Violations of Humanitarian Law (see p. 792). Other relevant developments concerned the work of international commission of enquiry and tribunals for countries where sexual abuse had occurred within the context of armed conflicts, including those for Darfur (the Sudan), the former Yugoslavia, Rwanda and Sierra Leone, the work of the International Criminal Court (see p. 1402) and the involvement of UN peacekeeping personnel in sexual abuse and exploitation (see p. 165). The report noted that, despite the remedial measures taken, obstacles, such as the under-representation of women at decision-making levels, the persistence of violence against women in various spheres of life and their lack of access to financial resources, employment, education and social services, still posed challenges. The High Commissioner noted the lack of awareness of the seriousness of crimes of sexual and gender-based violence at the national level and recommended that States adopt legislation prohibiting rape and other forms of sexual violence. The training of law enforcement officials and other authorities involved in investigations of crimes of sexual violence should be strengthened to ensure that they were equipped to respond to victims' needs.

Subcommission action. On 11 August [res. 2005/27], the Subcommission reiterated that States should provide effective criminal penalties and compensation for unremedied violations, in order to end the cycle of impunity with regard to sexual violence committed during armed conflicts. It asked the High Commissioner to submit an updated report in 2006 on the issues of systematic rape, sexual slavery and slavery-like practices during armed conflict and encouraged States to promote human rights education on those issues.

Vulnerable groups

Women

Violence against women

Report of Secretary-General. In accordance with General Assembly resolution 50/166 [YUN 1995, p. 1188], the Secretary-General submitted to the Commission on Human Rights and to the Commission on the Status of Women the report of the United Nations Development Fund for Women regarding the Fund's activities to eliminate violence against women [E/CN.6/2005/7-E/CN.4/2005/70].

Reports of Special Rapporteur. In her annual report [E/CN.4/2005/72], the Special Rapporteur

on violence against women, its causes and consequences, Yakin Ertürk (Turkey), analysed the in-
terconnections between violence against women
and HIV/AIDS. The report considered violence
both as a cause and consequence of the disease,
the many forms of discrimination affecting
women living with HIV, particularly female migrants, refugees and minorities, and the obstacles to women's access to medical care and justice.
Against that background, the report noted that
HIV, which was rising in all parts of the world, was
spreading particularly among women and girls.
Of some 39 million people around the world
living with the disease, the percentage of women
affected was increasing significantly, currently
accounting for almost half of that number. In
sub-Saharan African, up to 57 per cent of those
living with HIV/AIDS were women, and in other
regions, including Latin America and the Caribbean, Asia and the Pacific, Eastern Europe and
Central Asia, the number was increasing. The
pandemic illustrated the complex manifestations
of gender inequality as it affected women, and
which was compounded by such other sources of
oppression as discrimination and patriarchy, sub-
jugating women to continuous violence and making them susceptible to HIV/AIDS. Although HIV-
related human rights were protected under international human rights law, States had yet to respond effectively to gender inequality as the root
cause and consequence of the gender-specific
manifestations of the disease. The report concluded that programmes aimed at the prevention
and treatment of HIV/AIDS could not succeed
without challenging the structures of unequal
power relations between men and women. It recommended measures for eliminating violence
against women; addressing the gender dimension of HIV/AIDS, discrimination and stigma; ensuring equal access to health care for women; empowering women for the full enjoyment of
human rights; and promoting a global coalition
against HIV/AIDS.

An addendum to the report [E/CN.4/2005/
72/Add.1 & Corr. 1] summarized communications
and urgent appeals on alleged cases of violence
against women, which the Special Rapporteur
had transmitted to 45 Governments, and the replies received thereto.

The Special Rapporteur visited the Russian
Federation (17-24 December 2004) [E/CN.4/2006/
61/Add.2], where she addressed violence stemming from the insecurity in the North Caucus
and domestic violence in the Federation at large.
The Special Rapporteur found that violence
against women in the Federation posed a major
challenge in terms of the Government's human
rights obligations and sustained security. Al-

though the Government was well equipped to
mobilize society to end such violence, public discourse on policy regarding gender equality was
hampered by the lack of national machinery for
the advancement of women. The Special Rapporteur identified key measures and initiatives
needed to protect and promote women's rights
and to eliminate violence against them, including Government action to empower them and improve their access to justice.

In Iran (29 January–6 February) [E/CN.4/
2006/61/Add.3], the Special Rapporteur found that
violence against women was ingrained in gender
inequality, perpetuated by patriarchal values and
attitudes based on male supremacy, and by State-
promoted institutional structures founded on
gender-biased, hardline interpretations of religious principles. Although most Iranian women
had access to health care, education, and to some
extent, employment and political participation,
gender-based legal provisions and practices that
rendered them vulnerable to violence in the
country persisted. The ruling clergy's reading of
the *sharia* (Islamic) law, which shaped attitudes
and institutional structures, tended towards con-
servative and gender-based interpretations. Violence against women in that context was rarely
acknowledged as a serious problem by the authorities, and as such, was rarely reported by
the victims. While the Government had taken
some steps to address violence against women,
more needed to be done to deal with the full
spectrum of such violence. The Special Rapporteur addressed recommendations to the Government, advocating the adoption and observation
of international human rights standards; the enhancement of women's access to justice through
transparent legal and judicial reforms; the prioritization of the elimination of violence against
women as a public policy issue, to prevent, investigate and punish all acts of violence against
women, whether perpetrated by private individuals or State actors; and the promotion and
support of the empowerment of women in all
spheres of life.

In Mexico (21-25 February) [E/CN.4/2006/
61/Add.4], the Special Rapporteur also found that
the high level of violence against women was both
the consequence and symptom of widespread
gender discrimination and inequality. Official
records indicated that one out of every four
women had been the victim of physical violence
and one in six had experienced sexual violence.
The *machista* culture, which relegated women to
a subordinate role in their family and community, often denied them an independent existence and made it difficult for them to escape
abusive relationships. The most vulnerable to vi-

olence were migrant women, many of whom travelled unaccompanied and without appropriate travel documents or financial resources, as well as indigenous women. The Special Rapporteur also examined reports of murders and disappearances of women in the State of Chihuahua on Mexico's border with the United States, and found impunity for perpetrators continuing as a result of the indifferent and negligent investigations by the authorities. Despite some Government efforts to control violence against women, more needed to be done. The Special Rapporteur recommended that the Government end impunity for violence against women; investigate and prosecute the perpetrators; provide protective and support services; create a gender-sensitive information and knowledge base; strengthen institutional infrastructure for the advancement of women; and promote training, and awareness-raising programmes.

Commission action. On 19 April [res. 2005/41], the Commission, condemning all acts of violence against women and girls, stressed the importance of efforts to eliminate impunity in that regard in situations of armed conflict, including by prosecuting gender-related crimes and crimes of sexual violence, providing protective measures, counselling or other appropriate assistance to victims and witnesses and by integrating a gender perspective into efforts to end impunity. The Special Rapporteur was asked to cooperate with other special procedures of the Commission, regional and intergovernmental organizations and their mechanisms engaged in promoting the rights of women and girls, and to report orally to the General Assembly in 2005. The Secretary-General was asked to assist her.

On 25 July, the Economic and Social Council took note of the Commission's resolution and requested the Special Rapporteur to present an oral report to the Assembly at its sixtieth (2005) session (**decision 2005/266**).

Further report of Special Rapporteur. The Special Rapporteur visited Afghanistan (9-19 July) [E/CN.4/2006/61/Add.5], where domestic violence, rape, trafficking and other forms of violence against women had reportedly escalated, owing to the conflict and post-conflict situations affecting the country in recent years. The consequent destruction of State structures, poverty, the lack of human and institutional capacity, and insecurity in the country contributed to women's vulnerability and the perpetuation of severe violence against them, illustrated by reports of rape, trafficking and forced marriages, including child marriages. The prevailing power blocks tended to legitimize much of the transgression of women's rights, based on _sharia_ law or Islamic

code, and perpetrators enjoyed impunity because the law enforcement and justice systems were generally dysfunctional and biased against women. Although some changes in Afghanistan's legal and institutional framework, introduced after the fall of the Taliban regime, had relatively improved the situation of women, including the adoption of the new Constitution recognizing the equal rights of men and women [YUN 2004, p. 311], the Special Rapporteur noted that the extraordinary level of violence against women was embedded in a traditional system of male domination in which women had no status as independent persons. She addressed recommendations to the Government, the international community and NGOs on issues relating to: State-building and sense of citizenry; family and criminal law; public awareness and targeted information campaigns on women's rights; the situation of women in detention; expanding and strengthening safe houses; data collection and research; prioritizing women's human rights; and the elimination of discrimination against women in public policy.

Traditional practices affecting the health of women and girls

Report of Special Rapporteur. In response to a 2004 Subcommission request [YUN 2004, p. 777], the Special Rapporteur on traditional practices affecting the health of women and the girl child, Halima Warzazi (Morocco), submitted a July final report [E/CN.4/Sub.2/2005/36] synthesizing her previous work. The report examined the origins of those practices, reviewed related actions taken by the Subcommission and identified the main practices warranting close scrutiny by the international community and the current situation regarding those practices, including female genital mutilation; "son" preference and its impact on nutritional priorities and its consequences, such as female infanticide and prenatal selection; and forced marriage, early marriage and crimes and acts of violence associated with dowries. The Special Rapporteur concluded that the policies and actions aimed at terminating harmful practices had to be directed towards raising the status of women in society from the earliest stage. She urged States to accelerate the drafting of legislation that outlawed all forms of violence against women and girls, including harmful traditional practices, and which prescribed penalties commensurate with the gravity of such acts. Those measures should be accompanied by national information and awareness campaigns.

Subcommission action. On 11 August [res. 2005/28], the Subcommission, taking note of the

Special Rapporteur's decision that her July report (see above) would be her final report on the subject, invited the Commission to request the Special Rapporteur on violence against women, its causes and consequences to continue the systematic examination of harmful traditional practices affecting the health of women and girls. It called on Governments to give full attention to the implementation of the 1994 Plan of Action for the Elimination of Harmful Traditional Practices Affecting the Health of Women and Children [YUN 1994, p. 1123] in their countries. The Subcommission reiterated its 2003 proposal [YUN 2003, p. 778] that three seminars be held in Africa, Asia and Europe to review progress achieved and to explore ways of overcoming obstacles in implementing the Plan of Action and asked the High Commissioner to help raise funds towards that end.

The girl child

On 19 April [res. 2005/44], the Commission, by a recorded vote of 52 to 1, called upon States to take measures, including legal reforms, to ensure girls' enjoyment of human rights and fundamental freedoms and to eliminate discrimination and all forms of violence against them, including harmful traditional practices, sexual abuse, son preference and early marriages.

(See also p. 1256).

Mainstreaming women's rights

Reports of Secretary-General. In response to a 2004 Commission request [YUN 2004, p. 778], the Secretary-General, in a January report [E/CN.4/2005/68], described measures taken to integrate a gender perspective into the work of the UN system by Commission mechanisms and procedures, human rights treaty bodies, OHCHR and human rights field presences. It also examined the participation of women in human rights mechanisms and activities. The report noted that, while attention had steadily grown regarding women's human rights in the work of the UN human rights system, the use of gender analysis and integration of a gender perspective in that work had been more varied and less methodical. Gender balance continued to be a problem among individuals carrying out the Commission's thematic and country-specific mandates, as women accounted for only 26.4 per cent of Commission mandate-holders in 2004. Also, while four of the six Special Rapporteurs reporting to the Subcommission were women, only eight of its 26 members were female. The report concluded that the participation of women in the work of human rights mechanisms was important in en-

suring that sufficient attention was paid to women's rights and gender issues. However, the full implementation of the gender mainstreaming strategy required more regular training of human rights staff, support for the work of gender focal points, the availability of tools to facilitate the integration of a gender perspective, and engaging in gender analysis and monitoring of the implementation of the strategy in all human rights activities. The report suggested, among other things, that the Commission encourage greater gender balance in the nomination, designation and election of experts to human rights mechanisms and give greater attention to women's participation in human rights activities and the benefits they could derive from doing so.

A further report [E/CN.4/2005/69-E/CN.6/2005/6] of the Secretary-General presented the joint 2005 work plan of the UN Division for the Advancement of Women and OHCHR.

Commission action. On 19 April [res. 2005/42], the Commission decided to integrate a gender perspective into all of its agenda items, and encourage Member States to promote gender balance by regularly nominating more female candidates for election to human rights treaty bodies and for appointment to UN bodies. It also encouraged the Secretary-General to ensure implementation of the joint work plan (see above), elaborate his plan annually, identify obstacles/impediments and areas for further collaboration, and submit them regularly to the Commission and to the Commission on the Status of Women. The Secretary-General was further asked to report in 2007.

Trafficking in women and girls

Reports of Special Rapporteur. In response to a 2004 Commission request [YUN 2004, p. 779], the Special Rapporteur on trafficking in persons, especially women and children, Sigma Huda (Bangladesh), submitted her first report [E/CN.4/2005/71]. The report described the content and scope of the mandate, its legal framework and the methods of work proposed by the Special Rapporteur, including communication with Governments, country visits, the consideration of thematic issues and cooperation with relevant partners. The report also highlighted the Special Rapporteur's activities since her appointment in 2004 [YUN 2004, p. 779]. She observed that the majority of victims of trafficking, often for sexual exploitation, were women and girls, and that the phenomenon represented a denial of all human rights. As trafficking continued to be treated as a "law and order" problem in many contexts, she intended to highlight its causes and human rights implications and to recommend measures aimed at preventing it through a human rights approach and the upholding of the rights of victims.

The Special Rapporteur visited Bosnia and Herzegovina (21-28 February) [E/CN.4/2005/71/Add.1; E/CN.4/2006/62/Add.2] to gather lessons learned from combating trafficking, to further study the situation and to recommend measures to assist the Government in addressing its root causes and in protecting victims' rights. To combat the problem, the country had adopted the 2001 National Action Plan, which focused on prevention, detection and prosecution of crimes relating to human trafficking, as well as assistance to and protection of victims. The framework for implementing the plan involved institutional arrangements, anti-trafficking interventions, border controls, awareness-raising, legislative reform, prosecution of the perpetrators, and a review of the situation regarding trafficking in children. While acknowledging that the Action Plan had facilitated progress in tackling the problem, the Special Rapporteur drew attention to persisting weaknesses in coordination, harmonization, the provision of training on new legislation and procedures, awareness-raising and education to eliminate other gender-based stereotypes, sensitization of law enforcement officials and the judiciary, assistance to victims and witness protection. The lack of resources had also hampered efforts to implement anti-trafficking laws. The Special Rapporteur addressed a number of recommendations to the Government, civil society and the international community for tackling those weaknesses and supported the country's efforts to combat trafficking and protect its victims. She welcomed a revision of the Action Plan and encouraged the Government to take the lead in implementing it, including in supporting shelters and rehabilitation programmes.

The Special Rapporteur visited Lebanon (7-16 September) [E/CN.4/2006/62/Add.3], following allegations from that country and other Middle Eastern States of widespread exploitation of foreign nationals and significant human trafficking in the region. Identifying the most vulnerable as female migrants from such countries as Sri Lanka, the Philippines and Ethiopia, among others, working as domestic servants in Lebanese homes, the Special Rapporteur examined their situation and highlighted the manifestations of their exploitation, the lack of State protection, alternative mechanisms for protection, and the situation of runaway workers. Other vulnerable groups included women in the sex industry and children, who were trafficked into organized begging and other forms of exploitation, including early or

forced marriage. Despite some progress, the Government still fell short of fulfilling its international obligations with regard to human trafficking, having failed to adequately organize and regulate the large-scale migration, which the country had experienced since the end of the period of conflict in the country. In her recommendations, the Special Rapporteur called upon the Government to: enhance national and international cooperation; criminalize all forms of trafficking and strengthen the labour framework; identify, protect and safely repatriate trafficked persons; and ensure the effective prosecution of acts of trafficking and related crimes. She called upon the countries of origin of migrants to offer them consular protection, preferably on the basis of bilateral agreements concluded with Lebanon, and asked civil society and the international community to focus more on the situation of migrant workers, foreign women in the sex industry and street children.

Children

On 19 April [res. 2005/44], the Commission, by a recorded vote of 52 to 1, called upon States to ensure that children were entitled to civil, political, economic, social and cultural rights without discrimination; incorporate special measures in programmes to combat racial discrimination, in accordance with the principle of the best interests of the child in programmes to combat racial discrimination; and to protect children from all forms of violence, including physical, mental and sexual violence, and to especially protect the rights of the girl child in that regard. States were also urged to: intensify efforts to ensure the implementation of the rights of the child to birth registration and preservation of identity, as recognized by law; ensure that they were not separated from their parents against their will, except when consistent with the Convention on the Rights of the Child (see p. 730), and address the problem of children growing up without parents; cooperate with the international community in supporting and participating in global poverty eradication efforts, particularly regarding investments in children and the realization of their rights to contribute to their social and economic development; ensure children enjoyed the highest attainable standard of physical and mental health and support and rehabilitate them and their families affected by HIV/AIDS; ensure children had access to good quality education; protect the rights of children with disabilities, migrant children, street children, refugee or internally displaced children; ensure that those arrested, detained or imprisoned were provided legal assistance and not sentenced to forced labour, corporal punishment or deprived of access to healthcare; eliminate child labour; facilitate the social reintegration of children in difficult situations; and ensure those affected by natural disasters were provided with access to basic social services.

(Other aspects of the Commission's resolution—child labour, the prevention and eradication of the sale of children, child prostitution and child pornography, and protection of children affected by armed conflict—are covered below.)

On 23 December [meeting 69], the General Assembly, on the recommendation of the Third Committee [A/60/505 & Corr.1], adopted **resolution 60/231** by recorded vote (130-1-0) [agenda item 67].

Rights of the child

The General Assembly,

Recalling its previous resolutions on the rights of the child, the most recent of which is resolution 59/261 of 23 December 2004, as well as Commission on Human Rights resolution 2005/44 of 19 April 2005,

Emphasizing that the Convention on the Rights of the Child must constitute the standard in the promotion and protection of the rights of the child, and bearing in mind the importance of the Optional Protocols to the Convention, as well as other human rights instruments,

Reaffirming the Vienna Declaration and Programme of Action, the United Nations Millennium Declaration, the outcome document of the twenty-seventh special session of the General Assembly on children, entitled "A world fit for children", and the outcome document of the twenty-sixth special session of the General Assembly on HIV/AIDS, entitled "Global Crisis - Global Action",

Taking note with appreciation of the reports of the Secretary-General on progress made towards achieving the commitments set out in the outcome document of the twenty-seventh special session of the General Assembly and on the status of the Convention on the Rights of the Child and the issues raised in Assembly resolution 59/261, as well as the reports of the Chairman of the Committee on the Rights of the Child, the Special Representative of the Secretary-General for Children and Armed Conflict and the Independent Expert for the United Nations study on violence against children,

Reaffirming that the best interests of the child shall be a primary consideration in all actions concerning children,

Recognizing the importance of incorporating a child-protection perspective across the human rights agenda, as highlighted in the outcome of the 2005 World Summit,

Profoundly concerned that the situation of children in many parts of the world remains critical, in an increasingly globalized environment, as a result of the persistence of poverty, social inequality, inadequate social and economic conditions, pandemics, in particular HIV/AIDS, malaria and tuberculosis, environmental

damage, natural disasters, armed conflict, displacement, violence, abuse, exploitation, trafficking in children and their organs, child prostitution, child pornography and child sex tourism, neglect, illiteracy, hunger, intolerance, discrimination, racism, xenophobia, gender inequality, disability and inadequate legal protection, and convinced that urgent and effective national and international action is called for,

Underlining the need for mainstreaming a gender perspective in all policies and programmes relating to children, and recognizing the child as a rights holder in all policies and programmes relating to children,

I
Implementation of the Convention on the Rights of the Child and the Optional Protocols thereto

1. *Reaffirms* that the general principles of, inter alia, the best interests of the child, non-discrimination, participation and survival and development provide the framework for all actions concerning children, including adolescents;

2. *Urges* States that have not yet done so to become parties to the Convention on the Rights of the Child and the Optional Protocols thereto as a matter of priority and to implement them fully by, inter alia, putting in place effective national legislation and policies;

3. *Urges* States parties to withdraw reservations that are incompatible with the object and purpose of the Convention or the Optional Protocols thereto and to consider reviewing other reservations with a view to withdrawing them;

4. *Welcomes* the work of the Committee on the Rights of the Child, and calls upon all States to strengthen their cooperation with the Committee, to comply in a timely manner with their reporting obligations under the Convention and the Optional Protocols thereto, in accordance with the guidelines elaborated by the Committee, and to take into account its recommendations on implementation of the Convention;

5. *Requests* all relevant organs of the United Nations system and United Nations mechanisms regularly and systematically to incorporate a strong child rights perspective throughout all activities in the fulfilment of their mandates, as well as to ensure that their staff are trained in child rights matters, and calls upon States to continue to cooperate closely with all these mechanisms, in particular the special rapporteurs and special representatives of the United Nations system;

6. *Encourages* States to strengthen their national statistical capacities and to use statistics disaggregated, inter alia, by age, gender and other relevant factors that may lead to disparities and other statistical indicators at the national, subregional, regional and international levels to develop and assess social policies and programmes so that economic and social resources are used efficiently and effectively for the full realization of the rights of the child;

II
Promotion and protection of the rights of the child

Registration, family relations and adoption

7. *Once again urges* all States to intensify their efforts to comply with their obligations under the Convention on the Rights of the Child to preserve the child's identity, including nationality and family relations, as recognized by law, to allow for the registration

of the child immediately after birth, to ensure that registration procedures are simple, expeditious and effective and provided at minimal cost and to raise awareness of the importance of birth registration at the national, regional and local levels;

8. *Encourages* States to adopt and enforce laws and improve the implementation of policies and programmes to protect children growing up without parents or caregivers, recognizing that, where alternative care is necessary, family- and community-based care should be promoted over placement in institutions;

9. *Calls upon* States to guarantee, to the extent consistent with the obligations of each State, the right of a child whose parents reside in different States to maintain, on a regular basis, save in exceptional circumstances, personal relations and direct contact with both parents by providing means of access and visitation in both States and by respecting the principle that both parents have common responsibilities for the upbringing and development of their children;

10. *Also calls upon* States to address and pay particular attention to cases of international parental or familial child abduction, and encourages States to engage in multilateral and bilateral cooperation to resolve these cases, preferably by accession to the Hague Convention on the Civil Aspects of International Child Abduction, and to facilitate, inter alia, the return of the child to the country in which he or she resided immediately before the removal or retention;

11. *Further calls upon* States to take all necessary measures to prevent and combat illegal adoptions and all adoptions that are not in the best interests of the child;

Economic and social well-being of children

12. *Calls upon* States and the international community to create an environment in which the well-being of the child is ensured, inter alia, by:

(a) Cooperating, supporting and participating in global efforts for poverty eradication at the global, regional and country levels, recognizing that strengthened availability and effective allocation of resources are required at all these levels, in order to ensure that all the internationally agreed development and poverty eradication goals, including those set out in the United Nations Millennium Declaration, are realized within their time framework, reaffirming that investments in children and the realization of their rights are among the most effective ways to eradicate poverty;

(b) Taking all necessary measures to ensure the right of the child to the enjoyment of the highest attainable standard of health and developing sustainable health systems and social services, ensuring access to such systems and services without discrimination, paying particular attention to adequate food and nutrition and assigning priority to activities and programmes aimed at preventing addictions, in particular addiction to alcohol and tobacco, and the abuse of narcotic drugs, psychotropic substances and inhalants and by, inter alia, securing appropriate prenatal and post-natal care for mothers;

(c) Recognizing the right to education on the basis of equal opportunity and non-discrimination by making primary education compulsory and available free to all children, ensuring that all children have access to education of good quality, as well as making secondary education generally available and accessible to all, in particular through the progressive introduction of free education, bearing in mind that special measures to ensure equal access, including affirmative action, contribute to achieving equal opportunity and combating exclusion;

(d) Designing and implementing programmes to provide social services and support to pregnant adolescents and adolescent mothers, in particular by enabling them to continue and complete their education;

Violence against children

13. *Condemns* all forms of violence against children, including physical, mental and sexual violence, torture, child abuse and exploitation, hostage-taking, domestic violence, trafficking in or sale of children and their organs, paedophilia, child prostitution, child pornography and child sex tourism as well as the increasing phenomenon of gang-related violence;

14. *Also condemns* the abduction of children, in particular extortive abduction and abduction of children in situations of armed conflict, including for the recruitment and use of children in armed conflicts, and urges States to take all appropriate measures to secure their unconditional release, rehabilitation, reintegration and reunification with their families;

15. *Urges* States:

(a) To strengthen efforts to prevent and protect children from all forms of violence through a comprehensive approach;

(b) To end impunity for perpetrators of crimes against children, investigate and prosecute all acts of violence and impose appropriate penalties;

(c) To protect children from abuse by government officials such as the police, law enforcement authorities and employees and officials in detention centres or welfare institutions;

(d) To take measures to protect children from violence or abuse in schools, including sexual abuse and intimidation, maltreatment and bullying, to establish complaint mechanisms that are age- and gender-appropriate and accessible to children and to take measures to eliminate the use of corporal punishment in schools;

(e) To strengthen international cooperation and mutual assistance to end impunity for crimes against children;

16. *Recognizes* the contribution of the International Criminal Court in ending impunity for the most serious crimes against children, including genocide, crimes against humanity and war crimes, and calls upon States not to grant amnesties for such crimes;

Non-discrimination

17. *Calls upon* all States to ensure the enjoyment by children of all their civil, political, economic, social and cultural rights without discrimination of any kind;

18. *Notes with concern* the large number of children who are victims of racism, racial discrimination, xenophobia and related intolerance, stresses the need to incorporate special measures, in accordance with the principle of the best interests of the child and respect for his or her views, in programmes to combat racism, racial discrimination, xenophobia and related intolerance, and calls upon States to provide special support and ensure equal access to services for all children;

19. *Calls upon* States to take all necessary measures, including legal reforms where appropriate, to eliminate all forms of discrimination against girls and all forms of violence, including female infanticide and prenatal sex selection, rape, sexual abuse and harmful traditional or customary practices, including female genital mutilation, marriage without the free and full consent of the intending spouses, early marriage and forced sterilization, by enacting and enforcing legislation and by formulating, where appropriate, comprehensive, multidisciplinary and coordinated national plans, programmes or strategies to protect girls;

20. *Also calls upon* States to take the necessary measures to ensure the full and equal enjoyment of all human rights and fundamental freedoms by children with disabilities in both the public and the private spheres, including access to good quality education and health care and protection from violence, abuse and neglect, and to develop and, where it already exists, to enforce legislation to prohibit discrimination against them in order to ensure their inherent dignity, promote their self-reliance and facilitate their active participation and integration in the community, taking into account the particularly difficult situation of children with disabilities living in poverty;

Promoting and protecting the rights of children, including children in particularly difficult situations

21. *Calls upon* all States to prevent violations of the rights of children working and/or living on the street, including discrimination, arbitrary detention and extrajudicial, arbitrary or summary executions, torture, and all kinds of violence and exploitation, and to bring the perpetrators to justice, to adopt and implement policies for the protection, social and psychosocial rehabilitation and reintegration of those children and to adopt economic, social and educational strategies to address the problems of children working and/or living on the street;

22. *Also calls upon* all States to protect refugee, asylum-seeking and internally displaced children, in particular those who are unaccompanied, who are particularly exposed to risks in connection with armed conflict, such as recruitment, sexual violence and exploitation, stressing the need for States as well as the international community to continue to pay more systematic and in-depth attention to the special assistance, protection and development needs of those children through, inter alia, programmes aimed at rehabilitation and physical and psychological recovery, and to programmes for voluntary repatriation and, wherever possible, local integration and resettlement, to give priority to family tracing and family reunification and, where appropriate, to cooperate with international humanitarian and refugee organizations, including by facilitating their work;

23. *Further calls upon* all States to ensure, for children belonging to minorities and vulnerable groups, including migrant children and indigenous children, the enjoyment of all human rights as well as access to health care, social services and education on an equal basis with others and to ensure that all such children, in particular victims of violence and exploitation, receive special protection and assistance;

24. *Calls upon* all States to protect the inheritance and property rights of orphans in law and in practice, with particular attention to underlying gender-based discrimination, which may interfere with the fulfilment of these rights;

25. *Also calls upon* all States to translate into concrete action their commitment to the progressive and effective elimination of child labour that is likely to be hazardous or to interfere with the child's education or to be harmful to the child's health or physical, mental, spiritual, moral or social development, to eliminate immediately the worst forms of child labour, to promote education as a key strategy in this regard, including the creation of vocational training and apprenticeship programmes and the integration of working children into the formal education system and to examine and devise economic policies, where necessary, in cooperation with the international community, that address factors contributing to these forms of child labour;

26. *Urges* all States that have not yet done so to consider signing and ratifying or acceding to the Convention concerning Minimum Age for Admission to Employment, 1973 (Convention No. 138) and the Convention concerning the Prohibition and Immediate Action for the Elimination of the Worst Forms of Child Labour, 1999 (Convention No. 182) of the International Labour Organization;

27. *Calls upon* all States, in particular those States in which the death penalty has not been abolished:

(a) To abolish by law, as soon as possible, the death penalty for those below the age of 18 years at the time of the commission of the offence;

(b) To comply with their obligations as assumed under relevant provisions of international human rights instruments, including the Convention on the Rights of the Child and the International Covenant on Civil and Political Rights;

(c) To keep in mind the safeguards guaranteeing protection of the rights of those facing the death penalty and the guarantees set out in United Nations safeguards adopted by the Economic and Social Council;

28. *Also calls upon* all States to ensure that no child in detention is sentenced to forced labour or corporal punishment or deprived of access to and provision of health-care services, hygiene and environmental sanitation, education, basic instruction and vocational training;

29. *Encourages* States to promote actions, including through bilateral and multilateral technical cooperation and financial assistance, for the social reintegration of children in difficult situations, considering, inter alia, views, skills and capacities that those children have developed in the conditions in which they lived and, where appropriate, with their meaningful participation;

Prevention and eradication of the sale of children, child prostitution and child pornography

30. *Calls upon* all States:

(a) To criminalize and penalize effectively all forms of sexual exploitation and sexual abuse of children, including all acts of paedophilia, including within the family or for commercial purposes, child pornography and child prostitution, child sex tourism, trafficking in children, the sale of children and their organs and the use of the Internet for these purposes, and to take effective measures against the criminalization of children who are victims of exploitation;

(b) To ensure the prosecution of offenders, whether local or foreign, by the competent national authorities, either in the country in which the crime was committed, in the country of which the offender is a national or resident, in the country of which the victim is a national or on any other basis permitted under domestic law, and for these purposes to afford one another the greatest measure of assistance in connection with investigations or criminal or extradition proceedings;

(c) To increase cooperation at all levels to prevent and dismantle networks trafficking or selling children and their organs and, for those States that have not yet done so, to consider signing and ratifying or acceding to the Protocol to Prevent, Suppress and Punish Trafficking in Persons, Especially Women and Children, supplementing the United Nations Convention against Transnational Organized Crime;

(d) In cases of trafficking in children, the sale of children, child prostitution and child pornography, to address effectively the needs of victims, including their safety and protection, physical and psychological recovery and full reintegration into society, including through bilateral and multilateral technical cooperation and financial assistance;

(e) To combat the existence of a market that encourages such criminal practices against children, including through the adoption, effective application and enforcement of preventive, rehabilitative and punitive measures targeting customers or individuals who sexually exploit or sexually abuse children, as well as by ensuring public awareness;

(f) To contribute to the elimination of the sale of children, child prostitution and child pornography by adopting a holistic approach, addressing the contributing factors, including underdevelopment, poverty, economic disparities, inequitable socio-economic structures, dysfunctional families, lack of education, urban-rural migration, gender discrimination, criminal or irresponsible adult sexual behaviour, child sex tourism, organized crime, harmful traditional practices, armed conflicts and trafficking in children;

Children affected by armed conflict

31. *Strongly condemns* any recruitment or use of children in armed conflict contrary to international law, as well as other violations and abuses committed against children affected by armed conflict, and urges all States and other parties to armed conflict that are engaged in such practices to end them;

32. *Reaffirms* the essential roles of the General Assembly, the Economic and Social Council and the Commission on Human Rights for the promotion and protection of the rights and welfare of children, including children affected by armed conflict, and notes the increasing role played by the Security Council in ensuring protection for children affected by armed conflict;

33. *Calls upon* States:

(a) When ratifying the Optional Protocol to the Convention on the Rights of the Child on the involvement of children in armed conflict, to raise the minimum age for voluntary recruitment of persons into the national armed forces from that set out in article 38, paragraph 3, of the Convention, bearing in mind that under the Convention persons under 18 years of age are entitled to special protection, and to adopt safeguards to ensure that such recruitment is not forced or coerced;

(b) To take all feasible measures to ensure the demobilization and effective disarmament of children used in armed conflicts and to implement effective measures for their rehabilitation, physical and psychological recovery and reintegration into society, in particular through educational measures, taking into account the rights and the specific needs and capacities of girls;

(c) To protect children affected by armed conflict, in particular from violations of international humanitarian law and human rights law and to ensure that they receive timely, effective humanitarian assistance, in accordance with international humanitarian law, including the Geneva Conventions of 12 August 1949, and calls upon the international community to hold those responsible for violations accountable, inter alia, through the International Criminal Court;

(d) To take all necessary measures, in accordance with international humanitarian law and human rights law, as a matter of priority, to prevent the recruitment and use of children by armed groups, as distinct from the armed forces of a State, including the adoption of policies that do not tolerate the recruitment and use of children in armed conflict, and legal measures necessary to prohibit and criminalize such practices;

34. *Notes with appreciation* the adoption of Security Council resolution 1612(2005) of 26 July 2005 on the protection of children affected by armed conflict and the efforts of the Secretary-General to implement the monitoring and reporting mechanism called for in that resolution, with the participation of and in cooperation with national Governments and relevant United Nations and civil society actors, including at the country level;

35. *Recognizes* the progress achieved since the establishment of the mandate of the Special Representative of the Secretary-General for Children and Armed Conflict in paragraphs 35 to 37 of General Assembly resolution 51/77 of 12 December 1996, and, bearing in mind the report of the Secretary-General on the United Nations system-wide response to children and armed conflict, recommends that the Secretary-General extend the mandate of the Special Representative for a further period of three years;

36. *Recalls* the recommendation contained in resolution 51/77 that the Special Representative foster international cooperation to ensure respect for children's rights in situations of armed conflict and contribute to the coordination of efforts by Governments and relevant United Nations bodies, as well as the request to Governments and relevant United Nations bodies to cooperate with the Special Representative;

III
Children infected with and affected by HIV/AIDS

37. *Acknowledges* that prevention, care, support, including psychosocial support, and treatment for those infected with and affected by HIV/AIDS, including children, are mutually reinforcing elements of an

effective response and must be integrated in a comprehensive approach to combat the pandemic, reaffirms that the full realization of human rights and fundamental freedoms for all is an essential element in the global response to the HIV/AIDS pandemic, and reaffirms also the importance of the elimination of all forms of discrimination against people living with or at risk of HIV/AIDS, especially those most vulnerable;

38. *Calls upon* States:

(*a*) To ensure universal access to comprehensive information related to HIV/AIDS prevention by 2010 through education, life skills training for adolescents and the use of child-targeted media and to ensure that this information is relevant, gender- and age-appropriate and timely, engaging the meaningful participation of children and their parents or caregivers in its development and recognizing children as agents of change, to enable them to protect themselves from HIV infection;

(*b*) To support adolescents to be able to deal positively and responsibly with their sexuality in order to protect themselves from HIV/AIDS infection and to implement measures to increase their capacity to protect themselves from HIV/AIDS, through, inter alia, the provision of health care, including for sexual and reproductive health, and through prevention education that promotes gender equality;

(*c*) To put in place strategies, policies and programmes that identify and address those factors that make individuals particularly vulnerable to HIV infection in order to complement prevention programmes that address activities that place individuals at risk of HIV infection, such as risky and unsafe sexual behaviour and injecting drug use;

(*d*) To ensure that, in preventing and addressing HIV/AIDS, particular attention is paid to girls, deeply concerned that the global HIV/AIDS pandemic disproportionately affects women and girls, that the majority of new HIV infections occur among young people and that unequal legal, economic and social status, negative or judgemental attitudes that limit the ability of girls to take preventive measures and violence against girls increase their vulnerability to HIV/AIDS;

(*e*) To take measures to prevent mother-to-child transmission of HIV, including the provision of essential drugs, appropriate antenatal, delivery and postpartum care, voluntary and confidential counselling and testing services for pregnant women and their partners and support for mothers, such as counselling on infant feeding options and access to treatment, including antiretroviral treatment;

39. *Also calls upon* States:

(*a*) To ensure full and equal access for children to voluntary, free and confidential counselling, testing and care, including affordable and effective medication for the treatment of HIV and AIDS and associated opportunistic infections, recognizing the need for youth-friendly services, and urges States to work with the pharmaceutical industry and other stakeholders to ensure the development and universal availability of child-suitable medication and treatments;

(*b*) To strengthen partnerships and international cooperation at the national, regional and international levels in order to offer infected and affected children medicines and related technology which are affordable, easy to use and readily available, in supporting developing countries that may not have the financial or human resources capacity to mount an effective response to the HIV/AIDS pandemic;

(*c*) To integrate all aspects of HIV and AIDS prevention, treatment, care and support into all health-care programmes and services;

40. *Further calls upon* States to take effective measures to eliminate stigmatization and discrimination on the basis of the HIV or AIDS status, actual or presumed, of the child or parent and to ensure that HIV or AIDS status does not stand in the way of the enjoyment by the child of all human rights;

41. *Calls upon* States to make suitable provision for children affected by HIV/AIDS who can no longer live with their parents to retain links with their wider family and community, urges all States to implement the United Nations Framework for the Protection, Care and Support of Orphans and Vulnerable Children Living in a World with HIV and AIDS and its key strategies, inter alia, by adopting and implementing, as an integral part of their comprehensive national planning and budgeting processes, national action plans for the protection and care of orphans and vulnerable children, and requests donors, the United Nations system and civil society to support their efforts;

42. *Urges* donors:

(*a*) To ensure, by 2007, a complete and successful replenishment of the Global Fund to Fight AIDS, Tuberculosis and Malaria, as well as the HIV/AIDS component of the work programmes of the agencies and programmes of the United Nations system engaged in the fight against HIV/AIDS, and notes that a major part of the international HIV and AIDS financing gap relates to children orphaned or made vulnerable by HIV/AIDS;

(*b*) To improve the effectiveness of their programmes through better alignment and elimination of duplication, and calls upon donors and the United Nations system to take forward the recommendations of the Global Task Team on Improving AIDS Coordination among Multilateral Institutions and International Donors;

Follow-up

43. *Decides:*

(*a*) To request the Secretary-General to submit to the General Assembly at its sixty-first session a report on the rights of the child, containing information on the status of the Convention on the Rights of the Child and the issues contained in the present resolution;

(*b*) To request the Special Representative of the Secretary-General for Children and Armed Conflict to continue to submit reports to the General Assembly and the Commission on Human Rights;

(*c*) To request the Independent Expert for the United Nations study on violence against children to present his final report to the General Assembly at its sixty-first session;

(*d*) To reiterate its invitation to the Chairman of the Committee on the Rights of the Child to present an oral report on the work of the Committee to the General Assembly at its sixty-first session as a way to enhance communication between the General Assembly and the Committee;

(*e*) To pay particular attention to the rights of children infected with and affected by HIV and AIDS at its special session on HIV and AIDS in 2006;

(f) To continue its consideration of this question at its sixty-first session under the item entitled "Promotion and protection of the rights of children", focusing section III on "Children and poverty".

RECORDED VOTE ON RESOLUTION 60/231:

In favour: Algeria, Andorra, Antigua and Barbuda, Argentina, Armenia, Australia, Austria, Azerbaijan, Bahrain, Bangladesh, Barbados, Belarus, Belgium, Benin, Brazil, Brunei Darussalam, Bulgaria, Burkina Faso, Cambodia, Canada, Chile, China, Colombia, Comoros, Costa Rica, Croatia, Cuba, Cyprus, Czech Republic, Denmark, Djibouti, Dominican Republic, Ecuador, Egypt, El Salvador, Eritrea, Estonia, Finland, France, Gambia, Georgia, Germany, Ghana, Greece, Guatemala, Guinea, Guyana, Hungary, Iceland, India, Indonesia, Iran, Iraq, Ireland, Italy, Jamaica, Japan, Jordan, Kazakhstan, Kuwait, Kyrgyzstan, Lao People's Democratic Republic, Latvia, Lesotho, Libyan Arab Jamahiriya, Liechtenstein, Lithuania, Luxembourg, Malawi, Malaysia, Maldives, Mali, Malta, Mauritania, Mauritius, Mexico, Monaco, Morocco, Myanmar, Namibia, Nepal, Netherlands, New Zealand, Niger, Nigeria, Norway, Oman, Pakistan, Panama, Peru, Philippines, Poland, Portugal, Qatar, Republic of Korea, Romania, Russian Federation, Rwanda, Samoa, San Marino, Saudi Arabia, Serbia and Montenegro, Singapore, Slovakia, Slovenia, South Africa, Spain, Sri Lanka, Sudan, Sweden, Switzerland, Syrian Arab Republic, Thailand, The former Yugoslav Republic of Macedonia, Timor-Leste, Togo, Trinidad and Tobago, Tunisia, Turkey, Uganda, Ukraine, United Arab Emirates, United Kingdom, United Republic of Tanzania, Uruguay, Uzbekistan, Venezuela, Yemen, Zambia, Zimbabwe.

Against: United States.

Abstaining: None.

The Third Committee adopted by separate recorded votes, paragraph 15 *(d)* by 125 to 17, with 13 abstentions; paragraph 27 by 109 to 28, with 21 abstentions; and paragraph 28 by 123 to 14, with 20 abstentions. The Assembly retained those paragraphs by recorded votes, respectively, of 95 to 11, with 14 abstentions; 85 to 20, with 16 abstentions; and 93 to 10, with 17 abstentions.

Violence against children

Report of Secretary-General. In response to a 2004 Commission request [YUN 2004, p. 785], the Secretary-General submitted a March progress report [E/CN.4/2005/75] on the study on violence against children, in accordance with General Assembly resolution 56/138 [YUN 2001, p. 681]. He noted that the independent expert appointed to lead the study, Paulo Sérgio Pinheiro (Brazil), had focused on gathering information on the topic, in order to provide an in-depth and global picture of the problem, documenting its nature, incidence, causes and consequences. As at February, 87 Governments had responded to a 2004 questionnaire on legal, institutional and policy frameworks to address the issue, which would lay the groundwork for the study. To encourage the submission of relevant information by other stakeholders, the expert had also designed an indicative outline of his final report, which was annexed to the current one. The expert emphasized that the views of children and youth should be reflected in the submissions. The expert also paid particular attention to relevant information available within the UN system and encouraged contributions from OHCHR, UNICEF, WHO and ILO. Further contributions were being sought from

the Committee on the Rights of the Child, which had recommended the study, the Commission's special procedures, other human rights bodies and NGOs. The expert was also gathering additional information through participation in several regional, subregional and national conferences on relevant issues.

Report of independent expert. Pursuant to General Assembly resolution 59/261 [YUN 2004, p. 779], the Secretary-General, by an August note [A/60/282], transmitted the report of independent expert Paulo Pinheiro, which summarized his activities, including those mentioned in the Secretary-General's report (see above). In addition to his ongoing efforts to collate responses to the questionnaire he had sent out to Governments previously, 117 of which had been received as at 16 August, the expert conducted regional, subregional and national consultations, undertook field visits to identify country experiences of violence against children and how to deal with them, and participated in several other thematic meetings designed to provide a forum for identifying existing research and the most effective practical approaches to eliminating violence against children and measures to protect them. The report also analysed the work of the Commission and the Subcommission special procedure mandate holders relating to the topic, as well as the concluding observations of the Committee on the Rights of the Child, which raised such key concerns as the insufficient financial and human resources allocated and the inadequacy of programmes established to prevent and combat the problem. The Committee observed, among other things, that children were not provided with adequate mechanisms to file complaints, and that in many cases, there were obstacles to prosecuting persons for child abuse and neglect. Also, rehabilitation measures for victims were lacking, as were comprehensive information and data on the different manifestations of violence against children. In completing his final report, the expert planned to build on the information emerging from the consultations and other action he had undertaken and would accord particular attention to the outcome of the analysis of responses to the questionnaire he had sent to Governments.

Commission action. On 19 April [res. 2005/44], the Commission, by a recorded vote of 52 to 1, called on States to prevent and protect children from all forms of violence, investigate and prosecute such violence and cases of torture against children and eliminate the use of corporal punishment in schools. The Secretary-General was asked submit his final report on the study of violence against children in 2006.

Sale of children, child prostitution and child pornography

Reports of Special Rapporteur. In response to a 2004 Commission request [YUN 2004, p. 786], the Special Rapporteur on the sale of children, child prostitution and child pronography, Juan Miguel Petit (Uruguay), submitted a report [E/CN.4/2005/78] on the prevention of child pornography on the Internet, based on information received from 51 Governments and from international organizations and NGOs, in response to a questionnaire he had circulated. The report examined the definition of child pornography in international instruments and national legislation, with particular reference to the Optional Protocol to the Convention on the Rights of the Child on the sale of children, child prostitution and child pornography and the Council of Europe Convention on Cybercrime, the two main international instruments on the issue. In that context, the report described national legislation relating to child pornography on the Internet, the work of national law-enforcement agencies in dealing with the issue, and domestic initiatives to combat it. Pointing to the challenges and potentially harmful use of the Internet, the report noted that cyberspace hosted an alarming quantity of child pornographic material and that chat rooms were increasingly being used by sexual predators for contacting children. Many countries still lacked legislation on child pornography and the resulting legal vacuum left a dangerous gap that exposed children to the risk of abuse, which was exacerbated by related impunity. The Special Rapporteur recommended that States ratify the Optional Protocol; attach criminal consequences to the conduct of each participant in the chain of child pornography, from production to possession; introduce legislation against "Internet grooming or luring" and on the obligations of Internet Service Providers (ISPs); and ensure that legislation on child pornography protected all children under the age of 18, regardless of the age of consent to sexual activity. He noted that more efforts were needed to identify the victims of abuse and to provide them with rehabilitation programmes and adequate compensation. Other recommendations related to awareness-raising campaigns, international cooperation and self-regulatory initiatives by the private sector.

Between 1 January and 31 December, the Special Rapporteur sent 34 communications to 25 countries regarding alleged cases relating to the sale of children, child prostitution and child pornography. Of those, replies were received from four Governments, with six other responses addressing communications he transmitted in previous years. The communications sent and replies thereto were summarized in a separate report [E/CN.4/2006/67/Add.1].

The Special Rapporteur visited Albania (31 October–7 November) [E/CN.4/2006/67/Add.2], followed by a mission to Greece (see below), in order to better understand the transnational elements of the phenomena of child trafficking and migration flows of unaccompanied children involving both countries. In Albania, he examined the situation relating to child trafficking, forms of child exploitation and the root causes and factors that protected against related risks. Other concerns included the phenomenon of unaccompanied children, domestic violence and sexual abuse, the situation of the Roma and Egyptian communities and their children, child labour, the role of the media and corruption in the public service. The Special Rapporteur found that the country had become a source of human trafficking, including children, for the purpose of sexual exploitation and forced labour. The main destinations were Italy, Greece and various other European countries. Albanian children who fell victim to trafficking were made to beg, wash car windows or to sell small items and flowers in the streets of Greece. Some of them were trafficked with the consent of their parents, as they were seen as assets to help their families cope. The internal prostitution market also appeared to be growing, and against that background, child trafficking occurred for the purpose of sexual exploitation, affecting mostly girls and young women. Despite some progress by the authorities in addressing the problem, including through the establishment of related legislative, institutional and policy frameworks and increased societal awareness, many challenges remained. The Special Rapporteur recommended various measures to the Government relating to the need for a functioning child protection system, social programmes for communities, creating the profession of specialized social workers, legislation, investigation and prosecution, and unaccompanied child migrants, among others.

In Greece (8-15 November) [E/CN.4/2006/67/Add.3], the Special Rapporteur further examined the transnational dynamics of child trafficking between that country and neighbouring Albania (see above) and found that, while the number of street children in the former had declined considerably, the problem of transnational child trafficking persisted. An appropriate system was not yet in place for detecting victims of such trafficking, and the child victims, together with adults, continued to be arrested, detained and deported on the grounds of illegal entry. Other issues of concern related to the deportation procedures and detention conditions of unaccompanied children, the lack of an institutionalized protection system and the status of cooperation with NGOs. While acknowledging progress in the country's efforts to combat the problem, the Special Rapporteur urged the Government to address remaining challenges and recommended measures relating to, among other things, international standards, legislation and agreements, including the decriminalization of begging; clear rules and standards for identifying victims; the need to end the detention of alien minors for illegal entry; the establishment of a more efficient and cooperative relationship with NGOs; and the implementation of public policies to protect Roma children.

Commission action. On 19 April [res. 2005/44], the Commission, by a recorded vote of 52 to 1, called on States to take measures to eliminate the sale of children, child prostitution and child pornography by adopting a holistic approach and addressing the contributing factors, including underdevelopment, poverty, economic disparities, inequitable socio-economic structures, dysfunctional families, lack of education, urban-rural migration, gender discrimination, irresponsible adult sexual behaviour, harmful traditional practices, armed conflicts and trafficking in children.

Child labour

By a recorded vote of 52 to 1, the Commission, on 19 April [res. 2005/44], called on States to translate into concrete action their commitment to protect children from economic exploitation, or from work that was hazardous, interfered with a child's education or was harmful to the child's health, and to eliminate the worst forms of child labour urgently. It urged them to consider ratifying and implementing ILO Convention No. 182 concerning the prohibition and elimination of the worst forms of child labour (Worst Forms of Child Labour Convention), adopted in 1999 [YUN 1999, p. 1388], and Convention No. 138 concerning the minimum age for admission to employment (Minimum Age Convention), adopted in 1973 [YUN 1973, p. 885].

Children and armed conflict

Report of Special Representative. In accordance with General Assembly resolution 51/77 [YUN 1996, p. 665], the Secretary-General's Special Representative for Children and Armed Conflict, Olara A. Otunnu (Côte d'Ivoire), in a February report [E/CN.4/2005/77], discussed key issues and proposals for establishing a monitoring, reporting and compliance mechanism for protecting children affected by armed conflict. The

mechanism would enable the provision of reliable and objective information on grave violations against children, and ensure action on and compliance with protection standards relating to children and armed conflict. The report addressed the issues of the most grave violations that should be monitored; standards that constituted the basis for monitoring; parties whose activities should be monitored; the gathering and compilation of information at the country level; review, scrutiny and integration of information and the preparation of reports at the Headquarters level; and identification of bodies that constituted "destination for action", with responsibility for taking necessary action based on monitoring reports.

Drawing on resources at both the national and international levels, the mechanism would operate at three principal levels: information-gathering, coordination and action at the country level; review, scrutiny and integration of information and preparation of reports at Headquarters level; and concrete actions to ensure compliance, to be taken by the bodies that constituted "destinations for action". The Office of the Special Representative, UN peacekeeping missions and UN country teams would play important roles in the establishment and implementation of the mechanism. The bodies constituting "destination for action" included the Governments, the Security Council, the General Assembly, the Economic and Social Council, the International Criminal Court (ICC), UN human rights bodies, regional and subregional organizations and NGOs and civil society organizations. Those entities would undertake concrete and targeted measures to ensure compliance.

Report of Secretary-General. In response to Security Council resolution 1539(2004) [YUN 2004, p. 787], the Secretary-General, in a February report [A/59/695-S/2005/72], outlined an action plan for establishing a monitoring, reporting and compliance mechanism, as proposed in the Special Representative's report (see above). The plan contained proposed actions designed to create a critical mass of response to ensure compliance and bring about the "era of application" of related international norms and standards. It also provided information on compliance and progress in ending the recruitment and use of children and other violations being committed against them, in particular, on compliance and progress in situations on the Council's agenda in numerous countries. In addition, the report considered the question of sexual exploitation and abuse by UN peacekeeping personnel, updated information on best practices for disarmament, demobilization and reintegration programmes for children, and discussed measures to control illicit subregional cross-border activities that were harmful to children, including cross-border abduction and recruitment, the trafficking of small arms and light weapons and the illicit exploitation of natural resources. In view of the widespread and unacceptable patterns of violations highlighted in the report, the Secretary-General recommended that the Council take targeted and concrete measures where insufficient or no progress had been made by parties named in the lists annexed to his previous reports. Such measures should include the imposition of travel restrictions on leaders and their exclusion from any governance structures and amnesty provisions, the imposition of arms embargoes, a ban on military assistance and restrictions on the flow of financial resources to the parties concerned. Annexed to the report were lists of parties that recruited or used children in situations of armed conflict on the agenda of the Security Council and parties that engaged in the practice or were involved in other situations of concern that were not on the Council's agenda.

Commission action. By a recorded vote of 52 to 1, the Commission, on 19 April [res. 2005/44], strongly condemned any recruitment and use of children in armed conflicts, and urged all parties to armed conflict to end the practice. It called on States to raise the minimum age for voluntary recruitment into their armed forces to 18 and adopt safeguards to ensure that the recruitment of those under 18 was not forced or coerced. The Commission asked States, UN bodies and regional organizations to integrate the rights of the child into all activities in conflict and post-conflict situations, ensure adequate child protection training of their staff and personnel and support national and international efforts to deal with the issue of landmines.

SECURITY COUNCIL ACTION

On 23 February [meeting 5129], following consultation among Security Council members, the President made statement **S/PSRT/2005/8** on behalf of the Council:

The Security Council considered the matter of children and armed conflict and took note with deep concern of the continued recruitment and use of children by parties to armed conflict in violation of international obligations applicable to them, as reported by the Secretary-General in his fifth report. It reiterates its commitment to address in all its forms the impact of armed conflict on children.

The Council reaffirms its strong condemnation of the recruitment and use of child soldiers by parties to armed conflict in violation of international obligations applicable to them and of all other violations and abuses committed against children in situations

of armed conflict. It urges all parties to armed conflict to halt immediately such intolerable practices.

The Council recalls all its previous resolutions, which provide a comprehensive framework for addressing the protection of children affected by armed conflict. It reiterates its determination to ensure respect for its resolutions and other international norms and standards for the protection of children affected by armed conflict.

The Council recalls, in particular, paragraph 2 of its resolution 1539(2004) of 22 April 2004, requesting the Secretary-General, taking into account the proposals contained in his report as well as any other relevant elements, to devise urgently an action plan for a systematic and comprehensive monitoring and reporting mechanism, which utilizes expertise from the United Nations system and the contributions of national Governments, regional organizations, non-governmental organizations in their advisory capacity and various civil society actors, in order to provide timely, objective, accurate and reliable information on the recruitment and use of child soldiers in violation of applicable international law and on other violations and abuses committed against children affected by armed conflict, for consideration in taking appropriate action.

The Council takes note of the Secretary-General's proposal for an action plan for the establishment of a monitoring, reporting and compliance mechanism, in accordance with this request and with paragraph 15 (b) of resolution 1539(2004) and has started consideration of the Secretary-General's proposal.

The Council reiterates the crucial need for a systematic and comprehensive monitoring and reporting mechanism, and its determination to ensure compliance and to put an end to impunity. The Council further reiterates its intention to complete expeditiously the process of the establishing the mechanism.

In this regard, it has started work on a new resolution with the aim of its early adoption and with due consideration of views expressed by the States Members of the United Nations during the open debate of 23 February 2005, in order to take forward the implementation of its previous resolutions with a view to ending the recruitment or use of child soldiers in violation of applicable international law and other violations and abuses committed against children affected by armed conflict situations, and promoting their reintegration and rehabilitation.

In further action, on 26 July [meeting 5235], the Council unanimously adopted **resolution 1612 (2005)**. The draft [S/2005/477] was prepared in consultations among Council members.

The Security Council,

Reaffirming its resolutions 1261(1999) of 25 August 1999, 1314(2000) of 11 August 2000, 1379(2001) of 20 November 2001, 1460(2003) of 30 January 2003 and 1539(2004) of 22 April 2004, which contribute to a comprehensive framework for addressing the protection of children affected by armed conflict,

Noting the advances made for the protection of children affected by armed conflict, particularly in the areas of advocacy and the development of norms and standards, while remaining deeply concerned over the lack of overall progress on the ground, where parties to conflict continue to violate with impunity the relevant provisions of applicable international law relating to the rights and protection of children in armed conflict,

Stressing the primary role of national Governments in providing effective protection and relief to all children affected by armed conflict,

Recalling the responsibilities of States to end impunity and to prosecute those responsible for genocide, crimes against humanity, war crimes and other egregious crimes perpetrated against children,

Convinced that the protection of children in armed conflict should be regarded as an important aspect of any comprehensive strategy to resolve conflict,

Reiterating its primary responsibility for the maintenance of international peace and security and, in this connection, its commitment to address the widespread impact of armed conflict on children,

Stressing its determination to ensure respect for its resolutions and other international norms and standards for the protection of children affected by armed conflict,

Having considered the report of the Secretary-General of 9 February 2005, and stressing that the present resolution does not seek to make any legal determination as to whether situations which are referred to in the report of the Secretary-General are or are not armed conflicts within the context of the Geneva Conventions of 1949 and the Additional Protocols thereto, of 1977, nor does it prejudge the legal status of the non-State parties involved in these situations,

Gravely concerned by the documented links between the use of child soldiers in violation of applicable international law and the illicit trafficking of small arms and light weapons, and stressing the need for all States to take measures to prevent and to put an end to such trafficking,

1. *Strongly condemns* the recruitment and use of child soldiers by parties to armed conflict in violation of international obligations applicable to them and all other violations and abuses committed against children in situations of armed conflict;

2. *Takes note* of the action plan presented by the Secretary-General relating to the establishment of a monitoring and reporting mechanism on children and armed conflict, as called for in paragraph 2 of its resolution 1539(2004) and, in this regard:

(a) Underlines the fact that the mechanism is to collect and provide timely, objective, accurate and reliable information on the recruitment and use of child soldiers in violation of applicable international law and on other violations and abuses committed against children affected by armed conflict, and will report to the working group to be created in accordance with paragraph 8 below;

(b) Underlines further the fact that this mechanism must operate with the participation of and in cooperation with national Governments and relevant United Nations and civil society actors, including at the country level;

(c) Stresses that all actions undertaken by United Nations entities within the framework of the monitoring and reporting mechanism must be designed to support and supplement, as appropriate, the protection and rehabilitation roles of national Governments;

(d) Also stresses that any dialogue established under the framework of the monitoring and reporting mechanism by United Nations entities with non-State armed groups in order to ensure protection for and access to children must be conducted in the context of peace processes, where they exist, and the cooperation framework between the United Nations and the concerned Government;

3. *Requests* the Secretary-General to implement, without delay, the above-mentioned monitoring and reporting mechanism, beginning with its application, within existing resources, in close consultation with countries concerned, to parties in situations of armed conflict listed in the annexes to the report of the Secretary-General that are on the agenda of the Security Council, and then, in close consultation with countries concerned, to apply it to parties in other situations of armed conflict listed in those annexes, bearing in mind the discussion of the Council and the views expressed by Member States, in particular during the annual debate on children and armed conflict, and also taking into account the findings and recommendations of an independent review on the implementation of the mechanism to be reported to the Council by 31 July 2006. The independent review will include:

(a) An assessment of the overall effectiveness of the mechanism, as well as the timeliness, accuracy, objectivity and reliability of the information compiled through the mechanism;

(b) Information on how effectively the mechanism is linked to the work of the Security Council and other organs of the United Nations;

(c) Information on the relevance and clarity of the division of responsibilities;

(d) Information on the budgetary and other resource implications for United Nations actors and voluntary funded organizations contributing to the mechanism;

(e) Recommendations for the full implementation of the mechanism;

4. *Stresses* that the implementation of the monitoring and reporting mechanism by the Secretary-General will be undertaken only in the context of and for the specific purpose of ensuring the protection of children affected by armed conflict and shall not thereby prejudge or imply a decision by the Security Council as to whether or not to include a situation in its agenda;

5. *Welcomes* the initiatives taken by the United Nations Children's Fund and other United Nations entities to gather information on the recruitment and use of child soldiers in violation of applicable international law and on other violations and abuses committed against children in situations of armed conflict, and invites the Secretary-General to take due account of these initiatives during the initial phase of implementation of the mechanism referred to in paragraph 3 above;

6. *Notes* that information compiled by this mechanism, for reporting by the Secretary-General to the General Assembly and the Security Council, may be considered by other international, regional and national bodies, within their mandates and the scope of

their work, in order to ensure the protection, rights and well-being of children affected by armed conflict;

7. *Expresses serious concern* regarding the lack of progress in development and implementation of the action plans called for in paragraph 5 *(a)* of its resolution 1539(2004), and, pursuant to this, calls upon the parties concerned to develop and implement action plans without further delay, in close collaboration with United Nations peacekeeping missions and United Nations country teams, consistent with their respective mandates and within their capabilities, and requests the Secretary-General to provide criteria to assist in the development of such action plans;

8. *Decides* to establish a working group of the Security Council consisting of all members of the Council to review the reports of the mechanism referred to in paragraph 3 above, to review progress in the development and implementation of the action plans mentioned in paragraph 7 above, and to consider other relevant information presented to it, and decides further that the working group shall:

(a) Make recommendations to the Council on possible measures to promote the protection of children affected by armed conflict, including through recommendations on appropriate mandates for peacekeeping missions and recommendations with respect to the parties to the conflict;

(b) Address requests, as appropriate, to other bodies within the United Nations system for action to support implementation of the present resolution in accordance with their respective mandates;

9. *Recalls* paragraph 5 *(c)* of its resolution 1539 (2004), and reaffirms its intention to consider imposing, through country-specific resolutions, targeted and graduated measures, such as, inter alia, a ban on the export and supply of small arms and light weapons and of other military equipment and on military assistance, against parties to situations of armed conflict that are on the agenda of the Security Council and are in violation of applicable international law relating to the rights and protection of children in armed conflict;

10. *Stresses* the responsibility of United Nations peacekeeping missions and United Nations country teams, consistent with their respective mandates, to ensure effective follow-up to Council resolutions, ensure a coordinated response to concerns regarding children and armed conflict and to monitor and report to the Secretary-General;

11. *Welcomes* the efforts undertaken by United Nations peacekeeping operations to implement the Secretary-General's zero-tolerance policy on sexual exploitation and abuse and to ensure full compliance of their personnel with the United Nations code of conduct, requests the Secretary-General to continue to take all necessary action in this regard and to keep the Council informed, and urges troop-contributing countries to take appropriate preventive action, including predeployment awareness training, and to take disciplinary action and other action to ensure full accountability in cases of misconduct involving their personnel;

12. *Decides* to continue the inclusion of specific provisions for the protection of children in the mandates of United Nations peacekeeping operations, including the deployment, on a case-by-case basis, of child-protection advisers, requests the Secretary-General to ensure that the need for and the number and roles of child-protection advisers are systematically assessed during the preparation for each United Nations peacekeeping operation, and welcomes the comprehensive assessment undertaken on the role and activities of child-protection advisers, with a view to lessons learned and best practices;

13. *Welcomes* recent initiatives by regional and subregional organizations and arrangements for the protection of children affected by armed conflict, and encourages continued mainstreaming of child protection into their advocacy, policies and programmes; development of peer review and monitoring and reporting mechanisms; establishment, within their secretariats, of child-protection mechanisms; inclusion of child-protection staff and training in their peace and field operations; subregional and interregional initiatives to end activities harmful to children in times of conflict, in particular cross-border recruitment and abduction of children, illicit movement of small arms, and illicit trade in natural resources through the development and implementation of guidelines on children and armed conflict;

14. *Calls upon* all parties concerned to ensure that the protection, rights and well-being of children affected by armed conflict are specifically integrated into all peace processes, peace agreements and post-conflict recovery and reconstruction planning and programmes;

15. *Also calls upon* all parties concerned to abide by the international obligations applicable to them relating to the protection of children affected by armed conflict, as well as the concrete commitments they have made to the Special Representative of the Secretary-General for Children and Armed Conflict, the United Nations Children's Fund and other agencies of the United Nations system, and to cooperate fully with the United Nations peacekeeping missions and United Nations country teams, where appropriate, in the context of the cooperation framework between the United Nations and the concerned Government, in the follow-up to and implementation of those commitments;

16. *Urges* Member States, United Nations entities, regional and subregional organizations and other parties concerned, to take appropriate measures to control illicit subregional and cross-border activities harmful to children, including illicit exploitation of natural resources, illicit trade in small arms, abduction of children and their use and recruitment as soldiers, as well as other violations and abuses committed against children in situations of armed conflict in violation of applicable international law;

17. *Urges* all parties concerned, including Member States, United Nations entities and financial institutions, to support the development and strengthening of the capacities of national institutions and local civil society networks for the advocacy, protection and rehabilitation of children affected by armed conflict to ensure the sustainability of local child-protection initiatives;

18. *Requests* that the Secretary-General direct all relevant United Nations entities to take specific measures, within existing resources, to ensure systematic mainstreaming of issues concerning children and armed

conflict within their respective institutions, including by ensuring allocation of adequate financial and human resources towards the protection of war-affected children within all relevant offices and departments and on the ground, as well as to strengthen, within their respective mandates, their cooperation and coordination when addressing the protection of children in armed conflict;

19. *Reiterates its request* to the Secretary-General to ensure that, in all his reports on country-specific situations, the protection of children is included as a specific aspect of the report, and expresses its intention to give its full attention to the information provided therein when dealing with those situations on its agenda;

20. *Requests* the Secretary-General to submit a report by November 2006 on the implementation of the present resolution and resolutions 1379(2001), 1460 (2003) and 1539(2004) which would include, inter alia:

(a) Information on compliance by parties in ending the recruitment or use of children in armed conflict in violation of applicable international law and other violations being committed against children affected by armed conflict;

(b) Information on progress made in the implementation of the monitoring and reporting mechanism mentioned in paragraph 3 above;

(c) Information on progress made in the development and implementation of the action plans referred to in paragraph 7 above;

(d) Information on the assessment of the role and activities of child-protection advisers;

21. *Decides* to remain actively seized of the matter.

Further report of Special Representative. In a September report [A/60/335 & Corr.1], the Special Representative provided an overview of the agenda for war-affected children, highlighted the progress made in protecting and addressing their needs and identified the principal elements of the "era of application" campaign for the enforcement of existing international child protection norms and standards. The report also highlighted significant advances that had created a strong momentum for the children in armed conflict agenda, in particular the development and strengthening of norms and standards, the placement of the issue on the Security Council's agenda, the incorporation of children's concerns into peace negotiations and accords, the deployment of child protection advisers to UN peace-keeping operations, increased global awareness and advocacy on children affected by armed conflict issues, the engagement of civil society, the work of UN field missions, and the integration of the issue of the protection of children affected by war into the agendas and programmes of regional and other international organizations. The report also considered mainstreaming children affected by armed conflict in the UN system and the "era of application" campaign.

The Special Representative determined that, despite the advances made, the situation of children in armed conflict remained grave and unacceptable, prompting him to call for a vigorous campaign to ensure the enforcement of international norms and standards for protecting their rights. The key elements of the "era of application" campaign included the review, naming and listing of the parties committing grave child rights violations and the initiation of dialogue with them in order to halt the abuses; the implementation of a monitoring and reporting mechanism on those violations; and ensuring accountability through concrete action by key policymaking bodies and entities, such as the General Assembly. The Special Representative concluded that a higher level of commitment and more effective collaboration by all parties concerned would be required to achieve the "era of application", and recommended that the Assembly consider introducing a separate resolution on children and armed conflict, in order to ensure a sustained focus on the issue. Further recommendations advocated that Member States ensure that the concerns of war-affected children were prioritized in their advocacy, policies and programmes, particularly in the context of post-conflict recovery and development, and that relevant UN entities took specific measures to ensure the systematic mainstreaming of children and armed conflict issues within their respective institutions and assess periodically the progress made in those efforts.

In October [S/2005/659], the Security Council appointed Jean-Marc de La Sablière (France) as Chairman of the Working Group of the Security Council on Children and Armed Conflict, established in accordance with Council resolution 1612(2005) (see p. 865).

Abduction of children in Africa

Report of High Commissioner. In a February report [E/CN.4/2005/74], the High Commissioner summarized replies received from Member States, relevant international organizations, OHCHR field presences and NGOs to a questionnaire, which OHCHR had prepared and circulated in 2004.

Commission action. On 19 April [res. 2005/43], the Commission, condemning the abduction of children, called for the unconditional release and safe return of all abducted children to their families and called upon African states to prohibit and criminalize such practices. They were also requested, in cooperation with relevant UN agencies, to assist the victims and their families and support sustainable rehabilitation and integration programmes for them, taking into account the special needs of abducted girls. OHCHR, in cooperation with Member States, ILO, UNICEF and other relevant UN agencies, international organizations and NGOs, was asked to undertake a comprehensive assessment of the situation of the abduction of children throughout Africa, and to report thereon in 2006. The Commission urged States to submit information to OHCHR regarding the implementation of its resolution and further urged those states that had established national mechanisms to combat the abduction of children to report on progress made in that regard to OHCHR.

Freedom of movement

Mass exoduses

Report of High Commissioner. In response to a 2003 Commission request [YUN 2003, p. 791], the High Commissioner, in a January report [E/CN.4/2005/80], described measures taken by OHCHR and other relevant UN bodies to address the problem of mass exoduses, taking into account information and comments provided by Governments, intergovernmental organizations, specialized agencies and NGOs. In that context, the report highlighted developments concerning refugees and internally displaced persons (IDPs) and discussed the question of accession to relevant international instruments; the prevention of mass exoduses and displacement; and assistance and protection to affected persons; and the question of durable solutions, including return. The High Commissioner noted that, States were continuing to accede to relevant international instruments and that important steps had been taken at the national and international levels to prevent displacement. States around the world had hosted millions of refugees and as many IDPs had found some degree of safety and support in their own countries. Large scale returns were also continuing in many areas, owing to efforts by States and international actors, most notably the United Nations. Nonetheless, ongoing outflows indicated that more could and should be done to better address the problem of mass exoduses and displacement, as assistance and protection measures were being hampered by the fear of terrorism, resource constraints, institutional problems, issues of access and safety of humanitarian personnel and of forcible return and insufficient attention to potential solutions. Further cooperation among States, the United Nations and other international partners would be required to overcome those obstacles and ensure that the rights of persons in situations of mass exodus were respected, protected and fulfilled.

Also in response to the Commission's 2003 request [YUN 2003, p. 791], the High Commissioner provided, in an addendum [E/CN.4/2005/80/Add.1], a compilation of relevant Commission and Subcommission reports and resolutions.

Commission action. On 19 April [res. 2005/48], the Commission requested the High Commissioner to pay particular attention to human rights situations that caused or threatened to cause mass exoduses and to contribute to efforts to address such situations through promotion and protection measures, emergency preparedness and response mechanisms, early warning and information-sharing, technical advice and expertise and cooperation in countries of origin and host countries. She was further asked to report in 2007 on measures taken to implement the Commission's resolution and on obstacles thereto, taking into account information and comments provided by Governments, intergovernmental organizations, specialized agencies and NGOs, and to annex to the report a thematic compilation of relevant Commission and Subcommission reports and resolutions.

Report of Secretary-General. Pursuant to General Assembly resolution 58/169 [YUN 2003, p. 792], the Secretary-General, in a September report [A/60/325] on human rights and mass exoduses, described UN system efforts to protect better those affected and to facilitate their return and reintegration, enhance the system's capacity to avert new flows of refugees and IDPs and tackle the root causes of such flows. Highlighting the scope of the challenge as presented in his March report entitled "In larger freedom: towards development, security and human rights for all" (see p. 67), the Secretary-General examined efforts to monitor the human rights of persons in mass exodus; the role of early warning mechanisms in preventing displacement; the human rights of IDPs, consideration of which had influenced the establishment of the mandate of his Representative on IDPs (see below); and mass exodus caused by natural disasters. He concluded that the phenomena of mass exodus and displacement, in order to be fully understood, had to be viewed within the framework of his reform proposals, in which had outlined the interdependence of human rights, poverty and development. Recent examples of mass exoduses, both as a result of armed conflict and as a consequence of massive natural disasters, had demonstrated the need to address comprehensively the human rights of victims, given that persons had the right to be protected from displacement. As human rights issues were often at the core of the conflicts or situations resulting in mass exoduses, patterns of discrimination and disadvantage, if unchecked, could develop into levels of violence that might reach genocidal proportions. The report pointed out that substantial progress had been made over the years by human rights treaty bodies to address those issues, the Commission's special procedures and parts of the UN system entrusted with humanitarian mandates, which had broadened early warning mechanisms in order to identify patterns of disadvantage at an early stage when preventive remedial action was possible. With sustained attention to capacity gaps and measures needed to implement the Secretary-General's proposals for humanitarian reform, the United Nations was striving to avoid the development of mass exodus and respond better to the needs of those affected.

Internally displaced persons

Reports of Secretary-General's Representative. In his first annual report to the Commission [E/CN.4/2005/84], the Secretary-General's Representative on the human rights of internally displaced persons, Walter Kälin (Switzerland), described his activities and reflected on the meaning and challenges of protection for IDPs. The report accorded particular attention the special needs of IDPs in terms of physical security and integrity; basic necessities of life; other economic, social, cultural, civil and political protection needs; and the needs of IDPs with particular vulnerabilities, such as women and children. It also considered frameworks for protection activity and proposed a complementary categorization of actions to the International Committee of the Red Cross, including actions to prevent violations of IDPs' rights under human rights and humanitarian law, stop violations of those rights, prevent the recurrence of violations and ensure remedies (including rehabilitation, restitution, compensation and satisfaction) for persons whose rights had been violated. Under each of the categories, the report highlighted the Representative's proposed programme of protection-related activities. It noted that progress had been made at the international level in conceptualizing the protection of IDPs, including through a growing acceptance of the Guiding Principles on Internal Displacement [YUN 1998, p. 675] and the adoption of a new IDP policy by the United Nations Inter-Agency Standing Committee (IASC). However, there was still a lack of appreciation of the particular needs of IDPs and the role of UN agencies and human rights mechanisms in addressing them. While States bore the primary responsibility for protecting IDPs, little attention had been devoted to whether and how the international community's conceptual framework for protection could be applied by Governments in devel-

oping their own responses. Considerable work also remained to be done at the international level, as the basic notion that the protection needs of IDPs should be given specific attention was still not universally accepted or practiced. The Representative would contribute to efforts to address that aspect, in keeping with his mandate to strengthen international protection and mainstream the human rights of IDPs throughout the UN system, in collaboration with key actors.

The Representative visited Nepal (13-22 April) [E/CN.4/2006/71/Add.2], which faced a serious problem of conflict-induced internal displacement, owing to the armed conflict between the Government and the insurgency led by the Communist Party of Nepal-Maoist (CPN-M). It was estimated that up to 100,000 persons in the country had been displaced by the conflict. Those affected were fleeing mainly from direct acts of violence or threats by the CPN-M; to prevent their children from being forcibly recruited or forced to contribute to the insurgency; the fear of reprisals by the Royal Nepalese Army or of being caught in the crossfire; a general feeling of insecurity and uncertainty; the collapse of local infrastructure and coping mechanisms within villages; and the economic decline in the traditionally poorer areas of the country, reportedly hastened by the conflict. Displaced persons often moved to urban or semi-urban areas in the Terai region, and onward to Kathmandu or India. In some cases, whole villages were displaced within days or hours by vigilante of alleged CPN-M supporters. The main needs of the IDPs related to security and protection, discrimination, food, shelter and health, access to education for their children, documentation, protection from sexual abuse and domestic violence, the risk of increased child labour, the lack of protection of property rights and the denial of voting and electoral rights. Although the authorities had taken some action to address the situation, including the establishment of several compensation and resettlement funds for victims, and the active efforts to support the National Human Rights Commission, the Representative was concerned about several major limitations to those efforts, including the inadequacy of the resources made available for IDPs. He recommended, among other things, that the Government adopt a comprehensive national IDP policy based on non-discrimination; train national and local authorities on the Guiding Principles on the Rights of IDPs; ensure that IDP property left behind was adequately protected; and create conditions conducive to the safe and dignified return to their homes. Recommendations were also addressed to CPN-M forces, the UN country team in the country and other international actors.

The Representative visited Croatia (6-8 June) [E/CN.4/2006/71/Add.3] and found that, although problems relating to the return of refugees and internal displacement caused by the armed conflicts in the former Yugoslavia had been largely resolved, some 7,000 cases of internal displacement still remained. A key factor affecting the resolution of their cases was an overburdened court system and haphazard execution of court judgements. The Representative called on the Government to address those problems in order to consolidate the progress that had already been achieved. Other systematic and structural problems demanding attention included deep-rooted discrimination against returnees who were members of ethnic minorities, perceived exclusion from appropriate participation in local structures of governance and civil service, incidents of localized violence, economic and societal difficulties and the residual effects of the armed conflict in the country [YUN 1995, p. 566], including especially, the presence of landmines. The Representative recommended specific measures to the Government for tackling those problems.

In Bosnia and Herzegovina (9-15 June) [E/CN.4/2006/71/Add.4], where some 185,000 IDPs were registered in the course of the year, the Representative focused on identifying outstanding problems and durable solutions. He found that the main obstacles to the sustainable return of those affected were physical insecurity, delays in the return of property to the original owners, the reconstruction of buildings and a discouraging economic, social and political environment. While threats to life and limb had been largely reduced, a cause for concern was the insufficient protection of vulnerable groups who were particularly exposed to the risk of attacks, including war crimes victims and witnesses and ethnic minorities, such as the Roma. Acknowledging the efforts of the Government and the international community to have a large proportion of occupied property returned to their original owners, the Representative maintained that much remained to be done to resolve outstanding property disputes, reconstruct houses and reconnect them to water and electricity supplies and infrastructure. The main challenge was to create conditions for sustaining returns, given that many returnees had reportedly sold their repossessed property and opted to remain at their site of displacement rather than reintegrate into their original communities. The Representative recommended that the authorities avoid depriving IDPs of their current accommodation without offering an adequate alternative solution. The inter-

national community should concentrate efforts and resources on creating an environment conducive to sustainable return, and assist in human rights training and related capacity-building in such areas as administration of justice, employment policies and the harmonization of the health and education systems.

The Representative visited Serbia and Montenegro, including Kosovo (16-24 June) [E/CN.4/2006/71/Add.5], where the events, which had resulted in international intervention in 1999 [YUN 1999, p. 333] to stop massive human rights violations, had, in turn, led to massive displacement. Against that background, an estimated 248,000 IDPs continued to live in difficult conditions in collective centres and irregular settlements, among them, the elderly, ill, disabled, traumatized, witnesses in war crimes investigations and trial, female-headed households and families of missing persons. Many of those affected, particularly Roma and other minorities, suffered discrimination, as they often had difficulties providing proof of their origins, and many were also only marginally aware of their rights under domestic and international law, while others were unable, for practical reasons, to access entitlements and remedies provided by the Government. The efforts of the international community and national authorities had been almost exclusively focused on return as the only solution, which discouraged local integration. Yet, returns had been slow for several reasons, including the fact that many IDPs lacked appropriate information, felt disempowered and were overwhelmed by negative messages about their region of origin, which reinforced their feelings of insecurity. Since they were unlikely to return or to live on their own, the time had come to find a dignified solution to their situation, given especially that the international community was in the process of withdrawing its support from many IDP centres and that the buildings no longer offered acceptable living conditions. The Representative recommended that national and local authorities, in coordination with international agencies, seek durable solutions for those persons, including alternative housing and appropriate institutional arrangements, such as social housing, foster families or homes which respected their right to human dignity. A comprehensive plan of action in that regard should be developed. Specific conclusions and recommendations were addressed to the Republic of Serbia, the internationally-administered Serbian province of Kosovo, the Republic of Montenegro, the international community and donors.

In the Sudan (3-13 October) [E/CN.4/2006/71/Add.6], the Representative assessed the preparedness of both Government authorities and the international community to receive hundreds of thousands of IDPs whose return was anticipated after the signing of a Comprehensive Peace Agreement in January (see p. 302), marking the end of the 22-year civil war between the southern and northern parts of the country. The conflict, which had left more than two million dead, displaced up to four million southerners internally and drove another half a million people to seek asylum abroad. The Representative, after reviewing the domestic and international response to displacement in the country, as well as the protection needs of the returning population, concluded that local authorities were not in a position to protect the human rights of returnees. Of particular concern was the forcible relocation of Khartoum IDPs to the south in a disrespectful manner. He recommended to the national and southern Sudanese authorities that IDPs be given a free and meaningful choice on whether to return or integrate locally, by providing them with reliable and up-to-date information and by refraining from forcible relocations and exposing them to living conditions that fell short of international human rights standards. He also advocated that the authorities and the UN system establish protection mechanisms for IDPs en route, and provide humanitarian assistance to returnees urgently. The authorities should also ensure that obstacles to sustainable return to the south were removed and that adequate conditions were created, including protection of the full spectrum of human rights of IDPs.

In Georgia (21-24 December) [E/CN.4/2006/71/Add.7], where uprisings by nationalist groups and the related violent internal conflict following the 1991 collapse of the Soviet Union had resulted in mass displacements, the Representative sought dialogue with the Government and other relevant actors, with a view to finding durable, rights-based solutions for the country's estimated 221,597 registered IDPs. The lack of political solutions to regional conflicts, as well as discriminatory measures and widespread feelings of insecurity, posed major obstacles to the return of displaced populations, which was further hampered by the lack of infrastructure and basic services in return areas. In considering the protection needs of IDPs, the Representative noted that issues of safety, including armed attacks, abductions, forced disappearances, robberies and explosions, deterred IDPs from returning. Other needs related to land and property issues, the conditions for sustainable return and institutional and structural problems. While stressing that IDPs had the right to return voluntarily to their former homes in safety and dignity, the

Representative welcomed the Government's intention to support more effectively their local integration. Of great concern, however, were the living conditions of IDPs accommodated in temporary collective shelters for many years, including many vulnerable groups. The Representative encouraged the Government to expedite the creation and implementation of its proposed policy for addressing the displacement crisis, ensuring that it supported integration into society and the acquisition of adequate accommodation, while maintaining the IDP option to return. He urged the de facto authorities in Abkhazia and the authorities in Tbilisi to refrain from adopting measures incompatible with the right to return and with international human rights standards, such as discriminatory legislation, particularly regarding the "citizenship law".

Commission action. On 19 April [res. 2005/46], the Commission called on Governments to protect and assist IDPs, including integration and protection assistance, develop national policies aimed at addressing their plight and ensure that they benefitted from public services. Stressing the need to strengthen further inter-agency arrangements and the capacities of UN agencies and other relevant actors to meet the immense humanitarian challenge of internal displacement, the Commission encouraged the Emergency Relief Coordinator to lead efforts in promoting an effective, predictable and collaborative response among relevant international agencies and bodies with regard to protecting and assisting IDPs. The Representative of the Secretary-General was asked to address the complex problem of internal displacement, in particular by mainstreaming the human rights of the internally displaced into all relevant parts of the UN system. The Commission recommended that the Representative strengthen international response to situations of internal displacement and invited him to submit annual reports on his activities to the Commission and the General Assembly. The Secretary-General was asked to assist him.

Communication. On 5 April [E/CN.4/2005/G/33], Turkey transmitted a note on the issue of internally displaced persons in the country.

GENERAL ASSEMBLY ACTION

On 16 December [meeting 64], the General Assembly, on the recommendation of the Third Committee [A/60/509/Add.2], adopted **resolution 60/168** without vote [agenda item 71 (*b*)].

Protection of and assistance to internally displaced persons

The General Assembly,

Deeply disturbed by the alarmingly high numbers of internally displaced persons throughout the world, for reasons including armed conflict, violations of human rights and natural or human-made disasters, who receive inadequate protection and assistance, and conscious of the serious challenges that this is creating for the international community,

Recognizing the significant number of persons who have become internally displaced owing to natural disasters over the course of the past twelve months,

Conscious of the human rights and the humanitarian dimensions of the problem of internally displaced persons, including in long-term displacement situations, and the responsibilities of States and the international community to strengthen further their protection and assistance,

Emphasizing that States have the primary responsibility to provide protection and assistance to internally displaced persons within their jurisdiction as well as to address the root causes of the displacement problem in appropriate cooperation with the international community,

Noting the growing awareness of the international community of the issue of internally displaced persons worldwide and the urgency of addressing the root causes of their displacement and finding durable solutions, including voluntary return in safety and with dignity, or local integration,

Recalling the relevant norms of international human rights law, international humanitarian law and international refugee law, and recognizing that the protection of internally displaced persons has been strengthened by identifying, reaffirming and consolidating specific standards for their protection, in particular through the Guiding Principles on Internal Displacement,

Emphasizing the central role of the Emergency Relief Coordinator for the inter-agency coordination of protection of and assistance to internally displaced persons, and welcoming the continued initiatives taken in order to ensure better protection, assistance and development strategies for internally displaced persons, as well as better coordination of activities regarding them,

Commending the Representative of the Secretary-General on the human rights of internally displaced persons for the activities undertaken so far, for the catalytic role that he plays in raising the level of consciousness about the plight of internally displaced persons and his efforts to promote a comprehensive strategy that focuses on prevention as well as better protection and assistance and addressing the development and other specific needs of internally displaced persons, including through the mainstreaming of the human rights of internally displaced persons into all relevant parts of the United Nations system,

Taking note of Commission on Human Rights resolution 2005/46 of 19 April 2005, and recalling the Vienna Declaration and Programme of Action adopted by the World Conference on Human Rights on 25 June 1993, regarding the need to develop global strategies to address the problem of internal displacement,

Deploring practices of forced displacement and their negative consequences for the enjoyment of human rights and fundamental freedoms by large groups of populations, and noting that the Rome Statute of the International Criminal Court defines the deportation or forcible transfer of population as a crime against humanity and the unlawful deportation or transfer of the civilian population, as well as ordering the displacement of the civilian population, as war crimes,

Welcoming the increasing dissemination, promotion and application of the Guiding Principles when dealing with situations of internal displacement,

Welcoming also the cooperation established between the new Representative of the Secretary-General and the United Nations and other international and regional organizations, and encouraging further strengthening of his collaboration in order to promote better protection, assistance and development strategies for internally displaced persons,

Acknowledging with appreciation the important and independent contribution of the International Red Cross and Red Crescent Movement and other humanitarian agencies in protecting and assisting internally displaced persons, in cooperation with relevant international bodies,

Recalling its resolution 58/177 of 22 December 2003,

1. *Welcomes* the appointment of the new Representative of the Secretary-General on the human rights of internally displaced persons;

2. *Welcomes also* the report of the Representative of the Secretary-General, and takes note of his conclusions and recommendations;

3. *Expresses its appreciation* to those Governments and intergovernmental and non-governmental organizations that have provided protection and assistance to internally displaced persons and have supported the work of the Representative of the Secretary-General;

4. *Encourages* the Representative of the Secretary-General, through continuous dialogue with Governments and all intergovernmental and non-governmental organizations concerned, to continue his analysis of the causes of internal displacement, the needs and rights of those displaced, measures of prevention and ways to strengthen protection, assistance and solutions for internally displaced persons, taking into account specific situations, and to include information thereon in his reports to the Commission on Human Rights and the General Assembly;

5. *Expresses particular concern* at the grave problems faced by many internally displaced women and children, including violence and abuse, sexual exploitation, forced recruitment and abduction, and welcomes the commitment of the Representative of the Secretary-General to pay more systematic and in-depth attention to their particular assistance, protection and development needs, as well as to other groups with special needs, such as severely traumatized individuals, older persons and persons with disabilities, taking into account the relevant resolutions of the General Assembly and bearing in mind Security Council resolution 1325(2000) of 31 October 2000;

6. *Notes with appreciation* the increasing role of national human rights institutions in assisting internally displaced persons and in promoting and protecting their human rights;

7. *Notes* the importance of taking the human rights and the specific protection and assistance needs of internally displaced persons into consideration, when appropriate, in peace processes and reintegration and rehabilitation processes;

8. *Recognizes* the Guiding Principles on Internal Displacement as an important international frame-

work for the protection of internally displaced persons, welcomes the fact that an increasing number of States, United Nations agencies and regional and non-governmental organizations are applying them as a standard, and encourages all relevant actors to make use of the Guiding Principles when dealing with situations of internal displacement;

9. *Welcomes* the fact that the Representative of the Secretary-General continues to use the Guiding Principles in his dialogue with Governments and intergovernmental and non-governmental organizations and other relevant actors, and requests him to continue his efforts to further the dissemination, promotion and application of the Guiding Principles and to provide support for efforts to promote capacity-building and the use of the Guiding Principles, as well as the development of domestic legislation and policies;

10. *Urges* all Governments to continue to facilitate the activities of the Representative of the Secretary-General, in particular Governments with situations of internal displacement, and to give serious consideration to inviting the Representative to visit their countries so as to enable him to continue and enhance dialogue with Governments in addressing situations of internal displacement, and thanks those Governments that have already done so;

11. *Invites* Governments to give serious consideration, in dialogue with the Representative of the Secretary-General, to the recommendations and suggestions addressed to them, in accordance with his mandate, and to inform him of measures taken thereon;

12. *Calls upon* Governments to provide protection and assistance, including reintegration and development assistance, to internally displaced persons, and to facilitate the efforts of relevant United Nations agencies and humanitarian organizations in these respects, including by further improving access to internally displaced persons;

13. *Emphasizes* the central role of the Emergency Relief Coordinator for the inter-agency coordination of protection of and assistance to internally displaced persons, and notes with appreciation the work of the Inter-Agency Internal Displacement Division within the Office for the Coordination of Humanitarian Affairs of the Secretariat;

14. *Takes note* of the efforts currently under way by the United Nations humanitarian system, emphasizes the need to strengthen further inter-agency arrangements and the capacities of the United Nations agencies and other relevant actors to meet the immense humanitarian challenges of internal displacement, and underlines in this regard the importance of an effective, accountable and predictable collaborative approach;

15. *Encourages* all relevant United Nations agencies and humanitarian assistance, human rights and development organizations to enhance their collaboration and coordination, through the Inter-Agency Standing Committee and in countries with situations of internal displacement, and to provide all possible assistance and support to the Representative of the Secretary-General;

16. *Notes with appreciation* the increased attention paid to the issue of internally displaced persons in the consolidated inter-agency appeals process, and encourages further efforts in this regard;

17. *Recognizes* the relevance of the global database on internally displaced persons advocated by the Representative of the Secretary-General, and encourages the members of the Inter-Agency Standing Committee and Governments to continue to collaborate on and support this effort, including by providing relevant data on situations of internal displacement and financial resources;

18. *Welcomes* the initiatives undertaken by regional organizations, such as the African Union, the Organization of American States, the Organization for Security and Cooperation in Europe, the Intergovernmental Authority on Development, the Council of Europe, the Commonwealth and the Economic Community of West African States, to address the protection, assistance and development needs of internally displaced persons, and encourages them and other regional organizations to strengthen their activities and their cooperation with the Representative of the Secretary-General;

19. *Requests* the Secretary-General to provide his Representative, from within existing resources, with all necessary assistance to carry out his mandate effectively, and encourages the Representative to continue to seek the contributions of States, relevant organizations and institutions in order to create a more stable basis for his work;

20. *Requests* the Representative of the Secretary-General to prepare, for consideration by the General Assembly at its sixty-second session, a report on the implementation of the present resolution;

21. *Decides* to continue its consideration of the question of protection of and assistance to internally displaced persons at its sixty-second session.

Housing and property restitution

Reports of Special Rapporteur. In response to a 2004 Subcommission request [YUN 2004, p. 791], the Special Rapporteur on housing and property restitution in the context of the return of refugees and IDPs, Paulo Sérgio Pinheiro (Brazil), submitted a June final report [E/CN.4/Sub.2/2005/17], annexed to which was the finalized version of the Draft Principles on Housing and Property Restitution for Refugees and Displaced Persons. Designed to assist relevant national and international actors in addressing the legal and technical issues surrounding housing, land and property restitution in situations of unlawful or arbitrary displacement, the Principles determined that all refugees and displaced persons had the right to have restored to them, or to be compensated for, any housing, land and/or property of which they were arbitrarily or unlawfully deprived. Overarching principles in that regard related to the respective rights to non-discrimination, equality between men and women in protecting them from displacement, privacy and respect for the home, peaceful enjoyment of possessions, adequate housing, and freedom of movement. The principles also outlined legal, policy, procedural and institutional implementation mechanisms to protect those rights, and highlighted the role of the international community in promoting and protecting the right to housing, land and property restitution.

An addendum to the report [E/CN.4/Sub.2/2005/17/Add.1] contained explanatory notes to the Principles, meant to provide an overview of the international human rights, refugee and humanitarian law and related standards, which supported and informed the Principles themselves.

Subcommission action. On 11 August [res. 2005/21], the Subcommission welcomed the Special Rapporteur's final report (see p. 872), endorsed the Principles on Housing and Property Restitution for Refugees and Displaced Persons and encouraged their application and implementation by States, intergovernmental organizations and other relevant actors. The Special Rapporteur was asked to compile and update the study on housing and property restitution for refugees and IDPs so that it could be published in one volume as part of the Human Rights Study Series in the official languages of the United Nations. The Secretariat was requested to transmit the Principles and the explanatory notes to the Committee on the Elimination of Racial Discrimination (see p. 728) and other UN treaty monitoring bodies and regional human rights bodies, in order to assure their wide dissemination.

Persons with disabilities

Report of OHCHR. In response to a 2004 Commission request [YUN 2004, p. 801], OHCHR submitted a report [E/CN.4/2005/82] on the progress made in implementing the recommendations contained in the 2002 study on human rights and disability [YUN 2002, p. 771]. The report reviewed efforts by States, treaty bodies, the Commission, national human rights institutions and civil society, and addressed OHCHR's programme of work relating to the human rights of persons with disabilities. The report concluded that, since the study's publication, there had been encouraging developments in the way in which disability issues were addressed within the human rights treaty system. There were increasing references to the issue in the general comments and recommendations of treaty bodies and positive examples of collaboration between States, national institutions and human rights/disability NGOs. However, the degree of attention that States devoted to disability under existing human rights mechanisms varied from one treaty to another, and it was vital that they referred more systematically to the rights of persons with disabilities and focused on the specific situation and needs of those individuals rather than dealing with them as one of the groups vulnerable to dis-

crimination. As suggested in the study, thematic discussions on disability could help increase attention to the rights of disabled persons under each treaty and clarify the content of human rights standards with regard to that category of individuals. National human rights institutions and disability NGOs could also enhance their contribution to the work of relevant human rights treaty bodies. OHCHR supported the elaboration of a new international convention to promote and protect the rights and dignity of persons with disabilities and considered that such an instrument could strengthen the protection already afforded by existing human rights treaties.

Commission action. On 20 April [res. 2005/65], the Commission called on OHCHR to continue implementing the recommendations addressed to it in the study on human rights and disability and to report to the Commission in 2006 on progress in that regard and on the achievement of the objectives set forth in its programme of work relating to the human rights of persons with disabilities. OHCHR was also asked to prepare an expert paper focusing on the lessons learned from existing monitoring mechanisms and to make it available to the Ad Hoc Committee on a Comprehensive and Integral International Convention on the Protection and Promotion of the Rights and Dignity of Persons with Disabilities (see below). The Secretary-General and OHCHR were requested to include in relevant reports to the Assembly and the Commission information on progress to ensure the full recognition and equal enjoyment of all human rights by persons with disabilities, and to make such reports available to the Ad Hoc Committee.

The Special Rapporteur on disability of the Commission for Social Development (see p. 1190) was invited to address the Commission in 2006 on her experience in disability and human rights-related issues. The Commission urged Governments to address the human rights of persons with disabilities in their reporting obligations under relevant human rights instruments, and called on UN organizations and agencies and intergovernmental institutions for development cooperation to integrate a disability and human rights perspective into their activities and to reflected that in related reports.

On 21 July, the Economic and Social Council, in its **resolution 2005/9** (see p. 1196), encouraged States to participate actively in international cooperation for the equalization of opportunities for persons with disabilities.

Report of Ad Hoc Committee. In response to General Assembly resolution 59/198 [YUN 2004, p. 1100], the Secretary-General, in August [A/60/266], transmitted the report of the Ad Hoc Committee on a Comprehensive and Integral International Convention on the Protection and Promotion of the Rights and Dignity of Persons with Disabilities, established in Assembly resolution 56/168 [YUN 2001, p. 1012], on its sixth session (New York, 1-12 August). The Committee, mandated to consider proposals for the convention, recommended that it continue its work in 2006.

GENERAL ASSEMBLY ACTION

On 23 December [meeting 69], the General Assembly, on the recommendation of the Third Committee [A/60/509/Add.2], adopted **resolution 60/232** without vote [agenda item 71 (*b*)].

Ad Hoc Committee on a Comprehensive and Integral International Convention on the Protection and Promotion of the Rights and Dignity of Persons with Disabilities

The General Assembly,

Recalling its resolution 56/168 of 19 December 2001, by which it decided to establish an Ad Hoc Committee, open to the participation of all Member States and observers to the United Nations, to consider proposals for a comprehensive and integral international convention to promote and protect the rights and dignity of persons with disabilities, based on a holistic approach in the work done in the fields of social development, human rights and non-discrimination and taking into account the recommendations of the Commission on Human Rights and the Commission for Social Development,

Recalling also its resolution 59/198 of 20 December 2004, as well as relevant resolutions of the Commission for Social Development and the Commission on Human Rights,

Reaffirming the universality, indivisibility, interdependence and interrelatedness of all human rights and fundamental freedoms and the need for persons with disabilities to be guaranteed their full enjoyment without discrimination,

Convinced of the contribution that a convention will make in this regard, and encouraged by the increased support of the international community for such a convention,

Welcoming with satisfaction the progress achieved so far in the negotiations on a draft convention,

Stressing the importance of the active participation of intergovernmental and non-governmental organizations and national human rights institutions in the work of the Ad Hoc Committee, and their valuable contribution to the promotion of the full enjoyment of all human rights and fundamental freedoms by persons with disabilities,

Underlining the importance of the participation of the Special Rapporteur on disability of the Commission for Social Development in the work of the Ad Hoc Committee,

Recognizing the important contributions made thus far to the Ad Hoc Committee by all stakeholders,

1. *Welcomes* the reports of the Ad Hoc Committee on a Comprehensive and Integral International Convention on the Protection and Promotion of the Rights and Dignity of Persons with Disabilities on its fifth and sixth sessions;

2. *Requests* the Secretary-General to transmit the reports of the Ad Hoc Committee to the Commission for Social Development at its forty-fourth session and to the Commission on Human Rights at its sixty-second session, and requests both Commissions to continue to contribute to the work of the Ad Hoc Committee;

3. *Invites* Member States and observers to continue to participate actively and constructively in the work of the Ad Hoc Committee with the aim of concluding a draft text of a convention and submitting it to the General Assembly, as a matter of priority, for its adoption, preferably at the sixty-first session;

4. *Decides* that the Ad Hoc Committee shall hold, within existing resources, prior to the sixty-first session of the General Assembly, two sessions in 2006, one of fifteen working days, from 16 January to 3 February, in order to achieve a complete reading of the draft text of a convention prepared by the Chairman of the Ad Hoc Committee, and one of ten working days, from 7 to 18 August;

5. *Underlines* the importance of further strengthening the cooperation and coordination between the Office of the United Nations High Commissioner for Human Rights and the Department of Economic and Social Affairs of the Secretariat in order to provide technical support to the work of the Ad Hoc Committee, and invites them to provide, in advance of the meetings of the Ad Hoc Committee, background documentation to assist Member States and observers in the negotiation of a draft convention, and to organize, in close connection and timing with the dates and venue of the meetings of the Ad Hoc Committee, meetings of experts and seminars in relation to the draft convention, within existing resources;

6. *Requests* the Secretary-General to continue to provide the Ad Hoc Committee with the facilities necessary for the performance of its work, and in this context invites the Secretary-General to reallocate resources to the United Nations Programme on Disability so as to provide support to the negotiations on a draft convention;

7. *Stresses* the need for additional efforts to ensure accessibility at the United Nations, with reasonable accommodation regarding facilities and documentation, for all persons with disabilities, in accordance with General Assembly decision 56/474 of 23 July 2002;

8. *Requests* the Secretary-General to explore and implement innovative measures, within existing resources and in consultation with organizations of persons with disabilities and the Bureau of the Ad Hoc Committee, for the provision of selected documents of the Ad Hoc Committee in formats accessible to participants with visual and hearing disabilities;

9. *Encourages* Member States to continue to include in their delegations to the Ad Hoc Committee persons with disabilities and/or other experts in the field;

10. *Urges* Member States, observers, civil society, international organizations, financial institutions and the private sector to contribute to the voluntary fund established pursuant to its resolution 57/229 of 18 December 2002 to support the participation of non-governmental organizations and experts from developing countries, in particular least developed countries, in the work of the Ad Hoc Committee;

11. *Requests* the Secretary-General to disseminate widely to non-governmental organizations all available information on accreditation procedures, modalities and supportive measures for their participation in the work of the Ad Hoc Committee, as well as the criteria for the financial assistance that is available through the voluntary fund;

12. *Also requests* the Secretary-General to transmit a comprehensive report of the Ad Hoc Committee and to report on the implementation of paragraphs 5, 6, 7, 8 and 11 of the present resolution to the General Assembly at its sixty-first session.

Indigenous people

Reports of Special Rapporteur. In response to a 2004 Commission request [YUN 2004, p. 792], the Special Rapporteur on the situation of human rights and fundamental freedoms of indigenous people, Rodolfo Stavenhagen (Mexico), submitted a January report [E/CN.4/2005/88], which focused on the obstacles, disparities and challenges facing indigenous peoples regarding access to and quality of education and cultural appropriateness of educational approaches. The report also provided examples of good practice and initiatives aimed at solving the educational problems of indigenous peoples in various countries. It observed that, although the right to education was universally recognized, indigenous peoples still did not exercise it fully. Whereas the right was critical to them as a means of extricating themselves from exclusion and discrimination and for the enjoyment and maintenance of their cultures and traditions, formal education had been a two-edged sword for them. While it enabled their children and youth to acquire knowledge and skills to allow them to progress in life and connect with the broader world, it had been a means of forcibly changing or destroying their cultures, especially when the programmes, curricula and teaching methods were detached from indigenous cultures. Factors impeding indigenous peoples' access to education included their demographic dispersion and lack of adequate transport, which often made it difficult for their children to attend the few schools that existed in their areas. Other major limiting factors related to economic, social and cultural questions, discrimination against indigenous education and assimilationist models of education and ignorance of, or failure to appreciate indigenous languages and culture. The Special Rapporteur recommended, among other things, that Governments attach high priority to the objectives and principles of indigenous education and prepare, in close collaboration with indigenous communities, programmes for training an adequate number of bilingual and intercultural education teachers. In addition, courses on indigenous peo-

ples should be broadened at all levels of national education, with an anti-racist, multicultural focus that reflected respect for cultural and ethnic diversity and, in particular, gender equality.

A separate report of the Special Rapporteur [E/CN.4/2006/78/Add.1] summarized communications, including urgent appeals he had sent to 17 Governments on alleged violations of indigenous peoples' rights between 1 January and 31 December 2005, and the responses received.

Commission action. On 20 April [res. 2005/51], the Commission asked the Special Rapporteur to request, receive, exchange and respond to information on violations of indigenous peoples' rights, begin preparing a study of best practices in implementing his recommendations, and submit a progress report in 2006 and a final report in 2007. The Commission further requested the Special Rapporteur to report on his activities to the General Assembly in 2005 and to the Commission in 2006. The Secretary-General was asked to assist him. The Commission took note of the Special Rapporteur's intention to devote his next report to the topics of constitutional reform, legislation and implementation of laws regarding the protection of indigenous peoples' rights, as well as the intention of OHCHR and the Inter-Parliamentary Union (IPU) to organize a seminar on that topic (see p. 876) to assist the Special Rapporteur in examining related issues in his annual report to the Commission in 2006.

In related action on 20 April [res. 2005/52], the Commission, by a recorded vote of 35 to 13, with 4 abstentions, requested the Special Rapporteur to liaise with the Special Adviser for the Prevention of Genocide [YUN 2004, p. 730] regarding the protection of indigenous peoples from genocide, and to develop an emergency response mechanism as part of his mandate. The Secretary-General was asked to ensure that the Special Adviser took into account the need to protect indigenous peoples and their territories and ensure that UN forces protected them, their territories and objects indispensable to their survival.

On 25 July, the Economic and Social Council, taking note of Commission resolution 2005/51, requested the Special Rapporteur to submit a report to the General Assembly in 2005 and to the Commission in 2006 (**decision 2005/270**).

Further reports of Special Rapporteur. The Special Rapporteur visited South Africa (28 July–8 August) [E/CN.4/2006/78/Add.2], which continued to deal with the legacy of the racist apartheid policy. Six groups within the country had identified themselves as indigenous and the Government had declared its commitment to meet the demands of the indigenous groups in the country. Although indigenous people had access to Government social services, including education, health delivery systems and infrastructure, they tended to be more marginalized than other sectors, such that they were concentrated at the lower end of the socio-economic scale. The Special Rapporteur recommended measures for improving the human rights situation of indigenous peoples in the country, including their constitutional recognition and removal of the stigma of their classification as "coloureds" by the then apartheid regime. He also called for a systematic land needs and land rights study of indigenous communities, the acceleration of the land restitution process, and the end of the policy of limiting indigenous peoples' restitution claims to the 1913 cut-off date. The Special Rapporteur further recommended the use of economic, social and human development indicators for indigenous peoples and the improvement of their access to the justice system, among other measures.

In New Zealand (16-26 November) [E/CN.4/2006/78/Add.3], the Special Rapporteur considered the human rights situation of the indigenous Maori, who accounted for 15 per cent of the national population. He reviewed aspects of their political representation, land rights claims and resettlements and the human rights implications of the Foreshore and Seabed Act of 2004, some aspects of which many Maori considered to be discriminatory. He also considered the country's justice system and language, cultural and education policies as they related to indigenous issues. The Special Rapporteur observed that, while the Maori were well integrated into the national economy, and the Government had made efforts to reduce inequalities in the country, persistent disparities remained between Maori and European-descended New Zealanders in many areas, including healthcare and affordable housing. The Special Rapporteur recommended constitutional reforms to regulate the relationship between the Government and the Maori, based on the 1840 Treaty of Waitangi with Britain, which was considered a founding document of New Zealand and which guaranteed the Maori full exclusive and undisturbed possession of their lands and estates, forests, fisheries and other properties which they might collectively or individually possess. Other recommendations addressed further constitutional issues; human rights issues and the Waitangi Tribunal; treaty settlements; the environment; education and culture; social policy; and international indigenous rights.

In response to Commission resolution 2005/51 (see p. 875), the Secretary-General, by a September note [A/60/358], transmitted a report of the Special Rapporteur, which reviewed activities undertaken between August 2004 and August 2005, and highlighted issues of concern requiring urgent attention. The report described the Special Rapporteur's cooperation with other international and regional mechanisms and discussed the major human rights problems affecting indigenous peoples, which related to persistent poverty, access to education and armed conflicts, among other factors. The Special Rapporteur concluded that, while the living conditions and human rights of indigenous people had improved in some countries and regions owing to specific circumstances, in many other instances, their rights had not been respected. The main problem was rooted in shortcomings in terms of implementation, the efficiency of institutions and the procedures and mechanisms for the full realization of their human rights. The Special Rapporteur recommended that States adopt specific goals and policies for indigenous people with regard to achieving the Millennium Development Goals on the eradication of extreme poverty and hunger and on the achievement of universal primary education, respectively. They should adopt emergency measures to guarantee the provision of basic services to indigenous communities where access to such services was lacking, and attach high priority to the objectives and principles of indigenous education.

On 16 December, the General Assembly took note of the Secretary-General's note (**decision 60/530**).

International seminars. In accordance with Commission resolution 2005/51 (see p. 875), OHCHR organized two international seminars on constitutional reforms, legislation and implementation of laws regarding the rights of indigenous peoples, in collaboration with IPU (Geneva, 25-26 July) and the Indigenous Peoples Law and Policy Programme of the University of Arizona (Arizona, United States, 12-14 October) [E/CN.4/2006/78/Add.5]. The seminar discussed with parliamentarians, government representatives and other experts the role of legislators in protecting and promoting indigenous peoples' rights and analysed good practices and obstacles encountered in the implementation of relevant legislation. Participants adopted conclusions and recommendations designed to provide an input in the Special Rapporteur's annual report to the Commission.

Working Group on Indigenous Populations

Commission action. By a recorded vote of 39 to 13, with 1 abstention, the Commission, on 20 April [res. 2005/49], invited the Working Group on Indigenous Populations (see p. 877) to continue to consider ways in which indigenous peoples' expertise could contribute to its work, and to pay special attention to its standard-setting activities throughout the Second International Decade of the World's Indigenous People (1995-2004) (see p. 879). The Commission invited Governments, indigenous peoples' organizations and NGOs to ensure the full participation of indigenous people in the Group's activities, and further invited the Group and special procedure mandate holders to continue to consider ways to ensure that indigenous peoples' situation was properly reflected in their periodic reports. The Commission recommended that the Economic and Social Council authorize the Working Group to meet for five working days prior to the Commission's 2006 session and the Chairperson-Rapporteur of the Group's 2004 session to submit a report on that session to the Permanent Forum on Indigenous Issues (see below). The Secretary-General was asked to assist the Group and to transmit its reports to Governments, indigenous peoples' organizations, intergovernmental organizations and NGOs.

ECONOMIC AND SOCIAL COUNCIL ACTION

In July, the Economic and Social Council, on the recommendation of the Commission on Human Rights [E/2005/23 & Corr.1], adopted **decision 2005/268** by recorded vote (32-17-1) [agenda item 14 (g)].

Working Group on Indigenous Populations of the Subcommission on the Promotion and Protection of Human Rights

At its 38th plenary meeting, on 25 July 2005, the Economic and Social Council took note of Commission on Human Rights resolution 2005/49 of 20 April 2005, and endorsed the Commission's recommendation to authorize the Working Group on Indigenous Populations of the Subcommission on the Promotion and Protection of Human Rights to meet for five working days prior to the fifty-seventh session of the Subcommission.

The Council also authorized the Chairperson-Rapporteur of the twenty-second session of the Working Group to submit the report on that session to the Permanent Forum on Indigenous Issues at its fourth session in 2005.

RECORDED VOTE ON DECISION 2005/268:

In favour: Armenia, Azerbaijan, Bangladesh, Belize, Brazil, Canada, China, Colombia, Congo, Costa Rica, Cuba, Ecuador, Guinea, India, Indonesia, Jamaica, Kenya, Malaysia, Mauritius, Mexico, Mozambique, Namibia, Nicaragua, Pakistan, Panama, Russian Federation, Saudi Arabia, Senegal, Thailand, Tunisia, United Arab Emirates, United Republic of Tanzania.

Against: Albania, Australia, Belgium, France, Germany, Iceland, Ireland, Italy, Japan, Lithuania, Poland, Republic of Korea, South Africa, Spain, Turkey, United Kingdom, United States.

Abstaining: Denmark.

Working group activities. The Working Group on Indigenous Populations held its twenty-third session (Geneva, 18-22 July) [E/CN.4/

Sub.2/2005/26] to review developments pertaining to the promotion and protection of human rights and fundamental freedoms of indigenous populations and to give special attention to the evolution of relevant standards. In annotations to the provisional agenda [E/CN.4/Sub.2/AC.4/2005/1/Add.1], the Secretariat presented background information on indigenous peoples and the international and domestic protection of traditional knowledge; indigenous peoples and conflict prevention and resolution; cooperation with other UN bodies in the sphere of indigenous issues; standard-setting activities and the International Decade of the World's Indigenous Peoples (see p. 879).

The Group had before it a working paper prepared by the secretariat of the Convention on Biological Diversity and Traditional Knowledge [E/CN.4/Sub.2/AC.4/2005/CRP.2] and expanded working papers by Antoanella-Iulia Motoc (Romania) and the Tebtebba Foundation offering guidelines to govern the implementation of the principle of free, prior and informed consent of indigenous peoples in relation to developments affecting their lands and natural resources [E/CN.4/Sub.2/AC.4/2005/WP.1], and by Yozo Yokota (Japan) and the Saami Council on substantive proposals on the draft principles and guidelines on the heritage of indigenous peoples [E/CN.4/Sub.2/AC.4/2005/3]. The Group also considered a Joint Statement from the Indigenous World Association and Indigenous Media Network [E/CN.4/Sub.2/AC.4/2005/CRP.3]; working papers prepared by the secretariat of the Permanent Forum on Indigenous Issues [E/CN.4/Sub.2/AC.4/2005/CRP.4] (see p. 881) and the Indian Movement Tupac Katari [E/CN.4/AC.4/2005/CRP.5]; and a note by the UN Secretariat on the Human Rights component of the Comprehensive Programme of Action for the Second Decade [E/CN.4/AC.4/2005/WP.2].

In its recommendations, the Group decided to maintain on its agenda for 2006 a sub-item on future priorities for its standard-setting activities, and decided that the preparation of working papers relating to standard-setting would be expanded to other Group activities. The Group decided to continue the dialogue on the session's principle theme "indigenous peoples and the international and domestic protection of traditional knowledge", by inviting interested bodies to discuss it in depth in 2006, and invited UN treaty bodies to pay specific attention to the promotion and protection of traditional knowledge. The Group reiterated its decision to accept the invitation extended by representatives of indigenous peoples from parties to *Treaty 6 in Canada* to a seminar on the implementation of treaties, agreements and other constructive arrangements, scheduled to take place in 2006. Under that item, Member States were invited to submit information during the Group's 2006 session on their respective conflict prevention/resolution mechanisms. The Subcommission was requested to appoint one of its members to prepare a preliminary report on current sequels of colonialism that continued to affect the lives of indigenous people, for submission to the Subcommission and the Working Group in 2007. The Group recommended that the Subcommission request OHCHR to invite submissions from Governments on the implementation of the principle of free, prior and informed consent of indigenous peoples in relation to developments affecting their lands and natural resources, also for submission in 2007. It invited OHCHR to prepare a draft publication drawing on the working papers on legal commentary and guidelines prepared by Ms. Motoc and the Tebtebba Foundation, as well as on the information provided by States on best practices in that area, for the Group's consideration in 2006. They further asked OHCHR to organize, in consultation with indigenous organizations and UN bodies, an expert seminar on the draft principles and guidelines on the protection of the heritage of indigenous peoples. The Group decided to further strengthen its cooperation with the Special Rapporteur on the situation of human rights and fundamental freedoms of indigenous people. It also further decided that the principle theme for its twenty-fourth session would be the "utilization of indigenous peoples' land by non-indigenous authorities, groups or individuals for military purposes." Governments, indigenous peoples, the UN system and NGOs were invited to provide information in advance and to contribute to the discussion on that item.

Annexed to the Group's report was a list of activities that it recommended to the Subcommission for possible inclusion in the Programme of Action of the Second Decade of the World's Indigenous People (see p. 879).

Subcommission action. On 11 August [res. 2005/23], the Subcommission asked the Secretary-General to transmit the Working Group's report on its 2005 session to the High Commissioner, indigenous organizations, Governments, intergovernmental organizations, concerned NGOs, treaty bodies and all thematic rapporteurs, special representatives, independent experts and working groups, and requested that it be made available to the Commission in 2006. The Subcommission decided that the Group, in 2006, should adopt as its principal theme "utilization of indigenous peoples' lands by non-indigenous authorities, groups or individuals for military

purposes" and review the revised draft principles and guidelines on the heritage of indigenous people [YUN 1995, p. 780]. It requested the Commission to endorse the participation of the Chairperson/Rapporteur of the Working Group at the fifth session of the Permanent Forum on Indigenous Issues in 2006, to enable him present the Group's report on its 2005 session, and to recommend that the Economic and Social Council approve such participation. It decided on the Group's agenda for 2006, asked the Secretary-General to prepare an annotated agenda for it and invited States to submit to the Group at that session information regarding mechanisms for conflict resolution and prevention available to indigenous peoples under their jurisdiction. OHCHR was asked to forward to the Coordinator for the Second International Decade of the World's Indigenous Peoples the list of activities annexed to the Group's report for possible inclusion in the Decade's Programme of Action, to be submitted to the General Assembly in 2005. The Subcommission endorsed the Group's recommendation that the High Commissioner organize a workshop on indigenous peoples and conflict resolution and prevention to be held in Geneva no later than in autumn of 2007 and invited the High Commissioner to organize, in Spring 2006, a second workshop on indigenous peoples, mining and other private sector companies and human rights. Miguel Alfonso Martínez (Cuba) was asked to submit the additional working paper requested in 2004 [YUN 2004, p. 795] on indigenous people and conflict prevention and resolution, and to prepare, without financial implications, a working paper on the current sequels of the colonial era that continued to adversely affect the living conditions of indigenous peoples in various parts of the world, to be submitted to the Working Group and to the Subcommission in 2007. The Subcommission further requested OHCHR to submit to the Group in 2006 an updated compilation of all studies, reports and other research work on the situation of the rights of indigenous peoples that had been undertaken since 1982 by UN bodies, and those that were currently being undertaken, to serve as a point of reference for the Group in its future research action. The Commission was asked to request the Economic and Social Council to authorize 10 meetings for the Working Group prior to the beginning of the Subcommission's 2006 session.

Voluntary Fund for Indigenous Populations

The Board of Trustees of the United Nations Voluntary Fund for Indigenous Populations, at its eighteenth session (Geneva, 28 February–4 March) [E/CN.4/Sub.2/AC.4/2005/5], recommended

26 travel grants totaling $136,900 to enable indigenous representatives to attend the Permanent Forum on Indigenous Issues, 25 travel grants totaling $80,800 to enable representatives to attend the Working Group on Indigenous Populations, and nine travel grants totaling $62,400 for representatives to attend the working group on the draft UN declaration of the rights of indigenous peoples. The Board's recommendations were approved by the High Commissioner on the Secretary-General's behalf on 7 March. Annexed to the report were lists of the beneficiaries.

Subcommission action. On 11 August [res. 2005/23], the Subcommission appealed to Governments, indigenous peoples, intergovernmental organizations, NGOs and other potential donors in a position to do so, to contribute to the Fund.

Second International Decade of the World's Indigenous People

Commission action. On 20 April [res. 2005/49], the Commission, by a recorded vote of 39 to 13, with 1 abstention, urged States to continue working, in cooperation with the UN system, on the implementation of the conclusions and recommendations of the First International Decade of the World's Indigenous People, and to support the goals of the Second Decade (2004-2013), proclaimed by the General Assembly in resolution 59/174 [YUN 2004, p. 799]. It invited the Coordinator for the Second Decade to secure the effective participation of Governments, the Permanent Forum on Indigenous Issues and other relevant UN system bodies and mechanisms, as well as indigenous and non-governmental organizations, in the planning, execution and monitoring of the Second Decade's programme of action (see below). The Commission invited the Working Group on Indigenous Populations to submit to the Second Decade's Coordinator a list of activities to be considered for possible inclusion in the human rights component of its programme of action. The High Commissioner was requested to submit, in 2006, a report on the 2005 activities undertaken by her Office relating to indigenous people, as well as other relevant proposals.

Subcommission action. On 10 August [res. 2005/19], the Subcommission endorsed the list of activities recommended by the Working Group on Indigenous Populations (see p. 877), compiled in compliance with Commission resolution 2005/49 (see p. 662), and requested OHCHR to forward it to the Coordinator of the Second Decade. It stressed the need to continue giving particular attention to achieving the effective participation of indigenous peoples in the planning, organization and implementation of the activities of the Second Decade. The Working Group

was requested to follow closely the activities carried out as part of the human rights component of the Second Decade's programme of action, so as to be able to contribute to its mid-term and end-term reviews, to be carried out in 2010 and 2015, respectively. The Coordinator for the Second Decade was asked to appeal to Governments and other donors to contribute to the Voluntary Fund for the Second International Decade of the World's Indigenous People (see p. 881).

Programme of Action for the Second International Decade

Report of Secretary-General. In accordance with General Assembly resolution 59/174 [YUN 2004, p. 799], the Secretary-General submitted an August report [A/60/270] containing a draft programme of action for the Second International Decade of the World's Indigenous People. The report identified five key objectives for the Decade: promoting non-discrimination and inclusion of indigenous peoples in the design, implementation and evaluation of laws, policies, resources, programmes and projects; promoting full and effective participation of indigenous people in decisions directly or indirectly affecting various aspects of their lives; redefining development policies that departed from a vision of equity and that were culturally appropriate; adopting targeted policies, programmes, projects and budgets for the development of indigenous people, including concrete benchmarks, with a particular emphasis on indigenous women, children and youth; and developing strong monitoring mechanisms and enhancing accountability for the protection of indigenous people and the improvement of their lives.

The report examined each area of action and made recommendations for achieving them at the international and national levels. At the national level, States were urged to develop policies and focused programmes to reverse ethnocentric perceptions of indigenous cultures, which were often stereotypical, folklorized and biased. They should review also national legislation to eliminate possible discriminatory provisions, with the full and effective participation of indigenous experts. The international community was urged to continue to promote bilingual and cross-cultural education programmes for indigenous and non-indigenous peoples, while States, the UN system and other intergovernmental organizations were urged to ensure access to comprehensive, community-based and culturally appropriate healthcare services, education, adequate nutrition and housing without discrimination. They were asked to finalize negotiations on the draft declaration on the rights of indigenous peoples and to adopt it early in the Second Decade, as a priority action. Regarding the promotion and monitoring of the programme, the report urged the Coordinator of the Second Decade to collect information and submit annual reports to the General Assembly on progress made in achieving the goals, objectives and programme of action of the Second Decade. The Assembly was asked to hold a midterm and end-term assessment of the Decade to review its progress. The report also recommended that indigenous organizations establish national committees to monitor the implementation of the programme of action.

GENERAL ASSEMBLY ACTION

On 16 December [meeting 64], the General Assembly, on the recommendation of the Third Committee [A/60/506 & Corr.1], adopted **resolution 60/142** without vote [agenda item 68].

Programme of Action for the Second International Decade of the World's Indigenous People

The General Assembly,

Bearing in mind that, in the Vienna Declaration and Programme of Action, the 1993 World Conference on Human Rights recognized the inherent dignity and the unique contribution of indigenous peoples to the development and plurality of society and strongly reaffirmed the commitment of the international community to their economic, social and cultural wellbeing and their enjoyment of the fruits of sustainable development,

Reaffirming the commitment of States to continue making progress in the advancement of the human rights of the world's indigenous peoples at the local, national, regional and international levels, as well as in the areas of culture, education, health, environment and social and economic development,

Reaffirming also that States should, in accordance with international law, take concerted positive steps to ensure respect for all human rights and fundamental freedoms of indigenous peoples, on the basis of equality and non-discrimination, and recognizing the value and diversity of their distinctive identities, cultures and social organizations,

Recalling its resolution 48/163 of 21 December 1993, in which it proclaimed the International Decade of the World's Indigenous People, commencing on 10 December 1994, with the goal of strengthening international cooperation for the solution of problems faced by indigenous people in such areas as human rights, the environment, development, education and health,

Bearing in mind the internationally agreed development goals, including those contained in the United Nations Millennium Declaration and the draft programme of action for the Second International Decade of the World's Indigenous People, which are linked and which together promote actions to improve the standard of living of the indigenous peoples,

Recalling its resolution 59/174 of 20 December 2004 proclaiming the Second International Decade of the World's Indigenous People, 2005-2014,

Expressing its appreciation to the Coordinator of the Second Decade, the Under-Secretary-General for Eco-

nomic and Social Affairs, for having elaborated a concrete programme of action to be pursued during the Decade based upon equal participation and partnership between all actors involved,

Conscious that in its resolution 59/174 it requested the Coordinator to fulfil his mandate in full cooperation and consultation with, inter alia, the Permanent Forum on Indigenous Issues, other relevant bodies and mechanisms of the United Nations system and the Office of the United Nations High Commissioner for Human Rights,

Keeping in mind the need to continue, as appropriate, developing standard-setting activities on issues of particular interest to indigenous peoples,

Expressing its appreciation for all contributions and proposals submitted in the course of the drafting of the programme of action for the Second Decade, and also giving due consideration to the contributions of the Office of the United Nations High Commissioner for Human Rights and the Working Group on Indigenous Populations of the Subcommission on the Promotion and Protection of Human Rights to the draft programme of action,

1. *Adopts* the Programme of Action for the Second International Decade of the World's Indigenous People as a guideline for action for the Second Decade;

2. *Urges* all actors involved in the process to cooperate in a constructive and decisive manner in order to achieve rapid progress and concrete results in realizing the goals of the Second Decade;

3. *Appeals* to the international community at large to provide financial support to the Programme of Action for the Second International Decade of the World's Indigenous People, inter alia, through contributions to the Voluntary Fund for the Second Decade;

4. *Adopts* "Partnership for action and dignity" as the theme for the Second Decade;

5. *Requests* the Coordinator of the Second Decade to consult with Member States, agencies, organizations and other relevant bodies and mechanisms of the United Nations system, indigenous organizations and other non-governmental organizations about the possibility of undertaking midterm and end-of-term reviews of the Second Decade;

6. *Reaffirms* that, in accordance with its resolutions 40/131 of 13 December 1985, 52/108 of 12 December 1997 and 56/140 of 19 December 2001, the representatives of indigenous communities and organizations will continue to benefit from the financial assistance provided by the United Nations Voluntary Fund for Indigenous Populations to facilitate their participation in the deliberations of the Permanent Forum on Indigenous Issues, the working group of the Commission on Human Rights charged with elaborating the draft United Nations declaration on the rights of indigenous peoples and the Working Group on Indigenous Populations of the Subcommission on the Promotion and Protection of Human Rights, according to the terms of reference of the Fund;

7. *Urges* all Governments and indigenous organizations concerned to take every action necessary to facilitate the adoption of the draft United Nations declaration on the rights of indigenous peoples as soon as possible;

8. *Invites* Governments, the organs, organizations and bodies of the United Nations system, other inter-

governmental organizations, indigenous and other non-governmental organizations and civil society actors to draw up their own plans for the Second Decade, using as a guideline for action the goals, objectives and Programme of Action for the Second Decade, including integrating a gender perspective in such activities;

9. *Decides* to include in the provisional agenda of its sixty-first session, under the item entitled "Indigenous issues", a sub-item entitled "Second International Decade of the World's Indigenous People".

Voluntary Fund for International Decade

Efforts continued during the year to secure support for the Voluntary Fund for the Second International Decade of the World's Indigenous People, which the General Assembly had requested the Secretary-General to establish in resolution 59/174 [YUN 2004, p. 799]. The new Fund would serve as the successor to the Fund established for the First Decade, pursuant to Assembly resolution 48/163 [YUN 1993, p. 865]. In 2005, the Assembly, in resolution 60/142 (see p. 880), by which it adopted the Programme of Action for the Second Decade, appealed to the international community to provide international support to the Programme through contributions to the new Fund. The Subcommission, in its resolutions 2005/19 and 2005/23 (see p. 879), made similar pleas to Governments and donors.

Draft declaration of the rights of indigenous peoples

Commission action. On 20 April [res. 2005/50], by a recorded vote of 52 to 0, with 1 abstention, the Commission recommended that the working group established to elaborate a draft declaration on the rights of indigenous peoples (see below) meet for 10 working days prior to the Commission's 2006 session and report in 2006. It urged all parties involved in the negotiation to present for adoption, as soon as possible, a final draft of the United Nations declaration on the rights of indigenous people.

ECONOMIC AND SOCIAL COUNCIL ACTION

On 25 July, the Economic and Social Council, on the recommendation of the Commission on Human Rights [E/2005/23 & Corr.1], adopted **decision 2005/269** by recorded vote (49-0-1) [agenda item 14 *(g)*].

Working Group of the Commission on Human Rights to elaborate a draft declaration in accordance with paragraph 5 of General Assembly resolution 49/214 of 23 December 1994

At its 38th plenary meeting, on 25 July 2005, the Economic and Social Council took note of Commission on Human Rights resolution 2005/50 of 20 April 2005, and authorized the Working Group established in accordance with Commission resolution 1995/32 of 3 March 1995 to meet for a period of ten working days

prior to the sixty-second session of the Commission, stipulating that the costs of the meeting would be met from within existing resources.

RECORDED VOTE ON DECISION 2005/269:

In favour: Albania, Armenia, Australia, Azerbaijan, Bangladesh, Belgium, Belize, Brazil, Canada, China, Colombia, Congo, Costa Rica, Cuba, Denmark, Ecuador, France, Germany, Guinea, Iceland, India, Indonesia, Ireland, Italy, Jamaica, Japan, Kenya, Lithuania, Malaysia, Mauritius, Mexico, Mozambique, Namibia, Nicaragua, Pakistan, Panama, Poland, Republic of Korea, Russian Federation, Saudi Arabia, Senegal, South Africa, Spain, Thailand, Tunisia, Turkey, United Arab Emirates, United Kingdom, United Republic of Tanzania.
Against: None.
Abstaining: United States.

Subcommission action. On 11 August [res. 2005/23], the Subcommission recommended the completion of the final version of the draft declaration as early as possible.

Workshop. During the year, Mexico organized an international workshop (Michoacán, Mexico, 26-30 September) [E/CN.4/2005/WG.15/CRP.1], at which informal discussions were held towards resolving some of the obstacles to the adoption of the UN draft declaration on the rights of indigenous peoples before the next session of the Working Group negotiating that draft (see below). The workshop considered three themes: self-determination; land, territories and natural resources; and general provisions. It heard presentations by representatives of Governments, indigenous peoples and academic experts.

Working group activities. The working group established to consider a draft declaration on the rights of indigenous peoples, at its eleventh session (Geneva, 5-16 December) [E/CN.4/2006/79], discussed articles relating to self-determination; lands, territories and resources; and other articles where potential agreement might be reached. The group had before it the report of the September workshop that considered those articles (see above), sponsored by Mexico, and intended to help facilitate the Group's negotiations.

The group discussed preambular paragraphs 6, 13 and article 36 related to treaties, self-determination and land, territories and resources. The working group's session was to be reconvened in January 2006.

Permanent Forum on Indigenous Issues

Report of Permanent Forum. The 16-member Permanent Forum on Indigenous Issues, established by Economic and Social Council resolution 2000/22 [YUN 2000, p. 731] to address indigenous issues relating to economic and social development, the environment, health, education and culture, and human rights, at its fourth session (New York, 16-27 May) [E/2005/43 & Corr. 1, 2], considered as its theme "Millennium Development Goals and indigenous peoples" and recommended three draft decisions for adoption by the Council (see below). Matters brought to the Council's attention related to the eradication of extreme poverty and hunger, the achievement of universal primary education, the human rights and fundamental freedoms of indigenous people, data collection on indigenous peoples, indigenous children and youth and indigenous women and the Forum's future work.

ECONOMIC AND SOCIAL COUNCIL ACTION

On 22 July, the Economic and Social Council authorized a three-day international expert group meeting on the MDGs, indigenous participation and good governance, and requested the meeting to report to the Forum in 2006 (**decision 2005/252**). It decided that the Forum's fifth session would be held in New York from 15 to 26 May 2006 (**decision 2005/253**), and approved the provisional agenda and documentation for that session (**decision 2005/254**).

On 25 July, the Council took note of the Forum's report on its fourth session (**decision 2005/296**).

Indigenous peoples' permanent sovereignty over natural resources

On 20 April [dec. 2005/110], the Commission, by recorded vote (38-2-12), expressed appreciation to the Special Rapporteur on indigenous peoples' permanent sovereignty over natural resources, Erica-Irene A. Daes (Greece), for her 2004 final report [YUN 2004, p. 800] on a study on the topic. It recommended that the Economic and Social Council authorize OHCHR to convene an expert seminar on the theme, and give further attention to and discuss the political, legal, economic, social and cultural aspects and matters relating to the study. It also recommended that

studies that might be used as a basis for reconciliation between Governments and indigenous peoples be issued as UN publications and part of the *Human Rights Study Series.*

ECONOMIC AND SOCIAL COUNCIL ACTION

On 25 July, the Economic and Social Council, on the recommendation of the Commission on Human Rights [E/2005/23 & Corr. 1], adopted **decision 2005/289** by recorded vote (33-2-15) [agenda item 14 (*g*)].

Final report on the study on indigenous peoples' permanent sovereignty over natural resources

At its 38th plenary meeting, on 25 July 2005, the Economic and Social Council took note of Commission on Human Rights decision 2005/110 of 20 April 2005, and endorsed the Commission's recommendation to authorize the Office of the United Nations High Commissioner for Human Rights to convene an expert seminar during 2005, to which representatives of indigenous peoples and Governments as well as the Special Rapporteur of the Subcommission on the Promotion and Protection of Human Rights would be invited, in order to give further attention to and to discuss in detail the many political, legal, economic, social and cultural aspects and matters relating to the study on indigenous peoples' permanent sovereignty over natural resources as well as to the study entitled "Indigenous peoples and their relationship to land".

The Council also endorsed the Commission's recommendation that the studies of the Special Rapporteur be issued as United Nations publications as part of the *Human Rights Study Series.*

RECORDED VOTE ON DECISION 2005/289:

In favour: Armenia, Azerbaijan, Bangladesh, Belize, Brazil, Canada, China, Colombia, Congo, Costa Rica, Cuba, Ecuador, Guinea, India, Indonesia, Jamaica, Kenya, Malaysia, Mauritius, Mexico, Mozambique, Namibia, Nicaragua, Pakistan, Panama, Russian Federation, Saudi Arabia, Senegal, South Africa, Thailand, Tunisia, United Arab Emirates, United Republic of Tanzania.
Against: Australia, United States.
Abstaining: Albania, Belgium, Denmark, France, Germany, Iceland, Ireland, Italy, Japan, Lithuania, Poland, Republic of Korea, Spain, Turkey, United Kingdom.

Chapter III

Human rights violations

Alleged violations of human rights and international humanitarian law in a number of countries were examined in 2005 by the General Assembly, the Economic and Social Council, the Commission on Human Rights and its Subcommission on the Promotion and Protection of Human Rights, and by Special rapporteurs, special representatives of the Secretary-General and independent experts appointed to examine allegations.

General aspects

In accordance with a procedure established by Economic and Social Council resolution 1503 (XLVIII) (1503 procedure) [YUN 1970, p. 530] to deal with communications alleging denial or violation of human rights, the Working Group on Situations of the Commission on Human Rights, in closed meetings on 24 March and 1 April, examined human rights situations in Honduras, Kyrgyzstan and Uzbekistan, to decide whether or not to refer any of those situations to the Commission. The Commission decided to discontinue consideration of the situation on human rights in Honduras and to keep those in Kyrgyzstan and Uzbekistan under review. It appointed an independent expert to report to it on Uzbekistan, in accordance with the 1503 procedure and Council resolution 2000/3 [YUN 2000, p. 596]. Subsequently, Michèle Picard (France) was appointed independent expert.

(For information on the right to restitution, compensation and rehabilitation for victims of grave violations of human rights and fundamental freedoms, see p. 792.)

Africa

(For information on the human rights situation in Burundi, see p. 735; Chad, p. 736; the Democratic Republic of the Congo, p. 736; Liberia, p. 740; Sierra Leone, p. 742; and Somalia, p. 743.)

Sudan

Report of independent expert. In response to a 2004 request of the Commission on Human Rights [YUN 2004, p. 803], the independent expert on the situation of human rights in the Sudan, Emmanuel Akwei Addo (Ghana), in a February report on his 2004 mission to the Sudan [E/CN.4/2005/11], described Sudan's obligations under international human rights and humanitarian law, particularly within the context of the continuing armed conflict between the Government and the Sudan People's Liberation Movement/Sudan People's Liberation Army (SPLM/SPLA).

Commission action. On 21 April [E/2005/23 (res. 2005/82)], the Commission on Human Rights condemned the continuing violation of human rights and international humanitarian law in the Sudan, including sexual violence against women and girls, the destruction of villages and widespread displacement and attacks against civilians by all parties, particularly the Janjaweed and other militias. Emphasizing the need to control, disarm and disband the militias and to bring those responsible for human rights violations to justice, the Commission also condemned violations of the N'Djamena Humanitarian Ceasefire Agreement [YUN 2004, p. 235] and their impact on humanitarian efforts. It called on all parties to observe the humanitarian ceasefire and grant safe and unhindered humanitarian access to the Darfur region and elsewhere in the country; cease all acts of violence and protect women and girls from sexual and other forms of violence; respect the rights of refugees and internally displaced persons (IDPs), including their right of voluntary return in safety and dignity; cooperate with relevant human rights bodies and mechanisms of the African Union (AU) and the United Nations; prevent the recruitment of children as soldiers and combatants; refrain from the use of landmines; and stop the abduction and murder of relief workers by armed groups. The Government of the Sudan was called upon to investigate human rights violations, bring the perpetrators to justice and end impunity for crimes committed in Darfur; enhance access to the courts for all victims of human rights violations; and strengthen the independence and impartiality of the judiciary. The Commission also called on the international community to expand support for the AU's efforts and activities aimed at bringing peace to the Sudan and to continue relief assistance to the affected population in Darfur. The High Commissioner was requested to increase and speed up the deployment of human rights monitors in Darfur to complement the mission in the Sudan and to increase technical assistance and advisory services to the Government, with a view to enhancing the national human rights capacity. The Commission appointed for one year, a special rapporteur on the situation of human rights in the Sudan, who would, with the Secretary-General's assistance, monitor the situation and submit an interim report to the General Assembly in 2005 and a report to the Commission in 2006.

On 25 July, the Economic and Social Council approved the Commission's decision to establish the mandate of a Special Rapporteur, as well as its requests to the Special Rapporteur and the Secretary-General (**decision 2005/280**).

In July, Sima Samar (Afghanistan) was appointed as the Special Rapporteur.

Note by Secretary-General. By a 20 September note [A/60/356], the Secretary-General informed the General Assembly that the Special Rapporteur was scheduled to visit the Sudan in October (see below) and would, therefore, not be able to submit a written report, which the Commission had called for in resolution 2005/82 (see p. 883). She would, however, make an oral presentation.

On 16 December, the Assembly took note of the Secretary-General's note (**decision 60/533**).

Reports of Special Rapporteur. The Special Rapporteur, Ms. Samar, undertook her first visit to the Sudan (15-22 October) [E/CN.4/2006/111] to gather information on the human rights situation and on the Government's action to promote and protect those rights. Among the issues of concern she addressed were: alleged violations of the rights to life and physical integrity; women's rights and gender-based violence; physical abuse in State custody, the denial of fair trial standards and detention conditions; impunity, transitional justice and justice in Darfur; rebuilding the entire justice system; the death penalty; forced recruitment of children and forced relocations; economic, social and cultural rights; freedom of association, freedom of expression and the media; national security, power and practice; reconciliation and reparation in Darfur; and the efforts of the United Nations Mission in the Sudan to promote human rights.

The Special Rapporteur concluded that the framework for the protection and promotion of human rights had improved through the signing of the Comprehensive Peace Agreement between the north and the south (see p. 301), the establish-

ment of the Government of National Unity and the Government of southern Sudan, and the adoption of the interim national constitution and the constitution of South Sudan, both of which guaranteed human rights and fundamental freedoms. However, despite the optimism generated by those positive developments, there was no significant improvement in the human rights situation. While peace talks progressed, the conflict in the Darfur region continued.

Effective action was not taken to disarm the Government-backed militia or Janjaweed, and none of the serious crimes committed during the 2004 conflict had been seriously investigated, nor were the perpetrators brought to justice. Immunities in place for security forces had not been repealed, the state of emergency laws were maintained in certain areas, and security agents continued to detain and torture persons suspected of crimes. Access to detention facilities was generally denied and new laws were introduced limiting freedoms of expression and association. Discrimination and the marginalization of groups persisted and basic human rights such as access to food, shelter, health care and education were not guaranteed, while humanitarian aid was looted or blocked from being delivered.

The Special Rapporteur recommended that all parties to the conflict respect international humanitarian and human rights law, particularly regarding the protection of civilians and the recruitment and use of child soldiers. The Government of National Unity should undertake, as a priority, a comprehensive law reform to ensure conformity with the interim national constitution and international human rights law, focusing on legislation regulating the police, armed forces, the press, non-governmental organizations (NGOs) and criminal law. The Special Rapporteur proposed to the Government a series of other measures designed to strengthen the national justice system and to prevent and/or deter further human rights violations. Other recommendations called for a civilian police presence in all displaced persons' camps and returnees' villages and enjoined Member States and the international community to provide financial, logistical and other support to the AU Mission in the Sudan, and to the Government and people in creating a non-violent society that respected human dignity. Rebel groups were asked to prevent and punish human rights abuses and violations of international humanitarian law by their commanders and combatants.

The Special Rapporteur, in a 27 October oral report to the Third (Social, Humanitarian and Cultural) Committee [A/C.3/60/SR.26], highlighted several positive developments in the political process in the Sudan, but noted that the implementation of the Comprehensive Peace Agreement was encountering serious delays, as the Commission established to monitor the process had not yet been set up. Also, national legislation had not been harmonized with the interim national constitution, which recognized international human rights standards. Thus, the people of the Sudan had seen little change in their everyday life since the formation of the Government of National Unity. Civilians were being harassed and killed in villages and camps for IDPs in all three regions of Darfur, where sexual violence was committed with impunity. Although the Government was addressing the issue, there had not been any tangible results. Pointing out that it was unclear whether the Government was truly committed to bringing the perpetrators of human rights violations to justice, the Special Rapporteur made a series of recommendations to the Sudanese authorities and the international community for the effective protection of human rights throughout that country, particularly regarding IDPs and women.

In response, the representative of the Sudan promised his country's full cooperation with the Special Rapporteur, as confirmation of his country's commitment to work through multilateral diplomatic channels for the protection and enhancement of human rights. The conflict in Darfur had adversely affected the humanitarian situation and caused suffering to the people there, but the Government was taking steps to alleviate the situation, including through the establishment of a special criminal court in Darfur (see p. 326) to try human rights violators and national committees to investigate cases of violence against women.

(For information on the visit to the Sudan by the Representative of the Secretary-General on internally displaced persons, see p. 869.)

Communications. The Sudan, in a follow-up to its 2004 communication announcing the establishment by its President of a Commission of Inquiry into alleged human rights violations by armed groups in Darfur [YUN 2004, p. 804], circulated, on 28 January, a summary of the Commission's findings [E/CN.4/2005/G/14]. It also announced on 8 March, the subsequent creation of three committees on judicial investigation, damage assessment and administrative issues to address the implementation of the Commission's recommendations [E/CN.4/2005/G/17].

On 1 March, the Government of the Sudan circulated its plan for disarming armed militias in the Darfur region [E/CN.4/2005/G/15], and, on 8 March, issued information concerning the sub-versive and criminal activities of rebel movements in that region [E/CN.4/2005/G/16].

Americas

(For information on the human rights situation in Haiti, see p. 740.)

Colombia

The Commission's Chairperson, in a 22 April statement [E/2005/23], said the Commission was concerned about the situation of human rights and international humanitarian law in Colombia, particularly regarding vulnerable groups. It reported violations of the rights to life, personal integrity, freedom and security, due process, privacy and intimacy, as well as alleged breaches of the fundamental freedoms of movement, residence, opinion and expression.

Concerns were also expressed over problems relating to the justice system, including access to justice and judicial independence/impartiality; the role of unverified information from informants; breaches of international humanitarian law by security agents; and the increasing number of IDPs. In particular, the Commission condemned massacres and cruel violence in the country, especially the murder in February of eight members of the Community of Peace of San José de Apartadó (citizens who sought to separate themselves from the conflict), terrorism and other criminal attacks by illegally armed groups, the recruitment by those groups of a large number of children, kidnapping, violations of the rights of minorities and indigenous communities, and of women and girls.

The Commission, stressing its support for the Government's efforts to establish the rule of law throughout the country, urged dialogue and negotiations between the Government and all illegally armed groups, emphasized the importance of truth, justice and reparation in a comprehensive peace strategy and requested the Government to ensure the investigation of complaints relating to forced disappearances. The Commission stressed the need to further address poverty, exclusion, social injustice and the gap in wealth distribution and called on the Government to ensure that the recommendations of the High Commissioner were implemented swiftly. The High Commissioner was asked to report in 2006.

Report of High Commissioner. The High Commissioner's report on the 2005 human rights situation in Colombia, based on information gathered by the Office of the High Commissioner for Human Rights in Colombia (OHCHR/Bogotá) [E/CN.4/2006/9 & Corr. 1, 2], stated that OHCHR continued to cooperate with and assist the Government of Colombia to improve the protection and promotion of human rights, particularly through its contacts with State authorities, civil society organizations, NGOs, churches, the media and diplomatic representatives, and a May visit to that country by the High Commissioner. During the year, the Office undertook 300 observation missions and received 2,403 complaints, of which 1,789 were related to violations of human rights and/or breaches of international humanitarian law.

According to the High Commissioner, the human rights situation in Colombia was marked by grave violations of civil and political rights and unresolved challenges affecting economic, social and cultural rights. Extrajudicial executions and enforced disappearances persisted with impunity, as did arbitrary detentions, torture and other cruel, inhuman or degrading treatment and attacks on the freedom of expression. While such violations were not a deliberate State policy, they were difficult to deal with, owing to the failure of the authorities to recognize them as violations and the inadequacy of remedial action. The related issue of poverty affecting over half of the Colombian population, particularly ethnic groups, women and children, reflected a high degree of inequity, especially regarding the enjoyment of the rights to education, health, employment and housing. Illegally armed groups, especially the Revolutionary Armed Forces of Colombia–People's Army (FARC-EP) and the paramilitaries of the Autodefensas Unidas de Colombia (United Self-Defence Forces of Colombia) (AUC), continued to commit serious breaches of humanitarian rules, such as attacks on the civilian population. Most affected were vulnerable groups, including human rights defenders, displaced persons, trade unionists, ethnic minorities, journalists, leaders of political parties, conscientious objectors, detainees and local authorities. The situation was exacerbated by challenges relating to the demobilization of over 11,100 persons released by paramilitary groups since 2003. Not only was the legal framework for the demobilization exercise incompatible with international principles, it conferred certain benefits to most demobilized persons, including pardon, and did not adequately address the problem of the State's responsibility in crimes committed by paramilitaries. In addition, there was no mechanism to ensure the dismantling of illegal structures, thereby enabling the para-

militaries to maintain their strong influence in many regions in the country.

While encouraging the national authorities to implement her previous recommendations, the High Commissioner addressed 26 additional proposals to the Government, the illegally armed groups operating in the country, operatives of Colombia's internal justice system and human rights mechanisms, civil society representatives and the international community regarding prevention and protection measures, the internal armed conflict, the rule of law and impunity, economic and social policies, the promotion of a human rights culture and OHCHR's advisory and technical cooperation services.

Communication. On 1 April [E/CN.4/2005/G/29], Colombia, in its observations on the content of the High Commissioner's report, stated that the importance the Government attached to human rights in that country was reflected by its inclusion in the 2002-2006 national development plan adopted in 2003, as well as in the adoption of a specific Government policy containing nine guiding principles, the implementation of which was being coordinated by the Office of the Vice President. However, while the Government appreciated the fact that the High Commissioner's report had acknowledged the progress made in guaranteeing human rights in Colombia, it did not accept a number of other observations contained therein.

(For information on a visit to Colombia by the Working Group on Enforced or Involuntary Disappearances, see p. 811.)

Cuba

Report of Personal Representative. In a report to the Commission [E/CN.4/2006/33], the High Commissioner's Personal Representative, Christine Chanet (France), reviewed factors hindering the realization of human rights in Cuba, especially the impact of the economic, trade and financial embargo (see p. 394) on economic, social and cultural rights. She noted that the restrictions imposed by the embargo had deprived Cuba of vital access to medicines and related technology, food, chemical water-treatment and electricity and had led to the adoption by the Cuban authorities of repressive laws, under which some Cuban citizens were described as mercenaries and subject to punishment. The difficulties facing the population as a result of the embargo had been compounded since 2004 by the tightening of economic and financial restrictions imposed by the United States.

Despite positive efforts by the Government to maintain a sound health system, improve the quality of education and literacy rates, combat discrimination against women and promote human rights, issues of concern remained, primarily about the continuing detention of some 80 persons, including journalists, writers, human rights defenders, politicians and opposition trade unionists arrested since March/April 2003. Annexed to the report was a list of those persons who remain imprisoned. Most of the victims had supported changing the electoral system and other legislative reforms. In 2005, more people were arrested and convicted for openly expressing dissident political opinions and the Working Group on Arbitrary Detention (see p. 799) reported that 60 persons remained in arbitrary detention. The Personal Representative was alarmed at allegations of ill-treatment in detention facilities. Several prisoners had been on hunger strike and the European Union had issued an appeal in favour of three of the affected prisoners.

The Personal Representative recommended that the Cuban Government halt the prosecution of citizens exercising rights guaranteed under the Universal Declaration of Human Rights, adopted by the General Assembly in resolution 217 A (III) [YUN 1948-49, p. 535]; release detained persons who had not committed acts of violence against individuals or property; review laws which had led to criminal prosecutions of persons exercising their freedom of expression, demonstration, assembly and association; uphold, without exception, the moratorium on the application of the death penalty; reform the rules of criminal procedure; establish a standing independent body to receive complaints from persons whose rights had been allegedly violated; review the regulations relating to travel into and out of Cuba in order to guarantee the freedom of movement; authorize NGOs to enter Cuba; foster pluralism in respect of associations, trade unions, the media and political parties; and accede to the International Covenant on Civil and Political Rights and its Optional Protocols and to the International Covenant on Economic, Social and Cultural Rights, adopted by the General Assembly in resolution 2200 A (XXI) [YUN 1966, pp. 423 & 419], as well as the former Covenant's Second Optional Protocol, aimed at the abolition of the death penalty, adopted by Assembly resolution 44/128 [YUN 1989, p. 484].

Commission action. On 14 April [res. 2005/12], the Commission, by a recorded vote of 21 to 17, with 15 abstentions, invited the Personal Representative to report on the current situation of human rights in Cuba, as addressed in previous Commission resolutions.

A draft resolution [E/CN.4/2005/L.94/Rev.1], introduced in the Commission on 21 April, would have requested the United States to authorize an impartial and independent fact-finding mission by the Commission's special procedures on the situation of detainees at the United States naval base in Guantánamo Bay, Cuba, as well as the Chairperson-Rapporteur of the Working Group on Arbitrary Detention, the Special Rapporteur on the question of torture and other cruel, inhuman and degrading treatment or punishment, the Special Rapporteur on the right of everyone to the enjoyment of the highest attainable standard of physical and mental health, and the Special Rapporteur on the independence of judges and lawyers to visit the detention centres at the base. The resolution would have also requested the High Commissioner to report in 2006 on the situation of detainees there, based on the findings of the visits, which would have been conducted by the designated special procedures. By a recorded vote of 22 to 8, with 23 abstentions, taken at the request of the United States, the draft resolution was rejected.

Communications. During the year, Cuba transmitted to the Commission a series of documents on issues relating to human rights and fundamental freedoms [E/CN.4/2005/G/18, E/CN.4/2005/G/26, E/CN.4/2005/G/36, E/CN.4/2005/G/39, E/CN.4/2005/G/41, E/CN.4/2005/G/42, E/CN.4/2005/G/43, E/CN.4/2006/G/1, E/CN.4/2006/G/3].

Asia

(For information on the human rights situation in Afghanistan, see p. 733; Cambodia, p. 735; and Timor-Leste, p. 744.)

Democratic People's Republic of Korea

Note by Secretariat. In response to a 2004 Commission request [YUN 2004, p. 807], a note by the Secretariat [E/CN.4/2005/32] described efforts to provide human rights advisory services to the Democratic People's Republic of Korea (DPRK). In that context, OHCHR had explored ways of initiating technical cooperation with DPRK, but was yet to receive a response from the Government to its proposals on the subject.

In a 28 February response [E/CN.4/2005/G/13], DPRK stated that it rejected the 2004 Commission resolution [YUN 2004, p. 807] that had called for the provision of technical cooperation to DPRK in the area of human rights, adding that the resolution, which was initiated by the European Union, was based on political motivations and had nothing to do with genuine promotion and protection of human rights.

Reports of Special Rapporteur. In a January report [E/CN.4/2005/34], the Special Rapporteur, Vitit Muntarbhorn (Thailand), summarized the situation of human rights in the DPRK, noting some constructive developments in recent decades as well as a variety of discrepancies and transgressions warranting immediate action. According to the Rapporteur, the country was party to four key human rights treaties and had submitted a number of reports to the relevant monitoring committees. It had occasionally allowed human rights mechanisms, such as the Committee on the Rights of the Child (see p. 731) and UN agencies, to assess the status of human rights in that country and to address related issues. It had also established some legal and operational infrastructures, such as the national constitution, which could help promote and protect human rights. Moreover, there was a warming of relations between DPRK and a number of countries within and outside the region. Nonetheless, the situation of human rights in DPRK did not accord with international standards. The enjoyment of human rights was affected by the nature of the country's leadership, with power concentrated absolutely at the top, by the continuing effects of the war (1950-1953) on the peninsula, the related demilitarization problems and the need for broad-based popular participation. Against that background, human rights challenges included the right to food and life. The food shortages of the mid-1990s, brought about by floods and drought, were compounded by power imbalances and inadequate response from the power structure. It had affected the country's development and endangered many lives and livelihoods. According to several humanitarian agencies, there was a continuing need for food aid to help the population, some 6.4 million of whom, particularly women and children, had benefited to date.

Other challenges related to the realization of the rights to security of person, humane treatment, non-discrimination and access to justice; freedom of movement and protection of displaced persons; the highest attainable standard of health and education; self-determination/political participation, access to information, freedom of expression/belief/opinion, association and religion; and of specific persons/groups, including women and children.

The Special Rapporteur recommended that the Government abide by international human rights standards and reform laws and practices inconsistent with those standards; uphold human rights, democracy, peace, sustainable devel-

opment and demilitarization; respect the rule of law, build the capacity of law enforcement bodies and reform the justice system; address the root causes of displacement, prevent persecution and victimization of those displaced; provide redress for transgressions, such as those relating to the abduction of foreign nationals; issue a national human rights action plan with public participation for law enforcement bodies; ensure that humanitarian assistance reached targeted groups; and seek assistance from OHCHR and other agencies for promoting and protecting human rights. Additional recommendations were addressed to the international community.

Commission action. On 14 April [res. 2005/11], by a recorded vote of 30 to 9, with 14 abstentions, the Commission expressed deep concern about continuing reports of systemic, widespread and grave violations of human rights in DPRK, its non-acceptance of the mandate of the Special Rapporteur on the situation of human rights in that country, as contained in a 2004 Commission resolution [YUN 2004, p. 807], and its failure to engage in technical cooperation activities with OHCHR. The Commission urged the Government to address those concerns in an open and constructive manner and requested the High Commissioner to continue to engage DPRK authorities in a comprehensive dialogue, with a view to establishing technical cooperation programmes in human rights, and to submit her findings and recommendations to the Commission in 2006. The Commission extended the Special Rapporteur's mandate for a further year and requested him, with assistance from the Secretary-General, to continue efforts to establish direct contact with the Government and people of DPRK, to report on the human rights situation in that country and on the Government's compliance with its obligations under international human rights instruments, and to submit his findings and recommendations to the General Assembly in 2005, and to the Commission in 2006. All relevant special rapporteurs and special representatives were also asked to examine alleged human rights violations in DPRK and to report thereon to the Commission in 2006.

On 25 July, the Economic and Social Council endorsed the Commission's decision to extend the Special Rapporteur's mandate and its request to him to submit reports (**decision 2005/258**).

As requested in Commission resolution 2005/11 (see above), the Secretary-General, by a 29 August note [A/60/306], transmitted the Special Rapporteur's updated report to the General Assembly, which further described the human rights situation in DPRK and his visits to Japan and Mongolia.

During his visit to Japan (24 February–4 March), the Special Rapporteur examined the impact on that country of the human rights situation in DPRK, particularly the reported abductions by that country of Japanese nationals. Japan claimed that 15 individuals had been abducted, five of whom had been released. DPRK claimed that eight of the remaining 10 persons had died; a claim contested by Japan, and the victim's families in particular. Expressing concern over the issue, and recalling that the abduction of persons ("enforced disappearances") was generally forbidden in national and international law, the Special Rapporteur called on DPRK to respond effectively and expeditiously to Japan's claims that some of the abducted persons were still alive and should be returned to Japan immediately and safely; verify claims concerning the alleged deaths of abducted Japanese nationals and ascertain whether there had been additional abductions; respect and guarantee family unity/reunification; enable the victims of abductions and their families to access justice and seek redress; and resume dialogue with Japan to prevent further abductions.

In Mongolia (4-11 March), the Special Rapporteur also examined the consequences for that country of the human rights situation in DPRK, especially the displacement of people across the borders since 1999, seeking refuge from DPRK. Mongolia provided temporary shelter and treated them as humanitarian cases, without specifically calling them refugees, since they were in transit and later departed for long-term settlement in the Republic of Korea. Mongolia feared a mass influx of non-nationals into the country, particularly the potentially destabilizing effect, which had inevitably influenced the country's policy-making and security concerns. The Special Rapporteur recommended that Mongolia should sustain its humanitarian policy and practice in sheltering those seeking refuge in the country and to continue to abide by international human rights and refugee law.

GENERAL ASSEMBLY ACTION

On 16 December [meeting 64], the General Assembly, on the recommendation of the Third Committee [A/60/509/Add.3 & Corr.1], adopted **resolution 60/173** by recorded vote (88-21-60) [agenda item 71 *(c)*].

Situation of human rights in the Democratic People's Republic of Korea

The General Assembly,

Reaffirming that States Members of the United Nations have an obligation to promote and protect human rights and fundamental freedoms and to fulfil the obligations that they have undertaken under the various international instruments,

Mindful that the Democratic People's Republic of Korea is a party to the International Covenant on Civil and Political Rights, the International Covenant on Economic, Social and Cultural Rights, the Convention on the Rights of the Child and the Convention on the Elimination of All Forms of Discrimination against Women,

Recalling Commission on Human Rights resolutions 2003/10 of 16 April 2003, 2004/13 of 15 April 2004 and 2005/11 of 14 April 2005,

Recalling in particular that, in its resolution 2005/11, the Commission on Human Rights urged the General Assembly to take up the question of the situation of human rights in the Democratic People's Republic of Korea if the Government did not extend cooperation to the Special Rapporteur of the Commission on the situation of human rights in the Democratic People's Republic of Korea and if no improvement of the situation of human rights in the country was observed,

Taking note of the report of the Special Rapporteur,

1. *Expresses its serious concern* at:

(a) The refusal of the Government of the Democratic People's Republic of Korea to recognize the mandate of the Special Rapporteur of the Commission on Human Rights on the situation of human rights in the Democratic People's Republic of Korea or to extend cooperation to him;

(b) Continuing reports of systemic, widespread and grave violations of human rights in the Democratic People's Republic of Korea, including:

(i) Torture and other cruel, inhuman or degrading treatment or punishment, public executions, extrajudicial and arbitrary detention, the absence of due process and the rule of law, the imposition of the death penalty for political reasons, the existence of a large number of prison camps and the extensive use of forced labour;

(ii) Sanctions imposed on citizens of the Democratic People's Republic of Korea who have been repatriated from abroad, such as treating their departure as treason, leading to punishments of internment, torture, cruel, inhuman or degrading treatment or the death penalty;

(iii) All-pervasive and severe restrictions on the freedoms of thought, conscience, religion, opinion and expression, peaceful assembly and association, and on equal access to information and limitations imposed on every person who wishes to move freely within the country and travel abroad;

(iv) Continuing violation of the human rights and fundamental freedoms of women, in particular the trafficking of women for the purpose of prostitution or forced marriage, forced abortions, and infanticide of children of repatriated mothers, including in police detention centres and camps;

(v) Unresolved questions relating to the abduction of foreigners in the form of an enforced disappearance;

2. *Expresses its concern* that the Government of the Democratic People's Republic of Korea has not engaged in technical cooperation activities with the United Nations High Commissioner for Human

Rights and her Office, despite efforts by the High Commissioner to engage in a dialogue with the authorities of the Democratic People's Republic of Korea in this regard;

3. *Expresses its deep concern* at the precarious humanitarian situation in the country, in particular the prevalence of infant malnutrition, which still affects the physical and mental development of a significant proportion of children;

4. *Urges* the Government of the Democratic People's Republic of Korea, in this regard, to ensure that humanitarian organizations, including non-governmental organizations and United Nations organizations, in particular the World Food Programme, have full, free, safe and unimpeded access to all parts of the Democratic People's Republic of Korea so that they may ensure that humanitarian assistance is delivered impartially on the basis of need in accordance with humanitarian principles, this concern having been aggravated by the announcement by the authorities of the Democratic People's Republic of Korea of their intention not to accept humanitarian assistance from January 2006;

5. *Also urges* the Government of the Democratic People's Republic of Korea to respect fully all human rights and fundamental freedoms and, in this regard, to implement fully the measures set out in the above-mentioned resolutions of the Commission on Human Rights, in particular full cooperation with the Special Rapporteur.

RECORDED VOTE ON RESOLUTION 60/173:

In favour: Afghanistan, Albania, Andorra, Argentina, Australia, Austria, Azerbaijan, Belgium, Belize, Bhutan, Bolivia, Bosnia and Herzegovina, Brazil, Bulgaria, Canada, Chile, Costa Rica, Croatia, Cyprus, Czech Republic, Denmark, Dominica, Dominican Republic, Ecuador, El Salvador, Estonia, Fiji, Finland, France, Georgia, Germany, Greece, Guatemala, Guinea-Bissau, Haiti, Honduras, Hungary, Iceland, Iraq, Ireland, Israel, Italy, Japan, Kazakhstan, Latvia, Lebanon, Liechtenstein, Lithuania, Luxembourg, Maldives, Malta, Marshall Islands, Mexico, Micronesia, Monaco, Netherlands, New Zealand, Nicaragua, Norway, Palau, Panama, Papua New Guinea, Paraguay, Peru, Philippines, Poland, Portugal, Republic of Moldova, Romania, Saint Vincent and the Grenadines, Samoa, San Marino, Saudi Arabia, Serbia and Montenegro, Slovakia, Slovenia, Solomon Islands, Spain, Sweden, Switzerland, The former Yugoslav Republic of Macedonia, Timor-Leste, Tonga, Turkey, Ukraine, United Kingdom, United States, Uruguay.

Against: Belarus, China, Cuba, Democratic People's Republic of Korea, Egypt, Gambia, Guinea, Indonesia, Iran, Lao People's Democratic Republic, Libyan Arab Jamahiriya, Malaysia, Russian Federation, Sudan, Syrian Arab Republic, Tajikistan, Turkmenistan, Uzbekistan, Venezuela, Viet Nam, Zimbabwe.

Abstaining: Algeria, Angola, Antigua and Barbuda, Bahamas, Bahrain, Bangladesh, Barbados, Benin, Botswana, Brunei Darussalam, Burkina Faso, Burundi, Cameroon, Cape Verde, Colombia, Côte d'Ivoire, Democratic Republic of the Congo, Djibouti, Eritrea, Ethiopia, Ghana, Guyana, India, Jamaica, Jordan, Kenya, Kuwait, Kyrgyzstan, Lesotho, Mali, Mauritania, Mauritius, Morocco, Mozambique, Namibia, Nepal, Niger, Nigeria, Pakistan, Qatar, Republic of Korea, Rwanda, Saint Lucia, Senegal, Singapore, Somalia, South Africa, Sri Lanka, Suriname, Thailand, Togo, Trinidad and Tobago, Tunisia, Tuvalu, Uganda, United Arab Emirates, United Republic of Tanzania, Vanuatu, Yemen, Zambia.

Iran

By a May note [E/CN.4/2006/3], the Secretariat circulated a letter from Iran drawing the attention of the Bureau of the Commission to the request of the Transnational Radical Party, an NGO in consultative status with the Economic and Social Council, for the withdrawal as an official document, of its written statement [E/CN.4/2005/NGO/260] to the sixty-first session of the Commis-

sion on the situation in the Iranian province of Khuzestan.

(See pp. 851 and 843, respectively, for details of visits to Iran by the Special Rapporteurs on violence against women, its causes and consequences and on adequate housing as a component of the right to an adequate standard of living.)

GENERAL ASSEMBLY ACTION

On 16 December [meeting 64], the General Assembly, on the recommendation of the Third Committee [A/60/509/Add.3 & Corr.1], adopted **resolution 60/171** by recorded vote (75-50-43) [agenda item 71 (c)].

Situation of human rights in the Islamic Republic of Iran

The General Assembly,

Guided by the Charter of the United Nations, the Universal Declaration of Human Rights, the International Covenants on Human Rights and other international human rights instruments,

Reaffirming that all Member States have an obligation to promote and protect human rights and fundamental freedoms and to fulfil the obligations they have undertaken under the various international instruments in this field,

Mindful that the Islamic Republic of Iran is a party to the International Covenant on Civil and Political Rights, the International Covenant on Economic, Social and Cultural Rights, the International Convention on the Elimination of All Forms of Racial Discrimination and the Convention on the Rights of the Child,

Recalling its previous resolutions on the subject, the most recent of which is resolution 59/205 of 20 December 2004, and recalling also Commission on Human Rights resolution 2001/17 of 20 April 2001,

Noting the statements made by the Government of the Islamic Republic of Iran on strengthening respect for human rights in the country and promoting the rule of law,

1. *Welcomes:*

(a) The open invitation extended by the Government of the Islamic Republic of Iran to all human rights thematic monitoring mechanisms in April 2002 and the cooperation extended to the special procedures of the Commission on Human Rights during their visits;

(b) The visit of the Special Rapporteur of the Commission on Human Rights on violence against women, its causes and consequences to the Islamic Republic of Iran from 29 January to 6 February 2005;

(c) The visit of the Special Rapporteur of the Commission on Human Rights on adequate housing as a component of the right to an adequate standard of living to the Islamic Republic of Iran from 19 to 30 July 2005;

(d) The recommendation by the head of the judiciary of the Islamic Republic of Iran to judges in December 2002 that they choose alternative punishment in cases where the sentence of stoning would otherwise be imposed;

(*e*) The announcement by the head of the judiciary in April 2004 of the ban on torture and the subsequent passage of related legislation by the parliament, which was approved by the Guardian Council in May 2004;

(*f*) The compliance by the Islamic Republic of Iran with its obligation, as a party to the Convention on the Rights of the Child, to deliver its presentation to the Committee on the Rights of the Child in January 2005;

(*g*) The human rights dialogues between the Islamic Republic of Iran and a number of countries, while regretting that a number of these have not been held at regular intervals lately;

(*h*) The cooperation with United Nations agencies in developing programmes in the field of human rights, good governance and the rule of law;

2. *Expresses its serious concern* at:

(*a*) The continuing harassment, intimidation and persecution of human rights defenders, non-governmental organizations, political opponents, religious dissenters, political reformists, journalists, parliamentarians, students, clerics, academics and webloggers, including through undue restrictions on the freedoms of assembly, opinion and expression, the use of arbitrary arrest, targeted at both individuals and their family members, and the unjustified closure of newspapers and blocking of Internet sites, as well as the absence of many conditions necessary for free and fair elections, including by the arbitrary disqualification of large numbers of prospective candidates, including all women, during the presidential elections of June 2005;

(*b*) The persistent failure to comply fully with international standards in the administration of justice and, in particular, the absence of due process of law, the refusal to provide fair and public hearings, the denial of the right to counsel and access to counsel by those detained, the use of national security laws to deny human rights, the harassment, intimidation and persecution of defence lawyers and legal defenders, the lack of respect for internationally recognized safeguards, inter alia, with respect to persons belonging to religious, ethnic or national minorities, officially recognized or otherwise, the application of arbitrary prison sentences, and the violation of the rights of detainees, including the systematic and arbitrary use of prolonged solitary confinement, the failure to provide proper medical care to those imprisoned and the arbitrary denial of contact between detainees and their family members;

(*c*) The continuing use of torture and cruel, inhuman or degrading treatment or punishment such as flogging and amputations;

(*d*) The continuing of public executions, including multiple public executions, and, on a large scale, other executions in the absence of respect for internationally recognized safeguards, and, in particular, deplores the execution of persons who were under the age of 18 at the time their offence was committed, contrary to the obligations of the Islamic Republic of Iran under article 37 of the Convention on the Rights of the Child and article 6 of the International Covenant on Civil and Political Rights and in spite of the announcement of a moratorium on juvenile executions;

(*e*) The continuing violence and discrimination against women and girls in law and in practice, despite some minor legislative improvements, and the refusal of the Guardian Council to take steps to address this systemic discrimination, noting in this context its rejection, in August 2003, of the proposal of the elected parliament to accede to the Convention on the Elimination of All Forms of Discrimination against Women;

(*f*) The continuing discrimination, and other human rights violations against persons belonging to ethnic and religious minorities, recognized or otherwise, including Arabs, Kurds, Baluchis, Christians, Jews and Sunni Muslims, the escalation and increased frequency of discrimination and other human rights violations against the Baha'i, including cases of arbitrary arrest and detention, the denial of freedom of religion or of publicly carrying out communal affairs, the disregard of property rights, the destruction of sites of religious importance, the suspension of social, educational and community-related activities and the denial of access to higher education, employment, pensions, adequate housing and other benefits and recent violent crackdowns on Kurds;

3. *Calls upon* the Government of the Islamic Republic of Iran:

(*a*) To ensure full respect for the rights to freedom of assembly, opinion and expression, and the right to take part in the conduct of public affairs in accordance with its obligations under the International Covenant on Civil and Political Rights and, in particular, to end the harassment, intimidation and persecution of political opponents and human rights defenders, including by releasing persons imprisoned arbitrarily or on the basis of their political views;

(*b*) To ensure full respect for the right to due process of law, including the right to counsel and access to counsel by those detained, in criminal justice proceedings and, in particular, to ensure a fair and public hearing by a competent, independent and impartial tribunal established by law, to end harassment, intimidation and persecution of defence lawyers and legal defenders and to ensure equality before the law and the equal protection of the law without any discrimination in all instances, including for members of religious, ethnic, linguistic or other minority groups, officially recognized or otherwise;

(*c*) To eliminate, in law and in practice, the use of torture and other cruel, inhuman or degrading treatment or punishment, such as amputations and flogging, to end impunity for violations of human rights that constitute crimes by bringing the perpetrators to justice in accordance with international standards and, as proposed by the elected Iranian parliament, to accede to the Convention against Torture and Other Cruel, Inhuman or Degrading Treatment or Punishment;

(*d*) To abolish public executions and other executions carried out in the absence of respect for internationally recognized safeguards, in particular, as called for by the Committee on the Rights of the Child in its report of January 2005, executions of persons who, at the time of their offence, were under the age of 18, and to uphold the moratorium on executions by stoning and to introduce this moratorium as law as a first step towards the abolition of this punishment;

(*e*) To eliminate, in law and in practice, all forms of discrimination and violence against women and girls, and, as proposed by the elected Iranian parliament, to accede to the Convention on the Elimination of All Forms of Discrimination against Women;

(f) To eliminate, in law and in practice, all forms of discrimination based on religious, ethnic or linguistic grounds, and other human rights violations against persons belonging to minorities, including Arabs, Kurds, Baluchis, Christians, Jews, Sunni Muslims and the Baha'i, and to address this matter in an open manner, with the full participation of the minorities themselves, to otherwise ensure full respect for the right to freedom of thought, conscience, religion or belief of all persons, and to implement the 1996 report of the Special Rapporteur of the Commission on Human Rights on religious intolerance, which recommended ways in which the Islamic Republic of Iran could emancipate the Baha'i community;

4. *Encourages* the thematic mechanisms of the Commission on Human Rights, inter alia, the Special Rapporteur on extrajudicial, summary or arbitrary executions, the Special Rapporteur on torture and other cruel, inhuman or degrading treatment or punishment, the Special Rapporteur on the independence of judges and lawyers, the Special Rapporteur on freedom of religion or belief, the Special Rapporteur on the promotion and protection of the right to freedom of opinion and expression, the Special Representative of the Secretary-General on the situation of human rights defenders and the Working Group on Enforced or Involuntary Disappearances, to visit or otherwise continue their work to improve the situation of human rights in the Islamic Republic of Iran, and urges the Government of the Islamic Republic of Iran to cooperate with these special mechanisms and to illustrate how their subsequent recommendations have been addressed, including recommendations of special procedures that have visited the country in the past twelve months;

5. *Decides* to continue its examination of the situation of human rights in the Islamic Republic of Iran at its sixty-first session, under the item entitled "Human rights questions", in the light of additional elements provided by the Commission on Human Rights.

RECORDED VOTE ON RESOLUTION 60/171:

In favour: Albania, Andorra, Argentina, Australia, Austria, Belgium, Belize, Bolivia, Bosnia and Herzegovina, Bulgaria, Canada, Chile, Costa Rica, Croatia, Cyprus, Czech Republic, Denmark, Dominican Republic, Ecuador, El Salvador, Estonia, Fiji, Finland, France, Germany, Greece, Guatemala, Haiti, Honduras, Hungary, Iceland, Ireland, Israel, Italy, Japan, Latvia, Liechtenstein, Lithuania, Luxembourg, Malta, Marshall Islands, Mauritania, Mexico, Micronesia, Monaco, Netherlands, New Zealand, Nicaragua, Norway, Palau, Papua New Guinea, Paraguay, Peru, Poland, Portugal, Republic of Moldova, Romania, Saint Vincent and the Grenadines, Samoa, San Marino, Serbia and Montenegro, Slovakia, Slovenia, Solomon Islands, Spain, Sweden, Switzerland, The former Yugoslav Republic of Macedonia, Timor-Leste, Tonga, Tuvalu, Ukraine, United Kingdom, United States, Vanuatu.

Against: Afghanistan, Algeria, Armenia, Azerbaijan, Bahrain, Bangladesh, Belarus, Botswana, Brunei Darussalam, China, Cuba, Democratic People's Republic of Korea, Djibouti, Egypt, Gambia, Guinea, India, Indonesia, Iran, Kazakhstan, Kuwait, Kyrgyzstan, Lebanon, Libyan Arab Jamahiriya, Malaysia, Maldives, Morocco, Myanmar, Niger, Oman, Pakistan, Qatar, Russian Federation, Saint Lucia, Saudi Arabia, Senegal, Somalia, South Africa, Sri Lanka, Sudan, Syrian Arab Republic, Tajikistan, Togo, Tunisia, Turkmenistan, Uzbekistan, Venezuela, Viet Nam, Yemen, Zimbabwe.

Abstaining: Angola, Antigua and Barbuda, Bahamas, Barbados, Benin, Bhutan, Brazil, Burkina Faso, Burundi, Cameroon, Cape Verde, Colombia, Côte d'Ivoire, Democratic Republic of the Congo, Eritrea, Ethiopia, Ghana, Guinea-Bissau, Guyana, Iraq, Jamaica, Kenya, Lao People's Democratic Republic, Lesotho, Mali, Mauritius, Mongolia, Mozambique, Namibia, Nepal, Nigeria, Panama, Philippines, Republic of Korea, Rwanda, Singapore, Suriname, Thailand, Trinidad and Tobago, Uganda, United Arab Emirates, United Republic of Tanzania, Zambia.

Myanmar

Commission action. On 14 April [res. 2005/10], the Commission, while acknowledging encouraging developments in Myanmar, including the Government's release of some 19,906 prisoners, its establishment of a committee for the prevention of the recruitment of under-age soldiers, its ratification of several human rights instruments, its negotiation of a ceasefire agreement with the Karen National Union (KNU) and cooperation with humanitarian agencies, expressed grave concern at the systematic violation of human rights in the country. The Commission called on the Government to end those violations; lift all restraints on peaceful political activity by all persons; restore democracy and respect the results of the 1990 elections by releasing unconditionally, members of political parties and all political prisoners; ensure that future elections were conducted according to international standards for free and fair elections and that the National Convention included all political parties and major ethnic nationalities not represented by a political party; initiate an independent inquiry, with international cooperation, into the Depayin incident of 30 May 2003 [YUN 2003, p. 819], as called for in General Assembly resolution 58/247 [YUN 2003, p. 820]; restore the independence of the judiciary; consider becoming party to all relevant international human rights and humanitarian law instruments; and establish a national human rights commission to promote and protect human rights.

The Government was further called upon to pursue, through dialogue and peaceful means, the end of conflict with all ethnic groups in Myanmar, cooperate with the Special Envoy of the Secretary-General for Myanmar and with the Special Rapporteur to bring about the country's transition to civilian rule, and to eradicate the practice of forced labour by all Government organs. The Commission extended the Special Rapporteur's mandate for a further year and asked him, with assistance from the Secretary-General, to report to the Assembly in 2005 and to the Commission in 2006, and to integrate a gender perspective in his work.

On 25 July, the Economic and Social Council endorsed the Commission's decision to extend the Special Rapporteur's mandate and its request to him to submit reports (**decision 2005/257**).

Reports of Secretary-General. In response to Assembly resolution 59/263 [YUN 2004, p. 812], the Secretary-General submitted a March report

[E/CN.4/2005/130] on his good offices efforts and those of his Special Envoy, Razali Ismail, in facilitating national reconciliation and democratization in Myanmar. Acknowledging that Myanmar faced complex and difficult challenges in its transition to democracy and quest for national reconciliation, the Secretary-General cautiously welcomed the Government's seven-step road map aimed at democratic transition [YUN 2003, p. 820] and acknowledged the potential role that the National Convention could play in that regard. However, contrary to consistent advice that the process be all-inclusive and democratic to be credible, the National Convention fell short of those basic requirements and did not adhere to the recommendations of the Assembly and the Commission on Human Rights. The continued detention of Daw Aung San Suu Kyi and other members of her party, the detention and arrest of other ethnic national leaders, the restrictions on the activities of the country's political parties, and the mass imprisonment of people for expressing their political views were incompatible with the process of democratization and national reconciliation, however defined. The Secretary-General maintained that, unless the views of the National League for Democracy (NLD), other political parties and all the country's ethnic groups on Myanmar's future were sought, considered and taken into account, the National Convention and the road map process would be incomplete and lacking in credibility. He reiterated his call on Myanmar's authorities to make the road map process more inclusive and credible, and to resume substantive political dialogue with all ethnic groups and political leaders, including Daw Aung San Suu Kyi, in order to achieve a genuine process of national reconciliation. The Secretary-General emphasized the need for the remaining constraints on all political and ethnic leaders to be lifted and for political prisoners, including elected officials, to be released. The authorities should ensure that the third phase of the road map—the drafting of the constitution—was fully inclusive. A national referendum should be held subsequently, and unless that exercise adhered to internationally accepted standards of conduct and participation, it may be difficult for the international community to endorse the result. The authorities should demonstrate their commitment to a genuine and credible process of democratization and national reconciliation by allowing the Secretary-General's Special Envoy to resume his visits to Myanmar as soon as possible, in order to continue his facilitation efforts and to discuss ways to enhance Myanmar's cooperation with the UN good offices efforts. The Secretary-General maintained that the Government of Myanmar had an obligation to ensure that its people derived the same benefits of economic, social and political development as elsewhere in the region and underscored the UN system's parallel commitment to invest in the country's long-term future, by enhancing the scale and scope of its social and humanitarian engagement with the people and communities.

In October [A/60/422 & Corr.1], the Secretary-General further reported on his good offices efforts and those of his Special Envoy, aimed at facilitating national reconciliation and democratization in Myanmar. The report reiterated the shortcomings of the National Convention, which continued to exclude representatives from many political parties, including NLD, and failed to adhere to the Assembly's recommendations. The Secretary-General, therefore, called on the Myanmar authorities to make the reform efforts more inclusive and credible when the National Convention resumed later in the year and during subsequent phases of the road map process, including those for drafting the constitution and organizing a national referendum. The Secretary-General recalled that Daw Aung San Suu Kyi had expressed her readiness to cooperate with the Government for the good of the people, as had the representatives of ethnic nationality political parties. He promised to mobilize international assistance to support Myanmar's authorities, if progress occurred.

On 24 October [A/C.3/60/2], Myanmar stated that the Secretary-General's report contained factual errors and went beyond the parameters mandated by Assembly resolution 59/263. Myanmar claimed that the main thrust of the report seemed to question the National Convention process, the first important step of the seven-point political road map for transition to democracy.

On 7 November [A/60/422/Add.1], the Secretary-General clarified the issues raised by Myanmar.

Reports of Special Rapporteur. In response to Commission resolution 2005/10 and Economic and Social Council decision 2005/257 (see p. 892), the Secretary-General, by an August note [A/60/221], transmitted the interim report of Special Rapporteur Paulo Sérgio Pinheiro (Brazil) on the human rights situation in Myanmar, based on information he had received up to 22 July. The Special Rapporteur regretted that the situation regarding the exercise of fundamental rights and freedoms in Myanmar had not substantially changed, as many people continued to be harassed, arrested, tried and sentenced to prison for the peaceful exercise of basic civil and political rights and freedoms. Despite the welcome release in July of 249 political prisoners, there reportedly remained over 1,100 others, including monks, lawyers, teachers, journalists, farmers, politicians, student leaders, writers and poets. The Special Rapporteur was concerned at ongoing allegations of pervasive and systematic torture and ill-treatment of persons in pre-trial detention, the denial to detainees of access to their relatives, legal professionals and others, and the application of the 1975 State Protection Law permitting the Home Minister to detain without charge or trial anyone believed to constitute "a danger to the State". Among those detained under the law was Daw Aung San Suu Kyi, who had been under house arrest for over nine of the past 16 years, and her virtual solitary confinement and lack of access to her NLD colleagues ran counter to the spirit of national reconciliation. The situation regarding economic, social and cultural rights and the rights of ethnic minorities raised similar concerns. The humanitarian situation also remained dire, as the ongoing conflict between Government forces and non-State groups, combined with grave human rights violations, continued to result in mass population displacements.

The Special Rapporteur recommended that the Government demonstrate its commitment to implement political and constitutional reforms by guaranteeing: the full and effective participation of all political actors, including NLD, political parties and ethnic leaders, in a meaningful and substantive dialogue; the release of NLD General Secretary Daw Aung San Suu Kyi and other political prisoners; the protection and promotion of civil and political rights and that State institutions receive and investigate all complaints of human rights abuses; and the prosecution of those responsible in accordance with international standards. The Government should initiate fundamental reforms, with the assistance of the international community and multilateral organizations, so that Myanmar could successfully integrate into international financial and economic structures. In that context, policy initiatives which could be launched simultaneously during the transition process could include civil service reform, environmental protection, reform of the education sector and the judiciary, and the establishment of social safety nets for the most vulnerable groups, including the poor, women, youth, the elderly and persons with disabilities. As a matter of priority, however, the Government should ratify core international human rights instruments.

On 16 December, the General Assembly took note of the interim report of the Special Rapporteur (**decision 60/533**).

In a later report [E/CN.4/2006/34], the Special Rapporteur stated that the National Convention reconvened in December, but had made no progress towards genuine democratic reform and the situation regarding the exercise of fundamental human rights and freedoms remained grave. The intimidation, harassment, arbitrary arrest and imprisonment of civilians for peacefully exercising their civil and political rights and freedoms continued and the activities of political parties remained severely repressed by government agents. On 27 November, the Government issued a new executive order prolonging the detention of Daw Aung San Suu Kyi for a further six months and the number of political prisoners reached an estimated 1,144 persons. The socio-economic and humanitarian situation in the country had also further deteriorated.

The Special Rapporteur observed that the human rights concerns in the country were largely the same as those he had highlighted six years ago and regretted that early indications of the Government's willingness to address those problems had disappeared. He stated that his previous recommendations remained valid, and their implementation was even more essential, given the stagnation of the transition process, the lack of progress towards national reconciliation and the deteriorating humanitarian situation. He was convinced that progress in resolving the ethnic conflict in Myanmar might not be possible or sustainable without tangible political reform. The ongoing armed conflict in several ethnic minority areas continued to underpin the most grave human rights abuses in the country, to exacerbate its humanitarian decline and to inhibit socio-economic development. Without an inclusive reform process, such challenges could not be addressed by the Government's current road map process.

GENERAL ASSEMBLY ACTION

On 23 December [meeting 69], the General Assembly, on the recommendation of the Third Committee [A/60/509/Add.3 & Corr.1], adopted **resolution 60/233** without vote [agenda item 71 (c)].

Situation of human rights in Myanmar

The General Assembly,

Guided by the Charter of the United Nations and the Universal Declaration of Human Rights, and recalling the International Covenants on Human Rights and other relevant human rights instruments,

Reaffirming that all Member States have an obligation to promote and protect human rights and fundamental freedoms and the duty to fulfil the obligations they have undertaken under the various international instruments in this field,

Reaffirming also its previous resolutions on the situation of human rights in Myanmar, the most recent of which is resolution 59/263 of 23 December 2004, those of the Commission on Human Rights, the most recent of which is resolution 2005/10 of 14 April 2005, and the conclusions of the International Labour Conference of 4 June 2005,

Bearing in mind Security Council resolution 1325 (2000) of 31 October 2000 on women and peace and security, resolutions 1265(1999) of 17 September 1999 and 1296(2000) of 19 April 2000 on the protection of civilians in armed conflict and resolution 1612(2005) of 26 July 2005 on children in armed conflict, and the report of the Secretary-General on children and armed conflict,

Recognizing that good governance, democracy, the rule of law and respect for human rights are essential to achieving sustainable development and economic growth, and affirming that the establishment of a genuine democratic government in Myanmar is essential for the realization of all human rights and fundamental freedoms,

Affirming that the will of the people is the basis of the authority of government and that the will of the people of Myanmar was clearly expressed in the elections held in 1990,

1. *Welcomes:*

(*a*) The reports of the Special Rapporteur of the Commission on Human Rights on the situation of human rights in Myanmar and the reports of the Secretary-General;

(*b*) The personal engagement and statements of the Secretary-General with regard to the situation of Myanmar;

(*c*) The efforts of the United Nations and other international humanitarian organizations to deliver urgently needed humanitarian assistance to the most vulnerable people in Myanmar;

(*d*) The release by the Government of Myanmar of two hundred and forty-nine political prisoners on 6 July 2005, while noting that over one thousand, one hundred political prisoners remain incarcerated;

(*e*) The establishment by the Government of a committee for the prevention of military recruitment of underage soldiers and the adoption in November 2004 of an outline plan of action to address the issues of underage recruitment and child soldiers;

(*f*) The ratification by Myanmar on 30 March 2004 of the United Nations Convention against Transnational Organized Crime and two of the Protocols thereto, namely, the Protocol to Prevent, Suppress and Punish Trafficking in Persons, Especially Women and Children, and the Protocol against the Smuggling of Migrants by Land, Sea and Air, and the enactment by Myanmar on 13 September 2005 of an Anti-trafficking in Persons Law drawn up in accordance with the Convention;

2. *Expresses grave concern* at:

(*a*) The ongoing systematic violation of the human rights, including civil, political, economic, social and cultural rights, of the people of Myanmar, including violations of the right to an adequate standard of living, discrimination and violations suffered by persons belonging to ethnic nationalities, women and children, especially in non-ceasefire areas, including but not limited to extrajudicial killings, rape and other forms of sexual violence persistently carried out by members of the armed forces, continuing use of torture, deaths

in custody, political arrests and continuing imprisonment and other detentions; forced relocation; forced labour, including child labour; trafficking in persons; denial of freedom of assembly, association, expression and movement; wide disrespect for the rule of law, continuing recruitment and use of child soldiers, use of landmines, and the confiscation of arable land, crops, livestock and other possessions;

(*b*) The extension of the house arrest of the General Secretary of the National League for Democracy, Aung San Suu Kyi, and her deputy, Tin Oo, and the persistent denial of their human rights and fundamental freedoms, including freedom of movement and association, as well as the continuing detention, particularly incommunicado detention, of other senior leaders of the League and of the leadership of other political parties or ethnic nationalities, particularly the detention of Khun Htun Oo and Sai Nyunt Lwin, Chairman and General Secretary, respectively, of the Shan Nationalities League for Democracy, and Sao Hso Ten, Chairman of the Shan State Peace Council;

(*c*) The consistent harassment of members of the National League for Democracy and other politicians, and the fact that no full and independent inquiry, with international cooperation, into the attack perpetrated near Depayin on 30 May 2003 has been initiated, despite the decision taken thereon by the General Assembly in its resolution 58/247 of 23 December 2003;

(*d*) The absence of a substantive and structured dialogue with Aung San Suu Kyi and the National League for Democracy, and some representative ethnic groups, that facilitates national reconciliation, coupled with continuing restrictions placed on the League and other political parties, which have prevented them from participating in the National Convention, including the continued closure of the regional offices of the League;

(*e*) The renewed attacks by military forces on ceasefire groups in violation of ceasefire agreements, and the subsequent and continuing violations of human rights, and the deterioration of the enjoyment of human rights by the affected populations;

(*f*) The continuing denial of the freedom of human rights defenders to pursue their legitimate activities;

(*g*) The situation of the large number of internally displaced persons and the flow of refugees to neighbouring countries, and recalls in this context the obligations of Myanmar under international law;

(*h*) The fact that the Government of Myanmar, as noted by the 2005 International Labour Conference, has still not implemented the recommendations of the International Labour Organization Commission of Inquiry, has yet to demonstrate its stated determination to eliminate forced labour and take the necessary measures to comply with the International Labour Organization Convention concerning Forced or Compulsory Labour, 1930 (Convention No. 29), and has yet to demonstrate commitment at the highest level to a substantive policy dialogue that can address the forced labour problem;

(*i*) The fact that the Special Envoy of the Secretary-General for Myanmar and the Special Rapporteur of the Commission on Human Rights on the situation of human rights in Myanmar have been unable to visit the country for almost two years, despite repeated requests;

(j) The imposition of various travel restrictions on United Nations and other international organizations undertaking to enable access for the delivery of humanitarian assistance to all parts of Myanmar, and notes the related withdrawal of the Global Fund to Fight AIDS, Tuberculosis and Malaria;

3. *Strongly calls upon* the Government of Myanmar:

(a) To end the systematic violations of human rights in Myanmar and to ensure full respect for all human rights and fundamental freedoms;

(b) To end impunity and to investigate and bring to justice any perpetrators of human rights violations, including members of the military and other government agents in all circumstances;

(c) To consider as a matter of high priority becoming a party to all instruments of international human rights law and international humanitarian law, and to ensure that existing legal obligations are implemented;

(d) To promote the full enjoyment of all human rights and allow human rights defenders to pursue their activities unhindered and to ensure their safety, security and freedom of movement in that pursuit;

(e) To put an immediate end to the recruitment and use of child soldiers and to extend full cooperation to relevant international organizations in order to ensure the demobilization of child soldiers, their return home and their rehabilitation in accordance with Security Council resolutions 1539(2004) of 22 April 2004 and 1612(2005), and stresses the need for the Government of Myanmar to maintain close dialogue with the United Nations Children's Fund and to cooperate with the Special Representative of the Secretary-General for Children and Armed Conflict in accordance with Council resolutions 1539(2004) and 1612(2005);

(f) To end widespread rape and other forms of sexual violence persistently carried out by members of the armed forces, in particular against women belonging to ethnic nationalities, and to investigate and bring to justice any perpetrators in order to end impunity for those acts;

(g) To end the systematic forced displacement of persons and other causes of refugee flows to neighbouring countries, to provide the necessary protection and assistance to internally displaced persons, in cooperation with the international community, and to respect the right of refugees to voluntary, safe and dignified return monitored by appropriate international agencies in accordance with international law, including applicable international humanitarian law;

(h) To release all political prisoners immediately and unconditionally, including National League for Democracy leaders Aung San Suu Kyi and Tin Oo, and Shan Nationalities League for Democracy leader Khun Htun Oo and other Shan leaders, and to allow their full participation in an inclusive and credible process of national reconciliation;

(i) To lift all restraints on peaceful political activity of all persons, including former political prisoners, by, inter alia, guaranteeing freedom of association and freedom of expression, including freedom of the media, and to ensure unhindered access to information for the people of Myanmar and to desist from arresting and punishing persons for their peaceful political activities;

(j) To urgently resolve the serious issues identified by the very High-level Team and the International Labour Conference, including to give clear assurances that no action will be taken against persons lodging complaints of forced labour, to resolve outstanding allegations of forced labour, to issue the necessary visas to allow a strengthening of the International Labour Organization presence in Myanmar, and to respect the freedom of movement of the Liaison Officer ad interim;

(k) To cooperate fully with the Special Envoy and the Special Rapporteur in order to bring Myanmar towards a transition to civilian rule, and to ensure that they are both granted full, free and unimpeded access to Myanmar and that no person cooperating with the Special Envoy, the Special Rapporteur or any international organization is subjected to any form of intimidation, harassment or punishment, and to review as a matter of urgency the cases of those currently undergoing punishment in this regard;

(l) Without further delay, to cooperate fully with the Special Rapporteur to facilitate an independent international investigation of continuing reports of sexual violence and other abuse of civilians carried out by members of the armed forces in Shan, Karen, Mon and other states;

(m) To ensure immediately safe and unhindered access to all parts of Myanmar for the United Nations and international humanitarian organizations and to cooperate fully with those organizations so as to ensure that humanitarian assistance is delivered in accordance with humanitarian principles and reaches the most vulnerable groups of the population in accordance with international law, including applicable international humanitarian law;

(n) To ensure that discipline in prisons does not constitute torture or cruel, inhuman or degrading treatment or punishment, and that conditions of detention otherwise meet international standards, and to include the possibility of visiting any detainee, including Aung San Suu Kyi;

(o) To ensure that government forces do not engage in food and land requisition or the destruction of villages;

(p) To continue to take action to fight the HIV/AIDS epidemic;

4. *Calls upon* the Government of Myanmar:

(a) To ensure that the remainder of the National Convention, in particular the subsequent constitution-drafting exercise, becomes genuinely inclusive, through the unhindered participation of all political parties and representatives of ethnic nationalities;

(b) To ensure that the proposals tabled at the National Convention for the chapters of the draft constitution are consistent with the Universal Declaration of Human Rights, the International Covenants on Human Rights and other human rights instruments;

(c) To create the conditions for the free operation of existing and new political parties, in advance of the referendum and elections envisaged under the seven-step road map, and to ensure that all eligible citizens are registered to vote in any future referendum and elections and that these are conducted according to international standards with the full participation of all political parties;

(d) To pursue through dialogue and peaceful means the immediate suspension and permanent end of conflict with all ethnic groups in Myanmar, including by ensuring that the constitution-drafting process responds to the concerns of the ethnic nationalities, including the ceasefire groups attending the National Convention, and respects their rights, so as to increase the likelihood that the ceasefires will lead to lasting political settlements and peace;

(e) To fulfil its obligations to restore the independence of the judiciary and due process of law, and to take further steps to reform the system of the administration of justice;

5. *Requests* the Secretary-General:

(a) To continue to provide his good offices and to pursue his discussions on the situation of human rights and the restoration of democracy with the Government and the people of Myanmar, including all relevant parties to the national reconciliation process in Myanmar, and to offer technical assistance to the Government in this regard;

(b) To give all necessary assistance to enable his Special Envoy and the Special Rapporteur to discharge their mandate fully and effectively;

(c) To report to the General Assembly at its sixty-first session and to the Commission on Human Rights at its sixty-second session on the progress made in the implementation of the present resolution;

6. *Decides* to continue the consideration of the question at its sixty-first session.

Turkmenistan

Report of Secretary-General. In response to General Assembly resolution 59/206 [YUN 2004, p. 813], the Secretary-General submitted a September report on the situation of human rights in Turkmenistan [A/60/367]. The report described efforts to implement resolution 59/206, including the development of constructive dialogue between Turkmenistan and OHCHR on technical cooperation for the preparation of reports to human rights treaty bodies and the implementation of international human rights standards; the related activities of the Commission's special procedures; and the status of Turkmenistan's reporting to treaty bodies and efforts to implement their recommendations.

The Secretary-General concluded that, although the country had made some progress in addressing outstanding problems, the reported continuation of serious human rights violations indicated a lack of overall improvement in the human rights situation there. He encouraged the Government to continue to submit reports to UN treaty bodies, to maintain dialogue with the Committee on the Elimination of Racial Discrimination and to implement the recommendations made by those bodies. It should extend invitations to the Commission's thematic special mechanisms interested in visiting that country and to continue cooperation with OHCHR.

Communication. In an 11 April note to OHCHR [E/CN.4/2005/G/35], Turkmenistan described recent measures taken by the Government to improve human rights and to strengthen cooperation with international organizations.

GENERAL ASSEMBLY ACTION

On 16 December [meeting 64], the General Assembly, on the recommendation of the Third Committee [A/60/509/Add.3 & Corr.1], adopted **resolution 60/172** by recorded vote (71-35-60) [agenda item 71 *(c)*].

Situation of human rights in Turkmenistan

The General Assembly,

Reaffirming that all States Members of the United Nations have the obligation to promote and protect human rights and fundamental freedoms and the duty to fulfil the obligations that they have undertaken under the various international instruments in this field,

Recalling its resolutions 58/194 of 22 December 2003 and 59/206 of 20 December 2004, and Commission on Human Rights resolutions 2003/11 of 16 April 2003 and 2004/12 of 15 April 2004,

Noting the conclusion of the first needs-assessment mission of the Office of the United Nations High Commissioner for Human Rights to Turkmenistan in March 2004 and the ongoing consultations to finalize a possible technical cooperation project,

Noting with appreciation that the Government of Turkmenistan has received the Chairman-in-Office and the High Commissioner on National Minorities of the Organization for Security and Cooperation in Europe,

Welcoming the report of the Secretary-General of 20 September 2005, which concludes that, while the Government of Turkmenistan has made some progress in addressing human rights issues and has shown readiness to cooperate with the international community, there was a lack of overall improvement in addressing serious human rights violations,

Reaffirming that improving security and the fight against terrorism should be conducted in accordance with international law, in particular international human rights, humanitarian and refugee law, and democratic principles,

1. Welcomes:

(a) The fact that additional minority religious groups have been allowed to worship for the first time as a result of the removal of a legal impediment to the full realization of the right to freedom of thought, conscience, religion or belief, but notes that serious violations of these freedoms continue;

(b) The release in April 2005 of four Jehovah's Witnesses who had made conscientious objections to undertaking military service;

(c) The lifting of criminal penalties for the activities of non-registered non-governmental organizations in November 2004, while nevertheless noting that difficulties in the registration process for non-governmental organizations and private organizations continue and that other significant restrictions continue to hinder their activities;

(*d*) The submission, within the past year, of the national report under the International Convention on the Elimination of All Forms of Racial Discrimination to the Committee on the Elimination of Racial Discrimination, as well as the reports due under the Convention on the Rights of the Child and the Convention on the Elimination of All Forms of Discrimination against Women, while encouraging the Government of Turkmenistan to comply with its outstanding reporting obligations to the Human Rights Committee, the Committee on Economic, Social and Cultural Rights and the Committee against Torture;

(*e*) The demonstrated readiness of the Government of Turkmenistan to discuss human rights matters with interested third parties on an ad hoc basis and to agree on the desirability of continuing dialogue and practical cooperation;

(*f*) The statements made by the President of Turkmenistan in April 2005 on democratic reforms, and urges that those reforms be truly democratic, in line with established international norms;

(*g*) The accession by Turkmenistan to the following United Nations protocols and conventions, and urges the Government of Turkmenistan to implement its obligations under these instruments:

(i) The Optional Protocol to the Convention on the Rights of the Child on the involvement of children in armed conflict;

(ii) The Optional Protocol to the Convention on the Rights of the Child on the sale of children, child prostitution and child pornography;

(iii) The United Nations Convention against Transnational Organized Crime, its Protocol to Prevent, Suppress and Punish Trafficking in Persons, Especially Women and Children and its Protocol against the Smuggling of Migrants by Land, Sea and Air;

(*h*) The public statements of the President of Turkmenistan recommending the abolition of the practice of removing children from school for the cotton harvest and reprimanding a local governor for the use of child labour in the fields, as well as a law passed on 1 February 2005 prohibiting the employment of minors under the age of 15 and stipulating that no form of child labour should interfere with a child's education, and calls upon the Government of Turkmenistan to ensure that the law is fully implemented;

(*i*) The decision of the Government of Turkmenistan to grant citizenship or permanent resident status to more than sixteen thousand refugees, including a significant number of Tajik refugees, who had fled Tajikistan between 1992 and 1999 and whose naturalization under the Turkmen Nationality Law had been advocated for many years by the United Nations High Commissioner for Refugees;

(*j*) The abolition of exit visas as a requirement for leaving the country;

2. *Expresses its grave concern* at the continuing and serious human rights violations occurring in Turkmenistan, in particular:

(*a*) The persistence of a governmental policy based on the repression of all political opposition activities;

(*b*) The continuing abuse of the legal system through arbitrary detentions, imprisonment and surveillance of persons who try to exercise their freedom of expression, assembly and association, and harassment of their families;

(*c*) The poor conditions in prisons in Turkmenistan and credible reports of ongoing torture and mistreatment of detainees;

(*d*) The failure of the Government of Turkmenistan to grant access to detainees to the International Committee of the Red Cross, according to the usual terms of the Committee, as well as to international monitors;

(*e*) The complete control of the media by the Government of Turkmenistan, its censorship of all newspapers and access to the Internet and intolerance of independent criticism of government policy, as well as further restrictions on the freedom of expression and opinion, including shutting down of the last remaining Russian-language radio station, Radio Mayak, even if satellite television is permitted and widely used, harassing of local correspondents and collaborators of Radio Liberty and prohibition of all contact between local journalists and foreigners without the express consent of the Government;

(*f*) Continuing restrictions on the exercise of the freedom of thought, conscience, religion or belief, including the use of registration procedures as a means to limit the right to freedom of thought, conscience and religion of members of certain religious communities;

(*g*) Continuing discrimination by the Government of Turkmenistan against ethnic Russian, Uzbek and other minorities, inter alia, in the fields of education and employment and access to media, despite assurances by the Government that it will stop this discrimination, taking note in this regard of the concluding observations of the Committee on the Elimination of Racial Discrimination of August 2005;

(*h*) Forced displacement of its citizens, including a disproportionate displacement of ethnic minorities;

(*i*) Continuing restrictions on the exercise of the right of peaceful assembly, including increased constraints faced by civil society organizations, such as the slow progress in the registration of non-governmental organizations under the procedures set out in the law of 2003 on public associations;

(*j*) The continuing failure of the Government of Turkmenistan to respond to the criticisms identified in the report of the Rapporteur of the Moscow Mechanism of the Organization for Security and Cooperation in Europe with regard to the investigation, trial and detention procedures following the reported assassination attempt against the President of Turkmenistan in November 2002, as well as the failure of the Turkmen authorities to allow appropriate independent bodies, family members and lawyers access to those convicted, or to provide any kind of evidence to dispel rumours that some of those convicted have died in detention;

(*k*) Arbitrary or unlawful interference with individuals' privacy, family, home or correspondence and violations of the freedom to leave one's country;

(*l*) Reported instances of hate speech against national and ethnic minorities, including statements attributed to high-ranking government officials and public figures supporting an approach to Turkmen ethnic purity, as noted in the concluding observations of the Committee on the Elimination of Racial Discrimination of August 2005;

3. *Urges* the Government of Turkmenistan:

(*a*) To ensure full respect for all human rights and fundamental freedoms and, in this regard, to implement fully the measures set out in General Assembly resolutions 58/194 and 59/206 and Commission on Human Rights resolutions 2003/11 and 2004/12;

(*b*) To work closely with the Office of the United Nations High Commissioner for Human Rights with regard to the areas of concern and to cooperate fully with all the mechanisms of the Commission on Human Rights, in particular to consider favourably requests made by a number of special rapporteurs of the Commission to visit the country, as recalled in the report of the Secretary-General, and with all the relevant United Nations treaty bodies;

(*c*) To implement fully the recommendations outlined in the report of the Rapporteur of the Moscow Mechanism of the Organization for Security and Cooperation in Europe and to work constructively with the various institutions of the Organization, and to facilitate further visits of the Organization's Chairman-in-Office as well as his Personal Envoy for participating States in Central Asia, and of the Organization's High Commissioner on National Minorities;

(*d*) To follow through on the presentation of the Government of Turkmenistan to the Commission on Human Rights in April 2004 and the meetings of the Government of Turkmenistan with the International Committee of the Red Cross in 2005 by finalizing an agreement allowing the Committee to visit Turkmen prisons with full and repeated access to all places of detention in accordance with the usual modalities for that organization, and by providing international monitors, lawyers and relatives with full and repeated access to all those in detention, including those convicted of involvement in the coup attempt of 25 November 2002;

(*e*) To respect the right of everyone to freedom of thought, conscience, religion or belief, whether a member of a religious group or not, and to cease the harassment, detention and persecution of members of religious minorities, whether registered or unregistered;

(*f*) To bring laws and practices governing registration of public associations, including non-governmental organizations, into line with the standards of the Organization for Security and Cooperation in Europe and to enable non-governmental organizations, particularly human rights organizations, and other civil society actors, including independent media, to carry out their activities without hindrance;

(*g*) To submit reports to the United Nations treaty bodies to which it has assumed a reporting obligation and to give due regard to the recommendations and concluding observations of those treaty bodies, the most recent being the recommendations and concluding observations of the Committee on the Elimination of Racial Discrimination;

(*h*) To fulfil its responsibility to ensure that those responsible for human rights violations are brought to justice;

4. *Requests* the Secretary-General to submit a report to the General Assembly at its sixty-first session on the implementation of the present resolution.

RECORDED VOTE ON RESOLUTION 60/172:

In favour: Albania, Andorra, Argentina, Australia, Austria, Belgium, Bolivia, Bosnia and Herzegovina, Brazil, Bulgaria, Canada, Chile, Costa Rica, Croatia, Cyprus, Czech Republic, Denmark, Dominican Republic, Ecuador, El Salvador, Estonia, Finland, France, Germany, Greece, Guatemala, Haiti, Honduras, Hungary, Iceland, Ireland, Israel, Italy, Japan, Latvia, Liechtenstein, Lithuania, Luxembourg, Malta, Marshall Islands, Mauritania, Mexico, Micronesia, Monaco, Netherlands, New Zealand, Nicaragua, Norway, Palau, Papua New Guinea, Paraguay, Peru, Poland, Portugal, Republic of Korea, Republic of Moldova, Romania, Saint Vincent and the Grenadines, Samoa, San Marino, Serbia and Montenegro, Slovakia, Slovenia, Spain, Sweden, Switzerland, The former Yugoslav Republic of Macedonia, Timor-Leste, United Kingdom, United States, Uruguay.

Against: Afghanistan, Azerbaijan, Bahrain, Bangladesh, Belarus, Brunei Darussalam, China, Cuba, Democratic People's Republic of Korea, Egypt, Gambia, Indonesia, Iran, Jordan, Kazakhstan, Kuwait, Libyan Arab Jamahiriya, Malaysia, Maldives, Morocco, Myanmar, Oman, Pakistan, Qatar, Saudi Arabia, Sudan, Syrian Arab Republic, Tajikistan, Turkmenistan, United Arab Emirates, Uzbekistan, Venezuela, Viet Nam, Yemen, Zimbabwe.

Abstaining: Algeria, Angola, Antigua and Barbuda, Armenia, Bahamas, Barbados, Belize, Benin, Bhutan, Botswana, Burkina Faso, Burundi, Cameroon, Cape Verde, Colombia, Côte d'Ivoire, Democratic Republic of the Congo, Djibouti, Eritrea, Ethiopia, Fiji, Ghana, Guinea, Guinea-Bissau, Guyana, India, Iraq, Jamaica, Kenya, Kyrgyzstan, Lao People's Democratic Republic, Lesotho, Malawi, Mali, Mauritius, Mozambique, Namibia, Nepal, Niger, Nigeria, Panama, Philippines, Russian Federation, Rwanda, Saint Lucia, Senegal, Singapore, Somalia, South Africa, Sri Lanka, Suriname, Thailand, Togo, Tonga, Trinidad and Tobago, Tunisia, Uganda, United Republic of Tanzania, Vanuatu, Zambia.

Uzbekistan

According to a report of the High Commissioner [E/CN.4/2006/119], the outbreak of demonstrations in the Andijan city of Uzbekistan between 12 and 14 May, resulted in the deaths of over 176 people and caused some 500 survivors to flee to Kyrgyzstan. In the absence of a positive response from Uzbekistan to the call from the High Commissioner and the Secretary-General for an international investigation, OHCHR dispatched a mission to Kyrgyzstan from 13 to 21 June to collect information on the causes and circumstances of the incidents as a preparatory step to a possible independent international investigation into those events. Following extensive meetings and interviews with some of the eyewitnesses in Kyrgyzstan, the mission concluded that there was strong, consistent and credible testimony that grave violations of human rights, mostly of the right to life, were committed by Uzbek military and security forces, and that the incident resulted in mass killing. The demonstration at Babur Square was a public expression of discontent relating to the trial of 23 businessmen whose arrest had created financial and personal hardship to the population in and around Andijan, and while the demonstration might have constituted a serious threat to law and order, the armed forces appeared not to have taken any measures to protect life and did not warn people against gathering at the square.

The mission recommended the prompt establishment of an international commission of inquiry to investigate the alleged violations, to establish the facts and circumstances and, to the extent possible, prosecute those responsible. In the light of conflicting information on the death toll, such an inquiry should also establish what happened to the bodies of those killed, trace those who had disappeared and ensure that survivors were reunited with their families. The Government of Uzbekistan should ensure adequate compensation for the families of the victims and for those whose property was destroyed during those incidents.

Given the consistent pattern of human rights violations in Uzbekistan, the international community should consider appointing a country-based special rapporteur or independent expert, with the mandate to report on progress in implementing international human rights norms and in ensuring the rule of law in the country.

In December, the General Assembly called on the Government of Uzbekistan to implement promptly the recommendations contained in the mission's report, most notably with respect to granting permission for the establishment of an international commission of inquiry into the events in Andijan (see resolution 60/174 below).

Communication. By a 2 August communication [A/59/890], Uzbekistan circulated a decree of its President on the abolition of the death penalty.

GENERAL ASSEMBLY ACTION

On 16 December [meeting 64], the General Assembly, on the recommendation of the Third Committee [A/60/509/Add.3 & Corr.1], adopted **resolution 60/174** by recorded vote (74-39-56) [agenda item 71 (c)].

Situation of human rights in Uzbekistan

The General Assembly,

Reaffirming that all States Members of the United Nations have an obligation to promote and protect human rights and fundamental freedoms, and the duty to fulfil the obligations they have undertaken under the various international instruments in this field,

Mindful that Uzbekistan is a party to the International Covenant on Civil and Political Rights, the Convention against Torture and Other Cruel, Inhuman or Degrading Treatment or Punishment, the International Covenant on Economic, Social and Cultural Rights, the International Convention on the Elimination of All Forms of Racial Discrimination, the Convention on the Elimination of All Forms of Discrimination against Women and the Convention on the Rights of the Child,

Deeply concerned by the events that occurred in Andijan in May 2005 and the subsequent response of the Uzbek authorities,

1. *Welcomes:*

(*a*) The high-level talks of the Government of Uzbekistan with the Secretary General of the Organization for Security and Cooperation in Europe and with the Special Representative of the European

Union for Central Asia, and hopes that a real, constructive dialogue on human rights issues will be held soon;

(*b*) The steps, albeit limited, taken to date to implement the National Action Plan on Torture and the recommendations of the Special Rapporteur of the Commission on Human Rights on torture and other cruel, inhuman or degrading treatment or punishment, including the definition of torture by the Supreme Court in accordance with the Convention against Torture and Other Cruel, Inhuman or Degrading Treatment or Punishment, and the amendment of the Criminal Code to include torture as a punishable crime;

(*c*) The statement made by the President of Uzbekistan on 28 January 2005 in which he expressed, inter alia, the intention to provide for true independence of the judiciary, and calls upon the Government of Uzbekistan to take steps to allow for its practical independence, as outlined by the President;

(*d*) The decree of the President of Uzbekistan on 1 August 2005 that the death penalty shall be abolished in Uzbekistan as from 1 January 2008;

2. *Expresses its grave concern* at the continuing and serious human rights violations occurring in Uzbekistan, in particular:

(*a*) Eyewitness reports of indiscriminate and disproportionate force used by government troops to quell demonstrations in Andijan in May 2005 resulting in the death of many civilians;

(*b*) The pressure applied to prevent citizens of Uzbekistan with refugee status granted by the Office of the United Nations High Commissioner for Refugees from travelling to a third country;

(*c*) Reports of arbitrary arrest and detention, including of eyewitnesses to the events in Andijan;

(*d*) Prevention of the functioning of independent media and the intolerance of any form of dissent expressed therein, and increasing restrictions on freedom of expression, particularly harassment, beatings, arrests and threats made against journalists and civil society activists attempting to document and publicize information on the events in Andijan;

(*e*) Continuing refusal to permit the registration of opposition political parties, and their consequent inability to participate in the electoral process;

(*f*) A continuing pattern of discrimination, harassment and prosecution with regard to the exercise of freedom of thought, conscience and religion;

(*g*) Serious constraints on, and harassment and detention of, the members of non-governmental organizations and civil society, including human rights defenders;

3. *Deeply regrets* the decision of the Government of Uzbekistan to reject both the repeated calls of the United Nations High Commissioner for Human Rights for the establishment of an independent commission of inquiry into the events that occurred in Andijan on 13 May 2005 and the request of the Special Rapporteur of the Commission on Human Rights on extrajudicial, summary or arbitrary executions to visit Uzbekistan soon afterwards;

4. *Strongly calls upon* the Government of Uzbekistan:

(*a*) To implement fully without any delay the recommendations contained in the report of the mission of the Office of the United Nations High Commissioner for Human Rights to Kyrgyzstan from 13 to 21 June 2005, most notably with respect to granting permission for the establishment of an international commission of inquiry into the events in Andijan;

(b) To accede to the 1951 Convention relating to the Status of Refugees and its 1967 Protocol;

(c) To put an end to the harassment and detention of eyewitnesses to the events in Andijan;

(d) To ensure readily accessible and fair trials;

(e) To ensure full respect for all human rights and fundamental freedoms and, in this regard, to implement fully the recommendations of the independent expert on the situation of human rights in Uzbekistan appointed under the confidential 1503 procedure at the sixtieth session of the Commission on Human Rights and to extend full cooperation to the newly appointed independent expert;

(f) To permit the full freedom of practising religion;

(g) To implement fully the recommendations contained in the report of the Special Rapporteur of the Commission on Human Rights on the question of torture on his visit to Uzbekistan from 24 November to 6 December 2002;

(h) To work closely with the Office of the United Nations High Commissioner for Human Rights with regard to the areas of concern and to cooperate fully with all the mechanisms of the Commission on Human Rights and all the relevant United Nations treaty bodies;

(i) To allow the representatives of the International Committee of the Red Cross unimpeded access to persons detained, in accordance with its working procedures;

(j) To implement fully the commitments undertaken within the framework of the Organization for Security and Cooperation in Europe and to cooperate with the institutions of the Organization;

(k) To register independent opposition political parties and allow them to participate in the electoral process;

(l) To lift restrictions on the activities of civil society, including non-governmental organizations;

(m) To protect journalists, including those who write articles opposing government policy, in line with past appeals by the President for journalists to be more critical, and the functioning of independent media outlets, including, as the case may be, licensing and accreditation;

(n) To take legislative, judicial, administrative and other appropriate measures to actively protect human rights defenders against any violence, threats and other forms of harassment, and to withdraw all measures that restrict their freedom of action, assembly and speech or that hinder them in carrying out their legitimate activities according to the Declaration on the Right and Responsibility of Individuals, Groups and Organs of Society to Promote and Protect Universally Recognized Human Rights and Fundamental Freedoms;

(o) To place no restrictions on diplomats and representatives of the United Nations, the Organization for Security and Cooperation in Europe and other international bodies in respect of their travel to Uzbekistan;

5. *Requests* the Secretary-General to submit a report on the implementation of the present resolution to the General Assembly at its sixty-first session.

RECORDED VOTE ON RESOLUTION 60/174:

In favour: Albania, Andorra, Argentina, Armenia, Australia, Austria, Belgium, Bolivia, Bosnia and Herzegovina, Brazil, Bulgaria, Canada, Chile, Costa Rica, Croatia, Cyprus, Czech Republic, Denmark, Dominican Republic, Ecuador, El Salvador, Estonia, Finland, France, Georgia, Germany, Greece, Guatemala, Honduras, Hungary, Iceland, Ireland, Israel, Italy, Japan, Latvia, Liechtenstein, Lithuania, Luxembourg, Malta, Marshall Islands, Mauritania, Mexico, Micronesia, Monaco, Netherlands, New Zealand, Nicaragua, Norway, Palau, Papua New Guinea, Paraguay, Peru, Poland, Portugal, Republic of Moldova, Romania, Saint Vincent and the Grenadines, Samoa, San Marino, Serbia and Montenegro, Slovakia, Slovenia, Solomon Islands, Spain, Sweden, Switzerland, The former Yugoslav Republic of Macedonia, Timor-Leste, Turkey, United Kingdom, United States, Uruguay, Vanuatu.

Against: Afghanistan, Azerbaijan, Bahrain, Bangladesh, Belarus, Botswana, Brunei Darussalam, China, Cuba, Democratic People's Republic of Korea, Egypt, Gambia, India, Indonesia, Iran, Jordan, Kazakhstan, Kuwait, Kyrgyzstan, Libyan Arab Jamahiriya, Malaysia, Maldives, Morocco, Myanmar, Oman, Pakistan, Qatar, Russian Federation, Saudi Arabia, Sudan, Syrian Arab Republic, Tajikistan, Turkmenistan, United Arab Emirates, Uzbekistan, Venezuela, Viet Nam, Yemen, Zimbabwe.

Abstaining: Algeria, Angola, Antigua and Barbuda, Bahamas, Barbados, Belize, Benin, Bhutan, Burkina Faso, Burundi, Cameroon, Cape Verde, Colombia, Côte d'Ivoire, Democratic Republic of the Congo, Djibouti, Eritrea, Ethiopia, Fiji, Ghana, Guinea, Guinea-Bissau, Guyana, Haiti, Iraq, Jamaica, Kenya, Lao People's Democratic Republic, Lesotho, Malawi, Mali, Mauritius, Mozambique, Namibia, Nepal, Niger, Nigeria, Panama, Philippines, Republic of Korea, Rwanda, Saint Lucia, Senegal, Singapore, Somalia, South Africa, Sri Lanka, Suriname, Thailand, Togo, Tonga, Trinidad and Tobago, Tunisia, Uganda, United Republic of Tanzania, Zambia.

Europe

Belarus

Commission action. By a recorded vote of 23 to 22, with 7 abstentions, the Commission rejected a motion by the Russian Federation that the Commission take no decision on a draft resolution introduced in the Commission on 14 April [E/2005/23].

On the same day, the Commission, by a recorded vote of 23 to 16, with 14 abstentions, adopted a draft resolution [res. 2005/13], by which it expressed concern that Belarus Government officials were implicated in the forced disappearance and/or summary execution of three political opponents and a journalist; at findings that the 2004 parliamentary elections had fallen significantly short of commitments made under the Organization of Security and Cooperation in Europe (OSCE); at the grave situation of the independent media in Belarus; at reports that the Government was enforcing excessive legal requirements and requesting substantial monetary sums for the registration and operation of NGOs; at reports on the Government's level of observance of international conventions relating to freedom of association and related rights to organize and to collective bargaining; at persistent reports of harassment and closure of NGOs, national minority organizations, independent media outlets, opposition political parties, independent trade unions and religious organizations and the harassment of individuals engaged in democratic activities; at the continuing pressure exerted by the Government on academic institutions; at its failure to cooperate with the Commission's mechanisms; at the politically motivated prosecution of a leading opposition figure; and at the continuing reports of arbitrary arrest and detention. The Commission urged the Government to address those concerns.

The Commission extended the Special Rapporteur's mandate for a further year and asked him to continue efforts, with the Secretary-General's assistance, to establish direct contact with the Government and people of Belarus and to report in 2006.

On 25 July, the Economic and Social Council endorsed the Commission's decision to extend the Special Rapporteur's mandate (**decision 2005/259**).

Report of Special Rapporteur. The Special Rapporteur, Adrian Severin (Romania), submitted a report [E/CN.4/2006/36] on the human rights situation in Belarus, based on the findings of his missions to Estonia, Latvia, Lithuania and Poland, and discussions and consultations in Geneva, Strasbourg (France) and Brussels. The Special Rapporteur, noting the refusal of the Belarus Government to cooperate with him, stated that all efforts made to engage in constructive dialogue were futile.

Belarus, by obstructing United Nations special procedures from fulfilling their mandates, violated its obligations, as a Member State of the Organization, and as party to international human rights instruments to which it had adhered. The Government had not considered any of the Special Rapporteur's previous recommendations, nor those of other special procedures. The breach of social, economic and cultural rights in that country was a matter of concern, since an oligarchy, formed by managers of the former Soviet industrial-military-agricultural complex, had generated a political superstructure headed by the President, which preserved an obsolete command economy that was surviving only within a context of political oppression and social hardship. Workers' rights were violated and there were considerable imbalances between employment, wages and the provision of basic services, and between rural and urban settlements. The regime suppressed or brought under its control every independent civil or economic initiative, and the President reportedly disposed personally of a shadow budget that was larger than the State budget, without any civic or political

oversight, while the regime kept people quiet by meeting their basic needs from extra-economic resources. The regime had reinforced its authoritarian character and was rapidly turning into a dictatorship with clear totalitarian inclinations.

Emphasizing that the conclusions and recommendations contained in his 2004 report [YUN 2004, p. 815] remained valid, the Special Rapporteur urged the Government to give a clear sign of its readiness to cease human rights violations and to bring perpetrators to justice. He further recommended that the Commission request OHCHR to establish a group of legal experts to analyse the responsibility of senior Government officials in the disappearance or murder of public persons, political opponents and journalists and to make proposals for their prosecution. Also, the Secretary-General should investigate the apparent involvement of senior Government officials in international organized crime and illegal arms sales, monitor the international financial cash flows of Belarus, and, if necessary, freeze the foreign bank accounts of those involved in illicit trafficking, and prosecute criminals. In order to continue to raise international awareness of the situation of human rights in Belarus, the Special Rapporteur recommended that the Commission extend his mandate and enlarge its scope and means. Other recommendations were addressed to the Belarusian political opposition and civil society, the international community, Member States and regional organizations, particularly the Council of Europe and OSCE.

Communications. On 24 March, Belarus, referring to the Special Rapporteur's report (see above), submitted information on its contribution to strengthening international security, arms control and disarmament [E/CN.4/2005/G/27], and on social and economic developments in that country, based on the reports of international organizations [E/CN.4/2005/G/28].

Cyprus

Commission action. On 14 April [dec. 2005/103], the Commission retained the item on Cyprus on its agenda, with the understanding that previous resolutions would continue to remain operative, including its request to the Secretary-General to report on their implementation.

(See also p. 491.)

Note by Secretary-General. In response to a 2004 Commission request [YUN 2004, p. 816], the Secretary-General transmitted an OHCHR report [E/CN.4/2006/31 & Corr.1], which provided an overview of human rights issues in Cyprus covering the period up to 23 December 2005. Human rights concerns were rooted in the persisting division of the island, which affected the freedom of movement, property rights, the freedom of religion and the right to education, among other rights.

Limitations to the freedom of movement, owing notably to identity checks at crossing points, particularly affected the military zones in the northern part of the island. The crossing points had also given rise to other problems, including criminal activities, such as smuggling, drug and human trafficking and illegal immigration. Other issues of concern pertained to the question of missing persons, which the Security Council, in resolution 1642(2005) (see p. 496), asked the parties to assess and address with urgency and seriousness.

Regarding economic rights, the gap in the standards of living between the two parts of the island persisted. The report, emphasizing that the continuing de facto partition of the island constituted a major obstacle to the enjoyment of human rights, concluded that the situation would greatly benefit from a comprehensive settlement of the Cyprus problem.

Middle East

Lebanon

On 14 April [dec. 2005/102], the Commission deferred to its 2006 session consideration of a draft resolution on the human rights situation of Lebanese detainees in Israel.

(For information on a visit to Lebanon by the Special Rapporteur on trafficking in persons, especially women and children, see p. 854.)

Territories occupied by Israel

During 2005, the question of human rights violations in the territories occupied by Israel as a result of the 1967 hostilities in the Middle East was again considered by the Commission on Human Rights. Political and other aspects were considered by the General Assembly, its Special Committee to Investigate Israeli Practices Affecting the Human Rights of the Palestinian People and Other Arabs of the Occupied Territories (Committee on Israeli Practices) and other bodies (see PART ONE, Chapter VI).

Reports of Secretary-General. In response to a 2004 Commission request [YUN 2004, p. 817], the Secretary-General reported that he had brought the Commission's resolution on the occupied Syrian Golan to the attention of all Governments, the specialized agencies, regional intergovern-

mental organizations and international humanitarian organizations [E/CN.4/2005/26]. It was also communicated to the Committee on Israeli Practices, the Committee on the Exercise of the Inalienable Rights of the Palestinian People (Committee on Palestinian Rights) and the United Nations Relief and Works Agency for Palestine Refugees in the Near East (UNRWA).

The Secretary-General, in a further report [E/CN.4/2005/27], also submitted in response to a 2004 Commission request [YUN 2004, p. 817], said he had brought the Commission's resolution on the violation of human rights in the occupied Arab territories to the attention of the Government of Israel and all other Governments, relevant UN bodies, specialized agencies, regional intergovernmental organizations and international humanitarian organizations, the Committee on Israeli Practices, the Committee on Palestinian Rights and UNRWA. He received no reply from Israel.

A note of the Secretary-General [E/CN.4/2005/28] listed all General Assembly reports issued since 23 April 2004 on the situation of the population living in the occupied Arab territories.

Commission action. On 14 April [res. 2005/6], the Commission, by a recorded vote of 39 to 2, with 12 abstentions, expressed concern at the continuing Israeli settlement and related activities, in violation of international law, which had changed the physical character and demographic composition of the occupied territories, including East Jerusalem and the occupied Syrian Golan. It also expressed concern at the new construction plan announced by Israel on 18 April (see p. 509).

Taking note of the resumption of dialogue between the parties, the Commission urged them to seize the opportunity offered by the current political context to give renewed impetus to the peace process and to implement the 2003 road map aimed at a comprehensive settlement [YUN 2003, p. 464], endorsed by the Security Council in resolution 1515(2003) [ibid., p. 483]. The Commission asked Israel to implement measures, including the confiscation of arms and enforcement of criminal sanctions, to prevent violence by Israeli settlers and to guarantee the safety and protection of Palestinians. It further demanded that Israel comply with its legal obligations set out in the 2004 advisory opinion of the International Court of Justice (ICJ) [YUN 2004, p. 465] and implement the recommendations regarding settlements contained in the High Commissioner's report on her 2000 visit to the region [YUN 2000, p. 776].

Also, on 14 April [res. 2005/7], by a recorded vote of 29 to 10, with 14 abstentions, the Commission condemned Israel's continuing violations of the human rights of the Palestinian people in the Occupied Palestinian Territory and called on Member States to fulfil their obligations under international human rights and humanitarian law to ensure that Israel ceased killing, targeting, arresting and harassing Palestinians, particularly women and children. The High Commissioner was asked to address the issue of Palestinian pregnant women giving birth at Israeli checkpoints owing to Israel's denial of access to hospitals, with a view to ending that inhumane practice, and to report thereon to the General Assembly in 2005 and to the Commission in 2006. The Commission further requested the High Commissioner to demand the immediate release of Palestinian detainees, including women, children and the sick, investigate reported cases of torture, harassment or ill-treatment and bring to justice Israeli officers involved in the abuse of detainees.

Israel was asked to comply with its obligations under international law, as mentioned in the ICJ advisory opinion and as demanded in relevant General Assembly resolutions, to cease construction of the wall in the Occupied Palestinian Territory, dismantle the structure and make reparations for damage caused due to its construction.

The Special Rapporteur was asked to report to the General Assembly in 2005 and to the Commission in 2006.

On the same date [res. 2005/8], by a recorded vote of 32 to 2, with 19 abstentions, the Commission called on Israel to comply with UN resolutions on the Syrian Golan and demanded that it rescind its decision to impose its laws, jurisdiction and administration on the occupied territory. It also called on Israel to desist from changing the physical character, demographic composition, institutional structure and legal status of the area and from imposing Israeli citizenship and identity cards on the Syrian citizens of the Syrian Golan and to cease its repressive measures against them. The Secretary-General was requested to bring the Commission's resolution to the attention of all Governments, UN organs, specialized agencies, regional intergovernmental organizations and international humanitarian organizations, to widely publicize it and to report in 2006.

Reports of Special Rapporteur. A report of Special Rapporteur John Dugard (South Africa) [E/CN.4/2005/29] focused on Israel's military incursions into the Gaza Strip, the demolition of houses, violations of human rights and humanitarian law arising from the wall it was constructing in the Occupied Palestinian Territory and restrictions on freedom of movement. The report stated that the large-scale demolition of houses during the past year, resulting in many deaths and rendering hundreds of persons homeless in parts of Gaza, probably qualified as war crimes under the Geneva Convention relative to the Protection of Civilian Persons in Time of War (Fourth Geneva Convention).

Although Israel had announced that it would withdraw unilaterally from Gaza [YUN 2004, p. 455], in reality, it intended to retain ultimate control over the area by controlling its borders, territorial sea and airspace. Referring to the 2004 ICJ advisory opinion, which held that the wall Israel was building was contrary to international law, the Special Rapporteur noted that Israel had not dismantled the wall. Freedom of movement was severely curtailed in the West Bank and Gaza, with the inhabitants of Gaza being imprisoned by a combination of wall, fence and sea, and by roadblocks that had effectively divided the small territory. The Special Rapporteur reminded States of their obligation not to recognize the illegal situation resulting from the wall's construction and not to render aid or assistance in maintaining the situation. While acknowledging Israel's legitimate security concerns, the Special Rapporteur stressed that those concerns should be addressed within the parameters of the law and that Israel was both legally and morally obliged to bring its practice in line therewith.

In a March addendum [E/CN.4/2005/29/Add.1], the Special Rapporteur reported on his visit to the Occupied Palestinian Territory and Israel (13-20 February), following the announcement of a ceasefire agreement between Palestinian Authority President Mahmoud Abbas and Israeli Prime Minister Ariel Sharon (see p. 506), by which Palestine would stop all acts of violence against Israelis and Israel would cease all military activity against Palestinians. The Special Rapporteur observed that, despite violations, the ceasefire agreement continued to hold, resulting in important improvements in the human rights situation in the Palestinian Territory, including the release of some 500 Palestinian prisoners from Israeli jails; the return to the West Bank of many Palestinians deported to Gaza and overseas; the discontinuation by the Israeli Defence Forces (IDF) of the targeted killings or assassinations of militants and the announced cessation of the punitive demolition of houses belonging to persons who had committed acts of violence against Israelis; the increase in the number of Palestinian workers and merchants allowed to enter Israel from the Gaza Strip; and the removal of some checkpoints in the West Bank and plans to hand over the control of five cities to the Palestinian Authority.

Despite those developments and reforms, however, the main violations of human rights and humanitarian law in the Occupied Palestinian Territory had not been addressed, including settlements, checkpoints and roadblocks, the situation in Gaza and the continued incarceration of over 7,000 Palestinians. The Special Rapporteur concluded that there was still hope for both Israel and Palestine, and that if the ceasefire was to hold, the Palestinian Authority would have to exercise control over militant groups responsible for violence against IDF and settlers within Palestine and for suicide bombings within Israel. It was equally important that Israel kept its part of the bargain. In that regard, it was not sufficient for Israel merely to cease its military activity against Palestinians, but it also had to address the causes of Palestinian militancy. In the longer term, the questions of the return of refugees, the status of Jerusalem and the occupation had to be confronted, but in the short term, Israel needed to address the release of prisoners, the abandonment of checkpoints, the dismantling of the wall and the evacuation of all settlements in Palestinian territory. If it failed to do so, it would forfeit an opportunity for peace that might not arise again.

In a 29 March communication [E/CN.4/2005/G/30], Israel transmitted its response to the aforementioned reports of the Special Rapporteur.

An August note of the Secretary-General [A/60/271] transmitted a further report of the Special Rapporteur, based on his visit to the Occupied Palestinian Territory (Gaza and the West Bank, 26 June–3 July). The report focused on Israel's decision to withdraw Jewish settlers and troops from Gaza, its continuing construction of the wall in Palestinian territory, the expansion of settlements and the de-Palestinization of Jerusalem.

The report noted that Israel's withdrawal from Gaza would result in the decolonization of Palestinian territory, but would not end the occupation owing to its continuing control of Gaza's borders. In addition, Israel had ignored ICJ's advisory opinion that the construction of the wall was contrary to international law and should be dismantled, and was planning to expand Jewish settlements in the West Bank and parts of Jerusalem. The report also drew attention to the impact of the wall on the welfare of Palestinians, cutting thousands of them off their agricultural lands and forcing them to gradually leave land and homes they had occupied for generations.

Highlighting what he considered to be principal violations of human rights in the Occupied Palestinian Territory, the Special Rapporteur pointed out that the wall and settlements seriously undermined the Palestinian people's fundamental right to self-determination, upon which all other rights depended. Other key rights that continued to be violated included the freedom of the person, the freedom of movement, women's rights, economic and social rights and the right to a clean environment. He said that only a resolution to the conflict, which would end the Israeli occupation of the Occupied Palestinian Territory, the construction of the wall, the expansion of settlements and the de-Palestinization of Jerusalem, would restore hope for respect for human rights.

On 16 December, the General Assembly took note of the Special Rapporteur's report (**decision 60/533**).

(For information on a visit to the Occupied Palestinian Territory by the Special Representative of the Secretary-General on human rights defenders, see p. 718.)

Report of High Commissioner. In response to Commission resolution 2005/7 (see p. 904), the High Commissioner submitted a 31 August report [A/60/324] containing information from three UN entities on the issue of Palestinian pregnant women giving birth at Israeli checkpoints.

PART THREE

Economic and social questions

Chapter I

Development policy and international economic cooperation

Global economic growth continued into 2005, but at a slower pace than the 4 per cent recorded in 2004, and was expected to fall to around 3 per cent. Much of that deceleration was attributable to the slowdown in developed economies, although some developing countries were also showing signs of losing momentum. The moderate slowdown in the global economy was an indication that the world's main engine of growth, the United States economy, might not be able to drive global growth without support from other parts of the world, at a time when the euro was stagnating and Japan's growth showed a moderate deceleration.

Development issues were high on the global agenda in 2005, as world leaders attending the High-level Plenary Meeting of the General Assembly, in September (see p. 47) adopted the "2005 World Summit Outcome", in which they acknowledged that development was a central goal in itself and that sustainable development in its economic, social and environmental aspects constituted a key element of the overarching framework of United Nations activities.

During the year, the United Nations convened the International Meeting to Review the Implementation of the Programme of Action for the Sustainable Development of Small Island Developing States and adopted the Mauritius Declaration and Mauritius Strategy for the Further Implementation of the Programme of Action for the Sustainable Development of Small Island Developing States.

The United Nations also convened the second phase of the World Summit on the Information Society, which adopted the Tunis Commitment and Tunis Agenda for the Information Society. The Summit also called upon the Assembly to declare 17 May as World Information Society Day, to help raise awareness of the importance of the Internet as a global facility, of the issues dealt with at the Summit, as well as ways to bridge the digital divide.

The Commission on Sustainable Development considered the implementation of the outcomes of the 2002 World Summit on Sustainable Development, particularly the Johannesburg Declaration and Plan of Implementation, which outlined actions and targets for stepping up implementation of Agenda 21, a programme of action for sustainable development worldwide, adopted at the 1992 United Nations Conference on Environment and Development. As its contribution to the Assembly's High-level Plenary Meeting (see above), the Commission adopted a resolution on accelerating implementation of development goals and targets related to water, sanitation and human settlements—the thematic cluster of its 2004-2005 multi-year programme. In other development-related activities, the United Nations celebrated 2005 as the International Year of Microcredit; and launched the United Nations Decade of Education for Sustainable Development (2005-2014), and the International Decade for Action, "Water for Life" (2005-2015). The international community continued its observance of the United Nations Decade for the Eradication of Poverty (1997-2006), aimed at eradicating absolute poverty and substantially reducing overall poverty worldwide, and achieving the MDG of halving by 2015 the proportion of the world's people living in extreme poverty. The Assembly, for its part, adopted a resolution on the Decade, focusing on: a global response and policies for poverty eradication; specific initiatives in the fight against poverty; Africa, least developed, landlocked and island developing countries; and the United Nations and the fight against poverty.

In other actions regarding countries in special situations, the Assembly decided to convene a high-level meeting on the midterm comprehensive global review of the implementation of the Programme of Action for the Least Developed Countries for the Decade 2001-2010 in 2006, and welcomed the decision by the Commission on Sustainable Development to devote one day of its 2006 session to review the implementation of the Mauritius Strategy.

In addition, the Assembly noted the results of the sixth annual Ministerial Meeting of Landlocked Developing Countries, and a report of the Secretary-General on poor mountain countries.

International economic relations

Development and international economic cooperation

A number of UN bodies addressed development and international economic cooperation issues during 2005, including the General Assembly and the Economic and Social Council.

On 22 December, the Assembly took note of the report of the Second (Economic and Financial) Committee on its discussion of macroeconomic policy questions [A/60/486] (**decision 60/541**).

Economic and Social Council consideration. On 18 April, the Economic and Social Council held its eighth special high-level meeting with the Bretton Woods institutions (the World Bank Group and the International Monetary Fund), the World Trade Organization (WTO) and the United Nations Conference on Trade and Development (UNCTAD) [A/60/3]. It had before it a 6 April note [E/2005/50] by the Secretary-General on coherence, coordination and cooperation in the context of the implementation of the Monterrey Consensus: achieving the internationally agreed development goals, including those contained in the Millennium Declaration. A summary of the meeting by the Council President [A/59/823-E/2005/69] highlighted the critical importance of building momentum towards the 2005 High-level Plenary Meeting of the General Assembly (see p. 47), which would provide a unique opportunity to agree on actions to achieve the MDGs [YUN 2000, p. 51] and implement the Monterrey Consensus adopted at the 2002 International Conference on Financing for Development [YUN 2002, p. 953].

At its high-level segment (29 June–1 July, and 27 July) [A/60/3], the Council considered the theme of achieving the internationally agreed development goals, including the MDGs, and implementing the outcomes of the major UN conferences and summits: progress made, challenges and opportunities. Activities included a high-level policy dialogue on important developments in the world economy and international economic cooperation.

During its coordination segment (5-7 July) [A/60/3], the Council again discussed how to achieve the internationally agreed development goals, including the MDGs.

Globalization and interdependence

In response to General Assembly resolution 59/240 [YUN 2004, p. 822], the Secretary-General submitted a 1 September report on building institutions for achieving the development goals and integrating them into the global economy [A/60/322]. The report examined the features of effective institutional change, the challenges to be faced and ways to manage integration, while achieving sustainable development. According to the report, the process of globalization and interdependence, created by market reforms and openness, had made integration into the world economy imperative, particularly for developing countries. However, in many cases, particularly in Africa and Latin America, efforts at integration had fallen short of expectations, mainly due to the lack of appropriate and effective institutions around which economic activity and development could thrive. To achieve poverty eradication and sustainable development, institutions were needed that could put developing countries on the path to economic growth and mediate the goals of social equity and environmental sustainability. Institutional development and adaptation were therefore an enduring challenge. Institutional reform that narrowly focused on the role of markets and securing private property rights without attention to holistic and optimal development outcome might be inadequate. Markets, though critical, needed to be seen within the context of broader societal goals of social equity and environmental sustainability. The principal challenge for developing countries was creating sound institutional foundations for the effective functioning of markets within the framework of their social and environmental objectives. A central objective should be to ensure that institutional reforms responded to the needs of the poor as a key priority in poverty-reduction strategies, as well as in overall strategies to promote more rapid, broad-based and sustainable development. Making globalization work for all required the reshaping of rules governing trade, finance and technology transfer; filling the institutional gap in areas such as investment and migration; and giving developing countries a more effective voice and the means to participate in making the global decisions that affected them.

The report recommended that developing countries put institutional development high among their development priorities, and that Governments design their policies, regulatory regimes and agencies to flexibly balance social, economic and environmental objectives. It also recommended the development of flexible regulatory frameworks among Governments, the private sector and consumers, because of their crucial role in delivering development within the new dynamic of interdependence; and expand productive employment through measures that would enable, rather than constrain, the informal economy sector. At the regional level, countries could consider establishing and/or strengthening regional and interregional cooperation arrangements to pool their resources on major development issues. Internationally, a global sustained capacity and institutional development effort was required, supported by the UN system, the Bretton Woods institutions and WTO and other relevant international organizations, to promote the dissemination of institutional innovations that could be adapted by developing countries. Global institutional challenges in trade, finance, investment and technology should be reviewed in order to promote pro-development global rules and norms that gave developing countries a better chance of integrating beneficially in the global economy. Expert-level meetings should be organized to analyse and review institutional questions raised in the Secretary-General's report so as to bring greater clarity to the complex challenges of building inclusive, accountable, dynamic pro-poor and pro-development institutions.

GENERAL ASSEMBLY ACTION

On 22 December [meeting 68], the General Assembly, on the recommendation of the Second Committee [A/60/490/Add.1], adopted **resolution 60/204** without vote [agenda item 54 (*a*)].

Role of the United Nations in promoting development in the context of globalization and interdependence

The General Assembly,

Recalling its resolutions 53/169 of 15 December 1998, 54/231 of 22 December 1999, 55/212 of 20 December 2000, 56/209 of 21 December 2001, 57/274 of 20 December 2002, 58/225 of 23 December 2003 and 59/240 of 22 December 2004 on the role of the United Nations in promoting development in the context of globalization and interdependence,

Recalling also the 2005 World Summit Outcome,

Recalling further its resolution 57/270 B of 23 June 2003 on the integrated and coordinated implementation of and follow-up to the outcomes of the major United Nations conferences and summits in the economic and social fields,

Reaffirming the resolve expressed in the United Nations Millennium Declaration to ensure that globalization becomes a positive force for all the world's people,

Recognizing that globalization and interdependence have opened new opportunities for the growth of the world economy and development, that globalization offers new perspectives for the integration of developing countries into the world economy and that it can improve the overall performance of the economies of developing countries by opening up market opportunities for their exports, by promoting the transfer of information, skills and technology and by increasing the financial resources available for investment in physical and intangible assets, acknowledging that globalization has also brought new challenges for growth and sustainable development and that developing countries have been facing special difficulties in responding to them, recognizing that some countries have successfully adapted to the changes and benefited from globalization but that many others, especially the least developed countries, have remained marginalized in the globalizing world economy, and recognizing also that, as stated in the Millennium Declaration, the benefits are very unevenly shared, while the costs are unevenly distributed,

Recognizing also that all human rights are universal, indivisible, interdependent and interrelated,

Recognizing further that an enabling economic environment should, inter alia, foster a dynamic and well-functioning business sector and include efforts to further promote good corporate and public-sector governance, to combat corruption in the public and private sectors and to promote the strengthening of and respect for the rule of law,

Noting that particular attention must be given, in the context of globalization, to the objective of protecting, promoting and enhancing the rights and welfare of women and girls, as stated in the Beijing Declaration and Platform for Action,

Noting also that an overall commitment to multiculturalism helps to provide an environment for preventing and combating discrimination and promoting solidarity and tolerance in our societies,

Noting further the ongoing work on cultural diversity in the United Nations Educational, Scientific and Cultural Organization,

Reaffirming the commitment to eradicate poverty and hunger and promote sustained economic growth, sustainable development and global prosperity for all and to promote the development of the productive sectors in developing countries to enable them to participate more effectively in and benefit from the process of globalization,

Reaffirming also its strong support for fair globalization and its resolve to make the goals of full and productive employment and decent work for all, including women and young people, a central objective of relevant national and international policies as well as national development strategies, including poverty reduction strategies, as part of the efforts to achieve the Millennium Development Goals, and that these measures should also encompass the elimination of the worst forms of child labour, as defined in International Labour Organization Convention No. 182, and forced labour, and resolving to ensure full respect for the fundamental principles and rights at work,

Reaffirming further the commitment to broaden and strengthen the participation of developing countries and countries with economies in transition in international economic decision-making and norm-setting, and to that end stressing the importance of continuing efforts to reform the international financial architecture, and noting that enhancing the voice and participation of developing countries and countries with economies in transition in the Bretton Woods institutions is a continuing concern,

Reaffirming its commitment to governance, equity and transparency in the financial, monetary and trading systems and its commitment to open, equitable, rule-based, predictable and non-discriminatory multilateral trading and financial systems,

1. *Takes note* of the report of the Secretary-General;

2. *Reaffirms* the need for the United Nations to play a fundamental role in the promotion of international cooperation for development and the coherence, coordination and implementation of development goals and actions agreed upon by the international community, and resolves to strengthen coordination within the United Nations system in close cooperation with all other multilateral financial, trade and development institutions in order to support sustained economic growth, poverty eradication and sustainable development;

3. *Reaffirms also* that good governance is essential for sustainable development; that sound economic policies, solid democratic institutions responsive to the needs of the people and improved infrastructure are the basis for sustained economic growth, poverty eradication and employment creation; and that freedom, peace and security, domestic stability, respect for human rights, including the right to development, and the rule of law, gender equality, market-oriented policies and an overall commitment to just and democratic societies are also essential and mutually reinforcing;

4. *Reaffirms further* that good governance at the international level is fundamental for achieving sustainable development, that, in order to ensure a dynamic and enabling international economic environment, it is important to promote global economic governance through addressing the international finance, trade, technology and investment patterns that have an impact on the development prospects of developing countries, and that to this effect the international community should take all necessary and appropriate measures, including ensuring support for structural and macroeconomic reform, a comprehensive solution to the external debt problem and increasing the market access of developing countries;

5. *Reaffirms* that each country has primary responsibility for its own development, that the role of national policies and development strategies cannot be overemphasized in the achievement of sustainable development and that national efforts should be complemented by supportive global programmes, measures and policies aimed at expanding the development opportunities of developing countries, while taking into account national conditions and ensuring respect for national ownership, strategies and sovereignty;

6. *Recognizes*, at the same time, that domestic economies are now interwoven with the global economic system and that, inter alia, the effective use of trade and investment opportunities can help countries to fight poverty;

7. *Stresses* that, in the increasingly globalizing interdependent world economy, a holistic approach to the interconnected national, international and systemic challenges of financing for development, namely, sustainable, gender-sensitive and people-centred development, is essential and that such an approach must open up opportunities for all and help to ensure that resources are created and used effectively and that solid and accountable institutions are established at all levels;

8. *Stresses also* that development strategies have to be formulated with a view to minimizing the negative social impact of globalization and maximizing its positive impact, while striving to ensure that all groups of the population, in particular the poorest, benefit from it, and that at the international level, efforts should focus on the means to achieve the internationally agreed development goals, including the Millennium Development Goals;

9. *Stresses further* that, in the common pursuit of growth, poverty eradication and sustainable development, a critical challenge is to ensure the necessary internal conditions for mobilizing domestic savings, both public and private, sustaining adequate levels of productive investment and increasing human capacity, while a crucial task is to enhance the efficacy, coherence and consistency of macroeconomic policies and an enabling domestic environment is vital for mobilizing domestic resources, increasing productivity, reducing capital flight, encouraging the private sector and attracting and making effective use of international investment and assistance, and in this regard stresses also that efforts to create such an environment should be supported by the international community;

10. *Stresses* the special importance of creating an enabling international economic environment through strong cooperative efforts by all countries and institutions to promote equitable economic development in a world economy that benefits all people;

11. *Invites* developed countries, in particular major industrialized economies, to take into account the effect of their macroeconomic policies on international growth and development;

12. *Underlines* the fact that the increasing interdependence of national economies in a globalizing world and the emergence of rule-based regimes for international economic relations have meant that the space for national economic policy, i.e., the scope for domestic policies, especially in the areas of trade, investment and industrial development, is now often framed by international disciplines, commitments and global market considerations, that it is for each Government to evaluate the trade-off between the benefits of accepting international rules and commitments and the constraints posed by the loss of policy space and that it is particularly important for developing countries, bearing in mind development goals and objectives, that all countries take into account the need for appropriate balance between national policy space and international disciplines and commitments;

13. *Underlines also* the fact that in addressing the linkages between globalization and sustainable development, particular focus should be placed on identifying and implementing mutually reinforcing policies and practices that promote sustained economic growth, social development and environmental protection and that this requires efforts at both the national and international levels;

14. *Underlines further* the fact that the issue of enhancing the voice of developing countries and countries with economies in transition in the Bretton Woods institutions is of vital importance, stresses the importance of advancing ongoing work in this regard, taking into account progress in the context of the International Monetary Fund quota review, and invites the World Bank and the International Monetary Fund to continue to provide information on this issue, using

existing cooperation forums, including those involving Member States;

15. *Reaffirms* the commitments made in the Doha Ministerial Declaration and the decision of the General Council of the World Trade Organization of 1 August 2004 to fulfil the development dimensions of the Doha Development Agenda, which places the needs and interests of developing and least developed countries at the heart of the Doha work programme, and calls for the successful and timely completion of the Doha round of trade negotiations with the fullest realization of the development dimensions of the Doha work programme, and looks to the Sixth Ministerial Conference of the World Trade Organization, to be held in Hong Kong, China, from 13 to 18 December 2005, to constitute an important milestone to this end;

16. *Stresses* the importance of building a people-centred and inclusive information society so as to enhance digital opportunities for all people in order to help bridge the digital divide, putting the potential of information and communication technologies at the service of development and addressing the new challenges of the information society, and in this regard calls for the implementation of the outcomes of the World Summit on the Information Society;

17. *Reaffirms* that development is a central goal in itself and that sustainable development in its economic, social and environmental aspects constitutes a key element of the overarching framework of United Nations activities, stresses the importance of continuing efforts in this regard, and invites the World Bank, the International Monetary Fund, the regional development banks and other relevant institutions to further integrate development dimensions into their strategies and policies, consistent with their respective mandates;

18. *Reaffirms also* that gender equality is of fundamental importance for achieving sustained economic growth, poverty eradication and sustainable development, in accordance with the relevant General Assembly resolutions and United Nations conferences, and that investing in the development of women and girls has a multiplier effect, in particular on productivity, efficiency and sustained economic growth, in all sectors of economy, especially in key areas such as agriculture, industry and services;

19. *Invites* relevant organizations of the United Nations system and other relevant multilateral bodies to provide information to the Secretary-General on their activities to promote an inclusive and equitable globalization;

20. *Stresses* the importance of migration as a phenomenon accompanying increased globalization, including its impact on economies, and underlines further the need for greater coordination and cooperation among countries as well as relevant regional and international organizations;

21. *Recognizes* that science and technology, including information and communication technologies, are vital for the achievement of development goals and that international support can help developing countries to benefit from technological advancements and enhance their productive capacity, and in this regard reaffirms the commitment to promoting and facilitating, as appropriate, access to and the development, transfer and diffusion of technologies, including environmentally sound technologies and corresponding know-how, to developing countries;

22. *Recognizes also* the special needs of the least developed countries, the small island developing States, and the landlocked developing countries, within the new global framework for transit transport cooperation for landlocked and transit developing countries, as contained in the Almaty Programme of Action, and reaffirms continued support and assistance for their endeavours, particularly in their efforts to achieve the internationally agreed development goals, including those contained in the Millennium Declaration, and the implementation of the Brussels Programme of Action for the Least Developed Countries for the Decade 2001-2010, the Mauritius Strategy for the Further Implementation of the Programme of Action for the Sustainable Development of Small Island Developing States, and the Almaty Programme of Action;

23. *Emphasizes* the importance of recognizing and addressing the specific concerns of countries with economies in transition so as to help them to benefit from globalization, with a view to their full integration into the world economy;

24. *Recognizes* that the contribution of non-governmental organizations, civil society, the private sector and other stakeholders in national development efforts, as well as in the promotion of the global partnership for development, should be enhanced;

25. *Requests* the Secretary-General to submit to the General Assembly at its sixty-first session a report on the implementation of the present resolution under the item entitled "Globalization and interdependence".

Also on 22 December, the Assembly, by **decision 60/543**, took note of the report of the Second Committee on its consideration of the agenda item on globalization and interdependence [A/60/490].

Development through partnership

In response to General Assembly resolution 58/129 [YUN 2003, p. 836], the Secretary-General submitted an August report on enhanced cooperation between the United Nations and all relevant partners, particularly the private sector [A/60/214], which built upon his 2001 [YUN 2001, p. 743] and 2003 [YUN 2003, p. 835] reports on the subject. The report stated that much progress had been made on public-private partnerships in the last decade. The United Nations was successfully reaching out to and engaging business and civil society in its intergovernmental processes, and offering the private sector opportunities to bring its valuable perspective to the table. Partnerships had allowed the United Nations to become more creative and sophisticated in directing the skills and resources of business and civil society towards its own goals. The challenge was to learn from those experiences and move towards a more systematic approach to partnerships that included a greater focus on their impact and sustainability.

Despite the progress made by UN organizations in creating partnership units, only in a few cases was such work integrated into mainstream operations. Staff often lacked the incentives to become involved in partnership work and there was confusion in the UN system with regard to the legal issues governing partnership activities. Greater consistency and transparency were needed in selecting suitable business partners, and additional resources provided for training on the subject of partnerships to enable staff to work more effectively with businesses. Another impediment to more effective partnerships was a lack of understanding of corporate culture within the United Nations. To address that issue and enhance staff skills, some organizations were featuring staff exchange programmes. The Global Compact, launched in 2000 [YUN 2000, p. 989], which continued to be a magnet for businesses wanting to support UN goals, and the United Nations Fund for International Partnerships (UNFIP), the operational arm in the partnership between the UN system and the United Nations Foundation (UNF), the public charity administering the gift by Robert E. Turner to the United Nations of stock valued at some $1 billion to support UN causes, played a critical role in facilitating exchanges, particularly by reaching out to businesses and advocating business engagement within the United Nations.

The Secretary-General observed that one vital component of the ongoing UN transformative process was the progressive opening of the Organization to non-State actors. A variety of engagement mechanisms had been developed, but the challenge was finding ways to fully utilize the opportunities that partnerships afforded. Specific actions were required to scale up successful experiments and allow cooperative engagements with non-State actors to be a stronger force for institutional change.

The report recommended steps the UN system should take to build the environment for its private sector partnerships. Those included increasing institutional capacity in country offices; promoting the staff training at all levels; streamlining UN guidelines for partnerships; improving the coherence and practicality of the partner selection processes; building the foundation for smart selectivity through systematic impact assessment; and fostering transparency through improved learning and best practice exchanges.

GENERAL ASSEMBLY ACTION

On 22 December [meeting 68], the General Assembly, on the recommendation of the Second Committee [A/60/495 & Corr.1], adopted **resolution 60/215** without vote [agenda item 59].

Towards global partnerships

The General Assembly,

Recalling its resolutions 55/215 of 21 December 2000, 56/76 of 11 December 2001 and 58/129 of 19 December 2003,

Reaffirming the vital role of the United Nations, including the General Assembly and the Economic and Social Council, in the promotion of partnerships in the context of globalization,

Underlining the intergovernmental nature of the United Nations, and recalling the central role and responsibility of Governments in national and international policymaking,

Reaffirming its resolve to create an environment, at the national and global levels alike, that is conducive to sustainable development and the elimination of poverty,

Recalling the objectives formulated in the United Nations Millennium Declaration, notably the Millennium Development Goals, and the reaffirmation they have received in the 2005 World Summit Outcome, particularly in regard to developing partnerships through the provision of greater opportunities to the private sector, non-governmental organizations and civil society in general so as to enable them to contribute to the realization of the goals and programmes of the Organization, in particular in the pursuit of development and the eradication of poverty,

Underlining the fact that cooperation between the United Nations and all relevant partners, including the private sector, shall serve the purposes and principles embodied in the Charter of the United Nations and can make concrete contributions to the realization of the Millennium Development Goals and the other goals contained in the Millennium Declaration, as well as in the outcomes of major United Nations conferences and summits and their reviews, in particular in the area of development and the eradication of poverty, and shall be undertaken in a manner that maintains the integrity, impartiality and independence of the Organization,

Underlining also the importance of the contribution of the private sector, non-governmental organizations and civil society in general to the implementation of the outcomes of United Nations conferences in the economic, social and related fields,

Welcoming, in this regard, the participation of civil society and private-sector entities in the multi-stakeholder consultations on development finance issues, whose findings were presented at the High-level Dialogue on Financing for Development held in New York on 27 and 28 June 2005,

Emphasizing that all relevant partners, including the private sector, can contribute in several ways to addressing the obstacles confronted by developing countries in mobilizing the resources needed to finance their sustainable development and to the realization of the development goals of the United Nations through, inter alia, financial resources, access to technology, management expertise and support for programmes, including through the reduced pricing of drugs, where appropriate, for the prevention, care and treatment of HIV/AIDS and other diseases,

Welcoming the efforts and encouraging further efforts by all relevant partners, including the private sector, to engage as reliable and consistent partners in the development process and to take into account not only the economic and financial, but also the developmental, social, human rights, gender and environmental implications of their undertakings and, in general, towards accepting and implementing the principle of good corporate citizenship, that is, bringing social values and responsibilities to bear on a conduct and policy premised on profit incentives, in conformity with national laws and regulations,

Noting that, in line with Economic and Social Council resolution 2003/61 of 25 July 2003, the secretariat of the Commission on Sustainable Development is continuing its efforts to promote partnerships for sustainable development, inter alia, through the establishment of an interactive online database, the preparation of a report on partnerships for sustainable development to the Commission at its twelfth session, in 2004, the holding of a partnership fair at its twelfth and thirteenth sessions, in 2004 and 2005, respectively, and prospectively at its fourteenth session, in 2006, in line with the determination by the Council that partnerships for sustainable development, as voluntary multistakeholder initiatives, contribute to the implementation of Agenda 21 and the Plan of Implementation of the World Summit on Sustainable Development ("Johannesburg Plan of Implementation"),

Welcoming the implementation and expansion of the database of the Commission on Sustainable Development and its increasing use as a platform to provide access to information on partnerships and facilitate the exchange of experiences and best practices,

Taking note of the progress achieved in the work of the United Nations on partnerships, notably in the framework of various United Nations organizations, agencies, funds, programmes, task forces, commissions and initiatives, such as the Global Compact, launched by the Secretary-General, the Information and Communication Technologies Task Force and the United Nations Fund for International Partnerships, and welcoming the establishment of a multitude of partnerships at the field level, entered into by various United Nations agencies, non-public partners and Member States, such as the United Nations Public-Private Alliance for Rural Development,

1. *Takes note* of the report of the Secretary-General on enhanced cooperation between the United Nations and all relevant partners, in particular the private sector;

2. *Stresses* that partnerships are voluntary and collaborative relationships between various parties, both public and non-public, in which all participants agree to work together to achieve a common purpose or undertake a specific task and, as mutually agreed, to share risks and responsibilities, resources and benefits;

3. *Also stresses* the importance of the contribution of voluntary partnerships to the achievement of the internationally agreed development goals, including the Millennium Development Goals, while reiterating that they are a complement to, but not intended to substitute for, the commitments made by Governments with a view to achieving these goals;

4. *Further stresses* that partnerships should be consistent with national laws and national development strategies and plans, as well as the priorities of countries where their implementation takes place, bearing in mind the relevant guidance provided by Governments;

5. *Recalls* that the 2005 World Summit welcomed the positive contributions of the private sector and civil society, including non-governmental organizations, in the promotion and implementation of development and human rights programmes and also welcomed the dialogue between those organizations and Member States, as reflected in the first informal interactive hearings of the General Assembly with representatives of non-governmental organizations, civil society and the private sector;

6. *Also recalls* that the 2005 World Summit resolved to enhance the contribution of non-governmental organizations, civil society, the private sector and other stakeholders in national development efforts, as well as in the promotion of the global partnership for development, and encouraged public-private partnerships in the following areas: the generation of new investments and employment, financing for development, health, agriculture, conservation, sustainable use of natural resources and environmental management, energy, forestry and the impact of climate change;

7. *Encourages* the United Nations system to continue to develop, for those partnerships in which it participates, a common and systemic approach which places greater emphasis on impact, transparency, accountability and sustainability, without imposing undue rigidity in partnership agreements, and with due consideration being given to the following partnership principles: common purpose, transparency, bestowing no unfair advantages upon any partner of the United Nations, mutual benefit and mutual respect, accountability, respect for the modalities of the United Nations, striving for balanced representation of relevant partners from developed and developing countries and countries with economies in transition, sectoral and geographic balance, and not compromising the independence and neutrality of the United Nations system in general and the agencies in particular;

8. *Also encourages* responsible business practices, such as those promoted by the Global Compact;

9. *Further encourages* the Global Compact Office to promote the sharing of best practices and positive action through learning, dialogue and partnerships;

10. *Encourages* the relevant United Nations organizations and agencies, as well as the Global Compact Office, to share relevant lessons learned and positive experiences from partnerships, including with the business community, as a contribution to the development of more effective United Nations partnerships;

11. *Takes note with appreciation* of the appointment by the Secretary-General of a Special Adviser on the Global Compact;

12. *Requests* the Secretary-General to take further appropriate action to enhance partnership management through the promotion of: adequate training at all concerned levels; institutional capacity in country offices; strategic focus and local ownership; the sharing of best practices; the improvement of partner selection processes; and the streamlining of United Nations guidelines for partnerships between the United Nations and all relevant partners, including the private sector, and further requests the Secretary-General to report on these actions in the context of his

report under the item entitled "Towards global partnerships";

13. *Also requests* the Secretary-General, in consultation with Member States, to promote, within existing resources, impact-assessment mechanisms, taking into account best tools available, in order to enable effective management, ensure accountability and facilitate effective learning from both successes and failures;

14. *Welcomes* innovative approaches to use partnerships as a means to better implement goals and programmes, in particular in the pursuit of development and the eradication of poverty, and encourages relevant United Nations bodies and agencies and invites the Bretton Woods institutions and the World Trade Organization to further explore such possibilities, bearing in mind their different mandates, modes of operation and objectives, as well as the particular roles of the non-public partners involved;

15. *Recommends*, in this context, that partnerships should also foster the elimination of all forms of discrimination, including on gender grounds, in respect of employment and occupation;

16. *Reiterates its call upon*:

(a) All bodies within the United Nations system that engage in partnerships to ensure the integrity and independence of the Organization and to include information on partnerships in their regular reporting, as appropriate, on their websites and through other means;

(b) Partners to provide to and exchange relevant information with Governments, other stakeholders and the relevant United Nations agencies and bodies and other international organizations with which they engage, in an appropriate way, including through reports, with particular attention to the importance of sharing among partnerships information on their practical experience;

17. *Requests* the Secretary-General to report to the General Assembly at its sixty-second session on the implementation of the present resolution.

Coercive economic measures

In response to General Assembly resolution 58/198 [YUN 2003, p. 838], the Secretary-General submitted an August report [A/60/226] summarizing replies received from 14 Governments and two UN bodies, in response to his request for information on unilateral economic measures as a means of political and economic coercion against developing countries.

GENERAL ASSEMBLY ACTION

On 22 December [meeting 68], the General Assembly, on the recommendation of the Second Committee [A/60/486/Add.1], adopted **resolution 60/185** by recorded vote (120-1-50) [agenda item 50 (a)].

Unilateral economic measures as a means of political and economic coercion against developing countries

The General Assembly,

Recalling the relevant principles set forth in the Charter of the United Nations,

Reaffirming the Declaration on Principles of International Law concerning Friendly Relations and Cooperation among States in accordance with the Charter of the United Nations, which states, inter alia, that no State may use or encourage the use of unilateral economic, political or any other type of measures to coerce another State in order to obtain from it the subordination of the exercise of its sovereign rights,

Bearing in mind the general principles governing the international trading system and trade policies for development contained in relevant resolutions, rules and provisions of the United Nations and the World Trade Organization,

Recalling its resolutions 44/215 of 22 December 1989, 46/210 of 20 December 1991, 48/168 of 21 December 1993, 50/96 of 20 December 1995, 52/181 of 18 December 1997, 54/200 of 22 December 1999, 56/179 of 21 December 2001 and 58/198 of 23 December 2003,

Gravely concerned that the use of unilateral coercive economic measures adversely affects the economy and development efforts of developing countries in particular and has a general negative impact on international economic cooperation and on worldwide efforts to move towards a non-discriminatory and open multilateral trading system,

1. *Takes note* of the report of the Secretary-General;

2. *Urges* the international community to adopt urgent and effective measures to eliminate the use of unilateral coercive economic measures against developing countries that are not authorized by relevant organs of the United Nations or are inconsistent with the principles of international law as set forth in the Charter of the United Nations and that contravene the basic principles of the multilateral trading system;

3. *Requests* the Secretary-General to continue to monitor the imposition of measures of this nature and to study the impact of such measures on the affected countries, including the impact on trade and development;

4. *Also requests* the Secretary-General to submit to the General Assembly at its sixty-second session a report on the implementation of the present resolution.

RECORDED VOTE ON RESOLUTION 60/185:

In favour: Afghanistan, Algeria, Angola, Antigua and Barbuda, Argentina, Armenia, Azerbaijan, Bahamas, Bahrain, Bangladesh, Barbados, Belarus, Belize, Benin, Bhutan, Bolivia, Botswana, Brazil, Brunei Darussalam, Burkina Faso, Burundi, Cambodia, Cameroon, Cape Verde, Central African Republic, Chile, China, Colombia, Comoros, Congo, Costa Rica, Côte d'Ivoire, Cuba, Democratic People's Republic of Korea, Djibouti, Dominica, Dominican Republic, Ecuador, Egypt, Eritrea, Ethiopia, Fiji, Ghana, Grenada, Guatemala, Guinea, Guinea-Bissau, Guyana, Haiti, India, Indonesia, Iran, Iraq, Jamaica, Jordan, Kazakhstan, Kenya, Kuwait, Kyrgyzstan, Lao People's Democratic Republic, Lebanon, Lesotho, Liberia, Libyan Arab Jamahiriya, Madagascar, Malawi, Malaysia, Maldives, Mali, Mauritania, Mauritius, Mexico, Mongolia, Morocco, Mozambique, Myanmar, Namibia, Nepal, Nicaragua, Nigeria, Oman, Pakistan, Panama, Papua New Guinea, Paraguay, Peru, Philippines, Qatar, Russian Federation, Saint Kitts and Nevis, Saint Lucia, Saint Vincent and the Grenadines, Samoa, Saudi Arabia, Senegal, Sierra Leone, Singapore, Solomon Islands, Somalia, South Africa, Sri Lanka, Sudan, Suriname, Swaziland, Syrian Arab Republic, Tajikistan, Thailand, Togo, Tunisia, Tuvalu, Uganda, United Arab Emirates, United Republic of Tanzania, Uruguay, Uzbekistan, Venezuela, Viet Nam, Yemen, Zambia, Zimbabwe.

Against: United States.

Abstaining: Albania, Andorra, Australia, Austria, Belgium, Bulgaria, Canada, Croatia, Cyprus, Czech Republic, Denmark, Estonia, Finland, France, Georgia, Germany, Greece, Hungary, Iceland, Ireland, Israel, Italy, Japan, Latvia, Liechtenstein, Lithuania, Luxembourg, Malta, Marshall Islands, Monaco, Netherlands, New Zealand, Norway, Palau, Poland, Portugal, Republic of Korea, Republic of Moldova, Romania, San Marino, Serbia and Montenegro, Slovakia, Slovenia, Spain, Sweden, Switzerland, The former Yugoslav Republic of Macedonia, Turkey, Ukraine, United Kingdom.

The Assembly, on 8 November, adopted **resolution 60/12** on the necessity of ending the economic, commercial and financial embargo imposed by the United States against Cuba (see p. 394).

Sustainable development

Implementation of Agenda 21, the Programme for the Further Implementation of Agenda 21 and the Johannesburg Plan of Implementation

In 2005, various UN bodies, among them the General Assembly, the Economic and Social Council and the Commission on Sustainable Development, considered the implementation of the outcomes of the 2002 World Summit on Sustainable Development [YUN 2002, p. 821], particularly the Johannesburg Declaration and Plan of Implementation, which outlined actions and targets for stepping up implementation of Agenda 21—a programme of action for sustainable development worldwide, adopted at the 1992 United Nations Conference on Environment and Development [YUN 1992, p. 672]—and of the Programme for the Further Implementation of Agenda 21, adopted by the Assembly at its nineteenth special session in 1997 [YUN 1997, p. 792].

Commission on Sustainable Development consideration. As the main body responsible for coordinating and monitoring implementation of the Summit outcomes, the Commission on Sustainable Development, at its thirteenth session (New York, 11-22 April) [E/2005/29], discussed, in line with the multi-year programme adopted by the Economic and Social Council in resolution 2003/61 [YUN 2003, p. 842], the thematic cluster for the 2004-2005 implementation cycle—water, sanitation and human settlements.

Intersessional events. The Commission heard presentations on the following intersessional events that were held in preparation for its thirteenth session: Stockholm Water Week (Stockholm, Sweden, 16-20 August 2004); World Urban Forum (Barcelona, Spain, 13-17 September 2004); Global Water, Sanitation and Hygiene Forum (Dakar, Senegal, 29 November–3 December 2004); International Conference on Integrated Water Resources Management (Tokyo, Japan, 6-9 December 2004); World Conference on Disaster Reduction (Kobe, Japan, 18-22 January, 2005); International Meeting to Review the Implementation of the Programme of Action for the Sustainable Development of Small Island Developing States (Port Louis, Mauritius, 10-14 January); African Ministerial Conference on Housing and Urban Development (Durban, South Africa, 31 January–4 February); and the Second International Forum on Partnerships for Sustainable Development (Marrakesh, Morocco, 21-23 March).

Thematic issues. For its consideration of the thematic issues for 2004-2005—water, sanitation and human settlements, the Commission had before it reports of the Secretary-General on policy options and possible actions to expedite implementation of the goals, targets and commitments of Agenda 21, the Programme for the Further Implementation of Agenda 21 and the Johannesburg Plan of Implementation covering freshwater management [E/CN.17/2005/2] (see p. 1129), sanitation [E/CN.17/2005/3] and human settlements [E/CN.17/2005/4] (see p. 1165). It also considered a Secretariat note [E/CN.17/2005/5] containing the views of major groups (women, children and youth, indigenous peoples, NGOs, local authorities, workers and trade unions, business and industry, scientific and technological community, and farmers) on their priorities for action in the three thematic areas. Also before the Commission was the report of the Intergovernmental Preparatory Meeting for the thirteenth session [E/CN.17/2005/6], containing the Chairman's summary of interactive discussions on the three themes.

The Commission adopted some 30 policy options and 100 practical measures and actions to expedite implementation of commitments relating to water, sanitation and human settlements [A/60/261].

Implementation activities

In response to General Assembly resolution 59/227 [YUN 2004, p. 829], the Secretary-General submitted on 16 August the report on the implementation of Agenda 21, the Programme for the Further Implementation of Agenda 21 and the outcome of the World Summit on Sustainable Development [A/60/261 & Corr.1]. It reviewed activities at the intergovernmental, inter-agency, regional and country levels during 2005 to ensure a coordinated follow-up to the World Summit, and the progress made both in advancing partnerships for sustainable development and in integrating further major groups into the work of the Commission on Sustainable Development. The report showed that there was a broad range of implementation going on at all levels. At the intergovernmental level, the Commission, at its policy session, focused on water, sanitation and human settlements, and adopted policy options and practical measures to accelerate implementation in those three thematic areas (see above). The Economic and Social Council, at its substantive session, devoted its high-level segment to achieving the internationally agreed development goals, including the MDGs; its coordination segment focused on implementing those development goals; and its general segment reviewed, among other topics, the work of the functional commissions, including that of the Commission on Sustainable Development. At the inter-agency level, the United Nations System Chief Executive Board for Coordination (CEB) continued to coordinate system-wide activities in sustainable development and, through its High Level Committee on Programmes (HLCP), provided overall guidance to UN-Water, UN-Energy, UN-Oceans and other inter-agency cooperation initiatives in sustainable development.

Regionally, UN regional commissions, through their priority programme activities, as well as other offices, regional development banks and organizations had contributed to implementing sustainable development goals and targets. At the national level, Member States had made available to the Commission significant information relating to sustainable development. Major groups played multiple roles at various levels, promoting education, raising awareness of socio-economic and environmental issues and monitoring progress in implementing sustainable development. Some 300 voluntary, multi-stakeholder partnerships working towards sustainable development goals had registered with the Commission's secretariat.

The Secretary-General urged all concerned to stay on track concerning implementation, while aiming for accelerated progress. He urged Governments to continue implementing the 2005 World Summit Outcome (see p. 48) and supporting the Commission on Sustainable Development; requested HLCP to continue monitoring the operational effectiveness of UN-Water, UN-Energy, UN-Oceans and other inter-agency collaborative mechanisms; and called upon donor Governments and international financial institutions to target funding support to developing countries in key policy options and practical measures as identified in the policy decision of the Commission's thirteenth session (see p. 917).

GENERAL ASSEMBLY ACTION

On 22 December [meeting 68], the General Assembly, on the recommendation of the Second Committee [A/60/488/Add.1], adopted **resolution 60/193** without vote [agenda item 52 (a)].

Implementation of Agenda 21, the Programme for the Further Implementation of Agenda 21 and the outcomes of the World Summit on Sustainable Development

The General Assembly,

Recalling its resolutions 55/199 of 20 December 2000, 56/226 of 24 December 2001, 57/253 of 20 December 2002 and 57/270 A and B of 20 December 2002 and 23 June 2003, respectively, and its resolutions 58/218 of 23 December 2003 and 59/227 of 22 December 2004,

Recalling also the Rio Declaration on Environment and Development, Agenda 21, the Programme for the Further Implementation of Agenda 21, the Johannesburg Declaration on Sustainable Development and the Plan of Implementation of the World Summit on Sustainable Development ("Johannesburg Plan of Implementation"), as well as the Monterrey Consensus of the International Conference on Financing for Development,

Reaffirming the commitment to implement Agenda 21, the Programme for the Further Implementation of Agenda 21, the Johannesburg Plan of Implementation, including the time-bound goals and targets, and the other internationally agreed development goals, including those contained in the United Nations Millennium Declaration, and reaffirmed in the 2005 World Summit Outcome,

Recalling the 2005 World Summit Outcome,

Reaffirming the decisions taken at the eleventh session of the Commission on Sustainable Development,

Reaffirming also the continuing need to ensure a balance among economic development, social development and environmental protection as interdependent and mutually reinforcing pillars of sustainable development,

Reiterating that the Commission is the high-level body responsible for sustainable development within the United Nations system and serves as a forum for consideration of issues related to integration of the three dimensions of sustainable development,

Reaffirming that eradicating poverty, changing unsustainable patterns of production and consumption and protecting and managing the natural resource base of economic and social development are overarching objectives of and essential requirements for sustainable development,

Recognizing that good governance within each country and at the international level is essential for sustainable development,

Recognizing also that eradicating poverty is the greatest global challenge facing the world today and an indispensable requirement for sustainable development, particularly for developing countries, and that although each country has the primary responsibility for its own sustainable development and poverty eradication and the role of national policies and development strategies cannot be overemphasized, concerted and concrete measures are required at all levels to enable developing countries to achieve their sustainable development goals as related to the internationally agreed poverty-related targets and goals, including those contained in Agenda 21, the relevant outcomes of other United Nations conferences and the Millennium Declaration,

Recalling the decision taken by the Commission at its thirteenth session to devote one day of its review sessions to the review of the implementation of the Mauritius Strategy for the Further Implementation of the Programme of Action for the Sustainable Development of Small Island Developing States, focusing on that year's thematic cluster, as well as on any new developments regarding the sustainable development efforts of small island developing States using existing modalities,

Recalling also the decision of the Commission to request its secretariat to update the policy options and practical measures contained in the Chairman's summary of the interactive discussions held at the Intergovernmental Preparatory Meeting, on a regular basis, so as to make it a living document, and to develop web-based tools to disseminate information on implementation and best practices,

Looking forward to the upcoming cycles of the work programme of the Commission as adopted at its eleventh session and their contributions to the further implementation of Agenda 21, the Programme for the Further Implementation of Agenda 21 and the outcomes of the World Summit on Sustainable Development,

1. *Takes note* of the report of the Secretary-General on the activities undertaken in the implementation of Agenda 21, the Programme for the Further Implementation of Agenda 21 and the outcomes of the World Summit on Sustainable Development;

2. *Notes* that the Commission on Sustainable Development at its thirteenth session adopted policy decisions on options and practical measures aimed at accelerating progress in implementation in the areas of water, sanitation and human settlements;

3. *Reiterates* that sustainable development is a key element of the overarching framework for United Nations activities, in particular for achieving the internationally agreed development goals, including those contained in the United Nations Millennium Declaration and in the Plan of Implementation of the World Summit on Sustainable Development ("Johannesburg Plan of Implementation");

4. *Calls upon* Governments, all relevant international and regional organizations, the Economic and Social Council, the United Nations funds and programmes, the regional commissions and the specialized agencies, the international financial institutions, the Global Environment Facility and other intergovernmental organizations, in accordance with their respective mandates, as well as major groups, to take action to ensure the effective implementation of and follow-up to the commitments, programmes and time-bound targets adopted at the World Summit on Sustainable Development, and encourages them to report on concrete progress in that regard;

5. *Calls for* the effective implementation of the commitments, programmes and time-bound targets adopted at the World Summit on Sustainable Development and for the fulfilment of the provisions relating to the means of implementation, as contained in the Johannesburg Plan of Implementation;

6. *Encourages* Governments to participate at the appropriate level with representatives, including ministers, from the relevant departments and organizations working in the areas of energy for sustainable development, industrial development, air pollution/atmosphere and climate change, as well as finance, in the fourteenth session of the Commission;

7. *Recalls* the decision of the Commission at its eleventh session to invite the regional commissions, in collaboration with the secretariat of the Commission, to consider organizing regional implementation meetings in order to contribute to the work of the Commission, and, in this regard, welcomes the activities undertaken by the regional commissions and the secretariat of the Commission to organize the regional implementation meetings in preparation for the fourteenth ses-

sion of the Commission, and looks forward to their contributions, based on the discussions in the intergovernmental regional implementation meetings, to the preparation of the fourteenth session;

8. *Also recalls* the decision of the Commission at its eleventh session that activities during Commission meetings should provide for the balanced involvement of participants from all regions, as well as for gender balance;

9. *Invites* donor countries to consider supporting the participation of experts from the developing countries in the areas of energy for sustainable development, industrial development, air pollution/atmosphere and climate change in the fourteenth session of the Commission;

10. *Reaffirms* the objective of strengthening the implementation of Agenda 21, including through the mobilization of financial and technological resources, as well as capacity-building programmes, particularly for developing countries;

11. *Also reaffirms* the objective of enhancing the participation and effective involvement of civil society and other relevant stakeholders in the implementation of Agenda 21, as well as to promote transparency and broad public participation;

12. *Further reaffirms* the need to promote corporate responsibility and accountability as envisaged by the Johannesburg Plan of Implementation;

13. *Reaffirms* the need to promote the development of microenterprises and small- and medium-sized enterprises, including by means of training, education and skill enhancement, with a special focus on agro-industry as a provider of livelihoods for rural communities;

14. *Requests* the secretariat of the Commission to make arrangements to facilitate the balanced representation of major groups from developed and developing countries in the sessions of the Commission;

15. *Also requests* the secretariat of the Commission to coordinate the participation of the relevant major groups in the discussions at the fourteenth session of the Commission;

16. *Requests* the Secretary-General, in reporting to the Commission at its fourteenth session on the state of the implementation of Agenda 21, the Programme for the Further Implementation of Agenda 21 and the Johannesburg Plan of Implementation, on the basis of appropriate inputs from all levels, to submit thematic reports on the thematic cluster of issues for the fourteenth session of the Commission, in accordance with the decisions taken by the Commission at its eleventh session;

17. *Also requests* the Secretary-General to submit a report to the Commission, at its review session, on progress and obstacles in respect of sustainable development in small island developing States, including recommendations on how to enhance the implementation of the Mauritius Strategy for the Further Implementation of the Programme of Action for the Sustainable Development of Small Island Developing States, focusing on that year's thematic cluster;

18. *Encourages* Governments and organizations at all levels, as well as major groups, including the scientific community and educators, to undertake results-oriented initiatives and activities to support the work of the Commission and to promote and facilitate the

implementation of Agenda 21, the Programme for the Further Implementation of Agenda 21 and the Johannesburg Plan of Implementation, including through voluntary multi-stakeholder partnership initiatives;

19. _Notes_ the convening of the Second International Expert Meeting on the Ten-year Framework of Programmes for Sustainable Consumption and Production in San José, Costa Rica, from 5 to 8 September 2005;

20. _Also notes_ the work in inter-agency cooperation and coordination undertaken in the follow-up to the World Summit on Sustainable Development, and requests the Secretary-General to report, at its sixty-first session, on action taken by the United Nations system in the thematic areas being addressed by the Commission in its current two-year cycle, with a view to facilitating an in-depth consideration of system-wide inter-agency cooperation and coordination in the relevant thematic areas, in accordance with the mandates agreed upon in the Johannesburg Plan of Implementation;

21. _Decides_ to include in the provisional agenda of its sixty-first session the item entitled "Implementation of Agenda 21, the Programme for the Further Implementation of Agenda 21 and the outcomes of the World Summit on Sustainable Development", and requests the Secretary-General, at that session, to submit a report on the implementation of the present resolution.

Commission on Sustainable Development

The Commission on Sustainable Development held its thirteenth session in New York on 30 April 2004 and from 11 to 22 April 2005 [E/2005/29]. On 22 April, the Commission held the first meeting of its fourteenth session, at which it elected the members of its Bureau [E/2005/29]. The Commission's high-level segment interactive sessions focused on turning political commitments into action, with discussions on the MDGs and the impact of natural disasters on water, sanitation and human settlements and how to prevent and respond thereto. The session included an interactive dialogue with ministers and major groups; a policy session on regional perspectives, policy options and other measures in the three thematic areas; and a ministerial panel on the economic benefits of sound policies for water, sanitation and human settlements at all levels. A partnerships fair provided a venue for networking and exchanging lessons learned and best practices; and a learning centre offered 15 courses on goals and targets related to water, sanitation and human settlements.

The Commission recommended to the Economic and Social Council for adoption two draft resolutions: one on support to the Bureau in preparing for future Commission sessions (see below) and the other on support for the travel of representatives from developing countries and countries with economies in transition to future

Commission sessions. It also recommended to the Council for adoption decisions on the term of the Bureau; dates of meetings of the Commission during 2006/2007; and the Commission's report at its thirteenth session and provisional agenda for the fourteenth. The Commission also adopted a decision [dec. 13/1] on policy options and practical measures to expedite implementation in water, sanitation and human settlements, which it submitted to the Council for consideration as a significant contribution to the High-level Plenary Meeting of the General Assembly (see p. 47).

The Commission also had before it a 1 April letter from Morocco transmitting the executive summary of the Second International Forum on Partnerships for Sustainable Development (Marrakesh, Morocco, 21-23 March) [E/CN.17/2005/7].

ECONOMIC AND SOCIAL COUNCIL ACTION

On 20 July [meeting 32], the Economic and Social Council, on the recommendation of the Commission [E/2005/29], adopted **resolution 2005/5** without vote [agenda item 13 _(a)_].

Support to the Bureau in preparing for future sessions of the Commission on Sustainable Development

The Economic and Social Council,

Taking note of the decisions of the Commission on Sustainable Development adopted at its sixth, seventh and eighth sessions on matters related to the intersessional work of the Commission,

Recalling its resolution 2003/61 of 25 July 2003 concerning the mandate and new organization and programme of work for the Commission,

1. _Decides_ that, in order for members of the Bureau to carry out their functions effectively, consideration should be given to providing financial support consisting of travel and daily subsistence to members of the Bureau from developing countries and countries with economies in transition through designated extra-budgetary contributions to the Trust Fund to Support the Work of the Commission on Sustainable Development;

2. _Also decides_ that financial support to members of the Bureau from developing countries and countries with economies in transition should cover participation in one of the meetings of the Bureau to be held outside New York and the respective regional implementation meeting and other relevant meetings in the region;

3. _Invites_ donor Governments, institutions and other organizations to contribute to the Trust Fund.

At the same meeting, the Council, on the recommendation of the Commission [E/2005/29], adopted **resolution 2005/6** without vote [agenda item 13 _(a)_].

Support for the travel of representatives of developing countries and countries with economies in transition to future sessions of the Commission on Sustainable Development

The Economic and Social Council,

Recalling General Assembly resolution 59/227 of 22 December 2004, in which the Assembly encouraged, inter alia, broad-based participation of government representatives and experts in the meetings of the Commission on Sustainable Development,

Emphasizing that such broad participation of representatives and experts from developing countries is key to a balanced review of thematic clusters of issues of the implementation cycles,

1. *Invites* donor Governments, institutions and other organizations to provide contributions to the Trust Fund to Support the Work of the Commission on Sustainable Development;

2. *Recommends* that the General Assembly decide that support to participants from developing countries, with priority given to the least developed countries, as well as from countries with economies in transition, may be provided from the Trust Fund for travel from funds designated for that purpose.

On 20 July, the Council decided that the current term of the Bureau of the Commission should continue on the basis of a one-year term for its next cycle, comprising the fourteenth and fifteenth sessions of the Commission (**decision 2005/227**), and the Commission's fourteenth (review) session should take place from 1 to 12 May 2006, the intergovernmental preparatory meeting for the fifteenth session from 26 February to 2 March 2007, and the Commission's fifteenth (policy) session from 30 April to 11 May 2007 (**decision 2005/228**); took note of the Commission's report on its thirteenth session; and approved the provisional agenda for the fourteenth (2006) session (**decision 2005/229**).

Tourism

In response to General Assembly resolution 56/212 [YUN 2001, p. 752] and decision 58/573 [YUN 2004, p. 833], the Secretary-General, in July [A/60/167], transmitted to the Assembly a report prepared by the World Tourism Organization (UNWTO) [YUN 2004, p. 1513] on implementation of the 1999 Global Code of Ethics for Tourism—a set of basic principles to guide tourism development and serve as a frame of reference for stakeholders in the tourism sector, adopted by the UNWTO General Assembly in 1999. The Code of Ethics was not legally binding, the report pointed out, but its application could be advanced by incorporating its contents and provisions into appropriate legislation, regulations and professional codes. Part I of the Protocol of Implementation, adopted in 2001, created the World Committee on Tourism Ethics, tasked with interpreting, applying and evaluating the Global Code of Ethics

for Tourism. Part II, the conciliation mechanism for the settlement of disputes, was to be submitted for final adoption to the UNWTO General Assembly's sixteenth session in Dakar, Senegal, in 2005.

The World Committee conducted a survey between 2004 and 2005 of UNWTO members to assess the degree of implementation of the Code. It found that nearly three quarters of the 92 respondents had already incorporated its principles into their laws, regulations or tourism development plans. The Code had been translated into 33 countries. It was generally disseminated among various tourism stakeholders, and was applied in the promotion of responsible travel advisories. The World Committee planned to establish a short- and medium-term strategy to improve the promotion of the Code worldwide and strengthen its implementation. It endorsed the idea of regional tourism awards as a way of encouraging the implementation of the Code.

In the report's conclusions, the UNWTO Secretary-General observed that, five years after its adoption, the Global Code of Ethics had proved to be a valuable tool in developing environmentally and socially sound and sustainable tourism. UNWTO would report to the United Nations within five years on the progress achieved in implementing the Code by both the public and private tourism sectors.

GENERAL ASSEMBLY ACTION

On 22 December [meeting 68], the General Assembly, on the recommendation of the Second Committee [A/60/488], adopted **resolution 60/190** without vote [agenda item 52].

Global Code of Ethics for Tourism

The General Assembly,

Recalling its resolution 56/212 of 21 December 2001 and its decision 58/573 of 13 September 2004,

Recalling also its resolution 58/232 of 23 December 2003, by which it approved the Agreement between the United Nations and the World Tourism Organization,

Recalling further the Manila Declaration on World Tourism of 10 October 1980, the Rio Declaration on Environment and Development and Agenda 21 of 14 June 1992, the Amman Declaration on Peace through Tourism of 11 November 2000, the Johannesburg Declaration on Sustainable Development and the Plan of Implementation of the World Summit on Sustainable Development, the Declaration of Barbados and the Programme of Action for the Sustainable Development of Small Island Developing States, the Mauritius Declaration and the Mauritius Strategy for the Further Implementation of the Programme of Action for the Sustainable Development of Small Island Developing States, and the Brussels Declaration and the Programme of Action for the Least Developed Countries for the Decade 2001-2010,

Recognizing the important dimension and role of tourism as a positive instrument towards the eradication of poverty and the improvement of the quality of life for all people, its potential to make a contribution to economic and social development, especially of the developing countries, and its emergence as a vital force for the promotion of international understanding, peace and prosperity,

1. *Takes note* of the note by the Secretary-General transmitting the report by the World Tourism Organization on the implementation of the Global Code of Ethics for Tourism;

2. *Notes with interest* the establishment of the World Committee on Tourism Ethics as adopted by the General Assembly of the World Tourism Organization in 2001;

3. *Notes* the approval by the World Committee on Tourism Ethics of the Procedures for Consultation and Conciliation for the Settlement of Disputes concerning the Application of the Global Code of Ethics for Tourism;

4. *Reiterates* the invitation to Member States and other stakeholders to consider introducing, as appropriate, the contents of the Global Code of Ethics for Tourism in their relevant laws, regulations and professional practices, and, in this regard, recognizes with appreciation those Member States that have already done so;

5. *Recognizes* the need to promote sustainable tourism development, including non-consumptive tourism and ecotourism, taking into account the spirit of the International Year of Ecotourism, 2002, the United Nations Year for Cultural Heritage, 2002, the World Ecotourism Summit, 2002, and the Quebec Declaration on Ecotourism, and the Global Code of Ethics for Tourism as adopted by the World Tourism Organization in 1999, in order to increase the benefits from tourism resources for the population in host communities while maintaining the cultural and environmental integrity of the host communities and enhancing the protection of ecologically sensitive areas and natural heritages and to promote sustainable tourism development and capacity-building in order to contribute to the strengthening of rural and local communities;

6. *Invites* Member States and other stakeholders to give support to the activities undertaken by the World Tourism Organization in favour of sustainable tourism in developing countries for the eradication of poverty;

7. *Emphasizes* the need for the promotion of responsible and sustainable tourism for the protection and safeguarding of natural and cultural heritage that could be beneficial to all sectors of society and the natural environment towards the achievement of sustainable development;

8. *Requests* the Secretary-General to report to the General Assembly at its sixty-fifth session on the developments related to the implementation of the present resolution on the basis of the reports of the World Tourism Organization.

Eradication of poverty

UN Decade for Eradication of Poverty

In response to General Assembly resolution 59/247 [YUN 2004, p. 834] on implementation of the first United Nations Decade for the Eradication of Poverty (1997-2006) [A/60/314], the Secretary-General submitted a 30 August report on the centrality of employment to poverty eradication.

The report examined the relationship between growth and poverty reduction equation and discussed the key elements of employment strategy, including generating adequate levels of productive employment and work, enhancing productivity, choice of technique, sectoral shift and labour market interventions. It also looked at the employment dimensions of security and human rights, and their linkages to growth and poverty reduction.

The report concluded that the achievement of the MDG of eradicating poverty required more than just high economic growth. There should be a focus on creating better and more productive jobs by investing in labour-intensive industries, especially agriculture, encouraging a shift in the structure of employment to higher productivity occupations and sectors, and upgrading job quality in the informal economy. Employment also played a major role in maintaining peace and security. Respect for human rights and dignity was an essential element for poverty eradication and the foundation for providing access to and opportunities for productive employment. Of critical importance were promoting education, skill development, training and health care, and empowering workers through improving their protection, rights and voice, while expanding opportunities for quality jobs.

Recommendations for the Assembly's consideration included: ensuring that the creation of productive employment was a central objective of national and international macroeconomic policies, and that employment policies were fully integrated into national poverty reduction strategies; enhancing coherence within the multilateral system in promoting productive and decent work; promoting decent employment opportunities, rights at work, social protection and social dialogue, as well as raising the quality of work, skills and capabilities. Recommendations also included: increasing the demand for labour, raising the productivity and incomes of people living in poverty and improving their access to health care, education, skills development and training; integrating socially excluded groups into the labour market and overcoming discrimination and barriers to employment against women and girls.

GENERAL ASSEMBLY ACTION

On 22 December [meeting 68], the General Assembly, on the recommendation of the Second Committee [A/60/492/Add.1], adopted **resolution 60/209** without vote [agenda item 56 (a)].

Implementation of the first United Nations Decade for the Eradication of Poverty (1997-2006)

The General Assembly,

Recalling its resolutions 47/196 of 22 December 1992, 48/183 of 21 December 1993, 50/107 of 20 December 1995, 56/207 of 21 December 2001, 57/265 and 57/266 of 20 December 2002, 58/222 of 23 December 2003 and 59/247 of 22 December 2004,

Recalling also the United Nations Millennium Declaration, adopted by Heads of State and Government on the occasion of the Millennium Summit, and their commitment to eradicate extreme poverty and to halve, by 2015, the proportion of the world's people whose income is less than one dollar a day and the proportion of people who suffer from hunger,

Recalling further the 2005 World Summit Outcome,

Underlining the priority and urgency given by the Heads of State and Government to the eradication of poverty, as expressed in the outcomes of the major United Nations conferences and summits in economic and social fields,

Bearing in mind the outcomes of the World Summit for Social Development and the twenty-fourth special session of the General Assembly,

Expressing its deep concern that the number of people living in extreme poverty in many countries continues to increase, with women and children constituting the majority and the most affected groups, in particular in the least developed countries and in sub-Saharan Africa,

Encouraged by reductions in poverty in some countries in the recent past and determined to reinforce and extend this trend to benefit people worldwide,

Acknowledging the contribution of full and productive employment to poverty eradication and to the achievement of the internationally agreed development goals, including the Millennium Development Goals,

Recognizing that microcredit and microfinance programmes can generate productive self-employment and assist people in eradicating poverty and reducing their social and economic vulnerability,

Expressing deep concern that the number of women and girls living in poverty has increased disproportionately to the number of men, particularly in developing countries, and that the majority live in rural areas where their livelihoods are dependent on subsistence agriculture,

Aware that, to eradicate poverty and achieve sustainable development, women and men must participate fully and equally in the formulation of macroeconomic and social policies and strategies for the eradication of poverty,

Recognizing that the empowerment of women is a critical factor in the eradication of poverty and that the implementation of special measures aimed at empowering women can help to achieve this,

Recognizing also that improving women's economic status also improves the economic status of their families and their communities and thereby creates a multiplier effect for economic growth,

Recognizing further that mobilizing financial resources for development at the national and international levels and the effective use of those resources are central to a global partnership for development in support of the achievement of the internationally agreed development goals, including the Millennium Development Goals,

Recognizing the ongoing international efforts, contributions and discussions, such as the Action against Hunger and Poverty initiative, aimed at identifying and developing possible innovative and additional sources of financing for development from all sources, public and private, domestic and external, to increase and supplement traditional sources of financing within the context of the follow-up to the International Conference on Financing for Development, and recognizing that some of the sources and their use fall within the realm of sovereign action,

Noting with interest the International Conference on Poverty Alleviation and Development, to be hosted by the Government of Mauritius in 2006,

Reiterating the need to strengthen the leadership role of the United Nations in promoting development,

1. *Takes note* of the report of the Secretary-General;

2. *Reiterates* that eradicating poverty is the greatest global challenge facing the world today and an indispensable requirement for sustainable development, in particular for developing countries;

3. *Underlines* the fact that each country has the primary responsibility for its own sustainable development and poverty eradication, that the role of national policies and development strategies cannot be overemphasized, and that concerted and concrete measures are required at all levels to enable developing countries to eradicate poverty and achieve sustainable development;

4. *Acknowledges* that sustained economic growth, supported by rising productivity and a favourable environment, including for private investment and entrepreneurship, is necessary to eradicate poverty, achieve the internationally agreed development goals, including the Millennium Development Goals, and realize a rise in living standards;

5. *Reaffirms* the importance of the contributions and assistance made by developing countries to the other developing countries in the context of South-South cooperation in order to achieve development and eradicate poverty;

6. *Recognizes* that, for developing countries to reach the targets set in the context of national development strategies for the achievement of the internationally agreed development goals, including the Millennium Development Goals, in particular the goal on the eradication of poverty, and for such poverty eradication strategies to be effective, it is imperative that developing countries be integrated into the world economy and share equitably in the benefits of globalization;

7. *Reaffirms* that, within the context of overall action for the eradication of poverty, special attention should be given to the multidimensional nature of poverty and the national and international conditions and policies that are conducive to its eradication, fostering, inter alia, the social and economic integration of people living in poverty and the promotion and protection of all human rights and fundamental freedoms for all, including the right to development;

Global response for the eradication of poverty

8. *Stresses* the importance of the follow-up to the outcomes of the International Conference on Financing for Development and the World Summit on Sus-

tainable Development, and calls for the full and effective implementation of the Monterrey Consensus of the International Conference on Financing for Development and the Plan of Implementation of the World Summit on Sustainable Development ("Johannesburg Plan of Implementation"), as well as the outcomes of other major United Nations conferences and summits in the economic and social fields;

9. *Reaffirms* that good governance at the international level is fundamental for achieving poverty eradication and sustainable development; also reaffirms that, in order to ensure a dynamic and enabling international economic environment, it is important to promote global economic governance through addressing the international finance, trade, technology and investment patterns that have an impact on the development prospects of developing countries; to that end, reiterates that the international community should take all necessary and appropriate measures, including ensuring support for structural and macroeconomic reform and a comprehensive solution to the external debt problem and increasing market access for developing countries; and also reaffirms that a universal, rule-based, open, non-discriminatory and equitable multilateral trading system, as well as meaningful trade liberalization, can substantially stimulate development worldwide, benefiting countries at all stages of development;

10. *Also reaffirms* the commitment to broaden and strengthen the participation of developing countries and countries with economies in transition in international economic decision-making and norm-setting, and to that end stresses the importance of continuing efforts to reform the international financial architecture, noting that enhancing the voice and participation of developing countries and countries with economies in transition in the Bretton Woods institutions remains a continuous concern;

11. *Further reaffirms* that good governance at the national level is essential for poverty eradication and sustainable development; that sound economic policies, solid democratic institutions responsive to the needs of the people and improved infrastructure are the basis for sustained economic growth, poverty eradication and employment creation; and that freedom, peace and security, domestic stability, respect for human rights, including the right to development, and the rule of law, gender equality, market-oriented policies and an overall commitment to just and democratic societies are also essential and mutually reinforcing;

12. *Welcomes* the outcomes of the eleventh session of the United Nations Conference on Trade and Development, held in São Paulo, Brazil, from 13 to 18 June 2004, and the adoption of The Spirit of São Paulo, and the São Paulo Consensus;

13. *Reaffirms* the need for the United Nations to play a fundamental role in the promotion of international cooperation for development and the coherence, coordination and implementation of development goals and actions agreed upon by the international community, and also reaffirms the need to strengthen coordination within the United Nations system in close cooperation with all other multilateral financial, trade and development institutions in order to support sustained economic growth, poverty eradication and sustainable development;

14. *Stresses* that together with coherent and consistent domestic policies, international cooperation is essential in supplementing and supporting the efforts of developing countries to utilize their domestic resources for development and poverty eradication and in ensuring that they will be able to achieve the internationally agreed development goals, including the Millennium Development Goals;

15. *Recalls* that Member States redirected and recommitted themselves to fulfilling the development dimensions of the Doha Development Agenda, which places the needs and interests of developing countries at the heart of the Doha work programme, and recognizes the major role that trade plays as an engine of growth and development and in eradicating poverty;

16. *Recognizes* that fighting corruption at all levels is a priority and that corruption is a serious barrier to effective resource mobilization and allocation and diverts resources from activities that are vital for poverty eradication, the fight against hunger and economic and sustainable development;

17. *Reaffirms* the Monterrey Consensus, and recognizes that mobilizing financial resources for development and the effective use of those resources in developing countries and countries with economies in transition are central to a global partnership for development in support of the achievement of the internationally agreed development goals, including the Millennium Development Goals, and in this regard:

(*a*) Welcomes the increased resources that will become available as a result of the establishment of timetables by many developed countries to achieve the target of 0.7 per cent of gross national product for official development assistance by 2015 and to reach at least 0.5 per cent of gross national product for official development assistance by 2010 as well as, pursuant to the Brussels Programme of Action for the Least Developed Countries for the Decade 2001-2010, 0.15 per cent to 0.20 per cent for the least developed countries no later than 2010, and urges those developed countries that have not yet done so to make concrete efforts in this regard in accordance with their commitments;

(*b*) Recognizes the importance of official development assistance as an important source of financing development for many developing countries, and stresses the need to translate increases in official development assistance into real increases in resources for national development strategies, to achieve their national development priorities as well as the internationally agreed development goals and objectives including the Millennium Development Goals, taking into account the need for resource predictability including budget support mechanisms where appropriate; also, welcomes recent efforts and initiatives to enhance the quality of aid and increase its impact, including the Paris Declaration on Aid Effectiveness, and resolves to take concrete, effective and timely action in implementing all agreed commitments on aid effectiveness, with clear monitoring and deadlines, including through further aligning assistance with countries' strategies, building institutional capacities, reducing transaction costs and eliminating bureaucratic procedures, making progress on untying aid, enhancing the absorptive capacity and financial management of recipient countries and strengthening the focus of development results; also encourages the broadest possible participation of developing countries in future work on aid effectiveness;

(c) Recognizes the importance of developing innovative sources of financing for development, provided that such sources do not unduly burden developing countries, notes that some countries will launch the International Financial Facility, have launched its immunization pilot, and that some countries, utilizing their national authorities, will implement in the near future a contribution on airline tickets as a "solidarity contribution" to enable financing for development projects, and notes that other countries are considering whether and to what extent they will participate in those initiatives;

(d) Emphasizes the importance of microcredit and microfinance in the eradication of poverty and highlights that the observance of the International Year of Microcredit, 2005 has provided a significant opportunity to raise awareness, to share best practices and to further enhance financial sectors that support sustainable pro-poor financial services in all countries, in this regard urges member countries to put best practices into action, and invites the international community, including the United Nations system, to build on the momentum created by the Year;

(e) Acknowledges the vital role the private sector can play in generating new investments, employment and financing for development;

18. *Resolves* to continue to support the development efforts of middle-income developing countries by working, in competent multilateral and international forums and also through bilateral arrangements, on measures to help them meet, inter alia, their financial, technical and technological requirements;

19. *Also resolves* to address the development needs of low-income developing countries by working in competent multilateral and international forums, to help them meet, inter alia, their financial, technical and technological requirements;

20. *Recognizes* that an enabling domestic environment is vital for mobilizing domestic resources, increasing productivity, reducing capital flight, encouraging the private sector and attracting and making effective use of international investment and assistance, and that efforts to create such an environment should be supported by the international community;

21. *Emphasizes* that creditors and debtors must share responsibility for preventing unsustainable debt situations, and stresses that debt relief can play a key role in liberating resources that should be directed towards activities consistent with poverty eradication, sustained economic growth and sustainable development and the achievement of the internationally agreed development goals, including the Millennium Development Goals, and, in this regard, urges countries to direct those resources freed through debt relief, in particular through debt cancellation and reduction, towards these objectives;

22. *Calls upon* the developed countries, by means of intensified and effective cooperation with developing countries, to promote capacity-building and facilitate access to and transfer of technologies and corresponding knowledge, in particular to developing countries, on favourable terms, including concessional and preferential terms, as mutually agreed, taking into account

the need to protect intellectual property rights, as well as the special needs of developing countries;

23. *Recognizes* the crucial role that microcredit and microfinance could play in the eradication of poverty, the promotion of gender equality, the empowerment of vulnerable groups and the development of rural communities, encourages Governments to undertake policies to facilitate the expansion of microcredit and microfinance institutions in order to service the large unmet demand among poor people for financial services, including the identification and development of mechanisms to promote sustainable access to financial services, the removal of institutional and regulatory obstacles and the provision of incentives to microfinance institutions that meet established standards for delivering such financial services to the poor;

24. *Also recognizes* the potential of information and communication technologies to serve as a powerful tool for development and poverty eradication and to help the international community to maximize the benefits of globalization, and, in this regard, welcomes the Tunis Commitment and the Tunis Agenda for the Information Society adopted by the World Summit on the Information Society at its Tunis phase, and recalls the Geneva Declaration of Principles and the Geneva Plan of Action adopted by the Summit at its Geneva phase;

Policies for the eradication of poverty

25. *Reaffirms* that the eradication of poverty should be addressed in a multisectoral and integrated way, as set out in the Johannesburg Plan of Implementation, taking into account the importance of the need for the empowerment of women and sectoral strategies in such areas as education, the development of human resources, health, human settlements, rural, local and community development, productive employment, population, environment and natural resources, water and sanitation, agriculture, food security, energy and migration and the specific needs of disadvantaged and vulnerable groups in such a way as to increase opportunities and choices for people living in poverty and to enable them to build and to strengthen their assets so as to achieve development, security and stability, and, in that regard, encourages countries to develop their national poverty reduction policies in accordance with their national priorities, including, where appropriate, through poverty reduction strategy papers;

26. *Underlines*, in this context, the importance of further integration of the internationally agreed development goals, including the Millennium Development Goals, in the national development strategies and plans, including the poverty reduction strategy papers where they exist, and calls upon the international community to continue to support developing countries in the implementation of those development strategies and plans;

27. *Strongly supports* fair globalization, and resolves to make the goals of full and productive employment and decent work for all, including for women and young people, a central objective of the relevant national and international policies, as well as national development strategies, including poverty reduction strategies, as part of efforts to achieve the Millennium Development Goals, resolves that these measures should also encompass the elimination of the worst

forms of child labour, as defined in International Labour Organization Convention No. 182, and forced labour; and also resolves to ensure full respect for the fundamental principles and rights at work;

28. *Recognizes* the importance of disseminating best practices for the reduction of poverty in its various dimensions, taking into account the need to adapt those best practices to suit the social, economic, cultural and historical conditions of each country;

29. *Reaffirms* that all Governments and the United Nations system should promote an active and visible policy of mainstreaming a gender perspective in all policies and programmes aimed at the eradication of poverty, at both the national and international levels, and encourages the use of gender analysis as a tool for the integration of a gender dimension into planning the implementation of policies, strategies and programmes for the eradication of poverty;

30. *Also reaffirms* that all Governments and the United Nations system should emphasize the importance and encourage the mainstreaming of poverty eradication in all policies, at both the national and international levels;

31. *Further reaffirms* that poverty eradication, changing unsustainable patterns of production and consumption and protecting and managing the natural resource base of economic and social development are overarching objectives of, and essential requirements for, sustainable development;

32. *Emphasizes* the critical role of both formal and non-formal education, in particular basic education and training, especially for girls, in empowering those living in poverty, reaffirms in that context the Dakar Framework for Action adopted at the World Education Forum, and recognizes the importance of the United Nations Educational, Scientific and Cultural Organization strategy for the eradication of poverty, especially extreme poverty, in supporting the Education for All programmes as a tool with which to achieve the millennium development goal on universal primary education by 2015;

33. *Recognizes* the devastating effect of HIV/AIDS, malaria, tuberculosis and other infectious and contagious diseases on human development, economic growth, food security and poverty reduction efforts in all regions, in particular sub-Saharan Africa, and urges Governments and the international community to give urgent priority to combating those diseases;

34. *Also recognizes* that armed conflict results in the loss of human lives and the destruction of economic resources, and that countries emerging from conflict are faced with damaged physical and social infrastructure, scarce employment opportunities, reduced foreign investment and increased capital flight, and, in this regard, stresses that strategies, programmes and international assistance for reconstruction and rehabilitation should, inter alia, create employment and eradicate poverty;

35. *Emphasizes* the link between poverty eradication and improving access to safe drinking water, and stresses in that regard the objective to halve, by 2015, the proportion of people who are unable to reach or to afford safe drinking water and the proportion of people who do not have access to basic sanitation, as reaffirmed in the Johannesburg Plan of Implementation;

36. *Recognizes* that the lack of adequate housing remains a pressing challenge in the fight to eradicate extreme poverty, particularly in the urban areas in developing countries, expresses its concern at the rapid growth in the number of slum-dwellers in the urban areas of developing countries, particularly in Africa, stresses that, unless urgent and effective measures and actions are taken at the national and international levels, the number of slum-dwellers, who constitute one third of the world's urban population, will continue to increase, and emphasizes the need for increased efforts, with a view to significantly improving the lives of at least 100 million slum-dwellers by 2020;

37. *Also recognizes* that the eradication of rural poverty and hunger is crucial for the achievement of the internationally agreed development goals, including the Millennium Development Goals, and that rural development should be an integral part of national and international development policies;

38. *Further recognizes* that access to microcredit and microfinance can contribute to the achievement of the internationally agreed development goals, including the Millennium Development Goals, in particular the goals relating to poverty eradication, gender equality and the empowerment of women;

39. *Emphasizes* the important contribution the observance of the International Year of Microcredit, 2005, has made in raising awareness of the importance of microcredit and microfinance in the eradication of poverty, in sharing good practices and in enhancing financial sectors that support sustainable financial services for the poor, and calls upon Member States, the United Nations system and other international organizations to consolidate and further build on the momentum created by the Year with a view to providing microcredit and microfinance services to the poor;

40. *Recognizes* the important contribution that the observance of the International Year of Rice, 2004, has made in drawing world attention to the role that rice can play in providing food security and eradicating poverty in the attainment of the internationally agreed development goals, including the Millennium Development Goals;

Specific initiatives in the fight against poverty

41. *Also recognizes* the important potential contribution of the World Solidarity Fund to the achievement of the Millennium Development Goals, in particular the objective to halve, by 2015, the proportion of people living on less than one dollar a day and the proportion of people who suffer from hunger;

42. *Resolves* to operationalize the World Solidarity Fund established by the General Assembly, and invites Member States, international organizations, the private sector, relevant institutions, foundations and individuals in a position to do so to make voluntary contributions to the Fund;

43. *Recalls* that, in the Millennium Declaration, the Heads of State and Government, inter alia, identified solidarity as one of the fundamental and universal values that should underlie relations between peoples in the twenty-first century, and in that regard decides to proclaim 20 December of each year International Human Solidarity Day;

44. *Invites* Governments and relevant stakeholders to utilize entrepreneurship, taking fully into account

national interests, priorities and development strategies, to contribute to poverty eradication;

45. *Recognizes* that natural disasters remain a major impediment to sustainable development and poverty eradication, and, in this regard, invites Member States, the United Nations system, including international financial institutions, regional bodies and international organizations, as well as relevant civil society organizations, to support, implement and follow up the Hyogo Framework for Action 2005-2015: Building the Resilience of Nations and Communities to Disasters, adopted by the World Conference on Disaster Reduction, held in Kobe, Hyogo, Japan, from 18 to 22 January 2005;

Africa, least developed countries, landlocked developing countries and small island developing States

46. *Stresses*, as recognized in the Millennium Declaration and reiterated in the 2005 World Summit Outcome, the importance of meeting the special needs of Africa, where poverty remains a major challenge and where most countries have not benefited fully from the opportunities of globalization, which has further exacerbated the continent's marginalization;

47. *Reaffirms its support* for the New Partnership for Africa's Development, encourages further efforts in the implementation of the commitments contained therein in the political, economic and social fields, and calls upon Member States and the international community, and invites the United Nations system, to continue to support the implementation of the Partnership, the primary objective of which is to eradicate poverty and promote sustainable development on the basis of African ownership and leadership and enhanced partnerships with the international community, in accordance with the principles, objectives and priorities of the Partnership;

48. *Notes* the continuing role of the International Labour Organization in assisting African countries in implementing the Plan of Action for Promotion of Employment and Poverty Alleviation in Africa adopted at the extraordinary summit of the African Union on employment and poverty alleviation, held in Ouagadougou from 3 to 9 September 2004;

49. *Resolves* to promote a comprehensive and durable solution to the external debt problems of African countries, including through the cancellation of 100 per cent of multilateral debt consistent with the recent Group of Eight proposal for the heavily indebted poor countries, and, on a case-by-case basis, where appropriate, significant debt relief, including, inter alia, cancellation or restructuring for heavily indebted African countries not part of the Heavily Indebted Poor Countries Initiative that have unsustainable debt burdens;

50. *Calls upon* the Governments of the least developed countries and their development partners to implement fully the commitments contained in the Brussels Declaration and the Programme of Action for the Least Developed Countries for the Decade 2001-2010, adopted at the Third United Nations Conference on the Least Developed Countries, held in Brussels from 14 to 20 May 2001;

51. *Recognizes* the special needs and vulnerabilities of small island developing States, reaffirms the commitment to take urgent and concrete action to address those needs and vulnerabilities through the full and effective implementation of the Mauritius Strategy for the Further Implementation of the Programme of Action for the Sustainable Development of Small Island Developing States, the Programme of Action for the Sustainable Development of Small Island Developing States, and the outcome of the twenty-second special session of the General Assembly, and undertakes to promote greater international cooperation and partnership for the implementation of the Mauritius Strategy through, inter alia, the mobilization of domestic and international resources, the promotion of international trade as an engine for development and increased international financial and technical cooperation;

52. *Also recognizes* the special needs of and challenges faced by landlocked developing countries, and therefore reaffirms the commitment to urgently address those needs and challenges through the full, timely and effective implementation of the Almaty Programme of Action: Addressing the Special Needs of Landlocked Developing Countries within a New Global Framework for Transit Transport Cooperation for Landlocked and Transit Developing Countries and the São Paulo Consensus, encourages the work undertaken by the regional commissions and United Nations organizations towards establishing a time-cost methodology for indicators to measure the progress made in the implementation of the Almaty Programme of Action, and recognizes the special difficulties and concerns of landlocked developing countries in their efforts to integrate their economies into the multilateral trading system and that, in this regard, priority should be given to the full and timely implementation of the Almaty Declaration and Almaty Programme of Action;

The United Nations and the fight against poverty

53. *Calls* for the full implementation of General Assembly resolution 57/270 B of 23 June 2003 on the integrated and coordinated implementation of and follow-up to the outcomes of the major United Nations conferences and summits in the economic and social fields, which provides a comprehensive basis for the follow-up to the outcomes of those conferences and summits and contributes to the achievement of the internationally agreed development goals, including the Millennium Development Goals, in particular the eradication of poverty and hunger;

54. *Reaffirms* the role of United Nations funds and programmes, in particular the United Nations Development Programme and its associated funds, in assisting the national efforts of developing countries, inter alia, in the eradication of poverty, and the need for their funding in accordance with the relevant resolutions of the United Nations;

55. *Welcomes* the observance of the International Day for the Eradication of Poverty, established by the General Assembly in its resolution 47/196 of 22 December 1992 in order to raise public awareness to promote the eradication of poverty and extreme poverty in all countries, and in this regard recognizes the useful role the observance of the Day continues to play in raising public awareness and mobilizing all stakeholders in the fight against poverty, and requests the Secretary-General to undertake a review of the observ-

ance of the Day in order to identify lessons learned and ways to promote the mobilization of all stakeholders in the fight against poverty;

56. *Decides* to include in the provisional agenda of its sixty-first session the item entitled "Implementation of the first United Nations Decade for the Eradication of Poverty (1997-2006)".

Also on 22 December, the Assembly took note of the report of the Second Committee [A/60/492] on its discussion of the eradication of poverty and other development issues (**decision 60/545**).

Evaluation

By an April note [E/AC.51/2005/2], the Secretary-General transmitted to the Committee for Programme and Coordination (CPC) the report of the Office of Internal Oversight Services (OIOS) on the evaluation of linkages between headquarters and field activities: a review of best practices for poverty eradication in the framework of the United Nations Millennium Declaration.

OIOS concluded that those linkages were crucial to a comprehensive, multisectoral and coordinated approach to poverty eradication. Within the headquarters' field transmission line, a highly complex system of linkages connected and coordinated the poverty eradication activities of headquarters, regional and field offices, with linkages flowing in multiple directions and often dependent on personal connections and ad hoc agreements. That complexity was not conducive to the consistent and systematic transmission of knowledge, guidance and experience.

OIOS made recommendations to the Secretary-General, CEB, the United Nations Development Group, the UN Department of Economic and Social Affairs and the regional commissions. Those recommendations included enhancing collaboration among inter-agency coordinating bodies, introducing a more strategic approach to system-wide knowledge management networks, increasing the exchange of information between country teams and non-resident agencies and regional commissions, and strengthening management practices and the resident coordinator system.

At its forty-fifth session (6 June–1 July) [A/60/16], CPC recommended approval of those recommendations. It emphasized that the Secretary-General should enhance inter-agency coordination to fight hunger; UN programmes should be harmonized with the needs and priorities of national Governments; and the regional commissions and the country offices should establish mechanisms for the regular exchange of information and knowledge-sharing and strengthen their websites as platforms for the exchange of best practices.

International Year of Microcredit, 2005

The General Assembly, by resolution 53/197 [YUN 1998, p. 785], proclaimed 2005 the International Year of Microcredit to give impetus to microcredit programmes throughout the world. The goals of the year were to assess and promote the contributions of microcredit and microfinance towards the achievement of the MDGs; increase public awareness and understanding of them; promote inclusive financial systems; support sustainable access; and encourage innovation and partnership. The main message of the Year was building inclusive financial sectors to help poor people around the world gain access to affordable financial services.

Activities in observance of the Year were undertaken at the national and international levels. Among them were the "Blue Book" and data project, which had an important impact on further promoting the commitment to develop inclusive financial sectors. In addition, the Global Microentrepreneurship Award served to celebrate and reward microentrepreneurs around the world and contributed to promoting entrepreneurial culture, establishing strong partnerships and increasing the visibility of microentrepreneurs. An important outcome of the Year was the establishment of the United Nations Advisers Group on Inclusive Financial Sectors, which would provide advice and guidance to the United Nations and seek ways to make a broad variety of financial services accessible for the poor and small enterprises across the globe.

The Assembly had decided to devote a plenary meeting at its sixty-first (2006) session to consideration of the outcome and follow-up to the Year.

Rural development

On 27 July [meeting 40], the Economic and Social Council adopted **resolution 2005/45** [draft: E/2005/L.48] without vote [agenda item 7].

Promoting an integrated approach to rural development in developing countries for poverty eradication and sustainable development

The Economic and Social Council,

Reaffirming the ministerial declaration of the high-level segment of its substantive session of 2003,

Recalling its resolution 2004/48 of 23 July 2004,

Noting the offer of the Government of Brazil to host the International Conference on Agrarian Reform and Rural Development in 2006,

Reiterating that the eradication of rural poverty and hunger is crucial for the achievement of internationally agreed development goals, including those contained in the United Nations Millennium Declaration, and that rural development should be pursued through an integrated approach that encompasses economic, social and environmental dimensions, takes into account a gender perspective and consists of mutually reinforcing policies and programmes, which should be balanced, targeted, situation-specific, locally owned, should include local synergies and initiatives and should be responsive to the needs of rural populations,

Having considered progress, or the lack thereof, in the implementation of the ministerial declaration of the high-level segment of its substantive session of 2003 at its substantive session of 2005,

Decides to consider, at its regular organizational session in February 2006, the proposal to include a discussion on promoting an integrated approach to rural development in developing countries for poverty eradication and sustainable development at a future substantive session of the Council.

United Nations Alliance

On 26 July [meeting 39], the Economic and Social Council adopted **resolution 2005/42** [draft: E/2005/L.35, as orally amended] without vote [agenda item 13 *(a)*].

United Nations Public-Private Alliance for Rural Development

The Economic and Social Council,

Recalling the ministerial declaration adopted on 2 July 2003 at the high-level segment of the Economic and Social Council, which underlined the importance of alliances and partnerships among actors in different sectors for the promotion of integrated rural development,

Recalling also its resolution 2004/49 of 23 July 2004 on the United Nations Public-Private Alliance for Rural Development,

Underlining the importance of the contribution of the private sector, non-governmental organizations and civil society in general to the implementation of the outcomes of United Nations conferences in the economic, social and related fields,

Recalling the central role and responsibility of Governments in national and international policymaking,

Bearing in mind General Assembly resolution 58/129 of 19 December 2003, entitled "Towards global partnerships", in which the Assembly, inter alia, identified the principles and objectives of such partnerships and welcomed the establishment of a multitude of partnerships at the field level, entered into by various United Nations organizations, Member States and other stakeholders, such as the United Nations Public-Private Alliance for Rural Development (the United Nations Alliance),

1. *Encourages* the initiative of the Government of the Dominican Republic to serve as the second pilot country for the United Nations Public-Private Alliance for Rural Development (the United Nations Alliance);

2. *Invites* all Member States, the funds, programmes and agencies of the United Nations system, the Bretton Woods institutions, civil society, the private sector and other relevant stakeholders to support the programmes and activities of the United Nations Alliance in its mission to promote sustainable rural development, consistent with General Assembly resolution 58/129 and other relevant resolutions and decisions of the Assembly and the Economic and Social Council;

3. *Stresses* that activities of the funds, programmes and specialized agencies of the United Nations system at the country level in support of the United Nations Alliance should take into account the implementation of the United Nations Development Assistance Framework;

4. *Requests* the Secretary-General to report to the Economic and Social Council at its substantive session of 2007 on the work of the United Nations Alliance.

Science and technology for development

Commission on Science and Technology for Development

The Commission on Science and Technology for Development held its eighth session in Geneva from 23 to 27 May [E/2005/31]. It considered as its main substantive theme "Science and technology promotion, advice and application for the achievement of the internationally agreed development goals contained in the United Nations Millennium Declaration" (see below). The Commission had before it reports of the Secretary-General on science and technology promotion, advice and application for the achievement of the MDGs [E/CN.16/2005/2 & Corr.1,2] (see below) and on a review of the Commission's work methods [E/CN.16/2005/4 & Corr.1]. It also discussed a February note by the Secretariat on implementation of and progress made on decisions taken at the Commission's seventh (2004) session [E/CN.16/2005/3 & Corr.1]. The Commission heard national country reports on experiences in science and technology promotion, advice and application of the MDGs, as well as presentations by international organizations on their contribution to its work.

The Commission recommended a draft resolution and three draft decisions for adoption by the Economic and Social Council. It brought to the Council's attention a decision by which it took note of the reports that were before its eighth session [E/2005/31 (dec. 8/101)]. The Commission chose as the substantive theme for its 2005-2006 intersessional period "Bridging the technology gap between and within nations".

By **decision 2005/308** of 27 July, the Council decided that the Commission would adopt a biennial programme of work beginning at its ninth session, focusing, in the first year, on policy analyses and, in the second, on operational aspects and implementation. It should also strengthen the connection between its review of implementation and its policy recommendations. The Commission should encourage the active participation of civil society and the private sector in its activities, and strengthen collaboration with the other functional commissions.

The Council also took note of the Commission's report on its eighth (2005) session and approved the provisional agenda and documentation for the ninth (2006) session (**decision 2005/309**).

On 27 July [meeting 40], the Economic and Social Council, on the recommendation of the Commission [E/2005/31], adopted **resolution 2005/52** without vote [agenda item 13 (b)].

Science and technology for development

The Economic and Social Council,

Welcoming the work of the Commission on Science and Technology for Development on its theme "Science and technology promotion, advice and application for the achievement of the internationally agreed development goals contained in the United Nations Millennium Declaration",

Taking note of initiatives that call for substantial support for institutes of higher education and centres of excellence in developing countries, particularly in Africa, such as that of the Commission for Africa,

Expressing its appreciation for the support provided to the Commission for Africa by donors including the generous financial contributions of the Governments of Italy and Pakistan to the network of centres of excellence to be established, as well as the financial support provided by Austria to expand the Internet connectivity benchmarking tool and the financial and technical support provided by the Centre for Information Technology of the state of Geneva to assist the least developed countries for building capacity in information and communication technologies,

Taking note of General Assembly resolution 58/200 of 23 December 2003, in which the relevant bodies of the United Nations system engaged in biotechnology were urged to work cooperatively so as to ensure that countries received sound scientific information and practical advice to enable them to take advantage of those technologies, as appropriate, to promote economic growth and development,

1. *Takes note* of the findings contained in the report of the Commission on Science and Technology for Development on its eighth session and of the following recommendations of the Commission at its eighth session, and invites Governments to review these recommendations and to consider implementing them as they deem appropriate:

(a) To ensure that science, technology and innovation strategies are incorporated in international and national development strategies, especially those addressing the Millennium Development Goals and that science and technology education and research and technology are a major part of these strategies and are funded adequately;

(b) To support venture capital and encourage the establishment of business incubators and science and technology parks and, at the same time, strengthen linkages between public research and private industry

and tap into regional and international research and development networks;

(c) To create innovative compensation and reward structures to promote research and innovation directed towards solving development problems aligned with national objectives in such areas as agriculture, health, the environment, the mitigation of natural disasters and the protection of traditional knowledge;

(d) To strengthen science and technology educational systems, including through strong gender policies ensuring equal access to technological and scientific studies, appropriate funding, the introduction of entrepreneurial skills and attention to relevant intellectual property rights issues, and provide science and technology graduates with incentives and resources for starting innovative enterprises, with a view to improving gainful employment;

(e) To ensure that adequate funding is allocated for the infrastructure for science and technology development, taking into account national needs for technological upgrading and development and providing a favourable working environment for scientists and researchers to attract and keep them in their home countries;

(f) To involve representatives from industry, academia and public sectors in carrying out a comprehensive technology foresight exercise with the purpose of identifying technologies that are likely to help address pressing socio-economic issues, and establish priorities accordingly in science and technology policy and governmental programmes on research and education;

(g) To encourage the design and implementation of science and technology systems targeted at the poor and at adapting conventional science and technologies, such as those of the green revolution, as well as emerging technologies, such as information and communication technologies and biotechnology;

(h) To promote international cooperation and establish linkages aimed at sharing experiences and forging partnerships for the provision of financial assistance and expertise with a view to maximizing coverage of the socio-economic benefits of the progress achieved by modern science and technology;

2. *Decides* to make the following recommendations to the Commission, by which the Commission, within its existing mandate and within existing resources or through extrabudgetary resources, is:

(a) Encouraged to facilitate the establishment of a network of centres of excellence in developing countries with a view to allowing scientists and engineers to interact with each other and make use of state-of-the-art teaching and research facilities offered by these centres;

(b) Requested to collect and compile case studies of successful experiences and best practices in science, technology and innovation that showcase their positive impact on the internationally agreed development goals, including those contained in the United Nations Millennium Declaration, with a view to evaluating and benchmarking national science and technology policies;

(c) Requested to further develop its Internet connectivity benchmarking tool, using extrabudgetary sources;

(d) Encouraged to continue providing its expertise and analytical skills for science, technology and innovation policy reviews aimed at providing information-based policy recommendations to assist developing countries with their specific needs and circumstances;

New substantive theme and other activities

Recognizing that science and technology are essential in the implementation of the internationally agreed development goals contained in the United Nations Millennium Declaration and that many developing countries will need to enhance their capacity to harness the benefits of technology,

Welcoming the proposal to establish an informal working group for Africa as part of the Commission on Science and Technology for Development to address science and technology issues for Africa,

Endorses the decision of the Commission to select as its substantive theme for the intersessional period 2005-2006 "Bridging the technology gap between and within nations" and that specific emphasis should be placed on multi-stakeholder partnerships not only for bridging the technology gap but also to prevent it from growing wider; in this regard, the Commission will identify and address concrete aspects of this theme in cooperation with experts at its forthcoming panel meeting.

GENERAL ASSEMBLY ACTION

On 22 December [meeting 68], the General Assembly, on the recommendation of the Second Committee [A/60/490/Add.2], adopted **resolution 60/205** without vote [agenda item 54 (*b*)].

Science and technology for development

The General Assembly,

Recalling its resolutions 58/200 of 23 December 2003 and 59/220 of 22 December 2004,

Recognizing the vital role that science and technology can play in development and in facilitating efforts to eradicate poverty, achieve food security, fight diseases, improve education, protect the environment, accelerate the pace of economic diversification and transformation and improve productivity and competitiveness,

Recalling the 2005 World Summit Outcome,

Recognizing that international support can help developing countries to benefit from technological advances and can enhance their productive capacity,

Underscoring the role that traditional knowledge can play in technological development and in the sustainable management and use of natural resources,

Recognizing the catalysing role of information and communication technologies in promoting and facilitating the achievement of all development goals, and in this regard stressing the importance of the contribution of the World Summit on the Information Society process to the building of a people-centred, balanced and inclusive information society so as to enhance digital opportunities for all people in order to help bridge the digital divide,

Welcoming the Tunis Commitment and the Tunis Agenda for the Information Society of the second phase of the World Summit on the Information Society, and recalling the Geneva Declaration of Principles and the Geneva Plan of Action of the first phase of the Summit,

Acknowledging with appreciation the role played by the International Telecommunication Union in the organization of the two phases of the World Summit,

Welcoming the adoption of the Bali Strategic Plan for Technology Support and Capacity-building of the United Nations Environment Programme,

Noting with appreciation the hosting of the second World Information Technology Forum by Botswana from 31 August to 2 September 2005 in Gaborone,

Acknowledging the urgent need to bridge the digital divide and to assist developing countries to benefit from the potential of information and communication technologies,

Noting with appreciation the work of the Commission on Science and Technology for Development during its intersessional period 2004-2005 on the theme "Science and technology promotion, advice and application for the achievement of the internationally agreed development goals contained in the United Nations Millennium Declaration", in particular, the recommendation to facilitate the establishment of a network of centres of excellence in developing countries with a view to allowing scientists and engineers to interact with each other and make use of state-of-the-art teaching and research facilities offered by those centres,

Taking note of the selection by the Commission on Science and Technology for Development of the substantive theme "Bridging the technology gap between and within nations" for its work during the intersessional period 2005-2006,

Taking note also of the report of the Secretary-General on science and technology for development,

Taking note further of the United Nations Conference on Trade and Development publication entitled *The Digital Divide: ICT Development Indices 2004,*

Reaffirming the need to enhance the science and technology programmes of the relevant entities of the United Nations system,

Taking note with interest of the establishment of the interagency cooperation network on biotechnology, UN-Biotech, as described in the report of the Secretary-General,

1. *Affirms its commitment* to:

(*a*) Strengthen and enhance existing mechanisms and to support initiatives for research and development, including through voluntary partnerships between the public and private sectors, to address the special needs of developing countries in the areas of health, agriculture, conservation, sustainable use of natural resources and environmental management, energy, forestry and the impact of climate change;

(*b*) Promote and facilitate, as appropriate, access to, and development, transfer and diffusion of, technologies, including environmentally sound technologies and the corresponding know-how, to developing countries;

(*c*) Assist developing countries in their efforts to promote and develop national strategies for human resources and science and technology, which are primary drivers of national capacity-building for development;

(*d*) Promote and support greater efforts to develop renewable sources of energy, such as solar, wind and geothermal energy;

(*e*) Implement policies at the national and international levels to attract both public and private investment, domestic and foreign, that enhances knowledge, transfers technology on mutually agreed terms and raises productivity;

(f) Support the efforts of developing countries, individually and collectively, to harness new agricultural technologies in order to increase agricultural productivity through environmentally sustainable means;

2. *Requests* the Commission on Science and Technology for Development to provide a forum to address within its mandate the special needs of developing countries in areas such as agriculture, rural development, information and communication technologies and environmental management;

3. *Encourages* the United Nations Conference on Trade and Development and other relevant organizations to assist developing countries in their efforts to integrate science, technology and innovation policies in national development strategies;

4. *Recognizes* the contribution of the International Centre for Genetic Engineering and Biotechnology and its affiliated centres as well as the United Nations Industrial Development Organization, the United Nations Environment Programme, the Food and Agriculture Organization of the United Nations, the World Health Organization and the United Nations Conference on Trade and Development in the area of biotechnology, and encourages those and other relevant bodies of the United Nations system engaged in biotechnology to collaborate with a view to enhancing effectiveness in the implementation of programmes designed to assist developing countries in building capacity in all areas of biotechnology, including for industry and agriculture, as well as for risk assessment and management of biosafety;

5. *Reiterates its request* to the Secretary-General of the World Summit on the Information Society to transmit to the General Assembly at its sixtieth session the report of the Summit;

6. *Requests* the Secretary-General to submit to the General Assembly at its sixty-second session a report on the implementation of the present resolution.

Promoting the application of science and technology to meet the development goals

The Commission had before it an April report by the Secretary-General on science and technology promotion, advice and application for achieving the MDGs [E/CN.16/2005/2 & Corr.1 & 2], which focused on three sub-themes: infrastructure building as a foundation for scientific and technology development; the mutual interaction and dependency of science and technology education with research and development; and promoting gainful employment and enterprise development through the use of existing and emerging technologies. The report's main findings were that science, technology and innovations were crucial inputs to the competitiveness and growth prospects of countries and that science and engineering education was critical to developing countries in addressing development problems and helping enterprises remain competitive in the global economy. The report also found that:

research and development were under-funded in such critical areas as agriculture, health and environmental management; infrastructure development provided the foundation for technological activities and the opportunity for technological learning; and the development of enterprises was critical to economic growth and to achieving the MDGs. The report further found that the effective harnessing of existing and emerging technologies, particularly applications in information and communication technology (ICT) and biotechnologies, could increase the likelihood of achieving the MDGs. The opportunities for developing countries would be enhanced if national and international norms helped balance the interests of technology producers and users, and enhanced the transfer of relevant knowledge and technology.

The report recommended that the Commission, in collaboration with international scientific organizations, should help establish a network of centres of excellence in developing countries to allow scientists and engineers to interact and utilize the state-of-the-art research facilities offered by those centres, and compile best practices case studies of the link between science and technology and socio-economic development. Governments were called upon to consider other proposals relating to science and technology for development.

Biotechnology

In response to General Assembly resolution 58/200 [YUN 2003, p. 860], the Secretary-General submitted an August report [A/60/184], which reviewed UN system biotechnology-related activities in agriculture and food, health, biosafety and the environment, trade and development and capacity-building. It examined the status of collaboration among those UN entities, and recommended ways to strengthen system-wide coordination, especially through UN-Biotech—the interagency cooperation network on biotechnology established to complement and add value to existing programmes and projects by facilitating synergies and joint efforts to maximize system-wide coordination and coherence. The report proposed that UN-Biotech should serve as an advisory unit for developing countries on new trends in biotechnology innovations, policy and trade. It should focus on building productive capacity in all areas of biotechnology to help developing countries become leaders in formulating policies as the technology was developed. It should also explore mechanisms to help those countries build the human resources and infrastructure needed to participate in the bioeconomy.

Biotechnology had the potential to become a powerful tool in meeting the challenges posed by food insecurity, industrial underdevelopment, environmental degradation and disease. As most of the investment in modern biotechnology had occurred in developed countries, significant new investments and human resources development would be required in the developing world. The accelerated development and application of bio-technologies would also require all relevant UN agencies to coordinate their activities and help developing countries build their institutional capacities.

Information and communication technologies

During 2005, the United Nations continued to consider how the benefits of new technologies, especially ICT, could be made available to all, in keeping with recommendations contained in the ministerial declaration adopted by the Economic and Social Council at its 2000 high-level segment [YUN 2000, p. 799], the Millennium Declaration [ibid., p. 49] and the Geneva Declaration of Principles and Plan of Action [YUN 2003, p. 857], adopted at the first phase of the World Summit on the Information Society [ibid.]. Among the year's events, was the convening of the second phase of the World Summit on the Information Society in November, which adopted the Tunis Commitment and the Tunis Agenda for the Information Society (see below).

World Summit on the Information Society (second phase)

The second phase of the World Summit on the Information Society (Tunis, Tunisia, 16-18 November) [WSIS-05/TUNIS/DOC/9(Rev.1)-E] was attended by political leaders from 174 countries, including Heads of State or Government, and representatives of intergovernmental organizations, NGOs and the private sector. It adopted the Tunis Commitment and Tunis Agenda for the Information Society, recognizing that the time had come to move from principles to action on financial mechanisms for bridging the digital divide, on Internet governance, and on follow-up and implementation of the decisions (Declaration of Principles and Plan of Action) [YUN 2003, p. 857] of the first phase held in Geneva in 2003 [ibid.] and those of the second (see below) held in Tunis. In two round tables, the Summit discussed the overarching theme "From commitment to action: implementation after Tunis". It also held a high-level panel discussion on ICT for development. The Summit considered reports on a number of multi-stakeholder events and one outlining activities undertaken by Governments and stakeholders in implementing the decisions of the first phase of the Summit and assessing progress in building the Information Society [WSIS-05/TUNIS/DOC/5].

Tunis Commitment and Agenda for the Information Society

The Tunis Commitment, adopted on 18 November, reaffirmed Governments' commitment to building a people-centred, inclusive and development-oriented information society to enable people to achieve their full potential and the internationally agreed development goals and objectives, including the MDGs, and confirmed that the key principles for building an inclusive information society were those elaborated in the Geneva Declaration. It underlined the importance of removing barriers to bridging the digital divide, particularly those that hindered economic, social and cultural development especially of developing countries. It recognized that the ICT revolution could have a tremendous positive impact as an instrument of sustainable development, and underscored the effectiveness of ICTs as tools for promoting peace, security and stability, and enhancing democracy, social cohesion, good governance and the rule of law.

The Summit committed itself to evaluating and following up progress in bridging the digital divide and promoting universal access to ICTs. Calling on the international community to ensure that all countries had equitable and affordable access to those technologies, the Summit pledged to pay attention to the special needs of marginalized and vulnerable groups, countries in special situations and indigenous peoples and their cultural heritage. It recognized the existence of a gender divide, and reaffirmed the commitment to women's empowerment and their full participation in the information society; pledged to strengthen action to protect the rights of children in the context of ICTs; and reaffirmed the commitment to empower youth in ICT-based development programmes.

The Summit reaffirmed its desire to build affordable and accessible ICT networks and develop applications, and pledged to implement the Digital Solidarity Agenda, contained in the Geneva Plan of Action. The Summit was convinced that its goals could be accomplished through the involvement, cooperation and partnership of Governments and other stakeholders, and that international cooperation and solidarity at all levels were indispensable if the fruits of the information society were to benefit everyone. It reaffirmed its strong resolve to develop and implement an effective and sustainable response to the challenges and opportunities of building a truly global information society that benefited all peoples.

The Tunis Agenda for the Information Society addressed the financial mechanisms for meeting the challenges of ICT for development, Internet governance, and implementation and follow-up. The Summit recognized that bridging the digital divide would require sustainable investments for ICT infrastructure and services, capacity-building and transfer of technology over many years. It also recognized the Monterrey Consensus on Financing for Development [YUN 2002, p. 953] as the basis for creating financial mechanisms to promote ICT for development, in accordance with the Digital Solidarity Agenda. It agreed that the financing of ICT for development needed to be placed in the context of the growing importance of ICTs, not only as a medium of communication, but also as a development enabler and a tool for achieving development goals, including the MDGs. It encouraged Governments to give priority to ICTs in their national development strategies, and multilateral institutions and bilateral public donors to consider providing more financial support for regional and large-scale national ICT infrastructure projects. The Agenda listed areas where current approaches to ICT for development financing were insufficient, as well as other relevant issues that had not received adequate attention.

Acknowledging the prerequisites for access to financial mechanisms, the Summit recommended: improving mechanisms to make financial resources more predictable and sustainable; enhancing regional cooperation and creating multi-stakeholder partnerships; and providing affordable access to ICTs by reducing international Internet costs, and by encouraging the International Telecommunication Union (ITU) to continue studying the question of International Internet Connectivity as an urgent matter. It also recommended coordinating programmes among Governments and major financial players to mitigate investment risks and costs in rural and low-income market segments; helping to accelerate the development of domestic financial instruments; and improving access to facilities to finance ICT infrastructure and services. The Summit welcomed the Digital Solidarity Fund [YUN 2003, p. 858], a voluntary financial mechanism for transforming the digital divide into digital opportunities for the developing world by focusing on urgent needs at the local level.

The Summit recognized Internet governance as an essential element for a people-centred, inclusive, development-oriented and non-discriminatory information society, and committed itself to the stability and security of the Internet as a global facility and to ensuring the legitimacy of its governance, based on the full participation of all stakeholders. Regarding the management of the Internet, the Summit recognized that authority for Internet-related public policy issues was the sovereign right of States, and that all stakeholders should continue to play their respective roles in Internet-related matters. It reaffirmed the need to develop and implement a global culture of cybersecurity, underlined the importance of developing legislation to prosecute cybercrime, resolved to deal effectively with the growing problem posed by the abuse of unsolicited electronic bulk mail and underlined the importance of countering terrorism on the Internet.

The Summit reaffirmed its commitment to turn the digital divide into digital opportunity and called for strategies to increase affordable global connectivity, particularly among developing countries. It encouraged Governments and other stakeholders to promote ICT education and training in developing countries, and committed itself to working towards multilingualization of the Internet. It recognized that Internet governance included public policy, social, economic and technical issues, and that many cross-cutting issues were not adequately addressed by existing mechanisms. In view of the continuing internationalization of the Internet, the Summit agreed to implement the Geneva Principles on Internet Governance, and invited the UN Secretary-General to convene, in 2006, the Internet Governance Forum (IGF) for multi-stakeholder policy dialogue, and to examine the desirability of continuing the Forum. The Summit welcomed the offer by Greece to host the first IGF meeting.

The Summit committed itself to ensuring the sustainable implementation and follow-up of the outcomes and commitments reached during its Geneva and Tunis phases, and encouraged Governments which had not done so to elaborate sustainable national e-strategies, as part of their national development and poverty reduction plans, before 2010. It stated its commitment to working to achieve the indicative targets set out in the Geneva Plan of Action for improving ICT connectivity and access by 2015. The Summit established a mechanism for implementation and follow-up at the national, regional and international levels.

The Summit requested the UN Secretary-General to establish, within the UN System Chief Executives Board for Coordination, a UN Group on the Information Society to facilitate the implementation of the 2005 World Summit outcomes and to report to the General Assembly, by June 2006, on the modalities of inter-agency coordination. It requested the Economic and Social Council to oversee the system-wide follow-up of the Geneva and Tunis outcomes, and to review, in 2006, the mandate, agenda and composition of the Commission on Science and Technology for Development, including considering the strengthening of that body. The Summit requested the General Assembly to conduct an overall review of the implementation of the Summit outcomes in 2015, as well as periodic evaluations, using an agreed methodology for measuring and bridging the digital divide. It called upon the Assembly to declare 17 May as World Information Society Day to help raise awareness, annually, of the importance of the Internet as a global facility, of the issues dealt with in the Summit, as well as ways to bridge the digital divide.

Summit preparations

Preparations for the Tunis phase of the World Summit on the Information Society continued throughout 2005. The second meeting of the Preparatory Committee (Geneva, 17-25 February) heard progress reports on the drafting of the final documents and related activities. At its third meeting (Geneva, 19-30 September), the Preparatory Committee considered the text of the final documents of the Summit, which it adopted at the resumed session (Tunis, 13-15 November), and recommended them to the World Summit for adoption.

Four regional preparatory meetings were held in 2005: the African Regional Conference (Accra, Ghana, 2-4 February); the Pan Arab Conference on the World Summit on the Information Society Phase II (Cairo, Egypt, 8-10 May); the Asia-Pacific Regional Conference (Tehran, Islamic Republic of Iran, 31 May–2 June); and the Latin America and the Caribbean Regional Conference (Rio de Janeiro, Brazil, 8-10 June).

UN role

ICT Task Force. In June, the Secretary-General submitted to the Economic and Social Council the third annual report [E/2005/71] of the Information and Communication Technologies Task Force, which was established in 2001 [YUN 2001, p. 763] to provide a global forum on integrating ICT into development programmes and a platform for promoting public and private partnerships to help bridge the digital divide and foster digital opportunity. The second report was submitted to the Council in 2004 [YUN 2004, p. 846].

In its third year, the Task Force, through its core activities, working groups and regional nodes, contributed to advancing multi-stakeholder discussion on policy issues relating to the bench-marking of progress in ICT, Internet governance, promoting an enabling environment, supporting ongoing partnerships and strengthening support activities. It added to progress in measuring, monitoring and analysing the impact of ICT on the achievement of the internationally agreed development goals, supported and promoted collaborative initiatives at the regional, subregional and national levels, and provided significant input to the formulation of a comprehensive UN ICT strategy.

The Task Force continued to promote the mainstreaming of ICT into development. Within the context of the ongoing programme of reform and renewal of the United Nations, the Task Force provided advice to the Secretary-General on ICT.

By **decision 2005/301** of 27 July, the Economic and Social Council took note of the third annual report of the ICT Task Force, and welcomed its valuable contribution to preparations for the Tunis phase of the World Summit on the Information Society and to mainstreaming ICT into development.

CEB consideration. At its tenth session (10-11 October) [CEB/2005/5], the High-level Committee on Management (HLCM) of CEB noted that the true cost of large ICT-based systems comprised not only software licences, the major cost, but development costs as well. It established a task force to document existing global software licensing purchasing agreements and explore new ones for the resource planning system software products currently in use throughout the UN system.

UNCTAD report. In response to General Assembly resolution 58/200 [YUN 2003, p. 860], UNCTAD submitted a publication, *The Digital Divide: ICT Development Indices 2004* [UNCTAD/ITE/IPC/2005/4], which reviewed trends in the digital divide, and evaluated and updated ICT development indices using a range of indicators to benchmark connectivity, access, ICT policy and overall ICT diffusion in a cross-country analysis of 165 countries. It presented a number of policy options for fostering ICT development, and successful country case studies conducted in China, Egypt, the Republic of Korea and the Czech Republic, and described innovative grass-roots ICT programmes in Africa. The report underscored the importance and relevance of benchmarking ICT development for policymaking, and called for proactive policies to ensure effective utilization of ICT in bridging opportunity gaps for those with limited access to technology.

Report of Secretary-General. In response to General Assembly resolution 57/295 [YUN 2002, p. 836], the Secretary-General submitted a 1 September report [A/60/323] on progress in developing a comprehensive UN system ICT strategy. In 2005, the ICT Network, guided by CEB, worked to implement the 15 initiatives contained in the ICT strategic framework grouped into five categories of development, governance, information security, working together and sustaining the initiative. The ICT Network prioritized them, selecting eight for immediate attention, and developing a business case for each one. A steering group was created to advise the Network and ensure a business-oriented direction for the cases selected. While work was proceeding in many areas of the strategic framework, of particular note was the critical areas of knowledge-sharing and knowledge management, where UN system efforts remained uncoordinated and had limited support. To address that issue, the Network was creating a system-wide knowledge-sharing and knowledge management strategy to link and guide individual efforts in the area.

By **decision 60/540** of 22 December, the Assembly took note of the Secretary-General's report on ICT for development: progress in the implementation of resolution 57/295.

Economic and social trends

The _World Economic and Social Survey 2005_ [Sales No. E.05.II.C1] was devoted to the issue of financing for development (see p. 1052).

The _Trade and Development Report, 2005_ [Sales No. E.05.II.D.13], published by UNCTAD, stated that the world economy was still growing at a steady pace, but the risk of a relapse hung in the balance. However, the 4 per cent growth in 2004, the best performance since 2000, was expected to fall to around 3 per cent in 2005. Most of the deceleration was attributable to the slowdown in developed economies, although some developing economies were showing signs of losing momentum.

The annual growth of the United States economy, the world's main engine of growth, was forecast to be around 3.5 per cent in 2005, while Australia, Canada and the United Kingdom were expected to experience a moderate decline in the gross domestic product (GDP) growth in 2005 of close to 2.5 per cent. Growth in the euro area had slowed since mid-2004 and expectations were that it would only reach 1.5 per cent or lower due to a fall in the growth rate exports and sluggish domestic demand. Japan recorded a 2.6 per cent growth rate in 2004, driven by consumption, non-residential investment and brisk export performance. Developing economies as a whole were ex-

pected to grow by 5 to 5.5 per cent in 2005, down from 6.4 per cent in 2004. Africa's growth rate was expected to expand from about 4.5 per cent in 2004 to close to 5 per cent in 2005, fuelled mainly by higher prices of primary commodity exports, particularly petroleum, greater political stability and improved agricultural performance. However, the overall figures for Africa masked considerable differences across countries, with growth rates ranging from a 31 per cent expansion in Chad to a contraction of over 8 per cent in Zimbabwe.

West Asia performed strongly in 2004, reaching 6.2 per cent growth, compared to 5.3 per cent the previous year, due to the massive windfall revenues in oil-exporting countries, which also benefited most of the other countries in the region through increased demand for their exports, capital inflows and workers' remittances. In East and South Asia, China and India acted as the second engine of worldwide growth. With 7.1 per cent growth in 2004, that region recorded its strongest expansion since the 1997 financial crisis, led by China. Preliminary evidence for 2005 in Latin America pointed to a continuation of economic growth, but at a slower pace, because of monetary tightening in the two biggest economies (Brazil and Mexico), slower growth in others (Argentina, Uruguay and Venezuela), less investment in natural resources and little new production capacities coming on stream in the Andean countries. Central America would maintain a moderate growth pace in 2005, while Caribbean countries, some of which were hit by natural disasters in the second half of 2004, should benefit from the recovery of tourism in 2005.

The report on the _World Economic Situation and Prospects_ [Sales No. E.06.II.C.2], prepared jointly by the UN Department of Economic and Social Affairs and UNCTAD, stated that the slowdown in the world economic growth experienced in 2005 was expected to continue at a moderate pace in the near term. Part of that global slowdown resulted from the maturing of the cyclical recovery in a number of economies from recessions and the associated unwinding of earlier stimuli policy. Several exogenous shocks, including natural disasters and terrorist incidents, also left their imprint on the current pace of growth. In the developed economy region, the deceleration of GDP growth rates in 2005 was also due to the surge in energy prices. The still modest, but continuing, growth in Japan in 2005 pointed to an end of the long period of stagnation, while growth in the euro area remained weak. Recovery in Western Europe as a whole was weaker than expected, with GDP rising by 1.5 per cent. Growth in the economies in transition moderated in 2005, but still preserved its dynamism and continued to outpace that of the world economy. In the developing countries, economic growth slowed moderately, reaching 5.7 per cent in 2005, compared to 6.6 per cent in 2004. Africa was the exception to that general trend, with GDP estimated to grow by 5.2 per cent, roughly the same as in 2004, as the region was able to maintain its economic performance, owing to favourable conditions in agriculture and higher prices and volume for exports.

On a per capita basis, the income of developing countries was expected to grow by about 4 per cent in 2005 and 2006. Of the 107 developing countries for which data were available, 51 of them registered per capita growth in 2005 above the 3 per cent necessary for reducing poverty, 19 reached that benchmark, but 36 did not. Conversely, per capita GDP growth declined in 14 countries. Overall, the distribution of per capita GDP growth rates across developing countries in 2005 remained similar to that of 2004, with a large number of them having registered satisfactory growth, while others remained below the benchmark.

Human Development Report 2005

The *Human Development Report 2005* [Sales No. 05.III.B.1], prepared by UNDP, discussed the question of international cooperation at the crossroads: aid, trade and security in an unequal world. It took stock of human development and the scale of the challenge facing the international community at the start of the 10-year countdown to 2015—the target date for achieving the MDGs. It found that human development was faltering in some key areas and inequalities were widening. The year 2005 marked a crossroad, during which Governments would be invited to make it the start of a "decade for development", put the investment and policies in place and adopt bold action plans, not only to meet the 2015 goals, but to overcome those inequalities and forge a new pattern of globalization.

The report analysed the problems facing international cooperation and identified solutions. It ranked 177 countries in its human development index by combining indicators of life expectancy, educational attainment and adjusted per capita income, among other factors. Of the countries listed, 57 were in the high human development category, 88 in the medium category and 32 in the low category.

UNDP consideration. In response to General Assembly resolution 57/264 [YUN 2002, p. 841], UNDP submitted to its Executive Board an update

[DP/2005/19] on consultations that took place in the preparation of the *Human Development Report.*

In June [E/2005/35 (dec. 2005/30)], the Board took note of the update.

Development policy and public administration

Committee for Development Policy

The Committee for Development Policy (CDP), at its seventh session (New York, 14-18 March) [E/2005/33], considered three major themes: achieving the internationally agreed development goals, including the MDGs, as well as implementing the outcomes of the major UN conferences and summits: progress made, challenges and opportunities; reconstruction, development and sustainable peace in post-conflict countries; and improvements in the criteria for the identification of the least developed countries (LDCs), in preparation for the 2006 triennial review of the list of LDCs.

CDP believed that recent changes in both developing and developed countries held the promise that, given the right direction and effort, the MDGs were achievable. Success, particularly in sub-Saharan Africa, depended on responsible and accountable leadership, and on the ownership, planning and executing of the policies and programmes by the countries themselves. The capacity of those Governments to implement development policies and programmes needed to be strengthened, with international assistance. Considering the links between poverty and conflict, CDP called for special attention to be paid to the reintegration into society of people involved in violence, and proposed that a UN monitoring unit be set up to identify countries most at risk of conflict, and a UN post-conflict reconstruction facility created to serve as a prompt response instrument for donor coordination.

CDP also proposed "Coping with economic vulnerability and instability: national and international policy responses" as the theme for its 2006 session.

By **decision 2005/306** of 27 July, the Economic and Social Council deferred consideration of the CDP report on its seventh session, with a view to concluding its deliberations before commencement of the Committee's eighth (2006) session.

Public administration

Committee of Experts on Public Administration. In March, the Economic and Social Council considered the recommendations contained in the report of the Committee of Experts on Public Administration on its third session [YUN 2004, p. 849].

On 31 March [meeting 4], it adopted **resolution 2005/3** [draft: E/2005/L.8/Rev.1] without vote [agenda item 2].

Public administration and development

The Economic and Social Council,

Recalling its resolutions 2001/45 of 20 December 2001, 2002/40 of 19 December 2002 and 2003/60 of 25 July 2003,

Reaffirming the role of the public service in the attainment of national goals for social and economic development, including those contained in the United Nations Millennium Declaration,

Emphasizing the need to improve the efficiency, transparency and accountability of public administration,

Recognizing the important role played by public administration with respect to the planning and provision of public services and the positive contribution it can make to the creation of an enabling environment to promote sustainable development,

1. *Takes note* of the report of the Committee of Experts on Public Administration on its third session;

2. *Reiterates* that efficient, accountable, effective and transparent public administration, at both the national and international levels, has a key role to play in the implementation of the internationally agreed development goals, including those contained in the United Nations Millennium Declaration, and in that context stresses the need to strengthen national public sector administrative and managerial capacity-building, in particular in developing countries and countries with economies in transition;

3. *Requests* all Member States to abide by the principles of proper management of public affairs and public property, fairness, responsibility and equality before the law and the need to safeguard integrity and foster a culture of transparency, accountability and rejection of corruption at all levels and in all its forms, and in that regard urges Member States that have not yet done so to consider enacting laws to accomplish those ends;

4. *Encourages* the international community to increase financial, material and technical support to developing countries with a view to assisting them in their efforts to strengthen and revitalize their public administration institutions and managerial capacity through, inter alia, adopting methods, processes and systems that foster public participation in the governance and development process, and in that regard calls upon the United Nations to provide further substantive technical and advisory support to developing countries, at their request, aimed at strengthening their public service delivery, ensuring national ownership in the development of these programmes;

5. *Welcomes* the initiative of the African countries to strengthen their institutional capacities and their public service through appropriate mechanisms or institutions, in particular the New Partnership for Africa's Development;

6. *Encourages* Member States to consider, as appropriate, the recommendations made by the Committee of Experts on Public Administration;

7. *Requests* the Secretary-General to focus the work of the Organization on public administration according to the recommendations contained in Economic and Social Council decision 2004/302 of 23 July 2004, General Assembly resolution 58/231 of 23 December 2003 and the report of the Committee of Experts on Public Administration on its third session, in particular those aimed at strengthening the human capital in the public sector, facilitating access to information and best practices, promoting good governance and accountability in public administration, at the national and international levels, and strengthening public administration institutions in developing countries, in particular the least developed countries;

8. *Encourages* the Secretary-General to continue his consultations with Member States on a regular basis on the nomination of members of the Committee, keeping in mind its resolution 2001/45 and the annex thereto;

9. *Encourages* the United Nations system and Member States to celebrate United Nations Public Service Day in a more visible manner, and invites Member States to nominate candidates for the United Nations Public Service Awards.

The Committee of Experts on Public Administration, at its fourth session (New York, 4-8 April) [E/2005/44], had before it two reports of the Secretary-General: on revitalizing public administration: strategic directions for the future [E/C.16/2005/2]; and on promoting and rewarding innovations and excellence for revitalizing public administration and service delivery: the United Nations public service awards [E/C.16/2005/5]. The Committee also had before it a Secretariat report on bottom-up approaches and methodologies to develop foundations and principles of public administration: the example of criteria-based organizational assessment [E/C.16/2005/3].

To revitalize public administration, the Committee recommended that the Council encourage countries to ratify, adopt and implement commitments and conventions on integrity, transparency and accountability, including those on corruption, crime and forced or child labour; support a wider concept of security to include human security and human rights; reaffirm and deepen the participatory processes of Government and civil society dialogue and inclusion, in order to implement the MDGs; and support the Secretariat in providing the analytical tools, research findings and advisory services to that end.

Regarding the bottom-up approach in developing sound public administration principles, the Committee reaffirmed that there was no good governance without good government.

The Committee decided to focus on defining the basic concepts relating to governance and public administration and to provide an in-depth assessment of such concepts, their evolution and their use and application. To ascertain the values and qualities of public administration in effective service delivery, the Committee requested the Secretariat to prepare a questionnaire to elicit views from the recipients of public services on what constituted a well-performing, efficient and quality-oriented public administration.

The Committee called for the strengthening of the United Nations Public Service Awards to improve the process of granting the awards and their content and for consideration to be given to adapting or expanding the criteria and/or categories of the awards to recognize the special difficulties faced by public administration in LDCs, crisis or post-conflict countries or countries with special development challenges. The Committee reviewed the activities of the United Nations Programme on Public Administration, Finance and Development and welcomed the celebration of the tenth anniversary of the General Assembly's resumed fiftieth session [YUN 1996, p. 750] on public administration and development.

On 27 July, the Council deferred consideration of the report of the Committee of Experts on Public Administration until its resumed substantive session (**decision 2005/310**).

ECONOMIC AND SOCIAL COUNCIL ACTION

On 21 October [meeting 41], the Economic and Social Council adopted **resolution 2005/55** [draft: E/2005/L.51] without vote [agenda item 13 (g)].

Report of the Committee of Experts on Public Administration on its fourth session and dates, venue and provisional agenda for the fifth session of the Committee

The Economic and Social Council,

Recognizing the importance of good governance, which flows, inter alia, from a harmonious and balanced relationship of the State, the private sector and civil society, and recognizing the importance of State capacity, including institutional and human resource capacity, in securing steady and sustainable progress towards internationally agreed commitments and objectives,

Recognizing also that all Member States, in particular the developing countries, can greatly benefit from peer learning and the sharing of experiences about innovation and initiative in the public sector,

Recognizing further that the United Nations Public Service Award is an effective means of rewarding outstanding achievements in the area of public administration and encouraging their replication,

Recognizing recent regional initiatives that have led to successful actions to promote integrity, transparency and accountability,

Underscoring the importance of public administration as a tool to support progress on development and human rights in line with the United Nations Millennium Declaration,

Reaffirming the need to deepen the participatory processes of government to ensure citizens' engagement to achieve the internationally agreed development goals, including those contained in the Millennium Declaration, and to encourage the Secretariat to provide the analytical tools, research capacity and advisory services to that end,

1. *Takes note* of the report of the Committee of Experts on Public Administration on its fourth session;

2. *Encourages* countries to ratify, adopt and implement the relevant commitments and conventions in the areas of integrity, transparency and accountability, including those related to the prevention of corrupt policies and practices;

3. *Requests* the Committee of Experts on Public Administration to deepen its analysis of the relationships between State capacity, public administration and development by identifying, for the benefit of interested countries, successful examples, options and solutions in the area of public administration that have facilitated the achievement of the internationally agreed development goals, including those contained in the United Nations Millennium Declaration;

4. *Requests* the Secretary-General to disseminate and promulgate in a more systematic and coherent way innovations and successful practices recognized by the United Nations Public Service Award;

5. *Also requests* the Secretary-General to strengthen the capacity and the reach of the United Nations Online Network in Public Administration and Finance to serve as a vehicle for sharing knowledge, innovation and practices in public administration, in particular by associating more partner organizations from developing countries with the network;

6. *Approves* the convening of the fifth session of the Committee of Experts on Public Administration in New York from 3 to 7 April 2006;

7. *Also approves* the following agenda for the fifth session of the Committee:

1. Innovation in public administration for the achievement of the internationally agreed development goals, including those contained in the Millennium Declaration;

2. Searching for a bottom-up approach and methodologies for developing foundations and principles of sound public administration (continued from the fourth session);

3. Review of the work programme of the United Nations Programme in Public Administration, Finance and Development.

Report of Secretary-General. In response to General Assembly resolution 59/55 [YUN 2004, p. 851], the Secretary-General submitted a July report on public administration and development [A/60/114], which highlighted the development challenges facing Member States, and, based on responses from 40 countries to a questionnaire submitted to Governments reviewed the measures adopted to revitalize public administration systems. The future of public administration, it said, lay in instituting measures to reconfigure public service organizations into open, participative, knowledge-sharing, innovating and results-oriented service-delivery systems, and it stressed the need to strengthen the UN's role in public administration.

Future directions in revitalizing public administration should focus on consolidating the gains of the reform and revitalization measures instituted in the past 10 years, particularly in underscoring the role of public administration in development, to strengthen public administration knowledge-sharing networks and to invest in institutional capacity-building and human resource development. To ensure that the study of public administration did not lag too far behind developments in practice, a new programme of action should be launched, aimed at rehabilitating public administration education and training institutions.

The report concluded that the coming years would be crucial for public administration systems worldwide. Besides contributing to efforts to alleviate poverty, they would be required to create conditions for wealth creation and broad development objectives.

The United Nations had a key role to play in helping Member States meet the challenges outlined by: continuing to promote the adoption of public administration principles and standards; sharing information, knowledge and successful experiences by organizing global and regional forums and expanding the UN Online Network in Public Administration; and fostering horizontal exchanges between and among administrations. The Organization's role also included strengthening the UN Public Service Awards mechanism; launching a global initiative to enhance research, teaching and training in public administration schools and institutes; providing specialized technical assistance to developing countries to support their public administration revitalization; and strengthening partnerships with other organizations to maximize the impact of its activities.

Transmitted to the Secretary-General by the Republic of Korea was the text of the Seoul Declaration on Participatory and Transparent Governance [A/60/391], adopted at the Sixth Global Forum on Reinventing Government (Seoul, Republic of Korea, 24-27 May). The Forum welcomed the upcoming launch by the Republic of Korea, together with DESA, of a feasibility study on establishing the United Nations Governance Centre in Seoul, to serve as a regional and international focal point for advancing research, disseminating information and providing training

courses on reinventing government, as well as that Government's commitment to establishing a portal site for online sharing of information on innovations and best practices on good governance. The seventh Forum, to be hosted by the United Nations in 2007, would highlight the importance of improving public administration in order to achieve the internationally agreed development goals, including the MDGs.

On 30 November [meeting 58], the General Assembly adopted **resolution 60/34** [draft: A/60/L.24 & Add.1] without vote [agenda item 41].

Public administration and development

The General Assembly,

Recalling all pertinent resolutions, in particular its resolution 59/55 of 2 December 2004 on public administration and development,

Acknowledging the tenth anniversary of the resumed fiftieth session of the General Assembly, on public administration and development, held in April 1996,

Recognizing the important role played by public administration with respect to the planning and provision of public services and the positive contribution it can make to the creation of an enabling environment to promote sustainable development,

Emphasizing the need to improve the efficiency, transparency and accountability of public administration,

Reiterating that efficient, accountable, effective and transparent public administration, at both the national and international levels, has a key role to play in the implementation of the internationally agreed development goals, including the Millennium Development Goals,

Noting that the capacities of public institutions and human resources will play a vital role in the ability of Member States to effectively achieve the Millennium Development Goals,

Acknowledging, further, that measures that increase participatory and transparent governance will help Member States to build and strengthen state capacity to address development and other challenges,

Stressing the importance of participatory public administration responsive to the needs of the people, and good governance,

1. *Takes note* of the report of the Secretary-General;

2. *Emphasizes* that good governance and transparent and accountable public administration at the national and international levels will contribute to the achievement of the Millennium Development Goals;

3. *Recognizes* the importance of the efforts of Governments to foster public participation in governance and development processes through cooperating with all stakeholders in their societies, including the private sector, civil society and non-governmental organizations;

4. *Stresses* that national efforts to improve governance, public administration and institutional and managerial capacities are essential to enable Member States to achieve the internationally agreed development goals, including the Millennium Development Goals,

and encourages Member States to increase their efforts in this regard;

5. *Encourages* the international community to increase support for national efforts, including those of developing countries, in public administration, including through North-South cooperation, South-South cooperation and public-private partnership to, inter alia, provide financial, educational, material and technical support and cooperation as appropriate;

6. *Requests* all Member States to abide by the principles of proper management of public affairs and public property, fairness, responsibility and equality before the law and the need to safeguard integrity and foster a culture of transparency, accountability and rejection of corruption at all levels and in all its forms, consistent with the United Nations Convention against Corruption, and in that regard urges Member States that have not yet done so to consider enacting laws to accomplish those ends;

7. *Agrees* that the United Nations should promote innovation in government and public administration, and stresses the importance of making more effective use of United Nations Public Service Day and the United Nations Public Service Awards in the process of revitalizing public administration by building a culture of innovation, partnership and responsiveness;

8. *Requests* the Secretary-General to continue to facilitate, through the United Nations Online Network in Public Administration and Finance, the dissemination of information, knowledge and valuable practices in public administration;

9. *Stresses* the valuable contribution that the Global Forum on Reinventing Government has made to the exchange of lessons learned in public administration reform;

10. *Takes note with appreciation* of the Seoul Declaration on Participatory and Transparent Governance, which was adopted by the participants in the sixth Global Forum on Reinventing Government, held in Seoul from 24 to 27 May 2005;

11. *Expresses its appreciation* to the Government of the Republic of Korea for hosting the sixth Global Forum on Reinventing Government;

12. *Emphasizes* the importance of the seventh Global Forum on Reinventing Government, to be hosted by the United Nations in 2007, which will highlight the importance of improving public administration in order to achieve the internationally agreed development goals, including the Millennium Development Goals;

13. *Urges* the United Nations to maximize the effectiveness of its activities in the field of public administration and development by strengthening partnerships with other international and regional organizations, as appropriate, and by promoting the use of information and communications technology as a tool for development;

14. *Requests* the Secretary-General to submit a report to the General Assembly on the implementation of the present resolution and the result of the seventh Global Forum on Reinventing Government, to be held in 2007.

Groups of countries in special situations

By **decision 60/544** of 22 December, the General Assembly took note of the report of the Second Committee on groups of countries in special situations [A/60/491 & Corr.1].

Least developed countries

The special problems of the officially designated least developed countries (LDCs) were considered in several UN forums in 2005, particularly in connection with the implementation of the Brussels Declaration and Programme of Action for LDCs for the Decade 2001-2010, adopted at the Third United Nations Conference on LDCs in 2001 [YUN 2001, p. 770] and endorsed by the General Assembly in resolution 55/279 in July of that year [ibid., p. 771]. World leaders, in their 2005 World Summit Outcome document, reaffirmed their commitment to addressing the special needs of LDCs (resolution 60/1) (see p. 48), and urged all countries and the UN system to speedily meet the goals and targets of the Brussels Programme, particularly the official development assistance target. The Committee for Development Policy (CDP) and UNCTAD also considered LDC-related issues.

LDC list

The number of countries officially designated as LDCs remained at 50. Although Cape Verde and Maldives were recommended for graduation from the list, the process would take place over a three-year period, as decided by the General Assembly in resolution 59/209 [YUN 2004, p. 854]. With regard to Maldives, the Assembly, in resolution 60/33 (see below), deferred, until January 2008, the start of the three-year transition period for its graduation from the list of LDCs, following the destruction and damage caused by the 26 December 2004 Indian Ocean tsunami to the country's social and economic infrastructure and disruption of its development plans.

The full list of LDCs comprised: Afghanistan, Angola, Bangladesh, Benin, Bhutan, Burkina Faso, Burundi, Cambodia, Cape Verde, Central African Republic, Chad, Comoros, Democratic Republic of the Congo, Djibouti, Equatorial Guinea, Eritrea, Ethiopia, Gambia, Guinea, Guinea-Bissau, Haiti, Kiribati, Lao People's Democratic Republic, Lesotho, Liberia, Madagascar, Malawi, Maldives, Mali, Mauritania, Mozambique, Myanmar, Nepal, Niger, Rwanda, Samoa, Sao Tome and Principe, Senegal, Sierra Leone, Solomon Islands, Somalia, Sudan, Timor-Leste, Togo, Tuvalu, Uganda, United Republic of Tanzania, Vanuatu, Yemen, Zambia.

Smooth transition strategy

CDP consideration. At its seventh session (New York, 14-18 March) [E/2005/33], CDP, which was responsible for adding countries to or graduating them from the LDC list, considered the situation in Maldives—one of two countries it had recommended, in resolution 2004/67 [YUN 2004, p. 855], to be graduated from the LDC category—in the light of the December 2004 Indian Ocean tsunami [ibid., p. 952], which had affected that country. The Committee, in turn, recommended to the Economic and Social Council that, in the case of Maldives, the consultative mechanism envisaged in General Assembly resolution 59/209 [YUN 2004, p. 854] be organized to consider the exceptional circumstances of reconstruction in the aftermath of the tsunami.

The Committee agreed that flexibility should be exercised in the application of the three criteria for the identification of LDCs: gross national income (GNI) per capita; the human assets index (HAI); and the economic vulnerability index (EVI). In determining the eligibility of countries for inclusion or graduation, the Committee suggested considering simultaneously two structural handicaps (HAI and EVI), or even the three criteria in such a way as to take into account some degree of substitutability among them and the possible combined impact of the handicaps as captured by HAI and EVI.

The Committee agreed that, if the GNI of a LDC increased to an exceptionally high level (at least twice the threshold level), the country could be considered eligible for graduation even if it did not reach the graduation threshold for either of the other two criteria, recognizing that the sustainability of the higher income level had to be taken into account. It decided to replace the average daily calorie consumption per capita by the percentage of the population undernourished.

Re-emphasizing that the size of population was a major indicator of economic vulnerability, the Committee agreed to include the proportion of the population displaced by natural disasters, together with the instability of the agricultural production, in the EVI, and to include an indicator of remoteness to reflect likely high transportation costs and isolation from world markets and to replace the share of manufacturing and modern services by the share of agriculture, forestry and fisheries.

On 30 November [meeting 58], the General Assembly adopted **resolution 60/33** [draft: A/60/L.21] without vote [agenda item 41].

Deferral of the smooth transition period for the graduation of Maldives from the list of least developed countries

The General Assembly,

Recalling its resolutions 59/209 and 59/210 of 20 December 2004,

Reaffirming its commitment to the process for graduation from the list of least developed countries and to the smooth transition strategy for countries graduating from that list,

Giving due consideration to the unique destruction and damage caused by the Indian Ocean tsunami of 26 December 2004 to the social and economic infrastructure of Maldives, the homes of thousands of individuals and their livelihoods, the setback to the economy of the country and the disruption of its development plans,

Inviting the international community to provide comprehensive support for the rehabilitation, reconstruction and risk reduction efforts being undertaken by the Government of Maldives,

1. *Expresses its deep concern* at the consequences of the Indian Ocean tsunami on Maldives;

2. *Decides* to defer, in the case of Maldives, for a period of three years until 1 January 2008, the commencement of the three-year smooth transition period for graduation from the list of least developed countries;

3. *Underlines* the unique nature of this decision, taken in the context of the unprecedented natural disaster caused by the tsunami of 26 December 2004.

Programme of Action (2001-2010)

In response to Economic and Social Council resolution 2004/65 [YUN 2004, p. 856] and General Assembly resolution 59/244 [ibid., p. 857], the Secretary-General submitted in May the first results-oriented annual progress report [A/60/81-E/2005/68] on the implementation of the Programme of Action for the LDCs for the Decade 2001-2010.

According to the report, despite significant progress of some LDCs in meeting specific goals, progress, as a group, in meeting most of the goals had been slow and uneven, and insufficient to achieve·the Brussels Programme of Action goals and its objective of eradicating poverty and achieving sustained growth and sustainable development by 2010. If current conditions persisted, the number of people living in extreme poverty might increase from 334 million in 2000 to 471 million in 2015. Three major obstacles—country ownership, capacity and resources—continued to hamper implementation of the Programme by LDCs, and the lack of statistical data jeopardized monitoring and reporting on the national level. To strengthen ownership, LDCs needed to prepare a results-based poverty reduction strategy in which their public actions and donor support were aimed at achieving the Programme's goals. Addressing the challenges of capacity-building and resources mobilization required strengthening of the partnership between LDCs and their development partners. Achieving the Programme's goals by 2010 also required developed countries to fulfil their commitments on ODA, debt relief, trade and technology transfer. Development partners should integrate the Brussels Programme into their development policies, strategies and programmes, and UN country teams should support the preparation and implementation of national development strategies based on the Brussels Programme.

ECONOMIC AND SOCIAL COUNCIL ACTION

On 27 July [meeting 40], the Economic and Social Council adopted **resolution 2005/44** [draft: E/2005/L.46] without vote [agenda item 6 *(b)*].

Implementation of the Programme of Action for the Least Developed Countries for the Decade 2001-2010

The Economic and Social Council,

Recalling the Brussels Declaration and the Programme of Action for the Least Developed Countries for the Decade 2001-2010,

Recalling also its decision 2001/320 of 24 October 2001, in which it decided to establish, under the regular agenda item entitled "Integrated and coordinated implementation of and follow-up to the major United Nations conferences and summits", a regular sub-item entitled "Review and coordination of the implementation of the Programme of Action for the Least Developed Countries for the Decade 2001-2010",

Recalling further its resolution 2003/17 of 22 July 2003 and its decision 2003/287 of 24 July 2003, as well as the ministerial declaration of the high-level segment of its substantive session of 2004 on the theme "Resources mobilization and enabling environment for poverty eradication in the context of the implementation of the Programme of Action for the Least Developed Countries for the Decade 2001-2010",

Recalling paragraph 5 of General Assembly resolution 59/244 of 22 December 2004, in which the Assembly decided to hold the comprehensive review of the Programme of Action in 2006 during its sixty-first session, in accordance with paragraph 114 of the Programme of Action, and paragraph 6 of the same resolution, in which the Assembly decided to consider at its sixtieth session the modalities for conducting such a comprehensive review,

1. *Takes note* of the annual progress report of the Secretary-General on the implementation of the Programme of Action for the Least Developed Countries for the Decade 2001-2010;

2. *Expresses its deep concern* over the insufficient progress achieved in the implementation of the Programme of Action, and stresses the need to address areas of weakness in its implementation;

3. *Urges* the least developed countries and their bilateral and multilateral development partners to undertake increased efforts and to adopt measures rapidly, with a view to meeting the goals and targets of the Programme of Action in a timely manner;

4. *Urges* the least developed countries that have not yet done so to develop, adopt and implement national development strategies to achieve the goals and targets of the Programme of Action;

5. *Calls upon* development partners to assist the least developed countries in the development and implementation of their national development strategies based on the goals and targets of the Programme of Action;

6. *Also calls upon* development partners, including organizations of the United Nations system, to provide assistance to national statistical bodies of the least developed countries in order to strengthen monitoring and reporting on the implementation of the Programme of Action;

7. *Calls upon* the least developed countries, in preparation for the comprehensive review in 2006 by the General Assembly at its sixty-first session, to undertake their national reviews on the implementation of the Programme of Action, with a particular focus on progress, obstacles, constraints, actions and measures necessary to further the implementation of the Programme of Action;

8. *Requests* United Nations resident coordinators to assist the least developed countries in undertaking their national reviews in preparation for the comprehensive review of the implementation of the Programme of Action by the General Assembly at its sixty-first session;

9. *Requests* the regional commissions to assist the least developed countries in undertaking regional reviews of the implementation of the Programme of Action in their respective regions in preparation for the comprehensive review in 2006 by the General Assembly at its sixty-first session;

10. *Encourages* the organizations of the United Nations system and other international organizations to undertake, in preparation for the comprehensive review in 2006 by the General Assembly at its sixty-first session, sectoral reviews of the implementation of the Programme of Action by their governing bodies;

11. *Requests* the Secretary-General to include least developed country issues in all relevant reports in the economic, social and related fields, in particular those that analyse global development trends, such as *World Economic Situation and Prospects*, to ensure the follow-up of their development in a broader context;

12. *Reiterates* the critical importance of the participation of Government representatives from the least developed countries in the annual review of the Programme of Action by the Economic and Social Council, welcomes in this regard the establishment by the Secretary-General of a specific trust fund for the travel and daily subsistence allowance of two representatives from each least developed country to attend the annual review of the Programme of Action, calls upon Member States to contribute generously to that trust fund, and requests the Secretary-General to intensify his efforts to mobilize the resources necessary in order to ensure that the trust fund is adequately resourced;

13. *Calls upon* the Secretary-General, while stressing the central role of the Economic and Social Council in the coordination of actions in the United Nations system for the implementation of the Programme of Action, to take appropriate measures to strengthen the efficiency and effectiveness of the Office of the High Representative for the Least Developed Countries, Landlocked Developing Countries and Small Island Developing States so that it can carry out its functions, in accordance with General Assembly resolution 56/227 of 24 December 2001;

14. *Requests* the Secretary-General to submit an annual progress report on the implementation of the Programme of Action in a more analytical and results-oriented way, by placing emphasis on the progress achieved by the least developed countries and their development partners in its implementation.

UNDP action. The Executive Board of the United Nations Development Programme/ United Nations Population Fund, at its annual session (New York, 13-24 June), adopted decision [E/2005/35 (dec. 2005/29)], in which it welcomed the United Nations Capital Development Fund business plan, 2005-2007: Investing in the LDCs to achieve the MDGs.

Trade and Development Board action. The Trade and Development Board (TDB) of UNCTAD, at its sixtieth session (Geneva, 3-14 October) [A/60/15 (Part IV)], adopted agreed conclusions [A/60/15 (agreed conclusion 482 (LII))] on the review of progress in the implementation of the Programme of Action for the LDCs. The Board encouraged UNCTAD to further enhance the delivery and effectiveness of its technical cooperation and capacity-building activities so as to improve their development impact on the economies of LDCs. It encouraged the UNCTAD secretariat to implement fully the relevant decisions of the São Paulo Consensus, adopted by UNCTAD XI [YUN 2004, p. 955], including the annualization of the *Least Developed Countries Report,* and to further enhance efforts in favour of LDCs, landlocked and transit developing countries and small island developing States. It called on the secretariat to make available adequate resources for that purpose and to seek voluntary contributions. The secretariat should contribute also to the 2006 General Assembly comprehensive midterm review of progress in the implementation of the Programme of Action and the related preparatory process. TDB called for intensified international support measures to enable LDCs to enhance their productive capacities, diversify their economies into non-preference-dependent activities, and improve their utilization of the market access preferences available to them. It emphasized the need for continued contributions, broader donor participation to ensure effective and efficient delivery and implementa-

tion of existing and new technical assistance programmes and projects in those countries.

GENERAL ASSEMBLY ACTION

On 23 December [meeting 69], the General Assembly, on the recommendation of the Second Committee [A/60/491/Add.1], adopted **resolution 60/228** without vote [agenda item 55 *(a)*].

Third United Nations Conference on the Least Developed Countries: high-level meeting on the midterm comprehensive global review of the implementation of the Programme of Action for the Least Developed Countries for the Decade 2001-2010

The General Assembly,

Recalling its resolution 55/279 of 12 July 2001, in which it endorsed the Brussels Declaration and the Programme of Action for the Least Developed Countries for the Decade 2001-2010, and its resolutions 57/276 of 20 December 2002, 58/228 of 23 December 2003 and 59/244 of 22 December 2004 on the Third United Nations Conference on the Least Developed Countries,

Recalling also its resolution 57/270 B of 23 June 2003 on the integrated and coordinated implementation of and follow-up to the outcomes of the major United Nations conferences and summits in the economic and social fields,

Reaffirming its resolution 55/2 of 8 September 2000, by which it adopted the United Nations Millennium Declaration, in particular paragraph 15 thereof, in which the Heads of State and Government undertook to address the special needs of the least developed countries,

Recognizing the importance of the review of the progress achieved towards meeting the goals and targets contained in the Programme of Action, as well as other internationally agreed development goals, including those contained in the Millennium Declaration, as they address the special needs of the least developed countries,

Taking note of the ministerial declaration of the high-level segment of the 2004 substantive session of the Economic and Social Council on the theme "Resources mobilization and enabling environment for poverty eradication in the context of the implementation of the Programme of Action for the Least Developed Countries for the Decade 2001-2010",

Recalling paragraph 5 of its resolution 59/244, in which it decided to hold the midterm comprehensive global review of the Programme of Action in 2006 during its sixty-first session, in accordance with paragraph 114 of the Programme of Action, and recalling also paragraph 6 of the same resolution, in which it decided to consider at its sixtieth session the modalities for conducting such a midterm comprehensive review,

Taking note of Economic and Social Council resolution 2005/44 of 27 July 2005 on the implementation of the Programme of Action for the Least Developed Countries for the Decade 2001-2010,

Recalling the 2005 World Summit Outcome,

Taking note of the annual progress report of the Secretary-General on the implementation of the Programme of Action for the Least Developed Countries for the Decade 2001-2010,

1. *Reaffirms* the commitment to address the special needs of the least developed countries, and urges all countries and all relevant organizations of the United Nations system, including the Bretton Woods institutions, to make concerted efforts and adopt speedy measures for meeting in a timely manner the goals and targets of the Brussels Programme of Action for the Least Developed Countries for the Decade 2001-2010;

2. *Expresses its deep concern* over the insufficient implementation of the Programme of Action, and stresses the need to address the areas of weakness in its implementation;

3. *Stresses* that progress in the implementation of the Programme of Action will require effective implementation of national policies and priorities for the economic growth and sustainable development of the least developed countries, as well as strong and committed partnership between those countries and their development partners;

4. *Reiterates its request* to the Secretary-General to ensure at the secretariat level the full mobilization and coordination of all parts of the United Nations system to facilitate coordinated implementation as well as coherence in the follow-up to the Programme of Action at the national, subregional, regional and global levels, and in this context requests the Secretary-General to engage the United Nations Development Group, consistent with the respective mandates of its members, in the coordinated implementation of the Programme of Action;

5. *Decides* to convene a high-level meeting on the midterm comprehensive global review of the implementation of the Programme of Action for the Least Developed Countries for the Decade 2001-2010, in New York on 19 and 20 September 2006, to be chaired by the President of the General Assembly;

6. *Decides also* to convene a three-day preparatory meeting of experts during the sixtieth session of the General Assembly, preferably on 4, 5 and 6 September 2006, for the midterm comprehensive global review in order to propose, as appropriate, measures to advance the process of the implementation of the Programme of Action;

7. *Stresses* that the midterm comprehensive global review should assess the progress made in the implementation of commitments and provide the occasion to reaffirm the goals and objectives agreed upon at the Third United Nations Conference on the Least Developed Countries, to share best practices and lessons learned, and to identify obstacles and constraints encountered, actions and initiatives to overcome them and important measures for the further implementation of the Programme of Action, as well as new challenges and emerging issues;

8. *Requests* the Secretary-General to prepare, for consideration by Member States, a note on the organizational aspects of the high-level meeting;

9. *Requests* the regional commissions to assist the least developed countries in undertaking regional reviews of the implementation of the Programme of Action in their respective regions in preparation for the midterm comprehensive global review in 2006 by the General Assembly at its sixty-first session;

10. *Emphasizes* that the midterm comprehensive global review of the implementation of the Programme of Action is of particular significance as it will provide an opportunity for the international community, in particular the least developed countries and their development partners, to discuss the implementation of the Programme of Action with a view to ensuring support for the least developed countries in all areas, in order to ensure the timely, effective and full implementation of the Programme of Action during the remainder of the decade;

11. *Requests* the organs, organizations, funds and programmes of the United Nations system to undertake sectoral appraisals in their respective fields of competence on the implementation of the Programme of Action, with special emphasis on areas where implementation has remained insufficient, and to make proposals for new measures as necessary, as further inputs to the preparation for the midterm comprehensive global review, and in this regard affirms that appropriate inter-agency meetings should be convened to ensure the full mobilization and coordination of the entire United Nations system, including the Bretton Woods institutions;

12. *Recognizes* the importance of the contribution of civil society actors in the preparatory process, and in this regard requests the President of the General Assembly to organize, within existing resources, one-day informal interactive hearings in New York with representatives of non-governmental organizations, civil society organizations and the private sector, as an input to the midterm comprehensive global review;

13. *Calls upon* all Member States to take a positive interest in the preparation of the midterm comprehensive global review and to be represented at a high level in the plenary meeting of the review, with a view to reaching a successful outcome;

14. *Emphasizes* the importance of country-level preparations as a critical input to the preparatory process for the midterm comprehensive global review and to the implementation of and follow-up to its outcome, and in this context calls upon the least developed countries to undertake their national reviews on the implementation of the Programme of Action, with a particular focus on progress, obstacles, constraints, actions and measures necessary to further its implementation;

15. *Requests* the Administrator of the United Nations Development Programme, in his capacity as Chairman of the United Nations Development Group, to ensure the full involvement of the United Nations resident coordinators and country teams in the least developed countries in the preparations for the midterm comprehensive global review, in particular at the country level, including in the preparation of national reports;

16. *Requests* the Secretary-General to submit, in a timely manner, a comprehensive report for the midterm comprehensive global review;

17. *Reiterates* the critical importance of the full and effective participation of the least developed countries in the midterm comprehensive global review of the Programme of Action at the national, regional and global levels, stresses that adequate resources should be provided, and in this regard requests the Secretary-General to mobilize extrabudgetary resources in order to cover the cost of participation of two government representatives from each least developed country in the process of the high-level meeting on the midterm comprehensive global review;

18. *Welcomes* the pledges already made by the United Nations Development Programme and the United Nations Conference on Trade and Development to support the preparatory process, and calls upon Member States and invites other multilateral development partners, intergovernmental and nongovernmental organizations and the private sector to make voluntary contributions to the trust fund established by the Secretary-General in accordance with resolution 59/244;

19. *Requests* the Secretary-General, with the assistance of concerned organizations and bodies of the United Nations, including the Department of Public Information of the Secretariat, to take the necessary measures to intensify their public information efforts and other relevant initiatives to enhance public awareness in favour of the midterm comprehensive global review;

20. *Also requests* the Secretary-General to submit to the General Assembly at its sixty-second session a report on the implementation of the present resolution.

The Secretary-General, in December [A/C.5/ 60/24], informed the Fifth (Administrative and Budgetary) Committee that a total of $254,000 would be required for the activities set out in resolution 60/228 (above).

Island developing States

International Meeting on Implementation of Programme of Action for SIDS

The International Meeting to Review the Implementation of the 1994 Programme of Action for the Sustainable Development of Small Island States (SIDS) [YUN 1994, p. 783] (Barbados Programme of Action) (Port Louis, Mauritius, 10-14 January) [A/CONF.207/11] adopted the Mauritius Declaration and the Mauritius Strategy for the Further Implementation of the Programme of Action for the Sustainable Development of Small Island Developing States. The Meeting assessed the progress achieved in implementing the Barbados Programme of Action and considered how best to invest future effort for a more effective implementation. It was attended by political leaders from 120 countries and representatives of intergovernmental organizations, NGOs and the private sector. Two round tables, convened during the high-level segment, discussed the way forward in mobilizing resources for the further implementation of the Barbados Programme of Action, and building capacity for the sustainable development of SIDS. Five panels, held from 10 to12 January, discussed issues confronting small island developing States: environmental vulnerabilities; special challenges in trade and economic development; the role of culture in their sustainable development; addressing the emerging trends and social challenges for their sustainable

development; and resilience-building. There were also parallel and associated activities by NGOs and other major groups, as well as partnerships activities.

Mauritius Declaration and Mauritius Strategy for Implementation

The Mauritius Declaration reaffirmed the continued validity of the Barbados Programme of Action as the blueprint for action in support of SIDS, while taking account of new and emerging issues, and invoked renewed political commitment to support the sustainable development strategies of SIDS through technical and financial cooperation, regional and interregional institutional assistance and an improved international enabling environment. The importance of technology transfer, capacity-building and human resources development to building the resilience of SIDS and to advancing implementation of the Programme of Action was also recognized.

Additionally, the Declaration reaffirmed the commitment to implementing the outcomes of major UN conferences and summits as they related to the sustainable development of SIDS. Recognizing the importance of international trade, it called on international institutions to pay attention to the structural disadvantages and vulnerabilities of those States, and to focus on their trade- and development-related needs and concerns to enable them to integrate fully into the multilateral trading system.

The Declaration reaffirmed the commitment to conservation and the sustainable use of island and marine biodiversity; recognized the important roles of women, youth and civil society in promoting sustainable development; and reaffirmed the commitment to create a world fit for children and to assist in their protection and minimize the impacts of natural disasters and environmental degradation on them. It also recognized the importance of the cultural identity of people in SIDS and the increasing incidence of health issues, particularly HIV/AIDS, which had a disproportionate impact on women and youth in SIDS, and committed States to ensuring that the health needs of SIDS were addressed in all regional and global programmes. Governments committed themselves to the timely implementation of the Mauritius Strategy and to advancing implementation of the Barbados Programme of Action.

The preamble to the Mauritius Strategy for the Further Implementation of the Programme of Action for the Sustainable Development of Small Island Developing States indicated that the Programme of Action remained the blueprint for SIDS and the international community to address national and regional sustainable development. Those States acknowledged that sustainable development was primarily a national responsibility, but for them to succeed, the principles contained in the Rio Declaration on Environment and Development, adopted at the 1992 International Conference on Environment and Development [YUN 1992, p. 670], should be given specific expression. There was a need for strengthened cooperation and partnership in support of sustainable development of SIDS at all levels, which should be broad-based to ensure the involvement and participation of relevant stakeholders. In order to complement national and regional development efforts of SIDS, there was an urgent need to enhance coherence, governance and consistency of the international monetary, financial and trading systems. Implementation of the sustainable development agenda for SIDS should proceed, notwithstanding the current emphasis on international security. In that regard, the international community acknowledged the increased financial and administrative obligation placed on those States as part of the global fight against terrorism. The importance of culture, the role of youth and the promotion of gender equality in their sustainable development were also recognized.

The Mauritius Strategy, responding to the need for a more focused approach to implementation of the Programme of Action, identified critical areas for further attention within the established sectors, and highlighted new and emerging issues that had to be addressed if more effective implementation was to be achieved. Those issues included: HIV/AIDS and health-related issues; security concerns; the impact of the erosion of trade preferences on SIDS and the consequent need for improved market access and an international trading system that promoted economic growth, employment and development for all; support for information communication technology development; and the importance of protecting cultural diversity and promoting cultural industries as a vital component of sustainable development strategy in SIDS. Beyond specific sectoral issues identified for continued attention, the Strategy promoted the fullest participation of civil society and other stakeholder groups, advocated greater South-South and SIDS cooperation, and articulated a range of cross-sectoral measures, regional and interregional mechanisms and strategies for enhanced inter-institutional consultation and coordination, particularly within the UN system, as essential tools to be employed in strengthening implementation of the Programme of Action.

More specifically, the Strategy set out the commitments made by SIDS and the actions they needed to take, with international support, in 19 areas: climate change and sea-level rise; natural and environmental disasters; management of wastes; coastal and marine resources; freshwater resources; land resources; energy resources; tourism resources; biodiversity resources; transport and communication; science and technology; graduation from LDC status; trade: globalization and trade liberalization; sustainable capacity development and education for sustainable development; sustainable production and consumption; national and regional enabling environments; health; knowledge management and information for decision-making; and culture.

Defining the UN's role in the further implementation of the Programme of Action, the Strategy declared that the Commission on Sustainable Development would continue to be the primary intergovernmental body responsible for the implementation of and follow-up to the commitments related to SIDS. Other UN system organs, programmes and organizations should coordinate and rationalize their work in implementing the Strategy. The Secretary-General was requested to fully mobilize and coordinate the agencies, funds and programmes of the UN system to further mainstream SIDS issues to facilitate coordinated implementation of the follow-up to the Programme of Action at the national, regional, subregional and global levels. He should ensure that DESA continued to provide substantive support and advisory services to those States for the further implementation of the Programme of Action and the Johannesburg Plan of Implementation, and that the Office of the High Representative for the Least Developed Countries, Landlocked Developing Countries and Small Island Developing States continue to mobilize international support and resources for the further implementation of the Programme of Action.

Communication. On 14 February, Mauritius transmitted to the Secretary-General the communiqué adopted at the Fifth Summit of the Heads of State and Government of the Alliance of Small Island States (Port Louis, Mauritius, 12 January), requesting that it be annexed to the report of the International Meeting [A/CONF.207/10].

GENERAL ASSEMBLY ACTION

On 14 July [meeting 113], the General Assembly adopted **resolution 59/311** [draft: A/59/L.63 and Add.1] without vote [agenda item 85 *(b)*].

International Meeting to Review the Implementation of the Programme of Action for the Sustainable Development of Small Island Developing States

The General Assembly,

Reaffirming the Declaration of Barbados and the Programme of Action for the Sustainable Development of Small Island Developing States, adopted by the Global Conference on the Sustainable Development of Small Island Developing States, and recalling its resolution 49/122 of 19 December 1994 on the Global Conference,

Recalling Agenda 21, the Johannesburg Declaration on Sustainable Development and the Plan of Implementation of the World Summit on Sustainable Development ("Johannesburg Plan of Implementation"), in particular the emphasis given to small island developing States in chapter VII of the Johannesburg Plan of Implementation, as well as the references to the specific needs of small island developing States contained in the United Nations Millennium Declaration and the Monterrey Consensus of the International Conference on Financing for Development,

Welcoming the adoption by the International Meeting to Review the Implementation of the Programme of Action for the Sustainable Development of Small Island Developing States, held in Port Louis from 10 to 14 January 2005, of the Mauritius Declaration and the Mauritius Strategy for the Further Implementation of the Programme of Action for the Sustainable Development of Small Island Developing States ("Mauritius Strategy for Implementation") on 14 January 2005,

Expressing its satisfaction that the International Meeting and its preparatory process provided for the active participation of all States Members of the United Nations and members of the specialized agencies, observers and various intergovernmental organizations, including the funds, programmes and specialized agencies of the United Nations system, as well as the major groups representing all the regions of the world,

Noting with interest the partnership initiatives announced by some Governments, international organizations and major groups at the International Meeting, as well as those already undertaken,

Welcoming the decision taken by the Commission on Sustainable Development at its thirteenth session to devote one day of the review sessions of the Commission to the review of the implementation of the Mauritius Strategy for Implementation, focusing on that year's thematic cluster, as well as on any new developments in the sustainable development efforts of small island developing States using existing modalities, and to request the Secretary-General to submit a report to the Commission at its review session on progress and obstacles to sustainable development in small island developing States, including recommendations to enhance the implementation of the Mauritius Strategy,

Recognizing that it is crucial to mobilize resources from all sources for the effective implementation of the Mauritius Strategy for Implementation,

Expressing its profound gratitude to the Government and the people of Mauritius for the excellent arrangements made for hosting the International Meeting, for the hospitality extended to the participants and for the facilities, staff and services placed at their disposal,

Expressing its appreciation to the Secretariat of the United Nations, including the Secretary-General of the International Meeting, the specialized agencies, the United Nations regional commissions, funds and programmes, and donor countries as well as those countries that contributed to the Trust Fund for Small Island Developing States, for their contribution to the success of the International Meeting,

Also expressing its appreciation to the Facilitator of the outcomes of the International Meeting,

Having considered the report of the International Meeting,

1. *Takes note* of the note by the Secretary-General transmitting the report of the International Meeting to Review the Implementation of the Programme of Action for the Sustainable Development of Small Island Developing States;

2. *Endorses* the Mauritius Declaration and the Mauritius Strategy for the Further Implementation of the Programme of Action for the Sustainable Development of Small Island Developing States;

3. *Welcomes* the renewed commitment of the international community to the implementation of the Programme of Action for the Sustainable Development of Small Island Developing States;

4. *Urges* Governments and all relevant international and regional organizations, United Nations funds and programmes, the specialized agencies, regional economic commissions, international financial institutions, the Global Environment Facility, as well as other intergovernmental organizations and major groups, to take timely actions to ensure the effective implementation of and follow-up to the Mauritius Declaration and the Mauritius Strategy for Implementation;

5. *Calls for* the full and effective implementation of the commitments, programmes and targets adopted at the International Meeting and, to this end, for fulfilment of the provisions for the means of implementation, as contained in the Mauritius Strategy for Implementation;

6. *Encourages* the implementation of partnership initiatives, within the framework of the Mauritius Strategy for Implementation, in support of the sustainable development of small island developing States;

7. *Recommends* that the outcomes of the International Meeting be taken into consideration at the High-level Plenary Meeting of the General Assembly, to be held from 14 to 16 September 2005, and in its preparatory process;

8. *Requests* the Secretary-General, through the Department of Economic and Social Affairs of the Secretariat, to articulate a plan with recommendations for action and proposed activities for the coordinated and coherent implementation of the Mauritius Strategy for Implementation by the relevant United Nations bodies, the specialized agencies, regional commissions and other organizations of the United Nations system within their respective mandates, and to report thereon to the General Assembly at its sixtieth session;

9. *Supports* the convening by the Department of Economic and Social Affairs of regional meetings of small island developing States in 2005 or 2006, in partnership with relevant regional organizations and stakeholders, for the follow-up to the implementation of the Mauritius Strategy for Implementation, funded from voluntary contributions, and in this regard encourages Member States to contribute to the Trust Fund for Small Island Developing States;

10. *Reiterates its request* to the Secretary-General to strengthen the Small Island Developing States Unit of the Department of Economic and Social Affairs, as called for in its resolutions 57/262 of 20 December 2002, 58/213 A of 23 December 2003 and 59/229 of 22 December 2004 and taking into account paragraph 7 of the present resolution, and urges the Secretary-General to ensure that the Unit is sufficiently and sustainably staffed without delay to undertake its broad range of mandated functions with a view to facilitating the full and effective implementation of the Mauritius Strategy for Implementation, within existing resources, including by redeploying resources;

11. *Requests* the relevant agencies of the United Nations system, within their respective mandates, to mainstream the Mauritius Strategy for Implementation further in their work programmes and to establish a focal point for small island developing States within their respective secretariats;

12. *Decides* to include in the provisional agenda of its sixtieth session under the item entitled "Sustainable development", a sub-item entitled "Follow-up to and implementation of the Mauritius Strategy for the Further Implementation of the Programme of Action for the Sustainable Development of Small Island Developing States".

Conference follow-up. In response to General Assembly resolution 59/311 (see above), the Secretary-General submitted an October report [A/60/401], which described a comprehensive UN system approach to promote and strengthen implementation of the Mauritius Strategy by national, regional and international stakeholders. The report summarized actual and proposed programming support and workplans of UN System organizations and bodies under the respective headings of the Mauritius Strategy. Among the activities identified for advancing the implementation of the Mauritius Strategy were regional meetings for the Caribbean (Saint Kitts and Nevis, 5-7 October), the Pacific (Samoa, 17-19 October) and for the Atlantic, Indian Ocean, Mediterranean and South China Seas (Seychelles, 26-28 October) to facilitate broad consultation on mechanisms and strategies and allow for the pursuit of partnership initiatives with civil society, regional institutions, the UN system and the donor community.

GENERAL ASSEMBLY ACTION

On 22 December [meeting 68], the General Assembly adopted **resolution 60/194** [draft: A/60/488/ Add.2] without vote [agenda item 52 (*b*)].

Follow-up to and implementation of the Mauritius Strategy for the Further Implementation of the Programme of Action for the Sustainable Development of Small Island Developing States

The General Assembly,

Reaffirming the Declaration of Barbados and the Programme of Action for the Sustainable Development of Small Island Developing States, adopted by the Global Conference on the Sustainable Develop-

ment of Small Island Developing States, and recalling its resolution 49/122 of 19 December 1994 on the Global Conference,

Reaffirming also the Mauritius Declaration and the Mauritius Strategy for the Further Implementation of the Programme of Action for the Sustainable Development of Small Island Developing States ("Mauritius Strategy for Implementation"), adopted by the International Meeting to Review the Implementation of the Programme of Action for the Sustainable Development of Small Island Developing States on 14 January 2005, and recalling its resolution 59/311 of 14 July 2005, in which it endorsed the outcomes of the International Meeting,

Recalling the 2005 World Summit Outcome,

Welcoming the decision taken by the Commission on Sustainable Development at its thirteenth session to devote one day of its review sessions to the review of the implementation of the Mauritius Strategy for Implementation, focusing on that year's thematic cluster, as well as on any new developments in the sustainable development efforts of small island developing States using existing modalities, and to request the Secretary-General to submit a report to the Commission at its review session on progress in and obstacles to sustainable development in small island developing States, including recommendations to enhance the implementation of the Mauritius Strategy for Implementation,

Recognizing that it is crucial to mobilize resources from all sources for the effective implementation of the Mauritius Strategy for Implementation,

1. *Takes note* of the report of the Secretary-General;

2. *Welcomes* the renewed commitment of the international community to the implementation of the Programme of Action for the Sustainable Development of Small Island Developing States;

3. *Urges* Governments and all relevant international and regional organizations, United Nations funds, programmes, specialized agencies and regional commissions, international financial institutions and the Global Environment Facility, as well as other intergovernmental organizations and major groups, to take timely action for the effective implementation of and follow-up to the Mauritius Declaration and the Mauritius Strategy for Implementation, including the further development and operationalization of concrete projects and programmes;

4. *Calls for* the full and effective implementation of the commitments, programmes and targets adopted at the International Meeting to Review the Implementation of the Programme of Action for the Sustainable Development of Small Island Developing States and, to this end, for the fulfilment of the provisions for the means of implementation, as contained in the Mauritius Strategy for Implementation, and encourages small island developing States and their development partners to continue to consult widely in order to develop further concrete projects and programmes for the implementation of the Mauritius Strategy for Implementation;

5. *Encourages* the implementation of partnership initiatives, within the framework of the Mauritius Strategy for Implementation, in support of the sustainable development of small island developing States;

6. *Notes with interest* the convening by the Department of Economic and Social Affairs of the Secretariat, pursuant to resolution 59/311, of regional meetings of small island developing States, held in Saint Kitts and Nevis, Samoa and Seychelles, as well as the interregional meeting of small island developing States, held in Rome in November 2005, and requests the Secretary-General to transmit the reports of the regional and interregional meetings to the Commission on Sustainable Development at its fourteenth session;

7. *Notes* the recent efforts to strengthen the Small Island Developing States Unit in the Department of Economic and Social Affairs, and urges the Secretary-General to ensure that the Unit is sufficiently and sustainably staffed to undertake its broad range of mandated functions with a view to ensuring the full and effective implementation of the Mauritius Strategy for Implementation, within existing resources, including by redeploying resources;

8. *Requests* the relevant agencies of the United Nations system, within their respective mandates, to mainstream, as appropriate, the Mauritius Strategy for Implementation in their work programmes and to establish a focal point for matters related to small island developing States within their respective secretariats;

9. *Requests* the Secretary-General to submit a report to the General Assembly at its sixty-first session on the follow-up to and implementation of the Mauritius Strategy for Implementation;

10. *Decides* to include in the provisional agenda of its sixty-first session, under the item entitled "Sustainable development", the sub-item entitled "Follow-up to and implementation of the Mauritius Strategy for the Further Implementation of the Programme of Action for the Sustainable Development of Small Island Developing States".

Landlocked developing countries

Report of Secretary-General. In response to General Assembly resolution 59/245 [YUN 2004, p. 861], the Secretary-General submitted an August report [A/60/287 & Corr.1] on the progress made by the UN system and other organizations in implementing the Almaty Programme of Action: Addressing the Special Needs of Landlocked Developing Countries within a New Global Framework for Transit Transport Cooperation for Landlocked and Transit Developing Countries. The Programme of Action was adopted by the International Ministerial Conference of Landlocked and Transit Developing Countries and Donor Countries and International Financial and Development Institutions on Transit Transport Cooperation (Almaty, Kazakhstan, 28-29 August 2003) [YUN 2003, p. 875].

The report analysed the overall socio-economic situation in landlocked developing countries and action taken to implement the Almaty Programme of Action in the priority areas of fundamental transit policy issues, infrastructure development and maintenance, inter-

national trade and trade facilitiation, international support measures and implementation and review of the United Nations.

In its conclusions and recommendations, the report stated that high trade transaction costs, due to their lack of access to the sea, isolation and remoteness from international markets, remained the main factors responsible for the marginalization of landlocked and transit developing countries in international trade and for their poor economic performance. The international community should provide greater market access for goods originating in landlocked and transit developing countries to mitigate the high transaction costs stemming from their geographical disadvantages. Technical assistance should be extended to them to ensure their effective participation in WTO trade negotiations, particularly those related to trade facilitation. The triangular arrangements promoting South-South cooperation between landlocked and transit developing States should be fully utilized. UN system organizations should intensify efforts to articulate a methodology to measure progress in establishing efficient transit transport systems, and should also provide technical assistance in transit transport. With official development assistance (ODA) as the major source of investment in infrastructure development in LDCs, donor countries and financial and development institutions were invited to provide greater financial resources to transit transport infrastructure projects in landlocked and transit developing countries, and to contribute to the trust fund set up to facilitate follow-up and implementation of the outcome of the Almaty Programme of Action.

UNCTAD report. UNCTAD submitted a July report [UNCTAD/LDC/2005/3(PART II)], in response to a request contained in the communiqué of the Fifth Annual Ministerial Meeting of Landlocked Developing Countries [YUN 2004, p. 861] for help in preparing for a meeting of trade ministers on their effective participation in the new round of WTO trade negotiations (Doha Development Round). The report provided key elements of a road map for landlocked and transit developing countries' participation in WTO negotiations. It analysed the situation of landlocked and transit developing countries in the international trading system and made proposals for long-term policy strategies to mitigate the effects of remoteness from world markets and to address related constraints.

Communications. On 29 April [A/60/75], Kazakhstan transmitted the joint communiqué of the High-level Meeting on the Role of International, Regional and Subregional Organizations in the Implementation of the Almaty Programme of Action (Almaty, 29-31 March). On 25 August [A/60/308], Paraguay transmitted the report of the Meeting of the Ministers of Landlocked Developing Countries Responsible for Trade (Asunción, 9-10 August), and the Asunción Platform for the Doha Development Round. On 26 September [A/C.2/60/2], the Lao People's Democratic Republic transmitted the ministerial communiqué of the Sixth Annual Ministerial Meeting of Landlocked Developing Countries (New York, 19 September). On 4 October [A/60/419], Azerbaijan, Georgia and Turkey transmitted the joint declaration on the "Kars-Akhalkalaki-Tbilisi-Baky new railway connection" project (Baky, 25 May).

GENERAL ASSEMBLY ACTION

On 22 December [meeting 68], the General Assembly, on the recommendation of the Second Committee [A/60/491/Add.2], adopted **resolution 60/208** without vote [agenda item 55 (b)].

Specific actions related to the particular needs and problems of landlocked developing countries: outcome of the International Ministerial Conference of Landlocked and Transit Developing Countries and Donor Countries and International Financial and Development Institutions on Transit Transport Cooperation

The General Assembly,

Recalling its resolutions 56/180 of 21 December 2001, 57/242 of 20 December 2002, 58/201 of 23 December 2003 and 59/245 of 22 December 2004,

Recalling also the United Nations Millennium Declaration,

Recalling further the 2005 World Summit Outcome,

Recognizing that the lack of territorial access to the sea, aggravated by remoteness from world markets, and prohibitive transit costs and risks impose serious constraints on export earnings, private capital inflow and domestic resource mobilization of landlocked developing countries and therefore adversely affect their overall growth and socio-economic development,

Recognizing also that landlocked developing countries, with their small and vulnerable economies, are among the poorest of developing countries, and noting that, of the thirty-one landlocked developing countries, sixteen are also classified by the United Nations as least developed countries,

Recalling the Almaty Declaration and the Almaty Programme of Action: Addressing the Special Needs of Landlocked Developing Countries within a New Global Framework for Transit Transport Cooperation for Landlocked and Transit Developing Countries,

Recalling also the New Partnership for Africa's Development, an initiative for accelerating regional economic cooperation and development as most landlocked and transit developing countries are located in Africa,

Noting with interest the Meeting of the Ministers of Landlocked Developing Countries Responsible for Trade, held in Asunción, on 9 and 10 August 2005,

which adopted the Asunción Platform for the Doha Development Round,

Taking note of the Communiqué of the Sixth Annual Ministerial Meeting of Landlocked Developing Countries, held at United Nations Headquarters on 19 September 2005,

1. *Takes note* of the report of the Secretary-General on the implementation of the Almaty Programme of Action: Addressing the Special Needs of Landlocked Developing Countries within a New Global Framework for Transit Transport Cooperation for Landlocked and Transit Developing Countries;

2. *Recognizes* the special needs and challenges faced by landlocked developing countries, and therefore reaffirms the commitment to urgently address those needs and challenges through the full, timely and effective implementation of the Almaty Programme of Action;

3. *Reaffirms* the right of access of landlocked countries to and from the sea and freedom of transit through the territory of transit countries by all means of transport, in accordance with the applicable rules of international law;

4. *Also reaffirms* that transit countries, in the exercise of their full sovereignty over their territory, have the right to take all measures necessary to ensure that the rights and facilities provided for landlocked countries in no way infringe their legitimate interests;

5. *Invites* Member States, organizations of the United Nations system and other relevant international, regional and subregional organizations and multilateral financial and development institutions to implement the specific actions in the five priorities agreed upon in the Almaty Programme of Action;

6. *Invites* donor countries and multilateral and regional financial and development institutions, in particular the World Bank, the Asian Development Bank, the African Development Bank and the Inter-American Development Bank, to provide landlocked and transit developing countries with appropriate financial and technical assistance in the form of grants or concessional loans for the construction, maintenance and improvement of their transport, storage and other transit-related facilities, including alternative routes and improved communications, to promote subregional, regional and interregional projects and programmes;

7. *Recognizes* that most transit countries are themselves developing countries often of broadly similar economic structure and beset by similar scarcity of resources, including the lack of adequate transit transport infrastructure;

8. *Emphasizes* that assistance for the improvement of transit transport facilities and services should be integrated into the overall economic development strategies of the landlocked and transit developing countries and that donor countries should consequently take into account the requirements for the long-term restructuring of the economies of the landlocked developing countries;

9. *Stresses* the need for the implementation of the São Paulo Consensus, adopted at the eleventh session of the United Nations Conference on Trade and Development, held in São Paulo, Brazil, from 13 to 18 June 2004, in particular paragraphs 66 and 84 thereof, by

the relevant international organizations and donors in a multi-stakeholder approach;

10. *Encourages* Member States to support the special needs of landlocked developing countries within a new global framework for transit transport cooperation for landlocked and transit developing countries, as contained in the Almaty Programme of Action, with respect to trade facilitation, consistent with the decision adopted by the General Council of the World Trade Organization on 1 August 2004, according to their individual needs;

11. *Invites* the relevant organizations of the United Nations system and other international organizations, including the regional commissions, the United Nations Development Programme, the United Nations Conference on Trade and Development, the World Bank, the World Customs Organization, the World Trade Organization and the International Maritime Organization, to integrate the Almaty Programme of Action into their relevant programmes of work, encourages them to continue their support to the landlocked and transit developing countries, inter alia, through well-coordinated and coherent technical assistance programmes in transit transport, and in this regard takes note of the joint communique adopted at the High-level Meeting on the Role of International, Regional and Subregional Organizations in the Implementation of the Almaty Programme of Action, convened by the Office of the High Representative for the Least Developed Countries, Landlocked Developing Countries and Small Island Developing States of the Secretariat and hosted by the Government of Kazakhstan in Almaty from 29 to 31 March 2005;

12. *Requests* the United Nations system organizations, particularly the Office of the High Representative for the Least Developed Countries, Landlocked Developing Countries and Small Island Developing States and regional commissions, to continue their efforts to establish effective indicators to measure progress in the implementation of the Almaty Programme of Action;

13. *Encourages* the United Nations Conference on Trade and Development, in particular the Division for Services Infrastructure for Development and Trade Efficiency and the Special Programme on the Least Developed Countries, Landlocked Developing Countries and Small Island Developing States, to continue its technical assistance activities and analytical work related to transit transport cooperation between landlocked and transit developing countries;

14. *Requests* the Office of the High Representative for the Least Developed Countries, Landlocked Developing Countries and Small Island Developing States, in accordance with the mandate given by the General Assembly in its resolution 56/227 of 24 December 2001 and in the Almaty Programme of Action and the Almaty Declaration, to continue its cooperation and coordination with organizations within the United Nations system, particularly those engaged in operational activities on the ground in landlocked and transit developing countries, to ensure effective implementation of the Almaty Programme of Action in line with Assembly resolution 57/270 B of 23 June 2003, and also requests the Office to continue to carry out advocacy work to mobilize international awareness and fo-

cus attention on the implementation of the Almaty Programme of Action;

15. *Requests*, in this regard, the Secretary-General to take the necessary measures, within existing resources, including through reprioritization, to provide the Office with adequate resources so as to allow it to effectively carry out its added mandate as stipulated in the Almaty Programme of Action;

16. *Invites* donor countries and the international financial and development institutions to make voluntary contributions to the trust fund established by the Secretary-General to support the activities related to the follow-up to the implementation of the outcome of the Almaty International Ministerial Conference;

17. *Decides* to include in the provisional agenda of its sixty-first session the item entitled "Specific actions related to the particular needs and problems of landlocked developing countries: outcome of the International Ministerial Conference of Landlocked and Transit Developing Countries and Donor Countries and International Financial and Development Institutions on Transit Transport Cooperation";

18. *Requests* the Secretary-General to submit to the General Assembly at its sixty-first session a report on progress made in the implementation of the Almaty Programme of Action and the present resolution.

Poor mountain countries

In response to General Assembly resolution 58/216 [YUN 2003, p. 1063], the Secretary-General submitted a September report [A/60/309] on the status of sustainable development in mountain regions, with an analysis of future challenges and made recommendations on ways to promote and effectively sustain development in mountain regions.

The report found that, despite increased awareness and the achievement of many positive results, key challenges were still being faced by fragile mountain ecosystems to attain sustainable development and alleviate poverty, consistent with the targets of the MDGs, including the growing demand for water and other natural resources, the consequences of global climate change, the growth of tourism, increasing rates of migration, conflicts and pressures of industry, mining and agriculture in a world of increased globalization. Higher levels of funding and investment in mountain areas, better coordinated cooperation at all levels and a stronger enabling environment with more supportive laws, policies and institutions were required. The report described action taken at the national level in Africa, Asia, Europe, Latin America and the Near East to achieve progress in sustainable mountain development, regional cooperation and transboundary approaches and international initiatives. It also looked at communications and networking, mountain partnership, education, research and resource mobilization and funding.

The report recommended possible courses of action the Assembly might take to help poor mountain countries.

The Assembly, in **resolution 60/198** of 22 December, invited the UN system, international financial institutions, the Global Environment Facility, relevant UN conventions and their funding mechanisms, civil society and the private sector, to provide support, including financial, to local national and international programmes and projects for sustainable development in mountain regions.

Chapter II

Operational activities for development

In 2005, the UN system continued to provide development assistance to developing countries and countries with economies in transition through the United Nations Development Programme (UNDP), the central UN funding body for technical assistance. UNDP income in 2005 amounted to $5.1 billion, a 21 per cent increase over 2004. Total expenditure for all programme activities and support costs in 2005 was $4.4 billion, compared with $3.6 billion the previous year. Technical cooperation funded through other sources included $48.4 million provided through the programme executed by the UN Department of Economic and Social Affairs, $170.5 million through the United Nations Fund for International Partnerships, and $27.3 million through the United Nations Capital Development Fund (UNCDF).

In May, the General Assembly confirmed the appointment of Kemal Dervis (Turkey) as UNDP Administrator for a four-year term, beginning on 15 August.

The Secretary-General reported in May on an appropriate management process, in the form of a matrix, for the full implementation of resolution of 59/250 on the 2004 triennial comprehensive policy review of UN operational activities for development. The matrix included implementation targets for the UN system, actions planned to pursue those targets, specific system entities responsible for those actions and the time frames for their execution. In July, the Economic and Social Council requested the Secretary-General to update the matrix, including analytical reporting on results and outcomes achieved.

The United Nations Office for Project Services (UNOPS) had a record project delivery of $888.2 million, exceeding the approved targets for the year by 35.5 per cent. In September, the UNDP/United Nations Population Fund (UNFPA) Executive Board approved an action plan for restoring the viability of UNOPS as a separate, self-financing service provider in the UN system.

The High-level Committee on South-South Cooperation, at its May/June meeting, reviewed progress in implementing the 1978 Buenos Aires Plan of Action for Promoting and Implementing Technical Cooperation among Developing Countries (TCDC) and the new directions strategy for TCDC. In December, the Assembly invited

UNDP to rename the Voluntary Trust Fund for the Promotion of South-South Cooperation as the United Nations Fund for South-South Cooperation, and to designate it as the main UN trust fund for promoting and supporting South-South and triangular initiatives.

The United Nations Volunteers programme, administered by UNDP, expanded for the ninth consecutive year, with 8,122 volunteers carrying out 8,470 assignments in 144 countries. The Assembly, in a December resolution on follow-up to the International Year of Volunteers (2001), called for UN system organizations and bodies to integrate volunteerism in its various forms into their policies, programmes and reports.

In January, the UNDP/UNFPA Executive Board considered further options for a future strategic niche and a new business model for UNCDF, and decided to maintain it as an independent organization focused on reducing poverty and achieving the Millennium Development Goals in least developed countries (LDCs). In May, the UNDP Administrator presented the UNCDF 2005-2007 business plan, which proposed a trust fund for investing in LDCs.

System-wide activities

Operational activities segment of Economic and Social Council

The Economic and Social Council, during its 2005 substantive session [A/60/3], considered the question of operational activities of the United Nations for international development cooperation at meetings held from 8 to 12 July, as decided by the Council on 1 March (**decision 2005/210**); a further meeting was held on 20 July, to complete consideration of a draft resolution on progress in the implementation of General Assembly resolution 59/250 [YUN 2004, p. 868] on the triennial comprehensive policy review of operational activities for development of the UN system (see p. 955). On 4 February (**decision 2005/205**), the Council decided to devote the work of the operational activities segment to progress in the implementation of resolution 59/250. The Council held discussions on South-South cooperation for development (see p. 982); and the reports of the Executive Boards of the United Nations Development Programme (UNDP)/United Nations Population Fund (UNFPA), the United Nations Children's Fund (UNICEF) and the World Food Programme (WFP).

Among the documents before the Council were reports of the Secretary-General on funding options and modalities for financing operational activities for development of the UN system [A/60/83-E/2005/72], comprehensive statistical data on operational activities for development for 2003 [A/60/74-E/2005/57], and the management process for the implementation of resolution 59/250 [E/2005/58], as well as the report of the High-level Committee on South-South Cooperation [A/60/39] (see sections below).

On 8 July, the Council held an interactive dialogue on introducing operational reforms in the UN development system, in pursuit of the internationally agreed development goals, including the Millennium Development Goals (MDGs) [YUN 2000, p. 51]. On 11 July, it held a panel discussion on funding arrangements for achieving those goals, including those contained in the Millennium Declaration [ibid., p. 49]: alternative options and modalities for financing UN system operational activities for development; and a dialogue with heads of UN funds and programmes on strengthening the resident coordination system, programme alignment, the role of regional structures in supporting operational effectiveness, and sector programme and national capacity development.

Implementation of resolution 59/250

In May [E/2005/58], the Secretary-General, in response to resolution 59/250 on the 2004 triennial policy review of operational activities for development of the UN system [YUN 2004, p. 868], reported on an appropriate management process for the full implementation of that resolution. The management process, set out in the form of a matrix, provided details about the issues addressed in the resolution, corresponding targets for the UN system as a whole and/or its components, concrete actions planned to pursue those targets, specific entities of the system that were responsible for those actions, and the time frames for their execution. The elements of the matrix were grouped by individual themes. They included the basic approach to the role and functioning of UN system development cooperation to support national development strategies and priorities, and the achievements of internationally agreed development goals; funding for UN operational activities and statistical reporting; capacity-building; transaction costs and effi-

ciency; coherence, effectiveness and relevance of operational activities for development; country-level capacity of the UN system; evaluation of operational activities for development; regional dimensions of operational activities; South-South cooperation and development of national capacities; gender; transition from relief to development; and additional reporting requirements. The matrix resulted from extensive consultations between the Secretariat and the UN system, including close collaboration with the United Nations Development Group (UNDG) and the UN System Chief Executives Board for Coordination (CEB), and reflected the several initiatives promoted to implement relevant parts of the resolution.

The Secretary-General said that the management process should assist the Economic and Social Council in fulfilling its responsibility for improving the quality and impact of UN operational activities, promoting an integrated approach, and ensuring that policy directives formulated by the General Assembly at the triennial comprehensive policy review were implemented on a system-wide basis. The management process should be reviewed in conjunction with the work programme for the implementation of reforms by UN system funds, programmes and specialized agencies to further simplify and harmonize their rules and procedures in compliance with resolution 59/250, a report on which was being prepared in consultation with all UNDG members and would be submitted separately to the Council. The key aim of UN system development support was to respond flexibly to the needs of developing countries, shaping operational activities to better respond to their demands, in accordance with their policies and priorities. Through its operational activities for development, the UN system could contribute significantly to the country-level implementation of the commitments made in the 2000 Millennium Declaration, adopted by the Assembly in resolution 55/2 [YUN 2000, p. 49], and other conferences and summits. However, the system should align its activities to well-defined national development priorities. It was crucial that economic, social, environmental and humanitarian factors were taken into account in building stable and sustainable conditions for economic growth and social development.

The Secretary-General, in a May report [A/60/74-E/2005/57] issued to complement his report on the management process for the implementation of resolution 59/250, provided detailed data on resources channelled through, and spent by UN system organizations for 2003 and previous years, as well as a review of the multi-year trends in UN system operational activities for development from 1993 to 2003.

A June report of the Secretary-General [A/60/83-E/2005/72] examined various options for funding UN system operational activities for development, in order to increase its predictability, long-term stability and adequacy, while preserving the advantages of current funding modalities. It was intended to stimulate debate on funding modalities for the operational activities of the system as a whole, as a key component of the overall effort to further the implementation of the global development agenda emerging from UN conferences and summits.

The report described two alternative funding models: the negotiated replenishment used by the International Fund for Agricultural Development (IFAD) (see p. 1590) and the voluntary indicative scale of contributions applied by the United Nations Environment Programme on a trial basis. In IFAD's negotiated replenishment, contributions were first estimated on the basis of a review of the adequacy of available resources, after which the Governing Council might invite Fund members to make additional contributions. While complex, the negotiated replenishment modality had proved capable, given the necessary political will and the right environment, of mobilizing a significant volume of resources for the International Development Association and the Global Fund to fight AIDS, Tuberculosis and Malaria, which used it.

UNEP's experimental voluntary indicative scale of contributions helped guide Member States in setting their levels of voluntary contributions for programme expenditures. Experience with the indicative scale had been positive and led to a significant increase both in the number of countries making voluntary contributions to UNEP and in the level of their contributions.

The report also discussed the expansion of supplementary funding as a short-term solution and its consequences, future challenges and options with regard to UN development funding.

CEB action. The CEB High-level Committee on Programmes (HLCP), at its ninth session (Rome, 23-25 February) [CEB/2005/4], decided to appoint a task group to review the practical implication of resolution 59/250 relating to the CEB/HLCP work programme and to identify ways for HLCP and UNDG to complement each other's work in advancing the resolution's objectives. HLCP approved the terms of reference for the task group at its 2005 retreat (Manhasset, New York, United States, 19-21 July) [CEB/2005/6]. At its tenth session (Frascati, Italy, 6-8 October) [CEB/2005/7], the task group submitted a progress report, which contained two sets of proposals on

capacity development and on the evaluation of UN system operational activities for development. A revised proposal for the two distinct areas was presented and endorsed by HLCP. The Committee agreed to launch an analysis of UN system capacity development efforts and to promote the formulation of an overall policy statement for CEB's endorsement, which should provide broad guidance to all CEB member organizations in supporting the evaluation function and encouraging wide collaboration.

ECONOMIC AND SOCIAL COUNCIL ACTION

On 20 July [meeting 33], the Economic and Social Council adopted **resolution 2005/7** [draft: E/2005/L.29] without vote [agenda item 3 (a)].

Progress in the implementation of General Assembly resolution 59/250 on the triennial comprehensive policy review of operational activities for development of the United Nations system

The Economic and Social Council,

Recalling General Assembly resolutions 44/211 of 22 December 1989, 47/199 of 22 December 1992, 50/120 of 20 December 1995, 52/203 of 18 December 1997, 52/12 B of 19 December 1997, 53/192 of 15 December 1998, 56/201 of 21 December 2001 and 59/250 of 22 December 2004, Economic and Social Council resolutions 2002/29 of 25 July 2002, 2003/3 of 11 July 2003 and 2004/5 of 12 July 2004 and other relevant resolutions,

Recalling also the importance of the triennial comprehensive policy review of operational activities, through which the General Assembly establishes key system-wide policy orientations for the development cooperation and country-level modalities of the United Nations system,

Reaffirming its role in providing coordination and guidance to the United Nations development system to ensure that those policy orientations are implemented on a system-wide basis, in accordance with General Assembly resolutions 48/162 of 20 December 1993, 50/227 of 24 May 1996 and 57/270 B of 23 June 2003,

Reaffirming also that the fundamental characteristics of operational activities for development of the United Nations system should be, inter alia, their universal, voluntary and grant-based nature, their neutrality and their multilateralism and their ability to respond to the development needs of recipient countries in a flexible manner, and that operational activities are carried out for the benefit of recipient countries, at the request of those countries and in accordance with their own policies and priorities for development,

Stressing that the purpose of reform is to make the United Nations development system more efficient and effective in supporting developing countries to achieve the internationally agreed development goals, on the basis of their national development strategies, and stressing also that reform efforts should enhance organizational efficiency and achieve concrete development results,

Emphasizing that operational activities for development of the United Nations system should be valued and assessed on the basis of their impact on recipient countries as contributions to enhance their capacity to pursue poverty eradication, sustained economic growth and sustainable development,

1. *Takes note* of the report of the Secretary-General on the management process for the implementation of General Assembly resolution 59/250 on the triennial comprehensive policy review of operational activities for development of the United Nations system, and welcomes the efforts to establish the management process for the implementation of the resolution, as contained in that report;

2. *Notes* the response of the United Nations system in undertaking initiatives to implement resolution 59/250, as specified in the actions, targets, benchmarks and time frames identified at the agency and inter-agency levels that are contained in that report;

3. *Requests* the Secretary-General, in response to paragraph 102 of resolution 59/250, to update the matrix contained in that report, including analytical reporting on results and outcomes achieved through the implementation of all actions outlined in the report;

4. *Encourages* the use, within the matrix, of quantifiable targets and measurable benchmarks, with well-defined time frames at the system level, in accordance with resolution 59/250, taking into account section III of the resolution on capacity-building in its entirety, as well as increasing system-wide capacity in support of recipient countries and enabling and facilitating the access of recipient countries to the full range of services and accumulated experience available throughout the entire United Nations system, including the regional commissions, as appropriate and consistent with their mandates;

5. *Takes note* of the work programme related to the coordination of operational activities for development for 2005;

6. *Takes note also* of the report of the Secretary-General on funding options and modalities for financing operational activities for development of the United Nations system;

7. *Looks forward* to further consideration of that report, in accordance with paragraph 24 of resolution 59/250;

8. *Takes note* of the report of the Secretary-General on comprehensive statistical data on operational activities for development for 2003;

9. *Requests* the Secretary-General to further refine the data contained in that report to better reflect funding for operational activities for development, including a better distinction between contributions made for humanitarian assistance and for long-term development cooperation, and expenditures and actual contributions as received and channelled through the United Nations funds, programmes and specialized agencies and the Secretariat;

10. *Also requests* the Secretary-General to make use of the annual statistical compendium on operational activities for development submitted to the Council at the operational activities segment of its substantive session in its new format, as adopted in accordance with paragraph 22 of resolution 59/250;

11. *Reaffirms* the necessity for the full implementation by the United Nations funds and programmes of the relevant provisions of resolution 59/250.

The Second (Economic and Financial) Committee considered the Secretary-General's reports on comprehensive statistical data on operational activities for development for 2003 (see p. 955) and on funding options and modalities for financing operational activities for development of the UN system (see p. 956) on 9 November.

On 22 December (**decision 60/546**), the General Assembly took note of the Committee's report on operational activities for development [A/60/493].

Report of UNDP Administrator and UNFPA Executive Director. In response to resolution 59/250 [YUN 2004, p. 868], the UNDP Administrator and the UNFPA Executive Director submitted, in December [E/2006/5], a report on joint UNDP/UNFPA progress towards the implementation of resolution 59/250 and specific UNDP and UNFPA activities.

The UNDG working group on capacity development, in which both UNDP and UNFPA participated, was defining a framework that would enable UN country teams to engage in structured capacity development for national counterparts, which was essential if developing countries were to achieve the internationally agreed development goals, including the MDGs [YUN 2000, p. 51]. The working group was developing a system-wide matrix; mapping potential niches for the United Nations in country-level capacity development initiatives; and compiling an inventory of existing capacity development tools, which, by mid-2006, would become part of the operational methodologies to be used by country teams.

In July, UNDP and UNFPA, along with their UNDG partners, adopted an action plan to implement the Paris Declaration on Aid Effectiveness, adopted by the High-level Forum on Aid Effectiveness in March, which addressed the alignment of the work of the United Nations with national development plans, the strengthening of national capacities in a changing aid environment and increased efforts to strengthen and use national systems. It would follow up on commitments made in the Rome Declaration on harmonization adopted in 2003 [YUN 2003, p. 938]; advise country teams of their role in the new aid environment; and serve as a tool to monitor the UNDG response. In February, UNDG endorsed a common position on the role of the United Nations in sector support and, in April, launched a cash transfer framework that was consistent with the Paris Declaration and which sought to reduce transaction costs for national partners.

The UNDG working group on joint programming established a database of joint programmes based on information provided by country offices and headquarters, covering approximately 150 joint programmes, over 30 of which began in 2005. The working group also oversaw a review of joint programme experiences in a number of countries.

To facilitate programmatic coherence, the UNDG Executive Committee requested UN country teams to review the timing of their programme cycles and, where necessary, readjust them to national cycles. The UNDG programme group would propose, in 2006, that UNDG adopt a single United Nations Development Assistance Framework (UNDAF) and its results matrix in lieu of multiple country programme documents, as a means of strengthening the role of the UNDAF as the basis for one coherent UN country programme. To ensure the quality of common country assessments (CCAs), UNDAF and UNDG developed a quality support and assurance system. UNDG members, including UNDP, reviewed the UNDAF documents completed in 2005, prepared five UNDAF good practice notes and enumerated 10 lessons from the review. UNDG forwarded the results to the country teams scheduled to begin their UNDAF exercises in September.

As called for in resolution 59/250, UNDG was developing an accountability framework for resident coordinators, along with systems for mutual resident coordinator and country team performance appraisal, reinforcing the notion of the resident coordinator as the principal UN representative in a country.

During the previous biennium, UNDP increased threefold its contribution of core resources to the funds allocated to the resident coordinator system, thus permitting the creation of a special $2.25 million fund to support countries in transition from relief to development. In 2005, those funds provided some 20 countries with strategic planning and coordination support for recovery and transition and were used to support technical missions.

As a follow-up to the 2005 World Summit (see p. 47), UNDP and UNFPA, together with their UNDG partners, prepared a common plan to support countries in their efforts to adopt, by 2006, national development strategies to achieve the internationally agreed development goals and objectives, including the MDGs, and to implement those strategies.

GENERAL ASSEMBLY ACTION

On 22 December [meeting 68], the General Assembly, on the recommendation of the Second Committee [A/60/493/Add.1], adopted **decision 60/547** by recorded vote (172-1-0) [agenda item 57].

Operational activities for development of the United Nations system

At its 68th plenary meeting, on 22 December 2005, the General Assembly, by a recorded vote of 172 to 1, with no abstentions, and on the recommendation of the Second Committee:

(*a*) Recalled its resolution 59/250 of 22 December 2004, as well as Economic and Social Council resolution 2005/7 of 20 July 2005 and other relevant resolutions;

(*b*) Took note of the reports of the Secretary-General on comprehensive statistical data on operational activities for development of the United Nations system for 2003 and on funding options and modalities for financing operational activities for development of the United Nations system, and decided to request the Economic and Social Council at its substantive session of 2006 to further consider the above-mentioned reports in conjunction with paragraph 102 of General Assembly resolution 59/250 on the evaluation of the full implementation of that resolution;

(*c*) Also took note of the report of the Joint Inspection Unit on some measures to improve overall performance of the United Nations system at the country level, the related note by the Secretary-General transmitting the comments of the United Nations System Chief Executives Board for Coordination on that report and the note by the Secretary-General transmitting the report of the Administrator of the United Nations Development Programme on the activities of the United Nations Development Fund for Women.

In favour: Afghanistan, Albania, Algeria, Andorra, Angola, Antigua and Barbuda, Argentina, Armenia, Australia, Austria, Azerbaijan, Bahamas, Bahrain, Bangladesh, Barbados, Belarus, Belgium, Belize, Benin, Bhutan, Bolivia, Botswana, Brazil, Brunei Darussalam, Bulgaria, Burkina Faso, Burundi, Cambodia, Cameroon, Canada, Cape Verde, Central African Republic, Chad, Chile, China, Colombia, Comoros, Congo, Costa Rica, Côte d'Ivoire, Croatia, Cuba, Cyprus, Czech Republic, Democratic People's Republic of Korea, Denmark, Djibouti, Dominica, Dominican Republic, Ecuador, Egypt, El Salvador, Eritrea, Estonia, Ethiopia, Fiji, Finland, France, Georgia, Germany, Ghana, Greece, Grenada, Guatemala, Guinea, Guinea-Bissau, Guyana, Haiti, Hungary, Iceland, India, Indonesia, Iran, Iraq, Ireland, Israel, Jamaica, Japan, Jordan, Kazakhstan, Kenya, Kuwait, Kyrgyzstan, Lao People's Democratic Republic, Latvia, Lebanon, Lesotho, Liberia, Libyan Arab Jamahiriya, Liechtenstein, Lithuania, Luxembourg, Madagascar, Malawi, Malaysia, Maldives, Mali, Malta, Marshall Islands, Mauritania, Mauritius, Mexico, Micronesia, Monaco, Mongolia, Morocco, Mozambique, Myanmar, Namibia, Nepal, Netherlands, New Zealand, Nicaragua, Nigeria, Norway, Oman, Pakistan, Palau, Panama, Papua New Guinea, Paraguay, Peru, Philippines, Poland, Portugal, Qatar, Republic of Korea, Republic of Moldova, Romania, Russian Federation, Rwanda, Saint Lucia, Saint Vincent and the Grenadines, Samoa, San Marino, Saudi Arabia, Senegal, Serbia and Montenegro, Sierra Leone, Singapore, Slovakia, Slovenia, Solomon Islands, South Africa, Spain, Sri Lanka, Sudan, Suriname, Swaziland, Sweden, Switzerland, Syrian Arab Republic, Tajikistan, Thailand, The former Yugoslav Republic of Macedonia, Togo, Trinidad and Tobago, Tunisia, Turkey, Tuvalu, Uganda, Ukraine, United Arab Emirates, United Kingdom, United Republic of Tanzania, Uruguay, Uzbekistan, Venezuela, Viet Nam, Yemen, Zambia, Zimbabwe.
Against: United States.
Abstaining: None.

Following the vote, the United States said that throughout the discussion on funding for the UN operational activities for development, its position had been that voluntary funding was the most effective way to ensure results and accountability. During the year, an attempt had been made to turn the discussion to consideration of various schemes to compel funding, including the so-called "voluntary indicative scales of contributions". Those schemes were unacceptable to the United States, as they were unrelated to performance results and accountability and incompatible with the voluntary funding principle for operational activities for development enshrined in previous resolutions.

Improving country-level UN system performance

The Economic and Social Council, at its 2005 substantive session (29 June–27 July), considered the report of the Joint Inspection Unit (JIU) on measures to improve overall performance of the UN system at the country level. The report, which was reissued for technical reasons, comprised two parts [A/60/125-E/2005/85 (part I) & Add.1 (part II)], the first providing a historical perspective on UN reform with a focus on operational activities, and the second addressing selected issues regarding the UN system's operational activities, especially in relation to country-level performance.

The report stated that, measured by funding levels, the United Nations, its funds, programmes and specialized agencies played only a modest role in international development, accounting for only $4,705 million in Members' core contributions, out of the latest published official development assistance (ODA) figure of $69 billion, or less than 7 per cent of net ODA, not including the amounts for lending and grant assistance at the disposal of the Bretton Woods institutions (the World Bank Group and the International Monetary Fund (IMF)). The relevance of the UN system's technical assistance and operational activities in 135 countries was perceived as its ability to link national and international goals, both in advice and implementation. The implementation of the agreed development agenda continued to be hampered by the different decision-making structures, policies, procedures, and institutional and management cultures of bilateral, regional and multilateral actors. The United Nations and its funds, programmes and specialized agencies were not always good examples of coherence and consistency. The issue, therefore, was how to define more clearly their respective roles in development and technical assistance, in order to organize the working relations of all parts of the UN development system, including the Bretton Woods institutions, and to optimize efficiency in planning, programming and implementation to benefit partner countries.

Part I of the report recommended that the General Assembly request the Secretary-General to provide, on the UN website, a full inventory of all the reform proposals made by the UN system to date as a possible part of the United Nations Intellectual History Project, which was to be set up by the UN Department of Public Information, in cooperation with other UN system organizations.

Part II dealt with the following issues and contained recommendations to address them: fostering a culture of partnership for improved analysis, planning, programme implementation and results; simplifying and harmonizing procedures; rationalizing field presence; monitoring progress in operational activities for development; and improving transparency.

Among the recommendations made were that the General Assembly should request UN system organizations to consider ways to achieve a single core country analysis, as well as a single comprehensive implementation plan with partner countries. Executive heads should explore the feasibility of further delegating authority to their field representation and improving simplification and harmonization within the system. The Assembly should de-link the functions of the resident coordinator and UNDP resident representative and change the designation process of the resident coordinator. The grade structure and skills profile of field representatives and other staff should be reviewed and a report thereon submitted to the Assembly and the Economic and Social Council. The governing bodies of UNDG organizations should request their respective executive heads to examine ways to further rationalize their field presence. The Assembly should establish at its sixtieth session a task force on operational activities to oversee, support and monitor developments in operational activities, as identified by the triennial comprehensive policy review of operational activities for development of the UN system. CEB should set up an inter-agency task force to deal with the issue of fundraising for extrabudgetary/non-core funding.

Annexed to part II of the report were a list of the 13 indicators, developed by the Development Assistance Committee of the Organisation for Economic Co-operation and Development (OECD/DAC), to identify progress in harmonization and alignment, and an explanation of UNDG's new tools and processes.

In November [A/60/125/Add.2-E/2005/85/Add.2], the Secretary-General transmitted to the Assembly his comments and those of CEB on the JIU report. CEB generally found part I of the report useful and informative. As to part II of the report, CEB agreed in principle that greater emphasis on inter-agency coordination at the policy level was indispensable for ensuring enhanced country-level effectiveness, and concurred with the JIU Inspector's view that efforts could be better focused on optimizing the efficiency of operations at that level. CEB agreed with the general theme of the report—the desirability of stronger field representation by UN system organizations with appropriate support mechanisms at their headquarters as one of the pillars of enhanced country-level coherence and coordination, but pointed out that a number of UN system organizations were already moving in that direction. In CEB's view, the analysis and most of the recommendations contained in the report did not take into account the significant differences between the core activities of the UN funds and programmes and those of the specialized agencies and, consequently, did not advance approaches to address those differences.

CEB agreed that the starting point of UN reform at the country level had to be a common, coherent programme, firmly grounded in national priorities and responding to national needs. However, there was no agreement on what constituted "effective" development policy, or how to gauge such policy.

CEB pointed out that several emerging trends in development cooperation were not identified in the report, including those relating to the increasing concentration of UN aid and grant assistance in the areas of humanitarian, social and emergency operations; the proliferation of nongovernmental organizations (NGOs) competing with UN system organizations at the country level; the enlargement of the scope of World Bank technical cooperation in all areas of the Organization's economic and social agendas; and the shifting role of UNDP from being the main funding source of the UN system to providing direct programme delivery in areas already covered by other UN system organizations. CEB noted that the sections of the report on the simplification and harmonization of procedures and on rationalizing field presence did not take into consideration the situation of the non-resident agencies. Several CEB members expressed concern that conferring formal authority and accountability for the development and monitoring of the UNDAF results matrix to the resident coordinator might erode the authority of the respective organizations' governing boards and executive heads for programme orientation and implementation. CEB also provided comments on the specific recommendations put forth in the JIU report.

On 9 November, the Second Committee considered the JIU report and the Secretary-General's note transmitting CEB's comments thereon. On 22 December, the Assembly took note of the Committee's report [A/60/493] on op-

erational activities for development (**decision 60/546**) (see p. 957), and the JIU report and the note by the Secretary-General thereon (**decision 60/547**) (see p. 958).

Financing of operational activities in 2004

UN system expenditures on operational activities, excluding loans through the World Bank Group, totalled $10 billion in 2004 [A/61/77-E/2006/59], the most recent year for which figures were available (compared with $9.7 billion in 2003). Of that amount, $2,899.6 million was distributed in development grants by WFP, $2,816.8 million by UNDP and UNDP-administered funds, $2,126.3 million by specialized agencies and other organizations from extrabudgetary sources, $1,343.6 million by UNICEF, $496.8 million by specialized agencies and other organizations from regular budgets, and $317.6 million by UNFPA.

The UNDP Administrator, in an August report on UN system technical cooperation expenditures in 2004 [DP/2005/34 & Add.1], said that, although 2004 marked the first year that technical cooperation to the developing world reached the $10 billion mark, it represented only a modest increase of 3.4 per cent over 2003. While WFP remained the key player, with $2.9 billion in expenditure, that figure represented a decline of 11.5 per cent from 2003. Expenditure increases of 17.3 per cent (at $2.8 billion) were posted by UNDP; specialized agencies, funds and programmes, 4.5 per cent (at $2.62 billion); UNICEF, 11.2 per cent (at $1.34 billion); and UNDP, 16.4 per cent (at $317.6 million).

By region, Africa was the largest recipient (25.6 per cent, or $2.6 billion), followed by the Arab States (25 per cent, or $2.5 billion), Asia and the Pacific (19.6 per cent, or $2 billion), Latin America and the Caribbean (16.1 per cent, or $1.6 billion) and Europe and the Commonwealth of Independent States (CIS) (4.3 per cent, or $430 million). Other global and interregional activities received 9.4 per cent or $940 million. Five countries received one quarter of total technical cooperation expenditure: Iraq ($1.1 billion), Afghanistan ($539 million), the Sudan ($506 million), Brazil ($289 million) and Ethiopia ($257 million). The health and humanitarian assistance sectors together accounted for 45.7 per cent of the total expenditure, or $4.7 billion.

In September [E/2005/35 (dec. 2005/42)], the UNDP/UNFPA Executive Board took note of the Administrator's report on technical cooperation expenditure for 2004.

At the 2005 United Nations Pledging Conference for Development Activities (New York, 11

November) [A/CONF.208/2005/L.1], Governments made pledges to UN programmes and funds concerned with development. The Conference noted that several Governments would communicate their pledges to the Secretary-General as soon as they were able to do so.

The Secretary-General provided a statement of contributions pledged or paid at the 2004 Pledging Conference, as at 30 June 2005, to 24 funds and programmes [A/CONF.208/2005/2]. The total amounted to some $800.2 million.

Technical cooperation through UNDP

The UNDP report on its performance and results for 2005, in implementation of the multi-year funding framework (MYFF) for 2004-2007 [DP/2006/17], described performance against core goals and organizational strategies. Observations made in the report were derived from the performance analysis of 135 country programmes, reporting results achieved against planned annual targets towards intended outcomes in the five UNDP practice areas established by the MYFF, 2004-2007: reducing human poverty; fostering democratic governance; energy and environment for sustainable development; crisis prevention and recovery; and responding to HIV/AIDS. The report contained also performance information on programme focus and results, organizational strategies and expenditures to achieve MYFF objectives. In keeping with Executive Board decision 2005/20 (see p. 972), the report adopted capacity development as its main theme. It presented a broad analysis of the programme portfolio, examining the distribution of demand and expenditure and progress made against targets set by country programmes, and highlighted UNDP's capacity development work, challenges and notable achievements. It examined two critical strategies outlined in the MYFF, 2004-2007, namely, the integration of drivers of development effectiveness and partnerships and coordination.

In 2005, all 135 country programmes were working in the poverty practice. All but two country programmes were involved in governance, and 123 in energy and environment. HIV/AIDS and crisis prevention and recovery had lower rates of country activity, with 90 and 83 programmes, respectively. UNDP country programmes, in partnership with national stakeholders, pursued 1,653 development outcomes within the five practices. Thirty-three per cent of outcomes were under the poverty practice; 28 per

cent under governance; 22 per cent under energy and the environment; 9 per cent under crisis prevention and recovery; and 8 per cent under HIV/AIDS.

Programme expenditures totalled $3.7 billion, $3.3 billion of which were country programme expenditures. Ninety per cent, or $3 billion, of the country programme expenditure was directly linked to the five practices. The major share (46 per cent) of that amount was spent in the governance practice, followed by the poverty practice (25 per cent), the crisis prevention and recovery, and energy and the environment practices (12 per cent each), and the HIV/AIDS practice (5 per cent).

The analysis indicated that UNDP had met one of the key strategic objectives of the 2004-2007 MYFF cycle: concentrating programming activity and financial resources within the five practices and 30 service lines. Close to 100 per cent of UNDP programming fell within the service lines and was consistent across all regions. Nine outcomes (0.3 per cent) fell outside the service lines, accounting for $2.1 million (0.07 per cent). On average, programmes focused on 10 service lines and 12 outcomes, a slight improvement over 2004, but fell short of the 6 to 10 outcome target of the MYFF. The majority of country programmes either fully or partially met their targets, with minor variations across regional bureaux and practices. The HIV/AIDS practice had the highest percentage of fully achieved targets (61 per cent). On average, country programmes reported 54 per cent of targets fully achieved, 42 per cent partially achieved, and 4 per cent not achieved.

One of UNDP key corporate strategies for ensuring quality development results centred on the promotion and integration of six critical and cross-cutting development drivers into its programmatic work. The 2005 data suggested that the majority of country programmes had placed a medium to high level of emphasis on four drivers: forging national partnerships (85 per cent of country programmes); fostering an enabling environment (77 per cent); developing national capacities (75 per cent); and seeking South-South cooperation (57 per cent). More work needed to be done to integrate the remaining two drivers—promoting gender equality and enhancing national ownership—both of which showed low emphasis placed by the majority of country programmes. The data also suggested that emphasis on the other four drivers could be improved, as expected levels of high emphasis were not realized.

The report concluded that the 2005 review of UNDP performance suggested that the organization was on track to meeting the performance targets and executing the operational strategies of the MYFF, 2004-2007. The assessment of field operations confirmed that UNDP was operating in line with UN reform principles and mandates, while remaining aligned with, and responsive to, national priorities. With respect to capacity development work, UNDP conformed to the recommendations of the 2004 triennial comprehensive policy review [YUN 2004, p. 867] and the World Summit Outcome, adopted by the General Assembly in resolution 60/1 (see p. 48), with country programmes involved in a wide range of substantive capacity development programmes in each practice. Substantial support went into strengthening governance institutions to enhance the efficiency and effectiveness of both public and private sector entities and create more stable foundations for democracy.

The UNDP Administrator, in a December report [E/2006/5] on UNDP activities, issued jointly with the UNFPA Executive Director, stated that in recognition of the key role of communities in sustaining post-conflict assistance, UNDP launched an integrated community development programme in Burundi and a similar initiative, the Srebrenica regional recovery programme, in Bosnia and Herzegovina. It supported a transition and recovery programme for northern Uganda designed to reintegrate internally displaced persons, provided assistance for disarmament, demobilization and reintegration efforts in the Democratic Republic of the Congo (DRC), and worked with UN partners to develop joint programmes on disarmament, demobilization and reintegration in Haiti and the Sudan. UNDP worked with the UN Department of Peacekeeping Operations (DPKO) to develop the United Nations Integrated Office in Sierra Leone (see p. 281), which would replace the UN Mission in Sierra Leone in January 2006. The Office would be headed by a representative of the Secretary-General who would also serve as resident representative of UNDP and UN resident coordinator. In Haiti, Kosovo (Serbia and Montenegro), Liberia, Sierra Leone and the Sudan, UNDP supported the reform and rebuilding of the justice and security sectors, and emphasized developing the capacity of national and local institutions to work with civic, traditional and community leaders. It provided technical and logistical support to the truth and reconciliation commissions in Sierra Leone and Timor-Leste and to the Special Court for Sierra Leone. UNDP also supported rebuilding and reconciliation efforts at the community level in Côte d'Ivoire.

UNDP supported, in collaboration with several UN partners, a programme for building national conflict prevention, as well as some 80 countries in implementing the 2001 Programme of Action to Prevent, Combat and Eradicate the Illicit Trade in Small Arms and Light Weapons in All Its Aspects [YUN 2001, p. 499]. UNDP helped Mauritania, Senegal and Uganda in setting up national mine action programmes and collaborated with other UN organizations in establishing a completion initiative to resolve landmine issues in various countries. It also promoted South-South cooperation through the mine action exchange programme and helped launch a forum of mine-affected countries. UNDP intensified efforts in 2005 to build national capacity for natural disaster prevention, preparedness and recovery, drawing on lessons learned from the 2004 Indian Ocean tsunami [YUN 2004, p. 952] and other natural disasters.

UNDP/UNFPA Executive Board

In 2005, the UNDP/UNFPA Executive Board held its first (20-28 January) and second (6-9 September) regular sessions and an annual session (13-14 June), all in New York [E/2005/35].

At the first regular session, the Board adopted 14 decisions, including one giving an overview of the Board's actions taken at that session [E/2005/35 (dec. 2005/14)]. Other decisions dealt with a revision of UNDP financial regulations (see p. 976); the UNDP global programme, 2005-2007 (see p. 964); the UNDP report on the assessment mission to Myanmar (see p. 964); the UNDP corporate gender strategy and action plan (see p. 968); options for a future business model for the United Nations Capital Development Fund (UNCDF) (see p. 985); the progress report of the Executive Director of the United Nations Office for Project Services (UNOPS) (see p. 978); the third cooperation framework for South-South cooperation (see p. 984); implementation by UNDP and UNFPA of the recommendations of the Board of Auditors (see p. 975); the reports of the UNDP Administrator and the UNFPA Executive Director to the Economic and Social Council (see p. 963), and their report on joint programming (see p. 970); and revision of UNFPA financial regulations, recovery of indirect costs for co-financing by UNFPA, and the quinquennial review of the UNFPA system for the allocation of resources to country programmes (see PART THREE, Chapter VIII).

At its annual session, the Executive Board adopted 17 decisions. In addition to an overview decision that summarized the action taken at that session [dec. 2005/31] and a decision expressing appreciation to the outgoing UNDP Administrator (see p. 963), other decisions dealt with: the UNDP global programme, 2005-2007 (see p. 964); the revision of UNDP financial regulations (see p. 976); the UNDP strategic cost management and implications for cost recovery (see p. 974); the internal audit and oversight for UNDP, UNFPA and UNOPS (see p. 975); the report on UNDP performance and results for 2004 in implementing the MYFF, 2004-2007 (see p. 964); the UNDP Administrator's annual report on evaluation, 2004 (see p. 971); the midterm report on the United Nations Development Fund for Women (UNIFEM) MYFF, 2004-2007 (see p. 1275); the status of regular resources funding commitments to UNDP and its funds and programmes for 2005 and onwards (see p. 973); the funding commitments to UNFPA, and the report of its Executive Director for 2004 (see PART THREE, Chapter VIII); the midterm review of UNDP successor programming arrangements (see p. 969); the question of gender in UNDP (see p. 968); the progress in implementing UNDP decision 2001/11: addressing the time frame for developing country programme documents (see p. 970); UNCDF business plan 2005-2007 (see p. 986); and the UNDP and UNFPA programme performance information at the country level (see p. 970).

At its second regular session, the Board adopted 11 decisions, including an overview decision [dec. 2005/42]. The other decisions concerned the Board's working methods (see below); UNDP budget estimates for the 2006-2007 biennium (see p. 973); UNIFEM budget estimates for the 2006-2007 biennium (see p. 1275); UNDP report on evaluation of the regional cooperation framework for the Arab States, 2002-2005 (see p. 971); UNOPS plan of action (see p. 979); estimates for the UNFPA biennial support budget for 2006-2007, the UNFPA 2004 financial review, its Technical Advisory Programme, and its role in emergency preparedness, humanitarian response, and transition and recovery (see PART THREE, Chapter VIII); and follow-up to the decisions and recommendations of the Joint United Nations Programme on HIV/AIDS (UNAIDS) Programme Coordinating Board (see p. 967).

The Economic and Social Council, by **decision 2005/230** of 20 July, took note of the reports of the UNDP/UNFPA Executive Board on its work in 2004 [YUN 2004, p. 877] and the report on its 2005 first regular session.

Working methods

In a September report [DP/2005/CRP.13], the Bureau of the UNDP/UNFPA Executive Board identified proposals to improve the Board's working methods with regard to the election of the Bureau; its decision-making process; documenta-

tion; meeting procedures; joint consideration of draft country programme documents; draft field visits and meetings; strengthening ties with the Economic and Social Council; and MDG country reporting.

On 9 September [dec. 2005/32], the Board decided, in order to ensure continuity of its work, to encourage newly elected members to participate in its work soon after their election by the Council; and to establish the composition of the incoming Bureau at an early date to enable incoming members to consult with the outgoing Bureau and take part in its work. The Board requested that it be provided with the financial implications of draft decisions prior to its sessions. The Board encouraged the joint meetings of the Executive Boards of UNDP/UNFPA, UNICEF and WFP to discuss and comment on individual country cases as a practical illustration of joint UN work in the field, and invited the UN agencies, funds and programmes taking part in UNDAF to participate in that exercise. It continued discussion and consultations on making its working methods more efficient and effective, while expediting and facilitating the decision-making process.

Appointment of Administrator

By a 3 May note [A/59/240], the Secretary-General requested that the General Assembly confirm the appointment of Kemal Dervis (Turkey) as UNDP Administrator for a four-year term, beginning on 15 August 2005 and ending on 14 August 2009, to replace Mark Malloch Brown, who had taken up the post of Chief of Staff to the Secretary-General, effective 18 January. The Assembly confirmed the appointment on 5 May 2005 (**decision 59/417**). The UNDP/UNFPA Executive Board, on 14 June [dec. 2005/15], commended Mr. Malloch Brown for his effective management of UNDP from 1999 to 2005.

UNDP/UNFPA reports

In January [dec. 2005/9], the UNDP/UNFPA Executive Board took note of the reports of the UNDP Administrator [E/2005/4-DP/2005/13] and the UNFPA Executive Director [E/2005/5-DP/FPA/2005/2] to the Economic and Social Council and decided to transmit them to the Council with the comments and guidance of delegations. The Council requested UNDP and UNFPA to maintain a sharp focus with respect to following up on the triennial comprehensive policy review [YUN 2004, p. 866].

The Executive Board, at its annual session in June, had before it an April [DP/2005/19] update on the *Human Development Report* consultations, submitted in response to General Assembly reso-

lution 57/264 [YUN 2002, p. 841]. The Human Development Report Office, charged with preparing the report (see p. 937), held five consultations
with Board members on a concept note for the report and the report's outline, statistics, structure
and message.

The Board took note of the report in June [dec.
2005/31].

UNDP operational activities

Country and regional programmes

The UNDP/UNFPA Executive Board, at its January session [dec. 2005/14], reviewed the draft subregional programme document for the countries
of the Organisation of Eastern Caribbean States
and Barbados. It approved the country programme
documents for Angola, Argentina, Armenia,
Azerbaijan, Bosnia and Herzegovina, Burundi,
the Democratic People's Republic of Korea, Guatemala, Iran, Kazakhstan, Kyrgyzstan, Lesotho,
Madagascar, Mauritius, the Philippines, the Republic of Korea, Romania, Serbia and Montenegro, Tajikistan, the former Yugoslav Republic
of Macedonia, Turkmenistan and Uzbekistan.

Also in January [dec. 2005/3], the Board took
note of the UNDP Administrator's report on the
assessment mission to Myanmar [DP/2005/6] and
the report by the independent assessment mission to that country, in particular the key challenges
and recommendations mentioned therein. The
Board requested the Administrator to consider
and implement the findings of the independent
assessment mission. It asked UNDP, in expanding
the programme, to ensure that quality was maintained, taking into account the findings of the
2004 mission [YUN 2004, p. 878].

At its annual session in June [dec. 2005/31], the
Board took note of draft country programme
documents and the comments made thereon for
Albania, Belarus, Bulgaria, Burkina Faso, Cambodia, China, Ghana, Georgia, Namibia, Peru,
Turkey, the British Overseas Territory of Turks
and Caicos Islands, Uganda, Ukraine and Viet
Nam. It took note of the one-year extensions of
the country programmes for the Democratic Republic of the Congo (DRC) and Liberia, and the
draft regional programme document for Europe
and the Commonwealth of Independent States
(CIS), 2006-2010. The Board also approved the
subregional programme for the countries of the
Organisation of Eastern Caribbean States and
Barbados.

At its second regular session in September [dec.
2005/42], the Board took note of the draft country
programme documents and the comments made
thereon for Afghanistan, Bangladesh, Chad,
Guyana, Indonesia, the Libyan Arab Jamahiriya
and Swaziland. It also took note of the draft regional programme document for the Arab States,
2006-2009. The Board approved the two-year extension of phase IV of the Human Development
Initiative in Myanmar for the period 2006-2007;
the two-year extensions of the second country cooperation framework (CCF) for Mexico and the
country programme for Timor-Leste; the two-
year extension of the regional cooperation framework for Latin America and the Caribbean, from
1 January 2006 to 31 December 2007; and the
third-year extensions of the second CCFs for Chile
and Uruguay.

Global programme, 2005-2007

The UNDP/UNFPA Executive Board, at its January session, considered the UNDP global
programme, 2005-2007 [DP/GP/1], whose primary
objective was to support programme countries in
achieving the MDGs. The four priority areas outlined in the MYFF, 2004-2007, which was endorsed
by the Board in 2003 [YUN 2003, p. 901], made up the
substantive core of the programme: achieving the
MDGs and reducing human poverty; fostering
democratic governance; managing energy and
environment for sustainable development; and
responding to HIV/AIDS. Programme initiatives
would aim to accelerate progress towards the
realization of the MDGs through policy support
services, global learning, and knowledge management and capacity development.

On 28 January [dec. 2005/2], the Executive
Board extended until December 2005, the second global cooperation framework (GCF-II), approved in 2001 [YUN 2001, p. 793] and extended
previously in 2003 [YUN 2003, p. 893]. The Administrator was to ensure that the extension of GCF-II
did not have an adverse impact on programme
countries and to submit to the Board a revised
third global programme, together with a work
plan, at its annual session in June, concerning,
among other things, national ownership and
leadership of the development process. The
Board included an item on the global programme in the agenda of its June session.

In June [dec. 2005/16], the Board adopted the revised UNDP global programme, 2005-2007, and
workplan [DG/GP/1/Rev.1], and stressed the importance of fully aligning them with the MYFF,
2004-2007, and with the provision of the triennial
comprehensive policy review relating to national
ownership and development processes.

UNDP programme results

The establishment and implementation by
UNDP of its practice approach were an important

element of its strategy to provide knowledge services and part of its objective to develop the ability to provide high-quality support to programme countries. UNDP activities were organized under five practice areas: poverty reduction, fostering democratic governance, crisis prevention and recovery, energy and environment, and responding to HIV/AIDS.

Poverty reduction

In 2005, the poverty reduction practice registered the highest level of country demand for services, with 97 per cent of all country programmes reported having fully or partially met their targets in the practice. Fifty-seven per cent of the $761 million expenditure in the practice came from local resources, reflecting country commitment to achieving the MDGs and reducing poverty. The practice also accounted for the largest expenditure of regular resources in 2005 (32 per cent of the total), which was consistent with the country and global priority of focusing UNDP resources on the MDGs and reducing poverty, and with the demand for poverty practice advisory services.

UNDP supported the preparation of 50 of the 152 national MDG reports submitted in the build-up to the High-level Plenary Meeting of the General Assembly (World Summit) in September (see p. 47), as well as the national human development reports which complemented them. Significant capacity development was recorded in MDG reporting and monitoring. Priority interventions included: strengthening statistical capacity for data collection and monitoring poverty and inequality; using statistics to improve policy design and address gender issues and other social inequalities; setting benchmark indicators to monitor MDG progress; and promoting stakeholder involvement in policy dialogue and ownership of the development agenda. Despite progress made, a number of challenges remained, as the focus shifted from data collection to managing the growing amount of information on human development and the MDGs.

With respect to national ownership and local engagement in national development processes, UNDP supported countries in fostering civil society participation in policy formulation, implementation, and monitoring and evaluation of the MDGs. However, while many countries concentrated on building wide stakeholder support for the MDG agenda, advocacy and capacity-building for disadvantaged and marginalized groups to participate effectively in development dialogue and implementation processes were insufficient.

Work under the pro-poor policies service line focused on support for national capacity-building to help countries link their poverty reduction strategies to MDG-focused economic policies for pro-poor growth. Intensive capacity-building activities on MDG-based poverty reduction strategy papers were seen in all regions. While UNDP support for initiatives that connected and integrated the MDGs with national development strategies helped lay a foundation for follow-up to the World Summit, the limited absorptive capacity in many countries constrained efforts to transform national development plans into MDG-based development strategies.

Support for national aid coordination was an important element of UNDP's work under the globalization benefiting the poor service line, particularly in LDCs. The service line also covered support for trade and debt relief. In 2005, through regional programmes in Africa, Asia and the Arab States, UNDP assisted countries to utilize better development finance, improve their capacity to integrate into the global economy, and negotiate trade arrangements and debt relief for highly indebted poor countries. UNDP, in collaboration with other agencies, supported the coordinated delivery of trade-related capacity building technical assistance to over 29 LDCs. Despite progress in integrating trade into their respective anti-poverty strategies, various assessments indicated continuing constraints on the ability of many LDCs to enhance their supply-side response.

Within the private sector development and local poverty initiatives service lines, UNDP, in partnership with UNCDF, supported programme countries to access microfinance, productive resources and basic social services to help overcome poverty. In 2005, UNCDF supported programmes in 23 LDCs. At the regional level, UNCDF and UNDP approved a programme to build inclusive financial sectors in Africa.

Democratic governance

In 2005, 133 of 135 UNDP country programmes promoted democratic governance. UNDP was one of the largest providers of technical assistance in that area, with over $1.4 billion in expenditure worldwide. It played an important role in providing governance assistance in conflict and post-conflict countries, particularly in transitional justice and security sector reform, and helped countries to transition from UN peacekeeping operations to stability through electoral and constitutional processes and institution-building.

Of the 464 programme outcomes focusing on democratic governance, 23 per cent was in the area of justice and human rights, while decentralization, local governance and urban/rural development accounted for 22 per cent. The three service lines—public administration reform and anti-corruption; electoral systems and processes; decentralization and local governance—together accounted for approximately 83 per cent of the resources in governance. Projects falling under those service lines included electoral support programmes in Afghanistan, Cambodia, the DRC and Iraq, as well as large decentralization and local governance initiatives in other countries, including Haiti and Honduras.

UNDP's core results in each of the governance service lines included an emphasis on developing capacities. The practice increased focus on governance at the local level and decentralization more generally, with more than two thirds of country programmes reporting outcomes in the practice area and almost $1 billion in expenditure. UNDP continued to emphasize support for national decentralization policy making; local governance institution-building, including strengthening participation and partnerships in social service delivery; policy formulation and resource management; and urban and rural development. At the country level, progress was achieved in influencing national, sectoral and local development strategies to incorporate MDG targets; strengthening the capacity of public and civil society institutions to monitor and report resource use for development results; and facilitating policy dialogue among key stakeholders aimed at building broad-based consensus.

UNDP's development work was also visible in the public administration reform and anti-corruption service line, especially in the areas of reform for pro-poor public services, and the establishment of institutional, legal and policy frameworks to promote and enforce accountability, transparency and integrity in the public service. Capacity development also featured prominently in UNDP's justice and human rights work. It helped to increase human resources capacities through systematic training for legal, judicial and administrative officers in the justice system in the provision of human rights knowledge for the police, judiciary and the media and through the expansion of human rights advocacy networks.

In parliamentary development, UNDP capacity development support centred primarily on enhancing the representation function. It made significant progress in establishing legal and institutional frameworks that enabled free, fair, transparent and sustainable elections at all levels in 2005. E-governance and access to information were used to facilitate capacity development so as to increase opportunity and enhance the capacity of vulnerable groups to participate in policy-making processes.

Crisis prevention and recovery

The demand for services linked to the crisis prevention and recovery practice area increased in 2005, with 83 of 135 UNDP country offices working in that area. The most requested service line was natural disasters, followed closely by recovery. The natural disasters service line was especially prominent in the Asia and the Pacific and the Latin America and the Caribbean regions due to the 2004 Indian Ocean tsunami [YUN 2004, p. 952] and the 2004-2005 Atlantic hurricane seasons. The recovery service line was particularly in demand in Africa and to a lesser extent in Asia and the Pacific. Those two service lines also made up almost one third of the resources spent globally in the practice area in 2005, partly due to high investment and expenditure in post-tsunami recovery efforts. The highest expenditure was on the special initiatives for countries in transition, especially the Sudan and Afghanistan. Conflict prevention and peacebuilding accounted for a significant share of global expenditure in the practice area. In absolute numbers, UNDP was most active in crisis prevention and recovery in the African region (25 countries), followed by Asia and the Pacific (20), Europe and CIS (14), Latin America and the Caribbean (14), and the Arab States (10). When viewed proportionally, however, 80 per cent of all countries in Asia and the Pacific were active in crisis prevention and recovery, as were 59 per cent of countries in the Arab States region and around 56 per cent of the countries in each of the other regions.

UNDP contributied significantly to policy development and advocacy in crisis prevention and recovery, and its inputs and leadership role were reflected in many related fields. UNDP was designated the lead agency for early recovery within the framework of the Inter-Agency Standing Committee reform of humanitarian response and was charged with enhancing capacity at the global level to ensure integrated humanitarian and recovery responses. UNDP was also the lead agency for discussions with the Bretton Woods institutions and donor and landmine-affected countries on the need to integrate mine action concerns into development plans, programmes and budgets. It sought to foster an environment where national authorities could solve the problem of landmines by supporting the development of appropriate structures and policies for the coordination and implementation of mine action activities, as well as ensuring that adequate and sustainable human and financial resources were available to complete those activities.

With UNDP heavily involved in the mobilization and management of large amounts of official development assistance (ODA) in response to the 2004 Indian Ocean tsunami and several major hurricanes and earthquakes, particular emphasis was placed on supporting and facilitating national aid coordination arrangements and enhancing national ownership. Setbacks in recovery coordination were indicated in some areas of post-tsunami reconstruction, largely due to divergent views on priority setting between national and subnational levels; lengthy processes in resolving land allocation formalities; slow finalization of technical details for procurement processes; and the unfamiliarity of technical counterparts with certain UNDP and government procedures with regard to tsunami recovery.

Environment and energy

The energy and environment practice served 123 programme countries in 2005, with 22 per cent of total outcomes focusing on energy and environment for sustainable development. The distribution of demand was similar across all regions, with the lowest demand coming from Africa and the highest from Latin America and the Caribbean. The areas receiving priority attention were frameworks and strategies for sustainable development (96 countries), conservation and sustainable use of biodiversity (66 countries) and access to sustainable energy services (56 countries).

Country programme expenditure for the energy and environment practice was $327 million, including $103 million from the global environmental facility (GEF) (see p. 1141). An additional $77 million of GEF funding for energy and environment activities was reported under global initiatives and the small grants programme. The total GEF contribution of approximately $180 million represented 50 per cent of donor and trust fund contributions to total energy and environment expenditure for the year.

More than a third of the practice's outcomes (118) were focused on the integration of sustainable management of environment and natural resources in poverty reduction strategies and national development frameworks.

The most significant capacity development drivers within the energy and environment practice were developing national capacities and fostering an enabling policy environment. Activities were particularly strong in capacity development diagnostics for pro-poor responses and national, sectoral and local development strategies to incorporate MDG targets. Country programmes were working to ensure that activities under the practice supported countries in incorporating those targets into national, sectoral and local development strategies, and adapting them to national conditions and priorities.

While significant efforts were reported by most UNDP country programmes to support planning, target-setting and capacity development diagnostics to achieve the MDGs, that work was not sufficiently matched by efforts to increase the delivery of energy, water and sanitation services. However, some initiatives were paving the way in supporting such service delivery and implementation capacities. UNDP's support for access to safe water and sanitation services yielded significant results in Tajikistan, Myanmar, the Niger and Uzbekistan. Activities to support access to energy services, electricity or cleaner fuels in rural areas increased in 2005, with initiatives to improve access to energy services in remote areas of India and the United Republic of Tanzania.

Response to HIV/AIDS

UNDP continued to intensify capacity development efforts and build momentum at all levels of government and civil society to respond effectively to the HIV/AIDS epidemic. In 2005, 90 country programmes were involved in the fight against HIV/AIDS. UNDP undertook development support activities in 80 per cent of countries in Africa, and in 63 per cent of countries in the Asia and the Pacific region. Europe and CIS, Latin America and the Caribbean and the Arab States regions each contained roughly half of countries with HIV/AIDS programming. The focus of UNDP's HIV/AIDS interventions in the different regions mirrored the spread of the epidemic, reflecting both organizational focus and responsiveness to national demand. Development planning and implementation was the service line with the highest demand and expenditure, followed by leadership and capacity development, and advocacy and communication.

The majority of outcomes under the development planning and implementation service line centred on mainstreaming HIV/AIDS into national development plans, which was central to UNDP's HIV/AIDS work. The outcomes also reflected increased country demand for support in integrating HIV/AIDS into MDG-based poverty reduction strategies. In response to that demand, as well as the evolving global environment and the recommendations of the Global Task Team on improving AIDS coordination among multilateral and international donors (see p. 1327), UNDP was assigned the lead role, in collaboration with the World Bank, in supporting countries to mainstream HIV/AIDS more effectively into MDG-based poverty reduction strategy papers. In 2005, seven African countries benefited from capacity development support to plan, manage and deliver an increasingly robust response to the epidemic through the joint UNDP, World Bank and Joint United Nations Programme on HIV/AIDS (UNAIDS) initiative. Support would be expanded to meet demand from 13 more countries in 2006.

Another key area of growing demand was support to advance the "Three Ones" strategy endorsed by donor countries in 2004 [YUN 2004, p. 1219]. Those efforts helped to improve the capacity of national Governments in several countries in aid coordination and harmonization, including Indonesia, Kyrgyzstan, the Russian Federation and Zambia. In other countries, such as Mozambique and Rwanda, country efforts focused on strengthening national AIDS councils.

The leadership and capacity development service line continued to support efforts across all regions in both high and low prevalence settings. A key shift in the work under that service line was the adaptation of capacity development methodologies to targeted outcomes in development planning and human rights. Significantly fewer outcomes were reported under the advocacy and communication service line, possibly indicating a shift from making the case for action on HIV/AIDS to large-scale, multisectoral programmes.

The HIV/AIDS practice area continued to play an important role in developing country capacity for improved implementation of multilateral funding initiatives, including the Global Fund to Fight AIDS, Malaria and Tuberculosis, established in 2002 [YUN 2002, p. 1217]. While UNDP continued to act as principal recipient of last resort for Global Fund grants in 24 countries, the success of its engagement would ultimately be judged by the extent to which it built the capacity of local partners to implement the grants. That model had enabled the successful handover of its role as principal recipient to a local partner in Haiti, and similar results were expected in Benin and El Salvador.

Programme planning and management

Gender issues

The UNDP/UNFPA Executive Board, at its January session, considered a conference room paper updating the progress achieved in the partnership between UNDP and UNIFEM [DP/2005/CRP.2], submitted in response to 2004 Board decisions [YUN 2004, pp. 883 & 884, respectively]. The paper outlined four dimensions of a strengthened UNDP/UNIFEM partnership to enhance gender mainstreaming in UNDP and promote gender equality through: scaling up innovations piloted by UNIFEM; joint programming for enhanced development effectiveness; strengthening support to UNDP country programmes; and utilizing UNDP's role as coordinator of the resident coordinator system and chair of UNDG to advance gender mainstreaming. The Board took note of the paper on 28 January [dec. 2005/14].

Also before the Board in January was a report on the UNDP corporate gender strategy and action plan [DP/2005/7 & Corr.1]. The corporate gender strategy was designed to integrate the promotion of gender equality and women's empowerment fully into UNDP's core business and rested on three major dimensions: to develop capacities, both in-country and in-house, to integrate gender concerns in all practice areas and programmes; to provide gender-responsive policy advisory services that promoted gender equality and women's empowerment; and to support specific interventions that benefited women and scaled up and expanded innovative models, including those tested by UNIFEM.

Specific elements of the corporate gender action plan included: monitoring the MDGs from a gender perspective; gender-sensitive budgeting; reducing the incidence of HIV among vulnerable women; mainstreaming gender in macroeconomic policies and trade negotiations; promoting women's empowerment in democratic governance, decentralization and civil society participation; and developing capacities through training, knowledge sharing and networking. All UNDP bureaux and country offices were engaged in a mapping exercise, to produce a comprehensive review of gender-related interventions and planned activities, with a view to a possible partnership between UNIFEM and UNDP. The action plan would put emphasis on developing capacities; mainstreaming gender in the UNDP practice areas; and in MDG reporting, advocacy and implementation; coordinating UN system work on gender at the country level; mainstreaming gender in human development reports; providing financial and human resources to implement the plan; and developing performance indicators.

Annexed to the report were an assessment of substantive performance of the driver of development effectiveness on promoting gender equality, and a UNDP gender mainstreaming scorecard requested by the Board in 2004 [YUN 2004, p. 884].

On 28 January [dec. 2005/4], the Executive Board took note of the report and deferred further consideration of it to the Board's annual session in June.

In June, the Board considered an explanatory note on the implementation of the UNDP corporate gender strategy and action plan [DP/2005/

CRP.9], which indicated that UNDP continued to deliver on its gender programmes in all areas of the action plan, supported mainly by core resources. UNDP had developed an interim work plan to implement the corporate strategy and action plan in 2005. All UNDP regional bureaux, country offices, regional centres, the UNDP Learning Resource Centre, and the practice groups were working collaboratively to develop short- and long-term work plans with specific interventions to institutionalize gender equality as a core UNDP objective. The 2005 implementation plan focused on institutional capacities, including gender expertise and staff training for all units; a gender mainstreaming strategy implemented in 45 country offices, four regional centres and five headquarters units; knowledge sharing and tools development to strengthen internal capacities and learning; and mainstreaming gender in the CCA/UNDAF process, with support to the resident coordinator system. A results matrix on the implementation of the corporate strategy and action plan for 2005 was annexed to the note.

In June [dec. 2005/27], the Executive Board adopted the corporate gender strategy and action plan as set forth in the January report (see above). It took note of the explanatory note and urged UNDP to further expand its work in mainstreaming gender, including through the increase of financial and human resources to support the implementation of the action plan, and to take into account the comments of member States in that regard. The Board requested UNDP to promote and establish partnerships with all relevant UN organizations working in the area of gender to support the implementation of the plan. It requested the Administrator to develop the gender action plan through 2007, including the results matrix, taking into account the findings of the MYFF report on performance and results for 2004 [YUN 2004, p. 876], and the findings of the independent gender evaluation initiated that year [ibid., p. 883]. The Administrator was also asked to report to the Board on the medium-term action plan at its first regular session in 2006, building on the 2004 management response to the independent gender evaluation.

Programming arrangements

In May [DP/2005/18], the Administrator reported on the midterm review of UNDP programming arrangements for the period 2004-2007. In accordance with a 2002 Executive Board decision on programming arrangements [YUN 2002, p. 870], UNDP, for the first time within a programming period, conducted a full recalculation of target for resource assignment from the core

(TRAC) line 1.1.1 earmarkings for 2004-2007. In applying the distribution methodology approved in the Board's 2002 decision, the recalculation required a full redistribution of resources based on 2003 gross national income (GNI) per capita and population data, which was summarized in the report. The recalculation, like the initial calculation, was based on a $450 million regular programme resource base. Should regular programme resources fall below that base, TRAC 1.1.1 minimum allocations and fixed programme lines would be reduced in direct proportion to the shortfall; should regular programme resources exceed the $450 million base, TRAC 1.1.1 allocations not subject to the minimum allocation, and programme lines that were not fixed, would be increased on a pro rata basis.

Two options based on the midterm recalculation were presented in the report. Option 1 took into account all countries, reflecting either upward or downward revisions to their initial annual TRAC 1.1.1 earmarkings. Option 2 considered only those countries reflecting upward revisions to their annual TRAC 1.1.1 earmarkings. Under option 2, TRAC 1.1.1 resource flows to low-income countries during 2006-2007 were maximized. The initial annual TRAC 1.1.1 earmarkings, based on 2001 GNI, totalled $195.3 million; the recalculation, based on 2003 GNI, totalled $195.4 million under option 1 and $203.5 million under option 2. UNDP recommended the adoption of option 2.

The Administrator proposed changes in the earmarkings between TRAC lines 1.1.1 and 1.1.2 for available resources over the base total programming level of $450 million to provide UNDP with flexibility in supporting urgent programme country national capacity development needs towards achieving the MDGs. He also proposed a separate, predictable level of funding in the amount of $3 million for the Programme of Assistance to the Palestinian People.

In June [dec. 2005/26], the Executive Board took note of the report and reiterated that allocations from TRAC lines 1.1.1 and 1.1.2 to least developed countries (LDCs) should be fixed at a minimum of 60 per cent, and for low-income countries at a range of between 85 and 91 per cent. The Board maintained the current TRAC line 1.1.1 earmarkings for 2006 and 2007 and approved, subject to revision in 2007, the following temporary changes for available new resources over the base total programming level of $450 million: changing the ratio of internal earmarking between TRAC lines 1.1.1 and 1.1.2 from 60/40 per cent to 50/50 per cent; eliminating the current limitation on country allocations between TRAC lines 1.1.1 and 1.1.2, while fully adhering to the principle of priority allocation to low-income countries and LDCs; and introducing a flexibility of up to 10 per cent to facilitate some movement of TRAC 1.1.2 resources between regions, while retaining the regional limitation in principle. The Board also approved the proposed level of annual funding for the Programme of Assistance to the Palestinian People. UNDP was asked to assess the current programming arrangements, particularly the approved changes, in the context of proposing a successor programming arrangement for submission to the Board in 2007.

Joint programming

In January [dec. 2005/10], the Executive Board took note of the 2004 report [YUN 2004, p. 884] on joint programming submitted by the UNDP Administrator and the UNFPA Executive Director. The Board emphasized the importance that it attached to joint programming as a tool for supporting the implementation of national development plans, including poverty reduction strategies, through a more concerted approach under the CCA and UNDAF, towards achieving the internationally agreed development goals, including the MDGs. It requested the Administrator and the Executive Director, in managing their respective organizations' cooperation with other agencies, to ensure that the implementation of joint programming resulted in improved development impact, including the further harmonization of country programme preparation, implementation, monitoring and evaluation processes, and the improvement of communication between UN agencies during the programme cycle; effective delivery of programme goals and the reduction of transaction costs; and promotion of common monitoring and reporting processes to governing bodies and joint approaches to evaluations. The Board requested the Administrator and the Executive Director to report in June on joint programming and joint programmes in their respective annual reports, and to submit for the Board's consideration in 2006 a comprehensive report on the implementation of joint programming.

In response to a 2004 Executive Board decision [YUN 2004, p. 884], the UNDP Administrator and the UNFPA Executive Director reported, in April [DP/2005/28-DP/FPA/2005/10], on progress in the implementation of a 2001 Board decision that called for modifying the UNDP/UNFPA two-step programming process [YUN 2001, p. 799], addressing the issue of the time frame for developing country programme documents. The report indicated that, while the common country programming process had produced a more unified and strategic vision for country-level operational activities, the preparatory process was too cumbersome and its duration lengthy (two years in a typical five-year cycle). The report proposed shortening the preparation time for country programme documents as well as the time frame between preparation and implementation, in order to avoid those documents becoming outdated by the time of their approval; and ensuring high-quality processes and documents that improved the timeliness and relevance of UN programmes, while guaranteeing adequate formal approval for them. To do so, country teams would need to start the preparation process closer to the start of implementation and complete the CCA in three months. However, to maintain and improve the quality of strategic planning, it would be difficult to develop the UNDAF in less than three months. Shortening the preparation time for country programme documents, based on the UNDAF and its results matrix, could jeopardize the review with national partners and other stakeholders, undermine the quality of the products and affect the participation and ownership by Governments and their partners.

If the Executive Board wished, the time between the submission of the draft country programme documents and their approval by the Board could be reduced or, alternatively, the Board could approve the documents automatically within two months of the Board session at which they were submitted, unless five or more Board members wished to bring them before the Board for further discussion. That would reduce the approval period from seven to two months, and eliminate the need to schedule formal approval of the documents as an agenda item for Board sessions.

The report also discussed other options for further simplifying and streamlining the country programme preparation and approval process, but which would require further discussion among the agencies, as well as major changes in the current procedures of the respective Executive Boards.

In June [dec. 2005/28], the UNDP/UNFPA Executive Board took note of the report on the time frame for developing country programme documents and the proposals contained therein. It reconfirmed the validity of the current programming process approval procedure, while stressing the need to ensure the quality and results orientation of the country programme documents and their alignment with national priorities in the areas of competence of all agencies involved. It requested the UNDP Administrator and the UNFPA Executive Director, with UNICEF, to present to the Board in 2006 a joint report on options to further improve and streamline the current harmonized country programme approval procedure, so as to decrease the time frame for developing and approving country programmes and better synchronize them with the length of cycle of the respective national country programming instruments, bearing in mind the need to maintain the institutional integrity and organizational mandate of each agency.

Also in June [dec. 2005/30], the Executive Board requested UNDP and UNFPA to make a proposal at the Board's January 2006 session on cost-efficient approaches to providing programme-level data as part of their programming and reporting cycles.

Monitoring and evaluation

In April [DP/2005/25], the UNDP Administrator, in his annual report on evaluation covering the period from July 2004 to March 2005, addressed the progress and challenges in the area of evaluation. The report also identified the major findings of corporate evaluations, assessed UNDP's contribution to selected development results and highlighted the central organizational lessons. The analysis drew from 280 evaluations conducted during the year and a review of the function itself. The report, which integrated the evaluative work of all UNDP-associated funds and programmes, showed that the coverage of outcome evaluations improved dramatically in the reporting period, with 37 conducted, a proportional increase of 70 per cent over the 2003 figure.

The review of the UNDP evaluation function underscored that evaluation practices, as well as standards, capacities and demands, were highly variable across the organization. The results-oriented framework introduced in 2001 [YUN 2001, p. 803] was found to have only partial relevance in operational practice; some offices were planning, monitoring and evaluating around outcomes derived from national strategies, whereas others were still planning and conducting discrete project-based interventions, sometimes with weak review mechanisms and no evaluations. Evaluation budgeting had not been standardized at either the regional or the country-programme level and monitoring often took the largest share at the project level.

Evaluations conducted in 2004 revealed that UNDP's strategic positioning as an impartial and trustworthy organization and its ability to respond to major development concerns and provide access to expertise and global information were key to the organization's relevance. Wherever UNDP gained recognition as an impartial and legitimate broker, it mobilized support from Governments and international donors and made relevant contributions in facilitating dialogue and consensus-building on the rule of law and democratic practices.

Evaluations pointed to numerous poverty-reduction initiatives and public sector management efforts that concentrated on reform; UNDP programmes might yield greater benefits if they facilitated reform at a higher level of national importance. Evaluations also showed UNDP's gradual but uneven progress in the institutionalization and use of corporate results-based management and often highlighted the failure to situate projects within wider organizational and national frameworks, thus diminishing development results. They recommended that, at the country level, UNDP should focus on a small number of national priorities, with clear strategies for delivery as a basis for enhancing operational effectiveness and efficiency, as well as sustainability of benefits. UNDP would define its evaluation policy, which would be aligned with the norms and standards issued by the United Nations Evaluation Group in April, and situated within the priorities of General Assembly resolution 59/250 on the triennial comprehensive policy review of UN system operational activities for development [YUN 2004, p. 868].

In June [dec. 2005/21], the Executive Board encouraged the Evaluation Office to pay more attention to concrete development results achieved and follow-up on the recommendations of previous evaluations; highlighted the importance of seeking synergy through evaluation among UNDP and its associated funds and programmes in enhancing the accountability of the organization; and approved the codification of an evaluation policy during the 2005 reporting period and the formulation of a system for tracking evaluation recommendations.

Regional cooperation framework for Arab States region

At its September session, the Executive Board considered a July report [DP/2005/36] summarizing the findings of the independent evaluation of the regional cooperation framework for the Arab States, 2002-2005, carried out by the UNDP Evaluation Office. The report contained recommendations dealing with the design, relevance and positioning of future regional cooperation frameworks; management issues within the Regional Bureau for Arab States; and monitoring, evaluation and the systematic performance of UNDP regional programmes.

On 9 September [dec. 2005/35], the Executive Board took note of the report and welcomed the approach and methodology used in the evaluation. It requested the UNDP Evaluation Office to give more attention to the relevance of the regional programmes in their approach and conduct of independent evaluations of all regional programmes in the future. The Board expressed concern at the lack of outcome evaluations and requested UNDP to develop mechanisms for systematic monitoring and evaluation systems, and to collect baseline data and track indicators that could provide information on the outcomes and impact of UNDP regional programmes, in close cooperation with national authorities. The Board suggested that the Evaluation Office prioritize the conclusions and recommendations contained in the report. It urged UNDP to take into account the lessons learned in implementing the regional cooperation framework for the Arab States, 2002-2005, while developing and implementing the next regional programme for that region.

Funding strategy

Multi-year funding framework, 2004-2007

In June, the Executive Board had before it a report [DP/2005/16] on the multi-year funding framework, UNDP performance and results for 2004 [YUN 2004, p. 876] and a statistical annex [DP/2005/16/Add.2], as well as a report by the Joint Inspection Unit [DP/2005/16/Add.1], which provided a synopsis of 10 reports prepared by the Unit, with selected recommendations of relevance to UNDP.

In June [dec. 2005/20], the Executive Board took note of the UNDP report on its performance and results for 2004 in the implementation of the MYFF, 2004-2007. It encouraged UNDP to further advance its methodology for presenting its results and to continue to enhance and refine the quantitative and qualitative measures contained in the MYFF, so as to better analyse progress and results. The Board requested UNDP to include in subsequent MYFF reports an executive summary and a flow diagram showing the results chain it was reporting, and to take follow-up actions based on the report and the discussions following its presentation to the Board. UNDP should select capacity development as the theme for its in-depth analysis of the 2006 annual report, and present to the Board, in January 2006, a timeline for the preparation and discussion of its report on the end-of-cycle performance assessment of the MYFF, 2004-2007, as well as on the process leading to the preparation of the MYFF, 2008-2011. The Board called on donors to continue to increase voluntary contributions to UNDP regular resources and asked the Administrator to follow up on the recommendations contained in the JIU reports. The Board took note of the statistical analysis of the midterm report on the MYFF.

Financing

The UNDP Administrator, in his annual review of the financial situation for 2005 [DP/2006/37], said that consistent growth in resource contributions continued, reaching $4.8 billion in 2005, a 20 per cent increase over the 2004 level of $4 billion. Compared to 2004, regular resources income increased by 10 per cent to $914 million, exceeding the 2005 MYFF interim target of $900 million; exchange rate fluctuations accounted for approximately one quarter of the increase. Expenditures under regular resources increased 2 per cent, to $849 million. The resource balance, exclusive of operational reserves but including after-service health insurance, increased 31 per cent. Contributions from the top 15 bilateral donor members of the Development Assistance Committee of the Organisation for Economic Co-operation and Development (OECD/DAC) (Belgium, Canada, Denmark, Finland, France, Germany, Ireland, Italy, Japan, Netherlands, Norway, Sweden, Switzerland, United Kingdom, United States) increased by 8 per cent in nominal terms and 4 per cent in real terms.

Programme expenditure, including programme support to the resident coordinator system, development support services and the UNDP economist programme, increased 4 per cent, from $498 million to $520 million. By appropriation group, 56 per cent of expenditure went to programme support activities, 21 per cent to management and administration and 23 per cent to UN system operational activities. In terms of percentage share of programme expenditure among regions, Africa recorded the highest share of programme delivery ($205 million, or 41 per cent, and $517 million, or 16 per cent, for regular and other expenditures, respectively), followed by Asia and the Pacific ($149 million, or 30 per cent, and $644 million or 20 per cent, respectively), Latin America and the Caribbean ($38 million, or 7 per cent, and $1.2 billion, or 36 per cent, respectively), the Arab States ($41 million, or 8 per cent, and $273 million, or 9 per cent, respectively) and Europe and CIS ($36 million, or 7 per cent, and $238 million, or 8 per cent, respectively).

As at 31 December, the balance of unexpended regular resources stood at $238 million, an increase of 39 per cent over the 2004 figure of $171 million. UNDP held cash and investments for regular resources totalling $217 million, excluding the operational reserve.

For other resources activities—local resources (government, cost-sharing and cash-counterpart contributions), donor cost-sharing, trust funds, the United Nations Volunteers (UNV) programme (see p. 980), management services agreements, the Junior Professional Officer programme and the reserve for field accommodation—overall income increased by $820 million, from $3.3 billion in 2004 to $4.1 billion in 2005. Net contributions, interest and other income received totalled $3.8 billion, of which 32 per cent ($1.2 billion) were received from bilateral OECD/DAC donors; non-bilateral/multilateral sources and local resources shared 33 per cent ($1.3 billion) each. Overall expenditure increased by 29 per cent ($771 million). Contributions from OECD/DAC countries increased 31 per cent, from $900 million in 2004 to $1.2 billion in 2005.

In September [dec. 2005/42], the Executive Board took note of the Administrator's annual review of the financial situation for 2004 [YUN 2004, p. 887].

Regular funding commitments to UNDP

In June [DP/2005/17], UNDP submitted a report on the status of its regular funding commitments and its associated funds and programmes for 2005 and onward. Provisional data showed that contributions to regular resources for 2004 reached $842 million, a 9.4 per cent ($72 million) increase over the $770 million reached in 2003, marking the first time since 1996 that contributions exceeded $800 million. Current projections suggested that, based on the official UN exchange rate as at 1 May, contributions would exceed $900 million. Ten OECD/DAC members increased or resumed their contributions in local currency terms in 2004 and three donors increased their contributions by 10 per cent or more. Almost all OECD/DAC donors paid their contributions in full in 2004. Current estimates suggested that almost all OECD/DAC donors would either maintain or increase their contributions. Ten of those donors had indicated that they would increase their contribution in local currencies while one of them committed to increasing its contributions regularly over the full period of the MYFF, 2004-2007. Six programme countries made contributions in excess of $1 million to UNDP regular resources, indicating the high value such countries placed on UNDP work and the support they received from the organization. Eleven OECD/DAC donor countries provided fixed payment schedules in 2004. That same number had communicated their payment schedules for 2005. Of the 11 OECD/DAC donors that had provided schedules in 2003 and 2004, many did not contribute in accordance with the schedule provided. Although a number of donors delayed paying significant proportions of their pledges until the last quarter of 2004, the operational reserves did not have to be used.

In June [dec. 2005/23], the Executive Board took note of the report on the status of regular resources funding commitments to UNDP and its associated funds and programmes for 2005 and onwards. It also noted that UNDP had achieved the first (2004) annual funding target of the MYFF, 2004-2007, and that a stable and adequate base of regular resources was within reach, provided the organization continued to follow the directions of the MYFF, and improve programme design, implementation, monitoring and evaluation, as requested by the Board, and that UNDP member States not only sustained but increased their funding over the full period of the MYFF, 2004-2007. The Board requested member States to give priority to regular resources ("core" contributions) over other resources ("non-core" contributions). It requested UNDP to continue to reduce its dependency on a few large donors and to broaden its donor base. Countries that had already made their contributions to regular resources for 2005 were asked to consider supplementing them, if they were in a position to do so, in order to accelerate the momentum in rebuilding UNDP's regular resource base. The Board encouraged member States to announce multi-year pledges and payment schedules over the period of the MYFF, 2004-2007, and to adhere to those pledges and payment schedules.

Budget estimates for 2006-2007

In June [DP/2005/31], the Administrator submitted budget estimates for the 2006-2007 biennium, which underpinned the MYFF, 2004-2007, endorsed by the Executive Board in 2003 [YUN 2003, p. 901]. He proposed a budget in net terms of $658 million, an increase of $95 million over the net approved budget for 2004-2005 [ibid., p. 903], after adjustments made for security. The budget incorporated net cost increases of $86 million and net volume increases of $9 million, resulting primarily from the mainstreaming of United Nations Capital Development Fund (UNCDF) administrative costs into the UNDP budget proposals, and an increase of $1 million in projected income ($71 million, compared to $70 million in 2004-2005). The Administrator also proposed that UN-mandated security costs of $31 million be treated as a distinct requirement from regular resources. Despite expected programme delivery growth in both regular and other resources, the proposals represented a zero net real growth budget for 2006-2007, excluding the support budget requirements for UNCDF.

In August [DP/2005/32], the Advisory Committee on Administrative and Budgetary Questions (ACABQ) recommended that the process of harmonization towards implementing results-based budgeting for the next biennium, 2008-2009, be given high priority. While noting some improvement in channelling more funds to programmes in other resources, the Committee was of the opinion that further effort was needed to reduce expenditure on programme support and administration and management in respect of regular resources, so as to allocate more resources for programmes. It recommended that the Executive Board bear in mind its earlier recommendation that proposals for upward reclassification of UN posts in funds and programmes, particularly at the D-1 and D-2 levels, should be submitted only as a result of significant changes in the level and scope of responsibilities involved.

In September [dec. 2005/33], the Executive Board approved gross appropriations in the amount of $729,056,300 for the 2006-2007 biennial support budget, except the proposed new regional advocacy posts and the associated expenditure. It resolved that the income estimate of $71,210,000 should be used to offset the gross appropriations, resulting in estimated net appropriations of $657,846,300. The Board encouraged all host country Governments to meet their obligations for local office costs. Noting the increase in costs in the biennial support budget, it requested UNDP to report in more detail in the next budget on cost-containment strategies and measures. The Board authorized the incoming Administrator (see p. 963) to redeploy or reprioritize resources between appropriations lines up to a maximum of 5 per cent of the appropriation line to which the resources were redeployed, and urged him to continue to realign the UNDP support requirements funding modality with proportional cost sharing between regular and other resources. It endorsed the Administrator's proposal to reflect the UN-mandated security costs as a separate line in the UNDP resource plan and approved the amount of $31,243,700 from UNDP regular resources to cover such costs. The Board also endorsed ACABQ's concerns regarding the upward classifications of posts and asked UNDP to only submit such reclassifications as a result of significant changes in the level and scope of responsibilities involved and to better document such cases in the budget proposal. It endorsed the priority given to gender mainstreaming and requested that the financial implications of the gender action plan (see p. 968) for 2006 be reflected in the budgeting process. UNDP was asked to continue discussion with the

Board on the overall strategy to enhance the effectiveness of the resident coordinator system.

Strategic cost management and cost recovery

In response to a 2004 Board decision [YUN 2004, p. 890], UNDP submitted a January conference room paper [DP/2005/CRP.4] on current concepts for providing the Executive Board with additional options on extrabudgetary income reporting and preliminary elements for providing further transparency in such reporting. The current UNDP resource mobilization system was decentralized, as was the utilization of cost recovery income, with the bulk of such income remaining with country offices. As part of the new system design of the Atlas enterprise resource planning system, launched in 2004 [YUN 2004, p. 889], the various types of income from cost recovery were being tracked separately; however, as UNDP had not financially closed the 2004 financial year, aggregate figures for cost recovery by category were not yet available. Under the current reporting system, the ratio between the total support budget estimates and the total programme delivery estimates from other resources did not properly reflect the average cost recovery rate because no distinction was made between income earned through programme support and income earned through agency service. In addition, not all extrabudgetary income was earned on the basis of a percentage. Biennial support budget requirements were not based solely on income expected to be earned within the same biennium resulting from the cost recovery policy.

To make the reporting more transparent, UNDP proposed a two-step approach based on the availability of data from the Atlas system. First, the 2006-2007 biennial support budget could include a table for income earned from programme support and for services to UN organizations. Second, the 2008-2009 biennial support budget could include a more detailed breakdown of income earned from programme support to indicate the source of funds. The Administrator was committed to providing a more transparent report within the context of the UNDP budget estimates for the 2008-2009 biennium.

On 28 January [dec. 2005/14], the UNDP/UNFPA Executive Board took note of the conference room paper.

A May conference room paper [DP/2005/CRP.5] reported on the criteria for determining project-specific cost recovery rates, and established how the recovery rate for general management support (GMS) for a specific project was determined. The GMS rate of 5 to 7 per cent was set at the corporate level, based on an aggregate calculation of UNDP indirect variable costs and the required contribution of other resources to UNDP total operational costs. That approach was consistent with the harmonized principles and methodology of cost recovery agreed on among UN organizations. The criteria for determining the GMS rate within the 5 to 7 per cent range had to be based on the actual operational environment of the project, taking into account differences in the nature and complexity of projects and in costs among offices. UNDP established a fixed floor of 2 per cent in GMS for every trust fund and third-party cost-sharing project that was used to cover the indirect costs of central and headquarters units. UNDP recommended that the main criteria to guide the determination of a specific GMS rate above the 2 per cent fixed rate should be the proportional sharing of all indirect costs among regular and other resources at the individual unit level. That approach ensured that the Executive Board's requirement for the elimination of any subsidy from regular resources was fulfilled, while preserving a minimum of flexibility to adjust the GMS rate based on the project in question. UNDP also recommended that the incentives to donors to contribute both regular and other resources should be built on the focus of the intervention in line with the multi-year funding framework priorities; alignment to the programming cycle; and the development results achieved by each pool of funding, as long as the attributable management costs were proportionately split.

In June [dec. 2005/18], the Executive Board took note of the May conference room paper and reiterated that UNDP had to ensure that each funding source covered its proportional share of management and programme support. It stressed the need for flexibility within the established ranges of cost-recovery rates for contributions from both donor and recipient Governments so as to reflect the different execution modalities and management costs in different countries. The Board reaffirmed that UNDP had to ensure full recovery, at an aggregate level, of all actual costs for implementing activities financed from UNDP third-party cost-sharing, trust fund contribution and programme country cost-sharing. It noted that the May conference room paper did not outline a detailed proposal containing clear criteria that encouraged incentives for un-earmarked, timely and flexible contributions to trust funds, third-party cost-sharing and programme country cost-sharing, as requested by the Board in 2004 [YUN 2004, p. 890]. The Board asked UNDP to submit, at its second regular session in 2006, a report on the current practice of determining specific cost-recovery rates and clear cost-recovery criteria.

Audit reports

The Executive Board, at its January session, considered the Administrator's report [DP/2005/11] on implementation of the recommendations of the Board of Auditors for the 2002-2003 biennium [YUN 2004, p. 1396], which contained an update of actions taken by UNDP on the Board's recommendations, including the status of any follow-up action and the target date for completion. The Administrator said that progress had been achieved in most areas and outstanding issues were being addressed. The Executive Board also considered a conference room paper [DP/2005/CRP.3], which provided an update on the implementation of the recommendations.

In January [dec. 2005/8], the Executive Board took note of the Administrator's report and update, and stressed the importance of adequate follow-up to the Board of Auditors' recommendation, particularly regarding improving internal management control. It requested that future reports include an indication of the priority of the recommendations and an expected time frame for their implementation.

In May [DP/2005/26 & Corr.1], the Administrator submitted the annual report on the internal audit and oversight services provided by the UNDP Office of Audit and Performance Review (OAPR) for 2004. In response to a 2004 Executive Board decision [YUN 2004, p. 890], the report also contained information on the steps taken to address the issues contained in the 2003 audit report [ibid.], as well as the timeline for the completion of those efforts and indicators of progress or completion thereof.

As part of its efforts to improve effectiveness and client services, OAPR used an informal risk-assessment approach to prepare its strategy and work plan for 2005, taking into account recent audits conducted and the complexity, volume and level of operations of the various UNDP organizational units or of mission-critical projects. The risk-assessment process would be pursued further in 2005 and a more systematic and comprehensive system developed.

The number of UNDP audits/reviews undertaken in 2004 was 27, compared to 18 in 2003, while audit reports of national execution rose to 1,811, from 1,660 in 2003. OAPR issued a total of 16 internal audit reports on country offices, containing 485 recommendations, virtually all of which were accepted by management and were being implemented. At the end of 2004, OAPR started to prioritize the recommendations. Annexes to the report provided definitions of categories of recommendations, as well as definitions of standard audit opinion ratings used by OAPR and national execution audit areas.

In June [dec. 2005/19], the Executive Board took note of the reports of the Administrator, of OAPR to the UNOPS Executive Director [DP/2005/27] (see p. 980) and of the UNFPA Executive Director (see p. 957) on internal audit and oversight. It urged UNDP and UNFPA to base their oversight and accountability activities on a corporate risk model and develop risk-assessment functions in their audit offices; encouraged them to use monitoring and financial control data systems to better mitigate the risks related to programme implementation; and requested them to explain, in their next reports, the selection criteria of the country offices audited. The Board requested a further analysis of the underlying causes of audit remarks, and that the analysis and the presentation of audit recommendations by frequency of occurrence and by priority be maintained in future reports on internal audit and oversight. It asked UNDP and UNFPA to carry out an in-depth review of the level of internal audit resources, so as to align them with best practices and adequately cover the strategic areas identified in its current decision. The Board concurred with the need to strengthen the analysis of the outcomes of audits of nationally executed projects, and the follow-up actions taken to address audit observations and recommendations. UNDP, UNFPA and UNOPS should provide adequate training, particularly for field-based staff, to interpret and follow up on audit findings and recommendations, an analysis and presentation of the follow-up on previous internal audit recommendations in the 2003 and 2004 reports, and report on the status of the most frequent and highest-priority recommendations in the next report. The Administrator and the UNOPS and UNFPA Executive Directors were requested to provide a management response to their internal audit reports at the Board's annual session. UNDP was asked to arrange for the Board of Auditors to present their report to the Board.

Revision of financial regulations

In January, the Executive Board considered the Administrator's proposed revisions to the UNDP financial regulations [DP/2005/3]. The revisions reflected changes resulting from Board decisions that had affected the financial regulations since the last comprehensive revision in 2000 [YUN 2000, p. 838], including those dealing with the timing of the Board's special funding meeting [ibid., p. 836]; the treatment of support costs; and the elimination of the system of reimbursable target for resource assignment from the core (TRAC) earmarkings, with effect from 2001. They also reflected changes resulting from alignment with UNDG simplification and harmonization ini-

tiatives. The proposed substantive changes related to programming modalities, authority to commit resources against future receipt of contributions, separation of duties and previous Board decisions. Terminological and editorial changes to the financial regulations were also proposed. An annex to the report contained the text of the revised regulations.

ACABQ, in its report on the proposed revisions [DP/2005/4], emphasized the need for UNDP financial regulations to promote transparency and accountability. It recommended that the Board approve the revisions, as contained in the Administrator's report.

On 28 January [dec. 2005/1], the Board approved the proposed revised financial regulations, with the exception of changes to regulations 5.07 regarding commitment of resources against future receipt of contributions and 20.02 regarding exceptions to separation of duties. It requested the Administrator to establish risk guidelines with respect to the proposed changes to those regulations, as well as an independent expert assessment of the changes, and deferred consideration of them to the Board's annual session in June, pending the assessment. The Administrator was also requested to keep the financial regulations under review and to consult accordingly with the Board.

A June conference room paper [DP/2005/CRP.6], submitted in response to the Board's decision (see above), outlined in greater depth the rationale for the proposed changes to financial regulations 5.07 and 20.02, the associated risks and guidelines for mitigating those risks. The revisions and guidelines had been reviewed by the UNDP External Auditor of the United Nations Board of Auditors.

On 22 June [dec. 2005/17], the Executive Board approved, on a three-year provisional basis, the proposed changes to regulations 5.07 and 20.02, and requested that all transactions made during the period of waived separation of duties would be subject to ex post facto review. The Board also requested the Board of Auditors to assess the implementation of those changes at the end of the three-year trial period, within the context of their biennial audit.

Other technical cooperation

Review of UN regular programme of technical cooperation and Development Account

On 13 April (**decision 59/558**), the General Assembly decided to consider, as a matter of priority in 2005, the Secretary-General's 2004 report on the review of the regular programme of technical cooperation and the Development Account [YUN 2004, p. 891], which contained specific proposals for improving both programmes.

The Assembly, in **resolution 60/246** of 23 December (see p. 1489), having considered the Secretary-General's 2004 report, decided that the Development Account would be recosted for the 2006-2007 biennium and, to that end, requested the Secretary-General to pursue the relevant proposals contained in his report and provide to the Assembly at its sixty-first (2006) session recommendations on how additional resources of up to $5 million could be added to the Account.

UN activities

Department of Economic and Social Affairs

During 2005, the UN Department of Economic and Social Affairs (DESA) had approximately 500 technical cooperation projects under execution in a dozen substantive sectors, with a total project expenditure of $48.4 million. Projects financed by UNDP represented $9.7 million, and those by trust funds, $38.7 million.

On a geographical basis, DESA's technical cooperation programme included expenditures of $32 million for interregional and global programmes; $9.3 million in Africa; $3.7 million in Asia and the Pacific; $2.5 million in the Middle East; and $0.9 million in the Americas.

Distribution of expenditures by substantive sectors was as follows: associate expert programme, $23.8 million; socio-economic governance management, $8.8 million; governance and public administration, $6.9 million; programme support, $1.9 million; Information and Communication Technologies (ICT) Task Force, $1.8 million; infrastructure, $1.7 million; energy, $1.4 million; water, $1.1 million; social development, $0.5 million; knowledge management, $0.2 million; statistics, $0.2 million; and Forum on Forests, $0.1 million. Of the total delivery of $48.4 million, the associate expert programme comprised 50 per cent; socio-economic governance management, 19 per cent; and governance and public administration, 15 per cent.

On a component basis, DESA's delivery included $40.1 million for project personnel; $3.9 million for training; $2.2 million for equipment; $1.6 million for subcontracts; and $0.6 million for miscellaneous expenses.

The total expenditure for DESA against the UN regular programme of technical cooperation was $6.8 million. Distribution of expenditures by division was as follows: public administration and development management, $2.6 million; sustainable development, $1.7 million; statistics, $1.2 million; social policy and development, $0.8 million; advancement of women, $0.3 million; population, $0.1 million; and administrative support, $0.1 million. On a component basis, expenditure for the year included $4.9 million for advisory services; $0.8 million for meetings; $0.7 million for travel; and $0.4 million for consultancy services.

UN Fund for International Partnerships

The Secretary-General, in his report on the 2005 activities of the United Nations Fund for International Partnerships (UNFIP) [A/61/189], established in 1998 [YUN 1998, p. 1297] to manage the process of grant allocations through the United Nations Foundation, a public charity founded by Robert E. Turner to channel his gift to the United Nations of stock valued at some $1 billion, provided data on the seventeenth and eighteenth funding cycles and intersessional approvals in 2005, progress in each programme area, and a review of UNFIP activities in advocacy and partnership-building. A total of $170.5 million was programmed for 2005, $46.3 million in the seventeenth funding cycle and $1.5 million in the eighteenth. A further $122.7 million was approved between sessions of the United Nations Foundation Board of Directors. The difference in the level of grant approvals between the sessions resulted from the Board's decision to consolidate future investments by thematic area and use core resources to build partnerships and lead advocacy campaigns in support of key themes, instead of investing exclusively in projects or programmes. Of the total, $143.5 million was for six projects related to children's health; $2.7 million for three projects for population and women; $10.1 million for 18 projects for the environment; $3.7 million for four projects for peace, security and human rights; and $10.5 million for 23 strategic initiative projects. Since 1998, $809.5 million had been allocated to fund 376 projects in 121 countries, involving 39 UN organizations.

In 2005, UNFIP was given responsibility for the management and oversight of the United Nations Democracy Fund (UNDEF), established in Sirte, Libyan Arab Jamahiriya, on 4 July (see p. 655). UNDEF funding priorities were aimed at strengthening democratic dialogue and supporting constitutional processes; civil society empowerment; civic education; voter registration and strengthening of political parties; citizens' access to information; human rights and fundamental freedoms; and accountability, transparency and integrity. The Fund supported projects from governmental, non-governmental and UN system organizations. As at 31 December, UNDEF had received $41 million in pledges and contributions from 16 member States.

On 13 April (**decision 59/554**) and 23 December (**decision 60/550**), the General Assembly took note of the Secretary-General's reports on UNFIP activities in 2003 [YUN 2003, p. 905] and 2004 [YUN 2004, p. 892], respectively.

UN Office for Project Services

The United Nations Office for Project Services (UNOPS) was established in 1995 [YUN 1995, p. 900], in accordance with General Assembly decision 48/501 [YUN 1994, p. 806], as a separate, self-financing entity of the UN system to act as a service provider to UN organizations. It offered a broad range of services, from overall project management to the provision of single inputs.

2005 activities

The Executive Director, in his annual report on UNOPS activities for 2005 [DP/2006/22], said that the year was critical in the UNOPS multi-year turnaround programme, initiated in 2003 [YUN 2003, p. 906]. Project portfolio acquisition reached a record level of $1 million, with some 55 per cent attributable to post-conflict and emergency-related activities and 45 per cent to development activities.

Project delivery, which reached a record $888.2 million, exceeded the forecast of $641.4 million (38.5 per cent) submitted by the Executive Director in January.

In 2005, UNOPS generated $71.7 million in total revenue, exceeding the 2005 forecast of $53.8 million. Project services continued to provide the largest percentage of total UNOPS revenue ($58.8 million); including $27.6 million from UNDP core and trust funds, $4.1 million from UNDP management services agreements, and $26.8 million from other UN organizations. Service revenue totalled $9.9 million, and interest and rental income $2.3 million. For the first time since 1998, UNOPS achieved an operating surplus of $5.2 million, which, after reimbursements to the United Nations oil-for-food programme and to the World Food Programme, resulted in an ending balance of $5.1 million.

Administrative expenditures reached $66.5 million in 2005, $9.2 million above the 2004 level and $15.7 million above the approved level of $50.9 million. Of the 2005 total, salaries and benefits accounted for $30.4 million, exceeding the budgeted level by $2.4 million; $25.6 million was spent on general and administrative expenses.

Reimbursements to UNDP and the United Nations accounted for $5.1 million. UNOPS also set aside $5.5 million for after-service health insurance payments, write-offs and doubtful accounts.

Budget estimates

Projected 2004 budget performance and revised 2005 estimates

In a January progress report on UNOPS activities [DP/2005/9], the Executive Director provided an overview of projected 2004 budget performance, revised budget estimates for 2005, and updates on the evolving UNOPS corporate strategy. Projected expenditure was expected to exceed revenue by almost $14 million. The fund balance, as at 31 December 2004, was estimated at $9.2 million, comprising an operating reserve balance of $6 million and working capital in the amount of $3.2 million.

As at 30 November 2004, UNOPS estimated that total 2004 delivery would be $381.6 million and revenue $38.4 million.

Total expenditures for 2004 were estimated at $52.4 million, of which $26.2 million pertained to salaries and benefits and $12.1 million to general and administrative expenditures. Reimbursements to UNDP and other UN organizations were estimated to reach $8.5 million, $1 million higher than initially projected. Expenditures under the approved change management budget were projected at $4.9 million.

As at 30 November 2004, new business acquired under the project portfolio of services reached $663 million, $458 million of which related to business acquisition in post-conflict and transition environments.

The 2005 budget proposal estimated $53.8 million in revenues, comprising $42.1 million in project portfolio implementation; $9.8 million in service revenue derived from the IFAD loan portfolio and the Global Fund to Fight AIDS, Tuberculosis and Malaria; and $1.8 million in rental, interest and other miscellaneous income. Total 2005 expenditures were estimated at $50.9 million, comprising $28 million for salaries and benefits; $10.1 million for general administrative costs; $4.7 million for change management; $7.4 million for reimbursements to UNDP and other UN organizations; and $0.7 million for doubtful accounts. UNOPS would reduce ongoing operating expenses by $2 million in 2005, as compared to current estimates for 2004. The project delivery forecast for 2005 was $641.4 million. The 2005 year-end net income from operations was forecast at $2.9 million and a fund balance at $12.1 million.

In January [DP/2005/10], the UNOPS Management Coordination Committee (MCC), in response to a 2004 Executive Board decision [YUN 2004, p. 896], submitted its report on progress in UNOPS, including MCC's views on the Executive Director's January progress report on UNOPS activities (see p. 978), the 2005 budget proposals and recommendations for the future UNOPS operations. MCC noted the encouraging UNOPS business acquisition in 2004 for delivery during 2004 and 2005, and urged UNOPS management to ensure that new business generated higher income, with an emphasis on project management activities rather than limited loan-servicing activities. It expressed serious doubts as to whether the projected revenue for 2005, which were predicted to be 40 per cent more than the 2004 projections, would materialize, as recent revenue projections had not been accurate, or reliable. MCC also noted that the 2005 budget proposal offered only a narrow operating surplus of $2.9 million, and that the level of the 2005 fund balance was highly dependent on the final 2004 fund balance results, as well as on UNOPS ensuring that the 2005 income and expenditures reached projected levels. It observed that to date UNOPS had not demonstrated its ability to control expenditures within budgeted levels and had not been able to achieve the projected revenue. MCC therefore urged caution in the implementation of the 2005 budget proposal. Concerned that UNOPS might again incur an operating loss in 2005, it urged UNOPS senior management to monitor revenue and expenditures on a continuous basis and ensure adherence to the underlying principle that expenditure be below income in any single year.

MCC recognized the progress by UNOPS in implementing some important aspects of the change management process, but noted that a number of important change initiatives remained to be implemented, in particular the completion of a corporate strategy for achieving financial viability (see below). It discussed with UNOPS senior management various approaches for improving long-term financial performance and options to help ensure its sustainability.

MCC endorsed the 2005 budget proposal, provided that 2005 was viewed as a "survival year", during which UNOPS would consolidate the gains made in the implementation of the change management programme, while ensuring that expenditures remained below 95 per cent of actual income. During 2005, UNOPS should develop a plan of action to correct the persistent income volatility and high fixed costs, in order to become financially viable in 2006. MCC recommended that the UNDP/UNFPA Executive Board request UNOPS to outline, in the context of the ongoing development of a corporate strategy, a plan of action to improve financial performance, by realigning and reconfiguring its operations during the 2006-2007 period. UNOPS should submit a full plan of action for decision by the Executive Board at its annual session in 2005.

On 28 January [dec. 2005/6], the Executive Board took note of the Executive Director's progress report and MCC's report on the assessment of progress in UNOPS. It approved the 2005 budget estimates, and indicated that 2005 expenditures would be covered by revenues earned during that year, and the change management programme remained a priority and would be adjusted according to the availability of funds. It noted MCC concerns with regard to the attainment of 2005 targets and requested the Executive Director to provide periodic updates on the financial situation during 2005. He should continue to improve the UNOPS financial management and control systems and the required reporting. UNOPS should remain committed to its audit response and achieve a clean audit for the 2004-2005 biennium. The Executive Director was also asked to prepare, for the Board's September 2005 meeting, a comprehensive plan of action, based on consultations with MCC, on further measures to be implemented in 2006 to enhance the efficiency of business operations, ensure cost reductions, continue the change management process and achieve sustainable financial viability.

UNOPS action plan

In response to Executive Board decision 2005/6 (see above), the UNOPS Executive Director submitted an August report [DP/2005/39] providing two options for UNOPS to ensure the future viability of its operations as a self-financing, independent service provider in the UN system.

Option 1 proposed an immediate reduction in the range of services provided in UNOPS geographic coverage and fixed-cost structures around a core set of product offerings and skill sets. Its primary product lines would encompass engineering and infrastructure operations, complex operations management and supportive service lines. Primary market environments would comprise countries in post-conflict transition or recovering from natural disasters, and countries with poorly developed infrastructure and limited management or implementation capacities. The changes would be completed, for the most part, in 2006, enabling UNOPS to start rebuilding its reserves and return to sustained viability in 2007.

Option 2 would maintain the current range of UNOPS service offerings, but cut fixed costs, rationalize its structures and phase out portfolios that could not achieve full cost recovery. The support structure would be more geographically dispersed than for option 1, but portfolios would be subject to full cost recovery, assured by improved pricing through activity-based costing processes. Implementation of the changes would be completed by late 2007, enabling UNOPS to begin returning to sustained viability in 2008.

The report specified product lines, related product streams under option 1 and service lines under option 2, and included financial projections for each option, with explanatory notes about the data presented and the assumptions on which projections were developed.

An August conference room paper [DP/2005/CRP.14], submitted as a supplement to the action plan, provided updated financial projections for 2005 and for 2006-2008, taking into account revised revenue projections for 2005 and the impact of reimbursements required against fees for service earned in 2003 under the oil-for-food programme (see p. 434) and Security Council resolution 1483(2003) on the lifting of economic sanctions on Iraq [YUN 2003, p. 338].

In September [dec. 2005/36], the Executive Board took note of the Executive Director's report on the action plan for restoring the viability of UNOPS and the supplement thereto. It recognized the necessity for implementing the measures proposed under option 1. It emphasized that the measures to be taken in line with the decision were a foundation for the future, but did not exclude provision of services to clients in situations and circumstances other than those specified under option 1, so long as UNOPS could provide satisfactory services at full cost recovery. The Board expected that the reform measures would enable UNOPS to return to sustainable financial viability, rebuild its operational reserve and meet its statutory obligations with regard to staff post-service benefits and other areas. It requested the Executive Director to implement the reforms expeditiously and provide periodic updates to the Board in 2006 on the UNOPS financial situation and on progress in the implementation of the transition measures. The Board intended to engage in a continuing discussion on the role and mandate of UNOPS in the wider context of UN reform.

Audit reports

The Executive Board, at its January session [dec. 2005/8], took note of the Executive Director's report [DP/2005/12] on the implementation of the recommendations of the Board of Auditors [YUN 2004, p. 1397] for the 2002-2003 biennium.

In May [DP/2005/27], the UNDP Office of Audit and Performance Review (OAPR) reported that it conducted 20 internal audits covering operational activities at headquarters and in the field, including those under management and support services arrangements. Together, the audit reports contained 72 recommendations for improving internal controls and organizational efficiency. The organizational units concerned provided written comments on the contents of the draft audit reports. UNOPS provided comments on 61 of the recommendations. In general, the comments indicated that actions had been taken or were being taken to address the audit issues raised and recommendations made.

In June [dec. 2005/19] (see p. 976), the UNDP/UNFPA Executive Board took note of OAPR's May report.

UN Volunteers

The number of volunteers working for the UNDP-administered United Nations Volunteers programme (UNV) increased to 8,122, from 7,300 in 2004. The volunteers, representing 168 nationalities, carried out 8,470 assignments in 144 countries. Volunteers from developing countries represented 76.3 per cent of the total number of volunteers. Women accounted for 36.5 per cent of the total in 2005, compared to 35 per cent in 2004. By region, 47.3 per cent of assignments were carried out in Africa, 20.8 per cent in Latin America and the Caribbean, 18 per cent in Asia and the Pacific, 7.3 per cent in Europe and CIS, and 6.6 per cent in the Arab States.

The UNDP Administrator, in his annual report on the UNV financial situation [DP/2006/37 & Add.1], indicated that income for 2005 was $26.2 million, compared to $22.7 million in 2004. Taking into account that $3 million of the 2004 income related to 2003 contributions, the actual increase in total net income was $6.5 million, or 33 per cent compared to 2004. The increase in income was due mainly to a substantial increase in new trust funds, especially for recovery programmes related to the 2004 Indian Ocean tsunami [YUN 2004, p. 952]. Programme expenditure increased by $700,000 to $18.4 million, compared to $17.7 million in 2004. The balance of the operational reserve, as at 31 December, was $900,000.

Follow-up to the International Year of Volunteers (2001)

In response to General Assembly resolution 57/106 [YUN 2002, p. 881], the Secretary-General submitted a July report [A/60/128] on follow-up to the implementation of the International Year of Volunteers (2001) [YUN 2001, p. 814]. The report provided an overview of actions taken during the International Year and presented conclusions and recommendations for follow-up.

The Secretary-General said that the momentum built up during the Year continued to stimulate a vibrant and expanding volunteer movement. Most of the recommendations proposed by the Assembly in resolution 57/106 were being taken up by Governments and the UN system, as well as by civil society and the private sector. The World Volunteer Web portal, launched in 2002, encouraged global information sharing on how volunteerism could contribute to economic and social development. The first International Conference on Volunteerism and the Millennium Development Goals (Islamabad, Pakistan, 5-7 December 2004), organized jointly by UNDP, UNV and the National Commission for Human Development of Pakistan, outlined actions to enhance the environment for volunteer interventions in support of the MDGs [YUN 2000, p. 51]. Awareness was growing in many countries in all regions and was expected to lead to the participation of increased numbers of people in voluntary activity. Governments, the media and the private sector were increasingly vocal in their support for volunteering, and human resources and physical infrastructure were being developed to facilitate volunteerism.

Despite overall progress, positive global trends varied widely between countries and regions. In the least developed countries in Africa and in countries undergoing profound social, economic and political change, volunteering was lower on the agenda of Governments than in other parts of the world. The situation within the UN system was also mixed. Since 2001, UN system organizations were increasingly recognizing, facilitating and promoting volunteerism as an integral part of their work, but that trend needed to be reinforced and broadened.

In addition to raising awareness on the role and contribution of volunteerism, the International Year led, in many cases, to the introduction or strengthening of proactive measures at the national level to support voluntary action. Those developments needed to be sustained and extended to cover all countries if the potential of volunteerism to help meet the MDGs was to be fully realized.

GENERAL ASSEMBLY ACTION

On 16 December [meeting 64], the General Assembly, on the recommendation of the Third (Social, Humanitarian and Cultural) Committee

[A/60/501], adopted **resolution 60/134** without vote [agenda item 62].

Follow-up to the implementation of the International Year of Volunteers

The General Assembly,

Recalling its resolution 57/106 of 26 November 2002 on the follow-up to the International Year of Volunteers,

Recognizing the valuable contribution of volunteering, including traditional forms of mutual aid and self-help, formal service delivery and other forms of civic participation, to economic and social development, benefiting society at large, communities and the individual volunteer,

Recognizing also that volunteerism is an important component of any strategy aimed at, inter alia, such areas as poverty reduction, sustainable development, health, disaster prevention and management and social integration and, in particular, overcoming social exclusion and discrimination,

Noting with appreciation the efforts to increase understanding and awareness of volunteerism through research, global information-sharing and education, including efforts to develop an effective network for volunteers through, inter alia, the World Volunteer Web and linked national sites,

Acknowledging the existing contribution of the organizations of the United Nations system to supporting volunteering, including the work of United Nations Volunteers around the world,

Bearing in mind the need for an integrated and coordinated follow-up to the International Year of Volunteers to be pursued in the relevant parts of the United Nations system,

1. *Welcomes* the report of the Secretary-General;

2. *Takes note* of the report of the Secretary-General in response to the report of the Panel of Eminent Persons on United Nations-Civil Society Relations;

3. *Welcomes* the hosting of the first International Conference on Volunteerism and the Millennium Development Goals, organized jointly by the Government of Pakistan and the United Nations system and held in Islamabad from 5 to 7 December 2004, and takes note of its final report;

4. *Reiterates its call upon* Governments, with the active support of the media, civil society and the private sector, to observe the International Volunteer Day for Economic and Social Development on 5 December and to include activities, in particular on efforts to achieve the Millennium Development Goals;

5. *Reaffirms* the need to recognize and promote all forms of volunteerism as an issue that involves and benefits all segments of society, including children, young persons, older persons, persons with disabilities, minorities and immigrants and those who remain excluded for social or economic reasons;

6. *Recognizes* that volunteering, in particular at the community level, will help to achieve the internationally agreed development goals, including those contained in the United Nations Millennium Declaration;

7. *Also recognizes* the importance of supportive legislative and fiscal frameworks for the growth and development of volunteerism, and encourages Governments to enact such measures;

8. *Welcomes* the work of the United Nations Volunteers, and requests them to continue their efforts, together with other stakeholders, to raise awareness of volunteerism, increase reference and networking resources available, provide technical cooperation to developing countries, upon their request, in the field of volunteerism and enhance coordination among those operating on the ground;

9. *Invites* all stakeholders, especially from the private sector community and from private foundations, to support volunteerism as a strategic tool to enhance economic and social development, including by expanding corporate volunteering;

10. *Calls for* the relevant organizations and bodies of the United Nations system to integrate volunteerism in its various forms into their policies, programmes and reports, and encourages the recognition and inclusion of volunteer contributions in future United Nations and other relevant international conferences;

11. *Acknowledges* the importance of civil society organizations for the promotion of volunteerism, and in this respect recognizes that strengthening the dialogue and interaction between civil society and the United Nations contributes to the expansion of volunteerism;

12. *Encourages* Governments to establish partnerships with civil society in order to build up volunteer potential at the national level, given the important contribution that volunteerism makes to the fulfilment of the internationally agreed development goals, including those contained in the Millennium Declaration;

13. *Recognizes* the increasing attention being given to the economic dimension of volunteerism, and encourages Governments, with the support of civil society, to build up a knowledge base on the subject, to disseminate data and to expand research on other volunteer-related issues, including in developing countries;

14. *Welcomes* the work of the United Nations Volunteers in building up the capacity of the World Volunteer Web with a view to enhancing network capabilities and to expanding information, knowledge and resource management, and encourages Governments and all stakeholders, in particular the private sector, to contribute on a voluntary basis to this initiative;

15. *Requests* the Secretary-General to report to the General Assembly at its sixty-third session on the implementation of the present resolution under the item entitled "Social development, including questions relating to the world social situation and to youth, ageing, disabled persons and the family" and to include in the report proposals regarding possible ways to mark the tenth anniversary of the International Year of Volunteers in 2011.

Economic and technical cooperation among developing countries

South-South cooperation

In response to a 2004 UNDP/UNFPA Executive Board decision [YUN 2004, p. 898], the Special Unit for South-South Cooperation submitted, in January, an updated version of the third cooperation framework for South-South cooperation (2005-2007) [DP/CF/SSC/3/Rev.1 & Corr.1]. Through the framework, the Special Unit sought to strengthen UNDP's work in identifying and sharing knowledge and proven approaches to human development, particularly in efforts to meet the MDGs [YUN 2000, p. 51]. To that end, the framework elaborated the context, initiatives and strategy for sharing knowledge, experiences and technology through South-South cooperation. It was designed to respond to the emerging trends and changing fundamentals in southern development, with particular attention to the needs and priorities shared by LDCs, small island developing States (SIDS) and landlocked developing countries. In keeping with its mandate, the Special Unit would continue to support developing countries in addressing issues of common concern and in multicultural settings, so as to accelerate development through South-South approaches. The framework would place greater emphasis on establishing or strengthening self-sustaining mechanisms and platforms relevant to South-South cooperation, rather than supporting ad hoc forums and conferences. The Special Unit needed to become a South-South knowledge centre, complementing and linking with UNDP's global knowledge systems and those of UN organizations, developing countries and donor organizations. The framework would be designed to: support policy dialogue and follow-up to major intergovernmental conferences; help create an enabling environment and public-private partnership mechanisms for sustained intra-South business collaboration and technology exchanges; and support a more robust, South-specific system for managing and sharing development knowledge. The framework also included an implementation strategy.

The updated total resource mobilization target for the framework for 2005-2007 was $27,500, comprising $16,500 in UNDP regular resources and $11,000 in other resources.

On 28 January [dec. 2005/7], the Executive Board endorsed the third cooperation framework. It requested the UNDP Administrator to: include in his report to the High-level Committee on South-South cooperation in May (see p. 984) a detailed strategy for the implementation of the framework, including resource mobilization, and inform the Board thereon; hold periodic consultations with Member States; and report to the Board in June 2006 on progress achieved in implementing the framework.

An April report [SSC/14/2] reviewed the implementation of the revised Guidelines for the Review of Policies and Procedures concerning South-South Cooperation, including common indicators, as approved in 2003 by the thirteenth session of the High-level Committee on South-South cooperation. The report also reviewed the status, management and use of resources for the promotion of South-South cooperation, the development of a forward-looking strategy for resource mobilization, and supporting UNDP organizational, administrative and financial arrangements.

Among the recommendations made were that the Special Unit design and support the implementation of innovative projects that would serve as models for future replication in South-South development programmes, and that the Unit work more closely with UN development system organizations and UNDP country offices to further integrate South-South cooperation into their regular programmes. Other recommendations related to resource mobilization; South-South policy implementation; the use of information and communication technology; dissemination of information on specific problems and the needs of LDCs, SIDS and landlocked developing countries; and the use of the Web of Information for Development (WIDE).

Second South Summit. The Second South Summit of the Group of 77 and China (Doha, Qatar, 12-16 June) [A/60/111] adopted the Doha Declaration and Plan of Action, in which participating Heads of State and Government reaffirmed the role of South-South cooperation in confronting challenges faced by the South and as a valuable contribution to development, and the need to further strengthen it, including through enhancing the capacities of the institutions and mechanisms that promoted it. They called for a more energetic effort to deepen and revitalize South-South cooperation to take advantage of the new geography of international economic relations, while recognizing that such cooperation was complementary to, and not a substitute for, North-South cooperation. The participants reaffirmed that South-South trade should be enhanced and further market access from developing countries had to continue to stimulate such trade, and resolved to strengthen cooperation in the monetary and financial fields. In the Doha Plan of Action of the Second South Summit, participants decided to establish the South Fund for Development and Humanitarian Assistance for economic, social, health and educational development, as well as to address hunger, poverty and human catastrophes. The Plan of Action recommended the expansion of the Voluntary Trust Fund for the Promotion of South-South Cooperation, established in accordance with General Assembly resolution 50/119 [YUN 1995, p. 848], and requested the Assembly to review its struc-ture and modalities of operation in order to enable it to respond better to the needs of developing countries. Participants agreed to convene the third South Summit in 2010.

Report of Secretary-General. The Secretary-General, in response to Assembly resolution 58/220 [YUN 2003, p. 913], submitted an August report [A/60/257] on the state of South-South cooperation in the period since January 2003. The report reviewed its growing role and the opportunities and challenges of a globalizing world and provided an overview of trends in global and regional cooperation agreements. It also considered the contribution of developing and developed countries, the UN system, the private sector and civil society in support of South-South cooperation.

South-South cooperation received intense support from developing countries and the larger international community, as evidenced by a number of important summits and conferences organized by the Group of 77 and China, the Non-Aligned Movement and other entities. Its new vibrancy was reflected in increasing flows of South-South trade and investment and collaboration in the monetary and energy sectors. Movements towards regional and subregional integration also benefited South-South relations. The scope of South-South cooperation had also expanded beyond the traditional economic and technical areas. It was pervasive in UN development system activities, although there was little uniformity in the information available from different agencies. Despite signs of progress, however, the programmatic visibility of South-South cooperation in multilateral affairs continued to be generally low, which hampered improved coordination and synergy.

The report concluded that the emerging consensus of developed and developing countries on the value of South-South approaches to development presented a unique opportunity for the international community to scale up South-South and triangular initiatives that required the mobilization of complementary resources. Strategies and mechanisms for South-South coordination should be strengthened. To optimize the use of Southern capacities, the UN system should develop a more coordinated approach to the identification and use of the growing number of world-class experts and institutions in developing countries, in coordination with the Special Unit for South-South cooperation, which should be strengthened as the UN South-South cooperation focal point. As the private sector became the main source of foreign direct investment flows to developing countries, efforts should be made to expand and strengthen innovative, self-sustaining public-private partnership mechanisms to overcome obstacles to South-South cooperation.

High-level Committee
on South-South cooperation

The High-level Committee on South-South cooperation, formerly the High-level Committee on the Review of Technical Cooperation among Developing Countries, considered at its fourteenth session (New York, 31 May–3 June) [A/60/39] an April report [SSC/14/1 & Corr.1] reviewing progress in the implementation of the 1978 Buenos Aires Plan of Action for Promoting and Implementing Technical Cooperation among Developing Countries (TCDC) [YUN 1978, p. 467] and the new directions strategy for TCDC [YUN 1995, p. 902], as well as reports of the UNDP Administrator [SSC/14/2] (see p. 982). It also held a thematic discussion on the role of South-South cooperation in achieving the MDGs.

The Committee urged developed and developing countries, the organizations and agencies of the UN development system, including the regional commissions, and other development partners to intensify support for South-South initiatives, with a view to achieving economic growth, sustainable development and more equitable integration into the global economy. It stressed the need for intensifying triangular cooperation to facilitate educational and technical exchanges between developed and developing countries. The Committee called on UN development system entities to include in periodic reports on the internationally agreed development goals, including the MDGs, a section on South-South cooperation. The Committee requested the Special Unit to consult with Member States and UN organizations and agencies, with a view to updating the new directions strategy for technical cooperation among developing countries. The UNDP Administrator was asked to submit a comprehensive report to the High-level Committee at its fifteenth (2007) session on progress made in the implementation of the Buenos Aires Plan of Action and the new directions strategy.

In a decision on the overall framework for promoting and applying South-South cooperation [dec. 14/2], the Committee requested the Special Unit, in implementing its third cooperation framework (2005-2007) (see p. 982), to design and support the implementation of innovative South-South projects and programmes that would serve as models for replication or adaptation. The Committee called on the UN system to intensify the mainstreaming of South-South cooperation in development activities, in collabora-

tion with the Special Unit. It also called on the Unit to capitalize on the momentum generated by international conferences on South-South cooperation and initiatives in regional cooperation and integration to design specific follow-up and implementation actions that addressed the common concerns of developing countries. It should intensify support for national efforts to strengthen South-South policy implementation and continue to work with national South-South focal points to scale up well-coordinated South-South cooperation programmes to LDCs, landlocked developing countries and SIDS. The Committee encouraged the Special Unit to undertake initiatives to attract more resources, both financial and in kind, to supplement regular resources and other funds for South-South activities; and work more closely with UN development system organizations and agencies and the South Centre to maximize the potential of WIDE in addressing the need for information on best practices. The UNDP Administrator was asked to report to the High-level Committee on the implementation of the decision in 2007.

The Economic and Social Council, by **decision 2005/230** of 20 July, took note of the Committee's report on its twelfth session.

GENERAL ASSEMBLY ACTION

On 23 December [meeting 68], the General Assembly, on the recommendation of the Second Committee [A/60/493/Add.2], adopted **resolution 60/212** without vote [agenda item 57 (b)].

South-South cooperation

The General Assembly,

Recalling its resolution 58/220 of 23 December 2003,

Recalling also the 2005 World Summit Outcome,

Recalling further its resolution 59/250 of 22 December 2004, which, inter alia, called on organizations and bodies of the United Nations system to mainstream, in their programmes and through their country-level activities and country offices, modalities to support South-South cooperation,

1. *Welcomes* the report of the High-level Committee on South-South Cooperation at its fourteenth session and the decisions taken at that session;

2. *Takes note* of the report of the Secretary-General on the state of South-South cooperation;

3. *Stresses* that South-South cooperation, as an important element of international cooperation for development, offers viable opportunities for developing countries in their individual and collective pursuit of sustained economic growth and sustainable development;

4. *Recognizes* that developing countries have the primary responsibility for promoting and implementing South-South cooperation, not as a substitute for but rather as a complement to North-South cooperation, and in this context reiterates the need for the interna-

tional community to support the efforts of the developing countries to expand South-South cooperation;

5. *Encourages* the international community, including the international financial institutions, to support the efforts of developing countries, inter alia, through triangular cooperation;

6. *Recognizes* that regional integration initiatives between developing countries constitute an important and valuable form of South-South cooperation and that regional integration is a step towards beneficial integration into the world economy;

7. *Welcomes* the initiatives and partnerships being undertaken at the subregional, regional, interregional and global levels towards establishing public-private partnership mechanisms aiming to enhance and expand South-South cooperation in trade and investment;

8. *Takes note with appreciation* of the launching of the third round of negotiations on the Global System of Trade Preferences among Developing Countries as an important instrument to stimulate South-South cooperation;

9. *Recognizes* the considerable contribution of South-South cooperation arrangements, which promote development activities in developing countries;

10. *Also recognizes* the importance of initiatives and arrangements, including public-private mechanisms, in the undertaking of efforts to enhance cooperation between developing countries, including, inter alia, in the areas of information and communication technologies, science and technology, culture, health and education;

11. *Welcomes* the contributions made by developing countries in the context of South-South cooperation to countries and peoples stricken by natural disasters, including through the Voluntary Trust Fund for the Promotion of South-South Cooperation within the framework for the rehabilitation and reconstruction of countries affected by the Indian Ocean tsunami disaster and through the South Fund for Development and Humanitarian Assistance;

12. *Urges* all relevant United Nations organizations and multilateral institutions to intensify their efforts to effectively mainstream the use of South-South cooperation in the design, formulation and implementation of their regular programmes and to consider increasing allocations of human, technical and financial resources for supporting South-South cooperation initiatives, and in this regard takes note of the initiatives contained in the Havana Programme of Action adopted by the first South Summit, the Marrakesh Framework for the Implementation of South-South Cooperation and the Doha Plan of Action;

13. *Recognizes* the need to mobilize additional resources for enhancing South-South cooperation, reiterates in this context its decision, in its resolution 57/263 of 20 December 2002, to include the Voluntary Trust Fund for the Promotion of South-South Cooperation in the United Nations Pledging Conference for Development Activities, as long as it exists, recalls the decision to include the Pérez-Guerrero Trust Fund for Economic and Technical Cooperation among Developing Countries in the same Pledging Conference, and invites all countries, in particular developed countries, to support South-South and triangular cooperation through, inter alia, these funds, bearing in mind

the need for these funds to continue to use such resources in an effective manner;

14. *Invites* the United Nations Development Programme to rename the Voluntary Trust Fund for the Promotion of South-South Cooperation, which was established in accordance with General Assembly resolution 50/119 of 20 December 1995, as the United Nations Fund for South-South Cooperation, while maintaining its mandate and voluntary nature, and to designate it as the main United Nations trust fund for promoting and supporting South-South and triangular initiatives;

15. *Invites* the High-level Committee on South-South Cooperation and the United Nations Development Programme Executive Board, as appropriate, to consider measures to strengthen further the Special Unit for South-South Cooperation within the United Nations Development Programme as a separate entity and a focal point for South-South cooperation in the United Nations system, so as to enable it to carry out its full responsibilities, in particular through the mobilization of resources for the advancement of South-South cooperation, including through triangular cooperation;

16. *Decides* to include in the provisional agenda of its sixty-second session a sub-item entitled "South-South cooperation for development", and requests the Secretary-General to submit at that session a comprehensive report on the state of South-South cooperation and on the implementation of the present resolution.

UN Capital Development Fund

In 2005, contributions to the regular resources of the United Nations Capital Development Fund (UNCDF) declined by $7.7 million (45 per cent) to $9.5 million, from $17.2 million in 2004 [DP/2006/37 & Add.1]. Contributions to other resources increased to $10.3 million in 2005, from $6.2 million in 2004. Overall expenditure decreased by $3 million, from $30.3 million in 2004 to $27.3 million in 2005. Expenditure against regular resources decreased to $18.4 million, from $20.2 million in 2004. Other resources expenditures decreased by $1.2 million, from $10.1 million in 2004 to $8.9 million in 2005. Unexpended resources at the end of 2005 totalled $60.1 million, including an operational reserve of $22.6 million.

In June [DP/2005/21], UNCDF submitted to the UNDP/UNFPA Executive Board its 2004 results-oriented annual report (ROAR). Since no new strategic results framework was approved by the Executive Board in 2004, the 2002-2003 framework, which defined UNCDF sub-goals in local governance, microfinance and organizational strengthening, was automatically extended by one year.

UNCDF performance in 2004 continued to be affected by the low level of contributions to its core resources, which totalled $17.6 million, down from $26.9 million in 2003, and far below the target core contribution of $30 million called for by the Executive Board in 2002 [YUN 2002, p. 884]. Insufficient core funding affected UNCDF's capacity to scale up its programmes in local governance and microfinance and initiate new investments. The underlying causes for the gap between target and actual core resources prompted a reassessment of the UNCDF business model (see below).

Total programme expenditure from core and non-core resources in 2004 was $21 million, up from $16.7 million in 2003. Non-core programme expenditures continued their positive trend, reaching $6.6 million in 2004. Local governance remained the primary focus of UNCDF expenditure in 2004, accounting for 70 per cent of the total, followed by microfinance, 17 per cent. The remaining 13 per cent was spent on organizational strengthening. Disbursal rates averaged 73 per cent of planned expenditure in 2004 and were affected by the uncertainty surrounding the transition to a new business model and the rapid decline in core resources.

In 2004, UNCDF approved six new programmes under the local governance sub-goal with a total budget commitment of $10 million. Under the microfinance sub-goal, it approved six programmes applying its new sector development approach, with others in the pipeline for 2005. With regard to the organizational strengthening sub-goal, UNCDF reported improvement in its financial efficiency, resulting in a 9:1 ratio of programme delivery costs to staff support costs.

UNCDF future business model

In January, the UNDP/UNFPA Executive Board considered a report [DP/2005/8], issued in response to a 2004 Board decision [YUN 2004, p. 899], presenting four options for a future strategic niche and new business model for UNCDF. Those options were: maintaining an independent UNCDF focused on microfinance (option 1), first presented in 2004 [ibid.]; migrating current UNCDF programmes and activities in local development to a new UNDP centre for local development (option 2); maintaining an independent UNCDF focused on reducing poverty in LDCs (option 3); and migrating UNCDF microfinance programmes and activities to UNDP (option 4). Following consultation with Board members and private sector representatives, UNDP management proposed a fifth option, an independent UNCDF focused on private sector development. The Administrator established four working groups with representatives from UNCDF and UNDP to develop each of the options. The options were based on an evaluative framework setting out the guiding principles and strategic criteria. The Executive

Director would consult with the Board to seek its guidance on the proposed options.

On 28 January [dec. 2005/5], the Executive Board decided to maintain UNCDF as an independent organization focused on reducing poverty and achieving the MDGs in the LDCs (option 3). It requested the Administrator to provide a detailed implementation plan for that option and its sub-option 4, under which UNCDF would be gradually integrated financially into UNDP for decision at the Board's June session (see p. 986). The Administrator should also appoint a new Executive Secretary for UNCDF. The Board stressed that regular resources, because of their untied nature, would continue to be the foundation of UNCDF programme activities and that the Fund's effectiveness hinged on its access to predictable and sustained multi-year funding to finance its programmes. It called on UNDP to assist UNCDF in mobilizing the resources necessary to sustain its activities, and on donor countries and other countries in a position to do so to provide and sustain additional funding to UNCDF programmes and activities in the LDCs.

UNCDF business plan 2005-2007

A May report [DP/2005/22] presented the UNCDF 2005-2007 business plan: investing in LDCs to achieve the MDGs [YUN 2000, p. 51], including implementation arrangements, in accordance with UNDP/UNFPA Executive Board decision 2005/5 (see above). Building on the UNCDF niche and comparative advantages, the plan envisioned an expansion of UNCDF investments in and technical support to LDCs in the areas of local development and microfinance, thus supporting an increased number of LDCs to achieve the MDGs by 2015. It outlined strategies for generating increased business and resources and translating them into development results. The plan took as its key reference and starting point option 3, sub-option 4 (see above), selected by the Board in decision 2005/5 for the future UNCDF business model; that option was developed into a road map for UNCDF through a change management process that involved the participation of UNCDF staff and facilitation by UNDP.

Under the plan's business development strategy, UNCDF would establish, by mid-2005, a global trust fund for investing in LDCs, which, over time, would replace current UNCDF core resources as the primary source of predictable, multi-year funding. Its service lines would mirror the UNCDF strategic results framework and would be streamlined with UNDP/UNCDF partnerships within the overall UNDP multi-year funding framework (MYFF) (see p. 972). UNDP would support UNCDF in mobilizing resources for the trust fund, as well as specific global and regional initiatives, including the UNCDF-UNDP partnership for localizing the MDGs.

The administrative costs of UNCDF, to be funded through the UNDP biennium budget, were estimated at about $5 million per year for the 2006-2007 period. For UNCDF to fulfil its mandate, it would require predictable, multi-year programme resources in the order of $18 million per year, to be provided as either core or multi-year allocation under the global window of the trust fund for investing in LDCs. The total funding needed for administrative costs, technical expertise and investment purposes, including miscellaneous income, would amount to around $49 million in 2006 and $63 million in 2007.

In June [dec. 2005/29], the Executive Board welcomed the UNCDF business plan 2005-2007 and requested UNDP to report on the mainstreaming of UNCDF administrative costs in the 2006-2007 biennial support budget, as laid out in the plan. It also requested UNCDF to report to the Board at its first session in 2006 on its budgeting and programming decision-making processes. The Board reiterated its call to the Administrator to appoint, as soon as possible, a new UNCDF Executive Secretary. It called on donor countries, and other countries in a position to do so, to provide and sustain additional funding support for UNCDF programmes and activities in LDCs, including by providing funding to the proposed trust fund for investing in those countries. Member States, particularly LDCs, were encouraged to provide advocacy support to assist UNCDF in its resource mobilization efforts.

Chapter III

Humanitarian and special economic assistance

In 2005, the United Nations, through the Office for the Coordination of Humanitarian Affairs (OCHA), continued to mobilize and coordinate humanitarian assistance to respond to international emergencies. During the year, consolidated inter-agency appeals were launched for Angola, Benin, Burundi, the Central African Republic, Chad, Chechnya and neighbouring republics of the Russian Federation, the Congo, Côte d'Ivoire, Djibouti, the Democratic Republic of the Congo (DRC), Eritrea, the Great Lakes region, Guatemala, Guinea, Guyana, the Indian Ocean region, Malawi, the Niger, the Occupied Palestinian Territory, Somalia, the South Asia subregion, the Sudan, Uganda, and the West and Central Africa subregions. OCHA received contributions for natural disaster assistance totalling $7.6 billion.

The Ad Hoc Advisory Groups on Burundi, Guinea-Bissau and Haiti continued to develop long-term programmes of support for those countries.

The World Conference on Disaster Reduction (Kobe, Hyogo, Japan, 18-22 January) concluded a review of the 1994 Yokohama Strategy and Plan of Action and adopted the Hyogo Declaration and the Hyogo Framework for Action 2005-2015: Building the Resilience of Nations and Communities to Disasters. The Framework included strategic goals and priority actions aimed at the substantial reduction of disaster losses, in lives and in the social, economic and environmental assets of communities and countries over the following 10 years. The Conference also issued the common statement of the special session on the Indian Ocean disaster: risk reduction for a safer future.

Humanitarian assistance

Coordination

Humanitarian affairs segment
of the Economic and Social Council

The humanitarian affairs segment of the Economic and Social Council (13-15 July) considered, in accordance with Council **decision 2005/212**, the strengthening of UN humanitarian assist-ance coordination, including capacity, as well as organizational aspects, and convened panels on lessons learned from the 2004 Indian Ocean earthquake/tsunami disaster [YUN 2004, p. 921]. On 28 April (**decision 2005/216**), the Council decided to hold an informal event on 13 July to consider the issue of transition from relief to development.

The Council considered the Secretary-General's June report [A/60/87-E/2005/78] on strengthening the coordination of emergency humanitarian assistance, submitted in response to General Assembly resolutions 46/182 [YUN 1991, p. 421] and 59/141 [YUN 2004, p. 906], and Council resolution 2004/50 [ibid., p. 903]. The report summarized humanitarian developments and challenges, particularly capacity gaps experienced in complex emergencies and disasters over the preceding year. It also analysed the implementation and impact of Council resolutions 2002/32 [YUN 2002, p. 886], 2003/5 [YUN 2003, p. 916] and 2004/50, with a view to strengthening the policy guidance provided by those resolutions, and discussed the roles of and complementarity among UN entities with regard to multi-dimensional missions.

While the number of crises worldwide decreased from 31 in 2004 to 25 in 2005, the financial requirements to address them increased to nearly $6 billion, from $3.4 billion in 2004. Humanitarian concerns during the reporting period included major disasters in more than 12 nations caused by the 2004 Indian Ocean tsunami [YUN 2004, p. 952]; devastating hurricanes in the Caribbean; the decimation of crops by locusts in 10 West and North African countries; the outbreak of some 35 epidemics worldwide; ongoing fighting in the Darfur region of the Sudan, which resulted in the displacement of more than 2.4 million people and rendered 17 per cent of the region inaccessible to aid workers; and successive seasons of drought in the Horn of Africa, which left millions in need of food aid. While refugees in several parts of the world were able to find solutions, the number of internally displaced persons (IDPs) worldwide remained at 50 million.

Prospects for peace in nine African countries, including Angola, Sierra Leone and Somalia, presented opportunities for making progress on the humanitarian front. However, substantial humanitarian needs persisted and the challenges involved in addressing them remained significant. Despite the high levels of need and promising opportunities, donors still approached humanitarian crises unevenly and with insufficient resources. Funds to pay for prominent crises, including those in Afghanistan, Iraq and the aftermath of the Indian Ocean tsunami, were diverted from other areas, often to the detriment of African appeals; promises to replenish aid budgets depleted by large-scale crises were not generally kept.

The humanitarian community was capable of launching a massive response, but it was also apparent that the timeliness and efficacy of such a response could not be guaranteed. Some of the factors affecting response, such as lack of access and obstruction of aid, were specific to individual crises, while some of the key challenges seemed to be systemic in nature. Drawing on lessons learned from the crises in the Darfur region of the Sudan, the Indian Ocean region and elsewhere, the report highlighted limitations of the system and provided insight into possible improvements. In an effort to strengthen global humanitarian response capacities and improve the overall UN emergency response system, the Emergency Relief Coordinator initiated an independent, system-wide capacity review (see p. 991), which analysed potential resources to meet future demands for assistance and protection.

The Secretary-General evaluated the impact of humanitarian resolutions, including Council resolutions 2002/32, 2003/5 and 2004/50. The analysis suggested that the Council's value with respect to humanitarian assistance and coordination continued to be its inclusiveness as an annual platform that brought together UN agencies, non-governmental organizations (NGOs) and donor and recipient countries on issues that constrained humanitarian work. The Council also served as a means for tracking progress on humanitarian policy issues, but its effectiveness as a monitoring tool was contingent on its ability to promote accountability among all parts of the humanitarian system. The Council had failed to generate broad respect for humanitarian principles or promote compliance with them on the ground. It would benefit from a more strategic vision and approach with regard to humanitarian issues. Such an approach might better define its role vis-à-vis that of the General Assembly and the Security Council; clearly and systematically identify and address gaps in the system and improve humanitarian action; and promote broad

ownership of and accountability for issues of common concern.

The relationships between the humanitarian, development, political and military elements of UN missions were also reviewed. The "Report on Integrated Missions: Practical Perspectives and Recommendations", an independent study commissioned by the expanded Core Group of the Executive Committee on Humanitarian Affairs, identified ways in which the United Nations could improve its response in peacekeeping and peacebuilding situations. The study concluded that mission mandates needed to recognize humanitarian principles, and mission design had to be sufficiently flexible to allow for protection of the humanitarian operating environment. Mission structures had to enable human rights actors to meet their mandated obligations, while supporting transitional processes.

The Secretary-General recommended strengthening humanitarian response capacity by broadening the capacity base and improving expertise and performance benchmarks; improving coordination by making more efficient use of available resources; and expanding the use of the Central Emergency Revolving Fund (CERF) to include a grant facility component based on voluntary contributions (see p. 993).

Transition from relief to development

In response to General Assembly resolution 59/141 [YUN 2004, p. 906] and Economic and Social Council resolution 2004/50 [ibid., p. 903], the Secretary-General, in a June report [A/60/89-E/2005/79], discussed the issue of transition from relief to development. The report described key challenges in post-disaster, drought and conflict transitions, and highlighted lessons learned and best practices. The Secretary-General said that, while all transition situations were unique and required flexible responses adapted to the specific context and circumstances of the country, national ownership of the transition process was a key to successful and sustainable recovery and development efforts and to lasting peace. Managing recovery in any transition context required the investment of funds and efforts to build national capacity, empower communities and exploit the synergies among development, humanitarian and other actors. Post-disaster transition phases should include sustained support for the immediate restoration of livelihoods and basic social services, as well as for preparedness measures and activities that would reduce future disaster vulnerability. Disaster-recovery programming should be developed with affected Governments and communities and with an awareness of the existing socio-economic situation. The United

Nations needed to strengthen leadership and co-ordination support structures in the field and improve institutional accountability at Headquarters. That could include empowering the resident coordinator system to take on a more directive role during the transition phase and strengthening the UN country teams to ensure that support was provided in a timely, predictable and cost-effective manner. In addition, funding appeals should include support for early recovery needs and transition coordination.

Post-conflict transition operations involved a complex web of political, peacekeeping, human rights, humanitarian and development activities geared towards consolidating peace, supporting the restoration of State and Government institutions and reinforcing human security. It was critical, therefore, that the desired goal of those efforts be developed by and with affected Governments, civil society and communities. It was also essential to fully fund early recovery needs identified in the consolidated appeals process (CAP) and to support resident coordinators and UN country teams in issuing early transitional appeals for needs not covered by CAP.

ECONOMIC AND SOCIAL COUNCIL ACTION

On 15 July [meeting 28], the Economic and Social Council adopted **resolution 2005/4** [draft: E/2005/L.19, orally revised] without vote [agenda item 5].

Strengthening of the coordination of emergency humanitarian assistance of the United Nations

The Economic and Social Council,

Reaffirming General Assembly resolution 46/182 of 19 December 1991 and the guiding principles contained in the annex thereto, and recalling other relevant resolutions of the Assembly and Economic and Social Council and agreed conclusions of the Council,

Welcoming the fact that, at the humanitarian affairs segment of its substantive session of 2005, the Council considered the theme "Strengthening of the coordination of United Nations humanitarian assistance, including capacity as well as organizational aspects",

Also welcoming the fact, that the Council held a panel discussion on lessons learned from the recent Indian Ocean earthquake/tsunami disaster,

1. *Takes note* of the report of the Secretary-General;

2. *Also takes note* of the report of the Secretary-General on strengthening emergency relief, rehabilitation, reconstruction, recovery and prevention in the aftermath of the Indian Ocean tsunami disaster as well as of the report of the Secretary-General on the transition from relief to development;

3. *Requests* the relevant organizations of the United Nations system to strengthen, within their respective mandates, essential common humanitarian services that are coordinated through the Inter-Agency Standing Committee so that those services can be provided in a predictable, efficient and effective manner;

4. *Also requests* the relevant organizations of the United Nations system to engage systematically with relevant authorities and organizations at the regional and national levels to support efforts to strengthen humanitarian response capacities at all levels, in particular through preparedness programmes, with a view to improving the overall adequacy of the deployment of resources;

5. *Stresses* that the United Nations system should make efforts to enhance existing humanitarian capacities, knowledge and institutions, including, as appropriate, through the transfer of technology and expertise to developing countries and countries with economies in transition;

6. *Requests* the Secretary-General to encourage the relevant organizations of the United Nations system, within their respective mandates, to develop further appropriate mechanisms for the identification and/or development of specialist technical expertise and capacity to fill gaps in critical humanitarian programming sectors in order to improve the capacity of the United Nations system to respond to humanitarian needs;

7. *Also requests* the Secretary-General, in consultation with relevant United Nations humanitarian organizations and States, to discuss ways to help assess the effectiveness of the United Nations humanitarian response;

8. *Stresses* that the United Nations system should improve its ability to make the best use of existing humanitarian capacities at all levels;

9. *Requests* the Secretary-General to encourage the relevant organizations of the United Nations system to identify and use, as appropriate and available, local resources and expertise from within the affected country and/or its neighbours in response to humanitarian needs;

10. *Also requests* the Secretary-General, in consultation with States and relevant organizations, to further develop and improve, as required, mechanisms for the use of emergency standby capacities, including, where appropriate, regional humanitarian capacities, under the auspices of the United Nations, inter alia, through formal agreements with appropriate regional organizations, and to report on this issue to the General Assembly at its sixty-first session, through the Economic and Social Council;

11. *Further requests* the Secretary-General to develop more systematic links with Member States offering military assets for natural disaster response in order to identify the availability of such assets;

12. *Requests* the Secretary-General to strengthen the humanitarian response capacity of, and the support to, United Nations resident/humanitarian coordinators and United Nations country teams, including by providing the necessary training, identifying resources and improving the identification and selection of United Nations resident/humanitarian coordinators, to help provide a timely, predictable and appropriate response to humanitarian needs and to further improve United Nations coordination activities at the field level;

13. *Calls upon* the relevant United Nations entities, under the coordination mandate of the Office for the Coordination of Humanitarian Affairs of the Secretariat, to improve the development of common needs assessments and work towards more effective prioritiz-

ation, including reviewing the Consolidated Appeals Process Needs Assessment Framework and Matrix;

14. *Stresses* the importance of rapid access to funds for an effective United Nations humanitarian response in the initial phases of a humanitarian emergency, before an appeal is launched, or in cases of unanticipated humanitarian needs, as well as for addressing core needs in underfunded emergencies;

15. *Emphasizes* the need to establish reliable, predictable and timely funding to meet humanitarian needs, including those in underfunded emergencies;

16. *Requests* the Secretary-General to continue efforts, including through consultations with States, to address the need to establish finance mechanisms to enable timely allocation of humanitarian resources in response to the Consolidated Appeals Process so as to address gaps in the United Nations humanitarian response;

17. *Recommends* to the General Assembly that it improve functioning of the Central Emergency Revolving Fund, inter alia, through the possible inclusion of a grant facility component based on voluntary contributions, and requests the Secretary-General to submit a report on this issue for consideration by the Assembly at its sixtieth session;

18. *Requests* the Secretary-General to continue to strive to broaden the donor base for humanitarian response, including by engaging the private sector, as well as to strengthen efforts to further enhance transparency and accountability with respect to the channelling and utilization of resources;

19. *Recommends* to the General Assembly that it request the Secretary-General to ensure that United Nations humanitarian organizations work, as appropriate, with the Department of Peacekeeping Operations of the Secretariat in order to better ensure that humanitarian issues are accounted for from the earliest stages of planning and design of United Nations multidimensional integrated peacekeeping operations with humanitarian components and that the mandates of such operations continue to respect the need for their humanitarian activities to be carried out in accordance with humanitarian principles;

20. *Requests* the Secretary-General to reflect the progress made in the implementation of and follow-up to the present resolution in his next report to the Economic and Social Council and the General Assembly on the strengthening of the coordination of emergency humanitarian assistance of the United Nations.

Humanitarian Response Review. In an August report commissioned by the United Nations Emergency Relief Coordinator and the Under-Secretary-General for Humanitarian Affairs, independent consultants examined the humanitarian response capacities of the United Nations, NGOs, the Red Cross/Red Crescent movement and other key humanitarian actors. The evaluation, known as the Humanitarian Response Review, gauged the preparedness of international humanitarian organizations to predict, prevent and mitigate the impact of crises on vulnerable populations in complex emergencies and

natural disasters, and respond effectively to their needs. The major gap identified by the review was the low level of preparedness of humanitarian organizations in terms of human resources and sectoral capacities. The report recommended a global mapping of humanitarian response capacities covering international, national and regional action, the private sector and the military. Other key recommendations covered the development and application of performance benchmarks and indicators; strengthening response capacities; improving international response system coordination; and the adequacy of available funding to ensure timely response.

GENERAL ASSEMBLY ACTION

On 15 December [meeting 63], the General Assembly adopted **resolution 60/124** [draft: A/60/L.38 & Add.1] without vote [agenda item 73 (*a*)].

Strengthening of the coordination of emergency humanitarian assistance of the United Nations

The General Assembly,

Reaffirming its resolution 46/182 of 19 December 1991 and the guiding principles contained in the annex thereto, and recalling other relevant General Assembly and Economic and Social Council resolutions and agreed conclusions of the Council,

Taking note of the report of the Secretary-General on the strengthening of the coordination of emergency humanitarian assistance of the United Nations,

Also taking note of the report of the Secretary-General on the improvement of the Central Emergency Revolving Fund,

Reaffirming the principles of neutrality, humanity, impartiality and independence for the provision of humanitarian assistance,

Reiterating that independence means the autonomy of humanitarian objectives from the political, economic, military or other objectives that any actor may hold with regard to areas where humanitarian action is being implemented,

Expressing deep concern at the number and scale of natural disasters and their increasing impact within recent years, and reaffirming the need for sustainable measures at all levels to reduce the vulnerability of societies to natural hazards, using an integrated, multi-hazard and participatory approach to addressing vulnerability, risk assessment, and disaster prevention, mitigation, preparedness, response and recovery,

Reaffirming, in this regard, the Hyogo Declaration and the Hyogo Framework for Action 2005–2015: Building the Resilience of Nations and Communities to Disasters, as adopted by the World Conference on Disaster Reduction, held in Kobe, Hyogo, Japan, from 18 to 22 January 2005,

Noting with grave concern that violence, including sexual abuse and sexual and other violence against women, girls and boys, continues to be, in many emergency situations, deliberately directed against civilian populations,

Concerned about the need to mobilize adequate support, including financial resources, for emergency humanitarian assistance at all levels, including at the national, regional and international levels,

Recognizing the clear relationship between emergency, rehabilitation and development and that, in order to ensure a smooth transition from relief to rehabilitation and development, emergency assistance must be provided in ways that will be supportive of recovery and long-term development, and that emergency measures should be seen as a step towards long-term development,

Welcoming the ongoing efforts to strengthen international humanitarian response, including the emergency humanitarian assistance of the United Nations,

Emphasizing that the Office for the Coordination of Humanitarian Affairs of the Secretariat should benefit from adequate and more predictable funding, while stressing the importance for the Office to continue to make efforts to broaden its donor base,

1. *Takes note with appreciation* of the outcome of the eighth humanitarian affairs segment of the Economic and Social Council held during its substantive session of 2005;

2. *Calls upon* all Governments and parties in complex humanitarian emergencies, in particular in armed conflicts and in post-conflict situations, in countries in which humanitarian personnel are operating, in conformity with the relevant provisions of international law and national laws, to cooperate fully with the United Nations and other humanitarian agencies and organizations and to ensure the safe and unhindered access of humanitarian personnel and delivery of supplies and equipment in order to allow them to perform efficiently their task of assisting the affected civilian population, including refugees and internally displaced persons;

3. *Reaffirms* the obligation of all States and parties to an armed conflict to protect civilians in armed conflicts in accordance with international humanitarian law, and invites States to promote a culture of protection, taking into account the particular needs of women, children, older persons and persons with disabilities;

4. *Calls upon* States to adopt preventive measures and effective responses to acts of violence committed against civilian populations and to ensure that those responsible are promptly brought to justice, as provided for by national law and obligations under international law;

5. *Also calls upon* States to elaborate and implement strategies to report on, prevent and punish all forms of violence against women, girls and boys, in particular sexual violence and abuse;

6. *Recognizes* the Guiding Principles on Internal Displacement as an important international framework for the protection of internally displaced persons, and encourages Member States and humanitarian agencies to work together in endeavours to provide a more predictable response to the needs of internally displaced persons, and in that regard calls for international support, upon request, to capacity-building efforts of Governments;

7. *Emphasizes* the fundamentally civilian character of humanitarian assistance, reaffirms the leading role of civilian organizations in implementing humanitarian assistance, particularly in areas affected by conflicts, and affirms the need, in situations where military capacity and assets are used to support the implementation of humanitarian assistance, for their use to be in conformity with international humanitarian law and humanitarian principles;

8. *Encourages* the Emergency Relief Coordinator to continue his efforts to strengthen the coordination of humanitarian assistance, and calls upon relevant United Nations organizations and other humanitarian and development actors to work with the Office for the Coordination of Humanitarian Affairs of the Secretariat to enhance the coordination, effectiveness and efficiency of humanitarian assistance;

9. *Reiterates* the need for a more effective, efficient, coherent, coordinated and better performing United Nations country presence, with a strengthened role for the senior United Nations resident official responsible for the coordination of United Nations humanitarian assistance, including appropriate authority, resources and accountability;

10. *Requests* the Secretary-General to strengthen the support provided to United Nations resident/ humanitarian coordinators and to United Nations country teams, including through the provision of necessary training, the identification of resources, and improving the identification and selection of United Nations resident/humanitarian coordinators;

11. *Calls upon* the relevant organizations of the United Nations system and, as appropriate, other relevant humanitarian actors, to improve the humanitarian response to natural and man-made disasters and complex emergencies by strengthening the humanitarian response capacities at all levels, by strengthening the coordination of humanitarian assistance at the field level, including with national authorities of the affected State, as appropriate, and by enhancing transparency, performance and accountability;

12. *Calls upon* relevant United Nations organizations to continue to improve the transparency and reliability of humanitarian needs assessments and to engage in the improvement of the consolidated appeals process, inter alia, by further developing the process as an instrument for strategic planning and prioritization and by involving other relevant humanitarian organizations in the process, while reiterating that consolidated appeals are prepared in consultation with the affected State;

13. *Requests* the Secretary-General, in consultation with States and relevant organizations, to further develop and improve, as required, mechanisms for the use of emergency stand-by capacities, including, where appropriate, regional humanitarian capacities, under the auspices of the United Nations, inter alia, through formal agreements with appropriate regional organizations, and to report on that issue to the General Assembly at its sixty-first session through the Economic and Social Council;

14. *Calls upon* donors to take further steps to improve their policies and practices with respect to humanitarian action, and in that regard welcomes the continued efforts under the Good Humanitarian Donorship initiative;

15. *Decides* to upgrade the current Central Emergency Revolving Fund into the Central Emergency Response Fund by including a grant element based on voluntary contributions, to be replenished at regular intervals, so as to ensure a more predictable and timely response to

humanitarian emergencies, with the objectives of promoting early action and response to reduce loss of life, enhancing response to time-critical requirements and strengthening core elements of humanitarian response in underfunded crises, based on demonstrable needs and on priorities identified in consultation with the affected State as appropriate;

16. *Decides also* that the Fund will continue to operate in accordance with resolution 46/182 and the guiding principles contained in the annex thereto;

17. *Affirms* its role to provide overall policy guidance on the use of the Fund to maximize its impact and to improve its functioning, and encourages the Economic and Social Council to discuss the implementation of the Fund;

18. *Takes note* of the fact that an advisory group will be established, as an independent body, to provide advice to the Secretary-General on the use and impact of the Fund, and that the Inter-Agency Standing Committee will discuss the use and impact of the Fund;

19. *Calls upon* the Secretary-General, on the basis of his report on the improvement of the Central Emergency Revolving Fund and in consultations with all relevant stakeholders, to make the necessary managerial and administrative arrangements to facilitate the implementation of the grant element and set up appropriate reporting and accountability mechanisms to ensure that the funds allocated through the Fund are used in the most efficient, effective and transparent manner possible;

20. *Urges* all Member States and invites the private sector and all concerned individuals and institutions to consider making voluntary contributions to the Fund, welcomes the financial pledges already made, and emphasizes that contributions should be additional to current commitments to humanitarian programming and not to the detriment of resources made available for international cooperation for development;

21. *Requests* the Secretary-General to report to the General Assembly and the Economic and Social Council on the detailed use of the Fund;

22. *Also requests* the Secretary-General to commission an independent review of the Fund at the end of the second year of operation to assess, inter alia, both the grant and revolving elements of the Fund, its administration, criteria for resource allocation, actions and responses supported by it and its ability to meet its objectives, and to submit a report in that regard to the General Assembly at its sixty-third session;

23. *Emphasizes* the importance of the discussion of humanitarian policies and activities by the General Assembly and the Economic and Social Council and that those discussions should be continuously revitalized by Member States;

24. *Requests* the Secretary-General to report to the General Assembly at its sixty-first session, through the Economic and Social Council at its substantive session of 2006, on progress made in strengthening the coordination of emergency humanitarian assistance of the United Nations.

UN and other humanitarian personnel

In response to General Assembly resolution 59/211 [YUN 2004, p. 1435], the Secretary-General, in an August report [A/60/223 & Corr. 1], described

threats against humanitarian and UN personnel over the preceding year. He indicated that the apparent rise in the number of security incidents involving UN personnel was most likely due to the increased number of staff operating in the field and improved reporting capability within the UN security management system. It was evident that enhanced risk assessment skills, security training and adherence to minimum operating security standards had instilled greater confidence and capacity to operate safely in areas of higher risk.

The Assembly, in **resolution 60/123** of 15 December (see p. 1523), called on Governments and parties in complex humanitarian emergencies to ensure the safe and unhindered access of humanitarian personnel.

OCHA administrative functions

By **decision 60/551** of 23 December, the General Assembly deferred to its sixtieth (2006) session consideration of the Secretary-General's 2004 report on defining the administrative functions of the Office for the Coordination of Humanitarian Affairs (OCHA) [YUN 2004, p. 908].

Resource mobilization

Central Emergency Revolving Fund

In 2005, the Central Emergency Revolving Fund (CERF), established in 1992 [YUN 1992, p. 584] as a cash-flow mechanism for the initial phase of humanitarian emergencies, granted 13 advances, amounting to $36.5 million.

In response to General Assembly resolution 46/182 [YUN 1991, p. 421] and Economic and Social Council resolution 2005/4 (see p. 990), the Secretary-General submitted an October report [A/60/432] on improving CERF. Owing to its exclusively revolving nature, CERF increasingly faced difficulties in providing adequate resources for use in the initial phase of emergencies. To ensure a more predictable and timely response to humanitarian crises and address underfunded emergencies, the Secretary-General recommended that the Assembly upgrade CERF, which would be renamed the Central Emergency Response Fund, with a total target of $500 million, including the existing revolving element of $50 million and a grant element of $450 million. The Fund could be operational early in 2006. Up to two thirds of the Fund's total grant facility would be devoted to life-saving rapid response initiatives, providing financial liquidity to eligible humanitarian organizations to cover the core elements of immediate humanitarian need. An independent advisory group of experts would be formed to provide advice on the use of the Fund and the Inter-Agency Standing Committee would discuss its operation. Member States were encouraged to contribute generously to the Central Emergency Response Fund, ensuring that those contributions were additional to their current commitments to humanitarian programming.

The Assembly upgraded the Fund in resolution 60/124 of 15 December (see p. 991).

Consolidated appeals

The consolidated appeals process (CAP), an inclusive and coordinated programme cycle for analysing context, assessing needs and planning prioritized humanitarian response, was the humanitarian sector's main strategic planning and programming tool. In 2005, the United Nations and its humanitarian partners issued consolidated appeals seeking some $6 billion in assistance to Angola, the Central African Republic, Chad, Chechnya and neighbouring republics of the Russian Federation, the Congo, Djibouti, Eritrea, the Great Lakes region (Burundi, DRC, Rwanda, Uganda, the United Republic of Tanzania), Guatemala, Guyana, the Indian Ocean region (Indonesia, Maldives, Myanmar, Seychelles, Somalia, Sri Lanka), Malawi, the Occupied Palestinian Territory, the South Asia subregion (Pakistan), the Sudan and the West Africa subregion (Benin, Burkina Faso, Cape Verde, Côte d'Ivoire, Ghana, Guinea, Guinea-Bissau, Liberia, Mali, Mauritania, the Niger, Nigeria, Senegal, Sierra Leone, the Gambia, Togo), and collectively to countries in the West and Central Africa subregions (the Gambia, Guinea-Bissau, Mali, Mauritania, Sao Tome and Principe, and Senegal). Separate appeals were launched for Benin, Burundi, Côte d'Ivoire, the DRC, Guinea, the Niger, Somalia and Uganda.

The latest available data indicated that 67 per cent ($4.03 billion) of requirements had been met.

Mine clearance

On 8 December [meeting 62], the General Assembly, on the recommendation of the Fourth (Special Political and Decolonization) Committee [A/60/473], adopted **resolution 60/97** without vote [agenda item 27].

Assistance in mine action

The General Assembly,

Recalling its resolution 58/127 of 19 December 2003 and all its previous resolutions on assistance in mine clearance and mine action, all adopted without a vote,

Recalling all relevant treaties and conventions and their review processes,

Reaffirming its deep concern at the tremendous humanitarian and development problems caused by the presence of mines and explosive remnants of war that have serious and lasting social and economic consequences for the populations of countries affected by mines and explosive remnants of war,

Bearing in mind the serious threat that mines and explosive remnants of war pose to the safety, health and lives of local civilian populations, as well as of personnel participating in humanitarian, peacekeeping and rehabilitation programmes and operations,

Deeply alarmed by the number of mines that continue to be laid each year, as well as the presence of a decreasing but still very large number of, and area of square kilometres infested by, mines and explosive remnants of war as a result of armed conflicts, and therefore remaining convinced of the necessity and urgency of strengthening mine-action efforts by the international community with a view to eliminating the threat of landmines and explosive remnants of war to civilians as soon as possible,

Recognizing that, in addition to the primary role of States, the United Nations has a significant role to play in the field of assistance in mine action, and considering mine action to be an important and integrated component of United Nations humanitarian and development activities, as well as noting the inclusion of mine action in several United Nations peacekeeping operations,

Stressing the need to convince mine-affected States to halt new deployments of anti-personnel mines in order to ensure the effectiveness and efficiency of mine-clearance operations,

Stressing also the pressing need to urge non-State actors to halt immediately and unconditionally new deployments of mines and other associated explosive devices,

1. *Calls,* in particular, for the continuation of the efforts of States, with the assistance of the United Nations and relevant organizations involved in mine action, as appropriate, to foster the establishment and development of national mine-action capacities in countries in which mines and explosive remnants of war constitute a serious threat to the safety, health and lives of the local civilian population or an impediment to social and economic development efforts at the national and local levels;

2. *Urges* all States, in particular those that have the capacity to do so, as well as the United Nations system and relevant organizations and institutions involved in mine action, as appropriate, to provide:

(a) Assistance to countries affected by mines and explosive remnants of war for the establishment and development of national mine-action capacities;

(b) Support for national programmes, where appropriate, in cooperation with the relevant bodies of the United Nations system and relevant regional, governmental and non-governmental organizations, to reduce the risks posed by landmines and explosive remnants of war, including to women and children;

(c) Reliable, predictable and timely contributions for mine-action activities, including through national mine-action efforts and humanitarian mine-action programmes of non-governmental organizations, including those relating to victim assistance and mine risk education, especially at the local level, as well as through the Voluntary Trust Fund for Assistance in Mine Action and relevant regional trust funds for assistance in mine action;

(d) Necessary information and technical, financial and material assistance to locate, remove, destroy and otherwise render ineffective minefields, mines, booby traps, other devices and explosive remnants of war, in accordance with international law, as soon as possible;

(e) Technological assistance to countries affected by mines and explosive remnants of war;

and to promote user-oriented scientific research on and development of mine-action techniques and technology, within reasonable time frames;

3. *Encourages* efforts to conduct all mine-action activities in accordance with accepted national standards and with the International Mine Action Standards, where applicable, and emphasizes the importance of using an information management system, such as the Information Management System for Mine Action, to help facilitate mine-action activities;

4. *Encourages* all relevant multilateral, regional and national programmes and bodies to include, in coordination with the United Nations, activities related to mine action, including mine clearance, in their humanitarian, rehabilitation, reconstruction and development assistance activities, where appropriate, bearing in mind the need to ensure national and local ownership, sustainability and capacity-building, as well as to include a gender and age-appropriate perspective in all aspects of such activities;

5. *Stresses* the importance of cooperation and coordination in mine action, and emphasizes the primary responsibility of national authorities in that regard, also stresses the supporting role of the United Nations and other relevant organizations in that regard, and underlines the need for continuous assessment of the role of the United Nations in mine action;

6. *Notes* the potential that mine action can have as a peace and confidence-building measure in post-conflict situations among parties concerned;

7. *Declares* that 4 April of each year shall be officially proclaimed and observed as International Day for Mine Awareness and Assistance in Mine Action;

8. *Requests* the Secretary-General to submit to the General Assembly at its sixty-second session a report on the implementation of the present resolution and on follow-up to previous resolutions on assistance in mine clearance and assistance in mine action, including on relevant United Nations policies and activities;

9. *Decides* to include in the provisional agenda of its sixty-second session the item entitled "Assistance in mine action".

Humanitarian activities

Africa

Central African Republic

The UN Consolidated Inter-Agency Appeal for the Central African Republic, launched for $27.9 million in 2005, received 35 per cent of its target ($9.8 million).

The humanitarian crisis in the Central African Republic continued to spread, with the northern parts of the country, the most directly affected by the conflict, failing to recover from the destruction of the local economies and the consequent impact on sanitation, nutrition and education. Nevertheless, positive developments on the political front gave hope for an improvement in the Government's capacity as an effective partner for humanitarian action and a strengthening of external partnerships. UN system agencies identified four strategic priorities for the 2005 Appeal: access to basic health care, prevention of HIV/AIDS and psychological care for the victims of violence; food security; access to basic education; and ensuring and coordinating humanitarian action.

Chad

The UN Consolidated Inter-Agency Appeal for Chad sought $227.3 million in 2005, of which 61 per cent ($139.7 million) was received.

In 2005, the influx of Sudanese refugees into eastern Chad ended, the situation stabilized and agencies were able to address refugees' needs adequately. In addition, the international community provided more assistance to local host communities to mitigate the impact of the continued refugee presence in eastern Chad. In June, however, a new flow of refugees began to enter Chad from the Central African Republic, raising challenges comparable to those faced in the east. Other factors leading to instability included a tense political environment, the widespread proliferation of small arms, increasing levels of banditry and criminality, armed rebellion and danger from landmines and unexploded ordnance. On the economic front, State revenue remained low, the price of cotton fell on the international market, cattle export revenue was unpredictable, security expenditures increased due to the refugee crisis, and regular strikes and demonstrations were held by civil servants demanding the payment of salary arrears.

The Congo

The UN Consolidated Inter-Agency Appeal for the Congo for 2005, amounting to $24.1 million, received 38 per cent ($9.1 million) of its request.

Successive conflicts in the Congo over the preceding decade destroyed education, sanitation and roadway infrastructure and other means of survival, with the Pool region particularly affected, resulting in a humanitarian crisis. Apart from the consequences of war, the Congo was also affected by ebola virus epidemics and floods, and subregional instability, which caused an influx of some 65,000 refugees into the country.

In 2005, the principal strategic priorities for the humanitarian community included the improvement and rehabilitation of basic social services; revival of production and agricultural activities; the free movement of humanitarian actors and the rehabilitation of access routes; and the promotion of a culture of peace and human rights.

Eritrea

The UN Consolidated Inter-Agency Appeal for Eritrea, launched for $156.7 million in 2005, met 64 per cent ($100.8 million) of its requirements.

The food security situation continued to worsen in the early months of 2005, as a result of low production, inflation of market prices and insufficient distribution of food aid, exhausting further the already overstretched coping mechanisms of the poor. The stalemate in the peace process with Ethiopia (see p. 350) exacerbated the situation. Many investment programmes were postponed, and an unprecedented burden was placed on women and children as many families were without men as a result of conscription.

Great Lakes region

The UN Consolidated Inter-Agency Appeal for the Great Lakes region, launched for a total of $114.5 million to cover 2005, received 77 per cent ($88.1 million) of that amount. In addition to the regional appeal, individual country appeals were made for Burundi, the DRC and Uganda.

The thematic priorities identified in 2005 were providing basic needs assistance; preventing and addressing human rights violations, particularly sexual and gender-based violence and violations of children's rights; and improving humanitarian response policy, with a special focus on displaced populations and HIV/AIDS.

Burundi

The UN Consolidated Inter-Agency Appeal for Burundi, launched for $122 million in 2005, obtained 61 per cent ($74.3 million) of its goal.

Although Burundi did not fall back into a large-scale emergency, general living conditions for the majority of the population remained extremely fragile in 2005. The Government's lack of capacity to respond effectively to the population's needs showed the importance of sustaining support for early warning and rapid response programmes, and recurrent cycles of smaller emergencies highlighted entrenched vulnerabilities. The continuing stabilization of the political

and security situation allowed for sustained access to all parts of the country. However, persistent levels of extreme poverty, combined with declining agricultural production, were of major concern. Crop pests, lower land productivity and three years of drought, most apparent in the northern and eastern parts of the country, put an estimated 100,000 households at permanent risk of food insecurity and fragile nutritional conditions.

Democratic Republic of the Congo

The UN Consolidated Inter-Agency Appeal for the DRC sought $219.8 million in 2005, of which 65 per cent ($142.5 million) was received.

In 2005, significant progress was made towards improving the security situation in the eastern provinces, opening up large areas to humanitarian access. That allowed new opportunities for building protective environments for those communities. However, reaping the benefits in newly stabilized zones and disarming hard-liners became increasingly difficult in the second half of the year, and the potential remained for ongoing violence and rapid-onset emergencies in the eastern provinces. The physical isolation of vulnerable populations often impeded an adequate humanitarian response, and most provinces needed assistance on both humanitarian and structural levels.

Uganda

The UN Consolidated Inter-Agency Appeal for Uganda requested $188.8 million to cover 2005 requirements, of which 77 per cent ($146.2 million) was received.

The humanitarian and human rights situation in the northern and north-eastern conflict-affected districts remained dire, especially for women and children. Conditions varied greatly from area to area, however, and improved security conditions in the central portion of the country allowed the return of approximately 400,000 internally displaced persons to their villages. In the north-central area, approximately 1.7 million internally displaced persons continued to live in squalid conditions in overcrowded camps, facing poor water and sanitation, human rights abuses, disease outbreaks, wildfires and other perils. In the Karamoja subregion, unsustainable pastoral practices, intermittent drought and deteriorating security conditions combined to perpetuate a fragile food security situation.

Somalia

In response to General Assembly resolution 59/218 [YUN 2004, p. 913], the Secretary-General, in his August consolidated report [A/60/302], provided information on humanitarian assistance and relief provided by the United Nations and its partners in Somalia in 2005.

Insecurity continued to prevail in many parts of Somalia, particularly in the south and central regions; as a result, access to those communities was restricted, making them vulnerable to harassment, exploitation and extortion. Limited resources to strengthen security and safety measures for humanitarian actors severely affected the delivery of aid. However, humanitarian partners responded to the needs of an estimated 900,000 Somalis, including between 370,000 and 400,000 internally displaced persons. The north-eastern coast of Somalia was affected by the 2004 Indian Ocean tsunami [YUN 2004, p. 952], and heavy rains and flash floods caused widespread damage to infrastructure in Somaliland and Puntland; in both cases, the humanitarian response was rapid. The United Nations was working to update the inter-agency action plan for flood forecasting, preparedness and response for the Juba and Shabelle Rivers. In mid-April, cross-border and intra-clan fighting displaced an estimated 10,000 to 15,000 people in the Gedo region, which faced chronic food insecurity and showed the highest malnutrition rates in the country. While more than three years of drought had officially ended, an estimated 500,000 people remained in a state of humanitarian emergency, recovery from which was slowed by reduced herd sizes, excessive debt levels, civil strife and widespread destitution. UN agencies and NGOs continued to assist vulnerable communities in rehabilitating, operating and maintaining water supply systems, promoting hygiene and sanitation, and rebuilding infrastructure. However, the authorities and the aid community needed to strengthen longer-term strategies to find solutions to food and livelihood insecurity.

The UN Consolidated Inter-Agency Appeal for Somalia, launched for $162.8 million in 2005, met 61 per cent ($100 million) of requirements.

GENERAL ASSEMBLY ACTION

On 22 December [meeting 68], the General Assembly, on the recommendation of the Second (Economic and Financial) Committee [A/60/496 & Corr.1,2], adopted **resolution 60/219** without vote [agenda item 73 *(b)*].

Assistance for humanitarian relief and the economic and social rehabilitation of Somalia

The General Assembly,

Recalling its resolution 47/160 of 18 December 1992 and subsequent relevant resolutions, in particular resolutions 56/106 of 14 December 2001, 57/154 of 16 December 2002, 58/115 of 17 December 2003 and 59/218 of 22 December 2004,

Noting with serious concern the effects of the civil war in Somalia and in particular the destruction of the physical, economic and social infrastructure of Somalia,

Underlining the urgent need for the rehabilitation and reconstruction of the infrastructure,

Also underlining the urgency in rebuilding State institutions and in strengthening the capacity of those institutions,

Welcoming the continued efforts of the African Union and the Intergovernmental Authority on Development towards the successful conclusion of the peace process for Somalia,

Deeply concerned that the collateral effects of the ongoing drought continue to worsen, as evidenced by the high levels of malnutrition ranging from 19 to 22 per cent,

Noting with grave concern the effects of the 2004 tsunami, which threaten the livelihoods and environment of the coastal population and have had a negative impact on the Somali economy,

Underlining the urgent need for humanitarian assistance and continued relief, reconstruction and livelihood assistance, as well as equitable resource allocation to vulnerable communities, such as destitute pastoralists and internally displaced persons,

Concerned that shipments of illegal nuclear and toxic waste dumped along the coastline of Somalia and stirred up by the tsunami, as reported by the United Nations Environment Programme Asian Tsunami Disaster Task Force, have caused health and environmental problems and can cause serious long-term effects on human health, that they pose a very serious environmental hazard, not only in Somalia but in the eastern Africa subregion, and that they are contrary to international law, infringing on the sovereignty and territorial integrity of Somalia,

Recognizing the negative effects of the proliferation of small arms and light weapons on the humanitarian situation and on development in Somalia, and in this regard condemning the significant increase in the flow of weapons and ammunition supplies to and through Somalia,

Noting the intrinsic link between the search for peace and reconciliation and the alleviation of the humanitarian crisis in Somalia, and in this regard, underlining that a stable and secure environment in Somalia is essential to the future success of the national reconciliation process and that the improvement of the humanitarian situation is an essential component of support for the peace and reconciliation process,

Welcoming the continued focus of the United Nations, in partnership with the newly established Transitional Federal Government of Somalia,

Recalling the statements by the President of the Security Council of 31 October 2001 and 28 March 2002, by which the Council condemned attacks on humanitarian personnel and called upon all parties in Somalia to respect fully the security and safety of personnel of the United Nations, the International Committee of the Red Cross and non-governmental organizations, and to guarantee their complete freedom of movement and access throughout Somalia,

Re-emphasizing the crucial importance of the further implementation of its resolutions 47/160, 56/106, 57/154, 58/115 and 59/218 to rehabilitate basic social and economic services throughout the country,

Taking note of the reports of the Secretary-General,

1. *Expresses its appreciation* to the Secretary-General for his continued and tireless efforts to mobilize assistance for the Somali people, and welcomes the steps being taken to strengthen the capacity of the United Nations Political Office for Somalia, as well as the appointment of the Special Representative of the Secretary-General;

2. *Welcomes with great satisfaction* the formation of the transitional federal institutions and their relocation to Somalia, urges further progress, and calls upon the Somali leaders to continue to work towards establishing effective national governance through inclusive dialogue and consensus-building within the framework of those institutions, in accordance with the transitional federal charter of the Somali Republic adopted in February 2004;

3. *Urges*, in that regard, the Somali leaders to make every effort to create conditions to help to increase the effectiveness of humanitarian assistance by, inter alia, improving the security situation on the ground;

4. *Urges*, in that regard, donor countries and regional and subregional organizations to continue to contribute to the reconstruction and rehabilitation of Somalia, which is of fundamental importance, in particular through the mechanism of the rapid assistance programme and efforts coordinated by the United Nations;

5. *Urges* the United Nations to continue the implementation of the relief, rehabilitation and reconstruction programmes for Somalia in line with the priorities established by the Transitional Federal Government of Somalia;

6. *Commends* the Office for the Coordination of Humanitarian Affairs of the Secretariat, the funds and programmes of the United Nations as well as other humanitarian organizations for their response, especially in the wake of the 2004 tsunami, and underlines the urgent need to put into place practical measures aimed at alleviating the consequences of the drought in the most affected areas in Somalia;

7. *Urges* all States and intergovernmental and non-governmental organizations concerned to continue to implement further its resolutions 47/160, 56/106, 57/154, 58/115 and 59/218 in order to assist the transitional federal institutions in embarking on the rehabilitation of basic social and economic services, as well as institution-building aimed at the restoration of structures of civil governance at all levels in all parts of the country;

8. *Calls upon* the international community to assist in conducting critical assessments of the environmental impacts of the tsunami-affected areas, drought and flood-affected areas and of toxic and other wastes, and in putting into place aggressive programmes focusing on short-, medium- and long-term measures in the areas of institutional development, development of policy and legislation, land use and soil management, marine and coastal ecosystem management and disaster management (prevention, preparedness, assessment, response and mitigation);

9. *Calls upon* the Secretary-General to continue to mobilize rapid international financial assistance as well as humanitarian, rehabilitation and reconstruction relief for the Somali people and to help build capacity within the transitional federal institutions in support of a consensus agreement;

10. *Urges* the Somali parties to respect the security and safety of the personnel of the United Nations, the specialized agencies, the International Red Cross and Red Crescent Movement and non-governmental organizations, as well as all other humanitarian personnel, and to guarantee their complete freedom of movement and safe access throughout Somalia;

11. *Urges* the international community to support the need for peacebuilding measures and the speedy implementation of programmes for the disarmament, demobilization and reintegration of militias throughout Somalia in order to stabilize the entire country and thereby ensure the effectiveness of the Transitional Federal Government of Somalia;

12. *Calls upon* the international community to provide, as a matter of urgency, humanitarian assistance and relief to the transitional federal institutions and the Somali people to alleviate in particular the consequences of the civil war and the prevailing drought;

13. *Also calls upon* the international community to provide continuing and increased assistance in response to the United Nations 2004 Consolidated Inter-Agency Appeal for relief, rehabilitation and reconstruction assistance for Somalia;

14. *Commends* the Secretary-General for the establishment of the Trust Fund for Peacebuilding in Somalia, welcomes the contributions made thus far to the Fund, and appeals to Member States to contribute to it;

15. *Requests* the Secretary-General, in view of the critical situation in Somalia, to take all necessary and practicable measures for the implementation of the present resolution and to report thereon to the General Assembly at its sixty-first session.

Sudan

The UN Consolidated Inter-Agency Appeal for the Sudan sought $1.9 billion in 2005 and received 53 per cent ($1 billion) of that amount.

The January signing of the Comprehensive Peace Agreement (see p. 302) formally ended Africa's longest-running civil war, but significant political, economic and social challenges remained. In southern Sudan, increased activity by the Lord's Resistance Army, operating out of Uganda, affected aid and land transport and increased insecurity, threatening economic recovery and livelihoods. In the Darfur region, protracted insecurity, violations of human rights and drought led to an increase in the conflict-affected population, from 2.5 million in May to 3.4 million in August. The international aid community in Darfur provided sustained humanitarian assistance in the life-saving sectors of food, water, sanitation, shelter and health.

(For more information on the Sudan, see p. 301.)

West Africa

The UN Consolidated Inter-Agency Appeal for the West Africa subregion sought $202.2 million in 2005 to assist beneficiaries in Benin, Burkina Faso, Cape Verde, Côte d'Ivoire, the Gambia, Ghana, Guinea, Guinea-Bissau, Liberia, Mali, Mauritania, the Niger, Nigeria, Senegal, Sierra Leone and Togo, and received 69 per cent ($140.1 million) of the requirement.

Despite a recent shift towards peace in some countries in the subregion, the overall human security environment remained precarious. The Sahelian food security crisis, rising tensions in Côte d'Ivoire, political uncertainty in Guinea-Bissau (see p. 289), floods in five countries and the cholera epidemic in nine others were serious humanitarian concerns. Approximately 1.3 million people were displaced by conflicts in the region. An estimated 4 million children under the age of five suffered from acute malnutrition and 13 million from chronic malnutrition. Relatively stable countries that shared borders with countries in crisis continued to be affected by the deterioration of the security environment.

Côte d'Ivoire

The UN Consolidated Inter-Agency Appeal for Côte d'Ivoire sought $36.4 million to meet 2005 requirements, and received 55 per cent ($20.2 million) of that amount.

Côte d'Ivoire experienced a decline in all its key economic indicators, and humanitarian indicators pointed to a significant decrease in food security, administrative and judicial management of the territory, access to health and education, and protection and respect of human rights. The Pretoria Agreement on the Peace Process in Côte d'Ivoire (see p. 232) that ended the recent political-military crisis in the country was not fully respected, and the climate of violence and insecurity led to the forced displacement of an estimated 500,000 people. Local public administration and basic social services in the rebel-controlled north and in the buffer zone were weak, as exemplified by the declining access to education for children, especially girls. In the Government-controlled south, health and education systems were overburdened by the continued presence of displaced populations.

Guinea

The UN Consolidated Inter-Agency Appeal for Guinea, launched for $36.6 million in 2005, met 61 per cent ($22.5 million) of that target.

Guinea continued to cope with internally displaced persons, refugees and returnees from Côte d'Ivoire and nearly 1 million refugees from Sierra Leone and Liberia. A failed coup d'état against President Lansana Conté, in January, contributed to the sense of insecurity among Guineans. The linking of international assistance to Guinea's compliance with good governance and macroeconomic reforms resulted in increased poverty, high inflation and the breakdown of social services and infrastructure. The humanitarian situation was marked by rising mortality, morbidity and malnutrition rates. The outbreak of polio and yellow fever, a 50 per cent increase in fuel prices and the inability of the Government to provide basic social services further contributed to the deterioration of living conditions for an already vulnerable population, making Guinea's social indicators similar to those of a country emerging from prolonged war.

Asia

Afghanistan

The Secretary-General, in response to General Assembly resolution 59/112 B [YUN 2004, p. 917], submitted reports in March and August [A/59/744-S/2005/183 & A/60/224-S/2005/525] covering emergency international assistance activities in Afghanistan during the periods from 23 November 2004 to 15 March 2005 and 16 March to 12 August 2005, respectively. (For political aspects, see p. 397.)

Despite gains over the previous three years, State institutions remained limited in their capacity to deliver economic and social services. In December 2004, the Government merged the Ministries of Planning and of Reconstruction to form the Ministry of Economy, which was responsible for preparing a public sector development strategy and a macroeconomic framework for private sector development. Planning and aid coordination would be transferred to the Ministry once the required capacity was in place. In January 2005, the UN country team started developing the UN development assistance framework for Afghanistan, which aimed to improve its response to Afghan priorities and the Millennium Development Goals (MDGs). It also outlined the proposed development activities of individual UN agencies for the 2006-2008 period. Four critical areas of cooperation were identified under the framework: governance, rule of law and human rights; sustainable livelihoods; health and education; and environment and natural resources. Afghanistan's first national human development report, "Security with a Human Face", called on the Government and the international community to take a long-term view of Afghanistan's development, with the MDGs serving as a normative framework for the formulation of national policies.

In early 2005, heavy snow blocked district roads and prevented the movement of food, causing shortages, steep price rises and the outbreak of disease. The Government set up a disaster relief committee to coordinate the humanitarian response.

In his August report, the Secretary-General said that, while the previous three and a half years had seen significant economic growth in the urban centres, record crop yields and an improvement in food security, the economic and developmental challenges facing Afghanistan remained daunting. According to the International Monetary Fund (IMF), the economy had grown at a rate of 7.5 per cent in the 2004-2005 period, which, although steady, did not meet the estimated 9 per cent rate required to achieve recovery. Government revenues were expected to average less than $400 million per year—half the projected expenditures for public sector salaries and operations until 2008—and the Government was not expected to be able to cover its operating costs fully before 2013. The uncertain security situation, together with underdeveloped legal and regulatory frameworks, continued to discourage private sector investment. Afghanistan's development and rehabilitation needs far exceeded the preliminary estimates to which donors had committed themselves at the 2002 International Conference on Reconstruction Assistance to Afghanistan [YUN 2002, p. 258].

A smooth transition from relief to recovery had been hampered also by natural disasters, internal displacement, land rights issues and urban pressures due to the large influx of returnees; a lack of public sector capacity and access to vulnerable populations hindered attempts at a comprehensive response. The Government had increasingly assumed responsibility for disaster relief and humanitarian assistance, with the Ministry of Rural Rehabilitation and Development taking the lead in disaster-response management. Along with drought mitigation and winterization programmes, the Ministry coordinated the Government's response to nationwide floods in the spring and summer of 2005. On 28 June, the Tripartite Agreement between Afghanistan, Iran and UNHCR for the voluntary repatriation of Afghan refugees and displaced persons was renewed until the end of 2006. Over 3 million people had returned to Afghanistan since the beginning of the programme in March 2002.

On 30 November [meeting 58], the General Assembly adopted **resolution 60/32 B** [draft: A/60/L.27 & Add.1], without vote [agenda items 17 & 73 (e)].

Emergency international assistance for peace, normalcy and reconstruction of war-stricken Afghanistan

The General Assembly,

Recalling its resolution 59/112 B of 8 December 2004 and its previous relevant resolutions,

Recalling also the agreement reached among various Afghan groups in Bonn, Germany, on 5 December 2001, the International Conference on Reconstruction Assistance to Afghanistan, held in Tokyo on 21 and 22 January 2002, and the International Conference on Afghanistan held in Berlin on 31 March and 1 April 2004, and reminding donors to fulfil their commitments in this regard,

Welcoming the continuing and growing ownership of the rehabilitation and reconstruction efforts by the Government of Afghanistan through the National Development Framework, the "Securing Afghanistan's future" exercise and the national budget, and emphasizing the crucial need to achieve ownership in all fields of governance and to improve institutional capabilities in order to use aid more effectively,

Recognizing progress that has been made towards the Afghanistan national development strategy, and welcoming in this regard the adoption of the first report on the Millennium Development Goals by the Government of Afghanistan as well as its further efforts to achieve the Millennium Development Goals,

Welcoming, in this regard, the guarantee of human rights and fundamental freedoms for all Afghans in the new Constitution as a significant step towards an improved situation of human rights and fundamental freedoms, in particular for women and children,

Noting with concern, at the same time, reports of violations of human rights and of international humanitarian law and violent or discriminatory practices in parts of the country,

Noting with concern also that the lack of security in certain areas has caused some organizations to cease or curtail humanitarian and development operations in some parts of Afghanistan because limited access and inadequate security conditions for the delivery of aid continue to hamper their work substantially,

Welcoming the continuous return of refugees and internally displaced persons, while noting with concern that the conditions in parts of Afghanistan are not yet conducive to safe and sustainable returns to places of origin,

Remaining deeply concerned about the problem of millions of anti-personnel landmines and explosive remnants of war, which constitute a great danger for the population and a major obstacle for the resumption of economic activities and for recovery and reconstruction efforts,

Aware of the high vulnerability of Afghanistan to natural disasters, in particular drought or flooding, and emphasizing the need to prepare the population for extreme climate conditions through, for example, winterization measures,

Underlining the coordinating role of the Special Representative of the Secretary-General for Afghanistan and of the United Nations Assistance Mission in Afghanistan in ensuring a seamless transition, under Afghan leadership, from humanitarian relief to recovery and reconstruction,

Expressing its appreciation for the work of the executive steering committee of the provincial reconstruction teams, which provides guidance on management and coordination of provincial reconstruction teams and on the interaction of civilian and military actors,

Recognizing the need for a continued strong international commitment to humanitarian assistance and for programmes, under the ownership of the Government of Afghanistan, of recovery, rehabilitation and reconstruction, and expressing, at the same time, its appreciation to the United Nations system and to all States and international and non-governmental organizations whose international and local staff continue to respond positively to the humanitarian, transition and development needs of Afghanistan,

1. *Welcomes* the report of the Secretary-General and the recommendations contained therein;

2. *Urges* the Government of Afghanistan and local authorities to take all possible steps to ensure the safety, security and free movement of all United Nations, development and humanitarian personnel, as well as their safe and unhindered access to all affected populations, and to protect the property of the United Nations and of development or humanitarian organizations, including non-governmental organizations;

3. *Strongly condemns* all acts of violence and intimidation directed against development and humanitarian personnel and United Nations and associated personnel, regrets the loss of life and physical harm, and urges the Government of Afghanistan to make every effort to identify and to bring to justice the perpetrators of attacks;

4. *Welcomes* the completion of the disarmament and demobilization of child soldiers in the Afghan Military Forces, stresses the importance of the reintegration of child soldiers and of care for other war-affected children, commends the Government of Afghanistan for its efforts in this regard, and encourages continued efforts in cooperation with the United Nations;

5. *Expresses its concern* about the recruitment and use of child soldiers by illegal armed groups in Afghanistan, reiterates the importance of ending the use of children contrary to international law, and welcomes the accession by Afghanistan to the Convention on the Rights of the Child and the two optional protocols thereto;

6. *Reiterates* the necessity of providing Afghan children with educational and health facilities in all parts of the country, recognizing the special needs of girls, and encourages the Government of Afghanistan, with the assistance of the international community, to expand those facilities and to promote full and equal access to them by all members of Afghan society;

7. *Welcomes* the initiative of the Government of Afghanistan to formulate a national plan of action on combating child trafficking, encourages the Government to formulate the plan of action guided by the Protocol to Prevent, Suppress and Punish Trafficking in Persons, Especially Women and Children, supplementing the United Nations Convention against Transnational Organized Crime, and stresses the im-

portance of considering becoming a party to the Protocol;

8. *Calls for* the full respect of the human rights and fundamental freedoms of all, without discrimination of any kind, including on the basis of gender, ethnicity or religion, in accordance with obligations under the Afghan Constitution and international law;

9. *Stresses* the need to ensure respect for the right to freedom of expression and the right to freedom of thought, conscience or belief;

10. *Continues to emphasize* the necessity of investigating allegations of current and past violations of human rights and of international humanitarian law, including violations committed against persons belonging to ethnic and religious minorities, as well as against women and girls, of facilitating the provision of efficient and effective remedies to the victims and of bringing the perpetrators to justice in accordance with international law;

11. *Reiterates* the important role of the Afghan Independent Human Rights Commission in the promotion and protection of human rights and fundamental freedoms, and stresses the need to expand its range of operation in all parts of Afghanistan in accordance with the Afghan Constitution; welcomes the adoption by the Government of Afghanistan of key elements of the transitional justice action plan, and stresses the importance of judicial accountability of human rights offenders in accordance with international law;

12. *Stresses once again* the need for further progress on judicial reform in Afghanistan, and urges the Government of Afghanistan and the international community to devote resources also to the reconstruction and reform of the prison sector in order to improve respect for the rule of law and for human rights therein, while reducing physical and mental health risks to inmates;

13. *Recalls* Security Council resolution 1325(2000) of 31 October 2000 on women and peace and security, commends the efforts of the Government of Afghanistan to mainstream gender issues and to protect and promote the equal rights of women and men as guaranteed, inter alia, by virtue of its ratification of the Convention on the Elimination of All Forms of Discrimination against Women, and by the Afghan Constitution, welcomes the level of participation of Afghan women in the recent parliamentary and provincial council elections, including the election of female candidates to these bodies, and reiterates the continued importance of the full and equal participation of women in all spheres of Afghan life;

14. *Strongly condemns* incidents of discrimination and violence against women and girls, welcomes the significant efforts by the Government of Afghanistan to counter discrimination, urges the Government to actively involve all elements of Afghan society, in particular women, in the development and implementation of relief, rehabilitation, recovery and reconstruction programmes, and encourages the collection and use of statistical data on a sex-disaggregated basis to accurately track the progress of the full integration of women into the political, economic and social life of Afghanistan;

15. *Notes with concern* that opium poppy cultivation and the related drug production and trafficking pose a serious threat to security, the rule of law and develop-

ment in Afghanistan, and urges the Government of Afghanistan, supported by the international community, to work to mainstream counter-narcotics throughout all the national programmes; welcomes, in this context, the decrease in opium cultivation, commends the efforts of the Government of Afghanistan in this regard, and further urges it to increase its efforts against opium cultivation;

16. *Urges* in particular the Government of Afghanistan, in cooperation with the international community, to implement its comprehensive counter-narcotics implementation plan, aimed at eliminating illicit poppy cultivation, supporting increased law enforcement, interdiction, demand reduction, eradication of illicit crops, crop substitution and other alternative livelihood and development programmes, increasing public awareness and building the capacity of drug control institutions, and to promote the development of sustainable livelihoods in the formal production sector as well as other sectors, thus improving substantially the lives, health and security of the people, particularly in rural areas;

17. *Expresses its appreciation* to those Governments that continue to host Afghan refugees, acknowledging the huge burden they have so far shouldered in this regard, and reminds them of their obligations under international refugee law with respect to the protection of refugees, the principle of voluntary return and the right to seek asylum and to allow international access for their protection and care;

18. *Urges* the Government of Afghanistan, acting with the support of the international community, to continue and strengthen its efforts to create the conditions for the voluntary, safe, dignified and sustainable return and reintegration of the remaining Afghan refugees and internally displaced persons;

19. *Calls for* the provision of continued international assistance to the large numbers of Afghan refugees and internally displaced persons to facilitate their voluntary, safe and orderly return;

20. *Urges* the Government of Afghanistan to meet its responsibilities under the Convention on the Prohibition of the Use, Stockpiling, Production and Transfer of Anti-personnel Mines and on Their Destruction, to cooperate fully with the mine action programme coordinated by the United Nations, and to execute the destruction of all existing stocks of anti-personnel landmines;

21. *Endorses* the key principles for cooperation between the Government of Afghanistan and the international community during the post-Bonn process as set out in the report of the Secretary-General, including the leadership role of Afghanistan in the reconstruction process, the just allocation of domestic and international reconstruction resources across the country, regional cooperation, lasting capacity- and institution-building, combating corruption and the promotion of transparency and accountability, public information and participation, and the continued central role of the United Nations in the post-Bonn process, which should also include fields in which the United Nations offers the best expertise available;

22. *Invites* all States and intergovernmental and non-governmental organizations providing assistance to Afghanistan to focus on capacity-building and institution-building and to ensure that such work com-

plements and contributes to the development of an economy characterized by sound macroeconomic policies, the development of a financial sector that provides services, inter alia, to microenterprises, small and medium-sized enterprises and households, transparent business regulations and accountability;

23. *Urges* the Government of Afghanistan to continue to effectively reform the public administration sector in order to implement the rule of law, to ensure good governance and accountability at both national and local levels and to lead the fight against corruption;

24. *Also urges* the Government of Afghanistan to address, with the assistance of the international community, the question of claims for land property through a comprehensive land titling programme, including formal registration of all property and improved security for property rights, and welcomes the steps already taken by the Government of Afghanistan in this regard;

25. *Urges* the international community to channel assistance through the national budget, including by contributing to the Afghanistan Reconstruction Trust Fund and the Law and Order Trust Fund, and to generously support the national priority programmes of the Government of Afghanistan in order to strengthen ownership, transparency and the functioning of basic State institutions;

26. *Urgently appeals* to all States, the United Nations system and international and non-governmental organizations to continue to provide, in close coordination with the Government of Afghanistan and in accordance with its national development strategy, all possible and necessary humanitarian, recovery, reconstruction, financial, technical and material assistance for Afghanistan;

27. *Emphasizes* the need to maintain, strengthen and review civil-military relations among international actors, as appropriate, at all levels in order to ensure complementarity of action based on the different mandates and comparative advantages of the humanitarian, development, law enforcement and military actors present in Afghanistan;

28. *Requests* the Secretary-General to report to the General Assembly every six months during its sixtieth session on developments in Afghanistan, including on parliamentary and provincial elections and on consultations on the post-Bonn process as well as on the progress made in the implementation of the present resolution;

29. *Decides* to include in the provisional agenda of its sixty-first session an item entitled "The situation in Afghanistan".

Palestine

The UN Consolidated Inter-Agency Appeal for the Occupied Palestinian Territory, which sought $301.5 million in 2005, met 65 per cent ($195.7 million) of its requirements.

In 2005, the unfavourable humanitarian situation persisted in Palestine, despite the new momentum in the peace process resulting from the election of Palestinian President Mahmoud Abbas and Israel's disengagement from settlements in the Gaza Strip and parts of the northern West Bank. However, those developments did not affect the key humanitarian indicators. Poverty rates increased, largely because of lower work quality and increasingly fragile household coping mechanisms. Both the West Bank and the Gaza Strip remained strangulated by restrictions on free movement, diminishing prospects for indigenous Palestinian economic growth. Humanitarian assistance remained crucial, as survival strategies were unsustainable.

Europe

North Caucasus (Russian Federation)

The UN Consolidated Inter-Agency Appeal for Chechnya and Neighbouring Republics (North Caucasus–Russian Federation) sought $67.8 million in 2005, 67 per cent ($45.6 million) of which was received.

The security situation in Chechnya continued to cause humanitarian need and socio-economic uncertainty, both internally and in neighbouring republics. The infrastructure was largely destroyed and could not provide essential social services and normal living conditions. The unemployment rate was estimated at 80 per cent. Other areas of the North Caucasus, while not having suffered wide-scale destruction, shared Chechnya's economic stagnation and lack of opportunity. Basic health indicators in those areas were among the worst in the Russian Federation. The return of IDPs to Chechnya continued in 2005, but at a much slower rate than in 2004.

Special economic assistance

African economic recovery and development

New Partnership for Africa's Development

The General Assembly, by resolution 57/7 [YUN 2002, p. 910], endorsed the Secretary-General's recommendation [ibid., p. 909] that the New Partnership for Africa's Development (NEPAD), adopted in 2001 by the Assembly of Heads of State and Government of the Organization of African Unity [YUN 2001, p. 900], should be the framework within which the international community should concentrate its efforts for Africa's development.

Report of Secretary-General (March). The Secretary-General, responding to a 2004 request of the Committee for Programme and Coordina-

tion (CPC) [YUN 2004, p. 921], submitted a March report [E/AC.51/2005/6] on UN system support for NEPAD. That support was organized around seven clusters that broadly corresponded to the Partnership's priorities and strategies: infrastructure development; governance, peace and security; agriculture, trade and market access; environment, population and urbanization; human resources development, employment and HIV/AIDS; science and technology; and communication, advocacy and outreach. Institutional support was provided by the UN system to African countries, the African Union (AU) and subregional organizations, and the NEPAD secretariat, including through the secondment of staff to the various regional secretariats and helping them to prepare sectoral programmes; assisting in developing codes and standards; and providing technical expertise. Advocacy work and funding provided by the UN system complemented institutional support.

The Secretary-General concluded that opportunities for the UN system to aid Africa's development in general, and the implementation of NEPAD in particular, existed as much in working together to provide focused and coordinated support to NEPAD as in helping African countries to mobilize significant financial resources. As NEPAD's implementation gathered momentum, African countries would increasingly emphasize mobilizing those resources for NEPAD programme implementation; building technical expertise for the management of development programmes; and strengthening institutions to assist in achieving the NEPAD goals. The UN system should make an active contribution in support of those tasks.

CEB report. The United Nations System Chief Executives Board for Coordination (CEB), in its annual overview report for 2004-2005 [E/2005/63], discussed strengthening system-wide support for Africa and NEPAD. UN system efforts to increase support for NEPAD should place particular emphasis on: providing assistance in integrating NEPAD priorities into the African countries' national development frameworks; enhancing policy and operational coherence in supporting the implementation of NEPAD commitments at the regional, subregional and country levels; strengthening the UN system's technical support for the NEPAD secretariat; and expanding the UN system's technical and financial support for building institutional, managerial and technical capacities in Africa for domestic and external resource mobilization.

CPC action. CPC, at its forty-fifth session (6 June–1 July) [A/60/16 & Corr.1], endorsed the Secretary-General's recommendations on UN system support for NEPAD (see p. 1003). It called on the components of UN system to work together further to provide focused and coordinated support to NEPAD. The Economic Commission for Africa (ECA) and UN country offices should be utilized more actively to ensure broader understanding of and participation in NEPAD programmes. The General Assembly should request the UN system to explore innovative approaches for funding NEPAD priorities and programmes, and the Secretary-General should report to the Committee in 2006, and annually thereafter, on the system's progress, challenges and goals for NEPAD.

CPC requested CEB to ensure that support for NEPAD remained a UN system priority and to update information on its efforts to ensure effective and coordinated system-wide support for NEPAD in its next annual overview report. CEB member organizations were encouraged to further align their priorities with those of NEPAD and to scale up their efforts to support it.

Advisory Panel report. The Secretary-General, on 21 June [A/60/85], transmitted to the General Assembly the report of the Advisory Panel on International Support for NEPAD, established in 2004 [YUN 2004, p. 924]. The report, entitled "From rhetoric to action: mobilizing international support to unleash Africa's potential", carried a twofold central message: first, that NEPAD could not succeed without a significant increase in international support; and second, that unleashing Africa's development potential required harnessing the creativity and dynamism of private initiative in a range of areas, including agriculture, industry, science and technology and infrastructure development.

The Panel concluded that strengthening private initiative, including through the establishment of small enterprises at the grass-roots level, was the key to Africa's economic transformation, and that an efficient, supportive and capable public sector was vital to that goal. The Panel identified priority tasks to be carried out by African countries in the areas of rural development and agriculture, investment in human development, improvement in governance, private sector development, investment in physical infrastructure, and conflict resolution and peacebuilding.

The Panel endorsed the call for a substantial increase in aid levels, in accordance with the 2002 Monterrey Consensus [YUN 2002, p. 953], half of which should be channelled to sub-Saharan Africa. Donors should improve the coherence of their assistance objectives in individual country-supported development plans and strategies; better harmonize their administrative procedures; and commit themselves to an accelerated, time-bound programme for implementing measures contained in various aid-related declarations, including the Paris Declaration on Aid Effectiveness. The Panel supported the proposal that all debt should be cancelled for low-income countries and middle-income countries should receive substantial debt relief. It called for African and other nations to liberalize trade and recommended the establishment of adjustment assistance programmes in Africa to accompany import liberalization. Developed countries should promote policy measures to facilitate inward remittances and capital flows to Africa and, along with multilateral institutions, support the promotion of private business in Africa. In particular, development agencies needed to strengthen their technical cooperation with NEPAD and individual countries by assisting them in the design of country-specific strategies for improving investment climates. UN system organizations and agencies should improve collaboration to provide focused and coordinated support to NEPAD and help African countries mobilize significant financial resources for development at the national and regional levels. The United Nations should partner with the AU in a process of consultation and dialogue for following up on commitments.

Report of Secretary-General (August). In response to General Assembly resolution 59/254 [YUN 2004, p. 924], the Secretary-General submitted, in August, the third consolidated report [A/60/178] on progress in the implementation of and support for NEPAD, highlighting continuing challenges and constraints.

The Secretary-General said that, in addition to greater international response in support of Africa's development, 2005 was marked by important regional actions. Seven physical projects and two additional studies were being considered by the African Development Bank (ADB), and the number of regional infrastructure projects would increase, as projects under preparation with the support of the Canadian Infrastructure Project Preparation Facility (IPPF) became ready for financing and implementation. ADB had launched the preparation of four multinational projects under IPPF, and it was envisaged that approvals would be granted for the preparation of at least four additional projects under the Facility in 2005. The feasibility analysis for the East African Submarine Cable System (EASSy) project, to provide East African countries with a high bandwidth cable connection, was finalized in March. Fifteen African companies signed the memorandum regarding the cable, which would link Durban, South Africa, to Port Sudan, Sudan.

The first NEPAD e-schools demonstration, considered a critical element of the e-Schools Initiative, began in July, and would be launched in 20 countries over a four-month period. Several projects developed in 2004 [YUN 2004, p. 923] in the education and training sector were at various stages of completion.

Several countries used the NEPAD Health Strategy in advancing their health plans. The NEPAD secretariat was establishing multi-stakeholder platforms to help countries obtain developmental support to reach the MDG [YUN 2000, p. 51] on health. The issue of HIV/AIDS had been mainstreamed into the work of all NEPAD programmes, and the provision of antiretroviral treatment on the continent was expanding. The NEPAD secretariat and the AU Commissioner for Social Affairs submitted a joint report on HIV/AIDS, tuberculosis, malaria and polio to the Heads of State of the AU Summit (Abuja, Nigeria, 24-31 January), which endorsed the report's recommendations.

The NEPAD secretariat contributed to the implementation of the AU/NEPAD Tourism Action Plan [YUN 2004, p. 923] in the priority areas of strengthening institutional capacity and reinforcing human resources and quality assurance. That initiative culminated in the Tourism and Development Seminar (Johannesburg, South Africa, May-June), aimed at fostering awareness of tourism as a development tool and helping African countries to learn and share experiences on tourism development initiatives. The second meeting of the NEPAD African Ministerial Conference on Science and Technology (Dakar, Senegal, 29-30 September) approved a consolidated plan of action for promoting science and technology across Africa. Two specialized advisory panels—the AU/NEPAD high-level panel of eminent persons to advise on issues pertaining to biotechnology and an expert working group on science, technology and innovation indicators—were created to help provide policy guidance on matters of science and technology.

The NEPAD secretariat gender issues unit developed a framework and a three-year Comprehensive Strategic Plan, which provided a road map for gender mainstreaming and mobilizing civil society organizations to participate in NEPAD activities and processes. It launched a task force of experts on gender and development issues with the objective of incorporating gender issues into NEPAD programme implementation.

The Secretary-General observed that the central challenge was to grasp the opportunity for making progress and maintaining momentum in Africa's development. Related challenges included building the capacity of the national and regional institutions entrusted with NEPAD implementation; ensuring greater coherence and coordination between national development plans and NEPAD priorities; and promoting greater private sector implementation of NEPAD programmes and projects. African countries needed to continue to show their commitment to economic and social reforms through sound macroeconomic management, as well as focused emphasis on the implementation of NEPAD priorities. There was an urgent need to translate commitments made by Africa's development partners into results, and increased support for Africa should be matched by effective aid delivery and improved coordination among donors. Proposed debt relief needed to be broadened to cover all African low-income and middle-income countries. Compensatory and short-term adjustment-oriented aid flows should be provided to African countries seriously affected by the decline in trade revenue as a result of the extension of more-favoured-nation status to other countries.

GENERAL ASSEMBLY ACTION

On 23 December [meeting 69], the General Assembly adopted **resolution 60/222** [draft: A/60/L.16/Rev.1 & Add.1, orally revised] without vote [agenda item 66 (a)].

New Partnership for Africa's Development: progress in implementation and international support

The General Assembly,

Recalling its resolution 57/2 of 16 September 2002 on the United Nations Declaration on the New Partnership for Africa's Development,

Recalling also its resolution 57/7 of 4 November 2002 on the final review and appraisal of the United Nations New Agenda for the Development of Africa in the 1990s and support for the New Partnership for Africa's Development and resolutions 58/233 of 23 December 2003 and 59/254 of 23 December 2004 entitled "New Partnership for Africa's Development: progress in implementation and international support",

Recalling further the 2005 World Summit Outcome, including the recognition of the need to meet the special needs of Africa,

Bearing in mind that African countries have primary responsibility for their own economic and social development and that the role of national policies and development strategies cannot be overemphasized, and also the need for their development efforts to be supported by an enabling international economic environment, and in this regard recalling the support given by the International Conference on Financing for Development to the New Partnership,

Welcoming the report of the Secretary-General's Advisory Panel on International Support for the New Partnership for Africa's Development entitled "From rhetoric to action: mobilizing international support to unleash Africa's potential",

Having considered the report of the Secretary-General entitled "New Partnership for Africa's Development: third consolidated report on progress in implementation and international support",

1. *Takes note* of the report of the Secretary-General;

2. *Reaffirms its full support* for the implementation of the New Partnership for Africa's Development;

3. *Recognizes* the progress made in the implementation of the New Partnership as well as regional and international support for the New Partnership, while acknowledging that much needs to be done in the implementation of the New Partnership;

4. *Reaffirms its full support* for the implementation of the Declaration of Commitment on HIV/AIDS, adopted at the twenty-sixth special session of the General Assembly on 27 June 2001;

I
Actions by African countries and organizations

5. *Welcomes* the progress made by the African countries in fulfilling their commitments in the implementation of the New Partnership to deepen democracy, human rights, good governance and sound economic management, and encourages African countries, with the participation of stakeholders, including civil society and the private sector, to intensify their efforts in this regard by developing and strengthening institutions for governance, creating an environment conducive to attracting foreign direct investment for the development of the region;

6. *Welcomes and appreciates* the continuing and increasing efforts of African countries to mainstream a gender perspective and the empowerment of women in the implementation of the New Partnership;

7. *Welcomes* the good progress that has been achieved in implementing the African Peer Review Mechanism, in particular the completion of the self-assessment in some countries, the hosting of country support missions and the launching of the national preparatory process for the Peer Review in others, and urges African States as a matter of priority to join the Mechanism as soon as possible and to strengthen the Mechanism process for its efficient performance;

8. *Stresses* that conflict prevention, management and resolution and post-conflict consolidation are essential for the achievement of the objectives of the New Partnership, and in this regard welcomes the cooperation and support granted by the United Nations and development partners to the African regional and subregional organizations in the implementation of the New Partnership;

9. *Welcomes* the efforts made by African countries and regional and subregional organizations, including the African Union, in developing sectoral policy frameworks and implementing specific programmes of the New Partnership;

10. *Emphasizes* the importance for African countries to continue to coordinate, on the basis of national strategies and priorities, all types of external assistance, including that provided by multilateral organizations, in order to integrate effectively such assistance into their development processes;

11. *Encourages* the further integration of the priorities and objectives of the New Partnership into the programmes of the regional structures and organizations, and programmes for the African least developed countries;

12. *Recalls* that the African Union and the regional economic communities have a critical role to play in the implementation of the New Partnership, and in this regard encourages African countries, with the assistance of their development partners, to increase their support to enhance the capacities of these institutions;

13. *Emphasizes* that progress in the implementation of the New Partnership depends also on a favourable national and international environment for Africa's growth and development, including measures to promote a policy environment conducive to private sector development and entrepreneurship;

II
Response of the international community

14. *Welcomes* the efforts by development partners to strengthen cooperation with the New Partnership;

15. *Acknowledges* the various important initiatives of Africa's development partners in recent years, including those of the Organization for Economic Cooperation and Development, the Group of Eight Africa Action Plan, the European Union, the Tokyo International Conference on African Development, the report of the Commission for Africa entitled *Our Common Interest*, and the Africa Partnership Forum, and in this regard emphasizes the importance of coordination in such initiatives on Africa;

16. *Welcomes* the contribution made by Member States to the implementation of the New Partnership in the context of South-South cooperation, and in this regard encourages the international community, including the international financial institutions, to support the efforts of African countries, including through triangular cooperation;

17. *Acknowledges* the important role of the Africa Partnership Forum, as set out in the revised terms of reference dated 5 October 2005, which include catalysing action on the measures taken to meet the commitments that Africa and its development partners have made and coordinating support behind African priorities and the New Partnership, and encourages the Africa Partnership Forum to strengthen its efforts in this regard;

18. *Welcomes* the commitment of resources by some development partners for various New Partnership programmes, and in this regard notes with satisfaction that some developed countries have committed resources for the infrastructure project preparation facility and the Comprehensive Africa Agriculture Development Programme, and invites similar support to be extended to Africa in water and sanitation and in housing and urban development and other priority sectors specified in the New Partnership Programme of Action aiming at the achievement of sustainable development in the region;

19. *Urges* continuing support of measures to address the challenges of poverty eradication and sustainable development in Africa, including, as appropriate, debt relief, improved market access, support for the private sector and entrepreneurship, enhanced official development assistance and increased flows of foreign direct investment, and transfer of technology;

20. *Reiterates* the need for all countries and relevant multilateral institutions to continue efforts to enhance coherence in their trade policies towards African countries, and acknowledges the importance of efforts to fully integrate African countries into the international trading system through initiatives such as building Africa's trade capacity to compete and the provision of assistance to address the adjustment challenges of trade liberalization;

21. *Welcomes* the recent proposal of the Group of Eight, as endorsed by the Bretton Woods institutions at their 2005 annual meetings, to cancel 100 per cent of the outstanding debt of eligible heavily indebted poor countries owed to the International Monetary Fund, the International Development Association and the African Development Fund and to provide additional resources to ensure that the financing capacity of the international financial institutions is not reduced;

22. *Recognizes* the importance of a comprehensive and durable solution to the external debt problems of African countries, including through the cancellation of 100 per cent of multilateral debt, consistent with the recent Group of Eight proposal for the heavily indebted poor countries and, on a case-by-case basis, where appropriate, significant debt relief, including cancellation or restructuring for heavily indebted African countries not part of the Heavily Indebted Poor Countries Initiative that have unsustainable debt burdens, and welcomes the ongoing work undertaken by the International Monetary Fund and the World Bank to develop the debt sustainability framework for low-income countries, bearing in mind the importance of debt sustainability and sound budget management in the efforts to achieve national development goals, including the Millennium Development Goals;

23. *Welcomes* the recent increase in official development assistance pledged by many of the development partners, including the commitments of the Group of Eight and the European Union, that will lead to an increase in official development assistance to Africa of 25 billion dollars per year by 2010, and encourages all development partners to ensure aid effectiveness through the implementation of the Paris Declaration on Aid Effectiveness: Ownership, Harmonization, Alignment, Results and Mutual Accountability, adopted at the High-level Forum on the question of "Joint Progress toward Enhanced Aid Effectiveness: Harmonization, Alignment, Results", held in Paris from 28 February to 2 March 2005;

24. *Recognizes* the need for national Governments and the international community to make continued efforts to increase the flow of new and additional resources for financing for development, from all sources, public and private, domestic and foreign, to support the development of African countries;

25. *Welcomes* the efforts by development partners to align their financial and technical support to Africa more closely to the priorities of the New Partnership, as reflected in national poverty reduction strategies or in similar strategies, and encourages development partners to increase their efforts in this regard;

26. *Acknowledges* the activities of the Bretton Woods institutions and the African Development Bank in African countries, and invites those institutions to continue their support for the implementation of the priorities and objectives of the New Partnership;

27. *Requests* the United Nations system to continue to provide assistance to the African Union and New Partnership secretariats and to African countries in developing projects and programmes within the scope of the priorities of the New Partnership;

28. *Invites* the Secretary-General, as a follow-up to the 2005 World Summit, to urge the United Nations development system to assist African countries in implementing quick-impact initiatives, based on their national development priorities and strategies, to enable them to achieve the Millennium Development Goals, and in this respect acknowledges recent commitments by some donor countries;

29. *Notes* that the entities of the United Nations system have been actively using the regional consultation mechanism as a vehicle for fostering collaboration and coordination at the regional level, and encourages them to intensify their efforts in developing and implementing joint programmes in support of the New Partnership at the regional level;

30. *Encourages* the United Nations funds and programmes and the specialized agencies to continue to strengthen further their existing coordination and programming mechanisms, and the simplification and harmonization of planning, disbursement and reporting procedures, as a means of enhancing support for African countries in the implementation of the New Partnership;

31. *Notes* the growing collaboration among the entities of the United Nations system in support of the New Partnership, and requests the Secretary-General to promote greater coherence in the work of the United Nations system in support of the New Partnership, on the basis of the agreed clusters;

32. *Welcomes* the report of the Secretary-General's Advisory Panel on International Support for the New Partnership for Africa's Development, and looks forward to its supplementary report, including recommendations on the actions to be taken to enhance support for the implementation of the New Partnership;

33. *Requests* the Secretary-General to continue to take measures to strengthen the Office of the Special Adviser on Africa in order to enable it to effectively fulfil its mandate, including monitoring and reporting on progress related to meeting the special needs of Africa;

34. *Also requests* the Secretary-General to submit a comprehensive report on the implementation of the present resolution to the General Assembly at its sixty-first session on the basis of inputs from Governments, organizations of the United Nations system and other stakeholders in the New Partnership, such as the private sector and civil society.

Rwanda

In response to General Assembly resolution 59/137 [YUN 2004, p. 159], the Secretary-General, in his August consolidated report [A/60/302], updated the information on the implementation by UN agencies of programmes aimed at supporting groups left vulnerable by the 1994 genocide in Rwanda.

Rwanda, with support from the United Nations and the international community, had made significant progress in the areas of rehabilitation, reconstruction, reconciliation and social and political justice in the years following the genocide. The UN country team paid particular attention to the resettlement of vulnerable groups, including orphans, widows, returnees and IDPs during the rehabilitation and reconstruction process. Technical and financial support was provided by various UN agencies in the formulation and implementation of social and economic policies that benefited the poor and disadvantaged. That support resulted in the formulation of policies on good governance, gender equality and empowerment and stronger Government capacity to address economic and social challenges. The UN country team increased its commitment in the areas of institution-building and infrastructure development, health and education, the fight against HIV/AIDS, democratic governance, the reconciliation process and the justice system, and mobilized resources to scale up UN support to genocide survivors.

The Assembly, in **resolution 60/225** of 23 December (see p. 216), requested the Secretary-General to establish an outreach programme entitled "The Rwanda Genocide and the United Nations", as well as measures to mobilize civil society for Rwanda genocide victim remembrance and education.

African countries emerging from conflict

Burundi

On 4 February [E/2005/11], South Africa, Chairman of the Ad Hoc Advisory Group on Burundi, transmitted to the Economic and Social Council its statement made before the Council on the same day regarding the Group's activities. In September 2004, the Group met with President Domitien Ndayizeye of Burundi and Carolyn McAskie, the Secretary-General's Special Representative in Burundi. The President requested the Group's continued help in mobilizing support for the peace process, including the reform of security forces, the disarmament, demobilization and reintegration programme and international support to ensure the success of the transition process.

Burundi benefited from several positive developments, including the launching of the demobilization, reinsertion and reintegration programme to support up to 55,000 combatants; the provision of international support to the electoral process; a $40 million grant from the World Bank for agricultural rehabilitation and land management;

and ADB's decision to clear 35 per cent ($12 million) of Burundi's arrears, which allowed the Bank to resume operations in the country and facilitated the country's access to other multilateral facilities. Nevertheless, the level of international support was far below the approximately $1 billion commitment made at the 2004 Brussels Forum of Burundi's Development Partners [YUN 2004, p. 933]. The Group urged that the Council encourage Forum participants to increase their disbursements.

In response to Council resolution 2004/59 [YUN 2004, p. 932], the Group met with the UN Development Group/Executive Committee on Humanitarian Affairs (UNDG/ECHA) working group on transition issues to discuss UN system mechanisms for improving the coordination of activities during the transition phase, in particular the UN Development Assistance Framework, launched in January. Considering Burundi to be at a crossroads, the Group decided to continue its activities during the transition process, including a second mission to the country, in response to President Ndayizeye's September invitation.

ECONOMIC AND SOCIAL COUNCIL ACTION

On 1 March [meeting 3], the Economic and Social Council adopted **resolution 2005/1** [draft: E/2005/L.5] without vote [agenda item 2].

Ad Hoc Advisory Group on Burundi

The Economic and Social Council,

Recalling its resolutions 2002/1 of 15 July 2002, 2003/16 of 21 July 2003, 2003/50 of 24 July 2003, 2004/2 of 3 May 2004 and 2004/59 and 2004/60 of 23 July 2004, and its decision 2003/311 of 22 August 2003,

Having taken note of the oral report by the Chairman of the Ad Hoc Advisory Group on Burundi,

Recognizing the importance of maintaining the momentum in consolidating the peace process in Burundi,

1. *Commends* those donors that have provided support to Burundi, and calls for rapid disbursement of funds committed at the fourth Forum of Burundi's Development Partners, held in Brussels on 13 and 14 January 2004;

2. *Requests* the Ad Hoc Advisory Group on Burundi to continue to follow closely the humanitarian situation and economic and social conditions, to examine the transition from relief to development in Burundi and the way in which the international community supports the process and to report, as appropriate, to the Economic and Social Council at its substantive session of 2005;

3. *Decides* to consider the reports of the Advisory Group at its substantive session of 2005, requests that the report of the Group to that session describe, inter alia, how the Group has fulfilled its mandate, and decides also to hold a discussion on the work of the Group and on how it has fulfilled its mandate;

4. *Requests* the Secretary-General, the United Nations Development Group, the Office for the Coor-

dination of Humanitarian Affairs of the Secretariat and relevant United Nations funds and programmes and the specialized agencies to continue to assist the Advisory Group in accomplishing its mandate, and invites the Bretton Woods institutions to continue to cooperate to that end.

In response to Council resolution 2005/1 (above), the Advisory Group submitted a June report [E/2005/82] on the economic, social and humanitarian situation in Burundi, international donor support and the implementation of the Group's mandate. The Group was encouraged by the successful conduct of the referendum on the post-transition Constitution in February (see p. 202) and progress made in the disarmament, demobilization and reintegration programme. However, the return of refugees and IDPs continued to present a key challenge; food insecurity persisted; economic governance was weak and insufficient for developing public infrastructures; and the health situation was precarious. While international donor assistance failed to satisfy the country's enormous needs, it did support key steps in the peace process. Donors contributed close to $16 million to the election support trust fund set up by UNDP. In April, UNDP, the United Nations Population Fund (UNFPA) and UNICEF jointly signed cooperation agreements with Burundian authorities for the period from 2005 to 2007 for activities related to, among others, governance, poverty alleviation, water and sanitation, reproductive health, HIV/AIDS and youth-targeted programmes. Following the resumption of ADB activities in Burundi, the African Development Fund granted loans and made agreements for a total amount of $36 million. Operations were financed to reform the country's macroeconomic framework and civil service, to aid the socioeconomic reinsertion of disadvantaged groups, and to improve the social health and food situation in the Lake Tanganyika basin. Burundi was expected to complete its full poverty reduction strategy paper (PRSP) by September, after which it could reach the decision point for debt reduction under the Enhanced Heavily Indebted Poor Country Initiative as early as December.

The Group urged the international community and donors to provide additional assistance to answer short- and medium-term needs in the context of the transition from relief to development.

(For more information on the situation in Burundi, see p. 197.)

ECONOMIC AND SOCIAL COUNCIL ACTION

On 26 July [meeting 39], the Economic and Social Council adopted **resolution 2005/33** [draft: E/2005/L.37] without vote [agenda item 7 (*h*)].

Ad Hoc Advisory Group on Burundi

The Economic and Social Council,

Recalling its resolutions 2002/1 of 15 July 2002, 2003/16 of 21 July 2003, 2003/50 of 24 July 2003, 2004/2 of 3 May 2004, 2004/59 and 2004/60 of 23 July 2004 and 2005/1 of 1 March 2005 and its decision 2003/311 of 22 August 2003,

1. *Takes note with appreciation* of the report of the Ad Hoc Advisory Group on Burundi;

2. *Expresses its appreciation* to the Government and people of Burundi for the successful holding of the communal and legislative elections, and stresses the importance of concluding the transition period and further consolidating peace;

3. *Commends* those donors that have provided support to Burundi, calls for increased disbursement of funds committed at the fourth Forum of Burundi's Development Partners, held in Brussels on 13 and 14 January 2004, and encourages Member States to provide funds for the United Nations Consolidated Appeal for 2005;

4. *Encourages* the authorities of Burundi to finalize its poverty reduction strategy paper;

5. *Notes* the willingness of the authorities of Burundi to convene a further donor round table, and encourages the country's development partners to support the new Government with commensurate means and resources in the post-transition phase and through participation in the round table;

6. *Requests* the Ad Hoc Advisory Group to continue to follow closely the humanitarian situation and economic and social conditions, to examine the transition from relief to development in Burundi and the way in which the international community supports the process and to report to the Economic and Social Council at its substantive session of 2006;

7. *Notes* that the post-conflict recovery, reconstruction and rehabilitation, including the experience of the ad hoc advisory groups, are among the subjects being discussed in ongoing talks on United Nations reform;

8. *Recognizes* the importance of avoiding overlap and duplication with respect to existing mechanisms;

9. *Decides* that the work of the Ad Hoc Advisory Group on Burundi will be reviewed at the substantive session of 2006, with a view to considering whether to continue the mandate of the Advisory Group based on the Council's consideration of its report, which should be submitted no later than six weeks before the start of the substantive session of 2006, and of the situation prevailing in Burundi at that time.

Guinea-Bissau

On 1 March [meeting 3], the Economic and Social Council adopted **resolution 2005/2** [draft: E/2005/L.6] without vote [agenda item 2].

Ad Hoc Advisory Group on Guinea-Bissau

The Economic and Social Council,

Recalling its resolutions 2002/1 of 15 July 2002, 2003/1 of 31 January 2003, 2003/53 of 24 July 2003, 2004/1 of 3 May 2004 and 2004/59 and 2004/61 of 23 July 2004, and its decision 2002/304 of 25 October 2002,

Recognizing the link between political stability and economic and social development in Guinea-Bissau, as well as the persistent fragility of its democratic institutions,

Welcoming the positive and constructive role of the Ad Hoc Advisory Group on Guinea-Bissau in supporting the country to address its pressing short- and longer-term development objectives,

1. _Takes note_ of the report of the Ad Hoc Advisory Group on Guinea-Bissau;

2. _Welcomes_ the contributions of the Economic Community of West African States, the Community of Portuguese-speaking Countries and other partners to improving the situation in Guinea-Bissau;

3. _Welcomes also_ the recommendation by the Security Council, in its resolution 1580(2004) of 22 December 2004, to establish a voluntary emergency fund, to be administered by the United Nations Development Programme, to support efforts related to the planning and implementation of military reform;

4. _Welcomes further_ the commitment of the Government of Guinea-Bissau to hold presidential elections in accordance with the timetable in the Political Transition Charter, and in that regard invites the international community to provide financial and technical support to Guinea-Bissau in the holding of those elections;

5. _Expresses its appreciation_ to those organizations and countries that have provided assistance to Guinea-Bissau in controlling a locust invasion, which is undermining an already fragile economy, and appeals to the international community to provide additional assistance;

6. _Invites_ the donor community to consider providing budgetary support to meet emergency needs, including the payment of salaries, in particular by providing additional contributions through the Emergency Economic Management Fund;

7. _Recognizes_ that the key challenges for the Government of Guinea-Bissau will be to restore fiscal discipline, rebuild public administration and improve the climate for private investment and economic diversification and that meeting these challenges will require a combination of peace, firm commitment to sound policies by the authorities, improved governance and transparency, and the technical and financial support of the international community;

8. _Welcomes_ the progress in economic and financial management and accountability, as recognized by the International Monetary Fund and the World Bank at the meeting of Guinea-Bissau's partners to prepare for the round-table conference, held in Lisbon on 11 February 2005;

9. _Welcomes also_ the discussion at the International Monetary Fund on 19 November 2004 of the next steps in the Fund's engagement with Guinea-Bissau, which covered, inter alia, emergency post-conflict assistance, a poverty reduction and growth facility and a staff-monitored programme;

10. _Welcomes further_ the holding of the meeting of Guinea-Bissau's partners to prepare for the round-table conference, and stresses the importance of strong participation in the donor round-table conference scheduled for October 2005;

11. _Encourages_ the Government of Guinea-Bissau to give full consideration to the report of the Advisory Group;

12. _Reaffirms_ the need to create an enabling environment in Guinea-Bissau to promote economic and social development in the country, and in that regard renews its invitation to the Government of Guinea-Bissau, the organizations of the United Nations system, the Bretton Woods institutions, the donor community and the international community as a whole to give full consideration to the recommendations formulated by the Advisory Group in its first report and to take specific steps to give effect to the partnership approach set out therein with a view to implementing a long-term programme of support;

13. _Decides_ to extend the mandate of the Advisory Group until the substantive session of 2005 of the Economic and Social Council, and requests that, in its report to the Council at that session, the Group describe how it has fulfilled its mandate and, if necessary, include a discussion of the tasks remaining to be accomplished, as well as an estimated timetable for the completion of those tasks in the light of the prevailing situation and a discussion of the implementation of its recommendations;

14. _Decides also_ to consider the reports of the Ad Hoc Advisory Group on Guinea-Bissau at its substantive session of 2005.

In response to resolution 2005/2 (above), the Ad Hoc Advisory Group on Guinea-Bissau reported in June [E/2005/70] on the fulfilment of its mandate, including highlights of its work since 2002; remaining tasks; and challenges facing the country.

The Group continued its advocacy for Guinea-Bissau to ensure that it received adequate funds to meet its short-term needs and to help it secure longer-term assistance. In that regard, the Group participated in the meeting of Guinea-Bissau's partners (Lisbon, Portugal, 11 February), held in preparation for the full donors' round table conference later in the year, and to help mobilize resources for financing the $40 million fiscal gap in the 2005 budget. The Lisbon meeting confirmed that donors were not yet fully confident in the stability of Guinea-Bissau and were waiting until after the elections before providing non-emergency aid or agreeing on a date for the donors' round table. However, representatives of ADB, the Central Bank of West African States and the West African Economic and Monetary Union urged the international community not to subject Guinea-Bissau to the same conditionalities as other countries. In response, following the Lisbon meeting, the EU pledged an estimated 9.2 million euros in new budget support for 2005, disbursement of which could start by August. In the interim, the EU advanced 5 million of the 7.25 million euros compensation for fishing rights from June to April, to allow the payment of salaries in the sensitive period leading up to the elections. France contributed 0.5 million euros to the Economic Emergency Management Fund.

The World Bank Vice-President for Africa and the Managing Director visited Guinea-Bissau in January and February, respectively. Another World Bank team visited the country in May to discuss an economic recovery credit of $10 million to be disbursed in July. The Bank also intended to submit to its Board an interim support strategy package for a proposed $40 million credit devoted to energy, urban communications and community development projects, and for direct budget support.

An IMF mission visited the country in March to negotiate with national authorities a staff monitored programme, which could be transformed into an emergency post-conflict assistance programme. The IMF provisional data indicated that revenue had increased due to improved collection efforts and supervision. Nevertheless, despite budget support and the recent advance on fishing licences provided by the EU, the budget remained extremely tight. Salaries had been paid for January to April, but other expenditures, including those for the social sectors, had to be cut to far below minimum requirements. The budget gap for 2005 was approximately $16 million.

Two of the immediate tasks for the Group following the elections would be to expand the donor base for Guinea-Bissau and solicit support for the donors' round table. The Group recommended a comprehensive technical assistance plan for capacity-building; that the international community help Guinea-Bissau formulate a comprehensive economic diversification strategy to take advantage of its significant resources; that greater attention be paid to the issue of security sector reform; and that greater interaction and collaboration be promoted between the Group and regional organizations.

(For more information on the situation in Guinea-Bissau, see p. 289.)

ECONOMIC AND SOCIAL COUNCIL ACTION

On 26 July [meeting 39], the Economic and Social Council adopted **resolution 2005/32** [draft: E/2005/L.36] without vote [agenda item 7 *(h)*].

Ad Hoc Advisory Group on Guinea-Bissau

The Economic and Social Council,

Recalling its resolutions 2002/1 of 15 July 2002, 2003/1 of 31 January 2003, 2003/53 of 24 July 2003, 2004/1 of 3 May 2004, 2004/59 and 2004/61 of 23 July 2004 and 2005/2 of 1 March 2005 and its decision 2002/304 of 25 October 2002,

Welcoming the efforts of Guinea-Bissau, in particular the successful holding of the first round of presidential elections on 19 June 2005, looking forward to the continuing peaceful electoral process leading up to and including the second round of elections scheduled for 24 July 2005, and encouraging its efforts to consoli-

date democracy and further deepen transparency and good governance,

Recognizing the link between political stability and economic and social development in Guinea-Bissau,

Welcoming the positive and constructive role of the Ad Hoc Advisory Group on Guinea-Bissau in supporting the country in pursuing its pressing short- and long-term development objectives,

Also welcoming the efforts undertaken by the Secretary-General and his Special Envoy for Guinea-Bissau to assist all relevant actors in Guinea-Bissau to reach a peaceful conclusion of the transitional process in the country,

Recognizing the role played by partners of Guinea-Bissau in helping the country to return to constitutional order,

1. *Takes note with appreciation* of the report of the Ad Hoc Advisory Group on Guinea-Bissau;

2. *Expresses its appreciation* to those countries that have provided technical and financial support for the holding of the presidential elections;

3. *Also expresses its appreciation* to those countries and organizations that have shown flexibility in providing budget support to Guinea-Bissau in meeting its emergency needs, including through the Emergency Economic Management Fund, requests donors to continue to provide budgetary support to assist Guinea-Bissau in meeting the effective functioning of the State, and welcomes in this regard the decision of the United Nations Development Programme to extend the duration of the Fund until the end of 2005;

4. *Welcomes* the recommendation of the Security Council, in its resolution 1580(2004) of 22 December 2004, to establish a voluntary emergency fund, to be administered by the United Nations Development Programme, to support efforts related to the planning and implementation of military reform, and expresses appreciation to those countries and organizations that have provided technical and financial support, including through the United Nations Development Programme, for the definition and implementation of military sector reform;

5. *Also welcomes* the plan by the United Nations country team to design a transitional strategy for the country, and calls upon the United Nations system, and requests all other partners, to contribute to the implementation of the quick-impact microprojects envisaged therein;

6. *Calls upon* all participants at the meeting of partners of Guinea-Bissau, held in Lisbon on 11 February 2005, to ensure the implementation of its conclusions, including the fulfilment of their commitments, and to strongly support the donor round-table conference scheduled to be held in the last quarter of 2005, and encourages in this regard all traditional and non-traditional partners, in preparation for the conference, to identify lead donors for various sectors in an effort to coordinate assistance;

7. *Calls upon* the United Nations system, in collaboration with the Bretton Woods institutions and other multilateral and bilateral donors, to assist Guinea-Bissau in designing and implementing a comprehensive technical assistance plan that focuses on national priority areas, in particular on the public administration, health and education sectors;

8. *Encourages* the international community to find ways to support Guinea-Bissau in strengthening civil society organizations;

9. *Urges* the United Nations Conference on Trade and Development, the Common Fund for Commodities, where appropriate, and other relevant agencies to assist Guinea-Bissau in formulating and implementing a comprehensive economic diversification strategy;

10. *Notes* that post-conflict recovery, reconstruction and rehabilitation, including the experience of the ad hoc advisory groups, are among the subjects being discussed in ongoing talks on United Nations reform;

11. *Recognizes* the importance of avoiding overlap and duplication with respect to existing mechanisms;

12. *Decides*, in the light of the current situation in Guinea-Bissau, to extend the mandate of the Ad Hoc Advisory Group on Guinea-Bissau until the substantive session of 2006, with the understanding that the decision on whether to renew its mandate will be based on the Council's consideration of the report of the Ad Hoc Advisory Group, which should be submitted no later than six weeks before the start of the 2006 substantive session, and the situation prevailing in Guinea-Bissau at that time.

Other economic assistance

Haiti

In response to Economic and Social Council decision 2004/322 [YUN 2004, p. 939], the Ad Hoc Advisory Group on Haiti, reactivated in 2004 by Council resolution 2004/52 [ibid., p. 938], reported in May [E/2005/66] on its activities, the context for international support to Haiti in 2005 and planning for the country's long-term development.

In accordance with Security Council Presidential statement **S/PRST/2005/1** (see p. 378), the Group conducted its first mission to Haiti (12-16 April), in conjunction with the Security Council's mission to Haiti (see p. 379). The Group identified priority areas for action, including economic governance, transport, environment, energy, agriculture, education, justice, land titles and disarmament, demobilization and reintegration.

Haiti's Transitional Government prepared a two-year transitional programme, the Interim Cooperation Framework, extending from July 2004 to September 2006. In July 2004, donors pledged over $1 billion to support the Framework. At two meetings (Washington, D.C., December 2004, and Cayenne, French Guiana, March 2005), donors agreed to identify and fund projects for quick disbursement.

The Transitional Government made progress towards restoring financial and economic stability under an IMF Staff Monitored Programme, and in settling overdue service payments to the World Bank, using its own resources and a grant from Canada. Those steps made additional re-

sources available for the Interim Cooperation Framework and other activities. The IMF supported structural measures to enhance public sector governance and transparency, and the Inter-American Development Bank, in coordination with IMF and the World Bank, provided policy-based loans and technical assistance for key reforms and for anti-corruption initiatives.

The Group concluded that the first action of the new Government should be to determine its short-, medium- and long-term priorities. Work was under way to lay the foundation for a PRSP, which the Government could consider as its medium-term planning document. A broad range of national actors should be engaged to build an ongoing national dialogue on the way forward. The Government would need to focus on a few areas that would demonstrate to the Haitian people that action was being taken. The careful sequencing of activities would be critical to building stronger Government ministries and services, and ensuring that steps to modernize the economy had a positive effect on the poor. The report contained specific recommendations addressed to the Economic and Social Council, the United Nations Stabilization Mission in Haiti and the donor community regarding their respective roles in addressing Haiti's long-term development.

On 27 June [E/2005/86], Haiti informed the Economic and Social Council that it supported the recommendations of the Ad Hoc Advisory Group. It had made arrangements to establish a strategic think tank to identify the content of the long-term development programme and work in close collaboration with the Advisory Group.

ECONOMIC AND SOCIAL COUNCIL ACTION

On 27 July [meeting 40], the Economic and Social Council adopted **resolution 2005/46** [draft: E/2005/L.20/Rev.1] without vote [agenda item 7 (d)].

Ad Hoc Advisory Group on Haiti

The Economic and Social Council,

Recalling its resolution 2004/52 of 23 July 2004 and its decision 2004/322 of 11 November 2004 on the long-term programme of support for Haiti, in which the Council decided to reactivate the Ad Hoc Advisory Group on Haiti,

Recalling also its resolution 2004/46 of 22 July 2004 on support for the United Nations Stabilization Mission in Haiti,

Stressing the continued need for Member States, United Nations organs, bodies and agencies and other international organizations to contribute to the promotion of socio-economic recovery and stability in Haiti,

Taking into account the interaction and cooperation between the Economic and Social Council and the Security Council, within their respective mandates, on the situation in Haiti,

1. *Takes note* of the report of the Ad Hoc Advisory Group on Haiti;

2. *Encourages* the recent efforts by the Transitional Government of Haiti to focus on long-term development through the creation of a strategic planning unit in support of the Ministry of Planning and External Cooperation, and recognizes in this context the work of the United Nations country team and the Economic Commission for Latin America and the Caribbean to prepare the groundwork for a poverty reduction strategy;

3. *Decides* to extend the mandate of the Advisory Group until the substantive session of the Economic and Social Council in July 2006, with the purpose of following closely and providing advice on Haiti's long-term development strategy to promote socio-economic recovery and stability, with particular attention to the need to ensure coherence and sustainability in international support for Haiti, based on the long-term national development priorities, building upon the Interim Cooperation Framework and stressing the need to avoid overlap and duplication with respect to existing mechanisms;

4. *Expresses its satisfaction* to the Secretary-General for the support provided to the Advisory Group, and requests him to continue to support the Group's activities adequately;

5. *Requests* the Advisory Group, in accomplishing its mandate, to continue to cooperate with the Secretary-General, the United Nations Development Group, relevant United Nations funds and programmes and specialized agencies, the Bretton Woods institutions, regional organizations and institutions, including the Organization of American States and the Caribbean Community, the Inter-American Development Bank and other major stakeholders;

6. *Notes* that post-conflict recovery, reconstruction and rehabilitation, including the experience of the ad hoc advisory groups, are among the subjects being discussed in ongoing talks on United Nations reform;

7. *Requests* the Advisory Group to submit a report on its work, with recommendations, as appropriate, to the Economic and Social Council no later than six weeks before the start of the substantive session of 2006;

8. *Decides* that the work of the Advisory Group will be reviewed at the substantive session of 2006, with a view to considering whether to continue its mandate, based on the Council's consideration of the report of the Advisory Group and of the situation then prevailing in Haiti.

Kazakhstan

The Secretary-General, in his August consolidated report on humanitarian assistance and rehabilitation [A/60/302], provided information on cooperation and coordination for the human and ecological rehabilitation of the Semipalatinsk region of Kazakhstan, where nuclear tests were conducted by the Soviet Union between 1949 and 1989. An estimated 1,323,000 people were negatively affected by those tests and many were still suffering. The Semipalatinsk polygon had yet to be secured, the local economy was still suffering from the collapse of the Soviet Union, and morbidity and mortality levels were high.

The Secretary-General reported on progress made in implementing the Semipalatinsk Relief and Region Rehabilitation Programme since his previous report on the issue in 2002 [YUN 2002, p. 922], covering the health, humanitarian, environmental and economic sectors. In 2005, most donor programmes had ended or were coming to an end and fewer organizations were offering support, the magnitude of which was considerably smaller.

Arising out of a donors' meeting in Almaty in February 2004 to take stock of what had been accomplished and set priorities for further action, the Government of Kazakhstan launched a programme to address the problems of the former Semipalatinsk test site during the period 2005-2007. The main goal was to improve the ecological, economic, medical and social factors affecting living standards in the region. Kazakhstan was expected to provide approximately \$18.9 million to finance the programme.

GENERAL ASSEMBLY ACTION

On 22 December [meeting 68], the General Assembly, on the recommendation of the Second Committee [A/60/496 & Corr.1, 2], adopted **resolution 60/216** without vote [agenda item 73(b)].

International cooperation and coordination for the human and ecological rehabilitation and economic development of the Semipalatinsk region of Kazakhstan

The General Assembly,

Recalling its resolutions 52/169 M of 16 December 1997, 53/1 H of 16 November 1998, 55/44 of 27 November 2000 and 57/101 of 25 November 2002,

Taking note of the report of the Secretary-General,

Recognizing that the Semipalatinsk nuclear testing ground, inherited by Kazakhstan and closed in 1991, remains a matter of serious concern for the people and Government of Kazakhstan with regard to the long-term nature of its consequences for the lives and health of the people, especially children and other vulnerable groups, as well as for the environment of the region,

Taking into consideration the results of the international conference on the problems of the Semipalatinsk region, held in Tokyo in 1999, which have promoted the effectiveness of the assistance provided to the population of the region,

Recognizing the important role of national development policies and strategies in the rehabilitation of the Semipalatinsk region, and taking note with satisfaction of the elaboration of the Kazakhstan national programme entitled "Complex solution of the former Semipalatinsk nuclear test site problems for 2005-2007",

Recognizing also the contribution of different organizations of the United Nations system, donor States, intergovernmental and non-governmental organizations to humanitarian assistance and to the implementation of the projects aimed at the rehabilitation of the region and the role of the Government of Kazakhstan in this regard,

Recognizing further the challenges Kazakhstan faces in the rehabilitation of the Semipalatinsk region, in particular in the context of the efforts by the Government of Kazakhstan to ensure an effective and timely achievement of the Millennium Development Goals,

Taking note of the need for know-how in minimizing and mitigating radiological, health, socio-economic, psychological and environmental problems in the Semipalatinsk region,

Taking into account the fact that many international programmes in the Semipalatinsk region have been completed whereas serious social, economic and ecological problems continue to exist,

Conscious that the international community should continue to pay due attention to the issue of the human, ecological and socio-economic dimensions of the situation in the Semipalatinsk region,

Emphasizing the importance of support by donor States and international development organizations for the efforts by Kazakhstan to improve the social, economic and environmental situation in the Semipalatinsk region,

1. *Takes note* of the report of the Secretary-General and the information contained therein on measures taken to solve the health, ecological, economic and humanitarian problems and to meet the needs of the Semipalatinsk region;

2. *Welcomes and recognizes* the important role of the Government of Kazakhstan in providing domestic resources to help meet the needs of the Semipalatinsk region, including for the implementation of the Kazakhstan national programme entitled "Complex solution of the former Semipalatinsk nuclear test site problems for 2005-2007";

3. *Calls upon* the international community, including all Member States, in particular donor States, and United Nations institutions to continue to support Kazakhstan in addressing the challenges of the rehabilitation of the Semipalatinsk region and its population, taking additional action, including by facilitating the implementation of the Kazakhstan national programme on addressing the problems of the former Semipalatinsk nuclear testing ground in a comprehensive manner, and stresses the importance of regional cooperation in this regard;

4. *Urges* the international community to provide assistance to Kazakhstan in the formulation and implementation of special programmes and projects of treatment and care for the affected population as well as in the efforts to ensure economic growth and sustainable development in the Semipalatinsk region;

5. *Calls upon* all States, relevant multilateral financial organizations and other entities of the international community, including non-governmental organizations, to share their knowledge and experience in order to contribute to the human and ecological rehabilitation and economic development of the Semipalatinsk region;

6. *Invites* the Secretary-General to pursue a consultative process, with the participation of interested States and relevant United Nations agencies, on modalities for mobilizing the necessary support to seek appropriate solutions to the problems and needs of the Semipalatinsk region, including those prioritized in the report of the Secretary-General;

7. *Calls upon* the Secretary-General to continue his efforts to enhance world public awareness of the problems and needs of the Semipalatinsk region;

8. *Requests* the Secretary-General to report to the General Assembly at its sixty-third session, under a separate sub-item, on the progress made in the implementation of the present resolution.

Timor-Leste

In response to General Assembly resolution 58/121 [YUN 2003, p. 953], the Secretary-General, in his August consolidated report [A/60/302], provided information on humanitarian and rehabilitation assistance to Timor-Leste.

The Government and people of Timor-Leste had made significant progress towards consolidating democracy, strengthening State institutions, and building institutional capacity and social and economic development, especially meeting the MDGs [YUN 2000, p. 51]. However, ongoing challenges included the need for continued assistance to ensure sustained development, mainly in the areas of rule of law, justice, human rights and support for the police and other public administration institutions; continued infrastructure rehabilitation; the provision of health services to the general population; support to secondary and higher education; psychosocial support, particularly for children affected by violence; and greater participation of Timorese women in all aspects of society, including legislation to combat domestic violence and other gender-related crimes.

A strategic framework for broader sustainable development assistance was initiated, with specific focus on institutional capacity development in public financial management, the rule of law and justice, and democratic governance. A major objective of the renewed strategy was to continue to develop the capacity of Timorese civil servants and State institutions and improve coordination among all stakeholders.

Third States affected by sanctions

In a 13 May note [E/2005/62], the Secretary-General indicated that his 2004 report on the implementation of the provisions of the Charter of the United Nations related to assistance to third States affected by the application of sanctions [YUN 2004, p. 941] would be made available to the Economic and Social Council at its 2005 substantive session. By **decision 2005/312** of 27 July, the Economic and Social Council took note of the Secretary-General's 2004 report and his May note.

In response to General Assembly resolution 59/45 [ibid., p. 1346], the Secretary-General submitted an August report [A/60/320] highlighting measures for the further improvement of the procedures and working methods of the Security Council and its sanctions committees related to assistance to third States affected by the application of sanctions. It reviewed the Secretariat's capacity and modalities for implementing intergovernmental mandates and for addressing the main findings, including recommendations of the ad hoc expert group meeting on assistance to third States affected by the application of sanctions [YUN 1998, p. 1235]. The report also noted recent developments related to the role of the Assembly and the Economic and Social Council in the area of assistance to third States.

Disaster response

In 2005, the number of disasters, such as earthquakes, floods and droughts, increased by 18 per cent, killing some 92,000 people worldwide. The increase in such disasters, from 304 in 2004 to 360 in 2005, affected 157 million people who required immediate assistance, sustained injuries or lost their livelihoods. Natural disasters during the year cost an estimated $159 billion in damage, of which $125 billion were for losses caused by Hurricane Katrina in the United States.

In the Horn of Africa, West Africa and Southern Africa, drought, erratic rains, locust infestation and floods, coupled with chronic poverty, conflict, poor governance and HIV/AIDS, affected millions of people, including farmers and pastoral and agropastoral groups. As a result, more than 29 million people in those subregions required food assistance. In several countries, including Mali, Mauritania and the Niger, vulnerable populations suffered from severe malnutrition. In March, an epidemic of Marburg haemorrhagic fever was declared in Angola (see p. 1029), and by late June, 92 cases and 354 deaths had been recorded. A cholera outbreak in West Africa in June resulted in 42,390 cases of the disease and 702 deaths by late September (see p. 1035).

In early 2005, most of the Central Asia region suffered from adverse weather conditions; heavy rains and snowfall caused 486 deaths in Pakistan and over 100 deaths in Afghanistan, and affected 2 million people in Tajikistan. An earthquake measuring 6.4 on the Richter scale directly affected more than 32,000 people in Iran, with

612 confirmed dead. Following the 2004 Indian Ocean earthquake/tsunami [YUN 2004, p. 952], a powerful aftershock measuring 8.7 on the Richter scale struck the west coast of Sumatra on 28 March 2005. A 7.6-magnitude earthquake struck South Asia in October, killing close to 75,000 people, injuring an equal number, and leaving more than 3 million homeless (see p. 1034).

Twenty-two tropical storms were recorded in the Atlantic, with 12 becoming hurricanes, six of them major. The 2004-2005 hurricanes were directly responsible for the deaths of more than 6,000 people, with several million people affected and at least $100 billion in economic losses. In January, torrential rains caused severe flooding in the densely populated coastal regions of Guyana, affecting over 300,000 people—almost half of the country's population (see p. 1033). Floods and mudslides also caused devastation and displacement in El Salvador and in Guatemala (see p. 1030).

Disaster reduction

World Conference on Disaster Reduction (2005)

In accordance with General Assembly resolution 58/214 [YUN 2003, p. 958], the World Conference on Disaster Reduction was convened in Kobe, Hyogo, Japan, from 18 to 22 January [A/CONF.206/6]. The Conference adopted the Hyogo Declaration and the Hyogo Framework for Action 2005-2015: Building the Resilience of Nations and Communities to Disasters (see p. 1016). It also adopted the report of its Credentials Committee [A/CONF.206/5]. The Conference was attended by some 4,000 participants representing interested public and private entities from 168 States, 78 observer bodies, 161 NGOs and 152 media organizations. The Conference's Public Forum hosted 66 workshops. In three round tables, the Conference discussed disaster risk: the next development challenge; learning to live with risk; and emerging risks. The theme of the Conference, "Indian Ocean disaster: risk reduction for a safer future", was considered in a special session, which delivered a common statement (see p. 1016).

The Conference considered a Secretariat note [A/CONF.206/L.1], containing the review of the Yokohama Strategy and Plan of Action for a Safer World, adopted by the 1994 World Conference on Natural Disaster Reduction [YUN 1994, p. 851]. The review, which was prepared in accordance with Assembly resolutions 56/195 [YUN 2001, p. 863] and 57/256 [YUN 2002, p. 928], stressed the importance of underpinning disaster risk reduction with a more proactive approach to informing, motivating and involving people in all aspects of the issue in their own communities. It also highlighted the scarcity of resources allocated for risk reduction objectives. The review concluded that the Strategy's Principles remained valid as means to guide the development of policy frameworks for enhancing national and local disaster reduction capabilities. It identified gaps and challenges, including a lack of systematic implementation, co-operation and reporting of progress to reduce risk and vulnerability to disasters, which were addressed in the priorities for action outlined in the Hyogo Framework (see below).

Hyogo Declaration and Framework for Action

On 22 January, the Conference adopted the Hyogo Declaration and the Hyogo Framework for Action 2005-2015: Building the Resilience of Nations and Communities to Disasters. In the Declaration, Conference participants reaffirmed the vital role of the UN system in disaster risk reduction. They declared their intention to build on relevant international commitments and frameworks, as well as internationally agreed development goals, including those contained in the Millennium Declaration [YUN 2000, p. 49], to strengthen global disaster reduction activities for the twenty-first century. Participants affirmed that States had the primary responsibility for protecting people and property on their territory from hazards, and it was therefore vital to give high priority to disaster risk reduction in national policy. They resolved to develop indicators to track progress on disaster risk reduction activities and to further develop information-sharing mechanisms on programmes, initiatives, best practices, lessons learned and technologies in support of disaster risk reduction. The Conference called for action from all stakeholders to make the world safer from the risk of disasters within the next decade.

In the Hyogo Framework for Action, Conference participants resolved to pursue for the next 10 years the expected outcome of the Conference, namely, the substantial reduction of disaster losses in lives and the social, economic and environmental assets of communities and countries. To that end, the Conference adopted three strategic goals: more effective integration of disaster risk considerations into sustainable development policies, planning and programming at all levels, with a special emphasis on disaster prevention, mitigation, preparedness and vulnerability reduction; development and strengthening of institutions, mechanisms and capacities, particularly at the community level, that could systemati-

cally contribute to building resilience to hazards; and the systematic incorporation of risk reduction approaches into the design and implementation of emergency preparedness, response and recovery programmes in the reconstruction of affected communities. Drawing on the review of the Yokohama Strategy (see p. 1015), the Conference adopted five priorities for action: ensuring that disaster risk reduction was a national and local priority with a strong institutional basis for implementation; identifying, assessing and monitoring disaster risks and enhancing early warning; using knowledge, innovation and education to build a culture of safety and resilience at all levels; reducing underlying risk factors; and strengthening disaster preparedness for effective response at all levels. The Framework included specific key activities for each priority for implementation by States, regional and international organizations, and other relevant actors.

Common statement on the Indian Ocean disaster

In its common statement of the special session on the Indian Ocean disaster: risk reduction for a safer future, the World Conference on Disaster Reduction requested the Economic and Social Council to include regional disaster reduction mechanisms in the agenda of the humanitarian affairs segment of its 2005 substantive session (see p. 1015), and the secretariat of the International Strategy for Disaster Reduction to report on regional mechanisms for disaster reduction to that session and the sixtieth (2005) session of the General Assembly. The Secretary-General was invited to include regional mechanisms for disaster reduction in the agenda of the Assembly's sixtieth session and to submit to the Assembly a report thereon. The Conference recommended that regional disaster reduction mechanisms be established and strengthened as soon as possible for all relevant natural hazards. It called for the establishment of an effective and durable tsunami early warning system for the Indian Ocean and recommended elements of a forward strategy to achieve that goal.

International Strategy for Disaster Reduction

In response to General Assembly resolution 59/231 [YUN 2004, p. 946], the Secretary-General, in an August report [A/60/180], provided an overview of the implementation of the International Strategy for Disaster Reduction (ISDR), which was adopted by the programme forum of the International Decade for Natural Disaster Reduction (1990-2000) in 1999 [YUN 1999, p. 859] and endorsed by the Assembly in resolution 54/219 [ibid., p. 861]. The Inter-Agency Task Force for Disaster Reduction and the ISDR secretariat served as the main mechanisms for the Strategy's implementation by the UN system. The report also reviewed the follow-up to the World Conference on Disaster Reduction (see p. 1015).

The ISDR system, in collaboration with agencies and experts, was to assist in facilitating and coordinating action among stakeholders of the Hyogo Framework process (see p. 1016) and to further advocacy and resource mobilization, and in information sharing and reporting. As a first step in the follow-up to the World Conference, the ISDR secretariat presented to the eleventh session of the Inter-Agency Task Force (Geneva, 24-26 May) a set of strategic directions to assist in the implementation of the Hyogo Framework. The Task Force revised and adopted those directions and requested that guiding principles be specifically brought to the attention of States, national platforms and the constituencies of Task Force members, in order to support them in setting their implementation policy parameters. With the adoption of the strategic directions, the ISDR system was called upon to focus on institutional commitments, planning and programming, awareness and advocacy, and monitoring and reporting on progress.

In response to a decision of the eleventh session of the Task Force, a matrix showing commitments and initiatives supporting the implementation of the Hyogo Framework was developed under the coordination of the ISDR secretariat. Several UN agencies and programmes, as well as other international and regional organizations and bodies, initiated national and regional follow-up to the provisions of the Framework. Benchmarks, guidelines and generic indicators that could be adapted to national environments were being developed, facilitated by the ISDR secretariat, Task Force members and national experts. Thematic platforms and networks would be engaged or specifically developed to assist in the implementation of distinct components of the Framework.

The national ownership requirement endorsed by the Framework had stimulated follow-up activities, including national workshops for disaster risk reduction; reviews of national disaster risk reduction plans; the strengthening, or creation, of national platforms in support of broader national policy initiatives; and the development of sustainable institutional systems to deal with disaster risk. The Task Force requested the secretariat to prepare a review of regional and subregional strategies for the implementation of the Hyogo Framework and progress in strength-

ening the outreach of the ISDR system. To promote an integrated approach to climate change, the Task Force created the Working Group on Climate Change and Disaster Risk Reduction, co-chaired by UNDP and the World Meteorological Organization. A tsunami early warning system for the Indian Ocean region was being developed. A multipartner project coordinated by ISDR provided an integrated framework for strengthening early warning systems in the region. The United Nations Educational, Scientific and Cultural Organization (UNESCO) Intergovernmental Oceanographic Commission had put in place a mechanism to facilitate regional capacities for the detection of potential tsunamigenic events and to issue warnings, and other regional institutions were contributing to the establishment of a tsunami early warning system. The Secretary-General requested the ISDR secretariat to coordinate a global survey of early warning system capacities and gaps, with a view to achieving a comprehensive global capacity for systematic, people-centred early warning systems, as proposed in his report "In larger freedom: towards development, security, and human rights for all" [A/59/2005] (see p. 67).

The Secretary-General called on the Assembly to endorse the Hyogo Declaration (see p. 1016) and the Hyogo Framework for Action, and to invite States, civil society organizations, regional bodies and international organizations to comply with the request for implementation, follow-up and support, as set out in the Framework. The Assembly should endorse a proposed strengthening of the ISDR system as set out in the report, including its governance and secretariat and the distribution of roles and responsibilities among agencies, in support of the implementation of the Hyogo Framework. That would include the establishment of a management oversight board to advise and support the Under-Secretary-General for Humanitarian Affairs; a modified task force reformed into a global platform for disaster reduction, with a subsidiary programme advisory committee; and a strengthened ISDR secretariat to service the system at all levels. Member States were urged to fully support the work of the secretariat by contributing to the Trust Fund for Disaster Reduction. The Secretary-General also recommended the strengthening of regional mechanisms for collaboration and networking in support of national and local efforts to reduce disaster risk. He also called for greater political commitment for the systematic integration of risk reduction into development plans and increased provision of resources and application of knowledge of disaster reduction by Member

States, their communities and the wider international community.

ISDR reform. The proposal for strengthening the ISDR system in support of the implementation of the Hyogo Framework, as recommended by the Secretary-General in his August report (see p. 1016), was further discussed and refined at the ISDR stakeholder workshop (Geneva, 10-11 October) and the twelfth session of the Inter-Agency Task Force on Disaster Reduction (Geneva, 22-24 November). The Task Force established a reference group to develop guidance for the first session, scheduled for 2007, of the Global Platform for Disaster Risk Reduction, which was to succeed the Task Force. A revised reform proposal was presented by the Under-Secretary-General for Humanitarian Affairs on 19 December.

GENERAL ASSEMBLY ACTION

On 22 December [meeting 68], the General Assembly, on the recommendation of the Second Committee [A/60/488/Add.3], adopted **resolution 60/195** without vote [agenda item 52 *(c)*].

International Strategy for Disaster Reduction

The General Assembly,

Recalling its resolutions 44/236 of 22 December 1989, 49/22 A of 2 December 1994, 49/22 B of 20 December 1994, 53/185 of 15 December 1998, 54/219 of 22 December 1999, 56/195 of 21 December 2001, 57/256 of 20 December 2002, 58/214 of 23 December 2003 and 59/231 of 22 December 2004, and Economic and Social Council resolutions 1999/63 of 30 July 1999 and 2001/35 of 26 July 2001, and taking into due consideration its resolution 57/270 B of 23 June 2003 on integrated and coordinated implementation of and follow-up to the outcomes of the major United Nations conferences and summits in the economic and social fields,

Expressing its deep concern at the number and scale of natural disasters and their increasing impact within recent years, which have resulted in massive loss of life and long-term negative social, economic and environmental consequences for vulnerable societies throughout the world, in particular in developing countries,

Reiterating that, although natural disasters damage the social and economic infrastructure of all countries, the long-term consequences of natural disasters are especially severe for developing countries and hamper the achievement of their sustainable development,

Recognizing that disaster risk reduction is a crosscutting issue in the context of sustainable development,

Recognizing also the clear relationship between development, disaster risk reduction, disaster response and disaster recovery and the need to deploy efforts in all these areas,

Recognizing further the urgent need to further develop and make use of the existing scientific and technical knowledge to build resilience to natural disasters, and emphasizing the need for developing countries to

have access to technology so as to tackle natural disasters effectively,

Emphasizing that disaster risk reduction, including reducing vulnerability to natural disasters, is an important element that contributes to the achievement of sustainable development,

Stressing the importance of advancing the implementation of the Plan of Implementation of the World Summit on Sustainable Development and its relevant provisions on vulnerability, risk assessment and disaster management,

Expressing its profound gratitude to the Government and the people of Japan for the excellent arrangements made for hosting the World Conference on Disaster Reduction, held at Kobe, Hyogo, from 18 to 22 January 2005, for the hospitality extended to the participants and for the facilities, staff and services placed at their disposal, as well as for all the voluntary contributions made to facilitate the participation of representatives of developing countries, in particular those from the least developed countries,

Welcoming the Hyogo Declaration, the Hyogo Framework for Action 2005-2015: Building the Resilience of Nations and Communities to Disasters, and the common statement of the special session on the Indian Ocean disaster: risk reduction for a safer future, as adopted by the World Conference on Disaster Reduction,

Recognizing that the Hyogo Framework for Action complements the Yokohama Strategy for a Safer World: Guidelines for Natural Disaster Prevention, Preparedness and Mitigation and its Plan of Action,

Taking note that the scope of the Hyogo Framework for Action encompasses disasters caused by hazards of natural origin and related environmental and technological hazards and risks and thus reflects a holistic and multi-hazard approach to disaster risk management and the relationship between them, which can have a significant impact on social, economic, cultural and environmental systems, as stressed in the Yokohama Strategy for a Safer World: Guidelines for Natural Disaster Prevention, Preparedness and Mitigation and its Plan of Action,

Recalling the 2005 World Summit Outcome,

Recognizing the need to continue to develop an understanding of, and to address, socio-economic activities that exacerbate the vulnerability of societies to natural disasters and to build and further strengthen community capability to cope with disaster risks,

1. *Takes note* of the report of the Secretary-General on the implementation of the International Strategy for Disaster Reduction;

2. *Endorses* the Hyogo Declaration and the Hyogo Framework for Action 2005-2015: Building the Resilience of Nations and Communities to Disasters as adopted by the World Conference on Disaster Reduction, held at Kobe, Hyogo, Japan, from 18 to 22 January 2005, and recalls the common statement of the special session on the Indian Ocean disaster: risk reduction for a safer future;

3. *Calls for* a more effective integration of disaster risk reduction into sustainable development policies, planning and programming; for the development and strengthening of institutions, mechanisms and capacities to build resilience to hazards and for a systematic incorporation of risk reduction approaches into the

implementation of emergency preparedness, response and recovery programmes;

4. *Invites* Member States, the United Nations system, including international financial institutions, regional bodies and other international organizations, as well as relevant civil society organizations, to support, implement and follow up the Hyogo Framework for Action;

5. *Calls upon* the United Nations system, including international financial institutions and international organizations, to integrate the goals of and take into full account the Hyogo Framework for Action in their strategies and programmes, making use of existing co-ordination mechanisms, and to assist developing countries with those mechanisms to design disaster risk reduction measures with a sense of urgency;

6. *Calls upon* the international community to fully implement the commitments of the Hyogo Declaration and the Hyogo Framework for Action;

7. *Recalls* that the commitments of the Hyogo Declaration and the Hyogo Framework for Action include the provision of assistance for developing countries that are prone to natural disasters and disaster-stricken States in the transition phase towards sustainable physical, social and economic recovery, for risk-reduction activities in post-disaster recovery and for rehabilitation processes;

8. *Calls upon* the United Nations system, including the international financial institutions as well as regional banks and other regional and international organizations to support, in a timely and sustained manner, the efforts led by disaster-stricken countries for disaster risk reduction, in post-disaster recovery and rehabilitation processes;

9. *Takes note* of all the regional and subregional initiatives developed in order to achieve disaster risk reduction, reiterates the need to develop regional initiatives and risk reduction capacities of regional mechanisms and to strengthen them, wherever they exist, and encourages the use and sharing of all the existing tools;

10. *Notes* the importance of developing international mechanisms for the implementation of the actions established in the Hyogo Framework for Action, such as, for example, the International Recovery Platform launched to ensure the reduction of vulnerability during the post-disaster recovery phase;

11. *Recognizes* that each State has the primary responsibility for its own sustainable development and for taking effective measures to reduce disaster risk, including for the protection of people on its territory, infrastructure and other national assets from the impact of disasters, including the implementation of and follow-up to the Hyogo Framework for Action, and stresses the importance of international cooperation and partnerships to support those national efforts;

12. *Also recognizes* the need to strengthen the sharing of good practices, knowledge and technical support among all relevant stakeholders;

13. *Calls upon* the international community to support the development and strengthening of institutions, mechanisms and capacities at all levels, in particular at the community level, that can systematically contribute to building resilience to hazards;

14. *Stresses* the importance of further strengthening the capacity of the International Strategy for Disaster Reduction system in order to provide a solid basis for action as mandated by the Hyogo Framework for Action, and requests the Secretary-General to include this issue in his report to the General Assembly at its sixty-first session;

15. *Recognizes* the importance of integrating a gender perspective as well as engaging women in the design and implementation of all phases of disaster management, particularly at the disaster risk reduction stage;

16. *Expresses its appreciation* to those countries that have provided financial support for the activities of the Strategy by making voluntary contributions to the Trust Fund for the International Strategy for Disaster Reduction;

17. *Encourages* the international community to provide adequate voluntary financial contributions to the United Nations Trust Fund for Disaster Reduction, in the effort to ensure the adequate support for the follow-up activities to the Hyogo Framework for Action, and to review the current usage and feasibility for the expansion of the Fund, inter alia, to assist disaster-prone developing countries to set up national strategies for disaster risk reduction;

18. *Requests* the Secretary-General to allocate adequate financial and administrative resources, within existing resources, for the activities and effective functioning of the Inter-Agency Secretariat for the International Strategy for Disaster Reduction;

19. *Invites* Governments and relevant international organizations to consider disaster risk assessment as an integral component of development plans and poverty eradication programmes;

20. *Stresses* the importance of identifying, assessing and managing risks prior to the occurrence of disasters, for which it is necessary to combine the efforts at all levels from the development, humanitarian, scientific and environmental communities as well as the importance of integrating disaster risk reduction, as appropriate, into development plans and poverty eradication programmes;

21. *Also stresses* the need to foster better understanding and knowledge of the causes of disasters, as well as to build and strengthen coping capacities through, inter alia, the transfer and exchange of experiences and technical knowledge, access to relevant data and information and the strengthening of institutional arrangements, including community-based organizations;

22. *Recognizes* the importance of early warning as an essential element of disaster risk reduction and looks forward to the results of the Third International Conference on Early Warning, to be held from 27 to 29 March 2006, in Bonn, Germany;

23. *Requests*, in this context, the Inter-Agency Secretariat for the International Strategy for Disaster Reduction to complete the preparation of the global survey on early warning capacities and gaps, including an account of available technologies for early warning, and invites Member States to provide inputs that may assist the Inter-Agency Secretariat for the Strategy in preparing this survey;

24. *Reiterates its call upon* Governments to establish national platforms or focal points for disaster reduction and to strengthen them, wherever they exist, encourages the platforms to share relevant information

on standards and practices, urges the United Nations system, in this regard, to provide appropriate support for those mechanisms, and invites the Secretary-General to strengthen the regional outreach of the Inter-Agency Secretariat for the International Strategy for Disaster Reduction in order to ensure such support;

25. *Stresses* that continued cooperation and coordination among Governments, the United Nations system, other organizations, regional organizations, non-governmental organizations and other partners, as appropriate, are considered essential to address effectively the impact of natural disasters;

26. *Recognizes* the importance of linking disaster risk management to regional frameworks, as appropriate, such as the African Regional Strategy for Disaster Reduction developed within the New Partnership for Africa's Development, to address issues of poverty eradication and sustainable development;

27. *Emphasizes* the need for the international community to maintain its focus beyond emergency relief and to support medium- and long-term rehabilitation, reconstruction and risk reduction, and stresses the importance of implementing programmes related to the eradication of poverty, sustainable development and disaster risk reduction management in the most vulnerable regions, particularly in developing countries prone to natural disasters;

28. *Requests* the Secretary-General to submit to the General Assembly at its sixty-first session a report on the implementation of the present resolution, under the item entitled "Sustainable development".

On the same date, the Assembly, on the recommendation of the Second Committee [A/60/488/Add.3], adopted **resolution 60/196** without vote [agenda item 52 *(c)*].

Natural disasters and vulnerability

The General Assembly,

Recalling its decision 57/547 of 20 December 2002 and its resolutions 58/215 of 23 December 2003 and 59/233 of 22 December 2004,

Reaffirming the Johannesburg Declaration on Sustainable Development and the Plan of Implementation of the World Summit on Sustainable Development, adopted by the World Summit, held in Johannesburg, South Africa, from 26 August to 4 September 2002,

Reaffirming also the Hyogo Declaration and the Hyogo Framework for Action 2005-2015: Building the Resilience of Nations and Communities to Disasters, as adopted by the World Conference on Disaster Reduction, held at Kobe, Hyogo, Japan, from 18 to 22 January 2005,

Taking note that the scope of the Hyogo Framework for Action encompasses disasters caused by hazards of natural origin and related environmental and technological hazards and risks and thus reflects a holistic and multi-hazard approach to disaster risk management and the relationship between them, which can have a significant impact on social, economic, cultural and environmental systems, as stressed in the Yokohama Strategy for a Safer World: Guidelines for Natural Disaster Prevention, Preparedness and Mitigation and its Plan of Action,

Recalling the 2005 World Summit Outcome,

Recognizing the need to continue to develop an understanding of, and to address, the underlying risk factors, as identified in the Hyogo Framework for Action, including socio-economic factors, that exacerbate the vulnerability of societies to natural hazards, to build and further strengthen community capacity to cope with disaster risks and to enhance resilience against hazards associated with disasters, while also recognizing the negative impact of natural disasters on economic growth and sustainable development, in particular in developing countries and disaster-prone countries,

Noting that the global environment continues to suffer degradation, adding to economic and social vulnerabilities, in particular in developing countries,

Taking into account the various ways and forms in which all countries, in particular the more vulnerable countries, are affected by severe natural hazards such as earthquakes, tsunamis, landslides and volcanic eruptions and extreme weather events such as heat waves, severe droughts, floods and storms, and the El Niño/La Niña events which have global reach,

Expressing deep concern at the recent increase in the frequency and intensity of extreme weather events and associated natural disasters in some regions of the world and their substantial economic, social and environmental impacts, in particular upon developing countries in those regions,

Taking into account that geological and hydro-meteorological hazards and their associated natural disasters and their reduction must be addressed in a coherent and effective manner,

Noting the need for international and regional cooperation to increase the capacity of countries to respond to the negative impacts of all natural hazards, including earthquakes, tsunamis, landslides and volcanic eruptions and extreme weather events such as heat waves, severe droughts and floods, and associated natural disasters, in particular in developing countries and disaster-prone countries,

Bearing in mind the importance of addressing disaster risks related to changing social, economic, environmental conditions and land use, and the impact of hazards associated with geological events, weather, water, climate variability and climate change, in sector development planning and programmes as well as in post-disaster situations,

1. *Takes note* of the report of the Secretary-General on the implementation of the International Strategy for Disaster Reduction, in particular section II, entitled "Disasters associated with natural hazards and vulnerability: a development challenge";

2. *Recognizes* that each State has the primary responsibility for its own sustainable development and for taking effective measures to reduce disaster risk, including for the protection of people on its territory, infrastructure and other national assets from the impact of disasters, including the implementation of and follow-up to the Hyogo Framework for Action 2005-2015: Building the Resilience of Nations and Communities to Disasters, and stresses the importance of international cooperation and partnerships to support those national efforts;

3. *Urges* the international community to continue to address ways and means, including through cooperation and technical assistance, to reduce the ad-

verse effects of natural disasters, including those caused by extreme weather events, in particular in vulnerable developing countries, including least developed countries and in Africa, through the implementation of the International Strategy for Disaster Reduction, including the Hyogo Framework for Action, and encourages the Inter-Agency Task Force for Disaster Reduction to continue its work in this regard;

4. *Stresses* the importance of the Hyogo Declaration and the Hyogo Framework for Action and the priorities for action that States, regional and international organizations and international financial institutions as well as other concerned actors should take into consideration in their approach to disaster risk reduction and implement, as appropriate, according to their own circumstances and capacities, bearing in mind the vital importance of promoting a culture of prevention in the area of natural disasters, including through the mobilization of adequate resources for disaster risk reduction, and of addressing disaster risk reduction, including disaster preparedness, and the adverse effects of natural disasters in efforts to implement national development plans and poverty reduction strategies with a view to achieving the internationally agreed development goals, including the Millennium Development Goals;

5. *Encourages* Governments, through their respective International Strategy for Disaster Reduction national platforms and national focal points for disaster risk reduction, in cooperation with the United Nations system and other stakeholders, to strengthen capacity-building in the most vulnerable regions, to enable them to address the socio-economic factors that increase vulnerability, and to develop measures that will enable them to prepare for and cope with natural disasters, including those associated with earthquakes and extreme weather events, and encourages the international community to provide effective assistance to developing countries in this regard;

6. *Emphasizes*, in order to build resilience, particularly in developing countries, especially those vulnerable among them, the importance of addressing the underlying risk factors identified in the Hyogo Framework for Action and the importance of promoting the integration of risk reduction associated with geological and hydrometeorological hazards in disaster risk reduction programmes;

7. *Encourages* the Inter-Agency Task Force for Disaster Reduction to continue, within its mandate, particularly the Hyogo Framework for Action, to enhance the coordination of activities to promote disaster risk reduction and to make available to the relevant United Nations entities information on options for natural disaster risk reduction, including severe natural hazards and extreme weather-related disasters and vulnerabilities;

8. *Stresses* the importance of close cooperation and coordination among Governments, the United Nations system, other international and regional organizations as well as non-governmental organizations and other partners such as the International Red Cross and Red Crescent Movement, as appropriate, taking into account the need for the development of disaster management strategies, including the effective establishment of early warning systems that are, inter alia,

people-centred, while taking advantage of all available resources and expertise for that purpose;

9. *Encourages* the Conference of the Parties to the United Nations Framework Convention on Climate Change and the parties to the Kyoto Protocol to the United Nations Framework Convention on Climate Change to continue to address the adverse effects of climate change, especially in developing countries that are particularly vulnerable, in accordance with the provisions of the Convention, and also encourages the Intergovernmental Panel on Climate Change to continue to assess the adverse effects of climate change on the socio-economic and natural disaster reduction systems of developing countries;

10. *Requests* the Secretary-General to report to the General Assembly at its sixty-first session on the implementation of the present resolution, and decides to consider the issue of natural disasters and vulnerability at that session, under the sub-item entitled "International Strategy for Disaster Reduction" of the item entitled "Sustainable development".

International cooperation

In response to General Assembly resolution 59/212 [YUN 2004, p. 943], the Secretary-General, in an August report [A/60/227], provided an update on international cooperation in the field of disasters associated with natural hazards, highlighting the key challenges faced by the international community in strengthening the capacity of disaster-prone countries in disaster preparedness and response, post-disaster recovery and disaster risk reduction. In response to Assembly resolution 57/150 [YUN 2002, p. 926], the report also included information on the activities of the International Search and Rescue Advisory Group (INSARAG), an intergovernmental network established in 1991 [YUN 1991, p. 413] for international cooperation and coordination in earthquake response.

The report stated that, despite some worthwhile gains in the previous decade, the level of commitment and the resources available for preparedness remained inadequate at both the national and international levels. The participation of beneficiaries in the planning and implementation of relief programmes remained largely insufficient. National and international actors lacked a common approach and a shared understanding of terminology, definitions and standards. Governments of affected countries faced great difficulties in coordinating national and international relief assistance, and the capacity of UN country teams to coordinate international assistance was uneven. Coordination of recovery efforts remained a challenge and pointed to the need for more structured and systematic international support of national and local efforts.

International urban search and rescue teams belonging to the INSARAG network responded to the 2004 Indian Ocean earthquake and subsequent tsunami [YUN 2004, p. 952]. INSARAG organized an earthquake response exercise in Yerevan, Armenia, in June, and its methodology was introduced and practised in an exercise held in Geneva in April. It also conducted training courses in Hungary (February 2004), Tunisia (February 2004 and April 2005), Indonesia (May 2004) and Estonia (November 2004). In 2005, an international working group completed a revision of the INSARAG guidelines. The revised guidelines improved and updated the INSARAG coordination methodology and included agreed standards for classifying international search and rescue teams according to their capabilities in collapsed-structure rescue. The report also outlined challenges and recommendations in resolving administrative bottlenecks; safety and security of international staff; on-site coordination; and stopping the deployment of excess international search and rescue teams.

The Secretary-General recommended that UN organizations and donor Governments strengthen the capacity of disaster-prone countries in disaster mitigation, preparedness, response and post-disaster recovery within a risk reduction framework by supporting initiatives in that field and significantly increasing funding for preparedness activities. Regional organizations should play a greater role in disaster risk reduction and management by devising regional-level programmes and by supporting countries' efforts. Providers of relief assistance should maximize the participation of beneficiaries in planning and implementing relief programmes, and enhance the level of accountability to beneficiaries. The United Nations should strengthen civil-military coordination mechanisms and continue to develop and implement the UN humanitarian civil-military coordination concept, including the development of national standby teams, with Member States. Relevant UN organizations and Member States should enhance global capacity for sustainable post-disaster recovery. Member States should implement the priorities set out in the Hyogo Framework for Action 2005-2015 (see p. 1016). In particular, they should incorporate practical disaster reduction steps into sustainable development and poverty reduction strategies, as well as into disaster preparedness and response.

GENERAL ASSEMBLY ACTION

On 15 December [meeting 63], the General Assembly adopted **resolution 60/125** [A/60/L.39 & Add.1] without vote [agenda item 73 (a)].

International cooperation on humanitarian assistance in the field of natural disasters, from relief to development

The General Assembly,

Reaffirming its resolution 46/182 of 19 December 1991, the annex to which contains the guiding principles for the strengthening of the coordination of emergency humanitarian assistance of the United Nations system, as well as all its resolutions on international cooperation on humanitarian assistance in the field of natural disasters, from relief to development, and recalling the resolutions of the humanitarian segments of the substantive sessions of the Economic and Social Council,

Recognizing the importance of the principles of neutrality, humanity, impartiality and independence for the provision of humanitarian assistance,

Reiterating that independence means the autonomy of humanitarian objectives as distinct from the political, economic, military or other objectives that may be pursued by any actor with regard to areas where humanitarian action is being implemented,

Welcoming the Hyogo Declaration, the Hyogo Framework for Action 2005-2015: Building the Resilience of Nations and Communities to Disasters and the common statement of the special session on the Indian Ocean disaster: risk reduction for a safer future, as adopted by the World Conference on Disaster Reduction, held in Kobe, Hyogo, Japan, from 18 to 22 January 2005,

Emphasizing that the affected State has the primary responsibility in the initiation, organization, coordination and implementation of humanitarian assistance within its territory and in the facilitation of the work of humanitarian organizations in mitigating the consequences of natural disasters,

Emphasizing also the responsibility of all States to undertake disaster preparedness, response and mitigation efforts in order to minimize the impact of natural disasters, while recognizing the importance of international cooperation in support of the efforts of affected countries which may have limited capacities to fulfil this requirement,

Noting the critical role played by local resources, and by existing in-country capacities, in natural disaster management and risk reduction, disaster response, rehabilitation and development,

Recognizing the importance of international cooperation in support of the efforts of the affected States in dealing with natural disasters in all their phases, and of strengthening the response capacity of countries affected by disaster,

Noting with appreciation the important role played by Member States, including developing countries, that have granted necessary and continued generous assistance to countries and peoples stricken by natural disasters,

Recognizing the significant role played by national Red Cross and Red Crescent societies, as part of the International Red Cross and Red Crescent Movement, in disaster preparedness and risk reduction, disaster response, rehabilitation and development,

Emphasizing the importance of addressing vulnerability and integrating risk reduction into all phases of natural disaster management, post-natural disaster recovery and development planning,

Welcoming the work carried out by the Intergovernmental Oceanographic Commission of the United Nations Educational, Scientific and Cultural Organization in the setting up of regional tsunami early warning systems, in the Indian Ocean, the Mediterranean and the north-east Atlantic, and noting the proposed convening of a Third International Conference on Early Warning, to be held from 27 to 29 March 2006 in Bonn, Germany,

Recognizing that efforts to achieve economic growth, sustainable development and internationally agreed development goals, including the Millennium Development Goals, can be adversely affected by natural disasters, and noting the positive contribution that those efforts can make in strengthening the resilience of populations to such disasters,

Emphasizing, in this context, the important role of development organizations in supporting national efforts to mitigate the consequences of natural disasters,

1. *Takes note* of the reports of the Secretary-General entitled "International cooperation on humanitarian assistance in the field of natural disasters, from relief to development"; "Strengthening of the coordination of emergency humanitarian assistance of the United Nations"; "Strengthening emergency relief, rehabilitation, reconstruction, recovery and prevention in the aftermath of the Indian Ocean tsunami disaster"; "The transition from relief to development"; and "Improvement of the Central Emergency Revolving Fund";

2. *Expresses its deep concern* at the number and scale of natural disasters and their increasing impact, resulting in massive losses of life and property worldwide, in particular in vulnerable societies lacking adequate capacity to mitigate effectively the long-term negative social, economic and environmental consequences of natural disasters;

3. *Calls upon* States to fully implement the Hyogo Declaration and the Hyogo Framework for Action 2005-2015: Building the Resilience of Nations and Communities to Disasters, in particular those commitments related to assistance for developing countries that are prone to natural disasters and for disaster-stricken States in the transition phase towards sustainable physical, social and economic recovery, for risk-reduction activities in post-disaster recovery and for rehabilitation processes;

4. *Calls upon* all States to adopt, where required, and to continue to implement effectively, necessary legislative and other appropriate measures to mitigate the effects of natural disasters and integrate disaster risk reduction strategies into development planning, and in this regard requests the international community to continue to assist developing countries as well as countries with economies in transition;

5. *Welcomes* the effective cooperation among the affected States, relevant bodies of the United Nations system, donor countries, regional and international financial institutions and other relevant organizations, such as the International Red Cross and Red Crescent Movement, and civil society, in the coordination and delivery of emergency relief, and stresses the need to continue such cooperation and delivery throughout relief operations and medium- and long-term rehabilitation and reconstruction efforts, in a manner that reduces vulnerability to future natural hazards;

6. *Reiterates* the commitment to support the efforts of countries, in particular developing countries, to strengthen their capacities at all levels in order to prepare for and respond rapidly to natural disasters and mitigate their impact;

7. *Stresses* that, to increase further the effectiveness of humanitarian assistance, particular international cooperation efforts should be undertaken to enhance and broaden further the utilization of national and local capacities and, where appropriate, of regional and subregional capacities of developing countries for disaster preparedness and response, which may be made available in closer proximity to the site of a disaster, and more efficiently and at lower cost;

8. *Also stresses*, in this context, the importance of strengthening international cooperation, particularly through the effective use of multilateral mechanisms, in the timely provision of humanitarian assistance through all phases of a disaster, from relief and mitigation to development, including the provision of adequate resources;

9. *Welcomes* the role of the Office for the Coordination of Humanitarian Affairs of the Secretariat as the focal point within the overall United Nations system for the promotion and coordination of disaster response among United Nations humanitarian organizations and other humanitarian partners;

10. *Also welcomes*, so as to increase further the effectiveness of humanitarian assistance, the incorporation of experts from developing countries that are prone to natural disasters into the United Nations Disaster Assessment and Coordination system, and also the work of the International Search and Rescue Advisory Group in assisting such countries in strengthening urban search and rescue capacities and establishing mechanisms for improving their coordination of national and international response in the field, and recalls in this regard its resolution 57/150 of 16 December 2002 entitled "Strengthening the effectiveness and coordination of international urban search and rescue assistance";

11. *Requests* the Secretary-General, in consultation with States and relevant organizations, to continue to explore ways to strengthen the rapid response capacities of the international community to provide immediate humanitarian relief, building on existing arrangements and ongoing initiatives;

12. *Notes* the need to continue to improve the management and use of the Central Register of Disaster Management Capacities, including the Directory of Advanced Technologies for Disaster Response, which has the potential to support planning preparedness and response activities, and requests the Secretary-General to include information about the work of the Central Register in his report on the implementation of the present resolution;

13. *Requests* the Secretary-General to develop more systematic links with Member States offering military assets for natural disaster response in order to identify the availability of such assets;

14. *Encourages* donors to consider the importance of ensuring that assistance in the case of higher-profile natural disasters does not come at the expense of those natural disasters that may be relatively lower-profile, bearing in mind that the allocation of resources should be driven by needs;

15. *Encourages* States that have not acceded to or ratified the Tampere Convention on the Provision of Telecommunication Resources for Disaster Mitigation and Relief Operations, which entered into force on 8 January 2005, to consider doing so;

16. *Encourages* the further use of space-based and ground-based remote-sensing technologies, as well as the sharing of geographical data, for the prevention, mitigation and management of natural disasters, where appropriate;

17. *Encourages* Member States, relevant United Nations organizations and international financial institutions to enhance the global capacity for sustainable post-disaster recovery in areas such as coordination with traditional and non-traditional partners, identification and dissemination of lessons learned, development of common tools and mechanisms for recovery needs assessment, strategy development and programming, and incorporation of risk reduction into all recovery processes, and welcomes the ongoing efforts to this end;

18. *Requests* the United Nations system to improve its coordination of disaster recovery efforts, from relief to development, inter alia, by strengthening institutional, coordination and strategic planning efforts in disaster recovery, in support of national authorities;

19. *Stresses* the importance of rapid access to funds to ensure a more predictable and timely United Nations response to humanitarian emergencies;

20. *Requests* the Secretary-General to continue to improve the international response to natural disasters, and to report thereon to the General Assembly at its sixty-first session.

Disaster assistance

Indian Ocean tsunami aftermath

The massive Indian Ocean earthquake and resulting tsunami of December 2004 [YUN 2004, p. 952] killed 183,172 people in 12 countries. One year later, 43,320 people were still listed as missing and more than 1 million were displaced. Indonesia was the most affected country, as the coastline of its Aceh province was damaged by the initial force of the earthquake and then immediately engulfed by the tsunami. In Indonesia, Somalia and Sri Lanka, the disaster took place within the context of long-standing, complex crises, which had significant implications for the organization and delivery of humanitarian assistance. The disaster affected predominantly poor coastal communities, causing $10 billion in damages and destroying the livelihoods of some 1.4 million people, along with critical infrastructure, administrative capacity and basic services.

On 28 March 2005, a second earthquake off the island of Nias in Sumatra, measuring 8.7 on the Richter scale, left an additional 70,000 people displaced and nearly 1,000 dead.

The UN Consolidated Inter-Agency Flash Appeal for the Indian Ocean Earthquake-Tsunami 2005, covering the period from January to the end of June, sought $1.4 billion for humanitarian assistance and recovery efforts in Indonesia, Maldives, Myanmar, Seychelles, Somalia and Sri Lanka. At the Ministerial-level Meeting on Humanitarian Assistance to Tsunami-Affected Communities (Geneva, 11 January), 25 States pledged a total of $777 million towards the Flash Appeal and additional reconstruction activities. The latest available information indicated that the Appeal received 89 per cent ($1.25 billion) of the required amount.

ASEAN Declaration. On 11 January [A/59/669], Indonesia transmitted to the Secretary-General the Declaration on Action to Strengthen Emergency Relief, Rehabilitation, Reconstruction and Prevention in the Aftermath of the Earthquake and Tsunami Disaster of 26 December 2004, adopted at the special meeting of the Association of Southeast Asian Nations (ASEAN) leaders in the aftermath of the earthquake and tsunami (Jakarta, Indonesia, 6 January). The ASEAN leaders agreed to urgently mobilize additional resources to meet the needs of the victims; request the United Nations to mobilize the international community to support national emergency relief programmes; strengthen coordination and cooperation of national, regional and international relief efforts; and support the efforts of the affected countries as national coordinators to ensure an effective channelling and utilization of assistance. They also agreed to support national rehabilitation and reconstruction programmes; call on the international community to provide the necessary funds to sustain those programmes; establish a partnership involving donor countries and regional and international financial institutions to support national programmes; and promote private sector participation in rehabilitation and reconstruction efforts.

GENERAL ASSEMBLY ACTION

On 19 January [meeting 79], the General Assembly adopted **resolution 59/279** [draft: A/59/L.58 & Add.1, orally revised] without vote [agenda item 39].

Strengthening emergency relief, rehabilitation, reconstruction and prevention in the aftermath of the Indian Ocean tsunami disaster

The General Assembly,

Recalling its resolutions 46/182 of 19 December 1991, 57/152 of 16 December 2002, 57/256 of 20 December 2002, 58/25 of 5 December 2003, 58/214 and 58/215 of 23 December 2003, 59/212 of 20 December 2004, and 59/231 and 59/233 of 22 December 2004,

Expressing sincere condolences and deep sympathy to the victims, their families, the Governments and the peoples of those States that suffered huge losses of life and socio-economic and environmental damage from the unprecedented tsunami disaster that struck the Indian Ocean and Southeast Asian regions on 26 December 2004,

Commending the prompt response, support, generous contributions to and assistance of the international community, by Governments, civil society, the private sector and individuals, in the relief, rehabilitation and reconstruction efforts, which reflect the spirit of international solidarity and cooperation to address the disaster,

Commending also the leading role of the affected States and the role of the United Nations in addressing the disaster, and recognizing the importance of cooperation for effective mobilization, coordination and delivery of international assistance in the emergency relief phase,

Welcoming the Declaration on Action to Strengthen Emergency Relief, Rehabilitation, Reconstruction and Prevention in the Aftermath of the Earthquake and Tsunami Disaster of 26 December 2004, adopted at the special meeting of leaders of the Association of Southeast Asian Nations, held in Jakarta on 6 January 2005 in the aftermath of the earthquake and tsunami, and the pledges made by donor countries and international financial institutions for the affected countries,

Welcoming also the launching of the Indian Ocean earthquake-tsunami 2005 flash appeal by the Secretary-General to respond to the urgent and immediate needs of communities severely affected by the earthquake and tsunami and the outcome of the Ministerial-level Meeting on Humanitarian Assistance to Tsunami-affected Communities, held in Geneva on 11 January 2005,

Welcoming further the recent announcement by the Paris Club creditors that they will not expect debt payments from affected countries that request such forebearance until the World Bank and the International Monetary Fund have made a full assessment of their reconstruction and financing needs as well as specific initiatives from countries on this issue,

Welcoming the appointment by the Secretary-General of a Special Coordinator to coordinate international emergency relief operations in support of national emergency programmes of countries affected by the tsunami disaster and covered by the flash appeal,

Expressing concern over the medium- and long-term social, economic and environmental impacts of the disaster on the affected States,

Stressing the need to develop and implement risk-reduction strategies and to integrate them, where appropriate, into national development plans, in particular through the implementation of the International Strategy for Disaster Reduction, so as to enhance the resilience of populations in disasters and reduce risks to them, their livelihoods, the social and economic infrastructure and environmental resources,

Recognizing that the development of stronger institutions, mechanisms and capacities, including at the community level, that can systematically build resilience to hazards and disasters is essential to reducing the risks and the vulnerability of populations to disasters, including disaster preparedness, mitigation and early warning systems at all levels,

Recalling the need for continued commitment to assist the affected countries and their peoples, particularly the most vulnerable groups, to fully recover from the catastrophic and traumatic effects of the disaster, including in their medium- and long-term rehabilitation and reconstruction efforts, and welcoming Government and international assistance measures in this regard,

Emphasizing that disaster reduction, including reducing vulnerability to natural disasters, is an important element that contributes to the achievement of sustainable development,

Welcoming the convening of the World Conference on Disaster Reduction in Kobe, Japan, from 18 to 22 January 2005, with a view to updating the guiding framework on disaster reduction for the twenty-first century,

Noting the outcome of the International Meeting to Review the Implementation of the Programme of Action for the Sustainable Development of Small Island Developing States, held in Mauritius from 10 to 14 January 2005,

Stressing the importance of advancing the implementation of the Plan of Implementation of the World Summit on Sustainable Development ("Johannesburg Plan of Implementation") and its relevant provisions on vulnerability, risk assessment and disaster management,

Emphasizing the importance of establishing a partnership, upon the request and with the leadership of the country concerned, involving donor countries and regional and international financial institutions as well as the private sector and civil society, to support the respective national rehabilitation and reconstruction programmes of the affected countries,

Emphasizing also the importance of international cooperation in support of the efforts of the affected States in dealing with natural disasters in all phases, including prevention, preparedness, mitigation, recovery and reconstruction, as well as in strengthening the response capacity of affected countries,

1. *Expresses its deep concern* at the number and scale of natural disasters and their increasing impact within recent years, which have resulted in a massive loss of life and long-term negative social, economic and environmental consequences for vulnerable societies throughout the world, in particular in developing countries;

2. *Emphasizes* the need for the international community to maintain its focus beyond the present emergency relief, in order to sustain the political will to support the medium- and long-term rehabilitation, reconstruction and risk reduction efforts led by the Governments of the affected countries at all levels;

3. *Welcomes* the effective cooperation between the affected States, relevant bodies in the United Nations system, donor countries, regional and international financial institutions and civil society in the coordination and delivery of emergency relief, and stresses the need to continue such cooperation and delivery throughout the ongoing relief operations and rehabilitation and reconstruction efforts, in a manner that reduces vulnerability to future natural hazards;

4. *Encourages* the international community, particularly donor countries, international financial institutions and relevant international organizations, as well as the private sector and civil society, to deliver swiftly on their pledges and to continue to provide the neces-

sary funds and assistance to support the rehabilitation and reconstruction efforts;

5. *Welcomes* the increasing efforts to further enhance transparency and accountability with respect to the channelling and utilization of resources;

6. *Requests* the Secretary-General to appoint a special representative in order to, inter alia, sustain the political will of the international community to support medium- and long-term rehabilitation, reconstruction and risk reduction efforts led by the Governments of affected countries at all levels;

7. *Also requests* the Secretary-General to explore ways to further strengthen the rapid response capacities for immediate humanitarian relief efforts of the international community, building on the existing arrangements and ongoing initiatives, including the consideration of "standby arrangements" under the auspices of the United Nations;

8. *Invites* the World Bank and the Asian Development Bank, in collaboration with other international and regional financial institutions and the United Nations, to convene members of the international community, including affected countries, to address the medium- and long-term rehabilitation and reconstruction needs of the affected countries;

9. *Recognizes* the importance of the decision by the Association of Southeast Asian Nations to establish regional mechanisms on disaster prevention, preparedness and mitigation, encourages regional cooperation in this regard, and urges donor countries and regional and international organizations as well as other relevant institutions to provide, where appropriate, financial and technical assistance;

10. *Also recognizes* the importance of the promotion of public education, awareness and community participation in disaster prevention and preparedness, particularly at the local level, as well as the pressing need to develop and promote national and regional capacity and access to technology and knowledge in building and managing a regional early warning system and in disaster management, through national and regional efforts as well as through international cooperation and partnership;

11. *Emphasizes* the urgent need for the establishment of a regional early warning system, particularly for tsunamis, in the Indian Ocean and Southeast Asian regions, and notes the interest expressed by some Governments, bodies and organizations, including the Asian Disaster Preparedness Centre, to support the establishment of this system;

12. *Welcomes* the proposed convening of a regional ministerial meeting on regional cooperation with regard to a tsunami early warning system, to be held in Thailand on 28 January 2005;

13. *Also welcomes* the proposal of Germany to host a third international early warning conference, covering the complete range of natural hazards, with a focus on the urgent implementation of early warning systems for hydro-meteorological and geological hazards on a global scale;

14. *Further welcomes* the fact that the World Conference on Disaster Reduction will discuss the issue of a global and regional tsunami early warning system as part of its agenda;

15. *Requests* the Secretary-General to report to the General Assembly at its sixtieth session on the implementation of the present resolution under the item entitled "Strengthening of the coordination of humanitarian and disaster relief assistance of the United Nations, including special economic assistance" and to report to the Economic and Social Council at its substantive session in 2005.

Ministerial Declaration. The Ministerial Meeting on Regional Cooperation on Tsunami Early Warning Arrangements (Phuket, Thailand, 28-29 January), which included the participation of ministers and special envoys from 42 countries and the European Commission, adopted the Phuket Ministerial Declaration on Regional Cooperation on Tsunami Early Warning Arrangements. The Declaration committed participants to the early realization of an effective, real-time warning arrangement covering the Indian Ocean and South-East Asia. To that end, the participants would take immediate and practical steps to enhance early warning capabilities and cooperate towards the establishment of interim early warning arrangements and the strengthening of national systems. They would develop a system for, and undertake, the timely sharing of early warning information among their respective agencies and national centres, and establish timelines for implementing the elements for a regional tsunami early warning arrangement by mid-2006. The participants created an open-ended steering/coordinating group to promote implementation of the Declaration and made recommendations for further action. They welcomed the establishment of the Multi-donor Voluntary Trust Fund on Tsunami Early Warning Arrangements in the Indian Ocean and Southeast Asia, with the Economic and Social Commission for Asia and the Pacific (ESCAP) as administrator, and Thailand's pledge of $10 million in seed money.

Report of World Tourism Organization. In February [E/2005/48], the World Tourism Organization (UNWTO) (see p. 1595), reporting on its post-tsunami actions, stated that its Emergency Task Force, composed of senior tourism officials, industry leaders, high-level tourism experts and representatives of regional and international institutions, met (Phuket, Thailand, 31 January) to assess the damage caused by the tsunami and prepare a draft global tourism recovery action plan. The Phuket Action Plan, adopted by an extraordinary emergency session of the UNWTO Executive Council (Phuket, 1 February), focused on saving tourism jobs, relaunching small and medium-sized tourism enterprises, training or retraining the tourism workforce, repositioning tourism to be more sustainable and less vulnerable, and restoring consumer confidence in the affected tourism destinations. In collaboration with the international community, UNWTO initiated action to implement the Plan, including communications campaigns and workshops on risk management and repositioning tourism products.

A second meeting of the Emergency Task Force (Berlin, 10 March), convened to review progress towards the implementation of the Action Plan, announced that the tourism industry in the affected regions experienced a swifter than expected return to business. In its 2005 report "Tsunami: One Year On—A Summary of the Phuket Action Plan", UNWTO stated that it had earmarked over 40 Action Plan projects, the majority of which were completed.

By **decision 2005/223** of 15 July, the Economic and Social Council took note of the Secretary-General's note transmitting UNWTO's report on its post-tsunami actions.

Earth Observation Summit communiqué. The Third Earth Observation Summit (Brussels, Belgium, 16 February) adopted the "Communiqué relating to support for tsunami and multi-hazard warning systems within the context of the Global Earth Observation System of Systems". In the Communiqué, the Group on Earth Observations (GEO) was asked to support the expansion of multi-hazard capabilities for disaster reduction at national, regional and international levels, within the framework of the International Strategy for Disaster Reduction [YUN 1999, p. 859], by recognizing and building on existing and developing capabilities. GEO was also asked to support the UNESCO Intergovernmental Oceanographic Commission and related national and regional initiatives to realize effective tsunami warning systems in the Indian Ocean and elsewhere, as an integral part of a multi-hazard approach supported by the Global Earth Observation System of Systems.

Asian-African Leaders' Statement. In the Joint African-Asian Leaders' Statement on Tsunami, Earthquake and Other Natural Disasters, adopted at the Asian-African Summit 2005 (Jakarta and Bandung, Indonesia, 22-24 April) [A/59/841], participating Heads of State and Government agreed to establish an integrated strategy for the development of a multi-nodal early warning system with mechanisms for preparedness, prevention, mitigation and response, and to establish and upgrade national early warning systems.

Report of Secretary-General. In response to General Assembly resolution 59/279 (see p. 1024), the Secretary-General submitted a June report [A/60/86-E/2005/77] on strengthening emergency relief, rehabilitation, reconstruction, recovery and prevention in the aftermath of the Indian Ocean tsunami. The report highlighted key issues that had emerged from the tsunami recovery effort and lessons learned in the areas of national ownership and leadership, response capacity, coordination tactics and tools, resource mobilization, and displacement and protection of affected populations.

Following requests for assistance by the Governments of tsunami-affected countries, five UN Disaster Assessment and Coordination teams composed of 44 disaster-response experts from 18 countries and four international organizations were deployed to five of those countries. Sixteen UN agencies, 18 International Federation of Red Cross and Red Crescent Societies (IFRC) response teams, more than 160 international NGOs and countless private companies and civil society groups deployed to affected areas to provide emergency food, water and medical services. Some 35 countries provided military assets for the relief effort and the United Nations deployed civil-military coordination officers to key locations in the region. The disaster generated the contribution of more resources over a shorter period of time than any other crisis. The United Nations estimated that $6.8 billion had been pledged at the time of the report, some of which had been channelled through the UN Consolidated Inter-Agency Flash Appeal (see p. 994); media reports indicated that at least another $1 billion was contributed by private donors. Immediately following the disaster, the Secretary-General appointed the Deputy Emergency Relief Coordinator, Margareta Wahlstrom, as the Special Coordinator for humanitarian assistance to tsunami-affected communities.

Six months after the disaster, the immediate survival needs of those directly affected had been addressed. However, continuous seismic activity in the region caused further death and damage, slowed recovery efforts and continued to take a psychological toll on the population. It was clear that significant humanitarian needs would persist for many months. The Governments of several of the affected countries, in partnership with the World Bank, the Asian Development Bank and the United Nations, finalized medium- and long-term recovery and reconstruction plans.

To facilitate support for and implementation of national plans, the Secretary-General, in January, appointed former United States President William J. Clinton as his Special Envoy for Tsunami Recovery. The Special Envoy visited affected countries in May to assess progress in launching the recovery process. He also convened the Global Consortium for Tsunami-Affected Countries (New York, 3 June), which brought together affected Governments, UN agencies, international organizations and financial institutions, and NGOs to improve coordination among the main actors, particularly at the country level; facilitate the implementation of individual countries' reconstruction plans; and instil common transparency and accountability measures. The Consortium met again in Washington, D.C., on 22 September.

The Secretary-General recommended that the United Nations, Governments, and other members of the international community work to improve structures for national and international field response to major, sudden-onset emergencies; develop regional response capacity; build coherence within the civil-military response; invest in early warning and preparedness; enhance the coordination and capacity of the UN system for recovery; promote financial transparency and accountability; commit to reducing vulnerability and risk; and promote research and learning to guide recovery activities.

GENERAL ASSEMBLY ACTION

On 14 November [meeting 52], the General Assembly adopted **resolution 60/15** [draft: A/60/L.20 & Add.1] without vote [agenda item 73].

Strengthening emergency relief, rehabilitation, reconstruction and prevention in the aftermath of the Indian Ocean tsunami disaster

The General Assembly,

Recalling its resolutions 46/182 of 19 December 1991, 57/152 of 16 December 2002, 57/256 of 20 December 2002, 58/25 of 5 December 2003, 58/214 and 58/215 of 23 December 2003, 59/212 of 20 December 2004, 59/231 and 59/233 of 22 December 2004 and 59/279 of 19 January 2005,

Commending the prompt response, continued support, generous assistance and contributions of the international community, by Governments, civil society, the private sector and individuals, in the relief, rehabilitation and reconstruction efforts, which reflect the spirit of international solidarity and cooperation to address the disaster,

Noting the Declaration on Action to Strengthen Emergency Relief, Rehabilitation, Reconstruction and Prevention in the Aftermath of the Earthquake and Tsunami Disaster of 26 December 2004, adopted at the special meeting of leaders of the Association of Southeast Asian Nations, held in Jakarta on 6 January 2005,

Recalling the Hyogo Declaration and the Hyogo Framework for Action 2005-2015, as well as the common statement of the special session on the Indian Ocean disaster, adopted at the World Conference on Disaster Reduction, held in Kobe, Hyogo, Japan, from 18 to 22 January 2005,

Noting the communiqué relating to support for tsunami and multihazard warning systems within the context of the Global Earth Observation System of Systems, adopted at the third Earth Observation Summit, in Brussels, on 16 February 2005,

Taking note of the joint Asian-African leaders' statement on tsunami, earthquake and other natural disasters, adopted at the Asian-African Summit 2005, held in Jakarta on 22 and 23 April 2005,

Also taking note of the report of the Secretary-General on strengthening emergency relief, rehabilitation, reconstruction, recovery and prevention in the aftermath of the Indian Ocean tsunami disaster,

Welcoming the appointment of Mr. William Jefferson Clinton, former President of the United States of America, as the Secretary-General's Special Envoy for Tsunami Recovery and the establishment of the Global Consortium for Tsunami-Affected Countries to sustain the political will of the international community to support medium- and long-term rehabilitation, reconstruction and risk reduction efforts led by the Governments of affected countries,

Taking note with appreciation of the convening of the Global Consortium for Tsunami-Affected Countries in June and September 2005, aimed at improving coordination among relevant stakeholders and developing a common online tracking system and common indicators to monitor and evaluate the impact of tsunami relief and rehabilitation programmes, which emphasizes the need to promote national ownership of the tracking processes in tsunami-affected countries,

Welcoming ongoing efforts by the international system to capture, consolidate and disseminate lessons learned from the tsunami response and recovery to guide future disaster management at all levels,

Welcoming also the establishment of the Multi-Donor Voluntary Trust Fund on Tsunami Early Warning Arrangements in the Indian Ocean and Southeast Asia, which will contribute to setting up an early warning system and to building up the capacity of the region in dealing with natural disasters,

Welcoming further the proposed convening of a Third International Conference on Early Warning, in Bonn, Germany, from 27 to 29 March 2006, covering the complete range of natural hazards, with a focus on the urgent implementation of early warning systems for hydrometeorological and geological hazards on a global scale,

Stressing the need to develop and implement risk reduction strategies and to integrate them, where appropriate, into national development plans, in particular through the implementation of the International Strategy for Disaster Reduction, so as to enhance the resilience of populations in disasters and reduce risks to them, their livelihoods, the social and economic infrastructure and environmental resources,

Emphasizing that disaster reduction, including reducing vulnerability to natural disasters, is an important element that contributes to the achievement of sustainable development,

Stressing the need for continued commitment to assist the affected countries and their peoples, particularly the most vulnerable groups, to fully recover from the catastrophic and traumatic effects of the disaster, including in their medium- and long-term rehabilitation and reconstruction efforts, and welcoming Government and international assistance measures in this regard,

1. *Notes with appreciation* the efforts by the Governments of affected countries to complete the emergency relief phase and move forward to the rehabilitation and reconstruction phase, as well as in enhancing financial transparency and accountability with respect

to the channelling and utilization of resources, including, as appropriate, through the involvement of international public auditors;

2. *Takes note with appreciation* of the work of Mr. William Jefferson Clinton, former President of the United States of America, the Secretary-General's Special Envoy for Tsunami Recovery, and his various initiatives, and encourages his efforts to continue sustaining the political will of the international community, particularly regional and international financial institutions, civil society and the private sector, to support medium- and long-term rehabilitation, reconstruction and risk reduction efforts led by the Governments of affected countries;

3. *Encourages* donor countries and international and regional financial institutions, as well as the private sector and civil society, to strengthen partnerships and to continue supporting the medium- and long-term rehabilitation and reconstruction needs of the affected countries, including through the swift delivery of pledges made by donors;

4. *Emphasizes* the need to promote transparency and accountability among donors and recipient countries by means of, inter alia, a unified financial and sectoral information online tracking system—a development assistance database—with the support and participation of the Global Consortium for Tsunami-Affected Countries, and highlights the importance of timely and accurate information on assessed needs and the sources and uses of funds;

5. *Encourages* the continued effective coordination among the Governments of affected countries, relevant bodies of the United Nations system, international organizations, donor countries, regional and international financial institutions, civil society and private sectors involved in relief, rehabilitation and reconstruction efforts, in order to ensure adequate response to the remaining humanitarian needs and effective implementation of existing joint programmes and to prevent unnecessary duplication, as well as to reduce vulnerability to future natural hazards;

6. *Requests* the Secretary-General to strengthen the United Nations institutional mechanism and capacities in support of national and local authorities for the coordination of tsunami disaster recovery efforts;

7. *Reaffirms* that all regional efforts should serve the purpose of strengthening international cooperation aimed at the creation of a global multihazard early warning system, including the newly established Indian Ocean Tsunami Warning and Mitigation System;

8. *Stresses* the need for the development of stronger institutions, mechanisms and capacities at the regional, national and local levels, as affirmed in the Hyogo Declaration and the Hyogo Framework for Action 2005-2015, as well as through the promotion of public education, awareness and community participation, in order to systematically build resilience to hazards and disasters, as well as reduce the risks and the vulnerability of populations to disasters, particularly in developing countries;

9. *Urges* Governments and the United Nations system, in planning for disaster preparedness and responding to natural disasters, and implementing recovery, rehabilitation and reconstruction efforts, to integrate a gender perspective and to ensure that women take an active and equal role in all phases of disaster management;

10. *Requests* the Secretary-General to continue to explore ways to strengthen the rapid response capacities of the international community to provide immediate humanitarian relief, building on existing arrangements and ongoing initiatives;

11. *Also requests* the Secretary-General to report to the General Assembly at its sixty-first session on the implementation of the present resolution under the item entitled "Strengthening of the coordination of humanitarian and disaster relief assistance of the United Nations, including special economic assistance", through the Economic and Social Council at its substantive session in 2006.

Report of Special Envoy. In December [A/60/664], the Special Envoy for Tsunami Recovery reported on the status of the recovery effort in the affected countries, including India, Indonesia, Malaysia, Maldives, Myanmar, Seychelles, Somalia, Sri Lanka, Thailand and the United Republic of Tanzania. The recovery process was in its early phase, but much had been achieved in the first year, including the construction of transitional shelter, temporary schools and health clinics. Work on longer-term reconstruction was well under way, with permanent schools, highways and ports, and homes under construction across the region. The establishment of a regional early warning system was also progressing well. While significant progress was made in all the most affected countries, many hurdles remained. A major task for 2006 would be to sustain the level of commitment that had defined the international response up to that point.

The report also discussed key lessons learned with regard to coordination; national leadership in recovery; accountability and transparency; measuring recovery progress; disaster reduction and preparedness; the restoration of livelihoods and the economy; equity in recovery; and political reconciliation, reform and recovery. The Special Envoy said that affected Governments had to ensure that their national recovery plans incorporated disaster risk reduction and "building back better" objectives, with timelines for progress. All agencies, including UN agencies, should support national efforts and continue to give the tsunami recovery operation the institutional attention it deserved.

Other disaster assistance

Angola

In March, an epidemic of Marburg haemorrhagic fever was declared in Angola. By late June, 354 deaths out of 392 reported cases had been recorded, making the epidemic the deadliest and most intense Marburg fever outbreak ever. There was no cure, and in the case of the Angola outbreak, the virus was lethal in 90 per cent of the cases. The majority of the cases were concentrated in Uige province. The number of alert, suspect and confirmed cases was expected to increase as surveillance and reporting mechanisms improved. The Angolan Ministry of Health, which was responsible for coordinating the national response to the epidemic, was constrained by a lack of equipment and supplies, trained personnel and information systems to find cases and trace contacts.

The UN Consolidated Inter-Agency Flash Appeal for Angola was established to address the priority needs of case management; surveillance and epidemiology; social mobilization, risk reduction and health education; and logistics. The Appeal sought $4 million for the period from April to June, 78 per cent ($3.2 million) of which was received.

Benin

Elections held in Togo on 24 April sparked unrest in the border town of Aného, which in turn led to movements of people across the Mono River into Benin, beginning on 25 April. As at 5 May, 11,458 refugees, including 5,536 children, had entered Benin, 3,790 of whom were located at sites and camps in Hillacondji, Comé and Lokossa and 7,668 in Mono and Cotonou, the capital.

The UN Consolidated Inter-Agency Flash Appeal for Benin was aimed at supporting Government and civil society efforts to deal with the presence of 20,000 refugees in the country for the period from May to October. The Appeal sought $5.9 million and received 64 per cent ($3.8 million) of that amount.

Central America

El Salvador

In early October, El Salvador experienced two convergent and simultaneous emergency situations. One of the country's largest volcanoes, Ilamatepec, erupted on 1 October, causing damage and injuries up to 4 kilometres away, with ash falling in a much wider radius. Initially, 4,850 people were evacuated from the vicinity of the volcano following the first eruption and a second eruption, which occurred on 3 October. At the same time, heavy rains, in part brought on by the residual impact of Hurricanes Rita and Stan, caused flooding and deadly mud- and rockslides. By 6 October, 54,308 persons had been evacuated and it was estimated that the total at-risk popula-

tion stood at 160,485. The death toll from the two emergencies had reached 65.

The Joint UN Agency Appeal in El Salvador sought $13.7 million to be used by seven UN agencies, programmes and funds in their relief efforts. Of that total, 27 per cent ($3.7 million) was received.

Guatemala

In Guatemala, from 4 to 9 October, heavy rains brought by Hurricane Stan caused flooding and over 900 landslides in the southern coastal and western highlands regions, resulting in loss of life, injury and displacement of persons, as well as damage to housing and infrastructure, in 251 of 331 municipalities in 15 of the country's 22 departments. Preliminary information indicated that 652 people were killed and 130,179 were affected, particularly indigenous women and children in poor and isolated communities. The most vulnerable communities lost their livelihoods and incomes and faced precarious survival conditions in the subsequent months.

The UN Consolidated Inter-Agency Flash Appeal for Guatemala, launched in October for a period of six months, was intended to cover key actions in the areas of water, sanitation and hygiene; food security; shelter and non-food items; health services; communication and access to services; and inter-agency coordination and support. It sought $31.9 million, of which 69 per cent ($21.9 million) was received.

GENERAL ASSEMBLY ACTION

On 22 December [meeting 68], the General Assembly, on the recommendation of the Second Committee [A/60/496 & Corr.1 & 2], adopted **resolution 60/220** without vote [agenda item 73 *(b)*].

Humanitarian assistance and rehabilitation for El Salvador and Guatemala

The General Assembly,

Recalling its resolutions 53/1 B of 5 October 1998, 53/1 C of 2 November 1998, 54/96 E of 15 December 1999, 58/117 of 17 December 2003, 59/212 of 20 December 2004, and 59/231 and 59/233 of 22 December 2004,

Reiterating the need for the United Nations system to respond to requests for assistance by Member States and for humanitarian assistance to be provided in accordance with the principles of humanity, neutrality and impartiality,

Deeply regretting the loss of human lives and the scores of victims in the wake of Tropical Storm Stan, aggravated by other natural events, in El Salvador and Guatemala, from 3 to 12 October 2005,

Conscious of the huge material losses sustained to crops, homes, basic infrastructure and tourist and other areas,

Acknowledging the efforts of the Governments of El Salvador and Guatemala to protect the lives of their nationals and rapidly to assist the affected population, in particular the indigenous communities,

Conscious that the Central American countries are vulnerable to cyclical weather patterns and prone to natural hazards based on their geographical location and features, which impose additional challenges on their ability to achieve the Millennium Development Goals,

Noting the enormous effort that will be required to rebuild the affected areas and to alleviate the grave situation wreaked by these natural hazards,

Aware that the work of reconstruction requires the fullest coordinated support as well as the unwavering solidarity of the international community,

1. *Expresses its solidarity and support* to the Governments and the peoples of El Salvador and Guatemala;

2. *Expresses its appreciation* to the members of the international community that have offered their support to the rescue efforts and emergency assistance for the affected population;

3. *Appeals* to all Member States and all organs and bodies of the United Nations system, as well as international financial institutions and development agencies, to provide speedy support to the relief, rehabilitation and assistance effort for the affected countries;

4. *Calls upon* the international community to provide assistance in response to the flash appeal for Guatemala and to the joint United Nations agency appeal in El Salvador;

5. *Acknowledges* the efforts and progress made by El Salvador and Guatemala in strengthening their disaster-preparedness capacity, emphasizes the importance of investing in disaster risk reduction, and encourages the international community to cooperate with the Governments of El Salvador and Guatemala towards this end;

6. *Requests* the Secretary-General and all organs and bodies of the United Nations system, as well as international financial institutions and development agencies, to assist El Salvador and Guatemala, whenever possible, through continued effective humanitarian, technical and financial assistance that contributes to overcoming the emergency and achieving the rehabilitation and recovery of the economy and the affected population in the short, medium and long term, in conformity with the priorities identified at the national level;

7. *Requests* the relevant organs and organizations of the United Nations system and other multilateral organizations to increase their support and assistance for strengthening the disaster-preparedness capacity of the countries concerned;

8. *Requests* the Secretary-General to report to the General Assembly, through the Economic and Social Council, at the humanitarian affairs segment of its substantive session of 2006, on the implementation of the present resolution and on the progress made in the relief, rehabilitation and reconstruction efforts of the affected countries.

Djibouti

In 2005, Djibouti faced a severe food crisis in five out of six rural zones as a consequence of three consecutive failed rainy seasons and worsening drought conditions. Delayed rains and erratic rainfall patterns were insufficient to replenish water catchments or regenerate pastures, forcing pastoralists to continue seasonal grazing in coastal areas of Djibouti beyond the restorative capacities of the land. Consequently, pasture was overgrazed and exhausted in most areas.

Djibouti instituted policy measures to relieve high food prices and was working with the United Nations to increase access to food and water for the most vulnerable. However, with the remaining resources available to pastoralists depleted, the Government requested supplementary international assistance. Immediate needs included: food aid for 47,500 people; water for 18,000 people; supplementary feeding for 9,500 malnourished children; mobile health services for 5,000 people; animal feed, water and emergency veterinary care for 50,000 head of livestock; and support for disaster management structures at the national and local levels.

The UN Consolidated Inter-Agency Flash Appeal for Djibouti requested $7.49 million to cover requirements for a period of six months, beginning in April; it received 34 per cent ($2.6 million) of that amount.

GENERAL ASSEMBLY ACTION

On 22 December [meeting 68], the General Assembly, on the recommendation of the Second Committee [A/60/496 & Corr.1, 2], adopted **resolution 60/217** without vote [agenda item 73 *(b)*].

Economic assistance for the reconstruction and development of Djibouti

The General Assembly,

Recalling its resolution 58/116 of 17 December 2003 and its previous resolutions on economic assistance to Djibouti,

Recalling also the United Nations Millennium Declaration,

Recalling further the Brussels Declaration and the Programme of Action for the Least Developed Countries for the Decade 2001-2010, adopted by the Third United Nations Conference on the Least Developed Countries on 20 May 2001, as well as the mutual commitments undertaken on that occasion and the importance attached to the follow-up to and implementation of the Programme of Action,

Aware that Djibouti is included in the list of the least developed countries and that it is ranked one hundred fiftieth out of the one hundred seventy-seven countries studied in the *Human Development Report 2005,*

Noting that the economic and social development efforts of Djibouti are constrained by the extreme local climate conditions, in particular severe droughts and flash floods, and that the implementation of reconstruction and development programmes requires the deployment of substantial resources which exceed the limited capacity of the country,

Noting also that the situation in Djibouti has been made worse by the disastrous drought situation prevailing in the Horn of Africa and by the absence of natural resources, which continue to place serious constraints on the fragile economic, budgetary, social and administrative infrastructure of the country,

Expressing its concern at the severe shortage of drinkable water and the severe food crisis, as reflected in the report of the Secretary-General,

Noting that the Government of Djibouti has implemented a reform programme, including the approval of a poverty reduction strategy paper with the Bretton Woods institutions,

Noting with gratitude the support provided by various countries, as well as intergovernmental and nongovernmental organizations, to meet the humanitarian needs of the country,

1. *Takes note* of the report of the Secretary-General;

2. *Declares its solidarity* with the Government and the people of Djibouti, who continue to face critical developmental and humanitarian challenges owing to the scarcity of natural resources, coupled with harsh climatic conditions, including the acute issue of water supply and the severe food crisis impacting on the development aspirations of the country;

3. *Encourages* the Government of Djibouti, despite difficult economic and regional realities, to continue its important efforts towards the consolidation of democracy, the promotion of good governance, accountability and the eradication of poverty;

4. *Notes* the implementation of a reform programme and the adoption and endorsement of a poverty reduction strategy paper by Djibouti, encourages the Government of Djibouti to continue to work towards the attainment of the goals outlined in the poverty reduction strategy paper, and, in that context, appeals to all Governments, international financial institutions, the specialized agencies and nongovernmental organizations to respond adequately to the financial and material needs of the country in line with the poverty reduction strategy;

5. *Expresses its gratitude* to the intergovernmental organizations and the specialized agencies of the United Nations for their contributions to the national rehabilitation of Djibouti, and encourages them to continue their efforts;

6. *Expresses its appreciation* to the Secretary-General for his continued efforts to make the international community aware of the difficulties faced by Djibouti, and welcomes his coordinated response to the financial and technical needs of Djibouti and the process of aligning the United Nations Development Assistance Framework to the Djibouti poverty reduction strategy through the United Nations Development Assistance Framework midterm review of 2003-2007;

7. *Requests* the Secretary-General to continue, in close cooperation with the Government of Djibouti, his efforts to mobilize the resources necessary for an effective programme of financial, technical and material assistance to Djibouti;

8. *Also requests* the Secretary-General to report to the General Assembly at its sixty-second session on the progress made in the implementation of the present resolution.

Ethiopia

In Ethiopia, to differentiate between the chronically and acutely food-insecure popula-tions, two complementary action plans were developed in 2004: the 2005 humanitarian appeal to address the acute needs of the food-insecure population; and the Productive Safety Net Programme providing longer-term food security needs for approximately 5 million chronically food-insecure people with assistance in the form of cash or food for labour.

The humanitarian joint appeal intended to meet humanitarian needs for 7.8 million people was updated in May 2005 with a request for $345.2 million, including $240 million for food and $105.2 million in non-food assistance. An additional 471,510 beneficiaries would require food aid for the second half of 2005 due to localized failure of the mid-year harvest, and from August to December 2005, approximately 3.3 million people would continue to require emergency relief assistance. Extensive flooding in May affected an additional 55,000 vulnerable people in the Somali, Oromiya and Southern Nations, Nationalities and People's Regions. Conflict and ethnic tensions also caused displacement in eastern Oromiya and in the Somali and Gambella regions. Many IDPs in Gambella were left without food and other basic items due to limited access and lack of recognition and support.

GENERAL ASSEMBLY ACTION

On 22 December [meeting 68], the General Assembly, on the recommendation of the Second Committee [A/60/496 & Corr.1, 2], adopted **resolution 60/218** without vote [agenda item 73 *(b)*].

Humanitarian assistance and rehabilitation for Ethiopia

The General Assembly,

Recalling its resolutions 58/24 of 5 December 2003 on emergency humanitarian assistance to Ethiopia and 59/217 of 22 December 2004,

Recalling also the initiatives of the Secretary-General to improve food security, including the appointment of the Special Envoy for the Humanitarian Crisis in the Horn of Africa,

Concerned by the recurrent drought, which still affects millions owing to the serious crop failures in drought-prone parts of the country and the pastoralist areas that have weak infrastructures and low development capacities,

Bearing in mind the joint 2005 appeal of the United Nations and the Government of Ethiopia for emergency assistance for Ethiopia, to respond to the food and non-food requirements of households in need so as to prevent the worsening of the current humanitarian crisis,

Noting with serious concern the significant and persistent humanitarian needs in such areas as health, water and acute malnutrition that still exist in parts of the country,

Noting with serious concern also the dire humanitarian situation and its long-term socio-economic and environmental impacts,

Recognizing that the persistent problem of food insecurity is linked to inadequate progress in achieving and sustaining rural growth at levels required to build household and community assets needed to manage through the various shocks that induce food crises,

Welcoming the launch of the Productive Safety Nets Programme in 2005,

Emphasizing the need to address the crisis, bearing in mind the importance of the transition from relief to development, and acknowledging the underlying structural causes of recurrent drought in Ethiopia,

Recognizing that the main responsibility for improving the humanitarian situation and creating conditions for long-term development lies with the Government of Ethiopia, while bearing in mind the important role played by the international community,

Emphasizing the importance of establishing a strong early warning system for both food and non-food needs in order to better predict and respond as early as possible to disasters and to minimize their consequences,

1. *Takes note* of the report of the Secretary-General;

2. *Welcomes* the coordinated and collaborative efforts of the Government of Ethiopia, agencies, funds and programmes of the United Nations system, the donor community, non-governmental organizations and other entities, and their timely and generous response to the joint 2005 appeal so far, and, in this regard, encourages the international community to strengthen its response to non-food assistance;

3. *Also welcomes* the efforts of the Government of Ethiopia, the international community and civil society, including non-governmental organizations, to strengthen mechanisms already in place to respond to such emergency situations, expresses appreciation of their endeavours to increase the availability of food through the procurement of local produce and to ensure access of households in need to food, health and water facilities, sanitation, seeds and veterinary services, and strongly encourages the Government of Ethiopia to continue such efforts;

4. *Stresses* the need to address the underlying causes of food insecurity, and issues of recovery, asset protection and the sustainable development of the affected areas, welcomes in this regard the programme prepared by the Coalition for Food Security in Ethiopia, and encourages the international community to support the Coalition in realizing its main objective, namely, breaking the cycle of food aid dependency within the next three to five years, thereby enabling fifteen million vulnerable people to engage in sustainable productive activities;

5. *Welcomes* the Group of Eight action plan on ending the cycle of famine in the Horn of Africa, and looks forward to its full implementation;

6. *Encourages* the Government of Ethiopia to continue to strengthen its efforts to address the underlying structural causes of recurrent threats of drought as part of its overall economic development programme;

7. *Calls upon* all development partners, in cooperation with the Government of Ethiopia, to integrate relief efforts with recovery, asset protection and long-term development, including the structural and productive options needed to stimulate accelerated rural growth, and to address the underlying causes of recurrent drought in Ethiopia in a way that is, inter alia, in line with the poverty reduction strategy paper and the rural development strategy, bearing in mind the need to prevent such crises in the future and to improve the resilience of the population;

8. *Welcomes* the launch of the Productive Safety Nets Programme at the beginning of 2005, and emphasizes the importance of its effective implementation and its complementarity and coordination with activities undertaken in the context of the joint 2005 appeal of the United Nations and the Government of Ethiopia for emergency assistance for Ethiopia as well as with other food security operations;

9. *Welcomes* the initiative taken by the Secretary-General in appointing the Special Envoy for the Humanitarian Crisis in the Horn of Africa, with the objective of mobilizing resources to address the root causes of food insecurity as well as the sustainable development of the affected areas;

10. *Invites* the Office for the Coordination of Humanitarian Affairs of the Secretariat to continue its efforts to coordinate and develop a strategic response to recurrent humanitarian needs in Ethiopia and to consider ways to enhance the mobilization of emergency relief assistance in order to cover the remaining humanitarian needs in Ethiopia;

11. *Takes note* of the report on evaluation of the response to the 2002-2003 emergency in Ethiopia prepared jointly by the Government of Ethiopia and humanitarian partners, and urges the Government of Ethiopia, donors and all other stakeholders to continue to implement the recommendations contained therein;

12. *Requests* the Secretary-General to report to the General Assembly at its sixty-second session on the implementation of the present resolution.

Guyana

In January, torrential rains in Guyana caused serious flooding in the densely populated coastal area, affecting around 300,000 people. Thousands were forced to flee their homes in the capital city of Georgetown and coastal villages, and many families were trapped in their homes. Three weeks after the peak of the emergency, an estimated 92,000 people still had water in their homes, and the water level remained as high as 1.2 to 1.5 metres in some villages. Disease was a major threat, as poor sanitation, waste management and vector proliferation had rendered the waters highly infectious. The crisis had a serious impact on the normal coping mechanisms of families and communities, as many of the worst affected areas were also among the poorest.

The UN Consolidated Inter-Agency Flash Appeal for Guyana was established to address the country's humanitarian and community recovery needs for a period of six months, beginning in February. It sought $2.6 million and received 30 per cent ($779,730) of that amount.

Malawi

In Malawi, inadequate rainfall and insufficient access to agricultural inputs during the 2004-2005 season resulted in the country's worst food crisis since 1994. Approximately 4.2 million people were unable to meet their minimum food requirements from September 2005 until the next harvest in March 2006. Underlying the crisis were the mutually reinforcing factors of chronic poverty and a high prevalence of HIV/AIDS, compounded by poor general health conditions and malnutrition. Those factors, coupled with repeated shocks throughout the preceding five years, had exhausted the coping mechanisms of the most vulnerable households.

The UN Consolidated Inter-Agency Flash Appeal for Malawi was considered a "smart appeal", as it requested international support for Government leadership to address immediate humanitarian needs and action to minimize the likelihood of another food-shortage crisis the following year, through the distribution of subsidized or free seed and fertilizer. The Appeal was launched for $73.8 million to cover the period from September 2005 to March 2006, and it received 78 per cent ($57.8 million) of that amount.

Niger

In the Niger, the combined effect of drought and the 2004 desert locust infestation [YUN 2004, p. 941] negatively affected pasture and cereal production, compounding the structural factors of population growth, non-sustainable farming and the raising of livestock in an unpredictable environment. Nutritional surveys and food security data pointed to a critical situation in the Tillabéri, Tahoua, Maradi, Diffa, Agadez and Zinder regions. Subregional conflicts hindered the migration of labour that had always been the main coping mechanism during the lean season. Of the Niger's 12 million inhabitants, 3.6 million were adversely affected by the food crisis, of whom 2.5 million were thought to be extremely vulnerable and in need of food assistance. An estimated 32,000 children were severely malnourished and 160,000 were moderately malnourished.

The UN Consolidated Inter-Agency Flash Appeal for Niger covered the period from May to September and was later extended to December. It requested $81.4 million, of which 73 per cent was received ($59.2 million).

South Asia earthquake

On 8 October, an earthquake registering 7.6 on the Richter scale struck South Asia, totally devastating parts of northern Pakistan, India and Afghanistan. Close to 75,000 people were killed, an equal number injured, and more than 3 million left homeless. The earthquake affected the entire area of Pakistan-administered Kashmir and North-West Frontier Province, home to 4.5 million, wiping out hundreds of towns and villages and destroying the infrastructure. It was estimated that over 2 million people required life-saving assistance, including winterized shelter, medical care, food, water and sanitation facilities.

The UN Consolidated Inter-Agency Flash Appeal for South Asia, launched on 11 October and revised following the Conference on Assistance to Communities Affected by the Earthquake in South Asia (Geneva, 26 October), sought $561.3 million in assistance for a six-month period, beginning on 11 October. It received 67 per cent ($374.2 million) of that amount.

GENERAL ASSEMBLY ACTION

On 14 November [meeting 52], the General Assembly adopted **resolution 60/13** [draft: A/60/L.18 & Add.1] without vote [agenda item 73].

Strengthening emergency relief, rehabilitation, reconstruction and prevention in the aftermath of the South Asian earthquake disaster—Pakistan

The General Assembly,

Recalling its resolutions 46/182 of 19 December 1991, 57/152 of 16 December 2002, 57/256 of 20 December 2002, 58/25 of 5 December 2003, 58/214 and 58/215 of 23 December 2003, 59/212 of 20 December 2004, 59/231 and 59/233 of 22 December 2004 and 59/279 of 19 January 2005,

Expressing sincere condolences and deep sympathy to the victims, their families and the people of Pakistan, India, Afghanistan and other affected areas, who suffered huge losses of life and socio-economic and environmental damage from the massive earthquake that struck the South Asian region on 8 October 2005,

Deeply alarmed over the critical condition of millions of homeless and countless injured awaiting immediate response in desperation and pain, which is accentuated by extreme weather and difficult terrain,

Welcoming the assistance and contributions of the international community, including Governments, international organizations, civil society and the private sector, in the relief and rehabilitation efforts, which reflect the spirit of international solidarity and cooperation to address and meet the challenges of the disaster, and in this context also appreciating the role of the people and Government of Pakistan,

Welcoming also the launching of the South Asia earthquake 2005 flash appeal by the United Nations on 11 October 2005 and the continuous engagement by the Secretary-General to escalate the global relief efforts for the urgent and immediate needs of the affected people,

Welcoming further the convening by the United Nations of a high-level ministerial donors meeting in Geneva on 26 October 2005 to generate further relief assistance and support for recovery from the disaster,

Stressing the need to incorporate risk reduction approaches into development policies and recovery programmes, as set out in the Hyogo Framework for Action 2005-2015,

Recalling the need for continued commitment to assist the affected countries and their peoples, particularly the most vulnerable groups, to fully recover from the catastrophic and traumatic effects of the disaster, including in their medium- and long-term rehabilitation and reconstruction efforts, and welcoming measures announced by the Government of Pakistan and by the international agencies in this regard,

Emphasizing the importance of international cooperation in support of the efforts of the affected States in dealing with natural disasters and hazards in all phases, including prevention, preparedness, mitigation, recovery and reconstruction, as well as in strengthening the response capacity of affected countries,

1. *Expresses its sympathy* to the people affected by the earthquake in South Asia;

2. *Emphasizes* the need to give particular attention to helping the affected population, especially orphans and widows, in their physical and psychological trauma and to provide immediate medical assistance, in particular with regard to the vaccination of children and to long-term rehabilitation;

3. *Also emphasizes* the need for the international community to maintain its focus beyond the present emergency relief, in order to sustain the political will to support the medium- and long-term rehabilitation, reconstruction and risk reduction efforts led by the Government of Pakistan and other affected States at all levels;

4. *Welcomes* the effective cooperation between the authorities of Pakistan and the relevant bodies in the United Nations system, donor countries, regional and international financial institutions, relevant international organizations and civil society in the coordination and delivery of emergency relief, and stresses the need to continue such cooperation and delivery throughout the ongoing relief operations and rehabilitation and reconstruction efforts, in a manner that reduces vulnerability to future natural hazards;

5. *Encourages* the international community, particularly donor countries, international financial institutions and relevant international organizations, as well as the private sector and civil society, to deliver swiftly on their pledges and to continue to provide the necessary funds and assistance to support the rehabilitation and reconstruction efforts;

6. *Requests* the Secretary-General to appoint a special envoy in order to, inter alia, sustain the political will of the international community to support medium- and long-term rehabilitation, reconstruction and risk reduction efforts;

7. *Also requests* the Secretary-General to continue to explore ways to further strengthen the rapid response capacities for immediate humanitarian relief efforts of the international community, building on the existing arrangements and ongoing initiatives;

8. *Invites* the World Bank and the Asian Development Bank, in collaboration with donor countries, other international and regional financial institutions and the United Nations, to mobilize members of the international community, including affected countries, to address the medium- and long-term rehabilitation and reconstruction needs of the affected areas;

9. *Welcomes* the proposed convening of a reconstruction conference to generate assistance and commitments for long-term rehabilitation and reconstruction phases in the disaster-stricken areas, to be held in Islamabad on 19 November 2005;

10. *Requests* the Secretary-General to report to the General Assembly at its sixty-first session on the implementation of the present resolution under the item entitled "Strengthening of the coordination of humanitarian and disaster relief assistance of the United Nations, including special economic assistance", through the Economic and Social Council at its substantive session in 2006.

Donors' Conference. The Donors' Conference on Rehabilitation and Reconstruction of Earthquake-affected Areas was held in Islamabad, Pakistan, on 19 November to generate assistance and commitments for long-term rehabilitation and reconstruction in the wake of the 8 October South Asia earthquake. More than 80 countries and international agencies participated in the Conference.

Appointment of Special Envoy. On 15 December, in accordance with Assembly resolution 60/13 (above), the Secretary-General announced the appointment of former United States President George H. W. Bush as his Special Envoy for the South Asia Earthquake Disaster. The Special Envoy would lead overall UN system efforts in the aftermath of the earthquake and work to mobilize and sustain the political will of the international community to support recovery, reconstruction and emergency activities.

West Africa

A wave of cholera outbreaks in West and Central Africa started in June; by late September 42,390 cases, and 702 deaths, were reported in Burkina Faso, Guinea, Guinea-Bissau, Liberia, Mali, Mauritania, the Niger and Senegal. The epidemic also affected the Gambia and Sao Tome and Principe. The outbreaks caused suffering and panic, disrupted the social and economic fabric, strained already precarious health systems and hampered the development process. Limited resources impeded a more comprehensive and coherent approach to the epidemic at the local and subregional levels.

The UN Consolidated Inter-Agency Flash Appeal for West and Central Africa sought $3.3 million to assist the Governments of the Gambia, Guinea-Bissau, Mali, Mauritania, Sao Tome and Principe and Senegal. Of the required amount, 44 per cent ($1.4 million) was received.

Chernobyl aftermath

In response to General Assembly resolution 58/119 [YUN 2003, p. 963], the Secretary-General, in an October report [A/60/443], described international efforts to study, mitigate and minimize the consequences of the 1986 Chernobyl nuclear accident [YUN 1986, p. 584].

UN agencies continued to implement activities to promote a new recovery strategy for the affected territories, as outlined in "The human consequences of the Chernobyl nuclear accident: a strategy for recovery" [YUN 2003, p. 962]. In line with the strategy, responsibility for the coordination of Chernobyl issues across the UN system was shifted from OCHA to UNDP. UNDP planned to draw on the experience already amassed by its country offices in the three most-affected countries—Belarus, the Russian Federation and Ukraine—in designing programmes aimed at promoting economic development, community self-sufficiency and subregional coordination. It also aimed to promote and give high visibility to measures to revive community spirit and economic vitality, with a view to encouraging greater donor commitment to Chernobyl recovery. UN country teams were working to implement the recommendations of the recovery strategy, and were supported by broader agency initiatives tailored to the shared needs of the affected populations in the three countries. International assistance fell into five main categories: community-based development; infrastructure; health care and healthy lifestyles; radiation mitigation and standard setting; and reactor safety.

As a contribution to the recovery strategy, the International Atomic Energy Agency (IAEA), in 2003, established the Chernobyl Forum, which included the Governments of the three most-affected countries, OCHA, UNDP, the United Nations Environment Programme, the United Nations Scientific Committee on the Effects of Atomic Radiation, the World Bank and the World Health Organization (WHO). Its mandate was to review and reconcile scientific research on the environmental and health consequences of the Chernobyl accident by issuing authoritative statements and recommendations on the long-term impact. Two expert groups were established under the auspices of WHO and IAEA to address the human health consequences of the accident and the environmental impact, respectively. The groups reviewed the scientific evidence and prepared an assessment report, while UNDP prepared a summary of the socio-economic consequences of the accident and policy recommendations for the three Governments. The Forum also organized, through IAEA, an international conference on the theme "Chernobyl: looking back to go forward" (Vienna, 6-7 September 2005).

With funding from the Swiss Agency for Development and Cooperation and OCHA, the first phase of the International Chernobyl Research and Information Network (ICRIN) project, established in 2003 [YUN 2003, p. 963], was completed, and UNDP was seeking funding for the project's next phase. Owing to the parallel work concluded by the Forum, UNDP revisited the original plans for ICRIN and opted to shift focus to the adaptation and dissemination of available information.

The three most-affected countries were planning major events in April 2006 to commemorate the twentieth anniversary of the Chernobyl accident. The Secretary-General said that it would be appropriate for the Assembly President to convene a special commemorative meeting of the Assembly in April 2006 to call attention to the continuing needs of the region by designating the period from 2006 to 2016 as "the decade of rehabilitation and recovery of Chernobyl-affected areas". Annexed to the report were accounts by Belarus, the Russian Federation and Ukraine regarding their efforts to overcome the consequences of the accident.

GENERAL ASSEMBLY ACTION

On 14 November [meeting 52], the General Assembly adopted **resolution 60/14** [draft: A/60/L.19 & Add.1] without vote [agenda item 73 (c)].

Strengthening of international cooperation and coordination of efforts to study, mitigate and minimize the consequences of the Chernobyl disaster

The General Assembly,

Reaffirming its resolutions 45/190 of 21 December 1990, 46/150 of 18 December 1991, 47/165 of 18 December 1992, 48/206 of 21 December 1993, 50/134 of 20 December 1995, 52/172 of 16 December 1997, 54/97 of 8 December 1999, 56/109 of 14 December 2001 and 58/119 of 17 December 2003, as well as its resolution 55/171 of 14 December 2000 on closure of the Chernobyl nuclear power plant, and taking note of the decisions adopted by the organs, organizations and programmes of the United Nations system in the implementation of those resolutions,

Recalling Economic and Social Council resolutions 1990/50 of 13 July 1990, 1991/51 of 26 July 1991 and 1992/38 of 30 July 1992 and Council decision 1993/232 of 22 July 1993,

Conscious of the long-term nature of the consequences of the disaster at the Chernobyl nuclear power plant, which was a major technological catastrophe in terms of its scope and complexity and created humanitarian, environmental, social, economic and health consequences and problems of common concern, requiring for their solution wide and active international cooperation and coordination of efforts in this field at the international and national levels,

Expressing profound concern at the ongoing effects of the consequences of the accident on the lives and health of people, in particular children, in the affected areas of Belarus, the Russian Federation and Ukraine, as well as in other affected countries,

Noting the consensus reached among members of the Chernobyl Forum on the findings of the reports entitled "Environmental Consequences of the Chernobyl Accident and their Remediation: Twenty Years of Experience" and "Health Effects of the Chernobyl Accident and Special Health Care Programmes", and recognizing the important contribution made by the Forum to the overall assessment of the environmental, health and socio-economic effects of the Chernobyl disaster,

Acknowledging the importance of the national efforts being undertaken by the Governments of Belarus, the Russian Federation and Ukraine to mitigate and minimize the consequences of the Chernobyl disaster,

Recognizing the contribution of civil society organizations, including the national Red Cross Societies of Belarus, the Russian Federation and Ukraine and the International Federation of Red Cross and Red Crescent Societies, in response to the Chernobyl disaster and in support of the efforts of the affected countries,

Emphasizing the importance of the new developmental approach to tackling the problems caused by the Chernobyl accident aimed at normalizing the situation of the individuals and communities concerned in the medium and long term,

Stressing the exceptional Chernobyl-related needs, in particular in the areas of health, ecology and research, in the context of the transition from the emergency to the recovery phase of mitigation of the consequences of the Chernobyl disaster,

Noting the transfer of the functions of the United Nations Coordinator of International Cooperation on Chernobyl from the Under-Secretary-General for Humanitarian Affairs and Emergency Relief Coordinator to the Administrator of the United Nations Development Programme and Chairperson of the United Nations Development Group,

Stressing the need for further coordination by the United Nations Development Programme and improved resource mobilization by the United Nations system to support the activities of the International Chernobyl Research and Information Network as well as the efforts to disseminate the findings of the Chernobyl Forum,

Noting the completion of information needs assessments of the affected populations in Belarus, the Russian Federation and Ukraine under the aegis of the International Chernobyl Research and Information Network,

Stressing the significance of the upcoming twentieth anniversary of the accident for the further strengthening of international cooperation to study, mitigate and minimize the consequences of the Chernobyl disaster,

Taking note of the report of the Secretary-General concerning the implementation of resolution 58/119, as well as relevant parts of the reports of the agencies and organizations of the United Nations system,

1. *Welcomes* the contribution made by States and by organizations of the United Nations system to the development of cooperation to mitigate and minimize the consequences of the Chernobyl disaster, the activities of regional and other organizations and those of non-governmental organizations, as well as bilateral activities;

2. *Notes with appreciation* the efforts undertaken by the agencies of the United Nations system and other international organizations members of the Inter-Agency Task Force on Chernobyl to implement a new developmental approach to studying, mitigating and minimizing the consequences of the Chernobyl disaster, in particular through the development of specific projects, and stresses the need for the Inter-Agency Task Force to continue its activities to that end, including through coordinating efforts in the field of resource mobilization;

3. *Acknowledges* the difficulties faced by the most affected countries in minimizing the consequences of the Chernobyl disaster, and invites States, in particular donor States and all relevant agencies, funds and programmes of the United Nations system, in particular the Bretton Woods institutions, as well as non-governmental organizations, to continue to provide support to the ongoing efforts of Belarus, the Russian Federation and Ukraine to mitigate the consequences of the Chernobyl disaster, including through the allocation of adequate funds to support medical, social, economic and ecological programmes related to the disaster;

4. *Reaffirms* that the United Nations should continue to play an important catalytic and coordinating role in the strengthening of international cooperation to study, mitigate and minimize the consequences of the Chernobyl disaster;

5. *Requests* the Secretary-General and the United Nations Coordinator of International Cooperation on Chernobyl, in his capacity as Administrator of the United Nations Development Programme and as Chairperson of the United Nations Development Group, to take further appropriate practical measures to strengthen coordination of the international efforts in that area;

6. *Notes with satisfaction* the realization of the Cooperation for Rehabilitation Programme in Belarus and the Chernobyl Recovery and Development Programme in Ukraine, aimed at promoting better living conditions in and the sustainable development of the affected territories;

7. *Also notes with satisfaction* assistance rendered by the International Atomic Energy Agency to Belarus, the Russian Federation and Ukraine on remediation of agricultural and urban environments, cost-effective agricultural countermeasures and the monitoring of human exposure in areas affected by the Chernobyl disaster;

8. *Takes note with satisfaction* of the progress made by the Governments of the affected countries in implementing national strategies to mitigate the consequences of the Chernobyl accident, and calls upon United Nations agencies and multilateral and bilateral donors to continue to align their assistance with the priorities of the national strategies of the affected States, and stresses the importance of working together on their implementation in a common effort in the spirit of cooperation;

9. *Welcomes* the efforts of the Government of Ukraine and the international donor community to bring to completion the building of the shelter as well

as those efforts to provide for the environmentally sound collection and storage of nuclear waste, and encourages further efforts in this regard;

10. *Notes* the necessity of further measures to ensure the integration of the assessment by the Chernobyl Forum of the environmental, health and socio-economic consequences of the Chernobyl nuclear accident into the International Chernobyl Research and Information Network process through dissemination of the findings of the Forum, including in the form of practical messages on healthy and productive lifestyles, to the populations affected by the accident in order to empower them to maximize social and economic recovery and sustainable development in all its aspects;

11. *Recognizes* the role that the Commonwealth of Independent States plays in the process of preparing events in observance of the twentieth anniversary of the Chernobyl accident to be held in States participating in the Commonwealth;

12. *Welcomes,* in this context, the activities in observance of the International Day Commemorating Victims of Radiation Accidents and Catastrophes, 26 April, undertaken by the States participating in the Commonwealth of Independent States;

13. *Invites* Member States to observe this Day and to conduct appropriate activities to commemorate victims of radiation accidents and catastrophes and to enhance public awareness of their consequences for human health and the environment throughout the world;

14. *Welcomes* the initiatives of the Governments of Belarus, the Russian Federation and Ukraine to host international events on lessons learned and on future actions in response to the Chernobyl disaster to observe the twentieth anniversary of the Chernobyl accident, and invites organizations of the United Nations system, donor countries and other development agencies to contribute to their effective realization;

15. *Requests* the President of the General Assembly to convene, in April 2006, a special commemorative meeting of the Assembly in observance of the twentieth anniversary of the Chernobyl catastrophe;

16. *Requests* the Secretary-General to continue his efforts in the implementation of the relevant General Assembly resolutions and, through existing coordination mechanisms, in particular the United Nations Coordinator of International Cooperation on Chernobyl, to continue to maintain close cooperation with the agencies of the United Nations system, as well as with regional and other relevant organizations, while implementing specific Chernobyl-related programmes and projects;

17. *Requests* the United Nations Coordinator of International Cooperation on Chernobyl to organize, in collaboration with the Governments of Belarus, the Russian Federation and Ukraine, a further study of the health, environmental and socio-economic consequences of the Chernobyl accident, consistent with the recommendations of the Chernobyl Forum;

18. *Requests* the Secretary-General to submit to the General Assembly at its sixty-second session, under a separate sub-item, a report containing a comprehensive assessment of the implementation of all aspects of the present resolution.

Chapter IV

International trade, finance and transport

In 2005, the growth of world trade decelerated moderately, with the volume of merchandise exports slowing to 7.1 per cent, from 11 per cent in 2004. The deceleration was particularly evident in the developed economies. By contrast, many developing countries and economies in transition recorded relatively fast growing trade, albeit at a slower pace than in previous years. In the United States, import volume growth decelerated as the economy slowed with the maturing of the economic cycle, and the merchandise trade balance recorded a record deficit, despite faster export volume growth. Among developing countries, import growth outpaced export growth in Latin America and South Asia. Commodity prices continued to increase, boosting the export revenues of commodity exporters worldwide.

The net transfers of financial resources from developing to developed countries in 2005 rose to $483.4 billion. Transfers from economies in transition followed a similar pattern, reaching an estimated $95.5 billion. The General Assembly, recalling that trade was in many cases the most important external source of development financing, reiterated the role played by enhanced market access, balanced rules, appropriate adjustment facilities and technical assistance and capacity-building programmes. It reaffirmed the value of multilateralism to the global trading system and the commitment to a universal, rule-based, open, non-discriminatory and equitable multilateral trading system. It also stressed that the international financial system should promote economic growth and support sustainable development and hunger and poverty eradication, recognized the need to enhance the coherence, governance and consistency of the international monetary, financial and trading systems, as well as the need to ensure their openness, fairness and inclusiveness, and emphasized the importance of debt sustainability and debt relief to achieve internationally agreed development goals, including the Millennium Development Goals, adopted by the Assembly in 2000.

In April, the eighth high-level meeting between the Economic and Social Council and the Bretton Woods institutions (the World Bank Group and the International Monetary Fund), the World Trade Organization (WTO) and the United Nations Conference on Trade and Development (UNCTAD) discussed coherence, coordination and cooperation in the context of the implementation of the Monterrey Consensus, adopted at the 2002 International Conference on Financing for Development. In June, the Assembly held its second High-level Dialogue on Financing for Development under the overall theme "The Monterrey Consensus: status of implementation and tasks ahead". The Dialogue was in preparation for the special session of the sixtieth session of the Assembly on financing for development (see p. 67).

The Trade and Development Board, the governing body of UNCTAD, adopted agreed conclusions on the review of progress in the implementation of the Programme of Action for the Least Developed Countries for the Decade 2001-2010, and a decision on the review of UNCTAD technical cooperation activities. The Board adopted further agreed conclusions on economic development in Africa: the role of foreign direct investment in growth and development, and a decision on the venue for UNCTAD XII.

The International Trade Centre, operated jointly by UNCTAD and WTO, increased its delivery of technical assistance by 4.7 per cent to $22.1 million.

In May, the Assembly confirmed the appointment of Supachai Panitchpakdi as UNCTAD Secretary-General for a four year term beginning 1 September 2005.

International trade

The *Trade and Development Report, 2005* [Sales No. E.05.II.D.13] stated that the strong performance of the global economy in 2004 brought about an acceleration in world trade. Total merchandise exports grew by 22.5 per cent, as a result of both increasing volume (13 per cent) and rising dollar prices (9.5 per cent). The latter, partly caused by the depreciation of the dollar, increased the value of international trade in dollar terms within the euro area. In comparison to 2003, export volumes from developed countries made a strong recovery, growing by 11 per cent in 2004, compared to 3 per cent the previous year. In Europe, there was a widespread acceleration of export volume growth, largely due to the speeding up of intraregional trade with the new European Union (EU) acceding member countries, and expanding sales to East Asia and oil-exporters in West Asia and the Commonwealth of Independent States (CIS). Exports from the United States also recovered, as a result of a more competitive currency level, while Japan continued to benefit from dynamic Asian intraregional trade.

Exports from developing countries continued their rapid expansion in 2004, registering a growth rate of 16 per cent in volume terms. East and South Asia led that expansion, but Latin America and Africa also experienced significant increases. Exports increased at higher rates in developing countries than in the developed world. Increasing export volume, together with higher commodity prices, boosted the value of merchandise exports from developing countries, which grew by 26 per cent, particularly in regions with a large share of primary commodities in their total exports—Africa, CIS, South America and West Asia. As a whole, developing countries' share in world exports rose to 33.4 per cent.

The *World Economic Situation and Prospects 2006* [Sales No. E.06.II.C.2], jointly issued by the United Nations Conference on Trade and Development (UNCTAD) and the UN Department of Economic and Social Affairs (DESA), stated that, in 2005, growth of world merchandise trade decelerated moderately. After peaking at a growth rate of 11 per cent in 2004, the expansion in the volume of merchandise exports slowed to 7.1 per cent. In dollar value terms, world trade increased by 12.9 per cent in 2005. Prices of merchandise exports grew by 5.5 per cent, mainly reflecting higher prices for primary commodities, as the average price of traded manufactures remained flat during the year. The deceleration of international trade was particularly evident in the developed economies. In contrast, many developing countries and economies in transition recorded relatively fast growing trade, albeit at a slower pace than in 2003 and 2004.

In the United States, import volume growth decelerated and the merchandise trade balance recorded another record deficit, despite faster export volume growth. The rising deficit was explained both by higher oil prices and an increase in the deficit in the non-petroleum trade balance. The value of imports by the United States doubled that of exports. China became a major player in international trade, absorbing about 6 per cent of world imports in 2005, up from 3.3 per cent in 2000. Dependence on Chinese markets increased on a worldwide basis. The pace of growth of intra-Asian trade moderated alongside

that of China; Japan's exports also felt the slowdown. Western Europe absorbed about 40 per cent of world imports. Import demand decelerated in the euro zone in 2005, despite the boost brought about by the strength of the euro in the first half of the year. The deceleration in import volume growth in Europe was largely due to weak domestic demand. Japan registered similar developments, with imports slowing down in real terms. Partially offsetting the above trends, import demand by oil exporters, such as Norway, the Organization of Petroleum Exporting Countries (OPEC) members and the Russian Federation helped to sustain growth in trade.

Among developing countries, import growth outpaced export growth in Latin America and South Asia. African imports also increased strongly in real terms (at 11 per cent, up from 10 per cent in 2004), thanks to robust gross domestic product (GDP) growth, increased food imports in drought-affected countries and rising demand for capital goods. Exports of the new EU members continued to grow in real terms at a relatively fast pace in 2005. Conversely, manufactured exports by the Caribbean, Central America and Mexico suffered from slower demand in the United States, and increased competition by China in the United States market. Commodity prices continued to increase in 2005, thereby boosting the export revenues of commodity exporters worldwide. Major gains were observed in the prices of metals and minerals and agricultural raw materials, while food prices registered modest increases.

Multilateral trading system

Report of Secretary-General. In response to General Assembly resolution 59/221 [YUN 2004, p. 959], the Secretary-General submitted an August report [A/60/225] on international trade and development, prepared in collaboration with UNCTAD. The report reviewed developments in international trade and trading system, including the implications for developing countries of multilateral trade negotiations under the World Trade Organization (WTO) Doha work programme since the WTO General Council Decision of August 2004 ("July Package") [YUN 2004, p. 958], and identified the interlinkages between different negotiating areas and the Millennium Development Goals (MDGs) [YUN 2000, p. 51].

The report stated that, in 2004, developing countries' merchandise exports expanded by 25 per cent from 2003 to reach the value of $3 trillion, and their share in world merchandise exports increased to 33 per cent. Developing countries' exports grew faster than total world exports, which expanded by 20 per cent. The value of world exports amounted to $8.9 trillion. The largest share of developing countries' exports was accounted for by Asia, which represented 77 per cent of the total exports of developing countries (with a value of $2.3 trillion). Concerning trade in services, world exports in commercial services expanded by 16 per cent to reach a total value of $2.1 trillion in 2004. The share of developing countries' trade increased to 22.5 per cent, with an export value worth $485 billion.

The report noted that some 50 per cent of world trade took place within regional trade agreements. Developing countries participated in agreements with both developed and developing countries. The expansion of North-South agreements had transformed economic relationships based on pre-existing unilateral preferences into relationships based on reciprocity, such as in the free trade area of the Americas negotiations, the African, Caribbean Pacific/Europe economic partnership agreement negotiations and the Central American Free Trade Agreement. Such negotiations tended to result in deeper market access and higher regulatory standards than those at the multilateral level, and could have implications for developing countries. It was therefore important to ensure a positive interface and coherence between multilateralism and regionalism and an expeditious and meaningful outcome of the Doha work programme.

The report concluded that it was imperative for development and the viability and durability of the multilateral trading system that WTO members delivered on the development promises made in the Doha Ministerial Declaration (see below) to place the needs and interests of developing countries at the heart of negotiations and deliver an equitable and fair deal for developing countries.

Negotiating frameworks

On 13 July, the Second South Summit (Doha, Qatar, 14-16 June) of the Group of 77 and China adopted the Doha Declaration [TD/B(S-XXII)/2], which called for, among other things, enhanced market access for goods and services of export interest to developing countries to markets of developed countries, realization of the development dimension of the Doha work programme, the need for a solution to the question of commodities, and accelerating negotiations on the Trade Related Aspects of Intellectual Property Rights Agreement. It also adopted the Doha Plan of Action [TD/B(S-XXII)/3]. At the request of the Chairman of the Group, the texts of the Declaration and the Plan of Action were circulated as official documents of the twenty-second special

session and the thirty-seventh executive session (18 July) of the (UNCTAD) Trade and Development Board (TDB).

At the same session, TDB, for its consideration of the review of developments and issues in the post-Doha work programme of particular concern to developing countries, had before it an August note by the UNCTAD secretariat [TD/B/52/8] on the subject, providing an analysis of issues of concern in the post-Doha trade negotiations since the WTO General Council Decision of 1 August 2004 ("July Package") [YUN 2004, p. 958] and containing suggestions for policy makers and trade negotiators. The note stated that the Doha negotiations should fulfil their development promise and be concluded no later than 2006. TDB discussed the Post-July Package negotiations and the progress made towards the convening of the Sixth WTO Ministerial Conference in Hong Kong (see below); regional trade agreements and South-South cooperation; and the role of UNCTAD and TDB. The President reiterated the commitment made in the Millennium Declaration [YUN 2000, p. 47] to an open, rule-based, non-discriminatory, predictable and equitable multilateral trading system, supportive of economic growth and development and poverty alleviation. Progress in the multilateral trading system should be linked to progress in the accomplishment of internationally agreed development goals, including the MDGs. The importance of positive engagement by all members in the multilateral trading system was underscored, as well as the responsibility of all to a development-focus outcome of the Doha work programme and a strengthening of the multilateral trading system. It was also noted that special and differential treatment could be a cross-cutting issue and that technical assistance and capacity building could enable developing countries to participate in the negotiations and take advantage of the successful outcome of the Doha round.

The Sixth WTO Ministerial Conference was held in Hong Kong, China, from 13 to 18 December. On 18 December, it adopted the Ministerial Declaration, which outlined decisions on agriculture, non-agricultural market access (NAMA), services, development issues, trade facilitation and the rules aspects of the negotiations.

The deadline for eliminating agricultural export subsidies was set for 2013. Under NAMA, the Declaration called for a Swiss tariff cutting formula, which would cut high tariffs more than low tariffs, multi coefficients in the formula and sectoral negotiations. The Declaration also called for progress on market access negotiations for both agricultural and industrial goods. Other key provisions recommended continued work on non- tariff barriers, duty free/quota free access for 97 per cent of all goods originating from least developed countries and full negotiating modalities to be agreed upon by April 2006.

GENERAL ASSEMBLY ACTION

On 22 December [meeting 68], the General Assembly, on the recommendation of the Second (Economic and Financial) Committee [A/60/486/Add.1], adopted **resolution 60/184** by recorded vote (121-1-51) [agenda item 50 (a)].

International trade and development

The General Assembly,

Recalling its resolutions 56/178 of 21 December 2001, 57/235 of 20 December 2002, 58/197 of 23 December 2003 and 59/221 of 22 December 2004 on international trade and development,

Recalling also the provisions of the United Nations Millennium Declaration pertaining to trade and related development issues, as well as the outcomes of the International Conference on Financing for Development, held in Monterrey, Mexico, from 18 to 22 March 2002, and the World Summit on Sustainable Development, held in Johannesburg, South Africa, from 26 August to 4 September 2002,

Recalling further the Ministerial Declaration and decisions adopted at the Fourth Ministerial Conference of the World Trade Organization, held in Doha from 9 to 14 November 2001, the decision of 1 August 2004 of the General Council of the World Trade Organization and the full commitment of all members of the World Trade Organization to give effect to them, and the importance of the successful conclusion of the Doha work programme,

Recalling that trade is in many cases the single most important external source of development financing, and in this context reiterating the important role that enhanced market access, balanced rules, appropriate adjustment facility and well-targeted, sustainably financed technical assistance and capacity-building programmes can play in the economic development of developing countries, especially the least developed countries,

Bearing in mind the special needs of the least developed countries, the small island developing States and the landlocked developing countries, within a new global framework for transit transport cooperation for landlocked and transit developing countries, as identified, respectively, in the Brussels Programme of Action for the Least Developed Countries for the Decade 2001-2010, the Barbados Programme of Action and the Almaty Programme of Action,

Stressing the need to address adequately the vulnerabilities faced by developing countries, as a result of external shocks, particularly natural disasters, which can damage the social and economic infrastructure and have long-term consequences, especially hampering the achievement of their sustainable development,

Recalling its resolutions 57/250 of 20 December 2002 and 57/270 B of 23 June 2003, in which it invited the United Nations Conference on Trade and Development, as well as the Trade and Development Board, to contribute, within its mandate, to the implementation and the review of the progress made in the implemen-

tation of the outcomes of the major United Nations conferences and summits and invited the President of the Trade and Development Board to present the outcomes of such reviews to the Economic and Social Council,

Recalling also the Sno Paulo Consensus, adopted at the eleventh session of the United Nations Conference on Trade and Development, held in Sno Paulo, Brazil, from 13 to 18 June 2004, and reaffirming its commitment to its full and effective implementation,

Taking note of the review undertaken by the Trade and Development Board at its fifty-second session of developments and issues in the post-Doha work programme of particular concern to developing countries, and its contribution to an understanding of the actions required to forge consensus and help developing countries integrate, in a beneficial and meaningful manner, into the multilateral trading system and the global economy and to achieve a balanced, development-oriented and successful conclusion of the Doha negotiations,

Reaffirming the urgency, subject to national legislation, of recognizing the rights of local and indigenous communities that are holders of traditional knowledge, innovations and practices and, with the approval and involvement of the holders of such knowledge, innovations and practices, of developing and implementing benefit-sharing mechanisms on mutually agreed terms for the use of such knowledge, innovations and practices,

Reaffirming also the role of the United Nations Conference on Trade and Development as the focal point within the United Nations for the integrated treatment of trade and development and the interrelated issues in the areas of finance, technology, investment and sustainable development as reaffirmed by the Sno Paulo Consensus,

Noting the significant contribution of the multilateral trading system to economic growth, development and employment and the importance of maintaining the process of reform and liberalization of trade policies, as well as the importance of rejecting the use of protectionism, so that the system plays its full part in promoting recovery, growth and development, in particular of developing countries, bearing in mind paragraph 10 of its resolution 55/182 of 20 December 2000,

Taking note of the report of the Trade and Development Board and its statement, as well as the report of the Secretary-General,

1. *Reaffirms* the value of multilateralism to the global trading system and the commitment to achieving a universal, rule-based, open, non-discriminatory and equitable multilateral trading system that contributes to growth, development and employment generation, and emphasizes that bilateral and regional trading arrangements should contribute to the multilateral trading system;

2. *Underlines* the fact that the increasing interdependence of national economies in a globalizing world and the emergence of rule-based regimes for international economic relations have meant that the space for national economic policy, that is, the scope for domestic policies, especially in the areas of trade, investment and industrial development, is now often framed by international disciplines, commitments and global market considerations, that it is for each Gov-

ernment to evaluate the trade-off between the benefits of accepting international rules and commitments and the constraints posed by the loss of policy space and that it is particularly important for developing countries, bearing in mind development goals and objectives, that all countries take into account the need for appropriate balance between national policy space and international disciplines and commitments;

3. *Stresses* the importance of open, transparent, inclusive democratic and more orderly processes and procedures for the effective functioning of the multilateral trading system, including in the decision-making process, so as to enable developing countries to have their vital interests duly reflected in the outcome of trade negotiations;

4. *Reiterates* that development concerns form an integral part of the Doha Ministerial Declaration, and reaffirms the commitments made in the decision of 1 August 2004 of the General Council of the World Trade Organization to fulfil the development dimension of the Doha Development Agenda, which places the needs and interests of developing countries, especially the least developed among them, at the heart of the Doha work programme;

5. *Expresses its concern* over the lack of progress in areas of negotiations of particular concern to developing countries, which led to missing deadlines provided in the decision of the General Council of the World Trade Organization;

6. *Welcomes* the recent "aid for trade" initiative to address the adjustment challenges as well as to build the supply and trade capacities, infrastructure and institutions of developing countries, and stresses the need for the effective operationalization with sufficient and additional funding of the initiative to the benefit of the recipient countries;

7. *Reaffirms* that all countries have a shared interest in the success of the Doha work programme, which aims both at further increasing trading opportunities for developing countries and at making the trading system more conducive to development, and underscores the need for the major developed countries to make ambitious proposals in line with their commitments to make progress in all areas of negotiations, particularly in agriculture, non-agricultural market access, services, the trade-related intellectual property system and rules as well as operational and meaningful special and differential treatment for developing countries, and to adopt practical and concrete solutions to the outstanding implementation-related issues and concerns raised by developing countries;

8. *Calls for* the successful and timely conclusion of the negotiations on the Doha work programme in order to maximize the contribution of the trading system to raising standards of living, eradicating hunger and poverty, generating employment and achieving the internationally agreed development goals, including the Millennium Development Goals, and, in that context, underscores the fact that enhanced market access for goods and services of export interest to developing countries as well as strong, special and differential treatment in the outcome of negotiations in all areas, balanced rules and well-targeted sustainably financed technical assistance and capacity-building programmes for developing countries are needed for the realization of the development dimension highlighted in the Doha work programme, and stresses that the Sixth Ministerial Conference of the World Trade Organization, to be held in Hong Kong, China, from 13 to 18 December 2005, should constitute an important milestone to this end, and particularly for finalizing the negotiating modalities for successful conclusion of the Doha round by 2006;

9. *Recognizes* the need to ensure that the comparative advantage of developing countries is not undermined by any form of protectionism, including the arbitrary and abusive use of non-tariff measures, non-trade barriers and other standards to unfairly restrict the access of developing countries' products to developed countries' markets, reaffirms, in this regard, that developing countries should play an increasing role in the formulation of, inter alia, safety, environment and health standards, and recognizes the need to facilitate the increased and meaningful participation of the developing countries in the work of relevant international standard-setting organizations;

10. *Calls for* accelerating the negotiations on the development-related mandate concerning the Agreement on Trade-related Aspects of Intellectual Property Rights in the Doha Ministerial Declaration, especially the amendments of the Agreement, in order for intellectual property rules fully to support the objectives of the Convention on Biological Diversity as well as for trade-related aspects of intellectual property rights and public health to address the problems afflicting many developing countries, including the least developed countries, especially those resulting from HIV/AIDS, tuberculosis, malaria and other epidemics;

11. *Expresses its concern* about the adoption of a number of unilateral actions that are not consistent with the rules of the World Trade Organization, harm the exports of all countries, in particular those of developing countries, and have a considerable bearing on the ongoing World Trade Organization negotiations and on the achievement and further enhancement of the development dimension of the trade negotiations;

12. *Emphasizes* the need for further work to foster greater coherence between the multilateral trading system and the financial system, and urges the United Nations Conference on Trade and Development, in fulfilment of its mandate, to undertake the relevant policy analysis in those areas and to operationalize such work, including through its technical assistance activities;

13. *Reaffirms* the commitments made at the Fourth Ministerial Conference of the World Trade Organization and at the Third United Nations Conference on the Least Developed Countries, held in Brussels from 14 to 20 May 2001, calls, in this regard, upon developed countries that have not already done so to provide immediate bound duty-free, quota-free market access to all products originating from all least developed countries, calls upon developing countries that are in a position to do so to extend duty-free and quota-free market access to exports of these countries, and in this context reaffirms the need to consider additional measures for progressive improvement in market access for least developed countries;

14. *Also reaffirms* the commitment to actively pursue the work programme of the World Trade Organization with respect to addressing the trade-related issues and concerns affecting the fuller integration of countries

with small, vulnerable economies into the multilateral trading system in a manner commensurate with their special circumstances and in support of their efforts towards sustainable development, in accordance with paragraph 35 of the Doha Ministerial Declaration;

15. *Recognizes* the special problems and needs of the landlocked developing countries within a new global framework for transit transport cooperation for landlocked and transit developing countries, calls, in this regard, for the full and effective implementation of the Almaty Programme of Action, and stresses the need for the implementation of the Sno Paulo Consensus, in particular paragraphs 66 and 84 thereof, by the relevant international organizations and donors in a multistakeholder approach;

16. *Takes note with satisfaction* of the launch of the third round of negotiations on the Global System of Trade Preferences among Developing Countries and the progress achieved so far in these negotiations with the aim of concluding the third round by November 2006;

17. *Recognizes* the importance of addressing seriously the concerns of commodity-dependent developing countries, owing to the continuing volatility of world commodity prices and other factors, and of supporting the efforts of such countries to restructure, diversify and strengthen the competitiveness of their commodity sectors, and in this regard notes the formation of an international task force on commodities by the United Nations Conference on Trade and Development;

18. *Stresses* the importance of facilitating the accession of all developing countries, in particular the least developed countries, as well as countries with economies in transition, that apply for membership in the World Trade Organization, consistent with its criteria, bearing in mind paragraph 21 of resolution 55/182 and subsequent developments, and calls for the effective and faithful application of the World Trade Organization guidelines on accession by the least developed countries;

19. *Emphasizes* the importance of developing human, institutional, regulatory, research, trade policy and development capacities and infrastructures aimed at enhanced supply-side capacity and competitiveness, as well as ensuring a conducive international environment for the full and effective integration of developing countries into the international trading system;

20. *Invites* the United Nations Conference on Trade and Development, in accordance with its mandate, to monitor and assess the evolution of the international trading system and of trends in international trade from a development perspective, and, in particular, to analyse issues of concern to developing countries, supporting them in building capacities to establish their own negotiating priorities and negotiate trade agreements, including under the Doha work programme;

21. *Urges* donors, in this regard, to provide the United Nations Conference on Trade and Development with the increased resources necessary to deliver effective and demand-driven assistance to developing countries, as well as to enhance their contributions to the trust funds of the Integrated Framework for Trade-related Technical Assistance to Least Developed Countries and the Joint Integrated Technical Assistance Programme;

22. *Welcomes* the generous offer by the Government of Ghana to host the twelfth session of the United Nations Conference on Trade and Development in 2008, and expresses its gratitude to the African Union for its support for Ghana in this connection;

23. *Requests* the Secretary-General, in collaboration with the secretariat of the United Nations Conference on Trade and Development, to submit to the General Assembly at its sixty-first session a report on the implementation of the present resolution and on developments in the multilateral trading system, under the sub-item entitled "International trade and development" of the item entitled "Macroeconomic policy questions."

RECORDED VOTE ON RESOLUTION 60/184:

In favour: Afghanistan, Algeria, Angola, Antigua and Barbuda, Argentina, Armenia, Azerbaijan, Bahamas, Bahrain, Bangladesh, Barbados, Belarus, Belize, Benin, Bhutan, Bolivia, Botswana, Brazil, Brunei Darussalam, Burkina Faso, Burundi, Cambodia, Cameroon, Cape Verde, Central African Republic, Chile, China, Colombia, Comoros, Congo, Costa Rica, Côte d'Ivoire, Cuba, Democratic People's Republic of Korea, Djibouti, Dominica, Dominican Republic, Ecuador, Egypt, El Salvador, Eritrea, Ethiopia, Fiji, Ghana, Grenada, Guatemala, Guinea, Guinea-Bissau, Guyana, Haiti, India, Indonesia, Iran, Iraq, Jamaica, Jordan, Kazakhstan, Kenya, Kuwait, Kyrgyzstan, Lao People's Democratic Republic, Lebanon, Lesotho, Liberia, Libyan Arab Jamahiriya, Madagascar, Malawi, Malaysia, Maldives, Mali, Mauritania, Mauritius, Mexico, Micronesia, Mongolia, Morocco, Mozambique, Myanmar, Namibia, Nepal, Nicaragua, Nigeria, Oman, Pakistan, Panama, Papua New Guinea, Paraguay, Peru, Philippines, Qatar, Saint Kitts and Nevis, Saint Lucia, Saint Vincent and the Grenadines, Samoa, Saudi Arabia, Senegal, Sierra Leone, Singapore, Solomon Islands, Somalia, South Africa, Sri Lanka, Sudan, Suriname, Swaziland, Syrian Arab Republic, Tajikistan, Thailand, Togo, Tunisia, Tuvalu, Uganda, United Arab Emirates, United Republic of Tanzania, Uruguay, Uzbekistan, Venezuela, Viet Nam, Yemen, Zambia, Zimbabwe.

Against: United States.

Abstaining: Albania, Andorra, Australia, Austria, Belgium, Bulgaria, Canada, Croatia, Cyprus, Czech Republic, Denmark, Estonia, Finland, France, Georgia, Germany, Greece, Hungary, Iceland, Ireland, Israel, Italy, Japan, Latvia, Liechtenstein, Lithuania, Luxembourg, Malta, Marshall Islands, Monaco, Netherlands, New Zealand, Norway, Palau, Poland, Portugal, Republic of Korea, Republic of Moldova, Romania, Russian Federation, San Marino, Serbia and Montenegro, Slovakia, Slovenia, Spain, Sweden, Switzerland, The former Yugoslav Republic of Macedonia, Turkey, Ukraine, United Kingdom.

Trade policy

Trade in goods and services, and commodities

The Commission on Trade in Goods and Services, and Commodities, at its ninth session (Geneva, 14-18 March) [TD/B/COM.1/73], had before it the following documentation: a note by the UNCTAD secretariat on market entry for commodities: the role of trade and investment finance and competitiveness [TD/B/COM.1/72]; the report of the Expert Meeting on Financing of Commodity-based Trade and Development: Innovative Financing Mechanisms [YUN 2004, p. 964]; an UNCTAD secretariat note on trade in services and development implications [TD/B/COM.1/71]; the report of the Expert Meeting on Trade and Development Aspects of Professional Services and Regulatory Frameworks [TD/B/COM.1/EM.25/3]; the report of the Expert Meeting on Strengthening Participation of Developing Countries in Dynamic and New Sectors of World Trade: Trends, Issues and Policies [TD/B/COM.1/EM.26/3]; and an UNCTAD secretariat note on trade, environment and development [TD/B/COM.1/70].

In agreed recommendations adopted on 18 March, the Commission expressed appreciation to those donors contributing to the UNCTAD Trade Sub-programme and agreed that particular consideration should be given to the needs of least developed countries (LDCs). It called on UNCTAD to contribute to the mainstreaming of development into international trade and trade negotiations, in particular the Doha negotiations, through its work in consensus-building, analytical work, technical assistance and capacity building, in line with the mandate contained in the São Paulo Consensus [YUN 2004, p. 955]; support capacity building efforts in developing countries in trade policy formulation, trade negotiations, including WTO accession negotiations, and commodities; and strengthen technical assistance to address the special needs of developing countries. The Commission took note of the report of the Expert Meeting that launched the process of sectoral review of new and dynamic sectors in world trade and decided that the annual reviews should continue to be held. It recommended that UNCTAD undertake capacity building activities at national, subregional and regional levels through pilot projects to assist developing countries and invited donors to support such efforts. The Commission also recommended that UNCTAD enhance its work on the interrelationships between market access, market entry and competitiveness factors and their impact on the exports of developing countries; examine the effects of nontariff barriers; continue to work on the challenges and opportunities of trade liberalization, particularly in the area of preference erosion, as well as utilization and improvement of preferential schemes, and continue to support South-South trade initiatives, including the Global System of Trade Preferences (GSTP).

The Commission further recommended that UNCTAD continue to contribute to commodity sector development, diversification and more effective participation in the supply chain; establish the International Task Force on Commodities, announced at UNCTAD XI [ibid. p. 954]; enhance its work in the area of commodity finance; and implement strong and broad-based capacity- and institution-building programmes in that area. The international donor community was invited to enhance extrabudgetary support to UNCTAD in fulfilling its mandate in the area of commodities.

UNCTAD should continue to strengthen its policy-oriented analysis, consensus building and capacity-building activities on services to assist developing countries in: strengthening their domestic supply capacities and increasing their participation in services trade; carrying out assessments of trade in services in line with paragraph 95 of the São Paulo Consensus; undertaking sector-specific studies of interest to developing countries; deepening work on business and professional services in the areas identified in the report of the Expert Meeting on Trade and Development Aspects of Professional Services and Regulatory Frameworks (see above); helping develop capacities in developing countries to establish their own negotiating priorities and negotiate trade agreements, including on the General Agreement on Trade in Services (GATS) and regional trade agreements; and analysing domestic regulations and GATS rules from a development perspective.

UNCTAD should also continue its policy-oriented analysis, consensus building and capacity-building activities in the areas of trade, environment and development, including developing the Consultative Task Force (CTF) on Environmental Requirements and Market Access for Developing Countries; strengthening its work under the BioTrade Initiative, in particular national BioTrade programmes, and following up on partnerships launched at the World Summit on Sustainable Development [YUN 2002, p. 821] and at UNCTAD XI to promote trade, export diversification and investment in biotrade; assisting developing countries to make use of the trade and investment opportunities arising from the Kyoto Protocol [YUN 1997, p. 1048], including the Clean Development Mechanism (CDM), as well as in identifying tariffs and regulatory measures affecting trade in renewable energy goods and equipment, and exploring trading opportunities for environmentally preferable products.

On 18 March, the Commission took note of the reports of the expert meetings and the secretariat's progress report [TD/B/COM.1/69] on the implementation of agreed conclusions and recommendations of the Commission at its eighth (2004) session [YUN 2004, p. 963], including post-Doha follow-up.

At its thirty-sixth executive session (Geneva, 3 May) [A/60/15], TDB took note of the Commission's report and endorsed its recommendations.

Subsidiary bodies. In 2005, a number of expert meetings took place, all in Geneva, on issues to be considered by the Commission.

The Expert Meeting on Trade and Development Aspects of Professional Services and Regulatory Frameworks (17-19 January) [TD/B/COM.1/EM.25/3] had before it an UNCTAD secretariat note on the subject [TD/B/COM.1/EM.25/2], which discussed professional services and development; emergence of new regulatory frameworks and challenges facing developing countries; national experiences of trade in professional services; and experience with regional integration and mutual recognition agreements. In its policy conclusions, the Meeting agreed that developing countries needed to acknowledge the importance of promoting services trade. Unnecessary barriers to the supply of professional services should be removed and developed countries should open their markets to developing countries' professional services exports. Developing countries could benefit from liberalizing their professional services markets if liberalization was linked to human development, to the building of their domestic services capacities, and regulatory and institutional frameworks. Priority should be accorded to those regulatory policies that could yield broader gains, feed into human development and addressed poverty alleviation and income inequalities. Countries with strong regulatory and institutional frameworks should help developing countries in strengthening their domestic regulations, and multilateral and bilateral development agencies should shift attention to services and services trade. To increase the exports of developing countries through the global outsourcing of services, a number of preconditions needed to be met, including the creation of an efficient telecommunications infrastructure and the development of an education system in line with the needs of the market. UNCTAD should, among other things, facilitate the assessment of professional services at the sub-sectoral level; devise trade and development benchmarks for professional services; identify elements for disciplines on qualifications requirements and procedures, licensing requirements and procedures, and technical standards with regard to professional services; analyse trade opportunities arising from global outsourcing of professional services, and ways of facilitating such trade in order to enhance developing countries' exports and market entry barriers faced by developing country professional services supplier.

The Expert Meeting on Strengthening Participation of Developing Countries in Dynamic and New Sectors of World Trade: Trends, Issues and Policies (7-9 February) [TD/B/COM.1/EM.26/3] had before it an UNCTAD secretariat note on the subject [TD/B/COM.1/EM.26/2]. The Meeting reviewed policies and actions to enhance developing country participation in: information technology (IT)-enabled outsourcing of services; renewable energy products, including bio-fuels; and textiles and clothing. With regard to IT-enabled outsourcing of services, the experts stated that UNCTAD should complement its analytical work with capacity-building activities and consider a

programme of seminars/workshops in selected countries to identify and assess the capabilities of countries; developing countries concerned should identify and seek sources of funding for building the infrastructure necessary for offshore outsourcing' with special consideration given to the plight of LDCs. In the area of renewable energy products, the Meeting called on UNCTAD to assist developing country members in identifying tariff and non-tariff barriers affecting trade in renewable energy goods and equipment; analyse the implications of trade and environmental regimes for renewable energy markets; and review the various approaches to developing an international strategy for renewable energy. The experts stressed that an environment favourable to private sector initiatives in the bio-fuels sector should be created in developing countries and that the role of Governments in designing promotion policies for the production, use and local trade in bio-fuels should be defined. UNCTAD should assess the trade competitiveness of developing countries in the growing worldwide use of and trade in bio-fuels, as well as market access and market entry issues related to imports of bio-fuels in industrialized economies. As to textiles and clothing, UNCTAD could assist developing countries in strengthening their participation in the manufacture of dynamic textiles and clothing products.

The Expert Meeting on Methodologies, Classification, Quantification and Development Impacts of Non-Tariff Barriers (NTBs) (5-7 September) [TD/B/COM.1/EM.27/3] had before it an UNCTAD secretariat note on the subject [TD/B/COM.1/EM.27/2], which reviewed the scope, definition and classification of NTBs, their quantification, and the concerns of developing countries. The Meeting called on UNCTAD to improve its classification of NTBs and its Coding System of Trade Control Measures by identifying and adding new NTBs, and focus on better defining, classifying and quantifying NTBs, in cooperation with all relevant international and regional organizations and other stakeholders. In particular, its Trade Analysis and Information System required more precise and comprehensive data on NTBs. UNCTAD should maintain a case studies database on various aspects of NTBs; help trade negotiators of developing countries, especially LDCs, build their capacity to deal with NTB-related negotiating issues; give priority to the principal NTBs faced by LDC exporters and those of other developing countries; and improve its analysis of the effects of NTBs on supply capacity, competitiveness and market access/entry conditions. The experts also recommended that UNCTAD establish a Group of Eminent Persons on NTBs and a network of national focal points in developing countries to improve collection and analysis of data on NTBs.

The Expert Meeting on Dynamic and New Sectors of World Trade (24-26 October) [TD/B/COM.1/EM.28/5] had before it UNCTAD secretariat notes on promoting participation of developing countries in dynamic and new sectors of world trade: the electronic sector [TD/B/COM.1/EM.28/2], fishery products [TD/B/COM.1/EM.28/3], and steel and related specialty products [TD/B/COM.1/EM.28/4]. Particular attention was given to LDCs and African countries that specialized in sectors that were among the least market dynamic in world trade. Their inability to manage the challenges of changing global trading and economic processes and the resulting shifts in the international division of labour, were a source of concern. Recognizing that not all countries would be able to participate in the dynamic and new sectors, the experts called on developing countries, including LDCs and African countries, as well as their development partners, to pay attention to the opportunities presented by those sectors for greater diversification and improved domestic value-added from exports.

The Expert Meeting on Distribution Services (16-18 November) [TD/B/COM.1/EM.29/3] considered an UNCTAD secretariat note on the subject [TD/B/COM.1/EM.29/2], which discussed market overview and trends; development issues and challenges facing developing countries; business perspective; regulatory issues; competition-related issues; country experiences; distribution of other services: audiovisual and tourism; and issues for GATS negotiations. The Meeting concluded that measures should be taken at the bilateral, regional and international levels to ensure effective access for goods and services from developing countries to global distribution channels. Developed countries could play an important role in increasing the participation of developing countries in trade in distribution services. The experts called on UNCTAD to support developing countries in their assessment of trade liberalization in the area of distribution services; analyse the distribution value chain of a selected product; promote a better understanding of the classification and coverage of distribution services provided under the UN Central Product Classification and the GATS services classification; analyse to what extent lessons learned in Organisation for Economic Cooperation and Development countries could be applied as best practices in developing countries to promote the distribution of goods and services from those countries; identify ways to overcome challenges facing developing countries in accessing distribution channels and information networks and improve infrastruc-

ture, trade facilitation and conditions for traders in developing countries; and analyse to what extent trade agreements could help to achieve those objectives, thereby promoting South-South trade.

Interdependence and global economic issues

TDB, in October [A/60/15], considered interdependence and global economic issues from a trade and development perspective: new features in global interdependence. Participants agreed that, despite the growing importance of developing countries in international trade and finance and the expansion of South-South trade, the global economic environment continued to be shaped by macroeconomic and trade policies in developed countries. Asia was recognized as the most dynamic region in 2004/2005. Latin American economies recovered strongly in 2004 and prospects for 2005 pointed to a continuation of that recovery. Africa's growth performance, however, was reason for concern, particularly in sub-Saharan Africa, where it was still too low to allow for a strong increase in per capita income and a significant reduction of poverty. There was also concern about the increasing global current-account imbalances and the consequences of their eventual correction for the global economy, particularly for developing countries. It was recognized that a more balanced geographical pattern of demand growth would be helpful in correcting those imbalances, and that the necessary adjustments should be shared by the major surplus economies and the major deficit countries. Correction of the imbalances required broad-based multilateral policy coordination and counterbalancing action in major surplus economies. Attention was drawn to the continuing volatility of primary commodity prices, posing a serious risk for the sustainability of growth, and to the need for better international coordination to reduce the instability of commodity prices and exchange rates. A reexamination of mechanisms for reducing price instability in a wide range of commodities so as to minimize its adverse impact on national income could help strengthen a global partnership for development. The currently favourable external environment was a necessary but insufficient condition for sustained growth and development; continued domestic efforts for capital formation and structural change were needed, and developed countries could help developing countries by granting better market access and by facilitating the transfer of technology and increasing financial assistance and debt relief. The *Trade and Development Report 2005* (see p. 1039) analysed the new features of global interdependence and considered the recent trends in the global economy, especially the interplay between the imbalances in the global economy and the implications for developing countries of the emergence of East and South Asia as a new growth pole. TDB stressed the importance of UNCTAD in identifying the elements of a coherent global development strategy and providing alternative views on economic policies from a development perspective.

Trade promotion and facilitation

In 2005, UN bodies maintained assistance to developing countries and transition economies in promoting their exports and facilitating their integration into the multilateral trading system. The main originator of technical cooperation projects in that area was the International Trade Centre, under the joint sponsorship of UNCTAD and WTO.

International Trade Centre

In 2005, the UNCTAD/WTO International Trade Centre (ITC) increased its delivery of technical assistance by 4.7 per cent to $22.1 million, from $21.1 million in 2004 [ITC/AG/(XXXIX)/206]. Assistance to Africa and LDCs amounted to 36 per cent and 37 per cent of total delivery, respectively. A total of 184 projects were operational, some 130 publications and technical materials were issued and almost 1,000 advisory missions were carried out. Some 400 training workshops were held with over 17,000 participants.

ITC responded with renewed efforts to harness trade for development. It expanded its WTO-related field activities; increased its support to public-private sector dialogue; sharpened its tools and backstopping services for national and sectoral export strategies; enriched its programmes to boost South-South trade, enterprise competitiveness and the capacity of trade support institutions (TSIs); and improved the depth of its assistance to specific export products and services sectors. Progress was made in achieving greater understanding of trade issues, their business implications and the critical role of business advocacy; applying ITC tools for designing and managing export strategies; enhancing the capacity of export enterprises and TSIs; generating South-South trade and developing better ways to promote products and services from developing countries. New partnerships were launched and an important contribution was made to trade-related MDGs.

ITC focused its activities on its five corporate goals. Under the goal of facilitating the integration of enterprises into the multilateral trading system, the beneficial integration of the business community in developing countries and economies in transition remained ITC's primary focus through broad-based technical cooperation activities aimed at ensuring the development dimension of the Doha negotiations. ITC helped build capacity for participation in services trade negotiations at the national level, continued its support on technical barriers to trade and sanitary and phytosanitary measures, and helped identify new market opportunities after the phasing out of the WTO Agreement on Textiles and Clothing.

Under the goal of supporting the design of trade development strategies, support was provided to a large number of countries at national, sectoral and enterprise levels. Design methodologies were refined and assistance for preparing national export strategies reinforced. ITC provided assistance, under regional and national programmes, for the development of sectoral strategies in 20 countries. It initiated action to develop a methodology for strategy design for services to respond to the increasing number of requests to provide advisory- and capacity-building support to the services sector; provided support to strategy implementation and to ensure its incorporation into national economic and social development planning processes.

As to the goal of strengthening key trade support services (both public and private), international trade treaties were examined, and a regional arbitration network for Southern Africa was established. Activities to establish and strengthen trade promotion organizations continued in Brazil, Pakistan, the Russian Federation, Sierra Leone, Tajikistan and the United Arab Emirates.

On the goal of improving sector performance, ITC provided assistance to critical sectors, including textile and clothing, leather, organic and natural products, fresh fruit and vegetables, coffee, wood products, jute, fisheries, gems and jewellery, services and tourism. Business opportunities between companies were created in key sectors and to support export development work at the sector level; the South-South Trade Promotion Programme organized eight buyers-sellers meetings on services, horticultural and apicultural products, food and agro-processing products, pharmaceutical and natural products, wood and wood products and aid relief items. A record number of 67 business associations and 434 companies in the South concluded new business transactions worth $37.7 million, and a number of market orientation tours were organized for exporters from Benin, Burkina Faso and Senegal to prospect new markets in the South and in developed countries, resulting in business opportunities for small and medium-sized enterprise (SME) exporters from those countries.

Under the goal of building enterprise competitiveness, two new markets and supply assessment tools were developed to quantify the gap between SME needs and the provision of business development services in meeting those needs. ITC held 28 management training events, involving 830 enterprises and trainers. The training and counselling capacities created through ITC's regional hubs continued to demonstrate their viability, and thirty new publications were developed to support the delivery of integrated SME training programmes teaching management, exporting and e-business skills to enterprise managers, with specific support for women entrepreneurs.

JAG action. The ITC Joint Advisory Group (JAG), at its thirty-eighth session (Geneva, 18-22 April) [ITC/AG/(XXXVIII)/204], considered the reports on ITC 2004 activities [YUN 2004, p. 965] and on its technical cooperation projects in 2004 [ITC/AG/(XXXVIII)/202/Add.1,2], and the report of the Consultative Committee of the ITC Global Trust Fund [ITC/AG/(XXXVIII)/203].

The Group noted the increase in delivery of 82 per cent over a four-year period and encouraged ITC to implement its "managed growth" strategy, which emphasized both qualitative and quantitative growth. It endorsed ITC's work in promoting public-private sector dialogue and consultations on trade strategy and called upon it to provide assistance in formulating service sector strategies, building awareness of service exports among service associations and capacities within trade support institutions to promote service exports and organize networking meetings for industry associations. The Group encouraged ITC to maintain its role in increasing the international competitiveness of the textile and clothing sector and in addressing non-tariff barriers. ITC was encouraged to continue to move the Integrated Framework for Trade-related Technical Assistance to Least Developed Countries forward and to increase its support to promoting public-private sector dialogue. ITC's role in supporting sectors of importance to LDCs and in identifying non-tariff trade barriers among developing countries was welcomed. It was encouraged to help countries mainstream trade into national development and poverty reduction strategies and to increase its efforts to attract private-sector partnerships.

In terms of ITC's geographical coverage, the Group noted that the level of support to LDCs had been higher in earlier years than in 2004 and urged ITC to reverse that downward trend in view of the continued marginalization of LDCs from the benefits of world trade. It emphasized the importance of increasing support to the African region and noted that ITC had prepared a response paper on possible areas of support from ITC. It endorsed ITC's focus on building national capacities for trade promotion to ensure the sustainability of its operations and requested it to support SME rehabilitation in tsunami-affected countries in the Indian Ocean region.

Pledges of trust fund contributions to ITC were announced by Canada, China, Denmark, France, Germany, India, Italy, Japan, the Netherlands, Norway, Sweden and Switzerland.

In October [A/60/15], TDB took note of JAG's report on its thirty-eighth session.

ITC administrative arrangements

In March [A/60/6 (Sect. 13)], the Secretary-General submitted preliminary budget estimates for ITC for the 2006-2007 biennium. Requirements, expressed in Swiss francs (SwF) at 2004-2005 rates, were estimated at SwF 65,540,400. Since SwF 470,000 from various sources would be available to ITC during the 2006-2007 biennium, the contribution of each organization (the United Nations and WTO) was estimated at SwF 32,535,200 at 2004-2005 rates for the biennium.

The Advisory Committee on Administrative and Budgetary Question (ACABQ), in its first report on the proposed programme budget for the 2006-2007 biennium [A/60/7], recommended that the General Assembly take note of the resources proposed in the ITC preliminary budget estimates.

The Secretary-General, in November, submitted revised budget estimates for ITC for the 2006-2007 biennium [A/60/6 (Sect. 13)/Add.1]. Those requirements were estimated at SwF 66,058,600, before recosting, or SwF 68,369,400, at 2006-2007 rates, representing a decrease of 0.02 per cent compared with the approved budget for 2004-2005. Since the projected miscellaneous income was at SwF 470,000 for the 2006-2007 biennium, the biennial contribution of the United Nations and WTO was SwF 33,949,700, or $26,732,000, at the exchange rate of SwF 1.27 to $1.00.

In December [A/60/7/Add.16 & Corr.1], ACABQ recommended that the Assembly approve an amount of SwF 68,369,400, at 2006-2007 rates, under section 13, ITC UNCTAD/WTO, of the proposed programme budget for the 2006-2007 biennium.

The Assembly, in section I of **resolution 60/248**, of 23 December (see p. 1494), approved resources in the amount of $26,732,000 for the 2006-2007 biennium under section 13, ITC UNCTAD/WTO,

of the proposed programme budget for 2006-
2007.

Enterprise, business facilitation and development

The Commission on Enterprise, Business Facilitation and Development, at its ninth session
(Geneva, 22-25 February) [TD/B/COM.3/70], had
before it UNCTAD secretariat notes on linkages,
value chains and outward investment: internationalization patterns of developing countries'
SMEs [TD/B/COM.3/69]; efficient transport and
trade facilitation to improve participation by developing countries in international trade [TD/B/
COM.3/67]; e-commerce strategies for development: selected trade and development aspects of
information and communication technologies
(ICTs) [TD/B/COM.3/68]; a progress report on the
implementation of the Commission's agreed recommendations at its eighth session [TD/B/COM.3/
66]; and a number of 2004 expert meeting reports
[YUN 2004, p. 968].

In its agreed recommendations on improving
the competitiveness of SMEs, the Commission
agreed that the globalization process had affected
the business environment for SMEs in developing
countries, with international competitiveness
becoming increasingly difficult for them. It also
agreed that the internationalization of enterprises could strengthen the competitiveness of
developing country firms. It requested UNCTAD
to continue its work on policy analysis in the area
of enterprise competitiveness and its technical
assistance and capacity building efforts. It
should explore ways in which issues of SME development could be addressed and provide assistance to tsunami-affected countries in SME competitiveness rehabilitation. It should also study
the possible development of a competitiveness
analysis framework and relevant indicators for
SME sector development.

In its recommendation on efficient transport
and trade facilitation, the Commission asked
UNCTAD to: keep under review and monitor developments relating to efficient transport and
trade facilitation and examine their implications
for developing countries; provide technical assistance and capacity building activities in that
area; monitor developments and disseminate information on security measures affecting the international trade and transport of developing
countries; and cooperate with other intergovernmental and non-governmental organizations
(NGOs) in their work relating to the development
of international legal instruments.

On electronic commerce strategies for development, the Commission recommended that
UNCTAD should: carry out research and policy-

oriented analytical work on the implications for
trade and development of the different aspects of
ICT and e-business, with a focus on those sectors
of main interest to developing countries; continue, with an appropriate implementation strategy,
to provide a forum for international discussion
and exchange of experiences concerning ICT,
e-business and their applications, including dissemination of best practices and standards, in the
promotion of trade and development; continue
work on the measurement of ICT, including the
development of statistical capacity, to enable developing countries to measure the access, use and
impact of ICT and to monitor progress; contribute to capacity building in ICT for development,
particularly in trade sectors of special interest to
developing countries or those that could be enhanced through the use of ICT, such as tourism,
SME development and poverty alleviation, and
provide advisory services to developing countries
in the context of its capacity-building activities
and the multistakeholder partnerships launched
at UNCTAD XI [YUN 2004, p. 955], and facilitate a discussion on free and open source software, in partnership with private sector and civil society entities.

In May [A/60/15], TDB took note of the Commission's report and endorsed its recommendations.

Subsidiary bodies. A number of expert meetings were held in Geneva during the year. The
Expert Meeting on Trade Facilitation as an Engine for Development (21-23 September) [TD/B/
COM.3/EM.24/3] had before it an UNCTAD secretariat note on the subject [TD/B/COM.3/EM.24/2].
The meeting discussed trade and transport facilitation and development, trade facilitation and regional integration, private sector expectations
from the WTO negotiations on trade facilitation
and implementation of trade facilitation measures. It noted the general benefits of an efficient
trade and transport facilitation system and
agreed that trade facilitation and development
strategies should be tailored to the specific needs
of landlocked, least developed and small island
developing countries. Coordinated action was
also required to support those countries in their
effort to integrate into the world economy
through trade and transport facilitation. ITC
should continue to design and implement trade
and transport facilitation measures and programmes, and create or strengthen institutional
mechanisms to ensure the integration of trade
and transport facilitation into the development
process.

The Expert Meeting on ICT and Tourism for
Development (30 November–2 December)
[TD/B/COM.3/EM.25/3] had before it an UNCTAD

secretariat note on the subject [TD/B/COM.3/ EM.25/2]. The meeting examined current and future characteristics and the dynamics of the innovation process in the tourism industry, focusing on the role of ICTs in developing tourism, the innovation process in the tourism industry managing and promoting destinations online, and e-business challenges. In the light of the contribution of tourism to the economies of many developing countries, ICTs and e-business played a key role in helping destination management organizations (DMOs) and tourism suppliers in developing countries to promote their products and services worldwide. Tourism enterprise in developing countries, particularly SMEs, faced challenges in taking advantage of opportunities because of their slow adoption of ICTs. DMOs should create awareness of the potential offered by ICTs, provide business advice and facilitate access to technology and training. Experts also considered the relevance of destination management systems (DMSs) for Governments and for regional, national and local tourism providers and emphasized that the success of a DMS was related to the establishment of public and private partnerships. The experts concluded that e-tourism policies and strategies would play an increasing role in integrating enterprises, particularly SMEs, into global tourism markets. In developing countries, assistance with the development of e-tourism initiatives was urgently needed, along with capacity building programmes. In addition, experts proposed the development of a "virtual space" to share technical, marketing and strategic solutions, as well as best practices in managing destinations online. South Africa offered to host the "virtual space".

The Expert Meeting on Enhancing Productive Capacity of Developing Country Firms through Internationalization (5-7 December) [TD/B/COM.3/ EM.26/3] had before it an UNCTAD secretariat note on internationalization of developing country enterprises through outward foreign direct investment (OFDI) [TD/B/COM.3/EM.26/2] and five case studies prepared by the UNCTAD secretariat [TD/B/COM.3/EM.26/2/Add.1-5]. The meeting examined how enterprise competitiveness in developing countries and economies in transition could be enhanced through internationalization, with a focus on OFDI, particularly by SMEs, and identified policy options for helping developing countries strengthen their firms' competitiveness by investing abroad. It discussed the main trends of OFDI from developing countries, motivations, drivers, the impact on enterprise competitiveness, competitiveness gains and policies for OFDI, and programmes supporting enterprise internationalization. The challenges and risks of internationalization were discussed and risk factors identified. The experts identified also a wide range of trends, motivations, drivers, competitiveness gains and policies for OFDI which deserved further attention and in-depth analysis. They recognized that OFDI was a relatively new and little-studied phenomenon, and there was a need for more research on its impact on the competitiveness of domestic enterprises and home countries. In that regard, an awareness-building effort was needed to enhance understanding of developing countries' Governments and businesses regarding possible ways to increase the potential beneficial impact of OFDI and to minimize its possible negative effects.

Commodities

The UNCTAD/DESA report *World Economic Situation and Prospects 2006* [Sales No. E.06.II.C.2] stated that commodity prices continued on an upward trend in 2005. After an increase of 20 per cent in 2004, non-fuel commodity prices, as measured by the UNCTAD commodity index, rose by a further 10 per cent, on average, during the first 10 months of 2005. Higher nominal prices were supported by demand from Asia, in particular from China, and emerging supply constraints in some commodity markets. However, the pace of price increases decelerated during the year, and the increases in commodity prices did not offset the severe declines suffered in the past. Expressed in current United States dollars, non-fuel commodity prices were still lower than what they were in the early 1980s. In real terms, by the end of 2005, commodity prices were about 30 per cent lower than the average for the period 1975-1985. Average price increases concealed considerable diversity across commodity groups. Most of the increase in non-fuel commodity prices markets in 2005, was driven by developments in the minerals and metals markets. After reaching a peak in August 2005, oil prices declined, reflecting a deceleration of oil demand. Brent, one of the two key market references for light, sweet crude, was priced at $55 per barrel in late November, down from $63 in late August, when Hurricanes Katrina and Rita provoked serious disruptions in an already tight market.

Individual commodities

Timber. The United Nations Conference for the Negotiation of a Successor Agreement to the International Tropical Timber Agreement, 1994 [YUN 1994, p. 887] reconvened in 2005 (Geneva, 27 June–1 July). It had before it a final working paper [TD/TIMBER.3/L.4] resulting from the second part of the Conference which took place from 14 to 18 February. The Conference adopted a draft resolution [TD/TIMBER.3/10] requesting the UNCTAD Secretary-General to convene the Conference in January 2006 and, in cooperation with the Executive Director of the International Tropical Timber Organization, to prepare the necessary documentation, notably the working document resulting from the third part of the Conference.

Olive oil and table olives. As at 31 December, the International Agreement on Olive Oil and Table Olives, 1986, as amended and extended 1993 [YUN 1993, p. 760] until 31 December 2005, had 15 parties. On 16 March 2005, Monaco informed the Secretary-General of its decision to withdraw from the Agreement.

Sugar. As at 31 December, the International Sugar Agreement 1992 [YUN 1992, p. 625] had 22 signatories and 51 parties. During the year, Mozambique and Paraguay became parties.

Coffee. As at 31 December, the International Coffee Agreement 2001 [YUN 2001, p. 880] had 35 signatories and 63 parties. During the year, France, Italy and the United States became parties.

Cocoa. As at 31 December, the International Cocoa Agreement 2001 [YUN 2001, p. 880] had 11 signatories and 19 parties. During the year, the Dominican Republic and Venezuela became parties.

Common Fund for Commodities

The 1980 Agreement establishing the Common Fund for Commodities [YUN 1980, p. 621], a mechanism intended to stabilize the commodities market by helping to finance buffer stocks of specific commodities and such commodity development activities as research and marketing, entered into force in 1989, and the Fund became operational later that year. As at 31 December 2005, the number of parties to the Agreement remained at 110.

On 23 November, the General Assembly granted observer status to the Common Fund for Commodities (**resolution 60/26**) (see p. 1543).

Finance

Financial policy

The *World Economic and Social Survey 2005* [Sales No. E.05.II.C.1], which was devoted to financing for development, stated that improved economic conditions in developing countries, as well as the higher global growth and low interest rates, drove a recovery of private capital flows to developing countries in 2003 and 2004, perhaps signalling the beginning of a new cycle. However, periods of increased volatility in yield spreads on emerging market bonds, in 2004 and 2005, in response to uncertainty in the pace of interest rate increases in developed countries (particularly the United States), underscored the vulnerability of financial flows to acceleration in increases in interest rates. More importantly, net transfers of financial resources from developing countries did not experience a positive turnaround and continued to deteriorate in 2004, for the seventh year in a row, reaching an estimated $350 billion. Those transfers were explained by the combination of relatively low net financial flows and accumulation of very large foreign-exchange reserves, particularly in Asia. Divergence in regional trends in private financial flows also resulted in changes in regional distribution of those flows. The most striking aspect of such developments was the increased concentration of flows to Eastern and Southern Asia, in particular to China, at the expense of Latin America, where private financial flows remained far below the 1997 peak. Exhaustion of State assets available for privatization and mergers and acquisitions, joined by macroeconomic volatility in some developing countries, resulted in a brief decline in foreign direct investment (FDI) in 2002-2003, followed by a broad-based recovery across developing regions and economies in transition, owing to the improvement in a combination of cyclical, institutional and structural factors. As a result of the commitments contained in the Monterrey Consensus, adopted at the International Conference in Financing for Development [YUN 2002, p. 953], the decline in the share of official development assistance (ODA) in developed country gross national income (GNI) was reversed, rising to 0.25 per cent in 2003 and 2004. If all the commitments were met by the target date of 2006, total ODA was projected to reach $88 billion, an increase of almost 50 per cent in nominal terms, from the total recorded in 2002. Despite the positive trend since 2002, the projected ODA levels for 2006-2010 would fall short of the estimated $150 billion deemed necessary for developing countries to attain the Millennium Development Goals (MDGs) [YUN 2000, p. 51]. Furthermore, the recent reversal of the decline in aid flows barely brought real assistance back to the 1990 levels. The European Union (EU) and its member States, individually, which provided more than half of total ODA, undertook, in mid-2005, to achieve or maintain the 0.7 per cent ODA/GNI target by 2015.

The UNCTAD/DESA report *World Economic Situation and Prospects 2006* [Sales No. E.06.II.C.2], based on information available as at 30 November 2005, stated that macroeconomic policies and, in particular monetary policies, became less synchronized worldwide in 2005, in contrast to 2004, when many economies were unwinding the policy stimuli injected in earlier years. While central banks in some countries continued to raise policy interest rates, other countries reduced interest rates or maintained their policy stance for several months. Among the developed countries, the United States Federal Reserve Board raised interest rates by a total of 325 basis points from mid-2004, pushing up the Federal Funds rate to 4.25 per cent. No further monetary tightening was expected in the euro area, although it was not clear whether the increase in late 2005 was the beginning of a more prolonged restrictive stance. Signals from Japan were more clearly in the direction of maintaining the policy framework of quantitative easing, creating an environment where short-term interest rates could stay close to zero. The central banks in other developed countries would likely keep their policy stance at the current levels. In the developing countries and economies in transition, further monetary tightening was expected, although in measured steps. That strategy held, in particular for most Asian economies, along with continued intervention in foreign-exchange markets and sterilization. In contrast, in Latin America, room for easing remained in several countries with high interest rates and relatively low growth, such as Brazil and Mexico, as inflation was contained within the target range. While most African countries would maintain a cautious monetary policy stance, many economies in West Asia would raise interest rates. Meanwhile, monetary policy in most economies in transition would remain accommodative.

Financial flows

According to the UNCTAD/DESA report on the world economic situation and prospects, the magnitude of net transfers of financial resources from developing to developed countries had risen steadily from an estimated $8.1 billion in 1997 to $483.4 billion in 2005. The net transfer of resources from economies in transition had also followed a similar pattern since 1999, reaching an estimated $95.5 billion in 2005. The most important destination of the net outward transfer of financial resources from developing countries taken as a whole was to the United States, and more than offset the net outward transfer from other major developed countries, namely EU countries and Japan, to developing countries. Net private capital inflows to developing coun-

tries as a group fell substantially in 2005 to $95 billion from a peak of $184 billion reported in 2004. Most of the decline was due to falling inflows into East, South and Western Asia. However, inflows increased for Africa and Latin America and the Caribbean. There were substantial declines in portfolio and other investments. In contrast, FDI flows continued to increase and remained the largest type of net capital flow to developing countries.

Worldwide, FDI inflows increased by 18 per cent to $762 billion in 2005. In absolute terms, the bulk of the increase went to East and South Asia. FDI also increased strongly in Africa and Western Asia in relative terms. Total FDI flows to developing countries reached $278 billion in 2005, up from $233 billion in 2004. FDI related to the privatization process in the economies in transition slowed down as that process neared completion in many countries. More noteworthy, was the surge in FDI originating from developing countries, especially by Asian firms. In 2004, those outflows amounted to $83 billion, or about 12 per cent of worldwide FDI.

The role of FDI in Africa

A July report by the UNCTAD secretariat [TD/B/52/5] on economic development in Africa reviewed the role of FDI. It stated that many African countries had implemented policies for attracting FDI as a development finance vehicle of choice in an attempt to avoid further indebtedness, create jobs, acquire new technologies, build linkages with the rest of the economy and reduce poverty. Those policies did not, in many cases, increase FDI flows to productive sectors or ensure more rapid growth and reduce poverty. The report proceeded from the need for a more critical approach to evaluating the size, quality and impact of FDI in Africa and suggested that policy makers should pay attention to its costs and benefits as much as to ways of attracting it. It argued for a more balanced and strategic approach to FDI tailored to African economic conditions and development challenges. The report stressed the need to rethink the emphasis on attracting FDI and its replacement with a more balanced and strategic approach tailored to African conditions and challenges. It concluded that African policymakers should consider how the gains and costs from hosting FDI could be managed to strengthen profit-investment-export linkages and be aware of longer-term losses resulting from giving up policy space for subsequent industrialization and diversification efforts. Reversing the premature deindustrialization of the past two decades would shift resources away from traditional low-productivity activities and attract a more dynamic type of FDI to Africa. However, that would need the establishment of a more robust domestic accumulation process across the region, based on more linkages between the rural and urban economies, across sectors and among consumer, intermediate and capital-goods industries. The effectiveness of strategic trade and investment policies to encourage diversification into non-traditional exports should be complemented with a stronger regional focus.

TDB [A/60/15], in agreed conclusions adopted on 7 November [agreed conclusions 484 (LII)], noted that Africa's share of global FDI had declined over the past three years, 80 per cent of which was going into extractive sectors and had not generated the desired benefits. It underscored the need to encourage greater productive direct investment, including foreign investment, in African countries to support their development activities. Noting further that FDI could complement domestic investment by enhancing human and physical infrastructure, TDB encouraged the creation of an environment conducive to both domestic and foreign direct investment and urged policymakers to adopt a strategic and tailored approach to take into account African economic conditions and development challenges. It encouraged African Governments to adopt policies to attract FDI and increase its benefits for Africa, while achieving sustainable development, taking into account a regional coordinated approach. It underscored that rapid growth was a critical component in the design of African trade and development strategies, a contributor to which should be regional trade arrangements (RTAs) within the multilateral trading system. UNCTAD was urged to continue to undertake in-depth analysis and provide policy advice on African development.

International financial system

Report of Secretary-General. In response to General Assembly resolution 59/222 [YUN 2004, p. 973], the Secretary-General submitted a July report [A/60/163] on international financial system and development, which complemented his report [A/60/289] (see p. 1061) on follow-up to and implementation of the outcome of the International Conference on Financing for Development [YUN 2002, p. 953]. The report assessed the efficiency of the international financial system in allocating financial resources in a way that supported the mobilization of domestic resources and reviewed measures to improve its stability. It also reviewed policies to counter the pro-cyclicality of international capital flows, improve multilateral surveillance, create additional emergency official financing arrangements, strengthen the International Monetary Fund (IMF) financ-

ing of poor countries and streamline its lending conditionality, implement sovereign debt restructuring, improve the role of special drawing rights in the international financial system, support South-South cooperation in the international monetary system and enhance the voice and participation of developing countries in international financial decision-making.

In his conclusions, the Secretary-General stated that many countries were accumulating liquid foreign reserve balances to protect against the volatility of international capital flows and the resulting vulnerability to financial crisis. Measures to increase the stability of the international financial system and provide means to access liquidity in periods of turbulence would reduce the attractiveness of large individual country reserve balances. The reserves built up in multilateral development banks should continue to be used to support growth and poverty reduction in the poorest developing countries and provide liquidity support in middle-income countries. Although developing countries had taken measures to counter the pro-cyclicality of international capital flows, they remained vulnerable to global uncertainties and risks, and the transformation of the global financial system increased the likelihood of boom-bust cycles. It was essential to introduce a modified, system-wide approach to prudential regulation, taking into account the macroeconomic consequences of financial imbalances and the inherent pro-cyclicality of financial markets. Multilateral surveillance remained at the centre of crisis prevention efforts and should focus not only on crisis-prone countries, but also on the stability of the system as a whole, with special emphasis on the policy consistency of major economies. Since emergency financing at the international and regional levels contributed to crisis prevention and management, there was the need for easier, more automatic and rapid access to liquidity support in order to ease the burden of adjustment.

IMF/World Bank Development Committee. The joint International Monetary Fund (IMF)/World Bank Development Committee, in a communiqué issued following its 25 September meeting (Washington, D.C.), reiterated its support for the realization of the internationally agreed development goals, including the MDGs and reaffirmed the importance of sound policies in developing countries. The Committee stated that stronger country policies and more effective aid should be complemented with efforts to increase openness and market access, and stressed the importance of reforming agricultural trade policies to expand market access and eliminate trade-distorting subsidies. The Committee asked the

Bank and the Fund to examine the adequacy of mechanisms to address regional or cross-country aid for trade needs and explore new ones, and to integrate better trade-related needs into their support for country programmes. It welcomed the work on enhancing IMF instruments in support of its low-income members, and called for the strengthening of Bank-Fund collaboration.

In an earlier communiqué following a 17 April meeting (Washington D.C.), the Committee stated that macroeconomic stability remained critical, as was the need to strengthen public sector financial management, promote good governance, improve business climate and regulation and develop local financial markets. Development financing remained a challenge, requiring sustained action on domestic resource mobilization, private investment and trade. (See p. 1060 also.)

GENERAL ASSEMBLY ACTION

On 22 December [meeting 68], the General Assembly, on the recommendation of the Second Committee [A/60/486/Add.2], adopted **resolution 60/186** without vote [agenda item 50 *(b)*].

International financial system and development
The General Assembly,

Recalling its resolutions 55/186 of 20 December 2000 and 56/181 of 21 December 2001, both entitled "Towards a strengthened and stable international financial architecture responsive to the priorities of growth and development, especially in developing countries, and to the promotion of economic and social equity", as well as its resolutions 57/241 of 20 December 2002, 58/202 of 23 December 2003 and 59/222 of 22 December 2004,

Recalling also the United Nations Millennium Declaration and its resolution 56/210 B of 9 July 2002, in which it endorsed the Monterrey Consensus of the International Conference on Financing for Development, and the Plan of Implementation of the World Summit on Sustainable Development ("Johannesburg Plan of Implementation"),

Recalling further the 2005 World Summit Outcome,

Emphasizing that the international financial system should further sustain economic growth and support sustainable development and hunger and poverty eradication, while allowing for the coherent mobilization of all sources of financing for development, including the mobilization of domestic resources, international investment flows, official development assistance, external debt relief and an open, equitable, rule-based, predictable and non-discriminatory global trading system,

Stressing the importance of commitment to sound domestic financial sectors, which make a vital contribution to national development efforts, as an important component of an international financial architecture that is supportive of development,

Stressing also that good governance at the international level is fundamental for achieving sustainable development, in this regard reiterating the importance of promoting global economic governance by addressing the international finance, trade, technology and investment patterns that have an impact on the development prospects of developing countries in order to ensure a dynamic and enabling international economic environment, and reiterating also that, to this effect, the international community should take all necessary and appropriate measures, including ensuring support for structural and macroeconomic reform, finding a comprehensive solution to the external debt problem and increasing the market access of developing countries,

Reaffirming the commitment to broaden and strengthen the participation of developing countries and countries with economies in transition in international economic decision-making and norm-setting, and to that end stressing the importance of continuing efforts to reform the international financial architecture, noting that enhancing the voice and participation of developing countries and countries with economies in transition in the Bretton Woods institutions remains a continuous concern,

Recognizing the urgent need to enhance the coherence, governance and consistency of the international monetary, financial and trading systems and the importance of ensuring their openness, fairness and inclusiveness in order to complement national development efforts to ensure sustained economic growth and the achievement of the internationally agreed development goals, including the Millennium Development Goals,

Emphasizing the need for additional stable and predictable financing to help developing countries undertake investment plans to achieve internationally agreed development goals,

Recognizing, in this regard, the value of developing innovative sources of financing from various sources on a public, private, domestic and external basis to increase and supplement traditional sources of financing,

Reiterating the need to strengthen the leadership role of the United Nations in promoting development,

1. *Takes note* of the report of the Secretary-General;

2. *Notes* that global economic growth and a stable international financial system, inter alia, can support the ability of developing countries to achieve internationally agreed development goals, including the Millennium Development Goals, and stresses the importance of cooperative efforts by all countries and institutions to cope with the risks of financial instability;

3. *Emphasizes* that economic growth should be further strengthened and sustained, noting that global economic growth depends on national economic growth and that implementation of sound macroeconomic policies could significantly contribute to a revitalization of economic growth;

4. *Invites* the World Bank, the International Monetary Fund, the regional development banks and other relevant institutions to further integrate development dimensions into their strategies and policies, consistent with their respective mandates;

5. *Notes* that developing countries as a whole continue to experience a net outflow of financial resources, and requests the Secretary-General, in continuing collaboration with international financial institutions and other relevant bodies, to analyse the range of reasons for this in his report under this item;

6. *Underlines* the importance of promoting international financial stability and sustainable growth, and welcomes the efforts undertaken to this end by the International Monetary Fund and the Financial Stability Forum, as well as the consideration by the International Monetary and Financial Committee of ways to sharpen tools designed to promote international financial stability and enhance crisis prevention, inter alia, through an even-handed implementation of surveillance, including at the regional level, and a sharpening of surveillance of capital markets and systemically and regionally important countries, with a view, inter alia, to the early identification of problems and risks, integrating debt sustainability analysis, the fostering of appropriate policy responses, the possible provision of financing and other instruments designed to prevent the emergence or spread of financial crises and further improvements in the transparency of macroeconomic data and statistical information on international capital flows;

7. *Also underlines* the importance of efforts at the national level to increase resilience to financial risk, stresses in this regard the importance of better assessment of a country's debt burden and its ability to service that debt in both crisis prevention and resolution, and welcomes the ongoing work of the International Monetary Fund on assessing debt sustainability;

8. *Invites* developed countries, in particular major industrialized economies, to take into account the effect of their macroeconomic policies on international growth and development;

9. *Recognizes* the need for multilateral surveillance to remain at the centre of crisis prevention efforts and that surveillance should focus not only on crisis-prone countries but on the stability of the system as a whole;

10. *Reiterates* that measures to mitigate the impact of excessive volatility of short-term capital flows and to improve transparency of and information about financial flows are important and must be considered;

11. *Notes* the impact of financial crises or risk contagion in developing countries and countries with economies in transition, regardless of their size, and in this regard welcomes the efforts of the international financial institutions, in their support to countries, to continuously adapt their array of financial facilities and resources, drawing on a full range of policies, taking into account the effects of economic cycles, as and where appropriate, having due regard to sound fiscal management and the specific circumstances of each case, so as to prevent and respond to such crises in a timely and appropriate way;

12. *Underscores* the importance of competitive and inclusive private and public financial markets in mobilizing and allocating savings towards productive investment and thus making a vital contribution to national development efforts and to an international financial architecture that is supportive of development;

13. *Invites* the international financial and banking institutions to consider enhancing the transparency of risk-rating mechanisms, noting that sovereign risk assessments made by the private sector should maximize the use of strict, objective and transparent parameters, which can be facilitated by high-quality data and analysis, and encourages relevant development institutions, including the United Nations Conference on Trade and Development, to continue their work on this issue, including its potential impact on the development prospects of developing countries;

14. *Stresses* the importance of strong domestic institutions in promoting business activities and financial stability for the achievement of growth and development, inter alia, through sound macroeconomic policies and policies aimed at strengthening the regulatory systems of the corporate, financial and banking sectors, and also stresses that international cooperation initiatives in those areas should encourage flows of capital to developing countries;

15. *Underlines* the fact that the issue of enhancing the voice of developing countries and countries with economies in transition in the Bretton Woods institutions is of vital importance, stresses the importance of enhancing ongoing work in this regard, taking into account progress in the context of the International Monetary Fund quota review, and invites the World Bank and the International Monetary Fund to continue to provide information on this issue, using existing cooperation forums, including those involving Member States;

16. *Emphasizes* that it is essential to ensure the effective and equitable participation of developing countries in the formulation of financial standards and codes, underscores the need to ensure their implementation, on a voluntary and progressive basis, as a contribution to reducing vulnerability to financial crisis and contagion, and notes that more than one hundred countries have participated in or agreed to participate in the joint World Bank-International Monetary Fund financial sector assessment programme;

17. *Notes* the proposal to use special drawing rights allocations for development purposes, and considers that any assessment of special drawing rights allocations must respect the Articles of Agreement of the International Monetary Fund and the established rules of procedure of the Fund, which requires taking into account the global need for liquidity at the international level;

18. *Invites* the multilateral and regional development banks and development funds to continue to play a vital role in serving the development needs of developing countries and countries with economies in transition, including through coordinated action, as appropriate, and stresses that strengthened regional development banks and subregional financial institutions add flexible financial support to national and regional development efforts, thus enhancing their ownership and overall efficiency, and are an essential source of knowledge and expertise for their developing-country members;

19. *Calls for* the continued effort of the multilateral financial institutions, in providing policy advice, technical assistance and financial support to member countries, to work on the basis of nationally owned reform and development strategies, to pay due regard to the special needs and implementing capacities of developing countries and countries with economies in transition and to minimize the negative impacts of the adjustment programmes on the vulnerable segments of society, while taking into account the importance of gender-sensitive employment and hunger and poverty eradication policies and strategies;

20. *Stresses* the need to continuously improve standards of corporate and public sector governance, in-

cluding accounting, auditing and measures to ensure transparency, noting the disruptive effects of inadequate policies;

21. *Requests* the Secretary-General to submit a report to the General Assembly at its sixty-first session on the implementation of the present resolution;

22. *Decides* to include in the provisional agenda of its sixty-first session, under the item entitled "Macroeconomic policy questions", the sub-item entitled "International financial system and development".

Debt problems of developing countries

Report of Secretary-General. In response to General Assembly resolution 59/223 [YUN 2004, p. 977], the Secretary-General submitted a July report [A/60/139] on external debt crisis and development, which reviewed recent developments in the external debt of developing countries, the implementation of the Heavily Indebted Poor Countries (HIPC) Initiative, launched in 1996 [YUN 1996, p. 867], and the financing challenges for countries having reached the completion point. It also analysed new approaches within the Paris Club (a group of creditor countries), including the Evian approach, debt repayments, and the experiences of debt restructurings with private creditors. The principles of an orderly debt workout process were discussed in the light of those experiences.

The report concluded that, against the backdrop of better growth and export prospects in developing countries in general, recent trends revealed a smaller accumulation of debt and lower debt-service burden. However, some groups of countries continued to struggle for a durable solution to their serious debt problems. Despite notable progress in its implementation, the HIPC Initiative fell short of the MDG targets and would need additional development assistance, including full debt cancellation. In this respect, the G-8 (Group of most industrialized countries) agreed to provide additional resources to cover the cost of full cancellation of HIPC multilateral debt. However, the modalities of the implementation of the G-8 initiative needed to be clarified. For countries that had reached the completion point, it was important to achieve lasting debt sustainability and avoid falling into a new debt trap. Unfortunately, for many of them debt ratios had increased to unsustainable levels under the HIPC Initiative. In order to avoid debt-servicing difficulties and to achieve the MDGs by 2015, without an increase in debt ratios, exclusively grant-based finance for most HIPCs was called for, and donors were encouraged to fulfil their increased ODA commitments. However, in countries where additional loans were necessary, there was a need to promote responsible lending and borrowing and to link the grant element of such loans to the

capacity to pay. The question of debt-sustainability analysis was also key to the resolution of the debt crisis of other low- and middle-income countries. It should be part of the overall development strategy of a country, addressing debt, trade and finance issues in a coherent framework, and strengthening debt-management capacity should be an integral part of that strategy. It was essential to reach an international understanding on debt restructuring modalities, which would bring together official and private creditors in a dialogue, with a view to resolving debt problems in an expeditious and timely manner and protecting the interests of debtors and creditors.

Other actions. The joint IMF/World Bank Development Committee, in a communiqué issued following its 17 April meeting (Washington, D.C.), stressed the need to accelerate and sustain growth and development through sound policy frameworks and called upon the Bank to develop an action plan for Africa. It welcomed the agreement by the Bank and Fund on a joint framework for assessing debt sustainability in low-income countries, as well as proposals for additional debt and debt service relief, and agreed that further debt relief beyond HIPCs was needed in specific cases to secure long-term debt sustainability and support progress towards the fulfilment of the MDGs.

In a communiqué issued following its 25 September meeting (Washington, D.C.), the Committee welcomed the World Bank Group's Africa Action Plan, focusing on building state capacity and improving governance; strengthening the drivers of growth; and promoting broad participation in growth and sharing its benefits. It called for its timely implementation and urged the Bank to work closely with the African Union, the New Partnership for Africa's Development (see p. 1003), the African Development Bank, the African Partnership Forum and other partners. The Committee also welcomed the proposal adopted by the G-8 (Gleneagles, United Kingdom, July) for 100 per cent cancellation of debt owed by eligible HIPCs to the International Development Association (IDA), the African Development Fund, and IMF, and agreed on the need for an interdependent package that was additional to existing commitments and maintained the financial integrity and capacity of IDA to assist poor countries in the future. It also agreed on the need for additionality in donor resources for debt relief and emphasized the importance of maintaining sound economic performance and good governance by eligible countries.

The UNCTAD/DESA report *World Economic Situation and Prospects 2006* stated that, at the end of 2005, eighteen countries had reached the completion point under the HIPC Initiative and 10 had reached the decision point, making them eligible to receive interim debt relief. The implementation of the HIPC Initiative continued to progress slowly, owing mainly to the difficulty of eligible countries in complying with the conditions required to receive full debt relief. To many of them in the interim phase of the Initiative, maintaining macroeconomic stability was a major challenge.

The *World Economic and Social Survey 2005* stated that, by mid-April, 27 countries had received debt relief. Together with other debt relief initiatives, HIPC had provided two-thirds of the reduction in debt stocks of those countries. The total cost of providing debt relief to all of the 38 countries potentially eligible for assistance under the HIPC Initiative was estimated at $58 billion in 2004, in net current value terms. A little more than 50 per cent would come from debt forgiveness by bilateral creditors, while the rest would be provided by multilateral lenders.

GENERAL ASSEMBLY ACTION

On 22 December [meeting 68], the General Assembly, on the recommendation of the Second Committee [A/60/486/Add.3], adopted **resolution 60/187** without vote [agenda item 50 (c)].

External debt crisis and development

The General Assembly,

Recalling its resolutions 58/203 of 23 December 2003 and 59/223 of 22 December 2004 on external debt crisis and development,

Reaffirming the Monterrey Consensus of the International Conference on Financing for Development, which recognizes sustainable debt financing as an important element for mobilizing resources for public and private investment,

Recalling the United Nations Millennium Declaration adopted on 8 September 2000,

Recalling also the 2005 World Summit Outcome,

Recalling further its resolution 57/270 B of 23 June 2003,

Welcoming the fact that total debt service for developing countries decreased in the period from 2003 to 2004, leading to improvements in several traditional debt indicators, but concerned that some low- and middle-income developing countries that are not eligible for debt relief under the Heavily Indebted Poor Countries Initiative are still facing difficulties in finding a durable solution in meeting their external debt-servicing obligations, which could adversely affect their sustainable development,

Welcoming also the fact that the Heavily Indebted Poor Countries Initiative has enabled heavily indebted poor countries to markedly increase their expenditures on health, education and other social services consistent with national priorities and development plans, emphasizing in this regard the need to ensure that debt relief does not replace other sources of financing, stressing the importance of addressing the challenges of those heavily indebted poor countries that are facing difficulties in reaching the completion point under the Initiative, and expressing concern that some heavily indebted poor countries continue to face substantial debt burdens and need to avoid rebuilding unsustainable debt burdens after reaching the completion point under the Initiative,

Welcoming further the recent proposal of the Group of Eight, as endorsed by the Bretton Woods institutions at their 2005 annual meetings, to cancel 100 per cent of the outstanding debt of eligible heavily indebted poor countries owed to the International Monetary Fund, the International Development Association and the African Development Fund and to provide additional resources to ensure that the financing capacity of the international financial institutions is not reduced,

Emphasizing that debt sustainability is essential for underpinning growth, and underlining the importance of debt sustainability to the efforts to achieve national development goals, including the Millennium Development Goals, and that countries should direct those resources freed through debt relief, in particular through debt reduction and cancellation, towards activities consistent with poverty eradication, sustained economic growth and sustainable development and the achievement of the internationally agreed development goals, including the Millennium Development Goals,

Convinced that enhanced market access for goods and services of export interest to developing countries contributes significantly to debt sustainability in those countries,

1. *Takes note* of the report of the Secretary-General;

2. *Emphasizes* the special importance of a timely, effective, comprehensive and durable solution to the debt problems of developing countries, since debt financing and relief can be an important source of capital for economic growth and development;

3. *Stresses* the importance of promoting responsible borrowing and lending;

4. *Emphasizes* that creditors and debtors must share responsibility for preventing unsustainable debt situations;

5. *Underlines* the fact that the long-term sustainability of debt depends, inter alia, on the economic growth, mobilization of domestic resources and export prospects of debtor countries and, hence, on the creation of an enabling environment conducive to development, progress in following sound macroeconomic policies, transparent and effective regulatory frameworks and success in overcoming structural development problems;

6. *Reiterates its call upon* developed countries, as expressed in the Millennium Declaration, to complete the enhanced programme of debt relief for the Heavily Indebted Poor Countries Initiative and to ensure that it is fully financed, and in this regard underscores the importance of full participation by creditors in contributing their share to implementing the enhanced Heavily Indebted Poor Countries Initiative;

7. *Recognizes and encourages* the efforts of the heavily indebted poor countries, calls upon them to continue to improve their domestic policies and economic management, inter alia, through poverty reduction strategies, and to create a domestic environment conducive to private-sector development, economic growth and

poverty reduction, including a stable macroeconomic framework, transparent and accountable systems of public finance, a sound business climate and a predictable investment climate, and in this regard invites all creditors, both private and public, to encourage those efforts, for example, through further participation in the delivery of debt relief in the framework of the enhanced Heavily Indebted Poor Countries Initiative and continued provision of adequate and sufficiently concessional financing by international financing institutions and the donor community;

8. *Stresses* that debt relief can play a key role in liberating resources that should be directed towards activities consistent with poverty eradication, sustained economic growth and sustainable development and the achievement of the internationally agreed development goals, including the Millennium Development Goals, and in this regard urges countries to direct those resources freed through debt relief, in particular through debt cancellation and reduction, towards these objectives;

9. *Reiterates* that debt sustainability depends on a confluence of many factors at the international and national levels, emphasizes that country-specific circumstances and the impact of external shocks should be taken into account in debt sustainability analyses, underscores the fact that no single indicator should be used to make definitive judgements about debt sustainability, and in this regard, while acknowledging the need to use transparent and comparable indicators, invites the International Monetary Fund and the World Bank, in their assessment of debt sustainability, to take into account fundamental changes caused by, inter alia, natural disasters, conflicts, changes in global growth prospects or in the terms of trade, especially for commodity-dependent developing countries, and to continue to provide information on this issue using existing cooperation forums, including those involving Member States;

10. *Reiterates also* its invitation to the World Bank and the International Monetary Fund to keep the overall implications of the debt sustainability framework for low-income countries under review, calls for transparency in the computation of the country policy and institutional assessments, and welcomes the intention to disclose the country performance ratings of the International Development Association that form part of the framework;

11. *Welcomes* the Gleneagles proposal by the Group of Eight, as endorsed by the Bretton Woods institutions at their 2005 annual meetings, to cancel 100 per cent of the debt owed by heavily indebted poor countries to the International Monetary Fund, the International Development Association and the African Development Fund and their emphasis that it should be expeditiously implemented by the concerned multilateral financial institutions, also welcomes their efforts to proceed with steps to ensure all necessary arrangements to implement the proposal and ensure that the funds for this process are fully additional to existing aid commitments to the International Development Association and the African Development Fund, looks forward to the remaining heavily indebted poor countries with unsustainable debt burdens, including countries that may enter the Heavily Indebted Poor Countries Initiative process based on their debt burdens at the end of 2004, becoming eligible for such treatment as they reach the completion point, emphasizes that the key element of the proposal is that debt relief will be fully financed by donors to ensure that the financing capacity of international financial institutions is not reduced, and in particular that the financial integrity and capacity of the International Development Association and the African Development Bank to assist developing countries in the future is maintained, and also emphasizes the importance of eligible countries maintaining sound economic policies and performance;

12. *Notes with concern* that, in spite of the progress achieved, some countries that have reached the completion point of the Heavily Indebted Poor Countries Initiative have not been able to achieve lasting debt sustainability, stresses the importance of promoting responsible borrowing and lending and the need to help those countries to manage their borrowing and to avoid a build-up of unsustainable debt, including through the use of grants, and in this regard welcomes the ongoing work by the International Monetary Fund and the World Bank to develop a forward-looking debt sustainability framework for heavily indebted poor countries and low-income countries;

13. *Welcomes* the continued flexibility with regard to the application of eligibility criteria for the enhanced Heavily Indebted Poor Countries Initiative, in particular for low-income developing countries emerging from conflicts and/or affected by natural disasters, and on the computational procedures and assumptions underlying debt sustainability analysis, and in this regard takes note of the work on identifying low-income countries with unsustainable debt as of the end of 2004, with a view to finalization, by early 2006, of the list of countries potentially eligible for assistance under the Heavily Indebted Poor Countries Initiative;

14. *Emphasizes* that the Evian approach of the Paris Club, decided upon by creditors in October 2003, deals with the bilateral debt of non-heavily indebted poor countries and low- and middle-income countries, taking into account not only the financing gaps but also the medium-term debt sustainability of these countries, and welcomes the fact that its objective is to tailor debt restructuring to the financial needs of the country concerned and to ensure long-lasting debt sustainability for countries that have adopted policies that will secure an exit from Paris Club debt reschedulings;

15. *Calls upon* creditor countries, in this regard, to continue to ensure that a tailored response to debt restructuring is granted only in a case of imminent default and is not considered by debtor countries as an alternative to more expensive sources of finance, and takes into account country-specific circumstances, financial vulnerabilities and the objective of enhancing long-lasting debt sustainability, while emphasizing that creditors and debtors must share responsibility for preventing and resolving unsustainable debt situations in a timely and efficient manner;

16. *Acknowledges* the ongoing work towards a more comprehensive approach to sovereign debt restructuring, supports the increasing inclusion of collective action clauses in international bond issuing, takes note of the work on issues related to international arbitra-

tion and mediation mechanisms, and welcomes the efforts by borrowing countries and private-sector creditors to broaden the consensus on the Principles for Stable Capital Flows and Fair Debt Restructuring in Emerging Markets, which could contribute to strengthening crisis prevention and enhancing predictability of crisis management, bearing in mind the need not to preclude emergency financing in times of crisis, to promote fair burden-sharing and to minimize moral hazard;

17. *Stresses* the need to find a solution for the debt problems of low- and middle-income developing countries with unsustainable debt burdens that are not eligible for assistance under the Heavily Indebted Poor Countries Initiative, and in this regard invites creditors and debtors to continue to use, where appropriate and on a case-by-case basis, mechanisms such as debt swaps for alleviating their debt burden, and also stresses that this should be achieved in a fashion that does not detract from official development assistance resources, while maintaining the financial integrity of the multilateral financial institutions;

18. *Takes note* of the recent discussions and assessment by the Paris Club of the proposal for "Debt for Equity in Millennium Development Goal Projects";

19. *Invites* donor countries, taking into account country-specific debt sustainability analyses, to continue their efforts to increase bilateral grants to developing countries, which could contribute to debt sustainability in the medium to long term, and recognizes the need for countries to be able to invest, inter alia, in health and education while maintaining debt sustainability;

20. *Welcomes* the efforts of the international community to provide flexibility, and stresses the need to continue those efforts in helping post-conflict developing countries, especially those that are heavily indebted and poor, to achieve initial reconstruction for economic and social development;

21. *Welcomes also* the efforts by creditors to provide flexibility to developing countries affected by natural disasters on a case-by-case basis so as to allow them to address their debt concerns;

22. *Welcomes further* the efforts of, and further calls upon, the international community to support institutional capacity-building in developing countries and countries with economies in transition for the management of financial assets and liabilities and to enhance sustainable debt management as an integral part of national development strategies;

23. *Invites* the United Nations Conference on Trade and Development, the International Monetary Fund and the World Bank, in cooperation with the regional commissions, development banks and other relevant multilateral financial institutions, to continue cooperation in respect of capacity-building activities in developing countries in the area of debt management;

24. *Calls upon* all Member States and the United Nations system, and invites the Bretton Woods institutions as well as the private sector, to take appropriate measures and actions for the implementation of the commitments, agreements and decisions of the major United Nations conferences and summits, in particular those related to the question of the external debt problems of developing countries;

25. *Takes note* of the contribution provided by the multi-stakeholder dialogues on sovereign debt organized by the Financing for Development Office of the Department of Economic and Social Affairs of the Secretariat;

26. *Requests* the Secretary-General to submit to the General Assembly at its sixty-first session a report on the implementation of the present resolution and to include in that report a comprehensive and substantive analysis of the external debt and debt-servicing problems of developing countries;

27. *Decides* to include in the provisional agenda of its sixty-first session, under the item entitled "Macroeconomic policy questions", the sub-item entitled "External debt crisis and development".

Financing for development

Follow-up to the International Conference on Financing for Development

High-level meeting of the Economic and Social Council, Bretton Woods institutions, WTO and UNCTAD. In accordance with Economic and Social Council **decision 2005/211** of 1 March, the eighth special high-level meeting of the Council, the Bretton Woods institutions (the World Bank Group and IMF), WTO and UNCTAD was held in New York on 18 April. The meeting addressed the theme of coherence, coordination and cooperation in the context of the implementation of the Monterrey Consensus: achieving the internationally agreed development goals, including those contained in the Millennium Declaration. Before it was a note by the Secretary-General on the subject [E/2005/50], providing information and raising a number of questions on three subthemes: policies and strategies; trade, investment and private flows; and official development assistance (ODA), innovative sources of financing and debt.

The Council President, in his summary of the proceedings [A/59/823-E/2005/69], noted the participants' emphasis on the importance of a national development strategy towards achieving the MDGs. Such a strategy should be formulated within the country and respond to its specific needs and circumstances. The key role of an adequate policy space in formulating policy orientations was also emphasized. Governments needed to evaluate the trade-off between the benefits of accepting international rules and commitments and the constraints posed by a reduced policy space. It was necessary to pursue an appropriate balance between national policy orientations and international disciplines and commitments. As to policies and multilateral trade negotiations, it was agreed that international trade could make a substantial contribution to financing for development, the critical elements of which were: improved market access for developing countries in agriculture, manufactures and services; elimination of trade-distorting non-tariff barriers; and the provision of adequate preferential and differential treatment. Participants underscored the need to generate a favourable environment for business that included an adequate regulatory environment, rule of law, respect for property rights, transparency and an enabling infrastructure, as well as the need to adopt the appropriate kind of prudential regulations in developing countries. Concern was expressed about the stability of international private financial flows. Regarding the level and quality of ODA, the meeting considered that a rapid increase in aid flows was necessary and that for aid to be effective, recipient countries should receive more predictable, long-term, unconditional ODA that would allow them to better integrate aid flows into the design of their development strategy. The special aid needs of fragile countries were recognized.

By **decision 2005/224** of 19 July, the Economic and Social Council took note of the Secretary-General's note on coherence, coordination and cooperation in the context of the implementation of the Monterrey Consensus and of the summary, by the Council President, of the special high-level meeting of the Council, the Bretton Woods institutions, WTO and UNCTAD.

Reports of Secretary-General. In response to General Assembly resolution 59/225 [YUN 2004, p. 981], the Secretary-General submitted a September report [A/60/289] on follow-up to and implementation of the outcome of the International Conference on Financing for Development [YUN 2002, p. 953], providing updated information on the comprehensive review of the implementation of the Monterrey Consensus and reaffirming the policy actions contained in the Secretary-General's report prepared for the High-level Dialogue on Financing for Development [A/59/822] (see below); and a note on coherence, coordination and cooperation in the context of the implementation of the Monterrey Consensus: achieving the internationally agreed development goals, including those contained in the Millennium Declaration [E/2005/50] (see p. 1060), and the *World Economic and Social Survey 2005* (see p. 1052). The report considered measures to increase international financial and technical cooperation for development; proposals on external debt relief; progress in achieving the development dimension of the Doha round of WTO trade negotiations; and enhancing the coherence and consistency of the international monetary, financial and trading systems in support of development.

In an August report [A/60/289/Add.1], the Secretary-General reviewed multistakeholder consultations held in the second half of 2004 and the first half of 2005 to examine issues related to the mobilization of resources for financing development and to promote best practices and exchange of information on the implementation of the International Conference on Financing for Development. The consultations covered: building inclusive financial sectors for development; sovereign debt for sustained development; public-private partnerships for improving the reach and effectiveness of development assistance; improving the climate for private investment; and enhancing the coherence and consistency of the international financial, monetary and trading systems in support of development.

GENERAL ASSEMBLY ACTION

On 22 December [meeting 68], the General Assembly, on the recommendation of the Second Committee [A/60/487], adopted **resolution 60/188** without vote [agenda item 51].

Follow-up to and implementation of the outcome of the International Conference on Financing for Development

The General Assembly,

Recalling the International Conference on Financing for Development, held in Monterrey, Mexico, from 18 to 22 March 2002, and its resolutions 56/210 B of 9 July 2002, 57/250 of 20 December 2002, 57/270 B of 23 June 2003, 57/272 and 57/273 of 20 December 2002, 58/230 of 23 December 2003 and 59/225 of 22 December 2004, as well as Economic and Social Council resolutions 2002/34 of 26 July 2002, 2003/47 of 24 July 2003 and 2004/64 of 16 September 2004,

Taking note of the reports of the Secretary-General on the follow-up to and implementation of the outcome of the International Conference on Financing for Development, prepared in collaboration with the major institutional stakeholders,

Taking note also of other relevant reports of the Secretary-General on the follow-up to and implementation of the outcome of the International Conference on Financing for Development,

Having considered the *World Economic and Social Survey 2005: Financing for Development,*

Recalling the 2005 World Summit Outcome,

Having considered the summary by the President of the Economic and Social Council of the special high-level meeting of the Council with the Bretton Woods institutions, the World Trade Organization and the United Nations Conference on Trade and Development, held in New York on 18 April 2005,

Welcoming the High-level Dialogue on Financing for Development held in New York on 27 and 28 June 2005 and the separate meeting on financing for development held within the framework of the High-level Plenary Meeting of the General Assembly on 14 September 2005,

Having considered the summary by the President of the General Assembly of the High-level Dialogue on Financing for Development,

Reaffirming the commitment to the global partnership for development set out in the United Nations Millennium Declaration, the Monterrey Consensus of the International Conference on Financing for Development, the Plan of Implementation of the World Summit on Sustainable Development ("Johannesburg Plan of Implementation") and the 2005 World Summit Outcome,

Reaffirming also that each country must take primary responsibility for its own development and that the role of national policies and development strategies cannot be overemphasized for the achievement of sustainable development, and recognizing that national efforts should be complemented by supportive global programmes, measures and policies aimed at expanding the development opportunities of developing countries, while taking into account national conditions and ensuring respect for national ownership, strategies and sovereignty,

Recognizing the ongoing international efforts, contributions and discussions, such as the Action against Hunger and Poverty initiative, aimed at identifying and developing possible innovative and additional sources of financing for development from all sources, public and private, domestic and external, to increase and supplement traditional sources of financing within the context of the follow-up to the International Conference on Financing for Development, recognizing that some of the sources and their use fall within the realm of sovereign action,

Underlining that the increasing interdependence of national economies in a globalizing world and the emergence of rule-based regimes for international economic relations have meant that the space for national economic policy, that is, the scope for domestic policies, especially in the areas of trade, investment and industrial development, is now often framed by international disciplines, commitments and global market considerations; that it is for each Government to evaluate the trade-off between the benefits of accepting international rules and commitments and the constraints posed by the loss of policy space; and that it is particularly important for developing countries, bearing in mind development goals and objectives, that all countries take into account the need for appropriate balance between national policy space and international disciplines and commitments,

Reiterating the need to implement fully and build further on the commitments made and agreements reached at the International Conference on Financing for Development, and recognizing the strong link between financing for development and the achievement of the internationally agreed development goals, including the Millennium Development Goals,

Welcoming the recent decisions, commitments and proposals made in this regard to implement and build on the commitments made and agreements reached at the International Conference on Financing for Development,

1. *Underlines*, in accordance with the Monterrey Consensus:

(*a*) The importance of the implementation of the commitment to sound policies, good governance at all levels and the rule of law;

(*b*) The importance of the implementation of the commitment to create an enabling environment for mobilizing domestic resources and the importance of sound economic policies, solid democratic institutions responsive to the needs of the people and improved infrastructure as a basis for sustained economic growth, poverty eradication and employment creation;

(*c*) The importance, in order to complement national development efforts, of the implementation of the commitment to enhance the coherence and consistency of international monetary, financial and trading systems;

2. *Welcomes* the efforts by developing countries to adopt and implement national development strategies to achieve their national development priorities as well as the internationally agreed development goals and objectives, including the Millennium Development Goals; reaffirms the resolve, for those countries that have not yet done so, to adopt such strategies by 2006 and implement them; and also reaffirms the resolve to support these efforts as set out in the 2005 World Summit Outcome, including through increased resources;

3. *Stresses* the importance of a universal, rule-based, open, non-discriminatory and equitable multilateral trading system, as well as meaningful trade liberalization, that can substantially stimulate development worldwide, benefiting countries at all stages of development; in that regard reaffirms its commitment to trade liberalization and to ensuring that trade plays its full part in promoting economic growth, employment and development for all; thus welcomes the decisions of the World Trade Organization to place the needs and interests of developing countries at the heart of its work programme and commits itself to their implementation; and in this regard emphasizes the importance of fulfilling the development dimension of the Doha work programme and the successful completion of the Doha round as soon as possible;

4. *Notes* that, while foreign direct investment is a major source of financing development, the flow of such funds to developing countries and countries with economies in transition remains uneven, and in this regard calls upon developed countries to continue to devise source-country measures to encourage and facilitate the flow of foreign direct investment, inter alia, through the provision of export credits and other lending instruments, risk guarantees and business development services, and calls upon developing countries and countries with economies in transition to continue their efforts to create a conducive domestic environment for attracting investments by, inter alia, achieving a transparent, stable and predictable investment climate with proper contract enforcement and respect for property rights;

5. *Reaffirms* the Monterrey Consensus and recognizes that mobilizing financial resources for development and the effective use of those resources in developing countries and countries with economies in transition are central to a global partnership for development in support of the achievement of the internationally agreed development goals, including the Millennium Development Goals. In this regard:

(a) Welcomes the increased resources that will become available as a result of the establishment of timetables by many developed countries to achieve the target of 0.7 per cent of gross national product for official development assistance by 2015 and to reach at least 0.5 per cent of gross national product for official development assistance by 2010, as well as, pursuant to the Brussels Programme of Action for the Least Developed Countries for the Decade 2001-2010, 0.15 per cent to 0.20 per cent for the least developed countries by no later than 2010, and urges those developed countries that have not yet done so to make concrete efforts in this regard in accordance with their commitments;

(b) Recognizes the importance of official development assistance as a major source of financing development for many developing countries; stresses the need to translate increases in official development assistance into real increases in resources for national development strategies to achieve the national development priorities of developing countries as well as the internationally agreed development goals and objectives, including the Millennium Development Goals, taking into account the need for resource predictability, including budget support mechanisms where appropriate; welcomes recent efforts and initiatives to enhance the quality of aid and increase its impact, including the Paris Declaration on Aid Effectiveness; resolves to take concrete, effective and timely action to implement all agreed commitments on aid effectiveness, with clear monitoring and deadlines, including through further aligning assistance with countries' strategies, building institutional capacities, reducing transaction costs and eliminating bureaucratic procedures, making progress on untying aid, enhancing the absorptive capacity and financial management of recipient countries and strengthening the focus of development results; and encourages the broadest possible participation of developing countries in future work on aid effectiveness;

(c) Recognizes the importance of developing innovative sources of financing for development, provided that such sources do not unduly burden developing countries; notes that some countries will launch the International Financial Facility, some countries have launched the Facility's immunization pilot and some countries, utilizing their national authorities, will implement in the near future a contribution on airline tickets as a "solidarity contribution" to enable financing for development projects; and notes that other countries are considering whether and to what extent they will participate in those initiatives;

(d) Recognizes the progress achieved in this regard, and decides to give further consideration to the subject of innovative development financing from all sources, public and private, domestic and external;

(e) Emphasizes the importance of microcredit and microfinance in the eradication of poverty; highlights that the observance of the International Year of Microcredit 2005 has provided a significant opportunity to raise awareness, share best practices and further enhance financial sectors that support sustainable pro-poor financial services in all countries; in this regard urges member countries to put best practices into action; and invites the international community, including the United Nations system, to build on the momentum created by the Year;

(f) Acknowledges the vital role that the private sector can play in generating new investments, employment and financing for development;

6. *Stresses* the importance of investments in basic economic and social infrastructure, as set out in the Monterrey Consensus; notes that scaling up investment in infrastructure, alongside strong programmes for health and education, is a key element for faster growth and progress in reducing poverty; in this regard, calls for continued deepening and scaling up of support for infrastructure service delivery and removal of impediments in order to respond to the needs of developing countries, consistent with national development strategies; welcomes the progress made by the World Bank Group to strengthen public-private partnerships to leverage investment and maximize impact, including in the framework of the newly established Africa Infrastructure Consortium; and acknowledges the work of the World Bank in this area, including plans for a progress report to the Development Committee on the impact of fiscal space on growth and the achievement of the Millennium Development Goals;

7. *Emphasizes* the great importance of a timely, effective, comprehensive and durable solution to the debt problems of developing countries since debt financing and relief can be an important source of capital for economic growth and development, and also emphasizes that creditors and debtors must share responsibilities for preventing unsustainable debt situations;

8. *Welcomes,* in this regard, the recent proposal of the Group of Eight as endorsed by the Bretton Woods institutions at their 2005 annual meetings to cancel 100 per cent of the outstanding debt of eligible heavily indebted poor countries owed to the International Monetary Fund, the International Development Association and the African Development Fund, and to provide additional resources to ensure that the financing capacity of the international financial institutions is not reduced;

9. *Emphasizes* that corruption at all levels is a serious barrier to development and to effective resource mobilization and allocation; reaffirms the commitment expressed in the Monterrey Consensus to make the fight against corruption at all levels a priority; in this regard welcomes the entry into force on 14 December 2005 of the United Nations Convention against Corruption; and reiterates its invitation to all Member States and competent regional economic integration organizations, within the limits of their competence, to ratify or accede to and fully implement the Convention as soon as possible;

10. *Recognizes* the work of the Financing for Development Office of the Secretariat in organizing, within its mandate, workshops, multi-stakeholder consultations, panel discussions and other activities aimed at better enabling member countries to implement their commitments as agreed in the Monterrey Consensus, and requests the Office, in collaboration with experts from the public and private sectors, academia and civil society, to continue its work in this area;

11. *Reiterates its request* to the Secretary-General to consult with the Director-General of the World Trade Organization in order to expand existing cooperation between the two organizations on issues related to fi-

nancing for development and to build on the ad hoc modalities of interaction between the United Nations and the World Trade Organization that were undertaken in the preparations for the International Conference on Financing for Development held in 2002 by making better use of the possibilities offered by the existing framework of cooperation;

12. *Decides* in accordance with paragraph 73 of the Monterrey Consensus to hold a follow-up international conference on financing for development to review the implementation of the Consensus at a time between 2008 and 2009;

13. *Welcomes* the offer of the Government of Qatar to host the conference;

14. *Decides* that, in line with General Assembly resolution 57/270 B, the review conference should assess progress made; reaffirm goals and commitments; share best practices and lessons learned; and identify obstacles and constraints encountered, actions and initiatives to overcome them and important measures for further implementation, as well as new challenges and emerging issues;

15. *Also decides* to commence the preparatory process, including a decision on the exact date of the conference, at its sixty-first session;

16. *Resolves* to continue to make full use of the existing institutional arrangements for reviewing the implementation of the Monterrey Consensus, as set out in paragraph 69 of the Consensus and in line with resolution 57/270 B, including the high-level dialogues convened by the General Assembly and the spring meetings of the Economic and Social Council with the Bretton Woods institutions, the World Trade Organization and the United Nations Conference on Trade and Development;

17. *Stresses* the importance of the full involvement of all relevant stakeholders in the implementation of the Monterrey Consensus at all levels, and also stresses the importance of their full participation in the Monterrey follow-up process, in accordance with the rules of procedure of the General Assembly, in particular the accreditation procedures and modalities of participation utilized at the Conference and in its preparatory process;

18. *Decides* to include in the provisional agenda of its sixty-first session the item entitled "Follow-up to and implementation of the outcome of the International Conference on Financing for Development", and requests the Secretary-General to submit under that item an annual analytical assessment of the state of implementation of the Monterrey Consensus and of the present resolution, to be prepared in full collaboration with the major institutional stakeholders.

High-level Dialogue on Financing for Development

On 27 May [meeting 98], the General Assembly adopted **resolution 59/293** [draft: A/59/L.61] without vote [agenda item 84].

Modalities for the High-level Dialogue on Financing for Development

The General Assembly,

Recalling its resolution 57/250 of 20 December 2002,

Recalling also its resolution 59/145 of 17 December 2004, in which it decided to hold the High-level Dialogue on Financing for Development on 27 and 28 June 2005 in New York, and resolution 59/225 of 22 December 2004, in which it decided to consider, by the first part of 2005, the appropriate modalities for holding the High-level Dialogue, taking into account developments in the preparation for the High-level Plenary Meeting of the General Assembly to be held from 14 to 16 September 2005,

Recalling further its resolution 59/291 of 15 April 2005,

Bearing in mind that the results of the High-level Dialogue will be an input to the preparatory process for the High-level Plenary Meeting,

1. *Reiterates* that the High-level Dialogue on Financing for Development to be held on 27 and 28 June 2005 will be held at the ministerial level;

2. *Reaffirms* that the High-level Dialogue constitutes the intergovernmental focal point for the general follow-up to the International Conference on Financing for Development, held at Monterrey, Mexico, from 18 to 22 March 2002;

3. *Decides* that the overall theme of the High-level Dialogue will be "The Monterrey Consensus: status of implementation and tasks ahead";

4. *Decides also* that the High-level Dialogue will consist of a series of formal and informal meetings to constitute a policy dialogue and six interactive multi-stakeholder round tables to be held as follows:

(a) The first day will consist of a formal meeting chaired by the President of the General Assembly, at which the ministers and high-level officials attending the Dialogue will be able to make formal statements, on the understanding that the principle of precedence will be strictly applied, to allow participation at the ministerial level; the Secretary-General, the President of the Economic and Social Council, the President of the World Bank, the Managing Director of the International Monetary Fund, the Director-General of the World Trade Organization, the Secretary-General of the United Nations Conference on Trade and Development and the Administrator of the United Nations Development Programme, as the Chairman of the United Nations Development Group, will be invited to make statements;

(b) The second day will be devoted to six interactive multi-stakeholder round tables, divided into two sessions, each comprising three round tables, followed by an interactive dialogue in the form of an informal meeting with the participation of all relevant stakeholders, which will focus on the implementation of the results of the International Conference on Financing for Development and the link between financing for development and the achievement of the internationally agreed development goals, including those contained in the United Nations Millennium Declaration; the heads of relevant organizations of the United Nations system, the heads of regional and international intergovernmental organs that participated in the International Conference, as well as representatives of regional development banks, civil society and the business sector, will all be able to intervene, on the understanding that the principle of precedence will be strictly applied, to allow participation at the ministerial level;

5. *Decides further* that the central themes of the round tables will be based on sections of one chapter of the Monterrey Consensus adopted at the International Conference on Financing for Development, as follows:

Round table 1: Mobilizing domestic financial resources for development;

Round table 2: Mobilizing international resources for development–foreign direct investment and other private flows;

Round table 3: International trade as an engine for development;

Round table 4: Increasing international financial and technical cooperation for development;

Round table 5: External debt;

Round table 6: Addressing systemic issues–enhancing the coherence and consistency of the international monetary, financial and trading systems in support of development;

6. *Reiterates its invitation* to all Governments to enhance coordination among ministries of foreign affairs, finance, development cooperation and trade, as well as central banks and all other national stakeholders for the preparations for the High-level Dialogue;

7. *Invites* the Bretton Woods institutions, the World Trade Organization and relevant organizations of the United Nations system to participate in the High-level Dialogue, including in the preparatory phase, and invites the President of the Economic and Social Council, the President of the World Bank, the Managing Director of the International Monetary Fund, the Director-General of the World Trade Organization and the heads of other relevant regional and international intergovernmental organs to participate actively in the Dialogue;

8. *Invites* non-governmental organizations and business sector entities to participate at the interactive round tables and informal meetings of the High-level Dialogue, in accordance with the rules of procedure of the General Assembly, and decides that:

(a) Accreditation will be open to all non-governmental organizations that are in consultative status with the Economic and Social Council and to all non-governmental organizations and business sector entities accredited to the International Conference on Financing for Development or to its follow-up process;

(b) Interested non-governmental organizations and business sector entities that are not in consultative status with the Economic and Social Council or were not accredited to the International Conference on Financing for Development shall apply to the General Assembly for accreditation following the accreditation procedure established during the International Conference;

(c) The above arrangements concerning participation of non-governmental organizations and business sector entities in the High-level Dialogue will in no way create a precedent for other meetings of the General Assembly;

9. *Decides* that all issues regarding financing for development will be discussed during the informal interactive hearings, to be held on 23 and 24 June 2005, with representatives of non-governmental organizations, civil society organizations and the private sector, and requests the Secretariat to issue a summary of the hearings related to financing for development as an input to the High-level Dialogue;

10. *Requests* the Secretary-General to submit a report on the implementation of commitments and agreements reached at the International Conference on Financing for Development, to be prepared in full collaboration with the major institutional stakeholders, as an input to the High-level Dialogue;

11. *Also requests* the Secretary-General to prepare a note on the organization of work of the High-level Dialogue;

12. *Further requests* the Secretary-General to seek from the regional commissions their inputs on the regional and interregional aspects of the follow-up to the International Conference on Financing for Development and to report thereon to the High-level Dialogue;

13. *Requests* the Secretary-General to make available at the High-level Dialogue relevant inputs related to financing for development from all stakeholders, including the documents of the Economic and Social Council covering its 2005 special high-level meeting with the Bretton Woods institutions, the World Trade Organization and the United Nations Conference on Trade and Development;

14. *Reiterates its invitation* to countries to report by 2005, inter alia, through existing reporting mechanisms, on their efforts to implement the Monterrey Consensus, bearing in mind the need to achieve the internationally agreed development goals, including those contained in the Millennium Declaration;

15. *Decides* that the High-level Dialogue will result in a summary by the President of the General Assembly that will provide an input on financing for development to the preparatory process of the High-level Plenary Meeting of the General Assembly of September 2005.

In response to the Assembly's request, the Secretary-General submitted a June note [A/59/850] on the proposed organization of work of the High-level Dialogue.

In response to Assembly resolutions 59/145 [YUN 2004, p. 1364] and 59/293 (see above), the second High-level Dialogue on Financing for Development was held in New York on 27 and 28 June, under the overall theme "The Monterrey Consensus: status of implementation and tasks ahead". The High-level Dialogue, attended by Member States, institutional stakeholders, NGOs and business sector entities, consisted of a series of plenary and informal meetings to constitute a policy dialogue and of six interactive multi-stakeholder round tables on: mobilizing domestic financial resources for development; mobilizing international resources for development: FDI and other private flows; international trade as an engine for development; increasing international financial and technical cooperation for development; external debt; and addressing systemic issues: enhancing the coherence and consistency of the international monetary, financial and trading systems in support of development.

The High-level Dialogue had before it a Secretary-General report on the subject [A/59/822]; the Council President's summary of the high-level meeting of the Council, the Bretton Woods institutions, WTO and UNCTAD [A/59/823-E/2005/69] (see above); a Secretariat summary of the informal interactive hearings on issues related to financing for development [A/59/855], held in New York on 23 June; and a note by the Secretary-General [A/59/826] on implementation of the Monterrey Consensus, containing a review of the regional and interregional aspects of the follow-up to the International Conference on Financing for Development, prepared by the five regional commissions in compliance with resolution 59/293 (see above), and analysing the regional dimension in the implementation of the Monterrey Consensus; policies and measures to fulfil the commitments; and interregional aspects of the follow-up. It also had before the Secretary-General's May report on strengthening the role of the private sector and entrepreneurship in financing for development [A/59/800], prepared in response to Economic and Social Council resolution 2004/64 [YUN 2004, p. 979].

In August, the President of the Assembly prepared a summary of the High-level Dialogue [A/60/219] (see p. 67), which reviewed statements made by ministers and other high-level officials and which was to provide an input on financing for development to the preparatory process of the High-level Plenary Meeting of the Assembly (see p. 47).

Investment, technology and related financial issues

The UNCTAD Commission on Investment, Technology and Related Financial Issues held its ninth session in Geneva from 7 to 11 March [TD/B/COM.2/66].

For its consideration of policy issues related to investment and development, the Commission considered an UNCTAD secretariat note on emerging foreign direct investment (FDI) from developing countries [TD/B/COM.2/64]; the report of the Expert Meeting on Good Governance in Investment Promotion [YUN 2004, p. 984]; the report of the Expert Meeting on the Impact of FDI on Development [TD/B/ COM.2/EM.16/3]; and the *World Investment Report 2004: The Shift towards Services* [UNCTAD/WIR/ 2004]. For issues related to investment arrangements, the Commission had before it the UNCTAD secretariat note on the subject: Investor-State disputes and policy implications [TD/B/ COM.2/62]; a secretariat report on work undertaken under its work programme on international investment agreements in 2004 [UNCTAD/ ITE/IIT/2004/Misc.15/Rev.I]; the UN publication: Investor-State Dispute Settlement; and the UNCTAD Series on Issues on International In-

vestment Agreements [Sales No. E.00.II]. For its consideration of investment policy reviews (IPRs): exchange of national experiences, the Commission had before it a summary of deliberations on the issue by Algeria, Benin and Sri Lanka [TD/B/COM.2/65]. For its consideration of the implementation of its agreed conclusions and recommendations, including post-Doha follow-up, the Commission considered a progress report on the implementation of recommendations by the UNCTAD secretariat [TD/B/COM.2/63] and the 2004 Activities Report of the Division on Investment, Technology and Enterprise Development [UNCTAD/ITE/2005/1]. The Commission took note of the secretariat's progress report.

The Commission, in agreed recommendations, urged UNCTAD to continue its work on FDI and transnational corporations (TNCs) and their impact on development; further analyse emerging global and regional trends in FDI and their policy implications, especially in the context of South-South cooperation; and follow up on the work undertaken on FDI in services and support, in cooperation with other relevant international agencies, developing countries, especially LDCs in enhancing their FDI data collection and analysis capacity. It should also continue its work on international investment and technology transfer arrangements, with emphasis on bilateral and regional dimensions. Particular attention should be paid to monitoring emerging issues and developments, including in the field of investor-State dispute settlement. It recommended that the secretariat strengthen its programme on Good Governance in Investment Promotion and extend its assistance to more interested developing countries, in particular LDCs, in implementing measures to improve good governance in investment promotion.

The Commission noted that further support was needed to ensure that other countries also benefited from evaluations and improvement in their investment policy framework. Efforts should also be made to disseminate specific lessons arising from investment policy reviews and follow-up activities carried out by UNCTAD. The Commission welcomed the interaction with the World Association of Investment Promotion Agencies in supporting developing countries to attract beneficial FDI and encouraged the secretariat to enhance that cooperation. The Commission recommended that UNCTAD support country-level policy formulation and implementation, with a view to assisting countries in maximizing the benefits that FDI could bring to achieving the international development goals; assist developing countries in creating an enabling regulatory environment for public-private partnerships and investment in enterprises and projects providing basic services to the poor; assess ways in which developing countries could develop their domestic productive capability in the supply of essential drugs in cooperation with pharmaceutical companies; assist developing countries in promoting the application of science and technology in achieving the international development goals; and continue analytical work and the exchange of information and experiences in the area of positive corporate contributions to the social and economic development of host developing countries.

In May [A/60/15], TDB took note of the Commission's report and endorsed its recommendations.

Subsidiary bodies. In 2005, three expert meetings took place, all in Geneva. The Expert Meeting on the Impact of FDI on Development (24-26 January) [TD/B/COM.2/EM.16/3] considered an UNCTAD secretariat note on the globalization of research and development by TNCs and its implication for developing countries [TD/B/COM.2/EM.16/2]. The Meeting noted that, while most research and development activities remained in developed countries, developing countries were becoming more important as host and home countries of FDI in research and development. The Meeting identified a number of positive and negative impacts on host economies and concluded that active policies could create and facilitate the right conditions for countries to attract and benefit from FDI in research and development. Experts discussed the role of performance requirements in maximizing the benefits of research and development-related FDI in developing countries and the role of incentives in attracting it. They also addressed the role of home-country policies in encouraging TNCs to invest in research and development in developing countries, and, in the light of the importance of innovation and research and development for economic development, suggested that a list of indicators be created to assess and measure the contributions of TNCs to the transfer of technology to developing countries. The Experts also highlighted the need to explore the possibilities for the international community to support the strengthening of developing countries' national innovation systems.

The Expert Meeting on Positive Corporate Contributions to the Economic and Social Development of Host Developing Countries (31 October–2 November) [TD/B/COM.2/EM.17/3] had before it an UNCTAD secretariat note on the subject [TD/B/COM.2/EM.17/2]. The Meeting discussed investment in developing countries; provision of goods and services; employment creation, up-grading the skills of the local workforce and the creation of linkages; technology transfer, ethical business behaviour and minimizing the negative effects of business restructuring; and the role of policy. The Meeting suggested that UNCTAD provide a forum for dialogue between Governments, business and other development stakeholders to develop a common understanding of the role of business in development and to establish a common vision on how such a role could be enhanced through partnership among all stakeholders within the framework of the São Paulo Consensus [YUN 2002, p. 953]. UNCTAD should assess the effectiveness of existing practices in corporate contributions to development; help countries address issues related to the link between corporate contributions and development needs; and complement its work on corporate governance in the context of the Intergovernmental Group of Experts on International Standards of Accounting and Reporting.

The Expert Meeting on Capacity Building in the Area of FDI: Data Compilation and Policy Formulation in Developing Countries (12-14 December) [TD/B/COM.2/EM.18/3] had before it an UNCTAD secretariat note on FDI statistics: Data compilation and policy issues [TD/B/COM.2/EM.18/2]. The Meeting discussed key issues on FDI data compilation, analysis and policy formulation in developing countries and examined problems faced by those countries, particularly LDCs, in providing policy makers with timely and accurate FDI and TNC data that would enable them to design policies.

In its conclusions and recommendations, the Meeting stressed the need to collect reliable, accurate, timely and comparable statistical information on FDI and on the activities of TNCs, and to improve the data collecting and reporting systems of many developing countries to provide increased or enhanced information, including through international and regional cooperation. A mechanism should be established to enable developing and transition economies to submit data on FDI and the activities of TNCs to UNCTAD. UNCTAD could also play an expanded role in institutional capacity building in the field of FDI statistics. Experts called for more regional cooperation among relevant institutions in developing countries and economies in transition to promote a harmonized system for collecting and reporting statistics on FDI and TNCs and supported the creation of regional task forces. UNCTAD was asked to organize meetings on FDI statistics and policy formulation on a regular basis and to present the Expert Meeting's report to the UN Statistical Commission in 2007.

The Commission on Investment, Technology and Related Financial Issues, in March [TD/B/COM.2/66], took note of the report of the Expert Meeting on Good Governance in Investment Promotion [YUN 2004, p. 984] and the report of the Expert Meeting on the Impact of FDI on Development (see above).

Competition law and policy

The Intergovernmental Group of Experts on Competition Law and Policy did not meet in 2005. The Commission on Investment, Technology and Related Financial Issues, in March [TD/B/COM.2/66], took note of the report of the sixth (2004) session of the Group of Experts [YUN 2004, p. 984] and endorsed its agreed conclusions.

Fifth Review Conference

In accordance with General Assembly resolution 55/182 [YUN 2000, p. 895], the Fifth United Nations Conference to Review All Aspects of the Set of Multilaterally Agreed Equitable Principles and Rules for the Control of Restrictive Business Practices (known as the Set) was held in Antalya, Turkey from 14 to 18 November [TD/RBP/CONF.6/15]. It had before it three UNCTAD secretariat notes on the handbook on competition legislation [TD/RBP/CONF.6/2], a synthesis of recent cartel investigations [TD/RBP/CONF.6/4] and the review of capacity-building and technical assistance on competition law and policy [TD/RBP/CONF.6/6]; and two UNCTAD secretariat reports on presentation of types of common provisions to be found in international, particularly bilateral and regional, cooperation agreements on competition policy and their application [TD/RBP/CONF.6/3] and recent important cases involving more than one country [TD/RBP/CONF.6/5]. It also had before it two voluntary peer reviews on competition policy: Jamaica [TD/RBP/CONF.6/7] and Kenya [TD/RBP/CONF.6/8]; a report on ways in which possible international agreements on competition might apply to developing countries [TD/RBP/CONF.6/9]; an assessment of the application and implementation of the Set [TD/RBP/CONF.6/10]; an UNCTAD secretariat revised report on experiences gained on international cooperation on competition policy issues and the mechanisms used [TD/RBP/CONF.6/12]; an UNCTAD secretariat study on best practices for defining respective competencies and settling of cases which involved joint action of competition authorities and regulatory bodies [TD/RBP/CONF.6/13]; and an UNCTAD secretariat revised study on roles of possible dispute mediation mechanisms and alternative arrangements [TD/RBP/CONF.6/11].

By an 18 November resolution, the Conference, reaffirming the role of competition law and policy for economic development and the validity of the Set, called upon States to implement fully the provisions of the Set; increase cooperation between their competition authorities and Governments in order to strengthen international action against anticompetitive practices as covered by the Set; and assist UNCTAD in its technical cooperation by providing experts, training facilities or resources. It recommended that the Assembly convene the Sixth Conference in 2010; UNCTAD continue to work on the subjects indicated by the Fourth Conference and monitor trends and developments in the competition law and policy area; assist developing countries in their efforts to adopt competition laws and policies, establish competition authorities to tailor the laws and policies to their development needs; and facilitate stronger international cooperation. UNCTAD should provide technical assistance, advisory and training services and revise the commentary to the Model Law in the light of legislative developments and comments made by States. The Conference invited States to assist UNCTAD in connection with voluntary peer reviews and decided that UNCTAD should undertake: further reviews on competition law and policy of member States or regional groupings of States, back-to-back with sessions of the Group of Experts on Competition Law and Policy; arrangements for the conduct of voluntary peer reviews back-to-back with investment policy reviews conducted by UNCTAD; deliberations on the scope, criteria and conduct of such reviews; and periodic assessment and synthesis of the main issues encountered by countries or regions reviewed in developing and implementing their competition laws and policies. It also recommended the strengthening of the UNCTAD work programme to address competition law and policy issues; and requested the UNCTAD secretariat to continue publishing issues of the Handbook on Competition Legislation and an updated version of the Directory of Competition Authorities, and prepare an information note on recent important competition cases. It also decided on issues for consideration by the 2006 session of the Intergovernmental Group of Experts on Competition Law and Policy.

International standards of accounting and reporting

The Intergovernmental Working Group of Experts on International Standards of Accounting and Reporting, at its twenty-second session (Geneva, 21-23 November) [TD/B/COM.2/ISAR/31], had before it an UNCTAD secretariat note on the review of practical implementation issues of international financial reporting standards [TD/B/COM.2/ISAR/28], and two reports on guidance on corporate responsibility indicators in annual reports [TD/B/COM.2/ISAR/29 & Corr.1] and on guidance on good practices in corporate governance disclosure [TD/B/COM.2/ISAR/30]. The Experts also considered the survey on the "2005 Review of the implementation status of corporate governance disclosures" [TD/B/COM.2/ISAR/CRP.1].

In its agreed conclusions, the Working Group reiterated the importance of a common set of principles-based and high-quality financial reporting standards in support of the coherence and consistency of the international financial system. It agreed that a number of practical implementation challenges needed to be addressed to assist developing countries and economies in transition in meeting internationally recognized standards, particularly in the area of institutional and technical capacity-building. The Group suggested that efforts were needed to ensure broader participation of developing countries and economies in transition in the global standard-setting process, and agreed that the reporting needs of non-listed companies small and medium-sized enterprises (SMEs) should be one of the priorities. It also agreed to conduct further reviews of the practical implementation challenges of international financial reporting standards.

With regard to the comparability of indicators on corporate responsibility, the Group recognized the need for harmonized reporting on corporate responsibility as an important issue in the area of corporate transparency and suggested that the UNCTAD secretariat should conduct a review of enterprise reporting practices based on selected indicators and that follow up work on measurement methodology for selected indicators should be conducted. On the issue of corporate governance disclosure, the Group recognized that the updated "Guidance on good practice in corporate governance disclosure" included important developments in good disclosure practices and contributed to the promotion of convergence of the content of corporate governance disclosure, and agreed that it could be a useful voluntary tool for promoting increased transparency and improved governance. Consideration should be given to carrying out further work on the practical implementation of some of the good practices outlined. On the issue of accounting by SMEs, the Group agreed that the secretariat should continue to disseminate guidance to level 2 and 3 SMEs, as well as monitor and compile feedback on their implementation and field-testing of the guidance for level 3 SMEs. With regard to the Model Curriculum, the Group encouraged cooperation and coordination between UNCTAD and the Education Committee of the International Federation of Accountants and requested UNCTAD to assist States in meeting international qualification requirements. As to environmental accounting, the UNCTAD secretariat was requested to continue disseminating the Group's work on environmental accounting and eco-efficiency indicators and to compile feedback on the implementation experience of entities that were implementing the manual for preparers and users of eco-efficiency indicators.

The Commission on Investment, Technology and Related Financial Issues, in March [TD/B/COM.2/66], took note of the Intergovernmental Working Group' report on its twenty-first (2004) session [YUN 2004, p. 985] and endorsed its agreed conclusions.

Taxation

The Economic and Social Council, by **decision 2005/311** of 27 July, deferred consideration of the sub-item on international cooperation in tax matters to its 2006 organizational session.

Pursuant to Council resolution 2004/69 [YUN 2004, p. 985], the first session of the Committee of Experts on International Cooperation in Tax Matters was held in Geneva from 5 to 9 December [E/2005/45-E/C.18/2005/11]. The session discussed treaty abuses and treaty shopping; mutual assistance in collecting tax debts; international tax arbitration; earnings stripping; taxation of income derived by participants in development projects; modified permanent establishment definition; revision of the United Nations Model Double Taxation Convention between Developed and Developing Countries; and review and adoption of the revised draft Manual for the Negotiation of Bilateral Tax Treaties between Developed and Developing Countries.

In its conclusions and recommendations, the Committee recognized that treaty abuse needed to be dealt with in the United Nations Model Convention. It agreed on the importance of ensuring a balance between the need to provide certainty for investors and the need for tax administrations to combat treaty abuse. Further consideration should be given to addressing methods to combat specific treaty abuse issues. The Committee agreed that the proposed draft of article 27 of the Model Convention should be adopted in its current form, with the Commentary containing examples of situations where countries could decide to broaden its application and reflect the concerns raised by developing countries with respect to capacity and constitutional and legal difficulties in relation to the proposed article. It appointed a subcommittee to develop proposals for updating article 27 for discussion at the Committee's next session and decided to collect all data available on alternative methods for avoiding or solving disputes. The Committee agreed that further consideration should be given to the tax regime applied to donor-sponsored development projects and requested IMF to present a report within the framework of the International Tax Dialogue. Further consideration should also be given to the definition of permanent establishment; a subcommittee should propose improvements in the Commentary on article 5 of the Model and also propose language to update the Model and the Commentary on article 26 and present a report on the status of implementation by other international organizations. The Committee decided that its second session would be held in 2006, and requested the preparation of a shorter, revised version of the Manual for consideration at that session. The Committee would continue to organize training workshops for developing countries to provide capacity-building and technical assistance.

Transport

Maritime transport

The Review of Maritime Transport, 2005 [Sales No. E.05.II.D.14] reported that world seaborne trade increased strongly in 2004, reaching a record high of 6.76 billions tons. The annual growth rate reached 4.3 per cent, well below the 5.8 per cent increase in 2003. The world merchant fleet expanded to 895.8 million deadweight tons (dwt) at the beginning of 2005, a 4.5 per cent increase over 2004. New building deliveries increased marginally to 49.4 million dwt, and tonnage broken up and lost was more than halved to 10.6 million dwt, leaving a net gain of 38.8 million dwt.

The fleets of oil tankers and dry bulk carriers, which together made up 73.3 per cent of the total world fleet, increased by 6.1 per cent and 4.2 per cent, respectively. There was an 8.4 per cent increase, from 90.5 to 98.1 million dwt in the container ship fleet, and a 7.6 per cent increase, from 20.9 to 22.5 million dwt in the liquefied gas carriers fleet. Registration of ships by developed market economies and major open-registry countries accounted for 27 and 45.1 per cent of the world fleet, respectively. Open registries increased their tonnage marginally, two thirds of which was owned by market economy and developing countries. Developing countries' share reached 22.6

per cent, or 202.3 million dwt, of which 155.9 million dwt was registered in Asia.

Transport of dangerous goods

In response to Economic and Social Council resolution 2003/64 [YUN 2003, p. 993], the Secretary-General submitted a May report [E/2005/53] on the work, during 2003-2004, of the Committee of Experts on the Transport of Dangerous Goods and on the Globally Harmonized System of Classification and Labelling of Chemicals.

The report stated that the secretariat published the thirteenth revised edition of the *Recommendations on the Transport of Dangerous Goods: Model Regulations,* the fourth revised edition of the *Manual of Tests and Criteria* and the first edition of the *Globally Harmonized System of Classification and Labelling of Chemicals (GHS).* All main legal instruments or codes governing the international transport of dangerous goods by sea, air, road, rail or inland waterway were amended accordingly, with effect from 1 January 2005, and many Governments transposed the provisions of the *Model Regulations* into their own legislation for domestic traffic for application as from 2005. Many Governments and international organizations revised national and international legislation in order to implement the GHS by 2008. The Committee adopted amendments to the *Model Regulations,* the *Manual of Tests and Criteria* and the GHS. It also adopted a programme of work and planned sessions for the two Subcommittees of Experts and for the Committee for 2005-2006 and recommended a draft resolution for adoption by the Council.

The Committee's two subsidiary bodies held two sessions each, all in Geneva: the Subcommittee of Experts on the Transport of Dangerous Goods held its twenty-seventh (4-8 July) [ST/SG/AC.10/C.3/54] and twenty-eighth sessions (28 November–6 December) [ST/SG/AC.10/C.3/56 & Add.1]; and the Subcommittee of Experts on the Globally Harmonized System of Classification and Labelling of Chemicals held its ninth (11-12 July) [ST/SG/AC.10/C.4/18] and tenth (7-8 December) [ST/SG/AC.10/C.4/20] sessions.

A March annex [ST/SG/AC.10/32/Add.3 &Corr.1] to the 2004 report of the Committee of Experts on its second session [YUN 2004, p. 986] contained amendments to the GHS [ST/SG/AC.10/30] adopted by the Committee.

ECONOMIC AND SOCIAL COUNCIL ACTION

On 27 July [meeting 68], the Economic and Social Council adopted **resolution 2005/53** [draft: E/2005/53 & E/2005/L.42] without vote [agenda item 13 *(m)*].

Work of the Committee of Experts on the Transport of Dangerous Goods and on the Globally Harmonized System of Classification and Labelling of Chemicals

The Economic and Social Council,

Recalling its resolutions 1999/65 of 26 October 1999, 2001/34 of 26 July 2001, 2001/44 of 20 December 2001 and 2003/64 of 25 July 2003,

Having considered the report of the Secretary-General on the work of the Committee of Experts on the Transport of Dangerous Goods and on the Globally Harmonized System of Classification and Labelling of Chemicals during the biennium 2003-2004,

A. Work of the Committee regarding the transport of dangerous goods

Recognizing the importance of the work of the Committee for the harmonization of codes and regulations relating to the transport of dangerous goods,

Bearing in mind the need to maintain safety standards at all times and to facilitate trade, as well as the importance of this to the various organizations responsible for modal regulations, while meeting the growing concern for the protection of life, property and the environment through the safe transport of dangerous goods, including their security in transport,

Noting the increasing volume of dangerous goods being introduced into worldwide commerce, and the rapid expansion of technology and innovation,

Recalling its resolution 1973(LIX) of 30 July 1975 whereby it requested the Committee to study, in consultation with other bodies concerned, in particular the United Nations Conference on Trade and Development, the then Inter-Governmental Maritime Consultative Organization, the International Civil Aviation Organization, the International Air Transport Association and the regional commissions, the possibility of a joint approach to the drafting of an international convention on the transport of dangerous goods by all modes of transport which would take into account the general scope of a future convention on international intermodal transport,

Noting that the major international instruments governing the transport of dangerous goods by the various modes of transport and many national regulations are now harmonized with the Model Regulations annexed to the Committee recommendations on the transport of dangerous goods, but that the uneven progress in the updating process of national inland transport legislation in some countries of the world remains, inter alia, a reason for regulatory disharmony at the worldwide level and represents a serious legislative obstacle to international multimodal transport,

1. *Expresses its appreciation* for the work of the Committee of Experts on the Transport of Dangerous Goods and on the Globally Harmonized System of Classification and Labelling of Chemicals with respect to matters relating to the transport of dangerous goods, including their security in transport;

2. *Requests* the Secretary-General:

(*a*) To circulate the new and amended recommendations on the transport of dangerous goods to the Governments of Member States, the specialized agencies, the International Atomic Energy Agency and other international organizations concerned;

(*b*) To publish the fourteenth revised edition of the *Recommendations on the Transport of Dangerous Goods: Model Regulations* and the amendments to the fourth revised edition of the *Recommendations on the Transport of Dangerous Goods: Manual of Tests and Criteria* in all the official languages of the United Nations, in the most cost-effective manner, no later than the end of 2005;

(*c*) To make those publications available on the website of the secretariat of the Economic Commission for Europe, which also provides secretariat services to the Committee, and to make them available also on CD-ROM;

3. *Invites* all Governments, the specialized agencies, the International Atomic Energy Agency and the other international organizations concerned to transmit to the secretariat of the Committee their views on the Committee's work, together with any comments that they may wish to make on the amended recommendations;

4. *Invites* all interested Governments, the regional commissions, the specialized agencies and the international organizations concerned to take into account, when developing or updating appropriate codes and regulations, the recommendations of the Committee;

5. *Requests* the Committee to continue to study, in consultation with the International Maritime Organization, the International Civil Aviation Organization, the regional commissions and the intergovernmental organizations concerned, the possibilities of improving the implementation of the Model Regulations on the Transport of Dangerous Goods in all countries for the purposes of ensuring a high level of safety and eliminating technical barriers to international trade, including through the further harmonization of international agreements or conventions governing the international transport of dangerous goods, or a possible joint approach to the development of an effective international instrument on multimodal international transport of dangerous goods, as appropriate;

B. Work of the Committee regarding the Globally Harmonized System of Classification and Labelling of Chemicals

Bearing in mind that, in paragraph 23 (*c*) of the Plan of Implementation of the World Summit on Sustainable Development ("Johannesburg Plan of Implementation"), countries were encouraged to implement the Globally Harmonized System of Classification and Labelling of Chemicals as soon as possible with a view to having the system fully operational by 2008,

Bearing in mind also that the General Assembly, in its resolution 57/253 of 20 December 2002, endorsed the Johannesburg Plan of Implementation and requested the Economic and Social Council to implement the provisions of the Plan relevant to its mandate and, in particular, to promote the implementation of Agenda 21 by strengthening system-wide coordination,

Noting with satisfaction:

(*a*) That all United Nations programmes and specialized agencies concerned with chemical safety in the field of transport or of the environment, in particular the Economic Commission for Europe, the United Nations Environment Programme, the International Maritime Organization and the International Civil Aviation Organization, have taken appropriate steps to amend or consider amending their legal instruments in order to give effect to the Globally Harmonized System of Classification and Labelling of Chemicals;

(b) That the International Labour Office and the World Health Organization are also taking appropriate steps to adapt their existing chemical safety recommendations, codes and guidelines to the Globally Harmonized System, in particular in the areas of occupational health and safety and of the prevention and treatment of poisoning;

(c) That Member States participating in the activities of the Subcommittee of Experts on the Globally Harmonized System of Classification and Labelling of Chemicals, as well as the European Commission, are actively preparing revisions of national or regional legislation applicable to chemicals for implementation of the Globally Harmonized System;

(d) That several United Nations programmes, specialized agencies and regional organizations, in particular the United Nations Institute for Training and Research, the International Labour Organization, the World Health Organization, the Economic Commission for Europe, the Asia-Pacific Economic Cooperation Council, the Intergovernmental Forum on Chemical Safety, Governments, the European Commission and non-governmental organizations representing the chemical industry, have organized or contributed to multiple workshops, seminars and other capacity-building activities at the international, regional, subregional and national levels in order to raise administration, health sector and industry awareness and to prepare for the implementation of the Globally Harmonized System,

Aware that effective implementation by 2008 will require further cooperation between the Subcommittee of Experts on the Globally Harmonized System of Classification and Labelling of Chemicals and the international bodies concerned, continued efforts by the Governments of the Member States, cooperation with the industry and other affected parties, and significant support for capacity-building activities in countries with economies in transition and developing countries,

Recalling the particular significance of the United Nations Institute for Training and Research/International Labour Organization/Organization for Economic Cooperation and Development Global Partnership for Capacity-building to Implement the Globally Harmonized System for building capacities at all levels,

1. *Commends* the Secretary-General for the publication of the *Globally Harmonized System of Classification and Labelling of Chemicals (GHS)* in the six official languages of the United Nations, in book form and on CD-ROM, and the availability of that and related material on the website of the secretariat of the Economic Commission for Europe;

2. *Expresses its deep appreciation* to the Committee, United Nations programmes, specialized agencies and other organizations concerned for their fruitful cooperation and their commitment to the implementation of the Globally Harmonized System of Classification and Labelling of Chemicals;

3. *Requests* the Secretary-General:

(a) To circulate the amendments to the Globally Harmonized System to the Governments of Member States, the specialized agencies and other international organizations concerned;

(b) To publish the first revised edition of the *Globally Harmonized System of Classification and Labelling of Chemicals* in all the official languages of the United Nations in the most cost-effective manner no later than the end of 2005, and to make it available on CD-ROM and on the website of the secretariat of the Economic Commission for Europe, which provides secretariat services to the Committee;

4. *Invites* Governments that have not yet done so to take the necessary steps, through appropriate national procedures and/or legislation, to implement the Globally Harmonized System, as recommended in the Plan of Implementation of the World Summit on Sustainable Development;

5. *Reiterates its invitation* to the regional commissions, United Nations programmes, the specialized agencies and other organizations concerned to promote the implementation of the Globally Harmonized System and, where relevant, to amend their respective legal international instruments addressing transport safety, workplace safety, consumer protection or the protection of the environment so as to give effect to the Globally Harmonized System through such instruments;

6. *Invites* Governments, the regional commissions, United Nations programmes, the specialized agencies and other organizations concerned to provide feedback on implementation to the Subcommittee of Experts on the Globally Harmonized System of Classification and Labelling of Chemicals;

7. *Encourages* Governments, the regional commissions, United Nations programmes, the specialized agencies and other relevant international organizations and non-governmental organizations, in particular industry, to strengthen their support of the implementation of the Globally Harmonized System by providing financial contributions and/or technical assistance to capacity-building activities in developing countries and countries with economies in transition;

C. Programme of work of the Committee

Taking note of the programme of work of the Committee for the biennium 2005-2006 as contained in paragraphs 41 and 42 of the report of the Secretary-General on the work of the Committee of Experts,

Noting the relatively poor representation of experts from developing countries and countries with economies in transition in the work of the Committee and the need to promote their wider participation in its work,

Noting with concern that the General Service staff resources requested for the activities of the Subcommittee of Experts on the Globally Harmonized System of Classification and Labelling of Chemicals when it was established and which had been provided through general temporary assistance until the end of 2004 were suppressed in 2004, irrespective of the recommendations made by the Committee at its first session,

1. *Decides* to approve the programme of work of the Committee;

2. *Stresses* the importance of the participation of experts from developing countries as well as from countries with economies in transition in the work of the Committee, calls, in that regard, for voluntary contributions to facilitate their participation, including through support for travel and daily subsistence allow-

ance, and invites Member States and international organizations in a position to do so to contribute;

3. *Requests* the Secretary-General to reallocate appropriate General Service staff resources for the activities of the Committee;

4. *Also requests* the Secretary-General to submit a report to the Economic and Social Council in 2007 on the implementation of the present resolution, the recommendations on the transport of dangerous goods and on the Globally Harmonized System of Classification and Labelling of Chemicals.

UNCTAD institutional and organizational questions

In 2005, the Trade and Development Board (TDB), the governing body of UNCTAD, held the following sessions, all in Geneva: thirty-sixth executive session (3 May); twenty-second special session (18 July); thirty-seventh executive session (26 July); fifty-second session (3-14 October); and resumed fifty-second session (7 November) [A/60/15]. It also held hearings with civil society and private sector representatives (29 September) [TD/B/52/9] on the theme "Economic growth and poverty reduction in the 1990s: Lessons from a decade of economic reform for development strategies and global partnerships in the new millennium".

In May, TDB took note of the reports of its subsidiary bodies and the UNCTAD annual report, took action relating to the financing of experts and its contribution to the 2005 World Summit (see p. 47) and considered the outcome of the high-level meeting of the Economic and Social Council with the Bretton Woods institutions, WTO and UNCTAD.

On 18 July, TDB considered the contribution of UNCTAD to the follow-up to the relevant UN development conferences, including the Millennium Summit.

On 26 July, TDB considered UNCTAD activities relating to Africa, approved proposed amendments to the certificate of origin of the Generalized System of Preferences and decided to allow civil society organizations that had been accredited for UNCTAD XI to continue to participate in Board hearings for civil society. It also continued consideration of the financing of experts and took note of the report of the Working Party on the Medium-term Plan and Programme Budget on its resumed forty-fourth session.

In October, TDB adopted agreed conclusions on the review of progress in the implementation of the Programme of Action for the Least Developed Countries for the Decade 2001-2010 [agreed conclusions 482 (LII)] (see p. 942), and a decision on the review of UNCTAD technical cooperation

activities and their financing [dec. 483 (LII)] (see below). It requested the UNCTAD Secretary-General to consult further with member States on the financing of experts and the modalities for selecting them, and decided to hold a resumed session in November to finalize its agreed conclusions on economic development in Africa: the role of foreign direct investment in growth and development. TDB took note of: the report on UNCTAD contribution to the implementation of, and the review of progress made in the implementation of the outcomes of major UN conferences and summits [TD/B/52/6]; the reports on UNCTAD assistance to the Palestinian people (see p. 542) and on the hearings with civil society, in accordance with the São Paulo Consensus [YUN 2004, p. 955]; the oral report on multi- stakeholder partnerships for UNCTAD XI; the reports of the Working Party on the Medium-term Plan and Programme Budget on its forty-fifth session (see below) and of the UN Commission on International Trade Law on its thirty-eight session [A/60/17] (see p. 1456); and the reports of the Joint Advisory Group on ITC UNCTAD/WTO on its thirty-eighth session (see p. 1049) and of the Advisory Body on the implementation of courses by the secretariat in 2004-2005 and their impact, in accordance with the Bangkok Plan of Action [YUN 2000, p. 891].

In November, TDB adopted agreed conclusions on economic development in Africa: the role of foreign direct investment in growth and development [agreed conclusions 484 (LII)] (see p. 1054); and a decision on venue for UNCTAD XII [dec. 485 (LII)].

Working Party. The UNCTAD Working Party on the Medium-term Plan and Programme Budget (the Working Party) held three sessions in 2005, all in Geneva: the forty-fourth session (31 January–2 February) [TD/B/WP/179], the forty-fourth resumed session (30-31 May) [TD/B/WP/183] and the forty-fifth session (12-15 September) [TD/B/WP/184].

Technical cooperation

In a July report [TD/B/WP/181 & Add.1,2], the UNCTAD Secretary-General provided a review of technical cooperation activities in 2004, which were focused on enhancing the institutional and negotiating capacity of developing countries in the development of endogenous trade and development policies towards the implementation of the São Paulo Consensus [YUN 2004, p. 955]. In 2004, trust fund contributions for UNCTAD technical cooperation, the main source of funding, amounted to $26.9 million, about the same as in 2003. UNDP-supported activities reached their lowest level in 2004, accounting for 8.5 per cent, or $2.3 million of total expenditures; while the

UN regular programme budget accounted for 6.3 per cent.

UNCTAD technical cooperation activities continued to be carried out on the basis of inter-regional, regional and country-specific projects. Interregional projects, directed towards developing countries and regions, including LDCs, accounted for the bulk of UNCTAD's trust funds expenditures, at $15.5 million, and for 56 per cent of overall UNCTAD technical cooperation expenditures in 2004. Regional projects accounted for 9.5 per cent of expenditures, amounting to $2.6 million. Country projects amounted to $9.4 million, corresponding to more than one-third of expenditures.

By region, $4.2 million went to Africa, $4.5 million to Asia and the Pacific, $2.1 million to Latin America and the Caribbean, $1.2 million to Europe and $15.5 to interregional projects. LDCs continued to be the major beneficiaries of UNCTAD technical cooperation, with expenditures amounting to $9.2 million, reflecting an increase of 6.2 per cent over the previous year and representing one-third of total expenditures in 2004.

By programme, services infrastructure for development and trade efficiency accounted for 35.3 per cent of total expenditure; international trade in goods and services and commodities, 23 per cent; investment, enterprise development, and technology, 6.6 per cent; and globalization and development strategies, 12.5 per cent. The balance of 12.4 per cent went to programmes for executive direction and management and support services, cross-divisional advisory services; and least developed, landlocked and island developing countries.

Major technical assistance programmes in order of expenditures included Automated System for Customs Data($7.3 million); investment policy and capacity building ($3.2 million); Debt Management and Financial Analysis System ($3.2 million); trade negotiations and commercial diplomacy ($2.5 million); and trade, environment and development ($2.2 million).

Technical cooperation strategy

The Working Party on the Medium-term Plan and Programme Budget, at its forty-fifth session in September [TD/B/WP/184], considered the July report on UNCTAD technical cooperation activities in 2004 (see above) and adopted a draft decision for adoption by TDB on the review of UNCTAD technical cooperation activities and their financing.

On 7 October [A/60/15 (dec. 483 (LII))], TDB took note of the report on UNCTAD technical cooperation activities in 2004 and requested the secretariat to improve the information contained in annex I.

It underscored the importance of more effective and sustained capacity-building activities; expressed the need to ensure an equitable distribution of resources among developing country regions; and invited donors to continue to support interregional activities and UNCTAD's technical cooperation programme. It urged the secretariat to intensify consultations with potential beneficiaries of UNCTAD's assistance and to coordinate UNCTAD operational activities, the secretariat's research and analytical work and intergovernmental deliberations. The secretariat should report to the next session of the Working Party on technical cooperation relating to UNCTAD's contribution to the implementation of relevant Assembly resolutions and on progress made in operationalizing the São Paulo Consensus. Noting UNCTAD's efforts at raising funds, TDB requested the secretariat to provide further information on options for improving the system of funding technical assistance and making it more predictable; and called for strengthened cooperation among different providers of trade-related technical assistance. TDB requested the UNCTAD Secretary-General to enhance the coherence and the interdivisional nature of programmes and activities and to submit a progress report to the 2006 session of the Working Party. It also requested the secretariat to report on follow-up by no later than the forty-seventh (2007) session of the Working Party.

Evaluation

In August, an independent team submitted an evaluation of UNCTAD technical cooperation activities: in-depth evaluation of the training courses on key issues on the international economic agenda [TD/B/WP/182 & Add.1], in response to a request of the Working Party on the Medium-term Plan and Programme Budget, at its forty-third session [YUN 2004, p. 988]. The evaluation team reviewed all commitments contained in paragraph 166 of the Bangkok Plan of Action [YUN 2000, p.891] and assessed how they had been met. It stated that UNCTAD had developed an innovative product for technical assistance services in trade policy, and that the delivery of the courses had met their objectives. It stressed the positive impacts on some members' institutional capacity building in public agencies, research institutions and universities associated with foreign trade matters, and recommended that activities should continue to aim at excelling in the delivery of the training courses and building sustainable institutional and societal capacities.

At its forty-fifth session in September [TD/B/WP/184], the Working Party adopted agreed conclusions, noted the need for more predictable funding of the training courses and requested the secretariat to explore ways to regularly conduct six regional courses within the biennium and to report thereon to the Working Party in 2006. It encouraged the secretariat to ensure the sustainability of impact through, among other things, increased networking, and to provide courses in the UN language appropriate to the needs of the participants. The Working Party endorsed the recommendations contained in the evaluation report and requested the secretariat to submit a progress report to its forty-seventh (2007) session. It reiterated the importance of the UNCTAD evaluation process and requested that adequate human resources be provided for the coordination of future evaluations.

TDB, in October [A/60/15], endorsed the conclusions of the Working Party.

Participation in expert meetings

TDB, at its thirty-sixth executive session on 3 May [A/60/15], requested the Working Party to consider the outcome of informal consultations on the financing of experts.

On 31 May [TD/B/WP/183], the Working Party, in agreed conclusions on the financing of experts, requested its Chairman to continue consultations with a view to arriving at a solution within two months and to report to TDB. It recommended the designation by the UNCTAD Secretary-General of a focal point responsible for all matters related to the financing of experts and to report to TDB; and that the focal point assist in identifying appropriate modalities in accordance with UN administrative and financial and budgetary rules and regulations and relevant Assembly resolutions.

At its thirty-seventh executive session in July [A/60/15], TDB endorsed the Working Party's agreed conclusions and decided to include the issue of the financing of experts in the agenda of its fifty-second session and to request the secretariat to prepare a note thereon.

At its fifty-second session in October [A/60/15], TDB requested the UNCTAD Secretary-General to conduct, on an urgent basis, further consultations with member States on the financing of experts and the modalities for selecting them, and to report to the Board at an executive or special session.

Medium-term plan and programme budget

At its forty-fourth session [TD/B/WP/179], the Working Party reviewed the draft programme budget on trade and development for the 2006-2007 biennium [UNCTAD/EDM/MISC/2004/5/Rev.2]. In agreed conclusions, the Working Party considered that the review of the work programme could be more effective if it were provided with detailed information on financial and resource distribution. It therefore requested the UNCTAD secretariat to consult with the competent authorities in New York, with a view to sharing information needed or enhancing its proceedings. It invited the secretariat to enhance its contributions towards the implementation of the international development goals, including those contained in the Millennium Declaration, the follow-up to the High-level Plenary Meeting of the General Assembly to be held in September (see p. 47) and to major UN conferences and summits. It also called upon UNCTAD to explore ways in which it could help countries affected by the Indian Ocean earthquake and the tsunami in their recovery and rehabilitation efforts, in coordination with the international community. It also asked UNCTAD to further explore modalities for financing the participation of experts from developing countries in UNCTAD intergovernmental meetings on a predictable and sustainable basis.

At its forty-fourth resumed session [TD/B/WP/183], the Working Party further reviewed the proposed programme budget on trade and development for the 2006-2007 biennium [A/60/6 (Sect.12)]. In agreed conclusions, it requested the secretariat to provide an explanatory note containing information on the rationale for the allocation of resources to substantive subprogrammes, and to improve the quality and clarity of the expected accomplishments and indicators. Noting the two per cent decline in the allocation of resources for UNCTAD, it considered that UNCTAD should be provided with the resources necessary for the implementation of the outcomes of UNCTAD XI.

On 26 July [A/60/15], TDB took note of the Working Party's report on its resumed forty-fourth session and endorsed the agreed conclusions.

UNCTAD Secretary-General

By **decision 59/419** of 11 May, the General Assembly, on the proposal of the UN Secretary-General [A/59/110], confirmed the appointment of Supachai Panitchpakdi as Secretary-General of UNCTAD for a four year term of office, beginning on 1 September 2005 and ending on 31 August 2009.

Chapter V

Regional economic and social activities

In 2005, the five regional economic commissions of the United Nations continued to provide technical cooperation, including advisory services, to their member States. They also, among other activities, promoted programmes and projects and provided training to enhance national capacity-building in various sectors. Four of them—the Economic Commission for Africa (ECA), the Economic Commission for Europe (ECE), the Economic and Social Commission for Asia and the Pacific (ESCAP) and the Economic and Social Commission for Western Asia (ESCWA)—held regular sessions during the year. The Economic Commission for Latin America and the Caribbean (ECLAC) did not meet in 2005 but was scheduled to do so in 2006.

The Executive Secretaries of the commissions continued to meet periodically to exchange views and coordinate activities and positions on major development issues. In July, during its annual substantive session, the Economic and Social Council held an interactive dialogue with the Executive Secretaries on the theme: "Achievement of the internationally agreed development goals, including those contained in the Millennium Declaration: a regional perspective".

During the year, ECA and ECE continued to collaborate on the project for a Europe-Africa fixed link through the Strait of Gibraltar; cooperation and progress on the project were welcomed by the Council. The General Assembly, having considered a report by the Office of Internal Oversight Services on its inspection of ECA's subregional offices, urged the implementation of the recommendations contained therein. ECE examined domestic policies that had led to increased resources for development and the role of regional cooperation in financing for development. In December, it held an ad hoc session at which it adopted the workplan on ECE reform. ESCAP adopted revised statutes for its regional institutions so that their workplans were subject to the established intergovernmental review and approval process. It also established the Asian and Pacific Training Centre for Information and Communication Technology for Development (APCICT). The Council approved the revised statutes and the establishment of APCICT, and adopted a resolution on the midterm review of the functioning of ESCAP's conference structure.

In other action related to the regional commissions, the Council approved the admission of Germany as a member of ECLAC and adopted a resolution on ESCWA's Damascus Declaration on the Realization of the Millennium Development Goals.

Regional cooperation

During 2005, the United Nations continued to strengthen cooperation among its five regional commissions, between them and other UN entities, and with regional and international organizations.

On 4 February (**decision 2005/206**), the Economic and Social Council decided that the theme for the regional cooperation item of its 2005 substantive session would be "Achievement of the internationally agreed development goals, including those contained in the United Nations Millennium Declaration: a regional perspective". Accordingly, the Council held an interactive dialogue with the Executive Secretaries on that subject on 5 July.

Meetings of Executive Secretaries. The Executive Secretaries of the regional commissions met on 11 and 17 February (New York), 7-8 July (Beirut, Lebanon) and 24-27 October (New York) [E/2005/15, E/2006/15].

At their February meeting, the Executive Secretaries focused on progress made towards achieving internationally agreed development goals, including those contained in the United Nations Millennium Declaration, adopted at the Millennium Summit in 2000 [YUN 2000, p. 49], and the Secretary-General's reform initiatives for mainstreaming the regional dimension in the Organization's work in the economic and social sectors. They exchanged views on, among other things, the activities undertaken by the commissions on regional follow-up to the 2002 International Conference on Financing for Development [YUN 2002, p. 953]; the preparations for the thirteenth session of the Commission on Sustainable Development, to be held in April (see p. 920) in follow-up to the 2002 World Summit on Sustainable Development [YUN 2002, p. 821]; and preparations for the second phase of the World Summit on the Information Society, to be held in November (see p. 933).

The Executive Secretaries viewed the Economic and Social Council's 1 March decision to hold its dialogue with them immediately after the high-level segment of its substantive session (**decision 2005/210**) (see p. 954) as a positive step towards the Council's review of the regional dimensions of global issues, including coherent policies to address the varying degrees of achievement of the Millennium Development Goals (MDGs) [YUN 2000, p. 51] at the regional and subregional levels. They agreed that the MDGs and other international development goals were increasingly shaping the development agenda of the regions. Regional processes could bridge the gap between global perspectives and country-specific concerns, and could reinforce good practices through exchange of experiences. The Executive Secretaries were of the view that regional policies should focus, in particular, on the inter-linkages between growth, equity and poverty reduction; the conditions for a sustained process of poverty reduction; the links between economic policies and sustainable development; the combination of broad-based human capital formation with social protection and specific anti-poverty programmes; adherence to the principles of governance and accountability; and regional integration policies for reducing vulnerability to various external shocks, such as financial crises and natural or man-made disasters. They stressed that although national policies were crucial for achieving the MDGs, in a globalized world, a supportive international climate was indispensable. International commitments on aid, debt and trade issues for developing countries were essential for achieving the MDGs.

Together with other partners, including the United Nations Conference on Trade and Development (UNCTAD), the regional commissions continued to support their member States with regard to their effective integration into the global trading system. They assisted them in formulating trade policies and strategies that would ensure more equitable results of globalization and liberalization. In that regard, the Executive Secretaries noted that the regional commissions would prepare a joint report for the High-level Dialogue of the General Assembly on Financing for Development (see p. 1064), which would focus on obstacles to achieving the Monterrey Consensus, adopted at the 2002 International Conference on Financing for Development [YUN 2002, p. 953].

Concerning the report of the Secretary-General "In larger freedom: towards develop-

ment, security and human rights for all" [A/59/2005] (see p. 67), which observed that threats to peace and security in a globalized world included poverty, deadly infectious disease and environmental degradation, the Executive Secretaries agreed that those threats needed to be addressed by the international community at the global and regional levels in an integrated and preventative manner. They therefore decided to meet in July in Beirut, Lebanon, to address issues raised in the Secretary-General's report, including policy issues for greater coherence and harmony between bilateral, regional and global agreements, especially in areas relating to trade and development. Building on the experiences gained through their joint meetings, they were of the view that cooperation among the commissions should continue to be strengthened through knowledge sharing and networking.

Review and reform of the regional commissions

In a May report [E/2005/15], the Secretary-General updated the Economic and Social Council on actions taken by the regional commissions to implement the guidance given in Council resolution 1998/46 [YUN 1998, p. 1262] on mainstreaming the regional dimension into the work of the United Nations and enhancing the coherence of UN activities at the regional level. The report also provided a regional perspective on the achievement of internationally agreed development goals, including the MDGs, which was the theme for the regional cooperation item at the Council's substantive session.

An addendum to the report [E/2005/15/Add.1] contained the texts of resolutions and decisions adopted at recent meetings of the regional commissions and drawn to the Council's attention for consideration or action.

By **decision 2005/303** of 27 July, the Council took note of the Secretary-General's report and addendum. By the same decision, it took note of the report of the Secretary-General on the project for a Europe-Africa permanent link through the Strait of Gibraltar and of The Overview of the Economic Report on Africa 2005: "Meeting the Challenges of Unemployment and Poverty in Africa" [E/2005/17]; the summaries of: *the Economic and Social Survey of Asia and the Pacific, 2005* [E/2005/18]; the *Economic Survey of Europe, 2005*: the economic situation in Europe and the Commonwealth of Independent States in 2004-2005 [E/2005/16]; the *Economic Survey of Latin America and the Caribbean, 2004* [E/2005/19]; and the *Survey of Economic and Social Developments in the Economic and Social Commision for Western Asia, 2005* [E/2005/20].

The Council adopted resolutions on the Europe-Africa fixed link through the Strait of Gibraltar (resolution 2005/34); the midterm review concerning the functioning of the conference structure of ESCAP (resolution 2005/35); the statute of the Statistical Institute for Asia and the Pacific (resolution 2005/36); the statute of the UN Asian and Pacific Centre for Agricultural Engineering and Machinery (resolution 2005/37); the statute of the Asian and Pacific Centre for Transfer of Technology (resolution 2005/38); the Centre for Alleviation of Poverty through Secondary Crops Development in Asia and the Pacific (resolution 2005/39); the establishment of the Asian and Pacific Training Centre for Information and Communication Technology for Development (resolution 2005/40); the admission of Germany as a member of ECLAC (resolution 2005/41); and the Damascus Declaration and the role of ESCWA in the achievement of the internationally agreed development goals, including those contained in the Millennium Declaration (resolution 2005/50). It also adopted decisions on the implementation of resolutions concerning the participation of associate members of ECLAC in the follow-up to UN world conferences and in the work of the Council (decisions 2005/214 and 2005/302); and the venue of the sixty-second session of ESCAP (decision 2005/297).

(For the summaries of economic surveys covering the regions and the texts of the resolutions, see the relevant sections of this chapter.)

Audit of the regional commissions

In response to General Assembly resolution 59/271 [YUN 2004, p. 1369], the Secretary-General submitted a September report [A/60/378] on the implementation of the recommendations of the Office of Internal Oversight Services (OIOS) on its 2004 management audit of the regional commissions [YUN 2004, p. 992]. The report noted that the Executive Secretaries had undertaken follow-up action on all OIOS recommendations and provided details of those measures.

GENERAL ASSEMBLY ACTION

On 23 December [meeting 69], the General Assembly, on the recommendation of the Fifth (Administrative and Budgetary) Committee [A/60/604], adopted **resolution 60/239** without vote [agenda item 132].

Implementation of the recommendations of the Office of Internal Oversight Services on its management audit of the regional commissions

The General Assembly,

Recalling its resolution 59/271 of 23 December 2004,

Having considered the report of the Secretary-General on the implementation of the recommenda-

tions of the Office of Internal Oversight Services on its management audit of the regional commissions,

Takes note of the report of the Secretary-General on the implementation of the recommendations of the Office of Internal Oversight Services on its management audit of the regional commissions.

Africa

The Economic Commission for Africa (ECA) held its thirty-eighth session/Conference of African Ministers of Finance, Planning and Economic Development (Abuja, Nigeria, 14-15 May) under the theme "Achieving the MDGs in Africa". It considered the report and major recommendations of the twenty-fourth meeting of the Committee of Experts of the Conference of African Ministers of Finance, Planning and Economic Development [E/ECA/CM.38/8], which preceded the session (Abuja, 11-13 May), and discussed the session's agenda, statutory issues and the proposed programme of work and priorities for ECA for the 2006-2007 biennium [E/ECA/CM.38/3]. It also had before it: an issues paper on achieving the MDGs in Africa [E/ECA/CM.38/5]; the ECA annual report for 2005 [E/ECA/CM.38/2]; and an overview of a joint ECA/Organisation for Economic Co-operation and Development (OECD) paper: Mutual Review of Development Effectiveness in the Context of the New Partnership for Africa's Development (NEPAD) [E/ECA/CM.38/6].

The Ministers adopted a ministerial statement in which they recognized that strong political will and bold and decisive action were needed to achieve poverty eradication and promote sustainable development in Africa. The situation was particularly urgent as only 10 years remained until the target date for reaching the MDGs, which the Ministers reaffirmed as a vitally important framework for reducing poverty and advancing development. The Ministers were encouraged by progress in some parts of the continent and in several African countries on individual MDGs, including progress by countries with severe resource constraints. The wider picture was not satisfactory, however, and faster and broader progress was needed. The Ministers noted the importance of reviewing the advances made and obstacles encountered in implementing the MDGs; they supported the preparation of an African Common Position in that regard.

In consideration of a number of forthcoming high-level discussions, notably the African Union (AU) Summit (Sirte, Libyan Arab Jamahiriya, 4-5 July), the UN High-level Dialogue on Financing for Development (New York, 27-28 June) (see

p. 1064), the Summit of the Group of Eight (G-8) most industrialized countries (Gleneagles, United Kingdom, 6-8 July), and the General Assembly's World Summit (New York, 14-16 September) (see p. 47), the Ministers set out some key actions they needed to take in order to achieve the MDGs in Africa and highlighted what needed to be done by the international community to enable the African countries to meet the objectives. Those actions were detailed under the following headings: the fruits of growth must be increased and shared; towards local ownership and more effective national poverty reduction and growth strategies; greater focus needed on trade, infrastructure and agriculture; financing a "big push" for Africa; improving aid management and mutual accountability; and fostering greater institutional coherence and effectiveness.

Economic trends

In 2005, Africa's gross domestic product (GDP) grew by 5.3 per cent, a slight increase over the 5.2 per cent achieved in 2004, according to the Overview of the Economic Report on Africa 2006: "Recent economic trends in Africa and prospects for 2006" [E/2006/17]. A key driver of the economic recovery in recent years, after decades of decline and stagnation, was the improvement in macroeconomic management in many African countries, which resulted in controlled inflation rates and consolidation of fiscal balances. Another favourable factor was the increase in international prices of key African export commodities. East Africa led the continent with a GDP growth rate of 6.1 per cent, followed by Southern Africa at 5.8 per cent, North Africa at 5.3 per cent, West Africa at 4.9 per cent and Central Africa at 3.7 per cent. By country, 8 of the top 10 growth performers achieved the 7 per cent growth rate threshold estimated as needed to reach the MDGs: Angola, Equatorial Guinea, Ethiopia, the Libyan Arab Jamahiriya, Liberia, the Republic of the Congo, Mozambique and the Sudan. Lesotho, Malawi, Seychelles, Togo and Zimbabwe exhibited the weakest performance.

The average fiscal position on the continent improved from a deficit of 0.7 per cent of GDP in 2004 to a surplus of 0.7 per cent in 2005. That improvement was largely driven by the sizeable fiscal surpluses recorded by many oil-producing countries, however, and fiscal imbalances remained a critical problem in Africa, with as many as 28 countries recording fiscal deficits in 2005. The inflation outlook remained satisfactory, with a majority of countries recording single-digit inflation rates. The mean inflation rate for Africa increased slightly from 7.8 per cent in 2004 to

8.2 per cent in 2005. The continent's trade surplus increased to $27.7 billion in 2005 from $12.7 billion in 2004 as a result of a 45 per cent increase in the region's oil trade surplus. Africa's total debt stock stood at $285.8 billion in 2005 and debt-service payments rose to $31.8 billion.

Activities in 2005

The ECA programme of work in 2005 was organized under eight subprogrammes: facilitating economic and social policy analysis; fostering sustainable development; strengthening development management; harnessing information for development; promoting trade and regional integration; promoting the advancement of women; supporting subregional activities for development; and development planning and administration [E/ECA/CM.38/2; E/ECA/CM/39.2].

Facilitating economic and social policy analysis

In 2005, ECA continued its efforts to strengthen the capacity of member States to design and implement appropriate policies to achieve sustained economic growth for poverty reduction, in line with the priorities of the Millennium Declaration [YUN 2000, p. 49] and NEPAD [YUN 2001, p. 900]. Particular emphasis was placed on monitoring and tracking Africa's economic performance; conducting research and policy analysis on macroeconomic, financial and social issues; and strengthening the statistical capacities of African countries for monitoring progress towards the MDGs.

Activities included the organization of an ad hoc experts group meeting on capital flows and current account sustainability (Accra, Ghana, 21-25 September), which identified policies with respect to trade, capital flows and debt that could increase current account sustainability. In addition, a major research report was published, entitled *Unleashing the Private Sector in Africa*, which, in particular, underlined the role of African governments in promoting the development of the private sector by addressing the constraints to its growth and development, including strategies for increasing flows of foreign direct investment (FDI) and maximizing the contributions of the African diaspora to the continent's development. In the area of social policy and poverty analysis, ECA focused on support for member States in achieving the goals of NEPAD and the Millennium Declaration. The secretariat submitted to the Commission's May session an issues paper on achieving the MDGs in Africa [E/ECA/CM.38/5], which identified the main challenges in meeting the MDGs and provided policy recommendations on how they could be addressed.

New Partnership for Africa's Development

ECA continued to contribute to the implementation of NEPAD a programme for the continent's development that was initiated by African leaders in 2001 [YUN 2001, p. 900]. Most of NEPAD's priorities were at the core of ECA's own mandate and were supported through its analytical work and technical assistance in various areas. In response to NEPAD's emphasis on partnerships, ECA continued its work with the OECD secretariat on developing a framework for mutual accountability and policy coherence, which would form the basis for a new relationship between African countries and their development partners to increase aid effectiveness. It also supported the implementation of the African Peer Review Mechanism (APRM) by contributing to the development of some of the APRM codes and standards, providing country economic and governance data to the APRM secretariat and participating in support missions to nine countries. In addition, ECA carried out training and capacity-building activities to harness information and communication technologies (ICT) for development and increase Africa's participation in global ICT policy- and decision-making forums, as called for in NEPAD's Short-term Action Plan. NEPAD objectives were also supported through ECA assistance to the Regional Economic Communities (RECs) in the development and implementation of subregional policies and plans in order to ensure improved connectivity and unification of standards between member States. In December, an e-government strategy was completed for the East African Community.

In **resolution 60/222** of 23 December (see p. 1005), the General Assembly encouraged entities of the UN system to intensify their efforts in support of NEPAD at the regional level.

(For more information on NEPAD, see p. 1003.)

Information for development

ECA activities on harnessing information for development had the objective of further strengthening the growth of a sustainable information society in Africa that better addressed the continent's development challenges. Its work focused on: harnessing information technology for development through implementation of the African Information Society Initiative [YUN 1996, p. 880]; strengthening geoinformation systems for sustainable development; and improving access to information through enhanced library services.

In preparation for the second phase of the World Summit on the Information Society, to be held in November (see p. 933), ECA organized a meeting (Accra, 2-4 February), which, in addition to readying African countries for the Summit, addressed the challenges of achieving the information society in Africa and bridging the digital divide, capacity-building for Internet governance and operationalization of the Digital Solidarity Fund, which was established at the Summit's first phase in 2003 [YUN 2003, p. 858]. ECA organized a series of activities in the run-up to the November Summit, enabling African countries to participate actively in the global decision-making processes and reflect Africa's common concerns and perspectives in their outcomes, based on the African Regional Plan of Action on the Knowledge Economy, adopted by African ministers in charge of ICT (Geneva, 21 September).

The fourth meeting of the Committee on Development Information (Addis Ababa, 23-28 April), held under the theme "Information as an Economic Resource", sought to address key African development issues contained in the ECA workplan as they related to the information and knowledge economy. The Committee adopted a plan of action aimed at accelerating progress in building an effective information and knowledge economy that could enhance economic growth and sustainable development; it made recommendations in several key areas, such as statistics, geoinformation and library development.

Addressing the need to measure the impact of ICT in various sectors, ECA continued to implement its initiative, SCAN-ICT, which was aimed at building and strengthening the capacity of member States in the development of indicators and benchmarks for monitoring and assessing information society trends. The initiative entered its second phase in June with the launch of activities for collecting core ICT for development indicators in Cameroon, the Gambia, Ghana, Mauritius and Rwanda.

In the area of information and knowledge development, the ECA library launched the African Virtual Library Information Network portal in January as a platform for sharing development information and knowledge on Africa.

ECA was also a major geoinformation knowledge hub; it maintained a clearing house system for researchers and decision makers, providing space for member States to publicize their metadata holdings. Capacity-building activities remained central to ECA's mission of promoting awareness of the importance of harnessing and exploiting ICT for socio-economic development. ECA carried out a number of training courses and workshops throughout the year and continued to work through a number of bilateral and multilateral partnership mechanisms to carry out its activities.

Sustainable development

ECA activities in the area of fostering sustainable development aimed to promote awareness of the environmental foundations of sustainable development, with particular emphasis on integrating environmental sustainability into national development processes and poverty reduction strategies so that economic and social development would not be undermined by environmental degradation. They focused on: reinforcing the linkages among food security, population, environment and human settlements; improving stewardship of natural resources by strengthening capacities for sustainable exploitation; and building capacity in the use of science and technology to achieve sustainable development.

In the area of promoting agriculture and food security, ECA participated in five regional implementation meetings and in a summit (Accra, 5-6 May), which resulted in the adoption of the Accra Plan of Action to advance the implementation of the NEPAD Comprehensive African Agricultural Development Programme agenda at regional and country levels. Also in the framework of UN support for NEPAD, specifically the subcluster on water, the ECA secretariat organized workshops in Southern Africa (Pretoria, South Africa, 2-9 March) and North Africa (Cairo, Egypt, 14-17 April) for decision makers and technical personnel in water management to facilitate the development of an African regional water clearing house to strengthen cooperation in integrated water resources management. The inaugural issue of ECA's Sustainable Development Report on Africa highlighted significant environmental trends in the region with a view to increasing awareness of innovative ways to mainstream environment and sustainable development issues into national planning instruments. The fourth meeting of the Committee on Sustainable Development (Addis Ababa, 24-28 October) was held under the theme, "Managing land-based resources for sustainable development". In addition to discussing the theme issue, the Committee considered recent developments in science and technology policy for sustainable development and reviewed ECA's work programme in sustainable development.

ECA activities with regard to energy included a series of studies and reports on power sector reforms, particularly their environmental impact. Similarly, work undertaken in the area of science and technology was aimed at enhancing awareness of the role it could play in achieving sustainable development.

Development management

Addressing the challenge of establishing and sustaining good governance practices for broad stakeholder participation in the development process and strengthening the foundations for sustainable development in Africa remained the central objective of ECA's work under its subprogramme on strengthening development management.

During the year, ECA organized a series of subregional workshops on "Codes and standards for economic and corporate governance in Africa" in collaboration with its five subregional offices (SROs). The aim of the workshops was to provide a forum for experts and policy makers to review economic and corporate practices in member States; identify the main challenges, strategies and good practices; and make recommendations to enhance economic and corporate governance in the region. Each workshop ended with the adoption of a plan of action to promote better corporate governance in the public and private sectors.

The third meeting of the Committee on Human Development and Civil Society (Addis Ababa, 4-6 May) [E/ECA/CHDCS.3/7], held under the theme "Participation and Partnerships for Improving Development and Governance in Africa", underlined the importance of participation and partnerships among civil society, government and the private sector with a view to enhancing transparency, strengthening checks and balances in government and improving efficiency and accountability in the national budgeting process and the delivery of basic social services.

To address the challenge of achieving coherence of policy actions in international support for Africa, ECA and the Development Co-operation Directorate of OECD completed work on a framework for monitoring the progress of Africa and its development partners in support of the NEPAD objectives, and ensuring harmonization of donor policies. A draft of that document, the Mutual Review of Development Effectiveness in the Context of NEPAD, was presented at the fourth meeting of the Africa Partnership Forum (Abuja, 9-10 April), which brought together representatives of the G-8 countries, other OECD members, the 20 nations serving on the NEPAD Heads of State and Government Implementation Committee, the AU Commission and RECs.

The first annual African Governance Report (AGR) was issued in 2005. Even before its formal launching, scheduled for 2006, it was being used by several regional and subregional institutions to support their work on governance. AGR country case studies also served as inputs into the African Peer Review country self-assessment. A number of ad hoc expert group meetings and workshops were organized to review the results of research, analytical studies and publications prepared by the secretariat. Governance issues discussed at those meetings included: best practices in participatory development; public financial management and accountability in the context of budget transparency in Africa; and the role of Africa's civil society in the implementation of the APRM.

Promoting trade and regional integration

In 2005, ECA continued its efforts to accelerate the effective integration of Africa into the global economy and strengthen the process of regional integration on the continent through promoting intraregional and international trade and physical integration.

Throughout the year, ECA worked closely with other partners in supporting the member States in their preparations for the Sixth Ministerial Conference of the World Trade Organization (WTO) in December (see p. 1041). In that regard, ECA and the AU organized a meeting of African Ministers of Trade (Arusha, United Republic of Tanzania, 21-24 November) to assist them in defining and synchronizing their negotiating positions. Despite the failure of the WTO Ministerial Conference to reach agreement on key issues, Africa successfully defended its position, particularly on the crucial issue of agriculture, where it was agreed that various farm support measures would be eliminated by 2013.

ECA increased its support to member States in building a coherent strategy for negotiations between the African, Caribbean and Pacific States and EU countries on the Economic Partnership Agreements (EPAs). ECA undertook a comprehensive impact assessment of EPAs and organized three subregional expert group meetings to examine the main challenges of the negotiations and their potential implications for subregional economies. ECA presented the results of its technical studies, which highlighted the potential impact of concluding an EPA as proposed by the EU, and made recommendations on how Africa should respond. The subregional meetings were followed by a regional meeting (Mombasa, Kenya, 22-24 September) at which lessons and experiences from the various regions were shared and the way forward on EPAs agreed. In response to a request for ECA to examine how African countries could mitigate some of the possible im-

pacts of an EPA, it conducted studies on African countries that had concluded free trade agreements with the EU (Egypt, Morocco, South Africa, Tunisia) and distilled lessons for other African countries. In addition, ECA was undertaking country-specific studies on the likely impact of EPAs, working with national governments and research institutions so that they would gain the experience and skills necessary to conduct further studies. Studies had been completed for Djibouti, Ethiopia, Gabon, Mali, Rwanda, Senegal and Seychelles.

The work of the African Trade Policy Centre, established in 2004 [YUN 2004, p. 998] to strengthen ECA capacity on trade-related issues, continued in 2005. The Centre provided advisory services and training to African countries and regularly published analytical and policy-relevant research to assist member States in developing their negotiating positions.

The fourth session of the Committee on Trade, Regional Cooperation and Integration (Addis Ababa, 23-25 March) reviewed ECA's current and future work priorities in support of trade promotion and economic integration in Africa. The Committee also addressed policies and modalities for implementing regional integration at the national level, reviewed progress and prospects for greater inter-African trade and assessed the status of WTO and EPA negotiations.

Transport and communications

An important objective of ECA's work in the area of infrastructure development was to help establish an efficient, integrated and affordable transport and communications system. As part of the sub-Saharan Africa Transport Programme, a joint initiative of ECA and the World Bank, ECA co-organized the meeting of African Ministers of Transport (Bamako, Mali, 15-16 November). The Ministers adopted a declaration in which they committed themselves to integrating regional corridor treaties and relevant international transport conventions into national legislation, and to removing all non-physical barriers to transport.

In preparation for upcoming events, ECA was conducting a study on the status of transport development in Africa, the findings of which would feed into a 2006 symposium on financing transport infrastructure development in Africa.

Europe-Africa permanent link

In response to Economic and Social Council resolution 2003/52 [YUN 2003, p. 1004], the Secretary-General submitted an April report [E/2005/21] by the Executive Secretaries of ECA and ECE on the work done in connection with the project to establish a Europe-Africa permanent link through the Strait of Gibraltar. Work had taken place in the areas of geodesy, oceanography, geo-prospecting, deep borehole drilling and socio-economic research. Deep-drilling surveys were in progress, and their reports would help clarify geological uncertainties regarding the central portion of the project's undersea route and determine its longitudinal profile. The surveys would also provide information for construction strategies, first for an exploratory gallery and then for a rail tunnel. Future work would centre on the implementation of the 2004-2006 programme of work, giving special attention to the fourth borehole survey already in progress, and to updating the basic engineering and user traffic forecasting studies, in order to formulate the technical and financial feasibility appraisal.

ECONOMIC AND SOCIAL COUNCIL ACTION

On 27 July [meeting 40], the Economic and Social Council adopted **resolution 2005/34** [draft: E/2005/L.21] without vote [agenda item 10].

Europe-Africa fixed link through the Strait of Gibraltar

The Economic and Social Council,

Recalling its resolutions 1982/57 of 30 July 1982, 1983/62 of 29 July 1983, 1984/75 of 27 July 1984, 1985/70 of 26 July 1985, 1987/69 of 8 July 1987, 1989/119 of 28 July 1989, 1991/74 of 26 July 1991, 1993/60 of 30 July 1993, 1995/48 of 27 July 1995, 1997/48 of 22 July 1997, 1999/37 of 28 July 1999, 2001/29 of 26 July 2001 and 2003/52 of 24 July 2003,

Referring to resolution 912(1989) adopted on 1 February 1989 by the Parliamentary Assembly of the Council of Europe regarding measures to encourage the construction of a major traffic artery in south-western Europe and to study thoroughly the possibility of a fixed link through the Strait of Gibraltar,

Referring also to the Barcelona Declaration adopted at the Euro-Mediterranean Conference, held in Barcelona, Spain, in November 1995, and to the work programme annexed thereto, aimed at connecting the Mediterranean transport networks to the trans-European transport network so as to ensure their interoperability,

Referring further to the Lisbon Declaration adopted at the Conference on Transport in the Mediterranean, held in Lisbon in January 1997, and to the conclusions of the Pan-European Transport Conference, held in Helsinki in June 1997, on corridors in the Mediterranean incorporating the fixed link,

Taking note of the follow-up report prepared jointly by the Economic Commission for Europe and the Economic Commission for Africa pursuant to resolution 2003/52,

Taking note also of the conclusions of the second and third meetings of the Western Mediterranean Transport Group, held, respectively, in Rabat in September 1995 and in Madrid in January 1997, and of the conclusions of the meeting held in Brussels in 2000 by the Euro-Mediterranean Forum on Transport, which constitutes a framework for coordination among the coun-

tries of the Mediterranean basin for the development of integrated transport networks,

Taking note further of the conclusions of the studies launched by the European Commission (INFRAMED, MEDA TEN-T and DESTIN) for the development of an integrated transport network in the Mediterranean basin,

Taking note of the progress of the high-level committee on extension of the main trans-European transport arteries to neighbouring countries and regions, set up by the European Commission, which considers the France-Iberian peninsula-Morocco artery to be a corridor constituting a continuation of the trans-European network,

1. *Welcomes* the cooperation on the project for the link through the Strait of Gibraltar between the Economic Commission for Africa, the Economic Commission for Europe, the Governments of Morocco and Spain and specialized international organizations;

2. *Also welcomes* the progress made in deep-sea drilling project studies, and especially the work carried out, which have given a decisive impetus to geological and geotechnical explorations of undersea formations;

3. *Commends* the Economic Commission for Europe and the Economic Commission for Africa for the work done in preparing the project follow-up report requested by the Council in its resolution 2003/52;

4. *Notes with appreciation* the holding, in Madrid in January 2005, by the International Tunnelling Association, under the aegis of the Economic Commission for Europe and the Economic Commission for Africa, of a seminar on soundings and treatments;

5. *Renews its invitation* to the competent organizations of the United Nations system and to specialized governmental and non-governmental organizations to participate in the studies and work on the fixed link through the Strait of Gibraltar;

6. *Requests* the Executive Secretaries of the Economic Commission for Africa and the Economic Commission for Europe to continue to take an active part in the follow-up to the project and to report to the Council at its substantive session of 2007;

7. *Requests* the Secretary-General to provide formal support and, to the extent that priorities permit, the resources necessary, within the regular budget, to the Economic Commission for Europe and the Economic Commission for Africa, to enable them to carry out the activities mentioned above.

Integration of women in development

The overall objective of ECA's subprogramme on promoting the advancement of women was to mainstream gender into development policies, programmes and structures of member States. As a tool for gender mainstreaming, the secretariat completed work on the Easy Reference Guidebook on Mainstreaming Unpaid Work and Household Production in National Statistics, Policies and Programmes. Subregional workshops were organized for statisticians, planners and gender policy experts to assist member States in the effective use of the Guidebook. As a complement to the Guidebook, ECA took steps to increase the use of regular time-use surveys in Cameroon, Djibouti, Ghana, Morocco, Uganda and Zambia, with the aim of generating new, more accurate gender disaggregated statistics that addressed the MDGs.

In 2005, the results of the 12 pilot studies of the African Gender and Development Index, a monitoring mechanism to track progress towards gender equality and women's advancement, were produced. The countries had collected gender-disaggregated data in the social, economic and political areas and also reported on their achievements in reducing gender disparities and promoting the advancement of women. The studies revealed that the social sector had witnessed critical milestones in gender equality, particularly in primary and secondary education.

Other activities under the subprogramme included promoting the implementation of the Outcome and Way Forward document adopted at the seventh (2004) African Regional Conference on Women [YUN 2004, p. 998] and strengthening the capacity of ECA secretariat divisions and SROs in mainstreaming gender into ECA's activities and outputs.

Subregional offices

ECA's five subregional offices (SROs), located in Central, East, North, Southern and West Africa, continued to promote the harmonization of national policies in support of integration efforts and assist countries of the subregions to consolidate RECs in the overall framework of the AU and attain the goals set by NEPAD. A major priority was to support member States and the RECs in translating the priorities of NEPAD into concrete projects and programmes at the country and subregional levels, particularly in the areas of trade, infrastructure, human capacity development, gender mainstreaming, agriculture, food security and the environment.

The SROs, which served as the operational arms of ECA, facilitated subregional economic cooperation and integration and served as centres for policy dialogue through workshops, training, data collection and knowledge sharing. They also collaborated with other UN agencies in their subregions within the context of the UN Resident Coordinator system and the Common Country Assessment/United Nations Development Assistance Framework in the implementation of operational activities at the national level.

OIOS report. On 14 July, the Secretary-General submitted to the General Assembly a report of the Office of Internal Oversight Services (OIOS) on the inspection of programme and administrative management of the ECA's SROs [A/60/120]. OIOS stated that the SROs for East Af-

rica (Kigali, Rwanda), Southern Africa (Lusaka, Zambia), West Africa (Niamey, Niger), North Africa (Tangier, Morocco) and Central Africa (Yaoundé, Cameroon) were a vital part of ECA. However, their mandate was fulfilled only partially and their role was not clear. OIOS reviewed the progress and effectiveness of the implementation of all components of the SROs' mandate, focusing on coordination, cooperation and partnerships in operational activities and outreach. It learned that the activity of the SROs under each of their defined core functions was far more modest than mandated, and lack of resources limited their activity mainly to their countries of residence and restricted their ability to act as ECA's operational arm throughout their subregions. There was a lack of clarity regarding the balance between operational and analytical activities, and the SROs were weak facilitators of the integration activities of UN organizations and agencies in the subregions.

OIOS concluded that, while the resources of the SROs needed to be increased, resource growth needed to be drastically different in nature. The SROs needed operational expertise, skills that were geared to the specific requirements of their respective subregions, and specialist input to develop and maintain effective outreach and communications and establish a wide visibility in the subregions. Most of all, they needed an increased inflow of ICT resources in order to be effective collectors and disseminators of information relevant to the subregions. Another important challenge was to create a comprehensive, inclusive and dynamic system of coordination and cooperation among SROs; between SROs, UN agencies and other developmental partners; and with regional economic communities (RECs). A further challenge would be to prove convincingly to all concerned the unique value of SROs. Among other things, OIOS recommended that ECA: develop a separate subprogramme of work for each SRO in its biennial budgets; conduct an overall review of the function of regional advisers to ensure that their expertise was deployed correctly; establish a transparent, participatory and equitable mechanism for providing training to SROs; and develop a plan of evaluation and self-evaluation of the work of the SROs and consistently implement it.

GENERAL ASSEMBLY ACTION

On 23 December [meeting 69], the General Assembly, on the recommendation of the Fifth Committee [draft: A/60/609], adopted **resolution 60/235** without vote [agenda item 122].

Report of the Office of Internal Oversight Services on the inspection of programme and administrative management of the subregional offices of the Economic Commission for Africa

The General Assembly,

Recalling its resolutions 48/218 B of 29 July 1994, 54/244 of 23 December 1999 and 59/272 of 23 December 2004,

Having considered the report of the Office of Internal Oversight Services on the inspection of programme and administrative management of the subregional offices of the Economic Commission for Africa,

1. *Recalls* its resolution 59/287 of 13 April 2005 and its decision that the development of Africa shall be among the priorities of the Organization for the biennium 2006-2007;

2. *Recalls also* its resolutions 57/2 of 16 September 2002 and 57/7 of 4 November 2002, and stresses the important role played by the Economic Commission for Africa in coordinating the activities of the United Nations system at the regional level in support of the New Partnership for Africa's Development;

3. *Takes note* of the report of the Office of Internal Oversight Services on the inspection of programme and administrative management of the subregional offices of the Economic Commission for Africa, and welcomes the initial steps that the Commission has taken to implement the recommendations of the Office;

4. *Urges* the full and expeditious implementation of the recommendations of the Office of Internal Oversight Services, and requests the Secretary-General to support the efforts of the Economic Commission for Africa and its subregional offices to implement the recommendations of the Office;

5. *Also urges,* in particular, the appropriate integration of the subregional offices into the strategy for the Economic Commission for Africa to ensure increased coordination and the most effective management of resources and implementation of mandates;

6. *Requests* the Secretary-General to ensure that the information and communications technology capacity and strategy of the Economic Commission for Africa and its subregional offices are fully integrated with the information and communications technology strategy of the Organization and that it is used to its full capacity to disseminate information by electronic means;

7. *Also requests* the Secretary-General to intensify his efforts to fill vacancies in the subregional offices, inter alia, by recruiting staff with the appropriate operational skills and expertise that match the development priorities of the respective subregions;

8. *Takes note with concern* of the finding that the subregional offices of the Economic Commission for Africa have a restricted ability to act as the operational arm of the Commission throughout the countries of their respective subregions owing to the lack of adequate resources for core functions, the insufficient level of guidance and support from the headquarters of the Commission and the lack of a clear understanding as to the role of the subregional offices;

9. *Stresses* the important contribution that the Economic Commission for Africa and its subregional offices are making towards supporting the efforts of the regional economic communities of Africa to implement the priorities and objectives of the New Partnership for Africa's Development, and recognizes the need to strengthen the subregional offices;

10. *Requests* the Secretary-General to develop separate subprogrammes for the subregional offices of the Economic Commission for Africa;

11. *Also requests* the Secretary-General to enhance interaction between the regional advisers and subregional offices of the Economic Commission for Africa to ensure a closer link with subregional needs;

12. *Further requests* the Secretary-General to submit to the General Assembly at its sixty-first session a comprehensive plan of action to strengthen the subregional offices, based on the recommendations of the Office of Internal Oversight Services, with timelines and clear lines of managerial accountability and, in the context of the plan of action, to ensure that adequate resources are provided to the Economic Commission for Africa and its subregional offices to continue their support for the New Partnership for Africa's Development and the regional economic communities for Africa, as well as to ensure the full implementation of the recommendations of the Office of Internal Oversight Services.

Development planning and administration

The objective of the subprogramme on development planning and administration, implemented by the African Institute for Economic Development and Planning (IDEP), was to enhance national capacity for the formulation and implementation of development policies and economic management through training. IDEP contributed to strengthening the technical and analytical skills of experts in the public and private sectors of member States who performed the essential functions of strategic economic planning and management. To that end, IDEP conducted activities in the areas of training, seminars, workshops, conferences, library acquisition, documentation, networking and policy-oriented research.

Mid-career and senior officials from regional organizations and the public and private sectors were trained in the fields of economic policy and management, regional economic integration in Africa, applied econometrics for economic policy making, debt management and agricultural policies. The courses were organized in collaboration with several regional, continental and international institutions including the AU, the Arab Bank for Economic Development in Africa and the Government of the Netherlands.

IDEP staff members undertook six research studies on various policy-related issues, which were presented at international conferences, and 44 theses and graduate research papers were produced by trainees.

Construction of office facilities at ECA

In response to General Assembly resolution 56/270 [YUN 2002, p. 1458], the Secretary-General submitted a 3 November report [A/60/532] on progress in the construction of additional office facilities at ECA headquarters in Addis Ababa. He requested the Assembly to authorize the expansion of the new office building by two additional floors, endorse a proposed phased approach in financing of further requirements and approve an additional appropriation of funds in the amount of $3,671,500 for the project. The Assembly also had before it a report of the Advisory Committee on Administrative and Budgetary Questions (ACABQ) on the Secretary-General's proposals [A/60/7/Add.21]. ACABQ recommended approval of the total estimated additional costs of $3,671,500 if the Assembly were to approve the expansion.

On 23 December, the Assembly, in **resolution 60/248**, section VII (see p. 1495), took note of the Secretary-General's report and endorsed ACABQ's recommendations.

Regional cooperation

Cooperation between UN and ECCAS

On 14 July [meeting 113] the General Assembly, having considered the section of the Secretary-General's 2004 consolidated report on cooperation between the UN and regional organizations [YUN 2004, p. 999], which described cooperation between the UN and the Economic Community of Central African States (ECCAS), adopted **resolution 59/310** [draft: A/59/L.16/Rev.1] without vote [agenda item 56 (g)].

Cooperation between the United Nations and the Economic Community of Central African States

The General Assembly,

Recalling its resolutions 55/22 of 10 November 2000, 55/161 of 12 December 2000, 56/39 of 7 December 2001 and 57/40 of 21 November 2002 on cooperation between the United Nations and the Economic Community of Central African States,

Bearing in mind the treaty establishing the Economic Community of Central African States, by which the Central African countries have agreed to work for the economic development of their subregion, to promote economic cooperation and to establish a Common Market of Central Africa,

Recalling the United Nations Millennium Declaration, adopted on 8 September 2000 by the Heads of State and Government at the Millennium Summit of the United Nations, and especially section VII thereof,

Noting that, at the ninth regular session of the Economic Community of Central African States, held at Malabo on 24 June 1999, the Heads of State and Government of the member States decided to resume the activities of the Community, in particular by incorporating a collective security component, and by providing it with sufficient financial and human resources to enable it to become a real tool for the integration of their economies and to foster the development of cooperation between their peoples, with the ultimate aim of making it one of the five pillars of the African community and of helping Central Africa to meet the challenges of globalization,

Bearing in mind the report of the Secretary-General on the causes of conflict and the promotion of durable peace and sustainable development in Africa,

Welcoming the establishment of the Council for Peace and Security in Central Africa with a view to creating a climate of peace and security in the subregion and strengthening the rule of law essential to its development,

Welcoming also the efforts made by the Central African States, both on their own initiative and with the support of the international community, to focus on the difficulties afflicting this key region of Africa,

Noting the understanding of the States members of the Economic Community of Central African States regarding their undertaking to strengthen arrangements for cooperation within the Community,

Noting with deep concern that despite its enormous potential, which could make it one of the poles of development of the continent, Central Africa has yet to achieve the stability that would enable it to utilize its resources to the maximum benefit of its population in an equitable manner,

Welcoming the contribution made by the United Nations system to the efforts made at the national and subregional levels with a view to promoting the process of democratization, recovery and development in Central Africa,

Welcoming also the public meeting of the Security Council on 22 October 2002 devoted to strengthening cooperation between the United Nations system and the Central African region,

Recognizing the role that the private sector can play in the socio-economic development of Central African countries and their integration into the world economy, and stressing the importance of fostering a favourable environment for private investment and entrepreneurship,

Aware of the opportunities and challenges which globalization and liberalization can create for the economies of the countries of the subregion,

Noting with satisfaction that, as a result of the positive efforts of regional and subregional organizations, the subregion is gradually emerging from the conflicts that affect it, which offers an opportunity to build peace that must be seized by all parties and requires the mobilization of significant funds and increased resources to support demobilization, disarmament and reintegration programmes,

Welcoming the achievements of the Subregional Centre for Human Rights and Democracy in Central Africa,

Noting the positive measures taken by the Economic Community of Central African States to combat HIV/AIDS,

Noting also the important contribution of women to the development process,

Emphasizing the urgency of reaching an appropriate solution to the problem of refugees and internally displaced persons in Central Africa,

1. *Takes note* of the report of the Secretary-General on cooperation between the United Nations and the Economic Community of Central African States;

2. *Welcomes* the ongoing efforts of the Secretary-General to support the role of the subregional institutions, in particular his decision to dispatch, in June 2003, at the request of the Security Council, a multidisciplinary assessment mission to the Central African subregion with the task of implementing a global, holistic approach to the problems of peace, security and development in the subregion;

3. *Also welcomes* the efforts of States Members of the United Nations and United Nations organs, organizations and agencies which have maintained or strengthened their cooperation with the Economic Community of Central African States or have begun to cooperate with it with a view to achieving peace, security and development;

4. *Invites* the States Members of the United Nations and United Nations organs, organizations and agencies which have not yet established contact or relations with the Economic Community of Central African States to consider doing so in order to help the Community to strengthen its capacities in the area of the maintenance of peace and security and reconstruction;

5. *Commends* the international community for the financial, technical and material support given to the Economic Community of Central African States;

6. *Emphasizes* the importance of close cooperation between the United Nations system, including the Bretton Woods institutions, and the Economic Community of Central African States;

7. *Welcomes* the reforms undertaken by the Economic Community of Central African States, including the execution of its programme of action, in order to be better able to tackle the problems of cooperation and regional integration;

8. *Urges* all Member States and the international community to contribute to the efforts of the Economic Community of Central African States to achieve economic integration and development, promote democracy and human rights and consolidate peace and security in Central Africa and to implement the goals, targets and commitments of the United Nations conferences and the United Nations Millennium Declaration, in particular, to strengthen the role of women in the development process;

9. *Urges* the international community and the United Nations agencies to continue to provide those countries of the Economic Community of Central African States in which a process of national reconstruction is taking place with appropriate assistance to consolidate their efforts towards democratization and the consolidation of the rule of law and to support their national development programmes;

10. *Invites* the United Nations and the international community to coordinate their efforts to assist the Central African States in establishing demobilization, disarmament and reintegration programmes;

11. *Declares itself convinced* of the importance to conflict resolution of the implementation of global, integrated and concerted strategies on questions relating to peace, security and development, and aware of the value of international cooperation and efforts to restore and maintain peace, and emphasizes that the international community should continue to help those

countries which receive refugees to meet the resulting economic, social, humanitarian and environmental challenges;

12. *Urges* the United Nations and the international community as a whole to help to strengthen the means existing in the region to ensure that the Economic Community of Central African States has the necessary capacity with regard to prevention, monitoring, early warning and peacekeeping operations;

13. *Encourages* the countries of the Economic Community of Central African States to implement policies that promote sustained economic growth and sustainable development, including by promoting competition, regulatory reform, respect for property rights and expeditious contract enforcement;

14. *Stresses* the need to focus international assistance to countries of the Economic Community of Central African States in the areas of socio-economic growth and sustainable development, implementation of market-oriented reforms and the meeting of internationally agreed development goals, including those contained in the Millennium Declaration, and encourages the countries of the Community to improve governance and institutional capabilities in order to use aid more effectively;

15. *Requests* the Secretary-General to continue to enhance contacts with the Economic Community of Central African States with a view to strengthening cooperation between the United Nations system and the Community;

16. *Also requests* the Secretary-General to report to it at its sixty-first session on the implementation of the present resolution.

Asia and the Pacific

The Economic and Social Commission for Asia and the Pacific (ESCAP) held its sixty-first session in Bangkok, Thailand, in two parts: the senior officials segment from 12 to 14 May and the ministerial segment from 16 to 18 May [E/2005/39]. The session's theme topic was "Implementing the Monterrey Consensus in the Asian and Pacific Region: Achieving Coherence and Consistency". The Commission discussed policy issues for the ESCAP region; key developments and activities at the regional level; least developed, landlocked and island developing countries; management issues; technical cooperation activities; reports of regional intergovernmental bodies; and the activities of the Advisory Committee of Permanent Representatives and Other Representatives Designated by Members of the Commission [E/ESCAP/1352 & Add.1].

The Ministerial Round Table on Financing for Development was divided into two sessions. The first session consisted of presentations on the theme topic (see above) and on development, investment requirements and resource mobilization issues of the region; the second session heard presentations on domestic resource mobilization: role of the private sector and on an Asian investment fund: what it will do and why needed. The Round Table had before it a note by the secretariat [E/ESCAP/1332] on implementing the Monterrey Consensus [YUN 2002, p. 953], adopted at the 2002 International Conference on Financing for Development [ibid.], in the Asian and Pacific region.

A meeting of the High-level Panel on Tsunami Recovery Development also took place (see p. 1107).

Economic trends

According to the summary of the *Economic and Social Survey of Asia and the Pacific, 2006* [E/2006/18], the growth rate of the region's developing countries decelerated moderately in 2005. Those countries achieved a real GDP growth rate of 6.6 per cent compared to 7.4 per cent in 2004. The slowdown was primarily the result of high and volatile oil prices and a softening of global trade. More expensive oil also led to a very slight increase in inflation.

East and North-East Asia achieved an impressive average economic growth rate of 6.9 per cent in 2005, led by China, which achieved a rate of 9.6 per cent. The countries of North and Central Asia experienced the seventh successive year of growth in GDP, achieving 6.9 per cent for the year. Although high energy and commodity prices were driving such growth rates in the subregion, domestic demand also played an important role.

Not including Bangladesh, a least developed country (LDC), South and South-West Asia saw a rise in GDP of 7.0 per cent in 2005. South Asian countries maintained their growth momentum despite rising oil prices. Aided by normal monsoon rains, the reforms and structural changes initiated earlier had begun to pay off. The increasing integration of the subregion into the global economy, rising consumer spending and generally supportive policies were also helping the pace of growth. In South-West Asia, high energy prices continued to underpin the performance of Iran, but caused the economy to slow in Turkey.

Economic growth in the South-East Asian subregion, not including the LDCs, eased to 5.4 per cent in 2005 after an unusually good performance of 6.4 per cent in 2004, when strong global demand for manufactures, especially electronics and ICT products, had driven growth. Despite the doubling of oil prices between 2002 and 2004 and their continued rise in 2005, the region did not experience any marked increase in price pressures until the second quarter of 2005.

Lack of reliable data was a major constraint in reporting on the Pacific island countries, but there were indications that, despite continued political instability in the subregion, most of the economies expanded in 2005, due mainly to the growth of tourism, ongoing diversification in agriculture and the development of the aquaculture and fishing industries.

Among LDCs in the region, Bangladesh was experiencing steady growth. Inclement weather and internal conflict in Nepal led to slower growth in agriculture and in the broader economy. In Cambodia, the Lao People's Democratic Republic and Myanmar, the pace of GDP growth was broadly maintained, but price pressures increased. As a group, the LDCs in the region posted an economic growth rate of 5.2 per cent for the year.

The developed countries of the region saw an average growth of 2.5 per cent for 2005. Japan was witnessing a recovery in private consumption, which buttressed higher investment expenditures by corporations. In Australia and New Zealand, GDP growth eased in 2005 compared with 2004 but remained close to its long-term trend. Strong export growth was partly offset by weaker domestic demand.

Policy issues

The policy challenges facing Asia and the Pacific in 2005 included oil prices, which had doubled since the beginning of 2004 and tripled since 2002. As the region was highly dependent on oil, it remained vulnerable to any significant future increases. Both oil-importing and oil-exporting countries needed to develop a longer-term policy response to reduce oil dependency, improve energy efficiency and promote energy conservation.

Another policy issue was that of widening imbalances in the external accounts of the larger world economies, which posed a major economic risk for the ESCAP region. A precipitous spiralling of those imbalances could create large upheavals in the international financial markets and cause significant exchange rate instability involving not only the dollar but perhaps several currencies in the region as well. As there was only limited scope to address that problem at the national level, regional or international-level policy responses were required.

A further important issue was the potentially adverse impact on growth of a combination of tighter fiscal and monetary policies. The policy challenge was therefore to mix fiscal and monetary policies judiciously in order to ensure steady output growth over the following 12 to18 months. Governments were advised to develop medium-term scenarios for GDP growth, inflation, budgetary and balance-of-payments outcomes through a process of consultation with all relevant stakeholders.

Avian influenza presented a potential threat to the region in both human and economic terms. There was an urgent need for collective preparedness involving stockpiling medical supplies and taking joint action on possible control measures, such as travel restrictions. It was also important from the standpoint of cost-effectiveness to concentrate resources and action on controlling the disease at the source before it developed into a more rapidly spreading contagion.

Although the Asian and Pacific region had been growing faster economically than most parts of the world for two decades or more, the eradication of poverty remained its most important challenge. While rapid economic growth remained the surest route for reducing both income and non-income poverty, in countries where poverty was widespread, jobs and income growth alone would not have a positive impact on non-income poverty. Governments needed to intervene to make the growth process more equitable by expanding the provision of and access to public goods, particularly for and by the poor. Inequitable growth was a major issue in many smaller economies, including LDCs and Pacific island States. Their national efforts could be severely undermined by the paucity of financial and non-financial resources and further eroded by physical remoteness, as in the case of the Pacific island States. Without regional and international aid and support, the prospects for sustained long-term growth and poverty reduction were very limited.

Remittances sent by migrant workers on contract abroad had helped greatly to raise the standard of living of some of the poorest sections of society in South and South-East Asia and the Pacific. Countries with high levels of underemployment and with limited opportunities for formal sector employment could follow the example set by the Philippines and systematically promote the temporary export of workers as part of a national development and poverty-reducing strategy.

With regard to the WTO programme, developing economies in the ESCAP region were likely to be challenged in the upcoming months to make concessions of a commercial value so that developed countries would remain committed to the Doha Development Agenda, adopted by WTO in 2001 [YUN 2001, p. 1432]. The trade-dependent economies of the region would therefore need to

consider how they might harness the traditional reciprocity dynamics of WTO to move forward on their market access expectations.

At its 2005 session, ESCAP considered a report on the current economic situation in the region and related policy issues [E/ESCAP/1331] and the *Economic and Social Survey of Asia and the Pacific, 2005* [ST/ESCAP/2349].

While noting the importance of economic growth for sustained poverty reduction, the Commission pointed out that it was also necessary to ensure that economic benefits reached society's vulnerable groups, including women, children, young people, older persons and persons with disabilities. In that regard, the State was responsible for providing public goods and social safety nets to protect the neediest, and for enacting policies to ensure adequate investment in health and education. Given that demographic changes in most countries could result in older people constituting an increasingly large proportion of the population, the Commission asked the secretariat to consider the role of traditional support systems and identify ways to strengthen and weave those systems into broader national programmes to support ageing populations and formulate strategies to finance social security schemes and pensions.

In view of the crucial role that human resources development played in tackling poverty, the Commission urged that special measures be promoted to enhance access to livelihoods and the skills development and education of women, particularly women heading households and those with disabilities. It also urged the full implementation of the commitments made in the Beijing Declaration and Platform for Action [YUN 1995, p. 1170], adopted at the Fourth World Conference on Women [ibid., p. 1168], and the achievement of the MDG related to gender equality and the empowerment of women [YUN 2000, p. 51]. The Commission highlighted the need to increase women's political participation and economic opportunities and to eliminate violence against women and the trafficking of women and children. It asked the secretariat to examine the best practices of countries with effective programmes to combat human trafficking and issues related to international migration.

Drawing attention to the proclamation by the General Assembly, in resolution 53/197 [YUN 1998, p. 785], of 2005 as the International Year of Microcredit (see p. 928), the Commission emphasized the role of microfinance and microcredit in poverty reduction. It asked the secretariat to play a leading role in promoting microfinancing initiatives in the region, including by facilitating studies of best practices in member countries and sharing information on microcredit strategies.

Activities in 2005

Poverty reduction

The Commission had before it a note by the secretariat on key issues relating to poverty reduction [E/ESCAP/1334], which analysed the poverty situation in the region and discussed briefly the impact of the 2004 tsunami [YUN 2004, p. 000] on poverty in the affected countries. It also considered the reports of the first sessions of the Subcommittee on Poverty Reduction Practices [E/ESCAP/CPR(2)/4] and the Subcommittee on Statistics [E/ESCAP/CPR(2)/6], held in 2004 [YUN 2004, p. 1005]. The Commission endorsed the recommendations made at the 2004 sessions of the two subcommittees but observed that some prioritization was needed in terms of the areas on which the secretariat should focus. It noted that while significant progress had been made in reducing poverty, it still remained a major challenge. The 2004 tsunami and other natural disasters had had a negative impact on the poverty reduction process.

The Commission called for coherent policies and strategies, along with broad consensus, political will and a sense of purpose about the range of actions needed to reduce poverty. It called for greater collaboration between government, the private sector, civil society and the international community, so that stakeholders could play their vital roles in advocacy, planning and implementation of poverty reduction programmes. It urged that concrete steps be taken to support women's economic activities and called for comprehensive strategies and policies aimed at employment creation, community empowerment, capacity-building and social protection.

The secretariat was asked to place more emphasis on the development of the agricultural and rural sectors, as the prevalence of poverty and the so-called "hard-core poor" tended to be highest in them. As agricultural productivity had not increased, rural industrialization could be considered an alternative approach to poverty reduction in rural areas.

The Commission underscored the secretariat's role in promoting regional cooperation, exchange of information and experience and capacity-building to assist members in reducing poverty and promoting good governance. It invited the secretariat to continue its efforts to build the capacity of governments at the national, subnational and local levels. As data collection and analysis and utilization of geographical informa-

tion systems and other technologies were deemed important for sound policy formulation and programme planning, the secretariat and agencies of the UN system were called on to continue to provide technical and financial support to developing countries.

Given the fact that equitable trade, official development assistance (ODA) and debt relief were important in meeting the goals of poverty reduction and development, the Commission requested the secretariat to continue to follow, analyse and report on the issue of developed country subsidies and protection of agriculture and to examine innovative ways to address the chronic debt problem in the developing countries of the region. Some members of the Commission also urged developed countries to allocate 0.7 per cent of their GNP for ODA.

At its second session (Bangkok, 23-25 November), the Committee on Poverty Reduction [E/ESCAP/1364] discussed the process of decentralization and its implications for poverty reduction. It also addressed a number of issues related to the poverty reduction activities of ESCAP. It endorsed the reports of the Subcommittees on Poverty Reduction Practices and on Statistics on their 2004 sessions [YUN 2004, p. 1005]. The Committee further discussed the follow-up to the High-level Plenary Meeting of the sixtieth session of the General Assembly (see p. 47), issues related to the vital role of population and housing censuses in policy- and decision-making at local levels, and a revision of the international recommendations for statistics on economic activities. It also considered programme planning and the evaluation of a selected flagship project in the area of poverty reduction.

Statistics

Having considered the 2004 report of the Subcommittee on Statistics [E/ESCAP/CPR(2)/6], the Commission noted that the revision of the international standards on consumer price indices and household income and expenditure surveys would improve the accuracy of poverty measurement in the region. As household income and expenditure surveys were the most important instruments for collecting poverty data, the Commission recognized the need for them to be well designed and conducted in a manner that would permit poverty to be better understood. It commended efforts by the secretariat to develop its revised plan of action for poverty statistics and to strengthen the statistical capacity of the national and sectoral agencies of ESCAP members, especially the capacity necessary to measure achievements towards the MDGs.

The Commission also had before it the report of the Statistical Institute for Asia and the Pacific (SIAP) [E/ESCAP/1348], which reviewed SIAP's administrative and financial status, the implementation of the 2004 work programme and action taken by the SIAP Governing Board at its tenth (2004) session. On 18 May [E/2005/39 (res. 61/2)], the Commission adopted a revised statute of SIAP, which it recommended to the Economic and Social Council for adoption (see below).

ECONOMIC AND SOCIAL COUNCIL ACTION

On 26 July [meeting 39], the Economic and Social Council, on the recommendation of ESCAP [E/2005/15/Add.1], adopted **resolution 2005/36** without vote [agenda item 10].

Statute of the Statistical Institute for Asia and the Pacific

The Economic and Social Council,

Recalling Economic and Social Commission for Asia and the Pacific resolutions 50/5 of 13 April 1994 and 51/1 of 1 May 1995 on the Statistical Institute for Asia and the Pacific,

Recalling also the host country agreement between the Government of Japan and the United Nations, signed on 14 April 1995,

Noting with appreciation the significant financial and in kind resources that have been provided to the Institute, since its establishment, by the Government of Japan,

Taking into account the recommendations in the evaluation of the Institute carried out in 2003 and the need to integrate the work of the Institute into the programme of work of the Commission,

Taking note of the report on the Statistical Institute for Asia and the Pacific to the Commission at the current session,

Approves the revised statute of the Statistical Institute for Asia and the Pacific, as adopted by the Economic and Social Commission for Asia and the Pacific, the text of which is annexed to the present resolution.

Annex

Statute of the Statistical Institute for Asia and the Pacific

Establishment

1. The Statistical Institute for Asia and the Pacific (hereinafter referred to as "the Institute"), established in May 1970 as the Asian Statistical Institute, and accorded the legal status of a subsidiary body of the Economic and Social Commission for Asia and the Pacific (hereinafter referred to as "ESCAP" or "the Commission") pursuant to Commission resolutions 50/5 of 13 April 1994 and 51/1 of 1 May 1995, shall continue in existence under the terms of the present statute.

2. Participation in the training and other activities of the Institute is open to all members and associate members of the Commission.

3. The Institute has the status of a subsidiary body of ESCAP.

Objectives

4. The objectives of the Institute are to strengthen, through practically-oriented training of official statisticians, the capability of the developing members and associate members and economies in transition of the region to collect, analyse and disseminate statistics as well as to produce timely and high-quality statistics that can be utilized for economic and social development planning, and to assist those developing members and associate members and economies in transition in establishing or strengthening their statistical training capability and other related activities.

Functions

5. The Institute shall achieve the above objectives by undertaking such functions as:

(a) Training of official statisticians, utilizing existing centres and institutions for training available in member States;

(b) Networking and partnership with other international organizations and key stakeholders;

(c) Dissemination of information.

Status and organization

6. The Institute shall have a Governing Council (hereinafter referred to as "the Council"), a Director and staff. The Commission shall keep separate accounts for the Institute.

7. The Institute is located in the Tokyo Metropolitan Area, Japan.

8. The activities of the Institute shall be in line with relevant policy decisions adopted by the General Assembly, the Economic and Social Council and the Commission. The Institute shall be subject to the Financial and Staff Regulations and Rules of the United Nations and the applicable administrative instructions.

Governing Council

9. The Governing Council shall consist of a representative designated by the Government of Japan and eight representatives nominated by other members and associate members of ESCAP elected by the Commission. The members and associate members elected by the Commission shall be elected for a period of five years but shall be eligible for re-election. The Executive Secretary of ESCAP or his/her representative shall attend the meetings of the Council.

10. The Director of the Institute shall serve as Secretary of the Council.

11. Representatives of (a) States that are not members of the Council, (b) United Nations bodies and specialized and related agencies and (c) such other organizations as the Council may deem appropriate, as well as experts in fields of interest to the Council, may be invited by the Executive Secretary to attend meetings of the Council.

12. The Council shall meet at least once a year and shall adopt its own rules of procedure. Sessions of the Council shall be convened by the Executive Secretary of ESCAP, who may propose special sessions of the Council at his/her own initiative and shall convene special sessions at the request of a majority of the Council members.

13. A quorum for meetings of the Council shall be a majority of its members.

14. The nine representatives constituting the Council under paragraph 9 of the present statute shall have one vote each. Decisions and recommendations of

the Council shall be made by consensus or, when that is not possible, by a majority of the members present and voting.

15. The Council shall, at each regular session, elect a Chairperson and Vice-Chairperson, who shall hold office until the next regular session of the Council. The Chairperson or, in his/her absence, the Vice-Chairperson shall preside at the meetings of the Council. If the Chairperson is unable to serve for the full term for which he/she has been elected, the Vice-Chairperson shall act as Chairperson for the remainder of that term.

16. The Council shall review the administrative and financial status of the Institute and the implementation of its programme of work. The Executive Secretary of ESCAP shall submit an annual report, as adopted by the Council, to the Commission at its annual sessions.

17. The Council shall review and endorse annual and long-term workplans consistent with the programme of work.

Director and staff

18. The Institute shall have a Director and staff, who shall be ESCAP staff members appointed under the appropriate United Nations regulations, rules and administrative instructions. The Council will be invited to nominate candidates for the position of Director, once the vacancy is announced, and provide advice, as appropriate. Other members and associate members of the Commission may also submit nominations for the post. The Director and Professional staff shall be appointed for a total term, in principle, not exceeding five years. All appointments shall be for a fixed duration and shall be limited to service with the Institute.

19. The Director shall be responsible to the Executive Secretary of ESCAP for the administration of the Institute, the preparation of annual and long-term workplans and the implementation of the programme of work.

Resources of the Institute

20. All members and associate members of ESCAP should be encouraged to make a regular annual contribution to the operations of the Institute. The United Nations shall administer a joint contribution trust fund for the Institute, as referred to in paragraph 6, in which these contributions shall be deposited and utilized solely for the activities of the Institute, subject to paragraph 21 of the present statute.

21. United Nations bodies and specialized agencies and other entities should also be encouraged to make voluntary contributions to the operations of the Institute. The United Nations shall maintain separate trust funds for voluntary contributions for technical cooperation projects or other extraordinary voluntary contributions for activities of the Institute.

22. The financial resources of the Institute shall be administered in accordance with the Financial Regulations and Rules of the United Nations.

Amendments

23. Amendments to the present statute shall be adopted by means of a resolution of the Commission.

Matters not covered by the present statute

24. In the event of any procedural matter arising that is not covered by the present statute or rules of procedure adopted by the Governing Council under paragraph 12 of the present statute, the pertinent part of the rules of procedure of the Economic and Social Commission for Asia and the Pacific shall apply.

Entry into force

25. The present statute shall enter into force on the date of its adoption by the Commission.

Managing globalization

The Commission had before it four reports by the secretariat on key developments and activities at the regional level with regard to managing globalization [E/ESCAP/1335-1338]. Noting that many countries had not been able to benefit fully from the growth opportunities (increased trade flows, investment and information) that had opened up due to globalization, the Commission called on the secretariat to continue assisting members and associate members in enhancing and strengthening regional development cooperation and managing globalization more effectively. It recognized the importance of intersectoral projects in helping countries enhance capacity-building for the facilitation of trade and transport, formulating coherent trade and environment policies, promoting trade more effectively through knowledge management, and integrating ICT into the development process.

The Commission noted the adoption of the New Asian-African Strategic Partnership at the Asia-Africa Summit (Jakarta, Indonesia, 22-23 April) and requested the secretariat to support that partnership process. It expressed appreciation for the initiative taken by the secretariat in organizing the International Conference on Strengthening Regional Cooperation for Managing Globalization (Moscow, 28-30 September).

The second session of the Committee on Managing Globalization (Bangkok, 12-14 October) [E/ESCAP/1366] urged the secretariat to enhance its technical assistance activities in such areas as entrepreneurship promotion, FDI promotion and facilitation, brand name development and diversification, training in trade facilitation measures, particularly for LDCs and landlocked and transit developing countries, and other aspects of supply-side capacity-building. The secretariat was asked to continue its efforts to coordinate the regional preparations for the second phase of the World Summit on the Information Society (see p. 933) and to implement its outcome, and to consider undertaking a study to identify primary sources of air pollution in mega-cities to enable the formulation of effective abatement strategies. The Committee called on the secretariat to expand its capacity-building activities regarding the accession of ESCAP members to WTO and commended the secretariat for having organized, with the International Trade Centre, the meeting "Delivering on the WTO Round: High-level Government-Business Dialogue for Development (Macao, China, 4-6 October) in preparation for the Sixth WTO Ministerial Conference, to be held in December (see p. 1041). The Committee also asked the secretariat to continue to develop, promote and replicate the approach of public-private partnership initiatives, such as micro-hydropower electricity generation, and to facilitate the microfinancing of similar initiatives for the benefit of poor rural communities in the region. In view of rising oil prices, it further asked the Secretariat to initiate analytical work to develop policy options for energy security in order to improve eco-efficiency and promote commercial alternative energy options.

Least developed, landlocked and island developing countries

Special Body on Least Developed and Landlocked Developing Countries

The Commission had before it the report of the Special Body on Least Developed and Landlocked Developing Countries on its seventh session (Bangkok, 10-11 May) [E/ESCAP/1342], which considered: achieving the MDGs in the LDCs and landlocked developing countries through trade, debt relief and aid, in preparation for the Millennium +5 Summit (see p. 47); and information, communication and space technology (ICST) for meeting development challenges, in preparation for the second phase of the World Summit on the Information Society (see p. 933). It also reviewed the programme of work for the 2004-2005 biennium and requested the secretariat to conduct a mid-term review of the implementation of the Programme of Action for the LDCs for the Decade 2001-2010 [YUN 2001, p. 770].

The Commission stressed the importance of ICST policies and programmes for the development of education, health, business, commerce and disaster prevention and requested the secretariat to continue to assist members in the use of ICST. To ensure expansion of the economies in the region and secure their integration into the global economy, the Commission urged landlocked developing countries, transit developing countries and donor countries to deepen their cooperation in economic infrastructure development, trade facilitation and regional cooperation. In that regard, the 2003 Almaty Programme of Action [YUN 2003, p. 875] provided the frame-

work for partnership for the development of transit transport.

In an 18 May resolution [E/2005/39 (res. 61/11)], the Commission requested the Executive Secretary to integrate the implementation of the Almaty Programme of Action into the relevant work programmes of the secretariat. He was also asked to further expand the secretariat's programme to support the landlocked and transit developing countries in improving their transit transport systems and to report to the Commission in 2007 on progress in that regard.

By **resolution 60/208**, the General Assembly called for specific actions related to the particular needs of landlocked developing countries (see p. 951).

Economic and technical cooperation

In 2005, ESCAP received $25.4 million for technical cooperation activities [E/ESCAP/1383], representing an increase of almost 300 per cent over 2004. Of that amount, some $4 million was received from the UN system. Of the $20.1 million contributed by individual countries, $14 million came from three developing member countries: China, the Republic of Korea and Thailand. Other major donors were Japan and Sweden, which gave a total of $4.9 million. In addition to cash contributions, countries provided, on a non-reimbursable basis, a total of 137 work-months of the services of experts in various disciplines.

Transport, communications, tourism and infrastructure development

The Commission noted that the 2003 Intergovernmental Agreement on the Asian Highway Network [YUN 2003, p. 1010] would enter into force on 4 July 2005, thereby contributing to the improvement of transport infrastructure in participating countries. It requested the secretariat to continue to promote the development of the network and mobilize financial and technical assistance and urged it to continue to work towards the development of an integrated, international intermodal transport network in the region. The secretariat was requested to undertake capacity-building activities with regard to intermodal transport development and planning.

The Working Group on the Asian Highway, at its first meeting (Bangkok, 14-15 December) [TTD/WGAH/Rep.], requested member States to designate focal points responsible for matters related to the implementation of the Intergovernmental Agreement on the Asian Highway Network.

The third Expert Group Meeting on Developing Euro-Asian Transport Linkages (Istanbul, Turkey, 27-29 June), organized by ESCAP and ECE, considered progress already made with regard to identifying selected Euro-Asia routes for priority development, and discussed the main areas of focus for its next phase and the modalities to follow up on the project after its completion.

The Commission recognized the progress achieved at the November 2004 Regional Meeting to Draft an Intergovernmental Agreement on the Trans-Asian Railway Network [YUN 2004, p. 1008], and expressed support for the agreement. The Intergovernmental Meeting to Develop the Intergovernmental Agreement on the Trans-Asia Railway Network (Bangkok, 28-30 November) [E/ESCAP/TARN/Rep.] finalized the text of the Agreement.

With regard to the tourism industry in Asia and the Pacific, the Commission recognized the importance of its role in socio-economic development and poverty alleviation and eradication. It recommended that capacity-building for sustainable development in tourism be accorded high priority. Noting that the December 2004 tsunami [YUN 2004, p. 952] had severely affected tourism in several countries in the region, the Commission asked the secretariat to assist those countries in addressing the impact of the crises. The Commission endorsed the 2004 proposal of the Subcommittee on Transport Infrastructure and Facilitation and Tourism [YUN 2004, p. 1008] for a second phase (2006-2012) of the Plan of Action for Sustainable Tourism Development in the Asian and Pacific Region (1999-2005) [YUN 1999, p. 929].

The High-level Intergovernmental Meeting on Sustainable Tourism Development (Bali, Indonesia, 7-9 December) [E/ESCAP/1369] reviewed achievements resulting from the implementation of the Plan of Action for Sustainable Tourism Development in the Asian and Pacific Region (1999-2005). It also identified the challenges that lay ahead and addressed the strategies and approaches required to achieve sustainable tourism development. The Meeting proposed that a regional study on the role of tourism in socio-economic development be undertaken by the secretariat and include proposals for a common approach to monitoring the Plan of Action and measuring its benefits. It adopted the Bali Declaration on Sustainable Tourism Development, including phase II (2006-2012) of the Plan of Action and its Regional Action Programme for Sustainable Tourism Development. The Meeting was preceded by the Inter-agency/Expert Group Meeting on Tourism and Poverty Reduction (6 December).

Science and technology

Having considered the report of the Asian and Pacific Centre for Transfer of Technology (APCTT) on its 2004 activities and on the nineteenth session of its Governing Board (November 2004) [E/ESCAP/1345], the Commission recommended that the technical assistance activities of APCTT include the areas of ICT, biotechnology and nanotechnology, and that APCTT promote information exchange and collaboration among researchers in member countries.

The Commission adopted a resolution [E/2005/39 (res. 61/4)] on the Statute of the Asian and Pacific Centre for Transfer of Technology, which it recommended to the Economic and Social Council for adoption (see below).

The Commission also had before it the report of the Coordinating Committee for Geoscience Programmes in East and Southeast Asia (CCOP) [E/ESCAP/1353]. It took note of the high level of activities conducted by CCOP, including initiatives in response to the December 2004 tsunami. The forty-second session of CCOP (Beijing, 13-18 September) was followed by the forty-sixth meeting of the CCOP Steering Committee (19-20 September).

The Commission recognized the increasing role of the private sector in providing services based on space technology. It requested the secretariat to conduct studies of success stories with a view to advocating public-private partnerships that would help member countries to benefit from such services.

ECONOMIC AND SOCIAL COUNCIL ACTION

On 26 July [meeting 39], the Economic and Social Council, on the recommendation of ESCAP [E/2005/15/Add.1], adopted **resolution 2005/38** without vote [agenda item 10].

Statute of the Asian and Pacific Centre for Transfer of Technology

The Economic and Social Council,

Recalling Economic and Social Commission for Asia and the Pacific resolution 243(XLI) of 29 March 1985 on the statute of the Asian and Pacific Centre for Transfer of Technology,

Recalling also the agreement between the Government of India and the United Nations regarding the headquarters of the Centre, signed on 11 April 1994,

Noting with appreciation the significant financial resources and facilities that have been provided to the Centre, since its establishment, by the Government of India,

1. *Approves* the revised statute of the Asian and Pacific Centre for Transfer of Technology, as adopted by the Economic and Social Commission for Asia and the Pacific, the text of which is annexed to the present resolution;

2. *Requests* the Executive Secretary to seek regular budget resources for the Centre, including posts, within the proposed programme budget of the Economic and Social Commission for Asia and the Pacific for the biennium 2006-2007, to strengthen the research and

analytical capacity of the Centre, while recognizing the primary role of the Advisory Committee on Administrative and Budgetary Questions and the Fifth Committee in this regard, and recognizing also the principle that the technical assistance activities of the Centre should be funded by voluntary contributions;

3. *Also requests* the Executive Secretary to seek additional voluntary resources to strengthen the financial stability of the Centre.

Annex

Statute of the Asian and Pacific Centre for Transfer of Technology

Establishment

1. The Asian and Pacific Centre for Transfer of Technology (hereinafter referred to as "the Centre" or "APCTT"), established on 16 July 1977 pursuant to Economic and Social Commission for Asia and the Pacific resolutions 159(XXXI) of 6 March 1975 and 164 (XXXII) of 31 March 1976, shall continue in existence under the terms of the present statute.

2. The membership of the Centre is identical to the membership of the Economic and Social Commission for Asia and the Pacific (hereinafter referred to as "ESCAP" or "the Commission").

3. The Centre has the status of a subsidiary body of ESCAP.

Objectives

4. The objectives of the Centre are to assist the members and associate members of ESCAP through strengthening their capabilities to develop and manage national innovation systems; develop, transfer, adapt and apply technology; improve the terms of transfer of technology; and identify and promote the development and transfer of technologies relevant to the region.

Functions

5. The Centre shall achieve the above objectives by undertaking such functions as:

(a) Research and analysis of trends, conditions and opportunities;

(b) Advisory services;

(c) Dissemination of information and good practices;

(d) Networking and partnership with international organizations and key stakeholders;

(e) Training of national personnel, particularly national scientists and policy analysts.

Status and organization

6. The Centre shall have a Governing Council (hereinafter referred to as "the Council"), a Director and staff, and a Technical Committee.

7. The Centre is located in New Delhi.

8. The activities of the Centre shall be in line with relevant policy decisions adopted by the General Assembly, the Economic and Social Council and the Commission. The Centre shall be subject to the Financial and Staff Regulations and Rules of the United Nations and the applicable administrative instructions.

Governing Council

9. The Governing Council shall consist of a representative designated by the Government of India and no fewer than eight representatives nominated by other members and associate members of ESCAP

elected by the Commission. The members and associate members elected by the Commission shall be elected for a period of three years but shall be eligible for re-election. The Executive Secretary of ESCAP or his/her representative shall attend the meetings of the Council.

10. The Director of the Centre shall serve as Secretary of the Council.

11. Representatives of (a) States that are not members of the Council, (b) United Nations bodies and specialized and related agencies and (c) such other organizations as the Council may deem appropriate, as well as experts in fields of interest to the Council, may be invited by the Executive Secretary to attend meetings of the Council.

12. The Council shall meet at least once a year and adopt its own rules of procedure. Sessions of the Council shall be convened by the Executive Secretary of ESCAP, who may propose special sessions of the Council at his/her own initiative and shall convene such special sessions at the request of a majority of Council members.

13. A quorum for meetings of the Council shall be a majority of its members.

14. Each member of the Council shall have one vote. Decisions and recommendations of the Council shall be made by consensus or, when that is not possible, by a majority of the members present and voting.

15. The Council shall, at each regular session, elect a Chairperson and Vice-Chairperson. They shall hold office until the next regular session of the Council. The Chairperson or, in his/her absence, the Vice-Chairperson shall preside at the meetings of the Council. If the Chairperson is unable to serve for the full term for which he/she has been elected, the Vice-Chairperson shall act as Chairperson for the remainder of that term.

16. The Council shall review the administrative and financial status of the Centre and the implementation of its programme of work. The Executive Secretary of ESCAP shall submit an annual report, as adopted by the Council, to the Commission at its annual sessions.

Director and staff

17. The Centre shall have a Director and staff, who shall be ESCAP staff members appointed under the appropriate United Nations regulations, rules and administrative instructions. The Director shall be appointed in a manner consistent with United Nations regulations and rules. The Council will be invited to nominate candidates for the position of Director, once the vacancy is announced, and provide advice, as appropriate. Other members and associate members of the Commission may also submit nominations for the post.

18. The Director shall be responsible to the Executive Secretary of ESCAP for the administration of the Centre and the implementation of its programme of work.

Technical Committee

19. The Centre shall have a Technical Committee consisting of experts from members and associate members of ESCAP and from intergovernmental and non-governmental organizations. Members of the

Technical Committee shall be appointed by the Director in consultation with the Executive Secretary.

20. The Technical Committee shall be responsible for advising the Director on the formulation of the programme of work and on other technical matters concerning the Centre's operations.

21. Reports of meetings of the Technical Committee, and the Director's observations thereon, shall be submitted to the Council at its next session.

22. The Chairperson of the Technical Committee shall be elected by the Committee itself at each meeting.

Resources of the Centre

23. All members and associate members of ESCAP should be encouraged to make a regular annual contribution to the operations of the Centre. The United Nations shall administer a joint contribution trust fund in which those contributions shall be deposited.

24. The Centre will endeavour to mobilize sufficient resources to support its activities.

25. The United Nations shall maintain separate trust funds for voluntary contributions for technical cooperation projects or other extraordinary voluntary contributions for activities of the Centre.

26. The financial resources of the Centre shall be administered in accordance with the Financial Regulations and Rules of the United Nations.

Amendments

27. Amendments to the present statute shall be adopted by the Commission.

Matters not covered by the present statute

28. In the event of any procedural matter arising that is not covered by the present statute or rules of procedure adopted by the Governing Council under paragraph 12 of the present statute, the pertinent part of the rules of procedure of the Economic and Social Commission for Asia and the Pacific shall apply.

Entry into force

29. The present statute shall enter into force on the date of its adoption by the Commission.

Information and communication technologies

The Commission expressed appreciation for the secretariat's role in leading and coordinating the regional preparations for the first [YUN 2003, p. 857] and second (see p. 933) phases of the World Summit on the Information Society. In particular, it supported the outcomes of the subregional conferences (Fiji, Indonesia, Kyrgyzstan, Nepal) organized by the secretariat, in collaboration with the host Governments, the International Telecommunication Union and the Asia-Pacific Development Information Programme. It also expressed support for the formulation of a draft regional action plan towards the information society, and called for the early implementation of the Geneva Plan of Action and Declaration of Principles [ibid.]. The Commission called on all countries to participate actively in the High-level Asia-Pacific Conference for the World Summit on the Information Society (Tehran, Iran,

31 May–2 June). It took the view that the regional action plan to be finalized at the conference should take into account the need to bridge the digital divide by providing rural areas with Internet access and empowering socially disadvantaged groups. The Commission expressed the hope that the High-level Conference would result in the development of regional common principles to help define the meaning and scope of Internet governance; in that regard, the secretariat was asked to conduct a study of the principles common to Internet governance at both the international and domestic levels.

The High-level Asia-Pacific Conference for the World Summit on the Information Society adopted the Tehran Declaration and the Regional Action Plan towards the Information Society for Asia and the Pacific. The Regional Action Plan addressed key issues relating to the application of ICT and, among other things, outlined a plan for ICT projects and programmes at the regional level that would help to realize the vision of an inclusive and sustainable information society.

The Commission adopted an 18 May resolution [E/2005/39 (res. 61/6)] on the establishment of the Asian and Pacific Training Centre for Information and Communication Technology for Development, which it recommended to the Economic and Social Council for adoption (see below).

ECONOMIC AND SOCIAL COUNCIL ACTION

On 26 July [meeting 39], the Economic and Social Council, on the recommendation of ESCAP [E/2005/15/Add.1], adopted **resolution 2005/40** without vote [agenda item 10].

Establishment of the Asian and Pacific Training Centre for Information and Communication Technology for Development

The Economic and Social Council,

Recognizing the particularly rapid development in information and communication technology and its applications, and their implications for economic and social development, which have posed unprecedented challenges for developing countries in need of efficient, informed and timely access to information, information services, tools, best practices and other information and communication technology-related resources,

Expressing grave concern about the prevailing digital divide between countries and within countries and communities and its implications for development and the persistence of poverty,

Acknowledging the importance of information and communication technology for development and for building inclusive knowledge societies, as well as the role of the United Nations in promoting regional cooperation through partnerships with all relevant stakeholders,

Recalling the Declaration of Principles and the Plan of Action adopted by the World Summit on the Information Society on 12 December 2003 during its first phase, which called for capacity-building with an emphasis on creating a critical mass of qualified and skilled information and communication technology professionals and experts, the promotion of regional cooperation in the field of capacity-building by the United Nations and its specialized agencies and fostering effective international and regional cooperation among Governments, the private sector, civil society and other stakeholders, including international financial institutions,

Recalling also the Tokyo Declaration adopted on 15 January 2003 by Governments of the Asian and Pacific region as the region's input to the World Summit, which identified information and communication technology development, capacity-building and fostering of partnerships as priority areas for action in advancing the region's information society,

Recalling further Economic and Social Commission of Asia and the Pacific resolution 57/4 of 25 April 2001 on regional cooperation in information and communication technology for development as well as General Assembly resolution 55/279 of 12 July 2001 on the Programme of Action for the Least Developed Countries for the Decade 2001-2010,

Reaffirming General Assembly resolution 55/2 of 8 September 2000, by which the Assembly adopted the United Nations Millennium Declaration and resolved, inter alia, to ensure that the benefits of new technologies, especially information and communication technology, were available to all, and Assembly resolution 57/144 of 16 December 2002 on the follow-up to the outcome of the Millennium Summit,

Recalling General Assembly resolution 57/295 of 20 December 2002 on information and communication technology for development and Assembly resolution 56/189 of 21 December 2001 on human resources development, in which the Assembly made several references to information technologies,

Bearing in mind General Assembly resolution 57/270 of 20 December 2002 on integrated and coordinated implementation of and follow-up to the outcomes of the major United Nations conferences and summits in the economic and social fields,

Recalling its resolution 2002/2 of 19 July 2002 on restructuring the conference structure of the Economic and Social Commission for Asia and the Pacific, including the establishment of a subcommittee on information, communications and space technology,

Noting with satisfaction the outstanding success achieved by a number of countries in the region in the long-term development of their information and communication technology sectors and in harnessing new technologies for their national development,

Noting also with satisfaction the work of such international organizations as the International Telecommunication Union and the Asia-Pacific Telecommunity,

Acknowledging, in particular, the important work of the Asia-Pacific Telecommunity in facilitating capacity-building in the field of information and communication technology based on demand by its member States,

Recognizing the advantages of regional resource centres on information and communication technology development issues in Asia and the Pacific that may optimize the sharing of expertise on information and communication technology in the region and further improve the effectiveness of regional capacity-building activities and the sharing of tools and processes,

Expressing appreciation to the Government of the Republic of Korea for its offer to host the Asian and Pacific Training Centre for Information and Communication Technology for Development and to bear its institutional and operational costs,

Cognizant of the need to avoid any possible duplication between the work of the Training Centre and the human resources development work of the Asia-Pacific Telecommunity and other concerned international organizations,

1. *Decides* to establish the Asian and Pacific Training Centre for Information and Communication Technology for Development, which will contribute to the Economic and Social Commission for Asia and the Pacific programme of work in the area of training in information and communication technology as decided by the Commission in its resolution 61/6 of 18 May 2005;

2. *Approves* the statute of the Asian and Pacific Training Centre for Information and Communication Technology for Development, the text of which is annexed to the present resolution, as the basis for its operation;

3. *Requests* the Executive Secretary to take all necessary steps for the prompt establishment of the Training Centre, including the conclusion of a headquarters agreement between the host country and the United Nations;

4. *Encourages* the United Nations and other international organizations and agencies, as well as nongovernmental organizations in the field concerned, to provide support to the Training Centre and to cooperate in the implementation of its work programme;

5. *Calls upon* the Executive Secretary to establish mechanisms for close coordination between the Training Centre and the Asia-Pacific Telecommunity in its human resources development work programme, and to avoid possible duplication with the Telecommunity in the formulation of the Centre's workplans;

6. *Invites* all members and associate members to participate actively in monitoring and evaluating the work of the Training Centre in order to ensure that its activities do not duplicate those of other institutions and agencies in the region;

7. *Requests* the Executive Secretary to report annually to the Commission on the progress made by the Training Centre in: *(a)* capacity-building to bridge the digital divide; *(b)* creating a sustainable institutional framework for the training of trainers in the field of information and communication technology; and *(c)* enhancing regional cooperation in human resources development in that field;

8. *Also requests* the Executive Secretary to submit a report in 2008 on the performance of the Training Centre, in particular regarding the complementary and value-added contribution of its work to that of other relevant international organizations, which would serve as the basis for a midterm review by the Commission at its sixty-fourth session, in 2008;

9. *Further requests* the Executive Secretary to submit a comprehensive report on the work of the Training Centre based on the findings of the midterm review,

including an assessment of its financial sustainability and the complementary and value-added contribution of its work to that of other concerned international organizations, which would serve as the basis for a comprehensive review by the Commission at its sixty-sixth session, in 2010;

10. *Decides* to assess the performance of the Training Centre, on the basis of the findings of the comprehensive review by the Commission at its sixty-sixth session, and to determine whether to proceed with its operation thereafter.

Annex

Statute of the Asian and Pacific Training Centre for Information and Communication Technology for Development

Establishment

1. An Asian and Pacific Training Centre for Information and Communication Technology for Development (hereinafter referred to as "APCICT") is established, with a membership identical to the membership of the Economic and Social Commission for Asia and the Pacific (hereinafter referred to as "ESCAP" or "the Commission").

2. APCICT shall have the status of a subsidiary body of ESCAP.

Objective

3. The objective of APCICT is to build the capacity of members and associate members of ESCAP through training programmes in the use of information and communication technology (ICT) for the purposes of socio-economic development.

Functions

4. In pursuance of the objective stated in paragraph 3, APCICT shall have such functions as:

(*a*) Enhancing knowledge and skills in ICT for policymakers and ICT professionals;

(*b*) Enhancing the capacity of ICT trainers and ICT training institutions by providing for training-of-trainers programmes and exchanges of trainers and experts;

(*c*) Providing advisory services on human resources development programmes to members and associate members;

(*d*) Undertaking analytical studies related to human resources development in ICT, including identifying training needs and sharing best practices on human resources development programmes and training methods.

Status and organization

5. APCICT shall have a Governing Council (hereinafter referred to as "the Council"), a Director and staff.

6. APCICT shall be located in the Republic of Korea.

7. The activities of APCICT shall be in line with relevant policy decisions adopted by the General Assembly, the Economic and Social Council and the Commission. APCICT shall be subject to the Financial and Staff Regulations and Rules of the United Nations and the applicable administrative instructions.

Governing Council

8. APCICT shall have a Governing Council consisting of a representative nominated by the Government of the Republic of Korea and eight representatives of members and associate members of ESCAP elected by the Commission. The Council shall be elected for a pe-

riod of three years but shall be eligible for re-election. The Executive Secretary of the Commission or his/her representative shall attend the meetings of the Council. An interim Council shall be elected by ESCAP and constituted upon the adoption of the present statute. The Council shall be reconfirmed at the sixty-second session of the Commission.

9. The Director of APCICT shall serve as Secretary of the Council.

10. Representatives of (*a*) States that are not members of the Council, (*b*) United Nations bodies and specialized and related agencies and (*c*) such other organizations as the Council may deem appropriate, as well as experts in fields of interest to the Council, may be invited by the Executive Secretary to attend meetings of the Council.

11. The Council shall meet at least once a year and may adopt its own rules of procedure. Sessions of the Council shall be convened by the Executive Secretary of ESCAP, who may propose special sessions of the Council at his/her own initiative and shall convene such special sessions at the request of a majority of Council members.

12. A quorum for meetings of the Council shall be a majority of its members.

13. Each member of the Council shall have one vote. Decisions and recommendations of the Council shall be made by consensus or, when that is not possible, by a majority of the members present and voting.

14. The Council shall, at each regular session, elect a Chairperson and Vice-Chairperson. They shall hold office until the next regular session of the Council. The Chairperson or, in his/her absence, the Vice-Chairperson shall preside at the meetings of the Council. If the Chairperson is unable to serve for the full term for which he/she has been elected, the Vice-Chairperson shall act as Chairperson for the remainder of that term.

15. The Council shall be responsible for advising the Director on the formulation of the work programme. The Council shall review the administration and financial status of APCICT and the implementation of its programme of work. The Executive Secretary of ESCAP shall submit an annual report, as adopted by the Council, to the Commission at its annual sessions.

Director and staff

16. APCICT shall have a Director and staff, who shall be ESCAP staff members appointed under the appropriate United Nations regulations, rules and administrative instructions. The Director shall be appointed in a manner consistent with United Nations regulations and rules. The Council will be invited to nominate candidates for the position of Director, once the vacancy is announced, and provide advice, as appropriate. Other members and associate members of the Commission may also submit nominations for the post.

17. The Director shall be appointed for one year and be eligible for reappointment. The Director shall be responsible to the Executive Secretary of ESCAP for the administration of APCICT and the implementation of its programme of work.

Resources of the Centre

18. The operation of APCICT shall not involve additional regular budget resources of ESCAP. All members

and associate members of ESCAP should be encouraged to make a regular annual contribution, on a voluntary basis, to the operations of APCICT. The United Nations shall administer a joint contribution trust fund in which those contributions shall be deposited.

19. APCICT will endeavour to mobilize sufficient resources to support its activities.

20. The United Nations shall maintain separate trust funds for voluntary contributions for technical cooperation projects or other extraordinary voluntary contributions for activities of APCICT.

21. The financial resources of APCICT shall be administered in accordance with the Financial Regulations and Rules of the United Nations.

Amendments

22. Amendments to the present statute shall be adopted by the Commission.

Matters not covered by the present statute

23. In the event of any procedural matter arising that is not covered by the present statute or rules of procedure adopted by the Governing Council under paragraph 11 of the present statute, the pertinent part of the rules of procedure of the Economic and Social Commission for Asia and the Pacific shall apply.

Entry into force

24. The present statute shall enter into force on the date of its adoption by the Commission.

Environment and sustainable development

The fifth Ministerial Conference on Environment and Development in Asia and the Pacific (Seoul, Republic of Korea, 24-29 March) [E/ESCAP/ 1337] resulted in three main outcomes: the Ministerial Declaration on Environment and Development in Asia and the Pacific, 2005; the Regional Implementation Plan for Sustainable Development in Asia and the Pacific, 2006-2010; and the Seoul Initiative on Environmentally Sustainable Economic Growth (Green Growth).

In an 18 May resolution [E/2005/39 (res. 61/9)], the Commission requested all members and associate members to participate actively in the implementation of the recommendations of the Ministerial Conference in order to ensure the formulation of programmes and strategies to implement the Regional Implementation Plan at the national, regional and subregional levels; encourage Governments, the private sector and civil society to participate in activities forming part of the Seoul Initiative, including the establishment of the Seoul Initiative Network on Green Growth; and provide information on such programmes and activities to assist the ESCAP secretariat to review and assess the progress made in implementing the recommendations of the Ministerial Conference. All relevant UN bodies and specialized agencies, multilateral financial institutions, donor countries, agencies and NGOs were invited to contribute technical and financial resources to implement the Conference's recom-

mendations. The Commission called on the members of the Thematic Working Group on Environment and Development under the Regional Coordination Mechanism to play an effective role in the implementation of the Regional Implementation Plan and its regional initiatives, including the Seoul Initiative. The Executive Secretary was asked to mobilize human and financial resources to the greatest extent possible for the implementation of the Conference's recommendations; assist countries in the region by providing technical assistance in the realization of the Regional Implementation Plan and relevant national strategies and action; ensure effective coordination and joint pursuit of the activities of concerned UN bodies and specialized agencies in facilitating the implementation of the recommendations; encourage the active participation of all stakeholders in the implementation of the recommendations; and undertake a periodic review of progress made in implementing the Regional Implementation Plan and include an assessment of the results in the agenda of the sixth Ministerial Conference on Environment and Development, to be held by the year 2010.

In other action on environment and sustainable development, the Commission, in the light of rising oil prices, emphasized the need for joint efforts to reduce the use of fossil fuels and promote the use of alternative energy sources, including renewable energy. It requested the secretariat to strengthen its efforts to build national capacity and awareness among members and associate members in the areas of energy efficiency and renewable energy.

The Commission expressed support for the International Decade for Action, "Water for Life", 2005-2015 (see p. 1130), and requested the secretariat to strengthen cooperation in managing water resources in an integrated manner, particularly in order to reduce the effects of water shortages and drought. It encouraged the secretariat to take an active part in the preparations for the Fourth (2006) World Water Forum, which could be linked to regional efforts in connection with the Johannesburg Plan of Implementation [YUN 2002, p. 822] of the 2002 World Summit on Sustainable Development [YUN 2002, p. 821] with regard to water resources management. It also expressed support for an active role by the secretariat in providing a forum for and facilitating discussions at the regional level on a thematic cluster of issues, encompassing energy for sustainable development, industrial development, air pollution and climate change, as a modality for the regional preparations for the fourteenth (2006) and fifteenth (2007) sessions of the Commission on Sustainable Development.

Agriculture and development

The annual report of the Asian and Pacific Centre for Agricultural Engineering and Machinery (APCAEM) [E/ESCAP/1346] reviewed the major activities and implementation of the work programme of APCAEM in 2004, aimed at developing a research and analysis programme on agricultural engineering and machinery for increased food security and poverty reduction in the region. It contained the recommendations of the third session of the APCAEM Governing Board (December 2004) relating to the APCAEM plan of activities for 2005 and the programme of work for the 2006-2007 biennium.

By an 18 May resolution [E/2005/39 (res. 61/3)], the Commission adopted the revised Statute of the United Nations Asian and Pacific Centre for Agricultural Engineering and Machinery, which it recommended to the Economic and Social Council for adoption (see below).

The first session of the Governing Council of the Centre for Alleviation of Poverty through Secondary Crops Development in Asia and the Pacific (Bogor, Indonesia, 5-6 April) [E/ESCAP/1347] discussed the Centre's activities during the 2004-2005 biennium, plans for resource mobilization and the realigned programme of work for 2006-2007. It noted Indonesia's request that the Centre assist in tsunami reconstruction and rehabilitation in rural areas and recommended that resources be sought to follow up on that request.

On 18 May [res. 61/5], the Commission adopted a resolution on the Centre, which it recommended to the Council for action (see below). The Council also approved the revised Statute of the Centre (resolution 2005/39), which had been adopted by the Commission in 2004 [YUN 2004, p. 1009].

ECONOMIC AND SOCIAL COUNCIL ACTION

On 26 July [meeting 39], the Economic and Social Council, on the recommendation of ESCAP [E/2005/15/Add.1], adopted **resolution 2005/37** without vote [agenda item 10].

Statute of the United Nations Asian and Pacific Centre for Agricultural Engineering and Machinery

The Economic and Social Council,

Recalling Economic and Social Commission for Asia and the Pacific resolution 58/5 of 22 May 2002 on the establishment of the Asian and Pacific Centre for Agricultural Engineering and Machinery,

Recalling also the agreement between the Government of China and the United Nations regarding the headquarters of the Centre, signed on 19 November 2003,

Noting with appreciation the significant financial resources and facilities that have been provided to the Centre, since its establishment, by the Government of China,

1. *Approves* the revised statute of the United Nations Asian and Pacific Centre for Agricultural Engineering and Machinery, as adopted by the Economic and Social Commission for Asia and the Pacific, the text of which is annexed to the present resolution;

2. *Requests* the Executive Secretary to seek regular budget resources for the Centre, including posts, within the proposed programme budget of the Economic and Social Commission for Asia and the Pacific for the biennium 2006-2007, to strengthen the research and analytical capacity of the Centre, while recognizing the primary role of the Advisory Committee on Administrative and Budgetary Questions and the Fifth Committee in this regard, and also recognizing the principle that the technical assistance activities of the Centre should be funded by voluntary contributions;

3. *Also requests* the Executive Secretary to seek additional voluntary resources to strengthen the financial stability of the Centre.

Annex

Statute of the United Nations Asian and Pacific Centre for Agricultural Engineering and Machinery

Establishment

1. The Asian and Pacific Centre for Agricultural Engineering and Machinery, established on 22 May 2002 pursuant to Economic and Social Commission for Asia and the Pacific resolution 58/5 of the same date, shall continue in existence under the title "United Nations Asian and Pacific Centre for Agricultural Engineering and Machinery" (hereinafter referred to as "UNAPCAEM" or "the Centre") and under the terms of the present statute.

2. The membership of the Centre shall be identical to the membership of the Economic and Social Commission for Asia and the Pacific (hereinafter referred to as "ESCAP" or "the Commission").

3. The Centre has the status of a subsidiary body of ESCAP.

Objectives

4. The objectives of the Centre are to enhance technical cooperation among the members and associate members of ESCAP as well as other interested States Members of the United Nations, through extensive exchange of information and sharing of commercially successful machinery and technology, and to promote research and development and extension of agricultural engineering including machinery and rural industry for poverty reduction in the region.

Functions

5. The Centre shall achieve the above objectives by undertaking such functions as:

(a) Assistance in the improvement of agricultural engineering, mechanization, automation, biotechnology and genetic engineering;

(b) Enhancement of farm mechanization technologies in addressing issues related to subsistence farming for increased food security and poverty reduction and promoting agro-based small and medium-sized enterprise development and commercial farming to seize opportunities for increased market access and agro-food trade;

(c) A focus on an agro-based enterprise cluster concept and enterprise development activities to enhance the capabilities of members in identifying potential agricultural commodities in their respective countries on a clustering basis;

(d) Regional cooperation in technology transfer through networking of focal point national institutes in the Centre member countries and other relevant institutions;

(e) Setting up an interactive Internet website to allow members full access to information and technology databases, including the sharing of expert systems and decision support systems in financial management of small and medium-sized enterprises;

(f) Promotion of the technology transfer process from research and development institutes to the agricultural and farm machinery extension systems in member countries for poverty reduction;

(g) Dissemination and exchange of commercially successful machinery and drawings of appropriate tools, machines and equipment;

(h) Training workshops and advisory services on food safety standards and sanitary and phytosanitary issues under the World Trade Organization agricultural trade mandate;

(i) Tapping the resources of developed countries in building the capacity of member countries.

Status and organization

6. The Centre shall have a Governing Council (hereinafter referred to as "the Council"), a Director, a Deputy Director, subject to the availability of funds, other staff and a Technical Committee.

7. The Centre is located in Beijing.

8. The activities of the Centre shall be in line with relevant policy decisions adopted by the General Assembly, the Economic and Social Council and the Commission. The Centre shall be subject to the Financial and Staff Regulations and Rules of the United Nations and the applicable administrative instructions.

Governing Council

9. The Governing Council shall consist of a representative designated by the Government of China and eight representatives nominated by other members and associate members of ESCAP elected by the Commission. The members and associate members elected by the Commission shall be elected for a period of three years but shall be eligible for re-election. The Executive Secretary of the Commission or his/her representative shall attend the meetings of the Council.

10. The Director of the Centre shall serve as Secretary of the Council.

11. Representatives of *(a)* States that are not members of the Council, *(b)* United Nations bodies and specialized and related agencies and *(c)* such other organizations as the Council may deem appropriate, as well as experts in fields of interest to the Council, may be invited by the Executive Secretary to attend meetings of the Council.

12. The Council shall meet at least once a year and may adopt its own rules of procedure. Sessions of the Council shall be convened by the Executive Secretary of ESCAP, who may propose special sessions of the Council at his/her own initiative and shall convene such special sessions at the request of a majority of Council members.

13. A quorum for meetings of the Council shall be a majority of its members.

14. Each member of the Council shall have one vote. Decisions and recommendations of the Council shall be made by consensus or, when that is not possible, by a majority of the members present and voting.

15. The Council shall, at each regular session, elect a Chairperson and Vice-Chairperson. They shall hold office until the next regular session of the Council. The Chairperson or, in his/her absence, the Vice-Chairperson shall preside at the meetings of the Council. If the Chairperson is unable to serve for the full term for which he/she has been elected, the Vice-Chairperson shall act as Chairperson for the remainder of that term.

16. The Council shall review the administrative and financial status of the Centre and the implementation of its programme of work. The Executive Secretary of ESCAP shall submit an annual report, as adopted by the Council, to the Commission at its annual sessions.

Director and staff

17. The Centre shall have a Director, a Deputy Director subject to availability of funds, and staff, who shall be ESCAP staff members appointed under the appropriate United Nations regulations, rules and administrative instructions. The Director shall be appointed in a manner consistent with United Nations regulations and rules. The Council will be invited to nominate candidates for the position of Director, once the vacancy is announced, and provide advice, as appropriate. Other members and associate members of the Commission may also submit nominations for the post.

18. The Director shall be responsible to the Executive Secretary of ESCAP for the administration of the Centre and the implementation of its programme of work.

Technical Committee

19. The Centre shall have a Technical Committee consisting of experts from members and associate members of ESCAP and intergovernmental and nongovernmental organizations. Members and associate members of ESCAP will be invited to propose candidates for the Technical Committee. Members of the Technical Committee shall be appointed by the Director in consultation with the Executive Secretary. The Director may also invite governmental, intergovernmental and non-governmental institutions to propose experts who would best contribute to Technical Committee discussions on a specific topic.

20. The Technical Committee shall be responsible for advising the Director on the formulation of the programme of work and on other technical matters concerning the operations of the Centre.

21. Reports of meetings of the Technical Committee, with the Director's observations thereon, shall be submitted to the Council at its next session.

22. The Chairperson of the Technical Committee shall be elected by the Committee itself at each meeting.

Resources of the Centre

23. All members and associate members of ESCAP should be encouraged to make a regular annual contribution to the operations of the Centre. The United

Nations shall administer a joint contribution trust fund in which those contributions shall be deposited.

24. The Centre will endeavour to mobilize sufficient resources to support its activities.

25. The United Nations shall maintain separate trust funds for voluntary contributions for technical cooperation projects or other extraordinary voluntary contributions for activities of the Centre.

26. The financial resources of the Centre shall be administered in accordance with the Financial Regulations and Rules of the United Nations.

Amendments

27. Amendments to the present statute shall be adopted by the Commission.

Matters not covered by the present statute

28. In the event of any procedural matter arising that is not covered by the present statute or rules of procedure adopted by the Governing Council under paragraph 12 of the present statute, the pertinent part of the rules of procedure of the Economic and Social Commission for Asia and the Pacific shall apply.

Entry into force

29. The present statute shall enter into force on the date of its adoption by the Commission. Members and associate members elected to the Governing Board of the Centre at the fifty-ninth session of the Commission will serve as members of the Governing Council of the Centre until the sixty-second session of the Commission, in 2006.

Also on 26 July [meeting 39], the Council, on the recommendation of ESCAP [E/2005/15/Add.1], adopted **resolution 2005/39** without vote [agenda item 10].

Centre for Alleviation of Poverty through Secondary Crops Development in Asia and the Pacific

The Economic and Social Council,

Recalling Economic and Social Commission for Asia and the Pacific resolutions 174(XXXIII) of 29 April 1977, 220(XXXVIII) of 1 April 1982 and 60/5 of 28 April 2004 on the Centre for Alleviation of Poverty through Secondary Crops Development in Asia and the Pacific,

Noting with appreciation the significant financial resources that have been provided to the Centre, since its establishment, by the Government of Japan and the facilities that have been provided by the Government of Indonesia,

1. *Approves* the revised statute of the Centre for Alleviation of Poverty through Secondary Crops Development in Asia and the Pacific, as adopted by the Economic and Social Commission for Asia and the Pacific, annexed to the present resolution, which includes revised functions that strengthen the role of the Centre in coordinating research and analysis on secondary crops;

2. *Requests* the Executive Secretary to seek regular budget resources for the Centre, including posts, within the proposed programme budget of the Economic and Social Commission for Asia and the Pacific for the biennium 2006-2007, to strengthen the research and analytical capacity of the Centre, while recognizing the primary role of the Advisory Committee on Adminis-

trative and Budgetary Questions and the Fifth Committee in this regard, and recognizing also the principle that the technical assistance activities of the Centre should be funded by voluntary contributions;

3. *Also requests* the Executive Secretary to seek additional voluntary resources to strengthen the financial stability of the Centre.

Annex

Statute of the Centre for Alleviation of Poverty through Secondary Crops Development in Asia and the Pacific

Establishment

1. The Regional Coordination Centre for Research and Development of Coarse Grains, Pulses, Roots and Tuber Crops in the Humid Tropics of Asia and the Pacific (hereinafter referred to as "CGPRT Centre"), established in April 1981 pursuant to Economic and Social Commission for Asia and the Pacific resolution 174(XXXIII) of 29 April 1977 and its statute adopted by the Commission in its resolution 220(XXXVIII) of 1 April 1982, shall continue in existence under the title Centre for Alleviation of Poverty through Secondary Crops Development in Asia and the Pacific (hereinafter referred to as "CAPSA" or "the Centre") and under the terms of the present statute.

2. The membership of CAPSA is identical to the membership of the Economic and Social Commission for Asia and the Pacific (hereinafter referred to as "ESCAP" or "the Commission").

3. The Centre has the status of a subsidiary body of ESCAP.

Objective

4. The objective of CAPSA is to promote a more supportive policy environment in member countries to enhance the living conditions of rural poor populations in disadvantaged areas, particularly those who rely on secondary crops agriculture for their livelihood, and to promote research and development related to agriculture to alleviate poverty in the Asian and Pacific region.

Functions

5. The Centre shall achieve the above objective by undertaking such functions as:

(*a*) Coordination of socio-economic and policy research on secondary crops;

(*b*) Networking and partnership with other international organizations and key stakeholders;

(*c*) Research and analysis of trends and opportunities with regard to improving the economic status of rural populations;

(*d*) Production, packaging and dissemination of information and successful practices on poverty reduction;

(*e*) Dissemination of information and good practices on poverty reduction measures;

(*f*) Training of national personnel, particularly national scientists and policy analysts;

(*g*) Advisory services.

Status and organization

6. CAPSA shall have a Governing Council (hereinafter referred to as "the Council"), a Director and staff and a Technical Committee.

7. CAPSA is located in Bogor, Indonesia.

8. The activities of CAPSA shall be in line with relevant policy decisions adopted by the General Assembly, the Economic and Social Council and the Commission. CAPSA shall be subject to the Financial and Staff Regulations and Rules of the United Nations and the applicable administrative instructions.

Governing Council

9. The Governing Council shall consist of a representative nominated by the Government of Indonesia and eight representatives of members and associate members of ESCAP elected by the Commission. The members and associate members elected by the Commission shall be elected for a period of three years but shall be eligible for re-election. The Executive Secretary of the Commission or his/her representative shall attend the meetings of the Council.

10. The Director of the Centre shall serve as Secretary of the Council.

11. Representatives of (a) States that are not members of the Council, (b) United Nations bodies and specialized and related agencies and (c) such other organizations as the Council may deem appropriate, as well as experts in fields of interest to the Council, may be invited by the Executive Secretary to attend meetings of the Council.

12. The Council shall meet at least once a year and may adopt its own rules of procedure. Sessions of the Council shall be convened by the Executive Secretary of ESCAP, who may propose special sessions of the Council at his/her own initiative and shall convene such special sessions at the request of a majority of Council members.

13. A quorum for meetings of the Council shall be a majority of its members.

14. Each member of the Council shall have one vote. Decisions and recommendations of the Council shall be made by consensus or, when that is not possible, by a majority of the members present and voting.

15. The Council shall, at each regular session, elect a Chairperson and Vice-Chairperson. They shall hold office until the next regular session of the Council. The Chairperson or, in his/her absence, the Vice-Chairperson shall preside at the meetings of the Council. If the Chairperson is unable to serve for the full term for which he/she has been elected, the Vice-Chairperson shall act as Chairperson for the remainder of that term.

16. The Council shall review the administrative and financial status of CAPSA and the implementation of its programme of work. The Executive Secretary of ESCAP shall submit an annual report, as adopted by the Council, to the Commission at its annual sessions.

Director and staff

17. CAPSA shall have a Director and staff, who shall be ESCAP staff members appointed under the appropriate United Nations regulations, rules and administrative instructions. The Director shall be appointed in a manner consistent with United Nations regulations and rules. The Council will be invited to nominate candidates for the position of Director, once the vacancy is announced, and provide advice, as appropriate. Other members and associate members of the Commission may also submit nominations for the post.

18. The Director shall be responsible to the Executive Secretary of ESCAP for the administration of CAPSA and the implementation of its programme of work.

Technical Committee

19. CAPSA shall have a Technical Committee consisting of experts from members and associate members of ESCAP and intergovernmental and non-governmental organizations. Members of the Technical Committee shall be appointed by the Director in consultation with the Executive Secretary.

20. The Technical Committee shall be responsible for advising the Director on the formulation of the programme of work and on other technical matters concerning the operations of CAPSA.

21. Reports of meetings of the Technical Committee, and the Director's observations with respect thereto, shall be submitted to the Council at its next session.

22. The Chairperson of the Technical Committee shall be elected by the Committee itself at each meeting.

Resources of the Centre

23. All members and associate members of ESCAP should be urged to make a regular annual contribution to the operations of the Centre. The United Nations shall administer a joint contribution trust fund in which those contributions shall be deposited.

24. The Centre will endeavour to mobilize sufficient resources to support its activities.

25. The United Nations shall maintain separate trust funds for voluntary contributions for technical cooperation projects or other extraordinary voluntary contributions for the activities of CAPSA.

26. The financial resources of CAPSA shall be administered in accordance with the United Nations Financial Regulations and Rules.

Amendments

27. Amendments to the present statute shall be adopted by the Commission.

Matters not covered by the present Statute

28. In the event of any procedural matter arising that is not covered by the present statute or rules of procedure adopted by the Governing Council under paragraph 12 of the present statute, the pertinent part of the rules of procedure of the Economic and Social Commission for Asia and the Pacific shall apply.

Entry into force

29. The present statute shall enter into force on the date of its adoption by the Commission. Members and associate members elected to the Governing Board of the former CGPRT Centre at the fifty-ninth session of the Commission will serve as members of the Governing Council of CAPSA until the sixty-second session of the Commission, in 2006.

Social development

The Commission had before it reports on: key issues relating to emerging social issues [E/ESCAP/1339], which highlighted the outcomes of the first session of the Subcommittee on Socially Vulnerable Groups (Bangkok, 13-15 September 2004); the implementation of the 2001 Declaration of Commitment on HIV/AIDS, contained in General Assembly resolution S-26/2 [YUN 2001, p. 1126], and the Asia-Pacific Leadership Forum on HIV/AIDS and Development on its activities in 2003 and 2004 [E/ESCAP/1340]; the High-level Intergovernmental Meeting to Review Regional Implementation of the Beijing Platform for Action and Its Regional and Global Outcomes (Bangkok, 7-10 September 2004) [E/ESCAP/1341], which adopted the Bangkok Communiqué as the regional contribution to the review and appraisal of the implementation of the 1995 Beijing Declaration and Platform of Action, adopted at the Fourth World Conference on Women [YUN 1995, p. 1169]; and the Regional Framework for Strategic Action: Promoting Health and Sustainable Development [E/ESCAP/1358], which represented the key outcome of the first session of the Subcommittee on Health and Development (Bangkok, 1-3 December 2004).

The Commission called for continuous efforts to meet the goals and commitments made at the 1995 World Summit for Social Development [YUN 1995, p. 1113], and the twenty-fourth (2000) special session of the General Assembly [YUN 2000, p. 1012] that reviewed the implementation of the Copenhagen Declaration and the Programme of Action adopted at the Summit, especially in the three major areas of poverty reduction, employment expansion and social integration. It urged that the social impact of globalization and the interlinkages between economic and social policies be examined and asked the secretariat to assist members and associate members in achieving the internationally agreed development goals and commitments, particularly with regard to the social integration of disadvantaged groups, the strengthening of cross-generational linkages and social protection and security. The Commission emphasized the need to mainstream issues relating to youth, the family, ageing and disability into national development, particularly national poverty reduction strategies, and encouraged the adoption of socially oriented economic policies that reflected interlinkages among poverty reduction, social security, migration and the empowerment of women, youth and persons with disabilities.

The Commission called for assistance and protection to be extended to the family in recognition of its role as a fundamental unit of society, an untapped resource for economic and social development and a source of support for older persons. It emphasized the importance of the renewed commitment to combating the commercial sexual exploitation of children expressed at the Post-Yokohama Mid-term Review of the East Asia and Pacific Regional Commitment and

Action Plan against the Commercial Sexual Exploitation of Children (Bangkok, November 2004) and requested the secretariat to promote and coordinate regional initiatives on combating trafficking and the commercial sexual exploitation of women and girls. Noting that international migration was a consequence of globalization and had an impact on the development process of both sending and receiving countries, the Commission urged the adoption of policies and strategies to facilitate its management. It noted with concern the plight of migrant workers, the majority of whom, in some countries, were women. The Commission asked the secretariat to continue to provide assistance in addressing the issue of population ageing through technical assistance, advisory services and policy-oriented research and analysis, including an assessment of the future impact of population ageing on social services expenditure, pensions and long-term health-care and investment trends, and to develop regional projects on fostering supportive and enabling environments, in order to promote intergenerational support and reciprocity between older persons and their families.

In an 18 May resolution [E/2005/39 (res. 61/7)] on regional cooperation for the protection of vulnerable people through the promotion of economic and social aspects of human security as a follow-up to the Shanghai Declaration on cooperation in the Asia and Pacific region, which was endorsed by the Economic and Social Council in resolution 2004/6 [YUN 2004, p. 1001], the Commission requested the Executive Secretary to continue seeking means to support the secretariat's technical cooperation work in the area of community-building and human development in order to protect and enhance the capabilities of vulnerable people. He was also asked to report in 2006 on measures to support regional cooperation for the protection of vulnerable people through promoting economic and social aspects of human security as a follow-up to the Shanghai Declaration.

With regard to gender concerns, the Commission stressed the strategic role and responsibilities of national mechanisms for promoting gender equality and women's empowerment and asked the secretariat to provide technical assistance in strengthening the capacity of those mechanisms. It reaffirmed the urgent need to combat the spread of violence against women, including human trafficking, which was transnational in nature and required international cooperation by all stakeholders.

In an 18 May resolution [res. 61/10], the Commission reaffirmed its important role in implementing the 1995 Beijing Declaration and Platform for Action [YUN 2000, p. 1082], adopted at the Fourth

World Conference on Women, and the outcome of the twenty-third (2000) special session of the General Assembly (Beijing +5), adopted by resolution S/23-2 [YUN 2000, p. 1084]. ESCAP members and associate members were called on to: strengthen efforts to promote an active and visible policy to mainstream a gender perspective into the design, implementation and evaluation of programmes, especially in poverty reduction; continue to implement economic policies that were designed and monitored with the full and equal participation of women and enhance women's entrepreneurial potential by providing them with access to and control over resources; promote the protection of women in disaster areas and enhance the active role of women in disaster management; contribute to collaborative approaches and strategies aimed at protecting and promoting the rights and welfare of women migrant workers and forge international understanding and cooperation to combat trafficking in women; strengthen and improve the collection, processing and analysis of sex-disaggregated data and gender statistics at the local, national, regional and international levels for the effective monitoring and assessment of gains and gaps; and forge partnerships in further studying the positive and negative impacts of globalization on women and formulate a comprehensive and integrative strategy to address its effects on women. Members, associate members, agencies, regional and international financial institutions and the private sector were encouraged to provide countries in the region, particularly LDCs, with financial and technical support in implementing the Beijing Declaration and Platform for Action and the outcome of Beijing +5. The Commission requested the Executive Secretary to: continue promoting the implementation of the outcome of Beijing +5, specifically by intensifying efforts to build a database listing by region all programmes and projects by UN system organizations, and facilitate the dissemination of that information and evaluate their impact on women's empowerment; and mainstream gender assessments into all programmes to enable member countries to involve women in economic, social and political decision-making.

The Commission noted progress made in implementing the Biwako Millennium Framework for Action towards an Inclusive, Barrier-free and Rights-based Society for Persons with Disabilities in Asia and the Pacific during the Decade of Disabled Persons, 2003-2012 [YUN 2003, p. 1014]. It commended the secretariat on its efforts to promote a shift from a charity-based approach to a rights-based approach, which had a positive influence on disability policies and programmes at the local

and national levels. It emphasized the importance of introducing disability-sensitive, pro-poor development strategies. Noting discrepancies in the reporting of disability prevalence, the Commission urged the secretariat to continue its efforts to develop a common and standardized system for defining and classifying disability. It recommended that the secretariat assist in following up on the proposal to establish an Association of Southeast Asian Nations (ASEAN) disability commission.

In an 18 May resolution [res. 61/8], the Commission, noting that a mid-point review of the Biwako Millennium Framework should be conducted in 2007, called on members and associate members to renew their commitment to the implementation of the Framework and support and contribute to the ongoing work of the Ad Hoc Committee on a Comprehensive and Integral International Convention on the Protection and Promotion of the Rights and Dignity of Persons with Disabilities. They were encouraged to further strengthen their efforts to achieve the Framework's priorities, targets and strategies, with particular emphasis on: holistic and comprehensive approaches to disability-inclusive and responsive policies and programmes; support for capacity-building for persons with disabilities and their organizations; promotion of community approaches for empowerment and poverty alleviation; the mainstreaming of disability into overall national development plans, programmes and projects for poverty alleviation; and promotion of disability-inclusive international and regional cooperation. Governments and other stakeholders were invited to continue contributing to the ESCAP technical assistance trust fund for the Asian and Pacific Decade of Disabled Persons, 2003-2012 [YUN 2002, p. 991], and those that had not yet done so were asked to consider signing the Proclamation on the Full Participation and Equality of People with Disabilities in the Asian and Pacific Region [YUN 1992, p. 490]. The Commission requested the Executive Secretary to: provide Governments with technical support for the continued monitoring of the implementation of the Biwako Millennium Framework; hold in 2007 a high-level intergovernmental meeting on the mid-point review of the Decade; support the inclusion of disability in the regional preparations for the first five-year review of the UN Millennium Declaration and related outcomes of major UN conferences and summits; and further strengthen the partnership between ESCAP and the Asia-Pacific Development Centre on Disability.

The Commission broadly endorsed the recommendations contained in the Regional Framework for Strategic Action: Promoting Health and Sustainable Development [E/ESCAP/1358], which had been adopted by the Subcommittee on Health and Development at its first session [YUN 2004, p. 1010]. In the context of the tsunami disaster, concern was expressed over the emergence of non-communicable diseases and injuries as a leading cause of death, which were rapidly overtaking communicable diseases in the Asian and Pacific region, despite the recent outbreaks of SARS and avian influenza. The Commission requested enhanced secretariat action on the promotion in the region of financing of health for development. The continuous spread of HIV/AIDS and its linkages with poverty constituted a challenge to the region's socio-economic development. The Commission noted the need for increased technical and financial assistance in enhancing preventive efforts targeted at vulnerable populations, including youth, women, drug users, migrants and those working in the entertainment industry, and urged that regional collaboration in addressing HIV/AIDS be increased.

At the High-level Forum on Health Millennium Development Goals in Asia and the Pacific (Tokyo, 21-22 June) [A/60/337], health, development and finance ministers from the region and representatives from donor countries, international and regional organizations and relevant foundations and partnerships discussed progress made in achieving the health-related MDGs and identified remaining challenges.

In an 18 May resolution on a regional call for action to enhance capacity-building in public health [res. 61/12], the Commission urged members and associate members to: scale up their investments in the health sector through resource mobilization strategies; further integrate public health into their economic and social development strategies; raise professional and public awareness of the importance of public health and mobilize the participation of educational institutions, civil society and the mass media in promoting good public health practices; unite in securing a regional commitment to strengthening cooperation on capacity-building in public health; and improve regional public health preparedness and response systems to better cope with major diseases, such as in cases of global or regional outbreaks. Donors, including Governments, the private sector, UN bodies and specialized agencies, and regional and international financial institutions were encouraged to continue to support countries in the region by: providing funding and technical support to countries in their efforts to combat infectious diseases and epidemics; facilitating South-South and North-

South cooperation in order to build effective public health institutions and practices; integrating health dimensions into their strategies, work programmes, budget plans, projects and activities to strengthen regional public health capacity-building; and considering participation in the Global Fund to Fight AIDS, Tuberculosis and Malaria and encouraging the private sector to contribute to the Fund. The Commission requested the Executive Secretary to coordinate closely with the World Health Organization and other relevant organizations to: assist members and associate members in their capacity-building by mainstreaming health concerns into diverse development sectors in support of the fulfilment of the internationally agreed development goals; promote coordinated regional action in strengthening public health capacity-building through the Subcommittee on Health and Development and other ESCAP health-related institutions; and undertake advocacy for a public policy to create enabling environments for health promotion that strengthened physical, mental and spiritual health resilience and well-being, with an emphasis on community, school and workplace participation, towards a "healthy Asia-Pacific". The Executive Secretary was asked to report in 2006 on the implementation of the resolution.

The Committee on Emerging Social Issues, at its second session (Bangkok, 1-3 November) [E/ESCAP/CESI(2)/Rep.], requested the secretariat to, among other things: draw on good national experiences in implementing the MDGs related to social development to help developing members and associate members to map out strategies and build capacity to achieve their commitments; promote regional dialogue and cooperation through the exchange of information and best practices regarding the management of international migration; conduct a systematic regional study on international migration in order to identify knowledge gaps, determine its developmental impacts and ensure that migration policies were consistent with broad development goals; and provide technical support to member countries in strengthening publicly financed health schemes to achieve universal coverage, including social health insurance. The secretariat was further urged to: provide more opportunities for members and associate members to share national experiences on social protection and youth employment; assist members and associate members in implementing the Regional Framework for Strategic Action: Promoting Health and Sustainable Development; and work with UN agencies and international organizations to assist countries in strengthening their national capacity to develop effective responses to avian influenza and prevent the disease from becoming a pandemic.

Natural disasters

The Commission had before it a note by the secretariat [E/ESCAP/1333] that discussed emerging issues in response to tsunamis and other natural disasters. The report reviewed the economic and social losses incurred as a result of the 2004 tsunami [YUN 2004, p. 952], which killed around 300,000 people and affected several million. It examined national and regional experiences in disaster management and preparedness and made recommendations on formulating and adopting a regional strategy on disaster risk management and building community resilience in response to tsunamis and natural disasters in Asia and the Pacific.

The Commission also had before it the reports of the Mekong River Commission [E/ESCAP/1354], the Typhoon Committee [E/ESCAP/1355] and the Panel on Tropical Cyclones [E/ESCAP/1356] on their 2004 activities. It recommended that the secretariat organize workshops to facilitate the sharing of information, experience and lessons learned with regard to risk assessment, detection, warning and contingency planning. The secretariat was asked to conduct studies on the feasibility of enhancing detection and warning systems.

The Commission noted that the Panel on Tropical Cyclones, at its thirty-second session (New Delhi, India, February), had organized a technical conference on water-related disasters with special reference to storm surges and tsunamis and related early warning systems, as part of an effort to integrate possible regional activities related to tsunamis into the existing framework of cyclone-related disaster preparedness.

The High-level Panel on Tsunami Recovery Development met at the outset of the ministerial segment of the Commission's sixty-first session. The Commission was informed of the progress made by six tsunami-affected countries—India, Indonesia, Malaysia, Maldives, Sri Lanka and Thailand. It underlined the need to establish an effective regional tsunami early warning system and noted that several international initiatives had already been launched, many of them under the auspices of UN bodies. At the national level, good progress had been made on early warning systems in several countries, and some countries had expressed readiness to establish a regional, multi-hazard and multi-nodal early warning system, to be linked to their national systems as appropriate. The Commission noted with concern the limited capacity of small and less developed countries to effectively meet disaster preparedness needs and agreed that more urgent

efforts should be made to enhance disaster preparedness in the region. In that regard, it noted with appreciation Thailand's proposal to establish the Voluntary Trust Fund on Tsunami Early Warning Arrangements in the Indian Ocean and Southeast Asia, to be administered by the secretariat.

The Commission called on the United Nations to support all national efforts to create regional and multi-nodal systems whereby the rapid response capacities of States could be strengthened to save lives and reduce economic loss. In particular, the Commission endorsed the following recommended areas for priority activities to be undertaken by the secretariat: conducting regional assessments of socio-economic impacts by sector; organizing technical cooperation activities in natural disaster preparedness and management; assisting the Typhoon Committee in identifying ways to enhance its work on disaster preparedness; supporting national and regional efforts to link recovery to risk management for sustainable development and community resilience; promoting the application of space technology to disaster management; and promoting a regional standby arrangement for disaster relief.

Programme and organizational questions

The Commission endorsed ESCAP's draft work programme for 2006-2007 [E/ESCAP/1344], which included a new subprogramme on Pacific island developing countries and territories and fully incorporated the planned activities of the regional institutions into the relevant subprogrammes. It urged all development partners to support the implementation of the work programme and, to avoid duplication and achieve cost-effectiveness, encouraged the secretariat to coordinate its work with other UN agencies. It also encouraged further enhancement of the evaluation component. The Executive Secretary informed the Commission that the statutes of all the regional institutions (APCTT, APCAEM, CAPSA, SIAP) had been harmonized so that their workplans were subject to the established intergovernmental review and approval process.

Monitoring and evaluation

On 23 December, the General Assembly, in **resolution 60/248**, section IX (see p. 1495), welcomed ESCAP's efforts in rationalization of monitoring and evaluation in accordance with Assembly resolution 58/269 [YUN 2003, p. 1395], especially in carrying out self-evaluation activities in a systematic and comprehensive manner. It requested ESCAP to report on its activities in that area in the proposed programme budget for the 2008-2009 biennium.

OIOS report. The Commission had before it a 2004 OIOS report on its audit of the regional commissions [E/ESCAP/1349] and a summary of the key recommendations as they related to ESCAP and the actions taken to respond to them [E/ESCAP/1350]. The Commission urged the secretariat to further enhance its collaboration with other UN organizations and requested it to provide further information on the results of actions related to the OIOS audit.

ESCAP reform

Midterm review of ESCAP conference structure

On 18 May, the Commission, having considered a secretariat note on the midterm review concerning the functioning of its conference structure [E/ESCAP/1343], adopted a resolution [E/2005/39 (res. 61/1)] on the subject, which it recommended to the Economic and Social Council for adoption (see below).

ECONOMIC AND SOCIAL COUNCIL ACTION

On 26 July [meeting 39], the Economic and Social Council, on the recommendation of ESCAP [E/2005/15/Add.1], adopted **resolution 2005/35** without vote [agenda item 10].

Midterm review concerning the functioning of the conference structure of the Economic and Social Commission for Asia and the Pacific

The Economic and Social Council,

Recalling Economic and Social Commission for Asia and the Pacific resolutions 143(XXX) of 5 April 1974, 210(XXXVI) of 29 March 1980, 262(XLIII) of 30 April 1987, 47/3 of 10 April 1991, 48/2 of 23 April 1992, 51/3 of 1 May 1995 and 53/1 of 30 April 1997 on the conference structure of the Commission,

Recalling also General Assembly resolution 50/227 of 24 May 1996 on further measures for the restructuring and revitalization of the United Nations in the economic, social and related fields,

Recalling further General Assembly resolution 40/243 of 18 December 1985 on the pattern of conferences, in which the Assembly decided that United Nations bodies may hold sessions away from their established headquarters when a Government issuing an invitation for a session to be held within its territory has agreed to defray, after consultation with the Secretary-General as to their nature and possible extent, the actual additional costs directly or indirectly involved,

Recalling Economic and Social Commission for Asia and the Pacific resolution 58/1 of 22 May 2002 on restructuring the conference structure of the Commission, in particular paragraph 6 thereof on a midterm review to be conducted during the sixty-first session,

Recalling also Commission resolution 60/6 of 28 April 2004 on the revitalization of the United Nations ESCAP Pacific Operations Centre, in particular paragraphs 1 and 2 thereof regarding the terms of reference of the Special Body on Pacific Island Developing Countries and the establishment of an Advisory Council for the Centre,

Recalling further Commission resolution 60/5 of 28 April 2004 on the Centre for Alleviation of Poverty through Secondary Crops Development in Asia and the Pacific, by which it revised the statute of the Regional Coordination Centre for Research and Development of Coarse Grains, Pulses, Roots and Tuber Crops in the Humid Tropics of Asia and the Pacific and changed the name of the Centre,

Taking into account Commission resolutions 61/2 of 18 May 2005 on the statute of the Statistical Institute for Asia and the Pacific, 61/3 of 18 May 2005 on the statute of the United Nations Asian and Pacific Centre for Agricultural Engineering and Machinery, 61/4 of 18 May 2005 on the statute of the Asian and Pacific Centre for Transfer of Technology, in which it revised the statutes of the respective regional institutions, and 61/6 of 18 May 2005 on the establishment of the Asian and Pacific Centre for Information and Communication Technology for Development as a follow-up to the World Summit on the Information Society (all of the above-mentioned institutions being collectively referred to hereunder as "the regional institutions"),

Recognizing that a complete meeting cycle of the thirteen subsidiary bodies of the Commission was concluded at the end of 2004, which makes it possible at the current session of the Commission to review the efficiency and effectiveness of the new conference structure established in accordance with Commission resolution 58/1, while bearing in mind that the new conference structure came into effect only in 2003,

Recognizing also the need for the reporting process under the conference structure to be more streamlined so that the Commission can take timely action on the reports of its subsidiary bodies,

Taking note of the evaluations and recommendations of members and associate members concerning the outcomes of sessions of the Commission and its subsidiary bodies held under the new conference structure, which provide a useful basis for the midterm review,

Reiterating its support for keeping the work of the Economic and Social Commission for Asia and the Pacific focused on three key thematic areas: poverty reduction; managing globalization; and addressing emerging social issues,

Aware of the need for the conference structure to be kept in line with the process of overall reform of the United Nations,

1. *Notes with appreciation* that, since the adoption of Economic and Social Commission for Asia and the Pacific resolution 58/1 on 22 May 2002, a new conference structure has been established in accordance with the pattern set out in paragraph 1 of that resolution;

2. *Commends* the Executive Secretary of the Economic and Social Commission for Asia and the Pacific for his efforts to prepare and organize the conferences and meetings under the new structure in an effective and efficient way and to make them correspond more fully to the three key thematic areas of poverty reduction, managing globalization and addressing emerging social issues;

3. *Also commends* the Executive Secretary for having completed the reorganization of the secretariat as requested in paragraph 2 of Commission resolution 58/1;

4. *Decides* that, as a result of the midterm review of the functioning of the conference structure, the following points should override or be integrated into the present pattern of its conference structure, as prescribed in paragraph 1 of Commission resolution 58/1 and, where relevant, the respective terms of reference annexed to the resolution:

(a) Subsidiary structure

The thematic committees shall be retained to keep the work of the Economic and Social Commission for Asia and the Pacific focused on three key thematic areas: poverty reduction; managing globalization; and addressing emerging social issues. The work of the subcommittees shall be subsumed under the respective thematic committees beginning in 2006, as a means of strengthening their integration within their respective thematic contexts;

To ensure that the key sectoral issues formerly dealt with by the subcommittees can be addressed more effectively within a thematic framework, the format of the sessions of the thematic committees shall include segments as follows:

(i) Committee on Poverty Reduction: Poverty reduction practices and statistics;

(ii) Committee on Managing Globalization:
Part I: International trade and investment, and transport infrastructure and facilitation and tourism;
Part II: Information, communication and space technology, and environment and sustainable development;

(iii) Committee on Emerging Social Issues: socially vulnerable groups, and health and development;

To ensure timely review of emerging issues as well as reporting to the Commission, the thematic committees, including parts I and II of the Committee on Managing Globalization, shall meet separately and annually after the session of the Commission for a maximum duration of five days for each session, with the duration depending on the agenda of the committee in question;

The segments under three of the above committees shall be convened either consecutively or simultaneously. The segments under one of the above committees shall be convened consecutively. The secretariat will provide interpretation services in the working languages of the Commission;

(b) Special bodies

The Special Body on Pacific Island Developing Countries shall hold its sessions prior to the sessions of the Commission, in alternate years with the Special Body on Least Developed and Landlocked Developing Countries. The maximum duration of the sessions of each of the special bodies will be two days;

The Advisory Council of the United Nations ESCAP Pacific Operations Centre, comprising representatives of the Governments of Pacific island developing countries and territories, and also of Australia and New Zealand, shall meet biennially for a maximum duration of one day at the venue of the relevant session of the Special Body on Pacific Island Developing Coun-

tries to provide advice on the Centre's work programme priorities;

(c) Regional institutions of the Economic and Social Commission for Asia and the Pacific

The regional institutions of the Economic and Social Commission for Asia and the Pacific shall continue to function under the terms of reference stipulated in the relevant resolutions, namely, resolutions 60/5, 61/2, 61/3, 61/4 and 61/6;

The programmes of work of the regional institutions shall be aligned with the thematic priorities of the Commission under the strategic framework;

5. *Requests* the Executive Secretary to ensure that the thematic sessions of the committees are conducted in a results-oriented manner that yields concrete outcomes aimed at strengthening the focus and impact of the work of the Commission;

6. *Also requests* the Executive Secretary, in accordance with paragraph 6 of Commission resolution 58/1, to report to the Commission at subsequent sessions on the implementation of the present resolution, focusing in particular on whether the conference structure has served the purpose of improving efficiency and attracting higher and wider representation from members and associate members, which would serve in particular as the basis for the comprehensive review to be conducted during the sixty-third session concerning the functioning of the conference structure;

7. *Decides* to review the conference structure of the Commission, including its thematic and sectoral priorities and subsidiary structure, and to consider the possibility of further revising its structure at its sixty-third session.

ESCAP sixty-second session

The Commission welcomed the offer of Indonesia to host the sixty-second session from 20 to 26 April 2006. It endorsed "Enhancing regional cooperation in infrastructure development, including that related to disaster management" as the theme topic for that session.

By **decision 2005/297** of 26 July, the Economic and Social Council approved the holding of the sixty-second session of the Commission in Indonesia in 2006.

Europe

The Economic Commission for Europe (ECE), at its sixtieth session (Geneva, 22-25 February) [E/2005/37], considered the economic situation in Europe on the basis of the *Economic Survey of Europe, 2005, No. 1* [Sales No. E.05.II.E.7]. The Commission convened two round tables to discuss follow-up to the 2002 International Conference on Financing for Development [YUN 2002, p. 953]. The topic of the first was "Exchange of experiences with domestic policies that have successfully increased resources for development in the

ECE region" and that of the second, "The role of regional cooperation in financing for development in the ECE region". The Commission recognized the need to pursue implementation of the commitments made at the Conference.

With regard to sustainable development, the Commission stressed that there was a need to speed up efforts to meet the internationally agreed development goals and the commitments contained in the Johannesburg Plan of Implementation, adopted at the 2002 World Summit on Sustainable Development [YUN 2002, p. 822]. The Commission agreed to the proposal that a Chairperson's summary, based on the Executive Secretary's report on sustainable development in the ECE region [E/ECE/1421], be presented as ECE's contribution to the Intergovernmental Preparatory Meeting for the Commission on Sustainable Development (see p. 917). It decided to organize the second ECE Regional Implementation Forum in preparation for the fourteenth (2006) session of the Commission on Sustainable Development.

The Commission welcomed the signature, in 2004, of a memorandum of understanding between ECE and the Organization for Security and Cooperation in Europe (OSCE). It was emphasized, however, that support for OSCE should not detract from other ECE activities.

In the context of ECE reform, the Commission welcomed the start of work by a team of external evaluators on a comprehensive report on the state of ECE, which was expected to be delivered by the end of June 2005. It underlined that the outcome of the review should be taken into account in the 2006-2007 programme of work.

Having discussed a secretariat note on an e-strategy for ECE [E/ECE/1422], the Commission agreed that the use of ICT should be promoted in the ECE work programme with the aim of increasing efficiency and efficacy, but stressed that ICT was a tool to implement the programme and not a goal in itself. The secretariat was urged to put all materials available in the three languages of the Commission (English, French, Russian) on its website.

Following consideration of secretariat notes on the programme of work planning and evaluation processes [E/ECE/1423] and the recommendations of the Group of Experts on the Programme of Work on the programme planning processes [E/ECE/1423/Add.1], the Commission requested the Executive Secretary to provide clear and complete figures on the allocation of resources to all ECE activities. The Commission adopted the recommendations of the Group of Experts concerning new programme planning processes and stressed the need for the secretariat to expedite the preparation of the guide on evaluation meth-

ods, as outlined in its note on the programme of work planning and evaluation processes. The Commission took note of the reports of its Bureau on its meetings held between April and December 2004 [E/ECE/1428] and its Group of Experts on the Programme of Work on its meetings held between March and December 2004 [E/ECE/1429].

The Executive Secretary submitted a note on achieving the internationally agreed development goals, including the MDGs [E/ECE/1424], which reviewed ECE's contributions to achieving the goals within the region. The Commission noted the linkages between ECE activities and a number of major internationally agreed development goals, including the MDGs, and observed that ECE should continue to mainstream gender into its work.

The Commission also had before it a note by the Executive Secretary on major policy issues and their impact on the ECE work programme [E/ECE/1425], which highlighted the need for ECE to address issues such as globalization, transition and environmental policies within its mandate; and a report by the Executive Secretary on achievements of and constraints faced by ECE in 2004 [E/ECE/1426], which addressed, among other subjects, the difficulty of implementing the programme of work amid increasing demands for new activities and a zero-growth budget. The Commission stressed the importance of continuing to produce tangible results in keeping with the challenges and priorities of ECE's member States. In response to resource constraints, it asked the Executive Secretary to work with member States to ensure that the distribution of resources reflected the priorities set by the Commission.

The Commission also discussed ECE's technical cooperation activities in 2004 (see p. 1113). It stressed the need to increase assistance to low-income countries in a targeted and systematic manner and encouraged the development of joint technical cooperation projects in cooperation with other organizations.

The Commission held an ad hoc session on 2 December, at which it adopted the World Plan on ECE Reform [E/ECE/1434/Rev.1] (see p. 1114).

Economic trends

The ECE summary of main economic developments and risks and opportunities faced by the economies in its region in 2005 [E/2006/16] observed that the deceleration of economic growth in the United States in 2005 was expected to continue in 2006 and the growth outlook for Western Europe remained lacklustre. In the euro area, average annual economic growth was only 1.3 per cent in 2005, significantly below the estimated growth of potential output, which was itself moderate at some 2 per cent. Annual GDP growth rates of individual member countries of the euro area continued to diverge significantly: Italy and Germany achieved below-average growth of 0.1 per cent and 0.8 per cent, respectively, while France posted a somewhat stronger 1.6 per cent growth rate. Among non-euro EU members, economic growth in the United Kingdom slowed to 1.8 per cent in 2005, while Sweden and Denmark showed growth of 2.5 per cent and 2.4 per cent, respectively.

In contrast, economic activity in most of the eight new EU member States from Central Europe and the Baltic region continued to be dynamic in 2005. However, the pace of growth was uneven across countries. Aggregate GDP in the region grew by some 4 per cent in 2005, down from 5.4 per cent in 2004, but that decline reflected mainly the economic slowdown in Poland, where GDP grew by slightly more than 3 per cent. The Baltic States remained the fastest growing of the new EU members; on average, they posted a GDP growth rate of some 7 per cent in 2005.

Vibrant growth prevailed in South-East Europe in 2005, with aggregate GDP increasing by some 5 per cent. Bulgaria, Croatia and Romania, the EU accession candidates in the subregion, continued to benefit from rising investor and consumer confidence, while economic consolidation gained momentum in the remainder of South-East Europe.

The pace of economic expansion in the Commonwealth of Independent States (CIS) countries slowed somewhat in 2005, after two years of exceptionally strong growth. After achieving 8.1 per cent in 2004, the CIS countries posted an aggregate GDP of just over 6 per cent in 2005. That outcome reflected a moderation of growth of the two largest economies, the Russian Federation and Ukraine.

Activities in 2005

Trade, industry and enterprise development

The Committee for Trade, Industry and Enterprise Development, at its ninth session (Geneva, 23-27 May) [ECE/TRADE/360], approved: the renewal of the mandates of the Public-Private Partnership Alliance, and the Team of Specialists on Internet Enterprise Development; the change in the name of the Team of Specialists on Industrial Restructuring to the "Team of Specialists on Industrial Restructuring and Competitiveness", its updated terms of reference and the renewal of

its mandate; new activities on entrepreneurship and enterprise development directly under the Working Party on Industry and Enterprise Development; the changes to the 2004-2007 Programme of Work [TRADE/2004/4 & Add.1-5], as proposed in the summary of proposed changes to the draft programme of work, 2004-2007 [TRADE/2005/20]; and, for submission to the Group of Experts on the Programme of Work, the list of underfunded technical cooperation priorities contained in the annex to the secretariat note on capacity-building and technical cooperation in support of the Committee's programme of work [ECE/TRADE/2005/15].

The Committee requested the secretariat to prepare a document on the results of the 2005 Executive Forum on "After 15 Years of Market Reforms in Transition Economies: New Challenges and Perspectives for the Industrial Sector" (Geneva, 24-25 May) [TRADE/360/Add.1], invited its subsidiary bodies to follow up on the results, and requested the secretariat to report on the follow-up at the Committee's 2006 session. It approved the proposal for a 2007 forum on "The impact of the results from WTO Doha Development Round Negotiations on the Committee's work and, particularly, on Trade Facilitation" [TRADE/2005/21].

The Committee invited ECE to give its full attention to the importance of regional advisers to enable countries in transition to benefit fully from the programme of work. It also asked the secretariat to provide the Committee with written information on resources available and their use under the scope of the Industrial Restructuring and Enterprise Development programme budget. Having considered secretariat notes on building trade partnerships in the CIS region [TRADE/2005/17] and ECE instruments to address trade facilitation in the WTO Doha work programme: review of articles V, VIII and X of the General Agreement on Tariffs and Trade 1994 [TRADE/2005/18], the Committee requested the Bureau to define follow-up activities.

Timber

The Timber Committee, at its sixty-third session (Geneva, 27-30 September) [ECE/TIM/2005/2], held a policy forum on "Forest Certification—Do Governments Have a Role?" together with the Food and Agriculture Organization of the United Nations (FAO) European Forestry Commission. It asked the Working Party on Forest Economics and Statistics, with FAO, the International Tropical Timber Organization and other partners, to consider how to improve the quality of data on production, consumption and trade of certified forest products. Having reviewed the markets for forest products and considered forecasts for 2005 and 2006, with a focus on how forest certification policies influenced forest product markets in the ECE region, the Committee approved a market statement. It also reviewed the ECE/FAO contribution and role in the global and regional forest dialogues in a changing international environment.

The Committee adopted its 2008 work programme and approved a proposal for the strategic framework for its work for 2008-2009. In the context of ECE reform, the Committee considered a proposal by its Chairman that the Timber Subprogramme expand its monitoring and analysis activities to include policy and institutions of the forest and timber sector that were not monitored consistently by any body, in order to, among other things, support capacity-building in forest sector institutions through exchange of experience.

Transport

The sixty-seventh session of the Inland Transport Committee (Geneva, 15-17 February) [ECE/TRANS/162], reviewed, among other topics: intersectoral activities; the transport situation in ECE member countries and emerging development trends; transport and security; assistance to countries with economies in transition; status of application of international ECE transport agreements and conventions; transport trends and economics; road transport; road traffic safety; harmonization of vehicle regulations; rail and inland water transport; intermodal transport and logistics; border crossing facilitation; transport of dangerous goods and perishable foodstuffs; transport statistics; and the relationship between the Committee's strategic objectives and programme of work

The Committee adopted the final text of the draft Convention on International Customs Transit Procedures for the Carriage of Goods by Rail under Cover of SMGS Consignment Notes [TRANS/2005/13 & Corr.1] and decided that the Convention should be open for signature in Geneva from 1 August 2005 until 31 July 2006. The Committee also adopted the final version of the NST/2000 [TRANS/WP.6/2004/1/Rev.1], a new Pan European classification that linked the classes of goods in transport directly to the international classifications of production of goods by activity.

Energy

The Committee on Sustainable Energy, at its fourteenth session (Geneva, 27-30 June) [ECE/ENERGY/65], discussed the stabilization of the European energy market, focusing on South-East Europe and development of the energy market in that subregion. On 28 June, it held a High-level Meeting on Energy Security in the Caspian Sea Region. On 29 June, a special session took place on the implementation of the 1997 Kyoto Protocol [YUN 1997, p. 1048] to the 1992 UN Framework Convention on Climate Change [YUN 1992, p. 681], energy efficiency and climate change mitigation. The Committee also approved the recommendations of its Extended Bureau [ENERGY/2004/6] and reviewed the activities of its subsidiary bodies. It changed the name of its Ad Hoc Group of Experts on Supply of Fossil Fuels to the Ad Hoc Group of Experts on the Harmonization of Energy Reserves/Resources Terminology and endorsed the establishment of the Ad Hoc Group of Experts on Coal Mine Methane and of the Task Force on the Economic Benefits of Improving Mine Safety through Extraction and Use of Coal Mine Methane as part of the Group of Experts' programme of work.

Environment

The Committee on Environmental Policy, at its twelfth session (Geneva, 10-12 October) [ECE/CEP/127], considered the environmental performance reviews (EPRs) of Belarus and the Republic of Moldova and adopted their recommendations. It discussed mechanisms for enforcement and compliance and management of eco-funds in countries in transition. It agreed on the proposed structure of the second round of EPRs [CEP/2005/6] and provided guidance on the preparation of a progress report on the implementation of the Eastern Europe, the Caucasus and Central Asia Strategy. The Committee took note of the draft "Environment for Europe" communication strategy and asked the Working Group of Senior Officials to revise it for the sixth Ministerial Conference "Environment for Europe", to be held in 2007, after the Conference agenda had been defined. It welcomed the adoption of the ECE Strategy for Education for Sustainable Development (ESD) and the "Vilnius framework for implementation" by a High-level Meeting of Environment and Education Ministries (Vilnius, Lithuania, 17-18 March), and noted the preparations for the first meeting of the ESD Steering Committee (Geneva, 13-14 December). It also welcomed the cross-sectoral work on the environment and health, and transport, environment and health.

The third session of the Steering Committee for Transport, Health and Environment Pan-European Programme (Geneva, 11-12 April) [ECE/AC.21/2005/13] assessed progress made in implementing its work programme for 2003-2005 and adopted a new work programme, extending to

2007. It held preliminary discussions on preparations for the third High-level Meeting on Transport, Environment and Health, to be held in 2007.

The Second ECE Regional Implementation Forum on Sustainable Development (Geneva, 15-16 December) [E/ECE/1442] reviewed Europe's progress in implementing the commitments adopted at the 2002 World Summit on Sustainable Development [YUN 2002, p. 821]. It focused on the thematic cluster for the fourteenth (2006) and fifteenth (2007) sessions of the Commission for Sustainable Development (see p. 920): energy for sustainable development, industrial development, air pollution/atmosphere and climate change. The report of the Forum would be presented to the Commission in 2006.

Human settlements

The Committee on Human Settlements, at its sixty-sixth session (Geneva, 19-21 September) [ECE/HBP/136], having considered the question of its own reform, renamed itself the Committee on Housing and Land Management (subject to editorial changes) and agreed to further streamline its activities, putting emphasis on high-profile tasks and discontinuing two elements in the programme of work, namely, development of human settlements statistics; and major trends characterizing human settlements development. In consultation with the United Nations Human Settlements Programme (UN-Habitat), the Committee agreed to take an active part in the 2006 World Urban Forum and to organize ECE side events that would provide a platform for disseminating ECE experience and good practice in implementing major policy issues regarding the housing sector, land administration and, in particular, social housing and housing finance. The Committee supported the work on the main principles of Public/Private Partnership in land administration and noted its relevance to other areas of its work, such as housing and spatial planning. It adopted its programme of work for 2006-2007 and agreed on the draft biennial programme plan for 2008-2009.

Statistics

The Conference of European Statisticians, at its fifty-third session (Geneva, 13-15 June) [ECE/CES/68], considered the implications of the meetings of its parent bodies—the February session of ECE (see p. 1109) and the March session of the UN Statistical Commission (see p. 1368)—and agreed that the Bureau of the Conference, the Conference itself, and the Statistical Division should continue to contribute actively to strengthening ECE. The Conference, among other things, decided to follow the ECE external evaluation process and implement the recommendations for adjusting its work; asked the ECE Statistical Division to continue to be involved in technical cooperation activities through the Regional Adviser Programme, seek ways to increase its technical assistance and regularly draw the attention of Conference members to statistical areas where the less developed statistical offices in the ECE region needed help but the technical assistance activities were currently underfunded.

Having considered the Integrated Presentation (IP) of the international statistical work programmes and their coordination, the Conference adopted a revised classification for transport statistics, which was part of a new Pan-European classification, NST/2000 (see above). It also asked the Bureau to consider the appointment of a Steering Group to develop a workplan with regard to migration statistics. The possibility of eventually expanding that Steering Group into a global body would be explored within the Statistical Commission.

During the Conference session, seminars were held on improved data reporting and on sustainable development.

Operational activities

Operational activities in 2004, as described in a note by the Executive Secretary [E/ECE/1427], were mostly carried out through capacity-building workshops, seminars, study tours, policy advisory services and field projects. Activities were funded from the UN regular budget and the UN Development Account, together with extrabudgetary resources. Of the $1,119,028 from the regular budget, 25.7 per cent went to trade development, 16.2 per cent to transport, 15.6 per cent to sustainable energy, 14 per cent to industrial restructuring and enterprise development, 13.7 per cent to statistics, 13.5 per cent to environment and 1.3 per cent to management of technical cooperation activities. Extrabudgetary expenditure, from ECE general trust funds, local trust funds and other sources, totalled $5,736,623.

In accordance with the ECE technical cooperation strategy, adopted in 2004 [YUN 2004, p. 1014], which called for more focused and effective technical assistance to Central Asia, the Executive Secretary issued a report on the ECE/ESCAP Strategy for Central Asia and the future orientation of the UN Special Programme for the Economies of Central Asia (SPECA) [E/ECE/1427/Add.1], in which he stated that ECE and ESCAP had initiated consultations with the Governments of the subregion on a new joint strategic approach. Based on a lessons learned exercise, the two commissions had developed a broad range of proposals aimed at reforming and strengthening SPECA. Those proposals, together with the ECE/ESCAP workplan for 2005-2007 in support of SPECA, were considered at the International Conference on Strengthening Subregional Economic Cooperation in Central Asia and the Future Role of SPECA (Astana, Kazakhstan, 25-27 May) [ECE/TCU/CONF.1/2005/1].

Programme and organizational questions

ECE reform

On 30 June, the team of external evaluators, which the Commission had decided in 2004 [YUN 2004, p. 1014] to entrust with carrying out a comprehensive review of ECE, submitted its report "The state of UNECE". The evaluation team found that: the Commission's governance was too heavy and unnecessarily complex; the permanent subsidiary bodies had too much freedom to establish their own ad hoc working groups and task forces, and recommended that those bodies be streamlined and provided with clear mandates, time frames and budgets; a number of changes needed to be made to ECE's divisions and subprogrammes, including the discontinuation of the subprogrammes on human settlements, industrial restructuring and enterprise development, and economic analysis; and ECE should establish more partnerships with European organizations.

Having considered the report, the Commission, at an ad hoc session on 2 December, adopted the workplan on ECE Reform [E/ECE/1434/Rev.1], which contained a renewed mission statement and outlined changes to be made in: governance structure; priorities of the programme of work; technical cooperation; cross-sectoral issues; relations with other organizations; management; and resources. Under the workplan, the Commission established eight sectoral committees to replace the existing principal subsidiary bodies. The first session of the newly established Committee on Economic Cooperation and Integration would take place in 2006.

On 23 December, the General Assembly, in **resolution 60/248**, section X (see p. 1495), welcomed the ECE workplan on reform, decided that the Commission should implement the measures outlined therein and requested the Secretary-General to allocate the necessary resources from the proposed 2006-2007 programme budget [A/60/6].

Latin America and the Caribbean

The Economic Commission for Latin America and the Caribbean (ECLAC) did not meet in 2005. The Commission's thirty-first session was to be held in 2006.

Economic trends

A report on the economic situation in and outlook for Latin America and the Caribbean, 2005-2006 [E/2006/19], stated that the region's economy grew in 2005 for the third consecutive year and GDP expanded by an estimated 4.4 per cent, equal to a per capita GDP growth rate of almost 3 per cent. That satisfactory performance was reflected in most of the countries of the region, all of which, except Guyana, posted positive growth rates; the highest rates were achieved by Venezuela (9.3 per cent) and Argentina (9.1 per cent). However, there were sharp differences among subregions.

Regional economic expansion continued to be fuelled by exports, and the growth of the world economy once again had a positive impact on regional terms of trade, which improved by 4.8 per cent in 2005. Exports increased by 19.1 per cent and imports by 18 per cent, a slight slowdown compared with 2004. The merchandise trade balance was positive for the fourth consecutive year, standing at $77.8 billion. The most outstanding feature of the period of economic growth was the expanding surplus on the balance of payments current account. The surplus for 2005 was equivalent to 1.3 per cent of GDP. Those results were coupled with a positive flow of FDI into the Latin American countries.

The relatively rapid rate of job creation that began in the region in 2003 continued in 2005, with the employment rate estimated to have risen by 0.5 per cent. The accumulated increase over the 2003 to 2005 period was 1.5 per cent, a key factor in lifting 13 million people over the poverty line in the preceding two years. The unemployment rate dropped by more than 1 per cent to 9.1 per cent in 2005. Regional inflation continued its downward trend with a rate of 6.2 per cent, compared to 7.4 per cent in 2004.

Activities in 2005

Development policy and regional economic performance

The ECLAC Economic Development Division continued to report on the macroeconomic performance of both individual countries and the region as a whole in its publications *Economic Survey of Latin America and the Caribbean* and *Preliminary Overview of the Economies of Latin America and the Caribbean*. It also continued to publish working documents in the Macroeconomics of Development Series. The Division considered the implications of the proposed free trade area of the Americas for national macroeconomic policies and their regional coordination. In order to enhance decision-making in both the public and private sectors, it provided support to countries in the formulation of economic policy proposals, follow-up of results and expansion of information systems.

In the context of its project on integrating young people into the labour market, the Division conducted a seminar on analyses, challenges and proposals for youth employment (Santiago, Chile, 6-7 July) at which the main findings from the five countries under review (Chile, Ecuador, El Salvador, Paraguay, Peru) were presented. Work continued on the Macroeconomic Dialogue Network (REDIMA) project. The Network provided a high-level forum for discussion of macroeconomic issues linked to the integration process. Several meetings were held and a number of documents published under REDIMA II, the second phase of the project, which was launched in 2005.

The Latin American and Caribbean Institute for Economic and Social Planning (ILPES), which executed the ECLAC subprogramme on public administration planning, focused on: public administration; decentralization, land-use planning and management of territorial development; investment projects and planning; and cooperation between planning agencies in Latin America and the Caribbean. It organized several intergovernmental meetings, technical seminars and national, subregional and international courses, in addition to producing technical documents and teaching materials and carrying out technical assistance missions. The 16 international and subregional courses provided by ILPES in 2005 reached 519 participants from public, private, academic and other institutions; 6 courses were also provided by ECLAC, with ILPES support, and they reached 245 participants.

The twenty-third meeting of the Presiding Officers of the Regional Council for Planning of ILPES (Havana, Cuba, 29 June) reviewed the report of activities for the 2004-2005 period and the draft programme of work for 2006-2007. The States members adopted resolutions approving the ILPES programme of work for the 2006-2007 biennium and recommending that ILPES should incorporate planning issues more explicitly as part of its activities. ILPES also organized the seventeenth regional seminar on fiscal policy (Santiago, 24-27 January).

International trade and integration

The 2005 activities of the ECLAC Division of International Trade and Integration concentrated on: trade and regional integration trends; international trade regulations, regional integration and trade policies; analysis of specific markets of interest to the region; and trade facilitation. In response to challenges posed by changes in the world economy, it carried out analytical and empirical studies and formulated policy recommendations in order to help regional Governments to improve their linkages with the international economy and to encourage them to seize the opportunities offered by such changes. It also monitored multilateral, subregional and hemispheric negotiations and supported countries in the negotiation and implementation of trade agreements.

The Division's comparative study on East Asian and Latin American information technology industries culminated in the publication of a book detailing seven national case studies in Latin America and six in Asia. It also published *Latin America and the Caribbean in the World Economy, 2004: Trends 2005* [LC/G.2283-P], which contained a chapter devoted to the analysis of trends in world trade since the emergence of China as a major force in that sphere.

The Division set up a database, called the Interactive Graphic System on International Trade, with information on trade among 33 Latin American and Caribbean countries, 15 from the EU, and other selected countries. It also launched a database containing information on all cases being processed under the WTO Dispute Settlement Body and under various regional dispute settlement mechanisms.

The Division continued to implement a project on the application of ICT to trade facilitation and organized, with UNCTAD, an international seminar on trade facilitation and transport (Santiago, 29-30 November).

Social development and equity

The main activities of ECLAC's Social Development Division in 2005 consisted of improving the exchange and compilation of social information on the ECLAC region, producing social assessments to assist in the formulation of national social policies and programmes, supporting Governments with respect to the systems of management, monitoring and evaluation of social policies and programmes and promoting human rights, democracy and peace.

The 2005 edition of the *Social Panorama of Latin America* covered: the poverty dynamic and income distribution; demographic changes and their health implications; the socio-economic situation of youth; changes in household structure and the role of families; trends in social spending; and health policy reforms. On the basis of knowledge acquired from producing the Social Panorama, the Division's technical team continued to support and participate in the design and dissemination of methodologies, harmonization of objectives and training for the follow-up to the MDGs by UN system organizations and national agencies.

By 2005, the Latin American and Caribbean Network of Social Institutions formed a virtual network of 1,055 social institutions from 41 countries and territories in the region. The purpose of the Network was to facilitate the exchange of good practices, share experiences in the area of social policy and improve the capacity of national social institutions in terms of analysis and assessment of policies and programmes. Major activities in 2005 included virtual forums on early education, homeless people and violence against children and adolescents.

The third phase of the ECLAC/World Food Programme agreement began in 2005 with the preparation of studies on the cost of hunger and the cost-effectiveness, costs and benefits of reducing undernutrition in the region. Those studies considered the cases of Chile and Peru and assessed undernutrition in the Caribbean Basin. Requests were received for those studies to be repeated in the Central American countries.

Technical cooperation was provided to Brazil's National Education Development Fund in the form of training modules in management, supervision and evaluation of social programmes. ECLAC also collaborated with the UN Stabilization Mission in Haiti (see p. 389) to support the transition efforts.

Sustainable development and human settlements

During 2005 the ECLAC Sustainable Development and Human Settlements Division focused on: assessment of advances in sustainable development in the region; follow-up to public policies and international and regional agreements on sustainable development; analysis of the relationship between the economy and the environment; and land-use and human settlement development. It went online with a set of databases and georeferenced indicators from all the countries of the region to reflect the social, economic, environmental and institutional dimensions of sustainable development.

The Division organized various workshops and seminars, including a workshop on sustainable development indicators for Latin America and the Caribbean (Río de Janeiro, Brazil, 24-28 October), and a regional workshop on mainstreaming sustainability in carbon markets and in investment environments (Santiago, 13-14 September). It also offered the first distance-learning course on strategies to overcome poverty and substandard living conditions—a sustainable urban agenda (5 September–25 November) as part of the project "Urban Poverty: an Action Oriented Strategy for Urban Governments and Institutions in Latin America and the Caribbean".

The fourth Regional Meeting of Ministers and High-level Authorities of the Housing and Urban Development Sector in Latin America and the Caribbean (Santiago, November) exchanged knowledge and experience on human settlements at the sectoral level.

Population and development

In 2005, ECLAC's Latin American and Caribbean Demographic Centre (CELADE), or Population Division, focused on: technical cooperation and training in population and development; demographic analysis and population projections; activities relating to the development, adaptation and use of methodologies for generating and disseminating information on population; and incorporating socio-demographic variables into development policies and programmes. It also supported countries in the region to facilitate and coordinate their interactions and exchange of experiences in population and development and to assess progress in implementing the objectives of the Programme of Action of the 1994 International Conference on Population and Development [YUN 1994, p. 955].

As a follow-up to the regional strategy approved by the Regional Intergovernmental Conference on Ageing [YUN 2003, p. 1022], a governmental and expert meeting on ageing in South American countries (Buenos Aires, Argentina, 14-16 November) was organized in conjunction with other international organizations. An international seminar on indigenous peoples and Afrodescendants in Latin America and the Caribbean: relevance of sociodemographic information to policies and programmes (Santiago, 27-29 April) was organized by CELADE and the Fund for the Development of the Indigenous People of Latin America and the Caribbean.

CELADE worked with the ECLAC Subregional Headquarters for the Caribbean to organize an expert meeting on international migration in the Caribbean (Port of Spain, Trinidad and Tobago, 14-15 September). Other international migration activities included an expert meeting on international migration and development (Mexico City, 30 November–2 December), which was jointly organized by the National Population Council (Mexico), the United Nations Fund for Population Activities, the UN Department of Economic and Social Affairs and ECLAC in preparation for the High-level Dialogue on International Migration and Development to take place during the 2006 General Assembly.

Integration of women in development

The work of ECLAC's Women and Development Unit in 2005 focused on supporting Latin American and Caribbean countries in their efforts to mainstream the gender perspective in public policies and consolidate the role of institutions that sought to reduce gender inequality in various spheres of development. To that end, the Unit stepped up technical cooperation activities for the design of public policies aimed at achieving gender equality in the operation of markets, institutions and society as a whole. The Unit made significant advances at the technical level and in terms of cooperation with countries in the region, especially concerning the consultation processes on economic labour policies.

Newly established subregional networks focused on issues of political culture and reform of electoral systems; poverty, gender and race; and social policies, gender and poverty. A regional network of women experts was set up to deal with governance issues, and new virtual communication networks on gender issues were established between ministers and authorities, and between the latter and civil society. ECLAC continued to consolidate its role as inter-agency focal point for gender equity activities carried out in the region by organizations in the UN system.

The thirty-eighth meeting of the Presiding Officers of the Conference on Women in Latin America and the Caribbean (Mar del Plata, Argentina, 7-8 September) [LC/L.2430(MDM.38/4)] reviewed the activities carried out with regard to the implementation of the 2004 Mexico City Consensus [YUN 2004, p. 1024], adopted at the ninth session of the Regional Conference on Women in Latin American and the Caribbean.

Economic statistics and technical cooperation

During 2005, the work of the ECLAC Statistics and Economic Projections Division centred on: statistical databanks and the dissemination of statistics and regional indicators; economic statistics and the System of National Accounts; technical cooperation with member States and with regional and international statistical organizations;

evaluation and prospective analysis of the economic development process in countries of the region; and statistics and quantitative analysis of social processes.

In addition to publishing the Statistical Yearbook for Latin America and the Caribbean, the Division collaborated with various other parts of the ECLAC secretariat on reports such as the Economic Survey of Latin America and the Caribbean and the Social Panorama of Latin America. It contributed towards the aims of the REDIMA project (see p. 1115) by providing statistics and models for macroeconomic coordination. Databanks of statistics were updated and extended and user access enhanced.

In 2005, ECLAC convened two major meetings on statistical issues: the third meeting of the Statistical Conference of the Americas of ECLAC (Santiago, 1-3 June); and the fifth meeting of the Executive Committee of the Statistical Conference (Mexico City, 14-15 November). Participants adopted the revised draft strategic plan, 2005-2015, and defined the programme of regional statistical work for Latin America and the Caribbean, July 2005–June 2007.

Natural resources and infrastructure

The ECLAC Natural Resources and Infrastructure Division conducted work on: the participation of the private sector and regulation of the provision of public services; sustainable management of natural resources; natural resources and infrastructure in linkages with the global economy and regional integration processes; national and international legal instruments governing natural resources and infrastructure; and sustainability, efficiency and equity in land transport systems. One focus of the Division was the Initiative for the Integration of Regional Infrastructure in South America (IIRSA), through which the 12 South American States were collaborating on the construction of a new infrastructure network for the continent. In the context of IIRSA, ECLAC was actively involved in designing the guidelines for the Amazon Hub, which had the aim of building a multi-modal transport system to join the Atlantic and Pacific oceans, and in providing technical assistance to standardize regulations on the provision of infrastructure services, particularly intermodal transport, port infrastructure and maritime services.

As to the sustainable management of natural resources, priority was given to the process of energy integration, especially within the Andean Community and the Southern Common Market (MERCOSUR). The Division organized several workshops with other regional bodies, which resulted in the conclusion of a cooperation agreement to boost energy integration and the sustainable development of energy resources. Countries of the region exchanged experiences on mining environmental liabilities, and greater emphasis was placed on corporate responsibility, community relations and the equitable distribution of income from mining and exploitation of energy resources.

Production and management

The ECLAC Division of Production, Productivity and Management was responsible for activities regarding: analysis of production trends; policy design aimed at improving the business environment; strengthening the key agents of industrial and agricultural development; and fostering development and adapting and incorporating new technologies, in particular information technologies and biotechnologies. It continued to offer the annual Summer School on Latin American Economies to postgraduate students and collaborated with the World Intellectual Property Organization in organizing two regional courses on technological management and intellectual property in Latin America and the Caribbean. The Division improved and updated software containing information on export and industrial production patterns and developed a methodology that was used by 11 international organizations to harmonize a set of key indicators for household and business surveys on ICT. It produced several documents, such as Foreign Investment in Latin America and the Caribbean, which were disseminated widely on the Internet through the ECLAC portal.

The Division acted as technical secretariat for the Regional Preparatory Ministerial Conference of Latin America and the Caribbean (Río de Janeiro, 8-10 June) for the second phase of the World Summit on the Information Society (see p. 933). Regional Governments adopted the Plan of Action for the Information Society in Latin America and the Caribbean, which included concrete initiatives and activities and measurable targets based on the Plan of Action adopted at the World Summit's first (2003) phase [YUN 2003, p. 857] and the Río de Janeiro Commitment, a regional political declaration oriented towards sustainable development, digital inclusion and regional solidarity.

Subregional activities

Caribbean

The ECLAC subregional headquarters for the Caribbean in Port of Spain, which was also the secretariat of the Caribbean Development and

Cooperation Committee (CDCC), carried out activities in: macroeconomic policies and economic development; linkages with the international economy, integration and cooperation; statistics and information management for development; and sustainable development in the Caribbean. It organized training workshops on social and trade statistics and natural disaster impact assessment. Participants from member States, UN agencies and regional and subregional institutions took part in training exercises in the use of the Caribbean Social Statistics Database and the development of a social vulnerability index geared towards the formulation of social policy for small island developing States in the Caribbean.

In order to improve the timeliness and enhance the success of activities, the subregional headquarters constructed databases on: trade statistics; social statistics; and selected statistical indicators. It also constructed a bibliographic database, a database on women and development and the Caribbean Digital Library. The subprogramme contributed to the formulation of policies and programmes in the area of migration by intergovernmental bodies such as the Caribbean Community (CARICOM), the Regional Nursing Body and the Commonwealth Secretariat, particularly in relation to the brain drain in the health sector. During the 2004-2005 biennium, the subprogramme substantially increased the amount of technical assistance provided to member States and to regional and subregional institutions. Member and associate member States received substantive support in their preparations for participation in global conferences such as the International Meeting to Review the Implementation of the Programme of Action for the Sustainable Development of Small Island Developing States (see p. 946) and the second phase of the World Summit on the Information Society.

Mexico and Central America

The ECLAC subregional headquarters in Mexico provided analyses, training and technical assistance to countries of the subregion. It also helped to strengthen the trade-related and analytical capacities of member States through a project that included training on intellectual property, studies on fiscal impact in 13 member States and seminars on selected issues. The subregional headquarters facilitated the sharing of experiences and best practices by providing advisory services and organizing regional workshops with the Central American member States under a framework project being executed in conjunction with the International Development Research Centre. It undertook a new study on the impact of macroeconomic policies, exchange rates and external shocks in terms of poverty and inequality in Costa Rica, El Salvador and Honduras and on the effects of volatility in economic growth on employment, real income, public social expenditure and income distribution in Central America.

Analysis of oil supplies, prices, margins and the level of competition in national oil markets was expanded to respond to the urgent demand in that area. In addition, support was provided for the definition of projects for inclusion in the Meso-American Initiative for Energy Interconnection, which formed part of the Puebla-Panama Plan to promote regional integration and development. The subregional headquarters also executed a technical cooperation project on capacity-building in macroeconomic policy analysis for the central banks of the five Central American countries, the Dominican Republic and the Central American Monetary Council.

Under the subprogramme, ECLAC continued to act as a focal point for issues related to disasters, strengthening member States' capacity to evaluate and respond to natural disasters based on the disaster assessment methodology. It carried out training activities at the national level, conducted disaster evaluations, provided rapid quantifications of losses and their effects, and participated in the World Conference on Disaster Reduction (see p. 1015).

Programme and organizational questions

ECLAC associate member countries

At its resumed organizational session, the Economic and Social Council had before it a draft resolution on implementation of resolutions concerning the participation of associate member countries of ECLAC in the follow-up to UN world conferences and in the work of the Council [E/2004/15/Add.2]. By that draft, the Council would have noted the continued support of the international community for the addition of a category allowing for the participation of associate members of the regional commissions in world conferences and in special sessions of the General Assembly, and would have decided to establish the necessary mechanisms for the participation of associate members in the work of the Council and its subsidiary bodies. On 28 April, the Council deferred consideration of the draft until its 2005 substantive session (**decision 2005/214**).

On 27 July, the Council decided to take no further action on the matter (**decision 2005/302**).

Observer status

On 23 November, the General Assembly, by **resolution 60/25** (see p. 1542), granted observer status to the Latin American Integration Association in the work of the Assembly.

Admission of Germany

ECONOMIC AND SOCIAL COUNCIL ACTION

On 26 July [meeting 39], the Economic and Social Council, on the recommendation of ECLAC [E/2005/15/Add.1], adopted **resolution 2005/41** without vote [agenda item 10].

Admission of Germany as a member of the Economic Commission for Latin America and the Caribbean

The Economic and Social Council,

Bearing in mind that the Economic Commission for Latin America and the Caribbean was set up by Economic and Social Council resolution 106(VI) of 25 February 1948, which states that membership in the Commission shall be open to Members of the United Nations in North, Central and South America and in the Caribbean area, and to France, the Netherlands and the United Kingdom of Great Britain and Northern Ireland,

Bearing in mind also that the Commission was set up on the basis of the participation of all the countries of Latin America and the Caribbean and those which have had special relations of a historical, cultural, geographical or economic nature with the region,

Recalling that, in this spirit, the Commission subsequently admitted Spain in 1979, Portugal in 1984 and Italy in 1990,

Considering that the Government of Germany has communicated to the Commission, through the Executive Secretary of the Economic Commission for Latin America and the Caribbean, its desire to be admitted to membership in the Commission,

Taking into account the continuous historical, cultural and economic links that have existed between Germany and the Latin American and Caribbean countries throughout the history of the region and the important and growing contributions that German cooperation agencies have been making through the Commission to the development of Latin America and the Caribbean in recent years,

1. *Welcomes with satisfaction* the request of the Government of Germany for admission as a member of the Economic Commission for Latin America and the Caribbean;

2. *Approves* the admission of Germany as a member of the Commission and to this effect authorizes the amendment of paragraph 3 *(a)* of the terms of reference of the Commission by the insertion of the word "Germany", between the words "and to" and the word "France".

Western Asia

The Economic and Social Commission for Western Asia (ESCWA), at its twenty-third session (Damascus, Syrian Arab Republic, 9-12 May) [E/2005/41], adopted the Damascus Declaration on the Realization of the MDGs, which it submitted to the Economic and Social Council for action (see p. 1121). It also adopted a number of other resolutions, which it brought to the Council's attention (see below).

The main documents before the Commission were the report of the Executive Secretary on the activities of ESCWA since the Commission's twenty-second (2003) session [E/ESCWA/23/5, Part I & Adds. 1-4, Part II, Part III & Adds. 1-3 & Part IV] and a report by the ESCWA secretariat on priority issues in the Western Asia region [E/ESCWA/23/4 & Parts I, II & III].

The Commission decided that, as from 2006, it would hold its biennial sessions in even years in order to be in harmony with the submission of the UN strategic framework.

Economic and social trends

Economic trends

In 2005, the economies of ESCWA member countries grew for the third straight year after two decades of stagnation, according to the summary of the survey of economic and social developments in the ESCWA region, 2005-2006 [E/2006/20]. Excluding Iraq and Palestine, GDP growth in the ESCWA region stood at 6.3 per cent in 2005, compared to 6.4 per cent in 2004. However, the growth was relatively jobless and dependent on an unsustainable surge in the price of oil. For the members of the Gulf Cooperation Council (GCC) (Bahrain, Kuwait, Oman, Qatar, Saudi Arabia, United Arab Emirates), the oil boom was well into its third year. The GDP growth rates for those countries hovered around 7 per cent, whereas the per capita GDP rate for the year was 3.9 per cent. The demand-led portion of the economic expansion had benefited the non-oil private sectors, mainly in banking services, trade, construction and real estate. The more diversified economies (Egypt, Jordan, Lebanon, Syrian Arab Republic, Yemen) maintained their gradual acceleration in economic expansion during 2005 and, as a group, recorded a GDP growth rate of 4.8 per cent, with per capita income growth of 2.5 per cent. Favourable external conditions, a high level of global liquidity, rapid growth in trade in services such as tourism, and a stable inflow of workers' remittances from abroad loosened foreign exchange constraints, which allowed economic expansion to take place at a rapid pace. Positive external economic conditions helped Lebanon to avoid a large decline in its economy in the face of a deteriorating security situation. However, in the conflict-affected economies of Iraq and the Occupied Palestinian Territory, persistent security-related tensions blighted prospects for socio-economic stability and induced widespread poverty. Iraq's real GDP growth decreased from 23 per cent in 2004 to 10 per cent in 2005 and the Palestinian economy experienced weak growth, estimated at 4.9 per cent, up from 2 per cent in 2004.

Economic growth was unable to make a dent in the region's high unemployment rate, especially the high rate among young people. With unemployment holding steady at the 15 per cent mark, despite three successive years of economic growth, it was estimated that the ESCWA region needed to create 35 million jobs during the following decade in order to meet its development targets.

Oil

In 2005, the price of West Texas Intermediate Cushing (a representative brand of crude oil) averaged $56.6 per barrel, compared with $41.5 in 2004. The region's near-maximum level of oil production continued, with a slight increase of 2.3 per cent over its 2004 level. With the exception of Iraq, the region's member States of the Organization of Petroleum Exporting Countries (OPEC) (Kuwait, Qatar, Saudi Arabia, United Arab Emirates) produced 4.7 per cent more than their average crude oil production in 2004. Among the non-OPEC countries, Bahrain, Egypt, Oman, the Syrian Arab Republic and Yemen saw a 2.9 per cent decline in oil production compared to 2004. Gross oil export revenue in the region was estimated at $307 billion, a 40.4 per cent increase over 2004.

Trade

In 2005, the total gross value of ESCWA member countries' merchandise exports, including re-exports, was estimated at $462 billion, while merchandise imports were estimated at $273 billion. The GCC countries accounted for 87 per cent of those exports and 71 per cent of total imports. Oil and oil-related products continued to be the major export group of the ESCWA region and, despite the rise in oil prices, the 65 per cent share of oil exports in total exports barely changed from 2004. It was evident, therefore, that non-oil exports were growing at the same rate as oil exports.

The apparel sector in Jordan and the steel industry in Egypt became established as export revenue earners.

Activities in 2005

In 2005, ESCWA activities under its 2004-2005 work programme [YUN 2003, p. 1028] focused on four pivotal priorities: water and energy resources, social policies, globalization, and technology; and on the interdisciplinary issues of the empowerment and advancement of women, national statistical capacity-building, especially in monitoring the attainment of the MDGs, and the special needs of countries emerging from conflict.

Attainment of the MDGs

During the Commission's twenty-third session, a round-table discussion took place on the achievement of the MDGs, adopted by the General Assembly in 2000 [YUN 2000, p. 51], in ESCWA member countries. The round table had before it an ESCWA secretariat report [E/ESCWA/23/4 (Part II)], which reviewed progress made at the national level in ESCWA countries in implementing the goals and identified the most significant challenges confronting the countries of the region in that regard.

On 12 May, the Commission adopted the Damascus Declaration on the Realization of the MDGs and submitted it to the Economic and Social Council for action.

ECONOMIC AND SOCIAL COUNCIL ACTION

On 27 July [meeting 40], the Economic and Social Council, on the recommendation of ESCWA [E/2005/15/Add.1], adopted **resolution 2005/50** without vote [agenda item 10].

The Damascus Declaration and the role of the Economic and Social Commission for Western Asia in the achievement of the internationally agreed development goals, including those contained in the Millennium Declaration

The Economic and Social Council,

Reaffirming the United Nations Millennium Declaration, which was adopted by the General Assembly in its resolution 55/2 of 8 September 2000,

Also reaffirming the commitments made in partnership between developed and developing countries for the achievement of the internationally agreed development goals, including those contained in the Millennium Declaration,

Affirming the importance of intensifying cooperation between the countries of the region in order to realize the internationally agreed development goals, including those contained in the Millennium Declaration, by 2015,

Commending the efforts of the Economic and Social Commission for Western Asia in that field and the report on progress made towards realizing the Millennium Development Goals in that region, submitted to the Commission at its twenty-third session,

1. *Takes note* of the Damascus Declaration, adopted by the Economic and Social Commission for Western Asia at its twenty-third session;

2. *Affirms* the importance of increasing economic growth and linking that growth to the formulation of strategies for the eradication of poverty and unemployment and the achievement of social integration, with a view to realizing the internationally agreed development goals, including those contained in the Millennium Declaration, including by adopting the general policies necessary in respect of employment generation, social security, the improvement of living conditions, particularly for vulnerable persons, combating corruption and the strengthening of accountability;

3. *Stresses* the need for member countries of the Economic and Social Commission for Western Asia to coordinate at the regional level in support of the achievement of the internationally agreed development goals, including those contained in the Millennium Declaration;

4. *Urges* the United Nations organizations that are working in the Economic and Social Commission for Western Asia region to coordinate their activities in order to meet regional needs and to focus, in the meetings of the regional coordination group organized by the Commission, on the progress of the region towards the realization of those goals;

5. *Requests* the Economic and Social Commission for Western Asia to provide support to member countries in realizing the internationally agreed development goals, including those contained in the Millennium Declaration, including by building capacities to formulate policies, monitor the progress made, measure its impact and prepare regional reports;

6. *Requests* the Executive Secretary to submit a report on the progress made in this regard to the Commission at its twenty-fourth session.

Economic development and cooperation

The Technical Committee on Liberalization of Foreign Trade and Economic Globalization in the Countries of the ESCWA Region, at its fourth session (Beirut, 7-8 March) [E/ESCWA/GRID/2005/IG.2/5], discussed a number of issues on the WTO Doha Development Agenda [YUN 2001, 1432]; developments in foreign trade and economic globalization; and issues of concern to Arab countries, including agriculture, access to markets for non-agricultural products, trade facilitation, trade in services and trade-related aspects of intellectual property rights.

On 12 May [E/2005/41 (res. 254(XXIII))], the Commission, having considered the Executive Secretary's report on action taken in 2004-2005 in response to its 2003 resolution on science and technology [YUN 2003, p. 1026], requested her to produce a detailed study, financed by extrabudgetary resources, on the establishment of a technology centre to undertake activities aimed at building national technological capacities and harnessing those capacities to achieve the MDGs and strengthen economic and social development and regional and international cooperation in technological fields. She was also asked to submit that study to the ESCWA Consultative Committee on Scientific and Technological Development and Technological Innovation before reporting to the Commission's twenty-fourth (2006) session.

Development and unstable conditions

In response to a 2003 Commission request [YUN 2003, p. 1027], the ESCWA secretariat submitted a report on peace and security in the region [E/ESCWA/23/4(Part I)]. The Executive Secretary submitted a report [E/ESCWA/23/5(Part I)/Add.2/Supp.3] on progress made by ESCWA with regard to the requests made in the 2003 resolution. Also in response to a 2003 request [YUN 2003, p. 1027], the Executive Secretary submitted a report on rehabilitation and economic and social reconstruction in Palestine [E/ESCWA/23/5(Part I)/Add.2/Supp.13].

On 12 May [res. 260(XXIII)], the Commission, commending secretariat initiatives to support rehabilitation and development in Palestine, Iraq and Southern Lebanon, urged the Executive Secretary to provide early warning of the potential dangers posed by lack of security in the region to economic and social development and regional integration and to intensify endeavours to build capacities and support countries in the region that had suffered and were suffering from lack of stability, including through analytical activities in sustainable economic and social development fields. It urged member countries to produce policies that would strengthen regional cooperation and integration at the economic and social levels and appealed to them and to donor bodies to contribute to the rehabilitation and reconstruction of the countries of the region that had suffered or continued to suffer from instability. The Executive Secretary was asked to report in 2006 on progress made.

Technical cooperation

In response to a 2003 Commission request [YUN 2003, p. 1028], the Executive Secretary submitted the ESCWA Technical Cooperation Strategy [E/ESCWA/23/5(Part III)/Add.1] to help clarify the Commission's strategic position with respect to the provision of technical cooperation, improve its delivery, effectiveness and efficiency, and lay the ground for its development.

On 12 May [res. 258(XXIII)], the Commission approved the Strategy and requested the Executive Secretary to take all necessary measures to imple-

ment it. She was also asked to establish a technical cooperation information and knowledge-sharing network with member countries in order to strengthen and coordinate technical cooperation activities, to submit a progress report to the Commission in 2006 and to inform it of any amendments to the Strategy.

The Commission also considered reports by the Executive Secretary on strengthening consultancy services and technical cooperation activities in ESCWA [E/ESCWA/23/5(Part I)/Add.2/Supp.11] and on technical cooperation activities undertaken in 2004 [E/ESCWA/23/5(Part III)/Add.2].

In another 12 May resolution [res. 263(XXIII)], the Commission expressed the hope that member countries would provide all possible financial support to the ESCWA Trust Fund for Regional Activities with a view to enabling the secretariat to increase its operational activities. It requested donors at the national, regional and international levels to increase their financial support for ESCWA, including for technical cooperation activities. The Executive Secretary was asked to identify, establish and develop strategic partnerships and undertake collaborative initiatives with regional and international donors in the priority areas of work and to prepare a multi-year funding plan to submit to the Commission in 2006.

Transportation

The Committee on Transport, at its sixth session (Beirut, 22-24 March) [E/ESCWA/GRID/2005/IG.1/5], recommended the adoption by the Commission of three draft resolutions concerning: the selection of the routes to be given priority in the implementation of the Agreement on International Roads in the Arab Mashreq [YUN 2001, p. 928]; regional cooperation with respect to road traffic safety; and the adoption of the Memorandum of Understanding (MOU) on Maritime Transport Cooperation in the Arab Mashreq.

In other action, the Committee urged countries that had not signed or ratified the Agreement on International Railways in the Arab Mashreq [YUN 2002, p. 1019] to do so and asked the ESCWA secretariat to develop an action plan for the Agreement's implementation. It also recommended that the secretariat address member countries regarding the acceleration of the measures necessary for establishment and activation of national committees for the facilitation of transport and trade and stated that those committees should provide ESCWA with detailed reports on their activities. The Committee also made recommendations with regard to: organizational matters pertaining to the MOU on Maritime Transport Cooperation in the Arab Mashreq; the regional road transport information system; road safety; the amended strategic framework and proposed programme of work for the biennium 2006-2007; and the annual follow-up reports on the implementation of the Committee's recommendations.

On 12 May [res. 256(XXIII)], the Commission adopted the MOU on Cooperation in the Field of Maritime Transport in the Arab Mashreq [E/ESCWA/23/6] and urged members to sign and ratify it as soon as possible. The Executive Secretary was asked to report to the Commission in 2006 on implementation of the resolution.

By another resolution of the same date [res.257(XXIII)] on the selection of the routes to be given priority in the implementation of the Agreement on International Roads in the Arab Mashreq [YUN 2001, p. 928], the Commission adopted Agreement routes M40 and M45 as priority routes. It requested member countries through whose territories the routes passed to accelerate preparation of a detailed plan of action for the projects that needed to be carried out in respect of those routes, to be completed by 30 September 2007, and to begin taking measures to develop the routes to the standard required by the Agreement as soon as possible. The Executive Secretary was asked to provide technical assistance in the preparation of the plans of action, follow up their implementation and report to the Commission in 2008.

By a further 12 May resolution [res. 265(XXIII)], the Commission called on member countries to link the issue of road safety to their development programmes, with a view to increasing awareness of traffic safety measures through the audio-visual and written media, educational curriculums, cooperation with relevant regional and international institutions, and allocation of the necessary budgets. It also called on them to participate in the activities that ESCWA would undertake, including the preparation of studies, regional workshops on good traffic safety practices and preparations for the international traffic week that was scheduled for 2007, and to participate effectively in any General Assembly discussions on the issue. The Executive Secretary was asked to report to the Commission on implementation of the resolution in 2006.

Statistics

The Commission had before it reports by the Executive Secretary, submitted in response to the Commission's 2003 requests [YUN 2003, p. 1027], on the participation of ESCWA member countries in the International Comparison Programme (ICP) [E/ESCWA/23/5(Part I)/Add.2/Supp.10] and the development of statistical work in the ESCWA region [E/ESCWA/23/5(Part I)/Add.2/Supp.9].

On 12 May [res. 262(XXIII)], the Commission, having also considered the 2004 recommendations of the ESCWA Statistical Committee [YUN 2004, p. 1029] and of the UN Statistical Commission (see p. 1368), called on member countries to adopt national statistical strategies aimed at providing the data and indicators necessary to measure progress made towards economic and social development goals, particularly the MDGs, by carrying out censuses and household surveys, including surveys on the workforce and family income and expenditure. They were also called on to issue, at least once every two years, a national statistical report showing the progress made towards the MDGs and providing economic and social indicators for that purpose, in order to assist ESCWA in updating its databases. The Commission requested member countries to mainstream ICP operations in their national statistical programmes and organizational structures in the form of independent units or as part of units that produced price statistics, in order to formulate a purchasing power parity indicator and price comparison figures. Countries were further called on to strengthen the capacities of their statistical bodies to conduct the sectoral surveys necessary to apply the bases for the preparation of national accounts in accordance with the 1993 System of National Accounts [YUN 1993, p. 1112]. Surveys should also be carried out on the unofficial sector. The Executive Secretary was asked to provide consultancy services to member countries in the area of economic, social and environmental statistics and to report on progress made in implementing the Commission's resolution in 2006.

Natural resources, energy and environment

The Commission had before it a report by the Executive Secretary [E/ESCWA/23/5(Part I)/Add.2/Supp.6] on measures it had taken in response to the Commission's 2003 resolution [YUN 2003, p. 1027] on cooperation between ESCWA members with regard to water resources and the establishment of the Arab network for the integrated management of water resources.

On 12 May [res. 255(XXIII)], the Commission asked the Executive Secretary to prepare a feasibility study on the establishment of a regional mechanism for building member countries' capacities to manage shared water resources and to submit it to the ESCWA Committee on Water Resources. The Executive Secretary was also asked to continue her support for activities and programmes relevant to the aims of the proposed mechanism and to report to the Commission in 2006.

Social development

The Committee on Social Development, at its fifth session (Beirut, 29-30 March) [E/ESCWA/SDD/2004/IG.1/12], reviewed reports on social development policies and programmes in the ESCWA region, focusing on: social policies; local development; population and development; urban development; housing; and social statistics and indicators. Its recommendations included, among other things, that member countries be called on to: appoint permanent focal points on integrated social policies and adopt measures for their implementation and follow-up; adopt the country profiles on the social situation prepared by ESCWA; make use of the ESCWA programme on building the capacities of workers, trainers and researchers in the local community development field; use the Regional Campaign on Secure Housing and Land Tenure and Good Urban Governance as a guide and work to achieve its aims; implement the Arab Decade for Persons with Disabilities, 2004-2013; adopt the internationally recognized statistical concepts, definitions and classifications and employ them in the collation and presentation of data and in making regional and international comparisons, and allocate resources for the national statistical apparatus to provide precise and reliable data for the formulation and monitoring of the implementation of development policies and programmes; and follow up activities aimed at monitoring progress towards the MDGs and building national capacities to enable member countries to prepare the indicators necessary to produce national reports. The Committee further recommended that the needs of local communities be investigated and solutions put forward to the problems that they faced. In that regard, civil society should be encouraged to cooperate with Government institutions, and youth should be encouraged to contribute.

On 12 May [res. 259(XXIII)], the Commission noted that developments in the area of social policy in ESCWA countries were not keeping pace with the speed of economic and technological developments at the global level. It requested member countries to appoint permanent focal points to discuss the integrated social policies programme and adopt appropriate measures for its implementation and follow-up; they should also implement the next stage of that programme, which required national coordination in order to formulate social policies appropriate to each country. The Executive Secretary was asked to present to member countries for adoption the national reports on social policies being prepared by the Commission, with the proviso that those reports should be updated and submitted in their amended form to the Committee on Social Development.

Women

The Commission had before it a report by the Executive Secretary on the first and second (2004) sessions [YUN 2004, p. 1030] of the ESCWA Committee on Women, which was established by the Economic and Social Council by resolution 2003/9 [YUN 2003, p. 1028]. The report also reviewed the activities of the ESCWA subprogramme on the advancement and empowerment of women.

On 12 May [res. 264(XXIII)], the Commission requested member countries to adopt policies that took into consideration gender issues and to put in place national strategies for the empowerment of women and the institutional frameworks for their implementation, with a view to mainstreaming women's issues into activities, policies and programmes. It called on member countries to intensify efforts to implement the Beirut Declaration on Arab Women Ten Years after Beijing: Call for Peace [YUN 2004, p. 1030], the outcomes of the forty-ninth session of the Commission on the Status of Women (see p. 1274) and those of the 2000 comprehensive review and evaluation [YUN 2000, p. 1084] of the Beijing Platform for Action [YUN 1995, p. 1170], and to prepare national reports on progress made and obstacles faced in that regard. The Executive Secretary was asked to submit a progress report in 2006.

Programme and organizational questions

The Commission had before it a report by the Executive Secretary on progress made during 2004 in implementing the 2004-2005 programme of work [E/ESCWA/23/5(Part I)/Add.1]. The report also indicated major factors that had influenced modifications to the programme of work and described the resulting changes.

On 12 May [res. 267(XXIII)], the Commission adopted the amendments made to the 2004-2005 programme of work and requested the Executive Secretary to follow up its implementation and, if necessary, include activities to address any changes that might take place in the ESCWA region. She was also asked to include information on any further amendments in the progress report to be distributed to member countries.

By other resolutions of the same date, the Commission adopted the draft programme budget for the 2006-2007 biennium [E/ESCWA/23/7] and requested the Executive Secretary to distribute it to member countries following its adoption by the General Assembly and to submit a report in 2006 on progress made in its implementation, describing any amendments [res. 266(XXIII)]; and adopted the recommendations contained in the reports of ESCWA's subsidiary bodies and those relating to the convening of subcommittee meetings in the 2006-2007 biennium and called on member countries to cooperate with ESCWA in ensuring that those recommendations were implemented [res. 268(XXIII)].

Cooperation with LAS

On 12 May [res. 261(XXIII)], the Commission, having considered the Executive Secretary's report on cooperation between ESCWA and the League of Arab States (LAS) [E/ESCWA/23/8], called for a strategic partnership to be forged between the two organizations based on the comparative advantages enjoyed by each. It requested the Executive Secretary to submit to LAS her views on means of developing cooperation in all economic and social sectors and to provide the Commission with her proposals and a report on the progress of the cooperation arrangements. The Commission urged Governments and donor agencies, international financial institutions, members of the UN system and the private sector to support joint projects between ESCWA and LAS members in the economic and social development fields.

ESCWA twenty-fourth session

In an April note [E/ESCWA/23/9], the ESCWA secretariat invited the Commission to review the timing of its sessions. It recalled that in 2003 the General Assembly, by resolution 58/269 [YUN 2003, p. 1395], had replaced the four-year medium-term plan with a two-year strategic framework. Given that new context, the secretariat was of the view that, in order for the Commission to be actively involved in the review and appraisal of the strategic frameworks for 2008-2009 and subsequent bienniums, it should consider meeting in even years; its twenty-fourth session would therefore be held in 2006 instead of 2007. The Commission approved the suggestion.

Chapter VI

Energy, natural resources and cartography

The development of energy solutions through the promotion of renewable energy sources and the conservation of natural resources were discussed in 2005 by several UN bodies, including the Commission on Sustainable Development, which completed its initial two-year work cycle on the theme: water, sanitation and human settlements.

The energy concerns of both developed and developing nations were the main focus of many UN activities in 2005. Renewable energy issues were discussed at a number of international dialogues, including the UN Symposium on Hydropower and Sustainable Development (October) and the International Renewable Energy Conference (November), both held in Beijing, China.

A 2005 highlight was the award of the Nobel Peace Prize to the International Atomic Energy Agency (IAEA) and its Director General, Mr. Mohamed ElBaradei, for their efforts to prevent nuclear energy from being used for military purposes and to ensure that nuclear energy for peaceful purposes was used in the safest possible way. In his annual address to the General Assembly in October, the IAEA Director General said that nuclear energy was re-emerging in a way that few would have predicted.

After several years of planning, 2005 saw the beginning of the International Decade for Action, "Water for Life", 2005-2015. Several UN departments and agencies collaborated on programmes to develop better drinking water resources and to integrate water management solutions for all peoples. UN-Water, a UN system-wide mechanism, coordinated the efforts and defined a list of priorities for the Decade.

The Eighth United Nations Regional Cartographic Conference for the Americas, held in July/August, took action on the further development and dissemination of spatial data collection and on policy strategies to make cartographic data more accessible to all countries in the Americas.

Energy and natural resources

The Commission on Sustainable Development, at its thirteenth session (New York, 11-22 April) [E/2005/29] (see p. 917), considered the issue of natural resources, particularly safe and clean water resources, in line with its 2003 decision [YUN 2003, p. 1030] to focus on the overarching theme of water for its first two-year work cycle (2004-2005) and on energy for the second (2006-2007).

The Commission, at its high-level segment (20-22 April), discussed how to meet the Millennium Development Goals (MDGs) [YUN 2000, p. 52] that related to water, sanitation and human settlements. It agreed, among other things, that lack of financial resources was a main obstacle to achieving progress towards the agreed goals.

Documents before the Commission included the Chairman's summary of the Second International Forum on Partnerships for Sustainable Development (Marrakesh, Morocco, 21-23 March) [E/CN.17/2005/7], which was attended by stakeholders involved or interested in partnership initiatives, particularly those engaged in the day-to-day operations of existing water- or energy-related partnerships.

On 22 April, the Commission adopted a resolution on policy options and practical measures to expedite implementation in water, sanitation and human settlements (see p. 1130).

Also on 22 April, the Commission recommended to the Economic and Social Council the adoption of a draft decision approving the provisional agenda for the Commission's fourteenth (2006) session. The thematic cluster for the Commission's 2006/2007 implementation cycle would be: energy for sustainable development; industrial development; air pollution/atmosphere; and climate change. By **decision 2005/229** of 20 July, the Council adopted the draft.

In preparation for the fourteenth session, a number of international meetings were held in 2005 on the subject of energy for development: the fifth meeting of the Global Forum on Sustainable Energy (Vienna, 11-13 May) [E/CN.17/2006/13]; the UN Symposium on Hydropower and Sustainable Development (Beijing, 27-29 October) [E/CN.17/2006/10]; and the International Renewable Energy Conference 2005 (Beijing, 7-8 November) [E/CN.17/2006/9].

Energy

World Solar Programme (1996-2005)

In response to General Assembly resolution 58/210 [YUN 2003, p. 1031], the Secretary-General submitted a July report [A/60/154] on the promotion of new and renewable sources of energy, including the culmination of the World Solar Programme (1996-2005). He provided an overview of recent trends and advances in the development and use of new and renewable sources of energy and of international programmes to advance the use of such energy sources. He also provided a summary of the Programme and of follow-up efforts on renewable sources of energy under the Johannesburg Plan of Implementation, adopted in 2002 at the World Summit on Sustainable Development [YUN 2002, p. 821].

The Secretary-General noted that, in recent years, the share of energy derived from renewable resources had grown and policymakers in many countries had taken steps to increase the utilization of those energy sources. Many countries had intensified research and development efforts in support of energy from renewable sources, including electricity supply using grid and off-grid means, wind, solar photovoltaic, biomass and biogas co-generation, hydropower, tidal and geothermal solutions. Markets for modern renewable energy technologies were expanding at an annual rate of some 30 per cent for wind energy and about 20 per cent for solar photovoltaics, which had also experienced significant cost reductions over the years. Nevertheless, the total share of commercial energy gained from renewable sources remained far below its economic potential.

With regard to the World Solar Programme, launched at the World Solar Summit (Harare, Zimbabwe, 16-17 June 1996), endorsed by the Assembly in resolution 53/7 [YUN 1998, p. 976] and implemented by the United Nations Educational, Scientific and Cultural Organization (UNESCO), the Secretary-General stated that UNESCO's contribution to the Programme's implementation included a series of capacity-building projects and initiatives aimed at disseminating relevant scientific knowledge and technology. UNESCO had also carried out a number of training activities for participants from developing countries, particularly in Africa. Although the Programme's initial plan comprised a vast array of proposed projects, the number of projects eventually funded did not meet expectations. Nevertheless, the Programme had raised global awareness of renewable energy sources.

GENERAL ASSEMBLY ACTION

On 22 December [meeting 68], the General Assembly, on the recommendation of the Second (Economic and Financial) Committee [A/60/488/Add.6], adopted **resolution 60/199** without vote [agenda item 52 *(f)*].

Promotion of new and renewable sources of energy, including the implementation of the World Solar Programme

The General Assembly,

Recalling its resolutions 53/7 of 16 October 1998, 54/215 of 22 December 1999, 55/205 of 20 December 2000, 56/200 of 21 December 2001 and 58/210 of 23 December 2003 on the promotion of new and renewable sources of energy, including the implementation of the World Solar Programme 1996-2005,

Recalling also the 2005 World Summit Outcome,

Noting that the World Solar Programme 1996-2005 made a contribution to raising awareness of the increased role that new and renewable sources of energy can play in the global energy supply,

Recalling the recommendations and conclusions contained in the Plan of Implementation of the World Summit on Sustainable Development ("Johannesburg Plan of Implementation") concerning energy for sustainable development,

Welcoming initiatives that aim to improve access to reliable, affordable, economically viable, socially acceptable and environmentally sound energy services for sustainable development in order to contribute to the achievement of the internationally agreed development goals, including those set out in the United Nations Millennium Declaration,

Emphasizing that the increased use and promotion of all forms of new and renewable energy for sustainable development, including solar-thermal, photovoltaic, biomass, wind, hydro, tidal, ocean and geothermal forms, could make a significant contribution towards the achievement of sustainable development and the internationally agreed development goals, including the Millennium Development Goals,

Welcoming efforts by Governments and institutions that have embarked on policies and programmes that seek to expand the use of new and renewable energy for sustainable development, and recognizing the contributions of regional initiatives as well as of institutions in supporting the efforts of countries, in particular developing countries, in this respect,

1. *Takes note* of the report of the Secretary-General;

2. *Reaffirms* that the Johannesburg Plan of Implementation is the intergovernmental framework for energy for sustainable development agreed to at the World Summit on Sustainable Development, and calls for its full implementation;

3. *Emphasizes* the need to intensify research and development in support of energy for sustainable development, which will require increased commitment on the part of all stakeholders, including Governments and the private sector, to deploy financial and human resources for accelerating research efforts;

4. *Calls upon* Governments, as well as relevant regional and international organizations and other relevant stakeholders, to combine, as appropriate, the increased use of renewable energy resources, more efficient use of energy, greater reliance on advanced

energy technologies, including advanced and cleaner fossil fuel technologies, and the sustainable use of traditional energy resources, which could meet the growing need for energy services in the longer term to achieve sustainable development;

5. *Encourages* national and regional initiatives on new and renewable energies to promote access to energy, including new and renewable sources of energy, for the poorest and to improve energy efficiency and conservation by resorting to a mix of available technologies, taking into full account he provisions of the Johannesburg Plan of Implementation concerning energy for sustainable development;

6. *Calls upon* Governments to take further action to mobilize the provision of financial resources, technology transfer, capacity-building and the diffusion of environmentally sound technologies, as set out in the Johannesburg Plan of Implementation;

7. *Welcomes* the holding of the Beijing International Renewable Energy Conference 2005, organized by the Government of the People's Republic of China and supported by the Government of the Federal Republic of Germany, on 7 and 8 November 2005, in follow-up to the International Conference for Renewable Energies held in Bonn from 1 to 4 June 2004;

8. *Takes note* of ongoing activities related to the promotion of new and renewable sources of energy within the United Nations system;

9. *Encourages* the United Nations system to continue to raise awareness of the importance of energy for sustainable development, including the need for the promotion of new and renewable sources of energy and of the increased role they can play in the global energy supply, particularly in the context of sustainable development and poverty eradication;

10. *Requests* the Secretary-General, in his report on energy to the Commission on Sustainable Development at its fourteenth session, to present an overview of the implementation of the World Solar Programme 1996-2005;

11. *Stresses* that the wider use of available renewable sources of energy requires technology transfer and diffusion on a global scale, including through North-South and South-South cooperation;

12. *Requests* the Secretary-General to submit to the General Assembly at its sixty-second session a report on the implementation of the present resolution;

13. *Decides* to include in the provisional agenda of its sixty-second session, under the item entitled "Sustainable development", a sub-item entitled "Promotion of new and renewable sources of energy".

Nuclear energy

By an August note [A/60/204], the Secretary-General transmitted to the General Assembly the 2004 report of the International Atomic Energy Agency (IAEA). Presenting the report to the Assembly on 31 October [A/60/PV.40], the IAEA Director General said that he viewed the recent award of the 2005 Nobel Peace Prize as recognition of IAEA's ceaseless efforts to ensure that nuclear energy was used exclusively for peaceful purposes and as an affirmation of the value and importance of multilateral approaches to ad-

dressing global security challenges. The Director General outlined the Agency's progress on many fronts, including nuclear safety and security, health, food and environment. He underscored the re-emergence of nuclear energy as a source of power, stating that the renewed consideration of nuclear energy was being shaped by fast-growing global energy demands, an increased emphasis on the security of energy supplies and the risk of climate change. Near-term nuclear energy growth was centred in Asia and Eastern Europe: the Russian Federation intended to double its capacity by 2020; China planned a nearly sixfold expansion by the same date; and India anticipated a tenfold increase by 2022. The Director General hoped that, in the future, there would be an explicit focus on the need for energy for development. He observed that the IAEA International Project on Innovative Nuclear Reactors and Fuel Cycles was working to ensure that the future needs of all countries, including developing countries, were considered when innovative nuclear systems were evaluated.

The Director General described IAEA's nuclear verification efforts in connection with the Democratic People's Republic of Korea (see p. 1565) and Iran. He noted that the lack of agreement at the Review Conference of the States parties to the 1968 Treaty on the Non-Proliferation of Nuclear Weapons had spotlighted an unprecedented array of challenges to the non-proliferation and arms control regime (see p. 597).

GENERAL ASSEMBLY ACTION

On 31 October [meeting 41], the General Assembly adopted **resolution 60/6** [draft: A/60/L.13 & Add.1)] by recorded vote (137-1-0) [agenda item 84].

Report of the International Atomic Energy Agency

The General Assembly,

Having received the report of the International Atomic Energy Agency for 2004,

Taking note of the statement of the Director General of the International Atomic Energy Agency, in which he provided additional information on the main developments in the activities of the Agency during 2005,

Recognizing the importance of the work of the Agency,

Recognizing also the cooperation between the United Nations and the Agency and the Agreement governing the relationship between the United Nations and the Agency as approved by the General Conference of the Agency on 23 October 1957 and by the General Assembly in the annex to its resolution 1145(XII) of 14 November 1957,

1. *Takes note with appreciation* of the report of the International Atomic Energy Agency;

2. *Takes note* of resolutions GC(49)/RES/9A on measures to strengthen international cooperation in nuclear, radiation and transport safety and waste management, GC(49)/RES/9B on transport safety, GC(49)/

RES/10A on progress on measures to protect against nuclear and radiological terrorism, GC(49)/RES/10B on amendment to the Convention on the Physical Protection of Nuclear Material, GC(49)/RES/11 on strengthening of the Agency's technical cooperation activities, GC(49)/RES/12A on strengthening the Agency's activities related to nuclear science, technology and applications, GC(49)/RES/12B on the use of isotope hydrology for water resources management, GC(49)/RES/12C on the Programme of Action for Cancer Therapy, GC(49)/RES/12D on support to the African Union's Pan-African Tsetse and Trypanosomiasis Eradication Campaign, GC(49)/RES/12E on the plan for producing potable water economically using small and medium-sized nuclear reactors, GC(49)/RES/12F on Agency activities in the development of innovative nuclear technology, GC(49)/RES/12G on approaches to supporting nuclear power infrastructure development, GC(49)/RES/13 on strengthening the effectiveness and improving the efficiency of the safeguards system and application of the Model Additional Protocol, GC(49)/RES/14 on the implementation of the Agreement between the Agency and the Democratic People's Republic of Korea for the application of safeguards in connection with the Treaty on the Non-Proliferation of Nuclear Weapons, GC(49)/RES/15 on the application of Agency safeguards in the Middle East, GC(49)/RES/16A on staffing of the Agency's secretariat, and GC(49)/RES/16B on women in the secretariat, and decisions GC(49)/DEC/11 on Israeli nuclear capabilities and threat, GC(49)/DEC/12 on the amendment to article VI of the Statute, and GC(49)/DEC/13 on the amendment to article XIV.A of the Statute, adopted on 30 September 2005 by the General Conference of the Agency at its forty-ninth regular session;

3. *Reaffirms its strong support* for the indispensable role of the Agency in encouraging and assisting the development and practical application of atomic energy for peaceful uses, in technology transfer to developing countries and in nuclear safety, verification and security;

4. *Welcomes* resolution GC(49)/RES/2 approving the appointment of Mr. Mohamed ElBaradei as Director General of the Agency until 30 November 2009;

5. *Also welcomes* the award of the Nobel Peace Prize for 2005 to the Agency and its Director General, Mr. Mohamed ElBaradei, for their efforts to prevent nuclear energy from being used for military purposes and to ensure that nuclear energy for peaceful purposes is used in the safest possible way;

6. *Appeals* to Member States to continue to support the activities of the Agency;

7. *Requests* the Secretary-General to transmit to the Director General of the Agency the records of the sixtieth session of the General Assembly relating to the activities of the Agency.

RECORDED VOTE ON RESOLUTION 60/6

In favour: Albania, Algeria, Andorra, Argentina, Armenia, Australia, Austria, Azerbaijan, Bahamas, Bahrain, Bangladesh, Barbados, Belarus, Belgium, Belize, Bolivia, Bosnia and Herzegovina, Botswana, Brazil, Brunei Darussalam, Bulgaria, Cameroon, Canada, Chile, China, Colombia, Comoros, Costa Rica, Côte d'Ivoire, Croatia, Cuba, Cyprus, Czech Republic, Denmark, Djibouti, Egypt, Ethiopia, Finland, France, Gabon, Georgia, Germany, Ghana, Greece, Grenada, Guatemala, Guinea, Guyana, Haiti, Honduras, Hungary, Iceland, India, Indonesia, Iran, Iraq, Ireland, Israel, Italy, Jamaica, Japan, Jordan, Kazakhstan, Kenya, Kuwait, Lao People's Democratic Republic, Latvia, Liberia, Libyan Arab Jamahiriya, Liechtenstein, Lithuania, Luxembourg, Madagascar, Malay-

sia, Maldives, Malta, Marshall Islands, Mauritania, Mexico, Micronesia, Monaco, Mongolia, Morocco, Nepal, Netherlands, New Zealand, Nicaragua, Niger, Nigeria, Norway, Oman, Pakistan, Palau, Panama, Paraguay, Peru, Philippines, Poland, Portugal, Qatar, Republic of Korea, Republic of Moldova, Romania, Russian Federation, Saint Kitts and Nevis, Saint Lucia, Saint Vincent and the Grenadines, San Marino, Saudi Arabia, Senegal, Serbia and Montenegro, Singapore, Slovakia, Slovenia, South Africa, Spain, Sri Lanka, Suriname, Sweden, Switzerland, Syrian Arab Republic, Thailand, The former Yugoslav Republic of Macedonia, Timor-Leste, Togo, Tunisia, Turkey, Ukraine, United Arab Emirates, United Kingdom, United Republic of Tanzania, United States, Vanuatu, Venezuela, Viet Nam, Yemen, Zambia.

Against: Democratic People's Republic of Korea.

Abstaining: None.

Natural resources

Water resources

The Commission on Sustainable Development, at its thirteenth session (New York, 11-22 April) [E/2005/29], completed its two-year work cycle on the thematic cluster of water, sanitation and human settlements, in accordance with Economic and Social Council resolution 2003/61 [YUN 2003, p. 842]. The Commission had before it the Secretary-General's report on freshwater management: policy options and possible actions to expedite implementation [E/CN.17/2005/2], in which he presented proposals to achieve the goals on water set in Agenda 21—a programme of action for sustainable development worldwide, adopted at the 1992 United Nations Conference on Environment and Development [YUN 1992, p. 672]—and the Johannesburg Plan of Implementation, adopted at the 2002 World Summit on Sustainable Development [YUN 2002, p. 821]. The report noted that, while some progress had been made towards the goals, strengthened donor commitment and attention from national and local governments were needed, backed by adequate budgetary and aid allocations and strategies to raise low-cost financing. Resources were needed for infrastructure, and also for strengthening decentralized water governance and institutional capacity-building.

The Commission also considered the Secretary-General's report on sanitation: policy options and possible actions to expedite implementation [E/CN.17/2005/3], which suggested ways to meet the sanitation target contained in the Johannesburg Plan of Implementation. The report noted that sanitation was beginning to be recognized as a national development priority that needed to be supported by adequate policies and budgetary allocations. Giving small-scale service providers easier access to credit and service contracts could contribute to expanding sanitation coverage.

Other documents before the Commission on the thematic cluster included the report of the Commission's Intergovernmental Preparatory Meeting (New York, 28 February–4 March)

[E/CN.17/2005/6], a note by the Secretariat on major groups' (mainly non-governmental organizations) priorities for action in water, sanitation and human settlements [E/CN.17/2005/5], and the Secretary-General's report on human settlements: policy options and possible actions to expedite implementation [E/CN.17/2005/4] (see p. 1165).

On 22 April [E/2005/29 (res. 13/1)], the Commission adopted a resolution on policy options and practical measures to expedite implementation in water, sanitation and human settlements and recommended that the Economic and Social Council transmit it to the High-level Meeting of the General Assembly (see p. 47). The Commission called on Governments and the UN system and invited international financial institutions and other international organizations to take action on a series of recommendations concerning access to basic water services and integrated water resources management; access to basic sanitation, sanitation and hygiene education, and wastewater collection, treatment and reuse; and integrated planning and management of human settlements, access to affordable land, housing and basic services, and employment and enterprise promotion. The resolution also contained recommendations on interlinkages and cross-cutting issues and international institutional arrangements for monitoring and follow-up of the Commission's decisions on water, sanitation and human settlements.

International Decade for Action, "Water for Life", 2005-2015

In response to General Assembly resolution 59/228 [YUN 2004, p. 1034], the Secretary-General submitted a July report [A/60/158] on the activities planned within the UN system for the International Decade for Action, "Water for Life", 2005-2015, proclaimed by the Assembly in resolution 58/217 [YUN 2003, p. 1034]. The report outlined the activities that were organized for the launch of the Decade on 22 March, initial actions at the regional level, and proposals for a public information strategy and a communications plan for raising awareness. It also contained recommendations for action to be taken during the course of the Decade.

UN-Water, the UN system-wide mechanism for water-related issues, was responsible for coordinating the activities for implementing the Decade by the UN system and non–UN partners. It had defined a group of thematic initiatives for its work over the Decade, including coping with water scarcity and pollution; sanitation, safe drinking water and health; gender mainstreaming in water and sanitation; integrated

water resources management; transboundary issues; and disaster risk reduction.

The report also described Decade-related activities being undertaken by the Advisory Board on Water and Sanitation, established by the Secretary-General on World Water Day (22 March) 2004; the UN Inter-agency Task Force on Gender and Water; the Joint Monitoring Programme on water supply and sanitation; the Global Programme of Action for the Protection of the Marine Environment from Land-based Activities and associated programmes; UNESCO's International Hydrological Programme; the Water for African Cities and Water for Asian Cities programmes of the United Nations Human Settlements Programme (UN-Habitat); the United Nations International Strategy for Settlements Programme (UN-Habitat); the United Nations International Strategy for Disaster Reduction; regional initiatives being carried out by the five UN regional commissions; and assistance to country programmes. The report also described the communications strategy for the Decade and partnership initiatives.

In conclusion, the Secretary-General noted that Member States might wish to consider setting up national committees or designating focal points to facilitate and promote the Decade's activities. He also stated that special focus needed to be placed on Africa's water development and management and on gender, water and sanitation initiatives. Member States and national and international organizations were urged to make voluntary contributions to advance the Decade's goals, and interested stakeholders were encouraged to link their water-related activities to the Decade.

By **decision 60/542** of 22 December, the General Assembly took note of the Secretary-General's report.

Cartography

UN Regional Cartographic Conference for the Americas

In accordance with Economic and Social Council decision 2001/232 [YUN 2001, p. 941], the Eighth United Nations Regional Cartographic Conference for the Americas was held in New York from 27 June to 1 July [E/CONF.96/3]. In July, an excerpt of the Conference report [E/2005/83] was submitted to the Council. The Conference provided a forum for government officials, scientists and experts from the Americas to report on programmes undertaken to develop spatial data infrastructures in the region and to discuss common problems, needs and experiences in cartography and geographical information. The Conference was organized into three technical committees that addressed strategy, policy, economic and institutional issues; spatial data infrastructures and their development in the Americas; and geospatial data collection, management and dissemination.

The Conference adopted and recommended to the Council for adoption 14 draft resolutions covering: the benefits of developing a spatial data infrastructure; a partnership approach in developing a spatial data infrastructure; training, education and spatial standards discussion; policy and reform; outreach and related areas; global mapping and second administrative level boundaries projects; Geocentric Reference System for the Americas project; satellite data; spatial data dissemination; funding issues; the proposed 2006 meeting on geospatial data infrastructure and information of the Americas for sustainable development; the recommendation for an interregional meeting to consider, among other things, common problems; the recommendation for the Ninth United Nations Regional Cartographic Conference for the Americas to be convened in 2009; and a vote of thanks to those who had provided substantive and other support to the Conference.

By **decision 2005/231** of 20 July, the Council endorsed the recommendations contained in the excerpt from the Conference report.

Chapter VII

Environment and human settlements

In 2005, the United Nations and the international community continued to work towards protecting the environment through legally binding instruments and the activities of the United Nations Environment Programme (UNEP).

The twenty-third session of the UNEP Governing Council/sixth Global Ministerial Environment Forum adopted the Bali Strategic Plan for Technology Support and Capacity-building and an updated UNEP water policy and strategy. The Governing Council also adopted decisions on strengthening environmental emergency response and developing disaster prevention, preparedness, mitigation and early-warning systems in the aftermath of the 2004 Indian Ocean tsunami; chemicals management; poverty and the environment; and gender equality in the field of the environment. A summary of discussions on the environmental underpinnings of the Millennium Development Goals, held during the session by ministers and delegation heads, was submitted by the Governing Council President as a contribution to the High-level Plenary Meeting of the General Assembly (2005 World Summit) in September.

The Millennium Ecosystem Assessment (MA), a four-year international assessment to evaluate the state of major ecosystems and their links with human well-being, was completed in 2005, and two MA reports were released. The Global International Waters Assessment, which studied international waters and causes of environmental problems in 66 water regions, was also concluded and several reports on its findings were published. A second International Workshop on the regular process for global reporting and assessment of the state of the marine environment, including socio-economic aspects, known as the Global Marine Assessment, was convened in June. In November, the Assembly endorsed the Workshop's conclusions and decided to launch an "assessment of assessments", to be completed within two years.

The Montreal Protocol to the 1992 United Nations Framework Convention on Climate Change entered into force on 16 February; the first Conference of the Parties serving as the Meeting of the Parties to the Protocol was convened in November/December. The first meeting of the Conference of the Parties to the 2001 Stockholm Convention on Persistent Organic Pollutants was held in May.

The Assembly declared 2008 the International Year of Planet Earth and encouraged Member States, the UN system and other actors to take advantage of the Year to increase awareness of the importance of Earth sciences for the achievement of sustainable development and to promote action at the local, national, regional and international levels.

The United Nations Human Settlements Programme (UN-Habitat) continued to support the implementation of the 1996 Habitat Agenda, the Johannesburg Plan of Implementation of the 2002 World Summit on Sustainable Development and the Millennium Development Goals, with a focus on the Goal aimed at improving the lives of slum-dwellers. It supported local, national and regional human settlements development activities, including through the placement of Habitat Programme Managers in 32 countries. Among other measures, the Programme's Governing Council decided to accelerate the implementation of a cooperation framework with the World Bank Group and regional development banks, to increase resources and capacities for improving access to basic services for all and to strengthen the Slum Upgrading Facility of UN-Habitat.

Environment

UN Environment Programme

Governing Council/Ministerial Forum

The sixth Global Ministerial Environment Forum (GMEF), also serving as the twenty-third session of the Governing Council (GC) of the United Nations Environment Programme (UNEP), was held at UNEP headquarters in Nairobi, Kenya, from 21 to 25 February [A/60/25]. On 25 February [dec. 23/12], the Governing Council decided to hold its ninth special session in Dubai, United Arab Emirates, from 7 to 9 February 2006 and its twenty-fourth session in Nairobi, from 5 to 9 February 2007, and approved the provisional agendas for those sessions.

Ministerial consultations (21-23 February) discussed the implementation of the internationally agreed development goals of the Millennium Declaration, also known as the Millennium Development Goals (MDGs) [YUN 2000, p. 51], including the MDGs on the eradication of extreme poverty and hunger, environmental sustainability, and the promotion of gender equality and the empowerment of women [ibid., p. 52]. A summary of the discussions [A/60/25/Add.1], prepared by the Governing Council President as a contribution to the High-level Plenary Meeting of the United Nations General Assembly (2005 World Summit) (see p. 47), contained recommendations addressed to the international community and UNEP for the accelerated and sustainable implementation of the three goals.

The Committee of the Whole (21-25 February) [UNEP/GC.23/11] considered assessment, monitoring and early warning: state of the environment (see p. 1135); international environmental governance (see p. 1134); cooperation and coordination matters (see p. 1139); and the UNEP programme of work (see p. 1135), the Environment Fund (see p. 1143) and administrative and other budgetary matters (ibid.).

On 27 July, the Economic and Social Council took note of the Governing Council's report on its twenty-third session (**decision 2005/312**).

Subsidiary body

In 2005, the Committee of Permanent Representatives, which was open to representatives of all UN Member States and members of specialized agencies, held an extraordinary meeting on 1 February [UNEP/CPR/90/3] and regular meetings on 15 March [UNEP/CPR/91/2], 9 June [UNEP/CPR/92/2], 12 September [UNEP/CPR/93/2] and 28 December [UNEP/CPR/94/2]. The Committee discussed, among other matters, preparations for the Governing Council's ninth (2006) special session, the fourteenth (2005) session of the Commission on Sustainable Development (see p.920) and the 2005 World Summit (see p. 47); implementation of UNEP's programme of work and the relevant decisions of the Council's eighth special session [YUN 2004, p. 1036] and its twenty-second [YUN 2003, p. 1036] and twenty-third (2005) sessions; UNEP relations with the United Nations Office at Nairobi (UNON); and the status of the Environment Fund.

GENERAL ASSEMBLY ACTION

On 22 December [meeting 68], the General Assembly, on the recommendation of the Second (Economic and Financial) Committee [A/60/488], adopted **resolution 60/189** without vote [agenda item 52].

Report of the Governing Council of the United Nations Environment Programme on its twenty-third session

The General Assembly,

Recalling its resolutions 2997(XXVII) of 15 December 1972, 53/242 of 28 July 1999, 56/193 of 21 December 2001, 57/251 of 20 December 2002, 58/209 of 23 December 2003 and 59/226 of 22 December 2004,

Taking into account Agenda 21 and the Plan of Implementation of the World Summit on Sustainable Development ("Johannesburg Plan of Implementation"),

Reaffirming the role of the United Nations Environment Programme as the principal body within the United Nations system in the field of environment, which should take into account, within its mandate, the sustainable development needs of developing countries, as well as countries with economies in transition,

Reaffirming also that capacity-building and technology support to developing countries, as well as countries with economies in transition, in environment-related fields are important components of the work of the United Nations Environment Programme,

1. *Takes note* of the report of the Governing Council of the United Nations Environment Programme at its twenty-third session and the decisions contained therein;

2. *Notes* that the Governing Council, at its twenty-third session, discussed all components of the recommendations on international environmental governance as contained in its decision SS.VII/1, and notes also that reporting on international environmental governance is included in the agenda of its ninth special session;

3. *Welcomes* the adoption of the Bali Strategic Plan for Technology Support and Capacity-building, calls for the intensification of ongoing efforts to implement the Plan with regard both to mobilizing adequate resources, from all sources, as well as the strengthening of cooperation between the United Nations Environment Programme and other stakeholders, based on their comparative advantages, and invites Governments and other stakeholders in a position to do so to provide the necessary funding and technical assistance for its full implementation;

4. *Also welcomes* the continued efforts by the United Nations Environment Programme through the joint United Nations Environment Programme/Office for the Coordination of Humanitarian Affairs Environment Unit, taking into account the respective mandates of relevant United Nations entities towards the strengthening of environmental emergency response and disaster prevention, preparedness and early warning systems;

5. *Emphasizes* the need for the United Nations Environment Programme, within its mandate, to further contribute to sustainable development programmes, the implementation of Agenda 21 and the Johannesburg Plan of Implementation at all levels and to the work of the Commission on Sustainable Development, bearing in mind the mandate of the Commission;

6. *Recognizes* the need to strengthen the scientific base of the United Nations Environment Programme, as recommended by the intergovernmental consultation on strengthening the scientific base of the Pro-

gramme, including the reinforcement of the scientific capacity of developing countries, as well as countries with economies in transition, including through the provision of adequate financial resources;

7. *Recalls* the resolve of Member States to promote the sound management of chemicals and hazardous wastes throughout their life cycle, in accordance with Agenda 21 and the Johannesburg Plan of Implementation, aiming to achieve that by 2020 chemicals are used and produced in ways that lead to the minimization of significant adverse effects on human health and the environment using transparent and science-based risk assessment and risk management procedure, by adopting and implementing a voluntary strategic approach to international management of chemicals, and to support developing countries in strengthening their capacity for the sound management of chemicals and hazardous wastes by providing technical and financial assistance, as appropriate;

8. *Calls upon* the United Nations Environment Programme to continue within its mandate its activities related to small island developing States, in pursuance of the outcome of the International Meeting to Review the Implementation of the Programme of Action for the Sustainable Development of Small Island Developing States, held in Port Louis from 10 to 14 January 2005;

9. *Emphasizes* the need to further enhance coordination and cooperation among the relevant United Nations organizations in the promotion of the environmental dimension of sustainable development, and welcomes the continued active participation of the United Nations Environment Programme in the United Nations Development Group;

10. *Welcomes* the progress made in the implementation of the provisions of section III.B. of the appendix to decision SS.VII/1 of the Governing Council on strengthening the role and financial situation of the United Nations Environment Programme, including the significant broadening of the donor base and increasing total contributions to the Environment Fund, and in this regard notes that the Governing Council will review the implementation of those provisions at its twenty-fourth session;

11. *Reiterates* the need for stable, adequate and predictable financial resources for the United Nations Environment Programme, and, in accordance with resolution 2997(XXVII), underlines the need to consider the adequate reflection of all administrative and management costs of the Programme in the context of the United Nations regular budget;

12. *Emphasizes* the importance of the Nairobi headquarters location of the United Nations Environment Programme, and requests the Secretary-General to keep the resource needs of the Programme and the United Nations Office at Nairobi under review so as to permit the delivery, in an effective manner, of necessary services to the Programme and to the other United Nations organs and organizations in Nairobi;

13. *Decides* to include in the provisional agenda of its sixty-first session, under the item entitled "Sustainable development", a sub-item entitled "Report of the Governing Council of the United Nations Environment Programme on its ninth special session".

International environmental governance

The Governing Council considered a report of the Executive Director on international environmental governance [UNEP/GC.23/6], which discussed progress achieved with regard to the universal membership of GC/GMEF (see below); the Bali Strategic Plan on Technology Support and Capacity-building (see p. 1135); strengthening UNEP's scientific base (see p. 1136) and UNEP financing (see p. 1143); multilateral environmental agreements (see p. 1145); and enhanced coordination across the UN system, including the Environmental Management Group (see p. below).

The report summarized the divergent views on the universal membership of GC/GMEF submitted by Governments participating in an international seminar on the future of UNEP governance, hosted by Sweden (Stockholm, 22-23 November 2004). Those views related to strengthening UNEP, decision-making, voting rights, and administrative costs, among other issues.

On 25 February [A/60/25 (dec. 23/1, section III)], the Governing Council decided to review further and consider the issue of universal membership at its ninth (2006) special session, with a view to providing inputs to the Secretary-General's report to the General Assembly at its sixty-first (2006) session. Also before the Council was a report of the Executive Director on the outcomes of intergovernmental meetings of relevance to GC/GMEF [UNEP/GC.23/4].

Environmental Management Group

The Environmental Management Group (EMG), an inter-agency advisory group set up in 1999 to coordinate UN system activities in addressing the major challenges in the UNEP work programme [YUN 1999, p. 974], held its tenth meeting in Geneva on 8 February.

The Executive Director, in a report on environmental governance [UNEP/GC.23/6], reported that, with the assistance of an independent expert in institutional arrangements, he had conducted a comprehensive assessment on the secretariat's location. The assessment, in the form of an EMG study, examined the mandate and other aspects of EMG and suggested that EMG should address interests and issues of common concern to all of its members and that the Group be provided with the resources commensurate with its system-wide responsibilities. An excerpt from the study was included in the Executive Director's report.

On 25 February [dec. 23/1, sec. VI], the Governing Council acknowledged the 2004 report on EMG's work [YUN 2004, p. 1039] and the assessment of the location of the EMG secretariat. In that regard, it called upon the Executive Director to discuss the issue with EMG members and the Committee of Permanent Representatives and report to the Council on the outcome of those discussions in 2007. The Executive Director was asked to continue to promote UN system-wide coordination on environmental activities through EMG's work.

Bali Strategic Plan on Technology Support and Capacity-building

UNEP action. On 25 February [dec. 23/1, sec. I], the Governing Council adopted the Bali Strategic Plan on Technology Support and Capacity-building, first adopted by the High-level Open-ended Intergovernmental Working Group on an Intergovernmental Strategic Plan for Technology Support and Capacity-building in 2004 [YUN 2004, p. 1040]. The Council requested the Executive Director to: give high priority to the effective and immediate implementation of the Bali Strategic Plan; undertake, as a matter of priority, the necessary steps regarding coordination mechanisms, as provided for in the Plan; work out a resource-mobilization strategy and coordinate with other funding agencies to ensure immediate and sustained implementation; and report, in 2006, on measures taken for the full implementation the Plan and on the further implementation thereof in 2007. Governments in a position to do so were invited to provide additional financial resources for the Plan's full implementation.

The Governing Council took further action with regard to the Bali Strategic Plan in a decision on its budget and work programme [dec. 23/3] (see p. 1143).

Report of Executive Director. A December note by the Executive Director [UNEP/GCSS.IX/INF/14] contained the report of the high-level consultation on South-South Cooperation in environment in the context of the Bali Strategic Plan (Jakarta, Indonesia, 23-24 November). A central objective of the consultation was to examine the scope, extent and potential of South-South cooperation in environment; explore the means to build on existing experiences, capacities and programmes; and improve the coordination and participation of countries in the South. The consultation considered the modalities of a strategy to promote South-South cooperation in environment in the context of the Bali Strategic Plan and made a series of recommendations towards that end. UNEP was requested to develop a comprehensive programme of action for South-South cooperation, taking into consideration a number of elements presented in the report, to be submitted to the Governing Council in 2007. UNEP should incorporate the recommendations into the Executive Director's report on the implemen-

tation of the Bali Strategic Plan for submission to the Governing Council in 2006. The Governing Council President concluded that the recommendations would be used as the road map and programme of actions to be undertaken by UNEP in collaboration with relevant international organizations, and would constitute essential elements in the operationalization of the Bali Strategic Plan.

UNEP activities

In his February policy statement [UNEP/GC.23/2], the Executive Director discussed the outcomes of major intergovernmental meetings dealing with environmental issues; international environmental governance; and the proposed 2006-2007 UNEP programme and budget. The twenty-third (2005) GC/GMEF session would stress the twin themes of implementation and placing environment clearly in the context of development. UNEP would also continue its efforts in its five areas of concentration: environmental information, assessment and early warning; enhanced coordination of environmental conventions and development of environmental policy instruments; freshwater; technology transfer and industry; and support to Africa. The Bali Strategic Plan (see above) provided a blueprint for UNEP to assist in moving to a more stable future and its operationalization and adequate funding would be a lasting legacy of the twenty-third (2005) GC/GMEF session.

Monitoring and assessment

In response to a 2004 Governing Council decision [YUN 2004, p. 1041], the Executive Director submitted a report [UNEP/GC.23/3] evaluating the conclusions and recommendations of the intergovernmental consultation on strengthening UNEP's scientific base, also known as the Science Initiative. It proposed the development of a coherent, dynamic assessment framework, tentatively called "Environment Watch", for assessing the global environmental situation and providing policy-relevant recommendations to decision makers at all levels. The report also described priority actions for strengthening UNEP's scientific base, including efforts to: map the assessment landscape; design the fourth Global Environment Outlook report (see p. 1142); conduct thematic assessments; promote environmental early warning, observing and monitoring; strengthen regional dimensions of assessment, monitoring and early warning activities; promote the use of environmental indicators; revitalize networking structures for information and data management; and promote links between the ongoing multi-stakeholder consultative process to strengthen UNEP's scientific base, and the intergovernmental strategic plan for technology support and capacity-building (see p. 1135).

A note by the Executive Director [UNEP/GC.23/INF/18 & Corr.1] contained the evaluation of the conclusions and recommendations of the intergovernmental consultation on strengthening UNEP's scientific base and UNEP's response thereon; described in greater detail the characteristics and components of the proposed "Environment Watch" framework; outlined plans to revitalize networking structures to support the new framework; and provided more detailed information on proposed actions by UNEP with respect to environmental indicators as a key element of the framework. Other annexes provided information on ongoing thematic assessments undertaken by UNEP in collaboration with other partners; the regional dimensions of assessment and early warning activities; a progress report on the Global Assessment of the State of the Marine Environment (see p. 1158); a summary of the outcome of the First Plenary Meeting of the International Assessment of Agricultural Science and Technology for Development (Nairobi, Kenya, 30 August 2004); and background information on the ad hoc intergovernmental Group on Earth Observations and the Global Earth Observations System of Systems.

A further note by the Executive Director [UNEP/GC.23/INF/15] assessed the collection of data on environmental statistics conducted jointly by UNEP and the United Nations Statistics Division in 2004. It also detailed information on proposed actions by UNEP with respect to environmental statistics as a key element of the proposed new "Environment Watch" framework.

Governing Council action. On 25 February [dec. 23/1, sec. II], the Governing Council requested the Executive Director to update his proposal for the "Environment Watch" framework, taking into account the recommendations of the intergovernmental consultation on strengthening UNEP's scientific base (Nairobi, Kenya, 14-15 January 2004) [UNEP/SI/IGC/3] and the outcome of the intergovernmental and multi-stakeholder consultation on the fourth Global Environment Outlook (Nairobi, 19-20 February 2005) [UNEP/DEWA/GEO/IGC.1/2] (see p. 1142), and to submit that update to Governments for their views, so as to enable the submission of a report to the Governing Council in 2006. It invited Governments in a position to do so and other development partners to provide funding, including through in-kind support for the participation of national scientific experts and institutions, particularly from developing countries and countries with

economies in transition, for the further strengthening UNEP's scientific base.

Support to Africa

In a December report on the state of the environment and UNEP's contributions to addressing substantive environmental challenges [UNEP/GCSS.IX/10], the Executive Director said that the preparation of the second Africa Environment Outlook (AEO-2) report had been completed. AEO-2 highlighted the central role Africa's environment continued to play in sustaining livelihoods, and discussed opportunities for Africans to use their environmental resources to reduce absolute poverty. Its recommendations were adopted unanimously by African environment ministers at the second Partners' Conference on the Environment Initiative of the New Partnership for Africa's Development (NEPAD) (Dakar, Senegal, 15-16 March).

On 10 January, UNEP and the NEPAD secretariat signed a three-year agreement (2005-2008) aimed at enhancing the human and institutional capacities of the subregional African Economic Communities for the implementation of the NEPAD Environment Initiative. UNEP and the African Institute for Capacity Development jointly organized a technical workshop (Nairobi, Kenya, 21-25 November), which trained participants in environmental impact assessments, geographical information systems and tools, synergies and integrated reporting and coordinated response. From April to July, UNEP, in partnership with the NEPAD secretariat, the African Regional Economic Communities and the African Ministerial Conference on the Environment organized consultative meetings (Algeria, Botswana, Djibouti, Gabon, Nigeria) to review the first draft of the NEPAD subregional environmental action plan.

In 2005, 12 UNEP/Global Environment Facility (GEF) projects devoted exclusively to Africa were approved, with total funding of $106.1 million.

Water policy and strategy

Based on the discussions of the Committee of Permanent Representatives to UNEP and further informal consultations on UNEP's updated water policy and strategy, submitted in 2004 [YUN 2004, p. 1042], the Executive Director, in February [UNEP/GC.23/3/Add.5/Rev.1 & Add 1], submitted a revised (2005) version of the updated policy and strategy together with an explanatory note on the revisions. The section of the strategy dealing with the environmentally sound management of freshwater was substantially amended to provide a better indication of UNEP's intended freshwater-related activities for the 2005-2007 period, and the link between UNEP's work and that of other UN water-related activities and programmes. The revised text also included a new section dealing with coral reefs (see p. 1159).

On 25 February [dec. 23/2], the Governing Council adopted the 2005 updated water policy and strategy as a general framework and guidance for UNEP's activities in the field of water and sanitation for the period 2005-2007. It recommended that the Executive Director, in reviewing the updated policy and strategy, take into account ecosystem approaches to integrated water resource management; emerging concepts; global assessment and monitoring; innovative instruments; participation and water governance; support to regional and subregional water bodies; groundwater; the final report of the World Commission on Dams; and conceptual precision in the use of the terms "global waters", "international waters" and "transboundary waters" applied to oceans, seas and inland bodies of water. The Executive Director should, in respect of the updated water policy and strategy, monitor its implementation, intensify collaborative activities with Governments, organizations and agencies in that regard, and circulate a report on the implementation and resource allocation before the ninth (2006) GC/GMEF special session. He should also support developing countries and countries with economies in transition through UNEP's implementation of activities under the policy and strategy and ensure that it contributed to the achievement of the MDGs [YUN 2000, p. 51] and the Johannesburg Plan of Implementation of the 2002 World Summit on Sustainable Development [YUN 2002, p. 821]. He should revise, in collaboration with the United Nations Human Settlements Programme (UN-Habitat) and other agencies, the Strategic Action Plan on Municipal Wastewater [YUN 2002, p. 1055] of the Global Programme of Action (GPA) for the Protection of the Marine Environment from Land-based Activities (see p. 1158), for consideration by the Governing Council in its review of the updated water policy and strategy in 2007. The Executive Director was also asked to facilitate the further development of the UNEP Global Environment Monitoring System on Water to ensure its growing role in the development of water-quality indicators to support the achievement of the water-related MDGs and the goals contained in the Johannesburg Plan of Implementation; and its continued provision of inputs to the UN World Water Assessment Programme and its World Water Development Report. The Council asked the Executive Director to organize the second GPA Intergovernmental Review Meeting and urged Governments to support the costs associated with the meeting.

It also asked the Executive Director to ensure that UNEP in its environment-related water and sanitation activities, took into account the work of Governments, other organizations, multilateral environmental agreements and UN agencies, as well as the UNEP/United Nations Development Programme (UNDP) memorandum of understanding (see p. 1141), in order to avoid duplication and promote synergies. The Council requested that a draft updated water policy and strategy be circulated in time for the ninth (2006) GC/GMEF special session, and a final draft no later than September 2006 for consideration by the Council in 2007. Governments, intergovernmental bodies and international organizations were asked to respond positively to the Executive Director's resource-mobilization efforts to support implementation of the water policy and strategy, particularly by the relevant subprogrammes for 2005-2007. The Executive Director was asked to report to the Council in 2007.

The atmosphere

In 2005, UNEP assessed the impact of aerosol pollution on regional climate, the hydrological cycle, agriculture and human health in the Asia and Pacific region. The Atmospheric Brown Cloud project continued to study a three kilometre-deep pollution blanket that formed over parts of Asia during the monsoon season. UNEP capacity-building activities included the establishment of three observatory stations and training programmes for Asian scientists, and a team to assess the impact of the atmospheric brown cloud on agriculture, water resources and public health.

In June, UNEP, along with the World Bank's Community Development Carbon Fund and the UNEP Risoe Centre on Energy, Climate and Sustainable Development, launched the Carbon Finance for Sustainable Energy in Africa initiative. The $1.2 million, one-year project was designed to build public and private sector capacity in five sub-Saharan African countries to identify, develop and implement projects under the Clean Development Mechanism of the 1992 United Nations Framework Convention on Climate Change [YUN 1992, p. 681]. UNEP was implementing a $2.5 million project in the Asia and the Pacific region to reduce industrial greenhouse gas emissions.

Environment and sustainable development

In response to a 2004 Governing Council decision [YUN 2004, p. 1043], the Executive Director submitted, in January [UNEP/GC.23/3/Add.6/Rev.1], an updated report on the outcome of the International Meeting to Review the Implementation of the 1994 Programme of Action for the Sustainable Development of Small Island Developing States (SIDS) (Barbados Programme of Action) [YUN 1994, p. 783] (Port Louis, Mauritius, 10-14 January), which adopted the Mauritius Declaration and Strategy for the Further Implementation of the Programme of Action for the Sustainable Development of Small Island Developing States (see p.946). The report examined UNEP's mandate for SIDS-related activities and UNEP's contributions to the Review Meeting and follow-up activities.

In preparation for the review of the Programme of Action, UNEP provided SIDS with substantive and financial support for the preparation of national assessment reports, the organization of thematic workshops, participation in regional preparatory meetings and the elaboration and dissemination of technical reports. Together with partners, UNEP organized several side events with direct links to the Meeting, and was a major actor in the elaboration of the Mauritius Strategy and the Programme of Action. In terms of follow-up action, further attention would be paid within the UNEP programmatic areas during the 2004-2005 and 2006-2007 biennia to several elements of the Strategy, including good governance and South-South cooperation in capacity-building, disaster management and other environmental issues. UNEP would renew its cooperation with the South Pacific Regional Environment Programme; strengthen cooperation with the Atlantic, Indian Ocean, Mediterranean and South China Seas group of States; and link its cooperation with the Atlantic and Indian Ocean small island developing States with the NEPAD Environment Initiative. In the aftermath of the 2004 Indian Ocean tsunami disaster [YUN 2004, p. 952], it would concentrate on assessing damage to coastlines and coral reefs and on identifying restoration measures. In the Caribbean, UNEP's work would be framed within the context of a Caribbean small island developing States programme. The report also contained updated information on modalities for the effective implementation of the recommendations contained in the 2004 Governing Council decision on SIDS [ibid., p. 1043].

Governing Council action. On 25 February [dec. 23/5], the Council noted the outcomes of the International Meeting and requested the Executive Director to continue strengthening UNEP's SIDS-related activities and to rationalize UNEP's delivery in the Pacific, the Atlantic, the Indian Ocean, the South China Seas and the Caribbean regions. He should also ensure that UNEP's SIDS-

related activities contributed to the implementation of the Mauritius Strategy and report to the Council in 2007.

Commission on Sustainable Development action. The Commission on Sustainable Development, at its thirteenth session (New York, 11-22 April) [E/2005/29], considered the thematic cluster for its 2004/2005 implementation cycle in water, sanitation and human settlements, in accordance with Economic and Social Council resolution 2003/61 [YUN 2003, p. 842]. On 22 April [E/2005/29 (res. 13/1)], it adopted a resolution on policy options and practical measures to expedite implementation in water and sanitation (see p. 1129) and human settlements (see p. 1165).

Follow-up to World Summit on Sustainable Development (2002)

A report of the Executive Director [UNEP/GC.23/5] contained an overview of recent UNEP activities contributing to the implementation of the outcomes of the 2002 World Summit on Sustainable Development [YUN 2002, p. 821] with regard to water, sanitation and human settlements. It examined UNEP's contribution to the Commission on Sustainable Development; to poverty, gender and environment; technology support and capacity-building; regional support; international environmental governance; and other areas of progress.

On 25 February [dec. 23/10], the Governing Council requested the Executive Director to enhance UNEP's activities in all regions to promote understanding of the linkages between poverty and the environment, and assist Governments to integrate environmental decision-making into social and economic policy on poverty eradication, in accordance with UNEP's mandate and in line with its programme of work.

Policy and advisory services

Trade and the environment

In 2005, UNEP participated in sessions of the World Trade Organization (WTO) Committee on Trade and Environment. In cooperation with the Worldwide Fund for Nature, UNEP convened a high-level ministerial dialogue and a technical workshop on fisheries subsidies at the sixth WTO Ministerial Conference (Hong Kong, China, 13-18 December) (see p. 1041). It launched a four-year initiative on integrated assessment of trade-related policies and biodiversity to support the 1992 Convention on Biological Diversity [YUN 1992, p. 638].

Coordination and cooperation

Business and industry

In 2005, UNEP finalized a training package on the Global Compact Environmental Principles, which was launched at the Global Compact Summit (Shanghai, China, 30 November–1 December). UNEP continued its involvement in the Global Reporting Initiative (GRI), a multi-stakeholder process and independent institution launched in 2002 [YUN 2002, p. 1038] to develop and disseminate globally applicable, sustainable reporting guidelines. It participated in expert group meetings to develop the third revised version of the GRI guidelines [ibid.] for 2006. UNEP also released the first new tool developed by the Global e-Sustainability Initiative to help companies introduce their social and environmental expectations and engage with factory-level management of their supply chains.

Environmental emergencies

On 25 February [dec. 23/7], the Governing Council noted efforts to develop a five-pillar strategy for responding to the 2004 Indian Ocean tsunami disaster [YUN 2004, p. 952], in close coordination with the UN Office for the Coordination of Humanitarian Affairs (OCHA) and Governments of affected countries. It supported the efforts of Governments and the international community to develop a worldwide early-warning system for natural and human-induced disasters, taking into consideration the framework of the International Strategy for Disaster Reduction (ISDR) [YUN 1999, p. 859]. It invited Governments and UN agencies, funds and programmes to continue cooperating with UNEP and OCHA through the Joint UNEP/OCHA Environment Unit (see below) in providing emergency assistance to countries, in particular developing countries facing environmental emergencies and natural disasters with environmental impacts. The Council also invited Governments and relevant institutions to provide extrabudgetary resources for technical cooperation and capacity-building, within the context of the Bali Strategic Plan for Technology Support and Capacity-building, adopted by the Council in February (see p. 1135), for strengthening national- and local-level capacity for coping with the environmental aspects of hazard and risk reduction, early warning, preparedness, response and mitigation. The Executive Director should continue to cooperate with the Governments of countries affected by the Indian Ocean tsunami, the scientific community and other UN bodies, in providing expertise to support emergency environ-

mental planning and assistance; assessing environmental impacts of the tsunami and any subsequent risks to human health and livelihoods; promoting the integration of environmental considerations into wider mitigation, rehabilitation and reconstruction efforts; promoting international cooperation in the use of renewable energy technologies, particularly in reconstruction efforts; and supporting short- and long-term environmental restoration and management. He should also support the Intergovernmental Oceanographic Commission in coordinating UN efforts to establish the tsunami early-warning system for the Indian Ocean and South-East Asia regions and other high-risk areas. The Council asked the Executive Director to cooperate closely with Governments and relevant international organizations and inter-agency mechanisms, ISDR, OCHA and the United Nations Educational, Scientific and Cultural Organization (UNESCO) to promote the environmental components of such systems, including by making use of local observations and indigenous knowledge, and by assisting countries in developing strategies for enhancing ecosystems that mitigated the impact of tsunami and other disasters. The Executive Director was further asked to continue developing, in close consultation with Governments, relevant international institutions and secretariats of multilateral environment agreements, an environmental approach to the identification and assessment of areas potentially at risk from disasters, and guidelines outlining procedures and methodologies for environmental assessments of disasters; and to report to the Council in 2006.

Report of Executive Director. The Executive Director submitted a December report [UNEP/GCSS.IX/5] on environmental emergency response and disaster prevention, preparedness, mitigation and early-warning systems. The report summarized UNEP's assistance to the countries affected by the 2004 Indian Ocean tsunami; highlighted the activities of the Joint UNEP/OCHA Environment Unit; and noted UNEP's continuing role within the United Nations International Strategy for Disaster Reduction in reducing disaster vulnerability and implementing the Hyogo Framework for Action 2005-2015, adopted by the World Conference on Disaster Reduction (Kobe, Hyogo, Japan, 18-22 January) (see p. 1015).

In a joint workshop (Nairobi, Kenya, 31 October and 1 November), OCHA and UNEP reaffirmed their determination to enhance the international community's ability to assist countries affected by, and vulnerable to, natural disasters and environmental emergencies, and to strengthen further their collaboration through the Joint Unit. UNEP would continue to provide technical expertise to the UN system and affected countries to ensure that environmental issues were integrated into disaster response and post-disaster recovery and reconstruction plans.

In response to requests from Indonesia, Maldives, Seychelles, Somalia, Sri Lanka, Thailand and Yemen, UNEP established the Asian Tsunami Disaster Task Force (ATDTF) and deployed nearly 30 environmental experts to the countries affected by the Indian Ocean tsunami to assist environmental authorities in assessing damage and reconstruction needs. A preliminary report entitled "After the Tsunami—Rapid Environmental Assessment", containing a summary of the main impact and recovery needs, was released on 22 February. UNEP also provided expertise to support environmental assessments, strengthen the capacity of environmental authorities, promote sound environmental solutions and provide management tools for integrating environmental factors into recovery and reconstruction plans. It supported the implementation of environmental rehabilitation and recovery activities in Indonesia, Maldives, Sri Lanka and Thailand. In conjunction with ATDTF and GPA, the Regional Organization for the Conservation of the Environment of the Red Sea and Gulf of Aden hosted a meeting on coastal zone rehabilitation management for the tsunami-affected region (Cairo, 17 February), which adopted 12 guiding principles for environmentally-sound coastal rehabilitation and reconstruction, known as the Cairo Principles. As a follow-up to the Cairo meeting, the GPA coordinating office mobilized resources to support national-level dialogue in the Seychelles, Sri Lanka and Thailand. Through the flash appeal on strengthening early-warning systems in tsunami-affected countries, which was launched in January (see p. 1024), UNEP assisted Governments in building their capacity for early warning and disaster risk reduction. In February, UNEP organized a technical meeting on debris and waste management, as part of its contribution to the United Nations Post-tsunami Waste Management Plan. In Indonesia, Maldives and Sri Lanka, UNEP was helping build capacity to guide the reconstruction process and monitor the environmental situation, and to conduct environmental impact screening of reconstruction activities and strategic environmental assessments of proposed plans and programmes.

(For more information concerning post-tsunami recovery efforts, see p. 1024.)

In response to the South Asia earthquake of 8 October (see p. 1034), the Joint UNEP/OCHA Environment Unit deployed two United Nations Disaster Assessment and Coordination (UNDAC)-trained environmental experts with UNDAC teams to Islamabad, Mansehra and Muzaffarabad, Pakistan. The teams identified urgent environmental needs and recommended the immediate deployment of additional assistance in the areas of waste management, deforestation and landslides. With support from Sweden and Switzerland, the Joint Unit deployed two waste management experts to ensure that waste management was fully integrated into the response phase, especially in the areas of water and sanitation, camp management and health. In mid-October, UNEP was invited to contribute to the UN post-earthquake early recovery needs assessment and to lead the environment sector. At the request of Pakistan's Ministry of Environment, UNEP, in cooperation with OCHA, compiled a preliminary environmental assessment report, launched on 19 November in Islamabad, which was used to promote immediate recovery and meet longer-term environmental needs. Also in collaboration with the Ministry, UNEP was designing an environmental recovery programme.

Other activities of the Joint UNEP/OCHA Unit included interventions concerning forest fires in Indonesia and Peru; risk and needs assessments regarding a natural dam for retaining Lake Nyos in Cameroon, which was in danger of collapse; and floods and mudslides in Guatemala caused by Hurricane Stan. The Joint Unit also led a multi-stakeholder capacity-building mission to Iran in July to assist in the development of an environmental emergency centre; developed a chapter on environmental emergencies as part of the UNDAC Field Handbook; and facilitated, with the Swedish Rescue Services Agency, the North Atlantic Treaty Organization Partnership for Peace international course on environmental disaster operations. The Joint Unit facilitated training on secondary environmental impacts during natural disaster response at the UNDAC induction course for Asia, held in Singapore in August and September.

The sixth meeting of the Advisory Group on Environmental Emergencies (AGEE), convened jointly by UNEP and OCHA (Geneva, 22-24 June), discussed the UNEP Strategic Framework on Emergency Prevention, Preparedness, Assessment, Mitigation and Response, as well as the environmental response to the 2004 Indian Ocean tsunami. The UNEP Awareness and Preparedness for Emergencies at the Local Level (APELL) programme was strengthened as a key vehicle for local level disaster-related work. To further promote the APELL process, UNEP was revisiting, adapting and developing new tools and methods to repackage it as a multi-hazard disaster reduction programme. Pursuant to ISDR findings,

UNEP initiated the establishment of the Working Group on Environment and Disaster Risk Reduction, which aimed to foster understanding of environmental concerns and integrate them into the implementation of the Hyogo Framework for Action.

Global Environment Facility

The Global Environment Facility (GEF), a joint programme of UNDP, UNEP and the World Bank, established in 1991 [YUN 1991, p. 505] to help solve global environmental problems, was the designated financial mechanism for the 1992 Convention on Biological Diversity [YUN 1992, p. 683] (see p. 1148), the 1992 United Nations Framework Convention on Climate Change [ibid., p. 681] (see p. 1146), and the 1994 United Nations Convention to Combat Desertification [YUN 1994, p. 944] (see p. 1150), and served as the interim financial mechanism for the 2001 Stockholm Convention on Persistent Organic Pollutants (POPs) [YUN 2001, p. 971] (see p. 1162).

At the end of 2005, the cumulative UNEP/GEF work programme was financed to $1.1 billion, including $529 million in GEF resources, for activities in 153 countries. Through GEF enabling activities related to biodiversity, climate change, POPs and capacity-building needs assessment for global environmental management, UNEP assisted 139 countries in meeting their obligations to the global environmental conventions and building capacity to implement them.

Fifty new UNEP/GEF initiatives were approved in 2005, with funding of $325.8 million, including $96.8 million in GEF grant financing.

Memorandum of understanding

On 5 January [UNEP/GC.23/INF/13], UNEP signed a memorandum of understanding (MOU) with UNDP, by which the two Programmes would inform each other of their respective capacity development and other initiatives and actively seek mutual involvement. The MOU built on existing collaborative arrangements between them and sought to further enhance effectiveness and avoid duplication.

Participation of civil society

Under its Tunza strategy (2003-2008) for the engagement and involvement of young people in environmental issues [YUN 2002, p. 1040], UNEP organized the Children's World Summit for the Environment (Aichi, Japan, 26-29 July), which brought together 600 children between the ages of 10 and 14 from 65 countries. The Summit, part of the 2005 World Exposition (Aichi, Japan, 25 March–25 September), explored how to better

involve children in implementing decisions from the 1992 Conference on Environment and Development [YUN 1992, p. 670] and the 2002 World Summit on Sustainable Development [YUN 2002, p. 821]. Among the outcomes of the Children's World Summit were a declaration of commitments by participants and a petition challenging world leaders to set examples for sustainable development and create and enforce laws to improve efficiency in the production, consumption and conservation of energy.

The second Tunza International Youth Conference (Bangalore, India, 12-18 October), was organized by UNEP and India's Centre for Environmental Education (CEE) to discuss the MDGs [YUN 2000, p. 51] and cooperation among youth organizations. The Conference brought together 150 young adults aged 15 to 24, who shared experiences on community-based environmental action and developed joint strategies to promote environmental protection. Conference outcomes included individual commitments by participants, the establishment of partnership projects and model action plans for youth organizations, and a CEE international internship programme.

UNEP and the Global Sports Alliance co-organized the Sport Summit for the Environment (Nagoya, Japan, 30-31 July), which was also part of the 2005 World Exposition. UNEP and the International Olympic Committee organized the sixth World Conference on Sport and the Environment (Nairobi, Kenya, 9-11 November), which highlighted the link between sport, peace and the environment. The Declaration of the Conference called on the world of sport to identify and share examples of best practice in providing leadership and training in achieving peace and sustainable development through sport.

The sixth Global Civil Society Forum (Nairobi, 19-20 February) [UNEP/GCS/6/1] discussed draft Governing Council decisions; the UNEP programme of work and national committees; civil society engagement in GC/GMEF; and the aftermath of the 2004 Indian Ocean tsunami (see p. 1024).

A January note by the Executive Director [UNEP/GC.23/INF/16] contained the global civil society statement to the twenty-third (2005) session of GC/GMEF. A number of statement by regional civil society organizations from the African, Asia and the Pacific, European and Central Asian, Latin America and the Caribbean, North American, and West Asian regions were submitted also to the Forum [UNEP/GC.23/INF/16/Add.1-6].

Cooperation with UN-Habitat

A January report [UNEP/GC.23/INF/22] prepared jointly by the Executive Directors of UNEP and UN-Habitat described cooperation between the two organizations in the areas of assessment; policy; development and implementation of joint initiatives; cooperation in Africa, Europe, Asia and the Pacific and Latin America and the Carribean region; and opportunities for future cooperation.

Gender and the environment

Governing Council action. On 25 February [dec. 23/11], the Governing Council adopted a four-part decision on gender equality in the field of the environment. With regard to equal participation in decision-making, the Governing Council invited Governments to promote women's participation in environmental decision-making at all levels, with the aim of achieving broad gender balance. It encouraged the Executive Director to work with other UN agencies to assist Governments in promoting the equal participation of women and men in policy formulation, decision-making, implementation, monitoring and reporting on sustainable development; the sharing of good examples of gender-sensitive environmental initiatives; and the development of a mentorship programme to encourage young women to take an active role in environmental policy formulation and decision-making. He should also enhance the development and dissemination of gender-disaggregated analyses, and data and information on UNEP issues and activities, and strengthen further the involvement of women in those activities.

On the issue of gender mainstreaming in environmental policies and programmes, the Council called on the Executive Director to develop and promote gender-equality criteria for the implementation of programmes and to apply the UNEP gender-sensitivity guidelines. In the implementation of the Bali Strategic Plan on Technology Support and Capacity-building [YUN 2004, p. 1040], the Executive Director should take into account the Plan's objective with regard to gender-mainstreaming and the participation of women in environmental decision-making [ibid.]. He was also asked to give an account of lessons learned about gender-related aspects of environmental issues in conflict situations and to apply the conclusions drawn from them to UNEP's post-conflict assessment work.

As to assessing the effects of environmental policies on women, the Council requested the Executive Director, in collaboration with UNDP, to assist Governments in building capacity for gender mainstreaming in the context of the Bali Strategic Plan; collaborate with scientific institutions to promote research-exchange programmes on gender and the environment as an input to the

United Nations Decade of Education for Sustainable Development (2005-2014), proclaimed by the General Assembly in resolution 57/254 [YUN 2002, p. 826], and work with the Committee on the Elimination of Discrimination Against Women and other relevant human rights bodies in identifying lessons learned on gender-related aspects of environmental issues.

With regard to implementation, the Council invited Governments, in accordance with its 1999 decision on women in environment and development [YUN 1999, p. 979], to designate gender focal points and to notify the Executive Director thereof, and involve all stakeholders in their gender-equality and environment-related activities. The Executive Director was invited to explore options, in consultation with Governments, for developing an action plan for gender mainstreaming within UNEP's work, to integrate further gender-equality and environment activities into the Programme's work, communicate the current decision to the United Nations Commission on the Status of Women (see p. 1274) and report to the Council in 2007.

UNEP activities. The creation of a Gender and Environment Unit within UNEP's Major Groups and Stakeholders Branch in July 2005, strengthened women's capacity to participate in and shape environmental policy and action at all levels. Gender equality was a cross-cutting priority in all UNEP activities, and UNEP was systematically integrating gender perspectives into its programme design and implementation, along with measurable goals and indicators. The Capacity Building of Women for Energy and Water Management in the Himalayas project, conducted in Bhutan, India and Nepal, aimed to empower women to meet their water and energy needs.

General Assembly issues

In January [UNEP/GC.23/INF/3], the Executive Director provided information on the issues arising from resolutions adopted by the General Assembly in 2004 that called for action by, or were of relevance to, UNEP.

Global Environment Outlook

A February note by the Executive Director [UNEP/DEWA/GEO/IGC.1/2] addressed key aspects of the preparation, by 2007, of the fourth comprehensive Global Environment Outlook (GEO) report, as mandated by the Governing Council in 2003 [YUN 2003, p. 1039]. The note contained suggested elements for a proposed statement by the Global Intergovernmental and Multi-Stakeholder Consultation on the fourth GEO (Nairobi, Kenya, 19-20 February), reflecting its conclusions and recommendations on the GEO report's scope and process, and background information on the GEO process, the mandate for the report and its role in strengthening UNEP's scientific base. The note also outlined the proposed process, scope and overall structure of the fourth GEO report, together with proposed key questions to be considered by experts within the assessment process.

On 25 February [dec. 23/6], the Governing Council acknowledged the findings of the GEO *Yearbook 2004-2005* [YUN 2004, p. 1048], published in February, and welcomed its focus on gender, poverty and environment. It called on Governments and intergovernmental organizations to mainstream gender considerations into their relevant environmental policies, plans, programmes and activities, in particular through promoting: gender-balanced participation in environmental assessments, monitoring, policy and decision making; gender perspectives in the design of assessment, monitoring and early-warning processes and identifying priority environment-related data sets for gender disaggregation; and gender dimensions in the formulation of environmental policies, decisions and actions. The Council decided that the feature focus of the 2005-2006 GEO *Yearbook* should be energy and air pollution, which were also the corresponding thematic cluster of issues for the programme of work of the Commission on Sustainable Development for 2006-2007 (see p. 920). It noted the importance of environmental management in controlling emerging and re-emerging infectious diseases; in that connection, it called on Governments to promote cooperation between health and environmental authorities and requested the Executive Director to keep the human health aspects of environmental change under review in cooperation with the scientific community and relevant international organizations, in particular the World Health Organization (WHO). The Council noted emerging scientific evidence relating to global climate change and its impacts and encouraged the Intergovernmental Panel on Climate Change (see p. 1154) to take such evidence into account in its fourth assessment report. It encouraged Governments, the private sector and civil society to continue to address the serious challenges of global climate change, including through the implementation of international agreements. Noting the environmental indicators presented in the GEO *Yearbook* and the cooperation between the Executive Director and the United Nations Statistics Division on environment statistics, the Council called on Governments to undertake national networking for data collection and dissemination, provide data of

high quality and credibility for GEO *Yearbook* indicators, and respond to the United Nations Statistics Division/UNEP questionnaire on environment statistics. It invited Governments and international organizations to support capacity-building for data collection and management in support of the GEO *Yearbook* environmental indicators and for the broader collaboration between the United Nations Statistics Division and UNEP. The Executive Director was asked to establish a process for developing the fourth GEO report as an integrated assessment of the global environment. Governments and relevant institutions were called upon to provide extrabudgetary resources for technical cooperation and capacity-building.

UNEP secretariat

OIOS audit and inspection services

The Secretary-General submitted, in September [A/60/346], the report of the Office of Internal Oversight Services (OIOS) for the period from 1 July 2004 to 30 June 2005, which highlighted OIOS reports submitted to UNEP programme managers on: audit of the secretariat of the Convention on the Conservation of Migratory Species of Wild Animals and co-located agreement secretariats; audit of the Post-Conflict Assessment Unit; and Investigation into allegations of misconduct in that Unit.

Administrative and budgetary matters

Environment Fund

In a February note [UNEP/GC.23/INF/6], the Executive Director provided information on the status of the Environment Fund and other sources of UNEP funding, as well as an overview of the availability of resources and their use over the 2004-2005 biennium.

Following consideration of the proposed 2006-2007 biennial programme and support budget [UNEP/GC.23/8 & Corr.1] and the related report of the Advisory Committee on Administrative and Budgetary Questions (ACABQ) [UNEP/GC.23/8/Add.1], the Governing Council, on 25 February [dec. 23/3], approved appropriations for the Environment Fund in the amount of $144 million, including $16 million for the support budget and $6 million for the Fund programme reserve. It noted that an increase in funding from the UN regular budget for UNON or UNEP in 2006-2007 would decrease the requirement under the support budget, and the released resources should be reallocated for programme activities or the Environment Fund reserve. Governments were urged to support further strengthening of the Environment Fund through the options envisaged by the Council in its 2002 decision [YUN 2002, p. 1032], including the voluntary indicative scale of contributions. The Executive Director was authorized to reallocate resources between budget lines up to a maximum of 10 per cent of the appropriation to which the resources were reallocated, and up to 20 per cent, if needed, in consultation with the Committee of Permanent Representatives. He was also authorized to enter into forward commitments not exceeding $20 million for Fund programme activities for the 2008-2009 biennium, and to increase the level of the financial reserve to $20 million as and when carry-over resources became available over and above those needed to implement the programme approved for the 2004-2005 and 2006-2007 biennia. He should step up efforts to mobilize resources from all sources, in order to broaden further the donor base and to enhance income levels.

The Council requested the Executive Director to provide financial details of the work programme to Governments, as well as information on progress made in its implementation twice yearly and to the Committee of Permanent Representatives, on a quarterly basis, with comprehensive information on all financial arrangements made available for UNEP, including core funding, the Environment Fund, earmarked funds and payments by GEF and other sources. He was asked to: propose, in consultation with the Committee of Permanent Representatives, ways of addressing the balance between non-earmarked and earmarked funding of the work programme and ensure clarity with respect to resources and expected results; prepare for the 2008-2009 biennium a work programme consisting of Environment Fund programme activities amounting to $130 million; and submit, in consultation with the Committee of Permanent Representatives, a prioritized, results-oriented and streamlined draft budget and work programme for the 2008-2009 biennium for consideration and approval by the Governing Council in 2007. He was further asked to submit a detailed proposal for the further implementation of the Bali Strategic Plan for Technology Support and Capacity-building [YUN 2004, p. 1040] to the Council in 2006, including an assessment of the availability of requisite technical and financial resources, as well as the implications for UNEP's work programme and budget.

(For further information regarding the Bali Strategic Plan, see p. 1135.)

Trust funds

The Executive Director submitted a proposal [UNEP/GC.23/9] to reduce the number of trust funds in support of the UNEP work programme, and information on the management of the existing trust funds. Of the 70 trust funds reviewed to determine whether they should have their activities rapidly completed and be closed, the Executive Director expected, that by the end of the 2004-2005 biennium, that number would be reduced to about 31, and another five would have their activities completed and would be closed in 2006.

The Executive Director developed a new partnership agreement policy, whereby donor Governments would provide funding for a number of UNEP programmes and/or activities, and instead of several trust funds for each programme activity, a single trust fund was established for each partnership agreement. Through the new policy, the Executive Director expected to reduce to the minimum the number of trust funds in support of the work programme, especially since most of the trust funds to be closed would not be replaced.

Another possible option for the reduction of trust funds would be to merge into one the 14 personnel trust funds that were expected to be active in 2006-2007. However, the Executive Director was reluctant to reconsider that option, since there was no support for it.

Seventy-four UNEP-administered trust funds were active as at 15 November 2004, including those that supported the UNEP work plan.

On 25 February, the Governing Council approved the actions proposed by the Executive Director to reduce the number of trust funds in support of the work programme [dec. 23/4, section A]. It also approved the establishment of 16 trust funds, the extension of 24 and the closure of 20 others.

Financial reserve loan

On 25 February [dec. 23/4], the Governing Council noted the Executive Director's report on administrative and other budgetary matters [UNEP/GC.23/9], which included information on the loan from the Environment Fund financial reserve and the progress achieved in the implementation of the first phase of the construction of additional office accommodation at UNON [YUN 2002, p. 1041]. The Executive Director was asked to report to the Committee of Permanent Representatives on further progress on loan drawdowns and the status of the construction project.

Flow of financial information

On 25 February [dec. 23/4], the Governing Council requested the Executive Director, in conjunction with the executive secretaries of conventions for which UNEP was the trustee, to explore possibilities for further improving the financial information flows to ensure that accurate, up-to-date information was available to convention secretariats at all times, and to report to the Committee of Permanent Representatives thereon.

Strengthening UNEP's financing

The Executive Director, in a note on strengthening UNEP financing [UNEP/GC.23/INF/12], reported on measures taken in that regard, including implementation of the voluntary indicative scale of contributions pilot phase, which began in 2003 [YUN 2003, p. 1048] and was extended to 2004-2005 [YUN 2000, p.1049]; efforts to mobilize supplementary and earmarked funds; development of cooperation mechanisms, such as the partnership agreement; and efforts to secure increased contributions from the UN regular budget as an important element in the financing of UNEP core activities.

On 25 February [dec. 23/1], the Governing Council reaffirmed its support for the provision of adequate, stable and predictable financing of UNEP as a prerequisite for strengthening its capacity and functions, as well as effective coordination of the environmental component of sustainable development. It encouraged Governments to move towards contributions to the Environment Fund in preference to contributions to earmarked trust funds, with a view to enhancing the Council's role in setting UNEP's work agenda and priorities and to make their voluntary contributions to the Fund based on either the voluntary indicative scale of contributions or any of the other voluntary options identified in the Council's 2002 decision on international environmental governance [YUN 2002, p. 1032]. The Council requested the Executive Director, in accordance with that decision, to notify member States of the proposed voluntary indicative scale of contributions for the 2006-2007 biennium, and urged them to inform the Executive Director of their intention to use the proposed scale. He was also asked to: prepare a report to enable the Council at its twenty-fourth (2007) session to assess the operation of the extended pilot phase of the voluntary indicative scale of contributions and the other voluntary options identified in its 2002 decision; continue to seek an increase in funding from all sources to strengthen UNEP's financial base; and report on all aspects of financial strengthening for consideration by the Council in 2006.

General Assembly action. The General Assembly, in **resolution 60/189** of 22 December (see p. 1133), welcomed the progress made in strengthening UNEP's role and financial situation, including the significant broadening of its donor base and the increase in total contributions to the Environment Fund.

Environmental and equity considerations in procurement practices

On 25 February [dec. 23/8], the Governing Council invited Governments to share with UNEP their experiences, lessons learned and best practices related to environmental and equity considerations in procurement practices. It requested the Executive Director to prepare a compilation report on environmental and equity considerations regarding current UNEP procurement practices and an assessment of their performance, for the Council's consideration in 2007. He was also asked to report on the implementation of the Council's 1995 decision on environmental standards within the UN system [YUN 1995, p. 1089].

Extension of term of office of Executive Director

In a November note [A/60/553], the Secretary-General informed the General Assembly of Mr. Klaus Töpfer's decision not to seek a further term as UNEP's Executive Director, and his proposal to extend Mr. Töpfer's appointment, which was to end on 31 January 2006, for two months, to allow time to identify a suitable successor and ensure continuity in the work of UNEP and its Governing Council.

By **decision 60/409** of 23 November, the Assembly extended Mr. Töpfer's term of office until the end of March 2006.

International conventions and mechanisms

In a January note [UNEP/GC.23/INF/8], the Executive Director provided information on the status of new and existing conventions and protocols in the field of the environment, covering the period 1 January 2003 to 31 December 2004.

MEAs

On 25 February [dec. 23/1, sec. V], the Governing Council requested the Executive Director, in accordance with its 2002 decision on international environmental governance [YUN 2002, p. 1033], to continue to focus on improving coordination among, synergy between and effectiveness of multilateral environmental agreements (MEAs), taking into account the autonomous decision-making authority of the conferences of the parties to such agreements and the need to promote the environmental dimension of sustainable development among relevant UN organizations. He was also asked to intensify efforts to support implementation by parties to MEAs of their obligations under such agreements, including through the provision of technical assistance.

Report of Secretary-General. In response to General Assembly resolutions 59/234 [YUN 2004, p. 1051], 59/235 [ibid., p. 1055] and 59/236 [ibid., p. 1054], the Secretary-General, by a July note [A/60/171], transmitted reports submitted by the secretariats of the United Nations Framework Convention on Climate Change (see below), the United Nations Convention to Combat Desertification in Those Countries Experiencing Serious Drought and/or Desertification, Particularly in Africa (see p. 1150), and the Convention on Biological Diversity (see p. 1148), respectively.

Climate change convention

As at 31 December, the number of parties to the United Nations Framework Convention on Climate Change (UNFCCC), which was opened for signature in 1992 [YUN 1992, p. 681] and entered into force in 1994 [YUN 1994, p. 938], remained at 188 States and the European Community (EC).

As at 31 December, 156 States and the EC were parties to the Kyoto Protocol to the Convention [YUN 1997, p. 1048]. The Protocol entered into force on 16 February.

Conference of Parties

The eleventh session of the Conference of the Parties to UNFCCC and the first Conference of the Parties serving as the Meeting of the Parties to the Kyoto Protocol (Montreal, Canada, 28 November–10 December) [FCCC/CP/2005/5 & Add.1-2] adopted the five-year programme of work of the Subsidiary Body for Scientific and Technological Advice (SBSTA) on impacts, vulnerability and adaptation to climate change. It also adopted tables of the common reporting format for land use, land-use change and forestry. Other decisions related to: a dialogue on long-term cooperative action to address climate change by enhancing UNFCCC implementation; the operation of the Least Developed Countries Fund; extension of the mandate of the Least Developed Countries Expert Group; the development and transfer of technologies; review processes during the 2006-2007 period for parties included in the Convention's annex I list of industrialized countries and countries with economies in transition; submission of communications from parties not included in annex I; research needs related to the

Convention; flexibility for Croatia under article 4 of the Convention relating to commitments; institutional linkage of the Convention secretariat to the United Nations; adjustments under article 5 of the Protocol; and other administrative and financial matters.

In October, the Executive Board of the Kyoto Protocol's clean development mechanism issued its first annual report to the Conference of the Parties serving as the Meeting of the Parties to the Protocol [FCCC/KP/CMP/2005/4 & Add. 1.], covering the periods from November 2004 to September 2005 and from 30 September to 27 November 2005.

The twenty-second sessions of SBSTA (19-27 May) [FCCC/SBSTA/2005/4 & Amend.1 & Add.1] and of the Subsidiary Body for Implementation (SBI) (20-27 May) [FCCC/SBI/2005/10 & Add.1] were held in Bonn, Germany. In conjunction with those sessions, the UNFCCC secretariat organized a seminar of governmental experts (Bonn, 16-17 May) to discuss actions relating to the mitigation of, and adaptation to, climate change, and policies and measures adopted by the participants' respective Governments that supported the implementation of their commitments under UNFCCC and the Kyoto Protocol. SBSTA [FCCC/SBSTA/2005/10] and SBI [FCCC/SBI/2005/23] also held their twenty-third sessions (Montreal, Canada, 28 November–6 December).

GENERAL ASSEMBLY ACTION

On 22 December [meeting 68], the General Assembly, on the recommendation of the Second Committee [A/60/488/Add.4], adopted **resolution 60/197** without vote [agenda item 52 *(d)*].

Protection of global climate for present and future generations of mankind

The General Assembly,

Recalling its resolution 54/222 of 22 December 1999, its decision 55/443 of 20 December 2000 and its resolutions 56/199 of 21 December 2001, 57/257 of 20 December 2002, 58/243 of 23 December 2003 and 59/234 of 22 December 2004 and other resolutions relating to the protection of the global climate for present and future generations of mankind,

Recalling also the provisions of the United Nations Framework Convention on Climate Change, including the acknowledgement that the global nature of climate change calls for the widest possible cooperation by all countries and their participation in an effective and appropriate international response, in accordance with their common but differentiated responsibilities and respective capabilities and their social and economic conditions,

Recalling further the Johannesburg Declaration on Sustainable Development, the Plan of Implementation of the World Summit on Sustainable Development ("Johannesburg Plan of Implementation"), the Delhi Ministerial Declaration on Climate Change and Sustainable Development, adopted by the Conference of the Parties to the United Nations Framework Convention on Climate Change at its eighth session, held in New Delhi from 23 October to 1 November 2002, the outcome of the ninth session of the Conference of the Parties held in Milan, Italy, from 1 to 12 December 2003, and the outcome of the tenth session of the Conference of the Parties, held in Buenos Aires from 6 to 18 December 2004,

Recalling the 2005 World Summit Outcome,

Reaffirming the Mauritius Declaration and the Mauritius Strategy for the Further Implementation of the Programme of Action for the Sustainable Development of Small Island Developing States,

Remaining deeply concerned that all countries, in particular developing countries, including the least developed countries and small island developing States, face increased risks from the negative effects of climate change, and stressing the need to address adaptation needs relating to such effects,

Noting that one hundred and eighty-nine States and one regional economic integration organization have ratified the Convention,

Noting also that, to date, the Kyoto Protocol to the United Nations Framework Convention on Climate Change has attracted one hundred and fifty-six ratifications, including from parties mentioned in annex I to the Convention, which account for 61.6 per cent of emissions,

Noting further the work of the Intergovernmental Panel on Climate Change and the need to build and enhance scientific and technological capabilities, inter alia, through continuing support to the Panel for the exchange of scientific data and information, especially in developing countries,

Recalling the United Nations Millennium Declaration, in which Heads of State and Government resolved to make every effort to ensure the entry into force of the Kyoto Protocol and to embark on the required reduction in emissions of greenhouse gases,

Reaffirming its commitment to the ultimate objective of the Convention, namely, to stabilize greenhouse gas concentrations in the atmosphere at a level that prevents dangerous anthropogenic interference with the climate system,

Taking note of the report of the Executive Secretary of the United Nations Framework Convention on Climate Change on the work of the Conference of the Parties to the Convention,

1. *Calls upon* States to work cooperatively towards achieving the ultimate objective of the United Nations Framework Convention on Climate Change;

2. *Notes* that States that have ratified the Kyoto Protocol to the United Nations Framework Convention on Climate Change welcome the entry into force of the Kyoto Protocol on 16 February 2005 and strongly urge States that have not yet done so to ratify it in a timely manner;

3. *Notes with interest* the activities undertaken under the flexible mechanisms established by the Kyoto Protocol;

4. *Takes note* of the decisions adopted by the Conference of the Parties at its tenth session, and calls for their implementation;

5. *Notes* the importance of the eleventh session of the Conference of the Parties to the United Nations

Framework Convention on Climate Change and the first session of the Conference of the Parties serving as the Meeting of the Parties to the Kyoto Protocol, held in Montreal, Canada, from 28 November to 9 December 2005;

6. *Also notes* the ongoing work of the liaison group of the secretariats and offices of the relevant subsidiary bodies of the United Nations Framework Convention on Climate Change, the United Nations Convention to Combat Desertification in Those Countries Experiencing Serious Drought and/or Desertification, Particularly in Africa and the Convention on Biological Diversity, and encourages cooperation to promote complementarities among the three secretariats while respecting their independent legal status;

7. *Requests* the Secretary-General to make provisions for the sessions of the Conference of the Parties to the United Nations Framework Convention on Climate Change and its subsidiary bodies in his proposal for the programme budget for the biennium 2006-2007;

8. *Invites* the secretariat of the United Nations Framework Convention on Climate Change to report to the General Assembly at its sixty-first session on the work of the Conference of the Parties;

9. *Invites* the conferences of the parties to the multilateral environmental conventions, when setting the dates of their meetings, to take into consideration the schedule of meetings of the General Assembly and the Commission on Sustainable Development so as to ensure the adequate representation of developing countries at those meetings;

10. *Decides* to include in the provisional agenda of its sixty-first session the sub-item entitled "Protection of global climate for present and future generations of mankind".

Vienna Convention and Montreal Protocol

As at 31 December, 189 States and the EC were parties to the 1985 Vienna Convention for the Protection of the Ozone Layer [YUN 1985, p. 804], which entered into force in 1998 [YUN 1998, p. 810].

Parties to the Montreal Protocol, which was adopted in 1987 [YUN 1987, p. 868], numbered 188 States and the EC; to the 1990 Amendment to the Protocol, 179 and the EC; to the 1992 Amendment, 169 and the EC; to the 1997 Amendment, 138 and the EC; and to the 1999 Amendment, 102 and the EC.

The second Extraordinary Meeting of the Parties to the Montreal Protocol (Montreal, Canada, 1 July) [UNEP/OzL.Pro.ExMP/2/3] adopted a decision on the 2006 critical-use nominations for methyl bromide, an issue that had been left unresolved at the sixteenth Meeting of the Parties in 2004 [YUN 2004, p. 1052].

The combined seventh meeting of the Conference of the Parties to the Convention and seventeenth Meeting of the Parties to the Montreal Protocol was held in Dakar, Senegal, from 12 to 16 December [UNEP/OzL.Conv.7/7-UNEP/OzL.Pro.17/11]. The Conference of the Parties to the Convention approved a budget for the Convention Trust Fund of $897,672 for 2006, $589,691 for 2007 and $1,162,601 for 2008, and adopted decisions on other administrative and budgetary matters.

The Meeting of the Parties to the Montreal Protocol approved the request of Cyprus to be removed from the list of developing countries under the Protocol and adopted lists of controlled substances as process agents. Other decisions related to ratification issues; essential-use nominations for 2006-2007; process agents 2006-2007 critical-use exemptions for methyl bromide; laboratory and analytical critical uses of methyl bromide; recapturing/recycling and destruction of methyl bromide from space fumigation; minimizing production of chloroflourocarbons, as well as their use in metered-dose inhalers; laboratory and analytical uses of carbon tetrachloride; coordination between UNEP's Ozone secretariat and the International Plant Protection Convention secretariat; preventing illegal trade in controlled ozone-depleting substances; the environmentally sound destruction of concentrated and diluted sources of ozone-depleting substances; the assistance of the Ozone secretariat's Technology and Economic Assessment Panel for the meeting of experts on destruction of ozone-depleting substances, scheduled to take place in Montreal in February 2006; the 2005 report of the Assessment Panel and the Intergovernmental Panel on Climate Change, entitled *Safeguarding the Ozone Layer and the Global Climate System: Issues Related to Hydrofluorocarbons and Perfluorocarbons,* data and information provided by the parties to the Protocol; the 2006-2008 replenishment of the Multilateral Fund for the Implementation of the Montreal Protocol and the fixed-exchange-rate mechanism for the Fund's replenishment; compliance issues; and administrative and budgetary matters.

Convention on air pollution

As at 31 December, the number of parties to the 1979 Convention on Long-Range Transboundary Air Pollution [YUN 1979, p. 710], which entered into force in 1983 [YUN 1983, p. 645], stood at 49 States and the EC. Eight protocols to the Convention dealt with the programme for monitoring and evaluation of the pollutants in Europe (1984), the reduction of sulphur emissions or their transboundary fluxes by at least 30 per cent (1985), the control of emissions of nitrogen oxides or their transboundary fluxes (1988), the control of volatile organic compounds or their transboundary fluxes (1991), further reduction of sulphur emissions (1984), heavy metals (1998), persistent organic pollutants (POPs) (1998) and

the abatement of acidification, eutrophication and ground-level ozone (1999).

The twenty-third session of the Executive Body for the Convention (Geneva, 12-15 December) [ECE/EB.AIR/87 & Add.1] adopted decisions on emission data reporting under the 1998 Protocol on Heavy Metals, the 1998 Protocol on POPs and the 1999 Gothenburg Protocol to Abate Acidification, Eutrophication and Ground-level Ozone; the facilitation of participation of countries with economies in transition in the activities of the Executive Body; and compliance with reporting obligations.

Convention on Biological Diversity

As at 31 December, the number of parties to the 1992 Convention on Biological Diversity [YUN 1992, p. 638], which entered into force in 1993 [YUN 1993, p. 210], stood at 187 States and the EC.

At year's end, 129 States and the EC were parties to the Cartagena Protocol on Biosafety, which was adopted in 2000 [YUN 2000, p. 973] and entered into force in 2003 [YUN 2003, p. 1051]. During the year, 19 countries became parties.

The tenth (Bangkok, Thailand, 7-11 February) [UNEP/CBD/COP/8/2] and eleventh (Montreal, Canada, 28 November–2 December) [UNEP/CBD/COP/8/3] meetings of the Subsidiary Body on Scientific, Technical and Technological Advice adopted recommendations for consideration by the eighth (2006) meeting of the Conference of the Parties to the Convention.

Cartagena Protocol on Biosafety

The second meeting of the Conference of the Parties to the Convention serving as the Meeting of the Parties to the Cartagena Protocol on Biosafety (Montreal, Canada, 30 May–3 June) [UNEP/CBD/BS/COP-MOP/2/15] adopted rules of procedure for meetings of the Protocol's Compliance Committee, established in 2004 [YUN 2004, p. 1054], and a multi-year programme of work for the Biosafety Clearing-House. It established an Ad Hoc Technical Expert Group on Risk Assessment. Other decisions dealt with capacity building; cooperation with other organizations, conventions and initiatives; the implementation of article 8 of the Protocol on notification; article 18 on the handling, transport, packaging and identification of living modified organisms; the Ad Hoc Working Group of Legal and Technical Experts on Liability and Redress, established in 2004 [YUN 2004, p. 1054], and the report of its first meeting (Montreal, 25-27 May) [UNEP/CBD/BS/COP-MOP/2/11]; socio-economic considerations; public awareness of, and participation in the implementation of the Protocol; scientific and technical issues relating to the effective implementation of the Protocol; and administrative and budgetary matters.

GENERAL ASSEMBLY ACTION

On 22 December [meeting 68], the General Assembly, on the recommendation of the Second Committee [A/60/488/Add.8], adopted **resolution 60/202** without vote [agenda item 52 *(h)*].

Convention on Biological Diversity

The General Assembly,

Recalling its resolutions 55/201 of 20 December 2000, 56/197 of 21 December 2001, 57/253 and 57/260 of 20 December 2002, 58/212 of 23 December 2003 and 59/236 of 22 December 2004,

Recalling also the 2005 World Summit Outcome,

Reiterating that the Convention on Biological Diversity is the key international instrument for the conservation and sustainable use of biological resources and the fair and equitable sharing of benefits arising from the use of genetic resources,

Taking note of the reports of the Millennium Ecosystem Assessment,

Recalling the commitments of the World Summit on Sustainable Development to pursue a more efficient and coherent implementation of the three objectives of the Convention and the achievement by 2010 of a significant reduction in the current rate of loss of biological diversity, which will require action at all levels, including the implementation of national biodiversity strategies and action plans and the provision of new and additional financial and technical resources to developing countries,

Expressing its deep appreciation to the Government of Malaysia for hosting the seventh meeting of the Conference of the Parties to the Convention on Biological Diversity and the first meeting of the Conference of the Parties to the Convention serving as the Meeting of the Parties to the Cartagena Protocol on Biosafety, held in Kuala Lumpur from 9 to 20 and on 27 February, and from 23 to 27 February 2004, respectively,

Expressing its deep appreciation also to the Government of Brazil for its offer to host the eighth meeting of the Conference of the Parties to the Convention on Biological Diversity and the third meeting of the Conference of the Parties to the Convention serving as the Meeting of the Parties to the Cartagena Protocol on Biosafety, to be held in Curitiba from 20 to 31 March, and from 13 to 17 March 2006, respectively,

1. *Takes note* of the report of the Executive Secretary of the Convention on Biological Diversity, transmitted by the Secretary-General to the General Assembly at its sixtieth session;

2. *Notes* the recent progress made with respect to the achievement of the three objectives set out in the Convention on Biological Diversity;

3. *Urges* all Member States to fulfil their commitments to significantly reduce the rate of loss of biodiversity by 2010, and emphasizes that this will require an appropriate focus on the loss of biodiversity in their relevant policies and programmes and the continued provision of new and additional financial and technical resources to developing countries, including through the Global Environmental Facility;

4. *Reiterates* the commitment of States parties to the Convention on Biological Diversity and the Cartagena Protocol on Biosafety to support the implementation of the Convention and the Protocol, as well as other biodiversity-related agreements and the Johannesburg commitment for a significant reduction in the rate of loss of biodiversity by 2010, and to continue to negotiate within the framework of the Convention, bearing in mind the Bonn Guidelines, an international regime to promote and safeguard the fair and equitable sharing of benefits arising out of the utilization of genetic resources; and reiterates also the resolve of all States to fulfil commitments and significantly reduce the rate of loss of biodiversity by 2010 and to continue ongoing efforts towards elaborating and negotiating an international regime on access to genetic resources and benefit-sharing;

5. *Reaffirms* the commitment, subject to national legislation, to respect, preserve and maintain the knowledge, innovations and practices of indigenous and local communities embodying traditional lifestyles relevant to the conservation and sustainable use of biological diversity, promote their wider application with the approval and involvement of the holders of such knowledge, innovations and practices and encourage the equitable sharing of the benefits arising from their utilization;

6. *Notes* the holding of the tenth meeting of the Subsidiary Body on Scientific, Technical and Technological Advice of the Conference of the Parties to the Convention on Biological Diversity, as well as the meetings of the Ad Hoc Open-ended Working Group on Access to Genetic Resources and Benefit-sharing and the first meeting of the Ad Hoc Open-ended Working Group on Protected Areas;

7. *Notes also* the progress made at the second meeting of the Conference of the Parties to the Convention serving as the Meeting of the Parties to the Cartagena Protocol on Biosafety and the continuing efforts made towards the implementation of the Protocol, and stresses that this will require the full support of parties and of relevant international organizations, in particular with regard to the provision of assistance to developing countries as well as countries with economies in transition in capacity-building for biosafety;

8. *Invites* the countries that have not yet done so to ratify or to accede to the Convention;

9. *Invites* the parties to the Convention that have not yet ratified or acceded to the Cartagena Protocol on Biosafety to consider doing so;

10. *Invites* countries to consider ratifying or acceding to the International Treaty on Plant Genetic Resources for Food and Agriculture;

11. *Encourages* developed countries parties to the Convention to contribute to the relevant trust funds of the Convention, in particular so as to enhance the full participation of the developing countries parties in all of its activities;

12. *Urges* parties to the Convention on Biological Diversity to facilitate the transfer of technology for the effective implementation of the Convention in accordance with its provisions;

13. *Takes note* of the ongoing work of the liaison group of the secretariats and offices of the relevant subsidiary bodies of the United Nations Framework Convention on Climate Change, the United Nations

Convention to Combat Desertification in Those Countries Experiencing Serious Drought and/or Desertification, Particularly in Africa, and the Convention on Biological Diversity, and further encourages continuing cooperation in order to promote complementarities among the secretariats, while respecting their independent legal status;

14. *Stresses* the importance of reducing duplicative reporting requirements of the biodiversity-related conventions while respecting their independent legal status and their independent mandates;

15. *Invites* the States parties to the Convention on Biological Diversity to provide the new Executive Secretary of the Convention with full support for the fulfilment of his mandate and towards promoting the implementation of the Convention;

16. *Invites* the Executive Secretary of the Convention on Biological Diversity to continue reporting to the General Assembly on the ongoing work regarding the Convention, including its Cartagena Protocol;

17. *Decides* to include in the provisional agenda of its sixty-first session, under the item entitled "Sustainable development", the sub-item entitled "Convention on Biological Diversity".

Convention to combat desertification

As at 31 December, the total number of parties to the 1994 United Nations Convention to Combat Desertification in those Countries Experiencing Serious Drought and/or Desertification, particularly in Africa (UNCCD) [YUN 1994, p. 944], which entered into force in 1996 [YUN 1996, p. 958], stood at 190 States and the EC.

The third session of the Committee for the Review of the Implementation of the Convention (CRIC) (Bonn, Germany, 2-11 May) [ICCD/CRIC(3)/9] discussed thematic issues pertaining to the Convention implementation process in Africa and those under global review, and made recommendations relating to both of those issues and on the implementation of the Convention in Africa. At its fourth session (Nairobi, Kenya, 18-27 October), CRIC submitted further recommendations to the seventh session of the Conference of the Parties to the Convention (see below). The Committee on Science and Technology (Nairobi, 18-21 October), a Conference subsidiary body, also made a number of recommendations to the Conference.

The seventh session of the Conference of the Parties to the Convention (Nairobi, 17-28 October) [ICCD/COP(7)/16 & Add.1] renewed the mandate of CRIC as a subsidiary body of the Conference of the Parties, up to and including the eighth (2007) session of the Conference, and established an ad hoc working group make proposals to improve the procedures for the communication of information, particularly at the national level, as well as the quality and format of reports on the implementation of the Convention. The Conference also adopted decisions on strength-

ening the implementation of the Convention in Africa; follow-up to the outcome of the 2002 World Summit on Sustainable Development [YUN 2002, p. 821] relevant to UNCCD; adjustments to the elaboration process and the implementation of action programmes with regard to the Convention; mobilization of resources for the implementation of the Convention; collaboration between UNCCD and the Global Environment Facility (GEF); institutional arrangements for regional coordination units; the promotion and strengthening of relationships with other relevant conventions and international organizations, institutions and agencies; the roster of independent experts; the Millennium Ecosystem Assessment (see p. 1154); traditional knowledge; benchmarks and indicators; the development of early warning systems; the Land Degradation Assessment in Drylands; procedures and institutional mechanisms for the resolution of questions on implementation and arbitration and conciliation procedures; the International Year of Deserts and Desertification (2006) (see p. 1152), declared by the General Assembly in 2003 [YUN 2003, p. 1055]; relations between the UNCCD secretariat and the host country (Germany); and administrative and budgetary matters, including the 2006-2007 UNCCD programme and budget for the 2006-2007 biennium.

The Conference approved the continuation of the institutional linkage and related administrative arrangements between the UNCCD secretariat and the UN Secretariat for a further five years, to be reviewed by the General Assembly and the Conference no later than 31 December 2011. It decided to hold the eighth (2007) session of the Conference in Spain, and the fifth (2006) session of CRIC in Argentina. The Conference adopted the Nairobi Declaration on the Implementation of the United Nations Convention to Combat Desertification, in which participants declared their commitment to reduce poverty significantly as a prerequisite for promoting sustainable development, review progress on the implementation of the Convention after 10 years and mainstream national action plans into national development policies, programmes, strategies and implementation modalities. Annexed to the report of the session was the Declaration of the sixth Round Table of Members of Parliament (Nairobi, 25-26 October) on the role of members of parliament in enhancing implementation of UNCCD obligations.

JIU report. An August note by the UNCCD secretariat [ICCD/COP(7)/4] contained a report of the United Nations Joint Inspection Unit (JIU) reviewing the secretariat's management, administration and activities. The report contained recommendations for dealing with policy; governance; secretariat functions and activities; the relationship between the secretariat and the Global Mechanism, a UNCCD subsidiary body dealing with financial issues; financial, budgetary, administrative and management issues; and coordination and cooperation with relevant international bodies and conventions. JIU also compared the secretariats of UNCCD, UNFCCC and CBD, collectively referred to as the Rio Conventions. It concluded that, UNCCD was not provided with sufficient financial and human resources, as compared with the other two Conventions.

In a decision on follow-up to the JIU report, the seventh session of Conference of the Parties (see above) established an ad hoc, intergovernmental, intersessional working group to review the JIU report and develop a draft ten-year strategic plan and framework to enhance the implementation of UNCCD by addressing, among other things, the recommendations contained in the report.

GENERAL ASSEMBLY ACTION

On 22 December [meeting 68], the General Assembly, on the recommendation of the Second Committee [A/60/488/Add.7], adopted **resolution 60/201** without vote [agenda item 52 (g)].

Implementation of the United Nations Convention to Combat Desertification in Those Countries Experiencing Serious Drought and/or Desertification, Particularly in Africa

The General Assembly,

Recalling its resolution 59/235 of 22 December 2004 and other resolutions relating to the United Nations Convention to Combat Desertification in Those Countries Experiencing Serious Drought and/or Desertification, Particularly in Africa,

Reaffirming the Plan of Implementation of the World Summit on Sustainable Development ("Johannesburg Plan of Implementation"),

Recalling its resolution 58/211 of 23 December 2003, in which it declared 2006 the International Year of Deserts and Desertification,

Recalling also the 2005 World Summit Outcome,

Reaffirming the universal membership of the Convention, and acknowledging that desertification and drought are problems of a global dimension in that they affect all regions of the world,

Noting that timely and effective implementation of the Convention would help to achieve the internationally agreed development goals, including the Millennium Development Goals, and encouraging affected country parties to include, as appropriate, in their national development strategies measures to combat desertification,

Stressing the need for further diversification of funding sources to address land degradation, in accordance with articles 20 and 21 of the Convention,

Expressing its deep appreciation and gratitude to the Government of Kenya for hosting the seventh session of the Conference of the Parties to the Convention in Nairobi from 17 to 28 October 2005,

Welcoming the offer made by the Government of Spain to host the eighth session of the Conference of the Parties to the Convention in the autumn of 2007,

Welcoming also the offer made by the Government of Argentina to host the fifth session of the Committee for the Review of the Implementation of the Convention in September 2006,

1. *Takes note* of the report of the Secretary-General on the implementation of the United Nations Convention to Combat Desertification in Those Countries Experiencing Serious Drought and/or Desertification, Particularly in Africa;

2. *Resolves* to support and strengthen the implementation of the Convention to address causes of desertification and land degradation, as well as poverty resulting from land degradation, through, inter alia, the mobilization of adequate and predictable financial resources, the transfer of technology and capacity-building at all levels;

3. *Notes with interest* the decisions of the Conference of the Parties to the Convention at its seventh session on the outcomes of the third and fourth sessions of the Committee for the Review of the Implementation of the Convention;

4. *Invites* the donor community to increase its support to the implementation of the Convention with a view to bringing greater international attention to bear on the issue of land degradation and desertification, which will contribute to the improvement of the sustainable development of drylands and the global environment;

5. *Welcomes* the decision of the Conference of the Parties at its seventh session to conclude with the Council of the Global Environment Facility and to adopt the memorandum of understanding on enhanced collaboration between the Convention and the Facility;

6. *Invites* the Global Environment Facility to strengthen the focal area of land degradation, primarily desertification and deforestation;

7. *Also invites* the Global Environment Facility to continue to make resources available for capacity-building activities in affected country parties implementing the Convention;

8. *Takes note with interest* of ongoing efforts to diversify the availability of financial resources to support activities aimed at combating desertification and poverty;

9. *Calls upon* Governments, where appropriate, in collaboration with relevant multilateral organizations, including the Global Environment Facility implementation agencies, to integrate desertification into their plans and strategies for sustainable development;

10. *Stresses* the importance of the implementation of all decisions of the Conference of the Parties, in particular the decisions taken at its seventh session on strengthening of the Committee on Science and Technology and on the follow-up to the report of the Joint Inspection Unit, and supports the development of a ten-year strategy to foster the implementation of the Convention;

11. *Notes* steps taken by the Conference of the Parties at it seventh session to introduce the euro as the

budget and accounting currency as from the biennium 2008-2009;

12. *Recalls* the request of the Conference of the Parties at its seventh session that the Executive Secretary notify parties of their contributions for 2006 by 21 November 2005 and for 2007 by 1 October 2006 to encourage early payment, and urges all parties that have not yet paid their contributions for 1999 and/or the bienniums 2000-2001 and 2002-2003 to do so as soon as possible;

13. *Recognizes* the need to provide the secretariat of the Convention with stable, adequate and predictable resources in order to enable it to continue to discharge its responsibilities in an efficient and timely manner, and further recognizes the provision in section A on budget reform in the decision of the Conference of the Parties at its seventh session on the programme and budget for the biennium 2006-2007, including the request that the Executive Secretary take additional measures necessary to address those recommendations, ensure that the financial rules are fully respected in the future and report on this matter to the meeting of the Bureau and in the performance report for the biennium 2006-2007;

14. *Calls upon* Governments, and invites multilateral financial institutions, regional development banks, regional economic integration organizations and all other interested organizations, as well as nongovernmental organizations and the private sector, to contribute generously to the Supplementary Fund and the Special Fund, in accordance with the relevant paragraphs of the financial rules of the Conference of the Parties, and welcomes the financial support already provided by some countries;

15. *Takes note* of the ongoing work of the liaison group of the secretariats and offices of the relevant subsidiary bodies of the United Nations Framework Convention on Climate Change, the United Nations Convention to Combat Desertification in Those Countries Experiencing Serious Drought and/or Desertification, Particularly in Africa, and the Convention on Biological Diversity, and further encourages continuing cooperation in order to promote complementarities among the secretariats, while respecting their independent legal status;

16. *Approves* the continuation of the current institutional linkage and related administrative arrangements between the Convention secretariat and the United Nations Secretariat for a further five-year period, to be reviewed by both the General Assembly and the Conference of the Parties no later than 31 December 2011, as decided by the Conference of the Parties at its seventh session;

17. *Decides* to include in the calendar of conferences and meetings for the biennium 2006-2007 the sessions of the Conference of the Parties and its subsidiary bodies envisaged for the biennium;

18. *Requests* the Secretary-General to make provision for the sessions of the Conference of the Parties and its subsidiary bodies, including the eighth ordinary session of the Conference of the Parties and the meetings of its subsidiary bodies, in his proposal for the programme budget for the biennium 2006-2007;

19. *Decides* to include in the provisional agenda of its sixty-first session the sub-item entitled "Implementation of the United Nations Convention to Combat Desertification in Those Countries Experiencing Serious Drought and/or Desertification, Particularly in Africa";

20. *Requests* the Secretary-General to report to the General Assembly at its sixty-first session on the implementation of the present resolution.

International Year
of Deserts and Desertification

In response to General Assembly resolution 58/211 [YUN 2003, p. 1055], in which the Assembly declared 2006 the International Year of Deserts and Desertification, the Secretary-General submitted a July report [A/60/169] on the status of preparations for the observance of the International Year. The report provided information on the steps taken by the UNCCD Executive Secretary, the designated focal point for the Year, to implement resolution 58/211; described the objectives for the Year and the coordination and cooperation initiatives with institutional partners and parties to the Convention. The report contained also conclusions and recommendations to the Assembly.

GENERAL ASSEMBLY ACTION

On 22 December [meeting 68], the General Assembly, on the recommendation of the Second Committee [A/60/488/Add.7], adopted **resolution 60/200** by recorded vote (120-1-47) [agenda item 52 (g)].

International Year of Deserts
and Desertification, 2006

The General Assembly,

Recalling its resolution 58/211 of 23 December 2003, in which it declared 2006 the International Year of Deserts and Desertification,

Taking note of the decision of the seventh session of the Conference of the Parties to the United Nations Convention to Combat Desertification in Those Countries Experiencing Serious Drought and/or Desertification, Particularly in Africa, held in Nairobi from 17 to 28 October 2005, on the celebration of the International Year of Deserts and Desertification, 2006,

Deeply concerned by the exacerbation of desertification in all regions of the world, particularly in Africa, and its far-reaching implications for the implementation of the Millennium Development Goals, in particular on poverty eradication,

Deeply concerned also at the extensive destruction by Israel, the occupying Power, of agricultural land and orchards in the Occupied Palestinian Territory, including the uprooting of a vast number of fruit-bearing trees,

Conscious of the need to raise public awareness and to protect the biological diversity of deserts as well as indigenous and local communities and the traditional knowledge of those affected by this phenomenon,

Welcoming the decision of the Government of Algeria to convene and host an international conference with the participation of Heads of State and Government, dedicated to the protection of deserts and to combating desertification, in October 2006,

Welcoming also the decision of the Government of Israel to host, in cooperation with other stakeholders, an international conference entitled "Deserts and Desertification: Challenges and Opportunities" in Be'er Sheva, Israel, in November 2006,

Taking note of the report of the Secretary-General on the status of preparations for the International Year of Deserts and Desertification, 2006,

1. *Welcomes* the nomination of United Nations honorary spokespersons for the International Year of Deserts and Desertification, and encourages the Secretary-General to nominate additional personalities in that respect so as to promote a successful celebration of the Year worldwide;

2. *Reiterates its call upon* Member States and all relevant international organizations to support the activities related to desertification, including land degradation, to be organized by affected countries, in particular African countries and the least developed countries;

3. *Encourages* countries to contribute, as they are able, to the United Nations Convention to Combat Desertification in Those Countries Experiencing Serious Drought and/or Desertification, Particularly in Africa and to undertake special initiatives in observance of the Year with the goal of enhancing the implementation of the Convention;

4. *Invites* Member States to make voluntary contributions to the Special Fund of the Convention in order to achieve the objectives of resolution 58/211 entitled "International Year of Deserts and Desertification, 2006";

5. *Invites* Governments and all relevant stakeholders that have not yet done so to inform the secretariat for the Convention of activities envisaged for the observance of the Year;

6. *Requests* the Executive Secretary of the Convention to make available to the parties to the Convention and to observers a consolidated list of all activities reported, including lessons learned and best practices, in order to coordinate information and avoid overlapping of activities;

7. *Notes with interest* the decision of the Council of the Global Environment Facility to support, within its mandate, activities undertaken by affected developing countries parties to the Convention within the framework of the Year;

8. *Requests* the Secretary-General to report to the General Assembly at its sixty-second session on the celebration of the Year.

RECORDED VOTE ON RESOLUTION 60/200:

In favour: Afghanistan, Algeria, Andorra, Angola, Antigua and Barbuda, Argentina, Armenia, Azerbaijan, Bahamas, Bangladesh, Barbados, Belarus, Belize, Benin, Bhutan, Bolivia, Botswana, Brazil, Brunei Darussalam, Burkina Faso, Burundi, Cambodia, Cameroon, Cape Verde, Central African Republic, Chad, Chile, China, Colombia, Comoros, Congo, Costa Rica, Côte d'Ivoire, Cyprus, Dominica, Dominican Republic, Ecuador, Egypt, El Salvador, Eritrea, Ethiopia, Fiji, France, Ghana, Greece, Grenada, Guatemala, Guinea-Bissau, Guyana, Haiti, India, Iraq, Jamaica, Japan, Jordan, Kazakhstan, Kenya, Kuwait, Kyrgyzstan, Lao People's Democratic Republic, Lesotho, Liberia, Madagascar, Malawi, Malaysia, Maldives, Mali, Malta, Mauritania, Mauritius, Mexico, Monaco, Mongolia, Morocco, Mozambique, Myanmar, Namibia, Nepal, Nicaragua, Nigeria, Oman, Pakistan, Papua New Guinea, Paraguay, Peru, Philippines, Portugal, Qatar, Republic of Korea, Russian Federation, Saint Kitts and Nevis, Saint Lucia, Saint Vincent and the Grenadines, Samoa, Senegal, Sierra Leone, Singapore, Solomon Islands, South Africa, Spain, Sri Lanka, Sudan, Suriname, Swaziland, Tajikistan, Thailand, Togo, Tunisia, Tuvalu, Uganda, Ukraine, United Arab Emirates, United Republic of Tanzania, Uruguay, Uzbekistan, Venezuela, Viet Nam, Yemen, Zambia, Zimbabwe.

Against: Syrian Arab Republic.

Abstaining: Albania, Australia, Austria, Bahrain, Belgium, Bulgaria, Canada, Croatia, Cuba, Czech Republic, Democratic People's Republic of Korea, Denmark, Estonia, Finland, Georgia, Germany, Guinea, Hungary, Iceland, Indonesia, Ireland, Israel, Latvia, Lebanon, Libyan Arab Jamahiriya, Liechtenstein, Lithuania, Luxembourg, Marshall Islands, Micronesia, Netherlands, New Zealand, Norway, Palau, Poland, Republic of Moldova, Romania, San Marino, Saudi Arabia, Serbia and Montenegro, Slovakia, Slovenia, Sweden, Switzerland, The former Yugoslav Republic of Macedonia, United Kingdom, United States.

Environmental activities

Follow-up to the 2000 Millennium Summit

In January [UNEP/GC.23/10], the Executive Director submitted a background paper for the ministerial-level consultations held during the Governing Council's twenty-third session (21-23 February) (see p. 1133) on implementation of the internationally agreed development goals, known as the Millennium Development Goals (MDGs), of the Millennium Declaration, adopted by the General Assembly in resolution 55/2 [YUN 2000, p. 49]. The paper contained information on poverty reduction and environmental stability; water, sanitation and human settlements; and gender and the environment.

2005 World Summit

The Secretary General, in a March report, entitled "In larger freedom: towards development, security and human rights for all" [A/59/2005] (see p. 67), submitted to the High-level Plenary Meeting of the United Nations General Assembly (World Summit) in September (see.p. 47), discussed the implementation of the Millennium Declaration, including the MDG on ensuring environmental sustainability. He said that national poverty reduction strategies had to include investments in improved environmental management and make the structural changes required for environmental sustainability. In addition, regional and global efforts for environmental priorities, including shared waterways, forests, marine fisheries and biodiversity, had to be strengthened. The risk of harmful radiation appeared to be receding under the 1987 Montreal Protocol [YUN 1987, p. 686] to the 1985 Vienna Convention for the Protection of the Ozone Layer [YUN 1985, p. 804]. The international community had to support and implement the 1994 United Nations Convention to Combat Desertification in Those Countries Experiencing Serious Drought and/or Desertification, Particularly in Africa [YUN 1994, p. 944]. Governments should take steps to implement the 1992 Convention on Biological Diversity [YUN 1992, p. 638], and the commitment made in the Johannesburg Plan of Implementation [YUN 2002, p. 822] of the 2002 World Summit on Sustainable Development [ibid., p. 821] to reduce the loss of biodiversity by 2010. The 1997 Kyoto Protocol [YUN 1997, p. 1048] to the 1992 United Nations Framework Convention on Climate Change [YUN 1992, p. 681] came into force in February (see p. 1146), but was extended only until 2012; a more inclusive framework had to be developed beyond 2012, with broader participation by all major emitters of both developed and developing countries, to mitigate climate change, taking into account the principle of common but differentiated responsibilities.

The 2005 World Summit Outcome, adopted by the Assembly in **resolution 60/1** of 16 September (see p. 48), included measures for the management and protection of the environment in the context of sustainable development.

Millennium Ecosystem Assessment

The Millennium Ecosystem Assessment (MA), a four-year international assessment launched in 2001 [YUN 2001, p. 961] to evaluate the state of major ecosystems and their links with human well-being, was completed in 2005. The specific objectives of the MA were to identify priorities for action; provide tools for planning and management; provide foresight concerning the consequences of decisions affecting ecosystems; identify response options for achieving human development and sustainability; and help build individual and institutional capacity to undertake integrated ecosystem assessments and act on their findings. Two MA reports were released in 2005: *Living Beyond Our Means: Natural Assets and Human Well-being*, a statement by the MA Board containing 10 key messages and conclusions drawn from the Assessment; and *Ecosystems and Human Well-being: Synthesis*, a summary for decision-makers of the main MA synthesis report. Other synthesis reports issued dealt with biodiversity, desertification, opportunities and challenges for business and industry, wetlands and water, and health. The MA found that 60 per cent of the world's ecosystems were in decline or degraded to an extent that societies could no longer rely on them for climate regulation, clean air and water, fertile land and productive fisheries.

The atmosphere

Intergovernmental Panel on Climate Change

The twenty-third session of the Intergovernmental Panel on Climate Change (IPCC) (Addis Ababa, Ethiopia, 6-8 April), accepted the actions of the second joint session of IPCC Working Groups I and III held on the same dates. At its twenty-fourth session (Montreal, Canada, 26-28 September), IPCC discussed progress on its Fourth Assessment Synthesis Report, which was to be adopted and approved by IPCC in 2007; its National Greenhouse Gas Inventories Programme; further work on emissions scenarios; outreach; and administrative matters. It adopted the revised programme budget for 2006.

Terrestrial ecosystems

In 2005, UNEP launched An Ecosystem Approach to Restoring West African Drylands and Improving Rural Livelihoods through Agroforestry-based Land Management Interventions, a project to help build the scientific and technical capacity of some of the world's poorest dryland countries, including in the semi-arid lands of the West Africa subregion. In response to requests from Governments in northeast Asia, UNEP, the Asian Development Bank, the UN Economic and Social Commission for Asia and the Pacific and UNCCD developed a project on the prevention and control of dust and sandstorms, funded by GEF and the Asian Development Bank. The project included the establishment of a UNEP-led regional monitoring and early-warning network and an investment strategy to strengthen mitigation measures to address the root causes of dust and sandstorms.

Deforestation and forest degradation

United Nations Forum on Forests

The United Nations Forum on Forests (UNFF), at its fifth session (New York, 16-17 May) [E/2005/42], adopted two decisions that were brought to the attention of the Economic and Social Council. It decided to accredit two intergovernmental organizations: the Montreal Process and the secretariat of the Amazon Cooperation Treaty Organization [dec. 5/1]. In a decision on the review process of the fifth UNFF session [dec. 5/2], the Forum decided to complete consideration at its sixth (2006) meeting of items outlined in its multi-year programme of work, based on a draft text annexed to the decision. UNFF recommended a draft resolution for adoption by the Council on the report of its fifth session and the provisional agenda for its sixth session (see below).

The Forum had before it reports of the Secretary-General on a review of the effectiveness of the international arrangement on forests [E/CN.18/2005/6]; linkages between forests and the internationally agreed development goals, including the MDGs [YUN 2000, p. 51] [E/CN.18/2005/7]; and a review of progress and consideration of future UNFF actions [E/CN.18/2005/8]. Notes by the Secretary-General discussed the high-level ministerial segment of UNFF fifth session [E/CN.18/2005/4] and the parameters of a mandate for developing a legal framework on all types of forests [E/CN.18/2005/9]. Secretariat notes provided information on the Forum's fifth multistakeholder dialogue [E/CN.18/2005/3 & Add.1-8]; enhanced cooperation and policy and programme coordination [E/CN.18/2005/5]; and accreditation of intergovernmental organizations to UNFF [E/CN.18/2005/17]. A further secretariat note transmitted the statement from the Ministerial Meeting on Forests, convened by the Director-General of the Food and Agriculture Organization of the United Nations (FAO) (Rome, 14 March) [E/CN.18/2005/14]. The Forum considered reports of the workshop co-organized by Indonesia and Switzerland on decentralization, federal systems in forestry and national forest programmes, known as the Interlaken Workshop (Interlaken, Switzerland, 27-30 April 2004) [E/CN.18/2005/10], as well as reports on country-led initiatives in support of UNFF in forest landscape restoration implementation (Petrópolis, Brazil, 4-8 April 2005), submitted by Brazil and the United Kingdom [E/CN.18/2005/15]; innovative financial mechanisms: searching for viable alternatives to secure the basis for the financial sustainability of forests (San José, Costa Rica, 29 March–1 April), submitted by Costa Rica [E/CN.18/2005/13]; and the future of the International Arrangement on Forests (Guadalajara, Mexico, 25-28 January), submitted by Mexico and the United States [E/CN.18/2005/11]. Also before the Forum were the Collaborative Partnership on Forests Framework 2005 [E/CN.18/2005/INF/1]; an 11 April letter from the United Kingdom transmitting the report of the meeting of the Forests Dialogue on "Practical actions to combat illegal logging" (Hong Kong, China, 7-10 March) [E/CN.18/2005/12]; and the organizational initiative report, submitted by Costa Rica on 20 April [E/CN.18/2005/16], on the Expert Meeting on Traditional Forest-related Knowledge and the Implementation of Related International Commitments (San José, Costa Rica, 6-10 December 2004).

ECONOMIC AND SOCIAL COUNCIL ACTION

On 22 July [meeting 36], the Economic and Social Council, on the recommendation of the United Nations Forum on Forests [E/2005/42], adopted **resolution 2005/29** without vote [agenda item 13 (*i*)].

Report of the United Nations Forum on Forests on its fifth session and provisional agenda for its sixth session

The Economic and Social Council,

Recalling its resolution 2000/35 of 18 October 2000,

1. *Takes note* of the report of the United Nations Forum on Forests on its fifth session;

2. *Acknowledges* in particular the need to consider forest issues for the preparation of the input of the Economic and Social Council to the High-level Plenary Meeting of the sixtieth session of the General Assembly;

3. *Notes* that the United Nations Forum on Forests will continue its examination of its methods of work, as per General Assembly resolution 57/270B of 23 June 2003, through the implementation of decision 5/2, adopted by the Forum at its fifth session;

4. *Decides* to hold the sixth session of the Forum from 13 to 24 February 2006 in New York;

5. *Also decides* that the Forum, at its sixth session, should consider the venue and dates of its seventh session;

6. *Further decides* that the Forum, at its sixth session, should ensure the opportunity to receive and consider inputs from representatives of major groups as identified in Agenda 21, and in this regard that the Bureau should provide the opportunity for the major groups, as a priority, to hold side events during the sixth session of the Forum, to permit them to present their points of view on the issues to be addressed during the session;

7. *Approves* the provisional agenda for the sixth session of the Forum as set out below:

PROVISIONAL AGENDA FOR THE SIXTH
SESSION OF THE
UNITED NATIONS FORUM ON FORESTS

1. Election of officers.
2. Adoption of the agenda and other organizational matters.
3. Implementation of decision 5/2 of the fifth session of the United Nations Forum on Forests.
4. Date and venue for the seventh session of the Forum.
5. Provisional agenda for the seventh session of the Forum.
6. Adoption of the report of the Forum on its sixth session.

8. *Calls upon* interested donors to make voluntary financial contributions to the trust fund of the United Nations Forum on Forests in order to facilitate, in particular, travel of representatives from developing countries, with priority to the least developed countries, as well as from countries with economies in transition, taking into account General Assembly decision 58/554 of 23 December 2003.

Sustainable mountain development

In response to General Assembly resolution 58/216 [YUN 2003, p. 1063], the Secretary-General submitted a September report [A/60/309] describing the status of sustainable mountain development at the national, regional and international levels. The report also discussed communications and networking on mountain issues; the activities of the International Partnership for Sustainable Development in Mountain Regions, launched as an outcome of the 2002 World Summit on Sustainable Development [YUN 2002, p. 821]; education and research activities; and resource mobilization and funding mechanisms for sustainable mountain development. The report stated that, despite increased awareness and positive achievements, key challenges to sustainable development and poverty alleviation in mountains remained, including a growing demand for water and other natural resources; the consequences of global climate change; tourism growth; increasing rates of outmigration; conflicts; and the pressures of industry, mining and agriculture. Higher levels of funding and investment in mountain areas, better coordinated cooperation and a stronger enabling environment with more supportive laws, policies and institutions were also required. The report contained recommendations for the Assembly to promote and sustain development in mountain regions within the existing policy context, including chapter 13 of Agenda 21 [YUN 1992, p. 672] on sustainable mountain development, the Johannesburg Plan of Implementation of the World Summit on Sustainable Development [YUN 2002, p. 821] and the MDGs [YUN 2000, p. 51].

Mountain Partnership Declaration. A 25 October letter from Peru [A/C.2/60/4] contained the Declaration of the Andes, adopted by the Second Global Meeting of Members of the International Partnership for Sustainable Development in Mountain Regions (Cusco, Peru, 28-29 October 2004). In the Declaration, Partnership members reaffirmed their commitment to fulfil the goals of the United Nations Convention on Biological Diversity, the United Nations Framework Convention on Climate Change, the United Nations Convention to Combat Desertification, and other universally agreed multilateral instruments relevant to sustainable mountain development.

GENERAL ASSEMBLY ACTION

On 22 December [meeting 68], the General Assembly, on the recommendation of the Second Committee [A/60/488/Add.5], adopted **resolution 60/198** without vote [agenda item 52 *(e)*].

Sustainable mountain development

The General Assembly,

Recalling its resolution 53/24 of 10 November 1998, by which it proclaimed 2002 the International Year of Mountains,

Recalling also its resolutions 55/189 of 20 December 2000, 57/245 of 20 December 2002 and 58/216 of 23 December 2003,

Recalling further its resolution 59/238 of 22 December 2004 on rendering assistance to poor mountain countries to overcome obstacles in socio-economic and ecological areas,

Recognizing chapter 13 of Agenda 21 and all relevant paragraphs of the Plan of Implementation of the World Summit on Sustainable Development ("Johannesburg Plan of Implementation"), in particular para-

graph 42 thereof, as the overall policy frameworks for sustainable development in mountain regions,

Noting the International Partnership for Sustainable Development in Mountain Regions ("Mountain Partnership"), launched during the World Summit on Sustainable Development, with benefits from the committed support of forty-four countries, fourteen intergovernmental organizations and sixty-eight organizations from major groups, as an important approach to addressing the various interrelated dimensions of sustainable development in mountain regions,

Noting also the Bishkek Mountain Platform, the outcome document of the Bishkek Global Mountain Summit, held at Bishkek from 28 October to 1 November 2002, which was the concluding event of the International Year of Mountains,

1. *Takes note* of the report of the Secretary-General entitled "Sustainable mountain development";

2. *Notes with appreciation* that a growing network of Governments, organizations, major groups and individuals around the world recognize the importance of sustainable development of mountain regions for poverty eradication, as well as the global importance of mountains as the source of most of the Earth's freshwater, as repositories of rich biological diversity, as popular destinations for recreation and tourism and as areas of important cultural diversity, knowledge and heritage;

3. *Notes with concern* that there remain key challenges to achieving sustainable development, eradicating poverty in mountain regions and protecting mountain ecosystems, and that populations in mountain regions are frequently among the poorest of a given country;

4. *Notes* that the growing demand for natural resources, including water, the consequences of erosion, deforestation and other forms of watershed degradation, the occurrence of natural disasters, as well as increasing outmigration, the pressures of industry, transport, tourism, mining, agriculture and the consequences of global climate change are some of the key challenges in fragile mountain ecosystems to implementing sustainable development and eradicating poverty in mountains, consistent with the Millennium Development Goals;

5. *Expresses its deep concern* at the number and scale of disasters and their increasing impact within recent years, which have resulted in massive loss of life and long-term negative social, economic and environmental consequences for vulnerable societies throughout the world, in particular in mountain regions, especially those in developing countries;

6. *Underlines* the fact that action at the national level is a key factor in achieving progress in sustainable mountain development, welcomes its steady increase in recent years with a multitude of events, activities and initiatives, and invites the international community to support the efforts of developing countries to develop and implement strategies and programmes, including, where required, enabling policies and laws for the sustainable development of mountains, within the framework of national development plans;

7. *Encourages* the further establishment of committees or similar multi-stakeholder institutional arrangements and mechanisms at the national level to enhance

intersectoral coordination and collaboration for sustainable development in mountain regions;

8. *Also encourages* increased involvement of relevant stakeholders, including civil society and the private sector, in the development and implementation of programmes and activities related to sustainable development in mountains;

9. *Underlines* the need for improved access to resources for women in mountain regions as well as the need to strengthen the role of women in mountain regions in decision-making processes that affect their communities, cultures and environments;

10. *Stresses* that indigenous cultures, traditions and knowledge, including in the field of medicine, are to be fully considered, respected and promoted in development policy and planning in mountain regions, and underlines the importance of promoting full participation and involvement of mountain communities in decisions that affect them and of integrating indigenous knowledge, heritage and values in all development initiatives;

11. *Recognizes* that many developing countries as well as countries with economies in transition need to be assisted in the formulation and implementation of national strategies and programmes for sustainable mountain development, through bilateral, multilateral and South-South cooperation, as well as through other forms of collaborative approaches;

12. *Notes* that funding for sustainable mountain development has become increasingly important, especially in view of the greater recognition of the global importance of mountains and the high level of extreme poverty, food insecurity and hardship facing mountain communities;

13. *Invites* Governments, the United Nations system, the international financial institutions, the Global Environment Facility, all relevant United Nations conventions and their funding mechanisms, within their respective mandates, and all relevant stakeholders from civil society and the private sector to consider providing support, including through voluntary financial contributions, to local, national and international programmes and projects for sustainable development in mountain regions;

14. *Underlines* the importance for sustainable development in mountains of exploring a wide range of funding sources, such as public-private partnerships, increased opportunities for microfinance, including microinsurance, small housing loans, savings, education and health accounts, and support for entrepreneurs seeking to develop small and medium-sized businesses and, where appropriate, on a case-by-case basis, debt for sustainable development swaps;

15. *Underlines also* the importance of enhancing the sustainability of ecosystems that provide essential resources and services for human well-being and economic activity and developing innovative means of financing for their protection;

16. *Notes with satisfaction* the recent adoption by the Conference of the Parties to the Convention on Biological Diversity, of the programme of work on mountain biological diversity, the overall purpose of which is the significant reduction of the loss of mountain biological diversity by 2010 at the global, regional and national levels, and its implementation, which aims at making a significant contribution to poverty eradication in mountain regions;

17. *Recognizes* that mountain ranges are usually shared among several countries, and in this context encourages transboundary cooperation approaches, where the States concerned agree, to the sustainable development of mountain ranges and information-sharing in this regard;

18. *Notes with appreciation* in this context the Convention on the Protection of the Alps, which promotes constructive new approaches to integrated, sustainable development of the Alps, including through its thematic protocols on spatial planning, mountain farming, conservation of nature and landscape, mountain forests, population and culture, tourism, soil protection, energy and transport, and welcomes the recent membership of the Convention in the International Partnership for Sustainable Development in Mountain Regions;

19. *Also notes with appreciation* the Framework Convention on the Protection and Sustainable Development of the Carpathians, adopted and signed by the seven countries of the region to provide a framework for cooperation and multisectoral policy coordination, a platform for joint strategies for sustainable development and a forum for dialogue between all involved stakeholders;

20. *Stresses* the importance of capacity-building, institutional strengthening and educational programmes in order to foster sustainable mountain development at all levels and to enhance awareness of good practices in sustainable development in mountain regions and of the nature of relationships between highland and lowland areas;

21. *Encourages* the development and implementation of global, regional and national communication programmes to build on the awareness and momentum for change created by the International Year of Mountains and the opportunity provided annually by International Mountain Day on 11 December;

22. *Also encourages* Member States to collect and produce information and to establish databases devoted to mountains so as to capitalize on knowledge to support interdisciplinary research, programmes and projects and to improve decision-making and planning;

23. *Further encourages* all relevant entities of the United Nations system, within their respective mandates, to further enhance their constructive efforts to strengthen inter-agency collaboration to achieve more effective implementation of relevant chapters of Agenda 21, including chapter 13 and paragraph 42 and other relevant paragraphs of the Johannesburg Plan of Implementation, taking into account the inter-agency group on mountains and the need for the further involvement of the United Nations system, in particular the Food and Agriculture Organization of the United Nations, the United Nations Environment Programme, the United Nations University, the United Nations Development Programme, the United Nations Educational, Scientific and Cultural Organization and the United Nations Children's Fund, as well as international financial institutions and other relevant international organizations;

24. *Recognizes* the efforts of the Mountain Partnership implemented in accordance with Economic and Social Council resolution 2003/61 of 25 July 2003, in-

vites the international community and other relevant stakeholders, including civil society and the private sector, to consider joining the Mountain Partnership, and invites the Partnership Secretariat to report on its activities and achievements to the fourteenth meeting of the Commission on Sustainable Development in 2006, including in regard to the thematic cluster issues of energy, climate change, air pollution and atmosphere and industrial development;

25. *Notes with appreciation* in this context the efforts of the Mountain Partnership to cooperate with existing multilateral instruments relevant to mountains, such as the Convention on Biological Diversity, the United Nations Convention to Combat Desertification in Those Countries Experiencing Drought and/or Desertification, Particularly in Africa, the United Nations Framework Convention on Climate Change, the International Strategy for Disaster Reduction and mountain-related regional instruments such as the Convention on the Protection of the Alps and the Framework Convention on the Protection and Sustainable Development of the Carpathians;

26. *Takes note* of the conclusions of the second global meeting of the members of the Mountain Partnership, held in Cusco, Peru, on 28 and 29 October 2004, at the invitation of the Government of Peru;

27. *Requests* the Secretary-General to report to the General Assembly at its sixty-second session on the implementation of the present resolution, under a subitem entitled "Sustainable mountain development" of the item entitled "Sustainable development".

Marine ecosystems

Oceans and seas

The sixth meeting of the United Nations Open-ended Informal Consultative Process in Oceans and Law of the Sea (New York, 6-10 June) [A/60/99] (see p. 1436) discussed fisheries and their contribution to sustainable development and marine debris. Among the reports considered by the meeting, was an April overview report submitted by the UNEP Regional Seas Programme [A/AC.259/14], which described the issue of marine litter and UNEP's activities to address the problem. The meeting proposed actions to be taken by the General Assembly to address the issues of fisheries and marine debris. With regard to cooperation and coordination, the meeting proposed that the Assembly welcome the work of the secretariats of UN system agencies, programmes and funds, as well as those of international conventions, to enhance inter-agency coordination and cooperation on ocean issues. It also proposed that the Assembly encourage States to work closely with and through international organizations, funds and programmes, as well as UN system specialized agencies and relevant international conventions, to identify emerging areas of focus and the best way to address ocean issues.

The Assembly took action with regard to the Consultative Process and coordination and cooperation issues in parts XIII and XIV, respectively, of **resolution 60/30** (see p. 1443).

Report of Executive Director. In response to decisions adopted by the Governing Council in 2003 [YUN 2003, p. 1041 & pp. 1065-68], the Executive Director submitted a February progress report [UNEP/GC.23/3/Add.5/Rev.1/Add.2] on UNEP's water-related activities, including implementation of the Global Programme of Action for the Protection of the Marine Environment from Land-based Activities; the Regional Seas Programme; coral reefs; and activities related to marine safety and the protection of the marine environment from accidental pollution (see relevant sections below).

Global waters assessment

The Global International Waters Assessment (GIWA), inaugurated in 2000 [YUN 2000, p. 982] to assess international waters and causes of environmental problems in 66 water regions, focusing on the aquatic environment in transboundary waters, was concluded in 2005. In all, 14 reports were printed, 13 others were published on the Internet, and a further 11 were awaiting publication, including the project's final report. GIWA outputs were used by some new GEF projects, including the Lake Chad Basin Commission and the Pan African Global Change System for Analysis, Research and Training secretariat projects. The Assessment also provided input to intergovernmental processes, including the International Meeting to Review the Implementation of the 1994 Programme of Action for the Sustainable Development of Small Island States [YUN 1994, p. 783].

International Workshop. In June [A/60/91], the Secretary-General submitted a report on the results of the second international workshop convened in accordance with General Assembly resolution 59/24 [YUN 2004, p. 1333] on the regular process for global reporting and assessment of the state of the marine environment, known as the Global Marine Assessment (GMA), including the socio-economic aspects (New York, 13-15 June). The workshop considered the start-up phase, known as the "assessment of assessments" as a preparatory stage towards the establishment of the regular process of assessments. Before it was an 8 June note from Iceland [A/AC.271/1] to the Secretary General, indicating its intention not to participate in the second international workshop due to its concern over the mixing of scientific and management issues. In its conclusions, which were recommended to the Assembly for consideration, the workshop described the features and aims of, and organizational arrangements for, the "assessment of assessments".

The Assembly, in section XI of **resolution 60/30** (see p. 1442), endorsed the workshop's conclusions and decided to launch the "assessment of assessments", to be completed in two years. It established the Ad Hoc Steering Group to oversee the execution of the "assessment of assessments". The Assembly invited UNEP and the Intergovernmental Oceanographic Commission to jointly undertake the role of lead agencies, under the guidance of the Ad Hoc Steering Group, and determined the actions to be undertaken by the Group, including the establishment of a group of experts to assess the assessments and report to the Assembly. It decided that the execution of the "assessment of assessments", including the activities of the Ad Hoc Steering Group and the group of experts, would be financed through voluntary contributions and other resources available to participating organizations and bodies, and invited Member States in a position to do so to make contributions.

Global Programme of Action

A December note by the Executive Director [UNEP/GCSS.IX/INF/10] contained information on the Global Programme of Action (GPA) for the Protection of the Marine Environment from Land-based Activities. Key principles, directed mainly towards Governments, industrial/business associations and UN and intergovernmental bodies to provide guidance for the sustainable development and management of four economic sectors (aquaculture, ports and harbours, tourism and mining), were developed and adopted. The 12 Guiding Principles for Integrated Coastal Area and River Basin Management were finalized and published. UNEP was cooperating closely with China and other Governments, intergovernmental bodies, UN institutions and other stakeholders in preparing for the second Intergovernmental Review Meeting of GPA, scheduled to take place in Beijing, China, from 16 to 22 October 2006; a joint UN-Oceans/UN-Water task force was set up to provide guidance on the preparatory work for the Meeting. UNEP/GPA provided substantive support to Governments to develop national programmes of action (NPAs) for GPA implementation, including advice and assistance on GPA programme components and cross cutting issues. As a result of that support, over 40 countries were in the process of, or had finalized their NPAs. In May 2005, UNEP signed a memorandum of understanding with the South Pacific Regional Environment Programme.

In section IX of **resolution 60/30** of 29 November (see p. 1441), the General Assembly called on States to advance the implementation of GPA and the 2001 Montreal Declaration on the implementation of GPA [YUN 2001, p. 965].

Coral reefs

A December note by the Executive Director [UNEP/GCSS.IX/INF/10] provided information on UNEP's coral reef activities. Through its Coral Reef Unit (CRU) and UNEP-facilitated conventions, UNEP continued to support the implementation of coral reef activities by the International Coral Reef Initiative (ICRI), the International Coral Reef Network (ICRAN) and the Global Coral Reef Monitoring Network. During the International Meeting to Review the 1994 Programme of Action for the Sustainable Development of Small Island States [YUN 1994, p. 783], (Port Louis, Mauritius, 10-14 January) (see p. 946), CRU supported a side event entitled "Islands, Reefs and Communities: Committing to the Future", which highlighted the essential role of marine and coastal protected areas in human well-being and poverty alleviation. Palau and ICRI hosted another event "Benefits and Costs of Marine and Coastal Protected Areas for Islands", in June. UNEP, in partnership with ICRAN, implemented the ICRAN Mesoamerican Reef Alliance Project to address coral reef threats in relation to watershed management, sustainable fishing and sustainable tourism in the Mesoamerican subregion (Central America and nine south-eastern states of Mexico). In cooperation with the ICRAN Coordinating Unit, CRU expanded ICRAN activities to the Arabian Sea and was projecting the impact of climate change on coral reefs and the goods and services derived from them. CRU also secured $845,000 from the European Commission for capacity-building activities on coral reefs and marine protected areas in South Asia.

Regional Seas Programme

A December note by the Executive Director [UNEP/GCSS.IX/INF/10] provided information on the activities of the UNEP Regional Seas Programme. Under the Global Regional Seas Strategic Directions for 2004-2007, agreed to at the Sixth (2004) Global Meeting of Regional Seas Conventions and Action Plans [YUN 2004, p. 1060], a database providing an overview of all major actors and players in the conservation and management of marine and coastal environment of the various regional seas programmes was developed. The Mediterranean Strategy for Sustainable Development for the Mediterranean Action Plan, developed with the assistance of the UNEP Regional Seas Programme, was adopted by the Fourteenth Meeting of the Contracting Parties to the 1995 Barcelona Convention for the Protection of the Marine Environment and the Coastal Region of the Mediterranean, and its Protocols (Portoroz, Slovenia, 8-11 November) [UNEP(DEPI)/MED IG.16/13]. The Regional Seas Programme provided advice and guidance for translating regional seas conventions and protocols into national legislation in the Mediterranean, East Asia, Northwest Pacific and Caribbean regions. It conducted a training workshop on compliance and enforcement for regional seas conventions and related conventions in the wider Caribbean and Pacific regions. The Seventh Global Meeting of Regional Seas Conventions and Action Plans (Helsinki, Finland, 18-20 October) [UNEP(DEC)/RS.7] focused on strengthening the financial components of the regional seas programmes. In March, UNEP and the UNESCO Intergovernmental Oceanographic Commission signed an MOU which provided a framework for collaboration between the Global Ocean Observing System and the Regional Seas Programme. The seventh meeting of the Contracting Parties (Libreville, Gabon, 22-23 March) [UNEP(DEC)/WAF/CP.7/8] to the 1981 Abidjan Convention for Cooperation in the Protection and Development of the Marine and Coastal Environment of the West and Central African Regions [YUN 1981, p. 840] developed project proposals to coordinate with the New Partnership for Africa's Development Environmental Action Plan, strengthened linkages with large marine ecosystem programmes and supported small island developing States' projects. Under the South-east Pacific Action Plan, adopted in 1981 [ibid., p. 833], a workshop was held on GPA development and implementation at the regional and national levels (Chile, January). The Regional Seas Programme also worked to promote synergies and coordinated regional implementation of relevant multilateral environmental agreements and initiatives to develop and promote ecosystems-based marine and coastal management, and enhance its visibility.

In 2005, seven Regional Seas Programme national action plans were adopted by Governments for integration into sustainable development planning, and goals and targets developed for a regional strategic action plan.

Conservation of wildlife

In September, the Great Apes Survival Project (GRASP) held the First Intergovernmental Meeting on Great Apes and the Great Apes Survival Project and the first GRASP Council Meeting (Kinshasa, Democratic Republic of the Congo, 5-9 September). The Intergovernmental Meeting

adopted the Kinshasa Declaration on Great Apes to secure the long-term survival for all great ape species and their habitat. The GRASP Council adopted the Global Strategy for the Survival of Great Apes and their Habitat. UNEP's *World Atlas of Great Apes and their Conservation* was launched during the meetings.

Protection against harmful products and waste

Chemical safety

As at 31 December, 100 States and the EC were parties to the 1998 Rotterdam Convention on the Prior Informed Consent (PIC) Procedure for Certain Hazardous Chemicals and Pesticides in International Trade [YUN 1998, p. 997], which entered into force in 2004 [YUN 2004, p. 1063].

The Chemical Review Committee, established by the Conference of the Parties to the Rotterdam Convention as a subsidiary body in 2004 [ibid, p. 1064], held its first meeting (Geneva, 11-18 February) [UNEP/FAO/RC/CRC.1/28], during which it reviewed the notifications of final regulatory actions and the supporting documentation for 14 candidate chemicals submitted in accordance with article 5 of the Convention. The Committee also considered a note on the review of its role and mandate [UNEP/FAO/RC/CRC.1/3], as well as working procedures and policy guidance for the Committee, which were submitted by the Conference of the Parties.

The second meeting of the Conference of the Parties to the Convention (Rome, 27-30 September) [UNEP/FAO/RC/COP.2/19] established a compliance committee; adopted a work plan for regional and national delivery of technical assistance for 2006 and a process for the preparation of guidance documents; approved arrangements by the UNEP Executive Director and the FAO Director-General for the performance of Convention secretariat functions, to be concluded on the basis of a proposed MOU [UNEP/FAO/RC/COP.2/14/Add.1]; confirmed the appointment of members of the Chemical Review Committee; and amended the financial and budgetary arrangements for the 2005-2006 biennium. The Convention secretariat was asked to contribute to a study on cooperation and synergies with the secretariats of the 1989 Basel Convention on the Control of Transboundary Movements of Hazardous Wastes and their Disposal [YUN 1989, p. 420] and the 2001 Stockholm Convention on Persistent Organic Pollutants [YUN 2001, p. 971].

The Open-ended Ad Hoc Working Group on Non-Compliance held its first session (Rome, 26-27 September) [UNEP/FAO/RC/OEWG.1/3].

International chemicals management

In February, the UNEP Governing Council, having considered the Executive Director's 2004 report on chemicals management [YUN 2004, p. 1064], adopted a multi-part decision on that issue [dec. 23/9]. In the part dealing with cooperation between UNEP, relevant multilateral environmental agreements and other organizations [dec. 23/9 I], the Council requested the Executive Director to strengthen support for the 1989 Basel Convention on the Control of Transboundary Movements of Hazardous Wastes and their Disposal [YUN 1989, p. 420], the 1998 Rotterdam Convention on the Prior Informed Consent Procedure for Certain Hazardous Chemicals and Pesticides in International Trade [YUN 1998, p. 997] and the 2001 Stockholm Convention on Persistent Organic Pollutants [YUN 2001, p. 971], and to promote full cooperation and synergies between the secretariats of those Conventions and the UNEP Chemicals Branch. He was also asked to: promote cooperation between the secretariats of the 1987 Montreal Protocol on Substances that Deplete the Ozone Layer [YUN 1987, p. 686], the Basel, Rotterdam and Stockholm Conventions, the UNEP Chemicals Branch, and the World Customs Organization in addressing international illegal trafficking of hazardous chemicals and wastes; promote cooperation with the Basel Convention regional training centres in the implementation of activities of related multilateral environmental agreements and institutions; and report to the Council in 2007.

In the part of the decision dealing with the strategic approach to international chemicals management (SAICM) [dec. 23/9 II], the Council requested Governments in a position to do so and other stakeholders to contribute the extra-budgetary resources needed to support the further development of SAICM. The Executive Director was asked to provide funding towards that end and to report to the Governing Council in 2006 on the outcomes of that process of development. He should make preparations for a third and final meeting of the Preparatory Committee for the Development of SAICM, to be held in Vienna in September (see below), and, in cooperation with the other co-conveners, for the International Conference on Chemicals Management, scheduled to take place in conjunction with the ninth (2006) special session of the Governing Council. He was asked, as a matter of high priority, to provide for the implementation of UNEP's responsibilities under SAICM, once adopted, and to support developing countries and countries with economies in transition in implementing the strategic approach, taking into account the Bali Strategic Plan for Technology Support and Capacity-building (see p. 1135), and to report in 2007.

Preparatory Committee meeting. The third and final session of the Preparatory Committee for the Development of SAICM (Vienna, 19-24 September) [SAICM/PREPCOM.3/5] considered the SAICM global programme of action, its overarching policy strategy and a high-level declaration, which together were to form the tripartite structure for SAICM, as agreed by the Committee in 2004 [YUN 2004, p. 1064]. Draft texts of those three SAICM elements were annexed to the Committee's report and were to be forwarded to the 2006 International Conference on Chemicals Management for consideration.

In October [UNEP/GCSS.IX/6], the Executive Director reported that the third session of the Preparatory Committee agreed provisionally that he should be requested to perform secretariat functions for SAICM during its implementation phase. A number of issues remained to be resolved and various elements of the SAICM documents to be finalized, including sections of the policy strategy dealing with financial considerations and principles and approaches. The Committee President convened a meeting of an expanded bureau (Jongny, Switzerland, 4-5 November) to consider possible avenues for consensus, make final preparations for the International Conference on Chemicals Management and finalize and adopt SAICM and refer it to the governing bodies of relevant intergovernmental organizations, including GC/GMEF, for consideration.

Lead and cadmium

On 25 February [dec. 23/9 III], the Governing Council reaffirmed its 2003 decision on lead [YUN 2003, p. 1071] and requested the Executive Director to review available scientific information, focusing on long-range environmental transport, in order to inform future discussions on the need for global action in relation to lead and cadmium. Governments and other stakeholders were asked to increase contributions to facilitate the timely implementation of the decision, and the Executive Director was asked to report to the Council in 2007.

On 27 December, UNEP announced that vehicle fuels in sub-Saharan Africa would be lead-free as at 1 January 2006, meeting the phase-out date set by African Governments and their partners, including UNEP, in 2001.

Mercury

On 25 February [dec. 23/9 IV], the Governing Council reiterated the conclusion of the UNEP Global Mercury Assessment [YUN 2002, p. 1064] that there was sufficient evidence of significant global adverse impacts from mercury and its compounds to warrant further international action to reduce the risks to human health and the environment from the release of mercury and its compounds into the environment, and the Council's 2003 decision [YUN 2003, p. 1071] regarding the initiation of national, regional and global actions to reduce or eliminate such releases. It continued to urge all countries to adopt goals and to take national action to identify exposed populations and ecosystems and reduce anthropogenic mercury releases that affected human health and the environment. The Council requested the Executive Director to develop further the UNEP mercury programme and to prepare and publicize a report summarizing supply, trade and demand information for mercury, including in artisanal and small-scale gold mining. He should propose possible further actions in those areas for the Council's consideration in 2007, with the aim of facilitating and conducting technical assistance and capacity-building activities to support the efforts of countries in taking action regarding mercury pollution.

Governments were encouraged to promote and improve evaluation and communication methods, based on, among other things, guidance from WHO and FAO. Governments, the private sector and international organizations should take immediate action to reduce the risks to human health and the environment posed on a global scale by mercury in products and production processes. Governments in a position to do so should assist developing countries and countries with economies in transition through technology transfer, capacity-building and access to financial resources to achieve the goals of the Council's 2003 decision on mercury [ibid.], and with intergovernmental organizations, non-governmental organizations (NGOs) and the private sector develop and implement partnerships to reduce the risks to human health and the environment from the release of mercury and its compounds to the environment, with a view to achieving those goals. The Executive Director was asked to invite Governments, particularly of developing countries and countries with economies in transition, to identify, in consultation with stakeholders, a set of pilot partnerships by 1 September. He should also compile and report on needs identified to execute the partnerships and assist in mobilizing resources to support them; share and disseminate information submitted by partnerships on progress, lessons learned and emerging best practices and report on the results of those partnerships; report on the partnership programme at the third (2005) session of the SAICM Preparatory Committee (see p. 1161) and the 2006 International Conference on Chemicals Management and on partnership implementation, in 2007. The Council indicated a number of elements to be identified in each partnership and encouraged Governments, intergovernmental organizations, NGOs and the private sector to form a partnership to assist the Executive Director in resources mobilization. The Executive Director was asked to facilitate work between the UNEP mercury programme and Governments, other international organizations, NGOs, the private sector and the partnerships to: improve global understanding of international mercury emission sources, fate and transport; promote the development of inventories of mercury uses and releases and environmentally sound disposal and remediation practices; and increase awareness of environmentally sound recycling practices. Governments and stakeholders, especially in developed countries, and relevant international organizations, were encouraged to mobilize technical and financial resources to support partnerships.

The Council requested the Executive Director to report in 2007 on progress in implementing its decision and decided to assess, on the basis of the progress report, the need for further action on mercury, including the possibility of a legally binding instrument, partnerships and other actions.

Persistent organic pollutants

As at 31 December, 114 States and the EC were parties to the 2001 Stockholm Convention on Persistent Organic Pollutants (POPs) [YUN 2001, p. 971], which entered into force in 2004 [YUN 2004, p. 1066].

The first meeting of the Conference of the Parties to the Stockholm Convention (Punta del Este, Uruguay, 2-6 May) [UNEP/POPS/COP.1/31] accepted Switzerland's offer to host the Convention secretariat in Geneva and approved the operational budget of $5,366,136 for 2006 and an indicative operational budget of $4,213,264 for 2007. It adopted its rules of procedure; an arbitration procedure for the settlement of disputes among parties; and financial rules for the Conference of the Parties, its subsidiary bodies and the Convention secretariat. The Conference also adopted a memorandum of understanding between itself and Council of the Global Environment Facility; the guidance for assisting countries in preparing national implementation plans [UNEP/POPS/COP.1/INF/13 & Add.1]; guidance on technical assistance; the review process for entries in the Register of Specific Exemptions; the revised format for reporting under article 15 of the Convention; and formats for the Register of Specific Exemptions and the register for the synthetic pesticide dichloro-diphenyl-trichloroethane (DDT). It established the Persistent Organic Pollutants Review Committee as a subsidiary body and the Expert Group on Best Available Techniques and Best Environmental Practices. Other decisions dealt with evaluation; non-compliance; technical assistance provided to regional and subregional centres; enhancing synergies within the chemicals and waste cluster; best available techniques and best environmental practices; technical guidelines for the environmentally sound management of POPs waste; and financial and administrative matters.

The first meeting of the Persistent Organic Pollutants Review Committee (Geneva, 7-11 November) [UNEP/POPS/POPRC.1/10] adopted decisions on provisional confidentiality arrangements; a process for inviting experts to participate in Committee meetings; and the chemicals pentabromodiphenyl ether, chlordecone, hexabromobiphenyl, lindane, and perfluorooctane sulfonate.

Hazardous wastes

As at 31 December, the number of parties to the 1989 Basel Convention on the Control of Transboundary Movements of Hazardous Wastes and their Disposal [YUN 1989, p. 420], which entered into force in 1992 [YUN 1992, p. 685], rose to 166. The 1995 amendment to the Convention [YUN 1995, p. 1333], not yet in force, had been ratified, accepted or approved by 61 parties. During the year, the number of parties to the 1999 Basel Protocol on Liability and Compensation for Damage resulting from Transboundary Movements of Hazardous Wastes and their Disposal [YUN 1999, p. 998] rose to seven.

The first meeting (Geneva, 12-22 June) [UNEP/SBC/BUREAU/7/1/11] of the Expanded Bureau of the seventh (2004) meeting of the Conference of the Parties to the Convention discussed the Convention's partnership programme and resource mobilization strategy, the outcome of the first (2005) meeting of the Conference of the Parties to the 2001 Stockholm Convention on POPs (see p. 1162), and financial and administrative matters.

The fourth session of the Open-ended Working Group of the Convention (Geneva, 4-8 July) [UNEP/CHW/OEWG/4/18] agreed to the prioritization of its 2005-2006 work programme and approved, with amendments, the instruction manual for the implementation of the Basel Protocol on Liability and Compensation contained in a secretariat note [UNEP/CHW/OEWG/4/8]. Other decisions dealt with: the Basel Convention Partnership Programme; the Mobile Phone Partnership Initiative; the Joint Working Group of the International Labour Organization, the International Maritime Organization and the Convention on Ship Scrapping; the environmentally sound management of ship dismantling; the abandonment of ships on land or in ports; illegal traffic in hazardous wastes; sustainable financing and other financial matters; the preparation of technical guidelines on POPs and on the environmentally sound management of wastes resulting from surface treatment of metals and plastics; work on hazard characteristics; harmonization of the forms for the notification and movement of documents and related instructions; and resource mobilization.

Other matters

Occupied Palestinian and other Arab territories

In a February note [UNEP/GC.23/INF/30], the Executive Director provided information on the environment in the Occupied Palestinian Territory. UNEP organized, with the Palestinian Environment Quality Authority and the UNDP Programme of Assistance to the Palestinian People, three one-day workshops in Ramallah (29-31 January) on public awareness for senior Palestinian decision makers; solid waste for municipalities; and environmental education and awareness raising for schoolteachers. A capacity building seminar on hazardous waste in the Middle East (Helsinki, Finland, 7-9 February), organized in cooperation with Finland, was attended by Egyptian, Israeli, Jordanian and Palestinian participants.

Environment and security

A January note by the Executive Director [UNEP/GC.23/INF/21] provided information on UNEP's activities with regard to environment and security. The Executive Director said that the relationship between environmental degradation and political instability was poorly understood. A more systematic assessment of the links between environment and security and a more careful consideration of the links between environmental resources/degradation and development were needed. Efforts to address the relationship between environment and conflict were relatively undeveloped, with few major international institutions attempting to tackle that agenda collaboratively. Approaches that needed to be assessed, included conservation strategies that promoted cooperation; integration of development and environmental policy; incorporation of environmental security into urban development and planning; deepening the understanding of environmental policies in post-conflict situations; and rigorous assessment of the effectiveness and sustainability of interventions.

UNEP, UNDP and the Organization for Security and Co-operation in Europe launched the Environment and Security Initiative, a strategy to address conflict-prone environmental problems and implement opportunities that advanced and protected peace and the environment simultaneously, while promoting and securing sustainable development patterns.

UNEP intended to strengthen its role and involvement in environment and security issues, while expanding the scope of its work. Elements under consideration for UNEP's global agenda for environment and security included a global security assessment, a mapping exercise and an awareness campaign.

International Year of Planet Earth (2008)

On 22 December [meeting 68], the General Assembly, on the recommendation of the Second Committee [A/60/488/Add.1], adopted **resolution 60/192** without vote [agenda item 52 (a)].

International Year of Planet Earth, 2008

The General Assembly,

Reaffirming Agenda 21, the Plan of Implementation of the World Summit on Sustainable Development ("Johannesburg Plan of Implementation") and the Hyogo Framework for Action 2005-2015,

Noting that the wealth of scientific information available on planet Earth remains largely untapped and hardly known to the public or to policymakers and decision makers,

Convinced that education in Earth sciences provides humankind with tools for the sustainable use of natural resources and for building the scientific infrastructure essential for sustainable development,

Welcoming the decision of the General Conference of the United Nations Educational, Scientific and Cultural Organization to support the declaration of 2008 as the International Year of Planet Earth with a view to highlighting the importance of Earth sciences,

Taking into account the crucial role the Year could play, inter alia, in raising public awareness of the importance for sustainable development of the Earth's processes and resources; disaster prevention, reduction and mitigation; and capacity-building for the sustainable management of resources; and its important contribution to the United Nations Decade of Education for Sustainable Development,

1. *Decides* to declare 2008 the International Year of Planet Earth;

2. *Designates* the United Nations Educational, Scientific and Cultural Organization as the lead agency and the focal point for the Year to organize activities to be undertaken during the Year, in collaboration with the United Nations Environment Programme and other relevant entities of the United Nations system, as well as the International Union of Geological Sciences and other Earth science societies and groups through-

out the world, and in this regard agrees that the activities of the International Year of Planet Earth will be funded from voluntary contributions, including, inter alia, from industry and major foundations mobilized by a consortium of international organizations, led by the International Union of Geological Sciences;

3. *Encourages* all Member States, the United Nations system and all other actors to take advantage of the Year to increase awareness of the importance of Earth sciences for the achievement of sustainable development and to promote action at the local, national, regional and international levels;

4. *Requests* the Secretary-General to report to the General Assembly at its sixty-second session on the progress of the preparations for the International Year of Planet Earth.

Human settlements

Follow-up to the 1996 UN Conference on Human Settlements (Habitat II) and the 2001 General Assembly special session

Report of Secretary-General. In July [A/60/168], the Secretary-General, in response to General Assembly resolution 59/239 [YUN 2004, p. 1070], reported on follow-up to the Assembly's twenty-fifth (2001) special session [YUN 2001, p. 973] to review and appraise the implementation of the Habitat Agenda [YUN 1996, p. 994], adopted by the 1996 United Nations Conference on Human Settlements (Habitat II) [ibid., p. 992], and on the strengthening of the United Nations Human Settlements Programme (UN-Habitat). During the reporting period, UN-Habitat made significant progress in strengthening the United Nations Habitat and Human Settlements Foundation. General purpose funds from Governments rose from $8.3 million in 2003 to $10.5 million in 2004, while earmarked contributions rose from $17.2 million to $22.2 million. The twentieth session of the UN-Habitat Governing Council (see p. 1168) noted the imbalance between earmarked and non-earmarked contributions and called upon Governments and other Habitat Agenda partners to increase their funding to the Foundation and to give priority to non-earmarked, multi-year funding. UN-Habitat launched its newest subprogramme, the Human Settlements Financing Division, providing the Foundation with an operational platform for mobilizing resources at the country level. It also launched the Slum Upgrading Facility, a three-year pilot project. UN-Habitat expanded its efforts at the country level to build the capacity of States to achieve the Millennium Development Goals (MDGs) [YUN 2000, p. 51], especially the targets on slums. It expanded its technical assistance to over 80 States, and responded to demands for disaster mitigation and post-conflict humanitarian assistance and reconstruction. UN-Habitat placed national Habitat Programme Managers in 32 countries. The Programme adjusted its monitoring and research activities to support member States in monitoring implementation of the MDGs and in analysing policies and practices to help them achieve those targets, including documenting and disseminating best practices and undertaking seminal research on urban economic conditions, rural-urban linkages and effective strategies for improving urban self-employment and livelihood for the urban poor.

UN-Habitat created forums for global networking and established several strategic partnerships. It agreed to establish with the World Bank a cooperation agreement to provide greater coherence to urban development interventions at the country level, with an emphasis on promoting housing finance and placing urban development more squarely in the national development agenda. It signed agreements with the Asian Development Bank, the Inter-American Development Bank and the African Development Bank for joint projects and programmes in the areas of water, sanitation, housing and urban development, focusing on the living conditions of the urban poor. UN-Habitat also participated in regional ministerial meetings on housing and land and urban development in Latin America, Africa and Asia. It convened, with the African Union, the inaugural session of the African Ministerial Conference on Housing and Urban Development (Durban, South Africa, 31 January–4 February),which agreed to establish an enhanced implementation framework for promoting sustainable cities and towns in Africa. The Global Campaign for Secure Tenure and the Global Campaign on Urban Governance were launched in over 10 countries, within the framework of the MDG targets and the Plan of Implementation of the World Summit on Sustainable Development [YUN 2002, p. 821], with follow-up activities directed towards building local capacities. The Interagency Advisory Group on Forced Evictions, an international task force to facilitate negotiated policy alternatives to unlawful eviction, was established, and progress made in implementing the Water for African Cities and Water for Asian Cities programmes.

The Secretary-General noted that the crisis of rapid urbanization and the unique opportunity presented by slum upgrading for the attainment of the MDGs called for Governments to adopt pro-poor, urban policies and action plans. He encouraged Governments to strengthen UN-Habitat and the Human Settlements Foundation by providing non-earmarked, predicable funding and regular budget resources for core programme activities; and to contribute to the Water and Sanitation Trust Fund, the Slum Upgrading Facility and other technical cooperation trust funds.

Commission on Sustainable Development consideration. The Commission on Sustainable Development, at its thirteenth session (New York, 11–22 April) [E/2005/29] (see p. 920), considered policy options in the thematic areas of water, sanitation and human settlements. The Commission's intergovernmental preparatory meeting [E/CN.17/2005/6] discussed aspects of an integrated approach to land use, housing development, the delivery of water and sanitation services, transportation infrastructure, education and healthcare facilities and employment. It addressed the goals of providing improved housing and associated services to the urban poor; creating jobs and promoting enterprises; and developing finance institutions and financial products suitable to the needs of the urban poor. The Commission also considered the interlinkages among water, sanitation and human settlements.

The Commission had before it the reports of the Secretary-General on human settlements: policy options and possible actions to expedite implementation [E/CN.17/2005/4], and major groups' priorities for action in water, sanitation and human settlements [E/CN.17/2005/5]. The report on policy options discussed aspects of housing, tenure security and urban land management, including those relating to the urban poor, and considered the challenge of devising strategies and policies for increasing the productivity of urban areas, while supporting economic growth that benefitted the poor. Stating that such strategies needed to recognize the contribution of the informal sector to economic development and employment, the report also discussed issues relating to the development of a policy environment supportive of employment and enterprise. With respect to mobilizing the estimated $70 to $100 billion needed to achieve the MDG goal of improving the lives of at least 100 million slum-dwellers by 2020, the Secretary-General considered several options, including promoting community-based approaches to financing, promoting and scaling-up microfinancing schemes and developing market-based instruments and institutions. The report considered the participation of Governments, local authorities, UN agencies and other relevant actors in the development of a framework for action on the issue.

On 22 April [E/2005/29 (res. 13/1)], the Commission adopted a resolution on policy options and practical measures to expedite implementation in water, sanitation and human settlements. The resolution called upon Governments and the UN system, international financial institutions and other international organizations to provide an enabling policy and regulatory environment and to mobilize the requisite means of implementation for the promotion of sustainable human settlements development in both urban and rural areas, in accordance with national priorities. It supported integrated planning and management, among other activities, to prevent new slum dwellings and assist in providing access for the poor in urban and rural areas to descent and affordable housing and basic services, taking into account employment and enterprise promotion and other interlinkages and cross-cutting issues. The Commission requested UN-Habitat to facilitate effective global monitoring of progress in the implementation of human settlements goals and targets, as well as measures agreed at the current session of the Commission regarding human settlements. It also called upon member States to strengthen the UN-Habitat capacities to provide increased assistance to developing countries and countries with economies in transition, including through the pilot phase of the Slum Upgrading Facility.

Coordinated implementation of Habitat Agenda

In May [E/2005/60], in accordance with a 2004 Economic and Social Council request [YUN 2004, p. 1070], the Secretary-General reported on the coordinated implementation of the Habitat Agenda, in particular the work of UN-Habitat with regard to its four subprogrammes: shelter and sustainable human settlements development; monitoring of the Habitat Agenda; regional and technical cooperation; and human settlements financing. It also considered the UN-Habitat's cooperation and collaboration with its partners, including the World Bank and regional financial institutions and described innovations in its work, including on the debt-for-land swap programme between Kenya and Finland, the Slum Upgrading Facility, the launch of the UN-Habitat Water and Sanitation Trust Fund, and the implementation of an enabling strategy for civil society within cities. The report also reviewed UN-Habitat's financial, human resource and information management.

The Secretary-General encouraged Governments to include human settlements in their national development plans and to promote city and metropolitan planning in their poverty reduction strategies and their UN development assistance frameworks; assess conditions and trends in their urban slums and create a pro-poor

policy environment that placed the highest priority on improving the living environment of slum dwellers; participate and support the participation of Habitat partners from developing countries in the third session of the World Urban Forum, to be held in Vancouver, Canada in 2006; and increase the non-earmarked component of their contributions.

On 26 July, the Economic and Social Council, by **decision 2005/298**, took note of the Secretary-General's report and decided to transmit it to the General Assembly for consideration at its sixtieth (2005) session. It requested the Secretary-General to submit a further report for consideration by the Council in 2006.

In accordance with the Council's decision, the Secretary-General, by a September note [A/60/347], transmitted his May report on the coordinated implementation of the Habitat Agenda to the Assembly.

GENERAL ASSEMBLY ACTION

On 22 December [meeting 68], the General Assembly, on the recommendation of the Second Committee [A/60/489], adopted **resolution 60/203** without vote [agenda item 53].

Implementation of the outcome of the United Nations Conference on Human Settlements (Habitat II) and strengthening of the United Nations Human Settlements Programme (UN-Habitat)

The General Assembly,

Recalling its resolutions 3327(XXIX) of 16 December 1974, 32/162 of 19 December 1977, 34/115 of 14 December 1979, 56/205 and 56/206 of 21 December 2001, 57/275 of 20 December 2002, 58/226 and 58/227 of 23 December 2003 and 59/239 of 22 December 2004,

Taking note of Economic and Social Council resolutions 2002/38 of 26 July 2002 and 2003/62 of 25 July 2003 and Council decisions 2004/300 of 23 July 2004 and 2005/298 of 26 July 2005,

Recalling the goal contained in the United Nations Millennium Declaration of achieving a significant improvement in the lives of at least 100 million slum-dwellers by 2020 and the goal contained in the Plan of Implementation of the World Summit on Sustainable Development ("Johannesburg Plan of Implementation") to halve, by 2015, the proportion of people who lack access to safe drinking water and sanitation,

Recalling also the Habitat Agenda, the Declaration on Cities and Other Human Settlements in the New Millennium, the Johannesburg Declaration on Sustainable Development, the Johannesburg Plan of Implementation and the Monterrey Consensus of the International Conference on Financing for Development,

Recalling further the 2005 World Summit Outcome,

Recalling the decisions of the Commission on Sustainable Development at its thirteenth session related to the United Nations Human Settlements Programme (UN-Habitat) and human settlements,

Recognizing that the overall thrust and strategic vision of UN-Habitat and its emphasis on the two global campaigns on secure tenure and urban governance are strategic points of entry for the effective implementation of the Habitat Agenda, especially for guiding international cooperation in respect of adequate shelter for all and sustainable human settlements development,

Conscious of the unique opportunity provided by the Cities Without Slums Initiative mentioned in the Millennium Declaration for realizing economies of scale and substantial multiplier effects in helping to attain the other Millennium Development Goals,

Acknowledging the significance of the urban dimension of poverty eradication and the need to integrate water and sanitation issues within a broad-based approach to human settlements,

Expressing its appreciation to the regular Assembly of Ministers and High-level Authorities of the Housing and Urban Development Sector in Latin America and the Caribbean and its recent plan of action on the implementation of the Millennium Development Goals,

Expressing its appreciation also to the African Union, UN-Habitat and the Government of South Africa for convening and hosting the first African conference of housing and urban development ministers in Durban from 31 January to 4 February 2005, which established the African Ministerial Conference on Housing and Urban Development to promote sustainable human settlements in Africa,

Expressing its appreciation further to the Government of Canada and the city of Vancouver for their willingness to host the third session of the World Urban Forum in June 2006 and to the Government of China and the city of Nanjing for their willingness to host the fourth session of the World Urban Forum in 2008,

Taking note of the reports entitled *The State of the World's Cities 2004-2005: Globalization and Urban Culture* and *Global Report on Human Settlements 2005: Financing Urban Shelter,*

Noting the efforts by UN-Habitat to strengthen its collaboration with the United Nations Development Programme, the World Bank and other international organizations and its participation in the Executive Committee on Humanitarian Affairs,

Recognizing the continued urgent need for increased and predictable financial contributions to the United Nations Habitat and Human Settlements Foundation to ensure timely, effective and concrete global implementation of the Habitat Agenda, the Declaration on Cities and Other Human Settlements in the New Millennium and the relevant internationally agreed development goals, including those contained in the Millennium Declaration and the Johannesburg Declaration and Plan of Implementation, and the relevant decisions of the Commission on Sustainable Development at its thirteenth session,

1. *Takes note* of the report of the Governing Council of the United Nations Human Settlements Programme on the work of its twentieth session, the report of the Secretary-General on the coordinated implementation of the Habitat Agenda and the report of the Secretary-General on the implementation of the outcome of the United Nations Conference on Human Settlements (Habitat II) and strengthening of the United Nations Human Settlements Programme (UN-Habitat);

2. *Encourages* Governments to consider an enhanced approach to achieving the Cities Without Slums Initiative mentioned in the United Nations Millennium Declaration by upgrading existing slums and creating policies and programmes, according to national circumstances, to forestall the growth of future slums, and in this regard invites the international donor community and multilateral and regional development banks to support the efforts of developing countries, inter alia, through increased voluntary financial assistance;

3. *Recognizes* that Governments have the primary responsibility for the sound and effective implementation of the Habitat Agenda, the Declaration on Cities and Other Human Settlements in the New Millennium and the Millennium Declaration, and stresses the need for the international community to fully implement commitments to support Governments of developing countries and countries with economies in transition in their efforts, through the provision of the requisite resources, capacity-building, the transfer of technology and the creation of an international enabling environment;

4. *Calls for* continued financial support to UN-Habitat through increased voluntary contributions to the United Nations Habitat and Human Settlements Foundation, and invites Governments to provide multi-year funding to support programme implementation;

5. *Also calls for* increased, non-earmarked contributions to the Foundation;

6. *Requests* the Secretary-General to keep the resource needs of UN-Habitat under review so as to enhance its effectiveness in supporting national policies, strategies and plans in attaining the poverty eradication, gender equality, water and sanitation and slum upgrading targets of the Millennium Declaration and the Johannesburg Plan of Implementation;

7. *Emphasizes* the need for UN-Habitat to develop a results-based and less fragmented budget structure with a view to securing maximum efficiency, accountability and transparency in programme delivery regardless of funding source;

8. *Requests* the Secretary-General to keep the resource needs of UN-Habitat and the United Nations Office at Nairobi under review so as to permit the delivery, in an effective manner, of necessary services to UN-Habitat and the other United Nations organs and organizations in Nairobi;

9. *Invites* the international donor community and financial institutions to contribute generously to the Water and Sanitation Trust Fund, the Slum Upgrading Facility and the technical cooperation trust funds to enable UN-Habitat to assist developing countries to mobilize public investment and private capital for slum upgrading, shelter and basic services;

10. *Acknowledges* contributions of the regional consultative initiatives, including conferences of ministers in the area of human settlements, for implementation of the Habitat Agenda and the attainment of the Millennium Development Goals, and invites the international community to support such efforts;

11. *Stresses* the importance of publishing the financial rules and regulations of the United Nations Habitat and Human Settlements Foundation in time for their adoption no later than the end of 2005;

12. *Requests* UN-Habitat to intensify coordination in the framework of the United Nations Development Assistance Framework and the common country assessment and to continue to work with the World Bank, regional development banks, other development banks, regional organizations and other relevant partners to field-test innovative policies, practices and pilot projects in order to mobilize resources to increase the supply of affordable credit for slum upgrading and other pro-poor human settlements development in developing countries and countries with economies in transition;

13. *Invites* all Governments to participate actively in the third session of the World Urban Forum, and invites donor countries to support the participation of representatives from developing countries, in particular the least developed countries, and countries with economies in transition, including women and youth, in the Forum;

14. *Encourages* Governments to establish local, national and regional urban observatories and to provide financial and substantive support to UN-Habitat for the further development of methodologies for data collection, analysis and dissemination;

15. *Recognizes* the important role and contribution of UN-Habitat in supporting the efforts of countries affected by natural disasters and complex emergencies to develop prevention, rehabilitation and reconstruction programmes for the transition from relief to development, and in this regard requests UN-Habitat, within its mandate, to continue to work closely with other relevant agencies in the United Nations system, and invites the Inter-Agency Standing Committee to consider including UN-Habitat in its membership;

16. *Requests* UN-Habitat, through its involvement in the Executive Committee on Humanitarian Affairs and through contacts with relevant United Nations agencies and partners in the field, to promote the early involvement of human settlements experts in the assessment and development of prevention, rehabilitation and reconstruction programmes to support the efforts of developing countries affected by natural disasters and other complex humanitarian emergencies;

17. *Requests* the Secretary-General to submit a report to the General Assembly at its sixty-first session on the implementation of the present resolution;

18. *Decides* to include in the provisional agenda of its sixty-first session the item entitled "Implementation of the outcome of the United Nations Conference on Human Settlements (Habitat II) and strengthening of the United Nations Human Settlements Programme (UN-Habitat)".

UN Human Settlements Programme

Governing Council

In 2005, the Governing Council of the United Nations Human Settlements Programme (UN-Habitat) held its twentieth session (Nairobi, 4-8 April) [A/60/8]. The Council adopted 21 resolutions and one decision regarding various aspects of UN-Habitat's work and future sessions of the Governing Council. In a resolution on housing as a component to an adequate standard of living

for vulnerable or disadvantaged persons [res. 20/13], the Council requested the Executive Director to integrate the protection of such persons into all UN-Habitat activities, develop or strengthen mechanisms for monitoring the impact of human settlement policies and programmes on the lives and work of disadvantaged persons in cities, and report in 2007. Welcoming progress made in the work of UN-Habitat Best Practices and Local Leadership Programme [res. 20/6], the Council encouraged the Executive Director to make resources available in support of best practices, good urban practices and enabling legislation, and to report in 2007.

The Council took note of a draft strategy for enhancing the engagement of youth in UN-Habitat's work [HSP/GC/20/2/Add.5], and requested the Executive Director to finalize the Youth Strategy for Enhanced Engagement and to develop an action plan for its implementation, including an internal evaluation which would take into consideration input from youth organizations (res. 20/1). The Executive Director was also asked to strengthen and mainstream UN-Habitat's work on the engagement of young people in human settlements development and in addressing the problems of young people at risk, especially girls and young women; study the effects of social and economic conditions related to urbanization on the intergenerational transfer of values conducive to good citizenship and how national and local governments could assist that process; support youth organizations to develop partnerships with each other; facilitate the participation of youth representatives at important UN-Habitat meetings; and report in 2007. The Council also had before it a theme paper on enhancing the involvement of civil society in local governance [HSP/GC/20/4]. In a related resolution [res.20/16], the Executive Director was requested to continue compiling lessons learned and best practices and, in close collaboration with other parts of the UN system and with other partners, improve their dissemination and exchange, promote civil society involvement in UN-Habitat projects, and report to the Council in 2007.

The Council considered the Executive Director's report on progress made in implementing UN-Habitat's global campaign on secure tenure and urban governance, launched in 2000 [YUN 2000, p. 995] [HSP/GC/20/INF/6] and endorsed the conclusion of an independent evaluation of the campaign [HSP/GC/20/INF/7]. The Executive Director was asked to ensure that the campaign had a higher global visibility and to further mainstream its principles through UN-Habitat activities and programmes. She was further requested to report on the matter in 2007 [res. 20/12].

Welcoming the establishment of the African Ministerial Conference on Housing and Urban Development (see p. 1165) [res. 20/2], the Council requested the Executive Director to work closely with the Conference in achieving the aims of the Habitat Agenda and in accelerating the achievement of the MDGs in Africa; support the activities of the Conference and the implementation of the Cities Programme of the New Partnership for Africa's Development (NEPAD), and to report in 2007 on progress made by the Conference [res. 20/4]. The Executive Director was invited to mainstream the implementation of the Brussels Programme of Action for the Least Developed Countries [YUN 2001, p. 771] in UN-Habitat activities, as called for in General Assembly resolution 56/227 [ibid., p. 773], and to contribute to its effective implementation. Having considered a theme paper on post-conflict, natural and man-made disaster assessment and reconstruction [HSP/GC/20/5], the Council noted the guiding principles contained in the document and asked the Executive Director to elaborate them. She was requested to develop a strategic policy for UN-Habitat's role in addressing the sustainable human settlements aspect of human-made and natural disaster management for review by the Committee of Permanent Representatives before the end of 2005, and mobilize the financial resources required for such a strategy [res. 20/17]. In a further resolution [20/9], she was asked to assist in raising international awareness of the challenges faced by small island developing States with regard to sustainable human settlements development; assist those States in disaster preparedness, land registration, urban planning guidelines, and hurricane-resistant housing, among other areas; and to further strengthen cooperation with relevant UN agencies, funds and programmes related to small island developing States.

With regard to the sustainable development of Arctic cities [res. 20/8], the Council took note of the establishment of a North-North network for promoting and facilitating cooperation between cities located in the Arctic region. It requested the Executive Director to assist in raising international awareness of the sustainable development challenges of the far north and Arctic region, including those faced by indigenous people residing in those areas; consult with the United Nations and other partners and stakeholders on the matter; compile information on training activities in that region as a basis of further cooperation between UN-Habitat and relevant partners; and report on the implementation of the resolution to the Council in 2007.

Having considered the report of the Executive Director on progress in the implementation of the Special Human Settlements Programme for the Palestinian People [HSP/GC/20/2/Add.3], the Council welcomed progress made and reiterated its invitation to the donor community and financial institutions to support the programme [res. 20/14].

In a resolution on strengthening the Slum Upgrading Facility of UN-Habitat and the Human Settlements Foundation [res. 20/11], the Council invited Governments and others to continue to contribute financially to the Facility, capitalizing it to a minimum level of $30 million. It requested the Executive Director to accelerate efforts to implement a cooperation framework between UN-Habitat and the World Bank Group and similar framework agreements with regional development banks, and to report to the Council in 2007 on progress made regarding the Slum Upgrading Facility. As to the preservation and sustainable development of oases [res. 20/3], the Council asked the Executive Director to take into account the specific needs of oases in UN-Habitat global programmes, particularly in the Sustainable Cities and Localizing Agenda 21 programmes [YUN 1992, p. 672], and to strengthen consultation and partnership mechanisms on the matter. Having considered a report of the Executive Director [HSP/GC/20/7] on the decentralization and strengthening of local authorities, the Council took note of the draft guidelines prepared by the Advisory Group of Experts on Decentralization (AGRED) [YUN 2004, p. 1074]. It invited Governments to provide comments on the draft guidelines before the end of 2005 and requested the Executive Director, with AGRED support, to revise and finalize the guidelines during 2006 and to submit them to the Council in 2007. She was further requested to continue to develop the concept of a global observatory that would assess, monitor and evaluate the state of decentralization and accountability around the world [res. 20/18].

The Governing Council [res. 20/10] took note of the Executive Director's report [HSP/GC/20/2/Add.1,2] on the second session of the World Urban Forum [YUN 2004, p. 1073], and noted that the outcomes of the Forum had been taken into account in the preparation of the Secretary-General's report to the thirteenth session of the Commission on Sustainable Development on human settlements, and recommended that UN-Habitat be the focal point for following up and monitoring the outcomes of that session pertaining to human settlements. It invited the Executive Director to include the topic of interrelations between human settlements, energy and sustainable development in the agenda of the third World Urban Forum; prepare a report on energy consumption in human settlements, including examples of policy approaches for consideration by the Council and the Commission in 2007; inform Governments, through the Committee of Permanent Representatives, on the relevant outcomes of the thirteenth session of the Commission; and to report in 2007.

In further action, the Council [res. 20/19] approved the 2006-2007 draft integrated work programme and budget [HSP/GC/20/9], which included a general-purpose budget of $27,601,000, and a special-purpose budget of $55,148,000. It authorized the Executive Director to adjust the level of allocations for programme activities with the actual level of income, and to re-allocate general-purpose resources between subprogrammes up to a maximum 25 per cent of that budget. It requested the Executive Director to develop a resource-mobilization strategy for presentation to the Governing Council in 2007, including options for broadening the donor base and encouraging non-earmarked contributions. She was further requested to report periodically on the work programme.

The Council had before it a report of the Executive Director [HSP/GC/20/13] relating to the themes for the twenty-first (2007) and other future sessions of the Governing Council. The Council endorsed the recommendations of the Committee of Permanent Representatives on improving preparations for its sessions, and decided that its special themes would no longer be chosen two years in advance but by its Bureau at least six months before the start of each session, on the advice of the Executive Director, and in consultation with the Committee of Permanent Representatives. The Council requested the Committee of Permanent Representatives, in 2007, to recommend further proposals for improving the Committee's structure and organizational arrangements, and the Executive Director to prepare a background paper on the subject for use by the Committee [res. 20/21].

Among other documents, the Governing Council also considered a joint progress report of the Executive Directors of UN-Habitat and UNEP on their respective activities [YUN 2004, p. 1073]; a report on the work of the Committee of Permanent Representatives during the intersessional period [ibid., p. 1072]; and reports on implementing [HSP/GC/20/6] and monitoring the implementation of the MDG on improving the lives of slum dwellers [HSP/GC/20/6/Add.1].

Resolutions were also adopted on access to basic services for all within the context of sustainable human settlements [res. 20/5], regional and technical cooperation [res. 20/15] and gender equality in human settlements development [res. 20/7] (see below).

UN-Habitat activities

In 2005, UN-Habitat responded to the humanitarian challenges posed by the December 2004 Indian Ocean tsunami [YUN 2004, p. 953] and the earthquake in Pakistan on 8 October (see p. 1034). UN-Habitat was involved in rebuilding activities in Pakistan, Indonesia, Maldives, Sri Lanka and Thailand that were affected by the tsunami. UN-Habitat programmes in post-conflict areas, such as Afghanistan, Iraq, Kosovo (Serbia and Montenegro) and Somalia, remained active during the year, while new ground was broken for the Special Human Settlements Programme for the Palestinian People. In June, the Security Council appointed UN-Habitat's Executive Director, Anna Tibaijuka, as Special Envoy of the Secretary-General on Human Settlements in Zimbabwe. The Special Envoy visited that country (26 June–8 July) to assess reports of some 700,000 evictions of poor people by the Government (see p. 371). Following the submission of the mission's report, UN-Habitat reached an agreement with the Government to explore more equitable housing and land tenure solutions.

UN-Habitat accelerated implementation of its Water and Sanitation Slum Upgrading initiatives, with the aim of strengthening the UN-Habitat and Human Settlements Foundation and expanding working arrangements and partnerships with international and domestic financial institutions, the private sector, local government and the urban poor. During the year, UN-Habitat proposed innovative financial and institutional packages to help meet the slum upgrading and water and sanitation targets of the Millennium Declaration [YUN 2000, p. 49]. At the invitation of the United Kingdom, UN-Habitat participated in the work of the Commission for Africa [YUN 2004, p. 993] and continued its involvement in the annual meetings of Ministers of Housing and Urbanism of the Latin American and Caribbean Countries.

UN-Habitat's Global Campaign for Urban Governance and its Global Campaign for Secure Tenure continued to assist in implementing national Campaign activities. The Programme expanded its collaboration with the five UN regional commissions, with a view to expanding both Campaigns at the regional level. Within the framework of the Campaigns, UN-Habitat collaborated with partners, including advocacy groups, regional networks, UNDP, WHO, UNICEF and the World Bank to mainstream the Campaigns' objectives and more effectively synchronize UN-Habitat activities in the field. Collaboration with partners were initiated in producing toolkits, conducting capacity-building workshops and facilitating stakeholder consultations. The two Campaigns were also involved in a research project on transnational migration.

The Programme's operational activities focused on supporting Governments in formulating policies and strategies to create a self-reliant management capacity. As at 31 December, UN-Habitat was operating 95 technical programmes and projects in 60 countries around the world, with the majority in the least developed countries. The Programme's Monitoring and Research Division published the *Global Report on Human Settlements–Financing Urban Shelter*, as well as four issues of its magazine, *Habitat Debate*.

In October, the Secretary-General appointed Inga Bjork-Klevby (Sweden) as Assistant-Secretary-General and Deputy Executive Director of UN-Habitat.

Access to basic services

On 8 April [res. 20/5], the Governing Council, taking note of proposals made to the twelfth session of the Commission on Sustainable Development [YUN 2004, p. 831] to develop a set of codes and recommendations on partnerships and on the role of various actors regarding access to basic services for all, reaffirmed the importance of developing partnerships between central and local governments, the private sector, civil society and populations themselves, with a view to increasing national and local financial resources and capabilities for improving access to those services. The Executive Director, in cooperation with other relevant UN bodies, was asked to compile best practices on policies, norms and institutional capacities related to the delivery of basic services within the context of sustainable human settlements, focusing on the respective roles and responsibilities of national Governments, local authorities and other Habitat Agenda partners, and to identify underlying principles which could be drawn from them for discussion by the Committee of Permanent Representatives. She was requested also to invite relevant UN bodies, Governments and interested stakeholders to comment on her report on the issue, which should be taken into account in finalizing options on the way forward, including recommendations on guiding principles on the delivery of and access to basic services for all, for submission to the Council in 2007.

Regional and technical cooperation

The Governing Council, on 8 April [res. 20/15], acknowledged that Habitat Programme Manag-

ers reported to regional offices, while contributing to all normative, advocacy and monitoring activities of UN-Habitat, and to the UN resident coordinator on a regular basis. It stressed that all UN-Habitat activities at the national level, including the work of Habitat Programme Managers, should be aligned with host-country national development strategies and plans and that normative operational activities should respond to national challenges. The Council agreed that the work of Programme Managers would focus on promoting the integration of sustainable urbanization into UN development assistance frameworks and national development strategies and plans, as well as the global and normative mandate, programmes and campaigns of UN-Habitat; and support UN-Habitat operational activities at the national and local levels.

The Council requested the Executive Director to comply, in the deployment of Habitat Programme Managers, with the budgetary allocation from the Foundation's general-purpose contributions envisaged for that purpose in the 2006-2007 work programme and budget and to continue to deploy Programme Managers as other sources of funding were secured. She was further requested to undertake an independent strategic evaluation of the performance and impact of Habitat Programme Managers before the end of 2006, for submission to the Council in 2007, and to include the issue of their further deployment as part of the medium-term strategic and institutional plan, to be developed for the Council's 2007 session. Governments that were in a position to do so were invited to support the financial viability of the Habitat Programme Manager network, ideally through multi-year contributions, as well as UN-Habitat regional offices.

Role of women

On 8 April [res. 20/7], the Governing Council took note of the Executive Director's report [HS/GC/20/2] on progress made in the implementation of its 2003 resolution on women's roles and rights in human settlements and slum upgrading [YUN 2003, p. 1083]. Concerned by the persistence of discriminatory practices that limited women's participation in decision-making and prevented their ownership of land, the Council requested Governments and local authorities to involve women in decision-making at all levels of government and to encourage their participation in human settlements development planning, and to strengthen gender mainstreaming in local governance. Governments and local authorities should address violence and causes of violence against women in human settlements and develop partnerships with relevant organizations. Governments were urged to recognize and address, in a non-discriminatory way, the special needs, vulnerabilities, priorities and capacities of women in post-conflict and disaster situations, and review or revise discriminatory policies, laws and other practices, especially with regard to women's property rights.

The Executive Director was asked to ensure that all normative and operational activities of UN-Habitat addressed gender equality and women's empowerment in human settlements development by incorporating gender impact assessment and gender disaggregated data criteria in the design, implementation, monitoring and evaluation of their activities. In cooperation with Habitat Agenda partners, she should prepare information material and disseminate best practices on gender mainstreaming and women's empowerment in human settlements development at the local, municipal and national levels and report in 2007 on the implementation of the Council's resolution.

OIOS review

In an April note [E/AC.51/2005/3], the Secretary-General transmitted a report of the Office of Internal Oversight Services (OIOS) on the in-depth evaluation of UN-Habitat. The report, prepared in response to General Assembly resolution 59/272 [YUN 2004, p. 1370], reviewed the achievements and shortcomings of the Programme, considering such aspects as the advocacy of its norms, monitoring and research functions, operational activities, funding approaches, and executive direction and cross-cutting issues. With regard to its global campaigns, OIOS agreed that the Global Campaign on Urban Governance and the Global Campaign for Secure Tenure had raised awareness of the norms of good urban governance and secure tenure and led to changes at the policy and institutional levels in the countries in which the campaigns were launched. However, both Campaigns lacked clear strategies and plans and faced financial constraints. There were gaps in the Programme's research agenda and there was a need to establish clearer priorities and provide guidance to the network of academic and research institutions assisting UN-Habitat in its analytical work. OIOS also found that, despite some capacity, security and time frame constraints, clients were satisfied with the products of UN-Habitat's regional and technical cooperation projects, which had contributed to introduc-

ing new norms and policies at the national and local levels. The appointment of UN-Habitat Programme Managers (see p. 1171) had the potential to enhance the Programme's capacity to achieve its development goals and to help integrate shelter and urban poverty issues into UN development assistance frameworks.

With regard to financing, despite the fourfold increase in bilateral extrabudgetary contributions and the efforts to develop innovative approaches to financing, OIOS was concerned over the substantial proportion of bilateral governmental contributions and the reliance on a small number of donors. The new subprogramme on human settlement financing lacked clarity with respect to responsibility for coordinating and raising funds for the various programmes and activities. Other concerns included the continued absence of a full-time Deputy Executive Director and problems of capacity and funding of UN-Habitat's monitoring and evaluation functions. Recommendations were made to: further sharpen the focus of the Programme; improve the planning, management and funding of campaigns; mainstream housing rights; consolidate flagship reports; eliminate gaps in research; enhance the integration of the Best Practices and Local Leadership Programme into the UN-Habitat work programme; conduct an independent strategic evaluation of the role and effectiveness of UN-Habitat Programme Managers early in 2007; ensure the early involvement of human settlements experts in post-conflict and disaster assessment and reconstruction; improve the coordination of fund-raising activities; strengthen secretariat support to member States; and strengthen the capacity of the Evaluation and Monitoring Unit in its analytical work.

CPC action. On 10 and 13 June, the Committee for Programme and Coordination (CPC) [A/60/16 & Corr.1] considered the OIOS report. It urged UN-Habitat to continue to support the work of regional bodies, in particular the African Ministerial Conference on Housing and Urban Development (see p. 1165). It recommended that the General Assembly endorse the report's recommendations (see above), except those relating to the mainstreaming of housing rights and the consolidation of flagship reports; that the OIOS recommended deadline for an independent strategic evaluation of the role of the UN-Habitat Programme Managers be changed from before 2007 to the end of 2006; and that UN-Habitat Financial Rules and Regulations be adopted no later than the end of 2005.

Chapter VIII

Population

In 2005, the world's population reached 6.5 billion, as compared with 6.4 billion in 2004. Growing at the rate of about 1.2 per cent annually, world population was projected to reach the 7 billion mark in 2012, and long-range projections suggested that it could ultimately stabilize at about 9 billion people.

United Nations population activities continued to be guided, in 2005, by the Programme of Action adopted at the 1994 International Conference on Population and Development (ICPD) and the key actions for its further implementation adopted at the twenty-first special session of the General Assembly in 1999. The Commission on Population and Development, the body responsible for monitoring, reviewing and assessing the implementation of the Programme of Action, considered as its special theme "Population, development and HIV/AIDS, with particular emphasis on poverty". It also discussed how the implementation of the Programme of Action contributed to the achievement of internationally agreed development goals, including the Millennium Development Goals (MDGs); financial resources for implementing the Programme of Action; world population monitoring; world demographic trends; and the activities of the UN Population Division. The Population Division continued to analyse and report on world demographic trends and policies and to make its findings available in publications and on the Internet.

The United Nations Population Fund (UNFPA) continued, in 2005, to assist countries in implementing the ICPD agenda and the MDGs. It participated in the preparatory process leading to the 2005 World Summit review of progress made towards achieving the objectives and targets of the Millennium Declaration. In the World Summit Outcome, adopted by the General Assembly in September, world leaders reaffirmed the ICPD goal of achieving universal access to reproductive health as critical to the realization of the MDGs, and committed themselves to achieving universal access to reproductive health by 2015 and integrating that goal in strategies to attain the internationally agreed development goals aimed at reducing maternal mortality, improving maternal health, reducing child mortality, promoting gender equality, combating HIV/AIDS and eradicating poverty.

The United Nations made preparations, in 2005, for convening a High-level Dialogue on International Migration and Development. In December, the General Assembly decided that the High-level Dialogue would be held in New York on 14 and 15 September 2005 and would discuss the overall theme of the multidimensional aspects of international migration and development, in order to identify appropriate ways to maximize its development benefits and minimize its negative impacts. The Assembly also decided on the format of the session and the themes of four interactive round tables, as well as on related arrangements.

Follow-up to 1994 Conference on Population and Development

Implementation of the Programme of Action

Commission on Population and Development action. In follow-up to the recommendations of the 1994 International Conference on Population and Development (ICPD) [YUN 1994, p. 955], the Commission on Population and Development, at its thirty-eighth session (New York, 4-8 and 14 April) [E/2005/25], considered as its special theme "Population, development and HIV/AIDS, with particular emphasis on poverty", and discussed the flow of financial resources for assisting in the implementation of the Programme of Action. The Commission also considered the contribution of the implementation of the ICPD Programme of Action to the achievement of the internationally agreed development goals, including the United Nations Millennium Development Goals (MDGs) [YUN 2000, p. 51].

Population, development and HIV/AIDS

The special theme for the Commission's 2005 session was "Population, development and HIV/AIDS, with particular emphasis on poverty". For the Commission's discussion, the Secretary-General submitted a report [E/CN.9/2005/3] on world population monitoring, focusing on the theme of the session. The report provided an overview of population, HIV/AIDS and poverty, and examined the determinants of HIV/AIDS; mortality, population growth and orphanhood; fertility and sexual behaviour; geographical mobility; HIV/AIDS development and poverty; government views and policies; and prevention, treatment and care.

The report found that the HIV/AIDS pandemic had expanded rapidly since 1980 and had afflicted all regions of the world, both the rich and the poor. The hardest-hit countries were, however, among the poorest in the world, with a prevalence rate nine times higher than in the more developed regions.

Prevention was the central pillar of action against HIV/AIDS, the report concluded, and awareness of the behaviours that increased the risk of contracting HIV and resultant behavioural change were the key to prevention. When prevention actions failed, the next line of action was treatment with antiretroviral drugs to mitigate its effects and prolong life. Yet only about 1 in 10 of those needing treatment had access to antiretroviral therapy. During 2004, about 3 million people died of AIDS and 39 million people worldwide were infected with the disease. Households and families bore the burden of HIV/AIDS since they had to cope with the disease and its consequences. By placing heavy economic and social burden on families and households and eroding inter-generational support systems, AIDS increased poverty. In addition, it strained resources of the health and education sectors in poorer countries. Africa was the most affected, but steep increases in HIV infections had been recently observed in some countries in Asia and Eastern Europe. HIV prevalence in the Caribbean was the second highest in the world; and in some of the more developed countries, prevention efforts were not keeping pace with the growth of the epidemic. Most Governments reported having implemented HIV/AIDS prevention programmes, yet in many countries those most in need lacked access to basic prevention services.

The international community had recognized the terrible consequences of the epidemic and was taking steps to respond. However, unless more vigorous actions were undertaken to combat the disease and its effects, the HIV/AIDS epidemic portended a grim future for many countries, especially the poorer ones. There were, however, hopeful signs of improved HIV/AIDS awareness, of greater political commitment and of increased financial resources, particularly from the Global Fund to fight AIDS, Tuberculosis and Malaria, which by mid-2004 had approved over 300 grants in 128 countries totalling $3 bil-

lion. Nevertheless, financing for AIDS response was far short of the amount needed.

The Commission also considered the Secretary-General's report [E/CN.9/2005/4] on the monitoring of population programmes, focusing on population, development and HIV/AIDS, with particular emphasis on poverty. The report also discussed progress towards implementation of the ICPD Programme of Action, especially as it related to HIV/AIDS population and reproductive health, the five-year review of its implementation, the 2001 Declaration of Commitment HIV/AIDS, adopted at the twenty-sixth session of the General Assembly by resolution S-26/2 [YUN 2001, p. 1126], and the MDGs. It highlighted the effects of HIV/AIDS on population dynamics, including population losses, decreasing life expectancy, slower economic growth and greater extreme poverty.

The Secretary-General concluded that, since 1994 when the ICPD Programme of Action was adopted, the impact of HIV/AIDS in many countries had been devastating. While there had been some progress to increase access to antiretroviral treatment for those infected, much more needed to be done. Committed leadership, multisectoral approaches, partnerships, coordination and scaled-up efforts were all essential elements of an effective response. It was crucial also that prevention efforts be intensified, with strategies that addressed the wider issues of equality and social justice. Access to sexual and reproductive health information and services were essential for HIV prevention programmes. The Secretary-General encouraged countries to recognize and stress the linkages between reproductive health and HIV/AIDS in the various UN forums. AIDS had to be treated as both an emergency and a long-term development issue, and addressed through a wide array of efforts.

By a 14 April resolution [E/2005/25 (res. 2005/1)], which it brought to the attention of the Economic and Social Council, the Commission reaffirmed the ICPD Programme of Action, as well as the goals, targets and actions set forth in the Declaration of Commitment on HIV/AIDS; ICPD + 5 and internationally agreed development goals, including the MDGs; underscored the importance of actions by Governments and the international community to respond to the HIV/AIDS epidemic and reaffirmed the need for Governments to intensify national efforts and international cooperation in implementing the Declaration of Commitment on HIV/AIDS. Stressing that HIV/AIDS was contributing to the intensification of poverty in many countries, the Commission urged the international community to complement and supplement, through increased international development assistance, the efforts of developing countries that were committing increased national funds to fighting HIV/AIDS, particularly in Africa and the Caribbean. It also stressed the need for an integrated approach in national responses to the HIV/AIDS epidemic that would include an action framework to facilitate the coordination of work by all partners—one national HIV/AIDS framework, one national HIV coordinating body and one agreed country-level monitoring and evaluation system—the "Three Ones" strategy [YUN 2004, p. 1219] for the coordination of resources. The resolution also called for specified actions by Government, relevant United Nations and other international organizations and the international community to respond to the global HIV/AIDS epidemic.

Financial resources

In accordance with General Assembly resolution 50/124 [YUN 1995, p. 1094], the Secretary-General submitted to the Commission a January report [E/CN.9/2005/5] on the flow of financial resources for assisting in the implementation of the ICPD Programme of Action. It examined the flow of funds from donor countries and domestic expenditures for population activities in developing countries for 2003, as well as estimates for 2004 and projections for 2005. Although the financial targets of the Programme of Action for 2000 ($17 billion for reproductive health programme) were not met, it was encouraging that both international donor assistance and domestic expenditures for population activities had increased since then. Donor assistance was estimated at $4.2 billion in 2003, up from $3.2 billion in 2002, and domestic expenditures were estimated at almost $11 billion, up from 2000-2002 levels, for a total global estimate of just over $15 billion in 2003. To reach the 2005 target of $18.5 billion, the international community would have to increase levels of assistance and developing countries mobilize additional domestic resources. Estimates for 2004 and projections for 2005 were encouraging. Donor assistance was estimated to have increased to $4.5 billion in 2004 and was projected to increase to almost $6.4 billion in 2005. Resources mobilized by developing countries were estimated to reach $12.5 billion for 2004 and $12.7 billion in 2005. While the largest share of funding was currently going to AIDS-related activities, the increased resources were still not adequately addressing the growing AIDS pandemic.

The largest share of funding went to AIDS-related activities but funding for family planning and reproductive health, which had been lagging behind, needed to increase proportion-ately with current needs. The challenge for the international community was remaining on track to reach the 2005 target. Without a firm commitment to population, reproductive health and gender issues, and adequate allocation of financial resources in all areas, it was unlikely that any of the goals and targets of ICPD and the Millennium Summit [YUN 2000, p. 48] would be reached.

Implementing ICPD Programme of Action to achive development goals

In response to decision 2004/1 of the Commission on Population and Development [YUN 2004, p. 1086], the Secretary-General submitted a January report [E/CN.9/2005/6] on the contribution of the implementation of the ICPD Programme of Action, in all its aspects, to the achievement of the internationally agreed development goals, including those contained in the United Nations Millennium Declaration [YUN 2000, p. 49]. The report concluded that full implementation of the Programme of Action and related actions would contribute significantly to the achievement of universally agreed development goals. It would help accelerate the transition to low fertility in those developing countries with high fertility rates, and thus slow population growth, thereby improving the ability of those countries to adjust to future population increases, combat poverty, protect and repair the environment, and set the conditions for sustainable development. The reduction of fertility would result in a "demographic bonus", whereby the proportion of the population of working age would increase relative to that of children and the elderly—a change that could contribute significantly to economic growth and poverty reduction. Its fulfilment would also ensure the achievement of equivalent goals in the Millennium Declaration, in particular the reduction of child and maternal mortality, universal access to primary education, parity in access to secondary and higher education between boys and girls, reductions in the spread of HIV, and the achievement of gender equality and women's empowerment. Its implementation would also contribute to international objectives concerning urbanization, ageing and vulnerable groups. However, implementation depended on building a partnership for global development where all actors, including Governments, multilateral and donor agencies, civil society and the private sector, cooperated to realize its goals and objectives.

By a 14 April resolution [E/2005/25 (res. 2005/2)], which it brought to the attention of the Economic and Social Council, the Commission emphasized the importance of integrating the goal of universal access to reproductive health by 2015 into strategies to attain the development goals; the need to strengthen policy and programme linkages and coordination between HIV/AIDS and sexual and reproductive health and their inclusion in national development plans; and the importance of paying closer attention to the interrelations between population structure and trends, including population ageing, and poverty and development. It urged Member States and the UN system to strengthen international cooperation in international migration and development. The Commission welcomed the increase in domestic expenditures and international donor assistance for achieving ICPD goals, encouraged Governments, international organizations and financial institutions, and other relevant stakeholders to assist developing countries and countries with economies in transition in implementing the Programme of Action through technical assistance and capacity-building activities; and called for the provision of adequate resources to all areas of the Programme of Action.

International migration and development

In response to General Assembly resolution 59/241 [YUN 2004, p. 1077], the Secretary-General submitted an August report [A/60/205] on the organizational details of a high-level dialogue on international migration and development, to be held during the Assembly's sixty-first (2006) session. By resolution 58/208 [YUN 2003, p. 1087], the Assembly had decided to convene the high-level dialogue to discuss the multidimensional aspects of international migration and development, in order to identify appropriate ways to maximize its development benefits and minimize its negative impacts. The Secretary-General suggested that the high-level dialogue be held on 14 and 15 September 2006; that Member States be encouraged to participate at the ministerial level and other stakeholders at the highest possible level. He also suggested topics for five round tables. Annexed to the report was a proposed programme for the event.

GENERAL ASSEMBLY ACTION

On 23 December [meeting 69], the General Assembly, on the recommendation of the Second (Economic and Financial) Committee [A/60/490/ Add.3], adopted **resolution 60/227** without vote [agenda item 54 (c)].

International migration and development

The General Assembly,

Recalling its resolution 58/208 of 23 December 2003 and 59/241 of 22 December 2004,

Recalling also its resolution 57/270 B of 23 June 2003 on the integrated and coordinated implementation of

and follow-up to the outcomes of the major Untied Nations conferences and summits in the economic and social fields,

Recalling further the 2005 World Summit Outcome,

Taking note of the report of the Secretary-General,

1. *Decides* that the High-level Dialogue on International Migration and Development will be held in New York on 14 and 15 September 2006, and also decides that the High-level Dialogue will discuss the overall theme of the multidimensional aspects of international migration and development in order to identify appropriate ways and means to maximize its development benefits and minimize its negative impacts;

2. *Invites* Member States to participate in the High-level Dialogue at the ministerial level or highest level possible;

3. *Decides* that the Holy See, in its capacity as Observer State, and Palestine, in its capacity as observer, shall participate in the High-level Dialogue;

4. *Invites* those intergovernmental organizations and entities that have observer status with the General Assembly to participate in the High-level Dialogue;

5. *Invites* relevant United Nations agencies, funds and programmes, as well as the International Organization for Migration, to contribute to the preparation of, and participate in, the High-level Dialogue;

6. *Decides* that the participants in the High-level Dialogue will participate in accordance with the rules of procedure of the General Assembly;

7. *Also decides* that the High-level Dialogue will consist of four plenary meetings and four interactive round tables, within existing resources;

8. *Further decides* that the President of the General Assembly, the President of the Economic and Social Council and the Secretary-General will make introductory statements at the opening of the High-level Dialogue;

9. *Decides* that the round tables will be open to all Member States, the Holy See, in its capacity as Observer State, and Palestine, in its capacity as observer, and representatives of relevant entities of the United Nations system, including its relevant special rapporteurs, and the International Organization for Migration, as well as to other relevant regional and international intergovernmental organizations that have observer status, and also decides that the round tables will be organized as follows:

(a) The first set of two interactive round tables will be held concurrently in the afternoon of the first day of the High-level Dialogue;

(b) The second set of two interactive round tables will be held concurrently in the morning of the second day of the High-level Dialogue;

(c) Summaries of the deliberations of the four round-table sessions will be presented orally by the chairpersons of the round-table sessions during the concluding plenary meeting of the High-level Dialogue;

10. *Also decides* that the themes for each of the four round tables will be the following:

(a) Round table 1 will focus on the effects of international migration on economic and social development;

(b) Round table 2 will focus on measures to ensure respect for and protection of the human rights of all migrants, and to prevent and combat smuggling of migrants and trafficking in persons;

(c) Round table 3 will focus on the multidimensional aspects of international migration and development, including remittances;

(d) Round table 4 will focus on promoting the building of partnerships and capacity-building and the sharing of best practices at all levels, including the bilateral and regional levels, for the benefit of countries and migrants alike;

11. *Further decides* to hold, within existing resources, one-day informal interactive hearings in 2006 with representatives of non-governmental organizations, civil society organizations and the private sector, to be presided over by the President of the General Assembly, and requests the President of the Assembly to prepare a summary of the hearings prior to the High-level Dialogue in September 2006;

12. *Decides* that the President of the General Assembly will determine the list of invited participants and the exact format and organization of the hearings, in consultation with Member States and representatives of non-governmental organizations in consultative status with the Economic and Social Council, civil society organizations and the private sector;

13. *Also decides* that representatives of non-governmental organizations in consultative status with the Economic and Social Council, civil society organizations and the private sector, one from each grouping being selected during the informal interactive hearings, may also participate in each of the round tables of the High-level Dialogue, and that the President of the General Assembly will determine the list of such representatives, taking into account the principle of equitable geographical representation, in consultation with Member States;

14. *Further decides* that arrangements concerning the participation of non-governmental organizations, civil society and the private sector in the High-level Dialogue will in no way create a precedent for other meetings of the General Assembly;

15. *Requests* the Secretary-general, within existing resouces, to prepare a comprehensive overview of studies and analyses on the multidimensional aspects of migration and development, including the effects of migration on economic and social development in developed and developing countries, and on the effects of the movements of highly skilled migrants workers and those with advanced education;

16. *Invites* the Secretary-General to address also in his comprehensive overview in consultation with relevant United Nations organizations, short-term and seasonal workers within the issue of labour movements;

17. *Invites* the regional commissions to contribute to and coordinate dialogue at the regional level in preparation for the High-level Dialogue;

18. *Invites* the President of the General Assembly, within existing resources, in consultation with Member States, and with the assistance of the Secretariat, to organize prior to the High-level Dialogue up to two panel discussions with a focus on its overall theme;

19. *Notes* that the Commission on Population and Development, the Commission for Social Development and the Commission on the Status of Women will have considered the issue of international migration

within their respective mandates by the time of the High-level Dialogue, and invites their inputs through the Economic and Social Council;

20. *Also notes* that the Committee on the Protection of the Rights of All Migrant Workers and Members of Their Families will have considered the issue of protecting the rights of all migrant workers as a tool to enhance development, within its mandate, by the time of the High-level Dialogue, and invites the Secretary-General to make available for the High-level Dialogue the summary of the discussion in the Committee;

21. *Invites* appropriate regional consultative processes and other major initiatives undertaken by Member States in the field of international migration to contribute to the High-level Dialogue;

22. *Takes note* of the report of the Global Commission on International Migration, and notes its contribution to the debate on international migration and development, and also takes note of the report as an input for consideration at the High-level Dialogue;

23. *Reiterates* that the outcome of the High-level Dialogue will be a Chairperson's summary, which will be widely distributed to Member States, observers, United Nations agencies and other appropriate organizations;

24. *Requests* the Secretary-General to prepare a note on the organization of work of the High-level Dialogue;

25. *Recalls* its request to the Secretary-General to submit a report to the General Assembly at its sixty-first session on the implementation of resolution 59/241;

26. *Decides* to include in the provisional agenda of its sixty-first session the sub-item entitled "International migration and development".

Transfer costs of migrant remittances

On 22 December, the General Assembly, on the recommendation of the Second Committee [A/60/490/Add.3], adopted **resolution 60/206** without vote [agenda item 54 (c)].

Facilitation and reduction of the cost of transfer of migrant remittances

The General Assembly,

Recalling its resolutions 58/208 of 23 December 2003 and 59/241 of 22 December 2004,

Acknowledging the important nexus between international migration and development and the need to deal with the challenges and opportunities that migration presents to countries of origin, destination and transit, and recognizing that migration brings benefits as well as challenges to the global community,

Recognizing that remittance flows constitute sources of private capital and that remittances have increased over time, complement domestic savings and are instrumental in improving the well-being of recipients,

Recognizing also that remittance flows constitute one of the important aspects of international migration and that they particularly benefit the households of migrants and could impact the economies of recipient countries,

Recognizing further that there is a need to address and to promote conditions for cheaper, faster and safer transfers of remittances in both source and recipient countries, and the need to facilitate the potential of their productive use in recipient countries by beneficiaries that are willing and able to do so,

Noting that, despite some recent initiatives to facilitate and to reduce the costs of remittance transfers, the costs incurred by migrants remain high and could be reduced,

Noting also the fact that many migrants without access to regular financial services may resort to informal means of transferring remittances,

1. *Reaffirms* the importance of reducing the transfer costs of migrant remittances, facilitating their flow and, as appropriate, encouraging opportunities for development-oriented investment in recipient countries by beneficiaries that are willing and able to do so;

2. *Encourages* Governments and other relevant stakeholders to consider adopting measures, in accordance with national legislation, that facilitate migrant remittance flows to recipient countries, including through, inter alia:

(a) Simplifying procedures and facilitating access to formal means of remittance transfers;

(b) Promoting access to, and awareness of the availability and use of, financial services for migrants;

3. *Invites* development partners and relevant international organizations to support developing countries in their capacity-building efforts to facilitate the flows of migrant remittances;

4. *Looks forward* to the High-level Dialogue of the General Assembly on International Migration and Development to be held in 2006, which will offer an opportunity to discuss the multidimensional aspects of international migration and development in order to identify appropriate ways and means to maximize its development benefits and minimize its negative impacts;

5. *Invites* interested countries to voluntarily convey to the Secretary-General information on their practices, initiatives and proposals in regard to the facilitation and the reduction of the cost of migrant remittances, in the context of the preparation of the Secretary-General's comprehensive overview for the High-level Dialogue.

UN Population Fund

2005 activities

In accordance with a 2003 request by the Executive Board of United Nations Development Programme/United Nations Population Fund (UNDP/UNFPA) [YUN 2003, p. 1090] and its decision 2004/20 [YUN 2004, p. 1083] the UNFPA Executive Director submitted her report covering 2005 [DP/FPA/2006/2 (Part I & Add.1, Part II)], which discussed highlights and issues pertaining to organizational effectiveness. It also discussed the Fund's response to the new development aid environment, including follow-up to the 2005 World Summit (see p. 47), UN reform, and policy dialogue and national development frameworks.

It presented programme highlights from the Fund's three priority areas of work as defined in the multi-year funding framework (MYFF), namely, reproductive health, population and development, and gender (see below); and delineated UNFPA's efforts on investing in organizational effectiveness, including the emphasis on results-based programming and accountability.

The year 2005 was a banner one for UNFPA in terms of financial and political support, the Executive Director stated. The crowning achievement came at the 2005 World Summit, when Heads of State and Government reaffirmed the ICPD goal of achieving universal access to reproductive health as critical to the realization of the MDGs. In the 2005 World Summit Outcome (see p. 48), world leaders committed themselves to achieving universal access to reproductive health by 2015, and to integrating that ICPD goal into national development strategies. UNFPA's top priority for 2006 would be follow-up to the World Summit to ensure that population dynamics, reproductive health and gender equality were incorporated into national development strategies, policies and budgets.

Throughout 2005, UNFPA assisted countries in implementing the ICPD agenda and the MDGs. It worked within UN country teams to ensure that universal access to reproductive health by 2015 was integrated into national strategies and in monitoring at country and regional levels. In order to efficiently deliver assistance to countries in the MYFF priority areas of reproductive health, population and development, and gender, UNFPA strengthened its organizational effectiveness at all levels by advancing results-based management and aligning organizational processes, systems, structures and culture with its strategic direction. In response to the new aid environment, UNFPA focused attention on better equipping its country offices to effectively engage in national MDG situation analyses and strategy formulation. Towards that end, it developed an electronic package of support, which included software for costing reproduction services, guidance for engaging in poverty reduction strategies and a checklist for linking sexual and reproductive health and HIV/AIDS. It was also exploring regionalization options to enhance its ability to deliver high quality programming at the country level and strengthen its presence at the regional level, which would allow it to pursue simplification and harmonization through co-location and common services.

Regular income for UNFPA totalled $365.8 million in 2005, an increase of 11.6 per cent over 2004 income of $327.7 million. Contributions to other resources totalled $193.7 million, some 13 per cent over 2004. UNFPA expanded its donor base to 172 from 166 in 2004, and that number included all countries in sub-Saharan Africa. By programme area, the largest share of resources, 61.5 per cent, went to reproductive health activities; 21.3 percent to population and development strategies; 12 per cent to programme coordination and assistance; and 5.2 per cent to gender equality and women's empowerment. The highest priority for allocation of assistance, 67.5 per cent, was for Group A countries, which included all the least developed countries. By region, sub-Saharan Africa accounted for 33.3 per cent of programme assistance; Asia and the Pacific, 32.2 per cent; the Arab States and Europe, 12.1 per cent; and Latin America and the Caribbean, 9.1 per cent; and intercountry and interregional activities, 13.2 per cent.

The Executive Director reported jointly with UNDP [DP/FPA/2006/2 (Part II)] on the recommendations of the Joint Inspection Unit (JIU) in 2005. The report provided a synopsis of UNDP/UNFPA management responses to key JIU recommendations that were relevant to them. Of the nine reports issued by the JIU in 2005, four had cross-agency impact, with recommendations on how to improve country office performance; for a common payroll for UN system organizations; for the use of open-source software for development; and measures to strengthen UN system support for the New Partnership for Africa's Development (NEPAD) (see p. 1003).

On 28 January [E/2005/35 (dec. 2005/9)], the UNDP/UNFPA Executive Board took note of the report of the UNFPA Executive Director to the Economic and Social Council [E/2005/5-DP/FPA/2005/2], which addressed the implementation of the Secretary-General's reform programme, the provisions of the triennial comprehensive policy review and follow-up to the international conferences and the MDGs. It requested UNFPA to maintain a sharp focus in following up on the Triennial Comprehensive Policy Review contained in General Assembly resolution 59/250; and encouraged it to participate in the preparatory process leading to the 2005 review of the progress made towards achieving the objectives and targets contained in the 2000 Millennium Declaration and the MDGs.

On 23 June [ibid., (dec. 2005/25)], the Executive Board noted the report of the Executive Director for 2004 [YUN 2004, p. 1079] and emphasized the need to forge innovative partnerships among development partners, Governments, civil society and the private sector to achieve the ICPD goals and the MDGs. The Board recognized the progress being made to improve UNFPA's organizational effectiveness and encouraged it to continue to develop its managing-for-results framework

and to present a cumulative progress report in 2007.

By **decision 2005/230** of 20 July, the Economic and Social Council took note of the annual report of the UNFPA Executive Director [E/2005/5-DP/FPA/2005/2]; the report of the UNDP/UNFPA Executive Board on its work during 2004 [E/2004/35]; and the Board's report on its first regular session of 2005 [E/2005/35].

Reproductive health

In 2005, UNFPA invested 61.5 per cent of its financial resources in reproductive health, underscoring the ICPD goal of universal access to reproductive health information and services, including family planning and maternal health services. Reducing maternal mortality and morbidity remained a priority area for UNFPA, which, together with partners, supported safe motherhood interventions in some 90 countries and launched the Partnership for Maternal, Newborn and Child Health. It expanded the international initiative to mainstream emergency obstetric care. The Campaign to End Fistula grew significantly and was currently active in over 30 countries in Africa, Asia and the Arab States. Needs assessments were completed also in six new countries, and 15 countries were currently implementing strategies in prevention, treatment and rehabilitation. In the area of family planning, UNFPA focused its efforts on increasing the coverage of the population and service utilization, and collaborated with the World Health Organization (WHO) and other organizations in holding regional workshops and various activities. UNFPA and its partners were working to ensure that reproductive health, including family planning, was given high priority in national development planning for achieving the MDGs.

UNFPA provided reproductive health commodities to countries in all regions, and, with its partners, developed a global programme to enhance reproductive health commodity security. UNFPA was also working with its partners to intensify HIV prevention and strengthen HIV/AIDS and sexual and reproductive health linkages.

Population development and poverty

In monitoring progress towards the MDGs, UNFPA in 2005, focused support on data collection, analysis and use, specifically by strengthening the capacity of developing countries to monitor such progress. In collaboration with the UN Statistics Division, UNFPA increased its support to population and housing censuses, particularly the 2010 round, and was organizing regional workshops to sensitize developing countries on the importance of censuses and data collection.

Population ageing and international migration were important and emerging issues which needed to be accorded higher priority in policy dialogues and poverty reduction strategies. In 2005, UNFPA continued to provide technical guidance and financial support to train policymakers from developing countries to build national capacity to address the challenges of population ageing. In April, it convened an advisory group meeting on ageing issues in Malta. It worked closely with the UN programme on ageing, collaborated with WHO on a study of the determinants that impacted women's health and supported research into the social and economic policy implications of demographic transitions, including ageing. The Fund also supported country-level capacity development for formulating migration policy through its support for the International Migration Policy Programme review, and, together issued a publication entitled *"Meeting the Challenges of Migration: Progress Since the ICPD"*. In May, it hosted an expert group meeting on international migration and the MDGs in Marrakech, Morocco and collaborated with the United Nations Institute for Training and Research in organizing workshops on key migration issues.

Gender equality and empowerment of women

In 2005, UNFPA continued to mainstream gender concerns into all population and development programming as a primary means of achieving gender equality, equity and the empowerment of women, and supported capacity development of governments officials, NGOs and human rights institutions. It focused attention and technical and financial resources for addressing gender-based violence, particularly through the development of a regional programme for 20 countries in Africa. Under its Women, Peace and Security Initiative, UNFPA sponsored a workshop in Bucharest, Romania, in October, on reassessing institutional support for Security Council resolution 1325 (2000) [YUN 2000, p. 1113] on women, peace and security, and helped to institutionalize elements of that resolution in the armed forces and the police in 14 countries in Latin America and the Caribbean. Several initiatives were aimed at integrating gender mainstreaming and culturally sensitive and rights-based programming, and UNFPA and the United Nations Development Fund for Women were collaborating on a number of gender-related activities and studies. The involvement of men and boys was becoming a full component of the Fund's work on gender equal-

ity, with UNFPA-supported projects in Peru, Uganda and Viet Nam.

Country and intercountry programmes

UNFPA's provisional project expenditures for country and intercountry (regional and interregional) programmes in 2005 totalled $234.3 million, compared to $221.9 million in 2004, according to the Executive Director's statistical overview report [DP/FPA/2006/2 (Part I, Add.1)]. The 2005 figure included $186.7 million for country programmes and $47.6 million for intercountry activities. In accordance with the Board's procedure for allocating resources according to its categorization of countries laid down in 1996 [YUN 1996, p. 989], total expenditures in 2005 for Group A countries amounted to $126.1 million, compared to $121.1 million in 2004.

Africa. Provisional expenditures for UNFPA programmes in sub-Saharan Africa totalled $78 million in 2005, compared to $78.1 million in 2004. Most of that amount (57.1 per cent) went to reproductive health and family planning, followed by population and development strategies (22.9 per cent), programme coordination and assistance (13.9 per cent) and gender equality and women's empowerment (6.1 per cent). On 28 January [E/2005/35 (dec. 2005/14)], the UNDP/UNFPA Executive Board approved UNFPA country programmes for Angola, Burundi and Madagascar. On 23 June [dec. 2005/31], it took note of the draft country programme documents for Burkina Faso, Ghana, Namibia and Uganda; and on 9 September [dec. 2005/42], for Chad, Swaziland and Cape Verde, as well as the Cape Verde results and resources frameworks.

Arab States and Europe. Provisional expenditures for UNFPA programmes in the Arab States and Europe totalled $28.4 million, compared to $28.7 million on 2004. Most (63.1 per cent) was spent on reproductive health and family planning, followed by population and development strategies (21.5 per cent), programme coordination and assistance (10.8 per cent) and gender equality and women's empowerment (4.6 per cent). On 28 January [dec. 2005/14], the Executive Board approved UNFPA country programmes for Armenia, Azerbaijan, Kazakhstan, Kyrgyzstan, Romania, Tajikistan, Turkmenistan and Uzbekistan. On 23 June [dec. 2005/31], it took note of the draft country programme documents for Albania, Georgia, The Occupied Palestinian Territory, Turkey and Ukraine and on 9 September [dec. 2005/42], for Afghanistan.

Asia and the Pacific. Provisional expenditures for UNFPA programmes in Asia and the Pacific amounted to $75.5 million, compared to $65.9 million in 2004. Most of those expenditures (72 per cent) went to reproductive health and family planning, followed by population and development strategies (18.7 per cent), programme coordination and assistance (6.3 per cent) and gender equality and women's empowerment (3.1 per cent). On 28 January [dec. 2005/14], the Executive Board approved UNFPA country programmes for Iran and the Philippines. On 23 June [dec. 2005/31], it took note of the draft country programme documents for Bangladesh, Cambodia, China and Viet Nam, of the report on the implementation of the UNFPA special programme of assistance to Myanmar [DP/FPA/2005/11] and also of the first one-year extension of the first programme of special assistance to Myanmar [DP/FPA/2005/12]. The Board approved the two-year extension of the first country programme for Timor-Leste [DP/FPA/2005/12]; on 9 September [dec. 2005/42], it took note of the draft country programme documents for Afghanistan and Indonesia.

Latin America and the Caribbean. Provisional expenditures for UNFPA programmes in Latin America and the Caribbean totalled $21.4 million in 2005, compared to $21.1 million in 2004. As in other regions, most of the total (43.2 per cent) went to reproductive health and family planning, followed by population and development (27.4 per cent), programme coordination and assistance (15.1 per cent) and gender equality and women's empowerment (14.4 per cent). On 28 January [dec. 2005/14], the Executive Board approved a UNFPA country programme for Guatemala, and on 23 June [dec. 2005/31], took note of the draft country programme document for Peru.

Interregional programmes. Provisional expenditures for UNFPA intercountry and interregional programmes totalled $31 million in 2005 compared to $28.1 million in 2004. Most of that total (58 per cent) went to reproductive health and family planning, followed by programme coordination and assistance (20.4 per cent), population and development (19.2 per cent) and gender equality and women's empowerment (2.4 per cent).

Financial and management questions

Financing

UNFPA income from all sources totalled $565 million in 2005, compared to $502.1 million in 2004 [DP/FPA/2006/13], comprising $365.8 million from regular resources and $199.2 million from other resources. Expenditures totalled $523.3 million in 2005, up from $451.5 million in 2004, comprising $334.8 million from regular re-

sources and $188.6 million from other resources, resulting in an excess of $41.6 million.

Contributions to regular resources from donor Governments and a private contribution from the Mars Trust totalled $351.2 million in 2005, reflecting an 8.9 per cent increase over 2004. Contributions to trust funds, cost-sharing arrangements and other sources totalled $193.7 million, with interest income of $5.5 million, bringing to $199.2 million the total income from other sources.

On 8 September [E/2005/35 (dec. 2005/38)], the Executive Board took note of the annual financial review, 2004 [DP/FPA/2005/15]. It recognized the significance of increasing and achieving stability and predictability in contributions to regular resources, that timeliness in the payment of contributions was essential to maintaining liquidity and facilitating continuous programme implementation, and that more balanced burden-sharing was essential to UNFPA's long-term financial sustainability.

Estimates for 2006-2007 support budget

In a July report [DP/FPA/2005/13], the Executive Director submitted to the UNDP/UNFPA Executive Board the estimates for the 2006-2007 biennial support budget, totalling $209 million (gross) and $196.4 million (net). The estimates were based on a resource framework of $910 million for total income, consisting of $747 million in regular resources and $163 million in other resources. The regular resources projection was strong, despite the loss of funding from a major donor for the last four years. It was based on recent trends of a widening donor base and the large number of contributors from the euro area. Along with income for the biennium, there was an opening balance of over $1 billion in total resources available for programme and support activities in 2006-2007. The budget reflected a strategic investment in areas where needs were greatest: staffing in Africa and other country office locations; learning and training initiatives; staffing in strategic planning and resource mobilization; operational support for the Enterprise Resource Planning (Atlas) system; and staff costs, security and insurance.

Commenting, in August [DP/FPA/2005/14], on the estimates for the 2006-2007 biennial support budget, ACABQ noted UNFPA's commitment to implementing results-based budgeting and the steps being taken to ensure that by 2008, the Fund's MYFF document and the biennial support budget would be better integrated. ACABQ recommended that the harmonization process be given high priority, trusting that UNFPA would take into account lessons learned by other UN entities that had already implemented those techniques. Noting the increase in projected regular resource income for the 2006-2007 biennium, ACABQ encouraged UNFPA to continue to intensify its fund-raising activities, not only to maintain the level of resources but to attain further positive results. With regard to the estimated $400.6 million expenditure on programmes, ACABQ believed that there was greater potential for channelling more funds to programme activities by reducing costs on programme support and management and administration.

On 9 September [E/2005/35 (dec. 2005/37)], the Executive Board approved gross appropriations totalling $209 million ($196.4 net) for UNFPA's 2006-2007 support budget and resolved that income estimated of $12.6 million would be used to offset the gross appropriations, resulting in estimated net appropriations of $196.4 million. It authorized the Executive Director to redeploy resources between appropriation lines up to a maximum of 5 per cent; authorized extrabudgetary expenditures of $8.9 million for the Atlas project, as well as additional funding expenditures of $4.7 million to replenish the security reserve. The Board also took note of the ACABQ report [dec. 2005/42].

Revision of financial regulations and recovery of indirect costs

In January, the UNDP/UNFPA Executive Board considered reports by the Executive Director on revisions to UNFPA financial regulations, and on recovery of indirect costs for co-financing, as well as ACABQ's comments and recommendations thereon [YUN 2004, p. 1082].

On 28 January [E/2005/35 (dec. 2005/11)], the Board took note of those reports and approved the proposed revisions to the financial regulations, as amended. Regarding the financing of donor agreements, the Board requested the Executive Director to establish guidelines on standards for identifying and assessing risk factors, requirements for mitigating risk as a condition for approval and limitations on the actual disbursement of cash prior to the receipt of contributions.

On the same date [dec. 2005/12], the Board took note of the harmonized cost-recovery principles contained in the report on the recovery of indirect costs for co-financing, recognizing that their adoption by UN organizations constituted a step towards increased transparency and comparability of cost recovery throughout the UN system; and endorsed, on an interim basis, the UNFPA-specific implementation of those harmonized principles and their application in the recovery policy for indirect costs, consisting of a rate of 5 per cent on nationally executed cost-sharing ex-

penditures financed by programme countries and 7 per cent on all co-financed expenditures. It confirmed the current rate of 5 per cent for third-party procurement expenditures and the limits of indirect cost recovery by NGOS and UN agencies, as authorized by the Board in 2000 [YUN 2000, p. 1005]. The Board stressed that UNFPA should ensure full recovery of all actual costs for implementing activities financed from other (non-core) resources and requested the Executive Director to report, in 2007, on the indirect cost-recovery policy. It encouraged UNFPA to continue to refine its strategic cost-management system, including through the implementation of the Atlas system, in order to better attribute indirect costs to programmes and projects.

Audit reports

The Executive Director submitted to the UNDP/UNFPA Executive Board a report [DP/FPA/2005/1] on follow-up action by UNFPA to recommendations by the UN Board of Auditors for 2002-2003 [YUN 2004, p. 1397]. On 28 January [E/2005/35 (dec. 2005/8)], the Executive Board took note of the UNFPA report; stressed the importance of adequate follow-up to the Auditors' recommendations, particularly on improving internal management control; and requested that future reports indicate the priority of the recommendations and a time frame for their implementation.

In an April report [DP/FPA/2005/9], the Executive Director described UNFPA's internal audit and oversight activities carried out in 2004. Those included: management audits of eight offices (four in Africa, three in Latin America and the Caribbean, and one in the Arab States and Europe region); a review of 458 audit reports covering 2003 activities for projects executed by Governments and NGOS; management audits in eight country offices in the Africa region; and contracted audits in four country offices in the Asia and the Pacific region and six country offices in the Arab States and Europe region. Of the 18 reports issued in 2004, the level of internal controls and the compliance with financial, administrative and programme requirements were found to be satisfactory in four offices, partially satisfactory in 10 and deficient in four. A total of 743 recommendations were issued in 2004. UNFPA instituted several measures to strengthen its internal control systems, including the establishment of the Audit Services Branch and the posting of Operations managers in 44 country offices to enhance managerial capacity and ensure more consistent field control. It presented a framework for resolving issues contained in internal audit reports. The report also outlined the measures taken to address recommendations arising from previous audits, described the 2004 policy application review conducted by the Oversight and Evaluation Branch in the Asia and Pacific region; and summarized the 2004 activities of the Fund's organizational committees, established to improve oversight and accountability: the Oversight, Management and Programme Committees.

On 23 June [E/2005/35 (dec. 2005/19)], the Executive Board took note of the Executive Director's report and urged UNFPA to base its oversight and accountability activities on a corporate risk model and develop risk-assessment functions in its audit offices. It concurred with the need to strengthen analysis of the outcomes of audits, and requested UNFPA to provide adequate training to staff to interpret and follow up on audit findings and recommendations. UNFPA should explain the selection criteria of the country offices audited, and present an analysis of the follow-up to the 2003 and 2004 internal audit recommendations, and an in-depth review of the level of internal audit resources, as well as a management response to its internal audit reports at the Board's annual session, including the status of follow-up recommendations of previous audit reports.

Resource allocation

In response to Executive Board decision 2000/19 [YUN 2000, p. 1005], the UNFPA Executive Director submitted a quinquennial review of the system for allocating resources to country programmes [DP/FPA/2005/6]. The report provided an overview of the evolution of the Fund's resource allocation system and reviewed the experience with the current system. Proposals for updating the system included simplifying it by mainstreaming the countries with economies in transition into the country categories, harmonizing indicators with the MDGs and the 2004-2007 MYFF indicators, revising the threshold levels of indicators and simplifying the definitions of country categories. Annexed to the report were indicators used in the resource allocation system, the source data and the classification of countries resulting from the 2005 review of the resource allocation.

On 29 January [E/2005/35 (dec. 2005/13)], the Executive Board approved the approach, effective January 2005, for resource allocation, including the mainstreaming of the countries with economies in transition, synchronizing the resource allocation system cycle with the MYFF cycle, and amending the indicators and their threshold levels towards meeting the ICPD goals, ICPD+ 5 targets and the MDGs; endorsed the procedure

for categorizing countries into Groups A, B and C; requested the Executive Director to indicate in her annual reports the share of regular resources to Group A countries, LDCs and low-income countries, and recommended flexibility in the distribution of resources to individual countries, particularly to those changing categories, to ensure that the gains already made were not compromised.

Multi-year funding commitments

In May [DP/FPA/2005/8 & Corr.1], the Executive Director submitted to the UNDP/UNFPA Executive Board updated estimates of regular and other resources for 2005 and future years in the multi-year funding framework (MYFF). As at 1 April, 83 countries had submitted written pledges to UNFPA for 2005, 34 of which were multi-year pledges, five of them from major donors.

In 2004, UNFPA received regular contributions from a record 166 donor Governments. Total contributions received amounted to $331.6 million an increase of 13.4 per cent, as a result of substantially increased contributions from nine major donors and favourable exchange rates. Contributions for co-financing arrangements also increased by $41.2 million, to $131.1 milllion. Four countries (the Netherlands, Norway, Sweden and the United Kingdom) accounted for about half of UNFPA's regular resources. To achieve financial stability, UNFPA was focusing on maintaining its donor base and securing a higher level of pledges for 2005 from major donors. It was also trying to convince others that were contributing below the $1 million benchmark to become major donors. UNFPA anticipated that regular resources in 2005 would increase to $360 million or higher, with further increases expected in both 2006 and 2007. One proposal for increasing regular resources was for donor countries to increase the percentage of official development assistance allocated for population assistance. Discussions were ongoing with many major donor countries to increase their regular contributions in order to broaden the base of support to the Fund's regular resources.

On 23 June, [E/2005/35 (dec. 2005/24)], the UNDP/UNFPA Executive Board welcomed the substantial increase in 2004 regular income and co-financing income levels, the contributions made by programme countries which had enabled the Fund to reach its highest ever number of donors, and the projected increase in the 2005 regular income level. It recognized that sustaining and improving the UNFPA funding level would require countries able to do so to augment their funding efforts during MYFF 2004-2007.

Programming process

In 2005, the UNDP/UNFPA Executive Board considered the joint UNDP/UNFPA reports on experiences in joint programming [YUN 2004, p. 1084]; and on progress in implementing decision 2001/11 [YUN 2001, p. 1000] on the UNDP/UNFPA programming process, which addressed the issue of the time frame for developing country programme documents [DP/2005/28-DP/FPA/2005/10] (see p. 970). The Board took action on those reports in decisions [2005/35 (dec. 2005/10)] and [2005/35 (dec. 2005/28)].

In other action [dec. 2005/30] on UNDP/UNFPA programme performance information at the country level, the Board again took note of the joint report on progress in implementing decision 2001/11, and the Executive Director's report for 2004 on progress in implementing the MYFF, 2004-2007 [YUN 2004, p. 1083]; and requested UNDP and UNFPA, in consultation with relevant agencies, to make a proposal, at the first regular session in 2006, on cost-efficient approaches to providing programme-level data to their respective Boards as part of their programming and reporting cycles.

Technical Advisory Programme

In response to a 2004 Executive Board request [YUN 2004, p. 1084], the Executive Director submitted, in July [DP/FPA/2005/16], a review of the UNFPA Technical Advisory Programme against strategic goals contained in the MYFF 2004-2007. The Advisory Programme, an inter-agency arrangement for providing UNFPA assistance to countries for population and development activities, constituted the Fund's strategy for increasing the efficiency, effectiveness and impact of its technical support in reproductive health, population and development, and gender empowerment, and was composed of nine multi-disciplinary Country Technical Services Teams (CSTS).

The report described the main findings of an independent evaluation of the Programme, which revealed that it was beneficial to the effective implementation of the ICPD. The Programme provided UNFPA with a coherent system for delivering technical support to countries, increased the accessibility and use of technical information, was a cost-effective way of supporting capacity-building at all levels, and had been instrumental in supporting country office implementation of UN reform processes. However, the implementation of the Programme required ad-

justments to ensure more effectiveness and responded to the needs of a changing environment. Proposals for actions were made in five areas: managing multiple demands; participation of CSTS in national development frameworks and UN programming processes; contribution to capacity development; planning technical assistance; and the strategic partnerships programme.

It also proposed a two-year extension of the Programme, during which a vision of future UNFPA technical assistance would be articulated. Since the Programme would be harmonized with the UNFPA biennial support budget, the MYFF and the intercountry programme beginning in 2008, it also proposed a longer-term strategy to determine the appropriate structure of technical and strategic support consistent with UN reforms and the needs of partner countries, and define a cohesive format for the joint planning and delivery of technical assistance. It would also develop a corporate capacity development strategy and a clear vision for its technical support activities during the next cycle (2008-2011).

On 9 September [E/2005/35 (dec. 2005/39)], the Executive Board welcomed the UNFPA report and the proposals contained therein; approved the extension of the Technical Advisory Programme for a two year period, 2006-2007; authorized the Executive Director to maintain the current level of funding and to commit $40 million over that period for its implementation. It also requested the Executive Director to report on the implementation of the Programme during 2006-2007, as well as on the implementation of the recommendations of the external evaluation, and present to the Board in 2007 the new arrangements for providing technical assistance to programme countries during the period 2008-2011.

UNFPA role in emergency situations

In response to Executive Board decision 2000/13 [YUN 2000, p. 1003], UNFPA reported in August on its role in emergency preparedness, humanitarian response and transition and recovery [DP/FPA/2005/18]. According to the report, UNFPA, as a member of the Inter-Agency Standing Committee on Humanitarian Affairs and the United Nations Development Group, played a role in UN-wide policy deliberations on a range of peacebuilding and humanitarian issues. The growing recognition of data, gender and reproductive health needs in emergencies had resulted in increased demand for UNFPA technical and programme support in crisis situations. Activities included rapid assessments and other data collection, support for reproductive health through training, technical support and the deployment of reproductive health commodities and hygiene supplies, support for women's empowerment and the strengthening of emergency preparedness and response. However, a review of the environment and experience in the field had indicated that UNFPA had to adopt a paradigm shift in the way it worked. Through a series of consultative meetings a strategy was developed to strengthen UNFPA programming for humanitarian assistance and transition and recovery over a three-year period. The strategy identified steps for improving UNFPA capacity to adapt and respond to crises and for playing an integral role in national recovery processes. It was accompanied by workplans for action in five areas: enhancing human resources; strengthening strategic partnerships; increasing funding; reinforcing logistics, security and administration; and improving communication. The process was to be completed by January 2008, in time for the new MYFF cycle (2008-2011).

On 9 September [E/2005/35 (dec. 2005/40)], the Executive Board took note of the report and of the critical importance of UNFPA work in humanitarian and transition settings; recognized UNFPA plans to strengthen its institutional capacity in emergency preparedness, humanitarian response, and transition and recovery, and encouraged continued consultations with the Board in that regard. It requested the Executive Director to report, in 2007, on a comprehensive corporate strategy, including resource and staff implications, for those activities. The Board decided, as an interim measure, to raise the ceiling of the existing emergency fund from $1 million to $3 million to enable UNFPA to better respond to crisis situations, and requested the Executive Director to report on the utilization of the funds.

UN Population award

The 2005 United Nations Population Award was presented to Mercedes Concepcion (Philippines), Professor Emeritus at the College of Social Sciences and Philosophy, University of the Philippines, and a member of the Board of Commissioners of the Philippine Commission on Population, in the individual category, and to the Asociación Pro Bienestar de la Familia de Guatemala (APROFAM) in the institutional category. Professor Concepcion was selected for her significant contributions to population research and policy in the Philippines, where her studies on population growth were important in the formation of the national population policy. She ensured that valid and reliable systems were in place so that the national population could be monitored and evaluated on an ongoing basis. APROFAM was selected for providing excellent reproductive health services to lower-income families in Guatemala, including family planning, reproductive health education and sexual health counselling and training. It also undertook scientific investigations in the field of population and development and disseminated sociodemographic data in Guatemala to develop an information base for population policies and programmes.

The Award was established by General Assembly resolution 36/201 [YUN 1981, p. 792], to be presented annually to individuals or institutions for outstanding contributions to increasing awareness of population problems and to their solutions. In September, the Secretary-General transmitted to the Assembly the report of the UNFPA Executive Director on the Population Award [A/60/397].

Other population activities

Commission on Population and Development

The Commission on Population and Development, at its thirty-eighth session (New York, 4-8 and 14 April) [E/2005/25], considered as its special theme "Population, development and HIV/AIDS, with particular emphasis on poverty", which was discussed in the context of the follow-up to the 1994 ICPD (see p. 1173). Documents before the Commission included the report of its Bureau on the intersessional meeting (Lima, Peru, 16-19 October 2004) [E/CN.9/2005/2]; report of the Secretary-General on: world population monitoring, focusing on population, development and HIV/AIDS, with particular emphasis on poverty [E/CN.9/2005/3] (see p. 1173); monitoring of population programmes, focusing on population, development and HIV/AIDS, with particular emphasis on poverty [E/CN.9/2005/4] (see p. 1174); the flow of financial resources for implementation of the ICPD Programme of Action [E/CN.9/2005/5] (see p. 1175); the contribution of the implementation of the ICPD Programme of Action, in all its aspects, to the achievement of the internationally agreed development goals, including the MDGs [E/CN.9/2005/6] (see p. 1175); the working methods of the Commission on Population and Development [E/CN.9/2005/7]; world demographic trends [E/CN.9/2005/8]; and programme implementation and progress of work in the field of population in 2004 [E/CN.9/2005/9].

The Commission adopted and brought to the Economic and Social Council's attention resolutions on population, development and HIV/AIDS, with particular emphasis on poverty [E/2005/25 (res. 2005/1)] (see p. 1174) and on the contribution of the implementation of the ICPD Programme of Action, in all its aspects, to the achievement of the internationally agreed development goals, including those contained in the United Nations Millennium Declaration [res. 2005/2]. The Commission decided that the special theme for its fortieth (2007) session would be "The changing age structures of populations and their implications for development" [dec. 2005/1]. The Commission adopted a decision [dec. 2005/2] on improving its methods of work (see below). In other action [dec. 2005/3], the Commission took note of the documents it had considered at its thirty-eighth session. At a resumed meeting on 14 April, the Commission recommended to the Council the draft provisional agenda for its thirty-ninth (2006) session.

By **decision 2005/245** of 22 July, the Economic and Social Council took note of the report of the Commission on Population and Development on its thirty-eighth (2005) session, and approved the provisional agenda for its thirty-ninth (2006) session.

In preparation for its thirty-ninth session, the Commission's Bureau held an intersessional meeting (Banjul, Gambia, 19-20 December) [E/CN.9/2006/2].

Improving the Commission's methods of work

The Economic and Social Council, by **decision 2005/213** of 31 March, decided, in order to improve the work of the Commission on Population and Development, that with effect from the Commission's thirty-eighth (2005) regular session, and immediately following the closure of each regular session, the Commission would hold the first meeting of the subsequent session to elect a new Chairman and other members of the Bureau. It also decided that the terms of reference of Commission members would be for four regular sessions; and in that regard, extended the terms of office of those members that were to expire on 31 December 2005 to the conclusion of the thirty-ninth (2006) regular session, on 31 December 2006 until the conclusion of the fortieth (2007) regular session, on 31 December 2007 until the end of the forty-first (2008) regular session, and on 31 December 2008 until the end of the forty-second (2009) regular session. The pertinent provision of General Assembly resolution 1798(XVII) [YUN 1962, p. 558] would apply only to the substantive part of the Commission session.

In April, the Commission considered a Secretary-General's report on the working methods of the Commission [E/CN.9/2005/7], submitted in response to Assembly resolution 57/270 B [YUN 2003, p. 1468]. The report reviewed the Commission's work, particularly with respect to enhanc-

ing the implementation of, and follow-up to, ICPD and subsequent conferences and made recommendations for improving those methods.

The Commission decided [dec. 2005/2] that the regular geographical rotation of the chair would start with the election held at its thirty-ninth (2006) session, in alphabetical order; to establish, at that session, a multi-year programme of work for covering a series of general themes based on the ICPD Programme of Action and its implementation; and in examining the themes, to promote increased sharing of national, regional and international experiences through focused and interactive dialogues among experts and practitioners.

UN activities

In a report on programme implementation and progress of work of the UN Population Division in 2005 [E/CN.9/2006/6], the Secretary-General described the Division's major activities and outputs dealing with the analysis of fertility, mortality and international migration; world population estimates and projections; population policies, population and development interrelationship; and monitoring, coordination and dissemination of population information.

The Division's work in fertility and family planning analysis included a wallchart entitled *World Contraceptive Use 2005*, which showed the most recent data on selected contraceptive practice indicators. The data showed that 61 per cent of women age 15 to 49 who were married or in union were using contraceptives; and that the level of use (69 per cent) was higher in the more developed regions compared to 59 per cent in the less developed regions. Among the latter group, Africa had the lowest level of use, at 27 per cent, contrasted with Asia and Latin America and the Caribbean which had levels of use similar to that of the more developed regions. Overall, contraceptive use had increased in less developed regions, with contraceptive prevalence increasing by at least one percentage point every year in the majority of the developing countries, while remaining fairly stable at high levels in developed countries. The Division also issued a CD-ROM on the subject, and prepared the *Database on Marriage*, containing indicators of marital status for 202 countries or areas.

On mortality and health, the Division issued the *World Mortality Report 2005*, an overview of mortality changes in all countries in the latter half of the twentieth century. The report, the first of its kind produced by the Division, compiled and summarized available information about levels and trends of mortality and life expectancy for national populations, and presented estimates of key mortality indicators for 192 countries and areas, including countries with a population of 100,000, or greater in 2000.

Concerning international migration, the Division organized an expert group meeting to explore key aspects of international migration and development. The Division also organized a fourth coordination meeting on international migration (26 and 27 October), which focused on the implications of the report and recommendations of the Global Commission on International Migration for the United Nations system's work in international migration and for the General Assembly's high-level dialogue on international migration and development in 2006. The Division also issued a database entitled *Trends in Total Migrant Stock: The 2005 Revision,* and was finalizing the *International Migration Report 2005,* the second in a series that presented information on international migration levels and policies, as well as other related indicators.

With regard to world population projections, the Division issued the results of the *2004 Revision* of the biennial *World Population Prospects,* which showed that world population would continue to grow, increasing from 6.5 billion in 2005 to 9.1 billion in 2050; that currently 95 per cent of all population growth was absorbed by the developing world; and that by 2050, the population of the more developed countries as a whole would be declining slowly by about 1 million persons a year, while the developing world would still be adding 35 million annually, 22 million of them in the LDCs. The Division completed preparation of the *2005 Revision of World Urbanization Prospects,* which was also available on CD-ROM. Two wallcharts and an executive summary in all UN official languages were being prepared. The Division also organized, on 10 and 11 May, an expert meeting on software for demographic HIV/AIDS.

As to population policies, the Division's publication, *World Population Policies 2005,* found that Governments viewed HIV/AIDS as the most significant demographic issue facing them. Others

included high infant and child mortality and high maternal mortality in the developing countries. Of particular concern in the developed countries, were low fertility, population ageing and the small size of the working age population. The Division also completed evaluation and analysis of the *United Nations Ninth Inquiry among Governments on Population and Development,* the results of which had been incorporated into its publications. The wallchart *International Migration 2005* provided background information for the Commission on Population and Development and for the forthcoming high-level dialogue on international migration and development. Another wallchart, Population and HIV/AIDS 2005, provided an essential backdrop to the Assembly's high-level meeting on HIV/AIDS (see p. 1322) and focused on combating the disease.

With regard to population and development, the Division, along with co-sponsors, convened in Mexico City (30 November–2 December) [E/CN.9/2006/7], an expert group meeting on the social and economic implications of changing population age structures. A new version of the database *Population, Resources, Environment and Development* was released on CD-ROM and an Internet version would follow in 2006.

On monitoring population trends and policies, the Division updated and issued the latest edition of its annual monitoring report to the 2005 session of the Commission on population, development and HIV/AIDS, with particular emphasis on poverty (see p. 1173). In time for the 2005 World Summit (see p. 47), the Division issued Population Challenges and Development Goals. In disseminating population information and data, the Division continued to update and expand its website (www.unpopulation.org) to provide timely access by Governments and civil society to population information. Complementing the website was the Population Information Network (POPIN) (www.popin.org), which provided a portal to population information and data available throughout the UN system.

Chapter IX

Social policy, crime prevention and human resources development

In 2005, the United Nations continued to promote social, cultural, and human resources development, and to strengthen its crime prevention and criminal justice programme.

The Commission for Social Development considered as its priority theme the review of further implementation of the outcome of the 1995 World Summit for Social Development and the twenty-fourth (2000) special session of the General Assembly. It adopted a declaration on the tenth anniversary of the World Summit, as a contribution to the five-year review of the 2000 Millennium Declaration.

The Secretary-General reported on follow-up activities undertaken in regard to the tenth International Year of the Family. Work also continued by the Ad Hoc Committee on the Comprehensive and Integral International Convention on the Protection and Promotion of the Rights and Dignity of Persons with Disabilities. The United Nations Educational, Scientific and Cultural Organization promoted religious and cultural understanding. Various activities were undertaken to celebrate the International Year of Sport and Physical Education.

The Eleventh United Nations Congress on the Prevention of Crime and the Treatment of Offenders, held in Bangkok, Thailand, in April, adopted the Bangkok Declaration on Synergies and Responses: Strategic Alliances in Crime Prevention and Criminal Justice, which addressed major crime and criminal justice issues of concern to the international community. The Congress focused on five topics: effective measures to combat transnational organized crime; international cooperation against terrorism and links between terrorism and other criminal activities in the context of the work of the United Nations Office on Drugs and Crime (UNODC); threats and trends of corruption in the twenty-first century; economic and financial crimes; and making standards work, based on fifty years of standard-setting in crime prevention and criminal justice.

The Commission on Crime Prevention and Criminal Justice, at its fourteenth session, gave priority to the conclusions of the Eleventh Congress. It also focused, among other things, on bilateral agreement on the sharing of confiscated proceeds of crime or property, action against transnational organized crime and protocols related to terrorism within the UNODC framework.

The Secretary-General also reported on the work of the United Nations Institute for Training and Research.

Social policy and cultural issues

Social development

Follow-up to the 1995 World Summit and to the General Assembly special session

In response to General Assembly resolution 59/146 [YUN 2004, p. 1089], the Secretary-General submitted a May report [A/60/80] on the implementation of the Copenhagen Declaration on Social Development and the Programme of Action, adopted at the 1995 World Summit for Social Development [YUN 1995, p. 1113], and of the further initiatives for social development adopted by the Assembly's twenty-fourth (2000) special session [YUN 2000, p. 1012]. The report provided an overview of the activities for celebrating the tenth anniversary of the World Summit, which took place during the forty-third session of the Commission for Social Development (New York, 9-18 February) (see p. 1190). It noted that a number of trends had adversely affected social development since the convening of the Summit in Copenhagen. The broad concept of social development affirmed by all world leaders in Copenhagen had become less comprehensive and was severely weakened in global policymaking. While poverty was key in development policy and discourse, the other two core issues of the 1995 Summit—employment and social integration—had suffered from a general disconnect between economic and social policymaking. The report noted that the centrality of employment and the fundamental contribution of social integration to economic and social development were absent in the Millennium Development Goals (MDGs) [YUN 2000, p. 51] and that the injection of those missing links into the goals was needed to shore up efforts to build more inclusive, just and stable societies.

The panel discussion with the executive secretaries of the regional commissions on regional perspectives on the implementation of the outcome of the World Summit focused primarily on the core issues of poverty, employment and social integration. Mixed progress was reported by all of the commissions, especially since rising levels of income inequality within and among countries threatened the possibility of lifting people out of poverty, promoting employment and fostering social integration.

The Secretary-General's report on the world social situation in 2005 was transmitted to the Assembly in July (see p. 1193).

GENERAL ASSEMBLY ACTION

On 16 December [meeting 64], the General Assembly, on recommendations of the Third (Social, Humanitarian and Cultural) Committee [A/60/500], adopted **resolution 60/130** without vote [agenda item 61].

Implementation of the outcome of the World Summit for Social Development and of the twenty-fourth special session of the General Assembly

The General Assembly,

Recalling the World Summit for Social Development, held at Copenhagen from 6 to 12 March 1995, and the twenty-fourth special session of the General Assembly, entitled "World Summit for Social Development and beyond: achieving social development for all in a globalizing world", held at Geneva from 26 June to 1 July 2000,

Reaffirming that the Copenhagen Declaration on Social Development and the Programme of Action and the further initiatives for social development adopted by the General Assembly at its twenty-fourth special session, as well as a continued global dialogue on social development issues, constitute the basic framework for the promotion of social development for all at the national and international levels,

Recalling the United Nations Millennium Declaration and the development goals contained therein, as well as the commitments made at major United Nations summits, conferences and special sessions, including the commitments made at the 2005 World Summit,

Recalling also its resolution 57/270 B of 23 June 2003 on the integrated and coordinated implementation of and follow-up to the outcomes of the major United Nations conferences and summits in the economic and social fields,

1. *Takes note with appreciation* of the report of the Secretary-General;

2. *Also takes note with appreciation* of the report on the world social situation, 2005 and one of its main findings, that the development agenda cannot be advanced without addressing the challenges of inequality within and between countries and that the failure to address this inequality predicament will ensure that social justice and better living conditions

for all people will remain elusive and that communities, countries and regions will remain vulnerable to social, political and economic upheaval;

3. *Welcomes* the outcome of the ten-year review of the World Summit for Social Development, which took place during the forty-third session of the Commission for Social Development, in February 2005;

4. *Also welcomes* the reaffirmation by Governments of their will and commitment to continue implementing the Copenhagen Declaration on Social Development and the Programme of Action, in particular to eradicate poverty, promote full and productive employment and foster social integration to achieve stable, safe and just societies for all;

5. *Reaffirms* the recognition that the implementation of the Copenhagen commitments and the attainment of the internationally agreed development goals, including those contained in the United Nations Millennium Declaration, are mutually reinforcing and that the Copenhagen commitments are crucial to a coherent, people-centred approach to development;

6. *Recognizes* that, while action taken to implement the outcomes of the major United Nations summits, conferences and special sessions in the economic, social and related fields held during the past ten years will further promote social development, strengthened and effective international and regional cooperation and assistance for development and progress towards increased participation, greater social justice and improved equity in societies will also be required;

7. *Also recognizes* that the broad concept of social development affirmed by the World Summit for Social Development and the twenty-fourth special session of the General Assembly has been weakened in national and international policymaking and that, while poverty eradication is a central part of development policy and discourse, further attention should be given to the other commitments agreed to at the Summit, in particular those concerning employment and social integration, which have also suffered from a general disconnect between economic and social policymaking;

8. *Emphasizes* that poverty eradication policies should attack poverty by addressing its root and structural causes and manifestations, and that equity and the reduction of inequalities need to be incorporated in those policies;

9. *Reaffirms* the commitment to employment policies that promote full and productive employment and decent work for all under conditions of equity, equality, security and dignity, and also reaffirms that employment creation should be incorporated into macroeconomic policies;

10. *Reaffirms also* that social integration policies should seek to reduce inequalities, promote access to basic social services, education and health care, increase the participation and integration of social groups and address the challenges posed by globalization and market-driven reforms on social development in order for all people in all countries to benefit from globalization;

11. *Reaffirms further* that the Commission for Social Development will continue to have the primary responsibility for the follow-up and review of the

World Summit for Social Development and the outcome of the twenty-fourth special session of the General Assembly and that it serves as the main United Nations forum for an intensified global dialogue on social development issues, and encourages Governments, the relevant specialized agencies, funds and programmes of the United Nations system and civil society to enhance their support to its work;

12. *Reaffirms* the commitments made in "Meeting the special needs of Africa" at the 2005 World Summit, underlines the call of the Economic and Social Council for enhanced coordination within the United Nations system and the ongoing efforts to harmonize the current initiatives on Africa, and requests the Commission for Social Development to continue to give due prominence in its work to the social dimensions of the New Partnership for Africa's Development;

13. *Reaffirms also* that each country has the primary responsibility for its own economic and social development and that the role of national policies and development strategies cannot be overemphasized, and underlines the importance of adopting effective measures, including new financial mechanisms as appropriate, to support the efforts of developing countries to achieve sustained economic growth, sustainable development, poverty eradication and the strengthening of their democratic systems;

14. *Reaffirms further,* in this context, that international cooperation has an essential role in assisting developing countries, including the least developed countries, in strengthening their human, institutional and technological capacity;

15. *Reaffirms* that social development requires the active involvement of all actors in the development process, including civil society organizations, corporations and small businesses, and that partnerships among all relevant actors are increasingly becoming part of national and international cooperation for social development, and also reaffirms that, within countries, partnerships among the Government, civil society and the private sector can contribute effectively to the achievement of social development goals;

16. *Underlines* the responsibility of the private sector, at both the national and the international levels, including small and large companies and transnational corporations, regarding not only the economic and financial but also the development, social, gender and environmental implications of their activities, their obligations towards their workers and their contributions to achieving sustainable development, including social development, and emphasizes the need to take concrete actions within the United Nations system and through the participation of all relevant stakeholders on corporate responsibility and accountability, including for the prevention or prosecution of corruption;

17. *Invites* the Secretary-General, the Economic and Social Council, the regional commissions, the relevant specialized agencies, funds and programmes of the United Nations system and other intergovernmental forums, within their respective mandates, to continue to integrate into their work programmes and give priority attention to the Co-

penhagen commitments and the Declaration on the tenth anniversary of the World Summit for Social Development, to continue to be actively involved in their follow-up and to monitor the achievement of those commitments and undertakings;

18. *Decides* to include in the provisional agenda of its sixty-first session the item entitled "Implementation of the outcome of the World Summit for Social Development and of the twenty-fourth special session of the General Assembly", and requests the Secretary-General to submit a report on the question to the Assembly at that session.

Commission for Social Development

The Commission for Social Development, at its forty-third session (New York, 9-18 February) [E/2005/26], considered the priority theme, "Review of further implementation of the World Summit for Social Development and the outcome of the twenty-fourth special session of the General Assembly". The Commission held a two-day high-level segment devoted to the 10-year review of the 1995 World Summit for Social Development. It adopted the Declaration on the tenth anniversary of the World Summit (see below), reaffirming that the Copenhagen Declaration and Programme of Action and the further initiatives for social development adopted by the General Assembly at its twenty-fourth special session constituted the basic framework for the promotion of social development for all at the national and international levels. The Declaration recognized that the implementation of the 1995 Copenhagen commitments and the attainment of the MDGs were mutually reinforcing and that the Copenhagen commitments were crucial to a coherent, people-centred approach to development. As part of the high-level segment, the Commission held round table discussions on each of the core issues addressed by the Summit, namely, poverty eradication, promotion of full employment and fostering social integration. Annexed to the report were summaries of the round table discussions.

The Commission adopted a resolution on the implementation of the social objectives of the New Partnership for Africa's Development (NEPAD) (see p. 1003). It recommended to the Economic and Social Council for adoption two draft resolutions concerning persons with disabilities. In the first, on the further promotion of equalization of opportunities by, for, and with persons with disabilities and the protection of their human rights, the Commission recommended that the Council renew the mandate of the Special Rapporteur on Disability of the Commission for Social Development through 31 December 2008. In the second draft resolution, on the comprehensive and integral international convention to promote and protect the rights and dignity of persons with disabilities, the Commission recommended that the Council request the Commission for Social Development to continue to contribute to the process of negotiation of a draft convention.

In consideration of the situation pertaining to social groups, the Commission held its general debate and a panel discussion on youth in the context of the 10-year review of the World Programme of Action for Youth and the upcoming five-year review of the MDGs.

The Commission considered the Secretary-General's report [E/CN.5/2005/2] on the review of its work methods, submitted in accordance with Assembly resolution 57/270 B [YUN 2003, p. 1468].

Review of further implementation of the 1995 World Summit

The Secretary-General, in response to Economic and Social Council decision 2004/241 [YUN 2004, p. 1091], transmitted a report [E/CN.5/2005/6] on the review of further implementation of the World Summit for Social Development and the outcome of the twenty-fourth Special Session of the General Assembly. The report reviewed the implementation, from 1995 to 2005, of the ten commitments embodied in the Copenhagen Declaration on Social Development. The report consisted of four major chapters that included: comprehensive policy framework for people-centred development set forth by the Copenhagen Declaration; current prospects for an enabling environment for social development, as envisaged by the Summit; major trends in social development since the Summit with respect to poverty, employment, social integration, gender equality and education and health; and the way forward in terms of policy recommendations. Annexed to the report were the historical background on the international agenda on social development leading up to and including the World Summit; the ten commitments from the Copenhagen Declaration in their original wording; and an overview of the significance of the five-year review of implementation, after the Summit, at the twenty-fourth special session of the General Assembly held in 2000.

Declaration of the Commission for Social Development

On 21 July, the Economic and Social Council decided to transmit the Declaration of the Commission for Social Development on the tenth anniversary of the World Summit for Social Development to the General Assembly, including the Assembly's High-level Plenary Meeting on the re-

view of the United Nations Millennium Declaration (**decision 2005/234**).

Declaration on the tenth anniversary of the World Summit for Social Development

We, the representatives of Governments gathering at the forty-third session of the Commission for Social Development, in New York, on the occasion of the tenth anniversary of the World Summit for Social Development, held at Copenhagen in 1995, in the context of the review of the outcome of the Summit and of the twenty-fourth special session of the General Assembly and its contribution to the High-level Plenary Meeting of the General Assembly on the review of the United Nations Millennium Declaration, to be held from 14 to 16 September 2005,

1. *Reaffirm* that the Copenhagen Declaration on Social Development and the Programme of Action adopted by the World Summit for Social Development and the further initiatives for social development adopted by the General Assembly at its twenty-fourth special session constitute the basic framework for the promotion of social development for all at the national and international levels;

2. *Recognize* that the implementation of the Copenhagen commitments and the attainment of the internationally agreed development goals, including those contained in the Millennium Declaration, are mutually reinforcing and that the Copenhagen commitments are crucial to a coherent, people-centred approach to development;

3. *Stress* that policies and programmes designed to achieve poverty eradication should include specific measures to foster social integration, including by providing marginalized socio-economic sectors and groups with equal access to opportunities;

4. *Reaffirm* that an employment strategy that aims to promote full, freely chosen and productive employment with full respect for fundamental principles and rights at work under conditions of equity, equality, security and dignity should constitute a fundamental component of any development strategy. We further reaffirm that macroeconomic policies should, inter alia, support employment creation. The social impact and dimension of globalization deserve further attention;

5. *Recommit ourselves* to promoting social integration by fostering societies that are stable, safe and just and that are based on the promotion and protection of all human rights, as well as on non-discrimination, tolerance, respect for diversity, equality of opportunity, solidarity, security and participation of all people, including disadvantaged and vulnerable groups and persons;

6. *Reaffirm* the importance of promoting and attaining the goals of universal and equitable access to quality education, the highest attainable standard of physical and mental health and the access of all to primary health care as part of the effort to eradicate poverty, promote full and productive employment and foster social integration. We also recognize the continued need to address the impact of HIV/AIDS and other major infectious diseases on social and economic development;

7. *Recognize* that gender equality and the full participation of women in society are integral to building a society for all and must be at the centre of all economic and social development. We recommit ourselves to the urgent goal of achieving gender equality, to eliminating discrimination against women and to ensuring their full participation in all areas of life and at all levels;

8. *Reaffirm* that enhanced international cooperation and action at the national level are essential to the implementation of the Copenhagen Declaration and the Programme of Action. We underline the importance of adopting effective measures, including new financial mechanisms, as appropriate, to support the efforts of developing countries to achieve sustained economic growth, sustainable development, poverty eradication and strengthening of their democratic systems. We reaffirm that each country has primary responsibility for its own economic and social development and that national policies have the leading role in the development process. We also reaffirm that good governance is essential to sustainable development;

9. *Recognize* that ten years after Copenhagen, despite the efforts made and progress achieved in economic and social development, the situation of many developing countries, particularly in Africa and the least developed countries, as well as countries with economies in transition, requires further attention and action. We renew our commitment to support national efforts to promote a favourable environment for social and economic development, including the provision of technical and financial assistance, as appropriate, including through regional and other initiatives such as the New Partnership for Africa's Development;

10. *Dedicate ourselves,* a decade after Copenhagen, on the basis of our common pursuit of social development, to building solidarity, and renew our invitation to all people in all countries and in all walks of life, as well as the international community, to join in realizing our shared vision for a more just and equitable world. Therefore, we reaffirm our will and commitment to continue implementing the Copenhagen Declaration and the Programme of Action, in particular to eradicate poverty, promote full and productive employment and foster social integration to achieve stable, safe and just societies for all.

On 21 July, the Council took note of the Commission's report on its forty-third session and approved the provisional agenda and documentation for its forty-fourth (2006) session (**decision 2005/235**).

Future organization and methods of work of the Commission for Social Development

On 21 July [meeting 35], the Economic and Social Council, on the recommendation of the Commission for Social Development [E/2005/26], adopted **resolution 2005/11** without vote [agenda item 14 (b)].

Future organization and methods of work of the Commission for Social Development

The Economic and Social Council,

Recalling General Assembly resolution 57/270 B of 23 June 2003, in which the Assembly requested each functional commission of the Economic and Social Council to examine its methods of work in order to better pursue the implementation of the outcomes of the major United Nations conferences and summits, and to report to the Council no later than 2005 on the outcome of that examination,

Recalling also the primary responsibility of the Commission for Social Development for the follow-up to the World Summit for Social Development and the review of the Copenhagen Declaration on Social Development and Programme of Action of the World Summit for Social Development and the outcome of the twenty-fourth special session of the General Assembly,

1. *Recognizes* that the organization of work of the Commission for Social Development should contribute to advancing the implementation of the Copenhagen Declaration on Social Development and Programme of Action of the World Summit for Social Development and the outcome of the twenty-fourth special session of the General Assembly, bearing in mind links with the internationally agreed development goals, including those contained in the United Nations Millennium Declaration;

2. *Decides* that in order to fulfil its mandate, beginning with its forty-fifth session, the work of the Commission will be organized in a series of two-year action-oriented implementation cycles, which will include a review segment and a policy segment, and that the Commission should strengthen the connection between its review of implementation and its policy recommendations;

3. *Also decides* that, in its sessions, the Commission will also continue to review plans and programmes of action pertaining to social groups, including in relation to the priority theme;

4. *Further decides* that, in its review of the implementation of the Copenhagen Declaration and Programme of Action and the outcome of the twenty-fourth special session of the General Assembly, the Commission should emphasize increased exchange of national, regional and international experiences, focused and interactive dialogues among experts and practitioners, and sharing of best practices and lessons learned;

5. *Decides* that the Commission should invite all relevant stakeholders to continue to participate in its work at an appropriately high level;

6. *Invites* the regional commissions, in collaboration with the Department of Economic and Social Affairs of the Secretariat, to consider organizing regional meetings and activities, as necessary and appropriate, in order to contribute to the work of the Commission, in collaboration, as appropriate, with other regional and subregional intergovernmental organizations and bodies and the regional offices of funds and programmes of the United Nations system;

7. *Decides* that the Commission at its forty-fourth session should consider further its methods of work, bearing in mind its own experiences and those of

other functional commissions, and that its consideration should include the nature of its outcomes, negotiated and otherwise, the inclusion of emerging issues within its programme of work and the choice of themes for the 2007/2008 cycle;

8. *Also decides* that the Commission, at its forty-sixth session, should review the functioning of the two-year review and policy cycle, in order to ensure that this approach enhances the effectiveness and functioning of the Commission.

2005 Report on the World Social Situation

In July [A/60/117 & Rev.1], the Secretary-General transmitted to the General Assembly a report on the World Social Situation in 2005, which reviewed traditional aspects of inequalities in health, education, and opportunities for social and political participation. It also noted the impact of structural adjustment, market reforms, globalization and privatization on economic and social indicators. The report identified four areas of particular importance: addressing worldwide asymmetries derived from globalization; incorporating specific measures for reducing inequality in policies and programmes designed to achieve poverty reduction; expanding opportunities for employment, with particular attention to improving conditions in the informal economy; and promoting social integration and cohesion as a key development, peace and security.

By **decision 60/528** of 16 December, the Assembly took note of the Secretary-General's report.

Cooperatives in social development

Pursuant to General Assembly resolution 58/131 [YUN 2003, p. 1102], the Secretary-General, in July [A/60/138], submitted the replies he had received from Governments and international organizations on progress achieved in the resolution's implementation, particularly in promoting a supportive environment for the development of cooperatives and their contribution to poverty eradication, the generation of a full and productive environment and the enhancement of social integration.

The Secretary-General recommended promoting greater participation of cooperatives in poverty reduction. In order to enhance growth and sustainability of cooperatives, a legislative enactment, amendment or review was needed to broaden and deepen cooperatives' outreach among the poor, particularly for those in the rural or agriculture sector. In addition, he noted that greater impetus was needed to support programmes that entailed technology support from donors and created a political, social and economic environment conducive to autonomy and the democratic principles of cooperatives.

On 16 December [meeting 64], the General Assembly, on the recommendation of the Third Committee [A/60/501], adopted **resolution 60/132** without vote [agenda item 62].

Cooperatives in social development

The General Assembly,

Recalling its resolutions 47/90 of 16 December 1992, 49/155 of 23 December 1994, 51/58 of 12 December 1996, 54/123 of 17 December 1999, 56/114 of 19 December 2001 and 58/131 of 22 December 2003 concerning cooperatives in social development,

Recognizing that cooperatives, in their various forms, promote the fullest possible participation in the economic and social development of all people, including women, youth, older persons and persons with disabilities, and are becoming a major factor of economic and social development,

Recognizing also the important contribution and potential of all forms of cooperatives to the follow-up to the World Summit for Social Development, the Fourth World Conference on Women, the second United Nations Conference on Human Settlements (Habitat II) and their reviews, the World Food Summit, the Second World Assembly on Ageing, the International Conference on Financing for Development and the World Summit on Sustainable Development,

1. *Takes note* of the report of the Secretary-General;

2. *Draws the attention* of Member States to the recommendations contained in the report of the Secretary-General for further action to promote the greater participation of cooperatives in poverty reduction, in particular in the design, implementation and monitoring of poverty reduction strategy papers, where they exist;

3. *Encourages* Governments to keep under review, as appropriate, the legal and administrative provisions and requirements governing the activities of cooperatives in order to enhance the growth and sustainability of cooperatives in a rapidly changing socio-economic environment, to broaden and deepen the outreach of cooperatives among the poor, in particular those in rural areas or in the agricultural sector, and to promote the participation of women and vulnerable groups in cooperatives across all sectors;

4. *Urges* Governments, relevant international organizations and the specialized agencies, in collaboration with national and international cooperative organizations, to give due consideration to the role and contribution of cooperatives in the implementation of and follow-up to the outcomes of the World Summit for Social Development, the Fourth World Conference on Women, the second United Nations Conference on Human Settlements (Habitat II) and their reviews, the World Food Summit, the Second World Assembly on Ageing, the International Conference on Financing for Development, the World Summit on Sustainable Development and the 2005 World Summit by, inter alia:

(a) Utilizing and developing fully the potential and contribution of cooperatives for the attainment of social development goals, in particular the eradication of poverty, the generation of full and produc-

tive employment and the enhancement of social integration;

(b) Encouraging and facilitating the establishment and development of cooperatives, including taking measures aimed at enabling people living in poverty or belonging to vulnerable groups to engage on a voluntary basis in the creation and development of cooperatives;

(c) Taking appropriate measures aimed at creating a supportive and enabling environment for the development of cooperatives by, inter alia, developing an effective partnership between Governments and the cooperative movement, inter alia, through joint consultative councils and/or advisory bodies and by promoting and implementing better legislation, training, research, sharing of good practices and human resources development;

(d) Taking steps to improve the collection and dissemination of information and data on the role of cooperatives in poverty reduction and their contribution to social and economic development;

5. *Invites* Governments, in collaboration with the cooperative movement, to develop programmes aimed at enhancing capacity-building of cooperatives, including by strengthening the organizational, management and financial skills of their members, and to introduce and support programmes to improve the access of cooperatives to new technologies;

6. *Invites* Governments, relevant international organizations, the specialized agencies and local, national and international cooperative organizations to continue to observe the International Day of Cooperatives annually, on the first Saturday of July, as proclaimed by the General Assembly in its resolution 47/90;

7. *Requests* the Secretary-General, in cooperation with the relevant United Nations and other international organizations and national, regional and international cooperative organizations, to render support to Member States, as appropriate, in their efforts to create a supportive environment for the development of cooperatives, to continue to provide assistance for human resources development, technical advice and training and to promote an exchange of experience and best practices through, inter alia, conferences, workshops and seminars at the national and regional levels;

8. *Also requests* the Secretary-General to submit to the General Assembly at its sixty-second session a report on the implementation of the present resolution, focusing on the role of cooperatives in promoting full and productive employment.

Follow-up to and celebration of International Year of the Family (1994)

In accordance with General Assembly resolutions 59/147 [YUN 2004, p. 1096] and 59/111 [ibid.], the Secretary-General submitted a July report [A/60/155] on the follow-up to and celebration of the tenth anniversary of the International Year of the Family. The tenth anniversary was celebrated throughout 2004, and owing to the importance of the issue of the family to Member States, the United Nations and civil society organizations,

celebratory events continued into 2005. The Assembly noted that the follow-up to the tenth anniversary would form an integral part of the agenda of the Commission for Social Development until 2006.

According to the report, national coordination mechanisms were established and charged with creating and implementing a plan for observing the tenth anniversary, raising public awareness of family issues, and identifying priority issues for concrete actions. At the national level, Governments continued to work toward strengthening and empowering families by promoting social and economic well-being. Numerous countries also reviewed their constitutions and legal systems on issues relating to families, children, adolescents, older persons and people with disabilities.

The UN programme on the family within the Department of Economic and Social Affairs (DESA) undertook and supported a range of activities in family related issues, including the organization of seminars and policy workshops on HIV/AIDS and family well-being.

The Secretary-General recommended that the Assembly could encourage the programmes, funds and specialized agencies to consider how they could integrate a family perspective into their activities and to identify a focal point on family matters within their offices. The Assembly could further request DESA to disseminate a compilation of existing UN system development cooperation activities to strengthen cooperation in the area of the family. Acknowledging the need for additional capacity-building at the national level to promote and facilitate the development and implementation of family policies, the Assembly could also encourage Governments to support the United Nations Family Trust Fund to enable DESA to provide expanded assistance to countries. In addition, the Assembly could recommend that Governments encourage research activities that provided input for public policies with a family perspective, utilizing participatory methodologies and techniques to elaborate on priority issues and family needs, identify family structures and composition and collect opinions, attitudes and values of different generations.

GENERAL ASSEMBLY ACTION

On 16 December [meeting 64], the General Assembly adopted **resolution 60/133** [draft: A/60/501] without a vote [agenda item 62].

Follow-up to the tenth anniversary of the International Year of the Family and beyond

The General Assembly,

Recalling its resolutions 44/82 of 8 December 1989, 50/142 of 21 December 1995, 52/81 of 12 December 1997, 54/124 of 17 December 1999, 56/113 of 19 December 2001, 57/164 of 18 December 2002, 58/15 of 3 December 2003, 59/111 of 6 December 2004 and 59/147 of 20 December 2004 concerning the proclamation of the International Year of the Family and the preparations for, observance of and follow-up to the tenth anniversary of the International Year of the Family,

Noting that in paragraph 5 of its resolution 59/111 and paragraph 2 of its resolution 59/147, respectively, the General Assembly underlined the need to realize the objectives of the International Year of the Family and to develop concrete measures and approaches to address national priorities in dealing with family issues,

Noting also that the family-related provisions of the outcomes of the major United Nations conferences and summits of the 1990s and their follow-up processes continue to provide policy guidance on ways to strengthen family-centred components of policies and programmes as part of an integrated comprehensive approach to development,

Cognizant that the tenth anniversary of the International Year of the Family in 2004 provided an impetus for integrating family concerns into the national development planning process,

Aware that the basic objective of the follow-up to the tenth anniversary of the International Year of the Family is to support families in performing their societal and developmental functions and to build upon their strengths, in particular at the national and local levels,

Recognizing the need to assist families in their supporting, educating and nurturing roles in contributing to social integration,

Convinced of the necessity of ensuring an action-oriented follow-up to the tenth anniversary of the International Year of the Family beyond 2004,

Recognizing the important catalytic and supportive role of United Nations bodies, the specialized agencies and the regional commissions in promoting international cooperation by ensuring an action-oriented follow-up in the field of the family,

Cognizant of the need for continued inter-agency cooperation on the family in order to generate greater awareness of family issues among the governing bodies of the United Nations system,

Recognizing that civil society, including research and academic institutions, has a pivotal role in advocacy, promotion, research and policymaking in respect of family policy development,

Taking note with appreciation of the report of the Secretary-General,

1. *Encourages* Governments to continue to make every possible effort to realize the objectives of the International Year of the Family and to integrate a family perspective into policymaking;

2. *Invites* Governments to maintain the national coordination mechanisms established or revitalized during the observance of the tenth anniversary of the International Year of the Family to coordinate policies, programmes and strategies in order to bring about positive transformations by integrating family issues into national development planning;

3. *Recommends* that Governments, in cooperation with concerned academic and research centres as well as relevant non-governmental organizations, encourage action-oriented research that addresses public policies with a family perspective and contributes to the development of strategies, policies and programmes aimed at strengthening the economic and sustainable livelihood of families, and encourages the United Nations programme on the family to support and conduct action-oriented research, including through the issuance of research and publications on relevant topics, with the aim of supplementing the research activities of Governments;

4. *Encourages* Governments to support the United Nations Trust Fund on Family Activities to enable the Department of Economic and Social Affairs of the Secretariat to provide expanded assistance to countries, upon their request;

5. *Urges* States, the specialized agencies and intergovernmental and non-governmental organizations to address family-related concerns within the framework of the commitments undertaken at relevant major United Nations conferences and in their follow-up processes;

6. *Urges* Member States to create a conducive environment to strengthen and support all families, recognizing that equality between women and men and respect for all the human rights and fundamental freedoms of all family members are essential to family well-being and to society at large, noting the importance of the reconciliation of work and family life, and recognizing the principle that both parents have common responsibilities for the upbringing and development of the child;

7. *Encourages* continued and increased inter-agency cooperation within the United Nations system on family-related issues, and encourages the programmes, funds and specialized agencies of the United Nations system to identify focal points on family matters within their offices to support the integration of family issues in their work;

8. *Calls upon* the Secretariat to continue its important role on family issues within the United Nations system, and in this regard encourages the Department of Economic and Social Affairs to continue cooperation with Governments, the United Nations system and civil society in strengthening national capacities through the implementation of the mandated objectives of the International Year of the Family;

9. *Invites* Member States to undertake a review of the role and functions of existing national machineries for the family in order to better integrate family issues into national development programmes;

10. *Requests* the Secretary-General to submit a report on the implementation of the present resolution to the General Assembly at its sixty-second session;

11. *Decides* to consider the topic "Follow-up to the tenth anniversary of the International Year of the Family" at its sixty-second session under the item entitled "Social development, including questions relating to the world social situation and to youth, ageing, disabled persons and the family".

Persons with disabilities

World Programme of Action concerning Disabled Persons

The Secretary-General, in response to General Assembly resolution 58/132 [YUN 2003, p. 1105], transmitted an August report [A/60/290] on the implementation of the World Programme of Action concerning Disabled Persons. The report was based on contributions received from 26 Governments, 14 UN agencies or programmes and two non-governmental organizations (NGOs). It addressed the international policy framework on disability; progress made towards the equalization of opportunities for persons with disabilities; initiatives aimed at promoting a disability perspective in development; and actions to improve accessibility at the United Nations. Proposals for action to the Assembly included options for more effective synergy in monitoring the implementation of the two special international instruments—the World Programme of Action concerning Disabled Persons and the Standard Rules on Equalization of Persons with Disabilities [E/CN.5/ 2005/5].

ECONOMIC AND SOCIAL COUNCIL ACTION

On 21 July [meeting 35], the Economic and Social Council, on the recommendation of the Commission for Social Development [E/2005/26], adopted **resolution 2005/9** without vote [agenda item 14 (b)].

Further promotion of equalization of opportunities by, for and with persons with disabilities and protection of their human rights

The Economic and Social Council,

Recalling General Assembly resolution 37/52 of 3 December 1982, by which the Assembly adopted the World Programme of Action concerning Disabled Persons, resolution 48/96 of 20 December 1993, by which it adopted the Standard Rules on the Equalization of Opportunities for Persons with Disabilities, resolution 56/168 of 19 December 2001, by which it established the Ad Hoc Committee on a Comprehensive and Integral International Convention on the Protection and Promotion of the Rights and Dignity of Persons with Disabilities, resolutions 58/132 of 22 December 2003 and 59/198 of 20 December 2004, as well as Assembly decision 59/521 of 20 December 2004 on the issue of the proposed supplement to the Standard Rules,

Recalling also its resolutions 2002/26 of 24 July 2002 and 2004/15 of 21 July 2004 on further promotion of equalization of opportunities by, for and with persons with disabilities and protection of their human rights,

Encouraged by the elaboration of a convention carried out in the Ad Hoc Committee,

Mindful of the need to adopt and implement effective strategies and policies to promote the rights and the full and effective participation of persons with disabilities in economic, social, cultural and political life on the basis of equality in order to achieve a society for all,

Noting with satisfaction that the Standard Rules play an increasingly important role in the equalization of opportunities for persons with disabilities,

Noting with grave concern that persons with disabilities are, in some circumstances, among the poorest of the poor and that they continue to be excluded from the benefits of development, such as education and access to gainful employment,

Encouraging States to further participate actively in international cooperation for the equalization of opportunities for persons with disabilities,

1. *Welcomes* the work of the Special Rapporteur on Disability of the Commission for Social Development, and takes note of her report;

2. *Urges* Governments, the Secretary-General, intergovernmental organizations and non-governmental organizations, and invites relevant human rights treaty bodies, relevant bodies and organizations of the United Nations system, including the Bretton Woods institutions, multilateral development agencies and regional commissions, to create greater awareness of and support for the further implementation of the Standard Rules on the Equalization of Opportunities for Persons with Disabilities, to work closely with the United Nations programme on persons with disabilities, to promote the enjoyment of all human rights and fundamental freedoms of persons with disabilities and to improve consultation, exchange of information and coordination;

3. *Encourages* Governments, non-governmental organizations and the private sector to continue to contribute to the United Nations Voluntary Fund on Disability in order to support the activities of the Special Rapporteur as well as new and expanded initiatives to strengthen national capacities for equalization of opportunities by, for and with persons with disabilities;

4. *Decides* to renew the mandate of the Special Rapporteur through 31 December 2008 to further the promotion and monitoring of the Standard Rules in accordance with the provisions set down in section IV of the Standard Rules, including the human rights dimensions of disability;

5. *Requests* the Special Rapporteur to take into account the general ideas contained in the proposed supplement to the Standard Rules in the accomplishment of her mandate;

6. *Encourages* the Special Rapporteur to continue to participate in and contribute to the work of the Ad Hoc Committee on a Comprehensive and Integral International Convention on the Protection and Promotion of the Rights and Dignity of Persons with Disabilities;

7. *Requests* the Special Rapporteur to submit an annual report on the monitoring of the implementation of the Standard Rules to the Commission for Social Development.

GENERAL ASSEMBLY ACTION

On 16 December [meeting 64], the General Assembly, on recommendation of the Third Committee [A/60/501], adopted **resolution 60/131** without vote [agenda item 62].

Implementation of the World Programme of Action concerning Disabled Persons: realizing the Millennium Development Goals for persons with disabilities

The General Assembly,

Recalling the purposes and principles of the Charter of the United Nations, and reaffirming the obligations contained in relevant human rights instruments, including the Convention on the Elimination of All Forms of Discrimination against Women and the Convention on the Rights of the Child,

Recalling also its relevant resolutions, in particular resolution 37/52 of 3 December 1982, by which it adopted the World Programme of Action concerning Disabled Persons, resolution 48/96 of 20 December 1993, by which it adopted the Standard Rules on the Equalization of Opportunities for Persons with Disabilities, and resolution 58/132 of 22 December 2003, as well as the relevant resolutions of the Economic and Social Council and its functional commissions,

Recalling further the adoption of the United Nations Millennium Declaration on 8 September 2000 and of the 2005 World Summit Outcome on 16 September 2005 by Heads of State and Government, stressing the need to promote and protect the full enjoyment of all human rights and fundamental freedoms by persons with disabilities, and recognizing the importance of incorporating the disability perspective in the implementation of the outcomes of the major United Nations conferences and summits, with a view to achieving the internationally agreed development goals, including those contained in the Millennium Declaration,

Noting with appreciation the initiatives and actions of Governments to implement the World Programme of Action, the Standard Rules and relevant resolutions that give special attention to the questions of accessible environments and information and communication technologies, health, education and social services, employment and sustainable livelihoods, including the relevant activities of intergovernmental and non-governmental organizations, which reflect the strong commitment to the equalization of opportunities, the rights of persons with disabilities and the promotion and protection of the full enjoyment of all human rights by persons with disabilities, including in the context of development,

Reaffirming the outcomes of the major United Nations conferences and summits and their respective follow-up reviews,

Noting that the Madrid International Plan of Action on Ageing, 2002, adopted by the Second World Assembly on Ageing, considers "older persons and disabilities" as a specific issue for policy concern,

Welcoming the progress of the Ad Hoc Committee on a Comprehensive and Integral International Convention on the Protection and Promotion of the Rights and Dignity of Persons with Disabilities in preparing a draft text of the convention,

Acknowledging the complementary contributions of all existing international frameworks on disability,

Aware of the fact that there are at least 600 million persons with disabilities worldwide, of whom approximately 80 per cent live in developing countries,

Recognizing the important role of the World Programme of Action in the achievement of the Millennium Development Goals,

Recognizing also that the achievement of the purposes of the World Programme of Action is congruent with economic and social development, extended services provided to the whole population in the humanitarian area, the redistribution of resources and income and an improvement in the living standards of the population,

Acknowledging the important role of non-governmental organizations, in particular organizations of persons with disabilities, in the promotion and protection of the full enjoyment of all human rights by persons with disabilities, and noting in this regard their work in promoting the elaboration of an international convention on the rights of disabled persons,

Noting with appreciation the important contributions of regional intergovernmental organizations and the regional commissions of the United Nations in promoting awareness and building capacities for the full participation and equality of persons with disabilities, as well as the outcome of international conferences relating to persons with disabilities,

Mindful of the need to adopt and implement effective policies and strategies in all Member States, United Nations agencies, regional intergovernmental organizations and regional commissions of the United Nations to promote the rights and the full and effective participation of persons with disabilities at all levels,

Recognizing the importance of accessibility both of the physical environment and of information and communication in enabling persons with disabilities to enjoy fully their human rights and to play an active part in the development of society,

Reiterating that technology, in particular information and communication technologies, provides new possibilities for improving accessibility and employment for persons with disabilities and for facilitating their full and effective participation and equality, stressing in this regard the importance of enhancing cooperation among countries for the transfer of technology and technical and economic cooperation in the development and dissemination of appropriate disability-related technologies and know-how, and welcoming the initiatives of the United Nations and contributions from regional groups in promoting information and communication technologies as a means of achieving the universal goal of a society for all,

Recognizing the importance of timely and reliable data on disability-sensitive topics, programme planning and evaluation and the need for the further development of practical statistical methodology for the collection and compilation of data on populations with disabilities, and welcoming the initiatives of various United Nations agencies and regional groups in the area of collection of disability-related data and information,

Recognizing also the need to address the challenge of better incorporating the disability perspective in development and technical cooperation activities,

Recognizing further the need to improve the quality of life of persons with disabilities worldwide through the enhancement of awareness of and sensitivity to disability issues and respect for the full enjoyment of all human rights by persons with disabilities and by ensuring that the benefits of development programmes also reach them,

Recognizing that, because the vast majority of persons with disabilities continue to be excluded from the benefits of development and denied the full and equal recognition and enjoyment of their human rights, the impact of poverty on the conditions of persons with disabilities, especially in rural areas, should be given prominent consideration in the elaboration of national and international development strategies,

Expressing grave concern that situations of armed conflict continue to have especially devastating consequences for the human rights of persons with disabilities,

1. *Takes note* of the report of the Secretary-General on the implementation of the World Programme of Action concerning Disabled Persons, including his recommendations to mainstream the disability perspective in United Nations international and national development frameworks and to consider the effective synergy in monitoring the implementation of the existing international frameworks on disability;

2. *Welcomes* the work of the Special Rapporteur on disability of the Commission for Social Development to promote the full enjoyment of all human rights by, and the equalization of opportunities for, persons with disabilities, and encourages her to continue her work, bearing in mind the background of the World Programme of Action;

3. *Calls upon* Governments to take all necessary measures to advance beyond the adoption of national plans for persons with disabilities through, inter alia, the creation or reinforcement of arrangements for the promotion and awareness of disability issues and the allocation of sufficient resources for the full implementation of existing plans and initiatives, and emphasizes in this regard the importance of supporting national efforts through international cooperation;

4. *Urges* Governments and intergovernmental and non-governmental organizations to promote effective measures, as elaborated in the World Programme of Action, for the prevention of disability and the provision of appropriate habilitation and rehabilitation services for persons with disabilities in a manner respectful of the dignity and integrity of persons with disabilities;

5. *Encourages* Governments, intergovernmental and non-governmental organizations and the private sector, as appropriate, to continue to take concrete measures to mainstream the disability perspective in the development process and promote the implementation of relevant United Nations resolutions and agreed international standards concerning persons with disabilities, in particular the Standard Rules on the Equalization of Opportunities for Persons with Disabilities, and for the further equalization of opportunities for persons with disabilities;

6. *Encourages* Governments to continue and to strengthen their support to non-governmental organizations and other groups, including organizations of persons with disabilities, that contribute to the implementation of the World Programme of Action;

7. *Also encourages* Governments to involve persons with disabilities in the formulation of strategies and plans, in particular those pertaining to them;

8. *Urges* relevant organizations and bodies of the United Nations system, including the development agencies and funds, relevant human rights treaty bodies and the regional commissions, as well as intergovernmental and non-governmental organizations and institutions, to incorporate the disability perspective in their activities, as appropriate, and to continue to work closely with the Division for Social Policy and Development of the Secretariat for the equalization of opportunities for persons with disabilities and the promotion of the full enjoyment of all human rights and fundamental freedoms by persons with disabilities, including in activities at the field level;

9. *Stresses* the importance of improving data and statistics on persons with disabilities, in compliance with national legislation on the protection of personal data, so that they can be compared internationally and domestically for purposes of policy design, planning and evaluation from the disability perspective, urges Governments, in this regard, to cooperate with the Statistics Division of the Secretariat in the continuing development of global statistics and indicators on disability, and encourages them to avail themselves of the technical assistance of the Division to build national capacities for national data-collection systems;

10. *Urges* Governments and intergovernmental and non-governmental organizations to provide special protection to persons with disabilities from marginalized sectors of society, who may be vulnerable to multiple, intersecting or aggravating forms of discrimination, with special emphasis on integrating them into society and protecting and promoting their full enjoyment of all human rights;

11. *Urges* Governments to address the situation of persons with disabilities with respect to all actions taken to implement existing human rights treaties to which they are parties and in efforts taken towards achieving the Millennium Development Goals;

12. *Invites* Member States and observers to continue to participate actively and constructively in the Ad Hoc Committee on a Comprehensive and Integral International Convention on the Protection and Promotion of the Rights and Dignity of Persons with Disabilities, with a view to the early conclusion of a draft text of the convention, in order to present it to the General Assembly, as a matter of priority, for its adoption;

13. *Encourages* Governments, intergovernmental organizations, concerned non-governmental organizations and the private sector to continue to support the United Nations Voluntary Fund on Disability, with a view to strengthening its capacity to support catalytic and innovative activities to implement fully the World Programme of Action and the Standard Rules, including the work of the Special Rapporteur, and to support activities to build national capacities, with emphasis on priorities for action identified in the present resolution;

14. *Requests* the Secretary-General to continue to support the initiatives of relevant organizations and bodies of the United Nations system, as well as those of regional, intergovernmental and non-governmental organizations and institutions, for the further implementation of the World Programme of Action, including the promotion of the full enjoyment of all human rights by, and non-discrimination in respect of, persons with disabilities, as well as efforts to integrate persons with disabilities in technical cooperation activities, both as beneficiaries and as decision makers;

15. *Expresses its appreciation* to the Secretary-General for his efforts in improving the accessibility of the United Nations for persons with disabilities, and urges him to continue to implement plans to provide an accessible environment;

16. *Requests* the Secretary-General to submit a report to the General Assembly at its sixty-second session on the global implementation of the World Programme of Action, with respect to overall efforts being made to achieve the Millennium Development Goals, also including in the report possible options to improve the complementarity and synergy in the implementation of the World Programme of Action and other United Nations disability mechanisms and instruments, taking into account the strengths and main elements of the World Programme of Action as well as its important role in providing policy guidelines for States.

International convention on the rights of persons with disabilities

In accordance with General Assembly resolution 59/198 [YUN 2004, p. 1100], the Ad Hoc Committee on a Comprehensive and Integral International Convention on the Protection and Promotion of the Rights and Dignity of Persons with Disabilities, established by Assembly resolution 56/168 [YUN 2001, p. 1012], held its fifth (24 January–4 February) and sixth (1-12 August) sessions in 2005, both in New York.

At its fifth session [A/AC.265/2005/2], the Ad Hoc Committee recommended that the regional groups should hold consultations on the composition of its Bureau, and reiterated the need for additional efforts to ensure accessibility to facilities and documentation at the United Nations for all persons with disabilities. Burkina Faso transmitted to the Committee the summary proceedings of the subregional consultation on the draft convention on the protection and promotion of the rights and dignity of persons with disabilities [A/AC.265/2005/1].

At its sixth session [A/60/266], the Committee requested the Secretary-General to explore and implement innovative measures for the provision of selected documents in Braille. It also called upon UN system organizations and bodies, including the World Bank, to intensify their cooperation in support of the Committee's work.

Morocco [A/AC.265/2005/3] transmitted to the Committee the Casablanca Declaration, adopted at the conclusion of the regional consultative meeting of Arab States (Casablanca, Morocco, 15-17 June) on the comprehensive and integral international convention on the protection and promotion of the rights and dignity of persons with disabilities.

ECONOMIC AND SOCIAL COUNCIL ACTION

On 21 July [meeting 35], the Economic and Social Council, on the recommendation of the Commission for Social Development [E/2005/26], adopted **resolution 2005/10** without vote [agenda item 14 (*b*)].

Comprehensive and integral international convention on the protection and promotion of the rights and dignity of persons with disabilities

The Economic and Social Council,

Recalling General Assembly resolution 56/168 of 19 December 2001, by which the Assembly established an Ad Hoc Committee, open to the participation of all Member States and observers of the United Nations, to consider proposals for a comprehensive and integral international convention to promote and protect the rights and dignity of persons with disabilities, based on the holistic approach in the work carried out in the fields of social development, human rights and non-discrimination and taking into account the recommendations of the Commission on Human Rights and the Commission for Social Development,

Recalling also its resolution 2004/14 of 21 July 2004 on a comprehensive and integral international convention on the protection and promotion of the rights and dignity of persons with disabilities,

Welcoming the important contributions made so far to the work of the Ad Hoc Committee on a Comprehensive and Integral International Convention on the Protection and Promotion of the Rights and Dignity of Persons with Disabilities by all stakeholders,

Reaffirming the universality, indivisibility and interdependence of all human rights and fundamental freedoms and the need for their full enjoyment to be guaranteed to persons with disabilities, without discrimination,

Convinced of the contribution that a convention will make in this regard, and welcoming the firm support of the international community for such a convention and the continued engagement in its elaboration,

Recognizing the strong commitment and the positive steps taken by Governments to protect and promote the rights and dignity of persons with disabilities, including through collaboration and cooperation at the regional and international levels, with the aim of strengthening national capacities and supporting national efforts in order to improve the living conditions of persons with disabilities in all regions,

1. *Welcomes* the important progress achieved so far in the negotiation of a draft convention, and invites Member States and observers to continue to participate actively and constructively in the Ad Hoc Committee on a Comprehensive and Integral Inter-

national Convention on the Protection and Promotion of the Rights and Dignity of Persons with Disabilities, with a view to an early conclusion of a draft text of a convention in order to present it to the General Assembly, as a matter of priority, for adoption;

2. *Requests* the Commission for Social Development to continue to contribute to the process of negotiation of a draft international convention, bearing in mind its area of expertise and the experience in the implementation of the Standard Rules on the Equalization of Opportunities for Persons with Disabilities and the World Programme of Action concerning Disabled Persons;

3. *Welcomes* the contributions of the Special Rapporteur on Disability of the Commission for Social Development to the process of elaboration of a draft international convention, and requests the Special Rapporteur to contribute further to the work of the Ad Hoc Committee, drawing from her experience in the monitoring of the Standard Rules by, inter alia, providing her views on the elements to be considered in a draft international convention;

4. *Requests* the Department of Economic and Social Affairs of the Secretariat, through its Division for Social Policy and Development, to continue to support the work of the Ad Hoc Committee, in collaboration with the Special Rapporteur and other relevant United Nations bodies and agencies, through, inter alia, the provision of information on issues related to a draft international convention and the promotion of awareness of the work of the Ad Hoc Committee, from within existing resources;

5. *Underlines* the importance of strengthening cooperation and coordination between the Office of the United Nations High Commissioner for Human Rights and the Department of Economic and Social Affairs in order to provide technical support to the work of the Ad Hoc Committee, in accordance with General Assembly resolution 59/198 of 20 December 2004;

6. *Invites* bodies, organs and entities of the United Nations system to continue to participate, as appropriate, in the Ad Hoc Committee and to contribute to its work;

7. *Invites* non-governmental organizations, national disability and human rights institutions and independent experts with an interest in the matter to continue their active participation in and contributions to the work of the Ad Hoc Committee, and encourages the relevant bodies of the United Nations to continue to promote and support such active participation of civil society, in accordance with General Assembly resolutions 56/510 of 23 July 2002 and 57/229 of 18 December 2002;

8. *Invites* Governments, civil society and the private sector to contribute to the voluntary fund established by the General Assembly to support the participation of non-governmental organizations and experts from developing countries, in particular from least developed countries, in the work of the Ad Hoc Committee;

9. *Requests* the Secretary-General to disseminate widely to non-governmental organizations all available information on accreditation procedures, modalities and supportive measures to support their participation in the work of the Ad Hoc Committee,

as well as the criteria for the financial assistance that is available through the voluntary fund;

10. *Stresses* the need for additional efforts to ensure reasonable accessibility to facilities and documentation at the United Nations for all persons with disabilities, in accordance with General Assembly decision 56/474 of 23 July 2002;

11. *Requests* the Secretary-General and the Special Rapporteur to report to the Commission for Social Development at its forty-fourth session, on the implementation of the present resolution.

GENERAL ASSEMBLY ACTION

On 23 December [meeting 69], the General Assembly, on recommendation of the Third Committee [A/60/509/Add.2 (Part I)], adopted **resolution 60/232** without vote [agenda item 71 *(b)*].

Ad Hoc Committee on a Comprehensive and Integral International Convention on the Protection and Promotion of the Rights and Dignity of Persons with Disabilities

The General Assembly,

Recalling its resolution 56/168 of 19 December 2001, by which it decided to establish an Ad Hoc Committee, open to the participation of all Member States and observers to the United Nations, to consider proposals for a comprehensive and integral international convention to promote and protect the rights and dignity of persons with disabilities, based on a holistic approach in the work done in the fields of social development, human rights and non-discrimination and taking into account the recommendations of the Commission on Human Rights and the Commission for Social Development,

Recalling also its resolution 59/198 of 20 December 2004, as well as relevant resolutions of the Commission for Social Development and the Commission on Human Rights,

Reaffirming the universality, indivisibility, interdependence and interrelatedness of all human rights and fundamental freedoms and the need for persons with disabilities to be guaranteed their full enjoyment without discrimination,

Convinced of the contribution that a convention will make in this regard, and encouraged by the increased support of the international community for such a convention,

Welcoming with satisfaction the progress achieved so far in the negotiations on a draft convention,

Stressing the importance of the active participation of intergovernmental and non-governmental organizations and national human rights institutions in the work of the Ad Hoc Committee, and their valuable contribution to the promotion of the full enjoyment of all human rights and fundamental freedoms by persons with disabilities,

Underlining the importance of the participation of the Special Rapporteur on disability of the Commission for Social Development in the work of the Ad Hoc Committee,

Recognizing the important contributions made thus far to the Ad Hoc Committee by all stakeholders,

1. *Welcomes* the reports of the Ad Hoc Committee on a Comprehensive and Integral International Convention on the Protection and Promotion of the Rights and Dignity of Persons with Disabilities on its fifth and sixth sessions;

2. *Requests* the Secretary-General to transmit the reports of the Ad Hoc Committee to the Commission for Social Development at its forty-fourth session and to the Commission on Human Rights at its sixty-second session, and requests both Commissions to continue to contribute to the work of the Ad Hoc Committee;

3. *Invites* Member States and observers to continue to participate actively and constructively in the work of the Ad Hoc Committee with the aim of concluding a draft text of a convention and submitting it to the General Assembly, as a matter of priority, for its adoption, preferably at the sixty-first session;

4. *Decides* that the Ad Hoc Committee shall hold, within existing resources, prior to the sixty-first session of the General Assembly, two sessions in 2006, one of fifteen working days, from 16 January to 3 February, in order to achieve a complete reading of the draft text of a convention prepared by the Chairman of the Ad Hoc Committee, and one of ten working days, from 7 to 18 August;

5. *Underlines* the importance of further strengthening the cooperation and coordination between the Office of the United Nations High Commissioner for Human Rights and the Department of Economic and Social Affairs of the Secretariat in order to provide technical support to the work of the Ad Hoc Committee, and invites them to provide, in advance of the meetings of the Ad Hoc Committee, background documentation to assist Member States and observers in the negotiation of a draft convention, and to organize, in close connection and timing with the dates and venue of the meetings of the Ad Hoc Committee, meetings of experts and seminars in relation to the draft convention, within existing resources;

6. *Requests* the Secretary-General to continue to provide the Ad Hoc Committee with the facilities necessary for the performance of its work, and in this context invites the Secretary-General to reallocate resources to the United Nations Programme on Disability so as to provide support to the negotiations on a draft convention;

7. *Stresses* the need for additional efforts to ensure accessibility at the United Nations, with reasonable accommodation regarding facilities and documentation, for all persons with disabilities, in accordance with General Assembly decision 56/474 of 23 July 2002;

8. *Requests* the Secretary-General to explore and implement innovative measures, within existing resources and in consultation with organizations of persons with disabilities and the Bureau of the Ad Hoc Committee, for the provision of selected documents of the Ad Hoc Committee in formats accessible to participants with visual and hearing disabilities;

9. *Encourages* Member States to continue to include in their delegations to the Ad Hoc Committee persons with disabilities and/or other experts in the field;

10. *Urges* Member States, observers, civil society, international organizations, financial institutions and the private sector to contribute to the voluntary fund established pursuant to its resolution 57/229 of 18 December 2002 to support the participation of non-governmental organizations and experts from developing countries, in particular least developed countries, in the work of the Ad Hoc Committee;

11. *Requests* the Secretary-General to disseminate widely to non-governmental organizations all available information on accreditation procedures, modalities and supportive measures for their participation in the work of the Ad Hoc Committee, as well as the criteria for the financial assistance that is available through the voluntary fund;

12. *Also requests* the Secretary-General to transmit a comprehensive report of the Ad Hoc Committee and to report on the implementation of paragraphs 5, 6, 7, 8 and 11 of the present resolution to the General Assembly at its sixty-first session.

Cultural development

Dialogue among civilizations

In response to General Assembly resolution 56/6 [YUN 2001, p. 1014], the Secretary-General transmitted a report, in August [A/60/259], on the Global Agenda for Dialogue among Civilizations. The report discussed activities undertaken by the Member States and the United Nations Educational, Scientific and Cultural Organization (UNESCO), among others. It outlined a suggestion for a way forward, which could be achieved by securing the commitment of Governments; mobilizing role models in societies; and by changing shared narratives to reflect the increased interdependence among peoples, societies and youth. The Global Agenda for Dialogue had been a key initiative in the promotion of greater understanding among people around the world through activities, such as study tours, cultural festivals, educational exchange programmes, joint scientific research projects and conferences. The Secretariat received information on the implementation of the Global Agenda from 31 Member States and one Observer State.

On 14 July, following the proposals of Spain and Turkey, a major initiative entitled, "Alliance of Civilizations", was launched by the Secretary-General. It aimed to address efforts by the international community to bridge divides and overcome prejudice, misconceptions and polarization that potentially threatened world peace.

In the view of the Secretary-General, the most urgent task was to devise a strategy for creating a coalition of all those people who did not believe in inciting violence or supporting extremism and who made up the great majority of humankind. The Alliance of Civilizations initiative, which hopefully would receive the support of Governments, regional organizations and civil society, appeared to be the appropriate forum for the strategy. Movement towards such a coalition had to be driven by a new narrative in international relations, which would be based on the historical reality of continuous interaction among civilizations at the local, national and international levels, and on many societies where people of different cultures and religions had worked successfully together. It would recognize that confrontation was being pursued only by small (though determined) minorities. That narrative, in other words, would encompass aspirations for the future rather than the scars of the past; inclusion rather than the paradigm of "us and them"; a win-win paradigm rather than a zero-sum game. Dialogue among civilizations, like many ideas of global significance, needed to be pursued at a local level. The challenge was therefore to establish a dialogue within the confines of individual cities and countries, as well as to engage in dialogue across national and other boundaries. It was perhaps at that level that the lack of a real dialogue, between ethnically and culturally different groups sharing the same nationality, had proved most dangerous. Each culture had to develop its own narrative within its own boundaries. The hearts and minds of the next generation were the real object of a dialogue among civilizations. That meant that new narratives, if they were to catch on, needed to be validated by individuals who could inspire the young and fire their imagination. Those individuals—the role models of our societies—needed to be mobilized by the international community. They could be found in different social sectors: sport, entertainment, the media, science, education and business, and needed to be encouraged to take on an advocacy role.

Communications. On 13 May [A/60/77], the Islamic Republic of Iran transmitted to the Secretary-General a statement made by its President that was addressed to the UNESCO Conference on Dialogue among Civilizations (Paris, France, 5 April). In August [A/60/311], Iran also transmitted to the Secretary-General a national report on the implementation of the Global Agenda for Dialogue among Civilizations.

GENERAL ASSEMBLY ACTION

On 20 October [meeting 36], the General Assembly adopted **resolution 60/4** [draft: A/60/L.6 & Add.1, as orally revised] without vote [agenda item 42].

Global Agenda for Dialogue among Civilizations

The General Assembly,

Recalling its resolutions 53/22 of 4 November 1998, 54/113 of 10 December 1999 and 55/23 of 13 November 2000 entitled "United Nations Year of Dialogue among Civilizations" and its resolution 56/6

of 9 November 2001 entitled "Global Agenda for Dialogue among Civilizations",

Reaffirming the purposes and principles embodied in the Charter of the United Nations,

Recalling the United Nations Millennium Declaration adopted on 8 September 2000 which considers, inter alia, that tolerance is one of the fundamental values essential to international relations in the twenty-first century and should include the active promotion of a culture of peace and dialogue among civilizations, with human beings respecting one another in all their diversity of belief, culture and language, and neither fearing nor repressing differences within and between societies but cherishing them as a precious asset of humanity,

Recalling also the 2005 World Summit Outcome adopted at the High-level Plenary Meeting of the General Assembly, which considers, inter alia, that all cultures and civilizations contribute to the enrichment of humankind, acknowledges the importance of respect and understanding for religious and cultural diversity throughout the world and underlines the commitment of Member States to taking action to promote a culture of peace and dialogue at the local, national, regional and international levels,

Underlining the fact that all civilizations celebrate the unity and diversity of humankind and are enriched and have evolved through dialogue with other civilizations and that positive and mutually beneficial interaction among civilizations has continued throughout human history despite impediments arising from intolerance, disputes and wars,

Emphasizing that all peoples have the right of self-determination, by virtue of which they freely determine their political status and freely pursue their economic, social and cultural development,

Underlining the fact that the Global Agenda for Dialogue among Civilizations has been a key initiative in the promotion of greater understanding among civilizations and people around the world,

Reaffirming the objectives and principles of dialogue among civilizations, as elaborated in the Global Agenda,

Reiterating that dialogue among civilizations is a process between and within civilizations, founded on inclusion, and a collective desire to learn, uncover and examine assumptions, unfold shared meanings and core values, and integrate multiple perspectives through dialogue,

Emphasizing that the hearts and minds of the next generation are the real object of the dialogue among civilizations,

Welcoming the numerous initiatives and efforts to further promote dialogue among civilizations undertaken by States, the United Nations system, including the Personal Representative of the Secretary-General for the United Nations Year of Dialogue among Civilizations, and other international and regional organizations and civil society and non-governmental organizations, and the value of different initiatives on dialogue among cultures and civilizations, including the dialogue on interfaith cooperation and the initiative of the Alliance of Civilizations,

Commending the United Nations Educational, Scientific and Cultural Organization for its contribution to implementing the Global Agenda by including it in its medium-term strategy for 2002-2007 with a view to achieving its strategic objective of safeguarding cultural diversity and encouraging dialogue among cultures and civilizations,

1. *Takes note with appreciation* of the report of the Secretary-General submitted to the General Assembly at its sixtieth session in accordance with resolution 56/6;

2. *Expresses its firm determination* to further facilitate and promote dialogue among civilizations;

3. *Affirms* that, taking into account the Programme of Action of the Global Agenda for Dialogue among Civilizations, concrete and sustained activities should be designed and implemented in all regions by the widest possible range of partners and stakeholders;

4. *Reaffirms* that Member States have committed themselves to advancing human welfare, freedom and progress everywhere, and to encouraging tolerance, respect, dialogue and cooperation among different cultures, civilizations and peoples;

5. *Also reaffirms* that tolerance and respect for diversity and universal promotion and protection of human rights are mutually supportive, and recognizes that tolerance and respect for diversity effectively promote and are supported by, inter alia, the empowerment of women;

6. *Invites* States, international and regional organizations and civil society, including non-governmental organizations, to develop appropriate ways and means at the local, national, regional and international levels to further promote dialogue and mutual understanding among civilizations and to report on their activities to the Secretary-General;

7. *Invites* the United Nations system to continue to encourage and facilitate dialogue among civilizations and formulate ways and means to promote dialogue among civilizations in the activities of the United Nations in various fields;

8. *Requests* the Secretary-General to explore enhancing implementation mechanisms for the Global Agenda and for the present resolution and to report thereon to the General Assembly at its sixty-fifth session.

Culture of peace

In **resolution 60/3** of 20 October on the International Decade for a Culture of Peace and Non-Violence for the Children of the World, 2001-2010 (see p. 746), the General Assembly encouraged the appropriate authorities to provide education for children that included lessons in mutual understanding, tolerance, active citizenship, human rights and the promotion of a culture of peace. It also invited Member States to observe 21 September each year as the International day of peace, and as a day of global ceasefire and non-violence, in accordance with Assembly resolution 55/282 [YUN 2001, p. 575].

Religious and cultural understanding

By a 5 August report [A/60/201], the Secretary-General transmitted replies from 17 Member States and two UN agencies in response to a UN

Secretariat request for information on steps taken to implement General Assembly resolution 59/23 [YUN 2004, p. 1102], which dealt with the promotion of interreligious dialogue. The report also provided information on the implementation of Assembly resolution 59/142 [ibid.] on the promotion of religious and cultural understanding, harmony and cooperation.

UNESCO designated the promotion of interfaith dialogue as a flagship activity of the organization in its draft programme and budget for 2006 and 2007 and intensified its activities in the field of dialogue among civilizations, cultures and peoples. The United Nations Population Fund (UNFPA) was engaged in growing collaboration with members of religious communities to create, among other things, bridges of dialogue between the United Nations and the different religious establishments in the world.

The Secretariat's Department of Public Information launched a series of seminars in 2004 on the subject of "Unlearning Intolerance", which examined different manifestations of intolerance and explored ways to promote respect and understanding among peoples. The first two seminars focused on anti-Semitism and Islamophobia.

In related developments, the Assembly had before it UNESCO's midterm global review of the International Decade for a Culture of Peace and Non-Violence for the Children of the World, 2001-2010 [A/60/279] (see p. 746). The Assembly also took note of several initiatives on interreligious, intercultural and intercivilizational dialogues and cooperation for peace, including the Asia-Europe Meeting on Interfaith Dialogue (Bali, Indonesia, 21-22 July), co-hosted by Indonesia and the United Kingdom, which concluded with the Bali Declaration on Building Interfaith Harmony within the International Community [A/60/254]; the Conference on Interfaith Cooperation for Peace: Enhancing Interfaith Dialogue and Cooperation Towards Peace in the Twenty-first Century (New York, 22 June) [A/60/269-E/2005/91]; and the Informal Meeting of Leaders on Interfaith Dialogue and Cooperation for Peace (New York, 13 September) [A/60/383].

GENERAL ASSEMBLY ACTION

On 3 November [meeting 43], the General Assembly adopted **resolution 60/10** [draft: A/60/L.4/Rev.1 &Add.1], without vote [agenda item 43].

Promotion of interreligious dialogue and cooperation for peace

The General Assembly,

Reaffirming the purposes and principles enshrined in the Charter of the United Nations,

Recalling its resolutions 56/6 of 9 November 2001, on the Global Agenda for Dialogue among Civilizations, 57/6 of 4 November 2002, concerning the promotion of a culture of peace and non-violence, 57/337 of 3 July 2003, on the prevention of armed conflict, 58/128 of 19 December 2003, on the promotion of religious and cultural understanding, harmony and cooperation, 59/199 of 20 December 2004, on the elimination of all forms of religious intolerance, and 59/23 of 11 November 2004, on the promotion of interreligious dialogue,

Recalling also the 2005 World Summit Outcome of 16 September 2005, in which the Heads of State and Government reaffirmed the value of the dialogue on interfaith cooperation and committed themselves to taking action to promote a culture of peace and dialogue at the local, national, regional and international levels,

Affirming the need for all States to continue international efforts to enhance dialogue and broaden understanding among civilizations, in an effort to prevent the indiscriminate targeting of different religions and cultures,

Underlining the importance of promoting understanding, tolerance and friendship among human beings in all their diversity of religion, belief, culture and language, and recalling that all States have pledged themselves under the Charter to promote and encourage universal respect for and observance of human rights and fundamental freedoms for all without distinction as to race, sex, language or religion,

Taking note of several mutually inclusive and reinforcing initiatives on interreligious, intercultural and intercivilizational dialogues and cooperation for peace, including the Regional Summit on Interreligious and Inter-ethnic Dialogue, held in Tirana on 9 and 10 December 2004, the meeting on Intercultural and Interreligious Dialogue for the South-East Asia and the Pacific Region, held in Melbourne, Australia, from 12 to 14 April 2005, the initiative of Pakistan on "enlightened moderation", endorsed by the Organization of the Islamic Conference, the International Conference on Environment, Peace and the Dialogue among Civilizations and Cultures, held in Tehran on 9 and 10 May 2005, the launch of the Alliance of Civilizations by the Secretary-General on 14 July 2005, the launch of the World Summit on Christian-Muslim Relations, to be held in Senegal in 2007, the Congress of Leaders of World and Traditional Religions, held triennially in Astana, the Asia-Europe Meeting Interfaith Dialogue on the theme "Building Interfaith Harmony within the International Community", held in Bali, Indonesia, on 21 and 22 July 2005, the Conference on Interfaith Cooperation for Peace: Enhancing Interfaith Dialogue and Cooperation Towards Peace in the Twenty-first Century, held at United Nations Headquarters on 22 June 2005, and the Informal Meeting of Leaders on Interfaith Dialogue and Cooperation for Peace, held at United Nations Headquarters on 13 September 2005,

Recognizing the commitment of all religions to peace,

1. *Affirms* that mutual understanding and interreligious dialogue constitute important dimensions of the dialogue among civilizations and of the culture of peace;

2. *Takes note with appreciation* of the work of the United Nations Educational, Scientific and Cultural Organization on interreligious dialogue in the context of its efforts to promote dialogue among civilizations, cultures and peoples, as well as activities related to a culture of peace, welcomes its focus on concrete action at both the global and the regional and subregional levels and its new flagship activity on the promotion of interfaith dialogue, and encourages relevant bodies of the United Nations to work closely with the Organization and coordinate their efforts in this regard;

3. *Invites* the Secretary-General to continue to bring the promotion of interreligious dialogue to the attention of all Governments, regional organizations and relevant international organizations, including ways to strengthen the linkages and focus more on practical actions in the implementation of the initiatives on interreligious dialogue and cooperation for peace;

4. *Also invites* the Secretary-General, in the context of his report to the General Assembly at its sixty-first session under the item entitled "Culture of peace", to include information on the implementation of the present resolution.

Also on the same date, [meeting 43], the Assembly adopted **resolution 60/11** [draft: A/60/L.10 & Add.1] without vote [agenda item 43].

Promotion of religious and cultural understanding, harmony and cooperation

The General Assembly,

Reaffirming the purposes and principles enshrined in the Charter of the United Nations and the Universal Declaration of Human Rights, in particular the right to freedom of thought, of conscience and of religion,

Recalling the Global Agenda for Dialogue among Civilizations and the Universal Declaration on Cultural Diversity of the United Nations Educational, Scientific and Cultural Organization, as well as the principles contained therein,

Underlining the importance of promoting understanding, tolerance and friendship among human beings in all their diversity of religion, belief, culture and language, and recalling that all States have pledged themselves under the Charter to promote and encourage universal respect for and observance of human rights and fundamental freedoms for all, without distinction as to race, sex, language or religion,

Taking note of the adoption of the 2005 World Summit Outcome at the High-level Plenary Meeting of the General Assembly, which acknowledges the importance of respect and understanding for religious and cultural diversity throughout the world, and emphasizing the commitment contained therein to advance human welfare, freedom and progress everywhere, as well as to encourage tolerance, respect, dialogue and cooperation among different cultures, civilizations and peoples, in order to promote international peace and security,

Recalling its resolutions 59/23 of 11 November 2004 and 59/142 and 59/143 of 15 December 2004, and all other relevant resolutions,

Recognizing that interreligious dialogue and understanding, including the awareness of differences and commonalities among peoples and civilizations, contribute to the peaceful resolution of conflicts and disputes and reduce the potential for animosity, clashes and even violence,

Taking note of the valuable contribution of various initiatives at the national, regional and international level, such as the Alliance of Civilizations initiative, the Bali Declaration on Building Interfaith Harmony within the International Community, the Congress of Leaders of World and Traditional Religions, the Dialogue among Civilizations and Cultures, the strategy of "enlightened moderation", the Informal Meeting of Leaders on Interfaith Dialogue and Cooperation for Peace and the Islam-Christianity Dialogue, which are all mutually inclusive, reinforcing and interrelated,

Emphasizing the need, at all levels of society and among nations, for strengthening freedom, justice, democracy, tolerance, solidarity, cooperation, pluralism, respect for diversity of culture and religion or belief, dialogue and understanding, which are important elements for peace, and convinced that the guiding principles of democratic society need to be actively promoted by the international community,

Reaffirming that freedom of expression, media pluralism, multilingualism, equal access to art and to scientific and technological knowledge, including in digital form, and the possibility for all cultures to have access to the means of expression and dissemination are the guarantees of cultural diversity, and that in ensuring the free flow of ideas by word and image, care should be exercised that all cultures can express themselves and make themselves known,

Recognizing all efforts made by the United Nations system and other international and regional organizations to promote understanding, tolerance and friendship among human beings in all their diversity of culture, religion, belief and language,

Alarmed that serious instances of intolerance and discrimination on the grounds of religion or belief, including acts of violence, intimidation and coercion motivated by religious intolerance, are on the increase in many parts of the world and threaten the enjoyment of human rights and fundamental freedoms,

Considering that tolerance for cultural, ethnic, and religious and linguistic diversities, as well as dialogue among and within civilizations, is essential for peace, understanding and friendship among individuals and people of different cultures and nations of the world, while manifestations of cultural prejudice, intolerance and xenophobia towards different cultures and religions generate hatred and violence among peoples and nations throughout the world,

Emphasizing that combating hatred, prejudice, intolerance and stereotyping on the basis of religion or culture represents a significant global challenge that requires further action,

1. *Takes note* of the report transmitted by the Secretary-General in accordance with resolutions 59/142 and 59/143;

2. *Acknowledges* that respect for the diversity of religions and cultures, tolerance, dialogue and co-operation in a climate of mutual trust and understanding can contribute to the combating of ideologies and practices based on discrimination, intolerance and hatred and help to reinforce world peace, social justice and friendship among peoples;

3. *Reaffirms* the solemn commitment of all States to fulfil their obligations to promote universal respect for, and observance and protection of, all human rights and fundamental freedoms for all in accordance with the Charter of the United Nations, other instruments relating to human rights and international law; the universal nature of these rights and freedoms is beyond question;

4. *Also reaffirms* the importance for all peoples and nations to hold, develop and preserve their cultural heritage and traditions in a national and international atmosphere of peace, tolerance and mutual respect;

5. *Recognizes* that respect for religious and cultural diversity in an increasingly globalizing world contributes to international cooperation, promotes enhanced dialogue among religions, cultures and civilizations and helps to create an environment conducive to the exchange of human experience;

6. *Also recognizes* that, despite intolerance and conflicts that are creating a divide across countries and regions and constitute a growing threat to peaceful relations among nations, all cultures and civilizations share a common set of universal values and can all contribute to the enrichment of humankind;

7. *Further recognizes* that, while the significance of national and regional particularities and various historical, cultural and religious backgrounds must be borne in mind, it is the duty of States, regardless of their political, economic and cultural systems, to promote and protect all human rights and fundamental freedoms;

8. *Reaffirms* that the promotion and protection of the rights of persons belonging to national or ethnic, religious and linguistic minorities contribute to political and social stability and peace and enrich the cultural diversity and heritage of society as a whole in the States in which such persons live, and urges States to ensure that their political and legal systems reflect the multicultural diversity within their societies and, where necessary, to improve democratic and political institutions, organizations and practices so that they are more fully participatory and avoid the marginalization and exclusion of, and discrimination against, specific sectors of society;

9. *Encourages* Governments to promote, including through education, as well as the development of progressive curriculums and text books, understanding, tolerance and friendship among human beings in all their diversity of religion, belief, culture and language, which will address the cultural, social, economic, political and religious sources of intolerance, and to apply a gender perspective while doing so, in order to promote understanding, tolerance, peace and friendly relations among nations and all racial and religious groups, recognizing that education at all levels is one of the principal means to build a culture of peace;

10. *Calls upon* all States to exert their utmost efforts to ensure that religious and cultural sites are

fully respected and protected in compliance with their international obligations and in accordance with their national legislation, and to adopt adequate measures aimed at preventing acts or threats of damage to and destruction of these sites;

11. *Urges* States, in compliance with their international obligations, to take all necessary action to combat incitement to or acts of violence, intimidation and coercion motivated by hatred and intolerance based on culture, religion or belief, which may cause discord and disharmony within and among societies;

12. *Also urges* States to take effective measures to prevent and eliminate discrimination on the grounds of religion or belief in the recognition, exercise and enjoyment of human rights and fundamental freedoms in all fields of civil, economic, political, social and cultural life and to make all efforts to enact or rescind legislation, where necessary, to prohibit any such discrimination, and to take all appropriate measures to combat intolerance on the grounds of religion or beliefs;

13. *Further urges* States to ensure that, in the course of their official duties, members of law enforcement bodies and the military, civil servants, educators and other public officials respect different religions and beliefs and do not discriminate against persons professing other religions or beliefs, and that any necessary and appropriate education or training is provided;

14. *Welcomes* the efforts of States, relevant entities of the United Nations system and other intergovernmental organizations, civil society, including religion-based and other non-governmental organizations, and the media in developing a culture of peace, and encourages them to continue such efforts, including the promotion of interreligious and intercultural interaction within and among societies through, inter alia, congresses, conferences, seminars, workshops, research work and related processes;

15. *Requests* the Secretary-General to ensure the widest dissemination of the relevant United Nations material related to the present resolution in as many different languages as possible through the United Nations system, including the United Nations information centres, within available resources;

16. *Also requests* the Secretary-General, in the context of his report to the General Assembly at its sixty-first session under the item entitled "Culture of peace", to include information on the implementation of the present resolution.

Sports for development and peace

International Year of Sport and Physical Education (2005)

In response to resolution 58/5 [YUN 2003, p. 1111], in which the General Assembly proclaimed 2005 as the International Year of Sport and Physical Education, the Secretary-General reported, in August [A/60/217], on activities planned for the observance of the Year and on the status of the drafting of an international convention against doping in sport.

The activities and initiatives to commemorate the International Year highlighted the significant role that sport could play in accelerating progress towards the achievement of the MDGs by 2015 and added an impetus to efforts to better integrate sport into the development agenda. Sport-related activities of Governments and NGOs, undertaken with the United Nations and other partners within the framework of the International Year, were widespread and gaining momentum. Programmes promoting sport for development and peace had received greater attention and resources from Governments, civil society and private sector partners.

In order to capitalize on both the accomplishments and the potential for sport that the International Year was demonstrating, further initiatives were needed to incorporate sport as a useful tool in programmes for development and peace and to include sports-based initiatives in country programmes of the UN system, as appropriate and according to local needs. It was imperative that the programmes and institutional and advocacy initiatives that advanced sport for development and peace during the International Year lead to sustained long-term effects within the United Nations and among Governments, the private sector and civil society partners. Further steps included continuing to work according to the business plan of the United Nations Communications Group Working Group on Sport for Development and Peace and expanding and strengthening UN partnerships with Governments, international sports organizations and the private sector. Specific actions would include furthering efforts to encourage additional Member States to establish national focal points and national committees that would ideally become an integral part of governmental structures to ensure the sustainable continuation of mainstream sporting activities within society.

GENERAL ASSEMBLY ACTION

On 3 November[meeting 43], the General Assembly adopted **resolution 60/8** [draft: A/60/L.15 & Add.1] without vote [agenda item 48 *(a)*].

Building a peaceful and better world through sport and the Olympic ideal

The General Assembly,

Recalling its resolution 56/75 of 11 December 2001, in which it decided to consider the item entitled "Building a peaceful and better world through sport and the Olympic ideal" every two years in advance of each Summer and Winter Olympic Games,

Recalling also its resolution 58/6 of 3 November 2003, in which it decided to include in the provisional agenda of its sixtieth session the sub-item entitled "Building a peaceful and better world through sport and the Olympic ideal" and to consider this sub-item before the XX Olympic Winter Games,

Bearing in mind its resolution 48/11 of 25 October 1993, which, inter alia, revived the ancient Greek tradition of *ekecheiria* or "Olympic Truce" calling for a truce during the Games that would encourage a peaceful environment and ensuring the safe passage and participation of athletes and others at the Games and, thereby, mobilizing the youth of the world to the cause of peace,

Taking into account the inclusion in the United Nations Millennium Declaration of an appeal for the observance of the Olympic Truce now and in the future and support for the International Olympic Committee in its efforts to promote peace and human understanding through sport and the Olympic ideal,

Recalling its resolution 58/5 of 3 November 2003, in which it decided to proclaim 2005 the International Year for Sport and Physical Education, as a means to promote education, health, development and peace,

Recognizing that the goal of the Olympic movement is to build a peaceful and better world by educating the youth of the world through sport, practised without discrimination of any kind and in the Olympic spirit, which is based on mutual understanding, friendship, solidarity and fair play,

Welcoming the joint endeavours of the International Olympic Committee and the United Nations system in fields such as human development and poverty alleviation, humanitarian assistance, health promotion and HIV/AIDS prevention, combating malaria, tuberculosis and other infectious diseases, basic education, gender equality and environmental protection,

Recognizing the important role of sport in achieving internationally agreed development goals, including those contained in the Millennium Declaration, and reaffirming the commitments undertaken in this regard by the Heads of State and Government gathered at the World Summit of the General Assembly, held in New York from 14 to 16 September 2005,

Noting with satisfaction the flying of the United Nations flag at the Olympic Games,

1. *Urges* Member States to observe, within the framework of the Charter of the United Nations, the Olympic Truce, individually or collectively, during the XX Olympic Winter Games, to be held in Turin, Italy, from 10 to 26 February 2006, and the following Paralympic Winter Games, to be held also in Turin, from 10 to 19 March 2006, by ensuring the safe passage and participation of athletes at the Games;

2. *Welcomes* the decision of the International Olympic Committee to mobilize international sports organizations and the National Olympic Committees of the Member States to undertake concrete actions at the local, national, regional and world levels to promote and strengthen a culture of peace based on the spirit of the Olympic Truce and to cooperate with the national committees of the International Year for Sport and Physical Education;

3. *Requests* the Secretary-General to promote the observance of the Olympic Truce among Member States, drawing the attention of world public opinion

to the contribution such a truce would make to the promotion of international understanding, peace and goodwill, and to cooperate with the International Olympic Committee in the realization of this objective;

4. *Calls upon* Member States to cooperate with the International Olympic Committee and all concerned agencies and programmes of the United Nations in their efforts to use the Olympic Truce as an instrument to promote peace, during and beyond the Olympic Games period, and to implement projects using sport as a tool for development;

5. *Decides* to include in the provisional agenda of its sixty-second session the sub-item entitled "Building a peaceful and better world through sport and the Olympic ideal" and to consider this sub-item before the Games of the XXIX Olympiad, to be held in Beijing in 2008.

The Assembly, also on the same date [meeting 43], **adopted resolution 60/9** [draft: A/60/L.7 & Add.1], without vote [agenda item 48 *(b)*].

Sport as a means to promote education, health, development and peace

The General Assembly,

Recalling its resolutions 58/5 of 3 November 2003 and 59/10 of 27 October 2004, and its decision to proclaim 2005 the International Year for Sport and Physical Education, as a means to promote education, health, development and peace,

Recalling also its resolution 60/1 of 16 September 2005, in which it underlined that sport could foster peace and development and could contribute to an atmosphere of tolerance and understanding,

Acknowledging the major role of the United Nations, its funds and programmes, the United Nations Development Programme, the United Nations Educational, Scientific and Cultural Organization and other specialized agencies, in promoting human development through sport and physical education, through its country programmes,

Recalling the Convention on the Rights of the Child and the outcome document of the special session of the General Assembly on children, entitled "A world fit for children", stressing that education shall be directed to the development of children's personality, talents and mental and physical abilities to their fullest potential,

Acknowledging with concern the dangers faced by sportsmen and sportswomen, in particular young athletes, including child labour, violence, doping, early specialization, over-training and exploitative forms of commercialization, as well as less visible threats and deprivations, such as the premature severance of family bonds and the loss of sporting, social and cultural ties,

Considering the contribution of sport and physical education towards achieving the internationally agreed development goals, including those contained in the United Nations Millennium Declaration and the broader aims of development and peace,

Noting that sport and physical education is a lifelong activity and constitutes a major tool for health and physical development and for acquiring values necessary for social cohesion and intercultural dialogue,

Acknowledging that sport and physical education can present opportunities for solidarity and cooperation in order to promote tolerance, a culture of peace, social and gender equality, adequate responses to the special needs of persons with disabilities, dialogue and harmony,

Acknowledging also the contribution of the Olympic Games to understanding, peace and tolerance among and between peoples and civilizations,

Recognizing the need for greater coordination of efforts at the international level to facilitate a more effective fight against doping,

Noting the need for the development of a common framework within the United Nations to promote sport for education, health, development and peace,

Recognizing the need to maintain the momentum generated by the commemoration of the International Year for Sport and Physical Education, as a means to promote education, health, development and peace, through, inter alia, increased voluntary contributions and well-targeted communications-based activities,

1. *Takes note with appreciation* of the report of the Secretary-General entitled "Sport for peace and development: International Year of Sport and Physical Education";

2. *Welcomes* the widespread commitment demonstrated by Member States, sport-related organizations and the private sector for the successful commemoration of the International Year for Sport and Physical Education, as a means to promote education, health, development and peace, through the organization of activities and events at national, regional and international levels, including:

(*a*) The holding of international conferences emphasizing the role of sport as a means to promote education, health, development and peace;

(*b*) The setting up of a network of national focal points virtually in every region;

(*c*) The organization of youth leadership summits that highlight the use of sport as an entry point towards the achievement of the Millennium Development Goals;

(*d*) The strengthening of cooperation with the International Olympic Committee, sport-related associations and other partners;

(*e*) The appointment of sport celebrities as spokespersons for the International Year for Sport and Physical Education, as a means to promote education, health, development and peace;

3. *Notes* the elaboration of a business plan by the Working Group on Sport for Development and Peace of the United Nations Communications Group, as a common framework to foster coordination and cooperation for a more systematic and coherent use of sport as a means to promote education, health, development and peace, and requests the Secretary-General to disseminate the business plan as widely as possible among Member States, the United Nations system and sport-related organizations;

4. *Requests* the Secretary-General:

(*a*) To elaborate an action plan that will expand and strengthen United Nations partnerships with Governments, sport-related organizations and the private sector, on the basis, inter alia, of an assessment of progress achieved, steps taken and difficulties encountered in realizing the potential of sport as a tool for development and peace;

(*b*) To strengthen advocacy and social mobilization, especially at the national, regional and international levels, through well-targeted communications-based activities, and stresses the contribution of the United Nations Sport Bulletin as well as websites in this regard;

5. *Invites* Member States to provide voluntary contributions to ensure adequate execution of and follow-up to the activities being implemented by the Office of Sport for Development and Peace;

6. *Invites* Member States, the United Nations system, international sports bodies and sport-related organizations to promote further sport and physical education, including assistance for the building and restoration of sports infrastructures, the implementation of partnership initiatives and development projects, as a contribution towards achieving the internationally agreed development goals, including those contained in the United Nations Millennium Declaration, and the broader aims of development and peace;

7. *Invites* Governments and international sports bodies to assist developing countries, in particular the least developed countries and small island developing States, in their capacity-building efforts in sport and physical education, by providing financial, technical and logistic resources for the development of sports programmes;

8. *Welcomes* the adoption of the International Convention against Doping in Sport by the General Conference of the United Nations Educational, Scientific and Cultural Organization at its thirty-third session, and invites Member States to consider adhering to this Convention as early as possible;

9. *Requests* the Secretary-General to report to the General Assembly at its sixty-first session on the implementation of the present resolution and on the events organized at the national, regional and international levels to celebrate the International Year in 2005, under the item entitled "Sport for peace and development".

Crime prevention and criminal justice

Eleventh UN Crime Congress

The Eleventh United Nations Congress on Crime Prevention and Criminal Justice, held in Bangkok, Thailand from 18 to 25 April [A/CONF.203/18], adopted the Bangkok Declaration on Synergies and Responses: Strategic Alliances in Crime Prevention and Criminal Justice. The Declaration addressed major crime and criminal justice issues of concern to the international community, such as transnational organized crime, trafficking in human beings, corruption, terrorism, money-laundering, cybercrime, treatment of prisoners, juvenile justice and restorative justice, and called for enhanced international cooperation, including through the implementation of existing international instruments on crime prevention and terrorism and through the provision of technical assistance. The Congress also approved the report of the Credentials Committee.

The Congress was attended by 129 States, observers from UN offices, intergovernmental organizations, NGOs and over 1,100 experts. It was held under the theme "Synergies and responses: strategic alliances in crime prevention and criminal justice".

The Congress considered five major topics, with corresponding working papers prepared by the secretariat on: effective measures to combat transnational organized crime [A/CONF.203/4]; international cooperation against terrorism and links between terrorism and other criminal activities in the context of the work of UNODC [A/CONF.203/5]; corruption: threats and trends in the twenty-first century [A/CONF.203/6]; economic and financial crimes: challenges to sustainable development [A/CONF.203/7]; and making standards work: fifty years of standard-setting in crime prevention and criminal justice [A/CONF.203/8] (see p. 1235).

A report entitled "Fifty years of United Nations congresses on crime prevention and criminal justice: past accomplishments and future prospects" [A/CONF.203/15] was prepared by the secretary-general of the Congress as a background document. According to the report, past UN congresses on crime prevention and criminal justice had managed to develop material that might be regarded as "legislative", in the sense that it set out normative standards applicable to all States. Most of the material was "soft law", contained in resolutions of the relevant UN bodies. Increasingly, however, some of the material was being incorporated into treaty language or finding its way into the corpus of customary international law. Being the product of over a half a century of work, that material could hardly be described as a complete code of recommended practices. The instruments represented areas on which it was possible to gain a wide degree of consensus at a particular time. Their impact on the development of criminal justice, the strengthening of the notion of the rule of law and, more generally, a universal conscience of propriety, liberty and respect for common values was unquestionable. However, much work remained to be done and more challenges were emerging daily, such as new forms of economic crime or cybercrime.

The Congress also had before it a report on the state of crime and criminal justice worldwide [A/CONF.203/3], prepared by the Secretary-General in accordance with General Assembly resolution 59/151 [YUN 2004, p. 1108]. A more elaborate draft study on trends in crime and justice, carried out jointly by the United Nations Interregional Crime and Justice Research Institute and UNODC, was made available to the Congress for comment.

In accordance with Assembly resolution 59/151, a high-level segment of the Congress was held from 23 to 25 April. The government ministers and other high-level government officials who participated in the high-level segment highlighted the broad range of issues on the agenda of the Congress and the many changes that had taken place since the Tenth Congress, held in Vienna in April 2000 [YUN 2000, p. 1040]. It was noted that terrorism, weapons of mass destruction and organized crime had become global threats. The Congress offered the international community a unique opportunity to exchange experiences and views on how to deal with those new challenges, especially in view of their interconnected nature and their serious impact on security, stability and development, as reflected in the report of the High-level Panel on Threats, Challenges and Change entitled "A more secure world: our shared responsibility" [YUN 2004, p. 54], and the report of the Secretary-General entitled "In larger freedom: towards development, security and human rights for all" (see p. 67).

The Eleventh Congress elected Suwat Liptapanlop (Thailand) as its President.

The Secretary-General, in a statement read by the secretary-general of the Congress at the opening of the Eleventh Congress, said that organized crime was a leading threat to international peace and security and that the UN congresses on crime prevention and criminal justice should serve as a reminder of how much more needed to be done to tackle that threat. He noted the progress made in building a framework of international standards and norms for the fight against organized crime and terrorism, though he emphasized that a global strategy for that fight had to include the universal ratification and implementation of the United Nations Convention against Transnational Organized Crime and the Protocols thereto [YUN 2000, p. 1048], the United Nations Convention against Corruption [YUN 2003, p. 1127], and universal counter-terrorism instruments.

The Secretary-General submitted to the Assembly, in July, the report on the Eleventh Congress [A/60/172], highlighting the main features of the Congress, including the high-level segment, the discussions on the substantive items on its agenda and the outcome of the workshops held within the framework of the Congress.

On 16 December, the Assembly took note of the Secretary-General's report on the Eleventh Congress (**decision 60/536**).

Commission on Crime Prevention and Criminal Justice

The Commission on Crime Prevention and Criminal Justice, at its fourteenth session (Vienna, 23-27 May) [E/2005/30], considered the unedited report of the Eleventh Congress and a May note by the Secretariat [E/CN.15/2005/5] containing the Bangkok Declaration. The note recalled that the General Assembly, in resolution 59/151, had requested the Commission to give priority in 2005 to the conclusions and recommendations of the Eleventh Congress, with a view to recommending, through the Economic and Social Council, follow-up by the Assembly at its sixtieth (2005) session.

Following deliberations, the Commission recommended to the Council 6 draft resolutions for adoption by the Assembly and 4 draft resolutions and 3 draft decisions for adoption by the Council. The draft resolutions for adoption by the Assembly contained in Chapter I, Section A of the report related to the preparations for the Eleventh Congress, a bilateral agreement on the sharing of confiscated proceeds of crime or property, action against transnational organized crime, corruption and strengthening of international cooperation in the implementation of universal conventions, and protocols related to terrorism within the framework of UNODC activities. The draft resolutions and decisions for adoption by the Council related to witness protection, child victims, strengthening the rule of law and crime reporting, capital punishment and the holding of a roundtable on Africa. (see specific headings below.)

A thematic discussion was held on the conclusions and recommendations of the Eleventh Congress. The Commission also considered plans of action for the implementation of the Vienna Declaration on Crime and Justice (see p. 1211), strategic management and programme questions, and the provisional agenda for its fifteenth (2006) session.

On 22 July, the Council decided not to recommend for adoption by the Assembly the draft resolutions contained in chapter I, section A of the report of the Commission on Crime Prevention and Criminal Justice on its fourteenth session (**decision 2005/246**).

It took note of the Commission's report on its fourteenth session and approved the provisional agenda and documentation for the fifteenth session (**decision 2005/249**).

By a 19 December note [E/CN.15/2006/6], the Secretary-General transmitted to the Commission the report of the Board of Trustees of the United Nations Interregional Crime and Justice Research Institute. The Board, which held its fifteenth session (Turin, Italy, 17-18 November), reviewed and evaluated the Institute's 2005 activities and considered the 2006-2007 work programme and related budget proposals.

Strategic management and programme questions

At its fourteenth session, the Commission reviewed its strategic management and programme questions. It considered a March report [E/CN.15/2005/17] by the Secretary-General, submitted in response to General Assembly resolution 59/152 [YUN 2004, p. 1107], on assistance to least developed countries to ensure their participation in the sessions of the Commission and of States parties. The report stated that the review process of the implementation of crime prevention instruments at the conferences of States parties stood to benefit from the participation of all States parties to the instruments. By participating in the meetings of the Commission and the conferences, least developed countries would be able to express their concerns and also obtain information and knowledge to help them develop capacities for crime prevention and criminal justice.

In response to Economic and Social Council resolution 2003/24 [YUN 2003, p. 1123], the UNODC Executive Director presented a report [E/CN.15/2005/18] entitled "Work of the Centre for International Crime Prevention, including the management of the United Nations Crime Prevention and Criminal Justice Fund". The three intersessional meetings of the Commission, which were held in March 2005, discussed the status of preparations, as well as organizational matters for the Eleventh United Nations Congress on Crime Prevention and Criminal Justice and finalized the provisional agenda, documentation and arrangements for the fourteenth session of the Commission.

On the area of management, initiatives to maintain and strengthen dialogue with Member States continued, especially in the context of UNODC's programme management reforms. In addition, the Executive Director and senior staff met frequently with the chairmen of regional groups and representatives of Member States to update them on latest developments.

As at 15 March, total contributions and pledges to the United Nations Crime Prevention and Criminal Justice Fund from January 2004 to 2005 totalled $19,135,306. By June, the amount had increased to $27,825,470, or 104 per cent over the previous year. Of those contributions, $26,174,054 (or more than 94 per cent) were earmarked for specific projects.

Follow-up to Vienna Declaration on Crime and Justice

The Secretary-General, in response to General Assembly resolution 59/151 [YUN 2004, p.1108], submitted an April report [E/CN.15/ 2005/12] on the follow-up to the 2002 plans of action for the implementation of the Vienna Declaration on Crime and Justice: Meeting the challenges of the twenty-first century [YUN 2002, p. 1099]. The Vienna Declaration was adopted by the Assembly in December 2000 [YUN 2000, p. 1091]. The report highlighted the measures adopted by 22 Member States, 7 intergovernmental and 3 non-governmental organizations on the formulation of legislative policies and programmes in crime prevention and criminal justice at the national and international levels. The States adopted measures to address the problem of transnational organized crime, corruption, trafficking, smuggling of migrants, illicit manufacturing of firearms, money-laundering, terrorism, crime prevention, prison overcrowding, witnesses and victims of crime, high-technology and computer-related crime, juvenile justice, special needs of women in the criminal justice system, standards and norms, and restorative justice. Intergovernmental and non-governmental organizations affirmed the need for securing political, social and economic fairness in order to address the causes of criminality.

Crime prevention programme

At its fourteenth session, the Commission on Crime Prevention and Criminal Justice considered the UNODC Executive Director's report entitled "Development, security and justice for all" [E/CN.7/2005/6-E/CN.15/2005/2], and examined the Office's 2004 strategy to counter problems of organized crime and corruption, drug abuse, trafficking and terrorism. It highlighted UNODC's work in peace and security, poverty eradication, and the rule of law and good governance. UNODC assisted States in complying with international conventions on international drug control, organized crime, corruption and terrorism, through the provision of legal and technical assistance and law enforcement support in the context of its Global Programme against Corruption,

Global Programme against Money Laundering and Global Programme against Terrorism. Special emphasis was placed on HIV/AIDS prevention in the context of drug abuse.

UNODC advised Governments in enhancing their capacity to administer criminal law. In Afghanistan, legal assistance activities aimed at supporting the Afghan authorities in implementing a new drug control law and strengthening the drug control machinery were launched. In addition, UNODC helped major seaports in Africa, Asia and Latin America by establishing a container programme aimed at disrupting the flow of illicit commodities. In law enforcement, UNODC trained judges, magistrates, prosecutors and investigators from Eastern and Southern Africa on drug cases. It also supported improvements in the law enforcement capacity at points of entry in several countries in Eastern and Southern Africa, aimed at reducing the flow of drugs and other contraband, including precious metals, endangered species and stolen vehicles trafficked by organized crime syndicates.

The Commission also considered the Secretary-General's report [E/CN.15/2005/15] on action taken to promote effective crime prevention, submitted in response to Economic and Social Council resolution 2002/13 [YUN 2002, p. 1125]. The report stated that capacity in crime prevention was a renewable and sustainable resource that could flourish when community participation and democratic values were promoted. Crime prevention had to be a well-targeted technical cooperation activity that facilitated knowledge-based crime reduction. Towards that end, the Commission could invite Member States, intergovernmental and non-governmental organizations and the institutes of the United Nations Crime Prevention and Criminal Justice Programme network to apply the Guidelines for the Prevention of Crime and to support the development of the UNODC technical assistance programme in sustainable crime prevention, including pilot intervention projects for the generation and dissemination of knowledge.

ECONOMIC AND SOCIAL COUNCIL ACTION

On 22 July [meeting 36], the Economic and Social Council, on the recommendation of the Commission on Crime Prevention and Criminal Justice [E/2005/30], adopted **resolution 2005/22** without vote [agenda item 14 *(c)*].

Action to promote effective crime prevention

The Economic and Social Council,

Recalling the guidelines for cooperation and technical assistance in the field of urban crime prevention, annexed to its resolution 1995/9 of 24 July 1995, and the Guidelines for the Prevention of

Crime, annexed to its resolution 2002/13 of 24 July 2002,

Recalling also its resolutions 2003/26 of 22 July 2003 and 2004/31 of 21 July 2004, on the prevention of urban crime,

Taking note of the report of the Secretary-General entitled "Action to promote effective crime prevention" and the report of the Executive Director of the United Nations Office on Drugs and Crime entitled "Development, security and justice for all",

Mindful of the importance given to prevention in the United Nations Convention against Transnational Organized Crime and the Protocols thereto and the recognition in the Guidelines for the Prevention of Crime that crime prevention strategies should, where appropriate, take account of the links between local crime problems and transnational organized crime,

Recalling the Bangkok Declaration on Synergies and Responses: Strategic Alliances in Crime Prevention and Criminal Justice, adopted at the high-level segment of the Eleventh United Nations Congress on Crime Prevention and Criminal Justice, held in Bangkok from 18 to 25 April 2005,

Bearing in mind that the Bangkok Declaration recognizes that comprehensive and effective crime prevention strategies can significantly reduce crime and victimization and urges that such strategies be further developed and implemented at the local, national and international levels, taking into account, inter alia, the Guidelines for the Prevention of Crime,

Bearing in mind also that the Bangkok Declaration stresses the need to strengthen international cooperation in order to create an environment conducive to the fight against crime, including by promoting growth and sustainable development and eradicating poverty and unemployment through effective and balanced development strategies and crime prevention policies, and the need to consider measures to prevent the expansion of urban crime, including by improving international cooperation and capacity-building for law enforcement and the judiciary in that area and by promoting the involvement of local authorities and civil society, all of which would contribute to strengthening the rule of law,

Recalling the recommendations set out in the report of the Eleventh United Nations Congress on Crime Prevention and Criminal Justice, which, inter alia, stress the need for well-integrated, knowledge-based approaches, focusing on the most vulnerable areas and groups, and recognize the links between drugs and crime, including local, and transnational organized crime,

Acknowledging the range of approaches to crime prevention, and stressing the importance of exchanging knowledge and sharing successful practices within and between developing countries, developed countries and countries with economies in transition,

Mindful of the eighth World Conference on Injury Prevention and Safety Promotion, to be held in Durban, South Africa, from 2 to 5 April 2006, which is being organized jointly by the University of South Africa, the Medical Research Council of South Africa and the Foundation for Professional Development and co-sponsored by the World Health Organization, and the World Urban Forum III, to be convened by the United Nations Human Settlements Programme (UN-Habitat) in Vancouver, Canada, from 19 to 23 June 2006, both of which will provide an opportunity to exchange knowledge on crime prevention involving the health, urban development and justice sectors,

Noting that the forthcoming regional crime prevention forum for non-governmental organizations from Central and Eastern Europe which is being organized in Vienna on 27 and 28 October 2005 by the Conference of Non-Governmental Organizations in Consultative Relationship with the United Nations, in conjunction with the United Nations Office on Drugs and Crime, will address current problems and activities concerning the prevention of urban crime, human trafficking and corruption,

1. *Calls upon* Member States, intergovernmental and non-governmental organizations, local authorities and civil society to further develop and implement effective crime prevention strategies at national, regional and local levels that take into account, where appropriate, inter alia, the Guidelines for the Prevention of Crime;

2. *Invites* Member States, the United Nations Office on Drugs and Crime, institutes and other entities of the United Nations Crime Prevention and Criminal Justice Programme network, the United Nations Human Settlements Programme (UN-Habitat) and other intergovernmental and non-governmental organizations to support a more integrated approach to building capacity in crime prevention and criminal justice and to promote crime prevention cooperation as a contribution to the establishment and strengthening of the rule of law;

3. *Requests* the United Nations Office on Drugs and Crime, within available extrabudgetary resources, not excluding the use of existing resources from the regular budget of the United Nations Office on Drugs and Crime, to continue to undertake action pursuant to Economic and Social Council resolution 2004/28 of 21 July 2004 in relation to gathering information on standards and norms in crime prevention and criminal justice, given the importance of this as a platform for the exchange of information and successful practices in crime prevention, and calls upon Member States to make voluntary contributions to that end;

4. *Also requests* the United Nations Office on Drugs and Crime to pay due attention to crime prevention, with a view to achieving a balanced approach between crime prevention and criminal justice responses, to further developing initiatives on crime prevention, within available extrabudgetary resources, not excluding the use of existing resources from the regular budget of the United Nations Office on Drugs and Crime, and to promoting such work, where appropriate, with relevant international development organizations involved with sustainable livelihood;

5. *Requests* the Secretary-General to report to the Commission on Crime Prevention and Criminal Justice at its sixteenth session on progress made in rela-

tion to its actions on gathering information in respect of Member States and their crime prevention practices in order to promote effective crime prevention strategies.

On the same date, the Council, on the recommendation of the Commission on Crime Prevention and Criminal Justice [E/2005/30], adopted **resolution 2005/23** without vote [agenda item 14 (c)].

Strengthening reporting on crime

The Economic and Social Council,

Aware that regular collection and analysis of relevant information on crime may prove an invaluable tool for policymaking, technical cooperation and law enforcement,

Noting with appreciation the work of the United Nations Office on Drugs and Crime in the regular collection of information on crime trends and the operations of criminal justice systems in pursuance of General Assembly resolution 3021(XXVII) of 18 December 1972 on crime prevention and control and Economic and Social Council resolution 1984/48 of 25 May 1984 on crime prevention and criminal justice in the context of development, which resulted in the conducting of eight United Nations surveys on crime trends and operations of criminal justice systems, as well as the important contribution of the United Nations congresses on crime prevention and criminal justice as a forum for discussion and presentation of their findings,

Recalling General Assembly resolution 59/159 of 20 December 2004 on strengthening the United Nations Crime Prevention and Criminal Justice Programme, in particular its technical cooperation capacity, in which the Assembly called upon the Secretary-General to strengthen the United Nations Office on Drugs and Crime by providing it with the resources necessary for the full implementation of its mandate in crime prevention and criminal justice, including the preparation of an updated publication on world crime trends,

Recalling also its resolution 1997/27 of 21 July 1997 on strengthening the United Nations Crime Prevention and Criminal Justice Programme with regard to the development of crime statistics and the operations of criminal justice systems, in which it urged Member States to take action for the improvement of crime and criminal justice statistics and to provide support to the participation in the international surveys on victims of crime through extrabudgetary resources,

Considering the need to improve responses to crime, as emphasized in the Bangkok Declaration on Synergies and Responses: Strategic Alliances in Crime Prevention and Criminal Justice, adopted at the high-level segment of the Eleventh United Nations Congress on Crime Prevention and Criminal Justice, held in Bangkok from 18 to 25 April 2005,

Noting with appreciation the work done by the United Nations Office on Drugs and Crime and the institutes of the United Nations Crime Prevention and Criminal Justice Programme network in the area of trends in crime and justice,

1. *Recommends* that the Secretary-General convene an open-ended expert group, within available extrabudgetary resources, not excluding the use of existing resources from the regular budget of the United Nations Office on Drugs and Crime, to consider ways and means of improving crime data collection, research and analyses with a view to enhancing the work of the Office and other relevant international entities, in particular the United Nations Interregional Crime and Justice Research Institute, as appropriate, to enhance international cooperation and law enforcement;

2. *Invites* Member States to make voluntary contributions to support the work of the open-ended expert group;

3. *Requests* the Secretary-General to submit the results of the meeting of the open-ended expert group to the Commission on Crime Prevention and Criminal Justice at its fifteenth session.

ECONOMIC AND SOCIAL COUNCIL ACTION

On 22 July [meeting 36], the Economic and Social Council, on the recommendation of the Commission on Crime Prevention and Criminal Justice [E/2005/30], adopted **resolution 2005/15** without vote [agenda item 14 (c)].

Eleventh United Nations Congress on Crime Prevention and Criminal Justice

The Economic and Social Council,

Emphasizing the responsibility assumed by the United Nations in the field of crime prevention and criminal justice in pursuance of Economic and Social Council resolution 155 C(VII) of 13 August 1948 and General Assembly resolution 415(V) of 1 December 1950,

Acknowledging that the United Nations congresses on crime prevention and criminal justice, as major intergovernmental forums, have influenced national policies and practices and promoted international cooperation in this field by facilitating the exchange of views and experience, mobilizing public opinion and recommending policy options at the national, regional and international levels,

Recalling General Assembly resolution 46/152 of 18 December 1991, in the annex to which Member States affirmed that the United Nations congresses on crime prevention and criminal justice should be held every five years and should provide a forum for, inter alia, the exchange of views between States, intergovernmental and non-governmental organizations and individual experts representing various professions and disciplines, the exchange of experiences in research, law and policy development and the identification of emerging trends and issues in crime prevention and criminal justice,

Recalling also General Assembly resolution 57/270 B of 23 June 2003, on the integrated and coordinated implementation of and follow-up to the outcomes of major United Nations conferences and summits in the economic and social fields, in which it stressed that all countries should promote policies consistent and coherent with the commitments of the major United Nations conferences and summits, emphasized that the United Nations system had an important responsibility to assist Governments to stay fully engaged in the follow-up to and implementation of agreements and commitments reached at the major United Nations conferences and summits and invited its intergovernmental bodies to further promote the implementation of the outcomes of the major United Nations conferences and summits,

Recalling further General Assembly resolution 59/151 of 20 December 2004, in which it called upon the Eleventh United Nations Congress on Crime Prevention and Criminal Justice to formulate concrete proposals for further follow-up and action, paying particular attention to practical arrangements relating to the effective implementation of the international legal instruments pertaining to transnational organized crime, terrorism and corruption and technical assistance activities relating thereto, and requested the Commission on Crime Prevention and Criminal Justice at its fourteenth session to give high priority to considering the conclusions and recommendations of the Eleventh Congress, with a view to recommending, through the Economic and Social Council, appropriate follow-up by the General Assembly at its sixtieth session,

Bearing in mind the United Nations Millennium Declaration, adopted by the Heads of State and Government at the Millennium Summit of the United Nations on 8 September 2000, in which Heads of State and Government resolved to strengthen respect for the rule of law in international as well as in national affairs, to make the United Nations more effective in maintaining peace and security by giving it the resources and tools it needed for conflict prevention, peaceful resolution of disputes, peacekeeping, post-conflict peacebuilding and reconstruction, to take concerted action against international terrorism and accede as soon as possible to all the relevant international conventions, to redouble their efforts to implement their commitment to counter the world drug problem and to intensify their collective efforts to fight transnational crime in all its dimensions, including trafficking as well as smuggling in human beings and money-laundering,

Taking note of the report of the High-level Panel on Threats, Challenges and Change entitled "A more secure world: our shared responsibility" and the recommendations contained therein, as well as the report of the Secretary-General entitled "In larger freedom: towards development, security and human rights for all" and the proposals contained therein,

Recalling its decision 2004/242 of 21 July 2004, in which the Council decided that the prominent theme for the fourteenth session of the Commission on Crime Prevention and Criminal Justice should be "Conclusions and recommendations of the Eleventh United Nations Congress on Crime Prevention and Criminal Justice",

Having considered the report of the Eleventh United Nations Congress on Crime Prevention and Criminal Justice and the related recommendations made by the Commission on Crime Prevention and Criminal Justice at its fourteenth session,

1. *Expresses its satisfaction* with the results achieved by the Eleventh United Nations Congress on Crime Prevention and Criminal Justice, held in Bangkok

from 18 to 25 April 2005, including the Bangkok Declaration on Synergies and Responses: Strategic Alliances in Crime Prevention and Criminal Justice, adopted at the high-level segment of the Eleventh Congress;

2. *Takes note with appreciation* of the report of the Eleventh United Nations Congress on Crime Prevention and Criminal Justice, which contains the results of the Eleventh Congress, including the conclusions and recommendations made at the workshops and at the high-level segment held during the Eleventh Congress;

3. *Endorses* the Bangkok Declaration adopted by the Eleventh Congress, as approved by the Commission on Crime Prevention and Criminal Justice;

4. *Invites* Governments to take into consideration the Bangkok Declaration and the recommendations adopted by the Eleventh Congress in formulating legislation and policy directives and to make all efforts, where appropriate, to implement the principles contained therein, taking into account the economic, social, legal and cultural specificities of their respective States;

5. *Invites* Member States to identify areas covered in the Bangkok Declaration where further tools and training manuals based on international standards and best practices are needed, and to submit that information to the Commission on Crime Prevention and Criminal Justice so that it may take it into account when considering potential areas of future activity of the United Nations Office on Drugs and Crime;

6. *Requests* the Secretary-General to distribute the report of the Eleventh Congress, including the Bangkok Declaration, to Member States, intergovernmental organizations and non-governmental organizations, so as to ensure that its recommendations are disseminated as widely as possible, and to seek proposals by Member States for ways and means of ensuring appropriate follow-up to the Bangkok Declaration for consideration and action by the Commission on Crime Prevention and Criminal Justice at its fifteenth session;

7. *Notes* that the Governments of a number of States have offered to host the Twelfth United Nations Congress on Crime Prevention and Criminal Justice, to be held in 2010, and requests the United Nations Office on Drugs and Crime to engage in consultations with the Governments concerned and to report thereon to the Commission on Crime Prevention and Criminal Justice;

8. *Expresses its profound gratitude* to the people and Government of Thailand for the warm and generous hospitality extended to the participants of the Eleventh Congress and for the excellent facilities provided for the Congress;

9. *Requests* the Secretary-General to submit to the General Assembly, at its sixty-first session, a report on the implementation of the present resolution.

GENERAL ASSEMBLY ACTION

On 16 December [meeting 64], the General Assembly, on the recommendation of the Third (Social, Humanitarian and Cultural) Committee

[A/60/510 & Corr.1], adopted **resolution 60/177** without vote [agenda item 106].

Follow-up to the Eleventh United Nations Congress on Crime Prevention and Criminal Justice

The General Assembly,

Recalling its resolution 57/270 B of 23 June 2003, in which it emphasized that the United Nations system had an important responsibility to assist Governments to stay fully engaged in the follow-up to and implementation of agreements and commitments reached at the major United Nations conferences and summits and invited its intergovernmental bodies to further promote the implementation of the outcomes of the major United Nations conferences and summits,

Recalling also its resolution 59/151 of 20 December 2004, in which it requested the Secretary-General to ensure proper follow-up to the resolution and to report thereon, through the Commission on Crime Prevention and Criminal Justice, to the General Assembly at its sixtieth session,

Having considered the report of the Eleventh United Nations Congress on Crime Prevention and Criminal Justice and the related recommendations made by the Commission on Crime Prevention and Criminal Justice at its fourteenth session,

Bearing in mind its resolution 60/175 of 16 December 2005 on strengthening the United Nations Crime Prevention and Criminal Justice Programme, in particular its technical cooperation capacity, and the role of the United Nations Office on Drugs and Crime in the implementation of the measures outlined in the Bangkok Declaration on Synergies and Responses: Strategic Alliances in Crime Prevention and Criminal Justice,

1. *Endorses* the Bangkok Declaration on Synergies and Responses: Strategic Alliances in Crime Prevention and Criminal Justice, as contained in the annex to the present resolution, which was adopted by the Eleventh United Nations Congress on Crime Prevention and Criminal Justice and approved by the Commission on Crime Prevention and Criminal Justice at its fourteenth session and subsequently by the Economic and Social Council in its resolution 2005/15 of 22 July 2005;

2. *Invites* Governments to implement the Bangkok Declaration and the recommendations adopted by the Eleventh Congress in formulating legislation and policy directives, taking into account the economic, social, legal and cultural specificities of their respective States;

3. *Reaffirms* the readiness of Member States, in a spirit of common and shared responsibility, as acknowledged in the Bangkok Declaration, to seek to improve international cooperation in the fight against crime and terrorism, at the multilateral, regional and bilateral levels, in areas including, among others, extradition and mutual legal assistance;

4. *Invites* Member States to identify areas covered in the Bangkok Declaration in which further tools and training manuals based on international standards and best practices are needed, and to submit that information to the Commission on Crime Prevention and Criminal Justice so that it may take it into account when considering potential areas of future activity by the United Nations Office on Drugs and Crime;

5. *Requests* the Secretary-General to distribute the report of the Eleventh Congress, including the Bangkok Declaration, to Member States, intergovernmental organizations and non-governmental organizations, so as to ensure that its recommendations are disseminated as widely as possible, and to seek proposals by Member States for ways and means of ensuring appropriate follow-up to the Bangkok Declaration for consideration and action by the Commission on Crime Prevention and Criminal Justice at its fifteenth session;

6. *Also requests* the Secretary-General to submit to the General Assembly at its sixty-first session a report on strengthening the United Nations Crime Prevention and Criminal Justice Programme, in particular its technical cooperation capacity, including a chapter on the Bangkok Declaration, the recommendations adopted by the Eleventh Congress and the implementation of the present resolution.

Annex

Bangkok Declaration on Synergies and Responses: Strategic Alliances in Crime Prevention and Criminal Justice

We, the States Members of the United Nations,

Having assembled at the Eleventh United Nations Congress on Crime Prevention and Criminal Justice, held in Bangkok from 18 to 25 April 2005, to decide to take more effective concerted action, in a spirit of cooperation, to combat crime and seek justice,

Convinced that the United Nations congresses on crime prevention and criminal justice, which constitute a major intergovernmental forum, have contributed to national policies and practices by facilitating the exchange of views and experience, mobilizing public opinion and recommending policy options at the national, regional and international levels, thus making a significant contribution to progress and the promotion of international cooperation in crime prevention and criminal justice,

Recalling the work of the ten previous United Nations congresses,

Reaffirming the responsibility vested in the United Nations Crime Prevention and Criminal Justice Programme to work, together with Member States and regional and international organizations, in the fields of crime prevention and criminal justice,

Greatly concerned by the expansion and dimensions of transnational organized crime, including illicit drug trafficking, money-laundering, trafficking in persons, smuggling of migrants, illegal arms trafficking and terrorism, and any existing links among them, and by the increasing sophistication and diversification of the activities of organized criminal groups,

Emphasizing that enhancing dialogue among civilizations, promoting tolerance, preventing the indiscriminate targeting of different religions and cultures and addressing development issues and unresolved conflicts will contribute to international cooperation, which is among the most important elements to combat terrorism in all its forms and manifestations, and reaffirming that no terrorist act can be justified in any circumstance,

Reaffirming that States must ensure that any measures taken to combat terrorism comply with all of their obligations under international law and that they should adopt such measures in conformity with the Charter of the United Nations and international law, in particular international human rights, refugee and humanitarian law,

Alarmed by the rapid growth, geographical extent and effects of new economic and financial crimes, which have emerged as significant threats to national economies and the international financial system,

Highlighting the need for an integrated and systemic approach to combating corruption and money-laundering, within existing frameworks and instruments, in particular those under the aegis of the United Nations, since those crimes can be conducive to the perpetration of other criminal activities,

Noting with appreciation the work of the regional preparatory meetings for the Eleventh United Nations Congress on Crime Prevention and Criminal Justice,

Declare as follows:

1. We proclaim our political will and commitment to achieve the aspirations and objectives as set out in the present Declaration.

2. We reaffirm our continued support for and commitment to the United Nations and to the United Nations Crime Prevention and Criminal Justice Programme, especially the Commission on Crime Prevention and Criminal Justice and the United Nations Office on Drugs and Crime, the United Nations Interregional Crime and Justice Research Institute and the institutes of the Programme network, and resolve to strengthen the Programme further through sustained funding, as appropriate.

3. In a spirit of common and shared responsibility, we reaffirm our readiness to seek to improve international cooperation in the fight against crime and terrorism, at the multilateral, regional and bilateral levels, in areas including, among others, extradition and mutual legal assistance. We seek to ensure our national capacity and, where appropriate, the coherence of our international capacity, through the United Nations and other relevant global and regional organizations, to engage in international cooperation, in particular in the prevention, investigation, prosecution and adjudication of transnational organized crime and terrorism and in the discovery of any existing links among them.

4. We welcome the entry into force of the United Nations Convention against Transnational Organized Crime and two of its Protocols. We call upon all States that have not yet done so to seek to ratify or accede to and implement the provisions of that Convention and its Protocols, as well as the provisions of the United Nations Convention against Corruption and the international instruments against terrorism. In implementing the provisions of those instruments, we commit ourselves to full compliance with our obligations under international law, in particular international human rights, refugee and humanitarian law. We support every effort to facilitate the implementation of those instruments.

5. We call upon donor States and financial institutions to continue to make adequate voluntary contributions on a regular basis for the provision of technical assistance to developing countries and to countries with economies in transition, in order to help build their capacity to prevent and tackle crime in all its forms and apply the United Nations standards and norms in crime prevention and criminal justice and, in particular, to facilitate their becoming parties to and implementing the international instruments against terrorism and the relevant international instruments against crime, such as the United Nations Convention against Transnational Organized Crime and the Protocols thereto, the United Nations Convention against Corruption and the international drug control conventions.

6. We support a more integrated approach within the United Nations in relation to the provision of assistance for building capacity in crime prevention and criminal justice, and in cooperation in criminal matters of a transnational character, as a contribution to the establishment and strengthening of the rule of law.

7. We seek to improve our responses to crime and terrorism nationally and internationally, inter alia, by collecting and sharing information on crime and terrorism and on effective countermeasures, in accordance with national legislation. We welcome the important work done by the United Nations Office on Drugs and Crime and the United Nations Crime Prevention and Criminal Justice Programme network in the area of trends in crime and justice.

8. We are convinced that upholding the rule of law and good governance and proper management of public affairs and public property at the local, national and international levels are prerequisites for creating and sustaining an environment for successfully preventing and combating crime. We are committed to the development and maintenance of fair and efficient criminal justice institutions, including the humane treatment of all those in pretrial and correctional facilities, in accordance with applicable international standards.

9. We recognize the role of individuals and groups outside the public sector, such as civil society, non-governmental organizations and community-based organizations, in contributing to the prevention of and the fight against crime and terrorism. We encourage the adoption of measures to strengthen this role within the rule of law.

10. We recognize that comprehensive and effective crime prevention strategies can significantly reduce crime and victimization. We urge that such strategies address the root causes and risk factors of crime and victimization and that they be further developed and implemented at the local, national and international levels, taking into account, inter alia, the Guidelines for the Prevention of Crime.

11. We note that countries emerging from conflict are particularly vulnerable to crime, in particular organized crime and corruption, and therefore recommend that Member States, regional organizations and international entities such as the United Nations Office on Drugs and Crime, in coordination with the Department of Peacekeeping Operations of the Secretariat and other relevant entities, provide more effective responses to these problems, in order to re-establish, strengthen or sustain the rule of law and deliver justice in post-conflict situations.

12. With regard to the increased involvement of organized criminal groups in the theft of and trafficking in cultural property and illicit trafficking in protected species of wild flora and fauna, we recognize the importance of combating these forms of crime and, bearing in mind the relevant international legal instruments, such as the Convention on the Means of Prohibiting and Preventing the Illicit Import, Export and Transfer of Ownership of Cultural Property, the Convention on International Trade in Endangered Species of Wild Fauna and Flora and the Convention on Biological Diversity, we call upon Member States to take effective measures to strengthen international cooperation.

13. We note with concern the rise in kidnapping and trafficking in persons, which constitute serious, profitable and inhumane forms of organized crime, often committed with the objective of funding criminal organizations and, in some cases, terrorist activities, and hence recommend that measures be devised to combat these crimes and that attention be given to the creation of practical mechanisms for countering them. We recognize the need to implement measures intended to provide adequate assistance and protection to victims of kidnapping and trafficking in persons and their families.

14. Mindful of General Assembly resolution 59/156 of 20 December 2004 on preventing, combating and punishing trafficking in human organs, we note the serious concerns raised about the illicit removal of and trafficking in human organs and will examine with interest the report of the Secretary-General requested in that resolution.

15. We reaffirm the fundamental importance of the implementation of existing instruments and the further development of national measures and international cooperation in relation to criminal matters, such as consideration of strengthening and augmenting measures, in particular against cybercrime, money-laundering and trafficking in cultural property, as well as extradition, mutual legal assistance and the confiscation, recovery and return of proceeds of crime.

16. We note that, in the current period of globalization, information technology and the rapid development of new telecommunication and computer network systems have been accompanied by the abuse of those technologies for criminal purposes. We therefore welcome efforts to enhance and supplement existing cooperation to prevent, investigate and prosecute high-technology and computer-related crime, including through the development of partnerships with the private sector. We recognize the important contribution of the United Nations to regional and other international forums in the fight against cybercrime and invite the Commission on Crime Prevention and Criminal Justice, taking into account that experience, to examine the feasibility of providing further assistance in that area under the aegis of the United Nations, in partnership with other similarly focused organizations.

17. We recognize the importance of giving special attention to the need to protect witnesses and victims of crime and terrorism, and we commit ourselves to strengthening, where needed, the legal and financial framework for providing support to such victims, taking into account, inter alia, the Declaration of Basic Principles of Justice for Victims of Crime and Abuse of Power.

18. We call upon Member States to take steps, in accordance with their domestic laws, to promote access to justice, to consider the provision of legal aid to those who need it and to enable the effective assertion of their rights in the criminal justice system.

19. We note with concern the problem of trafficking in illicit drugs and the serious socio-economic consequences it entails, and therefore call for the strengthening of international cooperation in combating that form of organized crime.

20. We will strengthen international cooperation in order to create an environment that is conducive to the fight against crime, including by promoting growth and sustainable development and eradicating poverty and unemployment by means of effective and balanced development strategies and crime prevention policies.

21. We call upon States that have not yet done so to become parties to and implement the universal instruments against terrorism. In order to enhance the capacity of States to become parties to and implement those instruments and to comply with the relevant Security Council resolutions against terrorism, we express our support for the continuing efforts of the United Nations Office on Drugs and Crime, within its mandate and in coordination with the Counter-Terrorism Committee and the Counter-Terrorism Committee Executive Directorate of the Security Council, to assist States in their efforts to ratify and implement those instruments, through the provision of technical assistance upon request. This might include assistance to criminal justice systems to facilitate the effective implementation of those instruments.

22. We express the hope that the ongoing negotiation of the draft comprehensive convention on international terrorism will be concluded as soon as possible. In this context, we recognize that arriving at a possible definition of terrorism is one of the key issues to be resolved. We call upon Member States to consider signing and ratifying the International Convention for the Suppression of Acts of Nuclear Terrorism.

23. We are convinced that the expeditious entry into force and subsequent implementation of the United Nations Convention against Corruption are central to the efforts made at the international level to fight corruption and therefore accord high priority to supporting efforts to that end and call upon all States that have not yet done so to seek to sign, ratify or accede to the Convention.

24. We are also convinced that the proper management of public affairs and public property and the rule of law are essential to the prevention and control of corruption, including, inter alia, through effective measures for its investigation and prosecution. Furthermore, we recognize that, in order to curb corruption, it is necessary to promote a culture of integrity and accountability in both the public and the private sector.

25. We are convinced that asset recovery is one of the essential components of the United Nations Convention against Corruption and, for that reason, we

emphasize the need to adopt measures to facilitate asset recovery that are consistent with the principles of that Convention.

26. We are conscious of the challenge of investigating and prosecuting complex cases involving economic and financial crimes, including money-laundering. We call upon Member States to strengthen policies, measures and institutions for national action and international cooperation in the prevention, investigation and prosecution of economic and financial crimes, including money-laundering, and such crimes conducted by means of, or facilitated by, information technologies, in particular in connection with the financing of terrorism and trafficking in illicit drugs.

27. We are conscious of the crucial importance of tackling document and identity fraud in order to curb organized crime and terrorism. We seek to improve international cooperation, including through technical assistance, to combat document and identity fraud, in particular the fraudulent use of travel documents, through improved security measures, and encourage the adoption of appropriate national legislation.

28. We recommend that voluntary contributions and appropriate technical assistance be made available to developing countries to strengthen their capacity in order to support their efforts to fight effectively economic and financial crimes.

29. As appropriate, we endeavour to use and apply the United Nations standards and norms in our national programmes for crime prevention and criminal justice reform and to undertake, as needed, efforts to ensure their wider dissemination. We endeavour to facilitate appropriate training for law enforcement officials, including prison officials, prosecutors, the judiciary and other relevant professional groups, taking into account those norms and standards and best practices at the international level.

30. We recommend that the Commission on Crime Prevention and Criminal Justice give consideration to reviewing the adequacy of standards and norms in relation to prison management and prisoners.

31. We note with concern that the physical and social conditions associated with imprisonment may facilitate the spread of HIV/AIDS in pretrial and correctional facilities and thus in society, thereby presenting a critical prison management problem; we call upon States to develop and adopt measures and guidelines, where appropriate and in accordance with national legislation, to ensure that the particular problems of HIV/AIDS are adequately addressed in such facilities.

32. To promote the interests of victims and the rehabilitation of offenders, we recognize the importance of further developing restorative justice policies, procedures and programmes that include alternatives to prosecution, thereby avoiding possible adverse effects of imprisonment, helping to decrease the caseload of criminal courts and promoting the incorporation of restorative justice approaches into criminal justice systems, as appropriate.

33. We affirm our determination to pay particular attention to juvenile justice. We will consider ways to ensure the provision of services to children who are victims of crime and children in conflict with the law, in particular those deprived of their liberty, and to ensure that those services take into account their gender, social circumstances and developmental needs and the relevant United Nations standards and norms, as appropriate.

34. We stress the need to consider measures to prevent the expansion of urban crime, including by improving international cooperation and capacity-building for law enforcement and the judiciary in that area and by promoting the involvement of local authorities and civil society.

35. We express our profound gratitude to the people and the Government of Thailand for their warm and generous hospitality towards the participants and for the excellent facilities provided for the Eleventh Congress.

Strengthening technical cooperation

The Secretary-General, in response to General Assembly resolution 59/159 [YUN 2004, p. 1114], transmitted a July report [A/60/131] on strengthening the United Nations Crime Prevention and Criminal Justice Programme, in particular its technical cooperation capacity. It highlighted the features of the Eleventh United Nations Congress on Crime Prevention and Criminal Justice, the entry into force in 2003 [YUN 2003, p. 1126] of the United Nations Convention against Transnational Organized Crime and its supplementary Protocols and efforts to promote the entry into force of the United Nations Convention against Corruption (see below). The report covered the technical cooperation activities in providing assistance to States to respond more effectively to the challenges posed by transnational crime, trafficking in human beings, corruption and terrorism and to reinforce their institutional machinery for the maintenance of the rule of law. It also reviewed major initiatives related to the implementation of crime prevention and criminal justice standards and norms, research and dissemination of information, coordination and mobilization of resources.

The Commission on Crime Prevention and Criminal Justice, in response to resolution 2004/32 [YUN 2004, p. 1111], considered at its fourteenth session (see p. 1210), a report [E/CN.15/2005/3] on the implementation of technical assistance projects in Africa by UNODC. It welcomed UNODC efforts to improve the implementation of its projects in Africa, both at headquarters and in the field. It requested the Office to produce a concept paper analysing current drug and crime issues affecting the African continent, and to promote an exchange of views, based on the results of the analysis, among interested Member States and the African Union on technical assistance to Africa.

On 22 July [meeting 36], the Economic and Social Council, on the recommendation of the Commission on Crime and Criminal Justice [E/2005/30], adopted **resolution 2005/21** without vote [agenda item 14 (c)].

Strengthening the technical cooperation capacity of the United Nations Crime Prevention and Criminal Justice Programme in the area of the rule of law and criminal justice reform

The Economic and Social Council,

Recalling General Assembly resolution 46/152 of 18 December 1991 on the creation of an effective United Nations crime prevention and criminal justice programme and resolution 59/159 of 20 December 2004 on strengthening the United Nations Crime Prevention and Criminal Justice Programme, in particular its technical cooperation capacity,

Recalling also its resolution 2004/25 of 21 July 2004, in which it requested the United Nations Office on Drugs and Crime to consider specific practical strategies to assist in promoting the rule of law, and encouraged the Office to continue to provide technical assistance and advisory services to Member States upon request in support of criminal justice reform and to incorporate elements concerning the rule of law into such assistance,

Recalling further the Vienna Declaration on Crime and Justice: Meeting the Challenges of the Twenty-first Century, adopted by the Tenth United Nations Congress on the Prevention of Crime and the Treatment of Offenders, held in Vienna from 10 to 17 April 2000, and the plans of action for the implementation of the Vienna Declaration, and welcoming the progress made by Member States in implementing the Vienna Declaration and its plans of action,

Recalling the Bangkok Declaration on Synergies and Responses: Strategic Alliances in Crime Prevention and Criminal Justice, adopted at the high-level segment of the Eleventh United Nations Congress on Crime Prevention and Criminal Justice, held in Bangkok from 18 to 25 April 2005,

Conscious of the support expressed in the Bangkok Declaration for a more integrated approach within the United Nations in relation to the provision of assistance for building capacity in crime prevention and criminal justice, and in cooperation in criminal matters of a transnational character, as a contribution to the establishment and strengthening of the rule of law,

Conscious also of the commitment expressed in the Bangkok Declaration to the development and maintenance of fair and efficient criminal justice institutions, including the humane treatment of all those in pre-trial and correctional facilities, in accordance with applicable international standards,

Welcoming the commitment expressed in the Bangkok Declaration to strengthening the legal and financial framework for providing support to victims of crime and terrorism, to promoting access to justice, to considering the provision of legal aid, to facilitating training for prison officials, prosecutors, the judiciary and other relevant professional groups, taking into account the United Nations standards

and norms in crime prevention and criminal justice, to reviewing the adequacy of standards and norms in relation to prison management and prisoners, to ensuring that the problems of HIV/AIDS are addressed in pre-trial and correctional facilities, to further developing restorative justice policies, procedures and programmes that include alternatives to prosecution and to ensuring the provision of services to child victims and children in conflict with the law, in particular those deprived of their liberty,

Taking note of the report of the High-level Panel on Threats, Challenges and Change entitled "A more secure world: our shared responsibility",

Taking note also of the report of the Secretary-General entitled "In larger freedom: towards development, security and human rights for all",

Recognizing that effective criminal justice systems can only be developed based on the rule of law and that the rule of law itself requires the protection of effective criminal justice measures,

Recognizing also that effective criminal justice systems based on the rule of law are a prerequisite for combating transnational organized crime, trafficking in human beings, terrorism, corruption and other forms of transnational and domestic criminal activity,

1. *Emphasizes* the role of the United Nations Office on Drugs and Crime in developing and maintaining expertise on the rule of law in criminal justice systems and in providing advice and assistance on issues related to criminal justice and the rule of law, where appropriate, to Member States, other United Nations entities and intergovernmental organizations at their request;

2. *Reaffirms* the importance of the United Nations Crime Prevention and Criminal Justice Programme in promoting effective action to strengthen international cooperation in crime prevention and criminal justice and in assisting Member States in developing and maintaining fair and efficient criminal justice institutions, including through comprehensive and integrated approaches to criminal justice reform;

3. *Invites* relevant entities of the United Nations system, including the United Nations Development Programme, as well as the World Bank and other international funding agencies, to increase their cooperation and coordination with United Nations entities concerned with supporting the rule of law, including the United Nations Office on Drugs and Crime, in order to promote a more integrated approach to the provision of assistance for building capacity in crime prevention and criminal justice, and in cooperation in criminal matters of a transnational character, as a contribution to the establishment and strengthening of the rule of law;

4. *Reaffirms* the role of the United Nations Office on Drugs and Crime in responding to requests from Member States for technical cooperation, advisory services and other forms of assistance in the field of crime prevention and criminal justice, including in the area of criminal justice reform and reconstruction of national criminal justice systems, and recognizes the need to continue to enhance the provision of assistance in that field to Member States, upon request, in particular to least developed countries,

developing countries, countries with economies in transition and countries emerging from conflict;

5. *Invites* all States to support the operational activities of the United Nations Crime Prevention and Criminal Justice Programme, through voluntary contributions to the United Nations Crime Prevention and Criminal Justice Fund or through voluntary contributions in direct support of such activities, including, where appropriate, for the provision of technical assistance for the implementation of the commitments entered into at the Eleventh United Nations Congress on Crime Prevention and Criminal Justice, held in Bangkok from 18 to 25 April 2005;

6. *Expresses its appreciation* to non-governmental organizations and other relevant sectors of civil society for their support for the United Nations Crime Prevention and Criminal Justice Programme, and stresses the necessity to strengthen the role of civil society in criminal justice reform efforts;

7. *Encourages* the United Nations Office on Drugs and Crime to continue providing assistance to Member States, upon request, in particular to least developed countries, developing countries and countries with economies in transition, as well as to countries emerging from conflict, taking into account the leading role of other United Nations entities, such as the Department of Peacekeeping Operations of the Secretariat and the United Nations Development Programme in that area, in reinforcing the rule of law through technical cooperation, advisory services and other forms of assistance in the field of crime prevention and criminal justice reform and reconstruction of national criminal justice systems;

8. *Also encourages* the United Nations Office on Drugs and Crime to continue developing tools and training manuals on criminal justice reform, based on international standards and best practices;

9. *Requests* the Secretary-General to report on the implementation of the present resolution to the Commission on Crime Prevention and Criminal Justice at its sixteenth session.

On the same date, the Council mandated UNODC to organize, within available extrabudgetary resources, not excluding the use of existing resources from its regular budget, and in cooperation with the African Union and interested Member States, the Round Table for Africa for interested Member States, relevant agencies and institutes providing technical assistance to African States and promoting South-South cooperation. It also mandated UNODC to convene the Round Table before the end of 2005 (**decision 2005/248**).

The Round Table for Africa was held in Nigeria from 5 to 6 September. The programme of action endorsed at the Round Table charted a five-year plan to strengthen the rule of law on the continent. The programme suggested concrete steps to counter violence, corruption and crime, all of which were cause and consequence of Af-

rica's underdevelopment, according to a UNODC study discussed at the Round Table.

GENERAL ASSEMBLY ACTION

On 16 December 2005 [meeting 64], the General Assembly adopted **resolution 60/175** [draft: A/60/510 & Corr.1] without vote [agenda item 106].

Strengthening the United Nations Crime Prevention and Criminal Justice Programme, in particular its technical cooperation capacity

The General Assembly,

Recalling its resolution 46/152 of 18 December 1991 on the creation of an effective United Nations crime prevention and criminal justice programme, in which it approved the statement of principles and programme of action annexed to that resolution,

Recalling also its resolution 59/159 of 20 December 2004 on strengthening the United Nations Crime Prevention and Criminal Justice Programme, in particular its technical cooperation capacity,

Bearing in mind the United Nations Millennium Declaration, as well as the Vienna Declaration on Crime and Justice: Meeting the Challenges of the Twenty-first Century and its plans of action,

Reaffirming the commitment to combat transnational crime, undertaken by Heads of State and Government during the High-level Plenary Meeting of the General Assembly, held in New York from 14 to 16 September 2005,

Emphasizing the role of the United Nations in the field of crime prevention and criminal justice, specifically the reduction of criminality, more efficient and effective law enforcement and administration of justice, respect for human rights and the rule of law and promotion of the highest standards of fairness, humanity and professional conduct,

Recognizing that action against global crime is a common and shared responsibility, and stressing the need to work collectively to combat transnational crime,

Convinced of the need for closer coordination and cooperation among States in combating crime in all its forms and manifestations, including criminal activities carried out for the purpose of furthering terrorism, inter alia, through the development by the General Assembly of a comprehensive counterterrorism strategy, and bearing in mind the role that is played by both the United Nations and regional organizations in this respect,

Reaffirming, according to its resolution 60/177 of 16 December 2005, the commitment of the Member States to implement the Bangkok Declaration on Synergies and Responses: Strategic Alliances in Crime Prevention and Criminal Justice, adopted at the Eleventh United Nations Congress on Crime Prevention and Criminal Justice, held in Bangkok from 18 to 25 April 2005,

Recognizing existing efforts at the regional level that complement the work of the United Nations Crime Prevention and Criminal Justice Programme in combating corruption, the smuggling of migrants and trafficking in persons, especially women and children, noting in this context the ongoing work of the Bali and Puebla Processes, and recalling the major United Nations conferences and the pledge to encourage and support frameworks initiated at the regional level, such as the New Partnership for Africa's Development and similar efforts in other regions,

Welcoming the entry into force of the United Nations Convention against Corruption, which was opened for signature in Merida, Mexico, in December 2003,

Bearing in mind all its relevant resolutions, in particular those related to the urgent need to strengthen international cooperation and technical assistance in promoting and facilitating the ratification and implementation of the United Nations Convention against Transnational Organized Crime and the Protocols thereto and the United Nations Convention against Corruption, as well as the universal instruments against terrorism, including the International Convention for the Suppression of Acts of Nuclear Terrorism adopted by the General Assembly on 13 April 2005,

Bearing in mind also all relevant Economic and Social Council resolutions, in particular resolutions 2005/14, 2005/15, 2005/16, 2005/17, 2005/18 and 2005/19 of 22 July 2005 and all those relating to the strengthening of international cooperation as well as the technical assistance and advisory services of the United Nations Crime Prevention and Criminal Justice Programme of the United Nations Office on Drugs and Crime in the field of crime prevention and criminal justice, promotion and reinforcement of the rule of law and reform of criminal justice institutions, including in the context of post-conflict reconstruction, and on the implementation of technical assistance in Africa,

Acknowledging the role of United Nations standards and norms in crime prevention and criminal justice and their development, as reflected in Economic and Social Council resolution 2004/28 of 21 July 2004,

Aware of the continued increase in requests for technical assistance forwarded to the United Nations Office on Drugs and Crime by least developed countries, developing countries and countries with economies in transition, including in the context of post-conflict reconstruction, and recognizing the need to maintain a balance in the technical cooperation capacity of the Office between all priorities identified by the General Assembly and the Economic and Social Council,

Expressing its appreciation for the resources provided by certain Member States, which in recent years have permitted the United Nations Office on Drugs and Crime and the United Nations Interregional Crime and Justice Research Institute and institutes of the United Nations Crime Prevention and Criminal Justice Programme network and other relevant bodies to enhance their capacity to execute an increased number of projects in the field of crime prevention and criminal justice,

1. *Takes note with appreciation* of the report of the Secretary-General on the progress made in the implementation of General Assembly resolution 59/159;

2. *Reaffirms* the importance of the United Nations Crime Prevention and Criminal Justice Programme in promoting effective action to strengthen international cooperation in crime prevention and criminal justice, in responding to the needs of the international community in the face of both national and transnational criminality and in assisting Member States in achieving the goals of preventing crime within and among States and improving the response to crime;

3. *Reiterates its appreciation* of the work of the Commission on Crime Prevention and Criminal Justice to coordinate international cooperation efforts, and requests that a gender perspective continue to be integrated into all programmes and activities of the United Nations Office on Drugs and Crime;

4. *Reaffirms* the importance of the work of the United Nations Office on Drugs and Crime in the fulfilment of its mandate in crime prevention and criminal justice, including coordinating with and complementing the work of all relevant and competent United Nations bodies, including the Security Council Committee established pursuant to resolution 1373(2001) concerning counter-terrorism (the Counter-Terrorism Committee) and the Counter-Terrorism Committee Executive Directorate;

5. *Also reaffirms* the role of the United Nations Office on Drugs and Crime in providing to Member States, upon request and as a matter of high priority, technical cooperation, advisory services and other forms of assistance in the field of crime prevention and criminal justice, including in the areas of prevention and control of transnational organized crime, trafficking in human beings, in all its aspects, smuggling of migrants and corruption, as well as in the area of reconstruction of national criminal justice systems, and stresses the need to enhance, in accordance with its existing mandates, its operational activities to assist, in particular, least developed countries, developing countries and countries with economies in transition, including in the context of post-conflict reconstruction;

6. *Requests* the United Nations Office on Drugs and Crime to continue its efforts to provide Member States with technical assistance, upon request, to strengthen international cooperation in preventing and combating terrorism through the facilitation of the ratification and implementation of the universal conventions and protocols related to terrorism, including the International Convention for the Suppression of Acts of Nuclear Terrorism, in particular through training in the judicial and prosecutorial fields in their proper implementation, taking into account, in its programmes, the elements necessary for building national capacity in order to strengthen fair and effective criminal justice systems and the rule of law as an integral component of any strategy to counter terrorism;

7. *Expresses its grave concern* at the negative effects of transnational crime, including trafficking in persons and smuggling of migrants, the illicit trade in small arms and light weapons and trafficking in illicit drugs, on development, peace and security and human rights, and at the increasing vulnerability of States to such crime;

8. *Recognizes* the progress made in the implementation of the global programmes addressing trafficking in human beings, including support and protection of victims, corruption, organized crime, money-

laundering and terrorism, and calls upon the Secretary-General to enhance further the effectiveness of these programmes and to strengthen the focus of the United Nations Office on Drugs and Crime on these priority programmes in crime prevention and criminal justice;

9. *Reiterates its request* to the Secretary-General, as a matter of urgency, to provide the United Nations Crime Prevention and Criminal Justice Programme with sufficient resources for the full implementation of its mandates, in conformity with its high priorities;

10. *Invites* all States to increase their support to the operational activities of the United Nations Crime Prevention and Criminal Justice Programme through voluntary contributions to the United Nations Crime Prevention and Criminal Justice Fund or through voluntary contributions in direct support of such activities, including for the provision of technical assistance for the implementation of the plans of action of the Vienna Declaration on Crime and Justice: Meeting the Challenges of the Twenty-first Century as well as of the commitments undertaken at the Eleventh United Nations Congress on Crime Prevention and Criminal Justice and the measures outlined in the Bangkok Declaration on Synergies and Responses: Strategic Alliances in Crime Prevention and Criminal Justice;

11. *Also invites* all States to support, through voluntary contributions, the activities carried out by the United Nations Interregional Crime and Justice Research Institute and institutes of the United Nations Crime Prevention and Criminal Justice Programme network and other relevant bodies;

12. *Urges* States and relevant international organizations to develop national, regional and international strategies and other necessary measures to complement the work of the United Nations Crime Prevention and Criminal Justice Programme in addressing effectively transnational organized crime, including trafficking in persons and related criminal activities such as kidnapping and the smuggling of migrants, as well as corruption and terrorism;

13. *Urges* States and funding agencies to review, as appropriate, their funding policies for development assistance and to include a crime prevention and criminal justice component in such assistance;

14. *Encourages* relevant entities of the United Nations system, in particular the United Nations Development Programme, and invites the international financial institutions, in particular the World Bank and the International Monetary Fund, and regional and national funding agencies to further increase their support to and their interaction with the United Nations Office on Drugs and Crime in order to benefit from synergies and avoid duplication of effort, and to ensure that, as appropriate, activities on crime prevention and criminal justice, including activities related to the prevention of corruption and the promotion of the rule of law are considered in their sustainable development agenda and that the expertise of the Office is fully utilized;

15. *Welcomes* the efforts undertaken by the Commission on Crime Prevention and Criminal Justice to exercise more vigorously its mandated function of resource mobilization, and calls upon the Commis-

sion to strengthen further its activities in this direction;

16. *Also welcomes* the outcome of the round-table meeting on the theme "Crime and drugs as impediments to security and development in Africa", hosted by the Government of Nigeria in Abuja on 5 and 6 September 2005, pursuant to Economic and Social Council resolution 2004/32 of 21 July 2004, in the form of a comprehensive programme of action, 2006-2010, to strengthen the rule of law and the criminal justice systems in Africa, in which all African States, regional and subregional institutions, financial institutions and development partners are invited to integrate the issues of crime and drugs into their development strategies and into official development assistance for Africa;

17. *Expresses its appreciation* to non-governmental organizations and other relevant sectors of civil society for their support to the United Nations Crime Prevention and Criminal Justice Programme;

18. *Requests* the Secretary-General to continue to provide the United Nations Office on Drugs and Crime with adequate resources to enable it to promote in an effective manner and, as appropriate, under the guidance of the Conference of the Parties to the United Nations Convention against Transnational Organized Crime, the implementation of the Convention and the Protocols thereto and to discharge its functions as the secretariat of the said Conference of the Parties, in accordance with its mandate, and also requests the Secretary-General to transmit to the General Assembly the reports of the said Conference of the Parties;

19. *Also requests* the Secretary-General to take all necessary measures to provide adequate support to the Commission on Crime Prevention and Criminal Justice, as the principal policymaking body in this field, in performing its activities, including cooperation and coordination with the institutes of the United Nations Crime Prevention and Criminal Justice Programme network and other relevant bodies;

20. *Urges* all States and competent regional economic integration organizations that have not yet done so to sign, ratify or accede to the United Nations Convention against Transnational Organized Crime (Palermo Convention) and the Protocols thereto, as well as the United Nations Convention against Corruption and the international conventions and protocols related to terrorism, including the newly adopted International Convention for the Suppression of Acts of Nuclear Terrorism;

21. *Welcomes* the voluntary contributions already made, and encourages States to make adequate and regular voluntary contributions for the implementation of the United Nations Convention against Transnational Organized Crime and the Protocols thereto, through the United Nations funding mechanism specifically designed for that purpose in the Convention or in direct support of implementation activities and initiatives;

22. *Encourages* Member States to take into account the Model Bilateral Agreement on the Sharing of Confiscated Proceeds of Crime or Property annexed to Economic and Social Council resolution 2005/14 of 22 July 2005, as a useful model for those States interested in negotiating and concluding bi-

lateral agreements to facilitate the sharing of proceeds of crime, resulting in greater international cooperation in that area, such cooperation being one of the principal objectives of the United Nations Convention against Transnational Organized Crime;

23. *Encourages* States to make adequate and regular voluntary contributions for the implementation of the United Nations Convention against Corruption, which entered into force on 14 December 2005, through the Global Programme against Corruption of the United Nations Office on Drugs and Crime or in direct support of implementation activities and initiatives;

24. *Requests* the Secretary-General to submit a report on the implementation of the present resolution to the General Assembly at its sixty-first session.

UN Crime Prevention and Criminal Justice Programme

A March report [E/CN.15/2005/4 &Add.1] of the Secretary-General summarized the activities of the institutions comprising the United Nations Crime Prevention and Criminal Justice Programme network: the United Nations Interregional Crime and Justice Research Institute (UNRCRI); 13 regional and affiliated institutes; and the International Scientific and Professional Advisory Council.

UN African crime prevention institute

In a July report [A/60/123], submitted in response to General Assembly resolution 59/158 [YUN 2004, p. 1117], the Secretary-General highlighted activities of the African Institute for the Prevention of Crime and the Treatment of Offenders (UNAFRI) and discussed funding and support for the Institute, its future and strategies for sustaining it. He further pledged support for UNAFRI's emphasis on studying and developing remedial action to address crime problems by conducting advisory missions in Africa. The activities of the Institute focused on the individual needs of Member States and the growing awareness of the necessity of making crime prevention strategies a component of sustainable socio-economic development.

For the period January to June 2005, the total resources of the Institute amounted to $227,623, consisting of assessed contributions from Member States, UN grant portion and other income received from the rental of the Institute premises and interest on deposits.

The Institute would continue to develop new strategies for intervention in places affected by civil and armed conflicts. It would also continue its advocacy efforts to encourage development agencies working in Africa to incorporate crime prevention and criminal justice concerns into their cooperation programmes. The Institute would maintain a dialogue with Member States to mobilize political and material support for its programmes, as well as develop partnerships with the private sector, NGOs and UNODC.

GENERAL ASSEMBLY ACTION

On 16 December [meeting 64], the General Assembly, on recommendation of the Third Committee [A/60/510 & Corr.1], adopted **resolution 60/176** without vote [agenda item 106].

United Nations African Institute for the Prevention of Crime and the Treatment of Offenders

The General Assembly,

Recalling its resolution 59/158 of 20 December 2004 and all other relevant resolutions,

Taking note of the report of the Secretary-General,

Bearing in mind the urgent need to establish effective crime prevention strategies for Africa, as well as the importance of law enforcement agencies and the judiciary at the regional and subregional levels,

Noting that the financial situation of the United Nations African Institute for the Prevention of Crime and the Treatment of Offenders has greatly affected its capacity to deliver its services to African Member States in an effective and comprehensive manner,

1. *Commends* the United Nations African Institute for the Prevention of Crime and the Treatment of Offenders for its efforts to promote and coordinate regional technical cooperation activities related to crime prevention and criminal justice systems in Africa;

2. *Commends* the Secretary-General for his efforts to mobilize the financial resources necessary to provide the Institute with the core professional staff required to enable it to function effectively in the fulfilment of its mandated obligations;

3. *Reiterates* the need to strengthen further the capacity of the Institute to support national mechanisms for crime prevention and criminal justice in African countries;

4. *Urges* the States members of the Institute to make every possible effort to meet their obligations to the Institute;

5. *Calls upon* all Member States and nongovernmental organizations to adopt concrete practical measures to support the Institute in the development of the requisite capacity and to implement its programmes and activities aimed at strengthening crime prevention and criminal justice systems in Africa;

6. *Requests* the Secretary-General to intensify efforts to mobilize all relevant entities of the United Nations system to provide the necessary financial and technical support to the Institute to enable it to fulfil its mandate;

7. *Also requests* the Secretary-General to continue his efforts to mobilize the financial resources necessary to maintain the Institute with the core professional staff required to enable it to function effectively in the fulfilment of its mandated obligations;

8. *Calls upon* the United Nations Crime Prevention and Criminal Justice Programme and the

United Nations Office on Drugs and Crime to work closely with the Institute;

9. *Requests* the Secretary-General to enhance the promotion of regional cooperation, coordination and collaboration in the fight against crime, especially in its transnational dimension, which cannot be dealt with adequately by national action alone;

10. *Also requests* the Secretary-General to make concrete proposals, including the provision of additional core professional staff, to strengthen the programmes and activities of the Institute and to report to the General Assembly at its sixty-first session on the implementation of the present resolution.

Transnational organized crime

International convention

The entry into force, on 3 July 2005, of the Protocol against the Illicit Manufacturing of and Trafficking in Firearms, Their Parts and Components and Ammunition supplementing the United Nations Convention Against Transnational Organized Crime [YUN 2000, p. 1048], constituted a major milestone. As at 25 July, there were 107 States parties to the Organized Crime Convention, 86 States parties to the Protocol to Prevent, Suppress and Punish Trafficking in Persons, Especially Women and Children [ibid. p. 1063], 77 States parties to the Protocol against Smuggling of Migrants by Land, Sea and Air [ibid. p. 1063], and 43 States parties to the Firearms Protocol. A special treaty event was organized by UNODC, in close cooperation with the Office of Legal Affairs of the UN Secretariat, during the high-level segment of the Eleventh Crime Congress (see p. 1208). The event generated two accessions to the Organized Crime Convention, two accessions to the Trafficking in Persons Protocol, two accessions to and one ratification of the Migrants Protocol and one accession to the Firearms Protocol.

The Conference of the Parties to the United Nations Convention against Transnational Organized Crime, at its second session (Vienna, Austria, 10-21 October) [CTOC/COP/2005/8], reviewed and adopted decisions on the implementation of the Convention and its three supplementary Protocols and on technical assistance activities. The Conference aimed to promote those instruments and to improve the capacity of States to combat transnational organized crime.

Reports of Secretary-General. The Secretary-General submitted a March report [E/CN.15/2005/6] on the Convention and its Protocols and the activities and future work of UNODC, which was updated in a July report (see p. 1218) on strengthening the United Nations Crime and

Criminal Justice Programme, in particular its technical cooperation capacity.

On 22 July [meeting 36], the Economic and Social Council, on the recommendation of the Commission on Crime Prevention and Criminal Justice [E/2005/30], adopted **resolution 2005/17** without vote [agenda item 14 (c)].

International cooperation in the fight against transnational organized crime

The Economic and Social Council,

Recalling General Assembly resolution 55/25 of 15 November 2000, by which it adopted the United Nations Convention against Transnational Organized Crime, the Protocol to Prevent, Suppress and Punish Trafficking in Persons, Especially Women and Children, supplementing the United Nations Convention against Transnational Organized Crime, and the Protocol against the Smuggling of Migrants by Land, Sea and Air, supplementing the United Nations Convention against Transnational Organized Crime,

Recalling also General Assembly resolution 55/255 of 31 May 2001, by which it adopted the Protocol against the Illicit Manufacturing of and Trafficking in Firearms, Their Parts and Components and Ammunition, supplementing the United Nations Convention against Transnational Organized Crime,

Recalling further General Assembly resolution 59/157 of 20 December 2004 entitled "International cooperation in the fight against transnational organized crime: assistance to States in capacity-building with a view to facilitating the implementation of the United Nations Convention against Transnational Organized Crime and the Protocols thereto", and resolution 59/159 of 20 December 2004 entitled "Strengthening the United Nations Crime Prevention and Criminal Justice Programme, in particular its technical cooperation capacity",

Reaffirming its deep concern at the impact of transnational organized crime on the political, social and economic stability and development of societies,

Reaffirming that the adoption of the Convention and the Protocols thereto is a significant development in international criminal law and that they constitute important instruments for effective international cooperation, including regional and subregional cooperation, against transnational organized crime,

Taking note of the proposals of the Secretary-General on strengthening the United Nations Office on Drugs and Crime contained in his report entitled "In larger freedom: towards development, security and human rights for all",

1. *Takes note with appreciation* of the report of the Secretary-General on the United Nations Convention against Transnational Organized Crime and the Protocols thereto;

2. *Welcomes* the entry into force of the United Nations Convention against Transnational Organized Crime, the Protocol to Prevent, Suppress and Punish Trafficking in Persons, Especially Women and Children, supplementing the United Nations

Convention against Transnational Organized Crime, the Protocol against the Smuggling of Migrants by Land, Sea and Air, supplementing the United Nations Convention against Transnational Organized Crime, and the Protocol against the Illicit Manufacturing of and Trafficking in Firearms, Their Parts and Components and Ammunition, supplementing the United Nations Convention against Transnational Organized Crime;

3. *Notes* that the first session of the Conference of the Parties to the United Nations Convention against Transnational Organized Crime was held in Vienna from 28 June to 9 July 2004, and looks forward to the second session of the Conference of the Parties, to be held in Vienna from 10 to 21 October 2005;

4. *Commends* the United Nations Office on Drugs and Crime for its work in promoting the ratification of the Convention and the Protocols thereto, including, in particular, the preparation of legislative guides designed to facilitate the ratification and subsequent implementation of those instruments, and invites the Office to disseminate the legislative guides as widely as possible;

5. *Urges* all States and relevant regional economic integration organizations that have not done so to consider ratifying or acceding to the United Nations Convention against Transnational Organized Crime and the Protocols thereto, as soon as possible;

6. *Also urges* all States and relevant regional economic integration organizations to take all necessary measures to improve international cooperation, including regional and subregional cooperation, in criminal matters, especially extradition and mutual legal assistance, in accordance with their international obligations;

7. *Welcomes* the financial support provided by several donors to promote the entry into force and implementation of the Convention and the Protocols thereto, and encourages Member States to make sufficient voluntary contributions to the United Nations Crime Prevention and Criminal Justice Fund, as well as contributions in direct support of activities and projects of the United Nations Office on Drugs and Crime, including through contributions to the institutes of the United Nations Crime Prevention and Criminal Justice Programme network, for the provision of technical assistance to developing countries and countries with economies in transition for the implementation of those international legal instruments;

8. *Requests* the Secretary-General to continue to provide the United Nations Office on Drugs and Crime with the resources necessary to enable it to promote, in an effective manner, the implementation of the Convention and the Protocols thereto and to discharge its functions as the secretariat of the Conference of the Parties to the United Nations Convention against Transnational Organized Crime in accordance with its mandate;

9. *Requests* the United Nations Office on Drugs and Crime, building on the experience gained from the preparation of the legislative guides, to consult with the Conference of the Parties to the United Nations Convention against Transnational Organized Crime concerning the preparation of manuals and other tools to facilitate the implementation of the Convention and the Protocols thereto;

10. *Also requests* the United Nations Office on Drugs and Crime, within available extrabudgetary resources, not excluding the use of existing resources from the regular budget of the United Nations Office on Drugs and Crime, to continue to assist States, upon request, with capacity-building in the area of ratification as well as implementation of the Convention and its Protocols, in particular through international cooperation in criminal matters, including extradition and mutual legal assistance;

11. *Requests* the Secretary-General to transmit to the General Assembly the reports of the Conference of the Parties to the United Nations Convention against Transnational Organized Crime;

12. *Also requests* the Secretary-General to report on the implementation of the present resolution in his report on the work of the United Nations Office on Drugs and Crime to be submitted to the General Assembly at its sixty-first session.

Model agreement on disposal of confiscated proceeds of crime

Pursuant to Economic and Social Council resolution 2004/24 [YUN 2004, p. 1119], the Secretary-General submitted a February report [E/CN.15/2005/7] on the establishment of an intergovernmental expert group to prepare a draft model bilateral agreement on disposal of confiscated proceeds of crime covered by the United Nations Convention against Transnational Organized Crime and the United Nations Convention against Illicit Traffic in Narcotic Drugs and Psychotropic Substances of 1988 [YUN 1988, p. 690]. The expert group discussed how the confiscation of proceeds of crime or property and their disposal were regulated in their respective countries. The group unanimously agreed on the text of the draft model bilateral agreement as contained in the annex to the report and decided to submit it to the Commission on Crime Prevention and Criminal Justice. The Commission, at its fourteenth session (see p. 1210) recommended to the Economic and Social Council for approval a revised draft resolution for adoption by the General Assembly. However, the Council decided not to recommend the draft resolution for adoption by the Assembly. The Council adopted a resolution on the model bilateral agreement.

ECONOMIC AND SOCIAL COUNCIL ACTION

On 22 July [meeting 36], the Economic and Social Council, on the recommendation of the Commission on Crime Prevention and Criminal Justice [E/2005/30], adopted **resolution 2005/14** without vote [agenda item 14 (c)].

Model bilateral agreement on the sharing of confiscated proceeds of crime or property covered by the United Nations Convention against Transnational Organized Crime and the United Nations Convention against Illicit Traffic in Narcotic Drugs and Psychotropic Substances of 1988

The Economic and Social Council,

Recalling its resolution 2004/24 of 21 July 2004,

Recalling also the United Nations Convention against Transnational Organized Crime and the United Nations Convention against Illicit Traffic in Narcotic Drugs and Psychotropic Substances of 1988,

Recalling further the meeting of the intergovernmental expert group to prepare a draft model bilateral agreement on disposal of confiscated proceeds of crime covered by the United Nations Convention against Transnational Organized Crime and the United Nations Convention against Illicit Traffic in Narcotic Drugs and Psychotropic Substances of 1988, held in Vienna from 26 to 28 January 2005 with extrabudgetary resources provided for that purpose by the Government of the United States of America,

Convinced that a model bilateral agreement on sharing confiscated proceeds of crime or property could be a useful tool to facilitate greater international cooperation in that area, as one of the principal objectives of the United Nations Convention against Transnational Organized Crime and the United Nations Convention against Illicit Traffic in Narcotic Drugs and Psychotropic Substances of 1988,

Noting the importance of the reference in article 3 of the Model Bilateral Agreement on the Sharing of Confiscated Proceeds of Crime or Property to article 14, paragraph 2, of the United Nations Convention against Transnational Organized Crime, in which it is stated that States parties shall, to the extent permitted by domestic law, give priority consideration to returning the confiscated proceeds of crime or property to the requesting State party so that it can give compensation to the victims of the crime or return such proceeds of crime or property to their legitimate owners,

1. *Expresses its appreciation* to the intergovernmental expert group to prepare a draft model bilateral agreement on disposal of confiscated proceeds of crime covered by the United Nations Convention against Transnational Organized Crime and the United Nations Convention against Illicit Traffic in Narcotic Drugs and Psychotropic Substances of 1988 for having prepared the draft model bilateral agreement on the sharing of confiscated proceeds of crime or property;

2. *Adopts* the Model Bilateral Agreement on the Sharing of Confiscated Proceeds of Crime or Property, annexed to the present resolution, as a useful model that could be of assistance to States interested in negotiating and concluding bilateral agreements to facilitate the sharing of proceeds of crime;

3. *Stresses* that the Model Bilateral Agreement will not prejudice the principles set forth in the United Nations Convention against Corruption or the development, at a later stage, of any appropriate mechanism to facilitate the implementation of that Convention;

4. *Invites* Member States, in concluding agreements with other States in the area of sharing proceeds of crime pursuant to article 14 of the United Nations Convention against Transnational Organized Crime and article 5 of the United Nations Convention against Illicit Traffic in Narcotic Drugs and Psychotropic Substances of 1988 or in revising, where necessary or useful, existing bilateral agreements in that area, to take into account the Model Bilateral Agreement;

5. *Requests* the Secretary-General to bring to the attention of Member States the present resolution, together with the Model Bilateral Agreement;

6. *Encourages* Member States to inform the Secretary-General voluntarily of efforts undertaken in the area of sharing confiscated proceeds of crime or property, in particular the establishment of agreements in that area;

7. *Requests* the United Nations Office on Drugs and Crime to convey to the Commission on Crime Prevention and Criminal Justice information regarding efforts undertaken by Member States in the area of sharing confiscated proceeds of crime or property;

8. *Also requests* the United Nations Office on Drugs and Crime to provide to Member States, at their request, technical assistance and advice, within available extrabudgetary resources, not excluding the use of existing resources from the regular budget of the United Nations Office on Drugs and Crime, to give effect to the arrangements to be made pursuant to agreements to be negotiated on the basis of the Model Bilateral Agreement.

Annex

Model Bilateral Agreement on the Sharing of Confiscated Proceeds of Crime or Property

Agreement between the Government of _____ and the Government of _____ regarding the sharing of confiscated proceeds of crime or property

The Government of _____ and the Government of _____ (hereinafter referred to as "the Parties"),

Recalling the United Nations Convention against Transnational Organized Crime, in particular its article 12, paragraph 1, and articles 13 and 14,

Recalling also the United Nations Convention against Illicit Traffic in Narcotic Drugs and Psychotropic Substances of 1988, in particular article 5, paragraphs 1, 4 and 5,

Recognizing that this Agreement should not prejudice the principles set forth in the United Nations Convention against Corruption or the development, at a later stage, of any appropriate mechanism to facilitate the implementation of that Convention,

Reaffirming that nothing in the provisions of this Agreement should prejudice in any way the provisions and the principles on international cooperation set forth in the United Nations Convention against Illicit Traffic in Narcotic Drugs and Psychotropic Substances of 1988 and the United Nations Convention against Transnational Organized Crime, and that this Agreement is intended to enhance the effectiveness of international cooperation envisioned in those Conventions,

Considering [*reference to a treaty on mutual legal assistance if one exists between the Parties*],

Desiring to create an appropriate framework for sharing confiscated proceeds of crime or property,

Have agreed as follows:

Article 1. Definitions

For the purposes of this Agreement:

(a) The terms "proceeds of crime", "confiscation" and "property" shall be understood as defined in article 2 of the United Nations Convention against Transnational Organized Crime and article 1 of the United Nations Convention against Illicit Traffic in Narcotic Drugs and Psychotropic Substances of 1988;

(b) "Cooperation" shall mean any assistance described in articles 13, 16, 18-20, 26 and 27 of the United Nations Convention against Transnational Organized Crime or article 5, paragraph 4, and articles 6, 7, 9-11 and 17 of the United Nations Convention against Illicit Traffic in Narcotic Drugs and Psychotropic Substances of 1988, as well as cooperation between entities foreseen in article 7 of the United Nations Convention against Transnational Organized Crime, which has been given by one Party and which has contributed to, or facilitated, confiscation of proceeds of crime or property.

Article 2. Scope of application

This Agreement is intended solely for the purposes of mutual assistance between the Parties.

Article 3. Circumstances in which confiscated proceeds of crime or property [may] [shall] be shared

Where a Party is in possession of confiscated proceeds of crime or property and has cooperated with, or received cooperation from, the other Party, it [may] [shall] share such proceeds of crime or property with the other Party, in accordance with this Agreement, without prejudice to the principles enumerated in article 14, paragraphs 1, 2 and 3 (a), of the United Nations Convention against Transnational Organized Crime and article 5, paragraph 5 (b) (I), of the United Nations Convention against Illicit Traffic in Narcotic Drugs and Psychotropic Substances of 1988.

Article 4. Requests for sharing confiscated proceeds of crime or property

1. A request for sharing confiscated proceeds of crime or property shall be made within a time limit to be agreed between the Parties, shall set out the circumstances of the cooperation to which it relates and shall include sufficient details to identify the case, the confiscated proceeds of crime or property and the agency or agencies involved or such other information as may be agreed between the Parties.

Option 1

[2. On receipt of a request for sharing confiscated proceeds of crime or property made in accordance with the provisions of this article, the Party where confiscated proceeds of crime or property are located shall consider, in consultation with the other Party, whether to share such proceeds of crime or property, as set out in article 3 of this Agreement.]

Option 2

[2. On receipt of a request for sharing confiscated proceeds of crime or property made in accordance with the provisions of this article, the Party where confiscated proceeds of crime or property are located shall share with the other Party such proceeds of crime or property, as set out in article 3 of this Agreement.]

Article 5. Sharing of confiscated proceeds of crime or property

Option 1

[1. Where a Party proposes to share confiscated proceeds of crime or property with the other Party, it shall:

(a) Determine, at its discretion and in accordance with its domestic law and policies, the proportion of the confiscated proceeds of crime or property to be shared, which, in its view, corresponds to the extent of the cooperation afforded by the other Party; and

(b) Transfer a sum equivalent to that proportion set forth in subparagraph (a) above to the other Party in accordance with article 6 of this Agreement.

2. In determining the amount to transfer, the Party holding the confiscated proceeds of crime or property may include any interest and appreciation that has accrued on the confiscated proceeds of crime or property and may deduct reasonable expenses incurred in investigations, prosecution or judicial proceedings leading to the confiscation of the proceeds of crime or property.]

Option 2

[1. In sharing confiscated proceeds of crime or property in accordance with this Agreement:

(a) The proportion of the confiscated proceeds of crime or property to be shared shall be determined by the Parties on a *quantum meruit* basis or on any other reasonable basis agreed upon by the Parties;

(b) The Party holding the confiscated proceeds of crime or property shall transfer a sum equivalent to that proportion set forth in subparagraph (a) above to the other Party in accordance with article 6 of this Agreement.

2. In determining the amount to transfer, the Parties shall agree on any issues related to interest and appreciation that has accrued on the confiscated proceeds of crime or property and the deduction of reasonable expenses incurred in investigations, prosecution or judicial proceedings leading to the confiscation of the proceeds of crime or property.]

3. The Parties agree that it may not be appropriate to share where the value of the confiscated proceeds of crime or property is *de minimis*, subject to previous consultations between them.

Article 6. Payment of shared proceeds of crime or property

1. Unless the Parties agree otherwise, any sum transferred pursuant to article 5, paragraph 1 (b), of this Agreement shall be paid:

(a) In the currency of the Party where the proceeds of crime or property are located; and

(b) By means of an electronic transfer of funds or by cheque.

2. Payment of any such sum shall be made:

(*a*) In any case in which the Government of _____ is receiving payment, to [*identify the pertinent office or designated account as specified in the request*];

(*b*) In any case in which the Government of _____ is receiving payment, to [*identify the pertinent office or designated account as specified in the request*]; or

(*c*) To such other recipient or recipients as the Party receiving payment may from time to time specify by notification for the purposes of this article.

Article 7. Terms of transfer

1. In making the transfer, the Parties recognize that all right or title to and interest in the transferred proceeds of crime or property have already been adjudicated and that no further judicial proceedings are necessary to complete the confiscation. The Party transferring the proceeds of crime or property assumes no liability or responsibility for the proceeds of crime or property once they have been transferred and relinquishes all right or title to and interest in the transferred proceeds of crime or property.

2. Unless otherwise agreed, where a Party transfers confiscated proceeds of crime or property pursuant to article 5, paragraph 1 (*b*), of this Agreement, the other Party shall use the proceeds of crime or property for any lawful purpose at its discretion.

Article 8. Channels of communication

All communications between the Parties pursuant to the provisions of this Agreement shall be conducted through [*the central authorities designated pursuant to article [...] of the treaty on mutual legal assistance referred to in the preamble to the agreement]* or by the following:

(*a*) For the Government of _____, by the Office of _____;

(*b*) For the Government of _____, by the Office of _____; or

(*c*) By such other nominees as the Parties, for their own part, may from time to time specify by notification for the purposes of this article.

Article 9. Territorial application

This Agreement shall apply [*if applicable, designate any territories to which the agreement should be extended for each Government*].

Article 10. Amendments

This Agreement may be amended when both Parties have agreed in writing to such amendment.

Article 11. Consultations

The Parties shall consult promptly, at the request of either Party, concerning the interpretation, application or implementation of this Agreement, either generally or in relation to a particular case.

Article 12. Entry into force

This Agreement shall enter into force upon signature by both Parties or upon notification by the Parties that the necessary internal procedures have been completed.

Article 13. Termination of the Agreement

Either Party may terminate this Agreement, at any time, by giving written notice to the other Party. Termination shall become effective [...] months after receipt of the notice. The provisions shall, however, continue to apply in relation to confiscated proceeds of crime or property to be shared under this Agreement.

In witness whereof, the undersigned, being duly authorized by their respective Governments, have signed this Agreement.

Done in duplicate at [*location*], this _____ day of _____, ____.

For the Government of _____:

[*Signature*] _____

For the Government of _____:

[*Signature*] _____

Strategies for crime prevention

Corruption

UN Convention against Corruption

The Secretary-General, in a March report [E/CN.15/2005/9], highlighted the progress made towards the promotion of the entry into force of the United Nations Convention against Corruption [YUN 2003, p. 1127], which was adopted in 2003 by the General Assembly in resolution 58/4 [ibid.]. The report was submitted pursuant to Assembly resolutions 59/155 [YUN 2004, p. 1120], 59/159 [ibid., p. 1114] and 59/242 [ibid., p. 1121].

The Convention entered into force on 14 December.

ECONOMIC AND SOCIAL COUNCIL ACTION

On 22 July [meeting 36], the Economic and Social Council, on the recommendation of the Commission on Crime Prevention and Criminal Justice [E/2005/30], adopted **resolution 2005/18** without vote [agenda item 14 (*c*)].

Action against corruption: assistance to States in capacity-building with a view to facilitating the entry into force and subsequent implementation of the United Nations Convention against Corruption

The Economic and Social Council,

Deeply concerned about the impact of corruption on the political, social and economic stability and development of societies,

Bearing in mind that the prevention and combating of corruption is a common and shared responsibility of the international community, necessitating cooperation at the bilateral and multilateral levels,

Bearing in mind also that the prevention and elimination of corruption is a responsibility of all States and that they must cooperate with one another, with the support and involvement of individuals and groups outside the public sector, such as civil society, non-governmental organizations and community-based organizations, if their efforts to prevent and combat corruption are to be effective,

Reaffirming its support and commitment to the goals of the United Nations in the field of crime prevention and criminal justice, in particular the objectives set forth in the Vienna Declaration on Crime and

Justice: Meeting the Challenges of the Twenty-first Century,

Recalling General Assembly resolution 58/4 of 31 October 2003, in which it adopted the United Nations Convention against Corruption and urged all States and competent regional economic integration organizations to sign and ratify it,

Noting with appreciation the holding of the High-level Political Conference for the Purpose of Signing the United Nations Convention against Corruption in Merida, Mexico, from 9 to 11 December 2003,

Recalling General Assembly resolution 59/155 of 20 December 2004, entitled "Action against corruption: assistance to States in capacity-building with a view to facilitating the entry into force and subsequent implementation of the United Nations Convention against Corruption",

Noting with appreciation the initiative of the States that have made financial contributions to the United Nations Crime Prevention and Criminal Justice Fund to facilitate the ratification and implementation of the United Nations Convention against Corruption by developing countries and by countries with economies in transition,

1. *Takes note with appreciation* of the report of the Secretary-General on the United Nations Convention against Corruption;

2. *Welcomes* the signing of the United Nations Convention against Corruption by a large number of Member States and the ratification of the Convention by an increasing number of Member States, which reflects the high level of commitment on the part of the international community to the purpose of the Convention;

3. *Urges* Member States that have not yet done so to consider signing and ratifying the Convention as soon as possible, in order to allow its early entry into force and to facilitate its effective implementation;

4. *Also urges* Member States to promote a culture of integrity and accountability in both the public and the private sectors, and calls upon them to adopt measures to facilitate the recovery and return of assets that are consistent with the principles of the Convention;

5. *Calls upon* Member States to continue to make adequate voluntary contributions to the United Nations Crime Prevention and Criminal Justice Fund to provide developing countries and countries with economies in transition with the technical assistance that they may require to implement the Convention, including assistance for the preparatory measures required for implementation, taking into account article 62 of the Convention;

6. *Requests* the Secretary-General to provide the United Nations Office on Drugs and Crime with the resources necessary to enable it to promote, in an effective manner, the entry into force and implementation of the Convention, inter alia, through the provision of assistance to developing countries and countries with economies in transition for building capacity in the areas covered by the Convention;

7. *Also requests* the Secretary-General, within available extrabudgetary resources, not excluding the use of existing resources from the regular budget of the United Nations Office on Drugs and Crime, to finalize the legislative guide for the Con-

vention and, building on the experience gained in the preparation of the guide, to consider preparing manuals and other tools to facilitate implementation of the Convention;

8. *Further requests* the Secretary-General to report to the Commission on Crime Prevention and Criminal Justice at its fifteenth session on the implementation of the present resolution.

Funds of illicit origin

In response to General Assembly resolution 59/242 [YUN 2004, p. 1121], the Secretary General submitted, in July [A/60/157], a report on preventing and combating corrupt practices, and transfering assets of illicit origin and returning assets to countries of origin, which contained a summary of the responses received from 28 States on corruption issues, including on the scale of the transfer of assets of illicit origin and its impact on the economic and sustainable development of those states.

On 16 December, the Assembly took note of the Secretary-General's report (**decision 60/536**).

GENERAL ASSEMBLY ACTION

On 22 December [meeting 68], the General Assembly, on the recommendation of the Second Committee [A/60/490/Add.4], adopted **resolution 60/207** without vote [agenda item 54 *(d)*].

Preventing and combating corrupt practices and transfer of assets of illicit origin and returning such assets, in particular to the countries of origin, consistent with the United Nations Convention against Corruption

The General Assembly,

Recalling its resolutions 54/205 of 22 December 1999, 56/186 of 21 December 2001 and 57/244 of 20 December 2002, and recalling also its resolutions 58/205 of 23 December 2003 and 59/242 of 22 December 2004 on preventing and combating corrupt practices and transfer of assets of illicit origin and returning such assets to the countries of origin,

Recalling also the Monterrey Consensus of the International Conference on Financing for Development, which underlined that fighting corruption at all levels is a priority, and the Plan of Implementation of the World Summit on Sustainable Development ("Johannesburg Plan of Implementation"),

Recalling further the 2005 World Summit Outcome,

Emphasizing the need for solid democratic institutions responsive to the needs of the people and the need to improve the efficiency, transparency and accountability of domestic administration and public spending and the rule of law, to ensure full respect for human rights, including the right to development, and to eradicate corruption and build sound economic and social institutions,

Recognizing that fighting corruption at all levels is a priority and that corruption is a serious barrier to effective resource mobilization and allocation and diverts resources away from activities that are vital for poverty eradication, the fight against hunger, and economic and sustainable development,

Noting the particular concern of developing countries and countries with economies in transition regarding the return of assets of illicit origin derived from corruption to the countries from which they originated, consistent with the principles of the United Nations Convention against Corruption, in particular chapter V, in view of the importance that such assets can have to their sustainable development,

Recognizing the concern about the transfer and/or transaction of assets of illicit origin derived from corruption, and stressing the need to address this concern consistent with the principles of chapter V of the United Nations Convention against Corruption,

Recognizing also that the illicit acquisition of wealth can be particularly damaging to democratic institutions, national economies and the rule of law,

Convinced that a stable and transparent environment for national and international commercial transactions in all countries is essential for the mobilization of investment, finance, technology, skills and other important resources, and recognizing that effective efforts at all levels to prevent and combat corruption in all its forms in all countries are essential elements of an improved national and international business environment,

Concerned about the links between corruption in all its forms, including bribery, corruption-related money-laundering and the transfer of assets of illicit origin, and other forms of crime, in particular organized crime and economic crime,

Reiterating its concern about the seriousness of problems and threats posed by corruption to the stability and security of societies, undermining the institutions and the values of democracy, ethical values and justice and jeopardizing sustainable development and the rule of law, in particular when an inadequate national and international response leads to impunity,

Welcoming the initiatives taken by the Commonwealth Secretariat and the Group of Eight with regard to fighting corruption and improving transparency, including the initiative of the Group of Eight to support with bilateral technical assistance those countries committed to a partnership to increase transparency, good governance and the rule of law, and welcoming also the efforts of those Member States that have entered into "Compacts to Promote Transparency and Combat Corruption" with the Group of Eight,

1. *Condemns* corruption in all its forms, including bribery, money-laundering and the transfer of assets of illicit origin;

2. *Takes note* of the report of the Secretary-General;

3. *Welcomes* the entry into force on 14 December 2005 of the United Nations Convention against Corruption;

4. *Reiterates its invitation* to all Member States and competent regional economic integration organizations within the limits of their competence to ratify or accede to and fully implement the United Nations Convention against Corruption as soon as possible;

5. *Reaffirms* the commitment to make the fight against corruption a priority at all levels, and welcomes all actions taken in this regard at the national and international levels, including the adoption of policies that emphasize accountability, transparent public sector management and corporate responsibility and accountability, including efforts to return assets transferred through corruption, consistent with the United Nations Convention against Corruption;

6. *Welcomes* the efforts of Member States that have enacted laws and taken other positive measures in the fight against corruption in all its forms including, inter alia, in accordance with the United Nations Convention against Corruption, and in this regard encourages Member States that have not yet done so to enact such laws and to implement effective measures at the national level and, in accordance with domestic law and policies, at the local level, to prevent and combat corruption;

7. *Encourages* all Governments to prevent, combat and penalize corruption in all its forms, including bribery, money-laundering and the transfer of illicitly acquired assets, and to work for the prompt return of such assets through asset recovery consistent with the principles of the United Nations Convention against Corruption, particularly chapter V;

8. *Further encourages* subregional and regional cooperation, where appropriate, in the efforts to prevent and combat corrupt practices and the transfer of assets of illicit origin as well as for asset recovery consistent with the principles of the United Nations Convention against Corruption, particularly chapter V;

9. *Calls for* further international cooperation, inter alia, through the United Nations system, in support of national, subregional and regional efforts to prevent and combat corrupt practices and the transfer of assets of illicit origin, as well as for asset recovery consistent with the principles of the United Nations Convention against Corruption, particularly chapter V;

10. *Encourages* Member States to provide adequate financial and human resources to the United Nations Office on Drugs and Crime, including for the effective implementation of the United Nations Convention against Corruption, and further encourages the Office to give high priority to technical cooperation, upon request, inter alia, to promote and facilitate the ratification, acceptance, approval of or accession to and the implementation of the Convention;

11. *Notes* the imminent finalization by the United Nations Office on Drugs and Crime, in cooperation with the United Nations Interregional Crime and Justice Research Institute, of the legislative guide for the ratification and implementation of the United Nations Convention against Corruption;

12. *Reiterates its request* to the international community to provide, inter alia, technical assistance to support national efforts to strengthen human and institutional capacity aimed at preventing and combating corrupt practices and the transfer of assets of illicit origin as well as for asset recovery consistent with the principles of the United Nations Convention against Corruption, particularly chapter V, and

formulating strategies for mainstreaming and promoting transparency and integrity in both the public and private sectors;

13. *Urges* all Member States, consistent with the United Nations Convention against Corruption, to abide by the principles of proper management of public affairs and public property, fairness, responsibility and equality before the law and the need to safeguard integrity and to foster a culture of transparency, accountability and rejection of corruption;

14. *Welcomes* the actions by the private sector, at both the international and the national levels, including small and large companies and transnational corporations, to remain fully engaged in the fight against corruption, calls upon the private sector to continue to make efforts in this regard, takes note with appreciation of the work undertaken by the Global Compact in its consideration of its tenth principle, on anti-corruption, and emphasizes the need for all relevant stakeholders to continue to promote corporate responsibility and accountability;

15. *Encourages* all Member States that have not yet done so to require financial institutions to properly implement comprehensive due diligence and vigilance programmes, consistent with the principles of the United Nations Convention against Corruption and other applicable instruments, that could facilitate transparency and prevent the placement of illicitly acquired funds;

16. *Also encourages* Member States, relevant international organizations and the United Nations Office on Drugs and Crime to give prominence to 9 December as International Anti-Corruption Day, as established by the General Assembly in its resolution 58/4 of 31 October 2003;

17. *Expresses concern* about the magnitude of corruption at all levels, including the scale of the transfer of assets of illicit origin derived from corruption, and in this regard reiterates its commitment to preventing and combating corrupt practices at all levels;

18. *Requests* the Secretary-General to submit to the General Assembly at its sixty-first session a report on the implementation of the present resolution and to elaborate further on the magnitude of corruption at all levels, including the scale of the transfer of assets of illicit origin derived from corruption and the impact of corruption and such transfers on economic growth and sustainable development, and decides to include in the provisional agenda of its sixty-first session, under the item entitled "Globalization and interdependence", a sub-item entitled "Preventing and combating corrupt practices and transfer of assets of illicit origin and returning such assets, in particular to the countries of origin, consistent with the United Nations Convention against Corruption".

Protection of witnesses

On 22 July [meeting 36], the Economic and Social Council, on the recommendation of the Commission on Crime Prevention and Criminal Justice [E/2005/30], adopted **resolution 2005/16** without vote [agenda item 14 (c)].

Action against transnational organized crime: protection of witnesses

The Economic and Social Council,

Recalling General Assembly resolution 55/25 of 15 November 2000, by which it adopted the United Nations Convention against Transnational Organized Crime, the Protocol to Prevent, Suppress and Punish Trafficking in Persons, Especially Women and Children, supplementing the United Nations Convention against Transnational Organized Crime, and the Protocol against the Smuggling of Migrants by Land, Sea and Air, supplementing the United Nations Convention against Transnational Organized Crime,

Recalling also General Assembly resolution 55/255 of 31 May 2001, by which it adopted the Protocol against the Illicit Manufacturing of and Trafficking in Firearms, Their Parts and Components and Ammunition, supplementing the United Nations Convention against Transnational Organized Crime,

Concerned about the negative political, economic and social implications of the activities of organized criminal groups and the possible expansion of such activities,

Convinced of the need to strengthen local, regional and international cooperation in the effective prevention and combating of such activities wherever they occur,

Determined to facilitate the testimony of witnesses in order to ensure prosecution of those who participate in or profit from transnational organized crime, and thus to prevent the provision of safe havens for such persons,

Reaffirming the growing recognition of the key role of witnesses in criminal proceedings, especially in cases involving organized crime, and the need to encourage their collaboration and to provide them with effective protection from retaliation or intimidation,

1. *Takes note with appreciation* of the report of the Secretary-General on the United Nations Convention against Transnational Organized Crime and the Protocols thereto;

2. *Encourages* Member States to exchange their experiences with, and information on, action taken to provide effective protection for witnesses in criminal proceedings involving transnational and national organized crime and for their relatives and all other persons close to them;

3. *Requests* the Secretary-General to pay special attention, within the framework of technical assistance activities, to the issue of the protection of witnesses, in order to enable Member States to establish effective witness protection programmes;

4. *Also requests* the Secretary-General to convene, within available extrabudgetary resources, not excluding the use of existing resources from the regular budget of the United Nations Office on Drugs and Crime, an open-ended intergovernmental group of experts, the composition of which should reflect equitable geographical representation and the diversity of legal systems, to exchange experiences and put forward suggestions and recommendations with regard to protecting witnesses and encouraging them to collaborate in the judicial process, taking into account ongoing work in that area.

Terrorism

In April [E/CN.15/2005/13], the Secretary-General, in response to General Assembly resolution 59/153 [YUN 2004, p. 1125], submitted a report on strengthening international cooperation and technical assistance in promoting the implementation of the universal conventions and protocols related to terrorism within the framework of UNODC activities. The report reviewed the technical assistance activities of the Terrorism Prevention Branch of UNODC Division for Treaty Affairs and presented guidelines and proposals concerning the future approach to technical assistance for consideration by the Commission on Crime Prevention and Criminal Justice. The report also provided data on the status of ratification of the conventions and protocols related to terrorism and on voluntary contributions received by the Branch.

On 10 March, the Secretary-General presented to the International Summit on Democracy, Terrorism and Security (Madrid, Spain, 8-11 March) a report entitled "A Global Strategy for Fighting Terrorism", which included an examination of the role of the United Nations in implementing the Strategy. The Strategy was devised to complement the work of the UNODC Terrorism Prevention Branch in providing assistance to States in reviewing and revising national legislation against terrorism. UNODC developed a variety of technical tools, based on best practices identified by international experts that were used in training judicial and prosecutorial personnel in the proper implementation of the universal conventions and protocols related to terrorism. In international cooperation, UNODC continued to work on a series of specialized manuals and model laws on extradition and mutual legal assistance intended to allow States to make use of the guidance provided, in order to prepare bilateral agreements and to draft relevant legislation against terrorism.

In March [A/59/754-S/2005/197], Croatia transmitted to the Secretary-General the Zagreb Declaration on International Cooperation on Counter-Terrorism, Corruption and the Fight against Transnational Organized Crime, adopted at the expert workshop on "International cooperation on counter-terrorism, corruption and fight against transnational organized crime" (Zagreb, Croatia, 7-9 March).

ECONOMIC AND SOCIAL COUNCIL ACTION

On 22 July [meeting 36], the Economic and Social Council, on the recommendation of the Commission on Crime Prevention and Criminal Justice [E/2005/30], adopted **resolution 2005/19** without vote [agenda item 14 (c)].

Strengthening international cooperation and technical assistance in promoting the implementation of the universal conventions and protocols related to terrorism within the framework of the activities of the United Nations Office on Drugs and Crime

The Economic and Social Council,

Recalling all General Assembly and Security Council resolutions on terrorism,

Welcoming the adoption and the forthcoming opening for signature of the International Convention for the Suppression of Acts of Nuclear Terrorism,

Taking note with appreciation of the Bangkok Declaration on Synergies and Responses: Strategic Alliances in Crime Prevention and Criminal Justice, adopted at the high-level segment of the Eleventh United Nations Congress on Crime Prevention and Criminal Justice, held in Bangkok from 18 to 25 April 2005, which expresses the hope that the ongoing negotiation of the draft comprehensive convention on international terrorism will be concluded as soon as possible and recognizes that arriving at a possible definition of terrorism is one of the key issues to be resolved,

Recalling General Assembly resolution 59/46 of 2 December 2004, in which it reiterated that criminal acts intended or calculated to provoke a state of terror in the general public, a group of persons or particular persons for political purposes are in any circumstances unjustifiable, whatever the considerations of a political, philosophical, ideological, racial, ethnic, religious or other nature that may be invoked to justify them,

Stressing the need for Member States to ensure that any measures taken to combat terrorism comply with all their obligations under international law, in particular the Charter of the United Nations and international human rights, refugee and humanitarian law,

Mindful of the essential need to strengthen international, regional and subregional cooperation to effectively prevent and suppress terrorism in all its forms and manifestations, in particular by enhancing the national capacity of States,

Recalling Security Council resolution 1566(2004) of 8 October 2004, and reaffirming the obligation of States to cooperate fully in the fight against terrorism, especially with those States where or against whose citizens terrorist acts are committed, in accordance with their obligations under international law, in order to find, deny safe haven to and bring to justice, on the basis of the principle to extradite or prosecute, any person who supports, facilitates, participates or attempts to participate in the financing, planning, preparation or commission of terrorist acts or provides safe havens,

Mindful that acts, methods and practices of terrorism are contrary to the purposes and principles of the United Nations,

Reaffirming its unequivocal condemnation of terrorism in all its forms and manifestations, wherever and by whomsoever committed,

Noting that the Bangkok Declaration emphasizes that enhancing dialogue among civilizations, promoting tolerance, preventing the indiscriminate targeting of different religions and cultures and addressing development issues and unresolved conflicts will contribute to international cooperation, which is among the most important elements to combat terrorism in all its forms and manifestations, and reaffirming that no terrorist act can be justified in any circumstances,

Deeply concerned that acts of terrorism continue to be perpetrated, endangering the lives and well-being of individuals worldwide, and expressing its deepest sympathy and condolences to the victims of terrorist attacks and their families,

Noting the establishment of a working group pursuant to Security Council resolution 1566(2004),

Recalling General Assembly resolution 59/159 of 20 December 2004, in which it, inter alia, reaffirmed the importance of the work of the United Nations Office on Drugs and Crime in the fulfilment of its mandate in crime prevention and criminal justice, including to contribute to preventing and combating terrorism, and resolution 59/153 of 20 December 2004, in which it requested the Office to intensify its efforts to provide technical assistance, upon request, in preventing and combating terrorism, by facilitating the implementation of the universal conventions and protocols related to terrorism, including training of judicial and prosecutorial personnel, working in coordination with the Counter-Terrorism Committee and the Counter-Terrorism Committee Executive Directorate,

Mindful of General Assembly resolution 59/46 of 2 December 2004, in which it welcomed the continuing efforts of the Terrorism Prevention Branch of the United Nations Office on Drugs and Crime to assist States to become parties to and to work towards implementing the relevant international conventions and protocols related to terrorism,

Recalling that the Security Council, in its resolution 1535(2004) of 26 March 2004, recognized the need for the Counter-Terrorism Committee, where appropriate, to visit States, with the consent of the States concerned, and to engage in a detailed discussion to monitor the implementation of Council resolution 1373(2001) of 28 September 2001, and that such visits should be conducted, when appropriate, in close cooperation with relevant international, regional and subregional organizations and other United Nations bodies, including the United Nations Office on Drugs and Crime, in particular with its Terrorism Prevention Branch, taking special care of the assistance that might be available to address the needs of States,

Welcoming the initiative by the Secretary-General to establish a task force in his Office for the coordination of the counter-terrorism efforts of the Secretariat,

Welcoming also the adoption of Commission on Human Rights resolution 2005/80 of 21 April 2005, especially the appointment, for a period of three years, of a special rapporteur on the promotion and protection of human rights and fundamental freedoms while countering terrorism,

1. *Commends* the United Nations Office on Drugs and Crime for its contributions towards preventing and combating terrorism through the provision of technical assistance to States, upon request, in close consultation with the Counter-Terrorism Committee and the Counter-Terrorism Committee Executive Directorate, for the implementation of Security Council resolution 1373(2001), in particular for promotion of the ratification of, accession to and implementation of the universal conventions and protocols related to terrorism, as well as for its continuing close cooperation with international, regional and subregional organizations, and requests the Office to continue such work with international organizations, in particular the specialized agencies and other relevant entities of the United Nations system;

2. *Welcomes* the holding of regional and subregional workshops in San José, Tashkent, Port Louis, Praia and Lisbon to follow up on technical assistance activities conducted by the Terrorism Prevention Branch of the United Nations Office on Drugs and Crime in 2003 and 2004 by further familiarizing national experts and criminal justice officials with the requirements of Security Council resolution 1373(2001) and the requirements for becoming parties to and implementing the universal conventions and protocols related to terrorism and international cooperation agreements, and emphasizes the need for close cooperation, in that context, between the Terrorism Prevention Branch and the Counter-Terrorism Committee, the Counter-Terrorism Committee Executive Directorate and the Office of Legal Affairs of the Secretariat, as appropriate;

3. *Welcomes also* the holding of a subregional workshop in Zagreb from 7 to 9 March 2005, which resulted in the Zagreb Declaration on International Cooperation on Counter-Terrorism, Corruption and the Fight against Transnational Organized Crime, and encourages the Terrorism Prevention Branch, in coordination with the Counter-Terrorism Committee and within available extrabudgetary resources, not excluding the use of existing resources from the regular budget of the United Nations Office on Drugs and Crime, to continue to ensure proper follow-up to its technical assistance activities, in cases where such follow-up is requested by Member States;

4. *Calls upon* Member States that have not yet done so to consider becoming parties to, and to implement, the universal conventions and protocols related to terrorism as a matter of urgency and, where appropriate, to request assistance to that end from the United Nations Office on Drugs and Crime and relevant international, regional and subregional organizations, in coordination with the Counter-Terrorism Committee;

5. *Takes note* of the legislative assistance tools developed by the United Nations Office on Drugs and Crime, and requests the Office, within available extrabudgetary resources, not excluding the use of existing resources from the regular budget of the United Nations Office on Drugs and Crime, to finalize the draft guide for legislative incorporation and implementation of the universal instruments against terrorism and to develop it further to serve as a training tool when providing assistance to States, upon request, in capacity-building for the implementation of the universal instruments related to terrorism;

6. *Urges* Member States to strengthen, to the greatest extent possible, international cooperation

in order to prevent and combat terrorism, including, when necessary, entering into bilateral treaties on extradition and mutual legal assistance within the framework of the relevant Security Council resolutions, as well as the universal conventions and protocols related to terrorism and other relevant United Nations resolutions and in accordance with the Charter of the United Nations and international law, and to ensure adequate training of all relevant personnel in executing international cooperation, and calls upon Member States to request assistance to that end from the United Nations Office on Drugs and Crime and relevant international, regional and subregional organizations, when appropriate;

7. *Requests* the United Nations Office on Drugs and Crime, within available extrabudgetary resources, not excluding the use of existing resources from the regular budget of the United Nations Office on Drugs and Crime, to intensify its efforts to provide Member States with technical assistance, upon request, to strengthen international cooperation, including in international, national, regional and subregional forums, in preventing and combating terrorism through the facilitation of the implementation of the universal conventions and protocols related to terrorism, in particular through training in the judicial and prosecutorial fields in the proper implementation of the universal conventions and protocols related to terrorism, with particular emphasis on the need to coordinate such work with the Counter-Terrorism Committee and the Counter-Terrorism Committee Executive Directorate;

8. *Recognizes* the role of fair and effective criminal justice systems within the overall framework of the rule of law as an integral component of any strategy to counter terrorism, and requests the United Nations Office on Drugs and Crime, whenever appropriate, to take into account in its technical assistance programme to counter terrorism the elements necessary for building national capacity in order to strengthen criminal justice systems and the rule of law with a view to facilitating the effective implementation of the universal conventions and protocols related to terrorism and relevant Security Council resolutions;

9. *Notes* the discussions during the Eleventh United Nations Congress on Crime Prevention and Criminal Justice, held in Bangkok from 18 to 25 April 2005, on its agenda item entitled "International cooperation against terrorism and links between terrorism and other criminal activities in the context of the work of the United Nations Office on Drugs and Crime", and requests the Secretariat to take into account any existing links between terrorism and other forms of crime and to pursue an integrated, comprehensive approach in the delivery of technical assistance, emphasizing the transversal relevance of international cooperation;

10. *Urges* Member States to consider the early signing and ratifying of the International Convention for the Suppression of Acts of Nuclear Terrorism, and requests the United Nations Office on Drugs and Crime, upon request, to promote, in the course of its technical assistance activities, the

speedy ratification and full implementation of the Convention;

11. *Expresses its appreciation* to all Member States that have supported the technical assistance activities of the Terrorism Prevention Branch of the United Nations Office on Drugs and Crime, and invites all Member States to consider making voluntary financial contributions, in-kind contributions or both;

12. *Requests* the Secretary-General to report to the General Assembly at its sixty-first session on the implementation of the present resolution.

International commercial fraud

Pursuant to Economic and Social Council resolution 2004/26 [YUN 2004, p. 1123], the Secretary-General reported on the progress of preparation by the Intergovernmental Expert Group of a study on fraud, criminal misuse and falsification of identity. A preliminary meeting of the Intergovernmental Expert Group was held in Vienna on 17 and 18 March. A number of speakers emphasized that fraud was a serious concern for their Governments and echoed the concerns raised in the work of the United Nations Commission on International Trade Law (UNCITRAL), both in the range of frauds being committed and their expansive geographical scope and diversity. Delegates indicated that modern technologies had fuelled the evolution of offences, including the spread of offender expertise, the actual use of technologies by offenders to target victims and the use of technologies to transfer, conceal and launder proceeds. They also discussed the need for integrated public criminal law and private commercial law approaches, in particular in developing preventive measures involving commercial practices.

The Group recommended that the study should be conducted by volunteer experts and Member States and should encompass the full range of fraud offences, as well as offences involving criminal misuse and falsification of identity. The results of the study would be reviewed at a further meeting of the Intergovernmental Expert Group, subject to the availability of extrabudgetary resources.

Combating trafficking in persons

In response to General Assembly resolution 58/137 [YUN 2003, p. 1151], the Secretary-General, in a March report [E/CN.15/2005/8], highlighted steps taken to strengthen international cooperation in preventing and combating trafficking in persons and protecting victims of such trafficking. The report contained an analysis of the replies received from 37 States on the implementation of the resolution. The report also drew on information provided by relevant UN entities and international organizations within the framework of the activities of the United Nations System Chief Executives Board for Coordination on measures taken to curb trafficking in human beings.

The report noted that a considerable number of States had ratified or acceded to the 2000 Protocol to Prevent, Suppress and Punish Trafficking in Persons, Especially Women and Children, supplementing the United Nations Convention against Transnational Organized Crime (Trafficking in Persons Protocol) [YUN 2000, p. 1063], many of which had adopted legislation translating their obligations under the Protocol into national law. In addition, regional organizations had followed up with regional instruments and action plans. Nevertheless, in a considerable number of States, implementing legislation was lacking or only certain aspects of the Protocol were being addressed. As more than half of the Member States had not yet ratified the Protocol, the promotion of ratification remained an important issue. The challenge for States parties would be to ensure effective fulfilment of the Protocol obligations at the national level, including the provisions concerning international cooperation.

Although there had been a significant increase in information on trafficking in persons in recent years, such information generally related to individual cases or had been prepared for advocacy purposes. Reliability of data remained a major problem. A lack of a systematic collection of data made it hard to establish the magnitude of trafficking, whether on a national or a global scale. Even with legislation in place, many Governments did not yet have the necessary knowledge or capacity to address trafficking in persons in its multidimensional aspects, in particular as it related to the transnationality of such crimes. Only a limited number of Governments had adopted national action plans, created inter-agency coordination mechanisms or ombudspersons, addressed demand reduction or identified the role of all of the different departments concerned in countering trafficking crimes in a coordinated multidisciplinary way. Only some national services had the expertise and training to investigate and prosecute transnational crimes, including human trafficking, and convictions for such crimes were still rare. There was a strong need for curriculum development, preparation of training tools, training at the national, bilateral and international levels, gathering and sharing of police intelligence and coordination of investigations and prosecutions, including in relation to issues such as asset forfeiture, extradition and mutual legal assistance. In a number of coun-

tries, increased awareness of the seriousness of the violations of the human rights of victims of trafficking had led to the creation of victim protection and assistance schemes in line with the requirements of the Trafficking in Persons Protocol. However, most countries still had to establish proper victim protection schemes. Effective responses to trafficking in persons would also need to address the root causes, such as poverty, gender inequalities, unemployment and other socio-economic factors, which were major issues highlighted by a number of respondents. Apart from the need to secure proper funding for initiatives to combat trafficking in persons, the readiness of all actors concerned, countries of origin, transit and destination alike, to cooperate closely among themselves and with all relevant agencies and civil society would be key to countering trafficking in persons more effectively in the future.

UN standards and guidelines

The Eleventh United Nations Congress on Crime Prevention and Criminal Justice held a general discussion on a working paper prepared by the UN Secretariat entitled "Making standards work: fifty years of standard-setting in crime prevention and criminal justice" (see p. 1209). There was broad agreement among representatives on the need to continue giving priority to the implementation of standards and norms, both in developing and developed countries. There was also general agreement on the need for innovative approaches in the administration of justice, including the use of alternatives to imprisonment for minor offences, especially by first-time offenders, juvenile offenders and drug abusers, the use of restorative justice, including mediation and conciliation, and the need to take into consideration the rights of victims, in particular those of women and children.

The Committee in charge of reviewing the working paper recommended that the use and application of UN standards and norms in crime prevention and criminal justice should continue to be accorded high priority within the UN system and remain a standing item on the agenda of the Commission on Crime Prevention and Criminal Justice. In that context, the Congress commended the cluster approach in the assessment of the use and application of standards and norms, in accordance with Economic and Social Council resolution 2003/30 [YUN 2003, p. 1155]. Future reviews of their application should focus on identifying difficulties and problems, as well as best practices to overcome them, with a view to facilitating international cooperation through the sharing of such information and enhancing the impact of technical cooperation activities. In addition, States should ensure that relevant applicable human rights laws were integrated into their criminal justice systems and that the relevant international human rights instruments were consistently applied. States should also consider mechanisms to promote the widest possible application of UN standards and norms, including by coordinating the work of national authorities and agencies involved, as well as promoting the exchange of information between them. Such mechanisms should have the support of relevant non-governmental and civil society organizations. UNODC should publish an updated version of the *Compendium of United Nations Standards and Norms in Crime Prevention and Criminal Justice* in the six official languages of the Organization and, where possible, translate it into other languages to ensure its widest possible dissemination. UNODC should be provided with adequate resources to enable it to offer technical assistance in criminal justice reform to States, upon request. Considering that remand prisoners constituted the majority of the prison population in many countries and that, because of prison overcrowding, many prisoners were housed in inhumane conditions and often subjected to gross violations of human rights and even to torture and inhuman or degrading treatment, consideration should be given to the standards and norms in relation to prison management and prisoners. The Commission on Crime Prevention and Criminal Justice should consider the recommendations contained in the report of the Intergovernmental Expert Group Meeting to Develop Guidelines on Justice in Matters involving Child Victims and Witnesses of Crime (see below), and should give consideration to reviewing the adequacy of standards and norms in relation to prison management and prisoners. Furthermore, since mandatory sentences restricted the discretion of the courts in considering the circumstances of each offender and in applying alternative sanctions, States that had not yet done so should consider enacting legislation that provided for flexibility in sentencing, as well as for the imposition of non-custodial measures.

The Secretary-General submitted to the Commission an April report [E/CN.15/2005/14] on UN standards and norms in crime prevention and criminal justice, in response to Economic and Social Council resolution 2004/28 [YUN 2004, p. 1131]. The report provided an overview of activities undertaken to disseminate UN standards and norms in crime prevention and criminal justice and described advisory services and technical cooperation delivered.

Guidelines on justice for child victims and witnesses

Pursuant to Economic and Social Council resolution 2004/27 [YUN 2004, p. 1132], the Secretary-General submitted to the Commission on Crime Prevention and Criminal Justice the report of the Intergovernmental Expert Group Meeting to Develop Guidelines on Justice in Matters involving Child Victims and Witnesses of Crime (Vienna, Austria, 15-16 March) [E/CN.15/2005/14/Add.1 & Corr.1]. The report contained guidelines on justice in matters involving child victims and witnesses of crime that aimed to assist Governments and international organizations, NGOs and other interested parties in designing and implementing legislation and programmes to address those issues.

ECONOMIC AND SOCIAL COUNCIL ACTION

On 22 July [meeting 36], the Economic and Social Council, on the recommendation of the Commission on Crime Prevention and Criminal Justice [E/2005/30], adopted **resolution 2005/20** without vote [agenda item 14 *(c)*].

Guidelines on Justice in Matters involving Child Victims and Witnesses of Crime

The Economic and Social Council,

Recalling its resolution 1996/16 of 23 July 1996, in which it requested the Secretary-General to continue to promote the use and application of United Nations standards and norms in crime prevention and criminal justice,

Recalling also its resolution 2004/27 of 21 July 2004 on guidelines on justice for child victims and witnesses of crime, in which it requested the Secretary-General to convene an intergovernmental expert group in order to develop guidelines on justice in matters involving child victims and witnesses of crime,

Recalling further General Assembly resolution 40/34 of 29 November 1985, by which the Assembly adopted the Declaration of Basic Principles of Justice for Victims of Crime and Abuse of Power, annexed to the resolution,

Recalling the provisions of the Convention on the Rights of the Child, adopted by the General Assembly in its resolution 44/25 of 20 November 1989, in particular articles 3 and 39 thereof, as well as the provisions of the Optional Protocol to the Convention on the Rights of the Child on the sale of children, child prostitution and child pornography, adopted by the Assembly in its resolution 54/263 of 25 May 2000, in particular article 8 thereof,

Recognizing that justice for child victims and witnesses of crime must be assured while safeguarding the rights of accused persons,

Recognizing also that children who are victims and witnesses are particularly vulnerable and need special protection, assistance and support appropriate to their age, level of maturity and unique needs in order to prevent further hardship and trauma that may result from their participation in the criminal justice process,

Mindful of the serious physical, psychological and emotional consequences of crime and victimization for child victims and witnesses, in particular in cases involving sexual exploitation,

Mindful also of the fact that the participation of child victims and witnesses in the criminal justice process is necessary for effective prosecutions, in particular where the child victim may be the only witness,

Recognizing the efforts of the International Bureau for Children's Rights in laying the groundwork for the development of guidelines on justice in matters involving child victims and witnesses of crime,

Noting with appreciation the work of the Intergovernmental Expert Group Meeting to Develop Guidelines on Justice in Matters involving Child Victims and Witnesses of Crime, held in Vienna on 15 and 16 March 2005, for which extrabudgetary resources were provided by the Government of Canada, and taking note of the report of the Intergovernmental Expert Group,

Taking note of the report of the Eleventh United Nations Congress on Crime Prevention and Criminal Justice, held in Bangkok from 18 to 25 April 2005, regarding the item entitled "Making standards work: fifty years of standard-setting in crime prevention and criminal justice",

Welcoming the Bangkok Declaration on Synergies and Responses: Strategic Alliances in Crime Prevention and Criminal Justice, adopted at the high-level segment of the Eleventh United Nations Congress on Crime Prevention and Criminal Justice, in particular paragraphs 17 and 33 thereof, in which the importance of providing support and services to witnesses and victims of crime is recognized,

1. *Adopts* the Guidelines on Justice in Matters involving Child Victims and Witnesses of Crime, annexed to the present resolution, as a useful framework that could assist Member States in enhancing the protection of child victims and witnesses in the criminal justice system;

2. *Invites* Member States to draw, where appropriate, on the Guidelines in the development of legislation, procedures, policies and practices for children who are victims of crime or witnesses in criminal proceedings;

3. *Calls upon* Member States that have developed legislation, procedures, policies or practices for child victims and witnesses to make information available to other States, upon request and where appropriate, and to assist them in developing and implementing training or other activities in relation to the use of the Guidelines;

4. *Calls upon* the United Nations Office on Drugs and Crime to provide technical assistance, within available extrabudgetary resources, not excluding the use of existing resources from the regular budget of the United Nations Office on Drugs and Crime, as well as advisory services, to Member States, upon request, to assist them in the use of the Guidelines;

5. *Requests* the Secretary-General to ensure the widest possible dissemination of the Guidelines among Member States, the institutes of the United Nations Crime Prevention and Criminal Justice Programme network and other international, regional and non-governmental organizations and institutions;

6. *Recommends* that Member States bring the Guidelines to the attention of relevant governmental and non-governmental organizations and institutions;

7. *Invites* the institutes of the United Nations Crime Prevention and Criminal Justice Programme network to provide training in relation to the Guidelines and to consolidate and disseminate information on successful models at the national level;

8. *Requests* the Secretary-General to report to the Commission on Crime Prevention and Criminal Justice at its seventeenth session on the implementation of the present resolution.

Annex

Guidelines on Justice in Matters involving Child Victims and Witnesses of Crime

I. Objectives

1. The present Guidelines on Justice for Child Victims and Witnesses of Crime set forth good practice based on the consensus of contemporary knowledge and relevant international and regional norms, standards and principles.

2. The Guidelines should be implemented in accordance with relevant national legislation and judicial procedures as well as take into consideration legal, social, economic, cultural and geographical conditions. However, States should constantly endeavour to overcome practical difficulties in the application of the Guidelines.

3. The Guidelines provide a practical framework to achieve the following objectives:

(*a*) To assist in the review of national and domestic laws, procedures and practices so that these ensure full respect for the rights of child victims and witnesses of crime and contribute to the implementation of the Convention on the Rights of the Child, by parties to that Convention;

(*b*) To assist Governments, international organizations, public agencies, non-governmental and community-based organizations and other interested parties in designing and implementing legislation, policy, programmes and practices that address key issues related to child victims and witnesses of crime;

(*c*) To guide professionals and, where appropriate, volunteers working with child victims and witnesses of crime in their day-to-day practice in the adult and juvenile justice process at the national, regional and international levels, consistent with the Declaration of Basic Principles of Justice for Victims of Crime and Abuse of Power;

(*d*) To assist and support those caring for children in dealing sensitively with child victims and witnesses of crime.

4. In implementing the Guidelines, each jurisdiction should ensure that adequate training, selection and procedures are put in place to protect and meet the special needs of child victims and witnesses of crime, where the nature of the victimization affects categories of children differently, such as sexual assault of children, especially girls.

5. The Guidelines cover a field in which knowledge and practice are growing and improving. They are neither intended to be exhaustive nor to preclude further development, provided it is in harmony with their underlying objectives and principles.

6. The Guidelines could also be applied to processes in informal and customary systems of justice such as restorative justice and in non-criminal fields of law including, but not limited to, custody, divorce, adoption, child protection, mental health, citizenship, immigration and refugee law.

II. Special considerations

7. The Guidelines were developed:

(a) Cognizant that millions of children throughout the world suffer harm as a result of crime and abuse of power and that the rights of those children have not been adequately recognized and that they may suffer additional hardship when assisting in the justice process;

(b) Recognizing that children are vulnerable and require special protection appropriate to their age, level of maturity and individual special needs;

(c) Recognizing that girls are particularly vulnerable and may face discrimination at all stages of the justice system;

(d) Reaffirming that every effort must be made to prevent victimization of children, including through implementation of the Guidelines for the Prevention of Crime;

(e) Cognizant that children who are victims and witnesses may suffer additional hardship if mistakenly viewed as offenders when they are in fact victims and witnesses;

(f) Recalling that the Convention on the Rights of the Child sets forth requirements and principles to secure effective recognition of the rights of children and that the Declaration of Basic Principles of Justice for Victims of Crime and Abuse of Power sets forth principles to provide victims with the right to information, participation, protection, reparation and assistance;

(g) Recalling international and regional initiatives that implement the principles of the Declaration of Basic Principles of Justice for Victims of Crime and Abuse of Power, including the *Handbook on Justice for Victims* and the *Guide for Policy Makers*, both issued by the United Nations Office for Drug Control and Crime Prevention in 1999;

(h) Recognizing the efforts of the International Bureau for Children's Rights in laying the groundwork for the development of guidelines on justice for child victims and witnesses of crime;

(i) Considering that improved responses to child victims and witnesses of crime can make children and their families more willing to disclose instances of victimization and more supportive of the justice process;

(j) Recalling that justice for child victims and witnesses of crime must be assured while safeguarding the rights of accused and convicted offenders;

(k) Bearing in mind the variety of legal systems and traditions, and noting that crime is increasingly transnational in nature and that there is a need to ensure that child victims and witnesses of crime receive equivalent protection in all countries.

III. Principles

8. As stated in international instruments and in particular the Convention on the Rights of the Child as reflected in the work of the Committee on the Rights of the Child, and in order to ensure justice for child victims and witnesses of crime, professionals and others responsible for the well-being of those children must respect the following cross-cutting principles:

(a) *Dignity.* Every child is a unique and valuable human being and as such his or her individual dignity, special needs, interests and privacy should be respected and protected;

(b) *Non-discrimination.* Every child has the right to be treated fairly and equally, regardless of his or her or the parent's or legal guardian's race, ethnicity, colour, gender, language, religion, political or other opinion, national, ethnic or social origin, property, disability and birth or other status;

(c) *Best interests of the child.* While the rights of accused and convicted offenders should be safeguarded, every child has the right to have his or her best interests given primary consideration. This includes the right to protection and to a chance for harmonious development:

  (i) Protection: Every child has the right to life and survival and to be shielded from any form of hardship, abuse or neglect, including physical, psychological, mental and emotional abuse and neglect;

  (ii) Harmonious development: Every child has the right to a chance for harmonious development and to a standard of living adequate for physical, mental, spiritual, moral and social growth. In the case of a child who has been traumatized, every step should be taken to enable the child to enjoy healthy development;

(d) *Right to participation.* Every child has, subject to national procedural law, the right to express his or her views, opinions and beliefs freely, in his or her own words, and to contribute especially to the decisions affecting his or her life, including those taken in any judicial processes, and to have those views taken into consideration according to his or her abilities, age, intellectual maturity and evolving capacity.

IV. Definitions

9. Throughout these Guidelines, the following definitions apply:

(a) "Child victims and witnesses" denotes children and adolescents, under the age of 18, who are victims of crime or witnesses to crime regardless of their role in the offence or in the prosecution of the alleged offender or groups of offenders;

(b) "Professionals" refers to persons who, in the context of their work, are in contact with child victims and witnesses of crime or are responsible for addressing the needs of children in the justice system and for whom these Guidelines are applicable. This includes, but is not limited to, the following: child and victim advocates and support persons; child protection service practitioners; child welfare agency staff; prosecutors and, where appropriate, defence lawyers; diplomatic and consular staff; domestic violence programme staff; judges; court staff; law enforcement officials; medical and mental health professionals; and social workers;

(c) "Justice process" encompasses detection of the crime, making of the complaint, investigation, prosecution and trial and post-trial procedures, regardless of whether the case is handled in a national, international or regional criminal justice system for adults or juveniles, or in a customary or informal system of justice;

(d) "Child-sensitive" denotes an approach that balances the child's right to protection and that takes into account the child's individual needs and views.

V. The right to be treated with dignity and compassion

10. Child victims and witnesses should be treated in a caring and sensitive manner throughout the justice process, taking into account their personal situation and immediate needs, age, gender, disability and level of maturity and fully respecting their physical, mental and moral integrity.

11. Every child should be treated as an individual with his or her individual needs, wishes and feelings.

12. Interference in the child's private life should be limited to the minimum needed at the same time as high standards of evidence collection are maintained in order to ensure fair and equitable outcomes of the justice process.

13. In order to avoid further hardship to the child, interviews, examinations and other forms of investigation should be conducted by trained professionals who proceed in a sensitive, respectful and thorough manner.

14. All interactions described in these Guidelines should be conducted in a child-sensitive manner in a suitable environment that accommodates the special needs of the child, according to his or her abilities, age, intellectual maturity and evolving capacity. They should also be conducted in a language that the child uses and understands.

VI. The right to be protected from discrimination

15. Child victims and witnesses should have access to a justice process that protects them from discrimination based on the child's, parent's or legal guardian's race, colour, gender, language, religion, political or other opinion, national, ethnic or social origin, property, disability and birth or other status.

16. The justice process and support services available to child victims and witnesses and their families should be sensitive to the child's age, wishes, understanding, gender, sexual orientation, ethnic, cultural, religious, linguistic and social background, caste, socio-economic condition and immigration or refugee status, as well as to the special needs of the child, including health, abilities and capacities. Professionals should be trained and educated about such differences.

17. In certain cases, special services and protection will need to be instituted to take account of gender and the different nature of specific offences against children, such as sexual assault involving children.

18. Age should not be a barrier to a child's right to participate fully in the justice process. Every child should be treated as a capable witness, subject to examination, and his or her testimony should not be presumed invalid or untrustworthy by reason of the child's age alone as long as his or her age and maturity allow the giving of intelligible and credible testimony, with or without communication aids and other assistance.

VII. The right to be informed

19. Child victims and witnesses, their parents or guardians and legal representatives, from their first contact with the justice process and throughout that process, should be promptly and adequately informed, to the extent feasible and appropriate, of, inter alia:

(a) The availability of health, psychological, social and other relevant services as well as the means of accessing such services along with legal or other advice or representation, compensation and emergency financial support, where applicable;

(b) The procedures for the adult and juvenile criminal justice process, including the role of child victims and witnesses, the importance, timing and manner of testimony, and ways in which "questioning" will be conducted during the investigation and trial;

(c) The existing support mechanisms for the child when making a complaint and participating in the investigation and court proceedings;

(d) The specific places and times of hearings and other relevant events;

(e) The availability of protective measures;

(f) The existing mechanisms for review of decisions affecting child victims and witnesses;

(g) The relevant rights of child victims and witnesses pursuant to the Convention on the Rights of the Child and the Declaration of Basic Principles of Justice for Victims of Crime and Abuse of Power.

20. In addition, child victims, their parents or guardians and legal representatives should be promptly and adequately informed, to the extent feasible and appropriate, of:

(a) The progress and disposition of the specific case, including the apprehension, arrest and custodial status of the accused and any pending changes to that status, the prosecutorial decision and relevant post-trial developments and the outcome of the case;

(b) The existing opportunities to obtain reparation from the offender or from the State through the justice process, through alternative civil proceedings or through other processes.

VIII. The right to be heard and to express views and concerns

21. Professionals should make every effort to enable child victims and witnesses to express their views and concerns related to their involvement in the justice process, including by:

(a) Ensuring that child victims and where appropriate witnesses are consulted on the matters set forth in paragraph 19 above;

(b) Ensuring that child victims and witnesses are enabled to express freely and in their own manner their views and concerns regarding their involvement in the justice process, their concerns regarding safety in relation to the accused, the manner in which they prefer to provide testimony and their feelings about the conclusions of the process;

(c) Giving due regard to the child's views and concerns and, if they are unable to accommodate them, explain the reasons to the child.

IX. The right to effective assistance

22. Child victims and witnesses and, where appropriate, family members should have access to assistance provided by professionals who have received relevant training as set out in paragraphs 40 to 42 below. This may include assistance and support services such as financial, legal, counselling, health, social and educational services, physical and psychological recovery services and other services necessary for the child's reintegration. All such assistance should address the child's needs and enable him or her to participate effectively at all stages of the justice process.

23. In assisting child victims and witnesses, professionals should make every effort to coordinate support so that the child is not subjected to excessive interventions.

24. Child victims and witnesses should receive assistance from support persons, such as child victim/witness specialists, commencing at the initial report and continuing until such services are no longer required.

25. Professionals should develop and implement measures to make it easier for children to testify or give evidence to improve communication and understanding at the pre-trial and trial stages. These measures may include:

(a) Child victim and witness specialists to address the child's special needs;

(b) Support persons, including specialists and appropriate family members, to accompany the child during testimony;

(c) Where appropriate, to appoint guardians to protect the child's legal interests.

X. The right to privacy

26. Child victims and witnesses should have their privacy protected as a matter of primary importance.

27. Information relating to a child's involvement in the justice process should be protected. This can be achieved by maintaining confidentiality and restricting disclosure of information that may lead to identification of a child who is a victim or witness in the justice process.

28. Measures should be taken to protect children from undue exposure to the public by, for example, excluding the public and the media from the courtroom during the child's testimony, where permitted by national law.

XI. The right to be protected from hardship during the justice process

29. Professionals should take measures to prevent hardship during the detection, investigation and prosecution process in order to ensure that the best interests and dignity of child victims and witnesses are respected.

30. Professionals should approach child victims and witnesses with sensitivity, so that they:

(a) Provide support for child victims and witnesses, including accompanying the child throughout his or her involvement in the justice process, when it is in his or her best interests;

(b) Provide certainty about the process, including providing child victims and witnesses with clear expectations as to what to expect in the process, with as much certainty as possible. The child's participation in hearings and trials should be planned ahead of time and every effort should be made to ensure continuity in the relationships between children and the professionals in contact with them throughout the process;

(c) Ensure that trials take place as soon as practical, unless delays are in the child's best interests. Investigation of crimes involving child victims and witnesses should also be expedited and there should be procedures, laws or court rules that provide for cases involving child victims and witnesses to be expedited;

(d) Use child-sensitive procedures, including interview rooms designed for children, interdisciplinary services for child victims integrated in the same location, modified court environments that take child witnesses into consideration, recesses during a child's testimony, hearings scheduled at times of day appropriate to the age and maturity of the child, an appropriate notification system to ensure the child goes to court only when necessary and other appropriate measures to facilitate the child's testimony.

31. Professionals should also implement measures:

(a) To limit the number of interviews: special procedures for collection of evidence from child victims and witnesses should be implemented in order to reduce the number of interviews, statements, hearings and, specifically, unnecessary contact with the justice process, such as through use of video recording;

(b) To ensure that child victims and witnesses are protected, if compatible with the legal system and with due respect for the rights of the defence, from being cross-examined by the alleged perpetrator: as necessary, child victims and witnesses should be interviewed, and examined in court, out of sight of the alleged perpetrator, and separate courthouse waiting rooms and private interview areas should be provided;

(c) To ensure that child victims and witnesses are questioned in a child-sensitive manner and allow for the exercise of supervision by judges, facilitate testimony and reduce potential intimidation, for example by using testimonial aids or appointing psychological experts.

XII. The right to safety

32. Where the safety of a child victim or witness may be at risk, appropriate measures should be taken to require the reporting of those safety risks to appropriate authorities and to protect the child from such risk before, during and after the justice process.

33. Professionals who come into contact with children should be required to notify appropriate authorities if they suspect that a child victim or witness has been harmed, is being harmed or is likely to be harmed.

34. Professionals should be trained in recognizing and preventing intimidation, threats and harm to child victims and witnesses. Where child victims and witnesses may be the subject of intimidation, threats or harm, appropriate conditions should be put in place to ensure the safety of the child. Such safeguards could include:

(a) Avoiding direct contact between child victims and witnesses and the alleged perpetrators at any point in the justice process;

(b) Using court-ordered restraining orders supported by a registry system;

(c) Ordering pre-trial detention of the accused and setting special "no contact" bail conditions;

(d) Placing the accused under house arrest;

(e) Wherever possible and appropriate, giving child victims and witnesses protection by the police or other relevant agencies and safeguarding their whereabouts from disclosure.

XIII. The right to reparation

35. Child victims should, wherever possible, receive reparation in order to achieve full redress, reintegration and recovery. Procedures for obtaining and enforcing reparation should be readily accessible and child-sensitive.

36. Provided the proceedings are child-sensitive and respect these Guidelines, combined criminal and reparations proceedings should be encouraged, together with informal and community justice procedures such as restorative justice.

37. Reparation may include restitution from the offender ordered in the criminal court, aid from victim compensation programmes administered by the State and damages ordered to be paid in civil proceedings. Where possible, costs of social and educational reintegration, medical treatment, mental health care and legal services should be addressed. Procedures should be instituted to ensure enforcement of reparation orders and payment of reparation before fines.

XIV. The right to special preventive measures

38. In addition to preventive measures that should be in place for all children, special strategies are required for child victims and witnesses who are particularly vulnerable to recurring victimization or offending.

39. Professionals should develop and implement comprehensive and specially tailored strategies and interventions in cases where there are risks that child victims may be victimized further. These strategies and interventions should take into account the nature of the victimization, including victimization related to abuse in the home, sexual exploitation, abuse in institutional settings and trafficking. The strategies may include those based on government, neighbourhood and citizen initiatives.

XV. Implementation

40. Adequate training, education and information should be made available to professionals working with child victims and witnesses with a view to improving and sustaining specialized methods, approaches and attitudes in order to protect and deal effectively and sensitively with child victims and witnesses.

41. Professionals should be trained to effectively protect and meet the needs of child victims and witnesses, including in specialized units and services.

42. This training should include:

(a) Relevant human rights norms, standards and principles, including the rights of the child;

(b) Principles and ethical duties of their office;

(c) Signs and symptoms that indicate crimes against children;

(d) Crisis assessment skills and techniques, especially for making referrals, with an emphasis placed on the need for confidentiality;

(e) Impact, consequences, including negative physical and psychological effects, and trauma of crimes against children;

(f) Special measures and techniques to assist child victims and witnesses in the justice process;

(g) Cross-cultural and age-related linguistic, religious, social and gender issues;

(h) Appropriate adult-child communication skills;

(i) Interviewing and assessment techniques that minimize any trauma to the child while maximizing the quality of information received from the child;

(j) Skills to deal with child victims and witnesses in a sensitive, understanding, constructive and reassuring manner;

(k) Methods to protect and present evidence and to question child witnesses;

(l) Roles of, and methods used by, professionals working with child victims and witnesses.

43. Professionals should make every effort to adopt an interdisciplinary and cooperative approach in aiding children by familiarizing themselves with the wide array of available services, such as victim support, advocacy, economic assistance, counselling, education, health, legal and social services. This approach may include protocols for the different stages of the justice process to encourage cooperation among entities that provide services to child victims and witnesses, as well as other forms of multidisciplinary work that includes police, prosecutor, medical, social services and psychological personnel working in the same location.

44. International cooperation should be enhanced between States and all sectors of society, both at the national and at the international levels, including mutual assistance for the purpose of facilitating the collection and exchange of information and the detection, investigation and prosecution of transnational crimes involving child victims and witnesses.

45. Professionals should consider utilizing the present Guidelines as a basis for developing laws and written policies, standards and protocols aimed at assisting child victims and witnesses involved in the justice process.

46. Professionals should be enabled to periodically review and evaluate their role, together with other agencies in the justice process, in ensuring the protection of the rights of the child and the effective implementation of the present Guidelines.

Human resources development

In response to General Assembly resolution 58/207 [YUN 2003, p. 1159], the Secretary-General, in an August report [A/60/318], discussed the need for promoting comprehensive and cross-sectoral approaches to human resources development. The report emphasized the mutually reinforcing relationship between human resources development and the realization of the internationally agreed development goals, including those contained in the Millennium Declaration [YUN 2000, p. 49], and how both should be pursued in the context of national development strategies. The report focused on the need for investment in human resource development, gender mainstreaming and equality, the role of information and communication technologies, the role of the public sector and its broad-based engagement in the formulation and implementation of national and local policies to promote human resource development and the role of UN system support. It also addressed the impact of the movement of highly-skilled and educated people on human resources development in developing countries and made a number of related recommendations.

In a later report [A/60/687], the Secretary-General transmitted to the Assembly the report of the World Summit on the Information Society (Tunis, Tunisia, 16-18 November). The assembled world leaders, with the input of representatives from the private sector and civil society, agreed on the Tunis Commitment and Tunis Agenda for the Information Society (see p. 933).

GENERAL ASSEMBLY ACTION

On 22 December [meeting 68], the General Assembly, on the recommendation of the Second Committee [A/60/492/Add.3], adopted **resolution 60/211** without [agenda item 56 (c)].

Human resources development

The General Assembly,

Recalling its resolutions 52/196 of 18 December 1997, 54/211 of 22 December 1999, 56/189 of 21 December 2001 and 58/207 of 23 December 2003,

Recalling also the 2005 World Summit Outcome,

Stressing that human resources development is key to the efforts to achieve the internationally agreed development goals, including the Millennium Development Goals, and to expand opportunities for people, in particular for the most vulnerable groups of the population,

Recognizing that globalization and the evolution of information and communication technologies can make the challenge of human resources develop-

ment more complex for developing countries, and recognizing also the increasing development gap between developed and developing countries, including the gap in knowledge and in access to information and communication technologies, and the disparity of income within and among nations and its adverse impact on human resources development in developing countries,

Noting the impact of the movement of highly skilled people and those with an advanced education on human resources development and sustainable development in developing countries, and stressing the need for a global and comprehensive approach to maximize the positive impact of skilled labour mobility on human resources development,

Stressing that Governments have the primary responsibility for defining and implementing appropriate policies for human resources development and the need for greater support from the international community for the national efforts of developing countries,

Stressing also that health and education are at the core of human resources development and the need to ensure that, by 2015, children everywhere, boys and girls alike, will be able to complete a full course of primary schooling and will have equal access to all levels of education,

Emphasizing the continuing need for coordination and collaboration among the organizations of the United Nations system, within their mandates, in assisting developing countries, in particular the least developed countries, in fostering their human resources development,

1. _Takes note_ of the report of the Secretary-General;

2. _Recognizes_ the importance of human resources development in promoting sustainable development, and encourages Governments to integrate human resources development policies in their national development strategies;

3. _Stresses_ that investment in human resources development should be an integral part of national development policies and strategies, and in this regard calls for the adoption of policies to facilitate investment focused on infrastructure and capacity development, including, inter alia, education, health and science and technology, including information and communication technologies;

4. _States_ the importance of ensuring adequate resources for education as a fundamental aspect of eradicating poverty and promoting development with a view to achieving sustainable economic growth and human development, and, in this regard, encourages Governments to manage resources assigned to education in a responsible, accurate and transparent way and to ensure accountability;

5. _Calls for_ enhanced cooperation among all development partners, including those within the United Nations system, other international organizations, donors and private sector and non-governmental organizations, to support the human resources development efforts of developing countries as articulated in national development strategies;

6. _Also calls for_ steps to integrate gender perspectives in human resources development, including through policies, strategies and targeted actions aimed at promoting women's capacities and access to

productive activities, and in this regard emphasizes the need to ensure the full participation of women in the formulation and implementation of such policies, strategies and actions;

7. *Urges* the adoption of cross-sectoral approaches to human resources development, which combine, among other factors, economic growth, poverty eradication, the provision of basic social services, sustainable livelihoods, the empowerment of women, the involvement of young people, the needs of vulnerable groups of society and of local indigenous communities, political freedom, popular participation and respect for human rights, justice and equity, all of which are essential for enhancing human capacity in order to meet the challenge of development;

8. *Encourages* the strategic and innovative use of information and communication technologies in national development policies and programmes to facilitate education, training, knowledge-sharing, recruitment and job creation, stresses the importance of implementing the Tunis Commitment and the Tunis Agenda for the Information Society, adopted during the second phase of the World Summit on the Information Society, held at Tunis from 16 to 18 November 2005, as step towards addressing these challenges, and calls upon the international community to support the efforts of developing countries in this regard;

9. *Calls upon* the relevant entities of the United Nations system to give priority to the objectives of human resources development through, inter alia, integrating in their development programmes explicit support for building science and technology capacities compatible with local needs, resources, culture and practices;

10. *Calls upon* the international community, including the entities of the United Nations system, to support the efforts of developing countries to address the adverse effects of HIV/AIDS, malaria, tuberculosis and other infectious diseases on their human resources;

11. *Requests* the Secretary-General to submit to the General Assembly at its sixty-second session a report on the implementation of the present resolution with a focus on the role of science and technology in promoting human resources development;

12. *Decides* to include in the provisional agenda of its sixty-second session the sub-item entitled "Human resources development".

UN Institute for Training and Research

In response to General Assembly resolution 59/252 [YUN 2004, p. 1139], the Secretary-General submitted an August report [A/60/304] on the United Nations Institute for Training and Research (UNITAR). The report reviewed UNITAR's ongoing training and capacity-building programmes, highlighting recent methodologies such as e-learning and web-based interactive platforms, knowledge managements and new approaches to public-private partnerships. It also

proposed ways in which UNITAR could provide more systematically specialized common services to UN system, funds, programmes and organizations. While voluntary contributions remained low, UNITAR's financial situation improved, owing to the increase of special-purpose grants.

In a September report [A/60/360], submitted in response to Assembly resolution 59/276 [YUN 2004, p. 1383], the Secretary-General reviewed UNITAR's financial viability, including proposals to address long-term funding sources for rent and maintenance costs. In order to maintain and expand the current training programmes for international cooperation and multilateral diplomacy, the Secretary-General recommended providing UNITAR with an annual subvention. He further noted that the Assembly might wish to consider the report in the context of biennium proposed programme budget for the 2006-2007 biennium.

In accordance with Assembly resolutions 52/212 B [YUN 1998, p. 1288] and 58/249 A [YUN 2003, p. 1428], the Chairman of the Board of Auditors transmitted to the Assembly the Board's report [A/60/113] on implementation and recommendations relating to the 2002-2003 biennium. In the absence of any initiative by UNITAR to establish a new funding mechanism that allowed resources to be secured, the Board noted, among other things, that funding sources for UNITAR's General Fund remained fragile and dependent on UNITAR's level of activity and the interest of donors in its projects. The Board was of the view that the creation of an operating reserve would be prudent.

The Advisory Committee on Administrative and Budgetary Questions (ACABQ), in a related report [A/60/7/Add.4], considered the Secretary-General's September report and the Board of Auditors' report.

On 22 December [meeting 68], the General Assembly, on recommendation of the Second Committee [A/60/494/Add.1], adopted **resolution 60/213** without vote [agenda item 58 *(a)*].

United Nations Institute for Training and Research

The General Assembly,

Recalling its resolutions 51/188 of 16 December 1996, 52/206 of 18 December 1997, 53/195 of 15 December 1998, 54/229 of 22 December 1999, 55/208 of 20 December 2000, 56/208 of 21 December 2001, 57/268 of 20 December 2002, 58/223 of 23 December 2003 and 59/252 of 22 December 2004,

Taking note of the report of the Secretary-General,

Acknowledging the work of the Board of Trustees of the United Nations Institute for Training and Research on the functioning of the Institute,

Noting the continued progress made by the Institute in its various programmes and activities, including the strengthened cooperation with other organizations of the United Nations system and with regional and national institutions,

Expressing its appreciation to the Governments and private institutions that have made or pledged financial and other contributions to the Institute,

Noting the slight improvement in the financial situation of the Institute, and expressing its appreciation to those who have contributed to this improvement,

Noting also, however, that the bulk of the resources contributed to the Institute are directed to the Special Purpose Grants Fund rather than to the General Fund, stressing the need to address that unbalanced situation, and also noting that the participation of the developed countries in training programmes in New York and Geneva is increasing,

Noting further that the Institute is funded from voluntary contributions and that it delivers, free of charge, training courses to diplomats and delegates accredited to United Nations Headquarters in New York and to the United Nations offices at Geneva, Vienna and Nairobi,

Noting the various ongoing training programmes of the Institute, including those in the field of sustainable development,

Reiterating that training activities should be accorded a more visible and larger role in support of the management of international affairs and in the execution of the economic and social development programmes of the United Nations system,

1. *Reaffirms* the importance of a coordinated United Nations system-wide approach to research and training, based on an effective coherent strategy and an effective division of work among the relevant institutions and bodies;

2. *Also reaffirms* the relevance of the United Nations Institute for Training and Research, in view of the growing importance of training within the United Nations and the training requirements of States and local authorities, and the relevance of the training-related research activities undertaken by the Institute within its mandate;

3. *Welcomes* the progress made in building partnerships between the Institute and other organizations and bodies of the United Nations system with respect to their training programmes, and in this context underlines the need to develop further and to expand the scope of those partnerships, in particular at the country level;

4. *Requests* the Board of Trustees of the Institute to continue to ensure fair and equitable geographical distribution and transparency in the preparation of the programmes and in the employment of experts, and in this regard stresses that the courses of the Institute should focus primarily on development issues and the management of international affairs;

5. *Renews its appeal* to all Governments, in particular those of developed countries, and to private institutions that have not yet contributed financially or otherwise to the Institute to give it their generous financial and other support, and urges the States that have interrupted their voluntary contributions to consider resuming them in view of the successful restructuring and revitalization of the Institute;

6. *Encourages* the Board of Trustees to consider diversifying further the venues of the events organized by the Institute and to include among those venues the cities hosting regional commissions, in order to promote greater participation and reduce costs;

7. *Stresses* the need for the expeditious resolution of the issues related to the Institute's rent, rental rates and maintenance costs, taking into account its financial situation, as recommended in the report of the Secretary-General;

8. *Encourages* the Board of Trustees of the Institute to continue its efforts to resolve the critical financial situation of the Institute, in particular with a view to broadening its donor base and further increasing the contributions to the General Fund;

9. *Urges* the Board of Trustees of the Institute to complete expeditiously the implementation of the recommendations of the Board of Auditors made in respect of the biennium 2002-2003;

10. *Requests* the Secretary-General to submit to the General Assembly at its sixty-second session a report on the implementation of the present resolution, including details on the status of contributions to and the financial situation of the Institute;

11. *Invites* the Secretary-General, after consultation with the Board of Trustees of the Institute, in accordance with article XI of the statute of the Institute, to consider the desirability of reformulating article V, paragraph 2 *(j),* of the statute so that the report of the Secretary-General may be submitted to the Economic and Social Council rather than to the General Assembly, and include the findings in his report to the General Assembly at its sixty-second session.

On the same date, the Assembly took note of the report [A/60/494] of the Second Committee (**decision 60/548**).

On 23 December, the Assembly, in section XII of **resolution 60/248**, decided to provide UNITAR with the amount of $242,400, being the equivalent of the amount of rental, maintenance and other administrative costs associated with conducting the core training programme for the 2006-2007 biennium. It also reiterated that, in order to ensure stability of the funding for the General Fund and the viability of repaying the United Nations its debt, UNITAR should systematically charge 13 per cent of programme support costs to special purpose grants whenever possible.

United Nations System Staff College

On 22 December, the General Assembly, in **resolution 60/214** (see p. 1527) on the United Nations System Staff College, called upon all organizations of the United Nations system to make full and effective use of the facilities of the College and invited the College to strengthen further its engagement in knowledge-sharing and staff training and learning that could serve to advance the capacity of the United Nations system to contribute to the follow-up to the outcomes of major United Nations conferences and summits, as well as to support the timely and full realization of the internationally agreed development goals, including the Millennium Development Goals, with the aim of helping to provide multilateral solutions to problems in the areas of development, peace and collective security and reinforcing system-wide coherence.

It encouraged the College to continue to provide strategic leadership in order to increase operational effectiveness, promote inter-agency collaboration and strengthen management culture, including the development of new systems of performance management, flexible and collaborative work structures and cost-effective means of delivering services to clients and beneficiaries.

Chapter X

Women

During 2005, UN efforts to advance the status of women worldwide and ensure their rights continued to be directed by the principles and guidelines of the Beijing Declaration and Platform for Action, adopted at the Fourth (1995) World Conference on Women, and the outcome of the General Assembly's twenty-third (2000) special session, which reviewed progress in their implementation (Beijing+5). The occasion of the tenth anniversary of the World Conference inspired renewed efforts to implement the two instruments, which continued to be a driving force behind many high-level meetings and commemorative events throughout the year.

At its forty-ninth session in March, the Commission on the Status of Women convened a high-level plenary meeting focusing on the two thematic issues of the review of the implementation of the Beijing Platform for Action and the outcome documents of the twenty-third special session, and current challenges and forward-looking strategies for the advancement of women and girls. The Commission recommended to the Economic and Social Council for adoption a declaration on the occasion of the tenth anniversary of the Fourth World Conference on Women, which the Council endorsed in July. It also adopted resolutions on assistance to Palestinian women, women and girls in Afghanistan, and mainstreaming a gender perspective into all UN system policies and programmes.

In December, in follow-up to the Fourth World Conference and the outcome of the special session, the Assembly adopted a resolution requesting all UN bodies to ensure that programmes, plans and budgets visibly targeted the mainstreaming of gender perspectives, and calling on the UN system to play an active role in ensuring the effective and accelerated implementation of the Beijing Platform for Action and the outcome of the twenty-third special session. The Assembly also adopted resolutions on an in-depth study on all forms of violence against women; improvement of the situation of women in rural areas; violence against migrant workers; the girl child; women in development; and the Convention on the Elimination of All Forms of Discrimination against Women.

The United Nations Development Fund for Women focused on the implementation of its multi-year funding framework, which targeted goals in four key areas: feminized poverty, violence against women, the spread of HIV/AIDS and gender equality in democratic governance and in post-conflict countries. In July, the Economic and Social Council took action on the results of an independent assessment of UNIFEM, which had been commissioned by its Consultative Committee in 2004.

In 2005, the United Nations continued to strengthen and revitalize the International Research and Training Institute for the Advancement of Women (INSTRAW). The Office of Internal Oversight Services transmitted a report on the follow-up audit it conducted in December 2004, which revealed that, while there had been improvement in INSTRAW governance structure, further strengthening of programmatic and administrative oversight was needed. INSTRAW's financial situation remained precarious and a subcommittee was established to analyse a proposed fund-raising strategy.

Follow-up to the Fourth World Conference on Women and Beijing+5

During 2005, the Commission on the Status of Women, the Economic and Social Council and the General Assembly considered follow-up to the 1995 Fourth World Conference on Women, particularly the implementation of the Beijing Declaration and Platform for Action [YUN 1995, p. 1170] and the political declaration and further actions and initiatives to implement both instruments, adopted at the twenty-third (2000) special session of the Assembly (Beijing+5) by resolution S/23-2 [YUN 2000, p. 1084]. The Declaration had reaffirmed the commitment of Governments to the goals and objectives of the Fourth World Conference and to the implementation of the 12 critical areas of concern outlined in the Platform for Action: women and poverty; education and training of women; women and health; violence against women; women and armed conflict; women and the economy; women in power and decision-making; institutional mechanisms for the advancement of women; human rights and women; women and the media; women and the environment; and the girl child (see p. 1256 for action taken regarding the critical areas of concern). The issue of mainstreaming a gender perspective into UN policies and programmes continued to be addressed (see p. 1270).

Ten-year anniversary of Fourth World Conference

In 2005, the occasion of the ten-year anniversary of the Fourth (1995) World Conference on Women inspired renewed efforts to implement the Beijing Platform for Action and the outcome of the Assembly's twenty-third special session and was a driving force behind many meetings and commemorative events throughout the year, including the March high-level plenary meeting of the Commission on the Status of Women to review and appraise progress achieved in the implementation of those two instruments, which adopted a declaration reaffirming its commitment to ensure their implementation (see below). Other declarations adopted to commemorate the tenth anniversary of the Conference included one in February [E/CN.6/2005/10] by the European Conference of Ministers responsible for gender equality policy (Luxembourg, 4 February), and another, the "Beijing Plus 10 Declaration" [A/60/371], by representatives of Governments, intergovernmental organizations and civil society, including non-governmental organizations (NGOs), at the close of the Beijing Plus 10 Conference (29-31 August, Beijing).

Report of Secretary-General. Pursuant to General Assembly resolution S/23-2 [YUN 2000, p. 1084], the Secretary-General submitted a report [E/CN.6/2005/2 & Corr.1] to the Commission on the Status of Women, which appraised progress made in national level implementation of the Beijing Platform for Action and the outcome of the Assembly's special session. The report covered the two themes mandated in the Commission's multi-year work programme: "Review of the implementation of the Beijing Platform for Action and the outcome documents of the twenty-third session" and "Current challenges and forward-looking strategies for the advancement and empowerment of women and girls". The report gave an overview of the major trends in implementation of the Platform for Action; an analysis of the implementation of each of the 12 critical areas of concern and other related issues; an overview of progress achieved in institutional arrangements; and indicated priority areas for future action.

The overview of trends revealed that, over the past 10 years, the status and role of women had

changed significantly, although not at an equal pace in all regions. There was greater awareness of gender equality issues among Governments and the public at large; increased participation of women in public life; reduced child and maternal mortality; and improved worldwide access to education and the literacy of women and girls. Governments were tackling such issues as violence against women, human trafficking and the situation of women with special needs. There was a clear trend towards additional legislation to eliminate discrimination and promote gender equality. However, gaps remained between policy and practice and public attitudes towards the advancement of women had not changed at the same pace as policy, legal and institutional frameworks. Explicitly addressing persistent stereotypical attitudes and discriminatory practices would be critical to the full implementation of the Platform for Action and the outcome document. Achievements, obstacles and challenges were outlined for each of the 12 critical concerns, as well as for other issues, such as trafficking in women and girls; women and HIV/AIDS; indigenous women; information and communication technologies; the Millennium Development Goals (MDGs) [YUN 2000, p. 51]; and the role of men and boys in achieving gender equality. While many Governments identified priority areas for future action in relation to all critical areas of concerns, they gave considerable attention to the challenges and action required in relation to institutional development in support of gender equality and women's empowerment. A number of Governments cited the role of men and boys as critical for the achievement of gender equality and had elaborated plans for further work in that area.

Commission action. On 4 March [E/2005/27], the Commission on the Status of Women, meeting on the occasion of International Women's Day, adopted a draft declaration [E/CN.6/2005/L.1] in commemoration of the tenth anniversary of the Fourth World Conference on Women, which it transmitted to the Economic and Social Council for action.

ECONOMIC AND SOCIAL COUNCIL ACTION

On 21 July [meeting 34], the Economic and Social Council, on the recommendation of the Commission on the Status of Women [E/2005/27 & Corr.1], adopted **decision 2005/232** without vote [agenda item 14 (a)], by which it decided to transmit the following declaration to the General Assembly and its High-level Plenary Meeting on the review of the United Nations Millennium Declaration.

Declaration of the Commission on the Status of Women on the occasion of the tenth anniversary of the Fourth World Conference on Women

We, the representatives of Governments gathering at the forty-ninth session of the Commission on the Status of Women, in New York, on the occasion of the tenth anniversary of the Fourth World Conference on Women, held in Beijing in 1995, in the context of the review of the outcomes of the Conference and of the twenty-third special session of the General Assembly, entitled "Women 2000: gender equality, development and peace for the twenty-first century", and its contribution to the High-level Plenary Meeting of the General Assembly on the review of the United Nations Millennium Declaration, to be held from 14 to 16 September 2005,

1. *Reaffirm* the Beijing Declaration and Platform for Action adopted at the Fourth World Conference on Women and the outcome documents of the twenty-third special session of the General Assembly;

2. *Welcome* the progress made thus far towards achieving gender equality, stress that challenges and obstacles remain in the implementation of the Beijing Declaration and Platform for Action and the outcome documents of the twenty-third special session of the General Assembly, and, in this regard, pledge to undertake further action to ensure their full and accelerated implementation;

3. *Emphasize* that the full and effective implementation of the Beijing Declaration and Platform for Action is essential to achieving the internationally agreed development goals, including those contained in the Millennium Declaration, and stress the need to ensure the integration of a gender perspective in the High-level Plenary Meeting of the General Assembly on the review of the Millennium Declaration;

4. *Recognize* that the implementation of the Beijing Declaration and Platform for Action and the fulfilment of the obligations under the Convention on the Elimination of All Forms of Discrimination against Women are mutually reinforcing in achieving gender equality and the empowerment of women;

5. *Call upon* the United Nations system, international and regional organizations, all sectors of civil society, including non-governmental organizations, as well as all women and men, to fully commit themselves and to intensify their contributions to the implementation of the Beijing Declaration and Platform for Action and the outcome of the twenty-third special session of the General Assembly.

Communication. On 27 July [A/60/210], the Council President, pursuant to Council decision 2004/309 [YUN 2004, p. 1145], transmitted the Declaration to the Assembly.

Report of Secretary-General. In response to General Assembly resolution 59/168 [YUN 2004, p. 1145], the Secretary-General, in a July report [A/60/170], reviewed steps taken by the Assembly and its Main Committees during its fifty-ninth (2004) session to promote the achievement of gender equality through the gender mainstreaming strategy. The report reviewed outcomes of major events during the year, such as

the International Meeting to Review the Implementation of the Programme of Action for the Sustainable Development of Small Island Developing States (see p. 946); the World Conference on Disaster Reduction (see p. 1015); the Eleventh United Nations Congress on Crime Prevention and Criminal Justice (see p. 1208); and the high-level meeting on HIV/AIDS (see p. 1322). It also assessed the extent to which Assembly resolutions and reports of the Secretary-General had taken gender perspectives into account, particularly in relation to follow-up to major summits and conferences. The inclusion of gender perspectives in the preparations for the second phase of the World Summit on the Information Society (see p. 933) was also covered in the report.

The Secretary-General observed that the Assembly's Second (Economic and Financial) and Third (Social, Humanitarian and Cultural) Committees had paid greater attention to gender perspectives than other Assembly Committees. Although reports submitted to the various Committees contained a degree of gender analysis, they did not systematically include recommendations on further action. Resolutions also lacked qualitative analyses and specific recommended actions tended to reflect proposals made in reports of the Secretary-General. He recommended that the Assembly call for the integration of gender perspectives in reports submitted to it and in resolutions adopted by its subsidiary bodies, based on qualitative gender analysis and containing concrete recommendations for further action. The Assembly should request reporting on progress achieved, ensure gender mainstreaming in the implementation and follow-up to international conferences and summits, in particular in the context of the 2005 World Summit (see p. 47), as well as the outcome of the World Summit on the Information Society.

GENERAL ASSEMBLY ACTION

On 16 December [meeting 64], the General Assembly, on the recommendation of the Third Committee [A/60/504], adopted **resolution 60/140** without vote [agenda item 65].

Follow-up to the Fourth World Conference on Women and full implementation of the Beijing Declaration and Platform for Action and the outcome of the twenty-third special session of the General Assembly

The General Assembly,

Recalling its previous resolutions on the question, including resolution 59/168 of 20 December 2004,

Deeply convinced that the Beijing Declaration and Platform for Action and the outcome of the twenty-third special session of the General Assembly entitled "Women 2000: gender equality, development and peace for the twenty-first century", are important contributions to the achievement of gender equality and the empowerment of women and must be translated into effective action by all States, the United Nations system and other organizations concerned,

Reaffirming its commitment to the full, effective and accelerated implementation of the Beijing Declaration and Platform for Action and the outcome of the twenty-third special session,

Recalling the United Nations Millennium Declaration and the commitments to gender equality and the advancement of women contained therein, the commitments made at the major United Nations summits, conferences and special sessions, as well as the commitments made at the 2005 World Summit in this regard,

Welcoming progress made towards achieving gender equality, but stressing that challenges and obstacles remain in the implementation of the Beijing Declaration and Platform for Action and the outcome of the twenty-third special session,

Recognizing that the responsibility for the implementation of the Beijing Declaration and Platform for Action and the outcome of the twenty-third special session rests primarily at the national level and that strengthened efforts are necessary in this respect, and reiterating that enhanced international cooperation is essential for full, effective and accelerated implementation,

Reaffirming that gender mainstreaming is a globally accepted strategy for promoting the empowerment of women and achieving gender equality by transforming structures of inequality, and reaffirming also the commitment to actively promote the mainstreaming of a gender perspective in the design, implementation, monitoring and evaluation of policies and programmes in all political, economic and social spheres, as well as the commitment to strengthen the capabilities of the United Nations system in the area of gender equality,

Reaffirming also that the full realization of all human rights and fundamental freedoms is essential for the empowerment of women and girls,

Reaffirming further that the full representation and full and equal participation of women in political, social and economic decision-making in society enhances social and economic development policies and that the empowerment of women is a critical factor in the eradication of poverty,

1. *Welcomes* the report of the Secretary-General;

2. *Reaffirms* the Beijing Declaration and Platform for Action adopted at the Fourth World Conference on Women and the outcome of the twenty-third special session of the General Assembly, and welcomes the ten-year review and appraisal of the implementation of the Beijing Declaration and Platform for Action at the forty-ninth session of the Commission on the Status of Women and the outcome transmitted to the Assembly through the Economic and Social Council, including to the 2005 World Summit, in Council decision 2005/232 of 21 July 2005;

3. *Emphasizes* that the full, effective and accelerated implementation of the Beijing Declaration and Platform for Action and the outcome of the twenty-third special session is integral to achieving the internationally agreed development goals, including those contained in the United Nations Millennium Declaration and the outcomes of United Nations summits, confer-

ences and special sessions, as well as the commitments made at the 2005 World Summit;

4. *Calls upon* Governments, the United Nations system and other international and regional organizations, all sectors of civil society, including non-governmental organizations, as well as all women and men to fully commit themselves and to intensify their contributions to the implementation of the Beijing Declaration and Platform for Action and the outcome of the twenty-third special session;

5. *Recognizes* that the implementation of the Beijing Declaration and Platform for Action and the fulfilment of the obligations under the Convention on the Elimination of All Forms of Discrimination against Women are mutually reinforcing in achieving gender equality and the empowerment of women, and in this regard welcomes the contributions of the Committee on the Elimination of Discrimination against Women to promoting the implementation of the Platform for Action and the outcome of the twenty-third special session, and invites States parties to the Convention to include information on measures taken to enhance implementation at the national level in their reports to the Committee under article 18 of the Convention;

6. *Calls upon* States parties to comply fully with their obligations under the Convention on the Elimination of All Forms of Discrimination against Women and the Optional Protocol thereto and to take into consideration the concluding comments as well as the general recommendations of the Committee, and also calls upon those Member States that have not yet done so to consider signing, ratifying or acceding to the Optional Protocol;

7. *Reaffirms* that the Commission on the Status of Women will continue to play a central role in the follow-up to and review of the implementation of the Beijing Declaration and Platform for Action and the outcome of the twenty-third special session and in this regard welcomes their reaffirmation in the outcome of the forty-ninth session of the Commission, calls upon the Commission to give particular attention to the sharing of experiences and good practices in overcoming challenges to full implementation at the national and international levels, and in this regard encourages all actors, inter alia, Governments, the United Nations system, other international organizations and civil society, to continue to support the work of the Commission;

8. *Calls upon* Governments, the relevant funds and programmes, organs and specialized agencies of the United Nations system, within their respective mandates, and invites the international financial institutions and all relevant actors of civil society, including non-governmental organizations, to intensify action to achieve the full and effective implementation of the Beijing Declaration and Platform for Action and the outcome of the twenty-third special session, through:

(a) Sustained political will and commitment at the national, regional and international levels to take further action, inter alia, through the mainstreaming of gender perspectives, including through the development and use of gender equality indicators, as applicable, in all policies and programmes and the promotion of full and equal participation and empowerment of women, and enhanced international cooperation;

(b) Promotion and protection of, and respect for, the full enjoyment of all human rights and fundamental freedoms by women, including through the full implementation by States of their obligations under all human rights instruments, especially the Convention on the Elimination of All Forms of Discrimination against Women;

(c) Respect for the rule of law, including legislation, and continued efforts to repeal laws and eradicate policies and practices that discriminate against women and girls, and to adopt laws and promote practices that protect their rights and promote gender equality;

(d) Strengthening the role of national institutional mechanisms for gender equality and the advancement of women, including through financial and other appropriate assistance;

(e) Undertaking socio-economic policies that promote sustainable development and ensure poverty eradication programmes, especially for women, and strengthening the provision of and ensuring equal access to adequate, affordable and accessible public and social services, including education and training at all levels, as well as to all types of permanent and sustainable social protection/social security systems for women throughout their life cycle, and supporting national efforts in this regard;

(f) Adequate mobilization of resources at the national and international levels, as well as new and additional resources for the developing countries, including the least developed countries and countries with economies in transition, from all available funding mechanisms, including multilateral, bilateral and private sources;

(g) Increased partnerships among Governments, civil society and the private sector;

(h) Encouraging joint responsibility of men and boys with women and girls in the promotion of gender equality;

9. *Reaffirms* that States have an obligation to exercise due diligence to prevent violence against women and girls, provide protection to the victims and investigate, prosecute and punish the perpetrators of violence against women and girls, and that failure to do so violates and impairs or nullifies the enjoyment of their human rights and fundamental freedoms, and calls upon Governments to elaborate and implement strategies in this regard;

10. *Strongly encourages* Governments to continue to support the role and contribution of civil society, in particular non-governmental organizations and women's organizations, in the implementation of the Beijing Declaration and Platform for Action and the outcome of the twenty-third special session;

11. *Notes* that, at its fiftieth session, the Commission on the Status of Women will continue to discuss its working methods and develop a new programme of work to begin in 2007, and in this respect requests the Secretary-General to report to the Commission with recommendations for enhancing the work of the Commission as well as proposals for future themes;

12. *Encourages* the Economic and Social Council to continue its efforts to ensure that gender mainstreaming is an integral part of its work and that of its subsidiary bodies, through, inter alia, implementation of its agreed conclusions 1997/2 of 18 July 1997 and its resolution 2004/4 of 7 July 2004;

13. *Notes* the efforts of its Main Committees to pay attention to gender issues, and resolves to intensify such efforts to fully mainstream a gender perspective in their work, as well as in all future United Nations summits, conferences and special sessions and in their follow-up processes;

14. *Requests* all bodies that deal with programme and budgetary matters, including the Committee for Programme and Coordination, to ensure that programmes, plans and budgets visibly mainstream gender perspectives;

15. *Reaffirms* the primary and essential role of the General Assembly and the Economic and Social Council, as well as the central role of the Commission on the Status of Women, in promoting the advancement of women and gender equality;

16. *Also reaffirms* the commitment made at the 2005 World Summit to the full and effective implementation of Security Council resolution 1325(2000) of 31 October 2000, while noting the fifth anniversary of its adoption and the open debates in the Council on women and peace and security;

17. *Recognizes* the important role of women in the prevention and resolution of conflicts and in peacebuilding, and urges Governments and the United Nations system to take further steps to ensure the integration of a gender perspective and the full and equal participation of women in all efforts to promote peace and security, as well as to increase their role in decision-making at all levels, including through the development of national action plans and strategies;

18. *Calls upon* all parts of the United Nations system to continue to play an active role in ensuring the full, effective and accelerated implementation of the Beijing Platform for Action and the outcome of the twenty-third special session, as reaffirmed in the declaration adopted by the Commission on the Status of Women at its forty-ninth session, through, inter alia, the work of the Office of the Special Adviser on Gender Issues and Advancement of Women and the Division for the Advancement of Women and the maintenance of gender specialists in all entities of the United Nations system, as well as by ensuring that all personnel, especially in the field, receive training and appropriate follow-up, including tools, guidance and support, for gender mainstreaming;

19. *Requests* the Secretary-General to continue to report annually to the General Assembly, under the item entitled "Advancement of women", as well as to the Commission on the Status of Women and the Economic and Social Council, on the follow-up to and progress made in the implementation of the Beijing Declaration and Platform for Action and the outcome of the twenty-third special session, with an assessment of progress in gender mainstreaming, including information on key achievements, lessons learned and good practices, and to recommend further measures to enhance implementation.

Critical areas of concern

Violence against women

In compliance with General Assembly resolution 50/166 [YUN 1995, p. 1188], the Secretary-

General transmitted a December report [E/CN.6/ 2006/10-E/CN.4/2006/60] of the United Nations Development Fund for Women (UNIFEM), which covered its 2005 activities towards the elimination of violence against women (see p. 1276). Efforts focused on the implementation of the first year of UNIFEM's 2005-2008 revised strategy for the United Nations Trust Fund in Support of Actions to Eliminate Violence against Women. The strategy, based on lessons learned from the first eight years of the Trust Fund's operations, devolved decision-making to the subregional level. Grant-making during the year focused on providing support for the implementation of laws, policies and plans to combat violence against women and innovative approaches for addressing the interlinkages between HIV/AIDS and violence against women. In November, the Trust Fund, under the tenth grant-making cycle, provided $1.8 million to 24 initiatives in 30 countries. The Secretary-General concluded that violence against women was the most pervasive violation of human rights, occurring every day, in every country, in every region, regardless of income or level of development. His in-depth study on violence against women, to be released in 2006, would provide guidance to Governments, the UN system and the broader community on how to address the issue (see below). He also proposed that support for combating violence against women should be effective and be significantly increased, and that innovative approaches be replicated.

On 25 July, by **decision 2005/266**, the Economic and Social Council requested the Special Rapporteur on violence against women, its causes and consequences, to present an oral report to the Assembly at its sixtieth (2005) session (see p. 852).

In-depth study on violence against women

In response to General Assembly resolution 58/185 [YUN 2003, p. 1172], the Secretary-General submitted an August report [A/60/211], which provided a summary of the status of preparations for the in-depth study on all forms of violence against women and a preliminary discussion of substantive issues. It outlined the context, goals and scope of the study, and gave an overview of ongoing and planned preparatory activities.

Two consultative mechanisms, a task force, comprising representatives of UN system entities and NGOs and an advisory committee, consisting of 10 high-level, internationally recognized experts in the field of violence against women, were established to support the preparation of the study. The study would draw from contributions received from Member States, UN system enti-

ties, NGOs, as well as from research and literature available on the topic. Some 45 States had provided updates in response to a March 2005 note verbale and others were encouraged to provide such information by October 2005. Other activities furthering the preparatory process for the study included two expert group meetings (11-14 April and 17-20 May): one on the question of data and statistics on violence against women and another on good practices in combating and eliminating violence against women. The Division for the Advancement of Women convened a consultative workshop (6-7 September, New York) to discuss violence against women and its links with the MDGs and identify key issues to be addressed in the study. A preliminary outline of the study was annexed to the report. The Secretary-General, emphasizing that the preparation of the in-depth study was an opportunity to challenge a culture that allowed violence against women to persist, encouraged the active involvement and contributions of stakeholders during the preparatory process. He recommended that the Assembly take note of the interim report and consider the question of violence against women at its sixty-first (2006) session.

GENERAL ASSEMBLY ACTION

On 16 December [meeting 64], the General Assembly, on the recommendation of the Third Committee [A/60/503], adopted **resolution 60/136** without vote [agenda item 64].

In-depth study on all forms of violence against women

The General Assembly,

Recalling its resolution 58/185 of 22 December 2003 entitled "In-depth study on all forms of violence against women",

1. *Takes note* of the report of the Secretary-General on the status of preparations for the study;

2. *Welcomes:*

(*a*) The work undertaken so far in conducting the study, in particular at the expert group meeting on data and statistics on violence against women, held in Geneva from 11 to 14 April 2005, and the expert group meeting on good practices in combating violence against women, held in Vienna from 17 to 20 May 2005;

(*b*) The initiatives taken at the national, regional and international levels to highlight the study and contribute to its preparation, including the workshop on violence against women, held in Paris on 28 and 29 April 2005, and the consultation held at United Nations Headquarters on 6 and 7 September 2005;

3. *Stresses once again* the importance, when conducting the study, of close cooperation with:

(*a*) All relevant United Nations bodies, funds and programmes, including the United Nations Development Fund for Women, the United Nations Children's Fund, the United Nations Development Programme, the United Nations Population Fund, the World Health Organization and the International Research and Training Institute for the Advancement of Women;

(*b*) All relevant parts of the Secretariat, in particular the Office of the United Nations High Commissioner for Human Rights and the regional commissions;

(*c*) United Nations treaty bodies, in particular the Committee on the Elimination of Discrimination against Women;

(*d*) Special procedures of the Commission on Human Rights, in particular the Special Rapporteur on violence against women, its causes and consequences;

4. *Requests* the Secretary-General:

(*a*) To seize all opportunities to raise awareness of the conduct of the study and solicit contributions, and in this regard notes with appreciation the launch of a website dedicated to the study and the online discussion that took place from 26 September to 14 October 2005;

(*b*) To ensure that the conduct of the in-depth study on all forms of violence against women will be carried out in close cooperation with the in-depth study on the question of violence against children requested in its resolution 56/138 of 19 December 2001 so as to enable the exchange of appropriate information;

(*c*) To continue to provide opportunities for consultations with Member States and other stakeholders and to solicit information, including on strategies, policies, programmes and best practices, including from regional organizations;

(*d*) To continue and, where appropriate, to strengthen cooperation with relevant non-governmental organizations in the preparation of the study on all forms of violence against women;

5. *Urges* all relevant United Nations bodies, funds and programmes to cooperate fully with the Secretary-General in the conduct of the study and, whenever possible, draw attention to it, so as to expand opportunities for contribution to its preparation and follow-up;

6. *Encourages* Member States to contribute to the funding of the study in order to meet the budgetary requirements for the study and to provide, as applicable, the Secretary-General with updated information on issues to be covered by the study;

7. *Decides:*

(*a*) To extend the deadline for submission of the report mentioned in subparagraph (*d*) of its resolution 58/185 to its sixty-first session, at the latest by early September 2006, in time for an in-depth consideration at that session;

(*b*) To consider the report at its sixty-first session under the item entitled "Advancement of women".

Women migrant workers

In response to General Assembly resolution 58/143 [YUN 2003, p. 1173], the Secretary-General submitted a July report [A/60/137 & Corr.1] on violence against women migrant workers, which summarized the activities undertaken by UN system entities and other organizations to address the issue. As at 16 May, 23 Member States and one Observer State had provided information on measures taken. The Commission on Human Rights had also adopted resolutions relating to the elimination of violence against women and

the human rights of migrants. Many Member States also submitted information on legislative measures adopted to combat trafficking in women and girls. The feminization of migration was highlighted in several responses, as women constituted the highest percentage of workers who migrated annually, particularly in Indonesia, where 70 per cent of the 350,000 migrant workers were women. As to the human rights aspects, as at 17 June, 30 States had become parties to the International Convention on the Protection of the Rights of All Migrant Workers and Members of their Families [YUN 1990, p. 594]. Special rapporteurs of the Commission on Human Rights had devoted attention to the situation of migrant workers and migrant domestic workers (see p. 767); violence against women (see p. 1251); and trafficking in persons, especially women and children (see p. 1259). Some UN entities providing information on efforts to combat violence against women migrant workers included: the Division for the Advancement of Women, which launched the *World Survey on the Role of Women in Development 2004: Women and International Migration* on 3 March; the International Labour Organization (ILO), which published in May the report *A Global Alliance against Forced Labour;* and the United Nations Development Programme (UNDP), which reported on the implementation of several activities on migration and human trafficking.

The Secretary-General concluded that, while no specific legislation had been adopted by Member States during the period under review, legislation to protect migrant women from all forms of violence and to prevent discrimination and sexual harassment in relation to employment had benefited them. However, more information was needed on the impact of the measures taken, trends in violence against women migrant workers, settings in which violence occurred, and their use of available support services. Greater efforts were needed to monitor continuously and assess the effectiveness of legislative measures, as well as policy, prevention and support measures in order to take further corrective measures. Improvements were needed in the areas of research, surveys and data collection to design more effective and sustainable responses and in women's access to legal channels to reduce their vulnerability to exploitation, ill-treatment and human trafficking. Further exploration of the links between migration and trafficking was also stressed. The Secretary-General recommended that States provide sensitization training on violence against women migrant workers to government officials, law-enforcement agents, police officers, social workers, community leaders and other professionals likely to come in contact with that group and that Governments ratify international instruments, which addressed migration issues.

On 16 December [meeting 64], the General Assembly, on the recommendation of the Third Committee [A/60/503], adopted **resolution 60/139** without vote [agenda item 64].

Violence against women migrant workers

The General Assembly,

Recalling all of its previous resolutions on violence against women migrant workers and those adopted by the Commission on the Status of Women, the Commission on Human Rights and the Commission on Crime Prevention and Criminal Justice, and the Declaration on the Elimination of Violence against Women,

Reaffirming the provisions concerning women migrant workers contained in the outcome documents of the World Conference on Human Rights, the International Conference on Population and Development, the Fourth World Conference on Women and the World Summit for Social Development and their five-year reviews,

Noting with appreciation the various activities initiated by entities of the United Nations system, such as the Regional Programme on Empowering Women Migrant Workers in Asia of the United Nations Development Fund for Women and the high-level panel discussion held by the Commission on the Status of Women at its forty-ninth session on the integration of gender perspectives in macroeconomics, which included a discussion on the protection of women migrant workers, as well as other activities through which the plight of women migrant workers continues to be assessed and alleviated,

Recognizing the increasing feminization of international migration, which requires greater gender sensitivity in all policies and efforts related to the subject of international migration,

Noting the large numbers of women from developing countries and some countries with economies in transition who continue to venture forth to more affluent countries in search of a living for themselves and their families as a consequence of poverty, unemployment and other socio-economic conditions, and acknowledging the duty of the countries of origin, in cooperation with the international community, to try to create conditions that provide employment and economic security for their citizens,

Acknowledging the economic benefits that accrue to both the country of origin and the country of destination from the employment of women migrant workers,

Expressing deep concern at the continuing reports of grave abuses and acts of violence committed against women migrant workers, including, inter alia, sexual and gender-based violence, trafficking, domestic and family violence, racist and xenophobic acts and abusive labour practices,

Noting the tendency of many migrant women to be employed in the informal economy and in less skilled work compared with that of men, which puts those women at greater risk of abuse and exploitation,

Emphasizing the need for objective, comprehensive and broad-based information, possibly including a database for research and analysis, and a wide exchange of experience and lessons learned by individual Member States and civil society in the formulation of policies and concrete strategies to address the problem of violence against women migrant workers,

Encouraging the continuing participation of civil society in developing and implementing appropriate measures to support innovative partnerships among public agencies, non-governmental organizations and other members of civil society for combating violence against women migrant workers,

Realizing that the movement of a significant number of women migrant workers may be facilitated and made possible by means of fraudulent or irregular documentation and sham marriages with the object of migration, that this may be facilitated through, among other things, the Internet, and that those women migrant workers are more vulnerable to abuse and exploitation,

Recognizing the importance of joint and collaborative approaches and strategies at the bilateral, regional, interregional and international levels in protecting and promoting the rights and welfare of women migrant workers,

Recognizing also the importance of exploring the link between migration and trafficking in order to further efforts towards protecting women migrant workers from violence, discrimination, exploitation and abuse,

Encouraged by some measures adopted by some countries of destination to alleviate the plight of women migrant workers residing in their areas of jurisdiction, such as the establishment of protection mechanisms for migrant workers, facilitating their access to mechanisms for reporting complaints or providing assistance during legal proceedings,

Underlining the important role of relevant United Nations treaty bodies in monitoring the implementation of human rights conventions and the relevant special procedures, within their respective mandates, in addressing the problem of violence against women migrant workers and in protecting and promoting their rights and welfare,

1. *Takes note* of the report of the Secretary-General;

2. *Also takes note* of the reports of the Special Rapporteur of the Commission on Human Rights on the human rights of migrants and the Special Rapporteur of the Commission on violence against women, its causes and consequences, with regard to violence against women migrant workers, and encourages all special rapporteurs whose mandates relate to the subject of violence against women migrant workers to address the issue of violence against women migrant workers and their human rights, in particular the problems of gender-based violence and of discrimination, as well as trafficking in women;

3. *Notes* the findings contained in the World Survey on the Role of Women in Development, 2004: Women and International Migration, including its recommendations for concrete actions aimed at helping to empower migrant women, including women migrant workers, and reducing their vulnerability to abuse;

4. *Acknowledges with appreciation* the entry into force of the International Convention on the Protection of

the Rights of All Migrant Workers and Members of Their Families on 1 July 2003;

5. *Requests* all Governments to continue to co-operate fully with the Special Rapporteurs mentioned in paragraph 2 above in the performance of their tasks and mandated duties, including by making available to them requested information on violence against women migrant workers and by reacting promptly to their urgent appeals, and encourages Governments to give serious consideration to inviting them to visit their countries;

6. *Calls upon* all Governments to incorporate a gender perspective in all policies on international migration, including, inter alia, for the protection of migrant women from violence, discrimination, exploitation and abuse;

7. *Urges* concerned Governments, in particular those of the countries of origin and destination, to strengthen further their national efforts to protect and promote the rights and welfare of women migrant workers, including through sustained bilateral, regional, interregional and international cooperation, by developing strategies and joint action and taking into account the innovative approaches and experiences of individual Member States, and to establish and maintain continuing dialogues to facilitate the exchange of information;

8. *Also urges* concerned Governments, in particular those of the countries of origin and destination, to support and allocate appropriate resources for programmes aimed at strengthening preventive action, in particular information for target groups, education and campaigns to increase public awareness of this issue at the national and grass-roots levels, in cooperation with non-governmental organizations;

9. *Notes with appreciation* the adoption by Member States, including countries of origin, transit and destination, of measures to inform women migrant workers of their rights and the benefits to which they are entitled, and encourages other Member States to adopt appropriate measures in this regard;

10. *Calls upon* concerned Governments, in particular those of the countries of origin and destination, if they have not done so, to put in place penal and criminal sanctions to punish perpetrators of violence against women migrant workers and, to the extent possible, to provide, and to encourage non-governmental organizations to provide, victims of violence with the full range of immediate assistance and protection, such as counselling, legal and consular assistance, temporary shelter and other measures that will allow them to be present during the judicial process, as well as to establish reintegration and rehabilitation schemes for returning women migrant workers to their countries of origin;

11. *Encourages* concerned Governments, in particular those of the countries of origin and destination, to support and, if they have not done so, to formulate and implement training programmes for their law enforcers, prosecutors and service providers with a view to instilling among those public-sector workers the necessary skills and attitude to ensure the delivery of proper and professional interventions for women migrant workers who are subjected to abuse and violence;

12. *Also encourages* concerned Governments to adopt measures or strengthen existing ones that pro-tect the human rights of women migrant workers, regardless of their immigration status, including, inter alia, in policies that regulate the recruitment and deployment of women migrant workers and appropriate legal measures against intermediaries who deliberately encourage the clandestine movement of workers and who exploit women migrant workers, so as to reduce the vulnerability of migrant women to exploitation, ill treatment and trafficking, and to consider expanding dialogue among States on devising innovative methods to promote legal channels of migration, inter alia, in order to deter illegal migration;

13. *Invites* Governments, the United Nations system and non-governmental organizations to co-operate towards a better understanding of the problems of women and international migration, including to improve the collection, dissemination and analysis of the kind of data that can explain the causes and consequences of those problems, explore the links between migration and trafficking, and identify the causes of undocumented migration and its economic, social and demographic impact, as well as its implications for the formulation and application of social, economic and migration policies, including those relating to women migrant workers;

14. *Encourages* concerned Governments, in particular those of the countries of origin, transit and destination, to avail themselves of the expertise of the United Nations, including the Statistics Division of the Secretariat and other relevant bodies, such as the International Research and Training Institute for the Advancement of Women, to develop appropriate national data-collection methodologies that will generate comparable data on violence against women migrant workers as bases for research and analysis of the subject;

15. *Encourages* Member States to consider signing and ratifying or acceding to relevant International Labour Organization conventions and to consider signing and ratifying or acceding to the International Convention on the Protection of the Rights of All Migrant Workers and Members of Their Families, as well as all human rights treaties that contribute to the protection of the rights of women migrant workers;

16. *Welcomes* the entry into force of the Protocol to Prevent, Suppress and Punish Trafficking in Persons, Especially Women and Children, supplementing the United Nations Convention against Transnational Organized Crime on 25 December 2003, and the Protocol against the Smuggling of Migrants by Land, Sea and Air, supplementing the United Nations Convention against Transnational Organized Crime on 28 January 2004, and encourages Governments to consider signing and ratifying or acceding to the Protocols;

17. *Encourages* the Committee on the Elimination of Discrimination against Women to consider developing a general recommendation on the situation of women migrant workers;

18. *Requests* the Secretary-General to report to the General Assembly at its sixty-second session on the problem of violence against women migrant workers and on the implementation of the present resolution, taking into account updated information from the organizations of the United Nations system, in particular the International Labour Organization, the United Nations Development Programme, the United Nations Development Fund for Women and the International

Research and Training Institute for the Advancement of Women, and the International Organization for Migration, as well as the reports of the Special Rapporteurs mentioned in paragraph 2 above, and other relevant sources, including non-governmental organizations.

Women, peace and security

The Special Committee on Peacekeeping Operations, at its 2005 sessions [A/59/19 & Add.1] (see p. 128) encouraged Member States and the Secretariat to increase women's participation in all aspects and levels of peacekeeping operations, both civilian and military. The Committee also considered the report [A/59/710] by the Secretary-General's Adviser on Sexual Exploitation and Abuse by the United Nations Peacekeeping Personnel entitled "A comprehensive strategy to eliminate future sexual exploitation and abuse in UN peacekeeping operations" (see p. 119).

Report of Secretary-General. As requested by the Security Council in presidential statement S/PRST/2004/40 [YUN 2004, p. 1152], the Secretary-General submitted an October report [S/2005/636] on women and peace and security across the UN system, which provided information on the preparation of the system-wide action plan for the implementation of Council resolution 1325(2000) [YUN 2000, p. 1113], as well as conclusions and recommendations for moving forward. The action plan, which was annexed to the report, drew on contributions received from 37 entities and was structured according to 12 areas of action: conflict prevention and early warning; peacemaking and peacebuilding; peacekeeping operations; humanitarian response; post-conflict reconstruction and rehabilitation; disarmament, demobilization and reintegration; preventing gender-based violence in armed conflict; preventing sexual exploitation and abuse by UN staff, related personnel and UN partners; gender balance; coordination and partnership; monitoring and reporting; and financial resources.

The Secretary-General observed that the system-wide action plan provided a wealth of information on the activities being carried out by the UN system for women in conflict and post-conflict areas. It was a tool for better coordination and building synergies of the UN system and it would enable the system to align its activities with the goals of resolution 1325(2000) and provide an opportunity to draw on the expertise and resources of the entire system. He made recommendations for action to be undertaken at the intergovernmental, system-wide, UN entity and field levels for strengthening UN capacity to implement resolution 1325(2000) and related presidential statements. He also recommended that

the Security Council introduce a biennial report on the overall implementation of the system-wide action plan.

Communications. On 23 October [S/2005/664], Romania indicated that the Security Council was scheduled to hold a debate on the subject "Women's participation in peace processes" on 27 October, which would also commemorate the fifth anniversary of the adoption of resolution 1325(2000). On 24 October [A/60/444-S/2005/669], Sweden forwarded the report of the High-level meeting on "Building partnerships for promoting gender justice in post-conflict societies" (25-26 August, Stockholm), which was organized in cooperation with UNIFEM and the International Legal Assistance Consortium.

SECURITY COUNCIL ACTION

On 27 October [meeting 5294], following consultations among Security Council members, the President made statement **S/PRST/2005/52** on behalf of the Council:

> The Security Council reaffirms its commitment to the continuing and full implementation of its resolution 1325(2000) and recalls the statements by its President of 31 October 2001, 31 October 2002 and 28 October 2004, as reiterating that commitment.
>
> The Council recalls the 2005 World Summit Outcome, the Beijing Declaration and Platform for Action, the outcomes of the Conference and of the twenty-third special session of the General Assembly, entitled 'Women 2000: gender equality, development and peace for the twenty-first century', and the declaration of the Commission on the Status of Women at its forty-ninth session on the occasion of the tenth anniversary of the Fourth World Conference on Women.
>
> While welcoming the progress achieved so far, the Council stresses the importance and urgency of accelerating the full and effective implementation of resolution 1325(2000).
>
> The Council reaffirms the importance of full and equal participation of women in peace processes at all levels and urges Member States, regional and sub-regional organizations and the United Nations system to enhance the role of women in decision-making with regard to all peace processes and post-conflict reconstruction and rebuilding of societies.
>
> The Council welcomes the various initiatives and actions undertaken by Member States, the United Nations entities, civil society organizations and other relevant actors, focused on supporting and increasing the representation of women in peace negotiations and mainstreaming gender perspectives into peace agreements.
>
> The Council recognizes and welcomes the roles of, and contributions made by, women as mediators, educators, peacemakers, peacebuilders and advocates for peace, as well as their active contribution to reconciliation efforts and disarmament, demobilization and reintegration processes.

The Council recognizes the constant under-representation of women in formal peace processes and is deeply concerned about persistent obstacles and challenges resulting from situations such as violence against women, shattered economies and social structures, lack of rule of law, poverty, limited access to education and resources, various forms of discrimination and stereotypes. The Council believes that more must be done in order to achieve the greater participation and effective contribution of women at the negotiating table and in developing and implementing post-conflict strategies and programmes.

The Council encourages Member States and the Secretary-General to maintain regular contacts with local women's organizations and networks, to utilize their knowledge, expertise and resources and to ensure their involvement in reconstruction processes, particularly at the decision-making level.

The Council also encourages Member States, donors and civil society to provide financial, political and technical support, as well as adequate training for women's peacebuilding initiatives and networks.

The Council welcomes the system-wide action plan for the implementation of resolution 1325 (2000) across the United Nations system, contained in the report of the Secretary-General on women and peace and security, and requests the Secretary-General to update, monitor and review its implementation and integration on an annual basis, and report to the Council, starting in October 2006. In this context, the Council urges the Secretary-General to proceed with the appointment of a gender adviser within the Department of Political Affairs of the Secretariat and to continue to identify women candidates for senior-level positions within the United Nations system, including as special representatives. In this regard, the Council invites Member States to provide the Secretary-General with candidates, as appropriate.

The Council reiterates its call to Member States to continue to implement resolution 1325(2000), including through the development of national action plans or other national level strategies.

The Council welcomes the decision taken in the 2005 World Summit Outcome to establish the Peacebuilding Commission and looks forward to its contribution to the full implementation of resolution 1325(2000), inviting the Commission to pay particular attention to the knowledge and understanding that women can bring, through their participation and empowerment, to peacebuilding processes.

The Council requests the Secretary-General to ensure that all peace accords concluded with United Nations assistance address the specific effects of armed conflict on women and girls, as well as their specific needs and priorities in the post-conflict context. Within this framework, the Council underlines the importance of a broad and inclusive political consultation with various components of civil society, in particular women's organizations and groups.

The Council reaffirms its commitment to integrate gender perspectives into the terms of reference of Council visits and missions and to include gender specialists in its teams wherever possible.

The Council condemns sexual and other forms of violence against women, including trafficking in persons, calls upon all parties to armed conflict to ensure full and effective protection of women and emphasizes the necessity to end impunity of those responsible for gender-based violence.

The Council reiterates its condemnation, in the strongest terms, of all acts of sexual misconduct by all categories of personnel in United Nations peacekeeping missions. The Council welcomes the comprehensive report on sexual exploitation and abuse by United Nations peacekeeping personnel. The Council also welcomes the report of the Special Committee on Peacekeeping Operations on its 2005 resumed session and, taking into account General Assembly resolution 59/300, urges the Secretary-General and troop-contributing countries to ensure that the recommendations of the Special Committee which fall within their respective responsibilities are implemented without delay. In this connection, the Council expresses its support to the efforts of the United Nations to fully implement codes of conduct and disciplinary procedures to prevent and respond to sexual exploitation and enhance monitoring and enforcement mechanisms, and notes the strategies and actions included in the system-wide action plan to fully implement those codes of conduct and disciplinary procedures. The Council urges troop-contributing countries to take appropriate preventive action, including conducting predeployment awareness training, and to take disciplinary action and other action to ensure full accountability in cases of misconduct involving their personnel.

Women's health

Women, the girl child and HIV/AIDS

In a March resolution on women, the girl child and HIV/AIDS [E/2005/27 (res. 49/1)], the Commission on the Status of Women stressed that the HIV/AIDS emergency, with its devastating scale and impact, required urgent actions in all fields and at all levels. It welcomed the commitment by the World Health Organization (WHO) and the Joint United Nations Programme on HIV/AIDS (UNAIDS) to work with the international community to support developing countries in achieving the "3 by 5 target" of providing antiretroviral medicines to three million people infected with HIV/AIDS by the end of 2005 (see p. 1325). It called on Governments to ensure that the necessary resources were made available, in particular from donor countries and also from national budgets, in line with the Declaration of Commitment on HIV/AIDS, adopted by the twenty-sixth session of the General Assembly in resolution S-26/2 [YUN 2001, p. 1126].

The girl child

On 16 December [meeting 64], the General Assembly, on the recommendation of the Third Committee [A/60/505 & Corr.1], adopted **resolution 60/141** without vote [agenda item 67].

The girl child

The General Assembly,

Recalling its resolution 58/156 of 22 December 2003 and all relevant resolutions, including the agreed conclusions of the Commission on the Status of Women, in particular those relevant to the girl child,

Reaffirming the equal rights of women and men as enshrined, inter alia, in the Preamble to the Charter of the United Nations, the Convention on the Elimination of All Forms of Discrimination against Women and the Convention on the Rights of the Child,

Recalling all human rights and other instruments relevant to the rights of the child, in particular the girl child, including the Optional Protocols to the Convention on the Rights of the Child on the involvement of children in armed conflict and on the sale of children, child prostitution and child pornography, and the Protocol to Prevent, Suppress and Punish Trafficking in Persons, Especially Women and Children, supplementing the United Nations Convention against Transnational Organized Crime,

Reaffirming the United Nations Millennium Declaration adopted on 8 September 2000, and the commitments relevant to the girl child as contained in the 2005 World Summit Outcome adopted on 16 September 2005,

Reaffirming also the outcome document of the twenty-seventh special session of the General Assembly on children, entitled "A world fit for children", and the Declaration of Commitment on HIV/AIDS adopted at the twenty-sixth special session of the General Assembly on HIV/AIDS, entitled "Global Crisis—Global Action",

Reaffirming further all other relevant outcomes of major United Nations summits and conferences relevant to the girl child, as well as their five- and ten-year reviews, including the Beijing Declaration and Platform for Action adopted at the Fourth World Conference on Women, the outcome of the twenty-third special session of the General Assembly entitled "Women 2000: gender equality, development and peace for the twenty-first century", the Programme of Action of the International Conference on Population and Development and the Programme of Action of the World Summit for Social Development, and welcoming the declaration adopted on 4 March 2005 by the Commission on the Status of Women at its forty-ninth session,

Reaffirming the Dakar Framework for Action adopted at the World Education Forum,

Recognizing the efforts of the international community to strengthen the standards for combating sexual abuse and exploitation, and in this regard taking note of the Secretary-General's bulletin on special measures for protection from sexual exploitation and sexual abuse and other policies and codes of conduct developed by the United Nations system to prevent and address such incidents,

Recognizing also the need to achieve gender equality to ensure a just and equitable world for girls,

Deeply concerned about discrimination against the girl child and the violation of the rights of the girl child, which often result in less access for girls to education, nutrition and physical and mental health care and in girls enjoying fewer of the rights, opportunities and benefits of childhood and adolescence than boys and often being subjected to various forms of cultural, social, sexual and economic exploitation and to violence and harmful practices, such as female infanticide, rape, incest, early marriage, forced marriage, prenatal sex selection and female genital mutilation,

Deeply concerned also that, in situations of poverty, war and armed conflict, girl children are among those most affected and that their potential for full development is thus limited,

Concerned that the girl child has furthermore become the victim of rape, sexually transmitted diseases and, increasingly, of HIV, which have a serious impact on the quality of her life and leave her open to further discrimination, violence and neglect,

Emphasizing that increased access to education, including in the areas of sexual and reproductive health, for young people, especially girls, dramatically lowers their vulnerability to preventable diseases, in particular HIV/AIDS infection and sexually transmitted diseases,

Concerned by the increasing number of child-headed households, in particular those headed by orphan girls, including those orphaned by the HIV/AIDS pandemic,

Deeply concerned that early childbearing and limited access to sexual and reproductive health care, including in the area of emergency obstetric care, causes high levels of fistula and maternal mortality and morbidity,

Convinced that racism, racial discrimination, xenophobia and related intolerance reveal themselves in a differentiated manner for women and girls and can be among the factors leading to a deterioration in their living conditions, poverty, violence, multiple forms of discrimination and limitation or denial of their human rights,

1. *Stresses* the need for full and urgent implementation of the rights of the girl child as guaranteed to her under all human rights instruments, including the Convention on the Rights of the Child and the Convention on the Elimination of All Forms of Discrimination against Women, as well as the need for universal ratification of those instruments;

2. *Urges* States to consider signing, ratifying or acceding to the Optional Protocol to the Convention on the Elimination of All Forms of Discrimination against Women and the Optional Protocols to the Convention on the Rights of the Child;

3. *Urges* all States to take all necessary measures and to institute legal reforms to ensure the full and equal enjoyment by the girl child of all human rights and fundamental freedoms and to take effective action against violations of those rights and freedoms;

4. *Urges* all Governments and the United Nations system to strengthen efforts bilaterally and with international organizations and private-sector donors in order to achieve the goals of the World Education Forum, in particular that of eliminating gender disparities in primary and secondary education by 2005, and to implement the United Nations Girls' Education Initiative as a means of reaching this goal, and reaffirms the commitment contained in the United Nations Millennium Declaration in this regard;

5. *Calls upon* all States to take measures to address the obstacles that continue to affect the achievement of the goals set forth in the Beijing Platform for Action, as

contained in paragraph 33 of the further actions and initiatives to implement the Beijing Declaration and Platform for Action, where appropriate, including the strengthening of national mechanisms to implement policies and programmes for the girl child and, in some cases, to enhance coordination among responsible institutions for the realization of the human rights of girls, as indicated in the further actions and initiatives;

6. *Urges* States to enact and strictly enforce laws to ensure that marriage is entered into only with the free and full consent of the intending spouses, to enact and strictly enforce laws concerning the minimum legal age of consent and the minimum age for marriage and to raise the minimum age for marriage where necessary;

7. *Also urges* States to fulfil their obligations under the Convention on the Rights of the Child and the Convention on the Elimination of All Forms of Discrimination against Women, as well as the commitment to implement the Beijing Platform for Action and the outcomes of the twenty-third special session of the General Assembly entitled "Women 2000: gender equality, development and peace for the twenty-first century" and of the twenty-seventh special session on children;

8. *Urges* all States to promote gender equality and equal access to basic social services, such as education, nutrition, health care, including sexual and reproductive health care, vaccinations and protection from diseases representing the major causes of mortality, and to mainstream a gender perspective in all development policies and programmes;

9. *Also urges* all States to enact and enforce legislation to protect girls from all forms of violence and exploitation, including female infanticide and prenatal sex selection, female genital mutilation, rape, domestic violence, incest, sexual abuse, sexual exploitation, child prostitution and child pornography, trafficking and forced labour, and to develop age-appropriate safe and confidential programmes and medical, social and psychological support services to assist girls who are subjected to violence;

10. *Urges* States to formulate comprehensive, multidisciplinary and coordinated national plans, programmes or strategies to eliminate all forms of violence against women and girls, which should be widely disseminated and should provide targets and timetables for implementation, as well as effective domestic enforcement procedures through the establishment of monitoring mechanisms involving all parties concerned, including consultations with women's organizations, giving attention to the recommendations relating to the girl child of the Special Rapporteurs of the Commission on Human Rights on violence against women, its causes and consequences, and on trafficking in persons, especially women and children;

11. *Calls upon* all States and international and non-governmental organizations, individually and collectively, to implement further the Beijing Platform for Action, in particular the strategic objectives relating to the girl child, and the further actions and initiatives to implement the Beijing Declaration and Platform for Action;

12. *Urges* States to ensure that the right of children to express themselves and participate in all matters affecting them, in accordance with their age and maturity, is fully and equally enjoyed by girls;

13. *Recognizes* that a considerable number of children, including orphans, children living on the street, internally displaced and refugee children, children affected by trafficking and sexual and economic exploitation and children who are incarcerated, live without parental support, and in this regard urges States to take special measures to support such children and the institutions, facilities and services that care for them, and to build and strengthen children's abilities to protect themselves;

14. *Urges* States to take appropriate measures to address the needs of orphan girls by implementing national policies and strategies to build and strengthen governmental, family and community capacities to provide a supportive environment for orphans and girls and boys infected with and affected by HIV/AIDS, including by providing appropriate counselling and psychosocial support, and ensuring their enrolment in school and access to shelter, good nutrition and health and social services on an equal basis with other children; and to protect orphans and vulnerable children from all forms of abuse, violence, exploitation, discrimination, trafficking and loss of inheritance;

15. *Also urges* States to take special measures for the protection of girls affected by armed conflicts and by post-conflict situations and in particular to protect them from sexually transmitted diseases, such as HIV/AIDS, gender-based violence, including rape and sexual abuse, and sexual exploitation, torture, abduction and forced labour, paying special attention to refugee and displaced girls, and to take into account the special needs of girls affected by armed conflicts in the delivery of humanitarian assistance and disarmament, demobilization, rehabilitation assistance and reintegration processes;

16. *Deplores* all the cases of sexual exploitation and abuse of women and children, especially girls, in humanitarian crises, including those cases involving humanitarian workers and peacekeepers;

17. *Urges* all States and the international community to respect, protect and promote the rights of the child, taking into account the particular vulnerabilities of the girl child in pre-conflict, conflict and post-conflict situations, and calls for special initiatives designed to address all of the rights and needs of girls affected by armed conflicts;

18. *Calls upon* Governments, civil society, including the media, and non-governmental organizations to promote human rights education and the full respect for and enjoyment of the human rights of the girl child, inter alia, through the translation, production and dissemination of age-appropriate and gender-sensitive information material on those rights to all sectors of society, in particular to children;

19. *Calls upon* States and international and non-governmental organizations to mobilize all necessary resources, support and efforts to realize the goals, strategic objectives and actions set out in the Beijing Platform for Action and the further actions and initiatives to implement the Beijing Declaration and Platform for Action;

20. *Requests* the Secretary-General, as Chairman of the United Nations System Chief Executives Board for Coordination, to ensure that all organizations and

bodies of the United Nations system, individually and collectively, in particular the United Nations Children's Fund, the United Nations Educational, Scientific and Cultural Organization, the World Food Programme, the United Nations Population Fund, the United Nations Development Fund for Women, the World Health Organization, the United Nations Development Programme, the Office of the United Nations High Commissioner for Refugees and the International Labour Organization, take into account the rights and the particular needs of the girl child in country programmes of cooperation in accordance with national priorities, including through the United Nations Development Assistance Framework;

21. *Requests* all human rights treaty bodies, special procedures and other human rights mechanisms of the Commission on Human Rights and its Subcommission on the Promotion and Protection of Human Rights to adopt regularly and systematically a gender perspective in the implementation of their mandates and to include in their reports information on the qualitative analysis of violations of the human rights of women and girls, and encourages the strengthening of cooperation and coordination in that regard;

22. *Stresses* the importance of a substantive assessment of the implementation of the Beijing Platform for Action with a life-cycle perspective so as to identify gaps and obstacles in the implementation process and to develop further actions for the achievement of the goals of the Platform for Action;

23. *Requests* Member States to ensure that, in preventing and addressing HIV/AIDS, particular attention and support is given to the girl child infected with and affected by HIV/AIDS, including adolescent mothers;

24. *Urges* Member States to dramatically increase resources at all levels, particularly in the education and health sectors, to enable young people, especially girls, to gain the knowledge, attitudes and skills that they need to prevent HIV/AIDS and to enjoy the highest attainable standard of physical and mental health, including sexual and reproductive health;

25. *Requests* the Secretary-General to submit a report to the General Assembly at its sixty-second session on the implementation of the present resolution, including an emphasis on fistula, using information provided by Member States, the organizations and bodies of the United Nations system and non-governmental organizations, with a view to assessing the impact of the present resolution on the well-being of the girl child.

Women and human rights

Division for the Advancement of Women and OHCHR activities

In January, the Secretary-General submitted a report [E/CN.4/2005/68] (see p. 853) on integrating the human rights of women and the gender perspective throughout the UN system and indicated that it should be read together with the joint workplan of the UN Division for the Advancement of Women and the Office of the United Nations High Commissioner for Human Rights (OHCHR) [E/CN.4/2006/59-E/CN.6/2006/9], which provided a review of the implementation of the joint workplan for 2005 and the plan for 2006.

Special rapporteur on laws that discriminate against women

In a March resolution [E/2005/27 (res. 49/3)] on the appointment of a special rapporteur on laws that discriminate against women, the Commission on the Status of Women indicated that legislative and regulatory gaps, as well as the lack of implementation and enforcement of legislation and regulations had perpetuated inequality and discrimination, and in some cases, new laws discriminating against women had been introduced. It decided to consider, at its fiftieth (2006) session, the advisability of the appointment of a special rapporteur on laws that discriminate against women and requested the Secretary-General to report to the Commission on the implications of the creation of the position, including the views of Member States and relevant UN bodies.

Trafficking in women and girls

In March, the Commission on the Status of Women, in resolution [E/2005/27 (res. 49/2)] on eliminating demand for trafficked women and girls for all forms of exploitation, acknowledged that the majority of trafficked persons were women and girls, particularly from developing countries and countries with economies in transition. It welcomed the appointment of the Special Rapporteur of the Commission on Human Rights on trafficking in persons, especially women and children (see p. 853) and called on Governments to take appropriate measures to eliminate the demand for trafficked women and girls. It also encouraged Governments and civil society to increase their efforts to raise public awareness of human trafficking.

Women in Afghanistan

As requested by Economic and Social Council resolution 2004/10 [YUN 2004, p. 1163], the Secretary-General submitted to the Commission a report [E/CN.6/2005/5] on the situation of women and girls in Afghanistan, which contained information on political, social and economic developments affecting Afghan women in 2004, with particular focus on the new Constitution, and on women's participation in the electoral process. It included activities taken by the UN system in support of the Government of Afghanistan towards the advancement of women and gender equality. The Secretary-General reported that the Afghan Constitution, which was finalized in January 2004 [YUN 2004, p. 311], contained a number of articles imposing obligations on the State for the advancement of women. However, it did not include a comprehensive definition of equality and protection from discrimination on the basis of sex, neither did it explicitly address protections to ensure women's right to freely choose a spouse and to citizenship. In preparation for the Afghan elections, 4 million, or 41.3 per cent of the 10.5 million registered voters were women. However, women did not register evenly throughout the country, due to the overall security situation, high levels of illiteracy, cultural restrictions, hostility from male family members and household and family responsibilities. There were numerous reports of women being threatened when they attempted to register. For the presidential election in October, one woman ran as an independent candidate.

To strengthen the capacity for gender mainstreaming within line ministries, the Ministry of Women's Affairs conducted, with UNDP support, training for senior officials from several ministries. A gender adviser was also placed in the Ministry of Rural Rehabilitation and Development and Planning and gender units were to be established in other ministries.

Women and girls were specifically affected by the country's lack of security, limiting their freedom of movement to reach schools, health-care facilities and work. Many of them were subject to violent attacks, especially women government officials, journalists, potential candidates, teachers, NGO activists and humanitarian aid workers. Women and girls continued to be abducted for forced marriage, debt release, dispute settlement and honour crimes. Women's access to the judicial system remained a challenge to addressing violations of their rights. Their access to quality health care was also affected by restrictions on movement, security concerns and the lack of trained female health staff. Maternal mortality rates remained high, especially in Badakhshan province. The Ministry of Health, with the support of UNICEF and NGO partners, was establishing or upgrading one obstetric health facility per province, UNFPA was providing reproductive health kits and WHO was supporting the training of midwives and nurses. In the area of education, UNICEF estimated that 80 per cent of women over 15 years were illiterate and girls accounted for only 34 per cent of total enrolment in schools throughout the country. Further intensified efforts were needed to accelerate the building of schools, increase the number of teachers (especially female teachers), overcome the resistance to girls' education, increase their enrolment rates and support those women and girls who were excluded in the past.

The Secretary-General made a number of recommendations for strengthening the status of women and girls in Afghanistan.

On 22 March, the Commission on the Status of Women took note of the Secretary-General's report [E/2005/27 (dec. 49/103)].

ECONOMIC AND SOCIAL COUNCIL ACTION

On 21 July [meeting 34], the Economic and Social Council, on the recommendation of the Commission on the Status of Women [E/2005/27 & Corr.1], adopted **resolution 2005/8** without vote [agenda item 14 (a)].

Situation of women and girls in Afghanistan

The Economic and Social Council,

Reaffirming that all States have an obligation to promote and protect human rights and fundamental freedoms and the duty to fulfil the obligations they have undertaken under the various instruments in this field,

Recalling that Afghanistan is a party to several international human rights instruments, including the Convention on the Elimination of All Forms of Discrimination against Women,

Recalling also the importance of the implementation of Security Council resolution 1325(2000) of 31 October 2000 on women and peace and security, resolutions 1265(1999) of 17 September 1999 and 1296(2000) of 19 April 2000 on the protection of civilians in armed conflict, and resolution 1539(2004) of 22 April 2004 on children and armed conflict,

Recalling further that the new Constitution states that the citizens of Afghanistan, whether men or women, are equal before the law and that it guarantees the rights of women to serve in the National Assembly,

Recognizing that, in spite of recent improvements, women in Afghanistan continue to face serious violations of their human rights in many parts of the country, in particular in rural areas,

Strongly emphasizing that a safe environment, free from violence, discrimination and abuse, for all Afghans, is essential for a viable and sustainable recovery and reconstruction process,

Stressing the need to integrate a gender perspective when formulating and implementing programmes and policies,

1. *Welcomes*:

(a) The continuing commitment of the Government of Afghanistan to the full enjoyment of all human rights and fundamental freedoms by women and girls, the restoration of the active participation of Afghan women in political, economic and social life, the education of girls as well as boys and the opportunity for women to work outside the home;

(b) The provisions of the new Constitution, which state that the citizens of Afghanistan, whether men or women, are equal before the law and that at least two women are to be elected to the Wolesi Jirga (Lower House of Parliament) from each province, as a national average, and which provide that half of the President's nominees to the Meshrano Jirga (Upper House of Parliament) be women;

(*c*) The ongoing security sector reform processes being undertaken by the Government of Afghanistan with the support of the international community, including the demobilization, disarmament and reintegration of former combatants and the recruitment of a new cadre of women police;

(*d*) The peaceful and successful presidential election that took place on 9 October 2004 and the level of participation by women voters, who cast 40 per cent of the total number of votes;

(*e*) The candidacy of Afghan women in both the Presidential and Vice-presidential ballots, the appointment of three women to cabinet positions and the appointment of the first woman provincial governor on 2 March 2005;

(*f*) The recent publication of a report on transitional justice, entitled "A Call for Justice", by the Afghanistan Independent Human Rights Commission;

(*g*) The efforts by the Afghan Government to develop a national action plan on gender equality;

2. *Also welcomes* the report of the Secretary-General to the Commission on the Status of Women on the situation of women and girls in Afghanistan;

3. *Urges* the Government of Afghanistan:

(*a*) To fully implement the Constitution and all international treaties to which Afghanistan is a State party, including the Convention on the Elimination of All Forms of Discrimination against Women;

(*b*) To ensure that legislative, administrative and other measures support the full enjoyment by women and girls of human rights and fundamental freedoms, including by mainstreaming gender issues into policies and programmes at all levels, and to organize sustained awareness-raising campaigns on the equality of women and men;

(*c*) To enable the full, equal and effective participation of women and girls in civil, cultural, economic, political and social life throughout the country at all levels;

(*d*) To ensure that women, including through ensuring women's security, are able to register, run for office, campaign and vote in the upcoming National Assembly elections scheduled for 2005;

(*e*) To strengthen women's economic empowerment and their access to income-generating activities, credit, means of production, technology and resources, inter alia, by guaranteeing the property and inheritance rights of women and girls;

(*f*) To continue to strengthen the effective, full and equal access of women and girls to health care and education;

(*g*) To ensure that the Ministry of Women's Affairs, the Afghanistan Independent Human Rights Commission and the permanent Afghan judicial institutions have adequate human and financial resources to fulfil their mandates and address gender perspectives, in line with international standards;

(*h*) To continue its efforts to re-establish the rule of law, in accordance with international standards, inter alia, by ensuring the impartiality of the justice system and that law enforcement agencies respect and uphold human rights and fundamental freedoms, with particular emphasis on access to justice and redress mechanisms for women;

(*i*) To continue its efforts to reflect a gender perspective in the training and activities of the police, army, prosecutors and the judiciary and to promote the recruitment of Afghan women in all ranks;

(*j*) To raise awareness of and strengthen measures to prevent and eliminate violence, including domestic and sexual violence, against women and girls, with the aim of changing the attitudes that allow such crimes to take place and to develop support services for victims of such violence;

(*k*) To release women prisoners held in State detention centres for actions that do not constitute crimes under Afghan law and to provide them with adequate support for reintegration into their communities;

(*l*) To raise awareness of the need to prevent and eliminate enforced marriages, in accordance with article 16 (*b*) of the Convention on the Elimination of All Forms of Discrimination against Women;

(*m*) To support measures to ensure the full enjoyment of human rights and fundamental freedoms by women and girls, to hold accountable those who were responsible for gross violations of human rights in the past and to ensure that full investigations are conducted and perpetrators brought to justice, in accordance with international standards, in order to combat impunity;

4. *Invites* the United Nations system, international and non-governmental organizations, and donors:

(*a*) To ensure a human rights–based approach and coherent policy and resources for gender mainstreaming in all programmes and operations, based on the principles of non-discrimination and equality between women and men, and to ensure that women benefit equally with men from such programmes in all sectors;

(*b*) To reflect the needs of women and girls and the importance of their role in the process of peacebuilding, reconstruction and development;

(*c*) To support the elements of civil society active in the field of human rights and encourage the involvement of women therein;

(*d*) To ensure that all their international and national personnel, prior to beginning their service, receive training in gender equality, as well as appropriate training in the history, culture and traditions of Afghanistan, and are fully familiar with and guided by international standards of human rights;

(*e*) To integrate efforts to improve the health status of women within all reconstruction efforts, especially through access to skilled prenatal care, increasing access to skilled birth attendance, education programmes on basic health issues, community information activities and emergency obstetric care;

(*f*) To continue to support measures for the employment of women and the integration of a gender perspective into all social, development and reconstruction programmes, taking into account the special needs of widows and orphans and returning refugee and displaced women and girls, as well as those living in rural areas;

(*g*) To continue to provide financial and technical support to the Ministry of Women's Affairs and all line ministries in order to integrate gender perspectives into their programmes and budgets;

(*h*) To provide sufficient financial and technical support to the 2005 National Assembly elections process in order to facilitate the full participation of women as voters and candidates;

(i) To support the development of a long-term strategy to strengthen the judicial system, in line with international standards;

(j) To support measures to hold accountable those responsible for gross violations of women's human rights in the past and to ensure that full investigations are conducted and perpetrators brought to justice;

5. *Invites* the Commission on Human Rights to consider the report of the Secretary-General on the situation of women and girls in Afghanistan to the General Assembly at its sixty-first session and to fully include the situation of women and girls in any consideration of the human rights situation in Afghanistan;

6. *Requests* the Secretary-General to continue to review the situation of women and girls in Afghanistan and to submit to the Commission on the Status of Women at its fiftieth session a report on progress made in the implementation of the present resolution.

Palestinian women

In response to Economic and Social Council resolution 2004/56 [YUN 2004, p. 484], the Secretary-General reported [E/CN.6/2005/4] to the Commission on the Status of Women on the situation of and assistance to Palestinian women during the period from October 2003 to September 2004 (see p. 533). The Commission took note of the Secretary-General's report on 22 March [E/2005/27 (dec. 49/103)].

On 26 July, the Council took action on the situation of and assistance to Palestinian women in **resolution 2005/43** (see p. 534).

Women and development

In response to General Assembly resolution 58/206 [YUN 2003, p.1178], the Secretary-General submitted a July report [A/60/162 & Corr.1] on the impact of globalization on women's employment and empowerment, which reviewed the benefits and challenges faced by women as a result of service sector growth. It examined the gender perspectives of the World Trade Organization's General Agreement on Trade in Services and provided examples of activities to promote gender equality in the service sector, based on contributions from UN system entities.

The Secretary-General observed that, although the service sector had provided women with increased job opportunities, including in non-traditional sectors, such as information and communication technology and tourism, women continued to predominate in the traditionally female sectors of health and education. However, the impacts of globalization were complex and inequalities between men and women, including in terms of access to and control over productive resources and access to technology and market information, could limit women's employment options and restrict their participation in economic decision-making. An enabling environ-

ment should be created to ensure that both women and men could take advantage of globalization. He proposed for the Assembly's consideration a series of recommendations on gender equality in the economy, including developing policies, to enable both men and women to benefit from opportunities in the service sector and mitigate the negative effects on women; the gender wage gaps and segmentation of the labour market and improving the women's employment security; and identifying and addressing the gender perspectives of trade liberalization in the private sector and receiving national policies and practices to eliminate discrimination against migrant women's employment in the service sector.

GENERAL ASSEMBLY ACTION

On 22 December [meeting 68], the General Assembly, on the recommendation of the Second Committee [A/60/492/Add.2], adopted **resolution 60/210** without vote [agenda item 56 (b)].

Women in development

The General Assembly,

Recalling its resolutions 52/195 of 18 December 1997, 54/210 of 22 December 1999, 56/188 of 21 December 2001, 58/206 of 23 December 2003 and 59/248 of 22 December 2004 and all its other resolutions on the integration of women in development, and the relevant resolutions and agreed conclusions adopted by the Commission on the Status of Women, including the Declaration adopted at its forty-ninth session,

Reaffirming the Beijing Declaration and Platform for Action and the outcome of the twenty-third special session of the General Assembly, entitled "Women 2000: gender equality, development and peace for the twenty-first century", and recalling the outcomes of all other relevant major United Nations conferences and summits,

Reaffirming also the United Nations Millennium Declaration, which affirms that the equal rights and opportunities of women and men must be assured, and calls for, inter alia, the promotion of gender equality and the empowerment of women as being effective and essential to eradicating poverty and hunger, in combating diseases and in stimulating development that is truly sustainable,

Recognizing that access to basic affordable health care, preventive health information and the highest standard of health, including in the areas of sexual and reproductive health, is critical to women's economic advancement, that lack of economic empowerment and independence increases women's vulnerability to a range of negative consequences, including the risk of contracting HIV/AIDS, and that the neglect of the full enjoyment of human rights by women severely limits their opportunities in public and private life, including the opportunity for education and economic and political empowerment,

Reaffirming that gender equality is of fundamental importance for achieving sustained economic growth, poverty eradication and sustainable development, in accordance with the relevant General Assembly resolutions and United Nations conferences, and that investing in the development of women and girls has a multiplier effect, in particular on productivity, efficiency and sustained economic growth, in all sectors of the economy, especially in key areas such as agriculture, industry and services,

Reaffirming also the significant contribution that women make to the economy, that women are key contributors to the economy and to combating poverty through both remunerated and unremunerated work at home, in the community and in the workplace and that the empowerment of women is a critical factor in the eradication of poverty,

Recognizing that the difficult socio-economic conditions that exist in many developing countries, in particular the least developed countries, have resulted in the acceleration of the feminization of poverty,

Recognizing also that population and development issues, education and training, health, nutrition, the environment, water supply, sanitation, housing, communications, science and technology, and employment opportunities are important elements for effective poverty eradication and the advancement and empowerment of women,

Recognizing further, in this context, the importance of respect for all human rights, including the right to development, and of a national and international environment that promotes, inter alia, justice, gender equality, equity, civil and political participation and civil, political and fundamental freedoms for the advancement and empowerment of women,

Reaffirming the need to eliminate gender disparities in primary and secondary education by the earliest possible date and at all levels by 2015 and that equal access to education and training at all levels, in particular, inter alia, in business, trade, administration, information and communication technologies and other new technologies, as well as the need to eliminate gender inequalities at all levels, are essential for gender equality, the empowerment of women and poverty eradication and to allow women's full and equal contribution to, and equal opportunity to benefit from, development,

Recognizing that poverty eradication and the achievement and preservation of peace are mutually reinforcing, and recognizing also that peace is inextricably linked to equality between women and men and to development,

Aware that, while globalization and liberalization processes have created employment opportunities for women in many countries, they have also made women, especially in developing countries and in particular in the least developed countries, more vulnerable to problems caused by increased economic volatility, including in the agricultural sector, and that special support, particularly for women who are small-scale farmers, and empowerment are necessary to enable them to take advantage of the opportunities of agricultural market liberalization,

Recognizing that enhanced trade opportunities for developing countries, including through trade liberalization, will improve the economic condition of those societies, including women, which is of particular importance in rural communities,

Expressing its concern that, while women represent an important and growing proportion of business owners, their contribution to economic and social development is constrained by, inter alia, the denial and lack of equal rights and access of women to education, training, information, support services and credit facilities, and control over land, capital, technology and other areas of production,

Also expressing its concern about the underrepresentation of women in political and economic decision-making, and stressing the importance of mainstreaming a gender perspective in the formulation, implementation and evaluation of all policies and programmes,

Noting the importance of the organizations and bodies of the United Nations system, in particular its funds and programmes, including the United Nations Development Fund for Women, in facilitating the advancement of women in development, and noting the work done by the International Research and Training Institute for the Advancement of Women,

1. *Takes note* of the report of the Secretary-General;

2. *Also takes note* of the report of the Secretary-General entitled "World Survey on the role of women in development: women and international migration", and recommends that it be considered within the context of the High-level Dialogue on International Migration and Development, to be held in 2006;

3. *Calls upon* Governments, the United Nations system and other international and regional organizations, within their respective mandates, all sectors of civil society, including non-governmental organizations, as well as all women and men to fully commit themselves and to intensify their contributions to the implementation of the Beijing Declaration and Platform for Action and the outcome of the twenty-third special session of the General Assembly;

4. *Stresses* the importance of creating a favourable and conducive national and international environment in all fields of life for the effective integration of women in development;

5. *Urges* all Governments to develop and promote strategies to mainstream a gender perspective in the design and implementation of economic and development policies, including in budgetary policies and processes at all levels, and in the monitoring and evaluation of related programmes of action;

6. *Acknowledges* that the gender segmentation of the labour market creates an additional challenge for women in the economy, restricting opportunities for them in sectors traditionally dominated by men, and calls upon Governments and all other stakeholders, where appropriate, to make further efforts to address the gender wage gaps and gender segmentation of the labour market and to improve the conditions and security of women's employment in all sectors of the economy;

7. *Calls upon* all Governments to incorporate a gender perspective in all policies on international migration, including, inter alia, for the protection of women migrants from violence, discrimination, trafficking, exploitation and abuse;

8. *Requests* Governments to ensure the full and equal participation of women in decision-making and in policy formulation and implementation at all levels so that their priorities, skills and potentials can be adequately reflected in national policies;

9. _Recognizes_ the mutually reinforcing links between gender equality and poverty eradication, as well as the need to elaborate and implement, where appropriate, in consultation with civil society, comprehensive gender-sensitive poverty eradication strategies that address social, structural and macroeconomic issues;

10. _Recognizes also_ that violence against women and girls is one of the obstacles to the achievement of the objectives of equality, development and peace and the implications of violence against women and girls for the social and economic development of communities and States, and calls upon States to elaborate and implement, at all appropriate levels, plans of action to eliminate violence against women and girls;

11. _Recognizes further_ the need to strengthen the capacity of Governments to incorporate a gender perspective in policies and decision-making, and encourages all Governments, international organizations, including the United Nations system, and other relevant stakeholders to assist and support developing countries in integrating a gender perspective in all aspects of policymaking, including through the provision of technical assistance and financial resources;

12. _Stresses_ the importance of developing national strategies for the promotion of sustainable and productive entrepreneurial activities that will generate income among disadvantaged women and women living in poverty;

13. _Urges_ all Governments to ensure women's equal rights with men and their full and equal access to education, training, employment, technology and economic and financial resources, including credit, in particular for rural women and women in the informal sector, and to facilitate, where appropriate, the transition of women from the informal to the formal sector;

14. _Encourages_ Governments, the private sector, non-governmental organizations and other actors of civil society to promote and protect the rights of women workers, to take action to remove structural and legal barriers as well as stereotypical attitudes to gender equality at work and to initiate positive steps to promote equal pay for equal work or work of equal value;

15. _Urges_ all Governments to take all appropriate measures to eliminate discrimination against women with regard to their access to bank loans, mortgages and other forms of financial credit, giving special attention to poor, uneducated women, and to support women's access to legal assistance;

16. _Calls upon_ Governments and entrepreneurial associations to facilitate the access of women, including young women and women entrepreneurs, to education and training in business, administration and information and communication technologies;

17. _Recognizes_ the role of microfinance, including microcredit, in the eradication of poverty, the empowerment of women and the generation of employment, notes in this regard the importance of sound national financial systems, and encourages the strengthening of existing and emerging microcredit institutions and their capacities, including through the support of international financial institutions;

18. _Stresses_ the need for assistance to enable women in developing countries, particularly grass-roots women's groups, to have full access to and use of new technologies, including information technologies, for their empowerment;

19. _Urges_ States to design and revise laws that ensure that women are accorded full and equal rights to own land and other property, including through inheritance, and to undertake administrative reforms and other necessary measures to give women the same right as men to credit, capital and appropriate technologies and access to markets and information;

20. _Calls upon_ Governments to encourage the financial sector to mainstream gender perspectives in its policies and programmes;

21. _Also calls upon_ Governments to promote, inter alia, through legislation and family-friendly and gender-sensitive work environments, the facilitation of breastfeeding for working mothers and the provision of the necessary care for working women's children and other dependants and to consider promoting policies and programmes, as appropriate, to enable men and women to reconcile their work, social and family responsibilities;

22. _Recognizes_ the need to empower women economically and politically, particularly poor women, and in this regard encourages Governments, with the support of their development partners, to invest in appropriate infrastructure and other projects, as well as to create opportunities for economic empowerment, in order to alleviate for women and girls the burden of time-consuming everyday tasks;

23. _Expresses its concern_ that the HIV/AIDS pandemic reinforces gender inequalities, that women and girls bear a disproportionate share of the burden imposed by the HIV/AIDS crisis, that they are more easily infected, that they play a key role in care and that they have become more vulnerable to poverty as a result of the HIV/AIDS crisis;

24. _Reaffirms_ the commitment to achieve universal access to reproductive health by 2015, as set out at the International Conference on Population and Development, integrating this goal in strategies to attain the internationally agreed development goals, including those contained in the United Nations Millennium Declaration aimed at reducing maternal mortality, improving maternal health, reducing child mortality, promoting gender equality, combating HIV/AIDS and eradicating poverty;

25. _Calls upon_ the international community to make efforts to mitigate the effects of excess volatility and economic disruption, which have a disproportionately negative impact on women, and to enhance trade opportunities for developing countries in order to improve the economic situation of women;

26. _Urges_ the international community, the United Nations system and relevant organizations to give priority to assisting the efforts of developing countries to ensure the full and effective participation of women in deciding and implementing development strategies and integrating gender concerns into national programmes, including by providing adequate resources to operational activities for development in support of the efforts of Governments to ensure full and equal access of women to health care, capital, education, training and technology, as well as full and equal participation in all decision-making;

27. _Recognizes_ that a substantial increase in official development assistance and other resources will be

required if developing countries are to achieve the internationally agreed development goals and objectives, including those contained in the Millennium Declaration, and that in order to build support for official development assistance, cooperation will be needed in further improving policies and development strategies, both nationally and internationally, to enhance aid effectiveness;

28. *Encourages* the international community, the United Nations system, the private sector and civil society to continue to provide the necessary financial resources to assist national Governments in their efforts to meet the development targets and benchmarks agreed upon at the World Summit for Social Development, the Fourth World Conference on Women, the International Conference on Population and Development, the Millennium Summit, the International Conference on Financing for Development, the World Summit on Sustainable Development, the Second World Assembly on Ageing, the twenty-third and twenty-fourth special sessions of the General Assembly and other relevant United Nations conferences and summits;

29. *Encourages* the United Nations system and international and regional organizations, as appropriate, to assist Governments, at their request, in building institutional capacity and developing national action plans or further implementing existing action plans for the implementation of the Beijing Platform for Action;

30. *Urges* Governments to create and maintain a non-discriminatory and gender-sensitive legal environment by reviewing legislation, with a view to striving to remove discriminatory provisions as soon as possible and eliminating legislative gaps that leave women and girls without protection of their rights and without effective recourse against gender-based discrimination, and encourages assistance to countries in achieving this aim;

31. *Urges* multilateral donors, and invites international financial institutions, within their respective mandates, and regional development banks to review and implement policies to support national efforts to ensure that a higher proportion of resources reach women, in particular in rural and remote areas;

32. *Encourages* Governments, international organizations, including the United Nations system, the private sector and civil society to fully incorporate a gender perspective into the implementation of and follow-up to the World Summit on Sustainable Development and the International Conference on Financing for Development and to implement the specific recommendations on microfinance and microcredit for women and gender budget policies;

33. *Stresses* the importance of collecting and exchanging all relevant information needed on the role of women in development, including data on international migration, as well as the need to develop statistics disaggregated by sex, and in that regard encourages developed countries and relevant entities of the United Nations to provide support and assistance to developing countries, upon their request, with respect to establishing, developing and strengthening their databases and information systems;

34. *Calls upon* all organizations of the United Nations system, within their organizational mandates, to mainstream a gender perspective and to pursue gender equality in their country programmes, planning instruments and sector-wide programmes and to articulate specific country-level goals and targets in this field in accordance with the national development strategies;

35. *Calls upon* the United Nations system to integrate gender mainstreaming into all its programmes and policies, including in the integrated follow-up to United Nations conferences, in accordance with agreed conclusions 1997/2 on gender mainstreaming adopted by the Economic and Social Council at its substantive session of 1997;

36. *Encourages* all relevant United Nations funds and programmes and the specialized agencies, in accordance with their respective mandates, to assist Governments, at their request, in strengthening their capacity to promote and support the economic advancement of women through, inter alia, employment and entrepreneurship practices and programmes that affirm and empower women;

37. *Reiterates its request* to the Secretary-General to update the *World Survey on the Role of Women in Development* for the consideration of the General Assembly at its sixty-fourth session, noting that the survey should continue to focus on selective emerging development themes that have an impact on the role of women in the economy at the national, regional and international levels;

38. *Decides* that the theme for the next survey will be "Women's control over economic resources and access to financial resources, including microfinance";

39. *Requests* the Secretary-General to submit to the General Assembly at its sixty-second session a report on the progress made in the implementation of the present resolution, including women's increased participation in government decision-making bodies and its impact on the eradication of poverty;

40. *Decides* to include in the provisional agenda of its sixty-second session the sub-item entitled "Women in development".

Situation of women in rural areas

The Secretary-General submitted an October report [A/60/165] on the improvement of the situation of women in rural areas, in response to General Assembly resolution 58/146 [YUN 2003, p. 1181]. The report focused on women's empowerment, including in relation to access to education and training; control over resources; participation in decision-making processes; changes in household structure; and the impact of HIV/AIDS, migration and information and communication technologies. He also reported on activities undertaken by UN system organizations to respond to the challenges facing rural women by implementing policies and programmes addressing different aspects of their situation, such as land ownership, microfinance, access to markets and trade, trafficking and knowledge-sharing, education and training.

The Secretary-General concluded that the process of globalization had direct and indirect effects on the empowerment of rural women. Benefits included increased opportunities for off-farm activities, wage employment in non-agricultural sectors and participation in local decision-making and networking, including through information and communication technologies. On the other hand, rural women continued to experience the effects of unequal household divisions of labour, inaccessible education and health services, discriminatory and stereotypical attitudes and practices and violence. He stressed that the situation of rural women should be given explicit attention in the context of the High-level Plenary Meeting of the General Assembly (see p. 47), as well as, in the World Summit on the Information Society in Tunis, Tunisia (see p. 933). He emphasized the need for Governments, UN entities and other relevant stakeholders to support legislation, policies and programmes that strengthened the positive effects of globalization on the empowerment of rural women and made recommendations on specific interventions that could be undertaken towards that end.

GENERAL ASSEMBLY ACTION

On 22 December [meeting 64], the General Assembly, on the recommendation of the Second Committee [A/60/503], adopted **resolution 60/138** without vote [agenda item 64].

Improvement of the situation of women in rural areas

The General Assembly,

Recalling its resolutions 56/129 of 19 December 2001 and 58/146 of 22 December 2003,

Recalling also the importance attached to the problems of rural women in the Nairobi Forward-looking Strategies for the Advancement of Women, the Beijing Declaration and Platform for Action adopted by the Fourth World Conference on Women and their ten-year review and appraisal, the outcome documents of the twenty-third special session of the General Assembly and the Convention on the Elimination of All Forms of Discrimination against Women,

Recalling further the United Nations Millennium Declaration, in which Member States resolved, inter alia, to promote gender equality and the empowerment of women as effective ways to combat poverty, hunger and disease and to stimulate development that is truly sustainable, and the 2005 World Summit Outcome, in which they also resolved to promote gender equality and eliminate pervasive gender discrimination by taking all necessary resolute action,

Welcoming the declaration adopted by the Commission on the Status of Women at its forty-ninth session in the context of the review and appraisal of the Beijing Platform for Action and the outcome documents of the twenty-third special session of the General Assembly,

Welcoming also the agreed conclusions on women's participation in and access to the media, and information and communication technologies and their impact on and use as an instrument for the advancement and empowerment of women, adopted by the Commission on the Status of Women at its forty-seventh session,

Welcoming further the Monterrey Consensus of the International Conference on Financing for Development, as well as the Johannesburg Declaration on Sustainable Development and the Plan of Implementation of the World Summit on Sustainable Development ("Johannesburg Plan of Implementation"), in which Governments were called upon to mainstream the gender perspective into development at all levels and in all sectors,

Welcoming the ministerial declaration of the high-level segment of the substantive session of 2003 of the Economic and Social Council, adopted on 2 July 2003, which stressed the need for rural development to become an integral part of national and international development policies and of the activities and programmes of the United Nations system, and called for an enhanced role for rural women at all levels of rural development, including decision-making,

Recognizing the critical role and contribution of rural women, including indigenous women, in enhancing agricultural and rural development, improving food security and eradicating rural poverty,

Noting that some effects of globalization may deepen the socio-economic marginalization of rural women,

Noting also that the globalization process has had some benefits by providing opportunities for wage employment for rural women in new sectors,

Mindful of the fact that the available data and existing tools of measurement and analysis are insufficient for a full understanding of the gender implications of the processes of globalization and rural change and their impact on rural women,

Recognizing the urgent need to take appropriate measures aimed at further improving the situation of women in rural areas,

1. _Takes note_ of the report of the Secretary-General;

2. _Invites_ Member States, in collaboration with the organizations of the United Nations and civil society, as appropriate, to continue their efforts to implement the outcome of and to ensure an integrated and coordinated follow-up to United Nations conferences and summits, including their reviews, and to attach greater importance to the improvement of the situation of rural women, including indigenous women, in their national, regional and global development strategies by, inter alia:

(_a_) Creating an enabling environment for improving the situation of rural women and ensuring attention to their needs and contributions, including through enhanced cooperation and a gender perspective, and their full participation in the development, implementation and monitoring of macroeconomic policies and programmes and poverty reduction strategies, including poverty reduction strategy papers, based on the Millennium Development Goals;

(_b_) Pursuing the political and socio-economic empowerment of rural women and supporting their full and equal participation in decision-making at all levels, including through affirmative action, where appropriate, and support for women's organizations, labour unions or other associations and civil society groups promoting rural women's rights;

(c) Integrating a gender perspective into the design, implementation, monitoring and evaluation of development policies and programmes, including budget policies, paying increased attention to the needs of rural women so as to ensure that they benefit from policies and programmes adopted in all spheres and that the disproportionate number of rural women living in poverty is reduced;

(d) Ensuring that the perspectives of rural women are taken into account and that they participate in the design, implementation, monitoring and evaluation of policies and activities related to emergencies, natural disasters, humanitarian assistance, peacebuilding and post-conflict reconstruction;

(e) Investing in and strengthening efforts to meet the basic needs of rural women through improved availability, access to and use of critical rural infrastructure, such as energy and transport, capacity-building and human resources development measures and the provision of a safe and reliable water supply and sanitation, nutritional programmes, affordable housing programmes, education and literacy programmes and health and social support measures, including in the area of sexual and reproductive health and HIV/AIDS treatment, care and support;

(f) Designing and implementing policies that promote and protect the enjoyment by rural women and girls of all human rights and fundamental freedoms and creating an environment that does not tolerate violations of their rights, including domestic violence, sexual violence and other forms of gender-based violence;

(g) Developing specific assistance programmes and advisory services to promote economic skills of rural women in banking, modern trading and financial procedures and providing microcredit and other financial and business services to a greater number of women in rural areas, in particular female-headed households, for their economic empowerment;

(h) Considering adopting, where appropriate, national legislation to protect the knowledge, innovations and practices of women in indigenous and local communities relating to traditional medicines, biodiversity and indigenous technologies;

(i) Taking steps towards ensuring that women's unpaid work and contributions to on-farm and off-farm production, including income generated in the informal sector, are visible, and supporting remunerative non-agricultural employment of rural women, improving working conditions and increasing access to productive resources;

(j) Addressing the lack of timely, reliable and sex-disaggregated data, including by intensifying efforts to include women's unpaid work in official statistics, and developing a systematic and comparative research base on rural women that will inform policy and programme decisions;

(k) Designing and revising laws to ensure that, where private ownership of land and property exists, rural women are accorded full and equal rights to own land and other property, including through the right to inheritance, and undertaking administrative reforms and other necessary measures to give women the same right as men to credit, capital, appropriate technologies and access to markets and information;

(l) Promoting programmes to enable rural women and men to reconcile their work and family responsibilities and to encourage men to share equally with women household and childcare responsibilities;

(m) Mobilizing resources, including at the national level and through official development assistance, for increasing women's access to existing savings and credit schemes, as well as targeted programmes that provide women with capital, knowledge and tools that enhance their economic capacities;

(n) Supporting a gender-sensitive education system that considers rural women's specific needs in order to eliminate gender stereotypes and discriminatory tendencies affecting them;

3. *Invites* the Commission on the Status of Women to continue to pay due attention to the situation of rural women in the consideration of its priority themes;

4. *Invites* the relevant organizations and bodies of the United Nations system, in particular those dealing with issues of development, to address and support the empowerment of rural women and their specific needs in their programmes and strategies, including in the context of globalization;

5. *Stresses* the need to identify the best practices for ensuring that rural women have access to and full participation in the area of information and communication technologies, and invites the World Summit on the Information Society, at its second phase in Tunis, to take into consideration, while addressing gender issues, the priorities and needs of rural women and girls as active users of information and ensure their participation in developing and implementing global information and communication technology strategies;

6. *Invites* Member States, the United Nations and the relevant organizations of its system to ensure that the needs of rural women are mainstreamed into the integrated process of follow-up to the major summits and conferences in the economic and social fields, in particular the Millennium Summit, the World Summit on Sustainable Development, the International Conference on Financing for Development, the 2005 review of the progress achieved in implementing all the commitments made in the Beijing Platform for Action and the outcome documents of the twenty-third special session of the General Assembly entitled "Women 2000: gender equality, development and peace for the twenty-first century", and the 2005 World Summit;

7. *Invites* Member States to take into consideration the concluding comments and recommendations of the Committee on the Elimination of Discrimination against Women concerning their reports to the Committee when formulating policies and designing programmes focused on the improvement of the situation of rural women, including those to be developed and implemented in cooperation with relevant international organizations;

8. *Requests* the Secretary-General to report to the General Assembly at its sixty-second session on the implementation of the present resolution, addressing different aspects of the empowerment of rural women.

Eradication of poverty

In an 18 May letter [A/60/79] to the Secretary-General and the General Assembly President,

Qatar announced the establishment of a trust fund for non-governmental organizations (NGOs) to assist them in strengthening their capacities to eradicate poverty, ameliorate the livelihood of poor families and communities, and reinforce the role of women in sustainable development.

On 9 June [A/60/84], Burkina Faso transmitted to the Secretary-General the Plan of Action for Promotion and Employment and Poverty Alleviation, adopted at the extraordinary session of the African Union on employment and poverty alleviation (Ouagadougou, Burkina Faso, 3-9 September 2004). One of the 11 key priority areas identified for reversing the trend of persistent poverty and unemployment, included the empowerment of women by integrating them into labour markets and enabling them to participate in the development of poverty reduction strategies, policies and programmes.

Gender Advisory Board

On 26 May [E/2005/31], the Commission on Science and Technology for Development at its eighth session (23-27 May) (see p. 929) considered the mandate of the Gender Advisory Board, an expert group established in 1995 [YUN 1995, p. 849] by the Commission to facilitate its future deliberations on the gender implications of science and technology for developing countries.

The Commission recommended that the Economic and Social Council extend the Board's mandate for an additional five years, beginning from 1 January 2006.

The Council, by **decision 2005/307** of 27 July, extended the Board's mandate as recommended.

Economic advancement for women

The Commission on the Status of Women adopted a March resolution [E/2005/27 (res. 49/8)] on the economic advancement for women, in which it noted that hundreds of millions of women and girls worldwide lived in poverty, with the majority living in rural areas where their livelihoods were dependent upon subsistence and small-holder agriculture and employment in the informal sector. The Commission, among other actions, called on Member States to strengthen efforts to implement national and international commitments that would advance women's equality; promote gender mainstreaming in all phases of economic and social policy development. It further requested them to build the capacity for the effective collection, dissemination and analysis of gender-sensitive statistical indicators and statistics that were disaggregated by sex and other relevant factors to facilitate better policy development, monitoring and evaluation of the economic and social advancement of women. The Commission also re-

quested the Secretary-General to report on the implementation of the resolution at its fiftieth (2006) session.

Post-disaster relief and reconstruction

In a resolution [E/2005/27(res. 49/5)] on integrating a gender perspective in post-disaster relief, recovery, rehabilitation and reconstruction efforts, the Commission on the Status of Women, citing the Hyogo Framework for Action 2005-2015, adopted by the World Conference on Disaster Reduction (see p. 1015), which recognized that a gender perspective should be integrated into all disaster risk-management policies and stressing that women and children account for the majority of those adversely affected by natural disasters and their aftermath, called on UN entities and international and local humanitarian relief organizations to strengthen the gender dimensions of their responses to disaster situations. It also called on Governments to involve women in all levels of decision-making in disaster situations and to take the particular needs of women and girls into account. The Commission requested the Secretary-General to report on UN coordinated efforts to integrate gender dimensions in situations of natural disasters, including the Indian Ocean tsunami disaster, in his reports to the General Assembly at its sixtieth (2005) session.

Indigenous women

In a March resolution [E/2005/27 (res. 49/7)] on indigenous women: beyond the ten-year review of the Beijing Declaration and Platform for Action, the Commission on the Status of Women welcomed the fact that the theme of the third session of the Permanent Forum of Indigenous Issues [YUN 2004, p. 798] focused on indigenous women and took note of the recommendations, which emphasized equality, non-discrimination, the diversity of cultural identities and social organization of indigenous women and girls. It called on Governments, intergovernmental agencies, the private sector and civil society to ensure the full participation of indigenous women in all aspects of society.

Institutional mechanisms for the advancement of women

Inter-Agency Network. The United Nations Inter-Agency Network on Women and Gender Equality (IANWGE), at its fourth annual session (New York, 22-25 February) [IANWGE/2005/REPORT], endorsed decisions and recommendations made by task forces and working groups regarding the integrated and coordinated follow-up to major conferences on women as they related to the ten-year review of the Beijing Platform for Action at the forty-ninth session of the Commission on the Status of Women and beyond; the five-year review of the Millennium Declaration and the MDGs; gender statistics and indicators; human rights issues; human resources and the status of women in the UN system; women, peace and security; mainstreaming a gender perspective in the common country assessment/United Nations Development Assistance Framework (CCA/UNDAF); WomenWatch; gender and trade; gender and water; indigenous women; gender mainstreaming in evaluation, monitoring and programme reporting; and the ten-year review of the Beijing Platform for Action. The Network held a workshop entitled "Ten-year review of gender mainstreaming: focusing on results". On IANWGE methods of work, Network members concurred that the agenda covered too many areas, with insufficient time to analyse each issue. To allow for increased interaction among members and presenters and utilization of shared analyses on emerging issues, it recommended that the IANWGE agenda for its fifth (2006) session should correspond to that of the Commission on the Status of Women session for that year. Suggestions were also made on changing IANWGE timing to a much earlier date than the Commission on the Status of Women, reducing the duration of the meeting to three days and meeting in a location other than New York. The Network also made recommendations on the work methods of the task forces.

Report of Secretary-General. Responding to Commission resolution 48/4 [YUN 2004, p. 1167], the Secretary-General submitted a report [E/CN.6/2005/3] on measures taken and progress achieved in the follow-up to the Fourth World Conference on Women and to the General Assembly's twenty-third special session in mainstreaming a gender perspective throughout the UN system. The report provided information on achievements, lessons learned and best practices based on an analysis of inputs received from UN system entities.

The Secretary-General observed that many UN entities had shifted towards a more comprehensive approach to achieving gender equality, through the adoption of gender-sensitive policies, procedures and programming. Entities had developed institutional mechanisms to facilitate implementation and some of them incorporated gender perspectives into results-based planning and budgeting. Gender equality was increasingly incorporated into UN system programmes and operational activities. The Department of Public Information had raised awareness of gender equality, and several trust funds were established to support gender equality activities. Constraints

to full implementation of gender mainstreaming included high staff turnover; scepticism with regard to gender issues; lack of incentive to participate in training; underdeveloped reporting, monitoring and evaluation mechanisms; the lack of data disaggregated by sex; and the limited inclusion of existing data into mainstream statistical analysis. Lack of accountability and of financial resources were major challenges to effective implementation. The Secretary-General made recommendations to the Commission for encouraging UN entities to develop action plans with measurable goals and targets; establish mechanisms for holding staff and senior managers accountable for results; make gender training mandatory for all staff; and increase the exchange of experiences, good practices and lessons learned among entities of the UN system, as well as Governments and civil society.

Commission on the Status of Women. In March [E/2005/27 (res. 49/4)], the Commission on the Status of Women called on the international community, including the UN system and other regional organizations, to support Government efforts to strengthen their national mechanisms for gender mainstreaming; encourage donor and development agencies to include assistance activities for strengthening national machineries in their programmes; provide technical cooperation and other assistance to developing countries; and facilitate the sharing of information on guidelines, methodologies and best practices. It also requested that the Secretary-General report on progress in mainstreaming a gender perspective in the development, implementation and evaluation of national policies and programmes at the Commission's fiftieth (2006) session.

Further report of Secretary-General. Pursuant to Economic and Social Council resolution 2004/4 [YUN 2004, p. 1167] on the review of agreed conclusions 1997/2 on mainstreaming a gender perspective into all UN system policies and programmes, the Secretary-General submitted an April report [E/2005/54] on follow-up to the Fourth World Conference, which was based on the inputs of UN system bodies and organizations. The report outlined gaps between policy and practice and focused on action plans and other measures to promote gender mainstreaming. Approximately one fourth of the responding entities had adopted gender mainstreaming action plans and many of those that lacked corporate or overall action plans were guided by gender mainstreaming policies, strategies or frameworks, with the intent to draw up action plans in the future. The report concluded that, in response to the outcome of the review of the agreed conclusions 1997/2, UN entities continued to identify gaps between policy and practice in gender mainstreaming in their respective areas. Steps taken by entities to address those challenges, including the adoption of gender mainstreaming action plans, had been instrumental in moving them beyond policy formulation and towards implementation. Recommendations to the Council included encouraging UN entities to develop action plans with clear guidelines on the implementation of gender mainstreaming in policies and programmes; fully incorporate gender perspectives into programme budgets, multi-year funding frameworks and all results-based budgeting processes, as well as operational mechanisms; and strengthen accountability systems for all staff for gender mainstreaming, including through performance appraisals. The need to further develop and institutionalize monitoring and evaluation tools and gender impact analysis methodologies and to ensure the collection and use of sex-disaggregated data was also emphasized.

UNDP consideration. In response to United Nations Development Programme/United Nations Population Fund (UNDP/UNFPA) Executive Board decisions 2004/21, 2004/22 and 2004/38 [YUN 2004, p. 1167], UNDP presented respectively, its corporate gender strategy and action plan [DP/2005/7 & Corr.1], the UNDP gender mainstreaming scorecard [ibid.] and an update [DP/2005/CRP.2] on progress achieved in the partnership between UNDP and UNIFEM. The Executive Board requested UNDP to develop the gender action plan through 2007, including the results matrix, and to report on the medium-term action plan in 2006, building on the management response to the independent gender evaluation [E/2005/35 (dec. 2005/27)].

ECONOMIC AND SOCIAL COUNCIL ACTION

On 26 July [meeting 39], the Economic and Social Council adopted **resolution 2005/31** [draft: E/2005/L.38] without vote [agenda item 7 (e)].

Mainstreaming a gender perspective into all policies and programmes in the United Nations system

The Economic and Social Council,

Reaffirming its agreed conclusions 1997/2 of 18 July 1997 on mainstreaming a gender perspective into all policies and programmes in the United Nations system, and recalling its resolutions 2001/41 of 26 July 2001, 2002/23 of 24 July 2002, 2003/49 of 24 July 2003 and 2004/4 of 7 July 2004,

Reaffirming also that gender mainstreaming is a globally accepted strategy for promoting gender equality and constitutes a critical strategy in the implementation of the Beijing Platform for Action and the outcome of the twenty-third special session of the General Assembly,

Underlining the catalytic role played by the Commission on the Status of Women, as well as the important role played by the Economic and Social Council and the General Assembly, in promoting and monitoring gender mainstreaming within the United Nations system,

Welcoming the declaration adopted by the Commission on the Status of Women at its forty-ninth session,

1. *Welcomes* the report of the Secretary-General on follow-up to and progress in the implementation of the Beijing Declaration and Platform for Action and the outcome of the twenty-third special session of the General Assembly, especially in mainstreaming a gender perspective in entities of the United Nations system;

2. *Notes with appreciation* the progress and continued efforts by United Nations entities to address gaps between policy and practice in mainstreaming a gender perspective in their respective fields of work;

3. *Expresses concern* at the remaining gaps between policy and practice, with particular challenges relating to inadequate institutional mechanisms, including in the area of data collection, accountability, monitoring, reporting and training, as well as inadequate resource allocation;

4. *Calls upon* all entities of the United Nations system, including United Nations agencies, funds and programmes, to intensify efforts to address the challenges to the integration of gender perspectives in policies and programmes, including by:

(a) Developing action plans, where these do not yet exist, with clear guidelines on the practical implementation of gender mainstreaming in policies and programmes;

(b) Ensuring that action plans include timelines and specific provisions on institutional mechanisms at both headquarters and field offices and that they are fully coordinated with overall organizational goals and strategies;

(c) Fully incorporating a gender perspective in programme budgets and multi-year funding frameworks and into all results-based budgeting processes;

(d) Ensuring continuous awareness-raising and training on gender issues for all staff, including by integrating a gender perspective into all training programmes, as well as assessing the impact of the gender component of the existing training programmes to improve their effectiveness;

(e) Building the capacity of staff to undertake gender analysis and requiring staff to apply gender analysis to both policy formulation and programmatic work;

(f) Ensuring full and strong commitment by senior management officials to gender mainstreaming and its implementation in policies, programmes and projects;

(g) Strengthening accountability systems for all staff for gender mainstreaming, including through performance appraisals;

(h) Incorporating a gender perspective into operational mechanisms, in accordance with the national development strategies, including common country assessments and the United Nations Development Assistance Framework, poverty reduction strategy papers and reporting and implementation frameworks, such as those relating to the implementation of the internationally agreed development goals, including those contained in the United Nations Millennium Declaration;

(*i*) Continuing to support Governments and to work with civil society in their efforts to implement the Beijing Platform for Action and the outcome of the twenty-third special session of the General Assembly;

(*j*) Further developing and institutionalizing monitoring and evaluation tools and gender impact analysis methodologies, promoting the collection, compilation and analysis of sex-disaggregated data and ensuring the use by them of such data;

(*k*) Promoting the mainstreaming of gender perspectives into key macroeconomic and social development policies and national development programmes;

5. *Takes note* of the work already undertaken to implement General Assembly resolution 59/164 of 20 December 2004 on the improvement of the status of women in the United Nations system, and urges continued efforts towards its full implementation;

6. *Encourages* the Special Adviser on Gender Issues and Advancement of Women and the Division for the Advancement of Women of the Secretariat as well as other relevant United Nations entities to maintain their efforts to raise awareness of gender issues across the United Nations system;

7. *Recommends* that all entities of the United Nations system continue to promote cooperation, coordination and the sharing of methodologies and good practices, including through the development of tools and effective processes for monitoring and evaluation within the United Nations, in the implementation of agreed conclusions 1997/2, in particular through the Inter-Agency Network on Women and Gender Equality, and recommends further that all inter-agency mechanisms pay attention to gender perspectives in their work;

8. *Also recommends* that the Inter-Agency Network on Women and Gender Equality continues to provide practical support to its members in gender mainstreaming and to report regularly to the United Nations System Chief Executives Board for Coordination through its High Level Committee on Programme and its High Level Committee on Management in order to facilitate the incorporation of gender mainstreaming perspectives into their work;

9. *Calls upon* the United Nations system to strengthen inter-agency and country team collaboration on gender mainstreaming, including through the creation or expansion of electronic knowledge networks on gender mainstreaming;

10. *Requests* the Secretary-General to report to the Economic and Social Council at its substantive session of 2006 on progress in mainstreaming a gender perspective into all policies and programmes in the United Nations, with a focus on training activities.

UN machinery

Convention on the elimination of discrimination against women

As at 31 December 2005, 180 States were parties to the 1979 Convention on the Elimination of All Forms of Discrimination against Women, adopted by the General Assembly in resolution

34/180 [YUN 1979, p. 895]. During the year, Monaco acceded to the Convention. At year's end, 47 States parties had also accepted the amendment to article 20, paragraph 1, of the Convention in respect of the meeting time of the Committee on the Elimination of Discrimination against Women, which was adopted by the States parties in 1995 [YUN 1995, p. 1178]. The amendment would enter into force when accepted by a two-thirds majority of States parties.

The Optional Protocol to the Convention, adopted by the Assembly in resolution 54/4 [YUN 1999, p. 1100] and which entered into force in 2000 [YUN 2000, p. 1123], had 74 States parties as at 31 December 2005.

The Secretary-General submitted his annual report to the Assembly on the status of the Convention as at 31 July [A/60/206].

CEDAW

In 2005, the Committee on the Elimination of Discrimination against Women (CEDAW), established in 1982 [YUN 1982, p. 1149] to monitor compliance with the 1979 Convention, held two regular sessions in New York [A/60/38].

At its thirty-second session (10-28 January), CEDAW reviewed the initial or periodic reports of Algeria, Croatia, Gabon, Italy, the Lao People's Democratic Republic, Paraguay, Samoa and Turkey on measures they had taken to implement the Convention. CEDAW considered a Secretariat report on ways to expedite work [CEDAW/C/2005/I/4] and a report on the status of submission of reports by States parties under article 18 of the Convention, including a list of reports that had been submitted but not considered by the Committee [CEDAW/C/2005/I/2]. Three specialized agencies, the Food and Agriculture Organization of the United Nations (FAO), the United Nations Educational, Scientific and Cultural Organization (UNESCO) and the International Labour Organization (ILO) had submitted reports in accordance with article 22 of the Convention [CEDAW/C/2004/I/3 & Add.1, 3 & 4]. By two decisions, CEDAW adopted statements on the occasion of the ten-year review and appraisal of the Beijing Declaration and Platform for Action, to be brought to the attention of the forty-ninth session of the Commission on the Status of Women [A/60/38 (dec. 32/I)]; and on the gender aspects of the 2004 Indian Ocean tsunami disaster [YUN 2004, p. 952] [ibid. (dec. 32/II)].

In other actions, the Committee, in respect of issues arising from article 2 of the Optional Protocol, adopted views under article 7, paragraph 3, of the Optional Protocol (annexed to the report) and continued its work under article 8 of the Optional Protocol. In a summary of the Committee's activities concerning the inquiry into allegations of abduction, rape and murder of women in the Ciudad Juárez area of Chihuahua, Mexico, the Committee reiterated its 2004 decision [YUN 2004, p. 1170] to issue at a future date the substantive findings and recommendations emanating from its inquiry, which the Committee issued, together with the Mexican Government's observations, on 27 January [CEDAW/C/2005/OP8/Mexico]. The Committee requested the Government of Mexico to submit additional information on the follow-up to the Committee's recommendations, by 1 May. It invited the three NGOs that had submitted the information that led to the Committee's decision to conduct an inquiry and provide their views in a report to the Committee, also by that date, particularly their evaluation of the Government's actions in response to the Committee's findings and recommendations. It decided to consider Mexico's follow-up response, together with any information received from NGOs at its thirty-third session.

At its thirty-third session (5-22 July), CEDAW reviewed the initial or periodic reports of Benin, Burkina Faso, the Gambia, Guyana, Ireland, Israel, the Democratic People's Republic of Korea and Lebanon. It also considered reports on implementation of article 21 of the Convention [CEDAW/C/ 2005/II/3 and Add.1, 3 & 4] and on ways of expediting the Committee's work [CEDAW/C/2005/ II/2, CEDAW/C/2005/II/4]. The Committee requested the General Assembly: to authorize it to hold three annual sessions of three weeks each, with a one-week, pre-sessional working group for each session, effective January 2006; to meet on a temporary basis in 2006 and 2007, for part of its three annual sessions, in parallel working groups, to consider reports of States parties submitted under article 18 of the Convention; and to meet for up to seven days in parallel working groups during its third (2006), first and third (2007) annual sessions. The Committee intended to evaluate its experience, as well as the need for parallel working groups in July and August 2007. It further requested the Assembly to continue to authorize two annual sessions of the Working Group on Communications under the Optional Protocol to the Convention [A/60/38 (dec. 33/I)]. The Committee also adopted a statement on the situation of women in Iraq [ibid. (dec. 33/II)].

In other action, the Committee, in respect of issues arising from article 2 of the Optional Protocol, took note of the reports of the Working Group on Communications under the Optional Protocol on its fifth and sixth sessions (annexed to the report), and continued its work under article 8 of the Optional Protocol. Acting under article 9, paragraph 2 of the Optional Protocol, the Committee considered information received

from Mexico on measures taken in response to its recommendations concerning killing and abduction of women in the Ciudad Juárez area of Mexico, as well as from the three NGOs that had submitted the information that led the Committee to conduct an inquiry (see above). The Committee invited the Government of Mexico to include in its sixth periodic report, to be submitted by November 2005, details of any further measures taken in response to the Committee's findings, comments and recommendations.

In July, the Economic and Social Council took note of the report of CEDAW on the work of its thirty-second and thirty-third sessions by **decision 2005/296**.

GENERAL ASSEMBLY ACTION

On 23 December [meeting 69], the General Assembly, on the recommendation of the Third Committee [A/60/503], adopted **resolution 60/230** by recorded vote (127-1-0) [agenda item 64].

Convention on the Elimination of All Forms of Discrimination against Women

The General Assembly,

Recalling its resolution 58/145 of 22 December 2003 and its previous resolutions on the elimination of discrimination against women,

Bearing in mind that one of the purposes of the United Nations, as stated in Articles 1 and 55 of the Charter, is to promote universal respect for human rights and fundamental freedoms for all without distinction of any kind, including distinction as to sex,

Reiterating the need to intensify efforts to eliminate all forms of discrimination against women throughout the world,

Affirming that women and men should participate equally in social, economic and political development, should contribute equally to such development and should share equally in improved conditions of life,

Recalling the Vienna Declaration and Programme of Action adopted by the World Conference on Human Rights on 25 June 1993, in which the Conference reaffirmed that the human rights of women and the girl child were an inalienable, integral and indivisible part of universal human rights,

Acknowledging the need for a comprehensive and integrated approach to the promotion and protection of the human rights of women, which includes the integration of the human rights of women into the mainstream of United Nations activities system-wide,

Reaffirming the commitments made in the political declaration and the outcome document of the twenty-third special session of the General Assembly entitled "Women 2000: gender equality, development and peace for the twenty-first century", in particular paragraphs 68 *(c)* and *(d)* concerning the Convention on the Elimination of All Forms of Discrimination against Women and the Optional Protocol thereto,

Welcoming the declaration of the Commission on the Status of Women on the occasion of the tenth anniversary of the Fourth World Conference on Women, in which the Commission recognizes that the implementation of the Beijing Declaration and Platform for Action and the fulfilment of the obligations under the Convention are mutually reinforcing in achieving gender equality and the empowerment of women,

Recalling that, in the United Nations Millennium Declaration, Heads of State and Government resolved to implement the Convention,

Recognizing that the equal enjoyment by women of all human rights and fundamental freedoms will promote the realization of the rights of the child, bearing in mind the special needs of girls, and acknowledging the mutual reinforcement of the implementation of the Convention on the Elimination of All Forms of Discrimination against Women and the Convention on the Rights of the Child and the Optional Protocols thereto,

Noting that 18 December 2004 marked the twenty-fifth anniversary of the adoption by the General Assembly of the Convention on the Elimination of All Forms of Discrimination against Women, and welcoming the statement of the Committee on the Elimination of Discrimination against Women to commemorate the occasion,

Bearing in mind the recommendation of the Committee that national reports should contain information on the implementation of the Beijing Platform for Action, in accordance with paragraph 323 of the Platform,

Having considered the reports of the Committee on its thirtieth and thirty-first and thirty-second and thirty-third sessions,

Expressing concern at the great number of reports that are overdue (one hundred and eighty-seven), in particular initial reports, which constitutes an obstacle to the full implementation of the Convention,

1. *Welcomes* the report of the Secretary-General on the status of the Convention on the Elimination of All Forms of Discrimination against Women;

2. *Also welcomes* the growing number of States parties to the Convention, which now stands at one hundred and eighty, while expressing disappointment that universal ratification of the Convention was not achieved by 2000, and urges all States that have not yet ratified or acceded to the Convention to do so;

3. *Further welcomes* the rapidly growing number of States parties to the Optional Protocol to the Convention, which now stands at seventy-four, and urges other States parties to the Convention to consider signing and ratifying or acceding to the Optional Protocol;

4. *Urges* States parties to comply fully with their obligations under the Convention and the Optional Protocol thereto and to take into consideration the concluding comments as well as the general recommendations of the Committee on the Elimination of Discrimination against Women;

5. *Encourages* all relevant entities of the United Nations system, within their mandates, as well as Governments and intergovernmental and non-governmental organizations, in particular women's organizations, as appropriate, to strengthen assistance to States parties, upon their request, in implementing the Convention;

6. *Notes* that some States parties have modified their reservations, expresses satisfaction that some reservations have been withdrawn, and urges States parties to limit the extent of any reservations that they lodge to the Convention, to formulate any such reser-

vations as precisely and as narrowly as possible, to ensure that no reservations are incompatible with the object and purpose of the Convention, to review their reservations regularly with a view to withdrawing them and to withdraw reservations that are contrary to the object and purpose of the Convention;

7. *Welcomes* the adoption by the Committee of revised reporting guidelines, and urges States parties to adhere to the revised guidelines, in particular with regard to the content and length of reports;

8. *Recalls* the great number of overdue reports, in particular initial reports, and urges States parties to the Convention to make every possible effort to submit their reports on the implementation of the Convention in a timely manner, in accordance with article 18 thereof;

9. *Also recalls* its resolution 50/202 of 22 December 1995, in which it took note with approval of the amendment to article 20, paragraph 1, of the Convention, which has yet to enter into force;

10. *Strongly urges* States parties to the Convention to take appropriate measures so that acceptance of the amendment to article 20, paragraph 1, of the Convention by a two-thirds majority of States parties can be reached as soon as possible and the amendment can enter into force;

11. *Expresses its appreciation* for the efforts made by the Committee to improve the efficiency of its working methods, in particular the measures introduced following the informal meeting held in Utrecht, the Netherlands, from 5 to 7 May 2004, and encourages the Committee to enhance its activities in this regard, bearing in mind the need to increase the effectiveness of the work of the Committee;

12. *Notes* decision 33/I of the Committee, in which it requests an extension of its meeting time;

13. *Also notes* that in the three years since the holding of the exceptional session, in August 2002, a new backlog of reports of States parties has accumulated;

14. *Decides* to authorize the Committee to hold three annual sessions of three weeks each, with a one-week pre-sessional working group for each session, effective from January 2006 as a temporary measure, and to continue to authorize two annual sessions of the Working Group on Communications under the Optional Protocol to the Convention;

15. *Also decides* to authorize the Committee to meet on an exceptional and temporary basis in 2006 and 2007 for up to seven days in parallel working groups during its third (July/August) annual session in 2006 and its first (January) and third (July/August) annual sessions in 2007, taking due account of equitable geographical distribution, for the purpose of considering reports of States parties submitted under article 18 of the Convention;

16. *Urges* the Committee to evaluate progress, and decides to assess the situation with regard to the Committee's meeting time after two years, also taking into account the wider context of treaty body reform;

17. *Encourages* the Secretariat to extend further technical assistance to States parties, upon their request, to strengthen their capacity in the preparation of reports, in particular initial reports, and invites Governments to contribute to those efforts;

18. *Invites* States parties to make use of the technical assistance provided by the Secretariat to facilitate the preparation of reports, in particular initial reports;

19. *Encourages* the continued participation of members of the Committee in inter-committee meetings and meetings of persons chairing the human rights treaty bodies, including those on methods of work relating to the State reporting system;

20. *Encourages* the Committee, within its mandate, to continue to contribute to the efforts to strengthen cooperation and coordination between the treaty bodies;

21. *Requests* the Secretary-General, in accordance with General Assembly resolution 54/4 of 6 October 1999, to provide the resources, including staff and facilities, necessary for the effective functioning of the Committee within its full mandate, taking into account in particular the entry into force of the Optional Protocol to the Convention;

22. *Urges* Governments, organizations and bodies of the United Nations system and intergovernmental and non-governmental organizations to disseminate the Convention and the Optional Protocol thereto;

23. *Encourages* States parties to disseminate the concluding comments adopted in relation to the consideration of their reports, as well as the general recommendations of the Committee;

24. *Encourages* all relevant entities of the United Nations system to continue to build women's knowledge and understanding of and capacity to utilize human rights instruments, in particular the Convention and the Optional Protocol thereto;

25. *Urges* the specialized agencies, at the invitation of the Committee, to submit reports on the implementation of the Convention in areas falling within the scope of their activities;

26. *Welcomes* the contribution of non-governmental organizations to the work of the Committee;

27. *Invites* the Chairperson of the Committee on the Elimination of Discrimination against Women to address the General Assembly at its sixty-first and sixty-second sessions under the item on the advancement of women;

28. *Requests* the Secretary-General to submit to the General Assembly at its sixty-second session a report on the status of the Convention on the Elimination of All Forms of Discrimination against Women and the implementation of the present resolution.

RECORDED VOTE ON RESOLUTION 60/230:

In favour: Algeria, Andorra, Antigua and Barbuda, Argentina, Armenia, Australia, Austria, Azerbaijan, Bahrain, Bangladesh, Barbados, Belarus, Belgium, Benin, Brazil, Brunei Darussalam, Bulgaria, Burkina Faso, Canada, Chile, China, Colombia, Comoros, Costa Rica, Croatia, Cuba, Cyprus, Czech Republic, Denmark, Djibouti, Dominican Republic, Ecuador, Egypt, El Salvador, Eritrea, Estonia, Finland, France, Gambia, Georgia, Germany, Ghana, Greece, Guatemala, Guinea, Guyana, Hungary, Iceland, India, Indonesia, Iraq, Ireland, Italy, Jamaica, Japan, Jordan, Kazakhstan, Kuwait, Kyrgyzstan, Lao People's Democratic Republic, Latvia, Lesotho, Libyan Arab Jamahiriya, Liechtenstein, Lithuania, Luxembourg, Malawi, Malaysia, Maldives, Mali, Malta, Mauritania, Mauritius, Mexico, Monaco, Morocco, Myanmar, Namibia, Nepal, Netherlands, New Zealand, Niger, Nigeria, Norway, Oman, Pakistan, Panama, Peru, Poland, Portugal, Qatar, Republic of Korea, Romania, Russian Federation, Rwanda, Samoa, San Marino, Saudi Arabia, Serbia and Montenegro, Singapore, Slovakia, Slovenia, South Africa, Spain, Sri Lanka, Sudan, Sweden, Switzerland, Syrian Arab Republic, Thailand, The former Yugoslav Republic of Macedonia, Timor-Leste, Togo, Trinidad and Tobago, Tunisia, Turkey, Uganda, Ukraine, United Arab Emirates, United Kingdom, United Republic of Tanzania, Uruguay, Uzbekistan, Venezuela, Yemen, Zambia, Zimbabwe.

Against: United States.

Abstaining: None.

Commission on the Status of Women

The Commission on the Status of Women, at its forty-ninth session (New York, 28 February–1 and 12 March) [E/2005/27], recommended two draft resolutions to the Economic and Social Council for adoption on the situation of women and girls in Afghanistan (see p. 1260); and the situation of and assistance to Palestinian women (see p. 1262). It also recommended a draft decision for Council adoption on its report of the forty-ninth (2005) session and the provisional agenda for the fiftieth (2006) session (see below). The Commission also adopted and brought to the attention of the Council a declaration on the occasion of the tenth-anniversary of the Fourth World Conference on Women and resolutions on women, the girl child and HIV/AIDS (see p. 1256); eliminating demand for trafficked women and girls (see p. 1259); appointing a special rapporteur on laws that discriminated against women (see p. 1259); mainstreaming a gender perspective into all national policies and programmes (see p. 1270); integrating a gender perspective in post-disaster relief, recovery, rehabilitation and reconstructive efforts (see p. 1268); strengthening of the International Research and Training Institute for the Advancement of Women (INSTRAW) (see p. 1278); indigenous women (see p. 1268); and the economic advancement of women (see p. 1268). The Commission further adopted three decisions, which were brought to the Council's attention: one regarding the proposed 2006-2007 work programme of the Office of the Special Adviser on Gender Issues and Advancement of Women and the Division for the Advancement of Women 2006-2007 [dec. 49/102]; one to continue discussion of the Commission's working methods at its fiftieth (2006) session [dec. 49/101]; and one taking note of documents before it [dec. 49/103], among them the UNIFEM report on the elimination of violence against women [E/CN.6/2005/7-E/CN.4/2005/70] and the joint workplan of the Division for the Advancement of Women and OHCHR [E/CN.4/2005/69-E/CN.6/2005/6].

By **decision 2005/299** of 26 July, the Council took note of the Commission's report on its forty-ninth session and approved the provisional agenda for its fiftieth (2006) session.

Communications on the status of women

Working Group. At two meetings, one in February and a second in March [E/2005/27], the Commission considered the report [E/CN.6/2005/CRP.5] of the Working Group, which considered 18 confidential communications received directly by the Division for the Advancement of

Women (including one communication with allegations of 40 separate instances of discriminatory legislation) and three confidential communications received by the Office of the United Nations High Commissioner for Human Rights (OHCHR). No non-confidential communications were received. The Group noted that one communication that had been selected from the 1503 procedure material covered the same case as a communication that had been submitted directly to the Division. The Working Group also noted that Governments had replied to five of the 18 communications received and to all three of those transmitted by OHCHR. Replies were received alleging discriminatory legislation in 40 separate States. Communications were most frequently submitted on sexual violence against women; abduction and rape of young women by private individuals and the failure to provide protection and assistance to victims or investigate such cases; other forms of violence against women, including honour crimes, dowry-related violence and forced marriage and marital rape; threatening or pressuring victims of violence to retract complaints, and arbitrary prosecution and punishment of victims; torture and other cruel, inhuman or degrading treatment and violations of the rights to freedom of expression, association and movement, as well as the right to participate in political and public life; abuse of power, lack of due process, arbitrary detention and failure to grant a fair trial and inhumane treatment in detention; differential application of punishments in law based on sex without the right to appeal; and violations of human rights of women belonging to minorities. The Working Group was concerned about the climate of impunity in many cases where violence against women was perpetrated by security forces and police and the lack of commitment by some States to tackle impunity; their failure to exercise due diligence to prevent violence against women and adequately investigate crimes and punish perpetrators; the large number of cases where women victims and/or their family members who made complaints were pressured into retracting their statements or where victims were arbitrarily punished or detained instead of receiving redress for crimes committed against them; and the existence of legislation or practices intended to or with the effect of discriminating against women, despite the international obligations and commitment of States and their constitutional provisions to outlaw such discrimination. From the replies received, the Working Group noted that a number of Governments had already taken or were taking measures to repeal discriminatory laws.

UN Development Fund for Women (UNIFEM)

In June, the Executive Board of the United Nations Development Programme and of the United Nations Population Fund (UNDP/UNFPA), by decision [E/2005/35 (dec. 2005/22)], took note of the midterm report on the UNIFEM multi-year funding framework (MYFF), 2004-2007 [DP/2005/24] and encouraged UNIFEM to continue to track the progress of its MYFF according to the goals, outcomes and indicators in its results frameworks. It also encouraged countries to assist UNIFEM in reaching the targeted level of regular resources, including through multi-year pledges. In September [ibid. (dec. 2005/34)], the Board took note of the June report of the UNDP Administrator on the 2006-2007 budget estimates for UNIFEM [DP/2005/31] and approved a gross appropriation in the amount of $16,374,400 for UNIFEM.

Independent assessment. In 2004, the UNIFEM Consultative Committee submitted the report [A/60/62-E/2005/10] on an independent assessment of UNIFEM it had commissioned in 2004 [YUN 2004, p. 1172] entitled "Organizational Assessment: UNIFEM Past, Present and Future". The report examined a number of challenges facing UNIFEM, including the ambiguity in its autonomy, authority, status, resources and key constituencies. It made proposals for a stronger UNIFEM by enabling it to follow the course taken by UNFPA.

ECONOMIC AND SOCIAL COUNCIL ACTION

On 27 July [meeting 40], the Economic and Social Council adopted **resolution 2005/54** [draft: E/2005/L.44] without vote [agenda item 14 (a)].

United Nations Development Fund for Women

The Economic and Social Council,

Recognizing that mainstreaming a gender perspective into all aspects of the work of the United Nations is an ongoing process and that further concrete steps are required, as a matter of urgency, to ensure full implementation of its agreed conclusions 1997/2 of 18 July 1997, and its resolution 2004/4 of 7 July 2004,

Recalling General Assembly resolution 39/125 of 14 December 1984, in which the Assembly set forth the arrangements for association between the United Nations Development Fund for Women and the United Nations Development Programme,

Recalling also General Assembly resolution 59/250 of 22 December 2004, in which the Assembly called upon the United Nations development system to avail itself of the technical experience of the United Nations Development Fund for Women on gender issues,

Invites the Executive Board of the United Nations Development Programme to consider the report on the organizational assessment of the United Nations Development Fund for Women, as appropriate, in 2006.

UNIFEM activities. In 2005 [A/61/292], UNIFEM continued to focus on the implementation of its 2004-2007 MYFF, which contained a strategic results framework that highlighted the four key UNIFEM goals: reducing feminized poverty and exclusion; ending violence against women; halting and reversing the spread of HIV/AIDS; and achieving gender equality in democratic governance and in post-conflict countries. Reports from the second year of implementation of MYFF 2004-2007 indicated that UNIFEM provided support for legislative and policy change to strengthen gender equality through initiatives in more than 30 countries; strengthened the capacity of national and local partners to institutionalize tools, such as sex-disaggregated data in 39 instances and gender-responsive budgets in 20 countries; expanded the capacity of regional networks of gender equality advocates, such as ministries of gender or women's affairs in some 55 instances; supported women as candidates or parliamentarians in 16 countries; increased the reach of media organizations and professionals that generated messages in support of gender equality in 23 countries; and contributed to the establishment of more than 30 institutional mechanisms to address gender-based violence.

A UNIFEM task team worked with a UNDP management consultant team to conduct functional analyses and identify priorities for alignment and harmonization measures. UNIFEM will prioritize the strengthening of its human and operational capacities in early 2006.

In 2005, UNIFEM total income reached a record high of $57.6 million. It exceeded its overall multi-year funding framework target of $43.4 million. Core contributions in 2005 stood at $22 million, against the $25.4 million anticipated in the framework. In 2005, a total of 42 bilateral donors contributed to UNIFEM core funds, compared to 43 in 2004.

By **decision 60/547** of 22 December, the General Assembly took note of the report [A/60/274] on UNIFEM's 2004 activities [YUN 2004, p. 1172], transmitted by the Secretary-General in August.

GENERAL ASSEMBLY ACTION

On 16 December [meeting 64], the General Assembly, on the recommendation of the Second Committee [A/60/503], adopted **resolution 60/137** without vote [agenda item 64].

United Nations Development Fund for Women

The General Assembly,

Recalling its resolution 39/125 of 14 December 1984, by which it established the United Nations Development Fund for Women as a separate and identifiable entity in autonomous association with the United Nations Development Programme, as well as its resolution 56/130 of 19 December 2001,

Reaffirming the Beijing Platform for Action adopted by the Fourth World Conference on Women, which recognizes the special role of the Fund in the promotion of the economic and political empowerment of women, and the outcome of the twenty-third special session of the General Assembly entitled "Women 2000: gender equality, development and peace for the twenty-first century",

Welcoming the declaration adopted by the Commission on the Status of Women at its forty-ninth session, which emphasizes that implementation of the Beijing Platform for Action is essential to achieving the Millennium Development Goals,

Welcoming also the commitment of Heads of State and Government gathered at the 2005 World Summit to promote gender equality and the empowerment of women, as set out in the 2005 World Summit Outcome,

Reaffirming the primary and essential role of the General Assembly and the Economic and Social Council, as well as the central role of the Commission on the Status of Women, in promoting the advancement of women and gender equality,

Reaffirming also all relevant resolutions of the General Assembly, the Economic and Social Council and the Commission on the Status of Women, as well as Security Council resolution 1325(2000) of 31 October 2000 on women and peace and security,

Recognizing the importance of the Convention on the Elimination of All Forms of Discrimination against Women, and noting that the number of States parties to the Convention is among the highest for human rights conventions,

Welcoming the contributions that the Fund has made in supporting initiatives of Member States, United Nations organizations and non-governmental organizations to formulate and implement activities that promote gender equality and the empowerment of women,

Recalling its resolution 59/250 of 22 December 2004 on the triennial comprehensive policy review of operational activities for development of the United Nations system, and stressing the need for all organizations of the United Nations development system to implement their global, regional and country-level activities in accordance with their mandates,

Recalling also Economic and Social Council agreed conclusions 1997/2 of 18 July 1997 and Council resolution 2004/4 of 7 July 2004 on mainstreaming the gender perspective into all policies and programmes in the United Nations system,

Recalling further Economic and Social Council resolution 2005/54 of 27 July 2005 entitled "United Nations Development Fund for Women",

Noting the importance of the work of the Consultative Committee on the United Nations Development Fund for Women in policy and programme directions, as stipulated in the annex to resolution 39/125,

1. *Welcomes* the note by the Secretary-General on the activities of the United Nations Development Fund for Women, containing a results-focused report on progress in implementing its multi-year funding framework 2004-2007;

2. *Commends* the focus by the Fund on strategic programmes in its four core areas of work, namely, reducing feminized poverty, ending violence against women, halting and reversing the spread of HIV/AIDS and achieving gender equality in democratic governance and in post-conflict countries, and on supporting innovative programming in the context of the Beijing Platform for Action and commitments made at the twenty-third special session of the General Assembly and at the forty-ninth session of the Commission on the Status of Women;

3. *Notes with appreciation* the increased synergy between the United Nations Development Fund for Women and other funds, programmes and organizations of the United Nations system, as well as the Office of the Special Adviser on Gender Issues and Advancement of Women, the Division for the Advancement of Women of the Department of Economic and Social Affairs of the Secretariat and the International Research and Training Institute for the Advancement of Women, and calls upon those entities to continue their collaborative efforts;

4. *Calls upon* all organizations of the United Nations system, within their mandates, to mainstream a gender perspective and to pursue gender equality in their country programmes, planning instruments and sector-wide programmes and to articulate specific country-level goals and targets in this field in accordance with national development strategies;

5. *Encourages* the Fund to continue to contribute to the harmonization and coordination processes of United Nations reform through, inter alia, strengthened partnerships with other funds, programmes and organizations of the United Nations system and through the promotion of development, including technical cooperation, women's human rights and a gender-equality perspective in the policies, guidelines and tools developed by the United Nations Development Group;

6. *Emphasizes* the importance of continuing grassroots work, and, in order to achieve better coordination with other United Nations bodies, encourages the participation of the Fund in relevant high-level interagency coordination mechanisms;

7. *Recognizes* the efforts of the Fund and other United Nations funds and programmes to strengthen the gender-equality and women's empowerment perspective in formulation, implementation and evaluation processes related to national development plans and programmes aimed at eradicating poverty, including poverty reduction strategies, the Millennium Development Goals and the United Nations development assistance frameworks where they exist, and urges the Fund to support these processes;

8. *Encourages* the Fund to support strengthened and coordinated action on gender equality at the country level, in collaboration with the resident coordinator system, including by advocating and building the capacity of gender theme groups within United Nations country teams;

9. *Urges* the United Nations development system to avail itself of the technical and coordination experience of the Fund on gender issues while undertaking efforts to implement gender mainstreaming internally;

10. *Encourages* Member States and United Nations organizations to explore with the Fund possible innovative representational arrangements, including through the use of seconded staff, project offices and other means;

11. *Notes* the activities undertaken by the Fund in follow-up to resolution 56/130, including activities relating to the impact of armed conflict on women and the role of women in peacebuilding, and the support it provides for the participation of women in peace processes, and urges the Fund to increase its efforts and enhance its capacity to support a coordinated approach of the United Nations system to strengthen gender justice in peacebuilding and post-conflict recovery and reconstruction, including cooperation, as appropriate, with the Department of Political Affairs and the Department of Peacekeeping Operations of the Secretariat as well as Member States, regional organizations and other United Nations partners;

12. *Emphasizes* the importance of the Trust Fund in Support of Actions to Eliminate Violence against Women, established by General Assembly resolution 50/166 of 22 December 1995, as a critical response to the deep concern expressed at the fifty-ninth session of the Assembly regarding the persistence of violence and crimes against women in all parts of the world, and urges all Governments, non-governmental organizations and the public and private sectors to consider contributing or increasing contributions to the Trust Fund;

13. *Encourages* the Fund to continue to support the gender-equality and women's empowerment goals and targets of the Declaration of Commitment on HIV/AIDS adopted by the General Assembly at its twenty-sixth special session, by working closely with women who are affected by or infected with HIV/AIDS to develop their capacity to influence programmes and policies, building on its partnerships within the United Nations system, in particular with the Joint United Nations Programme on HIV/AIDS;

14. *Also encourages* the Fund to respond to country requests for the development or strengthening of accountability mechanisms for gender equality, including by building the capacity of Governments to undertake gender-responsive budget analysis and to use sex-disaggregated data as a basis for gender-responsive public policy formulation;

15. *Welcomes* the role of the Fund in promoting the strategic importance of the empowerment of women in all of the regions in which it operates, and notes with appreciation the enhanced programme activities of the Fund in the African region;

16. *Encourages* the Fund to strengthen cooperation with Member States and with United Nations programmes, funds and relevant agencies, as well as non-governmental organizations, and to provide assistance in order to implement the commitments on gender equality contained in the 2005 World Summit Outcome;

17. *Also encourages* the Fund to continue to assist Governments in implementing the Convention on the Elimination of All Forms of Discrimination against Women, in order to advance gender equality at all levels, including by reinforcing the cooperation between Governments and civil society, especially women's organizations, and by supporting efforts to follow up, as

appropriate, the concluding comments of the Committee on the Elimination of Discrimination against Women;

18. *Recognizes with appreciation* the increases in core contributions and, particularly, non-core contributions to the Fund made by Member States, private organizations and foundations, whose increased contributions demonstrate their commitment to the issues on which the Fund is working;

19. *Invites,* accordingly, Member States, non-governmental organizations and members of private organizations and foundations that have contributed to the Fund to continue to contribute and to consider increasing their financial contributions, and urges others that have not yet done so to consider contributing to the Fund to enable it to reach the targets for core resources in its multi-year funding framework.

INSTRAW

The report of the Executive Board of the United Nations International Research and Training Institute for the Advancement of Women (INSTRAW) (second session, New York, 1 June) [E/2005/75] provided a review of the implementation of the programme of work during the period October 2004–May 2005; the presentation of the proposed workplan, operational budget for 2006; and consideration of matters relating to fund-raising activities. The Board approved the proposed workplan, endorsed the operational budget for 2006 and agreed to consider recommendations for submission to the General Assembly regarding financial support for the Institute. It also agreed on the importance of seeking medium-term sustainable financial resources for the Institute and requested the Executive Director, in consultation with the UN Secretariat and the Board's President, to prepare a detailed report, including actions the Board could take and proposals for achieving the medium- and long-term sustainability of the Institute, and to consider recommendations to be submitted to the Assembly in 2006.

In July, by **decision 2005/296**, the Economic and Social Council took note of the report of the INSTRAW Executive Board.

Commission on the Status of Women. In a March resolution [E/2005/27 (res. 49/6)] on the revitalization and strengthening of INSTRAW, the Commission on the Status of Women welcomed INSTRAW's contributions to the ten-year review and appraisal of the Beijing Declaration and Platform for Action and the outcome of the twenty-third session. It invited voluntary contributions by Member States to the UN Trust Fund for INSTRAW. The Commission requested the Executive Director of the Institute to report to the Commission at its fiftieth (2006) session on the implementation of its work programme and

strategic plan 2004-2007, in particular as it related to the follow-up to the Fourth World Conference.

OIOS report. In August [A/60/281], the Office of Internal Oversight Services (OIOS) transmitted a report on the follow-up audit it conducted in December 2004 to determine the implementation status of recommendations contained in a previous OIOS report on the audit of INSTRAW [YUN 2002, p. 1165], which addressed issues concerning the sustainability and effectiveness of the Institute. The follow-up audit revealed that, although the establishment of an executive board had resulted in some improvements in the INSTRAW governance structure, further strengthening of programmatic and administrative oversight was needed. Concerns included inadequate documentation and the need for updated materials on the implementation of INSTRAW's work programme; the need to implement a training strategy and to improve website management; and non-performance on the OIOS recommendation to abolish the Institute's autonomous status, which had not been reflected in the revised INSTRAW statute in Economic and Social Council resolution 2003/57 [YUN 2003, p. 1195]. OIOS recommended that the Secretary-General should initiate consideration by intergovernmental bodies on ways to strengthen the Inter-Agency Network on Women and Gender Equality, and in that regard, suggested that delegation of formal authority for programme coordination beyond facilitation and information-sharing be given to the Secretary-General's Special Adviser on Gender Issues and Advancement of Women, as Chair of the Network. It also recommended a series of improvements in the strategic, programmatic and administrative management of INSTRAW.

By **decision 60/529** of 16 December, the General Assembly took note of the OIOS report.

Future of INSTRAW

Report of Secretary-General. In response to General Assembly resolution 59/260 [YUN 2004, p. 1173], the Secretary-General submitted a September report [A/60/372] on the future operation of INSTRAW. In efforts to further the revitalization process, INSTRAW undertook initiatives to implement its work programme, including developing a research framework for gender analysis on remittances and methodologies for conducting country case studies, expanding its collection of gender-training materials, strengthening its partnerships with other UN system entities and intensifying implementation of its fund-raising campaign. The implementation of INSTRAW strategic framework 2004-2007 and its 2005 work programme were making a contribution to programmes that benefited women in developing countries. Its two-pronged strategy to strengthen research and training capacities and to develop a comprehensive project portfolio for extrabudgetary funding provided the flexibility and increased efficiency of fund-raising efforts. The Secretary-General observed that, while the Institute had experienced increasing financial support, full implementation of the Institute's programmes and its ability to sustain its activities in 2006 would be contingent on Governments providing the required level of resources.

GENERAL ASSEMBLY ACTION

On 23 December [meeting 69], the General Assembly, on the recommendation of the Third Committee [A/60/503], adopted **resolution 60/229** by recorded vote (95-10-25) [agenda item 98].

Future operation of the International Research and Training Institute for the Advancement of Women

The General Assembly,

Recalling all of its previous resolutions on the situation of the International Research and Training Institute for the Advancement of Women, in particular resolutions 55/219 of 23 December 2000, 56/125 of 19 December 2001, 57/175 of 18 December 2002, 58/244 of 23 December 2003 and 59/260 of 23 December 2004,

Reaffirming its resolution 57/311 of 18 June 2003 on the financial situation of the Institute,

Welcoming the contributions of the Institute to the implementation of the Beijing Declaration and Platform for Action and the outcome document of the twenty-third special session of the General Assembly,

Taking note with appreciation of the progress report on the Institute by its Director with respect to the implementation of the programme of work for the period from October 2004 to May 2005, which measures progress through the utilization of indicators of achievement as established in the workplan for 2005,

Taking note of the letter dated 7 November 2005 from the Permanent Representative of Spain to the United Nations, in his capacity as President of the Executive Board of the International Research and Training Institute for the Advancement of Women, addressed to the President of the General Assembly,

Welcoming the approval by the Executive Board of the Institute of the proposed workplan for 2006 and its endorsement of the operational budget for 2006,

Recognizing the contributions of the Institute in promoting gender equality and the empowerment of women in the areas of security, international migration, in particular remittances and development, and governance and political participation,

Bearing in mind the importance of the medium- and long-term stability of the Institute, in order to strengthen the initiatives to be developed in the context of the fund-raising strategy and the consolidation of the revitalization of the Institute,

Reaffirming the importance of seeking medium-term sustainable financial resources for the Institute,

Welcoming the decision of the Executive Board to actively promote a fund-raising strategy for the Institute,

Bearing in mind the recommendation made by the Executive Board at its second session, held on 1 June 2005, that the report of the Director of the Institute, the proposed operational budget for 2006 and other relevant documents should be submitted to the General Assembly,

Recognizing that the implementation of the programme of work and strategic plan for the Institute will contribute to a comprehensive discussion on international migration and development from a gender perspective,

1. *Welcomes* the report of the Secretary-General;

2. *Requests* the International Research and Training Institute for the Advancement of Women, in accordance with its mandate, to coordinate further its activities and to develop its programme of work in collaboration with other relevant United Nations entities, such as the United Nations Development Fund for Women, the Office of the Special Adviser on Gender Issues and Advancement of Women, the Division for the Advancement of Women of the Department of Economic and Social Affairs of the Secretariat and the Committee on the Elimination of Discrimination against Women, and calls upon those entities to continue their collaborative efforts;

3. *Also requests* the Institute, in accordance with its mandate, to collaborate with the United Nations system, national machinery, non-governmental organizations and the private sector in promoting international cooperation to foster women's empowerment and gender equality, including through, inter alia, the promotion of better access to education for women and girls, and the mainstreaming of a gender perspective in all policies and programmes;

4. *Further requests* the Institute, in accordance with its mandate and in close coordination with the United Nations Population Fund, the United Nations Children's Fund and other relevant United Nations programmes and funds, to actively participate in and contribute to discussions on issues related to international migration and development, in particular in the preparations for and during the high-level dialogue thereon to be held in September 2006, during the sixty-first session of the General Assembly;

5. *Requests* the Institute, in accordance with its mandate and in close coordination with the United Nations Population Fund, the United Nations Children's Fund and the other relevant United Nations programmes and funds, to actively participate in and contribute to the examination of the special theme for the thirty-ninth session of the Commission on Population and Development in 2006, "International migration and development";

6. *Encourages* the Institute to continue, in close cooperation with other relevant United Nations bodies, to promote and undertake research and training programmes on gender mainstreaming, in the context of the Beijing Declaration and Platform for Action, as well as the commitments made at the twenty-third special session of the General Assembly;

7. *Requests* the Institute, within its mandate, to continue to assist countries in promoting and supporting

the political participation and economic and social advancement of women through training programmes;

8. *Stresses* the critical importance of voluntary financial contributions by Member States to the United Nations Trust Fund for the International Research and Training Institute for the Advancement of Women to enable it to carry out its mandate;

9. *Invites* Member States to make voluntary contributions to the Trust Fund, particularly during this critical transitional period;

10. *Decides* to provide its full support to the current efforts to revitalize the Institute and, in this regard, to provide it with the requisite funds to enable it to carry out its core functions for the biennium 2006-2007;

11. *Requests* the Secretary-General to report to the General Assembly at its sixty-second session on the implementation of the present resolution.

RECORDED VOTE ON RESOLUTION 60/229:

In favour: Algeria, Andorra, Antigua and Barbuda, Argentina, Armenia, Azerbaijan, Bahrain, Bangladesh, Barbados, Belarus, Benin, Brazil, Brunei Darussalam, Bulgaria, Burkina Faso, Chile, China, Colombia, Comoros, Costa Rica, Cuba, Cyprus, Djibouti, Dominican Republic, Ecuador, Egypt, El Salvador, Eritrea, Gambia, Ghana, Greece, Guatemala, Guinea, Guyana, India, Indonesia, Iran, Iraq, Jamaica, Jordan, Kazakhstan, Kuwait, Kyrgyzstan, Lao People's Democratic Republic, Lesotho, Libyan Arab Jamahiriya, Malawi, Malaysia, Maldives, Mali, Malta, Mauritania, Mauritius, Mexico, Morocco, Myanmar, Namibia, Nepal, Niger, Nigeria, Oman, Pakistan, Panama, Peru, Philippines, Portugal, Qatar, Rwanda, Samoa, San Marino, Saudi Arabia, Serbia and Montenegro, Singapore, Slovakia, South Africa, Spain, Sri Lanka, Sudan, Syrian Arab Republic, Thailand, The former Yugoslav Republic of Macedonia, Timor-Leste, Togo, Trinidad and Tobago, Tunisia, Turkey, Uganda, United Arab Emirates, United Republic of Tanzania, Uruguay, Uzbekistan, Venezuela, Yemen, Zambia, Zimbabwe.

Against: Australia, Canada, Denmark, Finland, Japan, Netherlands, New Zealand, Sweden, United Kingdom, United States.

Abstaining: Austria, Belgium, Croatia, Czech Republic, Estonia, France, Georgia, Germany, Hungary, Iceland, Ireland, Italy, Latvia, Liechtenstein, Lithuania, Luxembourg, Monaco, Norway, Poland, Republic of Korea, Romania, Russian Federation, Slovenia, Switzerland, Ukraine.

Financial situation

Report of Secretary-General. In a September report [A/60/366] on the financial situation of INSTRAW, the Secretary-General indicated that the available balance of the INSTRAW Trust Fund as at 1 January amounted to $959,675. For the period 1 January to 31 August 2005, $696,185 in additional income was received, comprising $691,295 in voluntary contributions and $4,890 in miscellaneous income. As the Fund balance as at 31 August was estimated at $896,368 and anticipated expenditures for September-December 2005 amounted to $424,208, it was determined that the Institute would have adequate resources

to function until the end of 2005, with a projected closing balance of $472,160. However, funds had been neither pledged nor received to finance operations in 2006. INSTRAW estimated the budget for 2006 core requirements at $1,314,352. The Secretary-General concluded that under the circumstances, the General Assembly would need to consider the future viability of the Institute.

Communication. On 15 November [A/C.3/60/11], Spain, on behalf of the INSTRAW Executive Board, informed the General Assembly that a Subcommittee had been established to analyse the proposed fund-raising strategy for INSTRAW [INSTRAW/EB/2005/R.6] and prepare recommendations for making the Institute financially stable. The Board called on the Assembly to provide sufficient financial assistance so that INSTRAW could carry out its activities until the suggestions in the strategy report had been examined and decided upon.

Statement of Secretary-General. In a November statement [A/C.5/60/16] on programme budget implications of draft resolution [A/C.3/60/L.15/Rev.1], the Secretary-General indicated that financial requirements for 2006 were estimated at $1,314,352. As it was anticipated that the balance available for allocation in the INSTRAW Trust Fund as at 1 January 2006 would amount to approximately $272,200, an additional amount of $1,042,200 might be required from the UN regular budget to maintain the Institute in 2006.

ACABQ report. In November [A/60/7/Add.20], the Advisory Committee on Administrative and Budgetary Questions, recommended that the Fifth (Administrative and Budgetary) Committee inform the Assembly that, should it adopt the draft resolution (above), additional requirements of up to $1,042,200 would arise under section 9, Economic and social affairs, of the 2006-2007 programme budget.

Fifth Committee consideration. The Fifth Committee, at its 23 December meeting [A/60/619], informed the Assembly accordingly and requested the Assembly to appropriate $1,042,200 against the contingency fund, to be used for the functioning of the Institute in 2006.

Chapter XI

Children, youth and ageing persons

In 2005, the United Nations Children's Fund (UNICEF) continued its efforts to ensure that every child received the best possible start in life; was fully immunized and protected from disease, including HIV/AIDS, and disability; had access to quality primary school education; and was protected from violence, abuse, exploitation and discrimination.

Further progress was made towards mainstreaming children's priorities into national policy. Of the 190 countries that had adopted "A world fit for children"—the outcome document of the General Assembly's 2002 special session on children—at least 172 had taken action on or planned to initiate policies to put the four major goals of the session into practice.

UNICEF's 2005 income was 40 per cent higher than in 2004, largely due to the significant increase in contributions, mostly from private sources, in response to the late 2004 Indian Ocean tsunami and the October 2005 earthquake in South Asia. UNICEF completed the final year of its medium-term strategic plan (MTSP) for 2002-2005 under its five organizational priorities. In September, the UNICEF Executive Board approved the MTSP for 2006-2009 with the same focus areas.

In observance of the tenth anniversary of its adoption of the World Programme of Action for Youth to the Year 2000 and Beyond, the Assembly, in October, devoted two plenary meetings to evaluating progress in implementing the 10 priority areas identified in the 1995 Programme of Action and the five new concerns recognized in 2003. The plenary meetings, at which many Member States were represented by youth delegates, culminated in the adoption of a resolution that called for strengthened efforts to implement the Programme of Action.

United Nations efforts to implement the 2002 Madrid International Plan of Action on Ageing continued during 2005. In December, the Assembly called on Governments and the UN system to ensure that the challenges of population ageing and the concerns of older persons were adequately incorporated into their programmes and projects.

Children

Follow-up to the 2002 General Assembly special session on children

In response to General Assembly resolution 59/261 [YUN 2004, p. 779], the Secretary-General submitted his third report [A/60/207] on the follow-up to the Assembly's twenty-seventh (2002) special session on children [YUN 2002, p. 1168]. The report provided an update on progress achieved in realizing the commitments set out in the session's final document, "A world fit for children", adopted in resolution S-27/2 [ibid., p. 1169]. That document, which consisted of a Declaration and a Plan of Action, committed Governments to a set of goals for children and young people, with a particular focus on health, education, protection from abuse, exploitation and violence, and combating HIV/AIDS.

Overall progress in 2005 in translating the commitments of "A world fit for children" into concrete actions was more encouraging than the previous year. By May, at least 172 countries had either taken or anticipated taking action to put the session's goals into operation; 41 countries had completed national plans of action for children, 45 national plans were under formulation and 14 countries planned doing so. In addition, many countries had chosen to incorporate the goals and commitments of the document into other national policy or planning instruments, such as poverty reduction strategies, national development plans and sector plans. In some cases, the follow-up process was slowed by external factors, including political instability, armed conflict and other crises. Nevertheless, some Governments faced with those problems had used the goals of "A world fit for children" and the Millennium Development Goals (MDGs) [YUN 2000, p. 51] to provide a unifying agenda in the process of social recovery. The report observed that regions had pursued the follow-up to the special session at different speeds and had shown varying preferences regarding the best way to proceed. Information on progress achieved was broken down by region and/or subregion. The report described the strengths and weaknesses in the special session follow-up process.

Noting that the Plan of Action of "A world fit for children" emphasized the importance of monitoring progress towards the adopted goals, the report stated that the broad international focus on the MDGs had led to the improvement of national monitoring systems. However, mechanisms in national plans of action for children were more variable, with some not including a central monitoring mechanism. Also, while many countries had well-established systems related to child health and education, data availability remained weak in the area of child protection.

UNICEF and other agencies were supporting a new round of Multiple Indicator Cluster Surveys (MICS) to provide the largest single source of data for reporting on progress towards the goals of "A world fit for children" and those of the MDGs. Comparable child-related data would also be produced by demographic and health surveys. Nearly 90 countries were engaged in household surveys during 2005 and 2006 to provide data for the commemorative plenary meeting devoted to the follow-up to the outcome of the special session for children that the Assembly had decided, in resolution 58/282 [YUN 2004, p. 1175], to hold in 2007. The surveys would also assist in closing some of the major information gaps, such as those related to child protection. Some 44 countries had adopted the *DevInfo* database system for compiling and presenting child-related data.

Following an analysis of progress in the four major areas of "A world fit for children", the Secretary-General concluded that most of the goals would only be achieved through a major intensification of action. While there were numerous, but often isolated, examples of rapid progress, many action plans had yet to be fully linked to national budgeting, implementation and monitoring mechanisms. Ongoing efforts needed to be expanded and better supported by resource allocations and at the political level.

The Secretary-General suggested that possible ways forward could include: the establishment of high-level national councils for children; capacity-building of national children's agencies and collaboration with parliamentarians and civil society organizations in the promotion of child-focused budgets; strengthening local government agencies to assist in the development, implementation and monitoring of child-centred programmes; and giving higher priority to developing structures and processes to facilitate ongoing involvement of civil society, including children and young people. The Secretary-General noted that regular reporting to the public on progress towards the goals was an important means of encouraging social mobilization and strengthening accountability. He also noted that, at the international level, the Committee on the Rights of the Child (see p. 731) had the potential to promote a closer linkage between follow-up on the special session goals, the MDGs and periodic reports by States parties on the Convention on the Rights of the Child. Use should be made of the Committee's concluding observations on State party reports to maintain government and public mobilization with respect to the goals for children. The Secretary-General observed that regional mechanisms could be further used to facilitate the intercountry exchange of experience and good practice in child-related programmes.

With regard to the commemorative plenary meeting to be held in 2007, the Secretary-General noted that all countries would be requested to hold a participatory review with stakeholders and provide a progress report before the end of 2006.

General Assembly action. The Assembly, in **resolution 60/231** on the rights of the child (see p. 855), taking note with appreciation of the Secretary-General's report (above), and called for action on a number of aspects of child welfare. In **resolution 60/1** on the World Summit Outcome (see. p. 48), the Assembly made commitments to protect children in situations of armed conflict and to respect and ensure the rights of each child without discrimination of any kind. The Assembly, in **resolution 60/3** (see p. 746), encouraged activities to promote the International Decade for a Culture of Peace and Non-Violence for the Children of the World 2001-2010 and, in **resolution 60/141** (see p. 1257), called for full respect for the human rights of the girl child.

United Nations Children's Fund

Throughout 2005, UNICEF continued its commitment to achieving the MDGs [YUN 2000, p. 51] and the goals contained in the outcome document, "A world fit for children", adopted in resolution S-27/2 [YUN 2002, p. 1169] by the General Assembly at its twenty-seventh (2002) special session on children [ibid., p. 1168] (see above). UNICEF's work was also guided by the 1989 Convention on the Rights of the Child, adopted by the Assembly in resolution 44/25 [YUN 1989, p. 560], and its Optional Protocols (see p. 730). Its mission was to defend children's rights, help meet their basic needs, ensure their survival and increase their opportunities to flourish. It was also mandated to rally political will and resources to invest in children's well-being; respond to emergencies to protect children and work with partners to provide a rapid response for those in need; and ensure special protection for the most disadvantaged children, such as victims of war, disasters, extreme poverty and all forms of violence and exploitation and those with disabilities. The Fund further aimed to promote equal rights for boys and girls and encourage their full participation in developing their communities; and work towards the human development goals adopted by the world community and the realization of the vision of peace, justice and social progress enshrined in the United Nations Charter. In 2005, UNICEF continued to focus its efforts on its five organizational priorities: girls' education; integrated early childhood development; immunization "plus"; fighting HIV/AIDS; and improved protection of children from violence, exploitation, abuse and discrimination.

UNICEF's annual flagship publication, *The State of the World's Children 2005*, focused on how poverty, conflict and HIV/AIDS threatened the ideal of childhood as a time for children to grow and develop to their full potential. It observed that the rights of over 1 billion children, as enshrined in the 1989 Convention on the Rights of the Child, were violated because they were denied one or more of the basic services required to survive and develop. It noted that millions of children were severely deprived of nutrition, water, sanitation facilities, access to basic health care services, shelter, education and information, while tens of millions were victims of exploitation, violence and abuse. In conflict situations, children who were not killed or injured could be abducted, orphaned or left with psychological and psychosocial distress, or suffering in conditions of inadequate shelter and from disease and poor nutrition. The HIV/AIDS pandemic had left some 15 million children under the age of 18 orphaned by the end of 2003, affecting their safety, health and development. The report stressed that children's rights would only be fulfilled when the world reaffirmed its moral and legal responsibilities to children; applied a human rights–based approach to social and economic development; adopted socially responsible policies that kept children specifically in mind; and invested additional funds in children, through increased official development assistance and improvements in national public finances.

UNICEF cooperated with 157 countries, areas and territories: 45 in sub-Saharan Africa; 35 in Latin America and the Caribbean; 35 in Asia; 20 in the Middle East and North Africa; and 22 in Central and Eastern Europe, the Commonwealth of Independent States (CIS) and the Baltic States.

Total expenditures, including write-offs, amounted to $2,197 million (compared to $1,606 million in 2004), of which 95.7 per cent ($2,103 million) was for programme assistance and support; 4 per cent ($88 million) for management and administration; and 0.3 per cent ($7 million) for write-offs. UNICEF operations in 2005, including an update on the mid-term review of the medium-term strategic plan (MTSP), were described in the UNICEF Annual Report, covering the period 1 January to 31 December 2005; the annual report of the Executive Director [E/2006/6]; and the report of the Executive Director on results achieved for children in support of the Millennium Summit agenda [YUN 2000, p. 49] through UNICEF's 2002-2005 MTSP [E/ICEF/2006/11].

In 2005, the UNICEF Executive Board held its first regular session (17-20 and 24 January), its annual session (6-10 June) and its second session (28-30 September), all in New York [E/2005/34/Rev.1], during which it adopted 20 decisions.

At its first regular session, the Board paid tribute to Carol Bellamy, whose second term as UNICEF's Executive Director expired on 30 April. She was succeeded by Ann Veneman.

By **decision 2005/230** of 20 July, the Economic and Social Council took note of the Board's report on the work of its first, second and annual sessions of 2004 [E/2004/34/Rev.1]; the Board's report on the work of its 2005 sessions [E/2005/34/Rev.1]; and the annual report of the Executive Director covering the year 2004 [E/2005/6], which was transmitted in accordance with a January decision of the Board [E/2005/34/Rev.1 (dec. 2005/1)].

On 29 September, the Executive Board adopted the programme of work and dates for its 2006 sessions [dec. 2005/17].

Programme policies

In her annual report to the Economic and Social Council covering 2005 [E/2006/6], the Executive Director described UNICEF's contribution towards implementing the MDGs [YUN 2000, p. 51], the Secretary-General's reform programme and the provisions of the triennial comprehensive policy review, adopted by the General Assembly in resolution 59/250 [YUN 2004, p. 868]. She described UNICEF's working relationships with UN agencies, non-governmental organizations (NGOs) and donor and programme countries as they collaborated in order to achieve the MDGs; gave an update on the funding of operational activities for development of the UN system; provided information on UNICEF's support for national capacity-building in the context of the MDGs and "A world fit for children" targets [YUN 2002, p. 1173]; and outlined efforts to strengthen the role of resident coordinators. She noted that, by the end of 2006, all countries, except those in crisis, were expected to have introduced the common country programming process, which placed UN system assistance in the context of the MDGs and national plans to achieve them, and indicated that UNICEF remained involved in training and technical support for countries implementing the new processes. The Executive Director also addressed the use of common premises and services with other UN organizations; monitoring and evaluation; gender mainstreaming; collaboration with the World Bank; and the follow-up to the Assembly's special session on children (see p. 1281).

Medium-term strategic plan (2002-2005)

In her third annual report on the 2002-2005 MTSP [E/ICEF/2005/6], the Executive Director provided information on progress, partnerships, constraints and key results achieved in 2002-2004 in the five organizational priority areas of the MTSP (see p. 1283), on cross-cutting strategies and on UNICEF income and expenditures for 2004.

On 10 June [dec. 2005/8], the Executive Board requested the Executive Director to strengthen the analytical content of her annual reports to the Board to include both qualitative and quantitative measures of progress against the MTSP targets.

Medium-term strategic plan (2006-2009)

The UNICEF Executive Board had before it a July report [E/ICEF/2005/11] on the 2006-2009 MTSP, which identified five focus areas for the four-year period: young child survival and development; basic education and gender equality; HIV/AIDS and children; child protection from violence, exploitation and abuse; and policy advocacy and partnerships for children's rights. The MTSP described UNICEF's support to the implementation of the MDGs [YUN 2000, p. 51]; elaborated on the links between the MDGs and the focus areas; gave details regarding the strategies, key results and targets for each of the focus areas; referred to the plan's major cross-cutting strategies; and outlined the plan's resource implications, fund-raising strategy and financial targets.

On 30 September [E/2005/34/Rev.1 (dec. 2005/18)], the Executive Board welcomed the 2006-2009 MTSP and approved: the organizational focus areas; the financial plan, including $697 million in programme expenditures from regular resources, to be submitted in 2006; and the transfer to the funded reserve of $20 million per year for after-service health insurance for 2005 and 2006 and $10 million per year for 2007-2009. The Executive Director was asked to assess progress to-

wards the key results established in the MTSP in her annual report to the Board.

Evaluation system

In her report on the 2002-2005 MTSP [E/ICEF/2005/6], the Executive Director informed the Executive Board that the scope of the evaluation function had expanded in 2004 through reviews of organizational performance and testing of methodologies for country programme evaluations. Studies were completed on immunization "plus", the African Girls' Education Initiative and external support to basic education. Evaluations were also undertaken of UNICEF preparedness and initial response in Iraq and Liberia.

On 10 June [dec. 2005/8], the Board recalled its 2004 decision on evaluations [YUN 2004, p. 1180], which requested that key findings be presented and discussed at the Board's meetings and that they be fully integrated into the Executive Director's annual report.

Emergency assistance

During the 2002-2005 period [E/ICEF/2006/11], approximately one third of the countries with which UNICEF cooperated were responding to crises and emergencies. In 2005, emergency funding reached $1 billion, in large part for the response to the Indian Ocean tsunami of December 2004 (see p. 1024) and other emergencies.

As a result of UNICEF's contribution to the tsunami response, child deaths from preventable diseases were avoided, most students were able to return to school rapidly and early fears of trafficking and exploitation were allayed. The crisis demonstrated the vital role of the private sector in providing funds, supplies and technical assistance and the importance of investing in early warning and preparedness at national and local levels. The earthquake that struck Pakistan, India and Afghanistan in October 2005 (see p. 1034) killed more than 75,000 people, over half of them children. Pre-positioned stocks enabled UNICEF to provide large-scale assistance within 48 hours. By the end of 2005, there had been no major disease outbreaks in Pakistan and systems were put in place to monitor the health, nutrition and protection status of affected children. UNICEF supported the Indian Government in immunizing children against measles, providing vitamin A and oral rehydration salts, water storage and treatment supplies for about 50,000 people.

In 2005, the Caribbean was affected by 14 hurricanes, three of which were classified as Category 5. UNICEF provided early assistance with water and sanitation materials, emergency kits, advocacy for child protection and psychosocial support. The Fund also provided technical support and supplies to families affected by Hurricane Katrina in the United States. In the Sudan, UNICEF and its partners reached 2 million people, some 60 per cent of the affected population, with essential health-care services, and it provided 900,000 people with safe water supplies. The Fund led the nutrition response to the emergency in the Niger, where insufficient rainfall and locust invasions placed nearly 3.3 million people in a situation of acute food insecurity.

In 2005, the Inter-Agency Standing Committee for the coordination of humanitarian assistance agreed upon a "cluster lead" approach, with UNICEF assuming the lead role for nutrition, water and environmental sanitation and data communications. The Fund also assumed a leadership role in some aspects of child protection and an important implementing role in health. The cluster lead approach was being tested and its initial performance reviewed. The Core Commitments for Children in Emergencies (CCCs) guided UNICEF's humanitarian response. The Fund continued to play a key role in building the capacities of Governments to protect children against natural disasters.

UNICEF programmes by region

In 2005 [E/ICEF/2006/11], UNICEF regional programme expenditure totalled $1,966 million, of which $872 million (45 per cent) went to sub-Saharan Africa (including programme assistance for Djibouti and the Sudan); $687 million (35 per cent) to Asia; $181 million (9 per cent) to the Middle East and North Africa; $99 million (5 per cent) to the Americas and the Caribbean; $62 million (3 per cent) to Central and Eastern Europe and CIS; and $64 million (3 per cent) to inter-regional programmes. Programme support costs amounted to an additional $137 million.

Programme expenditures were highest in countries with low income and high, or very high, under-five mortality rates. The 60 lowest income countries—defined as those with a per capita gross national income of $765 or less—which had a total child population in 2003 of 1.02 billion, or constituting 52 per cent of all children worldwide, received 62 per cent of total programme expenditures.

In September, the Executive Board considered summaries of midterm reviews and major evaluations of country programmes in Eastern and Southern Africa [E/ICEF/2005/P/L.23], West and Central Africa [E/ICEF/2005/P/L.24], Americas and the Caribbean [E/ICEF/2005/P/L.25], East Asia and the Pacific [E/ICEF/2005/P/L.26], South Asia [E/ICEF/2005/P/L.27], and Central and Eastern Europe, CIS and the Baltic States [E/ICEF/2005/P/L.28]. The reports reviewed the results achieved, the lessons learned and the need for adjustments in the country programmes.

(For information regarding the UNICEF country programme approval process, see p. 1293.)

Field visits

On a visit to Ethiopia (17-22 April) [E/ICEF/2005/CRP.5], Executive Board members observed that the implementation of UNICEF's country programmes focused on six areas: health and nutrition; water, sanitation and hygiene education; HIV/AIDS; basic education, with special interventions for girls' education; gender and child protection; and capacity-building of regional and *woreda* (district) institutions in programme monitoring and evaluation. Addressing emergencies that jeopardized food security and providing humanitarian assistance had become a major component of UNICEF operations in Ethiopia. The Board concluded that there was a need for more comprehensive, objective-oriented and clear-cut programming regarding children who lived or worked on the street, child trafficking, female genital mutilation, HIV/AIDS orphans and other vulnerable children. There was also an urgent need to scale up the focus on maternal health, since more than 80 per cent of women lacked adequate access to health and reproductive services. The Board emphasized the need to strengthen collaboration between UNICEF and the entire UN country team, the regional government and NGOs to combat chronic water shortage; low health indicators; poor sanitation; high rates of school dropout, especially among girls; food insecurity; and gender inequality.

Members of the Executive Boards of the United Nations Development Programme (UNDP)/United Nations Population Fund (UNFPA), UNICEF and the World Food Programme (WFP) made a joint field visit to Azerbaijan (8-15 May) [E/ICEF/2005/CRP.6]. They concluded that the UN country team should continue its advocacy with the Government to protect vulnerable groups through policy change. A pressing requirement was to increase and rationalize resources for health, education and child protection.

In Morocco (18-25 June) [E/ICEF/2005/CRP.11], UNICEF Executive Board members noted that the country programme comprised: support to national policies in education and health; support to children in rural environments; child protection; and promoting and monitoring implementation of the 1989 Convention on the Rights of the Child [YUN 1989, p. 560] (see also p. 730). They concluded that UNICEF added value in Morocco, not only because of the organization's financial contribution, but, more importantly, because of its strategic and policy contribution, technical cooperation, advocacy efforts, work in child rights, research activities and the development of intervention models and innovative tools.

UNICEF programmes by sector

In 2005, UNICEF programme expenditures, which were linked to the five organizational priorities established in 2001 under the 2002-2005 MTSP [YUN 2001, p. 1093], totalled $1,966 million [E/ICEF/2006/11], a 46 per cent increase over 2004. The largest share of total expenditure, $746 million (38 per cent), was spent on early childhood development (ECD), followed by $432 million (22 per cent) on girls' education; $367 million (19 per cent) on immunization "plus"; $196 million (10 per cent) on child protection; and $165 million (8 per cent) on HIV/AIDS. Some $60 million (3 per cent) was expended in other areas. Programme support costs amounted to an additional $137 million.

The shares for the five priority areas of the MTSP as part of total expenditure for programme assistance mostly remained stable during the four-year period. However, total programme spending for all five priority areas increased rapidly between 2002 and 2005, with ECD experiencing the highest percentage growth, followed by girls' education, HIV/AIDS, child protection and immunization "plus".

Early childhood development

In response to the findings of the 2004 MTSP mid-term review [YUN 2004, p. 1179], UNICEF worked increasingly with national partners in 2004-2005 to emphasize the convergence of initiatives for young children and to facilitate the efforts of national partners working across the social sectors. The focus on developing the capacities of families and communities to improve young child survival, growth and development was also strengthened.

In the area of child mortality reduction, UNICEF continued to implement the Accelerated Child Survival and Development Strategy (ACSD) in 11 African countries. It was estimated that the Strategy, which covered 17 million people, was preventing over 18,000 child deaths per year. Major gains were seen in the use of insecticide-treated bednets (ITNs) and routine preventive health services (immunization, vitamin A supplementation and antenatal care). UNICEF programme assistance for the ACSD strategy in the 11 countries came to less than $0.50 per beneficiary per year and the approximate average cost in

ACSD districts was $407 per life saved. The low cost was attributed to a dramatic increase in vitamin A supplementation, measles immunization and ITN coverage in very poor areas with very high mortality rates. In July, the African Union requested UNICEF and other partners to extend the programme to the whole continent, and called for its member States to integrate it into their national health policies, poverty reduction strategies and health sector reforms.

Child mortality reduction efforts also included parenting programmes and the Integrated Management of Childhood Illnesses (IMCI) approach. An independent review in 2004 and 2005 in Malawi, South Africa, the United Republic of Tanzania and Uganda showed that the IMCI approach had led to improved knowledge and family care practices in all areas. UNICEF-assisted parenting education programmes combined interventions for child survival, development and protection.

UNICEF doubled its annual resources for fighting malaria during the MTSP period, accelerating the coverage of known effective malaria prevention and control interventions. In 2005, UNICEF procured 17 million ITNs; played a lead role in bringing Roll Back Malaria partners [YUN 1998, p. 1384] together in support of country-led action plans; expanded household access to ITNs in a number of countries; and procured $10.5 million in antimalarial drugs, including $8.5 million worth of artemisinin-based combination therapies (ACT).

UNICEF also supported the introduction of improved formulations of both oral rehydration salts and zinc as part of the diarrhoea treatment package. Diarrhoea and pneumonia remained the two main killers of children. UNICEF's support for diarrhoea prevention was closely linked with water and sanitation programmes and the training of community health workers, and formed part of integrated approaches.

UNICEF's efforts to promote breastfeeding and complementary feeding during the MTSP period included the Baby-Friendly Hospital Initiative, advocacy for the International Code of Marketing of Breast-milk Substitutes and community approaches. By the end of 2005, 19,798 hospital and maternity facilities had been designated as "baby friendly" since the Initiative was launched in 1991 [YUN 1991, p. 693], compared to 15,165 in 2001. In 2005, UNICEF supported efforts to increase the registration of births in 83 countries.

In 2005, 23 per cent of Governments had a comprehensive policy on early childhood development, compared to 22 per cent in 2004; 52 per cent had an official national coordinating structure or mechanism for ECD, compared to 48 per cent in 2004; and 61 per cent had a national system for monitoring young child growth and/or development, compared to 53 per cent in 2004.

UNICEF continued to assist countries in reducing maternal mortality, supporting over 3,500 facilities in nearly 70 countries to provide emergency obstetric care services for pregnant women. The UNICEF contribution included: national-level advocacy; support to emergency obstetric care assessments and programme design; upgrading facilities with equipment, medications and staff training; support for communities in recognizing danger signs and providing transportation; and promoting integration with health sector plans. UNICEF was working with Governments to identify ways to integrate efforts for newborns into emergency obstetric care efforts, IMCI and community programmes, and had joined UNFPA and WHO to assist Governments in Africa to develop "road maps" for improving maternal health.

UNICEF increased its focus on integrated approaches to addressing anaemia, a major cause of maternal deaths and of cognitive deficits in young children. In Bhutan, UNICEF and WFP were supporting girls' education and iron supplementation in schools. UNICEF promoted food fortification as a strategy to prevent anemia and deficiencies in vitamin A and other micronutrients. With regard to the elimination of iodine deficiency disorders (IDD), UNICEF noted that 69 per cent of households in the developing world were consuming adequate amounts of iodized salt; 30 countries had reached the 2005 goal of sustainable elimination of IDD. UNICEF also stepped up its role in responding to nutritional emergencies in the second half of the MTSP period, including in Kenya, Malawi, the Niger and the Sudan, and worked with partners to dramatically expand an integrated package of child survival strategies for emergencies in Ethiopia.

Over the MTSP period, UNICEF expanded its support for water supply, sanitation and hygiene, assisting 95 countries by 2005, compared with 78 at the beginning of the decade. The Fund's assistance enabled large number of families in poverty to gain access to drinking water from protected sources in a number of countries, including the Democratic People's Republic of Korea, Ethiopia, Iraq, Nigeria and the Darfur region of the Sudan. More emphasis was placed on water quality, with a dramatic increase in the testing and protection of drinking water.

Immunization "plus"

Immunization was the only public health intervention to have consistently reached over 70 per cent of young children in recent years. It was making a significant contribution towards achieving the MDG on child mortality [YUN 2000, p. 52] and had the potential to prevent some 2.5 million child deaths each year.

In 2005, Governments were financing 100 per cent of routine vaccination costs in 73 countries; 89 countries had a national strategy for immunizing hard-to-reach groups; and 81 countries had a national communication strategic plan for immunization. However, 27 million children under one year and 40 million pregnant women, often among the poorest population groups, did not receive routine immunization services in 2004 and 19 countries had no government funding allocated to routine vaccinations.

Core UNICEF strengths for immunization continued to include its presence and capacities in vaccine procurement, supply management and programme communication. Since 2002, UNICEF and WHO had jointly promoted the Reaching Every District (RED) approach, whereby attention was shifted to low-performing areas based on local data. Evidence from the Democratic Republic of the Congo (DRC), Ethiopia, Kenya, Madagascar and Zimbabwe suggested an almost 50-per-cent fall in the number of unimmunized children after RED implementation.

Global coverage for three doses of the diphtheria/pertussis/tetanus vaccine (DTP3) reached 78 per cent worldwide in 2004, compared to 73 per cent in 2001. However, only 38 UNICEF-assisted countries met the target of 80 per cent DTP3 coverage in every district. Strong progress was observed in measles immunization; UNICEF and its other Measles Initiative partners surpassed the target to reduce measles mortality by half by 2005. Global measles mortality declined from an estimated 871,000 deaths in 1999 to 454,000 in 2004, with preliminary estimates suggesting an additional 9 per cent reduction in 2005. The Global Polio Eradication Initiative made significant progress towards the goal of interrupting endemic virus transmission; more than half of the 1,906 polio cases in 2005 occurred in non-endemic countries. India and Pakistan reduced the number of new polio cases by 50 per cent in 2005, setting the stage for final interruption of transmission. UNICEF facilitated the accelerated introduction of monovalent oral polio vaccines types 1 and 3, undertook targeted communications to reach marginalized children in Afghanistan, India, Nigeria and Pakistan—the last remaining polio-endemic countries— and, in Nigeria, focused on the northern states, where transmission was still high. UNICEF and the Maternal and Neonatal Tetanus (MNT) Elimination Partnership reduced the number of annual neonatal deaths from MNT from 215,000 in 1999 to

180,000 in 2002, although uncertainty about funding continued to affect their efforts. In 2005, 2.8 million women at risk received doses of the anti-tetanus vaccine in Ethiopia, 2.6 million in Bangladesh and over 1 million in both Mali and Myanmar.

UNICEF procured and distributed nearly 3 billion doses of vaccines worth $439 million in 2005, a 17 per cent increase from 2004, and an additional $53 million in cold-chain and safe injection equipment. Procurement of polio vaccine alone amounted to 2.1 billion doses, and the Micronutrient Initiative supplied 500 million vitamin A capsules through UNICEF. By improving its vaccine-supply forecasting, UNICEF exceeded 80 to 90 per cent accuracy across 90 countries. Where data was available, the number of countries affected by national stock-outs for any antigen in routine immunization fell to 37 in 2005, compared to 48 in 2004.

UNICEF continued to support safe injection practices, reporting that, in 2005, 85 programme countries exclusively used auto disable syringes for routine immunization, an increase from 72 in 2004.

Global Immunization vision and strategy

The Executive Board had before it a UNICEF secretariat note [E/ICEF/2005/9] on the draft global strategy on immunization, prepared jointly by UNICEF and WHO and presented to the Fifty-Eighth World Health Assembly (Geneva, 16-25 May). The strategy provided Governments and international organizations with a framework for planning and collaborating to meet the immunization challenges of the coming decade (2006-2015). Its aim was to protect people against disease, introduce new vaccines and technologies, and integrate immunization with other health interventions into the health system, with the goal of reaching at least an 80-per-cent immunization coverage in every district of every country by 2010.

On 9 June [dec. 2005/7], the Executive Board welcomed the UNICEF/WHO Global Immunization Vision and Strategy and urged countries to adopt it as a framework for strengthening national immunization programmes between 2006 and 2015. It requested the Executive Director to report regularly on progress in achieving the global immunization targets, and to strengthen relations with WHO, the Global Alliance for Vaccines and Immunization, and other partners to mobilize resources and support implementation. The World Health Assembly had adopted a similar resolution on 25 May.

Girls' education

The MDGs [YUN 2000, p. 51] continued to have a galvanizing effect in increasing investments and more efficient national implementation of strategies to meet the target of gender parity in primary education. UNICEF's role focused increasingly on the use of advocacy and partnerships to influence sector-based policies and to leverage resources. In the second half of the MTSP period, UNICEF played a greater role in helping countries prepare quality plans for support from the Education for All (EFA) Fast Track Initiative. An external evaluation of the African Girls' Education Initiative concluded that efforts by UNICEF and its partners had influenced the policy landscape and strengthened the profile of gender issues in education in all parts of Africa. The Fund also revitalized the United Nations Girls' Education Initiative for strengthening action on girls' education at all levels. The Initiative grew from just a few countries in 2002 to at least 25 in 2005.

In Liberia, a comprehensive Girls' Education Policy was completed with UNICEF support. In Mozambique, Nepal and Nigeria, new national policies to accelerate girls' education were also developed. In 52 per cent of UNICEF-assisted countries, Governments and/or the Fund had undertaken a gender review of the education sector. By 2005, 81 national EFA plans included explicit measures to help girls who were not in school and to reduce their number. The Governments of 54 countries were taking specific measures to boost the percentage of girls entering post-primary school. Three regions—the Middle East and North Africa, South Asia and West and Central Africa—did not meet the goal of gender parity in primary education by 2005; while 125 countries were on course to achieving gender parity, overall enrolment of both boys and girls remained unacceptably low.

Local UNICEF support sometimes took the form of single measures such as supplying learning materials, school meals, construction of classrooms or conditional cash transfers to households. However, those interventions were stop-gap solutions for highly disadvantaged populations. UNICEF also promoted models of good practice that could be adapted to country circumstances: major "back to school" campaigns were supported in 13 countries, resulting in significant increases in primary enrolment rates for girls and boys, and 93 countries developed or were developing standards for child-friendly, gender-sensitive school environments. In Haiti, a major "back to school" campaign brought back 38,000 children, 60 per cent of them girls; in Somalia, an enrolment drive registered 114,000 primary-school-aged children; and in Iraq,

4.6 million children received UNICEF-supplied educational kits. In Afghanistan, UNICEF support resulted in the new enrolment of 529,000 girls in schools. In Nepal, the "Welcome to School" initiative went nationwide in 2005, resulting in an almost 12 per cent increase in primary enrolment. The Fund also supported initiatives to increase enrolment in the Comoros, India and Nigeria.

In tsunami-affected countries, UNICEF constructed 213 temporary or semi-permanent schools and provided emergency education supplies to approximately 1.5 million children, helping to bring 90 per cent of them back to school within three months. It also supported initiatives in Nigeria, Uganda and the United Republic of Tanzania on sanitation and hygiene promotion in schools, which were associated with significant increases in girls' enrolment and retention rates. Other UNICEF-assisted education programmes included HIV/AIDS-prevention education and strategies to secure access for orphaned children. UNICEF procured a total of $86 million in education supplies in 2005, up 22 per cent from 2004. That growth was driven by emergency education (especially the "school in a box" and recreation kits, which were used as a first response for the restoration of education in emergencies) and ongoing support to girls' education activities.

Protection from violence, abuse, exploitation and discrimination

In 2005, UNICEF continued to expand partnerships with other UN agencies, intergovernmental organizations, regional bodies and national partners in order to enhance child protection efforts. It also promoted the close linkages between child protection and the MDGs. International experience remained weak in child protection compared to other priority areas for children within the Millennium agenda. However, almost all MTSP indicators for child protection showed a positive trend over the plan period: in 2005, 26 countries had national standards in place that adequately protected children deprived of liberty, double the number in 2002; public statements were made by 78 Governments recognizing the problem of child trafficking, compared to 64 in 2002, and by 85 Governments recognizing the problem of child sexual exploitation, 15 more than in 2002. In addition, 91 countries reviewed the legal standards that protected children from violence within the preceding three years, 30 more than in 2002; 118 countries initiated an analysis of the impact on children of violence, abuse, exploitation and discrimination, compared to 91 in 2002; and 57 Governments collected routine data on the worst forms of child la-

bour, 10 more than in 2002. UNICEF worked with the International Labour Organization and other partners to develop indicators for the worst forms of child labour, to be phased into the 2006-2009 MTSP. Indicators were also in use for monitoring children in public care, juvenile justice, child marriage, female genital mutilation/ cutting and violence. In Brazil, UNICEF promoted the inclusion of over 100,000 child workers in schools and supported a public awareness-raising campaign on child labour; in Senegal, the eradication of child labour was identified as a priority for the utilization of debt relief funds from Italy; and in the Middle East, 1,000 children formerly involved in camel racing were repatriated for family reunification.

UNICEF supported the development of action plans on commercially sexually exploited children and trafficking of women and children in Mongolia, Pakistan and Papua New Guinea, and worked with the tourism industry to take action against both child labour and the sexual and commercial exploitation of children. In Burkina Faso, Eritrea, Myanmar, Pakistan, the Sudan and elsewhere, UNICEF supported the reintegration of children who had been trafficked and/or exploited into communities. UNICEF reported that agreements against child trafficking were signed by nine West African countries; bilateral agreements were reached between Cambodia and China and between Cambodia and Viet Nam; and the new Council of Europe Convention on Action against Trafficking in Human Beings incorporated child trafficking provisions.

With regard to children in armed conflict, UNICEF led efforts for the disarmament, demobilization and reintegration (DDR) of children in many conflict-affected countries, particularly in West Africa, South Asia and Latin America. It trained humanitarian personnel and peacekeepers on child protection and the special needs of women and children in a number of countries. Working with 14 other UN agencies, the Fund led the preparation of an approach on children and DDR as part of the UN integrated system. Its assistance had reached over 2,500 child soldiers in Colombia since 1999, and nearly 800 child soldiers were demobilized in Burundi and 200 in Sri Lanka.

UNICEF made special efforts to build capacities for child protection in emergencies and supported the establishment of a practitioners' network to promote learning among humanitarian and academic organizations regarding the needs of children and families for psychosocial support following conflicts or natural disasters. In response to the Indian Ocean tsunami, UNICEF worked to ensure that all separated and unaccompanied children who lost one or both parents were rapidly registered, and nearly all were placed with extended family within a few months.

UNICEF also participated in the development and dissemination of guidelines and training on HIV/AIDS in emergencies. Partly due to its advocacy, the Maputo (Mozambique) Protocol to the African Charter on Human and People's Rights on the Rights of Women in Africa, which prohibited female genital mutilation, entered into force in November. UNICEF observed that in Burkina Faso the incidence of female genital mutilation had decreased from 66 per cent in 1996 to 40 per cent in 2005, and that several states in Nigeria had passed laws against the practice.

Limited growth of regular resources income over the MTSP period and some difficulties in raising other resources continued to affect overall performance in child protection.

On 10 June [dec. 2005/10], the UNICEF Executive Board requested the Executive Director to support Member States in their efforts to combat violence against children and adolescents and decided to consider in 2006 an oral report on activities on violence related to children and adolescents in conflict with the law.

(See also pp. 854-67.)

HIV/AIDS

The UNICEF Executive Director stated that a child under the age of 15 was dying of an AIDS-related illness every minute and almost 1,800 new paediatric infections were occurring per day [E/ICEF/ 2006/11]. Globally, 15 million children had lost at least one parent to HIV/AIDS. By 2010, there were expected to be 18 million such children in sub-Saharan Africa alone. In October, UNICEF launched the *Unite for Children, Unite against AIDS* campaign in partnership with the Joint United Nations Programme on HIV/AIDS (UNAIDS) (see p. 1305) and other partners. The campaign promoted a child-focused framework for action around the "four P" imperatives: preventing mother-to-child HIV (PMTCT); providing paediatric treatment; preventing infection among adolescents and young people; and protecting and supporting children affected by HIV/AIDS. UNICEF contributed to significant expansion of PMTCT services in a number of countries including Namibia, Nigeria, Swaziland, Uganda and Zambia. It also supported initiatives to increase PMTCT access to isolated and indigenous communities in Nicaragua and Peru. As UNAIDS co-sponsors, UNICEF and WFP moved towards joint programmes for making strategic use of food in support of scaling up PMTCT care and

treatment, and UNICEF continued to collaborate with the United States President Emergency Plan for AIDS Relief and with WHO on PMTCT and paediatric treatment issues.

UNICEF reported that the response to the HIV/AIDS epidemic was entering a new era. There was a distinct move from global-level advocacy to strong support for country-level implementation of comprehensive nationally led programmes in which UNICEF offices were increasingly playing a strategic role. In China, UNICEF assisted in the development of the first provincial-level policy on children affected by HIV/AIDS and a number of West and Central African countries established strategic national AIDS plans for 2006-2010.

Following agreement during the 2004 mid-term review [YUN 2004, p. 1179] that HIV/AIDS care and support needed greater attention, UNICEF convened consultations that identified a range of urgent actions: finalization of paediatric diagnosis and clinical staging guidelines; review of current treatment guidelines; expansion of PMTCT programmes; modelling of comprehensive care, support and treatment responses; negotiation of price reductions for paediatric formulations; and the development of information and forecasting systems. UNICEF also consulted with major pharmaceutical companies on the production of paediatric formulations for use in poor countries, which were expected to become available in mid-2006. The UNICEF/WHO paediatric care, support and treatment consultations on drug formulations, treatment guidelines and cotrimoxazole helped to provide guidance for implementation.

UNICEF provided leadership in developing a framework to guide the work of partners in assisting children orphaned or made vulnerable by HIV/AIDS (OVCs). It assisted in carrying out surveys of the situation of those children in several African countries, and supported a cash subsidy initiative for OVCs in Kenya; given that initiative's positive initial impact, a larger pilot was planned for 2006. By 2005, 60 countries had adopted strategies for the care and protection of OVCs, compared to 31 in 2002. However, major challenges remained, including aligning national responses to OVCs with existing HIV/AIDS plans and the weak capacities of social affairs ministries.

The Fund continued to sponsor a wide range of studies and assessments to improve national knowledge of HIV/AIDS, including national situation analyses in Bangladesh and Viet Nam; infant feeding and HIV/AIDS studies in Rwanda and the United Republic of Tanzania; and studies on awareness in schools in Djibouti and Zambia. At the end of 2005, national situation analyses on HIV/AIDS and children/youth had been conducted in 75 countries, compared to 70 in 2002.

UNICEF almost doubled the value of its anti-retroviral (ARV) drug procurement to $33.5 million in 2005, from $18.4 million in 2004, with an additional $8 million spent on other HIV/AIDS-related supplies and equipment, substantially increasing the number of children and adults with access to therapy. The Fund helped to achieve a major reduction in ARV costs in the Russian Federation.

(For further information on HIV/AIDS prevention and control, see p. 1322.)

UNAIDS programme coordination

In September, the UNICEF Executive Board had before it an August report [E/ICEF/2005/12] on UNICEF's contribution to the sixteenth (December 2004) [YUN 2004, p. 1219] and seventeenth (June 2005) meetings of the UNAIDS Programme Coordinating Board (see p. 1327). The report described its contribution to the Unified Budget and Work Plan for 2006-2007, and outlined the recommendations of the Global Task Team on Improving AIDS Coordination among Multilateral Institutions and International Donors (GTT) (see p. 1327). UNICEF's share of the UNAIDS core budget of $320 million amounted to $19.8 million.

On 30 September [dec. 2005/19], the Executive Board approved the GTT recommendations and requested the Fund to work with UNAIDS and other co-sponsors to develop annual priority action plans at the country level. UNICEF was encouraged to provide effective technical support to national Governments and to focus on areas of comparative advantage. It was also asked to intensify HIV prevention by developing an action plan based on the UNAIDS policy position paper entitled "Intensifying HIV prevention".

Operational and administrative matters

UNICEF finances

In 2005, UNICEF income totalled $2,762 million, an increase of $784 million (40 per cent) over 2004, a result of a significant increase in contributions to other resources, largely from private sources and in response to emergencies, which accounted for 71 per cent of total income in 2005. Income to regular resources increased by 3 per cent to $812 million. Total contributions were 20 per cent higher than forecast in the financial plan. UNICEF derived its income primarily from Governments, which contributed $1,472 million (53 per cent), and from private sector

sources, which contributed $1,235 million (45 per cent). The balance of $55 million came from other sources.

In January, the Executive Board took note of UNICEF's financial report and audited financial statements for the biennium ended 31 December 2003 [A/59/5/Add.2], action on which was deferred in 2004 [YUN 2004, p. 1187]. In September, the Board noted UNICEF's interim financial report and statements for the year ended 31 December 2004 [E/ICEF/2005/AB/L.4].

Budget appropriations

On 9 June [dec. 2005/4], the Executive Board approved recommendations for the aggregate indicative budgets for 19 country programmes for the period 2006-2010 and a programme for Palestinian children and women for the period 2006-2007, amounting to the following totals for regular and other resources, respectively, by region: Africa, $101,386,000 and $164,385,000; the Americas and the Caribbean, $4,500,000 and $18,170,000; Asia, $208,249,000 and $460,770,000; Central and Eastern Europe, CIS and the Baltic States, $27,094,000 and $76,160,000; and Middle East and North Africa, $4,000,000 and $24,240,000.

On the basis of the Executive Director's recommendation, contained in a 1 April report [E/ICEF/2005/P/L.21], the Board, on 9 June [dec. 2005/5], approved additional regular resources for 54 country programmes for 2005 and 2006, amounting to $80,397,731. On the same date [dec. 2005/6], the Board approved additional other resources for the approved country programmes of 20 countries, totalling $371,031,000.

On 29 September [dec. 2005/11], the Board approved the aggregate indicative budgets for five country programmes for 2006-2010, and for the DRC and Afghanistan for 2006-2007 for the following amounts from regular and other resources respectively: Swaziland, $3,755,000 and $21,250,000; Cape Verde, $3,300,000 and $2,150,000; Chad, $18,445,000 and $30,000,000; DRC $43,858,000 and $50,000,000; Guyana, $3,345,000 and $2,000,000; Indonesia, $26,500,000 and $100,000,000; and Afghanistan, $41,397,000 and $126,000,000. For the Cape Verde country programme, the Board only approved the UNICEF portion of the aggregate indicative budget.

The Board also considered a report recommending the allocation of funds to cover over-expenditures for 22 programmes, amounting to $1,061,196.63 [E/ICEF/2005/P/L.38]. On 29 September [dec. 2005/13], the Board approved the funding from regular resources.

Additionally, the Board considered a proposal for a supplementary appropriation for the 2004-

2005 biennium [E/ICEF/2005/AB/L.7] of $3 million for security-related costs. It also had before it a note from the Advisory Committee on Administrative and Budgetary Questions (ACABQ) [E/ICEF/2005/AB/L.8] recommending approval of the supplementary appropriation. On 29 September [dec. 2005/15], the Board approved the appropriation, increasing security-related costs from $14 million to $17 million.

On the recommendation of the Executive Director [E/ICEF/2005/P/L.37], the Board, on 29 September [dec. 2005/12], approved a five-year extension (2006-2010) of the programme of cooperation with the PolioPlus programme of Rotary International and an increase in funding from other resources of $10 million, subject to the availability of specific-purpose contributions from Rotary International. The Board also approved a five-year extension of the Vaccine Independence Initiative for the period 2006 to 2010.

Budget approval process

In accordance with a 2004 Executive Board decision [YUN 2004, p. 1187], whereby the UNICEF 2006-2007 biennial support budget would be reviewed at the Board's January 2006 session, the Executive Director, on 3 August [E/ICEF/2005/AB/L.3], recommended that the Board approve an interim one-month allocation for the support budget in the amount of $25,600,000 to cover January 2006, pending its approval of the biennial support budget. On 29 September [dec. 2005/16], the Board approved the allocation.

Audits

In an April report on internal audit activities in 2004, the Office of Internal Audit (OIA) stated that it had completed 35 audits in 2004 [E/ICEF/2005/AB/L.2]: 29 field audits; four headquarters audits; an audit of the termination of UNICEF activities and handover of assets related to the oil-for-food programme in Iraq; and one global summary report. In its audits of headquarters, OIA found that controls for the administration of travel services and the procurement of supplies and consultancy services were satisfactory. In country offices, controls were generally satisfactory, particularly for fund-raising and donor reporting, with considerable room for improvement in finance, basic programme management, cash assistance and supply assistance. The profile of country offices' risk-management practices in 2004 was similar to that of 2003, indicating that there was continuing scope for improving the programmatic and operational support from regional offices, and regional and global monitoring of the status of country offices' practices in areas of common weakness.

The Executive Board took note of the report in June.

In a July report [E/ICEF/2005/AB/L.6] to the UN Board of Auditors and ACABQ, UNICEF described steps taken to implement the recommendations of the Board of Auditors on the Fund's accounts for the 2002-2003 biennium. The report focused on those recommendations that either were not implemented or only partially implemented at the time of the previous report [YUN 2004, p. 1187].

Resource mobilization

UNICEF continued to collaborate with Governments to mobilize both regular and other resources. At the sixth annual pledging event in January, 50 countries pledged a total of $255.7 million. By year's end, 109 Governments had contributed $469 million in regular resources and $1,003 million in other resources, increasing their contributions to regular resources by 7 per cent, compared to 2004. However, there was a small decline in private sector contributions to regular resources that, combined with the unprecedented response to emergencies, left UNICEF with the lowest ever percentage of regular resources to total resources in 2005 at 29 per cent. The United States remained the largest donor to regular resources, with a contribution of $124 million, followed by Sweden ($55 million), Norway ($47 million), the Netherlands ($37 million), the United Kingdom ($35 million), Japan ($24 million), and Canada ($11 million).

Thematic funding in 2005 increased nearly fourfold over 2004, with the top 10 thematic donors (a mix of Governments and national committees) contributing a total of $495.4 million. The largest increase was for humanitarian response, with most thematic funding coming from the private sector. The number of government contributors to consolidated, flash and humanitarian action report appeals rose from 23 to 47.

Private Sector Division

Net income from UNICEF Private Sector Division (PSD) activities for the year ended 31 December 2005 totalled $288.6 million for regular resources, $2.6 million (0.9 per cent) lower than the $291.1 million raised in 2004 [E/ICEF/2006/AB/L.7]. The total included income of $255.7 million from private sector fund-raising activities, $63.6 million from the sale of UNICEF cards and gifts, deductions relating to a negative exchange rate adjustment of $14.3 million and investment fund expenditures of $16.4 million. In addition, $769.6 million ($218.8 million in 2004) was raised from private sector fund-raising activities for other resources, an increase of $550.8 million. That large increase was due to the unprecedented donor response to UNICEF emergency appeals for the Indian Ocean tsunami and the South Asian earthquake. Earmarked funding for non-emergencies also increased significantly, with $185.7 million raised in 2005, compared to $143.5 million in 2004. The net consolidated income for 2005, including both regular and other resources, amounted to $1,058.2 million, an increase of $548.3 million (107.5 per cent), compared with the 2004 net consolidated income of $509.9 million.

On 18 January [dec. 2005/2], the Executive Board approved budgeted expenditures of $96.9 million for the PSD work plan for 2005 [E/ICEF/ 2005/AB/L.1]. The Executive Director was authorized to redeploy resources between the various budget lines, up to a maximum of 10 per cent of the amounts approved, and to spend an additional amount between Executive Board sessions, up to the amount caused by currency fluctuations, to implement the 2005 approved work plan. The Board renewed investment funds with $17.1 million established for 2005; authorized the Executive Director to incur expenditures in 2005 related to the cost of goods delivered (production/purchase of raw materials, cards and other products) for 2006, up to $35 million; and approved the PSD medium-term plan for 2006 to 2009.

In September, the Board took note of the PSD financial report and statements for the year ended 31 December 2004 [E/ICEF/2005/AB/L.5].

Country programme approval process

The Executive Board had before it an April report [E/ICEF/2005/8] containing a review of the modified procedures for consideration and approval of proposals for country cooperation programmes, as requested by the Board in 2002 [YUN 2002, p. 1191]. The report gave an update on progress in implementing the modified procedures. A total of 35 country programme documents for new cooperation programmes had been approved by the Board, and a further 27 were expected to be presented for consideration and approval in 2005. The modified procedure supported better quality, result-oriented documents and promoted the harmonized and joint programming process with national partners and among UN agencies at the country level, while giving the Board the opportunity to provide substantive comments on new programmes.

On 10 June [dec. 2005/9], the Executive Board requested the Executive Director to present in 2006 a joint report with UNDP and UNFPA on possible options to further improve and streamline the current harmonized country programme approval procedure.

Joint programming

On 19 January [dec. 2005/3], the Executive Board considered the 2004 report of the Executive Director on the assessment of UNICEF experience in joint programming [E/ICEF/2004/10], which had been deferred in 2004 [YUN 2004, p. 1189]. The Board requested the Executive Director, in cooperation with the other agencies of the United Nations Development Group (UNDG), to ensure that joint programming had an improved impact on development by, where appropriate: further harmonizing country programme preparation, implementation, monitoring and evaluation processes and improving communication between UN agencies during the whole programme cycle; effective delivery of programme goals and reduction of transaction costs; and promotion of common monitoring and reporting processes to governing bodies and joint approaches to evaluations. The Executive Director was asked to submit a comprehensive report on the implementation of joint programming in 2006.

On 30 September [dec. 2005/20], the Board encouraged the joint meetings of the Executive Boards of UNICEF, UNDP/UNFPA and WFP to discuss and comment on one country case as a practical illustration of joint UN work in the field and invited UN agencies, funds and programmes to participate.

JIU reports

In January the Executive Board considered a secretariat note [E/ICEF/2005/4] on the activities of the Joint Inspection Unit (JIU) of specific relevance to UNICEF. The document provided information on reports prepared between September 2003 and September 2004, actions taken by the Fund in response to those reports, and the views of the Executive Director on the issues raised by the JIU inspectors.

Innocenti Research Centre

In July [E/ICEF/2005/13], UNICEF submitted to the Executive Board a progress report on the activities of its Innocenti Research Centre (IRC) (Florence, Italy), established in 1988 [YUN 1988, p. 649] as the International Child Development Centre to strengthen the capacity of UNICEF and its cooperating institutions to respond to the evolving needs of children and to promote a strong global ethic for them. The report reviewed IRC's implementation of its 2003-2005 work programme, focusing on its research on issues pertaining to the implementation of the 1989 Convention on the Rights of the Child [YUN 1989, p. 560] (see also p. 730), which assessed the impact of economic and social policies on children. An evaluation of the Centre's work over the previous three programme cycles found that its studies were used to influence strategic policy processes within and beyond UNICEF, and benefited from partnerships and cross-disciplinary expertise; and that collaboration between IRC and UNICEF headquarters, regional and country offices and national committees had been further consolidated. The report presented a proposed work programme for 2006-2008, which would include further research on the impact of socio-economic policies on child poverty, developing research on children's rights to raise awareness of the 1989 Convention on the Rights of the Child and its Optional Protocols, and supporting improved research methodologies in the areas of child trafficking, violence and the impact of armed conflict on children.

On 29 September [dec. 2005/14], the Executive Board authorized a three-year extension of the programme for the period 2006-2008, with a total allocation of $17 million in other resources, of which Italy pledged a minimum of 5.43 million euros (about $6.5 million) for its core activities. The Board invited all donors to contribute to the Centre's programme activities in order to meet the full cost of implementing its 2006-2008 programme.

Youth

World Programme of Action for Youth

Tenth anniversary

In 2005, the United Nations observed the tenth anniversary of its adoption, in resolution 50/81 [YUN 1995, p. 1211], of the World Programme of Action for Youth to the Year 2000 and Beyond.

As decided by the General Assembly in resolution 59/148 [YUN 2004, p. 1190], two plenary meetings, held on 6 October [A/60/PV.27, 28], were devoted to the evaluation of progress made in implementing the Programme of Action. During the debate, many Member States were represented by national youth delegates and representatives from youth organizations attended as observers. Also in accordance with Assembly resolution 59/148, the plenary sessions were preceded on 5 October by an interactive round table on the theme "Young people: making commitments matter".

The plenary sessions culminated in the adoption of resolution 60/2 (see p. 1296).

Implementation

UN policies and programmes on youth during the year continued to focus on the implementation of the 1995 World Programme of Action for Youth to the Year 2000 and Beyond, which addressed problems faced by youth worldwide and identified ways to enhance youth participation in national and international policy- and decision-making. The Programme of Action identified 10 priority issues for youth: education; employment; hunger and poverty; health; environment; drug abuse; juvenile delinquency; leisure-time activities; girls and young women; and participation in society and decision-making. The Assembly, by resolution 58/133 [YUN 2003, p. 1217], had noted five additional issues of concern to young people: globalization; the increased use of information and communication technology (ICT); HIV/AIDS; the increased participation of young people in armed conflict, both as victims and perpetrators; and the growing importance of intergenerational relations in an ageing global society. In resolution 60/2 (see p. 1296), the Assembly added those issues as additional priority areas for the implementation of the World Programme.

During the forty-third session of the Commission for Social Development (New York, 9-18 February) [E/2005/26], a panel discussion took place that highlighted the youth development agenda of the Programme of Action and its linkages to the MDGs [YUN 2000, p. 51] and internationally agreed targets. In addition, several workshops were organized in the Arab region on youth policies and strategies in the context of the MDGs (Bahrain, 28-29 May; Sana'a, Yemen, 21-23 June; Rabat, Morocco, 6-8 July). In order to develop a draft set of indicators to monitor and measure the global situation of youth, an expert group meeting on youth development indicators was organized (New York, 12-14 December).

Report of Secretary-General. In response to General Assembly resolution 58/133 [YUN 2003, p. 1217], the Secretary-General submitted a July report [A/60/156] summarizing the views and recommendations of young people regarding the 10-year review of the World Programme of Action for Youth to the Year 2000 and Beyond. The inputs were collected from young people through consultative meetings (Coimbra, Portugal, 31 January–4 February; New York, 14-17 February; Cairo, Egypt, 27-29 May) and in response to a booklet entitled "Making commitments matter: a toolkit for young people to evaluate national youth policy", published by the UN Department of Economic and Social Affairs in 2004. The views collected were grouped into three clusters, reflecting the 15 youth concerns identified by the Assembly (see p. 1294).

The report concluded that the response to the request for inputs to the 10-year review indicated that the World Programme of Action for Youth continued to have importance in the lives of young people. The process of gathering the inputs had generated a great deal of interest and commitment at regional and national levels.

World Youth Report 2005

In response to General Assembly resolution 58/133 [YUN 2003, p. 1217], the Secretary-General submitted an abridged version of the World Youth Report 2005 [A/60/61-E/2005/7], an overview of the global situation of young people on the occasion of the tenth anniversary of the adoption of the World Programme of Action for Youth to the Year 2000 and Beyond. The report was also considered at the forty-third session of the Commission for Social Development [E/2005/26] (see p. 1190). The report stated that between 1995 and 2005, the world's youth population (persons between 15 and 24 years of age) grew from 1,025 million to 1,153 million, 85 per cent of whom were living in developing countries. It also reviewed progress with regard to the 10 priority areas of the World Programme of Action and, in an annex, highlighted the five additional concerns (see p. 1294).

The report noted that the current generation of young people faced more complex challenges than previous generations. Over 200 million youth were living in poverty, 130 million were illiterate, 88 million were unemployed and 10 million were living with HIV/AIDS. While some progress had been achieved in a number of priority areas of the Programme of Action, the case for a renewed commitment to its goals was clear.

Recommendations presented by the Secretary-General for the Assembly's consideration included: the scaling-up of investments in youth; the inclusion of young people as partners in achieving the MDGs; the development of integrated youth policies by Governments, paying special attention to the various disadvantaged groups of young people, including those with disabilities, young migrants and indigenous youth; the continuous evaluation of youth policy by Governments and the involvement of young people in the evaluation; and the development of a verifiable set of indicators that would allow for better measurement of progress achieved for young people in the future. The Secretary-General further recommended that the Assembly endorse the five additional issues of concern (see

p. 1294) to complement the priority areas of the World Programme of Action and call on the UN system to enhance synergies among relevant system activities.

An expanded version of the Secretary-General's report, *World Youth Report 2005: Young People Today, and in 2015* [Sales No. E.05.IV.6], was launched as a UN sales publication on 4 October.

Youth employment

In response to General Assembly resolution 58/133 [YUN 2003, p. 1217], the Secretary-General submitted a July report [A/60/133 & Corr.1] containing a global analysis and evaluation of national action plans on youth employment. In an overview of the challenges relating to youth employment, the report observed that the International Labour Organization (ILO) estimated that around 88 million young people were unemployed worldwide. Of the 186 million unemployed persons in the world, young people accounted for 47 per cent, despite making up only 25 per cent of the global working-age population. ILO also reported an increase in intermittent work and insecure arrangements for young people in both industrialized and developing economies. As at 30 June 2005, 39 Member States had submitted a plan or progress report on the elaboration of national reviews and action plans on youth employment, and many others had prepared, or were in the process of preparing, national action plans or other documents addressing the matter.

The report noted that the urgency of the commitment to give young people access to decent and productive work had only increased since the adoption of the Millennium Declaration in 2000 [YUN 2000, p. 49]. Unemployment and underemployment of young people were not only a social concern, but also had economic and political dimensions. In countries with social protection, such as unemployment insurance, youth unemployment represented an enormous drain on budgets and a waste of capabilities. In others without social protection, the burden was felt by families and communities. Based on a review of national plans, the report presented a number of broad conclusions: policies to address youth employment required a coherent and integrated approach that prepared young people for the labour market and the labour market for young people; youth employment policies tended to focus on the supply side and needed to be accompanied by measures to create additional employment opportunities; policies favouring youth employment should be promoted with a view to improving the employment situation for people of all ages in the labour market; and the participation of representative youth organizations in the preparation of action plans was weak and the involvement of employers' and workers' organizations inadequate. In addition, most countries not only had a lot to learn from one another, but would welcome information and knowledge on how to address youth unemployment. The report also noted that meeting the Millennium Declaration commitment relating to youth employment required concerted and coordinated action at the local, national and international levels, and that developing strategies and programmes for youth employment provided a powerful tool for building political consensus and policy coherence in other areas, including security, peacebuilding and development. Finally, the report noted that the proposal of the High-Level Panel on Youth Employment of the Youth Employment Network (formed by the Secretary-General in collaboration with ILO and the World Bank in 2001 [YUN 2001, p. 1100]) for a major new policy and action-oriented initiative on the links between youth employment and collective security merited serious consideration and support.

Recommendations by the Secretary-General for the Assembly's consideration included: encouraging countries to prepare or implement national reviews and action plans on youth employment, and to submit their reports to the Youth Employment Network as soon as possible and encouraging countries to develop their plans in collaboration with youth, worker and employer organizations and civil society, and to integrate action plans into development and poverty reduction strategy documents. Governments were encouraged to develop appropriate policy-oriented indicators to monitor and evaluate progress in implementing national action plans. The Youth Employment Network should coordinate its core partners' work to improve indicators and Member States should be encouraged to consider youth employment as integral to their overall development and collective security strategies, giving renewed attention to the Millennium Declaration commitment concerning decent and productive work for young people. The Secretary-General also recommended that the Assembly renew its invitation, made in resolutions 57/165 [YUN 2002, p. 1192] and 58/133 [YUN 2003, p. 1217], to the Youth Employment Network to support Governments in the elaboration and implementation of national reviews and action plans; and to strengthen the Network's Youth Consultative Group so that its constituent youth organizations could play a more active role in the development of action plans. He further recommended that the Assembly invite new countries and organizations to join the Network; encourage

the lead countries to strengthen the Network as a peer exchange, support and review mechanism; and encourage Member States to provide additional financial resources to expand its work. He also recommended inviting ILO to update annually the global analysis of progress made in developing and implementing national reviews and action plans on youth employment.

At the fourth meeting of the High-Level Panel on Youth Employment (Beijing, 20-21 May), members concluded that the original vision for the Youth Employment Network [YUN 2001, p. 1100] had been achieved and proposed a strategy for its future direction, including the following three areas of action: capacity-building for sustainable partnership engagement; knowledge management and communication; and coordination and facilitation, including leveraging and pooling political, technical and financial resources for youth employment initiatives.

GENERAL ASSEMBLY ACTION

On 6 October [meeting 28], the General Assembly adopted **resolution 60/2** [draft: A/60/L.2 & Add.1] without vote [agenda item 62].

Policies and programmes involving youth

The General Assembly

1. *Reaffirms* the World Programme of Action for Youth to the Year 2000 and Beyond;

2. *Recognizes* that the implementation of the World Programme of Action and the achievement of the internationally agreed development goals, in particular those contained in the United Nations Millennium Declaration, require the full and effective participation of young people and youth organizations and other civil society organizations at the local, national, regional and international levels;

3. *Calls upon* Governments, organizations and bodies of the United Nations system and non-governmental organizations to develop strong partnerships to scale up investments in youth and to encourage youth-led contributions to achieving the internationally agreed development goals, in particular those contained in the Millennium Declaration;

4. *Urges* Governments, in consultation with youth organizations, to develop holistic and integrated youth policies based on the World Programme of Action and to evaluate them regularly as part of the follow-up action on and implementation of the Programme of Action;

5. *Requests* the United Nations regional commissions to organize, within their existing resources, regional consultations with Member States and youth organizations in order to evaluate the implementation of the World Programme of Action;

6. *Calls upon* the organizations, programmes and specialized agencies of the United Nations system to enhance inter-agency arrangements on youth policies and programmes with a view to improving coordination and enhancing synergies among relevant system activities in this regard;

7. *Welcomes* the commitment contained in the outcome document of the High-level Plenary Meeting of the sixtieth session of the General Assembly to make the goals of full and productive employment and decent work for young people a central objective of relevant national and international policies as well as national development strategies, including poverty reduction strategies, through, inter alia, the development of national action plans on youth employment, as well as by prioritizing therein the necessary resources for the implementation of these plans, and in this regard encourages relevant stakeholders to continue to assist and support, upon request, the efforts of Governments in the elaboration and implementation of national reviews and action plans;

8. *Stresses* the importance of the work of the Youth Employment Network as a peer exchange, support and review mechanism, and encourages Member States, the United Nations and partner organizations to strengthen and expand the Network at the national, regional and international levels;

9. *Welcomes* the participation of youth representatives in national delegations, and urges Member States to consider being represented by youth representatives on a continuing basis during relevant discussions in the General Assembly and the Economic and Social Council and its functional commissions, bearing in mind the principle of gender balance;

10. *Invites* all Governments and intergovernmental and non-governmental organizations to contribute, inter alia, to the United Nations Youth Fund for the participation of youth representatives in national delegations, in particular from developing countries;

11. *Welcomes* the decision to convene the informal, interactive round-table discussion, which created an opportunity for youth organizations to engage with Member States, and encourages the consideration of similar events in the future;

12. *Calls upon* Governments, the United Nations system, youth organizations and other relevant stakeholders to strengthen efforts aimed at the implementation of the ten priority areas contained in the World Programme of Action;

13. *Decides* to add the following as additional priority areas for the implementation of the World Programme of Action: the mixed impact of globalization on young women and men; the use of and access to information and communication technologies; the dramatic increase in the incidence of HIV infection among young people and the impact of the epidemic on their lives; the active involvement of young people in armed conflict, both as victims and as perpetrators; and the increased importance of addressing intergenerational issues in an ageing society;

14. *Requests* the Commission for Social Development at its forty-fifth session to elaborate the five priority areas mentioned above and to make recommendations on a supplement to the World Programme of Action to the General Assembly, to be adopted at its sixty-second session, taking into consideration other emerging issues of particular relevance to youth;

15. *Requests* the Secretariat, in collaboration with other relevant United Nations programmes and agencies, to establish a broad set of indicators related to youth, which Governments and other actors may choose to use to measure progress towards the implementation of the World Programme of Action;

16. *Takes note* of the three clusters presented in the report of the Secretary-General entitled "World Youth Report 2005", namely, youth in the global economy, youth in civil society, and youth and their well-being, and requests the Secretary-General to provide the General Assembly at its sixty-second session, through the Commission for Social Development at its forty-fifth session, with a comprehensive report on the implementation of the World Programme of Action, including the definition of goals and targets, in one of the three clusters mentioned above.

In other action, the Assembly, by **decision 60/528** of 16 December, took note of the reports of the Secretary-General on the World Youth Report 2005 [A/60/61-E/2007/7]; a global analysis and evaluation of national action plans on youth employment [A/60/133 & Corr.1]; and "Making commitments matter: young people's input to the 10-year review of the World Programme of Action for Youth to the Year 2000 and Beyond" [A/60/156].

Ageing persons

Follow-up to the Second World Assembly on Ageing (2002)

Report of Secretary General. In response to General Assembly resolution 59/150 [YUN 2004, p. 1193], the Secretary-General submitted a July report [A/60/151] on follow-up to the Second (2002) World Assembly on Ageing [YUN 2002, p. 1193]. He provided information on activities carried out by Member States at the national level in 2004/05 to implement the Madrid International Plan of Action on Ageing [ibid., p. 1194], which was adopted at the Second World Assembly. He also described action taken by the UN Secretariat and the funds and programmes of the UN system, and by major NGOs, in support of national implementation and their efforts to mainstream ageing issues into international programmes. The report described progress made by countries in implementing the Plan of Action's road map [YUN 2003, p. 1219], noting that action was being taken in several areas, including national capacity-building and promotion of institutional follow-up to the Madrid Plan; ageing-specific policy and programmes; and mainstreaming efforts.

The report noted that the UN Department of Economic and Social Affairs (DESA) was continuing to work on the technical assistance initiative, launched in 2003, to support Member States in implementing the Madrid Plan of Action, including undertaking advisory missions to Kyrgyzstan in 2004 and to Egypt in 2005. However, lack of awareness of the Madrid Plan or its contents remained an obstacle to implementation in some regions, and even among UN staff in field offices. Overall, there was a need to strengthen the strategy for raising the visibility of the Madrid Plan at both the national and international levels. The report observed that mainstreaming ageing in national plans and international strategies also remained a challenge. It also noted that ageing and the situation of older persons often continued to be addressed from a humanitarian perspective that ignored the potential of older persons to contribute to reaching national development objectives. It further noted that national capacity-building was essential for the implementation of the Madrid Plan, but the human and financial resources available to the UN system, and specifically to DESA, for providing technical assistance remained severely limited.

The Secretary-General suggested that the Assembly consider calling on States, UN system funds and agencies and NGOs to reinforce their advocacy campaigns aimed at informing major societal actors about the decisions taken at the Second World Assembly on Ageing. The Assembly should reiterate its recommendation that the situation of older persons should be taken into account in reaching development goals and stress the need for additional capacity-building at the national level in order to implement the Madrid Plan of Action.

International Conference. On 24 August [A/60/377-E/2005/92], Qatar transmitted to the Secretary-General and the General Assembly President the Declaration of the Doha International Conference on Ageing in View of Present-Day Changes (Doha, Qatar, 4-6 April). The Declaration contained recommendations relating to care and concern for the elderly and their participation in development, and appealed for the drafting of a universal declaration of the rights of the elderly, to be promulgated on the International Day of Older Persons (designated as 1 October by the Assembly in resolution 45/106 [YUN 1990, p. 820]).

GENERAL ASSEMBLY ACTION

On 16 December [meeting 64], the General Assembly, on the recommendation of the Third (Social, Humanitarian and Cultural) Committee [A/60/502 & Corr.1], adopted **resolution 60/135** without vote [agenda item 63].

Follow-up to the Second World Assembly on Ageing

The General Assembly,

Recalling its resolution 57/167 of 18 December 2002, in which it endorsed the Political Declaration and the Madrid International Plan of Action on Ageing, 2002, its resolution 58/134 of 22 December 2003, in which it took note, inter alia, of the road map for the implementation of the Madrid Plan of Action, and its resolution 59/150 of 20 December 2004,

Recalling also Economic and Social Council resolution 2003/14 of 21 July 2003, in which the Council invited Governments, the United Nations system and civil society to participate in a "bottom-up" approach to the review and appraisal of the Madrid Plan of Action,

Recalling further Commission for Social Development resolution 42/1 of 13 February 2004 entitled "Modalities for the review and appraisal of the Madrid International Plan of Action on Ageing, 2002", in which the Commission decided to undertake the review and appraisal of the Madrid Plan of Action every five years, with each review and appraisal cycle to focus on one of the priority directions of the Madrid Plan of Action,

Recognizing that in many parts of the world, awareness of the Madrid Plan of Action remains limited or non-existent, which limits the scope of implementation efforts,

1. *Calls upon* Governments, the organizations and bodies of the United Nations system and the non-governmental community to reinforce their advocacy campaigns aimed at informing all major societal actors, including older persons and their organizations, about the decisions taken at the Second World Assembly on Ageing;

2. *Recommends* that ongoing efforts to achieve the internationally agreed development goals, including those contained in the United Nations Millennium Declaration, take into account the situation of older persons;

3. *Calls upon* Governments and, within their mandates, the agencies and organizations of the United Nations system, and encourages the non-governmental community, to ensure that the challenges of population ageing and the concerns of older persons are adequately incorporated into their programmes and projects;

4. *Invites* Member States and the organizations and bodies of the United Nations system to take into account the needs and concerns of older persons in decision-making at all levels;

5. *Stresses* the need for additional capacity-building at the national level in order to promote and facilitate implementation of the Madrid International Plan of Action on Ageing, 2002, and in this connection encourages Governments to support the United Nations Trust Fund for Ageing to enable the Department of Economic and Social Affairs of the Secretariat to provide expanded assistance to countries, upon their request;

6. *Calls upon* Governments to consult and utilize the Research Agenda on Ageing for the Twenty-first Century, adopted by the Valencia Forum in April 2002, as a tool for strengthening national capacity on ageing for the implementation, review and appraisal of the Madrid Plan of Action;

7. *Invites* Governments, intergovernmental organizations and non-governmental organizations to encourage and support comprehensive, diversified and specialized research on ageing in all countries;

8. *Invites* the functional commissions of the Economic and Social Council to integrate the issues of population and individual ageing into their work in order to promote implementation of the Madrid Plan of Action;

9. *Recommends* that the Commission on the Status of Women continue to consider the situation of older women, in particular those who are most vulnerable, including those living in rural areas;

10. *Encourages* those regional commissions that have not yet done so to elaborate a regional strategy for the implementation of the Madrid Plan of Action;

11. *Takes note* of Commission for Social Development resolution 42/1, and in this context requests the Secretary-General to present his proposals for conducting the review and appraisal exercise at the regional and global levels to the Commission at its forty-fourth session;

12. *Requests* the organizations and bodies of the United Nations system to continue to strengthen the capacity of the focal points on ageing and to provide them with adequate resources for further implementation of the Madrid Plan of Action, in particular through appropriate mainstreaming action;

13. *Stresses* the importance of the collection of data and population statistics disaggregated by age and sex on all aspects of policy formulation by all countries, and encourages the relevant entities of the United Nations system to support national efforts in capacity-building, especially those of developing countries and countries with economies in transition, takes note in this context of the establishment by the United Nations of an Internet-accessible database on ageing, and invites States to submit, whenever possible, information for inclusion in the database;

14. *Takes note* of the report of the Secretary-General, and requests that it be forwarded to the Commission for Social Development at its forty-fourth session in order to assist the Commission in its deliberations;

15. *Requests* the Secretary-General to report to the General Assembly at its sixty-first session on the implementation of the present resolution.

Chapter XII

Refugees and displaced persons

In 2005, although the total number of persons of concern to the Office of the United Nations High Commissioner for Refugees (UNHCR) rose by 8 per cent to 20.8 million, from 19.2 million in 2004, the refugee population worldwide fell to its lowest level in almost a quarter century and mass refugee outflows into neighbouring countries were also the lowest in 29 years. Refugees accounted for 40 per cent of the 2005 population of concern, followed by internally displaced persons (IDPs), 32 per cent and stateless persons, 11 per cent. UNHCR maintained efforts to find durable solutions for those groups, encouraging voluntary repatriation or return as the preferred solution. In that regard, an estimated 1.1 million refugees returned to their countries of origin during the year. With UNHCR's assistance, thousands other refugees found solutions through resettlement elsewhere, or were integrated locally. To facilitate that process, the UNHCR Executive Committee had adopted a Conclusion on Local Integration, setting out a framework for related activities. New refugee outflows totalled some 136,000 recorded arrivals in 19 asylum countries, most notably in Chad (32,400), Benin (25,500), Ghana (13,600), Uganda (24,000) and Yemen (13,200). Those outflows resulted mainly from the ongoing conflict in Sudan's Darfur region and the consequent decline in the security situation in the Chad/Darfur area, instability in parts of the Central African Republic and violence in regions of Côte d'Ivoire, the Democratic Republic of the Congo (DRC) and Somalia, among other places. Overall, up to 5 million of the world's refugee population remained in protracted situations, including Afghans (1.7 million), Burundians (394,000), Congolese from the DRC (308,000), Somalis (229,000) and Sudanese (364,000). Others affected were Saharawi refugees in the Tindouf camps in Algeria, Bhutanese in Nepal and the Rohingyas in Bangladesh. UNHCR maintained efforts to find durable solutions for those caught in protracted situations, including through the restructuring of its Department of International Protection and the creation of a Solutions and operations support section, charged with reviewing such situations and enhancing resettlement services.

Despite improvements in many aspects of the protection environment during the year, UNHCR continued to face significant challenges in addressing protection gaps relating to sexual and gender-based violence and restrictive practices regarding reception and access to asylum procedures. Other difficulties included security-related concerns, as well as the major challenge of working with States to identify comprehensive approaches to using all durable solutions for persons of concern. Ongoing efforts to implement the "Convention Plus" initiative, launched in 2003 to help strengthen the commitment of States and UNHCR partners to resolving refugee situations through multilateral action plans, focused on concluding negotiations to better address secondary movements and target development assistance for durable solutions. During the year, the Commonwealth of Independent States (CIS) Conference process, launched in 1996 to address the unique and complex mix of problems facing refugees and other displaced people in those States, concluded with the adoption of a final statement and the examination of a successor framework for considering Euro-Asian cooperation on migration.

Appointment. On 27 May, the General Assembly, by **decision 59/420,** appointed Mr. Antônio Manuel de Oliveira Guterres as United Nations High Commissioner for Refugees for a period of five years.

Office of the United Nations High Commissioner for Refugees

Programme policy

Executive Committee Action. At its fifty-sixth session (Geneva, 3-7 October) [A/60/12/Add.1], the Executive Committee of the UNHCR Programme, in a conclusion on international protection, expressed concern at the human rights violations perpetuating displacement within and beyond national borders and called on States to promote and protect the rights of all refugees and other persons of concern, with special attention to those with specific needs, particularly children. It encouraged States, UNHCR, intergovernmental organizations and non-governmental organizations (NGOs) to redouble efforts to implement the Agenda for Protection [YUN 2002, p. 1205], the multi-year programme of action for enhancing the protection of refugees and asylum-seekers. Reflecting on the need for UNHCR to strengthen its presence in the field, the Committee called on States to support its efforts in that regard with the timely provision of resources and by ensuring the safety and security of all UNHCR personnel and property and that of other humanitarian organizations discharging UNHCR-mandated functions. The Committee noted proposals to strengthen the Programme's humanitarian system and encouraged it to explore the feasibility of assuming coordination responsibilities for the protection of internally displaced persons (IDPs), camp management and shelter in conflict situations. The Committee also adopted conclusions on the legal provision on international protection, including through complementary forms of protection and on local integration. It approved the creation of a post of Assistant High Commissioner (Protection) at the Assistant Secretary-General level, effective 1 January 2006; and adopted decisions on enhancing the independence of the Office of the Inspector-General; and on administrative, financial and programme matters.

In his opening statement to the Committee, the High Commissioner, highlighting aspects of the 2005 World Summit Outcome (see p. 48) that could open up new opportunities for addressing the root causes of the conflicts resulting in forced displacement, noted contradictions in areas crucial to UNHCR's work. Such a situation was at odds with UNHCR as a non-political humanitarian body. He stressed that the Office was primarily a protection agency concerned with the need to create a space where rights could be enjoyed fully and where the rule of law prevailed. That was one of the main reasons for his proposals to establish the position of Assistant High Commissioner for Protection [YUN 2004, p. 1200] and to reorganize UNHCR's field support services for effective protection delivery. The High Commissioner resolved to reform UNHCR's structures, rules and procedures, with the aim of ensuring that protection informed all its policies and activities, particularly regarding women, children and older persons of concern. From that perspective, mainstreaming the effective implementation of UNHCR policies, guidelines and actions on gender, age and diversity would be a top priority in 2006, as would continuing efforts to eradicate malnutrition and increase the capacity to combat HIV/AIDS and other serious health risks. The physical security of refugees and returnees also remained high on UNHCR's protection agenda, as was the security of its staff and partners. Its operational

priority was to build up the requisite capacity by 2007, to ensure a quick and effective response to unexpected refugee crises that might affect up to 500,000 people.

To further meet its challenges, UNHCR needed to demonstrate vision and results, strong partnerships, a viable funding base, transparency, accountability and structural reform. To that end, it was making efforts to strengthen the Office of the Inspector-General and its independence, and was committed to establishing a results-based management system, with clear objectives, a measurable process for achieving them and an organization-wide accountability framework. For the first time, the Office issued the Global Strategic Objectives at the beginning of the planning cycle to instruct and guide the budget and programming process.

GENERAL ASSEMBLY ACTION

On 16 December [meeting 64], the General Assembly, on the recommendation of the Third (Social, Humanitarian and Cultural) Committee [A/60/499], adopted **resolution 60/129** without vote [agenda item 39].

Office of the United Nations High Commissioner for Refugees

The General Assembly,

Having considered the report of the United Nations High Commissioner for Refugees on the activities of his Office and the report of the Executive Committee of the Programme of the United Nations High Commissioner for Refugees on the work of its fifty-sixth session and the conclusions and decisions contained therein,

Recalling its previous annual resolutions on the work of the Office of the High Commissioner since its establishment by the General Assembly,

Expressing its appreciation for the leadership shown by the High Commissioner, commending the staff and implementing partners of the Office of the High Commissioner for the competent, courageous and dedicated manner in which they discharge their responsibilities, and underscoring its strong condemnation of all forms of violence to which humanitarian personnel and United Nations and associated personnel are increasingly exposed,

1. *Endorses* the report of the Executive Committee of the Programme of the United Nations High Commissioner for Refugees on the work of its fifty-sixth session;

2. *Welcomes* the important work undertaken by the Office of the United Nations High Commissioner for Refugees and its Executive Committee in the course of the year, and notes in this context the adoption of the general conclusion on international protection, the conclusion on the provision of international protection, including through complementary forms of protection, and the conclusion on local integration, which are aimed at strengthening the international protection regime, consistent with the Agenda for Protection, and at assisting Governments in meeting their protec-

tion responsibilities in today's changing international environment;

3. *Reaffirms* the 1951 Convention relating to the Status of Refugees and the 1967 Protocol thereto as the foundation of the international refugee protection regime, recognizes the importance of their full and effective application by States parties and the values they embody, notes with satisfaction that one hundred and forty-six States are now parties to one instrument or to both, encourages States not parties to consider acceding to those instruments, underlines in particular the importance of full respect for the principle of non-refoulement, and recognizes that a number of States not parties to the international refugee instruments have shown a generous approach to hosting refugees;

4. *Notes* that fifty-eight States are now parties to the 1954 Convention relating to the Status of Stateless Persons and that thirty States are parties to the 1961 Convention on the Reduction of Statelessness, and encourages the High Commissioner to continue his activities on behalf of stateless persons;

5. *Notes with interest* the Mexico Plan of Action to Strengthen International Protection of Refugees in Latin America, endorsed by States participating in the meeting commemorating the twentieth anniversary of the Cartagena Declaration on Refugees convened in Mexico City on 15 and 16 November 2004, and expresses its support for the efforts of interested States and the Office of the High Commissioner to promote its implementation, with the cooperation and assistance of the international community;

6. *Welcomes* the successful conclusion of the follow-up process to the 1996 Geneva Conference on the problems of refugees, displaced persons, migration and asylum issues in the countries of the Commonwealth of Independent States, and encourages States, the Office of the High Commissioner and other relevant actors to continue to work collaboratively, building on the successes of the Conference process to date;

7. *Re-emphasizes* that the protection of refugees is primarily the responsibility of States, whose full and effective cooperation, action and political resolve are required to enable the Office of the High Commissioner to fulfil its mandated functions;

8. *Urges* all States and relevant non-governmental and other organizations, in conjunction with the Office of the High Commissioner, in a spirit of international solidarity and burden- and responsibility-sharing, to cooperate and to mobilize resources with a view to enhancing the capacity of, and reducing the heavy burden borne by, countries that have received large numbers of refugees and asylum-seekers, and calls upon the Office to continue to play its catalytic role in mobilizing assistance from the international community to address the root causes as well as the economic, environmental and social impact of large-scale refugee populations in developing countries, in particular the least developed countries, and countries with economies in transition;

9. *Emphasizes* that international protection of refugees is a dynamic and action-oriented function that is at the core of the mandate of the Office of the High Commissioner and that it includes, in cooperation with States and other partners, the promotion and facilitation of, inter alia, the admission, reception and treatment of refugees in accordance with internation-

ally agreed standards and the ensuring of durable, protection-oriented solutions, bearing in mind the particular needs of vulnerable groups and paying special attention to those with specific needs, and notes in this context that the delivery of international protection is a staff-intensive service that requires adequate staff with the appropriate expertise, especially at the field level;

10. *Notes* the activities undertaken in pursuit of the objectives of the Convention Plus initiative, and encourages the High Commissioner and interested States to strengthen the international protection regime through the development of specific, multilateral, comprehensive and practical approaches to resolving refugee situations, including improving international burden- and responsibility-sharing and realizing durable solutions within a multilateral context;

11. *Welcomes* the progress that has been achieved in increasing the number of refugees resettled and the number of States offering opportunities for resettlement, notes that the Multilateral Framework of Understandings on Resettlement sets out the strategic use of resettlement as part of a comprehensive approach to refugee situations aimed at improving access to durable solutions for a greater number of refugees, and invites interested States, the Office of the High Commissioner and other relevant partners to make use of the Multilateral Framework, where appropriate and feasible;

12. *Recalls* the important role of effective partnerships and coordination in meeting the needs of refugees and other displaced persons and in finding durable solutions to their situations, welcomes the efforts under way, in cooperation with countries hosting refugees and countries of origin, including their respective local communities, United Nations agencies and other development actors, to promote a framework for durable solutions, particularly in protracted refugee situations, which includes the "4Rs" approach (repatriation, reintegration, rehabilitation and reconstruction) to sustainable return, and encourages States, in cooperation with United Nations agencies and other development actors, to support, inter alia, through the allocation of funds, the development and implementation of the 4Rs and other programming tools to facilitate the transition from relief to development;

13. *Strongly reaffirms* the fundamental importance and the purely humanitarian and non-political character of the function of the Office of the High Commissioner of providing international protection to refugees and seeking permanent solutions to refugee problems, and recalls that these solutions include voluntary repatriation and, where appropriate and feasible, local integration and resettlement in a third country, while reaffirming that voluntary repatriation, supported by necessary rehabilitation and development assistance to facilitate sustainable reintegration, remains the preferred solution;

14. *Acknowledges* that the provision by States of complementary forms of protection to ensure that persons in need of international protection actually receive it is a positive way of responding pragmatically to certain situations, and affirms that measures to provide complementary forms of protection should be implemented in a manner that strengthens the existing international refugee protection regime;

15. *Notes* that local integration in the refugee context is a sovereign decision and an option to be exercised by States guided by their treaty obligations and human rights principles and that it is a dynamic and multifaceted two-way process that requires efforts by all parties concerned, including a preparedness on the part of refugees to adapt to the host society without having to forego their own cultural identity and a corresponding readiness on the part of host communities and public institutions to welcome refugees and to meet the needs of a diverse population, and acknowledges that the process of local integration is complex and gradual, comprising three distinct but interrelated legal, economic, and social and cultural dimensions, all of which are important to the ability of refugees to integrate successfully;

16. *Acknowledges* that the global refugee situation represents an international challenge requiring that international burden- and responsibility-sharing be addressed effectively, and recognizes that allowing for local integration, where applicable, is an act of States that is a durable solution for refugees, which contributes to the said burden- and responsibility-sharing, without prejudice to the specific situation of certain developing countries facing mass influxes;

17. *Emphasizes* the obligation of all States to accept the return of their nationals, calls upon States to facilitate the return of their nationals who have been determined not to be in need of international protection, and affirms the need for the return of persons to be undertaken in a safe and humane manner and with full respect for their human rights and dignity, irrespective of the status of the persons concerned;

18. *Condemns* all acts that pose a threat to the personal security and well-being of refugees and asylum-seekers, such as refoulement, unlawful expulsion and physical attacks, and calls upon all States of refuge, in cooperation with international organizations where appropriate, to take all necessary measures to ensure respect for the principles of refugee protection, including the humane treatment of asylum-seekers;

19. *Affirms* the importance of mainstreaming the protection needs of women and children to ensure their participation in the planning and implementation of programmes of the Office of the High Commissioner and State policies and the importance of according priority to addressing the problem of sexual and gender-based violence;

20. *Encourages* the Office of the High Commissioner to continue to improve its management systems and to ensure effective and transparent use of its resources, recognizes that adequate and timely resources are essential for the Office to continue to fulfil the mandate conferred upon it through its statute and by subsequent General Assembly resolutions on refugees and other persons of concern, recalls its resolutions 58/153 of 22 December 2003, 58/270 of 23 December 2003 and 59/170 of 20 December 2004 concerning the implementation of paragraph 20 of the statute of the Office, and urges Governments and other donors to respond promptly to annual and supplementary appeals issued by the Office for requirements under its programmes;

21. *Requests* the High Commissioner to report on his activities to the General Assembly at its sixty-first session.

Strengthening UNHCR

Oral report of High Commissioner. Pursuant to General Assembly resolution 58/153 [YUN 2003, p. 1226] on strengthening UNHCR's capacity to carry out its mandate, a UNHCR representative presented a 21 July oral update of the High Commissioner to the Economic and Social Council [E/2005/SR.35] on the coordination aspects of the work of the Office. UNHCR was working more closely with other actors within the UN system, as partnerships were the only means of helping conflict-torn countries create conditions for sustainable return. On the humanitarian front, UNHCR was collaborating with the Office for the Coordination of Humanitarian Affairs (OCHA) in a number of areas, including participation in an inter-agency process aimed at improving assistance and protection to internally displaced persons. It was cooperating with the World Food Programme (WFP) to secure adequate levels of food and water to refugees and exploring ways to enhance ties with the United Nations Children's Fund (UNICEF) and the Office of the High Commissioner for Human Rights. The Office was also strengthening its cooperation with the Department of Peacekeeping Operations in the field of disarmament, demobilization and reintegration in peacekeeping missions. It also supported the establishment of a Peacebuilding Commission (see p. 113) and hoped to contribute to the planned peacebuilding support office. In terms of longer-term recovery strategies, the Office's membership in the United Nations Development Group (UNDG) was beginning to show concrete results, as UNHCR was participating actively in the joint UNDG/World Bank needs assessments for countries emerging from conflict and in transition from relief to development.

Pursuant to Assembly resolution 59/172 [YUN 2004, p. 1208], which requested the Secretary-General to report orally to the Economic and Social Council on assistance to refugees, returnees and displaced persons in Africa (see p. 1311), the Representative noted that some 4.5 million people, including approximately 2.8 million refugees were of concern to UNHCR on the continent. Voluntary repatriation continued to be a key objective of its operations on the continent, and the challenge in such operations was to ensure the sustainability of returns by addressing the reintegration needs of returnees and IDPs, and the post-conflict reconstruction priorities of communities in the areas of return.

Coordination of emergency humanitarian assistance

In 2005 [A/61/12], UNHCR actively supported UN system reform and improvements to the global humanitarian response capacity through discussions on policy and implementation, notably regarding peace and security, system-wide coherence, development, and strengthening of the Resident Coordinator and Humanitarian Coordinator systems. It was engaged with the Peacebuilding Commission, whose work should play a crucial role in supporting the sustainable reintegration of returning refugees and IDPs. The Office also continued to participate in other key coordination bodies, including the United Nations Chief Executives Board for Coordination (CEB) and its subsidiary bodies, the UNDG and the Executive Committee for Humanitarian Affairs (ECHA). Together with the Joint United Nations Programme on HIV/AIDS (UNAIDS) and other partners, it maintained efforts to help combat HIV and AIDS among persons of concern and to ensure their inclusion within host country programmes on the disease. UNHCR continued to function as the secretariat of the UN sub-cluster on humanitarian response and post-conflict recovery in the African Union's (AU) New Partnership for Africa's Development (NEPAD) programme (see p. 1080). Bilateral collaboration helped make its interventions more effective in such areas as food security and nutrition, upholding human rights, advocacy in combating restrictive asylum measures, the rights of IDPs, and in respect of the many challenges posed by the asylum-migration nexus. Its partnerships with NGOs continued to evolve towards more comprehensive collaboration and involvement in the assessment, planning, implementation and evaluation phases of operations, as well as in revising various guidelines and policies. In 2005, over 20 per cent of UNHCR's budget was channelled through partnerships with nearly 650 NGOs, approximately 80 per cent of which were national NGOs. The bulk of the funding covered education, legal assistance and protection, health and nutrition, shelter and other infrastructure, community services, and transport and logistics.

Evaluation activities

UNHCR, in a July report [A/AC.96/1014], updated information on the activities of its Evaluation and Policy Analysis Unit (EPAU). During the year, the Unit published numerous evaluation reports, tools and reviews and worked on a variety of projects expected to be completed by year's end or early in 2006. Those included the revision of its urban refugee policy and fast-track programme; an evaluation of its protection staffing capacity, the Protection Information Section and vehicle fleet around the world; its joint evaluation of the Norwegian Refugee Committee's secondments to the Office and its pilot food dis-

tribution in five countries; and an update and follow-up to the 2004 evaluation of its Medical Service. The evaluation policy adopted in 2003 [YUN 2003, p. 1224] had been implemented, but showed distinct shortcomings owing to the lack of capacity to meaningfully train staff in evaluation, among other reasons. While noting the need for EPAU to also hone its policy analysis capacity, the report highlighted efforts to assess its practices and review UNHCR's evaluation policy and institutional framework, in order to meet the criteria set by the UN System-wide agreed Norms and Standards for Evaluation, contained in General Assembly resolution 59/250 [YUN 2004, p. 868]. Also in line with those norms and standards, the Unit intended to professionalize its team during 2005 and 2006. According to UNHCR's *Global Report 2005*, one of its key concerns was ensuring that evaluation findings and recommendations were effectively utilized by UNHCR. Thus, to support the use of lessons learned in programming and decision-making, the Unit designed a database which indexed all recommendations contained in evaluation reports, thereby allowing for better performance and accountability in planning and implementing UNHCR's operational activities.

Inspections

In 2005 [A/61/12], the High Commissioner revised the terms of reference of the role, functions and methods of work of the Inspector-General's Office (IGO), providing a new charter aimed at ensuring its independence. It also introduced a policy of wider dissemination of inspection reports and updating IGO's operational policies and procedures, in line with relevant administrative instructions from the Secretary-General. In October, the Executive Committee adopted a decision on enhancing IGO's independence to enable it to better fulfil its functions. IGO continued during the year to increase its investigation capacity through the training of 80 staff members in the Investigation Learning Programme. Quality standards were established to increase professionalism in the conduct of investigations and to provide the basis for quality assurance initiatives in the future.

During the year, IGO carried out ten inspections at the country level and one at headquarters, resulting in over 300 recommendations to address recurring problems. Those included patterns of use of United Nations Volunteers and United Nations Office for Project Services arrangements for meeting field staffing needs; assignment of critical front-line responsibilities in field operations to inexperienced staff; limited engagement of country offices with situations of statelessness; the lack of adequate information sharing with implementing partners in planning processes; and the lack of clarity in roles, responsibilities, authority levels and communication channels in field operations. IGO received 99 new reports of possible misconduct; investigative findings supported a conclusion of misconduct in 21 per cent of those cases.

During the reporting period, the UN Office of Internal Oversight Services (OIOS) audited operations and activities with expenditure amounting to $172 million in over 20 UNHCR field operations and several headquarters Units. It continued to use a measurement system to rate the effectiveness of the application of key internal controls in audited operations, which facilitated benchmarking between country operations, provided assurances that activities were adequately administered and assisted in identifying operations where prompt corrective action was required. UNHCR initiated a Risk Management Framework, which would help develop a risk-based audit plan for activities beginning in 2008.

Enlargement of the Executive Committee

On 22 July (**decision 2005/243**) and 21 October (**decision 2005/314**), respectively, the Economic and Social Council took note of the requests of Jordan [E/2005/46] and Portugal [E/2005/93] for membership in the UNHCR Executive Committee and recommended that the General Assembly take a decision at its sixtieth (2005) session on the question of enlarging the Committee's membership from 68 to 70 States.

GENERAL ASSEMBLY ACTION

On 16 December [meeting 64], the General Assembly, on the recommendation of the Third Committee [A/60/499], adopted **resolution 60/127** without vote [agenda item 39].

Enlargement of the Executive Committee of the Programme of the United Nations High Commissioner for Refugees

The General Assembly,

Taking note of Economic and Social Council decisions 2005/243 of 22 July 2005 and 2005/314 of 21 October 2005 concerning the enlargement of the Executive Committee of the Programme of the United Nations High Commissioner for Refugees,

Taking note also of the requests regarding the enlargement of the Executive Committee contained in the letter dated 8 March 2005 from the Permanent Representative of Jordan to the United Nations addressed to the Secretary-General and the letter dated 12 September 2005 from the Permanent Representative of Portugal to the United Nations addressed to the Secretary-General,

1. *Decides* to increase the number of members of the Executive Committee of the Programme of the

United Nations High Commissioner for Refugees from sixty-eight to seventy States;

2. *Requests* the Economic and Social Council to elect the additional members at its resumed organizational session for 2006.

Financial and administrative questions

UNHCR's initial annual programme budget target for 2005 was set at $974.6 million by the Executive Committee in 2004 [YUN 2004, p. 1200]. Total income for 2005 amounted to some $1,216 million. Contributions and miscellaneous income (including a carry-over from 2004) provided $843.6 million for the annual programme budget and $317.2 million for the supplementary programme budgets, with $16.1 million provided for the Junior Professional Officers (JPO) programme, and $39.3 million received from the UN regular budget. Expenditure totalled $1,141.6 million, with the highest amount going to Africa ($529 million), followed by Central Asia, South-West Asia, North Africa and the Middle East ($165.2 million), Europe ($108.3 million), Asia and the Pacific ($82.7 million) and the Americas ($31.4 million).

In October, the Executive Committee approved the revised annual programme budget for 2005, amounting to $980.5 million, including the UN regular budget contribution of $34.6 million, which, with the provisions for JPOs of $8.5 million and the needs under supplementary programmes of $370.2 million, brought total requirements in 2005 to $1,359.2 million.

The Committee also approved $1,136.8 million for the 2006 annual programme budget, including an operational reserve of $75.8 million, and agreed to continue on a further trial basis in 2006, to provide appropriation authority for fully funded additional activities. Together with $8.5 million for JPOs, those provisions brought requirements for 2006 to $1,145.3 million. The Committee authorized the High Commissioner, within the total appropriation, to effect adjustments in regional and global programmes and in headquarters budgets, create supplementary programmes and issue special appeals when emergency needs could not be met fully from the operational reserve.

The Committee decided to move to a biennial programme/budget cycle with effect from the 2008-2009 biennium and requested UNHCR to begin the necessary preparatory work, including the revision to its Financial Rules. The Committee extended the pilot period of the operational reserve, category II, to allow for an independent evaluation of its use and effectiveness, and enable a final decision on it to be made at the Committee's 2006 session. It also requested UNHCR, in

2006, to elaborate the criteria for and financial consequences of the non-inclusion of supplementary programmes in the annual programme budget.

Accounts (2004)

The audited financial statements of voluntary funds administered by UNHCR for the year ended 31 December 2004 [A/60/5/Add.5] showed total expenditures of $1,065.3 million and total available funds of $1,207 million, with a reserve balance of $141.7 million.

The Board of Auditors found that: expenditures had increased by 8 per cent, to $1,065 million, which exceeded the increase in income and led to a deficit of $58 million; the reserve and fund balance at year's end remained, at $142.4 million in real terms; and UNHCR was not able to obtain confirmation of the $4.5 million spent on its behalf by the United Nations Development Programme (UNDP), due to deficiencies in UNDP's new enterprise resource planning system. The Board further found that there was no proper segregation of financial duties in several instances for the posting of cash-related transactions; the amounts in previous subprojects covered by audit certificates decreased from 77 per cent in mid-June 2004 to 58 per cent in mid-June 2005; UNHCR failed to seek reimbursement to cover the cost of processing payments made for the United Nations Compensation Commission; and had not completely phased out the use of "project staff" by the 2001 deadline. In addition, the consistency and quality of public protection and resettlement activities and information could be further enhanced; results-based management and multi-year planning improved with regard to the definition of indicators of achievement and the evaluation process; and the management of field offices and the New York Office needed to be improved in the areas of delegation of authority, asset management and planning. The Board made recommendations to improve financial management and reporting and programme management. It observed that UNHCR had actively responded to most recommendations, although some had not yet been implemented.

UNHCR, in August [A/AC.96/1010/Add.1], reported on measures taken or proposed to respond to the Board's recommendations.

In a September report [A/60/387], the Advisory Committee on Administrative and Budgetary Questions (ACABQ) noted that UNHCR's financial situation was a continuing cause for concern, especially given its $58 million budget deficit, which was larger than in previous years. It expected the Board to address the underlying causes of the deficit and to develop management audit recommendations to assist UNHCR in reducing it without negatively affecting its operations. ACABQ expected the Office to prepare its budgets for 2007 and the 2008-2009 biennium using results-based budgeting guidelines, and asked for more details about its procurement activities. ACABQ expressed concern about unfunded liabilities for after-service health insurance, accrued annual leave and termination benefits amounting to $336 million. It noted, in that regard, that UNHCR had not fully implemented the Board's recommendation to phase out the use of project staff and requested an update on the situation of staff in between assignments in the Board's follow-up report.

The Executive Committee, in a decision on administrative, financial and programme matters [A/60/12/Add.1], requested that it be regularly informed on the measures taken to address the recommendations and observations made by the Board of Auditors and ACABQ.

GENERAL ASSEMBLY ACTION

On 23 December [meeting 69], the General Assembly, on the recommendation of the Fifth (Administrative and Budgetary) Committee [A/60/561], adopted **resolution 60/234 A** without vote [agenda item 121].

Financial reports and audited financial statements, and reports of the Board of Auditors

The General Assembly,

Recalling its resolutions 59/264 A of 23 December 2004 and 59/264 B of 22 June 2005,

Having considered the audited financial statements and the report of the Board of Auditors on the voluntary funds administered by the United Nations High Commissioner for Refugees for the year ended 31 December 2004, the note by the Secretary-General transmitting to the General Assembly the letter dated 1 July 2005 from the Chairman of the Board of Auditors transmitting the report of the Board on implementation of its recommendations relating to the biennium 2002-2003, and the related report of the Advisory Committee on Administrative and Budgetary Questions,

Recognizing the difficult conditions under which the Office of the United Nations High Commissioner for Refugees does its work,

1. *Accepts* the financial report and audited financial statements and the report and audit opinion of the Board of Auditors regarding the voluntary funds administered by the United Nations High Commissioner for Refugees for the period from 1 January to 31 December 2004;

2. *Endorses* the recommendations of the Board of Auditors contained in its report;

3. *Also endorses* the conclusions and recommendations contained in the report of the Advisory Committee on Administrative and Budgetary Questions, subject to the provisions of the present resolution;

4. *Takes note* of paragraph 18 of the report of the Advisory Committee on Administrative and Budgetary Questions, and invites the Advisory Committee, in its future consideration of the report on the implementation of the recommendations of the Board of Auditors, to provide further advice on this proposal;

5. *Commends* the Board of Auditors for the quality of its report and the streamlined format thereof;

6. *Recognizes* the efforts of the United Nations High Commissioner for Refugees in implementing the recommendations of the Board of Auditors, and requests the High Commissioner to intensify his efforts to continue to implement the recommendations of the Board and to report regularly to the relevant governing bodies on progress made in this regard;

7. *Notes* the concerns of the Board of Auditors about the general financial situation of the Office of the United Nations High Commissioner for Refugees, including the further depletion of the reserves of the Office, and encourages Member States to respond in a timely manner to the appeal of the Office for resources;

8. *Recalls* paragraph 7 of its resolution 58/249 A of 23 December 2003, by which the General Assembly requested the Secretary-General to report to it on the full extent of unfunded staff termination and post-service liabilities in the United Nations and its funds and programmes and to propose measures that would ensure progress towards fully funding such liabilities;

9. *Takes note* of the note by the Secretary-General transmitting to the General Assembly the letter dated 1 July 2005 from the Chairman of the Board of Auditors transmitting the report of the Board on implementation of its recommendations relating to the biennium 2002-2003;

10. *Requests* the Secretary-General, in accordance with paragraph 6 of its resolution 59/264 A, to take the necessary measures to ensure that the editing and translation of the reports of the Board of Auditors are completed in a manner that would ensure that they are submitted to the General Assembly in accordance with the six-week rule and thereby enable Member States to have adequate time to consider the large volume of reports prior to the sixty-first session of the General Assembly;

11. *Requests* the Secretary-General and the executive heads of the funds and programmes of the United Nations to include in future reports on the implementation of the recommendations of the Board of Auditors information on the setting of time frames, the identification of office holders and priorities for the implementation of the recommendations of the Board;

12. *Emphasizes* that the implementation of the recommendations of the Board of Auditors is essential to ensuring efficient operations and effective internal controls, and decides to monitor closely these efforts.

Management and administrative review

In connection with the High Commissioner's proposal for the establishment of the post of Assistant High Commissioner (Protection) [YUN 2004, p. 1200], UNHCR commissioned an independent study to review its senior management structure, in order to determine how such a position might affect that structure. The study, undertaken by the Geneva-based management consultancy firm, MANNET, examined the weaknesses and challenges facing UNHCR in carrying out its protection and durable solutions mandate; the relationship between the field, the UNHCR headquarters (the bureaux) and its Department of International Protection (DIP); the strategies and plans which the Office had adopted for its work; and the advantages and disadvantages of creating the proposed post.

The study found that UNHCR faced substantial problems regarding protection and durable solutions and that a persistent cause of those problems was related to the interface between its Operations Department and DIP. While reaffirming the status of the UNHCR headquarters as the primary platform for the management of operations, it held that DIP needed to be more operationally and field oriented and more dynamic on several policy and management issues. It acknowledged UNHCR's strategies and activities designed to strengthen protection and durable solutions but noted that better results would be achieved if those strategies and activities were brought together in a comprehensive organizational-strengthening or change-management context. The study raised questions pertaining to the advantages and disadvantages of the proposed post of Assistant High Commissioner, most notably in terms of its potential to help enhance UNHCR's ability to promote and advocate protection externally, strengthen its protection and durable solutions programme, enhance working relations between its operations department and DIP, reinforce the executive management group and strengthen its staffing situation. Other questions addressed the financial implications of creating the post and other alternatives. The study concluded that, although it did not find an overwhelming case for the proposed post of Assistant High Commissioner for Protection by upgrading the post of Director in DIP to that of Assistant Secretary-General level, such a position would be desirable, as it could significantly support UNHCR's overall capacity in protection and durable solutions and would also help improve the interface between operations and DIP. It therefore supported the High Commissioner's revised proposal for the new position, with the proviso that it be established within the context of a comprehensive organizational strengthening programme. That should not warrant any significant changes to UNHCR's structure, given that many of the problems preventing its headquarters from providing adequate support and guidance to the field were not primarily caused by organizational design but by cumbersome and inefficient processes rooted in the issues of organizational culture and leadership.

In October, the Executive Committee of the UNHCR Programme approved the creation of the post of Assistant High Commissioner (Protection) with effect from 1 January 2006, to oversee refugee protection and the related advocacy role of the Office.

Standing Committee

The UNHCR Standing Committee held three meetings in 2005: (8-11 March) [A/AC.96/1007]; (28-30 June) [A/AC.96/1017]; (21-22 September) [A/AC.96/1019]. It considered issues relating to UNHCR's programme budgets and funding; international protection; regional activities and global programmes; programme/protection policy; coordination; management, financial control, administrative oversight and human resources; governance; and consultations.

In October [A/60/12/Add.1], the Executive Committee reaffirmed its 2004 decision [YUN 2004, p. 1203] on the framework for the Standing Committee's programme of work for 2005, decided to integrate into its 2006 programme the work and activities of the High Commissioner's Forum and Convention Plus, and asked it to report on its work in 2006.

Staff safety

At the September meeting of the Standing Committee (21-22 September) [A/AC.96/1019], the Deputy Head of UNHCR Emergency and Security Service and the Chief of the Field Safety Section updated information on staff safety and security management, outlining the factors necessitating a comprehensive review of security management; the main issues of its two-year security work plan; the high priority accorded training and capacity building; a summary of the minimum operating security standards survey; collaboration with the UN Department of Safety and Security (DSS) and other UN organizations; and the future focus on staff safety. In response to questions regarding funding, notably a $10 million gap in funding, both executives clarified that the Office had not included security funding needs in the 2006 annual programme budget because field offices had not submitted up-to-date information. Of the options available, the highest priority was being given to seeking funding from UN common funds. Collaboration with DSS would be further strengthened, which should allow UNHCR to decrease the number of Field Safety Advisors deployed.

Refugee protection and assistance

Protection issues

In his annual report covering 2005 [A/61/12], the High Commissioner observed that, although the protection environment had improved in many areas, significant challenges persisted, including sexual and gender-based violence, often linked to limited livelihood alternatives and sub-standard food rations; restrictive practices regarding reception and access to asylum procedures; and instances of detention and refoulement in countries that had previously been strong adherents to refugee rights. UNHCR took steps to ensure that it could continue to strengthen its protection capacity in the light of changing developments, including systematizing dialogue on crosscutting issues at senior management levels, establishing a Field Reference Group on Protection Policies, developing a protection monitoring tool, and creating an innovative age, gender and diversity mainstreaming (AGDM) accountability framework (see p. 51). As the reporting period had witnessed further restrictions on access to and enjoyment of asylum, against a backdrop of growing national security concerns, UNHCR had intensified its advocacy, notably through training activities with border officials and the police. It continued to promote accession to the 1951 Convention relating to the Status of Refugees [YUN 1951, p. 520] and its 1967 Protocol [YUN 1967, p. 477].

In addition, UNCHR was engaging Governments to raise awareness of international protection needs and responsibilities, and to promote regional cooperation for protecting refugees within broader migration movements, cooperating as necessary with the International Organization for Migration (IOM). The Office worked with various other partners to ensure that legislation to criminalize trafficking included measures to protect and support the victims. The Office promoted ways of sharing burdens and responsibilities more equitably and building capacities to receive and protect refugees, and through its Strengthening Protection Capacity Project, consolidated and expanded its work to develop a comprehensive and sustainable capacity-building methodology. In a bid to address security-related concerns more effectively, it made efforts to sensitize refugees and local communities, as well as relevant government officials and the judiciary, on how best to address sexual and gender-based violence. It also stepped up its interventions against the military recruitment of children, in collaboration with UNICEF. As part of ongoing efforts to reinforce the search for durable solutions, the restructuring of UNHCR's Department of International Protection included the creation of a Solutions and Operations Support Section, charged primarily with reviewing protracted refugee situations. The restructuring also enhanced the Resettlement Service.

In a July note on international protection [A/AC.96/1008], the High Commissioner outlined the main challenges encountered by States and the international community, while addressing protection issues, and the actions taken to address them. He noted that, despite a reduction for the third consecutive year of the number of asylum-seekers in many industrialized countries and the fact that progress had been made in reducing decision-making backlogs in some countries and in building capacity in new asylum countries, refugees were not always safe in many asylum countries, owing to continuing conflicts. In some situations, the generosity of developing States that had hosted large numbers of refugees for many years showed signs of strain and the challenge was to maintain the momentum of the Agenda for Protection in an environment of "asylum fatigue". That could be done by making reporting on implementation a genuinely joint undertaking, whereby UNHCR, States and NGOs could jointly draft a comprehensive progress report five years after the Agenda's endorsement by the Executive Committee, outlining a common overview of gaps, challenges and future directions. Several of the recommendations contained in the Secretary-General's report entitled "In Larger Freedom" (see p. 68) could also significantly enhance the protection of the displaced.

The Executive Committee, in October [A/60/12/Add.1], noted the need for UNHCR to continue to strengthen its protection presence in the field, including female protection staff, and called on States to support its efforts through the timely and predictable provision of resources. It acknowledged the value of a focused range of activities aimed at strengthening the protection capacity of States, particularly those dealing with protracted refugee situations, and encouraged States, UNHCR, other intergovernmental organizations and NGOs to redouble their efforts to implement the Agenda for Protection and to explore the merits of a consolidated report to the Executive Committee on its implementation. In its conclusion on the provision of international protection, including through complementary forms of protection, it prescribed action and recommended measures for further strengthening the international refugee protection regime.

International instruments

In 2005, the number of States parties to the 1951 Convention relating to the Status of Refugees [YUN 1951, p. 520] and to its 1967 Protocol [YUN 1967, p. 477] rose to 143, following the accession of Afghanistan. Senegal's accession to the 1954 Convention relating to the Status of Stateless Persons [YUN 1954, p. 416] and the 1961 Convention on the Reduction of Statelessness [YUN 1961, p. 533] increased the number of States parties to those instruments to 58 and 30, respectively.

Convention Plus

In 2005, the "Convention Plus" initiative, launched in 2003 [YUN 2003, p. 1229] to help strengthen the commitment of States and UNHCR partners to resolving refugee situations, focused on concluding negotiations in order to address better secondary movements, target development assistance for durable solutions and explore opportunities for applying the Multilateral Framework of Understandings on Resettlement [YUN 2004, p. 1204]. The initiative encouraged UNHCR and the international community to place the resolution of protracted refugee situations higher on the international agenda, including through the adoption of comprehensive approaches to durable solutions, such as making more strategic use of resettlement and underpinning related durable solutions with development assistance. The initiative also engendered innovative methodologies for bridging gaps in protection, highlighted the complexity of addressing irregular secondary movements and provided a forum for clarifying the concerns and positions of States regarding those issues. At the meeting of the High Commissioner's Forum devoted to the "Convention Plus" (Geneva, 17 November), it was announced that the initiative would be mainstreamed into UNHCR's operations.

Assistance measures

The total population of concern to UNHCR increased from 19.5 million persons at the beginning of 2005 to 20.8 million by year's end. Of that number, stateless persons accounted for 11 per cent, IDPs 32 per cent and refugees, the largest group, 40 percent. However, the level of new refugee outflows during the year was the lowest since 1976, with a total of 136,000 *prima facie* refugee arrivals recorded in 19 asylum countries, notably Chad (32,400), Benin (25,500), Uganda (24,000), Ghana (13,600) and Yemen (13,200). Situations of particular concern included the ongoing conflict in the Sudan's Darfur region; a steady deterioration in the security situation in the Chad/Sudan border area and related military recruitments in refugee camps in eastern Chad, which chased 15,000 Chadians out of the country and displaced tens of thousands more inside; instability in parts of the Central African Republic, which resulted in further refugee movements into Chad; and continuing conflicts in parts of Côte d'Ivoire, the DRC, and Somalia uprooting people from their homes. IDPs worldwide numbered approximately 24 million, an increase of 22 per cent over the previous year and reflecting newly reported IDP situations in Iraq (1.2 million) and Somalia (400,000). Several countries reported a decrease in IDP numbers, including Bosnia and Herzegovina (126,500), Liberia (261,000) and the Russian Federation (164,000). No significant change, however, was recorded by Azerbaijan and Colombia, which had some 580,000 and 2 million IDPs, respectively. UNHCR assisted an estimated 1.1 million refugees to return to their places of origin, with the main returns occurring in Afghanistan (752,100), Angola (53,800), Burundi (68,300), Iraq (56,200) and Liberia (70,300). Many other refugees were resettled elsewhere, including Australia (11,700), Canada (10,400), Finland (770), the Netherlands (420), Norway (750), Sweden (1,300) and the United States (53,800). The main beneficiaries were from Afghanistan, Liberia, Myanmar, Somalia and the Sudan. Those assisted to find durable solutions through the local integration process of being granted citizenship by their host countries were absorbed by Armenia (2,300), Belgium (2,300), Ireland (580), Kyrgyzstan (3,400), Mexico (1,200), Turkmenistan (10,000) and the United States (58,900).

At year's end, there were an estimated 2.4 million stateless persons in 47 countries. That number was expected to increase as new data became available. During the year, UNHCR assisted concerned States to reduce protracted situations of statelessness by resolving the nationality status of stateless populations on their territories.

Refugees and the environment

During the year, UNHCR continued to implement its environmental policy and related activities, particularly with regard to safeguarding the institution of asylum in host countries where the presence of refugees had affected the environment. In accordance with its *Environmental Guidelines*, which were revised in 2005, it integrated environmental issues into field operations, which involved the dissemination of handbooks on forestry, livestock and sustainable agriculture. Repatriation operations in Africa would be assisted to develop country-specific rehabilitation strategies, in partnership with government authorities, NGOs, the World Conservation Union, the

United Nations Human Settlements Programme (UN-Habitat), the United Nations Environment Programme (UNEP) and other concerned agencies. UNHCR piloted various technologies and approaches to encourage the use of scarce natural resources more sustainably, including through the use of permaculture, techniques to reduce and substitute biomass materials for wood in cooking and construction, and the use of mud bricks and related construction materials needed by refugees. Other initiatives included the introduction of firewood-efficient stoves and of alternative energy sources, such as ethanol, biogas, solar and briquettes in Ethiopia, Nepal, Rwanda and Zambia. In November, the toolkit for the Framework for Assessing, Monitoring and Evaluation of Environment in Refugee Operations was completed. The mechanism, a pilot version of which was launched shortly thereafter, was benefitting refugee communities in Chad, Nepal, Uganda and the United Republic of Tanzania. According to the *UNHCR Global Report 2005*, funding for environmental impact-related projects in refugee-hosting countries was a fundamental issue that needed to be addressed in 2006.

Refugees and HIV/AIDS

In 2005, combating HIV/AIDS among persons of concern and ensuring full respect for the rights of those living with the disease remained policy priorities for UNHCR and were integral components of its strategic objective in programmes protection and assistance. It issued its 2005-2007 HIV/AIDS Strategic Plan, which drew on recent evidence on HIV/AIDS and forced displacement and on lessons learned from its previous strategic plan. Indicators of achievement in 2005 included the implementation of pilot projects and cooperation with UNAIDS co-sponsors for the inclusion and integration of refugees into host countries' HIV/AIDS policies and programmes. In addressing the linkage between sexual violence, protection and HIV/AIDS, UNHCR, together with the United Nations Population Fund (UNFPA), expanded its support to six country programmes in the area of post-exposure prophylaxis for rape victims. UNHCR gave technical and financial support to 29 country programmes. Globally, its HIV/AIDS interventions included voluntary counseling and testing in over 30 refugee camps in 11 countries for approximately 900,000 people; prevention of mother-to-child transmission programmes in over 18 camps in eight countries for approximately 650,000 people; and antiretroviral therapy to a number of refugees in 26 countries.

Refugee women

In 2005, UNHCR continued to implement its action plan to address the critical areas highlighted by the three evaluations it completed in 2002 [YUN 2002, p. 1201] on refugee women, refugee children and the role of community services, through targeted action to support groups facing discrimination. It continued to implement its pilot project on age, gender and diversity mainstreaming, launched in 2004 [YUN 2004, p. 1205]. It also dealt with the prevention of and response to sexual and gender-based violence, as well as gender equality.

Refugee children

The implementation of UNHCR's education policies was strengthened in 2005 through regional workshops on the application of field guidelines and strategic partnerships on education in Colombia, and on education and a community approach in Senegal. Some 1,000 students continued to receive university scholarships under the Albert Einstein German Refugee Initiative. UNHCR encouraged the establishment of national education committees to promote greater refugee access to quality education. To counter increasing trends of acute undernourishment among refugee children and women, it collaborated with the World Food Programme (WFP) in reducing the malnutrition rates among them to less than 10 per cent.

Report of Secretary-General. In response to General Assembly resolution 58/150 [YUN 2003, p. 1231], the Secretary-General submitted an August report on assistance to unaccompanied refugee minors [A/60/300]. The report addressed a rights-based approach to securing the interests of affected minors, and global priority issues relating to refugee children, including separation from family and caregivers, military recruitment, sexual exploitation, abuse and violence, education and the specific protection concerns of unaccompanied and separated adolescent girls and boys. It also highlighted other concerns and challenges, such as trafficking in refugee children, the situation of internally displaced girls and boys and unaccompanied children and HIV/AIDS.

The Secretary-General noted the strengthening of efforts and progress in addressing the protection of and assistance to unaccompanied and separated refugee children. Cooperation continued to be enhanced among UN agencies and with other partners, particularly the International Committee of the Red Cross, NGOs and government counterparts, largely as a result of the elaboration of common goals and principles in 2003-

2004. However, serious challenges remained, including a lack of accountability for violations, security concerns for both refugees and staff, insufficient human and financial resources, discrimination against girls and a lack of political will by States to implement or comply with relevant international norms and standards. The Secretary-General urged States to comply with those standards and to ensure that adequate resources were provided to allow girls and boys to enjoy their rights, including the right to education and to prevent the risk of being sexually abused, recruited into armed groups or trafficked. There was a continuing need for a clearer understanding of what constituted an effective child protection system, as well as for enhanced and more sustained attention by all actors to more adequate and effective identification, registration, tracing, and family reunification of unaccompanied girls and boys. There was also a need to strengthen all children-in-care arrangements to prevent abuse, neglect and the denial of other rights.

On 16 December, the Assembly took note of the Secretary-General's report (**decision 60/527**).

Regional activities

Africa

In 2005, the total population of concern to UNHCR in Africa, excluding North Africa, totalled 4.9 million, a slight increase over the 4.5 million recorded in 2004 [YUN 2004, p. 1206]. Of that number, 2.6 million were refugees, 1.5 million IDPs and 239,539 asylum-seekers.

The Secretary-General, in an August report [A/60/293], submitted in response to General Assembly resolution 59/172 [YUN 2004, p. 1208], updated information on assistance to refugees, returnees and displaced persons in Africa, covering 2004 and the first half of 2005. On a positive note, he observed that the end or prospects for resolving a number of difficult conflicts on the continent had provided large groups of African refugees with a unique opportunity for voluntary repatriation. Completed within the year were repatriation operations for Sierra Leonean and Somali refugees in Ethiopia, with those for Angolan, Burundian and Rwandan refugees underway. New operations were also launched for repatriating those from Liberia and the Congo, and it was expected that similar operations for Sudanese refugees would start within the year. Despite those encouraging developments, relentless political unrest and social tensions in other regions resulted in movements of refugees and IDPs, mainly in West Africa (Côte d'Ivoire, Togo), the Great Lakes region (Central African Republic, Democratic Republic of the Congo) and the Sudan. Overall, although the number of refugees in Africa declined slightly from 2.8 million in 2004 [YUN 2004, p. 1206] to 2.6 million in 2005, the continent still accounted for about one third of the global refugee population, and in that regard, the tragedy in Darfur (see p. 315) was of particular concern. Governmental, United Nations, international, regional and NGO partners reinforced cooperation to meet protection and assistance needs through improved coordination, joint missions, the development of field guidelines and improved methodologies and tools.

The report provided a regional overview of the refugee situation on the continent and described specific areas of inter-agency cooperation. Particularly positive developments were noted in the area of regional cooperation to reinforce protection for refugees on the continent, notably the decision of the African Union (AU) Heads of States (Abuja, Nigeria, 24-31 January) to convene in 2006, a ministerial conference on refugees, IDPs and returnees, as well as the reactivation of the Coordinating Committee on Assistance to Refugees, Returnees and Displaced Persons by AU leaders. UNHCR collaborated with the Economic Community of West African States (ECOWAS) to organize a regional experts' meeting on sustainable solutions to situations of forced displacement, aimed at identifying best practices. On behalf of refugees for whom voluntary repatriation remained elusive, the Office continued to pursue other durable solutions, particularly local integration in host countries and related resettlement. Nonetheless, chronic funding shortfalls and difficulties in bridging the gap between humanitarian assistance and development activities, especially in return situations, continued to pose problems. The Secretary-General concluded that, in order to end forced displacement and resolve the problem of refugees and other displaced persons in Africa, concerted efforts by the international community to address the root causes of conflicts on the continent should remain a priority, including those relating to socio-economic deprivation, political repression, inter-communal disputes, unemployment, the lack of basic infrastructure and services, and the depletion of natural resources.

Subregional developments

UNHCR report. According to UNHCR's *Global Report 2005*, in Central Africa and the Great Lakes subregion, UNHCR offered protection to some 750,000 refugees and asylum-seekers, assisted over 470,000 others, and facilitated the return of over 90,000 refugees to several States in that area. The main repatriation operations enabled 61,400 refugees from the United Republic of Tanzania to return to their homes in Burundi; 6,700 return to the DRC's South Kivu province, while over 7,000 others departed from the Congo to the Equateur province, also in the DRC. Patterns of return reflected political and humanitarian conditions in the countries of origin. Accordingly, the rate of return to Burundi, which peaked following the installation of the country's new Government, began to fall by year's end owing to a drought and consequent food insecurity, which undermined the scope of reintegration activities in the country. Political progress in the DRC had also encouraged a steady flow of returnees, especially towards the end of the year. On a negative note, a deteriorating security situation in the Central African Republic forced 18,000 people to flee to Chad. Of concern to UNHCR was the expulsion of some 5,000 Rwandan asylum-seekers from Burundi, following an agreement between the two Governments. Resettlement remained a tool for the international protection of refugees in the subregion, with some 300 cases submitted to third countries for that purpose. UNHCR provided support for processes and initiatives designed to address HIV/AIDS as it affected persons of concern in the subregion and led inter-agency efforts to tackle internal displacements there.

In East Africa and the Horn of Africa, the volatile security situation in some countries, compounded by the lack of sustainable development in that subregion, posed major challenges for UNHCR. Most of its operations were affected by problems relating to camp safety and security and by access and funding constraints. An estimated 7 million people in that subregion faced severe food shortages brought on by drought and other factors which could increase displacement and sharply reduce the likelihood for further returns. Following the signing of Sudan's Comprehensive Peace Agreement, UNHCR began to plan the voluntary return of some 380,000 Sudanese refugees from seven countries, but of the 64,000 it had expected to repatriate during the year, only 131 went home, owing mainly to the lack of infrastructure needed to absorb large numbers of returnees in South Sudan. During the year, preparations also continued for a multi-pronged Comprehensive Plan of Action for Somalia, designed to benefit some 350,000 returnees, 400,000 refugees, 400,000 IDPs and the local communities in which they lived. Within that framework, over 12,200 Somali refugees were assisted to return from Djibouti, Ethiopia and Kenya to Somaliland and Puntland, while some 6,500 refugees were resettled in countries outside the region, including Kenya, Ethiopia, Uganda and Eritrea. To facilitate the development of a favourable environment for durable solutions for refugees and other persons of concern in the subregion, UNHCR, through its regional office in Addis Ababa, strengthened its partnership with regional and subregional organizations and programmes, the private sector and Governments in addressing peace and security issues, educational and other training facilities for women, and in exploring ways of deepening the knowledge and understanding of the plight of refugees.

In West Africa, as the general refugee situation continued to improve, UNHCR facilitated the return of 38,000 Liberian refugees, mainly from Côte d'Ivoire, Ghana, Guinea, Nigeria and Sierra Leone, while 150,000 returned spontaneously. Some 260,000 IDPs also went back to their places of origin, with UNHCR's assistance. At the end of the year, UNHCR phased out its integration programme for Sierra Leonean returnees and handed over that responsibility to the country's Government and agencies. The overall number of persons of concern to UNHCR in the subregion decreased from 465,000 at the beginning of the year to 371,000 by year's end. One of the main challenges for the Office was the relatively slow return of Liberian refugees, owing to the decision of many refugees to await the end of the electoral process, and to the limited availability of basic services following 14 years of civil war. Other notable challenges and concerns included the socio-economic situation of most of the populations in that subregion, particularly regarding the problems of extreme poverty and massive youth unemployment. In April, violence surrounding presidential elections in Togo led to the exodus of approximately 40,000 refugees to Benin and Ghana, many of whom received UNHCR assistance, especially those who, by year's end, did not consider the political scene in Togo sufficiently changed to assure repatriation in safety and dignity. Despite continuous discussions in 2005, no change was observed in the status of the nearly 26,000 Mauritanian refugees in Mali and Senegal. In Cameroon, contingency plans were updated, as growing tensions in Chad and the Central African Republic highlighted the need for such preparation.

In Southern Africa, progress was made in safeguarding gender equality and in ensuring respect for the rights of refugee women and children. Another positive development was the repatriation of 52,000 Angolans from the DRC, Namibia and Zambia, organized by UNHCR. UNHCR extended the use of its registration system to more subregional States, which en-abled a reliable database of refugees to be set up, in order to improve the delivery of assistance and protection, implement durable solutions and underpin the planning of a phased-out strategy. UNHCR was not able to persuade host governments to enact less restrictive refugee legislation to pave the way for sustainable local integration. It was also of notable concern in the subregion that the HIV/AIDS pandemic was not abating, and in that regard, UNHCR focused on protection, rights-based advocacy, prevention, care and treatment, training and capacity-building to address the impact of the disease on refugees and host communities.

Other developments. The Executive Council of the AU, at its seventh ordinary session (Sirte, Libyan Arab Jamahiriya, 28 June–2 July), adopted a decision (EX.CL/Dec.127(V)) on the situation of refugees, returnees and displaced persons in Africa, by which the member States expressed concern over the persisting problem and undertook to promote mass voluntary repatriation, resettlement and rehabilitation of those affected.

GENERAL ASSEMBLY ACTION

On 16 December [meeting 64], the General Assembly, on the recommendation of the Third Committee [A/60/499], adopted **resolution 60/128** without vote [agenda item 39].

Assistance to refugees, returnees and displaced persons in Africa

The General Assembly,

Recalling its resolution 59/172 of 20 December 2004,

Recalling also the Organization of African Unity Convention governing the specific aspects of refugee problems in Africa of 1969 and the African Charter on Human and Peoples' Rights,

Reaffirming that the 1951 Convention relating to the Status of Refugees, together with the 1967 Protocol thereto, as complemented by the Organization of African Unity Convention of 1969, remains the foundation of the international refugee protection regime in Africa,

1. *Takes note* of the reports of the Secretary-General and the United Nations High Commissioner for Refugees;

2. *Notes* the need for African States to address resolutely the root causes of all forms of forced displacement in Africa and to foster peace, stability and prosperity throughout the African continent so as to forestall refugee flows;

3. *Notes with great concern* that, despite all of the efforts made so far by the United Nations, the African Union and others, the situation of refugees and displaced persons in Africa remains precarious, and calls upon States and other parties to armed conflict to observe scrupulously the letter and spirit of international humanitarian law, bearing in mind that armed conflict is one of the principal causes of forced displacement in Africa;

4. *Welcomes* decision EX.CL/Dec.197(VII) on the situation of refugees, returnees and displaced persons in Africa adopted by the Executive Council of the African Union at its seventh ordinary session, held at Sirte, Libyan Arab Jamahiriya, from 28 June to 2 July 2005;

5. *Expresses its appreciation* for the leadership shown by the Office of the United Nations High Commissioner for Refugees, and commends the Office for its ongoing efforts, with the support of the international community, to assist African countries of asylum and to respond to the protection and assistance needs of refugees, returnees and displaced persons in Africa;

6. *Recognizes* that, among refugees, returnees and internally displaced persons, women and children are the majority of the population affected by conflict and bear the brunt of atrocities and other consequences of conflict, and calls upon States to promote and protect the human rights of all refugees and other persons of concern, paying special attention to those with specific needs, and to tailor their protection responses appropriately;

7. *Reiterates* the importance of the full and effective implementation of standards and procedures, including the monitoring and reporting mechanism outlined in Security Council resolution 1612(2005) of 26 July 2005, to better address the specific protection needs of refugee children and adolescents and to safeguard rights and, in particular, to ensure adequate attention to unaccompanied and separated children and children affected by armed conflict, including former child soldiers in refugee settings, as well as in the context of voluntary repatriation and reintegration measures;

8. *Recognizes* the importance of early registration and effective registration systems and censuses as a tool of protection and as a means to enable the quantification and assessment of needs for the provision and distribution of humanitarian assistance and to implement appropriate durable solutions;

9. *Recalls* the conclusion on registration of refugees and asylum-seekers adopted by the Executive Committee of the Programme of the United Nations High Commissioner for Refugees at its fifty-second session, notes the many forms of harassment faced by refugees and asylum-seekers who remain without any form of documentation attesting to their status, recalls the responsibility of States to register refugees on their territories, reiterates in this context the central role which early and effective registration and documentation can play, guided by protection considerations, in enhancing protection and supporting efforts to find durable solutions, and calls upon the Office of the High Commissioner, as appropriate, to help States to conduct this procedure should they be unable to register refugees on their territory;

10. *Calls upon* the international community, including States and the Office of the High Commissioner and other relevant United Nations organizations, within their respective mandates, to take concrete action to meet the protection and assistance needs of refugees, returnees and displaced persons and to contribute generously to projects and programmes aimed at alleviating their plight and facilitating durable solutions for refugees and displaced persons;

11. *Reaffirms* the importance of timely and adequate assistance and protection for refugees, also reaffirms that assistance and protection are mutually reinforcing and that inadequate material assistance and food shortages undermine protection, notes the importance of a rights- and community-based approach in engaging constructively with individual refugees and their communities to achieve fair and equitable access to food and other forms of material assistance, and expresses concern in regard to situations in which minimum standards of assistance are not met, including those in which adequate needs assessments have yet to be undertaken;

12. *Also reaffirms* that respect by States for their protection responsibilities towards refugees is strengthened by international solidarity involving all members of the international community and that the refugee protection regime is enhanced through committed international cooperation in a spirit of solidarity and burden- and responsibility-sharing among all States;

13. *Further reaffirms* that host States have the primary responsibility to ensure the civilian and humanitarian character of asylum, and calls upon States, in cooperation with international organizations, within their mandates, to take all necessary measures to ensure respect for the principles of refugee protection and, in particular, to ensure that the civilian and humanitarian nature of refugee camps is not compromised by the presence or the activities of armed elements or used for purposes that are incompatible with their civilian character;

14. *Condemns* all acts that pose a threat to the personal security and well-being of refugees and asylum-seekers, such as refoulement, unlawful expulsion and physical attacks, calls upon States of refuge, in cooperation with international organizations, where appropriate, to take all necessary measures to ensure respect for the principles of refugee protection, including the humane treatment of asylum-seekers, notes with interest that the High Commissioner has continued to take steps to encourage the development of measures to better ensure the civilian and humanitarian character of asylum, and encourages the High Commissioner to continue those efforts, in consultation with States and other relevant actors;

15. *Deplores* the continuing violence and insecurity which constitute an ongoing threat to the safety and security of staff members of the Office of the High Commissioner and other humanitarian organizations and an obstacle to the effective fulfilment of the mandate of the Office and the ability of its implementing partners and other humanitarian personnel to discharge their respective humanitarian functions, urges States, parties to conflict and all other relevant actors to take all necessary measures to protect activities related to humanitarian assistance, prevent attacks on and kidnapping of national and international humanitarian workers and ensure the safety and security of the personnel and property of the Office and that of all humanitarian organizations discharging functions mandated by the Office, and calls upon States to investigate fully any crime committed against humanitarian personnel and bring to justice the persons responsible for such crimes;

16. *Calls upon* the Office of the High Commissioner, the African Union, subregional organizations and all African States, in conjunction with agencies of

the United Nations system, intergovernmental and non-governmental organizations and the international community, to strengthen and revitalize existing partnerships and forge new ones in support of the international refugee protection system, notes with interest the result of the Humanitarian Response Review, welcomes the proposals made by the Secretary-General and the General Assembly to strengthen the United Nations humanitarian system, and takes note of deliberations by the Inter-Agency Standing Committee aimed at following up on the Humanitarian Response Review and bringing about greater consistency in the response to humanitarian emergencies;

17. *Calls upon* the Office of the High Commissioner, the international community and other concerned entities to intensify their support to African Governments through appropriate capacity-building activities, including training of relevant officers, disseminating information about refugee instruments and principles, providing financial, technical and advisory services to accelerate the enactment or amendment and implementation of legislation relating to refugees, strengthening emergency response and enhancing capacities for the coordination of humanitarian activities;

18. *Reaffirms* the right of return and the principle of voluntary repatriation, appeals to countries of origin and countries of asylum to create conditions that are conducive to voluntary repatriation, recognizes that, while voluntary repatriation remains the pre-eminent solution, local integration and third-country resettlement, where appropriate and feasible, are also viable options for dealing with the situation of African refugees who, owing to prevailing circumstances in their respective countries of origin, are unable to return home, and welcomes in this regard the conclusion on local integration adopted by the Executive Committee of the Programme of the United Nations High Commissioner for Refugees at its fifty-sixth session;

19. *Also reaffirms* that voluntary repatriation should not necessarily be conditioned on the accomplishment of political solutions in the country of origin in order not to impede the exercise of the refugees' right to return, and recognizes that the voluntary repatriation and reintegration process is normally guided by the conditions in the country of origin, in particular that voluntary repatriation can be accomplished in conditions of safety and dignity;

20. *Welcomes* the development by the High Commissioner, in cooperation with other United Nations agencies and development actors, of the framework for durable solutions, aimed at promoting lasting solutions, particularly in protracted refugee situations, including the "4Rs" approach (repatriation, reintegration, rehabilitation and reconstruction) to sustainable return;

21. *Calls upon* the international donor community to provide financial and material assistance that allows for the implementation of community-based development programmes that benefit both refugees and host communities, as appropriate, in agreement with host countries and consistent with humanitarian objectives, and recognizes that promoting the self-reliance of refugees from the outset will contribute towards enhancing the ability of refugee communities to become self-reliant, as and when appropriate, with adequate

support from the international community for the host country and the refugees living there;

22. *Appeals* to the international community to respond positively, in the spirit of solidarity and burden- and responsibility-sharing, to the third-country resettlement needs of African refugees, notes in this regard the importance of using resettlement strategically, as part of situation-specific comprehensive responses to refugee situations, and to this end encourages interested States, the Office of the High Commissioner and other relevant partners to make full use of the Multilateral Framework of Understandings on Resettlement, where appropriate;

23. *Calls upon* the international donor community to provide material and financial assistance for the implementation of programmes intended for the rehabilitation of the environment and infrastructure affected by refugees in countries of asylum;

24. *Urges* the international community, in the spirit of international solidarity and burden-sharing, to continue to fund generously the refugee programmes of the Office of the High Commissioner and, taking into account the substantially increased needs of programmes in Africa, inter alia, as a result of repatriation possibilities, to ensure that Africa receives a fair and equitable share of the resources designated for refugees;

25. *Encourages* the Office of the High Commissioner and interested States to identify protracted refugee situations which might lend themselves to resolution through the development of specific, multilateral, comprehensive and practical approaches to resolving such refugee situations, including improvement of international burden- and responsibility-sharing and realization of durable solutions, within a multilateral context;

26. *Expresses grave concern* about the plight of internally displaced persons in Africa, calls upon States to take concrete action to pre-empt internal displacement and to meet the protection and assistance needs of internally displaced persons, recalls in that regard the Guiding Principles on Internal Displacement, and encourages the Office of the High Commissioner to continue to explore, with other relevant actors, the feasibility of taking on coordination responsibilities for clusters related to the protection of internally displaced persons, camp management and shelter in conflict situations as part of a broader United Nations coordination effort in support of United Nations humanitarian coordinators, without prejudice to its core mandate of refugee protection and assistance;

27. *Invites* the Representative of the Secretary-General on the human rights of internally displaced persons to continue his ongoing dialogue with Member States and the inter-governmental and non-governmental organizations concerned, in accordance with his mandate, and to include information thereon in his reports to the Commission on Human Rights and the General Assembly;

28. *Requests* the Secretary-General to submit a comprehensive report on assistance to refugees, returnees and displaced persons in Africa to the General Assembly at its sixty-first session, taking fully into account the efforts expended by countries of asylum, under the item entitled "Report of the United Nations High Commissioner for Refugees, questions relating to ref-

ugees, returnees and displaced persons and humanitarian questions", and to present an oral report to the Economic and Social Council at its substantive session of 2006.

The Americas

Important developments in North America and the Caribbean during 2005 included efforts by the United States to strengthen its refugee protection capacity through the creation of a new Refugee Corps to guide overseas adjudications for resettlement and the continuing improvement of its procedures for unaccompanied and separated children. Regarding its asylum policy and programmes, however, challenges remained, as legislators called for improved border security and the United States Congress passed legislations further restricting access to United States asylum procedures. The Congress increased, from $1 million to $2 million, its funding of the Legal Aid Orientation Programme for detained immigrants, which included refugees and asylum-seekers, and abolished limitations on the numbers of people granted asylum who could become eligible each year for permanent residency. With supplementary resettlement funding allocated by the Government, UNHCR referred 25,000 refugees to the United States, thereby exceeding its target of 20,000 referrals. In Canada, negative publicity in early 2005 of problems in the country's refugee system, including the failure to remove rejected asylum-seekers and alleged abuse of the asylum system, hardened public attitudes towards affected persons. The challenge for UNHCR and refugee advocates was to find ways to promote a more balanced view of asylum-seekers and counteract their negative portrayal as criminals. In that regard, refugees and others of concern to UNHCR featured prominently in Canada's new foreign policy statement. Canada achieved its overall government-assisted resettlement target for the year. In the Caribbean, instability in Haiti continued to preoccupy UNHCR, which launched a major contingency planning effort in neighbouring States. It continued to focus on its system of honorary liaison representatives, who played a key role in helping to maintain the rights of individuals seeking asylum. It also focused on refugee status determination and initiatives and made efforts to improve capacity-building there.

Central American countries and Mexico continued to receive a small but steady flow of asylum-seekers from Latin America and beyond, while the refugee population remained relatively stable at some 4,500. The principal durable solution promoted by UNHCR continued to be local integration, through permanent residency and naturalization. Efforts to improve access to asylum procedures yielded results, with Mexico receiving 687 asylum claims, 70 per cent more than in 2004 and more than twice as many in 2003. UNHCR promoted the protection of asylum-seekers and refugees in countries, such as El Salvador, Honduras and Guatemala. Of particular concern to the Office, was the increasing number of unaccompanied minors within mixed migratory flows. During the year, over 5,500 unaccompanied children, mainly from El Salvador, Guatemala and Honduras were intercepted and returned by Mexican migration authorities. As to urban refugees, UNHCR assisted some of them to find employment and began later in the year to implement its age, gender and diversity mainstreaming strategy, the results of which would be used to strengthen local integration and self-sufficiency strategies in 2006.

A major development in northern South America was the escalating conflict in Colombia, which caused an estimated 500,000 refugees to flee their homes but who did not officially seek protection for fear of deportation or discrimination, or because they were not aware of asylum procedures. UNHCR concentrated on finding solutions for those affected through local integration and resettlement. As the year marked the first year of implementation of the Mexico Plan of Action, launched in 2004 [YUN 2004, p. 1210] for strengthening the international protection of refugees in Latin America, UNHCR aligned its strategy with that of the Plan. Within that framework, UNHCR's Resettlement Units in Costa Rica and Ecuador referred some 955 refugees to an increasing number of resettlement countries, including Argentina, Brazil and Chile, which had just acquired that status. The community support and integration programmes in border areas helped UNHCR increase its protection presence through access to remote and underdeveloped border communities.

In southern South America, half of the subregion's 9,200 refugees and asylum-seekers received UNHCR support, with national and local authorities and social networks covering 40 per cent of their needs. Protection networks were strengthened to increase border monitoring and the region expanded its emerging resettlement programme. During the year, UNHCR's lobbying and advocacy resulted in the drafting or adoption of favourable refugee legislation in many subregional States, and the Office facilitated the functioning of national refugee commissions and promoted the implementation of procedures and criteria according to international standards. A number of recommendations to improve refugee status determination procedures were submitted to subregional Governments, with promising results. In 2005, total UNHCR expenditure in the Americas amounted to $31.4 million, for a population of concern of 3.2 million.

Asia and the Pacific and the Arab States

In 2005, UNHCR spent $82.7 million on activities in Asia and the Pacific, for a total population of concern of 2.2 million. Expenditures for operations in Central Asia, South-West Asia, North Africa and the Middle East amounted to $165.2 million, for a population of concern of 5.7 million.

South Asia

In 2005, progress towards solutions in the South Asian subregion was marked by the return of some 27,200 IDPs to their places of origin in Sri Lanka, in addition to 1,200 refugees who repatriated from India, with UNHCR's assistance. To address the protracted situation of Bhutanese refugees in Nepal, the Office encouraged an initiative by a number of subregional Governments to actively engage in finding comprehensive solutions, including the possibility of resettlement. That renewed hope for a revival of negotiations between Nepal and Bhutan, which should help resolve the situation of those refugees. UNHCR also made sustained efforts to define better access to naturalization as a durable solution for Hindu and Sikh Afghan refugees in India. However, the situation of the residual ethnic Afghan refugees remained problematic, highlighting the need for access to resettlement opportunities. A major concern for the Office was the lack of prospects for resolving the protracted situation of an estimated 20,000 refugees in camps in Bangladesh and Nepal. As a subregional priority, in its efforts to find durable solutions for those in need, UNHCR continued to expand its prevention and response capacities to sexual and gender-based violence.

East Asia and the Pacific

In 2005, UNHCR, increased its cooperation with subregional Governments and made significant progress in providing protection and finding solutions for persons of concern in that subregion. A January Memorandum of Understanding (MOU) signed by UNHCR, Vietnam and Cambodia allowed for the accommodation, for the first time, of the Montagnards (inhabitants of the Central Highlands) from Vietnam seeking asylum in Cambodia. Inside Vietnam, international access was granted to returnees areas, where micro projects were implemented. Elsewhere, the prospects for peace between the Indo-

nesian Government and the Free Aceh Movement paved the way for the eventual return of displaced people to the Province of Nanggroe Aceh Darussalam. There were also positive changes in Thailand and Malaysia, including improved asylum policies and standards, which enhanced the prospects for durable solutions for groups seeking refuge there. In Japan, refugee protection was enhanced through a legal amendment calling for the establishment of basic reception conditions and local integration schemes for refugees other than Indo-Chinese nationals. Progress was also made towards finding solutions for persons of concern in Australia, Papua New Guinea, Republic of Korea, the Philippines and Timor-Leste. Notable concerns in the subregion included the issue of nationals from the Democratic People's Republic of Korea attempting to seek refuge in China and Southeast Asian countries, for whom UNHCR maintained efforts to facilitate safe passage where the option existed. Additional challenges related to refugee status determination and resettlement in Hong Kong, China, and political uncertainty and restrictions to humanitarian agencies in Myanmar.

Central Asia, South-West Asia, North Africa and the Middle East

A major development in Central Asia was the cessation of refugee status, declared in December and to be implemented in 2006, regarding Tajik refugees who had fled the civil war in their country between 1992 and 1997. Many of them had been able to integrate into their countries of asylum, 9,500 of whom some were granted citizenship by Turkmenistan, while 3,370 others gained citizenship in Kyrgyzstan. With the support of key resettlement countries, UNHCR found durable solution for Afghan refugees in Central Asia, over 2,000 of whom were resettled in Tajikistan. Thereafter, the local integration of the remaining Afghans in Tajikistan became the priority of UNHCR and the Government. Activities addressing HIV/AIDS and sexual and gender-based violence were streamlined in all UNHCR operations in the Central Asian subregion, and the Office continued to provide legal and medical assistance to persons of concern there and to guarantee education for their children. Despite those achievements, the subregion experienced increasing protection challenges, most notably concerning the growing number of asylum-seekers and refugees, resulting in a highly politicized environment. Deportations and refoulement of those affected took place, in violation of human rights principles and minimum standards of international refugee law. Other challenges related to the Uzbek refugee crisis and continuing political volatility in much of Central Asia, the absence of national refugee legislation in Kazakhstan and tensions in Kyrgyzstan. In South-West Asia, major developments included the repatriation of over half a million Afghans from Pakistan and the Islamic Republic of Iran, with UNCHR assistance. However, Afghanistan's limited absorption capacity and lack of access to land undermined reintegration for the returnees. Finding that a considerable number of Afghans moved back and forth across borders in the subregion, UNHCR convened strategic consultations with the Governments there, international organizations and interested States, which resulted in an understanding that, while voluntary return would continue, many Afghans would probably remain in the neighbouring countries of asylum.

During the year, North African States witnessed a significant increase in the flow of asylum-seekers and economic migrants in transit from sub-Saharan Africa to Europe. To address better the situation, UNHCR developed a regional strategy to strengthen the institution of asylum in the area by increasing the capacity of national authorities to identify asylum-seekers and refugees among mixed migratory flows. However, structural deficiencies in the protection system in some of those States and UNHCR's limited resources were most evident towards year's end when hundreds of asylum-seekers in North African countries were expelled, including several recognized refugees. Considering that a solution to the plight of the Saharawi refugees in the Tindouf camps in Algeria did not seem imminent, UNHCR continued to assist them, making communication with their communities of origin possible by telephone and family visits. With a few exceptions, only a small number of refugees in North African countries opted for voluntary repatriation, and even fewer were resettled to third countries. Overall, no significant long-term solutions were identified for the asylum and migration problems facing the subregional States.

In the Middle East, the volatile security situation in Iraq remained the dominant issue, leading to uncertainty as to the future of thousands of Iraqi nationals still seeking refuge in neighbouring countries. The reintegration programme implemented during the year improved the conditions of up to 70,000 Iraqi returnees through infrastructure, housing and income generation projects and promotion of reconciliation. In terms of solutions, UNHCR focused on capacity building of local counterparts in the Gulf countries and on the promotion of refugee law, while the countries of the Gulf Cooperation Council (GCC) increased interest in partnership

with the Office. Although refugee status determination in Egypt remained suspended during the year, some 4,000 refugees in the country benefited from the resettlement programme that was implemented during the year. Elsewhere, thousands of Somali and Ethiopian asylum-seekers continued to undertake risky sea journeys to Yemen, where an estimated 78,000 refugees resided. Other concerns included security incidents in Yemen, which affected UNHCR's programme delivery, and several refugee demonstrations that resulted in violent clashes with the authorities and serious security problems in the subregion.

Europe

In 2005, UNHCR's expenditures in Europe amounted to $108.3 million, for a population of concern of 4.8 million. More than one third of that amount ($43.6 million) was spent on some 707,809 persons of concern in South-Eastern Europe.

Western, Central and Eastern Europe

In Western Europe, the downward trend in asylum applications continued, with the region as a whole showing a 14 per cent decrease. France remained the leading asylum destination with an estimated 50,000 asylum claims, although that represented a 15 per cent decrease compared to 2004. The majority of asylum-seekers came from Serbia and Montenegro, which accounted for some 20,000 applications, and Iraq, from where over 10,600 applications were filed. Others were from Bulgaria, China, Colombia, Eritrea, Haiti, Syria, the Russian Federation and Turkey. However, the political environment in Europe continued to resist attempts to stimulate constructive discussion on asylum and protection issues, as Governments maintained focus on irregular migration, the fight against terrorism and the related perception that increased security precautions were necessary. Measures to control migration and increasing doubts in some quarters about how readily non-Europeans would integrate in European society also influenced the consideration of asylum issues. UNHCR continued to cooperate closely with European Union (EU) institutions in addressing the EU's refugee policy and resource mobilization. In February, the High Commissioner and the European Commissioner for External Relations signed a strategic partnership agreement regarding protection and assistance to refugees and other persons of concern in third countries. Following the subsequent adoption of the first-phase asylum instruments at the EU level, focus shifted to the external dimension of refugee policy, particularly regarding improving protection in regions of origin. In that regard, UNHCR worked closely with the EU and its member States to elaborate concrete proposals. It also promoted and encouraged resettlement possibilities for refugees worldwide in European countries, provided support in the negotiation and implementation of tripartite agreements with several European countries for the return of Afghans, and helped to foster better integration programmes for refugees. Notable concerns for UNHCR related to the process of transforming EU directives into national law in EU countries, which the Office feared might lower standards, as European countries introduced more restrictive laws and administrative provisions for asylum-seekers. UNHCR monitored the process to ensure that asylum-seekers removed from one EU member State to another were not subjected to indirect refoulement owing to differences in standards.

Consistent with the situation in much of Europe during the year, Central Europe and the Baltic States recorded an overall decline of 38 per cent in the number of asylum claims. Slovenia was the only subregional State that witnessed a significant increase, with 1,600 applications, which was 25 per cent more than in 2004. UNHCR's efforts to promote burden sharing and resettlement in the area were bolstered by the resettlement of Uzbek refugees in Finland, Germany, Romania, the Netherlands, the Czech Republic, Sweden, Switzerland and the United States, with further resettlement scheduled in other countries in 2006. UNHCR continued to urge States to accept a broad and inclusive interpretation of the refugee definition, and in assisting them in addressing the complex challenges they faced, sharing lessons learned and best protection practices. Notable challenges and concerns in the subregion related to gaps in the right to access national territory and asylum procedures, inadequate scope for people to present their claim and the quality of decision-making, including the standards of interpretation and application of legal protection. Other concerns included the willingness and ability of EU member States to cope with the pressures they faced from asylum-seekers and the lack of a comprehensive integration strategy and limited expertise within the institutions responsible for refugee integration in the subregion. Such pressures had contributed to overcrowded reception facilities, increased detention of asylum-seekers and an unclear criteria for the imposition of immigration measures.

In Eastern Europe, with UNHCR support, all Governments undertook comprehensive analysis of the protection situation, aimed at identifying gaps in related capacity. The analysis gave a clear picture of the legislative and administrative institutions involved in refugee protection, established the constraints encountered in each country and constituted the basis for a regional analysis that was subsequently presented to the final meeting of the Commonwealth of Independent States (CIS) Conference process (see below). In Armenia, UNHCR helped analyse gaps in the protection and asylum framework, as well as needs and situations not sufficiently addressed by existing protection activities. It also formulated a burden-sharing strategy on housing solutions involving both governmental and non-governmental partners and assisted the Government in a national re-registration of refugees. In Azerbaijan, where the return of relative political and financial stability had raised hopes for the return of most of the country's IDPs, UNHCR and the Government took steps to design a return plan. In Belarus, the Republic of Moldova, and Ukraine, UNHCR continued to support governmental efforts to establish adequate reception facilities and advocated and facilitated the local integration of refugees as a durable solution. In the course of the year, the asylum authorities in those countries processed approximately 2,000 new asylum claims. In Ukraine in particular, UNHCR was engaged with the legal integration of formerly deported persons, of whom some 3,100 who had returned became naturalized citizens. In Georgia, where 235,000 IDPs lived in difficult conditions owing to the country's two unresolved internal conflicts, over 100 refugees were resettled in third countries and UNHCR continued to seek expanded resettlement opportunities for those who had no other durable solutions. It also urged the Government to promote local integration, including through granting citizenship or permanent residency to Chechen refugees with strong family ties in the country.

Follow-up to the 1996 Conference of CIS countries and neighbouring States

In response to General Assembly resolution 58/154 [YUN 2003, p. 1240], the Secretary-General submitted an August report [A/60/276] on follow-up to the 1996 Regional Conference to Address the Problems of Refugees, Displaced Persons, Other Forms of Involuntary Displacement and Returnees in the Countries of the Commonwealth of Independent States and Relevant Neighbouring States [YUN 1996, p. 1117]. The report provided information on progress in implementing the Conference's Programme of Action, the process of which was concluded in 2005 with a final meeting (see below). It concluded that, during the 10-year duration, the process had been successful in fulfilling many of the original goals by developing strategies and practical tools for more effective capacity-building and programme enhancement; promoting adherence to international standards and practices; and facilitating cooperation through partnerships at the regional and international levels. A second generation of intervention was being witnessed, informed by the full range of interests in the EU and by an overhauled global security agenda.

Final meeting of CIS Conference Process. The final meeting of the CIS Conference Process (Geneva, 10 October), held to conclude the ten-year initiative, adopted a final statement and considered a possible new framework for Euro-Asian cooperation on migration, asylum and displacement issues.

South-Eastern Europe

During the year, UNCHR provided protection and facilitated durable solutions for a total of some 600,000 people in South-Eastern Europe, of whom 164,000 were refugees and 436,000 IDPs. While that represented a significant drop from the 2004 total of some 870,000 people, the reduction had occurred almost entirely in the number of refugees and IDPs displaced by the conflicts in Croatia and Bosnia and Herzegovina, while the number of IDPs in Kosovo (Serbia and Montenegro) remained more or less stable at some 250,000. Persistent inter-ethnic violence in Kosovo, uncertainty over the province's future, unresolved disputes over property, restricted freedom of movement and limited access to basic services continued to hamper the return and sustainable integration of ethnic minorities originating from there. Only 2,500 returned in 2005, and the appointment of a Minister for Returns within the Kosovo Provisional Institutions of Self-Government did not result in significant positive change. Returns to Bosnia and Herzegovina decreased sharply in 2005 from 20,400 the previous year to 6,400 just as repatriation to Croatia from Serbia and Montenegro and Bosnia and Herzegovina decreased from approximately 7,500 in 2004, to nearly 5,300 in 2005. However, there was substantial local integration and naturalization of refugees from Croatia and Bosnia and Herzegovina in Serbia and Montenegro. At the regional level, UNHCR implemented the asylum component of the European Community Assistance for Reconstruction, Development and Stabilization project in Albania, Bosnia and Herzegovina, Croatia, The former Yugoslav Republic of Macedonia and Kosovo (Serbia and Montenegro). By so doing, the Office contributed to building the capacity of middle-level decision makers, NGOs and judges, and also strengthened regional cooperation on asylum issues and ensured the adoption of country progress reports. During the year, Ministers from Bosnia and Herzegovina, Croatia and Serbia and Montenegro signed the Sarajevo Declaration, by which they committed their countries to working together to solve outstanding displacement problems by the end of 2006.

Chapter XIII

Health, food and nutrition

In 2005, the United Nations continued to promote human health, coordinate food aid, promote food security, and support research in nutrition.

At the end of the year, about 40 million people globally were living with the human immuno-deficiency virus or the acquired immuno-deficiency syndrome (HIV/AIDS). An estimated 4.1 million people became infected with the virus, while 2.8 million died due to AIDS-related illnesses. *The Human Development Report 2005* identified AIDS as having inflicted the single greatest reversal in human development, although there were encouraging signs that the epidemic was beginning to be contained. The Joint United Nations Programme on HIV/AIDS (UNAIDS) continued to coordinate UN activities for AIDS prevention and control, appointing a Global Task Team to simplify and streamline multilateral procedures and practices to facilitate more effective country-led responses. UNAIDS also adopted a new policy approach to HIV prevention.

In 2005, the Roll Back Malaria Partnership conducted a comprehensive review of the epidemiological status of malaria and progress made in fighting the disease. It published the first World Malaria Report, which found that, while malaria remained a major global problem, substantial progress had been made in addressing the disease over the last several years.

Although tuberculosis trends were stable or in decline in the other World Health Organization (WHO) regions of the world, WHO Regional Committee for Africa declared tuberculosis an emergency in the African region, and urged member States in the region to step up interventions.

The United Nations Road Safety Collaboration defined a framework for collaboration on road safety issues, and initiated efforts to facilitate implementation of General Assembly resolution 58/289 on improving road safety and the recommendations of the *World Report on Road Traffic Injury Prevention.*

The WHO Framework Convention on Tobacco Control entered into force on 27 February and the World Health Assembly approved the revised International Health Regulations, which laid out the role of WHO and countries in identifying and responding to public health emergencies.

The year 2005 was very challenging for humanitarian aid according to the World Food Programme (WFP). The Indian Ocean tsunami, drought and locusts in the Niger, continuing conflict in the Darfur region of Western Sudan, hurricanes Katrina and Stan, and the earthquake in Kashmir took thousands of lives and destroyed many homes and livelihoods. In response to those and other crises, WFP distributed 4.2 million metric tons of food to 96.7 million people in 82 countries.

The Food and Agriculture Organization of the United Nations (FAO) continued to implement the Plan of Action adopted at the 1996 World Food Summit for meeting the commitments to halve the number of undernourished people worldwide by 2015. In support of an FAO resolution highlighting the importance of the potato as a staple food around the world, the Assembly declared 2008 the International Year of the Potato.

Health

2005 World Summit

The Secretary-General, in his March report [A/59/2005] entitled "In larger freedom: towards development, security and human rights for all" (see p. 67), discussed, among other subjects, progress and shortfalls in global public health, and made recommendations for improvement. The Secretary-General noted that the HIV/AIDS pandemic posed an unprecedented threat to human development and security and, in addition to being a public health crisis, undermined economic and social stability. Since 2000, some successes had been achieved in the fight against AIDS at the national level through integrated administrative structures, and at the international level through the Global Fund to Fight AIDS, Tuberculosis and Malaria [YUN 2002, p. 1217]. Nevertheless, the epidemic demanded an exceptional response and much remained to be done to reduce HIV incidence and provide antiretroviral treatment in the coming decade. He therefore called on the international community to provide urgently the resources needed for a comprehensive response to HIV/AIDS and to provide full funding for the Global Fund.

The Secretary-General also noted the slow and under-resourced international response to other evolving pandemics. He called for a concerted international response to strengthen existing mechanisms for timely and effective international cooperation and upon Member States to agree on the revision of the International Health Regulations at the World Health Assembly in May 2005 (see below).

The World Summit Outcome document, adopted by the Assembly in **resolution 60/1** (see p. 48), recognized that HIV/AIDS, malaria, tuberculosis and other infectious diseases posed severe risks for the entire world and serious challenges to the achievement of the Millennium Development Goals (MDGs) [YUN 2000, p. 51]. World leaders committed themselves to increasing investment and building on existing mechanisms to improve health systems in developing countries and those with economies in transition, in order to achieve the health-related MDGs by 2015. They further undertook to fully implement all the commitments established by the Declaration of Commitment on HIV/AIDS (see below), their obligations under the International Health Regulations (2005) adopted by the fifty-eighth World Health Assembly in May and the "Three Ones" principles, with the aim of coordinating the work of multiple institutions and international partners under one agreed HIV/AIDS framework.

AIDS prevention and control

Follow-up to the twenty-sixth special session
General Assembly 2005 High-level Meeting. In accordance with its resolution 58/313 [YUN 2004, p. 1216], the General Assembly held a High-level Meeting on 2 June to review progress achieved in realizing the commitments set out in the Declaration of Commitment on HIV/AIDS contained in resolution S-26/2 [YUN 2001, p. 1126], adopted by the Assembly's twenty-sixth special session.

The Meeting consisted of two plenary sessions and five interactive round tables covering areas related to the implementation of the Declaration of Commitment, particularly prevention, treatment, care and support, and human rights, including gender, orphans and resources. It was attended by representatives of Member States of all regions, multilateral organizations, especially those representing people living with HIV/AIDS, and civil society, in accordance with **decision 59/553** of 20 January. The meeting had before it for consideration the Secretary-General's April report [A/59/765], submitted in accordance with Assembly resolution 58/236 [YUN 2003, p. 1245],

summarizing progress achieved in realizing the obligations in the Declaration of Commitment, a discussion paper [A/59/CRP.1] for the round table on orphans and children made vulnerable by HIV/AIDS, and a note by the Assembly President transmitting the summaries of the discussions of the five round tables [A/59/852].

The Secretary-General's report observed that, although there were encouraging signs that the epidemic was beginning to be contained, overall, it continued to expand, with much of the world at risk of failing to reach the targets set forth in the Declaration. Eleven countries in sub-Saharan Africa were likely to lose more than one tenth of their labour force to AIDS by 2006, and its detrimental effect on agricultural sectors played a pivotal role in the recent food crisis in Southern Africa. The epidemic was also undermining the foundations of whole societies.

The report found that many of the most affected countries were falling short of the target of reducing by 2005 the level of infection among young people aged 15 to 24, and only 12 per cent of those needing antiretroviral therapy were receiving it as at December 2004; treatment programmes were insufficient; globally, 15 million children were orphaned by AIDS, and national efforts and donor support were currently insufficient to address the growing crisis; an acute shortage of trained personnel was a further hindrance to the implementation and expansion of essential AIDS programmes; many countries had yet to adopt legislation to prevent discrimination against people living with HIV, and few had enacted measures to promote and protect the human rights of vulnerable populations; and while political commitment to the AIDS response had become significantly stronger since 2001, it remained inadequate in many countries.

Since 2001, the resources available from all sources, including national spending in low- and middle-income countries, had increased dramatically and were projected to total some $8 billion in 2005 and $10 billion by 2007. Despite that increase, and successful efforts in mobilizing the funds called for in the Declaration, additional data analyses indicated that significantly increased resources would be required in future years to sustain a comprehensive response.

Among its recommendations, the report suggested scaling up successful prevention activities; reviewing national testing policies to encourage more widespread knowledge of serostatus and increasing donor financial support for testing initiatives; taking global action to further reduce the price and increase accessibility of antiretroviral therapy regimens; increasing accessibility to treatment through an integrated care approach; and using various approaches to target efforts towards vulnerable populations. The report called for the mobilization of international resources for an expanded, comprehensive response to the epidemic, including full funding for the Global Fund to Fight AIDS, Tuberculosis and Malaria, and for securing the commitment of low- and middle-income countries to increase allocations to AIDS from national budgets.

In his conclusions, the Secretary-General stated that in 2006, the Assembly would receive a comprehensive report on international progress in implementing the Declaration of Commitment on HIV/AIDS, with special reference to the targets set for 2005.

In accordance with resolution 58/313 [YUN 2004, p. 1216], the summaries of the round-table discussions were submitted to the Assembly's High-level Plenary Meeting in September (see p. 47).

Preparations for 2006 review meeting

On 23 December [meeting 69], the General Assembly adopted **resolution 60/224** [draft: A/60/L.43] without vote [agenda item 45].

Preparations for and organization of the 2006 follow-up meeting on the outcome of the twenty-sixth special session: implementation of the Declaration of Commitment on HIV/AIDS

The General Assembly,

Reaffirming its commitment to resolution S-26/2 of 27 June 2001 entitled "Declaration of Commitment on HIV/AIDS", and recalling its undertaking to devote sufficient time and at least one full day of the annual session of the General Assembly to review a report of the Secretary-General and make recommendations on action needed to achieve further progress,

Reaffirming the importance of the follow-up process prescribed in the Declaration of Commitment, which included the setting of specific time-bound targets, which fall due in 2005 and 2010, and noting in this regard the holding on 2 June 2005 of the High-level Meeting of the General Assembly to review progress achieved in realizing the commitments set out in the Declaration of Commitment,

Recalling the 2005 World Summit Outcome adopted at the meeting held from 14 to 16 September 2005, including the commitment to full implementation of the Declaration of Commitment,

Recognizing that progress has been made in containing the HIV/AIDS epidemic in a small but growing number of countries, but remaining deeply concerned by the overall expansion and feminization of the epidemic,

Recognizing also the primary role and responsibility of Governments in responding to HIV/AIDS and the essential need for the efforts and engagement of all sectors of society to generate an effective response,

Recognizing further the important role of the international community and international cooperation in order to assist Member States, particularly developing countries, and to complement national efforts for generating an effective response to HIV/AIDS,

Recognizing the essential role played in the response to AIDS by civil society, including national and international non-governmental organizations and organizations and networks representing people living with HIV/AIDS, women, men, young persons, girls and boys, orphans, community and faith-based organizations, families and the private sector,

1. *Decides* to undertake on 31 May and 1 June 2006 a comprehensive review of the progress achieved in realizing the targets set out in the Declaration of Commitment on HIV/AIDS and to convene on 2 June 2006 a high-level meeting aimed at continuing the engagement of world leaders in a comprehensive global response to HIV/AIDS;

2. *Invites* Member States and observers to be represented at the high-level meeting at the highest level;

3. *Decides* that the organizational arrangements for the comprehensive review should be as follows:

(*a*) The review meeting will comprise plenary meetings, an informal interactive hearing with civil society, panel discussions and round tables;

(*b*) The opening plenary meeting will feature statements by the President of the General Assembly, the Secretary-General, the Executive Director of the Joint United Nations Programme on HIV/AIDS and a representative of civil society;

(*c*) An informal interactive civil society hearing will be chaired by the President of the General Assembly or his representative and organized with the active participation of people living with HIV/AIDS and broader civil society, and will be attended by representatives of non-governmental organizations in consultative status with the Economic and Social Council, invited civil society organizations, the private sector, Member States and observers;

(*d*) In order to promote interactive and substantive discussions, participation in each round table will be limited to a maximum of forty to forty-five participants, including Member States, observers, representatives of entities of the United Nations system, civil society organizations and other invitees, and their participation will be limited to one round table; every effort will be made to ensure equitable geographical representation, taking into account the importance of ensuring a mix of countries in terms of size, HIV prevalence rates and levels of development; a representative of each of the regional groups will chair each round table with support from the co-sponsoring agencies of the Joint Programme; and between five and ten representatives of accredited and invited civil society organizations will participate in each round table, with due regard to equitable geographical representation after accommodation of all Member States;

(*e*) The chairpersons of the round tables and the informal interactive civil society hearing will present summaries of the discussions to the plenary meeting scheduled for 1 June 2006;

4. *Decides also* that the organizational arrangements for the comprehensive review and the high-level meeting, including the identification of the civil society representative to speak at the opening plenary meeting, the identification of themes for the round tables, the assignment of participants to round tables, the finalization of the panel discussions, the identification of chairpersons for the round tables and the format of the informal interactive hearing, will be finalized by the

President of the General Assembly, with support from the Joint Programme and in consultation with Member States;

5. *Encourages* Member States and observers to include in their national delegations to the meetings representatives of civil society, including non-governmental organizations and organizations and networks representing people living with HIV/AIDS, women, young persons, orphans, community organizations, faith-based organizations and the private sector;

6. *Invites* heads of entities of the United Nations system, including programmes, funds, specialized agencies and regional commissions, as well as the Global Fund to Fight AIDS, Tuberculosis and Malaria and the Special Envoys of the Secretary-General on HIV/AIDS, to participate in the review and the high-level meeting, as appropriate;

7. *Invites* intergovernmental organizations and entities that have observer status with the General Assembly, non-governmental organizations in consultative status with the Economic and Social Council and non-governmental members of the Programme Coordinating Board of the Joint Programme to participate in the review and the high-level meeting, including round tables and panel discussions as appropriate;

8. *Requests* the President of the General Assembly, following appropriate consultations with Member States, to draw up, not later than 15 February 2006, a list of other relevant civil society representatives, in particular associations of people living with HIV/AIDS, non-governmental organizations, including organizations of women and young people, girls and boys and men, faith-based organizations and the private sector, especially pharmaceutical companies and representatives of labour, including on the basis of the recommendations of the Joint Programme and taking into account the principle of equitable geographical representation, and to submit the list to Member States for consideration on a no-objection basis for a final decision by the Assembly on participation in the review and the high-level meeting, including round tables and panel discussions;

9. *Decides* that the arrangements outlined in paragraph 8 above shall not be considered a precedent for other similar events;

10. *Encourages* the timely submission of national reports by all Member States on their implementation of the Declaration of Commitment, noting the request for those submissions by 31 December 2005 as inputs to the report of the Secretary-General;

11. *Requests* the Secretary-General to submit a comprehensive and analytical report at least six weeks prior to its consideration by the General Assembly on progress achieved and challenges remaining in realizing the commitments set out in the Declaration of Commitment, in particular those set for 2005;

12. *Requests* that the secretariat of the Joint Programme and its co-sponsors assist in facilitating inclusive, country-driven processes, including consultations with relevant stakeholders, including non-governmental organizations, civil society and the private sector, within existing national AIDS strategies, for scaling up HIV prevention, treatment, care and support with the aim of coming as close as possible to the goal of universal access to treatment by 2010 for all

those who need it, including through increased resources, and working towards the elimination of stigma and discrimination, enhanced access to affordable medicines and the reduction of vulnerability of persons affected by HIV/AIDS and other health issues, in particular orphaned and vulnerable children and older persons; also requests, consistent with the timetable for the submission of the report of the Secretary-General, that the Joint Programme submit for the consideration of the review and the high-level meeting an assessment of these processes, based on inputs received from Member States, including an analysis of common obstacles to scaling up and recommendations for addressing such obstacles, as well as accelerated and expanded action;

13. *Invites* Member States to consider the adoption of a short declaration aimed at reaffirming and expressing recommitment to the full implementation of the Declaration of Commitment, including by giving due consideration to, inter alia, the assessment referred to in paragraph 12 above and the report of the Secretary-General.

Bangkok Declaration. The Eleventh United Nations Congress on Crime Prevention and Criminal Justice (Bangkok, Thailand, 18-25 April) adopted the Bangkok Declaration on Synergies and Responses: Strategic Alliances in Crime Prevention and Criminal Justice (see p. 1208). The Declaration addressed the problem of HIV/AIDS, noting with concern that the physical and social conditions associated with imprisonment might facilitate the spread of the disease in pre-trial and correctional facilities and thus in society, thereby presenting a critical prison management problem. The Declaration called upon States to develop and adopt measures and guidelines, in accordance with national legislation, to ensure that the particular challenges of HIV/AIDS were adequately addressed in prisons.

Declaration of San Salvador. On 28 December [A/60/672], El Salvador transmitted the Declaration of San Salvador, adopted by the Heads of State and Government of the Central American Integration System (SICA), meeting within the subregional framework for addressing sexually transmitted illnesses (STIs) and HIV/AIDS (San Salvador, El Salvador, 11 November). They firmly committed themselves to combating HIV/AIDS, ensuring that national and regional responses were harmonized and coordinated, and making progress towards the goal of universal access to treatment by 2010, as well as to refocusing HIV/AIDS prevention efforts.

Joint UN Programme on HIV/AIDS

The Joint United Nations Programme on HIV/AIDS (UNAIDS), which became fully operational in 1996 [YUN 1996, p. 1121], continued to serve as the main advocate for global action on

HIV/AIDS. UNAIDS was mandated to lead, strengthen and support an expanded response to the epidemic, with the aim of preventing the transmission of HIV, providing care and support, reducing the vulnerability of individuals and communities to HIV/AIDS, and alleviating the socio-economic and human impact of the epidemic.

Report of UNAIDS Executive Director. In response to Economic and Social Council resolution 2003/18 [YUN 2003, p. 1249], the Secretary-General, by a May note [E/2005/59], transmitted a report of the UNAIDS Executive Director, which provided an update on the status of the epidemic, summarized steps taken by UNAIDS to promote the implementation of the 2001 Declaration of Commitment on HIV/AIDS [YUN 2001, p. 1126] and other key developments in advancing a more effective and coordinated UN system response to the epidemic, and took account of the Programme Coordinating Board's (PCB) decisions, recommendations and conclusions taken following the Council's substantive session in 2003.

The Executive Director recommended that the Council endorse the PCB recommendation for intensified efforts by civil society groups, Governments and UN agencies to make the AIDS response work for women and girls, as well as the decision of the sixteenth meeting of PCB [YUN 2004, p. 1219] calling for a revitalized global approach to prevention. The Council should encourage UNAIDS and its partners to intensify efforts to reach the "3 by 5" target, and to strengthen monitoring and evaluation at the global and country levels, particularly through the provision of technical advice and the posting of specialist staff.

ECONOMIC AND SOCIAL COUNCIL ACTION

On 27 July [meeting 40], the Economic and Social Council adopted **resolution 2005/47** [draft: E/2005/L.20/Rev.1] without vote [agenda item 7(*g*)].

**Joint United Nations Programme
on HIV/AIDS (UNAIDS)**

The Economic and Social Council,

Recalling its resolution 2003/18 of 22 July 2003,

Having considered the report of the Executive Director of the Joint United Nations Programme on HIV/ AIDS (UNAIDS),

Recalling the goals and targets set forth in the Declaration of Commitment on HIV/AIDS, adopted by the General Assembly at its twenty-sixth special session in 2001, and the HIV/AIDS-related goals contained in the United Nations Millennium Declaration of 8 September 2000,

Reaffirming the importance of the follow-up process prescribed in the Declaration of Commitment, which included the setting of specific time-bound targets, which fall due in 2005 and 2010, and noting in this regard the holding on 2 June 2005 of the High-level Meeting of the General Assembly to review progress achieved in realizing the commitments set out in the Declaration of Commitment,

Noting with profound concern that 39.4 million people worldwide are living with HIV/AIDS, that the pandemic claimed 3.1 million lives in 2004, with 4.9 million new HIV infections, and that it has orphaned 15 million children to date,

Deeply concerned that the global HIV/AIDS pandemic has a disproportionate impact on women and girls and that the majority of new infections occur among young people,

Expressing serious concern about the continued global spread of HIV/AIDS, which exacerbates poverty and poses a major threat to economic and social development and to food security in heavily affected regions,

Noting the need for greater coherence and accountability in the responses to the HIV/AIDS pandemic,

Recognizing the importance of partnerships at the national, regional and international levels as part of the responses to HIV/AIDS, including for prevention, care, support and treatment, as well as the importance of enhanced support for human and institutional capacity development and of considerably increased financial resources,

Welcoming the World Food Programme and the Office of the United Nations High Commissioner for Refugees as the ninth and tenth co-sponsors of the Joint Programme,

1. *Urges* the Joint United Nations Programme on HIV/AIDS (UNAIDS) and the organizations and bodies of the United Nations system, within their respective mandates, to intensify their support to Governments, with a view to achieving the goals contained in the United Nations Millennium Declaration, as well as the goals and targets contained in the Declaration of Commitment on HIV/AIDS;

2. *Encourages* Governments to report fully in preparation for the report of the Secretary-General to the sixtieth session of the General Assembly on the implementation of the Declaration of Commitment on HIV/ AIDS;

3. *Welcomes* the support given by the Programme Coordinating Board of UNAIDS at its fifteenth, sixteenth and seventeenth meetings to the commitment of the Joint Programme to expanding technical support, building capacity and promoting coordinated and comprehensive responses at the country level, in particular through the implementation of the "three ones" principle for country-level coordination, and in taking into consideration the recommendations of the Global Task Team on Improving HIV Coordination among Multilateral Institutions and International Donors;

4. *Also welcomes* the intensification of joint regional United Nations action on HIV/AIDS, through improved communications between agencies at the regional level and through initiatives such as the regional support teams established by the Joint Programme to mobilize and leverage technical, financial and political support for the joint country-level efforts by the United Nations, largely through the country offices of the Programme in their respective regions, to assist national HIV/AIDS responses;

5. *Encourages* the Joint Programme and the World Health Organization to intensify their work with the international community in achieving the "3 by 5" target;

6. *Also encourages* the Joint Programme to continue to promote and support countries in the development of evidence-informed HIV/AIDS strategies, including efforts towards universal access to prevention, treatment and care services, recognizing the importance of a comprehensive approach to HIV/AIDS;

7. *Takes note with interest* of the endorsement by the Programme Coordinating Board at its seventeenth meeting, of the policy position paper of the Joint Programme entitled "Intensifying HIV Prevention", and urges the Programme to strengthen its leadership of global and regional efforts, as appropriate, and support national efforts to intensify HIV prevention as part of a comprehensive, coordinated and coherent response to HIV/AIDS;

8. *Encourages* the activities of the Joint Programme to strengthen, streamline and harmonize monitoring and evaluation efforts at the global, regional and country levels, in particular its efforts to rapidly improve monitoring and evaluation systems in priority countries through the provision of technical support and the posting of specialist staff in these and other countries;

9. *Commends* the Joint Programme and its partners for launching the Global Coalition on Women and AIDS, and calls for strengthened and improved action related to women and HIV/AIDS through intensified efforts by Governments, United Nations agencies, civil society and the private sector;

10. *Takes note with appreciation* of the endorsement of the Programme Coordinating Board, at its seventeenth meeting, of the recommendations of the Global Task Team on Improving AIDS Coordination among Multilateral Institutions and International Donors, and calls upon the Programme and the wider United Nations system and invites other multilateral institutions to implement the recommendations, as appropriate;

11. *Supports* the efforts of the Joint Programme to advocate that increased resources be devoted to the response to HIV/AIDS and to explore innovative options for expanding the funding base, both nationally and internationally;

12. *Commends* the Joint Programme for strengthening the results-based management framework and simplifying the 2006-2007 unified budget and work plan, as requested by the Programme Coordinating Board at its sixteenth meeting;

13. *Requests* the Secretary-General to transmit to the Economic and Social Council, at its substantive session of 2007, a report prepared by the Executive Director of the Joint Programme, in collaboration with other relevant organizations and bodies of the United Nations system, which should include information on progress made in implementing the coordinated response of the United Nations system to the HIV/AIDS pandemic as well as the decisions, recommendations and conclusions of the Programme Coordinating Board taken subsequent to the substantive session of the Council in 2005.

Trends

According to UNAIDS, at the end of 2005, close to 40 million people globally were living with HIV, of whom 36 million were adults and just over 2 million were children under the age of 15. An estimated 4.1 million new infections were recorded and approximately 2.8 million people died as a result of AIDS-related illnesses. While women made up 41 per cent of adults living with HIV in 1998, in 2005, that number had risen to nearly 50 per cent globally, and in sub-Saharan Africa the percentage was close to 60.

The epidemic continued to expand in sub-Saharan Africa, where an estimated 24.5 million people were living with the virus, resulting in a prevalence rate of 6.1 per cent. Around 2 million Africans died of AIDS-related illnesses in 2005, and some 2.7 million persons were newly infected with HIV. However, some declines were noted, especially among young people in Burkina Faso, Burundi, Ethiopia, Kenya, Uganda and Zimbabwe.

In Asia, approximately 8.3 million people were living with HIV, and 930,000 new infections were recorded. East Asia was experiencing the fastest growth in the world, mainly due to the growing epidemic in China, where an estimated 650,000 people were living with the disease. India's national prevalence rate stood at less than 1 per cent, which translated into around 5.7 million people living with the virus. Asian countries that had introduced large-scale prevention programmes—notably Cambodia and Thailand—had seen significant reductions in risk behaviour, and recorded declining levels of new HIV and other sexually transmitted infections.

The level of infection in Oceania was still very low, although Papua New Guinea was a country of concern, with the highest prevalence rate in the region of 1.8 per cent of the adult population or roughly 60,000 people living with HIV.

Available data from the Middle East and North Africa pointed to an increase in infection rates, and an estimated 440,000 people living with HIV.

In Eastern Europe and Central Asia, around 1.5 million people were living with HIV, and an estimated 53,000 people died of AIDS-related illnesses. Most of those infected were under the age of 30, with Estonia, Latvia, the Russian Federation and Ukraine being the worst-affected countries.

Latin America, which had around 1.6 million people living with HIV, recorded some 140,000 AIDS-related deaths in 2005. The Caribbean, the second most affected region of the world, with a prevalence rate of 1.6 per cent, had some 330,000 people living with the disease. At least three countries, the Bahamas, Haiti and Trinidad and Tobago, had far higher HIV prevalence rates of around 3 per cent.

An estimated 2 million people were living with HIV in high-income countries and some 30,000 died of AIDS-related illnesses, although the introduction of antiretroviral therapy dramatically reduced AIDS-related mortality. However, transmission of the disease among heterosexuals increased sharply and the epidemic was progressively shifting into poorer and marginalized sectors.

Since the establishment in 2003 of the "3 by 5" initiative [YUN 2003, p. 1248] for providing antiretroviral therapy to 3 million people in developing and transition countries by 2005, the number of people in those countries receiving therapy more than tripled to 1.3 million but was still substantially less than initially hoped. Access to antiretroviral therapy in sub-Saharan Africa, the world's hardest-hit region, had increased by more than 800 per cent. It was estimated that in 2005, between 250,000 and 350,000 deaths were averted because treatment was available. The ongoing effort to expand access to antiretroviral therapy had brought about positive change and paved the way for far greater advances towards the ultimate goal of universal access to HIV treatment and care.

UNAIDS activities

Leaders from donor and developing countries, civil society, UN agencies and other multilateral and international institutions met in London on 9 March to review the global response to AIDS under the theme "Making the Money Work: The Three Ones in Action". They agreed to form a Global Task Team to recommend ways the multilateral system could address duplication and gaps in the global response to AIDS and streamline, simplify and further harmonize procedures and practices to improve the effectiveness of country-led responses.

The Global Task Team, in its report issued in June [UNAIDS/PCB(17)/05.02], made recommendations to accelerate and improve AIDS response in the areas of: empowering inclusive national leadership and ownership; alignment and harmonization; reform for a more effective multilateral response; and accountability and oversight. Those recommendations were endorsed by the UNAIDS Programme Coordinating Board (PCB) at its seventeenth meeting (Geneva, 27-29 June), which also requested that action plans be developed to implement them and that the UNAIDS secretariat and co-sponsors, in cooperation with the Global Fund to Fight AIDS, Tuberculosis and Malaria [YUN 2002, p. 1217], report in 2006 on progress in their implementation.

HIV prevention strategy. In response to a 2004 PCB request regarding the development of a new strategy for intensifying HIV prevention [YUN 2004, p. 1219], UNAIDS, in a policy paper on the subject [UNAIDS/05.18E], outlined the principles, policy and programmatic actions that were needed to get ahead of the HIV epidemic. The new strategy was aimed at providing universal access to HIV prevention and treatment. It highlighted the gaps in HIV prevention actions and policies for bridging them, especially at the national level. The paper also identified UNAIDS's role in strengthening prevention. PCB endorsed the UNAIDS policy position paper and requested that UNAIDS create an action plan based thereon and on the Global Task Team recommendations (see above) and report to PCB by December 2005. It should also provide a progress report, in 2006, on efforts to intensify HIV prevention.

PCB, at its seventeenth meeting [UNAIDS/PCB(17)/05.10], also considered the report of its Executive Director [UNAIDS/PCB(17)/05.1.4], financial and budgetary updates as at 31 March 2005 [UNAIDS/PCB(17)/05.6.2], a progress report on implementation of the "Three Ones" approach [UNAIDS/PCB(17)/05.6.1], and the UN System Strategic Framework on HIV/AIDS 2006-2010 [UNAIDS/PCB(17)/05.5]. It endorsed the 2006-2007 unified budget and workplan [UNAIDS/PCB(17)/05.4], approved the core budget of $320.5 million. PCB also asked the UNAIDS secretariat to examine the possible establishment of a contingency fund and a midterm review; align the unified budget and workplan with the Global Task Team's recommendations (see above); and to identify the financial implications.

UNDP/UNFPA consideration. As a follow-up to the sixteenth [YUN 2004, p. 1219] and seventeenth (see above) PCB meetings, UNDP [DP/2005/40] and UNFPA [DP/FPA/2005/17] issued reports on their responses to and implementation of the PCB recommendations. The reports elaborated on their efforts in, among other areas, strengthening linkages between sexual and reproductive health and HIV/AIDS, the Global Task Team recommendations on Improving AIDS Coordination among Multilateral Institutions and International Donors, scaling up HIV treatment, the UNAIDS policy position paper on intensifying HIV prevention, the unified budget and workplan, 2006-2007, and women, gender and AIDS.

On 9 September [E/2005/35 (dec. 2005/41)], the UNDP/UNFPA Executive Board took note of both reports and requested that both agencies work with the UNAIDS secretariat and co-sponsors to develop action plans based on the recommendations of the Global Task Team and report on progress towards the implementation of those recommendations at the joint meeting of the UNDP/UNFPA, UNICEF and WFP Executive Boards in January 2006, and a special session of the PCB scheduled for June of the same year. The Board also asked both agencies to formulate an action plan based on the UNAIDS policy position paper on intensifying HIV prevention (see above).

HIV/AIDS and peacekeeping

On 18 July [meeting 5228], during the Security Council's consideration of HIV/AIDS and UN peacekeeping (see p. 116), the UNAIDS Executive Director gave an update on progress made in implementing Security Council resolution 1308 (2000) [YUN 2000, p. 82] on the provision of training for peacekeeping personnel in preventing the spread of HIV/AIDS. He stated that an Office on AIDS, Security and Humanitarian Response had been created in the UNAIDS secretariat, which, along with the Department of Peacekeeping Operations (DPKO), was pursuing a strategy to ensure that the United Nations set the highest possible standards in protecting both peacekeepers and the populations they served from HIV. In pursuit of that goal, one million AIDS-awareness cards had been distributed in 13 languages through peacekeepers and national forces, and a peer education kit, available in 11 languages, was currently part of the military training curricula in several troop-contributing countries. The Executive Director also pointed to the need to address HIV/AIDS among national uniformed services as a critical step in dealing with the larger issue of HIV/AIDS and peacekeeping. UNAIDS was assisting 53 Member States with comprehensive programmes to deal with returning national forces. However, two key challenges existed: the need to expand significantly access to HIV testing and counselling; and to ensure that the implementation of AIDS programmes consistently reached all levels of the uniformed services.

The Executive Director also presented the UNAIDS progress report "On the front line" [UNAIDS/05.16E], which detailed efforts made by UNAIDS in addressing AIDS and security.

The Security Council, in presidential statement **S/PRST/2005/33** (see p. 118), reaffirmed its commitment to the full implementation of resolution 1308(2000).

Tobacco

The World Health Organization (WHO) Framework Convention on Tobacco Control (FCTC), adopted in May 2003 by the World Health Assembly [YUN 2003, p. 1251], with WHO as the interim secretariat, entered into force on 27 February 2005, 90 days after the fortieth instrument of ratification was deposited. As at 31 December, 115

States and the European Community were parties to the Convention.

In preparation for the first session of the Conference of the Parties of the WHO FCTC, which, according to article 23 of the FCTC, was to be convened within one year of its entry into force, the Open-ended Intergovernmental Working Group on the Framework Convention held its second session (Geneva, 31 January–4 February) to: finalize its input to the first session of the Conference of the Parties to be held in Geneva from 6 to 17 February 2006, including recommendations for the designation of the permanent secretariat and arrangements for its functioning; propose a draft budget for the first financial period, draft rules of procedure and financial rules for the Conference of the Parties; and draw up the terms of reference for a study of potential sources and mechanisms of assistance.

Ad Hoc Inter-Agency Task Force

At its seventh session (Geneva, 30 November–1 December), the Ad Hoc Inter-Agency Task Force on Tobacco Control discussed smoke-free workplaces, illicit trade of tobacco products, the link between tobacco control and economic development, and preparations for FCTC implementation in member countries.

Roll Back Malaria initiative

The Secretary-General, pursuant to General Assembly resolution 59/256 [YUN 2004, p. 1222], transmitted an August report [A/60/208], prepared by WHO, on the Decade to Roll Back Malaria in Developing Countries, Particularly in Africa (2001-2010), which was proclaimed by the Assembly in resolution 55/284 [YUN 2001, p. 1139].

The report provided an update on activities undertaken and progress made to meet the 2010 malaria goals. The WHO report drew attention to the findings of the report published by the United Nations Millennium Project entitled "Coming to grips with malaria in the new millennium", which showed that five years after the launching of the Roll Back Malaria Initiative, country-level implementation of malaria efforts had been severely limited by a lack of resources and that more resources had to be mobilized to meet needs.

In terms of funding and resource mobilization, the WHO report stated that some $3 billion was needed worldwide to effectively roll back malaria. The Global Fund to Fight AIDS, Tuberculosis and Malaria had, by the end of 2004, allocated $1.8 billion on a five-year basis to 69 countries, including 38 in Africa. The Roll Back Malaria Partnership had worked to improve resource allocation for malaria at the country level to complement funding available through the Global Fund and external donors. In April, the World Bank announced a substantial increase in its support to combat malaria with a total commitment of $500 million to $1 billion over the next five years. In June, the United States Government announced a new international malaria initiative, targeting up to 35 high-burden countries over five years. It proposed increasing its current annual contribution of $200 million, through the bilateral Programme and the Global Fund, by $30 million in 2006, $135 million more in 2007 and an additional $300 million per year from 2008 to 2010. The United States asked major donors to provide $1.2 billion per year with the aim of exceeding the 2015 MDG goal for malaria.

The Summit of the Group of Eight (G-8) most industrialized countries (Scotland, United Kingdom, 6-8 July) called for an additional $1.5 billion annually to help ensure access to insecticide-treated nets, artemisinin-based combination therapies, intermittent preventive treatment for pregnant women and infants, indoor residual spraying and to build the capacity of African health services.

In terms of the treatment of malaria, the rapid shift to artemisinin-based combination treatment policies in 2004 and 2005 and the resulting surge in demand had led to a shortfall in artemisinin and artemisinin-based combination therapies. During the year, the industry made efforts to increase production and to ensure that the shortfall was remedied by the end of 2005. Projects in many African countries sought to establish the feasibility and effectiveness of using artemisinin-based combination therapies in the context of home management of malaria, a package that included education for mothers, training of community-level providers and the supply of pre-packaged medicines.

In the light of the need for new malaria medicines to replace those being lost to parasite resistance, the Drugs for Neglected Diseases Initiative and the drug company Sanofi Aventis announced plans to develop and seek pre-qualification for two new fixed-dose artemisinin-based combination therapies. In the meantime, research on the development of an effective malaria vaccine continued to be more complex than anticipated. The WHO Initiative for Vaccines Research and the Special Programme for Research and Training in Tropical Diseases continued to support those initiatives.

The WHO report also stated that the Roll Back Malaria Partnership had developed an overarching Roll Back Malaria Global Strategic Plan 2005-2015, aimed at achieving 80 per cent coverage of populations, a 50 per cent reduction of the malaria burden by 2010, and the achievement of the MDG for malaria by 2015. At a meeting with major partners, organized by WHO in November 2004, best practices for acute and chronic emergency situations were developed. As a follow-up to that meeting, the Malaria in Emergencies Network was set up in 2005. WHO also published in 2005 a handbook entitled *Malaria Control in Complex Emergencies: An Inter-agency Field Handbook* [WHO/HTM/MAL/2005.1107], which provided practical guidance on designing, implementing and monitoring measures to reduce malaria morbidity and mortality, addressing the needs of both the displaced and host populations in complex emergencies.

The Secretary-General urged the General Assembly to call on malaria-endemic countries to: increase domestic resource allocation for malaria control; ensure the recruitment, training and retention of health personnel; and establish national policies and operational plans to ensure that at least 80 per cent of those at risk or suffering from malaria benefited from major preventive and curative interventions by 2010. He called on the international community to: support the development of new medicines and technologies that prevented and treated malaria; increase financial support to the Global Fund to Fight AIDS, Tuberculosis and Malaria and other mechanisms so that insecticide-treated mosquito nets, insecticide for indoor spraying and effective antimalarial combination treatments were fully accessible and free; and establish universal protection of young children and pregnant women in malaria-endemic areas of Africa, providing them on a sustainable basis with insecticide-treated nets.

The first World Malaria Report [WHO/HTM/MAL/2005.1102], published by WHO and UNICEF in 2005, provided a global update on the epidemiological situation and progress made in the implementation of controls in all malaria-endemic countries throughout the world. It also examined global financing of malaria initiatives and discussed how to improve the Roll Back Malaria monitoring and evaluation.

GENERAL ASSEMBLY ACTION

On 23 December [meeting 69], the General Assembly adopted **resolution 60/221** [draft: A/60/L.44 & Add.1] without vote [agenda item 47].

2001-2010: Decade to Roll Back Malaria in Developing Countries, Particularly in Africa

The General Assembly,

Recalling that the period 2001-2010 has been proclaimed the Decade to Roll Back Malaria in Developing Countries, Particularly in Africa by the General Assembly, and that combating HIV/AIDS, malaria, tuberculosis and other diseases is included in the internationally agreed development goals, including those contained in the United Nations Millennium Declaration,

Recalling also its resolutions 49/135 of 19 December 1994, 50/128 of 20 December 1995, 55/284 of 7 September 2001, 57/294 of 20 December 2002, 58/237 of 23 December 2003 and 59/256 of 23 December 2004 concerning the struggle against malaria in developing countries, particularly in Africa,

Bearing in mind the relevant resolutions of the Economic and Social Council relating to the struggle against malaria and diarrhoeal diseases, in particular resolution 1998/36 of 30 July 1998,

Taking note of the declarations and decisions on health issues adopted by the Organization of African Unity, in particular the declaration and plan of action on the "Roll Back Malaria" initiative adopted at the Extraordinary Summit of Heads of State and Government of the Organization of African Unity, held in Abuja on 24 and 25 April 2000, as well as decision AHG/Dec.155(XXXVI) concerning the implementation of that declaration and plan of action, adopted by the Assembly of Heads of State and Government of the Organization of African Unity at its thirty-sixth ordinary session, held in Lomé from 10 to 12 July 2000,

Also taking note of the Maputo Declaration on Malaria, HIV/AIDS, Tuberculosis and Other Related Infectious Diseases, adopted by the Assembly of the African Union at its second ordinary session, held in Maputo from 10 to 12 July 2003,

Recognizing the linkages in efforts being made to reach the targets set at the Abuja Summit as necessary and important for the attainment of the "Roll Back Malaria" goal and the targets of the Millennium Declaration by 2010 and 2015, respectively,

Also recognizing that malaria-related ill health and deaths throughout the world can be substantially eliminated with political commitment and commensurate resources if the public is educated and sensitized about malaria and appropriate health services are made available, particularly in countries where the disease is endemic,

Emphasizing the importance of implementing the Millennium Declaration, and welcoming in this connection the commitment of Member States to respond to the specific needs of Africa,

Commending the efforts of the World Health Organization, the United Nations Children's Fund and other partners to fight malaria over the years, including the launching of the Roll Back Malaria Partnership in 1998,

Recalling resolution 58.2 adopted by the World Health Assembly on 23 May 2005 urging a broad range of national and international actions to scale up malaria control programmes,

Taking note of the Roll Back Malaria Global Strategic Plan 2005-2015 developed by the Roll Back Malaria Partnership,

1. *Takes note* of the note by the Secretary-General transmitting the report of the World Health Organization, and calls for support for the recommendations contained therein;

2. *Welcomes* the increased funding for malaria interventions and for research and development of preventative and control tools from the international community, including from the Group of Eight, the United States of America, the World Bank and the Bill and Melinda Gates Foundation, as well as the European Commission and other sources of bilateral funding;

3. *Calls upon* the international community to continue to support the "Roll Back Malaria" partner organizations, including the World Health Organization and the United Nations Children's Fund, as vital complementary sources of support for the efforts of malaria-endemic countries to combat the disease;

4. *Appeals* to the international community to work towards increased and sustained bilateral and multilateral assistance to combat malaria, including support for the Global Fund to Fight HIV/AIDS, Tuberculosis and Malaria, in order to assist States, in particular malaria-endemic countries, to implement sound national plans to control malaria in a sustained and equitable way that, inter alia, contributes to health system development;

5. *Urges* malaria-endemic countries to work towards financial sustainability, to increase, to the extent possible, domestic resource allocation to malaria control and to create favourable conditions for working with the private sector in order to improve access to good-quality malaria services;

6. *Calls upon* Member States, in particular malaria-endemic countries, to establish and/or strengthen national policies and operational plans, aspiring to ensure that at least 80 per cent of those at risk of or suffering from malaria may benefit from major preventive and curative interventions by 2010, in accordance with the technical recommendations of the World Health Organization, so as to ensure a reduction in the burden of malaria by at least 50 per cent by 2010 and 75 per cent by 2015;

7. *Urges* Member States to assess and respond to the needs for integrated human resources at all levels of the health system, in order to achieve the targets of the Abuja Declaration on Roll Back Malaria in Africa and the internationally agreed development goals of the United Nations Millennium Declaration, and to take actions, as appropriate, to effectively govern the recruitment, training and retention of health personnel;

8. *Calls upon* the international community, inter alia, by helping to meet the financial needs of the Global Fund to Fight HIV/AIDS, Tuberculosis and Malaria and through country-led initiatives with adequate international support, to create conditions for full access to insecticide-treated mosquito nets, insecticides for indoor residual spraying for malaria control and effective antimalarial combination treatments, including through the free distribution of such nets where appropriate;

9. *Requests* relevant international organizations, in particular the World Health Organization and the United Nations Children's Fund, to assist efforts of national Governments to establish universal protection of young children and pregnant women in malaria-endemic countries, particularly in Africa, with insecticide-treated nets as rapidly as possible, with due regard to ensuring sustainability through full community participation and implementation through the health system;

10. *Encourages* all African countries that have not yet done so to implement the recommendations of the Abuja Summit to reduce or waive taxes and tariffs for

nets and other products needed for malaria control, both to reduce the price of nets to consumers and to stimulate free trade in insecticide-treated nets;

11. *Expresses its concern* about the increase in resistant strains of malaria in several regions of the world;

12. *Encourages* all Member States experiencing resistance to conventional monotherapies to replace them with combination therapies, as recommended by the World Health Organization, in a timely manner;

13. *Recognizes* the importance of the development of effective vaccines and new medicines to prevent and treat malaria and the need for further and accelerated research, including by providing support to the United Nations Children's Fund/United Nations Development Programme/World Bank/World Health Organization Special Programme for Research and Training in Tropical Diseases and through effective global partnerships such as the various malaria vaccine initiatives and the Medicines for Malaria Venture, where necessary stimulated by new incentives to secure their development;

14. *Calls upon* the international community to support investment in the development of new medicines to prevent and treat malaria, especially for children and pregnant women, sensitive and specific diagnostic tests, effective vaccines, and new insecticides and delivery modes in order to enhance effectiveness and delay the onset of resistance, including through existing partnerships;

15. *Also calls upon* the international community to support ways to expand access to artemisinin-based combination therapy for populations at risk of exposure to resistant strains of falciparum malaria in Africa, including the commitment of new funds, innovative mechanisms for the financing and national procurement of artemisinin-based combination therapy and the scaling up of artemisinin production to meet the increased need;

16. *Applauds* the increased level of public-private partnerships for malaria control and prevention, including the financial and in kind contributions of companies operating in Africa, as well as increased engagement of non-governmental service providers;

17. *Calls upon* malaria-endemic countries to encourage regional and intersectoral collaboration, both public and private, at all levels, especially in education, agriculture, economic development and the environment, to advance malaria control objectives;

18. *Calls upon* the international community to support increased interventions, in line with the recommendations of the Roll Back Malaria Partnership, in order to ensure their rapid, efficient and effective implementation, to strengthen health systems, to monitor for counterfeit anti-malarial medicines and prevent the distribution and use of them, and to support coordinated efforts, inter alia, by providing technical assistance to improve surveillance, monitoring and evaluation systems and their alignment with national plans and systems so as to better track and report changes in coverage and the need for scaling up recommended interventions and subsequent reductions in the burden of malaria;

19. *Urges* Member States, the international community and all relevant actors, including the private sector, to promote the coordinated implementation and enhance the quality of malaria-related activities,

including via the Roll Back Malaria Partnership, in accordance with national policies and operational plans that are consistent with the technical recommendations of the World Health Organization and recent efforts and initiatives, including the Paris Declaration on Aid Effectiveness;

20. *Requests* the Secretary-General to report to the General Assembly at its sixty-first session on the implementation of the present resolution under the agenda item entitled "2001-2010: Decade to Roll Back Malaria in Developing Countries, Particularly in Africa".

Access to medication

On 15 April [E/2005/23 (res. 2005/23)] (see p. 848), the Commission on Human Rights, in a resolution on access to medication in the context of pandemics such as HIV/AIDS, tuberculosis and malaria, called on Governments to pursue policies that ensured access by all to pharmaceutical products and medical technologies for the prevention and treatment of pandemics, such as HIV/AIDS, tuberculosis and malaria. The Commission urged Governments to refrain from denying or limiting equal access to such products or technologies, and to consider enacting legislation in order to use to the fullest extent the flexibilities contained in the World Trade Organization Agreement on the Trade-Related Aspects of Intellectual Property Rights (TRIPS) and public health [YUN 2001, p. 1432].

In 2005, the fifty-eighth World Health Assembly and the United Nations Children's Fund (UNICEF) Executive Board approved a new strategy entitled "Global Immunization Vision and Strategy, 2006-2015" [WHO/IVB/05.05], aimed at addressing the challenges foreseen in immunization over that decade, including financing new and underused vaccines and ensuring adequate supply and access for all.

Global public health

On 23 May, the World Health Assembly, at its fifty-eighth session (Geneva, 16-25 May), adopted, by resolution 58.3, the revised International Health Regulations (International Health Regulations, 2005) for managing public health emergencies of international concern, which were to come into force on 23 May 2007, replacing the original regulations adopted in 1969 [YUN 1969, p. 876]. The revised regulations were to govern the roles of countries and WHO in identifying and responding to those emergencies and sharing information about them.

The Assembly also adopted resolution 58.5 on strengthening pandemic-influenza preparedness and response, including the avian influenza.

On 30 November [meeting 58], the General Assembly adopted **resolution 60/35** [draft: A/60/L.26 & Add.1] without vote [agenda item 120].

Enhancing capacity-building in global public health

The General Assembly,

Recalling the United Nations Millennium Declaration, adopted at the Millennium Summit of the United Nations, and the development goals contained therein, in particular the health-related development goals, and its resolutions 58/3 of 27 October 2003 and 59/27 of 23 November 2004,

Recalling also the 2005 World Summit Outcome, adopted by Heads of State and Government at the High-level Plenary Meeting of the sixtieth session of the General Assembly, held in New York from 14 to 16 September 2005, including the commitments on HIV/AIDS, malaria, tuberculosis and other health issues,

Recognizing that health is central to the achievement of the internationally agreed development goals, including all those contained in the Millennium Declaration, and that such goals create an opportunity to position health as a core part of the development agenda and to raise political commitment and financial resources for the sector,

Noting with concern the deleterious impact on humankind of HIV/AIDS, tuberculosis, malaria and other major infectious diseases and epidemics, and the heavy disease burden borne by poor people, especially in developing countries, including the least developed countries, as well as countries with economies in transition, and in this regard noting with appreciation the work of the Joint United Nations Programme on HIV/AIDS, its co-sponsoring agencies and the Global Fund to Fight HIV/AIDS, Tuberculosis and Malaria,

Also noting with concern the serious damage and loss of life caused by natural disasters and their negative impact on public health and health systems,

Bearing in mind the fact that the fight against new and re-emerging diseases, such as the severe acute respiratory syndrome and a human influenza pandemic arising from avian influenza, is far from over, and in this regard welcoming the efforts of the World Health Organization, the Food and Agriculture Organization of the United Nations and the World Organization for Animal Health in developing international strategies and collaboration, as well as the recent appointment by the Secretary-General of a Senior United Nations System Coordinator for Avian and Human Influenza,

Emphasizing that Member States have primary responsibility for strengthening their capacity-building in public health to detect and respond rapidly to outbreaks of major infectious diseases, through the establishment and improvement of effective public health mechanisms, while recognizing that the magnitude of the necessary response may be beyond the capabilities of many countries, in particular developing countries, as well as countries with economies in transition,

Convinced that strengthening public health systems is critical to the development of all Member States and that economic and social development are enhanced through measures that strengthen capacity-building in public health, including strategies for training, recruitment and retention of sufficient public health personnel, and systems of prevention and of immunization against infectious diseases,

Acknowledging that rapid progress will require political commitment and a scaling-up of more efficient and effective strategies and actions, greater investment of financial resources, adequately staffed and effective health systems, capacity-building in the public and private sectors, a clear focus on equity in access and outcomes, and collective action within and between countries,

Recognizing the need to strengthen national health and social infrastructures to reinforce measures to eliminate discrimination in access to public health, information and education for all people, especially for the most underserved and vulnerable groups,

Recognizing also the need for greater international and regional cooperation to meet new and existing challenges to public health, in particular in promoting effective measures such as safe, affordable and accessible vaccines, as well as assisting developing countries in securing vaccines against preventable infectious diseases and supporting the development of new vaccines,

Welcoming the Doha Declaration on the Agreement on Trade-Related Aspects of Intellectual Property Rights and Public Health, adopted on 14 November 2001, and noting the decision of the World Trade Organization General Council of 30 August 2003 on the implementation of paragraph 6 of the Declaration,

Recognizing the expertise of the World Health Organization and its role in, inter alia, coordinating actions with Member States in the areas of information exchange, personnel training, technical support, resource utilization, the improvement of global public health preparedness and response mechanisms and stimulating and advancing work on the prevention, control and eradication of epidemic, endemic and other diseases, as well as the work of the World Health Organization office dedicated to communicable disease surveillance and response,

Welcoming the efforts of the World Health Organization, in cooperation with Member States, the United Nations system, the Bretton Woods institutions, the private sector and civil society, in enhancing capacity-building in global public health and in promoting public health at the country level,

Underscoring the importance of the International Health Regulations (2005), adopted by the World Health Assembly in its resolution 58.3 of 23 May 2005, as an instrument for ensuring the maximum possible protection against the international spread of diseases with minimum interference in international traffic,

1. *Urges* Member States to further integrate public health into their national economic and social development strategies, including through the establishment and improvement of effective public health mechanisms, in particular networks of disease surveillance, response, control, prevention, treatment and information exchange and the recruitment and training of national public health personnel;

2. *Urges* Member States and the international community to increase investment, building on existing mechanisms and through partnership, to improve health systems in developing countries and countries with economies in transition with the aim of providing sufficient health workers, infrastructures, manage-

ment systems and supplies to achieve the health-related Millennium Development Goals by 2015;

3. *Calls upon* Member States and the international community to take action, as appropriate, to address shortages of human resources for health by, inter alia, developing, financing and implementing policies, within national development strategies, to improve training and management and effectively govern the recruitment, retention and deployment of health workers;

4. *Also calls upon* Member States and the international community to raise awareness of good public health practices, including through education and the mass media;

5. *Emphasizes* the importance of active international cooperation in the control of infectious diseases, based on the principles of mutual respect and equality, with a view to strengthening capacity-building in public health, especially in developing countries, including through the exchange of information and the sharing of experience, as well as research and training Programme focusing on surveillance, prevention, control, response, and care and treatment in respect of infectious diseases, and vaccines against them;

6. *Calls for* the improvement of the global public health preparedness and response systems, including systems of prevention and monitoring of infectious diseases, to better cope with major diseases, in particular a human influenza pandemic arising from avian influenza;

7. *Recognizes* World Health Assembly resolution 58.5 of 23 May 2005 on strengthening pandemic-influenza preparedness and response, and in this regard calls upon Member States to develop, implement and strengthen their national response plans, welcomes the ongoing collaboration across multiple forums to address issues to further national efforts and international cooperation on preparedness, contingency planning and response and containment of avian and pandemic influenza, and takes note with interest of the initiative of the International Partnership on Avian and Pandemic Influenza and its core principles;

8. *Calls upon* Member States to take all appropriate measures for furthering the purpose and eventual implementation of the International Health Regulations (2005), adopted by the World Health Assembly in its resolution 58.3 of 23 May 2005, pending their entry into force, including development of the necessary public health capacities and of legal and administrative provisions, and encourages them to implement the Regulations as early as possible and to support the Global Outbreak Alert and Response Network of the World Health Organization;

9. *Encourages* Member States to participate actively in the verification and validation of surveillance data and information concerning public health emergencies of international concern and, in close collaboration with the World Health Organization, to exchange information and experience in a timely and open manner on epidemics and the prevention and control of emerging and re-emerging infectious diseases that pose a risk to global public health;

10. *Urges* Member States and the international community to promote long-term funding, including public-private partnerships, where appropriate, for academic and industrial research as well as for the development of new vaccines and microbicides, diagnostic kits, drugs and treatments to address major pandemics, tropical diseases and other diseases, such as avian influenza and the severe acute respiratory syndrome, and to take forward work on market incentives, where appropriate, through such mechanisms as advance purchase commitments;

11. *Stresses* the importance of enhancing international cooperation in the area of public health in the aftermath of natural disasters to support national efforts to cope in all phases of the response, and urges Member States and the international community to strengthen their cooperation programmes, preparedness, mitigation, response and recovery in this regard;

12. *Invites* the regional commissions of the Economic and Social Council, as appropriate, to cooperate closely with Member States, the private sector and civil society, when requested, in their capacity-building in public health, as well as in regional cooperation to diminish and eliminate the deleterious impact of major infectious diseases;

13. *Encourages* Member States, as well as United Nations agencies, bodies, funds and programmes, in accordance with their respective mandates, to continue to address public health concerns in their development activities and programmes, and to actively support capacity-building in global public health and health-care institutions, such as through the provision of technical and other relevant assistance to the developing countries, as well as countries with economies in transition;

14. *Requests* the Secretary-General to submit to the General Assembly at its sixty-first session a report on the implementation of the present resolution.

Avian influenza

The World Health Assembly (Geneva, 16-25 May), in its resolution 58.5 on strengthening pandemic-influenza preparedness and response, stressed the need for all countries, especially those affected by highly pathogenic avian influenza, to collaborate with WHO and the international community to lessen the risk of a pandemic among humans that might be caused by the H5N1 influenza virus. The WHO Director-General was asked to develop plans and capacity for responding to a pandemic by providing capacity-building and technology transfer related to H5N1 influenza vaccines and diagnostics to developing countries.

The High-Level Committee on Programmes (HLCP) of the United Nations System Chief Executives Board for Coordination (CEB), in a briefing by WHO at its tenth session (Frascati, Italy, 6-8 October) [CEB/2005/7] on the latest developments regarding avian influenza, learned that, while several cases of transfer from birds to humans had been detected, there were no known cases in which the influenza had been transmitted from human to human. However, concern existed that the virus might mutate to acquire that capacity, which was an alarming possibility given the lack of vaccine and the limited quantities of medicine available to curtail the symptoms in humans. The influenza was already at a full-blown crisis stage among wild birds and poultry, with devastating economic effects on poor Asian farmers, many of whom were at risk of sliding back into extreme poverty.

On 29 September, the Secretary-General appointed Dr. David Nabarro of WHO to coordinate the UN response to the influenza.

Communication. The United States, on 31 October [A/60/530], transmitted to the Secretary-General a statement of core principles, adopted at a meeting (6-7 October) of the International Partnership on Avian and Pandemic Influenza, which dealt with the need for global cooperation to address the avian influenza and other international health emergencies.

Road safety

The Secretary-General transmitted to the General Assembly an August report [A/60/181 & Corr.1], prepared by WHO, which updated the status of implementation of the Assembly's recommendations contained in resolution 58/289 on improving global road safety [YUN 2004, p. 1224]. According to the report, the United Nations Road Safety Collaboration, a group developed by WHO in collaboration with the Economic Commission for Europe (ECE) and other regional commissions to address issues of road safety, comprised, as at March, 11 UN entities and 31 other international agencies working on road safety.

At its 2005 (16-17 March) meeting, participants of the Collaboration defined a common framework for collaboration on the implementation of Assembly resolution 58/289 and the recommendations of the 2004 World Report, on Road Traffic Injury Prevention [YUN 2004, p. 1223]; and agreed to concentrate on addressing a few specified areas identified in the World Report such as helmets, seat belts and child restraints, drinking and driving, speed and infrastructure. The Collaboration also identified a number of specific products, the creation of which would be directly relevant to achieving its objectives.

Among other initiatives, WHO developed an online global road safety legislation database and "The United Nations Road Safety Collaboration: a handbook of partner profiles". A series of "how to" manuals to guide countries on how to implement recommendations in the *World Report on Road Traffic Injury Prevention* were to be completed. A World Day of Remembrance for Road Crash Victims was called for the third Sunday in November, and the ECE was to host the First United Nations Global Road Safety Week, focusing on young road users, in April 2007.

The report concluded that, although the issue of road safety had not received the level of attention and resources commensurate with the magnitude of the problem, global awareness of the need for action and the momentum to do so had increased over the previous year. Groups that historically had not been very active in global dialogues on road safety had been engaged by the United Nations Road Safety Collaboration.

The recommendations in the report called upon the Assembly to encourage Member States to, among other national actions, bring national legislation in line with the Conventions on Road Traffic and Road Signs and Signals; continue using the *World Report on Road Traffic Injury Prevention* as a framework for road safety efforts; include road safety within projects aimed at tackling the MDGs; develop work programmes in road safety; support and participate in the Global Road Safety Week in 2007; and recognize the World Day of Remembrance for Road Crash Victims.

In other developments, the United Nations Road Safety Collaboration, at its third meeting (London, 14-15 November), finalized the goal and objectives for collaboration and discussed specific issues related to road safety, including data collection and indicators, policy, capacity development, alcohol and speed, seat belts and helmets.

GENERAL ASSEMBLY ACTION

On 26 October [meeting 38], the General Assembly adopted **resolution 60/5** [draft: A/60/L.8 & Add.1] without vote [agenda item 60].

Improving global road safety

The General Assembly,

Recalling its resolutions 57/309 of 22 May 2003, 58/9 of 5 November 2003 and 58/289 of 14 April 2004 on improving global road safety,

Having considered the report of the Secretary-General on the global road safety crisis,

Commending the World Health Organization for its role in implementing the mandate conferred upon it by the General Assembly in its resolution 58/289 to act, working in close cooperation with the United Nations regional commissions, as a coordinator on road safety issues within the United Nations system,

Also commending the United Nations regional commissions and their subsidiary bodies for having responded to the above-mentioned resolutions and to the report of the Secretary-General by accelerating or expanding their road safety activities,

Noting with satisfaction the progress made by the United Nations Road Safety Collaboration as described in the report of the Secretary-General, as well as the road safety initiatives undertaken by relevant United Nations agencies and international partners,

Underlining the importance for Member States to continue using the *World Report on Road Traffic Injury Prevention* as a framework for road safety efforts and implementing its recommendations by paying particular attention to the five risk factors identified, namely, the non-use of safety belts and child restraints; alcohol; the non-use of helmets; inappropriate and excessive speed; and the lack of infrastructure,

Welcoming the proposal of the Economic Commission for Europe to host the first United Nations Global Road Safety Week, in Geneva in April 2007, targeted at young road users, including young drivers,

Also welcoming the proposal to designate the third Sunday in November as the World Day of Remembrance for Road Traffic Victims, in recognition of road traffic victims and their families' loss and suffering,

Convinced that responsibility for road safety rests at the local, municipal and national levels,

Recognizing that many developing countries and countries with economies in transition have limited capacities to address these issues, and underlining, in this context, the importance of international cooperation towards further supporting the efforts of developing countries, in particular, to build capacities in the field of road safety and of providing the financial and technical support associated with such efforts,

1. *Expresses its concern* at the continued increase, in particular in developing countries, in traffic fatalities and injuries worldwide;

2. *Reaffirms* the importance of addressing global road safety issues and the need for the further strengthening of international cooperation, taking into account the needs of developing countries, by building capacities in the field of road safety, and providing financial and technical support for their efforts;

3. *Encourages* Member States and the international community, including international and regional financial institutions, to lend financial, technical and political support, as appropriate, to the United Nations regional commissions, the World Health Organization and other relevant United Nations agencies for their efforts to improve road safety;

4. *Invites* the United Nations regional commissions, relevant United Nations agencies and international partners to continue the existing road safety initiatives, and encourages them to take up new ones;

5. *Encourages* Member States to adhere to the 1949 Convention on Road Traffic and the 1968 Convention on Road Traffic and Convention on Road Signs and Signals, in order to ensure a high level of road safety in their countries, and also encourages them to strive to reduce road traffic injuries and mortality in order to achieve the Millennium Development Goals;

6. *Stresses* the importance of the improvement in the international legal road traffic safety norms, and welcomes in this regard the work of the Working Party on Road Traffic Safety of the Inland Transport Committee of the Economic Commission for Europe in the elaboration of a substantial package of amendments to the 1968 Conventions on Road Traffic and Road Signs and Signals;

7. *Invites* Member States to implement the recommendations of the *World Report on Road Traffic Injury Prevention*, including those related to the five main risk factors, namely, the non-use of safety belts and child restraints; the non-use of helmets; drinking and driving; inappropriate and excessive speed; as well as the lack of appropriate infrastructure;

8. *Also invites* Member States to establish a lead agency, on a national level, on road safety and to develop a national action plan to reduce road traffic injuries, by passing and enforcing legislation, conducting necessary awareness-raising campaigns and putting in place appropriate methods to monitor and evaluate interventions that are implemented;

9. *Invites* the United Nations regional commissions and the World Health Organization to organize jointly, within their resources as well as with voluntary financial assistance from concerned stakeholders from government, civil society and the private sector, the first United Nations Global Road Safety Week to serve as a platform for global and regional, but mainly national and local, activities to raise awareness about road safety issues and to stimulate and advance responses as appropriate for these settings, and to convene a second road safety stakeholders' forum in Geneva as part of the Global Road Safety Week to continue work begun at the first forum held at United Nations Headquarters in 2004;

10. *Invites* Member States and the international community to recognize the third Sunday in November of every year as the World Day of Remembrance for Road Traffic Victims as the appropriate acknowledgement for victims of road traffic crashes and their families;

11. *Requests* the Secretary-General to report to the General Assembly at its sixty-second session on the progress made in improving global road safety;

12. *Decides* to include in the provisional agenda of its sixty-second session the item entitled "Global road safety crisis".

Food and agriculture

Food aid

World Food Programme

At its 2005 substantive session in July, the Economic and Social Council had before it two reports pertaining to the World Food Programme (WFP): the annual report [E/2005/14] of the Executive Director for 2004 and a report [E/2005/36] of the Executive Board containing the decisions and recommendations of its 2004 sessions. By **decision 2005/230** of 20 July, the Council took note of those reports.

The WFP Executive Board, at its 2005 sessions [E/2006/36] held in Rome: first regular session (31 January–2 February), annual session (6-10 June), and second regular session (7-11 November), decided on organizational and programme matters and approved a number of projects. In November, the Board approved its biennial programme of work for 2006-2007 [WFP/EB.2/2005/10] and invited its Bureau, with the assistance of its secretariat, to update the programme of work in the light of the decisions taken at the sessions.

WFP activities

WFP's 2005 Annual Performance Report (APR) [WFP/EB.A/2006/4 & Corr.1] measured its activities during the year in line with the performance and results framework laid out in the 2004-2007 strategic plan and the 2004-2005 biennial management plan approved in October 2003 [YUN 2003, p. 1259].

At the close of 2005, the overall global food aid deliveries were 8.2 million tons, an increase of about 9 per cent from the 7.5 million tons delivered in 2004. Of that amount, WFP distributed 4.2 million metric tons of food to 96.7 million people in 82 countries, a decrease of about 16.8 per cent from the 113 million people reached in 2004. Of those assisted, 35 million were reached through emergency operations, 38.1 million through protracted relief and recovery operations and 23.6 million through development projects.

The Sudan was the single largest country operation in 2005. In Darfur alone, WFP reached 3.4 million people in an operation totalling $398.7 million. Natural disasters in 2005 challenged WFP to meet large unforeseen needs in demanding environments. Hurricanes Katrina, Rita and Stan, drought and locusts in the Niger and the earthquake in Kashmir prompted large-scale responses from WFP, which also continued to assist 2.2 million survivors of the 2004 Indian Ocean tsunami. Additionally, WFP was involved in addressing the food emergency in southern Africa.

WFP continued to focus assistance on children, with the aim of ending child hunger. It provided assistance to 58 million children, 30 per cent of whom were five years of age and under. Nearly 52 per cent of beneficiaries receiving food assistance were women or girls. Some 2.1 million beneficiaries were refugees, and 8.3 million were internally displaced persons.

With regard to direct expenses, at the regional level, sub-Saharan Africa received the largest share, 71 per cent, then Asia, 18 per cent, Latin America and the Caribbean, the Middle East and North Africa, 3 per cent each, and Eastern Europe and the Commonwealth of Independent States, 1 per cent.

Administrative and financial matters

Continued progress was made in addressing WFP's organizational weaknesses and strengthening core management processes. Sixty per cent of performance indicator targets aimed at strengthening management processes were either met or exceeded in 2005. Lessons from major operations were analysed and management decisions were made to improve responses. Further progress was made in reporting results by strategic priorities, allowing WFP to highlight outputs aligned with

corporate priorities. However, challenges remained in standardizing outcome-level reporting of food interventions. WFP was working to improve reporting on corporate outcome indicators in emergencies, and to develop, with humanitarian agencies, coordinated approaches and standards.

WFP's Executive Board, in a joint meeting (New York, 20-24 January) with the Executive Boards of UNDP/UNFPA and UNICEF, discussed, among other matters, simplification and harmonization relating to the United Nations Development Group initiatives on common country programming, common services and premises, and resource transfer modalities.

Resources and financing

In 2005, operational expenditures totalled $2.9 billion, the same as in 2004. Confirmed contributions reached $2.76 billion, a slight increase over the 2004 figure of $2.2 billion. The United States was again the largest contributor, providing some $1.2 billion to the Programme. Of the total contributions, $1.4 billion went to protracted relief and recovery operations, $756 million to the International Emergency Food Reserve, $269 million to development activities, $262 million to special operations, $18.6 million to the Immediate Response Account and $79.3 million to other initiatives.

Food security

Communication. On 11 August [E/2005/90], the Director-General of the Food and Agriculture Organization of the United Nations (FAO) confirmed that the FAO Council, at its one hundred and twenty-seventh session (Rome, 22-27 November, 2004), endorsed the Voluntary Guidelines to Support the Progressive Realization of the Right to Adequate Food in the Context of National Food Security, which were previously endorsed by the FAO Committee on World Food Security. The Guidelines, designed to facilitate Governments' efforts to implement the right to food, covered actions to be taken at the national level to enable people to feed themselves in dignity and establish safety nets for those unable to do so. Approval of the Voluntary Guidelines marked the first time an intergovernmental body agreed on the implications of the right to food for government policies and on how to implement such an approach.

Follow-up to the 1996 World Food Summit

At its one hundred and twenty-eighth session (Rome, 20-25 June) [CL 128/10], the FAO Council considered two reports of the FAO's Committee on World Food Security (CFS) on assessment of the world food security situation [CFS:2005/2] and a new reporting format for the follow-up to the implementation of the World Food Summit Plan of Action [CFS:2005/3]. The Council also considered a summary of the multi-stakeholder dialogue held in preparation for the 2006 Special Forum to review implementation of the Plan of Action, adopted at the 1996 World Food Summit [YUN 1996, p. 1129], which called on countries to halve the number of undernourished people by 2015.

According to the CFS assessment of world food security, as at March 2005, 36 countries, 23 in Africa, 7 in Asia/Near East, 5 in Latin America and 1 in Europe faced serious food shortages. Although various factors contributed to the shortages, civil strife and adverse weather were the most common. Concern was expressed that, at the current rate of progress, the goal of halving the world's hungry by 2015 might not be reached.

International Year of Rice

Communication. In a 24 August letter [A/C.2/60/3], the FAO Director-General transmitted to the General Assembly President a report on the outcome of the International Year of Rice, 2004, proclaimed by Assembly resolution 57/162 [YUN 2002, p. 1226]. The report noted that more than 800 activities in 68 countries marked the International Year of Rice, and the successful implementation of the Year had raised global awareness of the important role rice played in development and the fight against hunger. It also resulted in increased support for the development of sustainable rice-based production systems. The report recommended the broadening of research and development in rice-based production systems and further efforts by FAO and other relevant organizations to assist national Governments in the improvement and transfer of rice production technologies.

International Year of the Potato

On 25 November, the Conference of FAO (Rome, 19-26 November) adopted resolution 4/2005, declaring 2008 the International Year of the Potato. The potato was recognized as an important international staple food that played an important role in ensuring food security and alleviating poverty. The General Assembly, in resolution 60/191 (see below), joined FAO in declaring 2008 the International Year of the Potato.

GENERAL ASSEMBLY ACTION

On 22 Decmber 2005 [meeting 68], the General Assembly, on the recommendation of the Second

(Economic and Financial) Committee [A/60/488], adopted **resolution 60/191** without vote [agenda item 52].

International Year of the Potato, 2008

The General Assembly,

Noting that the potato is a staple food in the diet of the world's population,

Recalling resolution 4/2005 of the Conference of the Food and Agriculture Organization of the United Nations, adopted on 25 November 2005,

Affirming the need to focus world attention on the role that the potato can play in providing food security and eradicating poverty in support of achievement of the internationally agreed development goals, including the Millennium Development Goals,

1. *Decides* to declare 2008 the International Year of the Potato;

2. *Invites* the Food and Agriculture Organization of the United Nations to facilitate the implementation of the International Year of the Potato, in collaboration with Governments, the United Nations Development Programme, Consultative Group on International Agricultural Research centres and other relevant organizations of the United Nations system, as well as relevant non-governmental organizations.

Nutrition

Standing Committee on Nutrition

At its thirty-second session (Brasilia, Brazil, 14-18 March), the United Nations System Standing Committee on Nutrition (SCN) conducted a symposium on realizing the right to adequate food to help achieve the Millennium Development Goals (MDGs) [YUN 2000, p. 51]. Among other things, the symposium examined case studies of four countries, focusing on strengthening the food and nutrition aspects of national development plans in order to achieve the MDGs. The Committee also considered reports from working groups on nutrition, ethics and human rights; breastfeeding and complementary feeding; nutrition and HIV/AIDS; capacity development in food and nutrition; nutrition in emergencies; household food security; and nutrition throughout the life cycle. Plenary lectures were organized by working groups focusing on anaemia and iron deficiencies and the double burden of disease in developing countries.

UNU activities

The United Nations University (UNU), through its Food and Nutrition Programme for Human and Social Development (FNP), continued to assist developing regions to enhance individual, organizational and institutional capacity; carried out coordinated global research activities; and served as the academic arm for the UN system in areas of food and nutrition that were best addressed in a non-regulatory, non-normative environment.

In 2005, FNP was to finalize a global scientific review for harmonization of approaches for developing nutrient-based dietary standards that were to result in the resolution of differences arising in: the setting of national and international nutrient standards; the designing of national and international food policies; and enhancing the transparency of the application of national standards to trade and other regulatory/normative activities. Ten papers related to that issue were commissioned by FNP, which served as core documents for the jointly sponsored UNU/FAO/WHO consultation held in December.

During the year, FNP completed a global regional network of capacity development task forces in Southern, Eastern and West/Central Africa, Latin America, Asia, the Middle East and Eastern Europe. It also spearheaded the establishment of the African Nutrition Graduate Students Network, a cooperative network of African nationals enrolled in graduate nutrition programmes throughout the world.

Five UNU-Kirin Fellows from Asia completed their 12-month training programme at the National Food Research Institute in Tsukuba, Japan, in March, and five new Fellows began their training in April.

UNU continued its publication of the *Food and Nutrition Bulletin* and the *Journal of Food Composition and Analysis.*

Chapter XIV

International drug control

The United Nations continued in 2005 to strengthen international cooperation in countering the world drug problem, mainly through the Commission on Narcotic Drugs, the International Narcotics Control Board (INCB) and the United Nations Office on Drugs and Crime (UNODC). The UN system's drug control activities focused on carrying out the 1999 Action Plan for the Implementation of the Declaration on the Guiding Principles of Drug Demand Reduction.

UNODC coordinated the drug control activities of UN organizations and provided technical expertise to Member States. As the custodian of international conventions to counter the world drug problem, it assisted States in complying with those conventions and supported INCB in monitoring their implementation. States and the international community were assisted in improving data collection and analysis. UNODC also contributed to a strengthened international drug control system through its integrated portfolio of global programmes and regional and country projects. In addition, support was provided for the design and implementation of alternative development programmes and projects in all regions where illicit drugs were cultivated.

The Commission on Narcotic Drugs—the main UN drug control policymaking body—recommended a number of draft resolutions to the Economic and Social Council and adopted resolutions on the follow-up to the General Assembly's twentieth (1998) special session on countering the world drug problem, implementation of the international drug control treaties, demand reduction and the prevention of drug abuse, alternative development, illicit drug trafficking and supply, administrative and budgetary matters and strengthening UN machinery for international drug control. In July, the Council urged Governments to continue to contribute to maintaining a balance between the licit supply of and demand for opiate raw materials for medical and scientific needs, to prevent their illicit production or diversion and to remove barriers to the medical use of opioid analgesics. It encouraged the development, implementation and strengthening of measures for the prevention and suppression of illicit drug trafficking and to promote demand reduction in transit States. The Council called on the international community to support Afghanistan's counter-narcotics objectives and requested UNODC to ensure that multilateral support was provided. That call was echoed by the Assembly in December. Also in December, the Assembly adopted an omnibus resolution on international cooperation against the world drug problem that addressed data collection and research; community capacity-building; demand reduction; illicit synthetic drugs; control of substances; judicial cooperation; countering money-laundering; and illicit crop eradication and alternative development.

INCB reviewed the implementation of alternative development programmes, highlighting best practices and models for increasing their effectiveness. It continued to oversee the implementation of the three major international drug control conventions, analyse the drug situation worldwide and draw the attention of Governments to weaknesses in national control and treaty compliance, making suggestions and recommendations for improvements at the national and international levels.

Follow-up to the twentieth special session

Report of Secretary-General. In response to General Assembly resolution 59/163 [YUN 2004, p. 1229], the Secretary-General, in a July report [A/60/130], provided an overview of international cooperation aimed at combating the world drug problem, in particular the implementation of mandates relating to the outcome of the Assembly's 1998 twentieth special session on countering the world drug problem [YUN 1998, p. 1135], and the Action Plan for the Implementation of the Declaration on the Guiding Principles of Drug Demand Reduction, adopted by the Assembly in resolution 54/132 [YUN 1999, p. 1157]. The report reviewed follow-up action taken by the Commission on Narcotic Drugs and its subsidiary bodies and by Governments and through international cooperation to counter the world drug problem. It also described UN system activities, including work on drug demand reduction; supply reduction and law enforcement; alternative livelihoods and protecting the environment; and strengthening the drug programme of the United Nations Office on Drugs and Crime (UNODC).

The Secretary-General concluded that, although progress had been made to enhance international cooperation, much remained to be done with regard to the implementation of legislative measures. The countries most affected by illicit crop cultivation needed further capacity-building, programme coordination, monitoring and impact evaluation systems and long-term socio-economic development in order to sustain illicit crop eradication and alternative development and to prevent the re-emergence of illicit crops. Efforts were required to strengthen precursor control and combat the illicit manufacture of and trafficking in amphetamine-type stimulants (ATS). More should be done to develop systems to assess the problem of all illicit drugs and establish prevention programmes and treatment and rehabilitation services. The Secretary-General suggested that the Assembly call upon the Commission on Narcotic Drugs to monitor the progress made by Governments towards meeting the goals and targets set at the Assembly's twentieth special session and invite States to respond to the biennial reports questionnaire on those efforts and on the implementation of measures to enhance international cooperation to counter the world drug problem.

Commission on Narcotic Drugs. In January, the UNODC Executive Director submitted to the Commission on Narcotic Drugs his third biennial report on the world drug problem [E/CN.7/2005/2 & Add.1-6]. The report, prepared in response to Commission resolutions 42/11 [YUN 1999, p. 1191] and 44/2 [YUN 2001, p. 1143], was based on the replies from States to the third biennial reports questionnaire, for the period from June 2002 to June 2004. That information dealt with national drug control strategies; drug demand reduction; the Action Plan against Illicit Manufacture, Trafficking and Abuse of Amphetamine-type Stimulants and their Precursors, contained in resolution S-20/4 A, [YUN 1998, p. 1139]; countering money-laundering; the Action Plan on Eradication of Illicit Drug Crops and on Alternative Development, contained in resolution S-20 E [ibid., p. 1148]; judicial cooperation; and control of precursors. It also contained information on the implementation of the 2003 Commission resolution on supporting the international drug control system through joint action [YUN 2003, p. 1268].

The Commission, by an 11 March resolution [E/2005/28/Rev.1 (res. 48/8)], called on Member States to: identify and promote strategies for international cooperation in the development and

dissemination of best practices and relevant research, including the monitoring of drug trends; give attention to the development of their research workforces; and adopt, implement and evaluate best practices and research-based evidence for policy and workforce development and programme delivery. It urged UNODC to promote the transfer of knowledge across international borders by coordination and dissemination efforts; consider the role of multidisciplinary research structures in countering illicit drugs; and promote models of good practice. Governments and researchers were encouraged to disseminate best practices and relevant research.

World Summit Outcome. In the World Summit Outcome document, contained in **resolution 60/1** (see p. 48), the Assembly reaffirmed its determination to overcome the world narcotic drug problem and resolved to strengthen UNODC's capacity to assist Member States to eliminate both the supply of and demand for illicit drugs.

GENERAL ASSEMBLY ACTION

On 16 December [meeting 64], the General Assembly, on the recommendation of the Third (Social, Humanitarian and Cultural) Committee [A/60/511], adopted **resolution 60/178** without vote [agenda item 107].

International cooperation against the world drug problem

The General Assembly,

Recalling the United Nations Millennium Declaration, its resolution 59/163 of 20 December 2004 and its other previous resolutions,

Welcoming the unwavering determination and commitment of Heads of State and Government gathered at the 2005 World Summit, held in New York from 14 to 16 September 2005, as set out in the 2005 World Summit Outcome, to overcome the world drug problem through international cooperation and national strategies to eliminate both the illicit supply of and demand for illicit drugs, and taking note of the resolve they expressed to strengthen the capacity of the United Nations Office on Drugs and Crime, within its existing mandates, to provide assistance to States in those tasks upon request,

Reaffirming the Political Declaration adopted by the General Assembly at its twentieth special session and the importance of meeting the objectives targeted for 2008, the joint ministerial statement adopted at the ministerial segment of the forty-sixth session of the Commission on Narcotic Drugs, the Action Plan for the Implementation of the Declaration on the Guiding Principles of Drug Demand Reduction and the Action Plan on International Cooperation on the Eradication of Illicit Drug Crops and on Alternative Development,

Aware that significant progress continues to be made by Member States in meeting the goals set for 2008 at the twentieth special session of the General Assembly, as reflected in the biennial reports of the Executive Director of the United Nations Office on Drugs and

Crime, taking note of the fact that the third biennial report drew attention to areas requiring further efforts by the international community, and recognizing that the drug problem is still a global challenge that constitutes a serious threat to public health and safety and the well-being of humankind, in particular children and young people, and that it undermines socio-economic and political stability and sustainable development, including efforts to reduce poverty, and is linked to violence and crime, including in urban areas,

Concerned by the serious challenges and threats posed by the continuing links between illicit drug trafficking and terrorism and other national and transnational criminal activities, inter alia, trafficking in human beings, especially women and children, money-laundering, corruption, trafficking in arms and trafficking in chemical precursors, and reaffirming that strong and effective international cooperation is needed to counter these threats,

Concerned also that risk-taking behaviour, which can be increased by continued drug use, including injecting drug use and sharing of needles, is a significant route for the transmission of HIV/AIDS and other blood-borne diseases,

Acknowledging that community capacity-building is an essential component of effective drug policies and programmes,

Taking note of the adoption on 16 December 2005 of its resolution 60/179 entitled "Providing support to Afghanistan with a view to ensuring effective implementation of its Counter-Narcotics Implementation Plan", welcoming the ongoing efforts of Afghanistan in the fight against drug trafficking, and calling upon the Government of Afghanistan to intensify those efforts,

Bearing in mind that international cooperation in countering drug abuse and illicit production and trafficking has shown that positive results can be achieved through sustained and collective efforts, and expressing its appreciation for the initiatives in this regard,

I

Respect for the principles enshrined in the Charter of the United Nations and other provisions of international law in countering the world drug problem

1. *Reaffirms* that countering the world drug problem is a common and shared responsibility that must be addressed in a multilateral setting, requires an integrated and balanced approach and must be carried out in full conformity with the purposes and principles of the Charter of the United Nations and other provisions of international law, and in particular with full respect for the sovereignty and territorial integrity of States, the principle of non-intervention in the internal affairs of States and all human rights and fundamental freedoms, and on the basis of the principles of equal rights and mutual respect;

2. *Urges* all States to ratify or accede to, and States parties to implement all the provisions of, the Single Convention on Narcotic Drugs of 1961 as amended by the 1972 Protocol, the Convention on Psychotropic Substances of 1971 and the United Nations Convention against Illicit Traffic in Narcotic Drugs and Psychotropic Substances of 1988;

3. *Invites* all States, as a matter of priority, to sign, ratify or accede to, and States parties to fully implement, the United Nations Convention against Transnational Organized Crime and the Protocols thereto and the United Nations Convention against Corruption, in order to counter comprehensively the transnational criminal activities that are related to illicit drug trafficking;

II

International cooperation to counter the world drug problem and follow-up to the twentieth special session

1. *Emphasizes* that the world drug problem must be addressed in multilateral, regional, bilateral and national settings and that, in order to succeed, action to counter it has to involve all Member States, that action must be supported by strong international and development cooperation and must be further included in national development priorities, and that it requires a balance between supply reduction and demand reduction, as well as a comprehensive strategy that combines alternative development, including, as appropriate, preventive alternative development, eradication, interdiction, law enforcement, prevention, treatment and rehabilitation as well as education;

2. *Calls upon* all States to strengthen their efforts in the fight against the world drug problem, in order to achieve the objectives targeted for 2008 in the Political Declaration adopted by the General Assembly at its twentieth special session, and calls upon all relevant actors to promote and implement the outcome of the special session, as well as the outcome of the ministerial segment of the forty-sixth session of the Commission on Narcotic Drugs;

3. *Urges* Member States to fulfil their reporting obligations on the follow-up action to implement the outcome of the twentieth special session of the General Assembly on the world drug problem and to report fully on all measures agreed upon at the special session;

4. *Takes note with appreciation* of the outcome of the round-table meeting on the theme "Crime and drugs as impediments to security and development in Africa", held in Abuja on 5 and 6 September 2005, in the form of a comprehensive programme of action, 2006-2010;

Data collection and research

5. *Stresses* that data collection, analysis and evaluation of the results of ongoing national and international policies are essential tools for further developing sound, evidence-based drug control strategies, and therefore encourages Member States to further develop and institutionalize monitoring and evaluation tools and to utilize existing available data to exchange and share information at all levels;

6. *Calls upon* Member States to consider providing additional reporting and analysis on women-specific data relating to the use of illicit substances and access to appropriate treatment services;

Community capacity-building

7. *Encourages* all States to support community capacity-building through the development and dissemination of information on drug abuse trends and to provide training and encourage the formation of com-

munity networks at all levels, with a view to drawing on best practices and sharing experience;

Demand reduction

8. *Urges* all Member States to implement the Action Plan for the Implementation of the Declaration on the Guiding Principles of Drug Demand Reduction and to strengthen their national efforts to counter the abuse of illicit drugs in their population, in particular among children and young people;

9. *Calls upon* States and organizations with expertise in community capacity-building to provide, as needed, access to treatment, health care and social services for drug users, in particular those living with HIV/AIDS and other blood-borne diseases, and to extend support to States requiring such expertise, consistent with the international drug control treaties;

10. *Urges* States, in order to achieve a significant and measurable reduction of drug abuse by 2008:

(a) To further implement comprehensive demand reduction policies and programmes, including research, covering all the drugs under international control, in order to raise public awareness of the drug problem, paying special attention to prevention and education and providing, especially to young people and others at risk, information on developing life skills, making healthy choices and engaging in drug-free activities;

(b) To further develop and implement comprehensive demand reduction policies, including risk reduction activities, under the supervision of competent health authorities, that are in line with sound medical practice and the international drug control treaties and that reduce the adverse health and social consequences of drug abuse, and to provide a wide range of comprehensive services for the treatment, rehabilitation and social reintegration of drug abusers, with appropriate resources being devoted to such services, since social exclusion constitutes an important risk factor for drug abuse;

(c) To enhance early intervention programmes that dissuade children and young people from using illicit drugs, including, inter alia, polydrug use and the recreational use of substances such as cannabis and synthetic drugs, especially amphetamine-type stimulants, and to encourage the active participation of the younger generation and their families in campaigns against drug abuse;

(d) To consider strengthening and implementing broadly based prevention and treatment programmes and to ensure that such programmes adequately address the gender-specific barriers that limit access for young girls and women, taking into account all attendant circumstances, including social and clinical histories, in the context of education, the family and the community, as appropriate;

Illicit synthetic drugs

11. *Urges* States to renew their efforts, at the national, regional and international levels, to implement the comprehensive measures covered in the Action Plan against Illicit Manufacture, Trafficking and Abuse of Amphetamine-type Stimulants and Their Precursors, to make special efforts to counter the abuse and recreational use of amphetamine-type stimulants, especially by young people, and to disseminate infor-

mation on the adverse health, social and economic consequences of such abuse;

12. *Calls upon* Member States to transmit voluntarily information on emerging substances of abuse to the United Nations Office on Drugs and Crime so that it may quickly share the knowledge available about those substances, indications of their abuse and other health hazards, if known, as well as synthesis techniques, diversion channels and trafficking patterns;

Control of substances

13. *Encourages* States to establish or strengthen mechanisms and procedures to ensure strict control of substances used to manufacture illicit drugs, to support international operations aimed at preventing their diversion, including through coordination and cooperation between regulatory and enforcement services involved in precursor control, in cooperation with the International Narcotics Control Board, and to counter smuggling networks effectively, particularly in source and transit countries, by conducting, inter alia, backtracking law enforcement investigations;

14. *Urges* all States and relevant international organizations to cooperate closely with the International Narcotics Control Board, in particular in Operation Purple, Operation Topaz and Project Prism, in order to enhance the success of those international initiatives and to initiate, where appropriate, investigations by their law enforcement authorities into seizures and cases involving the diversion or smuggling of precursors and essential equipment, with a view to tracking them back to the source of diversion in order to prevent continuing illicit activity;

Judicial cooperation

15. *Calls upon* all States to strengthen international cooperation among judicial and law enforcement authorities at all levels in order to prevent and combat illicit drug trafficking and to share and promote best operational practices in order to interdict illicit drug trafficking, including by establishing and strengthening regional mechanisms, providing technical assistance and establishing effective methods for cooperation, in particular in the areas of air, maritime, port and border control and in the implementation of extradition treaties;

16. *Acknowledges* the work of the United Nations Office on Drugs and Crime in the field of international cooperation, in particular through the provision of legal advisory assistance and the development of best practice guidance, and encourages States to make use of those services and tools in the enhancement of national laws and practice;

17. *Urges* Member States, consistent with their legal systems, to cooperate with a view to enhancing the effectiveness of law enforcement action in relation to the use of the Internet to combat drug-related crime;

Countering money-laundering

18. *Urges* States to strengthen action, in particular international cooperation and technical assistance aimed at preventing and combating the laundering of proceeds derived from drug trafficking and related criminal activities, with the support of the United Nations system, international institutions such as the World Bank and the International Monetary Fund, as well as regional development banks and, where appropriate, the Financial Action Task Force on Money

Laundering and similarly styled regional bodies, to develop and strengthen comprehensive international regimes to combat money-laundering and its possible links with organized crime and the financing of terrorism and to improve information-sharing among financial institutions and agencies in charge of preventing and detecting the laundering of those proceeds;

19. *Calls upon* States to consider including provisions in their national drug control plans for the establishment of national networks to enhance their respective capabilities to prevent, monitor, control and suppress serious offences connected with money-laundering and the financing of terrorism, to counter in general all acts of transnational organized crime and to supplement existing regional and international networks dealing with money-laundering;

International cooperation in illicit crop eradication and alternative development

20. *Recognizes* the efforts made by States to implement innovative alternative programmes, inter alia, in reforestation, agriculture and small and medium enterprises, and stresses the importance of the United Nations system and the international community contributing to the economic and social development of the communities that benefit from such programmes;

21. *Calls* for a comprehensive approach integrating alternative development programmes, including, where appropriate, preventive alternative development, into wider economic and social development programmes;

22. *Calls upon* States, where appropriate:

(a) To enhance support, including, where appropriate, through the provision of new and additional resources, for alternative development; security and rule of law, as necessary; environmental protection and eradication programmes undertaken by countries affected by the illicit cultivation of cannabis, especially in Africa, of opium poppy and of coca bush, in particular national programmes that seek to reduce social marginalization and promote sustainable economic development;

(b) To enhance joint strategies, through international and regional cooperation, to strengthen, including by training, education and providing technical assistance, alternative development, eradication and interdiction capacity, with the aim of eliminating illicit crop cultivation and fostering economic and social development;

(c) To encourage international cooperation, including, as appropriate, preventive alternative development, to prevent illicit crop cultivation from emerging in or being relocated to other areas;

(d) To provide, in accordance with the principle of shared responsibility, greater access to their markets for products of alternative development programmes, which are necessary for the creation of employment and the eradication of poverty;

(e) To establish or reinforce, where appropriate, national mechanisms to monitor and verify illicit crops;

(f) To continue to contribute to the maintenance of a balance between the licit supply of and demand for opiate raw materials used for medical and scientific purposes and to cooperate in preventing the proliferation of sources of production of opiate raw materials;

(g) To share and disseminate their experience with alternative development, including, as appropriate, preventive alternative development, and with illicit crop eradication, and to involve both the benefiting communities and academic and research institutions in that process, with a view to deepening the knowledge base;

23. *Calls upon* Member States and national and international development organizations to increase their efforts to empower local communities and authorities in project areas and to enhance their participation in the decision-making process in order to increase their ownership of the development measures undertaken in accordance with national legislation and the sustainability of those measures and to create law-abiding and prosperous rural society;

24. *Calls upon* Member States and international organizations to strengthen their partnerships with the private sector and civil society, in accordance with national legislation, in order to support social and licit economic development in areas in which illicit drugs are produced, taking into account the role of the private sector and civil society in promoting social responsibility and in the production and marketing of products of alternative development programmes;

III

Action by the United Nations system

1. *Emphasizes* that the multidimensional nature of the world drug problem calls for the promotion of integration and coordination of drug control activities throughout the United Nations system, including in the follow-up to major United Nations conferences, as well as in other relevant multilateral institutions and organizations;

2. *Reaffirms its resolve* to continue to strengthen the United Nations machinery for international drug control, in particular the Commission on Narcotic Drugs, the United Nations Office on Drugs and Crime and the International Narcotics Control Board, in order to enable them to fulfil their mandates, bearing in mind the recommendations contained in Economic and Social Council resolution 1999/30 of 28 July 1999 and the measures taken and recommendations adopted by the Commission on Narcotic Drugs since its forty-fourth session, aimed at the enhancement of its functioning;

3. *Encourages* the Commission on Narcotic Drugs, as the global coordinating body in international drug control and as the governing body of the drug programme of the United Nations Office on Drugs and Crime, and the International Narcotics Control Board to continue their useful work on the control of precursors and other chemicals used in the illicit manufacture of narcotic drugs and psychotropic substances;

4. *Notes* that the International Narcotics Control Board needs sufficient resources to carry out all its mandates, including those that will enable it to perform effectively its task within the framework of Operation Purple, Operation Topaz and Project Prism, and therefore urges Member States to commit themselves in a common effort to assigning adequate and sufficient budgetary resources to the Board, in accordance with Economic and Social Council resolution 1996/20 of 23 July 1996, emphasizes the need to maintain its capacity, inter alia, through the provision of appropriate means by the Secretary-General and adequate technical support by the United Nations Office on Drugs and Crime, and calls for enhanced cooperation and

understanding between Member States and the Board in order to enable it to implement all its mandates under the international drug control conventions;

5. *Welcomes* the efforts of the United Nations Office on Drugs and Crime to implement its mandate, and requests the Office to continue:

(*a*) To strengthen dialogue with Member States and also to ensure continued improvement in management, so as to contribute to enhanced and sustainable programme delivery and further encourage the Executive Director to maximize the effectiveness of the drug programme of the United Nations Office on Drugs and Crime, inter alia, through the full implementation of Commission on Narcotic Drugs resolutions, in particular the recommendations contained therein;

(*b*) To strengthen cooperation with Member States and with United Nations programmes, funds and relevant agencies, as well as relevant regional organizations and agencies and non-governmental organizations, and to provide, upon request, assistance in implementing the outcome of the twentieth special session of the General Assembly;

(*c*) To increase its assistance, within the available voluntary resources, to countries that are deploying efforts to reduce illicit crop cultivation by, in particular, adopting alternative development programmes, and to explore new and innovative funding mechanisms;

(*d*) To allocate, while keeping the balance between supply and demand reduction programmes, adequate resources to allow it to fulfil its role in the implementation of the Action Plan for the Implementation of the Declaration on the Guiding Principles of Drug Demand Reduction, and support countries, upon their request, to further develop and implement drug demand reduction policies;

(*e*) To develop action-oriented strategies to assist Member States to implement the Action Plan for the Implementation of the Declaration;

(*f*) To strengthen dialogue and cooperation with multilateral development banks and with international financial institutions so that they may undertake lending and programming activities related to drug control in interested and affected countries to implement the outcome of the twentieth special session, and to keep the Commission on Narcotic Drugs informed of further progress made in this area;

(*g*) To take into account the outcome of the twentieth special session, to include in its report on the illicit traffic in drugs an updated, objective and comprehensive assessment of worldwide trends in illicit traffic and transit in narcotic drugs and psychotropic substances, including methods and routes used, and to recommend ways and means of improving the capacity of States along those routes to address all aspects of the drug problem;

(*h*) To publish the *World Drug Report*, with comprehensive and balanced information about the world drug problem, and to seek additional extrabudgetary resources for its publication in all the official languages;

(*i*) To provide technical assistance, from available voluntary contributions for that purpose, to those States identified by relevant international bodies as the most affected by the transit of drugs, in particular developing countries in need of such assistance and support;

(*j*) To provide assistance, at the request of States and respecting fully their sovereignty and territorial integrity, in monitoring illicit crop cultivation and in detecting on time its emergence or relocation;

6. *Welcomes also* the follow-up, led by the United Nations Office on Drugs and Crime, to the 2003 Paris Conference on Drug Routes from Central Asia to Europe (the Paris Pact), encourages the Office and other relevant international institutions to continue their efforts, and encourages the Office to develop similar strategies in other regions for countries affected by the transit of illicit drugs through their territory;

7. *Takes note* of the outcome of the "Thematic debate on drug abuse prevention, treatment and rehabilitation: (*a*) Community capacity-building; (*b*) Preventing HIV/AIDS and other blood-borne diseases in the context of drug abuse prevention", held by the Commission on Narcotic Drugs at its forty-eighth session;

8. *Requests* the United Nations Office on Drugs and Crime, subject to the availability of resources and the Commission on Narcotic Drugs guidelines for the use of general-purpose funds, together with international financial institutions and the organizations involved in preventing and suppressing money-laundering and drug trafficking, to facilitate the provision of training and advice through technical cooperation in States, when requested, taking into account, inter alia, the recommendations on money-laundering and the financing of terrorism formulated by the Financial Action Task Force on Money Laundering and its regional groups;

9. *Urges* all Governments to provide the fullest possible financial and political support to the United Nations Office on Drugs and Crime by widening its donor base and increasing voluntary contributions, in particular general-purpose contributions, to enable it to continue, expand and strengthen its operational and technical cooperation activities, and recommends that a sufficient share of the regular budget of the United Nations be allocated to the Office to enable it to carry out its mandates and to work towards securing assured and predictable funding;

10. *Encourages* the meetings of Heads of National Drug Law Enforcement Agencies and of the Subcommission on Illicit Drug Traffic and Related Matters in the Near and Middle East of the Commission on Narcotic Drugs to continue to contribute to the strengthening of regional and international cooperation, taking into account the outcome of the twentieth special session of the General Assembly and of the ministerial segment of the forty-sixth session of the Commission;

11. *Calls upon* the relevant United Nations agencies and entities, other international organizations and international financial institutions, including regional development banks, to mainstream drug control issues into their programmes, and calls upon the United Nations Office on Drugs and Crime to maintain its leading role by providing relevant information and technical assistance;

12. *Takes note* of the report of the Secretary-General, and, taking into account the promotion of integrated reporting, requests the Secretary-General to submit to the General Assembly at its sixty-first session

a report on the implementation of the present resolution with a focus on transit countries.

Conventions

International efforts to control narcotic drugs were governed by three global conventions: the 1961 Single Convention on Narcotic Drugs [YUN 1961, p. 382], which, with some exceptions of detail, replaced earlier narcotics treaties and was amended in 1972 by a Protocol [YUN 1972, p. 397] to strengthen the role of the International Narcotics Control Board (INCB); the 1971 Convention on Psychotropic Substances [YUN 1971, p. 380]; and the 1988 United Nations Convention against Illicit Traffic in Narcotic Drugs and Psychotropic Substances [YUN 1988, p. 690].

As at 31 December, 177 States were parties to the 1961 Convention, as amended by the 1972 Protocol. During the year, Bhutan acceded to the Convention.

The number of parties to the 1971 Convention stood at 179 as at 31 December, with the accession of Angola, Bhutan, Cambodia and Honduras during the year.

At year's end, 177 States and the European Community were parties to the 1988 Convention, with Angola, Cambodia, Cook Islands, the Democratic Republic of the Congo, Liberia, Micronesia, Samoa and Switzerland acceding in 2005.

Commission action. In March [E/2005/28/Rev.1], the Commission on Narcotic Drugs reviewed implementation of the international drug control treaties. It had before it the INCB report covering 2004 activities [YUN 2004, p. 1237] and the 2004 INCB technical report on the implementation of Article 12 of the 1988 Convention entitled "Precursors and Chemicals Frequently Used in the Illicit Manufacture of Narcotic Drugs and Psychotropic Substances" [E/INCB/2004/4].

The Commission welcomed INCB efforts to promote the maintenance of a global balance between the supply of and demand for opiate raw materials used for medical and scientific purposes, as required under the 1961 Convention as amended by the 1972 Protocol. However, it was concerned that some States used seized material for the licit manufacture of pharmaceuticals, despite several Economic and Social Council resolutions against that practice. The importance of adherence to and implementation of the international treaties was stressed, and INCB and UNODC were requested to assist States whose national systems for controlling drugs and substances used in illicit manufacture needed improvement. The Commission, noting with concern the increase in the illicit cultivation and production of, and trafficking in, opiates in Afghanistan (see p. 1356), agreed that support should be provided to that State and neighbouring and transit countries. It expressed concern at the increasing number of Internet sites that were illicitly selling pharmaceuticals containing internationally controlled substances and urged Governments to intensify their cooperation to investigate and prosecute such cases. Regarding article 12 of the 1988 Convention, the Commission emphasized the importance of its effective implementation and of universal adherence to it. The Commission noted the successes achieved by Project Prism, Operation Purple and Operation Topaz (see p. 1348). In view of the increasing illicit heroin manufacture in Afghanistan, it called on the international community to strengthen support for Operation Topaz and recommended that the Operation's Steering Committee should improve investigations of seized acetic anhydride in order to track its manufacturers and examine the feasibility of tagging products to determine at which points along the distribution chain diversions were taking place.

On 11 March [E/2005/28/Rev.1 (res. 48/11)], the Commission called on Member States to enact legislation to implement the 1988 Convention; develop the "know-your-client" principle referred to in Council resolution 2003/39 [YUN 2003, p. 1269] and Assembly resolution 59/162 [YUN 2004, p. 1234]; and strengthen the use of the pre-export notification mechanism. It urged States to investigate cases involving the diversion or smuggling of precursors; strengthen cooperation with associations, persons or companies engaged in activities involving precursors; and cooperate with INCB, in particular in Operation Purple, Operation Topaz and Project Prism. The Commission also encouraged States and INCB to address the use of substitute precursor chemicals by trafficking networks and urged INCB to follow up seizures and cases involving the diversion or smuggling of precursors; and to evaluate cases of attempted diversions and incorporate the findings in its annual Report on Precursors and Chemicals Frequently Used in the Illicit Manufacture of Narcotic Drugs and Psychotropic Substances. It called upon States to take note of the third biennial report of the Executive Director on the world drug problem (see p. 1340). The Executive Director was requested to report in 2006.

On the same date [res. 48/1], the Commission requested UNODC to gather from Member States information on emerging substances of abuse; called upon States to transmit that information voluntarily to UNODC and to share it at the bilateral, regional and international levels. The Commission encouraged States to use the monitoring mechanisms provided for by the limited international special surveillance list of non-scheduled substances, covering substitute and new chemicals for which information existed on their use in illicit drug manufacture, which was maintained and reviewed by INCB.

INCB action. In its report covering 2005 [Sales No. E.06.XI.2], INCB urged States that were not parties to any of the international drug control treaties to accede to them without delay. It also urged Governments to furnish in a timely manner all statistical reports required under the treaties and to establish their own estimates of narcotic drug requirements for medical needs. The Board urged manufacturing and exporting countries of psychotropic substances to submit annual statistical reports within the deadline, in conformity with the provisions of the 1971 Convention, and encouraged all Governments to update the assessments of their medical and scientific requirements for psychotropic substances. It also urged States that had not done so to comply with their treaty obligations and submit information on substances frequently used in the illicit manufacture of narcotic drugs and psychotropic substances, as required under article 12 of the 1988 Convention.

ECONOMIC AND SOCIAL COUNCIL ACTION

On 22 July [meeting 36], the Economic and Social Council, on the recommendation of the Commission on Narcotic Drugs [E/2005/28/Rev.1], adopted **resolution 2005/26** without vote [agenda item 14 (d)].

Demand for and supply of opiates used to meet medical and scientific needs

The Economic and Social Council,

Recalling its resolution 2004/43 of 21 July 2004 and previous relevant resolutions,

Recognizing that the medical use of narcotic drugs, including opiates, is indispensable for the relief of pain and suffering,

Emphasizing that the need to balance the global licit supply of opiates against the legitimate demand for opiates used to meet medical and scientific needs is central to the international strategy and policy of drug control,

Noting the fundamental need for international cooperation with the traditional supplier countries in drug control to ensure universal application of the provisions of the Single Convention on Narcotic Drugs of 1961 and that Convention as amended by the 1972 Protocol,

Reiterating that a balance between consumption and production of opiate raw materials was achieved in the past as a result of efforts made by the two traditional supplier countries, India and Turkey, together with established supplier countries,

Expressing deep concern at the level of licit global production of opiate raw materials and the significant accumulation of stocks over the past few years as a consequence of the operation of market forces, which has the potential to upset the delicate balance between the licit supply of and demand for opiates for medical and scientific purposes,

Emphasizing the importance of adhering to the estimates, based on actual consumption and utilization of narcotic drugs, furnished to and confirmed by the International Narcotics Control Board on the extent of cultivation and production of opiate raw materials, especially in view of the current oversupply,

Recalling the Joint Ministerial Statement adopted during the ministerial segment of the forty-sixth session of the Commission on Narcotic Drugs, in which ministers and other government representatives called upon States to continue to contribute to the maintenance of a balance between the licit supply of and demand for opiate raw materials used for medical and scientific purposes and to cooperate in preventing the proliferation of sources of production of opiate raw materials,

Considering that opiate raw materials and opiates derived therefrom are not just ordinary commodities that can be subjected to the operation of market forces, and that, therefore, market economy considerations alone should not determine the cultivation of opium poppy,

Reiterating the importance of medically appropriate use of opiates in pain relief therapy, as advocated by the World Health Organization,

Noting that countries differ significantly in their level of consumption of narcotic drugs and that in most developing countries the use of narcotic drugs for medical purposes has remained at an extremely low level,

1. *Urges* all Governments to continue to contribute to maintaining a balance between the licit supply of and demand for opiate raw materials used for medical and scientific purposes, the achievement of which would be facilitated by maintaining, insofar as their constitutional and legal systems permit, support to the traditional and established supplier countries, and to cooperate in preventing the proliferation of sources of production of opiate raw materials;

2. *Urges* Governments of all producer countries to adhere strictly to the provisions of the Single Convention on Narcotic Drugs of 1961 and that Convention as amended by the 1972 Protocol, and to take effective measures to prevent the illicit production or diversion of opiate raw materials to illicit channels, welcomes the study carried out by the International Narcotics Control Board on the relative merits of different methods of producing opiate raw materials, and encourages improvements in practices in the cultivation and production of opiate raw materials;

3. *Urges* Governments of consumer countries to assess their licit needs for opiate raw materials realistically on the basis of actual consumption and utilization of opiate raw materials and opiates derived therefrom and to communicate those needs to the International Narcotics Control Board in order to ensure easy supply, calls upon Governments of countries producing opium to limit the cultivation of opium poppy, taking into account the current level of global stocks, to the

estimates furnished to and confirmed by the Board, in accordance with the requirements of the Single Convention on Narcotic Drugs of 1961, and urges that, in providing estimates of such cultivation, producer countries consider the actual demand requirements of importing countries;

4. *Urges* the Governments of all countries where opium poppy has not been cultivated for the licit production of opiate raw materials, in the spirit of collective responsibility, to refrain from engaging in the commercial cultivation of opium poppy, in order to avoid the proliferation of supply sites;

5. *Commends* the International Narcotics Control Board for its efforts in monitoring the implementation of the relevant Economic and Social Council resolutions and, in particular:

(a) In urging the Governments concerned to adjust global production of opiate raw materials to a level corresponding to actual licit requirements and to avoid unforeseen imbalances between the licit supply of and demand for opiates caused by the exportation of products manufactured from seized and confiscated drugs;

(b) In inviting the Governments concerned to ensure that opiates imported into their countries for medical and scientific use do not originate in countries that transform seized and confiscated drugs into licit opiates;

(c) In arranging informal meetings, during the sessions of the Commission on Narcotic Drugs, with the main States that import and produce opiate raw materials;

6. *Requests* the International Narcotics Control Board to continue its efforts in monitoring the implementation of the relevant Economic and Social Council resolutions in full compliance with the Single Convention on Narcotic Drugs of 1961 and that Convention as amended by the 1972 Protocol;

7. *Requests* the Secretary-General to transmit the text of the present resolution to all Member States for consideration and implementation and to report to the Commission on Narcotic Drugs at its forty-ninth session on progress made in the implementation of the present resolution.

Also on 22 July [meeting 36], the Council, on the recommendation of the Commission [E/2005/28/Rev.1], adopted **resolution 2005/25** without vote [agenda item 14 (d)].

Treatment of pain using opioid analgesics

The Economic and Social Council,

Recalling its resolutions 1995/19 of 24 July 1995, 1996/19 of 23 July 1996, 1997/38 of 21 July 1997, 1998/25 of 28 July 1998, 1999/33 of 28 July 1999, 2000/18 of 27 July 2000, 2001/17 of 24 July 2001, 2002/20 of 24 July 2002, 2003/40 of 22 July 2003 and 2004/43 of 21 July 2004, in which it reiterated the importance of medically appropriate use of opiates in pain relief therapy as advocated by the World Health Organization,

Bearing in mind the report of the International Narcotics Control Board for 1999, especially its chapter I, entitled "Freedom from pain and suffering", in which the Board reminded all Governments that the medical use of narcotic drugs continued to be indispensable for the relief of pain and suffering and that adequate provision must be made to ensure the availability of narcotic drugs for such purposes,

Recalling the document entitled "Achieving balance in national opioids control policy: guidelines for assessment", prepared in 2000 by the World Health Organization in consultation with the International Narcotics Control Board to help Governments to achieve better pain management by identifying and overcoming the barriers to opioid availability, in which it was emphasized that opioids such as morphine were the drugs of choice in the treatment of severe pain and that they should be available at all times in adequate amounts and in the appropriate dosage forms to satisfy the health-care needs of the majority of the population,

Recalling also that, in May 2004, the Executive Board of the World Health Organization recommended for adoption by the Fifty-eighth World Health Assembly, to be held in May 2005, a draft resolution on cancer prevention and control, in which the Assembly would urge member States to ensure the medical availability of opioid analgesics according to international treaties and recommendations of the World Health Organization and the International Narcotics Control Board and subject to an efficient monitoring and control system,

Welcoming the fact that the World Health Organization is developing a strategy to integrate the availability of opioid pain medication into palliative care for HIV/AIDS, cancer and other chronic diseases,

Calling attention to the assessment of the International Narcotics Control Board in its report for 2004 according to which low consumption of opioid analgesics for the treatment of moderate to severe pain, especially in developing countries, continued to be a matter of great concern to the Board,

Noting, on the basis of that report, the disparities in the consumption of such medicines existing between developing and developed countries, and recalling that, in 2003, six countries together accounted for 79 per cent of global consumption of morphine, while developing countries, representing about 80 per cent of the world's population, accounted for only about 6 per cent of global consumption of morphine,

Bearing in mind that, in its report for 2004, the International Narcotics Control Board encouraged Member States that had not yet done so to examine the extent to which their health-care systems and laws and regulations permitted the use of opioids for medical purposes, to identify possible impediments to such use and to develop plans of action for the development of long-term pain management strategies, with a view to facilitating the supply and availability of narcotic drugs for all appropriate indications,

Recalling that, in its report for 1999, the International Narcotics Control Board stated that the development of a new, non-profit mechanism for the use of otherwise unused narcotic products should be considered and observed that the impediments to opioid availability that were frequently reported by government authorities were impediments originating in the regulatory and drug control system, medical/therapeutic impediments, economic impediments and social and cultural impediments,

1. *Recognizes* the importance of improving the treatment of pain, including by the use of opioid analge-

sics, as advocated by the World Health Organization, especially in developing countries, and calls upon Member States to remove barriers to the medical use of such analgesics, taking fully into account the need to prevent their diversion for illicit use;

2. _Invites_ the International Narcotics Control Board and the World Health Organization to examine the feasibility of a possible assistance mechanism that would facilitate the adequate treatment of pain using opioid analgesics and to inform the Commission on Narcotic Drugs at its forty-ninth session of the results of that examination;

3. _Requests_ the Secretary-General to transmit the text of the present resolution to all Member States for their consideration and implementation and to report on the implementation of the resolution to the Commission on Narcotic Drugs at its forty-ninth session.

In other action, the Council, by **resolution 2005/14** (see p. 1226), adopted the Model Bilateral Agreement on the Sharing of Confiscated Proceeds of Crime or Property covered by the United Nations Convention against Transnational Organized Crime and the United Nations Convention against Illicit Traffic in Narcotic Drugs and Psychotropic Substances of 1988.

International Narcotics Control Board

The 13-member International Narcotics Control Board held its eighty-second (31 January–4 February), eighty-third (2-13 May) and eighty-fourth (1-18 November) sessions, all in Vienna.

In performing the tasks assigned to it under the international conventions, the Board monitored the implementation of those conventions and maintained a permanent dialogue with Governments, using the information received to identify the enforcement of treaty provisions requiring them to limit to medical and scientific purposes the licit manufacture of, trade in and distribution and use of narcotic drugs and psychotropic substances. The Board, which was requested by the treaties to report annually on the drug control situation worldwide, noted weaknesses in national control and treaty compliance and made recommendations for improvements at the national and international levels.

The Board's 2005 report [Sales No. E.06.XI.2] examined the issue of alternative development, by which illegal drug crops could be substituted by legal cash crops to provide growers with similar or even higher incomes. It stated that alternative development programmes should take into account the context of livelihoods; be combined with law enforcement and drug prevention activities; and include drug abuse prevention and treatment and the development of infrastructure to transport legal crops to markets and to provide education and health care assistance. Alternative development should be integrated into broader development and investment efforts and long-term strategies. The Board recommended that Governments enhance joint strategies to strengthen alternative development programmes; ensure that those strategies were suited to the area concerned; anticipate changes in drug abuse and trafficking patterns; and ensure that law enforcement activities in illicit crop cultivation areas contributed to the building of trust between local communities and authorities and promoted the participation of crop growers in the formulation of policies.

With regard to the diversion of pharmaceutical products containing narcotic drugs, INCB urged Governments to collect information on their diversion and abuse and draw the attention of medical personnel to the good prescribing and dispensing practices recommended by the World Health Organization (WHO). It encouraged UNODC to assist Governments to monitor trends and prevent diversion and abuse. Noting that diversion of pharmaceuticals containing psychotropic substances was, together with illegally operating Internet pharmacies, the most important source for illicit drug suppliers (benzodiazepines and amphetamine-type stimulants (ATS) being the most abused), the Board urged Governments to collect information on the extent of diversion, monitor their consumption levels and raise awareness about the consequences of their abuse. INCB noted the increasing trafficking in and abuse of gamma-hydroxybutyric acid (GHB), a sedative-hypnotic, and called on Governments to increase their vigilance and develop appropriate abuse prevention programmes.

As to precursors, INCB remained the international focal point for the exchange of information under Project Prism, Operation Purple and Operation Topaz. Under Project Prism, the international initiative against diversion of ATS precursors, several diversion attempts were uncovered involving ephedra, the plant material not under international control from which ephedrine and pseudoephedrine were extracted. Also, efforts were made to gather information on the exports from South-East Asia of safrole-rich oils used in the illicit manufacture of methylenedioxymethamphetamine (MDMA) (Ecstasy and related drugs). Under Operation Purple, Governments continued to prevent the diversion of potassium permanganate for use in the illicit manufacture of cocaine. The Board called on them to investigate stopped shipments of the substance, improve information exchange on seizures and stopped shipments and dismantle the networks concerned. The monitoring of international trade under Operation Topaz, which tracked acetic anhydride used in heroin manufacture, continued. However, not all countries had appropriate mechanisms to report seizures. In October, the steering committees of Operations Purple and Topaz launched a new phase, named Project Cohesion, which introduced a regional approach to operational work and time-limited regional activities and provided for the exchange of real-time information, intelligence-gathering and backtracking investigations. Countries in West Asia were urged to develop counter-trafficking activities focusing on the substances used in the illicit manufacture of heroin and on acetic anhydride in particular. They were invited to use the mechanism established under Project Cohesion to receive advice and practical assistance in investigations.

With regard to ensuring the availability of drugs for medical purposes, INCB recommended that global stocks of opiate raw materials should be maintained at a level sufficient to cover global demand for about one year, in case of a production shortfall, and to reduce the risk of diversion associated with excessive stocks. It requested producer countries to submit cultivation estimates; to maintain cultivation within the limits of the estimates confirmed by the Board, or to furnish supplementary estimates; and to report the amounts of raw materials produced, as well as the alkaloids obtained from them. The Board welcomed Economic and Social Council resolution 2005/25 (see p. 1347) and requested Governments to promote the rational use of narcotic drugs for medical treatment, including the use of opioid analgesics, in accordance with WHO recommendations. It called on Governments to maintain a balance between the licit supply of and demand for opiate raw materials and to co-operate in preventing the proliferation of sources of their production. Having studied the relative merits of different methods of producing opiate raw materials, INCB invited producing countries to review their production systems and examine their production control measures.

INCB observed that the illicit sale of pharmaceuticals containing internationally controlled narcotic drugs and psychotropic substances through the Internet had increased. Noting that only a limited number of countries had adopted specific measures to prevent such misuse of the Internet, the Board called on Governments: to increase the awareness of law enforcement, regulatory and drug control authorities regarding the need to counteract those activities; identify focal points for activities related to illegal Internet pharmacies; and provide details of legislation and regulations related to such sites and to the use of the mail for shipping controlled drugs. Awareness-raising campaigns to alert the public to the dangers of illegal Internet pharmacies and close cooperative working relationships between the different agencies involved needed to be established at the national level. Increased international cooperation and networking were also required. The Board urged international organizations, particularly the Universal Postal Union, the International Criminal Police Organization (Interpol), the World Customs Organization and UNODC, to confront the problems of illicitly operating Internet pharmacies and the smuggling of controlled drugs by mail and to share their experiences with the Board. Governments should ensure the training of staff and the technical aid required for drug identification and provide information on seizures of drugs smuggled by mail to the countries of destination and international entities, in order to develop concerted international action. Every Government should also ensure that its national legislation provided for the control of all routes of international mail leading into and out of the country.

The INCB report was supplemented by three technical reports: Narcotic Drugs: Estimated World Requirements for 2006; Statistics for 2004 [E/INCB/2005/2]; Psychotropic Substances: Statistics for 2004; Assessments of Annual Medical and Scientific Requirements for Substances in Schedules II, III and IV of the Convention on Psychotropic Substances of 1971 [E/INCB/2005/3]; and Precursors and Chemicals Frequently Used in the Illicit Manufacture of Narcotic Drugs and Psychotropic Substances: Report of INCB for 2005 on the Implementation of Article 12 of the UN Convention against Illicit Traffic in Narcotic Drugs and Psychotropic Substances of 1988 [E/INCB/2005/4].

By **decision 2005/251** of 22 July, the Economic and Social Council took note of the INCB report for 2004 [YUN 2004, p. 1237].

World drug situation

In its 2005 report [Sales No. E.06.XI.2], INCB presented a regional analysis of world drug abuse trends and control efforts, so that Governments would be kept aware of situations that might endanger the objectives of international drug control treaties.

Africa

Cannabis remained the most widely grown, trafficked and abused drug in Africa. The region was the second largest producer of cannabis herb (after North America), accounting for 28 per cent of global production. It was abused by over 34 million people and illicitly produced in all subregions. In West and Central Africa, cannabis continued to be cultivated for commercial purposes, and constituted a significant commercial crop in Eastern Africa, especially in the Comoros, Ethiopia, Kenya, Madagascar, Uganda and the United Republic of Tanzania. The largest producers in Southern Africa were (in decreasing order) South Africa, Malawi, Lesotho and Swaziland. More than 40 per cent of the world's cannabis resin was produced in Morocco, which was the source of 80 per cent of the resin abused in Europe, the world's largest market. Illicit trafficking in cannabis resin continued to be a major problem in the Rif area of Morocco, where an eradication campaign was launched by the Government in May.

The African region, particularly Western and Northern Africa, was increasingly used for smuggling cocaine from South America into Europe and North America. There was an increased interdiction of cocaine (shipped from Brazil) in South Africa and on the eastern coast of Africa. Despite the increase in the volume of cocaine seized in Africa, its abuse remained low and was confined mainly to Nigeria, Senegal and South Africa. There was some concern, however, that as cocaine trafficking routes evolved, there would be a spillover effect and abuse would spread.

Although opiate abuse remained limited in Africa, it was becoming a cause for concern, particularly in countries along the Indian Ocean. Heroin interdiction rates remained low in the region, but significant seizures were made in Eastern Africa at the airports of Addis Ababa (Ethiopia), Nairobi (Kenya) and Dar es Salaam and Zanzibar City (United Republic of Tanzania); as countermeasures were taken, traffickers shifted their operations to other African countries, including Malawi, Rwanda, Uganda and Zambia. Heroin abuse had increased in Eastern Africa, particularly in Kenya, Mauritius and the United Republic of Tanzania, and in Rwanda, Somalia and Uganda. In Nigeria, there was growing abuse by injection. In Northern Africa, there were significant levels of heroin abuse in Egypt.

The availability of illicitly manufactured and diverted pharmaceutical products containing narcotic drugs and psychotropic substances in unregulated markets was a major problem. In most countries, a wide range of licit narcotic drugs and psychotropic substances were available without a prescription and on street markets following their diversion from licit channels.

In South Africa, the illicit manufacture of ATS, mainly cathinone, methcathinone, MDMA (Ecstasy) and methamphetamine, continued. Of particular concern was the emergence of abuse of methamphetamine (commonly called "tic") in the Cape Town area. Despite law enforcement efforts, methaqualone (Mandrax) abuse continued unabated. It was smuggled out of India and China, but some of it was also manufactured in South Africa. African countries were increasingly used by traffickers to divert precursor chemicals.

The widespread abuse of khat, a substance not under international control that was cultivated in Eastern Africa, had become a serious threat to reconstruction efforts in Somalia. With regard to regional cooperation, the African Union (AU) assigned to its Economic, Social and Cultural Council, an advisory body established in March, the responsibility of advising it on drug-related matters. The second Ministerial Conference on Drug Control in Africa (Grand Baie, Mauritius, December 2004), the theme of which was "Mainstreaming drug control in socio-economic development into Africa", was attended by experts from 28 AU member States. A regional meeting of the International Drug Enforcement Conference (Abuja, Nigeria, February) formulated a common position on money-laundering, international drug trafficking organizations and precursor chemicals control. The Arab Conference for Protecting Youth from Drug Abuse (Cairo, Egypt, June) formulated the Cairo Action Plan, containing recommendations on enhancing coordination among participating Arab countries in abuse prevention. For the first time in Africa, a subregional workshop on precursor control was held in Eastern Africa (Mombasa, Kenya, July), organized by UNODC, in cooperation with INCB. At the national level, Algeria and South Africa adopted national drug control master plans, while Lesotho prepared a comprehensive programme framework for abuse prevention, and Malawi took initiatives to address drug control issues. The Libyan Arab Jamahiriya enhanced programming and implementation capacities in demand reduction, and Kenya appointed a precursor control steering committee to address inadequate precursor control and to draft appropriate legislation.

In September, INCB sent a mission to Cape Verde, which had emerged as part of a major transit route for consignments of cocaine originating in South America en route to Europe. The Board encouraged the Government to strengthen the interdiction capabilities of its national drug law enforcement agencies and to assess the drug abuse situation. In January, the Board visited

Ghana, which it encouraged to update legislation on narcotic drugs and psychotropic substances, draft legislation on precursor chemical control and elaborate abuse prevention and demand reduction programmes. Following an August mission to Lesotho, INCB encouraged the Government to enact precursor control legislation, eradicate cannabis plant cultivation and introduce alternative development programmes. In August, an INCB mission visited Swaziland, where legislation used to control the licit and illicit movements of drugs dated back to the 1920s. The Board observed that a new drug bill was before the Parliament and encouraged the Government to adopt and implement it, as well as measures to control precursor chemicals. INCB urged the Government to take a stand against the legalization of cannabis plant cultivation, strengthen its eradication efforts and introduce alternative development programmes. Also in August, the Board visited Zambia and urged the Government to adopt and implement measures to control precursor chemicals; eradicate the illicit cultivation of cannabis; and introduce alternative development programmes. The Board encouraged the Government to provide drug law enforcement and pharmaceutical regulatory bodies with adequate resources.

Americas

Central America and the Caribbean

Central America and the Caribbean continued to be used as major trans-shipment points for consignments of illicit drugs, mainly cocaine, originating in South America and destined for the United States and Europe. The annual amount of cocaine seized in the region remained high (about 30 tons), with Panama accounting for the largest quantity seized (7 tons). The most significant increase in cocaine seizures was registered in Nicaragua, while seizures increased in Belize, Costa Rica and El Salvador.

The total volume of cannabis seized increased in Central America but declined in the Caribbean. In 2004, the largest total volume of cannabis seized (1,700 tons) was reported by Trinidad and Tobago. Jamaica remained the main producer and exporter of cannabis on a larger scale. Cannabis abuse continued to rise in the region.

To deal with the problem of opium poppy cultivation in Guatemala, the Government implemented a successful eradication programme during 2004, eliminating more than 5.4 million opium poppy plants. Guatemala saw the diversion of pharmaceutical preparations containing narcotic drugs from licit distribution channels for illicit use, and significant quantities of pharmaceutical preparations were smuggled from El Salvador, Honduras and Mexico. Heroin trafficking increased in El Salvador and Guatemala.

In 2004, cases involving MDMA (Ecstasy) from the Netherlands were reported in Costa Rica and the Dominican Republic.

With regard to regional cooperation, the Board welcomed the Meeting on Transnational Criminal Youth Gangs: Characteristics, Importance and Public Policies (Tapachula, Mexico, June), organized by the Inter-American Drug Abuse Control Commission (CICAD) of the Organization of American States. In October 2004, the Caribbean Epidemiology Centre, with UNODC and CICAD support, established drug information networks to guide efforts to reduce illicit drug supply and demand in the Caribbean. At the national level, almost all of the countries in Central America and the Caribbean had designed national plans to deal with the drug problem. However, they experienced difficulties in implementing them, mainly because of lack of human and financial resources. Most countries had no epidemiological studies on drug abuse, and measures for the control of pharmaceutical preparations, including rules regarding their prescription, distribution and sale, needed to be enhanced. The need for control measures had increased as pharmaceuticals, including pseudoephedrine, ATS, phentermine, hydrocodone and oxycodone, were sold over the Internet. In Honduras, the implementation of drug control legislation was hampered by corrupt practices. Also, the National Assembly had yet to adopt legislation to reform the statute covering illegal drugs and to make money-laundering a crime. Costa Rica promulgated a decree aimed at strengthening drug control. The Bahamas launched its first national drug control plan and signed a comprehensive maritime agreement to fight maritime drug trafficking. In Jamaica, the Board was concerned that illegal use of MDMA (Ecstasy) was subject to light penalties and encouraged the Government to include it in the list of drugs covered in the Dangerous Drugs Act.

North America

In the United States, declining abuse of cannabis, cocaine and MDMA (Ecstasy), particularly among adolescents and youth, was counteracted by an increase in the abuse of prescription drugs, in particular painkillers, and an increase in inhalant abuse. Methamphetamine manufacture, trafficking and abuse were on the rise, particularly in rural areas. Some 8 per cent of the population aged 12 and above were current users of illicit drugs; the main drug of abuse was cannabis, followed by prescription drugs and cocaine. Prescription drugs were diverted from domestic distribution channels or obtained from illegal Internet pharmacies. Most of the cocaine and much of the heroin, cannabis and methamphetamine available on the illicit markets in the United States were smuggled into the south-west from Mexico. Despite efforts by the Government to counter illicit drug manufacture and trafficking, Mexico remained the primary transit country for the cocaine and one of the main manufacturers of the heroin, methamphetamine and cannabis found in the United States. The smuggling of drugs over the border between Canada and the United States declined; however, cannabis and methamphetamine continued to be smuggled into the United States, while heroin and cocaine continued to be smuggled into Canada. Trafficking in and use of controlled synthetic drugs became entrenched in the drug culture in Canada, where the illicit market had evolved into a huge profit-making opportunity.

Cannabis remained the most abused drug in all three countries in the region. Its abuse increased in Canada and Mexico but declined in the United States. Domestic production increased in the United States, in part because of large-scale production by criminal groups, while Mexican cannabis was the principal type of foreign-produced cannabis available. Although Canada was not a primary source for cannabis found in the United States, 2 per cent of all cannabis seized on United States borders came through there. In Canada, cannabis plant cultivation continued to spread throughout the country due to the significant demand, particularly among youth.

In the United States, some 2.3 million persons were users of cocaine. In Canada, the annual prevalence of cocaine abuse increased between 1994 and 2004 from 0.7 to 1.9 per cent. The volume of cocaine passing through the corridor of Central America and Mexico to the United States increased, accounting for 92 per cent of the total volume entering the country. Most of the cocaine available on the illicit market in Canada was supplied by commercial trucks passing through the United States.

In the United States, heroin abusers represented 0.1 per cent of the population. The most prevalent types of heroin continued to be Colombian and Mexican. Despite its relatively small share of global opium production (less than 5 per cent), Mexico was the second largest supplier of heroin to the illicit market in the United States. About 60 per cent of the trafficked heroin was smuggled out of Colombia through Mexico, the remainder being manufactured in Mexico itself.

While most of the heroin available in Canada continued to originate in South-East and South-West Asia, heroin of Latin American origin was being encountered more frequently.

All three countries in North America experienced an increase in the abuse of pharmaceutical preparations containing narcotic drugs. In Mexico, it was nearly as frequent as cocaine abuse; in Canada, an illegal street market for many prescription drugs had been confirmed; and in the United States, the non-medical use of all major groups of prescription drugs, as well as illegal sale of prescription drugs via the Internet, often through Internet-based pharmacies, had increased sharply.

In the United States, over 3 million persons abused prescription drugs containing psychotropic substances, mostly tranquillizers, stimulants and, to a lesser extent, sedatives. Due to the high prescription level of stimulants used for the treatment of attention deficit disorder, those preparations were also found on the illicit market. In Mexico, the abuse of tranquillizers was higher and growing faster among women. GHB had become a matter of concern in the United States and Canada. In Mexico, the abuse of psychotropic substances was growing. The availability of MDMA (Ecstasy) decreased in the United States, while the demand for it increased in Canada, especially among adolescents and young adults. In the United States, the use of phencyclidine (PCP) and lysergic acid diethylamide (LSD) decreased to a very low level. In Canada, psilocybine, PCP and LSD continued to be available on the illicit market in small quantities.

While methamphetamine abuse among adolescents in the United States declined, its overall increase, particularly in rural areas, remained a matter of concern. The number of methamphetamine laboratories dismantled increased from over 9,000 in 2002 to more than 17,000 in 2004. Illicit drug markets in the United States were increasingly being supplied with methamphetamine manufactured in Mexico. The manufacture and distribution of a form of methamphetamine commonly called "ice" (with a higher purity level) by Mexican criminal groups increased sharply. The illicit manufacture of and trafficking in methamphetamine increased dramatically in Canada.

As to substances not under international control, ketamine abuse was reported in all three countries in North America. In Canada, ketamine was among the more popular drugs introduced in the "rave" subculture and stricter controls over it were implemented in Mexico. Inhalants abused in Mexico and the United States were easily accessible in the form of household and office products. In the United States, one out of 11 teenagers abused over-the-counter cough medications containing dextromethorphan.

The excellent cooperation between the three countries continued. The Canada–United States Cross-Border Crime Forum was the principal bilateral cooperative initiative between the two countries in fighting cross-border crime. Mexico and the United States improved cooperation in law enforcement, and a number of joint operations were conducted by Canada, Mexico and the United States. All three countries were members of the Financial Action Task Force on Money Laundering and of CICAD. As to national action, the United States National Drug Control Strategy included plans to increase drug abuse prevention and treatment efforts, to support drug court programmes, and to address the abuse of prescription drugs. In Canada, five provinces implemented programmes for tracking multiple-copy prescriptions in order to reduce the diversion of drugs at a high risk of being diverted and abused. In April, the Drug Strategy Community Initiatives Fund was launched to provide funds for illicit drug demand reduction and abuse prevention in Canada. Mexico increased the resources set aside for control of narcotic drugs and psychotropic substances.

An INCB mission to Mexico in January noted the efforts made in combating illicit drug production, manufacture, trafficking and abuse. However, the Board was concerned that trafficking organizations continued to impede drug control efforts and urged the Government to curb the influence of organized crime and to fight corruption at all levels. With regard to the illicit cultivation of cannabis plant and opium poppy, the Board recommended the adoption of means to prevent its resurgence.

South America

Cannabis continued to be the most abused narcotic drug in South America. The illicit cultivation of cannabis destined mainly for local or regional markets was taking place in most countries, as evidenced by increasing seizures. Paraguay was the principal source of the cannabis resin found in the region. Only 10 per cent of the cannabis cultivated within that country was abused locally; the rest was destined for Argentina, Brazil and Chile.

The level of illicit coca bush cultivation remained significantly lower in 2004 than in the peak year of 2000, although it increased compared with 2003. Intensified eradication and law enforcement efforts by Colombia led to a decrease in illicit coca bush cultivation in that country; however, cultivation increased in others, in particular in Bolivia and Peru.

In 2004, the area under coca bush cultivation in Bolivia, Colombia and Peru increased by 3 per cent (to 158,000 hectares) over 2003 and continued to spread to areas previously not affected. Significant replanting of coca bush was reported in Colombia at the end of 2004. In Peru, the total area under coca leaf cultivation was estimated at 50,300 hectares in 2004, an increase of 14 per cent over 2003. More than 10,000 hectares of coca bush were eradicated in 2004, but opposition to crop eradication was growing. Almost one quarter of the area cultivated with coca bush in Peru was in national parks and other locations not suitable for agriculture. Moreover, in 2005, several local governments issued ordinances legalizing the cultivation of coca bush for traditional purposes, such as chewing and making infusions. In Bolivia, where political and social tensions limited the Government's ability to deal with the increasing coca bush cultivation and the eradication policy was undermined by agreements with coca growers, the area under cultivation increased by 17 per cent to 27,700 hectares in 2004. Illicit coca bush cultivation was reported in Ecuador and Venezuela, near their borders with Colombia, although it was limited. Cocaine manufacture and drug trafficking continued to spread in the region despite intensified interdiction efforts. The bulk of the world's cocaine continued to be manufactured in Colombia, but illicit manufacture also took place in all other countries in the region except Paraguay. Drug traffickers responded to Colombia's intensified interdiction efforts by shifting manufacture to other countries and using new trafficking routes. Although cocaine abuse was a problem in South America, the amounts smuggled into the region were destined mainly for the United States or Europe. Brazil, Ecuador, Suriname and Venezuela were the countries most affected by cocaine trafficking, although Argentina and Chile were experiencing growing transit traffic. Precursor chemicals smuggled in South America continued to be from within the region. Cocaine was the second most abused narcotic drug in South America; however, the extent of abuse varied from country to country.

Illicit cultivation of opium poppy and trafficking in heroin did not diminish in South America. In Colombia in 2004, almost 4,000 hectares were used for opium poppy cultivation, which also continued in Peru and Venezuela. Heroin manufacture took place mainly in Colombia and, to a lesser degree, in Peru; it was mostly destined for the United States. Venezuela was one of the main transit countries for heroin shipments bound for the United States.

While the illicit manufacture of psychotropic substances in South America remained limited, their availability and abuse increased in a number of countries. The diversion and overprescribing of pharmaceuticals containing psychotropic substances continued. In Argentina, Chile and Uruguay, the abuse of sedatives (benzodiazepines) was second after cannabis and the abuse of stimulants (such as femproporex) was similar to or even higher than that of cocaine.

Ketamine was readily available in Peru on the illicit market and therefore abused extensively, despite the fact that officially its sale was restricted to hospitals. Its abuse was also detected in Uruguay.

With regard to regional cooperation, South American countries continued to participate in the multilateral cooperation mechanisms of CICAD for countries in the Americas. CICAD assisted them in preparing reports under the Multilateral Evaluation Mechanism and the development of the Inter-American Observatory on Drugs. It also carried out drug supply reduction and control activities and provided guidance in developing the integrated drug treatment system. Together with UNODC, CICAD was also establishing a drug information network to ensure common standards among countries and comparability of surveys. Regional cooperation included Operation Andes II, a regional tracking initiative for precursors carried out in collaboration with Interpol and the World Customs Organization, and joint activities carried out by Member States (Argentina, Brazil, Paraguay and Uruguay) and associated States (Bolivia and Chile) of the Common Market of the Southern Cone (MERCOSUR). In addition, multilateral and bilateral agreements between States with common geographical traits or shared borders continued to be upheld, and the United States and countries in Europe provided resources for drug control in South America through bilateral and multilateral agreements. At the national level, Argentina approved, in January, the Federal Plan for Integral Prevention of Drug Abuse and Drug Trafficking for 2005-2007. In Ecuador, a new national drug strategy for 2004-2008 and its implementation plan came into effect in 2004. In June, Guyana published a five-year drug control strategy for 2000-2005. Colombia strengthened its efforts in the area of law enforcement. A regional initiative aimed at combating the illicit use of chemicals in cocaine and heroin manufacture continued under Operation Seis Fronteras; it involved Bolivia, Brazil, Colombia, Ecuador, Peru and Venezuela, as well as the United States.

An INCB mission to Paraguay, in April, found that the legislative basis for the control of narcotic drugs and psychotropic substances was adequate. Nevertheless, the resources for drug control were insufficient and coordination between the agencies involved was lacking. The Board advised the Government to keep a balanced approach in its drug control policy, ensuring the reduction of both demand and supply of illicit drugs.

Asia

East and South-East Asia

Opiates, followed by ATS, continued to be the main drugs of abuse in East and South-East Asia. Heroin was the most commonly abused drug in the majority of countries, with the exception of Myanmar, where it was opium, and Japan, the Philippines, the Republic of Korea and Thailand, where it was methamphetamine. Heroin was the drug of choice in China (including the Hong Kong and Macao Special Administrative Regions (SARs) of China), Indonesia, Malaysia and Viet Nam. Some countries made progress in preventing opium abuse, particularly the Lao People's Democratic Republic.

In 2005, as a result of continued eradication efforts by Myanmar, the main source of illicit opium in the region, illicit opium poppy cultivation declined to 32,800 hectares, a decrease of 26 per cent compared with 2004. The Lao People's Democratic Republic further reduced illicit opium poppy cultivation from 6,600 hectares in 2004 to 1,800 hectares in 2005 and joined Thailand and Viet Nam as countries that were no longer significant suppliers of opiates on the world's illicit markets. However, it was faced with cannabis plant cultivation and trafficking and was emerging as a transit country for the smuggling of ATS and heroin. In 2004, several countries, such as Indonesia and Malaysia, reported an increase in the volume of opium seized.

The illicit manufacture of ATS continued mainly in China and the border area between China and Myanmar and, to a lesser extent, in Indonesia, Malaysia and the Philippines; many countries reported large seizures of ATS and other seizures of a significant quantity of sedatives and hallucinogens in 2004; Japan seized 310 kilograms of benzodiazepines and Indonesia over 1 million tablets of hallucinogens. Sizeable quantities of MDMA (Ecstasy) continued to be seized in Indonesia and Japan and also in the Hong Kong and Macao SARs of China. Although over half of the methamphetamine smuggled into the Republic of Korea originated in China, the Philippines was increasingly a significant source, and the Lao People's Democratic Republic emerged as a transit country for consignments of ATS originating in Myanmar. Pseudoephedrine and ephedrine continued to be seized in the region. Most countries reported increases in the abuse of methamphetamine and MDMA (Ecstasy).

The illicit cultivation of cannabis plants continued throughout East and South-East Asia, and several countries continued to seize substantial quantities. Indonesia, Japan, Myanmar and the Republic of Korea reported an increase in the volume of cannabis seized for 2004.

With regard to regional cooperation, the signatories of the 1993 memorandum of understanding on drug control between the countries in the Mekong area (Cambodia, China, the Lao People's Democratic Republic, Myanmar, Thailand and Viet Nam) adopted, in May, the Siemreap (Cambodia) Declaration, which focused on collaboration in many areas, including: the control of precursor chemicals and ATS; drug abuse treatment and prevention; the development of a package of interventions related to drug abuse and HIV/AIDS; sustainable alternative development; and technical and financial assistance. The second International Association of Southeast Asian Nations (ASEAN) and China Cooperative Operations in Response to Dangerous Drugs (ACCORD) Congress was held in Beijing in October. At the national level, China adopted new laws strengthening control over narcotic drugs, psychotropic substances and precursor chemicals. Japan continued to place high priority on drug control in its national planning. In March, Viet Nam approved a national drug control master plan for the period up to 2010. In December 2004, Cambodia approved a drug control master plan for 2005-2010.

South Asia

Drug trafficking and abuse problems in South Asia continued to be both serious and multifaceted. Owing to its proximity to opium poppy cultivation areas in West Asia and South-East Asia, there continued to be significant trafficking in and abuse of opiates, in particular heroin. In India, despite strict controls, some diversion from licit opium poppy cultivation continued, and the total area under licit opium poppy cultivation decreased in 2004, as a result of self-imposed restrictions by the Government. Some of the diverted opium was abused in India, and some was smuggled into other countries. Large quantities of heroin of West Asian origin were increasingly being seized in India, destined for illicit markets in that country, in Sri Lanka and in other regions, including Europe. Low-quality

heroin base known as "brown sugar" continued to be abused in Bangladesh, India, Maldives, Nepal and Sri Lanka. After declining for several years, the volume of heroin seized along the border between India and Pakistan was increasing. There was a shift in drug abuse patterns in India, from inhaling to injecting drugs (mainly heroin and buprenorphine).

The abuse of pharmaceutical preparations containing narcotic drugs and psychotropic substances diverted from licit channels remained one of the main drug control issues in South Asia. India was a major manufacturer of pharmaceuticals, accounting for approximately 10 per cent of global output. Despite strict controls, pharmaceuticals continued to be diverted in India and smuggled into countries in South Asia and other regions. Trafficking in such substances, particularly codeine-based cough syrups, dextropropoxyphene and buprenorphine, in India was a major concern for its neighbouring countries. There was also evidence of pharmaceuticals from India being smuggled into Myanmar, Pakistan (via Dubai) and States members of the Commonwealth of Independent States. Diazepam and nitrazepam were also diverted, to be abused in India or smuggled into other countries. In Bhutan, drug abuse was increasing, including abuse of cannabis and pharmaceutical preparations containing narcotic drugs and psychotropic substances.

India remained the main illicit manufacturer of methaqualone, most of which was smuggled into other countries, primarily South Africa, its main consumer. INCB noted the growing illicit trade in India in the substance commonly called "synthetic heroin", a drug prepared by crushing tablets of phenobarbital, a psychotropic substance in Schedule IV of the 1971 Convention.

Illicit cannabis plant cultivation and cannabis abuse continued in the region. The cannabis plant grew wild in several countries, including India, Sri Lanka, and Nepal; cannabis resin was produced in large quantities in Nepal and was abused locally and smuggled into other countries, primarily India. In Sri Lanka, the total volume of cannabis seized decreased in 2004. In Bangladesh, the decrease in the volume of seizures in 2004 was offset by a significant increase in trafficking in heroin and buprenorphine. According to a national household survey conducted in India, there were approximately 8.7 million cannabis abusers in the country.

With regard to regional cooperation, India and Pakistan, in August, agreed to enter into a memorandum of understanding to intensify mutual cooperation and liaison on drug control issues. Nationally, India imposed strict measures to control the sale of medicines in retail and wholesale establishments. INCB noted that Nepal needed to strengthen drug control legislation, particularly to regulate precursors, a major cause of concern, since the country was situated between China and India, two large precursor manufacturers. In June, Sri Lanka announced that controls would be strengthened at the international airport and its coast guard capabilities extended. Bangladesh expanded the capacity of its main centre for drug abuse treatment. The Board noted that drug abuse treatment facilities in the region remained inadequate and treatment programmes for female addicts were lacking in some countries.

In April, an INCB mission to Bangladesh noted that the Department of Narcotics Control did not receive sufficient resources from the Government and that cooperation between Government agencies involved in drug control was not adequate. The Board encouraged the Government to strengthen its capacity in drug abuse treatment and to conduct a survey on the scope of the drug addiction problem.

West Asia

Afghanistan remained the main producer of illicit opium poppy, accounting for 87 per cent of global production in 2005. Its share of the illicit manufacture of opiates, mainly heroin, increased, as the country continued to be a supplier of illicit morphine and heroin, as well as illicit opiate raw materials. Although the total area under illicit opium poppy cultivation in Afghanistan decreased by 21 per cent, from 131,000 hectares in 2004 to 104,000 in 2005, higher crop yields meant that actual opium production remained at almost the same level. Together, the central and provincial governments of Afghanistan eradicated 5 per cent of illicit poppy crops in 2005; not all provincial governments were committed to eradication efforts, however. According to the Government, the failure to provide alternative livelihoods for opium poppy growers, the security situation and the involvement of provincial officials in drug trafficking were the main reasons for the continuation of illicit opium poppy cultivation in the country. The abuse of drugs, including prescription drugs smuggled into the country, continued to increase. In Pakistan, illicit opium poppy cultivation, while not on the same scale as in Afghanistan, had increased; INCB urged the Government to intensify its eradication efforts. In Lebanon, despite eradication efforts and public information campaigns, illicit cultivation of the cannabis plant and, on a much smaller scale, opium poppy, took place. In several countries in Central Asia, opium poppy was culti-

vated on a small scale, and ephedra and cannabis plants continued to grow wild. The United Arab Emirates had become a trans-shipment point for heroin consignments destined for Europe from South Asia and South-West Asia. Cannabis, heroin and opium shipments originating in Afghanistan passed through Iran and Pakistan and were then sent overland through Oman and the United Arab Emirates to Europe. An estimated 60 per cent of Afghan opiates passed first through Iran and then Turkey before reaching Europe. Approximately 20 per cent passed through Central Asia, in particular Tajikistan, and 20 per cent was smuggled through Pakistan. Turkmenistan also continued to be used as a transit country. Uzbekistan continued to be an important transit country for consignments destined for Europe; they were smuggled mainly by road and rail through Kyrgyzstan and Tajikistan, as well as directly from Afghanistan. The increased availability of heroin and opium continued to fuel the abuse of narcotic drugs in West Asia and beyond. The southern Caucasus was emerging as an important transit area for trafficking and recent surveys revealed a significant increase in drug abuse in Azerbaijan and Georgia.

Seizure data for countries neighbouring Afghanistan showed an increase in the illicit manufacture of heroin and morphine since the 1990s. Pakistan remained the country with the largest seizures of opiates. However, seizures of heroin decreased significantly, from 6.4 tons in 2003 to 3.5 tons in 2004. Seizures of opiates in Turkey almost tripled, from 5.7 tons in 2003 to 14.7 tons in 2004. In Iran, the country with the largest volume of seized opium, seizures increased to 174 tons in 2004, nearly twice the figure recorded in 2003. The drug abuse situation in Iran worsened; opiates were the main drug of abuse, but crystalline methamphetamine and MDMA (Ecstasy) abuse had risen. In Central Asia, drug abuse increased, especially heroin.

Cannabis remained the main drug of abuse in countries on the Arabian peninsula, many of which continued to be used as transit countries for consignments of cannabis and opiates destined for Europe. Although the volume of drug seizures remained low in the southern Caucasus, drug abuse was increasingly becoming a problem.

While cocaine abuse was not a major issue in West Asia and INCB had no information regarding its illicit manufacture, a large amount of potassium permanganate continued to be imported into Iran.

The abuse of pharmaceuticals, especially benzodiazepines, remained of concern in West Asia. In Israel, a survey indicated that 6.1 per cent of students in secondary schools abused pharmaceuticals, a figure higher than that for cannabis or heroin. Fenetylline (Captagon) continued to be widely abused on the Arabian peninsula. As its licit manufacture had ceased, the substance was manufactured clandestinely, primarily in southern Europe, and trafficked into the Arabian peninsula through the Syrian Arab Republic and Jordan.

Regionally, the fight against trafficking of Afghan opiates remained central to cooperation between countries in West Asia and other countries. At the third annual Afghanistan Development Forum (Kabul, April), the development of legitimate alternative livelihoods in rural areas in Afghanistan was stressed. In 2005, countries in West Asia established a number of bilateral arrangements to combat drug trafficking. Turkey entered into agreements with Bosnia and Herzegovina, Kazakhstan and Kuwait to strengthen efforts against drug trafficking, terrorism and organized crime. In May, Iran and the United Arab Emirates signed a memorandum of understanding to combat drug trafficking. Jordan and the Syrian Arab Republic concluded a security agreement that provided for the redrawing of their common border and resulted in the seizure of large quantities of illicit drugs.

At the national level, Afghanistan continued to strengthen its administrative structures in the area of drug control. Following the establishment of the new Ministry of Counter-Narcotics in late 2004, the Cabinet Sub-Committee on Counter-Narcotics was formed. One of its key tasks in 2005 was the preparation of the alternative livelihood development plan, in which key areas requiring urgent assistance were identified. The Government strengthened its efforts in supply reduction and created the Counter-Narcotics Trust Fund, administered by the United Nations Development Programme (UNDP). The Fund would support legitimate alternative livelihoods for opium poppy growers. Iraq established a national drug control committee and was developing a national drug control plan; the Board welcomed its commitment to fight illicit drug trafficking and other criminal activities.

In September, an INCB mission visited Saudi Arabia. It noted the Government's commitment to drug control, reflected in its adoption of a new national drug control strategy in 2005. However, mechanisms for the collection of data and providing it to the Board needed to be improved.

Afghanistan

In a March report on the situation in Afghanistan and its implications for international peace and security [A/59/744-S/2005/183] (see also p. 397),

the Secretary-General noted that the illicit narcotics industry dominated Afghanistan's economy, generating income equivalent to an estimated 60 per cent of the legal gross domestic product; more than 350,000 families (10 per cent of the population) were economically dependent on the poppy economy. Anti-drug activities included the launching, on 16 February, by Afghanistan and the United Kingdom, of the 2005 Counter-Narcotics Implementation Plan, which concentrated on eradication and the creation of alternative livelihoods in the provinces most affected by opium production.

INCB, concerned that opium poppy cultivation and illicit drug trade continued to threaten the establishment of the rule of law and effective governance in Afghanistan, urged the Government to ensure that the situation was remedied. It also urged the international community to renew its efforts to combat opium production in the country and the associated corruption, so that the goals in the national drug control strategy could be achieved within the established time schedule.

ECONOMIC AND SOCIAL COUNCIL ACTION

On 22 July [meeting 36], the Economic and Social Council, on the recommendation of the Commission on Narcotic Drugs [E/2005/28/Rev.1], adopted **resolution 2005/24** without vote [agenda item 14 (d)].

Providing support to Afghanistan with a view to ensuring effective implementation of its Counter-Narcotics Implementation Plan

The Economic and Social Council
Recommends to the General Assembly the adoption of the following draft resolution:
[For text, see General Assembly resolution 60/179 below.]

GENERAL ASSEMBLY ACTION

On 16 December [meeting 64], the General Assembly, on the recommendation of the Third Committee [A/60/511], adopted **resolution 60/179** without vote [agenda item 107].

Providing support to Afghanistan with a view to ensuring effective implementation of its Counter-Narcotics Implementation Plan

The General Assembly,
Noting with concern the report of the United Nations Office on Drugs and Crime entitled "Afghanistan: Opium Survey 2004", which emphasizes that the cultivation of opium poppy in Afghanistan has increased to an unprecedented level, and stresses the threats to the security and stability of that country, neighbouring regions and the entire world that have emanated from the increased illicit cultivation of opium poppy and production of and trafficking in illicit drugs,
Recognizing the political will and continued commitment of Afghanistan to eliminate opium poppy cultivation by 2013, and welcoming in this context the Counter-Narcotics Implementation Plan of Afghani-

stan, launched in February 2005, which formalized the establishment of the new counter-narcotics ministry,

Taking note of the Constitution of Afghanistan, in article 7 of which the Government of Afghanistan expresses its strong resolve to fight against the illicit cultivation of opium poppy and the production of and trafficking in opium and other illicit narcotic drugs,

Encouraging the Government of Afghanistan to intensify its efforts to achieve an effective legislative counter-narcotics framework,

Welcoming the establishment by the Government of Afghanistan of a counter-narcotics police force in support of its counter-narcotics campaign, in the context of strengthening the law enforcement regime,

Noting with appreciation the achievements of the Government of Afghanistan during 2004 in implementing law enforcement measures leading to the elimination of thousands of acres of opium poppy cultivation, the interdiction of drug traffickers, the seizure of substantial amounts of illicit drugs, precursors and small arms and munitions and the dismantling of hundreds of clandestine laboratories used for illicit drug production, and noting the commitment of the Government to increasing its efforts substantially in those areas,

Noting the priority given by the Government of Afghanistan to ensuring a credible, targeted and reinforced illicit crop eradication campaign and to working with international partners through the national development budget and the newly established counter-narcotics trust fund in order to facilitate the provision of sustainable alternative livelihoods in targeted areas,

Bearing in mind that the fight against the illicit cultivation of opium poppy and the production of and trafficking in illicit narcotic drugs is a common and shared responsibility to be addressed through international efforts, as recognized by Member States in the Political Declaration adopted by the General Assembly at its twentieth special session,

Recalling the United Nations Millennium Declaration, and the goals contained therein, which focused on economic development, peace and security and the establishment of the required framework for international cooperation to achieve those goals,

Recalling also various other United Nations resolutions and recommendations, including General Assembly resolution 59/161 of 20 December 2004 and the recommendations of the International Narcotics Control Board in its report for 2004, requesting the international community to support the Government of Afghanistan in its fight against the illicit cultivation of opium poppy and trafficking in illicit narcotic drugs,

1. *Notes with appreciation* the bilateral and multilateral support being provided to Afghanistan by the international community through the United Nations Office on Drugs and Crime and other international entities;

2. *Commends* the Counter-Narcotics Implementation Plan of Afghanistan, which comprises an eight-point strategy that includes:

(*a*) Building counter-narcotics institutions and provincial structures;

(*b*) Increasing the awareness of the Afghan population about the problems and threats emanating from the illicit cultivation of opium poppy and the production of and trafficking in illicit narcotic drugs;

(*c*) Provision of alternative livelihoods and creation of the national development budget and the counter-narcotics trust fund to provide financial support;

(*d*) Interdiction and elimination of heroin-manufacturing laboratories through the national counter-narcotics police force;

(*e*) Strengthening legal and judicial institutions;

(*f*) A credible, targeted and verified eradication campaign;

(*g*) Demand reduction and treatment of addicts;

(*h*) Regional cooperation with neighbouring countries aimed at strengthening security belts in the region and countering the threat posed by the illicit cultivation of opium poppy and the production of and trafficking in illicit narcotic drugs;

3. *Calls upon* the international community to provide the necessary support to the counter-narcotics objectives of the Government of Afghanistan, by continued technical assistance and financial commitment, in particular, to all eight pillars of the Counter-Narcotics Implementation Plan;

4. *Encourages* all stakeholders to strengthen measures for global demand reduction, thereby enhancing efforts to combat illicit drug production and trafficking;

5. *Urges* Afghanistan to maintain illicit drug control among its highest priorities, as stipulated in its Constitution and the Counter-Narcotics Implementation Plan, with a view to enhancing its efforts to combat the illicit cultivation of opium poppy, the production of illicit drugs and trafficking in illicit drugs and precursors;

6. *Requests* the United Nations Office on Drugs and Crime to strengthen its efforts to ensure that multilateral support is provided to Afghanistan in line and in coordination with the Counter-Narcotics Implementation Plan.

Europe

Cannabis remained the most commonly abused drug in Europe. The plant was cultivated in several countries, in particular Albania and the Netherlands. Morocco continued to be a major source of cannabis resin, as well as Afghanistan, Pakistan and countries in Central Asia. Large amounts of cannabis resin were smuggled through Portugal. The European School Survey Project on Alcohol and Other Drugs found that the lifetime prevalence of cannabis among secondary school students 15-16 years old had risen by an annual average of almost 25 per cent between 1999 and 2003. In the Czech Republic, 44 per cent of students abused cannabis or cannabis resin.

The volume of cocaine seizures increased, particularly in Western Europe, partly as a result of strengthened law enforcement measures in the Netherlands. Although most of the cocaine smuggled into Europe entered through Spain or the Netherlands, the use of other countries had increased. New trends in cocaine trafficking included a route leading from the Andean subregion through Western Africa to Europe. Colombian trafficking groups were shipping cocaine to Spain through the islands off the coast of Mauritania and Senegal. Increased seizures of cocaine in Europe also reflected its increased abuse. In the Netherlands and Spain, cocaine was the second most commonly reported drug in specialist treatment centres after heroin. The annual prevalence rate for cocaine abuse rose among young persons in Denmark, Germany, Spain and the United Kingdom, as well as in some areas of Austria, Greece, Ireland and Italy.

The illicit demand for heroin was estimated to be about 170 tons, about half of which was abused in Western and Central Europe. Almost all of the heroin encountered on the illicit market in Europe was from Afghanistan. Most of the heroin seizures took place in the United Kingdom, Italy, Germany, the Netherlands, France and the Russian Federation (in that order). The smuggling of Afghan heroin into the Russian Federation increased significantly. Despite the increased availability of heroin in Europe as a whole, its abuse was stable or declining in Western Europe. Italy and the United Kingdom continued to report a high level of abuse. According to UNODC, the annual prevalence for the abuse of opiates in Europe was 0.8 per cent. In individual Eastern European countries, the rate was higher than the average for Europe as a whole. The number of drug abusers in the Russian Federation was as high as 6 million, or 4 per cent of the population.

It was estimated that up to 80 per cent of the MDMA (Ecstasy) abused worldwide was illicitly manufactured in laboratories in European countries. MDMA (Ecstasy) from Europe was smuggled into Australia, Canada, Japan and South Africa. It was the second most commonly abused drug in Europe after cannabis. The main sources of amphetamine found on the illicit markets in Europe were Belgium, the Netherlands and Poland. Bulgaria, Estonia and Lithuania also played an important role in illicit amphetamine manufacture. The illicit manufacture and abuse of methamphetamine remained limited to the Czech Republic and some of the Baltic States. Preparations containing buprenorphine were smuggled into Finland from France and, in 2005, Estonia emerged as a significant source of the buprenorphine preparations found on illicit markets in Finland. Tranquillizers or sedatives were most commonly abused in Poland (17 per cent), followed by Lithuania, France and the Czech Republic.

With regard to regional cooperation, the Council of the European Union (EU), in December 2004, endorsed the European Union Drugs Strategy for 2005-2012, which focused on illicit drug supply and demand reduction, and on international cooperation and research, information and evaluation. In June 2005, the EU Council endorsed the European Union Action Plan on Drugs for 2005-2008, covering the priority areas of the new strategy. In July, the Netherlands and the United States signed an agreement outlining areas for collaboration in drug demand reduction. In May, the EU Council adopted a decision on information exchange, risk assessment and the control of new psychoactive substances.

At the national level, the Drugs Act 2005 entered into force in the United Kingdom in April, giving new powers to drug law enforcement agencies. In September, the Russian Federation adopted a national programme for the prevention of drug abuse and trafficking for 2005-2009. Spain launched an action plan for 2005-2008 as part of the implementation of its national drug control strategy for 2000-2008.

INCB expressed concern over national drug control legislation and administrative mechanisms in Bosnia and Herzegovina, which had turned the country into a safe haven for traffickers. In June, the Board sent a mission to Bulgaria, where the percentage of persons who abused drugs by injection was a cause for serious concern. In order to address the problem of large-scale smuggling of counterfeit Captagon tablets from illicit laboratories in Bulgaria into the Arabian peninsula, INCB urged the Government to initiate a multilateral operation to investigate its trafficking. An INCB mission to the Russian Federation in May encouraged the Government to provide additional resources for drug control and to improve coordination among the drug control bodies. The Board noted with concern the extent of drug abuse in the country and requested the Government to facilitate the systematic collection and analysis of epidemiological data on drug abuse and to ensure the availability of drug dependence treatment.

Oceania

The illicit cultivation and abuse of cannabis continued to constitute serious problems in most countries in Oceania, including Australia, Fiji, Micronesia, New Zealand, Papua New Guinea and Samoa. Cannabis was the drug of choice throughout the region, due to its availability and low price. Cannabis originating in Papua New Guinea was seized in Australia and New Zealand. New Zealand reported a new form of cannabis resin commonly called "ice hash", which was manufactured from cannabis buds and smoked in pipes. Cannabis was often abused in combination with other drugs.

Both Australia and New Zealand reported increased seizures of cocaine. New Zealand appeared to be used increasingly as a major transit area for illicit drugs destined for Australia and the United States. In Australia, authorities continued to seize heroin in small quantities.

ATS continued to be illicitly manufactured in Oceania. Australia and New Zealand dismantled large numbers of clandestine laboratories and reported an increase in seizures of crystalline methamphetamine, mainly from China or Malaysia. In New Zealand, seizures of ephedrine and pseudoephedrine, precursor chemicals frequently used in the illicit manufacture of methamphetamine, increased. Australia reported that the lifetime prevalence rate for MDMA (Ecstasy) abuse was higher than the rate for all other drugs, except cannabis and methamphetamine. Trafficking in and abuse of MDMA (Ecstasy) became significant problems, in particular in Australia and New Zealand, where substantial quantities were seized. Seizures of ketamine, GHB and gamma-butyrolactone increased in New Zealand, which also reported increased seizures of khat.

Regionally, the Pacific Islands Forum continued to play a central role in promoting regional cooperation. At its annual meeting (Auckland, New Zealand, June) the Regional Security Committee of the Pacific Islands Forum discussed various security issues, including the need to strengthen legislation to prevent illicit drug manufacture and trafficking. At the national level, New Zealand strengthened its precursor control legislation by passing the Misuse of Drugs Amendment Bill in June. New Zealand also launched its Illicit Drug Monitoring System, a database containing information on drug abuse, illicit manufacture and trafficking.

UN action to combat drug abuse

UN Office on Drugs and Crime

The United Nations Office on Drugs and Crime (UNODC) implemented the Organization's drug and crime programmes in an integrated manner, addressing the interrelated issues of drug control, crime prevention and international terrorism in the context of sustainable development and human security. The drug programme continued to be implemented in accordance with General Assembly resolution 45/179 [YUN 1990, p. 874]. The Office served as the central drug control entity responsible for coordinating all UN drug control activities, and as the repository of technical expertise in international drug control

for the UN Secretariat. It acted on behalf of the Secretary-General in fulfilling his responsibilities under the terms of international treaties and resolutions relating to drug control, and provided services to the Assembly, the Economic and Social Council, and committees and conferences dealing with drug control matters.

The UNODC Executive Director described the Office's 2005 activities in a report to the Commission on Narcotic Drugs and to the Commission on Crime Prevention and Criminal Justice [E/CN.7/2006/5-E/CN.15/2006/2]. UNODC promoted the adoption and implementation of the three international drug control conventions and supported INCB in monitoring their implementation. The Office analysed, collected and published data on global drug problems. In 2005, it launched an investigation into the value of illicit drug markets and developed a global illicit drug index, which was presented in its World Drug Report 2005 [Sales No. E.05.XI.10]. In collaboration with Member States, UN agencies and national organizations, UNODC facilitated policymaking on drugs, suggested strategic directions and mobilized resources. It also delivered knowledge-based expertise to strengthen Member States' capacity to prevent and reduce drugs and crime. Technical assistance was crucial in reaching those goals.

In the area of illicit crop monitoring and eradication, UNODC surveys provided Governments and the donor community with data for the planning and design of alternative livelihoods and drug law enforcement assistance programmes. In 2005, surveys were conducted in Afghanistan, Bolivia, Colombia, the Lao People's Democratic Republic, Morocco, Myanmar and Peru. New coca surveys were launched in Ecuador and Venezuela, a price monitoring database was developed for Latin America and significant improvements were introduced in the use of remote sensing for illicit crop surveying. UNODC hosted an expert group meeting in December to review the thematic evaluation of alternative development and identify options for future activities. As part of its assistance to efforts to eliminate drug crops in Afghanistan, UNODC established a database on alternative livelihood projects and areas of investment to support local planning of alternative livelihoods. In Peru, the Office worked with over 6,000 families previously dependent on coca bush cultivation and assisted farmers' organizations in obtaining fair trade or organic certification for coffee and cacao crops. In Colombia, it expanded its alternative development programme and worked with the national forest warden family programme in the recovery of ecosystems affected by illicit economies. In the Lao People's Democratic Republic, support was provided to the Government in its efforts to eliminate opium poppy cultivation through community-based alternative development and the treatment and rehabilitation of opium addicts. During the year, UNODC published *Coca Cultivation in the Andean Region: a Survey of Bolivia, Colombia and Peru; Afghanistan: Opium Survey 2005; and Morocco: Cannabis Survey 2004.*

With regard to drug abuse prevention, UNODC continued to disseminate good practices through its Global Youth Network against Drug Abuse. It organized the regional forum for Central Asian mass media leaders (Almaty, Kazakhstan, 14 June), an initiative for drug abuse prevention with the help of mass media, civil society and non-governmental organizations. Pilot activities on drug abuse prevention targeting street children were undertaken, and 40 journalists were trained in the use of modern communication methodologies for advocating illicit drug supply and demand reduction. UNODC implemented a locally sustained evidence-based treatment and rehabilitation plan, building on its treatment and rehabilitation initiatives and networks in Africa, Central America, Central Asia and South-East Asia, as well as in the Russian Federation and its neighbouring countries.

In the area of data collection and drug abuse epidemiology, the Office, through the Global Assessment Programme on Drug Abuse, assisted 51 countries in training, situation analyses and network establishment.

UNODC supported the UN Reference Group on HIV/AIDS Prevention and Care among Injecting Drug Users in Developing and Transitional Countries. In 2005, it organized several consultative meetings on HIV/AIDS and undertook projects in cooperation with WHO and the Joint United Nations Programme on HIV/AIDS (UNAIDS) in Africa and the Middle East.

UNODC contributed to enhancing national capacity for drug testing and the quality of scientific support provided to national criminal justice systems and health services. It also supported member States of ASEAN and ACCORD through improving forensic capability in the profiling of ATS and their precursors. The Office focused on areas requiring further work, especially relating to drug abuse and implementation of legislative measures for international cooperation. It convened a workshop for experts (Vienna, 31 October–2 November) on measuring progress in drug demand reduction in relation to the 1998 twentieth special session of the General Assembly [YUN 1998, p. 1135].

UNODC supported health-care providers in five Eastern African countries with training on guidelines for estimating drug requirements. To counter the increasing problems of drug trafficking into and through the Persian Gulf area, UNODC and the United Arab Emirates cooperated in drug control coordination, training and policy development in that country and its neighbouring countries. In Cape Verde, a law enforcement initiative on promoting drug control and justice and countering money-laundering and organized crime was launched. In Asia, UNODC cooperation with ASEAN in drug control was strengthened with the second International ASEAN/ACCORD Congress (Beijing, October) and the renewed commitment to make ASEAN member States free of illicit drugs. In Central America, a partnership was forged with CICAD in the context of the subregional project on drug information systems, involving Argentina, Bolivia, Chile, Ecuador, Peru and Uruguay, as well as training for law practitioners.

In Central Asia and Afghanistan, UNODC and the World Bank cooperated under a joint action plan and shared information on the impact of the Afghan drug situation on neighbouring countries.

Administrative and budgetary matters

In a January report [E/CN.7/2005/8], the Executive Director presented to the Commission on Narcotic Drugs a consolidated outline of all UNODC activities planned for 2006-2007 and the resources required for their implementation. The 2006-2007 proposed budget for the United Nations Drug Control Programme (UNDCP) Fund totalled $194.7 million, an increase of $7.3 million (4 per cent), compared with the 2004-2005 budget. It was expected that the increase would be covered by voluntary resources, while funding from the UN regular budget would grow by only 1 per cent over the 2004-2005 biennium.

The Advisory Committee on Administrative and Budgetary Questions (ACABQ), in a March report [E/CN.7/2005/9], called on UNODC to examine which of its programme activities could be duplicative of programmes carried out by other UN entities and to ascertain the status of donor pledges so as to obtain more accurate information on support expected.

On 11 March [E/2005/28/Rev.1 (res. 48/13)], the Commission considered that the proposed outline and budget totalling $194.7 million provided a basis for the submission of the proposed initial 2006-2007 budget. Also on 11 March [res. 48/3], the Commission requested the Executive Director to broaden, in cooperation with Member States, the donor base; increase voluntary contributions to the UNDCP Fund; and monitor the ratio between the programme and the support budgets. It recommended that a sufficient share of the UN regular budget should be allocated to UNODC, and requested UNODC to examine whether its programme activities were duplicative of programmes carried out by other UN entities and to avoid such duplication. The Executive Director was asked to keep Member States informed on the use of general-purpose funds, to make proposals to donors, in accordance with the guidelines for the use of those funds, and to report in 2006 on progress made in securing assured and predictable voluntary funding.

The Executive Director, in a September report on the consolidated budget for the 2006-2007 biennium for UNODC [E/CN.7/2005/12 & Add.1], stated that the final 2004-2005 budget for UNDCP amounted to $170 million, representing a decrease of $17.4 million, or 9.3 per cent, over the initial budget. The initial 2006-2007 budget amounted to $182.4 million, reflecting an increase of $12.3 million, or 7.2 per cent, over the final 2004-2005 budget. In its financial overview, the report stated that, in the 2004-2005 biennium, special-purpose income for the Fund was stable at $128 million and programme expenditure increased by $21 million (20 per cent), from $104 million in 2002-2003 to $125 million. Owing to improved programme implementation, a further $14 million increase (12 per cent) was projected for 2006-2007 over 2004-2005. Core fund income was projected to decrease by $5 million (15 per cent), from $33.6 million in 2004-2005 to $28.6 million in 2006-2007. Core fund expenditure was also budgeted to decrease by $6.6 million (19 per cent), from $35.6 million in 2004-2005 to $29 million in 2006-2007.

In a November report [E/CN.7/2005/13], ACABQ commented on the consolidated budget outline for UNODC for 2004-2007.

The Commission on Narcotic Drugs [E/2005/28/Rev.1 (res. 48/14)] approved an appropriation of $41 million for the infrastructure for the 2004-2005 biennium funded under the UNDCP Fund for programme support and management and administration and an appropriation of $14.8 million for the final core programme budget; it also endorsed the final resource allocation for technical cooperation activities in the amount of $109.7 million for that biennium. The Commission approved an appropriation of $38.4 million for the initial infrastructure for the 2006-2007 biennium for programme support and management and administration and an appropriation of $16.7 million for the initial core programme budget. It authorized the Executive Director to redeploy resources between appropriation lines in the support and core budgets up to a maximum of 5 per cent of the appropriation to which

the resources were redeployed. The Commission endorsed the initial resource allocation for technical cooperation activities in the amount of $122.2 million. It also endorsed the programme and budget strategy for 2006-2007 and noted that implementation of the budget and additional priority programmes was subject to the availability of funding. The Commission urged UNODC to develop, in consultation with Member States, an overarching strategy, taking into account clearly defined objectives, improved benchmarks and performance indicators that would measure the impact of the Office's work. The Secretariat was asked to present a report on the matter in 2006.

Commission on Narcotic Drugs

The Commission on Narcotic Drugs, at its forty-eighth session, (Vienna, 7-11 March), recommended four resolutions and two decisions for adoption by the Economic and Social Council and one resolution to be recommended by the Council to the General Assembly for adoption. It also adopted thirteen resolutions, which it brought to the attention of the Council. It held a reconvened forty-eighth session on 7 and 8 December, also in Vienna, at which it adopted a resolution on the 2004-2005 final budget and the initial budget for 2006-2007 for the UNDCP Fund (see above) and brought it to the Council's attention.

Following the closure of its reconvened forty-eighth session on 8 December, the Commission opened its forty-ninth session to elect the new chairman and other bureau members.

By **decision 2005/250** of 22 July, the Council took note of the Commission's report on its forty-eighth session [E/2005/28/Rev.1] and approved the provisional agenda and documentation for the forty-ninth (2006) session, on the understanding that intersessional meetings would be held in Vienna, at no additional cost, to finalize the items to be included in the provisional agenda and the documentation requirements for the forty-ninth session.

Drug demand and abuse reduction

The Commission on Narcotic Drugs had before it a January Secretariat [E/CN.7/2005/3] report that provided an overview of trends in drug abuse for the period 1998-2003, based on information received from Member States, in response to the annual reports questionnaire. Analysis of the responses indicated the following trends: cannabis abuse increased in most of Asia, Africa and Europe, while remaining stable elsewhere; abuse of opioids decreased in Europe and

Oceania, increased in most of Asia and remained stable in North America; cocaine abuse was stable in the Americas, although still widespread, and was increasing and becoming problematic in Europe; abuse of ATS had increased in Asia and Europe and was stable in America and Oceania. The report also addressed the question of drug abuse treatment demand, basing its analysis on data provided by States between 2001 and 2003. The major issues were: opioid and cocaine abuse accounted for the majority of cases involving treatment, but the abuse of ATS and cannabis was regarded increasingly often as the primary reason for treatment; the mean age of people requiring treatment varied between 27 and 29, but demand for treatment by young cannabis users under 20 was increasing in many regions; men accounted for the majority of users and of seekers of treatment in all regions and, in many regions, women experienced difficulties in utilizing specialized treatment services; gender differences were smaller with regard to ATS abuse and larger with regard to cannabis and opioids; and, overall, there was a lack of standardized treatment data. As requested by the Commission in a 2004 resolution [YUN 2004, p. 1248], the report reviewed UNODC activities to improve the global information base on substance abuse in collaboration with other international agencies and expert bodies.

On 11 March [E/2005/28/Rev.1 (res. 48/6)], the Commission called on Member States to provide additional reporting and analysis on women-specific data relating to the use of illicit substances and access to appropriate treatment services; consider implementing broadly based prevention and treatment programmes for young girls and women; and give priority to providing both treatment for pregnant women who used illicit drugs and post-natal support services for mothers and children. It urged States to review barriers to treatment access by women and work towards their elimination, and requested UNODC to assist States in the elimination of such barriers by disseminating examples of programmes and policies that constituted good practice. The Commission requested UNODC to ensure that gender issues were given appropriate attention in future reporting on the world situation with regard to drug abuse.

Also on 11 March [res. 48/10], the Commission encouraged the international community to support developing countries in preventing drug abuse and treating and rehabilitating drug users, and to support producer, transit and consumer countries in their efforts to implement abuse prevention programmes, with an emphasis on children and adolescents. It encouraged Member States to share their experience with demand reduction programmes; strengthen the implementation of drug abuse prevention policies; and continue demand reduction programmes, paying attention to early intervention, rehabilitation and social reintegration, in order to prevent the transmission of HIV/AIDS and other diseases associated with drug abuse.

On the same date [res. 48/7], the Commission invited Member States to specify the skills and competencies needed to respond effectively to drug abuse and to assess the skills of personnel engaged in doing so. It recommended that Member States consider creating strategies to: recruit, support and retain workers with key skills; build the capacity and willingness of other relevant professional groups to respond effectively to people affected by drug abuse; and disseminate best practices and relevant research initiatives.

Also on 11 March [res. 48/4], the Commission urged Member States to monitor and update their policies for abuse prevention and to promote awareness among youth of the social and psychological problems that could result from drug abuse. Member States were also encouraged to promote lifestyles that were free from the use of illicit drugs.

HIV/AIDS and other blood-borne viruses

On 11 March [E/2005/28/Rev.1 (res. 48/12)], the Commission called on Member States to provide treatment, health care and social services for drug users living with HIV/AIDS and other blood-borne diseases and to strengthen advocacy programmes aimed at curbing prejudice against them. It called on Member States to: incorporate substance abuse prevention, treatment and health care into their national drug control strategies in order to reduce the spread of HIV/AIDS and other blood-borne diseases and drug abuse; and encourage linkages between national HIV/AIDS strategies and drug control strategies. They were also encouraged to incorporate prevention and treatment measures in relation to HIV/AIDS and other blood-borne diseases into their socio-economic development programmes, especially programmes designed to enhance the empowerment of women and child welfare, and to ensure that substance abuse treatment was accessible and affordable to drug users living with HIV/AIDS and other blood-borne diseases, and to eliminate barriers to access for drug users in need of HIV/AIDS care. The Commission called on UNODC and other entities involved in demand reduction and public awareness campaigns to design and implement their programmes in a sustainable manner, and requested UNODC to facilitate, in coordination with UNAIDS and other relevant UN entities, the collection and dissemination of information on the relationship between HIV/AIDS and drug abuse. The UNODC Executive Director was requested to report in 2007.

Drug control and related crime prevention assistance

In response to Economic and Social Council resolution 2004/39 [YUN 2004, p. 1249] and 2004/25 [ibid., p. 1111], the UNODC Executive Director submitted to the Commission on Narcotic Drugs a January report [E/CN.7/2005/10] on drug control and related crime prevention assistance for countries emerging from conflict. He described the nature and extent of UNODC projects being implemented in those countries and reviewed ongoing debates within the UN system on post-conflict restructuring and peacebuilding and UNODC's role therein. Technical assistance provided by UNODC increasingly recognized the importance of the links between issues related to drug control and trafficking, organized crime, corrupt practices and, possibly, terrorist activity in post-conflict areas. It therefore provided support in developing drug control and related crime strategies, including legal assistance, training and capacity-building, policy development, justice reform and HIV/AIDS prevention. A key challenge in many post-conflict countries was that State structures were not sufficiently developed to implement effective drug control plans or strategies. Therefore, an initial step was to build greater capacity within the State itself. An internal challenge for UNODC was to ensure that issues related to drug control, crime prevention and criminal justice were integrated into assistance programmes. The Office had therefore designed a programme of activities for Iraq and one for Afghanistan, aimed at capacity-building in the criminal justice system. Resources to provide for immediate assistance (advice, training and basic equipment) would facilitate work in post-conflict environments and enable UNODC to react to the needs of countries in transition, including those emerging from conflict. It was suggested that the Commission might provide guidance to UNODC by discussing how its position in the UN system as a specialized body dealing with drugs and crime could best be reflected in its operational activities in countries emerging from conflict. The Commission might also wish to urge States to increase their support for the work of the Office in such countries.

Illicit cultivation, manufacture and trafficking

On 22 July [meeting 36], the Economic and Social Council, on the recommendation of the Commission on Narcotic Drugs [E/2005/28/Rev.1], adopted **resolution 2005/27** without vote [agenda item 14 (d)].

International assistance to States affected by the transit of illicit drugs

The Economic and Social Council,

Recalling its resolutions 2001/16 of 24 July 2001, 2002/21 of 24 July 2002 and 2003/34 of 22 July 2003,

Recalling also the Political Declaration adopted by the General Assembly at its twentieth special session, the Action Plan for the Implementation of the Declaration on the Guiding Principles of Drug Demand Reduction and the measures to enhance international cooperation to counter the world drug problem,

Taking note of the third biennial report of the Executive Director of the United Nations Office on Drugs and Crime on the implementation of the outcome of the twentieth special session of the General Assembly and other relevant reports submitted to the Commission on Narcotic Drugs at its forty-eighth session, including the report on the world situation with regard to drug trafficking and the report on the world situation with regard to drug abuse,

Bearing in mind that all States are affected by the devastating consequences of drug abuse and trafficking in illicit drugs,

Taking into account the multifaceted challenges faced by States situated along international trafficking routes and the effects of trafficking in illicit drugs, including related crime and drug abuse, resulting from the transit of drugs through the territory of transit States,

Considering that a large number of transit States are developing countries or countries with economies in transition, which need international assistance to support their efforts to prevent and suppress illicit drug trafficking and reduce illicit drug demand,

Reiterating the principle of shared responsibility and the need for all States to promote and implement the actions necessary to counter the world drug problem in all its aspects,

1. *Reaffirms its commitment* to promoting coordinated drug control strategies and unified responses to drug trafficking, and, in that context, encourages the development, effective implementation and further strengthening of measures for the prevention and suppression of illicit drug trafficking and the reduction of illicit drug demand in transit States, as well as cooperation in areas such as border control, mutual legal assistance, law enforcement and exchange of information between transit States, countries of destination and countries of origin;

2. *Welcomes* the fact that the United Nations Office on Drugs and Crime has led the follow-up to the Paris Pact initiative that emerged from the Paris Statement, which was issued at the end of the Conference on Drug Routes from Central Asia to Europe, held in Paris on 21 and 22 May 2003, and encourages the Office to develop similar strategies in other regions for countries affected by the transit of illicit drugs through their territory;

3. *Calls upon* Member States and the United Nations Office on Drugs and Crime, subject to the availability of voluntary funds, which might be either from general-purpose funds, in accordance with the

guidelines for the use of general-purpose funds adopted by the Commission on Narcotic Drugs, or from earmarked funds, to further strengthen such initiatives by providing assistance and technical support to States affected by the transit of illicit drugs, in particular developing countries, as well as countries with economies in transition, that are in need of such assistance and support;

4. *Stresses* the need to integrate projects, where appropriate, for illicit drug demand reduction and to strengthen treatment and rehabilitation services for drug abusers in the programmes for international assistance to those transit States which are affected by drug abuse as a result of the transit of illicit drugs through their territory, to enable them to deal effectively with the problem;

5. *Urges* international financial institutions and other potential donors to provide financial assistance to States affected by the transit of illicit drugs through their territory, including for empowering and building the capacity of locally available human resources, so that those States may intensify their efforts to combat drug trafficking and drug abuse and deal with their consequences;

6. *Requests* the Executive Director of the United Nations Office on Drugs and Crime to report to the Commission on Narcotic Drugs at its forty-ninth session on the implementation of the present resolution.

Secretariat report. A report by the Secretariat [E/CN.7/2006/3] described global trends in illicit drug crop cultivation and the production of plant-based drugs during 2004-2005 and global and regional trends in illicit drug trafficking up to 2004. The trafficking trends described in the report were mainly based on drug seizures data. Information on cultivation and production was drawn from UNODC's crop monitoring surveys, and the primary sources of information on seizures were the replies submitted by Governments to the annual reports questionnaire for 2004 and previous years; other sources included reports on significant drug seizures and other reports received by UNODC or submitted to the Commission on Narcotic Drugs and its subsidiary bodies.

In 2005, the area under illicit poppy cultivation in Afghanistan declined by 21 per cent. However, because of good weather, opium production fell only slightly. In South-East Asia, cultivation continued to decline in both the Lao People's Democratic Republic and Myanmar, resulting in a fall in potential heroin manufacture to 467 tons. In the Andean countries, illicit coca bush cultivation increased in 2004, after three consecutive years of declines. Potential cocaine production was estimated at 687 tons in 2004, a 2 per cent increase over 2003.

Increased seizures of all drugs, except ATS, took place in 2004. Global seizures of Ecstasy-type substances increased by 77 per cent, however. Record-high volumes of both heroin (59 tons) and cocaine (578 tons) were seized. Global interdiction of cannabis herb rose by 7 per cent and that of cannabis resin by 6 per cent.

Internet drug sales

On 11 March [E/2005/28/Rev.1 (res. 48/5)], the Commission on Narcotic Drugs, expressing concern at the growing tendency of criminal groups to use modern technologies in their activities, urged Member States to cooperate in enhancing the effectiveness of law enforcement action in relation to the use of the Internet to combat drug-related crime, and to use modern law enforcement techniques to prevent drug-related crime through the Internet. It encouraged States to establish joint teams to identify illegal drug-related Internet sites and to strengthen cooperation among law enforcement agencies at the national and international levels. Member States with the appropriate expertise were invited to assist other States in planning and implementing training programmes designed to share expertise in preventing the use of the Internet to commit drug-related crime.

Alternative development

On 11 March [E/2005/28/Rev.1 (res. 48/9)], the Commission on Narcotic Drugs called on Member States and international development organizations to take into consideration the negative impact of illicit drug crop cultivation on development efforts, social and political stability and security and to integrate drug issues into their work. They were urged to foster a strong political commitment to alternative development programmes, including preventive alternative development, and to strengthen partnerships with the private sector and civil society. The Commission called for a comprehensive approach, integrating alternative development programmes into wider economic and social development programmes, to include: environmental conservation; access to financial mechanisms and micro-credit; access to land ownership; and capacity-building of local communities, institutions and authorities. States and the international community were called upon to promote a favourable economic environment and to provide access to their markets for products of alternative development programmes. The Commission reiterated that, in formulating and implementing drug control strategies, Member States and UN entities should ensure that measures of law enforcement, interdiction, eradication and alternative development were applied in a balanced manner and that there was coordination between the institutions involved. It urged States to review their policies and strategies in the light of the recent thematic evaluation of alternative development, and to share their experience with alternative development and illicit crop eradication. The Commission urged international financial institutions and other donors to provide financial assistance to States that were adopting and implementing measures to eradicate illicit drug crops, and called on UNODC to strengthen its capacity in alternative development. The Executive Director was asked to report in 2006. It decided to devote part of a future session of the Commission to alternative development.

Regional cooperation

In a December report [E/CN.7/2006/4], the Secretariat reviewed action taken by subsidiary bodies of the Commission on Narcotic Drugs in 2005. Following a review of drug trafficking trends and regional and subregional cooperation, each subsidiary body addressed drug law enforcement issues of priority in its region and made recommendations. The fortieth session of the Subcommission on Illicit Drug Traffic and Related Matters in the Near and Middle East (Baku, Azerbaijan, 12-16 September) [UNODC/SUBCOM/ 2005/5] considered strengthening border controls; countering money-laundering and controlling non-institutional financial and value transfer arrangements; and measures taken to counteract new trends in the use of technology by drug trafficking and organized criminal groups. It recommended to the Commission on Narcotic Drugs a draft resolution on the Baku Accord on Regional Cooperation against Illicit Drugs and Related Matters: a Vision for the Twenty-first Century, for adoption by the Economic and Social Council. The fifteenth meeting of Heads of National Drug Law Enforcement Agencies (HONLEA), Africa (Ouagadougou, Burkina Faso, 29 March–1 April) [UNODC/HONLAF/2005/5] considered the impact on African States of the transit traffic in illicit drugs; the underlying threat of illegal cannabis production in Africa; and the protection of witnesses. The fifteenth meeting of HONLEA, Latin America and the Caribbean (Santa Marta, Colombia, 17-21 October) [UNODC/ HONLAC/2005/5] examined drug trafficking trends and illicit drug distribution networks: law enforcement countermeasures; links between drug trafficking and other forms of organized crime; and measures to counteract new trends in the use of technology by groups engaged in drug trafficking and organized crime. The twenty-ninth meeting of HONLEA, Asia and the Pacific (Hanoi, Viet Nam, 7-11 November) [UNODC/HONLAP/ 2005/5] considered regional countermeasures

against heroin trafficking; measures to counteract new trends in the use of technology by drug trafficking and related organized criminal groups; responses to the threat posed by the manufacture of ATS within the region; and good practice procedures in law enforcement processing of drug abusers with HIV/AIDS.

A February report by the Secretariat [E/CN.7/2005/5 & Add.1] described action taken at the sixth meeting of HONLEA, Europe (Vienna, Austria, 7-11 February) [UNODC/HONEURO/ 2005/5]. The meeting considered illicit heroin in Europe: current trafficking trends, modus operandi and criminal organizations; reviewing controls over sea container traffic; the cocaine threat in Europe; and witness protection. It recommended to the Commission a draft resolution on the frequency of meetings of HONLEA, Europe, for adoption by the Council.

ECONOMIC AND SOCIAL COUNCIL ACTION

On 22 July [meeting 36], the Economic and Social Council, on the recommendation of the Commission on Narcotic Drugs [E/2005/28/Rev.1], adopted **resolution 2005/28** without vote [agenda item 14 (d)].

Frequency of meetings of Heads of National Drug Law Enforcement Agencies, Europe

The Economic and Social Council,

Recalling General Assembly resolutions 53/115 of 9 December 1998, 54/132 of 17 December 1999, 55/65 of 4 December 2000, 56/124 of 19 December 2001, 57/174 of 18 December 2002, 58/141 of 22 December 2003 and 59/163 of 20 December 2004, in which the Assembly stressed the importance of the meetings of heads of national drug law enforcement agencies in all regions of the world, and of the Subcommission on Illicit Drug Traffic and Related Matters in the Near and Middle East of the Commission on Narcotic Drugs, and encouraged them to continue to contribute to the strengthening of regional and international cooperation, taking into account the outcome of the twentieth special session of the Assembly,

Recalling also that, in its resolution 1990/30 of 24 May 1990, it decided to establish a Meeting of Heads of National Drug Law Enforcement Agencies, European Region, with the status of a subsidiary organ of the Commission on Narcotic Drugs,

Recalling further its resolution 1992/28 of 30 July 1992, entitled "Improvement of the functioning of the subsidiary bodies of the Commission on Narcotic Drugs", in which it requested the Commission to examine further, on a regular basis, the functioning of its subsidiary bodies,

Recalling its resolution 1993/36 of 27 July 1993, entitled "Frequency of and arrangements for meetings of Heads of National Drug Law Enforcement Agencies, Europe", in which it invited the Executive Director of the United Nations International Drug Control Programme to convene the Third Meeting of Heads of National Drug Law Enforcement Agencies, Europe, in

1995, and thereafter to convene such meetings every three years,

Alarmed at the serious and growing threat posed by organized criminal groups involved in drug trafficking, money-laundering and various other forms of organized crime and their potential and, in some cases, actual links with terrorist groups,

Convinced that further action is required to strengthen cooperation and coordination between the members of Heads of National Drug Law Enforcement Agencies, Europe, in order to effectively tackle drug trafficking within the region,

Also convinced that it is essential for the heads of all national drug law enforcement agencies in Europe to meet regularly to discuss trends in the illicit traffic in narcotic drugs and psychotropic substances and action taken to combat it,

Invites the Executive Director of the United Nations Office on Drugs and Crime to convene the Seventh Meeting of Heads of National Drug Law Enforcement Agencies, Europe, in 2007 and thereafter to convene such meetings every two years under the auspices of the Office.

Strengthening UN mechanisms

The Commission on Narcotic Drugs had before it a report by the Executive Director on strengthening UNODC and the role of the Commission [E/CN.7/2005/7]. The report, prepared in response to a 2004 Commission resolution [YUN 2004, p. 1254], described action taken to facilitate dialogue between Member States and UNDCP; operations and management; and UNDCP funding.

On 11 March [E/2005/28/Rev.1 (res. 48/2)], the Commission encouraged the process of UNODC reform, designed to create more effective and efficient organizational practices, and requested the Office to maintain a culture of continuous improvement in management practices. It asserted that the strength of UNODC continued to stem from staff of the highest competence and integrity, representing wide geographical distribution and gender balance, and requested the Executive Director to ensure that recruitment, selection and appraisal systems reflected that. It stressed that the effective functioning of UNODC country and regional offices depended on, among other things, their receiving the necessary administrative and managerial support and requested the Executive Director to ensure that such support was given. The Commission encouraged the Executive Director to implement the recommendations of the Independent Evaluation Unit and asked him to ensure that evaluation became an integral part of the design, monitoring and implementation of all UNODC projects. It welcomed the establishment of the Strategic Planning Unit in UNODC; encouraged the ongoing review of financial management; and supported the efforts of the Executive Director to ensure that issues relating to the world drug problem became an integral part of the sustainable development agenda. The Executive Director was requested to report in 2006.

Chapter XV

Statistics

The United Nations continued its statistical work programme in 2005, mainly through the activities of the Statistical Commission and the United Nations Statistics Division. In March, the Statistical Commission recommended to the Economic and Social Council the adoption of a draft resolution launching the 2010 World Population and Housing Census Programme; the Council adopted the resolution in July. The Commission also endorsed the 2006-2007 work programme for the Statistics Division, and approved the Commission's multi-year programme of work for 2005-2008.

The Commission reviewed the work of groups of countries and international organizations in various areas of economic, social, demographic and environment statistics and made specific recommendations and suggestions.

Work of Statistical Commission

The Statistical Commission, in accordance with Economic and Social Council decision 2004/236 [YUN 2004, p. 1255], held its thirty-sixth session in New York from 1 to 4 March [E/2005/24]. Among other actions, the Commission: recommended to the Council a draft resolution launching the 2010 World Population and Housing Census Programme (see p. 1372) and requested the Statistics Division to act as the umbrella organization for setting standards, providing technical expertise and training and setting priorities; requested the Statistics Division to revise and update the Principles and Recommendations for Population and Housing Censuses; endorsed the creation of a Committee on Environmental-Economic Accounting; recommended the creation of an intersecretariat working group on service statistics; and endorsed the recommendations of the Intersecretariat Working Group on National Accounts (ISWGNA) for enhancing the implementation of the System of National Accounts, 1993 (1993 SNA) [YUN 1993, p. 1112] and noted that the Statistics Division would take the lead in devising a strategy to address the impediments to implementing the 1993 SNA.

The Commission supported the proposed strategic focus for the technical cooperation activities of the Statistics Division; welcomed the start of data collection in the context of the International Comparison Programme (ICP) and the increase in participating countries; noted the progress in preparing the *United Nations Handbook on Poverty Statistics*; and welcomed the efforts of the Statistics Division to keep the revision of the International Standard Industrial Classification of All Economic Activities (ISIC) on schedule. It noted the work carried out by the Inter-Agency Expert Group on Millennium Development Goal Indicators; welcomed the efforts of the World Health Organization (WHO) to address the concerns expressed by the Commission at its thirty-fourth [YUN 2003, p. 1293] and thirty-fifth [YUN 2004, p. 1259] sessions; and reaffirmed the need for a better and more effective involvement of the international community of official statisticians at all stages of the development of health statistics. It also encouraged the Delhi Group on Informal Sector Statistics to continue to develop clearer definitions for producing data on the informal sector and to measure its contribution to gross domestic product and employment. The Commission endorsed the 2006-2007 Statistics Division work programme, and approved its own multi-year programme of work for 2005-2008.

On 22 July (**decision 2005/244**), the Council took note of the Commission's report on its thirty-sixth session [E/2005/24], decided that the thirty-seventh session should be held in New York from 7 to 10 March 2006 and approved the provisional agenda and documentation for that session.

Economic statistics

National accounts

In response to a 2004 Statistical Commission request [YUN 2004, p. 1256], the Secretary-General submitted the ISWGNA report [E/CN.3/2005/4] on progress made in updating the 1993 SNA [YUN 1993, p. 1112]. The report also described 1993 SNA implementation and addressed the Commission's 2004 request [YUN 2004, p. 1256] for an assessment of the factors impeding implementation in developing countries. ISWGNA provided information on the progress made on some of the 44 issues considered by the Advisory Expert Group on National Accounts in 2004 [ibid.], including balance of payments and public finance matters. It also discussed action taken to respond to the Statistical Commission's emphasis on transparency and broad involvement in the update programme [ibid.], which included the creation of the 1993 SNA website. ISWGNA also reviewed progress in implementing the 1993 SNA, including the results of a data availability analysis that reflected an improvement in both reporting on and implementation of the 1993 SNA in Member States. As requested by the Statistical Commission in 2004 [ibid.], the Statistics Division sent a questionnaire to all Member States and territories to enable it to determine the factors impeding implementation of the 1993 SNA. The survey revealed that the main factors impeding implementation were data inadequacy, lack of statistical training and inadequate staff resources, particularly in Africa. ISWGNA drew four main recommendations from the survey for the Commission's consideration: developing countries, particularly in Africa, might wish to increase the staffing of their national accounts departments; a study could be carried out among Member States on sharing human resources management experiences; another to determine best practices in operating domestic statistical training programmes; and a further one on data-collection best practices and strategies.

In March [E/2005/24], the Commission concluded that delivering the 1993 SNA update by 2008 would require focus, discipline and significant effort. It recommended maintaining the timetable for completing the 1993 SNA update and urged ISWGNA to prioritize the contingency plans for issues that might turn out to be intractable by applying the decision-making structure embedded in the governance structure.

The Commission endorsed the ISWGNA recommendations for enhancing implementation in developing countries and noted that the Statistics Division would take the lead in devising a strategy to address the impediments to implementation, which should focus on Africa. The Commission encouraged countries to intensify advocacy and reach out to high-level users and policy-makers in order to strengthen their awareness of the importance and usefulness of national accounts, thereby facilitating increased funding for the implementation of the 1993 SNA and for the budgets of National Statistical Offices or other agencies responsible for national accounts.

Service statistics

The Statistical Commission had before it a report of the Organisation for Economic Coopera-

tion and Development (OECD) on service statistics [E/CN.3/2005/5], which noted that services were increasingly important in modern economies, contributing some 68 per cent of value added to the world economy in 2002. OECD had submitted an interim report on the subject in 2004 [YUN 2004, p. 1256]. The report identified priority areas for improving service statistics, including engaging more countries in the service statistics agenda; improving implementation of existing guidelines within countries; and ensuring a clearer assignment of roles and responsibilities between organizations in addressing service statistics recommendations to countries. Annexed to the report was a document from the Voorburg Group on Service Statistics, which discussed its strategic vision for 2005-2008, focusing on classification issues, output measures and price indices.

In March [E/2005/24], the Commission recommended the creation of an intersecretariat working group on service statistics to identify the division of labour among international organizations regarding the maintenance and update of recommendations, such as those stemming from the Voorburg Group, and knowledge transfer. It would also promote the use of best practices. The Commission agreed that OECD should continue to coordinate international work on service statistics and provide a single annual report on the work undertaken by the various expert and city groups on service statistics, as mandated by the Commission in 2003 [YUN 2003, p. 1291]. The Commission agreed that the Voorburg Group should continue to develop internationally comparable concepts and methods in service statistics related to the measurement of output and prices and use of classifications.

The Commission also had before it the report of the Task Force on Statistics of International Trade in Services [E/CN.3/2005/6], which reviewed its own progress and that of its Technical Subgroup on the Movement of Natural Persons, and discussed future plans for increasing the quality of data, including promoting the implementation of the *Manual on Statistics of International Trade in Services*. The Task Force also outlined its continuing contribution to the current revisions of the basic economic statistics frameworks and classifications, as they affected trade in services, particularly the revision of the International Monetary Fund (IMF) *Balance of Payments Manual*, fifth edition.

In March [E/2005/24], the Commission noted the policy interest in improving data on remittances.

International Comparison Programme

The Statistical Commission had before it the Secretary-General's note transmitting a World

Bank report on the International Comparison Programme (ICP) [E/CN.3/2005/7], which discussed the Programme's financial and organizational status, described its research and development activities and the status of regional programmes, and reviewed data-collection and publishing plans. The report noted that the ICP Global Office was coordinating the Global Ring Comparison programme and was preparing the ICP Operational Manual and Price Collector's Guide for national coordinators. Other ICP activities included: overhauling the ICP website; development of an integrated software system, the ICP Tool Pack; revision of the ICP Handbook; and the generation of poverty-focused purchasing power parities (PPPs).

In March [E/2005/24], the Commission welcomed the start of data collection in most regions and the increase in the number of participating countries, which stood at over 150. It also welcomed the actions of the ICP Executive Board, the ICP Global Office of the World Bank and the African Regional Coordinator to ensure that price collection commenced in Africa as soon as possible. The Commission expressed satisfaction with the positive outlook for producing preliminary results by the end of 2006 in accordance with the current timetable.

Other economic statistics

Energy statistics

The Statistical Commission had before it a report prepared by Statistics Norway [E/CN.3/2005/3] reviewing the work undertaken in energy statistics by the main organizations involved in regional and international statistics. The report emphasized the need for high-quality energy statistics, and identified a number of problems regarding the quality of those statistics, including insufficient resources, duplication and differences in definitions and methodology. Statistics Norway's recommendations for addressing those problems included: reassessing the resources needed to meet the increased workload and objectives; better integration of the energy statistics and energy policy communities; and increased harmonization and integration of energy statistics activities of international/regional organizations, such as revising and updating the reference methodological handbooks and user manuals, and putting in place clear agreements on data sharing. It was also recommended that a forum be established for the main organizations involved in regional and international statistics with a mandate to strengthen international cooperation.

In March [E/2005/24], the Commission acknowledged the importance of quality energy statistics from both a socio-economic and an environmental perspective, particularly in terms of their timeliness, coverage, reliability and transparency. It emphasized the importance of energy statistics in greenhouse gas emissions inventories, particularly in the context of the implementation of the Kyoto Protocol [YUN 1997, p. 1048] to the United Nations Framework Convention on Climate Change [YUN 1992, p. 681]. The Commission noted the need to meet the international demand for energy statistics, while limiting the reporting burden on countries, and underlined the need to assist countries, particularly developing countries, in strengthening their capacity to produce energy statistics. It stressed the importance of the exchange of best practices in improving the quality of energy statistics, and recognized the Joint Oil Data Initiative as a good example of collaboration among countries and international organizations. The Commission also emphasized that energy statistics should be better integrated with other statistical systems, especially those linked to economic development, environment and national accounts.

The Commission recommended that the Statistics Division convene an ad hoc expert working group to: prioritize the wide range of technical and other issues covered in the Statistics Norway report; identify the most appropriate forums within which to address those issues; and report to the Bureau of the Commission, which would take up the group's recommendations to ensure that their implementation began in advance of the Commission's 2006 session.

As requested by the Commission, the ad hoc expert working group on energy statistics met in New York from 23 to 25 May [E/CN.3/2006/10]. It recommended the creation of a city group to contribute to the development of improved methods and international standards for national official energy statistics, and an intersecretariat working group to enhance international collaboration and coordination.

Price indexes and statistics

The Statistical Commission had before it the report of the Ottawa Group on Price Indexes [E/CN.3/2005/8], which indicated that, since its 2003 report to the Commission [YUN 2003, p. 1292], it had held two meetings. The Group noted the key role played by the Universal Standard Products and Services Classification (UNSPSC) in deriving price indexes for international comparison, and registered its support for the international statistics community to be involved in the development and maintenance of that classification under the supervision of the Statistics Division. The Group acknowledged the significant achievement of the Intersecretariat Working Group on Price Statistics (ISWGPS) in producing international manuals on consumer and producer price indexes, and supported the view that the manuals be seen as "living documents". Also before the Commission was the ISWGPS report [E/CN.3/2005/9], which focused on progress made in developing the series of price index manuals.

In March [E/2005/24], the Commission noted the existence of classification schemes related to electronic commerce, such as UNSPSC, and supported the Ottawa Group's proposal that the Statistics Division investigate its potential as a "derived" classification and consider the establishment of correspondence tables with existing international statistical classifications.

Informal sector statistics

The Statistical Commission had before it the report of the Delhi Group on Informal Sector Statistics [E/CN.3/2005/10], which outlined the issues discussed at the Group's seven meetings held between 1997 and 2004 and indicated its achievements in and plans for improving the quality and comparability of informal sector statistics.

In March [E/2005/24], the Commission encouraged the Delhi Group to continue its work on developing clearer definitions for producing data on the informal sector and measuring its contribution to the gross domestic product and employment. The Delhi Group should study the social aspects of the informal sector to supplement its current focus on the economic dimension. The Commission noted that ISWGNA would collaborate with the Delhi Group to improve the presentation of the concept of the informal sector in the updated 1993 SNA.

Environment statistics

The Statistical Commission had before it the Secretary-General's report on environmental-economic accounting [E/CN.3/2005/15], which discussed a proposal by a joint Statistics Division/United Nations Environment Programme (UNEP) meeting (Copenhagen, Denmark, 20-21 September 2004) for the creation of a Committee on Environmental-Economic Accounting. The new body would coordinate the further development of the Accounting Framework, ensure its successful implementation in Member States to meet policy needs and facilitate the systematic compilation of related environment statistics.

Also before the Commission was the report of the Intersecretariat Working Group on Environ-

ment Statistics [E/CN.3/2005/16], which described its 2004 activities and outlined plans for 2005/2006.

In March [E/2005/24], the Commission endorsed the creation of a Committee on Environmental-Economic Accounting, noting that its work programme should have a long-term perspective. It requested that the Committee's terms of reference be prepared and submitted to the Bureau of the Commission for approval. The Commission reconfirmed the role of the London Group on Environmental Accounting as the expert body in charge of methodological issues, which would support the role of the Committee. The Commission recognized the need for assisting countries in the implementation of environmental-economic accounting through the development of detailed compilation manuals and coordinated technical programmes, which should proceed in parallel with the improvement of environment statistics.

Demographic and social statistics

Population and housing censuses

The Statistical Commission had before it a Secretary-General's report on population and housing censuses [E/CN.3/2005/11 & Corr.1], which summarized the preparations carried out by the Statistics Division and the UN regional commissions with regard to the 2010 round of population and housing censuses, in response to the Commission's 2004 requests [YUN 2004, p. 1258]. Specifically, the report described actions taken to ensure the success of the 2010 round, including the initiation of the 2010 World Population and Housing Census Programme, to be implemented from 2005 to 2014. Annexed to the report were: the conclusions and recommendations of the United Nations Symposium on Population and Housing Censuses (New York, 13-14 September 2004); elements of a draft resolution on the 2010 World Population and Housing Census Programme for the Commission to recommend to the Economic and Social Council for adoption (see below); and the conclusions and recommendations of the United Nations Expert Group Meeting to Review Critical Issues Relevant to the Planning of the 2010 Round of Population and Housing Censuses (New York, 15-17 September 2004).

In March [E/2005/24], the Commission endorsed the recommendations of the Symposium and Expert Group Meeting and asked the Statistics Division to act as the umbrella organization for setting standards, providing technical expertise and training and setting priorities, as needed, for the 2010 round. It also asked that the umbrella strategy evolve around regional arrangements to the fullest possible extent. The Commission requested that work proceed on updating the *Principles and Recommendations for Population and Housing Censuses*. It noted the establishment of the Population and Housing Census Trust Fund, coordinated by the Statistics Division, which would be used, according to regional needs, to bridge the distance between national statistical offices in exchanging resources and support. The Commission was concerned that the Economic Commission for Africa was not undertaking activities directly related to population and housing censuses and requested the Statistics Division to explore the possibility of maintaining a focus on Africa in the context of the 2010 census round. The Commission requested the Statistics Division to report in 2006 on action taken in response to its requests.

ECONOMIC AND SOCIAL COUNCIL ACTION

On 22 July [meeting 36], the Economic and Social Council, on the recommendation of the Statistical Commission [E/2005/24], adopted **resolution 2005/13** without vote [agenda item 13 (c)].

2010 World Population and Housing Census Programme

The Economic and Social Council,

Recalling its resolution 1995/7 of 19 July 1995, in which it requested the Secretary-General to proceed with the development of the 2000 World Population and Housing Census Programme and urged States Members of the United Nations to carry out population and housing censuses during the period 1995-2004, as well as its earlier resolutions endorsing previous decennial programmes,

Having reviewed the efforts made by Member States to carry out population and housing censuses as part of the 2000 World Population and Housing Census Programme and also the activities of the United Nations and funding agencies in support of national efforts in that regard,

Recognizing the increasing importance of the 2010 round of population and housing censuses for meeting data needs for the follow-up activities to the Millennium Summit of the United Nations, held in New York from 6 to 8 September 2000, the International Conference on Population and Development, held in Cairo from 5 to 13 September 1994, the World Summit for Social Development, held in Copenhagen from 6 to 12 March 1995, the Fourth World Conference on Women, held in Beijing from 4 to 15 September 1995, and the United Nations Conference on Human Settlements (Habitat II), held in Istanbul from 3 to 14 June 1996, and to other regional and national meetings,

Considering the importance of the population and housing census to the preparation of a meaningful core set of national data and information necessary for socio-economic planning and governance,

Stressing that, for a country as a whole and for each administrative area therein, periodic population and housing censuses are one of the primary sources of data needed for effective development planning and for the monitoring of population issues and socio-economic and environmental trends, policies and programmes,

1. *Supports* the 2010 World Population and Housing Census Programme, consisting of a number of activities aimed at ensuring that Member States conduct a population and housing census at least once during the period from 2005 to 2014;

2. *Urges* Member States to carry out a population and housing census and to disseminate census results as an essential source of information for small-area, national, regional and international planning and development and to provide census results to national stakeholders as well as the United Nations and other appropriate intergovernmental organizations to assist in studies on population, environment and socio-economic development issues and programmes;

3. *Emphasizes* the importance of the 2010 World Population and Housing Census Programme for socio-economic planning, and requests increased support for the Programme;

4. *Requests* the Secretary-General to implement the 2010 World Population and Housing Census Programme.

Health statistics

In response to a 2004 Statistical Commission request [YUN 2004, p.1259], WHO submitted a report on health statistics [E/CN.3/2005/12], which described efforts to coordinate strategically the generation of health statistics and support countries in strengthening their health information systems. In particular, it covered: international programmes on the production of health statistics; support to statistical capacity-building at the country level; coordination of international programmes on the production of health statistics; harmonization of definitions, classifications and methodologies; collaboration at the regional level between WHO and other agencies involved in health statistics; and alternative methods of estimating the prevalence of HIV/AIDS. The report also described the future work of the WHO-based Health Metrics Network (the goal of which was to catalyse the development of country health information systems), which was awaiting the receipt of formal funding. WHO also reported that, in response to the Statistical Commission's 2004 request [YUN 2004, p. 1259], it had, together with the Statistics Division, established the Intersecretariat Working Group on Health Statistics to develop a coordinated and integrated agenda on the production of health statistics.

In March [E/2005/24], the Commission welcomed the WHO report and reaffirmed the need for better and more effective involvement of the community of official national and international statisticians at all stages of health statistics development. It recognized that the Health Metrics Network offered a promising approach for strengthening health information systems, particularly those of developing countries, while noting that the Network was not the appropriate forum for a strategic review of international programmes on the production of health statistics. The Commission stressed the need for the Intersecretariat Working Group on Health Statistics to continue its work on a coordinated and integrated agenda on the production of health statistics and asked for stronger involvement of country experts in its work; it agreed that WHO was best suited to lead the work of the Intersecretariat Working Group. The Commission welcomed WHO's announcement that it would make available a timetable regarding the planned release of microdata from the World Health Survey (2002-2003); it stressed the need for good metadata to accompany the publication of the microdata.

Poverty statistics

The Statistical Commission had before it the report of the Secretary-General on poverty statistics [E/CN.3/2005/13], which contained an update on the preparation of the *United Nations Handbook on Poverty Statistics*, including information on modifications made to the outline of the *Handbook* to address concerns raised by the Commission at its 2004 session [YUN 2004, p. 1259].

In March [E/2005/24], the Commission recognized that, while the current scope of the *Handbook* was adequate, future work might be needed to address new and emerging aspects of poverty. It welcomed the proposed work of the Statistics Division in poverty statistics, particularly capacity-building. The Commission also noted that the Rio Group on Poverty Statistics would publish a *Compendium on Poverty Statistics* in 2005, which would complement the *Handbook*. It further noted that the Rio Group intended to conclude its work in 2005.

Disability statistics

The Statistical Commission had before it the report of the Washington Group on Disability Statistics [E/CN.3/2005/14] summarizing the results of its 2004 meeting (Bangkok, Thailand, 29 September–1 October), which included agreement on a draft set of questions for the general disability measure, and the formation of a new working group to develop the protocols for implementing the general disability measure effectively.

In March [E/2005/24], the Commission thanked the World Bank for the grant to support the Group, noting that the funds would facilitate the participation of more developing countries in the Group's activities, help to develop disability

measures for generating comparable data, and pay for the testing of protocols in selected countries in every region of the world.

Other statistical activities

Information and communication technologies statistics

The Statistical Commission had before it the report of the Partnership on Measuring Information and Communication Technologies for Development [E/CN.3/2005/23], which gave an overview of the progress made internationally with respect to the collection of information and communication technologies statistical indicators, in particular in developing countries. It described international community action to harmonize those efforts and to agree on a set of core indicators as a basis for developing comparable statistics. Partnership activities would be brought to the attention of the World Summit on the Information Society in November (see p. 933).

International economic and social classifications

The Statistical Commission considered the Secretary-General's report on international economic and social classifications [E/CN.3/2005/19], which described the status of the revision of the International Standard Industrial Classification of All Economic Activities, the Central Product Classification, the International Standard Classification of Occupations, the Standard International Trade Classification, the Balance of Payments Manual and the Extended Balance of Payments Services Classification, and the agricultural classifications.

In March [E/2005/24], the Commission noted the progress made regarding the 2007 round of classifications revisions. It welcomed the expedited efforts of the Statistics Division to keep the revision of the International Standard Industrial Classification of All Economic Activities on schedule, and urged that similar efforts be made for the Central Product Classification. The Commission noted with concern that a technical expert group was no longer being convened to assist in the revision of the International Standard Classification of Occupations and urged the International Labour Organization to establish such a group.

Statistical capacity-building

The Statistical Commission had before it a report of the Secretary-General on statistical capacity-building [E/CN.3/2005/17], which described the 2004 technical cooperation programme of the Statistics Division and its funding mechanisms.

Also before the Commission was the report of the Partnership in Statistics for Development in the Twenty-first Century (PARIS 21) on statistical capacity-building [E/CN.3/2005/18], which outlined how national strategies for the development of statistics could assist a country to strengthen statistical capacity across the national statistical system. The report also described the support PARIS 21 could offer to countries in developing their national strategies.

In March [E/2005/24], the Commission reaffirmed the critical importance of statistical capacity-building, particularly in the context of increased national and international demand for development information. It supported the Statistics Division's proposed strategic focus for technical cooperation activities, and stressed the need for technical cooperation to be demand-driven, responsive to local conditions, nationally controlled and better coordinated. While recognizing the role of the Statistics Division in donor coordination, the Commission recommended that the Division work with the Committee for the Coordination of Statistical Activities to review what coordination mechanisms would be most suitable and effective.

The Commission also noted the effectiveness of the regional and subregional approach to statistical capacity-building programmes, which allowed for the exchange of practical experiences relevant to the local socio-economic context; it further noted that countries that did not belong to subregional groupings might require special attention. As part of the sustained capacity-building effort, the Commission emphasized the importance of strengthening statistical training centres and supporting in-house training; it also pointed to the need for training in management and programme planning skills alongside statistical training. The Commission requested a regular report, beginning in 2006, on the ability of countries to produce individual indicators on how metadata should be presented to accompany indicators on all Millennium Development Goals (MDGs) [YUN 2000, p. 51]. It agreed to form a Friends of the Chair group to define the modalities of the report and develop suggestions on processes for bridging the information gap between users and producers of MDG indicators; the group would report its recommendations to the Commission.

The Commission welcomed the activities of PARIS 21 in supporting statistical capacity-building in developing countries. It cautioned that efforts to formulate national statistical development strategies should not take away resources needed for core statistical activities, and stressed that the strategies should be flexible enough to accommodate local needs.

Follow-up to UN conferences and summits

The Statistical Commission had before it a report of the Secretary-General on indicators for monitoring the MDGs [YUN 2000, p. 51] and for follow-up to the outcomes of major UN conferences and summits in the economic and social fields [E/CN.3/2005/20]. The report described the work of the Inter-Agency and Expert Group on MDG Indicators in 2004-2005 in compiling and analysing those indicators, reviewing methodologies related to the agreed indicators, coordinating data compilation at the global level and coordinating support to countries that were establishing country-led programmes of data collection, analysis and reporting for indicators.

In March [E/2005/24], the Commission took note of the advances made by the Inter-Agency Expert Group on MDG Indicators in compiling indicators for global monitoring. Observing that many countries still lacked the capacity to produce the necessary data and that a review of indicators being produced at the national level was necessary for all the MDGs, the Commission stated that an opportunity was available to inform policymakers of the realistic level of statistical capacity necessary to produce the MDG indicators.

Presentation and standards for statistical data and metadata

The Statistical Commission had before it an OECD report on the presentation of statistical data and metadata [E/CN.3/2005/21], which outlined progress in developing the second draft of the _Data and Metadata Reporting and Presentation Handbook_, and included a timetable for its launching by the end of 2005.

The Commission also had before it the report of the task force to establish standards on data and metadata exchange [E/CN.3/2005/22], which described the Task Force's progress since March 2004, and outlined the next steps for the Statistical Data and Metadata Exchange initiative.

The Commission took note of the two reports.

Coordination and integration of statistical programmes

The Secretary-General submitted to the Statistical Commission the report of the Committee for the Coordination of Statistical Activities

(CCSA) on its third (New York, 1 March 2004) and fourth (New York, 1-3 September 2004) meetings [E/CN.3/2005/24]. Issues covered in the report included: progress in harmonizing the base year for index numbers to 2000 by the end of 2005; development of a draft declaration of principles for statistical activities in international organizations; information and communication technology indicators; statistics and the subnational level; and strategic issues related to the MDG indicators.

In March [E/2005/24], the Commission requested CCSA to make proposals regarding the use of national data by international organizations.

CCSA held two meetings in 2005: the fifth (New York, 28 February) and sixth (Rome, 12-14 September) [E/CN.3/2006/30]. Subjects discussed included: principles for statistical activities in international organizations; the implementation of good statistical practices in international organizations; and coordination of technical cooperation activities.

Follow-up to Economic and Social Council policy decisions

In response to a 2004 request by the Statistical Commission [YUN 2004, p. 1261], the Secretary-General submitted the report of the Bureau of the Statistical Commission on the review of the Commission's working methods [E/CN.3/2005/2], which suggested a number of improvements.

In March [E/2005/24], the Commission agreed to implement the suggested working procedures on a trial basis for its current (thirty-sixth) session, at the end of which their effectiveness would be reviewed. The Commission decided that there was no need to review its terms of reference as set out in Economic and Social Council resolution 1566(L) [YUN 1971, p. 331], as they were sufficiently broad to cover the Commission's current work.

Programme and institutional questions

In March [E/2005/24], the Commission approved changes to the Statistics Division's 2004-2005 work programme [YUN 2003, p. 1276], and endorsed its 2006-2007 proposed programme of work [E/CN.3/2005/25].

The Commission also approved its 2005-2008 multi-year programme of work [E/CN.3/2005/26]; recommended that the topic for the programme review in 2007 be education statistics; approved the provisional agenda and documentation for its thirty-seventh (2006) session; and recommended that the 2006 session be held in New York from 7 to 10 March.

PART FOUR

Legal questions

Chapter I

International Court of Justice

In 2005, the International Court of Justice (ICJ) delivered three Judgments, made four Orders and had 11 contentious cases pending before it.

In a 27 October address to the General Assembly, the ICJ President noted that the disputes resolved by the Court represented a level of activity unprecedented in its history. Faced with a growing caseload, ICJ had made efforts to increase its judicial efficiency, while maintaining the quality of its work. Among other reforms, it had modernized the organization of the Registry, reviewed and adapted its internal working methods, and modified its Rules where necessary. More States were accepting its jurisdiction to resolve their disputes with other nations. The ICJ President also noted that the Secretary-General, in his May report "In Larger Freedom: towards development, security and human rights for all" (see p. 67), had urged States to recognize ICJ's role in adjudicating their disputes and to consider how to further strengthen the Court's work.

Judicial work of the Court

During 2005, the Court delivered a Judgment on the merits of the case concerning *the Armed activities in the Territory of the Congo (Democratic Republic of the Congo v. Uganda)*, and a Judgment on the preliminary objections raised by the respondent Party in the case concerning *Certain Property (Liechtenstein v. Germany)*. The Chamber of the Court, formed to deal with the case concerning *Frontier Dispute (Benin/Niger)*, also delivered a Judgment on the merits in that case.

During the year, the Court was seized of one new case: *Dispute regarding Navigational and Related Rights (Costa Rica v. Nicaragua)*.

It held public hearings in the cases concerning *Frontier Dispute (Benin/Niger); Armed Activities on the Territory of the Congo (Democratic Republic of the Congo v. Uganda)* and *Armed Activities on the Territory of the Congo (New Application: 2002) (Democratic Republic of the Congo v. Rwanda)*.

The Court or its President further made Orders on the conduct of the proceedings in the cases concerning *Frontier Dispute (Benin/Niger); Sovereignty over Pedra Branca/Pulau Batu Puteh, Middle Rocks and South Ledge (Malaysia/Singapore); Certain Criminal Proceedings in France (Republic of the Congo v. France)*; and *Dispute regarding Navigational and Related Rights (Costa Rica v. Nicaragua)*.

During the year, there were no new developments in the cases concerning *Application of the Convention on the Prevention and Punishment of the Crime of Genocide (Bosnia and Herzegovina v. Serbia and Montenegro)* [YUN 1993, p. 1138]; *Gabcikovo-Nagymaros Project (Hungary/Slovakia)* [YUN 1998, p. 1186]; *Ahmadou Sadio Diallo (Guinea v. Democratic Republic of the Congo)* [ibid., p. 1190]; *Maritime Delimitation between Nicaragua and Honduras in the Carribean Sea (Nicaragua v. Honduras)* [YUN 1999, p. 1210]; *Territorial and Maritime Dispute (Nicaragua v. Colombia)* [YUN 2001, p. 1195]; and *Maritime Delimitation in the Black Sea (Romania v. Ukraine)* [YUN 2004, p. 1265].

ICJ activities in 2005 were covered in two reports to the General Assembly, for the periods 1 August 2004 to 31 July 2005 [A/60/4] and 1 August 2005 to 31 July 2006 [A/61/4]. On 27 October 2005, the Assembly took note of the 2004/2005 report (**decision 60/507**).

Application of the Convention on the Prevention and Punishment of the Crime of Genocide (Bosnia and Herzegovina v. Serbia and Montenegro)

Bosnia and Herzegovina instituted proceedings in 1993 [YUN 1993, p. 1138] against Serbia and Montenegro, then known as the Federal Republic of Yugoslavia, for alleged violations of the 1948 Convention on the Prevention and Punishment of the Crime of Genocide, adopted by the General Assembly in resolution 260 A (III) [YUN 1948-49, p. 959]. The Court delivered its Judgment in 1996 [YUN 1996, p. 1179], rejecting the preliminary objections raised by Serbia and Montenegro in 1995 [YUN 1995, p. 1307]. In 1997, Serbia and Montenegro filed a Counter-Memorial that included counterclaims against Bosnia and Herzegovina [YUN 1997, p. 1315]. Bosnia and Herzegovina filed a Reply in 1998 [YUN 1998, p. 1186], and Serbia and Montenegro filed a Rejoinder in 1999 [YUN 1999, p. 1204].

By an Order of 10 September 2001, the President of the Court placed on record the withdrawal by Serbia and Montenegro of the counterclaims submitted in its Counter-Memorial [YUN 2001, p. 1184].

Serbia and Montenegro had submitted to the Court, on 4 May 2001, a document entitled "Ini-

tiative to the Court to reconsider *ex officio* Jurisdiction over Yugoslavia". Submissions presented
in the document were, firstly, that the Court had
no jurisdiction *ratione persona* over Serbia and
Montenegro and, secondly, that the Court should
suspend proceedings regarding the merits of the
case until a decision on the jurisdictional issue
had been rendered. In a 12 June 2003 letter, the
ICJ Registrar informed the Parties that the Court
had decided that it could not effect a suspension
of the proceedings in the circumstances of the
case [YUN 2003, p. 1302].

Application for Revision of Judgment of 11 July 1996 concerning Application of the Convention on the Prevention and Punishment of the Crime of Genocide (Bosnia and Herzegovina v. Yugoslavia), Preliminary Objections (Yugoslavia v. Bosnia and Herzegovina)

On 24 April 2001 [YUN 2001, p. 1184], the Federal
Republic of Yugoslavia (FRY), currently known as
Serbia and Montenegro, filed an Application for
revision of the Judgment delivered by the Court
on 11 July 1996 in the case concerning *Application
of the Convention on the Prevention and Punishment
of the Crime of Genocide (Bosnia and Herzegovina v.
Yugoslavia), Preliminary Objections* [YUN 1996, p. 1179]
(see above).

Public hearings were held on the question of
the admissibility of the Application for revision
in 2002 [YUN 2002, p. 1264].

In its Judgment of 3 February 2003 [YUN 2003,
p. 1302], the Court found that the Application submitted by FRY for revision of the Judgment of 11
July 1996 was inadmissible.

The Court fixed 27 February 2006 as the date
for the opening of the hearings.

Armed activities on the territory of the Congo (Democratic Republic of the Congo v. Uganda)

The Democratic Republic of the Congo (DRC)
instituted proceedings against Burundi, Rwanda
and Uganda on 23 June 1999 [YUN 1999, p. 1209],
for acts of armed aggression perpetrated in flagrant violation of the Charter of the United
Nations and the Charter of the Organization of
African Unity (OAU). In 2001 [YUN 2001, p. 1191], the
DRC notified the Court that it wished to discontinue the proceedings against Burundi and
Rwanda. The President of the Court, in Orders
of 30 January 2001, placed the discontinuance by
the DRC on record and ordered the removal of
the case from the List.

In the case of Uganda, the Court, taking into
account an agreement of the Parties in 1999 [YUN
1999, p. 1210], fixed 21 January 2000 as the time
limit for the filing of a Memorial by the DRC and

21 April 2001 for the filing of a Counter-Memorial
by Uganda. The Memorial of the DRC was filed
within the prescribed time limit.

On 19 June 2000 [YUN 2000, p. 1218], the DRC requested the Court to indicate provisional measures requiring, among other things, the withdrawal of Uganda's army from Kisangani and the
cessation of military and other activities by
Uganda within the territory of the DRC. Public
sittings were held to hear the oral observations of
the parties on the request for the indication of
provisional measures. By an Order of 1 July both
Parties had to, forthwith, prevent and refrain
from any action, particularly armed action,
which might prejudice the rights of the other
Party in respect of whatever judgment the Court
might render, or which might aggravate or extend the dispute before the Court or make it
more difficult to resolve; both Parties had to,
forthwith, take measures to ensure full respect
within the zone of conflict for fundamental human rights and for the application of provisions
of humanitarian law. Judges Oda and Koroma
appended declarations to the Order.

Uganda filed its Counter-Memorial, which
contained counterclaims, within the time limit
set by the Court's Order of 21 October 1999 [YUN
1999, p. 1210].

By an Order of 29 November 2001 [YUN 2001,
p. 1192], the Court found that two of the counterclaims submitted by Uganda against the DRC
were "inadmissible as such and [formed] part of
the current proceedings", but that the third was
not. In view of those conclusions, the Court considered it necessary for the DRC to file a Reply
and Uganda a Rejoinder, addressing the claims
of both Parties, and fixed 29 May 2002 as the time
limit for the filing of the Reply and 29 November
2002 for the Rejoinder. Furthermore, in order to
ensure strict equality between the Parties, the
Court reserved the right of the DRC to present its
views in writing a second time on the Uganda
counterclaims in an additional pleading to be the
subject of a subsequent Order. The Reply was
filed within the time limit [YUN 2002, p. 1268]. By an
Order of 7 November 2002 [ibid.], the Court extended the time limit for the filing by Uganda of
its Rejoinder to 6 December 2002. The Rejoinder
was filed within the time limit.

By an Order of 29 January 2003 [YUN 2003,
p. 1303], the Court authorized the DRC's submission of an additional pleading relating solely to
the counterclaims submitted by Uganda, and
fixed 28 February 2003 as the time limit for its filing. The written pleading was filed within the
fixed time limit [ibid.]. The Court then fixed 10
November 2003 as the date for the opening of the
hearings.

In a 5 November 2003 letter, the DRC raised the question of whether the hearings might be adjourned to April 2004, to enable the diplomatic negotiations engaged by the Parties to be conducted in an atmosphere of calm. A 6 November 2003 letter by Uganda [ibid.] indicated that it supported the proposal and adopted the DRC's request.

By a 6 November 2003 letter, the ICJ Registrar informed the Parties that the Court had decided that the opening of the oral proceedings would be postponed and that a date would be fixed subsequently [ibid.].

Public hearings on the merits of the cases were held from 11 to 29 April 2005. At the conclusion of the hearings, the Parties presented submissions to the Court. The DRC requested the Court to adjudge and declare that Uganda, by engaging in military and paramilitary activities against it, by occupying its territory and by actively extending military, logistic, economic and financial support to irregular forces operating there, had violated principles of conventional and customary law, including that of non-use of force in international relations and the respect for the sovereignty of States; that it had committed acts of violence against nationals of the DRC, including by killing and injuring them or despoiling them of their property; that it had engaged in the illegal exploitation of Congolese national resources; and that it had violated the Order of the Court on provisional measures of 1 July 2000 [YUN 2000, p. 1218] by failing to comply with those measures. The DRC further requested the Court to declare that the stated violations of international law constituted wrongful acts attributable to Uganda, which had engaged its international responsibility, that Uganda cease forthwith all continuing internationally wrongful acts, that it provide specific guarantees and assurances that it would not repeat the wrongful acts complained of, and that Uganda was under obligation to the DRC to make reparation for all injury caused to the latter, with the nature, form and amount of the reparation to be determined by the Court.

Uganda requested the Court to declare the DRC requests inadmissible for the reasons set forth in Chapter XV of the Counter-Memorial [YUN 2001, p. 1192] and reaffirmed in the oral pleadings; that the requests of the DRC be rejected; and that Uganda's counterclaims, presented in Chapter XVIII of the Counter-Memorial, and reaffirmed in Chapter VI of the Rejoinder, as well as in the oral proceedings, be upheld. It further requested that Court reserve the issue of reparation in relation to Uganda's counterclaims for a subsequent stage of the proceedings.

In its Judgment of 19 December 2005, the Court, by four separate votes of 16 votes to 1, found that Uganda had violated the principle of non-use of force in international relations and the principle of non-intervention; that it had committed acts of killing, torture and other forms of inhuman treatment of the Congolese civilian population; that it had violated obligations owed to the DRC under international law relating to the exploitation of its natural resources; and upheld the objection of the DRC to the admissibility of the second counterclaim submitted by Uganda relating to the maltreatment of individuals other than Ugandan diplomats at Ndjili International Airport in 1998. By 15 votes to 2, it found that Uganda did not comply with the Order of the Court on provisional measures on 1 July 2000 [YUN 2000, p. 1218]. By 14 votes to 3, it found that the first counterclaim submitted by Uganda could not be upheld. In further votes, the Court found unanimously that the claim submitted by the DRC relating to alleged violations of international humanitarian and human rights law by Uganda in the course of hostilities between Ugandan and Rwandan military forces in Kisangani was admissible; that the DRC maltreated Ugandan diplomats and other individuals on the Embassy premises and at the Ndjili Airport; that Uganda was under obligation to make reparation to the DRC for the injury caused; and that, failing agreement between the Parties, the question of reparation due to the DRC would be settled by the Court. It rejected unanimously the objections of the DRC to the admissibility of Uganda's first counterclaim and to the admissibility of the part of the second counterclaim submitted by Uganda relating to the breach of the Vienna Convention on Diplomatic Relations of 1961. The Court found unanimously that the DRC was under obligation to make reparation to Uganda for the injury caused; and that, failing agreement between the Parties, the question of reparation due to Uganda would be settled by the Court.

Appended to the Judgment were: declarations by Judges Koroma and Tomka and by Judge ad hoc Vanhoeven; separate opinions by Judges Parra-Aranguren, Kooijmans, Elarby and Simma; and a dissenting opinion by Judge Kateka.

Certain property (Liechtenstein v. Germany)

On 1 June 2001 [YUN 2001, p. 1194], Liechtenstein filed an Application instituting proceedings against Germany's decisions to treat certain property of Liechtenstein nationals as German assets, seized for the purposes of restitution as a consequence of the Second World War, without ensuring any compensation.

In the Application, Liechtenstein requested the Court to adjudge and declare that Germany had incurred international legal responsibility and was bound to make appropriate reparation to Liechtenstein for the damage and prejudice suffered. Liechtenstein further requested that the nature and amount of such reparation should, in the absence of agreement between the Parties, be assessed and determined by the Court, if necessary, in a separate phase of the proceedings. As a basis for the Court's jurisdiction, Liechtenstein invoked article 1 of the European Convention for the Peaceful Settlement of Disputes, signed at Strasbourg, France, on 29 April 1957.

By an Order of 28 June 2001 [ibid.], the Court fixed 28 March and 27 December 2002, respectively, as the time limits for the filing of a Memorial by Liechtenstein and of a Counter-Memorial by Germany. The Memorial was filed within the fixed time limit.

On 27 June 2002 [YUN 2002, p. 1271], Germany filed certain preliminary objections to the jurisdiction of the Court and the admissibility of the Application; the proceedings on the merits were suspended in accordance with Article 79 of the Rules of the Court. Within the 15 November 2002 time limit fixed by the Court, Liechtenstein filed a written statement of its observations and submissions with regard to the preliminary objections raised by Germany.

Public hearings on those objections were held from 14 to 18 June 2004.

Germany requested the Court to adjudge and declare that it lacked jurisdiction over the claims brought against it and that those claims were inadmissible to the extent specified in its preliminary objections.

Liechtenstein requested the Court to adjudge and declare that the Court had jurisdiction over the claims presented in its Application and that they were admissible; and, accordingly, to reject Germany's preliminary objections in their entirety.

In its Judgment of 10 February 2005, the Court, by 15 votes to 1, rejected the preliminary objection that there was no dispute between Liechtenstein and Germany. By 12 votes to 4, it upheld the preliminary objection that Liechtenstein's Application should be rejected on the grounds that the Court lacked jurisdiction *ratione temporis* to decide the dispute. By 12 votes to 4, it found that it had no jurisdiction to entertain the Application filed by Liechtenstein on 1 June 2001 [YUN 2001, p. 1194].

Appended to the Judgment were dissenting opinions by Judges Kooijmans, Elaraby and Owada, and Judge ad hoc Berman; and a declaration by Judge ad hoc Fleischhauer.

Frontier dispute (Benin/Niger)

In 2002 [YUN 2002, p. 1271], Benin and the Niger jointly notified the Court of a Special Agreement, which was signed between them on 15 June 2001 and entered into force on 11 April 2002. Under article 1 of the Agreement, the Parties agreed to submit their boundary dispute to a chamber to be formed by the Court, pursuant to Article 26, paragraph 2, of the Court's Statute, and that each of them would choose a judge ad hoc. Article 2 of the Agreement stated that the Court was requested to determine the course of the boundary between Benin and the Niger in the River Niger sector; specify which State owned each of the islands in the River Niger, in particular Lété Island; and determine the course of the boundary between the two States in the River Mekrou sector. Article 10 contained a "special undertaking" as follows: "Pending the Judgment of the Chamber, the Parties undertake to preserve peace, security and quiet among the peoples of the two States".

By an Order of 27 November 2002 [ibid.], the Court decided to accede to the Parties' request and form a special chamber of five judges; the Court formed a Chamber of three members of the Court, together with two judges ad hoc chosen by the Parties. The Court fixed 27 August 2003 as the time limit for the filing of a Memorial by each Party. The Memorials were filed within the time limit.

By an Order of 11 September 2003 [YUN 2003, p. 1305], the President of the Court fixed 28 May 2004 as the time limit for the filing of a Counter-Memorial by each of the Parties; the Counter-Memorials were filed within the time limit fixed. On 20 November 2003 [ibid.], the Court held its first public sitting to enable the two judges ad hoc to make the solemn declaration required by the Statute and the Rules of Court.

By an Order of 9 July 2004 [YUN 2004, p. 1269], the President of the Chamber, taking into account the wish of the Parties to be authorized to submit a third pleading as provided for by the Special Agreement, authorized the submission of a Reply by each of the parties, and fixed 17 December 2004, as the time limit for the filing of that pleading. The Replies were deposited within the time limit thus prescribed.

Public hearings were held by the Court from 7 to 11 March 2005. Benin requested the Court to decide that the boundary between Benin and Niger took the course of a particular set of coordinates, and that sovereignty over all of the islands in the River Niger, and particularly Lété Island, lay with Benin. Niger requested the Court to adjudge and declare that the boundary between the countries took the course of another set of coordinates, insofar as that line could be established as it was at the date of independence and determine which islands belonged to each Party. It further requested the Court to declare that the attribution of islands to Benin and Niger according to the line of deepest soundings, as determined at the date of independence, should be regarded as final; that the boundary between the Parties passed through the middle of the Gaya and Malanville bridges; and that the line ran through the River Mekrou sector in two parts, with particular sets of coordinates.

In its Judgment of 12 July 2005, the Court, by 4 votes to 1, decided on the delimitation of the boundary between Benin and Niger in the River Niger and the coordinates thereof. By two further votes, each of 4 votes to 1, it found that the islands situated in the River Niger belonged to Benin or Niger as indicated in paragraph 117 of the Court's Judgment, and that the boundary between the countries on the bridges between Gaya and Malanville followed the boundary in the river. The Court found unanimously that the boundary between the two Parties in the River Mekrou sector followed the median line of that river, from the intersection of the said line with the line of deepest soundings of the main navigable channel of the River Niger as far as the boundary of the Parties with Burkina Faso.

Appended to the Judgment was a dissenting opinion by Judge ad hoc Bennouna.

Armed activities on the territory of the Congo (New Application: 2002) (Democratic Republic of the Congo v. Rwanda)

On 28 May 2002 [YUN 2002, p. 1271], the DRC filed an Application instituting proceedings against Rwanda in respect of a dispute concerning "massive, serious and flagrant violations of human rights and of international humanitarian law" resulting "from acts of armed aggression perpetrated by Rwanda on the territory of the Democratic Republic of the Congo in flagrant breach of the sovereignty and territorial integrity of the [latter], as guaranteed by the United Nations and OAU Charters." The DRC requested the Court to adjudge and declare that, by violating human rights, Rwanda had violated and was violating the UN Charter, as well as articles 3 and 4 of the OAU Charter; that it further violated a number of instruments protecting human rights; that, by shooting down a Boeing 727 owned by Congo Airlines on 9 October 1998 in Kindu, thereby causing the deaths of 40 civilians, Rwanda had violated certain conventions regarding international civil aviation; and that, by engaging in killing, slaughter, rape, throat-slitting and crucifying, Rwanda was guilty of genocide against more

than 3.5 million Congolese, including the victims of massacres in the city of Kisangani, and had violated the sacred right to life provided for in certain instruments protecting human rights, as well as the 1948 Convention on the Prevention and Punishment of the Crime of Genocide [YUN 1948-49, p. 959]. It further asked the Court to adjudge and declare that all Rwandan armed forces should be withdrawn from Congolese territory and that the DRC was entitled to compensation. In its Application, the DRC, in order to found the jurisdiction of the Court, relied on a number of compromissory clauses in treaties.

Also on 28 May 2002 [YUN 2002, p. 1272], the DRC submitted a request for the indication of provisional measures. Following public hearings on the request, the Court delivered its Order, by which, having found that it had no prima facie jurisdiction, it rejected the request of the DRC. In the Order, the Court also rejected the submissions by Rwanda seeking the removal of the case from the Court's List.

By an Order of 18 September 2002 [ibid.], the Court decided, in accordance with Article 79, paragraphs 2 and 3, of the revised Rules of the Court, that the written pleadings would first be addressed to the questions of the jurisdiction of the Court and the admissibility of the Application, and fixed 20 January 2003 as the time limit for the Memorial of Rwanda and 20 May 2003 for the DRC's Counter-Memorial. The pleadings were filed within the time limits [YUN 2003, p. 1306].

Public hearings addressed to the questions of the jurisdiction of the Court and the admissibility of the Application were held from 4 to 8 July 2005. At the conclusion of those hearings, the Parties presented their final submissions to the Court. Rwanda requested the Court to adjudge and declare that it lacked jurisdiction over the claims brought against Rwanda by the DRC, and that the claims brought against Rwanda by the DRC were inadmissible. The DRC asked the Court to find that the objections to jurisdiction and admissibility raised by Rwanda were unfounded, and that the Court had jurisdiction to entertain the case on those merits and that the Application of the DRC was admissible as submitted. It further asked the Court to proceed with the case on the merits.

Certain criminal proceedings in France (Republic of the Congo v. France)

On 9 December 2002 [YUN 2002, p. 1263], the Republic of the Congo filed an Application by which it sought to institute proceedings against France seeking the annulment of the investigation and prosecution measures taken by the French judicial authorities further to a complaint for crimes against humanity and torture filed by various associations against the President of the Congo, Denis Sassou Nguesso, the Congolese Minister of the Interior, Pierre Oba, and other individuals, including General Norbert Dabira, Inspector General of the Congolese Armed Forces. The Application further stated that, in connection with the proceedings, an investigating judge of the Meaux (France) tribunal de grande instance had issued a warrant for the President of the Congo to be examined as witness.

The Congo contended that by "attributing to itself universal jurisdiction in criminal matters and by arrogating to itself the power to prosecute and try the Minister of the Interior of a foreign State for crimes allegedly committed by him in connection with the exercise of his powers for the maintenance of public order in his country", France violated "the principle that a State may not, in breach of the principle of sovereign equality among all Members of the United Nations exercise its authority on the territory of another State". The Congo further submitted that, in issuing a warrant instructing police officers to examine the President of the Congo as witness in the case, France violated "the criminal immunity of a foreign Head of State, an international customary rule recognized by the jurisprudence of the Court".

In its Application, the Congo indicated that it sought to found the jurisdiction of the Court, pursuant to Article 38, paragraph 5, of the Rules of Court, "on the consent of the French Republic, which will certainly be given". In accordance with that provision, the Application by the Congo was transmitted to France and no further action was taken in the proceedings at that stage.

By an 8 April 2003 letter [YUN 2003, p. 1308], France stated that it "consent[ed] to the jurisdiction of the Court to entertain the Application pursuant to Article 38, paragraph 5. That consent made it possible to enter the case in the Court's List and to open the proceedings. In its letter, France added that its consent to the Court's jurisdiction applied strictly within the limits "of the claims formulated by the Republic of the Congo" and that "Article 2 of the Treaty of Co-operation signed on 1 January 1974 by the French Republic and the People's Republic of the Congo, to which the latter refers in its Application, does not constitute a basis of jurisdiction for the Court in the present case".

The Application of the Congo was accompanied by a request for the indication of a provisional measure "seek[ing] an order for the immediate suspension of the proceedings being conducted by the investigating judge of the Meaux tribunal de grande instance".

Taking into account the consent given by France and, in accordance with Article 74, paragraph 3, of the Rules of Court, the President of the Court fixed 28 April 2003 as the date for the opening of the public hearings on the request for the indication of a provisional measure submitted by the Congo. The hearings were held on 28 and 29 April 2003 [ibid.].

On 17 June 2003 [ibid.], the President of the Court read the Order, by which the Court found, by 14 votes to 1, that the circumstances, as they presented themselves to the Court, were not such as to require the exercise of its power under Article 41 of the Statute to indicate provisional measures. Judges Koroma and Vereshchetin appended a joint separate opinion to the Order, and Judge ad hoc de Cara a dissenting opinion.

By an Order of 11 July 2003 [ibid.], the President of the Court fixed 11 December 2003 as the time limit for the Memorial of the Congo and 11 May 2004 as the time limit for the Counter-Memorial of France. The Memorial was filed within the time limit.

By an Order of 17 June 2004 [YUN 2004, p. 1270], the Court, taking account of the agreement of the Parties and of the particular circumstances of the case, authorized the submission of a Reply by the Congo and a Rejoinder by France, and fixed 10 December 2004 and 10 June 2005 as the respective time limits for the filing of those pleadings. By Orders of 8 and 29 December 2004, the President of the Court, taking account of the reasons given by the Congo and of the agreement of the Parties, extended to 10 January and 10 August 2005, those respective timelimits [ibid.].

By an Order of 11 July 2005, the President of the Court again extended the respective time limits for the filing of the pleadings to 11 July 2005 and 11 August 2006 and later to 11 January 2006 and 10 August 2007.

Sovereignty over Pedra Branca/Pulau Batu Puteh, Middle Rocks and South Ledge (Malaysia/Singapore)

On 24 July 2003 [YUN 2003, p. 1308], Malaysia and Singapore jointly notified the Court of a Special Agreement, which was signed between them on 6 February 2003 at Putrajaya, Malaysia, and entered into force on 9 May 2003. In article 2 of the Special Agreement, the Parties requested the Court to determine whether sovereignty over Pedra Branca/Pulau Batu Puteh, Middle Rocks and South Ledge belonged to Malaysia or Singapore. In article 6, the Parties agreed to accept the judgment of the Court as final and binding upon them. The Parties further set out their views on the procedure to be followed.

By an Order of 1 September 2003 [ibid., p. 1309], the Court, taking into account the provisions of article 4 of the Special Agreement, fixed 25 March 2004 and 25 January 2005 as the respective time limits for the filing, by each of the Parties, of a Memorial and of a Counter-Memorial. The Memorials were filed within the time limit [YUN 2004, p. 1271].

By an Order of 1 February 2005, the Court, taking into account the provisions of the Special Agreement, fixed 25 November 2005 as the time limit for the filing of a Reply by each of the Parties.

Dispute regarding Navigational and Related Rights (Costa Rica v. Nicaragua)

On 29 September 2005, Costa Rica filed an Application instituting proceedings against Nicaragua in respect of a dispute concerning navigational and related rights on the San Juan River. Costa Rica stated in its Application that it sought "the cessation of [the] Nicaraguan conduct which prevent[ed] the free and full exercise and enjoyment of the rights that Costa Rica possess[ed] on the San Juan River, and which also prevent[ed] Costa Rica from fulfilling its responsibilities" under certain agreements between itself and Nicaragua. It stated that Nicaragua had, in particular since the late 1990s, imposed restrictions on the navigation of Costa Rican boats and their passengers on the San Juan River, in violation of Article VI of the Treaty of Limits, signed in 1858 between the two Parties, which granted Nicaragua sovereignty over the waters of the river, while recognizing at the same time important rights to Costa Rica. It maintained that those rights were confirmed and interpreted on 28 March 1888 by the then President of the United States, Grover Cleveland, and by a judgment of the Central American Court of Justice of 1916, as well as by the Agreement Supplementary to Article IV of the [1949] Pact of Amity of 9 January 1956. Costa Rica contended that the above-mentioned restrictions were "of a continuing character".

Costa Rica argued further that on 28 September 2005, the National Assembly of Nicaragua passed a resolution threatening to impose economic sanctions on Costa Rica in the event of its bringing the dispute to the Court, to which was annexed the text of a draft law imposing a 35 per cent import tax on all goods and services of Costa Rican origin. Costa Rica added that it had proposed many times to Nicaragua a diplomatic solution and the use of available mechanisms of peaceful resolution of differences, including mediation through the Organization of American States (OAS) and international arbitration, but that the Government of Nicaragua had rejected those alternatives.

Costa Rica requested the Court to adjudge and declare that Nicaragua had violated its obligations to facilitate and expedite traffic on the San Juan River within the terms of the 1858 Treaty and interpretation by the 1988 arbitration; to allow Costa Rican boats and their passengers to navigate freely and without impediment on the river for commercial purposes, and to moor freely on any of the river's banks without paying any charges, unless expressly agreed by both Governments. It further asked the Court to adjudge and declare that Nicaragua had violated its obligations not to require Costa Rican boats and their passengers to stop at any Nicaraguan post along the river; not to impose any charges or fees on Costa Rican boats and their passengers for navigating on the river; to allow Costa Rica the right to navigate the river in accordance with the Cleveland Award; to allow Costa Rica the right to navigate the San Juan River in official boats for supply purposes, for the exchange of personnel of the border posts along the river, and for the purposes of protection, as established in the pertinent instruments; to collaborate with Costa Rica in order to carry out those undertakings and activities which required a common effort by both States in order to facilitate and expedite traffic along the river, within the terms of the Treaty; and not to aggravate and extend the dispute by adopting measures against Costa Rica, including unlawful economic sanctions. Costa Rica requested the Court to determine the reparation to be made by Nicaragua.

As a basis for the Court's jurisdiction, Costa Rica invoked the declarations of acceptance of the Court's jurisdiction, made by Costa Rica in 1973 and by Nicaragua in 1979, as well as several other agreements between the parties.

By an Order of 29 November 2005, the Court fixed 29 August 2006 and 29 May 2007 as the time limits for the filing of a Memorial by Costa Rica and a Counter-Memorial by Nicaragua.

Communication. On 29 September [A/60/417-S/2005/632], Costa Rica informed the Secretary-General of its intention to bring the case concerning its navigational rights on the San Juan River (see above) before ICJ.

Other questions

Composition of the Court

Election of judges

By October 2004 notes [A/59/237, S/2004/830], the Secretary-General informed the General Assembly and the Security Council that Judge and former President of the Court, Gilbert Guillaume, whose term was to expire on 5 February 2009, intended to resign effective 11 February 2005. In accordance with the Statute of the Court, the Secretary-General invited the national groups of States parties to make nominations for a new member of the Court and fixed the deadline for nominations.

On 15 February 2005, the Assembly and the Council elected Ronny Abraham (France) to replace Mr. Guillaume as a member of the Court for a term of office beginning on 15 February and expiring on 5 February 2009 (**decision 59/415**).

By a July 2005 memorandum [A/60/186-S/2005/446], the Secretary-General informed the Assembly and the Council that, on 5 February 2006, the terms of office of five additional members of the Court would expire. He asked the Assembly, during its sixtieth (2005) session, to elect five judges for a term of office of nine years, beginning on 6 February 2006, and fixed the deadline for those nominations.

On 7 November, the Assembly and the Council elected five members of the Court to fill the vacancies occurring on 5 February 2006 (**decision 60/408**).

Trust Fund to Assist States in the Settlement of Disputes

In September [A/60/330], the Secretary-General reported on the activities and status of the Trust Fund to Assist States in the Settlement of Disputes through ICJ since the submission of his 2004 report [YUN 2004, p. 1274]. The Fund, established in 1989 [YUN 1989, p. 818], provided financial assistance to States for financial expenses incurred in connection with a dispute submitted to ICJ by way of a special agreement or the execution of a judgment resulting from such an agreement.

During the period under review (1 July 2004–30 June 2005), three States contributed to the Fund. As at 30 June, the Fund's balance stood at approximately $2 million.

The Fund did not receive any applications from States during the reporting period.

Noting that, since its inception, the Fund had had a decreasing level of resources, the Secretary-General urged States and other relevant entities to consider making substantial and regular contributions.

Chapter II

International tribunals and court

In 2005, the International Tribunal for the Prosecution of Persons Responsible for Serious Violations of International Humanitarian Law Committed in the Territory of the Former Yugoslavia since 1991 (ICTY) made significant progress in accomplishing its mandate by 2010. As part of that effort, a pilot e-Court system was implemented in February, integrating all documents into a central electronic database. In March, a Special War Crimes Chamber was established within the State Court of Bosnia and Herzegovina to receive cases from ICTY and take over cases of lower-level accused not being pursued by the Tribunal. In August, the Security Council amended ICTY Statute to extend the terms of office of some short-term judges, to allow them to finish adjudicating the cases on which they had begun working.

During the year, the International Criminal Tribunal for the Prosecution of Persons Responsible for Genocide and Other Serious Violations of International Humanitarian Law Committed in the Territory of Rwanda and Rwandan Citizens Responsible for Genocide and Other Such Violations Committed in the Territory of Neighbouring States between 1 January and 31 December 1994 (ICTR) rendered three judgments and commenced three new trials. The Tribunal was on course to completing all trials by 2008. Meanwhile, outreach programme activities continued to be a priority for ICTR, with the Information Centre in Rwanda being its focal point. To that end, seminars and workshops on international humanitarian and criminal law were held for Rwandan legal practitioners.

The International Criminal Court (ICC), in its second year of functioning, began its operational phase, conducting investigation into situations of concern in three countries. In June, the Security Council referred to it the situation in the Darfur region of the Sudan.

International Tribunal for the Former Yugoslavia

In 2005, the International Tribunal for the Former Yugoslavia (ICTY) advanced the implementa-

tion of its completion strategy [YUN 2002, p. 1275], adopting further reforms to ensure compliance with Security Council resolutions 1503 (2003) [YUN 2003, p. 1330] and 1534(2004) [YUN 2004, p. 1292]. In February, ICTY amended the following rules of its Rules of Procedure and Evidence: rule 11 bis requiring the President to designate a "Referral Bench" of three permanent judges selected from the Trial Chambers, rather than having the Trial Chamber alone determine whether a case should be referred to the authorities of a State, and rules 124 and 28. In July, ICTY amended rule 15 (B), relating to the disqualification of a judge at the request of a party, and to confer the decision on another Trial Chamber than the one of which the challenged judge was a member; rules 42 (A) and 43 (i) to harmonize them with rule 62, by removing the requirement that the accused speak the language in which he was informed of his rights; and rules 15 (C) and (D), 54 bis, 65 (D) and (E), 72 (E) and 127, to remove the requirement that a party seek leave from a bench of three judges for the right to appeal certain decisions.

The Referral Bench constituted by the President granted four transfers and denied one. ICTY conducted extensive training for judges and staff of the Special Chamber and assisted in its own investigations. It was also involved in building the region's national judicial capacity, hosting visits to Serbia and Montenegro and Croatia. The Tribunal was also active in the reconciliation process by making activities accessible, transparent and relevant. By the end of the year, one of the most notorious fugitives, Ante Gotovina, after evading justice for more than four years, was arrested and transferred to the Tribunal.

The activities of ICTY, established by Security Council resolution 827(1993) [YUN 1993, p. 440], were covered in two reports to the Council and the General Assembly, for the periods 1 August 2004 to 31 July 2005 [A/60/267-S/2005/532] and 1 August 2005 to 31 July 2006 [A/61/271-S/2006/666]. On 10 October, the Assembly took note of the 2004/2005 report (**decision 60/506**).

The Chambers

The judicial activities of the Tribunal's three Trial Chambers and of its Appeals Chamber included first instance and appeals proceedings against judgements, interlocutary decisions and State requests for review; proceedings regarding the Tribunal's primacy; and contempt cases. ICTY had a total of 30 judges—16 permanent judges, 2 ICTR judges in the Appeals Chamber and 12 ad litem judges.

New arrests and surrenders

Savo Todovic, whose initial indictment was made public in 2001, surrendered and was transferred to the Tribunal on 15 January. He was charged with crimes against humanity and violations of the laws or customs of war for events that took place at the Foca Kazneno-Popravni Dom prison, in Bosnia and Herzegovina. He pleaded not guilty to all charges on 17 February. On 25 July, the prosecution and Mr. Todovic filed notices of appeal against the partly confidential decision by the Referral Bench on 8 July, ordering that the case be referred to the authorities of the State of Bosnia and Herzegovina.

The indictment of Zdravko Tolimir, Radivoje Miletic and Milan Gvero was confirmed on 10 February. They were all charged with violations of the laws or customs of war and crimes against humanity allegedly committed against Muslim populations in the Srebrenica and Zepa enclaves. While Tolimir remained at large, both Miletic and Gvero surrendered to the authorities in February and were transferred to the Tribunal on 24 and 28 February, respectively. They pleaded not guilty to all counts and were given provisional release, following a Trial Chamber's decision of 19 July. Their trial was to commence in 2006. Earlier, on 10 June, the prosecution had filed a motion seeking joinder of the case concerning events in Srebrenica with those of Vujadin Popovic, Ljubisa Beara, Drago Nikolic, Ljubomir Borovcanin, Vinko Pandurevic and Milorad Trbic (see below). On 29 June, the Tribunal President issued an order referring the joinder motion to the Trial Chamber.

Rasim Delic, commander of the main staff of the Army of Bosnia-Herzegovina, was indicted on 15 February and charged, on the basis of his superior command responsibility, with four counts of violations of the laws or customs of war. Following his transfer to The Hague on 28 February, he pleaded not guilty to all charges at an initial appearance on 3 March, and was granted provisional release on 6 May. Momcilo Perisic, chief of the general staff of the Yugoslav Army, was transferred to the Tribunal on 7 March, and charged with eight counts of crimes against humanity and five counts of violations of the laws or customs of war for crimes allegedly perpetrated against civilians in Sarajevo. He pleaded not guilty to all charges at his initial appearance on

9 March. On 9 June, the Trial Chamber granted the accused provisional release.

Ramush Haradinaj and Lahi Brahimaj, who belonged to the Kosovo Liberation Army (KLA), surrendered to the Tribunal on 9 March 2005. Idriz Balaj, who was serving a sentence pursuant to a conviction in 2002, was also transferred to the Tribunal on the same day. The indictment, confirmed on 4 March, charged the accused with 37 counts of crimes against humanity and violations of the laws or customs of war. On 6 June, a motion filed by his counsel for provisional release was granted by the Trial Chamber.

The indictment against Ljube Boskoski and Johan Tarculovski was confirmed on 9 March 2005. Mr. Tarculovski was arrested in the former Yugoslav Republic of Macedonia (FYROM) and handed over to the Tribunal on 16 March. Mr. Boskoski, who was in custody in a Croatian prison, was transferred to the Tribunal on 24 March. In April, both pleaded not guilty to charges of three counts of violations of the laws or customs of war, allegedly committed in August 2001, in FYROM.

Gojko Jankovic, military police commander for Serb Forces, surrendered on 14 March. Following initial appearances before the Tribunal on 18 March and 15 April, he pleaded not guilty to all counts. On 22 July, the Referral Bench granted the transfer of the case, which took place on 8 December, to the authorities of the State of Bosnia and Herzegovina.

In August, two accused were located and arrested: Milan Lukic, in Argentina, who was originally indicted in 1998 for the killing of Muslim men, women and children in the eastern Bosnian town of Visegrad; and Dragan Zelenovic, in the Russian Federation, indicted for torture and rape in the Bosnian town of Foca. Both were awaiting transfer to the Tribunal. The indictment against Goran Borovnica, which was confirmed in 1995, was withdrawn, owing to the presumed death of the accused.

Josip Jovic and Marijan Krizic were indicted on 29 August for contempt of court for publishing the protected witnesses' testimony. Their trial was to commence in 2006.

After evading arrest for almost four years since his 2001 indictment [YUN 2001, p. 1199], Ante Gotovina, a former high-ranking Croatian military officer, was arrested on 7 December in the Canary Islands by the Spanish authorities, and transferred to The Hague.

Ongoing cases and trials

The trial of Vidoje Blagojevic and Dragan Jokic, charged jointly with other accused in 2001

[YUN 2001, p. 1199] for their alleged involvement in events in and around Srebrenica in 1995 [YUN 1995, p. 529], began in 2003 [YUN 2003, p. 1312] and ended in 2004 [YUN 2004, p. 1280]. In judgements passed against the two accused on 17 January 2005, the Trial Chamber acquitted Mr. Blagojevic on one count of extermination and Mr. Jokic on one count of murder. It found Mr. Blagojevic guilty for complicity to commit genocide, crimes against humanity and violations of the laws or customs of war and sentenced him to 18 years in prison. The Chamber found Mr. Jokic guilty for crimes against humanity and violations of the laws or customs of war and sentenced him to 9 years in prison.

On 25 January, Ivica Marijacic and Markica Rebic were indicted for disclosing information to a Croatian newspaper about the identity of a protected Tribunal witness revealed during the trial of Tihomir Blaskic [YUN 2004, p. 1282], in violation of a closed session order. Both respondents, who were charged with one count for contempt of the Tribunal, pleaded not guilty at their initial appearance on 14 June.

The trial of Sefer Halilovic, who was charged with one count of murder for the killing of Bosnian Croat civilians committed by subordinate brigades in Grabovica and Uzdol (Bosnia and Herzegovina) in September 1993, commenced on 31 January 2005. In a judgement issued on 16 November, the Trial Chamber found Mr. Halilovic not guilty.

By a 31 January judgement against General Pavle Strugar [YUN 2003, p. 1314; YUN 2004, p. 1279], the Trial Chamber found that it had not been established that the accused was responsible for having ordered or aided and abetted the unlawful shelling of the Old Town of Dubrovnik. He was, however, found guilty on two counts of failure to prevent or punish those involved in attacks on civilians and the destruction of, or wilful damage to, institutions dedicated to religion, charity and education, the arts and sciences, and historic monuments. He was sentenced to eight years' imprisonment. Appeals by the prosecution and the defence were currently pending before the Appeals Chamber.

In the case against Dragomir Milosevic, Chief Commander, Romanija Corps of the Bosnian Serb Army, who was indicted in 1999 for crimes in Sarajevo, a prosecution motion filed on 31 January for the indictment to be referred to the authorities of Bosnia and Herzegovina to be tried in their own courts was denied on 8 July. His trial was expected to commence towards the end of 2006.

Stjepan Seselj and Domagoj Margetic, publisher and editor, respectively, of a Croatian weekly magazine were indicted on 1 February for contempt for having disseminated excerpts of closed-session testimony of a protected witness in the Blaskic case [YUN 2004, p. 1282]. In an initial appearance before the Tribunal on 14 June, both accused pleaded guilty to two counts of contempt. The case was pending before the Trial Chamber.

Vladimir Lazarevic, Sreten Lukic and Nebojsa Pavkovic, indicted in 2003 [YUN 2003, p. 1312] on four counts of crimes against humanity (deportation; other inhumane acts; murder; and persecutions on political, racial and religious grounds) and one count of violations of the laws or customs of war (murder) for acts allegedly committed against Kosovo Albanians, were transferred to the Tribunal on 3 February and 4 and 24 April, respectively. All three accused pleaded not guilty to charges at their initial appearance. Mr. Lazarevic filed a request for provisional release, which was granted on 14 April. Mr. Pavkovic and Mr. Lukic applied for provisional release on 10 June and 20 May, respectively. On 1 April, the prosecution filed a motion seeking joinder of the case with that of former Serb officials Milan Milutinovic, Dragoljub Ojdanic and Nikola Sainovic [YUN 1999, p. 1214]. The Trial Chamber granted the motion on 8 July and ordered the prosecution to submit a consolidated indictment by 15 August.

In the appeal of Dragan Nikolic, filed in 2004 [YUN 2004, p. 1278] from the Trial Chamber sentencing judgement of 23 years in prison [YUN 2003, p. 1314], the Appeals Chamber, on 4 February, while supporting the appellant's position that the Trial Chamber had erred in taking into account the time he would actually serve in detention, dismissed the grounds of appeal in all other respects and imposed a new sentence on Mr. Nikolic of 20 years in prison.

In the case of Miroslav Kvoka and Others [YUN 2001, p. 1201], the Appeals Chamber, in a judgment issued on 28 February, allowed, in part, his fourth and fifth grounds of appeal, but dismissed the remaining grounds of appeal in all other aspects and affirmed his conviction and sentence of seven years' imprisonment as imposed by the Trial Chamber. In the case against Zoran Zigic, who was sentenced to 20 years in prison [YUN 2001, p. 1201], the Chamber, while allowing the accused grounds of appeal concerning his responsibility for crimes committed in the Omarska camp, affirmed his sentence. On 28 February, the Appeals Chamber dismissed all grounds of appeal of Mlado Radic and Dragoljub Prcac and affirmed the sentences of 20 years and 5 years' imprisonment imposed on them, respectively. Mr. Radic's request for provisional release was denied on 13

July and he was awaiting transfer to serve the remainder of his sentence.

Stanislav Galic, sentenced to 20 years' imprisonment in 2003 [YUN 2003, p. 1315], with one of the judges filing a separate and partially dissenting opinion, with an alternative recommendation of 10 years in prison, filed an appeal brief in 2004, including four rule 115 motions for the admission of additional evidence. On 22 March, the Appeals Chamber rejected the second rule motion. The following day, the Appeals Chamber granted him provisional release, from 31 March to 3 April, to attend the memorial service for his late sister. On 30 June, the Appeals Chamber rendered a consolidated decision and dismissed Mr. Galic's first and third motions for the admission of additional evidence. The Appeals Chamber was in the process of considering the fourth rule 115 motion.

In the case of Vinko Pandurevic and Milorad Trbic, Mr. Pandurevic, initially indicted in 2001 [YUN 2001, p. 1200], was transferred to the Tribunal on 23 March, and Mr. Trbic on 7 April. By an order dated 24 March, a new indictment was confirmed against them and both pleaded not guilty to all the charges on 3 and 11 May, respectively. On 10 June, the prosecution filed a motion seeking joinder of the case with those of Vujadin Popovic, Ljubisa Beara, Drago Nikolic, Ljubomir Borovcanin, Zdravko Tolimir, Radivoje Miletic and Milan Gvero and for all nine accused to be jointly charged and tried under one indictment. The motion was granted on 29 June.

The defence closed the cases for Enver Hadzihasanovic and Amir Kubura on 11 April and 15 July, respectively. Both of the accused had pleaded not guilty in 2001 [YUN 2001, p. 1199] and, by a third amended indictment, were further charged in 2003 with violations of the laws or customs of war [YUN 2003, p. 1314], and were provisionally released in 2004 [YUN 2004, p. 1278].

On 14 April, Milan Milutinovic, Dragoljub Ojdanic and Nikola Sainovic were granted provisional release, subject to a stay pending possible appeal by the prosecution. The following day, the prosecution decided not to appeal the Chamber's decision. On 1 April, it had filed a motion seeking joinder of the case with that of Nebojsa Pavkovic, Vladimir Lazarevic, Vlastimir Dordevic (who remained at large) and Sreten Lukic, and for all seven accused to be jointly charged and tried under one joint indictment. On 8 July, the Chamber granted the prosecution's motion and issued an order for a consolidated indictment by 15 August. The trial was to commence in 2006.

Vujadin Popovic, who was originally indicted in 2002, and charged, along with Ljubisa Beara, Drago Nikolic, Ljubomir Borovcanin, Vinko Pandurevic and Zdravko Tolimir, with genocide and conspiracy to commit genocide, as well as five counts of crimes against humanity and one count of violation of the laws or customs of war, surrendered on 14 April and was transferred to The Hague on the same day. At his initial appearance on 18 April, he pleaded not guilty to all charges. Mr. Popovic's request for provisional release, filed on 22 June, was refused by the Trial Chamber on 22 July, as it was not satisfied that the accused would appear for the trial if released. The defence submitted an application for leave to appeal against the decision of the Trial Chamber on 27 July. The trial was expected to commence in 2006.

The trial of Momcilo Krajisnik, charged in 2001 [YUN 2000, p. 1221] with eight counts of genocide, crimes against humanity, and violations of the laws or customs of war in more than 30 municipalities in Bosnia and Herzegovina during 1991 and 1992, began in 2004 [YUN 2004, p. 1279]. The Trial Chamber issued a scheduling order on 26 April, which allowed the prosecution's case to be completed by July. After hearing closing arguments by the defence, a judgement was expected to be rendered in 2006.

Kosta Bulatovic, a witness in the trial of Slobodan Milosevic, was charged with knowingly and wilfully interfering with the administration of justice on 19 and 20 April, by contumaciously refusing to answer the prosecution's questions. The trial was held on 6 May and a week later, the Trial Chamber found that the respondent was in contempt of the Tribunal. The Chamber imposed a sentence of four months' imprisonment; however, it suspended the operation of that sentence for a period of two years. On 27 May, Mr. Bulatovic filed an appeal, which was rejected by the Appeals Chamber.

Beqe Beqaj, indicted in 2004 [YUN 2004, p. 1277], was found guilty for contempt or attempted contempt for allegedly interfering or attempting to interfere with potential witnesses in the trial against Fatmir Limaj, Haradin Bala and Isak Musliu [YUN 2003, p. 1311]. He was provisionally released on 7 March and called back for trial on 22 April. The trial commenced on 25 April, and the Trial Chamber, in a judgement rendered on 30 April, found the accused guilty of contempt, but acquitted him for incitement to contempt. He was sentenced to four months' imprisonment, which he had already served in pre-trial detention and was released the following day.

In the case against Radovan Stankovic, who was charged in 2002, along with others [YUN 2002, p. 1277], of crimes against humanity and violations of the laws or customs of war for acts allegedly committed against Muslim women, the Prosecutor's motion [YUN 2004, p. 1281] requesting the referral of the case to the State Court of Bosnia and Herzegovina in Sarajevo was granted on 17 May. The decision was appealed on its merits by Mr. Stankovic, whereas the Prosecutor filed a notice of appeal on 30 May against the part of the decision requiring her to monitor the process in Sarajevo and report regularly to the Referral Bench. On 22 July, the Referral Bench granted the transfer of Mr. Stankovic.

On 8 June, Naser Oric, who had pleaded not guilty in 2004 [YUN 2004, p. 1280] to six counts of violations of law or customs of war, was acquitted by the Trial Chamber on both counts of alleged plunder of public or private property. The Chamber ordered the continuation of the case in relation to the other counts that were set out in the indictment. The Appeals Chamber granted an interlocutory appeal on 20 July that allowed the defence to call more witnesses and discuss more issues than originally outlined by the Trial Chamber.

On 29 June, the prosecution, in the case of Ljubisa Beara, who was indicted in 2004 [YUN 2004, p. 1277] for crimes committed in Srebrenica, filed a motion on 10 June, seeking a joinder of the case with those of Vujadin Popovic, Drago Nikolic, Ljubomir Borovcanin, Zdravko Tolimir, Radivoje Miletic and Milan Gvero and Vinko Pandurevic and Milorad Trbic (see p. 1390). On 29 June, the Tribunal President issued an order referring the joinder motion to the trial Chamber.

In the case against Zeljko Mejakic, Momcilo Gruban, Dusen Fustar and Dusko Knezevic, charged jointly in 2002 [YUN 2002, p. 1279], the Referral Bench, by its decision of 20 July, granted the Prosecutor's motion [YUN 2004, p. 1281] to refer the case to Bosnia and Herzegovina.

In the case against Milan Babic, sentenced to 13 years' imprisonment in 2004 for crimes against humanity and violations of the laws and customs of war [YUN 2004, p. 1277], the Appeals Chamber rendered its judgement in his appeal on 18 July and unanimously found that the Trial Chamber had erred in finding that the appellant's conduct subsequent to the crime of persecution could not be considered in mitigation solely because it did not include the alleviation of the suffering of victims, and had committed an error of law in not taking into account the appellant's attempts to further peace as a mitigating circumstance. While allowing the corresponding ground of appeal in part, the Appeals Chamber found that the error did not have an impact on the sentence. It unanimously dismissed each of the remaining grounds of appeal and affirmed the sentence of 13 years' imprisonment imposed by the Trial Chamber.

On 19 July, the Prosecutor filed a motion seeking a joinder of the case of Vojislav Seselj, charged in 2003 [YUN 2003, p. 1311; YUN 2004, p. 1277] in a 14-count indictment alleging crimes against humanity and violations of the laws or customs of war, with those of Milan Martic, Jovica Stanisic and Franko Simatovic [YUN 2003, p. 1311; YUN 2004, p. 1279], and for all four accused to be jointly charged and tried under one joint indictment.

Miroslav Deronjic, arrested in 2002 [YUN 2002, p. 1276], pleaded guilty in 2003 [YUN 2003, p. 1315] to charges brought against him and was sentenced in 2004 to 10 years' imprisonment [YUN 2004, p. 1278], which he appealed. On 20 July, the Appeals Chamber unanimously dismissed all the grounds of appeal filed by the appellant and affirmed the sentence imposed by the Trial Chamber.

In the case of Pasko Ljubicic [YUN 2001, p. 1200; YUN 2002, p. 1279; YUN 2003, p. 1313; YUN 2004, p. 1282], the Prosecutor, on 21 July, requested that it be referred to Bosnia and Herzegovina.

The trial against Mile Mrksic, Miroslav Radic and Veselin Sljivancanin commenced on 10 October. The three accused, who had been indicted jointly in 1997 [YUN 1997, p. 1322], were charged with five counts of crimes against humanity and four counts of violations of the laws or customs of war in relation to the mass killings in the Vukovar Hospital in November 1991. Earlier, on 8 February, the prosecution had filed a request with the Referral Bench to refer the case to Serbia and Montenegro or Croatia, which was later withdrawn.

Ivica Rajic pled guilty on 26 October to four counts of wilful killing, inhuman treatment, extensive destruction and appropriation of property in the area of Stupni Do in central Bosnia in 1993.

In the trial against Fatmir Limaj, Haradin Bala and Isak Musliu, who were arrested in 2003 [YUN 2003, p. 1311], the Trial Chamber in a judgement delivered on 30 November, acquitted Mr. Limaj and Mr. Musliu but found Mr. Bala guilty on three counts of violations of the laws or customs of war, torture, and cruel treatment and murder committed during 1998 in a Kosovo Liberation Army prison camp in the village of Llapushnik in central Kosovo (Serbia and Montenegro) and in the nearby Berisha mountains. He was sentenced to 13 years' imprisonment.

By a 7 December decision of the Trial Chamber, Miroslav Bralo was sentenced to 20 years' imprisonment, after he changed his plea of not guilty to guilty on 19 July, to charges including persecutions, murder and torture, for his role in an attack on the village of Ahmici in Bosnia and Herzegovina in 1993.

The trial of Milan Martic commenced on 13 December. He was indicted in 2002 [YUN 2002, p. 1276] for charges alleging crimes against humanity and violations of the laws or customs of war against Croat civilians committed by military and police organizations in the SAO Krajina (later Republic of Serbian Krajina) between 1991 and 1995. The trial was expected to conclude towards the end of 2006.

In the case against Slobodan Milosevic, the former President of the Federal Republic of Yugoslavia (FRY) (Serbia and Montenegro), whose trial commenced in 2002 [YUN 1999, p. 1214; YUN 2001, p. 1201; YUN 2002, p. 1277, YUN 2004, p. 1278], and who was charged with 66 counts of grave breaches of the 1949 Geneva Conventions, violations of the laws or customs of war, genocide or complicity in genocide and crimes against humanity, committed in Croatia, Bosnia and Herzegovina, and Kosovo, the Chamber ordered that the accused have the same amount of time to present his defence case as the prosecution. The parties indicated that they intended to bring cases in rebuttal and rejoinder, after the close of the defence case.

Judges of the Court

Ad litem judges

Extension of terms of office

The Secretary-General, on 7 January [A/59/666-S/2005/9], transmitted a letter to the General Assembly and Security Council Presidents, respectively, requesting the extension of the terms of office of seven short-term or ad litem judges of the Tribunal, which were expiring on 11 June, to allow them to finish adjudicating the cases on which they had begun working. Since those judges were not eligible for re-election, each trial would have to start anew with fresh panels of jurists, the rehearing of witnesses and representation of arguments if they were not allowed to continue, with substantial financial consequences and would negatively impact the target dates of the Tribunal's completion strategy. The Secretary-General also requested the appointment of two additional members from the current pool of ad litem judges to try cases anticipated to continue beyond 11 June.

SECURITY COUNCIL ACTION

On 18 January [meeting 5112], the Security Council unanimously adopted **resolution 1581(2005).** The draft [S/2005/31] was prepared in consultations among Council members.

The Security Council,

Taking note of the letter dated 6 January 2005 from the Secretary-General to the President of the Security Council,

Recalling its resolutions 1503(2003) of 28 August 2003 and 1534(2004) of 26 March 2004,

Bearing in mind the statement made to the Security Council at its 5086th meeting on 23 November 2004 by the President of the International Tribunal for the Former Yugoslavia, in which he expressed the commitment by the International Tribunal to the Completion Strategy,

Expressing its expectation that the extension of the terms of office of the ad litem judges concerned will enhance the effectiveness of trial proceedings and contribute towards ensuring the implementation of the Completion Strategy,

1. *Decides,* in response to the request by the Secretary-General, that:

(a) Judge Rasoazanany and Judge Swart, once replaced as ad litem judges of the International Tribunal for the Former Yugoslavia, finish the *Hadzihasanovic* case, which they have begun before expiry of their term of office;

(b) Judge Brydensholt and Judge Eser, once replaced as ad litem judges of the International Tribunal, finish the *Oric* case, which they have begun before expiry of their term of office;

(c) Judge Thelin and Judge Van den Wyngaert, once replaced as ad litem judges of the International Tribunal, finish the *Limaj* case, which they have begun before expiry of their term of office;

(d) Judge Canivell, once replaced as an ad litem judge of the International Tribunal, finish the Krajisnik case, which he has begun before expiry of his term of office;

(e) Judge Szenasi, if appointed to serve in the International Tribunal for the trial of the *Halilovic* case, proceed, once replaced as an ad litem judge of the International Tribunal, to finish that case, which he would have begun before expiry of his term of office;

(f) Judge Hanoteau, if appointed to serve in the International Tribunal for the trial of the *Krajisnik* case, proceed, once replaced as an ad litem judge of the International Tribunal, to finish that case, which he would have begun before expiry of his term of office;

2. *Takes note,* in this regard, of the intention of the International Tribunal to finish the Hadzihasanovic case before the end of September 2005, the *Halilovic* case before the end of October 2005, the *Oric* and *Limaj* cases before the end of November 2005 and the *Krajisnik* case before the end of April 2006.

The General Assembly, by **decision 59/406 B** of 20 January, endorsed the Secretary-General's recommendations, which were also endorsed by the Council in resolution 1581(2005) (see above).

Election of judges

The Secretary-General, on 24 February [S/2005/127], informed the Security Council that, in response to the request for nominations to replace the 27 ad litem judges whose terms of office were to expire on 11 June, 11 nominations had been received for the election of ad litem judges of the Trial Chambers within the statutory 60-day period. Since those nominations were short of the minimum number of 54 required by the Court's Statute, he requested the Council to extend the deadline for nominations by 30 days. On 14 March [S/2005/159], the Council agreed to extend the deadline until 31 March. On 11 April [S/2005/236], the Secretary-General forwarded to the Council and the General Assembly, respectively, the list of 22 nominations received, together with their curricula vitae.

SECURITY COUNCIL ACTION

On 20 April [meeting 5165], the Security Council unanimously adopted **resolution 1597(2005).** The draft [S/2005/261] was prepared in consultations among Council members.

The Security Council,

Reaffirming its resolutions 827(1993) of 25 May 1993, 1166(1998) of 13 May 1998, 1329(2000) of 30 November 2000, 1411(2002) of 17 May 2002, 1431(2002) of 14 August 2002, 1481(2003) of 19 May 2003, 1503(2003) of 28 August 2003 and 1534(2004) of 26 March 2004,

Having considered the letter dated 24 February 2005 from the Secretary-General to the President of the Security Council transmitting the list of candidates for election as ad litem judges of the International Tribunal for the Former Yugoslavia,

Noting that the Secretary-General had suggested that the deadline for nominations be extended until 31 March 2005 and that the President indicated in his reply of 14 March 2005 that the Security Council had agreed to the extension of the deadline,

Having considered the letter dated 11 April 2005 from the Secretary-General to the President of the Security Council, in which the Secretary-General suggested that the deadline for the nomination of candidates for election as ad litem judges be further extended,

Noting that the number of candidates continues to fall short of the minimum number required by the statute of the Tribunal to be elected,

Considering that the twenty-seven ad litem judges elected by the General Assembly at its 102nd plenary meeting on 12 June 2001 whose term of office expires on 11 June 2005 should be eligible for re-election, and wishing to amend the statute for that purpose,

Noting that, should the cumulative period of service of an ad litem judge of the Tribunal amount to three years or more, this will not result in any change in their entitlements or benefits and, in particular, will not give rise to any additional entitlements or benefits other than those that already exist and which will, in such an eventuality, be extended pro-rata by virtue of the extension of service,

Acting under Chapter VII of the Charter of the United Nations,

1. *Decides* to amend article 13 ter of the statute of the International Tribunal for the Former Yugoslavia and to replace that article with the provision set out in the annex to the present resolution;

2. *Decides,* further to the letter dated 11 April 2005 from the Secretary-General to the President of the Se-

curity Council to extend the deadline for nominations of ad litem judges under the amended provision of the statute for a further thirty days from the date of the adoption of the present resolution;

3. *Decides* to remain actively seized of the matter.

Annex

Article 13 ter Election and appointment of ad litem judges

1. The ad litem judges of the International Tribunal shall be elected by the General Assembly from a list submitted by the Security Council in the following manner.

(a) The Secretary-General shall invite nominations for ad litem judges of the International Tribunal from States Members of the United Nations and non-member States maintaining permanent observer missions at United Nations Headquarters;

(b) Within sixty days of the date of the invitation of the Secretary-General, each State may nominate up to four candidates meeting the qualifications set out in article 13 of the statute, taking into account the importance of a fair representation of female and male candidates;

(c) The Secretary-General shall forward the nominations received to the Security Council. From the nominations received the Security Council shall establish a list of not less than fifty-four candidates, taking due account of the adequate representation of the principal legal systems of the world and bearing in mind the importance of equitable geographical distribution;

(d) The President of the Security Council shall transmit the list of candidates to the President of the General Assembly. From that list the General Assembly shall elect the twenty-seven ad litem judges of the International Tribunal. The candidates who receive an absolute majority of the votes of the States Members of the United Nations and of the non-member States maintaining permanent observer missions at United Nations Headquarters shall be declared elected;

(e) The ad litem judges shall be declared elected for a term of four years. They shall be eligible for re-election.

2. During any term, ad litem judges will be appointed by the Secretary-General, upon request of the President of the International Tribunal, to serve in the Trial Chambers for one or more trials, for a cumulative period of up to, but not including three years. When requesting the appointment of any particular ad litem judge, the President of the International Tribunal shall bear in mind the criteria set out in article 13 of the statute regarding the composition of the Chambers and sections of the Trial Chambers, the considerations set out in paragraphs 1 *(b)* and *(c)* above and the number of votes the ad litem judge received in the General Assembly.

On 27 May [S/2005/346], the Secretary-General informed the Council that the number of nominations stood at 27 and requested that it extend further the deadline for nominations for the ad litem judges by another 30 days from the date of the Council's decision. The Council, by a 7 June letter to the Secretary-General [S/2005/371], postponed the deadline for nominations until 7 July. By a 1 August note [A/59/888], the Secretary-General submitted to the General Assembly the curricula vitae of the 34 candidates nominated.

SECURITY COUNCIL ACTION

On 26 July [meeting 5236], the Security Council unanimously adopted **resolution 1613(2005).** The draft [S/2005/478] was prepared in consultations among Council members.

The Security Council,

Recalling its resolutions 827(1993) of 25 May 1993, 1166(1998) of 13 May 1998, 1329(2000) of 30 November 2000, 1411(2002) of 17 May 2002, 1431(2002) of 14 August 2002, 1481(2003) of 19 May 2003, 1503(2003) of 28 August 2003, 1534(2004) of 26 March 2004 and 1597(2005) of 20 April 2005,

Having considered the nominations for ad litem judges of the International Tribunal for the Former Yugoslavia received by the Secretary-General,

Forwards the following nominations to the General Assembly in accordance with article 13 ter, paragraph 1 *(d)*, of the statute of the International Tribunal:

Mr. Tanvir Bashir Ansari (Pakistan)
Mr. Melville Baird (Trinidad and Tobago)
Mr. Frans Bauduin (The Netherlands)
Mr. Giancarlo Roberto Bellelli (Italy)
Mr. Ishaq Usman Bello (Nigeria)
Mr. Ali Nawaz Chowhan (Pakistan)
Mr. Pedro David (Argentina)
Mr. Ahmad Farawati (Syrian Arab Republic)
Ms. Elizabeth Gwaunza (Zimbabwe)
Mr. Burton Hall (Bahamas)
Mr. Frederik Harhoff (Denmark)
Mr. Frank Höpfel (Austria)
Ms. Tsvetana Kamenova (Bulgaria)
Mr. Muhammad Muzammal Khan (Pakistan)
Mr. Uldis Kinis (Latvia)
Mr. Raimo Lahti (Finland)
Ms. Flavia Lattanzi (Italy)
Mr. Antoine Mindua (Democratic Republic of the Congo)
Mr. Jawdat Naboty (Syrian Arab Republic)
Ms. Janet Nosworthy (Jamaica)
Ms. Chioma Egondu Nwosu-Iheme (Nigeria)
Ms. Prisca Matimba Nyambe (Zambia)
Ms. Michèle Picard (France)
Mr. Brynmor Pollard (Guyana)
Mr. Árpád Prandler (Hungary)
Ms. Kimberly Prost (Canada)
Sheikh Abdul Rashid (Pakistan)
Ms. Vonimbolana Rasoazanany (Madagascar)
Mr. Ole Bjrrn Strle (Norway)
Mr. Krister Thelin (Sweden)
Mr. Klaus Tolksdorf (Germany)
Mr. Stefan Trechsel (Switzerland)
Mr. Abubakar Bashir Wali (Nigeria)
Tan Sri Dato' Lamin bin Haji Mohd Yunus (Malaysia)

By a 9 August memorandum [A/59/887], the Secretary-General forwarded to the Assembly the list of 34 candidates for ad litem judges established by the Council in resolution 1613(2005)

(above). He also set out the procedure for the election of ad litem judges. On 23 August [A/59/887 & Add.1], he informed the Assembly that Mr. Muhammad Muzammal Khan and Sheikh Abdul Rashid (Pakistan) had withdrawn their candidature.

On 18 August [A/59/898], Liechtenstein, in a letter to the General Assembly President, proposed that the procedure for the election of ad litem judges set out in the Secretary-General's letter (see above) be modified to the effect that, if, in the first ballot, more than 27 candidates obtained an absolute majority of votes, the 27 with the highest number of votes should be considered elected. In the event of a tie for a remaining seat, there should be a restricted ballot limited to those candidates who had obtained an equal number of votes.

GENERAL ASSEMBLY ACTION

On 24 August [meeting 116], the General Assembly adopted **decision 59/406 C** without vote [agenda item 18].

Election of judges of the International Tribunal for the Prosecution of Persons Responsible for Serious Violations of International Humanitarian Law Committed in the Territory of the Former Yugoslavia since 1991

C

At its 116th plenary meeting, on 24 August 2005, the General Assembly, in accordance with article 13 ter of the statute of the International Tribunal for the Prosecution of Persons Responsible for Serious Violations of International Humanitarian Law Committed in the Territory of the Former Yugoslavia since 1991, elected the following twenty-seven ad litem judges for a four-year term of office beginning on 24 August 2005:

Mr. Melville BAIRD (Trinidad and Tobago)
Mr. Frans BAUDUIN (Netherlands)
Mr. Ali Nawaz CHOWHAN (Pakistan)
Mr. Pedro DAVID (Argentina)
Ms. Elizabeth GWAUNZA (Zimbabwe)
Mr. Burton HALL (Bahamas)
Mr. Frederik HARHOFF (Denmark)
Mr. Frank HÖPFEL (Austria)
Ms. Tsvetana KAMENOVA (Bulgaria)
Mr. Uldis KINIS (Latvia)
Mr. Raimo LAHTI (Finland)
Ms. Flavia LATTANZI (Italy)
Mr. Antoine MINDUA (Democratic Republic of the Congo)
Mr. Jawdat NABOTY (Syrian Arab Republic)
Ms. Janet NOSWORTHY (Jamaica)
Ms. Chioma Egondu NWOSU-IHEME (Nigeria)
Ms. Prisca Matimba NYAMBE (Zambia)
Ms. Michèle PICARD (France)
Mr. Brynmor POLLARD (Guyana)
Mr. Árpád PRANDLER (Hungary)
Ms. Kimberly PROST (Canada)
Ms. Vonimbolana RASOAZANANY (Madagascar)
Mr. Ole Bjrrn STRLE (Norway)
Mr. Krister THELIN (Sweden)
Mr. Klaus TOLKSDORF (Germany)

Mr. Stefan TRECHSEL (Switzerland)
Tan Sri Dato' Lamin Haji MOHD YUNUS (Malaysia)

Permanent judges

On 14 September [A/60/362-S/2005/593], the Secretary-General forwarded to the Security Council and the General Assembly a request from the President of the Tribunal to have Judge Christine Van Den Wyngaret (Belgium), whose term of office as an ad litem judge was extended by Council resolution 1581(2005) (see p. 1392) to 30 November, to commence her term of office as a permanent judge on 3 October for the *Mrksic et al* case; Judge Van Den Wyngaret had been elected by Assembly decision 59/406 [YUN 2004, p. 1283] to serve as a permanent judge of the Tribunal, beginning on 17 November.

SECURITY COUNCIL ACTION

On 30 September [meeting 5273], the Security Council unanimously adopted **resolution 1629 (2005).** The draft [S/2005/615] was prepared in consultations among Council members.

The Security Council,
Taking note of the letter dated 14 September 2005 from the Secretary-General to the President of the Security Council,
Decides that, notwithstanding article 12 of the statute of the International Tribunal for the Prosecution of Persons Responsible for Serious Violations of International Humanitarian Law Committed in the Territory of the Former Yugoslavia since 1991 and notwithstanding the fact that Judge Christine Van Den Wyngaert's elected term as a permanent judge of the Tribunal will, in accordance with article 13 bis of the statute of the Tribunal, only begin on 17 November 2005, she shall be assigned as a permanent judge to the *Mrksic et al.* case, which is due to commence on 3 October 2005.

The Assembly endorsed the Council's action on 4 October (**decision 60/402**).

Office of the Prosecutor

During the year, there was a significant increase in pretrial, trial and appellate work outputs. No new indictments (except for contempt of court) were issued. Efforts were made to obtain full cooperation of relevant countries, resulting in several arrests and better production of documents. The Office of the Prosecutor continued to assist in the reform of the judicial systems of the countries of the Former Yugoslavia. It continued to transfer cases to national courts and co-operated with the national authorities on non-referred war crimes cases. Altogether, 13 motions for the transfer of 21 accused were filed.

Cooperation continued with relevant Governments and international institutions to secure arrests or surrenders. Cooperation of the entity government of the Federation of Bosnia and Herzegovina, and the Government of Croatia, with regard to requests for assistance, information, archives, witnesses and suspects, were satisfactory. However, the authorities of Serbia and Montenegro, in particular the Government of Serbia, and the authorities of the entity government of the Republika Srpska (Bosnia and Herzegovina) failed to arrest a single fugitive.

The Registry

The Registry continued to provide administrative and judicial support to the Tribunal, and facilitated the work of the Chambers and the Office of the Prosecutor and the defence. It also managed the Detention Unit, the Victims and Witnesses Section, the legal aid office and the interpretation and translation service. The Registry also facilitated the implementation of the Tribunal's completion strategy, initiated in 2002 [YUN 2002, p. 1275], including the action plan to relocate protected witnesses and their families. In 2005, the Detention Unit successfully moved all detainees, staff and infrastructure from two physically separate units into a single facility of 84 cells, thereby facilitating a more cohesive programme of remand for all detainees and allowing for better flexibility to hold high-profile accused. The former Public Information Service and Outreach Programme were reorganized into the Communications Services. The Web Unit of the Media/Web Outreach Office continued to develop the Tribunal website in English, French and Bosnian/Croatian/Serbian as well as information in Albanian and Macedonian and maintained internet broadcast of courtroom proceedings.

Financing

2004-2005

Report of Secretary-General. The second performance report of ICTY for the 2004-2005 biennium [A/60/575], submitted in response to General Assembly resolution 59/274 [YUN 2004, p. 1285], reflected a net reduction of $21,962,900 in the overall resource requirement, as compared to the revised appropriation of $298,437,000 net for that biennium. The Assembly was being requested to further revise the appropriation for the biennium to $308,305,200 gross ($276,474,100 net).

ACABQ report. In December [A/60/591], the Advisory Committee on Administrative and Budgetary Questions (ACABQ) recommended approval of the revised appropriation for the 2004-2005 biennium.

On 23 December [meeting 69], the General Assembly, on the recommendation of the Fifth (Administrative and Budgetary) Committee [A/60/606], adopted **resolution 60/242** without vote [agenda item 134].

Second performance report for the biennium 2004-2005 on the International Tribunal for the Prosecution of Persons Responsible for Serious Violations of International Humanitarian Law Committed in the Territory of the Former Yugoslavia since 1991

The General Assembly,

Having considered the second performance report of the Secretary-General for the biennium 2004-2005 on the International Tribunal for the Prosecution of Persons Responsible for Serious Violations of International Humanitarian Law Committed in the Territory of the Former Yugoslavia since 1991 and the related report of the Advisory Committee on Administrative and Budgetary Questions,

Recalling its resolution 47/235 of 14 September 1993 on the financing of the International Tribunal for the Former Yugoslavia and its subsequent resolutions thereon, the latest of which were resolutions 58/255 of 23 December 2003 and 59/274 of 23 December 2004,

1. _Takes note_ of the second performance report of the Secretary-General for the biennium 2004-2005 on the International Tribunal for the Prosecution of Persons Responsible for Serious Violations of International Humanitarian Law Committed in the Territory of the Former Yugoslavia since 1991 and the related report of the Advisory Committee on Administrative and Budgetary Questions;

2. _Endorses_ the conclusions and recommendations contained in the report of the Advisory Committee on Administrative and Budgetary Questions;

3. _Resolves_ that, for the biennium 2004-2005, the amount of 329,317,900 United States dollars gross (298,437,000 dollars net) approved in its resolution 59/274 for the budget of the International Tribunal for the Former Yugoslavia shall be adjusted by the amount of 21,012,700 dollars gross (21,962,900 dollars net) for a total amount of 308,305,200 dollars gross (276,474,100 dollars net).

2006-2007

In August [A/60/264], the Secretary-General presented resource requirements for ICTY for the 2006-2007 biennium, which before recosting amounted to $310,884,100 gross ($280,782,700 net) and reflected a decrease in real terms of $17,597,600 net, or 5.9 per cent, compared to the revised appropriation for 2004-2005 (see above). The Secretary-General updated the costing parameters in December [A/60/600]. The revised figure of $305,137,300 took into account the effects of changes in the rates of exchange and inflation.

The recommendations of ACABQ were contained in its December report [A/60/591].

On 23 December [meeting 69], the General Assembly, on the recommendation of the Fifth Committee [A/60/606], adopted **resolution 60/243** without vote [agenda item 135].

Financing of the International Tribunal for the Prosecution of Persons Responsible for Serious Violations of International Humanitarian Law Committed in the Territory of the Former Yugoslavia since 1991

The General Assembly,

Having considered the reports of the Secretary-General on the financing for the biennium 2006-2007 of the International Tribunal for the Prosecution of Persons Responsible for Serious Violations of International Humanitarian Law Committed in the Territory of the Former Yugoslavia since 1991, on staff retention and legacy issues and on the revised estimates arising from changes in rates of exchange and inflation,

Having also considered the related reports of the Advisory Committee on Administrative and Budgetary Questions,

Recalling its resolution 47/235 of 14 September 1993 on the financing of the International Tribunal for the Former Yugoslavia and its subsequent resolutions thereon, the latest of which were resolutions 58/255 of 23 December 2003 and 59/274 of 23 December 2004,

1. _Takes note_ of the reports of the Secretary-General on the financing for the biennium 2006-2007 of the International Tribunal for the Prosecution of Persons Responsible for Serious Violations of International Humanitarian Law Committed in the Territory of the Former Yugoslavia since 1991, on staff retention and legacy issues and on the revised estimates arising from changes in rates of exchange and inflation;

2. _Endorses_ the conclusions and recommendations contained in the related reports of the Advisory Committee on Administrative and Budgetary Questions;

3. _Decides_ to appropriate to the Special Account for the International Tribunal for the Prosecution of Persons Responsible for Serious Violations of International Humanitarian Law Committed in the Territory of the Former Yugoslavia since 1991, a total amount of 305,137,300 United States dollars gross (278,559,400 dollars net) for the biennium 2006-2007, as detailed in the annex to the present resolution;

4. _Decides also_ that the total assessment for 2006 under the Special Account would amount to 152,443,900 dollars, being half of the estimated appropriation approved for the biennium 2006-2007 after taking into account 124,750 dollars, which is half of the estimated income for the biennium 2006-2007 of 249,500 dollars;

5. _Decides further_ to apportion the amount of 76,221,950 dollars gross (69,577,475 dollars net) among Member States in accordance with the scale of assessments applicable to the regular budget of the United Nations for 2006, as set out in General Assembly resolution 58/1 B of 23 December 2003;

6. _Decides_ to apportion the amount of 76,221,950 dollars gross (69,577,475 dollars net) among Member States in accordance with the scale of assessments applicable to peacekeeping operations for 2006;

7. *Decides also* that, in accordance with the provisions of its resolution 973(X) of 15 December 1955, there shall be set off against the apportionment among Member States, as provided for in paragraphs 5 and 6 above, their respective share in the Tax Equalization Fund of the estimated staff assessment income of 13,288,950 dollars approved for the International Tribunal for the Former Yugoslavia for 2006;

8. *Decides further* that the provisions for the application of credits under regulations 3.2 *(d)*, 5.3 and 5.4 of the Financial Regulations and Rules of the United Nations shall be suspended in respect of the amount of 21,012,700 dollars gross (21,962,900 dollars net), which otherwise would have to be surrendered pursuant to those provisions;

9. *Encourages* the International Tribunal for the Former Yugoslavia to continue its efforts to refer cases involving intermediate and lower-ranking accused to competent national jurisdictions in the former Yugoslavia pursuant to rule 11 bis of its Rules of Procedure and Evidence.

Annex

Financing of the International Tribunal for the Prosecution of Persons Responsible for Serious Violations of International Humanitarian Law Committed in the Territory of the Former Yugoslavia since 1991

	Gross	Net
	(United States dollars)	
Estimated appropriation for the biennium 2006-2007	320 842 900	289 925 300
Revised estimates: effect of changes in rates of exchange and inflation	(15 705 600)	(11 365 900)
Reductions made by the Advisory Committee on Administrative and Budgetary Questions (after recosting)	-	-
Reductions proposed by the Fifth Committee	-	-
Estimated initial appropriation for the biennium 2006-2007	305 137 300	278 559 400
Estimated income for the biennium 2006-2007	(249 500)	(249 500)
Assessment for 2006	152 443 900	139 154 950
Of which:		
Contributions assessed on Member States in accordance with the scale of assessments applicable to the regular budget of the United Nations for 2006	76 221 950	69 577 475
Contributions assessed on Member States in accordance with the scale of assessments applicable to peacekeeping operations of the United Nations for 2006	76 221 950	69 577 475

International Tribunal for Rwanda

In 2005, the International Criminal Tribunal for Rwanda (ICTR), in Arusha, the United Republic of Tanzania, delivered 3 trial judgements. In May [S/2005/336], the ICTR President submitted an updated and revised completion strategy (see p. 1402), which confirmed that the Tribunal was on course to complete the trials by 2008. The lifting of the freeze on the recruitment of new staff at the Tribunal at the beginning of 2005, allowed the Tribunal to recruit key personnel directly related to court proceedings. A fourth court room, inaugurated on 1 March through voluntary contributions from Norway and the United Kingdom, would allow full-day sessions of trials.

The activities of ICTR, established by Security Council resolution 955(1994) [YUN 1994, p. 299], were covered in two reports to the Council and the General Assembly, for the periods 1 July 2004 to 30 June 2005 [A/60/229-S/2005/534] and 1 July 2005 to 30 June 2006 [A/61/265-S/2006/658]. On 10 October, the Assembly took note of the 2004/2005 report (**decision 60/505**).

The Chambers

New cases

Following his indictment of 22 July, Joseph Serugendo, former Technical Chief of Radio Rwanda and Radio Télévision Libre des Milles Collines (RTLM), was arrested on 16 September in Libreville, Gabon, and transferred to the Tribunal's Detention Facility in Arusha on 23 September. According to the indictment, the accused acted in concert with others, to organize and conduct the 1994 genocide in Rwanda.

Callixte Kalimanzira, acting Minister of Interior of Rwanda in 1994, surrendered to the Tanzanian authorities on 8 November and was immediately transferred to the Detention Facility. He was charged with genocide, in the alternative complicity in genocide and with direct and public indictment to commit genocide.

Ongoing trials

On 25 January, the prosecution closed its case against Athanase Seromba, the Catholic priest of Nyange Parish in the Kivumu Commune, Kibuye Prefecture, whose trial commenced in 2004 [YUN 2004, p. 1288]. The defence case was scheduled to commence on 10 May; however, on 15 April, the accused requested a withdrawal of his assigned lead counsel, which resulted in a delay in the resumption of trial. On 8 June, the Registrar appointed a new lead counsel. The defence started its case on 31 October.

By a decision of 28 January, the Appeals Chamber in the case against Joseph Nzabirinda, disposed his notice of appeal of the Trial Chamber's "Decision on Joseph Nzabirinda's Motion to Set Aside the Registrar's Decision to Withhold the Amount Owed to Him in Meeting the Cost of His Defence". The Appeals Chamber held that the impugned decision was without interlocutory appeal and that it lacked jurisdiction to consider the Appellant's notice of appeal. Mr. Nzabirinda, a former investigator working for the defence team of Sylvain Nsabimana, was alleged to have carried out crimes in Ngoma commune together with Joseph Kanyabashi. He was arrested in 2001 [YUN 2001, p. 1208] and transferred to the Tribunal in 2002 [YUN 2002, p. 128].

In the joint trial against Pauline Nyiramasuhuko, Arsène Shalom Ntahobali, Sylvain Nsabimana, Alphonse Nteziryayo, Joseph Kanyabashi and Elie Ndayambaje, referred to as the "Butare" case, which began in 2001 [YUN 2001, p. 1208], the defence commenced its proceeding on 31 January following the prosecution's closure of its case in 2004. [YUN 2004, p. 1287].

A separate and amended indictment against André Rwamakuba, a former Minister of Primary and Secondary Education, who was indicted with three other accused in the case of *Karemera* and Others, was filed on 23 February. His trial commenced on 9 June and was expected to end in 2006.

On 14 March, Vincent Rutaganira, who had pleaded not guilty in 2002 [YUN 2002, p. 1285], but entered a guilty plea for crimes against humanity (extermination) in 2004 [YUN 2004, p. 1288], was sentenced to 6 years in prison.

The defence case of four senior Rwandan military officers (Théoneste Bagosora, Gratien Kabiligi, Anatole Nsengiyumva, Aloys Ntabakuze), which was originally scheduled for 12 January, had to be adjourned following the withdrawal of an assigned lead counsel by the Registrar. The trial, which began in 2002 [YUN 2002, p. 1285] and was referred to as the "Military I" case, resumed on 11 April. The presentation of defence evidence was scheduled to conclude in 2006.

The case against Mikaeli Muhimana, which commenced in 2004 [YUN 2004, p. 1287], closed on 20 January. On 28 April, he was convicted of genocide and crimes against humanity (murder and rape) and sentenced to imprisonment for life. Following the judgment, he was granted an extension of time for filing the notice of appeal until no more than 30 days from when the French text of the judgment, expected in 2006, would become available.

In a judgement delivered on 20 May, the Appeals Chamber, in the case against Laurent Semanza, whose trial began in 2000 [YUN 2000,

p. 1226, YUN 2001, p. 1208, YUN 2002, p. 1286, YUN 2004, p. 1288], partly reversed a conviction for complicity in genocide; reversed an acquittal for genocide and entered a conviction for genocide; partly reversed a conviction for aiding and abetting extermination as a crime against humanity and entered a conviction for ordering extermination; reversed acquittals for two counts of serious violations of common article 3 of the 1949 Geneva Conventions and the 1977 Additional Protocol thereto and entered convictions under those counts for aiding and abetting murders, instigating rape, torture and murder and for committing torture and intentional murder. It affirmed the remainder of the convictions entered by the Trial Chamber, quashed the sentence of 25 years' imprisonment and entered a new sentence of 35 years' imprisonment.

On 23 May, in the case of Juvénal Kajelijeli, the Appeals Chamber, vacating the convictions for genocide and extermination insofar as they were based on a finding of superior responsibility and having found that the accused rights were seriously violated during his arrest and pre-trial detention, set aside the two life sentences and one sentence of 15 years in prison imposed by the Trial Chamber in 2003 [YUN 2003, p. 1321], and converted them into a single sentence of 45 years' imprisonment.

On 23 June, the prosecution closed its case against Casimir Bizimungu, Justin Mugenzi, Jérôme Bicamumpaka and Prosper Mugiraneza, referred to as the "Government II" case [YUN 1999, pp. 1222 & 1223, YUN 2003, p. 1321]. The Appeals Chamber had earlier dismissed the prosecution's appeal against the Trial Chamber's decision denying leave to amend the indictment [YUN 2004, p. 1286]. The presentation by the defence for Mr. Mugenzi, the former Minister of Commerce of Rwanda, commenced on 1 November.

On 20 July, the prosecution closed its case against Tharcisse Muvunyi, the former colonel and commander of the École sous-officiers, whose trial commenced in 2004, after having called a total of 24 witnesses. The defence case started on 5 December and was expected to close by May 2006.

In the case of Jean de Dieu Kamuhanda, who had appealed the life sentences imposed on him by the Trial Chamber in 2004 [YUN 2004, p.1286], the Appeals Chamber, on 19 May, reaffirmed the convictions for genocide and extermination as crimes against humanity, vacated convictions for instigating and aiding and abetting genocide and extermination and affirmed the two concurrent sentences of imprisonment for life.

A fresh joint trial against Edouard Karemera, Andre Rwamakuba, Matthieu Ngirumpatse and

Joseph Nzirorera commenced on 19 September. The trial, which had originally started in 2003 [YUN 2003, p. 1321] and was referred to as the "Government I" case [YUN 1999, pp. 1222 & 1223], was terminated when the Appeals Chamber, in 2004 [YUN 2004, p. 1287], disqualified the judges and ordered a new trial to commence in 2005. However, Mr. Rwamakuba (see above), by a decision of 14 February, was severed from the case and was tried as a single accused (see below).

The trial against Jean Mpambara, former bourgmestre of Rukara commune, who was arrested in 2001 [YUN 2001, p. 1207], commenced on 19 September. He was charged with one count of genocide, and a judgment was expected in 2006.

The trial against Protais Zigiranyirazo commenced on 3 October. He was arrested in 2001 [YUN 2001, p. 1207], and charged with extermination or murder as a crime against humanity and held membership of the Akazu, the inner circle of the late President of Rwanda, Juvénal Habyarimana. The defence was expected to present its case in October 2006.

On 17 November, Paul Bisengimana, the former bourgmestre of Gikoro commune, who was arrested in 2001 and pleaded not guilty to charges in 2002 [YUN 2002, p. 1285], entered a guilty plea to murder and extermination as crimes against humanity. Following the Chamber's initial rejection of the plea, the prosecution filed an amended indictment on 7 December, to which he subsequently pleaded guilty.

On 13 December, Aloys Simba, a retired military officer who was convicted of genocide and crimes against humanity (extermination and murder) for his role in massacres in Gikongoro Prefecture, was sentenced to 25 years' imprisonment. He had earlier pleaded not guilty to charges made against him in 2002 [YUN 2002, p. 1285] and his trial commenced in 2004 [YUN 2004, p. 1287].

Office of the Prosecutor

The Prosecutor continued to implement the completion strategy, in consultation with the President of the Tribunal. Further efforts were made in identifying States willing to try Tribunal indictees that were referred to them. During the year, various measures were taken to improve the prosecution's information and evidence management capacity and implementation of prosecutorial best practices. In that regard, impetus was given towards staff training and continuing education in the pursuit of the completion strategy. The Office of the Prosecutor stepped up its tracking activities to ensure that as many fugitives as possible were arrested sufficiently early to enable the Chambers to complete their trials before the

end of 2008. In addition, the Prosecutor visited a number of African countries in which some of the fugitives were suspected to be and urged national authorities to cooperate more significantly in their arrest.

The Registry

The Registry continued to support the judicial process by servicing the Tribunal's other organs, participating in implementing the completion strategy and seeking support from States, international organizations and other stakeholders in the conduct of proceedings. During the year, it stepped up its outreach activities through judicial visits to the Tribunal and capacity-building training for members of the Rwandan judiciary and universities. It also maintained high-level diplomatic contacts and drafted numerous agreements with States or international organizations to ensure the continued cooperation of Member States and international organizations with the Tribunal. Meanwhile, the Press and Public Affairs Unit increased its monitoring and internal circulation of Tribunal-related media reports and continued to improve the Tribunal's website.

Financing

2004-2005

Report of Secretary-General. In December [A/60/573], the Secretary-General submitted, in response to General Assembly resolution 59/273 [YUN 2004, p. 1290], the second performance report of ICTR for the 2004-2005 biennium, which reflected a decrease in requirements of $3,307,300 gross ($3,875,900 net) as compared with the revised appropriation of $255,909,500 (gross) for the 2004-2005 biennium. The reduction in requirements was due to the combined effect of exchange rates and inflation ($1,285,100 gross) and decreases in post incumbency and other changes ($4,592,400 gross). The General Assembly was requested to revise the appropriation for 2004-2005 to $252,602,200 gross ($227,630,600 net) for the Special Account for ICTR.

ACABQ's comments and observations on the performance report were contained in its December report [A/60/591].

GENERAL ASSEMBLY ACTION

On 23 December [meeting 69], the General Assembly, on the recommendation of the Fifth Committee [A/60/605], adopted **resolution 60/240** without vote [agenda item 134].

Second performance report for the biennium 2004-2005 on the International Criminal Tribunal for the Prosecution of Persons Responsible for Genocide and Other Serious Violations of International Humanitarian Law Committed in the Territory of Rwanda and Rwandan Citizens Responsible for Genocide and Other Such Violations Committed in the Territory of Neighbouring States between 1 January and 31 December 1994

The General Assembly,

Having considered the second performance report of the Secretary-General for the biennium 2004-2005 on the International Criminal Tribunal for the Prosecution of Persons Responsible for Genocide and Other Serious Violations of International Humanitarian Law Committed in the Territory of Rwanda and Rwandan Citizens Responsible for Genocide and Other Such Violations Committed in the Territory of Neighbouring States between 1 January and 31 December 1994 and the related report of the Advisory Committee on Administrative and Budgetary Questions,

Recalling its resolution 49/251 of 20 July 1995 on the financing of the International Criminal Tribunal for Rwanda and its subsequent resolutions thereon, the latest of which were resolutions 58/253 of 23 December 2003 and 59/273 of 23 December 2004,

1. *Takes note* of the second performance report of the Secretary-General for the biennium 2004-2005 on the International Criminal Tribunal for the Prosecution of Persons Responsible for Genocide and Other Serious Violations of International Humanitarian Law Committed in the Territory of Rwanda and Rwandan Citizens Responsible for Genocide and Other Such Violations Committed in the Territory of Neighbouring States between 1 January and 31 December 1994 and the related report of the Advisory Committee on Administrative and Budgetary Questions;

2. *Endorses* the conclusions and recommendations contained in the report of the Advisory Committee on Administrative and Budgetary Questions;

3. *Resolves* that, for the biennium 2004-2005, the amount of 255,909,500 United States dollars gross (231,506,500 dollars net) approved in its resolution 59/273 for the budget of the International Criminal Tribunal for Rwanda shall be adjusted by the amount of 3,307,300 dollars gross (3,875,900 dollars net) for a total amount of 252,602,200 dollars gross (227,630,600 dollars net).

2006-2007

In August [A/60/265], the Secretary-General, as requested by the General Assembly in resolution 59/273 [YUN 2004, p 1290], submitted resource requirements for the 2006-2007 biennium for ICTR, in the amount of $261,640,400 gross ($237,265,600 net) before recosting, reflecting growth in real terms of $5,759,100 net or 2.5 per cent, compared with the revised appropriation for the 2004-2005 biennium. In December, [A/60/600], the Secretary-General submitted revised estimates amounting to $305,137,300, after recosting.

ACABQ, in December [A/60/591], recommended approval of the Secretary-General's proposals.

On 23 December [meeting 69], the General Assembly, on the recommendation of the Fifth Committee [A/60/605], adopted **resolution 60/241** without vote [agenda item 134].

Financing of the International Criminal Tribunal for the Prosecution of Persons Responsible for Genocide and Other Serious Violations of International Humanitarian Law Committed in the Territory of Rwanda and Rwandan Citizens Responsible for Genocide and Other Such Violations Committed in the Territory of Neighbouring States between 1 January and 31 December 1994

The General Assembly,

Having considered the reports of the Secretary-General on the financing for the biennium 2006-2007 of the International Criminal Tribunal for the Prosecution of Persons Responsible for Genocide and Other Serious Violations of International Humanitarian Law Committed in the Territory of Rwanda and Rwandan Citizens Responsible for Genocide and Other Such Violations Committed in the Territory of Neighbouring States between 1 January and 31 December 1994, on staff retention and legacy issues and on the revised estimates arising from changes in rates of exchange and inflation,

Having also considered the related reports of the Advisory Committee on Administrative and Budgetary Questions,

Recalling its resolution 49/251 of 20 July 1995 on the financing of the International Criminal Tribunal for Rwanda and its subsequent resolutions thereon, the latest of which were resolutions 58/253 of 23 December 2003 and 59/273 of 23 December 2004,

1. *Takes note* of the reports of the Secretary-General on the financing for the biennium 2006-2007 of the International Criminal Tribunal for the Prosecution of Persons Responsible for Genocide and Other Serious Violations of International Humanitarian Law Committed in the Territory of Rwanda and Rwandan Citizens Responsible for Genocide and Other Such Violations Committed in the Territory of Neighbouring States between 1 January and 31 December 1994, on staff retention and legacy issues and on the revised estimates arising from changes in rates of exchange and inflation;

2. *Endorses* the conclusions and recommendations contained in the related reports of the Advisory Committee on Administrative and Budgetary Questions;

3. *Decides* to appropriate to the Special Account for the International Criminal Tribunal for the Prosecution of Persons Responsible for Genocide and Other Serious Violations of International Humanitarian Law Committed in the Territory of Rwanda and Rwandan Citizens Responsible for Genocide and Other Such Violations Committed in the Territory of Neighbouring States between 1 January and 31 December 1994, a total amount of 269,758,400 United States dollars gross (246,890,000 dollars net) for the biennium 2006-2007, as detailed in the annex to the present resolution;

4. *Decides also* that the total assessment for 2006 under the Special Account would amount to 134,879,200 dollars gross, being half of the estimated appropriation for the biennium 2006-2007;

5. *Decides further* to apportion the amount of 67,439,600 dollars gross (61,722,500 dollars net) among Member States in accordance with the scale of assessments applicable to the regular budget of the United Nations for 2006, as set out in its resolution 58/1 B of 23 December 2003;

6. *Decides* to apportion the amount of 67,439,600 dollars gross (61,722,500 dollars net) among Member States in accordance with the scale of assessments applicable to peacekeeping operations for 2006;

7. *Decides also* that, in accordance with the provisions of its resolution 973(X) of 15 December 1955, there shall be set off against the apportionment among Member States, as provided for in paragraphs 5 and 6 above, their respective share in the Tax Equalization Fund of the estimated staff assessment income of 11,434,200 dollars approved for the International Criminal Tribunal for Rwanda for 2006;

8. *Decides further* that the provisions for the application of credits under regulations 3.2 *(d)*, 5.3 and 5.4 of the Financial Regulations and Rules of the United Nations shall be suspended in respect of the amount of 3,307,300 dollars gross (3,875,900 dollars net), which otherwise would have to be surrendered pursuant to those provisions;

9. *Welcomes* the continued efforts of the International Criminal Tribunal for Rwanda, in accordance with its statute, to assist the Government of Rwanda in strengthening its judiciary, and requests the Tribunal to increase its capacity-building efforts for the judiciary of Rwanda, including through recruitment, training and attachment programmes for Rwandan jurists, advocates and human rights practitioners, in view of the intention to transfer cases for prosecution to Rwanda;

10. *Reiterates* the importance of carrying out an effective outreach programme within the overall mandate of the International Criminal Tribunal for Rwanda and its completion strategy, and requests the Tribunal, in accordance with its mandate and in consultation with the Department of Public Information of the Secretariat, to develop and implement outreach programmes that are proactive, utilizing available resources optimally, and that contribute to the reconciliation process by effectively developing an increased understanding of its work among Rwandans.

Annex

Financing of the International Criminal Tribunal for the Prosecution of Persons Responsible for Genocide and Other Serious Violations of International Humanitarian Law Committed in the Territory of Rwanda and Rwandan Citizens Responsible for Genocide and Other Such Violations Committed in the Territory of Neighbouring States between 1 January and 31 December 1994

	Gross	Net
	(United States dollars)	
Estimated appropriation for the biennium 2006-2007	284 273 200	258 898 800
Revised estimates: effect of changes in rates of exchange and inflation	(14 514 800)	(12 008 800)

	Gross	Net
	(United States dollars)	
Reductions made by the Advisory Committee on Administrative and Budgetary Questions	-	-
Reductions proposed by the Fifth Committee	-	-
Estimated initial appropriation for the biennium 2006-2007	269 758 400	246 890 000
Assessment for 2006	134 879 200	123 445 000
Of which:		
Contributions assessed on Member States in accordance with the scale of assessments applicable to the regular budget of the United Nations for 2006	67 439 600	61 722 500
Contributions assessed on Member States in accordance with the scale of assessments applicable to peacekeeping operations of the United Nations for 2006	67 439 600	61 722 500

Communication. On 6 May [S/2005/303], Egypt transmitted to the Security Council a copy of the press release issued by ICTR on 29 April announcing that country's decision to provide voluntary financial support to the Tribunal.

Functioning of the Tribunals

Staff retention

In response to General Assembly resolutions 59/273 [YUN 2004, p. 1290] and 59/274 [ibid., p. 1286], the Secretary-General submitted an October report [A/60/436] on staff retention and legacy issues. According to the report, as the Tribunals moved closer to the completion of their mandates, it was expected that the number of staff departures would increase, as they sought more attractive benefits and/or longer-term appointments in other United Nations and common system organizations than those offered by the Tribunals. To ensure the timely completion of the mandates of the Tribunals, it was necessary to curtail the flow of departures of experienced staff, avoid the slow down of trials and the financial costs of recruiting and training new staff. The Secretary-General therefore proposed, in addition to a number of other measures, that a retention bonus be introduced for staff until specific posts were no longer needed.

On the question of legacy issues, the statutes of the Tribunals provided for the continuation of a number of functions after the completion of their mandates, which included judicial, legacy and administrative issues, such as, supervision of the enforcement of sentences, witness monitoring and their protection. On the administrative side, arrangements and related provisions were required for the payment of pensions to judges and surviving spouses after the closure of the Tribunals, and the liabilities associated with the after-service health insurance scheme for retired staff members; the legal nature, composition and location of the entity to be entrusted with the responsibility of carrying out those functions. Both Tribunals were currently considering those issues with a view to developing a final position and recommendation to the Assembly.

ACABQ, in its December report [A/60/591], believed that the idea of a retention bonus should be pursued and recommended that an analysis of the financial and other implications of introducing such a measure be provided to the Assembly.

Implementation of completion strategies

Progress assessment

ICTY

In response to Security Council resolutions 1503(2003) [YUN 2003, p. 1330] and 1534(2004) [YUN 2004, p. 1292], the President of ICTY submitted reports in May [S/2005/343 & Corr. 1] and December [S/2005/781] revising and updating the ICTY completion strategy and detailing progress made towards its implementation.

In May, the President outlined measures taken to implement the completion strategy, including the establishment of two working groups—the Working Group on Speeding up Trials and the Working Group on Speeding up Appeals—to examine procedures and practices, with a view to improving working methods. He reported that it was definitely not feasible to envisage an end of all trial activity at the Tribunal by the end of 2008 due to the large number of indictees and fugitives who had arrived at the Tribunal since his last report [YUN 2004, p. 1293], as well as the filing and confirmation of seven new trials or amended indictments by the prosecution involving 13 accused. He predicted that trials would have to run into 2009. In December, the President confirmed that fact. Moreover, whether trials would conclude by the end of 2009 was subject to several factors. Since the May report, four contempt cases involving six accused were in progress. Of primary importance were the trials of the Tribunal's three most notorious suspects—Radovan Karadzic, Ratko Mladic, both of whom were indicted in 1995 [YUN 1995, p. 1314], as well as the recently arrested Ante Gotovina, who was indicted in 2001 [YUN 2001, p. 1199]. If the other two fugitives were arrested in the near future, then the com-

pletion of all trials at the close of 2009 remained feasible. If not, their delivery date might well push the completion of all trials beyond that date.

ICTR

In response to Security Council resolutions 1503(2003) [YUN 2003, p. 1330] and 1534(2004) [YUN 2004, p. 1292], the President of ICTR submitted reports in May [S/2005/336] and December [S/2005/782] revising and updating the ICTR completion strategy and detailing progress made towards its implementation.

The reports reviewed recent judgments and trials in progress; cases for transfer to national jurisdictions for trial; the actual number of persons brought to trial at ICTR; and tracking and apprehension of fugitives. Although Council resolution 1503(2003) anticipated that all the work of ICTR and ICTY should be completed by 2010, the report noted that it was difficult at the current stage to indicate a completion strategy for the ICTR Appeals Chamber, as it was linked to the ICTY completion strategy. It was anticipated that the Appeals Chamber's workload would continue to increase. The report noted that the number of judges at the Appeals Chamber needed to be increased, if there were to be any reasonable prospects of completing the appeals by 2010. At the same time, 17 detainees were awaiting the commencement of their trials. Those cases would result in single-accused trials, some of which were expected to start in 2006, depending on Trial Chamber capacity. There were currently 26 accused in 10 cases, five of which were joint trials. It was estimated that by 2008, ICTR could complete trials and judgments involving sixty-five to seventy persons, depending on the progress of current and future trials. The Security Council considered those reports on 13 June [meeting 5199] and 15 December [meeting 5328].

International Criminal Court

The International Criminal Court (ICC), established by the Rome Statute [YUN 1998, p. 1209] as a permanent institution with jurisdiction over persons accused of the most serious crimes of international concern (genocide, crimes against humanity, war crimes and the crime of aggression), began the judicial phase of its operations in 2005. As at 31 December, the Statute had 139 signatories and 100 States parties.

In 2005, three States parties—Uganda, the Democratic Republic of the Congo (DRC) and the Central African Republic—referred situations in their respective territories to the Prosecutor. In March, following recommendations made by the International Commission of Inquiry for Darfur (see p. 323), the Security Council, by resolution 1593(2005) (see p. 324), referred the situation of Darfur to ICC.

One non-State party, Côte d'Ivoire, lodged a declaration accepting the jurisdiction of the Court. Based on available information, the Prosecutor initiated investigations in the DRC, Uganda and Darfur (the Sudan). The Prosecutor had also received more than 1,300 communications relating to situations that fell within the jurisdiction of the Court. In addition to the situations under investigation, the Prosecutor was monitoring eight other situations around the world, including in the Central African Republic and Côte d'Ivoire. The Pre-Trial Chamber began the first judicial proceedings and the first trial proceedings were expected to begin in 2006, provided the Court received sufficient cooperation from States in arresting and tranferring persons.

The activities of the Court were covered in an August report [A/60/177] transmitted by the Secretary-General to the General Assembly.

GENERAL ASSEMBLY ACTION

On 23 November [meeting 53], the General Assembly adopted **resolution 60/29** [draft: A/60/L.25 & Add.1] without vote [agenda item 81].

Report of the International Criminal Court

The General Assembly,

Recalling its resolutions 47/33 of 25 November 1992, 48/31 of 9 December 1993, 49/53 of 9 December 1994, 50/46 of 11 December 1995, 51/207 of 17 December 1996, 52/160 of 15 December 1997, 53/105 of 8 December 1998, 54/105 of 9 December 1999, 55/155 of 12 December 2000, 56/85 of 12 December 2001, 57/23 of 19 November 2002, 58/79 of 9 December 2003, 58/318 of 13 September 2004 and 59/43 of 2 December 2004,

Noting that the Rome Statute of the International Criminal Court was adopted on 17 July 1998 and entered into force on 1 July 2002,

Recalling that the Rome Statute reaffirms the purposes and principles of the Charter of the United Nations,

Noting the substantial progress that has been achieved so far in making the International Criminal Court fully operational, and also noting important milestones such as the decisions by the Prosecutor of the International Criminal Court to open investigations into the situation in Uganda and in the Democratic Republic of the Congo, the referral by the Security Council of the situation in Darfur since 1 July 2002 to the Prosecutor and the opening of an investigation into the situation in Darfur by the Prosecutor, as well as the issuance of arrest warrants for five leaders of the Lord's Resistance Army by the Court,

Recognizing the role of the International Criminal Court in a multilateral system that aims to end impunity, establish the rule of law and promote and encourage respect for human rights in accordance with international law and the purposes and principles of the Charter,

Expressing its appreciation to the Secretary-General for providing effective and efficient assistance in the establishment of the International Criminal Court,

Acknowledging the Relationship Agreement between the United Nations and the International Criminal Court ("Relationship Agreement") as approved by the General Assembly in its resolution 58/318, including paragraph 3 of the resolution with respect to the payment in full of expenses accruing to the United Nations as a result of the implementation of the Relationship Agreement, which entered into force on 4 October 2004 and which provides a framework for continued cooperation between the Court and the United Nations, which could include the facilitation by the United Nations of the Court's field activities, and encouraging the conclusion of supplementary arrangements and agreements, as necessary,

Having received the report of the International Criminal Court,

Reiterating the historic significance of the adoption of the Rome Statute of the International Criminal Court,

1. *Calls upon* all States from all regions of the world that are not yet parties to the Rome Statute of the International Criminal Court to consider ratifying or acceding to it without delay;

2. *Welcomes* the one-hundredth ratification of the Rome Statute, by Mexico on 28 October 2005;

3. *Calls upon* all States that have not yet done so to consider becoming parties to the Agreement on the Privileges and Immunities of the International Criminal Court;

4. *Encourages* States parties to the Rome Statute that have not yet done so to adopt national legislation to implement obligations emanating from the Rome Statute and to cooperate with the International Criminal Court in the exercise of its functions, and recalls the provision of technical assistance by States parties in this respect;

5. *Recalls* that, by virtue of article 12, paragraph 3, of the Rome Statute, a State which is not a party to the Statute may, by declaration lodged with the Registrar of the International Criminal Court, accept the exercise of jurisdiction by the Court with respect to specific crimes that are mentioned in paragraph 2 of that article;

6. *Looks forward* to the fourth session of the Assembly of States Parties to the Rome Statute of the International Criminal Court, to be held in The Hague from 28 November to 3 December 2005, as well as the resumed fourth session to be held in New York on 26 and 27 January 2006;

7. *Recalls* the establishment of the Special Working Group on the Crime of Aggression by the Assembly of States Parties, open to all States on an equal footing, and encourages all States to consider participating actively in the Working Group with a view to elaborating proposals for a provision on the crime of aggression;

8. *Encourages* States to contribute to the Trust Fund established for the benefit of victims of crimes within the jurisdiction of the International Criminal Court, and of the families of such victims, as well as to the Trust Fund for the participation of least developed

countries, and acknowledges contributions made to both trust funds so far;

9. *Welcomes* the report of the Secretary-General on the work of the Organization, in which reference is made to the important role of the International Criminal Court in advancing the cause of justice and the rule of law;

10. *Recalls* the referral by the Security Council of the situation in Darfur since 1 July 2002 to the Prosecutor of the International Criminal Court, and also recalls article 13 *(b)* of the Rome Statute;

11. *Notes* the significance of the conclusion and implementation of the Relationship Agreement between the United Nations and the International Criminal Court, which forms a framework for close cooperation between the two organizations and for consultation on matters of mutual interest pursuant to the provisions of that Agreement and in conformity with the respective provisions of the Charter of the United Nations and the Rome Statute;

12. *Welcomes* the report of the International Criminal Court for 2004, and invites the Court to submit, in accordance with article 6 of the Relationship Agreement, annual reports on its activities to the General Assembly;

13. *Recalls* that, pursuant to article 4, paragraph 2, of the Relationship Agreement, the International Criminal Court may attend and participate in the work of the General Assembly in the capacity of observer;

14. *Decides* to include in the provisional agenda of its sixty-first session the item entitled "Report of the International Criminal Court", which shall continue to be considered directly in plenary meeting, and under which shall be considered the annual report of the Court, the Court being invited to attend and to participate in these proceedings.

Assembly of States Parties

The Assembly of States Parties to the Rome Statute of the International Criminal Court met in The Hague for its fourth annual session (28 November–3 December [ICC-ASP/4/32].

The Assembly took note of its President's report on the activities of the Bureau, which had met 19 times since the last report [YUN 2004, p. 1296] to discuss the Court's progress and to review issues entrusted to it. In accordance with the Assembly's decision, the Bureau established two informal working groups: one, based in New York, to consider issues related to the relationship with the United Nations, including an ICC liaison office, the draft regulations of the trust fund for victims and the arrears of States parties to the Court; and the other, based in The Hague, to consider issues relating to the permanent premises of the Court, host country issues, including the Headquarters Agreement and the draft code of professional conduct for counsel.

The Assembly approved the programme budget for 2006 and the Working Capital Fund, with total appropriations of 82,464,400 euros. It took note of the reports of the external auditors on the audit of the financial statement of the Court and the Victims Trust Fund for the period ended 31 December 2004. It decided that if the term of office of members of the Board of the Trust Fund expired before the Assembly met to elect new members, those members would continue to serve until the election date.

The Assembly took note of the report to the Special Working Group on the Crime of Aggression and related reports and the report of the Working Group on the Trust Fund for Victims. It adopted the draft Code of Professional Conduct for Counsel. The Assembly agreed that the pension scheme for judges should be funded on an accrual basis and managed externally. It asked the Court to report on the most cost-effective option for managing the pension scheme, including the option of joining the United Nations Joint Staff Pension Fund. The Assembly requested that Committee on Budget and Finance to consider and report on the issue of including, for the purposes of determining pensions payable by the Court, pensions payable to individual judges who had served at other international tribunals and organizations. It established the guidelines for the selection and engagement of gratis personnel at the Court.

The Assembly decided to establish a Liaison Office in New York and took note of the report of the Working Group on the Permanent Premises.

The Chambers

The judicial activities of the Court were conducted by the Chambers, which consisted of 18 judges, organized in three divisions: the Appeals Division, the Trial Division and the Pre-Trial Division.

The Court began its first judicial proceedings at the pre-trial level. The Presidency constituted three Pre-Trial Chambers: Pre-Trial Chamber I–DRC, and Darfur (the Sudan); Pre-Trial Chamber II–Uganda; Pre-Trial Chamber III–Central African Republic. On 17 February, Pre-Trial Chamber I issued the first judicial decision in a case, deciding to convene a status conference with the Prosecutor and his representatives on the situation in the DRC. The other case before the Court was that of Joseph Kony, Vincent Otti, Okot Odhinambo and Dominic Ongwen (Uganda). Also before the Court was the situation in Darfur, the Sudan (see p. 1403).

Office of the Prosecutor

Investigations

The Office of the Prosecutor initiated investigations into three situations (the DRC, Uganda and Darfur, the Sudan) and was also collecting information on eight other situations of concern. Its investigations in the situation in Uganda involved allegations of large-scale abductions, killings, torture and sexual violence. The majority of alleged abductees were children. The investigation was at an advanced stage after 10 months. The Office concluded a cooperation agreement with the Government of Uganda and made several missions to engage with local groups to establish relationships for cooperation and assessing the interests of victims. The Office also invited community leaders to The Hague to discuss how to coordinate its efforts with those of community leaders. The Office of the Prosecutor and the Registry established a field office in Uganda.

The investigation of the situation in the DRC involved allegations of thousands of deaths by mass murder and summary execution since 2002, as well as large-scale patterns of rape, torture and use of child soldiers. Numerous armed groups active in the DRC were allegedly involved in crimes. Given the scale of the situation, the investigation of the cases would proceed in sequence; cases selected on the basis of gravity were prioritized in 2005, while others would be developed subsequently. The first investigations were progressing well. The Office of the Prosecutor and the Registry established a field office in Kinshasa and a field presence in Bunia and concluded a cooperation agreement with the Government. However, because of logistical challenges and the lack of effective control over many areas, the Government's ability to cooperate with the Office remained a great challenge for the investigation.

The Office of the Prosecutor was also investigating in the Darfur region of the Sudan, allegations of the killing of thousands of civilians and widespread destruction and looting of villages, leading to the displacement of approximately 1.9 million civilians, as well as allegations of a pervasive pattern of rape and sexual violence and persistent targeting and intimidation of humanitarian personnel. Following the referral of the case to ICC by the Security Council in resolution 1593(2005) (see p. 324), the Office collected more than 2,500 items from the International Commission of Inquiry for Darfur (see p. 323), as well as over 3,000 documents from other sources. The Office was in contact with more than 100 groups and individuals and interviewed more than 50 experts. On 1 June, the Prosecutor initiated an investigation and informed Pre-Trial Chamber I. The Prosecutor reported to the Security Council in June [meeting 5216] and December [meeting 5321] on progress made in the investigations. The Office would identify those individuals who bore the greatest responsibility for the crimes and assess the admissibility of the selected cases.

The Registry

The Registry worked to build the operational and administrative support structures for the Court, while also establishing mechanisms, policies and regulations to pursue its mandate in the areas of victim's participation and reparations, witness protection, defence and outreach. To enable the Court to operate efficiently and to work in a web-based environment, the Registry established a number of information systems. The Registry continued efforts to raise awareness of the Court and its activities. It strengthened the Court's public information capacity to support its outreach services in countries where the Court was active, including the establishment of a documentation centre and a website. It also undertook comparative studies relating to the establishment of the permanent premises of the Court, and developed a legal aid scheme to ensure sufficient means for the defence.

The Registry also provided administrative support to the Court's field operations, especially to support victims, witnesses, defence and outreach.

Support for those operations also entailed, among other things, providing security, which could vary between situations. The Registry undertook a number of training programmes for local authorities.

Chapter III

Legal aspects of international political relations

In 2005, the International Law Commission (ILC) continued to examine topics suitable for the progressive development of codification of international law. It considered aspects of State liability, the responsibility of States to cooperate in cases of mutual interest, and the scope of such questions as diplomatic protection and unilateral State actions, and reconstituted a study group to examine the increasing fragmentation of international law. Special Rapporteurs presented reports on the examination of treaties and international agreements. ILC also considered two new agenda items, the expulsion of aliens and the effects of armed conflicts on treaties.

United Nations instruments for the suppression of international terrorism continued their work during 2005. The Secretary-General's annual report on the implementation of the 1994 Declaration on Measures to Eliminate International Terrorism addressed the status of State and international organization participation in anti-terrorism measures. The Ad Hoc Committee on the convention for suppression of nuclear terrorism met for its ninth session, and recommending to the General Assembly a resolution on that topic. The Assembly adopted the International Convention on the Suppression of Acts of Nuclear Terrorism. It also adopted the Optional Protocol to the Convention on the Safety of United Nations and Associated Personnel.

International Law Commission

The International Law Commission (ILC) held its fifty-seventh session in Geneva in two parts (2 May–3 June; 11 July–5 August) [A/60/10]. During the second part, the International Law Seminar held its forty-first session, which was attended by 24 participants, mostly from developing countries. They observed ILC meetings, attended specially arranged lectures and participated in working groups on specific topics.

ILC, assisted by working groups and a Drafting Committee, continued to advance its work on reservations to treaties by adopting two draft guidelines dealing with the definition of objections to reservations and to the late formulation or widening of the scope of a reservation. It also heard a briefing from the Special Rapporteur on the topic of diplomatic protection and adopted nine draft articles on responsibility of international organizations and reviewed the work of previous sessions on international liability in the case of loss from transboundary hazardous activities. In addition, ILC considered the Special Rapporteur's report on shared natural resources and established a working group on transboundary groundwaters to review the 25 draft articles submitted by the Rapporteur. On the issue of the unilateral acts of States, the Commission considered analyses of 11 cases of State practice and conclusions thereon and reconstituted the working group on the topic. It exchanged views on the topic of the fragmentation of international law: difficulties arising from the diversification and expansion of international law, based on a briefing by the chairman of the study group on the subject.

ILC considered the Special Rapporteur's first report on the effects of armed conflicts on treaties, containing a set of 14 draft articles. It endorsed the Special Rapporteur's suggestion that a written request for information be circulated to Member Governments. ILC decided to include in its current programme of work the topic "the obligation to extradite or prosecute (*aut dedere aut judicare*)", and appointed Zdzislaw Galicki (Poland) as Special Rapporteur for that topic. ILC also reiterated that the reduction of the payment of honorarium to the nominal amount of one dollar by Assembly resolution 56/272 [YUN 2002, p. 1402] mostly affected Special Rapporteurs, particularly those from developing countries, as it compromised support for their research. It decided to hold its fifty-eighth session in two parts: from 1 May to 9 June and from 3 July to 11 August 2006.

GENERAL ASSEMBLY ACTION

On 23 November [meeting 53], the General Assembly, on the recommendation of the Sixth (Legal) Committee [A/60/516], adopted **resolution 60/22** without vote [agenda item 80].

Report of the International Law Commission on the work of its fifty-seventh session

The General Assembly,

Having considered the report of the International Law Commission on the work of its fifty-seventh session,

Emphasizing the importance of furthering the codification and progressive development of international law as a means of implementing the purposes and principles set forth in the Charter of the United Nations and in the Declaration on Principles of International Law concerning Friendly Relations and Cooperation among States in accordance with the Charter of the United Nations,

Recognizing the desirability of referring legal and drafting questions to the Sixth Committee, including topics that might be submitted to the International Law Commission for closer examination, and of enabling the Sixth Committee and the Commission to enhance further their contribution to the progressive development of international law and its codification,

Recalling the need to keep under review those topics of international law which, given their new or renewed interest for the international community, may be suitable for the progressive development and codification of international law and therefore may be included in the future programme of work of the International Law Commission,

Welcoming the holding of the International Law Seminar, and noting with appreciation the voluntary contributions made to the United Nations Trust Fund for the International Law Seminar,

Stressing the usefulness of focusing and structuring the debate on the report of the International Law Commission in the Sixth Committee in such a manner that conditions are provided for concentrated attention to each of the main topics dealt with in the report and for discussions on specific topics,

Wishing to enhance further, in the context of the revitalization of the debate on the report of the International Law Commission, the interaction between the Sixth Committee as a body of governmental representatives and the Commission as a body of independent legal experts, with a view to improving the dialogue between the two bodies,

Welcoming initiatives to hold interactive debates, panel discussions and question time in the Sixth Committee, as envisaged in resolution 58/316 of 1 July 2004 on further measures for the revitalization of the work of the General Assembly,

1. *Takes note* of the report of the International Law Commission on the work of its fifty-seventh session, and recommends that the Commission continue its work on the topics in its current programme, taking into account the comments and observations of Governments, whether submitted in writing or expressed orally in debates in the General Assembly;

2. *Expresses its appreciation* to the International Law Commission for the work accomplished at its fifty-seventh session, and encourages the Commission to complete its work on those topics that are near completion during its fifty-eighth session, taking into account the views expressed by Governments during the debates of the Sixth Committee, and any written comments that may be submitted by Governments;

3. *Draws the attention* of Governments to the importance for the International Law Commission of having their views on the following, which were adopted by the Commission at its fifty-sixth session:

(*a*) The draft articles and commentary on diplomatic protection;

(*b*) The draft principles on the allocation of loss in the case of transboundary harm arising out of hazardous activities;

4. *Invites* Governments to provide information to the International Law Commission, as requested in chapter III of its report, regarding:

(*a*) Shared natural resources;

(*b*) Effects of armed conflicts on treaties;

(*c*) Responsibility of international organizations;

(*d*) Expulsion of aliens;

(*e*) Unilateral acts of States;

(*f*) Reservations to treaties;

5. *Endorses* the decision of the International Law Commission to include the topic "The obligation to extradite or prosecute (*aut dedere aut judicare*)" in its programme of work;

6. *Invites* the International Law Commission to continue taking measures to enhance its efficiency and productivity;

7. *Encourages* the International Law Commission to continue taking cost-saving measures at its future sessions without prejudice to the efficiency of its work;

8. *Takes note* of paragraph 502 of the report of the International Law Commission, and decides that the next session of the Commission shall be held at the United Nations Office at Geneva from 1 May to 9 June and from 3 July to 11 August 2006;

9. *Welcomes* the enhanced dialogue between the International Law Commission and the Sixth Committee at the sixtieth session of the General Assembly, stresses the desirability of further enhancing the dialogue between the two bodies, and in this context encourages, inter alia, the continued practice of informal consultations in the form of discussions between the members of the Sixth Committee and the members of the Commission attending the sixty-first session of the Assembly;

10. *Encourages* delegations, during the debate on the report of the International Law Commission to adhere as far as possible to the structured work programme agreed to by the Sixth Committee and to consider presenting concise and focused statements;

11. *Encourages* Member States to consider being represented at the level of legal adviser during the first week in which the report of the International Law Commission is discussed in the Sixth Committee (International Law Week) to enable high-level discussions on issues of international law;

12. *Requests* the International Law Commission to continue to pay special attention to indicating in its annual report, for each topic, any specific issues on which expressions of views by Governments, either in the Sixth Committee or in written form, would be of particular interest in providing effective guidance for the Commission in its further work;

13. *Takes note* of paragraphs 503 to 509 of the report of the International Law Commission with regard to cooperation with other bodies, and encourages the Commission to continue the implementation of article 16, paragraph (*e*), and article 26, paragraphs 1 and 2, of its statute in order to further strengthen cooperation between the Commission and other bodies concerned with international law, having in mind the usefulness of such cooperation;

14. *Notes* that consulting with national organizations and individual experts concerned with interna-

tional law may assist Governments in considering whether to make comments and observations on drafts submitted by the International Law Commission and in formulating their comments and observations;

15. *Reaffirms* its previous decisions concerning the indispensable role of the Codification Division of the Office of Legal Affairs of the Secretariat in providing assistance to the International Law Commission;

16. *Approves* the conclusions reached by the International Law Commission in paragraph 498 of its report, and reaffirms its previous decisions concerning the documentation and summary records of the Commission;

17. *Expresses the hope* that the International Law Seminar will continue to be held in connection with the sessions of the International Law Commission and that an increasing number of participants, in particular from developing countries, will be given the opportunity to attend the Seminar, and appeals to States to continue to make urgently needed voluntary contributions to the United Nations Trust Fund for the International Law Seminar;

18. *Requests* the Secretary-General to provide the International Law Seminar with adequate services, including interpretation, as required, and encourages him to continue considering ways to improve the structure and content of the Seminar;

19. *Also requests* the Secretary-General to forward to the International Law Commission, for its attention, the records of the debate on the report of the Commission at the sixtieth session of the General Assembly, together with such written statements as delegations may circulate in conjunction with their oral statements, and to prepare and distribute a topical summary of the debate, following established practice;

20. *Requests* the Secretariat to circulate to States, as soon as possible after the conclusion of the session of the International Law Commission, chapter II of its report containing a summary of the work of that session, chapter III containing the specific issues on which the views of Governments would be of particular interest to the Commission and the draft articles adopted on either first or second reading by the Commission;

21. *Recommends* that the debate on the report of the International Law Commission at the sixty-first session of the General Assembly commence on 23 October 2006.

Unilateral acts of States

ILC considered the eighth report on unilateral acts of States [A/CN.4/557] by Special Rapporteur Victor Rodríguez Cedeño (Venezuela), which presented for consideration certain acts considered relevant for a more detailed study of practice relating to those acts and conclusions which could inform the practice. In an effort to formulate general rules applicable to all unilateral acts, and with a view to promoting the stability of relations between States, the Working Group on the topic examined several cases considered as unilateral acts: a note dated 22 November 1952 from the Minister for Foreign Affairs of Colombia; the declaration of the Minister for Foreign Affairs of

Cuba concerning the supply of vaccines to the Eastern Republic of Uruguay; Jordan's waiver of claims to the West Bank territories; the Egyptian declaration of 24 April 1957; statements made by France concerning the suspension of nuclear tests in the South Pacific; protests by the Russian Federation against Turkmenistan and Azerbaijan; statements made by nuclear-weapon States; the Ihlen Declaration of 22 July 1919; the Truman Proclamation of 28 September 1945; statements concerning the United Nations and its staff members (tax exemptions and privileges); and the conduct of Thailand and Cambodia with reference to the *Temple of Preah Vihear* case. The report noted that the acts considered were unilateral and expressed in very different ways, including official notes, public declarations, presidential proclamations, political speeches and even conduct signifying acceptance or acquiescence. It concluded that form was relatively unimportant in determining whether one was dealing with a unilateral legal act that could produce legal effects on its own without the need for its acceptance, or for any other reaction on the part of the addressee. However, it might be that the formality of the act had a role to play in determining the intent of the author. Also, in the cases considered, the addressee also varied widely, including States, the international community, an entity that had not yet been consolidated as a State, or an international organization. Acts with which the Committee was concerned involved only those formulated by States, including acts formulated by a State and addressed to an international organization. Another relevant question was the need to establish the moment at which the acts produced legal effects from the time of their formulation, without the need for their acceptance or for any reaction conveying such acceptance. In the cases considered, it seemed difficult to determine the moment at which an act produced legal effects. The Rapporteur said that the report might serve as a basis for progress on work on the topic, despite its complexity, and ILC might consider adopting a definition of unilateral acts and consider some of the draft articles already referred to the Drafting Committee separately from the study of practice relating to unilateral acts.

Responsibility of international organizations

ILC considered the third report on the topic of responsibility of international organizations [A/CN.4/553] by Special Rapporteur Giorgio Gaja (Italy). The report dealt with the breach of an international obligation on the part of an international organization and the responsibility of an international organization in connection with the act of a State or other international organization. It proposed draft articles 8 to 16 relating to the existence of a breach of an international obligation; international obligation in force for an international organization; extension in time of the breach of an international obligation; and breach consisting of a composite act; aid or assistance in the commission of an internationally wrongful act; direction and control exercised over the commission of an internationally wrongful act; and coercion of a State or another international organization. ILC adopted the report of the Drafting Committee on those articles, as well as the commentaries thereto.

ILC also had before it a May report [A/CN.4//556], submitted pursuant to General Assembly resolution 58/77 [YUN 2003, p. 1334], which contained information received from the UN Secretariat and five international organizations concerning their practice relevant to the topic of responsibility of international organizations, including cases in which States members of such organizations might be regarded as responsible for the organization's actions.

Fragmentation of international law

In 2005, ILC reconstituted the study group established in 2002 [YUN 2002, p. 1304] on the topic of fragmentation of international law: difficulties arising from the diversification and expansion of international law. The study group considered a memorandum on regionalism in the context of the study on "the function and scope of the *lex specialis* rule and the question of self-contained regimes and studies on the interpretation of treaties in the light of any relevant rules of international law applicable in the relations between the parties" (article 31 (3) (*c*) of the Vienna Convention on the Law of Treaties), in the context of general developments in international law and concerns of the international community; the application of successive treaties relating to the same subject matter (article 30 of the Vienna Convention on the Law of Treaties); the modification of multilateral treaties between certain of the parties only (article 41) of the Vienna Convention on the Law of Treaties); and hierarchy in international law: *jus cogens*, obligations *erga omnes*, Article 103 of the Charter of the United Nations, as conflict rules. It also had before it an informal paper on the "Disconnection Clause". The study group reaffirmed its approach to focus on the substantive aspects of fragmentation in the light of the 1969 Vienna Convention on the Law of Treaties. It reiterated its intention to attain an

outcome that would be concrete and of practical value. The study group reaffirmed its intention to develop a collective document for submission to ILC in 2006. The document would comprise a substantive study on fragmentation and a concise summary containing the proposed conclusions and, if appropriate, guidelines on how to deal with such fragmentation.

Shared natural resources

ILC considered the third report on shared natural resources [A/CN.4/551 & Corr.1 & Add.1] by Special Rapporteur Chusei Yamada (Japan), which proposed 25 draft articles for a convention on the law of transboundary aquifers, taking into account comments and suggestions previously offered by the Commission and the Sixth Committee. The addendum to the report contained important references to State practice and international instruments. The Special Rapporteur stated that he was aware of the scarcity of State practice and legal instruments on the subject and was making efforts to collect any available material. The replies from Governments and relevant international organizations [A/CN.4/555 & Add.1] to the Commission's 2004 questionnaire [YUN 2004, p. 1302] would facilitate the preparation of the study on groundwaters. Annexed to the report was the draft convention on the law of transboundary aquifers.

ILC took note of the report of its Working Group on Transboundary Groundwaters, which it had established to consider the Special Rapporteur's report, and expressed appreciation of the progress made in reviewing and revising eight draft articles. ILC took note of the Working Group's proposal that it be reconvened in 2006 to complete its work.

Expulsion of aliens

In June, ILC considered for the first time a preliminary report on the expulsion of aliens [A/CN.4/554] by Special Rapporteur Maurice Kamto (Cameroon). The report examined the issues raised by the idea of the "expulsion of aliens" and gave an overview of the right to expel in international law, the grounds for expulsion invoked in practice and the rights at stake during expulsion. It also examined the methodological problems associated with the consideration of the topic.

In examining the concepts of the expulsion of aliens and the right to expel, the Special Rapporteur held the view that customary international law was not in question. However, the reasons for expulsion could vary and were not all permissible under international law, bringing into play rights, particularly fundamental human rights, to which international law attached legal consequences to their violation. The Special Rapporteur looked at questions of terminology: whether to speak of "expulsion" of aliens, which in national legislation covered a more limited phenomenon, and whether the reference to "aliens" was sufficiently accurate and covered all the categories of persons under consideration. On the question of methodology, the Special Rapporteur sought the Commission's guidance on what treatment should be given to existing conventional rules, found in a number of human rights treaties. His inclination was to elaborate a complete regime, bearing in mind that, although treaty law would offer elements which might be included in the draft articles, a number of those rules arose initially from national legislation and international jurisprudence developed in the context of global and regional human rights judicial instances. The Special Rapporteur requested that the Secretariat prepare a compilation of applicable national and international instruments, texts and jurisprudence on the topic. ILC noted that its task was to consider carefully all the rules on the topic existing in customary international law, treaties and international agreements, State practice and internal laws; to develop them further where possible or appropriate; and to codify them for clearer and better application.

Effects of armed conflicts on treaties

In May, ILC considered the first report on the effects of armed conflicts on treaties by Special Rapporteur Ian Brownlie (United Kingdom) [A/CN.4/552], as well as a memorandum prepared by the Secretariat on the effect of armed conflict on treaties: an examination of practice and doctrine [A/CN.4/550 & Corr. 1]. The report presented a complete set of draft articles with commentaries, which were intended to clarify the legal position and promote and enhance the security of legal relations between States, thereby limiting the occasions on which the incidence of armed conflict had an effect on treaty relations. The draft articles were intended to be compatible with the Vienna Convention on the Law of Treaties. Acknowledging that the subject of a peaceful settlement of disputes was missing from the draft articles, the Special Rapporteur suggested that the subject be dealt with near the completion of a substantive draft, as there was a close relationship between the matters of substance and the appropriate type of dispute settlement mechanism.

The Special Rapporteur identified several policy questions requiring further consideration, in-

cluding the question of the applicable *lex specialis* in the draft articles and the question of a distinction between bilateral and multilateral treaties. Due to the preliminary nature of the current discussion, the Special Rapporteur opposed the referral of the draft articles to the Drafting Committee or the establishment of a working group and recommended that a request be circulated to Governments asking for information about their practice on the topic, especially contemporary practice.

During consideration of the Special Rapporteur's report, ILC supported the decision to present a complete set of draft articles and found the memorandum helpful in understanding the complexity of the issues. ILC endorsed the Special Rapporteur's request.

International State relations and international law

Jurisdictional immunities of States and their property

In 2004, the General Assembly, by resolution 59/38, adopted the Convention on Jurisdictional Immunities of States and Their Property [YUN 2004, p. 1304]. The Convention was opened for signature from 17 January 2005 until 17 January 2007 at UN Headquarters in New York. As at 31 December 2005, 17 countries had signed the Convention.

International terrorism

Conventions on international terrorism and for suppression of acts of nuclear terrorism

Ad Hoc Committee

In accordance with General Assembly resolution 59/46 [YUN 2004, p. 1311], the Ad Hoc Committee on the convention for suppression of nuclear terrorism, established by Assembly resolution 51/210 [YUN 1996, p. 1208], held its ninth session (New York, 28 March–1 April) to continue, within the framework of a working group of the Sixth Committee, the elaboration of a draft comprehensive convention on international terrorism, with appropriate time allocated to the continued consideration of outstanding issues.

The Ad Hoc Committee exchanged views on issues within its mandate and held informal consultations regarding the draft comprehensive convention on international terrorism and written amendments and four new proposals by Cuba relating to the draft international convention for the suppression of acts of nuclear terrorism, which were later withdrawn. The Committee finalized on 1 April the text of the draft international convention for the suppression of acts of nuclear terrorism, prepared by its Bureau [A/59/766] and recommended it to the Assembly for adoption. By resolution 59/290 of 13 April, the Assembly adopted the Convention (below), which was opened for signature from 14 September until 31 December 2006. As at 31 December 2005, 96 countries had signed the Convention.

Also on 1 April, the Ad Hoc Committee adopted its report [A/60/37], to which were annexed the text of the draft convention for the suppression of acts of nuclear terrorism, the Chairman's informal summary of the general discussion, the coordinators' reports and amendments and proposals submitted to the Committee in connection with the elaboration of a draft comprehensive convention on international terrorism and a draft international convention for the suppression of acts of nuclear terrorism.

GENERAL ASSEMBLY ACTION

On 13 April [meeting 91], the General Assembly, on the basis of the report of the Ad Hoc Committee established by Assembly resolution 51/210 of 17 December [A/59/766], adopted **resolution 59/290** without vote [agenda item 148].

International Convention for the Suppression of Acts of Nuclear Terrorism

The General Assembly,

Having considered the text of the draft international convention for the suppression of acts of nuclear terrorism elaborated by the Ad Hoc Committee established by General Assembly resolution 51/210 of 17 December 1996 and the Working Group of the Sixth Committee,

1. *Adopts* the International Convention for the Suppression of Acts of Nuclear Terrorism annexed to the present resolution, and requests the Secretary-General to open the Convention for signature at United Nations Headquarters in New York from 14 September 2005 to 31 December 2006;

2. *Calls upon* all States to sign and ratify, accept, approve or accede to the Convention.

Annex

International Convention for the Suppression of Acts of Nuclear Terrorism

The States Parties to this Convention,

Having in mind the purposes and principles of the Charter of the United Nations concerning the maintenance of international peace and security and the promotion of good-neighbourliness and friendly relations and cooperation among States,

Recalling the Declaration on the Occasion of the Fiftieth Anniversary of the United Nations of 24 October 1995,

Recognizing the right of all States to develop and apply nuclear energy for peaceful purposes and their legitimate interests in the potential benefits to be derived from the peaceful application of nuclear energy,

Bearing in mind the Convention on the Physical Protection of Nuclear Material of 1980,

Deeply concerned about the worldwide escalation of acts of terrorism in all its forms and manifestations,

Recalling the Declaration on Measures to Eliminate International Terrorism annexed to General Assembly resolution 49/60 of 9 December 1994, in which, inter alia, the States Members of the United Nations solemnly reaffirm their unequivocal condemnation of all acts, methods and practices of terrorism as criminal and unjustifiable, wherever and by whomever committed, including those which jeopardize the friendly relations among States and peoples and threaten the territorial integrity and security of States,

Noting that the Declaration also encouraged States to review urgently the scope of the existing international legal provisions on the prevention, repression and elimination of terrorism in all its forms and manifestations, with the aim of ensuring that there is a comprehensive legal framework covering all aspects of the matter,

Recalling General Assembly resolution 51/210 of 17 December 1996 and the Declaration to Supplement the 1994 Declaration on Measures to Eliminate International Terrorism annexed thereto,

Recalling also that, pursuant to General Assembly resolution 51/210, an ad hoc committee was established to elaborate, inter alia, an international convention for the suppression of acts of nuclear terrorism to supplement related existing international instruments,

Noting that acts of nuclear terrorism may result in the gravest consequences and may pose a threat to international peace and security,

Noting also that existing multilateral legal provisions do not adequately address those attacks,

Being convinced of the urgent need to enhance international cooperation between States in devising and adopting effective and practical measures for the prevention of such acts of terrorism and for the prosecution and punishment of their perpetrators,

Noting that the activities of military forces of States are governed by rules of international law outside of the framework of this Convention and that the exclusion of certain actions from the coverage of this Convention does not condone or make lawful otherwise unlawful acts, or preclude prosecution under other laws,

Have agreed as follows:

Article 1

For the purposes of this Convention:

1. "Radioactive material" means nuclear material and other radioactive substances which contain nuclides which undergo spontaneous disintegration (a process accompanied by emission of one or more types of ionizing radiation, such as alpha-, beta-, neutron particles and gamma rays) and which may, owing to their radiological or fissile properties, cause death, serious bodily injury or substantial damage to property or to the environment.

2. "Nuclear material" means plutonium, except that with isotopic concentration exceeding 80 per cent in plutonium-238; uranium-233; uranium enriched in the isotope 235 or 233; uranium containing the mixture of isotopes as occurring in nature other than in the form of ore or ore residue; or any material containing one or more of the foregoing;

Whereby "uranium enriched in the isotope 235 or 233" means uranium containing the isotope 235 or 233 or both in an amount such that the abundance ratio of the sum of these isotopes to the isotope 238 is greater than the ratio of the isotope 235 to the isotope 238 occurring in nature.

3. "Nuclear facility" means:

(a) Any nuclear reactor, including reactors installed on vessels, vehicles, aircraft or space objects for use as an energy source in order to propel such vessels, vehicles, aircraft or space objects or for any other purpose;

(b) Any plant or conveyance being used for the production, storage, processing or transport of radioactive material.

4. "Device" means:

(a) Any nuclear explosive device; or

(b) Any radioactive material dispersal or radiation-emitting device which may, owing to its radiological properties, cause death, serious bodily injury or substantial damage to property or to the environment.

5. "State or government facility" includes any permanent or temporary facility or conveyance that is used or occupied by representatives of a State, members of a Government, the legislature or the judiciary or by officials or employees of a State or any other public authority or entity or by employees or officials of an intergovernmental organization in connection with their official duties.

6. "Military forces of a State" means the armed forces of a State which are organized, trained and equipped under its internal law for the primary purpose of national defence or security and persons acting in support of those armed forces who are under their formal command, control and responsibility.

Article 2

1. Any person commits an offence within the meaning of this Convention if that person unlawfully and intentionally:

(a) Possesses radioactive material or makes or possesses a device:

(i)   With the intent to cause death or serious bodily injury; or

(ii) With the intent to cause substantial damage to property or to the environment;

(b) Uses in any way radioactive material or a device, or uses or damages a nuclear facility in a manner which releases or risks the release of radioactive material:

(i)   With the intent to cause death or serious bodily injury; or

(ii) With the intent to cause substantial damage to property or to the environment; or

(iii) With the intent to compel a natural or legal person, an international organization or a State to do or refrain from doing an act.

2. Any person also commits an offence if that person:

(a) Threatens, under circumstances which indicate the credibility of the threat, to commit an offence as set forth in paragraph 1 (b) of the present article; or

(b) Demands unlawfully and intentionally radioactive material, a device or a nuclear facility by threat, under circumstances which indicate the credibility of the threat, or by use of force.

3. Any person also commits an offence if that person attempts to commit an offence as set forth in paragraph 1 of the present article.

4. Any person also commits an offence if that person:

(a) Participates as an accomplice in an offence as set forth in paragraph 1, 2 or 3 of the present article; or

(b) Organizes or directs others to commit an offence as set forth in paragraph 1, 2 or 3 of the present article; or

(c) In any other way contributes to the commission of one or more offences as set forth in paragraph 1, 2 or 3 of the present article by a group of persons acting with a common purpose; such contribution shall be intentional and either be made with the aim of furthering the general criminal activity or purpose of the group or be made in the knowledge of the intention of the group to commit the offence or offences concerned.

Article 3

This Convention shall not apply where the offence is committed within a single State, the alleged offender and the victims are nationals of that State, the alleged offender is found in the territory of that State and no other State has a basis under article 9, paragraph 1 or 2, to exercise jurisdiction, except that the provisions of articles 7, 12, 14, 15, 16 and 17 shall, as appropriate, apply in those cases.

Article 4

1. Nothing in this Convention shall affect other rights, obligations and responsibilities of States and individuals under international law, in particular the purposes and principles of the Charter of the United Nations and international humanitarian law.

2. The activities of armed forces during an armed conflict, as those terms are understood under international humanitarian law, which are governed by that law are not governed by this Convention, and the activities undertaken by military forces of a State in the exercise of their official duties, inasmuch as they are governed by other rules of international law, are not governed by this Convention.

3. The provisions of paragraph 2 of the present article shall not be interpreted as condoning or making lawful otherwise unlawful acts, or precluding prosecution under other laws.

4. This Convention does not address, nor can it be interpreted as addressing, in any way, the issue of the legality of the use or threat of use of nuclear weapons by States.

Article 5

Each State Party shall adopt such measures as may be necessary:

(a) To establish as criminal offences under its national law the offences set forth in article 2;

(b) To make those offences punishable by appropriate penalties which take into account the grave nature of these offences.

Article 6

Each State Party shall adopt such measures as may be necessary, including, where appropriate, domestic legislation, to ensure that criminal acts within the scope of this Convention, in particular where they are intended or calculated to provoke a state of terror in the general public or in a group of persons or particular persons, are under no circumstances justifiable by considerations of a political, philosophical, ideological, racial, ethnic, religious or other similar nature and are punished by penalties consistent with their grave nature.

Article 7

1. States Parties shall cooperate by:

(a) Taking all practicable measures, including, if necessary, adapting their national law, to prevent and counter preparations in their respective territories for the commission within or outside their territories of the offences set forth in article 2, including measures to prohibit in their territories illegal activities of persons, groups and organizations that encourage, instigate, organize, knowingly finance or knowingly provide technical assistance or information or engage in the perpetration of those offences;

(b) Exchanging accurate and verified information in accordance with their national law and in the manner and subject to the conditions specified herein, and coordinating administrative and other measures taken as appropriate to detect, prevent, suppress and investigate the offences set forth in article 2 and also in order to institute criminal proceedings against persons alleged to have committed those crimes. In particular, a State Party shall take appropriate measures in order to inform without delay the other States referred to in article 9 in respect of the commission of the offences set forth in article 2 as well as preparations to commit such offences about which it has learned, and also to inform, where appropriate, international organizations.

2. States Parties shall take appropriate measures consistent with their national law to protect the confidentiality of any information which they receive in confidence by virtue of the provisions of this Convention from another State Party or through participation in an activity carried out for the implementation of this Convention. If States Parties provide information to international organizations in confidence, steps shall be taken to ensure that the confidentiality of such information is protected.

3. States Parties shall not be required by this Convention to provide any information which they are not permitted to communicate pursuant to national law or which would jeopardize the security of the State concerned or the physical protection of nuclear material.

4. States Parties shall inform the Secretary-General of the United Nations of their competent authorities and liaison points responsible for sending and receiving the information referred to in the present article. The Secretary-General of the United Nations shall communicate such information regarding competent authorities and liaison points to all States Parties and the International Atomic Energy Agency. Such authorities and liaison points must be accessible on a continuous basis.

Article 8

For purposes of preventing offences under this Convention, States Parties shall make every effort to adopt appropriate measures to ensure the protection of radioactive material, taking into account relevant recommendations and functions of the International Atomic Energy Agency.

Article 9

1. Each State Party shall take such measures as may be necessary to establish its jurisdiction over the offences set forth in article 2 when:

(a) The offence is committed in the territory of that State; or

(b) The offence is committed on board a vessel flying the flag of that State or an aircraft which is registered under the laws of that State at the time the offence is committed; or

(c) The offence is committed by a national of that State.

2. A State Party may also establish its jurisdiction over any such offence when:

(a) The offence is committed against a national of that State; or

(b) The offence is committed against a State or government facility of that State abroad, including an embassy or other diplomatic or consular premises of that State; or

(c) The offence is committed by a stateless person who has his or her habitual residence in the territory of that State; or

(d) The offence is committed in an attempt to compel that State to do or abstain from doing any act; or

(e) The offence is committed on board an aircraft which is operated by the Government of that State.

3. Upon ratifying, accepting, approving or acceding to this Convention, each State Party shall notify the Secretary-General of the United Nations of the jurisdiction it has established under its national law in accordance with paragraph 2 of the present article. Should any change take place, the State Party concerned shall immediately notify the Secretary-General.

4. Each State Party shall likewise take such measures as may be necessary to establish its jurisdiction over the offences set forth in article 2 in cases where the alleged offender is present in its territory and it does not extradite that person to any of the States Parties which have established their jurisdiction in accordance with paragraph 1 or 2 of the present article.

5. This Convention does not exclude the exercise of any criminal jurisdiction established by a State Party in accordance with its national law.

Article 10

1. Upon receiving information that an offence set forth in article 2 has been committed or is being committed in the territory of a State Party or that a person who has committed or who is alleged to have committed such an offence may be present in its territory, the State Party concerned shall take such measures as may be necessary under its national law to investigate the facts contained in the information.

2. .Upon being satisfied that the circumstances so warrant, the State Party in whose territory the offender or alleged offender is present shall take the appropriate measures under its national law so as to ensure that person's presence for the purpose of prosecution or extradition.

3. Any person regarding whom the measures referred to in paragraph 2 of the present article are being taken shall be entitled:

(a) To communicate without delay with the nearest appropriate representative of the State of which that person is a national or which is otherwise entitled to protect that person's rights or, if that person is a stateless person, the State in the territory of which that person habitually resides;

(b) To be visited by a representative of that State;

(c) To be informed of that person's rights under subparagraphs *(a)* and *(b)*.

4. The rights referred to in paragraph 3 of the present article shall be exercised in conformity with the laws and regulations of the State in the territory of which the offender or alleged offender is present, subject to the provision that the said laws and regulations must enable full effect to be given to the purposes for which the rights accorded under paragraph 3 are intended.

5. The provisions of paragraphs 3 and 4 of the present article shall be without prejudice to the right of any State Party having a claim to jurisdiction in accordance with article 9, paragraph 1 *(c)* or 2 *(c)*, to invite the International Committee of the Red Cross to communicate with and visit the alleged offender.

6. When a State Party, pursuant to the present article, has taken a person into custody, it shall immediately notify, directly or through the Secretary-General of the United Nations, the States Parties which have established jurisdiction in accordance with article 9, paragraphs 1 and 2, and, if it considers it advisable, any other interested States Parties, of the fact that that person is in custody and of the circumstances which warrant that person's detention. The State which makes the investigation contemplated in paragraph 1 of the present article shall promptly inform the said States Parties of its findings and shall indicate whether it intends to exercise jurisdiction.

Article 11

1. The State Party in the territory of which the alleged offender is present shall, in cases to which article 9 applies, if it does not extradite that person, be obliged, without exception whatsoever and whether or not the offence was committed in its territory, to submit the case without undue delay to its competent authorities for the purpose of prosecution, through proceedings in accordance with the laws of that State. Those authorities shall take their decision in the same manner as in the case of any other offence of a grave nature under the law of that State.

2. Whenever a State Party is permitted under its national law to extradite or otherwise surrender one of its nationals only upon the condition that the person will be returned to that State to serve the sentence imposed as a result of the trial or proceeding for which the extradition or surrender of the person was sought, and this State and the State seeking the extradition of the person agree with this option and other terms they may deem appropriate, such a conditional extradition or surrender shall be sufficient to discharge the obligation set forth in paragraph 1 of the present article.

Article 12

Any person who is taken into custody or regarding whom any other measures are taken or proceedings are carried out pursuant to this Convention shall be guaranteed fair treatment, including enjoyment of all rights and guarantees in conformity with the law of the State in the territory of which that person is present

and applicable provisions of international law, including international law of human rights.

Article 13

1. The offences set forth in article 2 shall be deemed to be included as extraditable offences in any extradition treaty existing between any of the States Parties before the entry into force of this Convention. States Parties undertake to include such offences as extraditable offences in every extradition treaty to be subsequently concluded between them.

2. When a State Party which makes extradition conditional on the existence of a treaty receives a request for extradition from another State Party with which it has no extradition treaty, the requested State Party may, at its option, consider this Convention as a legal basis for extradition in respect of the offences set forth in article 2. Extradition shall be subject to the other conditions provided by the law of the requested State.

3. States Parties which do not make extradition conditional on the existence of a treaty shall recognize the offences set forth in article 2 as extraditable offences between themselves, subject to the conditions provided by the law of the requested State.

4. If necessary, the offences set forth in article 2 shall be treated, for the purposes of extradition between States Parties, as if they had been committed not only in the place in which they occurred but also in the territory of the States that have established jurisdiction in accordance with article 9, paragraphs 1 and 2.

5. The provisions of all extradition treaties and arrangements between States Parties with regard to offences set forth in article 2 shall be deemed to be modified as between States Parties to the extent that they are incompatible with this Convention.

Article 14

1. States Parties shall afford one another the greatest measure of assistance in connection with investigations or criminal or extradition proceedings brought in respect of the offences set forth in article 2, including assistance in obtaining evidence at their disposal necessary for the proceedings.

2. States Parties shall carry out their obligations under paragraph 1 of the present article in conformity with any treaties or other arrangements on mutual legal assistance that may exist between them. In the absence of such treaties or arrangements, States Parties shall afford one another assistance in accordance with their national law.

Article 15

None of the offences set forth in article 2 shall be regarded, for the purposes of extradition or mutual legal assistance, as a political offence or as an offence connected with a political offence or as an offence inspired by political motives. Accordingly, a request for extradition or for mutual legal assistance based on such an offence may not be refused on the sole ground that it concerns a political offence or an offence connected with a political offence or an offence inspired by political motives.

Article 16

Nothing in this Convention shall be interpreted as imposing an obligation to extradite or to afford mutual legal assistance if the requested State Party has substantial grounds for believing that the request for extradition for offences set forth in article 2 or for mutual legal assistance with respect to such offences has been made for the purpose of prosecuting or punishing a person on account of that person's race, religion, nationality, ethnic origin or political opinion or that compliance with the request would cause prejudice to that person's position for any of these reasons.

Article 17

1. A person who is being detained or is serving a sentence in the territory of one State Party whose presence in another State Party is requested for purposes of testimony, identification or otherwise providing assistance in obtaining evidence for the investigation or prosecution of offences under this Convention may be transferred if the following conditions are met:

(a) The person freely gives his or her informed consent; and

(b) The competent authorities of both States agree, subject to such conditions as those States may deem appropriate.

2. For the purposes of the present article:

(a) The State to which the person is transferred shall have the authority and obligation to keep the person transferred in custody, unless otherwise requested or authorized by the State from which the person was transferred;

(b) The State to which the person is transferred shall without delay implement its obligation to return the person to the custody of the State from which the person was transferred as agreed beforehand, or as otherwise agreed, by the competent authorities of both States;

(c) The State to which the person is transferred shall not require the State from which the person was transferred to initiate extradition proceedings for the return of the person;

(d) The person transferred shall receive credit for service of the sentence being served in the State from which he or she was transferred for time spent in the custody of the State to which he or she was transferred.

3. Unless the State Party from which a person is to be transferred in accordance with the present article so agrees, that person, whatever his or her nationality, shall not be prosecuted or detained or subjected to any other restriction of his or her personal liberty in the territory of the State to which that person is transferred in respect of acts or convictions anterior to his or her departure from the territory of the State from which such person was transferred.

Article 18

1. Upon seizing or otherwise taking control of radioactive material, devices or nuclear facilities, following the commission of an offence set forth in article 2, the State Party in possession of such items shall:

(a) Take steps to render harmless the radioactive material, device or nuclear facility;

(b) Ensure that any nuclear material is held in accordance with applicable International Atomic Energy Agency safeguards; and

(c) Have regard to physical protection recommendations and health and safety standards published by the International Atomic Energy Agency.

2. Upon the completion of any proceedings connected with an offence set forth in article 2, or sooner if required by international law, any radioactive material, device or nuclear facility shall be returned, after consultations (in particular, regarding modalities of return and storage) with the States Parties concerned to the State Party to which it belongs, to the State Party of which the natural or legal person owning such radioactive material, device or facility is a national or resident, or to the State Party from whose territory it was stolen or otherwise unlawfully obtained.

3. (a) Where a State Party is prohibited by national or international law from returning or accepting such radioactive material, device or nuclear facility or where the States Parties concerned so agree, subject to paragraph 3 (b) of the present article, the State Party in possession of the radioactive material, devices or nuclear facilities shall continue to take the steps described in paragraph 1 of the present article; such radioactive material, devices or nuclear facilities shall be used only for peaceful purposes;

(b) Where it is not lawful for the State Party in possession of the radioactive material, devices or nuclear facilities to possess them, that State shall ensure that they are placed as soon as possible in the possession of a State for which such possession is lawful and which, where appropriate, has provided assurances consistent with the requirements of paragraph 1 of the present article in consultation with that State, for the purpose of rendering it harmless; such radioactive material, devices or nuclear facilities shall be used only for peaceful purposes.

4. If the radioactive material, devices or nuclear facilities referred to in paragraphs 1 and 2 of the present article do not belong to any of the States Parties or to a national or resident of a State Party or was not stolen or otherwise unlawfully obtained from the territory of a State Party, or if no State is willing to receive such items pursuant to paragraph 3 of the present article, a separate decision concerning its disposition shall, subject to paragraph 3 (b) of the present article, be taken after consultations between the States concerned and any relevant international organizations.

5. For the purposes of paragraphs 1, 2, 3 and 4 of the present article, the State Party in possession of the radioactive material, device or nuclear facility may request the assistance and cooperation of other States Parties, in particular the States Parties concerned, and any relevant international organizations, in particular the International Atomic Energy Agency. States Parties and the relevant international organizations are encouraged to provide assistance pursuant to this paragraph to the maximum extent possible.

6. The States Parties involved in the disposition or retention of the radioactive material, device or nuclear facility pursuant to the present article shall inform the Director General of the International Atomic Energy Agency of the manner in which such an item was disposed of or retained. The Director General of the International Atomic Energy Agency shall transmit the information to the other States Parties.

7. In the event of any dissemination in connection with an offence set forth in article 2, nothing in the present article shall affect in any way the rules of international law governing liability for nuclear damage, or other rules of international law.

Article 19

The State Party where the alleged offender is prosecuted shall, in accordance with its national law or applicable procedures, communicate the final outcome of the proceedings to the Secretary-General of the United Nations, who shall transmit the information to the other States Parties.

Article 20

States Parties shall conduct consultations with one another directly or through the Secretary-General of the United Nations, with the assistance of international organizations as necessary, to ensure effective implementation of this Convention.

Article 21

The States Parties shall carry out their obligations under this Convention in a manner consistent with the principles of sovereign equality and territorial integrity of States and that of non-intervention in the domestic affairs of other States.

Article 22

Nothing in this Convention entitles a State Party to undertake in the territory of another State Party the exercise of jurisdiction and performance of functions which are exclusively reserved for the authorities of that other State Party by its national law.

Article 23

1. Any dispute between two or more States Parties concerning the interpretation or application of this Convention which cannot be settled through negotiation within a reasonable time shall, at the request of one of them, be submitted to arbitration. If, within six months of the date of the request for arbitration, the parties are unable to agree on the organization of the arbitration, any one of those parties may refer the dispute to the International Court of Justice, by application, in conformity with the Statute of the Court.
2. Each State may, at the time of signature, ratification, acceptance or approval of this Convention or accession thereto, declare that it does not consider itself bound by paragraph 1 of the present article. The other States Parties shall not be bound by paragraph 1 with respect to any State Party which has made such a reservation.
3. Any State which has made a reservation in accordance with paragraph 2 of the present article may at any time withdraw that reservation by notification to the Secretary-General of the United Nations.

Article 24

1. This Convention shall be open for signature by all States from 14 September 2005 until 31 December 2006 at United Nations Headquarters in New York.
2. This Convention is subject to ratification, acceptance or approval. The instruments of ratification, acceptance or approval shall be deposited with the Secretary-General of the United Nations.
3. This Convention shall be open to accession by any State. The instruments of accession shall be deposited with the Secretary-General of the United Nations.

Article 25

1. This Convention shall enter into force on the thirtieth day following the date of the deposit of the twenty-second instrument of ratification, acceptance, approval or accession with the Secretary-General of the United Nations.
2. For each State ratifying, accepting, approving or acceding to the Convention after the deposit of the twenty-second instrument of ratification, acceptance, approval or accession, the Convention shall enter into force on the thirtieth day after deposit by such State of its instrument of ratification, acceptance, approval or accession.

Article 26

1. A State Party may propose an amendment to this Convention. The proposed amendment shall be submitted to the depositary, who circulates it immediately to all States Parties.
2. If the majority of the States Parties request the depositary to convene a conference to consider the proposed amendments, the depositary shall invite all States Parties to attend such a conference to begin no sooner than three months after the invitations are issued.
3. The conference shall make every effort to ensure amendments are adopted by consensus. Should this not be possible, amendments shall be adopted by a two-thirds majority of all States Parties. Any amendment adopted at the conference shall be promptly circulated by the depositary to all States Parties.
4. The amendment adopted pursuant to paragraph 3 of the present article shall enter into force for each State Party that deposits its instrument of ratification, acceptance, accession or approval of the amendment on the thirtieth day after the date on which two thirds of the States Parties have deposited their relevant instrument. Thereafter, the amendment shall enter into force for any State Party on the thirtieth day after the date on which that State deposits its relevant instrument.

Article 27

1. Any State Party may denounce this Convention by written notification to the Secretary-General of the United Nations.
2. Denunciation shall take effect one year following the date on which notification is received by the Secretary-General of the United Nations.

Article 28

The original of this Convention, of which the Arabic, Chinese, English, French, Russian and Spanish texts are equally authentic, shall be deposited with the Secretary-General of the United Nations, who shall send certified copies thereof to all States.

IN WITNESS WHEREOF, the undersigned, being duly authorized thereto by their respective Governments, have signed this Convention, opened for signature at United Nations Headquarters in New York on 14 September 2005.

Measures to eliminate terrorism

In accordance with General Assembly resolution 50/53 [YUN 1995, p. 1330], the Secretary-General, in August, issued his annual report [A/60/228] on measures taken by 26 States, 5 UN system entities and 5 intergovernmental organizations to implement the 1994 Declaration on Measures to Eliminate International Terrorism, approved by Assembly resolution 49/60 [YUN 1994, p. 1293] and Security Council resolution 1269(1999) [YUN 1999, p. 1240]. It listed 27 international instruments pertaining to terrorism, indicating the status of State participation in each, and provided information on workshops and training courses on combating terrorism by three UN bodies. The report noted the publication of the second volume of the United Nations Legislative Series, entitled *National Law and Regulations on the Prevention and Suppression of International Terrorism.*

In other action, the Commission on Crime Prevention and Criminal Justice, at its fourteenth session (23-27 May) [E/2005/30], recommended to the Economic and Social Council a resolution entitled "Strengthening international cooperation and technical assistance in promoting the implementation of the universal conventions and protocols relating to terrorism within the framework of the activities of the United Nations Office on Drugs and Crime". The resolution was approved on 22 July by the Council as **resolution 2005/19** (see p. 1232).

GENERAL ASSEMBLY ACTION

On 8 December [meeting 61], the General Assembly, on the recommendation of the Sixth Committee [A/60/519], adopted **resolution 60/43** without vote [agenda item 108].

Measures to eliminate international terrorism

The General Assembly,

Guided by the purposes and principles of the Charter of the United Nations,

Recalling the Declaration on the Occasion of the Fiftieth Anniversary of the United Nations,

Recalling also the United Nations Millennium Declaration,

Recalling further the 2005 World Summit Outcome, and reaffirming in particular the section on terrorism,

Recalling the Declaration on Measures to Eliminate International Terrorism, contained in the annex to General Assembly resolution 49/60 of 9 December 1994, and the Declaration to Supplement the 1994 Declaration on Measures to Eliminate International Terrorism, contained in the annex to resolution 51/210 of 17 December 1996,

Recalling also all General Assembly resolutions on measures to eliminate international terrorism, and Security Council resolutions on threats to international peace and security caused by terrorist acts,

Convinced of the importance of the consideration of measures to eliminate international terrorism by the General Assembly as the universal organ having competence to do so,

Deeply disturbed by the persistence of terrorist acts, which have been carried out worldwide,

Reaffirming its strong condemnation of the heinous acts of terrorism that have caused enormous loss of human life, destruction and damage, including those which prompted the adoption of General Assembly resolu-

tion 56/1 of 12 September 2001, as well as Security Council resolutions 1368(2001) of 12 September 2001, 1373(2001) of 28 September 2001 and 1377(2001) of 12 November 2001, and those that have occurred since the adoption of the latter resolution,

Recalling the strong condemnation of the atrocious and deliberate attack against the headquarters of the United Nations Assistance Mission for Iraq in Baghdad on 19 August 2003 in General Assembly resolution 57/338 of 15 September 2003 and Security Council resolution 1502(2003) of 26 August 2003,

Affirming that States must ensure that any measure taken to combat terrorism complies with all their obligations under international law and adopt such measures in accordance with international law, in particular international human rights, refugee and humanitarian law,

Stressing the need to strengthen further international cooperation among States and among international organizations and agencies, regional organizations and arrangements and the United Nations in order to prevent, combat and eliminate terrorism in all its forms and manifestations, wherever and by whomsoever committed, in accordance with the principles of the Charter, international law and the relevant international conventions,

Noting the role of the Security Council Committee established pursuant to resolution 1373(2001) concerning counter-terrorism in monitoring the implementation of that resolution, including the taking of the necessary financial, legal and technical measures by States and the ratification or acceptance of the relevant international conventions and protocols,

Mindful of the need to enhance the role of the United Nations and the relevant specialized agencies in combating international terrorism, and of the proposals of the Secretary-General to enhance the role of the Organization in this respect,

Mindful also of the essential need to strengthen international, regional and subregional cooperation aimed at enhancing the national capacity of States to prevent and suppress effectively international terrorism in all its forms and manifestations,

Reiterating its call upon States to review urgently the scope of the existing international legal provisions on the prevention, repression and elimination of terrorism in all its forms and manifestations, with the aim of ensuring that there is a comprehensive legal framework covering all aspects of the matter,

Emphasizing that tolerance and dialogue among civilizations, and enhancing interfaith and intercultural understanding, are among the most important elements in promoting cooperation and success in combating terrorism, and welcoming the various initiatives to this end,

Reaffirming that no terrorist act can be justified in any circumstances,

Recalling Security Council resolution 1624(2005) of 14 September 2005, and bearing in mind that States must ensure that any measure taken to combat terrorism complies with their obligations under international law, in particular international human rights, refugee and humanitarian law,

Taking note of the Final Document of the Thirteenth Conference of Heads of State or Government of Non-Aligned Countries, adopted in Kuala Lumpur on 25

February 2003, which reiterated the collective position of the Movement of Non-Aligned Countries on terrorism and reaffirmed the previous initiative of the Twelfth Conference of Heads of State or Government of Non-Aligned Countries, held in Durban, South Africa, from 29 August to 3 September 1998, calling for an international summit conference under the auspices of the United Nations to formulate a joint organized response of the international community to terrorism in all its forms and manifestations, as well as other relevant initiatives,

Bearing in mind the recent developments and initiatives at the international, regional and subregional levels to prevent and suppress international terrorism,

Noting regional efforts to prevent, combat and eliminate terrorism in all its forms and manifestations, wherever and by whomsoever committed, including through the elaboration of and adherence to regional conventions,

Recalling its decision in resolutions 54/110 of 9 December 1999, 55/158 of 12 December 2000, 56/88 of 12 December 2001, 57/27 of 19 November 2002, 58/81 of 9 December 2003 and 59/46 of 2 December 2004 that the Ad Hoc Committee established by General Assembly resolution 51/210 of 17 December 1996 should address, and keep on its agenda, the question of convening a high-level conference under the auspices of the United Nations to formulate a joint organized response of the international community to terrorism in all its forms and manifestations,

Aware of its resolutions 57/219 of 18 December 2002, 58/187 of 22 December 2003 and 59/191 of 20 December 2004,

Having examined the report of the Secretary-General, the report of the Ad Hoc Committee established by resolution 51/210 and the report of the Working Group of the Sixth Committee established pursuant to resolution 59/46,

1. *Strongly condemns* all acts, methods and practices of terrorism in all its forms and manifestations as criminal and unjustifiable, wherever and by whomsoever committed;

2. *Reiterates* that criminal acts intended or calculated to provoke a state of terror in the general public, a group of persons or particular persons for political purposes are in any circumstances unjustifiable, whatever the considerations of a political, philosophical, ideological, racial, ethnic, religious or other nature that may be invoked to justify them;

3. *Reiterates its call upon* all States to adopt further measures in accordance with the Charter of the United Nations and the relevant provisions of international law, including international standards of human rights, to prevent terrorism and to strengthen international cooperation in combating terrorism and, to that end, to consider in particular the implementation of the measures set out in paragraphs 3 *(a)* to *(f)* of resolution 51/210;

4. *Also reiterates its call upon* all States, with the aim of enhancing the efficient implementation of relevant legal instruments, to intensify, as and where appropriate, the exchange of information on facts related to terrorism and, in so doing, to avoid the dissemination of inaccurate or unverified information;

5. *Reiterates its call upon* States to refrain from financing, encouraging, providing training for or otherwise supporting terrorist activities;

6. *Urges* States to ensure that their nationals or other persons and entities within their territory that wilfully provide or collect funds for the benefit of persons or entities who commit, or attempt to commit, facilitate or participate in the commission of terrorist acts are punished by penalties consistent with the grave nature of such acts;

7. *Reminds* States of their obligations under relevant international conventions and protocols and Security Council resolutions, including Security Council resolution 1373(2001), to ensure that perpetrators of terrorist acts are brought to justice;

8. *Reaffirms* that international cooperation as well as actions by States to combat terrorism should be conducted in conformity with the principles of the Charter, international law and relevant international conventions;

9. *Welcomes* the adoption and opening for signature of the International Convention for the Suppression of Acts of Nuclear Terrorism, and notes the adoption of the Amendment to the Convention on the Physical Protection of Nuclear Material, the Protocol of 2005 to the Convention for the Suppression of Unlawful Acts against the Safety of Maritime Navigation and the Protocol of 2005 to the Protocol for the Suppression of Unlawful Acts against the Safety of Fixed Platforms Located on the Continental Shelf, and urges all States to consider, as a matter of priority, becoming parties to these instruments;

10. *Urges* all States that have not yet done so to consider, as a matter of priority, and in accordance with Security Council resolutions 1373(2001), and 1566 (2004) of 8 October 2004, becoming parties to the relevant conventions and protocols as referred to in paragraph 6 of General Assembly resolution 51/210, as well as the International Convention for the Suppression of Terrorist Bombings, the International Convention for the Suppression of the Financing of Terrorism and the International Convention for the Suppression of Acts of Nuclear Terrorism, and calls upon all States to enact, as appropriate, the domestic legislation necessary to implement the provisions of those conventions and protocols, to ensure that the jurisdiction of their courts enables them to bring to trial the perpetrators of terrorist acts, and to cooperate with and provide support and assistance to other States and relevant international and regional organizations to that end;

11. *Urges* States to cooperate with the Secretary-General and with one another, as well as with interested intergovernmental organizations, with a view to ensuring, where appropriate within existing mandates, that technical and other expert advice is provided to those States requiring and requesting assistance in becoming parties to and implementing the conventions and protocols referred to in paragraph 10 above;

12. *Notes with appreciation and satisfaction* that, consistent with the call contained in paragraph 9 of resolution 59/46, a number of States became parties to the relevant conventions and protocols referred to therein, thereby realizing the objective of wider acceptance and implementation of those conventions;

13. *Reaffirms* the Declaration on Measures to Eliminate International Terrorism and the Declaration to Supplement the 1994 Declaration on Measures to Eliminate International Terrorism, and calls upon all States to implement them;

14. *Calls upon* all States to cooperate to prevent and suppress terrorist acts;

15. *Urges* all States and the Secretary-General, in their efforts to prevent international terrorism, to make the best use of the existing institutions of the United Nations;

16. *Requests* the Terrorism Prevention Branch of the United Nations Office on Drugs and Crime in Vienna to continue its efforts to enhance, through its mandate, the capabilities of the United Nations in the prevention of terrorism, and recognizes, in the context of Security Council resolution 1373(2001), its role in assisting States in becoming parties to and implementing the relevant international conventions and protocols relating to terrorism, including the International Convention for the Suppression of Acts of Nuclear Terrorism, and in strengthening international cooperation mechanisms in criminal matters related to terrorism, including through national capacity-building;

17. *Welcomes* the publication by the Secretariat, as part of the United Nations Legislative Series, of the second volume of *National Laws and Regulations on the Prevention and Suppression of International Terrorism*, prepared by the Codification Division of the Office of Legal Affairs of the Secretariat pursuant to paragraph 10 *(b)* of the Declaration on Measures to Eliminate International Terrorism;

18. *Invites* regional intergovernmental organizations to submit to the Secretary-General information on the measures they have adopted at the regional level to eliminate international terrorism, as well as on intergovernmental meetings held by those organizations;

19. *Requests* the Secretary-General to submit proposals to strengthen the capacity of the United Nations system to assist States in combating terrorism and enhance coordination of United Nations activities in this regard;

20. *Notes* the progress attained in the elaboration of the draft comprehensive convention on international terrorism during the meetings of the Ad Hoc Committee established by General Assembly resolution 51/210 of 17 December 1996 and the Working Group of the Sixth Committee established pursuant to General Assembly resolution 59/46, and welcomes continuing efforts to that end;

21. *Decides* that the Ad Hoc Committee shall, on an expedited basis, continue to elaborate the draft comprehensive convention on international terrorism, and shall continue to discuss the item included in its agenda by General Assembly resolution 54/110 concerning the question of convening a high-level conference under the auspices of the United Nations;

22. *Decides also* that the Ad Hoc Committee shall meet from 27 February to 3 March 2006 in order to fulfil the mandate referred to in paragraph 21 above;

23. *Requests* the Secretary-General to continue to provide the Ad Hoc Committee with the necessary facilities for the performance of its work;

24. *Requests* the Ad Hoc Committee to report to the General Assembly at its sixtieth session in the event of the completion of the draft comprehensive convention on international terrorism;

25. *Also requests* the Ad Hoc Committee to report to the General Assembly at its sixty-first session on progress made in the implementation of its mandate;

26. *Welcomes* any update by the Secretary-General of the comprehensive inventory of the response of the Secretariat to terrorism as part of his report on measures to eliminate international terrorism;

27. *Decides* to include in the provisional agenda of its sixty-first session the item entitled "Measures to eliminate international terrorism".

Safety and security of United Nations and associated personnel

Ad Hoc Committee consideration. The Ad Hoc Committee on the Scope of Legal Protection under the 1994 Convention on the Safety of United Nations and Associated Personnel [YUN 1994, p. 1289], established by General Assembly resolution 56/89 [YUN 2001, p. 1227], held its fourth session (New York, 11-15 April) on ways to expand the scope of the legal protection under the Convention, including by means of a legal instrument.

The Committee had before it a revised proposal submitted by Costa Rica on the relationship between the Convention and international humanitarian law; a report by the Secretary-General [YUN 2004, p. 1315] on the scope of legal protection under the Convention; and a related proposal submitted by China, Japan, Jordan and New Zealand. The discussion focused on the text of a draft Protocol to the Convention compiled by the Committee's Chairman. Delegates considered the adoption of additional preambular paragraphs and sought further clarifications to articles II and III of the draft, in order to reflect the specific matters discussed at the meeting.

On 15 April, the Ad Hoc Committee adopted its report [A/60/52], to which was annexed the Chairman's revised text and the proposals by delegations, and recommended the report to the General Assembly for consideration. It also recommended work to expand the scope of the Convention during the Assembly's sixtieth (2005) session and that the revised text be used by the working group of the Sixth Committee. It further recommended that Costa Rica's proposal be considered separately by the Ad Hoc Committee.

Sixth Committee working group. On 3 October, the Sixth Committee established a working group to continue the work of the Ad Hoc Committee. The report on the group's work [A/C.6/60/L.4] contained details of its discussions on the expansion of the scope of legal protection under the Convention, based on the Chairman's text, which was annexed to the report. The working group did not have sufficient time to consider the proposals by Costa Rica and Venezuela. The working group adopted its report at its fourth meeting on 10 October.

GENERAL ASSEMBLY ACTION

On 8 December [meeting 61], the General Assembly, on the recommendation of the Sixth Committee [A/60/518], adopted **resolution 60/42** without vote [agenda item 83].

Optional Protocol to the Convention on the Safety of United Nations and Associated Personnel

The General Assembly,

Recalling its resolution 59/47 of 2 December 2004 on the scope of legal protection under the Convention on the Safety of United Nations and Associated Personnel,

Recalling also its resolution 49/59 of 9 December 1994, by which it adopted the Convention on the Safety of United Nations and Associated Personnel ("the Convention"),

Noting that the Convention, which entered into force on 15 January 1999, has been ratified or acceded to by seventy-nine States as at the date of the present resolution,

Reaffirming, in the context of the Convention and its Optional Protocol, the importance of maintaining the integrity of international humanitarian law,

Reaffirming also the obligation of all humanitarian personnel and United Nations and associated personnel to respect the national laws of the country in which they are operating, in accordance with international law and the Charter of the United Nations,

Deeply concerned by the increasing dangers and security risks faced by United Nations and associated personnel at the field level, and mindful of the need to provide the fullest possible protection for their security,

Having considered the report of the Ad Hoc Committee on the Scope of Legal Protection under the Convention on the Safety of United Nations and Associated Personnel, established pursuant to resolution 56/89 of 12 December 2001, and the report of the Working Group of the Sixth Committee,

Recalling paragraph 167 of the 2005 World Summit Outcome, which stressed the need to conclude negotiations on a protocol expanding the scope of legal protection of United Nations and associated personnel during the sixtieth session of the General Assembly,

Underlining the need to promote the universality of the Convention and thereby strengthen the safety and security of United Nations and associated personnel,

Encouraging States to enact national legislation, as necessary, in order to enable the implementation of the Convention and the Protocol,

1. *Adopts*, therefore, the Optional Protocol to the Convention on the Safety of United Nations and Associated Personnel, which is contained in the annex to the present resolution, and requests the Secretary-General as depositary to open it for signature;

2. *Invites* States to become parties to the Optional Protocol to the Convention on the Safety of United Nations and Associated Personnel.

Annex

Optional Protocol to the Convention on the Safety of United Nations and Associated Personnel

The States Parties to this Protocol,

Recalling the terms of the Convention on the Safety of United Nations and Associated Personnel, done at New York on 9 December 1994,

Deeply concerned over the continuing pattern of attacks against United Nations and associated personnel,

Recognizing that United Nations operations conducted for the purposes of delivering humanitarian, political or development assistance in peacebuilding and of delivering emergency humanitarian assistance which entail particular risks for United Nations and associated personnel require the extension of the scope of legal protection under the Convention to such personnel,

Convinced of the need to have in place an effective regime to ensure that the perpetrators of attacks against United Nations and associated personnel engaged in United Nations operations are brought to justice,

Have agreed as follows:

Article I
Relationship

This Protocol supplements the Convention on the Safety of United Nations and Associated Personnel, done at New York on 9 December 1994 (hereinafter referred to as "the Convention"), and as between the Parties to this Protocol, the Convention and the Protocol shall be read and interpreted together as a single instrument.

Article II
Application of the Convention to United Nations operations

1. The Parties to this Protocol shall, in addition to those operations as defined in article 1 (c) of the Convention, apply the Convention in respect of all other United Nations operations established by a competent organ of the United Nations in accordance with the Charter of the United Nations and conducted under United Nations authority and control for the purposes of:

(a) Delivering humanitarian, political or development assistance in peacebuilding, or

(b) Delivering emergency humanitarian assistance.

2. Paragraph 1 does not apply to any permanent United Nations office, such as headquarters of the Organization or its specialized agencies established under an agreement with the United Nations.

3. A host State may make a declaration to the Secretary-General of the United Nations that it shall not apply the provisions of this Protocol with respect to an operation under article II (1) (b) which is conducted for the sole purpose of responding to a natural disaster. Such a declaration shall be made prior to the deployment of the operation.

Article III
Duty of a State Party
with respect to article 8 of the Convention

The duty of a State Party to this Protocol with respect to the application of article 8 of the Convention to United Nations operations defined in article II of this Protocol shall be without prejudice to its right to take action in the exercise of its national jurisdiction over any United Nations or associated personnel who violates the laws and regulations of that State, provided that such action is not in violation of any other international law obligation of the State Party.

Article IV

Signature

This Protocol shall be open for signature by all States at United Nations Headquarters for twelve months, from 16 January 2006 to 16 January 2007.

Article V

Consent to be bound

1. This Protocol shall be subject to ratification, acceptance or approval by the signatory States. Instruments of ratification, acceptance or approval shall be deposited with the Secretary-General of the United Nations.

2. This Protocol shall, after 16 January 2007, be open for accession by any non-signatory State. Instruments of accession shall be deposited with the Secretary-General of the United Nations.

3. Any State that is not a State Party to the Convention may ratify, accept, approve or accede to this Protocol if at the same time it ratifies, accepts, approves or accedes to the Convention in accordance with articles 25 and 26 thereof.

Article VI

Entry into force

1. This Protocol shall enter into force thirty days after twenty-two instruments of ratification, acceptance, approval or accession have been deposited with the Secretary-General of the United Nations.

2. For each State ratifying, accepting, approving or acceding to this Protocol after the deposit of the twenty-second instrument of ratification, acceptance, approval or accession, the Protocol shall enter into force on the thirtieth day after the deposit by such State of its instrument of ratification, acceptance, approval or accession.

Article VII

Denunciation

1. A State Party may denounce this Protocol by written notification to the Secretary-General of the United Nations.

2. Denunciation shall take effect one year following the date on which notification is received by the Secretary-General of the United Nations.

Article VIII

Authentic texts

The original of this Protocol, of which the Arabic, Chinese, English, French, Russian and Spanish texts are equally authentic, shall be deposited with the Secretary-General of the United Nations, who shall send certified copies thereof to all States.

Done at New York this ... (day) ... (month) ... (year).

Diplomatic relations

Protection of diplomatic and consular missions and representatives

As at 31 December, the States parties to the following conventions relating to the protection of diplomatic and consular relations were: 184 States parties to the 1961 Vienna Convention on Diplomatic Relations [YUN 1961, p. 512], 51 parties to the Optional Protocol concerning the acquisition of nationality [ibid., p. 516] and 63 parties to the Optional Protocol concerning the compulsory settlement of disputes [ibid.].

The 1963 Vienna Convention on Consular Relations [YUN 1963, p. 510] had 168 parties, the Optional Protocol concerning acquisition of nationality [ibid., p. 512] had 39, and the Optional Protocol concerning the compulsory settlement of disputes [ibid.] had 45, after the United States withdrew from that Protocol in March 2005.

Parties to the 1973 Convention on the Prevention and Punishment of Crimes against Internationally Protected Persons, including Diplomatic Agents [YUN 1973, p. 775], numbered 153.

ILC consideration. ILC, at its fifty-seventh session [A/60/10], had before it the sixth report of Special Rapporteur Christopher John R. Dugard (South Africa) on diplomatic protection [A/CN.4/546]. The report examined the non-applicability of the clean hands doctrine (no action arises from wilful wrongdoing: *ex dolo malo non oritur actio*) to disputes involving inter-State relations properly so called, and cases of its application in the context of diplomatic protection, as well as the question of admissibility. According to the doctrine, a State which was guilty of illegal conduct might be deprived of the necessary *locus standi in judicio* for complaining of corresponding illegalities on the part of other States. In the context of diplomatic protection, the doctrine might be invoked to preclude a State from exercising diplomatic protection if the national it sought to protect had suffered an injury in consequence of his or her own wrongful conduct. The report addressed the arguments in support of the suggestion that the clean hands doctrine be included in the draft articles on diplomatic protection, approved by the Commission in 2004 [YUN 2004, p. 1317], according to which the doctrine did not apply to disputes relating to inter-State relations where a State did not seek to protect a national; it did apply to cases of diplomatic protection in which a State sought to protect an injured national; and it produced an effect only in the context of diplomatic protection.

The Special Rapporteur concluded that the evidence in favour of the clean hands doctrine was inconclusive and that there was no clear authority to support the applicability of the doctrine to cases of diplomatic protection. He saw no reason to include a provision dealing with the doctrine in the draft articles on diplomatic protection. General support was expressed in the Commission for the Special Rapporteur's conclusion on the clean hands doctrine, and that it was more appropriate for it to be invoked at the stage of the examination of merits since it related to the attenuation or exoneration of responsibility rather than admissibility.

Treaties and agreements

Reservations to treaties

ILC, at its sixtieth session [A/60/10], considered the tenth report of Special Rapporteur Alain Pellet (France) relating to the validity of reservations to treaties [A/CN.4/558, Add.1, Add.2], which complemented his ninth report [YUN 2004, p. 1319] on the object and definition of objections. ILC decided to send draft guidelines 3.1 (freedom to formulate reservations), 3.1.1 (reservations expressly prohibited by the treaty), 3.1.2 (definition of specified reservations), 3.1.3 (reservations implicitly permitted by the treaty) and 3.1.4 (non-specified reservations authorized by the treaty) to the Drafting Committee. It also sent to the Drafting Committee previously adopted draft guidelines (1.6 and 2.1.8) for revision in the light of the terms selected, and agreed to consideration of the tenth report in 2006. It provisionally adopted draft guidelines 2.6.1 (definition of objections to treaties) and 2.6.2 (definition of objections to the late formulation or widening of the scope of a reservation). It also adopted the commentary to those draft guidelines and reproduced in its report the text of draft guidelines on reservations to treaties provisionally adopted thus far by the Commission.

Treaties involving international organizations

The 1986 Vienna Convention on the Law of Treaties between States and International Organizations or between International Organizations [YUN 1986, p. 1006], which had not yet entered into force, had 40 States parties as at 31 December 2005.

Registration and publication of treaties by the United Nations

During 2005, 1,683 international agreements were received and 2,688 subsequent actions were registered or filed and recorded by the Secretariat. In addition, 1,382 formalities concerning agreements for which the Secretary-General performed depositary functions were registered. Twelve issues of the *Monthly Statement of Treaties and International Agreements* were published.

In addition, the texts of international agreements registered or filed and recorded were published in the UN *Treaty Series* (UNTS) in 72 volumes in the original languages, with translations into English and French where necessary. The United Nations Treaty Collection on the Internet (UNTC), which contained published UNTC volumes up to 2005, the *League of Nations Treaty Series*, the *Treaty Handbook, Multilateral Treaties Deposited with the Secretary-General*, the *Summary of Practice of the Secretary-General as Depositary of Multilateral Treaties*, the Focus Books, information on training and a range of materials on treaty law and practice received an average of 1.7 million hits per month in 2005.

Multilateral treaties

The UN *Treaty Series* and the regularly updated status of multilateral treaties deposited with the Secretary-General were available on the Internet at the UN Treaty Collection website.

New multilateral treaties concluded under UN auspices

The following treaties, concluded under UN auspices, were deposited with the Secretary-General during 2005:

Memorandum of Understanding on Maritime Transport Cooperation in the Arab Mashreq, adopted in Damascus, Syria, on 9 May 2005

International Convention for the Suppression of Acts of Nuclear Terrorism, adopted in New York on 13 April 2005

Multilateral treaties deposited with the Secretary-General

At the end of 2005, the Secretary-General performed depositary functions for 517 multilateral treaties. During the year, 104 signatures were affixed to treaties for which he performed depositary functions and 1,278 instruments of ratification, accession, acceptance and approval were deposited.

The following multilateral treaties, among others, in respect of which the Secretary-General acted as depositary, came into force in 2005:

Kyoto Protocol to the United Nations Framework Convention on Climate Change, adopted in Kyoto, Japan, on 11 December 1997

Tampere Convention on the Provision of Telecommunication Resources for Disaster Mitigation and Relief Operations, adopted in Tampere, Finland, on 18 June 1998

Protocol against the Illicit Manufacturing of and Trafficking in Firearms, Their Parts and Components and Ammunition, supplementing the United Nations Convention against Transnational Organized Crime, adopted in New York on 31 May 2001

Framework Convention on Tobacco Control, adopted in Geneva on 21 May 2003

United Nations Convention against Corruption, adopted in New York on 31 October 2003

Intergovernmental Agreement on the Asian Highway Network, adopted in Bangkok, Thailand, on 18 November 2003

Agreement on International Railways in the Arab Mashreq, adopted in Beirut on 14 April 2003

Protocol to the 1979 Convention on Long-range Transboundary Air Pollution to Abate Acidification, Eutrophication and Ground-level Ozone, adopted in Gothenburg, Sweden, on 30 November 1990

Protocol on Water and Health to the 1992 Convention on the Protection and Use of Transboundary Watercourses and International Lakes, adopted in London on 17 June 1999

1958 Motor Vehicle Agreement, adopted in Geneva on 20 March 1958

Information for 2005 regarding all multilateral treaties deposited with the Secretary-General was contained in *Multilateral Treaties Deposited with the Secretary-General: Status as at 31 December 2005*, vols. I & II [ST/LEG/SER.E/24], Sales No. E.06.V.2.

Chapter IV

Law of the sea

The United Nations continued in 2005 to promote universal acceptance of the 1982 United Nations Convention on the Law of the Sea and its two implementing Agreements on the conservation and management of straddling fish stocks and highly migratory fish and on the privileges and immunities of the International Tribunal for the Law of the Sea.

The three institutions created by the Convention—the International Seabed Authority, the International Tribunal for the Law of the Sea and the Commission on the Limits of the Continental Shelf—held sessions during the year.

UN Convention on the Law of the Sea

Signatures and ratifications

In 2005, Burkina Faso and Estonia ratified or acceded to the United Nations Convention on the Law of the Sea (UNCLOS), bringing the number of parties to 149. The Convention, which was adopted by the Third United Nations Conference on the Law of the Sea in 1982 [YUN 1982, p. 178], entered into force on 16 November 1994 [YUN 1994, p. 1301].

Meeting of States Parties

The fifteenth Meeting of States Parties to the Convention (New York, 16-24 June) [SPLOS/135] discussed the 2004 activities of the International Tribunal for the Law of the Sea [YUN 2004, p. 1330] and took action on a number of Tribunal-related financial and administrative issues. Also discussed were the 2004 activities of the International Seabed Authority (see p. 1433) and of the Commission on the Limits of the Continental Shelf (see p. 1434) and matters related to article 319 of the Convention, including issues relating to the implementation of the Convention.

Agreement relating to the Implementation of Part XI of the Convention

During 2005, the number of parties to the 1994 Agreement relating to the Implementation of Part XI of the Convention (governing exploitation of seabed resources beyond national jurisdic-

tion), adopted by the General Assembly in resolution 48/263 [YUN 1994, p. 1301], reached 122. The Agreement, which entered into force on 28 July 1996 [YUN 1996, p. 1215], was to be interpreted and applied together with the Convention as a single instrument, and in the event of any inconsistency between the Agreement and Part XI of the Convention, the provisions of the Agreement would prevail. Any ratification of or accession to the Convention after 28 July 1994 represented consent to be bound by the Agreement. Parties to the Convention prior to the Agreement's adoption had to deposit a separate instrument of ratification of or accession to the Agreement.

Agreement relating to conservation and management of straddling fish stocks and highly migratory fish stocks

As at 31 December, the number of parties to the 1995 Agreement for the Implementation of the Provisions of the United Nations Convention on the Law of the Sea of 10 December 1982 relating to the Conservation and Management of Straddling Fish Stocks and Highly Migratory Fish Stocks [YUN 1995, p. 1334] reached 56. Referred to as the Fish Stocks Agreement, it entered into force on 11 December 2001 [YUN 2001, p. 1232].

Report of Secretary-General. In response to General Assembly resolution 59/25 [YUN 2004, p. 1322], the Secretary-General submitted an August report [A/60/189] on the status of implementation of the Fish Stocks Agreement. The report contained information on initiatives taken or recommended to improve the conservation and management of fishery and other marine living resources, with a view to achieving sustainable fisheries and protecting marine ecosystems and biodiversity.

The report emphasized the importance of the full implementation by States of all international fishery instruments, whether legally binding or voluntary. It invited States to cooperate in all aspects of fishery conservation and management, including the establishment of regional fisheries management organizations; apply both the precautionary and ecosystem approaches; and collect and exchange fishery data and statistics. The report included information on actions taken to address lost or abandoned gear, marine debris, destructive fishing practices and the regulation of bottom fisheries. A report on the status and activities of the United Nations Fish Stocks Agreement Assistance Fund was included.

GENERAL ASSEMBLY ACTION

On 29 November [meeting 56], the General Assembly adopted **resolution 60/31** [draft: A/60/L.23 & Add.1] without vote [agenda item 75 (*b*)].

Sustainable fisheries, including through the 1995 Agreement for the Implementation of the Provisions of the United Nations Convention on the Law of the Sea of 10 December 1982 relating to the Conservation and Management of Straddling Fish Stocks and Highly Migratory Fish Stocks, and related instruments

The General Assembly,

Reaffirming its resolutions 46/215 of 20 December 1991, 49/116 and 49/118 of 19 December 1994, 50/25 of 5 December 1995 and 57/142 of 12 December 2002, as well as other resolutions on large-scale pelagic driftnet fishing, unauthorized fishing in zones of national jurisdiction and on the high seas, fisheries by-catch and discards, and other developments, its resolutions 56/13 of 28 November 2001 and 57/143 of 12 December 2002 on the Agreement for the Implementation of the Provisions of the United Nations Convention on the Law of the Sea of 10 December 1982 relating to the Conservation and Management of Straddling Fish Stocks and Highly Migratory Fish Stocks ("the Agreement"), and its resolutions 58/14 of 24 November 2003 and 59/25 of 17 November 2004,

Recalling the relevant provisions of the United Nations Convention on the Law of the Sea ("the Convention"), and bearing in mind the relationship between the Convention and the Agreement,

Recognizing that, in accordance with the Convention, the Agreement sets forth provisions concerning the conservation and management of straddling fish stocks and highly migratory fish stocks, including provisions on compliance and enforcement by the flag State and subregional and regional cooperation in enforcement, binding dispute settlement and the rights and obligations of States in authorizing the use of vessels flying their flags for fishing on the high seas, and specific provisions to address the requirements of developing States in relation to the conservation and management of straddling fish stocks and highly migratory fish stocks and the development of fisheries for such stocks,

Noting that the Code of Conduct for Responsible Fisheries of the Food and Agriculture Organization of the United Nations ("the Code") and its associated international plans of action set out principles and global standards of behaviour for responsible practices for the conservation of fisheries resources and the management and development of fisheries,

Noting with concern that effective management of marine capture fisheries has been made difficult in some areas by unreliable information and data caused by unreported and misreported fish catch and fishing effort and the contribution this lack of data makes to continued overfishing in some areas,

Noting with satisfaction the Strategy for Improving Information on Status and Trends of Capture Fisheries, recently adopted by the Food and Agriculture Organization of the United Nations, and recognizing that the long-term improvement of the knowledge and understanding of fishery status and trends is a fundamental basis for fisheries policy and management for implementing the Code,

Recognizing the need to implement, as a matter of priority, the Plan of Implementation of the World Summit on Sustainable Development ("Johannesburg Plan of Implementation"), in relation to achieving sustainable fisheries, including the objective to maintain or restore stocks to levels that can produce the maximum sustainable yield with the aim of achieving these goals for depleted stocks on an urgent basis and where possible not later than 2015,

Recognizing also the significant contribution of sustainable fisheries to food security, income and wealth for present and future generations,

Deploring the fact that fish stocks, including straddling fish stocks and highly migratory fish stocks, in many parts of the world are overfished or subject to sparsely regulated and heavy fishing efforts, as a result of, inter alia, unauthorized fishing, inadequate flag State control and enforcement, including monitoring, control and surveillance measures, inadequate regulatory measures, harmful fisheries subsidies and overcapacity,

Concerned that illegal, unreported and unregulated fishing threatens seriously to deplete certain fish stocks and to significantly damage marine habitats and ecosystems, to the detriment of sustainable fisheries as well as the food security and the economies of many States, particularly developing States,

Welcoming the outcomes of the twenty-sixth session of the Committee on Fisheries of the Food and Agriculture Organization of the United Nations, held from 7 to 11 March 2005,

Welcoming also the 2005 Rome Declaration on Illegal, Unreported and Unregulated Fishing, adopted by the Ministerial Meeting on Fisheries of the Food and Agriculture Organization of the United Nations on 12 March 2005, which renewed the resolve of the international community to prevent, deter and eliminate illegal, unreported and unregulated fishing,

Welcoming further the 2005 Rome Declaration on Fisheries and the Tsunami, adopted by the Ministerial Meeting on 12 March 2005, which addressed the issue of rehabilitation in relation to the tsunami disaster,

Noting the efforts of the International Labour Organization in relation to work in the fishing sector,

Recognizing that the interrelationship between ocean activities, such as shipping and fishing, and environmental issues needs further consideration,

Concerned that marine pollution from all sources, including vessels and, in particular, land-based sources, constitutes a serious threat to human health and safety, endangers fish stocks, marine biodiversity and marine habitats and has significant costs to local and national economies,

Recognizing that marine debris is a global transboundary pollution problem and that, due to the many different types and sources of marine debris, different approaches to its prevention and removal are necessary,

Recognizing also the need for appropriate measures to address lost or abandoned gear, including catches by derelict fishing gear, which adversely affects, inter alia, fish stocks and habitats,

Noting that the contribution of sustainable aquaculture to global fish supplies continues to respond to opportunities in developing countries to enhance local food security and poverty alleviation and, together with efforts of other aquaculture producing countries, will make a significant contribution to meeting future demands in fish consumption, bearing in mind article 9 of the Code,

Calling attention to the circumstances affecting fisheries in many developing States, in particular African States and small island developing States, and recognizing the urgent need for capacity-building, including the transfer of marine technology, to assist such States in meeting their obligations and exercising their rights under international instruments, in order to realize the benefits from fisheries resources,

Noting the obligation of all States, pursuant to the provisions of the Convention, to cooperate in the conservation and management of straddling fish stocks and highly migratory fish stocks, and recognizing the importance of coordination and cooperation at the global, regional, subregional as well as national levels in the areas, inter alia, of data collection, information-sharing, capacity-building and training for the conservation, management and sustainable development of marine living resources,

Recognizing the duty provided in the Convention, the Agreement to Promote Compliance with International Conservation and Management Measures by Fishing Vessels on the High Seas ("the Compliance Agreement"), the Agreement and the Code for flag States to exercise effective control over fishing vessels flying their flag and vessels flying their flag which provide support to such vessels, and to ensure that the activities of such vessels do not undermine the effectiveness of conservation and management measures taken in accordance with international law and adopted at the national, subregional, regional or global levels,

Recognizing also the urgent need for action at all levels to ensure the long-term sustainable use and management of fisheries resources through the wide application of a precautionary approach, and through appropriate measures to reduce waste, discards and other factors which adversely affect fish stocks,

Recognizing further the economic and cultural importance of sharks in many countries, the biological importance of sharks in the marine ecosystem, the vulnerability of certain shark species to over-exploitation and the need for measures to promote the long-term sustainability of shark populations and fisheries, and the relevance of the International Plan of Action for the Conservation and Management of Sharks, adopted by the Food and Agriculture Organization of the United Nations in 1999, in providing development guidance of such measures,

Reaffirming its support for the initiative of the Food and Agriculture Organization of the United Nations and relevant regional and subregional fisheries management organizations and arrangements on the conservation and management of sharks, while noting with concern that only a small number of countries have implemented the International Plan of Action for the Conservation and Management of Sharks,

Welcoming the Ministerial Declaration of the "Conference on the Governance of High Seas Fisheries and the United Nations Fish Agreement—Moving from Words to Action", held in St. John's, Canada, from 1 to 5 May 2005, acknowledging that it is an initiative to improve high seas fisheries governance, including effective implementation of the Agreement,

Noting with satisfaction the outcomes of the fourth round of informal consultations of States parties to the Agreement, held in New York from 31 May to 3 June 2005,

Taking note with appreciation of the report of the Secretary-General, in particular its useful role in gathering and disseminating information on or relating to the sustainable development of the world's marine living resources,

Expressing concern that the practice of large-scale pelagic drift-net fishing remains a threat to marine living resources, although the incidence of this practice has continued to be low in most regions of the world's oceans and seas,

Emphasizing that efforts should be made to ensure that the implementation of resolution 46/215 in some parts of the world does not result in the transfer to other parts of the world of drift nets that contravene the resolution,

Expressing concern over reports of continued losses of seabirds, particularly albatrosses and petrels, as well as other marine species, including sharks, fin-fish species and marine turtles, as a result of incidental mortality in fishing operations, particularly longline fishing, and other activities, while recognizing considerable efforts to reduce by-catch in longline fishing through various regional fisheries management organizations and arrangements,

Recognizing the endorsement of the Guidelines to Reduce Sea Turtle Mortality in Fishing Operations by the Committee on Fisheries at its twenty-sixth session,

Welcoming the fact that a growing number of States, and entities referred to in the Convention and in article 1, paragraph 2 *(b)*, of the Agreement, as well as regional and subregional fisheries management organizations and arrangements, have taken measures, as appropriate, towards the implementation of the provisions of the Agreement,

I
Achieving sustainable fisheries

1. *Reaffirms* the importance it attaches to the long-term conservation, management and sustainable use of the marine living resources of the world's oceans and seas and the obligations of States to cooperate to this end, in accordance with international law, as reflected in the relevant provisions of the Convention, in particular the provisions on cooperation set out in Part V and Part VII, section 2, of the Convention, and where applicable, the Agreement;

2. *Emphasizes* the obligations of flag States to discharge their responsibilities, in accordance with the Convention and the Agreement, to ensure compliance by vessels flying their flag with the conservation and management measures adopted and in force with respect to fisheries resources on the high seas;

3. *Calls upon* all States that have not done so, in order to achieve the goal of universal participation, to become parties to the Convention, which sets out the

legal framework within which all activities in the oceans and seas must be carried out, taking into account the relationship between the Convention and the Agreement;

4. *Calls upon* all States, directly or through regional fisheries management organizations and arrangements, to apply, in accordance with international law, the precautionary approach and an ecosystem approach widely to the conservation, management and exploitation of fish stocks, including straddling fish stocks and highly migratory fish stocks, and also calls upon States parties to the Agreement to implement fully the provisions of article 6 of the Agreement as a matter of priority;

5. *Welcomes and encourages* the work of the Food and Agriculture Organization of the United Nations and its Committee on Fisheries, in particular the recent call to effectively implement the various instruments already developed to ensure responsible fisheries;

6. *Urges* States to eliminate barriers to trade, including tariff peaks, high tariffs and non-tariff barriers and measures which are not consistent with their obligations under the World Trade Organization agreements, taking into account the importance of the trade of fisheries products, particularly for developing countries;

7. *Welcomes* the 2005 International Guidelines for the Ecolabelling of Fish and Fishery Products from Marine Capture Fisheries of the Food and Agriculture Organization of the United Nations, acknowledges the role of certification and ecolabelling schemes, which are to be consistent with international law, including relevant World Trade Organization agreements, and notes ongoing discussions in the World Trade Organization on such schemes;

8. *Urges* States and relevant international and national organizations to provide for participation of small-scale fishery stakeholders in related policy development and fisheries management strategies in order to achieve long-term sustainability for such fisheries, consistent with the duty to ensure the proper conservation and management of fisheries resources;

II
Implementation of the 1995 Agreement for the Implementation of the Provisions of the United Nations Convention on the Law of the Sea of 10 December 1982 relating to the Conservation and Management of Straddling Fish Stocks and Highly Migratory Fish Stocks

9. *Calls upon* all States, and entities referred to in the Convention and in article 1, paragraph 2 *(b)*, of the Agreement, that have not done so to ratify or accede to the Agreement and in the interim to consider applying it provisionally;

10. *Calls upon* States parties to the Agreement to harmonize, as a matter of priority, their national legislation with the provisions of the Agreement, and to ensure that the provisions of the Agreement are effectively implemented into regional fisheries management organizations and arrangements of which they are a member;

11. *Emphasizes* the importance of those provisions of the Agreement relating to bilateral, regional and subregional cooperation in enforcement, and urges continued efforts in this regard;

12. *Encourages* States, as appropriate, to recognize that the general principles of the Agreement should also apply to discrete fish stocks in the high seas;

13. *Calls upon* all States to ensure that their vessels comply with the conservation and management measures that have been adopted by subregional and regional fisheries management organizations and arrangements in accordance with relevant provisions of the Convention and of the Agreement;

14. *Urges* States parties to the Agreement, in accordance with article 21, paragraph 4, thereof to inform, either directly or through the relevant regional or subregional fisheries management organization or arrangement, all States whose vessels fish on the high seas in the same region or subregion of the form of identification issued by those States parties to officials duly authorized to carry out boarding and inspection functions in accordance with articles 21 and 22 of the Agreement;

15. *Also urges* States parties to the Agreement, in accordance with article 21, paragraph 4, to designate an appropriate authority to receive notifications pursuant to article 21 and to give due publicity to such designation through the relevant subregional or regional fisheries management organization or arrangement;

16. *Invites* States and international financial institutions and organizations of the United Nations system to provide assistance according to Part VII of the Agreement, including, if appropriate, the development of special financial mechanisms or instruments to assist developing States, in particular the least developed among them and small island developing States, to enable them to develop their national capacity to exploit fishery resources, including developing their domestically flagged fishing fleet, value-added processing and the expansion of their economic base in the fishing industry, consistent with the duty to ensure the proper conservation and management of fishery resources;

17. *Notes with satisfaction* that the Assistance Fund under Part VII of the Agreement has begun to operate and consider applications for assistance by developing States parties to the Agreement, and encourages States, intergovernmental organizations, international financial institutions, national institutions, nongovernmental organizations and natural and juridical persons to make voluntary financial contributions to the Fund;

18. *Welcomes* the inaugural meeting at Windhoek, from 28 to 30 September 2005 of the Scientific Committee of the South-East Atlantic Fisheries Organization and its Commission's subsequent adoption of new conservation measures for the resources that fall under its responsibility within the area of the Convention on the Conservation and Management of Fishery Resources in the South-East Atlantic Ocean, and urges signatory States and other States whose vessels fish in that Convention area for fishery resources covered by that Convention to become parties to that Convention as a matter of priority and, in the interim, to apply it and the measures adopted thereunder provisionally, to ensure that vessels entitled to fly their flags apply such measures;

19. *Also welcomes* the inaugural meeting in Pohnpei, Federated States of Micronesia, on 9 and 10 December 2004 of the Western and Central Pacific Fisheries

Commission, and further encourages relevant States to become parties to the Convention on the Conservation and Management of Highly Migratory Fish Stocks in the Western and Central Pacific Ocean and, in the interim, to apply that Convention and the measures adopted thereunder to vessels entitled to fly their flags;

20. *Reaffirms* paragraph 16 of resolution 59/25 concerning the convening by the Secretary-General, pursuant to article 36 of the Agreement, of a review conference ("the review conference"), to be held in New York from 22 to 26 May 2006;

21. *Takes note* of the report of the fourth round of informal consultations of States parties to the Agreement, requests that the Secretary-General, in preparing, in cooperation with the Food and Agriculture Organization of the United Nations, the comprehensive report referred to in paragraph 17 of resolution 59/25, take into account the specific guidance proposed by the fourth round of informal consultations regarding the comprehensive report, and also requests that an advance unedited version of such a report be made available in accordance with past practice via the website of the Division for Ocean Affairs and the Law of the Sea of the Office of Legal Affairs of the Secretariat ("the Division") as of 16 January 2006;

22. *Invites* States parties, as well as States and entities entitled to become parties, subregional and regional fisheries management organizations and arrangements, and other intergovernmental and non-governmental organizations, to submit information and views to the review conference on matters relevant to the mandate of the conference and which would inform its work;

23. *Recalls* paragraph 6 of resolution 56/13, and requests the Secretary-General to convene in March 2006 a fifth round of informal consultations of States parties to the Agreement, to serve as preparation for the review conference;

24. *Requests* the Secretary-General to prepare a draft provisional agenda and draft rules of procedure for the review conference, and to circulate them at the same time as the provisional agenda, proposed by the fourth round of informal consultations of States parties to the Agreement, for the fifth round of informal consultations, sixty days in advance of these consultations;

25. *Also requests* the Secretary-General to invite States, and entities referred to in the Convention and in article 1, paragraph 2 *(b)*, of the Agreement, which are not parties to the Agreement, to participate fully in the fifth round of informal consultations of States parties to the Agreement on an equal footing with those States parties, except without voting rights, and reaffirms that, in accordance with past practice, every effort will be made to adopt recommendations on the basis of consensus;

26. *Further requests* the Secretary-General to invite the United Nations Development Programme, the Food and Agriculture Organization of the United Nations and other specialized agencies, the Commission on Sustainable Development, the World Bank, the Global Environment Facility and other relevant international financial institutions, subregional and regional fisheries management organizations and arrangements, other fisheries bodies, other relevant intergovernmental bodies and relevant non-governmental organizations to attend the fifth round of informal consultations of States parties to the Agreement as observers;

27. *Encourages* wide participation in the review conference, in accordance with article 36 of the Agreement, and calls upon those States that are able to do so to become parties to the Agreement prior to the conference;

III
Related fisheries instruments

28. *Emphasizes* the importance of the effective implementation of the provisions of the Compliance Agreement, and urges continued efforts in this regard;

29. *Calls upon* all States and other entities referred to in article X, paragraph 1, of the Compliance Agreement that have not yet become parties to that Agreement to do so as a matter of priority and, in the interim, to consider applying it provisionally;

30. *Urges* States and subregional and regional fisheries management organizations and arrangements to implement and promote the application of the Code within their areas of competence;

31. *Urges* States to develop and implement, as a matter of priority, national and, as appropriate, regional plans of action to put into effect the international plans of action of the Food and Agriculture Organization of the United Nations;

32. *Welcomes* the adoption of the Code of Safety for Fishermen and Fishing Vessels as revised by the Food and Agriculture Organization of the United Nations, the International Labour Organization and the International Maritime Organization and encourages its effective application, and urges States to become parties to the 1993 Protocol to the Torremolinos International Convention for the Safety of Fishing Vessels;

IV
Illegal, unreported and unregulated fishing

33. *Emphasizes once again its serious concern* that illegal, unreported and unregulated fishing remains one of the greatest threats to marine ecosystems and continues to have serious and major implications for the conservation and management of ocean resources, and renews its call upon States to comply fully with all existing obligations and to combat such fishing and urgently to take all necessary steps to implement the International Plan of Action to Prevent, Deter and Eliminate Illegal, Unreported and Unregulated Fishing of the Food and Agriculture Organization of the United Nations;

34. *Calls upon* States not to permit vessels flying their flag to engage in fishing on the high seas or in areas under the national jurisdiction of other States, unless duly authorized by the authorities of the States concerned and in accordance with the conditions set out in the authorization, without having effective control over their activities, and to take specific measures, including deterring the reflagging of vessels by their nationals, in accordance with the relevant provisions of the Convention, the Agreement and the Compliance Agreement, to control fishing operations by vessels flying their flag;

35. *Affirms* the need to strengthen, where necessary, the international legal framework for intergovernmental cooperation, in particular at the regional and subregional levels, in the management of fish stocks and

in combating illegal, unreported and unregulated fishing, in a manner consistent with international law, and for States and entities referred to in the Convention and in article 1, paragraph 2 *(b)*, of the Agreement to collaborate in efforts to address these types of fishing activities, including, inter alia, the development and implementation of vessel monitoring systems and the listing of vessels in order to prevent illegal, unreported and unregulated fishing activities and, where appropriate and consistent with international law, trade monitoring schemes, including to collect global catch data, through subregional and regional fisheries management organizations and arrangements;

36. *Calls upon* flag and port States to take all measures consistent with international law necessary to prevent the operation of substandard vessels and illegal, unreported and unregulated fishing activities;

37. *Urges* States to exercise effective control over their nationals and vessels flying their flag in order to prevent and deter them from engaging in illegal, unreported and unregulated fishing activities;

38. *Recalls* the request to the Secretary-General to report to the General Assembly at its sixty-first session on the study undertaken by the International Maritime Organization, in cooperation with other competent international organizations, following the invitation extended to it in resolution 58/14 and resolution 58/240 of 23 December 2003, to examine and clarify the role of the "genuine link" in relation to the duty of flag States to exercise effective control over ships flying their flag, including fishing vessels, and the potential consequences of non-compliance with the duties and obligations of flag States prescribed in the relevant international instruments;

39. *Reaffirms* the appeal made by the Ministers of Fisheries of the Food and Agriculture Organization of the United Nations in their 2005 Rome Declaration on Illegal, Unreported and Unregulated Fishing, including for further international action to eliminate illegal, unreported and unregulated fishing by vessels flying "flags of convenience" as well as to require that a "genuine link" be established between States and fishing vessels flying their flags, and calls upon States to implement the Declaration as a matter of priority;

40. *Requests* States and relevant international bodies to develop, in accordance with international law, more effective measures to trace fish and fishery products to enable importing States to identify fish or fishery products caught in a manner that undermines international conservation and management measures agreed in accordance with international law, and at the same time to recognize the importance of market access, in accordance with provisions 11.2.4, 11.2.5 and 11.2.6 of the Code, for fish and fishery products caught in a manner that is in conformity with such international measures;

41. *Encourages* further work by competent international organizations, including the Food and Agriculture Organization of the United Nations and subregional and regional fisheries management organizations and arrangements, to develop guidelines on flag State control of fishing vessels;

42. *Recognizes* the need for enhanced port State controls to combat illegal, unreported and unregulated fishing, urges States to cooperate, in particular at the regional level and through regional and sub-regional fisheries management organizations and arrangements, and encourages States to apply the model scheme on port State measures endorsed by the Committee on Fisheries at its twenty-sixth session in March 2005 at the national and regional levels, to promote its application through regional fisheries management organizations and arrangements and bodies, and to consider, when appropriate, the possibility of developing a legally binding instrument;

43. *Calls upon* all States to ensure that vessels flying their flag do not engage in trans-shipments of fish caught by fishing vessels engaged in illegal, unreported and unregulated fishing, and, individually or through regional fisheries management organizations or arrangements, to develop more effective enforcement and compliance measures to prevent and suppress such trans-shipments in accordance with international law;

44. *Urges* States, individually and through relevant regional fisheries management organizations and arrangements, to establish mandatory vessel monitoring, control and surveillance systems for fishing vessels, including the sharing of information on fisheries enforcement matters, to join the existing voluntary International Monitoring, Control and Surveillance Network for Fisheries-Related Activities and to consider the possibility, when appropriate, of transforming the Network, in accordance with international law, into an international unit with dedicated resources that can assist fisheries enforcement agencies;

45. *Encourages and supports* the development of a comprehensive global record within the Food and Agriculture Organization of the United Nations of fishing vessels, including refrigerated transport vessels and supply vessels, that incorporates available information on beneficial ownership, subject to confidentiality requirements in accordance with national law, and urges flag States to require that all their large-scale fishing vessels operating on the high seas be fitted with vessel monitoring systems no later than December 2008, or earlier if so decided by the flag State or any relevant regional fisheries management organizations or arrangements, as called for in the 2005 Rome Declaration on Illegal, Unreported and Unregulated Fishing;

46. *Urges* States, individually and through regional fisheries management organizations and arrangements, to adopt and implement internationally agreed market-related measures in accordance with international law, including principles, rights and obligations established in World Trade Organization agreements, as called for in the International Plan of Action to Prevent, Deter and Eliminate Illegal, Unreported and Unregulated Fishing;

V

Fishing overcapacity

47. *Calls upon* States and relevant regional and sub-regional fisheries management organizations and arrangements, as a matter of priority, to take effective measures to improve the management of fishing capacity and to implement the International Plan of Action for the Management of Fishing Capacity of the Food and Agriculture Organization of the United Nations, taking into account the need, through these actions, to avoid the transfer of fishing capacity to

other fisheries or areas including, but not limited to, those areas where fish stocks are overexploited or in a depleted condition;

48. *Reaffirms* the 2005 Rome Declaration on Fisheries and the Tsunami, which emphasized, inter alia, the need for fisheries and aquaculture rehabilitation in the affected areas to be in line with the principles of the Code and stressed that rehabilitation efforts, including transfer of vessels, must proceed under the leadership and control of the affected nations and must ensure that the fishing capacity that is being re-built is commensurate with the productive capacity of the fisheries resources and their sustainable utilization;

49. *Urges* States to eliminate subsidies that contribute to illegal, unreported and unregulated fishing and to fishing overcapacity, while completing the efforts undertaken at the World Trade Organization in accordance with the Doha Declaration on the Agreement on Trade-Related Aspects of Intellectual Property Rights and Public Health to clarify and improve its disciplines on fisheries subsidies, taking into account the importance of this sector, including small-scale and artisanal fisheries and aquaculture, to developing countries;

VI
Large-scale pelagic drift-net fishing

50. *Reaffirms* the importance it attaches to continued compliance with its resolution 46/215 and other subsequent resolutions on large-scale pelagic drift-net fishing, and urges States and entities referred to in the Convention and in article 1, paragraph 2 (*b*), of the Agreement to enforce fully the measures recommended in those resolutions;

VII
Fisheries by-catch and discards

51. *Urges* States, regional and subregional fisheries management organizations and arrangements and other relevant international organizations that have not done so to take action to reduce or eliminate by-catch, catch by lost or abandoned gear, fish discards and post-harvest losses, including juvenile fish, consistent with international law and relevant international instruments, including the Code, and in particular to consider measures including, as appropriate, technical measures related to fish size, mesh size or gear, discards, closed seasons and areas and zones reserved for selected fisheries, particularly artisanal fisheries, the establishment of mechanisms for communicating information on areas of high concentration of juvenile fish, taking into account the importance of ensuring confidentiality of such information, and support for studies and research that will reduce or eliminate by-catch of juvenile fish;

52. *Encourages* States and entities referred to in the Convention and in article 1, paragraph 2 (*b*), of the Agreement to give due consideration to participation, as appropriate, in regional and subregional instruments and organizations with mandates to conserve non-target species taken incidentally in fishing operations;

53. *Requests* States and regional fisheries management organizations and arrangements to urgently implement, as appropriate, the measures recommended

in the Guidelines to Reduce Sea Turtle Mortality in Fishing Operations and the International Plan of Action for Reducing Incidental Catch of Seabirds in Longline Fisheries in order to prevent the decline of sea turtles and seabird populations by reducing by-catch and increasing post-release survival in their fisheries, including through research and development of gear and bait alternatives, promoting the use of available by-catch mitigation technology, and promotion and strengthening of data collection programmes to obtain standardized information to develop reliable estimates of the by-catch of those species;

VIII
Subregional and regional cooperation

54. *Urges* coastal States and States fishing on the high seas, in accordance with the Convention and the Agreement, to pursue cooperation in relation to straddling fish stocks and highly migratory fish stocks, either directly or through appropriate subregional or regional fisheries management organizations or arrangements, to ensure the effective conservation and management of such stocks;

55. *Urges* States fishing for straddling fish stocks and highly migratory fish stocks on the high seas, and relevant coastal States, where a subregional or regional fisheries management organization or arrangement has the competence to establish conservation and management measures for such stocks, to give effect to their duty to cooperate by becoming members of such an organization or participants in such an arrangement, or by agreeing to apply the conservation and management measures established by such an organization or arrangement;

56. *Invites,* in this regard, subregional and regional fisheries management organizations and arrangements to ensure that all States having a real interest in the fisheries concerned may become members of such organizations or participants in such arrangements, in accordance with the Convention and the Agreement;

57. *Encourages* relevant coastal States and States fishing on the high seas for a straddling fish stock or a highly migratory fish stock, where there is no subregional or regional fisheries management organization or arrangement to establish conservation and management measures for such stocks, to cooperate to establish such an organization or enter into another appropriate arrangement to ensure the conservation and management of such stocks, and to participate in the work of the organization or arrangement;

58. *Welcomes and urges* further efforts by regional fisheries management organizations and arrangements, as a matter of priority, to strengthen and modernize their mandates to include an ecosystem approach to fisheries management and biodiversity considerations, where those aspects are lacking, to ensure that they effectively contribute to long-term conservation and management of marine living resources;

59. *Urges* regional fisheries management organizations and arrangements to ensure that their decision-making processes rely on the best scientific information available, incorporate the precautionary approach, develop criteria for allocation which reflects, where appropriate, the relevant provisions of the Agreement, and strengthen integration, coordination and cooperation with other relevant fisheries organizations, re-

gional seas arrangements and other relevant international organizations;

60. *Encourages* States, through their participation in regional fisheries management organizations and arrangements, to initiate processes for their performance review, and welcomes the work of the Food and Agriculture Organization of the United Nations in the development of general objective criteria for such reviews;

61. *Calls upon* States, individually and through regional fisheries management organizations or arrangements, to strengthen or establish, consistent with national and international law, positive or negative lists of vessels fishing within the areas covered by relevant regional fisheries management organizations and arrangements in order to verify compliance with conservation and management measures and identify products from illegal, unreported and unregulated catches, including, where possible, establishing tracking and verification mechanisms to do so, and encourages improved coordination among all parties and regional fisheries management organizations and arrangements to share and use this information;

62. *Encourages* the establishment of regional guidelines for States to use in establishing sanctions, for non-compliance by vessels flying their flag and by their nationals, that are adequate in severity to effectively secure compliance, deter further violations and deprive offenders of the benefits deriving from their illegal activities;

IX
Responsible fisheries in the marine ecosystem

63. *Encourages* States to apply by 2010 the ecosystem approach, notes the Reykjavik Declaration on Responsible Fisheries in the Marine Ecosystem and decision VII/11 and other relevant decisions of the Conference of the Parties to the Convention on Biological Diversity, notes the work of the Food and Agriculture Organization of the United Nations related to guidelines for the implementation of the ecosystem approach to fisheries management, and also notes the importance to this approach of relevant provisions of the Agreement and the Code;

64. *Encourages* enhanced science for conservation and management measures that incorporate and strengthen, in accordance with international law, the precautionary approach and consideration of ecosystem approaches to fisheries management, including through implementation of the Strategy for Improving Information on Status and Trends of Capture Fisheries, and a greater reliance on scientific advice in adopting such measures;

65. *Calls upon* States and regional fisheries management organizations and arrangements to collect and, where appropriate, report to the Food and Agriculture Organization of the United Nations more timely and comprehensive catch and effort data, including for straddling fish stocks and highly migratory fish stocks within and beyond areas under national jurisdiction, discrete high seas stocks and by-catch and discards;

66. *Encourages* States, individually or through regional fisheries management organizations and arrangements and other relevant international organizations, to work to ensure that fisheries and other ecosystem data collection is performed in a coordinated and inte-

grated manner, facilitating incorporation into global observation initiatives, where appropriate;

67. *Also encourages* States to increase scientific research in accordance with international law on the marine ecosystem;

68. *Calls upon* States, the Food and Agriculture Organization of the United Nations and other specialized agencies of the United Nations, subregional and regional fisheries management organizations and arrangements, where appropriate, and other appropriate intergovernmental bodies, to cooperate in achieving sustainable aquaculture, including through information exchange, developing equivalent standards on such issues as aquatic animal health and human health and safety concerns, assessing the potential positive and negative impacts of aquaculture, including socio-economics, on the marine and coastal environment, including biodiversity, and adopting relevant methods and techniques to minimize and mitigate adverse effects;

69. *Reaffirms* the importance it attaches to paragraphs 66 to 71 of resolution 59/25 concerning the impacts of fishing on vulnerable marine ecosystems, and urges accelerated progress by States and regional fisheries management organizations and arrangements on implementing these elements of the resolution;

70. *Requests* regional fisheries management organizations and arrangements with the competence to regulate bottom fisheries to adopt, in accordance with paragraph 67 of resolution 59/25, and implement appropriate conservation and management measures, including spatial and temporal measures, to protect vulnerable marine ecosystems as a matter of urgency;

71. *Welcomes* progress made in the implementation of paragraphs 68 and 69 of resolution 59/25 calling for the expansion, where appropriate, of the competence of existing regional fisheries management organizations or arrangements to regulate bottom fisheries and the impacts of fishing on vulnerable marine ecosystems or for the establishment of new regional fisheries management organizations or arrangements with such competence to cover areas of the high seas where no such organization or arrangement currently exists;

72. *Calls upon* States urgently to accelerate their cooperation in establishing interim targeted protection mechanisms for vulnerable marine ecosystems in regions where they have an interest in the conservation and management of marine living resources;

73. *Requests* the Secretary-General, in cooperation with the Food and Agriculture Organization of the United Nations, to report to the General Assembly at its sixty-first session on the actions taken by States and regional fisheries management organizations and arrangements to give effect to paragraphs 66 to 69 of resolution 59/25, in order to facilitate the review referred to in paragraph 71 of the resolution of progress on action taken, with a view to further recommendations, where necessary, in areas where arrangements are inadequate, and further requests that an advance unedited version of the report be made available in accordance with past practice via the website of the Division as of 15 July 2006;

74. *Requests* States and regional fisheries management organizations and arrangements to submit detailed information to the Secretary-General in a timely manner on actions taken pursuant to paragraphs 66 to

69 of resolution 59/25 to facilitate a comprehensive review of such actions;

75. *Encourages* progress to establish criteria on the objectives and management of marine protected areas for fisheries purposes, and in this regard welcomes the proposed work of the Food and Agriculture Organization of the United Nations to develop technical guidelines in accordance with the Convention on the design, implementation and testing of marine protected areas for such purposes, and urges coordination and cooperation among all relevant international organizations and bodies;

76. *Notes* that 2005 marks the ten-year anniversary of the adoption of the Global Programme of Action for the Protection of the Marine Environment from Land-based Activities, and urges all States to implement the Global Programme of Action and to accelerate activity to safeguard the marine ecosystem, including fish stocks, against pollution and physical degradation;

77. *Calls upon* States, the Food and Agriculture Organization of the United Nations, the International Maritime Organization, the United Nations Environment Programme, in particular its Regional Seas programme, regional and subregional fisheries management organizations and arrangements and other appropriate intergovernmental organizations that have not yet done so to take action to address the issue of lost or abandoned fishing gear and related marine debris, including through the collection of data on gear loss, economic costs to fisheries and other sectors, and the impact on marine ecosystems;

78. *Encourages* close cooperation and coordination, as appropriate, between States, relevant intergovernmental organizations, United Nations programmes and other bodies, such as the Food and Agriculture Organization of the United Nations, the International Maritime Organization, the United Nations Environment Programme, the Global Programme of Action, and Regional Seas arrangements, regional and subregional fisheries management organizations and arrangements and relevant stakeholders, including nongovernmental organizations, to address the issue of lost and discarded fishing gear and related marine debris, through initiatives such as analysis of the implementation and effectiveness of the existing measures relevant to the control and management of derelict fishing gear and related marine debris, the development and implementation of targeted studies to determine the socio-economic, technical and other factors that influence the accidental loss and deliberate disposal of fishing gear at sea, the assessment and implementation of preventive measures, incentives and/or disincentives relating to the loss and disposal of fishing gear at sea, and the development of best management practices;

79. *Encourages* States, directly and through regional and subregional fisheries management organizations and arrangements, and in close cooperation and coordination with relevant stakeholders, to address the issue of lost and discarded fishing gear and related marine debris, through initiatives including developing and implementing joint prevention and recovery programmes, establishing a clearing-house mechanism to facilitate the sharing of information between States on fishing net types and other fishing gear, the regular, long-term collection, collation and dissemination of information on derelict fishing gear, and national inventories of net types and other fishing gear, as appropriate;

80. *Encourages* States, the United Nations Environment Programme, the Global Programme of Action, the Food and Agriculture Organization of the United Nations, the International Maritime Organization, subregional and regional fisheries management organizations and arrangements and other relevant intergovernmental organizations and programmes to consider the outcomes of the Asia-Pacific Economic Cooperation Education and Outreach Seminar on Derelict Fishing Gear and Related Marine Debris, held in January 2004, and how they may be implemented;

81. *Encourages* States to raise awareness within their fishing sector and subregional and regional fisheries management organizations and arrangements of the issue of derelict fishing gear and related marine debris and to identify options for action;

82. *Encourages* the Committee on Fisheries to consider the issue of derelict fishing gear and related marine debris at its next meeting in 2007, and in particular the implementation of relevant provisions of the Code;

X
Capacity-building

83. *Reiterates* the crucial importance of cooperation by States directly or, as appropriate, through the relevant regional and subregional organizations, and by other international organizations, including the Food and Agriculture Organization of the United Nations through its FishCode programme, including through financial and/or technical assistance, in accordance with the Agreement, the Compliance Agreement, the Code and the International Plan of Action to Prevent, Deter and Eliminate Illegal, Unreported and Unregulated Fishing and the International Plan of Action for the Conservation and Management of Sharks, to increase the capacity of developing States to achieve the goals and implement the actions called for in the present resolution;

84. *Welcomes* the work of the Food and Agriculture Organization of the United Nations in developing guidance on the strategies and measures required for the creation of an enabling environment for small-scale fisheries, including the development of a code of conduct and guidelines for enhancing the contribution of small-scale fisheries to poverty alleviation and food security that include adequate provisions with regard to financial measures and capacity-building, including transfer of technology, and encourages studies for creating possible alternative livelihoods for coastal communities;

85. *Encourages* increased capacity-building and technical assistance by States, international financial institutions and relevant intergovernmental organizations and bodies for fishers, in particular small-scale fishers, in developing countries, and in particular small island developing States, consistent with environmental sustainability;

86. *Encourages* the international community to enhance the opportunities for sustainable development in developing countries, in particular the least developed countries, small island developing States and coastal African States, by encouraging greater participation of

those States in authorized fisheries activities being undertaken within areas under their national jurisdiction, in accordance with the Convention, by distant-water fishing nations in order to achieve better economic returns for developing countries from their fisheries resources within areas under their national jurisdiction and an enhanced role in regional fisheries management, as well as by enhancing the ability of developing countries to develop their own fisheries, as well as to participate in high seas fisheries, including access to such fisheries, in conformity with international law, in particular the Convention and the Agreement;

87. *Requests* distant-water fishing nations, when negotiating access agreements and arrangements with developing coastal States, to do so on an equitable and sustainable basis, including by giving greater attention to fish processing, including fish processing facilities, within the national jurisdiction of the developing coastal State to assist the realization of the benefits from the development of fisheries resources;

88. *Encourages* greater assistance for developing States in designing, establishing and implementing relevant agreements, instruments and tools for the conservation and sustainable management of fish stocks, including the enhancement of research and scientific capabilities through existing funds, such as the Assistance Fund under Part VII of the Agreement, bilateral assistance, regional fisheries management organizations and arrangements assistance funds, the FishCode programme, the World Bank's global programme on fisheries and the Global Environment Facility;

XI
Cooperation within the United Nations system

89. *Requests* the relevant parts of the United Nations system, international financial institutions and donor agencies to support increased enforcement and compliance capabilities for regional fisheries management organizations and their member States;

90. *Invites* the Food and Agriculture Organization of the United Nations to continue its cooperative arrangements with United Nations agencies on the implementation of the international plans of action and to report to the Secretary-General, for inclusion in his annual report on sustainable fisheries, on priorities for cooperation and coordination in this work;

91. *Invites* the Division, the Food and Agriculture Organization of the United Nations and other relevant bodies of the United Nations system to consult and cooperate in the preparation of questionnaires designed to collect information on sustainable fisheries, in order to avoid duplication;

XII
Sixty-first session of the General Assembly

92. *Requests* the Secretary-General to bring the present resolution to the attention of all members of the international community, relevant intergovernmental organizations, the organizations and bodies of the United Nations system, regional and subregional fisheries management organizations and relevant non-governmental organizations, and to invite them to provide the Secretary-General with information relevant to the implementation of the present resolution;

93. *Also requests* the Secretary-General to submit to the General Assembly at its sixty-second session a report on "Sustainable fisheries, including through the 1995 Agreement for the Implementation of the Provisions of the United Nations Convention on the Law of the Sea of 10 December 1982 relating to the Conservation and Management of Straddling Fish Stocks and Highly Migratory Fish Stocks, and related instruments", taking into account information provided by States, relevant specialized agencies, in particular the Food and Agriculture Organization of the United Nations, and other appropriate organs, organizations and programmes of the United Nations system, regional and subregional organizations and arrangements for the conservation and management of straddling fish stocks and highly migratory fish stocks, as well as other relevant intergovernmental bodies and non-governmental organizations, and consisting, inter alia, of elements provided in relevant paragraphs in the present resolution;

94. *Decides* to include in the provisional agenda of its sixty-first session, under the item entitled "Oceans and the law of the sea", the sub-item entitled "Sustainable fisheries, including through the 1995 Agreement for the Implementation of the Provisions of the United Nations Convention on the Law of the Sea of 10 December 1982 relating to the Conservation and Management of Straddling Fish Stocks and Highly Migratory Fish Stocks, and related instruments".

Institutions created by the Convention

International Seabed Authority

Through the International Seabed Authority, established by UNCLOS and the 1994 Implementation Agreement [YUN 1994, p. 1301], States organized and conducted exploration of the resources of the seabed and ocean floor and subsoil beyond the limits of national jurisdiction. In 2005, the Authority, which had 149 members as at 31 December, held its eleventh session (Kingston, Jamaica, 15-26 August). Its subsidiary bodies, namely, the Assembly, the Council, the Legal and Technical Commission and the Finance Committee, also met during the session.

The Assembly considered the annual report of the Authority's Secretary-General [ISBA/11/A/4 & Corr.1], who reported that in 2005, the secretariat continued to develop a geological model of the polymetallic deposits of the Clarion-Clipperton fracture zone in the Pacific Ocean, as part of the 2005-2007 work programme [YUN 2004, p. 1330]. The project would be reviewed in 2006 and a workshop held in 2007 to examine its results. The Secretary-General drew the Assembly's attention to the Authority's efforts to promote marine scientific research in the Area, and his proposal to establish a trust fund to promote marine scientific research and to provide opportunities for qualified scientists from developing countries to participate in international research activities. The report also discussed the Authority's relations with the United Nations and other bodies.

The first meeting of Oceans and Coastal Agencies (UN-Oceans), an inter-agency coordination mechanism established by the General Assembly, in resolution 58/240 [YUN 2003, p. 1361] was held in Paris (25-29 January). A second meeting was held in New York in May preceding the sixth meeting of the United Nations Open-ended Informal Consultative Process on the Law of the Sea.

The Assembly considered the report of the Finance Committee and approved the recommendations contained therein [ISBA/11/C/8-ISBA/11/C/9].

The Legal and Technical Commission reported on its work during the eleventh session [ISBA/11/C/8]. The Commission considered the annual reports of contractors submitted pursuant to the Regulations on Prospecting and Exploration for Polymetallic Nodules in the Area [ISBA/6/A/18, annex] and explanatory notes to the draft regulations for prospecting and exploration for polymetallic sulphides and cobalt-rich ferromanganese crusts in the Area. The Commission reviewed the application for the approval of a plan of work for exploration for polymetallic modules submitted by Germany and considered recommendations of the workshop on polymetallic sulphides and cobalt-rich crusts: their environment and considerations for the establishment of environmental baselines and an associated monitoring programme for exploration. The Commission also considered an update on progress with the geological model of the Clarion-Clipperton Fracture Zone and on the Kaplan project on the study of the biodiversity in the Clarion-Clipperton Zone.

The Commission noted that its technical work was becoming more specialized and pointed to the need to strengthen its expertise in certain disciplines, including marine geology and geophysics, biology, oceanology, protection of the marine environment, and economic and legal matters relating to ocean mining. It recommended that the Council draw the attention of States parties to the issue and nominate such experts as candidates in the 2006 election of members of the Commission. It also requested that environmental issues be included in its agenda for 2006.

International Tribunal for the Law of the Sea

The International Tribunal for the Law of the Sea held its nineteenth (7-18 March) and twentieth (26 September–7 October) sessions, both in Hamburg, Germany [SPLOS/136].

In the *Case concerning The Conservation and Sustainable Exploitation of Swordfish Stocks in the South-Eastern Pacific Ocean* (*Chile/European Community*) [YUN 2003, p. 1353], the Special Chamber (28-29 December) established for that purpose, at the request of the parties, extended the time limit for making preliminary objections until 1 January 2008 and maintained the rights of the parties to revive the proceedings at any time.

In the *Juno Trader Case* (*Saint Vincent and the Grenadines v. Guinea-Bissau*) [YUN 2004, p. 1330], on 1 February, the Deputy Agent of Saint Vincent and the Grenadines informed the Tribunal of the difficulties encountered by the Juno Trader owner concerning the terms and posting of the bank guarantee with the Guinea-Bissau authorities. On 29 March, the counsel for Saint Vincent and the Grenadines informed the Registrar that, following an 18 March confidential agreement between Guinea-Bissau and the *Juno Trader*, the vessel was released and left Guinea-Bissau's exclusive zone on 27 March.

In the *Case concerning Land Reclamation by Singapore in and around the Straits of Johor (Malaysia v. Singapore)* [ibid., p. 1331], on 26 April, Malaysia and Singapore signed a settlement agreement to terminate the case upon agreed terms. On 1 September, upon the joint request of the parties, the arbitral tribunal rendered a final award in accordance with the terms specified in the settlement agreement.

Commission on the Limits of the Continental Shelf

In 2005, the Commission on the Limits of the Continental Shelf, established in 1997 [YUN 1997, p. 1362], held its fifteenth (4-22 April) [CLCS/44] and sixteenth (29 August–16 September) [CLCS/48 & Corr.1] sessions, both in New York.

At its fifteenth session, the Commission was informed that the training manual for the delineation of the outer limits of the continental shelf beyond 200 miles and for the preparation of submissions to the Commission had been prepared. The first training course based on the manual was conducted in Fiji (February/March) and others were planned. The Commission decided to seek a legal opinion from the UN Legal Counsel on the application of the Commission's rules of procedure regarding the additional material and information by Brazil to its 2004 submission [YUN 2004, p. 1331] relating to the limits of its continental shelf or substantial part thereof. The Commission also considered a submission from Australia, and established a subcommission to consider the matter. The Commission discussed its workload and was of the opinion that, under current arrangements, it might not be able to deliver on its functions. The Commission concluded that the matter should be brought to the attention of States parties at their next meeting.

At its sixteenth session, the Commission considered the submission by Ireland and continued consideration of submissions by Brazil and Australia. Following the request made at the fifteenth session (see above), the Commission considered the opinion of the Legal Counsel [CLCS/48], and acting accordingly, agreed to invite Brazil to transmit an addendum or corrigendum to its submission to the Commission through the Secretary-General. The Commission forwarded the legal opinion to the four States that had made submissions so far. The report discussed mechanisms by which coastal States might be apprised of the recommendations of a subcommission to the Commission and given the opportunity to express an opinion thereon. The Commission, based on the proposals of a working group established to examine the issue, adopted amendments to section III (6) and section VI (15) of annex III of its rules of procedure. The subject was to be considered further at its seventeenth session. The Commission also agreed to refer the matter of its heavy workload and the related financial implications to the General Assembly and the Meeting of States Parties.

Other developments related to the Convention

In response to General Assembly resolution 59/24 [YUN 2004, p. 1333], the Secretary-General submitted a March report, with later addenda, on oceans and the law of the sea [A/60/63 & Add.1, 2], describing the status of UNCLOS and its two implementing Agreements, and discussed issues related to maritime space; developments relating to institutions established by UNCLOS; capacity-building; developments relating to international shipping activities; maritime security and crimes at sea; the marine environment, marine resources and sustainable development; areas of focus at the sixth meeting of the Consultative Process; the Indian Ocean tsunami and international cooperation and coordination; and scientific, technical, economic, environmental, socio-economic and legal issues and the activities of the United Nations and other relevant international organizations.

The Secretary-General concluded that, to address the threats posed to the oceans and seas by climate change, natural disasters, environmental degradation, depletion of fisheries, loss of biodiversity and ineffective flag State control, and to achieve security and sustainability, concerted actions had to be taken by the international community. Those included ratification and full implementation of UNCLOS and other ocean-related instruments; more effective control by States over their vessels and refusal of registration to those vessels over which they could not exercise such control; encouragement by States to address the threat of climate change, including sea level rise and coral bleaching; increased implementation of the Global Programme of Action for the Protection of the Marine Environment from Land-based Activities; fostering environmentally sound waste management practices, including measures to deal with fisheries-related marine debris; support for work on preventing further destruction of marine ecosystems and associated losses of biodiversity and participation in discussions on the conservation and sustainable use of marine biodiversity in the General Assembly's ad hoc working group; and efforts by States to launch the initial phase of the process for global reporting and assessment of the state of the marine environment.

The Secretary-General noted that the United Nations Open-ended Informal Consultative Process on Oceans and Law of the Sea (see p. 1436) had reached the end of its second three-year cycle and was due for review and renewal by the Assembly. The tenth anniversary of the Global Programme of Action would be celebrated in 2006 and the International Maritime Organization had adopted instruments dealing with all aspects of international shipping. However, serious problems remained, including labour conditions, persons in distress at sea and incidents of piracy and armed robbery. He also noted the continuing work on waste management and ship recycling as well as international response to the tsunami disaster.

Marine environment: Global Marine Assessment

Responding to General Assembly resolution 59/24 [YUN 2004, p. 1333], the Secretary-General submitted a June report [A/60/91] providing an account of the second Global Marine Assessment (GMA) international workshop on the regular process for global reporting and assessment of the state of the marine environment, including socio-economic aspects (New York, 13-15 June). The workshop discussed the start-up phase, the Assessment of Assessments, as a preparatory stage towards the establishment of the regular process provided for in the Plan of Implementation of the World Summit on Sustainable Development (Johannesburg Plan of Implementation) [YUN 2002, p. 821] and resolutions 57/141 [YUN 2002, p. 1322] and 58/240 [YUN 2003, p. 1355]. The second international workshop established the modalities for conducting the Assessment of Assessments, particularly the establishment of an ad hoc steering group to oversee its execution, which were forwarded to the Assembly for consideration.

United Nations Open-ended Informal Consultative Process

In response to General Assembly resolution 59/24 [YUN 2004, p. 1333], the sixth meeting of the United Nations Open-ended Informal Consultative Process on Oceans and the Law of the Sea (New York, 6-10 June) [A/60/99] focused on fisheries and their contribution to sustainable development and marine debris. The meeting agreed on most of the elements relating to fisheries and their contribution to sustainable development. However, as it was unable to finalize the elements relating to marine debris and cooperation and coordination, it agreed that the co-Chairpersons' proposed elements, set out in section 2 of the report, would be forwarded to the Assembly. Delegations submitted proposals for additional issues to be considered by the Consultative Process; the application of an ecosystem approach to oceans management; integrated management approaches to address marine pollution; human and labour rights of those employed in the fishing and maritime sectors; short-, medium-, and long-term ecosystem management mechanisms to address and prevent the decline and extinction of associated species; promotion of marine scientific research, as well as capacity-building for the development of scientific information; international legal and institutional frameworks for the protection of marine mammals; naturally occurring mesoscale marine ecosystems; and coastal hazard preparedness.

The Informal Consultative Process reached the end of its second three-year cycle and was due for review and renewal by the Assembly at the sixtieth (2005) session.

On 29 November [meeting 56], the General Assembly adopted **resolution 60/30** [draft: A/60/L.22 & Add.1] by recorded vote (141-1-4) [agenda item 75 *(a)*].

Oceans and the law of the sea

The General Assembly,

Recalling its resolutions 49/28 of 6 December 1994, 52/26 of 26 November 1997, 54/33 of 24 November 1999, 57/141 of 12 December 2002, 58/240 of 23 December 2003, 59/24 of 17 November 2004 and other relevant resolutions concerning the United Nations Convention on the Law of the Sea ("the Convention"),

Having considered the report of the Secretary-General, the addendum thereto and also the reports on the sixth meeting of the United Nations Open-ended Informal Consultative Process on Oceans and the Law of the Sea ("the Consultative Process"), the second International Workshop on the regular process

for global reporting and assessment of the state of the marine environment, including socio-economic aspects, and the fifteenth Meeting of States Parties to the Convention,

Emphasizing the pre-eminent contribution provided by the Convention to the strengthening of peace, security, cooperation and friendly relations among all nations in conformity with the principles of justice and equal rights and to the promotion of the economic and social advancement of all peoples of the world, in accordance with the purposes and principles of the United Nations as set forth in the Charter of the United Nations, as well as for the sustainable development of the oceans and seas,

Emphasizing also the universal and unified character of the Convention, and reaffirming that the Convention sets out the legal framework within which all activities in the oceans and seas must be carried out, and that its integrity needs to be maintained, as recognized also by the United Nations Conference on Environment and Development in chapter 17 of Agenda 21,

Conscious that the problems of ocean space are closely interrelated and need to be considered as a whole through an integrated, interdisciplinary and intersectoral approach, and reaffirming the need to improve cooperation and coordination at national, regional and global levels, in accordance with the Convention, to support and supplement the efforts of each State in promoting the implementation and observance of the Convention, and the integrated management and sustainable development of the oceans and seas,

Reiterating the essential need for cooperation, including through capacity-building and transfer of marine technology, to ensure that all States, especially developing countries, in particular the least developed countries and small island developing States, as well as coastal African States, are able both to implement the Convention and to benefit from the sustainable development of the oceans and seas, as well as to participate fully in global and regional forums and processes dealing with oceans and law of the sea issues,

Emphasizing the need to strengthen the ability of competent international organizations to contribute, at the global, regional, subregional and bilateral levels, through cooperation programmes with Governments, to the development of national capacity in marine science and the sustainable management of the oceans and their resources,

Recalling that marine science is important for eradicating poverty, contributing to food security, conserving the world's marine environment and resources, helping to understand, predict and respond to natural events and promoting the sustainable development of the oceans and seas, by improving knowledge, through sustained research efforts and the evaluation of monitoring results, and applying such knowledge to management and decision-making,

Recalling also its decision, in resolutions 57/141 and 58/240, to establish a regular process under the United Nations for global reporting and assessment of the state of the marine environment, including socio-economic aspects, both current and foreseeable, building on existing regional assessments, as recommended by the World Summit on Sustainable Development, and noting the need for cooperation among all States to this end,

Reiterating its concern at the adverse impacts on the marine environment and biodiversity, in particular on vulnerable marine ecosystems, including corals, of human activities, such as overutilization of living marine resources, the use of destructive practices, physical impacts by ships, the introduction of alien invasive species and marine pollution from all sources, including from land-based sources and vessels, in particular through the illegal discharge of oil and other harmful substances, the loss or release of fishing gear and the dumping of hazardous waste such as radioactive materials, nuclear waste and dangerous chemicals,

Recognizing that hydrographic surveys and nautical charting are critical to the safety of navigation and life at sea, environmental protection, including the protection of vulnerable marine ecosystems, and the economics of the global shipping industry, and recognizing also in this regard that the move towards electronic charting not only provides significantly increased benefits for safe navigation and management of ship movement, but also provides data and information that can be used for sustainable fisheries activities and other sectoral uses of the marine environment, the delimitation of maritime boundaries and environmental protection,

Noting with concern the continuing problem of transnational organized crime and threats to maritime safety and security, including piracy, armed robbery at sea and smuggling, and noting the deplorable loss of life and adverse impact on international trade resulting from such activities,

Noting the important role of the Commission on the Limits of the Continental Shelf ("the Commission") in assisting States parties in the implementation of Part VI of the Convention, through the examination of information submitted by coastal States regarding the outer limits of the continental shelf beyond 200 nautical miles, and also noting the need to ensure the effective functioning of the Commission during a period of rapidly increasing workload, and noting in particular the need to ensure participation of the members of the Commission in its subcommissions,

Recognizing the importance and the contribution of the work over the past six years of the Consultative Process established by resolution 54/33 to facilitate the annual review of developments in ocean affairs by the General Assembly and extended for three years by resolution 57/141,

Noting the responsibilities of the Secretary-General under the Convention and related resolutions of the General Assembly, in particular resolutions 49/28, 52/26 and 54/33, and in this context the increase in activities of the Division for Ocean Affairs and the Law of the Sea of the Office of Legal Affairs of the Secretariat ("the Division"), in particular in view of the growing number of requests to the Division for additional outputs and servicing of meetings, the increasing capacity-building activities and assistance to the Commission, and the role of the Division in inter-agency coordination and cooperation,

Emphasizing that underwater archaeological, cultural and historical heritage, including shipwrecks and watercrafts, holds essential information on the history of humankind and that such heritage is a resource that needs to be protected and preserved,

I
Implementation of the Convention and related agreements and instruments

1. *Reaffirms* its resolutions 49/28, 52/26, 54/33, 57/141, 58/240, 59/24 and other relevant resolutions concerning the Convention;

2. *Calls upon* all States that have not done so, in order to achieve the goal of universal participation, to become parties to the Convention, and the Agreement relating to the Implementation of Part XI of the United Nations Convention on the Law of the Sea of 10 December 1982 ("the Agreement");

3. *Calls upon* all States that have not done so, in order to achieve the goal of universal participation, to become parties to the Agreement for the Implementation of the Provisions of the United Nations Convention on the Law of the Sea of 10 December 1982 relating to the Conservation and Management of Straddling Fish Stocks and Highly Migratory Fish Stocks ("the Fish Stocks Agreement");

4. *Reaffirms* the unified character of the Convention and the need to preserve its integrity;

5. *Once again calls upon* States to harmonize, as a matter of priority, their national legislation with the provisions of the Convention and, where applicable, relevant agreements and instruments, to ensure the consistent application of those provisions and to ensure also that any declarations or statements that they have made or make when signing, ratifying or acceding to the Convention do not purport to exclude or to modify the legal effect of the provisions of the Convention in their application to the State concerned and to withdraw any such declarations or statements;

6. *Calls upon* States parties to the Convention to deposit with the Secretary-General charts or lists of geographical coordinates, as provided for in the Convention;

7. *Urges* all States to cooperate, directly or through competent international bodies, in taking measures to protect and preserve objects of an archaeological and historical nature found at sea, in conformity with the Convention, and calls upon States to work together on such diverse challenges and opportunities as the appropriate relationship between salvage law and scientific management and conservation of underwater cultural heritage, increasing technological abilities to discover and reach underwater sites, looting and growing underwater tourism;

8. *Notes* the effort made by the United Nations Educational, Scientific and Cultural Organization with respect to the preservation of underwater cultural heritage, and notes in particular the rules annexed to the 2001 Convention on the Protection of the Underwater Cultural Heritage that address the relationship between salvage law and scientific principles of management, conservation and protection of underwater cultural heritage among parties, their nationals and vessels flying their flag;

II
Capacity-building

9. *Calls upon* donor agencies and international financial institutions to keep their programmes systematically under review to ensure the availability in all

States, particularly in developing States, of the economic, legal, navigational, scientific and technical skills necessary for the full implementation of the Convention and the objectives of the present resolution, as well as the sustainable development of the oceans and seas nationally, regionally and globally, and in so doing to bear in mind the interests and needs of landlocked developing States;

10. *Encourages* intensified efforts to build capacity for developing countries, in particular for the least developed countries and small island developing States, as well as coastal African States, to improve hydrographic services and the production of nautical charts, including electronic charts, as well as the mobilization of resources and building of capacity with support from international financial institutions and the donor community;

11. *Calls upon* States and international financial institutions, including through bilateral, regional and global cooperation programmes and technical partnerships, to continue to strengthen capacity-building activities, in particular in developing countries, in the field of marine scientific research by, inter alia, training the necessary skilled personnel, providing the necessary equipment, facilities and vessels and transferring environmentally sound technologies;

12. *Recognizes* the need to build the capacity of developing States to raise awareness of, and support implementation of, improved waste management practices, noting the particular vulnerability of small island developing States to the impact of marine pollution from land-based sources and marine debris;

13. *Also recognizes* the importance of assisting developing States, in particular the least developed countries and small island developing States, in implementing the Convention, and urges States, intergovernmental organizations and agencies, national institutions, nongovernmental organizations and international financial institutions, as well as natural and juridical persons, to make voluntary financial or other contributions to the trust funds, as referred to in resolution 57/141, established for this purpose;

14. *Encourages* States to use the Criteria and Guidelines on the Transfer of Marine Technology, adopted by the Assembly of the Intergovernmental Oceanographic Commission of the United Nations Educational, Scientific and Cultural Organization;

15. *Also encourages* States to assist developing States, and especially the least developed countries and small island developing States, as well as coastal African States, on a bilateral and, where appropriate, regional level, in the preparation of submissions to the Commission regarding the establishment of the outer limits of the continental shelf beyond 200 nautical miles, including the assessment of the nature and extent of the continental shelf of a coastal State through a desktop study, and the delineation of the outer limits of its continental shelf;

16. *Commends with satisfaction* the Division upon the completion of the training manual, notes with appreciation the successful conduct of two regional training courses, and welcomes the intention to conduct two additional training courses before mid-2006, the purpose of which is to train technical staff of coastal developing States on the delineation of the outer limits of the con-

tinental shelf beyond 200 nautical miles and on the preparation of submissions to the Commission;

17. *Requests* the Secretary-General, in cooperation with States and relevant international organizations and institutions, to continue making such training courses available at the regional and also the subregional and national levels, as appropriate;

18. *Invites* Member States and others in a position to do so to support the capacity-building activities of the Division, including, in particular, the training activities to assist developing States in the preparation of their submissions to the Commission, and invites Member States and others in a position to do so to contribute to the new trust fund established by the Secretary-General for the Office of Legal Affairs of the Secretariat to support the promotion of international law;

19. *Recognizes* the importance of the Hamilton Shirley Amerasinghe Memorial Fellowship Programme on the Law of the Sea, urges Member States and others in a position to do so to contribute to the further development of the Fellowship Programme, and takes note with satisfaction of the ongoing implementation of the United Nations and the Nippon Foundation Fellowship Programme, focusing on human resources development for developing coastal States parties and nonparties to the Convention in the field of ocean affairs and the law of the sea or related disciplines;

III
Meeting of States Parties

20. *Welcomes* the report of the fifteenth Meeting of States Parties to the Convention;

21. *Requests* the Secretary-General to convene the sixteenth Meeting of States Parties to the Convention in New York from 19 to 23 June 2006 and to provide the services required;

IV
Peaceful settlement of disputes

22. *Notes with satisfaction* the continued and significant contribution of the International Tribunal for the Law of the Sea ("the Tribunal") to the settlement of disputes by peaceful means in accordance with Part XV of the Convention, and underlines the important role and authority of the Tribunal concerning the interpretation or application of the Convention and the Agreement;

23. *Notes* that States parties to an international agreement related to the purposes of the Convention may submit to, inter alia, the Tribunal or the International Court of Justice any dispute concerning the interpretation or application of that agreement which is submitted to it in accordance with that agreement, and notes also the possibility, provided for in the statutes of the Tribunal and the Court, to submit disputes to a chamber;

24. *Equally pays tribute* to the important and longstanding role of the International Court of Justice with regard to the peaceful settlement of disputes concerning the law of the sea;

25. *Encourages* States parties to the Convention that have not yet done so to consider making a written declaration choosing from the means set out in article 287 of the Convention for the settlement of disputes concerning the interpretation or application of the Convention and the Agreement;

V
The Area

26. *Notes with satisfaction* the progress of the discussions on issues relating to the regulations for prospecting and exploration for polymetallic sulphides and cobalt-rich ferromanganese crusts in the Area, and reiterates the importance of the ongoing elaboration by the International Seabed Authority ("the Authority"), pursuant to article 145 of the Convention, of rules, regulations and procedures to ensure the effective protection of the marine environment, the protection and conservation of the natural resources of the Area and the prevention of damage to its flora and fauna from harmful effects that may arise from activities in the Area;

27. *Takes note* of the decision of the Council of the Authority to approve a plan of work for exploration of polymetallic nodules submitted by a new contractor, which is an important step towards the utilization of the resources in the Area;

28. *Also takes note* of the importance of the responsibilities entrusted to the Authority by articles 143 and 145 of the Convention, which refer to marine scientific research and protection of the marine environment respectively;

VI
Effective functioning of the Authority and the Tribunal

29. *Appeals* to all States parties to the Convention to pay their assessed contributions to the Authority and to the Tribunal in full and on time;

30. *Encourages* all States parties to the Convention to attend the sessions of the Authority, and calls upon the Authority to pursue all options, including the issue of dates, in order to improve attendance in Kingston and ensure global participation;

31. *Calls upon* States that have not done so to consider ratifying or acceding to the Agreement on the Privileges and Immunities of the Tribunal and to the Protocol on the Privileges and Immunities of the Authority;

VII
The continental shelf and the work of the Commission

32. *Encourages* States parties to the Convention that are in a position to do so to make every effort to submit information to the Commission regarding the establishment of the outer limits of the continental shelf beyond 200 nautical miles, in conformity with article 76 of the Convention and article 4 of annex II to the Convention, taking into account the decision of the eleventh Meeting of States Parties to the Convention;

33. *Notes with satisfaction* the progress in the work of the Commission, that it is giving current consideration to three new submissions that have been made regarding the establishment of the outer limits of the continental shelf beyond 200 nautical miles, and that a number of States have advised of their intention to make submissions in the near future;

34. *Approves* the convening by the Secretary-General of the seventeenth session of the Commission in New York from 20 March to 21 April 2006, and of the eighteenth session of the Commission in New York from 21 August to 15 September 2006, on the understanding that the following periods will be used for

the technical examination of submissions at the Geographic Information System laboratories and other technical facilities of the Division: 20 to 31 March 2006; 10 to 21 April 2006; 23 August to 5 September 2006; and 11 to 15 September 2006;

35. *Takes note* of the steps undertaken by the Secretariat to improve the facilities for the use by the Commission, as well as of the additional requirements of the Commission, and urges the Secretary-General to continue taking all necessary actions to ensure that the Commission can fulfil the functions entrusted to it under the Convention in light of its rapidly increasing workload;

36. *Encourages* States to make additional contributions to the voluntary trust funds established by resolution 55/7 of 30 October 2000, in its paragraphs 18 and 20, for the purpose of facilitating the preparation of submissions to the Commission for developing States, in particular the least developed countries and small island developing States, and compliance with article 76 of the Convention, and for the purpose of defraying the cost of participation of the members of the Commission from developing States in the meetings of the Commission;

37. *Expresses its firm conviction* about the importance of the work of the Commission, carried out in accordance with the Convention, including with respect to the participation of the coastal State in relevant proceedings concerning its submission;

38. *Takes note* of the amendment to annex 3 to the rules of procedure of the Commission that allows for enhanced interaction between submitting States and the Commission;

39. *Encourages* States to continue exchanging views in order to increase understanding of issues, including expenditures involved, arising from the application of article 76 of the Convention, thus facilitating preparation of submissions by States, in particular developing States, to the Commission;

40. *Requests* the Secretary-General, in cooperation with the Member States, to continue supporting and organizing workshops or symposiums on scientific and technical aspects of the establishment of the outer limits of the continental shelf beyond 200 nautical miles, taking into account the deadline for submission;

VIII
Maritime safety and security and flag State implementation

41. *Encourages* States to ratify or accede to international agreements addressing the safety and security of navigation and to adopt the necessary measures consistent with the Convention, aimed at implementing and enforcing the rules contained in those agreements;

42. *Also encourages* States to draw up plans and to establish procedures to implement the Guidelines on Places of Refuge for Ships in Need of Assistance;

43. *Welcomes* the convening of the ninety-fourth (Maritime) session of the International Labour Conference, from 7 to 23 February 2006, to adopt the consolidated maritime labour convention;

44. *Also welcomes* the efforts undertaken by the International Maritime Organization and the International Labour Organization to develop guidelines on fair treatment of seafarers in the event of a maritime accident, as a way of enhancing the protection of the

basic human rights of seafarers detained in connection with maritime accidents;

45. *Notes* the progress in the implementation of the Action Plan for the Safety of Transport of Radioactive Material, approved by the Board of Governors of the International Atomic Energy Agency in March 2004, and encourages States concerned to continue their efforts in the implementation of all areas of the Action Plan;

46. *Also notes* that cessation of the transport of radioactive materials through the regions of small island developing States is an ultimate desired goal of small island developing States and some other countries, and recognizes the right of freedom of navigation in accordance with international law. States should maintain dialogue and consultation, in particular under the aegis of the International Atomic Energy Agency and the International Maritime Organization, with the aim of improved mutual understanding, confidence-building and enhanced communication in relation to the safe maritime transport of radioactive materials. States involved in the transport of such materials are urged to continue to engage in dialogue with small island developing States and other States to address their concerns. These concerns include the further development and strengthening, within the appropriate forums, of international regulatory regimes to enhance safety, disclosure, liability, security and compensation in relation to such transport;

47. *Once again urges* flag States without an effective maritime administration and appropriate legal frameworks to establish or enhance the necessary infrastructure, legislative and enforcement capabilities to ensure effective compliance with, and implementation and enforcement of, their responsibilities under international law and, until such action is undertaken, to consider declining the granting of the right to fly their flag to new vessels, suspending their registry or not opening a registry, and calls upon flag and port States to take all measures consistent with international law necessary to prevent the operation of substandard vessels;

48. *Welcomes* the progress made by the International Maritime Organization on the establishment of a voluntary International Maritime Organization member State audit scheme, and looks forward to its further development within the International Maritime Organization;

49. *Looks forward* to the results of the ongoing work of the International Maritime Organization in cooperation with other competent international organizations, following the invitation extended to it in resolution 58/240 and resolution 58/14 of 24 November 2003, to examine and clarify the role of the "genuine link" in relation to the duty of flag States to exercise effective control over ships flying their flag, including fishing vessels, and the potential consequences of non-compliance with duties and obligations of flag States described in relevant international instruments;

50. *Encourages* States to cooperate to address threats to maritime safety and security, including piracy, armed robbery at sea, smuggling and terrorist acts against shipping, offshore installations and other maritime interests, through bilateral and multilateral instruments and mechanisms aimed at monitoring, preventing and responding to such threats;

51. *Urges* all States, in cooperation with the International Maritime Organization, to combat piracy and armed robbery at sea by adopting measures, including those relating to assistance with capacity-building through training of seafarers, port staff and enforcement personnel in the prevention, reporting and investigation of incidents, bringing the alleged perpetrators to justice, in accordance with international law, and by adopting national legislation, as well as providing enforcement vessels and equipment and guarding against fraudulent ship registration;

52. *Urges* States to become parties to the Convention for the Suppression of Unlawful Acts against the Safety of Maritime Navigation and the Protocol for the Suppression of Unlawful Acts against the Safety of Fixed Platforms Located on the Continental Shelf, takes note of the adoption of the 2005 Protocols amending those instruments on 14 October 2005, and also urges States parties to take appropriate measures to ensure the effective implementation of those instruments, through the adoption of legislation, where appropriate;

53. *Calls upon* States to effectively implement the International Ship and Port Facility Security Code and related amendments to the International Convention for the Safety of Life at Sea, and to work with the International Maritime Organization to promote safe and secure shipping while ensuring freedom of navigation;

54. *Also calls upon* States to ensure freedom of navigation and the rights of transit passage and innocent passage in accordance with international law, in particular the Convention;

55. *Welcomes* the work of the International Maritime Organization relating to the protection of shipping lanes of strategic importance and significance, and in particular in enhancing the safety, security and environmental protection in straits used for international navigation, and calls upon the International Maritime Organization, States bordering straits and user States to continue their cooperation efforts to keep such straits safe and open to international navigation at all times, consistent with international law, in particular the Convention;

56. *Calls upon* user States and States bordering straits for international navigation to cooperate by agreement on matters relating to navigational safety, including safety aids for navigation, and the prevention, reduction and control of pollution from ships;

57. *Welcomes* the progress in regional cooperation in some geographical areas, through the Jakarta Statement on Enhancement of Safety, Security and Environmental Protection in the Straits of Malacca and Singapore, adopted on 8 September 2005, and the Regional Cooperation Agreement on Combating Piracy and Armed Robbery against Ships in Asia, adopted on 11 November 2004 in Tokyo, and urges States to give urgent attention to adopting, concluding and implementing cooperation agreements at the regional level in high-risk areas;

58. *Urges* States that have not yet done so to become parties to the Protocol against the Smuggling of Migrants by Land, Sea and Air, supplementing the United Nations Convention against Transnational Organized Crime and the Protocol to Prevent, Suppress and Punish Trafficking in Persons, Especially Women and Children, supplementing the United Nations

Convention against Transnational Organized Crime, and to take appropriate measures to ensure their effective implementation;

59. *Calls upon* States to cooperate to ensure that persons are rescued at sea and delivered to a place of safety, and urges States to take all necessary measures to ensure the effective implementation of the amendments to the International Convention on Maritime Search and Rescue and to the International Convention for the Safety of Life at Sea relating to the delivery of persons rescued at sea to a place of safety, upon their entry into force, as well as of the associated Guidelines on the Treatment of Persons Rescued at Sea;

60. *Welcomes* the adoption by the International Hydrographic Organization of the "World Hydrography Day", to be celebrated annually on 21 June, with the aim of giving suitable publicity to its work at all levels and of increasing the coverage of hydrographic information on a global basis, and urges all States to work with that organization to promote safe navigation, especially in the areas of international navigation, ports and where there are vulnerable or protected marine areas;

IX

Marine environment, marine resources, marine biodiversity and the protection of vulnerable marine ecosystems

61. *Emphasizes once again* the importance of the implementation of Part XII of the Convention in order to protect and preserve the marine environment and its living marine resources against pollution and physical degradation, and calls upon all States to cooperate and take measures, directly or through competent international organizations, for the protection and preservation of the marine environment;

62. *Encourages* States to ratify or accede to international agreements addressing the protection and preservation of the marine environment and its living marine resources against pollution and physical degradation, as well as agreements that provide for compensation for damage resulting from marine pollution, and to adopt the necessary measures consistent with the Convention, aimed at implementing and enforcing the rules contained in those agreements;

63. *Also encourages* States to ratify or accede to the 1996 Protocol to the Convention on the Prevention of Marine Pollution by Dumping of Wastes and Other Matter, 1972, in order to ensure the timely entry into force of the Protocol;

64. *Further encourages* States, in accordance with the Convention and other relevant instruments, either bilaterally or regionally, to jointly develop and promote contingency plans for responding to pollution incidents, as well as other incidents that are likely to have significant adverse effects on the marine environment and biodiversity;

65. *Notes* the lack of information and data on marine debris, encourages relevant national and international organizations to undertake further studies on the extent and nature of the problem, also encourages States to develop partnerships with industry and civil society to raise awareness of the extent of the impact of marine debris on the health and productivity of the marine environment and consequent economic loss;

66. *Urges* States to integrate the issue of marine debris into national strategies dealing with waste management in the coastal zone, ports and maritime industries, including recycling, reuse, reduction and disposal, and to encourage the development of appropriate economic incentives to address this issue, including the development of cost recovery systems that provide an incentive to use port reception facilities and discourage ships from discharging marine debris at sea, and encourages States to cooperate regionally and subregionally to develop and implement joint prevention and recovery programmes for marine debris;

67. *Invites* the International Maritime Organization, in consultation with relevant organizations and bodies, to review annex V to the International Convention for the Prevention of Pollution from Ships, 1973, as modified by the Protocol of 1978 relating thereto, and to assess its effectiveness in addressing sea-based sources of marine debris;

68. *Welcomes* the continued work of the International Maritime Organization relating to port waste reception facilities, and notes the work done to identify problem areas and to develop an action plan addressing the inadequacy of such facilities;

69. *Calls upon* States to take all appropriate measures to control, reduce and minimize, to the fullest extent possible, marine pollution from land-based sources as part of their national sustainable development strategies and programmes, in an integrated and inclusive manner, and to advance the implementation of the Global Programme of Action for the Protection of the Marine Environment from Land-based Activities and the Montreal Declaration on the Protection of the Marine Environment from Land-based Activities;

70. *Welcomes* the convening in Beijing of the Second Intergovernmental Review Meeting of the Global Programme of Action for the Protection of the Marine Environment from Land-based Activities, from 16 to 20 October 2006, as an opportunity to discuss marine debris in relation to the source categories of the Global Programme of Action, and urges broad high-level participation;

71. *Also welcomes* the continued work of States, the United Nations Environment Programme and regional organizations in the implementation of the Global Programme of Action, and encourages increased emphasis on the link between freshwater, the coastal zone and marine resources in the implementation of international development goals, including those contained in the United Nations Millennium Declaration and of the time-bound targets in the Plan of Implementation of the World Summit on Sustainable Development ("Johannesburg Plan of Implementation"), in particular the target on sanitation, and the Monterrey Consensus of the International Conference on Financing for Development;

72. *Notes* the work under the Jakarta Mandate on Marine and Coastal Biological Diversity, and the Convention on Biological Diversity elaborated programme of work on marine and coastal biological diversity;

73. *Reaffirms* the need for States and competent international organizations to urgently consider ways to integrate and improve, based on the best available scientific information and in accordance with the Convention and related agreements and instruments, the management of risks to the marine biodiversity of seamounts, cold water corals, hydrothermal vents and certain other underwater features;

74. *Also reaffirms* the need for States to continue their efforts to develop and facilitate the use of diverse approaches and tools for conserving and managing vulnerable marine ecosystems, including the possible establishment of marine protected areas, consistent with international law and based on the best scientific information available, and the development of representative networks of any such marine protected areas by 2012;

75. *Notes* the work of States, relevant intergovernmental organizations and bodies, including the Convention on Biological Diversity, in the assessment of scientific information on, and compilation of ecological criteria for the identification of, marine areas that require protection, in light of the objective of the World Summit on Sustainable Development to develop and facilitate the use of diverse approaches and tools such as the establishment of marine protected areas consistent with international law and based on scientific information, including representative networks by 2012;

76. *Also notes* the Millennium Ecosystem Assessment Synthesis reports and the urgent need to protect the marine biodiversity expressed therein;

77. *Calls upon* States and international organizations to urgently take action to address, in accordance with international law, destructive practices that have adverse impacts on marine biodiversity and ecosystems, including seamounts, hydrothermal vents and cold water corals;

78. *Takes note* of the report of the Secretary-General relating to the conservation and sustainable use of marine biological diversity beyond areas of national jurisdiction, prepared and released in response to the request in paragraph 74 of resolution 59/24;

79. *Decides* that the meeting of the Ad Hoc Open-ended Informal Working Group established in paragraph 73 of resolution 59/24 shall be open to all States Members of the United Nations and all parties to the Convention, with others invited as observers in accordance with past practice of the United Nations, and noting that the meeting may be conducted in closed sessions, as appropriate;

80. *Decides also* that the meeting of the Working Group shall be coordinated by two co-chairpersons, who will be appointed by the President of the General Assembly in consultation with Member States and taking into account the need for representation from developed and developing countries;

81. *Reiterates its support* for the International Coral Reef Initiative, takes note of the International Coral Reef Initiative General Meeting, held in Mahe, Seychelles, from 25 to 27 April 2005, supports the work under the Jakarta Mandate on Marine and Coastal Biological Diversity and the elaborated programme of work on marine and coastal biological diversity related to coral reefs, and notes the progress that the International Coral Reef Initiative and other relevant bodies have made to incorporate cold water coral ecosystems into their programmes and activities and to promote the conservation and sustainable use of all coral reef resources;

82. *Encourages* States to cooperate, directly or through competent international bodies, in exchanging information in the event of accidents involving vessels on coral reefs and in promoting the development of economic assessment techniques for both restoration and non-use values of coral reef systems;

83. *Emphasizes* the need to mainstream sustainable coral reef management and integrated watershed management into national development strategies, as well as into the activities of relevant United Nations agencies and programmes, international financial institutions and the donor community;

84. *Encourages* further studies and consideration of the impacts of ocean noise on marine living resources;

X
Marine science

85. *Calls upon* States, individually, or in collaboration with each other or with relevant international organizations and bodies, to improve understanding and knowledge of the deep sea, including, in particular, the extent and vulnerability of deep sea biodiversity and ecosystems, by increasing their marine scientific research activities in accordance with the Convention;

86. *Notes* the contribution of the Census of Marine Life to marine biodiversity research, and encourages participation in this initiative;

87. *Takes note with appreciation* of the work of the Advisory Body of Experts on the Law of the Sea of the Intergovernmental Oceanographic Commission on the practice of States members of the Commission in the application of Parts XIII and XIV of the Convention, and notes the recommendations endorsed by the Commission as a result of this work;

88. *Welcomes* the adoption by the Assembly of the Intergovernmental Oceanographic Commission of the procedure for the application of article 247 of the Convention by the Commission;

XI
Regular process for global reporting and assessment of the state of the marine environment, including socio-economic aspects

89. *Endorses* the conclusions of the second International Workshop on the regular process for global reporting and assessment of the state of the marine environment, including socio-economic aspects ("the regular process");

90. *Decides* to launch the start-up phase, the "assessment of assessments", to be completed within two years, as a preparatory stage towards the establishment of the regular process;

91. *Decides also* to establish an organizational arrangement that includes an ad hoc steering group to oversee the execution of the "assessment of assessments", two United Nations agencies to co-lead the process, and a group of experts;

92. *Establishes* the Ad Hoc Steering Group with the following composition:

(*a*) One representative from each Member State to be appointed by the President of the General Assembly, in consultation with Member States and regional groups, ensuring an adequate range of expertise, and on an equitable geographical basis as follows: five Member States from the African Group, five Member States from the Asian Group, two Member States from the Eastern European Group, three Member States from the Latin American and Caribbean Group, and three Member States from the Western European and other States Group, with the understanding that agency funding support for such experts is subject to availability of funds;

(*b*) One representative from each of the following United Nations bodies and related international organizations: the Food and Agriculture Organization of the United Nations, the World Meteorological Organization, the International Maritime Organization, the Intergovernmental Oceanographic Commission and the United Nations Environment Programme, as well as the International Seabed Authority;

93. *Sets forth* the following functions to be performed by the Ad Hoc Steering Group:

(*a*) To approve the composition of the group of experts to be proposed by the lead agencies and communicate this composition to the States Members of the United Nations;

(*b*) To decide on a work programme for the "assessment of assessments", to be proposed by the group of experts through the lead agencies, and to distribute it to the States Members of the United Nations;

(*c*) To provide for an open-ended mid-term review of the work and progress made so far, in order to give all States Members of the United Nations an opportunity to comment on and contribute to the development of the ongoing work carried out under the "assessment of assessments";

(*d*) To give guidance, consistent with the conclusions of the second International Workshop, to the lead agencies and the group of experts, if required;

94. *Determines* that the lead agencies shall undertake the following actions, under the guidance of the Ad Hoc Steering Group, in addition to contributing to the work in accordance with their own mandate:

(*a*) To provide secretariat services to the Ad Hoc Steering Group;

(*b*) To coordinate the work in collaboration with relevant United Nations bodies, organizations and programmes and related international organizations;

(*c*) To establish a group of experts, upon approval by the Ad Hoc Steering Group, to undertake the actual work of assessing the various assessments, taking into account the importance of adequate participation of experts from developing countries within this group;

(*d*) To prepare a report on the results of the "assessment of assessments" for the General Assembly;

95. *Invites* the United Nations Environment Programme and the Intergovernmental Oceanographic Commission to jointly undertake the role of lead agencies, under the guidance of the Ad Hoc Steering Group;

96. *Decides* that the execution of the "assessment of assessments", including the activities of the Ad Hoc Steering Group and the group of experts, shall be financed through voluntary contributions and other resources available to participating organizations and bodies, and invites Member States in a position to do so to make contributions;

XII
Regional cooperation

97. *Notes* that there have been a number of initiatives at the regional level, in various regions, to further the implementation of the Convention, takes note in this context of the Caribbean-focused Assistance Fund, which is intended to facilitate, mainly through technical assistance, the voluntary undertaking of maritime delimitation negotiations between Caribbean States,

takes note once again of the Fund for Peace: Peaceful Settlement of Territorial Disputes, established by the General Assembly of the Organization of American States in 2000 as a primary mechanism, given its broader regional scope, for the prevention and resolution of pending territorial, land border and maritime boundary disputes, and calls upon States and others in a position to do so to contribute to these funds;

98. *Takes note* of the second Asia-Pacific Economic Cooperation Ocean-related Ministerial Meeting, held on 16 and 17 September 2005 in Bali, Indonesia, in particular the Joint Ministerial Statement and the Bali Plan of Action, which recognize the important contribution provided by the oceans and their resources to the sustainable economic growth and the well-being of the Asia-Pacific region;

XIII
Open-ended informal consultative process on oceans and the law of the sea

99. *Reaffirms* its decision to undertake an annual review and evaluation of the implementation of the Convention and other developments relating to ocean affairs and the law of the sea, welcomes the work of the Consultative Process over the past six years, notes the contribution of the Consultative Process to strengthening the annual debate of the General Assembly on oceans and the law of the sea, and decides to continue with the Consultative Process for the next three years, in accordance with resolution 54/33, with a further review of its effectiveness and utility by the Assembly at its sixty-third session;

100. *Recognizes* the need to strengthen and improve the efficiency of the Consultative Process, and encourages States, intergovernmental organizations and programmes to provide guidance to the co-chairpersons to this effect, particularly before and during the preparatory meeting for the Consultative Process;

101. *Requests* the Secretary-General to convene the seventh meeting of the Consultative Process, in New York, from 12 to 16 June 2006, to provide it with the necessary facilities for the performance of its work and to arrange for support to be provided by the Division, in cooperation with other relevant parts of the Secretariat, as appropriate;

102. *Encourages* States to make additional contributions to the voluntary trust fund, established pursuant to resolution 55/7, for the purpose of assisting developing countries, in particular least developed countries, small island developing States and landlocked developing States, in attending the meetings of the Consultative Process;

103. *Recommends* that, in its deliberations on the report of the Secretary-General on oceans and the law of the sea at its meeting, the Consultative Process should focus its discussions on the following topic/s: "Ecosystem approaches and oceans";

XIV
Coordination and cooperation

104. *Encourages* States to work closely with and through international organizations, funds and programmes, as well as the specialized agencies of the United Nations system and relevant international conventions to identify emerging areas of focus for improved coordination and cooperation and how best to address these issues;

105. *Requests* the Secretary-General to bring the present resolution to the attention of heads of inter-governmental organizations, the specialized agencies, funds and programmes of the United Nations engaged in activities relating to ocean affairs and the law of the sea, as well as funding institutions, and underlines the importance of their constructive and timely input for the report of the Secretary-General on oceans and the law of the sea and of their participation in relevant meetings and processes;

106. *Welcomes* the work done by the secretariats of relevant United Nations specialized agencies, programmes, funds and bodies and the secretariats of related organizations and conventions to enhance inter-agency coordination and cooperation on ocean issues, including through UN-Oceans, the inter-agency coordination mechanism on ocean and coastal issues within the United Nations system;

107. *Encourages* continued updates to Member States by UN-Oceans regarding its priorities and initiatives, in particular with respect to the proposed participation in UN-Oceans;

XV
Activities of the Division for Ocean Affairs and the Law of the Sea

108. *Expresses its appreciation* to the Secretary-General for the annual comprehensive report on oceans and the law of the sea, prepared by the Division, as well as for the other activities of the Division, which reflect the high standard of assistance provided to Member States by the Division;

109. *Requests* the Secretary-General to continue to carry out the responsibilities and functions entrusted to him in the Convention and by the related resolutions of the General Assembly, including resolutions 49/28 and 52/26, and to ensure the allocation of appropriate resources to the Division for the performance of its activities under the approved budget for the Organization;

XVI
Sixty-first session of the General Assembly

110. *Requests* the Secretary-General to prepare a comprehensive report, in its current comprehensive format and in accordance with established practice, for the consideration of the General Assembly at its sixty-first session, on developments and issues relating to ocean affairs and the law of the sea, including the implementation of the present resolution, in accordance with resolutions 49/28, 52/26 and 54/33, and to make the report available at least six weeks in advance of the meeting of the Consultative Process;

111. *Emphasizes* the critical role of the annual comprehensive report of the Secretary-General, which integrates information on developments relating to the implementation of the Convention and the work of the Organization, its specialized agencies and other institutions in the field of ocean affairs and the law of the sea at the global and regional levels, and as a result constitutes the basis for the annual consideration and review of developments relating to ocean affairs and the law of the sea by the General Assembly as the global institution having the competence to undertake such a review;

112. *Notes* that the report referred to in paragraph 110 above will also be presented to States parties pursu-ant to article 319 of the Convention regarding issues of a general nature that have arisen with respect to the Convention;

113. *Also notes* the desire to further improve the efficiency of, and effective participation of delegations in, the informal consultations concerning the annual General Assembly resolution on oceans and the law of the sea and the resolution on sustainable fisheries, decides to limit the period of the informal consultations on both resolutions to a maximum of four weeks in total and to ensure that the consultations are scheduled in such a way as to avoid overlap with the period during which the Sixth Committee is meeting and that the Division has sufficient time to produce the report referred to in paragraph 110 above;

114. *Decides* to include in the provisional agenda of its sixty-first session the item entitled "Oceans and the law of the sea".

RECORDED VOTE ON RESOLUTION 60/30:

In favour: Afghanistan, Algeria, Andorra, Angola, Antigua and Barbuda, Argentina, Armenia, Australia, Austria, Bahamas, Bahrain, Bangladesh, Barbados, Belarus, Belgium, Belize, Bolivia, Bosnia and Herzegovina, Botswana, Brazil, Brunei Darussalam, Bulgaria, Burkina Faso, Cambodia, Cameroon, Canada, Cape Verde, Central African Republic, Chile, China, Costa Rica, Côte d'Ivoire, Croatia, Cuba, Cyprus, Czech Republic, Denmark, Djibouti, Dominica, Dominican Republic, Egypt, Eritrea, Estonia, Ethiopia, Finland, France, Georgia, Germany, Greece, Grenada, Guatemala, Guinea, Guinea-Bissau, Honduras, Hungary, Iceland, India, Indonesia, Iran, Ireland, Israel, Italy, Jamaica, Japan, Kazakhstan, Kenya, Kuwait, Kyrgyzstan, Lao People's Democratic Republic, Latvia, Lebanon, Liberia, Liechtenstein, Lithuania, Luxembourg, Madagascar, Malaysia, Maldives, Mali, Malta, Marshall Islands, Mauritania, Mauritius, Mexico, Micronesia, Monaco, Mongolia, Morocco, Myanmar, Namibia, Netherlands, New Zealand, Nicaragua, Nigeria, Norway, Oman, Pakistan, Palau, Panama, Papua New Guinea, Paraguay, Peru, Philippines, Poland, Portugal, Qatar, Republic of Korea, Republic of Moldova, Romania, Russian Federation, Saint Kitts and Nevis, Saint Lucia, Saint Vincent and the Grenadines, Samoa, San Marino, Saudi Arabia, Serbia and Montenegro, Singapore, Slovakia, Slovenia, Solomon Islands, Spain, Sri Lanka, Sudan, Suriname, Sweden, Tajikistan, Thailand, Togo, Tonga, Trinidad and Tobago, Tunisia, Tuvalu, Ukraine, United Arab Emirates, United Kingdom, United Republic of Tanzania, United States, Uruguay, Viet Nam, Yemen.

Against: Turkey.

Abstaining: Colombia, Ecuador, Libyan Arab Jamahiriya, Venezuela.

Division for Ocean Affairs and the Law of the Sea

During 2005, the Division for Ocean Affairs and the Law of the Sea of the Office of Legal Affairs continued to fulfil its role as the substantive unit of the UN Secretariat responsible for reviewing and monitoring all developments related to the law of the sea and ocean affairs, as well as for the implementation of UNCLOS and related General Assembly resolutions.

The Division, in cooperation with intergovernmental bodies and host Governments, continued its capacity-building efforts through the organization of training courses. The Division held its first (Fiji, 28 February–4 March), second (Sri Lanka, 16-20 May) and third (Ghana, 5-9 December) regional workshops.

The twentieth Hamilton Shirley Amerasinghe Fellowship, established in 1981 [YUN 1981, p. 139], was awarded to Marvin T. Ngirutang of Palau.

Chapter V

Other legal questions

The Special Committee on the Charter of the United Nations and on the Strengthening of the Role of the Organization continued in 2005 to consider, among other items, proposals relating to the maintenance of international peace and security in order to strengthen the Organization and the implementation of Charter provisions on assistance to third States affected by the application of sanctions under Chapter VII.

The Committee on Relations with the Host Country continued to address a number of issues raised by permanent missions to the United Nations, including transportation and parking issues, acceleration of immigration and customs procedures, delays in issuing visas, travel regulations and tax exemption.

The General Assembly approved the United Nations Declaration on Human Cloning, in which it called upon Members States to: adopt all measures necessary to protect adequately human life in the application of life sciences; prohibit all forms of human cloning, that were incompatible with human dignity and the protection of human life; and adopt measures to prohibit the application of genetic engineering techniques that might be contrary to human dignity.

The Assembly adopted the United Nations Convention on the Use of Electronic Communications in International Contracts, as recommended by the United Nations Commission on International Trade Law (UNCITRAL). The Convention aimed to remove obstacles to electronic commerce in existing uniform law conventions and trade agreements.

In addition to finalizing and approving the draft convention on electronic commerce, UNCITRAL, at its thirty-eighth session, continued revisions of Model Laws on public procurement and on international commercial arbitration; and continued drafting an instrument on the carriage of goods wholly or partly by sea, as well as a legislative guide on security interests. It also reviewed implementation of the 1958 New York Convention on the Recognition and Enforcement of Foreign Arbitral Awards, the work on the collection and dissemination of case law on UNCITRAL texts, as well as training and technical assistance activities. The Commission approved a plan to hold, in 2007, a Congress to review the results of its past work programmes and the related

work of other organizations active in the field of international trade law, to assess current work programmes and to consider and evaluate topics for future work.

The Assembly granted observer status to the Hague Conference on Private International Law, an intergovernmental organization based at The Hague.

In other action, the Assembly approved the guidelines and recommendations for the United Nations Programme of Assistance in the Teaching, Study, Dissemination and Wider Appreciation of International Law for the 2006-2007 biennium.

International organizations and international law

Strengthening the role of the United Nations

Special Committee on United Nations Charter

In accordance with General Assembly resolution 59/44 [YUN 2004, p. 1344], the Special Committee on the Charter of the United Nations and on the Strengthening of the Role of the Organization, at its sixtieth session (New York, 14-18 March) [A/60/33], continued to consider proposals relating to: the maintenance of international peace and security, according priority to the implementation of the provisions of the Charter of the United Nations on assistance to third States affected by the application of sanctions; the peaceful settlement of disputes between States; proposals concerning the Trusteeship Council; the improvement of the Committee's working methods; and the status of the publications *Repertory of Practice of United Nations Organs* and *Repertoire of the Practice of the Security Council*.

With regard to the first item, the Russian Federation introduced revised provisions of its working paper, entitled "Declaration on the basic conditions and standard criteria for the introduction and implementation of sanctions and other coercive measures", which it had submitted in 2004 [YUN 2004, p. 1342]. The Special Committee's Working Group of the Whole reviewed the revised working paper. The Chairman invited the Russian Federation to consult with interested delegations on how to proceed further with the proposal.

The Special Committee also considered the revised working paper (2002) submitted by the Libyan Arab Jamahiriya on the strengthening of certain principles concerning the impact and application of sanctions [ibid.]. Libya reiterated that the Russian Federation's proposal (see above) shared two of the three central elements of its own proposal, and indicated that the third element was being considered by the International Law Commission in its work on the topic "Responsibility of international organizations" (see p. 1408). Should the Russian Federation's proposal be adopted, the two elements of Libya's proposal would be considered as covered. However, that should not be interpreted as withdrawal of its proposal. Some delegations suggested that the salient points raised in Libya's revised working paper be incorporated into the Russian proposal.

Discussion continued on the Russian Federation proposal (1998) entitled "Fundamentals of the legal basis for United Nations peacekeeping operations in the context of Chapter VI of the Charter of the United Nations". The sponsor reiterated the importance of elaborating a legal framework for peacekeeping operations under Chapter VI, which could serve as a useful guide in establishing future peacekeeping operations and proposed the elaboration of a standard classification of definitions for peacekeeping activities. While acknowledging that the issue was being discussed in other UN forums, the sponsor stressed that the Special Committee had a responsibility to address the question from a legal perspective and recalled the possibility of considering the matter jointly with the Special Committee on Peacekeeping Operations.

Regarding the working papers submitted by Cuba (1997 and 1998) entitled "Strengthening of the role of the Organization and enhancing its effectiveness", the sponsor explained that the objective was to analyse the respective functions and competencies assigned to the General Assembly and the Security Council under the Charter in the maintenance of international peace and security, with a view to enhancing the Assembly's role. It observed that the topic fell within the mandate of the Special Committee and its consideration would not duplicate the work of other bodies.

Libya emphasized the importance of its revised proposal (1998) on strengthening the role of the United Nations in the maintenance of international peace and security, which could be considered with those of Cuba on the same topic. Its proposal was aimed at analysing the relationship between the Council and the Assembly in the maintenance of international peace and security, focusing on the question of unanimity of the permanent members of the Council and defining decisions of a procedural nature under the Charter. Libya suggested that the Special Committee should recommend that the Sixth (Legal) Committee consider the legal aspects of the Libyan and Cuban proposals and make recommendation to the Assembly.

The Special Committee considered the revised working paper jointly submitted by Belarus and the Russian Federation (2001) proposing that an advisory opinion be sought from the International Court of Justice (ICJ) on the legal consequences of a State's resort to the use of force without prior Security Council authorization, except in the exercise of the right to self-defence. Belarus observed that, in the light of new approaches that had recently emerged concerning the use of armed force, including a unilateral use of force without Council authorization, an advisory opinion of the Court would contribute to the uniform interpretation and application of the relevant Charter provisions. On 17 March, both countries submitted a revised version of their working paper for consideration by the Special Committee in 2006.

During the exchange of views on the peaceful settlement of disputes, some delegations underscored the need to make use of the existing methods and procedures for doing so. The importance of fact-finding was acknowledged, as well as the role played by Special Representatives of the Secretary-General. It was also pointed out that discussion of the agenda item would continue to be of little practical value as long as there was no specific proposal for consideration by the Committee.

On the future of the Trusteeship Council, the views were expressed that it should either be abolished since its mandate had been fulfilled and a proposal to that end addressed to the Assembly and the Special Committee; or that it be assigned new functions in the context of future amendments to the Charter. Others held that it would be premature to abolish the Council or change its status, and that those matters be considered in the overall context of the reform of the Organization and the amendments to the Charter. It was suggested that those States whose territories or neighbouring territories were placed under trusteeship in the past be invited to present their views on the issue at future sessions of the Special Committee.

On the exchange of views on the *Repertory of Practice of United Nations Organs* and the *Repertoire of the Practice of the Security Council*, the representative of the Secretariat pointed out that, while the preparation of individual studies continued in 2004-2005 with regards to the *Repertory*, the work had slowed down considerably and had even stopped in some offices, owing to a lack of funds. Progress had been achieved in eliminating the backlog in regard to the *Repertoire*, including by posting the studies on the website and producing a more streamlined version. However, the trust fund for updating the *Repertoire* that had made that possible was depleted. The Special Committee recommended that the Assembly encourage voluntary contributions to the trust fund for updating the *Repertoire* and the trust fund for eliminating the backlog; the sponsoring, on a voluntary basis, and at no cost to the United Nations, of associate expert positions to assist in the preparation of the studies of both publications; and that the Secretary-General enhance cooperation with academic institutions and use the internship programme for the preparation of the studies for both publications.

Regarding the revised working paper (2004) submitted by Japan, Australia, the Republic of Korea, Thailand and Uganda on the importance of improving the working methods of the Special Committee and enhancing its efficiency, the Working Group of the Whole considered the revised provisions, after which the co-sponsors submitted a further revised working paper. The text of the agreed points was reproduced in the Committee's report.

Concerning the identification of new subjects, the Special Committee expressed its readiness to implement any decisions that might be taken at the 2005 High-level Plenary Meeting of the General Assembly (World Summit) (see p. 47) that concerned the UN Charter and any amendments thereto.

Report of Secretary-General. In response to General Assembly resolution 59/44 [YUN 2004, p. 1344], the Secretary-General submitted a July report [A/60/124] outlining the progress made in updating the *Repertory of Practice of United Nations Organs* and the *Repertoire of the Practice of the Security Council*. With respect to the *Repertory*, the Secretary-General concluded that the Assembly might wish to note the progress made in the preparation of *Repertory* studies and in their posting on the Internet in English, French and Spanish; and to consider the Special Committee's recommendations (see above). With regard to the *Repertoire*, the Secretary-General concluded that the Assembly might wish to: note the progress made towards its updating; encourage contributions to the trust fund, note Greece's further contribution and the support of Germany and Italy for associate experts; and encourage other States to consider providing such assistance.

On 23 November [meeting 53], the General Assembly, on the recommendation of the Sixth (Legal) Committee [A/60/517], adopted **resolution 60/23** without vote [agenda item 82].

Report of the Special Committee on the Charter of the United Nations and on the Strengthening of the Role of the Organization

The General Assembly,

Recalling its resolution 3499(XXX) of 15 December 1975, by which it established the Special Committee on the Charter of the United Nations and on the Strengthening of the Role of the Organization, and its relevant resolutions adopted at subsequent sessions,

Recalling also its resolution 47/233 of 17 August 1993 on the revitalization of the work of the General Assembly,

Recalling further its resolution 47/62 of 11 December 1992 on the question of equitable representation on and increase in the membership of the Security Council,

Taking note of the report of the Open-ended Working Group on the Question of Equitable Representation on and Increase in the Membership of the Security Council and Other Matters related to the Security Council,

Recalling the elements relevant to the work of the Special Committee contained in its resolution 47/120 B of 20 September 1993,

Recalling also its resolution 51/241 of 31 July 1997 on the strengthening of the United Nations system and its resolution 51/242 of 15 September 1997, entitled "Supplement to an Agenda for Peace", by which it adopted the texts on coordination and the question of sanctions imposed by the United Nations, which are annexed to that resolution,

Concerned about the special economic problems confronting certain States arising from the carrying out of preventive or enforcement measures taken by the Security Council against other States, and taking into account the obligation of Members of the United Nations under Article 49 of the Charter of the United Nations to join in affording mutual assistance in carrying out the measures decided upon by the Council,

Recalling the right of third States confronted with special economic problems of that nature to consult the Security Council with regard to a solution of those problems, in accordance with Article 50 of the Charter,

Recalling also that the International Court of Justice is the principal judicial organ of the United Nations, and reaffirming its authority and independence,

Taking note of the ongoing debate on the revised working papers on the working methods of the Special Committee,

Taking note also of the report of the Secretary-General on the *Repertory of Practice of United Nations Organs* and the *Repertoire of the Practice of the Security Council*,

Taking note further of paragraphs 106 to 110, 176 and 177 of the 2005 World Summit Outcome,

Mindful of the decision of the Special Committee, in which it expressed its readiness to engage, as appropriate, in the implementation of any decisions that may be taken at the High-level Plenary Meeting of the sixtieth session of the General Assembly in September 2005 that concern the Charter and any amendments thereto,

Recalling the provisions of its resolutions 50/51 of 11 December 1995, 51/208 of 17 December 1996, 52/162 of 15 December 1997, 53/107 of 8 December 1998, 54/107 of 9 December 1999, 55/157 of 12 December 2000, 56/87 of 12 December 2001, 57/25 of 19 November 2002, 58/80 of 9 December 2003 and 59/45 of 2 December 2004,

Recalling also its resolution 59/44 of 2 December 2004,

Having considered the report of the Special Committee on the work of its session held in 2005,

Noting with appreciation the work done by the Special Committee to encourage States to focus on the need to prevent and to settle peacefully their disputes which are likely to endanger the maintenance of international peace and security,

1. *Takes note* of the report of the Special Committee on the Charter of the United Nations and on the Strengthening of the Role of the Organization;

2. *Decides* that the Special Committee shall hold its next session from 3 to 13 April 2006;

3. *Requests* the Special Committee, at its session in 2006, in accordance with paragraph 5 of General Assembly resolution 50/52 of 11 December 1995:

(a) To continue its consideration of all proposals concerning the question of the maintenance of international peace and security in all its aspects in order to strengthen the role of the United Nations and, in this context, to consider other proposals relating to the maintenance of international peace and security already submitted or which may be submitted to the Special Committee at its session in 2006;

(b) To continue to consider, on a priority basis and in an appropriate substantive manner and framework, the question of the implementation of the provisions of the Charter of the United Nations related to assistance to third States affected by the application of sanctions under Chapter VII of the Charter based on all of the related reports of the Secretary-General and the proposals submitted on the question;

(c) To keep on its agenda the question of the peaceful settlement of disputes between States;

(d) To consider, as appropriate, any proposal referred to it by the General Assembly in the implementation of the decisions of the High-level Plenary Meeting of the sixtieth session of the Assembly in September 2005 that concern the Charter and any amendments thereto;

(e) To continue to consider, on a priority basis, ways and means of improving its working methods and enhancing its efficiency with a view to identifying widely acceptable measures for future implementation;

4. *Invites* the Special Committee at its session in 2006 to continue to identify new subjects for consideration in its future work with a view to contributing to the revitalization of the work of the United Nations;

5. *Notes* the readiness of the Special Committee to provide, within its mandate, such assistance as may be sought at the request of other subsidiary bodies of the General Assembly in relation to any issues before them;

6. *Requests* the Special Committee to submit a report on its work to the General Assembly at its sixty-first session;

7. *Recognizes* the important role of the International Court of Justice, the principal judicial organ of the United Nations, in adjudicating disputes among States and the value of its work, as well as the importance of having recourse to the Court in the peaceful settlement of disputes;

8. *Stresses* the desirability of finding practical ways and means to strengthen the Court, taking into consideration, in particular, the needs resulting from its workload;

9. *Takes note* of the progress made in the preparation of studies of the *Repertory of Practice of United Nations Organs* and their posting on the Internet in three languages, as well as the progress made towards updating the *Repertoire of the Practice of the Security Council* and posting advance versions of individual chapters on the Internet;

10. *Welcomes* the establishment of the trust fund to eliminate the backlog of the *Repertory of Practice of United Nations Organs*, and encourages States to make voluntary contributions to the trust fund and to bring the question of funding for the *Repertory* to the attention of private institutions and individuals that may wish to assist in that regard, as well as to consider the sponsoring, on a voluntary basis, and with no cost to the United Nations, of associate experts to assist in the preparation of the studies;

11. *Encourages* the enhanced cooperation with academic institutions and the use of the internship programme for the preparation of studies;

12. *Requests* the Secretary-General to continue his efforts, within the level of the currently approved budget, towards making available electronically all versions of the *Repertory of Practice of United Nations Organs* as early as possible;

13. *Endorses* the efforts of the Secretary-General to eliminate the backlog in the publication of the *Repertoire of the Practice of the Security Council*;

14. *Encourages* contributions to the trust fund for the updating of the *Repertoire of the Practice of the Security Council*;

15. *Requests* the Secretary-General to submit a report on both the *Repertory of Practice of United Nations Organs* and the *Repertoire of the Practice of the Security Council* to the General Assembly at its sixty-first session;

16. *Also requests* the Secretary-General to submit a report on the implementation of the provisions of the Charter of the United Nations related to assistance to third States affected by the application of sanctions to the General Assembly at its sixty-first session, under the item entitled "Report of the Special Committee on the Charter of the United Nations and on the Strengthening of the Role of the Organization";

17. *Decides* to include in the provisional agenda of its sixty-first session the item entitled "Report of the Special Committee on the Charter of the United Nations and on the Strengthening of the Role of the Organization".

Charter provisions relating to sanctions

Special Committee consideration. During the Special Committee's consideration of the implementation of the Charter provisions related to assistance to third States affected by sanctions [A/60/33], support was expressed for the continued consideration of the issue within the Committee and through a working group of the Sixth Committee. The view was expressed that attention should be paid to discussions of the subject in other UN forums, such as the Security Council's informal working group on general issues of sanctions and the Analytical Support and Sanctions Monitoring Team. It encouraged greater interaction between the various sanctions committees and the General Assembly. Noting that the report of the High-level Panel on Threats, Challenges and Change [YUN 2004, p. 54] contained recommendations relating to sanctions, the Committee said that, while it would be useful to explore different procedural measures aimed at reducing the impact of sanctions on States, generic efforts or controls that placed restrictions on the ability to impose sanctions would be unacceptable. Some delegations expressed disappointment that the recommendations and main findings of the ad hoc expert group had not yet been reviewed by the Special Committee, since those recommendations, together with the views of States and international organizations, constituted a solid basis for achieving concrete results in the Committee. Regret was expressed that none of the reports requested had been written, nor had the seminars, workshops or studies on the application of sanctions and their adverse effects taken place in, or focused on, Africa, even though 10 of the 13 States on which sanctions had been imposed by the Security Council in the last 15 years were in Africa.

The Special Committee recommended that the Assembly continue to consider the results of the 1998 expert group's deliberations and findings on developing a methodology for assessing the consequences incurred by third States as a result of preventive or enforcement measures [YUN 1998, p. 1235], taking into account the Committee's current debate; the views of States, UN system organizations, international financial institutions and other relevant organizations, as contained in the reports of the Secretary-General in 1999 [YUN 1999, p. 1252] and 2000 [YUN 2000, p. 1271]; his views on the main findings of the ad hoc expert group [YUN 2002, p. 1333]; and the information he was to submit on the follow-up to a 1999 Security Council note [YUN 1999, p. 1252]. The Committee also recommended that the Assembly address further the implementation of the Charter provisions related to assistance to third States affected by

the application of sanctions called for by Assembly resolutions yearly since 1995, the latest being resolution 59/45 [YUN 2004, p. 1346].

Report of Secretary-General. In response to General Assembly resolution 59/45, the Secretary-General submitted an August report [A/60/320] highlighting measures for further improving the procedures and working methods of the Security Council and its sanctions committees related to assistance to third States affected by the application of sanctions. It also reviewed the Secretariat's capacity and modalities for implementing intergovernmental mandates and the recommendations of the ad hoc expert group meeting [YUN 1998, p. 1235] on assistance to such States, and recent developments on the roles of the Assembly and the Economic and Social Council in that regard.

By **decision 2005/312** of 27 July, the Economic and Social Council took note of the Secretary-General's note [E/2005/62] on assistance to third States affected by the application of sanctions and of his 2004 report on the implementation of the Charter provisions related to such assistance [YUN 2004, p. 1345].

Security Council consideration. By a January note [S/2005/4], the President of the Security Council announced the Council's agreement that Augustine P. Mahiga (the United Republic of Tanzania) would serve as Chairman of the informal working group of the Security Council on general issues relating to sanctions, established in 2000 [YUN 2000, p. 1270], until 31 December 2005. In December [S/2005/842], the Council President transmitted to the Council the report submitted by the Chairman of the informal working group on the group's 2005 activities. He also announced, in a 29 December note [S/2005/841], that the Council had extended the working group's mandate [YUN 2004, p. 1345] until 31 December 2006.

UN Programme for the teaching and study of international law

In response to General Assembly resolution 58/73 [YUN 2003, p. 1370], the Secretary-General submitted an October report [A/60/441] on the United Nations Programme of Assistance in the Teaching, Study, Dissemination and Wider Appreciation of International Law during 2004 and 2005. Activities in the biennium included the holding of the forty-first session of the International Law Seminar (Geneva, 11-29 July) (see p. 1406). Under the International Law Fellowship Programme, the Secretary-General awarded, at the request of Governments of developing countries, 20 fellowships in 2004 and 17 in 2005. Lectures, seminars and study visits were organized by the UN Office of Legal Affairs (OLA) and the United Nations Institute for Training and Research (UNITAR). The Government of Thailand hosted a regional course on international law issues for countries of the Asian region (Bangkok, 25 October–5 November).

The OLA Codification Division participated in the electronic dissemination of information regarding UN work on the codification and progressive development of international law and its application and maintained a number of websites on other legal information. The United Nations Commission on International Trade Law (UNCITRAL) continued to expand its technical assistance programme, and organized seminars and symposiums in many developing countries to assist them in adopting and implementing UNCITRAL texts. The Treaty Section of OLA expanded its technical assistance programme on treaty law and practice. It organized, jointly with UNITAR, two training sessions at UN Headquarters and held training seminars in Viet Nam, Barbados and Geneva. At a treaty event "Focus 2005: responding to global challenges", held during the 2005 World Summit (see p. 75), 265 treaty actions were undertaken. Other programmes included the Hamilton Shirley Amerasinghe Memorial Fellowship on the Law of the Sea (see p. 1444), awarded annually by OLA; and the Fellowship Programme on the International Civil Service.

The report also described the legal publications issued during the year, proposed guidelines and recommendations regarding the execution of the Programme of Assistance in the 2006-2007 biennium, and outlined the administrative and financial implications of UN participation in the Programme for the 2004-2005 and 2006-2007 bienniums.

The Advisory Committee on the Programme held its thirty-ninth and fortieth sessions on 11 November 2004, and on 17 October 2005, respectively.

GENERAL ASSEMBLY ACTION

On 23 November [meeting 53], the General Assembly, on the recommendation of the Sixth Committee [A/60/514], adopted **resolution 60/19** without vote [agenda item 78].

United Nations Programme of Assistance in the Teaching, Study, Dissemination and Wider Appreciation of International Law

The General Assembly,

Taking note with appreciation of the report of the Secretary-General on the implementation of the United Nations Programme of Assistance in the Teaching, Study, Dissemination and Wider Appreciation of International Law and the guidelines and

recommendations on future implementation of the Programme which were adopted by the Advisory Committee on the Programme and are contained in section III of the report,

Considering that international law should occupy an appropriate place in the teaching of legal disciplines at all universities,

Noting with appreciation the efforts made by States at the bilateral level to provide assistance in the teaching and study of international law,

Convinced, nevertheless, that States and international organizations and institutions should be encouraged to give further support to the Programme and increase their activities to promote the teaching, study, dissemination and wider appreciation of international law, in particular those activities which are of special benefit to persons from developing countries,

Reaffirming its resolutions 2464(XXIII) of 20 December 1968, 2550(XXIV) of 12 December 1969, 2838 (XXVI) of 18 December 1971, 3106(XXVIII) of 12 December 1973, 3502(XXX) of 15 December 1975, 32/146 of 16 December 1977, 36/108 of 10 December 1981 and 38/129 of 19 December 1983, in which it stated or recalled that in the conduct of the Programme it was desirable to use as far as possible the resources and facilities made available by Member States, international organizations and others, as well as its resolutions 34/144 of 17 December 1979, 40/66 of 11 December 1985, 42/148 of 7 December 1987, 44/28 of 4 December 1989, 46/50 of 9 December 1991, 48/29 of 9 December 1993, 50/43 of 11 December 1995, 52/152 of 15 December 1997, 54/102 of 9 December 1999, 56/77 of 12 December 2001 and 58/73 of 9 December 2003, in which, in addition, it expressed or reaffirmed the hope that, in appointing lecturers for the seminars to be held within the framework of the fellowship programme in international law, account would be taken of the need to secure the representation of major legal systems and balance among various geographical regions,

1. *Approves* the guidelines and recommendations contained in section III of the report of the Secretary-General and adopted by the Advisory Committee on the United Nations Programme of Assistance in the Teaching, Study, Dissemination and Wider Appreciation of International Law, in particular those designed to achieve the best possible results in the administration of the Programme within a policy of maximum financial restraint;

2. *Authorizes* the Secretary-General to carry out in 2006 and 2007 the activities specified in his report, including the provision of:

(a) A number of international law fellowships in both 2006 and 2007, to be determined in the light of the overall resources for the Programme and to be awarded at the request of Governments of developing countries;

(b) A minimum of one scholarship in both 2006 and 2007 under the Hamilton Shirley Amerasinghe Memorial Fellowship on the Law of the Sea, subject to the availability of new voluntary contributions made specifically to the fellowship fund;

(c) Subject to the overall resources for the Programme, assistance in the form of a travel grant for one participant from each developing country, who

would be invited to possible regional courses to be organized in 2006 and 2007;

and to finance the above activities from provisions in the regular budget, when appropriate, as well as from voluntary financial contributions earmarked for each of the activities concerned, which would be received as a result of the requests set out in paragraphs 12 to 14 below;

3. *Expresses its appreciation* to the Secretary-General for his constructive efforts to promote training and assistance in international law within the framework of the Programme in 2004 and 2005, in particular for the organization of the fortieth and forty-first sessions of the International Law Seminar, held at Geneva in 2004 and 2005, respectively, and for the activities of the Office of Legal Affairs of the Secretariat related to the fellowship programme in international law and to the Hamilton Shirley Amerasinghe Memorial Fellowship on the Law of the Sea, carried out, respectively, through its Codification Division and its Division for Ocean Affairs and the Law of the Sea;

4. *Requests* the Secretary-General to consider the possibility of admitting, for participation in the various components of the Programme, candidates from countries willing to bear the entire cost of such participation;

5. *Also requests* the Secretary-General to consider the relative advantages of using available resources and voluntary contributions for regional, subregional or national courses, as against courses organized within the United Nations system;

6. *Further requests* the Secretary-General to continue to provide the necessary resources to the programme budget for the Programme for the next and the future bienniums with a view to maintaining the effectiveness of the Programme;

7. *Recognizes* the importance of the United Nations recurrent legal publications listed in the report of the Secretary-General, and strongly encourages their continued publication;

8. *Welcomes* the efforts undertaken by the Office of Legal Affairs to bring up to date the United Nations *Treaty Series* and the *United Nations Juridical Yearbook*, as well as efforts made to place on the Internet the *Treaty Series* and other legal information;

9. *Expresses its appreciation* to the United Nations Institute for Training and Research for its participation in the Programme through the activities described in the report of the Secretary-General;

10. *Also expresses its appreciation* to The Hague Academy of International Law for the valuable contribution it continues to make to the Programme, which has enabled candidates under the fellowship programme in international law to attend and participate in the Programme in conjunction with the Academy courses;

11. *Notes with appreciation* the contributions of The Hague Academy to the teaching, study, dissemination and wider appreciation of international law, and calls upon Member States and interested organizations to give favourable consideration to the appeal of the Academy for a continuation of support and a possible increase in their financial contributions, to enable the Academy to carry out its activities, particularly those relating to the summer courses, regional courses and programmes of the Centre for Studies and Research in International Law and International Relations;

12. *Requests* the Secretary-General to continue to publicize the Programme and periodically to invite Member States, universities, philanthropic foundations and other interested national and international institutions and organizations, as well as individuals, to make voluntary contributions towards the financing of the Programme or otherwise to assist in its implementation and possible expansion;

13. *Reiterates its request* to Member States and to interested organizations and individuals to make voluntary contributions, inter alia, for the International Law Seminar, the fellowship programme in international law, the Hamilton Shirley Amerasinghe Memorial Fellowship on the Law of the Sea and the United Nations Audiovisual Library in International Law, and expresses its appreciation to those Member States, institutions and individuals that have made voluntary contributions for this purpose;

14. *Urges in particular* all Governments to make voluntary contributions for the organization of regional refresher courses in international law by the United Nations Institute for Training and Research, especially with a view to covering the amount needed for the financing of the daily subsistence allowance for up to twenty-five participants in each regional course, thus alleviating the burden on prospective host countries and making it possible for the Institute to continue to organize the regional courses;

15. *Requests* the Secretary-General to report to the General Assembly at its sixty-second session on the implementation of the Programme during 2006 and 2007 and, following consultations with the Advisory Committee on the Programme, to submit recommendations regarding the execution of the Programme in subsequent years;

16. *Decides* to include in the provisional agenda of its sixty-second session the item entitled "United Nations Programme of Assistance in the Teaching, Study, Dissemination and Wider Appreciation of International Law".

Observer status for Hague Conference on Private International Law

On 23 November, the General Assembly, by **resolution 60/27** (see p. 1543) granted observer status for the Hague Conference on Private International Law in the work of the Assembly.

Host country relations

In four meetings held in New York (15 April, 6 July, 28 September and 28 October), the Committee on Relations with the Host Country considered the following aspects of relations between the UN diplomatic community and the United States, the host country: transportation issues regarding the use of motor vehicles, parking and related matters; acceleration of immigration and customs procedures; entry visas issued by the host country; exemption from taxes; and host country travel regulations. The recommendations and conclusions on those items, approved by the Committee at its October meeting, were incorporated in its report [A/60/26].

Transportation

The Committee heard complaints from Mali, Nigeria, the Russian Federation, Venezuela, Viet Nam and the Syrian Arab Republic regarding difficulties experienced in the implementation of the Parking Programme for Diplomatic Vehicles, in force since November 2002 [YUN 2002, p. 1338]. The complaints centred around the slow responses to parking ticket issues; the withholding of vehicle registration; insufficient parking spaces; the non-receipt of monthly reports on parking tickets; the distance between allocated parking spaces and the missions; and the unsatisfactory resolution of outstanding issues related to fines. Complaints were made about the authorities' refusal to renew licence plates when a mission had been issued more than two parking tickets and about the lack of clarity in parking signs.

The United States undertook to arrange trilateral meetings with the City of New York and delegations to discuss their parking complaints, and explained, with respect to the non-renewal of registrations for private vehicles belonging to mission staff, that in accordance with the Parking Programme, a mission-owned vehicle with too many outstanding tickets would prevent the renewal of another vehicle's registration. He referred to two recent diplomatic notes from the United States Mission requesting missions to notify the New York hotline, as well as the United States Mission, when encountering parking difficulties.

In its recommendations and conclusions, the Committee stated that it continued to review the implementation of the 2002 Parking Programme for Diplomatic Vehicles, with a view to ensuring that it was fair, non-discriminatory, effective and consistent with international law. It requested the host country to continue to bring to the attention of New York City officials, the problems experienced by the permanent missions or their staff with regard to the Programme, in order to improve its functioning and to promote compliance with international norms concerning diplomatic privileges and immunities.

Immigration and customs procedures

The Committee heard from Costa Rica, Jamaica, the Libyan Arab Jamahiriya, Malaysia, Mali, the Russian Federation, the Syrian Arab Republic and Venezuela about their experiences with US immigration and customs procedures. Requests were made for the exemption in the screening of official delegations at ports of entry to be extended to the staff of diplomatic missions, particularly the exemption from fingerprinting and photographing; that the exemption from body search applied at the ministerial level be extended to permanent representatives accredited to the United Nations, and that the host country should extend its review of the delays at airports to other ports of entry. Complaints were made that the new customs procedures were excessively lengthy and affected the departure of aircraft; and diplomats were being subjected to improper and unpleasant treatment and to secondary screening searches. Objections were also raised to the requirement of a 24-hour notice for travel plans. The Committee heard calls for the training of airport and airline personnel concerning diplomatic privileges and immunities, and for strengthened coordination between the Department of Homeland Security and the Department of State to ensure respect for privileges and immunities.

The United States representative responded that the new programme entitled "US Visit", which required all those entering the country to be fingerprinted, exempted "G" visa holders and their dependants, and asked to be informed of cases where that did not occur. He offered to direct the matter of the body search exemption for permanent representatives to the competent authorities. The procedures for airline arrivals were outside the scope of work of the Committee; however, where delays had occurred in the clearance of "G" visa holders, the United States Mission planned to meet with airport officials. A meeting between the Mission, the Department of Homeland Security and airport immigration authorities to discuss immigration procedures at the airports had resulted in a significant reduction of complaints.

At the September meeting, the United States representative acknowledged the positive comments made regarding the improvements introduced in connection with airport procedures and other areas; offered to meet with a representative of Venezuela to discuss that delegation's concerns; reported that United States authorities deemed it impossible to extend airport courtesies granted to cabinet-rank officials to permanent representatives, because airport security was under the control of transportation security agencies rather than the State Department; and pointed out that secondary screening at airports was determined by individual airlines based on certain booking characteristics, and not by the Department of Homeland Security or the State Department, and should be taken up with the airlines concerned. He underlined that the secondary screening was not directed at any particular diplomat or country, and invited all delegations to notify the Host Country Affairs Section of the United States Mission immediately of any incident at a port of entry or exit, rather than wait for the next meeting of the Committee to raise those complaints.

The Committee, considering that the maintenance of appropriate conditions for delegations and missions accredited to the United Nations was in the interest of the Organization and all Member States, appreciated the efforts made by the host country to that end, and anticipated that all the issues raised at its meetings would be duly settled in a spirit of cooperation and in accordance with international law.

Entry visas

The Committee heard complaints regarding delays in issuing entry visas from Cuba, Libyan Arab Jamahiriya, Nepal, Nigeria, the Russian Federation, Syrian Arab Republic and Venezuela.

Cuba deplored the fact that the President of the Cuban National Assembly had been prevented from participating in the second World Conference of Speakers of Parliament convened by the Inter-Parliamentary Union (IPU) at UN Headquarters from 7-9 September (see p. 76) and complained about the difficulties encountered by his delegation in relation to the High-level Plenary Meeting of the Assembly's sixtieth session (see p. 47). Venezuela complained about difficulties encountered by the delegation of President Hugo Chávez Frías regarding access to that same meeting and deplored the lack of compliance with the Headquarters Agreement and the rules and regulations on the attendance of Heads of State and high diplomatic officials at UN meetings. The Russian Federation reiterated that the 15-working-day time frame for granting visas was too long and constantly created difficulties for Russian representatives invited to perform official functions in the host country. The Libyan Arab Jamahiriya representative, while noting that a number of problems encountered previously had been overcome and all travel restrictions applicable to Libyan citizens had been lifted, the visa for the Prime Minister to attend the Assembly's High-level Plenary Meeting had been received two months after the application was submitted. Syria called upon the United States authorities to comply with international law and the Headquarters Agreement and suggested that the Committee should recommend a higher level of commitment from the host country in facilitating intergovernmental work.

The United States representative responded that its Mission was doing its utmost to ensure that visas were delivered on time. However, the 15-working-day application procedures for granting visas had to be maintained. He encouraged all delegations to contact the Mission when problems regarding the issuance of visas were anticipated or had occurred. He said that the Mission had worked very closely with the Cuban and Russian Missions, which had led to significant improvement. He suggested that unreasonable delays or emergency requests for visas be brought to the attention of the Host Country Affairs Section. More specifically, he said that the President of the Cuban National Assembly and other Cuban parliamentarians had been denied "B" (tourist) visas based on ineligibilities which were consistent with United States domestic immigration policies, and the National Assembly President was denied a "G" visa because the IPU Conference was not an official UN meeting. As for the Assembly's High-level Plenary Meeting, the Cuban Foreign Minister had been issued a visa on 13 September, and he regretted that the Minister had been unable to travel on that day. He also offered clarifications with respect to the entry on United States territory of the Venezuelan delegation.

The Committee anticipated that the host country would enhance its efforts to ensure the issuance, in a timely manner, of entry visas to representatives of Member States to travel to New York on official UN business, including to attend official UN meetings, noting that some delegations had requested shortening the time frame applied by the host country for issuing entry visas. The Committee also anticipated that the host country would enhance efforts to facilitate participation, including visa issuance, of representatives of Member States in other UN meetings, as appropriate.

Exemption from taxes

On the question of tax exemption, the Committee heard comments by Jamaica that many vendors refused to accept the tax exemption cards; as well as from Zambia and the Syrian Arab Republic.

The United States invited missions having problems with a particular vendor to contact the Office of Foreign Missions in New York, which was responsible for dealing with sales tax exemptions. The State of New York had declined the specific request of that Office to abandon the requirement for tax exemption forms. However, the issue would be revisited. In cases where sales taxes had been paid in New York State, there were possibilities of reimbursement, subject to the completion of formal procedures. He invited any mission not taking advantage of the utility tax and gasoline tax exemption programmes to apply.

Travel regulations

The Committee heard complaints, in July and September, from Cuba and the Russian Federation regarding the host country's policy of restrictions on their mission personnel and nationals working at the Secretariat. The United States explained that travel restrictions were applied to nationals of certain missions for national security reasons. Concerning the Russian Mission, a further relaxation of the travel restrictions had been introduced at border entry and exit points to include Atlanta, Georgia, and would also apply to Russian nationals working at the Secretariat.

The Committee, noting that some travel restrictions had been removed during the past year, continued to urge the host country to remove the remaining ones as soon as possible.

GENERAL ASSEMBLY ACTION

On 23 November [meeting 53], the General Assembly, on the recommendation of the Sixth Committee [A/60/520], adopted **resolution 60/24** without vote [agenda item 153].

Report of the Committee on Relations with the Host Country

The General Assembly,

Having considered the report of the Committee on Relations with the Host Country,

Recalling Article 105 of the Charter of the United Nations, the Convention on the Privileges and Immunities of the United Nations, the Agreement between the United Nations and the United States of America regarding the Headquarters of the United Nations and the responsibilities of the host country,

Recalling also that, in accordance with paragraph 7 of General Assembly resolution 2819(XXVI) of 15 December 1971, the Committee should consider, and advise the host country on, issues arising in connection with the implementation of the Agreement between the United Nations and the United States of America regarding the Headquarters of the United Nations,

Recognizing that effective measures should continue to be taken by the competent authorities of the host country, in particular to prevent any acts violating the security of missions and the safety of their personnel,

1. *Endorses* the recommendations and conclusions of the Committee on Relations with the Host Country contained in paragraph 72 of its report;

2. *Considers* that the maintenance of appropriate conditions for the normal work of the delegations and the missions accredited to the United Nations and the observance of their privileges and immunities, which is an issue of great importance, are in the interest of the United Nations and all Member States, and requests the host country to continue to solve, through negotiations, problems that might arise and to take all measures necessary to prevent any interference with the functioning of missions;

3. *Notes* that the Committee will continue to review the implementation of the Parking Programme for Diplomatic Vehicles, with a view to addressing the problems experienced by some permanent missions in that

respect and continuously ensuring its proper implementation in a manner that is fair, non-discriminatory, effective and therefore consistent with international law and that it shall remain seized of the matter;

4. *Expresses its appreciation* for the efforts made by the host country, and hopes that the issues raised at the meetings of the Committee will continue to be resolved in a spirit of cooperation and in accordance with international law;

5. *Notes* that during the reporting period some travel restrictions previously imposed by the host country on staff of certain missions and staff members of the Secretariat of certain nationalities were removed, and requests the host country to consider removing the remaining travel restrictions, and in this regard notes the positions of affected States, as reflected in the report of the Committee, and the positions of the Secretary-General and of the host country;

6. *Notes also* that the Committee anticipates that the host country will enhance its efforts to ensure the issuance, in a timely manner, of entry visas to representatives of Member States, pursuant to article IV, section 11, of the Agreement between the United Nations and the United States of America regarding the Headquarters of the United Nations, for travel to New York on United Nations business, and notes that the Committee anticipates that the host country will enhance efforts, including visa issuance, to facilitate the participation of representatives of Member States in other United Nations meetings as appropriate;

7. *Notes further* that a number of delegations have requested a shortening of the time frame applied by the host country for the issuance of entry visas to representatives of Member States, since the time frame poses difficulties for the full-fledged participation of Member States in United Nations meetings;

8. *Requests* the Secretary-General to remain actively engaged in all aspects of the relations of the United Nations with the host country;

9. *Requests* the Committee to continue its work in conformity with General Assembly resolution 2819 (XXVI);

10. *Decides* to include in the provisional agenda of its sixty-first session the item entitled "Report of the Committee on Relations with the Host Country".

International law

International bioethics law

Convention against cloning of human beings

Pursuant to General Assembly decision 59/547 [YUN 2004, p. 1351], the Sixth Committee met on 18 February to resume consideration of an international convention against the reproductive cloning of human beings. It had before it the report [A/C.59/L.27/Rev.1] of the open-ended Working Group established pursuant to Assembly decision 59/547 to finalize the text of a United Nations declaration on human cloning. Due to a lack of consensus, the Working Group was unable to agree on a draft text and submitted to the Committee for consideration draft proposals by Honduras and Italy and amendments by Belgium, together with an informal proposal, all of which were annexed to the report.

GENERAL ASSEMBLY ACTION

On 8 March [meeting 82], the General Assembly, on the recommendation of the Sixth Committee [A/59/516/Add.1], adopted **resolution 59/280** by recorded vote (84-34-37) [agenda item 150].

United Nations Declaration on Human Cloning

The General Assembly,

Recalling its resolution 53/152 of 9 December 1998, by which it endorsed the Universal Declaration on the Human Genome and Human Rights,

Approves the United Nations Declaration on Human Cloning annexed to the present resolution.

Annex

United Nations Declaration on Human Cloning

The General Assembly,

Guided by the purposes and principles of the Charter of the United Nations,

Recalling the Universal Declaration on the Human Genome and Human Rights, adopted by the General Conference of the United Nations Educational, Scientific and Cultural Organization on 11 November 1997, and in particular article 11 thereof, which states that practices which are contrary to human dignity, such as the reproductive cloning of human beings, shall not be permitted,

Recalling also its resolution 53/152 of 9 December 1998, by which it endorsed the Universal Declaration on the Human Genome and Human Rights,

Aware of the ethical concerns that certain applications of rapidly developing life sciences may raise with regard to human dignity, human rights and the fundamental freedoms of individuals,

Reaffirming that the application of life sciences should seek to offer relief from suffering and improve the health of individuals and humankind as a whole,

Emphasizing that the promotion of scientific and technical progress in life sciences should be sought in a manner that safeguards respect for human rights and the benefit of all,

Mindful of the serious medical, physical, psychological and social dangers that human cloning may imply for the individuals involved, and also conscious of the need to prevent the exploitation of women,

Convinced of the urgency of preventing the potential dangers of human cloning to human dignity,

Solemnly declares the following:

(a) Member States are called upon to adopt all measures necessary to protect adequately human life in the application of life sciences;

(b) Member States are called upon to prohibit all forms of human cloning inasmuch as they are incompatible with human dignity and the protection of human life;

(c) Member States are further called upon to adopt the measures necessary to prohibit the application of genetic engineering techniques that may be contrary to human dignity;

(d) Member States are called upon to take measures to prevent the exploitation of women in the application of life sciences;

(e) Member States are also called upon to adopt and implement without delay national legislation to bring into effect paragraphs (a) to (d);

(f) Member States are further called upon, in their financing of medical research, including of life sciences, to take into account the pressing global issues such as HIV/AIDS, tuberculosis and malaria, which affect in particular the developing countries.

RECORDED VOTE ON RESOLUTION 59/280:

In favour: Afghanistan, Albania, Andorra, Australia, Austria, Bahrain, Bangladesh, Belize, Benin, Bolivia, Bosnia and Herzegovina, Brunei Darussalam, Burundi, Chile, Comoros, Costa Rica, Côte d'Ivoire, Croatia, Democratic Republic of the Congo, Djibouti, Dominican Republic, Ecuador, El Salvador, Equatorial Guinea, Eritrea, Ethiopia, Georgia, Germany, Grenada, Guatemala, Guyana, Haiti, Honduras, Hungary, Iraq, Ireland, Italy, Kazakhstan, Kenya, Kuwait, Lesotho, Liberia, Liechtenstein, Madagascar, Malta, Marshall Islands, Mauritius, Mexico, Micronesia, Monaco, Morocco, Nicaragua, Palau, Panama, Paraguay, Philippines, Poland, Portugal, Qatar, Rwanda, Saint Kitts and Nevis, Saint Lucia, Saint Vincent and the Grenadines, Samoa, San Marino, Sao Tome and Principe, Saudi Arabia, Sierra Leone, Slovakia, Slovenia, Solomon Islands, Sudan, Suriname, Switzerland, Tajikistan, The former Yugoslav Republic of Macedonia, Timor-Leste, Trinidad and Tobago, Uganda, United Arab Emirates, United Republic of Tanzania, United States, Uzbekistan, Zambia.

Against: Belarus, Belgium, Brazil, Bulgaria, Cambodia, Canada, China, Cuba, Cyprus, Czech Republic, Democratic People's Republic of Korea, Denmark, Estonia, Finland, France, Gabon, Iceland, India, Jamaica, Japan, Lao People's Democratic Republic, Latvia, Lithuania, Luxembourg, Netherlands, New Zealand, Norway, Republic of Korea, Singapore, Spain, Sweden, Thailand, Tonga, United Kingdom.

Abstaining: Algeria, Angola, Argentina, Azerbaijan, Bahamas, Barbados, Burkina Faso, Cameroon, Cape Verde, Colombia, Egypt, Indonesia, Iran, Israel, Jordan, Lebanon, Malaysia, Maldives, Myanmar, Namibia, Nepal, Oman, Pakistan, Republic of Moldova, Romania, Serbia and Montenegro, Somalia, South Africa, Sri Lanka, Syrian Arab Republic, Tunisia, Turkey, Ukraine, Uruguay, Yemen, Zimbabwe.

The Sixth Committee, during consideration of the item, by a vote of 69 to 39 with 39, abstentions, voted to consider first the annex to the Committee's report containing the Honduras draft text, followed by the draft text by Italy. Amendments to the second preambular paragraph of the draft declaration contained in annex I were adopted by a single recorded vote of 59 to 47, with 41 abstentions; the amendment to delete operative paragraph (a) was rejected by a recorded vote of 57 to 48, with 42 abstentions, and to replace operative paragraph (b), by a recorded vote of 55 to 52, with 42 abstentions. The draft resolution [A.C.6/59/L.27/Rev.1], as amended, was adopted by the Committee by a recorded vote of 71 to 35, with 43 abstentions.

International economic law

In 2005, legal aspects of international economic law continued to be considered by the United Nations Commission on International Trade Law (UNCITRAL) and by the Sixth Committee of the General Assembly.

International trade law

At its thirty-eighth session (Vienna, 4-15 July), UNCITRAL finalized and approved the draft convention on the use of electronic communications in international contracts, and recommended it for adoption by the General Assembly at the sixtieth session. It continued its work on public procurement, arbitration, transport law, and security interests. It also reviewed the implementation of the 1958 New York Convention on the Recognition and Enforcement of Foreign Arbitral Awards (the New York Convention) [YUN 1958, p. 390], the work on the collection and dissemination of case law on UNCITRAL texts (CLOUT), and training and technical assistance activities.

The report of the session [A/60/17] described actions taken on those topics. (For details, see below.)

GENERAL ASSEMBLY ACTION

On 23 November [meeting 53], the General Assembly, on the recommendation of the Sixth Committee [A/60/515], adopted **resolution 60/20** without vote [agenda item 79].

Report of the United Nations Commission on International Trade Law on the work of its thirty-eighth session

The General Assembly,

Recalling its resolution 2205(XXI) of 17 December 1966, by which it established the United Nations Commission on International Trade Law with a mandate to further the progressive harmonization and unification of the law of international trade and in that respect to bear in mind the interests of all peoples, in particular those of developing countries, in the extensive development of international trade,

Reaffirming its belief that the progressive modernization and harmonization of international trade law, in reducing or removing legal obstacles to the flow of international trade, especially those affecting the developing countries, would contribute significantly to universal economic cooperation among all States on a basis of equality, equity and common interest and to the elimination of discrimination in international trade and, thereby, to the well-being of all peoples,

Having considered the report of the Commission on the work of its thirty-eighth session,

Reiterating its concern that activities undertaken by other bodies in the field of international trade law without adequate coordination with the Commission might lead to undesirable duplication of efforts and would not be in keeping with the aim of promoting efficiency, consistency and coherence in the unification and harmonization of international trade law,

Reaffirming the mandate of the Commission, as the core legal body within the United Nations system in the field of international trade law, to coordinate legal activities in this field, in particular to avoid duplication of efforts, including among organizations formulating rules of international trade, and to promote efficiency, consistency and coherence in the modernization and harmonization of international trade law, and to con-

tinue, through its secretariat, to maintain close cooperation with other international organs and organizations, including regional organizations, active in the field of international trade law,

1. *Takes note with appreciation* of the report of the United Nations Commission on International Trade Law on the work of its thirty-eighth session;

2. *Commends* the Commission for the finalization and approval of a draft convention on the use of electronic communications in international contracts;

3. *Also commends* the Commission for the progress made in its work on a revision of its Model Law on Procurement of Goods, Construction and Services, on model legislative provisions on interim measures in international commercial arbitration, on a draft instrument on transport law and on a draft legislative guide on secured transactions;

4. *Endorses* the efforts and initiatives of the Commission, as the core legal body within the United Nations system in the field of international trade law, aimed at increasing coordination of and cooperation on legal activities of international and regional organizations active in the field of international trade law, and in this regard appeals to relevant international and regional organizations to coordinate their legal activities with those of the Commission, to avoid duplication of efforts and to promote efficiency, consistency and coherence in the modernization and harmonization of international trade law;

5. *Reaffirms* the importance, in particular for developing countries, of the work of the Commission concerned with technical assistance in the field of international trade law reform and development, and in this connection:

(a) *Welcomes* the initiatives of the Commission towards expanding, through its secretariat, its technical assistance programme;

(b) *Expresses* its appreciation to the Commission for carrying out technical assistance activities in Azerbaijan, Brazil, China, Ethiopia (for the Common Market for Eastern and Southern Africa), Serbia and Montenegro, Slovenia, South Africa (for the Association of Law Reform Agencies of Eastern and Southern Africa) and Thailand;

(c) *Expresses* its appreciation to the Governments whose contributions enabled the seminars and briefing missions to take place, and appeals to Governments, the relevant bodies of the United Nations system, organizations, institutions and individuals to make voluntary contributions to the United Nations Commission on International Trade Law Trust Fund for Symposia and, where appropriate, to the financing of special projects, and otherwise to assist the secretariat of the Commission in carrying out technical assistance activities, in particular in developing countries;

(d) *Reiterates* its appeal to the United Nations Development Programme and other bodies responsible for development assistance, such as the World Bank and regional development banks, as well as to Governments in their bilateral aid programmes, to support the technical assistance programme of the Commission and to cooperate and coordinate their activities with those of the Commission;

6. *Takes note with regret* that, since the thirty-sixth session of the Commission, no contributions have been made to the trust fund established to provide travel as-

sistance to developing countries that are members of the Commission, at their request and in consultation with the Secretary-General, stresses the need for contributions to the trust fund in order to increase expert representation from developing countries at sessions of the Commission and its working groups, and reiterates its appeal to Governments, the relevant bodies of the United Nations system, organizations, institutions and individuals to make voluntary contributions to the trust fund;

7. *Decides*, in order to ensure full participation by all Member States in the sessions of the Commission and its working groups, to continue, in the competent Main Committee during the sixtieth session of the General Assembly, its consideration of granting travel assistance to the least developed countries that are members of the Commission, at their request and in consultation with the Secretary-General;

8. *Recalls* that the responsibility for the work of the Commission lies with the meetings of the Commission and its intergovernmental working groups, and stresses in this regard that information should be provided regarding meetings of experts, which bring an essential contribution to the work of the Commission;

9. *Also recalls* its resolutions on partnerships between the United Nations and non-State actors, in particular the private sector, and in this regard encourages the Commission to further explore different approaches to the use of partnerships with non-State actors in the implementation of its mandate, in particular in the area of technical assistance, in accordance with the applicable principles and guidelines and in cooperation and coordination with other relevant offices of the Secretariat, including the Global Compact Office;

10. *Reiterates its request* to the Secretary-General, in conformity with the General Assembly resolutions on documentation-related matters, which, in particular, emphasize that any reduction in the length of documents should not adversely affect either the quality of the presentation or the substance of the documents, to bear in mind the particular characteristics of the mandate and work of the Commission in implementing page limits with respect to the documentation of the Commission;

11. *Requests* the Secretary-General to continue providing summary records of the Commission's meetings relating to the formulation of normative texts;

12. *Stresses* the importance of bringing into effect the conventions emanating from the work of the Commission for the global unification and harmonization of international trade law, and, to this end, urges States that have not yet done so to consider signing, ratifying or acceding to those conventions;

13. *Takes note with appreciation* of the preparation of digests of case law relating to the texts of the Commission, in particular a digest of case law relating to the United Nations Convention on Contracts for the International Sale of Goods and a digest of case law relating to the Model Law on International Commercial Arbitration of the United Nations Commission on International Trade Law, which will assist in dissemination of information on those texts and promote their use, enactment and uniform interpretation;

14. *Welcomes* the decision of the Commission to hold, in the context of its fortieth session in 2007, a congress on international trade law in Vienna, with a view to reviewing the results of the past work of the Commission as well as related work of other organizations active in the field of international trade law, assessing current work programmes and considering topics and areas for future work, and acknowledges the importance of holding such a congress for the coordination and promotion of activities aimed at the modernization and harmonization of international trade law;

15. *Notes* that 2006 will mark the thirtieth anniversary of the adoption by the Commission of the Arbitration Rules of the United Nations Commission on International Trade Law, used worldwide in the settlement of disputes concerning international trade and investment, and in this regard welcomes initiatives being undertaken to organize conferences and other similar events to provide a forum for assessing the experience with the Rules, as well as discussing their possible revision;

16. *Recalls* its resolutions affirming the importance of high-quality, user-friendly and cost-effective United Nations websites and the need for their multilingual development, maintenance and enrichment, commends the Commission's restructured website in the six official languages of the United Nations, and welcomes the continuous efforts of the Commission to maintain and improve its website in accordance with the applicable guidelines.

Procurement

UNCITRAL [A/60/17] took note of the reports of Working Group I (Procurement) on its sixth (Vienna, 30 August–3 September 2004) [A/CN.9/568] and seventh (New York, 4-8 April) [A/CN.9/575] sessions relating to the revision of the UNCITRAL Model Law on Procurement of Goods, Construction and Services, in response to the Commission's 2004 request [YUN 2004, p. 1356]. UNCITRAL was informed that, at its sixth session, Working Group I had begun preparing proposals for the revision of the Model Law, with the preliminary consideration of 13 topics, and, at its seventh session, had started in-depth consideration of topics related to the use of electronic communications and technologies in the procurement process.

UNCITRAL noted the Working Group's decision to accommodate the use of electronic communications and technologies (including electronic reverse auctions), as well as the investigations of abnormally low tenders in the Model Law, and to consider those revisions to the Model Law at its eighth session. UNCITRAL commended the Working Group for the progress made, and reaffirmed its support for the review being undertaken and for the inclusion of novel procurement practices in the Model Law.

International commercial arbitration

UNCITRAL [A/60/17] took note of the progress made by Working Group II (Arbitration and

Conciliation) at its forty-first [YUN 2004, p. 1353] and forty-second (New York, 10-14 January) [A/CN.9/573] sessions, during which the Group continued discussions on a draft text for a revision of article 17 of the UNCITRAL Model Law on International Commercial Arbitration on the power of an arbitral tribunal to grant interim measures of protection on an ex parte basis; a draft provision on the recognition and enforcement of interim measures of protection issued by an arbitral tribunal (17 bis); and a draft article dealing with interim measures issued by state courts in support of arbitration (17 ter). UNCITRAL noted that the Group had yet to finalize its work on those draft articles, including the form in which the current and revised provisions could be presented in the Arbitration Model Law, and expressed its expectation that the Group would be able to present its proposals for final review and adoption to UNCITRAL's thirty-ninth (2006) session.

With respect to future work in the field of settlement of commercial disputes, UNCITRAL noted the Group's suggestion that priority consideration should be given to arbitrability of intra-corporate disputes and related issues, and those issues arising from online dispute resolution and the possible revision of the UNCITRAL Arbitration Rules. UNCITRAL was informed that 2006 would mark the thirtieth anniversary of the Arbitration Rules, and that conferences to celebrate that anniversary were expected to be organized in different regions, including one in Vienna on 6 and 7 April 2006, under the auspices of the International Arbitral Centre of the Austrian Federal Economic Chamber.

Implementation of the 1958 New York Convention

Under the ongoing project approved by UNCITRAL in 1995 [YUN 1995, p. 1364], aimed at monitoring the legislative implementation of the 1958 New York Convention [YUN 1958, p. 390], UNCITRAL [A/60/17] considered an interim report [A/CN.9/585] it had requested of the Secretariat in 2004 [YUN 2004, p. 1353]. The report set out the issues raised in the replies received to the questionnaire relating to the legal regime in States parties to the Convention governing the recognition and enforcement of foreign arbitral awards. It included additional questions UNCITRAL might want to put to States in order to obtain more comprehensive information regarding implementation practice.

UNCITRAL welcomed the progress reflected in the interim report. It was pointed out that, taking into account that questionnaires had been circulated since 1995, the work should be finalized in

due course, and that given the limited resources of the Secretariat, care should be taken to ensure that the project did not duplicate the extensive ongoing research on the implementation of the Convention. UNCITRAL considered the approach taken in preparing the interim report, including the naming of States and the possibility of appointing national experts on international arbitration, arbitration centres or academic organizations to assist the Secretariat in completing the work. UNCITRAL agreed that the Secretariat should have flexibility in determining the time frame for completing the project, the level of detail, whether individual States should be identified, the extent of references to case law, and in ensuring that the work was not duplicative of work in other forums.

Transport law

UNCITRAL [A/60/17] considered the reports of Working Group III (Transport Law) on its fourteenth [YUN 2004, p. 1354] and fifteenth (New York, 18-28 April) [A/CN.9/576] sessions, describing its continuing work on the provisions of a draft instrument on the carriage of goods wholly or partly by sea. UNCITRAL was informed that the Working Group had proceeded with its second reading of the draft instrument and had made good progress on a number of difficult issues, including those regarding the basis of liability pursuant to the draft instrument, as well as the scope of application of the instrument and related freedom of contract issues. The Group also considered the chapters of the draft instrument on jurisdiction and arbitration and had an initial exchange of views on the right of control and transfer of rights. Following consultations with Working Group IV (Electronic Commerce), the Group considered for the first time, at its fifteenth session, provisions in the draft instrument relating to electronic commerce. The Group was expected to complete its work at the end of 2006, with a view to presenting a draft instrument for possible adoption by UNCITRAL in 2007.

UNCITRAL commended the Working Group for the progress made. It noted that the Group's working methods should be compatible with the production of official documents in all official languages; that in meetings convened by the Secretariat, experts should be allowed to express themselves in UN working languages; and the translation of documents into all official languages should be considered by the Working Group. With respect to a time frame for completing the draft instrument, UNCITRAL agreed that 2007 would be a desirable goal for its completion and adoption, but that the matter should be revisited in 2006.

Electronic commerce

UNCITRAL, at its thirty-eighth session [A/60/17], considered the revised draft convention on the use of electronic communications in international contracts, which had been deliberated by Working Group IV at its forty-fourth session [YUN 2004, p. 1354]. It took note of the summary of the deliberations on the draft convention since the thirty-ninth session of the Working Group and of the background information provided [A/CN.9/577/Add.1], as well as of the comments on the draft convention submitted by Governments and international organizations [A/CN.9/578 & Add. 1-17]. After finalizing the draft convention, UNCITRAL requested the Secretariat to prepare, for its thirty-ninth session, the explanatory notes to the text. Also before UNCITRAL was a note by the Secretariat [A/CN.9/579] on current work by other international organizations in the area of electronic commerce.

On 15 July, UNCITRAL approved and submitted to the General Assembly for adoption at its sixtieth session, a UN convention on the use of electronic communications in international contracts, contained in an annex. The draft convention was aimed at removing possible legal obstacles to electronic commerce that might arise under existing international trade-related instruments.

GENERAL ASSEMBLY ACTION

On 23 November [meeting 53], the General Assembly, on the recommendation of the Sixth Committee [A/60/513], adopted **resolution 60/21** without vote [agenda item 79].

United Nations Convention on the Use of Electronic Communications in International Contracts

The General Assembly,

Recalling its resolution 2205(XXI) of 17 December 1966, by which it established the United Nations Commission on International Trade Law with a mandate to further the progressive harmonization and unification of the law of international trade and in that respect to bear in mind the interests of all peoples, in particular those of developing countries, in the extensive development of international trade,

Considering that problems created by uncertainties as to the legal value of electronic communications exchanged in the context of international contracts constitute an obstacle to international trade,

Convinced that the adoption of uniform rules to remove obstacles to the use of electronic communications in international contracts, including obstacles that might result from the operation of existing international trade law instruments, would enhance legal certainty and commercial predictability for international contracts and may help States gain access to modern trade routes,

Recalling that, at its thirty-fourth session, in 2001, UNCITRAL decided to prepare an international instrument dealing with issues of electronic contracting, which should also aim at removing obstacles to electronic commerce in existing uniform law conventions and trade agreements, and entrusted its Working Group IV (Electronic Commerce) with the preparation of a draft,

Noting that the Working Group devoted six sessions, from 2002 to 2004, to the preparation of the draft Convention on the Use of Electronic Communications in International Contracts, and that UNCITRAL considered the draft Convention at its thirty-eighth session in 2005,

Being aware that all States and interested international organizations were invited to participate in the preparation of the draft Convention at all the sessions of the Working Group and at the thirty-eighth session of the Commission, either as members or as observers, with a full opportunity to speak and make proposals,

Noting with satisfaction that the text of the draft Convention was circulated for comments before the thirty-eighth session of the Commission to all Governments and international organizations invited to attend the meetings of the Commission and the Working Group as observers, and that the comments received were before the Commission at its thirty-eighth session,

Taking note with satisfaction of the decision of the Commission at its thirty-eighth session to submit the draft Convention to the General Assembly for its consideration,

Taking note of the draft Convention approved by the Commission,

1. *Expresses its appreciation* to the United Nations Commission on International Trade Law for preparing the draft Convention on the Use of Electronic Communications in International Contracts;

2. *Adopts* the United Nations Convention on the Use of Electronic Communications in International Contracts, which is contained in the annex to the present resolution, and requests the Secretary-General to open it for signature;

3. *Calls upon* all Governments to consider becoming party to the Convention.

Annex

United Nations Convention on the Use of Electronic Communications in International Contracts

The States Parties to this Convention,

Reaffirming their belief that international trade on the basis of equality and mutual benefit is an important element in promoting friendly relations among States,

Noting that the increased use of electronic communications improves the efficiency of commercial activities, enhances trade connections and allows new access opportunities for previously remote parties and markets, thus playing a fundamental role in promoting trade and economic development, both domestically and internationally,

Considering that problems created by uncertainty as to the legal value of the use of electronic communications in international contracts constitute an obstacle to international trade,

Convinced that the adoption of uniform rules to remove obstacles to the use of electronic communications in international contracts, including obstacles that might result from the operation of existing international trade law instruments, would enhance legal certainty and commercial predictability for international contracts and help States gain access to modern trade routes,

Being of the opinion that uniform rules should respect the freedom of parties to choose appropriate media and technologies, taking account of the principles of technological neutrality and functional equivalence, to the extent that the means chosen by the parties comply with the purpose of the relevant rules of law,

Desiring to provide a common solution to remove legal obstacles to the use of electronic communications in a manner acceptable to States with different legal, social and economic systems,

Have agreed as follows:

Chapter I
Sphere of application

Article 1
Scope of application

1. This Convention applies to the use of electronic communications in connection with the formation or performance of a contract between parties whose places of business are in different States.

2. The fact that the parties have their places of business in different States is to be disregarded whenever this fact does not appear either from the contract or from any dealings between the parties or from information disclosed by the parties at any time before or at the conclusion of the contract.

3. Neither the nationality of the parties nor the civil or commercial character of the parties or of the contract is to be taken into consideration in determining the application of this Convention.

Article 2
Exclusions

1. This Convention does not apply to electronic communications relating to any of the following:

(*a*) Contracts concluded for personal, family or household purposes;

(*b*) (i) Transactions on a regulated exchange; (ii) foreign exchange transactions; (iii) inter-bank payment systems, inter-bank payment agreements or clearance and settlement systems relating to securities or other financial assets or instruments; (iv) the transfer of security rights in sale, loan or holding of or agreement to repurchase securities or other financial assets or instruments held with an intermediary.

2. This Convention does not apply to bills of exchange, promissory notes, consignment notes, bills of lading, warehouse receipts or any transferable document or instrument that entitles the bearer or beneficiary to claim the delivery of goods or the payment of a sum of money.

Article 3
Party autonomy

The parties may exclude the application of this Convention or derogate from or vary the effect of any of its provisions.

Chapter II
General provisions

Article 4
Definitions

For the purposes of this Convention:

(*a*) "Communication" means any statement, declaration, demand, notice or request, including an offer and the acceptance of an offer, that the parties are required to make or choose to make in connection with the formation or performance of a contract;

(*b*) "Electronic communication" means any communication that the parties make by means of data messages;

(*c*) "Data message" means information generated, sent, received or stored by electronic, magnetic, optical or similar means, including, but not limited to, electronic data interchange, electronic mail, telegram, telex or telecopy;

(*d*) "Originator" of an electronic communication means a party by whom, or on whose behalf, the electronic communication has been sent or generated prior to storage, if any, but it does not include a party acting as an intermediary with respect to that electronic communication;

(*e*) "Addressee" of an electronic communication means a party who is intended by the originator to receive the electronic communication, but does not include a party acting as an intermediary with respect to that electronic communication;

(*f*) "Information system" means a system for generating, sending, receiving, storing or otherwise processing data messages;

(*g*) "Automated message system" means a computer program or an electronic or other automated means used to initiate an action or respond to data messages or performances in whole or in part, without review or intervention by a natural person each time an action is initiated or a response is generated by the system;

(*h*) "Place of business" means any place where a party maintains a non-transitory establishment to pursue an economic activity other than the temporary provision of goods or services out of a specific location.

Article 5
Interpretation

1. In the interpretation of this Convention, regard is to be had to its international character and to the need to promote uniformity in its application and the observance of good faith in international trade.

2. Questions concerning matters governed by this Convention which are not expressly settled in it are to be settled in conformity with the general principles on which it is based or, in the absence of such principles, in conformity with the law applicable by virtue of the rules of private international law.

Article 6
Location of the parties

1. For the purposes of this Convention, a party's place of business is presumed to be the location indicated by that party, unless another party demonstrates that the party making the indication does not have a place of business at that location.

2. If a party has not indicated a place of business and has more than one place of business, then the place of business for the purposes of this Convention is that which has the closest relationship to the relevant contract, having regard to the circumstances known to or contemplated by the parties at any time before or at the conclusion of the contract.

3. If a natural person does not have a place of business, reference is to be made to the person's habitual residence.

4. A location is not a place of business merely because that is: (a) where equipment and technology supporting an information system used by a party in connection with the formation of a contract are located; or (b) where the information system may be accessed by other parties.

5. The sole fact that a party makes use of a domain name or electronic mail address connected to a specific country does not create a presumption that its place of business is located in that country.

Article 7
Information requirements

Nothing in this Convention affects the application of any rule of law that may require the parties to disclose their identities, places of business or other information, or relieves a party from the legal consequences of making inaccurate, incomplete or false statements in that regard.

Chapter III
Use of electronic communications in international contracts

Article 8
Legal recognition of electronic communications

1. A communication or a contract shall not be denied validity or enforceability on the sole ground that it is in the form of an electronic communication.

2. Nothing in this Convention requires a party to use or accept electronic communications, but a party's agreement to do so may be inferred from the party's conduct.

Article 9
Form requirements

1. Nothing in this Convention requires a communication or a contract to be made or evidenced in any particular form.

2. Where the law requires that a communication or a contract should be in writing, or provides consequences for the absence of a writing, that requirement is met by an electronic communication if the information contained therein is accessible so as to be usable for subsequent reference.

3. Where the law requires that a communication or a contract should be signed by a party, or provides consequences for the absence of a signature, that requirement is met in relation to an electronic communication if:

(a) A method is used to identify the party and to indicate that party's intention in respect of the information contained in the electronic communication; and

(b) The method used is either:

(i) As reliable as appropriate for the purpose for which the electronic communication was generated or communicated, in the light of all the circumstances, including any relevant agreement; or

(ii) Proven in fact to have fulfilled the functions described in subparagraph (a) above, by itself or together with further evidence.

4. Where the law requires that a communication or a contract should be made available or retained in its original form, or provides consequences for the absence of an original, that requirement is met in relation to an electronic communication if:

(a) There exists a reliable assurance as to the integrity of the information it contains from the time when it was first generated in its final form, as an electronic communication or otherwise; and

(b) Where it is required that the information it contains be made available, that information is capable of being displayed to the person to whom it is to be made available.

5. For the purposes of paragraph 4 (a):

(a) The criteria for assessing integrity shall be whether the information has remained complete and unaltered, apart from the addition of any endorsement and any change that arises in the normal course of communication, storage and display; and

(b) The standard of reliability required shall be assessed in the light of the purpose for which the information was generated and in the light of all the relevant circumstances.

Article 10
Time and place of dispatch and receipt of electronic communications

1. The time of dispatch of an electronic communication is the time when it leaves an information system under the control of the originator or of the party who sent it on behalf of the originator or, if the electronic communication has not left an information system under the control of the originator or of the party who sent it on behalf of the originator, the time when the electronic communication is received.

2. The time of receipt of an electronic communication is the time when it becomes capable of being retrieved by the addressee at an electronic address designated by the addressee. The time of receipt of an electronic communication at another electronic address of the addressee is the time when it becomes capable of being retrieved by the addressee at that address and the addressee becomes aware that the electronic communication has been sent to that address. An electronic communication is presumed to be capable of being retrieved by the addressee when it reaches the addressee's electronic address.

3. An electronic communication is deemed to be dispatched at the place where the originator has its place of business and is deemed to be received at the place where the addressee has its place of business, as determined in accordance with article 6.

4. Paragraph 2 of this article applies notwithstanding that the place where the information system supporting an electronic address is located may be different from the place where the electronic communication is deemed to be received under paragraph 3 of this article.

Article 11
Invitations to make offers

A proposal to conclude a contract made through one or more electronic communications which is not addressed to one or more specific parties, but is generally accessible to parties making use of information systems, including proposals that make use of interactive applications for the placement of orders through such information systems, is to be considered as an invitation to make offers, unless it clearly indicates the intention of the party making the proposal to be bound in case of acceptance.

Article 12
Use of automated message systems for contract formation

A contract formed by the interaction of an automated message system and a natural person, or by the interaction of automated message systems, shall not be denied validity or enforceability on the sole ground that no natural person reviewed or intervened in each of the individual actions carried out by the automated message systems or the resulting contract.

Article 13
Availability of contract terms

Nothing in this Convention affects the application of any rule of law that may require a party that negotiates some or all of the terms of a contract through the exchange of electronic communications to make available to the other party those electronic communications which contain the contractual terms in a particular manner, or relieves a party from the legal consequences of its failure to do so.

Article 14
Error in electronic communications

1. Where a natural person makes an input error in an electronic communication exchanged with the automated message system of another party and the automated message system does not provide the person with an opportunity to correct the error, that person, or the party on whose behalf that person was acting, has the right to withdraw the portion of the electronic communication in which the input error was made if:

(a) The person, or the party on whose behalf that person was acting, notifies the other party of the error as soon as possible after having learned of the error and indicates that he or she made an error in the electronic communication; and

(b) The person, or the party on whose behalf that person was acting, has not used or received any material benefit or value from the goods or services, if any, received from the other party.

2. Nothing in this article affects the application of any rule of law that may govern the consequences of any error other than as provided for in paragraph 1.

Chapter IV
Final provisions

Article 15
Depositary

The Secretary-General of the United Nations is hereby designated as the depositary for this Convention.

Article 16
Signature, ratification, acceptance or approval

1. This Convention is open for signature by all States at United Nations Headquarters in New York from 16 January 2006 to 16 January 2008.

2. This Convention is subject to ratification, acceptance or approval by the signatory States.

3. This Convention is open for accession by all States that are not signatory States as from the date it is open for signature.

4. Instruments of ratification, acceptance, approval and accession are to be deposited with the Secretary-General of the United Nations.

Article 17
Participation by regional economic integration organizations

1. A regional economic integration organization that is constituted by sovereign States and has competence over certain matters governed by this Convention may similarly sign, ratify, accept, approve or accede to this Convention. The regional economic integration organization shall in that case have the rights and obligations of a Contracting State, to the extent that that organization has competence over matters governed by this Convention. Where the number of Contracting States is relevant in this Convention, the regional economic integration organization shall not count as a Contracting State in addition to its member States that are Contracting States.

2. The regional economic integration organization shall, at the time of signature, ratification, acceptance, approval or accession, make a declaration to the depositary specifying the matters governed by this Convention in respect of which competence has been transferred to that organization by its member States. The regional economic integration organization shall promptly notify the depositary of any changes to the distribution of competence, including new transfers of competence, specified in the declaration under this paragraph.

3. Any reference to a "Contracting State" or "Contracting States" in this Convention applies equally to a regional economic integration organization where the context so requires.

4. This Convention shall not prevail over any conflicting rules of any regional economic integration organization as applicable to parties whose respective places of business are located in States members of any such organization, as set out by declaration made in accordance with article 21.

Article 18
Effect in domestic territorial units

1. If a Contracting State has two or more territorial units in which different systems of law are applicable in relation to the matters dealt with in this Convention, it may, at the time of signature, ratification, acceptance, approval or accession, declare that this Convention is to extend to all its territorial units or only to one or more of them, and may amend its declaration by submitting another declaration at any time.

2. These declarations are to be notified to the depositary and are to state expressly the territorial units to which the Convention extends.

3. If, by virtue of a declaration under this article, this Convention extends to one or more but not all of the territorial units of a Contracting State, and if the place of business of a party is located in that State, this place of business, for the purposes of this Convention, is considered not to be in a Contracting State, unless it is in a territorial unit to which the Convention extends.

4. If a Contracting State makes no declaration under paragraph 1 of this article, the Convention is to extend to all territorial units of that State.

Article 19
Declarations on the scope of application

1. Any Contracting State may declare, in accordance with article 21, that it will apply this Convention only:

(*a*) When the States referred to in article 1, paragraph 1, are Contracting States to this Convention; or

(*b*) When the parties have agreed that it applies.

2. Any Contracting State may exclude from the scope of application of this Convention the matters it specifies in a declaration made in accordance with article 21.

Article 20
Communications exchanged under other international conventions

1. The provisions of this Convention apply to the use of electronic communications in connection with the formation or performance of a contract to which any of the following international conventions, to which a Contracting State to this Convention is or may become a Contracting State, apply:

Convention on the Recognition and Enforcement of Foreign Arbitral Awards (New York, 10 June 1958);

Convention on the Limitation Period in the International Sale of Goods (New York, 14 June 1974) and Protocol thereto (Vienna, 11 April 1980);

United Nations Convention on Contracts for the International Sale of Goods (Vienna, 11 April 1980);

United Nations Convention on the Liability of Operators of Transport Terminals in International Trade (Vienna, 19 April 1991);

United Nations Convention on Independent Guarantees and Stand-by Letters of Credit (New York, 11 December 1995);

United Nations Convention on the Assignment of Receivables in International Trade (New York, 12 December 2001).

2. The provisions of this Convention apply further to electronic communications in connection with the formation or performance of a contract to which another international convention, treaty or agreement not specifically referred to in paragraph 1 of this article, and to which a Contracting State to this Convention is or may become a Contracting State, applies, unless the State has declared, in accordance with article 21, that it will not be bound by this paragraph.

3. A State that makes a declaration pursuant to paragraph 2 of this article may also declare that it will nevertheless apply the provisions of this Convention to the use of electronic communications in connection with the formation or performance of any contract to which a specified international convention, treaty or agreement applies to which the State is or may become a Contracting State.

4. Any State may declare that it will not apply the provisions of this Convention to the use of electronic communications in connection with the formation or performance of a contract to which any international convention, treaty or agreement specified in that State's declaration, to which the State is or may become a Contracting State, applies, including any of the conventions referred to in paragraph 1 of this article, even if such State has not excluded the application of paragraph 2 of this article by a declaration made in accordance with article 21.

Article 21
Procedure and effects of declarations

1. Declarations under article 17, paragraph 4, article 19, paragraphs 1 and 2, and article 20, paragraphs 2, 3 and 4, may be made at any time. Declarations made at the time of signature are subject to confirmation upon ratification, acceptance or approval.

2. Declarations and their confirmations are to be in writing and to be formally notified to the depositary.

3. A declaration takes effect simultaneously with the entry into force of this Convention in respect of the State concerned. However, a declaration of which the depositary receives formal notification after such entry into force takes effect on the first day of the month following the expiration of six months after the date of its receipt by the depositary.

4. Any State that makes a declaration under this Convention may modify or withdraw it at any time by a formal notification in writing addressed to the depositary. The modification or withdrawal is to take effect on the first day of the month following the expiration of six months after the date of the receipt of the notification by the depositary.

Article 22
Reservations

No reservations may be made under this Convention.

Article 23
Entry into force

1. This Convention enters into force on the first day of the month following the expiration of six months after the date of deposit of the third instrument of ratification, acceptance, approval or accession.

2. When a State ratifies, accepts, approves or accedes to this Convention after the deposit of the third instrument of ratification, acceptance, approval or accession, this Convention enters into force in respect of that State on the first day of the month following the expiration of six months after the date of the deposit of its instrument of ratification, acceptance, approval or accession.

Article 24
Time of application

This Convention and any declaration apply only to electronic communications that are made after the date when the Convention or the declaration enters into force or takes effect in respect of each Contracting State.

Article 25
Denunciations

1. A Contracting State may denounce this Convention by a formal notification in writing addressed to the depositary.

2. The denunciation takes effect on the first day of the month following the expiration of twelve months after the notification is received by the depositary. Where a longer period for the denunciation to take effect is specified in the notification, the denunciation takes effect upon the expiration of such longer period after the notification is received by the depositary.

DONE at New York, this [...] day of [...] 2005, in a single original, of which the Arabic, Chinese, English, French, Russian and Spanish texts are equally authentic.

IN WITNESS WHEREOF the undersigned plenipotentiaries, being duly authorized by their respective Governments, have signed this Convention.

Security interests

UNCITRAL [A/60/17] took note of the reports of Working Group VI (Security Interests) on its sixth [YUN 2004, p. 1355] and seventh (New York, 24-28 January) [A/CN.9/574] sessions, at which the Working Group continued the development of an efficient legal regime for security rights in goods involved in a commercial activity, in the form of a legislative guide.

UNCITRAL commended the Working Group for the progress it had achieved so far, noting that a complete consolidated set of legislative recommendations would be before the Working Group at its eighth (2006) session, including recommendations on inventory, equipment and trade receivables, as well as on negotiable instruments, negotiable documents, bank accounts and proceeds from independent undertakings. It also noted the progress made in the coordination of the Group's work with the Hague Conference on Private International Law, the International Institute for the Unification of Private Law (Unidroit), the World Bank and the World Intellectual Property Organization. UNCITRAL requested the Group to expedite its work so as to submit the draft legislative guide to the Commission for approval in principle, in 2006, and for final adoption in 2007.

Case law on UNCITRAL texts

UNCITRAL [A/60/17] noted the ongoing work under the system for the collection and dissemination of case law on UNCITRAL texts (CLOUT), consisting of the preparation of case abstracts and research aids and analytical tools, such as thesauri and indices, and the compilation of full texts of decisions. A total of 46 issues of CLOUT had been published, dealing with 530 cases.

UNCITRAL expressed its appreciation to the national correspondents for their work in selecting decisions and preparing case abstracts. It noted that the digest of the case law on the United Nations Sales Convention had been published in December 2004 [YUN 2004, p. 1356], and that the first draft of a digest of case law related to the Arbitration Model Law would be before CLOUT national correspondents at their July meeting.

Training and technical assistance

UNCITRAL [A/60/17] had before it a note by the Secretariat [A/CN.9/586] describing the technical assistance activities undertaken since 2004 and the direction of future activities. Among activities reported were 10 seminars organized to promote understanding of international commercial law conventions, model laws and other legal texts; assistance with legislative and other drafting; and participation in 43 seminars, conferences and courses examining UNCITRAL texts for possible

adoption or use. UNCITRAL also co-sponsored the twelfth Willem C. Vis International Commercial Arbitration Moot (Vienna, 19-24 March) to disseminate information about uniform law texts and the teaching of international trade law.

UNCITRAL noted that the technical assistance unit had identified its goals and taken steps to draft guidelines addressing the requirements for organizing, implementing and reporting on technical assistance activities, and was beginning to identify national and regional needs for technical assistance, as well as opportunities for developing joint programmes with, and participating in, programmes of organizations providing technical assistance in trade law reform.

UNCITRAL reiterated its appeal to all States, international organizations and other interested entities to contribute to its trust funds to enable it to meet the increasing demands for its training and technical legislative assistance and for travel assistance to Commission members from developing countries.

Future work

In 2005, UNCITRAL discussed its future work programme based on Secretariat notes on insolvency law [A/CN.9/582 & Add. 1-7], specifically on the treatment of corporate groups in insolvency, cross-border insolvency protocols in transnational cases, post-commencement financing and commercial fraud and insolvency, as well as on electronic commerce [A/CN.9/579].

UNCITRAL agreed to hold an international colloquium on insolvency in Vienna from 14 to 16 November, to facilitate further consideration and obtain the views and benefit from the expertise of international organizations and insolvency experts. As to future work on electronic commerce, UNCITRAL agreed that the Secretariat should prepare a more detailed study, with proposals as to the form and nature of the reference document that would be envisaged, and taking into account the recommendations for future work proposed by Working Group IV, for the Commission's consideration at its thirty-ninth (2006) session.

UNCITRAL approved a plan, in the context of its fortieth (2007) session, to hold a congress similar to the 1992 [YUN 1992, p. 1012] UNCITRAL Congress on Uniform Commercial Law in the Twenty-first Century. The 2007 Congress would review the results of UNCITRAL work programme, as well as the related work of other organizations active in the field of international trade law, assess current work programmes and consider and evaluate topics for future work.

PART FIVE

Institutional, administrative and budgetary questions

Chapter I

Strengthening and restructuring of the United Nations system

During 2005, the implementation of the Secretary-General's programme of reform of the Organization continued, with actions centred around the UN system's role in addressing the core challenges of development. In a report on the implementation of the Millennium Declaration, the Secretary-General considered issues relating to the use of monitoring, evaluation and reporting by the UN system, and stressed the importance of integrating and aligning UN development policies with the priorities and strategies of national Governments. In January, the Millennium Project, an independent advisory body commissioned by the Secretary-General in 2002, issued its final report on strategies for the implementation of the Millennium Development Goals (MDGs). A Development Cooperation Forum was established to review global, regional, and national strategies and policies for development cooperation and to provide guidance on the matter.

During the year, the Independent Inquiry Committee (IIC) established in 2004 to investigate the oil-for-food-programme issued several reports on its findings, including a September report on the programme's management. In response to the recommendations contained in the report, as well as the decisions of the General Assembly taken at its High-level Plenary meeting in September, action was taken to introduce reforms, such as the establishment of a new Ethics Office to serve as a focal point within the UN Secretariat for issues including financial disclosure, the protection of staff against retaliation for reporting misconduct, and the development of standards, training and education on ethics issues. Other changes in the UN's structure included the replacement of the Accountability Panel with the Management Performance Board, which would advise the Secretary-General on matters concerning the performance of individual senior managers, and the creation of an Audit Advisory Committee to assist the Secretary-General in his oversight responsibilities. A review of UN system governance arrangements, including an external evaluation of the auditing and oversight system, was to be conducted. The Assembly also adopted measures to strengthen its functioning.

Programme of reform

General aspects

In his annual report on the work of the Organization [A/61/1], the Secretary-General stated that, since 1997 [YUN 1997, p. 1389], when an ongoing UN reform package was first established, much of his reform agenda had been implemented. Changes had been made to work programmes, structures and systems, both at Headquarters and in the field, but not all reforms had been accepted by Member States and the Organization needed to continue to improve. Noting that Member States at the 2005 World Summit had reaffirmed their commitment to a more efficient and effective United Nations (see p. 63), the Secretary-General addressed issues relating to the Organization's intergovernmental machinery, as well as the Secretariat, its mandates, cooperation with regional organizations and system-wide coherence.

During 2005, reforms of the Secretariat included the introduction of measures to strengthen accountability and improve ethical conduct in the Organization. An Ethics Office was established in December (see p. 1476) to administer new policies on protection for reporting misconduct and financial disclosure, and procurement reforms efforts were validated by an independent review conducted by the United States National Institute of Government Purchasing. Following the revelation of criminal misconduct concerning a UN procurement official, the Secretary-General ordered a complete review of internal and financial controls. Two senior management committees were created to improve executive decision-making and a Management Performance Board established to improve senior managerial accountability.

To strengthen and update the UN programme of work, leaders at the World Summit, responding to the Secretary-General's proposal contained in his report "In larger freedom: towards development, security and human rights for all" (see p. 67), requested the General Assembly and other relevant organs to review all mandates that were older than five years. They also supported a stronger relationship between the United Nations and regional and subregional organizations and resolved to expand cooperation with such organizations. At the sixth high-level meeting with the heads of regional organizations, convened in July (see p. 96), a standing committee was established to provide overall guidance to the process of creating a more structured relationship between the United Nations and regional organizations. The World Summit outcome document also called for stronger UN system-wide coherence, in particular across development-related organizations, agencies, funds and programmes (see p. 65). It requested the Secretary-General to further strengthen the management and coordination of UN operational activities, as well as the governance, management and coordination of the Organization.

Agenda for change

Strengthening of the UN system

Report of the Secretary-General to the 2005 World Summit

In his March report "In larger freedom" (see p. 67), the Secretary-General noted that most of the reform elements contained in his 2002 "agenda for further change" [YUN 2002, p. 1353] had been implemented, resulting in a thoroughly revised programme budget for 2004-2005; a shorter, more efficient cycle of planning and budgeting for the 2006-2007 biennium; a reduction in the quantity of reports and meetings; and a greater integration of human rights elements in the work of the UN country teams. However, as progress in a number of other areas had been slow, the Secretary-General launched, in 2005, a two-track package of Secretariat reform: one to be pursued under his own authority; and another to be taken up in the context of the wider proposals contained in the report. The measures set for immediate implementation included initiatives to address serious concerns raised by UN staff in an integrity perception survey, the recommendations of the Independent Inquiry Committee investigating the oil-for-food programme (see p. 1475), and to improve the performance of senior management, enhance oversight and accountability and ensure ethical conduct and transparency.

In 2005, the Senior Management Group, an internal information-sharing and coordination tool established in 1997 [YUN 1997, p. 1390], was replaced with two smaller senior committees—one for policy issues and the other for management reform matters. A more transparent system for the selection of new UN leaders was introduced,

using an open selection process based on predetermined criteria, and a more structured system of induction put in place to ensure that senior officials were properly briefed on UN rules, regulations, codes of conduct and managerial systems. To address the need for better tools to ensure accountability, a Management Performance Board was created to assess the performance of individual managers and advise the Secretary-General on corrective action where necessary. A new Oversight Committee was also established to ensure that appropriate management action was taken to implement the recommendations of the various oversight bodies.

The Organization was moving ahead to strengthen ethical conduct, including introducing a new policy for the protection of whistleblowers and taking swift and appropriate disciplinary action against all proven cases of sexual misconduct. Measures to improve training, impose a new standard of conduct, establish credible complaint mechanisms and review welfare and recreational needs for personnel in the field were also underway, as were the introduction of a more expansive requirement for financial disclosure by senior officials and the better dissemination of code of conduct requirements. The Organization was also developing a clear and consistent policy for sharing different categories of UN information, which would increase transparency, while ensuring confidentiality. Alongside the proposed review of all mandates older than five years, the Secretary-General proposed a one-time buy-out for UN personnel whose skills and profiles no longer matched the needs of the Secretariat, and asked the General Assembly to approve a thorough review of all budgetary and human resources rules governing the Secretariat.

In the World Summit outcome document, world leaders asked the Secretary-General to submit, in early 2006, proposals for implementing management reforms to the Assembly for consideration and decisions in those areas of identified need (see p. 65).

Implementation of the Millennium Declaration

Reports of Secretary-General. In a May report to the Economic and Social Council [E/2005/56], the Secretary-General identified core issues relevant to the achievement of the Millennium Development Goals (MDGs), first elaborated in the section of the UN Millennium Declaration [YUN 2000, p. 49] that dealt with development and poverty eradication [ibid., p. 51], and reviewed progress made in implementing those

Goals. The MDGs, which were eight in number, were to eradicate extreme hunger; achieve universal primary education; promote gender equality and empower women; reduce child mortality; improve maternal health; combat HIV/AIDS, malaria and other diseases; ensure environmental sustainability; and develop a global partnership for development.

Noting that the achievement of the MDGs and the implementation of the wider development agenda were interlinked, the report also reviewed progress made in the integrated and coordinated implementation of the outcomes and commitments of major UN development conferences and summits. It highlighted the core challenges addressed by those meetings, including eradicating poverty, hunger and malnutrition; advancing education and literacy; providing health services, preventing disease and reducing mortality; promoting gender equality and empowering women; promoting employment; achieving social integration and addressing vulnerabilities of social groups; ensuring environmental sustainability and managing the natural resource base for development; promoting democracy, good governance and human rights; and addressing challenges of countries with special needs. Key instruments essential for the implementation of the MDGs—strengthening global partnership for development, making macroeconomic policies work for sustained employment-generating economic growth, promoting science and technology for development and enhancing the role of civil society and the private sector in development—were also examined. Those areas would serve as tools for developing integrated policy frameworks at the national and international levels, strengthening direct linkages with strategies to achieve the MDGs, and facilitating effective monitoring and evaluation of the implementation of the UN development agenda. The Secretary-General addressed the progress and gaps in the implementation of each of the core challenges highlighted in the report and considered the key instruments for achieving the UN development agenda.

The Secretary-General concluded that progress in the implementation of the development agenda had been made in several areas but was slow and uneven. Given the current pace, neither the MDGs, nor the broader UN development agenda, would be achieved, unless both were truly embraced at the national and international levels, backed by practical targets and long-term commitments; sectorial approaches to development replaced by a more integrated, synergistic and holistic framework; the necessary resources invested in pursuit of the agenda; institutional impediments at the national and international levels addressed; and constant monitoring and evaluation arrangements put in place to ensure that the process remained on track.

He outlined the principles guiding the implementation of the comprehensive UN development agenda, which included undertaking development and investment strategies, identifying and assessing needs, vulnerabilities and capacities; recognizing and building on interlinkages within the system; making the process particpatory and inclusive; mainstreaming the broader development objectives into macroeconomic policy; enhancing the role of civil society and the private sector in development; strengthening the role of science and technology; ensuring resources and international partnership for achieving the development agenda; and monitoring, evaluating and reporting in order to measure progress, identify impediments and take corrective actions.

To achieve the comprehensive UN development agenda, UN system organizations had to integrate and align fully their policies and programmes with the priorities of national Governments, international commitments and the agreed goals and targets embodied in that agenda, including the MDGs; develop coherent and integrated system-wide approaches to the achievement of key development objectives, which could be translated into national policies and strategies; design UN operational activities at the country level to support such strategies; strengthen the linkages between that work and the normative work of the Organization; and coordinate with other actors in the field.

At the intergovernmental level, there should be a coherent, coordinated and integrated monitoring and evaluation of the implementation of the development agenda. The Secretary-General recommended that the Economic and Social Council review progress in the implementation of the UN development agenda, particularly the MDGs, with a view to strengthening the system's capacity for a comprehensive monitoring and evaluation of its implementation and promoting effective policies and strategies at all levels. Towards that end, the Council should organize peer reviews of progress. An existing meeting or segment of the Council could be transformed once every two years into a Development Cooperation Forum, where global, regional and national strategies and policies for development cooperation could be reviewed and policy guidance provided. The Council should pursue a continuous policy dialogue within the UN system to enhance policy coherence, coordination and cooperation. It should mount coordinated responses to natural disasters and other actual or imminent threats to development and provide timely inputs or address developments in other forums that had major implications for achieving the development goals.

By **decision 2005/222** of 6 July, the Council noted the Secretary-General's report.

CEB action. The High-level Committee on Programmes (HLCP) of the United Nations System Chief Executives Board for Coordination (CEB), at its ninth session (Rome, Italy, 23-25 February) [CEB/2005/4], discussed the 2005 review of the implementation of the Millennium Declaration. It reviewed progress in the elaboration of a CEB report on the UN system response to the Declaration. It had before it a revised draft of that report, an updated annex on major collaborative initiatives to support the implementation of the Declaration and a summary of comments and suggestions by HLCP members on the draft. A revised version of the draft report was to be prepared for the April session of CEB, as part of the preparations for the high-level segment of the Economic and Social Council, as well as the discussions leading to the High-level Plenary Meeting of the General Assembly (World Summit). The report would also be brought to the attention of relevant agency governing bodies. HLCP established a task force to pursue a 2004 proposal [YUN 2004, p. 1364] of the United Nations Industrial Development Organization (UNIDO) to enhance the role of the UN system in economic development as a means of advancing the achievement of the MDGs. The task force should report in September and submit a final report in 2006.

CEB, at its first 2005 regular session (Mont Pèlerin, Switzerland, 9 April) [CEB/2005/1], in considering follow-up to the Millennium Declaration [YUN 2000, p. 49], discussed the Secretary-General's report to the World Summit entitled "In larger freedom: towards development, security and human rights for all" (see p. 67). The HLCP Chairman briefed CEB on the HLCP report entitled "One United Nations—catalyst for progress and change", the main purpose of which was to illustrate how the UN system had responded to the Millennium Declaration and the ways in which the follow-up to the Declaration was contributing to greater coherence and effectiveness in the system's work. CEB also considered UN system support for Africa's development, highlighting the challenges of mobilizing adequate resources to support the New Partnership for Africa's Development (NEPAD) (see p. 1003) and the implementation of the MDGs in Africa. CEB took note of the HLCP report "One United Nations" and endorsed its conclusions.

Final report of Millennium Project. In March [A/59/727], the Secretary-General transmitted an overview of the final report of the Millennium Project entitled *Investing in Development: A practical Plan to Achieve the Millennium Development Goals* (see p. 70), prepared by Professor Jeffrey D. Sachs, the Secretary-General's special adviser on the MDGs, who had been commissioned to conduct research to map out how those goals, based on the Millennium Declaration, could be achieved. The report was submitted to the 2005 World Summit.

(For the General Assembly's review of the Millennium Declaration, see chapter on the 2005 World Summit on p. 47.)

Managerial reform and oversight

Management reform

In accordance with General Assembly resolution 59/275 [YUN 2004, p. 1401], the Secretary-General, in a September report [A/60/342], examined the efforts of the Department of Management to improve its practices and reviewed the implementation of measures to reduce duplication, complexity and bureaucracy in UN administrative processes and procedures. Management improvement measures, which were in various stages of implementation, focused on improved practices in centralized support services, human resources management and budgetary and financial management. With regard to centralized support services, the Department of Management had implemented an automatic space management system for updating office space floor plans; an automated asset management system; a vehicle usage system; a requisition tracking system; inter-agency system for contracts; a global airline agreement for UN organizations, funds and programmes; a website for registering potential vendors, called the United Nations Global Marketplace; strengthened computer network operations; improved information and communication technology risk management; a reorganization of the UN Postal Administration; and the extension of the UN Integrated Management Information System (IMIS) to all peacekeeping missions.

Human resources management improvements centred around the implementation of a generic job profiles project intended to streamline vacancy announcements through a global database; new human resource data reports; an Electronic Performance Appraisal System (e-PAS); human resource action plans; and other projects. The Department's Office of Programme Planning, Budget and Accounts had improved a number of practices in the budget process, banking procedures and capacities, financial reporting and financial services to staff. Among other measures, it accomplished the linkage of the 2006-2007 budget with the biennial programme plan (see p. 1489), began providing system-wide access to pertinent budgetary information through the UN Intranet and was implementing a treasury banking project to assist peacekeeping missions.

The Secretary-General reviewed the implementation status of the efficiency measures recommended by OIOS and proposed time frames for their final implementation. Among those measures, the Procurement Service and DPKO were developing a common procurement management system to improve the efficiency and oversight of the Secretariat's global procurement activities. Legal requirements for the project had been initiated and would be submitted to the Information and Communications Technology Board Project Review Committee by the end of 2005. The proposed automation of the UN travel process had been given priority status by the IMIS User Group. A "My UN" portal was initiated in 2004, providing staff members with access to vacancy applications, emergency contact recordings and other human resources materials.

Managing for results

Note by Secretary-General. The Secretary-General, by a February note [A/59/617/Add.1], transmitted his comments and those of CEB on the Joint Inspection Unit (JIU) report on managing for results in the UN system [YUN 2004, p. 1372]. In its general comments, CEB found the JIU report to be useful and a valuable reference from a system-wide perspective. It was in broad agreement with the findings and conclusions. However, the two main recommendations on the use of benchmarks for measuring progress towards the effective implementation of results-based-management in respective UN system organizations, and that CEB should pay more attention to harmonizing that implementation, should be considered in the light of specific situations and requirements of the organizations of the system, as well as in relation to the inter-agency mechanisms in place within the CEB framework. While agreeing in principle with the practical benefits of utilizing benchmarks, the Secretary-General said that each organization should adapt them to its particular circumstances, programmes and outputs before they could be applied.

Procurement

By a March note [A/59/721], the Secretary-General transmitted to the General Assembly a JIU report reviewing procurement practices with-

in the UN system [YUN 2004, p. 1365]. In a June addendum [A/59/721/Add.1], he further transmitted his comments and those of CEB on the report. CEB was in general agreement with JIU'S findings and recommendations concerning the rationalization processes, establishment of unified reporting and accountability, training of staff, use of procurement manuals, common services, electronic methods and capacity-building in public procurement agencies in recipient countries.

The Assembly also considered the OIOS reports on the audit of safeguarding air safety standards while procuring air services for UN peacekeeping missions [YUN 2004, p.101] and on the audit of the functioning of the Headquarters Committee on Contracts [YUN 2003, p. 1386].

GENERAL ASSEMBLY ACTION

On 13 April [meeting 91], the General Assembly, on the recommendation of the Fifth (Administrative and Budgetary) Committee [A/59/652/Add.1], adopted **resolution 59/288** without vote [agenda item 107].

Procurement reform

The General Assembly,

Recalling its resolutions 54/14 of 29 October 1999, 55/247 of 12 April 2001 and 57/279 of 20 December 2002,

Having considered the report of the Secretary-General on procurement reform, the related report of the Advisory Committee on Administrative and Budgetary Questions and the reports of the Office of Internal Oversight Services on the audit of safeguarding air safety standards while procuring air services for the United Nations peacekeeping missions and on the audit of the functioning of the Headquarters Committee on Contracts,

A. Report of the Secretary-General on procurement reform

1. *Takes note* of the report of the Secretary-General and the related report of the Advisory Committee on Administrative and Budgetary Questions;

2. *Welcomes* the progress achieved in addressing the concerns expressed in its resolution 57/279 and the recent significant improvements made by the Secretary-General in procurement reform at Headquarters and in the field missions;

3. *Notes with appreciation* the progress achieved in the harmonization and streamlining of procurement practices;

4. *Calls upon* the executive heads of the funds and programmes of the United Nations to continue their efforts with a view to improving the efficiency of procurement by reducing duplication and harmonizing the procurement procedures in the United Nations system as a whole, in close cooperation with the Procurement Service of the Office of Central Support Services of the Secretariat;

5. *Requests* the Secretary-General to encourage all the organizations of the United Nations system, consistent with their respective mandates, to further improve their procurement practices, inter alia, by participating in the United Nations Global Marketplace

with a view to creating one common United Nations global procurement web site;

6. *Notes* the activities of the Inter-Agency Procurement Working Group and of the Common Services Procurement Working Group on enhancing the transparency and increasing the harmonization of procurement practices, and requests the Secretary-General, in consultation with the executive heads of the United Nations funds and programmes, to continue work in this regard;

7. *Requests* the Secretary-General to continue to simplify and streamline the vendor registration process and to share responsibilities among the various United Nations organizations;

8. *Notes* the efforts made by the Secretary-General to increase procurement opportunities for developing countries and countries with economies in transition, and requests the Secretary-General:

(a) To continue to simplify the vendor registration process, taking into account access to the Internet;

(b) To take further steps to sensitize the business community to procurement opportunities within the United Nations system, inter alia:

(i)   The holding of additional business seminars;
(ii) Inviting the Inter-Agency Procurement Working Group to hold more meetings in developing countries;
(iii) Including the issue of "Diversity of sources of procurement" as an agenda item at the annual meetings of the Inter-Agency Procurement Working Group;

9. *Notes also* the recent introduction of the principle of best value for money in relation to procurement, and requests the Secretary-General, when applying this principle, to continue safeguarding the financial interests of the Organization, consider best practices and ensure that adequate records are kept;

10. *Requests* the Secretary-General to submit to the General Assembly an overview and general analysis of the functioning of the principle of best value for money, within the framework of his regular reporting on procurement reform;

11. *Also requests* the Secretary-General to implement measures to reduce the time line associated with invoice payment;

12. *Further requests* the Secretary-General to issue ethical guidelines without delay for those involved in the procurement process, requests that those guidelines be shared with Member States through the procurement web site, and reiterates its request to the Secretary-General for the early adoption of a code of conduct for vendors and a declaration of ethical responsibilities for all staff involved in the procurement process;

13. *Encourages* the Inter-Agency Procurement Working Group to continue its efforts to produce comprehensive and generally applicable statistics encompassing the procurement activities of all United Nations entities;

14. *Welcomes* the training programmes for United Nations procurement staff that the Procurement Service has initiated, including in the field, and requests the Secretary-General to support these programmes and to evaluate and monitor their impact;

15. *Notes* the promotion by the Procurement Service of the voluntary principles of the corporate social responsibility initiative, the Global Compact, within the United Nations procurement framework, and requests the Secretary-General, as appropriate, to report to the General Assembly for further consideration;

16. *Requests* the Secretary-General, taking into account the comments and observations of the Board of Auditors and the Office of Internal Oversight Services, to ensure that information regarding the accountability factor within the procurement reform framework is provided in the next report of the Secretary-General on procurement reform;

17. *Also requests* the Secretary-General to continue to ensure that consistent non-compliance and poor performance by vendors is recorded and that appropriate action is taken with respect to their inclusion in the list of vendors;

18. *Takes note* of the agreements made with major companies, and urges the Secretary-General to continue to ensure adherence to the rules and procedures governing the procurement process and to enable more active participation by all vendors;

19. *Notes* the increase in the number of ex post facto cases, and requests the Secretary-General to continue to take appropriate action in order to minimize that practice to those cases which fully comply with the criteria of exigency;

20. *Requests* the Secretary-General, in his next report on procurement reform, to provide information on the implementation of the new delegations of authority, including mechanisms used to strengthen effective monitoring, oversight and accountability;

21. *Notes* the Secretary-General's plan to provide purchasing cards to departments and offices for the procurement of low-value items, and requests the Secretariat to develop strong internal control mechanisms that will safeguard against misuse, after consulting with the Office of Internal Oversight Services and outside organizations experienced in administering purchase card programmes.

B. Report of the Office of Internal Oversight Services on the audit of safeguarding air safety standards while procuring air services for the United Nations peacekeeping missions

1. *Takes note* of the report of the Office of Internal Oversight Services on the audit of safeguarding air safety standards while procuring air services for the United Nations peacekeeping missions;

2. *Requests* the Secretary-General, as recommended in the report of the Office of Internal Oversight, to fully document the reasons for not following up on the recovery of liquidated damages for contracts and to apply consistent methods to the collection of liquidated damages from vendors;

3. *Also requests* the Secretary-General to continue to ensure compliance with the standards and recommended practices of the International Civil Aviation Organization within the framework of the policy of the Department of Peacekeeping Operations of the Secretariat regarding the chartering of civilian registered aircraft, with the objective of ensuring the highest level of air safety when providing air services to the United Nations;

4. *Notes with concern* the delay and difficulties experienced in recruiting and appointing aviation safety officers in some peacekeeping operations, and requests

the Secretary-General to take all necessary measures to fill the vacancies expeditiously;

5. *Requests* the Secretary-General, in view of the limited number of site visits by aviation experts to operational bases of air carriers, to ensure that experts are able to conduct the necessary technical assessment of vendors;

6. *Notes with concern* that occurrences attributed to specific vendors were not included in the vendor performance reports, and requests the Secretary-General to take all necessary measures to ensure that such occurrences are reflected in the appropriate vendor performance reports;

7. *Requests* the Secretary-General to ensure that the Department of Peacekeeping Operations communicates the information on vendor performance to all aviation offices involved and the Procurement Service.

C. Report of the Office of Internal Oversight Services on the audit of the functioning of the Headquarters Committee on Contracts

1. *Takes note* of the report of the Office of Internal Oversight Services on the audit of the functioning of the Headquarters Committee on Contracts;

2. *Requests* the Secretary-General to review without delay options to better safeguard the independence of the Headquarters Committee on Contracts, including the option identified in recommendation 1 of the report of the Office of Internal Oversight Services;

3. *Also requests* the Secretary-General to examine the appropriateness of the current threshold for the review of procurement cases by the Headquarters Committee on Contracts with a view to improving the effectiveness and efficiency of the functioning of the Committee, taking into account the development of the delegation of authority to the field offices as described in paragraph 11 of the report of the Advisory Committee on Administrative and Budgetary Questions, and to report on action taken to the General Assembly in the context of the next report of the Secretary-General on procurement reform.

Oversight

Internal oversight

Appointment of Under-Secretary-General. In April [A/59/109], the Secretary-General informed the General Assembly of his proposal to appoint Inga-Britt Ahlenius (Sweden) as Under-Secretary-General for Internal Oversight Services for one fixed term of five years. The effective date of the appointment would be communicated to the Assembly later.

By **decision 59/418** of 5 May, the Assembly approved the appointment, beginning on 15 July 2005 and ending on 14 July, 2010.

In later addendum [A/59/109/Add.1], the Secretary-General confirmed those dates.

OIOS activities. In September, the Secretary-General transmitted the eleventh annual report of OIOS covering its activities from 1 July 2004 to 30 June 2005 [A/60/346 & Corr.1]. During that period, OIOS issued several reports, which the Secretary-General transmitted to the Assembly. In addition to reports on its own activities, those issued in 2005, were on: proposals on the strengthening and monitoring of programme performance and evaluation [A/60/73]; a review of operational capacity of United Nations Military Observers [A/59/764]; an audit of field security management [A/59/702]; an audit of mission subsistence allowance policies and procedures [A/59/698]; an investigation into allegations of sexual exploitation/abuse in the United Nations Organization Mission in the Democratic Republic of the Congo (MONUC) [A/59/661]; inspection of programmes and administrative management of the subregional office of the Economic Commission for Africa [A/60/120]; audit of the International Research and Training Institute for the Advancement of Women [A/60/281]; audit of the Capital Master Plan [A/60/288]; audit of the utilization and management of funds for strengthening the security and safety of UN premises [A/60/291]; review of effectiveness of military information management in peacekeeping operations [A/60/596]; and review of military involvement in civil assistance in peacekeeping operations [A/60/588]. OIOS reports transmitted to the Committee for Programme and Coordination (CPC) were on: an evaluation of linkages between Headquarters and field activities: a review of best practices for poverty eradication in the framework of the Millennium Declaration [E/AC.51/2005/2]; an in-depth evaluation of UN-Habitat [E/AC.51/2005/3]; a triennial review of the implementations made by CPC at its forty-second session on the in-depth evaluation of General Assembly and Economic and Social Council support and coordination [E/AC.51/2005.4]; and a triennial review of the implementation of the recommendations made by CPC at its forty-second session on the in-depth evaluation of legal affairs [E/AC.51/2005/5].

During the period under review, OIOS issued 2,167 recommendations to improve accountability mechanisms, internal controls and organizational efficiency and effectiveness, 779, or approximately 43.5 per cent of which were classified as critical. The overall implementation rate for all recommendations during the reporting period was approximately 50 per cent. As at 30 June 2005, the implementation of 34 recommendations issued in 2001/2002 (including two critical), 28 recommendations issued in 2002/2003 (including seven critical) and 124 recommendations issued in 2003/2004 (including 35 critical) had not yet started. The Office identified a total of $35.1 million in recommended savings, $18 million of which was actually saved and recovered. Approximately $3 million was identified as loss or waste of resources.

The report highlighted the oversight results of various risk areas, including management of peacekeeping operations; safety and security; human resources management; administration and finance; procurement; information and communication technology; programme management; the Office of the United Nations High Commission for Refugees, the UN Joint Staff Pension Fund and the UN Compensation Commission. During the reporting period, OIOS undertook a comprehensive risk assessment of the December 2004 Indian Ocean tsunami, in collaboration with Secretariat departments and UN funds and programmes. It was working with DPKO to ensure that serious cases of misconduct identified in MONUC were handled swiftly, in collaboration with troop-contributing countries. It conducted audits of procurement by peacekeeping missions and the risks associated with the capital master plan on the refurbishment of the UN Secretariat (see p. 1494). Investigations conducted dealt with allegations of corrupt behaviour by UN staff; accountability for theft of UN property; and collusion between UN staff and vendors. OIOS initiated a working group which prepared the drafts for the Organization's first whistleblower protection policy and conducted a thematic evaluation of poverty eradication. It collaborated with JIU to report to the General Assembly on strengthening the results-based management culture, produced a tutorial and glossary on the issue, and conducted training to enhance programme performance monitoring and reporting.

By **decision 60/551** of 23 December, the General Assembly deferred until its resumed sixtieth (2006) session consideration of the Secretary-General's report on OIOS activities.

GENERAL ASSEMBLY ACTION

On 13 April [meeting 91], the General Assembly, having considered the OIOS report on strengthening the investigative function in the United Nations [YUN 2004, p. 1374], adopted, on the recommendation of the Fifth Committee [A/59/652/Add.1], **resolution 59/287** without vote [agenda item 107].

Report of the Office of Internal Oversight Services on strengthening the investigation functions in the United Nations

The General Assembly,

Recalling its resolutions 48/218 B of 29 July 1994, 54/244 of 23 December 1999 and 59/272 of 23 December 2004, establishing the Office of Internal Oversight Services and its operational independence,

Recalling also its resolutions 57/282 of 20 December 2002 and 58/268 of 23 December 2003,

Having considered the report of the Office of Internal Oversight Services on strengthening the investigation functions in the United Nations,

Noting that independent investigation is in the best interests of the Organization,

Noting also that violations of the United Nations Financial Regulations and Rules and Staff Regulations and Rules and administrative instructions are considered misconduct and call for disciplinary action,

1. *Takes note* of the report of the Office of Internal Oversight Services on strengthening the investigation functions in the United Nations;

2. *Re-emphasizes* the principle of separation, impartiality and fairness on the part of those with responsibility for investigation functions;

3. *Re-emphasizes also* that the Office of Internal Oversight Services is the internal body entrusted with investigation in the United Nations;

4. *Notes* the need to enhance the capacity of the Office of Internal Oversight Services to conduct its mandated investigation functions efficiently;

5. *Recognizes* that the Office of Internal Oversight Services has established an efficient mechanism to enable all staff members and other persons engaged in activities under the authority of the Organization to convey directly their allegations to the Office of Internal Oversight Services;

6. Stresses that sexual exploitation and abuse constitute serious misconduct and fall under category I;

7. *Notes* that sexual harassment constitutes a serious concern to Member States, and, bearing in mind paragraph 12 of the present resolution, notes that the Office of Human Resources Management and programme managers may be entrusted to conduct investigations in this context;

8. *Decides* that the Office of Internal Oversight Services may entrust trained programme managers to conduct investigations on its behalf;

9. *Also decides* that in cases of serious misconduct and/or criminal behaviour, investigations should be conducted by professional investigators;

10. *Requests* the Secretary-General to implement the proposals of the Office of Internal Oversight Services to increase basic investigation training, as appropriate, for the handling of minor forms of misconduct, to develop written procedures for the proper conduct of investigations and to promote the concept of an independent investigation function within the United Nations;

11. *Decides* that the results of investigation conducted by programme managers should be reported to the Office of Internal Oversight Services;

12. *Requests* the Secretary-General to establish an administrative mechanism for the mandatory reporting by programme managers of allegations of misconduct to the Office of Internal Oversight Services and to report on the establishment of such a mechanism to the General Assembly at the resumed part of its sixtieth session;

13. *Also requests* the Secretary-General to ensure that the introduction of a mandatory reporting mechanism will not adversely affect the right of an individual staff member to report cases of allegations of misconduct directly to the Office of Internal Oversight Services;

14. *Further requests* the Secretary-General to ensure that where poor management practice is a contributory factor in cases of misconduct, appropriate managerial action is taken by the Office of Human Resources Management;

15. *Requests* the Secretary-General to ensure that an appropriate mechanism is in place to protect staff members who report misconduct within the Secretariat against retaliation;

16. *Also requests* the Secretary-General to ensure that, in case of proven misconduct and/or criminal behaviour, disciplinary action and, where appropriate, legal action in accordance with the established procedures and regulations will be taken expeditiously, and requests the Secretary-General to ensure that Member States are informed on an annual basis about all actions taken;

17. *Further requests* the Secretary-General to ensure that all staff of the Organization are informed of the most common examples of misconduct and/or criminal behaviour and their disciplinary consequences, including any legal action, with due regard to the protection of the privacy of the staff member(s) concerned;

18. *Requests* the Secretary-General to ensure that when conclusions of the Office of Internal Oversight Services are disputed by a programme manager, appropriate action will be taken to resolve the dispute and that information thereon will be included in the annual report of the Office of Internal Oversight Services.

External oversight

JIU activities. In its annual report to the General Assembly [A/61/34], JIU gave an overview of its activities in 2005, during which it issued reports on: review of management and administration in the World Intellectual Property Organization (WIPO) [JIU/REP/2005/1]; measures to improve overall performance of the UN system at the country level [JIU/REP/2005/2]; policies of UN system organizations towards the use of open source software in the secretariats [JIU/REP/2005/3] and in development [JIU/REP/2005/7 & Corr. 1]; a common payroll for UN system organizations [JIU/REP/2005/4]; review of management, administration and activities of the secretariat of the United Nations Convention to Combat Desertification [JIU/REP/2005/5]; external review of the implementation of strategic budgeting within a results-based framework in the International Labour Organization [JIU/REP/2005/6]; further measures to strengthen UN system support to the New Partnership for Africa's Development [JIU/REP/2005/8]; and common services in Vienna: Vienna Buildings Management Services [JIU/REP/2005/9]. It had also issued two notes on the review of the implementation of results-based management in the Pan American Health Organization [JIU/NOTE/2005/1] and review of the management of the United Nations laissez-passer [JIU/NOTE/2005/2].

During 2005, JIU's activity was marked by ongoing efforts to improve its method of work and the quality and relevance of its reports. The Unit continued to enhance its procedures for the selection of topics for the annual programme of work. It fine-tuned the methodology for management assessments of participating organizations and completed an additional seven assessments in 2005. To date, 14 assessments had been finalized, with nine planned for completion in 2006. In order to better determine and report on the impact of its recommendations, the Unit adopted a system which defined different categories of impact.

The Unit was revising its follow-up system in order to gather further information on the implementation status of accepted recommendations and the impact achieved. It continued to seek synergies with the work of OIOS and other oversight bodies.

Annexed to the report was the JIU work programme for 2006.

By **decision 60/551** of 23 December, the Assembly deferred until its resumed sixtieth (2006) session consideration of the JIU report for 2004 and its programme of work for 2005 [YUN 2004, p. 1372].

On the same date, by section XVI of **resolution 60/248** (see p. 1496), the Assembly approved the gross budget for JIU for the biennium 2006-2007 in the amount of $10,511,100.

Appointment of JIU members. By **decision 59/416 A** of 28 April, the Assembly appointed Juan Luis Larrabure as a member of JIU for a period of office beginning on 28 April 2005 and expiring on 31 December 2008, to replace Christopher Thomas, who had resigned.

In an August note [A/59/889], the Assembly President transmitted to the Assembly the names of four candidates for appointment as members of the Unit for a five-year term beginning on 1 January 2006 and expiring on 31 December 2010.

By **decision 59/416 B** of 24 August, the Assembly appointed those members.

Oil-for-food programme: Reports of Independent Inquiry Committee

The oil-for-food programme, established by Security Council resolution 986(1995) [YUN 1995, p. 475] authorizing the sale of Iraqi petroleum and petroleum products as a temporary measure to finance humanitarian assistance, thereby alleviating the adverse consequences of the sanctions regime imposed by the Council, was phased out on 21 November 2003 [YUN 2003, p. 362]. In April 2004, following public news reports and commentaries that had called into question the administration and management of the programme, including allegations of fraud and corruption, the Secretary-General established an independent high-level inquiry committee (IIC) on the matter [YUN 2004, p. 364].

During 2005, the IIC, headed by Paul A. Volcker, issued several reports on its findings: a February interim report on the initial procurement of UN contractors, Benon Sevan and oil allocations, internal programme audits and management of the programme's administrative account; a March interim report on the 1998 procurement of the humanitarian goods inspection contract and other conduct of UN officials; an August interim report on the conduct of Benon Sevan and Alexander Yakovlev; the Committee's main report, as well as the report of the Committee's independent working group to examine the impact of the programme on the Iraqi people, both issued in September; and an October report documenting the manipulation of the oil-for-food programme by Saddam Hussein. The first part of the main report issued in September gave an outline of the history of the programme, its framework and the key actors; examined the approval of contracts, the schemes to derive illicit income and the response of the Security Council; maladministration of the programme; the role of UN agencies in the three northern Governates; administrative costs; and control and oversight. Part two of the report examined the sources and amounts of illicit income to Iraq, including illicit payments on contracts, illicit income from smuggling, the impact of distorted prices and a summary of illicit income earned. The report, also contained the conclusions and recommendations of the Committee.

IIC found that the Security Council had struggled in clearly defining the broad purposes, policies and administrative control of the programme, leaving too much initiative and decision-making to the Iraqi regime, while retaining substantial elements of administrative, and therefore operational control. When questions of conflict between political objectives and administrative effectiveness arose, decisions were delayed, bungled, or avoided. The administrative and personnel structures of the programme were not adequate and the Organization and its Secretary-General needed a stronger structure at the top. Most notable among the administrative failures of the programme were an absence of effective controls and audits, and a palpable absence of authority and clear reporting lines, particularly in the Secretariat's senior management. Instances of corruption identified by the Committee reflected control weaknesses in the programme. A lack of effective coordination among UN agencies was also highlighted as there was no simple way to accurately track programme expenditures across agency lines.

Following its analysis, the Committee made a series of major recommendations to the UN system. It proposed the creation of the position of Chief Operating Officer, appointed by the Assembly and reporting to the Secretary-General, with authority over all aspects of administration; establishment of an Independent Oversight Board, which would have functional responsibility for all audits, investigation and evaluation activities, both external and internal across the UN Secretariat and agencies funded by the organization; improvement of coordination and the oversight framework for cross-agency programmes, including by establishing a high-level coordinating body for all major cross-agency relief and emergency programmes, ensuring that each programme had consolidated financial statements that were subject to external and internal audit, and other measures; reform and improvement of management performance, including through mandating periodic, high-level reviews of internal management review processes and through an overhaul of the management hiring, promotion, evaluation, and reward methodology, basing each on key tasks and agreed measures of performance; and the expansion of conflict-of-interest and financial disclosure requirements to lower levels of management. The Committee also proposed that agencies involved in the programme should return up to $50 million in excess compensation secured as a result of work performed under Security Council resolution 1483(2003) [YUN 2003, p. 338].

(See p. 435 for details on the Security Council's consideration of IIC findings.)

On 15 December, the General Assembly, on the recommendation of the General Committee [A/60/250/Add.3], decided to include in the agenda of its sixtieth session an item on the follow-up to the recommendations on administrative management and internal oversight of the Independent Inquiry Committee into the UN oil-for-food programme.

Implementation of 2005 World Summit decisions relating to oversight

In November [A/60/568 & Corr.1, 2], the Secretary-General, as requested in General Assembly resolution 60/1 (see p. 48) on the 2005 World Summit Outcome, presented his proposals for the establishment of an ethics office; a comprehensive review of governance arrangements, including an independent external evaluation of the auditing and oversight system; and the creation of an independent audit advisory committee.

The ethics office, whose objective would be to assist the Secretary-General in ensuring that all staff members observed and performed their functions with the highest standards of integrity, had as its main responsibilities: to administer the Organization's financial disclosure programme; undertake responsibilities assigned it under the UN policy for the protection of staff against retaliation for reporting misconduct; provide confidential advice and guidance to staff on ethical issues; and develop standards, training and education on ethics issues, in coordination with the Office of Human Resources Management. The Office would report regularly to the Secretary-General, giving an overview of its activities and any evaluations and assessments conducted. It would not replace existing mechanisms for reporting misconduct or the resolution of grievances.

The ethics office, which would be the focal point on ethics issues for the global UN Secretariat, would be headquartered in New York, with liaison offices in Geneva, Vienna and Nairobi. The head of the office would be appointed at the level of Assistant Secretary-General for a fixed, non-renewable five-year term.

The Secretary-General also submitted the terms of reference for the comprehensive review of governance arrangements, including an independent external evaluation of the auditing and oversight system within the United Nations and its funds, programmes and specialized agencies. The independent external evaluation to be conducted would consist of a review of best practice governance and oversight structures within the public and private sectors; a comparative analysis of those structures within the UN system; and the development of detailed options for model governance and oversight structures and mechanisms for the UN system. It would review also the Office of Internal Oversight Services (OIOS). The evaluation, be completed in two phases, would identify best international practices and models of governance, oversight and audit within the public and private sectors; study the mission, objectives and mandates of UN system bodies to determine the optimal models of governance and oversight; undertake a review of OIOS to provide a basis for decision-making, with respect to the appropriate level of independence for management; the adequacy of resources compared to its remit, the breadth of its functions, its reporting mechanisms and organization and structure.

Also submitted by the Secretary-General were his proposals for the creation of an independent oversight advisory committee, which he sug-gested be named the Independent Audit Advisory Committee. The Committee, which would assist the General Assembly in fulfilling its governance and oversight responsibilities, would have as it primary functions to review the OIOS budget and audit work plans, assess its work and effectiveness, and advise on the appointment of the Under-Secretary-General for Internal Oversight Services; review the system of internal control and risk management and any material weakness and compliance with corrective action plans; discuss with the United Nations Board of Auditors the audited financial statements, monitor the integrity of those statements and comment on and make input to the workplan of the Board of Auditors; and consider the effectiveness and objectivity of the internal audit process.

On 9 December [A/C.5/60/19], the Assembly President transmitted the Secretary-General's report to the Fifth (Administrative and Budgetary) Committee for consideration. In his letter, to the Fifth Committee Chairman, the President reported that the Assembly had held informal consultation on the report on 6 and 9 December, at the conclusion of which the co-chairs of the meeting stated that there was strong agreement of the need for comprehensive reform of the Organization and of the urgency of that process. Regarding the three proposals contained in the Secretary-General's report, there was agreement to create the ethics office, the proposal for which would be finalized in the budget process. There was recognition that the independent external review would take place. However questions were raised concerning the advisability of creating the independent advisory committee before completion of that review. As more technical work needed to be done on the latter two proposals, the Secretary-General was requested to submit his report to the Advisory Committee on Administrative and Budgetary Questions (ACABQ). The Assembly President should request Fifth Committee to consider the Secretary-General's proposals on an expedited basis and the recommendations brought to the attention of the Assembly by 19 December so that decisions could be made on all three proposals.

The comments of ACABQ on the three proposals were contained in its December report to the Assembly [A/60/7/Add.23].

On 23 December, by section XIII of **resolution 60/248** (see p. 1496), the Assembly approved the resources for the establishment of an ethics office and the conduct of the evaluation study. It decided to establish an Independent Audit Advisory Committee and requested the Secretary-General to propose its terms of reference, ensure coherence with the outcome of the ongoing review of oversight and report to the Assembly at the second part of its resumed sixtieth (2006) session on related resource requirements.

The Ethics Office was established by the Secretary-General's bulletin of 30 December [ST/SGB/2005/22].

Intergovernmental machinery

Revitalization of the work of the General Assembly

In his March report "In larger freedom" [A/59/2005], submitted to the 2005 World Summit, the Secretary-General addressed the strengthening of the Organization through a series of reform measures. He urged the Heads of State and Government to reform, restructure and revitalize the UN's major organs and institutions, including the General Assembly (see p. 69).

Report of Secretary-General. In June, at its resumed fifty-ninth session, the General Assembly had before it a report of the Secretary-General [A/59/860] on the revitalization of the work of the General Assembly. The report, submitted in accordance with Assembly resolution 58/316 [YUN 2004, p. 1374], outlined the draft programme of work of the plenary and the Main Committees of the General Assembly for its sixtieth session.

An addendum to the report [A/59/860/Add.1] contained the status of the documentation for Assembly's the sixtieth session, as at 2 August 2005.

GENERAL ASSEMBLY ACTION

On 12 September [meeting 117], the General Assembly adopted **resolution 59/313** [draft: A/59/L.69/Rev.1] without vote [agenda item 52].

A strengthened and revitalized General Assembly
The General Assembly,

Reaffirming the central position of the General Assembly as the chief deliberative, policymaking and representative organ of the United Nations,

Recalling its previous resolutions relating to the revitalization of its work,

Recognizing that the current interdependent international environment requires the strengthening of the multilateral system in accordance with the purposes and principles of the Charter of the United Nations and the principles of international law,

Recognizing also that the General Assembly is the universal and representative forum comprising all Members of the United Nations,

Recognizing further that, in order to be fully utilized, the General Assembly must fully play its role as set out in the Charter,

Stressing the need to strengthen the role and authority of the General Assembly,

Reaffirming the role and authority of the General Assembly on global matters of concern to the international community, as set out in the Charter,

Reaffirming also the role and authority of the General Assembly in encouraging the progressive development of international law and its codification in accordance with Article 13 of the Charter,

Stressing the need fully to respect and maintain the balance between the principal organs of the United Nations within their respective purviews and mandates, in accordance with the Charter,

Reaffirming that the plenary meetings of the General Assembly should constitute a forum for high-level policy statements, as well as for the consideration, inter alia, of agenda items of special political importance and/or urgency,

Underscoring the importance of providing adequate resources for the implementation of mandated programmes and activities,

Reaffirming its authority in the consideration of all budgetary issues, as stipulated in the Charter,

Role and authority of the General Assembly

1. *Stresses* the need to demonstrate political will to ensure the effective implementation of the resolutions adopted by the General Assembly;

2. *Decides,* in the context of further strengthening the role and authority of the General Assembly as set out in the Charter of the United Nations:

(a) To convene and organize major thematic debates in order to establish broad international understanding on current substantive issues of importance to Member States;

(b) To discuss issues pertaining to the maintenance of international peace and security in accordance with Articles 10, 11, 12, 14 and 35 of the Charter, where appropriate using the procedures set forth in rules 7, 8, 9 and 10 of the rules of procedure of the General Assembly, which enable swift and urgent action by the Assembly, bearing in mind that the Security Council has primary responsibility for the maintenance of international peace and security in accordance with Article 24 of the Charter;

(c) To consider the annual reports as well as special reports of the Security Council, in accordance with Article 15, paragraph 1, and Article 24, paragraph 3, of the Charter, through substantive and interactive debates;

(d) To invite the Security Council to submit periodically, in accordance with Article 24 of the Charter, special subject-oriented reports to the General Assembly for its consideration on issues of current international concern;

(e) To also invite the Security Council to update the General Assembly on a regular basis on the steps it has taken or is contemplating with respect to improving its reporting to the Assembly;

(f) To hold interactive debates on other reports submitted to the General Assembly in accordance with Article 15, paragraph 2, of the Charter;

President of the General Assembly

3. *Decides* to strengthen the role and leadership of the President of the General Assembly by:

(a) Authorizing the President of the General Assembly to propose interactive debates on current issues on the agenda of the Assembly, in consultation with Member States;

(b) Augmenting the resources available to the Office of the President of the General Assembly from within existing resources, subject to consideration by the Assembly of the proposed programme budget for the biennium 2006-2007, to provide for two further additional posts at management and senior levels to be filled on an annual basis following consultations with the incoming President, beginning at the sixtieth session of the Assembly;

(c) Making available to the President of the General Assembly adequate office and conference space with a view to enabling the President to carry out his/her functions in a manner commensurate with the dignity and stature of the Office;

(d) Requesting the Secretary-General to ensure that the President of the General Assembly is provided with proper protocol services at Headquarters and at other United Nations duty stations;

Agenda and working methods of the plenary Assembly and the Main Committees

4. *Decides* to establish an ad hoc working group open to all Member States to identify ways to further enhance the role, authority, effectiveness and efficiency of the General Assembly, inter alia, by building on relevant Assembly resolutions and reviewing the agenda and working methods of the Assembly;

5. *Decides also* that the ad hoc working group shall submit a report with specific recommendations to the General Assembly at its sixtieth session;

6. *Requests* the Secretary-General to provide the ad hoc working group with the necessary services;

7. *Encourages* the Main Committees to implement in full the provisions contained in paragraph 3 of the annex to resolution 58/316 of 1 July 2004, building upon the results of relevant discussions in each Committee;

8. *Encourages* the bureaux of the Main Committees to enhance their cooperation and to learn from each other's best practices;

9. *Requests* the Chairpersons of the Main Committees, at the end of their terms of office, to provide a short report on their observations and "lessons learned" to their immediate successors;

10. *Decides* that time limits on speeches in the plenary Assembly and in the Main Committees shall be applied in accordance with rules 72 and 114 of the rules of procedure of the General Assembly;

11. *Strongly urges* all officers presiding over meetings of the General Assembly to start such meetings on time;

12. *Encourages* the holding of interactive debates with a view to contributing to intergovernmental decision-making;

13. *Invites* Member States that are aligned with statements already made by the chair of a group of Member States, where possible, to focus additional interventions that they make in their national capacity on points that have not already been adequately addressed in the statements of the group in question, bearing in mind the sovereign right of each Member State to express its national position;

14. *Requests* the Secretary-General to issue the rules of procedure of the General Assembly in a consoli-

dated version in all official languages, in print and online;

15. *Recommends* consideration of the use of optical scanners as a means of expediting the counting of votes cast through secret ballots during elections, taking due account of the security requirements in this regard and the credibility, reliability and confidentiality of such means, and requests the Secretary-General to report on the modalities thereof to the General Assembly through the Committee on Conferences;

Documentation

16. *Requests* the Secretary-General to implement further the measures set out in paragraph 20 of resolution 57/300 of 20 December 2002 on the consolidation of reports and in paragraph 6 of the annex to resolution 58/316, on documentation;

17. *Encourages* Member States, when seeking additional information, to request that they be provided with the information either orally or, if in writing, in the form of information sheets, annexes, tables and the like, and encourages the wider use of this practice;

18. *Requests* the Secretary-General to ensure that documentation and reports are issued well in advance, in keeping with the six-week rule for the issuance of documentation simultaneously in all official languages, as set out in resolution 49/221 B of 23 December 1994 and in resolution 59/309 of 22 June 2005 on multilingualism;

19. *Also requests* the Secretary-General to submit a status report to the General Assembly at its sixtieth session on the implementation of all resolutions regarding the revitalization of its work, including resolutions 58/126 of 19 December 2003 and 58/316 and the present resolution.

In November, the General Assembly considered a report of the Fourth (Special Political and Decolonization) Committee [A/60/525] on the revitalization of the work of the General Assembly. The Committee Chairman drew the attention of the Committee to two related documents, regarding the approximate dates for the consideration of items by the Fourth Committee at the Assembly's sixty-first (2006) session [A/C.4/60/WP.1], and the revitalization of the Special Political and Decolonization Committee [A/C.4/60/WP.2].

By **decision 60/526** of 8 December, the Assembly took note of the report of the Fourth Committee.

Rotation of the post of Rapporteur of the Third Committee

By **decision 60/538** of 16 December, the General Assembly decided that, in order to rationalize its method of work, the Third Committee should elect its Rapporteur on the basis of their experience and personal competence, as well as the rotation among the regional groups. The Committee should elect a candidate nominated by the Group of Western European and Other States to serve as its Rapporteur at the Assembly's sixty-first (2006) session.

Review of Security Council membership and related matters

The Open-ended Working Group on the Question of Equitable Representation on and Increase in the Membership of the Security Council and Other Matters related to the Security Council submitted a report on its work during nine formal and four informal meetings held between 7 February and 1 September [A/59/47]. The Working Group considered the oral and written proposals and position papers of various delegations, which had been submitted in previous sessions and were set out in two clusters: cluster I, concerning increase in Security Council membership and related matters, and cluster II, dealing with the working methods of the Council and the transparency of its work. The discussions of the two clusters were summarized in conference room papers contained in annexes to the report.

At its first session (7 February), the Working Group endorsed the appointment of two Vice-Chairpersons. At its second (14 February) session, as well as at the four subsequent informal meetings (14-16 February), the Working Group considered six topics that were later discussed at length: accountability, in particular the relationship between the Security Council and the General Assembly, including reports of the Council to the Assembly; the relationship between the Council and other principal UN organs; consultations with troop-contributing countries; questions concerning the work of sanctions committees, including Article 50 of the Charter; subsidiary organs of the Council; and the question of the use of the veto. At its ninth meeting (1 September), the Working Group considered and adopted its report to the Assembly, including a recommendation that the Assembly adopt a draft decision on the matter.

By **decision 59/566** of 12 September, the Assembly took note of the Working Group's report and urged it to continue to exert efforts during the Assembly's sixtieth session, aimed at achieving progress on all the issues relevant to the question of equitable representation on and increase in the membership of the Security Council and other matters related to the Council. It decided that the question should be considered during the Assembly's sixtieth session, and that the Working Group should continue its work, taking into account progress achieved during the Assembly's forty-eighth (1993) and fifty-ninth (2004) sessions and drawing on the experience of the fifty-ninth session, as well as the views to be expressed in the sixtieth session, and report to the Assembly at its sixtieth (2005) session, including any agreed recommendations.

Revitalization of the United Nations in the economic, social and related fields

Work of the functional commissions

Report of Secretary-General. The Secretary-General, responding to Economic and Social Council resolution 2004/63 [YUN 2004, p. 1379] and earlier resolutions of the General Assembly and the Council, submitted a June report [E/2005/74] on the work of the functional commissions of the Council in 2005. The report focused on the substantive aspects of the commissions' activities and their role in the development and implementation of the internationally agreed development goals, including those contained in the Millennium Declaration [YUN 2000, p. 49]. During the period from 2001 to 2005, the Council's nine functional commissions made contributions towards the achievement of the internationally agreed development goals.

The Secretary-General recommended that the Council invite the commissions to continue to provide concise, action-oriented input to its substantive session in 2006, including to the Council's assessment of progress in achieving the agreed development goals. The Council should continue to consider the outcomes of the functional commissions on the basis of a thematic consolidated report. It should explore further avenues for promoting greater harmony and thematic unity, including through the conclusion of a multi-year programme and/or an indicative list of common themes. He recommended that the Council encourage a further deepening of collaboration among its commissions in advancing education and literacy. It invited the commissions to clearly identify the operational implications of their work in relation to HIV/AIDS and to bring them to the attention of the governing bodies of the UN funds and programmes for consideration and guidance; and consider ways of promoting closer and more effective overall interaction between the work of the commissions.

In other recommendations, the Council was encouraged to devote one of its coordination sessions to the issue of employment and the realization of the development goals, examine the ways in which the functional commissions were integrating that aspect into their work; stimulate substantive exchanges among its functional commissions on the social integration component of social development; and urge the commissions to mainstream the concept of sustainable development in their work. The Secretary-General further recommended that the Council recognize the development-related contributions of the United Nations Information and Communication Technology Task Force and the need to further build on such approaches; encourage Governments and the UN system, notably its commissions, to ensure that science and technology was incorporated into poverty reduction policies and strategies, and urge them to consider ways to strengthen linkages between public research and private industry; request the functional commissions to encourage the launching of multi-stakeholder initiatives on promoting technology transfer and development in the areas of interest to developing countries; and encourage its subsidiary bodies to incorporate a gender perspective in their follow-up to major UN conferences and summits, in their examination of their working methods and the development of themes for their multi-year programmes of work.

The Economic and Social Council, by **decision 2005/305** of 27 July, took note of the Secretary-General's report and requested him to submit a consolidated report on the work of the functional commissions in 2006.

Chapter II

United Nations financing and programming

While the overall financial position of the United Nations continued to improve in 2005, with an increasing number of Member States meeting their financial obligations to the regular budget in full, the situation remained fragile. Cash availability under the regular budget stood at $192 million from the beginning of the year through September, making cross-borrowing unnecessary. In October, aggregate assessments decreased to $5.4 billion, compared to $5.9 billion in 2004, due to significantly lower peacekeeping assessments. By the end of the year, unpaid assessments had fallen from $357 million in 2004 to $333 million, cash resources for peacekeeping activities amounted to over $1.6 billion and debt owed to Member States stood at $695 million. The number of Member States paying their regular budget assessments in full and on time increased to 140, up from 124 in 2004.

In December, the General Assembly adopted final budget appropriations for the 2004-2005 biennium, decreasing the amount of $3,737,508,800 approved in 2004 to $3,655,800,600 and increasing income estimates by $20,456,600 to $470,659,100. It also adopted revised budget appropriations for the 2006-2007 biennium of $3,798,912,500, an increase of $177,012,500 over the preliminary estimate in 2004 of $3,621,900,000.

The Committee on Contributions considered the methodology for preparing the scale of assessments for the period 2007-2009 and measures to encourage the payment of arrears, including multi-year payment plans.

Financial situation

Although the overall financial position of the United Nations showed signs of progress in 2005, particularly with regard to the increasing number of Member States meeting their financial obligations to the regular budget in full, the situation remained fragile. In October [A/60/427], the Secretary-General reported that aggregate assessments decreased to $5.4 billion as at 7 October (compared to $5.9 billion in 2004), due to significantly lower peacekeeping assessments. That

amount included assessments of $18 million for the capital master plan (see p. 1553). Cash availability under the regular budget and related reserve accounts at the beginning of the year stood at $192 million, making cross-borrowing unnecessary. It was projected that aggregate cash available would be over $100 million higher than at the end of 2004.

As at 7 October, unpaid assessments for the regular budget, peacekeeping and the two international tribunals totaled $2.9 billlion, which included: $2.1 million for peacekeeping (compared to $2.4 billion in 2004), $739 million for the regular budget ($14 million more than in 2004) and $73 million for the tribunals ($38 million less than in 2004). It was forecast that the Organization would owe Member States a total of $779 million as at 31 December 2005, due to a shortage of cash in some peacekeeping missions and delays in the phasing in of troops in the Sudan, the signing of memorandums of understanding with troop providers and the deployment of additional troops and police to missions in the Democratic Republic of the Congo, Côte d'Ivoire and Haiti. Member States that had paid their assessments in full as at 7 October numbered 126 (17 more than at 30 September 2004).

In his end-of-year review of the financial situation [A/60/427/Add.1], the Secretary-General noted that the performance of the four indicators of the Organization's financial health was reasonably good: unpaid assessments had fallen from $357 million in 2004 to $333 million; cash resources for peacekeeping activities amounted to over $1.6 billion; amounts outstanding for the tribunals fell from $30 million to $25 million; and the actual debt owed to Member States stood at $695 million. The number of Member States paying their regular budget assessments in full and on time had increased to 140, up from 124 in 2004.

On 12 September, the General Assembly deferred consideration of the agenda item on improving the financial situation of the United Nations and included it in the draft agenda of its sixtieth (2005) session (**decision 59/569**).

UN budget

Budget for 2004-2005

Final appropriation

In 2005, the General Assembly adopted final budget appropriations for the 2004-2005 biennium, decreasing the amount of $3,737,508,800 approved in resolutions 59/277 A [YUN 2004, p. 1381], 59/282 (see p. 1486), 59/294 (see p. 1488) and 60/244 (see p. 448) by $81,708,200 to $3,655,800,600, and increasing income estimates by $20,456,600 to $470,659,100.

Report of Secretary-General. In his second performance report on the 2004-2005 programme budget [A/60/572], the Secretary-General provided an estimate of the anticipated final levels of expenditure and income for the biennium, based on actual expenditures for the first 22 months of the biennium, projections for the last two months, changes in inflation and exchange rates and cost-of-living adjustments.

The anticipated final level of expenditures and of income represented a net decrease of $120.5 million, reflecting projected additional requirements of $69 million due to changes in exchange rates ($19.2 million), changes in inflation ($19.2 million), commitments entered into under the provisions of Assembly resolutions 58/273 [YUN 2004, p. 1422] and 59/276 [ibid., p. 1383] ($30.6 million); and reduced requirements of $171.5 million due to variations in posts costs and adjustments to other objects of expenditure and a decrease in income ($20.5 million).

The projected expenditure for the biennium was estimated at $3,655.5 million gross, a decrease of $82 million, compared with the revised appropriation of $3,737.5 approved in 2004 and April and June 2005. The projected income was

estimated at $470.7 million, an increase of $20.5 million, compared with the revised income of $450.2 million.

The Advisory Committee on Administrative and Budgetary Questions (ACABQ), in December [A/60/597], recalled that previously the analysis was based on 20 months' experience. It welcomed the progress achieved by the Secretariat in financial reporting and recommended that the Assembly take note of the Secretary-General's report.

GENERAL ASSEMBLY ACTION

On 23 December, the General Assembly [meeting 69], on the recommendation of the Fifth (Administrative and Budgetary) Committee [A/60/593/Add.2], adopted **resolution 60/245 A-B** without vote [agenda item 123].

Programme budget for the biennium 2004-2005

A

FINAL BUDGET APPROPRIATIONS FOR THE BIENNIUM 2004-2005

The General Assembly

1. *Takes note* of the second performance report of the Secretary-General on the programme budget for the biennium 2004-2005 and the related report of the Advisory Committee on Administrative and Budgetary Questions concerning the financial performance for the biennium 2004-2005;

2. *Notes* that paragraph 3 of the report of the Advisory Committee indicates that an additional cost of 257,200 United States dollars is required for the implementation of General Assembly decision 60/539 of 16 December 2005, partially offsetting the decrease of 81,965,400 dollars reflected under expenditure sections in the second performance report of the Secretary-General on the programme budget for the biennium 2004-2005;

3. *Resolves* that, for the biennium 2004-2005:

(a) The amount of 3,737,508,800 dollars appropriated by it in its resolutions 59/277 A of 23 December 2004, 59/282 of 13 April 2005, 59/294 of 22 June 2005 and 60/244 of 23 December 2005 shall be decreased by 81,708,200 dollars, as follows:

Budget section		Amount approved by the General Assembly in its resolutions 59/277 A, 59/282, 59/294 and 60/244	Increase/ (decrease)	Final appropriation
		(United States dollars)		
Part I. *Overall policy-making, direction and coordination*				
1. Overall policy-making, direction and coordination		61 543 200	1 915 500	63 458 700
2. General Assembly affairs and conference services		560 256 500	(4 407 100)	555 849 400
	Total, part I	621 799 700	(2 491 600)	619 308 100
Part II. *Political affairs*				
3. Political affairs		550 611 500	(59 847 300)	490 764 200
4. Disarmament		18 739 900	(1 038 300)	17 701 600
5. Peacekeeping operations		92 859 800	(4 003 300)	88 856 500
6. Peaceful uses of outer space		5 903 900	(62 200)	5 841 700
	Total, part II	668 115 100	64 951 100	603 164 00

Budget section	Amount approved by the General Assembly in its resolutions 59/277 A, 59/282, 59/294 and 60/244	Increase/ (decrease)	Final appropriation
		(United States dollars)	
Part III. *International justice and law*			
7. International Court of Justice	34 936 000	(1 105 100)	33 830 900
8. Legal affairs	40 634 000	(124 700)	40 509 300
Total, part III	**75 570 000**	**(1 229 800)**	**74 340 200**
Part IV. *International cooperation for development*			
9. Economic and social affairs	143 027 700	(2 124 800)	140 902 900
10. Least developed countries, landlocked developing countries and small island developing States	4 358 600	(260 600)	4 098 000
11. United Nations support for the New Partnership for Africa's Development	9 575 000	(1 306 800)	8 268 200
12. Trade and development	114 802 300	(3 207 100)	111 595 200
13. International Trade Centre UNCTAD/WTO	26 136 300	(540 300)	25 596 000
14. Environment	10 915 800	118 800	11 034 600
15. Human settlements	16 012 800	(61 900)	15 950 900
16. Crime prevention and criminal justice	10 040 200	658 300	10 698 500
17. International drug control	21 476 100	(674 300)	20 801 800
Total, part IV	**356 344 800**	**(7 398 700)**	**348 946 100**
Part V. *Regional cooperation for development*			
18. Economic and social development in Africa	96 242 000	(2 162 800)	94 079 200
19. Economic and social development in Asia and the Pacific	65 067 100	3 291 700	68 358 800
20. Economic development in Europe	54 761 800	999 800	55 761 600
21. Economic and social development in Latin America and the Caribbean	85 371 400	(1 151 100)	84 220 300
22. Economic and social development in Western Asia	50 995 600	(862 400)	50 133 200
23. Regular programme of technical cooperation	42 871 500	–	42 871 500
Total, part V	**395 309 400**	**115 200**	**395 424 600**
Part VI. *Human rights and humanitarian affairs*			
24. Human rights	64 571 300	(2 701 700)	61 869 600
25. Protection of and assistance to refugees	66 243 900	775 500	67 019 400
26. Palestine refugees	34 641 000	1 297 700	35 938 700
27. Humanitarian assistance	24 275 300	(359 800)	23 915 500
Total, part VI	**189 731 500**	**(988 300)**	**188 743 200**
Part VII. *Public information*			
28. Public information	162 322 600	(883 800)	161 438 800
Total, part VII	**162 322 600**	**(883 800)**	**161 438 800**
Part VIII. *Common support services*			
29A Office of the Under-Secretary-General for Management	11 518 000	204 500	11 722 500
29B Office of Programme Planning, Budget and Accounts	29 460 100	(529 400)	28 930 700
29C Office of Human Resources Management	58 562 300	(1 076 700)	57 485 600
29D Office of Central Support Services	229 894 300	(1 814 800)	228 079 500
29E Administration, Geneva	102 173 300	(85 800)	102 259 100
29F Administration, Vienna	32 025 300	(76 400)	32 101 700
29G Administration, Nairobi	13 512 500	2 021 700	15 534 200
Total, part VIII	**477 145 800**	**(1 032 500)**	**476 113 300**
Part IX. *Internal oversight*			
30. Internal oversight	24 187 000	(426 900)	23 760 100
Total, part IX	**24 187 000**	**(426 900)**	**23 760 100**
Part X. *Jointly financed administrative activities and special expenses*			
31. Jointly financed administrative activities	10 445 200	124 800	10 570 000
32. Special expenses	81 255 900	936 100	82 192 000
Total, part X	**91 701 100**	**1 060 900**	**92 762 000**
Part XI. *Capital expenditures*			
33. Construction, alteration, improvement and major maintenance	104 566 600	225 700	104 792 300
Total, part XI	**104 566 600**	**225 700**	**104 792 300**

Budget section	Amount approved by the General Assembly in its resolutions 59/277 A, 59/282, 59/294 and 60/244	Increase/ (decrease)	Final appropriation
	(United States dollars)		
Part XII. *Staff assessment*			
34. Staff assessment	417 544 800	11 806 200	429 351 000
Total, part XII	**417 544 800**	**11 806 200**	**429 351 000**
Part XIII. *Development Account*			
35. Development Account	13 065 000	–	13 065 000
Total, part XIII	**13 065 000**	**–**	**13 065 000**
Part XIV. *Safety and security*			
36. Safety and security	140 105 400	(15 513 500)	124 591 900
Total, part XIV	**140 105 400**	**(15 513 500)**	**124 591 900**
Grand total	**3 737 508 800**	**(81 708 200)**	**3 655 800 600**

(b) The Secretary-General shall be authorized to transfer credits between sections of the budget, with the concurrence of the Advisory Committee;

(c) In addition to the appropriations approved under subparagraph *(a)* above, an amount of 125,000 dollars is appropriated for each year of the biennium 2004-2005 from the accumulated income of the Library Endowment Fund for the purchase of books, periodicals, maps and library equipment and for such other expenses of the Library at the Palais des Nations as are in accordance with the objects and provisions of the endowment.

B
FINAL INCOME ESTIMATES FOR THE BIENNIUM 2004-2005

The General Assembly

Resolves that, for the biennium 2004-2005:

(a) The estimates of income of 450,202,500 United States dollars approved by it in its resolutions 59/277 B of 23 December 2004, 59/282 of 13 April 2005, 59/294 of 22 June 2005 and 60/244 of 23 December 2005 shall be increased by 20,456,600 dollars, as follows:

Income section	Amount approved by the General Assembly in its resolutions 59/277 B, 59/282, 59/294 and 60/244	Increase/ (decrease)	Final estimate
	(United States dollars)		
1. Income from staff assessment	421 964 300	11 024 100	432 988 400
Total, income section 1	**421 964 300**	**11 024 100**	**432 988 400**
2. General income	24 009 500	7 671 200	31 680 700
3. Services to the public	4 228 700	1 761 300	5 990 000
Total, income sections 2 and 3	**28 238 200**	**9 432 500**	**37 670 700**
Grand total	**450 202 500**	**20 456 600**	**470 659 100**

(b) The income from staff assessment shall be credited to the Tax Equalization Fund in accordance with the provisions of General Assembly resolution 973(X) of 15 December 1955;

(c) Direct expenses of the United Nations Postal Administration, services to visitors, catering and related services, garage operations, television services and the sale of publications, not provided for under the budget appropriations, shall be charged against the income derived from those activities.

Questions relating to the 2004-2005 programme budget

The Fifth Committee considered special subjects related to the 2004-2005 programme budget concerning estimates in respect of special political missions, good offices and other political initiatives authorized by the General Assembly and/ or the Security Council (see below), as well as revised estimates resulting from resolutions and decisions adopted by the Economic and Social Council in 2005. Other subjects considered included the UN information and communication technology strategy (see p. 1550); conditions of service and compensation for non-Secretariat officials (see p. 1508); and the UN security management system (see p. 1557).

Revised estimates in respect of matters of which the Security Council was seized

In March [A/59/534/Add.3 & Corr.1], the Secretary-General submitted additional resource requirements for the United Nations Assistance Mission for Iraq (UNAMI) and the United Nations Observer Mission in Bougainville (UNOMB) for the periods from 1 May to 31 December and 16 February to 15 August 2005, respectively. Those net requirements were estimated at $83,174,400 net, taking into account the unencumbered balance of $5,267,500 of the existing appropriation.

ACABQ recommended [A/59/569/Add.3] that the General Assembly appropriate that amount, noting that the charging of expenditures against the appropriation for UNAMI beyond 11 August 2005, would be subject to the extension of its current mandate.

In an April addendum [A/59/534/Add.4], the Secretary-General submitted estimated net requirements of $4,171,700 net for the expansion of the United Nations Political Office for Somalia (UNPOS) in 2005 and $13 million, as a subvention, for funding the Special Court for Sierra Leone for the period from 1 July to 31 December 2005, bringing the total appropriation for the period from 1 January to 31 December 2005 to $33 million. The combined requirements for UNPOS and the Court amounted to $37,171,700 net. A further subvention of $7 million for the Special Court would be submitted as a first charge against special political missions of the proposed 2006-2007 programme budget.

ACABQ, in an April report [A/59/569/Add.4], recommended approval of the resources requested for the expanded role of UNPOS but indicated that savings might be achieved, which should be included in the performance report. The Committee also recommended that the Secretary-General should intensify efforts to raise voluntary contributions to support the work of the Special Court for Sierra Leone and, should the Assembly agree to another subvention to meet the expenses of the Court, commitment authority should not exceed $13 million for the period from 1 July to 31 December 2005, bringing the total subvention to $33 million for that period.

GENERAL ASSEMBLY ACTION

On 13 April [meeting 91], the General Assembly, on the recommendation of the Fifth Committee [A/59/448/Add.3], adopted **resolution 59/282** without vote [agenda item 108].

Special subjects relating to the programme budget for the biennium 2004-2005
The General Assembly,

I

Estimates in respect of special political missions, good offices and other political initiatives authorized by the General Assembly and/or the Security Council
Having considered the report of the Secretary-General on the estimates in respect of special political missions, good offices and other political initiatives authorized by the General Assembly and/or the Security Council and the related report of the Advisory Committee on Administrative and Budgetary Questions,

1. *Takes note* of the report of the Secretary-General on estimates in respect of special political missions, good offices and other political initiatives authorized by the General Assembly and/or the Security Council and the related report of the Advisory Committee on Administrative and Budgetary Questions;

2. *Endorses* the observations and recommendations of the Advisory Committee on Administrative and Budgetary Questions contained in its report;

3. *Requests* the Secretary-General to consider ways and means of presenting the budgets of large missions in a manner that is more suitable for their size and complexity;

4. *Reiterates* that the charging of expenditures against the appropriation for special political missions is subject to the extension of the respective mandates;

5. *Notes* that an additional amount of 82,472,600 United States dollars is requested for the United Nations Assistance Mission for Iraq for the period from 1 May to 31 December 2005 and an additional amount of 701,800 dollars is requested for the United Nations Observer Mission in Bougainville for the period from 16 February to 15 August 2005, including the liquidation period;

6. *Approves* the budgets of the United Nations Assistance Mission for Iraq and the United Nations Observer Mission in Bougainville as set out in table 1 of the report of the Secretary-General;

7. *Decides* to appropriate, in accordance with the procedure set out in paragraph 11 of annex I to its resolution 41/213 of 19 December 1986, under section 3, Political affairs, of the programme budget for the biennium 2004-2005, the amount of 83,174,400 dollars for the United Nations Assistance Mission for Iraq and the United Nations Observer Mission in Bougainville;

8. *Also decides* to appropriate the amount of 4,131,200 dollars under section 34, Staff assessment, to be offset by a corresponding amount under income section 1, Income from staff assessment, of the programme budget for the biennium 2004-2005;

II

Information and communication technology strategy
Recalling its resolutions 57/295 of 20 December 2002, 58/270 of 23 December 2003, 59/126 B of 10 December 2004 and 59/265 of 23 December 2004,

Having considered the report of the Secretary-General on the information and communication technology strategy and the related report of the Advisory Committee on Administrative and Budgetary Questions,

Acknowledging that investment in information and communication technology is not an end in itself and should be aimed at improving the quality and timely delivery of mandates in a cost-effective manner,

1. *Takes note* of the report of the Secretary-General on progress in implementing the information and communication technology strategy and the related report of the Advisory Committee on Administrative and Budgetary Questions;

2. *Requests* the Secretary-General to develop and implement cost-neutral measures to provide Member States with secure access to the information currently accessible only on the Intranet ("iSeek") of the Secretariat in the working languages of the United Nations;

3. *Takes note* of the ongoing efforts in the field of disaster recovery and security threats in the new Department of Safety and Security of the Secretariat as well as in the Information Technology Services Division of the Office of Central Support Services of the Department of Management, and encourages all

decision-takers involved to elaborate a comprehensive approach in this matter;

4. *Requests* a more detailed analysis of the return on investment and the impact of such investment on the quality and timeliness of service delivery and of the resource requirements resulting from information and communication technology projects, as described in the annex to the report of the Secretary-General, in the context of the proposed programme budget for the biennium 2006-2007 and future budgets;

5. *Takes note* of the ongoing efforts for the elaboration of a comprehensive information and communication technology strategy, and reiterates the need for further integration and compatibility of administrative platforms of the inter-agency network and, in this regard, invites the United Nations System Chief Executives Board for Coordination to pay due attention to the issue;

6. *Recognizes* that technological infrastructures and supportive applications in the United Nations are based on Latin script, which leads to difficulties in processing non-Latin and bidirectional scripts, and requests the Secretary-General to continue his efforts to ensure that technological infrastructures and supportive applications in the United Nations fully support Latin, non-Latin and bidirectional scripts so as to enhance the equality of the official languages of the United Nations;

7. *Takes note* that some projects listed in the annex to the report of the Secretary-General are on hold, and requests the Secretary-General to ensure their implementation, as feasible;

8. *Recalls* section II, paragraphs 9 and 10, of its resolution 59/266 of 23 December 2004, takes note of paragraph 5 of the report of Advisory Committee on Administrative and Budgetary Questions, and requests the Secretary-General to report on measures to improve the Galaxy tool;

9. *Notes with appreciation* that public wireless Internet (Wi-Fi) hot spots have been made available in the Secretariat Building, and notes the intention of the Secretary-General to extend wireless coverage to the entire United Nations compound;

III

Conditions of service and compensation for officials other than Secretariat officials: members of the International Court of Justice and judges and ad litem judges of the International Tribunal for the Former Yugoslavia and the International Criminal Tribunal for Rwanda

Recalling section VIII of its resolution 53/214 of 18 December 1998, its resolution 56/285 of 27 June 2002 and its resolution 57/289 of 20 December 2002,

Recalling also Article 32 of the Statute of the International Court of Justice, as well as relevant General Assembly resolutions that govern the conditions of service and compensation for the members of the International Court of Justice and the judges of the International Tribunal for the Prosecution of Persons Responsible for Serious Violations of International Humanitarian Law Committed in the Territory of the Former Yugoslavia since 1991 and the International Criminal Tribunal for the Prosecution of Persons Responsible for Genocide and Other Serious Violations of International Law Committed in the Territory of

Rwanda and Rwandan Citizens Responsible for Genocide and Other Such Violations Committed in the Territory of Neighbouring States between 1 January and 31 December 1994,

Having considered the report of the Secretary-General and the related report of the Advisory Committee on Administrative and Budgetary Questions,

1. *Endorses* the recommendations of the Advisory Committee on Administrative and Budgetary Questions contained in its report, subject to the provisions of the present resolution;

2. *Reaffirms* the principle that conditions of service and compensation for non-Secretariat United Nations officials shall be separate and distinct from those of officials of the Secretariat;

3. *Requests* the Secretary-General, in future reports on the conditions of service of the members of the Court and the judges of the Tribunals, to present clearly information on annual salaries payable in both United States dollars and the applicable local currency, with full information on the actual dollar requirements for the budget concerned;

4. *Decides*, with retroactive effect from 1 January 2005, to increase the annual salary of the members of the Court and the judges and ad litem judges of the Tribunals by 6.3 per cent, as an interim measure and pending a decision based on the report requested in paragraph 8 below;

5. *Also decides* that, with retroactive effect from 1 January 2005, the annual value of all pensions in payment shall be increased by 6.3 per cent as an interim measure and pending a decision based on the report requested in paragraph 8 below;

6. *Further decides* that, in addition to the provisions of paragraph 2 of its resolution 40/257 C of 18 December 1985, with retroactive effect from 1 January 2005, those members of the Court who have taken up and maintained a bona fide primary residence at The Hague for less than five continuous years during their service with the Court shall be eligible, upon the completion of their appointment and resettlement outside the Netherlands, to receive a lump sum prorated on the basis of the ceiling of eighteen weeks of annual net base salary that is payable to members of the Court who have served for five continuous years, and also decides that those members of the Court who have similarly taken up and maintained a bona fide primary residence at The Hague for more than five but less than nine continuous years shall be eligible upon the completion of their appointment and resettlement outside the Netherlands for a lump sum prorated on the basis of the ceiling of twenty-four weeks of annual net base salary that is payable to members of the Court who have served for nine continuous years or more;

7. *Requests* the Secretary-General to report to the General Assembly on the additional expenditures resulting from the above decisions in the context of the second performance report on the programme budget for the biennium 2004-2005 and the second performance reports on the budgets of the International Tribunal for the Former Yugoslavia and the International Criminal Tribunal for Rwanda for the biennium 2004-2005;

8. *Also requests* the Secretary-General to submit a comprehensive report to the General Assembly at its sixty-first session, including proposals for a mechanism of remuneration based on market exchange rates

and local retail price fluctuations that limits the divergence of such remuneration from that of comparable positions of seniority within the United Nations system, on the protection of pensions in payment to former judges and their survivors as well as on the differences between the pension benefits of the judges of the International Tribunal for the Former Yugoslavia and the International Criminal Tribunal for Rwanda on the one hand and the members of the International Court of Justice on the other;

9. *Decides* that the conditions of service and compensation for the members of the International Court of Justice and the judges and ad litem judges of the International Tribunal for the Former Yugoslavia and the International Criminal Tribunal for Rwanda shall next be reviewed at its sixty-first session.

On 22 June [meeting 104], the Assembly, on the recommendation of the Fifth Committee [A/59/448/Add.4], adopted **resolution 59/294** without vote [agenda item 108].

Special subjects and questions relating to the programme budget for the biennium 2004-2005
The General Assembly,

I

Strengthened and unified security management system for the United Nations: standardized access control

Recalling paragraph 44 of section XI of its resolution 59/276 of 23 December 2004,

Having considered the report of the Secretary-General entitled "Strengthened and unified security management system for the United Nations: standardized access control" and the related report of the Advisory Committee on Administrative and Budgetary Questions,

Takes note of the report of the Secretary-General and endorses the observations and recommendation contained in the report of the Advisory Committee on Administrative and Budgetary Questions;

II

Estimates in respect of special political missions, good offices and other political initiatives authorized by the General Assembly and/or the Security Council

Recalling its resolution 58/284 of 8 April 2004 and section VII of its resolution 59/276 of 23 December 2004,

Having considered the report of the Secretary-General and the related report of the Advisory Committee on Administrative and Budgetary Questions concerning the requests of the Secretary-General for additional funding relating to the expansion of the United Nations Political Office for Somalia and for the subvention to the Special Court for Sierra Leone,

1. *Takes note* of the report of the Secretary-General and the related report of the Advisory Committee on Administrative and Budgetary Questions concerning the requests of the Secretary-General for additional funding relating to the expansion of the United Nations Political Office for Somalia and for the subvention to the Special Court for Sierra Leone;

2. *Endorses* the observations and recommendations of the Advisory Committee on Administrative and

Budgetary Questions contained in its report, subject to the provisions of the present resolution;

3. *Decides* to appropriate under the procedure provided for in paragraph 11 of annex I to resolution 41/213 of 19 December 1986 an amount of 24,171,700 United States dollars under section 3, Political affairs, of the programme budget for the biennium 2004-2005 for the United Nations Political Office for Somalia and for the subvention to the Special Court for Sierra Leone;

4. *Also decides* to appropriate an amount of 377,200 dollars under section 34, Staff assessment, to be offset by a corresponding amount under income section 1, Income from staff assessment, of the programme budget for the biennium 2004-2005;

5. *Notes* that the requirements arising under the regular budget in connection with the expansion of the United Nations Political Office for Somalia are estimated at 4,548,900 dollars gross (4,171,700 dollars net), after taking into account the unencumbered balance amounting to 845,700 dollars against the existing appropriation;

6. *Approves* the budget for the United Nations Political Office for Somalia in the amount of 5,394,600 dollars gross (5,017,400 dollars net) for the period from 1 June to 31 December 2005;

7. *Notes* the financial position of the Special Court for Sierra Leone as described in the report of the Secretary-General;

8. *Also notes* the request of the Secretary-General for an additional subvention of 13 million dollars to supplement the financial resources of the Special Court for Sierra Leone for the period from 1 July to 31 December 2005;

9. *Authorizes* the Secretary-General, as an exceptional measure, to enter into commitments in an amount not to exceed 13 million dollars to supplement the financial resources of the Special Court for Sierra Leone, for the period from 1 July to 31 December 2005, under special political missions in section 3, Political affairs, of the programme budget for the biennium 2004-2005, on the understanding that any regular budget funds appropriated for the Court would be refunded to the United Nations at the time of liquidation of the Court should sufficient voluntary contributions be received;

10. *Requests* the Secretary-General to provide relevant information regarding the utilization of funds appropriated from the regular budget for the Special Court for Sierra Leone in the context of the second performance report on the programme budget for the biennium 2004-2005;

11. *Also requests* the Secretary-General to keep the Member States informed, as appropriate, about the completion strategy of the Special Court for Sierra Leone;

12. *Appeals* to Member States, as a matter of urgency, to contribute voluntary funds in support of the Special Court for Sierra Leone;

13. *Requests* the Secretary-General, in concert with the Management Committee of the Special Court for Sierra Leone, to redouble efforts to raise voluntary contributions to support the work of the Court, and to report to the General Assembly at its sixtieth session on progress made;

14. *Also requests* the Secretary-General, in concert with the Registrar of the Special Court for Sierra Leone, to take fully into account the intentions of donors concerning their voluntary contributions without prejudice to the provisions of the present resolution.

Budget for 2006-2007

In introducing the proposed programme budget for the 2006-2007 biennium [A/60/6] before the Fifth Committee on 25 October, the Secretary-General said that the proposed budget, which amounted to approximately $3.6 billion before recosting, envisaged only a slight increase over the 2004-2005 biennium (less than 0.1 per cent). Growth in priority areas was to be funded largely through the reallocation of resources. The budget proposal, which was the first to be submitted in conjunction with a biennial programme plan under the arrangements for aligning the plan and the budget periods pursuant to resolution 59/275 [YUN 2004, p. 1401], included both a significant adjustment in staffing resources, as well as continued investment in information and communication technology and staff training.

With regard to the Organization's work and the changing environment in which it operated, the Secretary-General stated that the implementation of the 2005 World Summit Outcome (see p. 48) would provide an opportunity for programmatic and management changes and that Member States had already been informed about the work plan for that purpose, he announced that a senior adviser on management issues would soon be appointed. Other items to be addressed included the launch of the Peacebuilding Commission by December; budgetary requirements for a new Human Rights Council; financial implications of doubling the budget resources of the Office of the High Commissioner for Human Rights over the forthcoming five years; and proposals for strengthening oversight, including the creation of an independent oversight advisory committee and the new ethics office. During the first quarter of 2006, he would submit recommendations to ensure that all Secretariat policies, rules and regulations responded to the Organization's needs and increased its effectiveness. He also planned to facilitate the review of all mandates older than five years to eliminate outdated activities and reprioritize the Organization's plan of work; and to submit a proposal for a one-time staff buyout to establish a staffing profile, which would reflect the General Assembly's new priorities and allow the Secretariat to meet the needs of the twenty-first century. In that regard, over 3,000 obsolete, ineffective or marginally useful outputs had been discontinued. While sustained efforts over the past decade had led to structural, technical and managerial reforms, the process of management reform had to continue.

The Committee for Programme and Coordination (CPC) considered the proposed programme budget at its 2005 session (11 May and 6 June–1 July) [A/60/16 & Corr.1] and recommended that the Assembly approve the programme narratives of the majority of the budget sections subject to certain modifications. Noting that in some sections, the narratives in the budget fascicles, particularly the overview parts, differed from the overall orientation parts in the plan, CPC recommended that the Assembly ensure that the narratives were identical to the respective programmes of the plan and that the Secretary-General ensure the conformity, during implementation, of the overview parts of the budget with the 2006-2007 biennial programme plan. The Secretariat should also provide a list of outputs that would require revision or inclusion in the 2006-2007 programme budget due to legislative decisions taken at the Assembly's fifty-ninth (2004) session. The Committee welcomed the application of the results-based logical framework in several budget sections and requested the Secretary-General to submit proposals to the Assembly, in the context of the 2008-2009 proposed programme budget, for expanding that framework to enhance managerial responsibility for programme implementation. CPC further recommended that all legislative mandates be taken into account when preparing the strategic framework for the 2008-2009 biennium, to be submitted to the Assembly at its sixty-first (2006) session and that the Secretariat ensure the implementation of paragraph 12 of Assembly resolution 58/269 [YUN 2003, p. 1395] with regard to any new or revised mandates.

On 23 December [meeting 69], the General Assembly, on the recommendation of the Fifth Committee [A/60/608 & Corr.1], adopted **resolution 60/246** without vote [agenda item 124].

Questions relating to the proposed programme budget for the biennium 2006-2007

The General Assembly,

Recalling its resolutions 41/213 of 19 December 1986, 42/211 of 21 December 1987, 45/248 B, section VI, of 21 December 1990, 56/253 of 24 December 2001, 58/269 and 58/270 of 23 December 2003 and 59/275, 59/276 and 59/278 of 23 December 2004, and paragraphs 161 to 167 of its resolution 60/1 of 16 September 2005,

Reaffirming the respective mandates of the Advisory Committee on Administrative and Budgetary Questions and the Committee for Programme and Coordination in the consideration of the proposed programme budget,

Having considered the proposed programme budget for the biennium 2006-2007, as well as other reports and statements of programme budget implications submitted by the Secretary-General and the relevant reports of the Advisory Committee on Administrative and Budgetary Questions and the Committee for Programme and Coordination thereon,

1. *Reaffirms* that the Fifth Committee is the appropriate Main Committee of the General Assembly entrusted with responsibilities for administrative and budgetary matters;

2. *Also reaffirms* rule 153 of its rules of procedure;

3. *Endorses* the conclusions and recommendations of the Committee for Programme and Coordination as contained in paragraphs 61, 67 and 106 to 122 of its report;

4. *Notes* that consideration of the programme narratives contained in the revised estimates will follow consideration thereof by the Committee for Programme and Coordination no later than September 2006;

5. *Endorses*, subject to the provisions of the present resolution and without establishing a precedent, the recommendations of the Advisory Committee on Administrative and Budgetary Questions concerning posts and non-post resources as contained in chapter II of its first report on the proposed programme budget for the biennium 2006-2007, and the resource recommendations contained in its reports on revised estimates, including those on the 2005 World Summit Outcome, and on statements of programme budget implications relating to decisions taken by the Main Committees of the General Assembly;

6. *Decides* that the staffing table for the biennium 2006-2007 shall be as set out in the annex to the present resolution;

7. *Also decides* to extend for the biennium 2006-2007 the experiment approved under paragraph 14 of General Assembly resolution 58/270, and requests the Secretary-General to report to the Assembly at its sixty-first session on the implementation of the experiment;

8. *Requests* the Secretary-General to utilize the arrangements referred to in paragraph 7 above to identify available posts to provide for the new post requests referred to in paragraphs IV.2, IV.28 and IV.29 of the first report of the Advisory Committee on Administrative and Budgetary Questions on the proposed programme budget for the biennium 2006-2007, as well as in paragraph 5 of the second report of the Advisory Committee on the proposed programme budget;

9. *Recalls* its decision in paragraph 3 (*b*) of its resolution 59/313 of 12 September 2005 entitled "A strengthened and revitalized General Assembly", and endorses the proposals contained in paragraph 3 of the statement of the Secretary-General on the programme budget implications;

10. *Decides* to provide resources at the level sought by the Secretary-General in his statement of programme budget implications arising in respect of the draft resolution relating to Rwanda outreach and the amendment thereto;

11. *Recognizes* the need for limited discretion in budgetary implementation for the Secretary-General within defined parameters to be agreed by the General Assembly along with clear accountability mechanisms to the Assembly for its use, on the basis of recommendations of the Secretary-General to be provided to the Assembly at its resumed sixtieth session;

12. *Requests* the Secretary-General to achieve further efficiencies in non-post resources, and therefore decides to adjust non-post provisions covered in paragraph 5 above by a pro rata reduction of 1.75 per cent to be applied to all sections of the programme budget;

13. *Recognizes* that amendments to the provisions of the present resolution would stem from any decisions by the General Assembly in accordance with established procedures in response to proposals of the Secretary-General relating to paragraphs 161 to 167 of its resolution 60/1;

14. *Decides* that the Development Account shall be recosted for the biennium 2006-2007, and in this context requests the Secretary-General to pursue the relevant proposals contained in his report and to provide to the General Assembly at its sixty-first session recommendations on how additional resources in the region of 5 million dollars could be added to the Development Account.

Annex

Staffing table for the biennium 2006-2007

Category	2006–2007
Professional and above	
Deputy Secretary-General	1
Under-Secretary-General	29
Assistant Secretary-General	21
D 2	90
D 1	257
P 5	745
P 4/3	2 501
P 2/1	491
Subtotal	**4 135**
General Service	
Principal level	278
Other level	2 710
Subtotal	**2 988**
Other	
Security Service	306
Local level	1 849
Field Service	183
Trades and Crafts	176
Subtotal	**2 514**
Total	**9 637**

Appropriations

In his proposed programme budget for the 2006-2007 biennium [A/60/6], the Secretary-General recommended expenditures of $3,803.8 million and income of $26.5 million and staff assessment income of $437.9 million, an increase of $22.3 million, resulting in a net budget estimate of $3,339.3 million, or a 5.5 per cent real growth over the 2004-2005 budget.

Extrabudgetary resources for the 2006-2007 biennium were estimated at $5,631.1 million, comprising $883.7 million for support activities,

$1,676.7 million for substantive activities and $3,071 million for operational activities.

ACABQ, in its first report on the 2006-2007 programme budget [A/60/7 & Corr.1], noted that decisions yet to be taken on the Secretary-General's reform proposals might significantly affect estimates and that revised estimates would be submitted for the International Trade Centre of the United Nations Conference on Trade and Development/World Trade Organization (UNCTAD/WTO) and the Office of Internal Oversight Services (OIOS). The Committee agreed with the overall budget level proposed, and made specific recommendations in a number of areas where economies could be achieved.

In September [A/60/355], the Secretary-General submitted a statement on programme budget implications of the draft resolution [A/60/L.1] entitled "2005 World Summit Outcome" (see p. 48), estimated at $80 million. A detailed statement of programme budget implications would be submitted to the Assembly. In November [A/60/537], the Secretary-General submitted revised estimates of additional requirements totaling $73,368,800. ACABQ recommended reductions of $23,367,800 net [A/60/7/Add.13 & Corr.1, 2] to those estimates.

In December [A/60/599], the Secretary-General recommended revised estimates to reflect the latest data on actual inflation experience, the outcome of salary surveys, the movement of post adjustment indices in 2005, the effect of the evolution of operational rates of exchange in 2005 and the adjustment in staff assessment rates on the proposed 2006-2007 programme budget and the revised estimates to the proposed programme budget for the 2005 World Summit Outcome (see above). The recosted level of expenditure amounted to $3,795.8 million and total income was revised to $427.4 million.

Also in December [A/60/600], the Secretary-General recommended revised estimates in the amount of $269.8 million for the International Criminal Tribunal for Rwanda and $305.1 million for the International Tribunal for the Former Yugoslavia.

ACABQ, in its report on the 2006-2007 programme budget [A/60/7/Add.32], found no technical basis for objecting to the Secretary-General's revised estimates in the two reports and transmitted them to the Fifth Committee.

GENERAL ASSEMBLY ACTION

On 23 December [meeting 69], the General Assembly, on the recommendation of the Fifth Committee [A/60/608 & Corr.1], adopted **resolution 60/247 A-C** without vote [agenda item 124].

Programme budget for the biennium 2006-2007

A

BUDGET APPROPRIATIONS FOR THE
BIENNIUM 2006-2007

The General Assembly

Resolves that, for the biennium 2006-2007:

1. Appropriations totalling 3,798,912,500 United States dollars are hereby approved for the following purposes:

Section		Amount (Thousands of United States dollars)
Part I. *Overall policy-making, direction and coordination*		
1. Overall policy-making, direction and coordination		74 813 500
2. General Assembly and Economic and Social Council affairs and conference management		586 776 200
	Subtotal	**661 589 700**
Part II. *Political affairs*		
3. Political affairs		432 026 900
4. Disarmament		20 381 100
5. Peacekeeping operations		94 091 000
6. Peaceful uses of outer space		5 906 800
	Subtotal	**552 405 800**
Part III. *International justice and law*		
7. International Court of Justice		34 956 900
8. Legal affairs		42 289 400
	Subtotal	**77 246 300**
Part IV. *International cooperation for development*		
9. Economic and social affairs		157 930 900
10. Least developed countries, landlocked developing countries and small island developing States		5 056 800
11. United Nations support for the New Partnership for Africa's Development		10 791 900

Section		Amount *(Thousands of United States dollars)*
12. Trade and development		111 091 600
13. International Trade Centre UNCTAD/WTO		25 915 800
14. Environment		11 977 100
15. Human settlements		17 864 500
16. International drug control, crime prevention and criminal justice		31 527 800
	Subtotal	**372 156 400**
Part V. *Regional cooperation for development*		
17. Economic and social development in Africa		106 011 400
18. Economic and social development in Asia and the Pacific		71 858 100
19. Economic development in Europe		54 176 700
20. Economic and social development in Latin America and the Caribbean		94 630 400
21. Economic and social development in Western Asia		53 416 900
22. Regular programme of technical cooperation		45 622 000
	Subtotal	**425 715 500**
Part VI. *Human rights and humanitarian affairs*		
23. Human rights		83 088 400
24. Protection of and assistance to refugees		64 645 200
25. Palestine refugees		35 184 800
26. Humanitarian assistance		26 140 500
	Subtotal	**209 058 900**
Part VII. *Public information*		
27. Public information		177 302 500
	Subtotal	**177 302 500**
Part VIII. *Common support services*		
28. Management and support services		511 375 800
	Subtotal	**511 375 800**
Part IX. *Internal oversight*		
29. Internal oversight		31 330 100
	Subtotal	**31 330 100**
Part X. *Jointly financed administrative activities and special expenses*		
30. Jointly financed administrative activities		11 178 800
31. Special expenses		92 798 000
	Subtotal	**103 976 800**
PartXI. *Capital expenditures*		
32. Construction, alteration, improvement and major maintenance		74 841 300
	Subtotal	**74 841 300**
PartXII. *Safety and security*		
33. Safety and security		190 131 400
	Subtotal	**190 131 400**
PartXIII. *Development Account*		
34. Development Account		13 954 100
	Subtotal	**13 954 100**
35. Part XIV. *Staff assessment*		
34. Staff assessment		397 827 900
	Subtotal	**397 827 900**
	Total	**3 798 912 500**

2. The Secretary-General shall be authorized to transfer credits between sections of the budget with the concurrence of the Advisory Committee on Administrative and Budgetary Questions;

3. The budget for the biennium 2006-2007 amounts to 3,799 million dollars. Expected expenditure in the course of 2006 is 1,899 million dollars. The two-year budget will permit a full assessment on all Member States for 2006, in accordance with Article 17 of the Charter of the United Nations. The Secretary-General, while adhering to the existing procedures regarding the annual assessment on Member States, is authorized to enter into expenditure of a first tranche, limited to 950 million dollars, as an exceptional measure. The General Assembly, in order to ensure the availability of resources for programme delivery, will act in response to a request from the Secretary-General, at an appropriate time, for expenditure of the remaining funds;

4. The total net provision made under the various sections of the budget for contractual printing shall be administered as a unit under the direction of the United Nations Publications Board;

5. In addition to the appropriations approved under paragraph 1 above, an amount of 75,000 dollars is appropriated for each year of the biennium 2006-2007 from the accumulated income of the Library Endowment Fund for the purchase of books, periodicals, maps and library equipment and for such other expenses of the library at the Palais des Nations in Geneva as are in accordance with the objects and provisions of the endowment.

B

INCOME ESTIMATES FOR THE BIENNIUM
2006-2007

The General Assembly

Resolves that, for the biennium 2006-2007:

1. Estimates of income other than assessments on Member States totalling 427,355,200 United States dollars are approved as follows:

Income section	Amount (Thousands of United States dollars)
1. Income from staff assessment	401 734 800
2. General income	20 867 000
3. Services to the public	4 753 400
Total	**427 355 200**

2. The income from staff assessment shall be credited to the Tax Equalization Fund in accordance with the provisions of General Assembly resolution 973 (X) of 15 December 1955;

3. Direct expenses of the United Nations Postal Administration, services to visitors, the sale of statistical products, catering operations and related services, garage operations, television services and the sale of publications not provided for under the budget appropriations shall be charged against the income derived from those activities.

C

FINANCING OF APPROPRIATIONS FOR THE
YEAR 2006

The General Assembly

Resolves that, for the year 2006:

1. Budget appropriations consisting of 1,899,456,250 United States dollars, being half of the appropriation of 3,798,912,500 dollars approved for the biennium 2006-2007 by the General Assembly in paragraph 1 of resolution A above, plus 47,626,700 dollars, being the increase in revised appropriations for the biennium 2004-2005 approved by the Assembly in its resolutions 59/282 of 13 April 2005, 59/294 of 22 June 2005 and 60/244 and 60/245 A of 23 December 2005, shall be financed in accordance with regulations 3.1 and 3.2 of the Financial Regulations of the United Nations, as follows:

(a) 22,242,700 dollars, consisting of 12,810,200 dollars, being the net of half of the estimated income other than staff assessment approved for the biennium 2006-2007 under resolution B above, plus 9,432,500 dollars, being the increase in income other than staff assessment for the biennium 2004-2005;

(b) 1,924,840,250 dollars, being the assessment on Member States in accordance with its resolution 58/1 B of 23 December 2003;

2. There shall be set off against the assessment on Member States, in accordance with the provisions of General Assembly resolution 973 (X) of 15 December 1955, their respective share in the Tax Equalization Fund in the total amount of 218,242,100 dollars, consisting of:

(a) 200,867,400 dollars, being half of the estimated staff assessment income approved for the biennium 2006-2007 in resolution B above;

(b) 17,374,700 dollars, being the increase in income from staff assessment for the biennium 2004-2005 approved by the Assembly in its resolutions 59/282 of 13 April 2005, 59/294 of 22 June 2005 and 60/244 and 60/245 B of 23 December 2005.

Special subjects relating to the 2006-2007 programme budget

The Fifth Committee considered a number of special subjects relating to the 2006-2007 programme budget, among them revised estimates resulting from resolutions and decisions adopted by the Economic and Social Council at its resumed organizational and first substantive sessions of 2005; estimates in respect of special political missions, good offices and other political initiatives authorized by the General Assembly and/or the Security Council; the contingency fund; the effect of changes in rates of exchange and inflation; the Working Capital Fund; and unforeseen and extraordinary expenses (see sections below).

Other subjects concerned the International Trade Centre UNCTAD/WTO (see p. 1048); the capital master plan (see p. 1553); administrative expenses of the United Nations Joint Staff Pension Fund (see p. 1527); request for a subvention to the United Nations Institute for Disarmament Research (UNIDIR) (see p. 640); construction of additional office facilities at the Economic Commission for Africa (see p. 1552); possibility of operating guided tours, bookstores and gift shops at the United Nations Office in Nairobi (see p. 1551); Economic and Social Commission for Asia and the Pacific efforts in the rationalization of monitoring and evaluation (see p. 1107); workplan on reform of the Economic Commission for Europe (ECE) (see p. 1114); administrative and financial implications of the decisions and recommendations contained in the report of the International Civil Service Commission for 2005 (see p. 1505); financial viability of the United Nations Institute for Training and Research (UNITAR) (see p. 1243); establishment of the ethics office (see p. 1476); and the gross budgets for the Joint Inspection Unit (JIU) (see p. 1475), ICSC (see p. 1505) and the Department of Safety and Security.

On 23 December [meeting 69], the General Assembly, on the recommendation of the Fifth Committee [A/60/608 & Corr.1], adopted **resolution 60/248** without vote [agenda item 124].

Special subjects relating to the proposed programme budget for the biennium 2006-2007

The General Assembly,

I

International Trade Centre UNCTAD/WTO

Having considered the programme budget proposals for the International Trade Centre UNCTAD/WTO for the biennium 2006-2007 and the related report of the Advisory Committee on Administrative and Budgetary Questions,

Decides to approve resources in the amount of 26,732,000 United States dollars (at the exchange rate of 1.27 Swiss francs to 1 dollar) proposed for the biennium 2006-2007 under section 13, International Trade Centre UNCTAD/WTO, of the proposed programme budget for the biennium 2006-2007;

II

Capital master plan

Recalling its resolutions 54/249 of 23 December 1999, 55/238 of 23 December 2000, 56/234 and 56/236 of 24 December 2001 and 56/286 of 27 June 2002, section II of its resolution 57/292 of 20 December 2002 and resolution 59/295 of 22 June 2005 and its decision 58/566 of 8 April 2004,

Having considered the third annual progress report of the Secretary-General on the implementation of thecapital master plan and the related report of the Advisory Committee on Administrative and Budgetary Questions,

Having also considered the reports of the Board of Auditors and the Office of Internal Oversight Services for the period from August 2004 to July 2005,

1. *Recognizes* the urgent need to continue the implementation of the design and pre-construction phases of the capital master plan;

2. *Authorizes* the Secretary-General to proceed with design work, related project management and management of pre-construction services to the extent that those activities can be implemented without prejudice to the decision to be taken by the General Assembly at a later stage regarding its selection of the strategy for implementation of the capital master plan;

3. *Decides* to convert 8,198,000 dollars of the existing commitment authority into an appropriation with assessment for the year 2006 so as to provide for the continuation of design work and related project management and management of the pre-construction phase, including swing space requirements, as a minimum amount that would be required for capital master plan implementation during the first four months of 2006, irrespective of the strategy for the capital master plan to be endorsed by the General Assembly at a later stage;

4. *Also decides* to revert, as a matter of priority, to the issue of the capital master plan at the first part of its resumed sixtieth session, in March 2006;

III

Administrative expenses of the United Nations Joint Staff Pension Fund

Having considered the report of the Standing Committee of the United Nations Joint Staff Pension Board on the administrative expenses of the United Nations Joint Staff Pension Fund, the report of the Secretary-General on the administrative and financial implications arising from the report of the Standing Committee and the related reports of the Advisory Committee on Administrative and Budgetary Questions,

1. *Concurs* with the recommendations contained in the reports of the Advisory Committee on Administrative and Budgetary Questions on the administrative expenses of the United Nations Joint Staff Pension Fund and on the administrative and financial implications arising from the report of the Standing Committee of the United Nations Joint Staff Pension Board;

2. *Approves* expenses, chargeable directly to the Fund, totalling 91,722,700 dollars net for the biennium 2006-2007 and a revised estimate of 89,563,100 dollars net for the biennium 2004-2005 for the administration of the Fund;

3. *Also approves* an additional amount of 1,079,000 dollars above the level of resources set out in section 1, Overall policymaking, direction and coordination, of the proposed programme budget for the biennium 2006-2007 as the United Nations share of the cost of the administrative expenses of the central secretariat of the Fund;

4. *Authorizes* the United Nations Joint Staff Pension Board to supplement the voluntary contributions to the Emergency Fund for the biennium 2006-2007 by an amount not exceeding 200,000 dollars;

IV

Request for a subvention to the United Nations Institute for Disarmament Research

Recalling its resolution 59/276 of 23 December 2004,

1. *Takes note* of the note by the Secretary-General on the request for a subvention to the United Nations Institute for Disarmament Research resulting from the recommendations of the Board of Trustees of the Institute on the work programme of the Institute for 2006-2007 and the related report of the Advisory Committee on Administrative and Budgetary Questions;

2. *Endorses* the proposal that the request for a subvention to the Institute be submitted for review and approval by the General Assembly on a biennial basis in the context of its consideration of the proposed programme budget for the related biennium;

3. *Approves* the request for a subvention to the Institute of 468,100 dollars for the biennium 2006-2007 from the regular budget of the United Nations, on the understanding that no additional provision would be required under section 4, Disarmament, of the proposed programme budget for the biennium 2006-2007;

V

Revised estimates resulting from resolutions and decisions adopted by the Economic and Social Council at its resumed organizational and first substantive sessions of 2005

Takes note of the report of the Secretary-General, and endorses the observations and recommendations of the Advisory Committee on Administrative and Budgetary Questions contained in its report;

VI

Estimates in respect of special political missions, good offices and other political initiatives authorized by the General Assembly and/or the Security Council

1. *Takes note* of the report of the Secretary-General and endorses the observations and recommendations of the Advisory Committee on Administrative and Budgetary Questions contained in its report;

2. *Approves* for the 26 missions dealt with in the report of the Secretary-General the charge of 100 million dollars against the provision for special political missions requested under section 3, Political affairs, of the proposed programme budget for the biennium 2006-2007;

3. *Decides* to resume at the first part of its resumed sixtieth session its consideration of the report of the Secretary-General on the estimates in respect of special political missions, good offices and other political initiatives authorized by the General Assembly and/or the Security Council;

4. *Notes* that an unallocated balance of 255,949,300 dollars would remain against the provision of 355,949,300 dollars for special political missions under section 3, Political affairs, of the proposed programme budget for the biennium 2006-2007;

VII

Construction of additional office facilities at the Economic Commission for Africa in Addis Ababa

Takes note of the report of the Secretary-General and endorses the related recommendations of the Advisory Committee on Administrative and Budgetary Questions contained in its report;

VIII

Possibility of operating guided tours, bookstores and gift shops at the United Nations Office at Nairobi and the cost implications thereof

Recalling its resolution 58/263 of 23 December 2003,

Having considered the report of the Secretary-General and the related report of the Advisory Committee on Administrative and Budgetary Questions,

Requests the Secretary-General to organize, effective 1 January 2006, a guided tour operation at the United Nations Office at Nairobi, and in this context also requests him to report the actual income and expenditures of the guided tour operation at the United Nations Office at Nairobi in the budget performance reports for the biennium 2006-2007 under income section 3, Services to the public;

IX

Efforts of the Economic and Social Commission for Asia and the Pacific in rationalization of monitoring and evaluation

1. *Welcomes* the efforts of the Economic and Social Commission for Asia and the Pacific in rationalization of monitoring and evaluation in accordance with General Assembly resolution 58/269 of 23 December 2003, especially in carrying out self-evaluation activities in a systematic and comprehensive manner;

2. *Requests* the Commission, in this regard, to report on its activities in that area in the proposed programme budget for the biennium 2008-2009;

X

Workplan on reform of the Economic Commission for Europe

Welcomes the workplan on reform of the Economic Commission for Europe adopted by the Commission in its decision of 2 December 2005, decides that the Commission should implement the adopted measures outlined in its decision, and to that end requests the Secretary-General to allocate the requisite resources within section 19, Economic development in Europe, of the proposed programme budget for the biennium 2006-2007;

XI

Administrative and financial implications of the decisions and recommendations contained in the report of the International Civil Service Commission for 2005

Having considered the report of the Secretary-General and the related report of the Advisory Committee on Administrative and Budgetary Questions,

1. *Decides* to approve, with effect from 1 January 2006, the new scale of staff assessment recommended by the International Civil Service Commission in its report,

2. *Also decides* to revert to the other issues contained in the report of the Secretary-General at the first part of its resumed sixtieth session;

XII

Financial viability of the United Nations Institute for Training and Research

Recalling its resolution 59/252 of 22 December 2004 and section X of its resolution 59/276 of 23 December 2004,

Having considered the report of the Secretary-General and the related report of the Advisory Committee on Administrative and Budgetary Questions,

1. *Takes note* of the report of the Secretary-General and of the related report of the Advisory Committee on Administrative and Budgetary Questions;

2. *Decides* to provide the United Nations Institute for Training and Research with the amount of 242,400 dollars, being the equivalent of the amount of rental, maintenance and other administrative costs associated with conducting the core training programme for the biennium 2006-2007;

3. *Reiterates* that, in order to ensure stability of the funding for the General Fund and the viability of repaying the United Nations its debt, the Institute should systematically charge 13 per cent of programme support costs to special purpose grants whenever possible;

XIII

Ethics office; comprehensive review of the governance arrangements, including an independent external evaluation of the auditing and oversight system; and the independent audit advisory committee

Having considered the report of the Secretary-General and the related report of the Advisory Committee on Administrative and Budgetary Questions,

1. *Takes note* of the report of the Secretary-General and the related report of the Advisory Committee on Administrative and Budgetary Questions;

2. *Recalls* its resolution 60/246 of 23 December 2005;

3. *Notes* that the approved resources would provide for the establishment of an ethics office and the undertaking of the evaluation study called for pursuant to paragraph 164 (*b*) of General Assembly resolution 60/1 of 16 September 2005;

4. *Decides* to establish the Independent Audit Advisory Committee to assist the General Assembly in discharging its oversight responsibilities, and requests the Secretary-General to propose its terms of reference, ensure coherence with the outcome of the ongoing review of oversight and report to the Assembly at the second part of its resumed sixtieth session on related resource requirements;

XIV

Contingency fund

Notes that a balance of 4,966,000 dollars remains in the contingency fund;

XV

Effects of changes in rates of exchange and inflation

Having considered the report of the Secretary-General on the revised estimates resulting from the effect of changes in rates of exchange and inflation and the related report of the Advisory Committee on Administrative and Budgetary Questions,

Takes note of the revised estimates arising from recosting due to the effects of changes in the rates of exchange and inflation;

XVI

Joint Inspection Unit

Approves the gross budget for the Joint Inspection Unit for the biennium 2006-2007 in the amount of 10,511,100 dollars;

XVII

International Civil Service Commission

Approves the gross budget for the International Civil Service Commission for the biennium 2006-2007 in the amount of 16,211,300 dollars;

XVIII

Jointly financed gross budget of the Department of Safety and Security

Approves the gross budget for the Department of Safety and Security for the biennium 2006-2007 in the amount of 225,682,400 dollars, broken down as follows:

(*a*) Field security operations: 201,423,900 dollars;

(*b*) Security and safety services at the United Nations Office at Vienna: 24,258,500 dollars.

Contingency fund

The contingency fund, established by General Assembly resolution 41/213 [YUN 1986, p. 1024], accommodated additional expenditures relating to each biennium that derived from legislative mandates not provided for in the proposed programme budget or from revised estimates. Guidelines for its use were annexed to Assembly resolution 42/211 [YUN 1987, p. 1098].

The Fifth Committee considered the Secretary-General's December report [A/C.5/60/25] containing a consolidated statement of all programme budget implications and revised estimates falling under the guidelines for use of the fund. The consolidated amount of $22,098,100 would be within the approved level of the fund.

ACABQ, in its thirty-second report on the 2006-2007 programme budget [A/60/7/Add.31], said that, should the Assembly accept the assumptions and suggestions contained in the Secretary-General's report, the balance available in the fund would amount to $5,101,900.

Revised estimates in respect of matters of which the Security Council was seized

In December [A/60/585 & Corr.1], as a result of action taken or expected to be taken by the General Assembly and/or the Security Council, the Secretary-General submitted the proposed resource requirements for the period up to 31 December 2006 for 26 special political missions, except for the United Nations Assistance Mission in Afghanistan (UNAMA) and the United Nations Office in Timor-Leste (UNOTIL), which were estimated at $280,803,200 net ($297,498,900 gross). That amount would be charged against the $355,949,300 (before recosting) proposed for special political mission under section 3, Political affairs, of the 2006-2007 proposed programme budget.

In a later addendum [A/60/585/Add.2], in the context of decisions taken by the Security Council regarding three special political missions, (the Office of the Secretary-General's Special Envoy for the future status process for Kosovo, his Special Envoy for the implementation of Security Council resolution 1559(2004) [YUN 2004, p. 506] and the International Investigation Commission concerning the 14 February event in Lebanon), the Secretary-General proposed additional estimated requirements of $22,548,400 net ($25,022,800 gross).

ACABQ, in its thirty-eighth report [A/60/7/Add.37], noted that estimated requirements for the 29 special political missions totaled $303,351,600 for the period from 1 January to 31 December 2006. It recommended a reduction of $324,700 and approved resources amounting to $302,469,500.

Revised estimates resulting from Economic and Social Council action

In a September report [A/60/396], the Secretary-General submitted expenditure requirements resulting from resolutions and decisions adopted by the Economic and Social Council at its 2005 resumed organizational and first substantive sessions related to activities of the Commission on Sustainable Development, the United Nations Forum on Forests, The Ad hoc Advisory Group on Haiti, human rights, conference management, economic and social affairs and administration in Geneva. Those requirements were estimated at $4,143,300, $3,571,300 of which would be absorbed within resources provided for in the 2004-2005 or 2006-2007 programme budget, resulting in a net requirement of $572,700 under the 2006-2007 programme budget, to be charged against the contingency fund.

ACABQ, in its related report [A/60/7/Add.5], stated that, given the relatively minor amount involved, an additional appropriation might not be necessary, and therefore recommended any amount that might be required should be reported in the first performance report on the proposed programme budget for the 2006-2007 biennium.

Working capital fund

In December, the General Assembly established the Working Capital Fund for the 2006-2007 biennium at $100 million, the same level as for the 2004-2005 biennium [YUN 2003, p. 1421]. As in the past, the Fund was to be used to finance appropriations, pending the receipt of assessed contributions, to pay for unforeseen and extraordinary expenses, as well as for miscellaneous self-liquidating purchases and advance insurance premiums, and to enable the Tax Equalization Fund to meet current commitments pending the accumulation of credits.

GENERAL ASSEMBLY ACTION

On 23 December [meeting 69], the General Assembly, on the recommendation of the Fifth Committee [A/60/608 & Corr.1], adopted **resolution 60/250** without vote [agenda item 124].

Working Capital Fund for the biennium 2006-2007

The General Assembly

Resolves that:

1. The Working Capital Fund shall be established for the biennium 2006-2007 in the amount of 100 million United States dollars;

2. Member States shall make advances to the Working Capital Fund in accordance with the scale of assessments adopted by the General Assembly for contributions of Member States to the budget for the year 2006;

3. There shall be set off against this allocation of advances:

(*a*) Credits to Member States resulting from transfers made in 1959 and 1960 from the surplus account to the Working Capital Fund in an adjusted amount of 1,025,092 dollars;

(*b*) Cash advances paid by Member States to the Working Capital Fund for the biennium 2004-2005 in accordance with General Assembly resolution 58/274 of 23 December 2003;

4. Should the credits and advances paid by any Member State to the Working Capital Fund for the biennium 2004-2005 exceed the amount of that Member State's advance under the provisions of paragraph 2 above, the excess shall be set off against the amount of the contributions payable by the Member State in respect of the biennium 2006-2007;

5. The Secretary-General is authorized to advance from the Working Capital Fund:

(*a*) Such sums as may be necessary to finance budgetary appropriations pending the receipt of contributions; sums so advanced shall be reimbursed as soon as receipts from contributions are available for that purpose;

(*b*) Such sums as may be necessary to finance commitments that may be duly authorized under the provisions of the resolutions adopted by the General Assembly, in particular resolution 60/249 of 23 December 2005 relating to unforeseen and extraordinary expenses; the Secretary-General shall make provision in the budget estimates for reimbursing the Working Capital Fund;

(*c*) Such sums as may be necessary to continue the revolving fund to finance miscellaneous self-liquidating purchases and activities, which, together with net sums outstanding for the same purpose, do not exceed 200,000 dollars; advances in excess of 200,000 dollars may be made with the prior concurrence of the Advisory Committee on Administrative and Budgetary Questions;

(*d*) With the prior concurrence of the Advisory Committee, such sums as may be required to finance payments of advance insurance premiums where the period of insurance extends beyond the end of the biennium in which payment is made; the Secretary-General shall make provision in the budget estimates of each biennium, during the life of the related policies, to cover the charges applicable to each biennium;

(*e*) Such sums as may be necessary to enable the Tax Equalization Fund to meet current commitments pending the accumulation of credits; such advances shall be repaid as soon as credits are available in the Tax Equalization Fund;

6. Should the provision in paragraph 1 above prove inadequate to meet the purposes normally related to the Working Capital Fund, the Secretary-General is authorized to utilize, in the biennium 2006-2007, cash from special funds and accounts in his custody, under the conditions approved by the General Assembly in its resolution 1341(XIII) of 13 December 1958, or the proceeds of loans authorized by the Assembly.

Unforeseen and extraordinary expenses

Under specific circumstances, the Secretary-General was authorized by the General Assembly to enter into commitments for activities of an urgent nature, without reverting to it for approval under the terms of resolution 58/273 [YUN 2003, p. 1422].

GENERAL ASSEMBLY ACTION

On 23 December [meeting 69], the General Assembly, on the recommendation of the Fifth Committee [A/60/608 & Corr.1], adopted **resolution 60/249** without vote [agenda item 124].

Unforeseen and extraordinary expenses for the biennium 2006-2007

The General Assembly

1. *Authorizes* the Secretary-General, with the prior concurrence of the Advisory Committee on Administrative and Budgetary Questions and subject to the Financial Regulations and Rules of the United Nations and the provisions of paragraph 3 below, to enter into commitments in the biennium 2006-2007 to meet unforeseen and extraordinary expenses arising either during or subsequent to the biennium, provided that the concurrence of the Advisory Committee shall not be necessary for:

(*a*) Such commitments not exceeding a total of 8 million United States dollars in any one year of the biennium 2006-2007 as the Secretary-General certifies relate to the maintenance of peace and security;

(*b*) Such commitments as the President of the International Court of Justice certifies relate to expenses occasioned by:

(i)   The designation of ad hoc judges (Statute of the International Court of Justice, Article 31), not exceeding a total of 200,000 dollars;

(ii) The calling of witnesses and the appointment of experts (Statute, Article 50) and the appointment of assessors (Statute, Article 30), not exceeding a total of 50,000 dollars;

(iii) The maintenance in office for the completion of cases of judges who have not been re-elected (Statute, Article 13, paragraph 3), not exceeding a total of 40,000 dollars;

(iv) The payment of pensions and travel and removal expenses of retiring judges and travel and removal expenses and installation grant of members of the Court (Statute, Article 32, paragraph 7), not exceeding a total of 410,000 dollars;

(v)   The work of the Court or its Chambers away from The Hague (Statute, Article 22), not exceeding a total of 25,000 dollars;

(*c*) Such commitments not exceeding a total of 1 million dollars in the biennium 2006-2007 as the Secretary-General certifies are required for security measures pursuant to section XI, paragraph 6, of General Assembly resolution 59/276 of 23 December 2004;

2. *Resolves* that the Secretary-General shall report to the Advisory Committee and to the General Assembly at its sixty-first and sixty-second sessions all commitments made under the provisions of the present resolution, together with the circumstances relating thereto, and shall submit supplementary estimates to the Assembly in respect of such commitments;

3. *Decides* that for the biennium 2006-2007, if a decision of the Security Council results in the need for the Secretary-General to enter into commitments relating to the maintenance of peace and security in an amount exceeding 10 million dollars in respect of the decision, that matter shall be brought to the General Assembly, or, if the Assembly is suspended or not in session, a resumed or special session of the Assembly shall be convened by the Secretary-General to consider the matter.

Contributions

According to the Secretary-General's report on improving the financial situation of the United Nations [A/60/427/Add.1], unpaid assessed contributions to the UN budget at the end of 2005 totaled $333 million (compared to $357 million in 2004); outstanding peacekeeping arrears totaled $2,900 million (compared to over $2,500 million in 2004); and total unpaid assessments to the international tribunals were reduced to $25 million (compared to $30 million in 2004).

The number of Member States paying their regular budget assessment in full increased to 140 (compared to 124 at the end of 2004).

Assessments

The Committee on Contributions, at its sixty-fifth session (New York, 6-24 June) [A/60/11], considered a number of issues related to the payment of assessments, including the methodology for preparing the scale of assessments for the period 2007-2009, multi-year payment plans, measures to encourage the payment of arrears and the application of Article 19 of the Charter. The Committee decided to hold its sixty-sixth (2006) session from 5 to 30 June 2006. The General Assembly took action on the Committee's recommendations in July and December.

Application of Article 19

Committee on Contributions. The Committee on Contributions [A/60/11] reviewed requests from 10 Member States for exemption under Article 19, whereby a Member would lose its vote in the General Assembly if the amount of its arrears should equal or exceed the amount of contributions due from it for the preceding two full years. The Committee duly noted the Members' written and oral representations and evaluated them against their payment records and economic and political circumstances.

The Committee decided that it could take no action on the requests of Liberia and the Niger, as they were not submitted within the required two-week period prior to the Committee's session. It recognized the efforts of the Republic of Moldova to meet its financial obligations, despite the serious problems it continued to face and concluded that no action was required by the Assembly, since Moldova did not fall under the provisions of Article 19 in 2005. Determining that the failure of the Central African Republic, the Comoros, Georgia, Guinea-Bissau, Iraq, Somalia and Tajikistan to pay the full minimum amount of their arrears necessary to avoid the application of Article 19 was due to conditions beyond their control, and recalling the Article's provision that a Member might be permitted to vote if the Assembly was satisfied that its failure to pay was due to such conditions, the Committee recommended that they be allowed to vote until 30 June 2006. It urged the Central African Republic to make some payment to reduce or avoid an increase in its arrears and, acknowledging a payment of over $25,000 from the Comoros, urged it to do likewise. It noted Guinea-Bissau's intent to establish a multi-year payment plan and encouraged it to do so as soon as possible, as it was the second occasion that it had declared its intention to do that. The Committee welcomed Iraq's commitment to paying its obligations, as reflected in its multi-year payment plan and expressed its appreciation to the Niger for the payment of its second instalment under its 2005 multi-year payment plan. It also noted that Tajikistan, despite its continuing difficulties, had not only fulfilled the commitments it had made under the plan it submitted in 2000, but had exceeded the payments scheduled in the plan. With regard to Tajikistan's request that its arrears for peacekeeping activities that had accrued before 2000 be written off, the Committee indicated that such a request went beyond its competence as a technical advisory body.

Concerned that the nature and quality of the information provided by Member States requesting Article 19 exemptions varied widely, with some providing little, if any information, to support their requests, the Committee recalled the provisions of General Assembly resolution 54/237 C [YUN 1999, p. 1313] and recommended that the Assembly again urge all Member States requesting exemptions to submit as much information as possible in support of their requests. The Committee also recommended that every effort be made to remind Member States of the established deadline for exemption applications and requested the Secretariat to continue to include an early announcement in the *Journal* of the United Nations.

At the conclusion of the Committee's session on 24 June, only one Member State, Chad, was in arrears in the payment of its assessed contributions under the terms of Article 19 and had no vote in the Assembly. In addition, ten Members—the Central African Republic, the Comoros, Georgia, Guinea-Bissau, Iraq, Liberia, the Niger, Sao Tome and Principe, Somalia and Tajikistan—had been permitted to vote until 30 June 2005, pursuant to Assembly resolution 59/1 A [YUN 2004, p. 1394].

The Committee noted that Ethiopia and Pakistan, availing themselves of the opportunity afforded by Assembly resolution 58/1 B [YUN 2003, p. 1424], had paid the equivalent of $838,794.22 in currencies other than United States dollars.

Communications. On 24 June [A/59/864], the Chairman of the Committee on Contributions transmitted to the General Assembly the related section of the Committee's report dealing with those requests for exemption under Article 19 submitted to it (see above).

In letters to the Assembly President dated 29 June, and 8 and 13 July [A/59/869, A/59/868, A/59/871], respectively, Sao Tome and Principe, the Niger and Liberia made further requests for exemption under Article 19 and asked that the matter be taken up by the Assembly in plenary session at the beginning of July.

GENERAL ASSEMBLY ACTION

On 14 July [meeting 113], the General Assembly adopted **resolution 59/312** [draft: A/59/L.66 & Add.1, orally revised] without vote [agenda item 113].

Requests for exemption under Article 19 of the Charter of the United Nations

The General Assembly,

Having considered the letter dated 24 June 2005 from the Chairman of the Committee on Contributions addressed to the President of the General Assembly regarding the recommendations of the Committee on Contributions on requests for exemption under Article 19 of the Charter of the United Nations,

Reaffirming the obligation of Member States under Article 17 of the Charter to bear the expenses of the Organization as apportioned by the General Assembly,

1. *Reaffirms* its role in accordance with the provisions of Article 19 of the Charter of the United Nations and the advisory role of the Committee on Contributions in accordance with rule 160 of the rules of procedure of the General Assembly;

2. *Also reaffirms* its resolution 54/237 C of 23 December 1999;

3. *Agrees* that the failure of the Central African Republic, the Comoros, Georgia, Guinea-Bissau, Somalia and Tajikistan to pay the full minimum amount necessary to avoid the application of Article 19 of the Charter was due to conditions beyond their control;

4. *Decides* that the Central African Republic, the Comoros, Georgia, Guinea-Bissau, Somalia and Tajikistan should be permitted to vote in the General

Assembly until the Assembly takes a final decision during the main part of its sixtieth session;

5. *Takes note* of the information provided by Liberia, the Niger and Sao Tome and Principe;

6. *Agrees* that the failure of Liberia, the Niger and Sao Tome and Principe to pay the full minimum amount necessary to avoid the application of Article 19 of the Charter was due to conditions beyond their control, and invites Liberia, the Niger and Sao Tome and Principe to submit appropriate information to the Committee on Contributions if similar circumstances prevail in the future;

7. *Decides* that Liberia, the Niger and Sao Tome and Principe should be permitted to vote in the General Assembly until the Assembly takes a final decision during the main part of its sixtieth session.

Reports of Secretary-General. During the year, the Secretary-General reported to the Assembly on payments made by certain Member States to reduce their level of arrears below that specified in Article 19, so that they could vote in the Assembly. As at 11 January [A/59/668], 29 Member States were below the gross amount assessed for the preceding two full years (2003-2004). By 1 July [A/59/861], that number was reduced to 10 and remained at that level through 15 July [A/59/874], before dropping to 9 by 12 September [A/60/345].

Communication. On 12 October [A/C.5/60/2], the Assembly President transmitted to the Chairman of the Fifth Committee a 2 September request from the Niger for exemption under Article 19 to permit it to retain its vote in the Assembly, on account of its continuing economic and social difficulties and the commitment it had shown through the submission of a multi-year payment plan in March 2004 and the two instalment payments it had made, despite the grave economic conditions the country faced.

Statements by Liberia, the Niger and Sao Tome and Principe. During the Fifth Committee's consideration of the item on the scale of assessments for the apportionment of the expenses of the United Nations on 3 November [A/C.5/60/SR.7], Liberia said that its request for exemption under Article 19 had been received by the Committee on Contributions after the established deadline due to continued communication problems in the country. Liberia had not made much progress in paying its arrears due to conditions beyond its control, but hoped that, in 2006, the newly elected Government would be in a position to commit itself to a multi-year payment plan. In that regard, it requested that the Assembly grant an exemption so that Liberia could continue to exercise its vote during the Assembly's current session. The Niger also reiterated its request for exemption, citing the prolonged political instability, the 1999 coup d'état and subse-

quent humanitarian crisis, as factors contributing to the ongoing difficult economic situation, which had adversely impacted the country's ability to pay its arrears. Sao Tome and Principe said that the decline in world cocoa prices, combined with the increased prices for imports, had depressed incomes and living standards for the country and therefore, it was not in a position to pay its assessed contributions. Indicating that it would meet its financial obligations as soon as the economic situation improved, Sao Tome and Principe also trusted that the Assembly would accede to its request for an exemption.

Other matters related to payment of assessed contributions

The General Assembly also considered the recommendations of the Committee on Contributions on the methodology for future scale of assessments, multi-year payment plans, measures to encourage the payment of arrears, as well as the treatment of the outstanding assessed contributions of the former Yugoslavia [YUN 2003, p. 1428] (see sections below).

GENERAL ASSEMBLY ACTION

On 23 December [meeting 69], the General Assembly, on the recommendation of the Fifth Committee [A/60/602], adopted **resolution 60/237** without vote [agenda item 128].

Scale of assessments for the apportionment of the expenses of the United Nations

The General Assembly,

Recalling its resolutions 54/237 C of 23 December 1999, 57/4 B of 20 December 2002, 59/1 A of 11 October 2004, 59/1 B of 23 December 2004 and 59/312 of 14 July 2005,

Recalling also rule 160 of the rules of procedure of the General Assembly,

Having considered the report of the Committee on Contributions on the work of its sixty-fifth session,

Having also considered the letter dated 12 October 2005 from the President of the General Assembly addressed to the Chairman of the Fifth Committee,

Having further considered the report of the Secretary-General on multi-year payment plans,

Reaffirming the obligation of all Member States under Article 17 of the Charter of the United Nations to bear the expenses of the Organization as apportioned by the General Assembly,

A

1. *Reaffirms* its role in accordance with the provisions of Article 19 of the Charter and the advisory role of the Committee on Contributions in accordance with rule 160 of the rules of procedure of the General Assembly;

2. *Also reaffirms* its resolution 54/237 C;

3. *Requests* the Secretary-General to bring to the attention of Member States the deadline specified in resolution 54/237 C, including through an early an-

nouncement in the *Journal of the United Nations* and through direct communication;

4. *Urges* all Member States requesting exemption under Article 19 of the Charter to submit as much information as possible in support of their requests and to consider submitting such information in advance of the deadline specified in resolution 54/237 C to enable the collation of any additional detailed information that may be necessary;

5. *Agrees* that the failure of the Central African Republic, the Comoros, Georgia, Guinea-Bissau, Somalia and Tajikistan to pay the full minimum amount necessary to avoid the application of Article 19 of the Charter was due to conditions beyond their control;

6. *Decides* that the Central African Republic, the Comoros, Georgia, Guinea-Bissau, Somalia and Tajikistan should be permitted to vote in the General Assembly until the end of its sixtieth session;

7. *Takes note* of the information provided by the representatives of Liberia, the Niger and Sao Tome and Principe;

8. *Concludes* that the failure of Liberia, the Niger and Sao Tome and Principe to pay the full minimum amount necessary to avoid the application of Article 19 of the Charter was due to conditions beyond their control, and invites Liberia, the Niger and Sao Tome and Principe to submit appropriate information to the Committee on Contributions if similar circumstances prevail in the future;

9. *Decides* that Liberia, the Niger and Sao Tome and Principe should be permitted to vote in the General Assembly until the end of its sixtieth session;

10. *Decides also* that future exemptions under Article 19 of the Charter shall generally be granted through the end of the session of the General Assembly at which related requests are considered;

B

11. *Reaffirms* paragraph 1 of its resolution 57/4 B;

12. *Endorses* the conclusions and recommendations of the Committee on Contributions concerning multi-year payment plans, as contained in paragraphs 63 to 65 of its report, and encourages Member States with arrears to consider submitting such a plan;

13. *Takes note* of the report of the Secretary-General on multi-year payment plans;

14. *Urges* all Member States to pay their assessed contributions in full, on time and without imposing conditions;

C

15. *Takes note* of the conclusions and recommendations of the Committee on Contributions on measures to encourage the payment of arrears, as contained in paragraphs 68 to 70 of its report;

D

16. *Decides* to consider further at the first part of its resumed sixtieth session the methodology to be used in the preparation of the scale of assessments for the period 2007-2009, with a view to giving guidance to the Committee on Contributions on the matter.

Scale Methodology

Committee on Contributions. Pursuant to General Assembly resolution 58/1 B [YUN 2003, p. 1424], the Committee on Contributions contin-

ued to review [A/60/11] the different elements of the methodology for preparing future scales of assessments, focusing on elements relating to income measure; conversion rates; criteria for deciding when to replace market exchange rates (MERs); price-adjusted rates of exchange (PAREs); the base period; debt-burden adjustment; low per capita income adjustment; relief measures for Member States facing large scale-to-scale increases; and the annual recalculation of the scale. The Committee had before it additional information from the Statistics Division, as well as information gleaned from its discussion with a World Bank representative on issues related to data on external debt. Emphasizing the importance of its work, especially in the context of its consideration in 2006 of the scale of assessments for the period 2007-2009, the Committee requested the Secretary-General to ensure that sufficient resources were made available for that purpose. With regard to income measure, the Committee recommended that the scale of assessments for 2007-2009 should be based on the most current, comprehensive and comparable data available for the gross national income (GNI). Conversion rates should be based on MERs, and in instances where it would cause excessive fluctuations in the income of some Member States, PAREs or other appropriate conversion rates should be applied. The Committee considered a proposal for a more systematic approach to identifying which MERs should be replaced in preparing the scale of assessments. The Committee decided that it would use the proposed new approach in reviewing the scale of assessments for the period 2007-2009, with threshold figures of plus 50 per cent or minus 33 per cent, for changes in per capita GNI in United States dollars between 1999-2001 and 2002-2004, and MER valuation index levels of 1.2 and .08. However, final thresholds would be fixed after further analysis of the data to be used in preparing the 2007-2009 scale of assessments. The Committee agreed that application of any of the aforementioned criteria would not exclude consideration of other suitable cases for MERs replacement and that Member States could submit additional information to the Committee during its review of the scale. Concluding that, in general, relative PARE was the most technically sound method of adjusting MERs when distortions were identified, the Committee indicated that it would be the default method used when MERs were not appropriate. However, it recognized that other solutions might be needed in specific cases. With regard to the base year calculation of relative PARE, the Committee agreed that it should be decided on a case-by-case analysis.

The Committee decided to consider questions related to the base period, debt-burden adjustment and low per capita income adjustment at its sixty-sixth (2006) session. On the topic of large scale-to-scale increases in rates of assessment, it decided to consider the matter only if mandated to do so by the Assembly. The question of annual recalculation would be studied at its future sessions.

Measures to encourage payment of arrears

Report of Secretary-General. Pursuant to General Assembly resolution 59/1 B [YUN 2004, p. 1395], the Secretary-General submitted a March report [A/60/66] on multi-year payment plans/ schedules submitted by Georgia, the Niger, the Republic of Moldova, Sao Tome and Principe and Tajikistan and on the status of their implementation as at 31 December 2004. During the period 2000-2004, Tajikistan significantly exceeded the payments foreseen in its schedule, while payments for 2001-2004, for the Republic of Moldova fell short of its schedule. Sao Tome and Principe, during the period 2002-2004, also fell short of its schedule, with its foreseen payments exceeding the amounts actually received. Both Georgia and the Niger had payments and credits applied to the assessed contributions in 2004, which exceeded the amounts foreseen in their payment plans. The Secretary-General recommended that the Assembly should encourage Member States with significant arrears of contributions to consider submitting multi-year payment plans.

Committee on Contributions. The Committee on Contributions [A/60/11] concluded that, although results thus far were mixed, the system of multi-year payment plans had made a positive impact in encouraging Member States to reduce their unpaid assessed contributions and in providing a way for them to demonstrate their commitment to meeting their financial obligations to the United Nations. The Committee took note of the new payment plan submitted by Iraq, the completion of payments by the Republic of Moldova under its plan, as well as the payments of Georgia, the Niger and Tajikistan. The Committee also noted the considerable effort made by those Member States that had honoured their payment plan commitments and urged those that had not yet done so to do likewise so as to reduce their outstanding assessed contributions.

Noting that 2005 was the eighth year that it had considered the question of measures to encourage the payment of arrears, the Committee indicated that the only measure on which action had been taken was multi-year payment plans. It decided not to consider further the question of measures to encourage the payment of arrears, unless it received guidance thereon from the Assembly.

Outstanding assessed contributions

Pursuant to **decision 59/551 B** of 13 April, whereby the General Assembly deferred consideration of the question of the outstanding assessed contributions of the former Yugoslavia [YUN 2003, p. 1428], the Secretary-General, in a September report [A/60/140 & Corr.1], updated the information on the unpaid assessed contributions of the former Yugoslavia, consequent upon the admission in 2000 of the Federal Republic of Yugoslavia, renamed Serbia and Montenegro [ibid., p. 412] to membership of the United Nations. The report also outlined the options considered by the Assembly in earlier sessions and highlighted matters for consideration. The updated information reflected the application of credits arising in 2004 and 2005, bringing the total outstanding assessed amount to $16,135,838.

By **decision 60/551** of 23 December, the Assembly deferred until its resumed sixtieth (2006) session the reports of the Secretary-General on outstanding assessed contributions [YUN 2003, p. 1428] and unpaid assessed contributions (above) of the former Yugoslavia, as well as his letter dated 27 December 2001 to the Assembly President [YUN 2001, p. 1325].

Accounts and auditing

The General Assembly, at its resumed fifty-ninth (2005) session, considered the report of the Board of Auditors on UN peacekeeping operations for the period 1 July 2003 to 30 June 2004 [A/59/5 (Vol. II) & Corr.1], together with the Secretary-General's report on the implementation of the Board's recommendations [A/59/704], and related ACABQ comments and recommendations [A/59/736].

On 22 June, the Assembly, in **resolution 59/264 B**, endorsed the Board's report (see p. 143).

The Assembly, at its sixtieth session, had before it the reports of the Board of Auditors and audited financial statements of the voluntary funds administered by the Office of the United Nations High Commissioner for Refugees (UNHCR) [A/60/5/Add.5] (see p. 1300) and on the capital master plan [A/60/5 (Vol. 5)] (see p. 1554) for the period ended 31 December 2004, as well as the Secretary-General's July note, submitted pursuant to resolution 58/249 A [YUN 2003, p. 1428], transmitting the consolidated report of the Board of

Auditors on implementation of its recommendations relating to the 2002-2003 biennium [A/60/113] and covering the accounts of 15 organizations.

On 23 December, the Assembly, in **resolution 60/234**, endorsed the Board's recommendations on the voluntary funds administered by UNHCR.

By **decision 60/551** of the same date, it deferred consideration of the Board of Auditors' report on the capital master plan, as well as the related reports of the ACABQ [A/60/387, A/60/7/Add.12], until its resumed sixtieth (2006) session.

Review of UN administrative and financial functioning

On 13 April, by **decision 59/556**, the General Assembly took note of the Secretary-General's report on the review of the structure and functions of all liaison offices or representation in New York of organizations headquartered elsewhere but funded from the regular budget [A/59/395] and the related ACABQ report [A/59/552].

In compliance with Assembly resolution 54/236 [YUN 1999, p. 1317] and its endorsement of the CPC recommendation that a progress report on the review of the efficiency of the UN administrative and financial functioning be submitted biennially, the Secretary-General transmitted an April report [A/60/70] on progress and impact achieved by management improvement measures across the UN global Secretariat. The analysis drew on the second round of quantitative data from the Organization's online tool for tracking management reforms, the Progress and Impact Reporting System (PIRS). The report incorporated enhanced methodology, further advancing the quantitative assessment of impact and an expansion of the reporting so as to incorporate actions from the Secretary-General's 2002 reform agenda in the sphere of administrative and financial management improvements.

CPC, in June [A/60/16], took note of the Secretary-General's report, as well as the improvements to the presentation of information and the refinement to the methodology, which had taken into account previous comments of the Committee. It recommended that the Secretary-General implement the remaining recommendations, further refine the methodology and extend coverage of the data. The Committee invited the Assembly to review the appropriateness of continued consideration of the agenda item entitled "Review of the efficiency of the administrative and financial functioning of the United Nations" by the Committee, taking into account Assembly resolutions 54/236 and 59/275 [YUN 2004, p. 1401].

By **decision 60/503** of 20 September, the Assembly included the item in the agenda of its sixtieth session and allocated it to the Fifth Committee. The Committee had before it the reports of the Secretary-General on measures to strengthen accountability at the United Nations [A/60/312], the contribution made by the Department of Management to improve management practices [A/60/342] and the related ACABQ report [A/60/418].

On 23 December, the Assembly decided that the item on the review of the efficiency of the administrative and financial functioning of the United Nations would remain for consideration at its resumed sixtieth (2006) session (**decision 60/551**).

Programme planning

CPC, in informal consultations at its June/July session [A/60/16], resumed its consideration of the Secretary-General's report on priority-setting [YUN 2004, p. 1403]. Noting that Member States had been unable to reach an agreement on many aspects of the question, the view was expressed that it was the responsibility of Member States to designate priorities at the macro level for the Organization and that priority-setting was key to the UN programme planning and budgeting process. Difficulties to priority-setting were highlighted, such as the requirement to implement all legislative mandates, the non-sectoral structure of the strategic framework of the medium-term plan, the General Assembly's failure to designate priorities by programme or subprogramme, and the Assembly's decision in resolution 53/207 [YUN 1998, p. 1294] that the priorities contained in the budget outline should conform with those of the medium-term plan. The view was held that the Secretary-General should have the authority to make judgements at the subprogramme level, while others felt that priority-setting at all levels was the prerogative of Member States. It was noted that the majority of the conclusions in the report had been reflected in previous CPC reports.

In view of Assembly resolution 58/269 on strengthening of the United Nations: an agenda for further change [YUN 2003, p. 1395], it was felt that the Committee's recommendations should focus on issues relevant to the question of priority-setting within the context of more recent developments. In conclusion, the Committee emphasized that priority-setting in the Organization was an intergovernmental process and represented its longer-term objectives.

The Committee recommended that the Assembly approve the narrative of programme 27, safety and security, of the biennial programme plan for the 2006-2007 biennium [A/59/806], subject to modifications.

By **decision 60/551**, the Assembly deferred consideration of the report of the CPC on the work of its forty-forth (2005) session until the Assembly's resumed sixtieth (2006) session.

Programme performance

Evaluation

OIOS report. Pursuant to General Assembly resolution 58/269 [YUN 2003, p. 1395], OIOS, in collaboration with JIU, submitted a report [A/60/73] on proposals for strengthening and monitoring programme performance and evaluation, which contained the final report of the Working Group on Monitoring and Evaluation, established by OIOS to develop proposals and ensure broad support among departments and offices. JIU comments on the report of the Working Group were integrated into the conclusion and the annex to the report.

The Working Group found that, despite recent progress, the current monitoring and evaluation system required improvements in order to have a noticeable impact on future plans and decisions. The roles of the three main stakeholder groups, namely, the intergovernmental bodies, OIOS and programme and senior managers of the Secretariat needed to be clarified and their responsibilities enhanced. Other recommendations by the Working Group emphasized the need for intergovernmental bodies to use monitoring and evaluation findings as a basis for making action-oriented recommendations and decisions; programme planning to remain as a standing item on the agendas of the Assembly, its main committees and intergovernmental bodies; OIOS to strengthen its central monitoring and evaluation facility; and the integration and improvement of the existing results-based management tools and techniques, in particular the development of a new version of the Integrated Monitoring and Documentation Information System (IMDIS), in consultation with programme managers, to increase their use of IMDIS as a monitoring tool.

Concurring with the Working Group's proposals, JIU stressed that the complexity of the performance measurement system, as well as the burden placed on managers for data collection and on the governing bodies for data analysis, represented the largest risk threatening the successful implementation of results-based management. The Group urged the three main stakeholders to complete implementation of the action items contained in the report without delay.

OIOS reports to CPC. The Secretary-General transmitted to CPC a number of OIOS evaluation reports on linkages between headquarters and field activities: a review of best practices for poverty eradication in the framework of the UN Millennium Declaration [YUN 2000, p. 49] [E/AC.51/2005/2]; an in-depth evaluation of the United Nations Human Settlement Programme [E/AC.51/2005/3]; the triennial review of the implementation of CPC recommendations made at its forty-second session on the in-depth evaluation of General Assembly and Economic and Social Council affairs and Economic and Social Council support and coordination [E/AC.51/2005/4]; and the triennial review of the implementation of CPC recommendations made at its forty-second session on the in-depth evaluation of legal affairs [E/AC.51/2005/5].

CPC's comments and recommendations on those reports were contained in the report on its 2005 session [A/60/16]. By **decision 2005/225**, the Economic and Social Council took note of the CPC report.

On 20 October [A/C.5/60/11], the Assembly President transmitted to the Chairman of the Fifth Committee the deliberations of the Second (Economic and Financial) Committee on the first two reports and its additional comments thereon.

The Assembly deferred consideration of the CPC report on the work at its 2005 session and the OIOS report on proposals for strengthening and monitoring programme performance and evaluation, and the letter of its President to the Chairman of the Fifth Committee to its resumed sixtieth (2006) session (**decision 60/551**).

Chapter III

United Nations staff

During 2005, the General Assembly, through the International Civil Service Commission (ICSC), continued to review the conditions of service of staff of the UN common system. ICSC made recommendations to the Assembly on matters related to the conditions of service of the UN staff, including base/floor salary scale, mobility and hardship allowances and the scale of staff assessment. The Commission also conducted a study of the grade equivalencies between the United Nations and the United States federal civil service, as well as reviews of the pay and benefits system, hazard pay levels and best prevailing conditions of employment in Paris and Montreal.

The Secretary-General reported on: after-service health insurance; measures to strengthen accountability in the United Nations; staff composition; equitable geographic distribution; availability of skills in local labour markets; suspension of recruitment for staff in the General Service and related categories; staff rules and regulations; gratis personnel; financial accountability of staff; redeployment of posts; the UN System Staff College; headquarters agreements; protection from sexual abuse and exploitation; safety and security of UN personnel; conditions of travel; the Administrative Law Unit; the Office of the Ombudsman; criminal behaviour and disciplinary matters; the management review of the appeals process; and the work of the Joint Appeals Board (JAB). The Joint Inspection Unit issued reports on a common payroll and the harmonization of the conditions of travel for the UN system.

In continuing efforts to strengthen accountability in the United Nations, the Secretary-General proposed the establishment of an Oversight Committee to act as an independent advisory body. In April, the Assembly strengthened the investigation function of the Office of Internal Oversight services.

Conditions of service

International Civil Service Commission

The International Civil Service Commission (ICSC), a 15-member body established in 1974 by General Assembly resolution 3357(XXIX) [YUN 1975, p. 875], continued in 2005 to regulate and coordinate the conditions of service and the salaries and allowances of the UN common system.

ICSC held its sixtieth (Bangkok, Thailand, 28 February–11 March) and sixty-first (New York, 11-22 July) sessions, at which it considered, in addition to organizational matters, the conditions of service applicable to both Professional and General Service categories of staff, and those relating specifically to the Professional and higher categories and to the General Service and other locally recruited categories.

The deliberations, recommendations and decisions of ICSC on those matters were detailed in its thirty-first annual report to the Assembly [A/60/30 & Corr.1] (see sections below).

In a 10 October statement on the administrative and financial implications of ICSC decisions and recommendations for the 2006-2007 programme budget [A/60/421 & Corr.1], the Secretary-General estimated the additional resulting requirements at $5,669,300, net of staff assessment, which would be repleted in the recosting of the proposed programme budget.

On 18 October [A/60/7/Add.3], the Advisory Committee on Administrative and Budgetary Questions (ACABQ) indicated that it had no objection to the Secretary-General's approach and intention to reflect the additional requirements in the re-costing of the 2006-2007 proposed programme budget.

The Assembly, in section XVII of **resolution 60/248** of 23 December (see p. 1496) approved the amount of $16,211,300 for ICSC for the 2006-2007 biennium. On the same date, the Assembly deferred consideration of the 2005 ICSC report, the Secretary-General's statement on the programme budget implications of the ICSC recommendations and the related ACABQ report, until its resumed sixtieth (2006) session (**decision 60/551**).

Functioning of ICSC

The Commission had before it information submitted by its secretariat on the implementation or follow-up by common system organizations to its 2003-2004 decisions and/or recommendations. The Commission noted the high number of responses to its request for information and their clarity and hoped that the trend would continue. Expressing an interest in initiatives introduced by some organizations to encourage mobility and noting that the number of staff in the National Professional Officer category had increased, the Commission requested an update of mobility policies in organizations in 2007; a secretariat review of the status of National Professional Officers; and a report on the use of that category of staff to be presented at the Commission's (2006) session.

The Commission also considered a report on General Assembly actions taken at its fifty-ninth (2004) session concerning the UN common system, as well as details on resolutions and decisions adopted by the governing bodies of common system organizations. Commission members indicated that, while the information was useful, the report should have included a complete reference to specific decisions reflected in the text of the resolution. Emphasis was also placed on the need for quick and easy access to the Fifth (Administrative and Budgetary) Committee news briefs via the UN intranet.

Strengthening of ICSC

CEB consideration. At its ninth session (Geneva, 4-5 April) [CEB/2005/3], the High-level Committee on Management (HLCM) heard statements by the United Nations Chief Executives Board for Coordination (CEB) secretariat and the spokesperson of the Human Resources (HR) Network on the status of the Fifth Committee's consideration of the report of the High-level Panel on the Strengthening of ICSC [YUN 2004, p. 1410]. The Committee reaffirmed the view that the strengthening of ICSC and its functioning, pursuant to the Panel's recommendations, was of critical importance to the organizations and staff of the UN common system. It requested executive heads to convey that importance to Member States and to urge them to support a constructive review of the Panel's recommendations.

On 13 April, the General Assembly deferred consideration of the High-level Panel's report and the related comments by the Secretary-General and CEB [ibid., p. 1411] (**decision 59/551 B**). It also decided to consider, as a matter of priority, the question of the strengthening of the ICSC during its sixtieth (2005) session (**decision 59/561**).

On 23 December, the Assembly further deferred consideration of the High-level Panel's report and the related comments on the report by the Secretary-General and CEB (**decision 60/551**).

Remuneration issues

Pursuant to the standing mandate in General Assembly resolutions 47/216 [YUN 1992, p. 1055] and 55/223 [YUN 2000, p. 1331], ICSC continued to review the relationship between the net remuneration of UN staff in the Professional and higher categories (grades P-1 to D-2) in New York, and that of the current comparator, the United States federal civil service employees in comparable positions in Washington, D.C. (referred to as the margin). In its 2005 report to the Assembly [A/60/30 & Corr.1], ICSC noted that a net remuneration margin of 111.1 was forecast for 2005, based on existing grade equivalencies between United Nations and United States officials in comparable positions, as shown in annex V to its report. The actual year-to-year (2004 to 2005) gross increase for Washington, D.C., taking into account both the employment cost index and locality pay adjustment, was 3.71 per cent, effective 1 January 2005. In view of the rise in the comparator's civil service salaries as from 1 January 2005, the Commission found that an adjustment of the UN common system's scale of 2.49 per cent would be necessary in 2006 in order to maintain the base/floor scale in line with the comparator. ICSC, therefore, recommended that the base/floor salary scale for the Professional and higher categories be increased by 2.49 per cent through the standard consolidation procedures, on a no-loss/no-gain basis, with effect from 1 January 2006. The proposed staff assessment rates and associated base/floor salary scale were shown in annexes VI and VII of the report.

It further noted that the imbalances in the Tax Equalization Fund would require a reduction in staff assessment to lower the Fund by 20 per cent. While net salaries would not be impacted, gross salaries of the scale would be lower by 20 per cent.

On the basis of the 2003 revised methodology for surveys of best prevailing conditions of employment at Headquarters and non-Headquarters duty stations [YUN 2003, p. 1435], ICSC conducted two surveys of best prevailing conditions of service for the General Service category of staff: one in Paris, France, and the other in Montreal, Canada, with reference dates of October 2004 and April 2005, respectively. The surveys resulted in the recommendation of a new salary scale for each location, as reproduced in annexes IX and X of the ICSC report, and revised rates for dependency allowances. The financial implications associated with the revised salary scales and rates of dependency allowances in Paris were estimated at $750,000 per annum and in Montreal $1.17 million per annum.

The Commission also reviewed dependency allowances, including spouse benefits and the level of children's and secondary dependant's allowances (see p. 1509).

Statement by Secretary-General. In a 10 October statement [A/60/421 & Corr.1] on the administrative and financial implications of ICSC decisions and recommendations for the 2006-2007 programme budget, the Secretary-General indicated that the adjustment of the base/floor salary scale, implemented by standard method on a no-loss/no-gain basis, had been calculated by ICSC on an annual basis in the amount of $2,811,900, which included $2,380,000 for the mobility/hardship allowance and $431,900 for the scale of separation payments. Duty stations with low post adjustment that would otherwise fall below the level of the new base/floor would not be impacted. The financial implications of the ICSC recommendation for the proposed 2006-2007 programme budget would amount to $5,669,300 in additional requirements, net of staff assessment and would be reflected in the recosting of the proposed programme budget estimates, as well as the reduction of $48,890,000 in requirements for staff assessment.

ACABQ report. On 18 October [A/60/7/Add.3], ACABQ stated that it had no objection to the Secretary-General's approach. However, it concluded that the term "no-loss/no-gain" used in the Secretary-General's statement to substantiate a 2.49 per cent increase in the base/floor salary scale, needed further explanation to demonstrate whether or not an upward adjustment of the base/floor salary scale, when implemented through the method of consolidating post adjustment multiplier points, would actually result in no additional cost to United Nations. Questioning the cost neutrality beyond the date of implementation, particularly with regard to the management of the post adjustment system, ACABQ indicated that an explanation should be provided to the Fifth Committee and included in all future statements on ICSC recommendations. It also recommended that if necessary, the term "no-loss/no-gain" should be replaced with another term that would better describe the consolidation of post adjustment multiplier points into the base/floor salary scales.

On 23 December, the General Assembly, in section XI of **resolution 60/248** (see p. 1495), approved the new scale of staff assessment recommended by ICSC, with effect from 1 January 2006.

Post adjustment

ICSC continued to keep under review the operation of the post adjustment system, designed to measure cost-of-living discrepancies. It considered the report of its Advisory Committee on Post Adjustment Questions on the work of its twenty-seventh session (New York, 17-25 January). The report included recommendations on methodological issues of the post adjustment index calculations; preparatory activities for the next round of place-to-place surveys scheduled for 2005 at headquarters duty stations and Washington, D.C., and the practical aspects of conducting those surveys; guidelines on further studies to be carried out by the ICSC secretariat with respect to product comparability; and analyses of rent data from staff and external sources. The Commission endorsed the Advisory Committee's recommendations and agreed that it should review the survey results at its next (2006) meeting and submit a recommendation to the Commission in 2006.

Noblemaire principle

In 2005, following its 2004 in-depth review of the Noblemaire principle and its application [YUN 2004, p. 1412], ICSC commenced its study to determine the highest-paid national civil service, utilizing the two-phase methodology it had recommended in 1991 [YUN 1991, p. 905]. At its sixtieth session [A/60/30 & Corr.1], ICSC reviewed the data collected in phase I of the study, which had identified four national civil services for consideration in the phase II analysis, namely those of Belgium, Germany, Singapore and Switzerland. It decided to proceed with the analysis of those civil services and to collect information on remuneration levels of the World Bank and the Organisation for Economic Cooperation and Development (OECD) as a reference check only. At its sixty-first session, the secretariat presented the additional information on Germany, Singapore and Switzerland, but had yet to collect information from Belgium and the organizations earmarked for the reference check. In its discussion, the Commission recalled that both the German and Swiss civil services were included in its previous (1994-1995) Noblemaire study [YUN 1995, p. 1404] and that neither civil service had been deemed appropriate as the Noblemaire comparator. On the basis of current data collected from Germany, the Commission noted that benefit, leave and work-hour provisions had generally deteriorated, or at best had remained the same in a few cases, while salary levels had been subject to constraints since the 1995 exercise. As for Switzerland, the salary system had been revised—suggesting lower salary levels than those of the comparator—and the benefit structure had not indicated any significant improvement since 1995. With regard to Singapore, its confidentiality requirements had restricted the collection of all relevant salary data by the Commission, other than base salary, which made it difficult to adequately apply the Noblemaire principle. Furthermore, on the basis of a total compensation approach, ICSC did not find the Singaporean civil service better paid than the current comparator.

In the case of all three civil services, the Commission concluded that the resources required to conduct a full phase II study, particularly for the actuarial comparisons of the relevant benefit structures, would not be well spent. It took note of the progress made in the study and decided to discontinue any further study of Germany, Singapore and Switzerland. It would continue the study of Belgium and conduct the reference check with regard to the World Bank and OECD. The Commission requested its secretariat to provide a progress report on the item at its sixty-second (2006) session.

Grade equivalencies

In 2005, keeping with its practice to periodically review grade equivalencies every five years and pursuant to its 2004 decision to conduct a grade-equivalency study for the revised structure of the comparator's Senior Executive Service (SES) [YUN 2004, p. 1412], ICSC considered the item at its sixtieth and sixty-first sessions [A/60/30 & Corr.1]. The study involved the use of two comparison methods: one that assigned a midpoint or average salary to all members of the United States SES positions, and the other that linked the common system grades with the comparator's performance based SES salaries. However, as a result of ongoing changes in the structure of the United States federal civil service, and the consequential difficulties experienced by the secretariat in obtaining relevant data for the SES positions, the Commission deferred consideration of the issue to its sixty-first session.

A July update on progress indicated that during discussions held with the United States Office of Personnel Management, it had been noted that the application of performance pay was contingent on certification of a department's performance management system. Furthermore, there was no uniform application of the broadbanded salary structure, as agencies used different criteria, ranging from performance to responsibility, in order to work criticality for movement through the band. From a random sample of 51 SES positions reviewed, interviews were conducted on 44 positions in 10 departments. An independent evaluation of each position was also carried out. It was found that, if a certified performance management system was in place, the SES pay range was set at $107,550 to

$162,100 and where there was none in place, the range was $107,550 to $149,200. Departments were not allowed to utilize the full SES pay range, unless a certified performance system had been implemented. Inconsistencies and variances in banding configurations across departments were also indicated.

In the discussion, the Commission noted that, even though official certification of the performance management systems by the United States Office of Personnel Management was a requirement, decisions concerning the management of pay-for-performance systems, including the size of the payout, were the responsibility of the individual department and had resulted in variances. One member suggested the development of separate pay-for-performance systems for managers in the UN system. Other members questioned the validity of the United States Civil Service SES as an appropriate comparison, since the salaries were based on the person, whereas in the United Nations common system, it was based on the position.

The Commission took note of the progress made and looked forward to a report on the grade equivalency exercise from its secretariat in 2006.

Other remuneration issues

Conditions of service and compensation for non-Secretariat officials

Judges of ICJ and international tribunals

At its resumed fifty-ninth (2005) session, the General Assembly, pursuant to its decision 59/551 [YUN 2004, p. 1413], considered the Secretary-General's report [ibid., p. 1412] on the conditions of service and compensation of members of the International Court of Justice (ICJ), judges of the International Tribunal for the former Yugoslavia (ICTY) and of the International Criminal Tribunal for Rwanda (ICTR) and ad litem judges for both Tribunals, as well as the related ACABQ report [ibid., p. 1413], in which the Committee had recommended that the annual salary of ICJ members be set at $177,000 effective 1 January 2005.

The Assembly, in section III of **resolution 59/282** (see p. 1487), increased both the annual salary of the members of the Court and the judges and ad litem judges of the Tribunals and the annual value of all pensions in payment, by 6.3 per cent, pending a decision, based on the comprehensive report of the Secretary-General, on the question of pensions to be submitted to its sixty-first (2006) session. It also decided, with retroactive effect from 1 January 2005, that Members of the Court maintaining a bona fide primary residence at The Hague for up to nine continuous years during their Court service should be eligible, upon the completion of their appointment and resettlement outside the Netherlands, to receive a prorated lump sum.

Dependency allowances

Pursuant to a 2001 Commission decision [YUN 2001, p. 1341] to undertake a comprehensive review of allowances payable in the UN common system, ICSC conducted a review of dependency benefits in 2005 [A/60/30 & Corr.1], especially spouse benefits (including dependency and single rates, and salary structure) and children's and secondary dependant's allowances. The Commission re-examined the rationale and purpose of the spouse benefit for staff in the Professional and higher categories and identified the appropriate place of the spouse benefit in the overall pay and benefits package of common system staff. It noted that dependency benefits to staff in the Professional and higher categories were provided in the form of higher net salaries for staff with a primary dependant—as compared with those who had no primary dependant—and by flat-rate allowances for children and secondary dependants. While one salary scale was applied equally to staff with or without dependants, lower amounts of staff assessment were applied to gross salary for those staff with either a dependent spouse or child, resulting in a higher net base salary than that for single staff members. Agreeing with the Human Resources Network that one of the principles underlying the current system was that of "equal pay for equal work", the Commission emphasized that gross salary was the same for all UN staff, regardless of marital status or the number of children, and the system took into account the fact that additional expenditures were incurred by staff members with dependents. That principle was also recognized by the United States federal civil service (the current comparator) through its tax system, where single tax payers paid higher tax rates. Higher net salaries for dependency status were also the result of the tax system of most countries. It was noted that the system of base salary and allowances was developed nearly 30 years ago and as work realities and values had evolved, the Commission should examine how best to reflect that fact.

The Commission decided to maintain the distinction in remuneration between staff with and without primary dependants and the current ratios between the single and dependency rates of the base/floor salary scale. Pursuant to General Assembly resolution 59/268 [YUN 2004, p. 1408], the Commission reported to the Assembly that the rationale for doing so was directly linked to the practices of Member States that maintained such a differentiation in their tax systems.

Education grant

Practices of other civil services and international organizations

In response to a General Assembly request in resolution 59/268 [YUN 2004, p. 1408] that it be informed about the practices of other civil services and international organizations with regard to the provision of education grants, ICSC reviewed information that had been recently collected by OECD, which provided details of each education grant scheme for both international organizations and relevant national civil services. The data indicated that all international organizations and some national civil services provided for tertiary education under their schemes. However, as the OECD submission lacked details on UN comparator practices, separate information was provided by the ICSC secretariat, which compared comparator maximum education grant levels to UN common system maximum levels on a country-by-country basis. It also assessed the merits and disadvantages of adopting the comparator practices for UN common system purposes.

The Commission took note of the information provided and requested its secretariat to summarize the results for presentation to the Assembly.

Review of methodology

The Commission, under its ongoing review of the pay and benefits system continued to review the methodology for determining the level of the education grant. It considered its secretariat's proposals relating to the lump-sum approach, including the general outline of that approach, and specific issues relating to the selection of representative schools; the proposed new currency zoning for education grant ceilings; the adjustment of the maxima and cost controls; individual certification requirements; and the periodicity of the review of education grant levels.

The Commission asked its secretariat to continue its work, in collaboration with organizations and staff representatives, on developing proposals on education grant methodologies on the basis of current principles of the scheme, and in particular, the lump-sum approach. It should also develop models illustrating the practicality of the various review proposals, with a view to ensuring fairness, simplification and cost control, and report to the Commission on the issue at its sixty-third (2006) session.

Mobility and hardship allowance

ICSC continued its review of the current mobility and hardship scheme approved in 1989 [YUN 1989, p. 886] to compensate staff for service at difficult duty stations and to encourage operational mobility. At it's fifty-ninth (2004) session the Commission had decided to separate the mobility element from the hardship element and to delink both allowances from the base/floor salary scale [YUN 2004, p. 1415]. It also established a working group to develop options for compensating staff for services at hardship duty stations and for encouraging mobility, estimate the cost of those options and submit its recommendations to the Commission in 2005. The working group, using cost neutrality as the guiding principle and taking constraint into account, proposed the transference of funds from one element to another as an option for attaining cost neutrality. Although each element was treated separately, the group considered the proposal as a single package because of the integrated manner of its design.

For the mobility element, the proposed changes included flat amount payments to replace the percentages linked to the base/floor; the calculation of differentials for single and dependency rates by reference to flat amounts; clustering of the number of assignments for payment purposes; recognizing up to seven moves instead of the current five; no extension of payments for mobility after five years in the same location; and a review of payments every three years. A comparison between the current and proposed mobility scheme reflected a decrease of $22,392, which would be reallocated to support an increase to the hardship component.

Under the changes proposed for the hardship element, flat amount payments would replace the percentages linked to the base/floor; differentials for single and dependency rates would be calculated by reference to flat amounts; payments would be reviewed every three years; and higher payments would be made for assignments to more difficult duty stations. A comparison between the current and proposed hardship scheme reflected an increase of $4,385,069, which was accommodated through decreases in the mobility and the non-removal elements of the current scheme. Changes to the non-removal element were the same as for the hardship element, except that no distinction would be made between the amounts paid for the various duty stations and no extension of payment would be permitted beyond five years. Definitions for mobility and for hardship were also recommended. In determining the degree of hardship, consideration would be given to local conditions of safety and security, health care, education, housing, climate, isolation, or the availability of the basic amenities of life that resulted in less than acceptable standard of living for staff and their families. The concept of mobility would include movement within and across organizations, occupations and geographic locations. For the purpose of the scheme, mobility was defined as the geographic reassignment of a staff member for a period of one year or more from one duty station to another.

With regard to its consideration of assignment grant proposals, the Group recommended that two months' salary representing the assignment grant for the most dangerous duty stations should be paid in its entirety at the beginning of any assignment, which would be three or more years in duration.

The Commission approved the definitions proposed for mobility and hardship and endorsed the new arrangements for mobility, hardship, non-removal and assignment grant, as well as the modalities and review cycle proposed for updating allowances. It also recommended that the General Assembly approve the proposed arrangements and definitions and implement the new systems with effect from 1 July 2006.

CEB consideration. At its tenth session (New York, 10-11 October) [CEB/2005/5], HLCM adopted a statement on the new mobility and hardship scheme proposed by ICSC, which would replace the current matrix format. It was projected that the new scheme would continue to provide incentives to staff to serve at hardship duty stations and to be geographically mobile, as well as be easier to administer and more transparent to staff. The statement also reflected the Organization's disagreement with the decisions of ICSC [YUN 2004, p. 1415] and the General Assembly in resolution 59/268 [ibid. 1408] to decouple the adjustment of the mobility and hardship allowance from the base/floor salary scale.

The Committee approved the CEB statement for transmittal to the Assembly's sixtieth (2005) session, and was later issued as a note by the Secretary-General [A/60/273].

Hazard pay

The Commission, in reviewing the principle for granting hazard pay—payment for employment under conditions where war or active hostilities prevailed and the evacuation of families and non-essential staff had taken place—considered proposals on the level of such pay for locally and internationally recruited staff, for revising the criteria for its payment and for applying the same adjustment mechanism and periodicity for review as that for mobility, hardship and non-removal allowances.

The Commission decided to establish the level of hazard pay for internationally recruited staff at $1,300 per month as of 1 January 2006; retain the current level of hazard pay for locally recruited staff (25 per cent of the midpoint of the local salary scale for General Service staff); and approved a three-year review cycle, to be done simultaneously with the review of the allowances for mobility, hardship and non-removal; and to apply the same indicators used in updating those allowances when reviewing the level of hazard pay. The financial implications for the revised level of hazard pay were estimated at $1,440,990 per month.

Definition of hazard pay. The working group established to develop options for compensating staff for services at hardship duty stations and for encouraging mobility (see above) also considered proposals on hazard pay. The Group recommended to ICSC that the definition of hazard pay be revised to include the risk of life-threatening diseases, such as the severe acute respiratory syndrome (SARS) and the Ebola virus, to which medical personnel were directly exposed in the performance of their duties. The Commission approved the definition of the criteria for hazard pay as proposed in annex III of the report.

Entitlements of staff serving in non-family duty stations

In response to General Assembly resolution 59/266 [YUN 2004, p. 1418], ICSC considered the issue of harmonization of practices relating to the entitlements of staff serving at non-family duty stations. The Commission had before it detailed information on the practices of common system organizations on the subject, as well as a report by the organizations, which, inter alia, explained the rationale for the separate maintenance of the special operations approach and the mission subsistence approach. The special operations approach was used by the funds and programmes for staff assigned to longer but defined periods and with traditional entitlements, whereas mission subsistence allowance was used exclusively for those assigned to special peacekeeping operations and for political and peacebuilding missions. The rationale for maintaining two separate systems was the need to address two situations, which differed with regard to the mandate of the organization or mission, the duration of assignment, the type and limitation of employment, the manner and purpose of deployment, the number of staff in a duty station or mission area, family considerations and eligibility to receive entitlements. An increasing number of field-oriented organizations had applied the special operations approach. Organizations had agreed on a revised procedure to calculate the special operations living allowance,

which would be a monthly payment based exclusively on the daily subsistence allowance after 60 days. To help organizations make the adjustment, ICSC would have to update all non-capital-city daily subsistence allowance rates.

The Commission noted that the financial implications relating to the move from mission subsistence allowance rates, where applicable, to the after-60-day daily subsistence allowance were estimated at $2.98 million system-wide. It agreed with the rationale for maintaining two separate approaches under the special operations and mission subsistence regimes and endorsed the proposed change from mission subsistence allowance to the after-60-day daily subsistence allowance rate as the basis for calculating the special operations living allowance under the special operations approach.

After-service health insurance benefits

In response to resolution 58/249 A [YUN 2003, p. 1428], the Secretary-General submitted an October report [A/60/450 & Corr.1] on liabilities and proposed funding for after-service health insurance benefits, which provided overviews on the extent and recognition of liability, UN funding measures, revisions to the after-service health insurance provisions and the valuation reports of the ICTY, ICTR and the UN Compensation Commission. It also included details pertaining to action by funds, programmes and other organizations, along with a historical perspective on the after-service health insurance programme.

Actuarial studies had estimated that the current value of the accrued after-service health insurance liability, as at 31 December 2003, for the United Nations and common system organizations covered in the report, ranged from $0.5 million to $1,484.9 million, with a combined total of $4,022.9 million. Seven organizations had taken steps to both recognize and fund the actuarial liability from several sources, while others had not yet made provisions and were awaiting action by the United Nations prior to finalizing their plans to fund the liabilities.

The Secretary-General indicated that the UN external auditors and those of its agencies had stressed the need for organizations to fund their after-service health benefit obligations. A wide range of funding mechanisms would need to be put into place by the respective organizations with the approval of the appropriate governing bodies. Possible sources of funding for UN liabilities included the surplus held in reserves and special funds. However, if the General Assembly approved to fund the liability from a 4 per cent charge on payroll costs and from General Fund surpluses, it would result in Member States being required to pay more in assessed or pledged contributions.

The Secretary-General proposed changes in the after-service health insurance provisions, including increasing the eligibility requirements for subsidy from 10 to 15 years minimum participation with a "buy-in" provision after 10 years of participation; application of a theoretical pension of a minimum of 25 years of service as the basis for assessing retiree contributions, as opposed to using the actual number of years of service when less than 25; and introducing a minimum participation requirement for eligibility of dependants of at least five years at the time of retirement.

The Secretary-General requested the Assembly to approve, for initial funding of after-service health insurance benefits, an amount of $350,000; for ongoing funding, a charge equivalent to 4 per cent of salary costs; the utilization of unspent budget appropriations and the transfer of any excess income and savings; the proposed changes to the after-service health insurance provisions. It should authorize full recognition of the after-service health-insurance liability on financial statements and approve finding of liabilities as at 1 January 2006 for ICTY and ICTR and the United Nations Compensation Commission.

ACABQ report. In November [A/60/7/Add.11], ACABQ stated that, while the Secretary-General had estimated that the present value as at 31 December 2003 of accrued after-service health insurance liability of future benefits was $1,484.9 million, the underlying methodology for arriving at that estimate had not been clearly explained. Observing that after-service health insurance liabilities had probably escalated since 2003, the Committee stressed that updated data should be made available to the General Assembly before any decision on the matter was taken. It requested detailed information on how other estimates were derived, including those on provisions for current retirees and active employees currently eligible to retire with after-service health insurance benefits. ACABQ agreed in principle with the proposal to charge a certain percentage of salary costs as a means of building a fund for after-service health insurance payments, but wanted more detailed analysis before it could recommend a percentage. Special attention should be paid to the relationship between an additional charge on salary costs and programme support costs applied to extrabudgetary activities. Moreover, the proposal to utilize savings did not appear to be in line with the best management practices, was not transparent, might encourage overbudgeting and was not in keeping with Assembly resolution 56/237 [YUN

2001, p. 810], by which savings achieved through efficiency gains were to be directed to the Development Account. It recommended approval of the changes to the provision of the after-service health insurance programme.

The Assembly deferred consideration of the Secretary-General's report on after-service health insurance and the related ACABQ report until its resumed sixtieth (2006) session (**decision 60/551**).

Other staff matters

Managerial efficiency and strengthening accountability

Senior Management Network

CEB action. At it's ninth regular session [CEB/2005/3] (Geneva, 4-5 April), HLCM considered a progress report on the establishment of a Senior Management Service in the United Nations, which had been approved by CEB in 2004 [YUN 2004, p. 1415] as a means of strengthening managerial and leadership capacity throughout the Organization. Following consultations with members of the Human Resources Network and in response to a request of the General Assembly in resolution 59/268 [ibid., p. 1408], it was proposed to rename the Service as the Senior Management Network, in order to better reflect the purpose for the creation of a system-wide managerial network. Other developments included collaboration between the UN System Staff College and an inter-agency committee in evaluating proposals from institutions interested in developing the leadership programme to underpin the Service.

HLCM endorsed the redesignation of the Senior Management Service as the Senior Management Network and supported the development and implementation of the leadership development programme.

Note of Secretary-General. In an August note [A/60/209], the Secretary-General stated that the Senior Management Network would bring together senior managers throughout the UN system and executive heads would designate staff for participation in the Network and guide its direction. He emphasized that the Network did not involve any change in the conditions of service, compensation or contractual arrangements. The objectives of the Network included strengthening managerial and leadership capacity; building a common corporate culture; facilitating the devolution of responsibility and accountability in relation to core managerial functions; enhancing inter-agency cohesion and coordination and promoting mobility and learning across the system; and signalling a commitment to the professionalism of the management function. He also announced that a system-wide leadership programme being designed to support the Network was expected to be launched in 2006 for groups of senior managers from across the common system.

By **decision 60/551** of 23 December, the General Assembly deferred consideration of the Secretary-General's note until its resumed sixtieth (2006) session.

Strengthening accountability at the United Nations

Report of Secretary-General. Responding to General Assembly resolution 59/272 [YUN 2004, p. 1370], the Secretary-General submitted an August report [A/60/312] on measures taken to strengthen accountability at the United Nations, which outlined new measures developed, as well as those already initiated, under five thematic headings: measures for strengthening the accountability framework; strengthening oversight mechanisms; ensuring ethical conduct; enhancing transparency; and other measures. The report also provided information on the Secretariat's analysis of audit committees and the progress made on indicating time frames for the implementation of the recommendations of oversight bodies.

Among the measures adopted to strengthen the accountability framework was the replacement of the Accountability Panel with the Management Performance Board as of 13 May 2005 [ST/SGB/2005/13]. The Board, whose terms of reference and responsibilities were clearer and better defined than those of the Panel, would review the recommendations of the proposed oversight committee (see below); ensure that managers acted on issues identified by oversight bodies; monitor the manner in which senior managers exercised authority delegated to them, including their performance in achieving the objectives of human resources action plans; and review the outcome of the administration of justice proceedings in the Secretariat. As the Senior Management Group established in 1997 [YUN 1997, p. 1390] had proved to be too large for effective and timely decision-making, two smaller senior-level committees, a Policy Committee and a Management Committee, were created in 2005 to improve executive-level decision-making efforts. Mandatory induction programmes for senior officials were introduced, as well as a new method of defining performance expectations for programme delivery and results-based budgeting.

Performance indicators for all programmes, including peace-keeping missions were developed and performance measures—baselines and targets—were incorporated into the 2004-2005 and the proposed 2006-2007 programme budget. A revised e-PAS, an electronic enhancement of the original Performance Appraisal System (PAS), was also launched with new features, such as organizational core values and competencies, self-assessment by staff members, managerial competencies for supervisory staff, strengthened links between performance management and career development, and enhanced accountability measures, including an optional section for the comments of staff on supervision received. Conditions under which staff members might be held accountable and/or financially liable to the Organization for their actions were also defined.

The terms of condition for a United Nations oversight committee were also issued. The committee, an independent advisory panel to the Secretary-General, would ensure the systematic implementation of recommendations of oversight bodies; share audit-related information and lessons learned; and ensure that significant risks to the Organization were identified and mitigating measures taken. Other activities highlighted focused on efforts to enhance fraud and corruption prevention mechanisms and to strengthen the Office of Internal Oversight Services (OIOS). In April, by resolution 59/287 (see p. 1474), the Assembly strengthened the OIOS investigation function and decided that the results of all preliminary investigations conducted by programme managers should be reported to the Office. OIOS was thereby delegated independent, residual and exclusive authority to investigate the most serious cases (all "category one" cases involving high-risk complex matters and serious criminal crimes) and designated as the mandatory gateway of all "category two" (lower risk to the Organization) cases.

Efforts to enhance ethical conduct focused on the establishment of a UN Ethics Office (see p. 1476), broadening the financial disclosure policy, protecting against retaliation for reporting alleged misconduct, enhancing the codes of conduct and conflict-of-interest rules, incorporating ethics into staff training programmes, protecting against harassment in the workplace and aggressive pursuit of allegations of sexual abuse and exploitation by field personnel. Dissemination of information on the Secretary-General's decisions on disciplinary cases was emphasized to raise awareness and act as a deterrent, thereby enhancing ethical conduct.

In the area of enhancing transparency, the report summarized efforts to develop a new policy on access to UN information, implement the new process for the selection and appointment of senior officials, which utilized a Senior Appointment Group (SAG) for reviewing candidatures for appointment by the Secretary-General, constitute the Senior Review Group as a standing advisory body on the appointment and promotion to D-2 level posts and develop clear accounting standards.

In the light of issues raised by the Independent Inquiry Committee, which investigated the oil-for-food programme (see p. 1475), particularly the criticism of UN procurement practices, the Secretary-General commissioned a review, completed in June 2005, that compared existing procurement rules and regulations with the best global practices of outside organizations and companies to ensure that the improvements introduced since the mid to late 1990s met the highest global standards. The transparency achieved by the UN Procurement Service website was evaluated positively in the review. It indicated that the open approach of the Service to sourcing and vendor development was in line with that of leading public procurement agencies. In August 2005, the Secretary-General commissioned a full financial and internal control review of the current UN procurement system.

The Secretary-General also submitted a report on the efforts of the Department of Management to improve its practices, and a time-bound plan for the reduction of duplication, complexity and bureaucracy in UN administrative processes [A/60/342] (see p. 1470).

ACABQ report. In October [A/60/418], ACABQ, noting the Secretary-General's bulletin [ST/SGB/2005/18] establishing the Oversight Committee as of 15 September and outlining its role and functions, indicated that it would be difficult for the three internal members of the Oversight Committee to act in an independent capacity while performing their advisory role on the Committee, as specified in the report. Moreover, given the Oversight Committee's small membership, the absence of any one of its members could have a detrimental effect on its performance. ACABQ also expressed doubts over the appropriateness of the Oversight Committee's role in providing advice and suggestions on the priorities, long-term strategy and annual audit work plans of oversight bodies, as it questioned the independence of those bodies. It concluded that the terms of reference, composition and working methods of the Committee would need to be revisited in the light of any decision the General Assembly might take on the follow-up to the World Summit Outcome document (see p. 48).

On 23 December, the Assembly deferred until its resumed sixtieth (2006) session (**decision 60/551**) consideration of the reports of the Secretary-General and ACABQ on measures to strengthen accountability.

Personnel policies

Human resources management

The General Assembly, at its resumed fifty-ninth session in 2005, had before it reports and/or notes of the Secretary-General, consideration of which had been deferred from previous sessions on: implementation of multilingualism in the UN system [YUN 2003, p. 1451]; multilingualism [ibid.]; the report of ICSC on its fifty-sixth and fifty-seventh (2004) sessions [YUN 2004, p. 1408]; measures to prevent discrimination on the basis of nationality, race, gender, religion or language in the United Nations [ibid., p. 1432]; human resources management reform [ibid., p. 1416]; contractual agreements [ibid., p. 1424]; improving gender distribution in the Secretariat [ibid., p. 1428]; the study on the availability in local labour markets of the skills for which international recruitment for the General Service category takes place [ibid., p 1430]; and the review of the Headquarters Agreements concluded by organizations of the UN system on human resources issues affecting staff [ibid., p 1433]; and the list of staff of the United Nations Secretariat in 2004 [A/C.5/59/L.34].

In addition to those reports, the Assembly, at its sixtieth (2005) session, had before it the Secretary-General's reports on gratis personnel provided by Governments and other entities [A/59/716]; assessments of the system of geographical distribution and of the issues relating to possible changes in the number of posts subject to geographical distribution [A/59/724]; redeployment of posts [A/59/753]; special measures for protection from sexual exploitation and abuse [A/59/782]; amendments to staff rules [A/60/174]; safety and security of humanitarian personnel and protection of UN personnel [A/60/223 & Corr.1]; the study on the availability of skills in local labour markets for which international recruitment for the General Service category took place [A/60/262]; composition of the Secretariat [A/60/310]; coverage of staff by the malicious acts insurance policy on security spending by UN system organizations [A/60/317 & Corr.1]; report of the UN System Staff College on its work, activities and accomplishments [A/60/328]; suspension of recruitment for posts in the General Service and related categories [A/60/363]; amendments to the staff regulations [A/60/365]; and staffing of field missions, including the use of the 300 and 100 series of appointments [A/59/762] (see p. 150).

GENERAL ASSEMBLY ACTION

On 23 December [meeting 69], the General Assembly, on the recommendation of the Fifth (Administrative and Budgetary) Committee [A/60/603], adopted **resolution 60/238** without vote [agenda item 129].

Human resources management

The General Assembly,

Recalling Articles 8, 97, 100 and 101 of the Charter of the United Nations,

Recalling also its resolutions 49/222 A and B of 23 December 1994 and 20 July 1995, 51/226 of 3 April 1997, 52/219 of 22 December 1997, 52/252 of 8 September 1998, 53/221 of 7 April 1999, 55/258 of 14 June 2001, 56/280 of 27 March 2002, 57/305 of 15 April 2003, 58/296 of 18 June 2004 and 59/266 of 23 December 2004, as well as its other relevant resolutions and decisions,

Having considered the reports of the Secretary-General and the related report of the Advisory Committee on Administrative and Budgetary Questions, the report of the Office of Internal Oversight Services on the availability in local labour markets of the skills for which international recruitment for posts in the General Service category takes place and the report of the Joint Inspection Unit entitled "Review of headquarters agreements concluded by the organizations of the United Nations system: human resources issues affecting staff" and the comments of the Secretary-General and the United Nations System Chief Executives Board for Coordination thereon,

I

Composition of the Secretariat

1. *Requests* the Secretary-General to ensure that the highest standards of efficiency, competence and integrity serve as the paramount consideration in the employment of staff, with due regard for the principle of equitable geographical distribution, in accordance with Article 101, paragraph 3, of the Charter of the United Nations;

2. *Notes* that key human resources management targets are not being met by many departments;

3. *Also notes* the establishment of the Management Performance Board to replace the Accountability Panel as well as the functions and composition of the Board;

4. *Requests* the Secretary-General to submit to the General Assembly for consideration at its sixty-first session a report on the activities of the Management Performance Board since its inception, including how it has met the request of the General Assembly, contained in section I, paragraph 10, of its resolution 59/266, that the internal system of accountability with respect to human resources policies and objectives be strengthened in order to hold programme managers accountable for their performance in achieving the objectives contained in human resources action plans;

5. *Notes* that, owing to projected retirements, many Member States may become unrepresented and underrepresented during the period 2005-2009, and requests the Secretary-General to urgently take steps to address this matter;

6. *Recalls* section IV, paragraph 8, of its resolution 59/266, and reiterates its request that the Secretary-General include an analysis of the level of underrepresentation in his report on the composition of the Secretariat;

7. *Requests* the Secretary-General to provide to the General Assembly at its sixty-first session an assessment of recruitment to P-2 and P-3 posts, including the effect of the national competitive examinations and, if relevant, recommendations on how to improve this method of recruitment;

II

Amendments to the Staff Regulations and Rules

1. *Approves* the amendments to the Staff Regulations of the United Nations contained in the annex to the present resolution;

2. *Takes note* of the amendments to the Staff Rules;

III

Other matters

1. *Requests* the Secretary-General to report to the General Assembly at its sixty-first session on the practice of United Nations staff members having to renounce permanent residence status in a country outside the country of their nationality, including cases where staff members have been exceptionally authorized to retain permanent residence status in accordance with section 5.7 of the administrative instruction entitled "Visa status of non-United States staff members serving in the United States, members of their household and their household employees, and staff members seeking or holding permanent resident status in the United States", and the criteria used in making such exceptions;

2. *Also requests* the Secretary-General to report to the General Assembly at its sixty-first session on the implementation of the regulations governing the status, basic rights and duties of officials other than Secretariat officials and experts on mission, adopted in its resolution 56/280.

Annex

Amendments to the Staff Regulations

Regulation 1.2 Conflict of interest

For paragraph (n), substitute

(n) All staff members at the D-1 or L-6 level and above shall be required to file financial disclosure statements on appointment and at intervals thereafter as prescribed by the Secretary-General, in respect of themselves, their spouses and their dependent children, and to assist the Secretary-General in verifying the accuracy of the information submitted when so requested. The financial disclosure statements shall include certification that the assets and economic activities of the staff members, their spouses and their dependent children do not pose a conflict of interest with their official duties or the interests of the United Nations. The financial disclosure statements will remain confidential and will only be used, as prescribed by the Secretary-General, in making determinations pursuant to staff regulation 1.2 *(m)*. The Secretary-General may require other staff to file financial disclo-

sure statements as he deems necessary in the interest of the Organization.

Regulation 10.2

For the existing text, substitute

The Secretary-General may impose disciplinary measures on staff members whose conduct is unsatisfactory.

Sexual exploitation and sexual abuse constitute serious misconduct.

The Secretary-General may summarily dismiss a member of the staff for serious misconduct.

Pay and benefits system

In 2005, ICSC, continued its monitoring of the pilot study on pay-for-performance and broadbanding, initiated in 2004 [YUN 2004, p. 1424]. The Human Resources Network expressed concern on the need for flexibility in respect of the banding structure and the ability of organizations to set the bands to suit their individual needs, and on the participation of General Service together with Professional staff in the pilot studies, whereas the Commission's position was restrictive to the Professional category. In its discussion, the Commission addressed a number of issues raised by the volunteer organizations and consultants involved in the study, including study participants, control groups, the broadbanded model, duration of the pilot study, the competency component of the pilot study, peer review, client feed back and legal considerations. The Commission found the discussion useful and was encouraged by the progress made. However, concerned by the direction some of the test modalities had taken, it reminded the volunteer organizations that those modalities were the basis on which the study should be conducted, and any deviation required the Commission's prior approval.

Job Evaluation Master Standard

In 2005, ICSC continued its assessment of the implementation of the Job Evaluation Master Standard, a conceptual model of the new job evaluation system for the Professional and higher categories, presented at its fifty-seventh (2003) session [YUN 2003, p. 1445]. The system, designed to work from an automated platform, linked job design to the development of the competencies and supported performance management in an integrated manner. Having received an interim report in 2004 and a further update at its sixty-first (2005) session, the Commission indicated that of 18 organizations, twelve had implemented the new job evaluation system, resulting in the classification of approximately 1,400 posts, with the remaining six in the process of implementation. Organizations reported that, while the new system was simpler to use and allowed for faster

classification action, there were concerns with regard to the clarity of language and interpretation of terminology. Actions discussed and agreed upon by a number of organizations included, a glossary to address interpretation difficulties; updated training materials; alternative security provisions for the web-based job evaluation system; system-wide access to organizational post illustrations; and a virtual network of advisers.

The Commission encouraged organizations to increase the rate of implementation and endorsed the enhancements proposed by its secretariat. The Commission requested its secretariat to ensure that a random sample of UN jobs was classified by reference to the new job evaluation standard in preparation for the grade equivalency study (see p. 1508) with the United States federal civil service and to report in 2006, including on the number of grade levels of posts classified and any changes to those grade levels as a result of classification action taken.

Contractual arrangements

In follow-up to its 2004 decision [YUN 2004, p. 1425], ICSC considered the revised model contract for three contractual categories: continuing appointments, fixed-term appointments and temporary appointments. The Human Resources Network agreed that the proposed text was acceptable as a framework for contractual agreements. The Commission confirmed two types of requirements under temporary appointments: one of a short-term nature for less than one year and the other for functions required up to four years to accommodate urgent operational requirements for defined periods, such as peacekeeping, humanitarian assistance or special projects. Agreeing that it had a consensus on a viable framework that could be implemented by the organizations, the Commission decided to adopt the framework as amended and set out in annex IV of its report and submit its final report to the General Assembly's sixtieth (2005) session.

By **decision 60/551** of 23 December, the Assembly deferred consideration of the ICSC report and the Secretary-General's report on contractual arrangements [YUN 2004, p. 1424].

Staff composition

In an August annual report on the United Nations Secretariat's staff composition [A/60/310], the Secretary-General updated information on demographic characteristics of the Secretariat's staff and on the system of desirable ranges for geographical distribution. As at 30 June 2005, Secretariat staff numbered 15,989, some 1,166 more than at 30 June 2004. Of the total, 5,754 were in the Professional or higher categories, 9,226 were in the General Service and related categories, and 1,009 were project personnel; 7,753 were paid from the regular budget and 8,236 from extrabudgetary sources. Staff in posts subject to geographical distribution numbered 2,581, of whom 1,110 (43 per cent) were female. Seventeen Member States were unrepresented in all staff categories, while nine were underrepresented, compared to 15 and 10, respectively, in 2004. Appointments to posts subject to geographical distribution between 1 July 2004 and 30 June 2005 totalled 206. Of those, 25 (12.1 per cent) were nationals of underrepresented Member States, 142 (68.9 per cent) of within-range Member States, and 39 (18.9 percent) of overrepresented Member States.

The report also gave information on the demographic profile of Secretariat staff, staff movement between 1 July 2004 and 30 June 2005, and forecasts of anticipated retirements between 2005 and 2009.

Equitable geographical distribution assessment

In response to General Assembly resolution 57/305 [YUN 2003, p. 1440], the Secretary-General submitted a March report [A/59/724] on the comprehensive assessment of the system of geographical distribution and an assessment of the issues relating to possible changes in the number of posts subject to the system of geographical distribution. The report provided overviews on the origin and initial purpose of the concept of geographical distribution of the staff; current applicable definition of the concept; common factors in equitable geographic distribution in the UN common system; and modifications in the parameters of geographical status and their implications, which presented three scenarios for evaluation in terms of their impact on Member States' representation status.

In the first scenario, weights of the existing factors (membership, population and contribution) were varied within the limits of the existing base figure, which constituted the most common method of adjusting geographical distribution posts. Five variants were considered, with a baseline number of posts of 2,700 and the number of staff posts subject to geographical distribution, which stood at 2,545 as at 31 December 2004, held constant. The second scenario involved changing the number or posts in the base figure through the inclusion of new personnel categories. Four variants, which included staff posts under regular budget and extrabudgetary resources, were considered. Scenario three weighted ranges and posts within the context of the system of desirable ranges.

The Secretary-General noted that the various simulations using the variants described in the report showed that changing the weights of the factors (membership, population and contribution) would result in important changes in the representation status of Member States. The same was true when the base figure was expanded to include staff currently not having geographic status, which would have financial implications. It was projected that the inclusion of staff in the General Service and related categories would cost the Organization approximately $55.5 million annually. He recommended that the Assembly take note of the report.

By **decision 59/551 C** of 13 April, the Assembly deferred consideration of the Secretary-General's report to its resumed sixtieth (2006) session.

Gratis personnel

Report of Secretary-General. The Secretary-General, in February, submitted to the General Assembly his annual report [A/59/716] on the use of gratis personnel between 1 January 2003 and 31 December 2004. Type I gratis personnel serving under an established regime included interns, associate experts and technical cooperation experts obtained on non-reimbursable loans, while type II gratis personnel comprised personnel provided by a Government or other entity pursuant to Assembly resolution 51/243 [YUN 1997, p. 1469]. The Secretary-General reported that during 2004, the number of type I gratis personnel increased by 12.3 per cent from 1,149 to 1,290. The increase was attributable to an increase in interns, which constituted the majority (93 per cent) of that group of personnel. The number of interns had increased from 142 in 2002 to 1,057 in 2003 and reached 1,201 in 2004. The change in methodology for the compilation and statistical analysis of data for the report, which had been expanded to meet the requirements of Assembly resolution 57/281 B [YUN 2003, p. 1448] also had an impact on the reported number of interns. Associate experts decreased from 78 to 77 and technical cooperation experts from 14 to 12 from 2003 to 2004. The number of type II gratis personnel totalled 53 in 2003, up from one in 2002. Of the 53 persons, 34 served with OCHA relief operations, 21 were under standby arrangements, and the remaining individual was a hydrology expert, hired for a two-year- period that ended 31 December 2003. The increase in type II gratis personnel was primarily due to the expansion of emergency and humanitarian relief operations during the reporting period.

For the first time, as part of change of methodology, details on the breakdown by department, nationality and gender were included. Women comprised 63 per cent of type I gratis personnel in 2003 and 61 per cent in 2004; for type II gratis personnel, women comprised 19 per cent in 2003 and 26 per cent in 2004.

ACABQ report. In April [A/59/786], ACABQ noted that the Secretary-General's report on gratis personnel (see p. 1517) was the first such report presented on a biennial basis and that comparisons with the Committee's earlier report [YUN 2003, p. 1448] could not be drawn as a result of the change in methodology and new format of indicating information on the nationality, duration of service and functions performed of gratis personnel, as well as a breakdown by gender. It maintained that information concerning gratis personnel was a logical component of the Secretary-General's report on the composition of the Secretariat and requested once again that, details on gratis personnel be integrated into that report on a biennial basis, in the first year of the biennium. The Committee recommended that the Assembly take note of the report.

By **decision 59/551 C** of 13 April, the Assembly deferred until its resumed sixtieth (2006) session consideration of the Secretary-General's report on gratis personnel and the related ACABQ report.

Study of availability
of skills in local labour markets

In response to General Assembly resolution 59/266 [YUN 2004, p. 1418], the Secretary-General submitted an August report [A/60/262] covering the study on the availability of skills in local labour markets, for which international recruitment for the General Service category took place. The study, conducted by OHRM in cooperation with the Department for General Assembly and Conference Management (DGACM), took into account recommendations by OIOS in its report on the subject [YUN 2004, p. 1430]. The report provided background information, including a summary of skills required; described outreach efforts made to attract applications from labour markets; and analysed the results of the recruitment campaign.

For the practical purpose of identifying and testing candidates readily available in the local labour market, the recruitment campaign focused mainly on candidates residing in the New York metropolitan area, regardless of their legal status in the United States. The recruitment campaign, which was launched jointly by DGACM and OHRM in 2005, sought potential candidates by advertising vacancy announcements on the UN website and in English and foreign language newspapers, and by soliciting applications from the language departments of universities, language-training institutes, spouses of staff members and permanent missions to the United Nations.

The study presented projected requirements for editorial and desktop publishing assistants and for building a viable roster of qualified candidates. In response to the recruitment campaign, 1,303 applications were received as at 29 July, which included applicants seeking Arabic (166), Chinese (119), English (519), French (166), Russian (106) and Spanish (227) positions.

The Secretary-General concluded that the findings of the 2005 campaign reconfirmed the availability of a sufficient number of qualified candidates from the local labour market to meet the staffing needs of the English Text Processing Unit. For other languages, with the exception of Russian, the campaign indicated that it was possible to identify some qualified candidates locally, but not in sufficient numbers to meet the needs of DGACM. He invited the Assembly to provide guidance on whether a further study should be undertaken to conclusively determine if recruitment from outside the duty station area was necessary to meet the staffing needs of the Arabic, Chinese, French, Russian and Spanish text processing units. He also indicated that additional resources would be required for that study, as indicated in the OIOS report.

On 23 December, the Assembly deferred consideration of the Secretary-General's report on the study of the availability of skills in local labour markets and the related OIOS report to its resumed sixtieth (2006) session (**decision 60/551**).

Recruitment, promotion and placement

By **decision 59/560** of 13 April, the General Assembly decided that, in view of the fact that printed copies of vacancy announcements were not distributed to delegations, as required by resolutions 59/266 [YUN 2004, p. 1418] and 59/276 [ibid., p. 1383] on the establishment of the Department of Safety and Security, the D-2 posts of Deputy to the Under-Secretary-General, Director of the Division of Regional Operations, Director of the Division of Safety and Security Services and the D-1 post of Executive Officer, should on an exceptional basis, be readvertised for 30 days, while the process continued with respect to recruitment actions already under way. It further decided that with regard to the fourteen P-3 to P-5 posts in the Department, for which vacancy announcements were issued from 3 to 31 March in the Galaxy staff recruitment system, but were not distributed in printed form, the deadline for receipt of applications should be extended by 15 days, also on an exceptional basis.

Suspension of recruitment for posts in the General Service and related categories

Pursuant to General Assembly resolution 59/276 [YUN 2004, p. 1383], the Secretary-General submitted a September report [A/60/363] on the issue of lifting the suspension of recruitment for posts in the General Service and related categories for the remainder of the 2004-2005 biennium. The suspension, authorized by resolution 58/270 [YUN 2003, p. 1399] for the period 2004-2005, had resulted in high vacancy rates and staff turnover between offices and departments, as well as significant difficulties with programme implementation across the Secretariat. While the distribution of vacancies within and among programmes fluctuated over the course of the biennium, there had been a clear increase in the overall vacancy rate for posts subject to the suspension. Vacancies in areas requiring specialized skills had been difficult to fill and, as a short-term measure, increased reliance had been placed on individual contractors and overtime for existing staff. However, those interim measures were not sustainable in the long term. Moreover, the filling of vacant posts through the placement or promotion of existing staff members had created other vacancies.

The suspension had also adversely impacted succession planning, as no new entry-level staff were being recruited. Eligible candidates applying for a vacant post in one office were often selected by another office before the selection process was completed, which resulted in the vacancy being readvertised if no other candidate met the requirements of the position. An inordinate amount of time was spent on dealing with vacancies and training new staff.

The Secretary-General recommended that the Assembly lift the suspension of recruitment as from 1 December 2005, as it would not result in any additional costs for the 2004-2005 biennium or the upcoming one, as the normal General Service vacancy rate of 1.5 per cent had been used in the 2006-2007 proposed programme budget in anticipation of the lifting of the suspension.

ACABQ report. In October [A/60/7/Add.2], ACABQ indicated that it would be premature to approve the proposal to lift the suspension of recruitment as of 1 December 2005, while the comprehensive analysis of the functions performed by the General Service staff were still under way. The Committee recommended that the Secretary-General prepare a plan of action on the way forward, whether or not the freeze was continued past its scheduled termination date of 31 December 2005, and requested OHRM to establish a comprehensive list of specialized functions, based on those provided to the Committee. The Committee believed it was incumbent upon the Secretary-General to propose ways for selectively eliminating General Service posts whenever and wherever possible.

Review of General Service staffing

In view of the difficulties being experienced as a result of the suspension of recruitment posts in the General Service and related categories (see above), the Secretary-General submitted, in an August addendum [A/60/572/Add.4] to his second performance report for the 2004-2005 biennium (see p. 1483), a review of General Service staffing, which focused on determining whether the current ratios of General Service to Professional staff was too high; the factors that affected those ratios either positively or negatively; and the impact of technology on the work of General Service staff.

The Secretary-General stated that comparisons of UN staff ratios with other organizations were inherently problematic and not conclusive as to whether UN ratios were too high, as there was no standard or benchmark for determining what was too high. More importantly, the validity of the assumption that a high ratio of support staff to professional staff was a negative development, was questionable. Some organizations might view a high General Service-to-Professional ratio as effective staffing that resulted in a higher proportion of the work done by lower paid staff.

While internal comparisons indicated that nearly all departments had reduced their General Service-to-Professional ratios and that was perceived as a positive development, the Secretary-General emphasized that a much deeper analysis by function and job category would be needed to know how the reductions were achieved, what impact it had on programmes and products and how support staff reductions affected the work and workloads of professional staff.

With regard to technology, services had improved, response times were faster, products were better and information was more accessible internally and externally. It was reasonable to assume that technology was one factor contributing to the ability to handle more work with fewer staff, but further analysis was required to determine what other factors had an impact. He recommended that priorities for technology investments should be defined with regard to improved services and faster response times, expansion and improvement of products, redeployment or reductions of staff and that they be pursued in a rational order that maximized resources, minimized disruptions and maintained morale.

He concluded that it was tempting to seek standards and formulas to set staffing levels, but because of the dynamic nature of work, jobs, structures and staff programmes, the General Service-to-Professional staff ratio was difficult to apply. Each function would require a different standard that fluctuated with the impact of technology on the distribution of responsibilities and authorities and therefore it was not advisable to set rigid organizational standards or benchmarks for staffing ratios. The goal should be optimal staffing to meet the tasks assigned, irrespective of ratios and proportions. He emphasized that job descriptions and job titles would be updated to reflect the realities of General Service work and to conform to the generic job profiles. Attention would also be paid to the best practices and performance metrics of other UN organizations, non-UN organizations and professional associations for specific occupational categories. He indicated that CEB had already collected data on best practices and that ICSC might play a role in obtaining data from non-UN entities.

Redeployment of posts

In a March note [A/59/753], the Secretary-General presented, in accordance with General Assembly resolution 58/270 [YUN 2003, p. 1399], the guideline principles for the redeployment of posts, on an experimental basis, to meet the evolving needs of the Organization in attaining its mandated programmes and activities. He also reported that a total of 17 posts had been deployed during the 2004-2005 biennium. Of those, five posts were redeployed permanently and another 12 posts were redeployed between sections under temporary administrative arrangements to meet immediate needs. He indicated that no implications of the experiment for human resources had been noted thus far. The Secretariat intended to address the progress and lessons learned from the experiment in the comprehensive report to be considered at the General Assembly's sixtieth (2005) session.

Report of Secretary-General. In a December report [A/60/572/Add.3] on the progress of and lessons learned from the redeployment of posts experiment, the Secretary-General indicated that, of the 17 posts redeployed in the 2004-2005 biennium, five that had been previously reported in March (see above) had been taken into account in preparing the proposed 2006-2007 programme budget. The General Assembly would need to authorize the continuation of the 12 posts redeployed since the preparation of the pro-

gramme budget, where required, in the 2006-2007 biennium. Taking into account the experience thus far, it was proposed to account for five of the 12 redeployments in setting the initial staffing table for the 2006-2007 biennium. While the remaining seven would not be reflected in the initial staffing table for the biennium, provisions would be made for the continuation of those activities where required in the biennium, including the internal redeployment of authorized staffing for the programmes concerned. In addition to the 17 posts, 14 posts, consisting of six P-3 and eight P-2 posts, had been identified for possible redeployment, but were not redeployed during the 2004-2005 biennium and would remain in the respective budget process.

The Secretary-General noted the difficulties encountered in implementing the exercise, which included attempting to arrive at a definitive list of surplus staffing resources within a particular programme that might be available for redeployment. Measures were also taken to ensure that the redeployment policy did not target programmes with high vacancy rates. To ensure there were no resulting human resources implications, the internal reviews identified possible posts for outward redeployment and focused on current and forecasted vacancies and the rationalization of the staffing allocation.

Concluding that the experience to date was quite limited, the Secretary-General indicated that, should the Assembly decide to extend the authorization for deployment of posts to the 2006-2007 biennium, it would continue to monitor and report in the context of the performance reports. He recommended that the Assembly approve the redeployment of the five posts detailed in section II of the annex to the report and extend the authorization to the 2006-2007 biennium.

ACABQ report. In a December report [A/60/597] on the second performance report on the programme budget for the biennium, ACABQ recommended approval of the Secretary-General's proposal.

Common payroll

The Secretary-General, by a December note [A/60/582], transmitted the JIU report on a common payroll for the UN system organizations. The report addressed significant financial savings that would accrue to UN organizations and to Member States should they agree to establishing a common payroll. It examined payroll delivery in different organizations with a view to detecting major obstacles and developing recommendations for future improvement of payroll systems and processes, which would provide a starting point for a future cost-effective solution for payroll delivery across UN organizations system-wide.

Indicating that the UN system operated approximately 17 different payroll-processing systems, which were heavily influenced by organization-unique interpretation of common rules and regulations that unduly complicated payroll administration and modernization, the report projected $100 million in savings from a common payroll system over ten years. Other benefits included the elimination of redundant systems and processes; internal efficiencies and effectiveness; cost reductions; enabling agencies to focus on their core mission; and enhancing standardization, an opportunity to streamline payroll policies and procedures.

JIU recommended that the General Assembly should endorse the development of a common payroll system as the first step toward a common enterprise resource planning system and request the Secretary-General, as Chairman of CEB, to seek the highest level of commitment from UN system organizations by setting up a governance structure to oversee its development and implementation. He should also establish "leader" organizations or common service entities that could provide payroll services on a fee or financial basis to those with old or antiquated systems; harmonize, simplify and standardize the application across the UN system of common rules and regulations related to payroll and allowances; and report back to the Assembly on the status of implementation at its sixty-second (2006) session.

Multilingualism

On 22 June [meeting 104], the General Assembly, having considered the JIU report on the implementation of multilingualism in the UN system and the Secretary-General's report on multilingualism [YUN 2003, p. 1451] adopted **resolution 59/309** [draft: A/59/L.62, & Add.1] without vote [agenda item 156].

Multilingualism

The General Assembly,

Recognizing that the United Nations pursues multilingualism as a means of promoting, protecting and preserving diversity of languages and cultures globally,

Also recognizing that genuine multilingualism promotes unity in diversity and international understanding,

Recalling its resolution 47/135 of 18 December 1992, by which it adopted the Declaration on the Rights of Persons Belonging to National or Ethnic, Religious and Linguistic Minorities, and the International Covenant on Civil and Political Rights, in particular its article 27 concerning the rights of persons belonging to ethnic, religious or linguistic minorities,

Also recalling its resolutions 2(I) of 1 February 1946, 2480 B(XXIII) of 21 December 1968, 42/207 C of 11 December 1987, 50/11 of 2 November 1995, 52/23 of 25 November 1997, 54/64 of 6 December 1999, 56/262 of 15 February 2002, 59/126 B of 10 December 2004 and 59/265 and 59/266 of 23 December 2004,

1. *Takes note* of the report of the Secretary-General and the report of the Joint Inspection Unit;

2. *Also takes note* of the appointment of a new coordinator for multilingualism;

3. *Underlines* the need for full implementation of the resolutions establishing language arrangements for the official languages of the United Nations and the working languages of the Secretariat;

4. *Emphasizes* the paramount importance of the equality of the six official languages of the United Nations;

5. *Requests* the Secretary-General to continue to ensure, through the provision of documentation services and meeting and publishing services under conference management, including high-quality translation and interpretation, effective multilingual communication among representatives of Member States in intergovernmental organs and members of expert bodies of the United Nations equally in all the official languages of the United Nations;

6. *Notes with satisfaction* the willingness of the Secretariat to encourage staff members, in formal meetings with interpretation services, to use any of the six official languages of which they have a command;

7. *Recalls* its resolution 59/266, in which it reaffirmed the need to respect the equality of each of the two working languages of the Secretariat, reaffirms the use of additional working languages in specific duty stations as mandated, and in this regard requests the Secretary-General to ensure that vacancy announcements specify the need for either of the working languages of the Secretariat, unless the functions of the post require a specific working language;

8. *Also recalls* that in its resolution 59/266 it requested the Secretary-General to continue to take the steps necessary to ensure that the Galaxy e-staffing system was available in both of the working languages of the Organization;

9. *Encourages* United Nations staff members to continue to use actively existing training facilities to acquire and enhance their proficiency in one or more of the official languages of the United Nations;

10. *Recalls* its resolution 59/265, in which it reaffirmed the provisions relating to conference services of its resolutions on multilingualism;

11. *Also recalls* its resolution 59/126 B, and emphasizes the importance of multilingualism in United Nations public relations and information activities;

12. *Reaffirms* the need to achieve full parity among the six official languages on the United Nations website;

13. *Takes note with appreciation* of the work done by the United Nations information centres, including the regional United Nations information centres, in favour of the publication of United Nations information materials and the translation of important documents into languages other than the official languages of the United Nations, with a view to reaching the widest possible spectrum of audiences and extending the United Nations message to all the corners of the world in

order to strengthen international support for the activities of the Organization;

14. *Welcomes* the decision by the General Conference of the United Nations Educational, Scientific and Cultural Organization on 17 November 1999 that 21 February should be proclaimed "International Mother Language Day", and calls upon Member States and the Secretariat to promote the preservation and protection of all languages used by peoples of the world;

15. *Requests* the Secretary-General to report to it at its sixty-first session on the measures that can be taken by international organizations within the United Nations system in order to strengthen the protection, promotion and preservation of all languages, in particular languages spoken by persons belonging to linguistic minorities and languages facing extinction;

16. *Also requests* the Secretary-General to submit to it at its sixty-first session a comprehensive report on the implementation of its resolutions on multilingualism, including the implications of the present resolution;

17. *Decides* to include in the provisional agenda of its sixty-first session the item entitled "Multilingualism".

Staff rules and regulations

In accordance with staff regulation 12.3 stipulating that the full text of provisional staff rules and amendments should be reported annually to the General Assembly, the Secretary-General, in August [A/60/174], outlined amendments to the 100 and 200 series of Staff Rules, together with the rationale for the changes. Amendments to the 100 series related to annual and sick leave, appeals, the last day for pay purposes and maternity and paternity leave, while the amendments under the 200 series pertained to sick, maternity and paternity leave. The Secretary-General recommended that the Assembly take note of the amendments in the annex to the report, which he proposed to implement as from 1 January 2006.

In a September report [A/60/365], the Secretary-General also proposed amendments to the Staff regulations that were needed to enhance the accountability of UN staff with respect to both financial accountability of staff involved in the management of the Organization's resources and disciplinary accountability of staff members who committed acts of sexual exploitation and sexual abuse. The amendment relating to financial accountability extended the requirement to file financial disclosure statements, currently applicable to staff at the Assistant Secretary-General level and above, to all staff at the D1/L-6 and D2/L-7 levels. The Secretary-General further recommended that the Assembly amend staff regulation 1.2 authorizing him to require disclosure statements from additional staff as he deemed necessary.

In order to implement the recommendation in the report [A/59/710] on eliminating future sexual

exploitation and abuse in UN peacekeeping operations (see p. 119), to clarify in the Staff Regulations that sexual exploitation and sexual abuse constituted serious misconduct, the Secretary-General proposed the amendment of staff regulation 10.2.

The aforementioned amendments to the Staff Regulations were approved by the Assembly in **resolution 60/238** of 23 December (see p. 1515).

Headquarters agreements

JIU report. In February [A/59/526/Add.1], the Secretary-General transmitted his comments and those of CEB on the JIU report entitled "Review of the Headquarters Agreements concluded by the organizations of the United Nations system: human resources issues affecting staff", which had been submitted to the General Assembly in 2004 [YUN 2004, p. 1433].

Members of CEB welcomed the findings of the report and were broadly in agreement with its conclusions and recommendations. They strongly supported the recommendation that legislative bodies of organizations should bring to the attention of the host country the desirability of adopting more liberal policies with regard to work permits or similar arrangements for spouses of staff members and international organization officials, and that the issue of spousal employment remained one of the key factors still posing problems in attracting and retaining the right calibre of staff. The procedure whereby a spouse should have an offer of employment and then apply for a permit was not favoured by some employers. CEB members preferred either the automatic system, wherein the issuance of a visa to a staff accredits the staff member's spouse with a work permit or employment permits were offered prior to seeking employment.

Members also supported the implementation of all measures that would facilitate the exercise of the privileges and immunities relating to the work permits for children and visas for domestic helpers; the acquisition and rental of real property; retirement in the host country and tax exemption benefits. However, the Secretary-General seriously opposed integration into the social security system on the ground that mandatory contributions for social security schemes under national legislation were considered a form of direct taxation on the United Nations and therefore, contrary to article II, section 7, subparagraph (a) of the Convention on Privileges and Immunities of the United Nations [YUN 1946-47, p. 100].

Members expressed reservations with the recommendation that the Secretary-General should request CEB to coordinate the formulation of a model framework headquarters agreement, or standard articles ensuring uniformity for the approval of the Assembly. They noted that it would be difficult to implement system-wide, and unrealistic to expect that a model framework applicable to all organizations of the UN system would be able to capture all possible scenarios, including headquarters and field conditions and special circumstances. Moreover, various existing host country agreements covered fundamentally different activities and operations. Over time, different organizations had evolved customary regimes responsive to their particular activities, locations and unique circumstances, rendering a "one size fits all" approach inapplicable.

Safety and Security

Report of Secretary-General. In response to General Assembly resolution 59/211 [YUN 2004, p. 1435], the Secretary-General, in August [A/60/223 & Corr.1], updated information on the safety and security of UN personnel between 1 July 2004 to 30 June 2005. He noted that, since 1992, some 229 United Nations civilian staff members had been killed as a result of malicious acts, including 22 during the reporting period. The most significant threats to staff security continued to be physical attacks, threats, robbery and theft. There were three incidents of hostage-taking and 17 kidnappings, as well as four cases of rape and six sexual assaults. A total of 119 incidents of armed robbery involving significant UN assets were reported, as well as nine violent attacks against UN personnel on humanitarian convoys and operations, compared with seven such incidents during the previous reporting period. There were 123 incidents of harassment of humanitarian convoys, 220 incidents in which checkpoints or roadblocks prohibited access to UN personnel and 108 incidents of harassment, abuse or physical assault that had resulted in significant delays.

The Secretary-General said that, although the United Nations had not suffered another catastrophic attack, such as that which had taken place in Bagdad on 19 August 2003 [YUN 2003, p.1452], significant threats and risks remained. In Afghanistan, UN election activities were deliberately targeted throughout the lead-up to the 2004 elections, and were again at risk. Staff members in Iraq had continued to be subjected to the unrelenting hostility of armed groups opposed to their work. While the levels of organized violence had abated, humanitarian activities in Darfur, the Sudan, continued to be plagued by banditry. The security situation in Lebanon also remained fragile.

The report described the need for a more professional security management system that could respond flexibly, based on continuous analysis, with stronger staffing and a capacity to give to the Organization the technical guidance required to function safely in the face of a heightened global threat. It noted that the aim of the management system, under the leadership of the new Department of Safety and Security, was to enable the safe delivery by the Secretariat, as well as by UN agencies, funds and programmes, of mandated activities in the field. However, concern remained over the ongoing difficulties encountered in a few countries in obtaining permission to import communications equipment. Some host Governments continued to be unwilling to provide timely information in the event of the arrest or detention of locally recruited UN personnel, and very few countries had fully investigated attacks or other threats against international and locally recruited United Nations and associated staff members, or held the perpetrators accountable under international and national law. The increase in hostage-taking and kidnappings during the reporting period was particularly disturbing.

The Secretary-General concluded that, while the number of security incidents involving UN personnel appeared to have risen, that was most likely due to the increased number of staff operating in the field and improved reporting capability within the UN security management system. He urged Member States, local authorities and leaders at all levels to take the necessary action to enable UN staff to safely meet the needs of the world.

GENERAL ASSEMBLY ACTION

On 15 December [meeting 63], the General Assembly adopted **resolution 60/123** [draft: A/60/L.37] without vote [agenda item 73].

Safety and security of humanitarian personnel and protection of United Nations personnel

The General Assembly,

Reaffirming its resolution 46/182 of 19 December 1991 on strengthening of the coordination of humanitarian emergency assistance of the United Nations,

Recalling all relevant resolutions on safety and security of humanitarian personnel and protection of United Nations personnel, including its resolution 59/211 of 20 December 2004, as well as Security Council resolution 1502(2003) of 26 August 2003 and relevant statements by the President of the Council,

Recalling also all Security Council resolutions and presidential statements and reports of the Secretary-General to the Council on the protection of civilians in armed conflict,

Recalling further all relevant provisions of international law, including international humanitarian law and human rights law, as well as all relevant treaties,

Reaffirming the need to promote and ensure respect for the principles and rules of international law, including international humanitarian law,

Recalling that primary responsibility under international law for the security and protection of humanitarian personnel and United Nations and associated personnel lies with the Government hosting a United Nations operation conducted under the Charter of the United Nations or its agreements with relevant organizations,

Urging all parties involved in armed conflicts, in compliance with international humanitarian law, in particular their obligations under the Geneva Conventions of 12 August 1949 and the obligations applicable to them under the Additional Protocols thereto, of 8 June 1977, to ensure the security and protection of all humanitarian personnel and United Nations and associated personnel,

Welcoming the fact that the number of States parties to the Convention on the Safety of United Nations and Associated Personnel, which entered into force on 15 January 1999, has continued to rise, the number now having reached seventy-nine, and mindful of the need to promote universality of the Convention,

Deeply concerned by the dangers and security risks faced by humanitarian personnel and United Nations and associated personnel at the field level, as they operate in increasingly complex contexts, as well as the continuous erosion, in many cases, of respect for the principles and rules of international law, in particular international humanitarian law,

Commending the courage and commitment of those who take part in humanitarian operations, often at great personal risk, especially locally recruited staff,

Expressing profound regret at the deaths of international and national humanitarian personnel and United Nations and associated personnel involved in the provision of humanitarian assistance, and strongly deploring the rising toll of casualties among such personnel in complex humanitarian emergencies, in particular in armed conflicts and in post-conflict situations,

Strongly condemning acts of murder and other forms of violence, rape and sexual assault and all forms of violence committed in particular against women, and intimidation, armed robbery, abduction, hostage-taking, kidnapping, harassment and illegal arrest and detention to which those participating in humanitarian operations are increasingly exposed, as well as attacks on humanitarian convoys and acts of destruction and looting of property,

Expressing concern that the occurrence of attacks and threats against humanitarian personnel and United Nations and associated personnel is a factor that increasingly restricts the provision of assistance and protection to populations in need,

Recalling the inclusion of attacks intentionally directed against personnel involved in a humanitarian assistance or peacekeeping mission in accordance with the Charter as a war crime in the Rome Statute of the International Criminal Court, and noting the role that the Court could play in appropriate cases in bringing to justice those responsible for serious violations of international humanitarian law,

Reaffirming the need to ensure adequate levels of safety and security for United Nations personnel and associated humanitarian personnel, which constitutes an underlying duty of the Organization, and mindful of the need to promote and enhance the security consciousness within the organizational culture of the United Nations and a culture of accountability at all levels,

1. *Welcomes* the report of the Secretary-General;

2. *Urges* all States to take the necessary measures to ensure the full and effective implementation of the relevant principles and rules of international law, including international humanitarian law, human rights law and refugee law related to the safety and security of humanitarian personnel and United Nations personnel;

3. *Strongly urges* all States to take the necessary measures to ensure the safety and security of humanitarian personnel and United Nations and associated personnel and to respect and ensure respect for the inviolability of United Nations premises, which are essential to the continuation and successful implementation of United Nations operations;

4. *Calls upon* all Governments and parties in complex humanitarian emergencies, in particular in armed conflicts and in post-conflict situations, in countries in which humanitarian personnel are operating, in conformity with the relevant provisions of international law and national laws, to cooperate fully with the United Nations and other humanitarian agencies and organizations and to ensure the safe and unhindered access of humanitarian personnel and delivery of supplies and equipment in order to allow those personnel to perform efficiently their task of assisting the affected civilian population, including refugees and internally displaced persons;

5. *Calls upon* all States to consider becoming parties to and to respect fully their obligations under the relevant international instruments;

6. *Also calls upon* all States to consider becoming parties to the Rome Statute of the International Criminal Court;

7. *Takes note with appreciation* of the adoption of the Optional Protocol to the Convention on the Safety of United Nations and Associated Personnel, which expands the scope of legal protection under the Convention, and calls upon all States to consider signing and ratifying the Optional Protocol as soon as possible so as to ensure its rapid entry into force, and urges States parties to put in place appropriate national legislation, as necessary, to enable its effective implementation;

8. *Expresses deep concern* that, over the past decade, threats and attacks against the safety and security of humanitarian personnel and United Nations and associated personnel have escalated dramatically and that perpetrators of acts of violence seemingly operate with impunity;

9. *Strongly condemns* all threats and acts of violence against humanitarian personnel and United Nations and associated personnel, affirms the need to hold accountable those responsible for such acts, strongly urges all States to take stronger actions to ensure that any such acts committed on their territory are investigated fully and to ensure that the perpetrators of such acts are brought to justice in accordance with international law and national law, and urges States to end impunity for such acts;

10. *Calls upon* all States to provide adequate and prompt information in the event of the arrest or detention of humanitarian personnel or United Nations and associated personnel, so as to afford them the necessary medical assistance and to allow independent medical teams to visit and examine the health of those de-

tained, and urges them to take the necessary measures to ensure the speedy release of those who have been arrested or detained in violation of the relevant conventions referred to in the present resolution and applicable international humanitarian law;

11. *Calls upon* all other parties involved in armed conflicts to refrain from abducting humanitarian personnel or United Nations and associated personnel or detaining them in violation of the relevant conventions referred to in the present resolution and applicable international humanitarian law, and speedily to release, without harm or requirement of concession, any abductee or detainee;

12. *Reaffirms* the obligation of all humanitarian personnel and United Nations and associated personnel to observe and respect the national laws of the country in which they are operating, in accordance with international law and the Charter of the United Nations;

13. *Stresses* the importance of ensuring that humanitarian personnel and United Nations and associated personnel remain sensitive to national and local customs and traditions in their countries of assignment and communicate clearly their purpose and objectives to local populations;

14. *Requests* the Secretary-General to take the necessary measures to ensure full respect for the human rights, privileges and immunities of United Nations and other personnel carrying out activities in fulfilment of the mandate of a United Nations operation, and also requests the Secretary-General to seek the inclusion, in negotiations of headquarters and other mission agreements concerning United Nations and associated personnel, of the applicable conditions contained in the Convention on the Privileges and Immunities of the United Nations, the Convention on the Privileges and Immunities of the Specialized Agencies and the Convention on the Safety of United Nations and Associated Personnel;

15. *Recommends* that the Secretary-General continue to seek the inclusion of, and that host countries include, key provisions of the Convention on the Safety of United Nations and Associated Personnel, among others, those regarding the prevention of attacks against members of the operation, the establishment of such attacks as crimes punishable by law and the prosecution or extradition of offenders, in future as well as, if necessary, in existing status-of-forces, status-of-mission, host country agreements and other related agreements negotiated between the United Nations and those countries, mindful of the importance of the timely conclusion of such agreements, and encourages further efforts in this regard;

16. *Welcomes* ongoing efforts to promote and enhance the security consciousness within the organizational culture of the United Nations system, and requests the Secretary-General to continue to take the necessary measures in this regard, including by further developing and implementing a unified security management system, as well as by disseminating and ensuring the implementation of the security procedures and regulations and by ensuring accountability at all levels, and also welcomes the creation of the Department of Safety and Security of the Secretariat;

17. *Emphasizes* the importance of paying special attention to the safety and security of United Nations and associated personnel engaged in United Nations peacekeeping and peacebuilding operations;

18. *Also emphasizes* the need to pay particular attention to the safety and security of locally recruited humanitarian personnel, who are particularly vulnerable to attacks and who account for the majority of casualties;

19. *Requests* the Secretary-General to continue to take the necessary measures to ensure that United Nations and other personnel carrying out activities in fulfilment of the mandate of a United Nations operation are properly informed about and operate in conformity with the minimum operating security standards and relevant codes of conduct and are properly informed about the conditions under which they are called upon to operate and the standards that they are required to meet, including those contained in relevant national and international law, and that adequate training in security, human rights law and international humanitarian law is provided so as to enhance their security and effectiveness in accomplishing their functions, and reaffirms the necessity for all other humanitarian organizations to provide their personnel with similar support;

20. *Stresses* the need to ensure that all United Nations staff members receive adequate security training, including physical and psychological training, as well as training to enhance cultural awareness, prior to their deployment to the field, as well as the need to attach a high priority to stress management training and related counselling services for United Nations staff throughout the system;

21. *Takes note* of the report of the Secretary-General on a strengthened and unified security management system for the United Nations;

22. *Welcomes* the ongoing efforts of the Secretary-General to further enhance the security management system of the United Nations, and in this regard invites the United Nations and other humanitarian organizations to strengthen the analysis of threats to their safety and security in order to minimize security risks and to facilitate informed decisions on the maintenance of an effective presence in the field, inter alia, to fulfil their humanitarian mandate;

23. *Stresses* that the effective functioning at the country level of security operations requires a unified capacity for policy, standards, coordination, communication, compliance and threat and risk assessment;

24. *Recognizes* the need to continue efforts to achieve a strengthened and unified security management system for the United Nations, both at the headquarters and the field levels, and requests the United Nations system, as well as Member States, to take all appropriate measures to that end;

25. *Requests* the Secretary-General, inter alia, through the Inter-Agency Security Management Network, to continue to promote increased cooperation and collaboration among United Nations departments, organizations, funds and programmes and affiliated international organizations, including between their headquarters and field offices, in the planning and implementation of measures aimed at improving staff security, training and awareness, and calls upon all relevant United Nations departments, organizations, funds and programmes and affiliated international organizations to support these efforts;

26. *Recognizes* the need for continued efforts to enhance coordination and cooperation, both at the headquarters and the field levels, between the United Nations and other humanitarian and non-governmental organizations on matters relating to the safety and security of humanitarian personnel and United Nations and associated personnel, with a view to addressing mutual security concerns in the field;

27. *Underlines* the need to allocate adequate and predictable resources to the safety and security of United Nations personnel, including through the consolidated appeals process, and encourages all States to contribute to the Trust Fund for Security of Staff Members of the United Nations System;

28. *Recalls* the essential role of telecommunication resources in facilitating the safety of humanitarian personnel and United Nations and associated personnel, calls upon States to consider acceding to or ratifying the Tampere Convention on the Provision of Telecommunication Resources for Disaster Mitigation and Relief Operations of 18 June 1998, which entered into force on 8 January 2005, and urges them to facilitate and expedite, consistent with their national laws and international obligations applicable to them, the use of communications equipment in such operations, inter alia, through limiting and, whenever possible, lifting the restrictions placed on the use of communications equipment by United Nations and associated personnel;

29. *Requests* the Secretary-General to submit to the General Assembly at its sixty-first session a comprehensive and updated report on the safety and security of humanitarian personnel and protection of United Nations personnel and on the implementation of the present resolution.

Malicious acts insurance policy

Pursuant to General Assembly resolution 59/276 [YUN 2004, p. 1383], the Secretary-General submitted an August report [A/60/317 & Corr.1] on coverage of staff by the malicious acts insurance policy, which indicated that coverage of UN system staff under the malicious acts insurance policies was closely comparable system wide and most UN organizations maintained supplemental policies to provide coverage in 10 headquarters countries that were excluded under existing insurance policies. The Organization was looking into the possible expansion of the policy to those countries. Quotations were being sought from insurers and the financial implications for participating organizations of such expansion would be discussed by the CEB High-level Committee on Management.

ACABQ, in its November report [A/60/7/Add.9], recommended that the Assembly take note of the Secretary-General's report as an interim report.

Protection from sexual exploitation and abuse

Report of Secretary-General. In response to General Assembly resolution 57/306 [YUN 2003, p.

1237], the Secretary-General submitted an April report [A/59/782] containing information on the responses by 47 UN entities to the Secretariat's query regarding investigations into cases of sexual exploitation or sexual abuse. In 2004, 41 entities reported that they had received no reports of sexual exploitation or abuse, and 6 reported the opening of investigations into newly reported cases. A total of 121 allegations were reported, more than double the 53 allegations reported in 2003. As at 31 December 2004, the Department of Peacekeeping Operations reported 105 new allegations, of which 89 were against uniformed personnel and 16 were against civilian personnel. Fifteen allegations involved UN staff and one was related to a civilian. Seven of those allegations were sent to UN Headquarters for disciplinary action, seven were pending investigation and one was classified as unsubstantiated.

Of the two cases reported by UNICEF, one was dismissed due to insufficient evidence and the other was sent to UN Headquarters. WFP reported a case that was pending further investigation. OIOS reported a case, which was closed due to the staff member's resignation. UNHCR reported 10 cases; 6 had been classified as unsubstantiated or closed, and 4 were pending further investigation. The United Nations Volunteers Programme (UNV) reported two cases, one of which was dismissed after a preliminary investigation and the other was pending further investigation. It was reported that of all the allegations, 45 per cent involved sex with minors; 15 per cent, rape or sexual assault; 31 per cent, prostitution with women; and 6 per cent, exploitation and abuse of other forms.

The Secretary-General indicated that, while allegations had doubled since 2003, the Secretariat was aware that the data might still not reflect the true extent of those deplorable incidents. Complaints mechanisms needed to be developed in many remote field locations. Although some UN personnel were currently more willing to come forward with complaints as a result of newly implemented measures to prevent and respond to sexual exploitation and abuse, others were still inhibited by a lack of trust. Furthermore, in cases involving exchange of money or employment for sex, there was little incentive, economic or otherwise, for victims to come forward to report, which resulted in a probable under-reporting of those forms of misconduct. The Secretariat continued to work towards improving reporting measures, including designating focal points to facilitate the receipt of complaints and defining better the reporting procedures to encourage staff members to report allegations of misconduct.

The Secretary-General said the Organization remained committed to changing the organizational culture that permitted sexual abuse and exploitation. He also reiterated his commitment to implementing the recommendations made in the comprehensive strategy to eliminate future sexual exploitation and abuse in UN peacekeeping operations (see p. 119).

Staff College

In accordance with General Assembly resolution 55/207 [YUN 2000, p. 1354], the Secretary-General, by a September note [A/60/328], transmitted the second report of the Director of the United Nations System Staff College, covering the period from 1 July 2003 to 30 June 2005. The report outlined the Staff College's objectives and described its outputs, projects and other activities during the reporting period. Human and financial resources available to the College were also considered in the report.

In the 18 months covered by the report, the College organized and/or participated in 139 learning events. In November 2003, the Board of Governors of the College approved a budget for the biennium and a strategic plan, which focused on four thematic targets: training and continuous learning programmes for UN staff members; strengthening organizational capacities to increase operational effectiveness; raising awareness of management issues and promoting collaboration among UN agencies; and strengthening internal capacity-building systems.

The report concluded that the College had made considerable progress as an entity within the UN family, and had been supported in its work by Italy, the host-country. Additional support was provided by voluntary contributions received from other Member States.

In December, the Second Committee considered the report of the Secretary-General on the United Nations System Staff College (see above). On 22 December, the Assembly took note of the Second Committee's report [A/60/494 & Add.2] (**decision 60/548**).

GENERAL ASSEMBLY ACTION

On 22 December [meeting 68], the General Assembly, on the recommendation of the Second Committee [A/60/494/Add.2], adopted **resolution 60/214** without vote [agenda item 58(b)].

United Nations System Staff College in Turin, Italy

The General Assembly,

Recalling its resolutions 54/228 of 22 December 1999, 55/207 of 20 December 2000, 55/258 of 14 June 2001 and 58/224 of 23 December 2003,

Recalling also its resolution 55/278 of 12 July 2001, by which it approved the statute of the United Nations System Staff College,

Reaffirming the role of the Staff College as an institution for system-wide knowledge management, training and continuous learning for the staff of the United Nations system, in particular in the areas of economic and social development, peace and security and internal management,

1. *Takes note with appreciation* of the note by the Secretary-General and the accompanying report;

2. *Welcomes* the progress made by the United Nations System Staff College since the entry into force of its statute on 1 January 2002 in pursuing the objectives set forth therein;

3. *Calls upon* all organizations of the United Nations system to make full and effective use of the facilities of the Staff College;

4. *Invites* the Staff College to strengthen further its engagement in knowledge-sharing and staff training and learning that can serve to advance the capacity of the United Nations system to contribute to the follow-up to the outcomes of major United Nations conferences and summits, as well as to support the timely and full realization of the internationally agreed development goals, including the Millennium Development Goals, with the aim of helping to provide multilateral solutions to problems in the areas of development, peace and collective security and reinforcing system-wide coherence;

5. *Encourages* the Staff College to continue to provide strategic leadership in order to increase operational effectiveness, promote inter-agency collaboration and strengthen management culture by its own example, including the development of new systems of performance management, flexible and collaborative work structures and cost-effective means of delivering services to clients and beneficiaries;

6. *Calls upon* relevant institutions of the United Nations, including the United Nations University, the United Nations Institute for Training and Research and the Staff College, to collaborate closely to those ends;

7. *Welcomes* the financial and other support extended by Member States to the work of the Staff College, and invites the international community to strengthen its support to the College through voluntary contributions, in accordance with article VII of its statute, to enable the College to consolidate its distinctive contribution to fostering a cohesive management culture across the United Nations system that is responsive to the requirements of Member States;

8. *Decides* that article IV, paragraph 5, of the statute of the Staff College should be amended so that the biennial reports on the activities of the College are submitted to the Economic and Social Council rather than to the General Assembly.

UN Joint Staff Pension Fund

As at 31 December 2005, the United Nations Joint Staff Pension Fund (UNJSPF) had 93,683 active participants as compared to 88,356 at the end of 2004; the number of periodic payments in awards increased from 53,879 to 55,140 over the year. The breakdown of the periodic benefits in award was 17,992 retirement benefits; 12,392 early retirement benefits; 6,656 deferred retirement benefits; 8,923 widows' and widowers' benefits; 8,120 children's benefits; 1,015 disability benefits; and 42 secondary dependants' benefits. In the course of the biennium, 12,345 lump-sum withdrawal and other settlements were paid.

The Fund was administered by the 33-member United Nations Joint Staff Pension Board (UNJSB), which did not meet in 2005 because of the biennialization of the work of the Fifth Committee. Instead, the Board's Standing Committee met on its behalf (New York, 5-8 July) [A/60/183] and discussed, among other subjects, matters relating to Fund's administration and operation, revised budget estimates for the 2004-2005 biennium; budget estimates for the 2006-2007 biennium; and the authorization for contributions to the Emergency Fund for 2006-2007.

ACABQ report. In November [A/60/7/Add.7], having considered the Standing Committee's report, ACABQ recommended approval of the revised estimates of $89,563,100 for the 2004-2005 biennium and of the proposed budget of $108,262,500 for the Fund's administrative expenses for the 2006-2007 biennium. It also agreed with the Standing Committee's proposal to supplement voluntary contributions to the Emergency Fund by an amount not exceeding $200,000 for the 2006-2007 biennium.

In a 9 December report [A/C.5/60/18] on the administrative and financial implications arising from the report of the UNJSB Standing Committee, the Secretary-General indicated that, should the General Assembly approve the Committee's recommendations, as well as those of ACABQ, the revised overall requirements for the United Nations were estimated at $16,539,800 (at 2006-2007 rates). The cost to the regular budget for the biennium 2006-2007 would amount to $10,287,800, with the balance of $6,252,000 being reimbursed to the United Nations by UNDP, UNFPA and UNICEF, resulting in an additional appropriation requirement of $1,079,000 for the proposed 2006-2007 programme budget.

On 13 December [A/60/7/Add.22 & Corr.1], ACABQ recommended that the Fifth Committee report to the Assembly that an additional appropriation of $1,079,000 would need to be included under section 1 of the proposed 2006-2007 programme budget. The provision would represent a charge against the contingency fund.

The Assembly, in section III of **resolution 60/248** of 23 December (see p. 1494) approved expenses—chargeable directly to the Fund totaling $91,722,700 net for the 2006-2007 biennium—and a revised estimate of $89,563,100 net for the 2004-2005 biennium. It also approved an additional amount of $1,079,000 as the United Nations share of the cost of the administrative expenses and authorized UNJSB to supplement the voluntary contributions to the Emergency Fund by an amount not to exceed $200,000 for the 2006-2007 biennium.

Pension Fund investments

The market value of UNJSPF assets as at 31 December 2005 was $31.4 billion, an increase of 7.5 per cent from the previous year. The Fund's investment assets were distributed in equities (61.2 per cent), bonds (28.8 per cent), real-estate related instruments (4 per cent) and short-term holdings (5.5 per cent). The total investment return as at 31 March 2005, which took into account the timing of cash flows for the same period, was 10.4 per cent, representing a "real" or inflation-adjusted return of 7.3 per cent.

The Fund's investment income during the 2004-2005 biennium amounted to $4.4 billion, comprising $1.9 billion in interest, dividends, real estate and related securities and $2.5 billion in net profit on sales of investments. Investment management costs amounted to $44.2 million.

The Fund remained one of the most diversified pension funds in the world, with 49.2 per cent of its assets exposed to currencies other than the United States dollar, which was the Fund's unit of account.

Travel-related matters

By **decision 59/559** of 13 April, the General Assembly took note of the Secretary-General's 2004 report [YUN 2004, p. 1441] on standards of accommodation for air travel for the two-year period ended 30 June 2004 and the related ACABQ report [ibid.].

Conditions of travel

By a June note [A/60/78], the Secretary-General transmitted the JIU report entitled "Harmonization of the conditions of travel throughout the UN system", which provided a comprehensive analysis and historical review of the administration of travel in the UN system, including the impact of security measures on the time and conditions of travel. JIU found that, although travel practices were being shared among organizations, resulting in increased harmonization of the conditions of travel throughout the UN system, disparities still existed, such as the class of air travel and the lump-sum option. It proposed action for further improving the harmonization of travel policies and practices.

JIU recommended that the Assembly mandate the Secretary-General to review the criteria used to determine travel class for staff members, with a view to adopting a common policy, in particular the minimum travel time for entitlement to business class. On the use of lump-sum payment amounts for home leave, family visit and education travel, a 75 per cent benchmark figure of the full economy fare was suggested. It also recommended that the lump-sum option should be extended to family visit and education travel and the provisions requiring evidence of travel under the lump-sum option be discontinued. The practice of reporting exceptions to the approved class of travel should also be discontinued. Internal control mechanisms should remain in place and clear criteria established for upgrading travel to first class for reasons of eminency and on medical grounds. The use of alternative and more cost-effective modes of transportation was also emphasized, and the Secretary-General should review the current mileage system, with a view to replacing it by a standard rate to be applied worldwide. Other measures proposed related to the regulation of rental car use; the advance payment of subsistence and/or terminal expenses; increasing the threshold for the granting of stopovers for business and other classes of travel; review of standards of travel and entitlements for members of subsidiary organs of the United Nations and UN system organizations; and the adoption of provisions based on best practices with regard to reverse education travel, travel of breastfeeding mothers, travel of single parents, possibility of choosing an alternative place of home leave, taking the nationality of the spouse into account, and the minimum number of days to be spent in the country of home leave.

In August [A/60/78/Add.1], the Secretary-General transmitted his comments, as well as those of CEB on the JIU report. CEB members regarded the report as relevant and timely, particularly with regard to the ever-increasing need for staff members of UN organizations to undertake travel amid changing conditions in the global airline industry and the heightened awareness of the need to improve safety and security. They supported in general the conclusions contained in the report.

By **decision 60/551** of 23 December, the Assembly deferred to its resumed sixtieth (2006) session consideration of JIU report on the harmonization of the conditions of travel in the UN system and the Secretary-General's related note transmitting his comments and those of CEB.

Administration of justice

The General Assembly, at its resumed fifty-ninth (2005) session, had before it previously deferred reports of the Secretary-General on the administration of justice in the Secretariat [YUN 2004, p. 1441]; the role of the Panels on Discrimination and Other Grievances [ibid., p. 1442]; the outcome of the work of the Joint Appeals Board (JAB) during 2002 and 2003 [ibid., p. 1443]; the financial independence of the United Nations Administrative Tribunal (UNAT) from the Office of Legal Affairs [ibid.]; the OIOS report on the management review of the appeals process at the United Nations [ibid., p. 1442]; the UNAT report on its activities [ibid., p. 1443]; and the JIU report on the harmonization of the statutes of UNAT and the International Labour Organization Administrative Tribunal [ibid., p. 1444]. It also considered the Secretary-General's note on compensation for UNAT members [ibid. p. 1413] and the letter from the UNAT President to the Fifth Committee Chairman [ibid., p. 1441].

GENERAL ASSEMBLY ACTION

On 13 April [meeting 91], the General Assembly, on the recommendation of the Fifth Committee [A/59/773], adopted **resolution 59/283** without vote [agenda items 108 & 120].

Administration of justice at the United Nations

The General Assembly,

Recalling its resolutions 57/307 of 15 April 2003 and 59/266 of 23 December 2004,

Stressing that the system of justice in the United Nations as a whole should be independent, transparent, effective, efficient and fair,

Stressing also the importance of increased transparency in decision-making and increased accountability of managers for the system,

Noting that the existing system should respect the principle of due process and provide for appropriate peer review,

Noting with concern the continuing backlog of appeals in various parts of the system,

Emphasizing the necessity of informal mechanisms for the early and swift resolution of disputes in the Secretariat, in particular through a direct dialogue between managers and staff,

Emphasizing also the importance for the United Nations to have an efficient and effective system of internal justice so as to ensure that individuals and the Organization are held accountable for their actions in accordance with relevant resolutions and regulations,

Welcoming the increased focus on training for all participants in the system of administration of justice,

Recognizing that a transparent, impartial and effective system of administration of justice is a necessary condition for ensuring fair and just treatment of United Nations staff and important for the success of human resources reform in the Organization,

Having considered the reports of the Secretary-General on the administration of justice in the Secretariat, on the role of the Panels on Discrimination and Other Grievances, on the outcome of the work of the Joint Appeals Board during 2001 and 2002 and on the outcome of the work of the Joint Appeals Board during 2002 and 2003, the comprehensives report of the United Nations Administrative Tribunal on its activities, the reports of the Secretary-General on the possibility of the financial independence of the United Nations Administrative Tribunal from the Office of Legal Affairs and on measures to prevent discrimination on the basis of nationality, race, gender, religion or language in the United Nations, the note by the Secretary-General transmitting the report of the Office of Internal Oversight Services on the management review of the appeals process at the United Nations, the report of the Secretary-General containing the cost implications of the recommendations of the Office of Internal Oversight Services following its management review of the appeals processes, the note by the Secretary-General transmitting the report of the Joint Inspection Unit entitled "Administration of justice: harmonization of the statutes of the United Nations Administrative Tribunal and the International Labour Organization Administrative Tribunal", the note by the Secretary-General containing his comments on the report of the Joint Inspection Unit, the note by the Secretary-General on compensation for members of the United Nations Administrative Tribunal, the letter dated 18 November 2003 from the President of the United Nations Administrative Tribunal addressed to the Chairman of the Fifth Committee and the interim report of the Advisory Committee on Administrative and Budgetary Questions,

Regretting that the present system of administration of justice in the Secretariat continues to be slow, cumbersome and costly,

Regretting also that the related reports were not introduced at its fifty-eighth session, as requested in its resolution 57/307, and that, in addition, they were submitted and issued late at its fifty-ninth session,

1. *Notes* the importance of having a strong administration of justice mechanism that avoids duplication and overlap within the formal processes;

2. *Regrets* the continued serious delays in the appeals process, and stresses the need to implement measures to improve the appeals process to make it more efficient;

I

Cross-cutting issues - general guidelines

3. *Takes note* of the reports of the Secretary-General on the administration of justice in the Secretariat, on the role of the Panels on Discrimination and Other Grievances, on the outcome of the work of the Joint Appeals Board during 2001 and 2002, on the outcome of the work of the Joint Appeals Board during 2002 and 2003, on the possibility of the financial independence of the United Nations Administrative Tribunal from the Office of Legal Affairs, on measures to prevent discrimination on the basis of nationality, race, gender, religion or language in the United Nations and his report containing the cost implications of the recommendations of the Office of Internal Oversight Services following its management review of the appeals process;

4. *Takes note with interest* of the report of the Office of Internal Oversight Services on the management review of the appeals process at the United Nations;

5. *Endorses* the conclusions and recommendations of the Advisory Committee on Administrative and Budgetary Questions set out in its report, subject to the provisions of the present resolution;

6. *Stresses* that the administrative law framework of the Organization should allow all levels of United Nations staff to obtain due process, regardless of their location, grade or contractual arrangement;

7. *Appreciates* the efforts made by staff volunteering their services in the system of justice of the United Nations, and stresses the need to provide them with further training;

8. *Takes note with interest* of the option described in paragraph 30 of the report of the Secretary-General, and requests the Secretary-General to explore the implications of this option and to report thereon in the context of his annual report on the administration of justice in the Secretariat;

9. *Affirms* that the functions of staff members selected to serve under the new system are official in nature, and requests the Secretary-General to ensure that those staff members are given sufficient time off from their substantive responsibilities to perform their functions;

10. *Recognizes* that the system of administration of justice, being heavily dependent on volunteers, requires frequent and comprehensive training of participants, and calls upon the Secretary-General to organize periodic training at each of the headquarters duty stations for all staff involved in the system of administration of justice;

11. *Stresses* the importance of the proper implementation of a sound performance appraisal system as a potential means of avoiding conflict;

12. *Also stresses* the need to provide training in managerial skills to improve conflict resolution skills of managers;

13. *Further stresses* the need to link the ability of managers to respond in the course of a proceeding with their own individual performance appraisal;

14. *Notes* that staff rule 112.3, which relates to the financial liability of managers, has yet to be implemented, also notes the issuance of the Secretary-General's bulletin ST/SGB/2004/14, and requests the Secretary-General to report on its implementation to the General Assembly at its sixty-first session;

15. *Requests* the Secretary-General to expeditiously implement the recommendations of the Office of Internal Oversight Services, subject to the provisions of the present resolution;

16. *Decides* that the time limits recommended by the Office of Internal Oversight Services will be mandatory within the appeals process once adequate capacity is in place, and no later than 1 January 2006;

17. *Also decides* that measures should be taken to eliminate the appearance of conflict of interest, and towards this end requests the Secretary-General to proceed with the transfer of the responsibility for formulating decisions on appeals from the Department of Management of the Secretariat to the Office of the Secretary-General;

II

The informal mechanism of administration of justice

Ombudsman

18. *Stresses* the importance of the Office of the Ombudsman as the primary means of informal dispute resolution, and reaffirms General Assembly resolution 56/253 of 24 December 2001 on the establishment of the Office;

19. *Requests* that the Office of the Ombudsman continue and expand its outreach activities, in particular to local, national and General Service staff, in order to facilitate equal access and awareness-raising, bearing in mind the structure, activities and operational environment of the Organization;

20. *Requests* the Secretary-General to submit proposals for strengthening the Office of the Ombudsman through improved access to it for staff serving in different locations;

21. *Invites* the Office of the Ombudsman to reduce all possible delays in responding to the requests of staff in order to ensure that staff are encouraged to seek resolution of conflict in an informal way;

22. *Requests* the Secretary-General to submit, in the context of his annual report on the administration of justice in the Secretariat, information on the activities of the Ombudsman, including general statistical information and information on trends and comments on policies, procedures and practices that have come to the attention of the Ombudsman;

III

The formal mechanisms of administration of justice

Panel of Counsel

23. *Takes note* of the role of the Coordinator of the Panel of Counsel, in preliminary consultations before initiation of the formal appeals process, to support an informal resolution at an early stage;

24. *Stresses* the role of staff representatives in advising and assisting staff in addressing issues informally and formally;

25. *Recognizes* the need to strengthen the capacities of the Panels of Counsel by increasing the opportunity for training on the United Nations Staff Regulations and Rules, policies, procedures or precedents for staff serving on the Panels, in view of the urgent need to strengthen legal advice and administrative support for staff members submitting an appeal;

26. *Invites* staff representatives to explore the possibility of establishing a staff-funded scheme in the Organization that provides legal advice and support to the staff; staff representatives may consult with the Secretary-General as they deem appropriate;

27. *Invites* the Secretary-General to consider appropriate incentives to be built into the system to encourage staff members to serve on the Panels;

28. *Encourages* the Panel of Counsel to increase outreach activities, and requests the Secretary-General to consider the inclusion of travel costs in section 28A, Office of the Under-Secretary-General for Management, of the proposed programme budget for the biennium 2006-2007, for this purpose;

Administrative Law Unit

29. *Notes* that the Administrative Law Unit has the multiple functions of administrative review, appeals, disciplinary matters and advisory services;

30. *Requests* the Secretary-General to submit to the General Assembly by the end of its fifty-ninth session proposals to separate the above-mentioned functions, through the redeployment of resources, in order to avoid conflicts of interest, taking into account the following needs:

(a) To ensure the necessary means to collect evidence;

(b) To advise both the appellant and the respondent;

(c) To ensure the uniform application of administrative decisions;

(d) To ensure appropriate consultation with the Office of Human Resources Management of the Department of Management and legal experts;

(e) To relay all necessary information to the Office of Human Resources Management;

31. *Stresses* that increased accountability by managers would contribute to the elimination of the backlog of appeals cases, as stated in the report of the Secretary-General, and decides that as a means to facilitate early consideration of cases, the following procedures should be adopted:

(a) Staff members wishing to appeal an administrative decision should send a copy of their request to the executive head of their department;

(b) The Administrative Law Unit should clarify with managers the requirements for the respondent's reply and the contributions expected from managers, as well as time limits;

32. *Requests* the Secretary-General to ensure that written explanations by managers to the Administrative Law Unit are submitted within eight weeks with no possibility of extension, and decides that compliance with this responsibility shall constitute part of the performance appraisal of managers;

33. *Decides* to amend staff rule 111.2 (a) to provide that staff wishing to appeal an administrative decision shall submit to the executive head of their department, office, fund or programme a copy of the letter addressed to the Secretary-General requesting a review of the case;

Joint Appeals Board

34. *Stresses* the particular importance of providing adequate training to the members of the Joint Appeals Board;

United Nations Administrative Tribunal

35. *Recalls* paragraph 5 of its resolution 57/307, and regrets that the steps necessary to separate the secretariat of the United Nations Administrative Tribunal from the Office of Legal Affairs were not undertaken;

36. *Endorses* the proposal of the Secretary-General to transfer the resources of the Tribunal from section 8, Legal affairs, of the proposed programme budget to section 1, Overall policy-making, direction and coordination, effective from the beginning of the biennium 2006-2007;

37. *Reaffirms* paragraph 5 of its resolution 57/307, and requests the Secretary-General to guarantee the immediate independence of the Tribunal, including through ensuring the provision of administrative and

logistical services that are exclusive to the secretariat of the Tribunal;

38. *Recalls* the recent amendment to the statute of the Tribunal, which provides that members shall possess judicial or other relevant legal experience in the field of administrative law or its equivalent within their national jurisdiction;

39. *Acknowledges* the need for the further strengthening of professionalism in the Tribunal by increasing membership of professional judges;

40. *Decides* to amend article 3, paragraph 1, of the statute of the Tribunal, with effect from 1 January 2006, to read:

"The Tribunal shall be composed of seven members, no two of whom may be nationals of the same State. Members shall possess judicial experience in the field of administrative law or its equivalent within their national jurisdiction. Only three members shall sit in any particular case.";

41. *Also decides* that the amendment to article 3 will be applied in the election of new members of the Tribunal with effect from 1 January 2006;

42. *Requests* the Secretary-General to submit proposals on compensation for the members of the Tribunal once all its members meet the criteria set out in article 3 of the statute as amended in the present resolution;

43. *Notes* that the vast majority of appeals against administrative decisions concern termination of employment or non-renewal of employment contracts, and decides, with reference to recommendation 5 of the Office of Internal Oversight Services, to revert to the question of amendment of article 7 of the statute of the Tribunal following receipt of the report of the panel as described in section IV of the present resolution;

44. *Also notes* the report of the Joint Inspection Unit on administration of justice;

45. *Stresses* the importance of the eventual harmonization of the statutes of the United Nations Administrative Tribunal and the International Labour Organization Administrative Tribunal;

46. *Requests* the United Nations Administrative Tribunal to review the rules, practices and procedures of similar tribunals with a view towards enhanced effective management of caseloads;

IV

Review of the internal justice system

47. *Decides* that the Secretary-General shall form a panel of external and independent experts to consider redesigning the system of administration of justice;

48. *Also decides* that the panel shall be composed of a pre-eminent judge or former judge with administrative law experience, an expert in alternative dispute resolution methods, a leading legal academic in international law, a person with senior management and administrative experience in an international organization and a person with United Nations field experience;

49. *Further decides* that the terms of reference of the redesign panel shall be as follows:

(a) The redesign panel shall propose a model for a new system for resolving staff grievances in the United Nations that is independent, transparent, effective, ef-

ficient and adequately resourced and that ensures managerial accountability; the model should involve guiding principles and procedures that clearly articulate the participation of staff and management within reasonable time frames and time limits;

(b) The redesign panel shall:

(i) Consider the relevant resolutions of the General Assembly;

(ii) Receive and review information from all the relevant stakeholders regarding existing mechanisms for the administration of justice in the Organization;

(iii) Consult with United Nations staff, including individual staff members, the Staff Union and managers, in order to form an opinion as to how and why some aspects of the system function effectively while other aspects do not;

(c) The redesign panel shall, in particular:

(i) Consider alternative systems for resolving staff grievances by considering other models of organizational dispute resolution, while acknowledging the uniqueness of the United Nations system, in particular the immunity of United Nations staff from national laws and thus the lack of recourse to national courts;

(ii) In proposing a model, consider the value of creating an effective system for handling staff complaints that involves alternative forms of dispute resolution by which cases can be settled by mutual consent, such as mediation, conciliation, arbitration and/or an ombudsman;

(iii) Consider the peer review;

(iv) Identify proactive measures such as education and training, that the United Nations can implement to minimize the number of disputes that arise;

(v) Examine the functioning of the Office of the Ombudsman and, if needed, present models to provide services tailored to responding to the needs of the Organization;

(vi) Examine and develop the criteria to be used in the categorization of cases;

(vii) Review the functioning of the United Nations Administrative Tribunal and examine the further harmonization of its statute and that of the International Labour Organization Administrative Tribunal with a view to further professionalizing the United Nations Administrative Tribunal;

(viii) Examine the possibility of an integrated judicial system with a two-layer structure of first and second instance, taking into account existing structures;

(ix) Examine the legal representation of the Secretary-General in the system of administration of justice;

50. Decides that the panel shall start its functions no later than 1 February 2006 and shall submit its findings and recommendations by the end of July 2006;

51. Requests the Secretary-General to transmit the report and recommendations of the panel to the General Assembly as a matter of priority;

52. Also requests the Secretary-General to submit his comments on the recommendations contained in the panel's report, along with the estimate of time and

resources needed for their implementation, to the General Assembly at the first part of its resumed sixty-first session;

53. *Decides* that activities requested above that would give rise to additional resource requirements during the biennium 2004-2005 should be included in the proposed programme budget for the biennium 2006-2007.

Follow-up to resolution 57/307

Management review of the appeals process

In a February report [A/59/706], the Secretary-General, in response to an ACABQ request, provided the cost implications of the recommendations relating to the management review of the appeals process at the United Nations, conducted by OIOS in 2004 [YUN 2004, p. 1442]. For the 2004-2005 biennium, the total cost for addressing and eliminating the backlog in conducting administrative reviews and preparing respondents' replies to the Joint Appeals Board amounted to $462,100, which would be accommodated within existing 2004-2005 resources.

Additional resource requirements for the 2006-2007 biennium amounted to $1,021,600. Of that amount, $57,000 would be accommodated under existing resources, leaving a balance of $964,600 in additional resource requirements. The Secretary-General emphasized that those cost requirements represented the recurring resources needed to keep cases current and within time limits, thereby complying with the new timelines as recommended by OIOS.

ACABQ report. In an interim report [A/59/715], ACABQ indicated that the Secretary-General's report (see above) on the cost implications of the OIOS recommendations did not respond fully to the Committee's request for a clear justification of needs or provide a full exposé of what would be achieved through the provision of additional resources. ACABQ intended to revert to the issue in the context of the proposed 2006-2007 programme budget. Its examination would include the relevant activities of the Office of the Ombudsman, OLA, OHRM, the Office of the Under-Secretary-General for Management and UNAT.

In the meantime, ACABQ recommended that the Secretariat be authorized to eliminate the current backlogs using existing resources. Proposals for the 2006-2007 proposed programme budget should address the Committee's concerns for full justification and information provided on the implementation of the Assembly's requests to establish a clear linkage between the administration of justice and personal responsibility and accountability, and to develop an effec-

tive system for recovering financial losses to the Organization due to UNAT judgements caused by management irregularities, wrongful actions or negligence of UN Secretariat officials.

The Assembly took action on the Secretary-General's report and that of ACABQ in section I of **resolution 59/283** (see p. 1530).

Joint Appeals Board

In response to resolution 55/258 [YUN 2001, p. 1337], the Secretary-General submitted an April report [A/60/72 & Corr.1] on the outcome of the work of the Joint Appeals Board (JAB) in 2004. He stated that 74 appeals and suspension-of-action cases were filed with JAB in New York, Geneva, Vienna and Nairobi in 2004, as compared to 145 cases in the previous year. JAB disposed of 143 cases, compared to 121 in 2003. Regarding disciplinary cases, which were accorded priority, 11 such cases were considered in 2004, compared to 18 the previous year. The Secretary-General accepted fully or partially 87 per cent of unanimous JAB decisions favourable to appellants in 2004 and rejected 12 per cent, compared to 84 per cent acceptances and 17 per cent rejections in 2003.

Administrative Law Unit

Pursuant to a General Assembly request in resolution 59/283 (see p. 1529), the Secretary-General submitted a July report [A/59/883] on the administration of justice in the Secretariat, which considered separating the functions of the Administrative Law Unit to avoid the conflict of interest arising from the same Unit handling the multiple functions of administrative review, appeals, disciplinary matters and advisory services. The Secretary-General analysed the situation, taking into account the following requirements: to ensure the necessary means to collect evidence; to advise both the appellant and the respondent; to ensure the uniform application of administrative decisions; to ensure consultations with OHRM and legal experts; and to relay all necessary information to OHRM. He indicated that the Unit was an integral part of OHRM, acted on behalf of the Administration at all stages of the appeals process and made the Unit's role clear to all parties. If no mutually acceptable solution could be found, the staff member's right to proceed to formal litigation was unimpeded.

With regard to evidence collection, the Secretary-General reported that the combination of responsibilities discharged to the Unit resulted in a significant economy of resources at the stage of establishing the facts and legal issues of a case, far better than if those facts had to be established in two separate offices. Since the Unit represented the respondent, the Panel of Counsel and the appellants, the Secretary-General indicated that no conflict of interest existed in advising both parties. As an integral part of OHRM, the Unit had access to all relevant officials and a variety of internal and efficient means to provide or receive information and could ensure the uniform application of administrative decisions. Furthermore, a new system of communications would have to be implemented should the review functions be given to another office. Beyond the substantive aspects of whether the separation of the functions of the Unit was needed, the Secretary-General also determined that it would not be possible to do so through the redeployment of resources, as proposed by the Assembly.

The Secretary-General concluded that it would not be in interest of the Organization to separate the functions of the Unit. The issues raised would also be reviewed in a systematic manner by the redesigned Panel of Counsel, with a view to preparing a comprehensive solution for ensuring that the Organization had the most effective administration of justice system.

Office of Ombudsman

In September, pursuant to General Assembly resolution 59/283 (see p. 1529), the Secretary-General submitted the first report [A/60/376] on the activities of the Ombudsman, which covered the period from 25 October 2002 to 31 August 2005 and presented statistical information on trends and comments on policies, procedures and practices that had come to the attention of the Ombudsman. Since its inception in 2002, nearly 1,400 staff members had sought the assistance of the Office. A peer review conducted after its first year of operation, concluded that staff members generally had their concerns resolved in a timely manner. Feedback from staff who had used the services of the Office indicated that, in over 70 per cent of the closed cases, staff members were satisfied with the outcome. The most important type of issue raised by staff was promotion or career-related (316 cases), followed by termination of contracts (161), interpersonal conflicts (148), entitlement claims (119), conditions of service (103) and standards of conduct (83). The remaining cases were either found to be outside the terms of reference of the Ombudsman or those which the JAB had already commenced hearing, excluding intervention of the Office.

Challenges and issues identified through the review of cases included, disseminating information on existing rules and practices of the Organization; streamlining the various types of contracts; increasing transparency during the staff selection, recruitment and promotion process; fostering managerial excellence; ensuring training for new recruits; recognizing outstanding performance; strengthening the conflict resolution system; establishing a whistle-blower protection policy; addressing discrimination; reviewing the administration of justice system in the Secretariat; preparing mission personnel for deployment to the field; and addressing disparities of salaries, entitlements or security provisions between locally recruited staff and international staff.

The appointment and the terms of reference of the Office of the Ombudsman were annexed to the report.

Criminal behaviour and disciplinary action

In response to General Assembly resolution 59/287 (see p. 1474), the Secretary-General transmitted an August report [A/60/315] on disciplinary matters and cases of criminal behaviour, covering the period from 1 January 2004 to 30 June 2005, which provided information on the disciplinary and/or legal action taken in cases of established misconduct and/or criminal behaviour. An information circular [ST/IC/2005/51] was issued to inform all staff members of the most common examples of misconduct and criminal behaviour and their disciplinary consequences, including any legal action.

The report provided an overview of administrative machinery in disciplinary matters, describing the rules governing the conduct of staff members, the Secretary-General's authority to impose disciplinary measures for misconduct, due process for pursuing a matter as a disciplinary case, various forms of disciplinary measures that could be imposed, as well as non-disciplinary measures that could be applied. A summary was provided for each case that had led to the imposition of one or more disciplinary measures during the period covered, indicating the nature of the misconduct and measures imposed. Of the 24 cases detailed in the report, one dealt with theft and misappropriation, nine with fraud and misrepresentation, three with assault, six with sexual exploitation and abuse and five with other misconduct. However, not every case brought to the attention of the Secretary-General resulted in disciplinary measures being taken. If an OHRM review revealed that there was insufficient evidence to pursue a matter as a disciplinary one or if the staff member provided a satisfactory explanation in response to the allegations, the case was closed. Cases might also be closed if a staff member retired or separated from the Organization before disciplinary proceedings were concluded, as the Secretary-General had no authority to impose disciplinary action on former staff members. In such cases, a record would be placed in the official status file.

When an investigation showed that criminal activity might have occurred, the Secretary-General might decide to refer those cases to relevant national authorities for action. During the reporting period, the Secretary-General referred 32 such cases to national authorities, including 17 cases against identified individuals and 15 cases in which criminal behaviour was identified, but the individuals responsible were not.

UN Administrative Tribunal

In its annual note to the General Assembly [A/INF/60/5], the United Nations Administrative Tribunal (UNAT) reported in December, through the Secretary-General, that it delivered 59 judgements in 2005, relating to cases brought by staff against the Secretary-General or the executive heads of other UN bodies to resolve disputes involving terms of appointment and other issues. The Tribunal met in plenary in New York on 22 November and held two panel sessions (Geneva, 20 June–22 July and 24 October–23 November).

Chapter IV

Institutional and administrative matters

In 2005, the United Nations addressed administrative and institutional matters in order to ensure the efficient functioning of the Organization. The General Assembly resumed its fifty-ninth session and opened its sixtieth session on 13 September. A High-level plenary meeting was convened from 14 to 16 September to commemorate the sixtieth anniversary of the founding of the Organization. The Assembly granted observer status to the Latin American Integration Association, the Common Fund for Commodities, the Hague Conference on Private International Law and the Ibero-American Conference.

The Security Council held 235 formal meetings to deal with regional conflicts, peacekeeping operations and other issues related to the maintenance of international peace and security. The expansion of its membership was again considered by the Assembly.

In addition to its organizational and substantive sessions, the Economic and Social Council held a special high-level meeting with the Bretton Woods institutions (the World Bank Group and the International Monetary Fund), the World Trade Organization and the United Nations Conference on Trade and Development.

The Committee on Conferences examined requests for changes to the 2005 calendar of conferences and meetings and sought ways of optimizing the use of conference-servicing resources. As part of its reform process, it began using e-Meets, the electronic meetings management system.

The Secretary-General reported on progress in the implementation of the capital master plan for the refurbishment of the UN Headquarters complex in New York. The strategy for executing the project was re-examined and the Secretary-General recommended a phased approach to the renovations. The Secretary-General also reported on the establishment of the United Nations Department of Safety and Security.

Institutional machinery

General Assembly

The General Assembly met throughout 2005; it resumed and concluded its fifty-ninth session and held the major part of its sixtieth session. The fifty-ninth session was resumed in plenary meetings on 18-20 January; 15 February; 8, 21 and 29 March; 6-8, 13, 15, 21 and 28 April; 5, 9, 11 and 27 May; 2, 6, 13, 22, 23 and 27-28 June; 11-12, 14, 18 and 26 July. The sixtieth session opened on 13 September and continued until its suspension on 23 December.

A High-level plenary meeting of the Assembly (the 2005 World Summit) was held from 14 to 16 September to commemorate the sixtieth anniversary of the founding of the Organization and to chart its future course (see p. 47).

Organization of Assembly sessions

2005 sessions

By **decision 60/501** of 13 September, the General Assembly authorized the Committee on Relations with the Host Country, the Committee on the Exercise of the Inalienable Rights of the Palestinian People, the Working Group on the Financing of the United Nations Relief and Works Agency for Palestine Refugees in the Near East, the Executive Board of the United Nations Children's Fund (UNICEF), the Disarmament Commission, the Special Committee to Investigate Israeli Practices Affecting the Human Rights of the Palestinian People and Other Arabs of the Occupied Territories and the Committee on Conferences to meet during the main part of its sixtieth session. On 14 October, it authorized the Executive Board of the International Research and Training Institute for the Advancement of Women (INSTRAW) to do likewise.

By **decision 60/502** of 20 September, the Assembly adopted a number of provisions concerning the organization of the sixtieth session, as recommended by the General Committee [A/60/250 & Corr.1]. On 8 November, the Assembly extended the work of the Sixth (Legal) Committee until 29 November. On 8 December, it postponed the date of recess of the sixtieth session, originally fixed for 13 December, to 22 December. On 22 December, the Assembly further postponed the date of recess of the sixtieth session to 23 December.

Credentials

The Credentials Committee, at its first meeting on 13 December [A/60/595], had before it a memorandum by the Secretary-General indicating that, to date, 133 Member States had submitted the formal credentials of their representatives. Information concerning the representatives of 46 other Member States had been communicated also.

The Committee adopted a resolution accepting the credentials received and recommended a draft resolution to the General Assembly for adoption. On 20 December, the Assembly, by **resolution 60/181**, approved the Committee's report.

Agenda

During the resumed fifty-ninth (2005) session, the General Assembly, by **decision 59/503 B**, took a number of actions related to its agenda. It decided to reopen consideration of the item on the strengthening of the coordination of humanitarian and disaster relief assistance of the United Nations, including special economic assistance, in order to consider expeditiously a draft resolution [A/59/L.58]; the item on the election of judges of the International Tribunal for the Prosecution of Persons Responsible for Serious Violations of International Humanitarian Law Committed in the Territory of the Former Yugoslavia since 1991, and agreed to proceed immediately to its consideration in order to take action on the recommendations of the Secretary-General [A/59/666]; and the sub-item on the appointment of members of the Committee on Contributions, in order to consider expeditiously the report of the Fifth (Administrative and Budgetary) Committee [A/59/583/Add.1]. On the Secretary-General's proposal [A/59/239], the Assembly included in its agenda an additional item on the financing of the United Nations Mission in the Sudan and allocated it to the Fifth Committee, and decided to consider directly in plenary meeting the item on measures to eliminate international terrorism and to proceed immediately to its consideration in order to consider expeditiously a draft resolution [A/59/766] recommended by the Ad Hoc Committee established by Assembly resolution 51/210 [YUN 1996, p. 1208]. On the Secretary-General's proposal [A/59/240], the Assembly included in its agenda an additional sub-item on the confirmation of the appointment of the Administrator of the United Nations Development Programme and decided to consider it directly in plenary meeting; it agreed to proceed immediately to the consideration of the sub-item in order to take action on the appoint-

ment. The Assembly further decided to consider directly in plenary meeting the item on follow-up to and implementation of the outcome of the International Conference on Financing for Development, in order to consider expeditiously a draft resolution [A/59/ L.61]. On the Secretary-General's proposal [A/59/241], it included in its agenda the item on the election of the United Nations High Commissioner for Refugees and decided to consider it directly in plenary meeting. The Assembly decided to consider directly in plenary meeting the sub-item on the further implementation of the Programme of Action for the Sustainable Development of Small Island Developing States in order to consider expeditiously a draft resolution [A/59/L.63]; and the item on the scale of assessments for the apportionment of the expenses of the United Nations, in order to consider expeditiously a draft resolution [A/59/L.66].

On 13 April, the Assembly deferred for future consideration the agenda items on the programme budget for the 2004-2005 biennium, the scale of assessments for the apportionment of the expenses of the United Nations, and the UN common system (**decision 59/551 B**). On the same date, the Assembly decided to: defer until its sixtieth session consideration of the report of the Office of Internal Oversight Services (OIOS) [A/59/373] on the review of the operations and management of UN libraries (**decision 59/557**); consider, as a matter of priority at the earliest possible period, but no later than the main part of its sixtieth session, the Secretary-General's report [A/59/397] on the review of the regular programme of technical cooperation and the Development Account (**decision 59/558**); and consider, as a matter of priority during its sixtieth session, the question of the strengthening of the international civil service (**decision 59/561**).

On 22 June, the Assembly deferred until its sixtieth session consideration of the items on the scale of assessments for the apportionment of the expenses of the United Nations and on human resources management (**decision 59/551 C**), and decided to remove from its agenda the item on the financing of the United Nations Verification Mission and the United Nations Observer Mission in Angola (**decision 59/564**).

On 12 September, the Assembly deferred until its sixtieth session consideration of the agenda item on the programme budget for the 2004-2005 biennium (**decision 59/551 D**). On the same date, the Assembly deferred consideration of, and included in the draft agenda of its sixtieth session, the items on the prevention of armed conflict (**decision 59/568**); improving the financial situation of the United Nations (**decision 59/569**); financing of the United Nations Mission in East Timor (**decision 59/570**); and the situation in the occupied territories of Azerbaijan (**decision 59/571**).

The Assembly took a number of actions in respect of its sixtieth (2005) session agenda, as listed in **decision 60/503**. On 20 September, on the recommendation of the General Committee [A/60/250 & Corr.1], it adopted the agenda [A/60/251] and the allocation of agenda items [A/60/252] for the sixtieth session. On 25 October, the Assembly, also on the recommendation of the General Committee [A/60/250/Add.1], included in the agenda of its sixtieth session an additional item entitled "Observer status for the Hague Conference on Private International Law in the General Assembly" and allocated it to the Sixth Committee. On 31 October, the Assembly, on the recommendation of the General Committee [A/60/250/Add.2], included in the agenda of its sixtieth session an additional item entitled "Observer status for the Ibero-American Conference in the General Assembly" and allocated it to the Sixth Committee; and deferred consideration of the item "Question of the Comorian island of Mayotte" and included it in the provisional agenda of its sixty-second (2007) session. On 15 December, the Assembly, on the recommendation of the General Committee [A/60/250/Add.3], included in the agenda of its sixtieth (2005) session an additional item entitled "Follow-up to the recommendations on administrative management and internal oversight of the Independent Inquiry Committee into the United Nations oil-for-food programme" and decided to consider it directly in plenary meeting.

On 23 December, the Assembly, by **decision 60/551**, deferred until its resumed sixtieth (2006) session consideration of the items on the review of the efficiency of the administrative and financial functioning of the United Nations; the proposed programme budget for the 2006-2007 biennium; programme planning; the pattern of conferences; the scale of assessments for the apportionment of the expenses of the United Nations; the Joint Inspection Unit; the UN common system; the report of the Secretary-General on the activities of OIOS; and administrative and budgetary aspects of the financing of the UN peacekeeping operations. In section B of the decision, the Assembly deferred until its sixty-first (2006) session consideration of a series of documents related to the item on human resources management.

By **decision 60/508** of 31 October, the Assembly decided that the item "The situation in Central America: progress in fashioning a region of peace, freedom, democracy and development" should remain on its agenda, beginning with the sixty-first (2006) session, for consideration upon notification by a Member State. By **decision 60/509** of the same date, the Assembly deferred consideration of the item "Zone of peace and cooperation of the South Atlantic" and the related report of the Secretary-General [A/60/253 & Add.1]; included the item in the agenda of its sixty-first (2006) session; and decided to maintain biennial consideration of it thereafter.

The Assembly included in the provisional agenda of its sixty-first (2006) session the items "Missiles" (**decision 60/515**), "Establishment of a nuclear-weapon-free zone in Central Asia" (**decision 60/516**), "United Nations conference to identify ways of eliminating nuclear dangers in the context of nuclear disarmament" (**decision 60/517**), and "Convening of the fourth special session of the General Assembly devoted to disarmament" (**decision 60/518**).

On 8 December, the Assembly included in the provisional agenda of its sixty-second (2007) session the item "Review of the implementation of the Declaration on the Strengthening of International Security" (**decision 60/520**).

Resolutions and decisions of the General Assembly

By **decision 60/510** of 3 November, the Assembly deferred consideration of the agenda item "Implementation of the resolutions of the United Nations" and included it in the provisional agenda of its sixty-first (2006) session.

First, Third, Fifth and Sixth Committees

The General Assembly, on 8 December, noted that the Sixth (Legal) Committee had adopted its provisional programme of work for the sixty-first (2006) session of the Assembly as proposed by the Committee's Bureau (**decision 60/513**). On the same date, the Assembly approved the proposed programme of work and timetable of the First (Disarmament and International Security) Committee for 2006 (**decision 60/521**). On 16 December, the Assembly approved the programme of work of the Third (Social, Humanitarian and Cultural) Committee for the sixty-first session (**decision 60/537**). Also on 16 December, the Assembly, by a recorded vote of 81 to 33, and on the recommendation of the Fifth (Administrative and Budgetary) Committee [A/60/593/Add.1], decided to provide full conference services to the Committee's informal consultations beyond 6 p.m. and on weekends, until the end of the main part of its sixtieth session and to report on any related expenditure in the context of the second performance report on the programme budget for the 2004-2005 biennium (**decision 60/539**). On 22 December, the Assembly approved the programme of work of the Second (Economic and Financial) Committee for the sixty-first session (**decision 60/549**).

Security Council

The Security Council held 235 formal meetings in 2005, adopted 71 resolutions and issued 67 presidential statements. It considered 48 agenda items (see APPENDIX IV). In a September note [A/60/352], the Secretary-General, in accordance with Article 12, paragraph 2 of the Charter of the United Nations and with the consent of the Council, notified the General Assembly of 61 matters relative to the maintenance of international peace and security that the Council had discussed since his previous annual notification [YUN 2004, p. 1448]. The Secretary-General also listed 81 matters that the Council had not discussed since then. The Assembly, on 11 November, took note of the Secretary-General's note (**decision 60/512**).

Also on 11 November, the Assembly took note of the Council's report for the period 1 August 2004 to 31 July 2005 [A/60/2 & Corr.1] (**decision 60/511**).

Membership

The General Assembly continued to examine the question of expanding the Security Council's membership. It considered the report of the Open-ended Working Group on the Question of Equitable Representation on and Increase in the Membership of the Security Council and Other Matters related to the Security Council [A/59/47]. The Assembly took action with regard to the report in **decision 59/566** of 12 September (see p. 1480).

Economic and Social Council

The Economic and Social Council held its organizational session for 2005 on 19 January, 4 February, 1 and 31 March; a resumed organizational session on 27 and 28 April and 9 June; and a special high-level meeting with the Bretton Woods institutions (the World Bank Group and the International Monetary Fund), the World Trade Organization (WTO) and the United Nations Conference on Trade and Development (UNCTAD) on 18 April, all in New York. It held its substantive session from 29 June to 27 July and resumed substantive session on 21 October, in New York. The work of the Council in 2005 was covered in its report to the General Assembly [A/60/3].

On 19 January and 31 March, the Council elected its Bureau (a President and four Vice-Presidents) for 2005 (see APPENDIX III) and adopted the agenda of its organizational session [E/2005/2 & Corr.1 & Add.1 & Corr.1].

On 4 February, the Council approved the change in the dates of its 2005 substantive session from 4-29 July to 29 June–27 July (**decision 2005/202**), adopted the provisional agenda (**decision 2005/203**) and decided on the working arrangements for that session (**decision 2005/210**). On 29 June, it adopted the agenda [E/2005/100] and approved the proposed programme of work of that session [E/2005/L.9]. At the same meeting, it approved the requests for hearings from non-governmental organizations (NGOs) [E/2005/76] (**decision 2005/220**).

Sessions and segments

During 2005, the Economic and Social Council adopted 55 resolutions and 116 decisions. By **decision 2005/210** of 1 March, the Council decided that its high-level segment would be held from 29 June to 1 July; the coordination segment from 5 to 7 July; the operational activities segment from 8 to 12 July; the humanitarian affairs segment from 13 to 18 July; the general segment from 18 to 25 July; and to conclude its work on 26 and 27 July. By **decision 2005/211** of the same date, the Council decided that the special high-level meeting with the Bretton Woods institutions, WTO and UNCTAD would be held in New York on 18 April.

On 9 June, the Council deferred until the coordination segment of its 2005 substantive session consideration of the multi-year work programme for that segment (**decision 2005/218**).

2005 and 2006 sessions

On 4 February (**decision 2005/205**), the Council decided that the work of its 2005 operational activities segment would be devoted to the progress on and implementation of General Assembly resolution 59/250 [YUN 2004, p. 868] on the triennial comprehensive policy review of operational activities for development of the UN system. On the same date, it decided that the theme for the regional cooperation item at its 2005 substantive session would be "Achievement of the internationally agreed development goals, including those contained in the United Nations Millennium Declaration: a regional perspective" (**decision 2005/206**). On 31 March, it decided that the theme for the 2005 humanitarian affairs segment would be "Strengthening of the coordination of United Nations humanitarian assistance, including capacity, as well as organizational aspects", and that it would also convene a panel on the theme "Lessons learned from the recent earthquake/tsunami Indian Ocean disaster" (**decision 2005/212**). On 6 July, the Council adopted as its theme for the coordination segment of its 2006 substantive session "Sustained economic growth for social development, including the eradication of poverty and hunger". It decided that the establishment and implementation of a multi-year work programme for the segment would be guided by considerations set out in the decision, and to continue consultations on such a programme, with a view to finalizing it before the beginning of the 2006 substantive session (**decision 2005/221**).

On 27 July, the Council, by **decision 2005/300**, deferred until a later date consideration of the theme for its 2006 high-level segment. By **decision 2005/313** of 21 October, the Council adopted the following theme for that segment: "Creating an environment at the national and international levels conducive to generating full and productive employment and decent work for all, and its impact on sustainable development".

Work programme

On 4 February, the Economic and Social Council took note of the list of questions for inclusion in the programme of work of the Council for 2006 [E/2005/1], as orally revised (**decision 2005/204**).

Coordination, monitoring and cooperation

Institutional mechanisms

CEB activities

According to its annual overview report [E/2006/66], the work of the United Nations System Chief Executives Board for Coordination (CEB) was focused on the preparations for the 2005 World Summit (see p. 47) and the follow-up to its outcome (see p. 48). Those efforts culminated in the publication of the CEB report *One United Nations: Catalyst for Progress and Change— How the Millennium Declaration is Changing the Way the United Nations System Works*, which, in reviewing progress in implementing the Millennium Declaration, also charted the way forward for the UN system. CEB, through its High-level Committee on Programmes (HLCP) and High-level Committee on Management (HLCM), also addressed the cross-cutting issues of gender mainstreaming

and knowledge management. In the programme area, priority issues for inter-agency attention included employment, migration and system support to the New Partnership for Africa's Development (NEPAD), as well as follow-up to the World Summit on the Information Society. In the area of management and administration, efforts focused on: ensuring the safety and security of UN system personnel; promoting transparency and accountability as principles of good governance; improving the use of information and communication technologies in management and operations; enhancing financial and human resources management; and coordinating the UN system response to the threat of avian influenza.

CEB held two regular sessions in 2005: the first in Mont Pèlerin, Switzerland (9 April) [CEB/2005/1] and the second in New York (28 October) [CEB/2005/2]. Its principal subsidiary bodies met as follows: HLCM, ninth (Geneva, 4-5 April) [CEB/2005/3] and tenth (New York, 10-11 October) [CEB/2005/5] sessions; HLCP, ninth (Rome, 23-25 February) [CEB/2005/4] and tenth (Frascati, Italy, 6-8 October) [CEB/2005/7] sessions. HLCP also held its second retreat (Manhasset, United States, 19-21 July) [CEB/2005/6] to take stock of its accomplishments and draw conclusions to help guide its future orientation and work programme.

Report for 2004

The Committee for Programme and Coordination (CPC) [A/60/16 & Corr.1] considered CEB's annual overview report for 2004/2005 [YUN 2004, p. 1449]. It requested CEB to ensure that effective and coordinated support for NEPAD remained a UN system priority, and to update information on further efforts in that regard in its 2005/2006 overview report. CPC underlined the importance of effective coordination of system-wide efforts against hunger and recommended that CEB include in its 2005/2006 overview report information on the obstacles, problems and needs encountered by the inter-agency mechanisms dealing with the problem. It also recommended that the transfer of assets of illicit origin and their return to the countries of origin, as endorsed by the General Assembly in resolution 59/242 [YUN 2004, p. 1121], be added to the list of specific areas identified for joint work in the report. CEB recommended that the Assembly encourage the Secretary-General to improve the presentation of his report on the budgetary and financial situation of UN system organizations by providing information on all contributions, including core and non-core funding, as well as a clear definition of regular and voluntary funding. It also recommended that the Assembly review the inter-organizational mobility accord at its sixty-first

(2006) session under the agenda item on human resources management.

On 27 July, the Economic and Social Council took note of CEB's annual overview report for 2004/2005 (**decision 2005/225**).

Programme coordination

CPC held an organizational meeting on 11 May and its forty-fifth session from 6 June to 1 July, all in New York [A/60/16 & Corr.1].

CPC dealt with questions related to programme planning and the proposed programme budget for the 2006-2007 biennium. It considered OIOS reports on linkages between headquarters and field activities: a review of best practices for poverty eradication in the framework of the Millennium Declaration; the in-depth evaluation of the United Nations Human Settlements Programme; and two triennial reviews of the implementation of CPC recommendations on the in-depth evaluations of legal affairs and General Assembly and Economic and Social Council support and coordination. In addition to its review of CEB's annual overview report for 2004/2005 (see above), CPC considered the Secretary-General's reports on the progress and impact assessment of management improvement measures and UN system support for NEPAD, and a conference room paper on proposals for future thematic evaluations by OIOS.

On 19 July, the Council took note of CPC's report (**decision 2005/225**).

Joint Inspection Unit

The Joint Inspection Unit (JIU), in its annual report to the General Assembly covering the period 1 January to 31 December 2004 [A/60/34], described its process of reform, which began in 2003 [YUN 2003, p. 1388]. It discussed its 2005 work plan and its reports issued in 2004, the follow-up system for tracking the status of JIU recommendations and its relationship with other oversight bodies.

In section A of **decision 60/551** of 23 December, the Assembly deferred consideration of JIU's report until its resumed sixtieth (2006) session. In section XVI of **resolution 60/248** (see p. 1496), it approved a gross budget for JIU of $10,511,100 for the 2006-2007 biennium.

Other coordination matters

Follow-up to international conferences

Pursuant to Economic and Social Council resolution 2004/44 [YUN 2004, p. 1451], the Secretary-General submitted, in May [E/2005/61], an up-dated report on the role of the Council in the integrated and coordinated implementation of the outcomes of and follow-up to major UN conferences and summits. The report was submitted to the Assembly in August [A/60/275].

The review of the work methods of the Assembly and its Second and Third Committees was ongoing and further work would be needed to complete the consultations successfully. With regard to the Council and its subsidiary machinery, progress had been made in several areas, including strengthening thematic unity across the different segments of the Council's substantive session, reviewing the working methods of the functional commissions, and strengthening the role of the UN regional commissions in conference follow-up. Additional efforts were required to enhance cooperation among functional commissions and strengthen cooperation between the regional commissions and UN funds and programmes. The report contained recommendations for strengthening: the role of the Assembly and its Second and Third Committees in the coordinated and integrated follow-up to the comprehensive development agenda; the role of the Council and its subsidiary machinery in the implementation of Assembly resolutions 50/227, 52/12 B and 57/270 B; and the Council's cooperation with the funds and programmes, specialized agencies and inter-agency bodies, and international financial and trade institutions. The report also described efforts to comply with specific Council mandates related to recent international conferences and to enhance the Council's cooperation with, and the role of, civil society and the private sector.

ECONOMIC AND SOCIAL COUNCIL ACTION

On 27 July [meeting 40], the Economic and Social Council adopted **resolution 2005/48** [draft: E/2005/L.43] without vote [agenda items 6 and 8].

Role of the Economic and Social Council in the integrated and coordinated implementation of the outcomes of and follow-up to major United Nations conferences and summits

The Economic and Social Council,

Recalling its agreed conclusions 1995/1 of 28 July 1995 and 2002/1 of 26 July 2002 and its relevant resolutions on the integrated and coordinated implementation of and follow-up to the outcomes of major United Nations conferences and summits,

Recalling also General Assembly resolutions 50/227 of 24 May 1996, 52/12 B of 19 December 1997 and 57/270 B of 23 June 2003,

Recalling further the internationally agreed development goals, including those contained in the United Nations Millennium Declaration, the outcomes of the major United Nations conferences and summits and the reviews of their implementation in the economic, social and related fields,

Taking note of the report of the Secretary-General,

1. *Underlines* the unique opportunity provided by the High-level Plenary Meeting of the General Assembly in September 2005 to advance the implementation of all the commitments made in the United Nations Millennium Declaration and in the outcomes of the major United Nations conferences and summits;

2. *Takes note with appreciation* of the contributions of the functional commissions, the regional commissions and other relevant subsidiary bodies to the preparation of the input of the Economic and Social Council to the High-level Plenary Meeting of the General Assembly;

3. *Recalls* its decision 2005/221 of 6 July 2005, in which it decided to continue consultations on a multi-year work programme for the coordination segment, with a view to finalizing the work programme before the beginning of its substantive session of 2006;

4. *Welcomes* the progress made in the review of the working methods of several functional commissions, and invites those functional commissions and other relevant subsidiary bodies that have not yet done so to continue to examine their methods of work, as mandated by the General Assembly in its resolution 57/270 B, in order to better pursue the implementation of the outcomes of major United Nations conferences and summits, and to submit their reports to the Council in 2006;

5. *Recognizes* that progress has been made in several areas to enhance cooperation among the functional commissions and between the functional commissions and the funds and programmes, and invites the functional commissions to continue to work towards further strengthening this cooperation, including through the exchange of experiences, with the aim of contributing to the quality and impact of intergovernmental decisions;

6. *Requests* its commissions, in their reports, to clearly identify the operational implications of their work for consideration and appropriate action by the governing bodies of the United Nations funds and programmes;

7. *Decides* to further strengthen its linkages with the United Nations regional commissions, including through the contribution of the commissions to the preparation of reports on implementation reviews;

8. *Invites* the United Nations regional commissions, within their mandates, to continue to develop closer links among themselves through knowledge-sharing and to enhance cooperation, as appropriate, with the United Nations funds and programmes in order to ensure coherence in their work at the regional level while respecting the governance structures of the relevant bodies;

9. *Recognizes* the importance of an efficient reporting system in order to make better use of the information provided to the Economic and Social Council and to allow the Council to exercise its coordinating and policy guidance role, and encourages subsidiary bodies to adhere to the guidelines for documentation adopted by the General Assembly and the Council;

10. *Decides* to continue to promote integrated and coordinated implementation of and follow-up to the outcomes of the major United Nations conferences and summits;

11. *Stresses* the important contribution of civil society in the implementation of conference outcomes,

and emphasizes that the contribution of non-governmental organizations and the private sector to the work of the Economic and Social Council should be further encouraged and improved, in accordance with the rules and procedures of the Council;

12. *Decides* to continue to take the steps necessary for the effective implementation of the provisions of Assembly resolutions 50/227, 52/12 B and 57/270 B, which are relevant to the work of the Economic and Social Council and its subsidiary machinery;

13. *Requests* the Secretary-General to submit a report on the role of the Economic and Social Council in the implementation of Assembly resolutions 50/227, 52/12 B and 57/270 B for consideration by the Council at its substantive session of 2006.

The UN and other organizations

Observer status

Latin American Integration Association

On 15 July [A/60/141], Ecuador requested the inclusion in the agenda of the General Assembly's sixtieth session of an item on observer status for the Latin American Integration Association. In an explanatory memorandum annexed to the request, the Association stated that it was established by the 1980 Treaty of Montevideo and consisted of 12 member countries, which had agreed to pursue the regional integration process. Observer status would strengthen its interaction with the United Nations and expand the ability of both organizations to promote development and cooperation at the regional and global levels.

GENERAL ASSEMBLY ACTION

On 23 November [meeting 53], the General Assembly, on the recommendation of the Sixth Committee [A/60/521], adopted **resolution 60/25** without vote [agenda item 155].

Observer status for the Latin American Integration Association in the General Assembly

The General Assembly,

Wishing to promote cooperation between the United Nations and the Latin American Integration Association,

1. *Decides* to invite the Latin American Integration Association to participate in the sessions and the work of the General Assembly in the capacity of observer;

2. *Requests* the Secretary-General to take the necessary action to implement the present resolution.

Common Fund for Commodities

On 18 July [A/60/191], the United Republic of Tanzania requested the inclusion in the agenda of the General Assembly's sixtieth session of an item on observer status for the Common Fund for

Commodities. An explanatory memorandum annexed to the request stated that the Fund, which was negotiated under the auspices of the United Nations Conference on Trade and Development (UNCTAD) and entered into force in 1989, was an intergovernmental financial institution concerned exclusively with commodity development issues and projects. Its membership consisted of 106 countries and three intergovernmental institutions: the African Union, the European Community and the Common Market for Eastern and Southern Africa. Membership was open to UN Member States and specialized agencies, and to intergovernmental regional economic integration organizations that exercised competence in the Fund's fields of activity.

GENERAL ASSEMBLY ACTION

On 23 November [meeting 53], the General Assembly, on recommendation of the Sixth Committee [A/60/522], adopted **resolution 60/26** without vote [agenda item 156].

Observer status for the Common Fund for Commodities in the General Assembly

The General Assembly,

Wishing to promote cooperation between the United Nations and the Common Fund for Commodities,

1. *Decides* to invite the Common Fund for Commodities to participate in the sessions and the work of the General Assembly in the capacity of observer;

2. *Requests* the Secretary-General to take the necessary action to implement the present resolution.

The Hague Conference on Private International Law

On 12 October [A/60/232], the Netherlands requested the inclusion in the agenda of the General Assembly's sixtieth session of an item on observer status for The Hague Conference on Private International Law. An explanatory memorandum annexed to the request explained that the Conference, which had been an intergovernmental organization since 1955, comprised 65 member States. Its work covered international legal cooperation and litigation; international protection of children, families, family (property) relations and vulnerable adults; and international commercial and finance law. In each of those fields, the Conference had adopted a number of multilateral treaties, for which it provided assistance, monitoring and support. The Conference suggested that it be granted observer status to achieve more complementarity and to widen the potential for more systematic and programmatic cooperation.

GENERAL ASSEMBLY ACTION

On 23 November [meeting 53], the General Assembly, on the recommendation of the Sixth

Committee [A/60/533], adopted **resolution 60/27** without vote [agenda item 158].

Observer status for the Hague Conference on Private International Law in the General Assembly

The General Assembly,

Wishing to promote cooperation between the United Nations and the Hague Conference on Private International Law,

1. *Decides* to invite the Hague Conference on Private International Law to participate in the sessions and the work of the General Assembly in the capacity of observer;

2. *Requests* the Secretary-General to take the necessary action to implement the present resolution.

Ibero-American Conference

On 20 October [A/60/233], Spain requested the inclusion in the agenda of the General Assembly's sixtieth session of an item on observer status for the Ibero-American Conference. An explanatory memorandum annexed to the request stated that the first Ibero-American Summit of Heads of State and Government, held in Guadalajara, Mexico, in 1991, set up the Conference, with the participation of the sovereign Portuguese- and Spanish-speaking States of the Americas and Europe. Subsequent summits recognized that democracy and respect for human rights and fundamental freedoms were the pillars of the Ibero-American community. Cooperation programmes and projects conducted within the framework of the Conference in the areas of education, culture, science and technology promoted an Ibero-American identity, with a view to developing a sphere of cooperation.

GENERAL ASSEMBLY ACTION

On 23 November [meeting 53], the General Assembly, on the recommendation of the Sixth Committee [A/60/534], adopted **resolution 60/28** without vote [agenda item 159].

Observer status for the Ibero-American Conference in the General Assembly

The General Assembly,

Wishing to promote cooperation between the United Nations and the Ibero-American Conference,

1. *Decides* to invite the Ibero-American Conference to participate in the sessions and the work of the General Assembly in the capacity of observer;

2. *Requests* the Secretary-General to take the necessary action to implement the present resolution.

Participation in UN work

Intergovernmental organizations

The Economic and Social Council, on 28 April (**decision 2005/215**) and 9 June (**decision 2005/219**), respectively, included in the agenda of its 2005 substantive session the requests of the Global Water Partnership [E/2005/49] and the West African Economic and Monetary Union [E/2005/64] to participate as observers in the Council's work. The Council granted observer status to both organizations on 21 July (**decision 2005/233**).

Non-governmental organizations

Committee on NGOs

The Committee on Non-Governmental Organizations held its 2005 regular session (5-14 January) [E/2005/32 & Corr.1 (Part I)] and its resumed 2005 session (New York, 5-20 May) [E/2005/32 (Part II)], both in New York. In January, the Committee considered 144 applications for consultative status with the Council, including those deferred from its 1998-2004 sessions. It recommended 87 NGOs for consultative status and deferred consideration of 52 applications. The Committee closed its considerations of two applications and recommended the reclassification of one NGO from special to general consultative status. It took note of 72 quadrennial reports and deferred consideration of 12 others.

The Committee decided that an organization that resulted from the merger of organizations with consultative status with the Council should retain that status, and that the retained status should be the highest category given to the organizations that were party to the merger. It recommended general consultative status to two such NGOs and deferred consideration of three merged NGOs that did not have consultative status.

The Committee recommended four draft decisions on matters calling for action by the Council, including a decision related to the reinstatement of consultative status of an NGO (see below). By the third draft decision, the two days not used by the Committee at its regular session would be added to its resumed session in May (see below); the Council adopted the draft decision on 4 February (**decision 2005/209**).

The Committee reviewed its working methods relating to the implementation of Council resolution 1996/31 [YUN 1996, p. 1360], including the process of accreditation of NGO representatives. It considered the criteria for the reinstatement by the Council of consultative status to the Asociación para la Paz Continental (ASOPAZCO), an NGO suspended by the Council in 2000. The Committee recommended a draft decision for action by the Council, requesting ASOPAZCO to submit an updated application to be recognized as a consultative entity. The Council adopted the draft decision on 4 February (**decision 2005/208**).

Also on 4 February, the Council granted consultative status to 75 NGOs and placed 12 others on the Roster; reclassified one NGO from special to general consultative status; and noted that the Committee had taken note of 72 quadrennial reports and closed consideration of requests by two NGOs for consultative status (**decision 2005/207**).

At its resumed session, the Committee considered 148 applications for consultative status, including applications deferred from previous sessions. It recommended 105 NGOs for consultative status, deferred consideration of 40 applications, and closed consideration of three others. It recommended the reclassification of one NGO from special to general consultative status and one from roster to special consultative status. It deferred reclassification of one NGO. The Committee took note of 44 quadrennial reports and deferred consideration of 14 others.

The Committee adopted one decision for the Council's attention, and recommended five draft decisions for action by the Council. The Committee requested the Secretary-General to examine the causes for the persistent delays in the availability of documentation to the Committee and to report on it in 2006. On 21 July, the Council took note of the decision and requested the Secretary-General to take the actions requested by the Committee (**decision 2005/240**).

The Committee reviewed its working methods relating to the implementation of Council resolutions 1996/31, including the process of NGO accreditation, and decision 1995/304 [YUN 1995, p. 1445]. It considered implementation of Council decision 2001/295 [YUN 2001, p. 1377] relating to requests by those NGOs referred to in Council decision 1993/220 [YUN 1993, p. 668] to expand participation in other fields of the Council's work; and decision 2004/212 [YUN 2004, p. 831] concerning the participation of accredited NGOs in the 2002 World Summit on Sustainable Development [YUN 2002, p. 821] in future sessions of the Commission on Sustainable Development. The Committee also considered the strengthening of the NGO section of the Department of Economic and Social Affairs.

Following a proposal by Cuba, the Committee, by a role-call vote of 8 to 4, with 6 abstentions, recommended a draft decision for action by the Council to withdraw ASOPAZCO's consultative status. On 21 July, the Council adopted the draft decision (**decision 2005/239**).

The Committee considered a complaint by China against A Woman's Voice International; China proposed that the consultative status of that NGO be suspended for one year. A proposal by the United States to suspend debate on the issue was rejected by a roll-call vote of 10 to 2, with 5 abstentions. By a further roll-call vote of 15 to 1, with 1 abstention, the Committee recommended a draft decision for action by the Council to suspend the consultative status of A Woman's Voice International for one year. On 21 July, the Council adopted the draft decision (**decision 2005/238**).

Also on 21 July, the Council granted consultative status to 94 NGOs and placed 11 others on the Roster; reclassified one NGO from roster to general consultative status and another from roster to special consultative status; and noted that the Committee had taken note of 44 quadrennial reports and closed the case of complaints submitted by Member States against two NGOs (**decision 2005/237**). On the same day, the Council took note of the report of the Committee on its 2005 session (**decision 2005/242**). It decided that the Committee's 2006 regular session would be held from 19 to 27 January 2006 and its resumed session from 10 to 19 May 2006, and approved the provisional agenda for the Committee's 2006 session (**decision 2005/241**).

On 13 January, the Committee took note of the closure of the following NGOs that had informed the Secretariat of the termination of their activities: the Committee for European Security and Cooperation, International Family Health, and Oceans Institute of Canada.

Requests for hearing

On 13 May, the Committee on NGOs approved 27 requests from NGOs to be heard during the Council's high-level segment [E/2005/76].

Conferences and meetings

Committee on Conferences

The Committee on Conferences held an organizational meeting on 23 March and its substantive session on 19 and 27 September [A/60/32]. It examined requests for changes to the approved calendar of conferences for 2005 [A/AC.172/2005/2] and reviewed the draft biennial calender of conferences and meetings for 2006-2007 [A/AC.172/2005/CRP.2]. The Committee recommended that, pending confirmation by the Special Committee on Peacekeeping Operations of the possible shortening of its session, the draft calendar should indicate a four-week duration for it. It considered the utilization of conference-servicing resources and facilities; requests for exceptions to the Assembly's limitation on meet-

ings during Assembly sessions [YUN 1985, p. 1256]; improving the performance of the UN Department for General Assembly and Conference Management; documentation- and publication-related matters; translation and interpretation related matters; information technology; and other matters. (The Committee's deliberations and recommendations on those matters are detailed in the sections below.)

The Committee approved requests from several bodies for changes to the approved calendar for 2005.

On 19 July, the Economic and Social Council approved the calendar of conferences and meetings for 2006 and 2007 in the economic, social and related fields (**decision 2005/226**).

On 23 December, the Assembly deferred consideration of the Committee's report until its resumed sixtieth (2006) session (**decision 60/551**).

GENERAL ASSEMBLY ACTION

On 23 December [meeting 69], the General Assembly, on the recommendation of the Fifth Committee [A/60/601], adopted **resolution 60/236 A** without vote [agenda item 127].

Pattern of conferences

The General Assembly,

Reaffirming its relevant resolutions, including resolutions 40/243 of 18 December 1985, 41/213 of 19 December 1986, 43/222 A to E of 21 December 1988, 52/214 of 22 December 1997, 54/248 of 23 December 1999, 55/222 of 23 December 2000, 56/242 of 24 December 2001, 56/254 D of 27 March 2002, 56/262 of 15 February 2002, 56/287 of 27 June 2002, 57/283 A of 20 December 2002, 57/283 B of 15 April 2003, 58/250 of 23 December 2003 and 59/265 of 23 December 2004,

Reaffirming also its resolution 42/207 C of 11 December 1987, in which it requested the Secretary-General to ensure the equal treatment of the official languages of the United Nations,

Having considered the report of the Committee on Conferences and the relevant reports of the Secretary-General,

Having also considered the report of the Advisory Committee on Administrative and Budgetary Questions,

1. *Approves* the draft calendar of conferences and meetings of the United Nations for 2006 and 2007, as submitted by the Committee on Conferences, taking into account the observations of the Committee;

2. *Authorizes* the Committee on Conferences to make any adjustments to the calendar of conferences and meetings for 2006 and 2007 that may become necessary as a result of actions and decisions taken by the General Assembly at its sixtieth session;

3. *Notes with satisfaction* that the Secretariat has taken into account the arrangements referred to in General Assembly resolutions 53/208 A of 18 December 1998, 54/248, 55/222, 56/242, 57/283 B, 58/250 and 59/265 concerning Orthodox Good Friday and

the official holidays of Eid al-Fitr and Eid al-Adha, and requests all intergovernmental bodies to observe those decisions when planning their meetings;

4. *Requests* the Secretary-General to ensure that any modification to the calendar of conferences and meetings is implemented strictly in accordance with the mandate of the Committee on Conferences and other relevant resolutions of the General Assembly;

5. *Decides* to continue consideration of the item during the first part of its resumed sixtieth session;

6. *Also decides* to resume consideration of the reports of the Secretary-General on the pattern of conferences and on reform of the Department for General Assembly and Conference Management in order to take action on them.

Reform of the Department for General Assembly and Conference Management

In response to General Assembly resolution 59/265 [YUN 2004, p. 1463], the Secretary-General submitted a July report [A/60/112] on measures taken to reform the Department of General Assembly and Conference Management (DGACM) in the areas of conference management and integrated global management. Annexed to the report was a table containing compliance statistics on the submission of pre-session documents for 2004 and 2005.

The 2006-2007 draft calendar of conferences and meetings for New York-based bodies was generated by e-Meets, the electronic meetings management system, on an experimental basis. To facilitate the global planning of all sessions of calendar bodies, linkage between e-Meets and APG, a software for interpreter assignment, was completed in New York. At the United Nations Office at Geneva (UNOG), the first phase of e-Meets was implemented in February for meetings planning, and the second phase for the electronic processing of requests in June. At the United Nations Office at Vienna (UNOV), e-Meets was used for Vienna-based bodies meeting at headquarters; the system had been in operation at the United Nations Office at Nairobi (UNON) since 2003. APG was fully operational at all four duty stations.

In view of the lack of significant progress in 2004 in both the timely submission and adherence to page limits of documentation, heads of author departments and offices were reminded of the need to establish a transparent accountability system within the Secretariat. DGACM introduced vertical synchronization, which helped to match the capacity of each stage of downstream processing to its expected output. It also initiated horizontal synchronization, which ensured a balance of the processing capacity across languages in the simultaneous distribution of documents in the six official UN languages. The first pilot synchronization project involved the Central Planning and Coordination Service and the Translation Services. To increase transparency, DGACM was developing analytical instruments to identify more effectively the causes and impact of the late submission of documents. With the help of OIOS and the participation of author departments, DGACM also began a pilot self-evaluation project on the effectiveness of the slotting system for document forecasting and planning.

DGACM was establishing new reporting standards to provide greater transparency in documentation services to the intergovernmental bodies. Beginning with the 2005 substantive session of the Economic and Social Council and the sixtieth (2005) session of the General Assembly, DGACM would provide detailed advanced information on the status of pre-session documentation to the relevant intergovernmental bodies and author departments.

The first stage of DGACM's global management project had been completed. The use of common statistical indicators allowed for meaningful comparisons in the delivery of conference services by the four duty stations. A consolidated budget for the 2006-2007 biennium was prepared, which, for the first time, covered DGACM and conference servicing entities at UNOG, UNOV and UNON. DGACM proceeded with the second stage of the project, which aimed at the coordinating conference service operations at the four duty stations and at better utilizing allocated resources in the consolidated results-based budget. As recommended by OIOS in 2004 [YUN 2004, p. 1468], four task teams were established in January, on meeting servicing, examinations and training and documentation. DGACM was compiling a compendium of conference servicing policies, practices and procedures based in order to standardize them across duty stations, with a view to promoting comparability and strengthening planning and coordination. While the two-year global management project focusing on norm-setting would be completed by the end of the year, a long implementation process would continue to evolve in response to new challenges.

The Secretary-General said that DGACM intended to further refine the global management of the calendar and synchronize capacity with expected output, with greater focus on vertical synchronization; identify areas for further improvement following the completion of the self-evaluation project; analyse global information technology systems; and finalize the manual of policies, practices and procedures, and put in place mechanisms to ensure its effective implementation across duty stations.

The Committee on Conferences [A/60/32] supported DGACM's reform process but advised that, the Department should comply fully with relevant Assembly resolutions.

ACABQ report. In October [A/60/433], the Advisory Committee on Administrative and Budgetary Questions (ACABQ), having considered the Secretary-General's reports on DGACM reform (see above) and the pattern of conferences (see below), noted the continuing problems cited in those reports concerning the adherence to page limits and submission deadlines under the document slotting system. ACABQ was informed that of the 923 slotted documents in 2004, 236 (25.6 per cent) exceeded the page limit and 424 (45.9 per cent) were submitted late. In ACABQ's opinion, such findings raised the question of the accountability of author departments. ACABQ reiterated that, in order to function effectively, flexibility had to be built into the slotting system. It noted the proactive approach taken by DGACM to deal with compliance with deadlines and page limits, particularly its efforts to help enhance the drafting skills of Secretariat staff responsible for report preparation, and encouraged DGACM to continue to seek such creative solutions.

On 23 December, the Assembly deferred consideration of the Secretary-General's report on DGACM reform and ACABQ's report until its resumed sixtieth (2006) session (**decision 60/551**).

Use of conference services

The Committee on Conferences [A/60/32] considered the Secretary-General's July report on the pattern of conferences [A/60/93 & Corr.1], in which he discussed utilization of conference-servicing resources and facilities, documentation and publication, translation and interpretation, and information technology. The report also provided meeting statistics of a sample of UN bodies, statistics on conference services for meetings of regional and other groupings of Member States that met at the four duty stations from 1 May 2004 to 30 April 2005, and requests for meetings during the General Assembly's sixtieth (2005) session. The overall utilization factor in 2004 at the four duty stations was 83 per cent, six percentage points higher than in 2003 and exceeding the benchmark of 80 per cent for the first time since 2000. Both cancellations and time lost owing to late starting or early ending had been reduced markedly.

The Committee Chairman reported on his consultations with the bodies that had consistently utilized less than the applicable benchmark figure of their allocated resources for the previous three sessions. He recommended that consultations with those bodies be conducted on a more regular basis and that they be informed weekly of their meetings statistics. The Committee agreed that users should be encouraged to make more efficient use of conferences facilities, and the primary consideration for all users should be to ensure the best use of UN resources system-wide.

In October [A/60/433], ACABQ stated that it continued to be concerned that the methodology used for calculating the utilization factor had not changed significantly since 1993 and did not take into account the specific nature of work of the various bodies that were studied. It continued to believe that a more qualitative analysis was required and that the methodology should be revisited, with a view to developing a more results-based approach.

By **decision 60/551** of 23 December, the Assembly deferred until its resumed sixtieth (2006) session consideration of the Secretary-General's report.

Use of regional conference facilities

Nairobi

The Committee on Conferences [A/60/32] was informed that, as a result of vigorous marketing efforts, the United Nations Office at Nairobi (UNON) had been successful in attracting more meetings to its facilities. The utilization rate had increased by 28 per cent during the 2003/2004 period. Charges for conference services were reduced through streamlining, efficiency gains and increased client orientation. The Division of Conference Services intensified its efforts to become a major provider of conference services in the region.

Addis Ababa

The Secretary-General, in his July report on the pattern of conferences [A/60/93 & Corr.1], said that a notable increase in the level of activities at the conference centre at the Economic Commission for Africa (ECA) (Addis Ababa, Ethiopia) had been recorded in the last two years, with about 500 events hosted in 2004 as compared with 446 events in 2003. However, security considerations led to tighter control of access to and restrictions on the use of UN premises for commercial activities, thus limiting the potential to expand the use of the centre.

The Committee on Conferences [A/60/32] expressed concern about the impact of the security restrictions imposed on the conference centre. It requested information on the extent to which the application of headquarters minimum operating security standards had affected conference services at ECA and other duty stations.

Interpretation for regional and other groupings

In July [A/60/93 & Corr.1], the Secretary-General reported on the provision of interpretation services to meetings of regional and other major groupings of Member States for the period 1 May 2004 to 30 April 2005. The Committee on Conferences [A/60/32] noted that there had been a 29 per cent increase in the number of requests by such groupings for meetings held without interpretation, and a 21 per cent increase in the overall number of meetings requested by those groups. The percentage of meetings provided with interpretation during the reporting period decreased, in relative terms, to 85 per cent from 90 per cent during the previous period. In absolute terms, the total number of meetings also decreased. The introduction of the e-Meets electronic meetings management system as a tool for requesting conferences had brought about an improvement in the quality of services. However, there was little remaining capacity for accommodating additional meetings. The Committee expressed concern about the lack of capacity to provide for meetings of regional and other major groupings of Member States during peak periods.

Access of persons with disabilities to conferences services

In a 4 October letter to the General Assembly President [A/C.5/60/9], the Chairman of the Committee on Conferences said that the Committee had considered, at its 2005 substantive session [A/60/32] (see p. 1545), a letter from the Chairman of the Ad Hoc Committee on a Comprehensive and Integral International Convention on the Protection and Promotion of the Rights and Dignity of Persons with Disabilities, requesting assistance in ensuring that delegates with disabilities could participate meaningfully, and on an equal basis, with others in the work of the Ad Hoc Committee. The Committee on Conferences was addressed by the Secretary of the Ad Hoc Committee, who stated that the most urgent need was for official documentation relating to the work of the Ad Hoc Committee to be made available in both electronic format and in Braille. The Committee urged the Secretariat to continue to ensure that the special requirements of the Ad Hoc Committee were taken into account in conference room scheduling and to explore ways of providing the required documentation in electronic format and in Braille. It suggested that the Assembly consider those issues on a priority basis, as

well as the larger issue of the access of persons with disabilities to conference services.

By **decision 60/551** of 23 December, the Assembly deferred consideration of the letter until its resumed sixtieth (2006) session.

Construction of conference facilities

Additional conference rooms at Headquarters

By **decision 59/551 B** of 13 April, the General Assembly deferred for future consideration the Secretary-General's 2004 report [YUN 2004, p. 1469] on the plans for three additional conference rooms, to be created as part of the Capital Master Plan (see p. 1553), and viable solutions for allowing natural light into the rooms. By **decision 59/551 D** of 12 September, the Assembly deferred consideration of the report until its sixtieth (2005) session, and by **decision 60/551**, it deferred consideration of the report until its resumed sixtieth (2006) session.

Documentation

In response to General Assembly resolutions 58/270 [YUN 2003, p. 1399] and 59/276 [YUN 2004, p. 1476], the Secretary-General, in his July report on the pattern of conferences [A/60/93 & Corr.1], discussed issues related to documentation. Surveys of universities, depository libraries and other institutions, conducted in 2004 by the Dag Hammarskjöld Library, showed hesitancy on the part of institutions to abandon printed documentation to any degree. Although many of the institutions cited limitations in their technological capacity to provide customers with online access to documentation, a few clients were beginning to provide such access, and that trend was expected to continue.

DGACM set up a database to monitor decisions on policy issues, as well as individual cases on control and limitation of documentation, and explored ways to enhance the drafting skills of staff members involved in preparing reports. The Department of Public Information (DPI) continued the simultaneous distribution of documents in all official languages and the posting of parliamentary documentation on the Official Document System (ODS) and the UN website.

In response to resolution 59/265 [YUN 2004, p. 1463], the Secretary-General reported on options for improving the delivery of summary records, including those proposed in 2004 [ibid., p. 1467]. DGACM designed a pilot project to implement, for 2005, the option of concentrating précis-writing in the English Translation Service, which was expected to allow for shorter précis-writing times and records, as well as better planning of the translation capacity in other services involved in précis-writing during Assembly sessions. Under the option on setting a time frame for publication of summary records, DGACM conducted a pilot project aimed at translating the summary records of the main part of the Assembly's fifty-ninth (2004) session during the first quarter of 2005, with a deadline of 31 March for the simultaneous issuance of all records in all languages. The project was completed within the deadline. Experienced revisers conducted refresher courses on précis-writing under the option of shortening summary records. The response from bodies contacted by DGACM to indicate their willingness to review their entitlements to summary records, under the option of reducing the number of entitled bodies, was not encouraging, and further efforts were being made in that regard. Due to mixed reviews given by Member States to the option of replacing hard copies of summary records with digital recordings or electronic versions, that option was not explored further.

The Committee on Conferences [A/60/32] stressed that the timely issuance of documents was of fundamental importance to the work of intergovernmental bodies. Despite DGACM's efforts to meet mandated deadlines, the situation was not ideal. The problem, which appeared to lie in the late submission of documents by author departments, was being addressed by the interdepartmental task force on documentation, chaired by the Assistant Secretary-General for General Assembly and Conference Management. The Committee emphasized that strict adherence to page limits should not impede the provision of adequate information to Member States to enable them to make informed decisions. Similarly, the trend towards combining documents, while useful, could be taken too far. The Committee approved of the provision of training courses to enhance the drafting skills of staff members involved in preparing reports and welcomed the significant improvement in the timeliness of the issuance of summary records.

Workload standards

The Secretary-General, in his July report on the pattern of conferences [A/60/93 & Corr.1], said that a DGACM Task Force set up to review workload standards and performance measurement [YUN 2004, p. 1463] continued its work. The Task Force, which conducted a study in 2004 [ibid., p. 1467], found that the chief benefits of information technology (IT) use were enhanced consistency and accuracy of translation and interpretation. Productivity gains in one area were offset by changes in working methods. The Task Force

found no justification for any upward revisions of the existing workload standards at the current stage. Those standards should be supplemented by management data along the lines of the "balanced scorecard" used in public and private institutions, so as to provide a broader picture of DGACM performance from a full-system perspective.

The Committee on Conferences [A/60/32] considered the section of the Secretary-General's report concerning workload standards, as well as a non-paper, which contained a proposed methodology for evaluating the performance of conference services and information on IT tools and their impact on efficiency. The non-paper indicated that the matter required further elaboration.

In October [A/60/433], ACABQ took note of the Task Force findings and stated that the work of the Task Force should be further elaborated. The "balanced scorecard" approach should be expanded and a report submitted to the Assembly.

Translation and interpretation matters

Recruitment in language services

The Secretary-General reported in July [A/60/93 & Corr.1] that a demographic transition in the translation services at Headquarters continued to result in a high vacancy rate. A large number of retirements and the resulting influx of new staff were placing a heavy burden on training capacity and would have an impact on overall productivity. The situation was more stable in Geneva and Vienna. In compliance with General Assembly resolution 59/265 [YUN 2004, p. 1463], efforts were made to fill vacancies in the translation and interpretation services at Nairobi. Despite those efforts, filling vacant posts remained difficult, in particular extrabudgetary posts in Nairobi for language staff that could apply for regular budget posts in Geneva, New York and Vienna.

The Committee on Conferences [A/60/32] stressed the need to improve the quality of translation and interpretation, and to ensure that the terminology used by the translation and interpretation services reflected the latest linguistic norms. It expressed concern about the unequal distribution of resources among the language services and noted that all language services should be provided with equally favourable working conditions and resources, as stipulated in resolution 59/265.

In October [A/60/433], ACABQ welcomed the initiative by DGACM, working with the UN Office of Human Resources Management, to arrange an Arabic language interpretation examination aimed at filling vacant posts in Nairobi. It encouraged DGACM to intensify efforts in that regard, and, in the light of the prolonged vacancy situation, urged it to consider all possible approaches. DGACM was also encouraged to make a concerted effort to develop rosters of qualified applicants in all the official languages to fill posts that were likely to become vacant, after taking into account possible promotions and retirements.

Informational meetings

The Committee on Conferences [A/60/32] expressed support for the holding of informational meetings, organized in response to General Assembly resolution 57/283 B [YUN 2003, p. 1481], to brief Member States on terminology and consult with them on the improvement of language services. As requested in resolution 59/265 [YUN 2004, p. 1463], two such meetings were held in 2005.

UN information systems

Information and communication technology

In March [A/59/265/Add.1], the Secretary-General submitted an addendum to his 2004 report [YUN 2004, p. 1471] on the UN information and communication technology (ICT) strategy [YUN 2002, p. 1454]. The addendum contained proposals for the review of possible arrangements for the migration of financial and technical support to the Galaxy system from the UN Department of Peacekeeping Operations (DPKO) to the Department of Management. Despite the fact that Galaxy was a Secretariat-wide activity, DPKO continued to provide financial and technological support for its development and maintenance. Following a 2004 audit review of the system, OIOS recommended the migration of the technical development, maintenance and support functions from DPKO to the Information Technology Services Division of the Office of Central Support Services of the Department of Management. However, the auditors said that the transfer should not be effected until the Division could assure a continued level of service. A review would be conducted to establish the most appropriate technological infrastructure for the system. In the meantime, the UN Office of Human Resources Management (OHRM) and DPKO would continue their existing partnership to support and develop Galaxy.

On 13 April, the General Assembly, in section II of **resolution 59/282** (see p. 1486), took note of the Secretary-General's 2004 report and the related ACABQ report [YUN 2004, p. 1471]. It requested the Secretary-General to report on measures to improve the Galaxy system, and to develop and implement cost-neutral measures to provide Member States with secure access to the information accessible only on the Secretariat's Intranet, known as iSeek, in the working languages of the United Nations.

In a 22 April report [A/59/736], ACABQ recommended that lessons learned and experiences acquired during the development, implementation and roll-out phases of Galaxy should be fully documented and analysed and the results reflected in the Secretary-General's report to the Assembly at its sixtieth session. It recommended that the Assembly take note of the Secretary-General's report.

On 22 June, the Assembly, in section XVIII of **resolution 59/296** (see p. 139), having considered the addendum to the Secretary-General's report and the relevant section of ACABQ's report, requested the Secretary-General to ensure full implementation of the ICT strategy in order to avoid unnecessary redundancies.

International cooperation in informatics

In response to Economic and Social Council resolution 2004/51 [YUN 2004, p. 1472], the Secretary-General submitted a May report [E/2005/67] on international cooperation in the field of informatics, which highlighted the increased collaboration between the Secretariat and the Ad Hoc Open-ended Working Group on Informatics. Both the Working Group and the Secretariat considered areas where resources could be redirected to better serve the diplomatic community. The Working Group prioritized the needs of Member States and communicated them to the Secretariat. The Secretariat informed the Working Group about IT initiatives that would affect the diplomatic community and solicited input from the Working Group. The collaboration optimized the use of existing resources by focusing on practical issues.

WiFi technology, which allowed wireless Internet access, had been introduced extensively in Headquarters conference rooms, common hallways, lobbies and in the Dag Hammarskjöld Library. The Secretariat continued to provide electronic mail services and maintained the computer servers that supported services to the missions. It also implemented free ODS access worldwide. In collaboration with the Working Group, the Secretariat launched a new version of the primary web page for missions and produced a guide to Internet services for delegates.

On 22 July [meeting 36], the Economic and Social Council, adopted **resolution 2005/12** [draft: E/2005/L.33, orally amended] without vote [agenda item 7 (c)].

The need to harmonize and improve United Nations informatics systems for optimal utilization and accessibility by all States

The Economic and Social Council,

Welcoming the report of the Secretary-General on international cooperation in the field of informatics and the initiatives of the Ad Hoc Open-ended Working Group on Informatics,

Recognizing the interest of Member States in taking full advantage of information and communication technologies for the acceleration of economic and social development,

Recalling its previous resolutions on the need to harmonize and improve United Nations information systems for optimal utilization and access by all States, with due regard to all official languages,

Welcoming the intensification of efforts by the Information Technology Services Division of the Department of Management of the Secretariat to provide interconnectivity and unhindered Internet access to all Permanent and Observer Missions at the United Nations,

1. *Reiterates once again* the high priority that it attaches to easy, economical, uncomplicated and unhindered access for States Members and Observers of the United Nations, as well as non-governmental organizations accredited to the United Nations, to the computerized databases and information systems and services of the United Nations, provided that the unhindered access of non-governmental organizations to such databases, systems and services will not prejudice the access of Member States nor impose an additional financial burden for their use;

2. *Requests* the President of the Economic and Social Council to convene the Ad Hoc Open-ended Working Group on Informatics for one more year to enable it to carry out, from within existing resources, the due fulfilment of the provisions of the Council resolutions on this item, to facilitate the successful implementation of the initiatives being taken by the Secretary-General with regard to the use of information technology and to continue the implementation of measures required to achieve its objectives, and, in this regard, requests the Working Group to continue its efforts to act as a bridge between the evolving needs of Member States and the actions of the Secretariat;

3. *Expresses its appreciation* to the Information Technology Services Division for the continuing cooperation it is extending to the Working Group in the endeavour to further improve the information technology services available to all Permanent and Observer Missions at the United Nations and, in particular, for its work in the implementation of the following services: wireless Internet (WiFi) in United Nations conference rooms; revitalization of the website for United Nations delegations; implementation of the new global search in the Official Documents System of the United Nations; and unrestricted access to the Official Documents System;

4. *Requests* the Secretary-General to extend full cooperation to the Working Group and to give priority to implementing its recommendations;

5. *Also requests* the Secretary-General to report to the Economic and Social Council at its substantive session of 2006 on action taken to follow up the present resolution, including the findings of the Working Group and an assessment of its work and mandate.

Other matters

Common services

UN commercial activities

In response to General Assembly resolution 58/263 [YUN 2003, p. 1497], the Secretary-General reported in April [A/59/793] on the possibility and cost implications of operating bookstores, gift shops and guided tours at UNON. The location of UNON commercial operations within the security boundaries of the UNON compound was reviewed in the context of compliance with the Headquarters Minimum Operating Security Standards. The review indicated the need for the relocation of all commercial operations outside of the compound. The UN gift shop at UNON was temporarily closed for security reasons. UNON conducted a feasibility study for the operation of the gift shop, guided tours and other activities aimed at promoting the image of the United Nations at its premises. The study indicated the possibility of a resumption, in 2007, of the activities of the UN gift shop and the United Nations Children's Fund (UNICEF) card stand at a new, off-site building for UNON commercial operations, which would be part of the measures for strengthening security at the UNON compound. The construction of the new building, for which the Assembly approved funds in resolution 59/276 [YUN 2004, p. 1383], was expected to be completed by the end of 2006. It was envisaged that the gift shop would be run on a full cost-recovery basis, with no financial implications for the UN programme budget.

With regard to guided tours, it was determined that, given the limited number of tourists anticipated at UNON, the costs of operating a visitors' service would significantly exceed the potential revenue, requiring consistent subsidies to cover its financial deficit. The Secretary-General therefore recommended against operating guided tours at UNON.

ACABQ, in its first report on the proposed programme budget for the 2006-2007 biennium

[A/60/7 & Corr.1], concurred with the Secretary-General's recommendation concerning the operation of guided tours at UNON.

The Assembly, in section VIII of **resolution 60/248** of 23 December (see p. 1495), requested the Secretary-General to organize, effective 1 January 2006, a guided tour operation at UNON, and report the actual income and expenditures of the operation in the budget performance reports for the 2006-2007 biennium.

Outsourcing practices

On 13 April [meeting 91], the General Assembly, having considered the Secretary-General's 2004 report on outsourcing practices and the related ACABQ report [YUN 2004, p. 1472], and on recommendation of the Fifth Committee [A/59/652/Add.1], adopted **resolution 59/289** without vote [agenda item 107].

Outsourcing practices

The General Assembly,

Recalling its resolutions 54/256 of 7 April 2000, 55/232 of 23 December 2000 and 58/276 and 58/277 of 23 December 2003,

Having considered the report of the Secretary-General on outsourcing practices and the related report of the Advisory Committee on Administrative and Budgetary Questions,

1. *Takes note* of the report of the Secretary-General, and endorses the observations and recommendations of the Advisory Committee on Administrative and Budgetary Questions related thereto;

2. *Acknowledges* that outsourcing should be used in full compliance with the four criteria set out by the General Assembly, and requests the Secretary-General to monitor the quality of activities outsourced;

3. *Requests* the Secretary-General to continue to consider outsourcing actively in accordance with the guidance and goals mentioned in paragraphs 1 to 3 of resolution 55/232 and to ensure that programme managers satisfy all of the following criteria in their assessment of whether or not an activity of the Organization can be fully, or even partially, outsourced:

(*a*) Cost-effectiveness and efficiency: this is considered to be the most basic criterion; unless it can be adequately demonstrated that an activity can be done significantly more economically and, at the very least, equally efficiently, by an external party, outsourcing may not be considered;

(*b*) Safety and security: activities that could compromise the safety and security of delegations, staff and visitors may not be considered for outsourcing;

(*c*) Maintaining the international character of the Organization: outsourcing may be considered for activities in which the international character of the Organization is not compromised;

(*d*) Maintaining the integrity of procedures and processes: outsourcing may not be considered if it will result in any breach of established procedures and processes.

UN premises and property

Addis Ababa office facilities

By **decision 59/555** of 13 April, the General Assembly took note of Ethiopia's efforts to facilitate the construction of additional office facilities at the Economic Commission for Africa (ECA) in Addis Ababa, as well as the Secretary-General's 2004 report on the related construction project [YUN 2004, p. 1472]. It endorsed the recommendations contained in ACABQ's 2004 report on the project [ibid.].

In response to Assembly resolution 56/270 [YUN 2002, p. 1459], the Secretary-General submitted a November report [A/60/532] on progress made in the ECA construction project. Pursuant to recommendations made by ACABQ in 2004 [YUN 2004, p. 1472], ECA requested the UN offices in Addis Ababa located outside the ECA complex to provide updated estimates of their office space requirements. The survey verified the need for an increase of 2,780 square metres of office space in the new office building to be constructed at ECA headquarters as compared with the initial estimates reported in 2001 [YUN 2001, p. 1396]. The additional cost for the two additional floors was estimated at $2,390,600, bringing the total estimated cost of the project to $8,992,700, compared to the initial cost estimate of $7,711,800 approved by the Assembly in resolution 56/270.

It was anticipated that the bidding process and identification of a contractor could be finalized by March 2006, with construction starting in April 2006, which was expected to be completed by February 2008. If the proposed option to expand the building by two additional floors was approved by the Assembly (see below), completion of the construction would be envisaged for July 2008. It was recommended that the construction of the two additional floors be completed simultaneously with the originally approved project, as that option was the most cost effective. The Secretary-General requested the Assembly to: authorize the expansion of the new office building by two additional floors to a total capacity of 9,550 square metres and total estimated additional costs of $3,671,500; approve an additional appropriation for the additional costs under section 32 of the proposed programme budget for the 2006-2007 biennium (see p. 1489); and endorse a proposed phased approach in financing further requirements for the new building.

ACABQ, in December [A/60/7/Add.21], recommended approval of the total estimated additional costs indicated in the Secretary-General's report (see above) if the Assembly authorized the expansion of the new office building by two additional floors.

The Assembly, in section VII of **resolution 60/248** of 23 December (see p. 1495), took note of the Secretary-General's report on the construction of additional office facilities at ECA and endorsed ACABQ's recommendation.

Parking space at Headquarters

By **decision 59/551 B** of 13 April, the General Assembly deferred for future consideration the Secretary-General's 2004 report on viable options for ensuring sufficient parking space at UN Headquarters [YUN 2004, p. 1473]; by **decision 59/551 D** of 12 September, the Assembly deferred consideration of the report until its sixtieth (2005) session; and by section A of **decision 60/551** of 23 December, the Assembly further deferred consideration of the report until its resumed sixtieth (2006) session.

Capital Master Plan

Implementation of CMP

In May, the Secretary-General submitted an addendum [A/59/441/Add.1] to his 2004 report on the implementation of the capital master plan (CMP) [YUN 2004, p. 1475]. He said that by a 15 March letter, the United States had formally notified the United Nations of its loan offer of $1.2 billion to finance the CMP project and provided the details of the terms of the offer, which were essentially the same as those reported by the Secretary-General in 2004 [ibid.].

The Secretary-General reported that the Legislature of the State of New York did not pass legislation necessary for the United Nations Development Corporation (UNDC) to proceed with the construction of a new building to provide swing space during the CMP implementation, to be known as UNDC-5. In March, the Secretariat engaged a real estate consultant to identify alternatives. However, the commercial alternatives discussed in the report required further study and negotiations with landlords. The Secretary-General believed that the United Nations should proceed with leased space in the New York City area and set 2007 as the on-time refurbishment start date.

The Secretary-General recommended that the Assembly accept the host country's loan offer and authorize him to conclude an agreement with the host country to preserve the Organization's option to borrow up to $1.2 billion at an interest rate not to exceed 5.54 per cent per annum and a duration not to exceed 30 years, provided that the agreement did not create any legal or financial obligation for the United Nations to borrow any part of the $1.2 billion from the host country or

in any way restrict the Organization's discretion in deciding whether to borrow such funds, nor the authority of the United Nations to seek funds from any other source. He also recommended that the Assembly: request him to first seek the Assembly's authorization if the United Nations decided to draw down on any part of the loan amount; convert into an appropriation with assessment for the 2004-2005 biennium the full amount of the commitment authority of $26 million approved for that period in resolution 57/292 [YUN 2002, p. 1375]; and request him to report on CMP progress in 2006.

A further May addendum [A/59/441/Add.2] by the UN Legal Counsel stated that, if the United Nations accepted the offer, it would do so in a letter setting out the basic terms and understandings for the loan agreement to be negotiated, provided that acceptance of the offer was subject to the successful conclusion of the agreement. Thus, the letter created no legal obligation for the Organization regarding the loan offer.

ACABQ report. In an oral report presented to the Fifth Committee on 20 May [A/C.5/59/SR.53], the ACABQ Chairman recommended acceptance of the Secretary-General's proposals concerning the host country's loan offer, and that he be authorized by the Assembly to conclude an agreement on the offer and to draw down on the loan amount, with the understanding that if the Assembly's authorization was sought for that purpose, the Secretary-General would provide detailed information on the related conditions. As to the proposed conversion of the full amount of the commitment authority approved for the 2004-2005 biennium, ACABQ pointed out that the $26 million included a provision of $8.2 million budgeted for 2006. It therefore recommended that only $17.8 million should be appropriated and assessed. Commitment authority for the balance of $8.2 million should be renewed pending future action on the appropriation of that amount.

By **decision 59/551 B** of 13 April, the General Assembly deferred consideration of the following 2004 reports on the CMP: the Secretary-General's report on the status of possible funding arrangements for CMP [YUN 2004, p. 1473]; his second annual report on the implementation of CMP [ibid., p. 1475]; his report on cooperation with the City and State of New York related to CMP [ibid., p. 1474]; and ACABQ's report on CMP [ibid.]. By **decision 59/551 D** of 12 September, the Assembly deferred until its sixtieth (2005) session consideration of the above reports, along with the May 2005 addenda to Secretary-General's second annual report on CMP implementation and ACABQ's May 2005 oral report (see above).

On 22 June [meeting 104], the General Assembly, on recommendation of the Fifth Committee [A/59/448/Add.4], adopted **resolution 59/295** without vote [agenda item 108].

Capital master plan

The General Assembly,

Recalling its resolutions 54/249 of 23 December 1999, 55/238 of 23 December 2000, 56/234 and 56/236 of 24 December 2001 and 56/286 of 27 June 2002, section II of its resolution 57/292 of 20 December 2002 and its decision 58/566 of 8 April 2004,

1. *Decides* to convert 17,802,000 United States dollars of the existing commitment authority into an appropriation with assessment for the year 2005 and to renew the existing commitment authority for the balance of 8,198,000 dollars for the year 2006 so as to provide for the continuation of design work and related project management and management of preconstruction services for the baseline scope and scope options of the capital master plan;

2. *Requests* the Secretary-General to report to the General Assembly at the main part of its sixtieth session on all aspects of the capital master plan, including:

(a) Current estimate of costs and time line for implementation of the capital master plan;

(b) Viable options for swing space during construction, including the costs of all such options;

(c) The status of UNDC-5;

(d) An assessment of the viability of constructing a permanent building on the North Lawn of the premises of United Nations Headquarters to be used as a swing and/or consolidation space;

(e) The range of financing options for the capital master plan and overall cost and full analysis of such options, taking into account that direct assessment would be the simplest and cheapest option for meeting the costs of the capital master plan, as stated in the report of the Secretary-General and the oral report by the Chairman of the Advisory Committee on Administrative and Budgetary Questions;

(f) The progress of design and pre-construction work;

(g) Proposals on a working reserve fund;

3. *Decides* to revert to the issue of the capital master plan before the end of June 2005, including the relevant proposals contained in paragraph 39 of the report of the Secretary-General, not addressed in the present resolution, pertaining to the offer of the host country on an interest-bearing loan for the capital master plan.

Review of CMP

Report of Board of Auditors. In response to General Assembly resolution 57/292 [YUN 2002, p. 1375], the Secretary-General transmitted to the Assembly, in July [A/60/5 (vol. 5)], the report of the Board of Auditors on CMP for the year ended 31 December 2004. The review covered the overall implementation of CMP and nine contracts executed in 2004 for an aggregate amount of $12.4 million for the design development phase. The cumulative expenditure for CMP amounted to $26.2 million. For 2005, the estimated expenditures totalled $25.2 million, consisting of $7.4 million for the design development phase and $17.8 million for the construction documents phase. The Board found that the delay in the approval of the final scope confirmation reports and quality control plans for four design contracts had affected the schedule for the completion of the design development phase. Also, the Administration did not establish an advisory board, approved by the Assembly in 2002 [YUN 2002, p. 1375], to provide advice on financial matters and overall project issues. The Board recommended that the procedures for the coordination of work and activities among the firms engaged in the design phase should be reviewed to ensure that the work was completed within the envisaged time frame and budget, and that the Administration should consider establishing the planned advisory board on CMP financial matters.

OIOS report. In response to Assembly resolution 57/292, OIOS submitted an August report [A/60/288] on CMP for the period from August 2004 to July 2005. During that period, OIOS provided continuous audit coverage of activities related to CMP and the construction phase of the security strengthening project. Between 1 January 2004 and 30 June 2005, seven contracts were awarded, totalling $53,584,166.

OIOS concluded that the resources appropriated by the Assembly for CMP activities were generally utilized in accordance with UN Financial Regulations and Rules. However, UN operating procedures, documents related to construction contracts and contract language utilized by the CMP office needed to be improved. In the view of OIOS, the process used for selecting the real estate broker to provide real estate advisory services and to assist in identifying alternative swing space for occupancy in 2007 was transparent and fair. OIOS recommended that the Secretary-General establish the financial advisory board.

By **decision 59/551 B** of 13 April, the Assembly deferred consideration of the report of the Board of Auditors on CMP for the 2002-2003 biennium [YUN 2004, p. 1474] and the OIOS August 2003 to July 2004 report on CMP [ibid.], and by **decision 59/551 D** of 12 September, it deferred consideration of those reports until its sixtieth (2005) session. In section A of **decision 60/551** of 23 December, the Assembly deferred until its resumed sixtieth (2006) session consideration of the above reports, along with report of the Board of Auditors on CMP for the 2003-2004 biennium and the OIOS report on CMP for August 2004 to July 2005.

Re-examination of CMP alternatives

In accordance with General Assembly resolution 57/292 [YUN 2002, p. 1375], the Secretary-General submitted, in November, his third annual progress report on the implementation of CMP [A/60/550 & Corr.1,2]. The estimated alternative swing space costs were higher than initially projected, and construction cost had escalated to a new estimate of some $1.6 billion. That called for a re-examination of the strategy and alternatives for CMP and the development of new approaches and schedules to meet the defined scope.

Four main strategies were examined based on the assumption that the Assembly would approve the new approach at the main part of its sixtieth session. Strategy I included vacating the maximum amount of space at Headquarters, moving to four or more commercial swing space sites in Manhattan and the Dag Hammarskjöld Library to a space in Long Island City, Queens; building temporary conference facilities on the North Lawn and renovating the entire Headquarters complex in one major phase. Strategy II included the scope of strategy I for phasing and swing space, but it recommended cutting the approved renovation scope to stay within the initial $1.2 billion estimate.

Strategy III included construction of a new permanent office building on the North Lawn, leasing of space for the Dag Hammarskjöld Library in Long Island City, and building temporary conference facilities on the North Lawn. The Secretariat building would be relocated to the new office tower; the General Assembly building would be renovated, followed by renovation of the Conference building in two phases; and renovation of the Secretariat building deferred for a future project. The cost of strategy III was estimated at $1.5 billion, reflecting a $536 million increase.

Strategy IV represented a phased approach to the renovation. It included leasing approximately 10 floors of office space in Manhattan and space for the Dag Hammarskjöld Library in Long Island City, and building a temporary conference facility on the North Lawn. Ten floors of the Secretariat building would be vacated at each phase to allow for renovation in four phases. The entire General Assembly building would be renovated, followed by the Conference building, which would be renovated in two phases. The strategy would maintain a functional, visible UN Headquarters at its current site and minimize dependency on external elements, including the New York City real estate market. The estimated costs of the project under strategy IV amounted to $1.6 billion, including the costs covered by the amount of $8 million appropriated in 2001 for the preliminary phase and the $43.3 million approved by the Assembly for the design phase from 2002 to 2005. The projected completion date was late 2013, with some minor work in 2014. Following an evaluation of the four strategies, the Secretary-General recommended strategy IV.

An estimated expenditure pattern was also set out in the report, assuming that strategy IV was selected and that construction started in 2007. The accumulated requirements were expected to increase significantly from 2006 as the project moved to the development of construction documents and drawings and the preconstruction planning phase. From 2008, assuming a project duration of seven years, the construction costs would be between $200 million and $250 million annually, increasing to a peak of nearly $300 million in 2011.

The United Nations would be required to maintain a separate CMP funding facility within its accounting system. A working capital reserve was proposed in the amount of $45 million, representing 20 per cent of anticipated annual expenditures. The reserve would be financed through a separate assessment on Member States and phased out at the end of the construction phase, with related contributions credited back to Member States.

The Assembly made no decision at its fifty-ninth session on the CMP loan offer from the host country (see p. 1553). At a 9 September meeting of the Fifth Committee, the host country representative informed the Committee verbally that the offer would be renewed and adjusted. As at 11 November, the Secretary-General had not received formal notification from the host country of the loan offer renewal.

Total CMP expenditures as at 30 September amounted to $22.1 million, including $4.1 million in 2005. It was expected that an additional $3 million would be spent during the remainder of the year, bringing total 2005 estimated expenditures to $7.1 million. Anticipated requirements in 2006 were estimated at $126.9 million. In the light of the new strategic options, the initiation of the construction document phase would likely occur in 2006.

As to the selection of a financial consultant to design and develop the details of an implementation plan for CMP financing, an expression of interest was issued in April and a request for proposals was subsequently issued to 14 firms. Two firms responded, one of which was found to be technically qualified. However, the financial proposal submitted by that firm was considered excessive for the services required.

The Secretary-General recommended that the Assembly approve strategy IV for implementation of CMP, effective 1 January 2006; a revised project budget of $1.6 billion for the strategy, excluding potential scope options; and the CMP funding plan based on a multi-year assessment. The Assembly should endorse his proposal to maintain a separate CMP account for financing the plan and authorize him to proceed in 2006 with respect to early contracts required for the recommended strategy. It should appropriate $108,698,000 for 2006, including the conversion of the 2006 commitment authority in the amount of $8,198,000 into an appropriation for financing CMP design and preconstruction phases, and $45 million for the year 2006 for establishing a working operating reserve under the CMP account; and decide that both appropriations would be financed through an assessment on Member States. He further recommended that the Assembly request the Committee on Contributions to make recommendations to the Assembly at its sixty-first (2006) session on the possibility of imposing interest to be charged for the late payment of assessed contributions to the CMP account, and ask the Secretary-General to report on progress in the implementation of strategy IV in the context of annual progress reports on CMP.

A November addendum to the report [A/60/550/Add.1] contained an explanatory note on outside commercial borrowing.

ACABQ report. In its December report on CMP [A/60/7/Add.12], ACABQ stated that, while it saw merit in strategy IV, as recommended by the Secretary-General, it was of the opinion that the Assembly should be provided with a more comprehensive analysis of all options, particularly strategy III (see p. 1555). It recommended that, given the cost of building and removing a temporary structure on the North Lawn, full information be presented to the Assembly on the relative costs and merits of constructing a permanent structure. ACABQ requested that updated information on cost benefits for UN organizations located in New York that would result from the consolidation of office space into a permanent building be provided to the Fifth Committee, in addition to a detailed analysis and all relevant information on provisions made under strategy IV for contingencies and forward pricing escalation. ACABQ agreed in principle with the creation of a working capital reserve fund but it recommended that the issue be revisited whenever a decision on the main CMP strategy was taken. The Assembly should decide on which of the options should be chosen for CMP financing. In order to minimize further delay and provide for the smooth and continuous implementation of de-

sign and planning work, ACABQ recommended an appropriation of $102.7 million, including the existing 2006 commitment authority in the amount of $8.2 million.

In section II of **resolution 60/248** of 23 December (see p. 1494), the Assembly authorized the Secretary-General to proceed with CMP design work, related project management and management of pre-construction services to the extent to which those activities could be implemented without prejudice to the decision to be taken by the Assembly at a later stage regarding its selection of the strategy for CMP implementation. It decided to convert $8,198,000 of the existing commitment authority into an appropriation with assessment for 2006, so as to provide for the continuation of design work and related project management and management of the pre-construction phase. It also decided to revert, as a matter of priority, to the issue of CMP at the first part of its resumed sixtieth (2006) session.

In section A of **decision 60/551** of 23 December, the Assembly deferred until its resumed sixtieth (2006) session consideration of the Secretary-General's third annual progress report on the implementation of CMP; ACABQ's December report on CMP; and the reports deferred by the Assembly on 12 September (see p. 1553).

Security

Strengthening security of UN operations, staff and premises

OIOS report. In August [A/60/291], OIOS reported on the utilization and management of funds approved by the General Assembly in resolutions 58/295 [YUN 2004, p. 1476] and 59/276 [ibid., p. 1383] for strengthening security and safety at United Nations Headquarters in New York and at the United Nations Office at Geneva (UNOG).

As at 31 May, $35.4 million out of the $41.3 million approved by the Assembly had been obligated for projects at Headquarters and $16.2 million of the $35.1 million approved for one-time security upgrades at UNOG had been spent or pre-encumbered as at 30 April. Of the 18 projects at Headquarters, seven had been fully implemented, three were deferred to be incorporated into the capital master plan (CMP) project and eight were being implemented, with a target completion date of 31 December. Of those eight projects, one was proceeding satisfactorily, one had been delayed, and the remaining six projects were combined into one contract, which was being executed by a private contractor. That set of projects was at least six months behind schedule, at an additional cost of $2.6 million. The contractor submitted a claim for an additional $5.2 million in compensation and requested an eight-month contract extension to complete the construction work by February 2006. OIOS made a number of observations and recommendations regarding the inadequacy of guarantees, project management, change orders and contractor performance.

Project implementation at UNOG was progressing well, but the initial objectives and timelines were too ambitious, given that UNOG's capacity had not increased sufficiently, and at least $6.4 million in appropriations might not be expended by the end of the 2004-2005 biennium. UNOG submitted a draft security plan to the Department of Safety and Security detailing security requirements for the Palais des Nations in Geneva to be compliant with the Headquarters minimum operating security standards. In the view of OIOS, a comprehensive security strategy and detailed plan containing target dates and related cost estimates should be developed and used by UNOG to monitor project implementation.

For major contracts, OIOS found that UNOG had complied with UN procurement procedures, except in one case of a potential breach of confidentiality by the consortium of firms responsible for architectural/engineering work and supervision of the security projects. UNOG responded that the case was conducted in a transparent and fair manner within the Organization, and all contractors would be reminded of UN regulations and ethical standards.

As recommended by OIOS, UNOG conducted a survey of architectural and engineering fees payable in Switzerland, which concluded that the fees being paid by the Geneva office, as a percentage of the total construction cost applied at the time the contract was signed in 2002, were reasonable, but the rates had increased significantly. In the view of OIOS, the situation confirmed that the contract between UNOG and the consortium had not provided the flexibility and resulting savings envisaged by UNOG. The consortium was not fulfilling its responsibilities in a timely manner, and UNOG was encountering difficulties in controlling the resulting cost-determination decisions. In response to the OIOS audit, UNOG included, with effect from 15 August, the standard UN clause for liquidated damages in all tendering documents and resulting contracts related to construction, engineering and/or architectural services.

With the aim of increasing its sourcing, UNOG responded positively to the OIOS suggestion that it align itself to regional practices and publish invitations to bid for higher value construction and related services in national and official journals of the European Union.

Note by Secretary-General. In an October note [A/60/291/Add.1], the Secretary-General, in his supplementary comments on OIOS findings and recommendations, said that the recommendation concerning surrendering the unspent 2002-2003 appropriation relating to projects deferred to CMP, totalling $4.8 million, was inconsistent with the arrangements established by the Assembly for administering the multi-year accounts. Under the terms of the construction-in-progress account, the unspent provisions at the end of the financial period were to remain in the account and used in subsequent financial periods. Therefore, the recommendation should be withdrawn and the case should be closed.

In section A of **decision 60/551** of 23 December, the Assembly deferred until its resumed sixtieth (2006) session consideration of the OIOS report and the Secretary-General's note transmitting his comments thereon.

Report of Secretary-General. In response to resolution 59/276, the Secretary-General, in a December report [A/60/572/Add.2], summarized the work undertaken and planned by the Secretariat in 2004 and 2005 to implement approved security-strengthening projects. The total cost of the programme approved by the Assembly amounted to $105,705,100 at revised 2004-2005 rates; that amount was financed from the regular budget and, with respect to the United Nations Office at Vienna (UNOV), on a cost-shared basis with other organizations located at the Vienna International Centre. As at 30 September, $70,531,800, or 67 per cent of the total approved costs, had been committed with respect to that programme. The report detailed the implementation of individual projects at Headquarters, UNOG, UNOV, UNON, the Economic Commission for Africa, the Economic and Social Commission for Asia and the Pacific, and the Economic Commission for Latin America and the Caribbean.

ACABQ report. In December [A/60/597], ACABQ noted with concern the delayed implementation of security-strengthening projects at some duty stations and requested that increased attention be paid to the implementation of those projects as a priority.

Unified security management system

In response to resolution 59/276 [YUN 2004, p. 1383], the Secretary-General submitted an April report [A/59/776] on the strengthened and unified security management system for the United Nations. The report proposed a revised course of action for implementing the standardized access control system at all main duty stations and funding of the project's design phase. A project access control team was to be established to plan and, in the event the project was approved by the Assembly, coordinate the implementation of a comprehensive, fully integrated and standardized access control system, in consultation with the Office of Central Support Services. The team would be set up using existing resources and supplemented by additional resources of up to $180,000, which would be accommodated from within the resources approved for the 2004-2005 biennium and the proposed 2006-2007 programme budget.

In April [A/59/785], ACABQ recommended that the Assembly take note of the report with the expectation that a comprehensive progress report would be presented during the sixtieth session.

In section I of **resolution 59/294** of 22 June (see p. 1488), the Assembly took note of the Secretary-General's report on the strengthened and unified security management system for the United Nations and endorsed the observations and recommendation contained in the related ACABQ report (see above).

In October [A/60/424], the Secretary-General, reporting on progress achieved in establishing the strengthened and unified UN security management system, said that immediate action to establish the Department of Safety and Security was taken by the appointment, on 13 January, of the Under-Secretary-General for Safety and Security and the designation of officers-in-charge for the Divisions of Safety and Security Services and Regional Operations. The Under-Secretary-General laid out a number of key themes to govern the way ahead, including: a maximum reliance in safety and security on host Governments; a sharpened primary focus on operational effectiveness at the field level; a vigorous system-wide integration of existing UN security capacities; and a fundamental review of technical security policies, procedures and practices. The Division of Safety and Security Services, which unified the separate structures in New York and at offices away from Headquarters, became operational in April. Of the 383 additional posts authorized by the Assembly for uniformed officers, 116 security officers were recruited by May, with another 149 officers deployed in September and the majority of the remaining officers to be recruited by the end of the year. The Division of Regional Operations subsumed the four regional desks of the former Office of the United Nations Security Coordinator. The Executive Office was initiated on 1 January. The report also discussed field security operations, the Department's Field Support Service and a number of other security issues.

All UN civilian personnel in the field were under the authority of a single senior official, supported by one country security adviser. Heads of peacekeeping missions and special political missions supported by DPKO were appointed as designated security officials wherever appropriate. In Afghanistan, Iraq and the Sudan, DPKO and the Department of Safety and Security formed integrated security management structures so as to incorporate all UN civilian personnel into a single protection system.

At Headquarters, the Under-Secretaries-General for Peacekeeping Operations and for Safety and Security formed a standing committee on security to facilitate dialogue and decisions on matters of mutual concern, including the appointment of designated officials in peacekeeping missions and the further implementation of civilian security management in the field. A detailed procedure was formulated to support DPKO through the establishment of the Peacekeeping Operations Support Section within the Division of Regional Operations, which would be co-located with DPKO.

The Secretary-General concluded that the primary responsibility for the security of UN personnel rested with the host Governments, and to that end, the United Nations would work closely with those Governments. Considerable progress had been achieved in developing an integrated, system-wide security management system that ensured consistency, efficiency and effectiveness in safeguarding UN staff.

In November [A/60/7/Add.9], ACABQ said that, the Secretary-General's report fell short of meeting all requirements for the implementation report it had requested in 2004 [YUN 2004, p. 1478]. ACABQ expected that a comprehensive report on the implementation of resolution 59/276 would be submitted once the Department of Safety and Security became fully operational. It pointed out that expeditious recruitment for all authorized posts should be treated by the Secretariat with the highest priority and with due consideration given to equitable geographical distribution and other concerns expressed by the Assembly. ACABQ stressed the importance of reviewing the level of the post of the deputy to the Under-Secretary-General for Safety and Security in the context of the comprehensive implementation report and careful examination by the implementation management team of the organizational structure of the Department and of its operational requirements. It recommended that the Assembly take note of the Secretary-General's report as an interim report.

In section A of **decision 60/551** of 23 December, the Assembly deferred until its resumed sixtieth (2006) session consideration of the Secretary-General's October report on a strengthened and unified security management system for the United Nations and ACABQ's related report.

Security spending by UN organizations

In response to General Assembly resolution 59/276 [YUN 2004, p. 1383], the Secretary-General, in October [A/60/317 & Corr.1], reported on security spending by UN system organizations. A system-wide survey, by CEB, showed that security spending had increased significantly during the 2003-2005 period. The total security-related expenditure for 2005 was expected to reach $286.6 million, compared to $252.4 million in 2004, representing a 14 per cent increase. The largest increase appeared to have occurred in 2004, which showed a 49 per cent increase over 2003. However, since a significant part of the overall spending reported by the organizations was derived from estimates, rather than specific data, owing to the absence of standard budgeting and accounting systems across the UN system, the Secretary-General indicated that the presentation of security-related spending contained in the report should be considered a work in progress. The Secretary-General proposed the establishment of a standardized accounting and budgeting framework for security-related expenditure to improve the accuracy and the clarity of the analysis of expenditure patterns and trends, and to enhance policy review and formulation in that area.

The report discussed methodological issues concerning the collection and presentation of security-related expenditure data, and contained tables dealing with categories of expenditure relating to staff safety and security at the Office of the United Nations High Commissioner for Refugees and the 2003-2005 security-related expenditure of UN organization.

ACABQ, in November [A/60/7/Add.9], said that the data presented in the Secretary-General's report with regard to the organizations' 2003-2005 security-related expenditure raised a number of questions that were not addressed in the report, including the question of why some co-located organizations with seemingly similar security concerns had significantly different security expenditure patterns. ACABQ requested that information to that effect be provided to the Fifth Committee and that future reports on security-related spending contain information on salient factors underlying significant differences in security expenditures across the UN system.

PART SIX

Intergovernmental organizations related to the United Nations

Chapter I

International Atomic Energy Agency (IAEA)

In 2005, the International Atomic Energy Agency (IAEA) continued its work under the three pillars of its mandate—technology, safety and verification—with a specific focus to facilitate the development and transfer of peaceful nuclear technologies; to prevent the proliferation of nuclear weapons; and to maintain and expand a global nuclear safety regime, as well as strengthen the security of nuclear and radiological material and facilities.

The forty-ninth session of the IAEA General Conference (Vienna, Austria, 26-30 September) adopted resolutions and decisions on strengthening IAEA's activities in nuclear science, technology and applications; strengthening international cooperation in nuclear, radiation and transport safety and waste management; strengthening the effectiveness and efficiency of the safeguards system; strengthening IAEA technical cooperation activities; applying IAEA safeguards in the Middle East; implementing the safeguards agreement between IAEA and the Democratic People's Republic of Korea (DPRK); and measures to protect against nuclear terrorism.

In October, the 2005 Noble Peace Prize was awarded to IAEA and its Director-General, Mohamed ElBaradei, in recognition of their efforts to prevent nuclear energy from being used for military purposes and to ensure that nuclear energy for peaceful purposes was used in the safest possible way.

During the year, IAEA's membership rose to 139 member States, with the admission of Chad.

Activities

Nuclear safety and security

IAEA continued to support a global nuclear safety regime based on international legal instruments and regulatory infrastructures. During 2005, it conducted more than 120 safety review missions to member States. The Agency organized four international conferences and a number of training courses, seminars and workshops addressing nuclear safety and security. It set up an expanded Incident and Emergency Center to serve as the focal point for States to report emergencies and to facilitate the exchange of information between States on preparedness and re-

sponse, and the reporting of nuclear security incidents. The implementation of activities to protect against nuclear terrorism, approved by the Board of Governors in 2002 [YUN 2002, p. 1465], was completed in 2005, resulting in improved monitoring capabilities at border crossings; recovery of 70 radioactive sources; and an overall improvement in the preparedness of States in addressing the risk of malicious acts involving nuclear and radioactive materials. The Board approved a new Nuclear Security Plan for implementation between 2006-2009. In 2005, the Convention on the Physical Protection of Nuclear Material (CPPNM) [YUN 1979, p. 1239] was amended to protect nuclear facilities and material in peaceful domestic use, storage and transport. In addition, the amendment provided for expanded cooperation between States in locating and recovering stolen or smuggled nuclear material, mitigating any radiological consequences of sabotage, and preventing and combating related offences. By the end of 2005, there were 116 parties to CPPNM, compared to 109 in 2004.

Radiation Safety

IAEA's radiation safety programme continued to focus on the development of a unified set of safety standards and their application; the implementation of the Agency's radiation protection rules; and the provision of advice and services to member States. In 2005, IAEA published the *Guidance on the Import and Export of Radioactive Sources* as a supplementary guide to the revised Code of Conduct on the Safety and Security of Radioactive Sources, approved by the Board in 2003. Although neither the Code nor the guide was a legally binding instrument, the Director-General received written notification from 79 States expressing support for the Code and 17 States indicating their commitment to follow the supplementary guide.

Nuclear power

In 2005, IAEA continued to assist member States in planning and implementing programmes for the utilization of nuclear power, supported them in improving safety, and provided them with information and training. In March, IAEA held a conference in Paris, attended by high-level representatives of 74 Governments, to consider the future role of nuclear power. Participants affirmed the potential of nuclear power as a major means of meeting energy needs and sustaining development in the twenty-first century for a large number of both developed and developing countries. The Agency also undertook technical cooperation projects in providing scientific and technical support in the fields of nuclear power and the nuclear fuel cycle.

Nuclear fuel cycle

In February, IAEA transmitted a report on multilateral approaches to the civilian nuclear fuel cycle (MNAs), which cited five approaches to strengthen controls over sensitive nuclear technologies of proliferation concern—uranium enrichment and plutonium separation. In July, the Agency supported an international conference on MNAs in Moscow. IAEA also continued work on developing wide-ranging safety standards for fuel cycle facilities to address both generic and process-specific considerations. Initial guidelines made available in 2005 for evaluating facility safety allowed for self-assessment by a member State and implementation of a new IAEA peer review service entitled "Safety Evaluation During Operation of Fuel Cycle Facilities".

Radioactive waste management

In 2005, IAEA continued to provide guidance on the decommissioning of nuclear facilities. By the end of December, eight power plants worldwide had been completely decommissioned, 17 had been partially dismantled and safely enclosed, 31 were being dismantled prior to eventual site release and 30 were undergoing minimum dismantling prior to long-term enclosure. Regarding the disposal of low and intermediate level radioactive waste, Belgium, Hungary and the Republic of Korea agreed to host the sites for a national waste repository, which were expected to be licensed within the next decade. On safety matters, the Board of Governors approved the Safety Requirements for Geological Disposal in September. In October, the International Conference on the Safety of Radioactive Waste Material Disposal, held in Tokyo, Japan, fostered information exchange on related issues.

Marine environment and water resources

IAEA continued to promote the linkage between water and human development. Recent technological developments, resulting in easier and cheaper means for measuring isotopes in hydrological samples, combined with partnerships with other agencies, allowed the Agency to assist several member States in managing their water resources. A joint IAEA-World Bank isotope investigation had led to an alternative source of water in Bangladesh. The transfer of isotope and nuclear techniques through IAEA's technical cooperation programme also enabled member States to expand their capacity to map underground aquifers, detect and control pollution and monitor the safety of dams.

Food and agriculture

In 2005, the Agency made substantial progress in developing improved crop varieties through mutation induction. Over 25 new and improved varieties of staple food crops, including rice, wheat and millet, were introduced by member States using the technique of mutation induction by radiation, bringing the total number of crop varieties released to 2,300. IAEA cooperation with the Global Rinderpest Eradication Programme in the annual serological surveillance helped a number of African countries to achieve and maintain freedom from rinderpest, an infectious disease of ruminants. The surveillance tests utilized nuclear-related methods and technology, using radioisotopes for differential diagnosis.

Human health

IAEA continued to address needs related to the prevention, diagnosis and treatment of health problems in developing member States through the application of nuclear techniques. The Agency contributed to reducing child and infant mortality rates through technical assistance to member States in the use of stable (non-radioactive) isotope techniques as part of nutrition intervention programmes to combat malnutrition in children. Efforts were strengthened by the creation of the IAEA Nobel Cancer and Nutrition Fund (Nobel Fund) to expand human resources capacity and skills in developing regions of the world in cancer management, radiation oncology and nutrition. IAEA also established the Programme of Action for Cancer Therapy to enhance and expand its technical cooperation programme for improving cancer treatment in the developing world.

Technical cooperation

IAEA continued to transfer nuclear science and technology to developing member States through its technical cooperation programme, which provided training, expert advice and equipment. The Agency's programme focused on food and agriculture, human health, human resource development, nuclear science, physical and chemical applications, radiation and transport safety, radioactive waste management and water resources. In 2005, IAEA's secretariat completed $73.6 million worth of training, expert missions, fellowships and scientific visits, and delivered $33 million in equipment and other assistance to member States. Extrabudgetary resources rose to a new high of $14.9 million, compared to $10.9 million in 2004. The Agency also completed the phased restructuring of its Department of Technical Cooperation.

Safeguard responsibilities

During 2005, IAEA continued its verification programme and inspection activities to ensure States' compliance with their safeguards obligations. IAEA agreements were in force in 156 States and the Agency concluded that all declared nuclear material in those States remained in peaceful nuclear activities or had been accounted for, with the exception of DPRK, where no verification activities had taken place since 2003 and for which no safeguard conclusions could be drawn (see p. 606). In September, the Board of Governors found that Iran's failures and breaches of its obligations to comply with its comprehensive safeguards agreements constituted non-compliance. At the close of 2005, the origin of uranium found at various locations in Iran and the extent and nature of its enrichment programme remained major issues for which verification was ongoing.

Nuclear information

The International Nuclear Information System (INIS), IAEA's database to preserve and maintain nuclear knowledge, continued expanding at a record pace with 100,000 bibliographical records and more than 250,000 electronic text documents added in 2005. INIS had also grown to nearly one million authorized users. In December, IAEA established *Nucleus,* an information gateway allowing individuals in government, industry, the scientific community and the public to access to the Agency's nuclear knowledge and information resources.

Secretariat

At the end of 2005, IAEA secretariat staff totaled 2,312 for both the Professional and General Service categories.

Budget

The 2005 regular budget amounted to $322 million. A total of $39 million in extrabudgetary funds was provided by member States, the United Nations, international organizations and other sources.

NOTE: For further information, see *Annual Report 2005*, published by IAEA.

HEADQUARTERS AND OTHER OFFICE

HEADQUARTERS

International Atomic Energy Agency
P.O. Box 100
Wagramerstrasse 5
A-1400 Vienna, Austria
 Telephone: (43) (1) 2600-0
 Fax: (43) (1) 2600-7
 Internet: www.iaea.org
 E-mail: Official.Mail@iaea.org

NEW YORK LIAISON OFFICE

IAEA Office at the United Nations
1 United Nations Plaza, Room 1155
New York, NY 10017, United States
 Telephone: (1) (212) 963-6010/6011
 Fax: (1) (917) 367-4046
 Email: iaeany@un.org

Chapter II

International Labour Organization (ILO)

In 2005, the International Labour Organization (ILO) continued to promote social justice and economic stability and improve labour conditions. ILO's strategic objectives were to promote and realize fundamental principles and rights at work; create greater opportunities for women and men to secure decent employment and income; enhance the coverage and effectiveness of social protection; and strengthen tripartism and social dialogue.

In 2005, ILO membership remained at 178.

Meetings

The ninety-third session of the International Labour Conference (ILC) (Geneva, 31 May–16 June) discussed the urgent need to eliminate forced labour, create jobs for youth, improve safety at work and tackle the global jobs crisis. Other topics discussed at the annual meeting included the situation of workers in the occupied Arab territories, the state of labour standards in Belarus, Colombia and other countries and the Organization's ongoing efforts to stop the use of forced labour in Myanmar. Delegates also considered the current state of working hours and how to balance the need for flexibility with protecting workers' security, health and family life.

Confronted with record levels of youth unemployment in recent years, delegates from more than 100 countries discussed pathways to decent work for youth and the role of the international community in advancing the youth employment agenda. The Conference adopted resolutions relating to youth employment, occupational safety and health, and the arrears of member States. It marked the fourth World Day Against Child Labour by calling for the elimination of child labour in one of the world's most dangerous sectors—small-scale mining and quarrying—within five to 10 years.

Sectoral and other meetings convened in Geneva during 2005 included: Tripartite Meeting on Employment, Social Dialogue, Rights at Work and Industrial Relations in Transport Equipment Manufacturing (10-12 January); Meeting of Experts to Develop Guidelines for Labour Inspection in Forestry (24-28 January); Meeting of Experts to Develop a Revised Code of Practice on Safety and Health in the Iron and Steel Industry (1-9 February); the seventh European Regional Meeting (14-18 February); Tripartite Meeting of Experts to Develop Joint ILO/World Health Organization Guidelines on Health Services and HIV/AIDS (19-21 April); Tripartite Intersessional Meeting on the Follow-up to the Preparatory Technical Maritime Conference (21-27 April); and Tripartite Meeting on Promoting Fair Globalization in Textiles and Clothing in a Post-MFA Environment (24-26 October).

International standards

During the year, ILO activities with regard to Conventions and Recommendations included standard-setting and the supervision and promotion of the application of standards.

In 2005, the campaign for the ratification of ILO's core Conventions continued, with 11 ratifications by eight countries since June 2004, resulting in six countries being added to the list of member States having ratified all of ILO's core Conventions. As at 29 April, 109 States had ratified all eight fundamental Conventions, 26 had ratified seven of them and total ratifications obtained for the instruments had amounted to 1,236 or 87 per cent of the possible 1,424 ratifications.

Employment and development

ILO continued in 2005 to help constituents combat unemployment and poverty through the creation of employment opportunities and improvement of existing jobs. It provided advice and guidance on employment and labour market policies and information and statistical systems. Activities to promote employment included support to constituents to develop entrepreneurship through the creation of cooperatives and small- and micro-enterprises.

In March, the Office submitted to the Committee on Employment and Social Policy the *World Employment Report 2004-2005*, which found that were trade-offs to be made in striking the right policy balance between employment and income growth, and between productivity growth and poverty reduction. Focus needed to be on the parts of the economy where the majority of people worked, such as agriculture, small-scale activities in the urban and rural informal economy, and services and manufacturing. In relation to the implementation of the Global Employment Agenda and countries' efforts to place employment as a central goal in economic and social policy-making, the Committee also considered the issues of microfinance and decent work; the employment impact of HIV/AIDS; and technological change for higher productivity, job creation and improved standards of living.

Regarding human resources development, ILO emphasized the need for adaptating training policy and delivery to the rapidly changing skill requirements and special needs of vulnerable groups. It also responded to the needs of countries affected by conflict.

Field activities

In 2005, expenditure on technical cooperation programmes totaled $171.3 million, some $33 million more than in 2004. The leading fields of activity were: the standards and fundamental principles and rights at work sector, with 42.7 per cent ($73.2 million); the employment sector, with 29.4 per cent ($50.3 million); the social protection sector with 12 per cent ($20.5 million); and social dialogue with 10.9 per cent ($18.7 million).

In terms of regional distribution, Africa accounted for 24.2 per cent of total expenditure ($41.4 million); Asia and the Pacific, 28.9 per cent ($49.4 million); Latin America and the Caribbean, 16.7 per cent ($28.6 million); Europe, 6.7 per cent ($11.4 million); and the Arab States, 2.0 per cent ($3.4 million). Interregional and global activities accounted for 21.6 per cent ($36.9 million).

Educational activities

The Turin Centre and the International Institute for Labour Studies, both autonomous institutions within ILO, reported to the ILO Governing Body. The Centre continued to carry out training and related activities in a wide range of technical areas as an integral part of ILO technical cooperation activities. The Institute continued to conduct research, encouraged networking related to emerging labour policy issues, and acted as a catalyst for future ILO programme development.

Secretariat

As at 31 December, ILO employed a total of 2,596 full-time staff, of whom 1,213 were in the Professional and higher categories and 1,383 were in the General Service category.

Budget

ILO, in 2003, had adopted a budget of $529.6 million for the 2004-2005 biennium. At its 2005 session, ILC adopted a budget of $594.3 million for the 2006-2007 biennium.

NOTE: For further information on ILO, see *Report of the Director-General—ILO programme implementation, 2004-2005.*

HEADQUARTERS AND OTHER OFFICES

HEADQUARTERS

International Labour Organization
4, route des Morillons
CH-1211 Geneva 22, Switzerland
Telephone: (41) (22) 799-6111
Fax: (41) (22) 798-8685
Internet: www.ilo.org
E-mail: ilo@ilo.org

LIAISON OFFICE

International Labour Organization
Liaison Office with the United Nations
220 East 42nd Street, suite 3101
New York, NY 10017, United States
Telephone: (1) (212) 697-0150
Fax: (1) (212) 697-5218
E-mail: newyork@ilo.org

ILO maintained regional offices in Addis Ababa, Ethiopia; Bangkok, Thailand; Beirut, Lebanon; Geneva, Switzerland; and Lima, Peru.

Chapter III

Food and Agriculture Organization of the United Nations (FAO)

The Food and Agriculture Organization of the United Nations (FAO) continued to work towards achieving sustainable global food security by raising nutrition levels and living standards, improving agricultural productivity and advancing the condition of rural populations.

In 2005, FAO's Council held its one hundred and twenty-eighth (20-24 June), one hundred and twenty-ninth (16-18 November) and one-hundred and thirtieth (28 November) sessions, all in Rome, Italy. The FAO Conference, at its thirty-third session (Rome, 19-26 November), adopted reforms, including streamlining administrative and financial processes and restructuring and greater decentralization of staff and operations to developing countries. The Conference, on the occasion of FAO's sixtieth anniversary, also unanimously adopted a Declaration "Ensuring Humanity's Freedom from Hunger".

As part of the follow-up to the World Food Summits held in 1996 [YUN 1996, p. 1397] and 2002 [YUN 2002, p. 1225], FAO helped its members to prepare strategies towards meeting the goals of halving hunger by 2015 and medium-term food security and agricultural development programmes. With the collaboration of financial institutions, FAO also helped to formulate projects that would hasten a reversal of declining resources to agriculture.

At the Organization's November Conference, FAO member States voted to re-elect Jacques Diouf (Senegal) as Director-General for a third six-year term beginning in January 2006.

In 2005, FAO membership, with the admission of Belarus, increased to 188 countries and the European Union.

World food and hunger situation

In 2005, world cereal production increased sharply, reaching 2.065 billion tonnes, a 9 per cent increase over the previous year. World livestock production was estimated at 268.1 million tonnes of meat and 642.6 million tonnes of milk. World fish output in 2004, the latest year for which data were available, stood at 140.5 million tonnes, of which 45.5 were from aquaculture. World capture fisheries production was 95.0 million tonnes, a 5 per cent increase from 2003.

As at October, the number of countries facing serious food shortages world-wide, stood at 39, with 25 in Africa, 11 in Asia, two in Latin America and the Caribbean, and one in Europe. While causes varied, civil strife, adverse weather, including drought, predominated. The HIV/AIDS pandemic was another major contributing factor. Figures indicated that some 852 million people worldwide were chronically undernourished. The Organization calculated that every year that hunger persisted, it would cause death and disability that would affect developing countries future productivity to the value of $500 billion or more.

Activities

FAO continued to provide emergency assistance in the agricultural, livestock and fisheries sectors of developing countries affected by exceptional natural or man-made calamities. Over $400 million in funding for emergency and rehabilitation projects was approved for some 70 countries and regions in 2004-2005, including responses to hurricanes in the Caribbean, drought in the Horn of Africa, armed conflict in the Sudan and the December 2004 tsunami in Asia [YUN 2004, p. 952].

Through its field programmes, FAO provided technical assistance in food and agriculture, fisheries, forestry and rural development totalling $418.1 million, which comprised $170.5 million for emergency agricultural rehabilitation and $247.6 million for development and technical support. FAO's Investment Centre organized more than 600 field missions for some 140 investment projects in 100 countries. The Special Programme for Food Security assisted developing countries, particularly low-income food-deficit countries, to improve national and household food security on an economically and environmentally sustainable basis. By year's end, 102 countries were participating in the programme.

In 2005, FAO continued to participate in activities related to plant biological diversity; crop management and diversification; seed production and improvement; crop protection; agricultural engineering; prevention of food losses; and food and agricultural industries. It also contributed to the development of animal production and health programmes, improved processing and commercialization, as well as better control of animal diseases. The Global Rinderpest Eradication Programme continued its work to eliminate the fatal livestock virus by 2010. Asia was considered free of the disease and the only remaining suspect area was in the Horn of Africa.

The FAO Forestry Department continued its work in forest resource management, policy and planning, and products. It hosted the secretariat of the International Partnership for Sustainable Development in Mountain Regions and continued to work with non-governmental organizations, Governments and the private sector in promoting support for mountain livelihoods, especially for the 270 million mountain people living in developing and transition countries who were suffering from hunger.

The FAO Fisheries Department promoted the sustainable development of responsible fisheries and contributed to food security through activities in fishery resources, policy, industries and information. Implementation of the FAO Code of Conduct for Responsible Fisheries was a priority. At its 2005 meeting, the FAO Committee on Fisheries adopted a set of voluntary guidelines for the ecolabelling of fish products.

FAO provided technical assistance in plant breeding, the safe movement of germplasm, as well as associated systems. Following the 2004 entry into force of the International Treaty on Plant Genetic Resources for Food and Agriculture [YUN 2004, p. 1487], an FAO expert consultation in 2005 recommended that any responsible deployment of genetically modified crops should comprise the whole technology development process, from the pre-release risk assessment to biosafety considerations and post-release monitoring.

During the year, the Codex Alimentarius Commission, responsible for implementing the joint FAO/World Health Organization Food Standards Programme, adopted over 20 new and amended food standards, which included guidelines on vitamin and mineral food supplements and a code of practice to minimize and contain the use of antimicrobials drugs, such as antibiotics in the treatment of human illnesses and animal production.

Secretariat

As at 31 December, FAO employed 3,798 full-time staff, of whom 1,619 were in the Professional or higher categories and 2,179 were in the General Service category.

Budget

The regular programme budget for the 2004-2005 biennium totaled $749.1 million. In November, the FAO Conference approved a $765.7 million work programme for the 2006-2007 biennium.

HEADQUARTERS AND OTHER OFFICES

HEADQUARTERS

Food and Agriculture Organization of the United Nations
Viale delle Terme di Caracalla
00100 Rome, Italy
  Telephone: (39) (06) 57051
  Fax: (39) (06) 5705-3152
  Internet: www.fao.org
  Email: FAO-HQ@fao.org

NEW YORK LIAISON OFFICE

Food and Agriculture Organization Liaison
Office with the United Nations
1 United Nations Plaza, Room 1125
New York, NY 10017, United States
  Telephone: (1) (212) 963-6036
  Fax: (1) (212) 963-5425
  E-mail: FAO-LONY@fao.org

FAO also maintained liaison offices in Brussels, Geneva, Washington, D.C., and Yokohama, Japan; regional offices in Accra, Ghana; Bangkok, Thailand; Cairo, Egypt; and Santiago, Chile; and subregional offices in Apia, Samoa; Bridgetown, Barbados; Budapest, Hungary; Harare, Zimbabwe; and Tunis, Tunisia.

Chapter IV

United Nations Educational, Scientific and Cultural Organization (UNESCO)

In 2005, the United Nations Educational, Scientific and Cultural Organization (UNESCO) continued to promote cooperation in education, science, culture and communication among its member States. The biennial General Conference, at its thirty-third session (Paris, 3-21 October), adopted the organization's 2006-2007 programme budget. The 58-member Executive Board held its one hundred and seventy-first (12-28 April), one hundred and seventy-second (13-29 September) and one hundred and seventy-third (24 October) sessions, all in Paris.

In 2005, UNESCO membership increased to 191 member States, plus six associate members.

Activities

Education

As the lead agency for the United Nations Decade of Education for Sustainable Development (2005-2014) (DESD), launched on 1 March, UNESCO finalized and approved the International Implementation Scheme, providing DESD with a framework for integrating the principles, values and practices of sustainable development into all aspects of education and learning.

UNESCO convened the sixth meeting of the Education For All (EFA) Working Group (Paris, 19-21 July) and the fifth meeting of the EFA High-Level Group (Beijing, China, 28-30 November), which stressed the need for increased focus on basic education, particularly in neglected areas, such as adult literacy and education for rural people. A Ministerial Round Table on EFA (Paris, 7-8 October) emphasized the need for integrated partnerships between Governments and national and international partners. At the General Conference, UNESCO was asked to strengthen its advocacy for EFA and its coordination role by further developing the EFA Global Action Plan.

UNESCO organized the International Conference on the Right to Basic Education as a Fundamental Human Right and the Legal Framework for its Financing (Jakarta, Indonesia, 2-4 December), which adopted a set of recommendations made by high-level experts (Jakarta Declaration). It promoted cooperation between UN agencies and disability organizations on the right to edu-

cation and the importance of inclusion as a strategy for achieving EFA. In 2005, UNESCO issued reporting guidelines on the implementation of the Convention and the Recommendation against Discrimination in Education.

UNESCO and the Organisation for Economic Development and Cooperation (OECD), implemented a global policy review project on early childhood care and education to help countries identify measures to develop and implement policies to expand access, improve quality and ensure equity. It also provided capacity-building opportunities for government officials on EFA in early childhood and published the UNESCO Policy Brief series on early childhood.

Three core initiatives were launched in 2005 by UNESCO: the Literacy Initiative for Empowerment, which targeted countries with high illiteracy rates or illiterate populations of over 10 million; the Teacher Training Initiative for sub-Saharan Africa, which reinforced national capacities to attract and train quality teachers; and the Global Initiative on HIV/AIDS and Education, which assisted countries in moving towards a comprehensive education sector response to the epidemic.

Natural sciences

In 2005, UNESCO continued its involvement in the Global Earth Observation System of Systems to help countries identify and address challenges, such as climate change and natural disasters. Following the December 2004 Indian Ocean tsunami [YUN 2004, p. 952], the UNESCO Intergovernmental Oceanographic Commission [ibid., p. 1488] worked to coordinate a Tsunami Early Warning and Mitigation System for the region and to promote partnerships to develop warning systems for hazards in other ocean basins. UNESCO's disaster programme also contributed to the World Conference on Disaster Reduction (Kobe, Japan, 18-22 January) (see p. 1015). Other progress included the training of over 200 water specialists from developing countries by UNESCO's Institute for Water Education; the General Conference's approval of four additional water centres to cover ecohydrology, floods, arid lands, and water law and policy; and the publication of a 12-volume series entitled "Water and Ethics" in cooperation with the World Commission on the Ethics of Scientific Knowledge and Technology.

Social and human sciences

At its General Conference, UNESCO adopted the Universal Declaration on Bioethics and Human Rights, which dealt with ethical issues raised by medicine, life sciences and associated technologies as applied to human beings, taking into account their social, legal and environmental dimensions. The International Convention against Doping in Sport was also adopted.

UNESCO's Executive board adopted the *Intersectoral Strategy on Philosophy,* which would guide the social and human sciences sector in activities in the field of philosophy, based on three pillars of action: philosophy facing world problems; teaching philosophy in the world; and promotion of philosophical thought and research.

The European Regional Coalition, launched in 2004 [YUN 2004, p. 1489] as part of the International Coalition of Cities against Racism and Discrimination, became operational in 2005. Over 50 cities had joined the network and progress had been achieved toward the launch of other regional coalitions in Africa, Asia and the Pacific, and Latin America and the Caribbean in 2006.

Culture

UNESCO continued its activities to safeguard tangible cultural heritage in post-conflict situations. Within the framework of the 2003 Convention for the Safeguarding of the Intangible Cultural Heritage [YUN 2003, p. 1513], the Director-General proclaimed 43 Masterpieces of the Oral and Intangible Heritage of Humanity to raise awareness regarding the importance of safeguarding vulnerable expressions of cultural heritage. By December, 181 States were parties to the 1972 Convention Concerning the Protection of the World Cultural and Natural Heritage. Other activities included the launching of the UNESCO Cultural Heritage Laws Database in February, and the African World Heritage Fund at the twenty-ninth session of the World Heritage Committee (Durban, South Africa, 10-17 July). The General Conference also adopted the Convention on the Protection and Promotion of the Diversity of Cultural Expressions, devoted to those cultural expressions conveyed by cultural activities, goods and services.

Communication

In 2005, UNESCO participated in the second phase of the World Summit on the Information Society (Tunis, Tunisia, 16-18 November) (see p. 933), organizing three events and an exhibition to promote the concept of building "knowledge societies". UNESCO continued to promote freedom of expression and press freedom, worldwide and to lead major programmatic approaches to media assistance in conflict and post-conflict countries, including through its International Programme for the Development of Communication.

Supporting youth and a culture of peace

UNESCO continued its cooperation with youth and intergovernmental organizations. It convened the fourth UNESCO Youth Forum (Paris, 30 September–2 October), which focused on the theme "Young people and the Dialogue Among Civilizations, Cultures and Peoples—Ideas for Action in Education, Sciences, Culture and Communication." Discussions at the Youth Visioning for Island Living Youth Forum (Port Louis, Mauritius, 7-12 January), produced the "Youth Visioning Declaration".

Secretariat

As at 31 December, UNESCO employed 2,113 full-time staff, of whom 1,044 were in the Professional or higher categories and 1,069 were in the General Service category.

Budget

In October, the UNESCO General Conference approved a budget of $610 million for the 2006-2007 biennium.

HEADQUARTERS AND OTHER OFFICES

HEADQUARTERS

UNESCO House
7, Place de Fontenoy
75352 Paris 07 SP, France
 Telephone: (33) (1) 45-68-10-00
 Fax: (33) (1) 45-67-16-90
 Internet: www.unesco.org

UNESCO also maintained a liaison office in Geneva.

NEW YORK LIAISON OFFICE

2 United Nations Plaza, Room 900
New York, NY 10017, United States
 Telephone: (1) (212) 963-5995
 Fax: (1) (212) 963-8014
 E-mail: newyork@unesco.org

Chapter V

World Health Organization (WHO)

In 2005, the World Health Organization (WHO) continued to implement its corporate strategy to reduce mortality, morbidity and disability; promote healthy lifestyles and reduce health risk factors; develop health systems that were equitable and responsive to demands; develop an enabling policy and institutional environment in the health sector; and promote an effective health dimension to social, environmental and development policy. Priority areas included malaria, tuberculosis, cancer, cardiovascular diseases and diabetes, tobacco, mental health, making pregnancy safer and children's health, HIV/AIDS, health and the environment, food safety, health systems and blood safety.

The World Health Assembly, WHO's governing body, at its fifty-eighth session (Geneva, 16-25 May), adopted the revised International Health Regulations (2005), which provided a framework for global alert and response to public health emergencies of international concern and for strengthening national core capacities. The Assembly established World Blood Donor Day as an official annual event to be celebrated every 14 June and welcomed a new Global Immunization Strategy. It also adopted resolutions on a wide range of subjects, including strengthening pandemic-influenza preparedness, blood safety, international migration of health personnel, sustainable financing for tuberculosis prevention and control, elimination of iodine deficiency disorders, universal coverage of maternal, newborn and child health interventions, and adequate infant and young child nutrition. The importance of accelerating the achievement of the internationally agreed health-related goals, particularly those contained in the 2000 Millennium Declaration [YUN 2000, p. 49], was also stressed.

The one hundred and fifteenth session of the WHO Executive Board (Geneva, 17-24 January) considered the effects of the earthquake and tsunami in south Asia in December 2004 [YUN 2004, p. 952] and adopted a resolution to ensure strong support from the international community in humanitarian crises; endorsed the proposal for an expanded global smallpox vaccine reserve; and committed to the goal of eradicating poliomyelitis. At its one hundred and sixteenth session (Geneva, 26-27 May), the Board discussed international trade and health, genetic diseases con-

trol, nutrition and HIV/AIDS and the global public health response to accidental or deliberate use of biological and chemical agents that caused harm.

In 2005, WHO membership remained at 192, with two associate members.

2005 activities

During the year, WHO's epidemic alert and response operations were reinforced, the Global Outbreak Alert and Response Network was expanded and the WHO Strategic Health Operations Centre became fully operational. WHO provided effective leadership in surveillance, risk assessment, scientific research, capacity strengthening and operational response to the emerging threat of avian influenza and preparedness for a possible influenza pandemic. A senior WHO staff member was assigned to coordinate the UN system response to the avian influenza and a possible human influenza pandemic.

On 27 February, the WHO Framework Convention on Tobacco Control [YUN 2003, p. 1514] entered into force for its first 40 contracting Parties. The treaty provisions contained measures, such as tobacco advertising bans, tobacco price and tax increases, health warning labels on tobacco products and restrictions to protect people from second-hand tobacco smoke.

The WHO/UNAIDS "3 by 5 " initiative, with the goal of putting three million people living with HIV/AIDS on antiretroviral treatment (ARVs) by the end of 2005, provided evidence that it was possible to deliver such treatment in resource-limited settings and that major expansion of treatment was feasible in some of the poorest and most affected countries. The number of people receiving ARVs globally increased threefold between 2003 and 2005. Treatment and preventive efforts were also intensified for malaria and tuberculosis, including the formulation of a new strategy to stop tuberculosis (STOP TB), urgently needed in Africa where the WHO regional committee had declared the disease a regional emergency. Treatment was delivered to some 65 countries by the STOP TB Partnership's Global Drug Facility. WHO also procured and distributed insecticide-treated nets to protect vulnerable people from mosquitoes that transmitted malaria. Continuing WHO's global efforts to eradicate poliomyelitis, two countries had announced confirmation of no indigenous poliovirus for over 12 months, thereby reducing the number of polio-endemic countries to an all-time low of four. In addition, international efforts had stopped an epidemic in all but eight re-infected countries.

The year was marked by the need for unprecedented international response in the aftermath of natural disasters, and presented WHO and its partners with considerable logistical challenges. WHO was actively involved in the world's largest relief operation to help survivors of the Indian Ocean tsunami [YUN 2004, p. 952] by providing temporary health services, while efforts began to rebuild hospitals, clinics, pharmacies and medical stores. WHO also provided prompt support to the Government of Pakistan in the aftermath of the devastating South Asia earthquake. In both situations, WHO's early warning system, in relation to reports of infectious diseases, contributed to avoiding major disease outbreaks.

The WHO *World Health Report 2005—Make every mother and child count* emphasized that most of the deaths among children under five years of age were attributable to only a few conditions, which were avoidable through existing interventions, and called for a greater use of those interventions. It advocated a "continuum of care" approach for mother and child that would begin before pregnancy and extend through childbirth and into the baby's childhood. Working together with a wide range of partners, WHO launched a series of related initiatives. The Health Metrics Network was created to increase the availability and use of timely, reliable health information and a new Partnership for Maternal, Newborn and Child Health was launched, in which the world's leading professionals in that field formally joined forces to initiate efforts to achieve the international development goals for child and maternal health.

Secretariat

As at 31 December, WHO employed a staff of 4,329, including 1,704 in the Professional and higher categories and 2,347 in the General Service category. The remaining 278 were employed under other contracts. In addition, 3,968 staff held temporary appointments, including consultants.

Budget

WHO, in 2003, had adopted a budget of $880.1 million for the 2004-2005 biennium. Extrabudgetary resources were expected to reach approximately $1,824.5 million, leading to a total effective budget of $2,704.6 million. However, that was later revised to $2,824.1 million. In 2005, the World Health Assembly adopted a total effective budget of $3,313.4 million for the 2006-2007 biennium, an increase of 17 per cent over the previous biennium.

NOTE: For further details of WHO activities, see the *World Health Report 2005* published by the organization.

HEADQUARTERS AND OTHER OFFICES

HEADQUARTERS

World Health Organization
20, Avenue Appia
CH-1211 Geneva 27, Switzerland
Telephone: +41 (22) 791-21-11
Fax: +41 (22) 791-31-11
Internet: http://www.who.int
E-mail: info@who.int

WHO Office at the United Nations
2 United Nations Plaza, DC-2, Rooms 0956 to 0976
New York, N.Y. 10017, U.S.A.
Telephone: +1 (212) 963-43-88
Fax: +1 (212) 963-85-65

WHO is a decentralized organization, with regional offices in Brazzaville, Republic of the Congo; Cairo, Egypt; Copenhagen, Denmark; Manila, Philippines; New Delhi, India; and Washington, D.C., U.S.A.

Chapter VI

World Bank (IBRD and IDA)

The World Bank consisted of the International Bank for Reconstruction and Development (IBRD) and the International Development Association (IDA). Collectively, the following five institutions were known as the World Bank Group: IBRD, IDA, the International Finance Corporation (IFC) (see p. 1576), the Multilateral Investment Guarantee Agency (MIGA) and the International Centre for Settlement of Investment Disputes (ICSID). On 1 June, Paul Wolfowitz (United States) became the World Bank's tenth President.

In fiscal 2005 (1 July 2004–30 June 2005), the World Bank continued to promote sustainable economic development by providing loans, guarantees and related technical assistance for projects and programmes in developing countries. It also maintained a leading role in the debt relief process under the Heavily Indebted Poor Countries Initiative, in order to increase resources for poverty reduction. The second Global Monitoring Report, published by the Bank and IMF in April, assessed progress towards achieving the Millennium Development Goals (MDGs) [YUN 2000, p. 51]. The Bank had committed more than $2.5 billion to fighting HIV/AIDS in 67 countries. It provided support for expanding prevention, care, treatment, and advisory services to countries and promoted leadership through its global partnerships, especially as a co-sponsor of the Joint United Nations Programme on HIV/AIDS.

At the end of fiscal 2005, IBRD membership remained at 184.

Lending operations

IBRD continued to promote sustainable development through loans, guarantees, risk management products and non-lending, including analytical and advisory services. As at 30 June, its cumulative lending totalled $407.4 billion.

IBRD's lending in fiscal 2005 totalled $13.6 billion for 118 new operations in 37 countries, compared to $11 billion in 2004 for 87 operations in 33 countries. The figure represented the highest volume of IBRD lending in the previous six fiscal years. IBRD lending commitments were highest in Latin America and the Caribbean ($4.9 billion), followed by Europe and Central Asia ($3.6 billion) and South Asia ($2.1 billion). Public administration, including law and justice, re-

ceived the highest volume of IBRD lending, with $3.4 billion, followed by transportation, with $2.1 billion, and water, sanitation, and flood protection, with $1.6 billion.

In fiscal 2005, the four largest borrowers were Brazil, China, Colombia, India and Turkey, which collectively accounted for 53 per cent of total IBRD lending.

International Development Association

Established in 1960 as the Bank's concessional lending arm, IDA provided interest-free loans and other services to low-income countries to reduce poverty and improve the quality of life. In fiscal 2005, IDA commitments totalled $8.7 billion for 160 operations in 66 countries, compared with $9 billion for 158 operations in 62 countries in fiscal 2004 [YUN 2004, p. 1492]. In addition, IDA provided $2 billion in grants and a guarantee for $0.1 billion. Africa received the largest commitment of IDA resources with $3.9 billion, constituting 45 per cent of total IDA commitments. South Asia and East Asia and the Pacific followed, with $2.9 billion and $1.1 billion, respectively.

In fiscal 2005, about 21 per cent of total IDA financing was provided in the form of grants to the following clients and projects: debt-vulnerable poorest countries ($897 million); post conflict countries ($463 million); poorest countries ($316 million); HIV/AIDS projects ($133 million); and natural disaster reconstruction projects ($49 million).

Public administration, including law and justice, was the leading sector receiving IDA support, with $2.2 billion, or 26 percent of the total.

At the end of fiscal 2005, IDA membership remained at 165 countries.

International Centre for Settlement of Investment Disputes

ICSID, established in 1966, continued to encourage foreign investments by providing international facilities for coordination and arbitration of investment disputes. In fiscal 2005, 25 cases were registered with the Centre. ICSID also conducted research and publishing activities in arbitration and foreign investment law.

In 2005, ICSID membership increased to 142.

Multilateral Investment Guarantee Agency

The Multilateral Investment Guarantee Agency (MIGA), established in 1988, continued to encourage foreign direct investment in developing countries by providing guarantees to foreign investors against losses caused by non-commercial risks. It also provided technical assistance and advisory services to help developing countries strengthen the capacity of investment promotion intermediaries and disseminate information on investment opportunities. In fiscal 2005, MIGA issued $1.2 billion in guarantee coverage, for a cumulative total of $14.7 billion. Its membership remained at 165 countries.

World Bank Institute

The World Bank Institute continued to provide client countries with capacity development programmes, and used knowledge economy, governance and other diagnostic tools to assess critical country capacities. In fiscal 2005, the Institute helped civil society organizations from Benin, Guatemala, Guinea, Sierra Leone and Zambia to develop governance and anti-corruption assessments. Nearly 110,000 clients participated in more than 900 Institute activities, many through distance and e-learning.

Co-financing

Co-financing constituted an arrangement under which funds from the Bank were associated with funds provided by sources outside the recipient country for a specific lending project or programme. Major co-financing partners included the Inter-American Development Bank and the United Kingdom's Department for International Development. By region, most of the co-financing went to Latin America and the Caribbean ($3.3 billion), followed by Africa ($1.7 billion) and South Asia ($1.7 billion).

Financial activities

During fiscal 2005, IBRD raised $13 billion in medium- and long-term debt, roughly the same as in fiscal 2004. IBRD was able to borrow high volumes for long maturities on favorable terms, as a result of its prudent financial policies and practices. Debt securities, with a wide range of maturities and structures, were issued in 13 currencies. As at 30 June, IBRD's outstanding borrowings from capital markets were about $91.5 billion (net of swaps). Total disbursed and outstanding loans were $104.4 billion.

Capitalization

As at 30 June, the total authorized capital of IBRD was $190,811 million, of which $189,718 million had been subscribed. Of the subscribed capital, $11,483 million had been paid in and $178,235 million was callable.

Income and reserves

IBRD's net income was $1.3 billion in fiscal 2005, down from $2.4 billion in fiscal 2004. As at 30 June 2005, the Bank's liquid asset portfolio was $26.4 billion, down from $31 billion in fiscal 2004.

Secretariat

In 2005, the work of IBRD and IDA was performed by some 8,700 staff working in Washington, D.C., and in more than 100 country offices worldwide. A growing proportion of the Bank's work was being done in country offices.

NOTE: For further details regarding the Bank's activities, see *The World Bank Annual Report 2005.*

HEADQUARTERS AND OTHER OFFICES

HEADQUARTERS

The World Bank
1818 H Street, NW
Washington, D. C. 20433, United States
  Telephone: (1) (202) 473-1000
  Fax: (1) (202) 477-6391
  Internet: www.worldbank.org
  E-mail: feedback@worldbank.org

LIAISON OFFICE

The World Bank Mission to the United Nations
1 Dag Hammarskjöld Plaza
885 Second Avenue, 26th floor
New York, NY 10017, United States
  Telephone: (1) (212) 355-5112
  Fax: (1) (212) 355-4523

The World Bank also maintained offices in Brussels, Belgium; Frankfurt, Germany; Geneva; London; Paris; Sydney, Australia; and Tokyo, Japan.

Chapter VII

International Finance Corporation (IFC)

The International Finance Corporation (IFC), part of the World Bank Group, continued in fiscal 2005 (1 July 2004-30 June 2005) to promote sustainable growth in developing countries by financing private sector investments, helping to mobilize capital in international financial markets and providing technical assistance and advice to Governments and businesses. To address the environmental and social consequences of development, IFC continued to focus on sustainability as a priority in its investment and advisory activities.

During fiscal 2005, IFC membership increased to 178.

Financial and advisory services

In fiscal 2005, IFC's total committed portfolio amounted to $19.3 billion, of which $6.5 billion was committed to 236 new projects in 67 countries. Of the $6.45 billion, $5.37 billion came from IFC's own account, and the remaining $1.08 billion was mobilized from other financial institutions. IFC established the Global Trade Finance Programme, which helped banks deliver trade financing by providing risk coverage in difficult markets. It increased investments in renewable sources of energy and helped develop the market for carbon finance.

The Foreign Investment Advisory Service (FIAS) assisted Governments in developing policies and institutions to attract more foreign investment. FIAS completed 74 projects in fiscal 2005, including 16 knowledge management activities. Four regional learning events on investment climate issues were held in Bangkok, Thailand; Cape Town, South Africa; Istanbul, Turkey; and Washington, D. C.

Cumulative contributions to all donor-funded operations managed by IFC reached $1.1 billion through fiscal 2005. The donor community provided cumulative contributions of $203 million to support the Technical Assistance Trust Funds (TATF) programme, which included $17.8 million from IFC's own resources. Donors had approved more than 1,480 technical assistance projects through the programme since its inception in 1988. IFC created the Funding Mechanism for Technical Assistance and Advisory Services, which earmarked a portion of the Corporation's retained earnings as a contribution to support donor-funded operations and other technical assistance and advisory projects. Using funds designated from fiscal 2004 earnings, funding was approved for 46 activities and projects in the amount of $225 million over a six-year period. Expenditure in 2005 was $63 million.

Regional projects

In fiscal 2005, more than 55 per cent of IFC's new investments, for which IFC committed $6.5 billion, were in the financial sector, infrastructure, information technology and health and education.

IFC addressed Africa's development needs by expanding its programmes for smaller businesses, which constituted much of Africa's private sector. For larger projects, the strategy targeted more support at the formative stages of project development, thus expanding IFC's role beyond the provision of finance. IFC's commitments in the region totalled $1.9 billion for 30 projects in 14 countries.

In East Asia and the Pacific, IFC focused on developing stronger banks, strengthening the financial sector through technical assistance and investments in non-bank financial institutions, and promoting the growth of the region's domestic companies. IFC's commitments in the region totalled $3.8 billion for 40 projects in 11 countries.

In South Asia, which remained one of the world's fastest growing regions, IFC promoted sustainable private sector growth through investments in projects that had a high developmental impact. It also provided technical assistance, which helped improve client sustainability, strengthen smaller businesses and support community development programmes. IFC's commitments in the region totalled $2 billion for 20 projects in two countries.

In Europe and Central Asia, IFC was involved in the restructuring and privatization of the financial sector. It continued to support private banks, which improved access to finance for local private companies and smaller businesses. It also fostered the development of non-bank financial institutions, especially in housing finance and leasing. IFC's commitments in the region totalled $6.4 billion for 67 projects in 15 countries.

In Latin America and the Caribbean, IFC financed three operations totalling $96 million in the energy sector, with an emphasis on environmentally friendly sources of energy and on reducing harmful emissions. It also introduced innovative financial products into local capital markets, giving clients new sources of long-term financing, while helping them avoid foreign exchange risk. IFC's commitments in the region totaled $8.3 billion for 54 projects in 17 countries.

IFC's strategy in the Middle East and North Africa aimed to address the main challenges of the region, including employment creation and increased investment. In fiscal 2005, IFC focused on developmental sectors, such as housing and the development of smaller enterprises, and increased its activities related to infrastructure. It used technical assistance to reach its goals and introduce best practices. IFC's total commitment in the region amounted to $1.9 billion for 21 projects in eight countries.

Financial performance

In fiscal 2005, IFC's operating income was $2 billion, compared with $982 million in fiscal 2004. IFC's total committed portfolio at the end of fiscal 2005 was $19.3 billion, up from $17.9 billion in fiscal 2004. The portfolio consisted of loans, equity investments, guarantees and risk management products in 1,314 companies in 119 countries.

Capital and retained earnings

As at 30 June, IFC's net worth reached $9.8 billion, compared with $7.8 billion at the end of fiscal 2004.

Secretariat

IFC employed more than 2,400 staff, representing more than 120 nationalities.

NOTE: For further details of IFC activities, see *International Finance Corporation 2005 Annual Report*, published by the Corporation.

HEADQUARTERS AND OTHER OFFICE

HEADQUARTERS

International Finance Corporation
2121 Pennsylvania Avenue, NW
Washington, DC 20433, United States
Telephone: (1) (202) 473-3800
Fax: (1) (202) 974-4384
Internet: http://www.ifc.org
E-mail: webmaster@ifc.org

NEW YORK LIAISON OFFICE

International Finance Corporation
c/o The World Bank, Office of the Special Representative to the UN
1 Dag Hammarskjöld Plaza
885 Second Avenue, 26th floor
New York, NY 10017, United States
Telephone: (1) (212) 355-5112
Fax: (1) (212) 355-5523

Chapter VIII

International Monetary Fund (IMF)

In 2005, the International Monetary Fund (IMF) continued to work with its members to foster sustainable growth and financial stability through surveillance activities and policy advice; lending, in support of stabilization and reform programmes, and providing technical assistance in formulating sound policies and building robust institutions. IMF supported low-income developing countries through low-interest loans under the poverty reduction and growth facility (PRGF), and through debt relief under the enhanced Heavily Indebted Poor Countries (HIPC) Initiative. It also continued to counter money-laundering and combat the financing of terrorism.

In fiscal 2005 (1 May 2004–30 April 2005), which marked the sixtieth anniversary of the Bretton Woods Agreement establishing the IMF and the World Bank, the Fund's membership remained at 184.

IMF facilities and policies

In fiscal 2005, IMF continued to update its lending policies and policy conditionality—the conditions it attached to its financial assistance—to ensure that they met member country needs. In fiscal 2005, IMF appointed Roderigo de Rato as its new Managing Director. Under his leadership, IMF began a broad strategic review of its activities, focusing on how the Fund could best fulfil its mandate, develop priorities for future activities, and identify trade-offs and possible organizational changes. IMF also concluded a number of reviews targeting different aspects of its work, including a biennial review of Fund surveillance at the global, regional, and country levels, and a new review of conditionality. Reports from the Independent Evaluation Office provided the opportunity to review the growing role of IMF technical assistance and the Fund's overall role in relation to the 2001 capital account crisis in Argentina.

During the year, IMF policy advice provided by the Executive Board reflected concerns about rising oil prices and global imbalances.

Financial assistance

New IMF lending commitments in fiscal 2005 totalled 1.3 billion special drawing rights (SDR) compared with SDR 14.5 billion in fiscal 2004.

The decline in part reflected favourable financing conditions for emerging market sovereign borrowers.

IMF approved six new standby arrangements totalling over SDR 1.2 billion, and two existing commitments to Bolivia were augmented by SDR 85.8 million. Drawings under PRGF amounted to SDR 434.4 million, and the Executive Board approved augmentations in existing arrangements for Kenya and Bangladesh totalling SDR 53.3 million and SDR 50 million, respectively. IMF also committed SDR 1.8 billion in HIPC grants to 27 countries, of which SDR 1.5 billion was disbursed.

As at 30 April, 12 standby arrangements and extended arrangements, and 31 PRGF arrangements were in effect with members, while outstanding IMF credit amounted to SDR 49.9 billion, compared with SDR 62.2 billion a year earlier. During fiscal 2005, the Fund approved emergency post-conflict assistance to the Central African Republic, Haiti and Iraq. In addition, emergency natural disaster assistance was provided to Grenada, Maldives and Sri Lanka.

Liquidity

As at 30 April, IMF's usable resources totalled SDR 123 billion, a substantial increase from SDR 103.8 billion in fiscal 2004. Net uncommitted usable resources totalled SDR 99.9 billion at the end of fiscal 2005, compared with SDR 75 billion in fiscal 2004.

The Fund's liquid liability totalled SDR 49.8 billion compared with SDR 62.9 billion in 2004, while the ratio of the Fund's net uncommitted usable resource to its liquid liabilities increased to 200.4 per cent at the end of April 2005, from 119.4 per cent a year earlier.

SDR activity

In fiscal 2005, total transfer of SDRs decreased to SDR 10.6 billion, from SDR 13.8 billion in fiscal 2004.

IMF holdings of SDRs in the general resources account (GRA) increased to SDR 0.6 billion, from SDR 0.5 billion in fiscal 2004, while SDRs held by prescribed holders amounted to SDR 0.3 billion. SDR holdings by participants remained unchanged from fiscal 2004 at SDR 20.6 billion. SDR holdings of industrial and net creditor countries relative to their net cumulative allocations decreased from a year earlier. SDR holdings of non-industrial members amounted to 96 per cent of their net cumulative allocations compared with 76 per cent the previous year.

Policy on arrears

As at 30 April, financial obligations to IMF decreased from SDR 2.1 billion in 2004 to SDR 2 billion. The main reason for the decline was Iraq's settlement in September 2004 of its protracted arrears to the Fund. Most arrears were protracted (outstanding for more than six months), with about 45 per cent representing overdue principal and the remainder constituting of overdue charges and interest. Despite a decline in the Sudan's arrears, that country, together with Liberia, accounted for almost 79 per cent of the overdue financial obligations to the Fund, with Somalia and Zimbabwe accounting for the remainder. Under IMF's strengthened cooperative strategy on arrears, remedial measures were applied against the countries with protracted arrears.

Technical assistance and training

During fiscal 2005, IMF expanded and strengthened its technical assistance initiatives in priority areas, including trade facilitation, to stimulate economic growth in low-income countries. The Fund continued to review the effectiveness of its technical assistance programmes and centres, and sought to leverage its resources by cooperating with other technical assistance providers and mobilizing external funding. IMF spent about $80 million each year on technical assistance to member countries.

The IMF Institute continued to strengthen its training curriculum, delivering 124 courses and seminars to over 3,900 participants. Training was focused on four core areas: macroeconomic management, and financial, fiscal, and external sector policies.

Secretariat

As at 31 December, IMF employed 2,693 staff members, of whom 1,999 were Professional staff and 694 managerial and assistant staff.

Budget

The Fund's administrative budget for fiscal 2005 was approved at $905.1 million ($849.6 million, net of estimated reimbursements). In April, the Board approved $937 million ($876.1 million, net of reimbursements) for fiscal 2006.

NOTE: For further details of IMF activities, see *International Monetary Fund Annual Report 2005*, published by the Fund.

HEADQUARTERS AND OTHER OFFICES

HEADQUARTERS
International Monetary Fund
700 19th Street, NW
Washington, DC 20431, United States
Telephone: (1) (202) 623-7000
Fax: (1) (202) 623-4661
Internet: www.imf.org
E-mail: publicaffairs@imf.org

IMF also maintained offices in Geneva, Paris and Tokyo.

IMF OFFICE, UNITED NATIONS, NEW YORK
International Monetary Fund
885 Second Avenue, 26th floor
New York, NY 10017, United States
Telephone: (1) (212) 893-1700
Fax: (1) (212) 893-1715

Chapter IX

International Civil Aviation Organization (ICAO)

The International Civil Aviation Organization (ICAO) continued in 2005 to promote the safety, security and efficiency of civil air transport by prescribing standards and recommending practices and procedures for facilitating international civil aviation operations. Its objectives were set forth in annexes to the Convention on International Civil Aviation, adopted in Chicago, United States, in 1944 (the Chicago Convention).

In 2005, domestic and international scheduled traffic of the world's airlines increased to some 488 billion tonne-kilometres. Passenger traffic during the year increased by about 7 per cent to reach the 2 billion mark for the first time, while freight carriage remained at some 38 million tonnes. The passenger load factor on scheduled services in 2005 increased to about 75 per cent. Air freight increased by around 3 per cent to 142.5 billion tonne-kilometres, while there was little change in airmail traffic, which remained at about 4.6 billion tonne-kilometres. Overall passenger/freight/mail tonne-kilometres increased by some 6 per cent and international tonne-kilometres increased by about 7 per cent.

ICAO observed International Civil Aviation Day (7 December) under the theme "The Greening of Flight—maximizing compatibility between safe and orderly development of civil aviation and the quality of the environment".

In 2005, ICAO membership increased to 189 countries.

Activities

Air navigation

ICAO continued to update and implement international specifications and regional plans, with particular emphasis on aviation safety, efficiency improvements to the air navigation system, and communications, navigation and surveillance/air traffic management (CNS/ATM) systems. The specifications consisted of International Standards and Recommended Practices contained in 18 technical annexes to the Chicago Convention and Procedures for Air Navigation Services (PANS). In that regard, the ICAO Council adopted amendments to eight annexes and approved an amendment to one PANS document.

Other projects that were given special attention in 2005 included: the development of safety enhancement mechanisms, such as the Unified Strategy Programme to assist States; a procedure for transparency and disclosure of information regarding significant compliance shortcomings with respect to safety-related Standards and Recommended Practices; a new comprehensive systems approach to the Universal Safety Oversight Audit Programme; the harmonization of provisions relating to safety management; an increased emphasis on performance-based standards; the protection of the radio-frequency spectrum allocated to aeronautical safety services; aviation medicine issues, including global influenza preparedness; the integration of new, larger airplanes; and the modernization of the air navigation system, including a revision of the Global Air Navigation Plan for CNS/ATM systems.

Air transport

ICAO's air transport programmes were directed towards economic analysis and policy forecasting and planning; collection and publication of air transport statistics; financial management of airports and air navigation services, including user charges; economic aspects of CNS/ATM systems; environmental protection; facilitation of formalities for international air transport operations; and aviation security.

The seventh meeting of the Committee on Aviation Environmental Protection (Montreal, Canada, 3–7 October) reviewed the progress of ICAO's environmental work programme. The Committee was developing a framework to address the interdependencies of environmental measures and was also exploring tools to evaluate the impact of aircraft noise and local and global emissions related to aviation.

ICAO's Council adopted the nineteenth amendment to annex 9 on facilitation; new standards included obligations for all States to begin issuing machine readable passports no later than April 2010 and to allow non-machine readable passports to expire by 2015.

Progress was made in the implementation of the ICAO Aviation Security Plan of Action. Through the Universal Security Audit Programme, 41 States were audited by ICAO aviation security audit teams, bringing the total number of audited States to 105 by year's end. In November, ICAO launched a new programme to address the aviation security challenges faced by its member States. The Aviation Security Coordinated Assistance and Development Programme was established to assist States in aviation security from the perspective of sustainable development and capacity-building.

Legal matters

On 18 April, the 1989 Protocol relating to an amendment to the Convention on International Civil Aviation, which would increase the membership of the Air Navigation Commission from 15 to 19, entered into force.

The Special Group on the Modernization of the 1952 Rome Convention on Damage Caused by Foreign Aircraft to Third Parties on the Surface met from 10 to 14 January and from 4 to 8 July to refine the text of the draft Convention on Damage Caused by Foreign Aircraft to Third Parties. The Group also considered a supplementary compensation mechanism to cover payments to victims beyond the amounts which might be available through insurance to airlines and other aviation entities.

The Preparatory Commission for the International Registry of Mobile Assets held its third meeting (Montreal, 17-18 January), during which it approved regulations for the Registry, the user-fee schedule and the contract with the Registrar. In October, the Preparatory Commission approved procedures for the Registry.

In June, the ICAO Council established the Special Group on Legal Aspects of Emissions Charges, which met in Montreal in September. The Group agreed on key conclusions relating to emissions charges, in particular regarding the interpretation of article 15 of the Convention, on airport and similar changes.

In March, ICAO conducted a survey on legal measures to deal with new and emerging threats to civil aviation. The Council established a Secretariat study group to further examine the issue.

Technical cooperation

In 2005, ICAO undertook 277 technical cooperation projects in 105 countries. The technical cooperation programmes financed by the United Nations Development Programme (UNDP) trust funds, management service agreements and the Civil Aviation Purchasing Service had total expenditures of $115.9 million. Over 95 per cent of that amount was provided by Governments to fund their own projects.

A total of 509 fellowships were awarded in 2005, of which 473 were implemented. ICAO employed 463 experts from 44 countries, of whom 30 were on assignment under UNDP-funded projects and 433 worked on trust fund projects. There were 118 Governments and organizations registered with ICAO in 2005 under its Civil Aviation Purchasing Service. Total procurement for 2005 amounted to $88.5 million, compared with $102.5 million in 2004.

Secretariat

As at 31 December, ICAO employed 753 staff members, including 310 in the Professional and higher categories and 443 in the General Service and related categories.

Budget

Appropriations for the ICAO budget in 2005 amounted to $60,707,231.

NOTE: For further details on the activities of ICAO in 2005, see *Annual Report of the Council, 2005*.

HEADQUARTERS AND REGIONAL OFFICES

International Civil Aviation Organization
999 University Street
Montreal, Quebec, Canada H3C 5H7
Telephone: (1) (514) 954-8219
Fax: (1) (514) 954-6077
Internet: www.icao.int
E-mail: icaohq@icao.int

ICAO maintained regional offices in Bangkok, Thailand; Cairo, Egypt; Dakar, Senegal; Lima, Peru; Mexico, D.F.; Nairobi, Kenya; and Paris.

Chapter X

Universal Postal Union (UPU)

In 2005, the Universal Postal Union (UPU) worked to promote and develop a fast and reliable universal postal service through collaboration among its member countries. UPU's 190 members remained the largest physical distribution network in the world, with more than 5 million postal employees in some 660,000 post offices.

Activities of UPU organs

Universal Postal Congress

The Universal Postal Congress, UPU's supreme legislative authority, which last met in 2004 in Bucharest, Romania [YUN 2004, p. 1500], was scheduled to meet again in 2008, in Nairobi, Kenya.

Council of Administration

The Council of Administration (CA), which ensured the continuity of the Union's work between Congresses and studied regulatory, administrative, legislative and legal issues, held its annual session (Berne, Switzerland, 10-12 October). It adopted two resolutions on classification of countries for the Quality of Service Fund (QSF), as endorsed by the Terminal Dues Governance Issues Project Group. The terminal dues system involved payments postal services made to each other for the delivery of inbound foreign mail.

The first resolution provided the list of countries in the three categories that would receive 16.5 per cent, 8 per cent or 1 per cent QSF payments for 2006. The second resolution set strict criteria and procedures for countries that requested additional QSF resources under exceptional circumstances. The CA approved the current structure and composition of its bodies, as well as workplans for its project groups (2004) and working parties formed since the CA constituent meeting, held during the twenty-third UPU Congress [YUN 2004, p. 1500].

Postal Operations Council

The Postal Operations Council, at its annual session (Berne, 28 January), examined more than 400 proposals to modify the Letter Post and Parcel Post Regulations.

International Bureau

The UPU Bureau continued to provide support, liaison, information and consultation to the postal administrations of member countries. It studied developments in the postal environment, monitored the quality of global postal service and published information and statistics on international postal services. UPU's Postal Technology Centre continued to introduce new technology applications and information solutions to improve the quality, reliability and speed of national and international postal services.

Budget

Under UPU's self-financing system, contributions were payable in advance by member States based on the following year's budget. The CA approved a budget of 71.4 million Swiss francs for the 2005-2006 budget.

HEADQUARTERS

Universal Postal Union
Weltpoststrasse 4
3015 Berne, Switzerland
   Telephone: (41) (31) 350 31 10
   Fax: (41) (31) 350 31 10
   Internet: www.upu.int
   E-mail: info@upu.int

Chapter XI

International Telecommunication Union (ITU)

The International Telecommunication Union (ITU) continued in 2005 to promote the worldwide development and efficient operation of telecommunication systems.

At its annual session (Geneva, 12-22 July), the ITU Council discussed preparations for the second phase of the World Summit on the Information Society (WSIS) (see p. 933), the biennial budget for 2006-2007, the issue of cost-recovery of Satellite Network Filings and the financial consequences of eliminating cancellation fees, Internet issues, as well as general provisions regarding conferences.

During the year, the Union staged numerous events, including a number of WSIS-related thematic meetings, and a major trade exhibition showcasing the latest global technological trends (Salvador da Bahia, Brazil, 3-6 October).

ITU membership remained at 189 in 2005.

Radiocommunication Sector

ITU's Radiocommunication Sector (ITU-R) continued to ensure rational, equitable, efficient and economical use of the radio-frequency spectrum by all radiocommunication services, including those using satellite orbits, and to carry out studies and adopt recommendations on radiocommunication matters. Preparatory work for the 2007 Word Radiocommunication Conference began, and inter-sessional work for the Regional Radiocommunication Conference was implemented during 2005. The increased use of electronic documentation improved the efficiency of Study Group meetings and the Procedure for Simultaneous Adoption and Approval of Recommendations (PSAA) was increasingly implemented. During the year, 212 new and revised recommendations were published, covering such topics as the radiocommunication data dictionary for notification and coordination purposes, use of the Internet over satellite networks, technical characteristics of meteorological systems in the optical frequency range, and the future development of International Mobile Telecommunications 2000 and beyond. ITU-R continued to play a major role in the management of the radio-frequency spectrum and satellite orbits.

Telecommunication Standardization Sector

The Telecommunication Standardization Sector (ITU-T) continued to ensure the efficient and timely production of high-quality standards covering all areas of telecommunications. During the year, ITU-T focused on the next generation of information and communication technologies, cybersecurity, home networking, interactive televison, and international Internet connectivity.

ITU-T approved standards that would facilitate enhanced communication capabilities at lower cost, particularly by providing for interworking between dominant technologies in next generation networks (NGN). ITU-T announced a new NGN Global Standards Initiative that would deliver substantial cost savings through the economies of scale inherent in a single converged network providing mix-and-match implementation and global interoperability.

Telecommunication Development Sector

The Telecommunication Development Sector (ITU-D) continued in 2005 to promote investment and foster the expansion of telecommunication infrastructure in developing countries.

The Telecommunication Development Bureau (BDT) continued to assist countries to reform and restructure their telecommunication sectors through the introduction of new technologies, capacity development to ensure sustainability in management and operations, and by promoting financing and partnerships as a strategy to attract investment. Among other publications, the *World Telecommunication Indicators* report for 2004-2005 was published.

The sixth annual Global Symposium for Regulators (Hammamet, Tunisia, 14-15 November) gathered regulators, policy makers and service providers from 110 countries to develop a new regulatory framework to promote broadband deployment and access in developing countries.

Secretariat

As at 31 December 2005, ITU had 822 staff members, including 5 elected officials.

Budget

The 2006-2007 budget for ITU amounted to 339,435,000 Swiss francs.

NOTE: For further details regarding ITU activities, see the ITU website at www.itu.int.

HEADQUARTERS

International Telecommunication Union
Place des Nations
CH-1211, Geneva 20, Switzerland
Telephone: (41) (22) 730-5111
Fax: (41) (22) 733-7256
Internet: www.itu.int
E-mail: itumail@itu.int

Chapter XII

World Meteorological Organization (WMO)

In 2005, the World Meteorological Organization (WMO) continued to facilitate worldwide cooperation in the generation and exchange of meteorological and hydrological information and the application of meteorology to aviation, shipping, water problems, agriculture and other activities. During the fifty-seventh session of the WMO Executive Council (Geneva, 21 June–1 July), participants reviewed the activities of WMO and National Meteorological and Hydrological Services (NMHSs). It also addressed several issues, including WMO management reform; WMO Information System; locust menace in North and West Africa; strengthening regional and sub-regional offices; and strengthening contributions by NMHSs to hydrometeorological risk assessment at the national level.

WMO's membership remained at 181 States and six Territories at the end of 2005.

Observation systems

In 2005, WMO continued work on the redesign and establishment of an improved composite Global Observing System (GOS), which provided standardized observations of the atmosphere and ocean surfaces through surface- and space-based subsystems. Improvements were made in the availability of data produced by GOS's components, notably marine data and data transmitted from commercial aircraft via the Aircraft Meteorological Data Relay (AMDAR) programme.

Improvements in regional observation activities also continued, including: training seminars on climatological data reporting; the establishment of two new lead centres for global surface and upper-air data monitoring by Australia and Iran, respectively; and the revision of AMDAR training requirements for NMHSs. WMO also continued observation activities in the areas of atmospheric composition, the ozone, climate variability and water resources. In October, the Finnish Meteorological Institute and WMO signed a memorandum of understanding establishing a secretariat in Helsinki to develop an implementation plan for Integrated Global Atmospheric Observations of the ozone (IGACO-Ozone). To assist countries in maintaining their systems for acquiring water-related information and disseminating it to decision makers and various stake-

holders, WMO developed the World Hydrological Cycle Observing System (WHYCOS) programme.

World Climate Programme

The World Climate Programme continued to contribute to the infrastructure and human resources capabilities of NMHSs in climate monitoring, prediction and data management for improved climate services, especially in developing countries.

Natural disaster prevention and mitigation

In 2005, progress was made in the area of disaster prevention and mitigation. WMO contributed to the restructured and strengthened International Strategy for Disaster Reduction (ISDR) System for the implementation of the Hyogo Framework for Action: (2005-2015), adopted at the Second World Conference on Disaster Reduction (Kobe, Japan, 18-22 January) (see p. 1015). WMO ensured that strategic areas were reflected in all aspects of the Conference deliberations and outcome documents. Other efforts of WMO in the area of disaster prevention and mitigation included flood management and the coordination of emergency responses to technical and environmental disasters. WMO played an active role in the Indian Ocean tsunami aftermath (see p. 1024), and helped identify gaps in the development of an Indian Ocean Tsunami Early Warning System. It also provided emergency assistance to NMHSs in the South West Pacific and in Afghanistan, Iraq, and in Pakistan following the 8 October earthquake.

Research

In 2005, WMO established advisory boards and working groups for the Observing System Research and Predictability Experiment (THORPEX), and, with the assistance of WMO's regional commissions, programmes of work were developed for a Southern Hemisphere THORPEX Science Plan.

The World Climate Research Programme (WCRP), established in 1980 as a principal component of the World Climate Programme, pursued its objectives through research and observatorial and modelling activities that required international commitment, coordination and collaboration. Significant progress was made in the implementation of a new 10-year strategic framework entitled Coordinated Observation and Prediction of the Earth System. The main aim of that strategy was to facilitate the analysis and prediction of earth system variability and change for use in an increasing range of practical applications of direct relevance, benefit and value to society.

Applications of meteorology

The Applications of Meteorology Programme continued to focus on enhancing the capability of WMO members to provide comprehensive weather and related services, stressing public safety and welfare, and helping the public to understand better NMHS capabilities and how to benefit from them. A major event in 2005 was the Technical Conference on Public Weather Services (St. Petersburg, Russian Federation, 21-22 February), which discussed some of the key advances in technology that were impacting on the range and quality of public weather services provided by NMHSs. Among other developments, the World Area Forecasting System became fully operational on 1 July, providing high-quality forecasts of upper-level winds, temperatures and significant weather.

Hydrology and water resources

The International Decade for Action "Water for Life" (2005-2015), proclaimed by the General Assembly in 2003 [YUN 2003, p. 1034], was launched on 22 March by the Secretary-General, with the primary goal of fulfilling water-related MDGs. WMO participated actively in UN-Water (Global) meetings to ensure better coordination and collaboration with other UN agencies. In March, WMO was selected to chair the regional body in Africa of UN-Water for a period of two years, and worked to support the African Ministers Council on Water to assist African countries in promoting the concept of integrated water resources management. WMO also took part in the third session of the Committee for the Review of the Implementation of the United Nations Convention to Combat Desertification (Bonn, Germany, 2-11 May).

Technical cooperation

In 2005, WMO technical assistance, valued at $17.73 million, was financed by the Voluntary Cooperation Programme ($10.28 million), the United Nations Development Programme ($0.27 million), trust funds ($6.46 million) and WMO regular budget ($0.72 million).

Secretariat

As at 31 December 2005, WMO staff totalled 252.

Budget

A regular budget of 127,169,800 Swiss francs (SwF) for the 2004-2005 biennium was approved by the WMO Executive Council in 2003. The Fourteenth World Meteorological Congress, in 2003, approved a maximum expenditure of SwF 253,800,000 for the fourteenth financial period (2004-2007).

NOTE: For further details regarding WMO activities, see *World Meteorological Organization Annual Report 2005*, published by WMO.

HEADQUARTERS AND LIAISON OFFICE

World Meteorological Organization
7 bis, avenue de la Paix
(Case postale No. 2300)
CH-1211 Geneva 2, Switzerland
 Telephone: (41) 22-730-8111
 Fax: (41) (22) 730-8181
 Internet: www.wmo.ch
 E-mail: wmo@wmo.int

World Meteorological Organization Liaison Office at the United Nations
866 United Nations Plaza, Room A-302
New York, NY 10017, United States
 Telephone: (1) (212) 963-9444
 Fax: (1) (917) 367-9868
 E-mail: zbatjargal@wmo.int

Chapter XIII

International Maritime Organization (IMO)

In 2005, the International Maritime Organization (IMO) continued to facilitate cooperation to improve the safety and security of international shipping and to protect the maritime environment.

IMO's twenty-fourth Assembly (London, 21 November–2 December) adopted 22 resolutions on measures and procedures to strengthen maritime security. It also agreed that IMO should develop a new legally-binding instrument on ship recycling, for consideration and adoption in the 2008-2009 biennium.

In 2005, IMO membership increased to 166 with three associate members.

Activities in 2005

Prevention of pollution

In 2005, the IMO's Marine Environment Protection Committee (MEPC) approved new *Guidelines for the Facilitation of Response to a Pollution Incident*, which provided concrete guidance on the movement of equipment and personnel across national borders during an oil spill emergency. In addition, a series of web pages on oil spill resources was developed as part of IMO's website to facilitate access to technical information and assistance.

A revised scheme for phasing out single hull oil tankers and a new regulation that banned the carriage of heavy grade oil in single hull tankers entered into force on 5 April. *The Regulations for the Prevention of Air Pollution from Ships*, contained in Annex VI of the International Convention for the Prevention of Pollution from Ships, 1973, as modified by the Protocol of 1978 relating thereto (MARPOL 73/78), entered into force on 19 May. The regulations set limits on sulphur oxide and nitrogen oxide emissions from ship exhausts.

IMO designated the Torres Straight, the Canary Islands, the Galapagos Archipelago and the Baltic Sea as four new Particularly Sensitive Sea Areas (PSSA).

Ship security and safety at sea

In 2005, IMO's Maritime Safety Committee adopted a number of amendments to the International Convention for the Safety of Life at Sea, aimed at enhancing the safety of ships. In October, a Diplomatic Conference adopted the Protocol to the Convention for the Suppression of Unlawful Acts Against the Safety of Maritime Navigation, 1988 (SUA) [YUN 1988, p. 968], and the Protocol to the Suppression of Unlawful Acts against the Safety of Fixed Platforms Located on the Continental Shelf.

IMO's Secretary-General and the Government of the Republic of Indonesia convened a meeting on enhancing safety, security and environmental protection (Jakarta, Indonesia 7-8 September), which adopted the Jakarta Statement on the Enhancement of Safety, Security, and Environmental Protection in the Straits of Malacca and Singapore.

IMO published the Code of Safety for Fishermen and Fishing Vessels, 2005, and the Voluntary Guidelines for the Design, Construction, and Equipment of Small Fishing Vessels, 2005.

Secretariat

As at 31 December, IMO had 275 staff members, of whom 128 were in the Professional and higher categories and 147 were in the General Service category.

Budget

The IMO Assembly, in 2005, approved budget appropriations of 49,730,300 pounds sterling for the 2006-2007 biennium.

NOTE: For further information, see the organization's quarterly magazine, *IMO News.*

HEADQUARTERS

International Maritime Organization
4 Albert Embankment
London SE1 7SR, United Kingdom
Telephone: (44) (207) 735-7611
Fax: (44) (207) 587-3210
Internet: www.imo.org
E-mail: info@imo.org

Chapter XIV

World Intellectual Property Organization (WIPO)

The World Intellectual Property Organization (WIPO) continued to help ensure that the rights of creators and owners of intellectual property (IP) were protected worldwide, thus ensuring that inventors and authors were recognized and rewarded for their ingenuity.

During 2005, WIPO membership increased to 183. The number of States adhering to the treaties administered by WIPO also increased: as at 31 December, 168 States were parties to the Paris Convention for the Protection of Industrial Property, 160 to the Berne Convention for the Protection of Literary and Artistic Works, and 128 to the Patent Cooperation Treaty.

World Intellectual Property Day was celebrated on 26 April under the theme "Think, Imagine, Create".

Activities in 2005

Development cooperation

During 2005, WIPO undertook country- and sector-specific activities to assist developing countries in optimizing their protection systems for innovators, businesses, public research institutions and academia. Strategic sectors of the organization worked closely with its regional bureaux to develop programmes and events tailored to the needs of each member State. WIPO assisted the national intellectual property offices of Burkina Faso, Cameroon, Côte d'Ivoire, Ecuador, Guinea and Sri Lanka in placing geographical indications, or signs on goods that possessed qualities or a reputation due to their place of origin. It worked with Bhutan, Lebanon and Tanzania to develop national trademarks and branding strategies. WIPO also assessed the extent of IP use in selected African countries and carried out a peer review among members and potential members of the African Regional Intellectual Property Organization; assisted developing countries and economies in transition with national surveys assessing the economic contribution of their creative sectors; and carried out 68 office automation assistance projects in 53 member States. WIPO also helped to organize a Seminar on Intellectual Property and Development (Geneva, May 2-3) to address the establishment of a development-agenda for WIPO.

Intellectual property law

In 2005, the Standing Committee on the Law of Patents (SCP)—one of three WIPO committees dealing with legal matters—considered ways to advance discussions on the provisions of the draft Substantive Patent Law Treaty, which would provide common requirements for patent applications in different countries, improve the quality of granted patents, and facilitate the sharing of search and examination results between interested countries. At the General Assembly's sixtieth (2005) session, members decided to hold an Open Forum on the draft treaty in 2006 and convene an informal session of the Standing Committee on the Law of Patents to agree on a work programme.

Work continued in the Standing Committee on Copyright and Related Rights (SCCR) on proposals to update the IP rights of broadcasting organizations in the light of new technologies and a growing signal piracy problem, including piracy of pre-broadcast signals. SCCR held six regional consultation meetings on the protection of broadcasting organizations, and in November, at its thirteenth session, examined questions concerning the scope of the proposed new treaty on broadcasters' rights, the economic rights to be granted, and the duration of the protection.

On 28 April, the Patent Law Treaty, adopted in 2000 [YUN 2000, p. 1440] and designed to streamline national or regional requirements for the filing and prosecution of patent applications and the maintenance of patents, entered into force.

Arbitration and Mediation Centre

In 2005, WIPO's Arbitration and Mediation Center dealt with 39 arbitrations and 44 mediations involving parties from around the world. Mediation cases filed in 2005 included a complex dispute arising from an international collaboration agreement for the development of a cancer treatment that had led to prior litigation in several jurisdictions. In April, the Centre organized a Conference on Dispute Resolution in International Science and Technology Collaboration. Some 150 participants from 39 countries examined the types of disputes that could arise from complex international research collaborations between public and private research institutions and industry, and addressed the various options for resolving such disputes.

International registration activities

PCT. In 2005, international patent applications under the Patent Cooperation Treaty (PCT) increased by 9.3 per cent, reflecting international economic trends. Japan, the Republic of Korea and China showed the highest increases of 24.3 per cent, 33.6 per cent and 43.7 per cent, respectively.

Madrid System. WIPO received 33,565 international trademark applications under the Madrid System in 2005, a 13.9 per cent increase over 2004, due to the accession of the United States in 2003 and the European Community in 2004. By the end of 2005, WIPO's International Register contained over 450,000 trademark registrations in force, belonging to some 150,000 different holders. During the year, one country, Bahrain, acceded to the 1989 protocol to the Madrid Agreement concerning the International Registration of Trademarks.

Hague System. WIPO recorded 1,135 international registrations and 3,884 renewals of industrial designs under the Hague System in 2005. Two new States, Latvia and Singapore, joined the Geneva Act of the Hague Agreement, bringing the total number of members of the Hague System to 42.

Lisbon System. In 2005, Peru became party to the Lisbon Agreement and the Islamic Republic of Iran deposited an instrument of accession in December. By the end of the year, 23 States participated in the Lisbon System. The total number of registered international appellations of origin in force increased to 793.

Secretariat

As at 31 December, WIPO employed 855 staff members.

Budget

The approved programme and budget for 2006-2007 amounted to 531 million Swiss francs. About 89 per cent of WIPO's total income in 2005 was derived from global protection services fees, as well as fees related to arbitration and mediation services, while some 6 per cent came from member States' contributions. The remaining 5 per cent came mainly from the sale of WIPO publications, rental income and interest earnings.

NOTE: For further information, see *WIPO Annual Report 2005*, published by WIPO.

HEADQUARTERS AND OTHER OFFICE

HEADQUARTERS

World Intellectual Property Organization
34, Chemin des Colombettes (P.O. Box 18)
CH-1211 Geneva 20, Switzerland
   Telephone: (41) (22) 338-9111
   Fax: (41) (22) 733-5428
   Internet: www.wipo.int
   E-mail: wipo-mail@wipo.int

WIPO OFFICE AT THE UNITED NATIONS

2 United Nations Plaza, Suite 2525
New York, NY 10017, United States
   Telephone: (1) (212) 963-6813
   Fax: (1) (212) 963-4801
   E-mail: wipo@un.org

Chapter XV

International Fund for Agricultural Development (IFAD)

The International Fund for Agricultural Development (IFAD) continued in 2005 to promote the economic advancement of the rural poor by providing low-interest loans and grants.

The twenty-eighth session of the Governing Council (Rome, Italy, 15-18 February) focused on providing assistance in the processing and marketing of agricultural goods and responding to the needs created by the December 2004 Indian Ocean tsunami [YUN 2004, p. 952] and the October 2005 Pakistan earthquake (see p. 1034).

In 2005, IFAD membership increased to 164 states, of which 23 were in List A (developed countries), 12 in List B (oil-exporting developing countries) and 129 in List C (other developing countries). Of the latter, 49 were in Sub-List C1 (Africa), 49 in Sub-List C2 (Europe, Asia and the Pacific) and 31 in Sub-List C3 (Latin America and the Caribbean).

Resources

In 2005, IFAD was in the middle of its sixth replenishment (2004-2006). By the end of the year, member States had pledged a total amount equivalent to $509 million.

Activities

In 2005, IFAD responded to the exceptional needs created by the Indian Ocean tsunami and the Pakistan earthquake by developing fast-track projects to help survivors restore their livelihoods and strengthen their ability to face future disasters.

IFAD's Executive Board approved 31 new programmes and projects in 29 countries. The estimated total cost of those initiatives was over $1,053 million, of which $568.5 million would be provided by co-financiers, including Governments of the recipient countries.

As at 31 December, total IFAD investments were distributed as follows: Asia and the Pacific, $785 million for 41 projects; Eastern and Southern Africa, $590 million for 39 projects; the Near East and North Africa, Central and Eastern Europe and the Newly Independent States, $485 million for 33 projects; Latin America and the Caribbean, $461 million for 30 projects; and Western and Central Africa, $518 million for 41 projects.

Secretariat

As at 31 December, the IFAD secretariat had 317 staff members, comprising 150 Professional and higher-category positions and 167 General Service positions.

NOTE: For further details on IFAD activities in 2005, see *Annual Report 2005*, published by the Fund.

HEADQUARTERS AND OTHER OFFICES

HEADQUARTERS

International Fund for Agricultural Development
Via del Serafico, 107
00142 Rome, Italy
  Telephone: (39) (06) 54591
  Fax: (39) (06) 5043463
  Internet: www.ifad.org
  E-mail: ifad@ifad.org

IFAD also maintained offices in Eschbom, Germany, and Washington, D.C.

IFAD LIAISON OFFICE

2 United Nations Plaza, Room 1128-29
New York, NY 10017, United States
  Telephone: (1) (212) 963-0546
  Fax: (1) (212) 963-2787

Chapter XVI

United Nations Industrial Development Organization (UNIDO)

The United Nations Industrial Development Organization (UNIDO) continued in 2005 to promote the sustainable industrial development of developing countries and countries in transition.

The Industrial Development Board, at its thirtieth session (Vienna, 20-23 June), considered UNIDO's programme and budget for the 2006-2007 biennium. Member States discussed the implementation of a Cooperation Agreement with the United Nations Development Programme (UNDP) and the UNIDO strategic long-term vision.

The eleventh session of the UNIDO General Conference (Vienna, 28 November-2 December) appointed Kandeh K. Yumkella (Sierra Leone) as Director-General of UNIDO and adopted the strategic long-term vision statement for UNIDO for the period 2005-2015.

UNIDO membership remained at 171 in 2005.

Global forum activities

Through its global forum activities, UNIDO continued to promote industrial development and cooperation between countries, partnerships, knowledge-sharing, technology and investment. It also assisted developing countries and economies in transition in the implementation of multilateral environmental agreements.

Global forum activities included the compilation and dissemination worldwide of the 2005 edition of UNIDO's industrial statistics databases through various media, including CD-ROM, hard copy publication and the Internet; completion of a research programme on combating marginalization and poverty through industrial development; publication of research undertaken in the context of the medium-term programme framework 2004-2007 on productivity, technology diffusion, public goods, global value chains and of the 2005 *Industrial Development Report* entitled *Capability-building for catching-up: Historical, empiri-* *cal and policy dimensions*, and joint activities with selected multilateral organizations. UNIDO helped to organize the second International Conference on the Process of Innovation and Learning in Dynamic City Regions (Bangalore, India, 13-15 July) to examine case studies of dynamic city governance systems.

Technical cooperation

UNIDO continued to provide technical cooperation through its integrated programmes and country service frameworks, most of which dealt with capacity-building. Many were also geared towards increasing productivity and competitiveness, with a particular emphasis on small- and medium-sized enterprises and on environmental protection. During 2005, UNIDO achieved a record delivery of some $112.9 million in technical cooperation projects—compared to $98.8 million in 2004—due to efforts made to formulate and submit sound project proposals and replenish the stock of pipeline projects.

Secretariat

As at 31 December, UNIDO employed a total of 647 staff members: 246 were in the Professional or higher categories, 382 were in the General Service category and 19 were national officers.

Budget

The tenth (2003) session of the UNIDO General Conference approved the organization's 2004-2005 regular budget in the amount of 142,000,000 euros. The eleventh (2005) session approved the 2006-2007 regular budget in the amount of 154,009,900 euros.

NOTE: For further information on UNIDO, see *Annual Report of UNIDO 2005.*

HEADQUARTERS AND OTHER OFFICES

HEADQUARTERS
United Nations Industrial Development Organization
Vienna International Centre
P.O. Box 300
A-1400 Vienna, Austria
Telephone: (43) (1) 26026
Fax: (43) (1) 269-26-69
E-mail: unido@unido.org
Internet: http://www.unido.org

LIAISON OFFICES

UNIDO Office at Geneva
Palais des Nations
Le Bocage 1, Room 79
Avenue de la Paix 8-14
CH-1211 Geneva 10, Switzerland
  Telephone: (41) (22) 917-1434
  Fax: (41) (22) 917-0059
  E-mail: office.geneva@unido.org

UNIDO Office in New York
1 United Nations Plaza, Room DC1-1118
New York, NY 10017, United States
  Telephone: (1) (212) 963-6890
  Fax: (1) (212) 963-7904
  E-mail: office.newyork@unido.org

Chapter XVII

World Trade Organization (WTO)

During 2005, the World Trade Organization (WTO), the legal and institutional foundation of the multilateral trading system, continued to oversee the rules of international trade, settle trade disputes and organize trade negotiations.

The Sixth WTO Ministerial Conference (Hong Kong, China, 13-18 December), WTO's highest decision-making body, adopted a Declaration, which was intended to push the Doha Development Round negotiations, launched at the Fourth (2001) Ministerial Conference [YUN 2001, p. 1432], closer to completion (see below).

As at 31 December, WTO membership (members and observers) totalled 149.

General activities

In 2005, WTO observed its tenth anniversary. Doha Round negotiations continued throughout the year, involving some 450 meetings and 200 consultations held during the Sixth Ministerial Conference. The Conference reviewed the operation and functioning of the multilateral trading system and ongoing accession processes. Ministers from WTO's 149 member Governments approved a Declaration, which included: a 2013 end date for all export subsidies in agriculture; an agreement on cotton; duty- and quota-free market access for WTO's 32 least-developed country (LDC) members; an enhanced framework for full modalities in agriculture and non-agricultural market access; and a text in services that would facilitate ongoing negotiations.

The Committees and Working Groups of the WTO's General Council, the body overseeing WTO's work between Ministerial Conferences, received a number of mandates from the Council to follow up on issues and concerns related to the implementation of the Doha Development Agenda work programme, adopted in 2001 [YUN 2001, p. 1432]. The Committee on Trade and the Environment restructured its work to focus on the effect of environmental measures on market access and other issues. The Working Group on Trade, Debt and Finance examined themes, including better coherence in the design and implementation of trade-related reforms and monitoring, and trade liberalization as a source of growth.

During the year, the Trade Policy Body carried out reviews of Bolivia, Ecuador, Egypt, Guinea, Jamaica, Japan, Mongolia, Nigeria, Paraguay, the Philippines, Qatar, Romania, Sierra Leone, Trinidad and Tobago and Tunisia.

In May, the General Council appointed Pascal Lamy (France) as the next Director-General for a period of four years, beginning on 1 September.

Trade in goods

During 2005, the Committee on Agriculture continued to examine the implementation of members' commitments resulting from the Uruguay Round (1986-1994) of negotiations or from accession to WTO. It held the fourth transitional review of China's accession commitments, during which members raised concerns regarding the operation of Chinese trading enterprises and the implementation of its tariff quota commitments and taxation policies. The Agriculture and Commodities Division of the WTO secretariat undertook a number of technical assistance and training activities designed to assist members in implementing their existing commitments.

The Committee on Sanitary and Phytosanitary Measures considered specific trade concerns raised by members on a range of issues, including measures taken in response to the Avian influenza and the outbreak of foot-and-mouth disease, and those affecting trade in meat, fish and fresh fruit. In June, it completed its second review of the Agreement on the Application of Sanitary and Phytosanitary Measures, which set out the rights and obligations of members to ensure food safety, protect humans from plant- or animal-spread diseases, and protect plants and animals from pests and diseases.

The Committee on Safeguards continued to review national safeguard legislation and/or regulations.

Trade in services

In 2005, the Council for Trade in Services held four formal meetings, during which it continued its second review of most favoured nation exemptions, began its second review of air transport, and conducted its fourth transitional review of the Protocol on the Accession of the People's Republic of China to WTO, among other activities.

Intellectual property

The Council for the Trade-related Aspects of Intellectual Property Rights (TRIPS) Agreement followed up the reviews of the national implementing legislation of developing country members that were initiated in 2001 [YUN 2001, p. 1433] and 2002 [YUN 2002, p. 1497]. The completion of ten reviews was pending at the end of 2005. The Council continued its work on the preparation of an amendment to the TRIPS Agreement and undertook its fourth annual transitional review of the implementation by China of its WTO commitments regarding TRIPS.

Regional trade agreements

In 2005, the Special Session of the Committee on Regional Trade Agreements focused on the five remaining LDC Agreement-specific proposals, including one on the Understanding in Respect of Waivers of Obligations under the General Agreement on Tariffs and Trade (GATT) 1994, one on the Agreement on Trade-Related Investment Measures and three relating to the Decision on Measures in Favour of LDCs.

As at 31 December, WTO received notifications of 15 additional regional trade agreements, bringing the number of notified agreements to 241.

Trade and development

The Committee on Trade and Development continued to consider aspects of WTO's work in relation to development, including its technical assistance and training activities, the declining terms of trade for primary commodities and the developmental and environmental aspects of the Doha Round negotiations. Members also continued to pursue their work programmes on small economies and for LDCs.

Plurilateral agreements

At the end of the year, the Committee on Government Procurement continued negotiations on: the simplification and improvement of the text of the Agreement on Government Procurement; expansion of the coverage of the Agreement; and elimination of remaining discriminatory measures and practices that distorted open and competitive procurement.

International Trade Centre

The International Trade Centre, operated jointly by WTO and the United Nations Conference on Trade and Development (see p. 1048), continued to play a crucial role in trade-related technical cooperation and trade-related capacity-building. During the year, it focused its technical assistance for developing and transition economies on helping businesses understand WTO rules, strengthening enterprises, competitiveness and developing new trade promotion strategies.

Budget

The WTO budget for 2005 was 168.7 million Swiss francs.

Secretariat

As at 31 December, WTO staff numbered 594.

NOTE: For further information on WTO activities, see the organization's *Annual Report 2005*.

HEADQUARTERS

World Trade Organization
Centre William Rappard
154, rue de Lausanne
CH-1211 Geneva 21, Switzerland
Telephone: (41) (22) 739-5111
Fax: (41) (22) 731-4206
Internet: www.wto.org
*E-mail:*enquiries@wto.org

Chapter XVIII

World Tourism Organization (UNWTO)

In 2005, the World Tourism Organization (UNWTO), recognized by the UN General Assembly in resolution 58/232 [YUN 2003, p. 1475] as a specialized agency, continued to play a central role in promoting responsible, sustainable and universally accessible tourism, with particular attention to the interests of developing countries. In its second year as a UN agency, UNWTO assisted in rebuilding the tourism sector in destination countries affected by the 2004 Indian Ocean tsunami [YUN 2004, p. 952] and confirmed its role in fighting poverty around the world.

The UNWTO General Assembly, its governing body, held its sixteenth session (Dakar, Senegal, 3-6 December). The UNWTO Executive Council, which met between Assembly sessions, held its seventy-fifth session (Nessebar, Bulgaria, 13-14 June). Other meetings of UNWTO organs convened in 2005 included the first emergency session of the UNWTO Executive Council (Phuket, Thailand, 1 February); a conference on Harnessing Tourism for the Millennium Development Goals (MDGs) [YUN 2000, p. 51] (New York, 13 September); a World Tourism Forum for Peace and Sustainable Development (Rio de Janeiro, Brazil, 23-24 October); and meetings of the UNWTO Commissions for Africa (Gaborone, Botswana, April), Europe (Coimbra, Portugal, May), the Americas (Santiago, Chile, May), East Asia and the Pacific (Otsu, Japan, June) and the Middle East (Amman, Jordan, September).

World Tourism Day was commemorated on 27 September, under the theme "Travel and transport: from the imaginary of Jules Verne to twenty-first century reality".

As at 31 December, UNWTO comprised 150 member States, seven associate members, two observers and over 300 affiliate members, representing the private sector, educational institutions and destination management organizations. During the year, six States—the Bahamas, Belarus, Latvia, Papau New Guinea, Timor-Leste and the United Kingdom—became members of the Organization.

Activities

During 2005, UNWTO continued its work to develop sustainable tourism as a force for eliminating poverty, as part of its commitment to contribute to the implementation of the MDGs, in particular through its programme known as Sustainable Tourism—Eliminating Poverty (ST-EP) initiative, which was operated jointly with the United Nations Conference on Trade and Development (UNCTAD).

The UNWTO General Assembly (see above), considered, as one of its principle themes, tourism's contribution to the sustainable development of poorer countries and the elimination of poverty. During the session, the UNWTO Secretary-General highlighted the need for greater awareness of tourism in and to Africa.

The first emergency session of the UNWTO Executive Council, convened in February (see above), adopted the Phuket Action Plan (see p. 1026) to assist countries affected by the 2004 Indian Ocean tsunami [YUN 2004, p. 952] in the recovery of their tourism sectors.

The World Committee on Tourism Ethics, established by the UNWTO General Assembly in 2003 as an independent body to assist in implementing and monitoring the Global Code of Ethics for Tourism, at its third meeting (Tunis, Tunisia, 16-17 May), examined four disputes reported by individual applicants. Three of the four cases received did not qualify in terms of the Committee's criteria for the consideration of such cases. In the fourth case, the Committee was expected to make its recommendation towards the end of the year, after consulting all the parties concerned. The Committee agreed on a short and user-friendly extract of the Code entitled "The Responsible Tourist and Traveller", with the intention of creating awareness among ordinary travelers of their responsibilities.

During the year, UNWTO launched its UNWTO TedProm initiative, which encompassed all activities aimed at disseminating information about quality tourism through education, training and research programmes. The organization recognized and promoted those programmes and activities carried out by UNWTO Tourism Education Quality (TedQual) certified institutions, which were selected by means of a quality audit. UNWTO released the first edition of *TedQual: The World's Leading Tourism Programmes*, a publication aimed at promoting the academic programmes offered by TedQual certified institutions and helping to guide students in the tourism programme selection process.

Other UNWTO activities addressed cooperation for development; sustainable tourism development; statistics; market intelligence; support for tourism microbusiness; and other issues.

Regional activities to strengthen and support national tourism were undertaken by UNWTO in Africa, the Americas, Asia and the Pacific, the Middle East and Europe.

On 30 November, Franceso Frangialli (France) was re-elected for a third four-year term as Secretary-General of UNWTO, effective 1 January 2006.

Secretariat

As at 31 December 2005, UNWTO staff numbered 91, of whom 37 were in the Professional or higher categories and 54 were in the General Service category.

Budget

The UNWTO budget for 2005 amounted to 11,438,000 euros.

HEADQUARTERS AND OTHER OFFICE

World Tourism Organization
Capitán Haya, 42
28020 Madrid, Spain
  Telephone: (34) (91) 567-8100
  Fax: (34) (91) 571-3733
  Internet: www.world-tourism.org
  E-mail: omt@world-tourism.org

The UNWTO secretariat maintained a regional support office for Asia and the Pacific, in Osaka, Japan.

Appendices

Appendix I

Roster of the United Nations

There were 191 Member States as at 31 December 2005.

MEMBER	DATE OF ADMISSION	MEMBER	DATE OF ADMISSION	MEMBER	DATE OF ADMISSION
Afghanistan	19 Nov. 1946	El Salvador	24 Oct. 1945	Mauritania	27 Oct. 1961
Albania	14 Dec. 1955	Equatorial Guinea	12 Nov. 1968	Mauritius	24 Apr. 1968
Algeria	8 Oct. 1962	Eritrea	28 May 1993	Mexico	7 Nov. 1945
Andorra	28 July 1993	Estonia	17 Sep. 1991	Micronesia (Federated	
Angola	1 Dec. 1976	Ethiopia	13 Nov. 1945	States of)	17 Sep. 1991
Antigua and Barbuda	11 Nov. 1981	Fiji	13 Oct. 1970	Monaco	28 May 1993
Argentina	24 Oct. 1945	Finland	14 Dec. 1955	Mongolia	27 Oct. 1961
Armenia	2 Mar. 1992	France	24 Oct. 1945	Morocco	12 Nov. 1956
Australia	1 Nov. 1945	Gabon	20 Sep. 1960	Mozambique	16 Sep. 1975
Austria	14 Dec. 1955	Gambia	21 Sep. 1965	Myanmar	19 Apr. 1948
Azerbaijan	2 Mar. 1992	Georgia	31 July 1992	Namibia	23 Apr. 1990
Bahamas	18 Sep. 1973	Germany[3]	18 Sep. 1973	Nauru	14 Sep. 1999
Bahrain	21 Sep. 1971	Ghana	8 Mar. 1957	Nepal	14 Dec. 1955
Bangladesh	17 Sep. 1974	Greece	25 Oct. 1945	Netherlands	10 Dec. 1945
Barbados	9 Dec. 1966	Grenada	17 Sep. 1974	New Zealand	24 Oct. 1945
Belarus	24 Oct. 1945	Guatemala	21 Nov. 1945	Nicaragua	24 Oct. 1945
Belgium	27 Dec. 1945	Guinea	12 Dec. 1958	Niger	20 Sep. 1960
Belize	25 Sep. 1981	Guinea-Bissau	17 Sep. 1974	Nigeria	7 Oct. 1960
Benin	20 Sep. 1960	Guyana	20 Sep. 1966	Norway	27 Nov. 1945
Bhutan	21 Sep. 1971	Haiti	24 Oct. 1945	Oman	7 Oct. 1971
Bolivia	14 Nov. 1945	Honduras	17 Dec. 1945	Pakistan	30 Sep. 1947
Bosnia and Herzegovina	22 May 1992	Hungary	14 Dec. 1955	Palau	15 Dec. 1994
Botswana	17 Oct. 1966	Iceland	19 Nov. 1946	Panama	13 Nov. 1945
Brazil	24 Oct. 1945	India	30 Oct. 1945	Papua New Guinea	10 Oct. 1975
Brunei Darussalam	21 Sep. 1984	Indonesia[4]	28 Sep. 1950	Paraguay	24 Oct. 1945
Bulgaria	14 Dec. 1955	Iran (Islamic Republic of)	24 Oct. 1945	Peru	31 Oct. 1945
Burkina Faso	20 Sep. 1960	Iraq	21 Dec. 1945	Philippines	24 Oct. 1945
Burundi	18 Sep. 1962	Ireland	14 Dec. 1955	Poland	24 Oct. 1945
Cambodia	14 Dec. 1955	Israel	11 May 1949	Portugal	14 Dec. 1955
Cameroon	20 Sep. 1960	Italy	14 Dec. 1955	Qatar	21 Sep. 1971
Canada	9 Nov. 1945	Jamaica	18 Sep. 1962	Republic of Korea	17 Sep. 1991
Cape Verde	16 Sep. 1975	Japan	18 Dec. 1956	Republic of Moldova	2 Mar. 1992
Central African Republic	20 Sep. 1960	Jordan	14 Dec. 1955	Romania	14 Dec. 1955
Chad	20 Sep. 1960	Kazakhstan	2 Mar. 1992	Russian Federation[6]	24 Oct. 1945
Chile	24 Oct. 1945	Kenya	16 Dec. 1963	Rwanda	18 Sep. 1962
China	24 Oct. 1945	Kiribati	14 Sep. 1999	Saint Kitts and Nevis	23 Sep. 1983
Colombia	5 Nov. 1945	Kuwait	14 May 1963	Saint Lucia	18 Sep. 1979
Comoros	12 Nov. 1975	Kyrgyzstan	2 Mar. 1992	Saint Vincent and the	
Congo	20 Sep. 1960	Lao People's Democratic		Grenadines	16 Sep. 1980
Costa Rica	2 Nov. 1945	Republic	14 Dec. 1955	Samoa	15 Dec. 1976
Côte d'Ivoire	20 Sep. 1960	Latvia	17 Sep. 1991	San Marino	2 Mar. 1992
Croatia	22 May 1992	Lebanon	24 Oct. 1945	Sao Tome and Principe	16 Sep. 1975
Cuba	24 Oct. 1945	Lesotho	17 Oct. 1966	Saudi Arabia	24 Oct. 1945
Cyprus	20 Sep. 1960	Liberia	2 Nov. 1945	Senegal	28 Sep. 1960
Czech Republic[1]	19 Jan. 1993	Libyan Arab Jamahiriya	14 Dec. 1955	Serbia and Montenegro	1 Nov. 2000
Democratic People's		Liechtenstein	18 Sep. 1990	Seychelles	21 Sep. 1976
Republic of Korea	17 Sep. 1991	Lithuania	17 Sep. 1991	Sierra Leone	27 Sep. 1961
Democratic Republic of		Luxembourg	24 Oct. 1945	Singapore[5]	21 Sep. 1965
the Congo	20 Sep. 1960	Madagascar	20 Sep. 1960	Slovakia[1]	19 Jan. 1993
Denmark	24 Oct. 1945	Malawi	1 Dec. 1964	Slovenia	22 May 1992
Djibouti	20 Sep. 1977	Malaysia[5]	17 Sep. 1957	Solomon Islands	19 Sep. 1978
Dominica	18 Dec. 1978	Maldives	21 Sep. 1965	Somalia	20 Sep. 1960
Dominican Republic	24 Oct. 1945	Mali	28 Sep. 1960	South Africa	7 Nov. 1945
Ecuador	21 Dec. 1945	Malta	1 Dec. 1964	Spain	14 Dec. 1955
Egypt[2]	24 Oct. 1945	Marshall Islands	17 Sep. 1991	Sri Lanka	14 Dec. 1955

MEMBER	DATE OF ADMISSION	MEMBER	DATE OF ADMISSION	MEMBER	DATE OF ADMISSION
Sudan	12 Nov. 1956	Tonga	14 Sep. 1999	United Republic of	
Suriname	4 Dec. 1975	Trinidad and Tobago	18 Sep. 1962	Tanzania[7]	14 Dec. 1961
Swaziland	24 Sep. 1968	Tunisia	12 Nov. 1956	United States of America	24 Oct. 1945
Sweden	19 Nov. 1946	Turkey	24 Oct. 1945	Uruguay	18 Dec. 1945
Switzerland	10 Sep. 2002	Turkmenistan	2 Mar. 1992	Uzbekistan	2 Mar. 1992
Syrian Arab Republic[2]	24 Oct. 1945	Tuvalu	5 Sep. 2000	Vanuatu	15 Sep. 1981
Tajikistan	2 Mar. 1992	Uganda	25 Oct. 1962	Venezuela (Bolivarian	
Thailand	16 Dec. 1946	Ukraine	24 Oct. 1945	Republic of)	15 Nov. 1945
The former Yugoslav		United Arab Emirates	9 Dec. 1971	Viet Nam	20 Sep. 1977
Republic of Macedonia	8 Apr. 1993	United Kingdom of Great		Yemen[8]	30 Sep. 1947
Timor-Leste	27 Sep. 2002	Britain and Northern		Zambia	1 Dec. 1964
Togo	20 Sep. 1960	Ireland	24 Oct. 1945	Zimbabwe	25 Aug. 1980

[1]Czechoslovakia, which was an original Member of the United Nations from 24 October 1945, split up on 1 January 1993 and was succeeded by the Czech Republic and Slovakia.

[2]Egypt and Syria, both of which became Members of the United Nations on 24 October 1945, joined together—following a plebiscite held in those countries on 21 February 1958—to form the United Arab Republic. On 13 October 1961, Syria, having resumed its status as an independent State, also resumed its separate membership in the United Nations; it changed its name to the Syrian Arab Republic on 14 September 1971. The United Arab Republic continued as a Member of the United Nations and reverted to the name of Egypt on 2 September 1971.

[3]Through accession of the German Democratic Republic to the Federal Republic of Germany on 3 October 1990, the two German States (both of which became United Nations Members on 18 September 1973) united to form one sovereign State. As from that date, the Federal Republic of Germany has acted in the United Nations under the designation Germany.

[4]On 20 January 1965, Indonesia informed the Secretary-General that it had decided to withdraw from the United Nations. By a telegram of 19 September 1966, it notified the Secretary-General of its decision to resume participation in the activities of the United Nations. On 28 September 1966, the General Assembly took note of that decision and the President invited the representatives of Indonesia to take their seats in the Assembly.

[5]On 16 September 1963, Sabah (North Borneo), Sarawak and Singapore joined with the Federation of Malaya (which became a United Nations Member on 17 September 1957) to form Malaysia. On 9 August 1965, Singapore became an independent State and on 21 September 1965 it became a Member of the United Nations.

[6]The Union of Soviet Socialist Republics was an original Member of the United Nations from 24 October 1945. On 24 December 1991, the President of the Russian Federation informed the Secretary-General that the membership of the USSR in all United Nations organs was being continued by the Russian Federation.

[7]Tanganyika was admitted to the United Nations on 14 December 1961, and Zanzibar, on 16 December 1963. Following ratification, on 26 April 1964, of the Articles of Union between Tanganyika and Zanzibar, the two States became represented as a single Member: the United Republic of Tanganyika and Zanzibar; it changed its name to the United Republic of Tanzania on 1 November 1964.

[8]Yemen was admitted to the United Nations on 30 September 1947 and Democratic Yemen on 14 December 1967. On 22 May 1990, the two countries merged and have since been represented as one Member.

Appendix II

Charter of the United Nations and Statute of the International Court of Justice

Charter of the United Nations

NOTE: The Charter of the United Nations was signed on 26 June 1945, in San Francisco, at the conclusion of the United Nations Conference on International Organization, and came into force on 24 October 1945. The Statute of the International Court of Justice is an integral part of the Charter.

Amendments to Articles 23, 27 and 61 of the Charter were adopted by the General Assembly on 17 December 1963 and came into force on 31 August 1965. A further amendment to Article 61 was adopted by the General Assembly on 20 December 1971 and came into force on 24 September 1973. An amendment to Article 109, adopted by the General Assembly on 20 December 1965, came into force on 12 June 1968.

The amendment to Article 23 enlarges the membership of the Security Council from 11 to 15. The amended Article 27 provides that decisions of the Security Council on procedural matters shall be made by an affirmative vote of nine members (formerly seven) and on all other matters by an affirmative vote of nine members (formerly seven), including the concurring votes of the five permanent members of the Security Council.

The amendment to Article 61, which entered into force on 31 August 1965, enlarged the membership of the Economic and Social Council from 18 to 27. The subsequent amendment to that Article, which entered into force on 24 September 1973, further increased the membership of the Council from 27 to 54.

The amendment to Article 109, which relates to the first paragraph of that Article, provides that a General Conference of Member States for the purpose of reviewing the Charter may be held at a date and place to be fixed by a two-thirds vote of the members of the General Assembly and by a vote of any nine members (formerly seven) of the Security Council. Paragraph 3 of Article 109, which deals with the consideration of a possible review conference during the tenth regular session of the General Assembly, has been retained in its original form in its reference to a "vote of any seven members of the Security Council", the paragraph having been acted upon in 1955 by the General Assembly, at its tenth regular session, and by the Security Council.

WE THE PEOPLES
OF THE UNITED NATIONS
DETERMINED

to save succeeding generations from the scourge of war, which twice in our lifetime has brought untold sorrow to mankind, and

to reaffirm faith in fundamental human rights, in the dignity and worth of the human person, in the equal rights of men and women and of nations large and small, and

to establish conditions under which justice and respect for the obligations arising from treaties and other sources of international law can be maintained, and

to promote social progress and better standards of life in larger freedom,

AND FOR THESE ENDS

to practice tolerance and live together in peace with one another as good neighbours, and

to unite our strength to maintain international peace and security, and

to ensure, by the acceptance of principles and the institution of methods, that armed force shall not be used, save in the common interest, and

to employ international machinery for the promotion of the economic and social advancement of all peoples,

HAVE RESOLVED TO
COMBINE OUR EFFORTS TO
ACCOMPLISH THESE AIMS

Accordingly, our respective Governments, through representatives assembled in the city of San Francisco, who have exhibited their full powers found to be in good and due form, have agreed to the present Charter of the United Nations and do hereby establish an international organization to be known as the United Nations.

Chapter I
PURPOSES AND PRINCIPLES

Article 1

The Purposes of the United Nations are:

1. To maintain international peace and security, and to that end: to take effective collective measures for the prevention and removal of threats to the peace, and for the suppression of acts of aggression or other breaches of the peace, and to bring about by peaceful means, and in conformity with the principles of justice and international law, adjustment or settlement of international disputes or situations which might lead to a breach of the peace;

2. To develop friendly relations among nations based on respect for the principle of equal rights and self-determination of peoples, and to take other appropriate measures to strengthen universal peace;

3. To achieve international co-operation in solving international problems of an economic, social, cultural or humanitarian character, and in promoting and encouraging respect for human rights and for fundamental freedoms for all without distinction as to race, sex, language or religion; and

4. To be a centre for harmonizing the actions of nations in the attainment of these common ends.

Article 2

The Organization and its Members, in pursuit of the Purposes stated in Article 1, shall act in accordance with the following Principles:

1. The Organization is based on the principle of the sovereign equality of all its Members.

2. All Members, in order to ensure to all of them the rights and benefits resulting from membership, shall fulfil in good faith the obligations assumed by them in accordance with the present Charter.

3. All Members shall settle their international disputes by peaceful means in such a manner that international peace and security, and justice, are not endangered.

4. All Members shall refrain in their international relations from the threat or use of force against the territorial integrity or political independence of any state, or in any other manner inconsistent with the Purposes of the United Nations.

5. All Members shall give the United Nations every assistance in any action it takes in accordance with the present Charter, and shall refrain from giving assistance to any state against which the United Nations is taking preventive or enforcement action.

6. The Organization shall ensure that states which are not Members of the United Nations act in accordance with these Principles so far as may be necessary for the maintenance of international peace and security.

7. Nothing contained in the present Charter shall authorize the United Nations to intervene in matters which are essentially within the domestic jurisdiction of any state or shall require the Members to submit such matters to settlement under the present Charter; but this principle shall not prejudice the application of enforcement measures under Chapter VII.

Chapter II
MEMBERSHIP

Article 3

The original Members of the United Nations shall be the states which, having participated in the United Nations Conference on International Organization at San Francisco or having previously signed the Declaration by United Nations of 1 January 1942, sign the present Charter and ratify it in accordance with Article 110.

Article 4

1. Membership in the United Nations is open to all other peace-loving states which accept the obligations contained in the present Charter and, in the judgment of the Organization, are able and willing to carry out these obligations.

2. The admission of any such state to membership in the United Nations will be effected by a decision of the General Assembly upon the recommendation of the Security Council.

Article 5

A Member of the United Nations against which preventive or enforcement action has been taken by the Security Council may be suspended from the exercise of the rights and privileges of membership by the General Assembly upon the recommendation of the Security Council. The exercise of these rights and privileges may be restored by the Security Council.

Article 6

A Member of the United Nations which has persistently violated the Principles contained in the present Charter may be expelled from the Organization by the General Assembly upon the recommendation of the Security Council.

Chapter III
ORGANS

Article 7

1. There are established as the principal organs of the United Nations: a General Assembly, a Security Council, an Economic and Social Council, a Trusteeship Council, an International Court of Justice, and a Secretariat.

2. Such subsidiary organs as may be found necessary may be established in accordance with the present Charter.

Article 8

The United Nations shall place no restrictions on the eligibility of men and women to participate in any capacity and under conditions of equality in its principal and subsidiary organs.

Chapter IV
THE GENERAL ASSEMBLY

Composition

Article 9

1. The General Assembly shall consist of all the Members of the United Nations.

2. Each Member shall have not more than five representatives in the General Assembly.

Functions and Powers

Article 10

The General Assembly may discuss any questions or any matters within the scope of the present Charter or relating to the powers and functions of any organs provided for in the present Charter, and, except as provided in Article 12, may make recommendations to the Members of the United Nations or to the Security Council or both on any such questions or matters.

Article 11

1. The General Assembly may consider the general principles of co-operation in the maintenance of international peace and security, including the principles governing disarmament and the regulation of armaments, and may make recommendations with regard to such principles to the Members or to the Security Council or to both.

2. The General Assembly may discuss any questions relating to the maintenance of international peace and security brought before it by any Member of the United Nations, or by the Security Council, or by a state which is not a Member of the United Nations in accordance with Article 35, paragraph 2, and, except as provided in Article 12, may make recommendations with regard to any such questions to the state or states concerned or to the Security Council or to both. Any such question on which action is necessary shall be referred to the Security Council by the General Assembly either before or after discussion.

3. The General Assembly may call the attention of the Security Council to situations which are likely to endanger international peace and security.

4. The powers of the General Assembly set forth in this Article shall not limit the general scope of Article 10.

Article 12

1. While the Security Council is exercising in respect of any dispute or situation the functions assigned to it in the present Charter, the General Assembly shall not make any recommendation with regard to that dispute or situation unless the Security Council so requests.

2. The Secretary-General, with the consent of the Security Council, shall notify the General Assembly at each session of any matters relative to the maintenance of international peace and security which are being dealt with by the Security Council and shall similarly notify the General Assembly, or the Members of the United Nations if the General Assembly is not in session, immediately the Security Council ceases to deal with such matters.

Article 13

1. The General Assembly shall initiate studies and make recommendations for the purpose of:

a. promoting international co-operation in the political field and encouraging the progressive development of international law and its codification;

b. promoting international co-operation in the economic, social, cultural, educational and health fields, and assisting in the realization of human rights and fundamental freedoms for all without distinction as to race, sex, language or religion.

2. The further responsibilities, functions and powers of the General Assembly with respect to matters mentioned in paragraph 1 (b) above are set forth in Chapters IX and X.

Article 14

Subject to the provisions of Article 12, the General Assembly may recommend measures for the peaceful adjustment of any situation, regardless of origin, which it deems likely to impair the general welfare or friendly relations among nations, including situations resulting from a violation of the provisions of the present Charter setting forth the Purposes and Principles of the United Nations.

Article 15

1. The General Assembly shall receive and consider annual and special reports from the Security Council; these reports shall include an account of the measures that the Security Council has decided upon or taken to maintain international peace and security.
2. The General Assembly shall receive and consider reports from the other organs of the United Nations.

Article 16

The General Assembly shall perform such functions with respect to the international trusteeship system as are assigned to it under Chapters XII and XIII, including the approval of the trusteeship agreements for areas not designated as strategic.

Article 17

1. The General Assembly shall consider and approve the budget of the Organization.
2. The expenses of the Organization shall be borne by the Members as apportioned by the General Assembly.
3. The General Assembly shall consider and approve any financial and budgetary arrangements with specialized agencies referred to in Article 57 and shall examine the administrative budgets of such specialized agencies with a view to making recommendations to the agencies concerned.

Voting

Article 18

1. Each member of the General Assembly shall have one vote.
2. Decisions of the General Assembly on important questions shall be made by a two-thirds majority of the members present and voting. These questions shall include: recommendations with respect to the maintenance of international peace and security, the election of the non-permanent members of the Security Council, the election of the members of the Economic and Social Council, the election of members of the Trusteeship Council in accordance with paragraph 1 (c) of Article 86, the admission of new Members to the United Nations, the suspension of the rights and privileges of membership, the expulsion of Members, questions relating to the operation of the trusteeship system, and budgetary questions.
3. Decisions on other questions, including the determination of additional categories of questions to be decided by a two-thirds majority, shall be made by a majority of the members present and voting.

Article 19

A Member of the United Nations which is in arrears in the payment of its financial contributions to the Organization shall have no vote in the General Assembly if the amount of its arrears equals or exceeds the amount of the contributions due from it for the preceding two full years. The General Assembly may, nevertheless, permit such a Member to vote if it is satisfied that the failure to pay is due to conditions beyond the control of the Member.

Procedure

Article 20

The General Assembly shall meet in regular annual sessions and in such special sessions as occasion may require. Special sessions shall be convoked by the Secretary-General at the request of the Security Council or of a majority of the Members of the United Nations.

Article 21

The General Assembly shall adopt its own rules of procedure. It shall elect its President for each session.

Article 22

The General Assembly may establish such subsidiary organs as it deems necessary for the performance of its functions.

Chapter V

THE SECURITY COUNCIL

Composition

Article 23[1]

1. The Security Council shall consist of fifteen Members of the United Nations. The Republic of China, France, the Union of Soviet Socialist Republics, the United Kingdom of Great Britain and Northern Ireland and the United States of America shall be permanent members of the Security Council. The General Assembly shall elect ten other Members of the United Nations to be non-permanent members of the Security Council, due regard being specially paid, in the first instance to the contribution of Members of the United Nations to the maintenance of international peace and security and to the other purposes of the Organization, and also to equitable geographical distribution.
2. The non-permanent members of the Security Council shall be elected for a term of two years. In the first election of the non-permanent members after the increase of the membership of the Security Council from eleven to fifteen, two of the four additional members shall be chosen for a term of one year. A retiring member shall not be eligible for immediate re-election.
3. Each member of the Security Council shall have one representative.

Functions and Powers

Article 24

1. In order to ensure prompt and effective action by the United Nations, its Members confer on the Security Council primary responsibility for the maintenance of international peace and security, and agree that in carrying out its duties under this responsibility the Security Council acts on their behalf.
2. In discharging these duties the Security Council shall act in accordance with the Purposes and Principles of the United Nations. The specific powers granted to the Security Council for the discharge of these duties are laid down in Chapters VI, VII, VIII and XII.
3. The Security Council shall submit annual and, when necessary, special reports to the General Assembly for its consideration.

Article 25

The Members of the United Nations agree to accept and carry out the decisions of the Security Council in accordance with the present Charter.

Article 26

In order to promote the establishment and maintenance of international peace and security with the least diversion for armaments of the world's human and economic resources, the Security Council shall be responsible for formulating, with the assistance of the Military Staff Committee referred to in Article

47, plans to be submitted to the Members of the United Nations for the establishment of a system for the regulation of armaments.

Voting

Article 27[2]

1. Each member of the Security Council shall have one vote.

2. Decisions of the Security Council on procedural matters shall be made by an affirmative vote of nine members.

3. Decisions of the Security Council on all other matters shall be made by an affirmative vote of nine members including the concurring votes of the permanent members; provided that, in decisions under Chapter VI, and under paragraph 3 of Article 52, a party to a dispute shall abstain from voting.

Procedure

Article 28

1. The Security Council shall be so organized as to be able to function continuously. Each member of the Security Council shall for this purpose be represented at all times at the seat of the Organization.

2. The Security Council shall hold periodic meetings at which each of its members may, if it so desires, be represented by a member of the government or by some other specially designated representative.

3. The Security Council may hold meetings at such places other than the seat of the Organization as in its judgment will best facilitate its work.

Article 29

The Security Council may establish such subsidiary organs as it deems necessary for the performance of its functions.

Article 30

The Security Council shall adopt its own rules of procedure, including the method of selecting its President.

Article 31

Any Member of the United Nations which is not a member of the Security Council may participate, without vote, in the discussion of any question brought before the Security Council whenever the latter considers that the interests of that Member are specially affected.

Article 32

Any Member of the United Nations which is not a member of the Security Council or any state which is not a Member of the United Nations, if it is a party to a dispute under consideration by the Security Council, shall be invited to participate, without vote, in the discussion relating to the dispute. The Security Council shall lay down such conditions as it deems just for the participation of a state which is not a Member of the United Nations.

Chapter VI
PACIFIC SETTLEMENT OF DISPUTES

Article 33

1. The parties to any dispute, the continuance of which is likely to endanger the maintenance of international peace and security, shall, first of all, seek a solution by negotiation, enquiry, mediation, conciliation, arbitration, judicial settlement, resort to regional agencies or arrangements, or other peaceful means of their own choice.

2. The Security Council shall, when it deems necessary, call upon the parties to settle their dispute by such means.

Article 34

The Security Council may investigate any dispute, or any situation which might lead to international friction or give rise to a dispute, in order to determine whether the continuance of the dispute or situation is likely to endanger the maintenance of international peace and security.

Article 35

1. Any Member of the United Nations may bring any dispute, or any situation of the nature referred to in Article 34, to the attention of the Security Council or of the General Assembly.

2. A state which is not a Member of the United Nations may bring to the attention of the Security Council or of the General Assembly any dispute to which it is a party if it accepts in advance, for the purposes of the dispute, the obligations of pacific settlement provided in the present Charter.

3. The proceedings of the General Assembly in respect of matters brought to its attention under this Article will be subject to the provisions of Articles 11 and 12.

Article 36

1. The Security Council may, at any stage of a dispute of the nature referred to in Article 33 or of a situation of like nature, recommend appropriate procedures or methods of adjustment.

2. The Security Council should take into consideration any procedures for the settlement of the dispute which have already been adopted by the parties.

3. In making recommendations under this Article the Security Council should also take into consideration that legal disputes should as a general rule be referred by the parties to the International Court of Justice in accordance with the provisions of the Statute of the Court.

Article 37

1. Should the parties to a dispute of the nature referred to in Article 33 fail to settle it by the means indicated in that Article, they shall refer it to the Security Council.

2. If the Security Council deems that the continuance of the dispute is in fact likely to endanger the maintenance of international peace and security, it shall decide whether to take action under Article 36 or to recommend such terms of settlement as it may consider appropriate.

Article 38

Without prejudice to the provisions of Articles 33 to 37, the Security Council may, if all the parties to any dispute so request, make recommendations to the parties with a view to a pacific settlement of the dispute.

Chapter VII
ACTION WITH RESPECT TO THREATS TO THE PEACE, BREACHES OF THE PEACE, AND ACTS OF AGGRESSION

Article 39

The Security Council shall determine the existence of any threat to the peace, breach of the peace, or act of aggression and shall make recommendations, or decide what measures shall be taken in accordance with Articles 41 and 42, to maintain or restore international peace and security.

Article 40

In order to prevent an aggravation of the situation, the Security Council may, before making the recommendations or deciding upon the measures provided for in Article 39, call upon the parties concerned to comply with such provisional measures as it deems necessary or desirable. Such provisional measures shall be without prejudice to the rights, claims or position of the parties concerned. The Security Council shall duly take account of failure to comply with such provisional measures.

Article 41

The Security Council may decide what measures not involving the use of armed force are to be employed to give effect to its decisions, and it may call upon the Members of the United Nations to apply such measures. These may include complete or partial interruption of economic relations and of rail, sea, air, postal, telegraphic, radio and other means of communication, and the severance of diplomatic relations.

Article 42

Should the Security Council consider that measures provided for in Article 41 would be inadequate or have proved to be inadequate, it may take such action by air, sea or land forces as may be necessary to maintain or restore international peace and security. Such action may include demonstrations, blockade, and other operations by air, sea, or land forces of Members of the United Nations.

Article 43

1. All Members of the United Nations, in order to contribute to the maintenance of international peace and security, undertake to make available to the Security Council, on its call and in accordance with a special agreement or agreements, armed forces, assistance and facilities, including rights of passage, necessary for the purpose of maintaining international peace and security.

2. Such agreement or agreements shall govern the numbers and types of forces, their degree of readiness and general location, and the nature of the facilities and assistance to be provided.

3. The agreement or agreements shall be negotiated as soon as possible on the initiative of the Security Council. They shall be concluded between the Security Council and Members or between the Security Council and groups of Members and shall be subject to ratification by the signatory states in accordance with their respective constitutional processes.

Article 44

When the Security Council has decided to use force it shall, before calling upon a Member not represented on it to provide armed forces in fulfilment of the obligations assumed under Article 43, invite that Member, if the Member so desires, to participate in the decisions of the Security Council concerning the employment of contingents of that Member's armed forces.

Article 45

In order to enable the United Nations to take urgent military measures, Members shall hold immediately available national air-force contingents for combined international enforcement action. The strength and degree of readiness of these contingents and plans for their combined action shall be determined, within the limits laid down in the special agreement or agreements referred to in Article 43, by the Security Council with the assistance of the Military Staff Committee.

Article 46

Plans for the application of armed force shall be made by the Security Council with the assistance of the Military Staff Committee.

Article 47

1. There shall be established a Military Staff Committee to advise and assist the Security Council on all questions relating to the Security Council's military requirements for the maintenance of international peace and security, the employment and command of forces placed at its disposal, the regulation of armaments, and possible disarmament.

2. The Military Staff Committee shall consist of the Chiefs of Staff of the permanent members of the Security Council or their representatives. Any Member of the United Nations not permanently represented on the Committee shall be invited by the Committee to be associated with it when the efficient discharge of the Committee's responsibilities requires the participation of that Member in its work.

3. The Military Staff Committee shall be responsible under the Security Council for the strategic direction of any armed forces placed at the disposal of the Security Council. Questions relating to the command of such forces shall be worked out subsequently.

4. The Military Staff Committee, with the authorization of the Security Council and after consultation with appropriate regional agencies, may establish regional sub-committees.

Article 48

1. The action required to carry out the decisions of the Security Council for the maintenance of international peace and security shall be taken by all the Members of the United Nations or by some of them, as the Security Council may determine.

2. Such decisions shall be carried out by the Members of the United Nations directly and through their action in the appropriate international agencies of which they are members.

Article 49

The Members of the United Nations shall join in affording mutual assistance in carrying out the measures decided upon by the Security Council.

Article 50

If preventive or enforcement measures against any state are taken by the Security Council, any other state, whether a Member of the United Nations or not, which finds itself confronted with special economic problems arising from the carrying out of those measures shall have the right to consult the Security Council with regard to a solution of those problems.

Article 51

Nothing in the present Charter shall impair the inherent right of individual or collective self-defence if an armed attack occurs against a Member of the United Nations, until the Security Council has taken measures necessary to maintain international peace and security. Measures taken by Members in the exercise of this right of self-defence shall be immediately reported to the Security Council and shall not in any way affect the authority and responsibility of the Security Council under the present Charter to take at any time such action as it deems necessary in order to maintain or restore international peace and security.

Chapter VIII
REGIONAL ARRANGEMENTS

Article 52

1. Nothing in the present Charter precludes the existence of regional arrangements or agencies for dealing with such matters relating to the maintenance of international peace and security as are appropriate for regional action, provided that such arrangements or agencies and their activities are consistent with the Purposes and Principles of the United Nations.

2. The Members of the United Nations entering into such arrangements or constituting such agencies shall make every effort to achieve pacific settlement of local disputes through such regional arrangements or by such regional agencies before referring them to the Security Council.

3. The Security Council shall encourage the development of pacific settlement of local disputes through such regional arrangements or by such regional agencies either on the initiative of the states concerned or by reference from the Security Council.

4. This Article in no way impairs the application of Articles 34 and 35.

Article 53

1. The Security Council shall, where appropriate, utilize such regional arrangements or agencies for enforcement action under its authority. But no enforcement action shall be taken under regional arrangements or by regional agencies

without the authorization of the Security Council, with the exception of measures against any enemy state, as defined in paragraph 2 of this Article, provided for pursuant to Article 107 or in regional arrangements directed against renewal of aggressive policy on the part of any such state, until such time as the Organization may, on request of the Governments concerned, be charged with the responsibility for preventing further aggression by such a state.

2. The term enemy state as used in paragraph 1 of this Article applies to any state which during the Second World War has been an enemy of any signatory of the present Charter.

Article 54

The Security Council shall at all times be kept fully informed of activities undertaken or in contemplation under regional arrangements or by regional agencies for the maintenance of international peace and security.

Chapter IX
INTERNATIONAL ECONOMIC
AND SOCIAL CO-OPERATION

Article 55

With a view to the creation of conditions of stability and well-being which are necessary for peaceful and friendly relations among nations based on respect for the principle of equal rights and self-determination of peoples, the United Nations shall promote:

  a. higher standards of living, full employment, and conditions of economic and social progress and development;

  b. solutions of international economic, social, health, and related problems; and international cultural and educational co-operation; and

  c. universal respect for, and observance of, human rights and fundamental freedoms for all without distinction as to race, sex, language, or religion.

Article 56

All Members pledge themselves to take joint and separate action in co-operation with the Organization for the achievement of the purposes set forth in Article 55.

Article 57

1. The various specialized agencies, established by intergovernmental agreement and having wide international responsibilities, as defined in their basic instruments, in economic, social, cultural, educational, health, and related fields, shall be brought into relationship with the United Nations in accordance with the provisions of Article 63.

2. Such agencies thus brought into relationship with the United Nations are hereinafter referred to as specialized agencies.

Article 58

The Organization shall make recommendations for the co-ordination of the policies and activities of the specialized agencies.

Article 59

The Organization shall, where appropriate, initiate negotiations among the states concerned for the creation of any new specialized agencies required for the accomplishment of the purposes set forth in Article 55.

Article 60

Responsibility for the discharge of the functions of the Organization set forth in this Chapter shall be vested in the General Assembly and, under the authority of the General Assembly, in the Economic and Social Council, which shall have for this purpose the powers set forth in Chapter X.

Chapter X
THE ECONOMIC AND SOCIAL COUNCIL

Composition

Article 61[3]

1. The Economic and Social Council shall consist of fifty-four Members of the United Nations elected by the General Assembly.

2. Subject to the provisions of paragraph 3, eighteen members of the Economic and Social Council shall be elected each year for a term of three years. A retiring member shall be eligible for immediate re-election.

3. At the first election after the increase in the membership of the Economic and Social Council from twenty-seven to fifty-four members, in addition to the members elected in place of the nine members whose term of office expires at the end of that year, twenty-seven additional members shall be elected. Of these twenty-seven additional members, the term of office of nine members so elected shall expire at the end of one year, and of nine other members at the end of two years, in accordance with arrangements made by the General Assembly.

4. Each member of the Economic and Social Council shall have one representative.

Functions and Powers

Article 62

1. The Economic and Social Council may make or initiate studies and reports with respect to international economic, social, cultural, educational, health, and related matters and may make recommendations with respect to any such matters to the General Assembly, to the Members of the United Nations, and to the specialized agencies concerned.

2. It may make recommendations for the purpose of promoting respect for, and observance of, human rights and fundamental freedoms for all.

3. It may prepare draft conventions for submission to the General Assembly, with respect to matters falling within its competence.

4. It may call, in accordance with the rules prescribed by the United Nations, international conferences on matters falling within its competence.

Article 63

1. The Economic and Social Council may enter into agreements with any of the agencies referred to in Article 57, defining the terms on which the agency concerned shall be brought into relationship with the United Nations. Such agreements shall be subject to approval by the General Assembly.

2. It may co-ordinate the activities of the specialized agencies through consultation with and recommendations to such agencies and through recommendations to the General Assembly and to the Members of the United Nations.

Article 64

1. The Economic and Social Council may take appropriate steps to obtain regular reports from the specialized agencies. It may make arrangements with the Members of the United Nations and with the specialized agencies to obtain reports on the steps taken to give effect to its own recommendations and to recommendations on matters falling within its competence made by the General Assembly.

2. It may communicate its observations on these reports to the General Assembly.

Article 65

The Economic and Social Council may furnish information to the Security Council and shall assist the Security Council upon its request.

Article 66

1. The Economic and Social Council shall perform such functions as fall within its competence in connexion with the carrying out of the recommendations of the General Assembly.

2. It may, with the approval of the General Assembly, perform services at the request of Members of the United Nations and at the request of specialized agencies.

3. It shall perform such other functions as are specified elsewhere in the present Charter or as may be assigned to it by the General Assembly.

Voting

Article 67

1. Each member of the Economic and Social Council shall have one vote.

2. Decisions of the Economic and Social Council shall be made by a majority of the members present and voting.

Procedure

Article 68

The Economic and Social Council shall set up commissions in economic and social fields and for the promotion of human rights, and such other commissions as may be required for the performance of its functions.

Article 69

The Economic and Social Council shall invite any Member of the United Nations to participate, without vote, in its deliberations on any matter of particular concern to that Member.

Article 70

The Economic and Social Council may make arrangements for representatives of the specialized agencies to participate, without vote, in its deliberations and in those of the commissions established by it, and for its representatives to participate in the deliberations of the specialized agencies.

Article 71

The Economic and Social Council may make suitable arrangements for consultation with non-governmental organizations which are concerned with matters within its competence. Such arrangements may be made with international organizations and, where appropriate, with national organizations after consultation with the Member of the United Nations concerned.

Article 72

1. The Economic and Social Council shall adopt its own rules of procedure, including the method of selecting its President.

2. The Economic and Social Council shall meet as required in accordance with its rules, which shall include provision for the convening of meetings on the request of a majority of its members.

Chapter XI

DECLARATION REGARDING NON-SELF-GOVERNING TERRITORIES

Article 73

Members of the United Nations which have or assume responsibilities for the administration of territories whose peoples have not yet attained a full measure of self-government recognize the principle that the interests of the inhabitants of these territories are paramount, and accept as a sacred trust the obligation to promote to the utmost, within the system of international peace and security established by the present Charter, the well-being of the inhabitants of these territories and, to this end:

a. to ensure, with due respect for the culture of the peoples concerned, their political, economic, social, and educational advancement, their just treatment, and their protection against abuses;

b. to develop self-government, to take due account of the political aspirations of the peoples, and to assist them in the progressive development of their free political institutions, according to the particular circumstances of each territory and its peoples and their varying stages of advancement;

c. to further international peace and security;

d. to promote constructive measures of development, to encourage research, and to co-operate with one another and, when and where appropriate, with specialized international bodies with a view to the practical achievement of the social, economic, and scientific purposes set forth in this Article; and

e. to transmit regularly to the Secretary-General for information purposes, subject to such limitation as security and constitutional considerations may require, statistical and other information of a technical nature relating to economic, social, and educational conditions in the territories for which they are respectively responsible other than those territories to which Chapters XII and XIII apply.

Article 74

Members of the United Nations also agree that their policy in respect of the territories to which this Chapter applies, no less than in respect of their metropolitan areas, must be based on the general principle of good-neighbourliness, due account being taken of the interests and well-being of the rest of the world, in social, economic, and commercial matters.

Chapter XII

INTERNATIONAL TRUSTEESHIP SYSTEM

Article 75

The United Nations shall establish under its authority an international trusteeship system for the administration and supervision of such territories as may be placed thereunder by subsequent individual agreements. These territories are hereinafter referred to as trust territories.

Article 76

The basic objectives of the trusteeship system, in accordance with the Purposes of the United Nations laid down in Article 1 of the present Charter, shall be:

a. to further international peace and security;

b. to promote the political, economic, social, and educational advancement of the inhabitants of the trust territories, and their progressive development towards self-government or independence as may be appropriate to the particular circumstances of each territory and its peoples and the freely expressed wishes of the peoples concerned, and as may be provided by the terms of each trusteeship agreement;

c. to encourage respect for human rights and for fundamental freedoms for all without distinction as to race, sex, language, or religion, and to encourage recognition of the interdependence of the peoples of the world; and

d. to ensure equal treatment in social, economic, and commercial matters for all Members of the United Nations and their nationals, and also equal treatment for the latter in the administration of justice, without prejudice to the attainment of the foregoing objectives and subject to the provisions of Article 80.

Article 77

1. The trusteeship system shall apply to such territories in the following categories as may be placed thereunder by means of trusteeship agreements:

a. territories now held under mandate;
b. territories which may be detached from enemy states as a result of the Second World War; and
c. territories voluntarily placed under the system by states responsible for their administration.

2. It will be a matter for subsequent agreement as to which territories in the foregoing categories will be brought under the trusteeship system and upon what terms.

Article 78

The trusteeship system shall not apply to territories which have become Members of the United Nations, relationship among which shall be based on respect for the principle of sovereign equality.

Article 79

The terms of trusteeship for each territory to be placed under the trusteeship system, including any alteration or amendment, shall be agreed upon by the states directly concerned, including the mandatory power in the case of territories held under mandate by a Member of the United Nations, and shall be approved as provided for in Articles 83 and 85.

Article 80

1. Except as may be agreed upon in individual trusteeship agreements, made under Articles 77, 79 and 81, placing each territory under the trusteeship system, and until such agreements have been concluded, nothing in this Chapter shall be construed in or of itself to alter in any manner the rights whatsoever of any states or any peoples or the terms of existing international instruments to which Members of the United Nations may respectively be parties.

2. Paragraph 1 of this Article shall not be interpreted as giving grounds for delay or postponement of the negotiation and conclusion of agreements for placing mandated and other territories under the trusteeship system as provided for in Article 77.

Article 81

The trusteeship agreement shall in each case include the terms under which the trust territory will be administered and designate the authority which will exercise the administration of the trust territory. Such authority, hereinafter called the administering authority, may be one or more states or the Organization itself.

Article 82

There may be designated, in any trusteeship agreement, a strategic area or areas which may include part or all of the trust territory to which the agreement applies, without prejudice to any special agreement or agreements made under Article 43.

Article 83

1. All functions of the United Nations relating to strategic areas, including the approval of the terms of the trusteeship agreements and of their alteration or amendment, shall be exercised by the Security Council.

2. The basic objectives set forth in Article 76 shall be applicable to the people of each strategic area.

3. The Security Council shall, subject to the provisions of the trusteeship agreements and without prejudice to security considerations, avail itself of the assistance of the Trusteeship Council to perform those functions of the United Nations under the trusteeship system relating to political, economic, social, and educational matters in the strategic areas.

Article 84

It shall be the duty of the administering authority to ensure that the trust territory shall play its part in the maintenance of international peace and security. To this end the administering authority may make use of volunteer forces, facilities, and assistance from the trust territory in carrying out the obligations towards the Security Council undertaken in this regard by the administering authority, as well as for local defence and the maintenance of law and order within the trust territory.

Article 85

1. The functions of the United Nations with regard to trusteeship agreements for all areas not designated as strategic, including the approval of the terms of the trusteeship agreements and of their alteration or amendment, shall be exercised by the General Assembly.

2. The Trusteeship Council, operating under the authority of the General Assembly, shall assist the General Assembly in carrying out these functions.

Chapter XIII
THE TRUSTEESHIP COUNCIL

Composition

Article 86

1. The Trusteeship Council shall consist of the following Members of the United Nations:
    a. those Members administering trust territories;
    b. such of those Members mentioned by name in Article 23 as are not administering trust territories; and
    c. as many other Members elected for three-year terms by the General Assembly as may be necessary to ensure that the total number of members of the Trusteeship Council is equally divided between those Members of the United Nations which administer trust territories and those which do not.

2. Each member of the Trusteeship Council shall designate one specially qualified person to represent it therein.

Functions and Powers

Article 87

The General Assembly and, under its authority, the Trusteeship Council, in carrying out their functions, may:
a. consider reports submitted by the administering authority;
b. accept petitions and examine them in consultation with the administering authority;
c. provide for periodic visits to the respective trust territories at times agreed upon with the administering authority; and
d. take these and other actions in conformity with the terms of the trusteeship agreements.

Article 88

The Trusteeship Council shall formulate a questionnaire on the political, economic, social, and educational advancement of the inhabitants of each trust territory, and the administering authority for each trust territory within the competence of the General Assembly shall make an annual report to the General Assembly upon the basis of such questionnaire.

Voting

Article 89

1. Each member of the Trusteeship Council shall have one vote.

2. Decisions of the Trusteeship Council shall be made by a majority of the members present and voting.

Procedure

Article 90

1. The Trusteeship Council shall adopt its own rules of procedure, including the method of selecting its President.

2. The Trusteeship Council shall meet as required in accordance with its rules, which shall include provision for the convening of meetings on the request of a majority of its members.

Article 91

The Trusteeship Council shall, when appropriate, avail itself of the assistance of the Economic and Social Council and of the specialized agencies in regard to matters with which they are respectively concerned.

Chapter XIV
THE INTERNATIONAL COURT OF JUSTICE

Article 92

The International Court of Justice shall be the principal judicial organ of the United Nations. It shall function in accordance with the annexed Statute, which is based upon the Statute of the Permanent Court of International Justice and forms an integral part of the present Charter.

Article 93

1. All Members of the United Nations are *ipso facto* parties to the Statute of the International Court of Justice.

2. A state which is not a Member of the United Nations may become a party to the Statute of the International Court of Justice on conditions to be determined in each case by the General Assembly upon the recommendation of the Security Council.

Article 94

1. Each Member of the United Nations undertakes to comply with the decision of the International Court of Justice in any case to which it is a party.

2. If any party to a case fails to perform the obligations incumbent upon it under a judgment rendered by the Court, the other party may have recourse to the Security Council, which may, if it deems necessary, make recommendations or decide upon measures to be taken to give effect to the judgment.

Article 95

Nothing in the present Charter shall prevent Members of the United Nations from entrusting the solution of their differences to other tribunals by virtue of agreements already in existence or which may be concluded in the future.

Article 96

1. The General Assembly or the Security Council may request the International Court of Justice to give an advisory opinion on any legal question.

2. Other organs of the United Nations and specialized agencies, which may at any time be so authorized by the General Assembly, may also request advisory opinions of the Court on legal questions arising within the scope of their activities.

Chapter XV
THE SECRETARIAT

Article 97

The Secretariat shall comprise a Secretary-General and such staff as the Organization may require. The Secretary-General shall be appointed by the General Assembly upon the recommendation of the Security Council. He shall be the chief administrative officer of the Organization.

Article 98

The Secretary-General shall act in that capacity in all meetings of the General Assembly, of the Security Council, of the Economic and Social Council, and of the Trusteeship Council, and shall perform such other functions as are entrusted to him by these organs. The Secretary-General shall make an annual report to the General Assembly on the work of the Organization.

Article 99

The Secretary-General may bring to the attention of the Security Council any matter which in his opinion may threaten the maintenance of international peace and security.

Article 100

1. In the performance of their duties the Secretary-General and the staff shall not seek or receive instructions from any government or from any other authority external to the Organization. They shall refrain from any action which might reflect on their position as international officials responsible only to the Organization.

2. Each Member of the United Nations undertakes to respect the exclusively international character of the responsibilities of the Secretary-General and the staff and not to seek to influence them in the discharge of their responsibilities.

Article 101

1. The staff shall be appointed by the Secretary-General under regulations established by the General Assembly.

2. Appropriate staffs shall be permanently assigned to the Economic and Social Council, the Trusteeship Council, and, as required, to other organs of the United Nations. These staffs shall form a part of the Secretariat.

3. The paramount consideration in the employment of the staff and in the determination of the conditions of service shall be the necessity of securing the highest standards of efficiency, competence, and integrity. Due regard shall be paid to the importance of recruiting the staff on as wide a geographical basis as possible.

Chapter XVI
MISCELLANEOUS PROVISIONS

Article 102

1. Every treaty and every international agreement entered into by any Member of the United Nations after the present Charter comes into force shall as soon as possible be registered with the Secretariat and published by it.

2. No party to any such treaty or international agreement which has not been registered in accordance with the provisions of paragraph 1 of this Article may invoke that treaty or agreement before any organ of the United Nations.

Article 103

In the event of a conflict between the obligations of the Members of the United Nations under the present Charter and their obligations under any other international agreement, their obligations under the present Charter shall prevail.

Article 104

The Organization shall enjoy in the territory of each of its Members such legal capacity as may be necessary for the exercise of its functions and the fulfilment of its purposes.

Article 105

1. The Organization shall enjoy in the territory of each of its Members such privileges and immunities as are necessary for the fulfilment of its purposes.

2. Representatives of the Members of the United Nations and officials of the Organization shall similarly enjoy such privileges and immunities as are necessary for the independent exercise of their functions in connexion with the Organization.

3. The General Assembly may make recommendations with a view to determining the details of the application of paragraphs 1 and 2 of this Article or may propose conventions to the Members of the United Nations for this purpose.

Chapter XVII

TRANSITIONAL SECURITY ARRANGEMENTS

Article 106

Pending the coming into force of such special agreements referred to in Article 43 as in the opinion of the Security Council enable it to begin the exercise of its responsibilities under Article 42, the parties to the Four-Nation Declaration, signed at Moscow, 30 October 1943, and France, shall, in accordance with the provisions of paragraph 5 of that Declaration, consult with one another and as occasion requires with other Members of the United Nations with a view to such joint action on behalf of the Organization as may be necessary for the purpose of maintaining international peace and security.

Article 107

Nothing in the present Charter shall invalidate or preclude action, in relation to any state which during the Second World War has been an enemy of any signatory to the present Charter, taken or authorized as a result of that war by the Governments having responsibility for such action.

Chapter XVIII

AMENDMENTS

Article 108

Amendments to the present Charter shall come into force for all Members of the United Nations when they have been adopted by a vote of two thirds of the members of the General Assembly and ratified in accordance with their respective constitutional processes by two thirds of the Members of the United Nations, including all the permanent members of the Security Council.

Article 109[1]

1. A General Conference of the Members of the United Nations for the purpose of reviewing the present Charter may be held at a date and place to be fixed by a two-thirds vote of the members of the General Assembly and by a vote of any nine members of the Security Council. Each Member of the United Nations shall have one vote in the conference.

2. Any alteration of the present Charter recommended by a two-thirds vote of the conference shall take effect when ratified in accordance with their respective constitutional processes by two thirds of the Members of the United Na-

tions including all the permanent members of the Security Council.

3. If such a conference has not been held before the tenth annual session of the General Assembly following the coming into force of the present Charter, the proposal to call such a conference shall be placed on the agenda of that session of the General Assembly, and the conference shall be held if so decided by a majority vote of the members of the General Assembly and by a vote of any seven members of the Security Council.

Chapter XIX

RATIFICATION AND SIGNATURE

Article 110

1. The present Charter shall be ratified by the signatory states in accordance with their respective constitutional processes.

2. The ratifications shall be deposited with the Government of the United States of America, which shall notify all the signatory states of each deposit as well as the Secretary-General of the Organization when he has been appointed.

3. The present Charter shall come into force upon the deposit of ratifications by the Republic of China, France, the Union of Soviet Socialist Republics, the United Kingdom of Great Britain and Northern Ireland and the United States of America, and by a majority of the other signatory states. A protocol of the ratifications deposited shall thereupon be drawn up by the Government of the United States of America which shall communicate copies thereof to all the signatory states.

4. The states signatory to the present Charter which ratify it after it has come into force will become original Members of the United Nations on the date of the deposit of their respective ratifications.

Article 111

The present Charter, of which the Chinese, French, Russian, English, and Spanish texts are equally authentic, shall remain deposited in the archives of the Government of the United States of America. Duly certified copies thereof shall be transmitted by that Government to the Governments of the other signatory states.

IN FAITH WHEREOF the representatives of the Governments of the United Nations have signed the present Charter.

DONE at the city of San Francisco the twenty-sixth day of June, one thousand nine hundred and forty-five.

---

[1] Amended text of Article 23, which came into force on 31 August 1965.
(The text of Article 23 before it was amended read as follows:
    1. The Security Council shall consist of eleven Members of the United Nations. The Republic of China, France, the Union of Soviet Socialist Republics, the United Kingdom of Great Britain and Northern Ireland and the United States of America shall be permanent members of the Security Council. The General Assembly shall elect six other Members of the United Nations to be non-permanent members of the Security Council, due regard being specially paid in the first instance to the contributions of Members of the United Nations to the maintenance of international peace and security and to the other purposes of the Organization, and also to equitable geographical distribution.
    2. The non-permanent members of the Security Council shall be elected for a term of two years. In the first election of the non-permanent members, however, three shall be chosen for a term of one year. A retiring member shall not be eligible for immediate re-election.
    3. Each member of the Security Council shall have one representative.)

[2] Amended text of Article 27, which came into force on 31 August 1965.
(The text of Article 27 before it was amended read as follows:
    1. Each member of the Security Council shall have one vote.
    2. Decisions of the Security Council on procedural matters shall be made by an affirmative vote of seven members.
    3. Decisions of the Security Council on all other matters shall be made by an affirmative vote of seven members including the concurring votes of the permanent members; provided that, in decisions under Chapter VI, and under paragraph 3 of Article 52, a party to a dispute shall abstain from voting.)

[3] Amended text of Article 61, which came into force on 24 September 1973.
(The text of Article 61 as previously amended on 31 August 1965 read as follows:
    1. The Economic and Social Council shall consist of twenty-seven Members of the United Nations elected by the General Assembly.
    2. Subject to the provisions of paragraph 3, nine members of the Economic and Social Council shall be elected each year for a term of three years. A retiring member shall be eligible for immediate re-election.

3. At the first election after the increase in the membership of the Economic and Social Council from eighteen to twenty-seven members, in addition to the members elected in place of the six members whose term of office expires at the end of that year, nine additional members shall be elected. Of these nine additional members, the term of office of three members so elected shall expire at the end of one year, and of three other members at the end of two years, in accordance with arrangements made by the General Assembly.

4. Each member of the Economic and Social Council shall have one representative.)

[4] Amended text of Article 109, which came into force on 12 June 1968.

(The text of Article 109 before it was amended read as follows:

1. A General Conference of the Members of the United Nations for the purpose of reviewing the present Charter may be held at a date and place to be fixed by a two-thirds vote of the members of the General Assembly and by a vote of any seven members of the Security Council. Each Member of the United Nations shall have one vote in the conference.

2. Any alteration of the present Charter recommended by a two-thirds vote of the conference shall take effect when ratified in accordance with their respective constitutional processes by two thirds of the Members of the United Nations including all the permanent members of the Security Council.

3. If such a conference has not been held before the tenth annual session of the General Assembly following the coming into force of the present Charter, the proposal to call such a conference shall be placed on the agenda of that session of the General Assembly, and the conference shall be held if so decided by a majority vote of the members of the General Assembly and by a vote of any seven members of the Security Council.)

Statute of the International Court of Justice

Article 1

The International Court of Justice established by the Charter of the United Nations as the principal judicial organ of the United Nations shall be constituted and shall function in accordance with the provisions of the present Statute.

Chapter I
ORGANIZATION OF THE COURT

Article 2

The Court shall be composed of a body of independent judges, elected regardless of their nationality from among persons of high moral character, who possess the qualifications required in their respective countries for appointment to the highest judicial offices, or are jurisconsults of recognized competence in international law.

Article 3

1. The Court shall consist of fifteen members, no two of whom may be nationals of the same state.

2. A person who for the purposes of membership in the Court could be regarded as a national of more than one state shall be deemed to be a national of the one in which he ordinarily exercises civil and political rights.

Article 4

1. The members of the Court shall be elected by the General Assembly and by the Security Council from a list of persons nominated by the national groups in the Permanent Court of Arbitration, in accordance with the following provisions.

2. In the case of Members of the United Nations not represented in the Permanent Court of Arbitration, candidates shall be nominated by national groups appointed for this purpose by their governments under the same conditions as those prescribed for members of the Permanent Court of Arbitration by Article 44 of the Convention of The Hague of 1907 for the pacific settlement of international disputes.

3. The conditions under which a state which is a party to the present Statute but is not a Member of the United Nations may participate in electing the members of the Court shall, in the absence of a special agreement, be laid down by the General Assembly upon recommendation of the Security Council.

Article 5

1. At least three months before the date of the election, the Secretary-General of the United Nations shall address a written request to the members of the Permanent Court of Arbitration belonging to the states which are parties to the present Statute, and to the members of the national groups appointed under Article 4, paragraph 2, inviting them to undertake, within a given time, by national groups, the nomination of persons in a position to accept the duties of a member of the Court.

2. No group may nominate more than four persons, not more than two of whom shall be of their own nationality. In no case may the number of candidates nominated by a group be more than double the number of seats to be filled.

Article 6

Before making these nominations, each national group is recommended to consult its highest court of justice, its legal faculties and schools of law, and its national academies and national sections of international academies devoted to the study of law.

Article 7

1. The Secretary-General shall prepare a list in alphabetical order of all the persons thus nominated. Save as provided in Article 12, paragraph 2, these shall be the only persons eligible.

2. The Secretary-General shall submit this list to the General Assembly and to the Security Council.

Article 8

The General Assembly and the Security Council shall proceed independently of one another to elect the members of the Court.

Article 9

At every election, the electors shall bear in mind not only that the persons to be elected should individually possess the qualifications required, but also that in the body as a whole the representation of the main forms of civilization and of the principal legal systems of the world should be assured.

Article 10

1. Those candidates who obtain an absolute majority of votes in the General Assembly and in the Security Council shall be considered as elected.

2. Any vote of the Security Council, whether for the election of judges or for the appointment of members of the conference envisaged in Article 12, shall be taken without any distinction between permanent and non-permanent members of the Security Council.

3. In the event of more than one national of the same state obtaining an absolute majority of the votes both of the General Assembly and of the Security Council, the eldest of these only shall be considered as elected.

Article 11

If, after the first meeting held for the purpose of the election, one or more seats remain to be filled, a second and, if necessary, a third meeting shall take place.

Article 12

1. If, after the third meeting, one or more seats still remain unfilled, a joint conference consisting of six members, three appointed by the General Assembly and three by the Security Council, may be formed at any time at the request of either the General Assembly or the Security Council, for the purpose of choosing by the vote of an absolute majority one name for each seat still vacant, to submit to the General Assembly and the Security Council for their respective acceptance.

2. If the joint conference is unanimously agreed upon any person who fulfils the required conditions, he may be included in its list, even though he was not included in the list of nominations referred to in Article 7.

3. If the joint conference is satisfied that it will not be successful in procuring an election, those members of the Court who have already been elected shall, within a period to be fixed by the Security Council, proceed to fill the vacant seats by selection from among those candidates who have obtained votes either in the General Assembly or in the Security Council.

4. In the event of an equality of votes among the judges, the eldest judge shall have a casting vote.

Article 13

1. The members of the Court shall be elected for nine years and may be re-elected; provided, however, that of the judges elected at the first election, the terms of five judges shall expire at the end of three years and the terms of five more judges shall expire at the end of six years.

2. The judges whose terms are to expire at the end of the above-mentioned initial periods of three and six years shall be chosen by lot to be drawn by the Secretary-General immediately after the first election has been completed.

3. The members of the Court shall continue to discharge their duties until their places have been filled. Though replaced, they shall finish any cases which they may have begun.

4. In the case of the resignation of a member of the Court, the resignation shall be addressed to the President of the Court for transmission to the Secretary-General. This last notification makes the place vacant.

Article 14

Vacancies shall be filled by the same method as that laid down for the first election, subject to the following provision: the Secretary-General shall, within one month of the occurrence of the vacancy, proceed to issue the invitations provided for in Article 5, and the date of the election shall be fixed by the Security Council.

Article 15

A member of the Court elected to replace a member whose term of office has not expired shall hold office for the remainder of his predecessor's term.

Article 16

1. No member of the Court may exercise any political or administrative function, or engage in any other occupation of a professional nature.

2. Any doubt on this point shall be settled by the decision of the Court.

Article 17

1. No member of the Court may act as agent, counsel, or advocate in any case.

2. No member may participate in the decision of any case in which he has previously taken part as agent, counsel, or advocate for one of the parties, or as a member of a national or international court, or of a commission of enquiry, or in any other capacity.

3. Any doubt on this point shall be settled by the decision of the Court.

Article 18

1. No member of the Court can be dismissed unless, in the unanimous opinion of the other members, he has ceased to fulfil the required conditions.

2. Formal notification thereof shall be made to the Secretary-General by the Registrar.

3. This notification makes the place vacant.

Article 19

The members of the Court, when engaged on the business of the Court, shall enjoy diplomatic privileges and immunities.

Article 20

Every member of the Court shall, before taking up his duties, make a solemn declaration in open court that he will exercise his powers impartially and conscientiously.

Article 21

1. The Court shall elect its President and Vice-President for three years; they may be re-elected.

2. The Court shall appoint its Registrar and may provide for the appointment of such other officers as may be necessary.

Article 22

1. The seat of the Court shall be established at The Hague. This, however, shall not prevent the Court from sitting and exercising its functions elsewhere whenever the Court considers it desirable.

2. The President and the Registrar shall reside at the seat of the Court.

Article 23

1. The Court shall remain permanently in session, except during the judicial vacations, the dates and duration of which shall be fixed by the Court.

2. Members of the Court are entitled to periodic leave, the dates and duration of which shall be fixed by the Court, having in mind the distance between The Hague and the home of each judge.

3. Members of the Court shall be bound, unless they are on leave or prevented from attending by illness or other serious reasons duly explained to the President, to hold themselves permanently at the disposal of the Court.

Article 24

1. If, for some special reason, a member of the Court considers that he should not take part in the decision of a particular case, he shall so inform the President.

2. If the President considers that for some special reason one of the members of the Court should not sit in a particular case, he shall give him notice accordingly.

3. If in any such case the member of the Court and the President disagree, the matter shall be settled by the decision of the Court.

Article 25

1. The full Court shall sit except when it is expressly provided otherwise in the present Statute.

2. Subject to the condition that the number of judges available to constitute the Court is not thereby reduced below eleven, the Rules of the Court may provide for allowing one or more judges, according to circumstances and in rotation, to be dispensed from sitting.

3. A quorum of nine judges shall suffice to constitute the Court.

Article 26

1. The Court may from time to time form one or more chambers, composed of three or more judges as the Court may determine, for dealing with particular categories of cases; for example, labour cases and cases relating to transit and communications.

2. The Court may at any time form a chamber for dealing with a particular case. The number of judges to constitute such a chamber shall be determined by the Court with the approval of the parties.

3. Cases shall be heard and determined by the chambers provided for in this Article if the parties so request.

Article 27

A judgment given by any of the chambers provided for in Articles 26 and 29 shall be considered as rendered by the Court.

Article 28

The chambers provided for in Articles 26 and 29 may, with the consent of the parties, sit and exercise their functions elsewhere than at The Hague.

Article 29

With a view to the speedy dispatch of business, the Court shall form annually a chamber composed of five judges which, at the request of the parties, may hear and determine cases by summary procedure. In addition, two judges shall be selected for the purpose of replacing judges who find it impossible to sit.

Article 30

1. The Court shall frame rules for carrying out its functions. In particular, it shall lay down rules of procedure.

2. The Rules of the Court may provide for assessors to sit with the Court or with any of its chambers, without the right to vote.

Article 31

1. Judges of the nationality of each of the parties shall retain their right to sit in the case before the Court.

2. If the Court includes upon the Bench a judge of the nationality of one of the parties, any other party may choose a person to sit as judge. Such person shall be chosen preferably from among those persons who have been nominated as candidates as provided in Articles 4 and 5.

3. If the Court includes upon the Bench no judge of the nationality of the parties, each of these parties may proceed to choose a judge as provided in paragraph 2 of this Article.

4. The provisions of this Article shall apply to the case of Articles 26 and 29. In such cases, the President shall request one or, if necessary, two of the members of the Court forming the chamber to give place to the members of the Court of the nationality of the parties concerned, and, failing such, or if they are unable to be present, to the judges specially chosen by the parties.

5. Should there be several parties in the same interest, they shall, for the purpose of the preceding provisions, be reckoned as one party only. Any doubt upon this point shall be settled by the decision of the Court.

6. Judges chosen as laid down in paragraphs 2, 3 and 4 of this Article shall fulfil the conditions required by Articles 2, 17 (paragraph 2), 20, and 24 of the present Statute. They shall take part in the decision on terms of complete equality with their colleagues.

Article 32

1. Each member of the Court shall receive an annual salary.

2. The President shall receive a special annual allowance.

3. The Vice-President shall receive a special allowance for every day on which he acts as President.

4. The judges chosen under Article 31, other than members of the Court, shall receive compensation for each day on which they exercise their functions.

5. These salaries, allowances, and compensation shall be fixed by the General Assembly. They may not be decreased during the term of office.

6. The salary of the Registrar shall be fixed by the General Assembly on the proposal of the Court.

7. Regulations made by the General Assembly shall fix the conditions under which retirement pensions may be given to members of the Court and to the Registrar, and the conditions under which members of the Court and the Registrar shall have their travelling expenses refunded.

8. The above salaries, allowances, and compensation shall be free of all taxation.

Article 33

The expenses of the Court shall be borne by the United Nations in such a manner as shall be decided by the General Assembly.

Chapter II

COMPETENCE OF THE COURT

Article 34

1. Only states may be parties in cases before the Court.

2. The Court, subject to and in conformity with its Rules, may request of public international organizations information relevant to cases before it, and shall receive such information presented by such organizations on their own initiative.

3. Whenever the construction of the constituent instrument of a public international organization or of an international convention adopted thereunder is in question in a case before the Court, the Registrar shall so notify the public international organization concerned and shall communicate to it copies of all the written proceedings.

Article 35

1. The Court shall be open to the states parties to the present Statute.

2. The conditions under which the Court shall be open to other states shall, subject to the special provisions contained in treaties in force, be laid down by the Security Council, but in no case shall such conditions place the parties in a position of inequality before the Court.

3. When a state which is not a Member of the United Nations is a party to a case, the Court shall fix the amount which that party is to contribute towards the expenses of the Court. This provision shall not apply if such state is bearing a share of the expenses of the Court.

Article 36

1. The jurisdiction of the Court comprises all cases which the parties refer to it and all matters specially provided for in the Charter of the United Nations or in treaties and conventions in force.

2. The states parties to the present Statute may at any time declare that they recognize as compulsory *ipso facto* and without special agreement, in relation to any other state accepting the same obligation, the jurisdiction of the Court in all legal disputes concerning:

   a. the interpretation of a treaty;

   b. any question of international law;

   c. the existence of any fact which, if established, would constitute a breach of an international obligation;

   d. the nature or extent of the reparation to be made for the breach of an international obligation.

3. The declarations referred to above may be made unconditionally or on condition of reciprocity on the part of several or certain states, or for a certain time.

4. Such declarations shall be deposited with the Secretary-General of the United Nations, who shall transmit copies thereof to the parties to the Statute and to the Registrar of the Court.

5. Declarations made under Article 36 of the Statute of the Permanent Court of International Justice and which are still in force shall be deemed, as between the parties to the present Statute, to be acceptances of the compulsory jurisdiction of the International Court of Justice for the period which they still have to run and in accordance with their terms.

6. In the event of a dispute as to whether the Court has jurisdiction, the matter shall be settled by the decision of the Court.

Article 37

Whenever a treaty or convention in force provides for reference of a matter to a tribunal to have been instituted by the League of Nations, or to the Permanent Court of International Justice, the matter shall, as between the parties to the present Statute, be referred to the International Court of Justice.

Article 38

1. The Court, whose function is to decide in accordance with international law such disputes as are submitted to it, shall apply:
   a. international conventions, whether general or particular, establishing rules expressly recognized by the contesting states;
   b. international custom, as evidence of a general practice accepted as law;
   c. the general principles of law recognized by civilized nations;
   d. subject to the provisions of Article 59, judicial decisions and the teachings of the most highly qualified publicists of the various nations, as subsidiary means for the determination of rules of law.
2. This provision shall not prejudice the power of the Court to decide a case *ex aequo et bono*, if the parties agree thereto.

Chapter III
PROCEDURE

Article 39

1. The official languages of the Court shall be French and English. If the parties agree that the case shall be conducted in French, the judgment shall be delivered in French. If the parties agree that the case shall be conducted in English, the judgment shall be delivered in English.
2. In the absence of an agreement as to which language shall be employed, each party may, in the pleadings, use the language which it prefers; the decision of the Court shall be given in French and English. In this case the Court shall at the same time determine which of the two texts shall be considered as authoritative.
3. The Court shall, at the request of any party, authorize a language other than French or English to be used by that party.

Article 40

1. Cases are brought before the Court, as the case may be, either by the notification of the special agreement or by a written application addressed to the Registrar. In either case the subject of the dispute and the parties shall be indicated.
2. The Registrar shall forthwith communicate the application to all concerned.
3. He shall also notify the Members of the United Nations through the Secretary-General, and also any other states entitled to appear before the Court.

Article 41

1. The Court shall have the power to indicate, if it considers that circumstances so require, any provisional measures which ought to be taken to preserve the respective rights of either party.
2. Pending the final decision, notice of the measures suggested shall forthwith be given to the parties and to the Security Council.

Article 42

1. The parties shall be represented by agents.
2. They may have the assistance of counsel or advocates before the Court.
3. The agents, counsel, and advocates of parties before the Court shall enjoy the privileges and immunities necessary to the independent exercise of their duties.

Article 43

1. The procedure shall consist of two parts: written and oral.

2. The written proceedings shall consist of the communication to the Court and to the parties of memorials, counter-memorials and, if necessary, replies; also all papers and documents in support.
3. These communications shall be made through the Registrar, in the order and within the time fixed by the Court.
4. A certified copy of every document produced by one party shall be communicated to the other party.
5. The oral proceedings shall consist of the hearing by the Court of witnesses, experts, agents, counsel, and advocates.

Article 44

1. For the service of all notices upon persons other than the agents, counsel, and advocates, the Court shall apply direct to the government of the state upon whose territory the notice has to be served.
2. The same provision shall apply whenever steps are to be taken to procure evidence on the spot.

Article 45

The hearing shall be under the control of the President or, if he is unable to preside, of the Vice-President; if neither is able to preside, the senior judge present shall preside.

Article 46

The hearing in Court shall be public, unless the Court shall decide otherwise, or unless the parties demand that the public be not admitted.

Article 47

1. Minutes shall be made at each hearing and signed by the Registrar and the President.
2. These minutes alone shall be authentic.

Article 48

The Court shall make orders for the conduct of the case, shall decide the form and time in which each party must conclude its arguments, and make all arrangements connected with the taking of evidence.

Article 49

The Court may, even before the hearing begins, call upon the agents to produce any document or to supply any explanations. Formal note shall be taken of any refusal.

Article 50

The Court may, at any time, entrust any individual, body, bureau, commission, or other organization that it may select, with the task of carrying out an enquiry or giving an expert opinion.

Article 51

During the hearing any relevant questions are to be put to the witnesses and experts under the conditions laid down by the Court in the rules of procedure referred to in Article 30.

Article 52

After the Court has received the proofs and evidence within the time specified for the purpose, it may refuse to accept any further oral or written evidence that one party may desire to present unless the other side consents.

Article 53

1. Whenever one of the parties does not appear before the Court, or fails to defend its case, the other party may call upon the Court to decide in favour of its claim.
2. The Court must, before doing so, satisfy itself, not only that it has jurisdiction in accordance with Articles 36 and 37, but also that the claim is well founded in fact and law.

Article 54

1. When, subject to the control of the Court, the agents, counsel, and advocates have completed their presentation of the case, the President shall declare the hearing closed.

2. The Court shall withdraw to consider the judgment.
3. The deliberations of the Court shall take place in private and remain secret.

Article 55

1. All questions shall be decided by a majority of the judges present.
2. In the event of an equality of votes, the President or the judge who acts in his place shall have a casting vote.

Article 56

1. The judgment shall state the reasons on which it is based.
2. It shall contain the names of the judges who have taken part in the decision.

Article 57

If the judgment does not represent in whole or in part the unanimous opinion of the judges, any judge shall be entitled to deliver a separate opinion.

Article 58

The judgment shall be signed by the President and by the Registrar. It shall be read in open court, due notice having been given to the agents.

Article 59

The decision of the Court has no binding force except between the parties and in respect of that particular case.

Article 60

The judgment is final and without appeal. In the event of dispute as to the meaning or scope of the judgment, the Court shall construe it upon the request of any party.

Article 61

1. An application for revision of a judgment may be made only when it is based upon the discovery of some fact of such a nature as to be a decisive factor, which fact was, when the judgment was given, unknown to the Court and also the party claiming revision, always provided that such ignorance was not due to negligence.
2. The proceedings for revision shall be opened by a judgment of the Court expressly recording the existence of the new fact, recognizing that it has such a character as to lay the case open to revision, and declaring the application admissible on this ground.
3. The Court may require previous compliance with the terms of the judgment before it admits proceedings in revision.
4. The application for revision must be made at latest within six months of the discovery of the new fact.
5. No application for revision may be made after the lapse of ten years from the date of the judgment.

Article 62

1. Should a state consider that it has an interest of a legal nature which may be affected by the decision in the case, it may submit a request to the Court to be permitted to intervene.
2. It shall be for the Court to decide upon this request.

Article 63

1. Whenever the construction of a convention to which states other than those concerned in the case are parties is in question, the Registrar shall notify all such states forthwith.
2. Every state so notified has the right to intervene in the proceedings; but if it uses this right, the construction given by the judgment will be equally binding upon it.

Article 64

Unless otherwise decided by the Court, each party shall bear its own costs.

Chapter IV
ADVISORY OPINIONS

Article 65

1. The Court may give an advisory opinion on any legal question at the request of whatever body may be authorized by or in accordance with the Charter of the United Nations to make such a request.
2. Questions upon which the advisory opinion of the Court is asked shall be laid before the Court by means of a written request containing an exact statement of the question upon which an opinion is required, and accompanied by all documents likely to throw light upon the question.

Article 66

1. The Registrar shall forthwith give notice of the request for an advisory opinion to all states entitled to appear before the Court.
2. The Registrar shall also, by means of a special and direct communication, notify any state entitled to appear before the Court or international organization considered by the Court, or, should it not be sitting, by the President, as likely to be able to furnish information on the question, that the Court will be prepared to receive, within a time limit to be fixed by the President, written statements, or to hear, at a public sitting to be held for the purpose, oral statements relating to the question.
3. Should any such state entitled to appear before the Court have failed to receive the special communication referred to in paragraph 2 of this Article, such state may express a desire to submit a written statement or to be heard; and the Court will decide.
4. States and organizations having presented written or oral statements or both shall be permitted to comment on the statements made by other states or organizations in the form, to the extent, and within the time limits which the Court, or, should it not be sitting, the President, shall decide in each particular case. Accordingly, the Registrar shall in due time communicate any such written statements to states and organizations having submitted similar statements.

Article 67

The Court shall deliver its advisory opinions in open court, notice having been given to the Secretary-General and to the representatives of Members of the United Nations, of other states and of international organizations immediately concerned.

Article 68

In the exercise of its advisory functions the Court shall further be guided by the provisions of the present Statute which apply in contentious cases to the extent to which it recognizes them to be applicable.

Chapter V
AMENDMENT

Article 69

Amendments to the present Statute shall be effected by the same procedure as is provided by the Charter of the United Nations for amendments to that Charter, subject however to any provisions which the General Assembly upon recommendation of the Security Council may adopt concerning the participation of states which are parties to the present Statute but are not Members of the United Nations.

Article 70

The Court shall have power to propose such amendments to the present Statute as it may deem necessary, through written communications to the Secretary-General, for consideration in conformity with the provisions of Article 69.

Appendix III

Structure of the United Nations

General Assembly

The General Assembly is composed of all the Members of the United Nations.

SESSIONS
Resumed fifty-ninth session: 14 January–12 September 2005.
Resumed tenth emergency special session: 16, 19 and 20 July 2004 (suspended).
Sixtieth session: 13 September–23 December 2005 (suspended).

OFFICERS
Resumed fifty-ninth and tenth emergency special sessions
President: Jean Ping (Gabon).
Vice-Presidents: Algeria, Antigua and Barbuda, Australia, Azerbaijan, Bangladesh, Belgium, Burkina Faso, China, Djibouti, El Salvador, France, Ghana, Iran, Kazakhstan, Nicaragua, Russian Federation, Syrian Arab Republic, United Kingdom, United States, Uzbekistan, Zambia.

Sixtieth session
President: Jan Eliasson (Sweden).[1]
Vice-Presidents:[2] Angola, Armenia, Brazil, Central African Republic, China, France, Guinea-Bissau, India, Iran, Israel, Kenya, Malaysia, Mali, Myanmar, Pakistan, Paraguay, Russian Federation, Tunisia, United Kingdom, United States, Venezuela.

The Assembly has four types of committees: (1) Main Committees; (2) procedural committees; (3) standing committees; (4) subsidiary and ad hoc bodies. In addition, it convenes conferences to deal with specific subjects.

Main Committees

Six Main Committees have been established as follows:

Disarmament and International Security Committee (First Committee)
Special Political and Decolonization Committee (Fourth Committee)
Economic and Financial Committee (Second Committee)
Social, Humanitarian and Cultural Committee (Third Committee)
Administrative and Budgetary Committee (Fifth Committee)
Legal Committee (Sixth Committee)

The General Assembly may constitute other committees, on which all Members of the United Nations have the right to be represented.

OFFICERS OF THE MAIN COMMITTEES

Resumed fifty-ninth session

Fourth Committee[3]
Chairman: kyaw Tint Swe (Myanmar).
Vice-Chairpersons: Helfried Carl (Austria), Eduardo Calderon (Ecuador), Andrej Droba (Slovakia).
Rapporteur: Kais Kabtani (Tunisia).

Fifth Committee[3]
Chairman: John W. Ashe (Antigua and Barbuda)
Vice-Chairpersons: Dariusz Manczyk (Poland), Muhammad A. Muhith (Bangladesh), Eric Franck Saizonou (Benin)
Rapporteur: Katja Pehrman (Finland)

Sixth Committee[3]
Chairman: Mohamed Bennouna (Morocco)
Vice-Chairpersons: Ram Babu Dhakal (Nepal), Carlos Fernando Díaz Paniagua (Costa Rica), Csaba Simon (Hungary).
Rapporteur: Anna Sotaniemi (Finland)

Sixtieth session[4]

First Committee
Chairman: Choi Young-jin (Republic of Korea).
Vice-Chairmen: Gabriela Martinic (Argentina), Detlev Wolter (Germany), Lofti Bouchaara (Morocco).
Rapporteur: Elvina Jusufaj (Albania).

Fourth Committee
Chairman: Yashar Aliyev (Azerbaijan).
Vice-Chairmen: Subhas Gujadhur (Mauritius), Amparo Anguiano Rodriguez (Mexico), Alexander Gerts (Netherlands).
Rapporteur: Muhammed Shahrul Nizzam Umar (Brunei Darussalam).

Second Committee
Chairman: Aminu Bashir Wali (Nigeria).
Vice-Chairpersons: Selwin Charles Hart (Barbados), Juraj Koudelka (Czech Republic), Stefano Toscano (Switzerland).
Rapporteur: Abdulmalik Alshabibi (Yemen).

Third Committee
Chairman: Francis K. Butagira (Uganda).
Vice-Chairmen: Muhammad Anshor (Indonesia), Catarina Carvalho (Portugal), Eva Tomic (Slovenia).
Rapporteur: Pedro Cardoso (Brazil).

Fifth Committee
Chairman: John W. Ashe (Antigua and Barbuda).
Vice-Chairmen: Dariusz Manczyk (Poland), Muhammad A. Muhith (Bangladesh), Eric Franck Saizonou (Benin).
Rapporteur: Katja Pehrman (Finland).

Sixth Committee
Chairman: Juan Antonio Yañez-Barnuevo (Spain).
Vice-Chairmen: Mahmoud Hmoud (Jordan), Mahmoud Samy (Egypt), Grzegorz Zyman (Poland).
Rapporteur: Shermain Jeremy (Antigua and Barbuda).

Procedural committees

General Committee
The General Committee consists of the President of the General Assembly, as Chairman, the 21 Vice-Presidents and the Chairmen of the six Main Committees.

Credentials Committee

The Credentials Committee consists of nine members appointed by the General Assembly on the proposal of the President.

Resumed fifty-ninth session
Benin, Bhutan, China, Ghana, Liechtenstein, Russian Federation, Trinidad and Tobago, United States, Uruguay

Sixtieth session[5]
Cameroon, China, Panama, Portugal, Saint Lucia, Samoa, Sierra Leone, Russian Federation, United States.

Standing committees

The two standing committees consist of experts appointed in their individual capacity for three-year terms.

Advisory Committee on Administrative and Budgetary Questions (ACABQ)

To serve until 31 December 2005: Homero Luis Hernandez (Dominican Republic); Vladimir V. Kuznetsov, *Chairman* (Russian Federation); Thomas Mazet (Germany); Susan M. McLurg (United States); Mounir Zahran (Egypt).
To serve until 31 December 2006: Andrzej T. Abraszewski (Poland); Manlan Narcisse Ahounou (Côte d'Ivoire); Collen V. Kelapile (Botswana); E. Besley Maycock (Barbados); Murari Raj Sharma (Nepal).
To serve until 31 December 2007: Ronald Elkhuizen (Netherlands); Jorge Flores Callejas (Honduras); Jerry Kramer (Canada); Rajat Saha, *Vice-Chairman* (India); Sun Minqin (China); Jun Yamazaki (Japan).

On 23 November 2005 (dec. 60/410), the General Assembly appointed the following for a three-year term beginning on 1 January 2006 to fill the vacancies occurring on 31 December 2005: Guillermo Kendall (Argentina), Igor V. Khalevinsky (Russian Federation), Susan M. McLurg (United States), Tommo Monthe (Cameroon), Christina Vasak (France).

Committee on Contributions

To serve until 31 December 2005: Alvaro Gurgel de Alencar Netto (Brazil); Sergei I. Mareyev (Russian Federation); Bernard Meijerman (Netherlands); Hae-yun Park (Republic of Korea); Ugo Sessi, *Chairman* (Italy); Wu Gang (China).
To serve until 31 December 2006: Kenshiro Akimoto (Japan); Meshal Al-Mansour (Kuwait); Petru Dumitriu (Romania); Haile Selassie Getachew (Ethiopia); Ihor V. Humenny (Ukraine); David A. Leis (United States).
To serve until 31 December 2007: David Dutton (Australia); Paul Ekorong à Dong (Cameroon); Bernardo Greiver (Uruguay); Hassan Mohammed Hassan (Nigeria); Eduardo Iglesias (Argentina); Eduardo Manuel da Fonseca Fernandes Ramos (Portugal).

On 6 June 2005 (dec. 59/408) the General Assembly appointed Henrique da Silveira Sardinha Pinto (Brazil) for a six-month term beginning 6 June 2005 and ending 31 December 2005, as a result of the resignation of Alvaro Gurgel de Alencar Netto.
On 23 November 2005 (dec. 60/411), the General Assembly appointed the following for a three-year term beginning on 1 January 2006 to fill the vacancies occurring on 31 December 2005: Sujata Ghorai (Germany), Vyacheslav A. Logutov (Russian Federation), Richard Moon (United Kingdom), Hae-yun Park (Republic of Korea), Henrique da Silveira Sardinha Pinto (Brazil), Wu Gang (China).

Subsidiary and ad hoc bodies

The following is a list of subsidiary and ad hoc bodies functioning in 2005, including the number of members, dates of meetings/sessions in 2005, document numbers of reports (which generally provide specific information on membership), and relevant decision numbers pertaining to elections.

Ad Hoc Committee on a Comprehensive and Integral International Convention on Protection and Promotion of the Rights and Dignity of Persons with Disabilities

Session: Fifth, New York, 24 January–4 February
Chairman: Luis Gallegos Chiriboga (Ecuador)
Session: Sixth, New York, 1–12 August
Chairman: Don MacKay (New Zealand)

Membership: Open to all Member States and observers of the United Nations
Reports: A/AC.265/2005/2, A/60/266

Ad Hoc Committee established by General Assembly resolution 51/210 of 17 December 1996

Session: Ninth, New York, 28 March–1 April
Chairman: Rohan Perera (Sri Lanka)
Membership: Open to all States Members of the United Nations or members of the specialized agencies or of IAEA
Report: A/60/7

Ad Hoc Committee on the Indian Ocean

Meeting: New York, 26 July
Chairman: Prasad Kariyawasam (Sri Lanka)
Membership: 43
Report: A/60/29

Ad Hoc Committee on the Scope of Legal Protection under the Convention on the Safety of United Nations and Associated Personnel

Session: Fourth, New York, 11-15 April
Chairman: Christian Wenaweser (Liechtenstein)
Membership: Open to all States Members of the United Nations or members of the specialized agencies or of IAEA
Report: A/60/52

Advisory Committee on the United Nations Programme of Assistance in the Teaching, Study, Dissemination and Wider Appreciation of International Law

Session: Fortieth, New York, 17 October
Chairman: Robert Tachie-Menson (Ghana)
Membership: 25
Report: A/60/441

Board of Auditors

Session: Special session, New York, 7 December
Chairman: Guillermo N. Carague (Philippines)
Membership: 3
Report: A/60/543
Decision: GA 60/413

Committee on Conferences

Sessions: New York, 23 March (organizational), 19-27 September (substantive)
Chairman: Diego Simancas (Mexico)
Membership: 21
Report: A/60/32
Decision: GA 60/407

Committee on the Exercise of the Inalienable Rights of the Palestinian People

Meetings: Throughout the year
Chairman: Paul Badji (Senegal)
Membership: 23 (22 from 31 May)
Report: A/60/35

Committee on Information

Session: Twenty-seventh, New York, 18-28 April
Chairman: Mihnea Ioan Motoc (Romania)
Membership: 107 (108 from 8 December)

Report: A/60/21
Decision: GA 60/415

Committee on the Peaceful Uses of Outer Space
Session: Forty-eighth, Vienna, 8-17 June
Chairman: Adigun Ade Abiodun (Nigeria)
Membership: 67
Report: A/60/20 & Corr.1

Committee for Programme and Coordination (CPC)
Sessions: Forty-fifth, New York, 11 May (organizational), 6 June–1 July (substantive)
Chairman: Markiyan Kulyk (Ukraine)
Membership: 34
Report: A/60/16
Decisions: ESC 2005/201 E, GA 60/405

Committee on Relations with the Host Country
Meetings: New York, 15 April, 16 July, 28 September, 28 October
Chairman: Andreas D. Mavroyiannis (Cyprus)
Membership: 19 (including the United States as host country)
Report: A/60/26

Committee for the United Nations Population Award
Meetings: New York, 7 May, 7 June
Chairman: Judith Mbula Bahemuka (Kenya)
Membership: 10 (plus 5 honorary members, the Secretary-General and the UNFPA Executive Director)
Report: A/60/397

Disarmament Commission
Session: New York, 18-26 July (organizational) (resumed)
Chairman: Sylvester Ekundayo Rowe (Sierra Leone)
Membership: All UN Members
Reports: A/60/42

High-level Committee on the Review of Technical Cooperation among Developing Countries
Sessions: Organizational, New York, 10 May; fourteenth, New York, 31 May–3 June
President: Eladio Loizaga (Paraguay)
Membership: All States participating in UNDP
Report: A/60/39

International Civil Service Commission (ICSC)
Sessions: Sixtieth, Bangkok, Thailand, 8 February–11 March; sixty-first, New York, 11-22 July
Chairman: Mohsen Bel Hadj Amor (Tunisia)
Membership: 15
Report: A/60/30
Decision: GA 60/414

ADVISORY COMMITTEE ON POST ADJUSTMENT QUESTIONS
Session: Twenty-seventh, New York, 17-25 January
Chairman: Eugeniusz Wyzner (Poland)
Membership: 6

International Law Commission
Session: Fifty-seventh, Geneva, 2 May–3 June and 11 July–5 August
Chairman: Djamchid Momtaz (Iran)
Membership: 34
Report: A/60/10

Investments Committee
Meetings: New York, 7 February, 9 May, 12 September, 21 November
Chairman: William J. McDonough (United States)
Membership: 9
Decision: GA 60/412

Joint Advisory Group on the International Trade Centre UNCTAD/WTO
Session: Thirty-eighth, Geneva, 18-22 April
Chairman: Sarala Fernando (Sri Lanka)
Membership: Open to all States members of UNCTAD and all members of WTO
Report: ITC/AG(XXXVIII)/204

Joint Inspection Unit (JIU)
Chairman: Ion Gorita (Romania)
Membership: 11
Report: A/61/34
Decision: GA 59/416

Office of the United Nations High Commissioner for Refugees (UNHCR)

EXECUTIVE COMMITTEE OF THE HIGH COMMISSIONER'S PROGRAMME
Session: Fifty-sixth, Geneva, 3-7 October
Chairman: Juan Martabit (Chile)
Membership: 61
Report: A/60/12/Add.1
Decision: GA/60/129, GA/59/420

High Commissioner: Antônio Manuel de Oliveira Gutterres[6]

Panel of External Auditors
Membership: Members of the UN Board of Auditors and the appointed external auditors of the specialized agencies and IAEA

Special Committee on the Charter of the United Nations and on the Strengthening of the Role of the Organization
Meeting: New York, 14-18 March
Chairman: Andreas D. Mavroyiannis (Cyprus)
Membership: Open to all States Members of the United Nations
Report: A/60/33

Special Committee to Investigate Israeli Practices Affecting the Human Rights of the Palestinian People and Other Arabs of the Occupied Territories
Meetings: Geneva, 18-25 March and 24 June; Cairo, Egypt, 25 June–1 July; Amman, Jordan, 1-5 July; Damascus, Syrian Arab Republic, 5-9 July
Chairperson: Bernard A. B. Goonetilleke (Sri Lanka) (March), Prasad Kariyawasam (Sri Lanka) (April)
Membership: 3
Report: A/60/380

Special Committee on Peacekeeping Operations
Meetings: New York, 31 January–25 February; 4-8 April
Chairperson: Aminu Bashir Wali (Nigeria)
Membership: 117
Report: A/59/19/Rev.1

Special Committee on the Situation with regard to the Implementation of the Declaration on the Granting of Independence to Colonial Countries and Peoples
Session: New York, 17 February and 11 March (first part), 6, 7, 8, 13, 15, 16, 20 and 24 June (second part)
Chairman: Julian Robert Hunte (Saint Lucia)
Membership: 27
Report: A/60/23

United Nations Administrative Tribunal
Sessions: Geneva, 20 June–22 July; New York, 24 October–23 November
President: Julio Barboza (Argentina)
Membership: 7
Report: A/INF/60/5

United Nations Capital Development Fund (UNCDF)

EXECUTIVE BOARD

The UNDP/UNFPA Executive Board acts as the Executive Board of the Fund.

Managing Director: Mark Malloch Brown (UNDP Administrator) (until 13 August), Kemal Dervis (from 14 August)

United Nations Commission on International Trade Law (UNCITRAL)

Session: Thirty-eighth, Vienna, 4-15 July
Chairman: Jorge Pinzón Sánchez (Colombia)
Membership: 60
Report: A/60/17

United Nations Conciliation Commission for Palestine

Membership: 3
Report: A/60/277

United Nations Conference on Trade and Development (UNCTAD)

Session: Did not meet in 2005
Membership: Open to all States Members of the United Nations or members of the specialized agencies or of IAEA
Decision: GA 59/419

Secretary-General of UNCTAD: Supachai Panitchpakdi (Thailand)[7]

TRADE AND DEVELOPMENT BOARD

Sessions: Thirty-sixth executive, 3 May; twenty-second special, 18 July; thirty-seventh executive, 26 July; fifty-second, 3-14 October; all in Geneva
President: Mary Whelan (Ireland) (thirty-sixth and thirty-seventh executive and twenty-second special sessions), Ransford A. Smith (Jamaica) (fifty-second session)
Membership: Open to all States members of UNCTAD
Report: A/60/15

SUBSIDIARY ORGANS OF THE TRADE AND DEVELOPMENT BOARD

COMMISSION ON ENTERPRISE,
BUSINESS FACILITATION AND DEVELOPMENT
Session: Ninth, Geneva, 22-25 February
Chairperson: Sarala Fernando (Sri Lanka)
Membership: Open to all States members of UNCTAD
Report: TD/B/COM.3/70

COMMISSION ON INVESTMENT,
TECHNOLOGY AND RELATED FINANCIAL ISSUES
Session: Ninth, Geneva, 7-11 March
President: Love Mtesa (Zambia)
Membership: Open to all States members of UNCTAD
Report: TD/B/COM.2/66

Intergovernmental Group of Experts on Competition Law and Policy
Session: Did not meet in 2005
Membership: Open to all States members of UNCTAD

Intergovernmental Working Group of Experts on International Standards of Accounting and Reporting
Session: Twenty-second, Geneva, 21-23 November
Chairperson: Aziz Dieye (Senegal)
Membership: 34
Report: TD/B/COM.2/ISAR/31
Decisions: ESC 2005/201 C & E

COMMISSION ON TRADE IN
GOODS AND SERVICES, AND COMMODITIES
Session: Ninth, Geneva, 4-18 March
Chairperson: Dacio Castillo (Honduras)

Membership: Open to all States members of UNCTAD
Report: TD/B/COM.1/73 & Corr.1

WORKING PARTY ON THE
MEDIUM-TERM PLAN AND THE PROGRAMME BUDGET
Sessions: Forty-fourth, Geneva, 31 January–2 February and 30-31 May; forty-fifth, Geneva, 12-15 September
Chairperson: Enrique Manalo (Philippines) (forty-fourth session), Dmitri Godunov (Russian Federation) (forty-fifth session)
Membership: Open to all States members of UNCTAD
Reports: TD/B/WP/179, TD/B/WP/183, TD/B/WP/184

United Nations Development Fund for Women (UNIFEM)

CONSULTATIVE COMMITTEE

Session: Forty-fifth, New York, 17-18 February
Chairperson: Prince Zeid Ra'ad Zeid Al-Hussein (Jordan)
Membership: 5

Executive Director of UNIFEM: Noeleen Heyzer

United Nations Environment Programme (UNEP)

GOVERNING COUNCIL

Session: Twenty-third, Nairobi, Kenya
President: Rachmat Witoelar (Indonesia)
Membership: 58
Report: A/60/25

Executive Director of UNEP: Klaus Töpfer

United Nations Human Settlements Programme (UN-Habitat)

GOVERNING COUNCIL

Session: Twentieth, Nairobi, Kenya, 4-8 April
President: Petr Kopriva (Czech Republic)
Membership: 58
Report: A/60/8
Decisions: GA 60/406

Executive Director of UN-Habitat: Anna Kajumulo Tibaijuka

United Nations Institute for Disarmament Research (UNIDIR)

BOARD OF TRUSTEES

Sessions: Forty-fourth, New York, 23-25 February; forty-fifth, Geneva, 29 June–1 July
Chairman: Vicente Berasategui (Argentina)
Membership: 24, plus 1 ex-officio member (Director of UNIDIR)
Report: A/60/285

Director of UNIDIR: Patricia Lewis
Deputy Director: Christophe Carle

United Nations Institute for Training and Research (UNITAR)

BOARD OF TRUSTEES

Session: Forty-third, Geneva, 26-27 April
Chairman: Omar Hilale (Morocco)
Membership: 20, plus 4 ex-officio members
Report: A/60/304
Executive Director of UNITAR: Marcel A. Boisard

United Nations Joint Staff Pension Board

Session: Did not meet in 2005
Membership: 33

United Nations Relief and Works Agency for Palestine Refugees in the Near East (UNRWA)

ADVISORY COMMISSION OF UNRWA

Meeting: Amman, Jordan, 26 September
Chairperson: Rana Mokadden (Lebanon)

Membership: 10
Report: A/60/13
Decision: GA 60/522

WORKING GROUP ON THE FINANCING OF UNRWA
Meetings: New York, 8 September and 18 October
Chairman: Baki Ilkin (Turkey)
Membership: 9
Report: A/60/439

Commissioner-General of UNRWA: Peter Hansen (until 31 March), Karen Koning AbuZayd (from 28 June)
Deputy Commissioner-General: Filippo Grandi (from 25 September)

United Nations Scientific Committee on the Effects of Atomic Radiation

Session: Fifty-third, Vienna, 26-30 September
Chairman: Yasuhito Sasaki (Japan)
Membership: 21
Report: A/60/46

United Nations Staff Pension Committee

Meetings: New York, 18 May and 7 December
Chairperson: Jean-Michel Jakobowicz (France)
Membership: 12 (plus 8 alternates)

United Nations University (UNU)

COUNCIL OF THE UNITED NATIONS UNIVERSITY
Session: Fifty-second, Tokyo, Japan, 5-9 December
Chairperson: Vappu Taipale (Finland)
Membership: 24 (plus 3 ex-officio members and the UNU Rector)

Rector of the University: Hans J.A. van Ginkel

United Nations Voluntary Fund for Indigenous Populations

BOARD OF TRUSTEES
Session: Eighteenth, Geneva, 28 February–4 March
Chairperson: Victoria Tauli-Corpuz (Philippines)
Membership: 5
Report: E/CN.4/Sub.2/AC.4/2005/5

United Nations Voluntary Fund for Victims of Torture

BOARD OF TRUSTEES
Session: Twenty-fourth, Geneva, 13-22 April
Chairman: Ivan Tosevski (The former Yugoslav Republic of Macedonia)
Membership: 5
Report: A/60/215

United Nations Voluntary Trust Fund on Contemporary Forms of Slavery

BOARD OF TRUSTEES
Session: Tenth, Geneva, 7-11 March
Chairperson: Cheikh Saad-Bouh Kamara (Mauritania)
Membership: 5
Report: A/60/273

Conference
World Summit on the Information Society
Session: Tunis, Tunisia, 16-18 November (second phase)
President: Zine El Abidine Ben Ali (Tunisia)
Attendance: 174 States, European Community, regional commissions, UN bodies and programmes, regional organizations, specialized agencies, intergovernmental organizations, non-governmental organizations and business entities
Report: WSIS-05/TUNIS/DOC/9 (Rev.1)-E

Security Council

The Security Council consists of 15 Member States of the United Nations, in accordance with the provisions of Article 23 of the United Nations Charter as amended in 1965.

MEMBERS
Permanent members: China, France, Russian Federation, United Kingdom, United States.
Non-permanent members: Algeria, Argentina, Benin, Brazil, Denmark, Greece, Japan, Philippines, Romania, the United Republic of Tanzania.

On 10 October 2005 (dec. 60/403), the General Assembly elected the Congo, Ghana, Peru, Qatar and Slovakia for a two-year term beginning on 1 January 2006, to replace Algeria, Benin, Brazil, Philippines and Romania whose terms of office were to expire on 31 December 2005.

PRESIDENT
The presidency of the Council rotates monthly, according to the English alphabetical listing of its member States. The following served as President during 2005:

Month	Member	Representative
January	Argentina	Cesar Mayoral
		Rafeal Antonio Bielsa
February	Benin	Joel W. Adechi
		Rogatien Biaou
March	Brazil	Ronaldo Mota Sardenberg

Month	Member	Representative
April	China	Wang Guangya
		Zhang Yishan
May	Denmark	Ellen Margrethe Log
		Lars Faaborg-Andersen
		Per Stig Moller
June	France	Jean-Marc de la Sablière
		Michel Duclos
		Brigitte Collet
July	Greece	Adamantios Th. Vassilakis
		Petros Molyviatis
August	Japan	Kenzo Oshima
September	Philippines	Lauro L. Baja
		Gloria Macapagal-Arroyo
		Alberto G. Romulo
		Bayani S. Mercado
October	Romania	Mihnea Ioan Motoc
		Mihai-Razvan Ungureanu
		Gheorghe Dumitru
November	Russian Federation	Andrey I. Denisov
December	United Kingdom	Sir Emyr Jones Parry
		Adam Thomson
		Huw Llewellyn
		Vanessa Howe-Jones
		Paul Johnston

Military Staff Committee

The Military Staff Committee consists of the chiefs of staff of the permanent members of the Security Council or their representatives. It meets fortnightly.

Standing committees

Each of the three standing committees of the Security Council is composed of representatives of all Council members:

Committee of Experts (to examine the provisional rules of procedure of the Council and any other matters entrusted to it by the Council)
Committee on the Admission of New Members
Committee on Council Meetings Away from Headquarters

Subsidiary bodies

Counter-Terrorism Committee (CTC)

Chairman: Andrey I. Denisov (Russian Federation) (until March), Ellen Margrethe Log (Denmark) (from April)

United Nations Compensation Commission

Executive Secretary: Rolf Goran Knutsson

United Nations Monitoring, Verification and Inspection Commission (UNMOVIC)

Acting Executive Chairman: Demetrius Perricos

1540 Committee

Chairman: Mihnea Ioan Motoc (Romania)

Peacekeeping operations

United Nations Truce Supervision Organization (UNTSO)

Chief of Staff: Brigadier General Clive William Lilley

United Nations Military Observer Group in India and Pakistan (UNMOGIP)

Chief Military Observer: Major General Guido Palmieri (until September), Major General Draguyin Repinc (from December)

United Nations Peacekeeping Force in Cyprus (UNFICYP)

Special Representative of the Secretary-General and Head of Mission: Michael Moller
Force Commander: Major General Herbert Joaquin Figoli Almandos

United Nations Disengagement Observer Force (UNDOF)

Force Commander: Major General Bala Nanda Sharma

United Nations Interim Force in Lebanon (UNIFIL)

Personal Representative of the Secretary-General for Southern Lebanon: Geir O. Pedersen
Force Commander: Major General Alain Pellegrini

United Nations Mission for the Referendum in Western Sahara (MINURSO)

Personal Envoy of the Secretary-General: Peter van Walsum
Special Representative of the Secretary-General and Head of Mission: Alvaro de Soto (until August), Francesco Bastagli (from 1 September)
Force Commander: Major General Gyorgy Száraz (until 11 August), Brigadier General Kurt Mosgaard (from 12 September)

United Nations Observer Mission in Georgia (UNOMIG)

Special Representative of the Secretary-General and Head of Mission: Heidi Tagliavini
Chief Military Observer: Major General Hussein Ahmed Eissa Ghobashi (until July), Major General Niaz Muhammad Khan Khattak (from 13 August)

United Nations Interim Administration Mission in Kosovo (UNMIK)

Special Representative of the Secretary-General and Head of Mission: Soren Jessen-Petersen
Principal Deputy Special Representative: Lawrence Rossin
Deputy Special Representative for Police and Justice: Jean Dussourd (from 18 February)
Deputy Special Representative for Reconstruction: Joachim Rücker (from February)
Deputy Special Representative for Institutional Building: Werner Wnendt (from April)

United Nations Mission in Sierra Leone (UNAMSIL)[8]

Special Representative of the Secretary-General and Head of Mission: Daudi Nyelaulwa Mwakawago
Deputy Special Representative: José Vitor da Silva Angelo
Force Commander: Major General Sajjad Akram

United Nations Organization Mission in the Democratic Republic of the Congo (MONUC)

Special Representative of the Secretary-General and Chief of Mission: William Lacy Swing
Deputy Special Representatives: Ross Mountain, Haile Menkerios (from October)
Force Commander: Major General Samaila Iliya (until February) Lieutenant General Babacar Gaye (from March)

United Nations Mission in Ethiopia and Eritrea (UNMEE)

Special Envoy for Ethiopia and Eritrea: Lloyd Axworthy (until 16 August)
Special Representative of the Secretary-General: Legwaila Joseph Legwaila
Deputy Special Representatives: Joël W. Adechi (from 25 May), Azouz Ennifar (from 29 July)
Force Commander: Major General Rajender Singh

United Nations Mission of Support in East Timor (UNMISET)[9]

Special Representative of the Secretary-General and Head of Mission: Sukehiro Hasegawa
Force Commander: Lieutenant General Khairuddin Mat Yusof
Chief Military Observer: Brigadier General Pedro Rocha Pena Madeira

United Nations Mission in Liberia (UNMIL)

Special Representative of the Secretary-General and Head of Mission: Jacques Paul Klein (until April), Alan Claude Doss (from 15 August)
Deputy Special Representatives: Abou Moussa (until July), Steinar Bjornsson (from 10 January), Luiz Carlos da Costa (from 17 August)
Force Commander: Lieutenant General Joseph Olorungbon Owonibi

United Nations Operation in Côte d'Ivoire (UNOCI)

Special Representative of the Secretary-General and Head of Mission: Albert Tévoédjré (until March), Pierre Schori (from 1 April)
Principal Deputy Special Representative: Alan Claude Doss (until July), Abou Moussa (From 17 August)
Force Commander: Major General Abdoulaye Fall

United Nations Operation in Burundi (ONUB)

Special Representative of the Secretary-General and Chief of Mission: Carolyn McAskie
Deputy Special Representatives: Ibrahima Fall, Nureldin Satti
Force Commander: Major General Derrick Mbuyiselo Mgwebi

United Nations Stabilization Mission in Haiti (MINUSTAH)

Special Representative of the Secretary-General: Juan Gabriel Valdés
Principal Deputy Special Representative: Hocine Medili
Deputy Special Representative: Adama Guindo

Force Commander: Lieutenant General Augusto Heleno Ribeiro Pereira (until 1 September), Lieutenant General Urano Teixeira da Matta Bacellar (from 2 September)

United Nations Mission in Sudan (UNMIS)[10]

Special Representative of the Secretary-General and Head of Mission: Jan Pronk
Deputy Special Representatives: Taye-Brook Zerihoun, Manuel Aranda da Silva
Force Commander: Major General Fazle Elahi Akbar

Political, peace-building and other missions

United Nations Political Office for Somalia (UNPOS)

Representative of the Secretary-General and Head of UNPOS: Winston A. Tubman (until March), François Lonseny Fall (from 3 May)

Office of the Special Representative of the Secretary-General for the Great Lakes Region

Special Representative: Ibrahima Fall

United Nations Observer Mission in Bougainville (UNOMB)[11]

Head of Mission: Tor Stenbock

United Nations Peace-building Support Office in Guinea-Bissau (UNOGBIS)

Representative of the Secretary-General and Head of UNOGBIS: Joao Bernardo Honwana

Office of the United Nations Special Coordinator for the Middle East (UNSCO)

Special Coordinator for the Middle East Peace Process and Personal Representative of the Secretary-General to the Pales- *tine Liberation Organization and the Palestinian Authority:* Terje Roed-Larsen (until 2 January), Alvaro de Soto (from 6 May)

United Nations Peace-building Office in the Central African Republic (BONUCA)

Representative of the Secretary-General and Head of BONUCA: General Lamine Cissé

United Nations Tajikistan Office of Peace-building (UNTOP)

Representative of the Secretary-General: Vladimir Sotirov

Office of the Special Representative of the Secretary-General for West Africa

Special Representative of the Secretary-General: Ahmedou Ould-Abdallah

United Nations Assistance Mission in Afghanistan (UNAMA)

Special Representative of the Secretary-General and Head of UNAMA: Jean Arnault
Deputy Special Representatives: Ameerah Haq, Filippo Grandi (until 15 September)

United Nations Assistance Mission for Iraq (UNAMI)

Special Representative of the Secretary-General for Iraq: Ashraf Jehangir Qazi

United Nations Office in Timor-Leste (UNOTIL)[12]

Special Representative of the Secretary-General and Head of Mission: Sukehiro Hasegawa (from 21 May)
Deputy Special Representative: Anis Bajwa (from 15 August)

Economic and Social Council

The Economic and Social Council consists of 54 Member States of the United Nations, elected by the General Assembly, each for a three-year term, in accordance with the provisions of Article 61 of the United Nations Charter as amended in 1965 and 1973.

MEMBERS
To serve until 31 December 2005: Azerbaijan, Benin, Congo, Cuba, Ecuador, France, Germany, Greece, Ireland, Jamaica, Japan, Kenya, Malaysia, Mozambique, Nicaragua, Saudi Arabia, Senegal, Turkey.
To serve until 31 December 2006: Armenia, Bangladesh, Belgium, Belize, Canada, Colombia, Indonesia, Italy, Mauritius, Namibia, Nigeria, Panama, Poland, Republic of Korea, Tunisia, United Arab Emirates, United Republic of Tanzania, United States.
To serve until 31 December 2007: Albania, Australia, Brazil, Chad, China, Costa Rica, Democratic Republic of the Congo, Denmark, Guinea, Iceland, India, Lithuania, Mexico, Pakistan, Russian Federation, South Africa, Thailand, United Kingdom.

On 17 October 2005 (dec. 60/404), the General Assembly elected the following for a three-year term beginning on 1 January 2006 to fill the vacancies occurring on 31 December 2005: Angola, Austria, Benin, Cuba, the Czech Republic, France, Germany, Guinea-Bissau, Guyana, Haiti, Japan, Madagascar, Mauritania, Paraguay, Saudi Arabia, Spain, Sri Lanka, Turkey.

SESSIONS
Organizational session for 2005: New York, 19 January, 4 February and 1 and 31 March.
Resumed organizational session for 2005: New York, 27-28 April and 9 June.

Special high-level meeting with the Bretton Woods institutions and the World Trade Organization: New York, 18 April.
Substantive session of 2005: New York, 29 June–27 July.
Resumed substantive session of 2005: New York, 21 October.

OFFICERS
President: Munir Akram (Pakistan).
Vice-Presidents: Luis Gallegos Chiriboga (Ecuador), Johan C. Verbeke (Belgium), Ali Hachani (Tunisia), Agim Nesho (Albania).

Subsidiary and other related organs

SUBSIDIARY ORGANS
The Economic and Social Council may, at each session, set up committees or working groups, of the whole or of limited membership, and refer to them any item on the agenda for study and report.

Other subsidiary organs reporting to the Council consist of functional commissions, regional commissions, standing committees, expert bodies and ad hoc bodies.

The inter-agency United Nations System Chief Executives Board for Coordination also reports to the Council.

Functional commissions

Commission on Crime Prevention and Criminal Justice

Session: Fourteenth, Vienna, 23-27 May
Chairman: Oscar Cabello Sarubbi (Paraguay)
Membership: 40
Report: E/2005/30
Decision: ESC 2005/201 C

Commission on Human Rights

Sessions: Sixty-first, Geneva, 17 January and 14 March–22 April
Chairperson: Makarim Wibisono (Indonesia)
Membership: 53
Report: E/2005/23
Decision: ESC 2005/201 C

SUBCOMMISSION ON THE PROMOTION
AND PROTECTION OF HUMAN RIGHTS
Session: Fifty-seventh, Geneva, 25 July–12 August
Chairperson: Vladimir Kartashkin (Russian Federation)
Membership: 26
Report: E/CN.4/2006/2

Commission on Narcotic Drugs

Session: Forty-eighth, Vienna, 7-11 March
Chairperson: Sheel Kant Sharma (India)
Membership: 53
Report: E/2005/28
Decision: ESC 2005/201 C

Commission on Population and Development

Session: Thirty-eighth, New York, 4-8 and 14 April
Chairman: Crispin Grey-Johnson (Gambia)
Membership: 47
Report: E/2005/25
Decisions: ESC 2005/201 B & C

Commission on Science and Technology for Development

Session: Eighth, Geneva, 23-27 May
Chairman: Bernd Michael Rode (Austria)
Membership: 33
Report: E/2005/31

Commission for Social Development

Session: Forty-third, New York, 9-18 February
Chairperson: Dumisani Shadrack Kumalo (South Africa)
Membership: 46
Report: E/2005/26

Commission on the Status of Women

Session: Forty-ninth, New York, 28 February–11 and 22 March
Chairperson: Kyung-wha Kang (Republic of Korea)
Membership: 45
Report: E/2005/27
Decision: ESC 2005/201 C

Commission on Sustainable Development

Session: Thirteenth, New York, 11-22 April
Chairperson: John William Ashe (Antigua and Barbuda)
Membership: 53
Report: E/2005/29
Decision: ESC 2005/201 C

Statistical Commission

Session: Thirty-sixth, New York, 1-4 March
Chairman: Katherine Wallman (United States)
Membership: 24
Report: E/2005/24
Decision: ESC 2005/201 C

United Nations Forum on Forests

Session: Fifth, Geneva, 16-27 May
Chairman: Manuel Rodriguez Becerra (Colombia)
Membership: Open to all States Members of the United Nations and members of the specialized agencies
Report: E/2005/42 & Corr.1

Regional commissions

Economic Commission for Africa (ECA)

Session: Thirty-eighth session of the Commission/Conference of African Ministers of Finance, Planning and Economic Development, Abuja, Nigeria, 14-15 May
Chairman: Ngozi Okonjolweala (Nigeria)
Membership: 53

Economic Commission for Europe (ECE)

Session: Sixtieth, Geneva, 22-25 February
Chairman: Wolfgang Petritsch (Austria)
Membership: 55
Report: E/2005/37

Economic Commission for Latin America and the Caribbean (ECLAC)

Session: Did not meet in 2005
Membership: 41 members, 7 associate members

Economic and Social Commission for Asia and the Pacific (ESCAP)

Session: Sixty-first, Bangkok, Thailand, 12-18 May
Chairperson: Kassymzhomart Tokaev (Kazakhstan)
Membership: 53 members, 9 associate members
Report: E/2005/39

Economic and Social Commission for Western Asia (ESCWA)

Session: Twenty-third, Damascus, Syrian Arab Republic, 9-12 May
Chairman: Abdallah Al-Dardari (Syrian Arab Republic)
Membership: 13
Report: E/2005/41

Standing committees

Committee on Non-Governmental Organizations

Session: New York, 5-14 January
Chairperson: Paimaneh Hasteh (Iran)
Membership: 19
Report: E/2005/32 (Part I)

Committee for Programme and Coordination (CPC)

Sessions: Forty-fifth, New York, 11 May (organizational), 6 June–1 July (substantive)
Chairman: Markiyan Kulyk (Ukraine)
Membership: 34
Report: A/60/16
Decisions: ESC 2005/201 C & E, GA 60/405

Expert bodies

Committee of Experts on International Cooperation in Tax Matters

Session: First, Geneva, 5-9 December
Chairman: Noureddine Bensouda (Morocco)
Membership: 25
Report: E/2005/45
Decision: ESC 2005/201 E

Committee for Development Policy

Session: Seventh, New York, 14-18 March
Chairperson: Suchitra Punyaratabandhu (Thailand)
Membership: 24
Report: E/2005/33
Decision: ESC 2005/201 A

Committee on Economic, Social and Cultural Rights

Sessions: Thirty-fourth and thirty-fifth, Geneva, 25 April–13 May and 7-25 November
Chairperson: Virginia Bonoan-Dandan (Philippines)
Membership: 18
Report: E/2006/22
Decision: ESC 2005/201 C

Committee of Experts on Public Administration

Session: Fourth, New York, 4-8 April
Chairperson: Apolo Nsibambi (Uganda)
Membership: 24
Report: E/2005/44
Decision: ESC 2005/201 E

Committee of Experts on the Transport of Dangerous Goods and on the Globally Harmonized System of Classification and Labelling of Chemicals

Session: Did not meet in 2005
Membership: 35
Decision: ESC 2005/201 C

Permanent Forum on Indigenous Issues

Session: Fourth, New York, 16-27 May
Chairperson: Victoria Tauli-Corpuz (Philippines)
Membership: 16
Report: E/2005/43

United Nations Group of Experts on Geographical Names

Session: Did not meet in 2005 .
Membership: Representatives of the 22 geographical/linguistic divisions of the Group of Experts

Ad hoc body

United Nations System Chief Executives Board for Coordination

Sessions: Mont Pèlerin, Switzerland, 9 April; New York, 28 October
Chairman: The Secretary-General
Membership: Organizations of the UN system
Reports: CEB/2005/1, CEB/2005/2

Other related bodies

International Research and Training Institute for the Advancement of Women (INSTRAW)

EXECUTIVE BOARD

Session: Second, New York, 1 June, 31 October
President: Juan Antonio Yáñez-Barnuevo
Membership: 10 (plus 8 ex-officio members)
Report: E/2005/75, INSTRAW/EB/2005/R.7

Director of INSTRAW: Carmen Moreno

Joint United Nations Programme on Human Immunodeficiency Virus/Acquired Immunodeficiency Syndrome (UNAIDS)

PROGRAMME COORDINATING BOARD

Meeting: Seventeenth, Geneva, 27-29 June
Chairperson: Carlos Amtpmp da Rocha Paranhos (Brazil)

Membership: 22
Reports: UNAIDS/PCB(17)/05.10, UNAIDS/PCB(18)/06.18
Decisions: ESC 2005/201 C & D

Executive Director of UNAIDS: Dr. Peter Piot

United Nations Children's Fund (UNICEF)

EXECUTIVE BOARD

Sessions: First and second regular, New York, 17-20 and 24 January, 28-30 September; annual, New York, 6-10 June
President: Mehdi Danesh-Yazdi (Iran)
Membership: 36
Report: E/2005/34/Rev.1
Decision: ESC 2005/201 C

Executive Director of UNICEF: Carol Bellamy (until April), Ann M. Veneman (from 1 May)

United Nations Development Programme (UNDP)/ United Nations Population Fund (UNFPA)

EXECUTIVE BOARD

Sessions: First and second regular, and annual, New York, 20-28 January, 6-9 September; 13-24 June
President: Carmen María Gallardo Hernández (El Salvador)
Membership: 36
Report: E/2005/35
Decision: ESC 2005/201 C

Administrator of UNDP: Mark Malloch Brown (until 13 August), Kemal Dervis (from 14 August)
Associate Administrator: Zéphirin Diabré
Executive Director of UNFPA: Thoraya Ahmed Obaid

United Nations Research Institute for Social Development (UNRISD)

BOARD

Session: Forty-third, Geneva, 31 March
Chairperson: Emma Rothschild (United Kingdom)
Membership: 11 (plus 7 ex-officio members)
Decision: ESC 2005/236

Director of UNRISD: Thandika Mkandawire

World Food Programme (WFP)

EXECUTIVE BOARD

Sessions: First and second regular, Rome, Italy, 31 January–2 February, 7-11 November; annual, Rome, 6-10 June
President: Poul Skytte Christoffersen (Denmark)
Membership: 36
Report: E/2006/36
Decisions: ESC 2005/201 C

Executive Director of WFP: James T. Morris

Trusteeship Council[13]

Article 86 of the United Nations Charter lays down that the Trusteeship Council shall consist of the following:

Members of the United Nations administering Trust Territories;
Permanent members of the Security Council that do not administer Trust Territories;

As many other members elected for a three-year term by the General Assembly as will ensure that the membership of the Council is equally divided between United Nations Members that administer Trust Territories and those that do not.

Members: China, France, Russian Federation, United Kingdom, United States.

International Court of Justice

Judges of the Court

The International Court of Justice consists of 15 Judges elected for nine-year terms by the General Assembly and the Security Council.

The following were the Judges of the Court serving in 2005, listed in the order of precedence:

Judge	Country of nationality	End of term[14]
Shi Jiuyong, *President*	China	2012
Raymond Ranjeva, *Vice-President*	Madagascar	2009
Abdul G. Koroma	Sierra Leone	2012
Vladlen S. Vereshchetin	Russian Federation	2006
Rosalyn Higgins	United Kingdom	2009
Gonzalo Parra-Aranguren	Venezuela	2009
Pieter H. Kooijmans	Netherlands	2006
Francisco Rezek	Brazil	2006
Awn Shawkat Al-Khasawneh	Jordan	2009
Thomas Buergenthal	United States	2006
Nabil Elaraby	Egypt	2006
Hisashi Owada	Japan	2012
Bruno Simma	Germany	2012
Peter Tomka	Slovakia	2012
Ronny Abraham	France	2009

Registrar: Philippe Couvreur
Deputy Registrar: Jean-Jacques Arnaldez

Chamber of Summary Procedure

Members: Shi Jiuyong (ex officio), Raymond Ranjeva (ex officio), Gonzalo Parra-Aranguren, Awn Shawkat Al-Khasawneh, Thomas Buergenthal
Substitute members: Nabil Elaraby, Hisashi Owada

Chamber for Environmental Matters

Members: Shi Jiuyong (ex officio), Raymond Ranjeva (ex officio), Pieter H. Kooijmans, Francisco Rezek, Nabil Elaraby, Bruno Simma, Peter Tomka

Parties to the Court's Statute

All Members of the United Nations are ipso facto parties to the Statute of the International Court of Justice.

States accepting the compulsory jurisdiction of the Court

Declarations made by the following States, a number with reservations, accepting the Court's compulsory jurisdiction (or made under the Statute of the Permanent Court of International Justice and deemed to be an acceptance of the jurisdiction of the International Court) were in force at the end of 2005:

Australia, Austria, Barbados, Belgium, Botswana, Bulgaria, Cambodia, Cameroon, Canada, Costa Rica, Côte d'Ivoire, Cyprus, Democratic Republic of the Congo, Denmark, Dominican Republic, Egypt, Estonia, Finland, Gambia, Georgia, Greece, Guinea, Guinea-Bissau, Haiti, Honduras, Hungary, India, Japan, Kenya, Lesotho, Liberia, Liechtenstein, Luxembourg, Madagascar, Malawi, Malta, Mauritius, Mexico, Nauru, Netherlands, New Zealand, Nicaragua, Nigeria, Norway, Pakistan, Panama, Paraguay, Peru, Philippines, Poland, Portugal, Senegal, Serbia and Montenegro, Slovakia, Somalia, Spain, Sudan, Suriname, Swaziland, Sweden, Switzerland, Togo, Uganda, United Kingdom, Uruguay.

United Nations organs and specialized and related agencies authorized to request advisory opinions from the Court

Authorized by the United Nations Charter to request opinions on any legal question: General Assembly, Security Council.
Authorized by the General Assembly in accordance with the Charter to request opinions on legal questions arising within the scope of their activities: Economic and Social Council, Trusteeship Council, Interim Committee of the General Assembly, ILO, FAO, UNESCO, ICAO, WHO, World Bank, IFC, IDA, IMF, ITU, WMO, IMO, WIPO, IFAD, UNIDO, IAEA.

Committees of the Court

BUDGETARY AND ADMINISTRATIVE COMMITTEE
Members: Shi Jiuyong (ex officio) (Chair), Raymond Ranjeva (ex officio), Abdul G. Koroma, Vladlen S. Vereshchetin, Pieter H. Kooijmans, Awn Shawkat Al-Khasawneh, Thomas Buergenthal

COMMITTEE ON RELATIONS
Members: Gonzalo Parra-Aranguren (Chair), Francisco Rezek, Awn Shawkat Al-Khasawneh, Hisashi Owada

COMPUTERIZATION COMMITTEE
Members: Raymond Ranjeva (Chair); open to all interested members of the Court

LIBRARY COMMITTEE
Members: Abdul G. Koroma (Chair), Pieter H. Kooijmans, Francisco Rezek, Thomas Buergenthal, Peter Tomka

RULES COMMITTEE
Members: Rosalyn Higgins (Chair), Nabil Elaraby, Hisashi Owada, Bruno Simma, Peter Tomka, Ronny Abraham

Other United Nations–related bodies

The following bodies are not subsidiary to any principal organ of the United Nations but were established by an international treaty instrument or arrangement sponsored by the United Nations and are thus related to the Organization and its work. These bodies, often referred to as "treaty organs", are serviced by the United Nations Secretariat and may be financed in part or wholly from the Organization's regular budget, as authorized by the General Assembly, to which most of them report annually.

Committee on the Elimination of Discrimination against Women (CEDAW)

Sessions: Thirty-second and thirty-third, New York, 10-28 January and 5-22 July
Chairperson: Rosario Manalo (Philippines)

Membership: 23
Report: A/60/38

Committee on the Elimination of Racial Discrimination (CERD)

Sessions: Sixty-sixth and sixty-seventh, Geneva, 21 February–11 March and 2-19 August
Chairperson: Mario Jorge Yutzis (Argentina)
Membership: 18
Report: A/60/18

Committee on the Protection of the Rights of All Migrant Workers and Members of Their Families

Session: Second, Geneva, 25-29 April
Chairperson: Prasad Kariyawasam (Sri Lanka)

Membership: 10
Report: A/60/48

Committee on the Rights of the Child
Sessions: Thirty-eighth, thirty-ninth and fortieth, Geneva, 10-28 January, 17 May–3 June and 12-30 September
Chairperson: Jakob Egbert Doek (Netherlands)
Membership: 10
Reports: CRC/C/146, CRC/C/150, CRC/C/153

Committee against Torture
Sessions: Thirty-fourth and thirty-fifth, Geneva, 2-20 May and 7-25 November
Chairperson: Fernando Mariño (Spain)
Membership: 10
Reports: A/60/44

Conference on Disarmament
Meetings: Geneva, 24 January–1 April, 30 May–15 July, 8 August–23 September

President: Netherlands, New Zealand, Nigeria, Norway, Pakistan, Peru (successively)
Membership: 65
Report: A/60/27

Human Rights Committee
Sessions: Eighty-third, eighty-fourth and eighty-fifth, New York, 14 March–1 April, Geneva, 11-29 July and 17 October–3 November
Chairperson: Christine Chanet (France)
Membership: 18
Reports: A/60/40, vol. I

International Narcotics Control Board (INCB)
Sessions: Eighty-second, eighty-third and eighty-fourth, Vienna, 31 January–4 February, 2-13 May, and 1-18 November
President: Philip Onagewele Emafo
Membership: 13
Report: E/INCB/2005/1

Principal members of the United Nations Secretariat

(as at 31 December 2005)

Secretariat
The Secretary-General: Kofi A. Annan
Deputy Secretary-General: Louise Fréchette

Executive Office of the Secretary-General
Under-Secretary-General, Chef de Cabinet: Mark Malloch Brown
Under-Secretary-General, Special Adviser to the Secretary-General: Lakhdar Brahimi
   Assistant Secretary-General, Deputy Chef de Cabinet: Elisabeth Lindenmayer (until 8 February)
   Assistant Secretary-General for Policy Planning: Robert Orr

Office of Internal Oversight Services
Under-Secretary-General: Dileep Nair (until 23 April), Inga-Britt Ahlenius (from 15 July)

Office of Legal Affairs
Under-Secretary-General, Legal Counsel: Nicolas Michel
   Assistant Secretary-General: Ralph Zacklin

Department of Political Affairs
Under-Secretary-General: Kieran Prendergast (until 30 June), Ibrahim Gambari (from 1 July)
   Assistant Secretary-General, Executive Director, Counter-Terrorism Committee: Javier Rupérez
   Assistant Secretaries-General: Tuliameni Kalomoh, Danilo Türk (until July), Angela Kane (from December)

Department for Disarmament Affairs
Under-Secretary-General: Nobuyasu Abe

Department of Peacekeeping Operations
Under-Secretary-General: Jean-Marie Guéhenno
   Assistant Secretaries-General: Hédi Annabi, Jane Holl Lute

Office for the Coordination of Humanitarian Affairs
Under-Secretary-General for Humanitarian Affairs, Emergency Relief Coordinator: Jan Egeland
   Assistant Secretary-General, Deputy Emergency Relief Coordinator: Eva Margareta Wahlstrom

Department of Economic and Social Affairs
Under-Secretary-General: José Antonio Ocampo
   Assistant Secretary-General, Special Adviser on Gender Issues and Advancement of Women: Rachel Mayanja
   Assistant Secretary-General: Patrizio M. Civili

Department for General Assembly and Conference Management
Under-Secretary-General: Jian Chen
   Assistant Secretary-General: Angela Kane (until November)

Department of Public Information
Under-Secretary-General for Communications and Public Information: Shashi Tharoor

Department of Management
Under-Secretary-General: Catherine Bertini (until 30 April), Christopher Bancroft Burnham (from 1 June)

OFFICE OF PROGRAMME PLANNING, BUDGET AND ACCOUNTS
Assistant Secretary-General, Controller: Jean-Pierre Halbwachs (until February), Warren Sach (from 20 April)

OFFICE OF HUMAN RESOURCES MANAGEMENT
Assistant Secretary-General: Rosemary McCreery (until July), Jan Beagle (from 1 October)

OFFICE OF CENTRAL SUPPORT SERVICES
Assistant Secretary-General: Andrew Toh

CAPITAL MASTER PLAN PROJECT
Assistant Secretary-General, Executive Director: Louis Frederick Reuter IV

Office of the United Nations Ombudsman
Assistant Secretary-General, Ombudsman: Patricia M. Durrant

Economic Commission for Africa
Under-Secretary-General, Executive Secretary: K. Y. Amoako (until October), Abdoulie Janneh (from November)

Economic Commission for Europe
Under-Secretary-General, Executive Secretary: Brigita Schmö-gnerová

Economic Commission for Latin America and the Caribbean
Under-Secretary-General, Executive Secretary: José Luis Machinea

Economic and Social Commission for Asia and the Pacific
Under-Secretary-General, Executive Secretary: Kim Hak-Su

Economic and Social Commission for Western Asia
Under-Secretary-General, Executive Secretary: Mervat Tallawy

United Nations Office at Geneva
Under-Secretary-General, Director-General of the United Nations Office at Geneva: Sergei Ordzhonikidze

Office of the United Nations High Commissioner for Human Rights
Under-Secretary-General, High Commissioner: Louise Arbour
Assistant Secretary-General, Deputy High Commissioner: Mehr Khan Williams

United Nations Office at Vienna
Under-Secretary-General, Director-General of the United Nations Office at Vienna and Executive Director of the United Nations Office on Drugs and Crime: Antonio Maria Costa

International Court of Justice Registry
Assistant Secretary-General, Registrar: Philippe Couvreur

Secretariats of subsidiary organs, special representatives and other related bodies

International Trade Centre UNCTAD/WTO
Executive Director: J. Denis Bélisle

Office of the High Representative for the Least Developed Countries, Landlocked Developing Countries and Small Island Developing States
Under-Secretary-General, High Representative: Anwarul Karim Chowdhury

Office of the Special Adviser to the Secretary-General on Africa
Under-Secretary-General, Special Adviser: Mohamed Sahnoun

Office of the Special Adviser to the Secretary-General on Colombia
Under-Secretary-General, Special Adviser: James LeMoyne (until April).

Office of the Special Adviser to the Secretary-General for Special Assignments in Africa
Under-Secretary-General, Special Adviser: Ibrahim Gambari (until June).

Office of the Special Envoy of the Secretary-General for Myanmar
Under-Secretary-General, Special Envoy: Razali Ismail

Office of the Special Representative of the Secretary-General for Children and Armed Conflict
Under-Secretary-General, Special Representative: Olara A. Otunnu

Office of the Special Representative of the Secretary-General for the Great Lakes Region
Assistant Secretary-General, Special Representative: Ibrahima Fall

Office of the Special Representative of the Secretary-General for West Africa
Under-Secretary-General, Special Representative: Ahmedou Ould-Abdallah

Office of the United Nations High Commissioner for Refugees
Under-Secretary-General, High Commissioner: Ruud Lubbers (until 20 February), Antônio Manuel de Oliveira Gutterres (from 15 June)

Office of the United Nations Special Coordinator for the Middle East
Under-Secretary-General, Special Coordinator for the Middle East Peace Process and Personal Representative of the Secretary-General to the Palestine Liberation Organization and the Palestinian Authority: Terje Roed-Larson (until 2 January), Alvaro de Soto (from 6 May)

Special Adviser to the Secretary-General on Latin American Issues
Under-Secretary-General, Special Adviser: Diogo Cordovez

Special Envoy of the Secretary-General for the Commonwealth of Independent States
Under-Secretary-General, Special Envoy: Yuli Vorontsov

Special Envoy of the Secretary-General for the Humanitarian Crisis in the Horn of Africa
Under-Secretary-General, Special Envoy: Martti Ahtisaari (until 9 November)

Special Representative of the Secretary-General for the Sudan
Under-Secretary-General, Special Representative: Johannes Pronk
Assistant Secretary-General, Principal Deputy Special Representative: Taye-Brook Zerihoun

United Nations Assistance Mission in Afghanistan
Under-Secretary-General, Special Representative of the Secretary-General: Jean Arnault

United Nations Assistance Mission for Iraq
Under-Secretary-General, Special Representative of the Secretary-General for Iraq: Ashraf Jehangir Qazi

United Nations Children's Fund
Under-Secretary-General, Executive Director: Carol Bellamy (until April), Ann M. Veneman (from 1 May)
Assistant Secretaries-General, Deputy Executive Directors: Kul Gautam, Toshiyuki Niwa, Karin Sham Poo

United Nations Compensation Commission
Assistant Secretary-General, Executive Secretary: Rolf Goran Knutsson

United Nations Conference on Trade and Development
Assistant Secretary-General, Officer-in-Charge: Carlos Fortin Cabezas (until 31 August), Supachai Panitchpakdi (from 1 September)

United Nations Development Programme
Administrator: Mark Malloch Brown (until 13 August), Kemal Dervis (from 15 August)
Under-Secretary-General, Associate Administrator: Zéphirin Diabré
Assistant Administrator and Director, Bureau for Crisis Prevention and Recovery: Julia V. Taft (until 28 February), Kathleen Cravero (from 1 March)
Assistant Administrator and Director, Bureau of Management: Jan Mattsson
Assistant Administrator and Director, Bureau for Development Policy: Shoji Nishimoto
Assistant Administrator and Regional Director, UNDP Africa: Abdoulie Janneh
Assistant Administrator and Regional Director, UNDP Arab States: Khalaf Rima Hunaidi
Assistant Administrator and Regional Director, UNDP Asia and the Pacific: Hafiz Pasha

Assistant Administrator and Regional Director, UNDP Europe and the Commonwealth of Independent States: Kalman Mizsei

Assistant Administrator and Regional Director, UNDP Latin America and the Caribbean: Elena Martinez

United Nations Disengagement Observer Force

Assistant Secretary-General, Force Commander: Major General Bala Nanda Sharma

United Nations Environment Programme

Under-Secretary-General, Executive Director: Klaus Töpfer

Assistant Secretary-General, Deputy Executive Director: Shafqat S. Kakakhel

Assistant Secretary-General, Executive Secretary: Hamdallah Zedan

United Nations Human Settlements Programme (UN-Habitat)

Under-Secretary-General, Executive Director: Anna Kajumulo Tibaijuka

United Nations Institute for Training and Research

Assistant Secretary-General, Executive Director: Marcel A. Boisard

United Nations Interim Administration Mission in Kosovo

Under-Secretary-General, Special Representative of the Secretary-General and Head of Mission: Soren Jessen-Petersen

Assistant Secretary-General, Principal Deputy Special Representative: Lawrence Rossin

Assistant Secretaries-General, Deputy Special Representatives: Joachim Rucker (from 1 February), Jean Dussourd (from 18 February), Werner Wnendt (from April)

United Nations Interim Force in Lebanon

Assistant Secretary-General, Personal Representative of the Secretary-General for Southern Lebanon: Staffan de Mistura

Assistant Secretary-General, Force Commander: Major General Alain Pellegrini

United Nations Joint Staff Pension Fund

Assistant Secretary-General, Chief Executive Officer: Bernard G. Cochemé

United Nations Military Observer Group in India and Pakistan

Chief Military Observer: Major General Guido Palmieri (until September), Major General Dragutin Repinc (from December)

United Nations Mission in Ethiopia and Eritrea

Under-Secretary-General, Special Representative of the Secretary-General: Legwaila Joseph Legwaila

Assistant Secretaries-General, Deputy Special Representatives: Joël W. Adechi (from 25 May), Azouz Ennifar (from 29 July)

Force Commander: Major General Rajender Singh

United Nations Mission in Liberia

Under-Secretary-General, Special Representative of the Secretary-General and Head of Mission: Jacques Paul Klein (until April), Alan Claude Doss (from 15 August)

Assistant Secretary-General, Deputy Special Representative: Abou Moussa

Assistant Secretary-General, Force Commander: Lieutenant General Joseph Olorungbon Owonibi

United Nations Mission for the Referendum in Western Sahara

Under-Secretary-General, Special Representative of the Secretary-General and Chief of Mission: Alvaro de Soto (until August), Francesco Bastagli (from 1 September)

Force Commander: Major General Gyorgy Száraz (until 11 August), Brigadier General Kurt Mosgaard (from 12 September)

United Nations Mission in Sierra Leone

Under-Secretary-General, Special Representative of the Secretary-General and Chief of Mission: Daudi Ngelautwa Mwakawago

Assistant Secretary-General, Deputy Special Representative: José Vitor da Silva Angelo

Assistant Secretary-General, Force Commander: Major General Sajjad Akram

United Nations Mission of Support in East Timor

Assistant Secretary-General, Special Representative of the Secretary-General and Head of Mission: Sukehiro Hasegawa

Force Commander: Lieutenant General Khairuddin Mat Yusof

Chief Military Observer: Brigadier General Pedro Rocha Pena Madeira

United Nations Office in Timor-Leste

Special Representative of the Secretary-General and Head of Mission: Sukehiro Hasegawa

United Nations Monitoring, Verification and Inspection Commission

Assistant Secretary-General, Acting Executive Chairman: Demetrius Perricos

United Nations Observer Mission in Bougainville

Head of Mission: Tor Stenbock

United Nations Observer Mission in Georgia

Assistant Secretary-General, Special Representative of the Secretary-General and Head of Mission: Heidi Tagliavini

Chief Military Observer: Major General Hussein Ahmed Eissa Ghobashi (until July), Major General Niaz Muhammad Khan Khattak (from 13 August)

United Nations Office for Project Services

Assistant Secretary-General, Executive Director: Nigel Fisher

United Nations Operation in Burundi

Under-Secretary-General, Special Representative of the Secretary-General and Head of Mission: Carolyn McAskie

Assistant Secretary-General, Principal Deputy Special Representative: Nureldin Satti

United Nations Operation in Côte d'Ivoire

Under-Secretary-General, Special Representative of the Secretary-General and Chief of Mission: Albert Tévoédjré

Assistant Secretary-General, Principal Deputy Special Representative: Alan Claude Doss

Force Commander: Major General Abdoulaye Fall

United Nations Organization Mission in the Democratic Republic of the Congo

Under-Secretary-General, Special Envoy of the Secretary-General: Mustapha Niasse

Under-Secretary-General, Special Representative of the Secretary-General and Chief of Mission: William Lacy Swing

Assistant Secretary-General, Deputy Special Representative: Ross Mountain

Force Commander: Major General Samaila Iliya

United Nations Peace-building Office in the Central African Republic

Representative of the Secretary-General and Head of Office: General Lamine Cissé

United Nations Peace-building Support Office in Guinea-Bissau

Representative of the Secretary-General and Head of Office: Joao Bernardo Honwana

United Nations Peacekeeping Force in Cyprus

Assistant Secretary-General, Special Representative of the Secretary-General and Head of Mission: Zbigniew Wlosowicz (until 30 November), Michael Moller (from 1 December)
Force Commander: Major General Herbert Joaquin Figoli Almandos

United Nations Political Office for Somalia

Representative of the Secretary-General and Head of Office: Winston A. Tubman (until March), François Lonseny Fall (from 3 May)

United Nations Population Fund

Under-Secretary-General, Executive Director: Thoraya Ahmed Obaid
Deputy Executive Director, Management: Imelda Henkin
Deputy Executive Director, Programme: Kunio Waki

United Nations Relief and Works Agency for Palestine Refugees in the Near East

Under-Secretary-General, Commissioner-General: Peter Hansen (until 31 March), Karen Koning AbuZayd (from 28 June)
Assistant Secretary-General, Deputy Commissioner-General: Filippo Grandi (from 25 September)

United Nations Stabilization Mission in Haiti

Under-Secretary-General, Special Representative of the Secretary-General: Juan Gabriel Valdés

Assistant Secretary-General, Principal Deputy Special Representative: Hocine Medili
Assistant Secretary-General, Deputy Special Representative: Adama Guindo
Force Commander: Lieutenant General Augusto Heleno Ribeiro Pereira (until 1 September), Lieutenant General Urano Teixeira da Matta Bacellar (from September)

United Nations Tajikistan Office of Peace-building

Assistant Secretary-General, Representative of the Secretary-General: Vladimir Sotirov

United Nations Truce Supervision Organization

Assistant Secretary-General, Chief of Staff: Brigadier General Clive William Lilley

United Nations University

Under-Secretary-General, Rector: Hans J. A. van Ginkel
Director, World Institute for Development Economics Research: Anthony F. Shorrocks

On 31 December 2005, the total number of staff of the United Nations Secretariat with continuous service or expected service of a year or more was 16,176. Of these, 5,976 were in the Professional and higher categories, 1,044 were experts (200-series Project Personnel staff) and 9,156 were in the General Service and related categories.

---

[1]Elected on 13 June 2005 (dec. 59/421).
[2]Elected on 13 June 2005 (dec. 59/423).
[3]The only Main Committee to meet at the resumed session.
[4]Chairmen elected by the Committees; announced by the Assembly President on 13 June 2005 (dec. 59/422).
[5]Appointed on 13 September 2005 (dec. 60/401).
[6]Elected by the General Assembly for a period of five years from 15 June 2005 ending 14 June 2010 (dec.59/420).
[7]Appointed for a four-year term from 1 September 2005 to 31 August 2009, confirmed by the Secretary-General on 11 May 2005 (dec. 59/419).
[8]Completed on 31 December 2005
[9]Completed on 20 May 2005
[10]Established on March 2005
[11]Completed on 30 June 2005
[12]Established on 21 May 2005
[13]The General Assembly, in resolution 60/1 of 16 September, considering that the Trusteeship Council no longer met and had no remaining functions, decided to delete Chapter XIII of the Charter and references to the Council in Chapter XII.
[14]Term expires on 5 February of the year indicated.

Appendix IV
Agendas of United Nations principal organs in 2005

This appendix lists the items on the agendas of the General Assembly, the Security Council and the Economic and Social Council during 2005. For the Assembly, the column headed "Allocation" indicates the assignment of each item to plenary meetings or committees.

Agenda item titles have been shortened by omitting mention of reports, if any, following the subject of the item. Where the subject matter of an item is not apparent from its title, the subject is identified in square brackets; this is not part of the title.

General Assembly

Agenda items remaining for consideration at the resumed fifty-ninth session (18 January–11 September 2005)

Item No.	Title	Allocation
2.	Minute of silent prayer or meditation.	Plenary
4.	Election of the President of the General Assembly.	Plenary
6.	Election of the Vice-Presidents of the General Assembly.	Plenary
8.	Organization of work, adoption of the agenda and allocation of items.	Plenary
15.	Elections to fill vacancies in the principal organs:	
	(c) Election of a member of the International Court of Justice.	Plenary
16.	Elections to fill vacancies in subsidiary organs and other elections:	
	(b) Election of the United Nations High Commissioner for Refugees.[1]	Plenary
17.	Appointments to fill vacancies in subsidiary organs and other appointments:	
	(b) Appointment of members of the Committee on Contribution;	Plenary
	(h) Appointment of a member of the Joint Inspection Unit;	Plenary
	(i) Appointment of the Under-Secretary-General for Internal Oversight Services;	Plenary
	(j) Confirmation of the appointment of the Secretary-General of the United Nations Conference on Trade and Development;	Plenary
	(k) Confirmation of the appointment of the Administrator of the United Nations Development Programme.[1]	Plenary
18.	Elections of judges of the International Tribunal for the Prosecution of Persons Responsible for Serious Violations of International Humanitarian Law Committed in the Territory of The former Yugoslavia since 1991.	Plenary
39.	Strengthening of the coordination of humanitarian and disaster relief assistance of the United Nations, including special economic assistance.	Plenary
43.	Follow-up to the outcome of the twenty-sixth special session: implementation of the Declaration of Commitment on HIV/AIDS.	Plenary
45.	Integrated and coordinated implementation of and follow-up to the outcomes of the major United Nations conferences and summits in the economic, social and related fields..	Plenary
53.	Question of equitable representation on and increase in the membership of the Security Council and related matters.	Plenary
55.	Follow-up to the outcome of the Millennium Summit.	Plenary
56.	Cooperation between the United Nations and regional and other organizations:	
	(g) Cooperation between the United Nations and the Economic Community of Central African States.	Plenary
77.	Comprehensive review of the whole question of peacekeeping operations in all their aspects.	4th
84.	Follow-up to and implementation of the outcome of the International Conference on Financing for Development.	Plenary, 2nd
85.	Sustainable Development:	Plenary
	(b) Further implementation of the Programme of Action for the Sustainable Development of Small Island Developing States.	Plenary, 2nd

Item No.	Title	Allocation
105.	Human rights question:	
	(b) Human rights question, including alternative approaches for improving the effective enjoyment of human rights and fundamental freedoms.	Plenary
106.	Financial reports and audited financial statements, and reports of the Board of Auditors.	5th
107.	Review of the efficiency of the administrative and financial functioning of the United Nations.	5th
108.	Programme budget for the biennium 2004-2005.	5th
113.	Scale of assessments for the apportionment of the expenses of the United Nations.	Plenary, 5th
114.	Human resources management.	5th
116.	United Nations common systems.	5th
120.	Administration and justice at the United Nations.	5th
121.	Financing of the International Criminal Tribunal for the Prosecution of Persons Responsible for Genocide and Other Serious Violations of International Humanitarian Law Committed in the Territory of Rwanda and Rwandan Citizens Responsible for Genocide and Other Such Violations Committed in the Territory of Neighbouring States between 1 January and 31 December 1994.	5th
122.	Financing of the International Tribunal for the Prosecution of Persons Responsible for Serious Violations of International Humanitarian Law Committed in the Territory of the Former Yugoslavia since 1991.	5th
123.	Administrative and budgetary aspects of the financing of the United Nations peacekeeping operations.	5th
124.	Financing of the United Nations Angola Verification Mission and the United Nations Observer Mission in Angola.	5th
125.	Financing of the United Nations Mission in Bosnia and Herzegovina.	5th
126.	Financing of the United Nations Peacekeeping Force in Cyprus.	5th
127.	Financing of the United Nations Organisation Mission in the Democratic Republic of the Congo.	5th
129.	Financing of the United Nations Mission of Support in East Timor.	5th
130.	Financing of the United Nations Mission in Ethiopia and Eritrea.	5th
131.	Financing of the United Nations Observer Mission in Georgia.	5th
132.	Financing of the activities arising from Security Council resolution 687(1991):	
	(a) United Nations Iraq-Kuwait Observation Mission.	5th
133	Financing of the United Nations Interim Administration Mission in Kosovo.	5th
134.	Financing of the United Nations Mission in Liberia.	5th
135.	Financing of the United Nations peacekeeping forces in the Middle East.	
	(a) United Nations Disengagement Observer Force.	5th
136.	Financing of the United Nations Mission in Sierra Leone.	5th
137.	Financing of the United Nations Mission for the Referendum in Western Sahara.	5th
148.	Measures to eliminate international terrorism.	Plenary, 6th
150.	International convention against the productive cloning of human beings.	6th
153.	Financing of the United Nations Operation in Burundi.	5th
154.	Financing of the United Nations Mission in Côte d'Ivoire.	5th
155.	Financing of the United Nations Stabilization Mission in Haiti.	5th
156.	Multilingualism.	Plenary
158.	Declaration by the United Nations of 8 and 9 May as days of remembrance and reconciliation.	Plenary
164.	Financing of the United Nations Mission in the Sudan.[2]	5th

Agenda of the twenty-eighth special session
(24 January 2005)

Item No.	Title	Allocation
1.	Opening of the session by the Chairman of the delegation of Gabon.	Plenary
2.	Minute of silent prayer or meditation.	Plenary
3.	Credentials of the representatives of the special session of the General Assembly.	Plenary
4.	Election of the President.	Plenary
5.	Organization of the session.	Plenary
6.	Adoption of the agenda.	Plenary
7.	Commemoration of the sixtieth anniversary of the liberation of the Nazi concentration camps.	Plenary

Agenda of the sixtieth session[3]
(first part, 13 September–23 December 2005)

A. **Maintenance of international peace and security**

Item No.	Title	Allocation
9.	Report of the Security Council.	Plenary
10.	Support by the United Nations system of the efforts of Governments to promote and consolidate new or restored democracies.	Plenary
11.	The role of diamonds in fuelling conflict.	Plenary
12.	Prevention of armed conflict.	Plenary
13.	The situation in Central America: progress in fashioning a region of peace, freedom, democracy and development.	Plenary
14.	The situation in the Middle East.	Plenary
15.	Question of Palestine.	Plenary
16.	Zone of peace and cooperation of the South Atlantic.	Plenary
17.	The situation in Afghanistan and its implications for international peace and security.	Plenary
18.	Necessity of ending the economic, commercial and financial embargo imposed by the United States of America against Cuba.	Plenary
19.	Question of Cyprus.	Plenary
20.	Armed aggression against the Democratic Republic of the Congo.	Plenary
21.	Question of the Falkland Islands (Malvinas).	Plenary
22.	The situation of democracy and human rights in Haiti.	Plenary
23.	Armed Israeli aggression against the Iraqi nuclear installations and its grave consequences for the established international system concerning the peaceful uses of nuclear energy, the non-proliferation of nuclear weapons and international peace and security.	Plenary
24.	Consequences of the Iraqi occupation of and aggression against Kuwait.	Plenary
25.	Declaration of the Assembly of Heads of State and Government of the Organization of African Unity on the aerial and naval military attack against the Socialist People's Libyan Arab Jamahiriya by the present United States Administration in April 1986.	Plenary
26.	Implementation of the Declaration on the Granting of Independence to Colonial Countries and Peoples.	4th
27.	Assistance in mine action.	4th
28.	Effects of atomic radiation.	4th
29.	International cooperation in the peaceful uses of outer space.	4th
30.	United Nations Relief and Works Agency for Palestine Refugees in the Near East.	4th
31.	Report of the Special Committee to Investigate Israeli Practices Affecting the Human Rights of the Palestinian People and Other Arabs of the Occupied Territories.	4th
32.	Comprehensive review of the whole question of peacekeeping operations in all their aspects.	4th
33.	Questions relating to information.	4th
34.	Information from Non-Self-Governing Territories transmitted under Article 73 *e* of the Charter of the United Nations.	4th
35.	Economic and other activities which affect the interests of the peoples of the Non-Self-Governing Territories.	4th
36.	Implementation of the Declaration on the Granting of Independence to Colonial Countries and Peoples by the specialized agencies and the international institutions associated with the United Nations.	4th
37.	Offers by Member States of study and training facilities for inhabitants of Non-Self-Governing Territories.	4th
38.	Permanent sovereignty of the Palestinian people in the Occupied Palestinian Territory, including East Jerusalem, and of the Arab population in the occupied Syrian Golan over their natural resources.	2nd
39.	Report of the United Nations High Commissioner for Refugees, questions relating to refugees, returnees and displaced persons and humanitarian questions.	3rd
40.	The situation in the occupied territories of Azerbaijan.	Plenary

B. **Promotion of sustained economic growth and sustainable development in accordance with the relevant resolutions of the General Assembly and recent United Nations conferences**

41.	Report of the Economic and Social Council.	Plenary
42.	Global Agenda for Dialogue among Civilizations.	Plenary

Item No.		*Title*	*Allocation*
43.		Culture of peace.	Plenary
44.		Follow-up to the outcome of the special session on children.	Plenary
45.		Follow-up to the outcome of the twenty-sixth special session: implementation of the Declaration of Commitment on HIV/AIDS.	Plenary
46.		Integrated and coordinated implementation of and follow-up to the outcomes of the major United Nations conferences and summits in the economic, social and related fields.	Plenary
47.		2001-2010: Decade to Roll Back Malaria in Developing Countries, particularly in Africa.	Plenary
48.		Sport for peace and development:	
	(a)	Building a peaceful and better world through sport and the Olympic ideal;	Plenary
	(b)	International Year of Sport and Physical Education.	Plenary
49.		Information and communication technologies for development.	Plenary, 2nd
50.		Macroeconomic policy questions:	
	(a)	International trade and development;	2nd
	(b)	International financial system and development;	2nd
	(c)	External debt crisis and development.	2nd
51.		Follow-up to and implementation of the outcome of the International Conference on Financing for Development.	Plenary, 2nd
52.		Sustainable development:	
	(a)	Implementation of Agenda 21, the Programme for the Further Implementation of Agenda 21 and the outcomes of the World Summit on Sustainable Development;	2nd
	(b)	Follow-up to and implementation of the Mauritius Strategy for the Further Implementation of the Programme of Action for the Sustainable Development of Small Island Developing States;	2nd
	(c)	International Strategy for Disaster Reduction;	2nd
	(d)	Protection of global climate for present and future generations of mankind;	2nd
	(e)	Sustainable development in mountain regions;	2nd
	(f)	Promotion of new and renewable sources of energy, including the implementation of the World Solar Programme 1996-2005;	2nd
	(g)	Implementation of the United Nations Convention to Combat Desertification in Those Countries Experiencing Serious Drought and/or Desertification, Particularly in Africa;	2nd
	(h)	Convention on Biological Diversity;	2nd
	(i)	Rendering assistance to the poor mountain countries to overcome obstacles in socio-economic and ecological areas.	2nd
53.		Implementation of the outcome of the United Nations Conference on Human Settlements (Habitat II) and strengthening of the United Nations Human Settlements Programme (UN-Habitat).	2nd
54.		Globalization and interdependence:	
	(a)	Globalization and interdependence;	2nd
	(b)	Science and Technology for development;	2nd
	(c)	International migration and development;	2nd
	(d)	Preventing and combating corrupt practices and transfer of funds of illicit origin and returning such assets to the countries of origin.	2nd
55.		Groups of countries in special situations:	
	(a)	Third United Nations Conference on the Least Developed Countries;	2nd
	(b)	Specific actions related to the particular needs and problems of landlocked developing countries: outcome of the International Ministerial Conference of Landlocked and Transit Developing Countries and Donor Countries and International Financial and Development Institutions on Transit Transport Cooperation.	2nd
56.		Eradication of poverty and other development issues:	
	(a)	Implementation of the first United Nations Decade for the Eradication of Poverty (1997-2006);	2nd
	(b)	Women in development;	2nd
	(c)	Human resources development.	2nd
57.		Operational activities for development:	
	(a)	Operational activities for development of the United Nations system;	2nd
	(b)	South-South cooperation: economic and technical cooperation among developing countries.	2nd
58.		Training and research:	
	(a)	United Nations Institute for Training and Research;	2nd
	(b)	United Nations System Staff College in Turin, Italy.	2nd

Item No.	*Title*	*Allocation*
59.	Towards global partnership.	2nd
60.	Global road safety crisis.	Plenary
61.	Implementation of the outcome of the World Summit for Social Development and of the twenty-fourth special session of the General Assembly.	3rd
62.	Social development, including questions relating to the world social situation and to youth, ageing, disabled persons and the family.	Plenary, 3rd
63.	Follow-up to the International Year of Older Persons: Second World Assembly on Aging.	3rd
64.	Advancement of women.	3rd
65.	Implementation of the outcome of the Fourth World Conference on Women and of the twenty-third special session of the General Assembly, entitled "Women 200: gender equality, development and peace for the twenty-first century".	3rd

C. Development of Africa

66.	New Partnership for Africa's Development: progress in implementation and international support:	
	(a) New Partnership for Africa's Development: progress in implementation and international support;	Plenary
	(b) Causes of conflict and the promotion of durable peace and sustainable development in Africa.	Plenary

D. Promotion of human rights

67.	Promotion and protection of the rights of children.	3rd
68.	Indigenous issues.	3rd
69.	Elimination of racism and racial discrimination:	
	(a) Elimination of racism and racial discrimination;	3rd
	(b) Comprehensive implementation of and follow-up to the Durban Declaration and Programme of Action.	3rd
70.	Right of peoples to self-determination.	3rd
71.	Human rights questions:	
	(a) Implementation of human rights instruments;	3rd
	(b) Human rights questions, including alternative approaches for improving the effective enjoyment of human rights and fundamental freedoms;	3rd
	(c) Human rights situations and reports of special rapporteurs and representatives;	3rd
	(d) Comprehensive implementation of and follow-up to the Vienna Declaration and Programme of Action;	3rd
	(e) Report of the United Nations High Commissioner for Human Rights.	3rd
72.	Holocaust remembrance.	Plenary

E. Effective coordination of humanitarian assistance efforts

73.	Strengthening of the coordination of humanitarian and disaster relief assistance of the United Nations, including special economic assistance:	
	(a) Strengthening of the coordination of emergency humanitarian assistance of the United Nations;	Plenary
	(b) Special economic assistance to individual countries or regions;	2nd
	(c) Strengthening of international cooperation and coordination of to study, mitigate and minimize the consequences of the Chernobyl disaster;	Plenary
	(d) Assistance to the Palestinian people;	Plenary
	(e) Emergency international assistance for peace, normalcy and reconstruction of war-stricken Afghanistan.	Plenary

F. Promotion of justice and international law

74.	Report of the International Court of Justice.	Plenary
75.	Oceans and the law of the sea:	
	(a) Oceans and the law of the sea;	Plenary
	(b) Sustainable fisheries, including through the 1995 Agreement for the Implementation of the Provisions of the United Nations Convention on the Law of the Sea of 10 December 1982 relating to the Conservation and Management of Straddling Fish Stocks and Highly Migratory Fish Stocks, and related instruments.	Plenary
76.	Report of the International Criminal Tribunal for the Prosecution of Persons Responsible for Genocide and Other Serious Violations of International Humanitarian Law Committed in the Territory of Rwanda and Rwandan Citizens Responsible for Genocide and Other Such Violations Committed in the Territory of Neighbouring States between 1 January and 31 December 1994.	Plenary

Item No.	Title	Allocation
77.	Report of the International Tribunal for the Prosecution of Persons Responsible for Serious Violations of International Humanitarian Law Committed in the Territory of the Former Yugoslavia since 1991.	Plenary
78.	United Nations Programme of Assistance in the Teaching, Study, Dissemination and Wider Appreciation of International Law.	6th
79.	Report of the United Nations Commission on International Trade Law on the work of its thirty-eighth session.	6th
80.	Report of the International Law Commission on the work of its fifty-seventh session.	6th
81.	Report of the International Criminal Court.	Plenary
82.	Report of the Special Committee on the Charter of the United Nations and on the Strengthening of the Role of the Organisation.	6th
83.	Scope of legal protection under the Convention on the Safety of United Nations and Associated Personnel.	6th

G. Disarmament

Item No.	Title	Allocation
84.	Report of the International Atomic Energy Agency.	Plenary
85.	Reduction of military budgets:	
(a)	Reduction of military budgets;	1st
(b)	Objective information on military matters, including transparency of military expenditures.	1st
86.	Developments in the field of information and telecommunications in the context of international security.	1st
87.	Prohibition of the development and manufacture of new types of weapons of mass destruction and new systems of such weapons: report of the Conference on Disarmament.	1st
88.	Question of Antarctica.	1st
89.	Implementation of the Declaration of the Indian Ocean as a Zone of Peace.	1st
90.	African Nuclear-Weapon-Free Zone Treaty.	1st
91.	Consolidation of the regime established by the Treaty for the Prohibition of Nuclear Weapon in Latin America and the Caribbean (Treaty of Tlatelolco).	1st
92.	Verification in all its aspects, including the role of the United Nations in the field of verification.	1st
93.	Role of science and technology in the context of international security and disarmament	1st
94.	Establishment of a nuclear-weapon-free zone in the region of the Middle East.	1st
95.	Conclusion of effective international arrangements to assure non-nuclear-weapon States against the use or threat of use of nuclear weapons.	1st
96.	Prevention of an arms race in outer space.	1st
97.	General and complete disarmament:	
(a)	Notification of nuclear tests;	1st
(b)	Prohibition of the dumping of radioactive wastes;	1st
(c)	Reduction of non-strategic nuclear weapons;	1st
(d)	Transparency in armaments;	1st
(e)	National legislation on transfer of arms, military equipment and dual-use goods and technology;	1st
(f)	Missiles;	1st
(g)	Observance of environmental norms in the drafting and implementation of agreements on disarmament and arms control;	1st
(h)	Promotion of multilateralism in the area fo disarmament and non-proliferation;	1st
(i)	Convening of the fourth special session of the General Assembly devoted to disarmament;	1st
(j)	Implementation of the Convention on the Prohibition of the Development, Production, Stockpiling and Use of Chemical Weapons and on Their Destruction;	1st
(k)	Assistance to States for curbing the illicit traffic in small arms and collecting them;	1st
(l)	Towards a nuclear-weapon-free world: accelerating the implementation of nuclear disarmament commitments;	1st
(m)	Nuclear disarmament;	1st
(n)	Relationship between disarmament and development;	1st
(o)	Reducing nuclear danger;	1st
(p)	Measures to prevent terrorists from acquiring weapons of mass destruction;	1st
(q)	Follow-up to the advisory opinion of the International Court of Justice on the *Legality of the Threat or Use of Nuclear Weapons;*	1st
(r)	Implementation of the Convention on the Prohibition of the Use, Stockpiling, Production and Transfer of Anti-personnel Mines and on Their Destruction;	1st

Item No.	Title	Allocation
(s)	Nuclear-weapon-free southern hemisphere and adjacent areas;	1st
(t)	The illicit trade in small arms and light weapons in all its aspects;	1st
(u)	Confidence-building measures in the regional and subregional context;	1st
(v)	Conventional arms control at the regional and subregional levels;	1st
(w)	Regional disarmament;	1st
(x)	Prevention of the illicit transfer and unauthorized access to and use of man-portable air defence systems;	1st
(y)	The Hague Code of Conduct against Ballistic Missile Proliferation;	1st
(z)	Information on confidence-building measures in the field of conventional arms;	1st
(aa)	Bilateral strategic nuclear arms reductions and the new strategic framework;	1st
(bb)	Establishment of a nuclear-weapon-free zone in Central Asia;	1st
(cc)	United Nations conference to identify ways of eliminating nuclear dangers in the context of nuclear disarmament;	1st
(dd)	Problems arising from the accumulation of conventional ammunition stockpiles in surplus.	1st
98.	Review and implementation of the Concluding Document of the Twelfth Special Session of the General Assembly:	
(a)	Regional confidence-building measures: activities of the United Nations Standing Advisory Committee on Security Questions in Central Africa;	1st
(b)	United Nations regional centres for peace and disarmament;	1st
(c)	United Nations Regional Centre for Peace, Disarmament and Development in Latin America and the Caribbean;	1st
(d)	United Nations Regional Centre for Peace and Disarmament in Asia and the Pacific;	1st
(e)	United Nations Regional Centre for Peace and Disarmament in Africa;	1st
(f)	Convention on the Prohibition of the Use of Nuclear Weapons;	1st
99.	Review of the implementation of the recommendations and decisions adopted by the General Assembly at its tenth special session:	
(a)	Advisory Board on Disarmament Matters;	1st
(b)	United Nations Institute for Disarmament Research;	1st
(c)	Report of the Conference on Disarmament;	1st
(d)	Report of the Disarmament Commission.	1st
100.	The risk of nuclear proliferation in the Middle East.	1st
101.	Convention on Prohibitions or Restrictions on the Use of Certain Conventional Weapons Which May Be Deemed to Be Excessively Injurious or to Have Indiscriminate Effects.	1st
102.	Strengthening of security and cooperation in the Mediterranean region.	1st
103.	Comprehensive Nuclear-Test-Ban Treaty.	1st
104.	Convention on the Prohibition of the Development, Production and Stockpiling of Bacteriological (Biological) and Toxin Weapons and on Their Destruction.	1st
105.	Review of the implementation of the Declaration on the Strengthening of International Security.	1st

H. Drug control, crime prevention and combating international terrorism in all its forms and manifestations

106.	Crime prevention and criminal justice.	3rd
107.	International drug control.	3rd
108.	Measures to eliminate international terrorism.	6th

I. Organizational, administrative and other matters

1.	Opening of the session by the President of the General Assembly.	Plenary
2.	Minute of silent prayer or meditation.	Plenary
3.	Credentials of representatives to the sixtieth session of the General Assembly:	
(a)	Appointment of the members of the Credentials Committee;	Plenary
(b)	Report of the Credentials Committee.	Plenary
4.	Election of the President of the General Assembly.	Plenary
5.	Election of the officers of the Main Committees.	1st, 4th, 2nd, 3rd, 5th, 6th
6.	Election of the Vice-Presidents of the General Assembly.	Plenary
7.	Organization of work, adoption of the agenda and allocation of items: reports of the General Committee.	Plenary
8.	General debate.	Plenary

Item No.	Title	Allocation
109.	Notification by the Secretary-General under Article 12, paragraph 2, of the Charter of the United Nations.	Plenary
110.	Report of the Secretary-General on the work of the Organization.	Plenary
111.	Elections to fill vacancies in principal organs:	
	(a) Election of five non-permanent members of the Security Council;	Plenary
	(b) Election of eighteen members of the Economic and Social Council;	Plenary
	(c) Election of five member of the International Court of Justice.	Plenary
112.	Elections to fill vacancies in subsidiary organs and other elections:	Plenary
	(a) Election of twenty members of the Committee for Programme and Coordination;	Plenary
	(b) Election of twenty-nine members of the Governing Council of the United Nations Environment Programme;	Plenary
	(c) Election of the Executive Director of the United Nations Environment Programme;	Plenary
	(d) Election of the Executive Director of the United Nations Human Settlement Programme.	Plenary
113.	Appointments to fill vacancies in subsidiary organs and other appointments:	
	(a) Appointment of members of the Advisory Committee on Administrative and Budgetary Questions;	5th
	(b) Appointment of members of the Committee on Contributions;	5th
	(c) Confirmation of the appointment of members of the Investments Committee;	5th
	(d) Appointment of a member of the Board of Auditors;	5th
	(e) Appointment of members of the International Civil Service Commission;	5th
	(f) Appointment of members of the Committee on Conferences.	Plenary
114.	Admission of new Members to the United Nations.	Plenary
115.	Implementation of the resolutions of the United Nations.	Plenary
116.	Revitalization of the work of the General Assembly.	Plenary, 1st, 4th, 2nd, 3rd, 5th, 6th
117.	Question of equitable representation on and increase in the membership of the Security Council and related matters.	Plenary
118.	United Nations reform: measures and proposals.	Plenary
119.	Strengthening of the United Nations system.	Plenary
120.	Follow-up to the outcome of the Millennium Summit.	Plenary
121.	Financial reports and audited financial statements, and reports of the Board of Auditors:	
	(a) United Nations peacekeeping operations;	5th
	(b) Voluntary funds administered by the United Nations High Commissioner for Refugees;	5th
	(c) Capital master plan.	5th
122.	Review of the efficiency of the administrative and financial functioning of the United Nations.	5th
123.	Programme budget for the biennium 2004-2005.	5th
124.	Proposed programme budget for the biennium 2006-2007.	5th
125.	Programme planning.	2nd, 5th
126.	Improving the financial situation of the United Nations.	5th
127.	Pattern of conferences.	5th
128.	Scale of assessments for the apportionment of the expenses of the United Nations.	5th
129.	Human resources management.	5th
130.	Joint Inspection Unit.	5th
131.	United Nations common system.	5th
132.	Report of the Secretary-General on the activities of the Office of Internal Oversight Services.	5th
133.	Administration of justice at the United Nations.	5th
134.	Financing of the International Criminal Tribunal for the Prosecution of Persons Responsible for Genocide and Other Serious Violations of International Humanitarian Law Committed in the Territory of Rwanda and Rwandan Citizens Responsible for Genocide and Other Such Violations Committed in the Territory of Neighbouring States between 1 January and 31 December 1994.	5th
135.	Financing of the International Tribunal for the Prosecution of Persons Responsible for Serious Violations of International Humanitarian Law Committed in the Territory of the Former Yugoslavia since 1991.	5th
136.	Administrative and budgetary aspects of the financing of the United Nations peacekeeping operations.	5th
137.	Financing of the United Nations Operation in Burundi.	5th

Item No.	*Title*	*Allocation*
138.	Financing of the United Nations Operation in Côte d'Ivoire.	5th
139.	Financing of the United Nations Peacekeeping Force in Cyprus.	5th
140.	Financing of the United Nations Organization Mission in the Democratic Republic of the Congo.	5th
141.	Financing of the United Nations Mission in East Timor.	5th
142.	Financing of the United Nations Mission of Support in East Timor.	5th
143.	Financing of the United Nations Mission in Ethiopia and Eritrea.	5th
144.	Financing of the United Nations Observer Mission in Georgia.	5th
145.	Financing of the United Nations Stabilization Mission in Haiti.	5th
146.	Financing of the activities arising from Security Council resolution 687(1991):	
	(a) United Nations Iraq-Kuwait Observation Mission;	5th
	(b) Other activities.	5th
147.	Financing of the United Nations Interim Administration Mission in Kosovo.	5th
148.	Financing of the United Nations Mission in Liberia.	5th
149.	Financing of the United Nations peacekeeping forces in the Middle East:	
	(a) United Nations Disengagement Observer Force;	5th
	(b) United Nations Interim Force in Lebanon.	5th
150.	Financing of the United Nations Mission in Sierra Leone.	5th
151.	Financing of the United Nations Mission in the Sudan.	5th
152.	Financing of the United Nations Mission for the Referendum in Western Sahara.	5th
153.	Report of the Committee on Relations with the Host Country.	6th
154.	Cooperation between the United Nations and the Organization for Security and Cooperation in Europe.	Plenary
155.	Observer status for the Latin American Integration Association in the General Assembly.	6th
156.	Observer status for the Common Fund for Commodities in the General Assembly.	6th
157.	Election of judges of the International Tribunal for the Prosecution of Persons Responsible for Serious Violations of International Humanitarian Law Committed in the Territory of the Former Yugoslavia since 1991.	Plenary
158.	Observer status for the Hague Conference on Private International Law in the General Assembly.	6th
159.	Observer status for the Ibero-American Conference in the General Assembly.	6th
160.	Follow-up to the recommendations on administrative management and internal oversight of the Independent Inquiry Committee into the United Nations Oil-for-Food Programme.	Plenary

Security Council

Agenda items considered during 2005

Item No.[4]   *Title*

1. The situation in Afghanistan.
2. Report(s) of the Secretary-General on the Sudan.
3. The question concerning Haiti.
4. The situation in the Middle East, including the Palestinian question.
5. International Tribunal for the Prosecution of Persons Responsible for Serious Violations of International Humanitarian Law Committed in the Territory of the Former Yugoslavia since 1991.
6. Threats to international peace and security caused by terrorist acts.
7. Meeting of the Security Council with the troop-contributing countries [UNIFIL, UNMEE, MONUC, UNOCI, MINURSO, ONUB, MINUSTAH, UNDOF, UNOMIG, UNMIL, UNMIS, UNFICYP, UNIOSIL].
8. The situation in Georgia.
9. The situation in the Middle East.
10. The situation in Côte d'Ivoire.
11. Election of a member of the International Court of Justice.
12. The situation between Iraq and Kuwait.
13. Small arms.

Item
No.[4]   *Title*

14. Children and armed conflict.
15. Security Council resolutions 1160(1998), 1199(1998), 1203(1998), 1239(1999) and 1244(1999) [Kosovo].
16. Cross-border issues in West Africa.
17. The situation in Timor-Leste.
18. The situation concerning the Democratic Republic of the Congo.
19. Briefing by the Chairman-in-Office of the Organization for Security and Cooperation in Europe.
20. The situation between Eritrea and Ethiopia.
21. The situation in Burundi.
22. The situation in Bosnia and Herzegovina.
23. Wrap-up discussion on the work of the Security Council for the current month.
24. The situation in Guinea-Bissau.
25. Security Council mission [Haiti].
26. Briefings by Chairmen of subsidiary bodies of the Security Council.
27. The situation concerning Western Sahara.
28. The situation in Sierra Leone.
29. Post-conflict peace-building.
30. The situation concerning Iraq.
31. United Nations peacekeeping operations.
32. Letter dated 31 March 1998 from the Chargé d'affaires a.i. of the Permanent Mission of Papua New Guinea to the United Nations addressed to the President of the Security Council.
33. The situation in Cyprus.
34. The situation in Liberia.
35. Protection of civilians in armed conflict.
36. Africa's food crisis as a threat to peace and security.
37. The maintenance of international peace and security: the role of the Security Council in Humanitarian crises—challenges, lessons learned and the way ahead.
38. The responsibility of the Security Council in the maintenance of international peace and security: HIV/AIDS and international peacekeeping operations.
39. The situation in the Central African Republic.
40. Letters dated 26 July 2005 from the Permanent Representative of the United Kingdom of Great Britain and Northern Ireland to the United Nations addressed to the President of the Security Council (S/2005/485 and S/2005/489).
41. Threats to international peace and security.
42. Consideration of the draft report of the Security Council to the General Assembly.
43. The role of civil society in conflict prevention and the pacific settlement of disputes.
44. Cooperation between the United Nations and regional organisations in maintaining international peace and security.
45. Women and peace and security.
46. Election of five members of the International Court of Justice.
47. Report of the Secretary-General on the situation in Somalia.
48. The situation in Africa.

Economic and Social Council

Agenda of the organizational and resumed organizational sessions for 2005
(19 January, 4 February, 1 and 31 March; 27-28 April, 9 June)

Item
No.   *Title*

1. Election of the Bureau.
2. Adoption of the agenda and other organizational matters.
3. Basic programme of work of the Council.
4. Elections, nominations, confirmations and appointments.

Agenda of the substantive and resumed substantive sessions of 2005
(29 June–27 July; 21 October)

*Item
No.*   *Title*

1. Adoption of the agenda and other organizational matters.

   High-level segment

2. Achieving the internationally agreed development goals, including those contained in the Millennium Declaration, as well as implementing the outcomes of the major United Nations conferences and summits: progress made, challenges and opportunities.

   Operational activities of the United Nations for international development cooperation segment

3. Operational activities of the United Nations for international development cooperation:

   (a) Follow-up to policy recommendations of the General Assembly and the Council;

   (b) Reports of the Executive Boards of the United Nations Development Programme and of the United Nations Population Fund, the United Nations Children's Fund and the World Food Programme.

   Coordination segment

4. Towards achieving internationally agreed development goals, including those contained in the Millennium Declaration.

   Humanitarian affairs segment

5. Special economic, humanitarian and disaster relief assistance.

   General segment

6. Implementation of and follow-up to major United Nations conferences and summits:

   (a) Follow-up to the International Conference on Financing for Development;

   (b) Review and coordination of the implementation of the Programme of Action for the Least Developed Countries for the Decade 2001-2010.

7. Coordination, programme and other questions:

   (a) Reports of coordination bodies;

   (b) Proposed programme budget for the biennium 2006-2007;

   (c) International cooperation in the field of informatics;

   (d) Long-term programme of support for Haiti;

   (e) Mainstreaming a gender perspective into all policies and programmes in the United Nations system;

   (f) Information and Communication Technologies (ICT) Task Force;

   (g) Joint United Nations Programme on HIV/AIDS (UNAIDS);

   (h) Ad hoc advisory groups on African countries emerging from conflict;

   (i) Calendar of conferences and meetings in the economic, social and related fields.

8. Implementation of General Assembly resolutions 50/227, 52/12 B and 57/270 B.

9. Implementation of the Declaration on the Granting of Independence to Colonial Countries and Peoples by the specialized agencies and the international institutions associated with the United Nations.

10. Regional cooperation.

11. Economic and social repercussions of the Israeli occupation on the living conditions of the Palestinian people in the Occupied Palestinian Territory, including Jerusalem, and the Arab population in the occupied Syrian Golan.

12. Non-governmental organizations.

13. Economic and environmental questions:

    (a) Sustainable development;

    (b) Science and technology for development;

    (c) Statistics;

    (d) Human settlements;

    (e) Environment;

    (f) Population and development;

    (g) Public administration and development;

    (h) International cooperation in tax matters;

    (i) United Nations Forum on Forests;

    (j) Assistance to third States affected by the application of sanctions;

    (k) Cartography;

    (l) Women and development;

    (m) Transport of dangerous goods.

14. Social and human rights questions:

    (a) Advancement of women;

    (b) Social development;

(c)　Crime prevention and criminal justice;

(d)　Narcotic drugs;

(e)　United Nations High Commissioner for Refugees;

(f)　Comprehensive implementation of and follow-up to the Durban Declaration and Programme of Action;

(g)　Human rights;

(h)　Permanent Forum on Indigenous Issues.

[1]　Sub-item added at the resumed session.

[2]　Item added at the resumed session.

[3]　Further to resolution 58/316 of 1 July 2004, agenda items are organized under headings corresponding to the priorities of the Organization.

[4]　Numbers indicate the order in which items were taken up in 2005.

Appendix V

United Nations information centres and services

(as at January 2007)

ACCRA. United Nations Information Centre
Gamel Abdul Nassar/Liberia Roads
(P.O. Box GP 2339)
Accra, Ghana
  Serving: Ghana, Sierra Leone

ALGIERS. United Nations Information Centre
9a rue Emile Payen, Hydra
(Boîte postale 444, Hydra-Alger)
Algiers, Algeria
  Serving: Algeria

ANKARA. United Nations Information Centre
Birlik Mahallesi, 2 Cadde No. 11
06610 Cankaya
(P.K. 407)
Ankara, Turkey
  Serving: Turkey

ANTANANARIVO. United Nations Information Centre
22 rue Rainitovo, Antasahavola
(Boîte postale 1348)
Antananarivo, Madagascar
  Serving: Madagascar

ASUNCION. United Nations Information Centre
Avda. Mariscal López esq. Saraví
Edificio Naciones Unidas
(Casilla de Correo 1107)
Asunción, Paraguay
  Serving: Paraguay

BANGKOK. United Nations Information Service, Economic and Social Commission for Asia and the Pacific
United Nations Building
Rajdamnern Nok Avenue
Bangkok 10200, Thailand
  Serving: Cambodia, Lao People's Democratic Republic, Malaysia, Singapore, Thailand, Viet Nam, ESCAP

BEIRUT. United Nations Information Centre/ United Nations Information Service, Economic and Social Commission for Western Asia
UN House
Riad El-Solh Square
(P.O. Box 11-8575-4656)
Beirut, Lebanon
  Serving: Jordan, Kuwait, Lebanon, Syrian Arab Republic, ESCWA

BOGOTA. United Nations Information Centre
Calle 100 No. 8A-55, Piso 10
Edificio World Trade Center - Torre "C"
(Apartado Aéro 058964)
Bogotá 2, Colombia
  Serving: Colombia, Ecuador, Venezuela

BRAZZAVILLE. United Nations Information Centre
Avenue Foch, Case ortf 15
(Boîte postale 13210 or 1018)
Brazzaville, Congo
  Serving: Congo

BRUSSELS. Regional United Nations Information Centre
Résidence Palace
rue de la Loi/Wetstraat 155
Quartier Rubens, Block C2
1040 Brussels, Belgium
  Serving: Belgium, Cyprus, Denmark, Finland, France, Germany, Greece, Holy See, Iceland, Ireland, Italy, Luxembourg, Malta, Manaco Netherlands, Norway, Portugal, San Marino, Spain, Sweden, United Kingdom, European Union

BUCHAREST. United Nations Information Centre
c/o UN House
48 A Primaverii Blvd.
Bucharest 011975 1, Romania
  Serving: Romania

BUENOS AIRES. United Nations Information Centre
Junín 1940, 1er piso
1113 Buenos Aires, Argentina
  Serving: Argentina, Uruguay

BUJUMBURA. United Nations Information Centre
117 Avenue de la Révolution
(Boîte postale 2160)
Bujumbura, Burundi
  Serving: Burundi

CAIRO. United Nations Information Centre
1 Osiris Street, Garden City
(P.O. Box 262)
Cairo, Egypt
  Serving: Egypt, Saudi Arabia

CANBERRA. United Nations Information Centre
7 National Circuit, Level-1 Barton
(P.O. Box 5366, Kingston, ACT 2604)
Canberra ACT 2600
Australia
  Serving: Australia, Fiji, Kiribati, Nauru, New Zealand, Samoa, Tonga, Tuvalu, Vanuatu

COLOMBO. United Nations Information Centre
202/204 Bauddhaloka Mawatha
(P.O. Box 1505, Colombo)
Colombo 7, Sri Lanka
  Serving: Sri Lanka

DAKAR. United Nations Information Centre
Rues de Thann x Dagorne
(Boîte postale 154)
Dakar, Senegal
  Serving: Cape Verde, Côte d'Ivoire, Gambia, Guinea, Guinea-Bissau, Mauritania, Senegal

DAR ES SALAAM. United Nations Information Centre
Morogoro Road/Sokoine Drive
Old Boma Building (ground floor)
(P.O. Box 9224)
Dar es Salaam, United Republic of Tanzania
  Serving: United Republic of Tanzania

DHAKA. United Nations Information Centre
IDB Bhaban (8th floor)
Begum Rokeya Sharani
Sher-e-Bangla Nagar
(G.P.O. Box 3658, Dhaka-1000)
Dhaka-1207, Bangladesh
  Serving: Bangladesh

GENEVA. United Nations Information Service, United Nations Office at Geneva
Palais des Nations
1211 Geneva 10, Switzerland
  Serving: Switzerland

HARARE. United Nations Information Centre
Sanders House (2nd floor)
Cnr. First Street/Jason Moyo Avenue
(P.O. Box 4408)
Harare, Zimbabwe
  Serving: Zimbabwe

ISLAMABAD. United Nations Information Centre
House No. 26, Street 88 G-6/3
(P.O. Box 1107)
Islamabad, Pakistan
Serving: Pakistan

JAKARTA. United Nations Information Centre
Gedung Surya (14th floor)
Jl. M. H. Thamrin Kavling 9
Jakarta 10350, Indonesia
Serving: Indonesia

KATHMANDU. United Nations Information Centre
Pulchowk, Patan
(P.O. Box 107, UN House)
Kathmandu, Nepal
Serving: Nepal

KHARTOUM. United Nations Information Centre
United Nations Compound
Gamma'a Avenue
(P.O. Box 1992)
Khartoum, Sudan
Serving: Somalia, Sudan

LAGOS. United Nations Information Centre
17 Kingsway Road, Ikoyi
(P.O. Box 1068)
Lagos, Nigeria
Serving: Nigeria

LA PAZ. United Nations Information Centre
Calle 14 esq. S. Bustamante
Edificio Metrobol II, Calacoto
(Apartado Postal 9072)
La Paz, Bolivia
Serving: Bolivia

LIMA. United Nations Information Centre
Lord Cochrane 130
San Isidro (L-27)
(P.O. Box 14-0199)
Lima, Peru
Serving: Peru

LOME. United Nations Information Centre
107 boulevard du 13 janvier
(Boîte postale 911)
Lomé, Togo
Serving: Benin, Togo

LUSAKA. United Nations Information Centre
Revenue House (ground floor)
Cairo Road (Northend)
(P.O. Box 32905, Lusaka 10101)
Lusaka, Zambia
Serving: Botswana, Malawi, Swaziland, Zambia

MANAMA. United Nations Information Centre
United Nations House
Bldg. 69, Road 1901
(P.O. Box 26004, Manama)
Manama 319, Bahrain
Serving: Bahrain, Qatar, United Arab Emirates

MANILA. United Nations Information Centre
5th floor, Jaka II Building
150 Legaspi Street, Legaspi Village
(P.O. Box 7285 ADC (DAPO), Pasay City, Metro Minila
Makati City, Philippines
Serving: Papua New Guinea, Philippines, Solomon Islands

MASERU. United Nations Information Centre
United Nations Road
UN House
(P.O. Box 301, Maseru 100)
Maseru, Lesotho
Serving: Lesotho

MEXICO CITY. United Nations Information Centre
Presidente Masaryk 29-2do piso
Col. Chaputelpec Morales
11570 México D.F., Mexico
Serving: Cuba, Dominican Republic, Mexico

MOSCOW. United Nations Information Centre
4/16 Glazovsky Pereulok
Moscow 119002, Russian Federation
Serving: Russian Federation

NAIROBI. United Nations Information Centre
United Nations Office
Gigiri
(P.O. Box 30552)
Nairobi, Kenya
Serving: Kenya, Seychelles, Uganda

NEW DELHI. United Nations Information Centre
55 Lodi Estate
New Delhi 110 003, India
Serving: Bhutan, India

OUAGADOUGOU. United Nations Information Centre
14 Avenue de la Grande Chancellerie
Secteur no. 4
(Boîte postale 135)
Ouagadougou 01, Burkina Faso
Serving: Burkina Faso, Chad, Mali, Niger

PANAMA CITY. United Nations Information Centre
UN House Bldg. 154/155
Ciudad del Saber, Clayton
(P.O. Box 6-9083 El Dorado)
Panama City, Panama
Serving: Panama

PORT OF SPAIN. United Nations Information Centre
2nd floor, Bretton Hall
16 Victoria Avenue
(P.O. Box 130)
Port of Spain, Trinidad, W.I.
Serving: Antigua and Barbuda, Bahamas, Barbados, Belize, Dominica, Grenada, Guyana, Jamaica, Netherlands Antilles, Saint Kitts and Nevis, Saint Lucia, Saint Vincent and the Grenadines, Suriname, Trinidad and Tobago

PRAGUE. United Nations Information Centre
nam. Kinskych 6
15000 Prague 5, Czech Republic
Serving: Czech Republic

PRETORIA. United Nations Information Centre
Metro Park Building
351 Schoeman Street
(P.O. Box 12677)
Pretoria, South Africa
Serving: South Africa

RABAT. United Nations Information Centre
6 Angle avenue Tarik Ibnou Ziyad et Ruet Roudana
(Boîte postale 601, Casier ONU, Rabat-Chellah)
Rabat, Morocco
Serving: Morocco

RIO DE JANEIRO. United Nations Information Centre
Palácio Itamaraty
Av. Marechal Floriano 196
20080-002 Rio de Janeiro RJ, Brazil
Serving: Brazil

SANA'A. United Nations Information Centre
Street 5, off Al-Bonyia Street
Handlal Zone, beside Handhal Mosque
(P.O. Box 237)
Sana'a, Yemen
Serving: Yemen

SANTIAGO. United Nations Information Service, Economic Commission for Latin America and the Caribbean
Edificio Naciones Unidas
Avenida Dag Hammarskjöld, Vitacura
(Avenida Dag Hammarskjöld s/n, Vitacura Casilla 179-D)
Santiago, Chile
Serving: Chile, ECLAC

TEHRAN. United Nations Information Centre
No. 39, Shahrzad Blvd.
(P.O. Box 15874-4557, Tehran)
Darous, Iran
Serving: Iran

TOKYO. United Nations Information Centre
UNU Building (8th floor)
53-70 Jingumae 5-chome, Shibuya-Ku
Tokyo 150-0001, Japan
Serving: Japan

TRIPOLI. United Nations Information Centre
Khair Aldeen Baybers Street
Hay El-Andalous
(P.O. Box 286)
Tripoli, Libyan Arab Jamahiriya
  Serving: Libyan Arab Jamahiriya

TUNIS. United Nations Information Centre
61 boulevard Bab-Benath
(Boîte postale 863)
Tunis, Tunisia
  Serving: Tunisia

VIENNA. United Nations Information
  Service, United Nations Office at Vienna
Vienna International Centre
Wagramer Strasse 5
(P.O. Box 500, A-1400 Vienna)
A-1220 Vienna, Austria
  Serving: Austria, Hungary, Slovakia,
Slovenia

WARSAW. United Nations Information
  Centre
A. Niepodleglosci 186
(UN Centre P.O. Box 1, 02-514 Warsaw
  12)
00-608 Warszawa, Poland
  Serving: Poland

WASHINGTON, D.C. United Nations Information Centre
1775 K Street, N.W., Suite 400
Washington, D.C. 20006, United States
  Serving: United States

WINDHOEK. United Nations Information
  Centre
372 Paratus Building
Independence Avenue
(Private Bag 13351)
Windhoek, Namibia
  Serving: Namibia

YANGON. United Nations Information
  Centre
6 Natmauk Road, Tamwe Township
(P.O. Box 230)
Yangon, Myanmar
  Serving: Myanmar

YAOUNDE. United Nations Information
  Centre
Immeuble Tchinda, Rue 2044, derrière
  camp SIC TSINGA
(Boîte postale 836)
Yaoundé, Cameroon
  Serving: Cameroon, Central African
Republic, Gabon

For more information on UNICs, access the Internet: http://www.un.org/aroundworld/unics

Indexes

USING THE SUBJECT INDEX

To assist the researcher in reading and searching the *Yearbook* index, three typefaces have been employed.

ALL BOLD CAPITAL LETTERS are used for major subject entries, including chapter topics (e.g., **DEVELOPMENT, DISARMAMENT**), as well as country names (e.g., **TAJIKISTAN**), region names (e.g., **AFRICA**) and principal UN organs (e.g., **GENERAL ASSEMBLY**).

CAPITAL LETTERS are used to highlight major sub-topics (e.g., POVERTY), territories (e.g., MONTSERRAT), subregions (e.g., CENTRAL AMERICA) and official names of specialized agencies (e.g., UNIVERSAL POSTAL UNION) and regional commissions (e.g., ECONOMIC COMMISSION FOR EUROPE).

Regular body text is used for single entries and cross-reference entries, e.g., armed conflict, mercenaries, terrorism.

1—An asterisk (*) next to a page number indicates the presence of a text (reproduced in full) of General Assembly, Security Council or Economic and Social Council resolutions and decisions, or Security Council presidential statements.

2—Entries, which are heavily cross-referenced, appear under key substantive words, as well as under the first word of official titles.

3—United Nations bodies are listed under major subject entries and alphabetically.

Subject index

Index of resolutions and decisions

Resolution/decision numbers in italics indicate that the text is summarized rather than reprinted in full. (For dates of sessions, refer to Appendix III.)

Index of 2005 Security Council presidential statements

How to obtain volumes of the *Yearbook*

Recent volumes of the *Yearbook* may be obtained in many bookstores throughout the world, as well as from United Nations Publications, Room DC2-853, United Nations, New York, N.Y. 10017, e-mail (publications@un.org); or from United Nations Publications, Palais des Nations, CH-1211 Geneva 10, Switzerland, e-mail (unpubli@unog.ch).

Yearbook of the United Nations, 2004
Vol. 58. Sales No. E.0.I.1 $175.

Yearbook of the United Nations, 2003 Vol. 57. Sales No. E.05.I.1 $150.	**Yearbook of the United Nations, 1995** Vol. 49. Sales No. E.96.I.1 $150.
Yearbook of the United Nations, 2002 Vol. 56. Sales No. E.04.I.1 $150.	**Yearbook of the United Nations, 1994** Vol. 48. Sales No. E.95.I.1 $150.
Yearbook of the United Nations, 2001 Vol. 55. Sales No. E.03.I.1 $150.	**Yearbook of the United Nations, 1993** Vol. 47. Sales No. E.94.I.1 $150.
Yearbook of the United Nations, 2000 Vol. 54. Sales No. E.02.I.1 $150.	**Yearbook of the United Nations, 1992** Vol. 46. Sales No. E.93.I.1 $150.
Yearbook of the United Nations, 1999 Vol. 53. Sales No. E.01.I.4 $150.	**Yearbook of the United Nations, 1991** Vol. 45. Sales No. E.92.I.1 $115.
Yearbook of the United Nations, 1998 Vol. 52. Sales No. E.01.I.1 $150.	**Yearbook of the United Nations, 1990** Vol. 44. Sales No. E.98.I.16 $150.
Yearbook of the United Nations, 1997 Vol. 51. Sales No. E.00.I.1 $150.	**Yearbook of the United Nations, 1989** Vol. 43. Sales No. E.97.I.11 $150.
Yearbook of the United Nations, 1996 Vol. 50. Sales No. E.97.I.1 $150.	**Yearbook of the United Nations, 1988** Vol. 42. Sales No. E.93.I.100 $150.

Yearbook of the United Nations
Special Edition
UN Fiftieth Anniversary
1945-1995
Sales No. E.95.I.50 $95

The 1946-47; 47-48; 48-49; 1950 and 2004 editions are available online at:
unyearbook.un.org
or
www.un.org/unyearbook

NOTES

NOTES

NOTES

NOTES

NOTES

NOTES